P9-CEC-662

THE RIVERSIDE

Dictionary of Biography

THE RIVERSIDE Dictionary of Biography

BOSTON · NEW YORK

The inclusion of any word or phrase in this book is not an expression of the Publisher's opinion as to whether or not it is subject to proprietary rights. No word in this book is to be regarded as affecting the validity of any trademark.

Adapted and published by arrangement with Chambers Harrap Publishers Ltd.

Visit our website: www.houghtonmifflinbooks.com

ISBN-13: 978-0-618-49337-1
ISBN-10: 0-618-49337-9

Library of Congress Cataloging-in-Publication Data

The Riverside dictionary of biography.
p. cm.
ISBN 0-618-49337-9
1. Biography--Dictionaries.
CT103.R49 2005
920.02--dc22

2004014026

Manufactured in the United States of America
QUM 10 9 8 7 6 5 4 3 2 1

Contents

List of Illustrations

The portraits that accompany each letter opener in the dictionary are presented in alphabetical order from left to right. The persons illustrated at each letter opener, and the source of each portrait, are herewith identified.

Abdullah ibn Hussein Corbis-Brooks Kraft, **Kofi Annan** © The Nobel Foundation, **Susan B. Anthony** Corbis, **Aung San Suu Kyi** AP/WWP-Richard Vogel

Robert Ballard AP/WWP-Victoria Arocho, **Beatrix** Corbis/Bettmann, **Yogi Berra** AP/WWP, **Margaret Bourke-White** AP/WWP

Cab Calloway Corbis/Bettmann, **Rachel Carson** AP/WWP, **Miguel de Cervantes** Corbis, **Marie Curie** © The Nobel Foundation

Alexandra David-Néel Courtesy of Centre Culturel Alexandra David-Néel, **Inge de Bruijn** Corbis-AFP, **Frederick Douglass** Corbis/Bettmann, **Antonín Dvořák** Corbis/Bettmann

Umberto Eco Corbis-Peter Turnley, **Maria Edgeworth** Courtesy of the James Smith Noel Collection, Louisiana State University, Shreveport, **Gertrude Elion** AP/WWP-Karen Tam, **Friedrich Engels** Corbis-Archivo Iconografico, S.A.

Susan Faludi Globe Photos, **Enrico Fermi** Corbis, **Ella Fitzgerald** Globe Photos, **Benjamin Franklin** Art Resource, New York-National Portrait Gallery, Smithsonian Institution

Indira Gandhi Corbis/Bettmann, **Geronimo** Corbis, **John Grisham** AP/WWP, **Janet Guthrie** Globe Photos

Stephen Hawking AP/WWP-Richard Lewis, **Rosalyn Higgins** Courtesy Photo Van der Plas & Van den Eeden, **Grace Murray Hopper** AP/WWP-Department of Defense, **Gordie Howe** Corbis/Bettmann

Dolores Ibarruri AP/WWP, **Henrik Ibsen** Corbis/Bettmann, **Miguel Indurain** AP/WWP-Donald Stampfli, **Isabella I** Art Resource, New York-Erich Lessing

Steve Jobs AP/WWP-Remy De La Mauviniere, **Irène Joliot-Curie** Corbis/Bettmann, **Loïs Mailou Jones** Courtesy of Moorland-Spingarn Research Center, Howard University-Mohamed Mekkawi, **James Joyce** Corbis/Bettmann

Donna Karan AP/WWP, **Kim Dae-Jung** Corbis-Reuters NewMedia Inc., **Martin Luther King** Corbis/Bettmann, **Chandrika Kumaratunga** Corbis-Reuters NewMedia Inc.

Laozi (Lao Tzu) Art Resource, New York-Foto Marburg, **Andrew Lloyd-Webber** Globe Photos-Phil Roach, **Sophia Loren** Globe Photos-Paul Schmulbach, **Mary Mason Lyon**

Courtesy of the Mount Holyoke College Archives and Special Collections, South Hadley, Massachusetts; detail of a painting by an unknown artist; image number LD 7082.25 1837

Yo-Yo Ma Corbis-Richard Chung, Reuters NewMedia Inc., **Ellen MacArthur** AP/WWP-Thierry Martinez, **Naguib Mahfouz** © The Nobel Foundation, **Lise Meitner** Corbis

Martina Navratilova Corbis-Reuters NewMedia Inc., **Pablo Neruda** AP/WWP-Levy, **Julia Babette Neuberger** Globe Photos, **Nicholas II** Corbis/Bettmann

Annie Oakley AP/WWP, **Edna O'Brien** Globe Photos, **Kenzaburo Oë** © The Nobel Foundation, **Jesse Owens** Corbis/Bettmann

Louis Pasteur Corbis/Bettmann, **Edith Piaf** AP/WWP, **Pocahontas** Library of Congress, **Elvis Presley** Corbis

Bin Said Qaboos AP/WWP-Hamid Al Qasmi, **Mary Quant** AP/WWP, **Harriet Quimby** Library of Congress, **Anthony Quinn** AP/WWP

Jeanette Rankin Library of Congress, **Diego Rivera** Corbis/Bettmann, **Gene Roddenberry** Globe Photos, **Arundhati Roy** Globe Photos

Sitting Bull Corbis, **Emma Stebbins** Library of Congress, **Gloria Steinem** AP/WWP-Robert F. Bukaty, **Sting** AP/WWP-Kevork Djansezian

Norgay Tenzing Globe Photos, **Valentina Tereshkova** Corbis/Bettmann, **Harriet Tubman** Library of Congress, **Ted Turner** Corbis-Mitchell Gerber

Galina Ulanova AP/WWP, **Sigrid Undset** Corbis/Bettmann, **John Updike** AP/WWP-Peter Lennihan, **Jørn Utzon** Corbis/Bettmann

Gloria Vanderbilt-Cooper Corbis-Reuters NewMedia Inc., **Mario Vargas Llosa** AP/WWP-Barriopedro, **Jules Verne** Corbis-Rykoff Collection, **Élizabeth Vigée-Lebrun** Art Resource, New York-Scala

Derek Walcott Corbis-Reuters NewMedia Inc., **Ida Wells-Barnett** Courtesy of Chicago Historical Society, neg. no. ICHi-12868, **Eli Whitney** Corbis/Bettmann, **Laura Ingalls Wilder** Courtesy of Herbert Hoover Presidential Library and Museum

Xerxes I Corbis/Bettmann, **Babe Didrikson Zaharias** Corbis/Bettmann, **Emiliano Zapata** AP/WWP, **Khaleda Zia** AP/WWP-Pavel Rahman

Staff

Houghton Mifflin

Vice President, Publisher of Dictionaries
Margery S. Berube

Vice President, Executive Editor
Joseph P. Pickett

Senior Editor, Project Manager
Steven R. Kleinedler

Associate Editor
Uchenna Ikonné

Consulting Editor
Julia Penelope

Editorial Assistant
Nicholas Durlacher

Vice President, Managing Editor
Christopher Leonesio

Art & Production Supervisor
Margaret Anne Miles

Database Production Supervisor
Christopher Granniss

Editorial Production Associate
Brianne Lutfy

Administrative Coordinator
Kevin McCarthy

Proofreaders
Kathryn Blatt
Diane Fredrick
Katherine M. Isaacs

Chambers

Managing Editor of the Chambers Concise Biographical Dictionary (on which this book is based)
Una McGovern

Editor
Gary Dexter

Editorial Assistance
Helen Bleck
Amanda Jones
Louise McCreesh
Hazel Norris
Elaine O'Donoghue
David Pickering

Prepress
Kirsteen Wright

The editors would also like to acknowledge the contributions made by all those who have worked on the *Chambers Biographical Dictionary* and the *Houghton Mifflin Dictionary of Biography*.

Preface

History is populated with a wide range of personalities — from the famous, to the not so famous, to the obscure. Woven together, these lives form a narrative of the world in which we live and create the foundation for understanding larger patterns of history. They also allow us to situate ourselves as a part of those grand patterns.

The 10,000 biographical entries contained within this book span both history and geography, and include individuals from all fields of endeavor. The entries are written in a concise, yet informative and entertaining manner. They have a standard format for accessibility and ease of use, beginning with basic information about the person's life, such as birth date and nationality, and then explaining the person's most significant acts and achievements, along with their cultural background. The text also contains hundreds of quotations and nearly a hundred illustrations, which will both inform and entertain.

Although they lived in different centuries, spoke different languages, and traveled on various parts of the earth, those whose stories fill the pages that follow share the privilege of shaping our world. From Hannibal's trip across the Alps to Neil Armstrong's first step on the moon, from Marie Curie's experiments with radioactivity to Stephen Hawking's theories of the universe, from Homer's chronicles of the Trojan War to Wole Soyinka's narrative of the struggles in modern Africa, the lives that are documented in this Dictionary of Biography provide the context for our own.

Note on the Text

Order of entries

The entries are sorted into an alphabetical order that disregards spaces or hyphens between words in the surname (or in the entire name if there is no comma). Saints tend to precede rulers, who in turn precede popes and other people with the same name. Rulers are sorted into chronological sequences within countries, which are themselves sorted alphabetically. However, the rules are not set in stone, and have been disregarded in cases where it is thought that the reader would instinctively look for a person in a different order.

Foreign names

The Pinyin transliteration of Chinese names has been used in most cases, accompanied by the Wade–Giles version in parentheses. Exceptions to this rule occur when the subject is better known under his or her Wade–Giles spelling, e.g. Chiang Kai-shek, and the order is reversed. Arabic names containing the particle al- or ibn- will normally be found under the element following the particle. Names of kings will often be found under their original spelling, e.g. Karl instead of Charles. Cross-references will assist the reader who tries to find the entry under the anglicized or alternative spelling.

Foreign titles of works

Titles of books, films, musical works, paintings and such that appear in a foreign language have mainly been translated into English. Italicized translations imply that the work has been published or presented (in the case of films) under that English title, whereas the use of quotation marks implies the inclusion of a literal translation to assist the reader in understanding the reference.

Abbreviations

To help the reader, the use of abbreviations and acronyms has been kept to a minimum. Many abbreviations that are used are explained in the text, and others are explained below:

BA	Bachelor of Arts
BBC	British Broadcasting Corporation
CBS	Columbia Broadcasting System
CD-ROM	compact disk read-only memory
CIA	Central Intelligence Agency
DFC	Distinguished Flying Cross
DNA	deoxyribonucleic acid
EC	European Community
EEC	European Economic Community
EU	European Union
FBI	Federal Bureau of Investigation
fl.	*floruit* (Latin), flourished
GPO	General Post Office
HQ	headquarters
IRA	Irish Republican Army
LCC	London County Council
LLB	*Legum baccalaureus* (Latin), Bachelor of Laws
Lt	Lieutenant
m.	married
MA	Master of Arts
MGM	Metro-Goldwyn-Mayer
MIT	Massachusetts Institute of Technology
NATO	North Atlantic Treaty Organization
NFL	National Football League
OEEC	Organization for European Economic Cooperation
PLC	public limited company
POW	prisoner of war
RAF	Royal Air Force
RCA	Radio Corporation of America
RNA	ribonucleic acid
SI	Système International (d'Unités)
SS	Schutzstaffel
UCLA	University of California at Los Angeles
UK	United Kingdom
UN	United Nations
UNESCO	United Nations Educational, Scientific and Cultural Organization
US	United States ("American")
USA	United States of America
USSR	Union of Soviet Socialist Republics
VE Day	Victory in Europe Day
WASP	White Anglo-Saxon Protestant
YMCA	Young Men's Christian Association

Aalto, (Hugo Henrik) Alvar 1898–1976 •*Finnish architect and designer*• Born in Kuortane, he studied at Helsinki Polytechnic and evolved a unique architectural style based on irregular and asymmetric forms and the imaginative use of natural materials. Regarded as the father of Modernism in Scandinavia, Aalto designed numerous public and industrial buildings in Finland, including the sanatorium at Paimio and the Finlandia concert hall in Helsinki.

Aaron 15th–13th century BC •*Biblical patriarch*• The elder brother of **Moses**, he was the first high priest of the Israelites and said to be the founder of the priesthood. He and his sons were ordained as priests after the construction of the Ark of the Covenant and the Tabernacle, and Aaron was confirmed as hereditary high priest by the miracle of his rod blossoming into an almond tree (hence various plants nicknamed "Aaron's rod").

Aaron, Hank (Henry Lewis) 1934– •*US baseball player*• Born in Mobile, Alabama, he is regarded as one of the greatest batters ever. A right-handed-batting outfielder, he set almost every batting record in his 23-season career with the Milwaukee Braves and the Milwaukee Brewers: 2,297 runs batted in, 1,477 extra-base hits, and 755 home runs (he broke **Babe Ruth**'s long-standing record of 714 in 1974).

Aasen, Ivar Andreas 1813–96 •*Norwegian philologist, lexicographer and writer*• Born in Sunmøre, the son of a peasant, he was a fervent nationalist, and created the national language called *Landsmål* (later known as *Nynorsk*, New Norwegian), based on western Norwegian dialects. It eventually achieved recognition alongside *Riksmål* in 1885.

Abacha, Sani 1943–98 •*Nigerian soldier and politician*• Born in Kano, he became an officer in the Nigerian army in 1963, army Chief of Staff in 1985, chairman of the Joint Chiefs of Staff in 1989 and Secretary of Defense in 1993. He assumed the presidency in a bloodless coup in 1993, instituting military rule and banning all political parties and trade unions. International criticism of his regime peaked with the execution of writer and activist Ken Saro-Wiwa (1941–95) and Nigeria was suspended from the Commonwealth.

Abailard, Peter *See* **Abelard, Peter**

Abbado, Claudio 1933– •*Italian conductor*• Born in Milan, he made his debut as an opera conductor at La Scala in 1960, and went on to be musical director there (1968–86). His tenure was marked occasionally by controversy, but mostly by acclaim, and he established his standing as one of the leading conductors in the world. While at La Scala, he was also the principal conductor of the London Symphony Orchestra (1979–88), and was later musical director of the Vienna State Opera (1986–91) and chief conductor of the Berlin Philharmonic Orchestra (1989–1999). In 1994 he became artistic director of the Salzburg Easter Festival.

Abbas I (the Great) 1571–1629 •*Fifth Safavid shah of Persia*• After his accession (1587) he established a counterweight to the Turkmen tribal chiefs by creating a standing army. From 1598 he recovered Azerbaijan and parts of Armenia from the Ottomans, and Khurasan from the Uzbeks. He transferred his capital from Qazvin to Esfahan, which he developed with a program of public works. During his reign Persian artistic development reached its zenith.

'Abbas, al- c. 565–c. 653 •*Merchant and Islamic apostle*• He was the founder of the 'Abbasid dynasty of the Islamic Empire that ruled as caliphs of Baghdad (750–1258). The maternal uncle of the Prophet **Muhammad**, he was at first hostile to his nephew, but ultimately became one of the chief apostles of Islam and gave his name to the dynasty.

Abbas, Ferhat 1899–1985 •*Algerian nationalist leader*• Born in Taher in the Kabylie region, he served as a volunteer in the French army in 1939, but after France's defeat he produced in 1942 a "Manifesto of the Algerian People." In 1955 he joined the Front de Libération Nationale (FLN), the main Algerian resistance organization, and worked with **Ahmed Ben Bella** in Cairo, before founding in 1958 a "Provisional Government of the Algerian Republic" in Tunis. After independence in 1962 he became President of the National Constituent Assembly. He fell out of favor and was exiled but was restored to favor shortly before his death.

Abbas Hilmi Pasha 1874–1944 •*Last khedive of Egypt*• Born in Alexandria, he succeeded his father, **Tewfik Pasha** (1892), and attempted to rule independently of British influence. At the outbreak of war in 1914 he sided with Turkey and was deposed later that year when the British made Egypt a protectorate.

Abbe, Cleveland 1838–1916 •*US meteorologist*• Born in New York City, he published work on the atmosphere and climate, and was responsible for the introduction of the US system of standard time.

Abbe, Ernst 1840–1905 •*German physicist*• Born in Eisenach, he became professor at the University of Jena in 1870, and in 1878 director of the astronomical and meteorological observatories there. Consulted by optical instrument-maker **Carl Zeiss** in the 1860s, Abbe studied the resolution limit and manufacturing process of microscopes. Zeiss took Abbe into partnership, and arising out of his work on the microscope, Abbe founded the diffraction theory of optical imaging, from which modern optical imaging techniques have developed.

Abbott, Bud (William) 1898–1974 •*US comedian*• Born in Asbury Park, New Jersey, the son of a circus bareback rider, he led a life on the fringes of show business until 1931, when he teamed up with Lou Costello, originally Louis Francis Cristillo (1908–50), born in Paterson, New Jersey. They began performing as a comedy team in vaudeville and later brought their routines to films, radio, and television. Their films include *Buck Privates* (1941), *Lost in a Harem* (1944), and *The Naughty Nineties* (1945).

Abbott, Diane Julie 1953– •*English politician*• Educated at Harrow County Girls' Grammar School and Newnham College, Cambridge, she worked for the National Council for Civil Liberties, the Greater London Council (GLC) and Lambeth Borough Council. She joined the Labour Party in 1971 and served on the Westminster City Council (1982–86). Elected to parliament as MP for Hackney North and Stoke Newington in 1987, she became the first Black woman member of the House of Commons.

" "

> Forests of middle-aged men in dark suits ... all slightly redfaced from eating and drinking too much ... a nightmare of elderly white males.
>
> *1988 Of the House of Commons in the* ***New York Times****, June 3.*

Abbott, George Francis 1887–1995 •*US dramatist, director, producer and actor*• He was born in Forestville, New York, and began his career in 1913 as an actor. He wrote his first play, *The Head of the Family* (1912), for the Harvard Dramatic Club, and continued his career in New York, establishing himself with *The Fall Guy* (with James Gleason, 1925). He subsequently wrote and cowrote almost 50 plays and musicals, among them *Love 'em and Leave 'em* (1925); *Three Men on a Horse* (1935); *On Your Toes* (with **Richard Rodgers**

and **Lorenz Hart**, 1936); *The Pajama Game* (with Richard Bissell, 1954); and *Damn Yankees* (1955). In addition to an illustrious career as a producer, he directed over 100 theatrical pieces. He was awarded the Pulitzer Prize for drama (1960) for the hit musical *Fiorello!* (1959), along with cowriter Jerome Weidman (1913–98), lyricist Sheldon Harnick (1924–) and composer Jerry Bock (1928–). He also won six Tony awards for his work.

Abd-ar-Rahman I 731–88 •*Emir of Muslim Spain*• A member of the Umayyad dynasty, he survived the massacre of his family by the 'Abbasids (750), and conquered most of Muslim Spain, founding the emirate of al-Andalus (756) with its capital at Córdoba. Allying with the Christian Basques, he defeated Frankish incursions under **Charlemagne**.

Abd-ar-Rahman III 891–961 •*Emir of Córdoba*• He ruled from 912 and proclaimed himself caliph in 929. Under him the Umayyad emirate reached the peak of its power, extending its boundaries in successful campaigns against the Fatimids and the kings of León and Navarre. A great builder, he created a new city, Madimat az-Zahra, for his court and government.

Abd-ar-Rahman d. 732 •*Saracen leader*• He was defeated and killed by **Charles Martel** at the Battle of Tours.

Abd-ar-Rahman c. 1840–1901 •*Emir of Afghanistan*• The grandson of Dost Mohammed Khan, he was driven into exile in Russia (1869), but was brought back and proclaimed emir with British support (1880). He consolidated his power and arranged for the withdrawal of British troops, leaving Great Britain in control of foreign affairs, and in 1893 subscribed to the Durand Line (named after Sir Henry Durand, 1812–71) as the India-Afghanistan border.

Abd-el-Kader 1807–83 •*Algerian soldier, nationalist and emir*• Born in Mascara, after the French conquest of Algiers he was elected emir by the Arab tribes of Oran, and waged a long struggle with the French (1832–47). In 1835 he defeated a large French army at Makta. Eventually crushed by overpowering force, he took refuge in Morocco and began a crusade against the enemies of Islam, but was defeated at Isly in 1844 and finally surrendered in 1847.

Abd-el-Krim 1880–1963 •*Moroccan Berber chief*• Born in Ajdir, he began a career in the Spanish colonial government in Morocco before leading unsuccessful revolts against Spain and France (1921, 1924–25) and becoming known as the "Wolf of the Rif Mountains." He formed the Republic of the Rif and served as its President (1921–26), but was made to surrender by a large Franco-Spanish army under Marshal **Pétain** and was exiled to the island of Réunion. Granted amnesty in 1947, he went to Egypt where he formed the North African Liberation Committee.

Abd-ul-Aziz 1830–76 •*Sultan of Turkey*• Born in Constantinople (now Istanbul), he succeeded (1861) his brother **Abd-ul-Medjid**, whose liberal and westernizing reforms he continued, promulgating the first Ottoman civil code, and visiting western Europe (1871). Thereafter he became more autocratic, and after revolts in Bosnia, Herzegovina and Bulgaria, he was forced to abdicate.

Abd-ul-Hamid II, *known as* **the Great Assassin** 1842–1918 •*Sultan of Turkey*• Born in Constantinople (now Istanbul), he was the second son of Sultan **Abd-ul-Medjid** and successor to his brother Murad V. He promulgated the first Ottoman constitution (1876), but suspended it (1878) and ruled autocratically. His reign was notable for his cruel suppression of revolts in the Balkans, which led to wars with Russia (1877–78), and especially for appalling Armenian massacres (1894–96). A reform movement by the revolutionary Young Turks forced him to restore the constitution and summon a parliament (1908), but when he attempted a counterrevolution, he was deposed (1909) and exiled.

Abdul-Jabbar, Kareem, *originally* **Lewis Ferdinand Alcindor, Jr**, *known as* **Lew** 1947– •*US basketball player*• Born in New York City, he played with the Milwaukee Bucks and Los Angeles Lakers, earning numerous Most Valuable Player awards. He took the name Abdul-Jabbar when he converted to Islam in 1969. By the time of his retirement in 1989 he was recognized as one of the greatest players in the history of the game, holding several all-time records including most points scored (38,387).

Abdullah ibn Buhaina *See* **Blakey, Art**

Abdullah ibn Hussein 1882–1951 •*First king of Jordan*• Born in Mecca, the second son of **Hussein ibn Ali**, he took a prominent part in the Arab revolt against Turkey (1916–18), becoming emir of the British-mandated territory of Transjordan (1921). He became king when the mandate ended (1946), and was proclaimed King of Palestine (1948); but, with the formal establishment of the state of Israel, he had to be satisfied with sovereignty over the Hashemite Kingdom of Jordan (1949). He was assassinated in the presence of his grandson, who succeeded him.

Abdullah ibn Hussein 1962– •*King of Jordan*• Born in Amman, he was educated in Great Britain at St Edmund's School, Surrey, at Sandhurst and Oxford, and in the US at Georgetown University, Washington DC. He succeeded to the throne in 1999 on the death of his father **Hussein ibn Talal**.

Abdullah, Sheikh Muhammad 1905–82 •*Kashmiri politician*• Born in Soura, near Srinagar, he was a leading figure in the struggle for India's independence and the fight for the rights of Kashmir. Known as the "Lion of Kashmir," he participated actively in the Muslim struggle to overthrow the Hindu maharajah and substitute constitutional government, for which he was imprisoned (1931). For his championing the cause of an independent Kashmir and his subsequent treasonable refusal to pledge his loyalty to India, he was again imprisoned for most of the period 1953–68. As Chief Minister of Jammu and Kashmir from 1975 until his death, he was instrumental in persuading **Indira Gandhi** to grant Kashmir a degree of autonomy.

Abd-ul-Medjid 1823–61 •*Sultan of Turkey*• The successor to his father **Mahmud II** (1839), he continued the liberal reforms of the previous reign, reorganizing the court system and education, and granting various rights to citizens, including Christians. In 1850 he refused to give up the Hungarian political refugee **Lajos Kossuth** to the **Habsburg**s and in 1854 he secured an alliance with Great Britain and France to resist Russian demands, thus precipitating the Crimean War (1854–56). The Ottoman Empire was subsequently increasingly weakened by financial difficulties and internal nationalist problems.

Abdul Rahman, Tunka Putra 1903–90 •*Malaysian statesman*• Born in Alor Star, Kedah, the son of the sultan of Kedah, he studied law at Cambridge University. In 1945 he founded the United Malays' National Organisation (UMNO) and became Prime Minister on independence in 1957. He negotiated the formation of the Federation of Malaysia, embracing Singapore, Sarawak and Sabah (1961–62), and remained Prime Minister of the enlarged entity when it was established in 1963. He withdrew from active politics in 1970.

Abegg, Richard 1869–1910 •*German chemist*• He was born in Danzig (now Gdańsk, Poland). While a professor at Breslau (now Wrocław, Poland), he was one of the first chemists to perceive the chemical significance of the newly discovered (1897) electron, and his "rule of eight" (1904) concerning the electric basis of linkages between atoms was an important stage in the development of modern valence theory.

Abe Kobo 1924–93 •*Japanese novelist and playwright*• Born in Tokyo, he trained as a doctor, but turned to literature. His predominant theme of alienation is explored in a series of novels and plays. His novels include *Daiyon Kampyoki* (1959, Eng trans *Inter Ice Age 4*, 1971), *Suna no onna* (1962, Eng trans *The Woman in the Dunes*, 1965) and *Mikkai* (1977, Eng trans *Secret Rendezvous*, 1980).

Abel •*Biblical character*• The brother of **Cain** and second son of **Adam** and **Eve**, he was a shepherd, whose gift was accepted by God. He was murdered by his brother, Cain, whose gift God did not accept (Genesis 4:2–16).

Abel, Niels Henrik 1802–29 •*Norwegian mathematician*• Born in Finnøy, he showed mathematical genius by the age of 15, entered Oslo University in 1821, and in 1823 proved that there is no algebraic formula for the solution of a general polynomial equation of the 5th degree. Such a formula had been sought ever since the cubic and quartic equations had been solved in the 16th century by **Girolamo Cardano** and others. He developed the concept of elliptic functions independently of **Carl Gustav Jacobi**, and pioneered its extension to the theory of Abelian integrals and functions, which became a central theme of later 19th-century analysis, although his work was not fully understood in his lifetime.

Abelard or **Abailard, Peter** 1079–1142 •*French philosopher and scholar*• Peter Abelard was born near Nantes in Brittany, the eldest son of a noble Breton house. He studied under Johannes Roscellinus at Tours and William of Champeaux in Paris, and enjoyed great success as a teacher and educator. In 1115 he was appointed lecturer in the cathedral school of Notre Dame in Paris, where he became tutor to **Héloïse**, the beautiful and talented 17-year-old niece of the canon Fulbert, with whom he was lodging. They fell passionately in love, but when their affair was discovered, Fulbert threw Abelard out of the house. The couple fled to Brittany, where Héloïse gave birth to a son, Astrolabe, later returning to Paris where they were secretly married. Héloïse's outraged relatives took their revenge on Abelard by breaking into his bedroom one night and castrating him. He fled in shame to the abbey of St Denis to become a monk, and Héloïse took the veil at Argenteuil as a nun. In 1121, the Church condemned him for heresy, and he became a hermit at Nogent-sur-Seine. There his pupils helped him build a monastic school that he named the Paraclete. In 1125 he was elected abbot of St Gildas-de-Rhuys in Brittany, and the Paraclete was given to Héloïse and a sisterhood. He died at the priory of St Marcel, near Chalon; his remains were taken to the Paraclete at the request of Héloïse, and when she died in 1164 she was laid in the same tomb. In 1800 their ashes were taken to Paris, and in 1817 they were buried in one sepulcher at Père Lachaise.

Abelson, Philip Hauge 1913– •*US physical chemist*• Born in Tacoma, Washington, he was educated at Washington State College and the University of California at Berkeley. He worked at the Carnegie Institution, Washington DC, from 1939 to 1941. In 1940 Abelson assisted **Edwin Mattison McMillan** in bombarding uranium with neutrons, which led to the creation of a new element, neptunium, the first element discovered to be heavier than uranium and to be made synthetically. From 1941 on he worked on the Manhattan atomic bomb project. In 1946 he moved back to the Carnegie Institution, where he was appointed director of the Geophysical Laboratory in 1953, then president (1971–78), then trustee (1978–).

Abercrombie, Sir (Leslie) Patrick 1879–1957 •*English architect and pioneer of town planning in Great Britain*• He was Professor of Town Planning at Liverpool (1915–35) and University College London (1935–46). His major work was the replanning of London (*County of London Plan*, 1943, and *Greater London Plan*, 1944). His brother Lascelles Abercrombie (1881–1938) was a poet.

Abercromby, Sir Ralph 1734–1801 •*Scottish general*• Born in Menstrie in Clackmannanshire, he served in Europe in the Seven Years' War (1756–63). In 1793 he distinguished himself as a major general in Flanders under **Frederick**, Duke of York, and led successful operations against the French in St Lucia and Trinidad (1795–96). He led the Anglo-Turkish forces against the French at Aboukir Bay in 1801, but was mortally wounded.

Aberdeen, George Hamilton Gordon, 4th Earl of 1784–1860 •*Scottish statesman and prime minister*• Born in Edinburgh and educated at Harrow, he inherited a peerage at the age of seven. He was Foreign Secretary twice, under the Duke of **Wellington** (1828–30) and under Sir **Robert Peel** (1841–46). A confirmed free trader, he resigned with Peel over the repeal of the Corn Laws in 1846. In 1852, on the resignation of Lord **Derby**, he was made Prime Minister of a coalition government that was immensely popular until he committed Great Britain to an alliance with France and Turkey in the Crimean War in 1854. The gross mismanagement of the war aroused popular discontent, and he was forced to resign in 1855.

Abernathy, Ralph David 1926–90 •*US civil rights leader*• Born in Linden, Alabama, he became a Baptist minister in Montgomery where he was befriended by **Martin Luther King, Jr.** Together they organized a successful bus boycott to protest segregation (1955) and took part in many other civil rights demonstrations. Abernathy served as an officer of the Southern Christian Leadership Conference (SCLC), becoming president (1968–77) after King was assassinated. An advocate of nonviolence, he wrote in his autobiography, *And the Walls Came Tumbling Down* (1989), about his role in the civil rights movement.

Abington, Frances, *née* **Barton** 1737–1815 •*English actress*• Of obscure origins, she sold flowers in the street and was a street singer, milliner and kitchen maid before making her first appearance on the London stage at the Haymarket (1755). A versatile performer, she excelled not only in **Shakespeare** but also in a variety of comedic roles (Lady Teazle, Polly Peachum, Lucy Lockit).

Abney, Sir William de Wiveleslie 1844–1920 •*English chemist and educationist*• Born in Derby, he was educated at the Royal Military Academy at Woolwich and joined the Royal Engineers in 1861. He later became an instructor and then head at the School of Military Engineering. In 1899 he became assistant secretary to the Board of Education and, in 1903, its principal scientific adviser. Among other achievements he invented a gelatin emulsion which made instantaneous photography viable and an emulsion-coated paper from which modern photographic papers were developed. He was elected a Fellow of the Royal Society in 1876.

Abraham or **Abram** Early second millennium BC •*Old Testament father of the Hebrew people*• Born, according to Genesis, in the Sumerian town of Ur of the Chaldees (Ur, Iraq), he migrated with his family and flocks via the ancient city of Mari on the Euphrates (Haran) to the Promised Land of Canaan, where he settled at Shechem (Nablus). After a period in Egypt, he is said to have lived to be 175 years old, and was buried with his first wife, Sarah, in the cave of Machpelah in Hebron. By Sarah he was the father of Isaac (whom he was prepared to sacrifice for God) and grandfather of **Jacob** ("Israel"). By his second wife, Hagar (Sarah's Egyptian handmaiden), he was the father of **Ishmael**, the ancestor of twelve clans. By his third wife, Keturah, he had six sons who became the ancestors of the Arab tribes. He was also the uncle of Lot. Abraham is traditionally regarded as the father of the three great monotheistic religions: Judaism, Christianity and Islam.

Absalom 11th century BC •*Biblical figure*• He was the third and favorite son of King **David** of Israel in the Old Testament. He rebelled against his father and drove him out of Jerusalem. In an ensuing battle he was defeated, and as he was fleeing on a mule his hair was caught in the branch of an oak tree, leaving him dangling in the air, where he was killed by Joab (2 Samuel 18:15).

Abse, Dannie 1923– •*Welsh writer and physician*• Born in Cardiff, he was educated at the Welsh National School of Medicine, King's College London and Westminster Hospital. His literary output includes many volumes of poetry and several novels and plays. Autobiographical volumes are *A Poet in the Family* (1974), *A Strong Dose of Myself* (1982), and the novel *Ash on a Young Man's Sleeve* (1954).

" "

The theme of Death is to Poetry what Mistaken Identity is to Drama.

1984 Journal entry, collected in ***Journals from the Ant-Heap****.*

Abu 'Ali al-Hasan ibn al-Haytham *See* **Alhazen**

Abubakar, Abdulsalam 1942– •*Nigerian soldier and politician*• Born in Minna, he was educated at the Kaduna Technical Institute. After training in the US, he joined the Nigerian army and rose to become head of Nigeria's section of the UN peacekeeping force in Lebanon in 1978. By 1993 he was Nigeria's chair of the Joint Chiefs of Staff, and replaced **Sani Abacha** as head of state after the latter's sudden demise in 1998. He undertook to resolve Nigeria's outstanding problems of corruption and poverty, and set a date for democratic elections. These were held in 1999, when he was succeeded by **Olusegun Obasanjo**.

Abu Bakr c. 570–634 •*First Muslim caliph*• He was one of the earliest converts to Islam. He became chief adviser to the Prophet **Muhammad**, who married his daughter **Aïshah**, and on the death of the Prophet in 632 was elected leader of the Muslim community. In his short reign of two years he put down the "Apostasy," a religious and political revolt directed against the government at Medina, and set in motion the great wave of Arab conquests over Persia, Iraq and the Middle East.

Abu-Mashar *See* **Albumazar**

Abu Nuwas c. 760–c. 814 •*Arab poet*• He was a favorite at the court of the caliph **Harun al-Rashid** in Baghdad, and figures in the *Arabian Nights*.

Abzug, Bella, *originally* **Bella Savitzky** 1920–98 •*US feminist, lawyer and politician*• Born in the Bronx, New York, she was educated at Hunter College, New York, and Columbia University and practiced as a lawyer in New York (1944–70). She became noted for defending those accused of un-American activities and was a prominent peace campaigner, founding Women Strike for Peace (1961) and the National Women's Political Caucus. Winning a seat in Congress (1971), she vigorously championed welfare issues. She returned to her lawyer's practice in 1980, but continued her involvement in political issues. Her publications include *Gender Gap: Bella Abzug's Guide to Political Power for American Women* (1984).

Achebe, Chinua, *originally* **Albert Chinualumogo** 1930– •*Nigerian novelist, poet and essayist*• Born in Ogidi, the son of a mission teacher, he was educated at the University College of Ibadan. His early career was in broadcasting, but the publication of his first novel, *Things Fall Apart* (1958), at once heralded the emergence of a unique voice in African literature. Set in the second half of the 19th century and presenting an unsentimentalized picture of the Ibo people, it has since been translated into over 40 languages. Writing exclusively in English, he confirmed his early promise with four more novels, *No Longer At Ease* (1960), *Arrow of God* (1964), *A Man of the People* (1966) and *Anthills of the Savannah* (1987), which was short-listed for the Booker Prize.

Acheson, Dean Gooderham 1893–1971 •*US politician and lawyer*• Born in Middletown, Connecticut, he was educated at Yale and Harvard, and joined the Department of State in 1941, where he was undersecretary (1945–47) and secretary of state in the **Truman** administration (1949–53). He developed US policy for the containment of Communism, helped to formulate the **Marshall** Plan (1947–48) and participated in the establishment of NATO (1949). He was awarded the Pulitzer Prize for *Present at the Creation* (1969).

“ ”

Great Britain has lost an Empire and not yet found a role.

1962 Speech at West Point military academy, December 5.

Acheson, Edward Goodrich 1856–1931 •*US chemist and inventor*• He was born in Washington, Pennsylvania, and from 1880 to 1881 did research on electric lamps as an assistant to **Thomas Edison**. In 1891 he developed a process for manufacturing silicon carbide (carborundum), an extremely useful abrasive, and in 1896 devised a new way of making lubricants based on colloidal graphite.

Achurch, Janet 1864–1916 •*English actress*• Born in Lancashire, she made her London debut in 1883, and subsequently toured with the actor-manager **Frank Benson**, playing various Shakespearean roles. She is best known for her pioneering association with the works of **Ibsen**. She took the role of Nora in *The Doll's House* (1889), and both produced and starred in *Little Eyolf* (1896). After playing the title role in **George Bernard Shaw**'s *Candida* (1900), which he wrote for her, she was described by the playwright as a tragic actress of genius.

Ackerley, J(oseph) R(andolph) 1896–1967 •*English writer*• He was born in Herne Hill, Kent, educated at Rossall School, Lancashire, and studied law at Cambridge. His friendship with **E M Forster** resulted in his appointment as private secretary to the Maharajah of Chhokrapur, from which experience he wrote *Hindoo Holiday* (1932). From 1935 to 1959 he was literary editor of *The Listener*. His books include *My Dog Tulip* (1956) and *We Think the World of You* (1960), his only novel.

Ackroyd, Peter 1949– •*English novelist, biographer and critic*• He was born in London and educated at Clare College, Cambridge, and at Yale. He was literary editor of the *Spectator* (1973–77), and later (from 1986) chief book reviewer for *The Times* (London). He has published poetry, as well as critical and biographical works, including *Notes for a New Culture* (1976), *Ezra Pound and His World* (1981) and *T S Eliot* (1984). His novels are erudite, playful, and complex, and draw on literary and historical sources. Later works include *Milton in America* (1996), *The Life of Thomas More* (1998) and *London: The Biography* (2000).

Adair, John c. 1655–c. 1722 •*Scottish surveyor and cartographer*• He did notable work in mapping Scotland and its coast and islands. He prepared maps of counties in the central belt of Scotland (1680–86), and in 1703 published *Description of the Sea-Coast and Islands of Scotland* (Part 1). Elected a Fellow of the Royal Society in 1688, his maps and charts set new standards of quality and accuracy.

Adair, John Eric 1934– •*British leadership development consultant and writer*• Educated at Cambridge, London and Oxford, he developed his "Action-Centered Leadership" model while involved with leadership training as a senior lecturer at Sandhurst (1963–69) and as an associate director of the Industrial Society (1969–73). The model states that the leader of a group of people has to insure that needs are met in three interrelated areas—getting the task done, maintaining the team and satisfying the personal requirements of individual members.

Adam •*Biblical character, the first man*• The Book of Genesis describes God's creation of Adam from the dust of the earth, and of **Eve** from Adam's rib. In the biblical accounts Adam and Eve lived in the Garden of Eden until their disobedience by eating an apple from the tree of knowledge led to their banishment. Afterwards they had three sons, **Cain**, **Abel** and Seth. In the New Testament, Adam is seen as a precursor of **Jesus**, who is a second Adam (1 Corinthians 15:45 and elsewhere).

Adam of Bremen d. c. 1085 •*German ecclesiastical historian*• As a canon at Bremen Cathedral from c. 1066, he compiled the *Gesta Hammaburgensis ecclesiae pontificum* (c. 1075, "History of the Archbishopric of Hamburg"), based on church archives and interviews with learned men. It is the most important source for the history, geography and politics of northern Europe between the 8th and 11th centuries, and contains the first written reference to the discovery of *Vínland* (North America) by the Norse explorer, **Leif the Lucky**, around the year 1000.

Adam, Adolphe Charles 1803–56 •*French composer*• Born in Paris, he was the son of the pianist Louis Adam (1758–1848). He wrote successful operas, such as *Le postillon de Longjumeau* (1835, "The Postilion of Longjumeau") and *Si j'étais roi* (1852, "If I Were King"), but is chiefly remembered for the ballet *Giselle* (1841), from a story by **Théophile Gautier**.

Adam, James 1730–94 •*Scottish architect*• Born in Kirkcaldy, Fife, he was the brother and partner of **Robert Adam** and son of the architect William Adam of Maryburgh (1689–1748). His fame has been overshadowed by that of his elder brother, though their names are linked inextricably in their work and cemented by their publication of *The Works in Architecture of Robert and James Adam* (3 vols, 1773, 1779, 1822).

Adam, Paul Auguste Marie 1862–1920 •*French novelist and essayist*• He was born in Paris. Among his numerous novels are *Chair molle* (1885, "Weak Flesh"), *Le mystère des foules* (1895, "The Mystery of the Masses"), *Lettres de Malaisie* (1879, "Letters from Malaysia"), and *La force* (1899, "The Power"). He was cofounder of *Symboliste* and other French literary periodicals.

Adam, Robert 1728–92 •*Scottish architect*• Born in Kirkcaldy, Fife, the brother of **James Adam**, he studied at Edinburgh and in Italy (1754–58). He established a practice in London in 1758, and during the next 40 years he and his brother James succeeded in transforming the prevailing Palladian fashion in architecture by a series of romantically elegant variations on diverse classical originals. Their style of interior decoration was based on ancient Greek and Roman, characterized by the use of the oval, and lines of decoration in hard plaster, enlivened by painted panels in low relief. Surviving examples of their work are Home House in London's Portland Square, Lansdowne House, Derby House, Register House in Edinburgh, the Old Quad of Edinburgh University, and the oval staircase in Culzean Castle, Ayrshire.

Adamic, Louis 1899–1951 •*US writer*• He was born in Blato,

Austria-Hungary (now in Slovenia), and emigrated to the US in 1913. He served in the US Army, and became naturalized in 1918. He began writing short stories in the early 1920s, utilizing his experiences and personal observations in his books—as in *Laughing in the Jungle* (1932), about an immigrant. Other works include *Dynamite: The Story of Class Violence in America* (1931), *My America 1928–38* (1938) and *The Eagle and the Root* (1950).

Adamnan, St *See* **Adomnan, St**

Adams, Abigail, *née* **Smith** 1744–1818 •*US letter writer and first lady*• She was born in Weymouth, Massachusetts, and educated at home. After marrying **John Adams**, the vice president then second President of the new republic, she made observations in her letters that were lively and astute. She is considered to have been a strong political influence, and her letters, published in 1840 by her grandson, paint a vivid picture of the times and reflect her strong views on women's rights.

“ ”

It is not in the still calm of life, or the repose of a pacific station, that great characters are formed ... Great necessities call out great virtues.

1780 Letter to John Quincy Adams, January 19.

Adams, Ansel Easton 1902–84 •*US photographer*• Born in San Francisco, he initially trained as a musician but became a professional photographer in 1927. His work is notable for his broad landscapes of the western US. A devotee of straight, clear photography and print perfection, he was one of the founders with **Edward Weston** of the Group f/64 (1932) and helped set up the department of photography at the New York Museum of Modern Art (1940). His publications included *Taos Pueblo* (1930) and *Born Free and Equal* (1944).

Adams, Bryan Guy 1959– •*Canadian rock singer and guitarist*• Born in Kingston, Ontario, he played in bands in Canada, then in 1978 began his solo career as a songwriter, with writing partner Jim Vallance. He began recording in 1979, but had his first major success with his third album, *Cuts Like a Knife* (1983). His original hard rock credentials began to fade after the global success of "(Everything I Do) I Do For You," and he has since taken a more commercial approach. He remains a consistent bestseller.

Adams, Douglas Noel 1952–2001 •*English novelist and scriptwriter*• Born and educated in Cambridge, he worked as script editor on the popular television series *Doctor Who* (1978–80). Adams is best known for his humorous radio series (later adapted for television), *The Hitchhiker's Guide to the Galaxy*, which he also wrote as a sequence of novels: *The Hitchhiker's Guide to the Galaxy* (1979), *The Restaurant at the End of the Universe* (1980), *Life, the Universe and Everything* (1982) and *So Long, and Thanks for All The Fish* (1984). A further novel, *Mostly Harmless*, was added in 1992.

Adams, Gerry (Gerard) 1948– •*Northern Ireland politician*• Born in Belfast, he became politically active at an early age, joining the Irish Nationalist Party, Sinn Fein (We ourselves), the political wing of the IRA (Irish Republican Army). During the 1970s he was successively interned and then released because of his connections with the IRA, and in 1978 was elected vice president of Sinn Fein and later president. In 1982 he was elected to the Northern Ireland Assembly and in the following year to the UK parliament as member for Belfast West. He declined to take up his seat at Westminster and in the 1992 general election lost it to Joe Hendron of the Social Democratic and Labour Party, only to win it back in 1997. His publications include the autobiographies *Falls Memories* (1982), *Cage Eleven* (1990) and *Before the Dawn* (1996) as well as such books as *Politics of Irish Freedom* (1986), *Pathway to Peace* (1988) and *An Irish Voice: The Quest for Peace* (1997).

Adams, Henry Brooks 1838–1918 •*US historian*• He was born in Boston, the son of diplomat and author Charles Francis Adams (1807–86), and grandson of **John Quincy Adams**, sixth President of the US, and educated at Harvard. He edited the *North American Review* (1870–76) and wrote two novels, *Democracy* (1880) and *Esther* (1884). He also wrote historical works, including the monumental *History of the United States during the Administrations of Jefferson and Madison* (9 vols, 1870–77), and an autobiography, *The Education of Henry Adams* (1907), which was awarded the Pulitzer Prize in 1919.

Adams, James Truslow 1878–1949 •*US historian*• Born in Brooklyn, New York, he made his fortune as a stockbroker by 1912, then devoted himself to a life of scholarship. He wrote numerous popular and critically well received books on US history, including *The Founding of New England* (1921, Pulitzer Prize).

Adams, John 1735–1826 •*Second President of the US*• Born in Braintree (now Quincy), Massachusetts, the son of a farmer, he studied at Harvard, was admitted to the bar in 1758, and settled in Boston in 1768. Of strongly colonial sympathies, he led the protest against the Stamp Act (1765). He also led the debate that resulted in the Declaration of Independence. He served in Congress until 1777, after which he had an extensive diplomatic career in Europe. He took part in negotiating a peace treaty with Great Britain, and then served as minister to Great Britain (1785–88). He became the first US vice president, under **George Washington** (1789), an office he found frustrating. Both were re-elected in 1792, and in 1796 Adams succeeded Washington as President, with **Thomas Jefferson** as vice president. Adams's presidency was marked by factionalism within his cabinet and party, especially over the issue of war with France. He was defeated by Jefferson on seeking re-election in 1800. Both Jefferson and Adams died on the same day—July 4, 1826, the 50th anniversary of the Declaration of Independence.

“ ”

I agree with you that in politics the middle way is none at all.

1776 Letter to Horatio Gates, March 23.

Adams, John, *alias* **Alexander Smith** c. 1760–1829 •*English seaman*• He took part in the mutiny against Captain **William Bligh** on the *Bounty* in 1789. With **Fletcher Christian** and seven other mutineers he founded a colony on Pitcairn Island. By 1809 Adams was the sole European survivor (most of the mutineers had been killed by their Tahitian companions in 1794). Revered as the patriarch of the Pitcairn settlement, he was given a royal pardon for his part in the mutiny.

Adams, Sir John 1920–84 •*English nuclear physicist*• Educated at Eltham School, London, he went from school into the Siemens Research Laboratory at Woolwich before working on wartime radar development. His work on short wavelength systems took him to Harwell, where he engineered the world's first major postwar accelerator (the 180–MeV cyclotron) in 1949. At CERN (Conseil Européen pour la Recherche Nucléaire) at Geneva, he engineered the 25–GeV proton synchroton (1954) and he became director general in 1960. From 1969 to 1976 he oversaw the building of the 450–GeV super-proton-synchroton. He was director general of CERN for a second time from 1976 to 1980.

Adams, John Coolidge 1947– •*US composer*• Born in Worcester, Massachusetts, he studied the clarinet as a boy. While still a music student at Harvard, he conducted the Boston Symphony Orchestra and the Boston Opera. Later he moved to San Francisco and became head of the department of composition at the Conservatory. His music is sometimes described as minimalist—a style involving much repetition of melodies and phrases—but is actually more imaginative. His major works are the opera *Nixon in China* (1987), *Harmonium* (1980) for chorus and orchestra, and the *Grand Pianola Music* (1981–82). He has also written for films, including *Matter of Heart* (1985).

Adams, John Couch 1819–92 •*English astronomer*• Born in Lidcot, Cornwall, he graduated as Senior Wrangler and first Smith's Prizeman (1843) at St John's College, Cambridge, and was elected to a fellowship there. He studied the unexplained irregularities in the motion of the planet Uranus, assuming that these were due to an unknown perturbing body in the space beyond Uranus, and by 1845 he had derived elements for the orbit of such a body, named Neptune. His prediction of Neptune occurred almost simultaneously with that of the French astronomer Urbain Jean Joseph Leverrier, while the German astronomer **Johann Galle**, working on these calculations, actually observed Neptune in 1846.

Adams, John Quincy 1767–1848 •*Sixth President of the US*• Born in Braintree (now Quincy), Massachusetts, the son of **John Adams**, the second President of the US, at the age of 14 he became private secretary to the US envoy in St Petersburg. After accompanying his father in Paris for the peace negotiations with Great Britain, he began to study at Harvard in 1785 and was admitted to the bar in 1790. He had an extensive and brilliant diplomatic career between 1794 and 1817, except for a period serving in the US Senate (1803–08). As secretary of state under President **James Monroe**, he negotiated with Spain the treaty for the acquisition of Florida (1819), and was the principal author of the Monroe Doctrine. As President (1825–29), he failed to establish a strong base of public and political support and was therefore frustrated by executive and congressional factionalism. After his defeat by **Andrew Jackson** in 1828, he was elected to the House of Representatives, where through the 1830s and 1840s he became noted as a promoter of antislavery views.

Adams, Richard George 1920– •*English novelist*• Born in Berkshire, he was educated at Worcester College, Oxford, and after wartime service in the army worked as a civil servant with the Department of the Environment (1948–74). He made his name as a writer with the bestselling *Watership Down* (1972), an epic tale of a community of rabbits. Later books have included *Shardik* (1974), *The Plague Dogs* (1977), *The Iron Wolf* (1980), *The Bureaucats* and *The Outlandish Knight* (2000).

Adams, Samuel 1722–1803 •*American revolutionary politician*• Born in Boston, the second cousin of **John Adams**, second President of the US, he was chief agitator at the Boston Tea Party (1773). He anticipated **Napoleon I** by calling the English "a nation of shopkeepers" in 1776. He was lieutenant governor of Massachusetts from 1789 to 1794, and governor from 1794 to 1797.

Adams, Will(iam) 1564–1620 •*English navigator*• Born in Gillingham, Kent, he served with the Dutch in 1598 as pilot major of a fleet bound for the Indies. As pilot of the Dutch vessel *de Liefde* he was stranded off Japan in April 1600. The first Englishman to visit Japan, he was thrown into prison as a pirate but was freed after building two ships for the shogun **Tokugawa** Ieyasu and received a pension and the rank of samurai.

Adamson, Joy Friederike Victoria, *née* **Gessner** 1910–80 •*British naturalist and writer*• She was born in Austria. Living in Kenya with her third husband, British game warden George Adamson (1906–89), she studied and painted wildlife, and made her name with a series of books about the lioness Elsa: *Born Free* (1960), *Elsa* (1961), *Forever Free* (1962), and *Elsa and Her Cubs* (1965). She was murdered in her home by a disgruntled employee.

Adcock, (Kareen) Fleur 1934– •*New Zealand poet*• Born in Papakura, Auckland, she was educated in the UK and became resident there from 1963. Writing in a lucid, mostly narrative manner, and preferring invented situations to autobiographical matter, she is most successful when writing about apparently marginal or peripheral locations, such as New Zealand, Ulster, or the English Lakes. Her first collection was *The Eye of the Hurricane* (1964), and was followed by *In Focus* (1977), and *Below Loughrigg* (1977). She was editor of the influential *Oxford Book of Contemporary New Zealand Poetry* (1982), and her *Selected Poems* appeared in 1983. More recently she edited the *Faber Book of 20th Century Women's Poetry* (1987), and published *Poems 1960–2000* (2000).

Addams, Charles Samuel 1912–88 •*US cartoonist*• Born in Westfield, New Jersey, he was a regular contributor to the *New Yorker* magazine from 1935 on, specializing in macabre humor and a ghoulish group which was immortalized on television in the 1960s as *The Addams Family*.

Addams, Jane 1860–1935 •*US social reformer and feminist and Nobel Prize winner*• She was born in Cedarville, Illinois, and attended Rockford College, Illinois. In 1899 she founded the first US settlement house, Hull House in Chicago, dedicated to settlement work among the immigrant poor, where she made her home. Addams worked to secure social justice by sponsoring legislation relating to housing, factory inspection, female suffrage and pacifism. She also campaigned for the abolition of child labor and the recognition of labor unions. Many of these reforms were adopted by the Progressive Party as part of its platform in 1912; she seconded **Theodore Roosevelt**'s nomination for President and was an active campaigner on his behalf. She shared the 1931 Nobel Peace Prize, awarded in recognition of her efforts to end hostilities in World War I. Her many books include *Democracy and Social Ethics* (1902) and *Peace and Bread in Time of War* (1922).

Addin, Muslih *See* **Sádi**

Addington, Henry *See* **Sidmouth, 1st Viscount**

Addison, Joseph 1672–1719 •*English essayist and politician*• Born in Milston, Wiltshire, he was educated at Charterhouse and Queen's College and Magdalen College, Oxford, of which he became a Fellow. A distinguished classical scholar, he began his literary career in 1693 with a poetical address to **John Dryden** and an *Account of the Greatest English Poets* (1694). Elected Member of Parliament for Malmesbury in 1708, he kept the seat for life. A prominent member of the Kit-Kat Club, and a friend of **Jonathan Swift** and **Richard Steele**, he contributed to Steele's periodical *The Tatler*, and in March 1711 he and Steele founded the *Spectator*, 274 issues of which were the work of Addison. Satirized by **Pope** as "Atticus," he became Secretary of State under Sunderland in 1717, but resigned his post a year later, owing to failing health.

“ ”

A perfect tragedy is the noblest production of human nature.

*1711 In the **Spectator**, no. 18.*

Addison, Thomas 1793–1860 •*English physician*• Born near Newcastle upon Tyne, he graduated in medicine at Edinburgh in 1815. He then settled in London, and became assistant physician (1824), and physician (1837) to Guy's Hospital. His chief researches were on pneumonia, tuberculosis and especially on the disease of the adrenal glands, known as Addison's disease (first described in 1849).

Adelaide, St, *German* **Adelheid** 931–99 •*Holy Roman empress*• The daughter of **Rudolf II** of Burgundy, she married Lothair, son of Hugh of Italy, in 947. After his death (950) she was imprisoned by his successor, **Berengar II**, but was rescued by King **Otto I (the Great)**, of Germany, who married her in 951. They became emperor and empress in 962. Their son was **Otto II**, over whom Adelaide exercised considerable influence when he succeeded his father (973). She became joint regent with the Empress **Theophano** for her grandson Otto III (980–1002), and sole regent from 991 to 996. She retired to a convent she had founded at Seltz in Alsace. Her feast day is December 16.

Adelaide, Queen 1792–1849 •*Consort of William IV of Great Britain*• She was the eldest daughter of George, Duke of Saxe-Meiningen. In 1818 she married William, Duke of Clarence, who succeeded his brother, **George IV**, as **William IV** (1830–37). She acquired some unpopularity through her alleged political interference during the agitation (1831–32) preceding the 1832 Reform Act. Their two children, both daughters, died in infancy, and William was succeeded by his niece, Queen **Victoria**.

Adenauer, Konrad 1876–1967 •*German statesman*• Born in Cologne, he studied at Freiburg, Munich and Bonn, before practicing law in Cologne, where he became Lord Mayor in 1917. A member of the Center Party under the Weimar Republic, he was a member of the Provincial Diet and president of the Prussian State Council (1920–33). In 1933 he was dismissed from all his offices by the Nazis, and imprisoned in 1934 and 1944. In 1945, under Allied occupation, he became Lord Mayor again, and helped found the Christian Democratic Union (CDU). As the first Chancellor of the Federal Republic of Germany (1949–63), he established closer links with the French, and aimed to rebuild West Germany on the basis of partnership with other West European nations through NATO and the EEC. Although relations were restored with the USSR, relations with other countries in Eastern Europe remained frigid.

Ader, Clément 1841–1926 •*French engineer and pioneer of aviation*• Born in Muret, he built a steam-powered bat-winged airplane, the *Eole*, in 1890. It made the first powered takeoff in history, but could not be steered and flew for no more than 50 meters.

Adès, Thomas Joseph Edmund 1971– *•English composer, pianist, and conductor•* Born in London, he studied at the Guildhall School of Music and at King's College and St John's College, Cambridge. His professional appointments include Composer in Association for the Hallé Orchestra (1993–95), Benjamin Britten Professor of Music at the Royal Academy of Music (1997–99) and artistic director of the Aldeburgh Festival (1999–). Among the compositions that have brought him international recognition are *Darknesse Visible* (1992), *Powder Her Face* (1995) and *Piano Quintet* (2000).

Adie, Kate (Kathryn) 1945– *•English television reporter•* Born in Sunderland, she took a degree in Scandinavian studies at Newcastle University, joined BBC Radio in 1969 as a technician and then producer, and moved to television in 1977. A reporter on the BBC's national news since 1979, she has reported from trouble spots around the world and has been chief news correspondent since 1989. She has won numerous awards and was given the honorary title Officer, Order of the British Empire in 1993.

Adjani, Isabelle Jasmine 1955– *•French actress•* Born in Paris to an Algerian father and German mother, she was an artistic child and ran her own theater group before making her film debut in *Le petit bougnat* (1969, "The Little Coal Man"). Hailed as "the phenomenon of her generation" by *Le Figaro*, she went on to pursue a film career, winning acclaim for her performances in *L'histoire d'Adèle H* (1975, *The Story of Adèle H*), *L'été Meurtrier* (1983, *One Deadly Summer*) and *Camille Claudel* (1988). She had increasingly limited her screen appearances but after a lengthy absence returned in *Toxic Affair* (1993), *La Reine Margot* (1994) and *Diabolique* (1996).

Adler, Alfred 1870–1937 *•Austrian psychiatrist•* He was born and trained in Vienna. He became a prominent member of the psychoanalytical group that formed around **Sigmund Freud** in 1900. His best-known work was *Studie über Minderwertigkeit von Organen* (1907, "Study of Organ Inferiority and Its Psychical Compensation"), which aroused great controversy. In 1911 he broke with Freud and developed his own "individual psychology," investigating the psychology of the individual considered as different from others. His main contributions to psychology include the concept of the inferiority complex, and his special treatment of neurosis as the exploitation of shock.

Adler, Dankmar 1844–1900 *•US architect•* Born in Stadtlengsfeld, Prussia, he emigrated to the US with his father in 1854 and studied architecture in Detroit and Chicago. In 1881 he entered into a partnership with **Louis Sullivan**. Their work profoundly influenced 20th-century architecture, serving as a bridge between the classical revival of the 19th century and the simple, functional style of modern architecture. Among their designs were the Wainwright Building in St Louis (1890), considered the first true skyscraper, and the Transportation Building at the world's Columbia Exposition in Chicago (1893).

Adler, Larry (Lawrence Cecil) 1914–2001 *•US musician and self-taught harmonica virtuoso•* Educated at Baltimore City College, he won the Maryland Harmonica Championship at the age of 13 and began his show business career in New York the following year. He played as a soloist with some of the world's leading symphony orchestras, and had pieces composed for him by **Ralph Vaughan Williams**, **Malcolm Arnold** and others. He also wrote the music for several films. He emigrated to the UK after being blacklisted in the US for alleged pro-Communist leanings.

" "

His first choice had been Yehudi Menuhin; he was lucky he got me. Menuhin on the mouth-organ is a mess.

*1984 On Henry Koster's casting for the film **Music for Millions** (1944).*

Adler, Stella 1903–92 *•US actress and teacher•* She was born in New York City, the daughter of the Yiddish actor Jacob Adler. She worked as an actress in both Yiddish theater and on Broadway, including notable roles in **Clifford Odets**'s *Awake and Sing* and *Paradise Lost* (1935) for the Group Theatre (founded by her husband, **Harold Clurman**). She also directed plays, but is best known for her work as a teacher. She founded the Stella Adler Conservatory of Acting (1949), where she encouraged students to use imagination and the play itself as their inspiration, in opposition to the self-absorbed Method acting of **Lee Strasberg**.

Adomnan or **Adamnan, St** c. 625–704 *•Irish monk•* Born and educated in Donegal, Ireland, he joined the Columban brotherhood of Iona at the age of 27, becoming abbot in 679. *Adomnan's Vision*, a professed account of his visit to heaven and hell, is a work of the 10th or 11th century, but the *Vita Sancti Columbae* is undoubtedly his, and reveals a great deal concerning the remarkable community of Iona. His feast day is September 23.

Adorno, Theodor 1903–69 *•German social philosopher and musicologist•* Born in Frankfurt, he studied there and became an associate of the Institute for Social Research and a member of the movement known as the "Frankfurt School," which also included **Max Horkheimer** and **Herbert Marcuse**. His philosophy is most fully presented in *Negative Dialectics* (1966). He argues that the task of "critical theory" is to dissolve all conceptual distinctions so that they cannot deform the true nature of reality. His sociological writings on music, mass culture and art are generally much more accessible, and include *Philosophie der neuen Musik* (1949), *Versuch über Wagner* (1952) and *Mahler* (1960).

Adrian IV or **Hadrian**, *originally* **Nicolas Breakspear** 1100–59 *•English cleric and pope•* Born in Abbots Langley, near St Albans, Hertfordshire, he was educated at Merton Priory and Avignon. He became a monk himself in the monastery of St Rufus, near Avignon, and in 1137 was elected its abbot. Complaints about his strictness led to a summons to Rome, where the pope, **Eugenius III**, recognized his qualities and appointed him Cardinal Bishop of Albano in 1146. In 1152 he was sent as papal legate to Scandinavia to reorganize the Church, where he earned fame as the "Apostle of the North." He was elected pope in 1154, the only Englishman to attain the title. One of his early acts is said to have been the issue of a controversial bull granting Ireland to **Henry II**.

Adrian VI, *originally* **Adrian Dedel** 1459–1523 *•Dutch pope•* Born in Utrecht, he studied in Louvain, and was made a doctor of theology (1491). He was appointed tutor in 1507 to the seven-year-old Charles (later Charles I of Spain and the Emperor **Charles V**), who when he became king in 1516 made Adrian Inquisitor General of Aragon and effective coregent with the dying **Ferdinand the Catholic**'s choice **Ximénes**. On Ximénes's death, Charles worked closely with Adrian and made him regent in his absence from 1520, but in 1522 on the death of **Leo X**, Adrian was almost unanimously elected pope. He tried in vain to attack the sale of indulgences which had prompted **Martin Luther**'s first revolt, and demanded Luther's punishment for heresy. He allied with the emperor, England and Venice against France, thus failing to unite Christendom against the Ottoman Turks, who captured Rhodes.

Adrian (of Cambridge), Edgar Douglas Adrian, 1st Baron 1889–1977 *•English physiologist and Nobel Prize winner•* Born in London, he trained in the Physiological Laboratory, Cambridge, where he became a lecturer, and also a Fellow of Trinity College, Cambridge. Devoting his career to the study of the nervous system, he recorded the electrical activity of nerve fibers, and showed that neural information is conveyed by variations in the frequency at which nervous impulses are transmitted. He also developed techniques to study and understand the gross electrical activity of the brain, electroencephalography (EEG), used clinically for the study of epilepsy and other brain disorders. For his work on the function of neurons he shared the 1932 Nobel Prize for physiology or medicine with Sir **Charles Sherrington**.

AE or **A.E.** *See* **Russell, George William**

Aegidius, St *See* **Giles, St**

Ælfric, *known as* **Grammaticus ("the Grammarian")** c. 955–c. 1020 *•Anglo-Saxon churchman and writer of vernacular prose•* He was a pupil of Bishop Æthelwold of Winchester, became a monk and later abbot at the new monastery of Cerne Abbas in Dorset, and subsequently the first abbot of Eynsham in Oxfordshire. He composed two books of 80 *Homilies* (990–92) in Old English, a paraphrase of the first seven books of the Bible, and a book of *Lives of the Saints* (993–98). He also wrote a widely used Latin grammar and Latin-English glossary, accompanied by a Latin *Colloquium* between a master, his pupil, and various craftsmen.

Aeschylus c. 525–c. 456 BC •*Greek tragic dramatist*• Born in Eleusis, he served in the Athenian army in the Persian Wars, was wounded at Marathon (490 BC) and probably fought at Salamis (480). His first victory as a poet was gained in the dramatic competitions of 484 and he won 13 first prizes in tragic competitions before losing to **Sophocles** in 468. Of some 60 plays ascribed to him, only 7 are extant: *The Persians, Seven against Thebes, Prometheus Bound, The Suppliants*, and the *Oresteia*, which comprises three plays about the murder of Agamemnon and its consequences (*Agamemnon, Choëphoroe* and *Eumenides*) and was his last great success on the Athenian stage (458). He was the first great writer of tragedy and must be credited with devising its classical form and presentation.

Aesop or **Esop** 6th century BC •*Semilegendary Greek author of fables*• Tradition represents him as a slave in Samos, and as a confidant of King **Croesus** of Lydia, for whom he undertook various unlikely missions. The fables attributed to him are simple tales, often of animals, devised to illustrate moral lessons, and are probably derived from many sources. They were first popularized by the Roman poet **Phaedrus** in the first century AD. **Erasmus** published an edition in Latin in 1513 which was widely used in schools. They also served as models for the verse fables of **Jean de La Fontaine**.

Æthelbert *See* **Ethelbert**

Æthelflæd *See* **Ethelflæd**

Æthelred *See* **Ethelred**

Æthelstan *See* **Athelstan**

Æthelthryth, St *See* **Etheldreda, St**

Aëtius, Flavius c. 390–454 AD •*Roman general*• He was born in Moesia. In AD 433 he became patrician, consul, and general in chief, and as such maintained the empire for 20 years. His main achievements were the destruction of the Burgundian Kingdom in eastern Gaul, and the defeat of **Attila** the Hun in 451. Three years later the jealous emperor **Valentinian III** stabbed him to death.

Aflaq, Michel 1910–89 •*Syrian politician*• He was born in Damascus and educated at the University of Paris. A schoolteacher and then journalist in Damascus, he was, with **Salah al-Din Bitar**, the founder of the Ba'ath Socialist Party (1943). The ideology behind the party was essentially socialist, with an emphasis on Arab unity. It was also anti-Zionist and instrumental in the foundation, with **Gamal Abd al-Nasser**, of the United Arab Republic (1958–61). Aflaq was ousted from Syria in 1966.

Africanus, Leo *See* **Leo Africanus**

Africanus, Sextus Julius c. 160–c. 240 AD •*Roman traveler and historian*• Born in Libya, he wrote *Chronologia*, a history of the world from the creation to AD 221.

Aga Khan III, *in full* **Aga Sultan Sir Mohammed Shah** 1877–1957 •*Imam (leader) of the Ismaili sect of Muslims*• Born in Karachi, India (now in Pakistan), he succeeded to the title in 1885. He founded Aligarh University (1910). He worked for the British cause in both World Wars, and in 1937 was president of the League of Nations assembly. He was succeeded as 49th Imam by his grandson Karim, the son of Aly Khan, as **Aga Khan IV**.

Aga Khan IV, Karim 1936– •*Imam (leader) of the Ismaili sect of Muslims*• Born in Geneva, Switzerland, the grandson of **Aga Khan III** and son of the late Aly Khan, he succeeded his grandfather as 49th Imam (1957). He was educated at Le Rosey in Switzerland, and later studied Asian history at Harvard.

Agassi, Andre 1970– •*US tennis player*• Born in Las Vegas, Nevada, he defeated **Stefan Edberg** to win the inaugural ATP world championship in 1991, and went on to win the men's singles at Wimbledon in 1992. He won the US Open in 1994 and 1999, the French Open in 1999, and the Australian Open in 1995, 2000 and 2001. He won the gold medal at the Atlanta Olympics in 1996. In 2001 he married **Steffi Graf**.

Agassiz, (Jean) Louis (Rodolphe) 1807–73 •*US naturalist and glaciologist*• Born in Môtier-en-Vully, Switzerland, he studied at the medical school of Zurich and at the universities of Heidelberg and Munich. His main interest was zoology and while still a student he published *The Fishes of Brazil* (1829) which brought him to the attention of **Georges Cuvier**. In 1832 he was appointed Professor of Natural History at the University of Neuchâtel, where he became interested in glaciers. In *Études sur les glaciers* (1840) and *Système glacière* (1847) he demonstrated that glaciers are not static but move, and developed the theory of the ice ages, giving credibility to the previously unacceptable ideas of Horace Bénédict de Saussure (1740–99) and **James Hutton**. He later became a professor at Harvard where, in 1859, he founded the Museum for Comparative Zoology, to which he donated his collections.

Agate, James Evershed 1877–1947 •*English critic and essayist*• Born in Manchester, and educated at Manchester Grammar School, he wrote dramatic criticism for several newspapers including the *Manchester Guardian*, and for the BBC, before becoming drama critic of the *Sunday Times* (1923). He wrote also on literature and films, and was the author of essays, novels and, notably, a nine-part autobiography in the form of a diary, *Ego* (1935–48).

“ ”

Long experience has taught me that in England nobody goes to the theatre unless he or she has bronchitis.

Attributed.

Agatha, St d. 251 AD •*Christian martyr*• Born in Catania, Sicily, she is said to have dedicated herself to God, rejected the love of the Roman consul Quintinian, and suffered a cruel martyrdom. She is the patron saint of Catania, and is invoked against fire and lightning; she is also the patron saint of bell founders. Her feast day is February 5.

Agathocles 369–289 BC •*Tyrant of Syracuse*• He fought the Carthaginians and invaded Tunisia, and took on the royal title (305 BC) in imitation of the Macedonian generals who succeeded **Alexander the Great**. A ruthless tyrant according to the hostile tradition, he nevertheless enjoyed popular support, and under him Sicily achieved her last period of independent power before the Roman conquest.

Agee, James 1909–55 •*US novelist, poet, film critic and screenwriter*• He was born in Knoxville, Tennessee, and educated at Harvard. He worked for several magazines before being commissioned to rove the Southern states during the Depression with the photographer Walker Evans, an assignment that produced the documentary *Let Us Now Praise Famous Men* (1941). He then wrote classic film scripts including *The African Queen* (1951) and *The Night of the Hunter* (1955). His unfinished semiautobiographical novel *A Death in the Family* (1955) was awarded a posthumous Pulitzer Prize.

Agnelli, Giovanni 1866–1945 •*Italian manufacturer*• Born in Villa Perosa, Piedmont, he was educated at a military academy and became a cavalry officer. In 1899 he founded Fiat (Fabbrica Italiana Automobili Torino).

Agnes, St c. 292–c. 304 AD •*Roman Christian*• She was probably martyred in Rome during the persecutions of **Diocletian**. The patron saint of virgins, she is said to have refused to consider marriage. Her feast day is January 21.

Agnes of Assisi, St 1197–1253 •*Italian Christian*• The daughter of Count Favorino Scifi, she joined her sister, who became St **Clare**, in a convent in 1211, in the face of violent parental opposition. They became cofounders of the order of the Poor Ladies of San Damiano (Poor Clares, formerly called Minoresses).

Agnesi, Maria Gaetana 1718–99 •*Italian mathematician and scholar*• Born in Milan and educated privately, she published books on philosophy and mathematics, and her mathematical textbook *Istituzioni analitiche* (1784) became famous throughout Italy. She is mainly remembered for her description of a versed sine curve, which following an early mistranslation of Italian, became known as the "witch of Agnesi."

Agnew, Spiro T(heodore) 1918–96 •*US politician*• Born in Baltimore, Maryland, the son of a Greek immigrant, he served in

World War II and studied law at the University of Maryland. In 1966 he was elected governor of Maryland on a liberal platform, supporting antidiscrimination and antipoverty legislation, but by 1968 he had become considerably more conservative. He became **Richard Nixon**'s running mate in the 1968 election, and took office as vice president in 1969. He resigned in 1973 after charges of corruption during his years in Maryland politics were brought against him.

“ ”

To some extent, if you've seen one city slum, you've seen them all.
1968 Election campaign speech, Detroit, October 18.

Agnon, Shmuel Yosef, *originally* **Shmuel Josef Czaczkes** 1888–1970 •*Israeli novelist and Nobel Prize winner*• Born in Buczacz, Galicia (now Poland), he went to Palestine in 1907, studied in Berlin (1913–24), then settled in Jerusalem and changed his surname to Agnon. He wrote an epic trilogy of novels on Eastern Jewry in the early 20th century, culminating in *Tmol Shilshom* (1945, "The Day Before Yesterday") as well as several volumes of short stories. He was awarded the Nobel Prize for literature, jointly with the Swedish author **Nelly Sachs**, in 1966.

Agostini, Giacomo 1943– •*Italian motorcyclist*• Born in Lovere, Bergamo, he won a record 15 world titles between 1966 and 1975, including the 500-cc title a record eight times (1966–72, 1975). He won 10 Isle of Man TT Races (1966–75), including the Senior TT five times (1968–72).

Agricola, Gnaeus Julius AD 40–93 •*Roman general*• He was born in Forum Julii (now Fréjus, Provence). Rome's longest-serving and most successful governor in Britain (AD 78–84), he subdued northern England and Lowland Scotland, and actively encouraged the development of Roman-style towns in the south. The circumnavigation of Britain by his fleet greatly impressed contemporaries. His son-in-law **Tacitus** wrote his biography.

Agrippa, Marcus Vipsanius c. 63–12 BC •*Roman general and politician*• He played an important role in various of **Augustus**'s military campaigns, including his victory over Sextus, the son of **Pompey** in 36 BC, and over **Mark Antony** at Actium (31). The Emperors **Caligula** and **Nero** were descendants of his marriage with Augustus's daughter, **Julia**.

Agrippina the Elder c. 14 BC–AD 33 •*Roman noblewoman*• She was the daughter of **Marcus Vipsanius Agrippa** and granddaughter of the emperor **Augustus**. She married **Germanicus Caesar**, and was the mother of **Caligula** and **Agrippina the Younger**. Regarded as a model of heroic womanhood, she accompanied her husband on his campaigns, and took his ashes home when he was murdered (AD 19). **Tiberius** banished her (30) to the island of Pandataria, where she died of starvation.

Agrippina the Younger AD 15–59 •*Roman empress*• She was the daughter of **Agrippina the Elder** and the Roman soldier **Germanicus Caesar**. She married first Cnaeus Domitius Ahenobarbus, by whom she had a son, the future emperor **Nero**. Her third husband was her uncle, the emperor **Claudius**, who subsequently made Nero his successor, ousting **Britannicus**, his own son by his former wife, **Messalina**. Agrippina then proceeded to poison all her son's rivals and enemies, and finally (allegedly) the emperor himself. She ruled as virtual coregent with Nero, but he had her put to death.

Aguinaldo, Emilio 1870–1964 •*Philippine revolutionary*• He led the uprising against Spain in the Philippines (1896–98), and against the US (1899–1901), but after being captured in 1901 took an oath of allegiance to the US.

Aguirre, José Antonio 1904–60 •*Basque politician*• Born into a middle-class, Carlist family, he became leader of the conservative Basque Nationalist Party (PNV). He was elected as the first president (Lendakari) of the Basque country (Euzkadi) after the Second Spanish Republic passed the Autonomy Statute in 1936. After the fall of Bilbao (1937), he took the government into exile in France. Following the outbreak of World War II, he was denied passage to England, and so undertook an extraordinary journey via Nazi Germany (complete with artificial mustache and glasses), Sweden, and Brazil to Uruguay. After the war, he headed the government-in-exile in France.

Agutter, Jenny (Jennifer Anne) 1952– •*English actress*• Born in Taunton, Somerset, she made her film debut at the age of 11 in *East of Sudan* (1964) and appeared in the role of Bobbie in *The Railway Children* (1970), which she had already played in a BBC television serial (1968). Hollywood success followed, with appearances in *Logan's Run* (1976), *The Eagle Has Landed* (1976), *Amy* (1981) and *An American Werewolf in London* (1981). She has appeared in numerous TV series, and returned to *The Railway Children* in 2000, playing Mother in a new TV film adaptation.

Ahab 9th century BC •*King of Israel*• A warrior king (c. 889–850 BC) and builder, he extended his capital city of Samaria and refortified Megiddo and Hazor. He fought against the Assyrians at the Battle of Karkar (853). To extend his alliances in the north he married **Jezebel**, daughter of the King of Tyre and Sidon, who introduced the worship of the Phoenician god, Baal. This aroused the furious hostility of the prophet **Elijah**. Ahab was killed in battle against the Syrians at Ramoth Gilead.

Ahern, Bertie 1951– •*Irish politician*• Born in Dublin, he studied at University College, Dublin, and began his career as an accountant. He became a member of the Dáil in 1977, a Minister of State for Defence in 1982, Lord Mayor of Dublin in 1986–87, President of Fianna Fáil in 1994 and Taoiseach (Prime Minister of Ireland) in 1997. As Taoiseach he was widely credited as one of the architects of the Good Friday Agreement in 1998.

Ahidjo, Ahmadou 1924–89 •*Cameroonian politician*• Born in Garoua, and educated at the École Supérieure d'Administration, Yaoundé, he was a radio operator in the post office before entering politics in 1947, being elected to the Territorial Assembly. He represented Cameroon in the Assembly of French Union (1953–57). From 1957 to 1960 he held senior positions in the Territorial Assembly of Cameroon. In 1960 he became President and was re-elected to that post in 1972, 1975 and 1980. He resigned in 1982 and went into voluntary exile in France.

Ahmad ibn Ibrahim al-Ghazi, *also known as* **Ahmad Gran** c. 1506–1543 •*Sultan of Adal, Somalia*• He declared a jihad against Christian Ethiopia in the 1530s, and with assistance from the Ottomans, dominated the empire until his defeat and death in battle against the emperor **Galawdewos** in 1543.

Ahmad Khan, Sir Sayyid 1817–98 •*Indian lawyer and educator*• One of the most influential Indian Muslims of the 19th century, he was an employee of the British East India Company and later a judge. He worked to further the Muslim cause in India. His greatest legacy was his establishment of the Mohammedan Anglo-Oriental College (now Aligarh Muslim University) in 1875 and the development of the Muslim Educational Conference, which eventually spread across India.

Ahmad Shah Durrani c. 1722–73 •*Founder and first monarch of Afghanistan*• He was born in Multan, Punjab. A cavalry general under the Persian emperor **Nadir Shah**, he was elected king of the Afghan provinces when the emperor was assassinated (1745). He established his capital at Kandahar, and made nine successful invasions of the Punjab and plundered Lahore (1752) and Delhi (1757). He defeated the Marathas at Panipat (1761), and the Sikhs near Lahore (1762), when he razed the Temple of Amritsar. After his death the great Afghan empire he had founded soon disintegrated.

Ahmed Arabi, *also called* **Arabi Pasha** 1839–1911 •*Egyptian soldier and nationalist leader*• An officer in the Egyptian army, he fought in the Egyptian-Ethiopian War (1875–79), took part in the officers' revolt that deposed **Ismail Pasha** (1879), and was the leader of a rebellion against the new khedive, **Tewfik Pasha**, in 1881 that led to the setting up of a nationalist government, with Ahmed Arabi as War Minister. The British intervened to protect their interests in the Suez Canal, and he was defeated at Tel-el-Kebir (1882). Sentenced to death, he was exiled to Ceylon (Sri Lanka) instead and pardoned (1901).

Ahmet I 1590–1617 •*Sultan of Turkey*• The son of **Mehmet III**, he was born in Manisa, and succeeded in 1603. He waged an unsuccessful war with Persia (Iran) from 1602 to 1612 and internal rebellion weakened Ottoman authority. He built the Blue Mosque in Constantinople (Istanbul).

Ahmet II 1642–95 •*Sultan of Turkey*• The son of Ibrahim, he was born in Edirne and succeeded in 1691. A disastrous defeat at Slankamen (1691) by the Austrians lost him Hungary and his Arab provinces were plagued by unrest.

Ahmet III 1673–1736 •*Sultan of Turkey*• He was the son of **Mehmet IV**, and in 1703 succeeded his brother Mustafa II. He sheltered **Karl XII** of Sweden after Poltava (1709), thus annoying **Peter I (the Great)**, with whom he waged a successful war terminated by the Treaty of Adrianople (1713), by which he regained Azov. He defeated the Venetians (1715), gaining the Morea, but soon after was defeated by the Austrians, losing territories around the Danube, especially Belgrade. He was deposed by the janissaries (1730) and died in prison.

Ahmose I 16th century BC •*King of ancient Egypt*• He founded the 18th Dynasty and freed Egypt from the alien Shepherd Kings (Hyksos).

Ahmose II 6th century BC •*King of ancient Egypt*• He ruled from 569 to 525 BC, cultivated the friendship of the Greeks, and greatly promoted the prosperity of Egypt. He built the temple of Isis at Memphis.

Ai Ch'ing *See* **Ai Qing**

Aidan, St, *known as* **the Apostle of Northumbria** d. 651 •*Christian monk*• Born in Ireland, he became a monk in the Celtic monastery on the island of Iona. In 635, he was summoned by King **Oswald** of Northumbria to evangelize the north. He established a church and monastery on the island of Lindisfarne, of which he was appointed the first Bishop, and from there traveled throughout Northumbria founding churches. His feast day is August 31.

Aidid, Mohamed Farah c. 1930–96 •*Somali soldier and politician*• Born in a rural area of Italian Somaliland, he served in the colonial police force and transferred to the Somali army following the country's independence in 1960. During the war with Ethiopia over the possession of Ogaden province he was promoted to general by President **Siad Barre**. In the early 1970s he lost that support and was imprisoned. Freed, following Barre's overthrow, he was appointed ambassador to India. In 1993 he was elected leader of the Hebr Gader clan during a civil war which ruined Somalia and led to intervention by UN forces. He was reported dead in 1996 and his son assumed control of the country.

Aiken, Conrad Potter 1889–1973 •*US poet and novelist*• Born in Savannah, Georgia, he was educated at Harvard, where his roommate was **T S Eliot**, and his contemporaries were **Robert Benchley** and **Walter Lippmann**. He made his name with his first collection of verse, *Earth Triumphant* (1914), followed by other volumes, including *Turns and Intervals* (1917) and *Senlin* (1925). His *Selected Poems* won the 1930 Pulitzer Prize. He also wrote short stories and novels.

Aiken, Howard Hathaway 1900–73 •*US mathematician and computer engineer*• Born in Hoboken, New Jersey, he grew up in Indianapolis, Indiana, and was educated at the universities of Wisconsin and Chicago, before moving to Harvard (1939–61). He succeeded in persuading IBM to sponsor the building of a calculating machine, resulting in the Automatic Sequence-Controlled Calculator (ASCC), or Harvard Mark I. Completed in 1943 and weighing 35 tons, this was the world's first program-controlled calculator, which Aiken regarded as the realization of **Charles Babbage**'s dream. A Mark II was built in 1947, but by then Aiken's design was being overtaken by the development of the stored-program computer.

Aiken, Joan Delano 1924–2004 •*English author*• She was born in Rye, East Sussex, the daughter of the writer **Conrad Aiken**. Her prolific output has included historical, crime and children's novels as well as plays, poetry and short stories. Adult fiction includes *Trouble with Product X* (1966) and *Dangerous Games* (1999), and her best-known children's works are the quartet of books beginning with *The Wolves of Willoughby Chase* (1962).

Ailey, Alvin, Jr 1931–89 •*US dancer and choreographer*• Born in Texas, he became a member of **Lester Horton**'s company in 1950, assuming directorship after Horton's death in 1953. In New York he trained with **Martha Graham**, Charles Weidman (1901–75) and Hanya Holm (1893–1992), while dancing and acting on Broadway and elsewhere. He retired from the stage in 1965 to devote himself to the Alvin Ailey American Dance Theater, a popular, multiracial modern dance ensemble he had formed in 1958. His most famous dance is *Revelations* (1960), an alternately mournful and celebratory study of religious spirit.

Ainsworth, William Harrison 1805–82 •*English historical novelist*• Born in Manchester, he studied for the law but married a publisher's daughter and began a literary career instead. He is chiefly remembered for popularizing the story of the highwayman **Dick Turpin** in *Rookwood* (1834) and the legend of Herne the Hunter in *Windsor Castle* (1843).

Ai Qing (Ai Ch'ing), *originally* **Jiang Haicheng** 1910–96 •*Chinese poet*• Born in Jinhua County, Zhejiang (Chekiang) Province, he studied painting in France (1928–31), but returned to China when the Japanese invaded, and was arrested for leftist activities and imprisoned (1932–35). His first published poem, "Dayanhe" (1934), named after his wet nurse, and his collection of poetry, also *Dayanhe* (1936), brought him fame. He was an active propagandist for Communist-controlled literature, but at the time of the Hundred Flowers Campaign (1956–57) he was accused of revisionism and stripped of his party membership. In 1959 he was exiled to a remote district in the desert area of Xinjiang (Sinkiang) for 17 years but was allowed to publish again from 1978.

Airy, Sir George Biddell 1801–92 •*English astronomer and geophysicist*• Born in Alnwick, Northumberland, he graduated (1823) from Trinity College, Cambridge, and was elected a Fellow. He became Lucasian Professor of Mathematics in 1826, and Plumian Professor of Astronomy and director of the Cambridge Observatory in 1828. His research on optics earned him the Copley Medal of the Royal Society (1831), and his investigations in planetary theory earned him the Royal Astronomical Society's Gold Medal (1833). Two years later he was appointed Astronomer Royal and director of the Greenwich Observatory, which he completely reorganized, and he later achieved worldwide acceptance of the Greenwich zero meridian. He was president of the Royal Society in 1871, four times president of the Royal Astronomical Society and was knighted in 1872.

Aïshah or **Ayeshah**, *known as* **the Mother of Believers** c. 613–78 •*Wife of the prophet Muhammad*• The daughter of **Abu Bakr**, the first caliph, she married the prophet **Muhammad** at the age of nine, and became the third and favorite of his nine wives, but had no children. When Muhammad died (632) she resisted the claims to the caliphate of **Ali**, Muhammad's son-in-law, in favor of her father. She fomented opposition against the third caliph, **'Uthman** (which led to his death), and when Ali became the fourth caliph (656) she led a revolt against him, but was defeated, captured, and exiled to Medina.

Aitken, Sir Max (John William Maxwell) 1910–85 •*British newspaper publisher*• He was born in Montreal, Canada, and educated at Westminster School and Pembroke College, Cambridge. He was the son of the 1st Lord **Beaverbrook**. He established a reputation as a playboy and socialite before the war, but served with great distinction as a fighter pilot, ending the war as a group captain. He became a Conservative Member of Parliament briefly, for Holborn (1945–50), before joining his father in running Beaverbrook Newspapers (*Daily Express* and *Sunday Express*). The newspapers were already in decline, and in 1977 they were sold to Trafalgar House. A yachting enthusiast, he became a leading ocean-racing skipper.

Akbar the Great, *originally* **Jalal-ud-Din Muhammad Akbar** 1542–1605 •*Mughal emperor of India*• Born in Umarkot, Sind, he succeeded his father, Humayun (1556), and took over from his regent in 1560. The start of his reign was marred by civil war and rebellion, but he soon gained control of the whole of India north of the Vindhya Mountains. He constructed roads, established a uniform system of weights and measures, and adjusted taxation. He was unusually tolerant toward non-Muslims, and greatly encouraged science, literature and the arts.

Akerman, Chantal 1950– •*Belgian film director, screenwriter and actress*•Born in Brussels, she studied film in Brussels and Paris, and began making short films, inspired by **Jean-Luc Godard**. Her experimental visual style was sparse and her narratives minimal, but strongly defined. Her demanding and often controversial films seek to reverse traditional male perspectives, and include *Jeanne Dielman* (1975), *Les rendez-vous d'Anna* (1978, *Rendezvous with Anna*), and her first English language film, *Histoires d'Amérique* (1989, *American Stories*).

Akhenaten and **Nefertiti** 14th century BC •*Egyptian king and queen of the 18th Dynasty*• Akhenaten (also spelt Akhenaton) was the assumed name of Amenhotep IV. He was the son of **Amenhotep III** (with whom he may have ruled jointly for a time) and his wife Tiy. Six years into his reign (1379–1362 BC) he renounced the worship of the old gods, introduced a purified and monotheistic solar cult of the sun disk (Aten), and changed his name. For these actions he became known as the "Heretic Pharaoh." He built a new capital at Amarna (Akhetaten), where the arts flourished. He was married to Nefertiti (Nofretete), who is thought to have been an Asian princess born in Mitanni. She is immortalized in the beautiful sculptured head found at Amarna in 1912. Two of their six daughters were married to Akhenaten's successors Smenkhare and **Tutankhamun**.

Akhmatova, Anna, *pseudonym of* **Anna Andreyevna Gorenko** 1888–1966 •*Russian poet*• Born in Odessa, she studied in Kiev before moving to St Petersburg. In 1910 she married the poet Nikolai Gumilev (1886–1921), who at first influenced her style, and with him and **Osip Mandelstam** started the neoclassicist Acmeist movement. She was divorced from Gumilev in 1918. After her early collections of terse but lyrical poems, including *Vecher* (1912, "Evening"), she developed an impressionist technique. After the publication of *Anno Domini MCMXXI* (1922), she was officially silenced until 1940 when she published *Iz shesti knig* ("From Six Books"), but in 1946 her verse was banned. She was reinstated in the 1950s. Her later works include *Rekviem* (Munich, 1963, "Requiem"), a moving cycle of poems on the **Stalin** purges.

Akiba ben Joseph *See* **Akiva ben Joseph**

Akihito 1933– •*Emperor of Japan*•Born in Tokyo, the eldest son of **Hirohito** (Showa), he was educated among commoners at the élite Gakushuin school, unlike previous princes. In 1959 he married Michiko Shoda (1934–), the daughter of a flour company president, who thus became the first nonaristocrat to enter the imperial family. On his becoming emperor (1989), the new Heisei (Achievement of Universal Peace) era commenced.

Akins, Zoë 1886–1958 •*US dramatist, novelist and poet*• Born in Humansville, Montana, she trained as an actress in New York, and in 1912 published *Interpretations*, a collection of poetry. Later, she concentrated on writing plays. Her most popular were *Déclassée* (1919), a society melodrama, followed by *Daddy's Gone A-Hunting* (1921), a sentimental portrayal of a failing marriage. In 1935, Akins was awarded the Pulitzer Prize for her dramatization of **Edith Wharton**'s novel, *The Old Maid*. Among her other works are the two novels, *Forever Young* (1941) and *Cake upon the Water* (1951).

Akiva or **Akiba ben Joseph** c. 50–135 AD •*Jewish rabbi, scholar and teacher in Palestine*• A pupil of Rabbi Eliezer, he founded a rabbinical school at Jaffna. He is credited with extensive exegetical attempts to relate Jewish legal traditions to scriptural texts, and with providing the basis for the Mishnah by his systematic grouping and codification of the *halakhoth* (legal traditions). He apparently supported the revolt against Rome under **Simon Bar Kokhba** in 132 AD against the emperor **Hadrian**, and was martyred by the Romans soon afterward, by being flayed alive.

Alain-Fournier, *pseudonym of* **Henri-Alban Fournier** 1886–1914 •*French writer*• Born in La Chapelle d'Angillon, the son of a country schoolmaster, he became a literary journalist in Paris, but was killed at St Rémy, Haute Meuse, soon after the outbreak of World War I. He left a semiautobiographical fantasy novel, one of the outstanding French novels of the 20th century, *Le Grand Meaulnes* (first published in the *Nouvelle Revue Française*, 1913, Eng trans in the US *The Wanderer*, 1958, in UK *The Lost Domain*, 1966), and a few short stories, collected in *Miracles* (1924).

Alamán, Lucas 1792–1853 •*Mexican politician and historian*• Born in Guanajuato, he trained as a mining engineer, and once faced the Inquisition for possessing banned books. As a deputy to the Spanish Cortés (1820–21) summoned by **Ferdinand VII** in the wake of the Riego Revolt (1820), he spoke out for Mexican independence and in favor of monarchy. Mexico's most influential Conservative, Minister of State to Emperor **Iturbide** (1822), Foreign Minister and Minister of State for Antonio Bustamante and President **Santa Anna**, he founded the National Museum and died shortly after completing his monumental *Historia de Mexico* (1842–52, "History of Mexico").

Alanbrooke (of Brookeborough), Alan Francis Brooke, 1st Viscount 1883–1963 •*British field marshal and master of strategy in World War II*•Born in Bagnères-de-Bigorre, France, he trained at the Royal Military Academy, Woolwich. In World War II he commanded the 2nd Corps of the British Expeditionary Force (1939–40), covering the evacuation from Dunkirk in France. He became Commander-in-Chief Home Forces (1940–41), and Chief of the Imperial General Staff (CIGS) from 1941 to 1946. As principal strategic adviser to **Churchill**, he accompanied him to the conferences with **Franklin D Roosevelt** and **Stalin**. He became a field marshal in 1944, and was created baron in 1945 and viscount in 1946.

Alarcón, Juan Ruiz de, *in full* **Juan Ruiz de Alarcón y Mendoza** c. 1580–1639 •*Spanish dramatist*• Born in Taxco, Mexico, he was neglected for generations, except by plagiarists, but is now considered a leading playwright of the Golden Age of Spanish drama. He was a master of both heroic tragedies and, notably, character comedies, and his *La verdad sospechosa* ("The Suspicious Truth") was the model for **Corneille**'s *Le Menteur*.

Alarcón, Pedro Antonio de 1833–91 •*Spanish writer*• Born in Guadix, he served with distinction in the African campaign of 1859–60. He published a vivid war diary, travel notes and poems, but is best known for his novels, particularly *Sombrero de tres picos* (1874, Eng trans *The Three-Cornered Hat*), on which **Manuel de Falla** based his ballet, *The Three-Cornered Hat*.

Alaric I, *also called* **Alaric the Goth** c. 370–410 AD •*King of the Visigoths*•Born in Dacia, he led the Gothic auxiliaries of the eastern Roman Emperor **Theodosius I (the Great)** in AD 394. He was elected King of the Visigoths (395) and invaded Greece, but was eventually driven from the Peloponnese by **Flavius Stilicho** and the troops of the Roman western empire. In 408 he laid siege to Rome and in 410 he entered the city, which his troops looted for three days. The sack of Rome, the first capture of the city by foreigners in 800 years, is vividly described by **Edward Gibbon**. Both contemporaries and later historians consider 410 as the end of the Roman Empire. Alaric set off to invade Sicily, but died at Cosenza.

Alaric II AD 450–507 •*King of the Visigoths*• He reigned (from AD 485) over Gaul south of the Loire, and most of Spain. In 506 he issued a code of laws known as the Breviary of Alaric (*Breviarium Alaricianum*). An Arian Christian, he was routed and killed at the Battle of Vouillé, near Poitiers, by the Orthodox **Clovis**, King of the Franks.

Alba, Ferdinand Alvarez de Toledo *See* **Alva, Ferdinand Alvarez de Toledo**

Alban, St 3rd century AD •*Roman soldier and first Christian martyr in Britain*• He was, according to **Bede** and some earlier writers, a pagan Romano-Briton living in the town of Verulamium (now St Albans), who was scourged and beheaded, around 300 AD, for helping a fugitive Christian priest who had converted him. His feast day is June 22.

Albee, Edward Franklin, III 1928– •*US dramatist*• Born in Washington DC, he was adopted by a rich theater-owning family, and educated in Connecticut. His play *The Zoo Story* (1958) was influenced by the theater of the absurd and began his attack on the complacency of the US middle class. He continued this in further one-act plays, such as *The American Dream* (1960). He had an enormous success with *Who's Afraid of Virginia Woolf?* (1962, filmed 1966), which, with caustic wit, exposes a marriage built on illusions. Other works include *A Delicate Balance* (1966, Pulitzer Prize), *Box* and *Quotations from Chairman Mao Tse-Tung* (both

1968). His dramatizations include *Malcolm* (1965) and *Lolita* (1981). He had little success with his later plays until *Three Tall Women* (1991, Pulitzer Prize) revived his career.

“ ”

People would rather sleep their way through life than stay awake for it.

Quoted in Joseph F McCrindle (ed) ***Behind the Scenes*** *(1971).*

Albers, Josef 1888–1976 •*US painter and designer*• Born in Bottrop, Westphalia, Germany, he trained in Berlin, Essen and Munich, and from 1920 was involved with the Bauhaus, where he studied and later taught. In 1933 he emigrated to the US where he spread the Bauhaus ideas. He became a US citizen in 1939. As a painter he was interested chiefly in color relationships, and from 1950 he produced a series of wholly abstract canvases, *Homage to the Square*, exploring this theme.

Albert I c. 1255–1308 •*King of Germany*• The son of **Rudolf I** of Habsburg, he was elected King of Germany in opposition to the deposed Adolf of Nassau, whom he then defeated and killed at Göllheim (1298). He proceeded energetically to restore the power of the monarchy and reduce that of the electoral princes, but was murdered by his disaffected nephew, John.

Albert I 1875–1934 •*King of the Belgians*• Born in Brussels, the younger son of Philip, Count of Flanders, he succeeded his uncle, **Leopold II**, in 1909. At the outbreak of World War I he refused a German demand for the free passage of their troops, and after a heroic resistance led the Belgian army in retreat to Flanders. He commanded the Belgian and French army in the final offensive on the Belgian coast (1918), and reentered Brussels in triumph. He was killed in a climbing accident in the Ardennes, and was succeeded by his son, **Leopold III**.

Albert, *called* **the Bear** c. 1100–70 •*Count of Ballenstëdt*• Count of Ballenstëdt from 1123, he founded the House of Ascania which ruled in Brandenburg for 200 years. In 1134, in return for service in Italy, Emperor Lothar III granted him extensive lands between the Elbe and the Oder. He obtained Brandenburg itself (1150) by a treaty formerly made with Count Pribislav, and took the title margrave.

Albert 1490–1568 •*1st Duke of Prussia*• Born in Ansbach, he was the younger son of the Margrave of Ansbach, and was elected the last Grand Master of the Teutonic Order in 1511. He embraced the Reformation, and, on the advice of **Martin Luther**, declared himself secular Duke of Prussia (1519). He cultivated Protestant Denmark and Sweden against the Emperor **Charles V**, but had to surrender privileges to the nobles to sustain his finances.

Albert, Prince 1819–61 •*Prince consort to Queen Victoria of Great Britain*• Born at Schloss Rosenau, near Coburg, he was the younger son of the Duke of Saxe-Coburg-Gotha and Louisa, daughter of the Duke of Saxe-Gotha-Altenburg. He was educated in Brussels and Bonn, and in 1840 married his first cousin, Queen **Victoria**—a marriage that became a lifelong love match. He was given the title Prince Consort (1857) and throughout their marriage he was, in effect, the Queen's private secretary. He was interested in the encouragement of the arts and the promotion of social and industrial reforms. He designed Osborne House on the Isle of Wight, was a patron of Sir **Edwin Landseer**, and he planned and managed the Great Exhibition of 1851, whose profits enabled the building of museum sites in South Kensington (including the Victoria and Albert Museum, the Science Museum, and the Natural History Museum) and the Royal Albert Hall (1871). His death, possibly from cancer rather than typhoid, led to a long period of seclusion by his widow. The Albert Memorial in Kensington Gardens, designed by Sir **George Gilbert Scott**, was erected in his memory (1871).

“ ”

I have had wealth, rank and power, but, if these were all I had, how wretched I should be.

1861 Attributed last words.

Alberti, Leon Battista 1404–72 •*Italian architect*• Born in Genoa, he worked in Florence from 1428 and became one of the best-known figures of the Renaissance. His *Della Pittura* (1436) contains the first description of perspective construction. Influenced by **Marcus Vitruvius Pollio**, he wrote *De re aedificatoria* (10 vols, 1485), which stimulated interest in antique Roman architecture. His own designs, which include the churches of San Francesco in Rimini and Santa Maria Novella in Florence, are among the best examples of the pure classical style.

Alberti, Rafael Merello 1902–99 •*Spanish poet and dramatist*• A member of the great “Generation of '27,” which included **Federico García Lorca**, **Luis Cernuda** and Pedro Salinas, he began as a painter. He fought against General **Franco** and in 1939 went into exile to Argentina, then Rome, only to return home after Franco's death. His best poetry is considered to be his fifth collection *Sobre los ángeles* (1929, English version, *Concerning the Angels*, 1967), showing the influences of surrealism and the Spanish critic **José Ortega y Gasset**.

Albertus Magnus, St, Graf von Bollstädt, *known as* **Doctor Universalis** c. 1200–80 •*German philosopher and cleric*• Born in Lauingen, he studied in Padua, and, entering the newly founded Dominican order, taught theology in the schools of Hildesheim, Ratisbon, and Cologne, where St **Thomas Aquinas** was his pupil. In 1262 he retired to his convent in Cologne to write. He was a faithful follower of **Aristotle** as presented by Jewish, Arabian and Western commentators, and comprehensively documented 13th-century European knowledge of the natural sciences, mathematics and philosophy. Of his works the most notable are the *Summa theologiae* and the *Summa de creaturis*. He was canonized in 1931 and named Doctor of the Church by Pope **Pius XI**. His feast day is November 15.

Albinus *See* **Alcuin**

Albright, Madeleine Korbel, *née* **Korbel** 1937– •*US diplomat*• Born in Czechoslovakia, she was educated at Wellesley College and Columbia University. She was a staff member of the National Security Council during the administration of President **Carter**, and has been a senior adviser to prominent Democrats. She was the US's permanent representative to the United Nations (1993–96), the first US ambassador to the UN to have been born outside the US. She was appointed secretary of state in President **Clinton**'s cabinet in 1996—the first woman to hold that office.

Albumazar or **Abu-Mashar** 787–885 •*Arab astronomer and astrologer*• Born in Balkh, Afghanistan, he spent much of his life in Baghdad, where he became the leading astrologer of his day, and his books were widely circulated. Despite his fantastic theories about the beginning and end of the world, he did valuable work on the nature of the tides.

Albuquerque, Afonso de, *called* **the Great** 1453–1515 •*Portuguese viceroy of the Indies*• Born near Lisbon, he landed on the Malabar Coast, India, in 1502, conquered Goa and established what was to become, with Ceylon, Malacca and the island of Ormuz, the Portuguese East Indies. In 1515 he was replaced peremptorily by the king, and died shortly afterward.

Alcaeus c. 620–after 580 BC •*Greek lyric poet*• He was born and lived in Mytilene on the island of Lesbos, where he was a contemporary of **Sappho**. He wrote in a variety of meters, including the four-line Alcaic stanza named after him and used notably (in Latin) by **Horace**. He composed drinking songs, hymns, political odes and love songs, of which only fragments now remain.

Alcalá Zamora, Niceto 1877–1949 •*Spanish politician*• A lawyer and landowner from Andalusia, he was Liberal Minister of Development (1917) and Minister of War (1922). In opposing the dictatorship of **Miguel Primo de Rivera** (1923–30), he joined the Republican cause and, with the establishment of the Second Republic (1931), headed both the provisional government and the Constituent Cortes's first administration. He resigned in October of that year over the new constitution's anticlerical clauses, but accepted the presidency in December. He was removed in 1936 after a decisive vote of the Cortes against him (238–5), and died in exile in Buenos Aires.

Alcamenes 5th century BC •*Greek sculptor*• He was the pupil and rival of **Phidias** in Athens. A Roman copy of his *Aphrodite* is in the

Louvre, Paris, and his marble *Procne with Itys* has been restored to the Acropolis at Athens.

Alcibiades c. 450–404 BC •*Athenian statesman, a member of the powerful Alcmaeonid family*• After the death of his father Clinias in 447, Alcibiades was brought up in the house of **Pericles**. **Socrates** also exercised a considerable influence over him. Alcibiades was the principal mover in sending an expedition against Syracuse in 415 BC, which he jointly commanded. While the fleet was preparing to sail, all the "Herms" (small statues of Hermes) in Athens were mutilated in a single night. Alcibiades' enemies contrived to blame him for this, and he was recalled to stand trial for sacrilege. He fled to Sparta and advised the Spartans to send help to Syracuse, which contributed substantially to the Athenians' defeat in 413 and caused them economic problems at home. He fell out with the Spartans in 412 and rejoined the Athenian side, directing Athenian operations in the eastern Aegean, where he won several notable victories. He was unjustly blamed for the Athenian defeat off Notium (406), and went into voluntary exile, where he actively intrigued with the Persians. He was assassinated in 404 BC.

Alcindor, Lew *See* **Abdul-Jabbar, Kareem**

Alcmaeon fl. 520 BC •*Greek physician and philosopher, the first recorded anatomist*• Born in Crotona, Italy, he founded original medical theories based on empirical surgical practice. He was the true discoverer of the eustachian tubes, and the pioneer of embryology through anatomical dissection.

Alcock, Sir John William 1892–1919 •*English aviator*• Born in Manchester, he served in the Royal Naval Air Service in World War I and later became a test pilot for Vickers Aircraft, and with **Arthur Whitten Brown** as navigator, he was the first to fly the Atlantic Ocean nonstop (June 14, 1919). The journey, in a Vickers-Vimy biplane from Newfoundland to Ireland, took 16 hours and 27 minutes. Both men were knighted after the flight. Soon afterward Alcock was killed in an airplane accident in France.

Alcott, (Amos) Bronson 1799–1888 •*US teacher and Transcendentalist*• Born near Wolcott, Connecticut, he was the father of **Louisa M Alcott**. He started as a peddler, became an itinerant teacher, then opened an unorthodox, unsuccessful school in Boston, a vegetarian cooperative farming community (called Fruitlands), which also failed, and published books on the principles of education. An ardent Transcendentalist, and a brilliant teacher and educationist, he was eventually appointed Superintendent of Schools in Concord, Massachusetts, in 1859. In 1879 he established the Concord Summer School of Philosophy and Literature.

Alcott, Louisa May 1832–88 •*US writer*• Born in Germantown, Philadelphia, the daughter of **Bronson Alcott**, she was a nurse in a Union hospital during the Civil War, and published her letters from this period as *Hospital Sketches* in 1864. In 1868 she achieved enormous success with *Little Women*, which drew on her own home experiences, and became a children's classic. A second volume, *Good Wives*, appeared in 1869, followed by *An Old Fashioned Girl* (1870), *Little Men* (1871) and *Jo's Boys* (1886). She also wrote adult novels and was involved in women's suffrage and other reform movements.

Alcuin, *Anglo-Saxon name* **Ealhwine**, *known as* **Albinus** c. 737–804 •*Northumbrian scholar, and adviser to the emperor Charlemagne*• Born in York, he was educated at the cloister school, of which in 778 he became master. In 781, returning from Rome, he met **Charlemagne** at Parma, and joined the court at Aix-la-Chapelle (now Aachen). Here he devoted himself first to the education of the royal family, but through his influence the court became a school of culture for the Frankish empire, inspiring the Carolingian Renaissance. His works comprise poems, works on grammar, rhetoric, and dialectics, theological and ethical treatises, lives of several saints, and over 200 letters.

Alda, Alan, *originally* **Alphonso Joseph d'Abruzzo** 1936– •*US actor and director*• Born in New York City, the son of actor Robert Alda (1914–86), he performed with his father at the Hollywood Canteen (1945) and progressed, via summer stock and small television appearances, to his Broadway debut in *Only in America* (1959). He made his film debut in *Gone Are the Days* (1963), but it was his role as Captain "Hawkeye" Pierce in the Korean War comedy series *M*A*S*H* (1972–83), which he also wrote and directed at times, that brought him his greatest popularity. His acerbic sense of humor has been highlighted in films such as *Sweet Liberty* (1986) and *A New Life* (1988). He also appeared in the **Woody Allen** films *Crimes and Misdemeanors* (1989), *Manhattan Murder Mystery* (1993) and *Everyone Says I Love You* (1996).

Alden, John c. 1599–1687 •*Pilgrim leader*• Born in England, he traveled to America with the Pilgrims as a cooper on the *Mayflower* and became a leader of the Plymouth Colony, serving as assistant to the governor. **Henry Wadsworth Longfellow**'s poem *The Courtship of Miles Standish* gives a fictional account of the marriage of John Alden and Priscilla Mullins.

Alder, Kurt 1902–58 •*German organic chemist and Nobel Prize winner*• Born in Königshütte (now Chorźow, Poland), he studied chemistry at the universities of Berlin and Kiel and became a professor at Kiel in 1934. In 1928, in collaboration with **Otto Diels**, he reported a facile reaction between a diene and a compound with an activated double bond to give a cyclic product (the Diels-Alder reaction), a reaction valuable in synthetic organic chemistry. For its discovery, Alder and Diels were jointly awarded the Nobel Prize for chemistry in 1950.

Aldington, Richard, *originally* **Edward Godfree** 1892–1962 •*English poet, novelist, editor and biographer*• Born in Hampshire, he was educated at London University, and in 1913 became editor of *The Egoist*, the periodical of the imagist school. His first volume of poetry was called *Images 1910–1915* (1915). His experiences in World War I left him ill and bitter, and this led to his best-known novel *Death of a Hero* (1929). He also wrote many biographies, including *Wellington* (1946), which was awarded the James Tait Black Memorial Prize. He was married to the poet **Hilda Doolittle** 1913 to 1937.

Aldiss, Brian Wilson 1925– •*English science-fiction writer and novelist*• He was born in Dereham, Norfolk, and educated at Framlingham College. His prolific career began with his first novel, *The Brightfount Diaries*, in 1955. He was literary editor of the *Oxford Mail* (1958–69), and had considerable success with *The Hand-Reared Boy* (1970) and *A Soldier Erect* (1971). He is best known, however, as a writer of science fiction, such as *Non-Stop* (1958, entitled *Starship* in the US), *Frankenstein Unbound* (1973), *Helliconia Spring* (1982), *Helliconia Summer* (1983), *Helliconia Winter* (1985) and *Dracula Unbound* (1991). He also writes graphic novels, has edited many books of short stories, and produced histories of science fiction such as *Billion Year Spree* (1973). He collaborated with **Stanley Kubrick** in an unsuccessful attempt to bring his short story "Supertoys Last All Summer Long" (1969) to the big screen; it later appeared as *A.I. Artificial Intelligence* (2001) under the direction of **Steven Spielberg**.

" "

Science fiction is no more written for scientists than ghost stories are written for ghosts.

1961 ***Penguin Science Fiction****, introduction.*

Aldrin, Buzz (Edwin Eugene) 1930– •*US astronaut*• Born in Montclair, New Jersey, he was educated at West Point and the Massachusetts Institute of Technology. He was an air force pilot in the Korean War and became an astronaut in 1963. He set a space walking record in 1966 during the flight of Gemini 12, and during the 1969 expedition in Apollo 11 with **Neil Armstrong** and **Michael Collins** he became the second man to set foot on the moon. He published *Men From Earth* in 1989.

Aldus Manutius, *also called* **Aldo Manucci** or **Manuzio** c. 1450–1515 •*Italian scholar and printer*• He was born in Bassiano and was the founder of the Aldine Press, which produced the first printed editions of many Greek and Roman classics. He was first to use italics on a large scale.

Alea, Tomás Gutiérrez *See* **Gutiérrez Alea, Tomás**

Aleichem, Sholem or **Sholom** or **Shalom**, *pen name of* **Solomon J Rabinowitz** 1859–1916 •*Russian Jewish writer*• Born in Pereyaslev,

Ukraine, he worked for some years as a rabbi, then devoted himself to writing and Yiddish culture, contributing to the Hebrew magazine *Hamelitz*. In 1893 he moved to Kiev, but the pogroms of 1905 drove him to the US, where he attempted to establish himself as a playwright for the Yiddish theater in New York. He traveled widely, giving readings of his work in many European cities, and from 1908 to 1914 spent most of his time in Italy to improve his health. He returned to settle in New York in 1914. His short stories and plays portray Jewish life in Russia in the late 19th century with vividness, humor and sympathy. His other works include *Jewish Children* (Eng trans 1920), *Stories and Satires* (Eng trans 1959) and *Old Country Tales* (Eng trans 1966). The popular musical *Fiddler on the Roof* is based on his stories.

Aleixandre, Vicente 1898–1984 •*Spanish poet and Nobel Prize winner*• Born in Seville, he suffered from renal tuberculosis in his youth, which forced him to remain in Spain after the Civil War despite his Republican sympathies. Among his early works were *Ámbito* (1928, "Ambit") and *Pasión de la tierra* (1935, "Passion of the World"), but it was his collected poems, *Mis poemas mejores* (1937), that established his reputation as a major poet. His later publications include *Antología total* (1976, "Complete Works"). He was awarded the Nobel Prize for literature in 1977.

Alekhine, Alexander Alexandrovich 1892–1946 •*French chess player*• Born in Moscow, Russia, he gained his Master title at St Petersburg in 1909. The Russian Revolution left him without his legacy and he worked as a magistrate before taking up French citizenship. Having prepared more thoroughly than his opponent, he defeated **José Capablanca** in 1927 to win the world championship. Married four times to older women, and an alcoholic, he was successful in defenses of his title until he faced **Max Euwe** in 1935. Alekhine regained his title by beating Euwe in a return match two years later.

Alekseyevich, Pyotr *See* **Kropotkin, Peter**

Alemán, Mateo 1547–1610 or 1620 •*Spanish novelist*• Born in Seville, he led a disorderly, poverty-stricken life in Spain, and ultimately emigrated to Mexico in 1608. His great work is the important picaresque novel *Guzmán de Alfarache* (1599, second part 1604, Eng trans *The Spanish Rogue*, 1622, 1924), in which the decline and ultimate repentance of a runaway boy mirrors the sinful and corrupt state of Spain.

Alemán Lacayo, Arnoldo 1946– •*Nicaraguan politician*• Born in Managua, he studied law at the National Autonomous University and was leader of the pro-Somoza Liberal Student Youth Organization in the 1960s. He was imprisoned as a counterrevolutionary in 1980 and placed under house arrest in 1989. He served as Mayor of Managua (1990–95) and was president of the Federation of Central American Municipalities (1993–95). Having become leader of the Liberal Party Alliance in 1996, he became President of Nicaragua in 1997, defeating former President **Daniel Ortega**.

Alembert, Jean le Rond d' 1717–83 •*French philosopher and mathematician*• He was born in Paris and studied law, medicine and mathematics at the Collège Mazarin. In 1743 he published *Traité de dynamique*, developing the mathematical theory of **Newton**ian dynamics, including the principle named after him. Until 1758 he was **Diderot**'s principal collaborator on the *Encyclopédie*, of which he was scientific editor, and wrote the *Discours préliminaire*, proclaiming the philosophy of the French Enlightenment.

Alepoudelis, Odysseus *See* **Elytis, Odysseus**

Alexander I c.1077–1124 •*King of Scotland*• He was the fourth son of **Malcolm III Canmore** and Queen **Margaret**. In 1107 he succeeded his brother, Edgar, but only to the area north of the Forth (see **David I**). He married Sibylla, a natural daughter of **Henry I** of England.

Alexander II 1198–1249 •*King of Scotland*• Born in Haddington, East Lothian, the son of **William I**, he succeeded to the throne in 1214. He supported the English barons against King **John**, later concluding a peace treaty with **Henry III** (1217) and marrying Henry's eldest sister, Joan (1221). After the death of Joan in 1238 he married Marie (1239), a French noblewoman. His reign represents an important landmark in the making of the Scottish kingdom. He renounced his hereditary claims to Northumberland, Cumberland, and Westmoreland by the Treaty of York (1237), and concentrated on the vigorous assertion of royal authority in the north and west.

Alexander III 1241–86 •*King of Scotland*• In 1249 he succeeded his father, **Alexander II**, and in 1251 married Princess Margaret (1240–75). Soon after he had come of age, he defended the kingdom against the Norwegians, who were routed at Largs (1263). By the Treaty of Perth (1266), Scotland gained the Hebrides and the Isle of Man. In the later part of his reign, the kingdom enjoyed a period of peace and prosperity.

Alexander I 1777–1825 •*Emperor of Russia*• Born in St Petersburg, the grandson of **Catherine the Great**, he became emperor in 1801 and instituted a wide range of reforms, notably in administration, education, science, and the system of serfdom. In 1805 Russia joined the coalition against **Napoleon I**, but after a series of military defeats was forced to conclude the Treaty of Tilsit (1807) with France. When Napoleon broke the treaty by invading Russia in 1812, Alexander pursued the French back to Paris. He took an active part in the destruction of Napoleon's retreating army at Dresden and Leipzig in 1813 and entered Paris with the Allies in 1814. He claimed and received Poland at the Congress of Vienna (1814–15). During the last years of his reign his increased religious mysticism, influenced by the cosmopolitan religious mystic Madame von Krüdener (1764–1824), contributed to his founding of the Holy Alliance (1815), a document delineating Christian principles, and intended to exclude the House of **Bonaparte** from power in France, which was signed by Emperor Francis I (see **Francis II**), **Frederick William III**, and other European leaders. His mysterious death at Taganrog caused a succession crisis which led to the attempted revolutionary coup of the Decembrists.

Alexander II, *known as* **the Liberator** 1818–81 •*Czar of Russia*• Born in St Petersburg, he was educated by his father **Nicholas I**. In 1841 he married Princess Marie of Hesse-Darmstadt (1824–80). He succeeded to the throne (1855) during the Crimean War, and signed the Treaty of Paris that ended it (1856). The great achievement of his reign was the emancipation of the serfs in 1861 (hence his nickname), followed by judicial and social reforms. He maintained friendly relations with Prussia, especially in the Franco-Prussian War (1870–71), and married his only daughter Marie to Alfred, second son of Queen **Victoria**. Although he sold Alaska to the US (1867), he extended the Russian Empire in the Caucasus and central Asia, and successfully fought against Turkey (1877–78), winning the liberation of Bulgaria. In 1880, soon after the death of his first wife, he married his mistress, Katharina Dolgorukova (1847–1922). Despite his liberal views, his government was severe in repressing peasant unrest and revolutionary movements. After several assassination attempts he was mortally injured by a bomb thrown at him in St Petersburg.

“ ”

It is better to abolish serfdom from above than to wait for it to abolish itself from below.

1856 Speech, March 30.

Alexander III 1845–94 •*Czar of Russia*• Born in St Petersburg, he was the younger son and successor of **Alexander II** (1881). In 1866 he married Princess Marie Dagmar (1847–1928), daughter of King **Christian IX** of Denmark and sister of Queen **Alexandra** of Great Britain. He was openly critical of his father's reforming policies before his accession. He followed a repressive domestic policy, especially in the persecution of Jews, and promoted Russian language and traditions and the Orthodox Church. Abroad, his policy was cautious, and he consolidated Russia's hold on central Asia to the frontier of Afghanistan, provoking a crisis with Great Britain (1885). Despite several assassination attempts, he died a natural death and was succeeded by his son **Nicholas II**.

Alexander I 1888–1934 •*King of the Serbs, Croats and Slovenes, and king of Yugoslavia*• Born in Cetinje, the second son of **Peter I**, he distinguished himself in the Balkan War (1912–13), was Commander in Chief of the Serbian army in World War I, and acted as regent for his father (1914–21). He was King of the Serbs, Croats and Slovenes (1921–29), and tried to build up a strong and unified Yugoslavia, imposing a royal dictatorship (1929). In 1934 he set out on a state visit to France but was assassinated in Marseilles by a Macedonian terrorist in the pay of Croatian nationalists.

Alexander III, *originally* **Orlando Bardinelli** c. 1105–81 •*Italian pope*• Born in Siena, he taught law at Bologna, and became adviser to Pope **Adrian IV**. As pope (1159–81), he was engaged in a struggle with the Emperor **Frederick I (Barbarossa)**, who supported antipopes against him. The emperor was finally defeated at the Battle of Legnano (1176) and peace was concluded by the Treaty of Venice (1177). The other notable conflict of church and state in which he was involved was that between **Henry II** of England and **Thomas à Becket**. He also called the third Lateran Council (1179).

Alexander VI, *originally* **Rodrigo Borgia** 1431–1503 •*Spanish pope*• He was born in Játiva, Spain, and studied law at Bologna University. Father to **Cesare Borgia**, **Lucrezia Borgia**, and other children, he was made a cardinal by his uncle, Pope Calixtus III (1378–1458, pope from 1455), and became pope on the death of Innocent VIII as a result of flagrant bribery. The long absence of the popes from Italy had weakened their authority and curtailed their revenues. To compensate for this loss, Alexander endeavored to break the power of the Italian princes, and ruthlessly appropriate their possessions for the benefit of his own family. He apportioned the New World between Spain and Portugal and introduced the censorship of books. Under his pontificate **Savonarola** was executed as a heretic.

Alexander VII, *originally* **Fabio Chigi** 1599–1667 •*Italian pope*• He was born in Siena. As nuncio in Cologne, he had protested against the Treaty of Westphalia (1648), which ended the Thirty Years' War. His papal election (1655) was said to have been settled by belief in his opposition to nepotism, to which he later succumbed. He supported the Jesuits against the Jansenists and forbade the translation of the Roman Missal into French. He was also responsible for the construction of the colonnade in the piazza at St Peter's, Rome.

Alexander VIII, *originally* **Pietro Vito Ottoboni** 1610–91 •*Italian pope*• Born in Venice, he was an aristocrat who was elected (1689) in succession to the anti-French **Innocent XI** with the help of the French ambassador. Alexander, however, continued Innocent's policy of hostility to **Louis XIV**'s policy of Gallicanism, condemning the 1682 declaration by the French clergy in its favor. He was hostile to the Jesuits and was pleased at the defeat of Louis XIV's ally, the ousted **James VII and II** of Scotland, England and Ireland, at the Battle of the Boyne (1689).

Alexander Nevsky c. 1220–63 •*Russian grand prince, hero and saint*• Born in Vladimir, he received his surname from his victory over the Swedes on the River Neva (1240). He later defeated the Teutonic Knights (1242) and the Lithuanians (1245), and also helped maintain Novgorod's independence from the Mongol Empire. He was canonized by the Russian Orthodox Church in 1547, and is the subject of a film by **Sergei Eisenstein**.

Alexander of Battenberg *See* **Battenberg, Prince Alexander of**

Alexander of Hales, *known as the* **Irrefragable Doctor** c. 1170–1245 •*English scholastic philosopher*• Born in Hales, Gloucestershire, he studied in Paris and became Professor of Philosophy and Theology there, later entering the Franciscan order. His chief work was the *Summa universae theologiae*, a system of instruction for the schools of Christendom.

Alexander of Tralles 6th century •*Greek physician*• Born in Tralles, Huydra, he practiced in Rome, and was the author of *Twelve Books on Medicine*, a major work on pathology which was current for several centuries in Latin, Greek and Arabic.

Alexander Severus AD 208–35 •*Roman emperor*• He was the cousin and adopted son of **Heliogabalus**, whom he succeeded in AD 222. A weak ruler, under the influence of others, he failed to control the military. Though successful against the Sassanid Artaxerxes (233), he was murdered by mutinous troops during a campaign against the Germans. Fifty years of political and military instability in the Roman Empire followed his death.

Alexander the Great 356–323 BC •*King of Macedonia*• Alexander was born in Pella, the son of **Philip II** of Macedon, and **Olympias**. He was educated by eminent Greek teachers including **Aristotle**. He was only 16 when Philip appointed him regent in his absence on a campaign against Byzantium, and at the battle fought against an alliance of Greek cities at Chaeronea (338 BC), Alexander commanded the left wing of the Macedonian army and took a decisive part in the action. When Philip was assassinated in 336, Alexander, not yet 20, became king. He ruthlessly crushed rebellions in Illyria and razed Thebes to the ground as a warning to the Greeks (335). He waged successful military campaigns in Persia, and marched on to Palestine. In Egypt, where he was welcomed as a liberator from the Persians, he founded Alexandria, the first and most famous of his new cities (331). The great cities of Babylon, Susa and the Persian capital Persepolis opened their gates to Alexander. In 326 Alexander proceeded to the conquest of India, and at the Hydaspes (Jhelum) overthrew the local king Porus in a hard-fought and costly battle. At Babylon he was planning further ambitious conquests, of Arabia and to the west, when he was taken ill after a banquet, and died 11 days later. An unclear succession resulted in a long power struggle for parts of the empire between Alexander's leading generals. In later antiquity, Alexander was viewed variously as a ruthless conqueror and destroyer at one extreme, and as a farsighted statesman pursuing a civilizing mission for the world at the other. Modern scholarship continues to fluctuate between these opposing views.

“ ”

The end and object of conquest is to avoid doing the same thing as the conquered.

As given in Plutarch ***Alexander****, 40.2.*

Alexander, Bill, *originally* **William Alexander Paterson** 1948– •*English stage director*• He was born in Hunstanton, Norfolk, and worked at the Bristol Old Vic (1971–73) and the Royal Court Theatre, London, before joining the Royal Shakespeare Company (RSC) in 1977 as an assistant to **John Barton** and **Trevor Nunn**. He became resident (later associate 1984–91, and honorary associate) director at the RSC, directing new plays such as **Howard Barker**'s *The Hang of the Gaol* (1978) and *Country Dancing* (1986). His Shakespearean productions include *Richard III* (1984), *The Merry Wives of Windsor* (1985), *A Midsummer Night's Dream* (1986), *The Merchant of Venice* (1987), *Cymbeline* (1987, 1989) and *Much Ado About Nothing* (1990). He was artistic director of the Birmingham Repertory Theatre from 1993 to 2000.

Alexander, Franz Gabriel 1891–1964 •*US psychoanalyst*• He was born in Budapest, Hungary and received his MD from Budapest University. During World War I he was a medical officer, after which he studied and then worked at the Institute for Psychoanalysis in Berlin. He settled permanently in the US in 1932, where he founded the Chicago Institute for Psychoanalysis. His work on psychosomatic disorders, among which he included peptic ulcer, essential hypertension, and rheumatic arthritis, was especially influential.

Alexander, Grover Cleveland, *known as* **Pete** 1887–1950 •*US baseball player*• Born in Elba, Nebraska, he was one of the greatest right-handed pitchers in the history of the game. In a long and brilliant career, he played for the Philadelphia Phillies (1911–17), Chicago Cubs (1918–26) and St Louis Cardinals (1926–29). He shared (with Christy Mathewson, 1880–1925) a record of 373 wins. The story of his life was told in the film *The Winning Team* (1952).

Alexander (of Tunis), Sir Harold Rupert Leofric George Alexander, 1st Earl 1891–1969 •*Anglo-Irish field marshal and politician*• Born in Caledon, County Tyrone, in World War I he commanded a battalion of the Irish Guards on the Western Front. Between 1932 and 1939 he was a staff officer with the Northern Command and in India. In 1940 he was the last officer to leave Dunkirk. His North Africa command (1942–43) brought one of the most complete victories in World War II. He commanded the invasions of Sicily and Italy (1943), was appointed field marshal on the capture of Rome in June 1944 and became Supreme Allied Commander in the Mediterranean for the rest of the war. He later became Governor-General of Canada (1946–52) and Minister of

Defence in **Churchill**'s Conservative government (1952–54).

Alexander, Jean 1925– •*English actress*• She was born in Liverpool, and after working as a library assistant, she joined the Adelphi Guild Theatre in Macclesfield (1949) and toured for two years. She spent the next 11 years with a variety of repertory companies appeared in television plays like *Jacks and Knaves* (1961) before being cast in the long-running *Coronation Street* (1964–87). Her character of the dowdy, tactless gossip Hilda Ogden won her the Royal Television Society's Best Performance award (1984–85). She later appeared in the series *Last of the Summer Wine* (1988) and the film *Scandal* (1989).

Alexander, John White 1856–1915 •*US painter*• Born in Allegheny, Pennsylvania, he worked as an illustrator for *Harper's* magazine, and as a portrait painter, owning studios in Paris and New York. His many portraits include those of **Auguste Rodin**, **Mark Twain**, **Thomas Hardy**, **Grover Cleveland**, **Andrew Carnegie**, **Walt Whitman** and **Robert Louis Stevenson**.

Alexander, Samuel 1859–1938 •*Australian philosopher*• Born of Jewish parents in Sydney, he moved to England and studied at Balliol College, Oxford (1877). He was made a Fellow of Lincoln College, Oxford, where he was tutor in philosophy until 1893, when he was appointed Professor of Philosophy at Manchester University. His growing concern for the situation of European Jewry led him to introduce his colleague **Chaim Weizmann** (later to become leader of the Zionist movement) to **Arthur James Balfour**, a meeting which led to the Balfour Declaration (1917), establishing the principle of a Jewish national home, and eventually to the establishment of the state of Israel.

Alexander, William *See* **Stirling, 1st Earl of**

Alexandra, Queen 1844–1925 •*Queen consort of Edward VII of Great Britain and Northern Ireland*• Born in Copenhagen, the eldest daughter of King **Christian IX** of Denmark, she married Edward (1863) when he was Prince of Wales. She engaged in charity work, founding the Imperial (Royal) Military Nursing Service in 1902.

Alexandra, Princess, *in full* **Helen Elizabeth Olga Christabel**, *also known as* **the Hon Mrs Angus Ogilvy** 1936– •*British princess*• The daughter of George, Duke of **Kent** and Princess Marina of Greece, she married (1963) the Rt Hon Sir Angus Ogilvy (1928–). They have a son, James (1964–), and a daughter, Marina (1966–).

Alexandra (Alix) Fyodorovna 1872–1918 •*German princess, and empress of Russia as the wife of Nicholas II*• Born in Darmstadt, the daughter of Grand Duke Louis of Hesse-Darmstadt and **Alice Maud Mary** (the daughter of Queen **Victoria**), she married Nicholas in 1894 and tended to dominate him. Deeply pious and superstitious, she came under the evil influence of the fanatical **Rasputin** and meddled disastrously in politics. When the revolution broke out, she was imprisoned by the Bolsheviks with the rest of the royal family (1917), and later shot in a cellar at Yekaterinberg.

Alexis or **Aleksei**, *originally* **Sergei Vladimirovich Simansky** 1877–1970 •*Russian Orthodox ecclesiastic*• He accommodated to the Soviet regime to save Orthodoxy. First elected to a bishopric in 1913, he was made Metropolitan of Leningrad (now St Petersburg) in 1933 and, despite one spell of exile, was able to survive to earn a reputation for his courage during the Siege of Leningrad. He was then elected Patriarch of Moscow and All Russia in 1944, in succession to Patriarch Sergei (1876–1944). He generally supported Soviet attitudes to the world at large in order to protect his Christian flock at home, in which he had some success.

Alexis or **Aleksei I Mikhailovich** 1629–76 •*Second Romanov Czar of Russia*• He was born in Moscow, and succeeded his father **Michael Romanov** in 1645. Personally abstemious and benevolent, he had great interest in Western culture and technology. Abroad, he waged war against Poland (1654–67), regaining Smolensk and Kiev, while at home his attempts to place the Orthodox Church under secular authority brought him into conflict with the patriarch, Nikon. His new code of laws (1649) legitimized peasant serfdom in Russia and he generally strengthened the centralizing autocracy. He suppressed a great peasant revolt led by Stenka Razin (1670–71). His son became **Peter I (the Great)**.

Alexis or **Aleksei Petrovich** 1690–1718 •*Russian prince*• The eldest son of **Peter I (the Great)**, he was born in Moscow. A heavy drinker, having opposed the czar's reforms, he was excluded from the succession, and escaped to Vienna and then to Naples. Induced to return to Russia, he was condemned to death, but pardoned, only to die in prison a few days after. His son became czar, as **Peter II**.

Alexius I Comnenus 1048–1118 •*Byzantine emperor*• Born in Constantinople (Istanbul), he was founder of the Comnenian dynasty (see **Comnenus**). He strengthened the weakened Byzantine state, and defeated the attacking Turks and Normans. He was able to use the warriors of the First Crusade (1096–1100) to recover lands in Asia Minor, but relations with them were complicated by the setting up of the Latin states in Antioch, Edessa, Jerusalem and Tripoli. His reign is well known from the *Alexiad*, the biography written by his daughter **Anna Comnena**.

Alfarabius *See* **Farabi, Abu Nasr al-**

Alferov, Zhores I(vanovich) 1930– •*Russian physicist and Nobel Prize winner*• Born in Vitebsk, Belorussia (now Belarus), he was educated at the Leningrad Electrotechnology Institute and worked at the Ioffe Institute of Physics and Technology. His work on semiconductors and quantum electronics contributed to the development of fast transistors, as used in radio link satellites and mobile telephone base stations. In recognition of his achievements he shared the 2000 Nobel Prize for physics with **Herbert Kroemer** and **Jack S Kilby**.

Alfieri, Vittorio, Count 1749–1803 •*Italian poet and dramatist*• He was born in Asti, near Piedmont, inherited a vast fortune at the age of 14, and traveled throughout Europe before turning his hand to writing, achieving great success with his first play, *Cleopatra*, in 1775. In Florence in 1777 he met the Countess of Albany who became his mistress. He wrote numerous tragedies, six comedies, and *Abele*, a "tramelogedia," or mixture of opera and tragedy. He also wrote an autobiography, *Vita* (1803).

Alfonsin (Foulkes), Raul 1927– •*Argentine politician*• Born in Chascomas and educated at military and law schools, he joined the Radical Civil Union (UCR) in 1945. Following time spent in local government and imprisonment by the **Perón** government, he was elected President in 1983 and ensured that several leading military figures were brought to trial for human rights abuses. In 1986 he was joint winner of the Council of Europe's human rights prize. He was replaced as president by **Carlos Menem** in 1989 but remained leader of the UCR until 1991.

Alfonso I, *also called* **Affonso** or **Afonso Henriques** 1110–85 •*Earliest king of Portugal*• He was born in Guimarães. His mother, Theresa of Castile, ruled until 1128 in his name after his father, Henry of Burgundy, first Count of Portugal, had died. He attacked the Moors, defeated them at Ourique (1139), and proclaimed himself king, so securing Portuguese independence from León. He took Lisbon (1147), and later, all Galicia, Estremadura and Elvas.

Alfonso III, *called* **the Great** c. 838–910 •*King of León, Asturias and Galicia*• He ruled from 866 until his death. Helped by civil war in the Muslim eminate of Córdoba, he fought over 30 campaigns and gained numerous victories over the Moors, occupied Coimbra, and extended his territory as far as Portugal and Old Castile. His three sons conspired against him and eventually dethroned him.

Alfonso V, *called* **the Magnanimous** 1396–1458 •*King of León, Castile and Sicily*• He succeeded his father, Ferdinand I, in 1416. At home he faced a jealous aristocracy and a restless Catalonian peasantry. Abroad, after a series of campaigns against Corsica, Sardinia and Naples, he made himself King of Naples (1442), never returning to Spain.

Alfonso X, *called* **the Astronomer** or **the Wise** 1221–84 •*King of León and Castile*• Born in Burgos, Spain, he succeeded his father, Ferdinand III, in 1252. He captured Cádiz and Algarve from the Moors, and thus united Murcia with Castile. In 1271 he crushed an insurrection headed by his son Philip, but was defeated in a second uprising under another son, Sancho (1282). Alfonso was the founder of a Castilian national literature and fostered work on Spanish history and the Bible, as well as compiling a code of laws and a planetary table.

Alfonso XII 1857–85 •*King of Spain*• The son of **Isabella II**, he was born in Madrid and educated in Vienna and England. After a period of republican rule following the overthrow of his mother (1868), he was formally proclaimed king (1874) and in 1876 he suppressed the last opposition of the Carlists (supporters of the Spanish pretender **Don Carlos** de Bourbon and his successors). Tactful and judicious, if politically inexperienced, he summoned the Cortes (parliament) to provide a new constitution, and under the influence of his Prime Minister, Antonio Cánovas del Castillo, his reign was a time of peace and relative prosperity. In 1879 Alfonso XII married Maria Christina (1858–1929), daughter of Archduke Charles Ferdinand of Austria. He was succeeded by his posthumously born son, **Alfonso XIII**.

Alfonso XIII 1886–1941 •*King of Spain*• He was born in Madrid, the posthumous son of **Alfonso XII**, and his mother, Maria Christina of Austria, acted as regent until 1902, when he assumed full power. In 1906 he married Princess Ena of Battenberg, granddaughter of Queen **Victoria**. His reign was increasingly autocratic and unpopular. After neutrality during World War I, he was blamed for the Spanish defeat in the Moroccan War (1921), and from 1923 he associated himself with the military dictatorship of **Miguel Primo de Rivera** (1923–30). In 1931 Alfonso agreed to elections, which voted overwhelmingly for a republic. He refused to abdicate, but left Spain, and died in exile.

Alford, Kenneth, *pseudonym of* **Frederick J Ricketts** 1881–1945 •*English composer*• One of the world's best-known composers of military music, he was born in London and first proved his musical prowess as an organist. His gifts as a composer were first shown, however, at the military academy Kneller Hall. His best-known march, "Colonel Bogey," written in 1914, was later used to great effect in the film *The Bridge on the River Kwai* (1957).

Alfred, *called* **the Great** 849–99 •*Anglo-Saxon king of Wessex*• Born in Wantage, Berkshire, he was the youngest son of King Æthelwulf. As a child he traveled to Rome and the Frankish court of **Charles I** (the Bald). He succeeded his brother **Ethelred I** as king (871), when Viking invaders were occupying the north and east of England, and Wessex was under constant attack. Early in 878 the Danish army led by **Guthrum** invaded Wessex but Alfred defeated them at Edington, Wiltshire (878). He repelled another invasion (885), captured London (886), and made a treaty formalizing the partition of England, with the Danelaw under Viking rule. Modeling his kingship on **Charlemagne** and his Frankish successors, he created a ring of fortified strongholds (*burhs*) around his kingdom and built a fleet (hence his reputation as the "father of the English navy"). His strategy enabled his successors to reconquer the Danelaw. He promoted education in the vernacular, fostered all the arts, and inspired the production of the *Anglo-Saxon Chronicle*. He himself translated Latin books into Anglo-Saxon, including the *Pastoral Care* of Pope **Gregory I (the Great)**, the *Consolations of Philosophy* by **Boethius**, and the works of St **Augustine** and the Venerable **Bede**. He was buried in Winchester.

Alfvén, Hugo Emil 1872–1960 •*Swedish composer and violinist*• Born in Stockholm, he was a composer in the late Romantic tradition, and wrote five symphonies and the ballet *Prodigal Son* (1957) amongst many other works. He made much use of folk melodies and his best-known piece is *Midsommarvaka* (1904, "Midsummer Vigil," better known as the *Swedish Rhapsody*).

Alger, Horatio 1832–99 •*US writer and clergyman*• Born in Revere, Massachusetts, he was educated at Harvard. He became a Unitarian minister, and wrote boys' adventure stories on the "poor boy makes good" theme, such as *Ragged Dick* (1867) and *From Canal Boy to President* (1881).

Algren, Nelson 1909–81 •*US novelist*• Born in Detroit, he moved early to Chicago, where he trained as a journalist at the University of Illinois, before becoming a migrant worker during the Depression. In Chicago again from 1935, he became a leading member of the "Chicago school of realism." He produced a series of uncompromising novels, including *Somebody in Boots* (1935), *Never Come Morning* (1942) and *The Man with the Golden Arm* (1949), a novel about drug addiction regarded by some as his best work. He had a transatlantic affair with **Simone de Beauvoir**, which is described in her novel *Les Mandarins* (1954) and in her autobiography.

" "

I went out there for a thousand a week, and I worked Monday, and I got fired Wednesday. The guy that hired me was out of town Tuesday.

In Malcolm Crowley (ed) ***Writers at Work*** *(1958).*

Alhazen, *Latinized name of* **Abu 'Ali al-Hasan ibn al-Haytham** c. 965–c. 1040 •*Arab mathematician*• Born in Basra, Iraq, he wrote a work on optics (known in Europe in Latin translation from the 13th century) giving the first account of atmospheric refraction and reflection from curved surfaces, and the construction of the eye. In later life he turned to mathematics and wrote on **Euclid**'s treatment of parallels and on **Apollonius of Perga**'s theory of conics.

Ali, *properly* **'Alī ibn Abī Ṭālib** d. 661 •*Fourth Islamic caliph*• The cousin of the prophet **Muhammad**, whose daughter **Fatima** he married. He withdrew, or was excluded from, government during the caliphates of **Abu Bakr** and **Omar**, and disagreed with **'Uthman** on the interpretation of the Koran and application of the law. Although not involved in the death of 'Uthman he was elected caliph soon after, but encountered opposition, led by **Mu'Awiyah**, governor of Syria, which was the beginning of a major Sunni-Shiite division within Islam that has persisted to the present day.

Ali, Maulana Muhammad 1878–1931 and **Ali, Maulana Shaukat** 1873–1938 •*Muslim Indian political activists*• Both brothers were closely associated with the internal politics of Aligarh College prior to World War I. In 1911 Muhammad Ali founded *Comrade*, an English-language weekly paper espousing pan-Islamic views. Shortly afterward he moved the paper to Delhi, and also bought an Urdu paper, *Hamdard*, which he used to set forth his political views. In 1913 Shaukat Ali organized *Anjuman-i-Khuddam-i-Kaaba* to provide Indian support for Muslim causes in the Middle East. The continued activities of this movement after the outbreak of World War I resulted in the detention of both brothers between 1915 and 1919. On their release, they joined the Khilafat Conference, to protest against British policy toward the Sultan of Turkey, who was also Caliph of Islam. Muhammad soon became the leader. Because of **Mahatma Gandhi**'s support of the Khilafat Movement, the brothers allied with the Indian National Congress and Muhammad persuaded the Khilafat Conference to adopt Gandhi's strategy of Satyagraha (literally, "truth-force"–a philosophy of nonviolent resistance to evil). The brothers were again arrested in 1921. In 1923, Muhammad Ali was elected president of the Congress. **Kemal Atatürk**'s 1924 abolition of the caliphate undermined the Khilafat movement, which continued on with dwindling support and influence. During the late 1920s both brothers broke with Congress but remained highly influential national political leaders.

Ali, Muhammad *See* **Mehemet 'Ali**

Ali, (Chaudri) Muhammad 1905–80 •*Pakistani politician*• Born in Jullundur, India, he was educated at Punjab University. In 1947, on the partition of India, he became the first Secretary-General of the Pakistan government. In 1951 he became Finance Minister, and in 1955 Prime Minister. He resigned a year later because of lack of support from members of his own party, the Muslim League.

Ali, Muhammad, *formerly* **Cassius Marcellus Clay** 1942– •*US boxer*• Born in Louisville, Kentucky, he won the Olympic amateur light-heavyweight title in Rome in 1960. After turning professional, he won the world heavyweight title in 1964 by defeating Sonny Liston in seven rounds at Miami Beach (and subsequently in a rematch at Lewiston, Maine). He joined the Black Muslim sect in 1964, changed his name to Muhammad Ali, and refused military service on religious grounds. For this he was sentenced to prison and stripped of his title in 1967, but he was able to return to professional boxing in 1970 when the Supreme Court quashed his conviction. He lost to Joe Frazier in 1971, but defeated him in January 1974 and regained his title by beating **George Foreman** in October of that year in Zaire. He lost it again (to Leon Spinks) in February 1978 but regained it in a rematch in September of that year. He thus made history by regaining the world heavyweight title twice. He retired in 1981.

“ ”

Float like a butterfly, sting like a bee.

*c. 1964 Quoted in G Sullivan **Cassius Clay** (1964), chapter 8.*

Ali Bey 1728–73 •*Egyptian ruler*• Born a slave in Akkhasia in the Caucasus, he distinguished himself in the service of Ibrahim Katkhuda and became chief of the **Mamluks**. He became Sultan in 1768 and established in Egypt an adminstration independent of Ottoman overlordship. He conquered Syria and part of Arabia. He died soon after being defeated by an army raised by one of his sons-in-law. He was an excellent administrator, and under him Egypt briefly achieved independence for the first time in over 200 years, but after his death, it lapsed into virtual anarchy.

Alice Maud Mary 1843–78 •*British princess*• Born at Buckingham Palace, London, she was the second daughter of Queen **Victoria**. In 1862 she married Prince Louis of Hesse-Darmstadt, who succeeded his uncle as Grand Duke (1877). They had four daughters: the eldest became the mother of Louis, Earl **Mountbatten**; the youngest, **Alexandra (Alix) Fyodorovna** married **Nicholas II** of Russia.

Ali Pasha, *surnamed* **Arslan**, *also known as* **the Lion of Janina** c. 1741–1822 •*Turkish leader*• An Albanian brigand and assassin, he was born in Tepelene and became Pasha of Trikala (1787) and Janina, Greece (1788), and governor of Rumili (1803). At Janina he maintained a barbarous but cultured court which was visited by Lord **Byron** and other European travelers. He developed contacts with France and Great Britain, but he was deposed in 1820 by Sultan **Mahmud II**, and was put to death in 1822.

Allais, Maurice 1911– •*French economist, engineer and Nobel Prize winner*• Born in Paris, and educated at the École Polytechnique and the École Nationale Supérieure des Mines, he was appointed Professor of Economic Analysis at the latter institution (1944–88). His primary contributions have been in the reformulation of the theories of general economic equilibrium and maximum efficiency and in the development of new concepts, particularly in relation to capital and consumer choice. In 1977 he was named an officer of the Legion of Honor and in 1988 he was awarded the Nobel Prize for economics.

Allen, Ethan 1738–89 •*American soldier, Revolutionary leader, and writer*• He was born in Litchfield, Connecticut. Allen distinguished himself early in the Revolutionary War when he led Vermont's Green Mountain Boys with **Benedict Arnold** in the capture of Fort Ticonderoga from the British (May 10, 1775). He then assisted in an effort to capture Montreal, but was himself captured. He returned to Vermont and continued to campaign for its independence from New York. He wrote *The Narrative of Colonel Ethan's Captivity* (1779) and the deistical *Reason, the Only Oracle of Man* (1784).

Allen, Florence Ellinwood 1884–1966 •*US judge and feminist*• Born in Salt Lake City, Utah, she was educated at Western Reserve University in Cleveland, Ohio. Graduating from New York University Law School in 1913, she was admitted to the Ohio bar in 1914, and worked assiduously for women's rights. She became the first woman to sit on a general federal bench and the first on a court of last resort. In 1965 she published the autobiographical *To Do Justly*.

Allen, George 1832–1907 •*English publisher and engraver*• Born in Newark-on-Trent, Nothinghamshire, he was a pupil of **John Ruskin**, for whom he engraved many plates, and whose publisher he subsequently became. He started a business in Bell Yard, Fleet Street, which ultimately merged with others and became the well-known house of Allen and Unwin.

Allen, Gracie (Grace Ethel Rosalie) 1895–1964 •*US comedy actress*• Born in San Francisco, California, to a show-business family, she made her stage debut as a child and was a regular vaudeville performer from her teenage years onward. She met her future husband **George Burns** in 1922 and they subsequently formed a double act under the title "Sixty-Forty." Their own radio show, *The Adventures of Gracie*, began in 1932 and they eventually transferred to television with the long-running *The Burns and Allen Show* (1950–57). She also appeared in a number of films, often with Burns, including *We're Not Dressing* (1934) and *The Gracie Allen Murder Case* (1939).

Allen, Gubby, *properly* **Sir George Oswald Browning Allen** 1902–89 •*English cricket player*• Born in Sydney, Australia, he was educated at Eton and Trinity College, Cambridge, where he got a cricket Blue. He played for England in 25 Tests. He was captain in the tests against India in 1936, and on the tour of Australia that followed the controversial "Bodyline" series of 1932–33 under **D R Jardine**, in which he disapproved of his captain's tactics.

Allen, James Alfred van *See* **Van Allen, James Alfred**

Allen, Richard 1760–1831 •*US clergyman*• Born to slave parents in Philadelphia, he bought his freedom, became an itinerant preacher, and at the age of 27 founded the Free African Society of Philadelphia, the first organization of free African Americans. He was spiritual leader of the first African Methodist Episcopal Church, and throughout his life worked as a leader in many African-American institutions to improve the lives of newly freed slaves.

Allen, Steve (Stephen Valentine Patrick William) 1921–2000 •*US entertainer and author*• Born in New York City, he studied at Drake University, Des Moines. His childhood was spent in vaudeville entertaining with his parents, and his early career was as a radio disc jockey. In 1950 he was given his first television series for CBS, and by 1953 was host of *The Tonight Show*, which he made immensely popular with a mix of ad-libbing, man-on-the-street interviews and celebrity chat. He composed and recorded hundreds of songs and was a prolific author, writing poetry, philosophy and cultural criticism as well as books of humor.

Allen, Woody, *originally* **Allen Stewart Konigsberg** 1935– •*US screenwriter, actor, director, short-story writer and occasional jazz clarinetist*• He was born in Brooklyn, New York, and launched his career as a comedian in clubs and on television, developing the self-deprecating neurosis and "genetic dissatisfaction with everything" that were to become his stock-in-trade. He made his film debut scripting and acting in *What's New, Pussycat?* (1965). *Take the Money and Run* (1969) was the first of his own films, which are mainly comedies centered on modern US city life. His first movie projects—often coscripted with Marshall Brickman—were more obviously vehicles for his stand-up routines and included *Bananas* (1971), *Everything You Always Wanted to Know About Sex ... But Were Afraid to Ask* (1972) and *Love and Death* (1975). After *Annie Hall* (1977, three Academy Awards for Best Director, Best Script and Best Picture) and *Manhattan* (1979), his films took on a more fictive and structured aspect, as in *Stardust Memories* (1980), *Hannah and Her Sisters* (1986, Academy Award for Best Original Screenplay), *Crimes and Misdemeanours* (1989), and *Mighty Aphrodite* (1995). A frequent magazine contributor, he has also written plays and books of stories and sketches.

“ ”

It's not that I'm afraid to die. I just don't want to be there when it happens.

*1975 **Death: A Comedy in One Act**.*

Allenby, Edmund Henry Hynman, 1st Viscount 1861–1936 •*English field marshal*• Educated at Haileybury and Sandhurst, he joined the Inniskilling Dragoons. He served in South Africa (1884–85, 1888), and in the Second Boer War (1899–1902). As commander of the 3rd army during the Battle of Arras (1917), he came close to breaching the German line. He then took charge of the Egyptian expeditionary force, and conducted a masterly campaign against the Turks in Palestine and Syria, capturing Jerusalem (1917), Damascus and Aleppo (1918). Promoted to field marshal, he was High Commissioner in Egypt (1919–25), and granted independence to Ethiopia in 1922.

Allende, Isabel 1942– •*Chilean novelist*• She was born in Lima, Peru, the cousin and goddaughter of former Chilean president **Salvador Allende**. Several months after the overthrow of Chile's coalition government in 1973 by the forces of a junta headed by General **Pinochet**, she and her family fled Chile. She sought sanctuary in Venezuela, and her first novel, *La casa de los espíritus* (Eng trans *The House of the Spirits*, 1985), arose directly out of her exile and her estrangement from her family, in particular her aged grandfather, who remained in Chile. Further novels have included *De amor y de sombra* (Eng trans *Of Love and Shadows*, 1987) and *El plan infinito* (1993, Eng trans *The Infinite Plan*, 1993). Her first nonfiction work, *Paula* (1994, Eng trans, 1995), was written for her daughter who was lying in a coma. More recent works include *Retrato en sepia* (2000, Eng trans *Portrait in Sepia*, 2001).

Allende (Gossens), Salvador 1908–73 •*Chilean politician*• Born in Valparaíso, he took an early interest in politics and was arrested several times, while a medical student, for his radical activities. In 1933 he helped found the Chilean Socialist Party. He was elected to the Chamber of Deputies (1937–41), served as Minister of Health (1939–41) and was a senator (1945–70). He sought, and failed to win, the presidency in 1952, 1958 and 1964 but was narrowly successful in 1970. He tried to build a socialist society within the framework of a parliamentary democracy but met widespread opposition from business interests, supported by the US CIA. He was overthrown, in September 1973, by a military junta, led by General **Pinochet**, and died in the fighting in the presidential palace in Santiago.

Alleyn, Edward 1566–1626 •*English actor*• Born in London, he was a contemporary of **Shakespeare**, and acted in many of **Christopher Marlowe**'s plays. He founded Dulwich College (1619) and deposited in its library documents relating to his career (including the *Diary* of **Philip Henslowe**, whose stepdaughter he married), which give a unique insight into the financial aspects of Elizabethan theater.

Allgood, Sara 1883–1950 •*US actress*• She was born in Dublin, Ireland, and first appeared at the opening night of the Abbey Theatre there (1904) in Lady **Gregory**'s *Spreading the News*. She was later noted for her creations of the parts of Juno Boyle and Bessie Burgess in **Sean O'Casey**'s *Juno and the Paycock* (1924) and *The Plough and the Stars* (1926), respectively. Her performance of Juno in the **Alfred Hitchcock** film (1930, US title) *The Shame of Mary Boyle* gives a glimpse of the dignity and realism she brought to the part. In 1940 she settled in Hollywood, and became a US citizen in 1945. She appeared in over 30 films, including *Jane Eyre* (1943) and *Between Two Worlds* (1944), but was seldom offered parts suited to her talent, and died penniless.

Allingham, Margery Louise 1904–66 •*English detective-story writer*• Born in London, she was the creator of the fictional detective Albert Campion, and wrote a string of elegant and witty novels, including *Crime at Black Dudley* (1928), *Police at the Funeral* (1931), *More Work for the Undertaker* (1949), *The Tiger in the Smoke* (1952) and *The Mind Readers* (1965).

Alliss, Peter 1931– •*English golfer and commentator*• Born in Berlin, he enjoyed a career as a successful golfer in the 1950s and 1960s, winning some 20 major European competitions. He was selected for every Ryder Cup team except one between 1953 and 1969, achieving his most notable victory with the team of 1957 (the first to defeat the US in 24 years). He never fully realized his potential as a player, but following his retirement in 1969 established himself as television golf's most memorable commentator, working chiefly for the BBC. He has also published many books on the game.

Allston, Washington 1779–1843 •*US artist and writer*• Born in Waccamaw, South Carolina, he studied at Harvard and the Royal Academy in London before going on to Paris and Rome, where he formed a close friendship with **Coleridge**. He worked for a time in London, but returned to the US in 1820. The earliest American Romantic painter, he painted large canvases, such as *The Rising of a Thunderstorm at Sea* (1804), and religious scenes, such as *Belshazzar's Feast* (1817–43). He also published a book of poems and a gothic art novel.

Almagro, Diego de 1475–1538 •*Spanish conquistador*• Born in Almagro, Castile, he was on the first exploratory expedition from Peru against the Incas led by **Francisco Pizarro** (1524–28). In the second expedition (from 1532), he joined Pizarro in 1533 at Cajamarca, where the Inca chieftain **Atahualpa** was executed, and occupied the Inca capital of Cuzco. In 1535–36 he led the conquest of Chile, but came back to Cuzco in 1537, and after a dispute with Pizarro occupied it by force, thus beginning a civil war among the Spaniards. Early in 1538 he was defeated by an army led by Pizarro's brother, Hernando, and was captured and executed.

Almeida, Francisco de c. 1450–1510 •*Portuguese soldier and viceroy of the Indies*• He was 1st Viceroy of the Portuguese Indies (1505–09) until he was superseded by **Afonso de Albuquerque**. He was killed in South Africa on his voyage home in a skirmish with indigenous people at Table Bay, and buried where Cape Town now stands.

Almodóvar, Pedro, *originally* **Pedro Almodóvar Caballero** 1951– •*Spanish film director*• He was born in Calzada de Calatrava. He moved to Madrid in 1967, where he worked for a telephone company. He began making films in the mid-1970s and took full advantage of the post-**Franco** cultural freedom to develop a recognizable personal style. His first film to attain worldwide success was the frenetic farce *Mujeres al borde de un ataque de nervios* (1988, *Women on the Verge of a Nervous Breakdown*). Later films include *¡Átame!* (1990, *Tie Me Up, Tie Me Down!*) and *Todo sobre mi madre* (1999, *All About My Mother*), which won an Academy Award for Best Foreign Language Film.

Almohads, *Arabic* **al-Muwaḥḥidun ("the Unitarians")** 12th–13th century •*Arabic religious movement*• Founded around the year 1124 in the High Atlas mountains by the Berber Ibn Tumart (1091–1130), its principal tenets were the belief in the essential unity of God, an allegorical interpretation of the Koran, and moral reform. The movement gained rapid support among the Berber peasantry of Morocco, and proclaiming himself Mahdi, or divinely appointed leader, Ibn Tumart took the offensive against the perceived corruption and literalism of the **Almoravids**. His successor Abd al-Mu'min (d. 1163) gradually conquered Morocco and extended his rule as far as Tunisia and into Spain, establishing a hereditary monarchy. Art, architecture and the sciences flourished under Almohad rule, but the original faith rapidly declined, and disputes broke out. After the defeat of al-Naṣir (d. 1214) by the Christians at Las Navas de Tolosa (1212), the empire disintegrated under the pressure of local dynasties, its last remnant being finally extinguished in 1276.

Almoravids, *Arabic* **al-Murabaṭun**, *also known as* **al-mulaththamun ("the veiled ones")** 11th–12th century •*Nomadic Berber people of the western Sahara*• In the mid-11th century they were converted to a puritanical form of orthodox Islam by the Malikite jurist and missionary 'Abd Allah ibn Yasin (d. 1059). Assisted by their domination of the gold trade between West Africa and the Iberian peninsula, and an efficient military organization, they invaded Morocco in 1058 under the tribal chief Abu Bakr ibn Umar (d. 1088), founding a new capital at Marrakesh (c. 1070). His cousin Yusuf ibn Tashufin (1061–1106) conquered the rest of Morocco and Algeria, and crossed into Spain in response to the Iberian Muslims' appeals for assistance against the Christians. After defeating Alfonso VI of Castile (1086) he, and then his son Ali ibn Yusuf (d. 1143), annexed the Muslim kingdoms which had arisen after the collapse of the Umayyad caliphate in Spain, and took the offensive against the Christians. This vast, but politically unstable, empire barely survived Ali's death, however, unable to withstand the twin threat of an invigorated Reconquista under **El Cid** and Alfonso VII in Spain, and a new religious and political rival in Morocco, the **Almohads**.

al-Murabaṭun *See* **Almoravids**

al-Muwaḥḥidun *See* **Almohads**

al-Nasser, Gamal Abd *See* **Bar Hebraeus**

Aloysius, St *See* **Gonzaga, Luigi**

Alp Arslan, *literally* **"hero lion"** c. 1030–72 •*Seljuk sultan*• He succeeded his uncle, Muhammad Tüghrül Beg (c. 990–1063), in 1063. He concentrated on extending the frontiers of the Seljuk Empire, conquering Georgia, Armenia and much of Asia Minor. He entrusted the central administration to his capable vizier Nizam al-Mulk. He restored good relations with the 'Abbasid caliph and was about to launch a major offensive against the caliphate's rivals the Fatimids, when he was recalled to meet a Byzantine offensive in

Armenia. At Manzikert (1071) he defeated and captured the Emperor Romanus IV, opening up the interior of Anatolia to the nomadic Turkmen tribes. Killed in a struggle with a prisoner while on campaign in Persia (Iran), he was succeeded by his son Malik-Shah.

Alpher, Ralph Asher 1921– •*US physicist*• Born in Washington DC, he studied at George Washington University, spent World War II as a civilian physicist and later worked at Johns Hopkins University, Baltimore, and in industry. Together with **Hans Bethe** and **George Gamow**, he proposed in 1948 the "alpha, beta, gamma" theory which suggests that the abundances of chemical elements are the result of thermonuclear processes in the early universe. These ideas later became part of the "big bang" model of the universe.

Alsop, Will(iam Allen) 1947– •*English architect*• Born in Northampton, he trained at the Architectural Association in London before setting up his own practice. His most important projects have included designs for the Hôtel du Département government building in Marseilles (1990), North Greenwich Station (2000) and Peckham Library and Media Centre (2000), for which he was awarded the prestigious Stirling Prize.

Alston, Richard John William 1948– •*English choreographer*• Born in Stoughton, Sussex, he was educated at Eton and Croydon College of Art (1965–67), also studying at the London School of Contemporary Dance (1967–70). His first piece of choreography was performed at The Place, London, in 1968. From 1975 to 1977 he studied in New York with **Merce Cunningham**, who greatly influenced his technique. Returning to Great Britain, he spent three years as a freelance choreographer before joining Ballet Rambert as resident choreographer in 1980, becoming director (1986–92). He renamed the company Rambert Dance Company in 1987. Alston is currently artistic director of The Place and the Richard Alston Dance Company (1994–).

Alstyne, Mrs Van *See* **Crosby, Fanny**

Altdorfer, Albrecht c. 1480–1538 •*German painter, engraver and architect*• He was born in Regensburg and his most outstanding works are biblical and historical subjects set against highly imaginative and atmospheric landscapes. His *Landscape with a Footbridge*, in the National Gallery, London, is one of a pair of paintings which mark him as the first painter of pure landscape. He was a leading member of the Danube School of German painting, and also a pioneer of copperplate etching.

Althusser, Louis 1918–90 •*French philosopher*• Born in Birmandreis, Algeria, he was educated in Algiers and in France, and imprisoned in concentration camps during World War II. From 1948 he taught in Paris, and joined the Communist Party. He wrote influential works on the interpretation of Marxist theory, including *Pour Marx* (1965, "For Marx") and *Lénin et la philosophie* (1969, "Lenin and Philosophy"). In 1980 he murdered his wife, following which he was confined in an asylum.

Altman, Robert 1925– •*US film director*• Born in Kansas City, Missouri, he worked on industrial documentaries before directing his first feature film *The Delinquents* (1957). His first critical and commercial success was *M*A*S*H* (1970). Noted for his use of multi-track sound, overlapping dialogue and kaleidoscopic narratives, he has constantly explored the unheroic reality of cherished American myths. His films include *McCabe And Mrs Miller* (1971), *The Long Goodbye* (1973) and *Nashville* (1975). A neglected figure in the 1980s, he returned to favor with the television drama *Tanner* (1988) and the Hollywood satire *The Player* (1992). Subsequent films include *Short Cuts* (1993), *Cookie's Fortune* (1999) and *Gosford Park* (2001).

Alva or **Alba, Ferdinand Alvarez de Toledo, Duke of** 1508–82 •*Spanish general*• Born in Piedrahita, he was made Governor of Feuenterrabia at the age of 17, and he fought so well in the Battle of Pavia (1525), in Hungary against the Turks, in **Charles V**'s expedition to Tunis and Algiers, and in Provence, that he became general at 26, and Commander in Chief at 30. He defended Navarre and Catalonia (1542), and in 1547 contributed greatly to Charles V's victory at Mühlberg over the Elector of Saxony. After the abdication of Charles V in 1556, Alva overran the States of the Church, but was obliged by **Philip II** to conclude a peace and restore all his conquests. On the revolt of the Netherlands, he was sent as lieutenant general in 1567 to enforce Spanish control there. He established the so-called Bloody Council, which drove thousands of Huguenot artisans to emigrate to England. He executed Counts Egmont and Horn, then defeated **William** of Orange, and entered Brussels in 1568. Holland and Zeeland renewed their efforts against him, and succeeded in destroying his fleet, until he was recalled by his own wish in 1573. He later commanded the successful invasion of Portugal in 1581.

Alvarado, Pedro de c. 1485–1541 •*Spanish conquistador*• Companion of **Hernán Cortés** during the conquest of Mexico (1519–21), he became Governor of Tenochtitlán, where the harshness of his rule incited an Aztec revolt which drove the Spaniards out. In the following year Tenochtitlán was recaptured and razed, and Mexico City built in its place. From 1523 to 1527 he was sent by Cortés on an expedition to Guatemala, which also conquered parts of El Salvador. He returned to Spain, and in 1529 was appointed Governor of Guatemala. He embarked on an expedition to conquer Quito, Ecuador, in 1534, but was bought off by **Francisco Pizarro**.

Álvarez (Cubero), José 1768–1827 •*Spanish sculptor*• He was imprisoned in Rome for refusing to recognize **Joseph Bonaparte** as King of Spain, but was later released and employed by **Napoleon I** to decorate the Quirinal Palace. In 1816 he became court sculptor to **Ferdinand VII** in Madrid, where he executed, in the classical style, *Antilochus and Memnon* (Royal Museum) and portraits and busts of the nobility and of **Gioacchino Rossini**.

Alvarez, Luis Walter 1911–88 •*US experimental physicist and Nobel Prize winner*• Born in San Francisco, he studied physics at the University of Chicago where he worked together with **Arthur Compton** in the study of cosmic rays. He joined **Ernest Lawrence** at Berkeley University in 1936 where he worked on nuclear physics. During World War II he invented a radar guidance system for landing aircraft in conditions of poor visibility. After the war he returned to Berkeley where he became Professor of Physics in 1945. There he developed **Donald Glaser**'s bubble chamber technique in order to carry out a range of experiments in which a large number of subatomic particles were identified. These results ultimately led to the quark model invented by **Murray Gell-Mann** and George Zweig. In 1968 Alvarez was awarded the Nobel Prize for physics for this work.

Alzheimer, Alois 1864–1915 •*German psychiatrist and neuropathologist*• He was born in Markbreit, and studied medicine in Würzburg and Berlin. After posts in a couple of psychiatric hospitals, he became head of the anatomical laboratories of Emil Kraepelin's psychiatric clinic in Munich and, in 1912, Professor of Psychiatry and Neurology at the University of Breslau (now Wrocław, Poland). He made important contributions to the preparation of microscopic sections of brain tissue and left some clinical studies, but is best remembered for his full clinical and pathological description, in 1907, of presenile dementia (Alzheimer's disease).

Amadeus *See* **Hoffmann, Ernst Theodor Wilhelm**

Amadeus VIII (the Peaceful), *also known as* **Felix V** 1383–1451 •*Antipope and ruler of Savoy*• Born in Chambéry, Savoy, he became Count (1391) and Duke (1416) of Savoy, and ruler of Piedmont (1419). In 1434 he retired to the monastery of Ripaille, beside Lake Geneva, but was elected pope (1439) as Felix V (an antipope, in opposition to **Eugenius IV**). He resigned in 1449.

Amado, Jorge 1912–2001 •*Brazilian novelist*• Born on a cocoa plantation near Ilhéus, Bahia, he was expelled from Brazil in 1938 for his political beliefs and spent several years in exile, though he was briefly a Communist deputy of the Brazilian parliament (1946–47). His first novel, *O país do carnaval* (1932, "The Country of the Carnival"), follows a youthful member of the intelligentsia seeking political answers in the wake of the revolution of 1930. Amado's next few novels outlined his personal manifesto and highlighted the causes of various exploited groups in society. *Gabriela, cravo e canela* (1952, Eng trans *Gabriela, Clove and*

Cinnamon, 1962) marked a change in style and emphasis. Subsequent books, like *Doña Flor e seus dois maridos: História moral e de amor* (1966, Eng trans *Doña Flor and Her Two Husbands*, 1969) show equal social awareness and compassion, but are more subtle, and use irony to good effect.

Amanullah Khan 1892–1960 •*Ruler of Afghanistan 1919–29*• He was born in Paghman, and as Governor of Kabul he assumed the throne on the assassination of his father, Habibullah Khan (ruler 1901–19). He assumed the title of king in 1926. His push for westernizing reforms provoked rebellion (1928), and in 1929 he abdicated and went into exile in Rome. He was succeeded by **Mohammed Nadir Shah**.

Amati •*Italian family of violin makers in Cremona*• Andrea (c. 1520–1580) whose earliest known label dates from 1564, was the founder who developed the standard violin. Others were his younger brother Nicola (1530–1600), Andrea's two sons, Antonio (1550–1638) and Geronimo (1551–1635), and the latter's son, Niccolo (1596–1684), the master of **Guarnieri** and **Stradivari**. Geronimo (1649–1740) was the last important Amati.

Ambedkar, Bhimrao Ranji 1893–1956 •*Indian politician and champion of the depressed classes*• Born in a Ratnagiri village on the Konkan coast of Bombay, he was educated in Bombay, New York, and London. He became a London barrister and later a member of the Bombay Legislative Assembly and the leader of 60 million untouchables (members of the lowest caste). Appointed Law Minister in 1947, he was the principal author of the Indian Constitution. He resigned in 1951 and with some thousands of his followers he publicly embraced the Buddhist faith not long before his death. His dedicated work for the untouchables helped to secure a better life for them. His publications include *Annihilation of Caste* (1937).

Ambler, Eric 1909–98 •*English novelist and playwright*• Born in London, he was educated at Colfe's Grammar School and London University, then served an apprenticeship in engineering and worked as an advertising copywriter before turning to writing thrillers, invariably with an espionage background. He published his first novel, *The Dark Frontier*, in 1936. His best-known books are *Epitaph for a Spy* (1938), *The Mask of Dimitrios* (1939), *Dirty Story* (1967) and *The Intercom Conspiracy* (1970). He received the Crime Writers' Association award four times, and the **Edgar Allan Poe** award (1964). He also wrote a number of screenplays.

Ambrose, St c. 339–97 AD •*Italian bishop, writer and Doctor of the Church*• Born in Trier, Germany, the son of the prefect of Gaul. Though he was an unbaptized layman, his fairness in dealing with the Arian/Catholic controversy led to his appointment as Bishop of Milan in 374. One of the four Latin Doctors of the Church (with St **Augustine**, St **Jerome**, and **Gregory I** [**the Great**]), he is remembered for his preaching and literary works, for his introduction of the use of hymns, and for improvements in the service—the Ambrosian ritual and Ambrosian chant. His feast day is December 7.

Amdahl, Gene Myron 1922– •*US computer scientist and entrepreneur*• Born in Flandreau, South Dakota, he studied electrical engineering at South Dakota State University and later became project manager at an IBM plant in 1952, the year in which he was awarded a PhD in physics at the University of Wisconsin. From 1960 he managed the company's advanced data processing systems and led the design of several IBM computers, most notably the extremely successful System/360. He later set up several computer-related businesses.

Amenhotep II 15th century BC •*King of Egypt of the 18th Dynasty*• The son of **Tuthmosis III** and Queen **Hatshepsut**, he ruled from 1450 to 1425 BC, and fought successful campaigns in Palestine and on the Euphrates. His mummy was discovered at Thebes in a well-preserved tomb.

Amenhotep III c. 1411–c. 1375 BC •*King of Egypt of the 18th Dynasty*• The son of **Tuthmosis IV**, he ruled from 1417 to 1379 BC and consolidated Egyptian supremacy in Babylonia and Assyria. In a reign of spectacular wealth and magnificence, he built his great capital city, Thebes, and its finest monuments, including the Luxor temple, the great pylon at Karnak, and the colossi of Memnon.

Amenhotep IV *See* **Akhenaten**

Amery, John 1912–45 •*English pro-Nazi adventurer*• He was the elder son (later disowned) of the Conservative politician **L S Amery**. He was declared bankrupt in 1936, and became a gunrunner for General **Franco** in the Spanish Civil War. Recruited by the Nazis in France, where he had been living since the outbreak of World War II, he began pro-**Hitler** broadcasts from Berlin in 1942. Captured by Italian partisans in 1945 and handed over to the British authorities, he was tried in London for high treason. He was hanged in December 1945.

Amery, L(eopold Charles Maurice) S(tennett) 1873–1955 •*English Conservative politician*• Born in Gorakpur, India, he was educated at Harrow and Oxford. After ten years on the staff of *The Times* (London), he became Member of Parliament for Sparkbrook, Birmingham, a seat which he held for 34 years. He served in **Churchill**'s wartime administration as Secretary of State for India and Burma. He became famous for his exhortation to **Neville Chamberlain**, in May 1940, adapting **Cromwell**'s words, "In the name of God, go!"

Amherst, Jeffrey Amherst, 1st Baron 1717–97 •*English soldier*• He was born in Riverhead, Kent, and joined the army at the age of 14. He played an important part in the North American phase of the Seven Years War (1756–63), and was in command of the expedition against the French in Canada and captured Louisburg (1758). After the fall of Quebec the following year, he completed the conquest of Canada by taking Montreal in 1760. He became a peer in 1776, and served as Commander in Chief of the British army. Amherst College was named after him.

Amici, Giovanni Battista 1784–1863 •*Italian optician, astronomer and natural philosopher*• He was born in Modena. He constructed optical instruments, perfecting his own alloy for telescope mirrors and, in 1827, produced the dioptric, achromatic microscope that bears his name. He became director of the Florence Observatory in 1835.

Amies, Sir (Edwin) Hardy 1909–2003 •*English couturier and dressmaker by appointment to Queen Elizabeth II*• After studying languages in France and Germany, he worked as a trainee in Birmingham before becoming a managing designer in London in 1934, where he made a name for himself especially with his tailored suits for women. He founded his own fashion house in 1946, was awarded a royal warrant in 1955, started designing for men in 1959 and became known chiefly for his menswear. He retired in 2001 at the age of 92. His publications include *The Englishman's Suit* (1994).

Amin (Dada), Idi 1925–2003 •*Ugandan soldier and politician*• Born in Koboko of a peasant family, after a rudimentary education he rose rapidly to become Commander in Chief of the army and air force (1966). Originally a friend of Prime Minister **Milton Obote**, in 1971 he staged a coup, dissolving parliament and establishing a military dictatorship. He expelled 500 Israeli citizens, all Ugandan Asians with British passports, and the British High Commissioner, seized foreign-owned businesses and estates and ordered the killing of thousands of his opponents. His attempt to annex the Kagera area of Tanzania (1978) gave President **Nyerere** the opportunity to send his troops into Uganda. Amin was deposed within six months (1979). He fled to Libya and after expulsion from several countries settled in Saudi Arabia in 1980.

Amis, Sir Kingsley 1922–95 •*English novelist and poet*• Born in London, he was educated at the City of London School and at St John's College, Oxford, and was a lecturer in English literature at University College, Swansea (1948–61) and Fellow of Peterhouse, Cambridge (1961–63). He achieved huge success with his first novel, *Lucky Jim* (1954), the story of a comic antihero in a provincial university. "Jim" appeared again as a small-town librarian in *That Uncertain Feeling* (1955), and as a provincial author abroad in *I Like It Here* (1958). His later novels include *Ending Up* (1974), *Jake's Thing* (1978), *Stanley and the Women* (1984), *The Old Devils* (1986, Booker Prize), *The Folks That Live on the Hill* (1990), and *The Russian Girl*

(1992). He also published four books of poetry, and wrote nonfiction works. He was married (1965–83) to the novelist Elizabeth Jane Howard (1923–). His son is **Martin Amis**.

“ ”

He was of the faith chiefly in the sense that the church he currently did not attend was Catholic.

*1963 **One Fat Englishman**, chapter 14.*

Amis, Martin Louis 1949– •*English novelist and journalist*• Born in Oxford, the son of **Kingsley Amis**, he was educated at Exeter College, Oxford, and acted in the film *A High Wind in Jamaica* (1965). He worked for the *Times Literary Supplement* and *New Statesman*, but has been a full-time writer since 1979. He began precociously with his first novel, *The Rachel Papers* (1973), and followed it with two more witty satires, *Dead Babies* (1975) and *Success* (1978). Subsequent novels include *Money* (1984), *London Fields* (1989) and *Time's Arrow* (1991), which plays with concepts of time and history. His later works include *The Information* (1995) and a memoir, *Experience* (2000), for which he won the James Tait Black Memorial Prize. He has also written a great deal of literary journalism.

Amman, Jakob c. 1645–c. 1730 •*Swiss religious*• He was a Mennonite bishop, whose followers founded the Amish sect in the 1690s. Its members still practice an exclusively rural and simple way of life in various parts of the US and Canada.

Ammanati, Bartolommeo 1511–92 •*Italian architect and sculptor*• Born in Settignano, he executed the ducal palace in Lucca, working in the late Renaissance style. He also designed part of the Pitti Palace and the Ponte S Trinità (destroyed in World War II) in Florence.

Ammann, Othmar Hermann 1879–1965 •*US structural engineer*• Born in Schaffhausen, Switzerland, he emigrated to the US in 1904 to work with the Pennsylvania Steel Company. He became a US citizen in 1924. Later he designed some of the US's greatest suspension bridges, including the George Washington Bridge in New York (1931), Golden Gate Bridge in San Francisco (1937) and Verrazano Narrows Bridge in New York (1965).

Ammianus Marcellinus c. 330–90 AD •*Roman historian*• Born of Greek parents in Antioch, he fought in Gaul, Germany and the East, then settled in Rome and devoted himself to literature. He wrote in Latin a history of the Roman Empire from AD 98 (the death of **Domitian**). It comprised 31 books, of which only the last 18 are extant.

Ammonius, *surnamed* **Saccas** c. 160–242 AD •*Greek philosopher*• A sack carrier in Alexandria, Egypt, as a young man, he was the founder of Neo-Platonic philosophy, and was the teacher of **Plotinus**, **Origen** and **Longinus**.

Amontons, Guillaume 1663–1705 •*French instrument maker and physicist*• Born in Paris, and incurably deaf from adolescence, he studied geometry, mechanics and physical science. He designed many instruments, including a hygrometer (1687) and various air thermometers. Between 1699 and 1702 he discovered the interdependence of volume, temperature and pressure of gases, later demonstrated explicitly by **Joseph Gay-Lussac** and Jacques Charles (1746–1823). **Daniel Fahrenheit** owed much to his investigation of the thermal expansion of mercury (1704).

Amory, Derick Heathcoat Amory, 1st Viscount 1899–1981 •*English Conservative politician*• Born in Tiverton, Devon, and educated at Eton and Christ Church, Oxford, he entered parliament in 1945. He was Minister of Pensions (1951–53), at the Board of Trade (1953–54), Minister of Agriculture (1954–58) and was made viscount while he was Chancellor of the Exchequer (1958–60).

Amos 835–765 BC •*Old Testament prophet*• Born in Tekoa, near Bethlehem, he was the earliest prophet in the Bible to have a book named after him. He worked as a herdsman, and was an outspoken critic of the unjust acts of the northern kingdom of Israel.

Ampère, André Marie 1775–1836 •*French mathematician and physicist*• He was born in Lyons, where his father was a wealthy merchant. Educated by means of his father's library, Ampère held various academic posts, including ones at the École Polytechnique in Paris and at the Collège de France. Although he contributed to a number of fields, he is best known for laying the foundations of the science of electrodynamics through his theoretical and experimental work, following **Hans Christian Oersted**'s discovery in 1820 of the magnetic effects of electric currents, in *Observations électro-dynamiques* (1822, "Electrodynamic Observations") and *Théories des phénomènes électro-dynamiques* (1830, "Theory of Electrodynamic Phenomena"). Ampère was elected a Fellow of the Royal Society, and his name is given to the basic SI unit of electric current (ampere, amp).

Amr ibn al-'As d. 664 •*Arab soldier*• A convert to Islam, he joined the prophet **Muhammad** in 629, and took part in the conquest of Palestine in 638. In 639 he undertook the conquest of Egypt; in 642 he captured Alexandria after a 14-month siege and accepted the capitulation of Egypt. He became the first Muslim governor of Egypt (642–44) and helped **Mu'Awiyah** to seize the caliphate from **Ali** by capturing Alexandria again in 658. He was Governor of Egypt again from 661 to 663.

Amundsen, Roald Engelbreth Gravning 1872–1928 •*Norwegian explorer, the first man to navigate the Northwest Passage and to reach the South Pole*• Born in Borge, he abandoned his medical studies in favor of a life at sea. In 1897 he served with the Belgian Antarctic expedition as first mate of the *Belgica*, the first vessel to overwinter in Antarctica. From 1902 to 1906 he sailed the Northwest Passage from east to west in the smack *Gjöa* and located the magnetic North Pole. In 1910 he set sail in the *Fram* in an attempt to reach the North Pole, but hearing that **Robert Peary** had apparently beaten him to it, he switched to the Antarctic and reached the South Pole in December 1911, one month ahead of Captain **Scott**. He built a new ship, the *Maud*, and sailed her through the Northeast Passage in 1918. In 1926 he flew the airship *Norge* from Spitsbergen to Alaska across the North Pole with **Lincoln Ellsworth** and **Umberto Nobile**. In 1928 he disappeared when searching by plane for Nobile, whose airship, *Italia*, had gone missing on another flight to the Pole. He wrote several books, including *My Life As an Explorer* (1927).

“ ”

Beg leave to inform you proceeding Antarctica. Amundsen.

1910 Cable sent from Madeira to Captain Robert F Scott in Melbourne, October 12.

Anacreon c. 570–c. 475 BC •*Greek lyric poet*• From Teos, Asia Minor, he helped found the Greek colony of Abdera in Thrace (c. 540 BC). He was invited to Samos by **Polycrates** to tutor his son. After the tyrant's downfall, he was brought to Athens by Hipparchus, son of the tyrant **Pisistratus**, and later went to Thessaly. His work, which survives only in fragments, includes poems of love and wine, satires, dedications and epitaphs.

Anand, Mulk Raj 1905– •*Indian novelist and critic*• He was born in Peshawar (now in Pakistan), but left India for Great Britain, where he was beaten up for blacklegging during the General Strike (1926). His first novel, *Untouchable* (1935), was rejected by 19 publishers, the 20th agreeing to take it on if **E M Forster** would write a preface. This he did, sparking off a remarkable career for Anand. His humanist novels, such as *Coolie* (1936), *Two Leaves and a Bud* (1937) and *The Village* (1939, the first of a trilogy), depict life in the poverty-stricken Punjab. He later began an ambitious seven-volume autobiographical work of fiction, *The Seven Ages of Man*.

Anastasia, *in full* **Grand Duchess Anastasia Nikolayevna Romanov** 1901–1918? •*Russian duchess*• Born in Peterhof, the youngest daughter of Czar **Nicholas II**, she is believed to have perished when the **Romanov** family was executed by the Bolsheviks in a cellar in Yekaterinburg on July 19, 1918. Various people have claimed to be Anastasia, especially Mrs "Anna Anderson" Manahan, who died in Virginia, US (1984) at the age of 82. Her story inspired two films (*Anastasia*, with **Ingrid Bergman**, and *Is Anna Anderson Anastasia?* with Lilli Palmer), and several books.

Anaxagoras 500–428 BC •*Ionian philosopher*• Born in Clazomenae, Asia Minor, he taught for 30 years in Athens, where his many illustrious pupils included **Pericles** and **Euripides**. His explanations of physical phenomena by natural causes brought accusations of impiety, and he was banished from Athens. He withdrew to Lampsacus, on the Hellespont, and died there. He held that matter is infinitely divisible (that is, any piece of matter, regardless of how small it is, contains portions of all kinds of matter).

" "

The sun provides the moon with its brightness.

Fragment in Plutarch ***De facie in orbe lunae****, 929b.*

Anaximander 611–547 BC •*Ionian philosopher*• Born in Miletus, Asia Minor, he was successor and perhaps pupil of **Thales**. He posited that the first principle was not a particular substance like water or air but the "Boundless" (*apeiron*), which he conceived of in both physical and theological terms. He is believed to have used the gnomon (a sundial with a vertical rod) to measure the lengths of the seasons and he is also thought to have drawn the first map of the inhabited world (he recognized that the surface of the Earth must be curved, though he visualized it as a cylinder rather than a sphere).

Anaximenes d. c. 500 BC •*Greek philosopher*• Born in Miletus, Asia Minor, he became the third of the three great Milesian thinkers, succeeding **Thales** and **Anaximander**. He proposed that the first principle and basic form of matter was air, which could be transformed into other substances by a process of condensation and expansion. He also believed that the Earth and the heavenly bodies were flat and floated on the air like leaves.

Ancram, Michael Andrew Foster Jude Kerr, Earl of 1945– •*English Conservative politician*• Born in London, the son of the 12th Marquess of Lothian, he was educated at Ampleforth and at the universities of Oxford and Edinburgh. He became Member of Parliament for Berwickshire and East Lothian in 1974 and subsequently represented Edinburgh South (1979–87) and Devizes (from 1992). He served as Parliamentary Under-Secretary in the State Scottish Office (1983–87) and Northern Ireland Office (1993) and was Minister of State for Northern Ireland (1993–97). He then served as chairman of the Conservative Party (1998–2001) before becoming shadow Secretary of State for Foreign and Commonwealth Affairs.

Andersen, Hans Christian 1805–75 •*Danish writer*• Born in Odense, Fünen, the son of a shoemaker and a washerwoman, he had a talent for poetry, and at 14 went to Copenhagen to seek a job in the theater. He failed, but his writing attracted the attention of influential men and, application having been made to the king, he was given a place at an advanced school. He received a traveling pension from the king in 1833 and toured widely in Europe, writing poetry, travel books, novels and plays. In 1835 he began publishing the tiny pamphlets of fairy tales which are his greatest work (translated into English in 1846). There are more than 150 of them, including "The Emperor's New Clothes," "The Snow Queen," "The Little Mermaid" and "The Ugly Duckling." He is considered to be one of the world's greatest storytellers.

Anderson, Carl David 1905–91 •*US physicist and Nobel Prize winner*• Born in New York City, he studied at the California Institute of Technology (Caltech) under **Robert Millikan**, and in 1932 discovered the positron, the positively charged electron-type particle, thus confirming the existence of antimatter predicted by **Paul Dirac**. He did notable work on gamma and cosmic rays, and was awarded the 1936 Nobel Prize for physics (jointly with **Victor Hess**). Later he confirmed the existence of intermediate-mass particles known as mesons or muons.

Anderson, Elizabeth Garrett, *née* **Garrett** 1836–1917 •*English physician, the first English woman doctor*• Born in London, she was brought up at Aldeburgh in Suffolk. In 1860 she began studying medicine, in the face of prejudiced opposition to the admission of women, and eventually (1865) qualified as a medical practitioner by passing the Apothecaries' Hall examination. In 1866 she established a dispensary for women in London (later renamed the Elizabeth Garrett Anderson Hospital), where she instituted medical courses for women. In 1870 she was given the degree of MD by the University of Paris. Her sister was the suffragette **Millicent Fawcett**.

Anderson, Gerry 1929– •*British creator of television programs*• He entered the British film industry as a trainee with the Colonial Film Unit and later worked as an assistant editor before cofounding Pentagon Films (1955). He enjoyed his greatest success with a number of adventure series that combined puppet characters with technologically advanced hardware and special effects, the best known being *Fireball XL-5* (1962–63), *Thunderbirds* (1965–66) and *Captain Scarlet and the Mysterons* (1967–68). He later branched out into live action shows (with human actors) like *The Protectors* (1972–74) and *Space 1999* (1975–77) before returning to the use of puppetry in *Terrahawks* (1983–84). He switched back to live action for *Space Precinct* (1994–95). He was given the honorary title Member, Order of the British Empire in 2001.

Anderson, Dame Judith, *originally* **Frances Margaret Anderson** 1898–1992 •*Australian actress*• Born in Adelaide, South Australia, she made her Sydney stage debut in *A Royal Divorce* (1915) and first appeared in New York in 1918. She made her film debut in *Madame of the Jury* (1930) but preferred the stage, appearing in productions like *Mourning Becomes Electra* (1932), *Hamlet* (1936, with **John Gielgud**), and *Macbeth* (1937) at the Old Vic in London. Her chilling performance as the sinister Mrs Danvers in **Alfred Hitchcock**'s *Rebecca* (1940) earned her a cinema career portraying cruel and domineering women in films like *Laura* (1944) and *Diary of a Chambermaid* (1946). Her many theater credits include the title part in **Robinson Jeffers**'s adaptation of *Medea* (1947, 1982). Her later film appearances comprise *Cat on a Hot Tin Roof* (1958), *Inn of the Damned* (1974) and *Star Trek III* (1984). A Broadway theater was named in her honor in 1984.

Anderson, Lindsay Gordon 1923–94 •*British stage and film director*• Born in Bangalore, India, he was educated at Oxford, became a film critic, and was cofounder and editor of *Sequence* (1949–51). He made his directorial debut with the documentary *Meeting the Pioneers* (1948) and was a key figure in the "Free Cinema" movement of the 1950s, winning an Academy Award for *Thursday's Children* (1953). Later feature films include *This Sporting Life* (1963), *If…* (1968) and *Britannia Hospital* (1982). He was associate director at the Royal Court Theatre from 1969 to 1975.

" "

Perhaps the tendency is to treat the films of one's own country like the prophets—with less than justice.

1947 Comment, quoted in Ian Christie ***Arrows of Desire****.*

Anderson, Marian 1902–93 •*US contralto*• She was born into a poor African-American family in Philadelphia, and had her training financed by members of the church where she sang in the gospel choir. She studied in New York and spent most of her career as a concert singer. She overcame racial discrimination to sing at Carnegie Hall in 1929. However, in 1939 she was prevented from performing at Constitution Hall in Washington DC, but there was such a protest that **Eleanor Roosevelt** and others arranged for her to appear in concert at the Lincoln Memorial, where she performed triumphantly. Renowned for the range and rich tone of her voice, she became the first African-American singer at the White House and at the Metropolitan Opera. President **Eisenhower** made her a delegate to the United Nations in 1958, and she received many honors and international awards.

Anderson, Maxwell 1888–1959 •*US historical dramatist*• Born in Atlantic, Pennsylvania, he attended the University of North Dakota and Stanford University. He became a verse playwright, and was in vogue in the late 1920s to the early 1940s with numerous plays, including *Elizabeth the Queen* (1930), *Key Largo* (1939) and *The Eve of St Mark* (1942). Commercially successful, his plays had strong, simple themes. He also wrote screenplays, most notably that from **Erich Maria Remarque**'s novel *All Quiet on the Western Front* (1930). He won a Pulitzer Prize for *Both Your Houses* in 1933.

Anderson, Philip Warren 1923– •*US physicist and Nobel Prize winner*• Born in Indianapolis, Indiana, he studied antenna engineering at the Naval Research Laboratories during World War II and then at Harvard, where he received his PhD. As a student under **John H Van Vleck** he worked on pressure broadening in microwave and infrared spectra. He joined Bell Telephone Laboratories in 1949, where he demonstrated that it is possible for an electron in disordered materials to be trapped in a small region (1958). This process, later known as "Anderson localization," furthered our understanding of disordered materials and contributed to their extensive exploitation in modern applications such as solar cells, thin film transistors and xerography. He was appointed assistant director of Bell Telephone Laboratories in 1974, before moving to Princeton University. For his theoretical work on the electronic structure of magnetic and disordered systems he shared the 1977 Nobel Prize for physics with Sir **Nevill Mott** and Van Vleck.

Anderson, Sherwood 1876–1941 •*US fiction writer*• Born in Camden, Ohio, he had an uncertain childhood and irregular schooling, and at 17 enlisted to fight in the Spanish-American War. He later returned to Ohio and married, but in 1912 left his family and his lucrative position as head of a paint factory to devote all his time to writing. Settling in Chicago, he joined a literary circle that included **Carl Sandburg**, **Theodore Dreiser** and **Edgar Lee Masters**. His first novel was *Windy McPherson's Son* (1916), but his best-known work is *Winesburg, Ohio* (1919), a collection of interrelated short stories which portray the "secret lives" of marginal characters and the sensibilities of the young artist who observes them and then escapes. Subsequent books include *Poor White* (1920) and *The Triumph of the Egg* (1921). His *Memoirs* (1942) and *Letters* (1953) were published posthumously.

Anderson, Thomas 1819–74 •*Scottish organic chemist*• He studied at Edinburgh and Stockholm, became Professor of Chemistry at Glasgow, and discovered pyridine.

Andersson, Bibi (Birgitta) 1935– •*Swedish actress*• Born in Stockholm, she studied at the Kungliga Dramatiska Teatern there. She began her career in 1949 as a film extra and is best known for her roles in many **Ingmar Bergman** films such as *Sjunde inseglet* (1956, *The Seventh Seal*), *Persona* (1966) and *The Touch* (1971), for which she received the British Academy Award for Best Foreign Actress.

Ando, Tadao 1941– •*Japanese architect*• Born in Osaka, he had a brief career as a professional boxer and was largely self-taught as an architect through his observation of buildings in Africa, Europe and the US. He founded his own company in Osaka in 1969 and has since designed a wide range of buildings. Among his most notable works are the Church of Light in Osaka, the Water Temple in Osaka and the Rokko Housing complex near Osaka. He was awarded the Royal Institute of British Architects gold medal in 1997.

Andre, Carl 1935– •*US sculptor*• He was born in Massachusetts, and trained briefly at Phillips Art College, Andover, before gravitating to New York City, where he became close friends with **Frank Stella**. His initial experiments, with woodcutting, were inspired by **Constantine Brancusi**, then a job on the Pennsylvania Railroad in the 1960s led him to experiment with mass-produced materials. He is now best known for his minimalist sculptures of that period, such as *Equivalent VIII*, a floor piece consisting of 120 bricks stacked in two layers to form a rectangle (Tate Modern, London). His *144 Magnesium Square* (1969, Tate Modern) can be walked on, evidence of his increasing concern with the site itself as sculpture. In the 1970s his work was characterized by the use of flat metal plates enriched with color, as in *Twelfth Copper Corner* (1975). In the 1980s he returned to working in wood, for example *Bloody Angle* (1985, Stedelijk Museum, Amsterdam).

Andrea da Firenze, *originally* **Andrea Bonaiuti** fl. c. 1343–77 •*Italian painter*• His most famous work is the monumental fresco cycle in the Spanish chapel of the Dominican church of Santa Maria Novella in Florence, painted c. 1366–68. Many panel paintings of varying quality are attributed to him, but his only other documented work is the *Life of St Ranieri*, frescoes in the Camposanto in Pisa, completed in 1377.

Andrea del Sarto *See* **Sarto, Andrea del**

Andreä, Johann Valentin 1586–1654 •*German theologian*• Born near Tübingen, he was Protestant court chaplain at Stuttgart, and was long regarded as the founder or restorer of the Rosicrucians. He wrote *Chymische Hochzeit Christiani Rosencreutz* (1616).

Andreotti, Giulio 1919– •*Italian Christian Democrat politician*• Born in Rome and educated at the University of Rome he was elected to the first postwar Constituent Assembly in 1945 and to parliament in 1947. He held ministerial posts in almost all the postwar governments, and served as Prime Minister between 1972 and 1973, 1976 and 1979, and 1989 and 1992. He became a Life Senator in the Chamber of Deputies in 1992. In subsequent years he was investigated over allegations of complicity in the 1979 murder of a journalist, but was acquitted in 1999 after a three-year trial. He cofounded the political party Democrazia Europea ("European Democracy") in 2001.

Andretti, Mario Gabriele 1940– •*US racecar driver*• Born in Montona, Italy, he emigrated with his family to Nazareth, Pennsylvania, in the US in 1955 and began his career in stock car and midget car racing, then progressed to the US Auto Club circuit, in which he was champion three times (1965, 1966, 1969). In a Formula One career stretching from 1968 to 1982, he competed in 128 Grand Prix, winning 16. His most successful year was 1978, when he won the racing drivers' world championship. His son Michael (1962–) followed him into motor racing.

Andrew, St 1st century AD •*One of the 12 Apostles of Jesus*• He was a fisherman who had previously followed **John the Baptist**. According to tradition he preached the Gospel in Asia Minor and Scythia, and was crucified in Achaia (Greece) by order of the Roman governor. The belief that his cross was X-shaped dates only from the 14th century. He was the brother of Simon Peter (St **Peter**), and is the patron saint of Scotland and of Greece and Russia. His feast day is November 30.

Andrew, Prince *See* **York, Duke of**

Andrew, (Christopher) Rob(ert) 1963– •*English rugby union player*• Born in Richmond, Yorkshire, he is the world record holder, with 21, for international drop goals. As England's most capped fly-half he played 69 times between 1985 and 1995 and scored a record 396 points. He was one of the first to embrace union's professionalism when he left his club Wasps and signed for Newcastle Rugby Club. He retired from international rugby in 1995.

Andrews, Anthony 1948– •*English actor*• Born in North London, the son of a BBC music arranger, he acted in costume dramas such as *The Pallisers* (1974), *The Duchess of Duke Street* (1976–77) and *Upstairs, Downstairs* (1975), before starring as Brian Ash in *Danger U.X.B.* (1979). He became known worldwide in the role of Sebastian Flyte in *Brideshead Revisited* (1981), which won him a British Academy of Film and Television Arts Best Actor award. Television movies and mini-series followed, including *Mistress of Paradise* (1981), *Ivanhoe* (1982), *The Scarlet Pimpernel* (1983), *The Woman He Loved* (1988) and *Love in a Cold Climate* (2001). He also appeared in a stage production of Ibsen's *Ghosts* in 2001.

Andrews, Eamon 1922–87 •*Irish broadcaster*• Born in Dublin, he was an All-Ireland amateur juvenile middleweight boxing champion. He began sports commentating for Radio Éireann in 1939 and subsequently worked on various programs for BBC Radio, including *Sports Report* (1950–62). On television he hosted the parlor game *What's My Line?* (1951–63) and *This Is Your Life* (1955–87).

Andrews, Dame Julie, *originally* **Julia Elizabeth Wells** 1935– •*English singer and actress*• She was born in Walton-on-Thames, Surrey, into a showbusiness family. Trained as a singer, she made her London debut in the 1947 revue *Starlight Roof*. Radio and stage successes led to a role in the New York production of *The Boyfriend* (1954) and several long-running Broadway musicals, notably *My Fair Lady* (1956) and *Camelot* (1960), as well as the very successful film musicals *Mary Poppins* (1964, Academy Award for Best Actress), and *The Sound of Music* (1965). Other films include *S.O.B.* (1981), and *Victor/Victoria* (1982). A return to Broadway in the stage version of *Victor/Victoria* (1995–97) proved a personal triumph. Her voice was left severely damaged after routine throat surgery in 1997. She was created Dame Commander of the British Empire in 2000.

Andrews, Thomas 1813–85 •*Irish physical chemist*• Born in

Belfast, he studied medicine at Edinburgh University and he practiced as a physician in Belfast, where he was Professor of Chemistry at Queen's College (1849–79). He is noted for his discovery of the critical temperature of gases, above which they cannot be liquefied, however great the pressure applied.

Andrews Sisters, The •*US vocal harmony trio*• LaVerne (1915–67), Maxene (1918–95) and Patti (1920–) Andrews were born and raised in Minneapolis, and began to work on the RKO circuit when in their early teens, with the youngest sister, Patti, singing lead lines, and Maxene and LaVerne singing soprano and contralto harmonies. Their breakthrough record was *Bei mir bist du schön* (1939), a huge wartime success; others include "Pistol Packin' Mama" (1943) with **Bing Crosby**, and "Boogie Woogie Bugle Boy." They retired as a group in the late 1950s.

Andrianov, Nikolai Yefimovich, *nicknamed* **Old One-Leg** 1952– •*Russian gymnast*• Born in Vladimir, he won 15 Olympic medals (7 gold) between 1972 and 1980. In addition, he won 12 world championship medals, including the overall individual title in 1978.

Andrić, Ivo 1892–1975 •*Serbian author and diplomat and Nobel Prize winner*• Born near Travnik (now in Bosnia and Herzegovina), he was interned by the Austrian government as a Yugoslav nationalist during World War I. He later joined the diplomatic service and was minister in Berlin at the outbreak of World War II. His chief works are *Na Drini Ćuprija* (1945, Eng trans *The Bridge on the Drina*, 1959) and *Travnička hronika* (1945, Eng trans *Bosnian Story*, 1958). He received the 1961 Nobel Prize for literature.

Andronicus, *called* **Cyrrhestes** 1st century BC •*Greek architect*• Born in Cyrrhus, he constructed the Tower of the Winds in Athens, known in the Middle Ages as the Lantern of Demosthenes.

Andronicus I Comnenus c.1122–85 •*Byzantine emperor*• Born in Constantinople (Istanbul), the grandson of **Alexius I Comnenus**, he acted treasonably and created scandal until the death of Manuel (1182), when he became first guardian, then colleague, of the young Emperor Alexius II. Emperor from 1183, he massacred the westerners in Constantinople, and caused first the dowager empress to be strangled, then Alexius himself, and married his youthful widow. He was overthrown and killed in a popular uprising.

Andronicus II Palaeologus 1260–1332 •*Byzantine emperor*• He was born in Constantinople (Istanbul), and during his reign (1282–1328), he withdrew from the negotiations for the union of the Greek and Roman communions, and restored the Greek ritual in full. He was an intellectual theologian rather than a warrior, and the empire suffered much from Catalan mercenaries, hired for the wars with the Turks, and declined to the status of a minor state.

Andronicus III Palaeologus 1296–1341 •*Byzantine emperor*• Born in Constantinople (Istanbul), he was the grandson of **Andronicus II Palaeologus**. Excluded from the succession for the accidental murder of his brother, he compelled his grandfather to make him his colleague in the empire and then to abdicate (1328). During his reign (1328–41), which saw almost constant warfare, the Turks occupied the southern shores of the Bosporus, and the Serbians conquered Bulgaria, Epirus and Macedonia. He relied on Cantacuzenus, a future emperor, to reform the law courts and rebuild the imperial navy.

Andronicus of Rhodes fl. 70–50 BC •*Greek Aristotelian philosopher*• He lived in Rome in **Cicero**'s time and edited the writings of **Aristotle**.

Andronicus, Livius *See* **Livius Andronicus**

Andropov, Yuri 1914–84 •*Soviet politician*• Born in the village of Nagutskoye in Stavropol province of the North Caucasus region of southern Russia, the son of a railway official, he was appointed head of the KGB (1967–82) and, in 1973, became a full member of the politburo. His firm handling of dissident movements while he was at the KGB enhanced his reputation, enabling him to be chosen as General Secretary **Leonid Brezhnev**'s successor in 1973. In this post he proved to be more radical and reformist than his previous record would have suggested, but he died after less than 15 months in office. During that time he had successfully groomed a group of potential successors, one of whom was **Mikhail Gorbachev**.

Aneurin or **Aneirin** fl. 6th–7th century •*Ancient British poet*• The creator of the oldest surviving poetry composed in Scotland, his principal work, *Y Gododdin*, celebrates the British heroes who were annihilated by the Saxons in the bloody Battle of Cattraeth (Catterick, Yorkshire) c. 600. It contains one of the earliest mentions of King **Arthur**.

Anfinsen, Christian B(oehmer) 1916–95 •*US biochemist and Nobel Prize winner*• Born in Monessen, Pennsylvania, he was educated at Harvard, and from 1939 to 1944 worked at the Carlsberg Laboratory, a leading institute of protein chemistry. During 1947–48 he worked with **Hugo Theorell** at the Medical Nobel Institute before moving to the National Institutes of Health in Bethesda, Maryland (1950–82). He applied enzymic and chemical hydrolysis in the preliminary fragmentation of the protein insulin, eventually deducing the structure of the amino acids of the enzyme ribonuclease. The final primary sequence of ribonuclease reflected the combined research of several workers including **Stanford Moore** and **William Stein**, with whom he shared the Nobel Prize for chemistry in 1972.

Angas, George Fife 1789–1879 •*English shipowner*• Born in Newcastle upon Tyne, he is regarded as a founder of South Australia. He was appointed commissioner for the formation of the colony in 1834, and emigrated to Adelaide in 1851.

Angeles, Victoria de los *See* **de los Angeles, Victoria**

Angelico, Fra, *real name* **Guido di Pietro**, *monastic name* **Giovanni da Fiesole** c. 1387–1455 •*Italian painter*• Born in Vicchio, Tuscany, as a young man he entered the Dominican monastery of San Domenico at Fiesole, near Florence. The community was obliged to leave Fiesole (1409), and some time after its return in 1418 Fra Angelico began to paint. In 1436 he was transferred to Florence, where he worked for **Cosimo de' Medici**, and in 1445 he was summoned by the pope to Rome where he worked until his death. His most important frescoes are in the Florentine convent of San Marco, which is now a museum. Of his easel pictures, a *Coronation of the Virgin* is held by the Louvre, Paris, and a *Glory* by the London National Gallery. There are other notable examples in the Uffizi, Florence.

Angell, Sir Norman, *originally* **Ralph Norman Angell Lane** 1872–1967 •*English writer, pacifist and Nobel Prize winner*• Born in Holbeach, Lincolnshire, he wrote *The Great Illusion* (1910) and *The Great Illusion 1933* (1933) to prove the economic futility of war even for the victors. He won the Nobel Peace Prize in 1933.

Angelou, Maya (Marguerite Annie), *née* **Johnson** 1928– •*US writer*• She was born in St Louis, Missouri, and after the breakup of her parents' marriage, she and her brother lived with their grandmother in Stamps, Arkansas. She was raped by her mother's boyfriend when she was eight and for the next five years was mute. In her teens she moved to California to live with her mother, and at 16 gave birth to her son, Guy. In her twenties she toured Europe and Africa in the musical *Porgy and Bess*. In New York she joined the Harlem Writers Guild and continued to earn her living performing in **Jean Genet**'s *The Blacks*. In the 1960s she was involved in Black struggles and then spent several years in Ghana as editor of *African Review*. Her multivolume autobiography, commencing with *I Know Why the Caged Bird Sings* (1969), is imbued with optimism, humor and homespun philosophy, and was a critical and popular success. She has published several volumes of verse, including *And Still I Rise* (1978), and is the Reynolds Professor of American Studies at Wake Forest University in North Carolina. In 1993 she read her poem "On the Pulse of Morning" at President **Clinton**'s inauguration. Recent works include *Even the Stars Look Lonesome* (1998). She was awarded the National Medal of Arts in 2000.

“ ”

Self-pity in its early stage is as snug as a feather mattress. Only when it hardens does it become uncomfortable.

1974 ***Gather Together In My Name****, chapter 6.*

Angerville, Richard *See* **Aungerville, Richard**

Ångström, Anders Jonas 1814–74 •*Swedish physicist*• Born in Lödgö, he became Professor of Physics at the University of Uppsala in 1858, and from 1867 he was secretary to the Royal Society at Uppsala. He wrote on heat, magnetism, and especially optics; the angstrom unit, for measuring wavelengths of light, is named after him.

Ann, Mother *See* **Lee, Ann**

Anna Comnena 1083–1148 •*Byzantine princess*• The daughter of Emperor **Alexius I Comnenus**, she tried in vain to secure the imperial crown, and failed in her attempt to overthrow or poison her brother (1118). Disappointed and ashamed, she withdrew from the court, and sought solace in literature. On the death of her husband (1137), she wrote a life of her father, the *Alexiad*, which contains an account of the First Crusade.

Anna Ivanovna 1693–1740 •*Empress of Russia*• Born in Moscow, she was the younger daughter of Ivan V and niece of **Peter I (the Great)**. In 1710 she married the Duke of Courland, who died the following year. After the early death of **Peter II** she was elected to the throne by the Supreme Privy Council (1730), with conditions that severely limited her authority. She trumped the council by abolishing it and ruled as an autocrat with her German favorite, **Ernst Johann Biron**, who assumed the title of Duke of Courland and became the real power behind the throne. Together they established a reign of terror, in which 20,000 people are said to have been banished to Siberia.

Annan, James Craig 1864–1946 •*Scottish photographer*• The son of **Thomas Annan**, he went to Vienna and studied the art of photogravure, a photographic etching process, with its inventor, Karl Klic, and was to become a master of this medium. Among his friends was **David Young Cameron**; together they traveled to the Low Countries (1892) and Italy (1894), producing work complementary in character and subject. Annan gained an international reputation during his lifetime, exhibiting in Europe and the US. Examples of his work were published in **Alfred Stieglitz**'s influential magazine *Camera Work* (1903–17).

Annan, Kofi Atta 1938– •*Ghanaian civil servant, diplomat and Nobel Prize winner*• Born in Kumasi in the former Gold Coast (now Ghana), he was educated at the University of Science and Technology in Kumasi, and went on to further studies in the US and Switzerland. He began his career as a budget officer with the World Health Organization in 1962, and held key posts in a number of other UN agencies before becoming Secretary-General in 1997. He is particularly associated with his work as UN special envoy in negotiations with Iraq and Yugoslavia, and has put forward many proposals to reform the increasingly unwieldy bureaucracy of the United Nations. His efforts to bring new life to the UN were recognized in 2001 when he and the UN itself were jointly awarded the Nobel Peace Prize.

Annan, Thomas 1829–87 •*Scottish photographer*• He was born in Fife, the son of a farmer and flax spinner. After apprenticeship as a lithographer, he jointly set up a photographic studio in 1855 and opened his own printing works in 1859. Much encouraged and influenced by **David Octavius Hill**, Annan was known in his own day for the accurate reproduction of paintings, including Hill's enormous *Signing of the Deed of Demission*.... He took a particular interest in the question of permanence and purchased the Scottish rights to the carbon process in 1866 and the British rights to Karl Klic's photogravure process in the 1880s. His son was the photographer **James Craig Annan**.

Anne, St 50 BC–AD 50 •*Mother of the Virgin Mary*• She is first mentioned in the *Protevangelium* of James, in the second century. She is said to have been born in Nazareth or in Bethlehem, and to have lived with her husband Joachim from the age of 20. She is the patron saint of Brittany and of Canada, and her feast day is July 26.

Anne 1665–1714 •*Queen of Great Britain and Ireland from 1702*• Anne was born at St James's Palace in London, the second daughter of the Duke of York (later **James VII and II**) and his first wife, Anne Hyde. She was the younger sister of **Mary II** (wife of **William III**). Although her father became a Catholic and married the Catholic **Mary of Modena** in 1672, Anne was brought up a staunch Protestant. In 1683 she married Prince George of Denmark (1653–1708); she bore him 17 children, only one of whom survived infancy but died at the age of 12. For much of her life she was greatly influenced by her close friend and confidante, **Sarah Churchill**, the future Duchess of Marlborough. When her father was overthrown in the Glorious Revolution of 1688, Anne supported the accession of her sister Mary and her brother-in-law William, and was placed in the succession; but after quarrelling with Mary she was drawn by the Marlboroughs into Jacobite intrigues for the restoration of her father or to secure the succession of his son, **James Stuart**, the Old Pretender. In 1701, however, after the death of her own son, she signed the Act of Settlement designating the Hanoverian descendants of **James VI and I** as her successors, and in 1702 she succeeded William III on the throne. Queen Anne's reign was marked by a concern for national unity under the Crown, which was achieved with the union of the parliaments of Scotland and England in 1707. On her death in August 1714, she was succeeded by **George I**.

“ ”

I have changed my Ministers but I have not changed my measures. I am still for moderation, and I will govern by it.

1711 Addressing her new Tory administration, January.

Anne, Princess, *in full* **Anne Elizabeth Alice Louise**, *also called* **the Princess Royal** 1950– •*British princess*• The only daughter of Queen **Elizabeth II** of Great Britain and Northern Ireland, and Prince **Philip**, she married (1973) Lieutenant (now Captain) **Mark Phillips** of the Queen's Dragoon Guards. They have two children: Peter Mark Andrew (1977–) and Zara Anne Elizabeth (1981–). The couple separated in 1989 and divorced in 1992. In December 1992 Anne married Commander Timothy Laurence (1955–). An accomplished horsewoman, Anne has ridden in the British equestrian team, and was European cross-country champion (1972). She is a keen supporter of charities and overseas relief work, and as president of Save the Children Fund she has traveled widely promoting its activities.

Anne Boleyn 1501–36 •*English queen*• The daughter of Sir Thomas Boleyn and Elizabeth Howard, daughter of the Duke of Norfolk, she was at the French court from 1519 to 1521. On her return her suitors included King **Henry VIII**, who began to shower favors upon her father, having already had an affair with her sister. Anne became Henry's second wife in a secret ceremony in January 1533. **Thomas Cranmer** soon declared the marriage legal (May 1533) and Anne was crowned with great splendor in Westminster Hall on Whitsunday. Within three months Henry's passion had cooled. It was not revived by the birth (September 1533) of a princess (later **Elizabeth I**), still less by that of a stillborn son (1536). She was arrested and taken to the Tower of London, convicted of treason on fragile evidence, and beheaded on Tower Green on May 19. Henry married to **Jane Seymour** eleven days later.

Anne of Austria 1601–66 •*Queen of France*• Born in Valladolid, Spain, she was the eldest daughter of **Philip III** of Spain and wife of **Louis XIII** of France, whom she married in 1615. Their first son was born in 1638; he succeeded to the throne on his father's death in 1643, as **Louis XIV**, with Anne as regent (1643–51). She wielded power with her favorite, Cardinal **Mazarin**, as Prime Minister. They ruled France during the Frondes, and after Louis technically came of age in 1651, they continued to rule the country jointly until Mazarin's death (1661), when Anne retired to the convent of Val de Grâce, and Louis XIV became absolute monarch.

Anne of Bohemia 1366–94 •*Queen of England*• The daughter of the emperor **Charles IV**, she married **Richard II** as his first wife in 1382. Richard was devoted to her but the expenses of her household soured relations between king and parliament. She died of the plague, childless.

Anne of Brittany 1476–1514 •*Duchess of Brittany and twice queen of France*• The daughter of Duke Francis II of Brittany, she succeeded her father in 1488. She struggled to maintain Breton independence, but was forced to marry **Charles VIII** of France (1491), thus uniting Brittany with the French Crown. After his death, she married his successor, **Louis XII** in 1499.

Anne of Cleves 1515–57 •*German princess and queen of England*• She was the daughter of John, Duke of Cleves, a noted champion of Protestantism in Germany. She became the fourth queen of **Henry VIII** in January 1540, as part of **Thomas Cromwell**'s strategy of developing an alliance with German Protestant rulers. The marriage was declared null and void, on grounds of non-consummation, six months afterwards. On agreeing to the divorce, Anne was given a large income, and she remained in England until her death.

Anne of Denmark 1574–1619 •*Danish princess, and queen of Scotland and England*• The daughter of King **Frederik II** of Denmark, she married (1589) **James VI** of Scotland, the future **James I** of England. While much of her time was spent in planning extravagant court entertainments, she encouraged the arts and architecture, and appeared in dramatic roles in court masques by **Ben Jonson**.

Annigoni, Pietro 1910–88 •*Italian painter*• Born in Milan, he worked in England during the 1950s, and held a London exhibition in 1954. He was one of the few 20th-century artists to put into practice the technical methods of the old masters, and his most usual medium was tempera. His Renaissance manner is shown at its best in his portraits, for example of Queen **Elizabeth II** (1955, 1970) and President **Kennedy** (1961).

Anning, Mary 1799–1847 •*English fossil collector*• Born in Lyme Regis, Dorset, she was the daughter of a carpenter and vendor of fossil specimens who died in 1810, leaving her to make her own living. In 1811 she discovered in a local cliff the fossil skeleton of an ichthyosaur, now in the Natural History Museum, London. She also discovered the first plesiosaur (1821) and the first pterodactyl, *Dimorphodon* (1828).

Annunzio, Gabriele d' *See* **D'Annunzio, Gabriele**

Anouilh, Jean 1910–87 •*French dramatist*• He was born in Bordeaux, of French and Basque parentage, and studied law in Paris. His first play, *L'Hermine* (1931, Eng trans *The Ermine*, 1955), was not a success, but his steady output soon earned him recognition. He was influenced by the neoclassical fashion inspired by **Jean Giraudoux**, but his very personal approach to the reinterpretation of Greek myths was less poetic, and more in tune with the contemporary taste for artifice and stylization. Among his many successful plays are *Antigone* (1946, prod in English, New York 1946, London 1949), *Médée* (1946, Eng trans *Medea*, 1956), *Becket* (1959, first performed in London, 1961), *Cher Antoine* (1969, Eng trans *Dear Antoine*, 1971), and *La Culotte* (1978, "The Breeches").

Anquetil, Jacques 1934–87 •*French racing cyclist*• Born in Normandy, he was the foremost of the second wave of French cyclists to emerge after World War II. He won the Tour de France five times, including four successes in a row (1961–64). Excelling in time-trial stages, he could make ferocious attacks, or suddenly distance the field on a conventional stretch of road. He retired in 1969.

Anschütz, Ottomar 1846–1907 •*German photographer*• Born in Lissa, formerly Prussia, now Poland, he was a pioneer of instant photography. He also made an early series of pictures of moving animals and people, making a substantial contribution to the invention of the cinematograph.

Anselm, St 1033–1109 •*Italian theologian and philosopher*• He was born near Aosta, Piedmont. Appointed Archbishop of Canterbury in 1093 he was frequently in conflict over Church rights, first with **William II** (William Rufus), then with **Henry I**. A follower of **Augustine**, Anselm was a major figure in early scholastic philosophy, remembered especially for his theory of atonement and his ontological proof for the existence of God. He defined God as "something than which nothing greater can be conceived." Since anything that exists in reality is by nature greater than anything that exists only in the mind, God must exist in reality, for otherwise he would not be "the greatest conceivable being." His feast day is April 21.

Anson, George Anson, Baron 1697–1762 •*English naval commander*• Born in Shugborough Park, Staffordshire, he joined the navy in 1712, and was made a captain in 1724. In 1739, on the outbreak of war with Spain (the War of Jenkins' Ear, 1739–48), he received the command of a Pacific squadron of six vessels, and sailed from England in 1740. With one ship and less than 200 men, but with £500,000 of Spanish treasure, he returned to Spithead in 1744, having circumnavigated the globe. He was made First Lord of the Admiralty (1751). He wrote *Voyage Round the World* (1748).

Anstey, F, *pseudonym of* **Thomas Anstey Guthrie** 1856–1934 •*English writer*• Born in London, he studied at Trinity Hall, Cambridge, and in 1880 was called to the bar. A whimsical humorist, he wrote *Vice Versa* (1882), *The Tinted Venus* (1885), *The Brass Bottle* (1900), and many other novels and dialogues. He was on the staff of *Punch* from 1887 to 1930.

Antenor 6th century BC •*Greek sculptor*• He worked in Athens, and is known to have executed bronze statues of *Harmodius* and *Aristogiton*, and a majestic marble of *Kore* from the Acropolis (now in the Acropolis Museum).

Anthony of Padua *See* **Antony of Padua, St**

Anthony, C L *See* **Smith, Dodie**

Anthony, Susan B(rownell) 1820–1906 •*US social reformer and women's suffrage leader*• Born in Adams, Massachusetts, she attended schools in Battensville, New York, and Philadelphia. Her feminist activities began at 17 when she campaigned for equal pay for women teachers, and she was also an early supporter of the temperance and antislavery movements. In 1869 she founded the National American Woman Suffrage Association with **Elizabeth Stanton**. With Stanton and **Matilda Joslyn Gage** produced the four-volume *History of Woman Suffrage* (1881–1902).

“ ”

There will never be complete equality until women themselves help to make laws and to elect lawmakers.

*1897 In **The Arena**.*

Antigonus, *also called* **Monophthalmos ("the one-eyed")** d. 301 BC •*Macedonian general*• He was one of the generals of **Alexander the Great**. After Alexander's death, he received the provinces of Phrygia Major, Lycia and Pamphylia. On the regent Antipater's death in 319 BC he waged incessant wars against the other generals, making himself master of all Asia Minor and Syria. In 306 he assumed the title of king together with his son Demetrius Poliorcetes, but was defeated and slain by **Lysimachus** and his son, **Cassander**, and **Seleucus I** at Ipsus in Phrygia.

Antigonus II Gonatas c. 319–239 BC •*King of Macedonia*• He succeeded to the throne in 276 BC, seven years after the death of his father, Demetrius Poliorcetes. **Pyrrhus** of Epirus overran Macedonia in 274, but Antigonus soon recovered his kingdom, and consolidated it despite incessant wars.

Antiochus I, *called* **Soter** c. 323–c. 261 BC •*Seleucid king of Syria*• He was the son of **Seleucus I**, one of **Alexander the Great**'s generals, whose murder (280 BC) gave him the whole Syrian Empire, but left him too weak to assert his right to Macedonia. He gained the name of Soter ("Saviour") for a victory over the Gauls (275 BC).

Antiochus II, *called* **Theos ("God")** c. 286–246 BC •*Seleucid king of Syria*• The son and successor (261 BC) of **Antiochus I**, he married **Berenice Syra**, daughter of **Ptolemy II**, exiling his first wife, Laodice, and her children. On his death there followed a struggle between the rival queens; Berenice and her son were murdered and Laodice's son, Seleucus II, succeeded.

Antiochus III, *called* **the Great** 242–187 BC •*Seleucid king of Syria*• The grandson of **Antiochus II**, he waged war against **Ptolemy IV Philopator**, obtained Palestine and Coele-Syria (198), and married his daughter Cleopatra to the young King **Ptolemy V** of Egypt, which became almost a Seleucid protectorate. He afterward became involved in war with the Romans, but refused to invade Italy at **Hannibal**'s request. He entered Greece, but was defeated at Thermopylae (191), and by **Scipio** the Elder at Magnesia (190/189).

Antiochus IV, *called* **Epiphanes ("God Manifest")** c. 215–163 BC •*Seleucid king of Syria*• The son of **Antiochus III**, he fought against

Egypt and conquered a great part of it. He twice took Jerusalem, where his attempt to stamp out Judaism and establish the worship of Greek gods provoked the Jews to a successful insurrection under Mattathias and his sons, the **Maccabees**.

Antisthenes c. 455–c. 360 BC •*Greek philosopher*• He is thought to be cofounder, with his pupil **Diogenes of Sinope**, of the Cynic school. He was a rhetorician and a disciple of **Gorgias**, and later became a close friend of **Socrates**. Only fragments of his many works survive.

Antonello da Messina c. 1430–79 •*Italian painter*• Born in Messina, he was the only major 15th-century Italian artist to come from Sicily. An accomplished master of oil painting, he helped popularize the medium. His style is a delicate synthesis of the northern and Italian styles. In 1475 he was working in Venice, where his work influenced **Giovanni Bellini**'s portraits. There are fragments of his Venetian San Cassiano altarpiece in Vienna. His first dated work, the *Salvator Mundi* (1465), and a self-portrait are in the National Gallery, London.

Antonescu, Ion 1882–1946 •*Romanian general and dictator*• Born into an aristocratic family in Pitesti, he served as military attaché in Rome and London, and became Chief of Staff and Minister of Defense in 1937. Imprisoned in 1938 for plotting a right-wing revolt, he was a supporter of **Hitler**. In September 1940 he assumed dictatorial powers and forced the abdication of King **Carol II**. In 1944 he was overthrown, and then executed for war crimes.

Antoninus Pius, *originally* **Titus Aurelius Fulvus Boionius Arrius Antoninus**, *after adoption* **Titus Aelius Hadrianus Antoninus** AD 86–161 •*Roman emperor*• Born in Lanuvium, the son of a consul, he was sent as proconsul into Asia by the emperor **Hadrian**, was adopted by him (AD 138) and the same year came to the throne. His reign was proverbially peaceful and happy, as a result of his integrity and benevolence. In his reign the empire was extended, and the Antonine Wall, named after him, was built between the Forth and Clyde rivers in North Britain.

Antonioni, Michelangelo 1912– •*Italian film director*• He was born in Ferrara, Italy, and after taking a degree in political economy at Bologna University, began as a film critic before becoming an assistant director (1942). He made several documentaries (1945–50) before turning to feature films, often scripted by himself, and noted for character study rather than plot. He gained an international reputation with *L'Avventura* (1959, *The Adventure*), a long, slow-moving study of its two main characters. *Blow-Up* (1967) won the Palme d'Or at the Cannes Film Festival, while his other films include *La Notte* (1961, *The Night*) and *The Passenger* (1974). He received an Honorary Academy Award in 1995 and was made a Commander of the Legion of Honor in 1996.

Antony or **Anthony, St**, *also called* **Antony of Egypt** or **Antony the Great** c. 251–356 AD •*Egyptian ascetic and the father of Christian monasticism*• Born in Koman, Upper Egypt, he sold his possessions for the poor at 20, then spent 20 years in the desert, where he withstood a famous series of temptations, often represented in later art. In AD 305 he left his retreat and founded a monastery near Memphis and Arsinoë. His feast day is January 17.

Antony or **Anthony of Padua, St** 1195–1231 •*Portuguese friar*• He was born in Lisbon. In 1220 he joined the Franciscan order, and, noted for his preaching, became one of its most active proponents. Canonized in 1232 by **Gregory IX**, he is the patron saint of Portugal, the lower animals, and lost property. His feast day is June 13.

Antony, Mark, *also known as* **Marcus Antonius** c. 83–30 BC •*Roman politician and soldier*• He was related on his mother's side to **Julius Caesar**. In 47 he was made master of the horse, and was left to govern Italy during Caesar's absence in Africa. He held no further post until 44, when he was consul with Caesar. After Caesar's assassination, the conspirators fled, leaving Antony with almost absolute power. In the young Octavianus **Augustus** (named as heir in Caesar's will), he encountered a more ruthless and astute politician than himself. He was besieged and defeated at Mutina (43), and fled to Gaul. There he found support in the army of **Lepidus**, and returned to Rome. Augustus held a consultation with Antony and Lepidus, and it was decided that the three should share control of the Roman world as triumvirs. In Rome, a reign of terror began; among their first victims was **Cicero**, who had attacked Antony in the series of speeches called the Philippics. Antony went on to Athens, and then passed over to Asia, where he met and was captivated by **Cleopatra**. A new division of the Roman world was now arranged, Antony taking the east, and Augustus the west, while Lepidus had to be content with Africa; Antony also married Augustus's sister **Octavia** (40). Differences grew up between Antony and Augustus, and in 37 Antony separated from Octavia and rejoined Cleopatra. His position in the East, his relations with Cleopatra, and his unsuccessful campaigns against the Parthians (36 and 34), were seized upon by Augustus and misrepresented for propaganda purposes. Eventually Augustus declared war on Cleopatra (32) and in the naval engagement of Actium (31), Antony and Cleopatra were defeated. Antony returned to Egypt where, deserted by the navy and army and deceived by a false report of Cleopatra's death, he committed suicide.

Anza, Juan Bautista de 1735–88 •*Spanish explorer*• Born in Frontereas, Mexico, he made an expedition with the Spanish army from Sonora over the Colorado Desert to Spanish missions in California (1774), becoming the first to establish a land route to Spain's northern possessions, which were normally reached by sea. He founded San Francisco in 1776.

Anzilotti, Dionisio 1867–1950 •*Italian judge and jurist*• Born in Pistoia, he was educated at Pisa. Professor of Law at Rome University (1911–37), he was a founder of the positive school of international law; this derived the law from international precedent rather than from theory. He became a judge of the Permanent Court of International Justice (1921–30), and its president (1928–30).

Aouita, Said 1960– •*Moroccan track athlete*• Born in Rabat, he set world records at 1,500 meters and 5,000 meters in 1985, becoming the first man in 30 years to hold both records. He also broke world records at 2 miles, 2,000 meters, and 3,000 meters. He was the 1984 Olympic champion, 1986 overall Grand Prix winner, and 1987 world 5,000-meter champion.

Apelles 4th century BC •*Greek painter*• Probably born in Colophon, on the Ionian coast of Asia Minor, he is said to have accompanied **Alexander the Great** on his expedition to Asia and to have settled at Ephesus. None of his work has survived, but his fame is apparent from ancient writings.

Apollinaire, Guillaume, *pseudonym of* **Wilhelm Apollinaris de Kostrowitzky** 1880–1918 •*French poet*• Born in Rome of Polish descent, he settled in Paris in 1900, and became a leader of the movement rejecting poetic traditions in outlook, rhythm and language. His poetry includes *Alcools* (1913, Eng trans 1964) and *Calligrammes* (1918). He was wounded in World War I, and during his convalescence wrote the play *Les mamelles de Tirésias* (1918, "The Breasts of Tiresias"), for which he coined the term "surrealist," and the Modernist manifesto *L'esprit nouveau et les poètes* (1946, "The New Spirit and the Poets").

" "

Vienne la nuit sonne l'heure
Les jours s'en vont je demeure.
Let night come, ring out the hour,
The days go by, I remain.

1913 ***Alcools****, "Le Pont Mirabeau."*

Apollinaris, *called* **the Younger** c. 310–c. 390 AD •*Syrian prelate*• Bishop of Laodicea from AD 360, he was one of the sternest opponents of Arianism. He supported a doctrine (Apollinarianism) condemned by the Council of Constantinople (381) as denying the true human nature of **Jesus**.

Apollonius of Perga fl. 250–220 BC •*Greek mathematician*• Known as "the Great Geometer," he was the author of the definitive ancient work on conic sections that laid the foundations of later teaching on the subject. He also wrote on various geometrical problems, and put forward two descriptions of planetary motion.

Apollonius Rhodius b. c. 295 BC •*Greek poet and literary scholar*•

Born in Alexandria, Egypt, he was a pupil of **Callimachus** and became head of the Alexandrian library c. 260–247 BC. His great (and only surviving) work is the *Argonautica*, an epic poem on the Homeric model describing the quest for the Golden Fleece.

Appel, Karel Christian 1921– •*Dutch painter and sculptor*• Born in Amsterdam, he studied at the Royal College of Art there. He began his artistic career in 1938, and was one of an influential group of Dutch, Belgian and Danish expressionists known as "Cobra." His work, containing swirls of brilliant color and aggressively contorted figures, has affinities with American abstract expressionism and has won many prizes, including the UNESCO prize, the Venice Biennale (1953) and the Guggenheim International prize (1961).

Appert, Nicolas François 1749–1841 •*French chef and inventor*• He was born in Châlons-sur-Marne. A chef and confectioner, in 1795 he began experiments in preserving food in hermetically sealed containers, in response to a call from the French government for a solution to the problem of feeding the greatly expanded army and navy. He opened the world's first commercial canning factory in 1812. Initially he used glass jars and bottles, changing to tin-plated metal cans in 1822.

Appius Claudius Caecus fl. 312–308 BC •*Roman politician and general*• His fame rests primarily on his great reforming censorship (312–308 BC), during which he opened up the political process to the lower orders, made the Senate less exclusive and launched a number of projects to improve the quality of life in Rome, including the building of the city's first aqueduct, the Aqua Appia, as well as the first great Roman road, the Via Appia (Appian Way).

Appleton, Sir Edward Victor 1892–1965 •*English physicist and Nobel Prize winner*• Born in Bradford, he studied at St John's College, Cambridge. Following appointments at the Cavendish Laboratory in 1920 and London University, he returned to Cambridge (1936) as Jacksonian Professor of Natural Philosophy. In 1949 he was appointed Principal and Vice Chancellor of Edinburgh University. In 1947 he won the Nobel Prize for physics for his contribution toward exploring the ionosphere. His work revealed the existence of a layer of electrically charged particles in the upper atmosphere (the Appleton layer) which plays an essential part in making wireless communication possible between distant stations, and was also fundamental to the development of radar.

Apponyi, Albert Georg, Count 1846–1933 •*Hungarian statesman*• Born in Vienna, he entered the Hungarian Diet in 1872, and soon became leader of the moderate opposition which became the National Party in 1891. In 1899 he and his supporters went over to the Liberal government party, and from 1901 to 1903 he was President of the Diet.

Apuleius, Lucius 2nd century AD •*Roman writer, satirist and rhetorician*• Born in Madaura, in Numidia, Africa, he was educated at Carthage and Athens. He is best known as the author of the picaresque novel *Metamorphoses* (Eng trans *The Golden Ass*, 1566), a tale of adventure containing elements of magic, satire and romance, notably the story of Cupid and Psyche.

Aquila, *known as* **Ponticus** fl. 130 AD •*Translator of the Old Testament into Greek*• A native of Sinope, he is said to have been first a pagan, then a Christian, and finally a Jew.

Aquinas, St Thomas 1225–74 •*Italian scholastic philosopher and theologian*• Born in the castle of Roccasecca, near Aquino, and was a descendant of the family of the counts of Aquino. He was educated by the Benedictines of Monte Cassino, and at the University of Naples. In 1244 he entered the Dominican order of mendicant friars and later made his way to Cologne to become a pupil of the great Dominican luminary, **Albertus Magnus**. In 1252 he went to Paris, and taught there, with growing reputation, until in 1258 he was summoned by the pope to teach successively in Anagni, Orvieto, Rome and Viterbo. He died at Fossanuova on his way to defend the papal cause at the Council of Lyons, and was canonized in 1323. His prolific writings, which include *Summa contra gentiles* (1259–64) and the *Summa theologiae* (1266–73), have exercised enormous intellectual authority throughout the Church. He was the first among the metaphysicians of the 13th century to stress the importance of sense perception and the experimental foundation of human knowledge. Through his commentaries he made **Aristotle**'s thought available and acceptable in the Christian West, and in his philosophical writings he tried to combine and reconcile Aristotle's scientific rationalism with the Christian doctrines of faith and revelation. Aquinas was known as the "Doctor Angelicus" and the only other scholastic theologian who rivaled him was the "Doctor Subtilis," **Duns Scotus**. The Franciscans followed Scotus, and the Dominicans Thomas, with the result that medieval theologians were divided into two schools, Scotists and Thomists, whose divergencies penetrate more or less every branch of doctrine.

“ ”

Ars autem deficit ab operatione naturae.

Art pales when compared to the workings of nature.

c.1272 ***Summa Theologiae****, Book 3, question 66, article 4.*

Aquino, Benigno, *nicknamed* **Ninoy** 1932–83 •*Philippine politician*• Born into a political family, he rose rapidly through provincial politics to become a senator at the age of 35. He was the principal opposition leader during the period of martial law, declared by President **Ferdinand Marcos** in 1972. In 1977 Aquino was arrested and sentenced to death on charges of murder and subversion, but in 1980, suffering from a heart condition, he was allowed to leave for the US for surgery (and exile). On his return to the Philippines (1983), he was assassinated by a military guard at Manila airport. His death unleashed mass demonstrations against the Marcos order, which were to lead, in 1986, to the collapse of the Marcos presidency and the succession of Benigno's widow, **Cory Aquino**.

Aquino, Cory (Maria Corazón), *née* **Cojuango** 1933– •*Philippine politician*• The daughter of a wealthy sugar baron in Tarlac province, she studied in the US, where she gained a degree in mathematics at Mount St Vincent College, New York. In 1956 she married **Benigno Aquino**, and after his imprisonment in 1972 by President **Ferdinand Marcos** kept him in touch with the outside world. Following her husband's assassination, she took up his cause, and with widespread support claimed victory in the 1986 presidential elections. The nonviolent "people's power" movement which followed brought the overthrow of Marcos and Aquino's installation as president. Her presidency was, however, much troubled by internal opposition. In 1992 she did not run for the presidency again, but instead supported the successful bid of General **Fidel Ramos**.

Arabi Pasha *See* **Ahmed Arabi**

Arafat, Yasser, *real name* **Mohammed Abed Ar'ouf Arafat** 1929– •*Palestinian resistance leader*• He was born in Jerusalem, and educated at Cairo University (1952–56). He cofounded the Al Fatah resistance group in 1956, which later gained control of the Palestine Liberation Organization (PLO), which had itself been formed in 1964. Acknowledged (though not universally popular) as the PLO leader, he skillfully managed the uneasy juxtaposition of militancy and diplomacy, and gradually gained world acceptance of the PLO; the organization was formally recognized by the United Nations in 1974. Under his leadership, the PLO's original aim—to create a secular democratic state over the whole of the prewar Palestine—was modified to one of establishing an independent Palestinian state in any part of Palestine from which Israel would agree to withdraw. In 1985 he agreed with King **Hussein** of Jordan to recognize the state of Israel, provided that territory which had been seized was restored. This initiative failed but in July 1988 Hussein surrendered his right to administer the West Bank, indicating that the PLO might take over the responsibility. Arafat, to the surprise of many Western politicians, persuaded the majority of his colleagues to acknowledge the right of Israel to coexist with an independent state of Palestine. In 1993 Arafat and the Prime Minister of Israel **Yitzhak Rabin** negotiated a peace agreement at the White House (signed in Cairo in 1994), by which Israel agreed to withdraw from Jericho and the Gaza Strip. Arafat and Rabin, together with Israel's Foreign Minister **Shimon Peres**, were jointly awarded the Nobel Peace Prize in 1994. He was elected president of the Palestinian National Council, with 88 percent of the vote, in January 1996.

Aragon, Catherine of *See* **Catherine of Aragon**

Aragon, Louis 1897–1983 •*French writer and political activist*• Born in Paris, he became one of the most brilliant of the Surrealist group and cofounded the journal *Littérature* with **André Breton** in 1919. He published two volumes of poetry, *Feu de joie* (1920, "Bonfire") and *Le mouvement perpétuel* (1925, "Perpetual Motion"), and a Surrealist novel, *Le paysan de Paris* (1926, "The Peasant of Paris"). After a visit to the USSR in 1930 he became a convert to Communism. Thereafter he wrote socialist-realistic novels in a series entitled *Le monde réel* (1933–51, "The Real World").

Arana Goiri, Sabino de 1865–1903 •*Basque nationalist*• From a well-to-do Carlist family, he created much of the language and symbolism of Basque nationalism. Not only did he revive the Basque language, by publishing grammars, textbooks, histories, newspapers and magazines, but he also created the word *Euzkadi* for the Basque ethnic nation, designed the first Basque flag (the ikurrina), founded the first Basque cultural club, and coined many of its key political slogans. He founded the Basque Nationalist Party (PNV) in 1895. He was also the first Basque nationalist to win public office.

Arany, János 1817–82 •*Hungarian poet*• Born in Nagy-Szalonta, he was a leader with **Sándor Petőfi** of the popular national school, and is regarded as one of the greatest Hungarian poets. He was chief secretary of the Hungarian Academy from 1870 to 1879. His works include the satire *The Lost Constitution* (1845), which won the Kisfaludy Society Prize, and the *Toldi* trilogy (1847–54), the story of the adventures of a young peasant in the 14th-century Hungarian court.

Arber, Agnes, *née* **Robertson** 1879–1960 •*English botanist*• She was born in London and educated at University College London (UCL), and Newnham College, Cambridge. Her study of early printed herbals led to her first and most widely read book, *Herbals, Their Origin and Evolution* (1912), which became the standard work. She also published books on comparative plant anatomy and the philosophy of biology.

Arber, Werner 1929– •*Swiss microbiologist and Nobel Prize winner*• Born in Gränichen, he studied at the Swiss Federal Institute of Technology, Geneva University, and the University of Southern California, returning to Geneva and then to Basel University as Professor of Molecular Biology from 1970. In the 1960s he proposed that when bacteria defend themselves against phages (the viruses which attack bacteria) they use selective enzymes which cut the phage DNA at specific points in the DNA chain. He shared the Nobel Prize for physiology or medicine in 1978 with **Hamilton Smith** and **Daniel Nathans**.

Arbus, Diane, *née* **Nemerov** 1923–71 •*US photographer*• Born in New York City, she rebelled against the social norms of her privileged background and her work in conventional fashion photography. Her aim was to portray people "without their masks," and she became famous in the 1960s for her ironic studies of both the wealthy and the deprived classes.

Arbuthnot, John 1667–1735 •*Scottish physician and writer*• Born in Inverbervie, Kincardineshire, he studied at Aberdeen, Oxford and St Andrews universities. He became a close friend of **Jonathan Swift** and all the literary celebrities of the day, as well as a physician-in-ordinary to Queen **Anne** (1705). In 1712 he published five satirical pamphlets against the Duke of **Marlborough**, called *The History of John Bull*, which was the origin of the popular image of John Bull as the typical Englishman. With Swift, **Pope**, **John Gay** and others he founded the Scriblerus Club, and he was the chief contributor to the *Memoirs of Martin Scriblerus* (1741).

" "

Law is a bottomless pit.

1712 ***The History of John Bull**, title of pamphlet.*

Arcadius AD 377–408 •*First Roman emperor of the East alone*• He was born in Spain, and ruled with his father, the emperor **Theodosius I (the Great)** (AD 383–95). On Theodosius's death Arcadius received the eastern half of the Roman Empire, the western falling to his brother **Honorius**. Arcadius's held a vast empire, but the real rulers were the Gaul Rufinus, the eunuch Eutropius, and his wife, Empress Eudoxia, who persecuted and banished St **John Chrysostom** (404).

Arcaro, Eddie (George Edward) 1916–97 •*US jockey*• Born in Cincinnati, Ohio, he was five-times winner of the Kentucky Derby, the top horse race in the US (first run in 1875). He won 4,799 races in a career spanning 30 years, from 1931 to 1961. He also won the triple crown twice, in 1941 and 1948 (Kentucky Derby, Preakness and Belmont Stakes).

Arcesilaus or **Arcesilas** c. 316–c. 241 BC •*Greek philosopher*• He was born in Pitane, Aeolia, Asia Minor, and became the sixth head of the Athenian Academy founded by **Plato**. Under his leadership the school became known as the "Middle Academy" to distinguish it from the "Old Academy."

Archbold, John Frederick 1785–1870 •*English lawyer*• A prolific author of practical legal textbooks, he is best remembered for *Criminal Pleading, Evidence and Practice* (1822) a work which, repeatedly revised, is an essential handbook for lawyers in the English criminal courts.

Archelaus fl. c. 450 BC •*Greek philosopher and cosmologist*• Reputed to have been the pupil of **Anaxagoras** and the teacher of **Socrates**, he made some limited modifications to the physical theories of Anaxagoras and others.

Archelaus d. 399 BC •*King of Macedonia*• He ruled from 413 to 399 BC, and was a great patron of the arts. He was portrayed by **Plato** in the *Gorgias* as a cruel monster.

Archelaus 1st century AD •*Ethnarch of Judaea*• He was the son of **Herod the Great**, and succeeded his father in AD 1, when he maintained his position against an insurrection raised by the Pharisees. After a nine-year reign, he was deposed by Augustus for his tyranny, and banished to Vienne, in Gaul, where he died.

Archer (of Weston-Super-Mare), Jeffrey Howard Archer, Baron 1940– •*British writer and former politician*• He sat as Conservative Member of Parliament for the constituency of Louth (1969–74), but resigned from the House of Commons after a financial disaster that led to bankruptcy. In order to pay his debts he turned to writing fiction. His first book, *Not a Penny More, Not a Penny Less* (1975), was an instant bestseller, which he followed up with other blockbusters like *Kane and Abel* (1979), which was dramatized on television, and *First Among Equals* (1984, also televised). Despite critical reservations about their literary merits, his books continue to sell in vast numbers. He was Deputy Chairman of the Conservative Party (1985–86), but resigned following allegations over which he later cleared his name in a successful libel action against the *Daily Star* newspaper. He was made a life peer in 1992 and in 1999 ran as a candidate for the London mayoral elections, but withdrew from the race after allegations that he had committed perjury in a 1987 libel action. In 2001 he received a four-year jail sentence on charges of perjury and perverting the course of justice.

Archer, Robyn 1948– •*Australian singer and actress*• She was born in Adelaide, South Australia. Her name has particularly been linked with the German cabaret songs of **Kurt Weill**, Hanns Eisler and **Paul Dessau**. Her shows, *To Those Born Later* (1977) and *A Star is Torn* (1979), were also successes. From 1992 to 1995 she was Artistic Director of the National Festival of Australian Theatre and she continues to play a leading role in the Australian arts community and in 2000 was made an Officer of the Order of Australia.

Archer, Thomas c. 1668–1743 •*English baroque architect*• Born in Tamworth-in-Arden, Warwickshire, he studied abroad, and designed the churches of St John's, Westminster (1714–28), and St Paul's, Deptford (1712–30), as well as Roehampton House in Surrey.

Archilochus of Paros fl. 714–676 BC •*Greek poet*• From the island of Paros, his work was highly regarded by the ancients, who placed him on a level with **Homer**, **Pindar** and **Sophocles**. **Plato** called him "the very wise," but much of his renown is for vituperative satire. Only fragments of his work survive.

Archimedes c. 287–212 BC •*Greek mathematician and inventor*• He was born in Syracuse, the son of an astronomer, and probably studied at Alexandria. He is remembered in popular tradition for inventing the Archimedean screw (which is still used for raising water), and for the story that he discovered "Archimedes's principle" while in the bath and ran into the street with a cry of *Eureka!* ("I have found it!"). The principle states that a body immersed in a fluid displaces a volume of fluid equal to its own volume. He also demonstrated the power of levers in moving large weights, and in this context made his famous declaration: "Give me a firm spot on which to stand, and I shall move the Earth." His major importance in mathematics, however, lies in his discovery of formulae for the areas and volumes of spheres, cylinders, parabolas, and other plane and solid figures, in which the methods he used anticipated the theories of integration to be developed 1,800 years later. He is said to have devised weapons to defend Syracuse from attack by the Romans, but was killed during the Roman capture of the city, supposedly by a soldier whose challenge Archimedes ignored while immersed in a mathematical problem.

Archipenko, Alexander 1880–1964 •*US sculptor*• He was born in Kiev, Ukraine, and studied there and in Moscow and Paris. He took an active part in the Cubist movement, and introduced holes and voids into sculpture, as in *Walking Woman* (1912, Benveo Art Museum). After 1923 he lived in the US. His work is characterized by extreme economy of form, and shows the influence of **Constantin Brancusi**. From c. 1946 he experimented with new materials, such as Plexiglas, lit from within.

Ardashir I, *also called* **Artaxerxes** d. 241 AD •*Founder of the Persian dynasty of the Sassanids*• He overthrew Ardavan (Artabanus), the last of the Parthian kings (c. 226 AD). He next conquered Media and a large part of the Iranian highlands, and created the biggest threat faced by Rome in the East, but was defeated by **Alexander Severus** (233). He made Zoroastrianism the state religion.

Arden, Elizabeth, *née* **Florence Nightingale Graham** c. 1880–1966 •*US beautician and businesswoman*• Born in Woodbridge, Ontario, Canada, and a nurse by training, she went to New York City in 1908 and opened a beauty salon on Fifth Avenue in 1910, adopting the personal and business name of "Elizabeth Arden." She produced and advertised cosmetics on a large scale, and developed a worldwide chain of salons.

Arden, John 1930– •*British playwright*• He was born in Barnsley, Yorkshire, and educated at Sedbergh School, King's College, Cambridge, and the Edinburgh College of Art. The college dramatic society produced his first play, a romantic comedy entitled *All Fall Down*, in 1955. Subsequent plays include *Serjeant Musgrave's Dance* (1959), staged in the Brechtian tradition, and *The Workhouse Donkey* (1963), a caricature of local politics in the north of England. Arden has continually experimented with dramatic form and theatrical technique, both in the plays he has written alone and in the many pieces in which he has collaborated with his wife, Margaretta D'Arcy (1934–). He has also written television scripts, a volume of essays, and a novel, *Silence Among the Weapons* (1982).

Areios *See* **Arius**

Arendt, Hannah 1906–75 •*US philosopher and political theorist*• Born in Hanover, Germany, she was educated at Marburg, Freiburg and Heidelberg universities. She moved to the US in 1940 as a refugee from the Nazis and worked for various Jewish organizations and became chief editor at Schocken Books (1946–48). She became naturalized in 1950, and after the publication of her first major work, *The Origins of Totalitarianism* (1951), she held academic posts at Princeton, Chicago and in New York. Among her books are *The Human Condition* (1958), *Eichmann in Jerusalem* (1963) and *The Life of the Mind* (published posthumously, 1978).

Arensky, Anton Stepanovich 1861–1906 •*Russian composer*• Born in Novgorod, he studied under **Rimsky-Korsakov**, and from 1895 conducted the court choir at St Petersburg. His compositions, which show the influence of **Tchaikovsky**, include five operas, two symphonies, and vocal and instrumental pieces.

Aretaeus fl. 100 AD •*Greek physician*• Born in Cappadocia, he was considered to rank next to the great physician **Hippocrates**. The first four books of his great work, preserved nearly complete, discuss the causes and symptoms of diseases; the other four, the cure.

Argand, Jean-Robert 1768–1822 •*Swiss mathematician*• Born in Geneva, he gave his name to the Argand diagram, in which complex numbers are represented by points in the plane.

Argenson, René Louis Voyer, Marquis d' 1694–1757 •*French statesman*• The son of the Marquis d'Argenson (1652–1721), who created the secret police and established the *lettres de cachet*, he became Councillor to the Parlement of Paris in 1716, and Foreign Minister (1744–47). His *Mémoires* is an important source of information on the period. He fell a victim in 1747 to the machinations of Madame de **Pompadour**.

Argyll, Archibald Campbell, 5th Earl of 1530–73 •*Scottish nobleman*• The son of the 4th Earl, he was a Protestant follower of **Mary Queen of Scots**. He succeeded to the earldom in 1558 and was involved in the assassination of her huband, Lord **Darnley** (1567). He later supported King **James VI and I** and became Lord High Chancellor of Scotland in 1572.

Argyll, Archibald Campbell, Marquis and **8th Earl of**, *known as* **the Covenanting Marquis** or **Cross-Eyed Archibald** 1607–61 •*Scottish nobleman*• Son of Archibald, 7th Earl of **Argyll**, he became a member of **Charles I**'s Privy Council in 1626, but in 1638 joined the Covenanters in support of Scottish Presbyterianism. In 1641 he was reconciled with Charles and created Marquis of Argyll. In the English Civil War he joined the Parliamentary side, and after being defeated by the Marquis of **Montrose** at Inverlochy in 1645 took part in the defeat of Montrose and his royalists at Philiphaugh in 1645. He formed a Scottish government under **Cromwell**'s patronage, but after the execution of the king he repudiated Cromwell, accepted the proclamation of **Charles II** as King in Scotland (1649), but later submitted to Cromwell again. At the Restoration of Charles II in 1660 he was arrested and executed.

Argyll, Archibald Campbell, 9th Earl of 1629–85 •*Scottish nobleman*• Son of Archibald, 8th Earl of **Argyll**, he was imprisoned by **Cromwell** for a suspected royalist plot (1657–60). After the Restoration of **Charles II** in 1660, he came into favor, but his efforts on behalf of his father led to him being imprisoned again until 1663. In 1681 he refused to sign the Test Act that forced all public office holders to declare their belief in Protestantism, and was sentenced to death for treason. He escaped to Holland. In 1685, after the accession of **James VII and II**, he conspired with the Duke of **Monmouth** to overthrow the king. He returned to Scotland but was captured and executed.

Argyll, John Campbell, 2nd Duke of 1678–1743 •*Scottish politician*• He succeeded Archibald, 1st Duke of **Argyll** in 1703. A committed Unionist, he was a high commissioner to the Scottish parliament of 1704 and one of the strongest supporters of the Act of Union of 1707. At the time of the Jacobite Rising in Scotland (1715–16) he commanded the Hanoverian forces that dispersed the Jacobite troops without a battle. He was created Duke of Greenwich in 1719.

Arias Navarro, Carlos 1908–89 •*Spanish politician*• Notorious as the "Butcher of Málaga" for being state prosecutor there during the Nationalists' savage repression during the Spanish Civil War (1936–39). He became Prime Minister in December 1973 after the assassination of **Luis Carrero Blanco**. Following General **Franco**'s death (1975), he was confirmed as the first Prime Minister of the monarchy. He resigned in 1976 under King **Juan Carlos I**, having proven too hardline to effect the transition to democracy.

Arias Sanchez, Oscar 1940– •*Costa Rican politician and Nobel Prize winner*• Born in Heredia, Costa Rica, he was educated in England, then returned to Costa Rica, where he started a law practice. He entered politics, joining the left-wing National Liberation Party (PLN) and later became its secretary-general. Elected president of Costa Rica in 1986, on a neutralist platform, he was the major author of a Central American Peace Agreement aimed at securing peace in the region, and particularly in Nicaragua. He completed his term as president in 1990, and although enormously popular in Costa Rica was barred by the constitution from seeking reelection. He won the 1987 Nobel Peace Prize.

Aribau, Bonaventura Carles 1798–1862 •*Spanish economist and writer*• Born in Barcelona, he became a banker in Madrid, and was appointed director of the Mint and of the Spanish Treasury (1847). Aribau was the author of the *Oda a la Patria* (1833, "Ode to the Motherland"), one of the earliest and best modern poems in Catalan, which greatly influenced contemporary Catalan writers.

Ariosto, Ludovico 1474–1533 •*Italian poet*• He was born in Reggio nell'Emilia. At the court of Cardinal Ippolito d'Este, at Ferrara, he produced, over a period of ten years, his great poem, *Orlando furioso* (1516, "Orlando Enraged," enlarged 3rd edition, 1532), which takes up the epic tale of **Roland** (as Orlando) from the French *chansons de geste* and forms a continuation of **Matteo Boiardo**'s *Orlando innamorato* ("Orlando in Love").

“ ”

Natura il fece, e poi roppe la stampa.
Nature made him, and then broke the mold.

*1516 **Orlando Furioso**, canto 10, stanza 84.*

Aristarchos or **Aristarchus of Samos** fl. 270 BC •*Greek astronomer*• He worked in Alexandria, Egypt, and is famous for his theory of the motion of the Earth, maintaining not only that the Earth revolves on its axis but that it travels in a circle around the Sun, anticipating the theory of **Copernicus**.

Aristarchus of Samothrace c. 215–143 BC •*Alexandrian grammarian and critic*• Best known for his edition of **Homer**, Aristarchus also wrote many commentaries and treatises, edited **Hesiod**, **Pindar**, **Sophocles**, **Aeschylus** and other authors, and was the head of the Alexandrian Library from c. 180 to c. 145 BC.

Aristide, Jean-Bertrand 1953– •*Haitian political leader*• Born in Port-Salut, Haiti, he was ordained a Roman Catholic priest in 1982 and assigned to a small parish in the slums of Port-au-Prince. He became one of the leading critics of the **Duvalier** regime and was exiled (1982–85), but he returned and was elected president of Haiti in 1990. He was almost immediately forced into exile by the military, and began a three-year effort to regain the presidency with the backing of the US government, which recognized Aristide as the democratic alternative in Haiti despite its discomfort with his socialist rhetoric. In a last-minute effort before a planned US invasion, a US diplomatic team led by **Jimmy Carter** negotiated a peaceful occupation and transfer of power in 1994, and Aristide returned to serve out the final year of his presidency. Barred by the Haitian constitution from seeking a second consecutive term, he gave his backing to former premier Réne Préval, who was elected to succeed him as president in 1996. He formally left the priesthood in 1994. Aristide was reelected president in 2000 by a large majority, and went into exile in 2004 following a period of civil unrest.

Aristides c. 550–c. 467 BC •*Athenian general and politician*• A respected general in the Greco-Persian Wars, he held command under **Miltiades (the Younger)** at the Battle of Marathon (490 BC). He also served at Salamis (c. 480) and, with **Pausanias**, at Plataea (479). He altered the constitution so that all citizens were admitted to the archonship, and organized the Delian League after the defeat of the Persians.

Aristippus 410–350 BC •*Greek philosopher*• He was born in Cyrene, North Africa, and founded the Cyrenaic school of Hedonism, which was influential in the late fourth and early third centuries BC, and which argued that pleasure was the highest good. He became a pupil of **Socrates** in Athens, and taught philosophy both at Athens and Aegina, the first of the pupils of Socrates to charge fees for instruction.

Aristophanes c. 448–c. 385 BC •*Greek comic dramatist*• Aristophanes wrote some 50 plays, but only 11 are extant. His most sharply satirical works belong to his early period (up to c. 425 BC): *Knights*, *Clouds* and *Wasps* (422) (named from their respective choruses), and *Peace* (421). These were followed by *Birds* (414), *Lysistrata* (411), *Thesmophoriazusae* (411) and *Frogs* (405, which contains a burlesque poetic contest between **Aeschylus** and **Euripides**). Later come *Ecclesiazusae* (392) and *Plutus* (388). Aristophanes is the only writer of Old Comedy of whom complete plays survive. The objects of his often savage satire are social and intellectual pretension.

“ ”

Old age is second childhood.

423 BC Clouds l. 1417.

Aristotle 384–322 BC •*Greek philosopher and scientist*• Aristotle was born at Stagira, a Greek colony on the peninsula of Chalcidice. In about 342 he was appointed by **Philip II**, King of Macedon, to act as tutor to his 13-year-old son, **Alexander**. Aristotle finally returned to Athens in 335 to found his own school, the Lyceum, where he taught for the next 12 years. His followers became known as "peripatetics," supposedly from his restless habit of walking up and down while lecturing. When Alexander the Great died in 323 there was a strong anti-Macedonian reaction in Athens; Aristotle was accused of impiety and took refuge at Chalcis in Euboea, where he died the next year. Aristotle's writings represent a vast output covering many fields of knowledge: logic, metaphysics, ethics, politics, rhetoric, poetry, biology, zoology, physics and psychology. Most of the extant work consists of unpublished material in the form of lecture notes or students' textbooks, which were edited and published by **Andronicus of Rhodes** in the middle of the 1st century BC. His work exerted an enormous influence on medieval philosophy (especially through St **Thomas Aquinas**), Islamic philosophy (especially through **Averroës**), and on the whole Western intellectual and scientific tradition. The works most read today include the *Metaphysics* (the book written "after the *Physics*"), *Nicomachean Ethics*, *Politics*, *Poetics*, *De Anima* and the *Organon* (treatises on logic).

Arius, *Greek* **Areios** c. 250–336 AD •*Libyan theologian, founder of the heresy "Arianism"*• Trained in Antioch, he became a presbyter in Alexandria and c. 319 AD maintained, against his bishop, that in the doctrine of the Trinity the Son was not coequal or coeternal with the Father, but only the first and highest of all finite beings, created out of nothing by an act of God's free will. He secured some support, but was excommunicated in 321 by a synod of bishops at Alexandria, which instigated fierce controversy. To resolve it, the Council of Nicaea was called (325) which defined the absolute unity of the divine essence, and the absolute equality of the three persons. Arius was banished, but recalled in 334. In 336 he went to Constantinople (Istanbul), where he died suddenly, before he could be admitted to the sacrament. After his death the strife spread more widely abroad. The West was mainly orthodox, the East largely Arian or semi-Arian, but by the end of the fourth century the doctrine was largely suppressed.

Arkwright, Sir Richard 1732–92 •*English industrialist and inventor of mechanical spinning*• Born in Preston, Lancashire, in 1767 he patented his celebrated spinning frame—the first machine that could produce cotton thread of sufficient tenuity and strength to be used as warp. He entered into partnership with Jedidiah Strutt of Derby, and set up a large, water-powered factory at Cromford, Derbyshire (1771), and in 1775 took out a fresh patent for various additional improvements to the machinery. His success stimulated rival cotton spinners to use his designs, and in 1781 he prosecuted nine different manufacturers—the outcome, however, was that in 1785 his letters patent were canceled. His inventions diminished the demand for labor, and in 1779 his large mill near Chorley was destroyed by a mob. Despite this, he became rich and powerful.

Arlen, Harold, *originally* **Hyman Arluck** 1905–86 •*US composer*• Born in Buffalo, New York, he was one of the busiest composers in show business during the 1930s and 1940s, writing songs for Harlem's Cotton Club ("I've Got the World on a String," "Stormy Weather") and Broadway shows and working with lyricists such as E Y Harburg, **Ira Gershwin**, and Johnny Mercer. His numerous songs for films include "Over the Rainbow," "That Old Black Magic" and "One for My Baby."

Arlington, Henry Bennet, 1st Earl of 1618–85 •*English statesman*• He was born in Arlington, Middlesex. A member of the cabal ministry under **Charles II**, he was Secretary of State (1662–74), negotiated the Triple Alliance against France (1668), and helped to develop the English party system. In 1674 he was cleared of an embezzlement charge, but resigned and became Lord Chamberlain.

Arliss, George, *originally* **Augustus George Andrews** 1868–1946 •*English actor*• He was born in London and first appeared on the stage at the Elephant and Castle (1887), but made his reputation as an actor in the US, where he lived for 22 years from 1901, in plays like *The Second Mrs Tanqueray* (1901) and *Disraeli* (1911). His film career began in the US in 1920. He is remembered for his portraryals of famous historical characters, such as the Duke of **Wellington** and Cardinal **Richelieu**. He won an Academy Award for *Disraeli* (1929).

Arlott, (Leslie Thomas) John 1914–91 •*English writer and broadcaster*• Born in Basingstoke, Hampshire, he was a clerk in a mental hospital then became a detective with the Southampton Borough police (1934–45). He went on to gain popularity as a top cricket commentator, retiring eventually in 1980. He wrote numerous books about cricket.

“ ”

Most games are skin-deep, but cricket goes to the bone.

1977 ***Arlott and Trueman on Cricket.***

Armani, Giorgio 1935– •*Italian fashion designer*• Born in Piacenza, he studied medicine in Milan, and worked in a department store until he became a designer for Nino Cerruti in 1961. He also freelanced before setting up the Giorgio Armani company in 1975. He designed first for men, then women, and has won numerous awards.

Armatrading, Joan 1950– •*British singer and songwriter*• Born in St Christopher-Nevis in the Caribbean, she moved to Great Britain in 1958. Gaining a reputation as an amateur performer around Birmingham, she began writing songs with a friend, Pam Nester, and moved to London in 1971. They made one album, *Whatever's for Us*, before breaking up acrimoniously. Armatrading then signed to A&M and recorded *Back to the Night* (1975) and had great success with the often-reissued "Love and Affection" (1976). *Me, Myself, I* (1980) was a personal declaration of independence, and shortly afterward she was an honored guest at her native island's independence celebrations. She has continued to record and tour, and was given the honorary title Member, Order of the British Empire in 2001.

Arminius d. 19 AD •*Chief of the German Cherusci*• He served as an officer in the Roman army and acquired Roman citizenship. However, in AD 9 he allied with other German tribes against the Romans, and in the Teutoburg Forest ambushed and annihilated an entire Roman army of three legions commanded by **Publius Quintilius Varus**. Later murdered by some of his own kinsmen, **Tacitus** praised him as the "liberator of Germany."

Arminius, Jacobus, *properly* **Jakob Hermandszoon**, *also called* **Jacob Harmensen** 1560–1609 •*Dutch theologian*• Born in Oudewater, he was ordained in 1588 and was made Professor of Theology at Leyden in 1603. He opposed the Calvinistic doctrine of predestination, arguing that God forgives all who repent and believe in Christ. His teaching was formalized in the "remonstrance" of 1610, and refuted at the Synod of Dort (1618–19). The "Remonstrants" persisted in their belief, however, and Arminianism influenced the development of religious thought all over Europe.

Armitage, Edward 1817–96 •*English painter*• Born in London, he studied under **Paul Delaroche** and became professor at the Royal Academy Schools in 1875. He produced paintings on historical and biblical subjects, including the frescoes *Death of Marmion*, and *Personification of the Thames* in the House of Lords.

Armitage, Kenneth 1916–2002 •*English sculptor*• Born in Leeds, he studied at Leeds College of Art and at the Slade School in London (1937–39), and in 1952 he gained international recognition when he exhibited at the Venice Biennale. His bronzes are usually of semiabstract figures, united into a group by stylized clothing, such as *People in the Wind* (1950). In the 1970s he combined sculpture and painting in figures of wood, plaster and paper, as in *Figure and Clouds* (1972), but returned to bronze by the 1980s. He became a member of the Royal Academy in 1994.

Armstead, Henry Hugh 1828–1905 •*English sculptor*• He was born in London, and worked at first in gold and silver, but from 1863 he turned to sculpture. His best-known works include the marble reliefs and bronze statues of Astronomy, Chemistry, Rhetoric and Medicine for the **Albert** Memorial in London, the fountain at King's College, Cambridge, and the statues on the government offices in Whitehall (1875).

Armstrong, Edwin Howard 1890–1954 •*US electrical engineer and inventor*• Born in New York City, he graduated from Columbia University, having already discovered the principle of the feedback circuit, although the Supreme Court later awarded the patent priority to **Lee De Forest**. He devised the superheterodyne circuit, which became the basis for amplitude-modulation radio receivers. As Professor of Electrical Engineering at Columbia University (1935–54), he also perfected the frequency-modulation system of radio transmission that virtually eliminated the problem of interference from static. Engaged in many lawsuits, Armstrong eventually took his own life.

Armstrong, Gillian May 1952– •*Australian film director*• Born in Melbourne, she won a scholarship to the Film and Television School in Sydney. Her first feature film, *My Brilliant Career* (1979), won 11 Australian Film Institute awards. She enjoyed a change of pace in the breezy musical comedy *Starstruck* (1982), and continued to focus attention on the difficulties facing independent women in such films as *The Last Days of Chez Nous* (1993). Later works include her highly acclaimed dramatization of **Louisa May Alcott**'s *Little Women* (1994) and **Peter Carey**'s *Oscar and Lucinda* (1997).

Armstrong, Henry, *originally* **Henry Jackson** 1912–88 •*US boxer and Baptist minister*• Born in Columbus, Mississippi, he was the only man to hold world titles at three weights simultaneously. In August 1938 he held the featherweight, lightweight, and welterweight titles. In 1940 he fought a draw with Cerefino Garcia for the middleweight title.

Armstrong, Lance 1971– •*US cyclist*• Born in Plano, Texas, he won the US amateur cycling championship in 1990. He turned professional in 1992 and within a year was ranked fifth in the world. He won legs in the Tour de France in 1993 and 1995 but in 1996 was diagnosed with advanced cancer. Declared clear of cancer in 1997, he became the second American (after **Greg LeMond**) to win the Tour de France, in 1999. Armstrong won each year thereafter through 2004, setting a new record with six wins.

Armstrong, Louis (Daniel), *popularly known as* **Satchmo** (from **Satchelmouth**) *or* **Pops** 1901–71 •*US jazz trumpeter and singer*• Armstrong was born in New Orleans and brought up by his mother in extreme poverty. While serving a sentence for delinquency in the city's "home for colored waifs," he learned to play the cornet, and from that humble start developed into the first major jazz virtuoso. Released from the institution in 1914, he worked as a musician in local bars, getting encouragement from **King Oliver**, the city's leading cornettist. In 1919, Armstrong replaced Oliver in the band led by **Kid Ory**, and also played on Mississippi riverboats. In 1922, he joined Oliver's band in Chicago, and recordings by the Creole Jazz Band, featuring the cornet partnership, set new standards of musicianship in early jazz. These standards were surpassed by Armstrong himself a few years later, recording with his "Hot Five" and "Hot Seven" studio groups, when his playing moved beyond the constraints of New Orleans-style collective improvisation towards the virtuoso delivery for which he later gained world renown. A 1926 recording of his use of "scat singing" (imitating an instrument with the voice using abstract vocables) started a vogue in jazz, of which he became the most celebrated exponent. The group included his then wife, Lilian Armstrong (*née* Hardin, 1898–1971), who went on to a successful career as a jazz pianist after their divorce in 1931. From the late 1920s Armstrong, then playing trumpet, began two decades as a star soloist and singer with various big bands. In 1947 the formation of his first All Stars group marked a return to small-group jazz. Armstrong made the first of many overseas tours in 1933, and appeared in more than 50 films as a musician and entertainer.

“ ”

Musicians don't retire; they stop when there's no more music in them.
*1968 Quoted in the **Observer**, April 21.*

Armstrong, Neil Alden 1930– *•US astronaut•* Born in Wapakoneta, Ohio, he was educated there and at Purdue University. A fighter pilot in Korea and later a civilian test pilot, in 1962 he was chosen as an astronaut. In 1969 with **Buzz Aldrin** and **Michael Collins** he set out in Apollo 11 and on July 20, 1969, Armstrong and Aldrin became, in that order, the first men to set foot on the moon. Armstrong taught aerospace engineering at Cincinnati University (1971–79).

Armstrong (of Ilminster), Robert Armstrong, Baron 1927– *•English civil servant•* Educated at Eton and Christ Church, Oxford, he entered the Civil Service in 1950 and rose rapidly. In 1970 he became Principal Private Secretary to the Prime Minister, **Edward Heath** and, under **Margaret Thatcher**, Cabinet Secretary and head of the Civil Service (1983–87). He would have remained relatively anonymous had it not been for his testimony during the British government's disastrous attempt in the Australian courts in 1986 to halt publication of **Peter Wright**'s book *Spycatcher*, when Armstrong made the famous remark that he had perhaps been “economical with the truth.”

Armstrong, William George Armstrong, Baron 1810–1900 *•English inventor and industrialist•* He was born in Newcastle upon Tyne. Apprenticed to a solicitor, he became a partner, but turned to engineering, and in 1840 produced a much improved hydraulic engine, in 1842 an apparatus for producing electricity from steam, and in 1845 the hydraulic crane. In 1847 he founded the Elswick Engine-Works, Newcastle, where he also produced the “Armstrong” breech-loading gun.

Arnarson, Ingólfur late 9th century *•Norwegian Viking•* Originally from Hördaland, southwest Norway, he is honored as the first settler of Iceland, in 874. His descendants held the hereditary and honorary post of supreme chieftain (*allsherjargoði*) of the Icelandic parliament (Althing) after its foundation in 930.

Árnason, Jón, *known as* **the Grimm of Iceland** 1819–88 *•Icelandic collector of folktales•* Born in northern Iceland, he collected and published a huge collection of Icelandic folktales and fairytales (*Íslenskar þjóðsögur og œvintýri*, 2 vols, 1862–64), translated as *Icelandic Legends* by **Eiríkur Magnússon** (1864–66).

Arnaud, Yvonne Germaine 1892–1958 *•French actress•* Born in Bordeaux, and educated in Paris, she trained as a concert pianist and toured Europe as a child prodigy. With no previous acting experience, she took the role of Princess Mathilde in the musical comedy *The Quaker Girl* (1911), and was an instant success. Further success on the British stage followed with *The Girl in the Taxi* (1912) and many musicals and farces including *Tons of Money* (1922) and *Love for Love* (1943). She made several film adaptations of her stage successes as well as films like *On Approval* (1931) and *The Ghosts of Berkeley Square* (1947).

Arnauld, Antoine, *known as* **the Great Arnauld** 1612–94 *•French Jansenist philosopher, lawyer, mathematician and priest•* His attacks on the Jesuits and his activities as head of the Jansenist sect in France led to his expulsion from the Sorbonne, persecution, and ultimate refuge in Belgium. While at Port-Royal, where there was a Jansenist community, he collaborated with **Blaise Pascal** and Pierre Nicole (1625–95) on the work known as the *Port-Royal Logic* (1662).

Arne, Thomas Augustine 1710–78 *•English composer•* Born in London and educated at Eton, he began his musical career as a violinist. He produced his first opera, *Rosamond* in 1733. He wrote over 50 operas and other works, including (as composer of the Drury Lane Theatre) settings of Shakespearean songs. His best-known piece is “Rule, Britannia,” originally written for *The Masque of Alfred* (1740).

Arnim, Achim von, *real name* **Karl Joachim Friedrich Ludwig von Arnim** 1781–1831 *•German writer•* Born in Berlin, he was the author of fantastic but original romances. He published over 20 volumes, mainly tales and novels, including the folk-song collection *Des Knaben Wunderhorn* (1806, “The Boy's Magic Horn”) with **Clemens von Brentano**. His writing is overtly moralistic and his most ambitious work is the unfinished novel *Die Kronenwächter* (1817, “The Crown Minder”). His wife, Bettina (1785–1859), Brentano's sister, was as a girl infatuated with **Goethe**, and afterward published a (largely fictitious) *Correspondence* with him, as well as ten volumes of tales and essays.

Arnim, Jürgen, Baron von 1891–1971 *•German soldier•* Born of an old Silesian military family, he served in World War I, and in World War II was given command of a Panzer division in the Russian campaign. He took over the 5th Panzer Army in Tunisia in 1943 and succeeded **Erwin Rommel** in command of the Afrika Korps. In May 1943 he surrendered his troops to the Allies, and was interned in Great Britain and later the US.

Arnold, Aberhard 1883–1935 *•German pacifist, founder of the Bruderhof movement in Nazi Germany•* Born in Breslau, he studied theology at Halle. A convinced pacifist associated with the Student Christian Movement, he linked spiritual authenticity with an awareness of economic injustice. He visited Bruderhof colonies in Canada, and incurred the hostility of the Gestapo, which saw allegiance to the state as the highest priority. A selection of his writings and addresses, *God's Revolution*, was published in 1984.

Arnold, Benedict 1741–1801 *•American general and turncoat•* Born in Norwich, Connecticut. In the American Revolution he joined the colonial forces, and for his gallantry at the Siege of Quebec (1775) was made a brigadier general. He also fought with distinction at the Battles of Ridgefield and Saratoga, and in 1778 was placed in command of Philadelphia. His resentment at being passed over for promotion, followed by his marriage to a woman of Loyalist sympathies, led him to conspire with British adjutant general John André (1751–80) to betray West Point, but André was captured and Arnold then fled behind British lines. From 1781, he lived in obscurity in London.

Arnold, Eve 1913– *•US photojournalist•* Born in Philadelphia to Russian immigrant parents, she originally studied medicine but changed to photography studies. She was the first woman to photograph for Magnum Photos (1951). She moved to London in 1961, and traveled to such places as the USSR, Afghanistan, Egypt and China. Her photo-essays have appeared in publications like *Life* and the *Sunday Times*. The retrospective “Eve Arnold in Britain” was shown at the National Portrait Gallery, London, in 1991. Her books include *The Un-retouched Woman* (1976) and *All in a Day's Work* (1989).

Arnold, Sir Malcolm Henry 1921– *•English composer•* Born in Northampton, Northamptonshire, he studied composition at the Royal College of Music (1938–40) and was principal trumpet player with the London Philharmonic Orchestra until 1948. He has composed ten symphonies and other orchestral music including the overture *Tam O'Shanter* (1955), 18 concertos, six ballets, two one-act operas, and vocal, choral and chamber music. Of his film scores, *Bridge over the River Kwai* received an Academy Award (1957). Given the honorary title of Commander, Order of the British Empire in 1970, he was knighted in 1993.

Arnold, Matthew 1822–88 *•English poet and critic•* Born in Laleham, Middlesex, the eldest son of **Thomas Arnold** of Rugby, he was educated at Winchester, Rugby, and Balliol College, Oxford. He was an inspector of schools (1851–86), and from 1857 to 1867 he was Professor of Poetry at Oxford. He made his mark with *Poems: A New Edition* (1853–54), which contained “The Scholar Gipsy” and “Sohrab and Rustum,” and with *New Poems* (1867), which contained “Dover Beach” and “Thyrsis.” He published several distinguished works of criticism including *On the Study of Celtic Literature* (1867), *Culture and Anarchy* and *Literature and Dogma* (1873).

“ ”

Culture, the acquainting ourselves with the best that has been known and said in the world, and thus with the history of the human spirit.
*1873 **Literature and Dogma**, preface.*

Arnold, Thomas 1795–1842 •*English educationist and scholar*• Born in East Cowes, Isle of Wight, he was the father of **Matthew Arnold**, and was educated at Winchester and Corpus Christi College, Oxford. In 1828 he was appointed headmaster of Rugby, and reformed the school system, especially by introducing sports and ending bullying. His life inspired **Thomas Hughes**'s novel *Tom Browne's Schooldays*. He wrote sermons and works on classical and modern history, and in 1841, shortly before his death, he became Regius Professor of Modern History at Oxford. His second son, Thomas (1823–1900), was a literary scholar, and his daughter, Mary Augusta, was the novelist Mrs **Ward**.

Arnolfo di Cambio 1232–1302 •*Italian sculptor and architect*• Born in Colle di Val d'Elsa, he was a pupil of **Nicola Pisano** and his work includes the pulpit at Siena, a portrait of **Charles of Anjou**, and the tomb of Cardinal de Braye at Orvieto. He was also the designer of Florence Cathedral.

Arp, Hans or **Jean** 1887–1966 •*Alsatian sculptor and poet*• He was born in Strassburg. He was one of the founders, with **Hugo Ball**, of the Dada movement in Zurich in 1916. As a sculptor he began by producing abstract reliefs in wood, such as *Madame Torso in a Wavy Hat* (1916, Berne) and *Forest* (1916, Penrose Collection, London), with works including *Landmark* (1938) and *Ptolemy I* (1953, both in Paris).

Árpád d. c. 907 •*National hero of Hungary*• A Magyar chieftain in the Caucasus, in c. 896 he led the Magyars from the Black Sea and occupied modern Hungary. He founded the Árpád dynasty of Hungary, with **Stephen I** becoming the first King of Hungary, and the dynasty continuing until 1301.

Arrau, Claudio 1903–91 •*Chilean pianist*• Born in Chillan, he gave his first recital in Santiago at age five. His musical education was sponsored by the Chilean government, and he studied at the Stern Conservatory, Berlin (1912–18), with the **Liszt** pupil Martin Krause (1853–1918). Renowned as an interpreter of **Bach**, **Beethoven**, **Chopin**, **Schumann**, Liszt and **Brahms**, his musical thoughts were collected in *Conversations with Arrau* by Joseph Horowitz (1982).

Arrhenius, Svante August 1859–1927 •*Swedish physical chemist and Nobel Prize winner*• Born in Wijk, near Uppsala, he went to the University of Uppsala in 1876. He became professor in Stockholm (1895), and later director of the Nobel Institute there (1905). His theory of electrolytic dissociation explained electrolytic conductivity and elucidated many other properties of electrolyte solutions. He was awarded the Nobel Prize for chemistry in 1903.

Arriaga, Manoel José de 1840–1917 •*Portuguese statesman*• He took part in the revolution of 1910 which overthrew King Manuel II (1889–1932, ruled 1908–10), and from 1911 to 1915 was the first elected President of the Republic of Portugal.

Arrian, *Latin* **Flavius Arrianus** c. 95–180 AD •*Greek historian*• A native of Nicomedia, Bithynia, he became an officer in the Roman army, and was appointed Governor of Cappadocia by **Hadrian**. His chief work is the *Anabasis Alexandrou*, a history of the campaigns of **Alexander the Great**, which has survived almost complete.

Arrianus, Flavius *See* **Arrian**

Arrol, Sir William 1839–1913 •*Scottish engineer*• Born in Houston, Renfrewshire, he got his first job in a thread mill by lying about his age. He became an apprentice blacksmith at the age of 14, studied mechanics and hydraulics at night school, and started his own engineering business at the age of 29. He constructed the second Tay Railway Bridge (1882–87) to replace the ill-fated bridge that collapsed in 1879, the Forth Railway Bridge (1883–90), and Tower Bridge in London (1886–94).

Arrow, Kenneth Joseph 1921– •*US economist and Nobel Prize winner*• Born in New York City, he graduated from Columbia University and was professor at Stanford University (1949–68 and 1979–91, then emeritus) and Harvard (1968–79). His primary field is the study of collective choice based on uncertainty and risk. He shared the 1972 Nobel Prize for economics with Sir **John Hicks**.

Arsinoë c. 316–270 BC •*Macedonian princess*• She was the daughter of **Ptolemy I Soter** and one of the most conspicuous of Hellenistic queens. She married first (c. 300 BC) the aged **Lysimachus**, King of Thrace, secondly (and briefly) her stepbrother, Ptolemy Ceraunus, and finally (c. 276) her own brother, **Ptolemy II Philadelphus**, so becoming queen of Egypt. Several cities were named after her.

Artaud, Antonin Marie Joseph 1896–1948 •*French dramatist, actor, director and theorist of the surrealist movement*• He was born in Marseilles and became an active member of the surrealist movement (1924–26). In 1927 he cofounded the Théâtre **Alfred Jarry**. He wrote *Le théâtre et son double* (1938, Eng trans *The Theater and its Double*, 1958), in which he describes the Theater of Cruelty, and his influence on postwar theater was profound. His last years were spent in a mental institution, from where he continued to write.

Artaxerxes *See* **Ardashir I**

Artaxerxes I, *called* **Longimanus ("Long-Handed")** d. 425 BC •*King of Persia*• The second son of **Xerxes I**, he reigned from c. 464 to 425 BC. In a long and peaceful reign, he sanctioned the Jewish religion in Jerusalem, and appointed **Nehemiah** governor of Judea (445 BC).

Artaxerxes II, *called* **Mnemon ("Mindful")** d. c. 358 BC •*King of Persia*• The son of **Darius II**, he reigned from 404 to c. 358 BC. He lost control of Egypt, but became the arbiter of Greece. He rebuilt the royal palace at Susa.

Artaxerxes III, *originally* **Ochus** d. 338 BC •*King of Persia*• The son and successor of **Artaxerxes II**, he found the empire disintegrating at his accession (358 BC), but his cruel energy did much to build it up again. He was poisoned by his favorite eunuch, Bagoas.

Artedi, Peter 1705–35 •*Swedish ichthyologist and botanist*• Known as "the father of ichthyology," he wrote *Ichthyologia*, a very important systematic study of fishes; it was edited by **Linnaeus**, his closest friend, and was published in 1738, after Artedi had drowned in an Amsterdam canal. He inspired Linnaeus in the classification of animals and plants.

Artemisia II d. c. 350 BC •*Queen of Caria*• She was the sister and wife of Mausolus, ruler of Caria. She succeeded Mausolus (353–352 BC) and erected the magnificent Mausoleum at Halicarnassus (now Bodrum, Turkey) to his memory. It was one of the traditional Seven Wonders of the Ancient World.

Arthur fl. early 6th century •*Semilegendary king of the Britons*• He may have been a Romano-British war leader in the west of England called Arturus, but he is represented as having united the British tribes against the invading Saxons, and as having been the champion of Christendom. The *Anglo-Saxon Chronicle* makes no mention of him, however, and he first appears in the ninth-century Welsh chronicle, **Nennius**'s *Historia Britonum*. Other works in which he appears include the *Annales Cambriae* (tenth century), and *The Black Book of Camarthen* (12th century). He also figures in the Welsh romance *Culhwch and Olwen*, and in the *Gesta Regum Anglorum* of **William of Malmesbury**. The story of Arthur became interwoven with legends of the Holy Grail and the Knights of the Round Table at Camelot, told by such writers as **Geoffrey of Monmouth**, **Chrétien de Troyes**, **Layamon**, and Sir **Thomas Malory**.

Arthur, Prince 1187–1203 •*Duke of Brittany*• Born in Nantes, he was the posthumous son of Geoffrey, Duke of Brittany, and grandson of **Henry II**. On the death of his uncle, **Richard I** (1199), he claimed the English throne; the French king, **Philip II**, supported his bid for the throne. However, Arthur was captured and imprisoned by John (1202), and died, possibly on John's orders.

Arthur, Prince 1486–1502 •*English prince*• Born in Winchester, he was the eldest son of **Henry VII**. When he was less than two years old a marriage was arranged between him and **Catherine of Aragon** in order to provide an alliance between England and Spain. The wedding took place in November 1501, but Arthur, a sickly young man, died six months later at Ludlow before the marriage was consummated.

Arthur, Chester Alan 1830–86 •*21st President of the US*• Born in Fairfield, Vermont, the son of an Irish Baptist minister, he became the head of an eminent law firm and leader of the Republican Party in New York State. He was vice-president when **James A Garfield** became President (1881) and succeeded him on his assassination, holding the presidency from 1881 to 1885. During his administration he supported the Civil Service Reform Act of 1883 and vetoed a Chinese exclusion bill. His administration was known for its efficiency and integrity.

Arthur, Jean, *originally* **Gladys Georgianna Greene** 1905–91 •*US actress*• Born in New York City, she left school at the age of 15 to become a model, and later an actress. She made her film debut in *Cameo Kirby* (1923) followed by several unremarkable roles. Being a husky-voiced, vivacious actress, she survived the transition to sound, became adept at comedy and costarred with some of Hollywood's most prominent actors. Her best films include *Mr Deeds Goes to Town* (1936), *Mr Smith Goes to Washington* (1939) and *The More the Merrier* (1943, Academy Award nomination).

Artigas, José Gervasio 1764–1850 •*Uruguayan national hero*• Born in Montevideo, he was a gaucho in his youth, then an army officer in Spanish service. He became the most important local patriot leader in the wars of independence against Spain, and also resisted the centralizing pretensions of Buenos Aires. The last 30 years of his life were spent in exile in Paraguay.

Artin, Emil 1898–1962 •*Austrian mathematician*• Born in Vienna, he studied in Leipzig, Germany, and taught at the universities of Göttingen and Hamburg before emigrating to the US in 1937, where he held posts at Indiana and Princeton before returning to Hamburg in 1958. His work was mainly in algebraic number theory and class field theory, and has had great influence on modern algebra.

Arundel, Thomas 1353–1414 •*English prelate and statesman*• The third son of Richard Fitzalan, Earl of Arundel, he was Chancellor of England five times (1386–89, 1391–96, 1399, 1407–10, 1412–13). He became archdeacon of Taunton and Bishop of Ely (1374), then Archbishop of York (1388), and finally of Canterbury (1396). He supported the nobles opposed to **Richard II**, who banished him (1397), but he returned to help seat Henry of Lancaster (**Henry IV**) on the throne (1399). He was a vigorous opponent of the Lollards.

Arup, Sir Ove Nyquist 1895–1988 •*English civil engineer*• Born in Newcastle upon Tyne, of Danish parentage, he studied in Denmark before moving to London in 1923. He was responsible for the structural design of Coventry Cathedral (designed by Sir **Basil Spence**, 1962) and St Catherine's College, Oxford (by **Arne Jacobsen**, 1964). With his partner Jack Zunz, he evolved the structural design which permitted the realization of **Jørn Utzon**'s unique architectural conception of the Sydney Opera House (1956–73).

Arzner, Dorothy 1900–79 •*US film director*• Born in San Francisco, she studied medicine at the University of Southern California. She began her film career as a script typist in 1919. She was editor on such important silent features as *Blood and Sand* (1922). After making her directorial debut with *Fashions for Women* (1927), she directed Paramount's first sound feature *Wild Party* (1929). Her best-known films include *Merrily We Go to Hell* (1932) and *Dance, Girl Dance* (1940). She was the only major woman director in Hollywood in the 1930s.

Asad, Bashar al- *See* **Assad, Bashar al-**

Asad, Hafez al- *See* **Assad, Hafez al-**

Asbjørnsen, Peter Christian 1812–85 •*Norwegian folklorist*• Born in Christiania (now Oslo), he studied at the university there. On long journeys on foot he collected popular poetry and folklore, and, with his friend Jørgen Moe, Bishop of Christiansand, published the famous *Norske folke eventyr* (1841–44, Eng trans *Norwegian Folk Stories*, 1859).

Asbury, Francis 1745–1816 •*US churchman*• Born in Handsworth, Staffordshire, England, he was sent as a Methodist missionary to America in 1771. A key figure in the foundation of the Methodist Episcopal Church (1770–84), he became the first Methodist bishop in the US.

Ascham, Roger 1515–68 •*English humanist and scholar*• Born in Kirby Wiske near Thirsk, Yorkshire, he was educated at St John's College, Cambridge. From 1548 to 1550 he was tutor to the Princess Elizabeth (the future **Elizabeth I**), and later became Latin secretary to **Mary I** (1554). In defense of archery he published, in 1545, *Toxophilus* ("Lover of the Bow") and he is also noted for *The Scholemaster*, an influential treatise on education, published posthumously by his widow in 1570.

Asclepiades fl. 1st century BC •*Greek physician*• Born in Pruss, Bithynia, he seems to have been a peripatetic teacher of rhetoric before settling in Rome as a physician. There he advanced the doctrine that disease results from discord in the corpuscles of the body, and recommended good diet and exercise as a cure.

Ash'arī, al-, *in full* **Abū al-Ḥasan al-Ash'arī** 873/874–935/936 •*Islamic theologian and philosopher*• Born in Basra, he studied with the sect of Mutazilites, with whom he broke at the age of 40. His major work is *Maqalat*, and his major thesis was to defend the idea of God's omnipotence and to reaffirm traditional interpretations of religious authority within Islam.

Ashbee, Charles Robert 1863–1942 •*English designer, architect and writer*• Born in Isleworth, Surrey, he was educated at King's College, Cambridge, and was much influenced by the work and thinking of **William Morris** and **John Ruskin**. He founded the Essex House Press and the London Survey, and was founder and director of the Guild of Handicraft (1888–1908) in London's East End (later in Gloucestershire), attempting to put into practice the ideals of the Arts and Crafts Movement.

Ashbery, John Lawrence 1927– •*US poet, critic and novelist*• Born in New York City, he attended Harvard. He has worked as an art critic in France, and since 1980 in the US, where he has also been a professor of English. His volumes of verse, characterized by their abstract obscurity, include *The Tennis Court Oath* (1962), *Rivers and Mountains* (1966), *Self-Portrait in a Convex Mirror* (1975, Pulitzer Prize), and *A Wave* (1984). His only novel is *A Nest of Ninnies* (1969), coauthored with James Schuyler.

" "

There is the view that poetry should improve your life. I think people confuse it with the Salvation Army.

*1989 In the **International Herald Tribune**, October 2.*

Ashburner, Michael 1942– •*English geneticist*• He studied at Cambridge. Elected a Fellow of the Royal Society in 1990, he has been Professor of Biology at Cambridge since 1991, and has held research fellowships and visiting professorships in many countries. Ashburner is best known for his work on the heat shock genes of the fruit fly. These genes are activated by a short burst of increased temperature, and are thus useful in the study of gene control.

Ashby, Dame Margery Irene, *née* **Corbett** 1882–1981 •*English feminist*• The daughter of the Liberal Member of Parliament for East Grinstead, she was educated at home and studied classics at Newnham College, Cambridge. She attended the first International Women's Suffrage Congress in Berlin (1904) and subsequently worked with various women's organizations, traveling widely throughout the world and becoming president of the International Alliance of Women for 23 years (1923–46).

Ashcroft, John 1942– •*US Republican politician*• Born in Chicago, Illinois, he was educated at Yale University and the University of Chicago and subsequently embarked on a legal career. He served as Missouri's attorney general (1977–84) and governor (1984–93) before becoming a senator (1994–2000). In December 2000 he was appointed attorney general of the US under President **George W Bush**, promising to renew the war on drugs, reduce gun violence and fight discrimination.

Ashcroft, Dame Peggy (Edith Margaret Emily) 1907–91 •*English actress*• She was born in Croydon, Greater London. Her first major success in London was in *Jew Süss* (1929). Her great roles included Juliet in **John Gielgud**'s production of *Romeo and Juliet* (1935), *Cleopatra* (1935), and *Hedda Gabler* (1954). She received an Academy Award for Best Supporting Actress her role in the film, *A Passage to India* (1984), and in 1991 received the **Olivier** award for outstanding service to the theater. She was given the honorary title of Dame Commander, Order of the British Empire in 1956.

Ashdown (of Norton-sub-Hamdon), Paddy, Baron, *properly* **Jeremy John Durham Ashdown** 1941– •*English politician*• Born in

India, he joined the Royal Marines (1959–71) and served in the Special Boat Squadron (the navy's equivalent of the Special Air Service). He then worked in the diplomatic service (1971–76), before becoming Liberal Member of Parliament for Yeovil in 1983. From 1988 to 1999 he was the leader of the Liberal Democrats (formerly the Liberal and Social Democratic Party). He was elevated to the peerage upon his retirement from the House of Commons in 2001. His publications include *Making Change Our Ally* (1994) and two autobiographical volumes, *The Ashdown Diaries Volume One 1988–1997* (2000) and *The Ashdown Diaries Volume Two 1997–1999* (2001).

Ashe, Arthur Robert, Jr 1943–93 •*US tennis player*• Born in Richmond, Virginia, he won the US national singles championship in 1968 and the first US Open championship later the same year. He was a professional tennis player from 1969 to 1979 and won the men's singles at the Australian Open (1970) and at Wimbledon (1975) when he defeated **Jimmy Connors**. In his retirement (from 1980), he became a campaigner for AIDS awareness, having been diagnosed with AIDS himself, allegedly after a blood transfusion during his second heart bypass operation in 1983. He was the first male African-American tennis player to achieve world ranking.

Asher, Jane 1946– •*English actress and writer*• Born in London, she made her film debut at the age of five in *Mandy* (1952) and continued acting as a child. Other notable film appearances include *The Greengage Summer* (1961) and *The Winter's Tale* (1968). On television, she appeared in *Brideshead Revisited, Wish Me Luck* (1988–90) and *The Choir* (1995). She also runs Jane Asher Party Cakes and has written many books mainly on cookery. She is married to **Gerald Scarfe**.

Ashford, Evelyn 1957– •*US sprinter*• Born in Shreveport, Louisiana, she studied at UCLA. In the early 1980s she was dubbed the world's fastest woman, beating her East German rival for the title, Marlies Gohr, at Zurich in August 1984. She set two new world records in the 100 meters (10.79 seconds, 1983, and 10.76 seconds, 1984), and competed in four successive Olympic Games, winning gold for the 100 meters (1984) and 4 × 100 meters relay (1984, 1988, 1992).

Ashkenazy, Vladimir 1937– •*Icelandic pianist and conductor*• Born in Gorky (now Nizhny Novgorod) in the former USSR, he was joint winner (with **John Ogdon**) of the Tchaikovsky Piano Competition in Moscow (1962) and earned an international reputation as a concert pianist before concentrating more on conducting. He took Icelandic nationality in 1972. He was director of the Royal Philharmonic Orchestra, London (1987–94), Chief Conductor of the Berlin Radio Symphony Orchestra (now Deutsches Symphonie-Orchester Berlin, 1989–99), and Music Director of the Czech Philharmonic Orchestra (1998–).

Ashley, Laura, *née* **Mountney** 1925–85 •*Welsh fashion designer*• Born in Merthyr Tydfil, south Wales, she married Bernard Ashley in 1949 and they started up a business manufacturing furnishing materials and wallpapers. She then experimented with designing and making clothes, and this transformed the business from one small shop to an international chain selling clothes, furnishing fabrics and wallpapers. Ashley Mountney Ltd became Laura Ashley Ltd in 1968, and her work continued to be characterized by a romantic style and the use of natural fabrics, especially cotton.

Ashmole, Elias 1617–92 •*English antiquary*• Born in Lichfield, Staffordshire, he qualified as a lawyer in 1638 and subsequently combined work for the Royalist cause with the study of mathematics, natural philosophy, astronomy, astrology and alchemy. In 1677 he presented to the University of Oxford a fine collection of rarities, bequeathed to him by his friend John Tradescant, the Younger (1608–62), thus founding the Ashmolean Museum (built in 1682).

Ashoka *See* **Aśoka**

Ashton, Sir Frederick William Mallandaine 1904–88 •*English dancer and choreographer*• Born in Guayaquil, Ecuador, he was brought up in Peru where he saw **Anna Pavlova** dance. He trained in London under **Léonide Massine** and **Marie Rambert**, who commissioned his first piece, *A Tragedy of Fashion* (1926). After a year dancing under the direction of **Bronislava Nijinska** in the US, he returned to Britain to help found the Ballet Club, which later became Ballet Rambert (now Rambert Dance Company). During this time he partnered and created roles for dancers like **Alicia Markova**. He joined the Sadler's Wells Ballet in 1935 as a dancer/choreographer, where he later succeeded Dame **Ninette de Valois** as director (1963–70). He also worked with the New York City Ballet and the Royal Danish Ballet Company, and produced such works as *Façade* (1931), *Ondine* (1958), and *The Dream* (1964). He was knighted in 1962, and given many other honors around the world.

Ashton, Julian Rossi 1851–1942 •*Australian painter and teacher*• Born in Alderstone, Surrey, England, he emigrated to Australia in 1878. In 1896 founded the Sydney Art School. He is best known for his influence on later Australian artists including George Lambert, Sydney Long, Elioth Gruner and **William Dobell**, and for working strenuously for the recognition of Australian artists.

Ashurbanipal or **Assurbanipal**, *also called* **Sardanapalus** 7th century BC •*King of Assyria*• The eldest son of **Esarhaddon** and grandson of **Sennacherib**, he was the last of the great Assyrian kings and his reign (668–627 BC) marks the zenith of Assyrian splendor. A generous patron of the arts, he founded in Nineveh the first systematically gathered and organized library in the ancient Middle East.

Asimov, Isaac 1920–92 •*US novelist, critic and popular scientist*• Born in Petrovichi, Russia, he was taken to the US when he was three. He received a PhD in chemistry from Columbia University and led a distinguished career as an academic biochemist. As a science-fiction writer, he produced a prodigious body of work including *Foundation* (1951), *Foundation and Empire* (1952), *Second Foundation* (1953), *The Caves of Steel* (1954), *The Naked Sun* (1957), and the short stories which form the collection *I, Robot* (1950).

“ ”

If there is a category of human being for whom his work ought to speak for itself, it is the writer.

1976 Comment in D L Fitzpatrick (ed) ***Contemporary Novelists***.

Aske, Robert d. 1537 •*English rebel*• Originally from Yorkshire he became an attorney at Gray's Inn, London. He headed the Catholic uprising known as the Pilgrimage of Grace in protest of **Henry VIII**'s dissolution of the monasteries, and was subsequently hanged in York for treason.

Askew, Anne 1521–46 •*English Protestant martyr*• Born near Grimsby, Humberside, she was an early convert to the Reformed doctrines. Rejected because of this by her husband, she went to London to sue for a separation, but in 1545 was arrested on a charge of heresy. After examination and torture on the rack, she was burned in Smithfield, London.

Askey, Arthur 1900–82 •*English comedian*• Born in Liverpool, he made his professional debut in 1924. A small man (he stood only 5 ft 2 in tall), he became principal comedian in summer seasons at British seaside resorts. He achieved wide recognition on radio with *Band Wagon* (1938), and became known as "Big-Hearted Arthur." He had a button-holing style, a cheery manner, a harmless humor, and made a catch phrase of "I thank you!" He appeared regularly on television, and in several films.

Aśoka or **Ashoka** 3rd century BC •*Ruler of India*• The last major Mauryan emperor (c. 269–232 BC), and conqueror of Kalinga, he was a convert to Buddhism, and organized it as the state religion, while giving freedom to other religous sects. He gave up armed conquest in favor of disseminating *dharma* (broadly, moral principles), and inscribed his pronouncements on rocks and pillars.

Aspdin, Joseph 1779–1855 •*English bricklayer and inventor*• He was born in Leeds. In 1824 he patented what he called "Portland cement," manufactured from clay and limestone, a hydraulic cement which would set hard even under water.

Aspinall, Sir John Audley Frederick 1851–1937 •*English mechanical engineer*• Born in Liverpool, he rose from locomotive fireman to be chief mechanical engineer and general manager of the

Lancashire and Yorkshire Railway (1899–1919). He designed many types of locomotives and completed one of the first main-line railway electrification schemes in Great Britain from Liverpool to Southport (1904).

Asquith, H(erbert) H(enry), 1st Earl of Oxford and Asquith 1852–1928 •*English statesman*• He was born in Morley, Yorkshire, and educated at City of London School and Balliol College, Oxford. Called to the bar in 1876, he became a Queen's Counsel in 1890 and was Liberal Member of Parliament for East Fife (1886–1918). He became Home Secretary (1892–95) and, despite upsetting many of his fellow Liberals by his support for the anti-Boer imperialists during the South African War (1899–1902), Chancellor of the Exchequer (1905–08), succeeding Sir **Henry Campbell-Bannerman** as Prime Minister in April 1908. His administration was notable for the upholding of free trade, the introduction of old age pensions, payment for Members of Parliament, the Parliament Act of 1911, Welsh disestablishment, suffragette troubles, the declaration of war (1914), the coalition ministry (1915), and the Sinn Fein rebellion (1916). He was ousted in December 1916 by supporters of **Lloyd George** and some Conservatives who thought his conduct of the war was not sufficiently vigorous. He later led the Independent Liberals who rejected Lloyd George's continuing coalition with the Conservatives. Created an earl in 1925, he wrote his *Memories and Reflections* (1928) and his second wife **Margot Asquith** wrote a lively *Autobiography* (1922).

Asquith, Margot (Emma Alice Margaret), *née* **Tennant** 1864–1945 •*Scottish society figure*• She was born in Peebleshire, the daughter of Sir Charles Tennant, and received little formal education but possessed unusual literary, artistic and musical talents. She became a brilliantly witty hostess who led a group of young intellectuals and aesthetes called the "Souls" who advocated greater freedom for women. In 1894 she married **H H Asquith**, who became Prime Minister in 1908. When Asquith was forced to resign in 1916, she wrote two famously indiscreet autobiographies.

" "

David Lloyd George could not see a belt without hitting underneath it.

*1953 **The Listener**, June 11.*

Assad or **Asad, Bashar al-** 1965– •*Syrian politician*• He was born in Damascus, the son of **Hafez al-Assad**, President of Syria from 1971 to 2000, and originally trained as an ophthalmologist. He later entered the Syrian armed forces. On the death of his father in 2000 he took over as President and Secretary-General of the ruling Ba'ath Party.

Assad or **Asad, Hafez al-** 1928–2000 •*Syrian general and statesman*• He was born in Qardaha, near Latakia in northwest Syria, into a peasant family of nine children, and changed his family name of Wahsh ("boar" in Arabic), to Assad ("lion"). After a military career, he became Minister of Defense and Commander of the Air Force (1966–70), instigated a coup in 1970 and became Prime Minister and then President (1971–2000). He belonged to the minority Alawi sect of Islam. After the 1973 Arab-Israeli War, he negotiated a partial withdrawal of Israeli troops from Syria. In 1976 he sent Syrian troops into Lebanon, and did so again in early 1987. By 1989 he had imposed Syrian control over the greater part of Lebanon. He enjoyed Soviet support, and was one of the few Arab leaders to support Iran in its war with Iraq (1980–88). Following his sending of Syrian forces to join the UN coalition against Iran in the Gulf War, Syria's relationship with Western nations improved. He was a supporter of the Palestinian radicals against **Yasser Arafat**'s mainstream PLO (Palestine Liberation Organization) and in 1995 entered negotiations with Israel as part of the US-brokered peace process. He was succeeded as President by his son **Bashar al-Assad**.

Asselyn, Jan, *nicknamed* **Crabbetje ("Little Crab")** 1610–52 •*Dutch painter*• Born in Amsterdam, he traveled to Italy and became a successful painter of Italianate landscapes that depicted imaginary Arcadian vistas inspired by the Roman countryside. He was influenced by **Claude Lorrain** and is the subject of an etching by his friend **Rembrandt**.

Asser, Tobias Michael Carel 1838–1913 •*Dutch jurist and Nobel Prize winner*• He was born in Amsterdam and became a Professor of Law at Amsterdam University. He persuaded the Dutch government to call the first Hague Conference for the unification of International Private Law in 1893, and was awarded, jointly with the Austrian pacifist Alfred Fried (1864–1921), the Nobel Peace Prize in 1911 for his work in creating the Permanent Court of Arbitration at the Hague Peace Conference of 1899.

Assurbanipal *See* **Ashurbanipal**

Astaire, Adele, *professional name of* **Adele Austerlitz** 1898–1981 •*US dancer, actress and singer*• Born in Omaha, Nebraska, she was the older sister of **Fred Astaire**. Her career began in her teens, partnering with her brother in a song-and-dance act that reached Broadway in 1917. Their postwar show *For Goodness Sake* (1922) was a big success, and they went on to further success in 1924 in **Gershwin** shows, including *Lady, Be Good* and *Funny Face*—both now inextricably associated with Fred's name.

Astaire, Fred, *professional name of* **Frederick Austerlitz** 1899–1987 •*US actor, dancer and singer*• He was born in Omaha, Nebraska, and began his career teamed with his sister **Adele Astaire** as a touring vaudeville act (1916), rising to stardom with her on Broadway. When Adele married (1932), Fred went to Hollywood and continued with various partners, notably **Ginger Rogers**. His many films include *Top Hat* (1935) and *Follow the Fleet* (1936). He announced his retirement in 1946, but returned to create further classic musicals like *Easter Parade* (1948) and *The Band Wagon* (1953), then turned to straight acting, winning an Academy Award nomination for *The Towering Inferno* (1974). He revolutionized the film musical with a succession of original and innovative tap-dance routines. He was described as the world's greatest dancer by both **George Balanchine** and **Rudolf Nureyev**. He published his autobiography, *Steps in Time*, in 1960.

Astaire, Mrs Fred *See* **Smith, Robyn**

Astbury, William Thomas 1889–1961 •*English X-ray crystallographer*• Born in Longton, Stoke-on-Trent, Staffordshire, he studied at Cambridge and with Sir **William Bragg**'s team at University College London (1920–21) before becoming a lecturer in textile physics at the University of Leeds (1928), where he held the new chair of biomolecular structure from 1945. In 1926 he began taking X-ray diffraction photographs using natural protein fibers such as those of hair, wool and horn. Using the photographic techniques he had helped to develop, he showed that diffraction patterns could be obtained which changed when the fiber was stretched or wet. On this basis he classified fibrous proteins, and although his interpretation of their molecular structures proved incorrect, his pioneer work laid the basis for important work which followed, most notably by **Linus Pauling**. Astbury probably coined the phase "molecular biology" and, with Florence Bell, he attempted (wrongly) the first hypothetical structure for the key genetic material DNA (1938).

Aston, Francis William 1877–1945 •*English physicist and Nobel Prize winner*• Born in Birmingham and educated at Malvern, Birmingham and Cambridge, he invented the mass spectrograph in 1919, with which he investigated the isotopic structures of elements and for which he won the Nobel Prize for chemistry in 1922. The Aston dark space, in electronic discharges, is named after him.

Astor, John Jacob 1763–1848 •*US financier*• Born in Waldorf, Germany, the son of a butcher, he went to London at the age of 16 and worked with his brother, a maker of musical instruments. He emigrated to the US in 1783 and invested his small capital in a fur business in New York. He built up a fur-trading empire, first in Canada and then in the Far West, combining his holdings in the American Fur Company in 1808. His major philanthropic act was the endowment of the Astor Library, now the New York Public Library. The Astor family became one of the leading clans in the US's wealthy aristocracy.

Astor, John Jacob 1864–1912 •*US financier*• A great-grandson of **John Jacob Astor** (1763–1848), he served in the Spanish-American War, and built part of the Waldorf-Astoria Hotel in New York. He was drowned with the *Titanic*.

Astor (of Hever), John Jacob Astor, Baron 1886–1971 •*British newspaper proprietor*• Born in New York, he was the son of William Waldorf, 1st Viscount **Astor**. Educated at Eton and New College, Oxford, he was elected Member of Parliament for Dover in 1922, and became chairman of the Times Publishing Company after the death of Lord Northcliffe (**Alfred Harmsworth**), resigning his directorship in 1962.

Astor, Mary, *originally* **Lucille Langhanke** 1906–87 •*US film actress*• Born in Quincy, Illinois, she made her film debut in *The Beggar Maid* (1921) and was cast as beautiful ingénues in historical dramas like *Beau Brummell* (1924) and *Don Juan* (1926). She carved a special niche playing bitchy women of the world, winning an Academy Award for *The Great Lie* (1941), but her range also included the treacherous femme fatale of *The Maltese Falcon* (1941), comedy in *The Palm Beach Story* (1942) and tender drama in *Dodsworth* (1936). Despite press revelations of a scandalous private life and alcoholism, she moved into a phase playing warm-hearted matriarchs, most memorably in *Meet Me in St. Louis* (1944).

Astor, Nancy Witcher Astor, Viscountess, *née* **Langhorne** 1879–1964 •*British politician*• Born in Danville, Virginia, USA, the daughter of a wealthy tobacco auctioneer, she married **Waldorf Astor**, 2nd Viscount Astor, whom she succeeded as Conservative Member of Parliament for Plymouth in 1919, becoming the first woman Member of Parliament to sit in the House of Commons. She was known for her interest in social problems, especially women's rights and temperance.

“ ”

I married beneath me. All women do.

1951 Speech, Oldham.

Astor, Waldorf Astor, 2nd Viscount 1879–1952 •*British politician*• He was born in New York City, the son of **William Waldorf Astor**, 1st Viscount Astor. He moved to England with his family in 1889, was educated at Eton and New College, Oxford, and elected Member of Parliament for Plymouth in 1910. On passing to the House of Lords in 1919 he became parliamentary secretary to the local government board (subsequently Ministry of Health) and his wife, **Nancy Astor**, succeeded him in the House of Commons. He was proprietor of the *Observer* (1919–45).

Astor, William Waldorf Astor, 1st Viscount 1848–1919 •*British newspaper proprietor*• Born in New York, he was the great-grandson of the fur magnate **John Jacob Astor** (1763–1848). Defeated in the election for governor of New York State (1881), he was US minister to Italy (1882–85). He emigrated to Great Britain in 1892 and bought the *Pall Mall Gazette* and *Pall Mall Magazine*. Naturalized in 1899, he bought the *Observer* in 1911, and was made a viscount in 1917.

Asturias, Miguel Angel 1899–1974 •*Guatemalan fiction writer, poet and Nobel Prize winner*• A law graduate from the National University, he is best known for his novel, *El Señor Presidente* (1946, Eng trans *The President*, 1963) about the fall and trial of a hated dictator of an unnamed Latin-American country. Other books include *Hombres de maiz* (1949, Eng trans *Men of Maize*, 1975) and a trilogy on the foreign exploitation of the banana trade. He was awarded the Nobel Prize for literature in 1967.

Atahualpa c. 1502–33 •*Last emperor of the Incas*• On the death of his father Huayna-Capac (c. 1527) he ruled the northern half of the Inca Empire, the Kingdom of Quito, and in 1532 overthrew his elder brother, Huáscar, who ruled Peru from Cuzco. Brave, ambitious, and popular with his troops, he was captured (1532) by the Spaniards led by **Francisco Pizarro**, who invaded and conquered Peru. He was found guilty of treason and executed.

Atanasoff, John Vincent 1903–95 •*US physicist and computer pioneer*• Of Bulgarian extraction, he was born in Hamilton, New York, and was educated at the University of Florida, Iowa State College and the University of Wisconsin, where he received a PhD in physics. In 1942, with the help of Clifford Berry (1918–63), he built an electronic calculating machine—the ABC (Atanasoff-Berry Computer)–one of the first calculating devices utilizing vacuum tubes. His ideas entered the mainstream of computer development through **John W Mauchly**, who was influenced by Atanasoff in constructing the ENIAC (Electronic Numerical Integrator and Calculator). In 1972 a landmark court case ruled that Atanasoff—not **John Presper Eckert** and Mauchly—was the true originator of the electronic digital computer.

Atatürk, Mustapha Kemal, *originally* **Mustafa Kemal** 1881–1938 •*Turkish general and statesman*• He was born in Salonika and led the Turkish nationalist movement from 1909. He drove the Greeks from Anatolia (1919–22), raising a nationalist rebellion in protest against the postwar division of Turkey, and in 1921 he established a provisional government in Ankara. The following year the Ottoman sultanate was formally abolished, and in 1923 Turkey was declared a secular republic, with Kemal as President (1923–38). He became a virtual dictator, and launched a social and political revolution, introducing western fashions, the emancipation of women, educational reform, the replacement of the Arabic script with the Latin alphabet, and the discouragement of traditional Islamic loyalties in favor of a strictly Turkish nationalism. In 1935, he took the name Atatürk (Father of the Turks).

Atget, (Jean) Eugène (Auguste) 1857–1927 •*French photographer*• He was born in Libourne, near Bordeaux. Shunning modern methods, he continued to use gelatin dry-plate negatives and printing-out paper in order to achieve the extreme contrasts in light and dark that characterize his powerful, poetic photographs of Parisian scenes. He sold his work (he took over 10,000 photographs) cheaply to artists for use as source material, and to historical societies as records of Paris. Shortly before his death he was "discovered" and rescued from obscurity.

Athanaric d. 381 AD •*Visigothic chieftain*• As chieftain (from AD 364) he fought three campaigns against the emperor Valens (born c. 328, ruled 364–378), brother of Emperor **Valentinian I**, and was a fierce persecutor of the Christians in Dacia (Romania). Finally defeated by the Huns in 376, he was driven from the north of the Danube, and died at Constantinople (Istanbul).

Athanasius, St c. 296–373 AD •*Greek Christian theologian and prelate*• He was born in Alexandria. In his youth he often visited the celebrated hermit **St Antony**, and for a time embraced an anchorite's life himself. As a deacon, he was a distinguished participant at the great Council of Nicaea (Nice) in AD 325. In 326 he was chosen Patriarch of Alexandria and primate of Egypt. As a result of his stand against the heretic **Arius**, he was dismissed from his see on several occasions by emperors sympathetic to the Arian cause. His writings includes work on the Trinity, the Incarnation and the divinity of the Holy Spirit. The so-called *Athanasian Creed* (representing Athanasian beliefs) was little heard of until the seventh century. His feast day is May 2.

Athelstan or **Æthelstan** c. 895–939 •*Anglo-Saxon king*• The grandson of **Alfred the Great**, he was the son of **Edward the Elder**, whom he succeeded as King of Wessex and Mercia (924). A warrior king, he extended his rule over parts of Cornwall and Wales, and kept Norse-held Northumbria under control. In 937 he defeated a confederation of Scots, Welsh and Vikings from Ireland in a major battle at Brunanburh. He died unmarried and was succeeded by his half-brother, **Edmund I**.

Athenaeus 2nd century AD •*Greek writer*• Born in Naucratis, Egypt, he lived first in Alexandria, and later in Rome. He wrote the *Deipnosophistae* ("Banquet of the Learned"), a collection of anecdotes and excerpts from ancient authors arranged as scholarly dinner-table conversation. Thirteen of its 15 books survive more or less complete, together with a summary of the other two.

Athenais *See* **Eudocia**

Atherton, David 1944– •*English conductor*• Born in Blackpool, he studied at Fitzwilliam College, Cambridge. In 1968 he became the youngest-ever conductor of the Henry Wood Promenade Concerts; other appointments have included resident conductor at the Royal Opera House (1968–79), music director and principal conductor of the San Diego Symphony Orchestra (1980–87) and music director and principal conductor of the Hong Kong Philharmonic Orchestra (1989–2000). Atherton is the founder of the London Sinfonietta (1967), a leading ensemble for contemporary music, and the US-based Mainly Mozart festival (1989).

Atherton, Gertrude Franklin, *née* **Horn** 1857–1948 •*US novelist*• She was born in San Francisco. Left a widow in 1887, she traveled extensively, living in Europe most of her life, and the settings for her novels range from ancient Greece to California and the West Indies. The most popular of her many novels are *The Conqueror* (1902), a fictional biography of **Alexander Hamilton**, and *Black Oxen* (1923).

Atholl, Katharine Marjory Stewart-Murray, Duchess of, *née* **Ramsay** 1874–1960 •*Scottish Conservative politician*• Born in Bamff, Perthshire, daughter of historian Sir James Ramsay, she studied at Wimbledon High School and the Royal College of Music. Though an early opponent of women's suffrage, she became Member of Parliament for Kinross and Perthshire in 1923 and was the first Conservative woman minister as Parliamentary Secretary to the Board of Education (1924–29). She successfully resisted changes in policy which would have adversely affected the education of poorer children, and from 1929 to 1939 campaigned against ill-treatment of women and children in the British Empire. She was responsible for translating an unexpurgated edition of *Mein Kampf* to warn of **Hitler**'s intentions. Her publications include *Searchlight on Spain* (1938) and *Women and Politics* (1931).

Atiyah, Sir Michael Francis 1929– •*English mathematician*• Born in London, he graduated from Trinity College, Cambridge. After lecturing in Cambridge and Oxford he became Savilian Professor at Oxford (1963–69), and in 1966 was awarded the Fields Medal (the mathematical equivalent of the Nobel Prize). After three years at Princeton University he returned to Oxford as Royal Society research professor in 1973. He has worked on algebraic geometry, algebraic topology, index theory of differential operators, and most recently on the mathematics of quantum field theory, where he has been particularly concerned with bridging the gap between mathematicians and physicists. One of the most distinguished British mathematicians of his time, he was appointed to the Order of Merit in 1992. His *Collected Works* (5 vols) were published in 1988.

Atkins, Chet (Chester Burton) 1924–2001 •*US country music guitarist, producer and record executive*• Born in Luttrell, Tennessee, he began to play guitar as a child, and developed a distinctive style, influenced by Merle Travis's fingerpicking, but encompassing jazz, blues, and other colorings. He worked with the **Carter Family** and **Hank Williams** before signing with RCA. He took over the label's country roster in 1952, and brought in many important artists, including **Dolly Parton**, **Willie Nelson**, **Waylon Jennings** and **Charley Pride**. He was a virtuoso guitarist, and recorded many albums after his debut in 1953 with *Gallopin' Guitar*.

Atkinson, Rowan Sebastian 1955– •*English actor, writer and comic*• Born in Newcastle upon Tyne, he first appeared in Oxford University revues at the Edinburgh Festival Fringe. His shows have included *The Nerd* (1984) and *The Sneeze* (1988). On television he has starred in *Not the Nine O'Clock News* (1979–82), *Blackadder*, a comedy series set in various historical periods (1983–89), the silent comedy series *Mr Bean* (1990–95), and *The Thin Blue Line* (1995–96). Film appearances include *The Tall Guy* (1989), *The Witches* (1990), *Four Weddings and a Funeral* (1994), and *Bean* (1997).

Atlas, Charles, *originally* **Angelo Siciliano** 1894–1972 •*US physical culturist*• He was born in Acri, Italy, and emigrated to the US with his family in 1904. A "97-pound weakling" as a youth, he developed a system of muscle exercises that improved his physique until he resembled the statue of a Greek titan (Atlas). Billing himself as "the World's Most Perfectly Developed Man," he taught his bodybuilding system through a successful worldwide mail-order business.

Atta, Hakim ben *See* **Mokanna, al-**

Attenborough, Sir David Frederick 1926– •*English naturalist and broadcaster*• Born in London, he is the younger brother of filmmaker **Richard Attenborough**. He joined the BBC in 1952 as a trainee producer. For the series *Zoo Quest* (1954–64) he made expeditions to remote parts of the globe to capture intimate footage of rare wildlife in its natural habitat. From 1965 to 1968 he was Controller of BBC 2 and subsequently director of programs (1969–72) before returning to documentary making, with such series as *Life on Earth* (1979), *The Living Planet* (1984), *The Trials of Life* (1990), *Life in the Freezer* (1993), *The Private Life of Plants* (1995) and *The Life of Birds* (1998). He also narrated *The Blue Planet* (2001). He has also written books to accompany many of these series. Renowned as one of the world's most respected and popular wildlife documentary makers, he was given the honorary title of Commander, Order of the British Empire in 1974 and was knighted in 1985.

Attenborough (of Richmond upon Thames), Richard Samuel Attenborough, Baron 1923– •*English film actor, producer and director*• He was born in Cambridge and trained at the Royal Academy of Dramatic Art before making his first professional appearance in *Ah, Wilderness* (1941) and film debut in *In Which We Serve* (1942). At first typecast as weak and cowardly youths, he played the thug Pinkie in *Brighton Rock* on stage (1943) and on film (1947). He developed into a conscientious character actor, winning British Academy Awards as the kidnapper in *Séance on a Wet Afternoon* (1964) and the bombastic sergeant major in *Guns at Batasi* (1964). He was actor-producer of several feature films in the 1960s before turning to directing on *O What a Lovely War!* (1969). A 20-year crusade to film the life of **Mahatma Gandhi** led to *Gandhi* (1982) which won eight Academy Awards. His other directorial credits include *Cry Freedom* (1987) and *Shadowlands* (1993). After a lengthy absence, he returned to acting in *Jurassic Park* (1993), which he followed with *Miracle on 34th Street* (1994), and *Elizabeth* (1998), amongst other films. He married actress Sheila Sim (1922–) in 1944 and is the brother of Sir **David Attenborough**. He was given the honorary title of Commander, Order of the British Empire in 1967, knighted in 1976, and made a life peer in 1993.

Atticus, Titus Pomponius 110–32 BC •*Roman intellectual, businessman and writer*• He was born in Rome, of a wealthy family, and educated with **Cicero** and Gaius Marius the Younger. He acquired the surname Atticus because of his long residence in Athens (85–65 BC) to avoid the civil war. He was a wealthy and highly cultivated man, he amassed a large library, wrote histories of Greece and Rome (now lost), and was an intimate friend of Cicero, who used him as an editor and consultant. Cicero's *Letters to Atticus* form a famous and prolific correspondence.

Attila c. 406–53 AD •*King of the Huns*• Called the Scourge of God, he was the legendary king who appears as Etzel in the German *Nibelungenlied* and Atli in the Old Icelandic *Völsunga Saga* and the heroic poems of the *Edda*. His empire extended from the Rhine to the frontiers of China. Having murdered his brother (with whom he had been joint king) he devastated all the countries between the Black Sea and the Mediterranean (447), and defeated the emperor Theodosius. He invaded Gaul in 451, and though defeated there he invaded Italy in 452, where Rome itself was only saved by the intervention of Pope **Leo I**, who paid huge bribes to Attila. He died the night after his marriage to a Burgundian princess, Ildeco, and the Hunnish Empire decayed. His death, in a pool of blood in bed, led to stories of vengeance and murder by his bride, graphically described by **Edward Gibbon**.

Attlee, Clement Richard Attlee, 1st Earl 1883–1967 •*English Labour statesman*• Born in Putney, near London, he was educated at University College, Oxford, and was called to the bar in 1905. He converted to socialism, and 1919 he became the first Labour Mayor of Stepney. In 1922 he entered parliament and became **Ramsay MacDonald**'s parliamentary secretary (1922–24), Under-Secretary of State for War (1924), served on the Simon Commission on India (1927–30) and was Postmaster General (1931) but did not become a member of the coalition government. One of the few Labour MPs to retain his parliamentary seat in the following election, he became Deputy Leader of the Opposition (1931–35) under **George Lansbury**, whom he succeeded as Leader in 1935, and paved the way for **Churchill**'s wartime premiership by refusing to commit his party to a coalition under **Neville Chamberlain**. He was Dominions Secretary (1942–43) and Deputy Prime Minister (1942–45) in Churchill's War Cabinet. As Leader of the Opposition he accompanied Sir **Anthony Eden** to the San Francisco and Potsdam conferences (1945), and returned to the latter as Prime Minister after the 1945 Labour victory. He carried through a vigorous program of nationalization and reform—the National Health Service was introduced and independence was granted to India (1947) and Burma (1948). He was again Leader of the Opposition from 1951 to 1955 when he resigned and accepted an earldom. His many books include *The Labour Party in Perspective* (1937), with supplement *Twelve Years Later* (1949), and an autobiography, *As It Happened* (1954).

Attucks, Crispus c. 1723–70 •*American Revolutionary patriot*• Nothing is known with certainty of his early life, but some historians identify him as the Massachusetts-born son of an African slave and a Natick Indian, who escaped from slavery and found work as a sailor on whaling ships. Accounts of the Boston Massacre (March 5, 1770) describe him as a huge man, one of the foremost in the crowd of colonists that gathered to taunt a small group of British soldiers and the first to fall when the soldiers opened fire. He and the other four Americans killed in the massacre were hailed as martyrs by the independence movement and were buried in a common grave. His patriotism is honored by a statue on the Boston Common (erected 1888).

Attwell, Mabel Lucie 1879–1964 •*English artist and writer*• Born in London, she studied at Heatherley's and other art schools. She illustrated children's classics such as the *Water Babies* (1915) and *Peter Pan* (1921). Noted for her studies of children, both humorous and serious, she illustrated her own and others' stories for children. Her popular "cherubic" dimpled tots were continued in annuals and children's books by her daughter, working under her mother's name.

Atwell, Winifred 1914–83 •*Trinidadian pianist and entertainer*• Born in Trinidad, she was a piano player from early childhood. She became a pop cabaret performer and had a lucrative contract with the British Decca record label and a string of "ragtime" hits, featuring a jangly, public-bar piano sound, including "Black and White Rag," "Coronation Rag," and "Let's Have a Party."

Atwood, Margaret Eleanor 1939– •*Canadian writer, poet and critic*• She was born in Ottawa. After graduating from the University of Toronto and Radcliffe College, she held a variety of jobs ranging from waitress and summer-camp counselor to lecturer in English literature and writer-in-residence. Her first published work, a collection of poems entitled *The Circle Game* (1966), won the Governor-General's award. Since then she has published several volumes of poetry, collections of short stories, children's books, and critical works such as *Survival* (1972), an acclaimed study of Canadian literature. She is best known, however, as a novelist. *The Edible Woman* (1969) deals with emotional cannibalism and provoked considerable controversy within and beyond the women's movement. It was followed by such works as *Surfacing* (1972), *Life Before Man* (1979) and *Bodily Harm* (1982). Other novels include *The Handmaid's Tale* (1985), *Cat's Eye* (1989), *The Robber Bride* (1993), and *Alias Grace* (1996). She won the Booker Prize in 2000 for *The Blind Assassin*.

Aubrey, John 1626–97 •*English antiquary, biographer and folklorist*• Born in Easton Piercy, Wiltshire, he was educated at Malmesbury, Blandford, and Trinity College, Oxford. Of his works only *Miscellanies* (1696), containing stories and folklore, was printed in his lifetime, but he left a wealth of material. His biographical and anecdotal material on celebrities of his time like Hobbes, **Milton**, and **Francis Bacon**, collected for the antiquarian Anthony à Wood (1632–95), was published in *Letters by Eminent Persons* (1813), better known as *Brief Lives*.

Aubusson, Pierre d' 1423–1503 •*French soldier and prelate*• Grand Master of the Knights Hospitalers from 1476, his outstanding achievement was his defense of Rhodes (1480) against a besieging army of 100,000 Turks under Sultan **Mohammed II (the Conqueror)**. In 1481 he made a treaty with the Turks under the new sultan, **Bayezit II**, by agreeing to imprison the sultan's rebellious brother, Djem. In 1489 he was created cardinal.

Auchincloss, Louis Stanton 1917– •*US novelist, short-story writer and critic*• Born in Lawrence, New York, he trained as a lawyer and was admitted to the New York bar in 1941. He is a novelist of manners, at home with old money and a highly codified, traditional society, but also has a fine sense of intrigue. His first novel was *The Indifferent Children* (1947). *Pursuit of the Prodigal* (1959), *Portrait in Brownstone* (1962), *The Embezzler* (1966) and *A World of Profit* (1968) are often considered to be the best of his subsequent novels.

Auchinleck, Sir Claude John Eyre 1884–1981 •*English field marshal*• He joined the 62nd Punjabis in 1904, served in Egypt and Mesopotamia. In World War II, he commanded in northern Norway and India, and then moved to the Middle East (1941). He made a successful advance into Cyrenaica, but was later thrown back by **Erwin Rommel**. His regrouping of the 8th Army on El Alamein is now regarded as a successful operation, but at the time he was made a scapegoat for the retreat and replaced by General **Alexander** (1942). In 1943 he returned to India, serving subsequently as Supreme Commander in India and Pakistan (1947).

Auchterlonie, Willie 1872–1963 •*Scottish golf club maker*• Born in St Andrews, Fife, he won the Open Golf Championship at the age of 21, using only seven homemade clubs. In 1935 he was appointed professional to the Royal and Ancient at St Andrews, where his workshop and store became venerated by golfers.

Auden, W(ystan) H(ugh) 1907–73 •*US poet and essayist*• Born in York, England, he was educated at Gresham's School, Holt, and Christ Church, Oxford. His first volume of *Poems* (1930) was accepted for publication by **T S Eliot** at Faber and Faber. In the 1930s he wrote passionately on social problems of the time from a far-left standpoint. In 1935 he married Erika Mann, the daughter of **Thomas Mann**, in order to provide her with a passport out of Nazi Germany. He wrote *Spain* (1937) in support of the Spanish Republic's cause and (with **Christopher Isherwood**) published *Journey to a War* (1939), a report on Japanese aggression in China. He emigrated to New York in 1939 and was naturalized in 1946, but returned to live in England when he was Professor of Poetry at Oxford (1956–61). *Another Time* (1940) contains some of his best-known poems. In the US he converted to Anglicanism, tracing this in *The Sea and the Mirror* (1944) and *For the Time Being* (1944). He collaborated with Isherwood in three plays and also edited many anthologies and collections, wrote much literary criticism and several librettos. A master of verse form, using fresh and accessible language, his influence as a poet has been immense.

Audrey, St *See* **Etheldreda, St**

Audubon, John James 1785–1851 •*US ornithologist and bird artist*• Audubon was born in Les Cayes, Haiti, the illegitimate son of a French sea captain named Jean Audubon and a Creole woman. He was taken to France and adopted by Audubon and his wife, who died young. In 1803 he was sent to the US to look after his father's property near Philadelphia, where he spent time hunting and drawing birds. In 1808 he married and moved to Kentucky. There he had some unsuccessful business ventures, meanwhile devoting himself to his "Great Idea"—an ambitious project to make a comprehensive catalogue of every species of bird in America. He painted in pastel, watercolor and oils. In 1826 he took his work to Europe in search of a publisher, holding exhibitions in Paris, London, Liverpool and Edinburgh. In London he sought out the engraver and painter Robert Havell (1793–1878) to make the copperplate engravings of "double-elephant" plates, and 1827 saw the publication in England of the first of the 87 portfolios of his massive *Birds of America* (1827–38). It eventually comprised colored life-size plates of 1,065 birds, and cost $115,000. He also published, with the Scottish ornithologist William MacGillivray (1796–1852), an accompanying text, *Ornithological Biography* (1831–39). Between 1840 and 1844 he produced a "miniature" edition in seven volumes that became a bestseller. He eventually returned to the US to settle.

Auer, Karl, Baron von Welsbach 1858–1929 •*Austrian chemist*• Born in Vienna, he invented the gas mantle which bears his name and carried out important work on the rare metals, isolating the elements neodymium and praseodymium. He also developed the cerium-iron alloy known as "Auer metal" or "mischmetal." The first improvement over the flint and steel in use since medieval times, it is still used to strike sparks in cigarette lighters and gas appliances.

Auerbach, Frank 1931– •*British artist*• Born in Germany, he came to Great Britain in 1939. He studied in London at St Martin's

School of Art (1948–52) and the Royal College of Art (1952–55), but his most important formative influence was **David Bomberg**, who taught him briefly at the Borough Polytechnic, London. He works with oil paint of predominantly earth colors, thickly applied in layers, and his subject matter is figurative, including portraits of a few close friends and familiar views of Primrose Hill and Camden Town in London.

Auerbach, Red, *properly* **Arnold Auerbach** 1917– •*US basketball coach*• Born in Brooklyn, New York, he studied at George Washington University, Washington DC, and served in the US Navy during World War II. He is best known for coaching the Boston Celtics to eight straight NBA championships (1959–66), a record since unmatched, and was the first coach in history to preside over 1,000 wins. Among his many honors he was named the greatest coach in the history of the NBA by the Professional Basketball Writers of America (1980).

Auersperg, Anton Alexander, Graf von, *pseudonym* **Anastasius Grün** 1806–76 •*Austrian poet*• He was distinguished by his liberalism and ultra-German sympathies, and was one of the best-known epic and lyrical poets in the German language. His works include a volume of love poetry, *Blätter der Liebe* (1830, "Leaves of Love"), a collection of political poetry, *Spaziergänge eines Wiener Poeten* (1831, "A Viennese Poet's Walks"), and *Gedichte* (1837, "Poems"), a volume of lyrical poems.

Auger, Pierre Victor 1899–1993 •*French physicist*• Born in Paris, he was educated at the École Normale Supérieure and later became professor at the University of Paris. He discovered that an atom can de-excite from a state of high energy nonradiatively, by losing one of its own electrons rather than emitting a photon. He later investigated the properties of the neutron and worked on cosmic-ray physics, discovering extended air showers (also known as Auger showers) where the interaction of cosmic rays with Earth's upper atmosphere produces cascades of large numbers of secondary particles.

Augspurg or **Augsburg, Anita Johanna Theodora Sophie** 1857–1943 •*German feminist, pacifist and writer*• Born in Verden an der Aller, she studied law in Zurich (1893–97). She became a leading figure in the Bund Deutscher Frauenvereine (Federation of German Women's Associations) in Berlin, alongside **Lida Heymann**, **Minna Cauer** and Marie Stritt (1856–1928). In 1902, the four founded the Deutscher Verband für Frauenstimmrecht to campaign for women's suffrage. After German women gained the vote in 1919, Augspurg, Heymann and Cauer worked for civil rights, producing the newspaper *Die Frau im Staat* (1919–33, "Women in the State").

August, Bille 1948– •*Danish film director*• Born in Lundtofte, he studied photography in Stockholm before attending the Danish Film School. He made his feature debut with *Honning Måne*, (1979, *In My Life*). His international breakthrough came with a version of **Martin Andersen Nexö**'s novel *Pelle Erobreren* (1987, *Pelle the Conqueror*) which won the Palme D'Or at Cannes and an Academy Award for Best Foreign Film. Later films include *The House of the Spirits* (1993), *Smilla's Sense of Snow* (1996), *Les Misérables* (1998) and *En Sång för Martin* (2001, *A Song for Martin*).

Augusta, Julia *See* **Livia, Drusilla**

Augustine of Canterbury, St d. 604 •*Italian prelate and the first Archbishop of Canterbury*• Born probably in Rome, he was prior of a Benedictine monastery there, when in 596 Pope **Gregory I (the Great)** sent him with 40 other monks to convert the Anglo-Saxons to Christianity. He was kindly received by **Ethelbert**, King of Kent, whose wife was a Christian, and the conversion and baptism of the king contributed greatly to his success. As Bishop of the English from 597, he established his church at Canterbury, but did not succeed in extending his authority over the native British Church. He died at Canterbury, and in 612 his body was transferred to the Abbey of Saints Peter and Paul, now the site of St Augustine's Missionary College (1848). His feast day is May 26.

Augustine of Hippo, St, *originally* **Aurelius Augustinus** AD 354–430 •*Numidian Christian, one of the four Latin Doctors of the Church*• Born in Tagaste (now Souk-Ahras), Numidia, he was brought up a Christian by his devout mother, Monica (who became St Monica). He went to Carthage to study and had a son, Adeodatus (AD 372), by a mistress there. He became deeply involved in Manicheanism, which seemed to offer a solution to the problem of evil. In 383 he moved to teach in Rome, then in Milan, and became influenced by Skepticism and then by Neo-Platonism. He finally became converted to Christianity and was baptized (together with his son) by St **Ambrose** in 387. Ordained a priest in 391, he became Bishop of Hippo in 396, where he was a relentless antagonist of the heretical schools of Donatists, Pelagians and Manicheans. He wrote his autobiography *Confessions* (397), *De civitate Dei* (413–26, "The City of God"), a vindication of Christianity, and *De Trinitate* ("The Trinity"), a weighty exposition of the doctrine of the Trinity. The central tenets of his creed were the corruption of human nature through the fall of man, the consequent slavery of the human will, predestination and the perseverance of the saints. His feast day is August 28.

" "

Da mihi castitatem et continentiam, sed noli modo.

Grant me chastity and continence, but not yet.

AD 397 ***Confessions****, book 8, chapter 7 (translated by Henry Chadwick).*

Augustus II (the Strong) 1670–1733 •*Elector of Saxony and twice king of Poland*• Born in Dresden, he succeeded to the electorship as Frederick Augustus I (1694) on the death of his brother, John George IV. After fighting against France and the Turks, he renounced his Lutheranism and became a Roman Catholic (1696), to secure his election to the Polish throne as Augustus II (1697–1704). With **Peter I (the Great)** of Russia and Frederik IV of Denmark, he planned the partition of Sweden, invading Livonia in 1700. Defeated by **Karl XII** of Sweden, Augustus was deposed (1704) and replaced by **Stanisław Leszczyński**. Although he recovered the throne in 1709, by the end of his reign Poland was little more than a Russian protectorate.

Augustus, (Gaius Julius Caesar) Octavianus 63 BC–AD 14 •*The first Roman emperor*• Augustus was the son of the senator and praetor Gaius Octavius, and Atia, **Julius Caesar**'s niece. At the time of Caesar's assassination (March 44), Augustus abandoned his studies in Illyricum and returned to Italy where, using Caesar's money and name, he raised an army, defeated **Mark Antony**, and gained the consulship. When Antony returned from Gaul with **Lepidus**, Augustus joined them in forming a triumvirate. He received Africa, Sardinia and Sicily; Antony received Gaul; and Lepidus received Spain. Their power was soon made absolute by their reign of terror in Italy, and by their victory at Philippi over the republicans under **Brutus** and **Cassius** (42). The Roman world was divided again, Augustus taking the western half and Antony the eastern, while Lepidus had to be content with Africa. Augustus gradually built up his position in Italy and the West, ingratiating himself with the Roman people and misrepresenting the actions of Antony in the East. War was declared against **Cleopatra**, whom Antony had joined in 37, and after his naval victory at Actium (31) Augustus became the sole ruler of the Roman Empire. Antony and Cleopatra committed suicide. In 29, after settling affairs in Egypt, Greece and the East, Augustus returned to Rome in triumph, and proclaimed universal peace. At home and abroad the declared policy of Augustus was one of national revival and restoration of traditional Roman values. He legislated to mold the fabric of Roman society, and beautified the city of Rome. Abroad, he pursued a policy of calculated imperial conquest, and considerably extended the territory of the Roman Empire in central and northern Europe.

Augustus, Romulus *See* **Romulus Augustulus**

Aulén, Gustaf Emmanuel Hildebrand 1879–1977 •*Swedish Lutheran theologian and composer*• He was born in Ljungby, Kalmar. Professor of Systematic Theology at Lund (1913–33), and Bishop of Strängnäs (1933–52), he was a leading representative of the Scandinavian school of theology that sought Christian truth behind doctrines rather than in the form in which they were presented. He wrote several books, including his most famous study, *Christus Victor* (1931), which presented the death of Christ as a triumph over the powers of evil, following the approach of **Irenaeus** and **Martin Luther**. Aulén's second love was music and he was president of the Royal Swedish Academy of Music (1944–50).

Aulenti, Gae(tana) 1927– *•Italian architect•* Born in Palazzolo dello Stella, she trained at Milan Polytechnic. She taught at Venice and Milan in the 1960s before spending three years researching with Luca Roncini in Florence. Her works include the Palazzo Grassi, Venice (1985), Museo del Arte Catalana, Barcelona (1985), and the redesign of the Musée d'Orsay in Paris (1980–86), which was nominated by the International Union of Architects as one of the ten most important works in the previous three years. She has also worked with corporate clients and theatrical stage design.

Aungerville or **Angerville, Richard**, *also called* **Richard de Bury** 1287–1345 *•English churchman•* Born in Bury St Edmunds, Suffolk, he studied at Oxford and became a Benedictine monk at Durham. Having been tutor to **Edward III**, he was made successively Dean of Wells and Bishop of Durham. He collected manuscripts and books, and his own principal work, *Philobyblon*, describes the state of learning in England and France.

Aung San 1915–47 *•Burmese nationalist•* He was the dominant figure in the nationalist movement during and after World War II in the Pacific theater. At the beginning of the 1940s, Aung San, working with Japanese agents, formed the anti-British Burma Independence Army, which entered Burma (now Myanmar) with the invading Japanese in January 1942. He rapidly became disillusioned with the Japanese, however, and, as a leading figure in the Anti-Fascist People's Freedom League (AFPFL), turned his troops against them (1945). In the immediate postwar period he became president of the AFPFL and, in 1946, was effectively Prime Minister in the Governor's Executive Council. In January 1947 he traveled to London to negotiate, with success, Burma's independence. On July 19, however, he was assassinated by a political rival. His death removed the one figure who might have held together Burma's warring political interests as the country achieved independence (1948). His daughter is **Aung San Suu Kyi**.

Aung San Suu Kyi 1945– *•Burmese political leader and founder of the National League for Democracy•* Aung San Suu Kyi was born in Rangoon, the daughter of Burmese nationalist hero General **Aung San**. She went to Oxford University to study politics, philosophy and economics, and in 1969 worked for the United Nations in New York. In 1988 she returned to Burma (now Myanmar) and after appeals to the government for more open consultation on the country's future, she cofounded the National League for Democracy (NLD) and became its General Secretary. The government had established its State Law and Order Restoration Council (SLORC), introduced martial law and imprisonment without trial, and banned public meetings, forbidding Suu Kyi to hold her office. Nonetheless, she toured the country and addressed supporters, who attended in large numbers. As a result, in 1989 she was placed under house arrest by the military junta. Her release in July 1995 did not change her long-standing conviction that the military had no place in politics, but she was careful not to provoke violent reactions, emphasizing the need for dialogue and reconciliation and appealing to exiled Burmese opposition groups to practice patience. She was reappointed General Secretary of the NLD in October 1995. Following her release her movements were restricted, but she continued to address supporters at the gates of her compound to work towards the framing of a new constitution. She was placed under house arrest again in 2000 when she tried to travel to Mandalay in defiance of the restrictions placed upon her and was finally released unconditionally in 2002. She was awarded the Nobel Peace Prize (1991) and the Presidential Medal of Freedom (2000).

Aurangzeb 1618–1707 *•Mughal emperor of India•* Born in Dhod, Malwa, he was the third son of Emperor **Shah Jahan** and struggled for power with his three brothers, finally putting them to death. During his reign (1659–1707), the empire remained outwardly prosperous, but his puritanical and narrow outlook alienated the various communities of the empire, particularly the Hindus. Opposed by his own rebellious sons and by the Mahratha Empire in the south, he died a fugitive.

Aurelian, *properly* **Lucius Domitius Aurelianus** c. 215–75 AD *•Roman emperor•* He was born of humble origins in Dacia or Pannonia. He rose through the army and on the death of Claudius II (AD 270), was elected emperor by the army. During his reign, he restored good discipline in the army, order in domestic affairs, and political unity to the Roman dominions, he was entitled Restitutor Orbis—"Restorer of the World." He was assassinated by his own officers near Byzantium during a campaign against the Persians.

Aurelius, Marcus *See* **Marcus Aurelius**

Auric, Georges 1899–1983 *•French composer•* Born in Lodève, Hérault, he studied under **Vincent d'Indy** and became one of the group of young French composers known as Les Six. Inspired by both **Erik Satie** and **Igor Stravinsky**, his compositions range from orchestral pieces to ballets, songs and film scores, including **Jean Cocteau**'s *La belle et la bête* (1946) and several British films, including *Passport to Pimlico* (1949).

Auriol, Jacqueline 1917–2000 *•French aviator•* The daughter-in-law of **Vincent Auriol**, she broke the women's jet speed record in 1955 by flying at 715 miles per hour in a French *Mystère*. She published *I Live to Fly* in 1970.

Auriol, Vincent 1884–1966 *•French socialist statesman•* He studied law, and was a Deputy (1914–40, 1945–47), Minister of Finance in the Popular Front government (1936–37) and Minister of Justice (1937–38). He opposed the granting of power to Marshal **Philippe Pétain** in 1940, and joined the French Resistance, escaping to Algeria in 1943, where he became president of the Foreign Affairs Committee of the Consultative Assembly. He represented France at the first meeting of the UN, was elected president of the Constituent Assembly in 1946, and was first president of the Fourth Republic (1947–53).

Aurobindo, Sri, *originally* **Sri Aurobindo Ghose** 1872–1950 *•Indian philosopher, poet and mystic•* Born in Calcutta into a high-caste Bengali family, he was educated in England at Cambridge. A proficient linguist, he returned to India in 1892 and became a professor in Baroda and Calcutta. In 1908 he was imprisoned by the British authorities in India for sedition, and studied yoga in jail. Renouncing nationalism and politics for yoga and Hindu philosophy, he founded an ashram in 1910 at Pondicherry. His books include *The Synthesis of Yoga* (1948) and *Aurobindo on Himself* (1953) among many others.

Austen, Jane 1775–1817 *•English novelist•* Jane Austen was born in Steventon, Hampshire; her father was an able scholar and served as her tutor. She spent the first 25 years of her life in Steventon, and the last eight in nearby Chawton (moving to Winchester just a few months before her death), and did almost all of her writing in those two places. During the intervening years in Bath, which appears to have been an unsettled time in her otherwise ordered and rather uneventful life, her writing was more sporadic, and she abandoned an early novel, *The Watsons*, following the death of her father in 1805. She never married, although she had a number of suitors, and wrote perceptively on the subjects of courtship and marriage in her novels. Her characteristic subject was the closely observed and often ironically depicted morals and mores of country life, which she rendered with genius. Her best-known works in this vein are *Sense and Sensibility* (1811), *Pride and Prejudice* (1813), *Emma* (1816), and the posthumously published *Persuasion* (1818). *Mansfield Park* (1814) is a darker and more serious dissection of her chosen fictional territory, and although never as popular, it is arguably her masterpiece.

“ ”

It is a truth universally acknowledged, that a single man in possession of a good fortune, must be in want of a wife.

*1813 **Pride and Prejudice**, opening line.*

Auster, Paul, *pseudonym* **Paul Benjamin** 1947– *•US novelist and poet•* Born in Newark, New Jersey, by the time of his first novel, *Squeeze Play*, in 1982, he had already produced several volumes of poetry, a selection of which appeared with some essays in *Ground Work* (1990). The cerebral mystery novels which make up *The New York Trilogy* (1985–87) were followed by *In the Country of Last Things*

(1987). Other novels include *The Music of Chance* (1991) and *Mr Vertigo* (1994). He also wrote the film *Smoke* (1995) and cowrote and codirected its follow-up, *Blue in the Face* (1995).

Austin, Alfred 1835–1913 •*English poet*• Born in Leeds, he was educated at Stonyhurst and Oscott College, and graduated from London University. He published *The Season: A Satire* (1861), *The Human Tragedy* (1862), *The Conversion of Winckelmann* (1862) and a dozen more volumes of poems of little merit, and an autobiography (1911). From 1883 to 1893 he edited the *National Review*. His appointment as Poet Laureate (1896) brought public derision. He was much parodied as a poet.

Austin (of Longbridge), Herbert Austin, 1st Baron 1866–1941 •*English car manufacturer*• Born in Buckinghamshire and educated at Rotherham Grammar School and Brampton College, he went to Australia in 1884 and worked in engineering shops there. He went back to England in 1893 and joined the Wolseley Sheep-Shearing Company in Birmingham. In 1895, with the Wolseley Company, he produced his first three-wheel car, and in 1905 he opened his own works near Birmingham, which rapidly developed and whose considerable output included, in 1921, the popular "Baby" Austin 7. He was Conservative Member of Parliament for King's Norton (1918–24).

Austin, John 1790–1859 •*English jurist*• He was born in Creeting Mill, Suffolk, was called to the bar in 1818, and in 1826 was appointed Professor of Jurisprudence at the newly founded University of London (now University College). His *Province of Jurisprudence Determined* (1832), defining (on a utilitarian basis) the field of ethics and law in time had a great influence on English views of the subject, and introducing a precise terminology previously unknown.

Austin, J(ohn) L(angshaw) 1911–60 •*English philosopher*• Born in Lancaster, Lancashire, he was educated at Balliol College, Oxford. A leading figure in the "Oxford Philosophy" movement, his distinctive contribution was the meticulous examination of ordinary linguistic usage to resolve philosophical questions. He pioneered the analysis of speech acts, and his best-known works are *Philosophical Papers* (1961), *Sense and Sensibilia* (1962) and *How to Do Things with Words* (1962).

Austral, Florence, *originally* **Florence Wilson** 1894–1968 •*Australian soprano*• Born in Richmond, Victoria, she adopted the name of her country as a stage name prior to her debut in 1922 at Covent Garden, London. She toured the US and Canada in the 1920s, and appeared in the complete cycles of *The Ring* at Covent Garden, London, and at the Berlin State Opera, which she joined as a principal in 1930. Also appearing frequently in the concert hall, she made many recordings with other leading singers of her day.

Auteuil, Daniel 1950– •*French actor*• Born in Algeria, he grew up in France, beginning his career on stage with the Théâtre National Populaire, and making his screen debut in *L'Agression* (1974). He came to international attention playing the treacherous farmer Ugolin in two films by the director Claude Berri, *Jean de Florette* (1986) and *Manon des sources* (1986). Subsequent films have included *Un Coeur en hiver* (1992) and *Sade* (2000).

Avedon, Richard 1923– •*US photographer*• Born in New York City, he studied at Columbia University and the Design Laboratory of the New School for Social Research, New York, before becoming a staff photographer on *Harper's Bazaar* (1945–65). Famous for his photographs of fashion models and celebrities, he originally concentrated on dramatic, motion photographs out of doors, and later developed an uncompromisingly realistic and stark style which has great emotional impact. His publications include *Nothing Personal* (1964), *Avedon: Photographs 1947–77* (1978, text by Rosamond Bernier) and an autobiography (1993).

Aventinus, *Latin name of* **Johannes Thurmayr** 1477–1534 •*German humanist scholar and historian*• Born in Abensberg (Latin *Aventinum*), Bavaria, he taught Greek and mathematics at Kraków, and wrote a history of Bavaria. He was known as the "Bavarian Herodotus."

Avenzoar, *Arabic name* **Ibn Zohr** c. 1072–1162 •*Arab physician*• Born in Seville, he published influential medical works describing such conditions as kidney stones and pericarditis, and was considered the greatest clinician in the western caliphate.

Averlino, Antonio de Pietro *See* **Filarete, Antonio**

Averroës or **Averrhoës**, *also called* **Ibn Rushd**, *Arabic in full* **Abū al-Walīd Muḥammad ibn Aḥmad ibn Muḥammad ibn Rushd** 1126–98 •*Islamic philosopher and physician*• Born in Córdoba, Spain, the son of a distinguished family of jurists, he served as kadi (judge) and physician in Córdoba and Seville, and in Morocco. He wrote extensive *Commentaries* on many of **Aristotle**'s works, which were both influential and controversial in the development of scholastic philosophy in the Middle Ages, they offered a partial synthesis of Greek and Arabic philosophical traditions. He was the most famous of the medieval Islamic philosophers.

Avery, Milton Clark 1893–1965 •*US painter*• He was born in Sand Bank, New York. A figurative painter who worked with bold, flat masses of color, he was influenced by **Henri Matisse**. His major works, reflecting his interest in people, beaches, and landscapes, include *Sea and Sand Dunes* (1955), *Moon Path* (1958), *Beach Blankets* (1960) and *Dunes and Sea II* (1960).

Avery, Oswald Theodore 1877–1955 •*US bacteriologist*• Born in Halifax, Nova Scotia, Canada, he studied medicine at Colgate University and spent his career at the Rockefeller Institute Hospital, New York (1913–48). He became an expert on pneumococci, and in 1928 investigated a claim that a nonvirulent, rough-coated strain could be transformed into the virulent smooth strain by the mere presence of some of the dead smooth bacteria. Avery confirmed this result, and went on in 1944 to show that the transformation is caused by the presence of DNA in the dead bacteria, although he did not suggest that the molecules which carry the whole reproductive pattern of any living species (the genes) are simply DNA, a concept which was to emerge only later.

Avery, Tex, *originally* **Frederick Bean** 1908–80 •*US animated-cartoon director*• He was born in Texas and in 1929 joined the **Walter Lantz** animation studio. Moving to Warner Brothers to direct his first cartoon, Porky Pig in *Goldiggers of '49* (1935), he soon was noticed for his zany comedy, creating Daffy Duck in *Porky's Duck Hunt* (1937), and developing Bugs Bunny in *A Wild Hare* (1940). Moving to MGM he created Droopy (*Dumb Hounded*, 1943), Screwy Squirrel (*Screwball Squirrel*, 1944) and many other characters.

Avicebrón, *Arabic name* **Solomon ben Yehuda ibn Gabirol** c. 1020–c. 1070 •*Jewish poet and philosopher*• He was born in Málaga, Spain. Most of his prose work is lost, but a Latin translation of his most famous work, *Fons vitae* ("The Fountain of Life") survives. Neo-Platonist in character, it was very influential among later Christian scholastics. His poetry became part of the mystical tradition of the Kabbalah.

Avicenna, *Arabic name* **Abū 'Alī al-Ḥusayn ibn 'Abd Allāh ibn Sīnā** 980–1037 •*Persian philosopher and physician*• Born near Bokhara, Persia (Iran), he was renowned for his precocious and prodigious learning, becoming physician to several sultans, and for some time vizier in Hamadan. He was one of the main interpreters of **Aristotle** to the Islamic world, and was the author of some 200 works on science, religion and philosophy. His medical textbook, *al-Qānūn fī aṭ-ṭibb* ("Canon of Medicine"), long remained a standard work.

Ávila, St Teresa of *See* **Teresa of Ávila, St**

Ávila Camacho, Manuel 1897–1955 •*Mexican soldier and politician*• Born in Tezuitlán, Mexico, he studied accounting, then joined the revolutionary army of **Venustiano Carranza**. As President of Mexico from 1940 to 1946, he brought stability to the country, pursuing a policy of moderate social reform, expanding the school system, and sponsoring social security legislation.

Avogadro, (Lorenzo Romano) Amedeo Carlo 1776–1856 •*Italian physicist and chemist*• Born in Turin, Piedmont region, he trained as a lawyer. From 1806 he concentrated on science, and soon became Professor of Mathematics and Physics at the College of Vercelli (1809). He published widely on physics and chemistry and, in 1811, seeking to explain **Joseph Gay-Lussac**'s law of combining gaseous volumes (1809), he formulated the famous hypothesis that equal volumes of all gases contain equal numbers of molecules when at the same temperature and pressure (Avogadro's law). The hypothesis was practically ignored for around 50 years, and universal acceptance did not come until the 1880s.

Awdry, W(ilbert) V(ere) 1911–97 •*English author and Church of England clergyman*• He was born in Ampfield, Hampshire. His railway stories for young people, especially those featuring Thomas the Tank Engine, delighted generations of small children. The first, *The Three Railway Engines*, appeared in 1945, and *Thomas, the Tank Engine*, a year later. Over 25 books followed, until *Tramway Engines* appeared in 1972, following which Awdry's son, Christopher, succeeded to the authorship.

Axel, Gabriel Mørch 1918– •*Danish film director*• He was born in Denmark, lived as a child in France, and trained as an actor at Copenhagen Royal Theater. He began directing films in the 1950s, and his Danish films include *Den røde kappe* (1966, "The Red Cape"). In 1987 he made his international breakthrough with *Babettes gæstebud* (*Babette's Feast*), an adaptation of a short story by **Karen Blixen**, which in 1988 won the Academy Award in the Best Foreign Language Film category. He participated in the *Lumière et compagnie* (1995, *Lumière and Company*) project alongside other great directors.

Axel, Richard 1946– •*US molecular biologist*• Born in New York City, he graduated in medicine from Johns Hopkins University in 1970. He has held various positions at Columbia University and is now both Professor of Pathology and of Biochemistry and Molecular Biophysics there. In 1975 he showed that when DNA is combined with cellular proteins as chromatin it can be split at specific regions, regions later shown to contain genes which are transcriptionally active. This was an essential step in understanding gene activation and regulation. In 1979 he was responsible for developing the technique which made it possible to mutate cloned genes in specific ways, reintroduce the mutated genes into cells and then determine the effect of mutations on gene activity.

Axelrod, Julius 1912– •*US pharmacologist and Nobel Prize winner*• Born in New York City, he qualified in biology and chemistry, and worked for some years as a laboratory analyst before entering research; he obtained his PhD at the age of 45. As chief of the pharmacological section of the Clinical Sciences Laboratory at the National Institutes for Mental Health (1955–84), his research focused on the chemistry and pharmacology of the nervous system, especially the role of the catecholamines, adrenaline and noradrenaline. His work accelerated investigations into the links between brain chemistry and psychiatric disease, and in the search for psychoactive drugs. He jointly won the 1970 Nobel Prize for physiology or medicine with **Ulf von Euler** and **Bernard Katz**.

Ayala, Francisco 1906– •*Spanish author*• Born in Granada, he studied at the University of Madrid, where he later taught. He served with the republican government during the Spanish Civil War and at its end was forced into exile in Argentina, later living and teaching in the US and returning to Spain in 1976. He is noted particularly for novels such as *Death As a Way of Life* (1958) and *The Bottom of the Glass* (1962), which explore with humor the conflicts between dictatorship and democracy. *Things Remembered and Things Forgotten* (1982–88) are experimental memoirs.

Ayckbourn, Sir Alan 1939– •*English playwright*• Born in London and educated at Haileybury School, Hertfordshire, he was an acting stage manager in repertory before joining the Stephen Joseph Theatre Company at Scarborough. A founder-member of the Victoria Theatre, Stoke-on-Trent, in 1962, he returned in 1964 to Scarborough, where most of his plays have premiered and where he has been the artistic director since 1971. The first of a torrent of West-End successes was *Relatively Speaking* in 1967, and he was quickly established as a master of farce. His plays often shrewdly observe the English class structure, and he has made considerable experiments with staging and dramatic structure: *Way Upstream* (1982), for example, necessitates the flooding of the stage. Among his most successful farces are *Time and Time Again* (1972), *Bedroom Farce* (1977) and *Joking Apart* (1979). He has also written musicals and plays for children, and was a BBC radio drama producer (1964–70). Later plays include *Woman in Mind* (1985) and *Henceforward* (1987), which reflect an increasingly bleak vision of society. He was given the honorary title of Commander, Order of the British Empire in 1987 and was knighted in 1997.

Ayer, Sir A(lfred) J(ules) 1910–89 •*English philosopher*• Born in London and educated at Eton and Oxford, he was a pupil of **Gilbert Ryle**. He became Grote Professor at University College London (1947) and was later Wykeham Professor of Logic at Oxford (1959–78). His first and most important book, *Language, Truth and Logic* (1936), was a lucid, concise and forceful account of the anti-metaphysical doctrines of the Vienna Circle of philosophers, whom he visited in 1932. His later publications include *The Problem of Knowledge* (1956) and *The Central Questions of Philosophy* (1972). He was knighted in 1970.

“ ”

The traditional disputes of philosophers are, for the most part, as unwarranted as they are unfruitful.

*1936 **Language, Truth and Logic**, chapter 1.*

Ayers, Sir Henry 1821–97 •*Australian politician*• Born in Portsea, Hampshire, England, he emigrated to South Australia in 1841 and took up a post with the South Australia Mining Association, with which he was associated for 50 years. Elected in 1863 to the first Legislative Council for the state under responsible government, he was a member of the council for 36 years. He was premier four times, and Ayers Rock, a giant monolith in the south of the (then) Northern Territories of South Australia, was named after him by **William Gosse** in 1873.

Ayeshah *See* **Aïshah**

Aylward, Gladys 1902–70 •*English missionary in China*• Born in London, in 1930, she spent all her savings on a railway ticket to Tientsin in northern China, and with a Scottish missionary, Mrs Jeannie Lawson, founded the Inn of the Sixth Happiness in Yangcheng. From there in 1938 she made a great trek across the mountains leading over 100 children to safety during the war with Japan. After nine years with the Nationalists caring for the wounded, she returned to England in 1948, preached for five years, then in 1953 settled in Taiwan as head of an orphanage. The 1958 film *The Inn of the Sixth Happiness*, starring **Ingrid Bergman**, was based on her life.

Aylwin (Azòcar), Patricio 1919– •*Chilean lawyer and politician*• Born in Santiago, after a successful early legal career, he was elected president of the Christian Democratic Party in 1973, and as leader of the opposition coalition triggered the national plebiscite of October 1988 that brought down General **Pinochet** in the 1989 elections. Power was formally transferred from the military regime to Aylwin in 1990, but his inability to secure the two-thirds majority in Congress necessary to amend the 1980 constitution allowed the outgoing junta to nominate almost one-fifth of the Senate's membership and thus to thwart Aylwin's efforts to lift press censorship and to abolish the death penalty. Continuing revelations about the previous regime's record on human rights triggered violent demonstrations, but Pinochet still resisted attempts to remove him as military Commander in Chief, a post he held until 1998. Aylwin was President until 1994.

Ayres, Gillian 1930– •*English painter*• Born in Barnes, London, she trained at Camberwell School of Art, and first exhibited in 1952. Her free, abstract style, with its emphasis on color and the active properties of paint, was influenced by seeing photographs of **Jackson Pollock** at work. During the 1980s she introduced gold into her pictures and turned from acrylics to oils, the titles of her paintings expressing the essential literary Britishness of her inspiration—*Green Grow the Rushes, O!* (1990), *May Day Games* (1990), *Go and Catch a Falling Star* (1990). She was given the honorary title Officer, Order of the British Empire in 1986 and was made a Royal Academician in 1991, later resigning in protest over the "Sensation" exhibition but accepting reelection in 2000.

Ayrton, Michael 1921–75 •*English painter, sculptor, illustrator, art critic, translator and novelist*• He was born in London. His early painting falls into the wartime English Neo-Romantic movement along with that of **Graham Sutherland**, **John Minton** and **John**

Craxton. His sculpture dates from 1954, when he began treating subjects from classical mythology, especially Daedalus and Icarus, which led to his building a maze in brick and stone in the Catskill Mountains, New York. He produced a huge number of now highly prized book illustrations, including **Thomas Nashe**'s *The Unfortunate Traveller.* He wrote several books, including the novels *The Maze Maker* (1967)—based on the Daedalus story—and *The Midas Consequence* (1974), and he translated and illustrated the work of **Archilochos of Paros**.

Ayton, Sir Robert 1570–1638 •*Scottish poet and courtier*• Born in Kinaldie, near St Andrews, he was educated at St Andrews University and studied law in Paris. A courtier of **James VI and I** in London, he wrote lyrics in English and Latin, and is credited with the prototype of "Auld Lang Syne."

Aytoun, William Edmonstoune 1818–65 •*Scottish poet and humorist*• Born in Edinburgh, he was educated at the Edinburgh Academy and Edinburgh University. He published a collection of romantic pastiches, *Poland, Homer and Other Poems* (1832), and in 1836 began a lifelong connection with *Blackwood's Magazine*, to which he contributed countless parodies and burlesque reviews. His works include *Bon Gaultier Ballads* (1845), *Lays of the Scottish Cavaliers and Other Poems* (1848) and *Norman Sinclair* (1861), a semi-autobiographical novel.

" "

'He is coming! he is coming!'
Like a bridegroom from his room,
Came the hero from his prison
To the scaffold and the doom.

1848 ***Lays of the Scottish Cavaliers and Other Poems,*** *"The Execution of Montrose," stanza 14.*

Ayub Khan, Mohammed 1907–74 •*Pakistani field marshal and politician*• He was born in Abbottabad and educated at Aligarh Moslem University and at Sandhurst. He served in World War II, became first Commander in Chief of Pakistan's army (1951) and later field marshal (1959). He became President of Pakistan in 1958 after a bloodless army coup, and established a stable economy and political autocracy. In March 1969, after widespread civil disorder and violent opposition from both the right and left wings, he relinquished power and martial law was reestablished. He published his autobiography, *Friends, Not Masters*, in 1967.

Azaña (y Díaz), Manuel 1880–1940 •*Spanish politician and intellectual*• He was born in Alcalá de Henares. A qualified lawyer, he founded a political party, *Acción Republicana* in 1925. With the advent of the Second Republic (1931), he became Minister of War and then Prime Minister (1931–33) of a reforming government. An outstanding orator and thinker, he himself was closely identified with army reform and anticlericalism. During a period of opposition (1933–36) when he was the chief architect of the Popular Front coalition which triumphed in the general election of February 1936, he resumed the premiership. In May of that year he became President, and remained throughout the Spanish Civil War until February 1939, when General **Franco** forced him into exile in France, where he died.

Azcona del Hoyo, José Simon 1927– •*Honduran politician*• Born in La Ceiba, he trained as a civil engineer in Honduras and Mexico. He became interested in politics and ran in the 1963 general election as a candidate for the Liberal Party of Honduras (PLH) but his career was interrupted by a series of military coups. He served in the governments of Roberto Suazo and Walter Lopez (1982–86), which were ostensibly civilian administrations but, in reality, were controlled by the army commander in chief, General Gustavo Alvarez. The latter was removed by junior officers in 1984 and in 1986 Azcona narrowly won the presidential election. A moderate conservative, he served as President of Honduras until 1990, signing the Central American Peace Accord of 1987 despite his government's quiet acceptance of the presence in Honduras of Nicaraguan Contras backed by the US. He was barred by law from seeking a second term.

Azhari, Ismail al- 1900–69 •*Sudanese politician*• He was the leader of the Sudanese Unionist Party which was the victor of the first Sudanese parliamentary elections in 1953. He formed the first government in 1954. Opposed by the Mahdists, he was nonetheless able to guide the Sudan toward independence (1956). He became President of the Supreme Council of the Sudan in 1964, but a military coup in 1969 resulted in his being placed under house arrest and he died during this confinement.

Azharuddin, Mohammad 1963– •*Indian cricket player*• Born in Hyderabad, India, he emerged as a formidable batsman, making his Test debut for India in 1985 and scoring three centuries in his first three consecutive matches. Within a year he had brought his Test run total to over 1,000. Named captain of India in 1989, he went on to become his country's most successful captain, with 14 Test victories. In 2000, with a total of 99 Test appearances, he was banned for life by the Indian Board of Control for involvement in match fixing.

Azikiwe, Nnamdi, *known as* **Zik of Africa** 1904–96 •*Nigerian journalist and politician*• He was born in Zungeri, in north Nigeria. He studied in the US, at Storer College, Lincoln University and Howard University. He then taught at Lincoln. He returned to Africa in 1934 and edited the *African Morning Post* (1934–37) in Accra before going back to Nigeria to take up the editorship of the *West African Pilot* (1937–45). He was a member of the Nigerian Youth Movement (1934–41) and helped found the National Council of Nigeria and the Cameroons (NCNC) of which he was Secretary (1944–46) and President (1946–60). A member of the Nigerian Legislative Council (1947–51), he became Prime Minister of the Eastern Region (1954–59) after two years as Leader of the Opposition. He was appointed the first Black Governor-General of Nigeria in 1960 and was the President of the first Nigerian Republic from 1963 to 1966. He was in Britain at the time of the 1966 military uprising, but returned as a private citizen to Nigeria soon afterward. He became leader of the Nigerian People's Party (1979–96), and was a member of the Council of State (1979–83).

Aznar López, José María 1953– •*Spanish politician*• Born in Madrid, he was educated at Madrid University, and began his career as a tax inspector. He joined the Alianza Popular (later the Partido Popular) in 1978 and became a member of the Spanish Cortes in 1982. After holding several high offices in his party and in regional government, he was elected Prime Minister in 1996. His platform was one of modernized conservatism, promising to institute reforms of the Civil Service and tax system as well as to root out Basque terrorism.

Azorín, *pseudonym of* **José Martinez Ruiz** 1873–1967 •*Spanish novelist and critic*• Born in Monóvar, and educated at Valencia, he belongs to the generation of Pío Baroja y Nessi and **Unamuno**, and his early novel *La voluntad* (1902, "Willpower") reflects their pessimism. His lucid essays rebelled against the prevailing florid manner, but they are uneven in their insights. His other novels include *Don Juan* (1922) and *Doña Inés* (1925).

B

Baade, (Wilhelm Heinrich) Walter 1893–1960 •*US astronomer*• Born in Schröttinghausen, Germany, he studied at the universities of Münster and Göttingen, and from 1919 to 1931 worked at the Hamburg Observatory, Bergedorf. In 1931 he moved to the Mount Wilson Observatory (now part of Hale Observatories) in California. Baade's major interest was the stellar content of various systems of stars. He discovered two discrete stellar types or "populations," which are characterized by blue stars in spiral galaxies and fainter red stars in elliptical galaxies. In 1944, helped by the wartime blackout in the Pasadena area, he resolved the center of the Andromeda galaxy and its two companions into stars. He was awarded the Gold Medal of the Royal Astronomical Society in 1954. After retirement he became Gauss Professor at the University of Göttingen (1959).

Baader, Andreas 1943–77 •*West German terrorist*• Born in Munich, into a middle-class family, he became associated with the student protest movement of the late 1960s and was imprisoned for setting fire to department stores in Frankfurt in 1968. Critical of Germany's postwar materialism and military dominance by the US, he formed, with **Ulrike Meinhof**, the underground guerrilla group Rote Armee Fraktion (Red Army Faction), which carried out a series of political assassinations and terrorist outrages. He was captured and sentenced to life imprisonment in 1977 and later committed suicide.

Baal-Shem-Tov, *properly* **Israel ben Eliezer** 1699–1760 •*Polish Jewish teacher and healer*• He was born probably in Thiste, Podolia, but little is known of his humble origins. He became the founder of modern Hasidism.

Babangida, Ibrahim 1941– •*Nigerian politician and soldier*• He was born in Minna, Niger state. Educated at military schools in Nigeria, he was commissioned in 1963 and, after training in the UK, became an instructor at the Nigerian Defense Academy. He took part in the overthrow of the government of **Shehu Shagari** in 1983 and was made Commander in Chief of the army. In 1985 he led a coup against President **Muhammadu Buhari** and assumed the presidency himself. In 1993 he was replaced by General Sani Abacha (1943–98) following military intervention in the general elections.

Babbage, Charles 1791–1871 •*English mathematician*• Born in Teignmouth, Devon, and educated at Trinity and Peterhouse Colleges, Cambridge, he spent most of his life attempting to build two calculating machines. The first, the "difference engine," was designed to calculate tables of logarithms and similar functions by repeated addition performed by trains of gear wheels. A small prototype model described to the Astronomical Society in 1822 won the Society's first gold medal, and Babbage received government funding to build a full-sized machine. However, by 1842 he had spent large amounts of money without any substantial result, and government support was withdrawn. Meanwhile he had conceived the plan for a much more ambitious machine, the "analytical engine," which could be programmed by punched cards to perform many different computations. The idea can now be seen to be the essential germ of today's electronic computer, with Babbage regarded as the pioneer of modern computers.

Babbitt, Milton Byron 1916– •*US composer*• Born in Philadelphia, he studied music and mathematics at New York and Princeton Universities. He used his flair for mathematical reasoning in formulating his musical theories and helped to evolve a "Princeton school" of Modernist composition; this applied the principles of twelve-note music, not only to melody and harmony, but to other musical parameters such as rhythm. Babbitt was director of the Columbia-Princeton Electronic Music Center in New York City from 1959. His work includes *Three Compositions* for piano (1947), *Philomel* for voice and magnetic tape (1964) and *Triad* for clarinet, viola and piano (1994).

Bāb-ed-Din, *literally* **"Gate of Righteousness,"** *originally* **Mirza Ali Mohammed** 1819–50 •*Persian religious leader*• He was born in Shiraz. In 1844 he declared himself the Bab ("Gateway") to the prophesied 12th Imam; he then claimed to be the Imam himself. He was imprisoned in 1847 and later executed at Tabriz. The religion he founded (Babism) was the forerunner of the Baha'i faith (see **Bahaullah**).

Babel, Isaak Emmanuilovich 1894–c. 1941 •*Russian short-story writer*• Born in the Jewish ghetto of Odessa, he worked as a journalist in St Petersburg, served in the czar's army on the Romanian front and, after the Revolution, in various Bolshevik campaigns as a Cossack supply officer. A protégé of **Maxim Gorky**, he is remembered for his stories of the Jews in Odessa in *Odesskie rasskazy* (1916, Eng trans *Odessa Tales*, 1924), and stories of war in *Konarmiya* (1926, Eng trans *Red Cavalry*, 1929), but also wrote plays, albeit less successfully. He was exiled to Siberia in the mid-1930s, and died in a concentration camp there.

“ ”

No iron can stab the heart with such force as a full stop put just at the right place.

1932 **Guy de Maupassant**.

Babington, Antony 1561–86 •*English conspirator*• Born into a wealthy Catholic family in Dethick, Derbyshire, he served as a page to **Mary Queen of Scots** during her imprisonment at Sheffield. In 1586 he was induced by John Ballard and other Catholic emissaries to lead a conspiracy aiming to murder **Elizabeth I** and release Mary (the Babington Plot). Coded messages in which Mary approved the plot were intercepted by **Francis Walsingham**, and were later used against her. Babington fled but was captured at Harrow and executed with the others.

Babrius fl. c. 2nd century AD •*Greek writer*• Little is known of him except that he collected **Aesop**ic fables, which he turned into popular verse. Almost all of these were thought to have been lost, but in 1841 a Greek discovered 123 of them at Mount Athos. A translation of these and those by **Phaedrus** was made by Ben Edwin Perry and was published in 1965.

Babur 1483–1530 •*First Mughal emperor of India*• Born in Fergana, Central Asia, a descendant of **Genghis Khan** and nephew of Sultan Mahmud Mirza of Samarkand, he attempted unsuccessfully as a young man to establish himself as ruler there. He had greater success in Afghanistan, entering Kabul in 1504, but later again failed to win Samarkand (1511–12). The death of Sikandir Lodi (1517) brought civil war to the Afghan Lodi Empire in India and Babur took advantage of this to invade. He defeated Ibrahim Lodi decisively at Panipat, north of Delhi (1526), and founded the Mughal Empire. As well as being a distinguished soldier, he was also a poet and diarist, with interests in architecture, gardens and music. Himself a Muslim, he initiated the policy of toleration toward non-Muslims that became a hallmark of the Mughal Empire at its height.

Bacall, Lauren, *originally* **Betty Perske** 1924– •*US film actress*• Born in New York City, she became a student at the American Academy of Dramatic Arts and made her stage debut in *Johnny*

Two-by-Four (1942). She also worked as a model. Seen on the cover of *Harper's Bazaar*, she was signed to a contract by director **Howard Hawks** and launched as "Slinky! Sultry! Sensational!" in the film *To Have and Have Not* (1944). Husky-voiced and with a feline grace, she appeared as tough, sophisticated and cynical as her costar **Humphrey Bogart**, whom she married in 1945. They costarred in such thrillers as *The Big Sleep* (1946), *Dark Passage* (1947) and *Key Largo* (1948), and she displayed a gift for light comedy in *How to Marry a Millionaire* (1953). After Bogart's death in 1957, she turned increasingly to the theater, but later film appearances include *Murder on the Orient Express* (1974). She was married to the actor **Jason Robards, Jr** (1961–69) and has written two volumes of autobiography: *By Myself* (1979) and *Now* (1994).

Bacchylides 5th century BC •*Greek lyric poet*• He was born on the island of Ceos and was a nephew of the poet **Simonides**. Little of his poetry was thought to have survived, until the end of the 19th century, when papyri containing substantial victory odes were acquired by the British Museum. He was a rival of **Pindar** and wrote odes celebrating patrons' victories in the Olympic and other games.

Bach, C(arl) P(hilipp) E(manuel), *known as the* **Berlin** or **Hamburg Bach** 1714–88 •*German composer*• Born in Weimar, he was educated at the Thomasschule, Leipzig, where his father, **J S Bach**, was cantor, and at Frankfurt University. In 1740 he became cembalist (a cembalo is an instrument like a harpsichord) to the future **Frederick II (the Great)**. Later, he was Kapellmeister at Hamburg (1767). He was left-handed and therefore found it easiest to play the organ and clavier, for which his most accomplished pieces were composed. He introduced the sonata form, wrote numerous concertos, keyboard sonatas, church and chamber music, and bridged the transitional period between his father and **Franz Haydn** with his homophonic, formal, yet delicate compositions.

Bach, Johann Christian, *known as the* **London Bach** 1735–82 •*German composer*• Born in Leipzig, he was the 11th and youngest son of **J S Bach**, and studied under his brother **C P E Bach** in Berlin and, from 1754, in Italy. After becoming a Catholic, he was appointed organist at Milan (1760) where he composed ecclesiastical music, including two masses, a requiem and a Te Deum, as well as operas. In 1762 he settled in London and was appointed composer to the London Italian opera. He became musician to Queen **Charlotte Sophia** (1763) and later collaborated with Karl Friedrich Abel (1723–87). The young **Mozart** on his London visit (1764) took to him and was influenced by his style.

Bach, Johann Sebastian 1685–1750 •*German composer*• Born in Eisenach, he was orphaned before he was ten, and placed in the care of his elder brother, Johann Christoph Bach (1671–1721), organist at Ohrdruf, who taught him to play the organ and clavier. In 1704, he was appointed organist at Arnstadt, but found his official duties as choirmaster increasingly tedious, and in 1707, he became organist at Mühlhausen. In 1717 he took the post of Kapellmeister to Prince Leopold of Anhalt-Cöthen, where he wrote mainly instrumental music, including the *Brandenburg Concertos* (1721) and *The Well-Tempered Clavier* (1722). Having been widowed and left with four children, in 1722 Bach married Anna Magdalena Wilken (1701–60), an accomplished singer, harpsichordist and copyist, for whom he wrote a collection of keyboard pieces. For his six surviving children by her, Bach wrote a keyboard instruction book, and with Anna he completed a second *Notebook*. In 1723 he was appointed cantor of the Thomasschule in Leipzig, and produced nearly 300 church cantatas, the *St Matthew Passion*, the *Mass in B Minor* (begun in 1733), and the *Christmas Oratorio*. At the time of his death when he had become almost totally blind, he was engaged on a masterly series of fugues for keyboard, *The Art of the Fugue*. His work stands midway between the old and the new, his main achievement being his remarkable development of polyphony. To his contemporaries he was known mainly as an organist, and a century was to pass before he was to achieve due recognition as a composer.

Bach, Wilhelm Friedemann, *known as the* **Halle Bach** 1710–84 •*German composer*• Born in Weimar, he was the eldest and most gifted son of **J S Bach**. Educated in Leipzig at the Thomasschule and the university, he became organist at Dresden (1733) and Halle (1747). However, his way of life became increasingly dissolute and from 1764 he lived without fixed occupation at Brunswick, Göttingen and Berlin. He was a very distinguished organist, but few of his compositions, which include church cantatas and several instrumental pieces, were published, since he rarely wrote them down.

Bachman, Richard *See* **King, Stephen Edwin**

Baciccia, *originally* **Giovanni Battista Gaulli** 1639–1709 •*Italian painter*• Born in Genoa, he is best known for his spectacular baroque illusionistic ceiling frescoes. Their illusionism is enhanced by the combination of painted figures and stucco work which breaks down the barrier between two- and three-dimensional representation. His flamboyant and colorful style is indebted to **Rubens** and **Correggio**, but the most forceful qualities of his work, best seen in the ceiling of the Jesuit church of the Gesù in Rome, were probably encouraged by his friend **Gian Bernini**.

Backley, Steve 1969– •*English javelin thrower*• He was born in Sidcup, Kent. He established a new Commonwealth record of 91.46 meters in 1992, winning Commonwealth gold medals in 1990, 1994 and 2002, and silver in 1998. His other medals have included golds in the European Cup in 1989 and 1997, in the World Cup in 1989, 1994 and 1998, and in the European championships in 1990, 1994, 1998 and 2002. The Olympic gold medal has eluded him, although he won bronze in 1992 and silver in 1996 and 2000.

Backus, John 1924– •*US computer programmer*• He studied mathematics at Columbia University, before joining IBM in 1950 as a computer programmer. After developing an assembly language for IBM's 701 computer, Backus then suggested the development of a compiler and higher-level language for the IBM 704. This was approved as the FORTRAN (FORmula TRANslation) project, which was not completed until 1957. FORTRAN was a landmark programming language that opened the computer up to the nonspecialist, allowed computers to talk to each other, and paved the way for other computer languages such as COBOL, ALGOL and BASIC.

Bacon, Delia Salter 1811–59 •*US writer*• She was born in Tallmadge, Ohio, and spent the years 1853–58 in England trying to prove the theory that **Shakespeare**'s plays were written by **Francis Bacon**, Sir **Walter Raleigh**, **Edmund Spenser**, and others. She did not originate the idea herself, but was the first to give it currency in her *Philosophy of the Plays of Shakspeare Unfolded* (1857, with a preface by **Nathaniel Hawthorne**).

Bacon, Francis, Baron Verulam of Verulam and **Viscount St Albans** 1561–1626 •*English philosopher and statesman*• Born in London, the younger son of Sir Nicholas Bacon, and nephew of **William Cecil**, Lord Burghley, he studied at Trinity College, Cambridge, and at Gray's Inn, being called to the bar in 1582. A Member of Parliament from 1584, he was appointed Solicitor General (1607), Attorney General (1613), Privy Councilor (1616), Lord Keeper (1617), and Lord Chancellor (1618). He was raised to the peerage as Lord Verulam, and created viscount in 1621. However, complaints were made that he accepted bribes from suitors in his court, and he was publicly accused before his fellow peers, fined, imprisoned, and banished from parliament and the court. Although soon released, and later pardoned, he never returned to public office, and died deeply in debt. In March 1626 he caught cold while stuffing a fowl with snow in order to observe the effect of cold on the preservation of flesh, and died. His philosophical works include *The Advancement of Learning* (1605), a review of the state of knowledge in his own time and its chief defects, *De augmentis scientiarum* (1623), and *Novum organum* (1620), which stresses the scientific method of induction.

“ ”

The wisest, brightest, meanest of mankind.

*From Alexander Pope, **An Essay on Man**, Epistle 4 (1734).*

Bacon, Francis 1909–92 •*British artist*• Born in Dublin of English parents, he settled permanently in England in 1928. After working as an interior designer he began painting in about 1930 without any formal training. He first made a major impact in 1945 with his *Three*

Figures at the Base of a Crucifixion. Although the initial inspiration for his work was surrealism he made frequent use of imagery annexed from old masters such as **Velázquez** and **Eadweard Muybridge**'s photographs of figures in motion. These are usually translated into blurred and gory figures imprisoned in unspecific architectural settings. His pictures frequently evoke atmospheres of terror and angst. He is widely regarded as Great Britain's most important postwar artist.

Bacon, Roger c. 1214–1292 •*English philosopher and scientist*• Born probably in Ilchester, Somerset, he studied at Oxford and Paris, later gaining a reputation for unconventional learning in philosophy, magic and alchemy, becoming known as *Doctor Mirabilis* ("Wonderful Teacher"). In 1247 he began to devote himself to experimental science and also joined the Franciscan Order, returning to Oxford in 1250. Again in Paris, he compiled (1266–67) his *Opus majus* ("Greater Work") along with two other works, a summary of all his learning. In 1277 his writings were condemned by the Franciscans for "suspected novelties," and he was imprisoned. He died in Oxford soon after his eventual release. He has been (mistakenly) credited with scientific inventions like the magnifying glass and gunpowder, but he published some remarkable speculations about lighter-than-air flying machines, the circumnavigation of the globe and the construction of microscopes and telescopes. His views on the primacy of mathematical proof and on experimentalism have often seemed strikingly modern, and he published many works whose importance was only recognized in later centuries.

Badarayana •*Indian philosopher*• This unknown Indian philosopher is the reputed author of the *Vedanta* (or *Brahma*) *Sutra*, and is sometimes identified with the fifth-century sage Vyasa, who is traditionally credited with compiling the *Mahabharata*. The *Vedanta Sutra* is the foundation text of *Vedanta*, one of the six classic systems of Hindu philosophy. Its varied interpretation is the basis of the schools founded by **Śankara**, **Ramanuja** and **Madhva**.

Baden-Powell, Robert Stephenson Smyth Baden-Powell, 1st Baron 1857–1941 •*English soldier and founder of the Boy Scouts*• He was born in London and educated at Charterhouse. He joined the army in 1876, served in India and Afghanistan, was on the staff in Ashanti and Matabeleland, and won fame as the defender of Mafeking (1899–1900) in the Boer War. He was promoted to lieutenant general in 1907. He is best known, however, as the founder of the Boy Scouts (1908) and, with his sister Agnes (1858–1945), of the Girl Guides (1910). He published *Scouting for Boys* (1908), founded the Wolf Cubs (1916), and was acclaimed World Chief Scout in 1920.

“ ”

The scouts' motto is founded on my initials, it is: BE PREPARED, which means, you are always to be in a state of readiness in mind and body to do your DUTY.

1908 ***Scouting for Boys***.

Bader, Sir Douglas Robert Stuart 1910–82 •*English aviator*• Born in London, he lost both legs in a flying accident in 1931 and was invalided out of the RAF, but overcame his disability and returned in 1939. He commanded the first RAF Canadian Fighter Squadron, evolving tactics that contributed to victory in the Battle of Britain, but was captured in 1941 after a collision with an enemy aircraft over Béthune. He received many honors, and he was knighted in 1976.

Badoglio, Pietro 1871–1956 •*Italian general*• He was born in Piedmont. As Governor of Libya (1929–34), he achieved the pacification of the Sanusi tribesmen by 1932. In 1935 he replaced **Emilio De Bono** at the head of the conquest of Abyssinia and became Viceroy of the new colony in May 1936. On Italy's entry into World War II (1940) he was made Commander in Chief, but resigned after humiliating defeats in Greece and Albania (December 1940). In 1943 he was asked by **Victor Emmanuel III** to form an anti-Fascist government after the arrest of **Mussolini**. He signed an armistice with the Allies at Malta and declared war on Germany. Badoglio formed a broad coalition government in 1944, but after the liberation of Rome in June he was obliged to resign under pressure from the Americans and politicians with better anti-Fascist credentials. He was replaced by **Ivanoe Bonomi**.

Baeck, Leo 1873–1956 •*German Jewish religious leader*• Born in Lissa, Prussia, he was rabbi in Berlin (1912–42), and when the Nazis came to power became the political leader of German Jewry. He spent three years in the Theresienstadt concentration camp (1942–45). After the war he lectured in Great Britain. His chief publications were *Das Wesen des Judentums* (1905, Eng trans *The Essence of Judaism*, 1948) and *The Pharisees and Other Essays* (1947).

Baeda, St *See* **Bede, St**

Baedeker, Karl 1801–59 •*German publisher*• He was born in Essen and started his own publishing business in Koblenz in 1827. He is best known for the authoritative guidebooks which still bear his name.

Baekeland, Leo Hendrik 1863–1944 •*US chemist*• He was born in Ghent, Belgium, and studied there and at other Belgian universities before becoming Professor of Physics and Chemistry at Bruges in 1885. He emigrated to the US in 1889 and founded a chemical company to manufacture one of his inventions: photographic printing paper which could be used with artificial light. Subsequently he made the first synthetic phenolic resin, known as Bakelite, which replaced hard rubber and amber as an insulator. Its success led to the founding of the Bakelite Corporation in 1910. Baekeland wrote on many topics in organic chemistry and electrochemistry and on the reform of patent law.

Baer, Karl Ernst Ritter von 1792–1876 •*German naturalist and pioneer in embryology*• Born in Piep, Estonia, he graduated in medicine from Dorpat University. He was appointed professor at Königsberg University (1817–34), and from 1834 taught at St Petersburg University. From 1826 he investigated the mammalian ovary, research which finally established that reproduction necessarily involved an egg (ovum). Investigating embryo development, he was the first to differentiate the notochord, the gelatinous cord that in vertebrates becomes the backbone and skull. He also drew attention to the neural folds which develop into the central nervous system, and formulated the "biogenetic law," which states that in embryonic development general characters appear before special ones.

Baeyer, Johann Friedrich Wilhelm Adolf von 1835–1917 •*German organic chemist and Nobel Prize winner*• Born in Berlin, he discovered a new double salt of copper and sodium at the age of 12. He studied at Heidelberg and became Professor of Chemistry at Strasbourg (1872) and Munich (1875–1915). His research covered many aspects of chemistry, notably the synthesis of the dye indigo and the elucidation of its structure, and the mechanism of photosynthesis. He was awarded the 1905 Nobel Prize for chemistry.

Baez, Joan 1941– •*US folksinger and civil rights campaigner*• She was born in Staten Island, New York. Her strong, pure soprano was one of the major voices of the folk revival of the 1960s. She broadened her traditional and ballad repertoire to include songs that were written by contemporary writers like **Bob Dylan** (with whom she had a much-publicized relationship), Phil Ochs and Tim Hardin, and was writing her own songs by the end of the decade. A Quaker, she was active in the civil rights and peace movements, and she has continued to combine humanitarian work with music. Her later recordings were aimed at a more mainstream rock market.

Baffin, William c. 1584–1622 •*English navigator*• He was born probably in London, and from 1612 to 1616 was the pilot on several expeditions in search of the Northwest Passage. The most significant of these were the voyages under the command of Robert Bylot on the *Discovery*, during which they examined Hudson Strait (1615), discovered Baffin Bay (1616), and discovered Lancaster, Smith, and Jones Sounds (1616), which were later shown to lead to the Arctic Ocean and the Pacific Ocean. These were to be the most important explorations of the Passage for nearly two centuries and were largely ignored by future Arctic explorers until confirmed by Sir **John**

Ross in 1818. He later carried out extensive surveys of the Red Sea (1616–21), and was killed at the Siege of Ormuz.

Bagaza, Jean-Baptiste 1946– *•Burundian politician and soldier•* Born in Rutovu, Bururi Province, he attended military schools in Belgium. In 1976 he led a coup to overthrow President Micombero and was appointed President by a Supreme Revolutionary Council. In 1984 the post of Prime Minister was abolished and Bagaza was elected head of state and government. In 1987 he was himself ousted in a coup led by Major Pierre Buyoya. During the civil war in Burundi in 1996 he was a leading supporter of the Tutsis' demands to control the country, and as leader of the hardline pro-Tutsi PARENA party he remains an important figure in Burundi's troubled political scene.

Bagehot, Walter 1826–77 *•English economist and journalist•* Born in Langport, Somerset, he graduated in mathematics at University College, London, and was called to the bar in 1852. After a spell as banker in his father's firm, he succeeded his father-in-law James Wilson (1805–60) as editor of *The Economist* in 1860. His *English Constitution* (1867) became a standard work. He followed Thomas Hill Green (1836–82) and others in applying the theory of evolution to politics, as in *Physics and Politics* (1872). He advocated many constitutional reforms, including the introduction of life peers.

" "

Writers, like teeth, are divided into incisors and grinders.

*1858 **Estimates of Some Englishmen and Some Scotchmen**, "The First Edinburgh Reviewers."*

Bahaullah or **Baha-Allah**, *literally* **"Glory of God,"** *originally* **Mirza Huseyn Ali** 1817–92 *•Persian religious leader and founder of the Islamic Baha'i movement•* Born in Tehran, he became a follower of the Shiraz merchant Mirza Ali Mohammed (see **Bāb-ed-din**), founder of the Persian Babi sect. Persecuted and imprisoned in 1852, he was exiled to Baghdad, Constantinople (Istanbul) and Acre. In 1863 he proclaimed himself as the prophet that Bāb-ed-din had foretold, and became the leader of the new Baha'i faith.

Bailey, David Royston 1938– *•English photographer•* Born in London's East End, he became interested in photography while on national service in Singapore. Upon his return to Britain he became an assistant fashion photographer and by 1960 was working with *Vogue*, where his eye for striking photographs and even more striking women, notably his then-lover Jean Shrimpton (1942–), made his name. Capturing the Zeitgeist of the 1960s with his photographs of cultural icons such as **Mick Jagger** and the **Rolling Stones**, the **Kray brothers**, and **Catherine Deneuve** (the second of his four wives), he became as famous as many of his subjects. He has published numerous books, including *David Bailey's Rock and Roll Heroes* (1997) and a retrospective, *David Bailey: Birth of the Cool* (1999), and has also made commercials, documentaries and films. He was given the honorary title of Commander, Order of the British Empire, in 2001.

Bailey, Sir Donald Coleman 1901–85 *•English engineer•* Born in Rotherham, South Yorkshire, he graduated from Sheffield University. During World War II he designed the prefabricated, mobile, rapidly erected bridge named for him. He was knighted in 1946.

Bailey, F(rancis) Lee 1933– *•US criminal lawyer•* Born in Waltham, Massachusetts, he studied at Harvard and Boston University. He had a high-profile career as a defense attorney, defending Dr Sam Sheppard (the inspiration for the 1960s television series and 1993 film *The Fugitive*), **Albert Desalvo** (the Boston Strangler) and the kidnapped heiress Patty Hearst (1954–), who was convicted of bank robbery with her left-wing terrorist abductors. More recently he defended OJ Simpson at his 1995 murder trial. In late 2001 he was disbarred by the Florida Supreme Court from practicing law in Florida due to the alleged mishandling of a client's forfeited assets.

" "

The guilty never escape unscathed. My fees are sufficient punishment for anyone.

*1972 In the **Los Angeles Times**, January 9.*

Bailey, Nathan or **Nathaniel** d. 1742 *•English lexicographer•* He was the compiler of *An Universal Etymological English Dictionary* (1721; supplementary volume 1727), used by **Samuel Johnson** as the basis of his own dictionary. Apart from this, all that is known about him is that he was a Seventh-day Baptist, and that he ran a boarding school in Stepney, near London, where he died.

Baillie, Dame Isobel 1895–1983 *•Scottish soprano•* Born in Hawick, in the Scottish Borders, she moved with her family to Manchester. She made her debut with the Hallé Orchestra under Sir **Hamilton Harty** in 1921, and, after studies in Milan, won immediate success in her opening season in London in 1923. She regularly performed with such conductors as Sir **Thomas Beecham**, **Arturo Toscanini** and **Bruno Walter**, and gave over 1,000 performances of the *Messiah*.

Baily, Francis 1774–1844 *•English astronomer•* Born in Newbury, Berkshire, he made a large fortune as a stockbroker. On his retirement in 1825 he devoted himself to astronomy and was president of the Royal Astronomical Society when he died. He detected the phenomenon known as "Baily's beads" during an eclipse of the sun in 1836 and calculated the mean density of the earth.

Bain, Aly 1945– *•Shetland fiddler•* Born in Lerwick, Shetland, he studied with the great fiddler Tom Anderson before leaving Shetland in 1968 to play traditional music professionally. His extraordinary gifts emerged initially with singer/guitarist Mike Whellans. In 1972, they joined Cathal McConnell and Robin Morton in The Boys of the Lough, a group which remains a vital force, albeit with several changes of personnel. His television work includes *Aly Meets the Cajuns* (1988) and *The Transatlantic Sessions* (1996). He was given the honorary title Member, Order of the British Empire, in 1994.

Bainbridge, Dame Beryl Margaret 1934– *•English novelist and actress•* Born in Liverpool, she attended ballet school in Tring, Hertfordshire, and was a repertory actress (1949–60). Her novels, beginning with *A Weekend with Claude* (1967, revised 1981), are marked by concision, caustic wit, and carefully turned prose. She has also written short stories, essays and a number of television plays. Her 1996 novel *Every Man for Himself* reached the Booker Prize shortlist and won the Whitbread Novel award. *Master Georgie* (1998) also reached the Booker Prize shortlist and won the James Tait Black Memorial Prize, while her later works include *According to Queeney* (2001). She was given the honorary title of Dame Commander, Order of the British Empire, in 2000.

Bairakdar, Mustafa 1755–1808 *•Turkish grand vizier, pasha of Rustchuk•* After the revolt of the janissaries (1807) by which Selim III was deposed in favor of Mustapha IV, he marched his troops in 1808 to Constantinople (Istanbul), but found Selim already dead. He executed the murderers, deposed Mustapha, and proclaimed his brother, **Mahmud II**, sultan. The janissaries counterattacked, however, and Mustafa Bairakdar defended himself bravely until, strangling Mustapha and throwing his head to the besiegers, he then blew himself up.

Baird, John Logie 1888–1946 *•Scottish electrical engineer and television pioneer•* Born in Helensburgh, Strathclyde, he studied electrical engineering in Glasgow. Poor health compelled him to give up the post of engineer to the Clyde Valley electric power company. He finally settled in Hastings, East Sussex (1922), and began research into the possibilities of television. Hampered by continuing ill health and lack of financial support, he nevertheless succeeded in building a television apparatus, almost entirely from scrap materials, and in 1926 gave the first demonstration of a television image. His 30-line mechanically scanned system was adopted by the BBC in 1929, being superseded in 1936 by his 240-line system. In the following year the BBC chose a rival 405-line system with electronic scanning made by Marconi-EMI. He continued his research up to the time of his death and succeeded in producing three-dimensional and colored images (1944), as well as projection onto a screen and stereophonic sound.

Baird, Spencer Fullerton 1823–87 *•US naturalist•* Born in Reading, Pennsylvania, of Scottish descent, he was educated at Dickinson College, Carlisle, and studied medicine in New York. However, he turned to ornithology, encouraged by **John Audubon**

and others. In 1850 he was appointed assistant secretary to **Joseph Henry** at the Smithsonian Institution in Washington DC (secretary from 1878), and published *Catalogue of North American Mammals* (1857) and *Catalogue of North American Birds* (1858). Baird's sandpiper and Baird's sparrow are named in his honor.

Bairnsfather, (Charles) Bruce 1888–1959 •*British cartoonist*• Born in Murree, India, he served in France during World War I, and became famous for his war cartoons featuring the character "Old Bill." During World War II, he was an official war cartoonist attached to the US army in Europe. His drawings appeared in various periodicals, war books, in his *Fragments from France* (6 vols, 1916), and in *Jeeps and Jests* (1943).

Baker, Sir Benjamin 1840–1907 •*English civil engineer*• Born in Frome, Somerset, he entered into a long association with **John Fowler** in 1861, designing the London Metropolitan Railway, Victoria Station and many bridges. Their greatest achievement was the Forth Rail Bridge (1883–90). Baker was also consulting engineer for the Aswan Dam in Egypt and its subsequent heightening, and the Hudson River Tunnel in New York (1888–91). He also designed the vessel that carried Cleopatra's Needle to London.

Baker, Chet (Chesney Henry) 1929–88 •*US jazz trumpet player*• He was born in Yale, Oklahoma. He first came to wide attention in **Gerry Mulligan**'s famous pianoless quartet in 1953, but drug addiction severely interrupted his career at many points. Nonetheless, his limpid horn tone and fragile singing won him a following throughout his career, and he continued to perform in his highly distinctive style until his death in a fall from a hotel window in Amsterdam. His life was chronicled in a moving documentary film, *Let's Get Lost* (1989).

Baker, George *See* **Divine, Father**

Baker, Howard Henry, Jr 1925– •*US politician*• Born in Huntsville, Tennessee, he studied law at the University of Tennessee and represented his native state in the Senate from 1967 to 1985. A Republican, he was vice chairman of the committee investigating the Watergate scandal (1973), and served as Senate minority leader (1977–81), majority leader (1981–85) and White House Chief of Staff (1987–88). He became the US ambassador to Japan in 2001 in the **George W Bush** administration.

“ ”

Never speak more clearly than you think.

*1987 On becoming President Reagan's third Chief of Staff. In the **New York Times**, September 6.*

Baker, James Addison, III 1930– •*US politician*• Born in Houston, Texas, he studied at Princeton and the University of Texas Law School, served in the US Marines and became a successful corporate lawyer. He entered politics as a Republican county manager of the unsuccessful 1970 campaign for the Senate by his close friend, **George Bush**. Later he was appointed undersecretary of commerce (1975–76) in the **Gerald Ford** administration and managed Ford's 1976 presidential and Bush's 1979 Republican Party nomination campaigns. President **Ronald Reagan** made him his White House Chief of Staff in 1981 and secretary of the treasury in 1985. After directing Bush's victorious presidential campaign in 1988, he was secretary of state (1989–92). In the final year of the Bush administration he was once again Chief of Staff, and he ran Bush's unsuccessful reelection campaign. He also played a key role in **George W Bush**'s election campaign in 2000.

Baker, Dame Janet Abbott 1933– •*English mezzo-soprano*• Born in Hatfield, Yorkshire, she studied music in London (1953). She made her debut in 1956 as Roza in **Bedřich Smetana**'s *The Secret*. During the 1960s she worked as a soloist for Sir **John Barbirolli**, after which she had an extensive operatic career, specializing in early Italian opera and the works of **Benjamin Britten**. Also a concert performer, she was a noted interpreter of **Mahler** and **Elgar**. In 1982 she retired from the operatic stage and published her autobiography, *Full Circle*. She was given the honorary title of Dame Commander, Order of the British Empire, in 1976 and Companion of Honour in 1994.

Baker, Josephine, *originally* **Freda Josephine McDonald** 1906–75 •*French entertainer and campaigner*• Born in St Louis, Missouri, she ran away from home at the age of 13. In 1925 she went to Paris with La Revue Nègre, where her singing and dancing ability captured the attention of the French as an example of the African-American jazz scene. She became a French citizen in 1937, and during World War II worked for the Red Cross and the French Resistance, for which she was awarded the Croix de Guerre, the Rosette de la Résistance and was appointed a Chevalier of the Legion of Honor. After the war, she campaigned for civil rights in the US and worked to achieve a Global Village. She was NAACP (National Association for the Advancement of Colored People) Woman of the Year in 1951.

Baker (of Dorking), Kenneth Wilfred Baker, Baron 1934– •*English Conservative politician*• He was born in Newport, Monmouth, and studied history at Magdalen College, Oxford, entering local politics in 1962 as a Conservative councilor in Twickenham. In 1968 he was elected to the House of Commons, representing Acton, then St Marylebone and later Mole Valley (1983–97), and became Parliamentary Private Secretary to **Edward Heath** when he was Leader of the Opposition. In the **Thatcher** administration he rose from Minister of State in the Department of Trade to become Secretary of State for the Environment (1985) and for Education (1986), responsible for introducing a controversial education reform bill. He was appointed chairman of the Conservative Party in 1989, and under **John Major** was Home Secretary (1990–92). He later turned his attention to writing, editing several poetry anthologies and publishing a volume of memoirs, *The Turbulent Years: My Life in Politics* (1993). He was made a life peer in 1997.

Baker, Sir Samuel White 1821–93 •*English explorer*• Born in London, he went in 1845 to Ceylon (Sri Lanka), where he established an agricultural settlement at Nuwara Eliya, and afterward supervised the construction of a railway across the Dobrudja. In 1860 he undertook the exploration of the Nile sources. At Gondokoro (1863), he met the explorers **John Speke** and **James Grant**, who told Baker of a great lake, Luta Nzige, described to them by the local people. In 1864 Baker reached this inland sea into which the Nile flows and named it Albert Nyanza. He was knighted in 1866, and was subsequently invited to command an expedition, organized by the pasha of Egypt, for the suppression of slavery and the annexation of the equatorial regions of the Nile Basin. He later traveled in Cyprus, Syria, India, Japan and the US.

Bakewell, Joan Dawson, *née* **Rowlands** 1933– •*English broadcaster and writer*• Born in Stockport, she studied at Newnham College, Cambridge. She has presented television series on current affairs and the arts including *Meeting Point* (1964), *Late Night Line-Up* (1965–72) and *Heart of the Matter* (1988–), and has worked widely in radio. Her publications include *The Complete Traveller* (1977) and *The Heart of Heart of the Matter* (1996). She was appointed chair of the British Film Institute in 1999.

Bakewell, Robert 1725–95 •*English agriculturist*• Born in Dishley, Leicestershire, he improved the standard and methods of the management of sheep, cattle, and draft horses by selection and inbreeding. He established the Leicester breed of sheep and the Dishley breed of longhorn cattle, and aroused wide interest in breeding methods.

Bakey, Michael Ellis De *See* **DeBakey, Michael Ellis**

Bakst, Leon 1866–1924 •*Russian painter*• Born in St Petersburg, he painted religious and genre works in Moscow, then turned to scenery design at Hermitage Court Theater in St Petersburg. In 1908 he went to Paris, where he was associated with **Sergei Diaghilev**, designing the décor and costumes for numerous ballet productions (1909–21). His rich, exuberant colors, seemingly uncontrolled, in reality produced a powerful theatrical effect which revolutionized fashion and decoration in general.

Bakunin, Mikhail Aleksandrovich 1814–76 •*Russian revolutionary*• Born near Moscow, of aristocratic descent, he took part in the German revolutionary movement (1848–49) and was condemned to death. Sent to Siberia in 1855, he escaped to Japan, and arrived in England in 1861. In 1870 he attempted an abortive uprising at Lyons. As a leading anarchist he was the opponent of **Karl Marx** in the Communist International, but at the Hague Congress in 1872 he was outvoted and expelled. He believed that Communism, with its theoretical "withering away of the state," was an essential step toward anarchism.

Balaguer, Joaquín (Vidella) 1907– •*Dominican Republic politician*• He was Professor of Law at Santo Domingo University from 1938, and ambassador to Colombia and Mexico in the 1940s before entering politics. He served in the dictatorial regime of Rafael Trujillo, after whose assassination in 1961 he fled to the US (1962). Returning in 1965, he won the presidency in 1966, and was reelected in 1970, 1974, 1986, 1990 and 1994. He ran again in 2000 at the age of 93 but was unsuccessful.

Balakirev, Mili Alekseyevich 1836–1910 •*Russian composer*• Born in Nizhny Novgorod, he turned to composing after an early career as a concert pianist. **César Cui**, **Mussorgsky**, **Rimsky-Korsakov**, **Aleksandr Borodin**, and **Tchaikovsky** were all influenced by him. He founded the Petersburg Free School of Music (1862), and was director of the Imperial Capella (from 1883). His compositions include two symphonies, a symphonic poem *Tamara* (1867–82) and the oriental fantasy for piano, *Islamey* (1869).

Balanchine, George, *originally* **Georgi Melitonovich Balanchivadze** 1904–83 •*US choreographer, a major figure in 20th-century dance*• Born in St Petersburg, Russia, he enrolled at the Petrograd Conservatory to study composition, but he turned to ballet and formed his own small company whose innovations were frowned on by the theater authorities. During a European tour in 1924, he defected with a group of dancers who performed for a time in London as the Soviet State Dancers. Eventually they were taken into **Sergei Diaghilev**'s Ballets Russes in Paris. In 1925 he succeeded **Bronislava Nijinska** as choreographer and ballet master. His ballets *Apollo* (1928) and *The Prodigal Son* (1929) are regarded as his masterpieces of that period. He opened the School of American Ballet in New York in 1934 and was director of the New York City Ballet from 1948. He also choreographed many Broadway shows and Hollywood musicals.

Balboa, Vasco Núñez de 1475–1519 •*Spanish explorer*• He was born in Jerez de los Caballeros, and in 1511 joined an expedition to Darién (Central America) as a stowaway. Taking advantage of an insurrection, he took command, founded a colony at Darién, and extended Spanish influence into neighboring areas. On one of these expeditions he climbed a peak and sighted the Pacific Ocean, the first European to do so, and took possession for Spain. The governorship was granted in 1514 to Pedro Ariar de Ávila, whose daughter he married. However, after a disagreement in 1519 Balboa was beheaded.

Balch, Emily Greene 1867–1961 •*US social reformer, pacifist and Nobel Prize winner*• She was born in Jamaica Plain, Massachusetts, and educated at Bryn Mawr College. From 1896 to 1918 she taught economics at Wellesley College, and her innovative courses included coverage of **Karl Marx** and women's place in the economy. An active pacifist, she openly opposed World War I and was viewed by the authorities with increasing suspicion. In 1919 her academic appointment was not renewed. She helped establish the Women's International League for Peace and Freedom (1919) and subsequently proved an indefatigable administrator, writer and promoter for peace. She shared the 1946 Nobel Peace Prize with **John Mott**. Her works include *Our Slavic Fellow Citizens* (1910) and *Toward Human Unity* (1952).

Balcon, Sir Michael Elias 1896–1977 •*English film producer*• Born in Birmingham, he was rejected for military service because of a flaw in his left eye and spent World War I employed by the Dunlop Rubber Company. He subsequently formed a modest distribution company, moved into film production with advertising films and documentaries, and in 1921 helped found Gainsborough Pictures. In 1931 he took charge of production at Gaumont British and backed British films that could compete in the international market, among them *Rome Express* (1932) and *The Thirty-Nine Steps* (1935). After a brief spell as head of British production for the Hollywood studio MGM, he became head of production at Ealing Studios (1938–58). Among the many classic films created under his control are *Whisky Galore* (1948), *The Blue Lamp* (1949), *The Lavender Hill Mob* (1951), and *The Cruel Sea* (1953). He was knighted in 1948.

Baldwin I c. 1171–c. 1205 •*Emperor of Constantinople*• Born in Valenciennes, he succeeded his parents as Count of Hainault and Flanders in 1195. In 1202 he joined the Fourth Crusade, and in 1204 was made the first Latin Emperor of Constantinople (Istanbul). The Greeks, with the aid of the Bulgarians, rose up and took Adrianople. Baldwin laid siege to the town, but was defeated and executed.

Baldwin II 1217–73 •*Emperor of Constantinople*• Born in Constantinople (Istanbul), the nephew of **Baldwin I**, he succeeded his brother Robert as emperor in 1228. To raise money he sold alleged relics, including **Jesus**'s crown of thorns and part of the True Cross, to **Louis IX** of France. The Greeks, under **Michael VIII Palaeologus**, took Constantinople in 1261, extinguishing the Latin Empire. Thereafter Baldwin lived as a fugitive, having sold his rights to **Charles of Anjou**.

Baldwin II, *known as* **Baldwin du Bourg** d. 1131 •*King of Jerusalem*• He was a son of Count Hugh of Rethel. He succeeded his cousin Baldwin I as Count of Edessa (1100) and King of Jerusalem (1118). He expanded his territory and attacked Muslim Damascus, with assistance from the Templars and Hospitalers.

Baldwin III c. 1130–62 •*King of Jerusalem*• The grandson of **Baldwin II of Bourg**, he succeeded his father, Fulk of Anjou, in 1143, but enjoyed sole authority (1152) only after long disputes and civil war with his mother Melisende. His main achievement was the capture of Ascalon, the last Fatimid stronghold in Palestine, in 1153.

Baldwin, James Arthur 1924–87 •*US writer*• Born in Harlem, New York City, into a strongly religious African-American family, he was preaching in churches at the age of 14, an experience that inspired his novel *Go Tell It on the Mountain* (1954). He moved to Europe, living mainly in Paris from 1948 to 1957, in a conscious rejection of US society and its racism, before returning to the US as a civil rights activist. His novels are often strongly autobiographical but marked by a **Flaubert**ian attention to form. *Giovanni's Room* (1957) is a study of gay relationships, and *Another Country* (1963) examines the sexual dynamics of US racism. He also wrote *Tell Me How Long the Train's Been Gone* (1968), *Just Above My Head* (1979), *Notes of a Native Son* (1955), *The Fire Next Time* (1963), and the plays *The Amen Corner* (1955), *Blues for Mr Charlie* (1964) and *The Women at the Well* (1972).

Baldwin (of Bewdley), Stanley Baldwin, 1st Earl 1867–1947 •*English Conservative politician and prime minister*• Born in Bewdley, Worcestershire, he was educated at Harrow and Trinity College, Cambridge, and became vice chairman of the family iron and steel business. A Member of Parliament in 1906, he became president of the Board of Trade (1921), and he unexpectedly succeeded **Bonar Law** as premier in 1923, being preferred to **George Curzon**. Shortly afterward he brought down the Liberal coalition with a speech that revealed his distrust of **David Lloyd-George**, despite criticism of his handling, as Chancellor of the Exchequer, of the US debt. His period of office included the General Strike (1926) and was interrupted by the **Ramsay MacDonald** Coalition (1931–35), in which he served as Lord President of the Council. He skillfully avoided a party split by his India Act (1935), but his disavowal of the **Hoare**-Laval pact, ceding Ethiopian territory to Italy, and the policy of nonintervention in Spain (1936) came to be regarded as betrayals of the League of Nations. He was noted for his reluctance to rearm Great Britain's defenses and for his tact and resolution during the constitutional crisis culminating in **Edward VIII**'s abdication (1936). Criticism of his failure to recognize the threat from Nazi Germany brought his resignation in 1937.

Balenciaga, Cristóbal 1895–1972 •*Spanish couturier*• He was born in Guetaria in the Basque country, the son of a seamstress. In 1915 he opened dressmaking and tailoring shops in Madrid and Barcelona, but left Spain during the Spanish Civil War to become a couturier in Paris. A perfectionist, he designed clothes that were noted for their dramatic simplicity and elegant design.

Balfa, Dewey 1927–92 •*Cajun musician and teacher*• Born in Mamou, Louisiana, he was the leading figure in a Cajun family that made an enormous contribution to the preservation and dissemination of the authentic music of the French-based Louisiana Cajun community. Taught by their father Charles, the Balfa Brothers band also featured his brothers Rodney and Will, both killed in a road accident (1979), as well as the great accordionist Nathan Abshire. The family tradition is maintained in the band Balfa Toujours.

Balfour, Arthur James Balfour, 1st Earl of 1848–1930 •*Scottish statesman and philosopher*• Born into an ancient Scottish family, he succeeded to the family estate in East Lothian in 1856. Educated at Eton and Trinity College, Cambridge, he entered parliament in 1874, becoming Secretary for Scotland (1886) and Chief Secretary for Ireland (1887–91), where his policy of suppression earned him the name "Bloody Balfour." A Conservative, he succeeded his uncle **Robert Cecil** (3rd Marquis of Salisbury) as Prime Minister (1902–05), and later served as First Lord of the Admiralty (1915–16). As Foreign Secretary (1916–19), he was responsible for the Balfour Declaration (1917), which promised Zionists a national home in Palestine. He resigned in 1922, was created an earl, but served again as Lord President (1925–29).

" "

Nothing matters very much, and very few things matter at all.

Attributed.

Balfour, Lady Frances 1858–1931 •*Scottish suffragist, churchwoman and author*• Born in London, she had political ambitions that were stifled by the role of women at that time, but she had strong connections with both the Whig and Tory parties, the former through her own family, and the latter through her marriage to Eustace Balfour, the brother of **Arthur James Balfour**. A tireless worker for women's rights, she lectured on behalf of the National Union of Woman's Suffrage Societies. She also spoke out on such issues as Irish home rule and free trade. Working for the Church of Scotland, she fought for the Reunion of 1929. She wrote a number of memoirs.

Balfour, George 1872–1941 •*Scottish electrical engineer and pioneering contractor*• Born in Portsmouth, he founded his own construction company, Balfour Beatty Ltd, in 1909 with an accountant, Andrew Beatty. They built and operated the tramway systems for Dunfermline, Llanelly, and many towns in the Midlands, and designed the first major hydroelectric schemes in Scotland, as well as pioneering the National Grid in the 1930s. Balfour also built the giant Kut Barrage on the Tigris for Iraq. He was Unionist Member of Parliament for Hampstead, London, from 1918.

Baliol *See* **Balliol**

Ball, Hugo 1886–1927 •*German artist*• He was born in Pirmasens, Germany. Soon after the outbreak of World War I he emigrated to Zürich, where in 1916 he cofounded the Dada movement with **Hans Arp** and **Tristan Tzara**. In the same year he established the Cabaret Voltaire, which opposed the war and the cultural values that had begotten it and espoused an anarchic individualism and freedom from artistic convention. Among his better-known works are his sound poems and the diary excerpts of his Dada period published as *Flight out of Time* (1927).

Ball, John d. 1381 •*English rebel*• Born in St Albans, Hertfordshire, he was an excommunicated priest who was executed as one of the leaders in the Peasants' Revolt of 1381, led by **Wat Tyler**.

Ball, John 1818–89 •*Irish botanist and alpinist*• Born in Dublin, he was taken to Switzerland at the age of seven. The following year, at Ems, he spent much time trying to measure the height of the hills with a mountain barometer. After a period at Cambridge, Ball visited Sicily and published a valuable paper on its botany. He was the first president of the Alpine Club (1857), wrote the *Alpine Guide* (1863–68), and in 1871 accompanied Sir **Joseph Dalton Hooker** and George Frederick Maw to Morocco to investigate the flora of the Great Atlas Mountains. In 1882 he visited South America. He proposed one theory on the antiquity of the alpine flora, and another claiming that most endemic South American plants originated on a hypothetical ancient mountain range in Brazil.

Ball, Lucille Desirée 1910–89 •*US comedienne*• Born in Celoron, New York, she was an amateur performer as a child. After moving to Hollywood she spent several years in bit parts and B movies before more substantial roles were offered. A lively redhead with a raspy voice and infallible timing, she began working in television in 1951 and became one of its best-loved characters, starring in situation comedies such as *I Love Lucy* (1951–55), *The Lucy Show* (1962–68) and *Here's Lucy* (1968–73). She bought her own studio with her first husband, Desi Arnaz, and also became a successful production executive, making films such as *The Facts of Life* (1960) and *Yours, Mine and Ours* (1968).

Balla, Giacomo 1871–1958 •*Italian artist*• Born in Turin, he was one of the founders of Futurism and a signatory to the 1910 Futurist Manifesto. Primarily concerned with conveying movement and speed in painterly terms, he achieved this by imitating time-lapse photography; *Dog on a Leash* (1912) exemplifies this technique. Although Futurism outlived World War I, by 1930 Balla was painting in a more conventional style.

Balladur, Edouard 1929– •*French politician*• Born in Smyrna, Turkey, he was educated in France at Marseilles, Aix-en-Provence and Paris. In 1966 he became technical adviser to Prime Minister **Georges Pompidou**, and his many public schemes included the construction of a road under Mont Blanc. He became Minister of Economy in 1986 and Prime Minister in 1993. Following the death of President **Mitterrand** he ran in the French presidential election in 1995 but lost to **Jacques Chirac**.

Ballantyne, James 1772–1833 and **John** 1774–1821 •*Scottish printers*• They were born in Kelso and were both at Kelso Grammar School with Sir **Walter Scott**. In 1797 James started the Tory *Kelso Mail*, and in 1802, having already printed some ballads for Scott, he produced the first two volumes of the *Border Minstrelsy*. In 1805 Scott became a secret partner in the business, which in 1808 expanded into the printing, publishing and bookselling firm of John Ballantyne & Co. As early as 1813 bankruptcy threatened the firm, and it was deeply involved in **Archibald Constable**'s ruin (1826). John had died bankrupt five years earlier, and James was employed by the creditors' trustees in editing the *Weekly Journal* and in the literary management of the printing office.

Ballantyne, Robert Michael 1825–94 •*Scottish children's writer*• He was born in Edinburgh, a nephew of **John** and **James Ballantyne**, the printers and publishers of Sir **Walter Scott**. Educated at The Edinburgh Academy, he joined the Hudson's Bay Company in 1841, and worked as a clerk at the Red River Settlement in northern Canada until 1847, returning to Edinburgh in 1848. His adventure stories include *The Young Fur Traders* (1856), about his experiences in Canada, *The Coral Island* (1857), his most famous work, and *The Dog Crusoe* (1861).

Ballard, J(ames) G(raham) 1930– •*British fiction writer*• Born in Shanghai, China, he was educated at Cambridge. Until recently he was better known for his science fiction, fashioning a series of novels at once inventive, experimental and, in several cases, bizarre. He has commented that "science fiction is the authentic literature of the 20th century, the only fiction to respond to the transforming nature of science and technology." His early novels, including his first, *The Drowned World* (1962), offer a view of the world beset by elemental catastrophe, a theme also taken up in *The Drought* (1965) and *The Day of Creation* (1985). The more experimental side of his fiction is seen in the "fragmented novels," like *The Atrocity Exhibition* (1970) and *Crash* (1973, filmed 1996). He has been admired for his short stories, particularly those included in such collections as *The Terminal Beach* (1964), *The Disaster Area* (1967) and *War Fever* (1990). *Empire of the Sun* (1984, filmed 1987), an autobiographical novel, was shortlisted for the Booker Prize. Its sequel, *The Kindness of Women* (1991), is also autobiographical. He won the Guardian Fiction prize in 1984, the James Tait Black Memorial Prize in 1985 and the Commonwealth Writers Prize (Eurasia) in 2001. His recent works include *Rushing to Paradise* (1994), *A User's Guide to the Millennium* (1996), *Cocaine Nights* (1996) and *Super-Cannes* (2000). *The Complete Short Stories* was published in 2001.

“ ”
The only truly alien planet is Earth.
*1962 "Which Way to Inner Space," in **New Worlds**, May.*

Ballard, Robert Duane 1942– •*US underwater explorer*• Born in Wichita, Kansas, and educated at the Universities of California, Hawaii and Rhode Island, he served as a commander with the US Navy in Vietnam before becoming director of the Center for Marine Exploration, Woods Hole Oceanographic Institute, Cape Cod, which he joined in 1969. He left Woods Hole in 1997 to found and head the Institute for Exploration in Mystic, Connecticut, as a center for deep-sea archaeology. He has led or taken part in numerous deep-sea expeditions, including the location and exploration via submersibles and remote-controlled cameras of the wrecks of the German battleship *Bismarck*, RMS *Titanic*, the *Lusitania* and USS *Yorktown*. His publications include *Exploring Our Living Planet* (1983) and *The Eternal Darkness: A Personal History of Deep-Sea Exploration* (with Will Hively, 2000).

Ballesteros, Seve(riano) 1957– •*Spanish golfer*• Born in Santander, he started as a caddy for foreign players and became one of the world's leading golfers. A highly combative, adventurous player, he has continually set records, and has an uncanny ability to produce recovery shots. When he won the British Open championship in 1979 he was the youngest player in the 20th century to do so, and he took the title again in 1984 and 1988. He was the youngest player ever to win the US Masters in 1980 (a position usurped by **Tiger Woods** in 1997). In 1997 he captained the European team for the Ryder Cup.

Balliol or **Baliol** •*Anglo-Norman family*• The founder, Guido or Guy, held Bailleul, Harcourt, and other fiefs in Normandy, and received large possessions in Durham and Northumberland from **William II (Rufus)**. Bernard, Guy's son (d. c. 1167), built the fortress of Barnard Castle, and Bernard's great-grandson, John de Balliol, founded Balliol College, Oxford (c. 1263). His wife, Devorguilla, the great-great-granddaughter of **David I**, founded Sweetheart Abbey, Kirkcudbrightshire (1275). Their third son, John, became King of Scotland (1292–96).

Balliol or **Baliol, Edward de** c. 1283–1364 •*King of Scotland*• The elder son of **John de Balliol**, he landed with 3,400 followers at Kinghorn, Fife (1332), accompanied by the barons displaced by **Robert Bruce**, who were bent on recovering their forfeited Scottish estates. At Dupplin Moor, Perthshire, they surprised and routed the Scottish army under the new regent, the Earl of Mar, and in September he was crowned King of Scotland at Scone. Less than three months later, he was himself surprised at Annan and fled across the Border. Two attempts to regain Scotland (1334–35) were unsuccessful and he eventually resigned his claims to the Scottish throne to **Edward III** (1356) in return for a pension of £2,000.

Balliol or **Baliol, John de**, *also known as* **Toom Tabard** c. 1250–1315 •*King of Scotland*• The son of the founder of Balliol College, Oxford, he succeeded to his mother's estates and her right to the lordship of Galloway, as well as to his father's vast possessions in England and Normandy. On the death of **Margaret** the Maid of Norway (1290), he became a claimant to the Crown of Scotland. His claim was pronounced superior to that of **Robert Bruce**, Lord of Annandale, by **Edward I** of England. Balliol swore allegiance to Edward, was invested at Scone (1292) and was forced to repudiate the Treaty of Bingham (1290), which guaranteed Scottish liberties. By 1295 a council of 12 magnates had taken control of government out of Balliol's hands and concluded an alliance with France, which was then at war with England. Edward invaded Scotland, took Balliol prisoner, stripped him of his royal insignia (hence the name Toom Tabard, or "empty jacket") and forced him to surrender his crown (1296). Imprisoned for three years, Balliol was eventually allowed to retire to his estates in France (1302), where he died.

Balmain, Pierre Alexandre 1914–82 •*French couturier*• Born in St Jean-de-Maurienne, he was the son of a draper. He studied architecture in Paris, then turned to dress design, opening his own fashion house in 1945. His designs were famous for elegant simplicity and included evening dresses, sportswear and stoles. He also designed for the theater and cinema.

Balthus, Count Balthasar Klossowski de Rola 1908–2001 •*French painter*• Born in Paris, of Polish descent, he had no formal training, but received early encouragement from **Pierre Bonnard** and **André Derain**. His work includes landscapes and portraits, but he is chiefly known for his interiors with adolescent girls, languidly erotic scenes painted in a highly distinctive naturalistic style with a hint of surrealism. He grew in fame and popularity in later years, despite the fact that he lived for many years as a virtual recluse.

Baltimore, David 1938– •*US microbiologist and Nobel Prize winner*• Born in New York City, he studied chemistry at Swarthmore College, the Massachusetts Institute of Technology (MIT) and Rockefeller University. He conducted research into virology at the Salk Institute (1965–68), and in 1970 discovered the "reverse transcriptase" enzyme which can transcribe DNA into RNA. His research into the connection between viruses and cancer earned him the 1975 Nobel Prize for physiology or medicine, jointly with **Renato Dulbecco** and **Howard Temin**. In the 1980s he chaired a US National Academy of Sciences committee on AIDS, and from 1997 chaired the AIDS Vaccine Advisory Committee of the US National Institutes of Health.

Balzac, Honoré de 1799–1850 •*French novelist*• Born in Tours, he was educated at the Collège de Vendôme, and studied law at the Sorbonne, Paris. His father wished him to become a notary, but he left Tours in 1819 to seek his fortune as an author in Paris. His first success was with *Le dernier Chouan* in 1829 (Eng trans *The Chouans*, 1893), followed in the same year by *La peau de chagrin* (Eng trans *The Magic Skin*, 1888). After writing several other novels, he conceived the idea of the *La Comédie humaine* (1842, "The Human Comedy"), a complete picture of modern civilization. Among the masterpieces which form part of Balzac's vast scheme are *Le Père Goriot* (1835, Eng trans *Père Goriot*, 1886), *Illusions perdues* (1837–43, 3 vols, Eng trans *Lost Illusions*, 1893) and *Eugénie Grandet* (1833, Eng trans 1859). The *Contes drolatiques* (1832–37, "Droll Tales"), a series of **Rabelais**ian stories, stand by themselves. He worked regularly for up to 18 hours a day, and wrote 85 novels in 20 years. However, as a young man he had incurred a heavy burden of debt and his work failed to bring him wealth, which may help account for his obsession with the workings of money in his novels. In 1850, only three months before his death, he married Eveline Hanska, a rich Polish lady he had corresponded with for more than 15 years.

“ ”
L'amour n'est pas seulement un sentiment, il est un art aussi.
Love is not only a feeling; it is also an art.
*1831 **"La Recherche de l'absolu."***

Bancroft, Anne, *originally* **Anna Maria Louisa Italiano** 1931– •*US actress*• Born in New York City, she was a child actress and dancer, and made her television debut in 1950 under the name Anna Marno. Her film debut, as Anne Bancroft, followed in 1952. She won a Tony award for her performance in *Two for a Season* on Broadway (1958), and another for *The Miracle Worker* (1959), gaining an Academy Award for the film version in 1962. Her major films include *The Pumpkin Eater* (1964), *The Graduate* (1967) and *The Elephant Man* (1980). She has been married to **Mel Brooks** since 1964 and has appeared in a number of his films.

Bancroft, Richard 1544–1610 •*English prelate*• Born in Farnworth, Lancashire, he graduated from Cambridge in 1567, and was consecrated Bishop of London in 1597. He attended Queen **Elizabeth I** during her last illness, and took the lead at the Hampton Court Conference. Succeeding John Whitgift (c. 1530–1604) as Archbishop of Canterbury in 1604, he worked hard to make the Roman Catholics faithful to the Crown by supporting the secular clergy rather than the Jesuits, and assisted in reestablishing episcopacy in Scotland.

Banda, Hastings Kamuzu 1898–1997 •*Malawian politician and physician*• Born near Kasungu, Nyasaland, he achieved an education by self-help in South Africa, graduating in philosophy and in medicine in the US and obtaining further honors at the Universities of Glasgow and Edinburgh. He practiced medicine in Liverpool during the whole of World War II and then ran a successful London practice before returning to his homeland in 1958 to lead the Malawi African Congress. He was jailed for a year in 1959 but, given an unconditional pardon, became Minister of National Resources (1961), then Prime Minister (1963), President of the Malawi Republic (1966) and Life President (1971). He established a strong, one-party control of Malawi, while at the same time following a pragmatic foreign policy line, recognizing both the white regime in South Africa and the socialist government in Angola. Banda lost his presidency in 1994 in the first all-party elections and was later put on trial following the murder of three Cabinet members and one Member of Parliament in 1983; however, in December 1995 he was acquitted.

Bandaranaike, Sirimavo Ratwatte Dias 1916–2000 •*Sri Lankan politician*• She was born in Ratnapura. The widow of Prime Minister **S W R D Bandaranaike**, who was assassinated in 1959, she became the leader of the Sri Lanka Freedom Party (SLFP) and the first woman Prime Minister in the world when she was elected in 1960. She held office from 1960 to 1965, and again from 1970 to 1977, although her second term was marred by insurrection and economic problems. In 1980 the United National Party (UNP) government of **Junius Jayawardene** stripped her of her civil rights, forcing her to relinquish temporarily the leadership of the SLFP to her son, Anura. In 1994 Bandaranaike was reelected as Prime Minister.

Bandaranaike, S(olomon) W(est) R(idgeway) D(ias) 1899–1959 •*Ceylonese politician*• Born in Colombo, and educated there and at Oxford. He helped to found the United National Party (UNP). He was Leader of the House in Ceylon's first parliament. In 1951 he resigned from the government and organized the Sri Lanka Freedom Party (SLFP). In 1956 he was the main partner in a populist coalition that defeated the UNP in an election dominated by the issue of national language and the spirit of Buddhist revivalism, and became Prime Minister. Bandaranaike's Sinhala-only proposals were opposed by representatives of the Tamil minority, and Sinhala-Tamil violence swiftly followed. When he was assassinated by a Buddhist monk, he was succeeded by his wife, **Sirimavo Bandaranaike**.

Banerji, Bibhuti Bhusan 1894–1950 •*Indian (Bengali) author*• He is best known for his novel *Pather Panchali* (1928–29, Eng trans *Chronicle of the Street*, 1969), made famous by **Satyajit Ray**'s great trilogy of films under the same title. It is essentially the story of the author's own childhood in rural Bengal.

Ban Gu (Pan Ku) AD 32–92 •*Chinese historian*• He initiated a tradition of dynastic histories under imperial patronage unparalleled in other civilizations. In AD 82 he completed a history of the Western Han dynasty (202 BC–AD 9). The tradition pioneered by Ban Gu served a crucial political and moral role in imperial China. The history of a preceding dynasty highlighted its shortcomings in providing wise and benevolent government, thus serving as lessons for the future and enhancing the legitimacy of the current ruling dynasty.

Bani-Sadr, Abolhassan 1935– •*Iranian politician*• The son of a preacher and landowner, he was associated with the **Ayatollah Khomeini** from 1966. He studied economics and sociology at the Sorbonne in Paris, having fled there in 1963 after a brief imprisonment in Iran. He was an important figure in the Iranian Revolution of 1978–79 and was elected first president of the Islamic Republic of Iran in 1980. He was soon criticized, however, by the fundamentalists and was eventually dismissed (1981) by Ayatollah Khomeini for failing to establish a "truly Islamic country." He fled to France where he was granted political asylum. The same year, he formed the National Council of Resistance to oppose the Iranian government and was chairman until 1984.

Bankhead, Tallulah 1903–68 •*US actress*• She was born in Huntsville, Alabama. She made her stage debut in 1918, and appeared in many plays and films, her two most famous stage roles being Regina in *The Little Foxes* (1939) and Sabina in *The Skin of Our Teeth* (1942). Her best film performance was in *Lifeboat* (1944). She also performed on radio and television.

Banks, Gordon 1937– •*English soccer player*• Born in Sheffield, he started his career as a goalkeeper with Chesterfield and Leicester City but was transferred to Stoke City. His performances in the 1966 and 1970 World Cups were outstanding and England might well have retained the trophy in Mexico had he been able to play in the crucial match against West Germany. He was given the honorary title Officer, Order of the British Empire, in 1970, and was voted Footballer of the Year in 1972, but an eye injury from a car crash later that year effectively ended his career.

Banks, Iain Menzies 1954– •*Scottish novelist and science-fiction writer*• Born in Dunfermline, Fife, he studied at the University of Stirling. He made a major impact with his controversial first novel, *The Wasp Factory* (1984), a study of insanity which shifted between psychological acuity and grotesque fantasy. A subsequent novel, *The Crow Road* (1992), incorporated familiar motifs and themes of Scottish writing, viewed from a slightly displaced perspective. He writes science-fiction novels using the name Iain M Banks, including *The State of the Art* (1989, rev ed 1991), *Against a Dark Background* (1993) and *Look to Windward* (2000). His other works include *Complicity* (1993), *Whit* (1995) and *The Business* (1999).

Banks, Sir Joseph 1744–1820 •*English botanist*• He was born in London, and educated at Harrow, Eton, and Christ Church, Oxford. In 1766 he made a voyage to Newfoundland collecting plants, and between 1768 and 1771 accompanied Captain **James Cook**'s expedition around the world in a vessel, the *Endeavour*, equipped at his own expense. In 1778 he was elected president of the Royal Society, an office he held for 41 years. His significance lies in his far-reaching influence, rather than in any single personal contribution to science. He founded the African Association, and the colony of New South Wales owed its origin mainly to him. Through him the breadfruit was transferred from Tahiti to the West Indies, the mango from Bengal, and many fruits of Ceylon and Persia. He was made a baronet in 1781, and his name is commemorated in the genus *Banksia*.

Banks, Lynne Reid 1929– •*English novelist*• Born in London, she trained at the Royal Academy of Dramatic Art and worked as an actress, journalist and teacher before turning to writing full-time in 1971. She was widely acclaimed for the novel *The L-Shaped Room* (1960, filmed 1962), which added a female perspective to other novels of the time, similarly dealing with young working- and lower-middle-class people in a grim postwar Great Britain. *The Backward Shadow* (1970) and *Two Is Lonely* (1974) complete the trilogy. In addition to many novels, she has also published plays, biographical fiction and children's books, most notably *The Indian in the Cupboard* (1980, filmed 1995).

Banneker, Benjamin 1731–1806 •*US mathematician and astronomer*• Born in Ellicott, Maryland, the son of a slave father and free mother, he was interested in mathematics and science, and as a young man constructed an entirely wooden clock that kept perfect time. He was recommended by **Thomas Jefferson** to assist with surveying the site of the District of Columbia and the city of Washington, and in his correspondence with Jefferson he defended the intellectual equality of African Americans. Banneker also published an almanac containing astronomical and tide calculations.

Bannerman, Helen Brodie, *née* **Boog Watson** 1862–1946 •*Scottish children's writer and illustrator*• Born in Edinburgh, she married a doctor in the Indian Medical Service and spent much of her life in India. It was there that she wrote the children's classic *The Story of Little Black Sambo* (1899), the tale of a Black boy and his adventures with the tigers. Phenomenally popular when it first appeared, it was judged by some after her death to be racist and demeaning to Blacks. She wrote several other illustrated books for children.

Bannister, Sir Roger Gilbert 1929– •*English athlete and neurologist*• Born in Harrow, he was the first man to break the "four-minute mile." He was educated at Merton College, Oxford, and completed his medical training at St Mary's Hospital, London. He won the mile event in the Oxford vs. Cambridge match four times (1947–50), and was a finalist in the 1,500-meter race in the 1952 Olympic Games in Helsinki. At an athletics meeting at Iffley

Road, Oxford, in 1954, he ran the mile in under four minutes (3 minutes 59.4 seconds). He was knighted in 1975.

“ ”

I leapt at the tape like a man taking his last spring to save himself from the chasm that threatens to engulf him.

*1955 Of the end of his record-breaking run, **First Four Minutes**.*

Banting, Sir Frederick Grant 1891–1941 •*Canadian physiologist and Nobel Prize winner*• Born in Alliston, Ontario, he studied medicine at Toronto University and later became professor there (1923). Working under **John Macleod**, in 1921 he discovered (with his assistant **Charles H Best**) the hormone insulin, still the principal remedy for diabetes. For this discovery he was jointly awarded the Nobel Prize for physiology or medicine in 1923 with Macleod. He was knighted in 1934.

Bantock, Sir Granville 1868–1946 •*English composer*• He was born in London, and was Professor of Music at Birmingham University (1908–34). His inspiration was often drawn from Asian life, as in his *Omar Khayyám* (in three parts, 1906, 1907, 1909). His works include the choral work *Atalanta in Calydon* (1912) and the *Hebridean Symphony* (1916).

Banville, John 1945– •*Irish author*• He was born in Wexford and educated at St Peter's College there. His many novels, often dealing with men suffering personal crises, include *Ghosts* (1993), *The Untouchable* (1997) and *Shroud* (2002). He has also published novels about the lives of **Copernicus**, **Kepler** and Sir **Isaac Newton**, and his numerous awards include the Guinness Peat Aviation Prize for *The Book of Evidence* (1989).

Ban Zhao (Pan Chao) AD 45–c. 114 •*Chinese historian and moralist*• Born in Anling, Gufang (now called Xianyang, Shaanxi [Shensi] province), the sister of the military commander, Ban Chao (Pan Ch'ao), and **Ban Gu**, she helped complete Ban Gu's history of the former Han dynasty and became a tutor to empresses and court ladies. Ban Zhao compiled a book of moral admonitions for women, emphasizing the virtues of deference and modesty, which exerted a lasting influence on attitudes toward women in China. A crucial assumption underpinning these admonitions was that women should not play any public role.

Bao Dai, *originally* **Nguyen Vinh Thuy** 1913–97 •*Indo-Chinese ruler*• Born in Hue, the son of Emperor Khai Dai (d. 1925), he succeeded as Emperor of Annam on his father's death, and ascended the throne in 1932. In 1945 he was forced to abdicate by the Viet Minh under **Ho Chi Minh**. In 1949, having renounced his hereditary title, he returned to Saigon as head of the state of Vietnam within the French Union. After the French Indo-China War he was deposed in 1955 by **Ngo Dinh Diem**. South Vietnam then became a republic, and Bao Dai went to live in France.

Barak, Ehud 1942– •*Israeli soldier and politician*• Born in the Mishmar Hasharon kibbutz, he was educated at the Hebrew University, Jerusalem, and Stanford University, California. He joined the Israeli army in 1959 and served as a commander in the Six-Day War (1967) and Yom Kippur War (1973), becoming Chief of General Staff in 1991. He entered the government as Minister of the Interior in 1995, and became head of the Labor Party in 1997 and Prime Minister in 1999. While in office he tried to push forward the peace process with the Palestinians and met with Syria to discuss the Golan Heights issue; his comparatively emollient approach was overtaken by events and he was replaced by the more hardline **Ariel Sharon** in 2001.

Baraka, Amiri, *adopted name of* **LeRoi (Everett LeRoy) Jones** 1934– •*US poet, playwright, prose writer and essayist*• Born in Newark, New Jersey, into a middle-class African-American family, he moved from his bourgeois roots into Black nationalism (he took the name "Amiri Baraka" in 1967) and later Marxism-Leninism. A prolific poet and dramatist with over 50 titles to his name, he is best known for work dating from the early 1960s, when his anger spilled out in poetry collections like *Preface to a Twenty Volume Suicide Note* (1961) and *Black Magic* (1967), and in plays like *The Toilet* and *The Slave* (both 1964). His other works include a volume of stories, *Tales* (1967), and a seminal study of the social significance of African-American music, *Blues People* (1963). He is professor emeritus at SUNY-Stony Brook, where he taught for 17 years until his retirement in 1996.

“ ”

A man is either free or he is not. There cannot be any apprenticeship for freedom.

*1962 "Tokenism," in **Kulchur**, Spring issue.*

Barat, St Madeleine Sophie 1779–1865 •*French nun*• Born into a peasant family in Joigny, Burgundy, she was educated by her highly religious brother Louis. In 1800 she was persuaded by Louis and his superior, Abbé Joseph Varin, to form the Society of the Sacred Heart of Jesus, an institute which would promote educational work among all classes. The first Convent of the Sacred Heart opened at Amiens in 1801, with Barat as superior from 1802. During her 63-year rule the convent grew and established 100 further foundations in Europe, North Africa and the US. She was canonized in 1925 and her feast day is May 25.

Barbarossa, Khair-ed-din, *known as* **Redbeard** d. 1546 •*Barbary pirate*• Born in Mitylene, he was a Turkish corsair along with his brother, attacking shipping in the Mediterranean. After the execution of his brother Horuk (1518), Barbarossa captured Algiers (1529) and was made admiral of the Homan fleet (1533).

Barber, Chris (Donald Christopher) 1930– •*English jazz trombonist and bandleader*• Born in Welwyn Garden City, Hertfordshire, he was a leading figure in the trad movement, having taken over the Ken Colyer band in 1953. His successes include "Rock Island Line" (1956) and "Petite Fleur" (1959), which feature skiffle pioneer Lonnie Donegan (1931–2002) and clarinettist Monty Sunshine (1928–), respectively, rather than his own characteristic trombone sound. Recent work with New Orleans vocalist Dr John (born Malcolm Rebennack, 1941–) underlined his ability to synthesize and package styles, and he is also a fine musicologist. He was given the honorary title Officer, Order of the British Empire, in 1991.

Barber, Samuel 1910–81 •*US composer*• Born in West Chester, Pennsylvania, he studied at the Curtis Institute, Philadelphia, and won two Pulitzer traveling scholarships (1935, 1936) as well as the US Prix de Rome. His early music, which includes the setting for voice and string quartet of **Matthew Arnold**'s *Dover Beach* (1931), the overture to *The School for Scandal* (1931), and the well-known *Adagio for Strings* (1936) is traditionally Neo-Romantic. However, after 1939 his work became increasingly individual, with more emphasis on chromaticism and atonality, as in the *Capricorn Concerto* (1944), the ballet *Medea* (1946), and several vocal pieces, including *Nuvoletta* (1947) from **James Joyce**'s *Finnegans Wake* and *Hermit Songs* (1952–53). His first full-length opera, *Vanessa*, was performed at the Salzburg Festival (1958), followed by *Antony and Cleopatra* at the Metropolitan Opera in New York (1966).

Barbera, Joseph Roland *See* **Hanna-Barbera**

Barbirolli, Sir John 1899–1970 •*British conductor and cellist*• Born in London of Franco-Italian origin, he served in World War I, and played in several leading string quartets (1920–24). He succeeded **Arturo Toscanini** as conductor of the New York Philharmonic Orchestra (1937), and returned to England as permanent conductor (1943–58) of the Hallé Orchestra in Manchester which, under his direction and with his promotion of the works of modern composers, regained its place among the world's finest. He married the oboist Evelyn Rothwell (1911–) in 1939. He was awarded the Gold Medal of the Royal Philharmonic Society in 1950 and given the Freedom of Manchester in 1958, when he became the Hallé's principal conductor.

Barbusse, Henri 1873–1935 •*French novelist*• He was born in Asnières of an English mother. He fought as a volunteer in World War I, which inspired his masterpiece, *Le feu* (1916, Eng trans *Under Fire*, 1917), in which a powerful realism is accompanied by a deep feeling for all human suffering. Other works include *Le couteau entre les dents* (1921, "Knife Between the Teeth") and *Le Judas de Jésus* (1927, "Jesus's Judas"). A noted pacifist, and an increasingly militant Communist, he later settled in the USSR.

Barca *See* **Hamilcar**

Barclay, Robert 1648–90 •*Scottish Quaker*• Born in Gordonstoun, he was educated at the Scots College in Paris, where his uncle was rector. In 1664 he returned to Scotland, and became a Quaker in 1667. He married a fellow Quaker in Aberdeen in 1670, the first Quaker wedding in Scotland, and took over his father's estate at Ury. In 1672 he startled Aberdeen by walking through its streets in sackcloth and ashes. Frequently imprisoned for attending illegal meetings, he at last found a protector in the Duke of York (the future **James VII and II**), because of distant family connections. He made several journeys to Holland and Germany, the latter with **William Penn** of Pennsylvania and **George Fox**. He became one of the proprietors of East New Jersey in 1682, and was appointed its nominal nonresident governor. Among his many scholarly and lucid tracts in defense of Quakerism is his *Apology for the True Christian Divinity* (1678).

Barclay, Robert 1843–1913 •*English banker*• Under him, the merger of 20 banks formed Barclay and Company Limited (1896). In 1917 the name was changed to Barclay's Bank Limited.

Bardeen, John 1908–91 •*US physicist and double Nobel Prize winner*• Born in Madison, Wisconsin, he studied electrical engineering at the University of Wisconsin, worked as a geophysicist at the Gulf Research Laboratories for three years, then obtained his PhD in mathematical physics at Harvard (1936). Together with **Walter Brattain** and **William Shockley** he developed the point-contact transistor (1947), for which they shared the Nobel Prize for physics in 1956. Bardeen was professor at the University of Illinois (1951–75), and with **Leon Cooper** and **John Schrieffer** he won the Nobel Prize for physics again in 1972 for the first satisfactory theory of superconductivity (the Bardeen-Cooper-Schrieffer, or BCS, theory).

Bardot, Brigitte, *originally* **Camille Javal** 1934– •*French film actress*• Born in Paris, the daughter of an industrialist, she was a ballet student and model, and her appearance on the cover of *Elle* magazine led to her film debut in *Le trou normand* (1952, *Crazy for Love*). It was *Et Dieu créa la femme* (1956, *And God Created Woman*), made with the director Roger Vadim (1928–2000), later her husband, that established her reputation as an international sex symbol. Her many screen credits include *La vérité* (1960, *The Truth*) and *Viva Maria* (1965), while *Vie privée* (1962, *A Very Private Affair*) was an autobiographical depiction of a young woman trapped by the demands of her stardom. Her last major film was *Si Don Juan était une femme* (1973, "If Don Juan Were a Woman"). Since then she has become closely concerned with animal welfare and the cause of endangered animal species, forming the Brigitte Bardot Foundation to work for animal rights in 1986. In 1996 she published a controversial autobiography, *Initiales B. B.*

Barenboim, Daniel 1942– •*Israeli pianist and conductor*• He was born in Buenos Aires, Argentina, and studied with Igor Markevich (1912–83) and **Nadia Boulanger**. A noted exponent of **Mozart** and **Beethoven**, he gained his reputation as pianist/conductor with the English Chamber Orchestra, then became musical director of the Orchestre de Paris (1975–89) and of the Chicago Symphony Orchestra (1991–), and musical and artistic director of the Deutsche Staatsoper, Berlin (1992–). He married the cellist **Jacqueline du Pré** in 1967, and became an Israeli citizen. His autobiography, *A Life in Music*, was published in 1991.

Barents, Willem d. 1597 •*Dutch navigator*• He was pilot to several Dutch expeditions in search of the Northeast Passage, and died off Novaya Zemlya. His winter quarters were found undisturbed in 1871, and in 1875 part of his journal was recovered by another expedition.

Barham, Richard Harris 1788–1845 •*English humorist*• He was born in Canterbury, and had a near-fatal coach accident in 1802 that partially crippled his right arm for life. He entered Brasenose College, Oxford (1807), was ordained (1813) and in 1821 received a minor canonry of St Paul's Cathedral, London. He began a series of burlesque metrical tales in 1837 under the pen name "Thomas Ingoldsby," which, collected under the title *The Ingoldsby Legends* (3 vols, 1840–47), at once became popular for their droll humor and esoteric learning.

“ ”

His eye so dim,
So wasted each limb,
That, heedless of grammar, they all cried, "That's him!"

1840–47 "The Jackdaw of Rheims" in ***The Ingoldsby Legends.***

Baring •*English family of financiers*• John (1730–1816) and Francis (1740–1810) Baring were the sons of John Baring (1697–1748), a German cloth manufacturer who in 1717 had started a small business at Larkbear, near Honiton, Devon. In 1770 they established the financial and commercial house Baring Brothers & Co., now known as Barings. In February 1995 Nick Leeson, a 28-year-old derivatives trader based in Singapore, lost over £600 million trading on the Tokyo stock market and caused the collapse of what had become a 200-year-old merchant banking empire. He was sentenced to six and a half years' imprisonment in Singapore, and Barings was bought by the Dutch bank ING.

Barker, George Granville 1913–91 •*English poet, novelist, playwright and scriptwriter*• Born in Loughton, Essex, he lived much of his life in the US and Italy and enjoyed a long, prolific career. However, from 1933 he suffered due to an association with **Dylan Thomas**, and from the inference that he was a member of the prewar New Apocalyptics. He was an energetic and eloquent writer, whose publications culminated in *Collected Poems* (1987). *Street Ballads* was published posthumously in 1992.

Barker, Harley Granville *See* **Granville-Barker, Harley**

Barker, Howard 1946– •*English dramatist*• Born in London, he studied history at the University of Sussex. His first play, *Cheek*, was produced at the Royal Court Theatre, London, in 1970. He has written over 20 plays on ambitious themes such as the nature of history and the degradation of political morality. They include *Stripwell* (1975), *The Hang of the Gaol* (1978), *Crimes in Hot Countries* (1983) and *Golgo* (1990). Some, such as *Scenes from an Execution* (1984, staged 1990) and *A Hard Heart* (1992), were written for radio and then adapted for the stage. His poetry includes *The Ascent of Monte Grappa* (1991). He formed The Wrestling School in 1989, a company that performs only his works.

Barker, Pat(ricia) Margaret, *née* **Drake** 1943– •*English author*• Born in Thornaby-on-Tees, Cleveland, she studied at the London School of Economics and Durham University. Her novels include *Union Street* (1982), *The Man Who Wasn't There* (1989) and the highly acclaimed trilogy of World War I novels *Regeneration* (1991, filmed 1997), *The Eye in the Door* (1993) and *The Ghost Road* (1995), the last of which won the Booker Prize. *Border Crossing*, a novel about a young boy who commits a murder and later confronts the psychiatrist who helped convict him, was published in 2001.

Barker, Ronnie (Ronald William George) 1929– •*English comic actor*• Born in Bedford, Bedfordshire, he made his professional debut at Aylesbury Repertory Theatre in *Quality Street* (1948), and his London debut in *Mourning Becomes Electra* (1955). An affable figure, adept at precisely detailed characterizations, tongue-twisting comic lyrics and saucy humor, he made many television appearances including *The Frost Report* (1966–67) and the sitcoms *Hark at Barker* (1969–70), *Open All Hours* (1976, 1981–85), the hugely popular *Porridge* (1974–77), *Going Straight* (1978) and *Clarence* (1988). With **Ronnie Corbett**, he made the long-running *The Two Ronnies* (1971–87). His films include *Wonderful Things* (1958), *Robin and Marian* (1976) and *Porridge* (1979). A keen collector of Victoriana, he has written light-hearted books on the subject, including *Book of Boudoir Beauties* (1975) and *Ooh-la-la!* (1983). He was given the honorary title Officer, Order of the British Empire, in 1978.

Barkla, Charles Glover 1877–1944 •*English physicist and Nobel Prize winner*• Born in Widnes, Lancashire, he studied at the universities of Liverpool and Cambridge. He left his early work on electromagnetic waves to study X-rays, which he researched for 40 years. Barkla deduced from the scattering of X-rays by gases that more massive atoms contain more electrons, thus taking the first steps toward the concept of the atomic number. Much of his work concerned secondary X-rays, which he found to consist of X-rays scattered from the incident beam and a fluorescent radiation characteristic of the scattering substance. By 1911 he was recognized as a world leader in the field and in 1917 was awarded the Nobel Prize for physics.

Barkley, Charles 1963– •*US basketball player*• Born in Leeds, Alabama, he established a reputation as one of the most talented and volatile players of the 1980s and 1990s, playing for the Philadelphia 76ers, the Phoenix Suns and the Houston Rockets. Barkley became widely known for his fierce playing style, which resulted in many fines for fouls. On retiring as a player in 2000 he became a television basketball analyst.

Bar Kokhba, Simon, *also spelled* **Cochba** or **Kochbas** d. 135 AD •*Jewish leader in Palestine*• He led, with the rabbi **Akiba ben Joseph**, a rebellion of Jews in Judea from AD 132, in response to the founding of a Roman colony (Aelia Capitolina) in Jerusalem, with a temple of Jupiter on the ruins of their own temple. The rebellion was suppressed by the emperor **Hadrian** with ruthless severity, and Simon Bar Kokhba was killed at the Battle of Bethar. In 1960 some of his letters were found in caves near the Dead Sea.

Barlow, Mrs *See* **Walter, Lucy**

Barnard, Christiaan Neethling 1922–2001 •*South African surgeon*• Born in Beaufort West, he graduated from Cape Town Medical School. After a period of research in the US he returned to Cape Town in 1958 to work on open-heart surgery and organ transplantation. In December 1967 at Groote Schuur Hospital he performed the first successful human heart transplant. The recipient, Louis Washkansky, died of pneumonia 18 days later, drugs given to prevent tissue rejection having heightened the risk of infection. A second patient, Philip Blaiberg, operated on in January 1968, survived for 594 days.

Barnard, Edward Emerson 1857–1923 •*US astronomer*• Born in Nashville, Tennessee, into a poor family, he had little education in his early years, but developed a strong amateur interest in astronomy. After discovering a number of comets and becoming skilled in astronomical work, he became both a teacher and a student at the observatory at Vanderbilt University and was appointed professor at Yerkes Observatory at the University of Chicago in 1895. He correctly concluded with **Maximilian Wolf** that those areas of the Milky Way which appear to be devoid of stars are in fact clouds of obscuring matter. His wide-ranging research included studies of novae, binary stars and variable stars. He discovered the fifth satellite of Jupiter (1892), later named Amalthea, and in 1916 identified the star with the greatest known apparent motion across the sky, now known as Barnard's star.

Barnardo, Thomas John 1845–1905 •*Irish doctor and philanthropist*• Born in Dublin, he was the founder of homes for destitute children. A clerk by profession, he converted to Christianity in 1862, and after a spell of preaching in the Dublin slums went to London (1866) to study medicine. Instead, while still a student, he founded the East End Mission for impoverished children in Stepney (1867) and a number of homes in Greater London, which came to be known as "Dr Barnardo's Homes." The organization now flourishes under the name of Barnardos, and is the largest child-care charity working in the UK.

Barnes, Djuna 1892–1982 •*US novelist, poet and illustrator*• Born in Cornwall-on-Hudson, New York, she began her career as a reporter and illustrator for magazines, then became a writer of one-act plays and short stories, published in a variety of magazines and anthologies. Her works, many of which she illustrated, range from the outstanding novel *Nightwood* (1936) to her verse play *The Antiphon* (1958), both included in *Selected Works* (1962).

Barnes, Dame (Alice) Josephine (Mary Taylor) 1912–99 •*English obstetrician and gynecologist*• Born in Sheringham, Norfolk, she studied physiology at Lady Margaret Hall, Oxford, before completing her clinical training at University College Hospital, London (1937). After various obstetrics, gynecology and surgery appointments in London and Oxford, she became deputy academic head of the Obstetric Unit of University College Hospital (1947–52), and surgeon at the **Marie Curie** Hospital (1947–67). She served in many medical positions, such as in the British Medical Association (first woman president, 1979–80) and the National Association of Family Planning Doctors, and also served on many national and international committees. She published extensively on obstetrics, gynecology and family planning, and was given the honorary title of Dame Commander, Order of the British Empire, in 1974.

Barnes, Julian Patrick 1946– •*English novelist*• He was born in Leicester. The crisp precision of his prose is partly explained by his having worked both as a journalist and as a lexicographer on the *Oxford English Dictionary Supplement*. His intellect, wit and love of France are reflected in his third novel, *Flaubert's Parrot* (1984), in which a retired doctor discovers the stuffed parrot which was said to have stood upon **Gustave Flaubert**'s desk. Later novels include *A History of the World in 10½ Chapters* (1989), a confection of fictional narrative, philosophical deliberation and art criticism, *Talking It Over* (1991) and its later sequel *Love, etc* (2000), *The Porcupine* (1992) and *England, England* (1998). He has also published short stories, collected articles and essays.

“ ”

You can have your cake and eat it: the only trouble is you get fat.

1984 ***Metroland****, chapter 7.*

Barnum, Phineas Taylor 1810–91 •*US showman*• Born in Bethel, Connecticut, he began his career of entertaining and deluding an eager public with the exhibition of an elderly former slave billed as the 160-year-old nurse of **George Washington**. From 1841 he ran Barnum's American Museum in New York City, exhibiting such curiosities as the Fiji mermaid and the dwarf "General Tom Thumb" (**Charles Stratton**) and promoting them with flamboyant publicity. In 1871 he opened a three-ring touring circus that he called the "Greatest Show on Earth." In 1881 he joined with his rival James Anthony Bailey (1847–1906) to found the famous Barnum and Bailey Circus.

Barr, Roseanne *See* **Roseanne**

Barras, Paul François Jean Nicolas, Comte de 1755–1829 •*French revolutionary*• He was born in Fox-Amphoux. An original member of the Jacobin Club, he was chiefly responsible for the overthrow of **Robespierre**, and was given dictatorial powers by the National Convention. In 1795, acting against a royalist uprising, he was aided by his young friend Napoleon Bonaparte (later **Napoleon I**), who fired on the rebels (the historical "whiff of grapeshot"). Barras became one of the five members of the Directory (1795). Once more dictator in 1797, he guided the state almost alone, until his hedonism and corruption made him so unpopular that Napoleon overthrew him easily (1799).

Barrault, Jean-Louis 1910–94 •*French actor and producer*• Born in Le Vesinet, he made his Paris stage debut in *Volpone* (1931). A member of the Comédie-Française (1940–46), he formed the Compagnie Renaud-Barrault with his actress wife Madeleine Renaud (1903–94). Director of the Théâtre de France (1959–68), Théâtre des Nations (1965–67, 1972–74) and the Théâtre d'Orsay (1974–81), he was renowned for a sensitive, poetic style of acting that included a fluidity born of his training in mime with Étienne Decroux. He made his film debut in *Les beaux jours* (1935) and gave significant performances in *Les enfants du Paradis* (1945, "The Children of Paradise"), *La ronde* (1950) and *La nuit de Varennes* (1981). The actress Marie-Christine Barrault (1944–) is his niece. He published an autobiography, *Reflections on Theater*, in 1951, and a volume of memoirs in 1974 entitled *Memories for Tomorrow*.

Barre, Mohamed Siad 1919– •*Somali soldier and politician*• Educated locally and at an Italian military academy, he was a police officer in Somaliland, under both Italian and British trusteeship, before joining the Somali army in 1960. He led a successful coup in 1969. Using a KGB-trained secret service and manipulating the clan divisions of the Somalis, he was backed first by the USSR and then by the US. When uprisings took place in 1989, he attempted to stamp out the opposition, but was unsuccessful. Forced to leave Mogadishu in 1991, he left behind an impoverished country divided into competing warring factions. In 1992 US troops attempted to restore order in Somalia; however, two years later they were forced to pull out, leaving the country in chaos.

Barre, Raymond 1924– •*French conservative politician*• Born in St Denis on the French dependency of Réunion, he made his reputation as an influential neoliberal economist at the Sorbonne and as vice president of the European Commission (1967–72). He was Minister of Foreign Trade under President **Giscard d'Estaing** and was appointed Prime Minister (1976–81) after the resignation of **Jacques Chirac** in 1976. With unemployment mounting between 1976 and 1981, he became deeply unpopular, but his term as Prime Minister was later favorably reassessed after the failure of the 1981–83 socialist administration's reflationary experiment. During the 1980s he represented the center-right Union for French Democracy (UDF). He ran in the 1988 presidential election but was eliminated in the first ballot.

Barrie, J M, *properly* **Sir James Matthew Barrie** 1860–1937 •*Scottish novelist and dramatist*• Born in Kirriemuir, Angus, the son of a weaver, he graduated from Edinburgh University in 1882, then settled in London and became a journalist. He wrote a series of autobiographical prose works, including *The Little Minister* (1891, dramatized 1897), set in his native village disguised as "Thrums." From 1890 he wrote for the theater. Works like the successful *The Admirable Crichton* (1902), a good-humored social satire, established his reputation, but it is as the creator of *Peter Pan* (1904) that he will be chiefly remembered. Aware of the popular demand for dramatic sentimentality on the London stage, Barrie provided surface romance within dramatic structures that indirectly suggested a bleaker vision of life. He continued his excursions into fairyland in later plays such as *Dear Brutus* (1917) and *Mary Rose* (1920).

" "

I have always found that the man whose second thoughts are good is worth watching.

1908 ***What Every Woman Knows*** *(published 1918), act 3.*

Barrios, Eduardo 1884–1963 •*Chilean novelist and dramatist*• Born in Valparaíso of a Chilean father and a Peruvian mother, he worked variously as a weightlifter, officer cadet, nitrate company accountant, academic and acrobat, and served as Minister of Education during the dictatorship of Ibáñez del Campo. He was one of the earliest psychological novelists of South America, and his *El niño que enloqueció de amor* (1915, "The Boy Who Went Mad for Love") is often cited as the first novel of this kind. *El hermano asno* (1922, Eng trans as *Brother Ass* in *Fiesta in November*, 1942) is often taken to be his best novel.

Barron, Clarence Walker 1855–1928 •*US editor and publisher*• Born in Boston, he began his career in journalism with the *Boston Evening Transcript*. He founded the Boston News Bureau (1887) and the Philadelphia News Bureau (1897) to give businessmen reliable financial information. In 1901, when he bought Dow Jones and Co, he became publisher of the *Wall Street Journal*, which he augmented with *Barron's National Business and Financial Weekly* (1921).

Barrow, Clyde 1909–34 •*US thief and murderer*• Born in Texas, he was the partner of **Bonnie Parker**. Despite their popular romantic image, they and their gang were responsible for a number of murders. The pair met in 1932. When Barrow first visited Parker's house, he was arrested on seven counts of burglary and car theft. Parker smuggled a gun to him and he escaped. Recaptured a few days later after robbing a railway office, he was sentenced to 14 years' imprisonment. He persuaded a fellow prisoner to chop off two of his toes and was subsequently released. With their gang, Parker and Barrow continued to rob and murder until they were shot dead at a police roadblock in Louisiana in May 1934. Their end was predicted by Parker in a poem, variously called *The Story of Bonnie and Clyde* and *The Story of Suicide Sal*.

Barrow, Errol Walton 1920–87 •*Barbadian politician*• Born in Barbados, he flew in the RAF (1940–47), then studied at London University and Lincoln's Inn. Returning to Barbados, he became active in the Barbados Labour Party (BLP), but in 1955 he left the BLP and cofounded the Democratic Labour Party (DLP). In the elections following independence in 1961 the DLP was victorious and Barrow became the first Prime Minister. His unbroken tenure was ended in 1976 by the BLP, led by "Tom" Adams. In 1986, a year after Adams's death, Barrow returned to power with a decisive majority but he died the following year and was succeeded by Erskine Lloyd Sandiford.

Barrow, Sir John 1764–1848 •*English naval administrator and traveler*• Born in Dragley Beck, Morecambe Bay, Lancashire, in 1792 he was appointed private secretary to Lord **Macartney**, the British envoy to China, accompanying him to Cape Colony, South Africa, in 1797. Barrow wrote about his experiences in these countries in *Travels in China* (1804) and *Account of Travels into the Interior of Southern Africa* (2 vols, 1801–04). He was appointed second secretary of the admiralty (1804–45), and promoted Arctic expeditions by Sir **John Ross**, Sir **James Clark Ross** and Sir **John Franklin**, and was a founder and vice president of the (Royal) Geographical Society (1830). Barrow Strait and Point Barrow in the Arctic, and Cape Barrow in the Antarctic, were named in his honor, as was the northern duck, Barrow's goldeneye.

Barry, Sir Charles 1795–1860 •*English architect*• Born in London and educated privately, he was apprenticed to a firm of surveyors before going to Italy (1817–20). On his return, he designed the Travellers' Club (1831), the Manchester Athenaeum (1836), the Reform Club (1837), and the new Palace of Westminster (1840), completed after his death by his son Edward Middleton Barry (1830–80). His work showed the influence of the Italian Renaissance. His fifth son, Sir John Wolfe-Barry (1836–1918), was engineer of the Tower Bridge and Barry Docks.

Barry, Elizabeth 1658–1713 •*English actress*• Her patron was the Earl of **Rochester** and her many roles included the chief characters in the plays of **Thomas Otway** and **William Congreve**.

Barry, Marie Jeanne, Comtesse du, *née* **Bécu** 1741–93 •*French courtesan*• Born in Vaucouleurs, the illegitimate daughter of a dressmaker, she married Comte Guillaume du Barry and became the official mistress of **Louis XV**. She wielded much influence, helped to bring about the downfall of the Finance Minister, the Duc de **Choiseul** (1770), and was notorious for her extravagance, though she was a generous patron of the arts. She was banished from court after Louis's death (1774), and was guillotined during the French Revolution.

Barry, Philip 1896–1949 •*US dramatist*• Born in Rochester, New York, he is now remembered for such plays as *The Philadelphia Story* (1939), a bright comedy of manners which was a hit for the actress **Katharine Hepburn**. *Holiday* (1929) and *The Animal Kingdom* (1932) contain sharper satire but are still, at heart, affectionate comedies.

Barrymore, Ethel 1879–1959 •*US actress*• She was born in Philadelphia, the daughter of the actor-playwright Maurice Barrymore and the actress Georgiana Drew Barrymore. In 1897–98 she scored a great success in London with Sir **Henry Irving** in *The Bells*. Her film appearances include *Rasputin and the Empress* (1932), the only production in which she and her brothers, **Lionel Barrymore** and **John Barrymore**, appeared together, and *None But the Lonely Heart* (1944, Academy Award, Best Supporting Actress). She also appeared on radio and television.

Barrymore, John 1882–1942 •*US actor*• He was born in Philadelphia. He spent some time studying art, but eventually returned to the family profession, making his name in Shakespearean roles, his Hamlet being particularly famous. He also appeared in many films. His classical nose and distinguished features won for him the nickname of "The Great Profile," the name of the last film in which he appeared (1940), but his screen appearances never fully reflected his talents. John was the younger brother of **Ethel Barrymore** and **Lionel Barrymore** and the grandfather of actress Drew Barrymore (1975–).

Barrymore, Lionel 1878–1954 •*US actor*• He was born in Philadelphia. He appeared in small parts in the early films of **D W Griffith** before making his name in **Gerald du Maurier**'s *Peter Ibbetson* (1917) and in *The Copperhead* (1918). He subsequently took many roles in films and radio plays, notably *A Free Soul* (1931, Academy Award for Best Actor), *Grand Hotel*, *Dinner at Eight* and

Duel in the Sun. After twice accidentally breaking a hip he was confined to a wheelchair, but continued to act, playing Dr Gillespie in the original *Dr Kildare* film series. He also had etchings exhibited and was a talented musician, musical arranger and composer. The elder brother of **Ethel Barrymore** and **John Barrymore**, he wrote *We Barrymores* (1951).

Barstow, Stan(ley) 1928– •*English novelist*• Born in Yorkshire into a mining community that provided much material for his fiction, he achieved a major success with his first novel, *A Kind of Loving* (1960), which later grew into a trilogy with *The Watchers on the Shore* (1966) and *The Right True End* (1976). His other novels include *Joby* (1964), *A Raging Calm* (1968), *Just You Wait and See* (1986) and *Next of Kin* (1991). His autobiography, *In My Own Good Time*, was published in 2001. He has also written short stories and plays for theater, radio and television.

Bart, Jean *See* **Barth, Jean**

Bart, Lionel 1930–99 •*English composer and lyricist*• He was born in London. In 1959 his *Lock Up Your Daughters*, a musical based upon **Henry Fielding**'s 1730 play, *Rape upon Rape*, ended the US domination of the musical theater in London. He followed it with *Fings Ain't Wot They Used T'be* (1959), *Oliver!* (1960) and *Blitz!* (1962), a cavalcade of East End life during World War II. *Maggie May*, a between-the-wars story of a Liverpool prostitute, followed in 1964, but his Robin Hood musical, *Twang!* (1965), was a flop, as was *La Strada* (1969).

Barth or **Bart, Jean** 1651–1702 •*French privateer*• Born in Dunkirk, he served first in the Dutch navy, but on the outbreak of war with Holland (1672) joined the French service. In 1691, in command of a small squadron in the North Sea, he destroyed many English vessels. In 1694, after a desperate struggle with a superior Dutch fleet, he recaptured a convoy of 96 ships and took them to Dunkirk. Soon after he was taken prisoner but escaped from Plymouth to France where in 1697 **Louis XIV** appointed him to the command of a squadron.

Barth, John Simmons 1930– •*US novelist and short-story writer*• Born in Cambridge, Maryland, he was educated at Johns Hopkins University, and was a professional drummer before turning to literature and teaching. His earliest novels—*The Floating Opera* (1956), *End of the Road* (1958), *The Sot-Weed Factor* (1960) and *Giles Goat-Boy* (1966)—combined realism, formidable learning and fantastic humor. Later novels such as *Letters* (1979), *Tidewater Tales* (1988) and *The Last Voyage of Somebody the Sailor* (1991) are prolix and less assured. Since 1991 he has been professor emeritus at Johns Hopkins University.

“ ”

Everyone is necessarily the hero of his own life story.

1958 ***The End of the Road***, *chapter 1.*

Barth, Karl 1886–1968 •*Swiss theologian*• He was born in Basel, and studied at Berne, Berlin, Tübingen and Marburg. While pastor at Safenwil, Aargau, he wrote a commentary of St **Paul**'s epistle to the Romans (1919) which established his theological reputation. He became professor at Göttingen (1921), Münster (1925) and Bonn (1930), refused to take an unconditional oath to **Hitler**, was dismissed and became professor at Basel (1935–62). He played a leading role in the German Confessing Church and Barmen Declaration (1934). His theology begins with the realization of human wickedness, the principal sin being man's endeavor to make himself, rather than God, the center of the world, and reemphasized God's unquestionable authority and "otherness." However, Barth was criticized on the grounds that his own reasoned exposition of antiphilosophical theology itself constitutes philosophy and that he prescribed belief in a divinity that failed to explain the nature of humanity. His many works include *Knowledge of God and the Service of God* (1938) and the monumental *Church Dogmatics* (1932–67).

Barthelme, Donald 1931–89 •*US novelist and short-story writer*• Born in Philadelphia, Pennsylvania, he worked as a journalist and magazine editor before turning to fiction. An experimentalist who rejected the traditions of the conventional novel form and was inventive in his use of language, he was associated with the mid-1960s avant-garde. The short stories in *Come Back, Dr Caligari* (1964) and *Unspeakable Practices, Unnatural Acts* (1968) are regarded as his most characteristic work. Other collections include *City Life* (1970) and *Sadness* (1972), and share the broader humor of his novels *Snow White* (1967) and *The Dead Father* (1975). He was the brother of the novelist Frederick Barthelme (1943–).

Barthes, Roland 1915–80 •*French writer, critic and teacher*• He was born in Cherbourg, and after researching and teaching he began to write. His collection of essays entitled *Le degré zéro de l'écriture* (1953, Eng trans *Writing Degree Zero*, 1967) immediately established him as France's leading critic of Modernist literature. His literary criticism avoided the traditional value judgments and investigation of the author's intentions, addressing itself instead to analysis of the text as a system of signs or symbols. Despite criticism from more traditional scholars he continued with this method and produced *Mythologies* (1957), a semiological exploration of such diverse cultural phenomena as wrestling, children's toys and film stars' faces. Though influenced by Marxism, **Sigmund Freud**, existentialism and structuralism, he remained a versatile individualist and a fierce critic of what he saw as stale and oppressive bourgeois thinking. He gained international recognition as a developer of semiology and structuralism and produced an imaginative autobiography, *Roland Barthes by Roland Barthes*.

“ ”

Tout refus du langage est une mort.

Any refusal of language is a death.

1957 ***Mythologies***, *"La nouvelle Citroën."*

Bartholdi, (Frédéric) Auguste 1834–1904 •*French sculptor*• He was born in Colmar, Alsace, and specialized in enormous monuments, such as the red sandstone *Lion of Belfort* (1880, Belfort) and the colossal bronze *Statue of Liberty* on Bedloe's Island, New York Harbor. Unveiled in 1886, it was a present to the US from the French Republic.

Bartholomew 1st century AD •*One of the 12 Apostles of Jesus*• Little is known of his family, but his name is linked with St **Philip**'s in all but one list of the Apostles in the Gospels. He is often considered identical with Nathaniel of Cana. If this is correct, **Jesus** described him as "a true Israelite in whom there is nothing false." According to **Eusebius of Caesarea** in his *Ecclesiastical History*, Bartholomew had left behind the Hebrew Gospel according to St **Matthew** in India. He is reported to have worked as a missionary in Ethiopia and in Mesopotamia, where tradition holds that he was martyred. His feast day is August 24.

Bartlett, John 1820–1905 •*US bookseller*• Born in Plymouth, Massachusetts, he was for many years the owner of the University Book Store at Harvard (1849–63). He compiled *Familiar Quotations* (1855) and also published a *Complete Concordance to Shakespeare's Dramatic Works and Poems* (1894).

Bartók, Béla 1881–1945 •*Hungarian composer*• Born in Nagyszentmiklós (now Sînnicolau Mare, Romania), he learned to play the piano mainly from his mother and first performed in public in 1892. Among his teachers was István Thomán, a former pupil of **Liszt**. He toured widely as a pianist, during which a growing interest in folk song led him to study Hungarian and Balkan folk-music traditions that greatly influenced his own compositions. He was Professor of the Pianoforte at the Budapest Academy from 1907 to 1934 and later became known throughout Europe as a composer, but was driven into exile by World War II and settled in the US. His many works include *The Miraculous Mandarin* and the *Concerto for Orchestra*.

Bartolommeo, Fra, *real name* **Baccio della Porta** 1475–1517 •*Italian painter*• Born near Florence, he was a pupil of Cosimo di Rosselli (1439–1507), in whose studio he met Mariotto Albertinelli (1474–1515), with whom he later often collaborated. Under the influence of **Savonarola** he publicly burned many of his paintings and in 1500 became a Dominican novice, but **Raphael**'s visit to Florence in 1504 encouraged him to take up painting again, and they became close friends, helping one another with their work.

Later, overwhelmed by the work of Raphael in the Vatican apartments and **Michelangelo** in the Sistine Chapel, he refused all entreaties to collaborate with them. Most of his work is still in Florence, but there is a notable Annunciation by him in the Louvre.

Barton, Clara (Clarissa Harlowe) 1821–1912 •*US founder of the US Red Cross*• Born in Oxford, Massachusetts, she was a schoolteacher from 1836 to 1854, worked in the Patent Office in Washington DC (1854–57), and during the Civil War (1861–65) helped to obtain and distribute supplies and comforts for the wounded. In Europe for health reasons (1869–73), she worked for the International Red Cross in the Franco-Prussian War (1870–71). Back in the US she established the US branch of the Red Cross in 1881 and became its first president (1881–1904). As a result of her campaigning, the US signed the Geneva Convention in 1882.

Barton, Sir Derek Harold Richard 1918–98 •*English chemist and Nobel Prize winner*• Born in Gravesend, Kent, he studied at Imperial College, London. After work in military intelligence he returned to Imperial College as assistant lecturer and then Imperial Chemical Industries Fellow. In 1949 he spent a year at Harvard and produced a seminal paper on the relationship between conformation and chemical reactivity for which he shared the 1969 Nobel Prize for chemistry with **Odd Hassel**. By 1960, X-ray crystallography had largely replaced degradative studies in the determination of structure, and Barton turned his attention to synthetic and biosynthetic work, also pioneering the use of photochemical reactions in synthesis. In 1977 he was appointed director of the French National Center for Scientific Research (CNRS) at the Institute for the Chemistry of Natural Substances in Gif-sur-Yvette, and from 1986 to 1995 was appointed distinguished professor at Texas Agricultural and Mechanical University. He was knighted in 1972 and made an Officer of the French Legion of Honor in 1985.

Barton, Sir Edmund 1849–1920 •*Australian jurist and statesman*• Born in Sydney, he was elected to the New South Wales legislature in 1879. He was leader of the Federation movement from 1896, headed the committee that drafted the Commonwealth Constitution Bill and led the delegation that presented it to the British parliament in 1900. He was the first Prime Minister of the Australian Commonwealth (1901–03). From 1903 until his death he served as a high court judge.

Barton, Elizabeth, *known as* **the Maid of Kent** or **the Nun of Kent** c.1506–34 •*English prophet*• Born in Kent, she was a domestic servant at Aldington. After an illness in 1525, she began to go into trances and make prophecies against the authorities. The archbishop sent two monks to examine her, and one of these, Edward Bocking, convinced that she was directly inspired by the Virgin **Mary**, became her confessor at the Priory of St Sepulchre at Canterbury. She denounced **Henry VIII**'s divorce and marriage to **Anne Boleyn**, and was hanged for treason at Tyburn with Bocking.

Barton, John Bernard Adie 1928– •*English stage director*• He was born in London and educated at King's College, Cambridge. He joined the newly created Royal Shakespeare Company at Stratford-upon-Avon in 1960 and was associate director there from 1964 to 1991, when he became advisory director. He wrote and directed *The Hollow Crown* (1961), an anthology about English monarchs, and adapted the three parts of *Henry VI* into two plays, *Henry VI* and *Edward VI*, for the monumental Wars of the Roses sequence (1963–64). He also adapted and directed a series of ten plays titled *The Greeks* (1980), based on the *Oresteia* legend. He is the author of *Playing Shakespeare* (1984), based on his television series (1982).

Bartram, John 1699–1777 •*American botanist*• Born near Darby, Pennsylvania, he became a successful farmer and also built up an unrivaled collection of North American plants, which he sold to European botanists and horticulturists. In 1743 the British Crown commissioned him to visit the Indian tribes of the "League of Six Nations," the results of which were published, and in 1765 he was named King's Botanist. He was considered to be the "father of American botany," and **Carolus Linnaeus** called him "the greatest natural botanist in the world."

Baruch *See* **Spinoza, Benedict de**

Baryshnikov, Mikhail Nikolayevich 1948– •*US dancer and choreographer*• Born in Riga, Latvia, of Russian parents, he first trained at the Riga Choreography School and then with the Kirov Ballet in Leningrad (now St Petersburg). In 1976 he defected to the West while on tour in Canada and then went to the US. His new career began at the American Ballet Theater, where he partnered **Gelsey Kirkland**. He then moved to New York City Ballet, where he worked with **George Balanchine** and had roles created for him by Balanchine, **Jerome Robbins**, **Frederick Ashton** and others. In 1980, he returned to the American Ballet Theater, taking over as artistic director. He has always maintained an interest in ballet as a popular art form and has taken part in several Hollywood films, including *The Turning Point* (1977). *White Knights*, with choreography by **Twyla Tharp**, followed in 1985, and *Dancers* in 1987. In 1990 he founded the White Oak Dance Project, a touring modern-dance company.

Baselitz, Georg, *originally* **Hans-Georg Kern** 1938– •*German avant-garde artist*• Born in Deutschbaselitz, Saxony, he studied art in East Berlin (1956–57) before moving to West Berlin in 1957. His violent subject matter and his "wild expressionist" style show affinities with **Edvard Munch** and **Oskar Kokoschka**. Although he often paints sets, such as the *Strassenbild* cycle (1979–80), with a shouting or gesticulating figure at a window repeated from canvas to canvas, his real forte is painting figures, trees, animals, and other objects, upside down.

Basho, Matsuo, *pseudonym of* **Matsuo Munefusa** 1644–94 •*Japanese poet*• He was born in Ueno. He took his pen name from the banana tree, after settling down in his hermitage near Tokyo. He was responsible for turning the 17-syllable haiku from a lighthearted diversion into a serious art form. After being apprenticed to a samurai, he led a wandering life, partly documented in his book of travels, *Oku no hosomichi* (1689, The Narrow Road to the Deep North," Eng trans by Nobuyuki Yuasa, 1966), written in a mixture of poetic prose and haiku. Basho's verse has a modern and almost existential quality, which influenced **Ezra Pound** and the imagists.

" "

An old pond
A frog jumps in
The sound of water

c. 1689 Quoted in Hugh Cortazzi, ***The Japanese Achievement*** *(1990).*

Basie, Count (William) 1904–84 •*US jazz pianist, organist and bandleader*• Born in Red Bank, New Jersey, he drifted away from his studies to take casual jobs as a musician and was given some coaching by **Fats Waller** in New York. In 1927 he reached Kansas City, then emerging as the center of a distinct style of orchestral jazz to which Basie was to remain true during his half-century as a bandleader. In 1929 began a five-year involvement as pianist and coarranger with the Bennie Moten band. When Moten died in 1935 the band was largely re-formed under Basie's leadership, at first being called the Barons of Rhythm, and including the important tenor saxophone stylist **Lester Young** as a featured soloist. A radio broadcast was heard by record producer John Hammond, who organized a major tour for the band, which led to recording and booking contracts. Now called the Count Basie Orchestra and established in New York, the band quickly achieved national fame and worked heavy touring schedules—as well as making film and television appearances—until 1950 when big bands appeared to be no longer viable. However after two years of leading an octet, Basie re-formed a 16-piece orchestra and continued to lead it until his death. During his 50-year career he employed some of the most eminent swing musicians. Among his most popular compositions are "One O'Clock Jump" and "Jumpin'" at the Woodside.

Basil I (the Macedonian) c.812–86 •*Byzantine emperor*• Born in Thrace, he rose in the imperial service from obscure origins to become coruler (866) with Michael III, whom he murdered in 867. He recovered parts of Calabria, developed the navy and revised **Justinian** I's law code. The dynasty he founded ruled Constantinople (Istanbul) until 1056.

Basil II (Bulgaroctonus) c. 958–1025 •*Byzantine emperor*• He came to the throne as sole ruler in 976. A revolt (989), involving the army and aristocracy, was quelled with the support of **Vladimir I**, who married Basil's sister Anna and converted to Christianity. Vladimir's Russian troops became the core of the future Varangian Guard, the élite unit of the Byzantine army. His 15-year war against the Bulgarians culminated in victory in the Belasica Mountains. Fourteen thousand prisoners were blinded and in groups of a hundred, each led by a one-eyed man, sent back to their czar, Samuel, who died of shock (1015). Bulgaria was annexed to the empire by 1018, while the eastern frontier was extended to Lake Van in Armenia. Austere and irascible, Basil II died unmarried, and left no leader to consolidate his work.

Basil the Great, St c. 329–79 AD •*Bishop of Caesarea and Doctor of the Church*• Born in Caesarea, Cappadocia, he studied at Byzantium and Athens. He lived for a time as a hermit, and in AD 370 succeeded **Eusebius of Caesarea** as bishop of his native city. Along with his brother, St **Gregory of Nyssa**, he defended Christian philosophy against Arianism. He is regarded as one of the greatest of the Greek Fathers. His feast day is January 1 or 2.

Basilides fl. c. 125 AD •*Syrian Gnostic philosopher*• He founded a sect in Alexandria, Egypt, and his esoteric doctrines seem to have blended Christian thought with elements from **Zoroaster**, Indian philosophy and magic. His disciples (Basilidians) were active in Egypt, Syria, Italy and even Gaul into the fourth century.

Basilius, John *See* **Bessarion, John**

Baskerville, John 1706–75 •*English printer*• Born at Sion Hill, Wolverley, Worcestershire, he began as a footman, became a writing master in Birmingham, and from 1740 carried on a successful japanning business there. Around 1750, following experiments in letter founding, he produced several types, one of which bears his name, and manufactured his own paper and ink. In 1758 he became printer to Cambridge University. Unaffected by superstition, he chose to be buried in his own garden, but his remains were exhumed.

Baskin, Leonard 1922–2000 •*US artist*• Born in New Brunswick, New Jersey, he studied the Talmud with the intent of becoming a rabbi but turned to sculpture and graphic art instead. His strongly molded figures and black-and-white engravings convey a concern for the vulnerability and mortality of humans and the threat of spiritual decay; he often used birds of prey to symbolize evil and death. He taught at Smith College (1953–73) and founded and operated the Gehenna Press, publishing illustrated books.

" "

Pop art is the inedible raised to the unspeakable.

1965 In ***Publisher's Weekly****, April 5.*

Basov, Nikolai Gennadevich 1922–2001 •*Russian physicist, inventor and Nobel Prize winner*• Born in Voronezh, he served in the Red Army during World War II, and became director (c. 1973–89) of the Lebedev Physics Institute, Moscow. His work provided the theoretical basis for the development of the maser (microwave amplification by stimulated emission of radiation) in 1955. In 1958 he proposed the use of semiconductors for the creation of lasers (light amplification by stimulated emission of radiation), subsequently successfully producing numerous types of these devices (1960–65). For his work on amplifiers and oscillators used to produce laser beams he was awarded the 1964 Nobel Prize for physics jointly with his colleague **Aleksandr Prokhorov** and the US physicist **Charles Townes**.

Bass, George 1771–1803/12 •*English naval surgeon*• He was born at Aswarby, Lincolnshire, and joined the navy. With **Matthew Flinders** he explored (1795–1800) the strait between Tasmania and Australia that bears his name. He died at sea either on the journey to South America or while mining there.

Bass, Michael Thomas 1799–1884 •*English brewer*• Born in Burton-on-Trent, Staffordshire, he joined the family business (founded by his grandfather, William Bass, in 1777), which he expanded considerably. He helped to improve the lot of workers both as employer and as Liberal Member of Parliament (1848–83). His son, Michael Arthur Bass (1837–1909), became Baron Burton in 1886.

Bassani, Giorgio 1916–2000 •*Italian novelist and poet*• Born in Bologna, he lived until 1943 in Ferrara, where much of his fiction is set. *Cinque storie ferraresi* ("Five Stories of Ferrara") appeared in 1956, most of them composed in the aftermath of World War II. A sensitive chronicler of Italian Jews and their suffering under Fascism, he was a realist who wrote elegiacally. One of the outstanding Italian novelists of the 20th century, he was at his most exquisite in *Gli occhiali d'oro* (1958, *The Gold-Rimmed Spectacles*, 1960) and *Il giardino dei Finzi-Contini* (1962, *The Garden of the Finzi-Continis*, 1965).

Bassano, Jacopo da, *properly* **Giacomo da Ponte** 1510–92 •*Venetian painter*• Born in Bassano, he is regarded as the founder of genre painting in Europe. His best paintings are of peasant life and biblical scenes, and include the altarpiece of the Nativity at Bassano, *Jacob's Return to Canaan* and *Portrait of a Gentleman*. His four sons also became painters, notably Francesco (1549–92) and Leandro (1557–1662), who, like their father, anticipated the Mannerist style.

Bassey, Dame Shirley 1937– •*Welsh singer*• Born in Tiger Bay, Cardiff, she began making records in the late 1950s, gaining popularity for her dramatic cabaret-style performances in songs such as *As I Love You* (1958), *Hey Big Spender* (1967) and the theme songs from the two James Bond films *Goldfinger* (1964) and *Diamonds Are Forever* (1971). In 1996 she appeared in the film *La passione*. Her many awards include 20 gold disks, and she was given the honorary title of Dame Commander, Order of the British Empire, in 2000.

Bastos, Augustos Roa *See* **Roa Bastos, Augusto**

Batchelor, Joy 1914–1991 •*English animated-cartoon producer*• Born in Watford, Hertfordshire, she became a fashion artist for *Harper's Bazaar* magazine. She tried animation with *Robin Hood* (1935), and in 1941 married fellow producer **John Halas**, and formed the Halas-Batchelor animation unit. In World War II they made propaganda films for the Ministry of Information, followed by the first British feature-length cartoon, *Handling Ships*, in 1945. Other films have included *The Owl and the Pussycat* (1952) and **George Orwell**'s *Animal Farm* (1954).

Bateman, Henry Mayo 1887–1970 •*Australian cartoonist*• Born in Sutton Forest, New South Wales, he lived in England from infancy. From 1906, influenced by the French cartoonist **Caran d'Ache**, he developed a purely visual style of comic strip for *Punch* and other periodicals. He is best known for a series of humorous drawings depicting embarrassing "The Man Who ... " situations such as *The Guardsman Who Dropped His Rifle*. He wrote *The Art of Drawing* (1926) and *Himself* (1937).

Bates, Alan, *originally* **Arthur Bates** 1934–2003 •*English actor*• He was born in Allestree, Derbyshire, and after national service in the RAF, he studied at the Royal Academy of Dramatic Art. Following his London stage debut in *The Mulberry Bush* (1956) he appeared in *Look Back in Anger* (1956), *Long Day's Journey into Night* (1958) and *The Caretaker* (1960). He was then seen in some of the most popular British films of the decade, including *A Kind of Loving* (1962), *Georgy Girl* (1966), *Far from the Madding Crowd* (1967) and *Women in Love* (1969). Other films include *The Fixer* (1968), *The Go-Between* (1971) and *Secret Friends* (1992). His television work includes the series *The Mayor of Casterbridge* (1978) and *An Englishman Abroad* (1982, British Academy of Film and Television Arts award). He was given the honorary title of Commander, Order of the British Empire, in 1995.

Bates, Daisy May, *née* **O'Dwyer** 1863–1951 •*Australian anthropologist*• Born in Tipperary, Ireland, she arrived in Australia in 1884, and the same year married Harry Morant(1865–1902). After a period in England as a London journalist she was commissioned by *The Times* to investigate the condition of Aboriginals. She returned to Australia in 1899, and from that time spent most of her life in the north and west of the country with remote tribes, by whom she was known as Kabbarli (grandmother). Her work included making detailed notes of Aboriginal life and customs, and working for Aboriginal welfare, setting up camps for the aged. She published an account of her life in 1938. In her 80s, she returned to live with a tribe in South Australia, but illness forced her return to Adelaide and her retirement in 1945.

Bates, H(erbert) E(rnest) 1905–74 •*English novelist, playwright, and short-story writer*• Born in Rushden, Northamptonshire, he began his working life as a solicitor's clerk, provincial journalist and warehouse clerk. His first play, *The Last Bread*, and his first novel, *The Two Sisters*, both appeared in 1926. He is one of the greatest exponents of the short-story form, and his essay of literary criticism, *The Modern Short Story*, is regarded as a classic. His best-known works are *Fair Stood the Wind for France* (1944), *The Jacaranda Tree* (1949) and *The Darling Buds of May* (1958).

Bates, Henry Walter 1825–92 •*English naturalist*• Born in Leicester, with his friend **Alfred Wallace** he left to explore the Amazon in 1848, and continued until 1859, when he returned with 14,700 specimens, including almost 8,000 species of insect new to science. In 1861 his *Contributions to an Insect Fauna of the Amazon Valley* described the phenomenon now known as Batesian mimicry, in which harmless, edible species of animals resemble others which are distasteful or poisonous, and thus gain protection from predators. This discovery provided strong evidence in support of natural selection.

Bateson, Gregory 1904–80 •*US anthropologist*• Born in Grantchester, Cambridgeshire, England, the son of geneticist William Bateson, he studied physical anthropology at Cambridge, but made his career in the US. His first major monograph, *Naven* (1936), based on fieldwork in New Guinea, was an innovative work introducing many themes that have since become central to the anthropological study of ritual and symbolism. With **Margaret Mead** he was involved with the culture-and-personality movement, publishing *Balinese Character* in 1942. The anthology *Steps to an Ecology of Mind* (1973) and his book *Mind and Nature* (1978) reflect the extraordinary range of his interests.

“ ”

Information is any difference that makes a difference.

1984 Quoted in ***Scientific American****, no. 41, September.*

Bathsheba born c. 970 BC •*Biblical character*• She was the daughter of Eliam and the wife of Uriah the Hittite, an army officer. After King **David** had committed adultery with Bathsheba, Uriah was sent to his death, in order to hide the king's crime, enabling him to take the beautiful Bathsheba for himself. Nathan the prophet forced David to condemn his own action, and prophesied the death of their first child. Their second child was **Solomon**, David's successor.

Batista y Zaldivar, Fulgencio 1901–73 •*Cuban dictator*• Born in Oriente province, a laborer's son, he rose from sergeant-major to colonel in the army coup against President Machado (1931–33) and himself became President (1940–44). In 1952 he overthrew President Prio, and, with himself as sole candidate, was reelected President (1954). He ruled as a ruthless, embezzling dictator until his overthrow by **Fidel Castro** in 1959, when he found refuge in the Dominican Republic.

Batman, John 1801–39 •*Australian pioneer*• Born in Rose Hill, New South Wales, he settled in Tasmania but in 1835 sailed to the mainland looking for grazing land. He explored the area where Melbourne now stands and said: “This will be the place for a village.” With **John Pascoe Fawkner** he is regarded as the founder of Melbourne.

Batten, Jean 1909–82 •*New Zealand pioneer aviator*• Born in Rotorua, she abandoned a possible career in music, went to England in 1929 and at 21 took her pilot's and ground engineer licenses. In 1934, in a Gypsy Moth, she broke **Amy Johnson**'s record for the flight from England to Australia by nearly five days. She became the first woman to complete the return journey and in 1935 flew over the South Atlantic Ocean to Argentina. Her autobiography was republished as *Alone in the Sky* in 1979.

Battenberg, Prince Alexander of 1857–93 •*First prince of Bulgaria*• Born in Verona, Austria (now in Italy), he was the second son of Prince Alexander of Hesse, and his morganatic wife, the Polish Countess von Hauke. He was also uncle of Louis, 1st Earl **Mountbatten**, and nephew of Czar **Alexander II** of Russia. He was elected prince of the new principality of Bulgaria (1879). In 1885 he annexed eastern Romania after an uprising there, provoking the hostility of Serbia, whose army he defeated in two weeks. In 1886 he was overpowered by pro-Russian army conspirators in his Sofia palace and forced to abdicate, retiring to Darmstadt in Austria.

Battenberg, Prince Henry of 1858–96 •*German prince*• The third son of Prince Alexander of Hesse, in 1885 he married Princess Beatrice (1857–1944), youngest daughter of Queen **Victoria**, and died at sea of fever caught in the Ashanti campaign.

Battenberg, Prince Louis Alexander *See* **Mountbatten**

Battutah, Ibn *See* **Ibn Battutah**

Baudelaire, Charles Pierre 1821–67 •*French Symbolist poet*• Born in Paris, he had an unhappy childhood quarreling with his stepfather, and was sent on a voyage to India. He stopped off at Mauritius, where Jeanne Duval became his mistress and inspiration. On his return to Paris in 1843 he spent much of his time in the studios of **Eugène Delacroix** and **Honoré Daumier**, and wrote art criticism. In 1847 he published an autobiographical novel, *La Fanfarlo*. His major work is an influential collection of poems, *Les fleurs du mal* (1857, Eng trans *Flowers of Evil*, 1909), for which author, printer and publisher were prosecuted for impropriety in 1864. He translated (1856–65) the works of **Thomas De Quincey** and **Edgar Allan Poe**. Having written a critical work on his literary associates **Honoré de Balzac**, Théophile Gautier and **Gérard de Nerval**, published posthumously in 1880, he took to drink and opium, became paralyzed, and died in poverty.

“ ”

Les parfums, les couleurs et les sons se répondent.

Scents, colors and sounds echo one another.

1857 ***Les fleurs du mal****, “Correspondances.”*

Baudouin I 1930–93 •*King of the Belgians*• Born near Brussels, the elder son of **Leopold III** and his first wife, Queen Astrid, he succeeded to the throne (1951) on the abdication of his father over the controversy of the latter's conduct during World War II. In 1960 he married the Spanish Doña Fabiola de Mora y Aragon. He was succeeded by his brother, Albert II (1934–).

Baugh, Sammy (Samuel Adrian) 1914– •*US football player*• He was born near Temple, Texas, and played college football for Texas Christian University. He signed with the Washington Redskins in 1937 and led his team to NFL championships in 1937 and 1942. His skill in passing earned him the nickname “Slingin' Sammy,” and he led the NFL in passing six times. His punting average of 51.4 yards a kick in 1940 remains a record.

Baum, L(yman) Frank 1856–1919 •*US writer*• Born in Chittenango, New York, he worked as a magazine editor until the publication and tremendous success of his second children's book, *The Wonderful Wizard of Oz* (1900), which was staged as a musical in 1901. (The classic movie version, starring **Judy Garland**, was made in 1939.) Baum traveled in Europe, then settled in California, where he continued to write stories about the land of Oz, a total of 14 books in all.

Baum, Vicki, *originally* **Vicki Hedvig** 1888–1960 •*US novelist*• She was born in Vienna, Austria, and studied music at the Vienna Conservatory. After writing several novels and short stories in German, she made her name with *Menschen im Hotel* (1930, Eng trans *Grand Hotel*), which became a best seller and a popular film. She emigrated to the US in 1931, where she published her later novels, including *Falling Star* (1934), *Headless Angel* (1948) and *The Mustard Seed* (1953). She was naturalized in 1938.

Bausch, Pina 1940– •*German dancer and choreographer*• Born in Solingen, West Germany (Germany), from 1955 she trained with **Kurt Jooss** in Essen, and then with **José Limón** and **Antony Tudor** in New York in 1959. After a season with the Metropolitan Opera Ballet Company (1960–61) and another with US choreographer **Paul Taylor**, she returned to Essen where she staged several operas for the Wuppertal Theater. Her success led to an invitation to found her own company. After staging **Stravinsky**'s *Le sacre du printemps*

(1975, *The Rite of Spring*) and **Brecht** and **Weill**'s *Seven Deadly Sins*, she began to produce her own work in the late 1970s. Her choreography and particularly her unusual stagings mark a turning point in contemporary dance and have remained a powerful influence.

Bawden, Nina 1925– •*English writer*• Born in London, she writes primarily on the domestic issues of the middle classes, such as friendships, marriages, divorces and family life. *Anna Apparent* (1972) is a study of an illegitimate child evacuee, while the middle-aged narrator of *Afternoon of a Good Woman* (1976) reflects on a life of disappointment and emotional betrayal before turning to face her future with renewed resilience. *The Ice House* (1983) casts a discriminating eye on a 30-year female friendship, with all its confidences and rivalries. She also writes children's books, including *Carrie's War* (1973). Her autobiography, *In My Own Time*, was published in 1994.

Bax, Sir Arnold Edward Trevor 1883–1953 •*English composer*• Born in London, he studied piano at the Royal Academy of Music there. A visit to Russia in 1910 inspired such piano pieces as *Gopak* (1911) and *In a Vodka Shop* (1915), but much more influential on Bax was the Celtic revival. He wrote several Irish short stories (under the name of Dermot O'Byrne), and composed orchestral pieces (1912–13), and many songs set to the words of revival poets. Between 1921 and 1939 he wrote seven symphonies, and his *Mater Ora Filium* (1921) is a highly accomplished English choral work. He was prolific in many other areas, encompassing tone poems, such as *In the Faery Hills* (1909), chamber music, piano solos and concertos, and in 1942 he was appointed Master of the King's Musick. He published an autobiography, *Farewell, My Youth* (1943). His brother Clifford (1886–1962) was a playwright and author.

“ ”

One should try everything once, except incest and folk-dancing.

1943 ***Farewell, My Youth***

Baxendale, Leo 1930– •*English cartoonist*• Born in Lancashire, he worked as a journalist and illustrator before freelancing strips to the *Beano* comic, beginning with *Little Plum* (1953) and *Minnie the Minx*. A large cartoon series, *When the Bell Rings* (1954), evolved into *The Bash Street Kids*, a riotous gang of juvenile delinquents. He designed the new weekly comic *Wham* (1964), and despite leaving the field in 1975 remains the most imitated artist in British comics. In later years, he has continued to draw strips for newspapers, has taken part in numerous exhibitions and has published books including the autobiographical *Pictures in the Mind* (2000).

Baxter, James Keir 1926–72 •*New Zealand poet, dramatist and critic*• Born in Dunedin, he led a bohemian life until he converted to Roman Catholicism. Subsequently he founded a religious community on the Wanganui River. He published more than 30 books of poetry, his first volume, *Beyond the Palisade* (1944), appearing when he was 18. The poems he wrote before his conversion are collected in *In Fires of No Return* (1958). Latterly he was less productive but his appointment to the Burns Fellowship at the University of Otago in 1966 inspired him to produce some of his best work. His *Collected Poems* (1979) was edited by J E Weir who, since Baxter's death, has produced editions of previously unpublished verse. His plays include *The Band Rotunda* (1967), *The Sore-Footed Man* (1967) and *The Temptation of Oedipus* (1967).

Baxter, Stanley 1926– •*Scottish comic actor*• Born in Glasgow, he made his professional debut as Correction's Varlet at the Edinburgh Festival production of *The Thrie Estates* in 1948. He made his television debut in *Shop Window* (1951) and his film debut in *Geordie* (1956), following with pictures such as *Crooks Anonymous* (1962) and *The Fast Lady* (1962). A proven favorite on the small screen, his many television series include *On the Bright Side* (1959), *Baxter On …* (1964) and *The Stanley Baxter Show* (1968–71). He subsequently created glittering comic extravaganzas such as *The Stanley Baxter Picture Show* (1972), *Stanley Baxter's Christmas Box* (1976) and *Stanley Baxter on Television* (1979).

Bayard, Pierre du Terrail, Chevalier de 1476–1524 •*French soldier*• Born in the Château Bayard, near Grenoble, he accompanied **Charles VIII** to Italy in 1494–95 and was knighted after the Battle of Fornovo. In the service of **Louis XII** he fought with legendary bravery at Milan (1501) and Barletta (1502), and campaigned in Spain and against the Genoese and Venetians, taking Brescia by storm in 1512. At Marignano he won a brilliant victory for **Francis I**, and when **Charles V** invaded Champagne with a large army in 1521, Bayard defended Mézières, saving France from invasion. While fighting in Italy, he was mortally wounded and died facing the foe, reciting the *Miserere*. He was known as *le Chevalier sans peur et sans reproche* ("the knight without fear and without reproach").

Bayer, Johann 1572–1625 •*German astronomer and celestial mapmaker*• Born in Rhain, Bavaria, he was by profession a lawyer, but had a keen interest in astronomy. He published a celestial atlas, *Uranometria* (1603), in which the positions of nearly 1,000 stars are depicted in addition to a similar number recorded in **Tycho Brahe**'s famous catalog. Bayer added 12 new constellations to the 48 defined by Ptolemy in the second century; this part of the atlas incorporated observations of the Dutch navigator Petrus Theodori (d. 1596). Bayer also introduced the mode of designating stars in each constellation in order of magnitude by letters of the Greek alphabet, a system which remains in use for stars visible with the naked eye.

Bayes, Thomas 1702–61 •*English mathematician*• He was born in London, and in 1731 became Presbyterian minister in Tunbridge Wells. He is principally remembered for his posthumously published *Essay Toward Solving a Problem in the Doctrine of Chances* (1763), in which he was the first to study the idea of statistical inference, and to estimate the probability of an event from the frequency of its previous occurrences.

Bayezit I, *also spelled* **Bayezid** or **Bajazet** c. 1360–c. 1403 •*Sultan of the Ottoman Empire*• In 1389 he succeeded his father, Murat I, and swiftly conquered Bulgaria, parts of Serbia, Macedonia and Thessaly, and most of Asia Minor, earning him the name of Yildirim ("Thunderbolt"). For ten years he blockaded Constantinople (Istanbul), and inflicted a crushing defeat on King **Sigismund** of Hungary at Nicopolis, on the Danube (1396). Bayezit would have entirely destroyed the Greek Empire if he had not in turn been completely defeated by **Timur** near Ankara in 1402. Bayezit himself fell into the hands of the conqueror, who treated him with great generosity (his incarceration in an iron cage being a myth), and in whose camp he died. He was succeeded by his son Süleyman.

Bayezit II 1448–1512 •*Sultan of the Ottoman Empire*• Born in Thrace, he succeeded his father, **Mehmet II**, the conqueror of Constantinople (Istanbul), in 1481. During his reign a succession of wars against Hungary, Poland, Venice, Egypt and Persia (Iran) served, on the whole, to establish Ottoman power in the Balkans, Asia Minor and the eastern Mediterranean.

Bayle, Pierre 1647–1706 •*French Protestant philosopher and critic*• Born in Carlat, Languedoc, he studied under the Jesuits at Toulouse. Forced into exile for his Calvinist beliefs, he became a professor at the University of Rotterdam (1681), and he started a popular journal of literary criticism, *Nouvelles de la république des lettres* (1684, "News from the Republic of Letters"). He wrote a strong defense of liberalism and religious toleration, but was dismissed from the university in 1693 and attacked by the theologian Jurieu as an agent of France and an enemy of Protestantism. He then concentrated on his major work, the encyclopedic *Dictionnaire historique et critique* (1697, "Historical and Critical Dictionary"). He was further persecuted for the work's alleged profanity, and for the claim in it that morality was independent of religion, but his writings later influenced **Voltaire** and others.

Baylis, Lilian Mary 1874–1937 •*English theatrical manager*• She was born in London, the daughter of musicians. In 1898, she helped with the management of the Royal Victoria Hall (the Old Vic), becoming sole manager in 1912 and establishing its reputation for Shakespearean theater. In 1931 she reopened Sadler's Wells Theatre for the exclusive presentation of opera and ballet, founding the companies that were to become the English National Opera and the Royal Ballet.

Bayliss, Sir William Maddock 1860–1924 •*English physiologist*• Born in Wednesbury, West Midlands, he studied science at

University College London (UCL), where he remained for most of his career, from 1912 as Professor of General Physiology. Much of his research was conducted in collaboration with **Ernest Starling**. In studies of pancreatic secretion they showed that the discharge is induced by a chemical substance that they called secretin, the first known hormone. His celebrated book *Principles of General Physiology* first appeared in 1914 and is considered a classic. In 1903 he took out an action for libel against the secretary of the National Antivivisection Society, who had accused Bayliss of carrying out experiments on unanesthetized animals, and he donated the damages he won to the furtherance of research in physiology. He was elected a Fellow of the Royal Society in 1903, and knighted in 1922.

Baylor, Elgin 1934– •*US basketball player*• Born in Washington DC, he studied at Seattle University. He signed with the Minneapolis (later Los Angeles) Lakers in 1958, and stayed with the team until forced out by injury in 1971. In his 14 NBA seasons, he scored 23,149 points, averaging 27.4 per game, making him the highest-scoring forward in the game and third-highest player ever behind **Michael Jordan** and **Wilt Chamberlain**.

Bazalgette, Sir Joseph William 1819–91 •*English engineer*• Born in Enfield, Middlesex, he constructed London's drainage system and the Thames embankment, and was a notable pioneer of public health engineering.

Bazán, Emilia Pardo *See* **Pardo Bazán, Emilia**

Baziotes, William 1912–63 •*US painter*• Born in Pittsburgh, Pennsylvania, he studied at the National Academy of Design in New York from 1933 to 1936. His early work was influenced by **Picasso**, but in the 1940s he was one of a number of US painters, including **Jackson Pollock**, **Arshile Gorky** and **Robert Motherwell**, whose art developed from European surrealism. His dreamlike images often contain suggestions of animal forms.

Beach, Frank Ambrose 1911–88 •*US comparative psychologist and endocrinologist*• Born in Emporia, Kansas, he studied at Kansas State University, the University of Chicago, and Harvard University. He worked at the American Museum of Natural History in New York in its Department of Experimental Biology, which under his direction became the Department of Animal Behavior (1936–46), and he subsequently became Professor of Psychology first at Yale (1946–58) and then at the University of California at Berkeley (1958–78). One of the first US biologists to appreciate the work of European ethologists, in his research he has been concerned with the hormonal regulation of reproductive behavior. He developed the concept of "gender role" to account for aspects of human sexuality, and wrote *Hormones and Behavior* (1948) and *Sex and Behavior* (1965).

Beach, Moses Yale 1800–68 •*US journalist and inventor*• Born in Wallingford, Connecticut, he experimented with engines and invented, but failed to patent, a rag-cutting machine widely used in paper mills. After beginning his career in journalism with the *New York Sun* in 1834, he bought the newspaper in 1838, and it flourished under his editorship. Preoccupied with speed, he introduced ingenious ways to get news (such as having boats meet ships from Europe, using carrier pigeons, and using pony express riders). He also originated syndicated news stories and established the first European edition of a US paper (*American Sun*, 1848).

Beach Boys, The *See* **Wilson, Brian**

Beadle, George Wells 1903–89 •*US biochemical geneticist and Nobel Prize winner*• Born in Wahoo, Nebraska, he became interested in agricultural genetics, studying the genetics of maize, the fruit fly (*Drosophila*) and the bread mold *Neurospora*. At Stanford University (1937–46), in association with **Edward Tatum**, he developed the idea that specific genes control the production of specific enzymes. Beadle and Tatum shared the Nobel Prize for physiology or medicine in 1958 with **Joshua Lederberg**.

Beale, Dorothea 1831–1906 •*English pioneer of women's education*• Born in London, she was educated at Queen's College, London, and taught there from 1849. In 1857 she was appointed head teacher of Clergy Daughters' School in Westmoreland, and from 1858 to 1906 was principal of Cheltenham Ladies' College. In 1885 she founded St Hilda's College, Cheltenham, the first English training college for women teachers, and sponsored St Hilda's Hall in Oxford for women teachers in 1893. An ardent suffragette, she was immortalized in verse with **Frances Mary Buss**: "Miss Buss and Miss Beale, Cupid's darts do not feel."

Beale, Lionel Smith 1828–1906 •*English physiologist and microscopist*• He was born in London and entered King's College London to study medicine. A master of the techniques of vital staining and a fine investigator of cellular tissue, "Beale's cells" (the pyriform nerve ganglion cells) commemorate his researches. He attracted greatest notice, however, for his opposition to the theories of **T H Huxley** and **Charles Darwin**.

Beals, Jessie Tarbox, *née* **Tarbox** 1870–1942 •*US photographer*• Born in Hamilton, Canada, and a daughter of the inventor Nathaniel Tarbox, she became a teacher in Massachusetts in 1887, carrying out portrait photography in the summers of the 1890s. She married machinist Alfred T Beals in 1897, and after she had taught him photography, they became itinerant photographers (1900). She became a journalist in upstate New York (1902) and then established a studio in New York City (1905). In 1910–12 she made documentary photographs of children in the New York slums. In 1928–29 she visited Southern California, photographing mainly celebrities and gardens. She is considered to be among the very first women press photographers.

Beamon, Bob (Robert) 1946– •*US athlete*• Born in New York City, he became a noted long jumper. He smashed the world record at the 1968 Olympic Games in Mexico City, with a jump of 8.90 meters (29 feet 2.5 inches)—55 centimeters (21.5 inches) farther than the previous record. The high altitude increased the difficulty of the jump and made the achievement all the more impressive. The record stood until 1991, when it was broken by Mike Powell in Tokyo.

Bean, Roy c.1825–1903 •*US frontiersman*• Born in Mason County, Kentucky, he served with Confederate irregulars in New Mexico during the Civil War and was a blockade runner in San Antonio, Texas. In 1882 he moved to the sparsely populated region west of the Pecos River and opened a saloon. Doubling as a justice of the peace, he styled himself the "law west of the Pecos" and presided over a barroom court, often interrupting the proceedings to serve liquor. His arbitrary and sometimes bigoted rulings made him a legend in a state that admired the unconventional. After falling in love with a picture of the British actress **Lillie Langtry**, he named his Texas settlement for her.

Beard, James 1903–85 •*US chef*• He was born in Portland, Oregon. An influential teacher of cooking, he wrote numerous cookbooks on American cuisine, including *The James Beard Cookbook* (1959), *American Cookery* (1972), and *Beard on Bread* (1973), as well as an autobiography of his early years, *Delights and Prejudices* (1964).

Beard, Mary Ritter 1876–1958 •*US feminist and historian*• She was born in Indianapolis, Indiana, and educated at DePauw University. In 1900 she married Charles Austin Beard and became involved in women's suffrage, first in Oxford, England, where her husband was a student, then in New York (from 1902) where they both enrolled at Columbia University. After the birth of her son (1907) she joined the National Women's Trade Union League, helping to run strikes and protests. She worked assiduously (1913–17) for the Congressional Union (later the National Women's Party) under **Alice Paul**'s leadership, but gradually became more interested in teaching and writing. Her publications include *Woman's Work in Municipalities* (1915), *On Understanding Women* (1931) and, most famously, *Women as a Force in History* (1946). With her husband she wrote several influential works on American history.

Bearden, Romare 1914–88 •*US artist*• He was born in Charlotte, North Carolina, and raised in Harlem, New York City. A painter whose vibrant works express the theme of the experience of African Americans in the US, he is represented in numerous US museums. In the 1960s he was a founder of the Cinque Gallery, for young artists, and the Spiral Group to aid African-American artists.

Beardsley, Aubrey Vincent 1872–98 •*English illustrator*• Born in Brighton, Sussex, he worked in architectural and fire insurance offices. He became famous by his fantastic posters and illustrations for *Morte d'Arthur*, **Oscar Wilde**'s *Salomé*, **Pope**'s *Rape of the Lock*, *Mlle de Maupin*, *Volpone*, as well as for the *Yellow Book* magazine (1894–96) and his own *Book of Fifty Drawings*, mostly executed in black and white, in a highly individualistic asymmetrical style. With Wilde he is regarded as leader of the Decadents of the 1890s. He died of tuberculosis at Menton, having become a Roman Catholic.

The Beatles •*English pop band*• The Beatles became the best-known group in popular music in the 1960s. They formed in Liverpool in 1960; three of the founder-members, **John Lennon**, **Paul McCartney** and **George Harrison**, were later joined by Ringo Starr (originally Richard Starkey, 1940–), who replaced the original drummer, Pete Best, before their breakthrough. The group learned their trade through grueling engagements at the city's Cavern Club and at venues in Hamburg, West Germany. Under the management of Brian Epstein, a local record-shop owner, they signed a recording contract in 1962 and their regional popularity quickly spread across the country with such records as "Love Me Do," "She Loves You" and "I Want to Hold Your Hand." In 1964 the last two titles were released in the US, and "Beatlemania" spread rapidly around the world, with the group consistently surpassing all previous figures for concert attendances and record sales. As teen idols, they provoked hysteria wherever they played in the first half of the decade, then became the first mature rock icons in the second. Their music ranged from the lyrically beautiful "Yesterday" to the complex rhythms of "Paperback Writer," the nostalgia of "Penny Lane," and the surrealism of "Strawberry Fields Forever." In 1967 they released *Sergeant Pepper's Lonely Hearts Club Band*, an album which, with its long musically and thematically linked songs, achieved a new maturity for pop and became perhaps the most influential recording since the advent of **Elvis Presley**. The group dissolved in 1970 amid complex legal wranglings. Paul McCartney went on to record alone and with Wings. John Lennon wrote and recorded in the US with his wife, **Yoko Ono**, and was murdered in New York (1980), and George Harrison made further recordings and became a successful film producer. Other major recordings of the Beatles include *Please Please Me* (1963), *Rubber Soul* (1965), *Revolver* (1966), *The Beatles* (1968, also known as *The White Album*), *Abbey Road* (1969) and *Let It Be* (1970). They also made the films *A Hard Day's Night* (1964), *Help!* (1965) and *Magical Mystery Tour* (1967).

Beaton, Sir Cecil Walter Hardy 1904–80 •*English photographer and designer*• He was born in London, and educated at Harrow and Cambridge. In the 1920s, as a staff photographer for *Vanity Fair* and *Vogue*, he became famous for his society portraits, including those of royalty. After World War II, he designed scenery and costumes for many ballet, operatic, theatrical and film productions, including *My Fair Lady* (1964) and *Gigi* (1958). His publications include *The Book of Beauty* (1930), *The Glass of Fashion* (1959) and *The Magic Image* (1975). He also wrote several volumes of autobiography (1961–78).

Beaton or **Bethune, David** 1494–1546 •*Scottish statesman and Roman Catholic prelate*• Born in Balfour, Fife, he was educated at St Andrews, Glasgow, and Paris universities. In 1525 he took his seat in the Scots parliament as abbot of Arbroath and became Privy Seal. Elevated to cardinal (1538), he was made Archbishop of St Andrews in 1539. On **James V**'s death, he produced a forged will, appointing himself and three others regents of the kingdom during the minority of the infant **Mary Queen of Scots**. The nobility, however, elected the Protestant **James Hamilton**, 2nd Earl of Arran, regent. Beaton was arrested, but soon regained favor and was made Chancellor (1543). A persecutor of the Scottish Protestants, he had the reformer **George Wishart** burned at St Andrews (1546), but was murdered in revenge three months later by a group of Protestant conspirators. He was the nephew of **James Beaton**.

Beaton or **Bethune, James** 1470–1539 •*Scottish prelate and statesman*• He graduated from St Andrews in 1493, and rose rapidly to be Archbishop of Glasgow (1509), and of St Andrews (1522). One of the regents during **James V**'s minority, Beaton upheld the **Hamilton** against the **Douglas** faction, and in 1526 had "to keep sheep in Balgrumo," while the Douglases plundered his castle. He was soon, however, reinstated in his see. He was an opponent of the Reformation, and he initiated the persecution of Protestants: **Patrick Hamilton** and three other Protestants were burned at the stake during his primacy. He was the uncle of Cardinal **David Beaton**.

Beatrix, *in full* **Beatrix Wilhelmina Armgard** 1938– •*Queen of the Netherlands*• Born in Soestdk, the eldest daughter of Queen **Juliana** and Prince **Bernhard Leopold**, she married (1966) a West German diplomat, Claus-Georg von Amsberg (1926–2002). Their son, Prince Willem-Alexander (1967–) is the first male heir to the Dutch throne in over a century; their other sons are Johan Friso (1968–) and Constantijn (1969–). She acceded to the throne on her mother's abdication in 1980.

Beatty, David Beatty, 1st Earl 1871–1936 •*English naval commander*• Born in Nantwich, Cheshire, he joined the navy in 1884 and served in the Sudan (1896–98). As commander of a battleship he took part in the China War (1900) and in 1912 was appointed to command the 1st Battle Cruiser Squadron. In January 1915 he pursued German battle cruisers near the Dogger Bank, sinking the *Blücher*, and took part in the Battle of Jutland (1916). He succeeded Lord **Jellicoe** as Commander in Chief of the Grand Fleet in 1916 and became First Sea Lord in 1919.

Beatty, Warren, *originally* **Warren Beaty** 1937– •*US film actor, director and producer*• Born in Richmond, Virginia, the brother of actress **Shirley MacLaine**. His film debut was in *Splendor in the Grass* (1961). He appeared as a broodingly handsome leading man in several comedies as well as portraying more complex combinations of naivety and cynicism in films like *Lilith* (1964) and *Mickey One* (1965). He acted in and produced *Bonnie and Clyde* (1967), cowrote *Shampoo* (1975) and codirected *Heaven Can Wait* (1978), and was the producer, cowriter and star of *Reds* (1981), which won him an Academy Award as Best Director. His enduring Casanova image has often detracted from his many political interests and consistent efforts to expand the scope of his talents. In 1992 he married the actress Annette Bening (1958–). He subsequently made *Bulworth* (1997).

Beau Brummell *See* **Brummell, George Bryan**

Beaufort, Sir Francis 1774–1857 •*British naval officer and hydrographer*• Born in Navan, County Meath, Ireland, he joined the Royal Navy in 1787, fought in the retreat of Cornwallis (1795), and was severely wounded near Málaga. After a period working on shore telegraphs in Ireland he held three commands, and was seriously wounded while surveying the coast of Asia Minor and suppressing piracy. From 1829 to 1855 he was hydrographer to the navy, devising the Beaufort scale of wind force. He was promoted to rear admiral in 1846.

Beaufort, Henry 1377–1447 •*English cardinal and politician*• He studied at Oxford and Aix-la-Chapelle, was consecrated Bishop of Lincoln (1398) and Winchester (1405), and became a cardinal in 1426. He was Lord Chancellor on three occasions (1403–05, 1413–17, 1424–26). He strongly opposed **Henry V**'s proposition to levy a new impost on the clergy for the war against France, but he lent the King (1416–21), out of his own private purse, £28,000—a sum which justifies the belief that he was the wealthiest subject in England. During the 1430s he controlled the government of the young King **Henry VI** of England.

Beaufort, Lady Margaret, Countess of Richmond 1443–1509 •*English noblewoman*• The daughter of John Beaufort, 1st Duke of Somerset, she married Edmund Tudor, Earl of Richmond in 1455. The Lancastrian claim to the English Crown was transferred to her when the male line died out, and it was because of her descent from **John of Gaunt** that her son Henry (**Henry VII**) ascended the throne after the defeat of **Richard III** (1485). During the Wars of the Roses she was imprisoned at Pembroke by the Yorkists. She was a benefactress of Oxford and Cambridge Universities, where she endowed two divinity professorships. She also founded Christ's College and St John's College, Cambridge, and was a patron of **William Caxton**. She translated Thomas à Kempis into English.

Beaumarchais, Pierre Augustin Caron de 1732–99 •*French playwright*• Born in Paris, the son of a watchmaker, he was brought up in his father's trade, and invented, at 21, a new escapement that was pirated by a rival. The affair brought him to notice at court, where his good looks and fine speech and manners quickly procured him advancement. He was engaged to teach the harp to **Louis XV**'s daughters, and made a fortune through two judicious marriages and profitable speculation. He made his reputation with *Mémoires du Sieur Beaumarchais par lui-même* (1774–78, "Autobiography"), a work which united the bitterest satire with the sharpest logic. The same brilliant satire burns in his two famous comedies, *Le barbier de Séville* (1775, Eng trans *The Barber of Seville*, 1776) and *La folle journée ou le mariage de Figaro* (1784, Eng trans *The Follies of a Day; or, The Marriage of Figaro*, 1785). The Revolution cost Beaumarchais his vast fortune, and, suspected of an attempt to sell arms to the émigrés, he had to take refuge in Holland and England (1793).

“ ”

Je me presse de rire de tout, de peur d'être obligé d'en pleurer.
I am quick to laugh at everything so as not to be obliged to cry.
*1775 **Le Barbier de Séville**, act 1, scene 2.*

Beaumont, Francis c.1584–1616 •*English Elizabethan dramatist*• Born in Gracedieu, Leicestershire, he was educated at Broadgates Hall (now Pembroke College), Oxford, and entered the Inner Temple in 1600. He soon became a friend of **Ben Jonson** and **John Fletcher**. With the latter, Beaumont was to be associated closely until he married Ursula Isley (1613) and retired from the theater. He and Fletcher are said to have shared everything: work, lodgings, and even clothes. Their dramatic works, compiled in 1647, contained 35 pieces, and another folio, published in 1679, 52 works. Modern research finds Beaumont's hand in only about 10 plays, which include, however, the masterpieces. *The Woman Hater* (1607) is attributed solely to Beaumont, and he had the major share in *The Knight of the Burning Pestle* (1609), a burlesque of knight errantry and a parody of **Thomas Heywood**'s *Four Prentices of London*. *Philaster* (1610), *The Maid's Tragedy* (1611) and *A King and No King* (1611) established their joint popularity.

Beau Nash *See* **Nash, Richard**

Beauvoir, Simone de 1908–86 •*French socialist, feminist and writer*• Born in Paris, she was educated at the Sorbonne, where she later lectured. She will probably be remembered chiefly for the enormous impact made by *Le Deuxième sexe* (1949, Eng trans *The Second Sex*, 1953), a study of women's social situation and historical predicament; it was one of the first feminist tracts which, despite its alleged shortcomings, remains authoritative for its intelligence and the forcefulness of the case it presents. It inspired many women to salutary writings and actions and led several to refer to its author as "the mother of us all." She was also a notable novelist and autobiographer. The lifelong companion of **Jean-Paul Sartre**, with him she contributed to the existentialist movement of the mid-20th century. Her more autobiographical writings and novels include *Les Mandarins* (1954), a winner of the Prix Goncourt; *Mémoires d'une jeune fille rangée* (1958, Eng trans *Memoirs of a Dutiful Daughter*, 1959); *La force de l'âge* (1960, Eng trans *The Prime of Life*, 1963); *Une mort très douce* (1964, Eng trans *A Very Easy Death*, 1972); *Toute compte fait* (1972, Eng trans *All Said and Done*, 1974); and *La cérémonie des adieux* (1981, Eng trans *Adieux: A Farewell to Sartre*).

Beaverbrook, Max (William Maxwell Aitken), 1st Baron 1879–1964 •*British newspaper magnate and politician*• Born in Maple, Ontario, Canada, he was educated in Newcastle, New Brunswick. By 1910 he had made a fortune out of the amalgamation of Canadian cement mills. He went to Great Britain in 1910, entered Parliament (1911–16), and became private secretary to **Bonar Law**. He was an observer at the Western Front early in World War I and wrote *Canada in Flanders* (1917). When **Lloyd George** became premier, he was made Minister of Information (1918). In 1919 he plunged into journalism and took Fleet Street by storm by taking over the *Daily Express* and making it into the most widely read daily newspaper in the world. He founded the *Sunday Express* (1921) and bought the *Evening Standard* (1929). The "Beaverbrook press" fully expressed the ebullient, relentless, and crusading personality of its owner. In World War II **Churchill** successfully harnessed Beaverbrook's dynamic administrative powers for the production of much-needed aircraft. He was made Minister of Supply (1941–42), Lord Privy Seal, and lend-lease administrator in the US. He became Chancellor of the University of New Brunswick in 1947. He wrote *Politicians and the Press* (1925), *Men and Power* (new edn 1956), and *The Decline and Fall of Lloyd George* (1963).

Beccafumi, Domenico, *originally* **di Pace** c.1486–1551 •*Italian painter*• Born in Siena, he was influenced by High Renaissance artists such as **Michelangelo** and **Raphael** without forsaking the traditionally Sienese qualities of decorative color and sinuous line. His paintings are characterized by unusual perspective, complicated figure poses and complex color effects, and are considered an early manifestation of the post-Renaissance style known as Mannerism. Much of his best work remains in the Pinacoteca, Siena.

Bechet, Sidney Joseph 1897–1959 •*US jazz musician*• Born in New Orleans, he was already an outstanding jazz clarinettist as a teenager. He took up the soprano saxophone in 1919, his forceful style making him the first significant saxophone voice in jazz. As the New Orleans style declined in popularity, Bechet spent much of the 1930s in obscurity, emerging in 1940 as a figurehead of the traditional jazz revival. The warmth of his reception during many tours in Europe led him to make his permanent home in Paris.

Bechstein, Karl 1826–1900 •*German manufacturer*• He was born in Gotha. In 1856 he founded his famous piano factory in Berlin. His grand pianos were of a very high standard, and were produced in large quantities.

Beckenbauer, Franz 1945– •*German soccer player*• Born in Munich, he captained the West German national team to European Nations Cup success in 1972 and to the World Cup triumph of 1974, and won three successive European Cup winner's medals with Bayern Munich (1974–76). His masterful style earned him the nickname "the Kaiser," while his tactical innovations changed both the role of sweeper and the game itself. He retired from playing in 1983, and from 1984 to 1990 was manager of the West German national team, coaching them to consecutive World Cup finals as runners-up in 1986 and then (with a united German team) as winners in 1990. He thus became the first man to win the World Cup both as player and manager. He became President of Bayern Munich in 1994, and led Germany's successful bid to host the 2006 World Cup.

Becker, Boris 1967– •*German tennis player*• Born in Leimen, he first came to prominence in 1984 when he finished as runner-up in the US Open. In 1985 he became the youngest-ever winner of the men's singles at Wimbledon, as well as the first unseeded winner. He successfully defended his title in 1986, won it for a third time in 1989, and was a beaten finalist in 1988, 1990, 1991 and 1995. He also won the US Open in 1989, the Australian Open in 1991 and 1996 and the Grand Slam Cup in 1996. In 1991 he was named the world number one player.

Becket, Thomas (à) 1118–70 •*English saint and martyr, Archbishop of Canterbury*• He was born in London, the son of a wealthy Norman merchant. Educated at Merton Priory and in London, he trained in knightly exercises at Pevensey Castle, studied theology in Paris, and became a notary. About 1142 he entered the household of **Theobald**, Archbishop of Canterbury, who sent him to study canon law at Bologna and Auxerre. In 1155 he became Chancellor, the first Englishman since the Norman Conquest who had filled any high office. A brilliant figure at court, he showed his knightly prowess in the Toulouse campaign (1159) and was also a skilled diplomat. He changed dramatically when he was created Archbishop of Canterbury in 1162. He resigned the chancellorship, turned a rigid ascetic, showed his liberality only in charities, and became a zealous servant of the Church. He soon championed its rights against the king and had courtiers, several nobles and other laymen excommunicated for their alienation of Church property. **Henry II**, who, like all the Norman kings, endeavored to keep the clergy in subordination to the state, in 1164 convoked the Council of Clarendon, which adopted the so-called Constitutions, or laws relating to the respective powers of Church and State. Initially Becket refused to consent, but afterward was induced to give his unwilling approval. Henry now began to perceive that Becket's notions and his own were utterly antagonistic, and exhibited his hostility to Becket, who tried to leave the country. For this offense Henry confiscated his goods, and sequestered the revenues of his see. Becket escaped to France, spending two years at the Cistercian abbey of Pontigny in Burgundy, then went to Rome and pleaded personally before the pope. In 1170 an agreement was reached and Becket returned to England, entering Canterbury amid the rejoicings of the people, who regarded him as a shield from the oppressions of the nobility. Fresh quarrels soon broke out however and Henry's impetuously voiced wish to be rid of "this turbulent priest" led to Becket's murder in Canterbury cathedral in 1170, by four knights, Hugh de Merville, William de Tracy, Reginald Fitzurse, and Richard le Breton. Becket's martyrdom forced confessions from the king; he was canonized in 1173 and Henry did public penance at his tomb in 1174. In 1220 his bones were transferred to a shrine in the Trinity chapel, until it was destroyed during the Reformation in 1538. It was the place of pilgrimage described by **Chaucer** in the Prologue to the *Canterbury Tales*. His feast day is December 29.

Beckett, Gilbert Abbott À *See* **À Beckett, Gilbert Abbott**

Beckett, Margaret Mary, *née* **Jackson** 1943– •*English Labour politician*• Born in Ashton-under-Lyne, she trained as an engineer at Manchester College of Science and Technology, and worked as a metallurgist before entering Parliament as Labour Member of Parliament of Lincoln (1974–79). In 1979 she joined Granada Television as chief researcher until 1983, when she was elected Member of Parliament for Derby South. A fiercely pragmatic politician, she rose to the deputy leadership by 1992. After the sudden death of Labour leader **John Smith** (1994), she was acting Leader for a few months until **Tony Blair** took over and she was given the shadow health portfolio again. She was shadow front bench spokesperson for trade and industry (1995–97), and after Labour's landslide win in the 1997 general election, entered the Cabinet as President of the Board of Trade and Secretary of State for Trade and Industry. In 1998 she became President of the Privy Council and Leader of the House of Commons, and was appointed Secretary of State for the Environment, Food and Rural Affairs in 2001.

Beckett, Samuel Barclay 1906–89 •*Irish writer, playwright and Nobel Prize winner*• Born in Dublin and educated at Portora Royal School, Enniskillen, and Trinity College, Dublin, he became a lecturer in English at the École Normale Supérieure in Paris and later in French at Trinity College, Dublin. From 1932 he lived mostly in France and was, for a time, secretary to **James Joyce**. His early poetry and first two novels, *Murphy* (1938) and *Watt* (1953), were written in English, but many subsequent works first appeared in French: the trilogy *Molloy, Malone Meurt* and *L'innommable* (translated in 1955, 1956 and 1958), and the plays *En attendant Godot* (1955, Eng trans *Waiting for Godot*, 1956), which took London by storm, and *Fin de partie* (1957, Eng trans *End Game*, 1958), for example. *Godot* best exemplifies the Beckettian view of the human predicament, the poignant bankruptcy of all hopes, philosophies, and endeavors. His later works include *Happy Days* (1961), *Not I* (1973) and *Ill Seen Ill Said* (1981). He was awarded the 1969 Nobel Prize for literature. Although there were one or two increasingly short pieces in later years—*Breath* (1970) shows a heap of rubbish on the stage and has a soundtrack which consists of a single breath—he wrote very infrequently toward the end of his life.

“ ”

VLADIMIR: That passed the time.
ESTRAGON: It would have passed in any case.
VLADIMIR: Yes, but not so rapidly.

*1955 **Waiting for Godot**, act 1.*

Beckford, William Thomas 1759–1844 •*English writer and art collector*• He was born in Fonthill, Wiltshire, and at 16 revealed remarkable intellectual precocity in his satirical *Memoirs of Extraordinary Painters*. From 1777 he spent much time on the Continent, meeting **Voltaire** in 1778. He wrote, in French, *Vathek*, an Arabian tale of gloomy imaginative splendor modeled on Voltaire's style, which was published in France in 1787 and in an unauthorized English version in 1786. After spending three years in Portugal (1793–96) he returned to England and erected Fonthill Abbey, designed by James Wyatt (1746–1813). Its chief feature was a tower, 276 ft (83.6 m) high, in which Beckford lived in mysterious seclusion until 1822. In 1834 he published *Italy, with Sketches of Spain and Portugal*, and in 1835 another volume of *Recollections* of travel.

Beckham, David Robert Joseph 1975– •*English soccer player*• Born in Leytonstone, London, he joined Manchester United as a trainee in 1991 and made his full team debut with the club in 1995. He first turned out for England in 1996, but incurred the hostility of the press when he was sent off for kicking an opponent during England's ill-fated 1998 World Cup campaign. He gradually clawed his way back into favor, however, and in 2000 was appointed captain of the national team. A midfielder admired for his attacking skills and ability to score from free kicks, he became the most famous British soccer player of his generation and a popular icon, a reputation boosted by his photogenic good looks and marriage (1999) to pop star Victoria Beckham (1974–), formerly of The Spice Girls.

Beckmann, Max 1884–1950 •*German painter, draftsman and printmaker*• Born in Leipzig, he moved to Berlin in 1904, where he began painting large-scale, dramatic works. The suffering he experienced as a hospital orderly in World War I led him to develop a highly individual, distorted, expressive style influenced by Gothic art. A series of self-portraits reflects the anguish caused by contemporary events, and nine monumental triptychs painted between 1932 and his death form a similar moral commentary. On learning that his work was to be included in an exhibition of Degenerate Art to be mounted by the Nazis in 1937, he fled to Holland, where he lived until finally emigrating to the US in 1947. He taught at various US universities until his death.

Becquerel, Antoine Henri 1852–1908 •*French physicist and Nobel Prize winner*• Born in Paris, he studied at the École Polytechnique and the School of Bridges and Highways, and later succeeded his father **Alexandre-Edmond Becquerel** to the chair of physics at the Natural History Museum. He was an expert in fluorescence and phosphorescence, continuing the work of his father and grandfather. During his study of fluorescent uranium salt, pitchblende, he accidentally left a sample that had not been exposed to light on top of a photographic plate, and noticed later that the plate had a faint image of the pitchblende. He concluded that these "Becquerel rays" were a property of atoms, thus discovering radioactivity and prompting the beginning of the nuclear age. His work led to the discovery of radium by **Marie** and **Pierre Curie** and he subsequently shared with them the 1903 Nobel Prize for physics.

Bede or **Baeda, St**, *also called* **the Venerable Bede** c. 673–735 •*Anglo-Saxon scholar, theologian and historian*• Born near Monkwearmouth, Durham, in 682 he moved to the new monastery of Jarrow, Tyne and Wear, where he was ordained priest in 703 and remained a monk for the rest of his life. Besides Latin and Greek literature, he studied Hebrew, medicine, astronomy and prosody. He wrote homilies, biographies, hymns, epigrams, works on chronology, grammar and physical science, commentaries on the Old and New Testaments, and translated the Gospel of St John into Anglo-Saxon just before his death. His greatest work was his Latin *Historia ecclesiastica gentis Anglorum* ("Ecclesiastical History of the English People"), which he finished in 731, and is the single most valuable source for early English history. It was later translated into Anglo-Saxon by, or under, King **Alfred**. Bede was canonized in 1899 and his feast day is May 27.

Bedford, John of Lancaster, Duke of 1389–1435 •*English soldier, statesman and prince*• The third son of **Henry IV**, he was made Duke of Bedford (1414) by his brother, **Henry V**, and during the war with France he was appointed Lieutenant of the Kingdom. After Henry's death (1422), Bedford became Guardian of England and virtual Regent of France during the minority of his nephew, **Henry**

VI. In the Hundred Years' War, helped by alliance with Burgundy, he defeated the French in several battles, but in 1428–29 he failed to capture Orleans. He had **Joan of Arc** burned at the stake in Rouen (1431), and had Henry VI crowned King of France (1431), but in 1435 a treaty was negotiated between **Charles VII** and the Duke of Burgundy, which, together with English insolvency, was to ruin English interests in France. Yet, single-minded, consistent and clear-sighted, at his death he presided over more French territory than Henry V had possessed.

Bednorz, (Johannes) Georg 1950– •*German physicist and Nobel Prize winner*• Born in West Germany, he studied at Münster University and at the Swiss Federal Institute of Technology in Zurich. He then joined the IBM Zurich Research Laboratory (1982–) and investigated, with **Alex Müller**, a new range of material types based on oxides. In 1986 they observed superconductivity at a temperature 12 kelvin higher than the previous record of 23 kelvin. Within two years superconductivity at temperatures as high as 90 kelvin had been achieved, and with superconductors now able to operate using inexpensive and plentiful coolants, the practical applications of superconducting devices multiplied enormously. Bednorz was awarded the 1987 Nobel Prize for physics jointly with Müller.

Beebe, (Charles) William 1877–1962 •*US naturalist and explorer*• Born in Brooklyn, New York, he was curator of ornithology for the New York Zoological Society from 1899, wrote many widely read books, including *Galápagos* (1923) and *The Arcturus Adventure* (1925), and explored ocean depths down to 3,028 feet (923 meters) in a bathysphere (1934).

Beecham, Sir Thomas 1879–1961 •*English conductor and impresario*• Born in St Helens, Lancashire, he was educated at Rossall School and Wadham College, Oxford. He began his career as a conductor with the New Symphony Orchestra at Wigmore Hall in 1906 and became principal conductor (1932) and artistic director (1933) of Covent Garden. In 1946 he founded the Royal Philharmonic Orchestra, and conducted at Glyndebourne from 1948 to 1949. Beecham did much to champion the works of **Frederick Delius**, **Jean Sibelius** and **Richard Strauss**, and was noted for his candid pronouncements on musical matters, his "Lollipop" encores (of popular works of classical music), and his after-concert speeches. He was the son of the famous "pill millionaire," Sir Joseph Beecham (1848–1916).

" "

The English may not like music—but they absolutely love the noise it makes.

Quoted in L Ayre ***The Wit of Music*** *(1930).*

Beecher, Henry Ward 1813–87 •*US Congregationalist clergyman and writer*• Born in Litchfield, Connecticut, he was the son of **Lyman Beecher**. Educated at Amherst College, Massachusetts, he preached at Indianapolis, and in 1847 became the first pastor of Plymouth Congregational Church, in Brooklyn, New York, where he preached temperance and denounced slavery. On the outbreak of the Civil War in 1861 his church raised and equipped a volunteer regiment. At the end of the war in 1865 he became an earnest advocate of reconciliation. His many writings include *Seven Lectures to Young Men* (1844), *Summer in the Soul* (1858), *Yale Lectures on Preaching* (1874) and *Evolution and Religion* (1885). He was the brother of **Harriet Beecher Stowe**.

Beecher, Lyman 1775–1863 •*US Presbyterian minister*• Born in New Haven, Connecticut, he studied at Yale, and became a minister. His evangelical preaching aroused opposition among conservative Presbyterians, and he was charged with heresy but acquitted. He then became leader of the New School Presbyterians. He was the father of 13 children, including **Harriet Beecher Stowe** and **Henry Ward Beecher**.

Beeching, Richard Beeching, Baron 1913–85 •*English engineer and administrator*• Born in Maidstone, Kent, and educated at Imperial College, London, he became chairman of the British Railways Board (1963–65) and deputy chairman of Imperial Chemical Industries (1966–68). He is best known for the scheme devised and approved under his chairmanship (the Beeching Plan) for the substantial contraction of the rail network of the UK. He identified 5,000 miles of track and 2,000 stations for closure, and this had a tremendous effect on the future of the railways. He was created a life peer in 1965.

Beerbohm, Sir (Henry) Max(imilian), *called* **the Incomparable Max** 1872–1956 •*English writer and caricaturist*• Born in London, the son of a Lithuanian corn merchant, and half-brother of Sir **Herbert Beerbohm Tree**, he was educated at Charterhouse and Merton College, Oxford. He published his first volume of essays (some of which had appeared in the *Yellow Book*) under the ironic title *The Works of Max Beerbohm* (1896). He succeeded **George Bernard Shaw** as drama critic of *The Saturday Review*, until 1910, when he married a US actress, Florence Kahn (d. 1951), and went to live, except during the two world wars, in Rapallo, Italy. His delicate, unerring, aptly captioned caricatures were collected in various volumes beginning with *Twenty-five Gentlemen* (1896) and *Poet's Corner* (1904). Further volumes of parodies and stories were *Happy Hypocrite* (1897) and *A Christmas Garland* (1912), full of gentle humor, elegance, and rare wit, and ending with *And Even Now* (1920). His best-known work was his only novel, *Zuleika Dobson* (1912), an ironic romance of Oxford undergraduate life.

Beerbohm Tree, Sir Herbert *See* **Tree, Sir Herbert Beerbohm**

Beethoven, Ludwig van 1770–1827 •*German composer*• He was born in Bonn, where his father was a tenor in the service of the Elector of Cologne, and his grandfather a bass singer and Kapellmeister. He had his first music lessons from his father, who was ambitious on his behalf and saw him as a second **Mozart**. He first appeared as a keyboard prodigy at Cologne in 1778. In 1787 he visited Vienna, where he is thought to have received lessons from Mozart, but he hurried back to Bonn on his mother's death. He came into contact with **Haydn** in 1790, and two years later Haydn agreed to teach him in Vienna, which Beethoven made his permanent home. He was also taught by **Antonio Salieri**. In 1795 he played in Vienna for the first time, performing the B-flat Piano Concerto, and published his op 1 trios and op 2 piano sonatas. He went on to perform in Prague, Dresden and Berlin, and earned a growing reputation as a pianist and improvisor. His creative output is traditionally divided into three periods. By 1802 he had composed three piano concertos, two symphonies, the String Quartets op 29, and op 31, but already suffered deeply from depression caused by his increasing deafness. The first works of his "middle period" show him as the heroic, unbounded optimist, determined to strive creatively in the face of despair. His third symphony, a much longer work than was usual at the time, was originally dedicated to **Napoleon Bonaparte**, but on learning that he had proclaimed himself emperor, Beethoven defaced the title page and called the work *Eroica* (1804). In the opera *Fidelio* the themes of fidelity, personal liberation, and symbolic passage from darkness to light dominate; in association with this work he composed the three *Leonora* overtures. The final version of *Fidelio* was produced in 1814, by which time the rich corpus of the middle years was complete: piano sonatas including the *Waldstein*, *Appassionata* and *Lebewohl*; the Symphonies nos. 4–8; the *Razumovsky* quartets; the fourth and fifth piano concertos; incidental music to **Goethe**'s *Egmont*, and the *Archduke* Trio. As time went on, his domestic life declined: according to the accounts of contemporaries he was ill-kempt, unhygienic, argumentative, and arrogant; and he was disordered in business dealings, quarrelsome with friends, and tormented more and more by illness. Yet the last decade of Beethoven's life saw the most extraordinary and supremely great achievements: the *Diabelli* Variations, the last piano sonatas, the last five string quartets, the Mass in D (*Missa Solemnis*) and the *Choral* Symphony (no. 9). The Romantics embraced Beethoven as their supreme precursor; and his influence on succeeding generations of musicians has been immense.

Beeton, Mrs Isabella Mary, *née* **Mayson** 1836–65 •*English cookery writer*• She was educated in Heidelberg and became an accomplished pianist. In 1856 she married Samuel Orchard Beeton, a publisher, and her *Book of Household Management*, first published in parts (1859–60) in a cookery and domestic science magazine founded by her husband, made her name a household word. She died after the birth of her fourth son.

" "

There is no more fruitful source of family discontent than a housewife's badly-cooked dinners and untidy ways.

1861 ***The Book of Household Management****, preface.*

Begin, Menachem 1913–92 •*Israeli statesman and Nobel Prize winner*• Born in Brest-Litovsk, Russia (later Poland, now Brest, in Belarus), he studied law at Warsaw University. An active Zionist, he became head of the Betar Zionist movement in Poland in 1931. On the invasion of Poland in 1939 he fled to Lithuania, where he was arrested by the Russians. He was released in 1941, enlisted in the Free Polish Army, and was sent to British-mandated Palestine in 1942. After being discharged from the army the following year, he became Commander in Chief of the Irgun Zvai Leumi resistance group in Israel and gained a reputation as a terrorist. He founded the right-wing Herut Freedom Movement in 1948, became chairman of the Herut Party, and was a member of the first, second and third Knessets. In 1973 three parties combined to form the Likud Front, a right-of-center nationalist party with Begin as its leader, and in the 1977 elections he became Prime Minister at the head of a coalition government. Throughout his life he was a man of hard-line views concerning the Arabs, but in the late 1970s he sought a peaceful settlement with the Egyptians and attended peace conferences in Jerusalem (1977) and at Camp David (1978) at the invitation of President **Jimmy Carter**. In 1978 he and President **Sadat** of Egypt were jointly awarded the Nobel Prize for peace. He resigned the premiership in 1983.

Behan, Brendan 1923–64 •*Irish author*• Born in Dublin, he left school at 14 and soon joined the IRA. In 1939 he was sentenced to three years in Borstal for attempting to blow up a Liverpool shipyard, and soon after his release was given 14 years by a Dublin military court for the attempted murder of two detectives. He was released in a general amnesty (1946), but was in prison again in Manchester (1947) and was deported in 1952. His first play, *The Quare Fellow* (1954; filmed 1962), starkly dramatized the prison atmosphere prior to a hanging. His exuberant Irish wit, spiced with balladry and bawdry and a talent for fantastic caricature, found scope in his next play, *The Hostage* (1958, first produced in Irish as *An Giall*). It is also evident in the autobiographical novel, *Borstal Boy* (1958), and in *Brendan Behan's Island* (1963). He was the brother of **Dominic Behan**.

Behan, Dominic 1928–89 •*Irish novelist and folklorist*• Born in Dublin, the brother of **Brendan Behan**, he adapted old airs and poems into contemporary Irish Republican material, notably in *The Patriot Game*. Resentfully overshadowed for much of his life by the legend of his brother, he lived largely outside Ireland from 1947 as a journalist and singer. He ultimately settled in Scotland, where for the first time he won acceptance in his own right as a writer, and as an Irish and Scottish nationalist. His only novel, *The Public Life of Parable Jones*, was published just before his death.

Behn, Aphra, *née* **Johnson** 1640–89 •*English writer and adventuress*• Born in Wye, Kent, Behn was brought up in Surinam, where she made the acquaintance of the enslaved African prince Oroonoko, the subject afterward of her novel *Oroonoko* (1688), in which she anticipated **Jean Jacques Rousseau**'s "noble savage." Returning to England in 1663, she married a merchant called Behn, who died within three years. She then turned professional spy at Antwerp, sent back political and naval information, but received little thanks, and on her return was imprisoned for debt. She turned to writing, as perhaps the first professional woman author in England, and wrote many coarse but popular Restoration plays, such as *The Forced Marriage* (1670) and *The Feigned Courtizans* (1678).

Behrens, Peter 1868–1940 •*Pioneering German architect and designer*• Born in Hamburg, he trained as a painter, and was appointed director of the Düsseldorf Art and Craft School (1903–07). In 1907 he became artistic adviser to **Walther Rathenau** at the AEG electrical company in Berlin, and he also designed workers' apartment houses in Vienna and Stuttgart, and the German embassy in St Petersburg (1912). He was professor at Düsseldorf and Vienna, and trained several notable modern architects, including **Le Corbusier**, **Ludwig Mies van der Rohe** and **Walter Gropius**.

Behring, Emil von 1854–1917 •*German bacteriologist, pioneer in immunology and Nobel Prize winner*• Born in Hansdorf, West Prussia, he enrolled in the Army Medical College in Berlin. In 1888 he went to join the Institute of Hygiene in Berlin, where his major contribution was the development of a serum therapy against tetanus and diphtheria (1890), which became instrumental in counteracting these diseases. Behring's recommendations for reducing the occurrence of tuberculosis in animals and for disinfecting milk were important public health measures, and he was awarded the first Nobel Prize for physiology or medicine in 1901. During World War I, the tetanus vaccine developed by him helped to save so many lives that he received the Iron Cross, very rarely awarded to a civilian.

Beiderbecke, (Leon) Bix 1903–31 •*US cornettist*• The archetypal white youngster smitten by early jazz (and the posthumous subject of Dorothy Baker's novel *Young Man with a Horn*, 1938), he was born to musical parents in Davenport, Iowa, and was largely self-taught on piano and cornet. On being expelled from a military academy at the age of 19, he began the short career that made him one of the most celebrated jazz performers of the 1920s. His bell-like tone and lyrical solo improvisations were heard to best effect in various small groups, but he also transformed the commercial sound of such big bands as the **Paul Whiteman** and Jean Goldkette orchestras. His later career was ravaged by alcoholism, and he died of pneumonia at the age of 28.

Béjart, Maurice, *originally* **Maurice Jean Berger** 1927– •*French dancer and choreographer*• Born in Marseilles, he trained at the Marseilles Opera Ballet and then in Paris and London. He moved to the Royal Swedish Ballet (then under **Roland Petit**) where he both performed and choreographed. In 1954 he founded the Mudra School and his own company, which was invited to remain as the Ballet of the 20th Century in Brussels after a major success there. He developed a physical style which displays the talents of the male dancer, and was the first to present a ballet in a sports arena. His works include *The Firebird* (1970), in which a ballerina becomes the leader of the partisans, *Notre Faust* (1975, "Our Faust"), a black mass set to **J S Bach** and tango music, *Choreographic Offering* (1971) and *Kabuki* (1986). In 1987 the company moved to Lausanne, Switzerland, and changed its name to Béjart Ballet Lausanne.

Belafonte, Harry (Harold George) 1927– •*US singer and actor*• Born in New York City, he spent part of his childhood in Jamaica, returning to New York in 1940. His lilting calypso songs of the 1950s brought him superstar status, and his album *Calypso*, with the popular "Banana Boat Song," was the first to sell over a million copies. An award-winning performer on television and in films, he has worked for civil rights in the US as a director of the Southern Christian Leadership Conference (SCLC), in South Africa, and as a UNICEF goodwill ambassador.

Belasco, David 1853–1931 •*US playwright, director and theater manager*• Born in San Francisco and one of the most powerful figures on Broadway, he owned the Belasco Theater where, from 1906 until his death, he directed numerous plays. Belasco, nicknamed the "Bishop of Broadway," also found time to write over 50 plays, both alone and in collaboration, most of them sentimental domestic and historical dramas. As an author, though, he is chiefly remembered for writing *Madame Butterfly* (1900, with John L Long) and *The Girl of the Golden West* (1905). Both were transformed into operas by **Puccini**, the former becoming one of the composer's most celebrated works.

Belaúnde Terry, Fernando 1912–2002 •*Peruvian statesman*• Born in Lima, the son of a Prime Minister, he was an architect before entering politics and becoming leader of the Popular Action Party (AP) in 1956. He campaigned for the presidency in 1956 and 1962, eventually winning it in 1963, but was deposed by the army in a bloodless coup in 1968. He won the presidency again in 1980, and was the first civilian to leave office and be succeeded by another constitutionally elected civilian (1985).

Belisarius 505–65 •*Byzantine general*• Born in Germania, Illyria, he served Emperor **Justinian I**. He defeated a great Persian army at Dara in 530, and in 532 suppressed a dangerous insurrection in Constantinople (Istanbul) by the destruction of 30,000 of the "Green" faction. In Africa he twice defeated the Vandals (534–35), conquered the Ostrogoths in Italy (535), conquered Sicily (536), and occupied Rome, which he defended for a year (537–38). In 540 he captured the Ostrogothic capital, Ravenna, but in 542 he was campaigning against the Persians, and from 544 to 548 he was again sent to Italy to deal with the resurgent Ostrogoths. In 562 he was falsely accused of conspiracy against the emperor, but in 563 he was restored to honor.

Bell, Alexander Graham 1847–1922 •*US inventor*• Born in Edinburgh, Scotland, he was educated there and in London, and first worked as an assistant to his father in teaching elocution (1868–70). In 1872 he opened a school in Boston for training teachers of the deaf, and in 1873 he was appointed Professor of Vocal Physiology at Boston University, where he devoted himself to the teaching of people who could not hear or speak and to spreading his father's system of "visible speech." After experimenting with various acoustical devices he produced the first intelligible telephonic transmission with a message to his assistant on June 5, 1875. He patented the telephone in 1876, defended the patent against **Elisha Gray** (1835–1901), and formed the Bell Telephone Company in 1877. In 1880 he established the Volta Laboratory, and invented the photophone (1880) and the graphophone (1887). He also founded the journal *Science* (1883).

Bell, Andrew 1753–1832 •*Scottish educationist and founder of the Madras System of education*• Born in St Andrews, Fife, he took Episcopal orders, and went to India in 1787, and in 1789 became superintendent of the Madras military orphanage, where he taught with the aid of the pupils themselves by introducing the monitorial system. His methods attracted little attention in Great Britain until in 1803 **Joseph Lancaster** also published a tract recommending the monitorial system. Lancasterian schools began to spread over the country and in 1811 the National Society for the Education of the Poor was founded, of which Bell became superintendent, and whose schools soon numbered 12,000.

Bell, Sir Charles 1774–1842 •*Scottish anatomist, surgeon and neurophysiological pioneer*• Born in Edinburgh, he studied at Edinburgh University, moving to London in 1804, where he became proprietor of an anatomy school and rose to prominence as a surgeon. Today he is remembered for his pioneering neurophysiological research, first set out in his *Idea of a New Anatomy of the Brain* (1811). Bell demonstrated that nerves consist of separate fibers sheathed together and that fibers convey either sensory or motor stimuli but never both. His work on the functions of the spinal nerves triggered disputes with **François Magendie**. Bell's experimental work led to the discovery of the long thoracic nerve ("Bell's nerve"), and the type of facial paralysis known as "Bell's palsy" is named after him.

Bell, (Arthur) Clive Heward 1881–1964 •*English art and literary critic*• He studied at Trinity College, Cambridge, and stated his aesthetic theory of "significant form" in *Art* (1914). Another version of this was formulated in 1920 by **Roger Fry**, a fellow member of the Bloomsbury Group, described in his *Old Friends* (1956). His critical essays include *Since Cézanne* (1922) and *An Account of French Painting* (1931). In 1907 he married **Vanessa Bell**, sister of **Virginia Woolf** and daughter of Sir **Leslie Stephen**. Their son Julian (1908–37), also a writer, was killed in the Spanish Civil War.

“ ”

Art and Religion are, then, two roads by which men escape from circumstance to ecstasy.

*1914 **Art**, part 2, chapter 1.*

Bell, James Thomas, *known as* **"Cool Papa"** 1903–91 •*US baseball player*• Born in Starkville, Mississippi, he entered the Negro Leagues in 1922 with the St Louis Stars. Barred from the major leagues by segregation, he spent his career with a number of Negro League teams, earning his nickname for coolness as a pitcher. His remarkable fleetness of foot led him to be dubbed the fastest base runner of all time, and he once circled the bases in 12 seconds. He retired a year before the color bar was ended in 1947 and resisted attempts to lure him back into major league playing.

Bell, Lawrence Dale 1894–1956 •*US aircraft designer and constructor*• Born in Mentone, Indiana, he began his career as a mechanic to two exhibition pilots in 1913. In 1935 he formed the Bell Aircraft Corporation and among its more notable aircraft were the Airacuda, Airacobra, Kingcobra and, in 1942, the P-59 Airacomet, the first US jet-propelled aircraft. From 1941 he produced a famous line of helicopters, and in 1947 he created the first rocket-propelled airplane, the Bell X-1, the first manned aircraft to exceed the speed of sound.

Bell, Vanessa, *née* **Stephen** 1879–1961 •*English painter and decorative designer*• Born in Kensington, London, she was the daughter of Sir **Leslie Stephen** and elder sister of **Virginia Woolf**, and a leading member of the Bloomsbury Group. She married the critic **Clive Bell** in 1907, but left him in 1916 to live with **Duncan Grant**, a fellow contributor to **Roger Fry**'s Omega Workshops (1913–20). Elected to the London Group in 1919, she exhibited with them regularly from 1920.

Bellamy, David James 1933– •*English botanist, writer and broadcaster*• Born in London, he earned a doctorate in botany and was senior lecturer in the department of botany at Durham University (1960–80). His television career began with *Life in Our Sea* in 1970 and he became widely known as a presenter of the popular science series *Don't Ask Me* (1974–78). His own series have included *Bellamy on Botany* (1972), *Bellamy's Britain* (1974), *Bellamy's Bugle* (1986–88), and *Bellamy Rides Again* (1991–92). He has published widely, is a director of numerous environmental and conservation organizations, and was given the honorary title Officer, Order of the British Empire, in 1994.

Bellany, John 1942– •*Scottish painter and etcher*• Born in Port Seton, he studied at Edinburgh College of Art (1960–65) and at the Royal College of Art (1965–68). Like many Scots of his generation, he adopted an expressive form of realism in the 1970s inspired by **Fernand Léger** and by German art. He was elected a Royal Academician in 1991 and was given the honorary title of Commander, Order of the British Empire, in 1994.

Bellarmine, St Francis, *properly* **San Roberto Francesco Romolo Bellarmino** 1542–1621 •*Italian Jesuit theologian*• Born in Montepulciano, near Siena, he joined the Jesuits at Rome in 1560, and studied theology at Padua and Louvain in the Spanish Netherlands. He was made a cardinal in 1599 against his own inclination, and in 1602, Archbishop of Capua. After the death of Clement VIII, he evaded the papal chair, but was induced by **Paul V** to hold an important place in the Vatican from 1605 until his death. In the 17th century, stone beer jugs with a caricature of his likeness, called bellarmines, were produced by Flemish Protestants to ridicule him. He was canonized in 1930, and his feast day is May 17.

Bellay, Joachim du 1522–60 •*French poet and prose writer*• Born in Liré, he was, after his friend and fellow student **Pierre de Ronsard**, the most important member of the Pléiade. His *Défense et illustration de la langue française* (1549, "Defense and Illustration of the French Language"), the manifesto of the Pléiade, advocating the rejection of medieval linguistic traditions and a return to classical and Italian models, had a considerable influence at the time.

Bellingshausen, Fabian Gottlieb Benjamin, von 1778–1852 •*Russian explorer*• He was born in Oesel and joined the Russian navy at the age of ten. In 1819–21 he led an expedition around the world which made several discoveries in the Pacific Ocean, and sailed as far south as 70° in the Antarctic. The Bellingshausen Sea there is named after him.

Bellini, Gentile *See* **Bellini, Giovanni**

Bellini, Giovanni c. 1430–1516 •*Venetian painter*• One of a family of painters, he became the greatest Venetian artist of his time and was instrumental in making Venice an artistic center to rival Florence. His father Jacopo Bellini (c. 1400–70) had studied under

Gentile da Fabriano and painted a wide range of subjects, of which a few Madonnas in Italy and drawings in the Louvre, Paris, and the British Museum, London, remain, showing Jacopo's interest in architectural and landscape setting. Giovanni's style progressed from the sharp and stylized manner inherited from his father to the more sensuous, painterly one for which he is famous. His sense of design was learned from the severe classical style of his brother-in-law **Andrea Mantegna** and his fluid oil technique from **Antonello da Messina**. His art is essentially calm and contemplative; one of his chief contributions to Italian art was his successful integration of figures with landscape background. Another is his naturalistic treatment of light. Almost all his pictures are religious and he remains best known for a long series of Madonnas to which he brought a humanistic sensibility. All the most talented younger painters of his day, including **Titian**, came to his studio and through them his innovations were perpetuated. His own style continued to develop to the end, and his later work is influenced by the youthful genius **Giorgione**.

Bellini, Jacopo *See* **Bellini, Giovanni**

Bellini, Vincenzo 1801–35 •*Italian operatic composer*• Born in Catania, Sicily, he was an organist's son, and was sent by a Sicilian nobleman to the San Sebastians Conservatorio in Naples. He wrote many operas, but international success came with *Il pirata* (1827, "The Pirate"), and was followed by *I Capuleti ed i Montecchi* (1830, "The Capulets and the Montagues," based on *Romeo and Juliet*) and his two great works of lyrical expression, *La sonnambula* (1831, "The Sleepwalking Girl") and *Norma* (1831).

Bello, Andrés 1781–1865 •*Venezuelan writer and polymath*• He was born and educated in Caracas. He lived in London (1810–29) before settling in Chile, where he became a senior public servant, senator, and first Rector of the university (1843). Considered the most remarkable Latin American intellectual of the 19th century, his writings embrace language, law, education, history, philosophy, poetry, drama and science.

Belloc, (Joseph) Hilaire P(ierre) 1870–1953 •*British writer and poet*• He was born in St Cloud, near Paris. His family moved to England during the Franco-Prussian War, and settled there in 1872. He was educated at the Oratory School, Birmingham, under **John Newman**, and Balliol College, Oxford, but did military service in the French army. He became a naturalized British subject (1902) and a Liberal Member of Parliament (1906–10). Disapproving of modern industrial society and socialism, he wrote *The Servile State* (1912), advocating a return to the system of medieval guilds. He was a close friend of **G K Chesterton**, who illustrated many of his books. He is best known for his nonsensical verse for children, *The Bad Child's Book of Beasts* (1896) and *Cautionary Tales* (1907), and also wrote travel books, historical studies, and religious books. He was an energetic Roman Catholic apologist. His sister Marie Belloc Lowndes (1868–1947) was a novelist and playwright.

“ ”

When I am dead, I hope it may be said,
"His sins were scarlet, but his books were read."

1923 "On His Books."

Bellow, Saul 1915– •*US writer and Nobel Prize winner*• He was born in Lachine, Quebec, Canada, the son of immigrant Russian parents, and spent his childhood in Montreal. In 1924 his family moved to Chicago, a city that was to figure largely in his fiction, and he attended university there and at Northwestern in Evanston, Illinois. He abandoned his postgraduate studies at the University of Wisconsin to become a writer, and his first novel, *The Dangling Man*, a study of a man in predraft limbo, appeared in 1944. Other works include *The Victim* (1947), *The Adventures of Augie March* (1953), *Henderson the Rain King* (1959), *Herzog* (1964), *Humboldt's Gift* (1975), and *More Die of Heartbreak* (1986). Most are concerned with the fate of liberal humanism in a violent and absurd environment that has severed the present from an intellectually and emotionally nourishing past. In 1962 he was appointed a professor at the University of Chicago, and in 1976 was awarded the Nobel Prize for literature. His recent publications include a volume of three tales, *Something to Remember Me By* (1991), a novel, *The Actual* (1997) and *The Collected Stories* (2001). *Ravelstein* (2000) caused controversy in its thinly disguised account of the author's friendship with writer Allan Bloom.

Belo, Carlos Filipe Ximenes 1948– •*East Timorese priest and campaigner*• He was born in the village of Wailakama and ordained as a priest in 1980, becoming Papal Administrator in the East Timorese capital Dili in 1983. Indonesian control in East Timor following the invasion of 1975 had led to widespread abuse of human rights, and Belo became a spokesman for nonviolent opposition to the military government. He won the Nobel Peace Prize (1996; with **José Ramos-Horta**) for his work toward a just and peaceful solution to the conflict in East Timor, where free elections leading to independence were held in 2001.

Belteshazzar *See* **Daniel**

Bely, Andrei, *pseudonym of* **Boris Nikolayevich Bugayev** 1880–1934 •*Russian novelist, poet and critic*• He was born in Moscow. A leading Symbolist writer, he early met **Vladimir Soloviev**, the religious philosopher, and fell under his influence. While at Moscow University Bely wrote Decadent poetry, but his reputation rests on his prose. *Serebryany golub* (1909, Eng trans *The Silver Dove*, 1974), his first and most accessible novel, was followed by his masterpiece, *Petersburg* (1916, Eng trans *St Petersburg*, 1959), in which the action centers on a bomb camouflaged as a tin of sardines. The autobiographical *Kotik Letayev* (1922, Eng trans *Kotik Letaev*, 1971) is a stream-of-consciousness attempt to show how children become aware of what is going on in the world. His later novels are more overtly satirical of the prerevolutionary Russian scene. He is regarded as one of the most important Russian writers of the 1920s.

Beman, Deane R 1938– •*US golf administrator*• Born in Washington DC, he was a member of the US Walker Cup team (1959–65) and the Eisenhower trophy team (1960–66), and became a moderately successful professional golfer in the early 1970s. As commissioner of the US Professional Golfers' Association Tour (1974–94), his success has been due partly to combining the US Tour with both corporate America and television. His supporters claim he has generated a huge increase in prize money for the players, but some critics argue that in the process he has sold golf's soul.

Benacerraf, Baruj 1920– •*US immunologist and Nobel Prize winner*• He was born in Caracas, Venezuela. His family moved to the US (1940) and he entered the Medical College of Virginia, becoming Professor of Pathology in 1960. In New York, he showed that response to antigens was genetically determined, and named the determining genes as the immune-response genes. He later clarified how genetically determined structures on cell surfaces regulate responses to diseased cells and in organ transplants. For this work he shared the 1980 Nobel Prize for physiology or medicine with **Jean Dausset** and **George Snell**. In 1990 he was awarded the National Medal of Science.

Ben Ali, Zine el Abidine 1936– •*Tunisian politician*• Born in Hammam Sousse, he studied in France and the US, then began a career in military security. He became Minister of the Interior and then Prime Minister under "President-for-Life" **Habib Bourguiba**, who had been in power since 1956. In 1987 he forced Bourguiba to retire and assumed the presidency himself; he immediately embarked on constitutional reforms, promising a greater degree of democracy. He has, however, been criticized for his government's human rights record. Reelected for a third term in 1999, he announced his intention in 2001 to reverse his previous constitutional reforms, thus allowing his candidacy in future presidential elections.

Benaud, Richie (Richard) 1930– •*Australian cricket player and commentator*• Born in Penrith, New South Wales, he first played for New South Wales in 1948 and went on to appear in 63 Test matches for Australia, serving as captain on 28 occasions and participating in three successful tours of England (1953, 1956 and 1961). In all he took 248 Test wickets and scored 2,201 Test runs, becoming the first man to achieve 2,000 runs and 200 wickets in Test cricket. He has since become widely familiar as a cricket commentator and has also worked as an international sports consultant. His books include *Anything But ... An Autobiography* (1998).

Benavente y Martinez, Jacinto 1866–1954 •*Spanish dramatist and Nobel Prize winner*• Born in Madrid, he meant to enter the legal profession but turned instead to literature. He won recognition as a playwright with *El nido ajeno* (1893, "The Other Nest"), which was followed by some satirical society comedies. His masterpiece is *Los intereses creados* (1907, "Human Concerns"), an allegorical play in the commedia dell'arte style. He also wrote children's plays. He won the Nobel Prize for Literature in 1922.

Ben Bella, Ahmed 1916– •*Algerian politician*• Born in Maghnia, on the Moroccan border, he served with distinction in the French army in World War II. In 1949 he became leader of the extremist independence movement, the Organisation Spéciale (Special Organization), the paramilitary wing of the Algerian nationalist Parti du Peuple Algérien (Party of the Algerian People). In 1950 he founded the National Liberation Front (FLN). The FLN then embarked on a long war (1954–62) ending in independence and Ben Bella's election in 1963 as President. He was deposed in 1965 in a coup led by General **Houari Boumédienne** and kept under house arrest until 1979. Between 1981 and 1990, he went into exile, but afterward returned to Algeria.

Bench, Johnny Lee 1947– •*US baseball player*• Born in Oklahoma City, he played in the National League with the Cincinnati Reds and was the outstanding catcher of the 1970s. He had great ability with the bat, hit over 350 home runs, and led the league three times in seven years for runs batted in. He was the National League's Most Valuable Player (MVP) on several occasions and almost monopolized the Gold Glove award for his particular position.

Benchley, Robert Charles 1889–1945 •*US humorist, critic and parodist*• He was born in Worcester, Massachusetts, and studied at Harvard where he edited the *Lampoon* and starred in the Hasty Pudding shows. While working for *Vanity Fair* he met **Dorothy Parker** and together with **Robert Sherwood**, **James Thurber**, **George Kaufman** and Franklin P Adams, they formed the notorious Algonquin Round Table. He was at his most brilliant in the sketches collected in *20,000 Leagues Under the Sea, or, David Copperfield* (1928), *From Bed to Worse* (1934) and *My Ten Years in a Quandary, and How They Grew* (1936). His humor derives from the predicament of the "Little Man," himself writ large, beset on all sides by the complexity of existence in the modern world. **E B White** and Thurber thought him a finer humorist even than **Mark Twain**, and Parker described him as a "kind of saint." He appeared in cameo roles in many films.

“ ”

One square foot less and it would be adulterous.

On the tiny office he shared with Dorothy Parker, quoted in the ***New Yorker****, January 5, 1946.*

Benda, Julien 1867–1956 •*French philosopher and essayist*• Born in Paris and educated at the university there, he found fame writing in opposition to **Henri Bergson**, just before World War I. He then caused a sensation in 1927 with *La Trahison des clercs* ("The Treachery of the Intellectuals") in which he accuses modern thinkers of abandoning philosophical neutrality to support doctrines of class and race hatred, such as Marxism and Fascism. Later publications included *Tradition de l'existentialisme* (1947, "Tradition of Existentialism") and *La dialectique materialiste* (1948, "Materialist Dialectique"). He wrote two novels, *L'Ordination* (1911, "The Ordination") and *Les amorandes* (1922).

Benedetto, Anthony Dominick *See* **Bennett, Tony**

Benedict VIII d. 1024 •*First of the Tusculan popes*• Born probably in the county of Tusculum, Italy, he was elected in 1012. He was temporarily driven from Rome by the antipope Gregory VI, of the Crescenti family, but was restored to the papal chair by the emperor **Henry II**, whom he crowned in 1014. Later he defeated the Saracens and the Greeks in northern Italy, and introduced clerical and monastic reforms. The uncle of Pope **Benedict IX**, he was succeeded by his brother, John XIX.

Benedict IX d. c. 1065 •*Last of the Tusculan popes*• He succeeded his uncle, John XIX, in 1032, obtaining the papal throne by simony. In 1036 the Romans banished him on account of his licentiousness. Several times reinstalled, he was as often deposed.

Benedict XIII •*Title assumed by two popes*• Pedro de Luna (c. 1328–1423), born in Illneca, Kingdom of Aragon, Spain, was elected as antipope by the French cardinals in 1394 in succession to the antipope Clement VII at Avignon after the Great Western Schism of 1378; and Pietro Francesco Orsini (1649–1730), an Italian Dominican cardinal, was elected pope in 1724. A learned man of simple habits and pure morals, he placed himself under the guidance of the unscrupulous Cardinal Niccolo Coscia.

Benedict XIV, *originally* **Prospero Lambertini** 1675–1758 •*Italian pope*• Born in Bologna, he studied theology and law at Rome, and became pope in 1740. He urged that restraint be exercised by those responsible for compiling the index of prohibited literature, and he was also keen to avoid too open a breach with Jansenism. However, he was not merely a doctrinal pragmatist: in the *Ex quo singulari* (1742) and the *Omnium sollicitudinum* (1744) he denounced, and prohibited, the various traditional practices which Jesuits had tolerated among converts in India and China, saying they were incompatible with the Catholic faith. Distinguished by his learning and ability, Benedict XIV founded chairs of physics, chemistry and mathematics in Rome, and revived the academy of Bologna.

Benedict XV, *originally* **Giacomo Della Chiesa** 1854–1922 •*Italian pope*• Born of a noble Italian family, he was ordained at 24, became secretary to the papal embassy in Spain (1883) then secretary to Cardinal Rampolla, bishop (1900), Archbishop of Bologna (1907), and cardinal (May 1914). Although a junior cardinal, he was elected to succeed **Pius X** in September 1914, soon after the outbreak of World War I. He made repeated efforts to end the war, and organized war relief on a munificent scale.

Benedict of Nursia, St c. 480–c. 547 AD •*Italian founder of Western monasticism*• Born in Nursia, near Spoleto, he was educated at Rome, and as a boy of 14 lived alone for three years in a cave near Subiaco, praying and meditating. Appointed the abbot of a neighboring monastery at Vicovaro, he soon left it to found 12 small, highly disciplined monastic communities. He ultimately established a monastery on Monte Cassino, near Naples, later one of the richest and most famous in Italy. In 515 he is said to have composed his *Regula monachorum*, which became the common rule of all Western monasticism. He was declared the patron saint of all Europe by Pope **Paul VI** in 1964. His feast day is July 11.

Benedict, Ruth, *née* **Fulton** 1887–1948 •*US anthropologist*• Born in New York City, she studied philosophy and English literature at Vassar before going on to study anthropology under Alexander Goldenweiser and **Franz Boas** at Columbia University. She became a leading member of the culture-and-personality movement in US anthropology during the 1930s and 1940s. Her most important contribution lay in her "configurational" approach to entire cultures, according to which each culture tends to predispose its individual members to adopt an ideal type of personality. Thus every culture, she believed, could be characterized in terms of its own distinctive ethos. Her best-known works include *Race: Science and Politics* (1940), a book against racism, and *The Chrysanthemum and the Sword: Patterns of Japanese Culture* (1946).

Beneš, Eduard 1884–1948 •*Czechoslovak statesman*• Born in Kožlany, a farmer's son, he studied law and became Professor of Sociology at Prague. As an émigré during World War I he worked in Paris with **Tomáš Masaryk** for Czech independence, becoming Foreign Minister of the new state (1918–35), and for a while premier (1921–22). In 1935 he succeeded Masaryk as President, but resigned in 1938 following the Munich Agreement. He then left the country, setting up a government in exile, first in France, then in Great Britain. Returning to Czechoslovakia in 1945, he was reelected President the following year, but resigned after the Communist takeover in 1948.

Benesh, Rudolph 1916–75 and **Joan Benesh**, *née* **Rothwell** 1920– •*English dance notators*• Born in London and Liverpool, respectively, Rudolph was first a painter and Joan a member of the Sadler's Wells Ballet. Together they copyrighted (1955) a dance notation system, called choreology, that has been included in the syllabus of London's Royal Academy of Dancing and is used to document all important Royal Ballet productions. They opened their own institute in 1962 and their influence on a great number of notators and educators has been incalculable.

Benét, Stephen Vincent 1898–1943 •*US poet and novelist*• Born in Bethlehem, Pennsylvania, his work was often inspired by American history and folklore, and he is best known for his long poems *John Brown's Body* (1928), on the Civil War, and *Western Star* (1943). He wrote several volumes of evocative poems in traditional form, including the collection *Ballads and Poems 1915–30* (1931) and *Burning City* (1936). His other writings include four more novels, short stories and two one-act folk operas. He was awarded the 1929 and the 1943 Pulitzer prizes. His brother William Rose Benét (1886–1950) was also a writer.

Ben-Gurion, David, *originally* **David Gruen** 1886–1973 •*Israeli statesman*• Born in Plonsk, Poland, he emigrated to Palestine in 1906. Expelled by the Turks during World War I, he recruited Jews to the British Army in North America. In Palestine in 1919 he founded a socialist party and became Secretary to the Histadrut in 1921. He led the Mapai (Labor) Party from its formation in 1930, and became Prime Minister after independence (1948–53), when he was responsible for Israel absorbing large numbers of refugees from Europe and Arab countries. He was Prime Minister again from 1955 to 1963.

Benigni, Roberto 1952– •*Italian comic actor and director*• Born in Misericordia, he moved swiftly from local cabaret to national television where he earned the description "dung-heap **Woody Allen**." He made his film debut in *Berlinguer, ti voglio bene* (1977) and made his directorial debut with *Tu mi trubi* (1983). Subsequent films like *Il piccolo diavolo* (1985, *The Little Devil*) and *Il mostro* (1994, *The Monster*) broke box-office records across Europe and established him as one of Italy's favorite film comics. His English-language films include *Down by Law* (1986) and *Night on Earth* (1991). He won three Academy Awards in 1999 for *La vita è bella* (1997, *Life Is Beautiful*), becoming the first person to win the Best Actor award for a non-English-speaking role.

Benincasa, Caterina *See* **Catherine of Siena, St**

Benjamin of Tudela d. 1173 •*Spanish rabbi and traveler*• He was born in Navarre, and from 1159 to 1173 made a journey from Saragossa through Italy and Greece, to Palestine, Persia (Iran), and the borders of China, returning by way of Egypt and Sicily. He was the first European traveler to describe the Far East.

Benjamin, Paul *See* **Auster, Paul**

Benjamin, Walter 1892–1940 •*German literary and Marxist critic*• Born in Berlin, he was educated at the Friedrich-Wilhelm Gymnasium in Thuringia. His early work includes the 1925 study *Trauerspiel* (Eng trans *The Origin of German Tragic Drama*, 1977), an attempt to understand the 17th century from a German standpoint, and the so-called Arcades Project, which focused upon post-Napoleonic France. Toward the end of the 1920s, Benjamin, encouraged by his encounter with **Bertolt Brecht**, turned toward Marxian materialism, producing essays like "The Work of Art in an Age of Mechanical Reproduction" (1936), which is included in the posthumous 1969 collection, *Illuminations* (ed Hannah Arendt). Benjamin's reputation was revived by this and the aphoristic and autobiographical *Reflections* (published first in English, 1978), making him a central figure in neo-Marxist and materialist criticism, and an icon of heroic resistance against totalitarianism. He committed suicide.

Benn, Gottfried 1886–1956 •*German poet*• Born in Mansfeld, West Prussia, he embraced the philosophy of nihilism as a young man, and became one of the few intellectuals to favor Nazi doctrines, although his poems were banned by the Nazis in 1938. (Ironically, they were banned again by the Allies in 1945 for his earlier pro-Nazi sympathies.) Trained in medicine as a venereologist, he began writing expressionist verse that dealt with the uglier aspects of his profession, such as *Morgue* (1912). Later his work became more versatile, though still pessimistic, and his postwar poetry won him a place among the leading poets of the century.

Benn, Tony (Anthony Neil Wedgwood) 1925– •*English Labour politician*• Born in London, the son of Viscount Stansgate, he was educated at Westminster School and New College, Oxford. A Labour Member of Parliament from 1950 to 1960, he was debarred from the House of Commons on succeeding to his father's title, but was able to renounce it in 1963 and was reelected to parliament the same year. He held a number of ministerial posts in the Wilson government, and on Labour's return to power was made successively Secretary of State for Industry, Minister for Posts and Telecommunications, and Secretary of State for Energy, a position he held until the Conservative victory in the 1979 elections. Representing the left wing of Labour opinion he unsuccessfully stood for the deputy leadership of the party in 1981. He lost his seat in the general election of 1983, but returned to represent Chesterfield from 1984 until his retirement at the 2001 general election. He was the main focus for the left-wing challenge to the Labour leadership in the late 1970s and 1980s, which ultimately failed but which led some on the right to leave and form the Social Democratic Party. He remains an outspoken political critic and active defender of his socialist and democratic ideals. Among his publications are *Arguments for Socialism* (1979), *Arguments for Democracy* (1981) and *Years of Hope* (1994).

“ ”

It is as wholly wrong to blame Marx for what was done in his name, as it is to blame Jesus for what was done in his.

Quoted in Alan Freeman ***The Benn Heresy*** *(1982).*

Bennet, Henry *See* **Arlington, 1st Earl of**

Bennett, Alan 1934– •*English dramatist, actor and director*• Born in Leeds, he studied modern history at Oxford. He came to prominence as a writer and performer in *Beyond the Fringe*, a revue performed at the Edinburgh Festival in 1960, and wrote a television series, *On the Margin* (1966), before his first stage play, *Forty Years On* (1968). He is essentially a humanist, noted for his wry, self-deprecating humor, which combines a comic-tragic view of life, and later plays include *Getting On* (1971, about a Labour MP), *Single Spies* (1988) and *The Madness of George III* (1991). The latter was rewritten as a screenplay entitled *The Madness of King George* in 1995 and then made into an award-winning film. He has also written much for television, including *An Englishman Abroad* (1983), *The Insurance Man* (1986), and a series of six monologues, *Talking Heads* (1988). His memoirs, entitled *Writing Home*, were published in 1994. His recent works include *Father! Father! Burning Bright* (2000) and *The Laying On of Hands* (2001).

Bennett, (Enoch) Arnold 1867–1931 •*English novelist*• Born near Hanley, Staffordshire, the son of a solicitor, he was educated locally and at London University. He became a solicitor's clerk in London, and published his first novel, *The Man from the North*, in 1898. In 1902 he moved to Paris, where he lived for ten years, and from then on was engaged exclusively in journalistic and creative writing. His claims to recognition as a novelist rest mainly on the early *Anna of the Five Towns* (1902), the more celebrated *The Old Wives' Tale* (1908), and the *Clayhanger* series—*Clayhanger* (1910), *Hilda Lessways* (1911), and *These Twain* (1916), subsequently issued (1925) as *The Clayhanger Family*—in all of which novels the "Five Towns," centers of the pottery industry, feature not only as background, but almost as dramatis personae. His genial, humorous streak shows in works like *The Card* (1911), *The Grand Babylon Hotel* (1902), *Imperial Palace* (1930), and the play *The Great Adventure* (1913). *Lord Raingo* (1926) is a political novel. He was a sound and influential critic, and as "Jacob Tonson" on *The New Age* he was a discerning reviewer. His *Journals*, written in the manner of the brothers **Edmond** and **Jules de Goncourt**, were published posthumously.

Bennett, Floyd 1890–1928 •*US aviator*• Born near Warrensburg, New York, he became a naval pilot during World War I. He accompanied **Richard Evelyn Byrd** on an expedition to Greenland (1925). In May 1926 he piloted Byrd on the first airplane flight over the

North Pole, and received the Congressional Medal of Honor. He died while planning Byrd's flight over the South Pole in 1929.

Bennett, Jill 1931–90 •*English actress*• Born in London, she made her debut at Stratford in 1949, and in London in 1950. She scored her first major success in **Jean Anouilh**'s *Dinner with the Family* (1957), and went on to establish a considerable reputation as an elegant, sharp-witted actress, both in classical and contemporary drama. She married the playwright **John Osborne** in 1968, and played in a number of his works, as well as an acclaimed title role in his version of **Ibsen**'s classic drama *Hedda Gabler* (1972).

Bennett, Louise Simone, *also known as* **Miss Lou** 1919– •*Jamaican poet*• Born in Kingston, and educated at Excelsior High School, she studied journalism by correspondence course before going to the Royal Academy of Dramatic Art in London in 1945. After graduating she taught drama in Jamaica, performed in theaters in Great Britain and the US, and lectured widely on Jamaican folklore and music. In 1954 she married the Jamaican actor and impresario, Eric Coverley. Her numerous books include retellings of Jamaican folk stories, collections of her own ballads and *Jamaican Labrish* (1966), a poetry collection, of which she was the editor. Her use of Jamaican dialect and speech rhythms, humor and satirical wit for the purposes of social and political comment have made her one of the outstanding performance poets of the 20th century. In 2001 she was awarded the Order of Merit, one of Jamaica's highest honors.

Bennett, Sir Richard Rodney 1936– •*English composer*• Born in Broadstairs, Kent, he was educated at the Royal Academy of Music in London (1953–56), and in Paris under **Pierre Boulez** and **Olivier Messiaen**. Well known for his music for films (1963, *Billy Liar*, 1973, *Murder on the Orient Express*), he has also composed operas, orchestral works, chamber music, and experimental works for one and two pianos. Some of his music uses the twelve-tone scale, and his interest in jazz has prompted such works as *Jazz Calendar* (1963) and *Jazz Pastoral* (1969). His more recent work shows a growing emphasis on internal rhythmic structure. Among his other pieces are the operas *The Mines of Sulphur* (1965), *A Penny for a Song* (1968) and *Victory* (1970), and a birthday present for pianist Susan Bradshaw entitled *A Book of Hours* (1991). He was knighted in 1998.

Bennett, Tony, *stage name of* **Anthony Dominick Benedetto** 1926– •*US jazz and popular singer*• Born in New York, he began performing under the name "Joe Bari," but changed to Tony Bennett at the suggestion of **Bob Hope** in 1950. He had a series of hit singles during the 1950s and early 1960s which established his reputation as a powerful interpreter of sophisticated popular songs, including his signature tune, "I Left My Heart in San Francisco" (1962). He worked in more jazz-oriented settings in the 1960s, and recorded two fine albums with pianist **Bill Evans** in the mid-1970s. Bennett's career took an unexpected late turn with a highly successful MTV *Unplugged* show in 1994, which brought him to a much younger audience. His autobiography, *The Good Life*, appeared in 1998.

Benny, Jack, *originally* **Benjamin Kubelsky** 1894–1974 •*US comedian*• Born in Waukegan, Illinois, he was a child prodigy violinist, performing as part of a vaudeville double-act, "Salisbury and Benny," and also appearing as "Ben Benny, the Fiddlin' Kid." After naval service during World War I, he returned to the stage and toured extensively before making his film debut in the short *Bright Moments* (1928). Following his Broadway success in *The Earl Carroll Vanities* (1930) and his radio debut on the *Ed Sullivan Show* (1932), he earned his own radio series which, combined with its subsequent television incarnation, *The Jack Benny Show* (1950–65), won him the loyalty and warm affection of a mass audience. A gentle, bemused, self-effacing figure, his humor lacked malice, relying for its effect on his grasp of timing and an act based on his ineptitude as a fiddler, his perennial youth and an unfounded reputation as the world's stingiest man. A sporadic film career included *Charley's Aunt* (1941) and *It's in the Bag* (1945).

Benoît de Sainte-Maure fl. c. 1150 •*French poet*• Born in either Sainte-Maure, near Poitiers, or Sainte-More, near Tours, he wrote a vast romance, *Roman de Troie* ("Tale of Troy"); it became a source book for many later writers, notably **Boccaccio**, who in turn inspired **Chaucer** and **Shakespeare** to use Benoît's episode of Troilus and Cressida.

Benoit Samuelson, Joan 1957– •*US marathon runner*• Born in Cape Elizabeth, Maine, she studied at Bowdoin College, Maine, and while there entered the 1979 Boston marathon, setting a surprise American women's record of 2:35:15. She went on to lower it in 1983 and gain the world record with a time of 2:22:43. In 1984 she won the first Olympic women's marathon, and in 1985 won the Sullivan Award as the most outstanding US amateur athlete.

Bentham, Jeremy 1748–1832 •*English philosopher, writer on jurisprudence and social reformer*• Born in London, he went to Queen's College, Oxford, at the age of 12 and was called to the bar at the age of 15. He was more interested in the theory of the law, and is best known as a pioneer of utilitarianism in his works *A Fragment on Government* (1776) and *Introduction to the Principles of Morals and Legislation* (1789), which argued that the aim of all actions and legislation should be "the greatest happiness of the greatest number." He held that laws should be socially useful and not just reflect the status quo, and developed a "hedonic calculus" to estimate the effects of different actions. He planned a special prison (the Panopticon) and a special school (the Chrestomathia), and helped start the *Westminster Review* (1823). He also founded University College London, where his clothed skeleton can still be seen.

" "

The greatest happiness of the greatest number is the foundation of morals and legislation.

1789 ***An Introduction to the Principles of Morals and Legislation****, chapter 13.*

Bentham, Sir Samuel 1757–1831 •*English inventor and naval architect*• He was born in London, and apprenticed as a shipwright. Unable to find work at home, he went to Russia (1783) where he introduced some revolutionary heavy naval armaments that enabled a much smaller Russian force to defeat the Turks in 1788. For nearly 20 years after 1795 he devoted his energies to building up Great Britain's naval strength during the critical period of the Napoleonic Wars, introducing advances in naval architecture, shipbuilding, large-caliber nonrecoil carronades, the use of steam dredgers, and dockyard administration. His campaign against corruption and maladministration in the Admiralty dockyards aroused such bitterness that in 1812 he was forced to resign. He was the brother of **Jeremy Bentham**.

Bentinck, William, 1st Earl of Portland 1649–1709 •*English soldier and courtier*• He was born in Holland. The boyhood friend of **William III**, he was entrusted with the secrets of his foreign policy, and after the revolution was created an English peer, and given large estates.

Bentinck, William Henry Cavendish, 3rd Duke of Portland 1738–1809 •*English statesman*• He became a Member of Parliament in 1761, succeeding to the dukedom in 1762. His first Cabinet post was as Lord Chamberlain of the Household under the Marquis of **Rockingham** (1765–66). Along with other aristocratic Whigs, he maintained connection with Rockingham which kept him in opposition until 1782, when he was Lord Lieutenant of Ireland. He was nominal head of the ministry usually known as the **Fox-North** coalition (1783), which **George III** hated and rapidly dismissed. He led the Whigs in opposition to **William Pitt** the Younger until 1794, when he agreed to join him in a coalition government. He served as Home Secretary (1794–1801) during a period of considerable radical disturbance in England and rebellion in Ireland (1798), and as Lord President of the Council under Henry Addington (Viscount **Sidmouth**) in 1801–03. He was summoned by George III in 1807 to head an administration of Pittites after the fall of the "Ministry of all the Talents"; by now old, frail and gouty, he was little more than titular leader until his death in office.

Bentine, Michael 1921–96 •*English comedy performer*• Born in Watford, Hertfordshire, of Peruvian parentage, after wartime service in the RAF he worked at the Windmill Theatre (1946) and in the show *Starlight Roof* (1947). One of the early members of The

Goons (1951–52), he left the popular radio series to pursue a solo career and on television made the animated children's series *The Bumblies* (1954), before appearing in *After Hours* (1959–60), *It's a Square World* (1960–64) and *All Square* (1966–67), which allowed him to indulge his penchant for surreal humor, mechanical jokes and illustrated lectures in which anything could happen. Later television series, often for children, included *The Golden Silents* (1965) and *Mad About It* (1981). He also cowrote and appeared in the films *The Sandwich Man* (1966) and *Bachelor of Arts* (1969), and wrote numerous novels and autobiographies.

Bentley, Charles Raymond 1929– •*US geophysicist and glaciologist*• Born in Rochester, New York, he studied physics at Yale and geophysics at Columbia, becoming in 1968 A P Crary Professor of Geophysics (now emeritus). In west Antarctica he discovered that the ice rests on a floor far below sea level, which means that the region would be open ocean if the ice melted. He has pioneered the application of geophysical techniques such as radioglaciology, the use of electromagnetic waves to measure the thickness and properties of ice. He has contributed to the understanding of the Antarctic crust, and in the 1980s his research group investigated the soft sediment beneath an Antarctic ice stream that is now believed to be a critical factor in the movement of the ice surface.

Bentley, Derek William c. 1933–53 •*English alleged murderer*• Born in south London, he was a man of low intelligence who worked variously as a furniture mover, a garbageman and a road sweeper. On Sunday, November 2, 1952, when he was 19 and his friend **Christopher Craig** was 16, they broke into a confectionery warehouse in Croydon. They were seen climbing over the fence, and the police were alerted. Bentley, who was carrying a knife and brass knuckles, and Craig, who was armed with a gun, were approached by the police. Craig fired several shots, initially wounding one policeman and then killing another. Both were arrested and charged and Bentley was found guilty and given the death sentence. Craig, who was too young to receive the death penalty, was detained indefinitely. Despite a series of appeals to the government and to the queen, all of which received vigorous public support, Bentley was hanged on January 28, 1953. Craig was released in 1963 and Bentley's conviction was overturned in 1998.

Bentley, Edmund Clerihew 1875–1956 •*English journalist and novelist*• Born in London, he worked on the *Daily News* (1901–12) and the *Daily Telegraph* (1912–34). He is chiefly remembered as the author of *Trent's Last Case* (1913; US, *The Woman in Black*, 1912), which is regarded as a milestone in the transformation of the detective novel. A close friend of **G K Chesterton**, he originated and gave his name to the humorous verse form known as the "clerihew."

Benz, Karl Friedrich 1844–1929 •*German engineer and car manufacturer*• Born in Karlsruhe, he developed a two-stroke engine from 1877 to 1879, and founded a factory for its manufacture, leaving in 1883 when his backers refused to finance a mobile engine. He then founded his second company, Benz & Co, Rheinische Gasmotorenfabrik, at Mannheim. His first car—one of the earliest gasoline-driven vehicles—was completed in 1885 and sold to a French manufacturer. In 1926 the firm was merged with the Daimler-Motoren-Gesellschaft to form Daimler-Benz and Co.

Berberian, Cathy (Catherine) 1925–83 •*US soprano and composer*• Born in Attleboro, Massachusetts, of Armenian extraction, she studied music and drama at Columbia and at New York Universities. She was married to the composer **Luciano Berio** from 1950 to 1966, who wrote many works for her. Other composers, including **Igor Stravinsky** and Henri Pousseur, wrote pieces for her and she performed work as diverse as **Claudio Monteverdi** and **John Lennon** and **Paul McCartney**. Her own compositions include *Stripsody* (1966), an unaccompanied "cartoon" for vocalist, and *Morsicat(h)y* (1971) for piano.

Berceo, Gonzalo de c. 1180–c. 1246 •*Spanish poet*• Born in Verceo, he was the earliest known Castilian poet. He became a deacon and wrote more than 13,000 verses on devotional subjects, of which the best is a biography of St Oria. He was also the author of *Milagros de la Virgen*, a collection of legends of the Virgin Mary's appearances on earth. His poems were not discovered and published until the late 18th century.

Berchem or **Berghem, Nicholas** 1620–83 •*Dutch landscape painter*• He was born in Haarlem and worked mainly there. His early training was by his father, the still-life painter Pieter Claesz (c. 1596–1661), but he developed a very different style. On visiting Italy in his twenties he made landscape studies for which, when he painted them, he was to become famous and influential. His work is represented in most European collections.

Berengar I d. 924 •*King of Italy and emperor of the Romans*• He succeeded his father Eberhard, a count of Frankish origin, as Margrave of Friuli. He was King of Italy from 888 and Emperor of the Romans from 915. He died at the hands of his own men.

Berengar II c. 900–66 •*King of Italy*• He was the grandson of **Berengar I**. He succeeded his father as Margrave of Ivrea in 928 and became king in 950. In 951/2 he was dethroned by the emperor **Otto I** and later, after three years' refuge in a mountain fortress, was sent as a prisoner to Bavaria (963) where he died.

Berengar of Tours 999–1088 •*French scholastic theologian*• Born probably in Tours, Touraine (now in France), he studied under Fulbert at Chartres. An opponent of the doctrine of transubstantiation, he was excommunicated by Pope Leo IX in 1050. Finally, in 1078, he was cited to appear at Rome, where he repeatedly renounced, but apparently never abandoned, his "error." He spent his last years in a cell on an island in the Loire, near Tours.

Berenice, *known as* **Berenice Syra** c. 280–c. 246 BC •*Queen of Syria as the wife of Antiochus II*• The daughter of **Ptolemy II, Philadelphus**, her marriage to **Antiochus II** of Syria in 252 BC brought about a hiatus in the fighting between the Egyptians and the Seleucids. When Antiochus died, however, Antiochus's divorced wife Laodice (who had been exiled with her children on his marriage to Berenice) plotted the death of the queen and her young son, enabling her own son to succeed as Seleucus II. Berenice's brother Ptolemy III, Euergetes came from Egypt to Syria to avenge his sister's death, an act which resulted in the Third Syrian War.

Berenice 1st century BC •*Princess of the Jewish Idumean dynasty*• She was the daughter of Costobarus and **Salome**, who was a sister of **Herod the Great**. She was married to Aristobulus, her cousin, from c. 17 BC and their children were Herod of Chalcis, **Herod Agrippa I** (father of the Jewish **Berenice**), Aristobulus, Herodias and Mariamne. She allegedly set in motion the plot to murder her husband by her uncle Herod, whose brother-in-law Theudion she later married. Her third husband was Archelaus, whom she married when Theudion was executed for scheming against Herod.

Berenice, *known as* **the Jewish Berenice** c. 28–c. 79 AD •*Princess of the Jewish Idumean dynasty*• She was the daughter of **Herod Agrippa I** and Cypros, and was married to her uncle Herod of Chalcis. After she had given birth to two sons, he died (AD 48) and Berenice moved to the court of her brother, **Herod Agrippa II**, with whom she allegedly had an incestuous relationship. After the recapture of Jerusalem by Rome (AD 70), she became the mistress of **Flavius Titus**, who had noticed her some years earlier during a visit to Judea. They made no secret of living together in Rome, but Titus was advised, on account of Berenice's race, to send her away. The love affair continued but never culminated in marriage, even when Berenice returned to Rome around 79, the year Titus became emperor. She is the model for the tragic heroine of **Racine**'s *Berenice* (1670) and **Pierre Corneille**'s *Tite et Bérénice* (1670).

Berenice I fl. c. 317–c. 275 BC •*Macedonian princess and queen of Egypt*• Born in Macedonia, she went to Egypt as a lady-in-waiting to Eurydice, who became the second wife of **Ptolemy I, Soter**. Ptolemy married Berenice as his third wife (c. 317 BC) and made her Queen of Egypt in 290. Their son became **Ptolemy II, Philadelphus** when he succeeded his father in 283, and their daughter **Arsinoë** married Ptolemy II as his second wife.

Berenice II c. 269–221 BC •*Princess of Cyrene*• The daughter of Magas, King of Cyrene, she married Ptolemy III, Euergetes (247 BC), thus uniting Cyrene (in modern Libya) with Egypt. When her husband went to fight in the Third Syrian War to avenge the murder of his sister (**Berenice** Syra), Berenice dedicated a lock of her hair to Aphrodite for his safe return. According to the court astronomer, the hair ended up in heaven and became the constellation Coma Berenices ("Hair of Berenice"). Berenice's son Ptolemy IV, Philopator succeeded his father and began his reign by having her poisoned; he married his sister Arsinoë III.

Berenice III d. c. 80 BC •*Egyptian princess*• The daughter of Ptolemy IX and either Cleopatra Selene or Cleopatra IV, she first married her uncle, Ptolemy X, and became queen after the death (101 BC) of the dowager queen Cleopatra III, Ptolemy VIII's widow. The people of Alexandria, thinking that Ptolemy had murdered Cleopatra, rebelled and expelled him in 87, so he raised an army in Syria and returned to Egypt, where he plundered the tomb of **Alexander the Great** to pay his soldiers. Expelled again, he fled to Asia Minor, taking Berenice with him. She returned to Egypt after his death (80) and became sole ruler of Egypt, but was murdered by Ptolemy Alexander, the son of Ptolemy X.

Berenice IV d. 55 BC •*Egyptian princess*• She was the daughter of Ptolemy XII Auletes and the elder sister of **Cleopatra**. While her father was forced by impending insurrection away from Egypt (58–55 BC), his wife died and Berenice was proclaimed queen. Toward the end of her reign, Alexandria was attacked by Aulus Gabinius, the Roman proconsul of Syria. Ptolemy XII was recalled in 55, whereupon he had his daughter murdered.

Beresford, Jack 1899–1977 •*English oarsman*• Educated at Bedford School, he served in the army during World War I. He competed for Great Britain at five Olympics (1920–36) as sculler and oarsman, winning three gold and two silver medals, and received the Olympic Diploma of Merit in 1949. He won the Diamond Sculls at Henley four times, and was elected president of the Thames Rowing Club in 1971.

Berg, Alban 1885–1935 •*Austrian composer*• Born in Vienna, he studied under **Arnold Schoenberg**, and allied the twelve-tone technique to a traditional style. He is best known for his opera *Wozzeck* (first performed 1925), his Violin Concerto (1935), and the *Lyric Suite* for string quartet (1926). His unfinished opera *Lulu* was posthumously produced from 1978 to 1979.

Berg, David Brandt *See* **David, Moses**

Berg, Patty (Patricia Jane) 1918– •*US golfer*• Born in Minneapolis, Minnesota, she began playing in amateur competitions in 1933, and won the Minnesota state championships in 1935, 1936 and 1938. Considered the foremost female golfer in the US, she won the US amateur title in 10 of the 13 tournaments she entered in 1938. She was named Outstanding Female Athlete by the Associated Press for 1938, 1943 and 1955. She cofounded the Ladies Professional Golf Association (LPGA).

Berg, Paul 1926– •*US molecular biologist and Nobel Prize winner*• Born in Brooklyn, New York, he was educated at Pennsylvania State and Western Reserve Universities, although his studies were interrupted by World War II, which he spent in the US Navy. In the 1960s, he purified several transfer RNA molecules (tRNAs), and in the 1970s he developed techniques to cut and splice genes from one organism into another. Concerned about the effects of mixing genes from different organisms, he organized a yearlong moratorium on genetic engineering experiments, and in 1975 chaired an international committee to draft guidelines for such studies. These techniques are now widely used in biological research. In 1978 Berg enabled gene transfer between cells from different mammalian species for the first time. He shared the 1980 Nobel Prize for chemistry with **Frederick Sanger** and **Walter Gilbert**.

Bergen, Candice 1946– •*US actress*• Born in Beverly Hills, California, the daughter of the ventriloquist Edgar Bergen, she attended school in Switzerland but dropped out to become an actress. After making her film debut in *The Group* (1966), she became a leading lady of 1970s cinema, appearing in films such as *Carnal Knowledge* (1971), *Starting Over* (1979) and *Gandhi* (1982). She is best known for playing a single mother in the television series *Murphy Brown* (1988–98) for which she won five Emmy awards. She published an autobiography, *Knock Wood*, in 1984.

Berger, Hans 1873–1941 •*German psychiatrist, inventor of electroencephalography*• Born in Neuses bei Coburg, he studied medicine at Jena University, where he remained for the rest of his career, becoming Professor of Psychiatry in 1919. His research attempted (mostly unsuccessfully) to establish relationships between psychological states and various physiological parameters, such as heartbeat, respiration and the temperature of the brain itself. Although precise correlations between electrical brain activity and psychic processes have not emerged, Berger's electroencephalograph, has become a useful tool of research and diagnosis into brain functions and diseases.

Berger, John Peter 1926– •*English novelist, playwright and art critic*• Born in London, he studied at the Central and Chelsea Schools of Art and began his working life as a painter and a drawing teacher, but soon turned to writing. His novels reflect his Marxism and artistic background, and have been well-received. Titles include *A Painter of Our Time* (1958) and *Corker's Freedom* (1964). His fame was enhanced with the publication of *G* (1972), a story of migrant workers in Europe, which won the Booker Prize. In his acceptance speech, Berger denounced the sponsors and announced that he would donate half of the prize money to the militant Black Panthers Party. Among his other writings the best known are *Ways of Seeing* (1972), on the visual arts, and *Pig Earth* (1979), a collection of short stories of French peasant life. More recent works include *To the Wedding* (1995), *Photocopies* (1996) and *King: A Street Story* (1999).

“ ”

If we could all live a thousand years ... we would each, at least once during that period, be considered a genius.

1972 ***G****, part 3, chapter 6.*

Berger, Maurice Jean *See* **Béjart, Maurice**

Bergerac, Savinien Cyrano de *See* **Cyrano de Bergerac, Savinien**

Berghem, Nicholas *See* **Berchem, Nicholas**

Bergius, Friedrich 1884–1949 •*German chemist and Nobel Prize winner*• He was born in Goldschmieden, near Breslau (now Wrocław, Poland). After studying chemistry at Leipzig, he received his doctorate in 1907. He was appointed assistant lecturer at Hanover in 1909 and developed a process for the conversion of coal into oil. He continued this work when he became head of the research laboratory of the Goldschmidt company in Essen in 1914. Finding himself unable to continue these studies after World War I, he turned his attention to the acidic hydrolysis of wood to sugar. He shared the 1931 Nobel Prize for chemistry with **Carl Bosch** for his work on coal.

Bergman, (Ernst) Ingmar 1918– •*Swedish film and stage director and writer*• He was born in Uppsala, and became a trainee theater director in Stockholm. His films include the elegiac *Sommernattens leende* (1955, *Smiles of a Summer Night*), the somber *Det sjunde inseglet* (1957, *The Seventh Seal*), *Smultronstället* (1957, *Wild Strawberries*), *Ansiktet* (1958, *The Face*), *Skammen* (1968, *Shame*), *Viskningar och rop* (1972, *Cries and Whispers*) and the British-Norwegian coproduction *Autumn Sonata* (1978). They became a cult for art-cinema audiences, winning many international prizes. Preoccupied with guilt, emotional repression and death, he created a succession of bleak masterpieces, outstanding for their photographic artistry and haunting imagery. His last film, *Fanny and Alexander* (1982), was an unexpectedly life-affirming evocation of autobiographical elements from his own childhood. Still active in the theater, he has continued to write screenplays, including *The Best Intentions* (1992), winner of the Palme D'Or at the Cannes Film Festival. He has published an autobiography, *The Magic Lantern* (1988), and a number of novels, including *Private Confessions* (1994).

Bergman, Ingrid 1915–82 •*Swedish film and stage actress*• Ingrid Bergman was born in Stockholm. After studying at the Royal Dramatic Theater, she was offered a contract by Svenskfilmindustri and made her film debut in *Munkbrogreven* (1934, "The Count of Monk's Bridge"). Unaffected and vivacious, she was signed by **David O Selznick** to appear in an English-language remake of *Intermezzo* (1939, with **Leslie Howard**), the story of a tragic romance between a concert pianist and a married violinist, and became an immensely popular romantic star in such films as *Casablanca* (1942), *For Whom the Bell Tolls* (1943), *Gaslight* (1944), which won her a first Oscar for best actress, *Spellbound* (1945) and *Notorious* (1946, with **Cary Grant**). In 1950 she gave birth to the illegitimate child of director **Roberto Rossellini**. The ensuing scandal led to her being ostracized from the US film industry. She continued her career in Europe, making films with Rossellini that included *Stromboli* (1950) and *Viaggio in Italia* (1954, "Journey to Italy"). After separating from Rossellini she was welcomed back by Hollywood in 1956, won an Academy Award for her part in *Anastasia*, and played missionary **Gladys Aylward** in *The Inn of the Sixth Happiness* (1958). Her last film was **Ingmar Bergman**'s *Autumn Sonata* (1978), a deeply felt exploration of a mother-daughter relationship. She was nominated seven times for an Academy Award, and won a third award for best supporting actress in *Murder on the Orient Express* (1974). In 1982 she played Israeli Prime Minister **Golda Meir** in a television production *A Woman Called Golda*, for which she won an Emmy award. Her daughter **Isabella Rossellini** is also an actress.

Bergson, Henri 1859–1941 •*French philosopher and Nobel Prize winner*• Born in Paris, the son of a Polish Jewish musician and an English mother, he was educated in Paris. He became professor at the Collège de France (1900–24), and was an original thinker who became something of a cult figure. He asserted that the *élan vital*, or "creative impulse," not a deterministic natural selection, is at the heart of evolution, and intuition, not analysis, reveals the real world of process and change. His own writings are literary, suggestive and analogical rather than philosophical in the modern sense, and he greatly influenced such writers as **Marcel Proust** (to whom he was connected by marriage), **Georges Sorel** and **Samuel Butler**. His most important works were *Essai sur les données immédiates de la conscience* (1889, Eng trans *Time and Free Will*, 1910), *Matière et mémoire* (1896, Eng trans *Matter and Memory*, 1911) and *L'évolution créatrice* (1907, Eng trans *Creative Evolution*, 1911). He was awarded the Nobel Prize for literature in 1927.

Beria, Lavrenti Pavlovich 1899–1953 •*Soviet secret police chief*• Born near Sukhumi, Georgia, into a peasant family, from 1921 to 1931 he served as a member of the OGPU (a forerunner of the KGB) in the Caucasus, before becoming First Secretary of the Georgian Communist Party in 1931. In 1938 he was appointed Soviet Commissar for Internal Affairs by his patron, **Stalin**, and was active in purging Stalin's opponents during World War II. He gained the title of Marshal in 1945. On Stalin's death in 1953, he attempted to seize power, but the coup was foiled by fearful military and party leaders. Following arrest by Marshal **Georgi Zhukov**, he was tried for treason and executed. Described as the "**Himmler** of Russia," he was a plotter of ruthless ambition and a notoriously skilled organizer of forced labor, terror and espionage.

Bering, Vitus Jonassen 1681–1741 •*Danish navigator*• Born in Horsens, he joined the navy of **Peter I (the Great)** in 1703. For his bravery in the wars with Sweden he was appointed to lead an expedition of discovery in the Sea of Kamchatka to determine whether the continents of Asia and America were joined. After an inconclusive expedition in 1728, in 1733 he was given command of the 600-strong Great Northern expedition to explore the Siberian coast and Kuril Islands. In 1741 he sailed from Okhotsk toward the American continent, and sighting land, followed the coast northward. However, sickness and storms forced him to return, and he was wrecked on the island of Avatcha (Bering Island), where he died of scurvy. Bering Sea and Bering Strait are also named after him. His discoveries were confirmed by Captain **James Cook**.

Berio, Luciano 1925–2003 •*Italian composer and teacher of music*• Born in Oreglia, he studied at the Music Academy in Milan, and at Tanglewood, Massachusetts. He and **Bruno Maderna** founded an electronic studio in Milan (1954–61), and in 1962 Berio moved to the US. He taught composition at the Juilliard School in New York and then returned to Italy in 1972 to continue his musical work. He is particularly interested in the combining of live and prerecorded sound, and the use of tapes and electronic music, as in his compositions *Mutazioni* (1954, "Mutations"), *Omaggio a James Joyce* (1958, "Homage to James Joyce") and *Questo vuol dire che ...* (1969–70, "This Means That ..."). His *Sequenza* series for solo instruments (1958–75) are striking virtuoso pieces. Pieces such as *Passaggio* (1963), for one female performer and two choruses, one in the pit and one in the audience, show the same pleasure in the dramatic tension of musical expression as his larger-scale stage works, *Laborintus II* (1965) and *Opera* (1969–70, revised in three acts in 1977). Between 1950 and 1966 he was married to the US soprano **Cathy Berberian**, for whom he wrote many works. *Continuo* (1991) is one of his later compositions.

Berkeley, Busby, *originally* **William Berkeley Enos** 1895–1976 •*US choreographer and director*• He was born in Los Angeles. He directed his first Broadway show, *A Night in Venice*, in 1928 and was subsequently hired by **Samuel Goldwyn** to devise the musical number for the film *Whoopee* (1930). He stayed in Hollywood to become one of the cinema's most innovative choreographers, noted for his mobile camerawork and kaleidoscopic routines involving great numbers of chorus girls and much sexual innuendo. His work enhanced films like *42nd Street* (1933), *Dames* (1934) and *Lady Be Good* (1941). In later years, ill health restricted his opportunities, but he directed *Take Me Out to the Ball Game* (1948), contributed imaginatively to *Small Town Girl* (1953) and enjoyed a Broadway success as the supervising producer of the 1971 revival of *No, No, Nanette*.

Berkeley, George 1685–1753 •*Irish Anglican bishop and philosopher*• Born at Dysert Castle, Kilkenny, he was educated at Kilkenny College and Trinity College, Dublin (where he remained, as Fellow and tutor, until 1713). In 1724 he became dean of Derry, in 1734 Bishop of Cloyne, and in 1752 moved to Oxford. His most important books were published in his early years: *Essay Toward a New Theory of Vision* (1709), *A Treatise Concerning the Principles of Human Knowledge* (1710) and *Three Dialogues Between Hylas and Philonous* (1713). His remaining literary work was divided between questions of social reform and of religious reflection.

" "

It is impossible that a man who is false to his friends and neighbors should be true to the public.

1750 ***Maxims Concerning Patriotism.***

Berkeley, Sir Lennox Randall Francis 1903–89 •*English composer*• Born in Oxford, he was a pupil of **Nadia Boulanger**. His early compositions, the largest of which is the oratorio *Jonah* (1935), show the influence of his French training in their conciseness and lucidity. Later works, notably the *Stabat Mater* (1946), the operas *Nelson* (1953) and *Ruth* (1956), and the orchestral *Windsor Variations* (1969), have won him wide recognition for their combination of technical refinement and emotional appeal. He was knighted in 1974.

Berkeley, Michael Fitzhardinge 1948– •*English composer*• Born in London, the son of **Lennox Berkeley**, he studied at the Royal Academy of Music and with **Richard Rodney Bennett**. He has composed concertos, and orchestral, chamber and choral works, including a powerful plea for peace in a nuclear age, the oratorio *Or Shall We Die?* (1983, text by **Ian McEwan**). He is well known for his introductions to music on radio and television.

Berkoff, Steven 1937– •*English dramatist, actor and director*• He was born in London, and after studying at the École Jacques Lecoq in Paris, he founded the London Theatre Group, for whom he directed his own adaptations from the classics, including **Franz Kafka**'s *Metamorphosis* (1969). His own plays include *Greek* (1979, a variant of the Oedipal myth transferred to contemporary London) and *West* (1983, an adaptation of the Beowulf legend); *Decadence* (1981) counterpoints the sexual and social activities of an upper-class couple with that of a working-class woman and a private detective, and in *Kvetch* (1987) the anxieties of a group of West End Jews are metamorphosed into a comic dinner party. He has also played film villains, as in *Beverly Hills Cop* (1984). Other plays and adaptations include *Agamemnon* (1977), *Sink the Belgrano* (1986), *In the Penal Colony* (1988) and *Brighton Beach Scumbags* (1991).

Berkowitz, David, *also known as* **Son of Sam** c. 1953– •*US murderer*• He dubbed himself "Son of Sam" in a note to the New York Police Department. He terrorized the city for a year in 1976 and 1977, preying on courting couples and women. He shot dead six people and wounded another seven. A special squad of 200 detectives was set up to trace him, but he avoided detection. At one time he was thought to have been a policeman. He was finally caught because of a parking ticket: he watched as it was stuck on his car, and then tore it to pieces. A woman witnessed this, noticed a strange smile on his face and reported him to the police. Pleading insanity, he claimed at his trial that Satanic voices told him to kill. Pronounced sane, he received a prison sentence of 365 years in August 1977.

Berle, Milton, *originally* **Milton Berlinger** 1908–2002 •*US entertainer*• Born in New York City, he began his career as a child performer in vaudeville, and later appeared as a comic actor in silent films and on Broadway. His zany but accessible style of comedy won him a loyal following, and he was a regular on several radio programs. Because his variety show *Texaco Star Theater* (1948–56) made the new medium of television popular, he was nicknamed "Mr Television."

Berlichingen, Götz von *See* **Götz von Berlichingen**

Berlin, Irving, *originally* **Israel Baline** 1888–1989 •*US composer*• Born in Temun (Tyumen), Russia, he was taken to the US as a child. He worked for a time as a singing waiter in a Bowery beerhall, introducing some of his own songs like "Alexander's Ragtime Band" and "Everybody's Doin It." A "soldier show" in 1918 led to musical comedy and films in the 1920s and 1930s. In 1939 he wrote "God Bless America," which achieved worldwide popularity in World War II and has become America's unofficial national anthem. The 1940s saw him at the peak of his career, with the hit musical *Annie Get Your Gun* (1946) and a stream of songs like "Anything You Can Do," "There's No Business Like Show Business" and the enduring "White Christmas." In all, he wrote the words and music for more than 900 songs.

Berlin, Sir Isaiah 1907–97 •*British philosopher and historian of ideas*• Born in Riga, Latvia, he emigrated to England with his Russian-speaking Jewish family in 1921 and was educated at Corpus Christi College, Oxford, where he spent most of his academic career. He also served as a diplomat in the British embassies in Moscow and in Washington. His works include *Karl Marx* (1939), *Historical Inevitability* (1954), *The Age of Enlightenment* (1956), *Two Concepts of Liberty* (1958), *Vico and Herder* (1976), *Magnus of the North* (1993), four volumes of essays (1978–80) and translations of **Ivan Turgenev**. Considered one of the leading liberal thinkers of the century, he was knighted in 1957 and appointed to the Order of Merit in 1971.

Berlinguer, Enrico 1922–84 •*Italian politician*• Born in Sardinia into a wealthy landowning family, he devoted himself from his early twenties to making the Italian Communist Party (PCI) a major force in Italian politics. In 1976, under his leadership, it won more than a third of the Chamber of Deputies' seats, prompting Berlinguer to propose the "historic compromise" with the Christian Democrat Party (DC) by which, in return for social reforms and an increased say on policy formation, the PCI agreed to respect the Church and constitutional institutions and discourage labor militancy. Under Berlinguer's influence, Italian Communism flourished in the 1970s but the coalition was undermined by the traditional DC suspicion of the left, the anti-Communist attitude of Pope **John Paul II** and the anti-Soviet feeling which was caused by the invasion of Afghanistan.

Berlioz, (Louis) Hector 1803–69 •*French composer*• Born in Côte-Saint-André, he first studied medicine, but produced some large-scale works before entering the Paris Conservatoire in 1826. He fell in love with the Irish Shakespearean actress Harriet Smithson (1800–54) and wrote the *Symphonie fantastique* (1830) for her; they married in 1833. His other works include the *Grande messe des morts* (1837, "High Mass for the Dead"), the dramatic symphony *Roméo et Juliette* (1839, "Romeo and Juliet"), the cantata *La damnation de Faust* (1846, "The Damnation of Faust"), and his operas *Les Troyens* (1856–58, "The Trojans") and *Béatrice et Bénédict* (1860–62). Despite a considerable reputation in Germany, Prussia and Great Britain, he failed to win respect in France, and that, together with the deaths of his second wife and his son, and his own ill health, overshadowed his later years.

Berlitz, Charles Frambach 1914– •*US educationist*• He was born in New York City, the grandson of Maximilian Delphinus Berlitz, who had founded the Berlitz School in 1878 as a German émigré to the US and developed what became known as "the Method." This consists of demonstrations and the identification of objects, with the instructors speaking only in the language being taught. By 1914 there were over 300 schools throughout the world, but large financial losses caused by World War I led to the sale of all the schools outside North and Central America in 1921. Charles graduated from Yale *magna cum laude* in 1936 and went on to restore the Berlitz company's fortunes through commissions for the services in World War II and business courses for employees going overseas afterward.

Berlusconi, Silvio 1936– •*Italian businessman and politician*• He was born in Milan. One of Italy's richest men, he has interests in television stations, housing, financial services, a cinema chain, and AC Milan soccer club. He is leader of the right-wing Forza Italia Party, which won more seats (155) in the 1994 election than any other (though not an absolute majority). He formed a government that included neo-Fascist ministers but resigned at the end of that year having received a vote of no-confidence. He returned to power in 2001, again including neo-Fascist ministers in his government, and promised to resolve the conflict of interest between his business empire and the office of Prime Minister.

Bernadette, St, *originally* **Marie Bernarde Soubirous** 1844–79 •*French nun and visionary*• Born in Lourdes, she claimed to have received 18 apparitions of the Blessed Virgin in 1858 at the Massabielle Rock, near Lourdes, a well-known place of pilgrimage. Attending a local school run by the Sisters of Charity of Nevers, she became a nun in 1866, and was beatified in 1925 and canonized in 1933. Her feast day is February 18 or April 16.

Bernadotte •*Swedish royal dynasty*• Jean Baptiste Jules Bernadotte founded the House in 1818 and later became King **Karl XIV Johan** of Sweden. On his death he was succeeded by his son, **Oskar I**, and the reigning monarchs of Sweden, Norway, Denmark and Belgium are his direct descendants. In 1794 Bernadotte's future wife Désirée met **Napoleon I**, who later described her as his "first love," and her elder sister, Julie, married **Joseph Bonaparte**. Désirée's eventual marriage to Bernadotte (1798) eased his strained relations with Bonaparte.

Bernal, John Desmond, *nicknamed* **Sage** 1901–71 •*Irish crystallographer*• Born in Nenagh, County Tipperary, he was educated by the Jesuits at Stonyhurst College, Lancashire, won a scholarship to Emmanuel College, Cambridge, and from the first showed himself a polymath. He developed modern crystallography and was a founder of molecular biology, pioneering work on the structure of water. He progressed from a lectureship at Cambridge to a professorship of physics and then crystallography at Birkbeck College, London (1937–68), and included among his major works *The Origin of Life* (1967). A communist from his student days, his hopes for communism's possibilities for science were first shown in his *The Social Function of Science* (1939) and *Marx and Science* (1952).

Bernard of Clairvaux, St, *also known as* **the Mellifluous Doctor** 1090–1153 •*French theologian and reformer*• Born near Dijon, he entered the Cistercian monastery of Cîteaux in 1113. In 1115 he became the first abbot of the newly founded monastery of Clairvaux, in Champagne. He led a studious, ascetic life and founded more than 70 monasteries. Known for his eloquence, an antidote to the dry scholasticism of the age, he drew up the statutes of the Knights Templars in 1128, and secured the recognition of Pope Innocent II. His writings comprise more than 400 epistles, 340 sermons, and several theological treatises. The monks of his reformed branch of the Cistercians are often called Bernardines. He was canonized in 1174, and his feast day is August 20.

Bernard of Menthon, St, *also called* **the Apostle of the Alps** 923–1008 •*Italian churchman*• Born in Savoy, he founded, as archdeacon of Aosta, the hospices in the Alpine passes that were named after him, as were St Bernard dogs, trained by the monks to go to the aid of travelers. He was canonized in 1115 and his feast day is May 28 or June 15.

Bernard, Jessie Shirley, *née* **Ravitch** 1903–96 •*US sociologist and writer*• Born in Minneapolis, Minnesota, she studied at the University of Minnesota where she met Luther Lee Bernard, whom she married in 1925. She worked alongside him, and together they produced works which included *Origins of American Sociology* (1943). She later pursued a career as an influential and groundbreaking feminist writer. Her pertinent analyses include *The Sex Game* (1968), *Women, Wives and Mothers* (1975) and *The Female World from a Global Perspective* (1987).

Berners-Lee, Tim(othy) 1955– •*English computer scientist*• Born in London, the son of two computer scientists, he studied at Queen's College, Oxford. At CERN (Conseil Européen pour la Recherche Nucléaire) from 1980 he developed the hypertext system Enquire as a tool for linking documents held on different computers. This became the World Wide Web, which was launched within CERN in 1990 and made available to the public on the Internet in 1991. He subsequently became director of the World Wide Web Consortium at the Massachusetts Institute of Technology (1994–) and holds the 3Com Founders Chair there (1999–).

Bernhard Leopold 1911– •*Prince of the Netherlands*• Born in Jena, the son of Prince Bernhard Casimir of Lippe-Biesterfeld, in 1937 he married **Juliana**, the only daughter of **Wilhelmina**, Queen of the Netherlands, and the title of Prince of the Netherlands was conferred on him. During World War II he escaped to England, where he helped to organize the Dutch Resistance. He was involved (1976) in a controversy over the activities of Lockheed Aircraft Corporation, and this produced a constitutional crisis that harmed the monarchy.

Bernhardt, Sarah, *originally* **Sarah-Marie-Henriette Rosine Bernard** 1844–1923 •*French actress*• She was born in Paris and entered the Paris Conservatoire in 1859. Bernhardt won fame as Zanetto in **François Coppée**'s *Le Passant* (1869), and as the Queen of Spain in **Victor Hugo**'s *Ruy Blas* (1872). She was recalled to the Comédie Française and after 1876 she made frequent appearances in London, the US and Europe. Her most famous roles include *Phèdre* (1877) and Marguerite in *La dame aux camélias* (1884). She founded the Théâtre Sarah Bernhardt in 1899. In 1915 she had a leg amputated, but did not abandon the stage. A legendary figure in the theater world, she was considered to be the greatest *tragédienne* of her day.

“ ”

For the theatre one needs long arms; it is better to have them too long than too short. An artiste with short arms can never, never make a fine gesture.

1907 ***Memories of My Life.***

Bernières, Louis de *See* **de Bernières, Louis**

Bernini, Gian Lorenzo 1598–1680 •*Italian sculptor, architect and painter*• Born in Naples, the son of a sculptor, he went to Rome at an early age, and there attracted the attention of Cardinal Scipione Borghese who became his patron. For him he sculpted a series of life-size marble statues that established his reputation as the leading sculptor of his day (1618–25, Borghese Gallery, Rome). Under Pope **Urban VIII**, he designed the famous baldacchino for St Peter's, and there is much other sculptural and architectural work by him still in the Vatican. However, under the next pope, Innocent X, he fell out of favor, partly because of the structurally unsound towers on the facade of St Peter's for which he was responsible. In 1647 he designed the fountain of the four river gods in the middle of the Piazza Navona. Superseded in papal favor by the sculptor Alessandro Algardi, Bernini concentrated on private commissions, the most famous of which is the Cornaro Chapel in the Church of Santa Maria della Vittoria. The central element of the design, the sculpture depicting *The Ecstasy of Saint Theresa*, is one of the great works of the baroque period. The dominant figure of the baroque period in Rome, he did his last work on the tomb of **Alexander VII** in St Peter's and the small Jesuit Church of San Andrea della Quirinale.

Bernoulli, Daniel 1700–82 •*Swiss mathematician*• Born in Groningen, the Netherlands, the son of **Jean Bernoulli**, he studied medicine and mathematics at the universities of Basel, Strasbourg and Heidelberg He worked on trigonometric series, mechanics and vibrating systems, and pioneered the modern field of hydrodynamics. His *Hydrodynamica* (1738) explored the physical properties of flowing fluids, and anticipated the kinetic theory of gases, pointing out that pressure would increase with increasing temperature. He solved a differential equation proposed by Jacopo Riccati, now known as Bernoulli's equation.

Bernoulli, Jacques or **Jakob** 1654–1705 •*Swiss mathematician*• He was born in Basel, the brother of **Jean Bernoulli**. He investigated infinite series, the cycloid, transcendental curves, logarithmic spiral and the catenary. In 1690 he applied **Gottfried Leibniz**'s newly discovered differential calculus to a problem in geometry, and introduced the term "integral." His *Ars conjectandi* (1713), an important contribution to probability theory, included his "law of large numbers," his permutation theory and the "Bernoulli numbers," coefficients found in exponential series.

Bernoulli, Jean or **Johann** 1667–1748 •*Swiss mathematician*• Born in Basel, the younger brother of **Jacques Bernoulli**, he graduated in medicine but turned to mathematics. He wrote on differential equations, both in general and with respect to the length and area of curves, isochronous curves and curves of quickest descent. He founded a dynasty of mathematicians that continued for two generations, and was employed by the Marquis de l'Hospital to help him write the first textbook on the differential calculus.

Bernstein, Carl 1944– •*US journalist and author*• He was born in Washington DC. With journalist Bob Woodward (1943–) he was responsible for unmasking the Watergate cover-up (1972), which resulted in a constitutional crisis and the resignation of President **Richard Nixon** (August 9, 1974). For their coverage, Bernstein and Woodward earned virtually every major journalism award, and won for the *Washington Post* the 1973 Pulitzer Prize for public service. Together they wrote the bestseller *All the President's Men* (1974), which became a successful film, and *The Final Days* (1976), an almost hour-by-hour account of President Nixon's last months in office. In 1989 Bernstein published *Loyalties: A Son's Memoirs*.

Bernstein, Leonard 1918–90 •*US conductor, pianist and composer*• Born in Lawrence, Massachusetts, he was educated at Harvard and the Curtis Institute of Music. He achieved fame suddenly in 1943, when he conducted the New York Philharmonic Orchestra as a substitute for **Bruno Walter**. His compositions include three symphonies, a television opera, a mass, a ballet, and many choral works and songs, but he is best known for his two musical comedies *On the Town* (1944) and *West Side Story* (1957), and for his concerts for young people.

Berra, Yogi (Lawrence Peter) 1925– •*US baseball player and coach*• Born in St Louis, Missouri, he played with the New York Yankees from 1946 to 1963, including 14 World Series (a record). He also set the record for most home runs by a catcher in the American League (313). He went on to manage and coach the Yankees and then did the same for their archrivals, the New York Mets, then coached the Houston Astros from 1986 to his retirement in 1992. Known for his illogical sayings, his most famous quote was "It ain't over 'til it's over."

“ ”

It ain't over 'til it's over.

Attributed.

Berri, Nabih 1938– •*Lebanese politician and soldier*• Born in Freetown, Sierra Leone, he studied law at Lebanese University. In 1980 he became leader of Amal ("Hope"), a branch of the Shiite nationalist movement founded by Iman Musa Sadr. He has held a number of ministerial posts in governments since 1984, and in 1992 became Speaker of the Lebanese Parliament. He was reelected for a third term in 2000.

Berry, Chuck (Charles Edward Anderson) 1926– •*US rock singer*• Born in St Louis, Missouri, he learned to play the guitar in high school, then served three years in a reform school for armed robbery (1944–47) before moving to Chicago in 1955 and launching his professional career. He had his first success with "Maybellene" (1955). With songs such as "School Days" (1957), "Rock and Roll Music" (1957) and "Johnny B Goode" (1958), he appealed to teenagers of all races. Jailed in 1962 for two years on a charge (1959) of transporting a minor over state lines for immoral purposes, he never fully recovered his creativity thereafter, although "My Ding a Ling" (1972) was the most successful single of his career. His influence was pivotal both to 1950s rock and roll and to the British pop renaissance of the early 1960s, and is evident in much of the **Beatles**' and the **Rolling Stones**' work. "Johnny B Goode" was one of the songs on the Voyager spacecraft's "Greetings to the Universe" record in 1977, carried into space as a message to possible alien life-forms.

Berryman, John, *originally* **John Allyn Smith** 1914–72 •*US poet, biographer, novelist and academic*• Born in McAlester, Oklahoma, he adopted his stepfather's name at the age of 12. Educated at Columbia University and Clare College, Cambridge, he taught at several US universities. His biography of **Stephen Crane** (1950) is rated highly but his reputation rests on his poetry. His first collection, *Poems*, appeared in 1942, and was followed by *Homage to Mistress Bradstreet* (1956, inspired by the 17th-century New England poet, **Anne Bradstreet**), which established his reputation. His major work is his *Dream Songs*, begun in 1955: *77 Dream Songs* (1964) won the Pulitzer Prize in 1965, and *His Toy, His Dream, His Rest: 308 Dream Songs* (1968) received the National Book award in 1969. The complete sequence was published in 1969. His other books include the novel *Recovery* (1973), concerning alcoholism. Unable to overcome his own drinking problem and mental illness, he committed suicide.

“ ”

The artist is extremely lucky who is presented with the worst possible ordeal which will not actually kill him.

*1972 Interview in **The Paris Review**, Winter issue.*

Berthollet, Claude Louis, Comte de 1749–1822 •*French chemist*• Born in Talloires, Savoy, he studied medicine at Turin and Paris. He helped **Antoine Lavoisier** with his research on gunpowder and also with the creation of a new system of chemical nomenclature which is still in use today. He accepted Lavoisier's antiphlogistic doctrines, but disproved his theory that all acids contain oxygen. He was the first chemist to realize that there is a connection between the manner in which a chemical reaction proceeds and the mass of the reagents; this insight led others to formulate the law of definite proportions. He also demonstrated that chemical affinities are affected by the temperature and concentration of the reagents. Following **Joseph Priestley**'s discovery that ammonia is composed of hydrogen and nitrogen, Berthollet made the first accurate analysis of their proportions. After accompanying **Napoleon I** to Egypt he remained there for two years, helping to reorganize the educational system. He voted for Napoleon's deposition in 1814, and on the restoration of the **Bourbon**s was created a count.

Bertolucci, Bernardo 1941– •*Italian film director*• He was born in Parma, and was an amateur filmmaker and poet. His collection of poetry, *In cerca del mistero* (1962, "In Search of Mystery"), won the Premio Viareggio prize and he made his directorial debut the same year with *La commare secca* (*The Grim Reaper*). A member of the Italian Communist Party, he makes films which depict the tension between conventionality and rebellion, exploring the complex relationships between politics, sex and violence. The success of *Il conformista* (1970, *The Conformist*) and *Ultimo tango a Parigi* (1972, *Last Tango in Paris*) allowed him to make the Marxist epic *Novecento* (1976, *1900*). He won a Best Director Academy Award for the epic *The Last Emperor* (1987). Other films include *The Sheltering Sky* (1990), *Little Buddha* (1993), *Stealing Beauty* (1996), which marked his return to Italy, and *Besieged* (1998).

Berwald, Franz Adolf 1796–1868 •*Swedish composer*• Born in Stockholm, into a musical family, he made his reputation with four symphonies he composed, the *Sérieuse* and *Capricieuse* in 1842 and the *Singulière* and *Eb* in 1845. In 1847 **Jenny Lind**'s appearance in his *Ein ländlisches Verlobungsfest in Schweden* ("A Swedish Country Betrothal") in Vienna brought him great acclaim. He returned to Sweden in 1849 and divided his time between music, business concerns and increasing involvement in social issues until 1867, when he was made Professor of Composition at the Swedish Royal Academy. His fiery expression and original inspiration made him the most impressive Swedish composer of the 19th century.

Berwick, James Fitzjames, 1st Duke of 1670–1734 •*French and Jacobite general*• He was the illegitimate son of **James VII and II**. Educated in France as a Catholic, he was created Duke of Berwick (1687), but fled from England at the Glorious Revolution of 1688. He fought in his father's Irish campaign (1689–91), and then in Flanders and against the Camisards. In 1706 he was created a Marshal of France, and in Spain established the throne of **Philip V** by the decisive victory of Almanza (1707) in the War of the Spanish Succession. Appointed Commander in Chief of the French forces (1733), he was killed while besieging Phillippsburg.

Berzelius, Jöns Jacob 1779–1848 •*Swedish chemist*• Born in Väfversunda, East Götland, he studied medicine at Uppsala and worked as an unpaid assistant in the College of Medicine at Stockholm before succeeding to the chair of medicine and pharmacy in 1807. In 1815 he was appointed Professor of Chemistry at the Royal Caroline Medico-Chirurgical Institute in Stockholm, retiring in 1832. Soon after **Alessandro Volta**'s invention of the electric battery, Berzelius began in 1802 to experiment with the voltaic pile. Working with Wilhelm Hisinger he discovered that all salts are decomposed by electricity. He went on to suggest that all compounds are made up of positive and negative components, a theory which laid the foundations for our understanding of radicals. In 1803 he and Hisinger discovered cerium; Berzelius also discovered selenium and thorium and was the first person to isolate silicon, zirconium and titanium. His greatest achievement, however, was his contribution to atomic theory. Matching the idea of constant proportions with **John Dalton**'s atomic theory, and persuaded of the central importance of oxygen from his studies of **Antoine Lavoisier**'s work, he drew up a table of atomic weights using oxygen as a base, devising the modern system of chemical symbols. He also made significant contributions to organic chemistry. A pioneer of gravimetric analysis, he has had few rivals as an experimenter. As a result of the poverty of his early years, he had to improvise much of his apparatus and some of his innovations are still standard laboratory equipment, for example, wash bottles, filter paper and rubber tubing. He was elected to the Stockholm Royal Academy of Sciences in 1808 and became its secretary in 1818. He was awarded the Gold Medal of the Royal Society of London, and in 1835 he was created a baron by Charles XIV.

Besant, Annie, *née* **Wood** 1847–1933 •*English theosophist*• She was born in London of Irish parentage. In 1874 she became vice president of the National Secular Society and she was an ardent proponent of birth control and socialism. In 1889, after meeting Madame **Blavatsky**, she developed an interest in theosophy, and went to India, where she became involved in politics, being elected president of the Indian National Congress from 1917 to 1923. Her publications include *The Gospel of Atheism* (1877) and *Theosophy and the New Psychology* (1904).

Besant, Sir Walter 1836–1901 •*English novelist and social reformer*• Born in Portsmouth, he studied at King's College London and at Christ's College, Cambridge, and after a few years as a professor in Mauritius, devoted himself to literature. In 1871 he entered into a literary partnership with James Rice, and together they produced many novels. Besant himself wrote *All Sorts and Conditions of Men* (1882) and *Children of Gibeon* (1886), describing conditions in the slums of the East End of London, and other novels advocating social reform, resulting in the establishment of the People's Palace, London (1887), for popular recreation. He was the brother-in-law of **Annie Besant**.

Bessarion or **Basilius, John** 1403–72 •*Byzantine theologian*• Born in Trebizond (Trabzon), he was educated in Constantinople

(Istanbul). As Archbishop of Nicaea (Iznik) from 1437, he accompanied the Greek emperor, John Palaeologus, to the Councils of Ferrara and Florence in Italy, to bring about union between the Byzantine and Latin Churches (1438). He joined the Roman Church, was made a cardinal by Pope **Eugenius IV** (1439), served as papal governor of Bologna (1450–55). He was one of the earliest scholars to transplant Greek literature and philosophy into the West.

Bessel, Friedrich Wilhelm 1784–1846 •*German mathematician and astronomer*• Born in Minden, Westphalia, he started as a ship's clerk but in 1810 was appointed director of the observatory and professor at Königsberg. He cataloged stars and was the first to identify the nearest stars and determine their distances. He predicted the existence of a planet beyond Uranus as well as the existence of dark stars. In the course of this work he systematized the mathematical functions involved, which today bear his name, although **Joseph Fourier** had worked on them earlier.

Bessemer, Sir Henry 1813–98 •*English metallurgist and inventor*• Born in Charlton, Hertfordshire, he learned metallurgy in his father's type foundry, and at the age of 17 set up his own business in London to produce small castings and artwork. In 1855, as a result of his efforts to find a method of manufacturing stronger gun barrels for use in the Crimean War (1853–56), he patented an economical process by which molten pig iron can be turned directly into steel by blowing air through it in a "Bessemer converter." Bessemer established a steelworks at Sheffield in 1859, which expanded from armaments to meet the worldwide demand for steel rails, locomotives and bridges. He was elected a Fellow of the Royal Society in 1877 and knighted in 1879. Other English steelmasters were reluctant to accept Bessemer's process, but in the United States entrepreneurs including **Andrew Carnegie** made a fortune from it.

Bessmertnova, Natalia 1941– •*Russian ballerina*• Born in Moscow, she trained at the Bolshoi Ballet School (1952–61), joining the company on graduation. She has become famous for her interpretation of all the major roles of the classical repertory. She has also taken important roles in ballets devised by her husband **Yuri Grigorovich**, particularly *Ivan the Terrible* (1975). She was awarded the Lenin prize in 1986.

Besson, Luc 1959– •*French film director*• Born in Paris, he directed a number of short films and commercials before his feature debut *Le Dernier combat* (1983, "The Last Battle"). He enjoyed great popular success with the thriller *Subway* (1985) and the globetrotting saga *The Big Blue* (1988). Telling original stories with remarkable visual flair and technical virtuosity, his subsequent feature films include *Nikita* (1990), *Leon* (1994), *The Fifth Element* (1997) and *The Messenger: The Story of Joan of Arc* (1999). He has also written and produced other films, and has directed documentaries and pop videos.

Best, Charles Herbert 1899–1978 •*Canadian physiologist*• He was born in West Pembroke, Maine, and graduated in physiology and biochemistry from the University of Toronto. As a research student there in 1921 he helped **Frederick Banting** to isolate the hormone insulin, used in the treatment of diabetes. (Banting gave him a share of his 1923 Nobel Prize for physiology or medicine.) He enjoyed considerable success during his later career. He discovered choline (a vitamin that prevents liver damage) and histaminase (the enzyme that breaks down histamine), introduced the use of the anticoagulant heparin, and continued to work on insulin, showing in 1936 that the administration of zinc with insulin can prolong its activity.

Best, George 1946– •*Northern Irish soccer player*• Born in Belfast, he is considered the greatest individual soccer player ever produced by Northern Ireland. He was the leading scorer for Manchester United in the Football League First Division in 1967–68, and in 1968 won a European Cup medal and the title of European Footballer of the Year. However, he became increasingly unable to cope with the pressure of top-class soccer, and was virtually finished by the time he was 25 years old. His attempted comebacks with smaller clubs in England, the US and Scotland were unsuccessful, but in his short time as a player he had made himself one of the game's immortals. His life was the subject of the film *Best* (2000), and he published *Blessed: My Autobiography* in 2001.

Bestall, A(lfred) E(dmeades) 1892–1986 •*English illustrator and author*• He was born in Mandalay, Burma. He is mainly remembered for having illustrated and written the Rupert Bear cartoon strip in the *Daily Express* newspaper for 30 years (1935–65), taking over from Rupert's creator, **Mary Tourtel**. He also illustrated and wrote 41 volumes of the *Rupert Bear Annual* (1936–76).

Betancourt, Rómulo 1908–81 •*Venezuelan statesman and reformer*• He was born in Guatire, Miranda. One of the founders of the Acción Democrática Party, he held power from 1945 to 1947. On the fall of the Pérez Jiménez dictatorship (1950–58), he was elected president (1959–64) of the new Venezuelan democracy. He chose a moderate course, adopting an agrarian law (1960), and ambitious economic development plans which provided for a transition from the dictatorship.

Bethe, Hans Albrecht 1906– •*US physicist and Nobel Prize winner*• Born in Strassburg, Germany (now Strasbourg, France), he was educated at the Universities of Frankfurt and Munich. During World War II he was director of theoretical physics for the Manhattan atomic bomb project based at Los Alamos. In 1939 he proposed the first detailed theory for the generation of energy by stars through a series of nuclear reactions. He also contributed with **Ralph Alpher** and **George Gamow** to the "alpha, beta, gamma" theory of the origin of the chemical elements during the early development of the universe. He was awarded the 1967 Nobel Prize for physics.

Bethlen, Gábor or **Gabriel** 1580–1629 •*King of Hungary*• Born into a Hungarian Calvinist family, he was elected Prince of Transylvania (1613). Fierce, unscrupulous, yet astute, in 1619 he invaded Hungary and, although he soon lost the royal title, he forced Emperor **Ferdinand II** to grant religious freedom to the Hungarian Protestants and to recognize his authority in several Hungarian provinces, making him titular king (1620–21). Gábor resumed hostilities against the empire (1623, 1626), but his declining health precluded further success.

Bethlen, István (Stephen), Count 1874–1951 •*Hungarian statesman*• Born in Gernyeszeg (Cornesti), Transylvania, he was a leader of the counterrevolutionary movement after World War I, and as Prime Minister (1921–31) promoted Hungary's economic reconstruction.

Bethmann Hollweg, Theobald von 1856–1921 •*German statesman*• Born in Hohenfinow, Brandenburg, he qualified in law, then rose in the service of Prussia and the German Empire, becoming Imperial Chancellor in 1909. Although not identified with the German elite's most bellicose elements, and fearing the effects of war upon German society, he nevertheless played an important part in the events which brought about general war in 1914. Anxious for a negotiated peace in 1917, he was forced from office. He wrote *Reflections on the World War* (1920).

Bethune, David *See* **Beaton, David**

Bethune, James *See* **Beaton, James**

Bethune, Mary McLeod, *née* **McLeod** 1875–1955 •*US educator and administrator*• Born in Mayesville, South Carolina, to parents who had been slaves before the Civil War, she began her career by teaching in Southern schools. In 1904 she opened the Daytona Normal and Industrial Institute for Girls, which merged in 1923 with the Cookman Institute to become the coeducational Bethune-Cookman College, of which Bethune was president. She was also founding president of the National Council of Negro Women (1935–49). She was director of the division of Negro Affairs within the National Youth Administration, and insisted that the number of African Americans enrolled in the program be increased. She also administered the Special Negro Fund, which assisted many African-American college students, and was sent by the State Department to attend the San Francisco Conference to establish the United Nations (1945).

Betjeman, Sir John 1906–84 •*English poet, broadcaster and writer on architecture*• Born in Highgate, London, he was educated at

Highgate Junior School (where **T S Eliot** was one of his teachers), Marlborough School and Magdalen College, Oxford (where he met and got to know **W H Auden** and **Louis MacNeice**). The early period of his life is dealt with in his blank-verse autobiography, *Summoned by Bells* (1960). He left the university without a degree, and marked time as a cricket master in a preparatory school. He was dismissed as the *Evening Standard's* film critic, but went on to write for the *Architectural Review* and became general editor of the *Shell Guides* in 1934. He wrote the bleak "Death in Leamington" for the *London Mercury* in 1930 and a year later his first collection of verse, *Mount Zion; or, In Touch with the Infinite* was published. Other collections include *Continual Dew: A Little Book of Bourgeois Verse* (1937), *Old Lights for New Chancels* (1940), *New Bats in Old Belfries* (1945), *A Few Late Chrysanthemums* (1954) and *Collected Poems* (1958). Betjeman's passionate interest in architecture (especially of Victorian churches) and topography led to the publication of a number of books, including *Ghastly Good Taste* (1933), *Vintage London* (1942) and *Cornwall* (1965), and is also reflected in his poetry. He was the quintessential poet of the suburbs, particular, jolly, nostalgic and wary of change, preferring the countryside to the city. He was knighted in 1969 and succeeded **Cecil Day Lewis** as poet laureate in 1972.

" "

Come, friendly bombs, and fall on Slough
It isn't fit for humans now
There isn't grass to graze a cow
Swarm over, Death!

*1937 **Continual Dew**, "Slough."*

Beuys, Joseph 1921–86 •*German avant-garde artist*• Born in Kleve, he served as a pilot in the Luftwaffe in World War II, during which he was shot down. He studied art at the Düsseldorf Academy, where he later became Professor of Sculpture (1961–71). His sculpture consisted mainly of assemblages of bits and pieces of rubbish, which were also included as elements of "happenings" which he organized. His work, which had links with the Italian movement known as Arte Povera, flouted the conventions even of modern art, being deliberately antiformal and banal. He was also a prominent political activist and crusader for direct democracy, and helped to found the Green Party in Germany.

Bevan, Aneurin 1897–1960 •*Welsh Labour politician*• Born in Tredegar, Monmouthshire, he was one of 13 children of a miner. He began work in the pits at the age of 13. Six years later he was chairman of a Miners' Lodge of more than 4,000 members, and led the Welsh miners in the 1926 General Strike. Elected as the Independent Labour Party (ILP) Member of Parliament for Ebbw Vale (1929), he joined the more moderate Labour Party in 1931, establishing a reputation as a brilliant, irreverent and often tempestuous orator. In 1934 he married **Jennie Lee**. During World War II he was frequently a "one-man Opposition" against **Churchill**. Appointed Minister of Health in the 1945 Labour government, he introduced the revolutionary National Health Service in 1948. He became Minister of Labour in 1951, but resigned the same year over the National Health charges proposed in the budget. From this period dated "Bevanism," the left-wing movement aimed at making the Labour Party more socialist and less "reformist," though he himself ceased to be a "Bevanite" at the 1957 Brighton party conference when he opposed a one-sided renunciation of the hydrogen bomb by Great Britain. The most publicized Labour politician of his time, he brought to the House of Commons radical fervor, iconoclastic restlessness and an acute intellect. He published *In Place of Fear* (1952).

Beveridge, William Henry Beveridge, 1st Baron 1879–1963 •*British economist, administrator and social reformer*• Born of Scottish descent in Rangpur, Bengal, he was educated at Charterhouse and Balliol College, Oxford. As leader writer on the *Morning Post*, he made himself the leading authority on unemployment insurance, and compiled his notable report, *Unemployment* (1909, revised 1930). From 1934 he served on several commissions and committees and was the author of the *Report on Social Insurance and Allied Services* (1942), known as "The Beveridge Report." This was a comprehensive scheme of social insurance, covering the whole community without income limit. Published at the height of World War II, it was a remarkable testimony to Great Britain's hopes for the future, and provided the basis for the creation of the welfare state. He was elected as a Liberal Member of Parliament in 1944, but defeated in 1945. He was made a baron in 1946. He wrote the autobiographical *Power and Influence* (1953), and books on unemployment and social security.

Bevin, Ernest 1881–1951 •*English Labour politician*• He was born in Winsford, Somerset, and orphaned by the age of seven. Self-educated, he came early under the influence of trade unionism and the Baptists, and was for a time a lay preacher. At the age of 30 he was a paid official of the dockers' union and in 1920 he earned himself a national reputation by his mostly successful handling of his union's claims before a wage tribunal at which he was opposed by an eminent barrister. This won him the title "the dockers' KC." He built up the gigantic National Transport and General Workers' Union from 32 separate unions and became its general secretary (1921–40). He was one of the leaders in the General Strike (1926), and in 1940 he became Minister of Labour and National Service in **Churchill**'s coalition government, successfully attaining complete mobilization of Great Britain's manpower by 1943. He began to take a keen interest in foreign affairs and became Foreign Secretary in **Clement Attlee**'s Labour government (1945–51). He accepted the necessity for the Western powers to establish a federal government in Western Germany, and by the Berlin air lift (June 1948–May 1949) accepted and met the Soviet challenge for the control of that city. He was largely responsible for the successful conclusion of mutual assistance (1948) and defense agreements (1949) with other European powers and the US, but opposed total integration of European states, believing that Great Britain had special Commonwealth obligations, acquiescing reluctantly in the formation of a Council of Europe. Ill health made him relinquish office in March 1951, and he died a month later. The pioneer of modern trade unionism, Bevin was essentially a skilled and moderate negotiator, robust, down-to-earth, a "John Bull" of trade unionists. His realism earned him the censure of the more left-wing elements in his party as well as the esteem of many of his political opponents. He wrote *The Job to Be Done* (1942).

" "

If you open that Pandora's box, you never know what Trojan 'orses will appear.

*1948 Expressing doubts about the value of the newly formed Council of Europe. Recalled by his secretary Sir Roderick Barclay in Michael Charlton **The Price of Victory** (1983).*

Bewick, Thomas 1753–1828 •*English wood engraver*• Born in Ovingham, Northumberland, he was apprenticed at age 14 to Ralph Beilby (1744–1817), a Newcastle engraver; he became his partner in 1776 and, taking his brother John (1760–95) as an apprentice, consolidated his reputation with his woodcuts for *Gay's Fables* (1779). His other works include *History of Quadrupeds* (1790) and *History of British Birds* (1797–1804). He later produced *Aesop's Fables* (1818), in which he was assisted by his son, Robert Elliott (1788–1849), who became his partner in 1812. Bewick's swan was named in his honor shortly after his death.

Bezos, Jeff(rey P) 1964– •*US businessman*• Born in Albuquerque, New Mexico, he studied electrical engineering and computer science at Princeton University before entering investment banking. In 1994 he founded his own virtual bookstore, which he called Amazon.com after the world's longest river, and concentrated on designing software to facilitate business using the Internet. His company rapidly became the biggest retailer on the Internet, worth millions of dollars by the end of the 1990s, and had won international recognition as a pioneer in electronic commerce.

Bhartrihari fl. 7th century •*Hindu poet and philosopher*• He was the author of three *satakas* (centuries) of stanzas on practical conduct, love, and renunciation of the world, and a Sanskrit grammarian.

Bhasa fl. 3rd century AD •*Sanskrit dramatist*• He was the author of plays on religious and legendary themes.

Bhave, Vinoba 1895–1982 •*Indian land reformer*• Born in a Maharashtra village, he was taken into the care of **Mahatma Gandhi** as a young scholar, an event which changed his life. Distressed by the land hunger riots in Telengana, Hyderabad (1951), he began a walking mission throughout India to persuade landlords to give land to the peasants. A barefoot, ascetic saint, his silent revolution led to 4,000,000 acres of land being redistributed in four years.

Bhindranwale, Sant Jarnail Singh 1947–84 •*Indian politician and Sikh extremist leader*• Born into a poor Punjabi Jat farming family, he trained at the orthodox Damdani Taksal Sikh missionary school, becoming its head priest in 1971 and assuming the name Bhindranwale. He campaigned violently against the heretical activities of Nirankari Sikhs during the later 1970s, demanding a separate state of "Khalistan" during the early 1980s and precipitating a bloody Hindu-Sikh conflict in Punjab. After taking refuge in the Golden Temple complex at Amritsar and building up an arms cache for terrorist activities, with about 500 devoted followers he died at the hands of the Indian Security Forces who stormed the temple in "Operation Blue Star."

Bhumibol Adulyadej 1927– •*King of Thailand*• Born in Cambridge, Massachusetts, he is the grandson of King **Chulalongkorn** (Rama V). He became monarch as King Rama IX (1946) after the assassination of his elder brother, King Ananda Mahidol. He married Queen Sirikit in 1950 and has one son, Crown Prince Vajiralongkorn (1952–), and three daughters. As king, he has been the focus of unity and a stabilizing influence in a country noted for its political turbulence. Now the longest-reigning monarch in Thailand's history, he is a highly respected figure, viewed in some quarters as semidivine, and he wields considerable political influence.

Bhutto, Benazir 1953– •*Pakistani politician, the first modern-day woman leader of a Muslim nation*• She was born in Karachi, the daughter of the former Prime Minister **Zulfikar Ali Bhutto**, and of Begum Nusrat Bhutto, also a politician. After an education at Oxford University, she returned to Pakistan and was frequently placed under house arrest (1977–1984) by General **Mohammed Zia ul-Haq**, who had executed her father following the 1977 coup against him. Between 1984 and 1986, she and her mother lived in England, and she became the joint leader in exile of the opposition Pakistan People's Party (PPP). Martial law was lifted in Pakistan in December 1985, and she returned the following April to launch a nationwide campaign for open elections. In 1988 she was elected Prime Minister, after the death of Zia in mysterious circumstances. In her first term, she achieved an uneasy compromise with the army and improved relations with India; and she led Pakistan back into the Commonwealth in 1989. In 1990 her government was removed from office by presidential decree, and she was accused of corruption. She was later defeated in the elections, but was returned to power in the elections of 1993. In September 1995 the armed forces were discovered to have hatched a plot to remove her; and a year later her brother Murtaza was killed during a gun battle with police. Defeated in the 1997 election, she was later sentenced to five years' imprisonment for corruption and disqualified from politics. She went into exile and her appeal against the conviction was upheld in 2001, but further charges followed and she faces jail if she returns to Pakistan.

Bhutto, Zulfikar Ali 1928–79 •*Pakistani statesman*• Born in Larkana in the province of Sind in British-ruled India, he was the son of a landed aristocrat. A graduate of the universities of California and Oxford, he began a career in law and joined the Pakistani Cabinet in 1958 as Minister of Commerce, and became Foreign Minister in 1963. He founded the Pakistan People's Party (PPP) in 1967. After the secession of East Pakistan (Bangladesh) in 1971, he became President (1971–73) and Prime Minister (1973–77). Opposition to his policies, especially from right-wing Islamic parties, led to the army (under General **Zia ul-Haq**) seizing control after the 1977 elections. Tried for corruption and murder, he was sentenced to death in 1978. In spite of worldwide appeals for clemency, the sentence was carried out in 1979. His elder daughter, **Benazir Bhutto**, became PPP leader.

Biandrata, Giorgio *See* **Blandrata, Giorgio**

Bias 6th century BC •*Greek orator*• A native of Priene, Ionia, he became famous for his pithy sayings, and was one of the "Seven Wise Men" of Greece (the others were Chilon, Cleobulus, **Periander**, Pittacus of Mitylene, **Solon** and **Thales**).

Bidault, Georges 1899–1983 •*French statesman*• He was born and educated in Paris, where he became a professor of history and edited the Catholic newspaper *L'Aube*. He served in both world wars, was taken prisoner in World War II, was released, and took part in the French Resistance movement. He then became leader of the Mouvement Républicain Populaire (MRP) and was Prime Minister (1946, 1949–50), deputy Prime Minister (1950, 1951), and Foreign Minister (1944, 1947, 1953–54). Prime Minister again in 1958, he opposed General **de Gaulle** over the Algerian War, and was charged with plotting against the security of the state. He was in exile 1962–68.

Biddle, John 1615–62 •*English preacher and the founder of English Unitarianism*• Born in Wotton-under-Edge, Gloucestershire, he studied at Magdalen Hall, Oxford. In 1641 he was elected master of the Gloucester Free School, but in 1645 was imprisoned for rejecting in his preaching the deity of the Holy Ghost, and was banished to the Scilly Isles in 1655. On release in 1658, he continued to preach in London until after the Restoration. Arrested again in 1662, he could not pay his fine of £100, and was sent to jail where he died.

Bierce, Ambrose Gwinnett 1842–1914 •*US short-story writer and journalist*• Born in Meigs County, Ohio, he grew up in Indiana and fought for the Union in the Civil War. He wrote *Tales of Soldiers and Civilians* (1892) including his most celebrated story, "An Occurrence at Owl Creek Bridge," which is a haunted, near-death fantasy of escape influenced by **Edgar Allan Poe** and in turn influencing **Stephen Crane** and **Ernest Hemingway**. He compiled the much-quoted *Cynic's Word Book* (published in book form in 1906), now better known as *The Devil's Dictionary*. He moved to Washington DC, and in 1913 went to Mexico to report on **Pancho Villa**'s army and disappeared.

" "

Acquaintance, n. A person whom we know well enough to borrow from, but not well enough to lend to.

1906 ***The Cynic's Word Book.***

Biermann, Ludwig 1907–86 •*German astronomer*• Born in Hamm, he was educated at the University of Berlin, where he graduated in 1932 and was later a lecturer (1938–45). His early work on stellar atmospheres led to studies of magnetic phenomena in sunspots and the solar corona, but his greatest achievement was his theoretical prediction (1951) of the existence of a continuous stream of high-speed particles flowing from the sun, which acted as the driving force behind the ionic tails of comets. The existence of this "solar wind" was confirmed in 1959. Biermann was awarded the gold medal of the Royal Astronomical Society in 1974.

Bigelow, Jacob 1787–1879 •*US physician and botanist*• Born in Sudbury, Massachusetts, he was educated at the universities of Harvard and Pennsylvania, and practiced medicine in Boston. He helped to compile the single-word nomenclature of the American Pharmacopoeia of 1820, subsequently adopted in England. He published a study of all of the plants growing within the Boston area, and with Francis Booth he later extended the range of his work, this enlarged work becoming a standard manual of botany for many years. The genus *Bigelovia* is named after him.

Bigelow, Kathryn 1952– •*US film director*• She began her career as a painter, but switched to filmmaking after enrolling at Columbia University graduate film school in New York. Her first commercial success arrived with the contemporary horror film *Near Dark* (1987). Her stylish direction earned her attention, and her reputation was enhanced by her best film, the tense police thriller *Blue Steel* (1990). Her other films include *Point Break* (1991) and *Strange Days* (1995).

Biggers, Earl Derr 1884–1933 •*US novelist and playwright*• Born in Warren, Ohio, he was educated at Harvard, and entered journalism as a staff writer on the Boston *Traveler*. He introduced the famous character "Charlie Chan" in a series of detective novels starting with *The House Without a Key* (1925) and finishing with *Keeper of the Keys*, which appeared a year before his death.

Biggs, Ronald 1929– •*English thief*• He was a member of the gang who carried out the Great Train Robbery. On August 8, 1963, the night mail train from Glasgow to London was stopped at Sears Crossing in Buckinghamshire. The robbers escaped with 120 mailbags, containing over £2.5 million. Biggs was traced by fingerprints left on a ketchup bottle and on a Monopoly board at the gang's farm hideout. He was convicted and sentenced to 25 years for conspiracy and 30 years (to run concurrently) for armed robbery. He escaped from Wandsworth Prison on July 8, 1965 and fled to Australia. Pursued by the police, he eventually settled in Brazil. There, saved from extradition because his girlfriend was pregnant (under Brazilian law, fathers of Brazilian children cannot be extradited), he continued to live, supported by an income generated largely by press interviews. In ill health, he returned to the UK in May 2001 to serve the remainder of his sentence in Belmarsh Prison.

Bigordi, Domenico di Tommaso *See* **Ghirlandaio, Domenico**

Bihzad, Ustad Kamal al-Din born c. 1440 •*Persian painter*• Born in Herat, he was the most famous Persian painter of the end of the 15th century (the Timurid period), known as "the Marvel of the Age." He worked under the patronage of Shah Baisunkur Mirza at his academy for painters, calligraphers, illuminators and bookbinders; only a few of his works remain. Bihzad lost the stiffness and detail of the paintings of the earlier 15th century and his works are masterpieces of composition, full of action and realism, and introducing entirely new color combinations.

Bikila, Abebe 1932–73 •*Ethiopian athlete*• Born in Ethiopia, he was the first Black athlete to win a gold in an Olympics marathon when he ran barefoot in Rome in 1960 and set a new world record of 2 hours, 15 minutes and 16.2 seconds. He went on to run in the 1964 Tokyo Olympics and, this time wearing socks and shoes, won again and beat his own Olympic record by three minutes. He had undergone an appendectomy only 40 days before. A car crash in 1969 paralyzed him and he was confined to a wheelchair for the rest of his life.

Biko, Steve (Stephen) 1946–77 •*South African Black activist*• Born in King William's Town, Cape Province, he was one of the founders (as well as the first president) of the all-Black South African Students Organization (1969). His encouragement of Black self-reliance and his support of Black institutions made him a popular figure, and in 1972 he became honorary president of the Black People's Convention, a coalition of over 70 Black organizations. The following year he was served with a banning order severely restricting his movements and freedom of speech and association. He was detained four times in the last few years of his life, and died in police custody as a result of beatings received. His story was the basis for **Richard Attenborough**'s 1987 film *Cry Freedom*. In 1997 five former security policemen confessed to having been involved in his murder.

Bill, Max 1908–94 •*Swiss artist and teacher*• Born in Winterthur, he trained at the Zurich School of Arts and Crafts (1924–27), and was a fellow student with **László Moholy-Nagy** and **Josef Albers** at the Bauhaus in Dessau (1927–29). Working as an architect as well as a painter, sculptor and product designer, he developed the essential Bauhaus principles of cooperative design along abstract (or "concrete") and purely functionalist lines; he designed typewriters, tables, chairs, lamps and electric wall plugs.

Billings, Josh, *pseudonym of* **Henry Wheeler Shaw** 1818–85 •*US humorist*• He was born in Lanesboro, Massachusetts, and worked as a land agent in Poughkeepsie, New York. He published facetious almanacs and collections of witticisms, relying heavily on deliberate misspelling. The first of these was *Josh Billings, His Sayings* (1866).

" "

Man was kreated a little lower than the angells and has bin gittin a little lower ever since.

1866 ***Josh Billings, His Sayings***, *chapter 28.*

Billington-Greig, Teresa, *née* **Billington** 1877–1964 •*English suffragette, socialist and writer*• Born in Blackburn, Lancashire, she became secretary of the Manchester Equal Pay League, and first met **Emmeline Pankhurst** when her job was threatened for refusing to teach religious instruction. A friend of the Pankhursts and **Annie Kenney**, Billington-Greig joined the Women's Social and Political Union in 1903 and became its London organizer (1907). However, in 1907, in dispute with the Pankhursts, she founded the Women's Freedom League with **Charlotte Despard** and **Edith How-Martyn**. Though an ardent suffragette, twice imprisoned for her activities, she became a critic of the more militant suffragists, as she indicates in *The Militant Suffrage Movement* (1911).

Billroth, (Christian Albert) Theodor 1829–94 •*Austrian surgeon*• Born in Bergen auf Rügen, Prussia (now in Germany), he became Professor of Surgery at Zurich (1860–67) and Vienna (1867–94). A pioneer of modern abdominal surgery, he performed the first successful excision of the larynx (1874) and the first resection of the intestine (1881). A brilliant musician, he was a friend of **Brahms**.

Billy the Kid *See* **Bonney, William H**

Binchy, Maeve 1940– •*Irish novelist, playwright and short-story writer*• Born in Dublin and educated at University College, Dublin, she has had plays staged in Dublin and won awards in Ireland and Prague for her television play *Deeply Regretted By* (1979). Her collections of short stories include *Victoria Line, Central Line* (1987) and *Dublin 4* (1982), and her novels include *Light a Penny Candle* (1982), *Firefly Summer* (1987), *Circle of Friends* (1990, film version 1995), *The Copper Beech* (1992), *The Glass Lake* (1994), *Evening Class* (1996), *Tara Road* (1998) and *Scarlet Feather* (2000). In 2000 she announced that she would no longer write novels.

Binet, Alfred 1857–1911 •*French psychologist, the founder of "intelligence tests"*• He was born in Nice. Director of physiological psychology at the Sorbonne from 1892, his first tests were used on his children. Later, with Théodore Simon (1873–1961), he expanded the tests (1905) to encompass the measurement of relative intelligence among deprived children (the Binet-Simon tests). These were later developed further by **Lewis Terman**.

Binford, Lewis Roberts 1930– •*US archaeologist, pioneer of the "processual" school ("New Archaeology")*• Trained originally in forestry and wildlife conservation, he studied anthropology at Michigan University. An ethnoarchaeologist rather than an excavator, he has worked to striking effect among the Navajo, the Nunamiut Inuit, and the Alyawara Aboriginals of Australia. He directs particular attention to the systemic nature of human culture and the ever-changing interaction between the technological, social and ideological subsystems of all societies, ancient and modern, and his work has powerfully influenced the intellectual development of archaeology. His original manifesto *New Perspectives in Archaeology* (1968, with Sally R Binford) has subsequently been elaborated in the autobiographical *An Archaeological Perspective* (1972), *Bones* (1981) and *In Pursuit of the Past* (1983).

Bing, Ilse 1899–1998 •*German photojournalist*• Born in Frankfurt am Main, she trained in music and art and attended the university there from 1920. Studying for a PhD in the history of art, she began photographing in 1928 to illustrate her dissertation on the architect **Friedrich Gilly**. She first went to New York City in 1936, refused the offer of a staff position on *Life* magazine, and thereafter saw her work included in important exhibitions in the US. She emigrated to New York in 1941. She gave up photography in 1959, but her work was "rediscovered" in 1976 when it was included in two major exhibitions in New York at the Museum of Modern Art and the Witkin Gallery. Her publications include *Words As Visions* (1974).

Bingham (of Cornhill), Thomas Henry Bingham, Baron 1933– •*English judge*• He was educated at Sedbergh School and

Balliol College, Oxford. Called to the bar in 1959, he became a Queen's Counsel (1972), a judge of the High Court of Justice (1980), a Lord Justice of Appeal (1986), Master of the Rolls (1992), Lord Chief Justice (1996) and Senior Law Lord (2000). Notable cases over which he presided include the Court of Appeal case in 1998 that resulted in the overturning of the conviction of **Derek Bentley**.

Bingzhi, Jiang *See* **Ding Ling**

Bin Laden, Osama bin Mohammad c. 1957– •*Saudi Arabian terrorist leader*• Born in Riyadh, the son of a Yemeni-born construction billionaire, he was educated at the King Abdul Aziz University in Jiddah. During the 1980s he used his wealth to support rebels resisting the Soviet occupation of Afghanistan, establishing centers to recruit and train fighters. In 1988 he founded the Al-Qaeda organization to support Islamic opposition movements across the world and by 1991 had identified the US as his chief enemy. He was expelled from Saudi Arabia in 1991 and had to leave Sudan in 1996 after pressure from the US and the United Nations. In 1998 he called upon Muslims everywhere to attack Americans and US interests and was strongly suspected of being linked with various terrorist attacks against the West. In 2001 he was identified as the man behind the destruction of the World Trade Center in New York after two aircraft were flown into the twin towers by Muslim hijackers on September 11, causing thousands of deaths. He was also blamed for an attack on the Pentagon. The US responded by declaring war on international terrorism, organizing assaults against Bin Laden's bases in Afghanistan and against the Taliban regime accused of sheltering him.

Binnig, Gerd Karl 1947– •*German physicist and Nobel Prize winner*• Born in Frankfurt am Main, he was educated at Goethe University there, and then joined IBM's Zurich research laboratories (1978). There he started work with Heinrich Rohrer (1933–) on a new form of high-resolution electron microscope, the scanning tunneling electron microscope, which used the tunneling electron current between a scanning needle and the surface of a sample to profile the sample's surface. For this work Binnig and Rohrer shared the 1986 Nobel Prize for physics with Ernst Ruska (1906–88), who had invented the electron microscope some 55 years earlier.

Binoche, Juliette 1964– •*French actress*• She was born in Paris and studied at the National Conservatory of Drama. Her understated and powerful screen presence attracted international attention in films such as *The Unbearable Lightness of Being* (1988) and *Damage* (1992), and she went on to star in the *Three Colors* trilogy (1992–94) of **Krzysztof Kieslowski**. *The English Patient* (1996) won her both an Academy Award and a British Academy of Film and Television Arts award for Best Supporting Actress, and subsequent films have included *Chocolat* (2001).

Bintley, David Julian 1957– •*English ballet director*• Born in Huddersfield, West Yorkshire, he studied at the Royal Ballet School. He began his career as a professional choreographer in the late 1970s with works including *The Outsider* (1978) and *The Swan of Tuonela* (1982), becoming company choreographer and then resident choreographer at the Sadler's Wells Theatre Ballet (1983–86) and resident choreographer and principal dancer at the Royal Ballet (1986–93). He became director of the Birmingham Royal Ballet in 1995.

Binyon, (Robert) Laurence 1869–1943 •*English poet and art critic*• Born in Lancaster, he was educated at Oxford. His study *Painting in the Far East* (1908) was the first European treatise on the subject, and *Japanese Art* (1909), *Botticelli* (1913) and *Drawings and Engravings of William Blake* (1922) followed. Meanwhile he had achieved a reputation as a poet in the tradition of **Wordsworth** and **Matthew Arnold**. His poetry includes *Lyric Poems* (1894) and *Odes* (1901), containing some of his best work, especially "The Sirens" and "The Idols." He also wrote plays and translated **Dante**'s *Divine Comedy* into terza rima (1933–43). Extracts from his elegy "For the Fallen" (set to music by **Elgar**) adorn war memorials throughout the British Commonwealth.

Biondi, Matt(hew) 1965– •*US swimmer*• Born in Morego, California, he won a record seven medals at the 1986 world championships, including three golds, and at the 1988 Olympics won seven medals, including five golds. He set the 100-meter freestyle world record of 48.74 seconds in Orlando, Florida, in 1986. He won silver in the 50-meter freestyle at the 1992 Olympics, and announced his retirement in 1993.

Bird, Dickie (Harold Dennis) 1933– •*English cricket player and umpire*• Born in Barnsley, Yorkshire, he played for Yorkshire (1956–59) and Leicestershire (1960–64) and by the end of his playing career had scored 3,314 runs in first-class cricket. He became better known, however, as an umpire (1970–98), celebrated as much for his sense of humor and eccentricities as for his authority on the pitch. He umpired a record 67 Test matches in the years 1973–96, 93 limited-overs internationals and the first three finals of the Cricket World Cup.

Bird, Larry (Joe) 1956– •*US basketball player*• Brought up in French Lick, Indiana, in 1979 he became a professional with the Boston Celtics, leading the team to a National Basketball Association (NBA) championship (1980–81 season). He was most valuable player (MVP) in the 1984 and 1986 NBA championship finals and MVP for the NBA three times (1984–86). He retired from the game in 1992, after playing on the gold-medal-winning US Olympic team.

Bird, Vere Cornwall 1910–99 •*Antiguan statesman*• Born in St John's, Antigua, he was a founder-member of the Antigua Trades and Labour Union (1939) and then leader of the Antigua Labour Party (ALP). In the preindependence period he was elected to the Legislative Council and became Chief Minister (1960–67) and then premier (1967–71, 1976–81). When full independence as Antigua and Barbuda was achieved in 1981, he became Prime Minister, and he and his party were reelected in 1984 and 1989.

Birdseye, Clarence 1886–1956 •*US businessman and inventor*• Born in Brooklyn, New York, he became a fur trader in Labrador, where he observed that food kept well in the freezing winter conditions. On his return to the US he developed a process for freezing food in small packages suitable for retailing, and in 1924 he helped found the General Seafoods Company, marketing quick-frozen foods. He sold the company in 1929. He was president of Birdseye Frosted Foods (1930–34) and of Birdseye Electric Company (1935–38). Some 300 patents are credited to him, his other inventions including infrared heat lamps, the recoilless harpoon gun and a method for removing water from food.

Birdwood (of Anjac and Totnes), William Riddell Birdwood, 1st Baron 1865–1951 •*British field marshal*• He was born in Kirkee, India, where his father was an official of the government of Bombay. Trained at Sandhurst, in 1914 he was put in command of the Australian and New Zealand contingents then arriving in Egypt for the Dardanelles offensive. He planned the landing at Gallipoli, and upon evacuation from the peninsula, he took his troops to the Western Front, through the battles of the Somme and Ypres in 1916 and 1917. After the war he returned to India to command the Northern Army, becoming Commander in Chief in 1925, and retiring in 1930.

Birendra, Bir Bikram Shah Dev 1945–2001 •*King of Nepal*• The son of King Mahendra, he was born in Kathmandu, and educated at St Joseph's College, Darjeeling, Eton, and Tokyo and Harvard Universities. He married Queen Aishwarya Rajya Laxmi Devi Rana (1970), and became king on his father's death (1972). During his reign there was gradual progress toward political reform, but Nepal remained essentially an absolute monarchy, with political activity banned, until 1990, when Birendra was forced to concede much of his power. He was killed when his son Crown Prince Dipendra massacred his parents and seven other royals.

Birgitta or **Bridget, St** c. 1303–73 •*Swedish visionary and author*• Born in Finsta, Uppland, she was married at the age of 13, gave birth to eight children, and gained considerable political insight through travel and service at the Swedish court. Widowed in 1344, she subsequently moved to Rome. Her monastery at Vadstena in Sweden was founded toward the end of her life. Her numerous revelations were recorded by her confessors and very widely published in Latin after her death as *Revelationes coelestes*. They are characterized by vivid realistic detail and abundant imagery, frequently inspired by her experiences as a mother. She was canonized in 1391.

Birkbeck, George 1776–1841 •*English physician and educationist*• He was born in Settle, Yorkshire, and in 1799 became Professor of Natural Philosophy at Anderson's College, Glasgow, where he delivered his first free lectures to the working classes. He was the founder and first president of the London Mechanics' or Birkbeck Institute (1824), which developed into Birkbeck College, a constituent college of London University.

Birkenhead, Frederick Edwin Smith, 1st Earl of 1872–1930 •*English lawyer and statesman*• Born in Birkenhead, Cheshire, he attended Birkenhead Grammar School, studied at Wadham College, Oxford, and was called to the bar in 1899. He entered parliament as a Conservative in 1906 and by his provocative maiden speech established himself as a considerable orator and wit. In the Irish crisis (1914) he vigorously supported **Edward Carson**'s organized resistance to Home Rule. He became Attorney General (1915–19), and Lord Chancellor (1919–22). His extraordinary ability was seen at its best in the trial of **Roger Casement** (1916), when he appeared for the Crown. He played a major part in the Irish settlement of 1921 and was created earl in 1922. **Stanley Baldwin** appointed him Secretary of State for India (1924–28), but his conduct caused much criticism and he resigned. His greatest achievements as a lawyer were the preparation of the series of acts reforming land law, and a textbook on international law.

“ ”

I do not deal with subtleties; I am only a lawyer.

Quoted in Richard Fountain ***The Wit of the Wig*** *(1968).*

Birkhoff, George David 1884–1944 •*US mathematician*• Born in Overisel, Michigan, he studied at Harvard and the University of Chicago, and was professor at several US universities. In 1913 he proved "**Poincaré**'s last theorem," which Jules Poincaré had left unproven at his death. This was a crucial step in the analysis of motions determined by differential equations, and opened the way to modern topological dynamics. Later he extended Poincaré's work and developed ergodic theory, where the methods of probability theory are applied to particle motion. He is regarded as the leading US mathematician of the early part of the 20th century.

Birmingham Six •*Alleged IRA terrorists unjustly imprisoned*• This is the familiar collective name for the six men found guilty of the IRA bombing of the Mulberry Bush and Tavern in the Town pubs in Birmingham in 1974, in which 21 people were killed and 160 injured; each man was sentenced to 21 life sentences. However, the prosecution case at their 1975 trial was based mainly on confessions, which the defense claimed had been extracted after severe beatings, and one of which was shown to have been forged. Also, the forensic evidence relied on the now discredited Geiss test for determining whether an individual has recently handled explosive substances. In February 1991 the Director of Public Prosecutions announced that he could no longer argue that the convictions were safe, and the following month the Birmingham Six were set free after 16 years of wrongful imprisonment. Their names are Hugh Callaghan (1931–), Patrick Hill (1944–), Gerard Hunter (1949–), Richard McIlkenny (1934–), William Power (1947–) and John Walker (1936–).

Birt, John Birt, Baron 1944– •*English television executive and controller*• Born in Bootle, Merseyside, he studied engineering at St Catherine's College, Oxford. He trained with Granada Television, working on *World in Action*, then started to successfully produce programs. Moving to London Weekend Television, he rose to director of programs (1982–87). He joined the BBC in 1987 as deputy director general, and caused controversy with his criticism of the news and current affairs programs. He became director general in 1992, and had a commercial tenure in office until he stood down in 2000 and took up a life peerage.

Birtwistle, Sir Harrison 1934– •*English composer*• Born in Accrington, Lancashire, he began his career as a clarinettist. While in Manchester he formed, with other young musicians including **Peter Maxwell Davies** and **John Ogdon**, the New Manchester Group for the performance of modern music. In 1967 he formed the Pierrot Players, again with Maxwell Davies, and much of his work was written for them and for the English Opera Group. It was two works of 1965, the instrumental *Tragoedia* and the vocal/instrumental *Ring a Dumb Carillon*, that established him as a leading composer. He became the composer-in-residence at the London Philharmonic Orchestra in 1993, and was Henry Purcell Professor of Composition at King's College London (1994–2001). Among his works are the operas *Punch and Judy* (1966–67) and *The Masque of Orpheus* (1974–82), *The Fields of Sorrow* (1971), *Earth Dances* (1986) and the opera *Gawain* (1990). He was knighted in 1988 and created Companion of Honour in 2000.

Biscop, Simon *See* **Episcopius, Simon**

Bishop, Elizabeth 1911–79 •*US poet*• Born in Worcester, Massachusetts, she grew up in New England and Nova Scotia, and graduated from Vassar College. She lived in Brazil from 1952 to 1967, published several travel books, including *Brazil* (1967), and taught at Harvard from 1970. She was noted for her verse, which often evokes images of nature. Her first collection, *North and South* (1946), was reprinted with additions as *Poems: North and South—A Cold Spring* (1955) and received the 1956 Pulitzer Prize for poetry. Later works include *Complete Poems* (1969) and *Geography III* (1976).

Bishop, (John) Michael 1936– •*US molecular biologist, virologist and Nobel Prize winner*• Born in York, Pennsylvania, he was educated at Harvard Medical School. In 1972 he became Professor of Microbiology and Immunology at the University of California, then in 1982 Professor of Biochemistry and Biophysics, and Chancellor in 1998. He has received many major awards, including the Nobel Prize for physiology or medicine in 1989 (jointly with **Harold Varmus**) for his discovery of oncogenes, normal cellular genes involved in the normal growth and development of all mammalian cells. Certain faults in oncogene regulation can severely damage the growth of the affected cell type and cause cancer.

Bismarck, Prince Otto Edward Leopold von, Duke of Lauenburg 1815–98 •*Prusso-German statesman, the first chancellor of the German Empire*• He was born in Schönhausen, Brandenburg, and studied law and agriculture at Göttingen, Berlin and Greifswald. In 1847 he became known in the new Prussian parliament as an ultraroyalist, and opposed equally the constitutional demands of 1848 and the scheme of a German empire, as proposed by the Frankfurt parliament of 1849. In 1851, as Prussian member of the resuscitated German diet of Frankfurt, he resented the predominance of Austria, and demanded equal rights for Prussia. In 1862 he became Prime Minister. The death of the king of Denmark (1863) fueled the Schleswig-Holstein question, and excited a fever of German nationalism, which led to the defeat of Denmark by Austria and Prussia, and the annexation of the duchies. This provoked the "Seven Weeks' War" between Prussia and Austria, which ended in the defeat of Austria (1866), and the reorganization of Germany under the leadership of Prussia. During this Bismarck was an influential figure, and, from being universally disliked, became highly popular and a national hero. He further unified German feeling during the Franco-Prussian War (1870–71), which he deliberately provoked. Created a count in 1866, he was then made a prince and became the first chancellor of the new German Empire (1871–90). His domestic policy was marked by universal suffrage, reformed coinage, codification of the law, nationalization of the Prussian railways, repeated increase of the army, and various attempts to combat socialism. To counteract Russia and France, in 1879 he formed the Austro-German Treaty of Alliance (published in 1888), which Italy joined in 1886. The phrase "man of blood and iron" was used by the "Iron Chancellor" in a speech in 1862. Two attempts were made on his life (1866, 1874). Disapproving the initially liberal policy of the emperor **Wilhelm II**, he resigned the chancellorship in March 1890, becoming Duke of Lauenburg. He was finally reconciled with Wilhelm in 1894.

“ ”

Anyone who has ever looked into the glazed eyes of a soldier dying on the battlefield will think hard before starting a war.

1867 Speech, Berlin, August.

Bizet, Georges, *originally* **Alexandre Césare Léopold** 1838–75 •*French composer*• Born in Paris, he studied at the Conservatoire there under **Ludovic Halévy**, whose daughter he married in 1869, and in Italy. Although he won the Prix de Rome in 1857 with *Le Docteur Miracle* ("Doctor Miracle"), his efforts to achieve a reputation as an operatic composer with such works as *Les pêcheurs de perles* (1863, "The Pearl-Fishers") and *La jolie fille de Perth* (1867, "The Fair Maid of Perth") were largely unsuccessful. His charming incidental music to Daudet's play *L'Arlésienne* (1872, "The Maid of Arles") was successful and survived in the form of two orchestral suites. Bizet's reputation is based on these and on the four-act opera *Carmen*, completed just before his death of heart disease, although *Les pêcheurs* and *La jolie fille* have enjoyed recent revivals.

Bjerknes, Vilhelm F(riman) K(oren) 1862–1951 •*Norwegian mathematician, meteorologist and geophysicist*• Born in Christiania (Oslo), he graduated from the University of Christiania. He initially collaborated with his father (a mathematics professor) on theories of hydrodynamical forces. While continuing this work, he produced his famous circulation theorem (1898) and applied his thorough knowledge of hydrodynamics to a study of atmospheric and ocean processes. He devised equations which enabled both the thermal energy and that due to baroclinicity to be calculated for a developing cyclone. In 1912 he moved to Leipzig where Bjerknes became Professor of Geophysics, though soon after **Fridtjof Nansen** persuaded him to set up a geophysical institute in Bergen.

Bjørnson, Bjørnstjerne Martinius 1832–1910 •*Norwegian writer, politician and Nobel Prize winner*• Born in Kvikne, Österdalen, the son of a pastor, and educated in Molde, Christiania (Oslo) and Copenhagen, he was a playwright and novelist of wide-ranging interests, a lifelong champion of liberal causes and constantly active politically as a Home Ruler and republican. An ardent patriot, he sought to free the Norwegian theater from Danish influence and revive Norwegian as a literary language. He was named Norway's national poet, and his poem, *Ja, vi elsker dette landet* (1870, "Yes, We Love This Land of Ours") became the national anthem. His other major works include the novel *Fiskerjenten* (1868, "The Fisher Girl"), the epic poem *Arnljot Gelline* (1870), and his greatest plays, *Over Evne I* and *II* (1893, 1895, "Beyond One's Powers"), about a clergyman capable of working miracles but incapable of responding to his wife's love. He was awarded the 1903 Nobel Prize for literature.

Black, Adam 1784–1874 •*Scottish publisher*• He was born in Edinburgh, the son of a master builder, and was apprenticed at 15 to an Edinburgh bookseller. He set up his own bookshop in 1807, and started publishing in 1817. In 1826 he bought the *Encyclopaedia Britannica* after **Archibald Constable**'s failure and in 1854 he bought the rights to **Walter Scott**'s novels from the estate of Robert Cadell (1788–1849). He was Lord Provost between 1843 and 1848, and Liberal Member of Parliament for the burgh (1856–65).

Black, Cilla, *originally* **Priscilla Maria Veronica White** 1943– •*English singer and television host*• Born in Liverpool, she made her debut at the city's legendary Cavern Club and had No. 1 singles with "Anyone Who Had a Heart" (1964) and "You're My World" (1964). Subsequent chart hits included "You've Lost That Lovin' Feelin" (1965), "Alfie" (1966), "Step Inside Love" (1968) and "Surround Yourself with Sorrow" (1969). She also appeared in the films *Ferry Cross the Mersey* and *Work Is a Four-Letter Word* (1967). Turning to television, she became the host of *Surprise, Surprise* (1984–) and *Blind Date* (1985–). She was given the honorary title Officer, Order of the British Empire, in 1997.

Black, Clementina Maria 1853–1922 •*English suffragist, trade unionist and novelist*• Born in Brighton, East Sussex, she was educated at home. On her mother's death she moved to London, where she did research for her novels and lectured on 18th-century literature. She set up the militant Women's Trade Union Association (1889), which merged with the Women's Industrial Council (1897), and as its president, she played an important part in collecting data on women's work and campaigning against sweatshop industries. Her publications include *Sweated Industry and the Minimum Wage* (1907) and her best-known book, *Married Women's Work* (1915), as well as a number of novels.

Black, Sir James Whyte 1924– •*Scottish pharmacologist and Nobel Prize winner*• Born in Uddingston, Strathclyde, he graduated in medicine at St Andrews University. Following appointments at Imperial Chemical Industries Pharmaceuticals (1958–64) and the Wellcome Research Laboratories (1978–84) as director of therapeutic research, he was appointed Professor of Pharmacology and departmental head at University College London (1973–77). He was Professor of Analytical Pharmacology at King's College Medical School in London (1984–93, now emeritus). In 1962 while at Imperial Chemical Industries, he discovered the drug netherlide (Alderlin®), the first beta-blocking drug, which opened the way to new treatments for certain types of heart disease (angina, tachycardia), and led to his development of safer, more effective drugs. At the Wellcome Laboratories he produced burimamide and cimetidine, new drugs with which he distinguished classes of histamine receptor, used in the treatment of ulcers. He was elected a Fellow of the Royal Society in 1976 and knighted in 1981, and shared with **Gertrude Elion** and **George Hitchings** the 1988 Nobel Prize for physiology or medicine.

Black, Joseph 1728–99 •*Scottish chemist*• Born in Bordeaux, France, the son of a wine merchant, he was educated at Belfast, Glasgow and Edinburgh. In his MD thesis of 1754 he showed that the causticity of lime and the alkalis is due to the absence of the "fixed air" (carbon dioxide) present in limestone and the carbonates of the alkalis. With this discovery he was the first person to realize that there are gases other than air, and his experimental method laid the foundations of quantitative analysis. Between 1756 and 1761 he evolved the theory of "latent heat" on which his scientific fame chiefly rests.

Blackadder, Elizabeth 1931– •*Scottish painter*• Born in Falkirk, Stirlingshire, she studied at Edinburgh University and Edinburgh College of Art, where she later taught (1962–86). Her early work was mainly landscape, but from the 1970s she began to concentrate on still life, for which she is now best known. In both oil and watercolor she paints recognizable objects with apparently random associations (e.g., cats, fans, ribbons, flowers and plants) on an abstract empty background. Her interest in calligraphic gesture and the space between motifs shows considerable Japanese influence. She was the first woman to hold the prestigious post of Her Majesty's Painter and Limner in Scotland (2001–).

Blackbeard *See* **Teach, Edward**

Blackburn, Helen 1842–1903 •*Irish social reformer*• Born in Knightstown, County Kerry, in 1859 she moved with her family to London. A staunch believer in the vote as the key to women's equality, she was secretary of the National Society for Women's Suffrage from 1874 to 1895. Her many publications include a *Handbook for Women Engaged in Social and Political Work* (1881) and *Women's Suffrage: A Record of the Movement in the British Isles* (1902). In 1899, with Jessie Boucherett, she founded the Freedom of Labour Defence League, aimed at maintaining women's freedom and their powers of earning.

Blackburn, Jemima 1823–1909 •*Scottish painter*• She was born in Edinburgh, and showed a precocious talent from an early age. Her animal drawings greatly impressed Sir **Edwin Landseer**, whom she met in 1843. One of the most popular illustrators in Victorian Britain, she illustrated 27 books, the most important being *Birds from Nature* (1862, 1868), which demonstrates her great skill with brush and lithographic crayon. Her most enduring works are the albums containing hundreds of watercolors depicting the day-to-day events of late-19th-century family life in the Scottish Highlands.

Blackett, Patrick Maynard Stuart, Baron 1897–1974 •*English physicist and Nobel Prize winner*• Born in London and educated at Dartmouth College, he served in the Royal Navy during World War I. He was the first to photograph, in 1925, nuclear collisions involving transmutation, and was awarded the Nobel Prize for physics in 1948 for developing the Wilson cloud chamber, using it to confirm the existence of the positron (the antiparticle of the electron). He pioneered research on cosmic radiation and, in World War II, operational research. He also contributed to the theories of particle pair production, and the discovery of "strange" particles.

Black Hawk 1767–1838 •*Native American leader*• Born in Saukenuk, a village of the Sauk people in Illinois, he became a Sauk chief and opposed US expansion into his people's ancestral lands. He sided with the British in the War of 1812 and fought US forces until 1815. In the ensuing decade he and his people were forced to move westward, but they kept revisiting their homeland. Their effort to plant crops there in 1832 led to a conflict with federal troops and began the Black Hawk War, which lasted from April to August of that year. Black Hawk and his followers were finally defeated at Bad Axe River in Wisconsin, and he was captured and imprisoned. After his death his bones were displayed in an Iowa museum.

Blackmore, Richard Doddridge 1825–1900 •*English novelist*• Born in Longworth, Berkshire, he was educated at Exeter College, Oxford. After publishing several collections of poetry, he found his real niche in fiction. *Clara Vaughan* (1864) was the first of 15 novels, mostly with a Devonshire background, of which *Lorna Doone* (1869) is his masterpiece and an accepted classic of the West Country. Other novels include *The Maid of Sker* (1872), *Alice Lorraine* (1875) and *Tommy Upmore* (1884).

Blackstone, Tessa Ann Vosper Evans, Baroness, *née* **Blackstone** 1942– •*English sociologist*• Born in Bures, Suffolk, she was educated at the London School of Economics. After several lecturing posts she became adviser to the Central Policy Review Staff in the Cabinet Office (1975–78), then director of education at the Inner London Education Authority, and was master of London University's Birkbeck College (1987). Awarded a life peerage in 1987, she has served in the House of Lords as Opposition front bench spokesperson on education and science (1988–92), on foreign affairs (1992–97), and has since become Minister of State for Education and Employment (1997–2001) and Minister of State for the Arts (2001–).

Blackwell, Sir Basil Henry 1889–1984 •*English publisher and bookseller*• Born in Oxford, he was the son of the chairman of the famous Oxford bookshop (founded in 1846). He was educated at Magdalen College School and Merton College, and joined the family business in 1913, but also published independently, founding the Shakespeare Head Press (1921). He succeeded to the chairmanship in 1924 and from that time joined the family bookselling interest with that of publishing, mostly on academic subjects.

Blackwell, Elizabeth 1821–1910 •*US physician, the first woman doctor in the US*• She was born in Bristol, England, the sister of **Emily Blackwell**. Her family emigrated to the US in 1832, where her father died six years later, leaving a widow and nine children. Elizabeth helped to support the family by teaching, devoting her leisure to the study of medical books. After fruitless applications for admission to various medical schools, she entered that in Geneva, New York, and graduated in 1849. She next visited Europe and, after much difficulty, was admitted into La Maternité in Paris, and St Bartholomew's Hospital in London. She was responsible for opening the field of medicine to women.

Blackwell, Emily 1826–1910 •*US physician*• She was born in Bristol, England, the sister of **Elizabeth Blackwell**. Her family emigrated to the US in 1832, and she was educated at Cleveland (Western Reserve) University, followed by work in Europe where she was assistant to Sir **James Simpson**. From 1869 to 1899 she was Dean and Professor of Obstetrics and Diseases of Women at the Women's Medical College in New York. She was the first woman doctor to undertake major surgery on a considerable scale.

Blackwood, Algernon Henry 1869–1951 •*English novelist*• Born in Shooters Hill, Kent, he was educated at Edinburgh University before working his way through Canada and the US, as related in his *Episodes Before Thirty* (1923). His novels, which reflect his taste for the supernatural and the occult, include *The Human Chord* (1910) and *The Wave* (1916). He also published the collections of short stories, *Tongues of Fire* (1924) and *Tales of the Uncanny and Supernatural* (1949).

Blackwood, William 1776–1834 •*Scottish publisher*• Born in Edinburgh, he was apprenticed to a bookseller at the age of 14 and established himself as a bookseller in Edinburgh—principally of antiquarian books—in 1804. In 1817 he started *Blackwood's Magazine* as a Tory rival to the Whig *Edinburgh Review*, and from the seventh number assumed the editorship with **John Gibson Lockhart**, **James Hogg**, and others as contributors.

Blair, Cherie *See* **Booth, Cherie**

Blair, Tony (Anthony Charles Lynton) 1953– •*British Labour politician*• Born in Edinburgh, he was educated at Fettes College and St John's College, Oxford. After graduating he became a barrister specializing in trade union and employment law. He was elected to parliament as Labour Member of Parliament for Sedgefield in 1983 and achieved success as opposition Home Affairs spokesman in 1992 by promoting law and order, traditionally a Conservative interest. In 1994 he succeeded **John Smith** as Leader of the Labour Party and instituted a series of reforms to streamline and modernize the Labour Party. In 1997 Labour's landslide win in the general election made Blair Prime Minister, the third youngest, after **Pitt** the Younger and Lord **Liverpool**, to take office. He was reelected in 2001. In 2003, despite large-scale anti-war protests, British forces joined a US-led coalition in military action in Iraq.

Blaise or **Blasius, St** d. c. 316 AD •*Armenian churchman and martyr*• Born in Sebastea in Cappadocia, Asia Minor, he became Bishop of Sebastea and is said to have suffered martyrdom during a period of persecution. He is the patron saint of woolcombers, and is invoked in cases of throat trouble and cattle diseases. His feast day is February 3.

Blake, Eubie (James Hubert) 1883–1983 •*US pianist and composer*• He was born in Baltimore, Maryland, and began working with bandleader Noble Sissle in 1915. They scored a significant success with *Shuffle Along* (1921), one of the earliest African-American Broadway productions. He contributed to numerous musicals, notably *Chocolate Dandies* (1929, with Sissle), and was the subject of the Broadway musical *Eubie* (1978). His most important legacy lay in his mastery of ragtime piano, and he was increasingly recognized as a major practitioner. During his long career he wrote, recorded and performed numerous songs, such as "I'm Just Wild About Harry" and "Memories of You." He marked his hundredth birthday with the wry observation: "If I'd known I was gonna live this long I would have taken better care of myself."

Blake, Peter 1932– •*English painter*• He was born in Dartford, Kent. From the mid-1950s, while still a student at the Royal College of Art, he was a pioneer of the Pop Art movement in Great Britain, using media imagery from sources such as comics, advertisements and popular magazines. His most widely known work is the cover design for the **Beatles**' album *Sergeant Pepper's Lonely Hearts Club Band* (1967). In 1975 he was a founder-member of the Brotherhood of Ruralists. He became a member of the Royal Academy in 1980 and was given the honorary title of Commander, Order of the British Empire, in 1983.

Blake, Sir Peter James 1948–2001 •*New Zealand yachtsman*• He was born in Auckland, and made his name in the Whitbread Round the World Race, which he won on his fifth attempt in 1989–90. In 1994 he was coskipper with **Robin Knox-Johnston** on a record-breaking circumnavigation, and in 1995, for only the second time in its 144-year history, he took the America's Cup away from America with a non-US crew. Given the honorary title Member, Order of the British Empire, in 1983 and the honorary title Officer, Order of the British Empire, in 1991, he was then knighted in 1995. In 2001 he was named Special Envoy to the United Nations Environment Program. He was killed by pirates on the Amazon River later that year.

Blake, Quentin Saxby 1932– •*English artist, illustrator and teacher*• Born in Sidcup, Kent, he studied at Downing College, Cambridge. Since the late 1950s he has illustrated the work of a wide range of children's authors including **Roald Dahl**, **Russell Hoban**, **Joan Aiken** and others, as well as illustrating books for adults by **Evelyn Waugh**, **George Orwell** and **Stella Gibbons**. His books as both writer and illustrator include *Clown* (1995) and *Zagazoo* (1998). He was appointed Children's Laureate in 1999.

Blake, Robert 1599–1657 •*English naval commander*• Born in Bridgwater, Somerset, he was educated at Wadham College,

Oxford. In the English Civil War he took part in the defense of Bristol (1643), Lyme Regis (1644) and Taunton (1644–45). Appointed admiral in 1649, he blockaded Lisbon, destroyed Prince **Rupert**'s fleet, and captured the Scilly Isles and Jersey. In the first Dutch War (1652–54) he defeated **Maarten Tromp** at the Battle of Portland (1653) and shattered Dutch supremacy at sea. His greatest victory was in 1657 at Santa Cruz off Tenerife, where he destroyed a Spanish treasure fleet. He is considered one of the greatest English admirals.

Blake, William 1757–1827 •*English poet, painter, engraver and mystic*• Born in London, the son of an Irish hosier, he did not go to school, but was apprenticed in 1771 to the engraver James Basire. After studying at the Royal Academy School he began to produce watercolor figure subjects and to engrave illustrations for magazines. His first book of poems, *Poetical Sketches*, appeared in 1783. He went on to produce many "illuminated books," in which the text is interwoven with his imaginative designs. These were printed from engraved copper plates and then either hand-colored or printed in color by himself or his wife, Catherine Boucher. Such books include *Songs of Innocence* (1789) and *Songs of Experience* (1794), collections of delicate lyrics which express his ardent belief in the freedom of the imagination and his hatred of rationalism and materialism; and mystical and prophetical works such as the *Book of Thel* (1789) and *The Marriage of Heaven and Hell* (1793). Epic poems include *The Four Zoas* (1795–1804, begun as *Vala*), *Milton* (1804–08) and *Jerusalem* (1804–20). His figure designs include a highly acclaimed series of 537 colored illustrations to **Edward Young**'s *Night Thoughts* (1797) and 12 to **Robert Blair**'s *The Grave* (1808). His finest artistic work is to be found in the 21 *Illustrations to the Book of Job* (1826), completed when he was almost 70. At his death he was employed on the illustrations to the *Divina Commedia* of **Dante**. He is also known as a wood engraver. Among the most important of his paintings are *The Canterbury Pilgrims*, which the artist himself engraved; *The Spiritual Form of Pitt Guiding Behemoth* (now in the National Gallery, London); *Jacob's Dream*; and *The Last Judgement*. Blake's poetry has also been used as a basis for many musical compositions. Notable among these are: *Ghost of Abel* (Dennis Arundell), *Songs and Proverbs* (**Benjamin Britten**), *Seasons* (Eric Fogg), *Job* (**Ralph Vaughan Williams**), *Jerusalem* (**Hubert Parry**), and *Song of Liberty* (**Michael Tippett**).

" "

Tyger! Tyger! burning bright
In the forests of the night,
What immortal hand or eye
Could frame thy fearful symmetry?

*1794 **Songs of Experience**, "The Tyger."*

Blakemore, Colin Brian 1944– •*British physiologist*• After a period at Cambridge (1968–79), he was appointed Waynflete Professor of Physiology at Oxford University in 1979. He has worked on the physiology of the brain, and published *Mechanics of the Mind* in 1977. He gave the BBC Reith Lectures in 1976. A high-profile supporter of experiments on animals, he has become the object of fierce criticism by animal-rights activists.

Blakey, Art(hur), *also known as* **Abdullah ibn Buhaina** 1919–90 •*US jazz drummer and bandleader*• Born in Pittsburgh, Pennsylvania, he began as a pianist, but switched to drums. His early engagements included work with the Billy Eckstine Orchestra (1944–47), which featured many of the emerging bebop musicians. Blakey adopted the new style, and recorded with the first of his many versions of The Jazz Messengers in 1947. The group, initially co-led with Horace Silver, became the most important band in the development of the influential hard bop style of the 1950s, and its exmembers constitute a virtual "who's who" of the form.

Blamey, Sir Thomas 1884–1951 •*Australian field marshal*• He was born near Wagga Wagga, New South Wales, and became Chief of Staff of the Australian Corps in 1918. At the outbreak of World War II he commanded the Australian Imperial Forces in the Middle East. He served as deputy Commander in Chief to **Archibald Wavell** and had command of Commonwealth operations in Greece (1941). He became Commander in Chief of Allied land forces in Australia (1942) and received the Japanese surrender in 1945. In 1950 he was made a field marshal, the first Australian soldier to hold this rank.

Blanc, Raymond René 1949– •*French chef and restaurateur*• He was born near Besançon, and after training as a waiter he went to England in 1972 to manage a pub on the River Thames, the Rose Revived, where he began to cook in 1975. He opened a small restaurant in Oxford in 1977, Les Quat' Saisons, and progressed through more elaborate premises before opening Le Manoir aux Quat' Saisons in 1984. He is a popular broadcaster whose publications include *Cooking for Friends* (1991), *Blanc Mange* (1994) and *Blanc Vite* (1999).

Blanchard, Jean Pierre François 1753–1809 •*French balloonist, inventor of the parachute*• He was born in Les Andelys. With John Jeffries (1744–1819) he was the first to cross the English Channel by balloon, from Dover to Calais, in 1785. He was killed at La Haye during practice parachute jumps from a balloon.

Blanchett, Cate (Catherine Elise) 1969– •*Australian actress*• Born in Melbourne, she studied at the National Institute of Dramatic Art. She began her career with the Sydney Theatre Company, winning the 1993 Newcomer award with *Kafka Dances*, then moved to the screen, appearing in films such as *Oscar and Lucinda* (1997), *Elizabeth* (1998; Golden Globe award), *The Talented Mr Ripley* (1999), *An Ideal Husband* (1999) and *The Lord of the Rings* trilogy (2001, 2002, 2003).

Blanchflower, Danny (Robert Dennis) 1926–93 •*Northern Irish soccer player and broadcaster*• Born in Belfast, he was a powerful influence on the Northern Irish team that reached the World Cup quarterfinals in 1958. Transferring from Aston Villa to Tottenham Hotspur, he masterminded the London club's double success of 1960–61 in the League and the Football Association Cup, the first time the double was achieved in the 20th century. He was British Footballer of the Year in 1960–61, and won a European Cupwinners' Cup medal with Tottenham. His influence on the game was immortalized in the British film *The Glory, Glory Days*.

" "

We try to equalize before the others have scored.

*1958 Explaining his tactics as captain of Northern Ireland. Quoted in Colin Jarman **The Guinness Dictionary of Sports Quotations** (1990).*

Blanco, Serge 1958– •*French rugby union player*• Born in Venezuela, he represented Biarritz at club level. He played 93 times for France and became the second most capped international player behind **Philippe Sella**. His position as fullback allowed him to score 38 international tries. Pacy and glamorous, he was revered as a national figure. He retired in 1991.

Blanda, (George) Frederick 1927– •*US football player*• Born in Youngwood, Pennsylvania, he held (until 2000) the record for the most points (2,002) in any National Football League (NFL) career. He played for the Chicago Bears, Baltimore Colts, Houston Oilers and Oakland Raiders (1949–75).

Blandrata or **Biandrata, Giorgio** c. 1515–c. 1590 •*Italian physician, theologian and founder of Unitarianism in Poland and Transylvania*• Born in Saluzzo, Piedmont, he was compelled to flee to Geneva in 1556 due to the freedom of his religious opinions, but in 1558 **John Calvin**'s displeasure at his anti-Trinitarianism drove him to Poland. Finally, in 1563, he became physician to John Sigismund, Prince of Transylvania. He is said to have been strangled in his sleep by his nephew.

Blankers-Koen, Fanny (Francina) 1918– •*Dutch athlete*• She was born in Amsterdam and achieved success at the comparatively late age of 30, when she dominated women's events in the London Olympics of 1948. She won four gold medals: the 100 meters (11.9 seconds), 200 meters (24.4 seconds), 80-meter hurdles (11.2 seconds) and the 4 × 100-meter relay, and earned the nickname "the flying Dutch housewife." At various times she also held world records for both the high and long jumps.

Blanqui, (Louis) Auguste 1805–81 •*French revolutionary*• Born in Puget-Théniers, he worked from 1830 at building up a network of secret societies committed to violent revolution. He spent 37 years in prison, and was in prison in 1871 when he was elected president of the revolutionary Commune of Paris. He was released in 1879. In 1881 his followers, known as Blanquists, joined the Marxists.

Blashford-Snell, Colonel John 1936– •*English explorer and youth leader*• Born in Hereford, he was educated at Victoria College, Jersey, and the Royal Military Academy, Sandhurst, and was commissioned into the Royal Engineers in 1957. He participated in over 40 expeditions, and led the Blue Nile (1968), British Trans-Americas (1972) and Zaire River (1975) expeditions under the aegis of the Scientific Exploration Society (SES), of which he is honorary chairman. He then went on to lead two major youth projects: Operation Drake (1978–80) and Operation Raleigh, which involved over 10,000 young people in adventurous, scientific and community projects in over 73 countries (1984–92) before being established as the Raleigh International.

Blasis, Carlo 1797–1878 •*Italian dancer, choreographer and teacher*• Born in Naples, he danced in France, Italy, London and Russia, and became director of the Dance Academy in Milan in 1837. The author of noted treatises on the codification of ballet technique (1820, 1840, 1857), he is regarded as the most important ballet teacher of the 19th century.

Blasius, St *See* **Blaise, St**

Blatch, Harriot (Eaton) Stanton, *née* **Stanton** 1856–1940 •*US suffrage leader*• Born in Seneca Falls, New York, the daughter of **Elizabeth Cady Stanton**, she was educated at Vassar College. She moved to Basingstoke, England, on her marriage (1882) to William Blatch, and after her return to the US she founded the Equality League of Self-Supporting Women (1907) and became an activist for women's rights, founding the Women's Political Union in 1908. Her published works include *Mobilizing Woman-Power* (1918) and *A Woman's Point of View* (1920).

Blavatsky, Helena Petrovna, *known as* **Madame Blavatsky**, *née* **Hahn** 1831–91 •*US theosophist*• Born in Yekaterinoslav, Russia (now Dnipropetrovs'k, Ukraine), she traveled widely in the East, including Tibet, and came to the US in 1873. In 1875, with **Henry Steel Olcott**, she founded the Theosophical Society in New York City and later carried on her work in India. Her psychic powers were widely acclaimed but did not survive investigation by the Society for Psychical Research, although this did not deter her large following, which included **Annie Besant**. Her writings include *Isis Unveiled* (1877).

Bleasdale, Alan 1946– •*English dramatist*• He was born in Liverpool and was educated at Wade Deacon Grammar School, Widnes, and Padgate Teacher Training College. His television play *The Blackstuff* (1980), and the ensuing television series *The Boys from the Blackstuff* (1982), about a group of unemployed Liverpudlians, were an enormous success, and established his reputation. *The Monocled Mutineer*, a television series set during World War I, followed in 1986 but was less well received. He enjoyed another success with *GBH* (1991), a television drama about corruption in local politics. His stage plays include *Are You Lonesome Tonight?* (1985) and *On the Ledge* (1993).

Blériot, Louis 1872–1936 •*French aviator*• Born in Cambrai, he made the first flight across the English Channel (July 25, 1909) from Baraques to Dover in a small 24-hp monoplane. He later became an aircraft manufacturer.

Blessed, Brian 1936– •*English actor and adventurer*• Born in Mexborough, South Yorkshire, he made his name on television as PC Fancy Smith in *Z Cars* (1962–65) and later played Emperor Augustus in *I, Claudius* (1976) and Long John Silver in *Return to Treasure Island* (1989). His film roles include Prince Vultan in *Flash Gordon* (1980), Lord Locksley in *Robin Hood: Prince of Thieves* (1991) and Boss Nass in *Star Wars: Episode 1—The Phantom Menace* (1999). He climbed 25,400 feet (7,700 m) without oxygen for the BBC documentary *Galahad of Everest* in 1990 and returned to climb Everest three years later, reaching 28,000 feet (8,500 m) without oxygen, the oldest man to do so. He was also the oldest man to reach the magnetic North Pole on foot.

Blessington, Marguerite Gardiner, Countess of, *née* **Marguerite Power** 1789–1849 •*Irish literary hostess, memoirist and novelist*• She was born in Knockbrit, near Clonmel, County Tipperary. Sold into marriage at 14 by her dissolute father, she abandoned her husband, and when her spouse fell to his death from a window, she married the Earl of Blessington, with whom she had been living for some time. After his death from apoplexy in 1829, she became one of London's most vivacious hostesses, a prolific author, and a dreadful debtor. Her books include *Journal of Conversations with Lord Byron* (1832), two travel books, *The Idler in Italy* (1839) and *The Idler in France* (1841), and a number of three-volume novels concerning upper-middle-class manners.

Blethyn, Brenda Anne, *née* **Bootle** 1946– •*English actress*• She was born in Ramsgate, Kent, and studied at the Guildford School of Acting. She worked with the National Theatre from 1975 to 1990 and appeared increasingly in cinema roles from the early 1990s in films such as *A River Runs Through It* (1992), *Secrets and Lies* (1996; Best Actress, Cannes Film Festival) and *Little Voice* (1999). Her extensive television work has included roles in *The Buddha of Suburbia* (1993) and *First Signs of Madness* (1996).

Bleuler, Eugen 1857–1939 •*Swiss psychiatrist who coined the word "schizophrenia"*• He was born in Zollikon, near Zurich, studied medicine at the University of Bern, and became Professor of Psychiatry at Zurich (1898–1927). He researched epilepsy and other physiological conditions, then turned to psychiatry, and in 1911 published an important study on what he called schizophrenia, or "splitting of the mind." One of his pupils was **Carl Gustav Jung**.

Bley, Carla, *née* **Borg** 1938– •*US jazz composer, bandleader and pianist*• Born in Oakland, California, she moved to New York City as a teenager. She founded the Jazz Composers Orchestra with Michael Mantler in 1964, which she subsequently developed into a distribution network for commercially difficult music. Composition was always her major artistic concern, and she has produced significant works for important jazz musicians like Gary Burton and Charlie Haden, as well as many pieces for her own ensembles. One of the most distinctive figures in contemporary jazz, she has made a major impact in a traditionally male-dominated field.

Bligh, William 1754–c. 1817 •*English naval officer*• Born in Plymouth, he went to sea at the age of 15 and was picked by Captain **James Cook** as sailing master of the *Resolution* on his third voyage (1776–80). In 1787 he commanded the *Bounty* on a voyage to Tahiti to collect plants of the breadfruit tree and introduce them to the West Indies. On the return voyage, on April 28, 1789, **Fletcher Christian** led a mutiny, and Bligh and 18 men were cast adrift in an open boat without charts. In June they reached Timor, in the East Indies, having traveled nearly 4,000 miles. Bligh served under Lord **Nelson** in command of the *Glatton* at the Battle of Copenhagen in 1801. In 1805 he was appointed Governor of New South Wales and was imprisoned (1808–10) by mutinous soldiers during the so-called Rum Rebellion. Bligh was exonerated of all blame, and promoted to admiral on his retirement in 1811.

Blind Harry *See* **Harry, Blind**

Bliss, Sir Arthur (Drummond) 1891–1975 •*English composer*• Born in London, he studied under **Gustav Holst**, **Charles Stanford** and **Ralph Vaughan Williams** at the Royal College of Music, and in 1921 became Professor of Composition there. After a year, he resigned to devote himself to composition, including music for the film *Things to Come* (1935), based on the 1933 novel by **H G Wells**; the ballets *Checkmate* (1937) and *Miracle in the Gorbals* (1944); the opera *The Olympians* (1949); chamber music; and piano and violin works. He was music director of the BBC (1942–44), and in 1953 succeeded Sir **Arnold Bax** as Master of the Queen's Musick.

" "

The jazz band can be used for artificial excitement and aphrodisiac purposes, but not for spreading eternal truths.

1941 "Music Policy."

Blixen, Karen, Baroness, *pseudonym* **Isak Dinesen** 1885–1962 •*Danish storyteller and novelist*• Born in Rungsted, she was educated at home and in France, Switzerland and England, and adopted English as her main literary language, translating some of her most important works back into Danish. In 1914 she married her cousin, Baron Bror Blixen Finecke, from whom she contracted syphilis. Their life on an unproductive coffee plantation in Kenya is recounted in *Den afrikanske farm* (1937, Eng trans *Out of Africa*, 1938), which was also the basis of a Hollywood film. After her divorce and the death of her lover Denys Finch-Hatton in a plane crash, she returned to Denmark and began writing the brooding, existential tales for which she is best known, among them *Winter's Tales* (1942), *Last Tales* (1957) and *Anecdotes of Destiny* (1958). "Babette's Feast" (1950), also successfully filmed, shows a lighter side to her artistic nature.

Blobel, Günter 1936– •*US cell biologist and Nobel Prize winner*• Born in Waltersdorf, Silesia (then in Germany, now in Poland), he was educated at the universities of Tubingen and Wisconsin, emigrated to the US in 1960 and later became a naturalized US citizen. In recognition of his discovery that proteins have intrinsic signals that direct their transport and position within the cell, he was awarded the Nobel Prize for physiology or medicine in 1999.

Bloch, Felix 1905–83 •*US physicist and Nobel Prize winner*• Born in Zurich, Switzerland, he was educated at the University of Leipzig in Germany, where he obtained his PhD in 1928. For his PhD, he solved **Erwin Schrödinger**'s equation to explain the conduction of metals, giving rise to the band model of solids which forms the basis of much of solid-state physics. He left Germany for the US in 1933 and became Professor of Theoretical Physics at Stanford University (1934–71). During World War II he worked on radar, and after the war he developed the technique of nuclear magnetic resonance (NMR). He was awarded the 1952 Nobel Prize for physics jointly with **Edward Mills Purcell** for this work. Bloch was the first director general of CERN (Conseil Européen pour la Recherche Nucléaire) in Geneva (1954–55).

Bloch, Konrad Emil 1912–2000 •*US biochemist and Nobel Prize winner*• Born in Neisse, Germany (now Nysa in Poland), he was educated at Columbia University, and emigrated to the US in 1936. Bloch's findings on glucose underlie our present-day understanding that, in animals, fatty acids cannot be converted into sugars. In 1943 he revealed the direct metabolic relationship between cholesterol and bile acids, and in the 1950s his discovery that the mold *Neurospora* required acetate for growth resulted in the recognition of mevalonic acid as the first-formed building block. For his work on cholesterol, Bloch shared the 1964 Nobel Prize for physiology or medicine with **Feodor Lynen**. He was awarded the US National Medal of Science in 1988.

Bloch, Martin 1883–1954 •*British painter*• Born in Neisse, Germany (now Nysa in Poland), he was forced to leave Germany by the Nazis in 1934, and went to Denmark, and later to England, where he opened a school of painting with Roy de Maistre. He interpreted the English landscape through his brilliant colors and expressionist technique.

Block, Herbert Lawrence, *pen name* **Herblock** 1909–2001 •*US cartoonist*• He was born in Chicago, and his first job as an editorial cartoonist was with the *Chicago Daily News* (1929–33). He joined the *Washington Post* in 1946 and syndicated his cartoons to more than 200 other newspapers. He satirized **McCarthy**ism, the Vietnam War, and the arms race, winning Pulitzer Prizes in 1942, 1954, and 1979, and he was awarded the Presidential Medal of Freedom in 1994.

Blok, Aleksandr Aleksandrovich 1880–1921 •*Russian poet*• Born in St Petersburg, he married (1903) the daughter of the famous chemist **Dmitri Mendeleev**. His poetry collections include *Stikhi o prekrasnoi dame* (1904, "Songs about the Lady Fair") and *Nochnye chasy* (1911, "Nocturnal Hours"). He welcomed the 1917 Revolution and wrote two poems, *Dvenadtsat'* (1918, Eng trans *The Twelve*, 1920), a symbolic sequence of revolutionary themes, and *Skify* (1918, "The Scythians"), an ode inciting Europe to follow Russia. Soon disillusioned, however, he suffered greatly in the hard times that followed the Revolution.

Blondel, *also called* **Blondel de Nesle** fl. 12th century •*French troubadour*• According to legend, he accompanied **Richard I**, Cœur de Lion, to Palestine on the Crusades, and located him when imprisoned in the Austrian castle of Dürrenstein (1193) by means of the song they had jointly composed. He is featured in Sir **Walter Scott**'s *The Talisman* (1825).

Blondin, Charles, *properly* **Jean François Gravelet** 1824–97 •*French acrobat and tightrope walker*• He was born in Hesdin, near Calais, and trained at Lyons. In 1859 he crossed Niagara Falls on a tightrope. He later performed several variations on his feat, making crossings blindfolded, with a wheelbarrow, with a man on his back, and on stilts.

Blood, Thomas c. 1618–80 •*Irish adventurer*• A Parliamentarian during the English Civil War, he was deprived of his estate at the Restoration. In 1663 he put himself at the head of a plot to seize Dublin Castle and James Butler Ormonde, the Lord Lieutenant. The plot was discovered and his chief accomplices executed. On May 9, 1671, together with three others, he broke into the Tower of London and stole the crown, while one of his associates took the orb. They were pursued and captured, but Blood was later pardoned by King **Charles II**, who also restored his estate.

Bloom, Claire, *originally* **Patricia Claire Blume** 1931– •*English actress*• Born in London, her stage roles include Cordelia opposite **John Gielgud** in a West End production of *King Lear* (1955) and Blanche du Bois in **Tennessee Williams**'s *A Streetcar Named Desire* (1974). Her many film appearances include *Look Back in Anger* (1959) and *Crimes and Misdemeanors* (1989). On television, she has played many classical roles, as well as Edith Galt Wilson in *Backstairs at the White House* (1979) and Lady Marchmain in *Brideshead Revisited* (1981). She won a British Academy of Film and Television Arts award for her performance in *Shadowlands* (1985).

Bloomer, Amelia, *née* **Jenks** 1818–94 •*US champion of women's rights and dress reform*• Born in Homer, New York, she founded and edited the feminist paper *The Lily* (1849–55), and worked closely with **Susan Anthony**. In her pursuit of dress equality she wore her own version of trousers for women which came to be called "bloomers."

Bloomfield, Leonard 1887–1949 •*US linguist*• He was born in Chicago and after holding several university posts became Sterling Professor of Linguistics at Yale in 1940. His early interest was in Indo-European, especially Germanic, phonology and morphology, but he later made studies of Malayo-Polynesian languages (especially Tagalog) and of Native American languages (particularly Menomini and Cree). Although he had in his *Introduction to the Study of Language* (1914) indicated his adherence to **Wilhelm Wundt**'s mentalistic psychology, in his major work on linguistic theory, *Language* (1933), he advocated and himself adopted behaviorism as the theoretical framework for linguistic analysis and description. This led to the almost total neglect of the study of meaning within the "Bloomfieldian" school of linguistics, and a concentration on phonology, morphology and syntax.

Bloor, Ella, *known as* **Mother Bloor**, *née* **Reeve** 1862–1951 •*US radical and feminist*• Born on Staten Island, New York, she married at the age of 19, and was a mother of four by 1892. In 1901 she joined the Socialist Party. She first wrote under the name Ella Bloor in 1906, reporting for **Upton Sinclair**. She was the party organizer for Connecticut for many years, attracting support for various labor causes. In 1919 she helped found the American Communist Party. Arrested more than 30 times during her career, she became a distinguished party speaker and was a member of the party's central committee (1932–48). Her works include *Women of the Soviet Union* (1930) and *We Are Many* (1940).

Blount, Charles, 8th Lord Mountjoy and **Earl of Devonshire** 1563–1606 •*English soldier*• He came from a declining family whose fortunes he was determined to revive. He served in the Low Countries, in Brittany, and in the Azores (1597). In 1600 he accepted the Irish command against the rebellion of **Hugh O'Neill**, Earl of Tyrone, winning a decisive victory at Kinsale (1601), laying Munster waste and ultimately receiving Tyrone's surrender at Mellifont, in 1603. Made Lord Lieutenant of Ireland, he reduced disaffected towns, and returned to England where he was rewarded by King **James VI and I** with an earldom, mastership of the ordnance, and lands, and by King **Philip III** of Spain with a pension.

Blücher, Gebhard Leberecht von, Prince of Wahlstadt, *known as* **Marshal Forward** 1742–1819 •*Prussian field marshal*• Born in Rostock, Mecklenburg, after two years in the Swedish service (1756–58), he fought with the Prussian cavalry (1760–70), but was discharged for dissipation and insubordination, and for 15 years farmed his own estates. He fought against the French in 1793 on the Rhine and in 1806 at Auerstädt, and fought also at Lübeck and Stralsund. When the Prussians rose against France in 1813 Blücher took chief command in Silesia. At the Katzbach he repulsed the enemy, and at Leipzig (1813) won important successes. In January 1814 he crossed the Rhine, and though once routed by **Napoleon I** won several battles, and on March 31 entered Paris. After Napoleon's return in 1815, Blücher assumed the general command; he suffered a severe defeat at Ligny, but completed **Wellington**'s victory at the Battle of Waterloo (1815) by his timely appearance on the field. At the second taking of Paris, he wanted to inflict on Paris what other capitals had suffered, but was restrained by Wellington.

Blum, Léon 1872–1950 •*French Socialist statesman*• He was born in Paris into a Jewish family. A lawyer, he was radicalized by the **Dreyfus** Affair (1899), becoming one of the leaders of the Socialist Party. In 1924 he lent his support to **Édouard Herriot**, a policy which resulted in great electoral advances by the Left and as a consequence the elections of 1936 gave France its first socialist Prime Minister since 1870. In 1938 Blum formed a second "popular front" government that had a stormy existence. During World War II he was interned in Germany. On his return in 1946 he was elected Prime Minister of the six-week caretaker government. As a writer he worked on magazines with **Marcel Proust** and most of the other leading authors of his day, wrote a play, *La colère* (1902, "Anger"), and theatrical criticism. After World War I he turned to political writings.

Blum, René 1878–1942 •*French impresario and critic*• Born in Paris, he became critic and editor of the literary journal *Gil Blas*. While he was director of the Theater of the Monte Carlo Casino he took over the administration of the Ballets Russes immediately after **Sergei Diaghilev**'s death in 1929, with **Léonide Massine** as director. During World War II he was arrested in France while the company was on tour in the US, and he died within a week of being sent to Auschwitz.

Blumberg, Baruch Samuel 1925– •*US biochemist and Nobel Prize winner*• Born in New York City, he studied at Columbia University and at Oxford. Blumberg discovered the "Australia antigen" in 1964 and reported its association with hepatitis B (known as the HBV virus). The finding was very rapidly applied to screening blood donors. His study of the distribution of the HBV virus in the population revealed that apparently healthy people could carry and transmit the live virus. In 1969 Blumberg introduced a protective vaccine, now widely used. He shared the 1976 Nobel Prize for physiology or medicine with **Daniel Gajdusek**. In 1999 he became director of the Astrobiology Institute of NASA.

Blume, Judy Sussman 1938– •*US writer for teenagers*• She was born in New Jersey, and educated at New York University. Her third book, *Are You There, God? It's Me, Margaret* (1970), brought acclaim for her candid approach to the onset of puberty and for her natural, if unsubtle, style. As with subsequent books, attempts were made to restrict its circulation. Her explicitness brought her into conflict with parents, but she has a remarkable rapport with her readers and confronts subjects that previously were ignored. Her other books include *It's Not the End of the World* (1972), *Deenie* (1973), *Blubber* (1974), *Forever* (1975), *Superfudge* (1980), and *Here's to You, Rachel Robinson* (1993).

Blundell, Sir Michael 1907–93 •*Kenyan farmer and politician*• Born in London, he emigrated to Kenya in 1925 to farm, and he served throughout World War II. He then involved himself in settler politics, being a member of the Legislative Council (1948–63) and leader of the European members (1952–54) and then Minister of Agriculture (1955–59, 1961–63). He broke with the dominant white group to espouse political change involving Black Kenyans in national politics, and he was much vilified for this. However, Blundell was an essential bridge between the white-dominated colonial years and the Black majority rule of independent Kenya.

Blunden, Edmund Charles 1896–1974 •*English poet and critic*• Born in Yalding, Kent, he was educated at Christ's Hospital and Queen's College, Oxford. He served in France in World War I and won the Military Cross. He was Professor of English Literature at Tokyo (1924–27), Fellow of Merton College, Oxford, from 1931, joined the staff of the *Times Literary Supplement* in 1943, returned to the Far East and from 1953 lectured at the University of Hong Kong. He was professor at Oxford from 1966 to 1968. A lover of the English countryside, he is essentially a nature poet, as is evident in *Pastorals* (1916) and *The Waggoner and Other Poems* (1920), but his prose work *Undertones of War* (1928) is perhaps his best. Other works include *The Bonadventure* (1922), on his visit to the US, a biography of **Leigh Hunt**, and books on **Charles Lamb** and **Keats**.

" "

Mastery in poetry consists largely in the instinct for not ruining or smothering or tinkering with moments of vision.

1930 ***Leigh Hunt.***

Blunkett, David 1947– •*English Labour politician*• He was born in Sheffield and, blind from birth, attended the Royal Normal College for the Blind in Shrewsbury; he joined the Labour Party at the age of 16. He studied politics at Sheffield University under Professor Bernard Crick (1929–), who has described him as a realist with the "conscience of the old Left." Blunkett became a member of Sheffield City Council in 1970 and was its leader by 1978. In 1983 he won a place on the Labour Party's national executive committee (NEC). As NEC chairman in 1993–94, he announced the first one-member-one-vote election for the Labour leadership. Member of Parliament for Sheffield (Brightside) since 1987, he rose to hold several posts in the Shadow Cabinet. Following Labour's general election victory in 1997, he became Secretary of State for Education and Employment and became Home Secretary in 2001.

Blunt, Anthony Frederick 1907–83 •*English art historian and Soviet spy*• Born in Bournemouth, Hampshire, he was educated at Marlborough and Trinity College, Cambridge, where he was made a Fellow in 1932. At Cambridge he became a Communist and met **Guy Burgess**, **Kim Philby** and **Donald Maclean**. He acted as a "talent-spotter" for Burgess, supplying names of likely recruits to the Russian Communist cause, and while serving in British Intelligence during World War II he passed on information to the Russian government. In 1964, after the defection of Philby, Blunt confessed in return for his immunity, and he continued as Surveyor of the Queen's Pictures (1945–72). Blunt had been Director of the Courtauld Institute of Art (1947–1974) and among his publications were *Art and Architecture in France 1500–1700* (1953) and his study of **Poussin** (1966–67). His knighthood awarded in 1956 was annulled in 1979.

Bly, Nellie *See* **Seaman, Elizabeth Cochrane**

Bly, Robert Elwood 1926– •*US poet, critic, translator and editor*• He was born in Madison, Minnesota, and was educated at Harvard and the University of Iowa. As a critic he is caustic, and as a poet, for a man so aware of foreign literature (he has translated **Pablo Neruda** among others), his poetry is surprisingly American in tone and locale. His first collection was *Silence in the Snowy Fields* (1962), followed by such volumes as *The Shadow-Mothers* (1970), *Sleepers Joining Hands* (1972), *Talking All Morning* (1980) and *The Apple Found in the Plowing* (1989). In 1991 he published *Iron John*, a controversial study of maleness and its frustrations, and he became a leading figure in the "men's movement." *The Sibling Society* (1997) examines adolescence.

Blyth, Sir Chay (Charles) 1940– •*British yachtsman*• He was educated in Hawick before joining the Parachute Regiment (1958–67). In 1966 he rowed across the North Atlantic with John Ridgeway, and in 1970–71 became the first person to sail solo around the world in the difficult westward direction. He circumnavigated the globe again in the 1973–74 Round the World Yacht Race, and won the Elapsed Time prize. He has also sailed the Atlantic from Cape Verde to Antigua in record-breaking time (1977), and organized the British Steel Challenge Round the World

Yacht Race (1992–93) and the BT Global Challenge Round the World Yacht Race (1996–97) with which he continues to be associated. He was given the honorary title of Commander, Order of the British Empire, in 1972 and knighted in 1997.

Blyth, Edward 1810–73 •*English naturalist and zoologist*• He was born in London, where he became a pharmacist, but spent so much time on ornithology that his business failed. His many articles on survival and natural selection of bird species anticipated **Charles Darwin**. He was curator of the museum of the Asiatic Society in Bengal (1841–62). Several birds are named after him, including Blyth's kingfisher, Blyth's pipit and Blyth's warbler.

Blyton, Enid Mary 1897–1968 •*English children's writer*• Born in London, she trained as a Froebel kindergarten teacher, then became a journalist, specializing in educational and children's publications. It was in the late 1930s that she began writing her many children's stories featuring such characters as Noddy, the Famous Five, and the Secret Seven. She identified closely with children, and always considered her stories highly educational and moral in tone, but has recently been criticized for racism, sexism and snobbishness, as well as stylistic inelegance and oversimplification. She published over 600 books, and is one of the most translated British authors. Her works also include school readers and books on nature and religious study.

Boabdil, *properly* **Abu Abdallah Muhammad** d. c. 1493 •*Last Moorish king of Granada*• He dethroned his father, Abu-al-Hasan (1482), but while he continued to struggle for power against his father and uncle the Christians gradually conquered the kingdom. Málaga fell in 1487, and after a two-year siege Granada itself capitulated to **Ferdinand the Catholic** and **Isabella of Castile** (1492). He was granted a small lordship in the Alpujarras, but sold his rights to the Spanish Crown (1493) and retired to Morocco where he died.

Boadicea *See* **Boudicca**

Boardman, Chris(topher Miles) 1968– •*English cyclist*• Born in Clatterbridge on the Wirral, he was reigning British champion in the 25-mile, 50-mile and pursuit events. He created a sensation at the 1992 Olympics at Barcelona riding a revolutionary streamlined cycle and took the gold medal in the 4,000-meter event. He captured the world championship titles in both the pursuit and time trial events in 1994 and also won the 4,000-meter title at the 1996 world championships.

Boas, Franz 1858–1942 •*US anthropologist*• He was born in Minden, Germany, and studied at the universities of Heidelberg, Bonn and Kiel. His expeditions to the Arctic and to British Columbia shifted his interest to the tribes there and thence to ethnology and anthropology, and prompted his emigration to the US in 1886, where he made his career, ultimately as Professor of Anthropology at Columbia from 1899. He sought to bring together ethnology, physical anthropology, archaeology and linguistics, and rejected the simple determinism and eugenic theories of the time, as outlined in his collection of papers, *Race, Language and Culture* (1940). His other books include *The Mind of Primitive Man* (1911) and *Anthropology and Modern Life* (1928). He was the dominant figure in establishing modern anthropology in the US.

Boateng, Paul Yaw 1951– •*British Labour politician*• He began his education in the international school at Accra, Ghana, and completed it in England, graduating in law and qualifying as a solicitor. He became politically active as a member of the Greater London Council (GLC) in 1981 and entered the House of Commons, representing Brent South, in 1987. In 1989 he became the first Black member of the Labour Shadow Cabinet as Treasury and Economic Affairs Spokesman (1989–92), then was appointed Legal Affairs Spokesman (1992–97). He became a Minister of State in 1998, Deputy Home Secretary in 1999 and Financial Secretary in 2001.

Boccaccio, Giovanni 1313–75 •*Italian writer*• Born in Tuscany or Paris, he abandoned commerce and the study of canon law, and in Naples (1328) he turned to storywriting in verse and prose. The *Teseide* ("Book of Theseus") is a graceful version in ottava rima of the medieval romance of Palamon and Arcite, which was partly translated by **Chaucer** in the *Knight's Tale*. The *Filostrato*, also in ottava rima, deals with the loves of Troilus and Cressida, also in great part translated by Chaucer. After 1350 he became a diplomat and a scholar, formed a lasting friendship with **Petrarch**, and visited Rome, Ravenna, Avignon and Brandenburg as Florentine ambassador. In 1358 he completed his major work, the *Decameron*, begun some ten years before, with medieval subject matter and classical form. He wrote in Latin an elaborate work on mythology, *De genealogia deorum gentilium* ("The Genealogies of the Gentile Gods"), and treatises, for example *De claris mulieribus* ("Famous Women") and *De montibus* ("On Mountains").

Boccioni, Umberto 1882–1916 •*Italian artist and sculptor*• Born in Reggio, he was the most original artist of the futurist school, and its principal theorist. After working with **Giacomo Balla**, **Gino Severini**, and **Emilio Marinetti** in Rome and Paris from 1898 to 1914, he wrote a comprehensive survey of the movement, *Pittura, scultura futuriste* (1914, "Futurist Painting and Sculpture"). An important bronze sculpture, *Unique Forms of Continuity in Space* (1913), is in the Museum of Modern Art, New York.

Bock, Fedor von 1880–1945 •*German field marshal*• Born in Küstrin, he was educated at Potsdam Military School. He served with distinction as a staff officer in World War I and later commanded the German armies invading Austria (1938), Poland (1939) and the Lower Somme, France (1940). Promoted to field marshal in 1940, he participated in the invasion of the USSR with remarkable success (1941), but was dismissed by **Hitler** for failing to capture Moscow (1942). He was killed with his wife and daughter in an air raid.

Böcklin, Arnold 1827–1901 •*Swiss painter*• Born in Basel, he combined classical themes involving nymphs and satyrs and mythological subjects with the dark romantic landscapes, rocks and castles characteristic of 19th-century German painting.

Bodhidharma 6th century •*Indian monk and founder of Zen Buddhism*• Born near Madras, he traveled to China in 520, where he had a famous audience with the emperor. He argued that merit leading to salvation could not be accumulated through good deeds, and taught meditation as the means of return to Buddha's spiritual precepts.

Bodichon, Barbara, *née* **Leigh Smith** 1827–91 •*English champion of women's rights*• Born in London, the daughter of a radical Member of Parliament who believed strongly in women's rights, she studied at Bedford College there, and in 1852 opened a primary school in London. She wrote *Women at Work* (1857) and with **Bessie Rayner Parkes** was a founder of the feminist magazine *The Englishwoman's Journal* (1858). She helped to found the college for women that became Girton College, Cambridge, and was also a landscape watercolorist.

Bo Diddley, *stage name of* **Elias Bates**, *later* **McDaniel** 1928– •*US rock and roll singer and guitarist*• Born in McComb, Mississippi, he was a boxer for a time, where he picked up his stage name. He began singing blues in Chicago clubs in the early 1950s, but established his trademark style with his first single, "Bo Diddley," in 1955. His chugging rhythms and custom-made guitar, with its rectangular sound box and distorted amplification, gave him a distinctive if limited style, and he had a number of hits in the rock and roll era, notably with his version of "Who Do You Love." He was a highly influential figure for later rock artists.

Bodin, Jean c. 1530–96 •*French political philosopher*• He was born and educated in Angers. His major work, *Les six livres de la république* (1576, *The Six Bookes of a Commonweale*, 1606), expounds the belief that property and the family form the basis of society, and that a limited monarchy is the best possible form of government. His *Colloqium heptaplomeres* (1587) presented a plea for religious tolerance through the device of a conversation between a Jew, a Muslim, a Lutheran, a Zwinglian, a Roman Catholic, an Epicurean and a Theist. Despite his enlightened views he shared the general belief of the time in sorcery and witchcraft, which he propounded in his influential *Démonomanie des sorciers* (1580, "Demonomania of Sorcerers").

Bodley, Sir Thomas 1545–1613 •*English scholar and diplomat*• Born in Exeter, he studied languages and divinity at Geneva, where his Protestant family had been forced to take refuge during the persecutions of Queen **Mary I**, but in 1558 he went to Magdalen College, Oxford, and was appointed Greek lecturer at Merton College in 1564. In the service of Queen **Elizabeth I** of England he was ambassador to Denmark, France and Holland. In 1587 he married a wealthy widow, and then spent huge sums on the repair and extension of the university library originally established by Humphrey, Duke of **Gloucester**, and collected books from all over Europe. The library, renamed the Bodleian, was opened in 1602. He was knighted by King **James VI and I** in 1604.

Bodmer, Sir Walter Fred 1936– •*English geneticist*• Born in Frankfurt, Germany, and educated at Clare College, Cambridge, he held a number of professorial posts before becoming Professor of Genetics at the University of Oxford (1970–79), and director general of the Imperial Cancer Research Fund (1991–96). He was elected a Fellow of the Royal Society in 1974 and knighted in 1986. Bodmer has published extensively on the genetics of the HLA histocompatibility system, which distinguishes foreign cells in the animal body and is a vital factor in transplant surgery. He has also published on somatic cell genetics, cancer genetics and human population genetics. In 1996 Bodmer was appointed Principal of Hertford College, Oxford.

Bodoni, Giambattista 1740–1813 •*Italian printer*• Born in Saluzzo, he designed (1790) a modern typeface still widely used today. His press in Parma published editions of the classics widely admired for their elegance.

Boehm or **Böhm, Theobald** 1794–1881 •*German flautist and inventor*• Born in Munich, he became a member of the Bavarian Court Orchestra in 1818 while working in the family trade as a goldsmith. In 1828 he opened a flute factory in Munich, and in 1831 determined to make a flute that would be acoustically perfect. As this involved making holes in places where they could not be fingered, he devised a key mechanism to overcome the problem, and in 1847 produced the model on which the modern flute is based.

Boeing, William Edward 1881–1956 •*US aircraft manufacturer*• He was born in Detroit, Michigan, and studied at Yale's Sheffield Scientific School. Having learned to fly in Los Angeles in 1915, he formed the Pacific Aero Products Co. in 1916 to build seaplanes he had designed with Conrad Westerfelt. Renamed the Boeing Airplane Company in 1917, it eventually became the largest manufacturer of military and civilian aircraft in the world. In 1927 he formed the Boeing Air Transport Company that introduced many novelties, including flying passengers by night, having two pilots and a flight attendant, and the use of constant two-way radiotelephone. He retired in 1934, when his air transport company became United Air Lines.

Boerhaave, Hermann 1668–1738 •*Dutch physician and botanist*• He was born in Voorhout, near Leiden, and took his degree in philosophy at Leiden in 1689. In 1690 he began the study of medicine. The two works on which his medical fame chiefly rests, *Institutiones medicae* (1708, "Medical Principles") and *Aphorismi de cognoscendis et curandis morbis* (1709, "Aphorisms on the Recognition and Treatment of Diseases"), were translated into various European languages, and even into Arabic. He pointed out that both plants and animals show the same law of generation, and by 1718 he was teaching sexual reproduction in plants, his international stature ensuring widespread acceptance of these ideas. In 1724 he also became Professor of Chemistry, and his *Elementa chemiae* (1724, "Elements of Chemistry") is a classic.

Boethius, Anicius Manlius Severinus c. 475–524 AD •*Roman philosopher and politician*• Born of a patrician Roman family, he studied in Athens and later produced the translations of and commentaries on **Aristotle** and **Porphyry** that became the standard textbooks on logic in medieval Europe. He was made consul in AD 510 and later Chief Minister to the ruler **Theodoric**, but in 523 he was accused of treason and imprisoned in Pavia, and was executed the following year. It was during his imprisonment that he wrote the famous *De consolatione philosophiae* ("The Consolation of Philosophy"), in which Philosophy personified solaces the distraught author by explaining the mutability of all earthly fortune and the insecurity of everything except virtue. The *Consolation* was for the next thousand years probably the most widely read book after the Bible.

“ ”

Nam in omni adversitate fortunae infelicissimum est genus infortunii, fuisse felicem.

In all adversity of fortune, the most wretched kind is once to have been happy.

523 ***De consolatione philosophiae****, book 2, part 4 (translated by V E Watts).*

Bogarde, Sir Dirk, *originally* **Derek Jules Ulric Niven van den Bogaerde** 1921–99 •*English actor and novelist*• Born in Hampstead, London, he acted in repertory theater and made his film debut as an extra in *Come On George* (1940). After service in World War II, he was signed to a long-term contract with Rank Films, spending many years playing small-time crooks, military heroes and romantic or light comedy roles, until he was voted Britain's top box-office star (1955 and 1957). Ambitious to tackle more challenging material, he played a blackmailed gay man in *Victim* (1961) and a sinisterly manipulative valet in *The Servant* (1963). Subsequently favoring European cinema, he has created a series of distinguished characterizations, subtly portraying decadence, enigma and ambiguity, notably in *Death in Venice* (1971), *The Night Porter* (1973) and *Providence* (1977). After a break of 13 years from the big screen he appeared as a dying father in *Daddy Nostalgie* (1990, *These Foolish Things*). Knighted in 1991, he published seven volumes of autobiography and a number of novels.

Bogart, Humphrey DeForest 1899–1957 •*US film actor*• Born in New York City, after serving briefly with the US Navy he became a stage manager and walk-on actor, graduating to juvenile leads before making his film debut in *Broadway's Like That* in 1930. Alternating between stage and screen, he was frequently cast as a vicious hoodlum, most memorably in *The Petrified Forest* (1936), on the strength of which he was given a long-term contract with Warner Brothers. After further gangster roles, notably in *Angels with Dirty Faces* (1938), he achieved stardom with his roles in *High Sierra* (1941), playing the part of an aging mobster, *The Maltese Falcon* (1941), *Casablanca* (1942, with **Ingrid Bergman**), playing the cynical nightclub owner Rick, which won him his first Oscar nomination for best actor, and *To Have and Have Not* (1944), which also marked the début of **Lauren Bacall**, who became his fourth wife in 1945. Over the next 15 years he created an indelible and enduring screen persona of the lone wolf: cynical but heroic, abrasive, romantic and stubbornly faithful to his own code of ethics, as in *The Big Sleep* (1946), in which he memorably played **Raymond Chandler**'s private detective Philip Marlowe, and in *Key Largo* (1948, with **Edward G Robinson**). His considerable acting prowess was also displayed when he played the selfish prospector in *The Treasure of the Sierra Madre* (1948), the gin-sodden boatman in *The African Queen* (1951), which won him an Oscar for Best Actor, and the psychopathic captain in *The Caine Mutiny* (1954). He died after a long struggle with cancer.

Bogdanov, Michael 1938– •*English stage director*• He was born in London and educated at the universities of Dublin, Munich and the Sorbonne. At the Royal Shakespeare Company he directed *The Taming of the Shrew* (1978), *Romeo and Juliet* (1986) and **Sean O'Casey**'s *Shadow of a Gunman* (1980). His National Theatre productions include **Howard Brenton**'s *The Romans in Britain* (1980) and **Thomas Kyd**'s *The Spanish Tragedy* (1982). In 1986, with actor **Michael Pennington**, he became cofounder and artistic director of the touring English Shakespeare Company.

Bohemond I c. 1056–1111 •*Prince of Antioch*• The eldest son of **Robert Guiscard**, he distinguished himself in his father's war against the Byzantine emperor, **Alexius I Comnenus** (1081–85). His brother Roger took the Apulian throne, and Bohemond joined the First Crusade (1096). While the other crusaders advanced to storm Jerusalem, he established himself as first Latin prince in Antioch (1098). He was taken prisoner by the Turks (1100–03), and then returned to Europe to collect troops, and after defeating Alexius (1107) was acknowledged by him as Prince of Antioch in return for his vassalage.

Böhm, Theobald *See* **Boehm, Theobald**

Böhme, Jakob 1575–1624 •*German mystical writer and alchemical thinker*• He was born near Görlitz, and for many years worked as a cobbler. He was persecuted for the profoundly gnostic elements in his wild but seminal thinking, and from 1618 was forbidden to circulate his writings. He is the chief heir of **Meister Eckhart**, and of **Paracelsus**. He regarded God as possessing both love and anger, and therefore as containing the seeds of both good and evil. He influenced the work of Angelus Silesius and **Goethe**, Romantic thinkers such as **Hegel**, **Friedrich Schelling** and, later, **Carl Gustav Jung**, and his writings were studied by **Isaac Newton**.

Bohr, (Aage) Niels 1922– •*Danish physicist and Nobel Prize winner*• Born in Copenhagen, he was the son of the Nobel prize-winning physicist **Niels Bohr**. Educated at the universities of Copenhagen and London, he worked from 1946 at his father's Institute of Theoretical Physics in Copenhagen where he became Professor of Physics (1956–92). From 1963 to 1970 he was also director there and from 1975 to 1981 he was director of Nordita (the Nordic Institute for Theoretical Atomic Physics). Together with **Benjamin Roy Mottelson** he developed the collective model of the nucleus, which combined the quantum-mechanical shell model of the nucleus and the classical liquid drop model. He shared the 1975 Nobel Prize for physics with Mottelson and **James Rainwater** for this work.

Bohr, Niels Henrik David 1885–1962 •*Danish physicist and Nobel Prize winner*• Born in Copenhagen and educated at Copenhagen University, he went to England to work with Sir **J J Thomson** at Cambridge and **Ernest Rutherford** at Manchester University, and returned to Copenhagen University as professor (1916). He greatly extended the theory of atomic structure when he explained the spectrum of hydrogen by means of Rutherford's atomic model and the quantum theories of **Albert Einstein** and **Max Planck** (1913). During World War II he escaped from German-occupied Denmark and assisted atom bomb research in the US, returning to Copenhagen in 1945. He later worked on nuclear physics and developed the liquid drop model of the nucleus. He was awarded the Nobel Prize for physics in 1922. His son, **Aage Niels Bohr**, won the 1975 Nobel Prize for physics.

Boileau, Nicolas, *known as* **Boileau Despréaux** 1636–1711 •*French poet and critic*• Born in Paris, he studied law and theology at Beauvais, before devoting himself to literature. In 1677 the king appointed him, along with **Racine**, official royal historian. His first publications (1660–66) were satires, some of which got him into trouble. *L'art poétique* ("The Art of Poetry"), imitated by **Pope** in the *Essay on Criticism*, was published in 1674. Between 1669 and 1677 he published nine epistles, written, like his satires, on the Horatian model. His works include several critical dissertations, a collection of epigrams, a translation of **Longinus**'s *On the Sublime* and a series of letters (many to Racine). His influence as a critic has been profound.

“ ”

Often, the fear of one evil leads us into inflicting one that is worse.

*1674 **L'Art poétique***

Boito, Arrigo 1842–1918 •*Italian composer and poet*• Born in Padua, he studied at the Milan Conservatorio. His first important work was the opera *Mefistofele* (1868), which survived its initial failure and later grew in popularity. Thereafter he concentrated mainly on writing libretti, the best-known of which are those for **Verdi**'s *Otello* (1884–86) and *Falstaff* (1889–92).

Bo Juyi or **Bai Juyi (Po Chü-i)** 772–846 •*Chinese poet of the Tang dynasty*• He was born in Shaanxi (Shensi) province, of which he became governor in 831. He was so admired as a lyric poet that his poems were collected by imperial order and engraved on stone tablets.

Bokassa, Jean Bédel 1921–96 •*Central African Republic soldier and politician*• He was born in Bobangui, Lobay, and joined the French army in 1939. After independence he was made army Commander in Chief. On January 1, 1966, he led the coup which overthrew his cousin President **David Dacko**, making himself Life President and, in 1977, crowning himself Emperor Bokassa I of the renamed Central African Empire. His rule was noted for its gratuitous violence and in September 1979 he was overthrown. Sentenced to death (in absentia) in 1980, he returned to the Central African Republic in 1986, was retried and, found guilty of murder and other crimes, was again sentenced to death. His sentence was commuted to life imprisonment and he was freed in 1993.

Bolam, James 1938– •*English actor*• Born in Sunderland, he starred alongside Rodney Bewes (1938–)in the television sitcom *The Likely Lads* (1964–66), as well as in its sequel, *Whatever Happened to the Likely Lads?* (1973–74) and in a cinema version (1976), before playing strong-willed Jack Ford in the gritty Northern drama *When the Boat Comes In* (1976–81). He has since starred in the *Beiderbecke* trilogy (1985–88), *Room at the Bottom* (1986–88) and *Second Thoughts* (1991–94), among other television programs, and in films including *A Kind of Loving* (1962), *The Loneliness of the Long Distance Runner* (1962) and *O Lucky Man!* (1973).

Boleyn, Anne *See* **Anne Boleyn**

Bolger, James Brendan 1935– •*New Zealand National Party politician*• Born on a farm at Taranaki, he became a National Party Member of Parliament in 1972. His farming interests led to his appointment as Associate Minister of Agriculture in 1977; he became leader of the National Party in 1986. In 1990 he was elected Prime Minister and introduced a number of free market reforms and cuts in public spending. He was returned in the 1996 general election but resigned as party leader in 1997.

Bolingbroke, Henry St John, 1st Viscount 1678–1751 •*English statesman and writer*• He was born in Battersea, London, and became the Tory Member of Parliament for Wootton Bassett in 1701. He was successively Secretary for War (1704–08) and Foreign Secretary (1710), and he shared the leadership of the party with **Robert Harley**. He was made a peer and in 1713 he negotiated the Treaty of Utrecht. After engineering Harley's downfall, he was plotting a Jacobite restoration when Queen **Anne** died, and **George I** succeeded. He fled to France, where he served **James Edward Stuart**, the Old Pretender, as Secretary of State and wrote *Reflections on Exile*. In 1723 he obtained permission to return to England, where he became the associate of **Pope**, **Jonathan Swift**, and other men of letters. His last years were spent in Battersea, where he wrote his *Letters on the Spirit of Patriotism* and *Idea of a Patriot King* (1749), which had a profound political influence. He was much admired as an orator.

Bolívar, Simón, *known as* **the Liberator** 1783–1830 •*South American revolutionary leader*• Born in Caracas, Venezuela, of a noble family, he studied law in Madrid. After the declaration of independence by Venezuela in 1811, he fled to New Granada and raised an army. In 1813, he entered Caracas as conqueror and proclaimed himself dictator of western Venezuela. Driven out in 1814, he made repeated descents on Venezuela from the West Indies, but it was only in 1821 that the victory of Carabobo virtually ended the war. In 1819 Bolívar became President of the new republic of Colombia (comprising modern Venezuela, Colombia and, from 1822, Ecuador). In 1824 he joined with other rebel leaders including **Antonio de Sucre** and **José de San Martin** to drive the Spaniards out of Peru, and made himself dictator there for a time. Upper Peru was made a separate state, and called Bolivia in his honor, while he was named perpetual protector, but his Bolivian constitution provoked political dissension, and led to the expulsion of the Colombian troops. His assumption of supreme power, after his return to Colombia in 1828, roused the apprehension of the republicans there, and in 1829 Venezuela separated itself from Colombia. Bolívar resigned in 1830.

Bolkiah, Sir Hassanal 1946– •*Sultan of Brunei*• The son of Sultan Sir Omar Ali Saifuddin, he was educated at the Victoria Institute in Kuala Lumpur, Malaysia, and Sandhurst. Appointed crown prince (1961), he became sultan (1967) on his father's abdication. On independence (1984), Sultan Bolkiah also became Prime Minister and Defense Minister, governing in a personalized, familial manner.

Böll, Heinrich 1917–85 •*German writer and Nobel Prize winner*•

Born in Cologne, he served as an infantryman in World War II before becoming a full-time writer. A trilogy, *Und sagte kein einziges Wort* (1953, Eng trans *Acquainted with the Night*, 1954), *Haus ohne Hüter* (1954, Eng trans *The Unguarded House*, 1957) and *Das Brot der frühen Jahre* (1955, Eng trans *The Bread of Our Early Years*, 1957), depicting life in Germany during and after the Nazi regime, gained him a worldwide reputation. His later novels, characteristically satirizing modern German society, included *Die vorlorene Ehre der Katherina Blum* (1974, Eng trans *The Lost Honor of Katherina Blum*, 1975). He also wrote a number of plays, and a volume of poems. He was awarded the 1972 Nobel Prize for literature.

Bolt, Robert Oxton 1924–95 •*English playwright*• Born in Manchester, he was educated at Manchester University, and worked as a schoolmaster. He achieved success with the Academy Award-winning *A Man for All Seasons* (1960), about the moral courage of Sir **Thomas More**. His later plays include *The Tiger and the Horse* (1960) and *State of Revolution* (1977), and among his screenplays are *Lawrence of Arabia* (1962), *Dr. Zhivago* (1965, Academy Award), *Ryan's Daughter* (1970) and *The Mission* (1986).

“ ”

To be human at all, we must stand fast a little, even at the risk of being heroes.

1960 Thomas More ***A Man for All Seasons.***

Boltwood, Bertram Borden 1870–1927 •*US radiochemist*• Born in Amherst, Massachusetts, he was educated at Yale, Munich and Leipzig. From 1904 onward he concentrated on radiochemistry, becoming the leading American in this field and laying the foundations for the study of isotopes. In 1906 he returned to Yale and became Professor of Radiochemistry in 1910. By showing that there is a constant ratio of radium to uranium in unaltered minerals, he confirmed the work of **Ernest Rutherford** and **Frederick Soddy** which suggested that radioactive elements decay and transmute into other elements. The radiometric dating methods developed from his work eventually revolutionized geology and archaeology. In 1907 he discovered the element ionium, since renamed thorium 230. He committed suicide.

Boltzmann, Ludwig 1844–1906 •*Austrian physicist*• Born in Vienna, he studied at the University of Vienna. Although his interests were diverse he is most celebrated for the application of statistical methods to physics and the relation of kinetic theory to thermodynamics. In 1868 he extended **James Clerk Maxwell**'s theory of the velocity distribution for colliding gas molecules to derive the "Maxwell-Boltzmann distribution." In 1877 he presented the famous "Boltzmann equation" which showed how increasing entropy corresponded to increasing molecular randomness, and in 1884 he derived the law for black-body radiation found experimentally by **Josef Stefan**, his teacher in Vienna. Boltzmann's work came under attack from positivists in Vienna, and partly because of the unpopularity of his views, he suffered severe depression from 1900 and committed suicide.

Bolyai, János 1802–60 •*Hungarian mathematician*• Born in Kolozsvár, he took up a military career, but retired due to ill health in 1833. After attempting to prove **Euclid**'s parallel postulate, that the straight line which passes through a given point and is parallel to another given line is unique, he realized that it was possible to have a consistent system of geometry in which this postulate did not hold, and so became one of the founders of non-Euclidean geometry, together with **Nikolai Lobachevski**.

Bomberg, David 1890–1957 •*English painter*• Born in Birmingham, he trained as a lithographer before studying painting in London at the City and Guilds School, at the Westminster School of Art (1908–10) under **Walter Sickert**, and at the Slade (1911–13). He was a founding member of the London Group (1913). His compositions, such as *The Mud Bath* and *In the Hold* (1913–14), combine abstract and vorticist influences.

Bombois, Camille 1883–1970 •*French primitive painter*• Born in Venarey-les-Laumes, Côte d'Or, the son of a bargeman, he had no academic training, and worked in a traveling circus, as a porter on the Paris Métro, a construction worker and a longshoreman, while painting as a hobby. By 1923 he had been discovered by collectors and was able to devote all his time to painting his very personal landscapes (e.g., of the *Sacré Cœur*) and pictures of wrestlers and acrobats. They are uncompromisingly realistic, with a childlike frankness and simplicity of technique.

Bonaparte •*Influential Corsican family*• They were active from the 16th century. The name was spelled Buonaparte until 1768.

Bonaparte, (Maria Annunciata) Caroline 1782–1839 •*Queen of Naples*• Born in Ajaccio, Corsica, the youngest surviving daughter of **Charles** and **Marie Bonaparte**, she married **Joachim Murat** (1800), becoming Queen of Naples in 1808. She brought a brilliant court life to the Neapolitan palaces of Caserta and Portici. After her husband's execution she lived, under surveillance, at Frohsdorf in Austria (1815–24) and Trieste (1824–31) before settling in Florence for the last seven years of her life.

Bonaparte, Charles Louis Napoléon *See* **Napoleon III**

Bonaparte, Charles Marie 1746–85 •*Corsican lawyer*• He was born in Ajaccio, and in 1773 was appointed Royal Counselor and Assessor to **Louis XVI** in Ajaccio. Married to **Marie Bonaparte**, he was father of **Napoleon I**.

Bonaparte, (Marie-Anne) Élisa 1777–1820 •*Grand Duchess of Tuscany*• Born in Ajaccio, Corsica, the eldest surviving daughter of **Charles** and **Marie Bonaparte**, she married Felix Baciocchi in 1797. As Duchess of Lucca (from 1806), she managed the economy of her small state so profitably that in 1809 **Napoleon I** made her Grand Duchess of Tuscany, where she revived the court glories of the Pitti Palace.

Bonaparte, François Charles Joseph *See* **Napoleon II**

Bonaparte, Jérôme 1784–1860 •*King of Westphalia*• Born in Ajaccio, Corsica, he was the son of **Charles** and **Marie Bonaparte**, and brother of **Napoleon I**. He was given a high military command in the Prussian campaign (1806), led an army corps at Wagram (1809), incurred his brother's displeasure during the invasion of Russia (1812), but fought with tenacity at Waterloo (1815). He became sovereign of Westphalia (1807–13) and married Princess Catherine of Württemberg in 1807. After exile in Rome, Florence and Switzerland, he returned to Paris (1847). His nephew **Napoleon III** appointed him Governor of the Invalides, created him a Marshal of France, and consulted him over the strategy of the Crimean War. His great-grandson Louis, Prince Napoleon (1914–97), became head of the House of Bonaparte in 1926.

Bonaparte, Joseph 1768–1844 •*King of Naples and Sicily, and king of Spain*• Born in Corte, Corsica, he was the eldest surviving son of **Charles** and **Marie Bonaparte**, and brother of **Napoleon I**. He married (1794) Julie Clary (1771–1845), elder sister of Desirée **Bernadotte**. He served Napoleon on diplomatic missions and was a humane sovereign in southern Italy, where he finally abolished feudalism, and reorganized justice, finance and education. In Spain he faced continuous rebellion and in 1813 his army was defeated by **Wellington** at Vittoria.

Bonaparte, Louis 1778–1846 •*King of Holland*• Born in Ajaccio, Corsica, he was the son of **Charles** and **Marie Bonaparte**, and the brother of **Napoleon I**. He was a soldier, serving originally in the artillery but later in the cavalry. He married Napoleon's stepdaughter, **Hortense de Beauharnais**, in 1802. After becoming Governor of Paris (1805), he ruled Holland as King Lodewijk I (1806–10) but abdicated because Napoleon had complained that he was too attached to the interests of the Dutch. He became Count of Saint-Leu, settled in Austria, Switzerland, and later in Florence, and mainly pursued literary interests. He was the father of **Napoleon III**.

Bonaparte, Lucien 1775–1840 •*Prince of Canino*• A younger brother of **Napoleon I**, he was born in Ajaccio, Corsica. He was made a member of the Council of Five Hundred (1798), and was later elected its president, saving his brother's career (1799) by refusing his outlawry. He was offered the crowns of Italy and Spain on condition that he divorce his second wife, but he refused them, and lived in his state of Canino, in the papal states. Essentially a republican, he denounced the arrogant policy of his brother toward the court of Rome, and was "advised" to leave Roman territory. In 1810, on his way to the US, he was captured by the English and kept a prisoner at Ludlow and Thorngrove, Worcestershire, till 1814. He spent the rest of his life in Italy.

Bonaparte, Marie Letizia, *née* **Ramolino** c. 1749–1836 •*Corsican noblewoman*• Born in Ajaccio, the daughter of a French army captain, she married **Charles Marie Bonaparte** in 1764. Of her 12 children, five died in infancy; the fourth child became **Napoleon I**. She was accorded official status as "Madame Mère de l'Empereur" (1804) and encouraged her son to seek reconciliation with the Church. She supported the fallen Napoleon on Elba (1814) but spent the last 18 years of her life in dignified retirement in Rome.

Bonaparte, Napoleon *See* **Napoleon I**

Bonaparte, Napoléon Joseph Charles Paul, *nicknamed* **Plon-Plon** 1822–91 •*French politician*• The son of **Jérôme Bonaparte** and nephew of **Napoleon I**, he was born in Trieste, Italy, and grew up in Italy. He entered military service in Württemberg (1837), and was expelled from France (1845) for republicanism. In 1851 he was named as the successor to **Napoleon III**. He fought in the Crimean War (1854), but was recalled by the emperor, and made Minister for the Colonies and Algeria (1858). In 1859 he married Princess Clotilda, daughter of **Victor Emmanuel II** of Sardinia. The death of the Prince Imperial (1879) made him head of the family, and in 1886, as pretender to the throne, he was exiled from France with his eldest son, Victor (1862–1926).

Bonaparte, (Marie) Pauline 1780–1825 •*Princess Borghese*• Born in Ajaccio, Corsica, she was the daughter of **Charles** and **Marie Bonaparte**, and was **Napoleon I**'s favorite sister. She married General Leclerc (1772–1802) in 1797 and accompanied him on an expedition to Haiti (1802) on which he contracted yellow fever and died. In 1803 she married Prince Camillo Borghese; her private life soon shocked the patrician family into which she married, not least because of her willingness to pose as a nude Venus for the sculptor **Antonio Canova**. She loyally supported Napoleon in his exile on Elba.

Bonaventure or **Bonaventura, St**, *originally* **Giovanni di Fidanza**, *known as* **Doctor Seraphicus** 1221–74 •*Italian theologian and Doctor of the Church*• Born near Orvieto, Tuscany, he became a Franciscan in 1243, a professor of theology at Paris in 1253, the General of his order in 1257, and Cardinal Bishop of Albano in 1273. He died during the Council of Lyons from ascetic exhaustion. His most important works are the *Breviloquium* (a dogmatic); the *Itinerarium mentis in Deum*; *De reductione artium ad theologiam*, a commentary on **Peter Lombard**; and his *Biblia pauperum* ("Poor Man's Bible"). His feast day is July 14.

Bond, Edward 1934– •*English dramatist and director*• He was born in London. His work uses a variety of metaphors for the corruption of capitalist society. His first play, *The Pope's Wedding*, was given a Sunday night reading at the Royal Court Theatre, London, in 1962 and aroused great controversy. *Saved* (1965) achieved notoriety through a scene in which a baby in a pram is stoned to death. Other plays include *The Fool* (1976), based on the life of the "peasant poet" **John Clare**, *The Woman* (1978), in which the characters are drawn from Greek tragedy, *The War Plays* (1985), and *Coffee: A Tragedy* (1995). He has also written for television and radio.

Bond, (Thomas) Michael 1926– •*English children's author*• He was born in Newbury, Berkshire, and worked for many years as a BBC cameraman. The creator of several fictional animal characters, his most popular creation is Paddington Bear, a small bear so named because he was discovered at Paddington Station in London. Hapless, vulnerable and good-natured, Paddington has so far been the hero of around 40 stories since his first appearance in *A Bear Called Paddington* (1958); his enormous popularity shows no sign of waning. Another creation is Monsieur Pamplemousse, about whom he has written a series of books for adults (1983–93). He published his autobiography, *Bears and Forebears: A Life So Far*, in 1996 and was given the honorary title Officer, Order of the British Empire, in 1997.

Bondfield, Margaret Grace 1873–1953 •*English Labour politician and trade unionist*• Born in Somerset, she became chairman of the Trades Union Congress (TUC) in 1923 and as Minister of Labour (1929–31) was the first woman to be a British Cabinet Minister.

Bondi, Sir Hermann 1919– •*British mathematical physicist*• Born in Vienna, he moved to England in 1937 to study at Trinity College, Cambridge, where he later became a Fellow (1943–49, 1952–54). Bondi served with great distinction as director general of the European Space Research Organization (1967–71), as chief scientific adviser to the Ministry of Defense and as chairman of the National Environmental Research Council (1980–84). Scientifically he is best known for his seminal book *Cosmology*, published in 1952, and for his proposal, with Sir **Fred Hoyle** and **Thomas Gold**, that the universe was in a steady state, matter being continuously created to fill the gaps left by the expansion. In 1962 Bondi wrote a keynote paper showing how the emission of gravitational waves is a necessary consequence of **Albert Einstein**'s general theory of relativity. He was knighted in 1973.

Bongo, Omar, *originally* **Albert-Bernard Bongo** 1935– •*Gabonese statesman*• Born in Lewai, Franceville, and educated in Brazzaville, he held various ministerial positions from 1960 to his appointment as vice president in 1966. When President M'ba died in 1967, he became President, establishing a one-party state in 1968. He has presided over the exploitation of Gabon's rich mineral resources (it has the highest per capita income of any African country) without notably diminishing inequalities. Reelected for the third time in 1986, he then won the multiparty presidential election in 1993 (after opposition parties were legalized in 1990), and was reelected again in 1998.

Bonham Carter, Helena 1966– •*English actress*• Granddaughter of **Lady Violet Bonham Carter**, she was born in London and educated at Westminster School. Her early films include the **E M Forster** adaptations *A Room with a View* (1985) and *Howards End* (1992), and she later diversified from these rather delicate "Edwardian" roles into films such as *Mighty Aphrodite* (1995), *Fight Club* (1999) and *Big Fish* (2003). She has appeared widely in theater and on television.

Bonham Carter, Lady Violet, Baroness Asquith (of Yarnbury) 1887–1969 •*English Liberal politician and publicist*• Daughter of **H H Asquith** by his first marriage, in 1915 she married Sir Maurice Bonham Carter (d. 1960), a scientist and civil servant. She was prominent in cultural and political movements, serving as president of the Liberal Party Organization (1944–45) and as a governor of the BBC (1941–46). She was created a life peeress in 1964. **Jo Grimond** was her son-in-law.

Bonhoeffer, Dietrich 1906–45 •*German Lutheran pastor and opponent of Nazism*• He was born in Breslau (now Wrocław, Poland), the son of an eminent psychiatrist, and was educated at Tübingen and Berlin. He left Germany in 1933 in protest aginst the Nazi enforcement of anti-Jewish legislation, and worked in German parishes in London until 1935, when he returned to Germany, to become head of a pastoral seminary of the German Confessing Church until its closure by the Nazis in 1937. He became deeply involved in the German resistance movement and in 1943 was arrested and imprisoned until 1945, when he was hanged at Flossenbürg. His best-known and most-interpreted writings are *Ethik* (1949, "Ethics") and *Widerstand und Ergebung* (1951, Eng trans *Letters and Papers from Prison*, 1953), on the place of Christian belief and the concept of Christ in the modern world.

" "

The cross is God's truth about us, and therefore it is the only power that can make us truthful. When we know the cross we are no longer afraid of the truth.

1937 Nachfolge (translated as ***The Cost of Discipleship***).

Boniface, St *See* **Bruno, St**

Boniface, St, *originally* **Wynfrith**, *also known as* **the Apostle of Germany** c. 680–c. 754 •*Anglo-Saxon missionary*• Born in Wessex (probably in Crediton in Devon), he became a Benedictine monk in Exeter as a child, and taught in the monastery of Nursling near Romsey. In 718 he set out with a commission from Pope **Gregory II** to preach the gospel to all the tribes of Germany. He met with great success and was consecrated Bishop (723), Archbishop and Primate of Germany (732). His goal was to impose Roman Catholic order on the whole Frankish kingdom and to suppress the irregularities of Irish, or Columban, Christianity. He had resumed his missionary work among the Frisians when he was attacked and killed at Dokkum, near Leeuwarden, by pagans. His feast day is June 5.

Bonington, Sir Chris(tian John Storey) 1934– •*English mountaineer and photojournalist*• Born in Hampstead, London, he was educated at University College School, London, and the Royal Military Academy, Sandhurst. His early mountaineering ascents include Nuptse (1961), Central Pillar of Freney, Mont Blanc (1961), Central Tower of Paine (1963), Brammah (1973), Changabang (1974), Mount Kongur, China (1981), Shivling West (1983) and the first British ascents of the north wall of the Eiger (1962) and Mt Vinson in Antarctica (1983). He led or co-led many successful expeditions, including Annapurna South Face (1970) and Everest (1972 and 1975, the southwest face), and reached the summit of Everest himself in 1985. He was knighted in 1996.

Bonington, Richard Parkes 1801–28 •*English painter*• Born near Nottingham, he moved to Calais around 1817, and there and at Paris he studied art. From 1824 he experimented increasingly in romantic subjects taken from history. His best-known works followed: *Francis I and Marguerite of Navarre, Henry IV Receiving the Spanish Ambassador, Entrance to the Grand Canal*, and *Ducal Palace*. He excelled in light effects achieved by the use of a large expanse of sky, broad areas of pure color and the silhouetting of dark and light masses, as well as his rich coloring of heavy draperies and brocades.

Bon Jovi, Jon, *originally* **John Francis Bongiovi, Jr** 1962– •*US rock singer*• Born in Perth Amboy, New Jersey, he is the singer and charismatic frontman of Bon Jovi, one of the most commercially successful rock bands of the 1980s, and whose album, *Slippery When Wet* (1986), established them as major players on the rock scene. He has worked on solo and acting projects in later years but has continued to tour and record with Bon Jovi.

Bonnard, Pierre 1867–1947 •*French painter and lithographer*• Born in Paris, he joined the group called "Les Nabis," which included **Maurice Denis** and **Édouard Vuillard**, with whom he formed the Intimist group. His style was formed under the influence of Impressionism, Japanese prints and the works of **Paul Gauguin** and **Toulouse-Lautrec**. Ignoring the movement toward abstraction, he continued to paint interiors and landscapes, in which everything is subordinated to the subtlest rendering of light and color effects.

Bonnat, Léon Joseph Florentin 1833–1922 •*French painter*• Born in Bayonne, he was well known as a painter of religious subjects, and as a portraitist of notable contemporaries, e.g., *Madame Pasca* (1874, Musée d'Orsay, Paris). He taught **Toulouse-Lautrec** and **Georges Braque**. He used his earnings from painting to collect old masters, which he donated to form the nucleus of the Musée Bonnat at Bayonne.

Bonner, Edmund c.1500–69 •*English prelate*• The reputation he earned at Oxford recommended him to **Thomas Wolsey**, who made him his chaplain. Imprisoned, however, from 1549 to 1553 for refusing to recognize royal supremacy during the minority of **Edward VI**, he was restored to office later, under **Mary I**, and pronounced sentence on several Protestant martyrs. On **Elizabeth I**'s accession (1558), he went with his episcopal colleagues to pay homage at Highgate, but was excepted from the honor of kissing her hand. In May 1559 he refused the Oath of Supremacy, so was deposed and imprisoned in the Marshalsea, where he died.

Bonner, Yelena 1923– •*Russian civil rights campaigner*• She was born in Moscow. After the arrest of her parents in **Stalin**'s "great purge" of 1937, she was brought up in Leningrad (St Petersburg) by her grandmother. During World War II she served in the army, but suffered serious eye injuries. In 1965 she joined the Communist Party (CPSU), but became disillusioned after the Soviet invasion of Czechoslovakia (1968). She married **Andrei Sakharov** in 1971 and resigned from the CPSU a year later. During the next 14 years she and her husband led the Soviet dissident movement. The couple was finally released from Gorky in 1986, as part of a new "liberalization" policy by the **Gorbachev** administration, and remained prominent campaigners for greater democratization. Following Sakharov's death in 1989 she continued to campaign on human rights issues.

Bonney, William H, *also known as* **Billy the Kid** 1859–81 •*US outlaw*• Born in New York City, he grew up in bad company in Kansas, Colorado and New Mexico, and killed his first man at the age of 12. In 1876 he began a series of crimes and killings in the Southwest and Mexico, and two years later he gathered a band of followers and began rustling cattle. He had killed 21 men, one for each year of his life, when he was finally tracked down and shot in Fort Sumner, New Mexico.

Bonnie and Clyde *See* **Barrow, Clyde and Parker, Bonnie**

Bonny Dundee *See* **Dundee, 1st Viscount**

Bono *See* **U2**

Bono, Edward de *See* **de Bono, Edward Francis Charles Publius**

Bono, Emilio de *See* **De Bono, Emilio**

Bonomi, Ivanoe 1873–1952 •*Italian politician*• A graduate in natural sciences and law, in 1909 he was elected to parliament. Expelled from the Italian Socialist Party in 1912, he founded a reformist socialist movement. In 1916–21 he was a minister on a number of occasions, and was briefly premier himself (1921–22). From 1942, he was a leading figure in the anti-Fascist struggle, replacing **Pietro Badoglio** as Prime Minister (1944) and establishing a broad, anti-Fascist coalition government. In 1945 he was forced to resign in favor of the more radical Ferruccio Parri. He became president of the Senate in 1948.

Bononcini or **Buononcini, Giovanni Maria** 1642–78 •*Italian composer*• Born near Modena, he became a violinist in the court orchestra there in 1671, and subsequently maestro di cappella of the cathedral. From 1666 he published a great quantity of chamber and vocal music, together with a treatise, the *Musico prattico*, which was influential in its day. His sons Giovanni Battista (1670–1755) and Marc Antonio (1675–1726) were notable composers, the former especially remembered for his rivalry with **Handel**.

Bontemps, Arna Wendell 1902–73 •*US writer*• Born in Alexandria, Louisiana, he became a leading figure in the Harlem Renaissance of the 1920s and 1930s. He wrote poems such as "Southern Mansion" and "A Black Man Talks of Reaping" and the novels *God Sends Sunday* (1931), *Black Thunder* (1936), and *Drums at Dusk* (1939). His anthologies of African-American verse and folklore and his nonfiction historical works helped establish a much wider appreciation of the richness and the validity of African-American culture.

Boole, George 1815–64 •*English mathematician and logician*• Born in Lincoln, Lincolnshire, he was largely self-taught. He was one of the first to direct attention to the theory of invariants, expressions in several variables that do not change when the coordinates change. His algebraic treatment of differential operators gradually led him to consider the operations of logic algebraically also, resulting in the work for which he is best remembered, his *Mathematical Analysis of Logic* (1847) and *Laws of Thought* (1854). In these he employed mathematical symbolism to express logical relations, thus becoming an outstanding pioneer of modern symbolic logic. Boolean algebra is a generalization of the familiar operations of arithmetic, and it is particularly useful in the design of circuits and computers.

Boom, Corrie ten *See* **ten Boom, Corrie**

Boone, Daniel 1735–1820 •*US frontiersman*• He was born in Pennsylvania to Quaker parents and moved with them to western North Carolina. He had little formal education but learned to hunt and trap. After working as a blacksmith in North Carolina he traveled to Kentucky in 1767–68 through the Cumberland Gap in the Appalachian Mountains (1769–71), becoming one of the first to explore the area. In 1775 he marked out the Wilderness Road and founded Boonesborough on the Kentucky River. Twice captured by Native Americans, he repeatedly (1775–78) repelled their attacks and became famed for his heroism. He played a crucial role in extending US settlement beyond the Allegheny Mountains and many legends have grown up around his life. He appears in **Byron**'s *Don Juan*.

Boorman, John 1933– •*English film director*• Born in Shepperton, Middlesex, his first feature film, *Catch Us If You Can* (1965), was followed by the stylish US thriller *Point Blank* (1967). Heavily influenced by the **Arthur**ian legends, his films often include mythological resonances or involve some form of quest, as in *Deliverance* (1972) and *Excalibur* (1981). *Hope and Glory* (1987), an affectionate re-creation of his wartime childhood, was both a critical and commercial success. Recent films include *Where the Heart Is* (1990), *Beyond Rangoon* (1995) and *The Tailor of Panama* (2001). He was given the honorary title of Commander, Order of the British Empire, in 1994.

Boorstin, Daniel Joseph 1914–2004 •*US academic and librarian*• Born in Atlanta, he attended Harvard, then won a Rhodes scholarship to Oxford. He was admitted to the English bar in 1937. He became senior historian of the Smithsonian Institution, Washington DC, director of the National Museum of History and Technology, Washington DC (1969–73), and Professor of American History at the University of Chicago (1944–69). He wrote many works which explore and explicate his native land, including *A History of the United States* (1980), *The Americans* trilogy (1965, 1968, 1973) and *The Discoverers* (1983).

Boot (of Trent), Jesse Boot, 1st Baron 1850–1931 •*English drug manufacturer*• Born in Nottingham, he inherited his father's herbalist's shop at 13 and studied pharmacy in his leisure hours. In 1877 he opened his first pharmacy in Nottingham and, by mass selling at reduced prices, introduced the modern chain store. In 1892 he began large-scale drug manufacture and by the early 1900s was controlling the largest pharmaceutical retail trade in the world, with over 1,000 branches in 1931. Knighted in 1909, he was created a peer in 1929.

Booth, Catherine, *née* **Mumford** 1829–90 •*English cofounder of the Salvation Army*• Born in Derbyshire, the daughter of a Wesleyan preacher, she married **William Booth** in 1855. She became a gifted preacher herself, and shared in her husband's evangelistic work. Following preaching tours around the country, they returned to London (1864) to start the work that became the Salvation Army. Their eight children all became active in the Salvation Army movement, and she also started the Army's women's work. Her funeral was attended by 36,000 people.

Booth, Cherie 1954– •*English barrister*• Born in Bury, Lancashire, she studied at the London School of Economics. She was called to the bar at Lincoln's Inn in 1976, and in 1980 married the future Prime Minister **Tony Blair**. In 1995 she was appointed a Queen's Counsel and in 1999 a Recorder, or part-time judge, and cofounded the human rights law firm Matrix in 2000. Among several public appointments, she is a trustee of the domestic violence charity Refuge (1995–) and a governor of the London School of Economics (1998–).

Booth, John Wilkes 1839–65 •*US assassin*• Born in Baltimore, he became a successful actor in Washington DC. In 1865 he entered into a conspiracy to avenge the defeat of the Confederacy, and shot President **Lincoln** at Ford's Theater, Washington DC, on April 14. He managed to escape to Virginia, but was tracked down and, refusing to surrender, was shot dead.

Booth, Margaret 1898–2002 •*US film editor*• Born in Los Angeles, she began cutting film for **D W Griffith**, and in 1921 moved to the Mayer studio, which became MGM in 1924. She was one of their leading film editors, and was supervising film editor at MGM from 1939 to 1968. The first woman to achieve success in her field, her film credits include *The Mutiny on the Bounty* (1935), *The Way We Were* (1973) and *California Suite* (1978). She received an Academy Award for overall career achievement in 1977 and only retired in 1986, aged 88 years.

Booth, William 1829–1912 •*English religious leader, founder and "General" of the Salvation Army*• Born in Nottingham, he married Catherine Mumford (**Catherine Booth**) in 1855 and became a Methodist New Connexion minister on Tyneside (1855–61). The couple went on preaching tours abroad and returned in 1864 to begin the Christian Mission in London's East End (1865), which in 1878 became the Salvation Army. Though often imprisoned for preaching in the open air, his men and women waged war on such evils as sweated labor and child prostitution, and a worldwide network of social and regenerative agencies was established. Opinion changed, and Booth was made freeman of London, honorary doctor of Oxford, was a guest at **Edward VII**'s coronation, and opened the US Senate with prayer. His book, *In Darkest England and the Way Out* (1890), describes his philosophy and motivation. He and Catherine had eight children who all became active in the Salvation Army movement.

Boothroyd, Betty, Baroness 1929– •*English Labour politician*• Born in Dewsbury, Yorkshire, she was a member of the dance troupe the Tiller Girls, and a political assistant before becoming a Hammersmith borough councilor in 1965. She was elected as Member of Parliament for West Bromwich in 1973 (West Bromwich West since 1974). Becoming deputy Speaker of the House of Commons in 1987, she commanded wide respect by her magisterial, even-handed performances. She then became the first woman Speaker of the House of Commons in 1992. She has been Chancellor of the Open University since 1994. She retired as Speaker and as a Member of Parliament in 2000 and was elevated to the peerage.

Bopp, Franz 1791–1867 •*German philologist*• Born in Mainz, after four years' study in Paris—paid for by the Bavarian government—he produced his first study of Indo-European grammar, *Über das Conjugationssystem der Sanskritsprache* ... (1816, "On the System of Conjugation in Sanskrit"), in which he traced the common origin of the grammatical forms of these languages. In 1821 he was appointed Professor of Sanskrit and Comparative Grammar in Berlin. His greatest work is *A Comparative Grammar of Sanskrit, Zend, Greek, Latin, Lithuanian, Old Slavonic, Gothic and German* (6 vols, 1833–52; trans 1856), a revised edition of which (publ 1856–61) included Classical Armenian.

Borden, Lizzie Andrew 1860–1927 •*US alleged murderess*• Born in Fall River, Massachusetts, she was accused of murdering her wealthy father and hated stepmother with an ax, in August 1892. In one of the most highly publicized murder trials in US history, she claimed to have been outside in the barn at the time of the murder, and despite a great deal of circumstantial evidence, was acquitted. She lived out her life in Fall River and was buried alongside her father and stepmother. The case is immortalized in a children's nursery rhyme.

Borden, Sir Robert Laird 1854–1937 •*Canadian statesman*• Born in Grand Pré, Nova Scotia, he practiced as barrister and became leader of the Conservative Party in 1901. In 1911 he overthrew Sir **Wilfrid Laurier**'s ministry over the question of reciprocity with the US and was Prime Minister of the Dominion until 1920. He organized Canada for war, and was the first overseas premier to attend a Cabinet meeting in London (1915).

Border, Allan 1955– •*Australian cricket player*• Born in Cremorne, Sydney, he made his Test debut for Australia in 1978, and captained the team from 1984 to 1994. He established a world record of most Test-match and one-day international appearances, and in 1993 set a new world record for runs scored in Test matches when his career total reached 10,161. He has played county cricket in England for Gloucestershire and Essex. He retired from Test cricket in 1995 and from Sheffield Shield cricket in 1996.

Bordet, Jules Jean Baptiste Vincent 1870–1961 •*Belgian physiologist and Nobel Prize winner*• Born in Soignies, he graduated from the University of Brussels in 1892, and in 1894 went to Paris to work at the Pasteur Institute. He explained the mechanics of bacteriolysis as being due to the action of two substances: a specific antibody present only in immunized animals, and a nonspecific, heat-labile substance which he identified as Hans Buchner's "alexin." This work made possible new techniques for the diagnosis and control of infectious diseases. He went on to discover the whooping cough bacillus, extracted an endotoxin, and prepared a vaccine (1906). An authority on serology, he was awarded the 1919 Nobel Prize for physiology or medicine.

Borg, Björn Rune 1956– •*Swedish tennis player*• A talented all-round sportsman in his youth, he left school at age 14 to concentrate on tennis, and at 15 was selected for the Swedish Davis Cup team. He was Wimbledon junior champion at 16, and became the dominant men's player in world tennis in the 1970s, winning a record five consecutive Wimbledon singles titles (1976–80). He also won the Italian championship twice and the French Open six times between 1974 and 1981. His Wimbledon reign ended in 1981 when he lost in the final to **John McEnroe**. He retired in 1983 and turned to business interests.

Borge, Victor 1909–2000 •*US entertainer and pianist*• Born in Denmark, he was educated at the Royal Danish Academy of Music, Copenhagen, and in Vienna and Berlin. He made his debut as a pianist in 1926 and as a revue actor in 1933. From 1940 he worked in the US for radio, television and theater, and performed with leading symphony orchestras on worldwide tours from 1956. He became a US citizen in 1948.

Borges, Jorge Luis 1899–1986 •*Argentine writer*• Born in Buenos Aires, he was educated there and at Geneva and Cambridge. From 1918 he was in Spain, where he was a member of the avant-garde Ultraist literary group, returning to Argentina in 1921. From 1923, he published poems and essays, and in 1941 the first collection of the intricate and fantasy-woven short stories for which he is famous appeared. Later collections include *Ficciónes* (1944 and 1956, Eng trans 1962), *El aleph* (1949, Eng trans *The Aleph and Other Stories 1933–1969*, 1970), and the verse collection *El hacedor* (1960, Eng trans *Dreamtigers*, 1963). Some stories from *El aleph* appear in the collection of translations, *Labyrinths* (1962). He became director of the National Library in 1955, after losing his sight. His last book was *Atlas* (1986), written with his companion, Maria Kodama.

“ ”

The Falklands thing was a fight between two bald men over a comb.

*1983 In **Time**, February 14.*

Borgia, *Italian form of* **Borja** •*Ancient Spanish family in the province of Valencia*• Alfonso de Borgia (1378–1458), bishop, accompanied Alfonso of Aragon to Naples, and was elected pope as Calixtus III (1455). His nephew Rodrigo Borgia (1431–1503) ascended the papal throne (1492) as **Alexander VI**. Before this, he had had a number of children by a Roman girl, Giovanna Catanei, known as Vanozza. Two of these children, **Cesare** and **Lucrezia Borgia**, became notorious as ambitious, murderous public figures.

Borgia, Cesare c. 1476–1507 •*Italian soldier*• He was the illegitimate son of Rodrigo Borgia (later Pope **Alexander VI**) and brother of **Lucrezia Borgia**. He was appointed Archbishop of Valencia (1492) and a cardinal (1493) after his father's election to the papacy (1492). He relinquished his cardinal's hat to marry Princess Charlotte d'Albret, sister of the king of Navarre (1498), and succeeded his elder brother Juan (whom he may have murdered) as Captain General of the papal army (1499). In two campaigns, with French help (1499–1501), he became master of the Romagna, and was made Duke of Romagna by his father. His ambitious plans for a Kingdom of Central Italy spread terror in an atmosphere of constant treachery and cruelty. In 1502 he and his father were mysteriously taken ill at a banquet, believed to have been poisoned. Though his father died, Cesare survived, but his enemies forced him to relinquish the Romagna and imprisoned him. He escaped (1506) and fled to the court of Navarre, but was killed at the siege of Viana. He was praised by **Machiavelli** in *Il principe* as a model prince and the savior of Italy: opportunistic, aggressive and ruthless. He encouraged art, and was the friend of **Pinturicchio** and the protector of **Leonardo da Vinci**.

Borgia, Lucrezia 1480–1519 •*Italian noblewoman*• Born in Rome, the illegitimate daughter of Rodrigo Borgia (later Pope **Alexander VI**), she was married off three times by her father for political reasons: first, at the age of 12 to Giovanni Sforza, Lord of Pesaro (1493), but this marriage was annulled by her father (1497); second, to Alfonso of Aragon, nephew of the King of Naples (1498), but this marriage was ended (1500) when Alfonso was murdered by her brother **Cesare Borgia**; and third (1501), to Alfonso d'Este (1486–1534). The son of the Duke of Este, Alfonso inherited the duchy of Ferrara, where Lucrezia established a brilliant court of artists and men of letters, including **Ariosto** and **Titian**. In legend she has become notorious, quite unfairly, for wantonness, vice and crime (including incest with her brother and father).

Borglum, (John) Gutzon (de la Mothe) 1867–1941 •*US sculptor*• He was born in Idaho, of Danish descent, and won renown for works of vast proportions such as the famous Mount Rushmore National Memorial portraying **George Washington**, **Abraham Lincoln**, **Thomas Jefferson**, and **Theodore Roosevelt**, hewn out of the solid rock of the mountainside (completed in 1939). His other monumental works include the head of Lincoln in the US Capitol rotunda, and the *Twelve Apostles* in the Cathedral of St John the Divine in New York.

Boris Godunov c. 1551–1605 •*Czar of Russia*• Of Tatar stock, he became a close friend of **Ivan IV**, and during the reign of Ivan's feeble son Fyodor (1584–98), Godunov was virtual ruler of the country; he colonized western Siberia and created the patriarchate (1589). He became czar on Fyodor's death (1598), and continued the expansionist policies of Ivan, going to war against both Poland and Sweden. At home, he disposed of the Tatar threat but was involved in the last years of his reign in a civil war against a pretender, claiming to be **Dmitri**, younger son of Ivan IV.

Borja *See* **Borgia**

Borlaug, Norman Ernest 1914– •*US plant pathologist and geneticist*• He was born in Cresco, Iowa. As director of the Wheat Program at the International Center for Maize and Wheat Improvement, he developed "dwarf" wheats that dramatically increased yields and made possible the "green revolution." He was awarded the 1970 Nobel Peace Prize.

Bormann, Martin 1900–45 •*German Nazi politician*• Born in Halberstadt, he participated in the abortive Munich putsch of 1923 and became one of **Hitler**'s closest advisers. He was appointed Reichsminister ("party chancellor") in May 1941 and was with Hitler to the last. His own fate was uncertain for a time, but he is now known to have committed suicide by a poison capsule during the breakout by Hitler's staff from the Chancellory (May 1, 1945). He was sentenced to death in absentia by the Nuremberg Court (1946).

Born, Max 1882–1970 •*German physicist and Nobel Prize winner*• Born in Breslau (now Wrocław, Poland) and educated at the universities of Breslau, Heidelberg, Zurich and Göttingen. In 1925, with his assistant **Pascual Jordan**, he built upon the earlier work of **Werner Heisenberg** to produce a systematic quantum theory. He used **Erwin Schrödinger**'s wave equation to show that the state of a particle (including its energy or position) could only be predicted in terms of probabilities, deducing from this the existence of quantum jumps between discrete states. This led to a statistical approach to quantum mechanics. He shared the 1954 Nobel Prize for physics with **Walther Bothe** for their work in the field of quantum physics.

“ ”

Science ... is so greatly opposed to history and tradition that it cannot be absorbed by our civilization.

*1968 **My Life and Views**.*

Borodin, Aleksandr Porfirevich 1833–87 •*Russian composer and scientist*• Born in St Petersburg, he was an illegitimate son of Prince Gedeanov, who registered him as the child of a serf. Borodin trained in medicine and distinguished himself as a chemist, then in 1862 began to study music. His works include the unfinished opera *Prince Igor* (1869–70, 1874–87, which contains the Polovtsian Dances), three symphonies, and the symphonic sketch *In the Steppes of Central Asia* (1880). From 1872, he lectured in chemistry at the St Petersburg School of Medicine for Women.

Borodin, Mikhail Markovich, *originally* **Mikhail Markovich Grusenberg** 1884–1951 •*Russian and Soviet politician and political adviser*• He participated in the Jewish worker movement in his native Russia and met **Lenin** in 1904. When the United Front was formed between the Guomindang (Kuomintang) and the Chinese Communist Party in 1923 Borodin, as the representative of both the Comintern and the Soviet Communist Party, became a personal adviser to **Sun Yat-sen**, but when the United Front broke down in 1927 Borodin was compelled to leave China. Made the scapegoat for the failure of **Stalin**'s policy in China, Borodin was henceforth given only minor posts. He died in a Siberian prison camp.

Borotra, Jean, *nicknamed* **the Bounding Basque** 1898–1994 •*French tennis player*• Born near Biarritz, he was the most famous of the so-called Four Musketeers (with Lacoste, Cochet and Brugnon) who emerged in the 1920s. He won the men's singles title at Wimbledon in 1924, and his extraordinary fitness enabled him to compete in veterans' events at that same venue when he was almost 80. He also won the French and Australian championships, as well as several Davis Cup medals between 1927 and 1932. He was secretary of Physical Education in the Vichy government (1940–42), but was imprisoned by the Nazis from 1943 to 1945.

Borromeo, St Carlo 1538–84 •*Italian prelate*• Born in his father's castle of Arona, on Lake Maggiore, he gained a PhD in canon and civil law from the University of Padua in 1559. At the age of 22, he was appointed a cardinal and Archbishop of Milan by his uncle, Pope **Pius IV**. He did much to bring the Council of Trent (1545–63) to a successful conclusion, and had the principal part in drawing up the famous *Catechismus Romanus* (1566). He was renowned for his determined efforts to maintain ecclesiastical discipline and for his relief of the poor during the famine of 1570 and the plague of 1576, and founded in 1570 the Helvetic College at Milan. In 1578 he founded the community later known as the Oblates of St Ambrose. He was canonized in 1610 and his feast day is November 4.

Borromini, Francesco 1599–1667 •*Italian baroque architect and sculptor*• Born in northern Italy, he spent all his working life in Rome, where he was associated with his great rival **Gian Bernini** in the Palazzo Berberini (1620–31) and the Baldacchino in St Peter's (1631–33). His own chief buildings were the San Carlo alle Quattro Fontane (1641), San Ivo della Sapienza (1660), Sant'Andrea delle Fratte (1653–65), and the oratorio of San Filippo Neri (1650). He is particularly noted for his command of spatial effects.

Borrow, George Henry 1803–81 •*English writer*• Born in East Dereham, Norfolk, he was educated at the High School, Edinburgh, and at Norwich Grammar School (1816–18). He was an accomplished linguist and traveled widely as an agent for the Bible Society, visiting St Petersburg (1833–35), Portugal, Spain, and Morocco (1835–39) and touring southeastern Europe (1844) and Wales (1854). He wrote numerous books in which romantic fiction and autobiography often overlapped, among them *The Zincali or an Account of the Gypsies of Spain* (1840), *The Bible in Spain* (1843), which was an instant success as a travel book, *Lavengro* (1851) and its sequel, *The Romany Rye* (1857), both novels about his own gypsy life.

Boscawen, Edward, *known as* **Old Dreadnought** 1711–61 •*English naval commander*• He distinguished himself at the sieges of Porto Bello (1739) and Cartagena (1741), and in command of the *Dreadnought* in 1744, he captured the French *Médée*. In command of the East Indian expedition, he displayed great military skill in the retreat from Pondicherry, and in 1755 he intercepted the French fleet off Newfoundland, capturing two ships and 1,500 men. He was appointed Commander in Chief of the successful expedition against Cape Breton (1758) and also gained victory over the French Toulon fleet in Lagos Bay (1759).

Bosch, Carl 1874–1940 •*German industrial chemist and Nobel Prize winner*• Born in Cologne, he studied at Leipzig. In 1909 he began work to adapt the laboratory process for synthesizing ammonia for commercial production. Bosch invented the process that bears his name, in which hydrogen is produced on an industrial scale by passing steam and water gas over a catalyst at high temperatures. He became president of I G Farbenindustrie. In 1931 he shared the Nobel Prize for chemistry with **Friedrich Bergius** for his part in the invention and development of chemical high-pressure methods, and in 1935 succeeded **Max Planck** as director of the Kaiser Wilhelm Institute.

Bosch, Hieronymus, *real name* **Jerome van Aken** c. 1450–1516 •*Dutch painter*• Named after the town in which he was born, 's Hertogenbosch in northern Brabant, he probably spent the whole of his life there. It is difficult to trace the development of his work because none of it is dated, but there are some quite conventional pictures that contrast with the depictions of a bizarre, nightmarish world for which he is famous. Although the roots of his work can be traced to devotional woodcuts of the period, the extravagance of his vision is hard to explain, as is its acceptance by local churches for which he worked. After his death, **Philip II** of Spain avidly collected his works and the majority of them are now in the Prado, Madrid, including his masterpiece, *The Garden of Earthly Delights*. He had many imitators in his lifetime but only **Pieter Brueghel** the Elder, had the ability to incorporate the imagery of Bosch into his own art.

Bose, Sir Jagadis Chandra 1858–1937 •*Indian physicist and botanist*• He was born in Mymensingh, Bengal (now in Bangladesh), and studied at Cambridge. He returned to Calcutta where he was appointed Professor of Physics at Presidency College. Bose became known for his study of electric waves, their polarization and reflection, and for his experiments demonstrating the sensitivity and growth of plants. In some of his ideas he foreshadowed **Norbert Wiener**'s cybernetics. He founded the Bose Research Institute in Calcutta for physical and biological sciences in 1917, was knighted in the same year and became the first Indian physicist to be elected a Fellow of the Royal Society (1920).

Bose, Satyendra Nath 1894–1974 •*Indian physicist*• Born in Calcutta and educated at Presidency College there, he became professor at Dacca University before being appointed to another chair at Calcutta University in 1952. In 1924 he succeeded in deriving the **Planck** blackbody radiation law, without reference to classical electrodynamics. **Albert Einstein** generalized his method to develop a system of statistical quantum mechanics, now called Bose-Einstein statistics, for integral spin particles which **Paul Dirac** named "bosons." Bose also contributed to the studies of X-ray diffraction and the interaction of electromagnetic waves with the ionosphere.

Bose, Subhas Chandra 1897–1945 •*Indian nationalist leader*• He managed the Calcutta newspaper *Forward*, and became the Chief Executive Officer of the Calcutta Corporation when Congress won its control in 1924. In 1928 Bose formed an Independence League with **Jawaharlal Nehru** in opposition to Congress's objective of dominion status. Throughout the 1930s Bose took part in the civil disobedience movement, but became increasingly dissatisfied with the nonviolent methods of **Mahatma Gandhi** and increasingly radical in his beliefs. He was twice in succession President of the Indian National Congress (1938). Having resigned from the organization (1939), he formed Forward Bloc, a militant nationalist party. With the outbreak of World War II, he supported the Axis Powers. Escaping from detention, he fled to Nazi Germany, then (1943) sailed to Singapore to take command of the Indian National Army (INA), a force formed of prisoners of war of the Japanese army. This force fought against the British in Burma and participated in the disastrous Japanese attempt to invade India from Burma. In 1943 he announced the formation of the Provisional Government of Free India. He was reported killed in an aircrash in Formosa (Taiwan).

Boston Strangler *See* **Desalvo, Albert**

Boswell, James 1740–95 •*Scottish writer and biographer of Samuel Johnson*• Born in Edinburgh, he was educated privately and at the University of Edinburgh. He studied civil law at Glasgow, but his true goal was literary fame and the friendship of the famous. In the spring of 1760 he ran away to London, where he hobnobbed with the young Duke of York and with **Richard Brinsley Sheridan**'s father. He first met Dr **Samuel Johnson** on his second visit to London, on May 16, 1763. In 1764 Boswell went to Utrecht to continue his legal studies, but stayed only for the winter and then toured Germany, France, Switzerland, and Italy. By an astounding process of literary gatecrashing Boswell introduced himself to **Voltaire** and **Jean Jacques Rousseau**. From Rousseau he procured an introduction to the hero of Corsica **Pasquale de Paoli**, whom he

"Boswellized" in *Account of Corsica* (1768), which was an immediate success. In 1773 Boswell was elected to Johnson's famous literary club, and took the great doctor on a memorable journey to the Hebrides. He was called to the English bar in 1786, but he hardly practiced. Boswell's wife died in 1789, leaving him six children, and thereafter his drinking habits got the better of him. The discoveries of Boswell's manuscripts, at Malahide Castle in Ireland in 1927 and at Fettercairn House in Scotland in 1930, which have been assembled by Yale University, are proof of his literary industry and integrity. A major literary enterprise (1777–83) was a series of 70 monthly contributions to the *London Magazine* under the pseudonym "The Hypochondriak." After Johnson's death *The Journal of the Tour of the Hebrides* (1785) appeared. Its great success made Boswell plan his masterpiece, *The Life of Samuel Johnson* (1791), of which *The Journal* served as a first installment.

" "

JOHNSON: Well, we had a good talk.
BOSWELL: Yes, Sir; you tossed and gored several persons.
1768 Conversation, recorded in ***The Life of Samuel Johnson****, vol. 2.*

Both, Andries c. 1612–41 •*Dutch painter*• Born in Utrecht, he was traditionally thought to have collaborated with his brother **Jan Both** by painting the figures in his landscapes, but he is now recognized as the author of paintings and drawings of scenes more akin to the work of **Adriaen Brouwer**. With his brother he traveled to Italy where, returning home from a party in Venice, he fell into a canal and was drowned.

Both, Jan c. 1618–52 •*Dutch painter*• Born in Utrecht, he lived in Italy from 1638 to 1641 and there perfected his style of painting views of the Roman countryside bathed in a golden light and populated by picturesque peasants. He became a leading exponent of "Italianate" landscape, and his style shows the influence of **Claude Lorrain**. Back in Utrecht, Both became a prominent member of the painters' guild, and his idyllic style was adapted by other Dutch painters to their views of Dutch landscape. He was the brother of **Andries Both**.

Botha, Louis 1862–1919 •*South African statesman and soldier*• He was born in Greytown, Natal. A member of the Transvaal Volksraad, he succeeded **Piet Joubert** (1900) as Commander in Chief of the Boer forces during the war, and in 1907 became Prime Minister of the Transvaal colony under the new constitution. In 1910 he became the first premier of the Union of South Africa. He suppressed **Christiaan De Wet**'s rebellion in 1914, and conquered German Southwest Africa in 1914–15.

Botha, P(ieter) W(illem) 1916– •*South African statesman*• The son of an internee in the Anglo-Boer War, he was steeped in politics. An advocate of apartheid before the National Party gained power, he entered parliament in 1948. Leader of the Cape section of the National Party, in 1966 he was chosen as leader of the party on **John Vorster**'s resignation on the second ballot only because the Transvaal Nationalists were divided. He thus became Prime Minister. Having built up the defense forces and supported the invasion of Angola in 1975, he now sought constitutional changes, but his ideas, although too progressive for some of his party (some members defected in 1982 to form the Conservative Party), were too cautious to appeal to the Black opposition. He suffered a stroke in 1989 and resigned later that year.

Botha, Pik (Roelof Frederik) 1932– •*South African politician*• After a career in the diplomatic service (1953–70), he entered politics and was elected to parliament. In 1977 he became Foreign Minister in the government of State President **P W Botha** and that of **F W De Klerk**. He brought his influence as a sounding board of international opinion strongly to bear in supporting the notable reforms that were introduced at the end of the 1980s. In 1992 he became leader of the Transvaal National Party and from 1994 to his retirement from politics in 1996 was Minister of Energy.

Botham, Ian Terence 1955– •*English cricket player*• Born in Heswall, Merseyside, he was regarded as an extremely talented all-rounder. He played for England in 102 Test matches, took 383 wickets, and scored 5,200 runs. He held the record number of Test wickets (373 wickets at an average of 27.86 runs until overtaken by **Richard Hadlee**), and his performance in 1981 won the Test series against Australia almost single-handedly. He played for Worcestershire (1987–91) and Durham (1992–93), before his retirement in 1993. Off-the-field brushes with authority alternated with successful charity fundraising campaigns. In 1996 he and teammate Allan Lamb lost a libel suit brought against **Imran Khan** who had accused them of ball tampering.

" "

Cricket is full of theorists who can ruin your game in no time.
1980 ***Ian Botham on Cricket****.*

Bothe, Walther Wilhelm Georg 1891–1957 •*German physicist and Nobel Prize winner*• Born in Oranienburg, Brandenburg, he studied at the University of Berlin. He developed an electric circuit to replace the laborious process of counting scintillations by eye used by **Hans Geiger** and Ernest Marsden. He also developed the coincidence technique, which allowed two particles to be associated with each other, and used this to study cosmic rays and nuclear physics. His work on the development of the coincidence technique in counting processes brought him the Nobel Prize for physics in 1954, shared with **Max Born**.

Bothwell, James Hepburn, 4th Earl of c. 1535–78 •*Scottish nobleman*• One of the greatest nobles in 16th-century Scotland, he succeeded his father as earl and hereditary Lord High Admiral (1556). A professed Protestant, he nevertheless was a staunch supporter of **Mary of Guise**, regent for her daughter **Mary, Queen of Scots**. In France in 1560, he met the young Mary, and on her return to Scotland (1561) she appointed him a Privy Councillor. In the following year he was accused of plotting to kidnap her, and imprisoned, but she recalled him (1565), shortly after her marriage to Lord **Darnley**. Shortly afterward (March 1566), Mary's secretary, **David Rizzio**, was murdered by Darnley, and Bothwell became her protector and chief adviser. The year 1567 was to be a year of high drama. Darnley himself was murdered in an explosion in Edinburgh (February 9), the chief suspect being Bothwell, who underwent a rigged trial and was acquitted (April 12). He then made a show of abducting Mary (April 23), who was pregnant (probably by him). Divorcing his wife, he married Mary as her third husband, but the marriage did not last long. Mary was forced to surrender to an army of rebellious Scottish noblemen at Carberry Hill (June 20), and he fled to Norway, where he was arrested on a trumped-up charge and imprisoned. On July 24, Mary miscarried (twins), and on the same day was forced to abdicate in favor of her infant son, **James VI**. The marriage was annulled in 1570. By then, Bothwell was imprisoned, first at Malmö in Sweden and subsequently at Dragsholm (1573) in Zeeland, Denmark, where he died, apparently insane.

Botticelli, Sandro, *originally* **Alessandro Filipepi** 1445–1510 •*Florentine painter*• Born in Florence, he learned his distinctive linear style from **Fra Filippo Lippi**, with whom he studied, but added to it something very personal and graceful. By 1480 he had his own workshop and was responsible for frescoes that form part of the 1482 scheme of decoration of the Sistine Chapel. He produced mostly religious works but is best known for his treatment of mythological subjects, *The Birth of Venus* (c. 1482–84) and the *Primavera* (c. 1478), both of which are in the Uffizi, Florence. During the last decade of the 15th century, his style became more severe and emotional, as in his *Mystic Nativity* (1500, National Gallery, London). By the time of his death, his linear style was out of fashion, but during the Victorian period it became a source of inspiration for the Pre-Raphaelite movement and art nouveau.

Bottomley, Virginia Hilda Brunette Maxwell 1948– •*English Conservative politician*• Born in Scotland, she was educated at Essex University and the London School of Economics. She worked as a researcher for a child poverty action group and as a lecturer in a college of further education before becoming Member of Parliament for Surrey South-West in 1984. Appointed Minister at the Department of the Environment (1988–89), she tackled such issues as the dumping of toxic waste, lead-free gasoline and litter. She became Secretary of State for Health in 1992 and was involved in the controversial closure of several hospitals. In 1998 she became a vice chair of the British Council.

Botvinnik, Mikhail Moiseyevich 1911–95 •*Soviet chess player*• Born in Leningrad (now St Petersburg), he was an electrical engineer by training. He won the 1948 tournament organized by FIDE (Fédération Internationale des Échecs) to fill the world championship, vacant after the death of **Alexander Alekhine**, and was world champion 1948–57, 1958–60 and 1961–63. He led Soviet domination of world chess for most of the remainder of the 20th century, contested only by the US player **Bobby Fischer**. After regaining his title twice, from **Vasili Smyslov** and **Mikhail Tal**, Botvinnik lost in 1963 to **Tigran Petrosian** and devoted most of his remaining career to training Soviet players and to the development of chess computers.

Boucher, François 1703–70 •*French painter*• Born in Paris, he was the purest rococo painter at the court of **Louis XV**. From 1727 to 1731 he was in Italy, and he was received into the academy in 1734. He worked on a range of material from stage design to tapestry, and from 1755 was director of the famous Gobelins factory. A refined portrait painter also, he produced several portraits of the king's most famous mistress, Madame de **Pompadour**, and it was she who bought his greatest pictures, *The Rising* and *The Setting of the Sun*. In 1765 he became *premier peintre du Roi*, but by this time his style was under attack from **Diderot**. His work is usually considered, along with that of his pupil, **Jean Fragonard**, to be wholly representative of the frivolous spirit of his age. Some of it can be seen in the London Wallace Collection.

Boudicca, *incorrectly called* **Boadicea** d. 61 AD •*British warrior-queen*• She was queen of the native tribe of Iceni (Norfolk, Suffolk and part of Cambridgeshire). Her husband, Prasutagus, an ally of Rome, had made the emperor **Nero** his coheir, but when he died (AD 60) the Romans annexed and pillaged all the Iceni territory. According to **Tacitus**, Boudicca was flogged and her daughters raped. The Iceni rebelled, led by Boudicca, and destroyed Camulodunum (Colchester), Londinium (London) and Verulamium (St Albans), killing up to 70,000 Romans. The Roman governor of Britain, Suetonius Paulinus, overwhelmed the Iceni in a bloody battle. Some 80,000 of the tribesmen were slaughtered, against only 400 Roman dead, and Boudicca herself is said to have taken poison.

Bougainville, Louis Antoine de 1729–1811 •*French navigator, mathematician and soldier*• Born in Paris, he studied law and then mathematics, publishing an important treatise on integral calculus, and was elected a Fellow of the Royal Society. Joining the French navy in 1763, he was responsible for colonizing the Falkland Islands for France, and for their transfer to Spain, and accomplished the first French circumnavigation of the world (1766–69), which he described in his valuable *Voyage autour du monde* (1771, Eng trans *A Voyage Round the World*, 1772). The largest of the Solomon Islands is named after him, as is the plant bougainvillea. In the American Revolution he commanded several ships of the line, and was made a field marshal in 1780 and a vice admiral in 1791. **Napoleon I** made him a senator, count of the empire, and member of the Legion of Honor.

Bouillon, Godfrey of *See* **Godfrey of Bouillon**

Boulanger, Georges Ernest Jean Marie 1837–91 •*French general and politician*• Born in Rennes, he served in Italy, China, and in the Franco-Prussian War (1870–71), and helped suppress the Paris Commune (1871). In 1886, as the protégé of **Clemenceau**, he was appointed Minister of War. He introduced many reforms in soldiers' pay and living conditions and became a popular national figure. Although deprived of his command in 1888, he was immediately elected Deputy for Dordogne and Nord, and demanded a revision of the constitution. Boulangism became most influential in 1889, and was supported with large sums of money by leading royalists for their own ends. Fearing a coup d'état, the government prosecuted Boulanger, who lost courage and fled the country in 1889. He was condemned in his absence, and eventually shot himself on his mistress's grave in Brussels.

Boulanger, Lili 1893–1918 •*French composer*• Born in Paris, and encouraged and supervised by her elder sister **Nadia Boulanger**, she studied at the Paris Conservatoire. In 1913, she was the first woman to win the Prix de Rome. She returned from Rome to look after the families of musicians fighting in World War I but died, leaving unfinished an opera based on **Maurice Maeterlinck**'s *La princesse Maleine* (1918). Among the many pieces she composed are *Pour les funérailles d'un soldat* (1912, "For the Funeral of a Soldier"), *Du fond de l'abîme* (1914–17, "From the Bottom of the Abyss") and *Vieille prière bouddhique* (1917, "Old Buddhistic Prayer").

Boulanger, Nadia 1887–1979 •*French musician*• Born in Paris, she studied at the Conservatoire there (1879–1904), where she won several prizes. She went on to write many vocal and instrumental works, winning second prize at the Prix de Rome in 1908 for her cantata, *La sirène* ("The Siren"). After 1918 she devoted herself to teaching, first at home, and later at the Conservatoire and at the École Normale de Musique. She was also a noted organist and conductor.

“ ”

Do not take up music unless you would rather die than not do so.

Advice to her pupils. Quoted in Alan Kendall ***The Tender Tyrant: Nadia Boulanger*** *(1976).*

Boulez, Pierre 1925– •*French conductor and composer*• Born in Montbrison, he studied at the Paris Conservatoire (1943–45) under **Olivier Messiaen**. His early work, notably the sonatine for flute and piano (1946), and two piano sonatas (1946, 1948), rebelled against what he saw as the conservatism of such composers as **Igor Stravinsky** and **Arnold Schoenberg**. In later compositions he developed the very individual view of music already apparent in the sonatine, namely, that whereas tonal music of the past can be seen as a straightforward progression from a point of departure, contemporary music describes a fluid and infinite universe out of which it is the composer's task to make a coherent work of art. Such works as *Le marteau sans maître* (1955, "The Hammer Without a Master") established his reputation worldwide. Among his numerous conducting posts, he became in the early 1990s the regular guest conductor with the Cleveland (Ohio) and Chicago Symphony orchestras and in 1992 participated in the 150th anniversary concert of the New York Philharmonic.

Boult, Sir Adrian Cedric 1889–1983 •*English conductor*• Born in Chester, he studied at Oxford and Leipzig. He conducted the City of Birmingham Orchestra from 1924 to 1930, when he was appointed musical director of the BBC and conductor of the newly formed BBC Symphony Orchestra. Extensive tours in Europe and the US won him a high reputation as a champion of English music, and this had a great influence upon the musical policy of the BBC. He was conductor-in-chief of the London Philharmonic Orchestra until 1957 and its president from 1965. He continued to conduct regularly until 1981.

Boulting Brothers •*English film directors and producers*• John Edward (1913–85) and Roy (1913–2001) Boulting were twins, born in Bray, Berkshire. Together they produced and directed a series of films. Among the most notable are *Brighton Rock* (1947, based on the novel by **Graham Greene**), *Lucky Jim* (1957, based on the novel by **Kingsley Amis**) and several comedies of postwar English life, including *I'm All Right, Jack* (1959) and *The Family Way* (1966). Roy Boulting was married five times, once (1971–76) to the actress Hayley Mills (1946–).

Boumédienne, Houari, *originally* **Mohammed Bou Kharrouba** 1927–78 •*Algerian soldier and statesman*• Born in Guelma in eastern Algeria, he was educated in Cairo and became a teacher. In 1954 he joined the FLN (Algerian National Liberation Front) to conduct guerrilla operations against the French. When Algeria gained independence in 1962, he became Minister of National Defense. In 1965 he led a military coup against President **Ben Bella** and established an Islamic socialist government, presiding over the Council of Revolution as effective head of state until he formally accepted election as president in 1976.

Bourassa, Robert 1933–96 •*French-Canadian politician*• He was born in Montreal, and became leader of the Quebec Liberal Party when it won an emphatic election victory in 1970, secured by means of its refusal to give prominence to the constitutional and language controversies and its promise to help the unemployment crisis. During the "October crisis" he was accused of being too ready to hand over power to Ottawa by those who suspected that he hoped to undermine his nationalist and left-wing opponents. He responded by reinforcing his demands for a special status for Quebec within the Confederation. He resigned as party leader when the Liberals lost the 1976 provincial elections to the Péquistes (Parti Québecois), but was reelected in 1983 and led the party to victory in 1985, serving as Prime Minister until 1993.

Bourbon •*French royal house*• For generations it occupied the thrones of France and Naples, and until 1931 that of Spain. Adhémar, sire of Bourbon in the 10th century, traced his descent from **Charles Martel**. In 1272 the Bourbon heiress married the sixth son of **Louis IX** of France. The family divided, the elder branch ended with the Constable de Bourbon (**Charles Bourbon**) in 1527. His son, Antoine (1518–62), obtained by marriage the throne of Navarre, and Antoine's son was Henry of Navarre (**Henry IV**), who became heir to the Crown of France in 1589 (see **Louis XIII–XVIII**, **Charles X** and the Comte de **Chambord**). The Orléans branch descends from a younger son of **Louis XIII** (Philippe, 1640–1701). From **Louis XIV** descend also the branches that formerly held the thrones of Spain, Parma and Naples. A younger brother of Antoine de Bourbon (Henri IV's father) founded the houses of Condé and Conti. The sons and grandsons of **Louis Philippe** held titles derived from Paris, Chartres, Nemours, Eu, Joinville, Aumale and Montpensier.

Bourbon, Charles, *known as* **Conestable** or **Constable de Bourbon** 1490–1527 •*French soldier*• The son of the Count of Montpensier and the only daughter of the Duke of Bourbon, he thus united the vast estates of both these branches of the Bourbon family. For his bravery at the Battle of Marignano in 1515 he was made Conestable of France by **Francis I**. Having lost royal favor, he renounced the service of France, and concluded a private alliance with the emperor **Charles V** (1523), and with **Henry VIII** of England. In 1524 he was chief commander at the great victory of Pavia, in which Francis I was taken prisoner. Along with Georg von Frundsberg, he led the mixed army of Spanish and German mercenaries that stormed and plundered Rome in 1527, but was struck down in the fierce struggle—by a bullet fired by **Benvenuto Cellini**, as the latter asserted.

Bourgeois, Jeanne Marie *See* **Mistinguett**

Bourgeois, Léon Victor Auguste 1851–1925 •*French socialist statesman and Nobel Prize winner*• Born in Paris, he studied law and served as Minister of Public Instruction (1890–92, 1898), Minister of Labor (1912–13, 1917) and as Prime Minister (1895–96). He was one of the founders of the League of Nations and in 1920 was awarded the Nobel Peace Prize. He advocated a form of socialism (called solidarism) that stressed the responsibilities and obligations of individuals as members of society.

Bourgeois, Louise 1911– •*US sculptor*• Born in Paris, she studied at the École du Louvre, the Académie des Beaux-Arts and at private art schools before emigrating to the US in 1938. She began painting, and had a one-woman show at the Bertha Schaefer Gallery in New York in 1945. In the late 1940s she turned to woodcarving, and in the 1960s to stone and metal, creating abstract sculptures which suggest figures, or parts of figures, such as *Labyrinthine Tower* (1963). Her forms became increasingly fantastical in the 1970s, and included weirdly colored totem forests or cavelike environments, like *Destruction of the Father* (1974). Her work of the 1980s and 1990s, filled with potent sexual imagery, celebrated femininity without sentiment or polemicism, as in her *Spiders* (1995), a collection of large metal spiders spiked with knitting needles.

Bourget, Paul 1852–1935 •*French poet, essayist and novelist*• He was born in Amiens, and began by writing verse. His *Essais* (1883) indicated his true strength, however. The second series, *Nouveaux essais de psychologie contemporaine* (1886, "New Essays on Contemporary Psychology"), was a subtle inquiry into the causes of pessimism in France. His first novel, *L'irréparable* (1884, "Beyond Repair"), was followed by a steady stream of works which placed him in the front rank of modern French novelists. *L'étape* (1902, "The Halting Place") marked the crystallization of his talent. His works after 1892 showed a marked reaction moving from realism and skepticism toward mysticism.

Bourguiba, Habib ibn Ali 1903–2000 •*Tunisian statesman*• Born in Monastir, Tunisia, he studied law in Paris and became a radical Tunisian nationalist in 1934. Over the next 20 years he served three prison sentences imposed by the French authorities. In 1956, however, the government of **Pierre Mendès-France** in Paris recognized that, in contrast to other Arab leaders, Bourguiba was moderate in his demands and he was accepted as Tunisia's first Prime Minister, becoming President in 1957. By 1962 he had secured the withdrawal of the French. His authority, however, was threatened by riots instigated by Islamic fundamentalists in 1983 and 1984, and subsequently he exercised little influence on policy. In 1987 he was deposed by his Prime Minister, General **Ben Ali**, on the grounds of senility.

Bourke-White, Margaret, *originally* **Margaret White** 1906–71 •*US photojournalist who pioneered the photo-essay*• Born in New York City, she studied photography at Columbia University. She started her career in 1927 as an industrial and architectural photographer, but was engaged by *Fortune* magazine in 1929 and became a staff photographer and associate editor at *Life* magazine when it started publication in 1936. Her 70 photographs for the study by **Erskine Caldwell** of rural poverty in the southern US, *You Have Seen Their Faces* (1937), were highly individual, in contrast to the more dispassionate records of the US government's Farm Security Administration workers. She was married to Caldwell from 1939 to 1942. She covered World War II for *Life* and was the first woman photographer to be attached to the US armed forces, producing outstanding reports of the Siege of Moscow (1941) and the opening of the concentration camps (1944). After the war, she recorded the troubles in India, Pakistan and South Africa, and was an official UN war correspondent during the Korean War. From 1952 she suffered from Parkinson's disease, but she continued to produce many photojournalistic essays until her retirement from *Life* in 1969. Her books include *Eyes on Russia* (1931), *Halfway to Freedom* (1946) and an autobiography, *Portrait of Myself* (1963).

" "

The beauty of the past belongs to the past.

1986 On modern photojournalism, quoted in ***Christian Science Monitor**, December 5.*

Bourne, Hugh 1772–1852 •*English founder of the Primitive Methodists*• He was born in Fordhays, Staffordshire, and his zeal as a Wesleyan preacher for large open-air meetings—carried on once from 6 AM till 8 PM—received no approbation from the leaders of the denomination, and in 1808 he was cut off from the Wesleyan connection. But he quickly gathered around him many devoted followers, and in 1810 a committee of ten members was formed at Standley, near Bemersley. The title of Primitive Methodists was adopted in 1812; colloquially, they were also called Ranters.

Bourne, Matthew Christopher 1960– •*English ballet director*• Born in London, he studied at the Laban Centre for Dance and Movement there. He was a cofounder of the dance company Adventures in Motion Pictures (1987) and has created and directed a number of works for it, including the award-winning version of *Swan Lake* (1995) with an all-male *corps de ballet*, and the "auto-erotic" **Bizet** tribute *Car Man* (2000). He has directed many works for other companies, as well as numerous television and film productions.

Bourque, Raymond 1960– •*Canadian hockey player*• Born in Montreal, he joined the Boston Bruins in 1979 as a starting defenseman. In 1980 he won the Calder Trophy as the National Hockey League's rookie of the year, and was the Norris Trophy winner as the League's outstanding defenseman in 1987, 1988, 1990, and 1991. In the 1999–2000 season he won both the Orr Trophy and the Harvey Trophy, and among numerous records he is the only defenseman ever to score 400 goals.

Boussingault, Jean Baptiste Joseph Dieudonné 1802–87 •*French agricultural chemist*• Born in Paris, he demonstrated that legumes increase nitrogen in soil by fixing atmospheric nitrogen, but that all other plants have to absorb nitrogen from the soil. He further showed that all green plants absorb carbon from the atmosphere in the form of carbon dioxide. His work laid the basis for modern advances in microbiology.

Boutros-Ghali, Boutros 1922– •*Egyptian politician and diplomat*• Born in Cairo, he received a doctorate in international law from the University of Paris. He traveled with President **Anwar Sadat** to Jerusalem on the diplomatic mission that resulted in the Camp David Accords (1978), and was appointed Minister of State for Foreign Affairs (1977–91). From 1992 to 1996 he was Secretary-General of the United Nations.

Bovet, Daniel 1907–92 •*Italian pharmacologist and Nobel Prize winner*• Born in Neuchâtel, Switzerland, he studied chemistry at Geneva before being invited, with his wife and collaborator Philomena Nitti, to establish the Laboratory of Chemotherapeutics at the Superior Institute of Health in Rome. He discovered the first antihistamine drugs in 1939. His second major study involved drugs blocking the action of adrenaline and noradrenaline, thereby preventing hypertension (high blood pressure), one of the most common medical disorders, and vasoconstriction. While visiting Brazil he became interested in the Indian neuromuscular poison curare, of which he later made synthetic analogues, which have been much used as muscle relaxants in anesthesia since 1950. He was awarded the 1957 Nobel Prize for physiology or medicine.

Bowdler, Thomas 1754–1825 •*English doctor and man of letters*• Born in Ashley, Bath, he retired from medical practice and settled on the Isle of Wight to devote himself to literary pursuits. He is immortalized as the editor of the "Family Shakespeare" (10 vols, 1818), in which "those words and expressions are omitted which cannot with propriety be read aloud in a family." "Bowdlerizing" has become a synonym for prudish expurgation.

Bowe, Riddick, *nicknamed* **Big Daddy** 1967– •*US boxer*• Born in Brooklyn, New York, he became a high earner, and is considered to be the world's best heavyweight after **Mike Tyson**, whom he never fought because of management disagreements. He fought **Evander Holyfield** three times, and won twice. His only loss, in a career total of 38 fights, was to Holyfield in 1993, when the hard bout was interrupted by a paraglider crashing into the Caesar's Palace ring. Since he was reputedly a hamburger junkie, Bowe's defeat was attributed by the press to a fast-food overdose. However, he beat Herbie Hide to win the World Boxing Organization heavyweight title in 1995.

Bowen, Elizabeth Dorothea Cole 1899–1973 •*Irish novelist and short-story writer*• She was born in County Cork, the daughter of a wealthy barrister and landowner, and was brought up in Dublin. Educated in England at Downe House School in Kent, she married in 1923 and in the same year published her first collection of short stories, *Encounters*, followed by *Anne Lee's* (1926). Her first novel, *The Hotel* (1927), began a string of delicately written explorations of personal relationships, of which *The Death of the Heart* (1938) and *The Heat of the Day* (1949), a war story, are the best known. She was also a perceptive literary critic.

Bowes-Lyon, Lady Elizabeth *See* **Elizabeth**

Bowie, David, *real name* **David Robert Jones** 1947– •*English rock singer*• He was born in Brixton, London. His early career was undistinguished, and he came close to becoming a Buddhist monk before the success of "Space Oddity" (1969). His career blossomed throughout the 1970s as he adopted a range of extreme stage images to suit a variety of musical styles and concepts. His albums have included *Hunky Dory* (1971), *The Rise and Fall of Ziggy Stardust and the Spiders from Mars* (1972), *Diamond Dogs* (1974), *Heroes* (1977), *Let's Dance* (1983) and *Heathen* (2002). He has also acted on Broadway in *The Elephant Man* (1980) and in films, including *The Man Who Fell to Earth* (1976), *Merry Christmas Mr Lawrence* (1983) and *Labyrinth* (1986).

Bowie, James 1790–1836 •*Mexican pioneer*• Born in Kentucky, US, he went to Texas in 1828 and settled in San Antonio. Although he became a naturalized Mexican citizen (c. 1831), he joined the agitation for Texas independence and became a colonel in the Texan army (1835–36). He fell ill during the siege of the Alamo and was found dead in his cot when the Mexicans stormed the citadel. He is sometimes said to be the inventor of the curved dagger or sheath knife named after him.

Bowles, Paul Frederick 1910–99 •*US novelist, composer, poet, travel writer and translator*• He was born in New York City. After studying at the University of Virginia, he went to Europe in 1928 and returned to study music with **Aaron Copland** in New York, and became a composer and music critic. He did not devote himself to writing until after World War II. His first novel, *The Sheltering Sky*, set in Morocco, appeared in 1949 and was immediately influential, sparking a US literary exodus to Tangier. He wrote three other novels, *Let It Come Down* (1952), *The Spider's House* (1955) and *Up Above the World* (1966), as well as several collections of short stories, including *Pages from Cold Point* (1968) and *Midnight Mass* (1981), and a collection of poems, *Scenes* (1968). He also translated and taped original stories of indigenous lives. He was married to the writer Jane Bowles (1918–73).

" "

The only effort worth making is the one it takes to learn the geography of one's own nature.

*1989 In **The Sunday Times**, July 23.*

Bowles, William Lisle 1762–1850 •*English clergyman and poet*• Born in King's Sutton vicarage, Northamptonshire, and educated at Trinity College, Oxford, he became vicar of Bremhill in Yorkshire and prebendary of Salisbury in 1804, and later chaplain to the prince regent (1818). He was a forerunner of the Romantic movement in English poetry, his *Fourteen Sonnets, Written Chiefly on Picturesque Spots during a Journey* (1789, published anonymously), had **S T Coleridge**, **Wordsworth** and **Robert Southey** among their enthusiastic admirers. His best poetical work is *The Missionary of the Andes*.

Bowman, Scotty (William Scott) 1933– •*Canadian hockey coach*• Born in Montreal, he won his first National Hockey League coaching position in 1967 with the St Louis Blues. He moved to the Montreal Canadiens as Head Coach in the 1971–72 season, winning five Stanley Cups for the team in eight seasons. Other notable successes have included a 1992 Stanley Cup for the Pittsburgh Penguins and another three Stanley Cups for the Detroit Red Wings in 1997, 1998, and 2002. He is the most successful coach in NHL history, with most career victories (1244) and most Stanley Cups (9).

Bowman, Sir William 1816–92 •*English physician and ophthalmic surgeon*• He was born in Nantwich, Cheshire. Working with Richard B Todd (1809–60), his most significant discoveries concerned the function of the kidney, part of which is now called Bowman's capsule, in particular the fact that urine is a by-product. He also gained a high reputation by his *Lectures on Operations on the Eye* (1849), describing the ciliary muscle. His *Collected Papers* appeared in 1892.

Bowring, Sir John 1792–1872 •*British diplomat*• Born in Exeter, on leaving school he entered a merchant's office, and acquired a knowledge of 200 languages. He visited Switzerland, Italy, Egypt, Syria, and the states of Germany, and prepared valuable government reports on their commerce. He sat in parliament from 1835 to 1849, actively promoting free trade. From 1849 he was British consul in Hong Kong, and in 1854 he was knighted and made Governor. In 1856, in retaliation for an insult to the British by a Chinese pirate ship, he ordered the bombardment of Canton, an event which almost caused the downfall of the **Palmerston** ministry. He published *The Kingdom and People of Siam* in 1857.

Box, (Violette) Muriel, *née* **Baker** 1905–91 •*English screenwriter*• Born in Tolworth, Surrey, she made her writing debut with *Alibi Inn* (1935). She married Sydney Box (1907–83) in 1935, with whom she established a very successful writing partnership until 1958. They shared an Oscar for *The Seventh Veil* (1945). An active women's rights campaigner during the 1960s, Muriel Box founded the feminist press Femina Books in 1966. Following her remarriage in 1970 to the Lord Chancellor, **Gerald Gardiner**, she turned her attention to political causes.

Boyce, William 1711–79 •*English composer*• Born in London, he was appointed composer (1736) and organist (1758) to the Chapel Royal, and in 1757 became Master of the King's Musick. A leading composer of church music, his works include the song "Hearts of Oak" and the serenata *Solomon* (1743), and he compiled a valuable collection of *Cathedral Music* (1760).

Boycott, Charles Cunningham 1832–97 •*English soldier*• Born in Burgh St Peter, Norfolk, as land agent for Lord Erne in County Mayo he was one of the first victims in 1880 of **Charles Stewart Parnell**'s system of social excommunication: on his refusal to lower rents, his tenants were advised to stop communicating with him. He thus gave, in the verb "to boycott," a new word to most European languages.

Boycott, Geoffrey 1940– •*English cricket player*• Born in Fitzwilliam, Yorkshire, he is the most celebrated batsman in postwar English cricket. He gained his county cap for Yorkshire (1963) and was capped for England in 1964. He played 108 times for England between 1964 and 1982, and scored more than 150 centuries, but there was controversy over his value as a player. His publications include *Boycott, the Autobiography* (1987) and *Boycott on Cricket* (1990).

Boyd, Arthur Merric 1862–1940 •*Australian painter*• He was born in Opoho, New Zealand. He arrived in Australia in 1886 and in that year married Emma Minnie à Beckett, granddaughter of Sir William à Beckett, first chief justice of Victoria (1852–57). He is particularly known for his watercolors.

Boyd, Arthur Merric Bloomfield 1920–99 •*Australian painter, sculptor and potter*• Born in Murrumbeena, Victoria, the son of **Merric Boyd**. After World War II he exhibited with the Contemporary Arts Society in Melbourne, then returned to Murrumbeena and the pottery established by his father. He moved to London in 1959, where he established his position as a painter of international significance. He was also noted as an etcher and as a theater and ballet designer.

Boyd, Martin à Beckett 1893–1972 •*Australian novelist and poet*• Born in Lucerne, Switzerland, the son of **Arthur Merric Boyd**, he was brought up in Melbourne, and lived for much of his life in Great Britain. His first three novels appeared under a pseudonym, "Martin Mills," as did his fourth, *Dearest Idol* (1929), for which he adopted the name "Walter Beckett." Thereafter he acknowledged his authorship, and produced his best work, to be seen in what is now referred to as the "Langton tetralogy": *The Cardboard Crown* (1952), *A Difficult Young Man* (1955), *Outbreak of Love* (1957) and *When Blackbirds Sing* (1962).

Boyd, (William) Merric 1888–1959 •*Australian ceramic artist*• Born in St Kilda, Victoria, he was the son of **Arthur Merric Boyd**. He studied at the pioneering porcelain works at Yarraville, Victoria, and later founded a famous studio at Murrumbeena, outside Melbourne, where he experimented with new ceramic techniques. His pottery is sought after by collectors.

Boyd, (Theodore) Penleigh 1890–1923 •*Australian landscape artist and dry-point etcher*• He was born in Westbury, Wiltshire, the son of **Arthur Merric Boyd**, and studied under **Frederick McCubbin**. He exhibited at the Royal Academy, London, in 1922.

Boyd, Robin Gerard Penleigh 1919–71 •*Australian architect, critic and writer*• Born in Melbourne, he reached a wide and popular audience with his books *Australia's Home* (1952), *The Australian Ugliness* (1960) and *The Great Australian Dream* (1972). His work shaped the future direction of Australian architecture and was acknowledged with several awards.

Boyd, William Andrew Murray 1952– •*British author*• He was born in Accra, Ghana, and educated at Glasgow University and Jesus College, Oxford. His first novel, *A Good Man in Africa* (1981), won the Whitbread Prize, and was followed by books such as *An Ice-Cream War* (1982) and *Brazzaville Beach* (1990), both of which continued the African theme and garnered prestigious awards. He has written several screenplays.

“ ”

It seems to me that there are statements about the world and our lives that have no need of formal proof procedures.

*1990 **Brazzaville Beach**, "Fermat's Last Theorem II."*

Boyer, Charles 1897–1978 •*French actor*• Born in Figeac, he was educated at the Sorbonne. His film debut was in *L'homme du large* (1920, "The Seafarer"). A popular matinee idol, he moved to Hollywood where his handsome looks, bass voice and expressive eyes made him the world's ideal Frenchman. Adept at comedy and drama, he appeared in such films as *Love Affair* (1939) and *Gaslight* (1944). He developed into an urbane, scene-stealing character actor of great charm in films like *Barefoot in the Park* (1967) and *Stavisky* (1974). He committed suicide two days after the death of his wife of 44 years.

Boyer, Herbert Wayne 1936– •*US biochemist*• Born in Pittsburgh, Pennsylvania, he studied there and worked at the University of California at San Francisco from 1966. A pioneer of genetic engineering, he showed in the 1970s that these methods could be used to make insulin and other costly biochemicals commercially, and in 1976 formed Genentech, Inc., for this purpose.

Boyer, Jean Pierre 1776–1850 •*Haitian politician*• Born a mulatto in Port-au-Prince, he was sent to France when young, and in 1792 joined the army. He fought against the British on their invasion of Haiti, and established an independent republic in the western part of the island. President Pétion, on his deathbed, recommended him as his successor (1818). After the death of **Henri Christophe**, he united the Black district with the mulatto (1820). The following year he also added the eastern district. He governed Haiti well for 15 years, but his partiality to the mulattos caused a Black uprising in 1843, and he fled.

Boyle, Danny 1956– •*English film director*• He was born in Bury, Lancashire, and began his career in theater, becoming artistic director of the Royal Court Theatre in 1982–87. He subsequently worked in television making dramas such as *Mr Wroe's Virgins* (1993), and made a much-acclaimed break into films with chic black comedies including *Shallow Grave* (1994) and *Trainspotting* (1996).

Boyle, Jimmy 1944– •*Scottish murderer and sculptor*• Born in the Gorbals, then a notorious slum area of Glasgow, he was involved in crime from a very early age. In 1967, he was convicted for the murder of Babs Rooney and given a life sentence. In 1973 he became one of the first offenders to participate in Barlinnie Prison Special Unit's rehabilitation program. He went on to produce many sculptures, which were exhibited in several countries, and to write his autobiography, *A Sense of Freedom* (1977). After his release in 1982, he published his prison diaries, *The Pain of Confinement* (1984), and worked with young offenders. He has become Scotland's most celebrated reformed criminal, has a successful career as a sculptor, and published his first novel, *Hero of the Underworld*, in 1999.

Boyle, Kay 1902–92 •*US novelist, short-story writer, poet and essayist*• Born in St Paul, Minnesota, she was brought up and educated in the US, then lived in Europe for 30 years as part of the literary expatriate fraternity of Paris's Left Bank in the 1920s and later as the *New Yorker*'s foreign correspondent (1945–53). Influenced by **Henry James**, she used her experience of expatriation most effectively in *Plagued by the Nightingale* (1931) and *Generation without Farewell* (1960), but her novels are generally inferior to her stories, which are amassed in several volumes, including *The Smoking Mountain* (1951). Her poems were collected in 1962.

Boyle, Mark 1934– •*Scottish artist*• Born in Glasgow, he began as a law student at Glasgow University. In 1964 he organized an event called "Street," in which a group of people looked out through an ordinary shop window into an ordinary street. His *London Study* of 1969 was a piece of fiberglass pavement left lying for 17 years to gather real dust. His ongoing project, *Journey to the Surface of the Earth*, began in 1969 with 1,000 darts thrown at a map of the world by blindfolded people. Boyle visits each site in turn, selects a six-foot square and makes a cast of it. He works with his partner Joan Hills and their two children, all artists; they exhibit as The Boyle Family.

Boyle, Richard, 1st Earl of Cork, *known as* **the Great Earl** 1566–1643 •*Anglo-Irish administrator*• Born in Canterbury, England, he studied at Cambridge and the Middle Temple, and then went to Ireland (1588) to make his fortune. He married an heiress, purchased large estates in Munster, promoted the immigration of English Protestants, and won the favor of Queen **Elizabeth I**. In 1620 he became Earl of Cork, and was made hereditary Lord High Treasurer in 1631. Although sidelined by Lord Deputy Wentworth (from 1633), he helped to secure his execution, and defended Munster against the Irish rebels (1641).

Boyle, Robert 1627–91 •*Irish physicist and chemist*• The seventh son of **Richard Boyle**, 1st Earl of Cork, he was born at Lismore Castle, Waterford. He was one of the first members of the antischolastic "invisible college," an association of Oxford intellectuals opposed to the prevalent doctrines of scholasticism, which became the Royal Society in 1645. Settling at Oxford in 1654, with **Robert Hooke** as his assistant, he carried out experiments on air, vacuum, combustion and respiration. In 1661 he published his *Sceptical Chymist*, in which he criticized the current theories of matter and defined the chemical element as the practical limit of chemical analysis. In 1662 he arrived at Boyle's law, which states that the pressure and volume of gas are inversely proportional. He also researched the calcination of metals, properties of acids and alkalis, specific gravity, crystallography and refraction, and first prepared phosphorus. As a director of the East India Company (for which he had procured the charter) he worked for the propagation of Christianity in the East, circulated at his own expense translations of the Scriptures, and by bequest founded the "Boyle Lectures" in defense of Christianity. He was, surprisingly, an alchemist, but his alchemy was a logical outcome of his atomism. If every substance is a rearrangement of the same basic elements, transmutations should be possible. Modern atomic physics has proved him right.

Boyle, Roger, Baron Broghill and **1st Earl of Orrery** 1621–79 •*Irish soldier and politician*• He was the third son of **Richard Boyle**, 1st Earl of Cork. In the English Civil War he first took the royalist side, but after the death of **Charles I** he came under the personal influence of **Cromwell**, and distinguished himself in the Irish campaign. He became one of Cromwell's special council and a member of his House of Lords. On Cromwell's death, he crossed to Ireland, and secured it for King **Charles II**. Four months after the Restoration he was made Earl of Orrery. He wrote poems, eight heroic plays, two comedies, a romance, *Parthenissa* (1654–65), and a *Treatise on the Art of War* (1677).

Brabham, Sir Jack (John Arthur) 1926– •*Australian racecar driver*• Born in Sydney, after service with the Royal Australian Air Force he started his racing career in 1947, in "midget" cars. He won the Australian Grand Prix in 1955 (and again in 1963 and 1964), then went to the UK where he joined the successful Cooper team. He won his first Formula 1 World Drivers' championship at Sebring, Florida, in 1959 by pushing his car over the finishing line and won the title again in 1960. In 1966 he won his third world title, and also the Constructor's championship, with a car of his own design, the Repco-Brabham. He was given the honorary title Officer, Order of the British Empire, in 1966 and knighted in 1979.

Bracegirdle, Anne c. 1663–1748 •*English actress*• She was renowned for her beauty, and for her performances (1688–1707) at Drury Lane and Lincoln's Inn Fields, particularly in the plays of **William Congreve**.

Bracton, Henry de c. 1210–68 •*English ecclesiastic and jurist*• He was born possibly in Exeter. In 1264 he became Archdeacon of Barnstaple and Chancellor of Exeter Cathedral. *De legibus et consuetudinibus Angliae*, the earliest attempt at a systematic treatment of English law, based on decided cases and the practice of royal courts, is attributed to him.

Bradbury, Sir Malcolm Stanley 1932–2000 •*English novelist and critic*• Born in Sheffield, he graduated from University College, Leicester. With Angus Wilson, he cofounded a creative writing program at the University of East Anglia. He was the author of numerous critical works embracing Modernist and post-Modernist ideas, and his own novels, many of them inspired by academia, include *Eating People Is Wrong* (1959), *The History Man* (1975), *Rates of Exchange* (1982) and *Dr Criminale* (1992). He also wrote short stories and television plays, and made several television productions, including the Emmy award-winning *Porterhouse Blue*.

" "

I like the English. They have the most rigid code of immorality in the world.

1959 ***Eating People Is Wrong****, chapter 5.*

Bradbury, Ray(mond Douglas) 1920– •*US science-fiction writer*• He was born in Waukegan, Illinois, and began early to contribute to pulp magazines, graduating to more literary magazines and short-story anthologies. He has written such notable novels as *Fahrenheit 451* (1953), *Dandelion Wine* (1957) and more recently *A Graveyard for Lunatics* (1990). However, he is primarily a short-story writer, creating some of the finest examples in the genre, among them "The Day It Rained Forever," "R Is for Rocket" and those included in *The Martian Chronicles* (1950). A prolific and wide-ranging writer, he has been the recipient of numerous awards.

Braddon, Mary Elizabeth 1835–1915 •*English novelist*• Born in London, she attained fame with a Victorian thriller, *Lady Audley's Secret* (1862), the story of a charming, golden-haired woman who concealed her murderous intents. Of some 75 popular novels, perhaps the best is *Ishmael* (1884). *The Doctor's Wife* (1864) is an adaptation of the theme of **Gustave Flaubert**'s *Madame Bovary*.

Bradfield, John Job Crew 1867–1943 •*Australian civil engineer and designer*• Born in Sandgate, Queensland, he was educated at Sydney University. In 1913 his original plan for a bridge across Sydney Harbor was adopted but, because of World War I, work did not begin until 1923. The widest and heaviest bridge of this type, it was opened in 1932.

Bradford, Barbara Taylor 1933– •*English novelist*• Born in Leeds, she worked as a journalist specializing in interior design, then left for the US, where she now lives. She became internationally known for her bestselling romantic trilogy, *A Woman of Substance* (1979), *Hold the Dream* (1985) and *To Be the Best* (1988). A prolific and extremely commercially successful writer, Bradford writes about strong, adaptable women triumphing in a man's world due to their intellect and indomitable spirit.

Bradford, William 1590–1657 •*American colonist and religious leader, one of the Pilgrim Fathers*• Born in Austerfield, Yorkshire, England, he was a nonconformist from boyhood, and went to Holland with a separatist group in 1609, seeking freedom of worship. In Leiden he became a tradesman and read widely. One of the moving spirits in the Pilgrim Fathers' expedition to the New World in 1620, he sailed on the *Mayflower*, and in 1621 took over from **John Carver** as elected governor of Plymouth colony. He was reelected 30 times between 1622 and 1656, and was perceived as a fair, but firm leader. He wrote a *History of Plimoth Plantation* (completed c. 1651, printed in 1856).

Bradford, William 1663–1752 •*American printer*• He was born in Barnwell, Leicestershire, England. A Quaker, he emigrated to the US in 1685 and founded the country's first paper mill, in Philadelphia in 1690. After moving to New York in 1693, he printed official papers, money, books, plays, and the first New York newspaper (*New York Gazette*, 1725).

Bradlee, Benjamin Crowninshield 1921– •*US journalist and author*• Born in Boston, he joined the *Washington Post* (1948) as a police and federal court reporter, and worked for *Newsweek* where, because of a close friendship with President **John F Kennedy**, he regularly filed scoops. In 1965 he became managing editor of the *Washington Post* and encouraged the investigative journalism which reached an apotheosis in the Watergate scandal. His *Conversations with Kennedy* was published in 1975, and he announced his retirement in 1991.

Bradley, Francis Herbert 1846–1924 •*Welsh philosopher*• Born in Glasbury, Brecknockshire (Powys), he became a Fellow of Merton College, Oxford, in 1870 but lived as a semi-invalid most of his life. He was probably the most important figure in the British idealist movement of this period. His most important works are *Ethical Studies* (1876), *Principles of Logic* (1883) and the highly original and influential *Appearance and Reality* (1893).

Bradley, Henry 1845–1923 •*English philologist and lexicographer*• In 1886 he became joint editor of the *Oxford English Dictionary* with Sir **James Murray**, and senior editor in 1915. He wrote *The Making of English* (1904) and *English Place-Names* (1910).

Bradley, James 1693–1762 •*English astronomer*• Born in Sherborne, Gloucestershire, he was educated at Northleach Grammar School and Balliol College, Oxford. His genius for mathematics and astronomy won him the friendship of **Edmond Halley** and **Isaac Newton**. He was Savilian Professor of Astronomy at Oxford (1721) and in 1742 succeeded Halley as Regius Professor of Astronomy at Greenwich. In 1729 he published his discovery of the aberration of light, providing the first observational proof of the Copernican hypothesis. In 1748 he discovered that the inclination of the Earth's axis to the ecliptic is not constant. He was appointed Astronomer Royal in 1742.

Bradley, Omar N(elson) 1893–1981 •*US general*• He was born in Clark, Missouri. Trained at West Point, he entered the army in 1915 and served in World War I. He commanded the II Corps in Tunisia and Sicily (1943), and in 1944 he commanded the US forces at the Normandy invasion, and later the US 12th Army Group through France. He became the first permanent chairman of the US Joint Chiefs of Staff (1949–53), and in 1950 was promoted to a five-star General of the Army.

Bradman, Sir Don(ald George) 1908–2001 •*Australian cricket player*• Born in Cootamundra, New South Wales, he is regarded as one of the greatest batsmen in the history of the game. He played for Australia from 1928 to 1948 (captain, 1936–48). A prodigious scorer, he made the highest aggregate and largest number of centuries in Tests against England, and holds the record for the highest Australian Test score against England (334 at Leeds in 1930). His batting average in Test matches was an astonishing 99.94 runs per innings. He was the first Australian cricket player to be knighted, in 1949.

Bradshaw, George 1801–53 •*English printer and Quaker*• Born in Salford, Greater Manchester, he was educated locally then was apprenticed to an engraver. A Manchester mapmaker, he is best remembered for the series of railway guides (Bradshaws) which he originated in 1839. He died of cholera in Christiania (now Oslo).

Bradshaw, Terry Paxton 1948– •*US football player*• Born in Shreveport, Louisiana, he played college football at Louisiana Tech. The first pick of the 1970 NFL draft, he signed with the Pittsburgh Steelers as quarterback. He led his team to four Super Bowl titles between 1974 and 1979 and was named Most Valuable Player in Super Bowls XIII and XIV. NFL player of the year in 1978, Bradshaw retired after the 1983 season, holding numerous records, and now works as a television commentator and motivational speaker.

Bradstreet, Anne, *née* **Dudley** 1612–72 •*American Puritan poet*• Born in Northampton, England, in 1628 she married a Nonconformist minister, Simon Bradstreet (1603–97), who later became governor of Massachusetts. She emigrated with her husband to New England in 1630. Her first volume of poems, *The Tenth Muse Lately Sprung up in America*, written in the style of Phineas Fletcher, was published by her brother-in-law in London in 1650 without her knowledge. She is considered the first English poet in America.

Bradwell, Myra R, *née* **Colby** 1831–94 •*US lawyer and campaigner for women's rights*• Born in Manchester, Vermont, she became a schoolteacher because universities were closed to women. Despite passing her legal examinations in 1869, she was debarred from practicing until 1892 on grounds of gender. She argued her case in both state and national supreme courts, procuring state legislation in 1882 that granted all persons, irrespective of sex, the right to select a profession. In 1868 she established, managed and edited the *Chicago Legal News* and in 1869 organized the first Women's Suffrage Convention in Chicago.

Brady, Ian 1938– •*Scottish murderer*• Born in Glasgow, he was a clerk with a fascination for Nazi memorabilia. He was found guilty of the murder of two children, John Kilbride and Lesley Ann Downey, and a 17-year-old boy, Edward Evans, on May 6, 1966. The harrowing case details revealed that Brady, with his lover **Myra Hindley**, lured young children into their home in Manchester and tortured them before killing them. They were described as the "Moors Murderers" because they buried most of their victims on Saddleworth Moor in the Pennines. Hindley made a private confession to two other murders in 1986, and the body of Pauline Reade was found in August 1987, 24 years after her disappearance. The body of 12-year-old Keith Bennett has never been found.

Brady, James Buchanan, *nicknamed* **Diamond Jim** 1856–1917 •*US financier*• Born in New York City, he began as a hotel bellhop, then worked for the New York Central Railroad, and later amassed a fortune as a salesman of railroad equipment, becoming famous for his extravagant tastes and display of diamond jewelery. His endowment to Johns Hopkins Hospital established the Brady Urological Institute.

Brady, Mathew B 1823–96 •*US photographer*• Born near Lake George, New York, he operated a portrait studio in New York City, first using daguerrotype and then switching to wet-plate photography in 1855. He built a thriving business, photographing numerous public figures such as **Abraham Lincoln**, but gave this up to take on a major project to record the Civil War with the Union armies. In 1862 he organized a team that covered all the major engagements and camp life. Though widely acclaimed, this effort ruined him financially and, despite a belated government grant, he died in poverty in a New York almshouse.

Brady, Matthew 1799–1826 •*Australian thief and bushranger*• Born in Manchester, England, of Irish descent, he was convicted in 1820 of stealing a basket of groceries. Transported for seven years to New South Wales, he was sent in 1823 to the penal colony of Macquarie Harbor in Van Diemen's Land (now Tasmania). Brady escaped with a small group in the following year, and they terrorized the island. After many exploits, including capturing an entire township, some of his gang turned informers. He was eventually captured and hanged in Hobart.

Bragg, Sir (William) Lawrence 1890–1971 •*British physicist and Nobel Prize winner*• Born in Adelaide, Australia, the son of Sir **William Bragg**, he was educated at Adelaide University from the age of 15, and Trinity College, Cambridge, where he discovered the Bragg law (1912), which describes the conditions for X-ray diffraction by crystals. Like his father, he became director of the Royal Institution (1954–65) and did much to popularize science. He shared the 1915 Nobel Prize for physics with his father, became Professor of Physics at Victoria University, Manchester (1919–37), and then succeeded **Ernest Rutherford** as head of the Cavendish Laboratory in Cambridge (1938–53). There he supported **Francis Crick** and **James Watson** in their work. He was knighted in 1941.

Bragg, Melvyn Bragg, Baron 1939– •*English novelist and television arts host*• Born in Lovell, near Carlisle, he produced and hosted several television programs before becoming host and and editor of the arts series *The South Bank Show* (1978–). He was head of arts at London Weekend Television from 1982 to 1990, when he became controller of arts there. He was also chairman of Border Television from 1990 to 1995. He hosted BBC Radio 4's *Start the Week* from 1988 to 1998, among other radio and television series. He co-wrote the films *Isadora* (1969), *Jesus Christ Superstar* (1973) and *Clouds of Glory*, as well as the stage musical *The Hired Man* (1984), adapted from his novel, and other plays. His novels include *Without a City Wall* (1968), *The Nerve* (1971), *The Silken Net* (1974), *A Time to Dance* (1990, adapted for television, 1992) and *The Soldier's Return* (1999). He was made a peer in 1998.

“ ”

Patriotism is seen not only as the last refuge of the scoundrel but as the first bolt-hole of the hypocrite.

*1976 **Speak For England**, introduction.*

Bragg, Sir William Henry 1862–1942 •*English physicist and Nobel Prize winner*• He was born in Westward, Cumberland, and educated at Trinity College, Cambridge. His extraordinary scientific career only really began when in 1904 he gave a lecture on radioactivity that inspired him to research this area. He became professor at Leeds in 1909 and from 1912 worked in conjunction with his son, **Lawrence Bragg**, on determining the atomic structure of crystals from their X-ray diffraction patterns. Their efforts won them a joint Nobel Prize for physics in 1915, the only father-son partnership to share this honor. William Bragg moved to University College London the same year and became director of the Royal Institution in 1923. His works include *Studies in Radioactivity* (1912), *X-rays and Crystal Structure* (1915, with his son) and *The Universe of Light* (1933). During World War I he directed research on submarine detection for the admiralty. He was knighted in 1920.

Brahe, Tycho or **Tyge** 1546–1601 •*Danish astronomer*• Born into a noble family in Knudstrup, South Sweden (then under Danish rule), he studied at the University of Copenhagen and then at Leipzig, Wittenberg, Rostock and Augsburg (1562–69). From the age of 14, when he saw the partial solar eclipse of 1560, he was obsessed by astronomy. In 1563 he discovered serious errors in the existing astronomical tables, and in 1572 carefully observed a new star in Cassiopeia (the supernova now known as Tycho's star), a significant observation which made his name. In 1576, with royal aid, he established his Uraniborg (Castle of the Heavens) Observatory on the island of Ven (formerly Hven), in The Sound (between Zealand Island and Sweden). There, for 20 years, he successfully carried out his observations, measuring the positions of 777 stars. In 1596, on the succession of **Christian IV**, he was forced to leave the country; after traveling for three years he accepted an invitation from the emperor **Rudolf II** to Benatky, near Prague, where he assisted **Johannes Kepler**. Brahe did not subscribe to **Copernicus**'s theory of a sun-centered planetary system, but his data allowed Kepler to prove that Copernicus was essentially correct. Brahe lost most of his nose in a duel at the age of 19, and wore a false silver nose for the rest of his life. He is considered the greatest pretelescope observer.

Brahms, Johannes 1833–97 •*German composer*• Born in Hamburg, the son of a poor orchestral musician, he showed early talent as a pianist, and as a young boy was compelled by family poverty to earn his living playing in the dockside inns of Hamburg. Although his reputation spread rapidly, it was not until 1853 that Brahms was able to concentrate on composition. He toured with the Hungarian refugee violinist Ede Reményi (1828–98) and met **Franz Liszt**. Brahms was introduced to **Clara** and **Robert Schumann**, whose enthusiasm for Brahms's early works, especially his assistance in publishing the piano sonatas, helped establish his reputation. In 1863 he settled in Vienna, and his life was uneventful except for occasional public appearances in Austria and Germany at which he played his own works. He was adopted by the anti-Wagnerian faction as the leader of traditional principles aginst "modern" iconoclasm, and his fame as a composer spread rapidly. Firmly based on classical foundations, his works contain hardly any program music apart from a few pieces such as the *Tragic Overture* (1886) and the C minor quartet (1855–75, inspired by **Goethe**'s *Werther*). He waited many years before venturing into great orchestral works: the first, *Variations on a Theme of Haydn*, appeared when he was 40, and his first symphony when he was 43. His greatest choral work is the *German Requiem*, which had its first full performance in 1869. He wrote much chamber music and many songs. He was prolific in all fields except opera, and the quality of his work is extraordinarily even, largely because of his ruthless destruction of early efforts and his refusal to publish any work which failed to measure up to his self-imposed standards of excellence.

Braid, James 1870–1950 •*Scottish golfer*• Born in Earlsferry, Fife, he trained as a joiner and went to work in St Andrews, where he became an impressive player. In 1893 he became a professional golfer. He won the Open championship five times between 1901 and 1910 (when he became the first player to break 300 for 72 holes at St Andrews), four *News of the World* matchplay championships between 1903 and 1911, and the French Championship in 1910. With **Harry Vardon** and John Henry Taylor (1871–1963) he formed the so-called Great Triumvirate of British golf in the Edwardian era.

Braille, Louis 1809–52 •*French educationist*• Born in Coupvray, near Paris, he was blind from the age of three, and at ten entered the Institution des Jeunes Aveugles in Paris. He studied organ playing, and became professor of the institution in 1826. In 1829 he devised a system of raised-point writing that the blind could both read and write.

Braine, John Gerard 1922–86 •*English novelist*• Born in Bradford, he had various jobs, including service in the Royal Navy, before following his mother's profession of librarian. In 1951 he went to London to become a full-time writer, but returned north the same year, after his mother's death in a highway accident. He then spent 18 months in the hospital suffering from tuberculosis, and it was during this period of enforced rest that he began to write his first successful novel, *Room at the Top*. The theme of aggressive ambition and determination to break through rigid social barriers identified him with the "angry young men" of the 1950s. His other novels include *The Vodi* (1959), *Life at the Top* (1962), *The Jealous God* (1964), *The Crying Game* (1964), *Stay with Me Till Morning* (1968) and *One and Last Love* (1981).

Bramah, Joseph 1748–1814 •*English inventor*• Born in Stainborough, Yorkshire, the son of a farmer, he was lamed at 16, so was apprenticed to the village carpenter, and later became a cabinetmaker in London. He made numerous inventions, including a beer machine for use at the bar of public houses, a safety lock (patented 1788) which he manufactured in partnership with Henry Maudslay, a hydraulic press (1795), and an ingenious machine for printing bank notes (1806). He was one of the first to propose the application of the screw propeller.

Bramante, Donato or **Donino**, *originally* **Donato di Pasuccio d'Antonio** or **Donato d'Agnolo** or **D'Angelo** 1444–1514 •*Italian High Renaissance architect*• Born near Urbino, he started as a painter, and from 1477 to 1499 worked in Milan, where he executed his first building projects, such as S Maria delle Grazie (1488–99). He spent the last 15 years of his life, from 1499, in Rome, where he was employed by popes **Alexander VI** and **Julius II** and where his most important work was done. He designed the new Basilica of St Peter's (begun in 1506), the Belvedere courtyard, the Tempietto di S Pietro in Montorio (1502), the Palazzo dei Tribunali (1508) and the Palazzo Caprini (c. 1510).

Branagh, Kenneth Charles 1960– •*Northern Irish actor and director*• He was born in Belfast and moved to England with his family when young. He studied at the Royal Academy of Dramatic Art and went straight to the West End, playing the Communist public schoolboy, Judd, in *Another Country* (1981). In 1984 he joined the Royal Shakespeare Company (RSC), and in 1987 he cofounded and became codirector of the Renaissance Theatre Company. He has appeared in television drama, directed productions in the West End, written plays, and both appeared in and directed several films, including *Henry V* (1989), *Dead Again* (1991), *Peter's Friends* (1992), *Much Ado About Nothing* (1993), *Mary Shelley's Frankenstein* (1994), *Hamlet* (1996) and *Love's Labour's Lost* (2000). He was married to **Emma Thompson** (1989, separated 1995) with whom he often costarred on stage and screen. He published an autobiography, *Beginning*, in 1989.

Brancusi, Constantin 1876–1957 •*Romanian sculptor*• He was born in Hobiţa and moved to Tîrgu Jiu, near Pestisani, as a boy. After several different jobs, he won a scholarship to the Bucharest Academy, and went to Paris in 1904, where he developed his highly individual style. Brancusi's *The Kiss* (1901–21, various versions) was the most abstract sculpture of the period, representing two block-like figures. His *Sleeping Muse* (1910, Pompidou Center, Paris) is the first of his many characteristic, highly polished egg-shaped carvings. *The Prodigal Son* (1925) shows the influence of African sculpture. His aim was simplification, to identify the essence, which he saw as being objective, and he was therefore outside the subjective expressionist schools of the day. Other works include *Bird in Space* (1925) and *The Sea-Lions* (1943).

Brand, Dollar *See* **Ibrahim, Abdullah**

Brand, Hennig 17th century •*German alchemist*• He was born in Hamburg and was active in the second half of the century. He began his career as a military officer and subsequently practiced as a physician. Around 1669 he discovered in urine a white waxy substance that glowed in the dark and which he named phosphorus ("light bearer"). He is the first scientist known to have discovered an element, the names of earlier discoverers being lost. He did not publicize his discovery, and phosphorus was discovered independently by **Robert Boyle** in 1680.

Brand, Sir Jan Hendrik 1823–88 •*South African statesman*• Born in Capetown, he was President of the Orange Free State from 1864 until his death. He defeated the Basutos (1865–69), and favored friendship with Great Britain.

Brand, Max, *pseudonym of* **Frederick Schiller Faust** 1892–1944 •*US novelist and short-story writer*• Born in Seattle, he was orphaned at the age of 13, but after leading a nomadic lifestyle as an agricultural worker, became a Western writer, contributing stories to around 24 pulp magazines using many pseudonyms. His first novel, *The Untamed*, appeared under the Brand name in 1919. Other novels include *Trailin'* (1919) and *Destry Rides Again* (1930). He died in Italy, where he was serving as a war correspondent with the US 88th Infantry Division.

Brandan, St *See* **Brendan, St**

Brando, Marlon 1924–2004 •*US film and stage actor*• Born in Omaha, Nebraska, he trained in Method acting at the New York Actors Studio. He appeared in several plays before achieving fame as the inarticulate and brutal Stanley Kowalski in **Tennessee Williams**'s *A Streetcar Named Desire* on stage (1947) and on film (1951). His varied film parts include the original motorcycle rebel in *The Wild One* (1953), the singing gambler Sky Masterson in *Guys and Dolls* (1955), a Western outlaw in *One-Eyed Jacks*, which he also directed (1961), a convincingly English **Fletcher Christian** in *Mutiny on the Bounty* (1962) and the US widower in the controversial *Last Tango in Paris* (1972). He won an Academy Award for *On the Waterfront* (1954) but refused to accept a second for *The Godfather* (1972), in protest against the film industry's treatment of Native Americans. He was a prominent campaigner for the Civil Rights movement. Following *Apocalypse Now* (1977) he grew reclusive, but ended an eight-year absence from the screen with the anti-apartheid drama *A Dry White Season* (1989). Other recent films include *Don Juan De Marco* (1995) and *The Island of Dr Moreau* (1996).

"

An actor is a kind of guy who if you ain't talking about him ain't listening.

*Quoted in Bob Thomas **Brando** (1973), chapter 8.*

Brandt, Bill (William) 1904–83 •*British photographer*• Born in Germany, he studied with **Man Ray** in Paris in 1929, and went to London in 1931. During the 1930s he made a series of striking social records, contrasting the lives of the rich and the poor, and during World War II he worked for the Ministry of Information recording conditions in London during the Blitz. His greatest creative work was his treatment of the nude, in which his essays on pure form, as published in *Perspective of Nudes* (1961) and *Shadows of Light* (1966), approached the surreal.

Brandt, Georg 1694–1768 •*Swedish chemist*• Born in Riddarhyttan, he studied medicine and chemistry at Leiden and Rheims. In 1727 he was made director of the chemical laboratory at the Bureau of Mines, Stockholm, and in 1730 he became Assay Master of the Swedish Mint. Around 1730 he discovered cobalt. He systematically investigated arsenic and its compounds, publishing the results in 1733, and he discovered the difference between potash and soda. He was also one of the first chemists to decry alchemy and to expose its fraudulent practices.

Brandt, Willy, *originally* **Karl Herbert Frahm** 1913–92 •*German statesman and Nobel Prize winner*• Born in Lübeck and educated there, he joined the Social Democrats at age 17 and, as a fervent anti-Nazi, fled in 1933 to Norway and worked as a journalist. On the occupation of Norway in 1940, he went to Sweden, continuing as a journalist in support of the German and Norwegian resistance movements. In 1945 he returned to Germany and from 1949 to 1957 was a member of the Bundestag, being president of the Bundesrat (1955–57). Notably a pro-West, anti-Communist leader, he became Mayor of West Berlin (1957–66), achieving international renown during the Berlin Wall crisis (1961). He was Chairman of the Sozialdemokratische Partei Deutschlands (SPD) in 1964, playing a key role in the party's remolding as a more moderate and popular force. In 1966 he led the SPD into a "Grand Coalition" government with the Christian Democrats and, as Foreign Minister, instituted the new policy of *Ostpolitik* (reconciliation between eastern and western Europe). This culminated in the signing of the Basic Treaty with East Germany in September 1972. Brandt was awarded the Nobel Peace Prize in 1971, but was forced to resign the chancellorship in April 1974, following the discovery that his close aide, Gunther Guillaume, had been an East German spy. He continued to serve, however, as SPD chairman until 1987, and headed an influential international commission (the Brandt Commission) on economic development between 1977 and 1983. The commission's main report, entitled *North-South: A Program for Survival* (1980), advocated urgent action by the rich North to improve conditions in the poorer Southern Hemisphere.

Branson, Sir Richard Charles Nicholas 1950– •*English entrepreneur and businessman*• Born in London he was educated at Stowe School, but left at the age of 16 to devote himself to his first enterprise, a magazine called *Student*. This was at first successful, but in the end proved unprofitable and was discontinued. In 1969 Branson began the Virgin mail-order business; two years later he opened the first branch of his record chain; and in 1973 he founded the Virgin record label. The success of these ventures, combined with some shrewd commercial judgments (he signed a contract with **The Sex Pistols** in 1977), soon gained him a reputation in youth culture as the acceptable face of capitalism. He founded Virgin Atlantic Airlines in 1984, and, with his business continuing to grow, floated the company in 1986 (and bought it back two years later). He sold Virgin Music for £560 million to Thorn EMI in 1992, and in 1993, with TV-am, he launched Virgin Radio, the UK's second independent national radio station. In 1995 Virgin acquired a chain of cinemas and 1996 saw the creation of the Virgin Rail Group. Branson's diverse business interests now also include retail, communications and financial services. The motto of all this activity has been "organic expansion" into areas where there is a perceived need. A grinning, outwardly informal and ebullient man, he has proved himself to be an astute self-publicist. In 1986 he won the Blue Riband title for the fastest sea crossing of the Atlantic. The following year, he became, with Per Lindstrand, the first to cross the Atlantic in a hot-air balloon, and he repeated the feat across the Pacific in 1991. His attempt to circumnavigate the world in 1997 was unsuccessful. *Losing My Virginity: The Autobiography* was published in 1998 and he was knighted in 2000.

Brant, Joseph, *Mohawk name* **Thayendanegea** 1742–1807 •*Mohawk chief*• The brother-in-law of the Irish fur trader, Sir William Johnson, he learned English and converted to Anglicanism. He served the British in the French and Indian War (1754–63), and during the uprising led by the Ottawa chief **Pontiac** (1763–66). In the American Revolution (1775–83), he commanded the Mohawks on the British side. After the Revolution he was assigned land in Canada by the British, and in 1785 went to England to persuade the British government to indemnify the Indians for their losses in the war. He translated St Mark's Gospel and the Prayer Book into Mohawk, and founded the first Episcopal church in upper Canada.

Branting, Karl Hjalmar 1860–1925 •*Swedish politician and Nobel Prize winner*• Born in Stockholm, he was cofounder of the Social Democratic Party of Sweden in 1889 and was its first parliamentary representative in 1896. He became chairman of the party in 1907 and helped to lead it away from revolutionary Marxism toward a more moderate "revisionist" program. He was Prime Minister in 1920, and again from 1921–23 and 1924–25. In 1921 he shared the Nobel Peace Prize for his work in international diplomacy, and was Sweden's first representative at the League of Nations (1922–25).

Brantôme, Pierre de Bourdeilles, Seigneur de c.1540–1614 •*French soldier and writer*• Born in Périgord, he was educated at Paris and Poitiers. In 1561 he accompanied **Mary Queen of Scots** to Scotland, and in 1565 he joined the expedition sent to Malta to assist the Knights of St John against the sultan. He also served in Italy, Africa and Hungary, and was made chamberlain to **Charles IX** and

Henry III, and fought against the Huguenots. About 1594 he was injured after a fall from a horse and retired to write his memoirs. His works, first published posthumously in 1665–66, comprise *Vies des grands capitaines* ("Lives of the Great Captains"), *Vies des dames galantes* ("Lives of the Courtesans") and *Vies des dames illustres* ("Lives of the Illustrious Ladies"). They provide a vivid, often scandalous, picture of the Valois court, and their literary merit and historical interest are considerable.

Braque, Georges 1882–1963 •*French painter*• Born in Argenteuil, the son of a house painter, he spent his boyhood in Le Havre. In Paris (from 1900), he studied at the École des Beaux-Arts, and became one of the founders of classical Cubism, working with **Picasso** from 1908 to 1914. After World War I (in which he was wounded) he developed a personal, nongeometric, semiabstract style. In 1924 and 1925 he designed scenes for two **Diaghilev** ballets, *Les fâcheux* and *Zéphyr et flore*. His paintings are mainly of still life, the subject being transformed into a two-dimensional pattern. They are among the outstanding decorative achievements of the 20th century and have had a pervasive influence on other painters. He was made a Commander of the Legion of Honor in 1951.

Brasch, Charles Orwell 1909–73 •*New Zealand poet, critic and editor*• Born in Dunedin, he established *Landfall*, a periodical of art, literature and politics, in 1947, and was its editor for 20 years, exercising great influence on the form and direction of contemporary New Zealand poets. His own verse includes *The Land and the People* (1939), *Not Far Off* (1969) and the posthumous *Home Ground* (1974, edited by Alan Roddick). His *Collected Poems* were published posthumously in 1984.

Brassaï, *properly* **Gyula Halasz** 1899–1984 •*French painter and photographer*• Born in Brasso, Hungary, and trained as an artist, he went to Paris in 1923 and worked as a journalist. From 1930 he made candid photographic records of the underworld and nightlife of 1930s Paris. His first collection, *Paris de nuit* (1933, "Paris at Night"), caused a sensation. He refused to photograph during the German occupation but worked in **Picasso**'s studio. His photographic work after the war retained its Parisian ethos.

Bratby, John Randall 1928–92 •*English artist and writer*• Born in Wimbledon, London, he was a leading protagonist of the English New Realist school, noted for being the enfant terrible of the artistic establishment. In the 1950s he was associated with the "kitchen sink" school because of his preoccupation with working-class domestic interiors, and he is considered to be a precursor of pop art. He was a prolific painter with a bold, colorful and vigorous style that often had distinctive white overdrawing. He wrote several novels, including the autobiographical *Breakdown* (1960), with his own illustrations. Notable paintings include *Still Life with Chip-Frier* (1956) and the mural *The Feeding of the Five Thousand* (1963).

Brathwaite, Edward Kamau, *originally* **Lawson Edward Brathwaite** 1930– •*West Indian poet and historian*• Born in Bridgetown, Barbados, he made his reputation with the three long poems reprinted together in 1973 as *The Arrivants: A New World Trilogy.* Each of the three analyzes a different aspect of West Indian Blacks' dispossession and their attempts to reconstitute an African-cum-Caribbean culture. His historical research, for works such as *The Folk Culture of the Slaves of Jamaica* (1970), has complemented his creative output, which has continued with *Mother Poem* (1977) and *Sun Poem* (1982), both celebrations of his native island.

Brattain, Walter Houser 1902–87 •*US physicist and Nobel Prize winner*• Born in Amoy, China, of US parents, he grew up on a cattle ranch in Washington, and was educated at the Universities of Oregon and Minnesota. He then joined Bell Telephone Laboratories where he worked as a research physicist until his retirement in 1967. With **John Bardeen** and **William Shockley** he developed the point-contact transistor, using a thin germanium crystal. He shared the Nobel Prize for physics with Bardeen and Shockley in 1956.

Brauchitsch, Walther von 1881–1948 •*German field marshal*• Born in Berlin, he was commissioned into the 3rd Guards Regiment of Foot in 1900. After studying at the War Academy he was promoted to captain and served on the General Staff during World War I. Between 1939 and 1941 he was Commander in Chief of the Germany army, a period of spectacular triumphs, but was dismissed by **Hitler** following the failure of the attack on Moscow.

Brauer, Adriaen *See* **Brouwer, Adriaen**

Braun, Emma Lucy 1889–1971 •*US botanist*• Born in Cincinnati, Ohio, she studied at the University of Cincinnati. She remained in academic positions at the university, becoming Professor of Plant Ecology in 1946, until taking early retirement in 1948. Her ecological work focused on detailed case studies of the vegetation in a variety of habitats in Ohio and Kentucky. She contributed to the growing conservation movement, stressing the importance of preserving natural habitats, and became the first woman to be elected president of the Ecological Society of America.

Braun, Eva 1912–45 •*German mistress of Adolf Hitler*• Born in Munich, she was secretary to **Hitler**'s staff photographer, became Hitler's mistress in the 1930s and is said to have married him before they committed suicide together in the air-raid shelter of the Chancellery during the fall of Berlin.

Braun, (Karl) Ferdinand 1850–1918 •*German physicist and Nobel Prize winner*• Born in Fulda, Hessen, he studied at the universities of Marburg and Berlin, and held posts at the universities of Würzburg, Leipzig, Marburg, Karlsruhe, Tübingen and Strasbourg. Although his main contributions were in pure science, he is best known for the first cathode-ray (the "Braun tube") oscilloscope introduced in 1897, providing a basic component of the television. In 1909 he shared with **Gugliemo Marconi** the Nobel Prize for physics for his practical contribution to wireless telegraphy.

Braun, Lily, *née* **von Kretschmann** 1865–1916 •*German socialist author and feminist*• Born in Halberstadt, she married the socialist writer and politician Heinrich Braun (1854–1927) in 1895 and became a member of the Social Democratic Party in 1896. Her best-known book is *Im Schatten der Titanen* (1908, "In the Shadow of the Titans"), and she is known for her novel *Liebesbriefe der Marquise* (1912, "Love Letters of the Marquise") and her *Memoiren einer Sozialistin* (1909–11, "Memoirs of a Woman Socialist").

Braun, Wernher von 1912–77 •*US rocket pioneer*• Born in Wirsitz, Germany, he studied engineering at the universities of Berlin and Zurich and founded in 1930 a society for space travel which maintained a rocket-launching site near Berlin. The German army authorities became interested in rockets, and by 1936, with **Hitler**'s backing, von Braun was director of the German rocket research station at Peenemünde, on the Baltic coast, where he perfected and launched the famous V-2 rockets against Great Britain in September 1944. At the end of the war he surrendered, with his entire development team, to the US. He was chiefly responsible for the manufacture and successful launching of the first US artificial earth satellite, *Explorer I*, in 1958, and became director of the Marshal Space Flight Center (1960–70), where he developed the Saturn rocket for the *Apollo 11* moon landing (1969). His books include *Conquest of the Moon* (1953) and *Space Frontier* (1967).

Brazil, Angela 1868–1947 •*English children's writer*• Born in Preston, Lancashire, she was a governess for some years before beginning to write. She never married, and lived with her brother and sister, describing her adult self as "an absolute schoolgirl." She wrote a series of stories of school life, all heavily moralistic, and notable for their healthy realism. Among the best of them are *The New Girl at St Chad's*, *A Fourth Form Friendship* and *Captain Peggie*.

Brazza, Pierre Savorgnan de 1852–1905 •*French explorer*• Born in Rio de Janeiro, Brazil, of Italian extraction, he joined the French navy in 1870, and served in western Africa in Gabon, where he explored the Ogowe River (1876–78). He became a French citizen in 1874, and in 1878 the French government gave him 100,000 francs for exploring the country north of the Congo, where he secured vast grants of land for France, and founded stations, including that of Brazzaville on the north shore of Stanley Pool.

Bréal, Michel 1832–1915 •*French comparative philologist and mythologist*• Born in Rhenish Bavaria, in 1858 he settled in Paris, and in 1866 became Professor of Comparative Grammar at the Collège de France. He founded the science of semantics with his *Essai de Sémantique* (1897, "Essay on Semantics"), an exposition of principles for the study of the meaning of words.

Bream, Julian Alexander 1933– •*English guitarist and lutenist*• Born in London, he made his debut there in 1950. A protégé of **Andrés Segovia**, he has edited much music for guitar and lute. He formed the Julian Bream Consort in 1961. Many works have been specially written for him, by **Benjamin Britten**, **Hans Werner Henze**, **Michael Tippett**, **William Walton** and others. He was given the honorary title of Commander, Order of the British Empire, in 1985.

Breasted, James Henry 1865–1935 •*US archaeologist and historian, the founder of US Egyptology*• Born in Rockford, Illinois, he studied at Yale and Berlin before joining the faculty at Chicago in 1894. His five-volume *Ancient Records of Egypt* (1906) transcribed every hieroglyphic inscription then known, and he led expeditions to Egypt and Nubia (1905–07) to copy inscriptions that were perishing or had hitherto been inaccessible. He set up his own Oriental Institute at the University of Chicago (1919) to promote research on ancient Egypt and western Asia, and under his directorship the Institute undertook notable excavations in the 1920s and 1930s in northern Palestine, at Khorsabad and Tell Asmar in Iraq, and (from 1931) at Persepolis, the Achaemenid capital of Iran.

Brecht, (Eugen) Bertolt Friedrich 1898–1956 •*German playwright and poet*• Born in Augsburg, he studied medicine and philosophy at Munich and Berlin Universities, and served briefly as a medical orderly in 1918. He won the Kleist drama prize in 1922 for his first two expressionist plays, *Trommeln in der Nacht* (1918, Eng trans *Drums in the Night*, 1966) and *Baal* (1918, Eng trans 1964). He was keenly interested in the effects produced by combining drama and music, and consequently collaborated with **Kurt Weill**, Hanns Eisler (1898–1962) and **Paul Dessau** in his major works. His reputation was established by the *Dreigroschenoper* (1928, Eng trans *The Threepenny Opera*, 1958), an adaptation of **John Gay**'s *Beggar's Opera* in a sham Victorian London setting, with music by Weill. A Marxist, Brecht regarded his plays as social experiments, requiring critical detachment, not emotional involvement, from the observing audience. He began to experiment with *Verfremdungseffekt* ("alienation effects") and introduced "epic" theater, requiring the audience to see the stage as a stage, actors as actors, instead of adhering to the traditional make-believe of the theater. With Hitler's rise to power in 1933, Brecht left Germany, and lived in exile for 15 years (1933–48), during which time he wrote some of his greatest plays, including *Mutter Courage und ihre Kinder* (1941 Eng trans *Mother Courage and Her Children*, 1961). His abiding hatred of Nazi Germany found expression in a series of short, episodic plays and poems collected under the title *Furcht und Elend des dritten Reiches* (1945, "Fear and Loathing Under the Third Reich"), and in *Der aufhaltsame Aufstieg des Arturo Ui* (1957, Eng trans *The Resistible Rise of Arturo Ui*, 1976). He denied membership in the Communist Party before a US Senate subcommittee on un-American activities in 1946, and in 1948 accepted the East German government's offer of a theater in East Berlin. The *Berliner Ensemble* was founded, producing under his direction his later plays, such as *Der gute Mensch von Sezuan* (1943, Eng trans *The Good Person of Szechuan*, 1948) and *Der kaukasische Kreidekreis* (1947, Eng trans *The Caucasian Chalk Circle*, 1948). By this time he was established as a major figure in 20th-century theater.

“ ”

One observes, they have gone too long without a war here. Where is morality to come from in such a case, I ask? Peace is nothing but slovenliness, only war creates order.

1941 ***Mother Courage****, scene 1.*

Breckinridge, John Cabell 1821–75 •*US politician*• Born near Lexington, Kentucky, he practiced law there until 1847, when he was appointed major of a volunteer regiment for the Mexican War. He sat in Congress from 1851 to 1855, and in 1856 was elected vice president, with **James Buchanan** as President. In 1860 he was the proslavery candidate for the presidency, but was defeated by **Abraham Lincoln**. A senator from March to December 1861, he was appointed a Confederate major general in 1862, was Secretary of War in **Jefferson Davis**'s Cabinet, and escaped to Europe, returning in 1868.

Brenan, Gerald, *originally* **Edward Fitz-Gerald Brenan** 1894–1987 •*English travel writer, Hispanophile and novelist*• He was born in Malta, the son of an officer in an Irish regiment, and after an itinerant boyhood he set off with a donkey, traveling across Europe to the Balkans and back again. He then went to Spain and settled in Yegen, the isolated village which became the focus of his classic *South from Granada* (1957). This was preceded by his best-known book, *The Spanish Labyrinth* (1943), still regarded as one of the most profound and perceptive studies of modern Spain. Other books include *The Literature of the Spanish People* (1951) and a novel, *Thoughts in a Dry Season* (1978).

Brendan or **Brandan, St** 484–577 •*Irish abbot and traveler*• Born in Tralee, now in County Kerry, he is traditionally regarded as the founder of the monastery of Clonfert in County Galway (561), and other monasteries in Ireland and Scotland. The *Navigation of St Brendan* (c. 1050) recounts his legendary voyage to a land of saints far to the west and north, possibly the Hebrides and the Northern Isles, or even Iceland. In old maps "St Brendan's country" is placed west of the Cape Verde Islands. His feast day is May 16.

Brendel, Alfred 1931– •*Austrian pianist*• Born in Wiesenberg, Moravia, he made his debut in Graz (1948), and is a distinguished interpreter of **Mozart**, **Schubert**, **Beethoven**, **Liszt** and **Schoenberg**. He tours internationally, giving master classes and making frequent television appearances, and has written many perceptive essays on music.

Brenner, Sydney 1927– •*British molecular biologist*• He was born in Germiston, South Africa, and educated at Witwatersrand University and Oxford. He joined the staff of the Medical Research Council (MRC) in 1957. With **Francis Crick**, Brenner worked to unravel the genetic code, working out the nucleotide codes for the 20 amino acids in 1961. He went on to research the embryology of the nematode worm, with the objective of relating the anatomy of an animal to the genetic basis of its structure. Brenner was a member of the Scripps Research Center at La Jolla, California (1992–94) and then director of the Molecular Sciences Institute at Berkeley, California (1996–2001).

Brentano, Clemens von 1778–1842 •*German poet, novelist and dramatist*• Born in Ehrenbreitstein, he led a somewhat irresponsible early life, before withdrawing to the monastery of Dülmen, near Münster (1818–24), where he recorded the revelations of the nun, **Anna Katharina Emmerich**. In his earliest poems the peculiarities of the Romantic school are carried to excess. His writing for the stage is characterized by great dramatic power and a wonderful humor, but he was mostly successful in his novellas, particularly in the *Geschichte vom braven Kasperl* (1817, "Tale of Honest Kasper").

Brentano, Lujo (Ludwig Josef) 1844–1931 •*German political economist and Nobel Prize winner*• He was born in Aschaffenburg, Bavaria. In 1868 he went to England to study the condition of the working classes. The outcome of this was his *English Guilds* (1870) and *Die Arbeitergilden der Gegenwart* (2 vols, 1871–72, "Workers' Guilds of the Present"). He became Professor of Economics in five universities and wrote on wages, labor in relation to land, compulsory insurance for workmen, and an *Economic History of England* (1929). A prominent pacifist, he was awarded the Nobel Peace Prize in 1927. He was the nephew of **Clemens von Brentano**.

Brent-Dyer, Elinor M(ary) 1894–1969 •*English children's writer*• Born in South Shields, Tyne and Wear, she became headmistress of the Margaret Roper Girls' School in Hereford. The first of her 98 schoolgirl novels, *Gerry Goes to School*, appeared in 1922. Her fourth book, *The School at the Chalet* (1925), established her famous "Chalet School" series, set in an English school in the Austrian Tyrol. Centered on Jo Bettany, the series sought to preach against English parochialism and xenophobia. Perhaps the best single title was *The Chalet School in Exile* (1940), a judicious account of the school's flight from Nazi rule with a grim depiction of persecution of Jews.

Brent of Bin *See* **Franklin, (Stella Marian Sarah) Miles**

Brenton, Howard 1942– •*English dramatist*• Born in Portsmouth, he wrote for fringe theater companies during the late 1960s, and was resident dramatist at the Royal Court Theatre,

London, from 1972 to 1973, where his play *Magnificence*, dealing with urban terrorism, was staged. *The Churchill Play* (1974) takes a bleak look at a future Great Britain governed by hardliners using troops to brutalize trade unionists. It was followed by *Weapons of Happiness* (1976, *The Romans in Britain*, premiered 1980), and *The Genius*, on the nuclear arms race (premiered 1983). He has also collaborated with **David Hare** on a number of projects, the most outstanding being *Pravda* (1985), a furiously ebullient satire on the cravenness of the national press.

Brenz, Johann 1499–1570 •*German Lutheran reformer*• Born in Weil, Swabia, he studied at Heidelberg University, and was ordained in 1520. He was coauthor of the Württemberg Confession of Faith, and his Catechism (1551) stands next to **Martin Luther**'s in Protestant Germany.

Breshko-Breshkovskaya, Yekaterina Konstantinovna 1844–1934 •*Russian revolutionary*• She was the daughter of a Polish landowner and a Russian aristocrat, and associated with various liberal and revolutionary groups in the more open society of St Petersburg under **Alexander II**. In the 1870s she worked with the Narodniki revolutionaries and was arrested and sent to Siberia (1874–96). In 1901 she helped to found the Socialist revolutionaries but in 1908 she was again exiled to Siberia, from which she was able to return only in 1917. Colorful and independent-minded, though dubbed the "Grandmother of the Revolution," she fell out with the Bolsheviks after their victory in October 1917, and died in Prague a firm anti-Communist.

Bresson, Robert 1901–99 •*French film director*• Born in Bromont-Lamothe, he made his directorial debut with *Les affaires publiques* (1934, "Public Affairs"). A prisoner of war in Germany, he subsequently directed *Les anges du péché* (1943, *Angels of the Streets*) and *Les dames du bois de Boulogne* (1946, *Ladies of the Park*). His distinctive style emerged during the 1950s, when his use of nonprofessional actors and restrained emotions created austere narratives dealing with redemption and salvation. His notable films include *Journal d'un curé de campagne* (1950, *Diary of a Country Priest*) and *Pickpocket* (1959). Later, equally rigorous films explored the concept of saintliness, the attraction of suicide and humankind's innate sense of greed. These include *Au hasard, Balthazar* (1966, *Balthazar*), *Une femme douce* (1969, "A Gentle Woman") and *L'argent* (1983, "Money").

Breton, André 1896–1966 •*French poet, essayist and critic, founder and theorist of the surrealist movement*• Born in Tinchebray, Normandy, he joined the Dadaist group in 1916 and was cofounder of the Dada magazine *Littérature* (1919). In 1930 he joined the Communist Party for a time, and spent the war years in the US. He collaborated with Philippe Soupault to write *Les champs magnétiques* (1920, "Magnetic Fields"), one of the first experiments in automatic writing. In 1922 he turned to surrealism, and in 1924 he published *Manifeste du surréalisme-poisson soluble* ("Soluble Fish"), and became editor of *La révolution surréaliste* (1924–30). His major novel was *Nadja* (1928, Eng trans 1960), which mingles the irrational and the everyday.

Breton, Nicholas c. 1555–c. 1626 •*English poet*• Born in London, the son of a merchant, and stepson of **George Gascoigne**, he was educated at Oxford and became a prolific writer of all kinds of verse, prose and pamphlets. His best-known poem is *The Passionate Shepheard* (1604). His prose work *Wits Trenchmour* (1597) is a fishing idyll on which **Izaak Walton** drew for *The Compleat Angler*. He also wrote a prose romance, *The Strange Fortune of Two Excellent Princes* (1600), and a collection of character observations, *Fantasticks* (1626).

Brett, Jeremy, *originally* **Jeremy Huggins** 1933–95 •*English actor*• Born in Berkswell, Warwickshire, he won acclaim for his classical performances with the Old Vic. On television, he played various leading parts before his definitive portrayal of Sir **Arthur Conan Doyle**'s Victorian sleuth in *The Adventures of Sherlock Holmes* (1984–85), *The Return of Sherlock Holmes* (1986–88), *The Casebook of Sherlock Holmes* (1991) and *The Memoirs of Sherlock Holmes* (1994), as well as several specials.

Breuer, Marcel Lajos 1902–81 •*US architect and designer*• Born in Pécs, Hungary, he was a student at the Bauhaus in Germany from 1920, and by 1924 had taken charge of the furniture workshop. He designed probably the first modern tubular steel chair, the "Wassily" (1925), and the well-known "Cesca" cantilevered chair (1928). In 1937 he joined **Walter Gropius** in the US as Associate Professor of Architecture at Harvard University (1937–46) and in architectural practice. Working independently after 1947, he designed buildings such as the UNESCO building in Paris (with Bernard Zehrfuss and **Pier Luigi Nervi** in 1958) and the Whitney Museum in New York City (1966).

Breughel *See* **Brueghel**

Breuil, Henri Édouard Prosper 1877–1961 •*French archaeologist*• Born in Mortain, he trained as a priest, became interested in cave art in 1900, and was responsible the following year for the discovery of the famous decorated caves at Combarelles and Font-de-Gaume in the Dordogne. Noted for his studies of artistic technique, he later became professor at the Collège de France (1929–47), and his work marked the beginning of the study of Paleolithic art, as shown by his *Quatre cents siècles de l'art pariétal* (1952, "Four Hundred Centuries of Cave Art").

Brewer, Ebenezer Cobham 1810–97 •*English clergyman*• Born in London, he took a first-class degree in law at Trinity Hall, Cambridge, in 1835, one year after receiving orders. He then became a London schoolmaster. His most enduring work is his *Dictionary of Phrase and Fable* (1870), still a standard work of reference.

Brewster, Sir David 1781–1868 •*Scottish physicist*• Born in Jedburgh, Roxburghshire, he was interested in the study of optics, and in 1815 he observed that measurement of the angle at which reflected light is polarized enables the calculation of the refractive index of a glass surface (Brewster's law). In the same year he showed that stress on transparent materials can alter the way in which they transmit light. In 1816 he invented the kaleidoscope, and later improved Sir **Charles Wheatstone**'s stereoscope by fitting refracting lenses. He was one of the chief originators of the British Association for the Advancement of Science (1831), and was knighted in 1832.

Brezhnev, Leonid Ilyich 1906–82 •*Soviet statesman*• Born in Kamenskoye (then called Dneprodzerzhinsk), Ukraine, the son of a steelworker, he joined the Komsomol (Communist Youth League) in 1923 and, having trained as an agricultural surveyor, worked on the collectivization programs in Belorussia (Belarus) and the Urals region during the 1920s. He was accepted into the Communist Party (CPSU) in 1931, and in 1938 was appointed party propaganda chief at Dnepropetrovsk. Between 1941 and 1945 he served as a political commissar to the Southern Army and after the war was sent to Moldavia (Moldova) as party chief (1950–52) to "sovietize" the newly ceded republic. The CPSU leader, **Joseph Stalin**, inducted Brezhnev into the secretariat and the politburo as a "candidate" member (1952). Brezhnev was removed from these posts following Stalin's death in 1953, but, with **Khrushchev**'s patronage, returned to favor in 1954, being sent to Kazakhstan to oversee implementation of the new "virgin lands" agricultural program. He was elected the new CPSU General Secretary in 1964, when Khrushchev was ousted. He emerged as an international statesman during the early 1970s, although during the later 1970s, as his health deteriorated, policymaking became paralyzed and economic difficulties mounted. The Brezhnev era saw the Soviet Union establish itself as a military and political superpower, extending its influence in Africa and Asia. At home, however, it was a period of caution and, during the 1970s, of economic stagnation.

“ ”

She is trying to wear the trousers of Winston Churchill.

1979 Of Margaret Thatcher. Speech.

Brian c. 926–1014 •*King of Ireland*• The "Brian Boroimhe" or "Boru" ("Brian of the tribute") of the annalists, he became chief of Dál Cais in 976, and after much fighting he made himself king of Leinster (984). After further campaigns in all parts of the country, his rule was acknowledged over the whole of Ireland (1002). He was killed after defeating the Vikings at Clontarf.

Briand, Aristide 1862–1932 •*French socialist statesman and Nobel Prize winner*• Born in Nantes, he began his political career on the extreme left, advocating a revolutionary general strike, but soon moved to the center as a "republican socialist," refusing to join the United Socialist Party (SFIO, Section Française de l'Internationale Ouvrière), which did not allow its members to participate in "bourgeois" governments. He held ministerial office almost continuously from 1906, being a Cabinet Minister 25 times, and Prime Minister 11 times. With **Jean Jaurès** he founded the socialist paper *L'humanité* (1904). He was a fervent advocate of the League of Nations, and of Franco-German reconciliation. He shared the 1926 Nobel Peace Prize with **Gustav Stresemann**, concluded the **Kellogg**-Briand Pact which proscribed war as a means of solving disputes (1928), and launched the idea of a United States of Europe (1929).

Brice, Fanny, *originally* **Fanny Borach** 1891–1951 •*US singer and actress*• Born in New York, she sang as a child in her parents' saloon, then won a singing contest at 13. She toured in the comedy *College Girls*, and was signed by **Florenz Ziegfeld** for the *Follies of 1910*, where her vivacious style made her a star. She performed in many other shows and revues, and was adept at both comic and torch songs. She married a well-known gangster, Nicky Arnstein, and her life story provided the basis of the hit musical *Funny Girl* (1964, filmed 1968).

Brickhill, Paul Chester Jerome 1916–91 •*Australian writer*• Born in Melbourne, and educated at Sydney University, he worked in journalism before serving with the Royal Australian Air Force during World War II. Shot down in North Africa, he was for two years a prisoner of war in Germany, in Stalag Luft III from which the intrepid escape was made, later described by him in *The Great Escape* (1951, filmed 1963). His first published book, *Escape to Danger* (1946), collected many stories of prison-camp life. He went on to become one of the most successful nonfiction writers of the postwar period, with *The Dam Busters* (1951, filmed 1956), *Escape—or Die* (1952), and the story of the amputee air ace **Douglas Bader**, *Reach for the Sky* (1954, filmed 1956).

Bridger, James, *usually known as* **Jim** 1804–81 •*US frontiersman and scout*• Born in Richmond, Virginia, he was apprenticed to a blacksmith but abandoned the trade to become a fur trapper in the frontier wilderness of the 1820s. A famous mountain man and the first white man to see the Great Salt Lake (1824), he operated the Rocky Mountain Fur Co. until the fur trade began to decline in the 1830s. Using Fort Bridger on the Oregon Trail as his home base, he later served as scout and guide for exploring and surveying expeditions.

Bridges, Jeff 1949– •*US actor*• Born in Los Angeles, the son of actor Lloyd Bridges (1913–98), he received Academy Award nominations for *The Last Picture Show* (1971), *Thunderbolt and Lightfoot* (1974), *Starman* (1984) and *The Contender* and has proved himself a versatile actor, mixing populist mainstream fare with more offbeat character roles. Later films include *Jagged Edge* (1985), *The Fabulous Baker Boys* (1989), in which he costarred with his brother Beau (1941–), *The Fisher King* (1991), *The Big Lebowski* (1998) and *Seabiscuit* (2003).

Bridges, Robert Seymour 1844–1930 •*English poet and critic*• Born in Walmer, Kent, he was educated at Eton and Corpus Christi College, Oxford, then studied medicine at St Bartholomew's Hospital. At university he met **Gerard Manley Hopkins** and arranged for the posthumous publication of his poems in 1918. Bridges's first collection, *Poems*, appeared in 1873, and was followed by two long poems, *Prometheus the Firegiver* (1883) and *Eros and Psyche* (1885), and several plays, only one of which was performed in his lifetime. He contributed to criticism with studies of **Milton** (1893) and **Keats** (1895). In 1912 he published his *Collected Poems* and in 1913 was appointed Poet Laureate, producing *The Spirit of Man* (1916) and the long poem *The Testament of Beauty* (1929).

Bridget, St, *also called* **St Brigid** or **St Bride** c. 453–523 •*Irish abbess*• Born (according to tradition) in Fochart, County Louth, she is said to be the daughter of a peasant woman and an Ulster prince. She entered a convent at Meath at 13, and founded four monasteries for women, the chief at Kildare (c. 470), where she was buried. Her legendary history includes many miracles, some of which were apparently transferred to her from the Celtic goddess, Ceridwen. One of the three great saints of Ireland (with **St Patrick** and **St Columba**), she is patron saint of Leinster and was also revered in Scotland (as St Bride). Her feast day is February 1.

Bridget, St *See also* **Birgitta, St**

Bridgman, Laura Dewey 1829–89 •*US teacher, devoid of sight, hearing and speech*• Born in Hanover, New Hampshire, at the age of two a violent fever destroyed her sight, hearing, smell, and to some degree taste. Dr **Samuel Howe** educated her systematically using a kind of raised alphabet at his Perkins School for the Blind, and she became a skillful teacher of others with the same disabilities. She is referred to in **Charles Dickens**'s *American Notes* (1842).

Bridgman, P(ercy) W(illiams) 1882–1961 •*US physicist and Nobel Prize winner*• Born in Cambridge, Massachusetts, he studied and taught at Harvard. Soon after completing his PhD in 1908 he initiated experiments on the properties of solids and liquids under high pressure, obtaining a new form of phosphorus, and demonstrated that at high pressures viscosity increases with pressure for most liquids. He was awarded the Nobel Prize for physics in 1946. In 1961 he became increasingly debilitated and incurably ill with cancer, and took his own life.

Bridport, 1st Viscount *See* **Hood, Alexander**

Brierley, Sir Ron(ald Alfred) 1937– •*New Zealand entrepreneur*• Born in Wellington and educated at Wellington College, he founded what was to become Brierley Investments Limited in 1961 and moved his operations to Sydney in the early 1970s. He sold his Industrial Equities conglomerate just before the 1987 crash and later became chairman of the UK-based Guinness Peat Group (1990–). He has also played a significant role in New Zealand's cricket fraternity. He was knighted in 1988.

Briers, Richard David 1934– •*English actor*• Born in Merton, Surrey, he studied at the Royal Academy of Dramatic Art. His stage work is extensive, encompassing roles in plays by **Shakespeare**, **Chekhov** and **Stoppard**, and he has acted in films including *Hamlet* (1996) and *Unconditional Love* (2000). He is perhaps best known for his roles in British television sitcoms such as *The Good Life* (1975–78) and *Ever-Decreasing Circles* (1984–89). He was given the honorary title Officer, Order of the British Empire, in 1989.

Briggs, Barry 1934– •*New Zealand speedway rider*• Born in Christchurch, he appeared in a record 17 consecutive world championship finals (1954–70), during which he scored a record 201 points and took part in 87 races, winning the title in 1957–58, 1964, and 1966. He won the British League Riders' championship six times (1965–70). Given the honorary title Member, Order of the British Empire, in 1973, he retired in 1976.

Briggs, Raymond Redvers 1934– •*English children's illustrator and writer*• He was born in London. His early publications, such as *Midnight Adventure* (1961), were conventional, but his *Mother Goose Treasury* (1966), with over 900 illustrations, established his reputation for eccentric comedy, and won him the **Kate Greenaway** Medal. He was awarded a second Greenaway Medal for *Father Christmas* (1973), which uses the comic-strip format, and features a grumpy, expletory Santa. *Fungus the Bogeyman* (1977) brought Briggs love and loathing, and *The Snowman* (1979, animated film 1982) enchanted adults and children alike. A provocative as well as an entertaining artist, he expressed his anxiety for the future well-being of the planet in *When the Wind Blows* (1982). In 1992 he was awarded the Kurt Maschler award for *The Man*. Later works include *The Bear* (1994) and *Ethel and Ernest* (1998).

Brighouse, Harold 1882–1958 •*English playwright*• He was born near Manchester, one of the first 20th-century English authors to write plays that were both popular and set beyond the metropolitan and country-house world of the fashionable and wealthy. Between 1909 and his death he completed over 70 plays, many of them amiably folksy one-act comedies set in Lancashire. His reputation depends on only one play, *Hobson's Choice* (1915). It was highly popular at the time, and is frequently revived.

Bright, John 1811–89 •*English orator and radical politician*• Born in Rochdale, Lancashire, he was the son of a Quaker cotton spinner. When the Anti-Corn Law League was formed in 1839 he was a leading member, and, with **Richard Cobden**, engaged in free-trade agitation. He became Member of Parliament for Durham (1843) and strongly opposed the Corn Laws until they were repealed. He was elected Member of Parliament for Manchester in 1847. Elected in 1857 for Birmingham, he seconded the motion against the Conspiracy Bill which led to the overthrow of Lord **Palmerston**'s government. His name was closely associated with the Reform Act of 1867. He retired from the **Gladstone** ministry in 1882, opposing his Home Rule policy (1886–88).

Brigid, St *See* **Bridget, St**

Brillat-Savarin, (Jean) Anthelme 1755–1826 •*French lawyer, gastronome and writer*• Born in Belley, he became a deputy there in 1789, and mayor in 1793. During the French Revolution he took refuge in Switzerland, and later the US, where he played in the orchestra of a New York theater. From 1796 until his death he was a member of the Court of Cassation, the French high court. His *Physiologie du goût* (1825, "The Physiology of Taste"), an elegant and witty compendium on the art of dining, has appeared in numerous editions and translations, including *A Handbook of Gastronomy*.

“ ”

Tell me what you eat and I will tell you what you are.

*1825 **Physiologie du goût**, aphorism 4 (translated by Anne Drayton, 1970).*

Brink, André 1935– •*South African writer, critic and translator*• He was born in Vrede, Orange Free State, educated in both South Africa and France, and became Professor of Afrikaans and Dutch Literature at Rhodes University, Grahamstown (1980–90), before going on to become Professor of English at the University of Cape Town. An Afrikaner dissident, he emerged as a writer in the 1950s but it was not until his seventh novel, *Kennis van die aand* (1973)—which he later translated into English as *Looking on Darkness* (1974)—was banned by the South African authorities that he began to attract international attention. Relating the story of a Black actor who makes good in London and returns to South Africa to confront the apartheid regime, it won the author admiration, though more for his courage than his style. Subsequent books have been criticized for their sentimentality and sensationalism but the best, such as *Rumours of Rain* (1978), *A Chain of Voices* (1982) and *States of Emergency* (1988), are powerful narratives which highlight conditions in South Africa without resorting to propaganda. Later works include *The Rights of Desire* (2001) and *The Other Side of Silence* (2002).

Brinkley, David McClure 1920–2003 •*US news commentator*• Born in Wilmington, North Carolina, he began his career as a reporter for his hometown newspaper. In 1943 he became a newswriter and television broadcaster for NBC in Washington DC. From 1951 to 1981 he was the network's Washington correspondent, and from 1956 to 1970 he coanchored a popular NBC nightly news program, the *Huntley-Brinkley Report*, with Chet Huntley (1911–74). From 1981 to 1997 he hosted *ABC This Week*, a weekly news program. He was the recipient of numerous journalism awards, including the Presidential Medal of Freedom (1992).

Brinster, Ralph Lawrence 1932– •*US molecular biologist*• Born in Montclair, New Jersey, he was educated at Rutgers University and at the University of Pennsylvania. With Richard Palmiter (1942–), he was the first to successfully inject the human growth hormone gene into a mouse embryo and replace the embryo into the mother's uterus. These mice proved to be significantly larger than their normal counterparts, indicating that the human growth hormone gene had been active. It is hoped that the technique can be extended to replace faulty genes in human genetic diseases such as cystic fibrosis.

Brisley, Stuart 1933– •*English sculptor and performance artist*• Born at Grayswood, near Haslemere, Surrey, he studied at Guildford School of Art and the Royal College of Art, then at the Universities of Munich and Florida. He came to public notice with his ritualistic performances; in 1972 he lay in a bath while meat rotted on the floor until after 10 days, his fellow artists begged him to stop. In 1973 he performed *Ten Days* over the Christmas period in Berlin, refusing *haute cuisine* food and leaving it to rot, as a comment on overconsumption in the West. Other shows include *Survival in Alien Circumstances*, in which he dug a hole and lived in it for two weeks. In 1985 his sound installation on the subject of nuclear attack, *Normal Activities May Be Resumed*, was held at the Institute of Contemporary Arts, London. Later works and exhibitions include *Black* (1996), *Trash* (1997) and *Legs* (2000).

Brissot (de Warville), Jacques Pierre 1754–93 •*French revolutionary*• Born near Chartres, he was a lawyer and journalist who wrote on criminal law. In 1789 he was present at the storming of the Bastille, and was elected Representative for Paris in the National Assembly, where he influenced the early movements of the Revolution. He became leader of the Girondins (or Brissotins), and contributed to the fall of the monarchy, but in the Convention his moderation made him suspect to **Robespierre**, and, with 20 other Girondins, he was guillotined.

Britannicus, *in full* **Claudius Tiberius Britannicus Caesar** AD 41–55 •*Emperor's son*• He was the son of the emperor **Claudius** and **Messalina**, and was surnamed in honor of his father's triumph in Britain (AD 43). Claudius's fourth wife, **Agrippina the Younger**, caused her husband to adopt her son **Nero**, and treat Britannicus as an imbecile. Nero, after his accession, had his stepbrother poisoned, claiming he was subject to epileptic fits. He is the subject of a tragedy by **Racine**.

Brittain, Vera Mary 1893–1970 •*English writer, feminist and pacifist*• She was born in Newcastle-under-Lyme, Staffordshire. After studying at Oxford she served as a nurse in World War I, recording her experiences in her best-known book, *Testament of Youth* (1933, republished 1978). *Testament of Friendship* (1940) and *Testament of Experience* (1957) followed. As well as writing a number of novels, she made several lecture tours in the US, promoting feminism and pacifism. Her daughter is the English politician **Shirley Williams**.

Brittan, Leon Brittan, Baron 1939– •*English Conservative politician*• Born in London and educated at Trinity College, Cambridge, and Harvard, he qualified as a barrister. He was chairman of the Conservative Bow Group (1964–65) and elected as a Member of Parliament in 1974. From 1979 he held ministerial posts under **Margaret Thatcher**, but resigned from the Cabinet in 1986 after a conflict with **Michael Heseltine** (Secretary for Defense) over the takeover of Westland Helicopters. He was vice president of the European Commission (1989–93, 1995–99) and a Member of the European Parliament (1989–99), and is Chancellor of the University of Teeside (1993–). He was knighted in 1989 and became a life peer in 2000.

Britten (of Aldeburgh), (Edward) Benjamin Britten, Baron 1913–76 •*English composer*• Born in Lowestoft, he studied the piano under Harold Samuel (1879–1937) and composition under Frank Bridge (1879–1941). Awarded a scholarship to the Royal College of Music, he worked there under **John Ireland** and was already a prolific composer. During the 1930s Britten wrote a great deal of incidental music for plays and documentary films, collaborating at times with **W H Auden**, whose poetry provided texts for the song cycles *Our Hunting Fathers* (1936) and *On This Island* (1937). From 1939 to 1942 Britten worked in the US, producing his large-scale instrumental works, the Violin Concerto (1939) and the *Sinfonia da Requiem* (1940). After his return to the UK, his works were mostly vocal and choral; significant exceptions are the Variations and Fugue on a Theme of Purcell (*The Young Person's Guide to the Orchestra*, 1946), the String Quartets no. 1 (1941) and no. 3 (1945), the Cello Symphony (1963), the Cello Sonata (1961) and three suites for solo cello (1964, 1967, 1972). After 1945, in addition to his choral and vocal works, Britten's reputation was due largely to his achievement in opera. His first operatic success was *Peter Grimes* (1945). Britten wrote two further operas on a large scale, *Billy Budd* (1951) and *Gloriana* (1953), the latter for the coronation of Queen **Elizabeth II**, and five "chamber operas," including *The Turn of the Screw* (1954, based on the **Henry James** novella), which are on a smaller scale and employ a basic orchestra of 12 players. Britten also composed a number of "children's operas," including *Let's Make an Opera!* (1949) and *Noye's Fludde* (1958). His later operas include *A Midsummer Night's Dream* (1960), *Owen Wingrave* (1970) and *Death in Venice* (1973). In addition to his enormous activity as a composer, Britten was an accomplished pianist, usually heard as an accompanist, particularly of his partner **Peter Pears**, with whom he and Eric Crozier founded in 1948 the annual Aldeburgh Festival. He was awarded a life peerage in 1976.

" "

I remember the first time I tried the result looked rather like the Forth Bridge.

1964 Of his first attempts at composition. Quoted in the ***Sunday Telegraph***.

Britton, Alison 1948– •*English potter*• Born in Harrow, Middlesex, she was trained at Leeds School of Art, the Central School of Art and Design and the Royal College of Art. Her unique hand-built, high-fired earthenware, often with hand-painted and inlaid patterns, broke new ground in an era when many of the traditional values of wheelmade pottery gave way to a more expressive generation of potters.

Broadbent, Jim 1949– •*British actor*• Born in Lincolnshire, he studied at the London Academy of Music and Dramatic Arts, later becoming a member of both the National Theatre and the Royal Shakespeare Company. He was cofounder of the comedy team the National Theatre of Brent and has appeared in films such as *Life Is Sweet* (1991), *Enchanted April* (1992), *Bullets over Broadway* (1994), *Little Voice* (1998), *Bridget Jones's Diary* (2001), *Moulin Rouge* (2001) and *Iris* (2001; Academy Award for Best Supporting Actor). His television credits include appearances in *Not the Nine O' Clock News* (1972–82) and *Blackadder* (1983–89).

Broca, (Pierre) Paul 1824–80 •*French surgeon and anthropologist*• Born in Sainte-Foy-la-Grande, Gironde, he was educated at the University of Paris, where he later taught medicine. He first located the motor speech center in the brain (1861), since known as the convolution of Broca or Broca's gyrus, and did research on prehistoric surgical operations. His anthropological investigations gave strong support to **Charles Darwin**'s theory of the evolutionary descent of man.

Broch, Hermann 1886–1951 •*Austrian novelist and essayist*• Born in Vienna, he spent his early adult life working in his father's textile business and was over 40 when he went to Vienna University to study philosophy and mathematics. When the Nazis invaded Austria in 1938 he was imprisoned, but influential friends, including **James Joyce**, obtained his release and facilitated his emigration to the US in 1940. His masterpiece is *Der Tod des Virgil* (1945, Eng trans *The Death of Virgil*, 1946). Other notable books include *Die Schlafwandler* (3 vols, 1931–32, Eng trans *The Sleepwalkers*) and *Der Versucher* (Eng trans *The Spell*) published posthumously in 1953 and first translated into English in 1987.

Brockhurst, Gerald Leslie 1891–1979 •*English artist and etcher*• Born in Birmingham, he studied at the Birmingham School of Art. His etchings and lithographs are mainly concerned with the themes of young womanhood and portraiture. He was influenced by the early Italian Renaissance painters and his masterpiece, *Adolescence*, was exhibited at the Royal Academy, London, in 1933.

Brockway, (Archibald) Fenner Brockway, Baron 1888–1988 •*English politician, pacifist and a founder of the Campaign for Nuclear Disarmament*• He was born in Calcutta, India, into a missionary family, and educated at the School for the Sons of Missionaries (now Eltham College) at Blackheath in England. As a young journalist he was converted to socialism by an interview with **Keir Hardie**. He joined the Independent Labour Party and became a militant pacifist, and was imprisoned during World War I. In the 1930s he claimed to have been the last socialist to speak publicly in Germany before **Hitler** came to power (1933). He was elected to parliament for the first time in 1929–31, and again in 1950–64. He was made a life peer in 1964, and wrote more than 20 books, including several autobiographical volumes. He died six months before his hundredth birthday.

Brod, Max 1884–1968 •*Austrian novelist, biographer, essayist, poet and dramatist*• Born in Prague, he became a Zionist and emigrated to Palestine in 1939, where he became the literary director of the Habimah Theater in Tel Aviv. Although he is known in the English-speaking world as the long-time friend, editor and biographer of **Franz Kafka**, he was a versatile and prolific writer in his own right, publishing, among others, *Die Frau, nach der man sich sehnt* (1927, Eng trans *Three Loves*), *Zauberreich der Liebe* (1928, The Magic Realm of Love") and *Tycho Brahes Weg zu Gott* (1916, Eng trans *The Redemption of Tycho Brahe*). He also produced plays, autobiographical writings and literary criticism.

Brodie, William, *known as* **Deacon Brodie** 1741–88 •*Scottish cabinetmaker and burglar*• Born in Edinburgh, the son of a wealthy wright (carpenter) and cabinetmaker, he followed his father in business and also became a deacon on the town council. Though highly regarded in society, his private life, which included two mistresses and five children, and a predilection for gambling, put him under financial pressure. By 1785 he had squandered his inheritance and so turned to burgling the homes of his acquaintances. In 1786 he enlisted the help of three professional criminals. Together they carried out a number of thefts, including that of the silver mace from the University of Edinburgh. In 1788 the gang was unsuccessful in its attempt to break into the Excise Office of Scotland, and Brodie fled to Holland. He was brought back to Edinburgh, stood trial and was hanged outside St Giles High Kirk, on a new gallows which he himself had designed.

Brodsky, Iosif Aleksandrovich 1940–96 •*US-Russian poet, translator and critic, and Nobel Prize winner*• Born in Leningrad (now St Petersburg), he was tried as a "social parasite" in 1964, and sent into exile. Although not known generally, he had poetry circulated in *samizdat* form, and various critics and poets interceded on his behalf. His cause was taken up in the US, but in 1972 he was expelled from Russia. In 1977 he became a US citizen, and in 1987 he was awarded the Nobel Prize for literature. Some of his later work was written in English and he also translated his own Russian poems into English. His many collections include *Stikhotvoreniya i poemy* (1965, "Longer and Shorter Poems"), *Uraniya: Novaya kniga stikhov* (1985, "Urania: A New Book of Poems," published in English as *To Urania: Selected Poems 1965–1985*, 1988) and *Pereshchyonnaya mesnost'* (1995, "Broken Country"). His translations of **John Donne** and **Andrew Marvell** into Russian are particularly prized. He became US Poet Laureate in 1991 and in 1992 published *Watermark*, a prose work on Venice.

Broglie, Louis-Victor Pierre Raymond, 7th Duc de 1892–1987 •*French physicist and Nobel Prize winner*• Born in Dieppe, he studied at the Sorbonne. Influenced by **Einstein**'s work on the photoelectric effect, which he interpreted as showing that waves can behave as particles, Broglie put forward the converse idea—that particles can behave as waves. The waves were detected experimentally by **Clinton Davisson** and Lester Germerin 1927, and separately by Sir **George Thomson**, and the idea of wave-particle duality was used by **Erwin Schrödinger** in his development of quantum mechanics. Broglie was awarded the Nobel Prize for physics in 1929.

Brome, Richard c. 1590–1652 •*English dramatist*• Little is known of him except that a note in the Biographica Dramatica of 1764 records he had "originally been no better than a menial servant to the celebrated **Ben Jonson**." Brome specialized in satirical comedies, and his works include *The Northern Lass* (1629), *The City Wit* (1630), about a man taking revenge on his mother-in-law and his wife's suitors, and *A Jovial Crew* (1641).

Bromfield, Louis 1896–1956 •*US novelist*• Born in Mansfield, Ohio, he was educated at Cornell Agricultural College and Columbia University, then served in the French army (from 1914), winning the Croix de Guerre. He returned to the US and published a number of novels on US life, including *Early Autumn* (1926, Pulitzer Prize), *The Rains Came* (1937), *Colorado* (1947), and *Mr Smith* (1951). His other works include the short story, *Awake and Rehearse* (1929), and the play, *The House of Women* (1927).

Bronhill, June, *originally* **June Gough** 1929– •*Australian soprano*• Born in Broken Hill, New South Wales, she adapted her stage name from this place. In 1954 she was an immediate success at Sadler's Wells in musicals such as *Robert and Elizabeth* and *The Sound of Music*, and in operetta, particularly as *The Merry Widow* (*Die lustige Witwe*). Later, she took the lead in *The Bride of Lammermoor* (*Lucia di Lammermoor*) at Covent Garden, London (1959). More recently she has appeared in speaking roles, especially in comedy, such as in *Arsenic and Old Lace* (1991).

Bronowski, Jacob 1908–74 •*Polish mathematician, poet and humanist*•Born in Łódź, Poland, he spent World War I with his grandparents in Germany, and went with them to live in England in 1920. He was educated at Jesus College, Cambridge, and became a lecturer at University College, Hull (1934–42), then left to develop operations research methods for the government. He became director of the Coal Research Establishment of the National Coal Board, and oversaw the development of smokeless fuel. He was a popular broadcaster, particularly in the BBC's *Brains Trust* and *The Ascent of Man* (1973).

“ ”

That is the essence of science: ask an impertinent question and you are on the way to a pertinent answer.

1973 ***The Ascent of Man****, chapter 4.*

Bronson, Charles, *originally* **Charles Buchinsky** 1922–2003 •*US actor*• He was born in Ehrenfield, Pennsylvania, and after service during World War II as a tailgunner, studied at California's Pasadena Playhouse. He made his reputation with *The Magnificent Seven* (1960), and was thereafter known for violent action films, especially the *Death Wish* series (beginning 1974). Other films include *The Dirty Dozen* (1967), *Breakheart Pass* (1975), *Murphy's Law* (1986), *The Indian Runner* (1991) and *Dead to Rights* (1995).

Brønsted, Johannes Nicolaus 1879–1947 •*Danish physical chemist*• Born in Varde, Jutland, he studied chemistry at the University of Copenhagen, where in 1908 he was appointed to the new chair of physical chemistry. In 1930 he became director of a new Physico-Chemical Institute in Copenhagen. Most of his contributions to physical chemistry concerned the behavior of solutions. His studies of the effect of ionic strength on the solubilities of sparingly soluble salts provided strong experimental support for the **Debye-Hückel** theory (1923) and his analogous studies of rates of reaction involving ions were also interpreted in terms of the same theory (1920–24). He is known for a novel and valuable definition of acids and bases, the Brønsted-**Lowry** definition, which describes an acid as a substance with a tendency to lose a proton, and a base as a substance that tends to gain a proton.

Brontë, Anne, *pseudonym* **Acton Bell** 1820–49 Born in Thornton, Yorkshire, the daughter of Patrick Brontë (1777–1861), a clergyman of Irish descent, and his Cornish wife, Maria (1783–1821), and the sister of **Charlotte** and **Emily Brontë** and Branwell (1817–48), Anne worked as a governess, but had to leave her second post because of her brother's infatuation with her employer. As well as sharing in the collection of poems which the sisters published in 1846 (under the names Currer Bell (Charlotte), Ellis Bell (Emily) and Acton Bell (Anne)), she wrote two novels, *Agnes Grey* (1845) and *The Tenant of Wildfell Hall* (1848); these are generally regarded as lesser works than those of her sisters, although *Wildfell Hall*, with its controversial subject matter and questioning of the status of married women, had a certain success.

Brontë, Charlotte, *pseudonym* **Currer Bell** 1816–55 Born in Thornton, Yorkshire, the daughter of Patrick Brontë (1777–1861), a clergyman of Irish descent, and his Cornish wife, Maria (1783–1821), and the sister of **Anne** and **Emily Brontë** and Branwell (1817–48), Charlotte worked for a time as a teacher and governess. In Brussels (1843–44), she formed an attachment to a married man, M Constantin Heger, who rejected her; she later scornfully satirized him in *Villette* (1852). Charlotte wrote four complete novels. *The Professor*, which was not published until after her death, dwells on the theme of moral madness, possibly inspired by Branwell's degeneration. It was rejected by her publisher, but with sufficient encouragement for her to complete her masterpiece, *Jane Eyre* (1847). This in essence, through the master-pupil love relationship between Rochester and Jane, constituted a magnificent plea for feminine equality with men in the avowal of their passions. It was followed in 1849 by *Shirley*, a novel set against the background of the Luddite riots. By now her brother and two sisters were dead, and she was left alone at Haworth with her father. *Villette*, founded on her memories of Brussels, was published in 1853. In 1850 she met and formed a friendship with **Elizabeth Gaskell**, who wrote a memoir of her. She married her father's curate, Arthur Bell Nicholls, in 1854 but died in pregnancy the following year, leaving the fragment of another novel, *Emma*. Two stories, *The Secret* and *Lily Hart*, were published for the first time in 1978.

Brontë, Emily Jane, *pseudonym* **Ellis Bell** 1818–48 Born in Thornton, Yorkshire, the daughter of Patrick Brontë (1777–1861), a clergyman of Irish descent, and his Cornish wife, Maria (1783–1821), and the sister of **Charlotte** and **Anne Brontë** and Branwell (1817–48), Emily worked as a governess in Halifax. She went to Brussels with Charlotte and in 1845 embarked on a joint publication of poems after Charlottte's discovery of her *Gondal* verse, including such fine items as "To Imagination," "Plead for Me" and "Last Lines." Her single novel, *Wuthering Heights* (1847), is an intense and powerful tale of love and revenge set in the remote wilds of 18th-century Yorkshire; it has much in common with Greek tragedy, and no real counterpart in English literature.

Bronterre *See* **O'Brien, James**

Bronzino, Agnolo, *also called* **Il Bronzino**, *properly* **Agnolo Tori di Cosimo di Moriano** 1503–72 •*Italian Mannerist painter*• Born in Monticelli, he was a pupil of **Jacopo da Pontormo**, who then adopted him. He decorated the chapel of the Palazzo Vecchio in Florence, and painted the *Christ in Limbo* (1552) in the Uffizi, Florence. His *Venus, Folly, Cupid and Time* (1542–45) is in the National Gallery, London, and his portraits include most of the **Medici** family, **Dante**, **Boccaccio** and **Petrarch**.

Brook, Peter Stephen Paul 1925– •*English theater and film director*• He was born in London and educated at Westminster, Greshams and Magdalen College, Oxford. In 1944 he joined a film company but left the following year to direct **Jean Cocteau**'s *The Infernal Machine*, after which he directed many classical plays at the Birmingham Repertory Theatre, including a notable production of *King John* by **Shakespeare**. In Brook's first season at Stratford (1947), his highly original production of *Romeo and Juliet* did not meet with wide critical acclaim. From 1947 to 1950 he was also director of productions at the Royal Opera House, Covent Garden, London, and during the 1950s he worked on many productions in Great Britain, Europe and the US. In 1962 he returned to Stratford to join the newly established Royal Shakespeare Company for which he directed, among other productions, the legendary **Paul Scofield**'s *King Lear* (1963), *Marat/Sade* (1964), *U.S.* (1966), and in 1970 his greatly acclaimed *Midsummer Night's Dream*. Most of his work in the 1970s was done with the Paris-based Center for Theater Research, which he helped to set up in 1970 and with which he has traveled widely in Africa and Asia; in 1978 he again returned to Stratford to direct *Antony and Cleopatra*. Among his films are *The Beggar's Opera* (1952), *Lord of the Flies* (1962), *Marat/Sade* (1967) and *Meetings with Remarkable Men* (1979). Later Paris productions include a nine-hour adaptation of *The Mahabharata*. In 2001 his London production of *Hamlet* was highly acclaimed. Brook's work is difficult to categorize and difficult to assess, although he is acknowledged to be "the director's director." He was made Companion of Honour in 1998.

Brooke, 1st Baron *See* **Greville, Sir Fulke**

Brooke, Sir Basil Stanlake *See* **Brookeborough, 1st Viscount**

Brooke, Edward William 1919– •*US politician*• He was born in Washington DC. After serving with distinction as attorney general of Massachusetts, where he worked to expose corruption in state government, he became the first African American elected to the US Senate since Reconstruction. A Republican, he served from 1967 to 1979.

Brooke, Sir James 1803–68 •*English soldier, and raja of Sarawak*• He was born in Benares, India, and educated in Norwich, Norfolk. In 1838 he sailed in a schooner-yacht from London for Sarawak, a province on the northwest coast of Borneo, with the aim of defeating piracy. Made Raja of Sarawak (1841) for assisting the local sultan against Dayak rebel tribes, he framed a new code of laws, declared the Dayak custom of headhunting a capital crime, and vigorously set about suppressing piracy. In 1857 Brooke repelled, with native forces, a series of attacks by a large body of Chinese, who had been irritated by his efforts to prevent opium smuggling.

Brooke, Peter Leonard, Baron 1934– •*English Conservative politician*• He was born in London, educated at Marlborough and Balliol College, Oxford, and entered the House of Commons as Member of Parliament for the City of London and Westminster South in 1977. He then advanced through a series of ministerial posts to replace **Norman Tebbit** as chairman of the Conservative Party in 1987. He was Secretary of State for Northern Ireland (1989–92), Secretary of State for National Heritage (1992–94), then chaired the House of Commons Select Committee on Northern Ireland from 1997, before retiring as a Member of Parliament and receiving a life peerage in 2001. He was created Companion of Honour in 1992.

Brooke, Rupert Chawner 1887–1915 •*English poet*•He was born at Rugby school, where his father was a master, and educated at King's College, Cambridge. In 1909 he settled in Granchester, and began to publish his poetry in journals, and also traveled in Germany, later visiting the US and Tahiti. His *Poems* appeared in 1911, and he also contributed to the first and second volumes of *Georgian Poetry.* Five war sonnets were published in 1915 and brought him great public recognition, which was increased by *1914 and Other Poems*, published in 1915, after his death. He died a commissioned officer on Skyros on his way to the Dardanelles and was buried there.

Brookeborough, Sir Basil Stanlake Brooke, 1st Viscount 1888–1973 •*Northern Irish statesman*• Born in Fermanagh, he was elected to the Northern Ireland parliament in 1929. He became Minister of Agriculture in 1933, Minister of Commerce in 1941, and Prime Minister from 1943 until his resignation in 1963. A staunch supporter of Unionist policy, he exhibited an unswerving determination to preserve the ties between Northern Ireland and Great Britain. He retired from politics in 1968.

Brookes, Sir Norman Everard 1877–1968 •*Australian tennis player*• Born in Melbourne, he went to Wimbledon in 1905, winning the all-comers' singles title, and returned the following year to win the singles, doubles, and mixed doubles titles. In the same year, he and Anthony Wilding achieved Australasia's first victory in the Davis Cup. He won again at Wimbledon in 1914 and, after service in World War I, played Davis Cup tennis until 1921, and captained six winning teams. He was also a national golf champion. He was knighted in 1939.

Brookner, Anita 1928– •*English novelist and art historian*• She was born in London. An authority on 18th-century painting, she was the first woman Slade Professor at Cambridge (1967–68), and was a Reader at the Courtauld Institute of Art (1977–88). She is the author of *Watteau* (1968) and *Jacques-Louis David* (1981). As a novelist she was a late starter, but in 12 years (1981–92) she published as many novels, elegant, witty and imbued with cosmopolitan melancholy. Invariably, her main characters are women, self-sufficient in all but love. By winning the Booker Prize, *Hôtel du lac* (1984) has become her best-known novel, and it is regarded by many as her most accomplished. Other titles include *Brief Lives* (1990), *Fraud* (1992), *Visitors* (1997), *Undue Influence* (1999) and *The Bay of Angels.*

“ ”

It is my contention that Aesop was writing for the tortoise market ... hares have no time to read.

*1984 **Hôtel Du Lac**, chapter 2.*

Brooks, Cleanth 1906–94 •*US academic and critic*• A Rhodes scholar at Exeter College, Oxford, he taught at Louisiana State University (1932–47) and Yale University, where he became Gray Professor of Rhetoric (1960–75). He was crucial in establishing New Criticism as an academic method, in part by jointly editing, with **Robert Penn Warren**, *The Southern Review* (1935–42). Also influential were his works, which included *Understanding Poetry* (1938; written with Warren) and *Literary Criticism: A Short History* (1957; written with William K Wimsatt, Jr).

Brooks, (Troyal) Garth 1962– •*US country music singer*•He was born in Yukon, Oklahoma, and his mother, Colleen Carroll, was a country singer. He has achieved astonishing success, his album sales of over 100 million making him the top-selling solo country artist. *No Fences* (1990) and *Ropin' the Wind* (1991) smashed all previous sales records for country music, and put him alongside the biggest rock and pop acts. His sincerity, spectacular rock-style stage shows and subsequent albums have served to confirm that eminence. In 2000 he announced his retirement from performing to concentrate on low-key projects.

Brooks, Gwendolyn Elizabeth 1917–2000 •*US poet and novelist*• Born in Topeka, Kansas, and brought up in the slums of Chicago, she taught English in a number of colleges, and was Publicity Director of the NAACP (National Association for the Advancement of Colored People) for a time in the 1930s. Her first collection, *A Street in Bronzeville* (1945), established the central theme of her work, chronicling the woes of urban African Americans, and her novel *Annie Allen* (1949) made her the first African American to win the Pulitzer Prize. Subsequent works in both poetry and prose have been increasingly radical in tone, as in *Riot* (1969). Other works include the novel *Maud Martha* (1953), an autobiography, *Report from Part One* (1972), *Winnie* (1988) and *Children Coming Home* (1991).

Brooks, Mel, *originally* **Melvin Kaminsky** 1926– •*US film actor and director*• Born in New York City, after service with the US Army, he performed as a comic in nightclubs and secured employment as a writer for radio and television. He wrote for the comic Sid Caesar on such television programs as *Your Show of Shows* (1950–54) and *Caesar's Hour* (1954–57), won an Academy Award for the short film *The Critic* (1963) and devised the popular series *Get Smart* (1965–70). He made his feature-length cinema debut with *The Producers* (1968), for which he also won an Academy Award, and has proven adept at comedies that spoof the major cinematic genres and skirt the boundaries of good taste. His films include *Blazing Saddles* (1974), *Young Frankenstein* (1974) and *High Anxiety* (1977). His company Brooksfilms has also been responsible for such offbeat fare as *The Elephant Man* (1980) and *The Fly* (1986). A Broadway production of *The Producers* in 2001 won a record 12 Tony awards. He has been married to **Anne Bancroft** since 1964.

Brooks, Van Wyck 1886–1963 •*US author and critic*•He was born in Plainfield, New Jersey, and graduated from Harvard. He spent much of his life as a writer in tracing the cultural and literary history of the US, and in early works such as *The Wine of the Puritans* (1909) he attacked the narrow-mindedness and materialism in US society that he regarded as the legacy of the Puritans. He also wrote biographical studies of US writers, and won the Pulitzer Prize with his *Flowering of New England* (1936), which chronicled the birth of a national literature in the early and mid-19th century.

Broonzy, Big Bill, *real name* **William Lee Conley Broonzy** 1893–1958 •*US blues singer, composer and musician*• Born in Scott, Mississippi, he began his musical life as a fiddler, but switched to guitar when he moved to Chicago in 1920. One of the most eclectic stylists among the great blues performers, he encompassed American folk songs and jazz as well as rural and urban blues. For much of his career his appearances were confined to small clubs and bars throughout the US, but in the 1950s he toured extensively, performing in Europe, Africa and South America.

Brophy, Brigid Antonia 1929–95 •*English writer and critic*• She was born in London and educated at St Paul's Girls' School and at Oxford. Her novels include *Hackenfeller's Ape* (1953), dealing with vivisection, *In Transit* (1969) and *Palace Without Chairs* (1978), on themes of lesbianism and transsexuality, and *The Snow Ball* (1964), in which the characters dress up for a ball as characters from **Mozart**'s *Don Giovanni*. Her critical works include *Mozart the Dramatist* (1964), the controversial *Fifty Works of English Literature We Could Do Without* (1967, jointly with her husband Sir Michael Levey and Charles Osborne) and a study of **Aubrey Beardsley** (1968). She campaigned vigorously against vivisection and in

1972 began a successful campaign for the establishment of a Public Lending Right. In the early 1980s she was afflicted with multiple sclerosis; she wrote about her illness in a collection of essays called *Baroque 'n' Roll* (1985).

Brosnan, Pierce 1953– •*Irish actor*• He was born in Navan and left Ireland at the age of 15 to study at the Drama Center, London. He became well known as the eponymous detective in the television series *Remington Steele* (1982–87), and his early films included *Victim of Love* (1991) and *The Lawnmower Man* (1992). It was as the new James Bond that he gained international stardom, in the films *Goldeneye* (1995), *Tomorrow Never Dies* (1997), *The World Is Not Enough* (1999) and *Die Another Day* (2002).

Brothers, Richard 1757–1824 •*English religious fanatic*• He was born in Newfoundland, of English parents. In 1793 he declared himself to be the "nephew of the Almighty," an apostle of a new religion, the Anglo-Israelites. In 1795, for prophesying the destruction of the monarchy, he was sent to Newgate prison, London, and subsequently to an asylum, but not before he had acquired a number of disciples, some of them men of influence and standing.

Brougham and Vaux, Henry Peter Brougham, 1st Baron 1778–1868 •*Scottish jurist and politician*• Born in Edinburgh, in 1802 he cofounded the influential *Edinburgh Review*. Aware that his liberal views were ahead of their time for Scotland, he moved to London, was called to the bar in 1808, and entered Parliament in 1810. As a barrister, his greatest triumph was the successful defense of Queen **Caroline of Brunswick** in 1820, and, as Lord Chancellor from 1830, he was one of the greatest reformers of the courts, establishing the judicial committee of the Privy Council and the Central Criminal Court. In 1834 he enraged King **William IV** by taking the Great Seal with him on a tour and using it as the centerpiece of a house party game. The brougham carriage was named after him.

" "

A legal gentleman who rescues your estate from your enemies, and keeps it himself.

His definition of a lawyer. Quoted in Richard Fountain ***The Wit of the Wig*** *(1968).*

Broun-Ramsay, James Andrew *See* **Dalhousie, Marquis of**

Brouwer or **Brauer, Adriaen** c. 1605–38 •*Flemish painter*• Born in Oudenarde, he studied at Haarlem under **Frans Hals**, and about 1630 settled at Antwerp. His favorite subjects were scenes from tavern life, country merrymaking, card players and smoking and drinking groups. He was also a notable landscape painter.

Brouwer, Luitzen Egbertus Jan 1881–1966 •*Dutch mathematician*• Born in Overschie, he entered Amsterdam University at the age of 16, where he was professor from 1912 to 1951. His doctoral thesis was on the foundations of mathematics, an area in which he worked throughout his life. He founded the intuitionist or constructivist school of mathematical logic, in which the existence of a mathematical object can only be proved by giving an explicit method for its construction. He also made fundamental advances in topology, and formulated the fixed point theorem named after him.

Brown, Sir Arthur Whitten 1886–1948 •*British aviator*• He was born in Glasgow of US parents. As navigator with Sir **John William Alcock** he made the first nonstop crossing of the Atlantic, in a Vickers-Vimy biplane on June 14, 1919, and shared a £10,000 prize given by the London *Daily Mail*. Both men were knighted after the flight.

Brown, Capability *See* **Brown, Lancelot**

Brown, Ford Madox 1821–93 •*British historical painter*• Born in Calais, France, he studied art at Bruges, Ghent, and Antwerp. In Paris he produced his *Manfred on the Jungfrau* (1841), a work intensely dramatic in feeling, but somber in coloring. He settled in England in 1846. He contributed verse, prose, and design to the Pre-Raphaelite *Germ*, was a close associate of **William Morris**, and in 1861 was a founder-member of Morris, Marshall, Faulkner & Company (later Morris & Company) for which he produced some designs for furniture and stained glass. Among his more mature works are *Christ Washing Peter's Feet*, *The Entombment* and his best-known painting, *The Last of England* (1855).

Brown, George 1818–80 •*Canadian politician and journalist*• Born in Alloa, Scotland, he emigrated to New York City in 1837 and to Canada in 1843. He became a member of the Canadian legislative assembly in 1851. As editor of the *Toronto Globe* he used his considerable influence to press the case for representation by population, to give Canada West a majority of seats in the legislature. After the Liberal-Conservatives took over government in 1854, Brown reorganized the party, and won the 1857 elections. He played a major role in a coalition government established to devise the constitutional reforms required for confederation. This he continued to support even after resigning (1865). Brown was also an antislavery activist, involved in the settlement of fugitive slaves during the 1850s. He was shot and killed by an employee fired from the *Globe*.

Brown, George Mackay 1921–96 •*Scottish poet, novelist and short-story writer*• Born in Stromness, Orkney, the "Hamnavoe" of his stories and poems, he suffered early from tuberculosis and was unable to work when he left school. He published his first collection, *The Storm*, in 1954, and it was followed by *Loaves and Fishes* (1959). His work draws on old sea yarns, myths, Scandinavian sagas and the folklore of Orkney, and his conversion to Catholicism in 1961 brought his concern with religion into relief. His works include the short-story collections *A Calendar of Love* (1967) and *A Time to Keep* (1969), and the novels *Greenvoe* (1972), *Magnus* (1973), and *Beside the Ocean of Time* (1994), which was shortlisted for the Booker Prize. His *Selected Poems* was published in 1991.

Brown, (James) Gordon 1951– •*Scottish Labour politician*• He was born in Kirkcaldy, Fife, the son of a Church of Scotland minister, and educated at Edinburgh University. After working as a lecturer and television journalist, he entered the House of Commons in 1983, as Labour Member of Parliament for Dunfermline East. He rose rapidly in the parliamentary party's hierarchy, becoming its senior Front Bench Spokesman on Treasury Affairs under **John Smith** in 1987. He became Opposition Spokesman for Trade and Industry (1989–92) and the Treasury (1992–97), and Chancellor of the Exchequer in 1997 when Labour came to power. His publications include *John Smith: Life and Soul of the Party* (1994, with **James Naughtie**).

Brown, Helen Gurley, *née* **Gurley** 1922– •*US journalist and commentator on gender affairs*• Born in Green Forest, Arkansas, she studied at Texas State College and Woodbury College, and after working in junior management for three years embarked on a career in advertising. In 1965 she was appointed editor in chief of the ailing *Cosmopolitan* magazine, which she transformed into an international success, remaining at *Cosmopolitan* until she retired in 1996 at the age of 73. Her first book was the bestseller *Sex and the Single Girl* (1962), which reflected a new mood of female independence. Other works include *Outrageous Opinions* (1966), *Sex and the New Single Girl* (1970), *Having It All* (1982) and *I'm Wild Again* (2000).

Brown, James 1928– •*US soul singer, songwriter and producer*• He was born in Barnwell, South Carolina. He began his professional career backed by a former gospel group, The Famous Flames, with whom he recorded his first "cry" ballads, "Please, Please, Please" and "Try Me" (1958). Mixing gospel and blues roots with his own aggressive energy, he put together a band and roadshow which by 1962 had made him America's leading rhythm and blues star and earned him the nickname "Soul Brother Number One." "Out Of Sight" (1964) brought him his first international success. An enduring influence on pop music, he was one of the first entertainers to assume complete control of his own career. His songs have included "Papa's Got a Brand New Bag" (1965), "It's a Man's Man's Man's World" (1966), "Ain't It Funky Now" (1969), "Sex Machine" (1970) and "Get Up Offa That Thing" (1976). Known as the "Godfather of Soul," he remains one of the most successful R & B artists ever, and his work has provided countless samples for the new generation of rap and hip hop artists. In 1988 he was jailed for six years on charges that included aggravated assault, but resumed his career on his early release.

Brown, Jim (James Nathaniel) 1936– •*US football player*• Born in St Simon Island, Georgia, he won attention as an All-American halfback at Syracuse University (1956) and went on to become a National Football League (NFL) star with the Cleveland Browns (1957–66). Fast and powerful, he scored a total of 126 touchdowns and led the league eight times in rushing. After retiring as a player he established a film career in Hollywood.

Brown, Joe (Joseph) 1930– •*English mountaineer*• Born in Manchester, he is one of the finest British rock climbers of the postwar period. In the 1950s, he formed a partnership with **Don Whillans**, and together they set new standards, putting up many original routes on rock faces in the Peak District and most notably on the huge face of Clogwyn Du'r Arddu in North Wales. In 1954 they made the first British ascent of the west face of the Petit Dru in the Alps, reducing the recorded ascension time from six days to 25 hours. With George Band, Brown reached the summit of Kangchenjunga, the world's third-highest mountain (1955). In 1966 he pioneered a series of extremely difficult routes on the sea cliffs of Gogarth in Anglesey.

Brown, John 1800–59 •*US abolitionist*• Born in Torrington, Connecticut, of Pilgrim descent, he was successively tanner and land surveyor, shepherd and farmer. A fervent abolitionist, he wandered through the country on antislavery enterprises. In 1854, five of his sons moved to Kansas, and, joining them after the border conflict had begun, he became a leader in the strife. His home was burned in 1856 and one of his sons killed. In 1859 he seized the federal arsenal at Harpers Ferry in Virginia, intending to launch a slave insurrection, and took several citizens prisoner. The arsenal was stormed by Colonel **Robert E Lee** with a company of marines. Brown and six men, barricading themselves in an engine house, continued to fight until two of Brown's sons were killed and he was severely wounded. Tried by a Virginia court for insurrection, treason and murder, he was convicted and hanged at Charlestown, Virginia. The song "John Brown's body lies a-moldering in the grave" (attributed to Thomas B Bishop [1835–1905]), commemorating the Harpers Ferry raid, was highly popular with Republican soldiers as a marching song in the Civil War. Provided with more fitting words by **Julia Ward Howe**, it became "The Battle Hymn of the Republic."

“ ”

I am as content to die for God's eternal truth on the scaffold as in any other way.

1859 Letter to his children on the eve of his execution, December 2.

Brown, John 1826–83 •*Scottish retainer*• He was born in Craithenaird, Balmoral, Aberdeenshire, the son of a crofter, and for 34 years was Queen **Victoria**'s personal attendant at Balmoral.

Brown, Lancelot, *also known as* **Capability Brown** 1715–83 •*English landscape gardener*• Born in Kirkharle, Northumberland, he established a purely English style of garden layout, using simple means to produce natural effects, as in the gardens of Blenheim, Kew, Stowe, Warwick Castle, Chatsworth, and others. He got his nickname from telling clients that their gardens had great "capabilities."

Brown, Michael Stuart 1941– •*US molecular geneticist and Nobel Prize winner*• Born in New York City, he was educated at the University of Pennsylvania. With **Joseph Goldstein**, he worked on cholesterol metabolism, studying how cholesterol is carried in the bloodstream by proteins called LDLs (low-density lipoproteins). Working on the genetic disease hypocholesterolemia, which results in abnormally high levels of cholesterol in the bloodstream, Brown found that sufferers of the disease lack a receptor to which the LDLs bind, thereby stopping cholesterol production. In 1984 Brown and Goldstein opened up the possibility of synthesizing drugs to control cholesterol metabolism, and they were jointly awarded the 1985 Nobel Prize for physiology or medicine.

Brown, Olympia 1835–1926 •*US Universalist minister and woman suffragist*• Born in Prairie Ronde, Michigan, she was educated at Antioch College and at St Lawrence University theological school. In 1863 she became the first US woman to be ordained by full denominational authority. As a supporter of women's rights, she served as president of the Woman Suffrage Association (1884–1912) and was also vice president of the National Woman Suffrage Association in 1892.

Brown, Paul 1908–91 •*US football coach*• Born in Norwalk, Ohio, he played college football for Miami University. The Browns, a team named after him, were among the first teams of the nascent National Football League, and under his guidance won championship titles in 1950, 1954 and 1955. His many revolutionary coaching practices, including film analysis and intelligence testing for players, earned him a place in the Hall of Fame in 1967. He went on to coach the Cincinnati Bengals to division titles in 1970 and 1973.

Brown, Rachel Fuller 1898–1980 •*US biochemist*• Born in Springfield, Massachusetts, she was educated at the University of Chicago, and began her career as a chemist at the New York State Department of Health in 1926. She made important studies of the causes of pneumonia and the bacteria involved. Shortly after the end of World War II, when methods of controlling bacterial forms of disease had been introduced, she isolated the first antifungal antibiotic, nystatin (1949).

Brown, Robert 1773–1858 •*Scottish botanist*• He was born in Montrose and educated at Aberdeen and Edinburgh. In 1798 he visited London, where his ability so impressed Sir **Joseph Banks** that he was appointed naturalist to **Matthew Flinders**'s coastal survey of Australia in 1801–05. He brought back nearly 4,000 species of plants for classification. In 1810 he received charge of Banks's library and collections, and when they were transferred to the British Museum in 1827 he became botanical keeper there. He is renowned for his investigation into the impregnation of plants and for being the first to note that, in general, living cells contain a nucleus. In 1827 he first observed the movement of fine particles in a liquid, which was named the "Brownian movement."

Brown, Thomas 1663–1704 •*English satirist*• He was born in Shifnal, Shropshire. As a student at Christ Church, Oxford, he produced his famous extempore adaptation of **Martial**'s 32nd epigram, "Non amo te, Sabidi," at the demand of Dr **John Fell**, the dean: "I do not love thee, Dr Fell." After teaching at Kingston-on-Thames, he settled in London, where he made an uncertain living by writing scurrilous satirical poems and pamphlets.

Brown, Tina 1953– •*English writer and editor*• Born in Maidenhead, Berkshire, and educated at Oxford, she won the 1978 Young Journalist of the Year award, and became editor in chief of *Tatler* magazine in 1979. She married the English journalist and *Sunday Times* editor **Harold Evans** in 1981. After leaving *Tatler* in 1983, she moved with Evans to New York City, where she became editor in chief of Condé-Nast's *Vanity Fair* magazine in 1984. From 1992 to 1998 she was the fourth editor of the *New Yorker* (founded 1925). Brown immediately implemented changes that brought censure and praise, enlivening the magazine through the use of more color and increased focus on current events, and improving its circulation by over 25 percent. In 1998 she founded *Talk* magazine, which closed down in 2002. She currently writes a weekly column for *The Times* (London).

Brown, Trisha 1936– •*US choreographer*• She was born in Aberdeen, Washington. With **Yvonne Rainer** and others she founded the experimental Judson Dance Company in 1962, and throughout the 1960s and 1970s she created a series of daringly original "equipment pieces" where dancers were rigged in harness to allow them to walk on walls or down the trunks of trees. Between 1970 and 1976 she ran an improvisational group, Grand Union, and founded the Trisha Brown Dance Company in 1970. In the late 1970s she began to work in traditional theaters, adding design and music to her pieces for the first time. **Robert Rauschenberg** created elements such as costumes, sets and electrical scores for several of her works, including *Glacial Decoy* (1979), *Set and Reset* (1983) and *If You Couldn't See Me* (1994).

Brown, William Wells c.1816–84 •*US writer*• Born into slavery in Kentucky, he was raised in St Louis, but after gaining his freedom helped runaway slaves in Ohio. He achieved fame with his autobiographical *Narrative of William W Brown, a Fugitive Slave* (1847), and became a leading advocate of abolition. He is best known for his novel *Clotelle; or, The President's Daughter* (1853), the story of an illegitimate mulatto girl born to President **Jefferson**'s housekeeper. His other works were a play, *The Escape* (1858), and an account of the history and culture of *The Black Man* (1863), later expanded as *The Rising Son* (1874).

Browne, Hablot K(night), *pseudonym* **Phiz** 1815–82 •*English illustrator*• Born in Kennington, London, he was apprenticed to a line engraver, but soon started etching and watercolor painting, and in 1833 earned a medal from the Society of Arts for an etching of "John Gilpin." In 1836 he became illustrator of *The Pickwick Papers*, and he maintained his reputation by his designs for other works by **Dickens**.

Browne, Sir Samuel James 1824–1901 •*British soldier*• Born in India, the son of a doctor, he joined the Indian army in 1849 and fought in the battles of Chilianwalla and Goojerat in the Second Sikh War (1848–49). During the Indian Mutiny (1857–58) he saw much service, including action at Lucknow and at Seerporah, where he lost his left arm and won a Victoria Cross. He was promoted to general in 1888; the "Sam Browne" sword belt is attributed to him.

Browne, Sir Thomas 1605–82 •*English writer and physician*• He was born in London. Educated at Pembroke College, Oxford, he studied medicine, traveled in Ireland, France, and Italy, graduated as Doctor of Medicine at Leiden in the Netherlands and at Oxford, and settled in 1637 at Norwich, where he lived and practiced the rest of his life. He was knighted by **Charles II** on his visit to Norwich in 1671. His greatest work is his earliest, the *Religio Medici* (c. 1635, authorized edition 1643)—a sort of confession of faith, revealing a deep insight into the mysteries of the spiritual life. In the 1650s he wrote *Hydriotaphia, or Urn Burial* (1658), considered to be the first archaeological treatise in English, and *The Garden of Cyrus* (1658), the most fantastic of Browne's writings, which aims to show that the number five pervaded not only all the horticulture of antiquity, but that it recurs throughout all plant life, as well as in the "figurations" of animals.

Browning, Elizabeth Barrett, *née* **Barrett** 1806–61 •*English poet*• Born in Coxhoe Hall, Durham, she spent her childhood at Hope End, Herefordshire. At 10 she read **Homer** in the original, and at 14 wrote an epic titled *The Battle of Marathon*. In her teens she damaged her spine, and was an invalid for a long time. Her *Essay on Mind, and Other Poems*, was published in 1826, and in 1833 she issued a translation of **Aeschylus**'s *Prometheus Bound*, succeeded by *The Seraphim, and Other Poems* (1838), in which was republished the poem on **William Cowper**'s grave. In 1845 she met **Robert Browning**, and married him the following year. They settled in Pisa (1846) and then Florence (1847), where they became the center of a literary circle. Her other works include *Casa Guidi Windows* (1851), *Aurora Leigh* (1856), her best-known work *Sonnets from the Portuguese* (published in the *Poems* of 1850), and *Last Poems* (1851).

" "

How do I love thee? Let me count the ways! —

1850 ***Sonnets from the Portuguese***, *sonnet 43, opening line.*

Browning, John Moses 1855–1926 •*US gunsmith and inventor*• Born in Ogden, Utah, the son of a Mormon gunsmith, he produced his first gun from scrap metal at the age of 13. He patented a breech-loading single-shot rifle in 1879, and the Browning automatic pistol in 1911. The Browning machine gun (1917) and the Browning automatic rifle (1918) were standard army weapons for many years.

Browning, Robert 1812–89 •*English poet*• Born in Camberwell, he attended lectures briefly at University College London and then traveled abroad. He made a visit to St Petersburg, and on his return *Paracelsus* (1835) won him some recognition in literary circles. He wrote several dramas and collections of shorter dramatic poems and published them under the title *Bells and Pomegranates* (1841–46). This work included *Dramatic Romances and Lyrics* (1845), which contained "My Last Duchess" and "The Pied Piper of Hamelin." From 1846 he was married to **Elizabeth Barrett Browning**, settling first in Pisa (1846) and then in Florence (1847), where their son, Robert Wiedemann Barrett Browning (1849–1912), the sculptor, was born. In 1855 Browning published *Men and Women*, which contained such poems as "Fra Lippo Lippi," "Childe Roland to the Dark Tower Came" and "Andrea del Sarto." After the death of his wife (1861) he settled in London with his son, and wrote the famous *The Ring and the Book*, published in four volumes (1868–69). Browning's poetry is distinguished by its spiritual insight and psychological analysis, and he invented new kinds of narrative structure to take the place of the epic and the pastoral. In his play *Pippa Passes* (1841), for example, a girl's song binds together a variety of scenes. Among his other chief works are *Dramatis Personae* (1864), *Pacchiarotto* (1876) and *Asolando* (1889).

Brubeck, Dave (David Warren) 1920– •*US pianist, composer and bandleader*• He was born in Concord, California, and studied music at the College of the Pacific, Stockton, California, leading a twelve-piece jazz band. Toward the end of World War II he was stationed in Europe, leading a service band, but in 1946 he resumed his studies and began to make his reputation as an experimental musician with his Jazz Workshop Ensemble. He reached a wider public with the Dave Brubeck Quartet, formed in 1951, including alto saxophonist Paul Desmond. Desmond's composition "Take Five," in 5/4 time, became one of the most popular recordings in jazz. He has composed larger-scale works such as ballets, a mass, and pieces for jazz group and orchestra, and continued to tour and record with small groups into the 1990s.

Bruce, Christopher 1945– •*English dancer and choreographer*• He was born in Leicester. On graduating from the Ballet Rambert School, he immediately joined the company. In 1967 he established his reputation in **Glen Tetley**'s *Pierrot lunaire* (1962). Within two years he had choreographed his first piece for Rambert, *George Frideric*, an abstract dance laced with drama. Later works include *Cruel Garden* (1977, with **Lindsay Kemp**), *Ghost Dances* (1981), *Swansong* (1987) and *His Grinning in Your Face* (2001), produced to celebrate Ballet Rambert's 75th anniversary. His work is a fusion of classical and modern dance idioms, with a strong undercurrent of social consciousness. Among many appointments he was artistic director of the Rambert Dance Company from 1994 to 2001. He was given the honorary title of Commander, Order of the British Empire, in 1998.

Bruce, Sir David 1855–1931 •*Scottish microbiologist and physician*• Born in Melbourne, Australia, while serving as an officer in the Royal Army Medical Corps (1883–1919), he identified in Malta the bacterium that causes undulant fever (brucellosis) in humans, named *Brucella* (1887). In 1895 in South Africa he discovered that the tsetse fly was the carrier of the protozoal parasite (*Trypanosoma brucei*) responsible for the cattle disease nagana, and sleeping sickness in humans. Elected a Fellow of the Royal Society in 1899 and knighted in 1908, he was Commandant of the Royal Army Medical College during World War I.

Bruce, James, *nicknamed* **the Abyssinian** 1730–94 •*Scottish explorer*• Born in Kinnaird House, Stirlingshire, and educated at Harrow, he became consul general in Algiers (1763–65), and in 1768 traveled to Abyssinia (Ethiopia). In 1770 he reached the source of the Abbai, or headstream of the Blue Nile, then considered the main stream of the Nile. His *Travels to Discover the Sources of the Nile* was published in 1790, but contained such extraordinary accounts of Abyssinia that many considered them fictitious at the time. Their truth was later confirmed by **Richard Burton** and other travelers.

Bruce, Lenny, *originally* **Leonard Alfred Schneider** 1925–66 •*US satirical comedian*• Born in New York, he first appeared as a nightclub performer in Baltimore, Maryland. The satire and black humor of his largely improvised act often overstepped the limits of what was considered permissible. In 1961 he was imprisoned for obscenity, and in 1963, a year after his first appearance at the Establishment Club in London, he was refused permission to enter Great Britain. In May 1963 he was found guilty of illegal possession of drugs; his death three years later was drug related. He was one of the first comedians who tried to disturb rather than amuse with his observation of the brutalities of the mid-20th century.

Bruce, Robert, *later* **Robert I**, *commonly known as* **Robert the Bruce** 1274–1329 •*King of Scotland from 1306, hero of the Scottish War of Independence*• He was born either at Turnberry in Ayrshire or in Essex. In 1296, as Earl of Carrick, he swore fealty to **Edward I** at Berwick, but soon joined the Scottish revolt under **William Wallace**. He was appointed one of the four guardians of Scotland in 1298, but did not fight against Edward again until the final uprising in 1306. His stabbing of John Comyn ("the Red Comyn"), the nephew of **John de Balliol** and a rival with a better claim to the throne, in the church of the Minorite Friars in Dumfries (February 10, 1306), allowed him to assert his own claim and two months later he was crowned king at Scone. Two defeats in 1306, one by an English army at Methven, near Perth, the other by the Lord of Argyll, a kinsman of the **Comyns**, at Dalry, near Tyndrum in Perthshire, forced him to flee, probably to Ireland, but he returned and defeated the English at Loudoun (May 1307). The death of Edward I the following July brought to the English throne a king, **Edward II**, who lacked his father's iron will and drive. By 1309 Robert was able to hold his first parliament (in St Andrews), which was, however, attended only by Bruce supporters. Spectacular military success between 1310 and 1314, when he won control of northern Scotland, resolved the doubts of many. A series of strongholds were recaptured, leaving only Lothian outside his control. In early 1314 the castles of Edinburgh and Roxburgh also fell to him, leaving Stirling as the only English stronghold north of the Forth. The victory (June 24, 1314) at Bannockburn, near Stirling, over a larger English army of nearly 20,000 men, did not end the Anglo-Scottish war, which went on until 1328 or later, but it did virtually settle the Scottish civil war, leaving Robert I unchallenged. He was succeeded by **David II**, his son by his second wife.

Bruce I, Robert de, *also spelled* **Bruis** or **Breaux** or **Brus** d. c. 1094 •*Norman knight*• He accompanied **William the Conqueror** to England in 1066. The name is traced to the domain of Bruis, near Cherbourg. He received extensive lands in Yorkshire.

Bruce II, Robert de c. 1078–1141 •*Scottish nobleman*• He was the son of **Robert de Bruce**, and a companion in arms of Prince David of Scotland, afterward **David I**, from whom he got the lordship of Annandale. He renounced his allegiance to David in the war in England between **Stephen** and **Matilda**, niece of the King of Scots, so forfeiting Annandale (1138).

Bruce V, Robert de, 4th Lord of Annandale d. 1245 •*Scottish nobleman*• He married Isabel, second daughter of David, Earl of Huntingdon and Chester, brother of King **William I** (the Lion), and thus founded the royal house of Bruce.

Bruce VI, Robert de, 5th Lord of Annandale 1210–95 •*Scottish nobleman*• He did homage to **Henry III** (1251), and was made Sheriff of Cumberland and Constable of Carlisle. When the Scottish throne became vacant at the death (1290) of **Margaret, Maid of Norway**, granddaughter of **Alexander III**, **John de Balliol** and Bruce claimed the succession. **Edward I** of England decided in favor of Balliol (1292). To avoid swearing fealty to his successful rival, Bruce resigned Annandale to his eldest son, **Robert de Bruce** (1253–1304).

Bruce VII, Robert de 1253–1304 •*Scottish nobleman*• The eldest son of **Robert de Bruce**, 5th Lord of Annandale, he is said to have accompanied **Edward I** of England on crusade to Palestine (1269). He married Marjory, Countess of Carrick (1271), and thus became Earl of Carrick, but resigned the earldom (1292) to his eldest son, **Robert Bruce**, the future King Robert I. On the death of his father (1295) he did homage to Edward for his English lands, was made constable of Carlisle, and fought for the English against **John de Balliol**. On Balliol's defeat he applied to Edward for the Crown of Scotland, but was refused it.

Bruce (of Melbourne), Stanley Melbourne Bruce, 1st Viscount 1883–1967 •*Australian statesman*• Born in St Kilda, Victoria, he was educated at Cambridge, and spent much time in England because of business interests. After service in World War I with a British regiment, he entered Australian federal politics in 1918, and was Treasurer in **William Morris Hughes**'s Nationalist government, but in 1923 joined with the Country Party in a coalition with himself as Prime Minister and Minister for External Affairs (1923–29). He became Australia's High Commissioner in London (1933–45), and played a leading part in **Churchill**'s War Cabinet. He became Viscount Bruce in 1947.

Bruch, Max 1838–1920 •*German composer*• Born in Cologne, he became musical director at Koblenz in 1865, and conducted the Liverpool Philharmonic Orchestra (1880–83), introducing many of his choral works. He is best known, however, for his Violin Concerto in G minor (1868), the *Kol Nidrei* (1881), variations in which he employs the idioms of Hebrew and Celtic traditional melodies, and the *Konzertstück*.

Bruckner, Anton 1824–96 •*Austrian composer and organist*• Born in Ansfelden, his early sacred choruses reflect a highly religious background. Following a rigorous, self-imposed training, and several posts as an organist, he wrote his Symphony no. 1 in 1865–66, becoming Professor of Composition at the Vienna Conservatory (1868–91). His fame rests chiefly on his nine symphonies (the last unfinished), but he also wrote four impressive masses, several smaller sacred works, and many choral works.

Brudenell, James Thomas *See* **Cardigan, 7th Earl of**

Brueghel or **Breughel, Jan the Elder**, *also called* **"Velvet" Brueghel** 1568–1625 •*Flemish artist*• He was born in Brussels, the younger son of **Pieter Brueghel** the Elder. He painted still life, flowers, landscapes and religious subjects, generally on a small scale. His son, Jan the Younger (1601–78), imitated him closely.

Brueghel, Pieter the Elder, *also spelled* **Breughel** or (after 1559) **Bruegel**, *also called* **"Peasant" Brueghel** c. 1520–69 •*Flemish artist*• He was born in the village of Bruegel, near Breda, and was the pupil of Pieter Coecke van Aelst (1502–50). An early influence on his work was **Hieronymus Bosch**. His work was highly regarded, particularly by **Rubens**, and much was bought for royal collections, but his reputation went into decline until the early 20th century. His pictures, often highly sophisticated moral commentaries derived from everyday proverbs, mainly depict earthy peasants engaging in various activities against a backdrop of well-observed landscape, and the truthfulness of his rendering of peasant life and weather conditions marks his work out from the Italianate style of his Netherlandish contemporaries. This genre reached its highest expression in his later works, *The Blind Leading the Blind* (1568), *The Peasant Wedding* (1568) and *The Peasant Dance* (1568).

Brueghel or **Breughel, Pieter the Younger**, *also called* **"Hell" Brueghel** c. 1564–1638 •*Flemish painter*• Born in Brussels and educated by his grandmother, then in Antwerp, he was the son of **Pieter Brueghel** the Elder. He was called "Hell" Brueghel because he painted *diableries*, scenes with devils, hags or robbers.

Bruijn, Inge De *See* **De Bruijn, Inge**

Brumby, Colin James 1933– •*Australian composer and teacher*• Born in Melbourne, he studied at the Conservatorium of Music there and in Europe. His considerable output includes operas, operettas for younger audiences, concertos, *Alice: Memories of Childhood* for the Queensland Ballet, choral works, film scores and chamber music, much of which has been recorded. Major works include a flute concerto and his *Festival Overture on Australian Themes* (1982), a symphony (1982), *Ballade for St Cecilia* (1971) and *The Phoenix and the Turtle* (1974).

Brummell, George Bryan, *known as* **Beau Brummell** 1778–1840 •*English dandy*• He was born in London, the son of Frederick, Lord **North**'s private secretary. At Eton, and during a brief period at Oxford, he was less distinguished for studiousness than for the exquisiteness of his dress and manners. Having come into a fortune, he entered on his true vocation as arbiter of taste and leader of early 19th-century fashionable society. A close friend and protégé of the Prince Regent (the future **George IV**), he quarreled with him in 1813, and in 1816 gambling debts forced Brummell to flee to Calais. From 1830 to 1832 he held a sinecure consulate at Caen. He died there in the pauper lunatic asylum.

" "

Who's your fat friend?

c. 1813 Of the Prince Regent. Quoted in Jesse ***Life of George Brummell*** *(1844), vol. 1.*

Brun, Charles le *See* **Le Brun, Charles**

Bruna, Dick 1927– •*Dutch artist and writer*• The creator of a highly successful series of picture books for young children, he started in the book trade in Utrecht, London and Paris, but he gave this up to concentrate on graphic art. His first book was *The Apple*, published in England in 1966, 13 years after it appeared in Holland. His great success came from 1959 onward when his books began to appear in their present format. Many of these featured Miffy, others the small dog Snuffy.

Brundtland, Gro Harlem 1939– •*Norwegian Labour politician*• Born in Oslo, she studied medicine at Oslo and Harvard, qualifying as a physician. In 1969, after working in public medicine services in Oslo, she joined the Labour Party and entered politics. She was appointed Environment Minister (1974–79) and then, as leader of the Labour Party group, became Prime Minister for a short time in 1981, the first woman Prime Minister of Norway. She was reelected Prime Minister in 1986, 1990 and 1993, but stepped down in 1996. In 1987 she chaired the World Commission on Environment and Development which produced the report *Our Common Future*. In 1998 she became Director General of the World Health Organization.

Brune, Guillaume Marie Anne 1762–1815 •*French soldier*• Born in Brive-la-Gaillarde, he commanded the revolutionary army in the Netherlands (1799) and defeated the Russo-British forces (the latter under the command of **Frederick Augustus**, Duke of York) at two battles of Bergen. He commanded under **Napoleon I** in Italy (1800). On the emperor's return from Elba in 1815 Brune joined him, and was murdered by a royalist mob at Avignon.

Brunel, Isambard Kingdom 1806–59 •*English engineer and inventor*• Born in Portsmouth, he was the son of Sir **Marc Isambard Brunel**, and in 1823 he entered his father's office. He helped to plan the Thames Tunnel, and in 1829–31 planned the Clifton Suspension Bridge. He designed the *Great Western* (1838), the first steamship built to cross the Atlantic Ocean, and the *Great Britain* (1845), the first ocean screw steamer. The *Great Eastern*, until 1899 the largest vessel ever built, was constructed to his design in collaboration with John Scott Russell, from whose yard in Millwall the "Great Ship" was launched on the second attempt in January 1858. In 1833 he was appointed engineer to the Great Western Railway, and constructed all the tunnels, bridges, and viaducts on that line. Among docks constructed or improved by him were those at Bristol, Monkwearmouth, Cardiff, and Milford Haven.

Brunel, Sir Marc Isambard 1769–1849 •*French engineer and inventor*• He was born in Hacqueville, Rouen, but during the French Revolution fled from Paris to the US (1793), where he worked as a surveyor and architect. Returning to Europe in 1799, he married and settled in England. He constructed public works in Woolwich arsenal and Chatham dockyard, and made experiments in steam navigation on the Thames in 1812, but his scheme for steam-driven tugboats was declined by the navy board. The destruction of his sawmills at Battersea by fire (1814) led to his bankruptcy in 1821, when he was imprisoned for debt. He was later released on receiving a £5,000 grant from the government. His most remarkable undertaking was the Thames Tunnel from Rotherhithe to Wapping (1825–43), for which he used the tunneling shield he had patented in 1818.

Brunelleschi, *properly* **Filippo di Ser Brunellesco** 1377–1446 •*Italian architect, goldsmith and sculptor*• Born in Florence, he began as a goldsmith. He is said to have turned his talents to architecture after his defeat by **Ghiberti** in the competition for the Florence Cathedral baptistery doors in 1402. He designed the dome of the cathedral in Florence: erected between 1420 and 1461, it is (measured diametrically) the largest in the world and served as the model for **Michelangelo**'s design for Saint Peter's in Rome. Other well-known buildings by him in Florence include Santo Spirito, San Lorenzo, and the Spedale degli Innocenti (Foundling Hospital). He was one of the figures responsible for the development of the Renaissance style in Florence, and is also to be noted for his innovations in the use of perspective.

Brunhilde c. 534–613 •*Frankish queen*• The daughter of the Visigothic King Athanagild, she married King Sigbert of Austrasia. After his assassination (575), as regent for her two grandsons, Theodebert II, King of Austrasia, and Theodoric II, King of Burgundy, she divided the government of the whole Frankish world with her rival **Fredegond**, who governed Neustria for **Clotaire II**. On Fredegond's death (598) she seized Neustria, and for a time united under her rule the whole Merovingian dominions, but was overthrown by the Austrasian nobles under Clotaire II, and was put to death by being dragged at the heels of a wild horse.

Brunhoff, Jean de 1899–1937 •*French writer and illustrator of children's books*• He was born in Paris. His creation Babar the Elephant is one of the most enduring characters of 20th-century children's literature. *L'histoire de Babar, le petit éléphant* (1931, Eng trans *The Story of Babar the Little Elephant*, 1934), which de Brunhoff both wrote and illustrated, was visually outstanding, produced on large pages with colored lithographic drawings and a hand-written text. De Brunhoff wrote seven *Babar* books in all, three of which were published posthumously. His son, Laurent de Brunhoff (1925–), continued to write and illustrate *Babar* stories after World War II.

Bruni, Leonardo, *styled* **Aretino** 1369–1444 •*Italian humanist*• Born in Arezzo, he was papal secretary from 1405 to 1415. He then wrote *Historiarum Florentini populi libri XII* (1610, "12 Books of Histories of the Florentine People"), and was made Chancellor of Florence in 1427. Bruni aided the advance of the study of Greek literature, mainly by his literal translations into Latin of **Aristotle**, **Demosthenes**, **Plato**, and others. He also wrote lives of **Petrarch** and **Dante** in Italian.

Brüning, Heinrich 1885–1970 •*German politician*• Born in Münster, he studied at Bonn and the London School of Economics. During the Weimar Republic he became in 1929 leader of the predominantly Catholic *Zentrum* (Center Party) and then Chancellor (1930–32). Faced with the problems of economic depression, he attempted to rule by decree, but was eventually replaced by the more conservative **Franz von Papen**.

Brunner, (Heinrich) Emil 1889–1966 •*Swiss Reformed theologian*• He was born in Winterthur, near Zurich. The author of nearly 400 books and articles, his reputation outside the Continent was established by translations of *The Mediator* (1927) and *The Divine Imperative* (1937). *The Divine-Human Encounter* (1944) reveals his debt to **Martin Buber**'s "I-Thou" understanding of the relationship between God and humans, but he parted company in 1934 with the dialectical theology of the early **Karl Barth** by holding that there *was* a limited universal revelation of God in creation.

Bruno, St, *known as* **Bruno the Great** 925–65 •*German prelate*• Born in Cologne, he was Imperial Chancellor in 940. In 953 he crushed a rebellion against his brother, **Otto I** (the Great), became Archbishop of Cologne the same year, and Duke of Lorraine in 954. He was distinguished both for piety and learning. He was the son of **Henry the Fowler**. His feast day is October 11.

Bruno, St, *also known as* **Boniface** 970–1009 •*German missionary*• Born in Querfurt, he was educated at Magdeburg Cathedral School, and entered the monastery in Ravenna in 997. He worked as a missionary bishop in Poland, Hungary and Ukraine. When he reached Prussia, he met fierce opposition, and was put to death with his companions. His feast day is June 19.

Bruno of Cologne, St c. 1030–1101 •*German churchman*• Born in Cologne, he became rector of the cathedral school at Rheims, but withdrew in 1084 to the mountains of Chartreuse, near Grenoble. Here with six friends he founded the austere Carthusian order on the site of the present Grande Chartreuse. In 1091, at the invitation of Pope **Urban II**, he founded a second Carthusian monastery at Della Torre, Calabria. His feast day is October 6.

Bruno, Frank(lin Roy) 1961– •*English boxer*• Born in London, he won the Amateur Boxing Association heavyweight championship when he was 18 years old. Early successes as a professional soon propelled him into the world top ten, and in October 1985 he took the European championship. In 1986 he challenged the World Boxing Association world championship, but lost to the holder, Tim Witherspoon, and a second attempt at the world crown, against **Mike Tyson** in 1989, also failed. In 1993 he unsuccessfully challenged **Lennox Lewis** for the World Boxing Council world title which he eventually won in 1995. He retired in 1996 and was given the honorary title Member, Order of the British Empire, in 1990.

Bruno, Giordano, *originally* **Filippo Bruno**, *nicknamed* **Il Nolano** 1548–1600 •*Italian hermetic thinker*• Born in Nola, near Naples, he became a Dominican friar but was too unorthodox to stay in the order, and fled to Geneva (1578). His pantheistic philosophy—whereby God animated the whole of creation as "world-soul"—and his sympathy with **Copernicus**'s theory of the universe brought him into conflict with the Inquisition. He was arrested in 1592 in Venice and after an eight-year trial was burned at the stake in Rome. His most famous works are *De l'infinito universo et mondi* (1584, "On the Infinite Universe and Worlds") and *Spaccio de la bestia trionfante* (1584, "The Expulsion of the Triumphant Beast").

Brusilov, Aleksei 1856–1926 •*Russian soldier*• He was born in Tiflis (now Tbilisi), Georgia. In World War I he led the invasion of Galicia (1914) and the Carpathians. From 1916 he distinguished himself on the Eastern Front, notably in command of the South Western Army Group in the only partly successful "Brusilov Offensive" against the Austrians in 1916. He became Chief of Staff in 1917, but the second "Brusilov Offensive" was frustrated, and many of his troops mutinied and added to the unrest that produced the Bolshevik Revolution. After the Revolution he commanded forces in the war against Poland (1920).

Bruton, John Gerard 1947– •*Irish Fine Gael politician*• Born in Dublin and educated at University College, Dublin, he was elected to the Dáil Éireann as a Fine Gael member in 1969 and became Minister of Finance in 1981. He became leader of Fine Gael in 1990 and was elected Prime Minister in 1994. He led Fine Gael in opposition from 1997 until his resignation after a vote of no confidence in 2001. During the discussions over the future of Northern Ireland he proved to be conciliatory to Unionist feelings and has been a constant critic of republican terrorism.

Brutus, Lucius Junius fl. 500 BC •*Roman hero*• He established republican government in Rome. The son of a rich Roman, on whose death **Tarquinius Superbus** seized the property and killed an elder brother, he himself escaped by feigning idiocy, from which he got his name (*Brutus* means "stupid"). When popular indignation was roused at the outrage on **Lucretia** by Sextus, son of Tarquinius Superbus, Brutus drove the royal family from Rome. He was elected as one of the first two consuls (509 BC). He fell repelling an attack led by one of Tarquin's sons.

Brutus, Marcus Junius c. 85–42 BC •*Roman politician*• He sided with **Pompey** when the civil war broke out in 49 BC, but, after the defeat at Pharsalia, submitted to **Julius Caesar**, and was appointed Governor of Cisalpine Gaul. He divorced his wife to marry Portia, the daughter of his master **Cato**. Cassius persuaded him to join the conspiracy to assassinate Caesar (44 BC), and, defeated by **Mark Antony** and Octavian (**Augustus**) at Philippi, he killed himself.

Bryan, W(illiam) J(ennings) 1860–1925 •*US politician*• Born in Salem, Illinois, he graduated from Illinois College in 1881 and studied law at Chicago. He served in the US House of Representatives as a Democrat from Nebraska (1891–95), and in 1896 captured the presidential nomination. He lost to **William McKinley** in that year and in 1900; in 1908 he gained the nomination for the third time but lost to **William Howard Taft**. In the course of his campaigns he became known as a great populist stump orator, styling himself as an advocate of the common people. He was appointed secretary of state by **Woodrow Wilson** (1913), but as an ardent pacifist resigned in June 1915 over America's second *Lusitania* note to Germany. His last public act was assisting the antievolutionist prosecutor in the Scopes Monkey Trial in Dayton, Tennessee. He was the father of the feminist **Ruth Rohde**.

Bryant, Bear, *properly* **Paul William Bryant** 1913–83 •*US football coach*• Born in Kingsland, Arkansas, he played college football for the University of Alabama and gained his nickname by wrestling a bear in a theater. He became Head Coach at the University of Maryland in 1935 and followed it with stints at the Universities of Kentucky and Texas A&M, but it was with his return to Alabama (1958–82) that he achieved his greatest successes, winning six National Championships and breaking Amos Alonzo Stagg's (1862–1965) record of 314 coaching victories by 1981.

Bryce, David 1803–76 •*Scottish architect*• He was born and educated in Edinburgh and entered partnership with William Burn (1789–1870) there. One of the preeminent architects of Victorian Scotland, he evolved and perfected the Scottish baronial style for his country houses, drawing inspiration from 16th-century Scottish architecture. He also used Italianate and French styles, as in Fettes College (1864–70), and designed several classical banks in Edinburgh.

Bryden, Bill (William Campbell Rough) 1942– •*Scottish stage director and dramatist*• He was born in Greenock, Renfrewshire, and began his career as a documentary scriptwriter before becoming associate director of the Royal Lyceum Theatre, Edinburgh (1971–74). From 1975 to 1985 he was an associate of the National Theatre, and from 1984 to 1993 he was head of drama for BBC Television Scotland. He has directed three films from his own screenplays: *Ill Fares the Land* (1982), *The Holy City* (1985) and *Aria* (1987), as well as *Parsifal* (1988) and *The Cunning Little Vixen* (1990) at Covent Garden. Also in 1990, he directed *The Ship*, a large-scale epic play about the Glasgow shipbuilding industry, set at a Clydeside shipyard, in the course of which a ship was built and launched. In 1994, he wrote and directed *The Big Picnic*, which was also performed at a Clydeside shipyard.

Bryson, Bill 1951– •*US author*• Born in Des Moines, Iowa, he moved to the UK as a young man and worked as a psychiatric nurse and business journalist. He turned to full-time writing in 1987, publishing a number of humorous travel memoirs including *Neither Here Nor There* (1993), *Notes from a Small Island* (1996), *A Walk in the Woods* (1998) and *In a Sunburned Country* (2001), all bestsellers. *Mother Tongue* (1990) and *Made in America* (1995) deal with the theme of the English language. He returned to live in the US in 1996.

Buber, Martin 1878–1965 •*Austrian Jewish theologian, philosopher and novelist*• Born in Vienna, he studied philosophy at Vienna, Berlin and Zurich, then became interested in Hasidism. He was Professor of Comparative Religion at Frankfurt (1923–33), then director of the Central Office for Jewish Adult Education until 1938 when he fled to Palestine to escape the Nazis and became Professor of the Sociology of Religion at Jerusalem. He is best known for his religious philosophy expounded most famously in *Ich und du* (1922, Eng trans *I and Thou*, 1958), contrasting personal relationships of mutuality and reciprocity with utilitarian or objective relationships. Both his philosophy and his reworkings of Hasidic tales, collected in English translation in *Tales of Rabbi Nachman* (1956) and elsewhere, have had a subtle influence on European and US literature.

Bubka, Sergei 1963– •*Ukrainian field athlete*• Born in Donetsk, he made his international debut as a pole vaulter at the 1983 world championship in Helsinki, where he won the gold medal. He retained this title in 1987, 1991, 1993, 1995 and 1997, and also won gold at the 1988 Olympics. In his career he has broken 35 world records and in 1992 took the world pole vault record to 6.12 m.

Bucer or **Butzer, Martin** 1491–1551 •*German Protestant reformer*• Born in Schlettstadt, Alsace, he entered the Dominican Order, and studied theology at Heidelberg. In 1521 he left the order, married a former nun, and in 1523 settled in Strasbourg. In the disputes between **Martin Luther** and **Huldreich Zwingli** he adopted a middle course. At Wittenberg in 1536 he made an agreement with the Lutherans, but when attacked for his refusal to sign the *Interim* in 1548, he came to England on **Thomas Cranmer**'s invitation (1549) as Regius Professor of Theology at Cambridge. In **Mary I**'s reign his remains were exhumed and burned.

Buchan, Alexander 1829–1907 •*Scottish meteorologist and oceanographer*• Born in Kinnesswood, near Kinross, he was educated at Edinburgh University. It was largely through his efforts that observatories were established at the summit of Ben Nevis (1883) and near its base at Fort William, and in 1868 he produced the first charts of storm tracks across the Atlantic. In his major work, *Report on Atmospheric Circulation* (1889), he presented global charts of monthly mean temperature, pressure and wind direction for the whole year. His studies of weather charts led him to conclude that the British climate is subject to warm and cold spells falling approximately between certain dates each year, the so-called Buchan spells.

Buchan, John, 1st Baron Tweedsmuir 1875–1940 •*Scottish writer and statesman*• Born in Perth, the son of a Free Church minister, he was educated at Glasgow University and at Brasenose College, Oxford. In 1901 he was called to the bar and became private secretary to Lord **Milner**, High Commissioner for South Africa. During World War I he served on HQ staff until 1917, when he became Director of Information. He was raised to the peerage in 1935, when he became Governor-General of Canada. His strength as a writer was for fast-moving adventure stories, which include *Prester John* (1910) and *Witch Wood* (1927). He became best known, however, for his spy thrillers featuring Richard Hannay: *The Thirty-Nine Steps* (1915), *Greenmantle* (1916) and others. He also wrote biographies.

“ ”

To live for a time close to great minds is the best kind of education.

1940 ***Memory Hold-the-Door***, *chapter 2.*

Buchanan, George c.1506–82 •*Scottish scholar and humanist*• He was born near Killearn in Stirlingshire. In 1537, King **James V** appointed him tutor to one of his illegitimate sons, the future Earl of **Moray**, but he was soon charged with heresy at St Andrews after writing a satirical poem about friars, *Franciscanus*. He fled to France, then to Coimbra in Portugal, where he was arrested by the Inquisition as a suspected heretic. During his confinement (1547–53) he made a Latin paraphrase of the Psalms, which was published in 1566 with a dedication to **Mary Queen of Scots**. He returned to Scotland in 1561 and was appointed classical tutor to the 19-year-old queen, but abandoned the queen's cause after the murder of Lord **Darnley** in 1567, and charged her with complicity in a scurrilous pamphlet, *Ane Detectioun of the Duings of Mary Quene* (1571). In 1567 he was elected Moderator of the newly formed General Assembly of the Church of Scotland, and later was appointed tutor to the four-year-old King **James VI** of Scotland (1570–78). His main works were *De juri regni apud Scotos* (1579, an attack on the divine right of monarchs and a justification for the deposition of Mary), and a monumental but unreliable history of Scotland, *Rerum scoticarum historia* (20 vols).

Buchanan, James 1791–1868 •*15th President of the US*• Born in Stony Batter, near Mercersburg, Pennsylvania, in 1812 he was admitted to the bar. Initially a Federalist and later a conservative Democrat, he served in the US House of Representatives (1821–31) and was minister to Russia for two years before returning to the Senate (1834–45). As Secretary of State (1845–49) under President **James K Polk**, he dealt with the annexation of Texas and the Mexican War as well as the Oregon boundary negotiations. He helped draft the Ostend Manifesto while minister to Great Britain (1853–56), and on his return to the US in 1856 gained the Democratic nomination and was elected President. His administration was plagued by rising sectional tensions, which his stand on slavery—he believed it wrong in principle but valid under the Constitution—did nothing to defuse.

Buchanan, Pat(rick Joseph) 1938– •*US Republican politician*• Born in Virginia, he was educated at Georgetown and Columbia universities before taking up a career in journalism. In 1969 he became a special assistant to the Republican leader **Richard Nixon**. He contested the Republican presidential nomination in 1992 and 1996 and ran as the Reform Party candidate in 2000.

Buchman, Frank Nathan Daniel 1878–1961 •*US evangelist*• He was born in Pennsburg, Pennsylvania, of devout Lutheran parents. Ordained in 1902, he became minister in charge of a hospice for underprivileged boys in Philadelphia (1902–07), traveled extensively, and in 1921, believing that there was an imminent danger of the collapse of civilization, founded at Oxford the "First Century Christian Fellowship." In 1938 it began to rally under the slogan "Moral Rearmament" (MRA), which emphasized constant adherence to the four cardinal principles of honesty, purity, unselfishness, and love, fostered by compulsory, public "sharing" of their shortcomings. After World War II the movement emerged in a more political guise as an alternative to capitalism and communism.

Büchner, Georg 1813–37 •*German dramatist and pioneer of expressionist theater*• He was born in Goddelau near Darmstadt, the brother of the physician and philosopher Ludwig Büchner (1824–99). After studying medicine and science, he became involved in revolutionary politics and fled to Zurich, where he died of typhoid fever at the age of 24. His best-known works are the poetical dramas *Dantons Tod* (1835, Eng trans *Danton's Death*, 1958) and *Woyzeck* (1837, Eng trans 1979). The latter is the true story of an uneducated and mentally backward army private who killed his girlfriend in a fit of jealousy. It was used by **Alban Berg** as the basis for his opera *Wozzeck*.

Buck, Pearl S(ydenstricker), *née* **Sydenstricker**, *pseudonym* **John Hedges** 1892–1973 •*US novelist and Nobel Prize winner*• Born in Hillsboro, West Virginia, the daughter of Presbyterian missionaries, she lived in China from her childhood, but was educated in the US. She returned to China as a missionary and teacher in 1921. Her earliest novels are colored by her experiences while living in China, and *The Good Earth* (1931) was a runaway bestseller. In 1935 she returned to the US, and most of her output after that date was concerned with contemporary US life. She was awarded the 1938 Nobel Prize for literature.

“ ”

Praise out of season, or tactlessly bestowed, can freeze the heart as much as blame.

1967 ***To My Daughters, With Love***, *"First Meeting."*

Buckingham, George Villiers, 1st Duke of 1592–1628 •*English politician and court favorite*• Born at his father's seat of Brooksby, Leicestershire, he was brought to the notice of **James VI and I** in 1614 and soon succeeded Robert Carr, Earl of Somerset, as favorite. He was knighted, then raised to the peerage as Viscount Villiers in 1616, and also became Earl of Buckingham in 1617, and Marquis in 1618. The abortive expedition against Cádiz exposed him to impeachment by the House of Commons, however, and only a dissolution rescued him. His expedition against France in 1627 failed, and while he was planning a second, he was assassinated by John Felton, a discontented subaltern.

Buckingham, George Villiers, 2nd Duke of 1627–87 •*English politician*• He was born in London, son of the 1st Duke. After his father's assassination in 1628 he was brought up with **Charles I**'s children. At the outbreak of the Civil War he joined the Royalists. He went with **Charles II** to Scotland, and after the Battle of Worcester went into exile. Returning secretly to England, in 1657 he married the daughter of Lord **Fairfax**, the Parliamentary general to whom his forfeited estates had been assigned. At the Restoration he recovered his estates, became a Privy Councilor, and for the next 25 years excelled the other courtiers in debauchery and wit. In 1667 he killed in a duel the Earl of Shrewsbury, whose countess, his lover, watched disguised as a page. He was involved in **Clarendon**'s downfall and was a member of the infamous Cabal of Charles II. In 1674 he was dismissed from government for alleged Catholic sympathies. He was the author and part-author of several comedies, the wittiest of them being *The Rehearsal* (1671), a parody of **Dryden**'s tragedies, but he is better known as the "Zimri" of Dryden's *Absalom and Achitophel*.

Buckland, William 1784–1856 •*English geologist and clergyman*• Born in Axminster, Devon, he was educated at Oxford, and became a reader in mineralogy there. He is known for his description of Kirkdale Cave, and his attempts to relate geology to the biblical description of the Creation. In 1845 he became dean of Westminster.

Buckley, William 1780–1856 •*Australian thief*• Born near Macclesfield, England, he was a bricklayer, then joined the army, but was transported to Australia in 1802 for stealing. He escaped the following year from a new convict settlement at Port Phillip, near Melbourne, was adopted by an Aboriginal tribe, and lived with them for 32 years before being found by an expedition. He became a bodyguard to the colonel in command of the new colony, then moved to Van Diemen's Land (later renamed Tasmania).

Buckley, William F(rank), Jr 1925– •*US political writer and journalist*• He was born in New York City. After serving in the military and the Central Intelligence Agency, he dedicated himself to combating creeping liberalism in US life. *Up from Liberalism* (1959) indicated his political position, but his best writing has been in a syndicated column called "On the Right." An author of fiction and nonfiction, he wrote many books including *God and Man at Yale* (1951), *Saving the Queen* (1976), *Marco Polo, If You Can* (1982) and *A Very Private Plot* (1993).

Buckner, Simon Bolivar, Jr 1886–1945 •*US soldier*• Born in Munfordville, Kentucky, he was the son of a Civil War general. Trained at West Point, he commanded the Alaska Defense Force (1940) and took part in operations for the recapture of the Aleutian Islands (1942–43). He commanded the 10th Army in the Central Pacific command, and led the invasion of the island of Okinawa in 1945. He was killed in action during the final stages of the capture of this key objective of US Pacific strategy.

Budaeus, *Latinized form of* **Guillaume Budé** 1467–1540 •*French scholar*• He was born in Paris. Of his works on philology, philosophy, and jurisprudence, the best known are his *Annotationes in XXIV libros pandectarum*, a work on ancient coins (1514), and the *Commentarii linguae Graecae* (1519). **Louis XII** and **Francis I** also employed him in diplomacy. Though suspected of a leaning toward Lutheranism, he was royal librarian and founded the royal collection at Fontainebleau, which, moved to Paris, became the Bibliothèque Nationale. His collected works were published in 1557.

Buddha ("the enlightened one") c. 563–c. 483 BC •*The title of Prince Siddhartha Gautama, the founder of Buddhism*• He was born the son of the rajah of the Sakya tribe ruling in Kapilavastu, 100 miles (160 km) north of Benares, in Nepal. When about 30 years old, he left the luxuries of the court, his beautiful wife, and all earthly ambitions in exchange for the life of an ascetic; after 6 years of extreme self-mortification he saw in the contemplative life the perfect way to self-enlightenment. According to tradition, he achieved enlightenment when sitting beneath a banyan tree near Buddh Gaya in Bihar. For the next 40 years he taught, gaining many disciples and followers, and died at the age of about 80 in Kusinagara in Oudh. His system was perhaps a revolutionary reformation of Brahmanism rather than a new faith, the keynote of it being that existence necessarily involves suffering, and that "Nirvana," or nonexistence, the chief good, is to be attained by diligent devotion to Buddhistic rules. The death of the body does not bring Nirvana: the unholy are condemned to transmigration through many existences. Buddhism spread steadily over India, and during the 3rd century BC was dominant from the Himalayas to Cape Comorin. It later began to decline; it was relentlessly persecuted by triumphant Brahmanism in the 7th and 8th centuries, and stamped out of continental India (except Nepal) by invading Islam. Meanwhile it had spread to Tibet, Ceylon (Sri Lanka), Burma (Myanmar), Siam (Thailand), China, and Japan, where it is still popular.

Buddhaghosa 5th century AD •*Indian Buddhist scholar*• He was born near Buddh Gaya, or Ghosa, East India, the place of the **Buddha**'s enlightenment. He studied the Buddhist texts in Ceylon (now Sri Lanka) and is best known for the *Visuddhimagga* ("The Path of Purity"), a compendium of the Buddhist doctrines.

Budé, Guillaume *See* **Budaeus**

Budenny, Semyon Mikhailovich 1883–1973 •*Russian and Soviet soldier*• He was the son of a Cossack farmer. He fought in the Russo-Japanese War (1904–05) and in World War I, and after the Russian Revolution (1917) became a Bolshevik and defeated the Whites in the battles of Tsaritsyn (1918–19). He served in the war against Poland (1920), and was made a marshal in 1935. In 1941 he commanded the southwest front against the German invasion, but was relieved after a disaster at Kiev.

Budge, Don (John Donald) 1915–2000 •*US tennis player*• Born in Oakland, California, the son of an immigrant Scot, he retains his reputation as one of the greatest tennis players ever. He was the first player to win all four Grand Slam events in the same year (1938). He won the Wimbledon singles, men's doubles (with Gene Mako) and, with US player Alice Marble, the mixed doubles (1937, 1938).

Bueno, Maria Esther 1939– •*Brazilian tennis player*• Born in São Paulo, she won Wimbledon in 1959 and 1960 and again in 1964, and was US champion on four occasions. Her graceful style disguised a classic backhand and powerful serve. With the US player Darlene Hard, she won the Wimbledon doubles title five times and the US doubles four times.

Buerk, Michael Duncan 1946– •*English television reporter*• Born in Solihull, West Midlands, he began working as a BBC television news correspondent from 1973. He became a household name in 1984, when his reports on the famine in Ethiopia provided the impetus for vast fundraising movements. After several more years as a foreign reporter he returned home to anchor the BBC's *Nine O'Clock News* (1988–2000), later rescheduled as the *Ten O'Clock News* (2000–). He was the Royal Television Society Journalist of the Year in 1984, and received the James Cameron Memorial award in 1987.

Buffalo Bill *See* **Cody, William F(rederick)**

Buffon, George-Louis Leclerc, Comte de 1707–88 •*French naturalist*• He was born in Montbard, Burgundy, and after studying law at the Jesuit college in Dijon, he devoted himself to science. In 1739 he was appointed director of the Jardin du Roi and the Royal Museum, and formed the design of his monumental *Histoire naturelle* (44 vols, 1749–67), in which all the known facts of natural science were discussed. After receiving various high honors, he was made Comte de Buffon by **Louis XV**. His work was inclined to generalization, but he proposed several new theories (including a greater age to the Earth than proposed in Genesis). His writings were influential in arousing interest in natural history, and foreshadowed the theory of evolution, although he never entirely broke with the ideas of the Church. He was made Comte de Buffon by **Louis XV**.

Bugatti, Ettore Arco Isidoro 1882–1947 •*Italian car manufacturer*• Born in Milan, he began designing cars in 1899 and set up his works in Strasbourg in 1907. World War I caused him to move to Italy and later to France, where his racing cars won international fame in the 1930s.

Bugeaud, Thomas 1784–1849 •*French soldier*• Born in Limoges, he served in the Napoleonic campaigns and in Algeria and Morocco (1836–44). In the February Revolution of 1848 he commanded the army in Paris.

Buhaina, Abdullah Ibn *See* **Blakey, Art(hur)**

Buhari, Muhammadu 1942– •*Nigerian soldier and politician*• Trained at military academies in Nigeria, England and India, he was Military Governor of North-Eastern State (1975–76), of Bornu State (1976), and then Federal Commissioner for Petroleum Resources (1976–78) and chairman of the Nigerian National Petroleum Corporation (1976–79). He returned to army duties (1976) but in 1983 led the military coup which ousted Shehu Shagari (1925–), when he became President. He was himself removed in a coup led by **Ibrahim Babangida** in 1985 and detained before being released in 1988.

Buick, David Dunbar 1854–1929 •*US auto manufacturer*• Born in Arbroath, Tayside, Scotland, he was taken to the US when he was two years old. In 1899 he sold his wholesale plumbing supply business and three years later established the Buick Manufacturing Company to make car engines. He built his first car in 1903 and formed the Buick Motor Company, but in 1908 it was taken over by the General Motors Corporation. At the time of his death, he was a clerk in a Detroit trade school.

Bujones, Fernando 1955– •*US dancer*• Born in Miami, of Cuban extraction, in 1972 he joined American Ballet Theater, becoming principal in 1974, when he was one of the first western dancers to win a gold medal at Varna International Competition in Bulgaria. Capable of both elegance and volatility, he has danced all the major classical roles for companies the world over and is equally at home in the modern repertoire.

Bukharin, Nikolai Ivanovich 1888–1938 •*Russian Marxist revolutionary and political theorist*• Born in Moscow, he was active in the Bolshevik underground (1905–17), and after the February Revolution returned to Russia. He played a leading role in the organization of the October Revolution in Moscow and was dubbed by **Lenin** "the darling of the party." He was a member of the Central Committee of the Communist Party in Russia and a member of the politburo (1924–29), in which position he came around to supporting Lenin's New Economic Policy, but had an ambivalent attitude toward **Stalin**'s collectivization campaign. In 1937 he was arrested in Stalin's Great Purge, expelled from the party, tried and shot.

Bukowski, Charles 1920–94 •*US poet and fiction writer*• Born in Andernach, Germany, he was taken to the US at the age of two, endured an unhappy childhood with an abusive father, and worked variously as a dishwasher and truck driver while learning to write. His first poetry collection was published in 1959, and he later published more than 40 other books of poetry, novels and short stories. A cult success as an underground writer, he evoked a world of lowlifers in a pared-down style influenced by **Ernest Hemingway**. He had a sardonic sense of humor and a liking for long titles, such as *Play the Piano Drunk Like a Percussion Instrument Until the Fingers Begin to Bleed a Bit* (1979). He also wrote the screenplay for the 1987 film *Barfly*, dramatizing his own younger days as a hard-drinking writer.

“ ”

You begin saving the world by saving one man at a time; all else is grandiose romanticism or politics.

*1967 **Tales of Ordinary Madness**, "Too Sensitive."*

Bulfinch, Charles 1763–1844 •*US architect*• Born in Boston, he graduated from Harvard. Ambitious to improve his native city, he returned to Boston and designed well-proportioned neoclassical buildings such as the Massachusetts State House (1798), New South Church (1814), and Massachusetts General Hospital (1820). Other works include the Connecticut State House (1796) and the Maine State Capitol (1831). Bulfinch succeeded **Benjamin Latrobe** as architect of the US Capitol in Washington DC.

Bulgakov, Mikhail Afanasevich 1891–1940 •*Russian novelist and dramatist*• Born in Kiev, he studied at the Theological Academy and the university there. He settled in Moscow in 1921, and began a stormy association with the Moscow Art Theater when he adapted part of his novel *Belaya gvardiya* (1925, Eng trans *The White Guard*, 1971) for the stage in 1926. His political attitudes in that play and in others brought him much criticism, and only a personal appeal to **Stalin** restored him to some favor. He described his tribulations with the theater in *Teatral'nyi roman* (1965, Eng trans *Black Snow, A Theatrical Novel*, 1967). His masterpiece is the novel *Master i Margarita* (1966, Eng trans *The Master and Margarita*, 1967), a remarkable fantasy.

Bulganin, Nikolai Aleksandrovich 1895–1975 •*Soviet politician*• Born in Nizhny Novgorod, he became an early member of the Communist Party, was mayor of Moscow (1933–37) and a member of the Military Council during World War II. Made a marshal at the end of the war, he succeeded **Stalin** as Minister for Defense in 1946. After Stalin's death he became vice premier in **Giorgi Malenkov**'s government and was made premier after the latter's resignation in 1955, though **Nikita Khrushchev** held the real power as First Secretary. Khrushchev ousted Bulganin from his nominal position in 1958 and, his authority totally eclipsed, he retained only the minor post of chairman of the Soviet State Bank.

Bull, John c. 1563–1628 •*English organist and composer*• Born in Somerset, he was appointed organist in the Queen's Chapel in 1586, first music lecturer at Gresham College in 1597 and organist to **James VI and I** in 1607. A Catholic, he fled to Belgium in 1613. Considered one of the founders of contrapuntal keyboard music, he has been credited with composing "God Save the King."

Bull, Phil, *pseudonym* **William Temple** 1910–89 •*English racing information service founder*• He made racing accessible to everyone by starting the Timeform organization in Halifax, Yorkshire. Today it is the world's largest information service for racing form. Bull operated under his pseudonym and was considered to be one of the most influential racing personalities of the 20th century. His opinions and shrewd judgment on form were highly regarded.

Bullard, Sir Edward Crisp 1907–80 •*English geophysicist*• Born in Norwich, Norfolk, he was educated at Clare College, Cambridge. He initiated the measurement of heat flux from the interior of the Earth (1940) and made the first effective measurement of the heat flow through oceanic crust. During World War II he worked on degaussing ships to protect them from German magnetic mines. In Toronto as Professor of Physics (1946–49), he worked on the dynamo theory of the Earth's magnetic field (1949). Then, as director of the National Physical Laboratory in London (1950–55), he employed the laboratory's early computer in the first numerical approach to dynamo theory. His computer-fit of the continents (1965) was instrumental in bringing the theory of continental drift back into favor. The geophysical laboratories at Cambridge are named after him, and he was given a knighthood in 1953.

Bullen, Frank Thomas 1857–1915 •*English writer*• He was a sailor until 1883, and made notable additions to the literature of the sea, including *Cruise of the Cachalot* (1898). He also wrote *Recollections* (1915).

Bullen, Keith Edward 1906–76 •*New Zealand mathematician and geophysicist*• Born in Auckland, he received his PhD at Cambridge. As a research student under **Harold Jeffreys**, he studied the arrival times for primary and secondary waves and the locations for the epicenters of global earthquakes to revise the travel-time tables. This work resulted in the *Jeffreys-Bullen Tables* (1940) which are still in use. Bullen divided the Earth into seven density layers consistent with the distribution of mass and seismic shadow zones. He was elected a Fellow of the Royal Society in 1949.

Buller, Sir Redvers Henry 1839–1908 •*English general*• He was born in Crediton, Devon. Educated at Eton, he joined the army in 1858 and fought in the war with China (1860), the Red River expedition (1870), the Ashanti War (1874), the Kaffir War (1878) and the Zulu War (1879), where his rescue of fellow soldiers in action at Inhlobane won him the Victoria Cross. He was Chief of Staff in the First Boer War (1881), and served in Egypt and the Sudan. As Commander in Chief in the Second Boer War (1899–1900), he raised the siege of Ladysmith (1900). He went on to command the 1st Army Corps (1901–06).

Bullock, Alan Louis Charles Bullock, Baron 1914–2004 •*English historian*• Educated at Bradford Grammar School and Wadham College, Oxford, he was Vice Chancellor of Oxford (1969–73), and Master of St Catherine's College, Oxford (1960–80). He was chairman of the Committee on Reading and Other Uses of English Language from 1972 to 1974, and the Bullock report (*A Language for Life*, 1975) was a response to suggestions that reading standards were declining. He also authored numerous works on 20th-century Europe, including *Hitler: A Study in Tyranny* (1952) and *Hitler and Stalin: Parallel Lives* (1991). He was made a life peer in 1976.

Bultmann, Rudolf Karl 1884–1976 •*German Protestant theologian*• He was born in Wiefelstede, Oldenberg. As Professor of New Testament at Marburg (1921–51), he maintained that while form criticism of the Gospels showed it was next to impossible to know anything about the historical **Jesus**, faith in Christ, rather than belief about him, was what mattered. The Gospels' existential challenge was, however, blunted for modern humanity by difficulties with miracles and other aspects of the New Testament worldview, which therefore needed to be "demythologized." His books include *The History of the Synoptic Tradition* (1921), *Jesus and the Word* (1934), *Theology of the New Testament* (2 vols, 1952–55), Gifford Lectures on *History and Eschatology* (1957), *Jesus Christ and Mythology* (1960) and *Existence and Faith* (1964).

Bulwer, Sir (William) Henry Lytton Earle, Baron Dalling and Bulwer 1801–72 •*English diplomat and author*• Born in London, he was educated at Harrow and Cambridge and entered the diplomatic service in 1827. As minister plenipotentiary in Madrid, he negotiated the peace between Spain and Morocco (1849). His outspokenness resulted in his expulsion, and in 1849 he proceeded to Washington DC, where he concluded the **Clayton**-Bulwer Treaty. He was ambassador to the Ottoman Porte

(1858–65), and ably carried out Lord **Palmerston**'s policy on the Eastern question. Among his works are *An Autumn in Greece* (1826) and *Historical Characters* (1868–70). He was the elder brother of **Edward Bulwer-Lytton**.

Bulwer-Lytton, Edward George *See* **Lytton, Bulwer**

Bunau-Varilla, Philippe Jean 1859–1940 •*French engineer*• He was born in Paris. The chief organizer of the Panama Canal project, he was instrumental in getting the waterway routed through Panama instead of Nicaragua, and worked to bring about the sale of the canal to the US. After inciting the Panama revolution (1903) to further this end, he was made Panamanian minister to the US and negotiated the Hay-Bunau-Varilla Treaty (1903) giving the US control of the canal zone.

Bunche, Ralph Johnson 1904–71 •*US diplomat and Nobel Prize winner*• Born in Detroit, the grandson of a slave, he studied at Harvard, Capetown, the London School of Economics, then became assistant Professor of Political Science at Howard University, Washington DC (1928). As director (1947–54) of the UN Trusteeship Department, he followed Count Folke **Bernadotte**, after the latter's assassination (1948), as UN mediator in Palestine and arranged for a cease-fire. Awarded the Nobel Peace Prize (1950), he became a UN Under-Secretary for Special Political Affairs (1954–67) and played an important role in Suez, the Congo, and the Indo-Pakistani War of 1965. He was Under-Secretary-General of the UN from 1968.

Buncho, Tani 1763–1840 •*Japanese painter*• Born in Edo (now Tokyo), the son of a poet, he was familiar with the styles of various schools and with Chinese works, and attempted a synthesis of these with European techniques. An illustrator of books and a prolific painter, he excelled in landscapes. He also introduced the Nanga style of painting to Edo, which encouraged individualism and the expression of the artist's own feelings, a revolutionary concept for the period.

Bundy, Ted (Theodore Robert), *assumed name* **Christopher Hagen** 1946–89 •*US lawyer and serial killer*• He was born in Vermont. An articulate and handsome man, he studied psychology and law. In 1974 he began a series of up to 40 murders in which he habitually raped and beat his victims. He stood trial in 1977 but escaped from custody, fleeing to Florida and assuming the name of Christopher Hagen. There he murdered a 12-year-old girl and, three days later, when the police checked the license plates of his van, they found it to have been stolen, and arrested Bundy. His trial took place in July 1979 in Miami, and was televised and watched by millions of people. He conducted his own defense with skill but was convicted and ten years later executed in Florida.

Bung Karno *See* **Sukarno, Ahmed**

Bunin, Ivan Alekseyevich 1870–1953 •*Russian author and Nobel Prize winner*• Born in Voronezh, he wrote lyrics and novels about the decay of the Russian nobility and of peasant life, and the disintegration of traditional rural patterns of life under the pressure of a changing world. They include *Gospodin iz San-Frantsisko* (1914, Eng trans *The Gentleman from San Francisco*, 1922), his best-known work, which has the vanity of all things earthly as its theme, and the autobiographical *The Well of Days* (1933, Eng trans 1946). He lived in Paris after the Russian Revolution (1917), and received the 1933 Nobel Prize for literature.

Bunsen, Robert Wilhelm 1811–99 •*German chemist and physicist*• Born in Göttingen, he studied at the university there and after a number of appointments became a professor (1852) at Heidelberg, where he remained until his retirement. He was a talented experimentalist, although the eponymous burner, for which he is best known, is a modification of something developed in England by **Michael Faraday**. He did invent the grease-spot photometer, a galvanic battery, and an ice calorimeter. He shared with **Gustav Robert Kirchhoff** the discovery, in 1859, of spectrum analysis, which facilitated the discovery of new elements, including cesium and rubidium. His most important work was his study of organoarsenic compounds such as cacodyl oxide. Following the partial loss of sight in one eye during an experiment, he forbade the study of organic chemistry in his laboratory.

Bunting, Basil 1900–85 •*English poet*• Born in Northumberland, he was neglected for most of his career, and until the publication of *Loquitur* (1965), **Ezra Pound** seemed to be his sole aficionado. However, Bunting attracted more admirers with his long poem, *Briggflatts* (1966). He has a greater following in the US than in Great Britain despite attempts to revive interest. His *Collected Poems* appeared in 1968.

Buñuel, Luis 1900–83 •*Spanish film director*• He was born in Calanda, Spain, and educated at Madrid University. His first films, *Un chien andalou* (1928, *An Andalusian Dog*) and *L'age d'or* (1930, *The Golden Age*), both made with **Salvador Dalí**, were a sensation with their surrealistic, macabre, poetic approach. He settled in Mexico (1947), his career in eclipse, but *Los olvidados* (1950, *The Young and the Damned*), a realistic study of juvenile delinquency, reestablished him, and later films, such as *Nazarin* (1958), *Viridiana* (1961), *Belle de jour* (1967), *La Voie Lactée* (1969, *The Milky Way*), *Le charme discret de la bourgeoisie* (1972, *The Discreet Charm of the Bourgeoisie*) and *Cet obscur objet de désir* (1977, *That Obscure Object of Desire*), illustrate his poetic, often erotic, use of imagery, his black humor, and his hatred of Catholicism, often expressed in blasphemy.

“ ”

Grâce à Dieu, je suis toujours athée.
Thanks be to God, I am still an atheist.

*1959 In **Le Monde**, December 16.*

Bunyan, John 1628–88 •*English writer and preacher*• Born in Elstow, Bedfordshire, he worked as a tinker. From 1644–45, he fought in the Parliamentary army, and in 1653 joined a Christian fellowship and became a preacher. In 1660 he was arrested while preaching in a farmhouse near Ampthill. During the 12 years' imprisonment in Bedford county jail which followed, Bunyan wrote *Profitable Meditations* (1661), *Christian Behavior* (1663), *The Resurrection of the Dead* (1665), *Grace Abounding* (1666) and some other works. Briefly released after the Declaration of Indulgence of 1672, Bunyan was then reimprisoned for six months, during which period he wrote the first part of *The Pilgrim's Progress* (1678). There followed the *Life and Death of Mr Badman* (1680), the *Holy War* (1682), and *The Pilgrim's Progress, Second Part* (1684), containing the story of Christiana and her children. Bunyan became pastor at Bedford for 16 years until his death after a ride through the rain from Reading to London.

Buononcini, Giovanni Maria *See* **Bononcini, Giovanni Maria**

Burbage, Richard c.1567–1619 •*English actor*• He was the son of the actor James Burbage, who built the Shoreditch and Blackfriars Theaters in London. Richard made his debut early, and had earned a considerable reputation as an actor when the death of his father (1597) brought him a share in the Blackfriars Theater. With his brother Cuthbert, he pulled down the Shoreditch house, and built the famous Globe Theater as a summer playhouse (1599), taking as partners **Shakespeare**, Heminge, Condell, and others.

Burbank, Luther 1849–1926 •*US horticulturist*• Born in Lancaster, Massachusetts, he received little formal education. He developed the Burbank potato, and in 1875 moved to Santa Rosa, California, where he spent over 50 years experimenting on the breeding of new fruits, flowers, grasses and vegetables. The city of Burbank is named after him.

Burbidge, Geoffrey 1925– •*English astrophysicist*• Born in Chipping Norton, Oxfordshire, he studied at Bristol University and University College London. He then went to the US, working at the Universities of Harvard (1951–52) and Chicago (1952–53, 1957–64), at Mount Wilson and Palomar (1955–57), and at the University of California at San Diego (1963–), where he is currently Professor of Physics. His most famous paper was published in 1957 and was written in conjunction with his wife **Margaret Burbidge**, Sir **Fred Hoyle** and **William Fowler**, in which they solved the problem of the creation of the higher elements in evolved stars. In 1967, again with his wife, Burbidge published an early and important book on quasars. In 1970 he showed that light-emitting stars only account for 25 percent of the total mass of their galaxies, highlighting the "missing mass" mystery which continues to this day—most of the matter in the universe cannot be detected by its radiation.

Burbidge, (Eleanor) Margaret, *née* **Peachey** 1923– •*English astronomer*• She was born in Davenport, Cheshire, and educated at University College London (1941–47), and her lifelong interest in astronomical spectroscopy began in London, where she was assistant director of the university observatory (1948–51). In 1951 she moved to the US, taking up appointments at Yerkes Observatory, the California Institute of Technology (Caltech) and the University of California at San Diego, where she was appointed Professor of Astronomy (1964–90), now emeritus, University Professor (1984–90), now emeritus, and, since 1990, Research Professor in the Physics Department. In collaboration with her husband, **Geoffrey Burbidge**, Sir **Fred Hoyle** and **William Fowler**, she published the results of theoretical research on nucleosynthesis, the processes whereby heavy chemical elements are built up in the cores of massive stars.

Burchfield, Robert William 1923–2004 •*English scholar and lexicographer*• He was born in Wanganui, New Zealand, becoming lecturer in English language at Oxford (1952–63), Tutorial Fellow (1963–79), and Senior Research Fellow (1979–90). From 1957 to 1986 he was editor of a new *Supplement to the Oxford English Dictionary*, which appeared in four volumes between 1972 and 1986. Among his other works are *The Oxford Dictionary of English Etymology* (1966, with **Charles Onions** and G W S Friedrichsen) and *The English Language* (1985).

Burckhardt, Jacob Christopher 1818–97 •*Swiss historian*• Born in Basel, he studied theology and art history in Berlin and Bonn. He became editor of the *Baselr Zeitung* (1844–45), and from 1858 to 1893 was Professor of History at Basel University. He is known for his works on the Italian Renaissance and on Greek civilization.

Burdett-Coutts, Angela Georgina, Baroness 1814–1906 •*English philanthropist*• Born in London, the daughter of Sir Francis Burdett, and granddaughter of **Thomas Coutts**, she inherited her grandfather's fortune in 1837 and used it to mitigate suffering. She established a shelter for "fallen" women, built model homes, and endowed churches and colonial bishoprics. In 1871 she received a peerage, and in 1872 she became the first woman to be given the freedom of the City of London. In 1881 she married William Ashmead-Bartlett (1851–1921), who assumed her name.

Buren, Martin van *See* **Van Buren, Martin**

Burgess, Anthony, *pseudonym of* **John Anthony Burgess Wilson** 1917–93 •*English novelist, critic and composer*• He was born in Manchester, into a Catholic family of predominantly Irish background, and was educated at the University of Manchester. In World War II he served in the Royal Army Medical Corps and entertained the troops with his compositions. He married in 1942, and after the war taught in England before becoming an education officer (1954–59) in Malaya and Brunei, where his experiences inspired the three novels which became *The Long Day Wanes: Time for a Tiger* (1956), *The Enemy in the Blanket* (1958), and *Beds in the East* (1959). Invalided out of the Colonial Service with a suspected brain tumor, he was given a year to live and wrote five novels in a year to provide for his prospective widow, but it was she who died first. In 1968 he married the Contessa Pasi and went to live abroad, first in Italy, later in Monte Carlo and Switzerland. Among his many novels are his dark and violent vision of the future, *A Clockwork Orange* (1962), *Earthly Powers* (1980), *The Kingdom of the Wicked* (1985), *Mozart and the Wolfgang* (1991) and *A Dead Man in Deptford* (1993). He was fascinated by language, as his various works of exegesis demonstrate. He also wrote biographies, books for children, and libretti.

“ ”

Death, like the quintessence of otherness, is for others.

1987 ***Little Wilson and Big God****, chapter 6.*

Burgess, Guy Francis de Moncy 1910–63 •*British double agent*• Born in Devonport, Devon, he was educated at Eton, at the Royal Naval College, Dartmouth, and at Trinity College, Cambridge, where he became a communist, and met **Donald Maclean**, **Kim Philby** and **Anthony Blunt**. Recruited as a Soviet agent in the 1930s, he worked with the BBC (1936–39), wrote war propaganda (1939–41), and again joined the BBC (1941–44) while working for MI5. After World War II he joined the Foreign Office and in 1950 became secretary of the British embassy in Washington DC, where Philby was chief MI6 liaison officer. Recalled in 1951 for "serious misconduct," he and Maclean disappeared, resurfacing in the USSR in 1956.

Burgh, Hubert de, Earl of Kent d. 1243 •*English statesman*• He was the Chief Justice of England, under Kings **John** and **Henry III** (1215–32), and was virtual ruler for the last four years, but now is chiefly remembered as the jailer of Prince **Arthur**. He was imprisoned (1232–34) after falling from favor, but later pardoned.

Burghley, 1st Baron *See* **Cecil, William**

Burgin, Victor 1941– •*English photographer*• Born in Sheffield, Yorkshire, he studied at the Royal College of Art, London, and at Yale in the US. Concerned with the social and cultural uses of photography, particularly in advertising, his pictures contain pieces of text superimposed on images of everyday urban life.

Burgkmair, Hans 1473–1531 •*German painter and wood engraver*• Born in Augsburg, a friend of **Albrecht Dürer**, he is best known for his nearly 700 woodcuts. He was also an accomplished fresco painter.

Burgos Seguí, Carmen de, *pseudonym* **Colombine** c. 1870–1932 •*Spanish feminist*• Born in the remote province of Almeria, the daughter of the consul of Portugal, she married young and then moved to Madrid after being abandoned by her husband. She was an outstanding advocate of women's rights and published a vast quantity of journalism both in Spain and Latin America (being the first Spanish female war correspondent in 1909) as well as many books on women's issues under the pseudonym "Colombine." Her novels include *Los inadaptados* (1909, "The Misfits") and *El último contrabandista* (1920, "The Last Smuggler").

Buridan, Jean c. 1300–c. 1358 •*French scholastic philosopher*• Born probably in Béthune, Artois, he studied under **William of Ockham** and taught in Paris. He published works on mechanics, optics, and, in particular, logic. He gave his name to the famous problem of decision making called "Buridan's Ass," where an ass faced with two equidistant and equally desirable bales of hay starves to death because there are no grounds for preferring to go to one bale rather than the other.

Burke, Edmund 1729–97 •*Irish statesman and philosopher*• Born in Dublin, he was educated at a Quaker boarding school and at Trinity College, Dublin. In 1750 he entered the Middle Temple, London, but soon abandoned law for literary work. His early works include *Vindication of Natural Society* (1756) and *Philosophical Inquiry into the Origin of Our Ideas of the Sublime and Beautiful* (1757). He was appointed Secretary for Ireland, and in 1765 entered parliament for the pocket borough of Wendover. Burke's eloquence soon earned him a high position in the Whig Party. The best of his writings and speeches belong to the turbulent and corrupt period of Lord **North**'s long administration (1770–82), and may be described as a defense of sound constitutional statesmanship against prevailing abuse and misgovernment. *Observations on the Present State of the Nation* (1769) was a reply to **George Grenville**. Perhaps the finest of his many efforts are the speech on *American Taxation* (1774), the speech *On Conciliation with America* (1775) and the *Letter to the Sheriffs of Bristol* (1777)—all advocating wise and liberal measures, which might have averted the troubles that ensued. Burke never systematized his political philosophy, which emerges with inconsistencies out of these writings and speeches. Opposed to the doctrine of "natural rights," he takes over the concept of "social contract," and attaches to it a divine sanction. After the fall of the Whig ministry in 1783 Burke was never again in office and, misled by party feeling, he opposed **William Pitt**'s measure for free trade with Ireland and the Commercial Treaty with France. In 1788 he opened the trial of **Warren Hastings** with the speech that will always rank among the masterpieces of English eloquence. His *Reflections on the Revolution in France* (1790) was read all over Europe.

“ ”
The age of chivalry is gone.—That of sophisters, economists, and calculators, has succeeded; and the glory of Europe is extinguished for ever.
*1790 **Reflections on the Revolution in France**.*

Burke, John 1787–1848 •*Irish genealogist*• Born in Tipperary, he was the compiler of *Burke's Peerage*—the first dictionary of baronets and peers of the UK in alphabetical order, published in 1826.

Burke, Robert O'Hara 1820–61 •*Irish explorer*• Born in St Clerans, County Galway, he emigrated to Australia in 1853. While an inspector of police in Victoria he accepted the leadership, with **William Wills**, of an expedition to cross the continent. They set off from Melbourne in 1860, and, after many hardships, Burke, Wills, **John King** and another man reached the tidal marshes of the Flinders River at the edge of the Gulf of Carpentaria. They were the first white men to cross the Australian continent from south to north but only King survived the return journey. Burke and the others died of starvation.

Burke, William 1792–1829 •*Irish murderer*• Born in County Cork, he moved to Scotland in 1818. With his partner William Hare (1790–1860) he committed a series of murders in Edinburgh, supplying dissection subjects to Dr **Robert Knox**, the anatomist. Hare turned king's evidence, and probably died sometime in the 1860s, a blind beggar in London, while Burke was hanged, to great public satisfaction.

Burks, Arthur Walter 1915– •*US computer scientist and philosopher*• Born in Duluth, Minnesota, by the end of World War II he had joined **John Presper Eckert** and **John Mauchly** in the design and construction of the ENIAC (Electronic Numerical Integrator and Computer) and the EDVAC (Electronic Discrete Variable Computer) computing machines. He conducted pioneering work on cellular automata and was coauthor of *The First Electronic Computer: The Atanasoff Story* (1971), in which he examined the birth of the electronic digital computer.

Burlington, Richard Boyle, 3rd Earl of 1695–1753 •*Anglo-Irish politician and patron of the arts*• A great admirer of **Andrea Palladio**, he was himself an enthusiastic architect. He redesigned the Burlington House in Piccadilly, and by his influence over a group of young architects fostered the Palladian style that was to govern English building for half a century.

Burne-Jones, Sir Edward Coley 1833–98 •*English painter*• Born in Birmingham of Welsh ancestry, he studied at Exeter College, Oxford, where he became the close friend of **William Morris** and **Dante Gabriel Rossetti** and abandoned his studies for the Church. In 1861 he became a founding member of Morris, Marshall, Faulkner & Company (later Morris & Company), for which he designed tapestries and stained glass. His early works, mostly watercolors, such as *The Merciful Knight* (1864) and *The Wine of Circe* (1867), are brighter than his later oils which, inspired by the early art of the Italian Renaissance, are characterized by a romantic and contrived Mannerism. His subjects, drawn from the Arthurian romances and Greek myths, include *The Days of Creation*, *The Mirror of Venus* (1877) and *Pan and Psyche* (1878).

Burnet, Sir Alastair, *originally* **James William Alexander Burnet** 1928– •*English journalist and broadcaster*• Born in Sheffield, South Yorkshire, he became leader-writer for *The Economist* (1958–62), before entering television as political editor of Independent Television News (ITN) (1963–65). He returned to *The Economist* as editor (1965) but continued to work for ITN as a newscaster, helping to launch *News at Ten* in 1967, before moving to the BBC as anchorman of *Panorama* in 1972. In 1974 he left television to become editor of the *Daily Express* but returned to ITN as a newscaster in 1976 and became associate editor on *News at Ten* in 1982. He retired in 1991.

Burnet, Sir (Frank) Macfarlane 1899–1985 •*Australian immunologist and virologist and Nobel Prize winner*• Born in Traralgon, eastern Victoria, he graduated in medicine from Melbourne University. From 1931 to 1934, he began working on viruses at the National Institute for Medical Research in London, and for the next 20 years made important contributions to our understanding of many animal viruses, especially the influenza virus. From the end of the 1950s he turned his attention to immunological problems, particularly the phenomenon of graft rejection. His work transformed the understanding of how the entry of foreign substances (antigens) into the body results in the production of specific antibodies that bind and neutralize the invader. **Peter Medawar**'s work provided the experimental evidence to support Burnet's theory, and in 1960 the two men shared the Nobel Prize for physiology or medicine. Burnet was elected a Fellow of the Royal Society in 1942, knighted in 1951, and appointed to the Order of Merit in 1958.

Burnett, Carol 1933– •*US comedienne and dramatic actress*• Born in San Antonio, Texas, she studied at the University of California, Los Angeles, then moved to New York City, where she found work on children's television. She became a television regular in *Stanley* (1956–57) and *The Garry Moore Show* (1959–62), for which she received her first Emmy award. A versatile comedy performer, she enjoyed enormous success with *The Carol Burnett Show* (1967–78, 1991) and *Carol and Company* (1990–91).

Burnett, Frances Hodgson, *née* **Frances Eliza Hodgson** 1849–1924 •*US novelist*• Born in Manchester, England, the daughter of a manufacturer, she emigrated with her family to Knoxville, Tennessee, in 1865, and there turned to writing to help out the family finances. Her first literary success was *That Lass o' Lowrie's* (1877). Later works include plays, her most popular story *Little Lord Fauntleroy* (1886), *The One I Knew Best of All* (1893, autobiographical), *The Little Princess* (1905) and *The Secret Garden* (1909), still one of the best-loved classics of children's literature. In her lifetime she was rated one of the foremost writers in the US, and was a friend of **Henry James**.

Burney, Charles 1726–1814 •*English musicologist*• Born in Shrewsbury, Shropshire, he studied music there, at Chester and London. After composing three pieces for Drury Lane (1745–50), he went as organist to King's Lynn, Norfolk (1751–60). He traveled (1770–72) in France, Italy, Germany, and Austria to collect material for his *Present State of Music in France and Italy* (1771), and his *General History of Music* (4 vols, 1776–89). His *General History* was long considered a standard work. He was the father of **Fanny Burney**, and knew many of the eminent men of his day, including **Edmund Burke**, Dr **Johnson** and **David Garrick**.

Burney, Fanny (Frances), *later* **Madame d'Arblay** 1752–1840 •*English novelist and diarist*• Born in King's Lynn, Norfolk, the daughter of **Charles Burney**, she educated herself by reading English and French literature and observing the distinguished people who visited her father. By the age of 10 she had begun scribbling stories, plays, and poems, and *Evelina*, her first and best novel, published anonymously in 1778, describes the entry of a country girl into the gaieties of London life. Her father at once recognized his daughter's talent and confided the secret to Mrs **Hester Piozzi**, who, as well as **Samuel Johnson**, championed the gifted young author. *Cecilia* (1782), though more complex, is less natural, and her style gradually declined in *Camilla* (1796) and *The Wanderer* (1814). She was appointed a second keeper of the robes to Queen **Charlotte** in 1786, but her health declined, and she retired on a pension and married a French émigré, General d'Arblay, in 1793. Her *Letters and Diaries* (1846) give a vivid and lively account of her life.

Burnham, Forbes 1923–85 •*Guyanese politician*• British-educated, he represented the African element in the Guyanese population and was coleader with **Cheddi Jagan** of the multiracial People's Progressive Party until 1955. In that year he split with Jagan over the latter's support for international communism and set up a rival African-based party, the People's National Congress (PNC), in 1964 becoming Prime Minister. He negotiated an independence constitution in 1966, and in 1970 established Guyana as a "cooperative socialist republic," remaining its President until his death.

Burningham, John 1936– •*English illustrator and children's writer*• Born in Farnham, Surrey, he was educated at **A S Neill**'s Summerhill and the Central School for Arts and Crafts, London. Popular and amusing, he draws children with round, cherubic faces which belie their highly aware resourcefulness, as in *The*

Shopping Basket (1982). Distinctions include illustrating **Ian Fleming**'s *Chitty Chitty Bang Bang* (1964) and receiving the **Kate Greenaway** award for *Borka* (1964) and *Mr Gumpy's Outing* (1970). Later publications include *Harvey Slumfenburger's Christmas Present* (1993) and *Whadayamean* (1999).

Burns, George, *originally* **Nathan Birnbaum** 1896–1996 •*US comedian*• Born in New York City, he broke into vaudeville as a comedian. He and his wife, **Gracie Allen**, performed as a comedy team (1923–58), in which he played the straight-man role of a sometimes patient, sometimes exasperated husband to her scatterbrained wife. Burns retired from show business after Allen's death in 1964, but he returned to acting in the late 1970s, winning an Academy Award for his performance as an old vaudevillian in *The Sunshine Boys* (1975), and appearing in numerous other films and television specials.

Burns, Robert 1759–96 •*Scottish poet and songwriter*• Robert Burns was born in Alloway, near Ayr. The son of a poor farmer, he nonetheless received a literary education. His father died bankrupt in 1784 and, with his brother Gilbert, Burns took a small farm at Mossgiel, near Mauchline, but his husbandry was beset by problems. As his farm went to ruin in 1785, he produced a prolific output of poetry celebrating love, lust and country life. Poems written in this year include the "Epistle to Davie," "Death and Dr Hornbook," "Halloween," "The Cotter's Saturday Night," "Holy Willie's Prayer," "The Holy Fair" and "The Address to a Mouse." Also in 1785, Elizabeth Paton, who had been a servant girl on his father's farm, gave birth to Burn's first illegitimate child. Around the same time, his entanglement with Jean Armour (1767–1834), the daughter of a stonemason, began. But when Jean's father refused to accept him as a son-in-law, he took up (1786) with a Mary Campbell ("Highland Mary"), who died not long after their liaison had begun. He decided to emigrate to Jamaica and, having produced a further output of verse, he published the famous Kilmarnock edition of his poetry, *Poems, Chiefly in the Scottish Dialect* (1786), to try to raise money for his journey. This edition includes the well-known poems "The Twa Dogs," "Address to the Deil" and "To a Louse"; "Address to the Unco Guid" and "Address to a Haggis" were among the poems added to the 1787 Edinburgh edition. The praise and admiration that his poetry received persuaded Burns to stay in Scotland, and he was greeted with acclaim on visiting Edinburgh in the winter of 1786. After a Highland tour, he returned to Edinburgh and began the epistolary flirtations with "Clarinda" (**Agnes Maclehose**). In 1788, he married Jean Armour. He leased a farm at Ellisland, near Dumfries, and in 1789 was made an excise officer. From 1788 until 1792 he worked on James Johnson's *Scots Musical Museum* (1787–1803), collecting, editing, writing and rewriting songs and music for the six-volume publication. The best-known songs accredited to him therein include "John Anderson My Jo," "Ye Jacobites By Name," "The Banks o' Doon," "A Red Red Rose" and "Auld Lang Syne." In 1790, by which time his farm was failing, he wrote his long narrative poem "Tam o'Shanter." He left his farm in 1791 and moved to Dumfries, flirted with the sentiments and fervor of the French Revolution, continued collecting and writing Scottish songs set to traditional airs, expressed radical opinions and made himself unpopular with the local lairds. He died of endocarditis induced by rheumatism, and is buried in Dumfries. Burns Suppers are held annually worldwide on his birthday (January 25).

" "

Some books are lies frae end to end,
And some great lies were never penn'd.

1785 "Death and Doctor Hornbook," stanza 1.

Burnside, Ambrose Everett 1824–81 •*US soldier and senator*• Born in Liberty, Indiana, he commanded a brigade at Bull Run, and in 1862 captured Roanoke Island. His corps was repulsed with heavy losses in the Battle of Antietam later that year. Commanding the army of the Potomac he crossed the Rappahannock to attack **Robert E Lee** near Fredericksburg, but was driven back with a loss of more than 10,000 men (1862). In 1863 he successfully held Knoxville, and in 1864 led a corps through the battles of the Wilderness and Cold Harbor. He gave his name to a style of side-whiskers called "burnsides" (now "sideburns").

Burr, Aaron 1756–1836 •*US politician*• Born in Newark, New Jersey, he was a graduate of Princeton, and was called to the bar in 1782. After serving as a US senator from New York (1791–97), he tied with **Thomas Jefferson** in the presidential election of 1800, and by decision of the House of Representatives became Vice President (1801–05) under Jefferson. For 20 years he carried on a personal and political rivalry with **Alexander Hamilton**, whom he mortally wounded in a duel (1804). Burr fled to South Carolina, and though indicted for murder, returned and completed his term as Vice President. He then devised a secret plan to establish an independent nation in the Southwest, but when rumors of this scheme leaked out, he was arrested and tried for treason (1807). Acquitted, he spent some years in Europe, and in 1812 resumed his law practice in New York but was shunned by society.

Burra, Edward 1905–76 •*English artist*• Born in London, he traveled widely in Europe and the US. He is well known as a colorist, and his surrealist paintings of figures against exotic (often Spanish) backgrounds are invariably in watercolor. His picture *Soldiers at Rye* (1941) is in Tate Britain, London. He also designed for the ballet.

Burrell, Sir William 1861–1958 •*Scottish shipowner and art collector*• He was born in Glasgow, the son of a shipping agent. He entered his father's business at the age of 15, and during his lifetime he accumulated a magnificent collection of 8,000 works of art from all over the world, including modern French paintings, which he gave in 1944 to the city of Glasgow. The Burrell Collection was finally opened to the public in 1983 in a new gallery built for it on the south side of Glasgow.

Burroughs, Edgar Rice 1875–1950 •*US popular author, creator of Tarzan*• Born in Chicago, he served in the US Cavalry and fought against the Apache but was discharged when it was discovered he was under age. Thereafter he had several colorful occupations before he took to writing, his aim being to improve on the average "dime" novel. *Tarzan of the Apes* (1914) was his first book to feature the jungle hero. It spawned many sequels, as well as films, radio programs and comic strips, making Burroughs a millionaire.

Burroughs, William S(eward) 1914–97 •*US writer*• He was born into a wealthy family in St Louis, Missouri. After graduating from Harvard in 1936, he traveled throughout the US and Europe. While in New York in 1944 he became a heroin addict and in 1953 he published *Junkie*, an account of this experience. His novels *The Naked Lunch* (1959) and *The Soft Machine* (1961) established him as a leading figure of the Beat movement, though one who stood somewhat apart. Intensely interested in the juxtaposition of apparently random ideas and observations, he was concerned in his later work with innovations in the novel form, such as the techniques of "cut-up" and "fold-in," by which words and phrases are either cut out and pasted together or formed by cross-column reading. Other works include *The Ticket That Exploded* (1962), *Dead Fingers Talk* (1963), *The Wild Boys* (1971), *Cities of the Red Night* (1981) and *My Education: A Book of Dreams* (1995).

" "

You can't fake quality any more than you can fake a good meal.

1987 ***The Western Lands****, chapter 2.*

Burstyn, Ellen, *née* **Edna Rae Gillooly** 1932– •*US actress*• Born in Detroit, she studied acting in California and New York City. Her notable stage roles include *Same Time, Next Year* (1975, Tony award), *The Three Sisters* (1977), and *Shirley Valentine* (1989). She made her film debut in *Goodbye Charlie* (1964) and has received Academy Award nominations for *The Last Picture Show* (1971), *The Exorcist* (1973), *Same Time, Next Year* (1978) and *Resurrection* (1980). She won a Best Actress Academy Award for *Alice Doesn't Live Here Anymore* (1974). Recent films include *The Cemetery Club* (1993) and *Requiem for a Dream* (2000), which earned her an Academy Award nomination.

Burt, Sir Cyril Lodowic 1883–1971 •*English psychologist*• Born in London, he was educated at Christ's Hospital and Jesus

College, Oxford, and at Würzburg. He became Professor of Education at London (1924–31) and then Professor of Psychology (1931–50). He was highly influential in the theory and practice of intelligence and aptitude tests, ranging from the psychology of education to the problems of juvenile delinquency. Since his death the authenticity of some of his research data has been questioned.

Burton, Decimus 1800–81 •*English architect*• Born in London, at the age of 23 he planned the Regent's Park colosseum, an exhibition hall with a dome larger than that of St Paul's Cathedral, and in 1825 designed the new layout of Hyde Park and the triumphal arch at Hyde Park Corner. He designed the Palm House at Kew Gardens (1844–48) with engineer Richard Turner.

Burton, Richard, *originally* **Richard Walter Jenkins** 1925–84 •*Welsh stage and film actor*• Born in Pontrhydfen, Wales, the son of a coal miner, he was adopted by his English teacher, Philip H Burton, and gained a scholarship to Exeter College, Oxford. He made his stage reputation in **Christopher Fry**'s *The Lady's Not for Burning* (1949), which was enthusiastically received on Broadway. A triumphant season at Stratford (1951) was followed by his first Hollywood film, *My Cousin Rachel* (1952), for which he received one of his six Academy Award nominations, and *The Robe* (1953), for which he was also nominated. In 1954 he was the narrator in the famous radio production of **Dylan Thomas**'s *Under Milk Wood.* Hailed as one of the most promising Shakespearean actors of his generation, a well-publicized romance with his costar in *Cleopatra*, **Elizabeth Taylor**, whom he eventually married (twice), projected him into the "superstar" category. His highly successful films include *Cleopatra* (1963), *The Spy Who Came in from the Cold* (1965) and *Where Eagles Dare* (1969), *Who's Afraid of Virginia Woolf?* (1968), *Equus* (1977) and *1984* (released in 1984, after his death).

Burton, Sir Richard Francis 1821–90 •*English explorer, linguist and diplomat*• Born in Torquay, Devon, he was largely self-educated and won a place at Oxford, where he began to study Arabic. He is said to have mastered approximately 30 languages, many with various dialects. In 1842 he served in Sind, India (now Pakistan) under Sir **Charles Napier**, and having mastered Hindustani, Persian, and Arabic, made a pilgrimage to Mecca disguised as a Pathan (1853). He was then commissioned by the Foreign Office to search for the sources of the Nile, and in 1856 set out with **John Hanning Speke** on the journey which led to the discovery (1858) of Lake Tanganyika. He was knighted in 1886. His most important books include *First Footsteps in East Africa* (1856), *The Lake Regions of Central Africa* (1860) and his translation of *The Arabian Nights* (16 vols, 1885–88).

Burton, Robert 1577–1640 •*English writer and clergyman*• Born in Lindley, Leicestershire, he was educated at Brasenose College, Oxford. In 1616 he was appointed to the Oxford vicarage of St Thomas, and about 1630 to the rectory of Segrave, Leicestershire. He kept both livings, but spent his life at Christ Church, where he died. The first edition of his great work, *Anatomy of Melancholy*, was written under the pseudonym "Democritus Junior," and appeared in quarto in 1621 (final, sixth edition, 1651–52). This strange book is a vast and witty compendium of Jacobean knowledge about the "disease" of melancholy, gathered from classical and medieval writers, as well as folklore and superstition. One of the most interesting parts is the long preface, "Democritus to the Reader," in which Burton gives indirectly an account of himself and his studies.

Burton, Tim 1960– •*US film director*• Born in Burbank, California, he worked for Walt Disney Studios where he made the inventive short films *Vincent* (1982) and *Frankenweenie* (1984). In 1985 he made his feature-length directorial debut with *Pee Wee's Big Adventure* and subsequently directed *Beetlejuice* (1988), *Batman* (1989), *Edward Scissorhands* (1990), *Ed Wood* (1994), *Mars Attacks!* (1996) and *Planet of the Apes* (2001). He has also produced the stop-motion animation films *The Nightmare Before Christmas* (1993) and *James and the Giant Peach* (1996).

Bury, Richard de *See* **Aungerville, Richard**

Busby, Sir Matt 1909–94 •*Scottish soccer player and manager*• Born in Bellshill, Lanarkshire, he became manager of Manchester United in 1945 after a comparatively undistinguished playing career with Manchester City and Liverpool. Almost immediately the club won the Football Association Cup in 1948 and the League Cup shortly afterward. Rebuilding the team, he seemed likely to win the European Cup for Great Britain for the first time in 1958 but his young team (known as the "Busby babes") was largely wiped out in an air crash at Munich airport. He himself was severely injured, but patiently reconstructed the team until European Cup success eventually came in 1968.

Bush, Alan Dudley 1900–95 •*English composer and pianist*• Born in London, he studied at the Royal Academy of Music (1918–22), and was founder of the Workers' Music Association (1936), of which he was president from 1941. His political and philosophical beliefs underlie much of his work, which includes four operas, four symphonies, concertos for violin and piano, choral works, including *The Winter Journey* (1946), songs, including the cycle *Voices of the Prophets* (1952), many chamber works and a considerable quantity of piano music and organ works.

Bush, George Herbert Walker 1924– •*41st President of the US*• Born in Milton, Massachusetts, the son of a Connecticut senator, he served in the US Navy (1942–45), and after the war received a degree in economics from Yale and established an oil-drilling business in Texas. In 1966 he devoted himself to politics, and was elected to the House of Representatives. During the Watergate scandal he was chairman of the Republican National Committee (1973–74) under President **Nixon**, and during the **Ford** administration he served as US envoy to China (1974–75), and then became director of the CIA (1976). In 1980 he sought the Republican presidential nomination, but lost to **Ronald Reagan**, later becoming his Vice President. He became President in 1988, defeating the Democratic candidate, **Michael Dukakis**. His administration (1989–93) was marked by his aggressive foreign policy, which included ordering the invasion of Panama (1989) to oust **Manuel Noriega** and presiding over the US-led UN coalition to drive Iraqi forces from Kuwait in the Gulf War (1991). He signed nuclear arms limitation treaties with the USSR and Russia and the North American Free Trade Agreement (1992) with Canada and Mexico. In the 1992 presidential elections he lost the presidency to Democrat **Bill Clinton**. His son, **George W Bush**, became US President in 2001.

Bush, George W(alker) 1946– •*43rd President of the US*• He was born in New Haven, Connecticut, the son of **George Bush**, 41st US President, and studied at Yale University and Harvard Business School. His early career was in the oil industry as founder of the Spectrum 7 Energy Corporation, and in 1989 he was manager of a consortium that bought the Texas Rangers baseball team. He was elected Governor of Texas in 1994 and proved a popular choice, winning reelection four years later. In 2000 he ran as the Republican presidential candidate against **Al Gore**, winning by the tightest margin in more than a century. In reaction to the **Clinton** years, his policies were notably right of center, particularly including tax cuts and support for a national missile defense system. As a President with little experience in foreign affairs, most commentators anticipated a withdrawal of the US from the world stage, but in 2001, following terrorist attacks on New York and Washington DC, Bush aggressively moved into the international arena and committed the US to a war on terrorism. This included the military invasion of Afghanistan and Iraq and the overthrow of the political regimes in these countries.

Bush, Kate (Catherine) 1958– •*English pop singer and songwriter*• Born in Plumstead, Surrey, she enjoyed immediate success with her debut single "Wuthering Heights" (1978), which became the first single written and performed by a woman to top the British charts. The album *Wuthering Heights* also topped the charts and Bush's many subsequent recordings have been characterized by the same emotional romanticism and unique soaring vocal style. Later albums have included *Never For Ever* (1980), *Hounds of Love* (1985) and *The Red Shoes* (1993).

Bush, Vannevar 1890–1974 •*US electrical engineer and inventor*• Born in Everett, Massachusetts, he graduated from Tufts College and the Massachusetts Institute of Technology. He devoted most of his considerable research effort from 1925 on to the development of calculating machines that led directly to the digital computers universally used today. He also devised a cipher-breaking machine that was successful in breaking Japanese codes during World War II, and he was instrumental in setting up the "Manhattan Project" in 1942 that led to the creation of the US atomic bomb.

Busoni, Ferruccio Benvenuto 1866–1924 •*Italian pianist and composer*• Born in Empoli, Tuscany, he was an infant prodigy. In 1889 he became Professor of Pianoforte at Helsinki. The influence of **Franz Liszt** is apparent in his piano concerto, and of his four operas, *Doktor Faust*, completed posthumously by a pupil in 1925, is his most impressive work. He was a noted editor of the keyboard music of **J S Bach** and Liszt.

“ ”

Music is the art of sounds in the movement of time.

1923 ***The Essence of Music.***

Buss, Frances Mary 1827–94 •*English pioneer of higher education for women*• Born in London, at the age of 23 she founded the North London Collegiate School for Ladies and was headmistress (1850–94)—the first woman to give herself the title. She also campaigned for women to be admitted to university. She appears in verse with **Dorothea Beale** of Cheltenham Ladies' College ("Miss Buss and Miss Beale, Cupid's darts do not feel").

Bustamante, Sir (William) Alexander, *originally* **William Alexander Clarke** 1884–1977 •*Jamaican politician*• Born near Kingston, he was adopted at the age of 15 by a Spanish seaman called Bustamante and spent an adventurous youth abroad before returning in 1932 to become a trade union leader. In 1943 he founded the Jamaica Labour Party (JLP) and in 1962, when Jamaica achieved independence, became its first Prime Minister.

Butcher, Rosemary 1947– •*English choreographer*• Born in Bristol, she studied at Dartington College in Devon. She began choreographing her own work in 1976 and has made over 30 pieces, often performing them in unusual places—in art galleries and once on a Scottish mountainside. The fast-moving *Flying Lines* (1985) incorporates music by **Michael Nyman** and an installation by Peter Noble. Other work includes *Touch the Earth* (1986) and *Spaces 4* (1997).

Bute, John Stuart, 3rd Earl of 1713–92 •*Scottish statesman*• He succeeded his father in 1723, and about 1737 became a lord of the bedchamber of **Frederick Louis**, Prince of Wales. On the Prince's death (1751), Bute strongly influenced **George III**. He was the main instrument in breaking the power of the Whigs and establishing the personal rule of the monarch through parliament. He was made Prime Minister in 1762, but resigned the following year.

Butenandt, Adolf Friedrich Johann 1903–95 •*German biochemist and Nobel Prize winner*• Born in Wesermuende, he studied medicine in Göttingen, and in 1929 he and **Edward Doisy** independently determined the structure of the female steroid hormone estrone. In 1931 Butenandt isolated the male hormone androsterone. The work for which he became truly famous, however, was the isolation of a few milligrams of progesterone and the determination of its structure. Butenandt was awarded the 1939 Nobel Prize for chemistry jointly with **Leopold Ružička**, although he was forbidden to accept it by the Nazi regime.

Buthelezi, Chief Mangosuthu Gatsha 1928– •*South African Zulu leader and politician*• Born in Mahlabatini, he was expelled from Fore Hare University College in 1950 where he was a member of the ANC (African National Congress). Officially appointed as chief of the Buthelezi in 1953, he was assistant to the Zulu king Cyprian (1953–68) before being elected leader of the Zulu Territorial Authority in 1970. A political moderate, he became in 1976 chief minister of KwaZulu, the Black South African homeland (which ceased to exist on May 1, 1994). He is founder-president of the Inkatha Freedom Party, a paramilitary organization for achieving a nonracist democratic political system. In 1994 he became Minister of Home Affairs in South Africa.

Butkus, Dick (Richard) 1942– •*US football player*• Born in Chicago, he played college football at the University of Illinois, joining the Chicago Bears in 1965. Initially a starting linebacker, then a middle linebacker, he became the team's defensive star with a combination of agility, swiftness and strength, appearing in seven All-Pro teams and eight consecutive Pro Bowl teams. A serious knee injury ended his career in 1973, after which he appeared widely on television and in films.

Butler, Alban 1710–73 •*English hagiographer*• Born in Appletree, Northampton, he was educated at Douai in France. He later became head of the English College at St Omer. His great work, the *Lives of the Saints* (1756–59), primarily intended for edification, makes no distinction between fact and fiction.

Butler, Benjamin Franklin 1818–93 •*US lawyer, general and congressman*• Born in Deerfield, New Hampshire, he was admitted to the bar in 1840, and became noted as a criminal lawyer, champion of the working classes and an ardent Democrat. As an army officer during the Civil War (1861–65), in 1862 he took possession of New Orleans, where prompt and severe measures crushed all opposition, and in 1863 received a command in Virginia. Elected to Congress in 1866, he was prominent in Republican efforts for the reconstruction of the Southern states and the impeachment of President **Andrew Johnson**. In 1882 he was elected Governor of Massachusetts.

Butler, Josephine Elizabeth, *née* **Grey** 1828–1906 •*English social reformer*• Born in Millfield Hill, Northumberland, she promoted women's education and successfully crusaded against licensed brothels and the white-slave traffic, and against the Contagious Diseases Acts which made women in seaports and military towns liable for compulsory examination for venereal disease.

Butler, Nicholas Murray 1862–1947 •*US educator and Nobel Prize winner*• Born in Elizabeth, New Jersey, he studied philosophy at Columbia University and in Berlin and Paris. Working for peace throughout his life, he established the Carnegie Endowment for International Peace and served as its president from 1925 to 1945. He shared the Nobel Peace Prize with **Jane Addams** in 1931.

Butler, Reg(inald) Cotterell 1913–81 •*English sculptor*• He was born in Buntingford, Hertfordshire, and trained as an architect and engineer. In 1953 he won first prize in the international *Unknown Political Prisoner* sculpture competition with a steel and bronze working model (1955–56). He was recognized as one of the leading exponents of "linear" sculpture, and produced many constructions in wrought iron, although he later turned to a more realistic style.

Butler, R(ichard) A(usten) Butler, Baron, *also called* **Rab** 1902–82 •*English Conservative politician*• Born in Attock Serai, India, the son of a distinguished administrator, he was educated at Marlborough and Cambridge, and became Member of Parliament for Saffron Walden, Essex in 1929. After a series of junior ministerial appointments from 1932, he was Minister of Education (1941–45). His name will always be associated with the Education Act of 1944 that reorganized the secondary school system and introduced the 11-plus examination for the selection of grammar school pupils. In the 1951 **Churchill** government he was Chancellor of the Exchequer, and in 1955 became Lord Privy Seal (until 1959) and Leader of the House of Commons (until 1961). He was widely expected to succeed **Anthony Eden** as Prime Minister in 1957, but **Harold Macmillan** was chosen and Butler became Home Secretary (until 1962). He again narrowly lost the premiership to **Alec Douglas-Home** in 1963, and became Foreign Secretary (1963–64). Once described as "both irreproachable and unapproachable," he will go down as one of the most progressive, thoughtful, and dedicated of Tory leaders. In 1965 he was made a life peer.

Butler, Samuel 1612–80 •*English satirist*• Born in Strensham, Worcestershire, he was educated at Worcester Grammar School, and perhaps Oxford or Cambridge. After the Restoration, he became secretary to the Earl of Carbery, Lord President of Wales, by whom he was appointed steward of Ludlow Castle (1661). From 1670 to 1674 he was secretary to George Villiers, 2nd Duke of **Buckingham**. He is best known as the author of the poem *Hudibras* (published in three parts: 1663, 1664, 1678). A burlesque satire on Puritanism, it secured immediate popularity, and was a special favorite of **Charles II**.

Butler, Samuel 1835–1902 •*English author, painter and musician*• He was born in Langar Rectory, near Bingham, Nottinghamshire, and educated at Shrewsbury and St John's College, Cambridge. Always quarreling with his clergyman father, he abandoned the idea of taking orders and instead became a sheep farmer in New Zealand (1859–64). On returning to England he lived in London and wrote *Erewhon* (1872), a Utopian satire in which, for example, machines have been abolished for fear of their mastery over men's minds. The dominant theme of its supplement, *Erewhon Revisited* (1901), is the origin of religious belief. Butler also studied painting and loved music, composing extensively. He later published translations of the *Iliad* (1898) and the *Odyssey* (1900), and his essay *The Humour of Homer* (1892) is a remarkable piece of literary criticism. He is best known, however, for his autobiographical novel *The Way of All Flesh*, published posthumously in 1903, a work of moral realism on the causes of strife between different generations, which left its mark on much 20th-century literature.

“ ”

The advantage of doing one's praising for oneself is that one can lay it on so thick and exactly in the right places.

1903 ***The Way of All Flesh****, chapter 34.*

Butler-Sloss, Dame (Ann) Elizabeth Oldfield, *née* **Havers** 1933– •*English judge*• Born at Kew Gardens, Richmond, Surrey, she was called to the bar in 1955 and practiced for 15 years. She was a divorce registrar from 1970, until her appointment in 1979 to the Family Division of the High Court. Also that year she was given the honorary title of Dame Commander, Order of the British Empire. After chairing the Cleveland Sex Abuse Inquiry (1987–88), she became the first woman Lord Justice of Appeal. In 1999 she became President of the Family Division.

Butlin, Sir William Edmund, *known as* **Billy Butlin** 1899–1980 •*British vacation camp promoter*• Born in South Africa, he moved with his parents to Canada. After serving in World War I, he worked his passage to England with only £5 capital. In 1936 he opened his first camp at Skegness, followed by others at Clacton and Filey. During World War II he served as director general of hostels to the Ministry of Supply. After the war more camps and hotels were opened both in Britain and abroad.

Butor, Michel Marie François 1926– •*French writer*• Born in Mons-en-Baroeul, he studied at the Sorbonne. He came to prominence during the 1950s, together with **Alain Robbe-Grillet**, **Nathalie Sarraute**, **Claude Simon** and others, who were known collectively as the “New Novelists.” His novels include *L'emploi du temps* (1956, Eng trans *Passing Time*, 1960), *Le génie du lieu* (1960, “The Spirit of the Place”), *Matière de rêves* (4 vols, 1975–77, “The Stuff of Dreams”) and *Transit* (1992). He also wrote poetry, plays and criticism.

Butt, Dame Clara Ellen 1872–1936 •*English concert and operatic contralto*• She was born in Southwick, Sussex. Her career was principally one of the concert hall and especially of the English music festivals, which seemed incomplete without her imposing presence. **Elgar** wrote his *Sea Pictures* for her, which she premiered at the Norwich Festival of 1899. In 1900 she married the English baritone R(obert) Kennerley Rumford (1870–1957); they often performed together, toured the US and Canada, and made four visits to Australia and New Zealand.

Butterley, Nigel Henry 1935– •*Australian composer and pianist*• Born in Sydney, he studied at the New South Wales Conservatorium, and later in London. He won the prestigious Italia prize in 1966 with *In the Head the Fire*, a musical work for radio. Other major works include *Fire in the Heavens*, which was performed at the opening of the Sydney Opera House in 1973, a violin concerto, *Meditations of Thomas Traherne*, *Letter from Hardy's Bay* and *Explorations for Piano and Orchestra*.

Butterworth, George 1885–1916 •*English composer, critic, and folk-song collector*• Born in London, he is remembered for his songs from *A Shropshire Lad* (1913) and the orchestral *The Banks of Green Willows* (1914). He was killed in action at Pozières.

Button, Dick (Richard Totten) 1929– •*US figure skater*• Born in Englewood, New Jersey, he studied at Harvard and competed nationally from an early age, winning seven consecutive national championships from 1946 to 1952 and five consecutive world championships from 1948 to 1952. He secured Olympic gold in 1948 and 1952, and the 1949 Sullivan Award as the US's outstanding amateur athlete. He later worked in television production.

Buttrose, Ita Clare 1942– •*Australian journalist, publisher and broadcaster*• Born in Sydney, she edited several women's magazines during the 1970s. Having been women's editor at the age of 28 for the *Daily Telegraph* and the *Sunday Telegraph*, she returned in 1981 as editor in chief, the first woman in Australia to be editor of either a daily or a Sunday newspaper. In 1985 she became host of *Woman's Day* on television, and in 1988 chief executive of Capricorn Publishing Pty Ltd and editor in chief of the *Sun Herald*, launching her own magazine, *Ita*, the following year and editing it until 1994.

Butzer, Martin *See* **Bucer, Martin**

Buxtehude, Diderik, *German* **Dietrich** c. 1637–1707 •*Danish organist and composer*• Born in Oldesloe or Hälsingborg (Helsingborg, now in Sweden), he was appointed to the coveted post of organist at the Marienkirche, Lübeck, in 1668. Here he began the famous *Abendmusiken*—evening concerts during Advent of his own sacred choral and orchestral music and organ works. In 1705 **J S Bach** walked 200 miles across Germany from Arnstadt and **Handel** traveled from Hamburg to attend the concerts and to meet Buxtehude, who was highly respected in his time as an organist and as a composer.

Buys Ballot, Christoph Hendrik Diederik 1817–90 •*Dutch meteorologist*• Born in Kloetinge, Zeeland, he studied and taught at Utrecht University. From 1852 onward he compiled maps which were among the first weather charts, showing wind direction and speed and temperature anomalies in graded shadings. In 1857 he produced Buys Ballot's law. He organized the first service of weather forecasts and storm warnings (1860) and designed the aeroclinoscope, which indicates the position of the center of a depression and the pressure gradient.

Byars, Betsy Cromer 1928– •*US children's writer*• Born in Charlotte, North Carolina, she was educated at Queen's College, New Jersey. She began to write in the 1960s but made no great impact until *The Summer of the Swans* (1970), the story of a girl and her retarded brother, which was awarded the **Newbery** Medal. Her other titles include *The Eighteenth Emergency* (1973), *Goodbye, Chicken Little* (1979) and *The Animal, the Vegetable, and John D Jones* (1982).

Byatt, Dame A(ntonia) S(usan), *née* **Drabble** 1936– •*English novelist and critic*• She was born in Sheffield and educated at Newnham College, Cambridge. After some years as a teacher and academic, she published *Degrees of Freedom* (1965), the first full-length study of **Iris Murdoch**'s novels. Further highly respected critical works followed. She made her reputation as a novelist with her third novel, *The Virgin in the Garden* (1978). This was followed by novels including *Possession* (1990), which won the Booker Prize, and *The Biographer's Tale* (2000). Her interests extend to art and art history, literary and social history, and philosophy, all of which feature in her novels. She published a volume of short stories and a collection of fairy tales, and was given the honorary title of Dame Commander, Order of the British Empire, in 1999. She is the elder sister of the novelist **Margaret Drabble**.

“ ”

He's one of those men who argues by increments of noise—so that as you open your mouth he says another, cleverer, louder thing.

1990 ***Possession****, chapter 15.*

Byers, Stephen John 1953– •*English Labour politician*• Born in Wolverhampton, West Midlands, he attended Liverpool Polytechnic before becoming a lecturer in law at Newcastle Polytechnic (1977–92). In 1992 he became Member of Parliament for Wallsend (renamed Tyneside North in 1997), and after the Labour landslide of 1997 became Minister for School Standards (1997–98), Chief Secretary to the Treasury (1998) and Secretary for Trade and Industry (1998–2001). As Secretary of State for

Transport, Local Government and the Regions (from 2001), he came under pressure following the collapse of Railtrack, the company running the railway network, and resigned (2002).

Bygraves, Max, *originally* **Walter William Bygraves** 1922– •*English singer and entertainer*• Born in London, he gained his stage name doing impressions of the legendary **Max Miller** and later won a part in BBC Radio's hugely popular *Educating Archie*. Seminovelty songs like "The Cowpuncher's Cantata," "Deck of Cards," and the Manning-Hoffman tongue-twister "Gilly Gilly Ossenfeffer Katzenellen Bogen by the Sea" were inexplicably successful and he had straight hits, too, with "You Need Hands" and "Fings Ain't Wot They Used to Be." He recorded a hugely successful sequence of standards albums, starting with *Singalongamax* in 1971. His television successes include *Max Bygraves* and *Singalongamax*. He was also in films such as *Skimpy in the Navy* (1949), *Tom Brown's Schooldays* (1951) and *Spare the Rod* (1961).

Byng, George, 1st Viscount Torrington 1663–1733 •*English naval commander*• Born in Wrotham, Kent, he joined the navy at 15, and as a supporter of William of Orange (the future **William III**), gained rapid promotion. As rear admiral, he captured Gibraltar in 1704, and for his gallant conduct at Málaga was knighted. In 1708 he commanded a squadron that frustrated a threatened landing in Scotland by the Old Pretender, **James Francis Edward Stuart**, and again in 1715. In 1718, as Admiral of the Fleet, he destroyed the Spanish fleet off Messina.

Byng (of Vimy), Julian Hedworth George Byng, 1st Viscount 1862–1935 •*English field marshal*• Commissioned in the 10th Hussars in 1883, he served in the Sudan (1884) and South Africa (1899–1902). In World War I he commanded the 9th Army Corps in Gallipoli (1915), the Canadian Army Corps in France at the capture of Vimy Ridge (1916–17), and thereafter the 3rd Army (1917–18), executing the first large-scale tank attack at Cambrai (November 1917). He later became Governor-General of Canada (1921–26) and was appointed field marshal in 1932.

Byrd, Richard Evelyn 1888–1957 •*US explorer and aviator*• Born in Winchester, Virginia, he graduated from the US Naval Academy, Annapolis, in 1912 and joined the navy's aviation service. With **Floyd Bennett** he made the first airplane flight over the North Pole (1926), for which they received the Congressional Medal of Honor. In 1929 he established a base, "Little America," in the Antarctic and was the first to fly over the South Pole.

Byrd, William 1543–1623 •*English composer*• He was born probably in Lincoln, and his early life is obscure, but it is likely that he was one of the children of the Chapel Royal, under **Thomas Tallis**. At the age of 20 he became organist of Lincoln Cathedral, where he remained until 1572, when he was made joint organist with Tallis of the Chapel Royal. Byrd was associated with **John Bull** and **Orlando Gibbons** in *Parthenia* (1611), the first printed music for virginals. A firm Catholic, Byrd was several times prosecuted as a recusant, but he wrote music of power and beauty for both the Catholic and the Anglican services, as well as madrigals, songs, and music for strings.

Byrne, John 1940– •*Scottish dramatist and stage designer*• He was born in Paisley, trained at Glasgow Art School, and designed stage sets for the 7:84 Theatre Company before writing his first play, *Writer's Cramp*, produced at the Edinburgh Festival Fringe (1977). Other plays include *The Slab Boys* (1978), *Normal Service* (1979) and *Cara Coco* (1982). He wrote the highly acclaimed *Tutti Frutti* (1987), a BBC Scotland television series about an aging pop group for which he won a British Academy of Film and Television Arts award, and followed it with *Your Cheatin' Heart* (1989). He returned to writing for the stage in 1992 with *Colquhoun and MacBryde*.

Byron, Annabella (Anne Isabella), *known as* **Lady Byron** or **Lady Noel Byron**, *née* **Milbanke** 1792–1860 •*English philanthropist*• Born at Elmore Hall, Durham, she married **Byron** in 1815, but the couple separated the following year after the birth of their daughter Ada (later the Countess of **Lovelace**). Lady Byron moved in radical circles and was a close friend of the art critic Anna Jameson (1794–1860) and **Barbara Bodichon**. She is noted particularly for her commitment to schemes for improving women's education, many of which she funded. Lady Byron was also involved in agricultural and industrial reforms, cooperative movements, the antislavery movement (she was a friend of **Harriet Beecher Stowe**) and other radical causes.

Byron (of Rochdale), George Gordon Noel Byron, 6th Baron *known as* **Lord Byron** 1788–1824 •*English poet of Scottish antecedents*• He was born in London, the grandson of naval officer **John Byron**, and the son of Captain "Mad Jack" Byron (1756–91). He was lame from birth, and this, together with his early years in shabby surroundings and exposed to the violent temper of his deserted mother, produced a repression in him which is thought to explain many of his later actions. In 1798 he succeeded to the title on the death of his great-uncle. He was educated at Aberdeen grammar school, then privately at Dulwich and at Harrow School, and went on to Trinity College, Cambridge, in 1805, where he read much but led a dissipated life. An early collection of poems under the title *Hours of Idleness* was badly received, and Byron replied with his powerful Popian satire *English Bards and Scotch Reviewers* (1809). He then set out on a grand tour, visiting Spain, Malta, Albania, Greece, and the Aegean, returning after two years with "a great many stanzas in Spenser's measure relative to the countries he had visited"; these appeared under the title *Childe Harold's Pilgrimage* in 1812 and were widely popular. This was followed by a series of oriental pieces, including the *Giaour* (1813), *Lara* (1814) and the *Siege of Corinth* (1816). During this time he dramatized himself as a man of mystery, a gloomy romantic figure, derived from the popular fiction of the day and not least from *Childe Harold*. He became the darling of London society, and lover of Lady Caroline Lamb, and gave to Europe the concept of the "Byronic hero." In 1815 he married an heiress, Anne Isabella Milbanke (**Annabella Byron**), who left him in 1816 after the birth of a daughter, Ada (later Countess of **Lovelace**). He was also suspected of a more than brotherly love for his half-sister, Augusta Leigh, and was ostracized. He left for the Continent, traveled through Belgium and the Rhine country to Switzerland, where he met **Percy Bysshe Shelley**, and on to Venice and Rome, where he wrote the last canto of *Childe Harold* (1817). He spent two years in Venice and there met the Countess Teresa Guiccioli, who became his mistress. Some of his best works belong to this period, including *Beppo* (1818), *A Vision of Judgment* (1822) and the satirical *Don Juan* (1819–24), written in a new meter (ottava rima) and in an informal conversational manner which enabled him to express the whole of his complex personality. He gave active help to the Italian revolutionaries and founded with **Leigh Hunt** a short-lived journal, *The Liberal*. In 1823 he joined the Greek insurgents who had risen against the Turks, and died of marsh fever at Missolonghi.

C

Caballé, Montserrat 1933– •*Spanish soprano*• Born in Barcelona, she enjoys, in addition to her concert repertoire, great acclaim in a wide variety of stage roles from **Rossini** to **Puccini**, in contemporary opera, in zarzuela, and in the German tradition. She has sung at Covent Garden, Glyndebourne, the Metropolitan Opera, La Scala, Mexico City and at many other major houses, and has made numerous recordings.

Cabell, James Branch 1879–1958 •*US novelist and critic*• Born in Richmond, Virginia, he made his name with his romance *Jurgen* (1919), the best known of a sequence of 18 novels, collectively entitled *Biography of the Life of Manuel*. Set in the imaginary medieval kingdom of Poictesme, and written in an elaborate, sophisticated style, they show Cabell's fondness for archaisms.

Cable, George Washington 1844–1925 •*US writer*• Born in New Orleans, at the age of 19 he volunteered as a Confederate soldier. After the Civil War he earned a precarious living in New Orleans, before taking up a literary career in 1879. In 1884 he went to New England. His Creole sketches in *Scribner's* made his reputation. Among his books are *Old Creole Days* (1879), *The Silent South* (1885), *Bylow Hill* (1902), *Kincaid's Battery* (1908) and *Lovers of Louisiana* (1918).

Cabot, John, *originally* **Giovanni Caboto** 1425–c. 1500 •*Italian navigator and explorer, the discoverer of mainland North America*• Born in Genoa, he moved to England and settled in Bristol around 1490. In 1497 under letters patent from King **Henry VII**, he sailed from Bristol with two ships in search of a route to Asia, accompanied by his three sons. On June 24, after 52 days at sea, he sighted land and claimed North America for England. He is thought to have made further voyages in search of the Northwest Passage, and after setting out in 1498, died at sea.

Cabot, Sebastian 1474–1557 •*Venetian navigator and cartographer*• Born in Venice, Italy, or Bristol, England, he is thought to have sailed with his father, **John Cabot**, on expeditions in search of the Northwest Passage to Asia. In 1544 he published an engraved map of the world (the only surviving copy is in the Bibliothèque Nationale in Paris). In 1548 he returned to England where he was made inspector of the navy by King **Edward VI**, and in 1551 founded the company of Merchant Adventurers of London.

Cabral or **Cabrera, Pedro Álvarez** c. 1467–c. 1520 •*Portuguese navigator*• Born in Belmonte, he sailed from Lisbon in 1500 in command of a fleet of 13 vessels bound for the East Indies. Drifting into the South American current of the Atlantic Ocean, he was carried (in the same year as **Vincente Pinzón**) to the unknown coast of Brazil, which he claimed on behalf of Portugal. From there he landed at Mozambique. He next sailed to Calicut (Kozhikode, Kerala), where he made the first commercial treaty between Portugal and India. He returned to Lisbon in 1501.

Cabrera, Pedro Álvarez *See* **Cabral, Pedro Álvarez**

Cabrera Infante, Guillermo 1929– •*Cuban novelist*• Born in Gibara, and educated at Havana University, he emigrated to England in 1966 and became a British citizen. He is best known for *Tres tristes tigres* (1967, Eng trans *Three Trapped Tigers*,1971), and *Vista del amanecer en el trópico* (1974, Eng trans *A View of Dawn in the Tropics*,1978). *La Habana para un infante difunto* (1979, Eng trans *Infante's Inferno*, 1984) is set in Havana during the 1940s and 1950s. He translated **James Joyce**'s *Dubliners* into Spanish (1972), has also written journalism, and, writing as "Guillermo Cain," film criticism (collected in *A Twentieth Century Job*, 1991) and screenplays.

Cabrini, St Francesca Xavier, *originally* **Maria Francesca** 1850–1917 •*US nun, the country's first saint*• Born in Sant 'Angelo, Lodigliano, Italy, she founded the Missionary Sisters of the Sacred Heart (1880), emigrated to the US in 1889 and became renowned as "Mother Cabrini" for her social and charitable work. She founded 67 houses in the US, Buenos Aires, Paris and Madrid. She was canonized in 1946. Her feast day is November 13.

Cadbury, George 1839–1922 •*English Quaker businessman and social reformer*• Born in Birmingham, he was the son of **John Cadbury**. In partnership with his elder brother, Richard Cadbury (1835–99), he took over his father's Birmingham-based cocoa business in 1861 and built it into the highly successful firm Cadbury Brothers. In 1894, guided by their Quaker and liberal principles, they established for the workers the model village of Bournville, near Birmingham. In 1902 George Cadbury became proprietor of the *Daily News* and campaigned actively for social reform through the newspaper.

Cadbury, John 1801–89 •*English Quaker businessman*• He was born in Birmingham, the son of Richard Tapper Cadbury, who had settled in Birmingham in 1794. He founded the cocoa and chocolate manufacturing firm which his sons Richard and **George Cadbury** took over in 1861.

Cade, Jack d. 1450 •*Irish rebel*• After an unsettled early career, he lived in Sussex, England, possibly as a physician. He then settled in Kent, and led the insurrection of 1450 against King **Henry VI**. With a great many followers he marched on London, but after a promise of pardon, his forces began to disperse. Cade attempted to reach the coast but was killed on the way.

Cadwallon d. 634 •*Pagan Welsh king of Gwynedd*• He ruled from c. 625. Having been driven out of his kingdom by **Edwin** (St Edwin), king of Northumbria, with **Penda**, king of Mercia, he invaded Northumbria (633) and killed Edwin at the Battle of Heathfield (Hatfield Chase), near Doncaster. He ravaged the kingdom, according to the Venerable **Bede**, but was himself defeated and killed by King **Oswald** (St Oswald) of Bernicia at the Battle of Heavenfield, near Hexham (634).

Caecilius, Firmianus *See* **Lactantius, Lucius Caelius**

Caedmon 7th century •*Anglo-Saxon poet*• He is the earliest Christian English poet known by name. According to **Bede**, he was an uneducated herdsman who in his old age received a divine call in a dream to sing of the Creation. He then became a monk at Whitby under the rule of **St Hilda**, where he turned other biblical themes into vernacular poetry.

Caesalpinus *See* **Cesalpino, Andrea**

Caesar, (Gaius) Julius 100 or 102–44 BC •*Roman general, statesman and dictator*• He was a member of the Julii, an ancient patrician family. His career progressed after service in Asia and Spain until, in 60 BC he reconciled Pompey and **Crassus**, and with them established the informal alliance known as the "First Triumvirate." Caesar gave Pompey his daughter Julia in marriage, while he married Calpurnia (Cornelia had died in 67, and Caesar had divorced his second wife Pompeia because the wife of Caesar, according to **Plutarch**, "must be above suspicion"). He was elected consul (59), and for a period of nine years (58–50) Caesar was occupied with military campaigns which extended Roman power to most of Gaul. He invaded Britain in 55 and 54. The triumvirate came to an end in 50 and the Senate called upon Caesar, now in Cisalpine Gaul, to resign his command and disband his army, and entrusted Pompey with large powers. Caesar refused and, supported by his victorious troops, he moved southward (49) and (famously) crossed the Rubicon, the boundary between Cisalpine Gaul and Italy. Pompey withdrew to Brundisium, pursued by Caesar, and from there to Greece (49); in three months Caesar was master of all Italy. After defeating Pompey's legates in Spain, he was appointed dictator. Pompey had gathered a powerful army in the east, and his fleet controlled the sea. Caesar, crossing the Adriatic, was driven back with heavy losses from Dyrrhachium. But in a second battle at Pharsalia (48), the senatorial army was routed, and Pompey himself fled to Egypt, where he was murdered. Caesar, again appointed dictator for a year, and consul for five years, instead of returning to Rome, went to Egypt where he engaged in the "Alexandrine War" on behalf of **Cleopatra**, who was now his mistress (47). After his victories in Gaul, Egypt, Pontus and Africa he had still to put down an insurrection by Pompey's sons in Spain (45). He received the title of "Father of his Country," was made dictator for life, and consul for 10 years; his person was declared sacred, his statue placed in temples, his portrait struck on coins, and the month Quintilis renamed Julius in his honor. Ambitious plans were ascribed to him. He proposed to codify the whole of Roman law, to found libraries, to drain the Pontine Marshes, to enlarge the harbor at Ostia, to dig a canal through the Isthmus, and to launch a war against the Dacians in central Europe and the Parthians in the east. In the midst of these vast designs he was assassinated on the Ides (15th) of March. The Republican conspirators were mostly aristocrats led by **Marcus Junius Brutus** and **Cassius**. A talented and successful orator and general, Caesar also left historical writings (on the Gallic and Civil Wars), which are simple and direct.

Cage, John 1912–92 •*US composer*• Born in Los Angeles, he was a pupil of **Schoenberg** and of Henry Cecil. Developing as an avant-garde composer, he not only used such experimental resources as indeterminacy (where a dice might be thrown to determine the elements of a composition), chance, electronics and the "prepared piano" (distorting the sound of the instrument with objects placed inside), but produced pieces, such as *4'33* (1952, silent throughout) and *Radio Music* (1956, for one to eight radios), that challenge established ideas about what music is. He carried on a lifelong collaboration with choreographer **Merce Cunningham**, composing music for his dances and often serving as his music director.

“ ”

Which is more musical, a truck passing by a factory or a truck passing by a music school?

1961 ***Silence.***

Cage, Nicolas, *originally* **Nicholas Coppola** 1964– •*US actor*• Born in Long Beach, California, he studied at the American Conservatory Theater in San Francisco before making his film debut in *Fast Times at Ridgemont High* (1982). He was then seen in *Rumble Fish* (1983) directed by his uncle **Francis Ford Coppola**. An adventurous performer, he has brought an intensity and individuality to a range of films including *Birdy* (1984), *Peggy Sue Got Married* (1986) and *Wild at Heart* (1990). He received an Academy Award for his performance as a dying alcoholic in *Leaving Las Vegas* (1995). Later films include *Con Air* (1997), *Snake Eyes* (1998) and *Adaptation* (2002).

Cagney, James Francis 1899–1986 •*US film actor*• Born on New York City's Lower East Side, he spent 10 years as an actor and dancer in vaudeville, in musicals and on Broadway. Seen there in *Penny Arcade* (1929), he was signed to a contract with Warner Brothers, making his film debut in *Sinner's Holiday* (1930). His film performance as the gangster in *The Public Enemy* (1931) brought him stardom, and it was followed by performances in *Angels with Dirty Faces* (1938), *The Roaring Twenties* (1939) and *Yankee Doodle Dandy* (1942), for which he won an Academy Award. Later, he offered an incisive psychological portrait of a hoodlum in one of his best films, *White Heat* (1949), and displayed his comic skills in the frenetic *One, Two, Three* (1961). He retired in 1961, but returned for *Ragtime* (1981) and the television film *Terrible Joe Moran* (1984). A farmer, painter and poet, he wrote an autobiography, *Cagney on Cagney* (1976).

Caillaux, Joseph Marie Auguste 1863–1944 •*French radical politician*• Born in Le Mans, he trained as a lawyer. As Prime Minister (1911–12), he negotiated the treaty with Germany following the Agadir Incident, by which France was given a free hand to subjugate Morocco. He was attacked for being too conciliatory toward Germany, and was arrested in 1918 on a charge of contacting the enemy. Tried by the Senate, he was sentenced in 1920 to three years' imprisonment. Amnestied in 1925, he resumed his political career in the influential post of President of the Finance Committee of the Senate. In 1914 his second wife shot and killed Gaston Calmette, editor of *Le Figaro*, who had published letters written to her by Caillaux while he was married to his first wife. She was acquitted after a sensational trial.

Cain •*Biblical character*• The eldest son of **Adam** and **Eve**, he was the brother of **Abel** and Seth. He is portrayed (in Genesis 4) as a farmer whose offering to God was rejected, in contrast to that of his herdsman brother Abel. He murdered Abel, and God's punishment was to make him a vagrant.

Cain, James M(allahan) 1892–1977 •*US thriller writer*• He was born in Annapolis, Maryland, and his earliest ambition was to emulate his mother and become a professional singer. He subsequently tried various jobs, was a reporter for many years and also taught journalism, but hankered after "the great American novel." After moving to California he found the style which is his hallmark, publishing *The Postman Always Rings Twice* (1934), in which an adulterous couple murder the woman's husband but betray each other, as well as *Serenade* (1937), *Mildred Pierce* (1941), *Double Indemnity* (1943) and *The Butterfly* (1947).

Caine, Sir Michael, *originally* **Maurice Micklewhite** 1933– •*English film actor*• Born in the East End of London, he spent many years as a struggling small-part actor before winning attention for his performance as an aristocratic officer in *Zulu* (1963). His belated stardom continued with roles as down-at-heel spy Harry Palmer in *The Ipcress File* (1965) and its two sequels, as the Cockney romeo *Alfie* (1966), and in *The Italian Job* (1969) and *Get Carter* (1971). A prolific performer, his reputation for consummate professionalism has withstood several inferior films and enhanced superior material like *California Suite* (1978) and *Educating Rita* (1983). Nominated four times, he won an Academy Award for *Hannah and Her Sisters* (1986, Best Supporting Actor) and again for *The Cider House Rules* (1999). He was knighted in 2000.

Cairncross, John 1913–95 •*Scottish double agent*• Born in Lesmahagow, he studied at Trinity College, Cambridge, and was recruited by the KGB in 1936. He was posted to the Cabinet Office on the outbreak of World War II and used the opportunity to pass secrets to the Soviet Union. He was dubbed "the Fifth Man," along with **Guy Burgess**, **Kim Philby**, **Anthony Blunt** and **Donald Maclean**, and although his role was discovered in the early 1950s he did not make a full public disclosure of his activities until 1991.

Cairns, Sir Hugh William Bell 1896–1952 •*Australian surgeon*• He was born in Port Pirie, South Australia. His medical studies at Adelaide University were interrupted by military service, but after World War I, a Rhodes Scholarship allowed him to continue his medical work, at Oxford and after, at the London Hospital. In 1937 he became Nuffield Professor of Surgery at Oxford. During World War II he became an adviser on head injuries to the Ministry of Health, and neurosurgeon to the army. He played a crucial role in organizing the evacuation and treatment of soldiers with neurological injuries and persuaded the army to make crash helmets compulsory for dispatch riders. Among his patients was **T E Lawrence**.

Caitanya c. 1486–1533 •*Indian Hindu mystic*• Born in Nadia, Bengal, he was a Sanskrit teacher before becoming an itinerant holy man. He was converted in 1510 to a life of devotion to Krishna. He spent the latter part of his life in Puri, inspiring disciples in both Bengal and Orissa with his emphasis on joy and love of Krishna, and the place of singing and dancing in worship.

Caius, John 1510–73 •*English physician and scholar*• Born in Norwich, Norfolk, he studied at Gonville Hall, Cambridge, then at Padua under **Andreas Vesalius**, then was a lecturer on anatomy in London (1544–64). President of the College of Physicians nine times, he was physician to **Edward VI**, **Mary I**, and **Elizabeth I**. In 1557 he obtained a charter to refound and enlarge his old

Cambridge college, Gonville Hall (founded by Edmund Gonville in 1348), and in 1559 became the first master of Gonville and Caius College. He was the author of various critical, antiquarian and scientific books, notably *A Boke or Counseill against the Disease Commonly Called the Sweate, or Sweatying Sicknesse* (1552).

Calamity Jane, *originally* **Martha Jane Burke** c. 1852–1903 •*US frontierswoman*• Born possibly in Princeton, Missouri, she was celebrated for her bravery and her skill at riding and shooting. She teamed up with the renowned US marshal **Wild Bill Hickok** at Deadwood, Dakota, before he was murdered. She is said to have threatened "calamity" for any man who tried to court her.

Caldecott, Randolph 1846–86 •*English artist and illustrator*• Starting as a bank clerk in Whitstable and Manchester, he moved to London to follow an artistic career. He illustrated **Washington Irving**'s *Old Christmas* (1876), and several children's books such as *The House That Jack Built* (1878) and **Aesop**'s *Fables* (1883). Since 1938 the Caldecott Medal has been awarded annually to the best US artist-illustrator of children's books.

Calder, Alexander 1898–1976 •*US artist, pioneer of kinetic art*• Born in Lawnton, Pennsylvania, he studied art in New York (1923–26). In 1926 he exhibited paintings in the Artists' Gallery, New York, and in 1929 he had a one-man show in Paris. A pioneer of kinetic art, from 1925 he increasingly specialized in abstract hanging wire constructions (**Marcel Duchamp** christened them "mobiles" in 1932). Some of these were connected to motors and were inspired by his fascination with the motion of animals and acrobats at the Ringling Brothers—**Barnum** and Bailey Circus.

Calderón de la Barca, Pedro 1600–81 •*Spanish dramatist*• Born in Madrid, he was educated by the Jesuits, studied at Salamanca (1613–19), and for 10 years served in the army in Italy and Flanders. In 1635 he was summoned by **Philip IV** to Madrid, and appointed a sort of master of the revels. The Catalonian rebellion in 1640 made him return to the army, but in 1651 he entered the priesthood, and in 1653 withdrew to Toledo. Ten years later he was recalled to court and to the resumption of his dramatic activity, and he continued to write for the court, the Church, and the public theaters till his death. His *autos sacramentales*, outdoor plays for the festival of Corpus Christi, number 72, have been divided into seven classes—biblical, ethical, "cloak and sword plays," dramas of passion, and so forth. The finest of them is *El divino Orfeo* ("Divine Orpheus"). Of his regular dramas 118 are extant, of which the most famous are *La vida es sueño* ("Life's a Dream") and *El alcalde de Zalamea* ("The Mayor of Zalamea"), both probably written in the 1630s.

Caldwell, Erskine 1903–87 •*US writer*• Born in White Oak, Georgia, he worked among the "poor whites" in the southern states, where he absorbed the background for his best-known work *Tobacco Road* (1932), of which the dramatized version by Jack Kirkland (1933) had a record run in New York. Other books include *God's Little Acre* (1933), *Sure Hand of God* (1947), *A Lamp for Nightfall* (1952), *Love and Money* (1954) and *Close to Home* (1962).

Calgacus, *also called* **Galgacus** 1st century AD •*Caledonian chieftain in northern Britain*• He was leader of the tribes defeated by **Agricola** at the Battle of Mons Graupius (AD 83). Agricola's biographer, **Tacitus**, attributes to him a heroic speech on the eve of a battle, with a ringing denunciation of Roman imperialism ("They make a desolation, and call it peace").

Calhoun, John Caldwell 1782–1850 •*US politician*• Born near Calhoun Mills (now Mount Carmel), South Carolina, he became a successful lawyer. In Congress he supported the measures which led to the war of 1812–15 with Great Britain, and promoted the protective tariff. In 1817 he joined **Monroe**'s Cabinet as Secretary of War. He was vice president under **John Q Adams** (1825–29) and **Andrew Jackson** (1829–37). In 1844, as Secretary of State, he signed a treaty annexing Texas, but strenuously opposed the war of 1846–47 with Mexico. He, **Henry Clay**, and **Daniel Webster** were the "great triumvirate" of US political orators.

Caligula, *properly* **Gaius Julius Caesar Germanicus** AD 12–41 •*Roman emperor*• The youngest son of **Germanicus Caesar** and **Agrippina** the Elder, he was born in Antium. He was nicknamed Caligula from his little soldier's boots (*caligae*). He ingratiated himself with **Tiberius**, and, on his death (AD 37), was coheir alongside the emperor's grandson Gemellus. The Senate, however, conferred imperial power on Caligula alone. His rule then developed into an erratic despotism. He banished or murdered his relatives, excepting his uncle **Claudius** and sister Drusilla (with whom he was suspected of committing incest), executed and confiscated the property of many citizens of Rome, and awarded himself extravagant honors, having aspirations toward deification. His brief but traumatic reign ended when he was assassinated.

“ ”

Utinam populus Romanus unam cervicem haberet!
Would that the Roman people had but one neck!

*c. 40 AD Quoted in Suetonius's **Lives of the Caesars**, "Gaius Caligula," section 30.*

Calisher, Hortense 1911– •*US novelist and short-story writer*• She was born in New York City, and educated at Barnard College there (graduated 1932); her fictional characters are usually drawn from the city's upper-middle class. Her novels, though frequently of novella length, are less successful than her powerfully and precisely written short stories, which include "In Greenwich There Are Many Gravelled Walks." Her memoirs were published in 1988 entitled *Kissing Cousins*.

Calixtus or **Callistus I** d. 222 AD •*Italian pope*• According to **Hippolytus**, his bitter opponent who became antipope in AD 217, he was originally a slave, who had twice undergone severe punishment for his crimes before he became a priest under Zephyrinus, whom he succeeded as pope (218). He was martyred.

Callaghan of Cardiff, (Leonard) James Callaghan, Baron, *also called* **Jim Callaghan** 1912– •*English Labour politician and prime minister*• Born in Portsmouth and educated at Portsmouth Northern Secondary School, he joined the staff of the Inland Revenue in 1929. In 1945 he was elected Labour Member of Parliament for South Cardiff and from 1950 represented Southeast Cardiff, and was made Chancellor of the Exchequer under **Harold Wilson** (1964–67). In this capacity he introduced some of the most controversial taxation measures in British fiscal history, including the corporation and selective employment taxes. He was Home Secretary (1967–70) and Foreign Secretary (1974–76), and was elected Prime Minister on Wilson's resignation (1976), remaining in office until the general election of 1979. A failure to anticipate or check the growing power of left-wing extremists within his party and in trade unionism is said to have contributed greatly to Labour's defeat by **Margaret Thatcher**. He resigned as Leader of the Opposition in 1980 and was made a life peer in 1987. His autobiography *Time and Chance* was published in 1987.

Callas, Maria, *stage name of* **Maria Meneghini**, *née* **Kalogeropoulos** 1923–77 •*US soprano*• Born in New York City of Greek parents, she studied at Athens Conservatory, and in 1947 appeared in Verona in *La Gioconda* ("The Joyful Girl"), where she won immediate recognition. She sang with great authority in all the most exacting soprano roles, and was particularly impressive in the intricate *bel canto* style of pre-Verdian Italian opera. The fierce but truthful drama of her performances, her tumultuous personal life (including a long relationship with **Aristotle Onassis**), and her transformation into an exceptional beauty all added to her fascination for the public. Driven perhaps too hard, her voice began to fail early, and she gave her last operatic performance at the Metropolitan in *Tosca* in 1965.

Calles, Plutarco Elias 1877–1945 •*Mexican political leader*• Born in Guaymas, Sonora, he became a schoolmaster and tradesman. He took part in the revolt against **Porfirio Díaz** (1910) and became Governor of Sonora (1917–19) and Secretary of the Interior (1920–24). From 1924 to 1928 he was President of Mexico. Known for his fanatical anticlericalism and for his efforts to restrict foreign influence in the oil industry, he was defeated by **Lázaro Cárdenas** and was exiled to the US in 1936, but allowed to return in 1941.

Callil, Carmen Thérèse 1938– •*Australian publisher*• Born and educated in Melbourne, of Irish-Lebanese descent, she went to

London in 1960. In 1972, with Ursula Owen and Rosie Boycott, she founded the feminist publishing house, Virago Press, with the intention of securing a place for women in the publishing and writing of literature in English. The company earned renown for promoting successful female authors like **Maya Angelou**, **Edith Wharton** and **Margaret Atwood**. When Virago joined the publishing group of Chatto and Windus, Bodley Head and Cape in 1982, Callil remained chairman but also became managing director of Chatto and Windus and The Hogarth Press, where she remained for 11 years. She resigned her chairmanship of Virago in 1995.

Callimachus c. 305–c. 240 BC •*Hellenistic poet, grammarian and critic*• Born in Cyrene, Libya, he became head of the Alexandrian library, and prepared a catalogue of it, in 120 volumes. He wrote a number of hymns and epigrams and a long elegiac poem, the *Aitia*. Some 64 of his epigrams remain, including one to his friend Heraclitus of Halicarnassus, made familiar in the translation by **William Cory** ("They told me, Heraclitus, they told me you were dead").

Callistratus 4th century BC •*Athenian orator and statesman*• His eloquence is said to have fired the imagination of the young **Demosthenes**. In 366 BC he allowed the Thebans to occupy Oropus, and was prosecuted, but defended himself successfully in a brilliant speech. He was prosecuted again in 361 BC for his Spartan sympathies and then was condemned to death, but fled before the sentence was pronounced. He returned from exile in Macedonia, hoping to win public support, but was instead executed.

Callistus I *See* **Calixtus I**

Callow, Simon Phillip Hugh 1949– •*English actor, director and writer*• He was born in London and made his London debut in *The Plumber's Progress* (1975). He joined the Joint Stock theater company in 1977. His extensive stage work has included performances in *Titus Andronicus*, **Brecht**'s *The Resistible Rise of Arturo Ui*, **Peter Shaffer**'s *Amadeus* (1979) and **Alan Bennett**'s *Single Spies*. In 1991 he directed the **Rodgers** and **Hammerstein** musical *Carmen Jones* at the Old Vic and made his debut as a film director with **Carson McCullers**'s *Ballad of the Sad Café*. His film appearances include *Four Weddings and a Funeral* (1994) and *Jefferson in Paris* (1995). He has directed widely in the theater and in opera, and written biographies of **Charles Laughton** (1987) and **Orson Welles** (1995).

Calloway, Cab(ell) 1907–94 •*US jazz bandleader and singer*• Born in Rochester, New York, he became a national figure when his band succeeded **Duke Ellington**'s at Harlem's Cotton Club in 1931, and had hits that year with the songs "Minnie the Moocher" (his signature tune) and "Kicking the Gong Around," both containing streetwise drug references. His scat-style catchphrases (for example, substituting nonsense syllables such as "hi-de-ho" for words) and flamboyant presentation remained characteristic throughout a long career, in which he also acted in stage musicals and in films, including *Stormy Weather* (1943) and *The Blues Brothers* (1980).

Calmette, (Léon Charles) Albert 1863–1933 •*French bacteriologist*• Born in Nice, he was a pupil of **Louis Pasteur** and founder of the Pasteur Institute in Saigon, where he discovered an antisnake-bite serum. In 1895 he founded the Pasteur Institute, Lille (director, 1895–1919). He is best known for the BCG vaccine (Bacille Calmette-Guérin), used in the inoculation against tuberculosis, which he discovered jointly with Camille Guérin (1908).

Calvi, Robert, *originally* **Gian Roberto Calvini** 1920–82 •*Italian banker and financier*• Born in Milan, he worked his way up through Banco Ambrosiano, becoming its chairman in 1975. In 1978, a report by the Bank of Italy on Ambrosiano concluded that several billion lire had been illegally exported. In May 1981, Calvi was indicted and arrested along with 10 others, and on July 20 he was found guilty and sentenced to four years' imprisonment and was fined 16 billion lire. Calvi was released pending his appeal. Throughout the 1970s, he had become increasingly involved in Propaganda 2 (P2), a secret masonic lodge, and became entangled in the P2 scandal when the extent of its influence became publicly known. By 1982, the bank hovered on the verge of financial collapse, but it was temporarily saved by patronage letters from the Vatican's bank which, under the leadership of Paul Marcinckus, had jointly perpetrated with Ambrosiano several dubious business deals. On June 18, his body was found hanging from scaffolding under Blackfriars Bridge in London, his pockets weighted down with bricks and concrete, and containing a large amount of cash. A verdict of suicide was recorded, which was overturned in 1983, when an inquest delivered an open verdict on the death.

Calvin, John 1509–64 •*French theologian, one of the most important reformers of the 16th century*• Calvin was born in Noyon, in Picardy. He studied Latin in Paris from 1523 and later, while studying law in Orléans, received from the Scriptures his first impulse to study theology. From Orléans he went to Bourges, where he learned Greek and began to preach the reformed doctrines. After a short stay (1533) in Paris, which had become a center of the "new learning" and of religious excitement, he visited Noyon. He went to Nerac, Saintonge, Angoulême, the residence of **Margaret of Angoulême**, Queen of Navarre, and then to Paris again. Calvin fled France to escape persecution; and at Basel in 1536 he issued his *Christianae religionis institutio* ("Institutes of the Christian Religion"). In Geneva, Guillaume Farel (1489–1565) persuaded Calvin to assist in the work of reformation. A Protestant Confession of Faith was proclaimed, and moral severity took the place of license. The strain, however, was too sudden and too extreme. A spirit of rebellion broke forth under the "Libertines," and Calvin and Farel were expelled from the city (1538). Calvin, withdrawing to Strasbourg, devoted himself to a critical study of the New Testament. In 1542 he was invited to return to Geneva, where, through his College of Pastors and Doctors, and his Consistorial Court of Discipline, he founded a theocracy, which was virtually to direct all the affairs of the city, and to control the social and individual life of the citizens. His struggle with the Libertines lasted 14 years, when the reformer's authority was confirmed into an absolute supremacy (1555). Calvin rendered a double service to Protestantism: he systematized its doctrine, and organized its ecclesiastical discipline. His commentaries encompass the greater part of the Old Testament and the whole of the New except the Revelation.

Calvin, Melvin 1911–97 •*US chemist and Nobel Prize winner*• He was born in Minnesota. In 1948 he helped elucidate the Thunberg-Wieland cycle by which some bacteria, unlike animals, synthesize four-carbon sugars, and hence glucose, from acetate as shown by **Konrad Bloch**. The idea that the cycle, operating in reverse, might fix carbon dioxide gas led him to investigate this process in photosynthesis (1950). The outcome was the Calvin cycle, for which he was awarded the Nobel Prize for chemistry in 1961.

Calvino, Italo 1923–85 •*Italian novelist, essayist and journalist*• Born in Santiago de las Vegas, Cuba, of Italian parents, he grew up in San Remo, Italy, and was educated at the University of Turin. A reluctant member of the Young Fascists, he participated in the Italian occupation of the French Riviera, but in 1943 he was able to join the Resistance. Throughout the 1940s he wrote for the communist paper *L'unità*. His first novel, *Il sentiero dei nidi di ragno* (1947, Eng trans *The Path to the Nest of Spiders*, 1956), was dubbed neorealist, but he became increasingly interested in fantasy, folktales and the nature of narrative. His early works include three fantastic "historical" novels, collectively titled *I nostri antenati* (1960, Eng trans *Our Ancestors*, 1980). Regarded as one of the most inventive of the European Modernists, he combined fantasy and surrealism with a hard, satirical wit. His later books include *Si una notte d'inverno un viaggiatore* (1979, Eng trans *If on a Winter's Night a Traveler*, 1981) and *Palomar* (1983).

Cam or **Cão** 15th century •*Portuguese explorer*• In 1482 he discovered the mouth of the Congo, near which an inscribed stone erected by him as a memorial was found in 1887. His voyages southward along the west African coast later enabled **Bartolomeu Diaz** to find the sea route to the Indian Ocean around the cape.

Cambio *See* **Arnolfo di Cambio**

Cambrensis, Giraldus *See* **Giraldus Cambrensis**

Cambridge, Ada 1844–1926 •*Australian novelist and poet*• Born in Norfolk, England, she was educated privately, and by the time she met and married George Cross at the age of 26, she had already published short stories, poems and a book of hymns. They left almost immediately for Australia where her husband was to be a missionary priest. A woman with a strong sense of class, she drew attention through her writing to women's social position and encouraged them to think for themselves. Her best work includes *A Marked Man* (1890), *Not All in Vain* (1892) and *Materfamilias* (1898).

Cambyses II, *Persian* **Kambujiya** d. 522 BC •*Second king of the Medes and Persians*• He succeeded his father, **Cyrus** the Great, in 529 BC. He put his brother Smerdis to death and invaded and conquered Egypt (525 BC), establishing Persian rule there for two centuries. Further attempts at expansion failed, however. When news came in 522 BC that Gaumáta the Magian had usurped the Persian throne, Cambyses marched against him from Egypt, but died in Syria, either by accident or suicide.

Camerarius or **Camerer, Joachim**, *originally* **Joachim Liebhard** 1500–74 •*German classical scholar and Lutheran theologian*• He was born in Bamberg. A friend of **Philip Melanchthon**, he embraced the Reformation at Wittenberg in 1521, and helped to formulate the Augsburg Confession of 1530. Professor of Greek and Latin at Tübingen (1535) and Leipzig (from 1541), Camerarius produced several editions of the classical authors, wrote a biography of Melanchthon (1566) and edited his letters (1569), and wrote *Epistolae familiares* (3 vols, 1583–95) on contemporary affairs.

Camerarius or **Camerer, Joachim** 1534–98 •*German botanist*• The son of **Joachim Camerarius**, he wrote *Hortus medicus et philosophicus* (1588) and *Symbola et emblemata* (1590), and was one of the most learned physicians and botanists of his age. His most distinguished descendant was **Rudolph Jacob Camerarius**.

Camerarius or **Camerer, Rudolph Jacob** 1665–1721 •*German physician and botanist*• Born in Tübingen, he was director of the botanic garden at Tübingen University and Professor of Botany, and was renowned for his experimental proof of sexuality in plants (*De sexu plantarum*, 1694).

Cameron, Sir David Young 1865–1945 •*Scottish artist*• Born in Glasgow, he studied at the Glasgow School of Art (1881–85). A noted landscape painter, he was also one of the most romantic of British etchers, following the lead of **James McNeill Whistler** and Francis Haden (1818–1910). Turning to his native landscape for inspiration, he introduced dry point to produce some of the most memorable images in 20th-century British printmaking.

Cameron (of Lochiel), Donald, *known as* **Gentle Lochiel** c. 1695–1748 •*Scottish Highland chieftain*• He was the grandson of Sir **Ewen Cameron of Lochiel** and succeeded to the clan chieftancy in 1719. His reluctant support of the Young Pretender (**Charles Edward Stuart**) in 1745 encouraged other chieftains. Seriously wounded at Culloden (1746), he died in exile in France. His brother Alexander was captured after Culloden and died in a prison hulk on the Thames, London, and his brother Archibald was executed in 1753, the last man to die for the Jacobite cause.

Cameron (of Lochiel), Sir Ewen 1629–1719 •*Scottish Jacobite and chief of clan Cameron*• A huge figure, famous for his ferocity and prodigious feats of strength, he led his clan against the parliamentary forces of the English Commonwealth, then fought with Claverhouse (Viscount **Dundee**) at Killiecrankie (1689), and supported the Earl of **Mar** in the 1715 Rebellion. He is said to have killed the last wolf in Scotland.

Cameron, (Mark) James 1911–85 •*Scottish journalist*• He was born of Scottish parents in Battersea, London. An accomplished reporter, he covered some of the great events in world affairs, from the Vietnam War to ill treatment of the underprivileged in India. He was also a writer and host of television programs, including *Men of Our Time* (1963), *Cameron Country* and the autobiographical *Once upon a Time* (1984). His radio play *The Pump* (1973) won the Prix Italia and was dramatized for television in 1980.

Cameron, James 1954– •*Canadian film director*• Born in Kapuskasing, Ontario, he studied physics at California State University and began his career as an art director for Roger Corman. His first major success was *The Terminator* (1984), and he went on to make several other highly successful action films with a sci-fi slant, including *Aliens* (1986), *The Abyss* (1989) and *Terminator 2* (1991). In 1996 he made *Titanic*, which won 11 Academy Awards, equaling the all-time record set by *Ben Hur* in 1959.

Cameron, Julia Margaret, *née* **Pattle** 1815–79 •*British photographer*• Born in Calcutta, India, at the age of 48 she was given a camera and she became a noted amateur photographer in the 1860s, making acclaimed close-up portraits of such Victorian public figures as **Tennyson**, **Charles Darwin**, **Thomas Carlyle** and Cardinal **Newman**. Her style was influenced by her friend **G F Watts** and the Pre-Raphaelites.

Camillus, Marcus Furius 447–365 BC •*Roman general and statesman*• He is best known for the capture and destruction, in 396 BC, of Rome's greatest rival of the day, the Etruscan city of Veii, and for driving the Gauls under Brennus out of Rome (387–386). For this he came to be regarded as the savior and second founder of Rome. There is a life of him by **Plutarch**.

Camm, Sir Sydney 1893–1966 •*English aircraft designer*• Born in Windsor, Berkshire, he joined the Hawker Engineering Company (which later became Hawker Siddeley Aviation) in 1923, and became their chief designer (1925–66), a post he retained until his death. He had a unique design record of highly successful single-engine military aircraft, notably the Fury, Hart and Demon biplanes, and his first monoplane, the Hurricane. He also designed the Tornado, Typhoon, Tempest, and the jet-engined Sea Hawk, Hunter and the jump-jet Harrier.

Camoëns or **Camões, Luis de** 1524–80 •*Portuguese poet*• Born in Lisbon, he studied for the church at Coimbra, but declined to take orders. Returning to Lisbon, probably in 1542, he fell in love with Donna Caterina Ataide, but her father opposed the marriage. He was banished from Lisbon for a year, and joining a Portuguese force at Ceuta, served there for two years, losing an eye. In 1550 he returned to Lisbon, where he was thrown into prison for participating in a street brawl, and was released only after volunteering to go to India. While in Goa (1553–55) his denunciations of the Portuguese officials led to a further spell of imprisonment, but after an exile of 16 years, he returned to Lisbon to spend the remainder of his life. He is best remembered for his *Os Lusiadas*, which was published in 1572 and an immediate success. It took as its subject the history of Portugal, and the Portuguese came to regard it as their national epic.

Camp, Walter Chauncy 1859–1925 •*US football coach and promoter*• He was born in New Britain, Connecticut. At Yale University (1888–92) he helped to shape American football rules, introducing the 11-man team (as against 15), the concept of "downs" and "yards gained," and the creation of a new point-scoring system. He also pioneered the notion of the All-American team, a somewhat bizarre concept since such a selection had no opposition abroad against which it could be measured. He is known as the "father of American football."

Campanella, Tommaso 1568–1639 •*Italian philosopher*• Born in Stilo, Calabria, he entered the Dominican order in 1583, and taught at Rome and Naples. He evolved an empirical, anti-Scholastic philosophy, presented in his work *Philosophia sensibus demonstrata* (1591, "Philosophy Demonstrated by the Senses"), for which he was imprisoned and tortured by the Inquisition. From prison he wrote his famous utopian work, *La città del sole* (c. 1602, *City of the Sun*), as well as other religious works and some poetry. He eventually fled to Paris in 1634, as a protégé of Cardinal **Richelieu**.

Campbell, Alexander 1788–1866 •*US pastor, leader of the Disciples of Christ, or Campbellites*• Born near Ballymena, Antrim, Northern Ireland, he emigrated with his family to the US in 1809, his father, **Thomas Campbell** (1763–1854), having emigrated earlier in 1807. In 1813 he succeeded his father as pastor of an independent church at Brush Run, Pennsylvania. He advocated a return to the simple church of New Testament times, and in 1826 published a translation of the New Testament. In 1841 he founded Bethany College in West Virginia.

Campbell, Sir Colin, Baron Clyde 1792–1863 •*Scottish field marshal*• Born in Glasgow, he assumed the name of Campbell from his mother's brother. He served throughout the Peninsular War (1804–14) against **Napoleon I**, and was twice badly wounded. He took part in the expedition to the US (1814), then spent nearly 30 years in garrison duty at Gibraltar, Barbados, Demerara, and England. He fought in the brief Chinese campaign of 1842, and in the second Sikh War (1848–49), afterward commanding for three years at Peshawar against the frontier tribes. On the outbreak of the Crimean War (1854) he commanded the Highland Brigade, bringing about the victory of Alma and repulsing the Russians with the celebrated "thin red line" at the Battle of Balaclava. On the outbreak of the Indian Mutiny (1857), Lord **Palmerston** offered him command of the forces in India: he effected the final relief of Lucknow (1857), was created Baron Clyde (1858), and brought the rebellion to an end (December 1858). He returned the next year to England and was made a field marshal.

Campbell, Donald Malcolm 1921–67 •*English car and speedboat racer*• He was born in Horley, Surrey. An engineer by training, he sought to emulate the achievements of his father, Sir Malcolm Campbell (1885–1949), and set new world speed records several times on both land and water, culminating in 1964 with a water speed record of 276.33 mph on Lake Dumbleyung in Australia, and a land speed record of 403.1 mph at Lake Eyre salt flats in Australia. He was killed when his *Bluebird* turbojet hydroplane crashed on Lake Coniston in England.

Campbell, Kim (Avril Phaedra) 1947– •*Canadian politician*• Born in British Columbia, she studied at the University of British Columbia and then at the London School of Economics. After returning to Vancouver she trained in law and practiced there, at the same time becoming involved in provincial politics. In the 1988 election she was elected a parliamentary member of the Progressive Conservative Party under **Brian Mulroney**. She soon became a Cabinet member as Justice Minister (1990–93) then Defence Minister (1993). She succeeded Mulroney in June 1993, becoming Canada's first woman Prime Minister, but in October that year she and all but two of her party's candidates lost their parliamentary seats in the national election, and the Liberal Party under **Jean Chrétien** took over.

Campbell, Mrs Patrick, *née* **Beatrice Stella Tanner** 1865–1940 •*English actress*• She was born in Kensington, London, of mixed English and Italian parentage. Though her mercurial temperament made her the terror of managers, she possessed outstanding charm and talent, and leapt to fame in *The Second Mrs Tanqueray* (1893). She played Eliza in **George Bernard Shaw**'s *Pygmalion* (1914) and formed a long friendship with the author.

" "

When you were quite a little boy somebody ought to have said "hush" just once.

1912 Letter to George Bernard Shaw, November 1.

Campbell-Bannerman, Sir Henry 1836–1908 •*Scottish Liberal statesman*• Born in Glasgow, he was educated at Glasgow and Trinity College, Cambridge, becoming Liberal Member of Parliament for Stirling in 1868. He was Chief Secretary for Ireland (1884), Secretary for War (1886, 1892–95), Liberal leader (1899), and Prime Minister (1905–08). A "pro-Boer," he granted the ex-republics responsible government, out of which grew the Union of South Africa. He launched the campaign against the House of Lords to reduce its power, which culminated in the passing of the momentous Parliament Act of 1911 after the Lords had blocked **David Lloyd George**'s "Peoples Budget." He resigned on April 4, 1908, and died April 11.

Campen, Jacob van 1595–1657 •*Dutch architect and painter*• Born in Haarlem, he was greatly influenced by Italian style and built the first completely classical building in Holland. His masterpiece was the Maurithuis, The Hague (1633). Other works include Amsterdam Theater (1637), based on **Andrea Palladio**'s Theatro Olympico, and Amsterdam Town Hall (1647–55, now the royal palace), a large classical building around two courts with a huge sculptured pediment depicting the oceans paying homage to Amsterdam, which was both a monument to the Peace of Munster and to the city itself.

Campese, David Ian 1962– •*Australian rugby player*• Born in Queanbeyan, New South Wales, he established a reputation as one of fastest wingers in modern rugby, making his debut for Australia in 1982. He was the captain and undisputed star of the World Cup–winning Australian team in 1991 and went on to represent Australia a record 101 times before his retirement in 1999, becoming in the process the leading try scorer in international rugby, with a total of 64 tries to his name.

Campin, Robert, *usually identified as the* **Master of Flémalle** c. 1375–1444 •*Netherlandish artist*• He has been identified as probably the Master of Flémalle from three paintings in the Städelsches Kunstinstitut in Frankfurt that were erroneously held to have originated in Flémalle. About 1400 he settled in Tournai, where **Rogier van der Weyden** and Jaques Daret (1406–c. 1468) were his pupils. His *Madonna* and the pair of portraits of a man and his wife in the National Gallery, London, show him to have been a painter of rude vigor who made innovative use of realism.

Campion, St Edmund 1540–81 •*English Jesuit*• Born in London, he was educated at Christ's Hospital and St John's College, Oxford. He became a deacon in the Church of England (1569), but his Roman Catholic sympathies were noticed, so he escaped to Douai in France, and in 1573 joined the Society of Jesus in Bohemia. Returning to England in 1580 he circulated his *Decem rationes* (Ten Reasons) against Anglicanism in 1581, was arrested, tortured, tried on a charge of conspiracy, and hanged in London. He was beatified in 1886 and canonized in 1970. His feast day is October 25.

Campion, Jane 1954– •*New Zealand film director*• Born in Wellington, she was trained at the Australian Film, Television and Radio School in Sydney, Australia, and her debut short, *Peel* (1982), won the Cannes Palme D'Or for Best Short Film. She made her feature film debut with *Sweetie* (1989), and then directed the three-part television series *An Angel at My Table* (1990), a dramatization of the autobiographies of **Janet Frame**. She won seven awards at the Venice Film Festival of 1990, and shared the Cannes Palme D'Or for *The Piano* (1993), the first such award for an Australian production as well as for a woman director. The film also secured her an Academy Award for Best Original Screenplay. Later films include *Portrait of a Lady* (1996), *Holy Smoke* (1999) and *In the Cut* (2003).

Campion, Thomas 1567–1620 •*English physician, poet and composer*• Born in Witham, Essex, he studied at Cambridge and abroad, and set his own lyrics to music. As well as poetry in Latin and English he left several books of "ayres" for voice and lute. He also wrote a treatise, *Observations in the Art of English Rhyme* (1602).

Campoamor, Clara 1888–1972 •*Spanish politician and feminist*• Of working-class origins, she graduated in law in 1924. In 1931 she was elected to the Constituent Cortes of the Second Republic as a deputy for the Radical Republican Party, and was largely responsible for the inclusion of women's suffrage in the Constitution of 1931. During the legislature of 1931–33 she was vice president of the Labor Commission and participated in the reform of the Civil Code. She also represented Spain at the League of Nations and founded the Republican Feminine Union. During the 1930s she wrote extensively on women's rights and aspirations. In 1938 she chose exile in Buenos Aires, moving in 1955 to Lausanne, where she died.

Campos Salles, Manuel Ferraz de 1841–1913 •*Brazilian politician*• Regarded as the "political architect of the Republic," he was a slave owner, fazendeiro and lawyer in Campinas, then the center of the coffee-growing region of Brazil. He became a Republican in the 1870s and was Minister of Justice in the Provisional Government of the Republic (1889–91), when he was responsible for the separation of church and state and the introduction of civil marriage. He was Governor of São Paulo (1896–98), and then President (1898–1902).

Camus, Albert 1913–60 •*French writer and Nobel Prize winner*• Born in Mondovi, Algeria, the son of a farm laborer, he studied philosophy at Algiers and became an actor, schoolmaster, playwright and journalist there and in Paris. Active in the French Resistance during World War II, he became coeditor with **Jean-Paul Sartre** of the left-wing newspaper *Combat* after the liberation. Having earned an international reputation with his existentialist novel, *L'étranger* (1942, Eng trans *The Outsider*, 1946), "the study of an absurd man in an absurd world," he set himself in his subsequent work the aim of elucidating some values for man confronted with cosmic meaninglessness. *Le mythe de Sisyphe* (1942, Eng trans *The Myth of Sisyphus*, 1955), concerning suicide, *L'homme révolté* (1951, Eng trans *The Rebel*, 1954), on the harm done by surrendering to ideologies, and a second masterpiece, *La peste* (1947, Eng trans *The Plague*, 1948), were followed by a return to extreme ironical pessimism in *La chute* (1956, Eng trans *The Fall*, 1957). His political writings are collected in *Actuelles I* (1950, "Chronicles of Today I") and *II* (1953). He was awarded the 1957 Nobel Prize for literature. Three years later he died in a car accident and in his briefcase was found an unfinished autobiographical novel, *Le premier homme* (Eng trans *The First Man*, 1995), which was then edited and published by his daughter Cathérine Camus in 1995.

“ ”

A novel is never anything but a philosophy put into images.
Recalled on his death, January 4, 1960.

Canaletto, *properly* **Giovanni Antonio Canal** 1697–1768 •*Italian painter*• Born in Venice, he studied in Rome but returned to Venice in 1730. Between 1746 and 1756 he worked in England where his views of London and elsewhere proved popular, and on his return to Venice his dramatic and picturesque views of that city became immensely popular with foreign visitors, especially the English. He is essentially a topographical painter—even today the views of Venice he depicts are remarkably unchanged—but he often shows a poetic response to his subjects. His nephew and pupil **Bernardo Bellotto** became known as Canaletto the Younger.

Canetti, Elias 1905–94 •*Bulgarian writer and Nobel Prize winner*• He was born in Rutschuk, Bulgaria, into a community of Spanish-speaking Jews. In his formative years he moved between England, Switzerland, Austria and Germany and was educated in Zurich and Frankfurt and at the University of Vienna. From 1938 Canetti lived in Great Britain. The works for which he is best known are his novel on the growth of totalitarianism, *Die Blendung* (1935–36, Eng trans *Auto-da-Fé*, 1946), and a speculative study of the psychology of mass behavior, *Masse und Macht* (1960, Eng trans *Crowds and Power*, 1962). He was awarded the Nobel Prize for literature in 1981.

Caniff, Milt(on Arthur) 1907–88 •*US cartoonist*• Born in Hillsboro, Ohio, he joined the Associated Press in 1922 to draw the daily jokes, *Mr Gilfeather* and *Gay Thirties*. In 1933 he created his first daily strip, *Dickie Dare*, then joined the *New York Daily News* to create a similar serial, *Terry and the Pirates* (1934). In World War II, Caniff drew a sexy strip, *Male Call*, for servicemen. Suddenly abandoning *Terry*, he created a new series about an expilot, *Steve Canyon* (1947), which continued until his death.

Canmore, Malcolm *See* **Malcolm III**

Canning, George 1770–1827 •*English statesman*• Born in London, he was raised and educated by his uncle after the death of his father when Canning was only one year old. He attended Eton and Christ Church, Oxford, and was admitted to the bar before entering Parliament in 1794 and becoming Under-Secretary of State under **William Pitt** the Younger (1796). He was navy treasurer (1801), and as Foreign Affairs Minister from 1807 in Lord **Portland**'s Cabinet he planned the seizure of the Dutch fleet that prevented **Napoleon I**'s planned invasion. His dispute with Lord **Castlereagh** over the Walcheren expedition resulted in a duel between them in which Canning was slightly wounded. After Castlereagh's suicide in 1822, he became Foreign Minister again, and on the death of Liverpool in 1827 he became Prime Minister in a coalition with the Whigs, but died later the same year. A notable orator, he was buried in Westminster Abbey near Pitt.

Cannizzaro, Stanislao 1826–1910 •*Italian organic chemist and legislator*• Born in Palermo, he studied in Palermo, Pisa and Turin. Condemned to death for his part in the Sicilian Revolution in 1848, he fled to Paris, but later returned to hold professorial posts throughout Italy. He did much to coordinate organic and inorganic chemistry, showing that the same laws apply to both. His greatest achievement was to recognize the difference between atomic weight and molecular weight, a discovery fundamental to the future development of chemistry. He also discovered that benzaldehyde reacts with potassium hydroxide to form benzoic acid and benzyl alcohol (the Cannizzaro reaction) and gave the name "hydroxyl" to the OH radical. An inspiring teacher, he devoted much energy to matters of public health and other civic duties and was made a senator in 1871.

Cannon, Annie Jump 1863–1941 •*US astronomer*• Born in Dover, Delaware, the daughter of a wealthy shipbuilder, she studied at Wellesley and Radcliffe Colleges. In 1896 she joined the staff of Harvard College Observatory in a major program of classification of stellar spectra. She classified the spectra of 225,300 stars brighter than magnitude 8.5, published in the nine volumes of the *Henry Draper Catalogue*. The catalog was later extended to fainter stars, of which she classified 130,000. She was inducted into the National Women's Hall of Fame in 1994.

Cano or **Elcano, Juan Sebastian del** d. 1526 •*Basque navigator*• He was born in Guetaria, on the Bay of Biscay. In 1519 he sailed with **Ferdinand Magellan** in command of the *Concepción*, and, after Magellan's death in the Philippines, safely navigated the *Victoria* home to Spain, arriving in 1522. He was the first man to circumnavigate the globe.

Canova, Antonio 1757–1822 •*Italian sculptor*• Born in Possagno, he studied in Venice and Rome, and after his *Theseus* (1782, Victoria and Albert Museum, London), came to be regarded as the founder of a new neoclassical school. He created the tombs of popes **Clement XIII** (1787–92) and **Clement XIV** (1783–87), and in 1802 he was appointed curator of works of art by **Pius VII**. Other works include a statue of **Pauline Bonaparte** (Princess Borghese) reclining as Venus Victrix (1805–07, Borghese Gallery, Rome), and the sculpture *The Three Graces* (begun 1814, National Gallery of Scotland, Edinburgh, and Victoria and Albert Museum, London).

Cantelupe, St Thomas de, *also called* **St Thomas of Hereford** c. 1218–82 •*English prelate*• Born near Henley-on-Thames, Oxfordshire, he studied at Oxford, Paris and Orleans, and was made Chancellor of Oxford University (1262). He supported the barons against **Henry III**, and was appointed Chancellor of England by **Simon de Montfort** (1264–65). Made Bishop of Hereford (1275), he became well known for his sense of justice and his kindness. He was canonized by Pope **John XXII** in 1320.

Cantona, Eric 1966– •*French soccer player*• He was born in Paris. Known for his outstanding flair and fiery temperament, he became the first player to win two successive Premier League Championship titles with two different clubs. After 45 caps for France, a dispute with the coach led to suspension from his national team. He played for the French clubs, then moved to England and joined Leeds United (1991–92), then Manchester United (from November 1992), and became a cult hero. In 1994 he was suspended from Manchester United for a year after he kicked a fan kung-fu style. He later retired from soccer to develop an acting career.

Cantor, Charles Robert 1942– •*US molecular geneticist*• Born in Brooklyn, New York, he was educated at Columbia University and the University of California at Berkeley. He taught at Columbia University from 1966, and in 1981 became chairman of the department of genetics and development. In 1984 he developed a pulse field gel technique to separate very large DNA molecules. He was director of the Human Genome Project at the University of California at Berkeley (1989–90) before becoming its principal scientist in 1990. He holds professional appointments at Boston University and is also director of the Center for Advanced Biotechnology there.

Cantor, Georg Ferdinand Ludwig Philipp 1845–1918 •*German mathematician*• Born in St Petersburg, Russia, he studied in Berlin and in 1877 became Professor of Mathematics at Halle University. He worked out a highly original arithmetic of the infinite, extending the concept of cardinal and ordinal numbers to infinite sets. Other aspects of his ideas on the theory of sets of points have become fundamental in topology and modern analysis. He also did important work on classical analysis, particularly in trigonometric series. His friend **Julius Dedekind** simultaneously developed a naive theory of sets, and their work was fused together around 1900 to become the setting for much subsequent work on the foundations of mathematics.

Canute *See* **Knut Sveinsson**

Cão *See* **Cam**

Cao Yu (Ts'ao Yü), *pseudonym of* **Wan Jiabao (Wan Chia-pao)** 1910–96 •*Chinese playwright*• Born in Tianjin (Tientsin), he studied Western literature at Qinghua University, where he was profoundly influenced by **Ibsen** and **George Bernard Shaw** to attack the corruption of traditional society. His best-known work, *Thunderstorm*, was staged in 1935. His other major plays are *Sunrise* (1935), *Wilderness* (1936), *Peking Man* (1940) and *The Family* (1941), adapted from the novel by Ba Jin. In 1979 he wrote the play *The Consort of Peace*. He is considered by many to be the most significant 20th-century dramatist in China.

Capa, Robert, *originally* **Andrei Friedmann** 1913–54 •*US photojournalist*• Born in Budapest, Hungary, he recorded the Spanish civil war (1935–37) and China under the Japanese attacks of 1938. In 1939 he emigrated to the US and covered World War II in Europe from the invasion of Normandy. Subsequently he reported on the early days of the state of Israel. He was killed by a land mine in the Indo-China fighting which preceded the war in Vietnam. His images of war were a compassionate portrayal of the suffering of both soldiers and civilians.

Capablanca, José Raúl 1888–1942 •*Cuban chess player*• He was born in Havana. At the age of four he learned chess by watching his father's games, and within nine years he had defeated the Cuban champion, Corzo, in a match. A local industrialist sponsored his education in the US, and in 1909 he achieved a sensational win in a match against US champion Marshall. On his first appearance in Europe he defeated most of the world's leading masters at the San Sebastian tournament, 1909, but he had to wait until 1921 for an opportunity to play for the world championship, defeating **Emanuel Lasker** without losing a game. He maintained a record of near invincibility from 1921 to 1927. His defeat by **Alexander Alekhine** in 1927 was a major surprise, and despite further tournament successes he never received the opportunity to regain his title.

Čapek, Karel 1890–1938 •*Czech novelist and playwright*• He was born in Malé Svatoňovice, Bohemia, and educated in Prague, Paris and Berlin. Several early works, including the novel *Zářivé hlubiny* (1916, "The Shining Depths"), were collaborations with his brother Josef Čapek (1887–1945), but he gained international attention with the play *R.U.R.* (1920, Eng trans 1923), a satirical vision of a dehumanized postindustrial society. The title stands for "Rossum's Universal Robots," and the play led the way for a new kind of science fiction, as well as introducing the word *robot* (Czech *robota*, "drudgery") into the English language. The brothers later collaborated on *Ze života hmyzu* (1921, Eng trans *The Insect Play*, 1923), which has a similar theme. Karel also wrote *Věc Makropulos* (1922), which formed the basis for his countryman **Leoš Janáček**'s 1925 opera *The Makropulos Affair*.

Capet, Hugo or **Hugh** c. 938–96 •*King of France*• As Duke of Francia, he was elected king of France on the death of the last Carolingian **Louis V** (987). The Capetian dynasty he founded ruled France until 1328.

Capistrano, Giovanni da *See* **John of Capistrano**

Capone, Al(phonse) 1899–1947 •*US gangster*• Born in Brooklyn, New York, the son of immigrants from Naples, Italy, he joined a street gang as a boy and, while working as a bartender and bouncer, received the razor slash across his cheek that led to his nickname "Scarface." He achieved worldwide notoriety as a racketeer during the Prohibition era in Chicago in the 1920s, amassing enormous profits from gambling, bootlegging and prostitution, buying off police and warring with rival gangs, most notoriously in the St Valentine's Day Massacre (1929). In 1931 he was indicted for income-tax evasion and on his conviction was sentenced to 11 years in prison. He was released on health grounds in 1939 and retired to his estate in Florida.

Capote, Truman 1924–84 •*US writer*• Born in New Orleans, of Spanish descent, he spent much of his childhood in Alabama. His short story "Miriam," published in the magazine *Mademoiselle*, was selected for the **O Henry** Memorial Award volume in 1946. *Other Voices, Other Rooms* (1948), his first novel, revealed his talent for sympathetic description of small-town life in the deep South and centers on the homosexual awakenings of a young boy. *The Grass Harp* (1951) is a fantasy performed against a background of the Alabama of his childhood. Other works are *Breakfast at Tiffany's* (1958) and *In Cold Blood* (1966). Latterly, he published a collection of short pieces, *Music for Chameleons* (1980) and the long-promised but unfinished novel *Answered Prayers*, extracts of which appeared in *Esquire* magazine in 1975.

“ ”

I don't care what anybody says about me as long as it isn't true.

Quoted in David Frost ***The Americans*** *(1970), "When Does a Writer Become a Star."*

Capp, Al, *originally* **Alfred Gerald Caplin** 1909–79 •*US cartoonist*• Born in New Haven, Connecticut, he studied at a series of art schools in Pennsylvania and Massachusetts, then entered comic strips as assistant to **Bud Fisher** on *Mutt and Jeff* (1930). Joining the Associated Press he took on a daily joke, *Mr Gilfeather* (1932), then became assistant to Ham Fisher on *Joe Palooka* (1933). In 1934 he began his own strip *L'il Abner*, featuring a cast of hillbilly characters as well as frequent caricatures of public officials. Capp's chunky artwork and gift for satire made the strip an enduring success, and he continued to draw it until his retirement in 1977.

Capra, Frank 1897–1991 •*US film director*• He was born in Palermo, Italy, but his family emigrated to California when he was six. He studied chemical engineering at the California Institute of Technology before moving into the film industry (1921), initially as a gag writer for silent comedies. His films include *It Happened One Night* (1934), *Mr Deeds Goes to Town* (1936), *You Can't Take It with You* (1938), which won Academy Awards, *Arsenic and Old Lace* (1942), *It's a Wonderful Life* (1946), *State of the Union* (1948), and his last, *A Pocketful of Miracles* (1961). His best-known work as a director celebrates the decency and integrity of the common man as he combats corruption and wrongdoing in high places. He retired in 1964.

Capriati, Jennifer 1976– •*US tennis player*• Born in New York City, she was 24 days short of her 14th birthday when she became a professional tennis player, and at age 14 she became the youngest Grand Slam semifinalist. She reached the finals in her third tournament, and won her eleventh, the Puerto Rican Open. By the age of 15, she had become one of the world's highest-paid athletes, but by the age of 18 she had never progressed beyond the semifinal of any Grand Slam, and had begun to have difficulty in raising her game. She withdrew from tennis and created controversy through her rebellious lifestyle, but later made a determined return to form, winning the Australian and French Open titles in 2001 and becoming one of the highest-ranked players once more.

Caprivi, Georg Leo, Graf von 1831–99 •*German soldier and statesman*• Born in Berlin, he fought in the campaigns of 1864 and 1866, and was Chief of Staff to the 10th Army Corps in the Franco-Prussian war (1870–71). He became Imperial Chancellor (1890–94) on **Bismarck**'s fall, and Prussian Prime Minister. His principal measures were the army bills of 1892–93 and the commercial treaty with Russia in 1894. He was dismissed in 1894.

Caracalla, *properly* **Marcus Aurelius Antoninus** AD 188–217 •*Roman emperor*• The son of the emperor **Septimius Severus**, he was born in Lyons, France. Caracalla was a nickname given him from his long hooded Gaulish tunic. He succeeded his father (AD 211) as joint emperor with his brother Publius Septimius Antoninius Geta, whom he murdered in 212. He next turned against all Geta's associates, killing many. Cruel and obsessed with advancing his martial dreams, in imitation of his hero **Alexander the Great**, he campaigned extensively in Germany, on the Danube, and in the East, and was assassinated as he was preparing for war against the Parthians. He is remembered for his edict of 212 (the *Constitutio Antoniniana*) which granted Roman citizenship to all free members of the empire.

Caractacus *See* **Caratacus**

Caramanlis, Konstantinos *See* **Karamanlis, Konstantinos**

Caran d'Ache, *pseudonym of* **Emmanuel Poire** 1858–1909 •*French caricaturist*• Born in Moscow, he studied there and then moved to Paris. He contributed to many periodicals, and was a pioneer in the development of the *bande dessinée* (comic strip), and a major influence on **H M Bateman**. Several collections of his works were published. His pseudonym came from the Russian word for *pencil*.

Caratacus or **Caractacus** or **Caradoc** fl. 40–52 AD •*British chieftain*• The son of **Cymbeline**, he fought against the Romans (AD 43–50), but was eventually defeated by Publius Ostorius Scapula near Ludlow. His wife and daughters were captured, his brothers surrendered, and he himself was handed over by Cartimandua, Queen of the Brigantes. He was taken to Rome (51), and exhibited in triumph by the emperor **Claudius**, but eventually pardoned. According to **Tacitus**, his forceful oratory saved his life.

Carausius, Marcus Aurelius Mausaeus d. 293 AD •*Roman emperor in Britain*• He was born in Menapia (Belgium). Originally a Batavian pilot, Carausius had been put in command of the Roman fleet (*Classis Britannica*) in the Channel to ward off pirates. A usurper, he ruled from AD 287, and was murdered by one of his officers, Allectus, who later set himself up as emperor in Britain in his stead.

Caravaggio, *properly* **Polidoro Caldara da Caravaggio** c. 1492–1543 •*Italian painter*• Born in Caravaggio, he aided **Raphael** in his Vatican frescoes. His *Christ Bearing the Cross* is in Naples. He was murdered by his servant at Messina.

Caravaggio, *properly* **Michelangelo Merisi da Caravaggio** 1573–1610 •*Italian painter*• Born in Caravaggio, near Bergamo, he trained in Milan, but moved to Rome in the 1590s. His early work is strikingly homoerotic, characterized by voluptuously portrayed young men in various guises. With his first two commissions, however, his style changed. The *Life of Saint Matthew* cycle in the Contarelli Chapel of the church of San Luigi dei Francese and the *Conversion of Saint Paul* and the *Crucifixion of Saint Peter* in the Cerasi Chapel of Santa Maria del Popolo, both in Rome, incorporate highly original, strongly lit, intensely realistic figures emerging dramatically from dark shadow. In 1606 he fled Rome after killing a man in a brawl, and spent the rest of his life wandering between Naples, Sicily and Malta. In the hope of a pardon, he tried to return to Rome, but on the journey he was wounded, lost all his baggage, and caught a fever and died. He had no pupils, but his influence throughout the rest of the century was immense, and he is widely regarded as the greatest Italian painter of the 17th century.

Caraway, Hattie (Ophelia) Wyatt, *née* **Wyatt** 1878–1950 •*US Democratic politician*• Born near Bakerville, Tennessee, she was married to Senator Thaddeus Horatius Caraway and, when he died in 1931 before his term had expired, she was appointed by the governor of Arkansas to fill his Senate seat. She ran successfully for the same seat in 1932, becoming the first woman ever elected to the US Senate. She served until 1945. An independent-minded Democrat, she sponsored an early version of the Equal Rights Amendment in 1943.

Card, Andrew 1947– •*US Republican politician*• Born in Holbrook, Massachusetts, he studied engineering at the University of South Carolina and attended the United States Merchant Marine Academy. He emerged as a leading figure in the Republican Party, running for the Republican nomination for governor of Massachusetts in 1982 and subsequently serving in the **Reagan** administration and becoming deputy Chief of Staff and then Secretary of Transportation under **George Bush**. After **George W Bush** became President in 2001 he was appointed Presidential Chief of Staff.

Cardano, Girolamo, *also called* **Jerome Cardan** or **Hieronymus Cardanus** 1501–76 •*Italian mathematician, naturalist, physician, philosopher, gambler and astrologer*• Born in Pavia, he became famous as a physician and teacher of mathematics in Milan and became Professor of Medicine at Pavia (1543) and Bologna (1562). In 1551 he visited Scotland to treat the archbishop of St Andrews and in London cast the horoscope of **Edward VI**. In 1570 he was imprisoned by the Inquisition for heresy, recanted and went to Rome in 1571 where he was given a pension by Pope **Pius V**. He died a few weeks after finishing his candid autobiography *De propria vita* (Eng trans, *Book of My Life*, 1930). A strange mixture of polymath and charlatan, he wrote over 200 treatises on, among other things, physics, mathematics, astronomy, astrology, philosophy, music and medicine. His most famous work is his treatise on algebra, the *Ars magna* ("The Great Skill"), in which the formulas for solving cubic and quartic equations were published for the first time.

Carden, Joan Maralyn 1937– •*Australian soprano*• Born in Melbourne, Victoria, she has been a principal artist with the Australian Opera since 1971. She made her debut at Covent Garden, London, in 1974 as Gilda in *Rigoletto*, a role she has since made her own. Renowned for her performances of **Mozart**, she has appeared at the Glyndebourne Festival, as Donna Anna in **Peter Hall**'s production of *Don Giovanni*, and with the English National Opera and the Metropolitan, New York. Her repertoire extends from **Handel** to **Richard Strauss** and **Benjamin Britten**, and one of her most celebrated performances is of the four heroines in *Les contes d'Hoffmann* ("The Tales of Hoffmann").

Cárdenas, Lázaro, *properly* **Lázaro Cárdenas del Rio** 1895–1970 •*Mexican general and politician*• Born in the Michoacán, the son of a peasant, he joined the revolutionary army in 1913, was a general by 1923 and became Governor of Michoacán (1928–32). He seized control of the government from his patron, President **Plutarco Calles**. His presidency (1934–40) shaped modern Mexico, and witnessed the creation of PEMEX (*Petroléos Mexicanos*) from nationalized foreign (mainly British) companies, and the PRM (Partido de la Revolución Mexicana, Mexican Revolutionary Party). Left-wing in his sympathies, he introduced many social reforms.

Cardigan, James Thomas Brudenell, 7th Earl of 1797–1868 •*English general*• Born in Hambleden, Buckinghamshire, he was Member of Parliament for Marlborough (1818–29) and North Northamptonshire (1832). In 1824 he joined the army, and in 1830 bought himself a command in the 15th Hussars as a lieutenant colonel. His fiery temper brought him into conflict with fellow officers, and he was forced to resign in 1833. From 1836 to 1847 he commanded the 11th Hussars, on which he lavished his own money to make it a crack squadron; after a duel with one of his officers in 1841 he was acquitted on a legal technicality by the House of Lords. Appointed major general in 1847, he commanded the Light Brigade ("the Six Hundred") in the Crimea, and led it to destruction in the charge against enemy guns at Balaclava (October 25, 1854). Received home as a hero, he was appointed Inspector-General of the cavalry (1855–60). The knitted woolen jacket he wore against the cold of a Crimean winter is named after him.

Cardin, Pierre 1922– •*French fashion designer*• Born in Venice, Italy, after working during World War II for a tailor in Vichy, he went to Paris in 1944, where he worked in fashion houses and on costume design. He opened his own house in 1953 and has since been prominent in fashion for both women and men, as well as in other fields of design and business. A retrospective of his work was shown at the Victoria and Albert Museum, London, in 1990, and in 1997 he was made a Commander of the Legion of Honor.

Cardoso, Fernando Enrique 1931– •*Brazilian politician*• Born into a wealthy military family in Rio de Janeiro, he became a sociologist and an opponent of the military regime. After the restoration of Brazilian democracy in the mid-1980s, he entered politics, serving as a senator (1986–92) and as Foreign Minister (1992). He became Finance Minister in 1993 and in 1994 he was elected President. His moderate free-market reforms won broad popular support by 1996, and he sought to curb the human rights abuses still rampant in Brazil. He was succeeded in 2002 by the left-wing candidate Luiz Inacio Lula da Silva.

Carducci, Giosuè 1835–1907 •*Italian poet and Nobel Prize winner*• Born in Valdicastello, he became Professor of Italian Literature at Bologna (1860), and set a new standard in scholarship. In 1876 he was returned to the Italian parliament as a Republican, and in 1890 became a senator. He published several volumes of verse, and was considered Italy's national poet. He was awarded the Nobel Prize for literature in 1906.

Carew, Thomas 1595–1639 •*English Cavalier poet*• Born in West Wickham, Kent, he studied at Merton College, and entered the Inner Temple to study law in 1612. He visited Holland as secretary to the ambassador (1613–16), but was dismissed for slandering his employers. After three years in London he went to France (1619–24) as secretary to the ambassador, and won the favor of **Charles I**. A friend of **Ben Jonson** and **John Donne**, he wrote witty songs and lyrics in the Cavalier tradition, as well as longer poems, notably the love poem "A Rapture."

“ ”

Here lies a king, that ruled as he thought fit
The universal monarchy of wit

1633 "An Elegy upon the Death of the Dean of Paul's, Dr. John Donne."

Carey, George Leonard 1935– •*English prelate and Archbishop of Canterbury*• Born in London to working-class parents, he left school at the age of 15 without any qualifications. After National Service spent in Egypt and Iraq, he graduated from the London School of Divinity, became curate of St Mary's, Islington (1962–66), and then spent 10 years teaching in theological colleges. As vicar of St Nicholas's, Durham, he became interested in charismatic renewal, and introduced new forms of worship. Appointed Archbishop of Canterbury in 1991 after four years as Bishop of Bath and Wells, he frequently emphasized his origins, and represented the liberal and modern aspects of the Church of England; he was a strong supporter of the ordination of women. He announced his retirement in 2002. He has published several books, including *I Believe in Man* (1975) and *Jesus 2000* (1999).

Carey, Peter 1943– •*Australian novelist*• Born in Bacchus Marsh, Victoria, he was educated at Geelong Grammar School, began a career as an advertising copywriter, then lived in London. His first book, *The Fat Man in History* (1974), was a collection of short stories, and he was quickly recognized as an innovative force in Australian writing. Other books include *Bliss* (1981), which explored the advertising world, and *Illywhacker* (1985). He won the Booker Prize with *Oscar and Lucinda* (1988), in which a compulsive gambler and a Sydney heiress fascinated with the manufacture of glass are bizarrely united. His other books include *The Tax Inspector* (1991), *The Big Bazoohley* (1995) and *Jack Maggs* (1997). In 2001 he again won the Booker Prize with *True History of the Kelly Gang*. He has also written screenplays, and now lives in New York.

“ ”

The declared meaning of a spoken sentence is only its overcoat, and the real meaning lies underneath its scarves and buttons.

1988 ***Oscar and Lucinda****, chapter 43, "Leviathan."*

Carl *See also* **Karl**

Carl XVI Gustaf 1946– •*King of Sweden*• Born in Stockholm, the grandson of King **Gustav VI**, he is the seventh sovereign of the House of **Bernadotte**. His father, Prince Gustav Adolf (1906–47), the heir apparent, was killed in an air crash, so Carl Gustaf became crown prince on his grandfather's accession (1950). Educated at boarding school, he did military service, and studied at Uppsala and Stockholm Universities. On his accession (1973), in accordance with the new constitution being discussed by the Riksdag (parliament), he became a democratic monarch like his grandfather. He is head of state, but does not preside at cabinet meetings and is not supreme commander of the armed forces. In 1976 he married a commoner, Silvia Sommerlath (1943–), daughter of a West German businessman. They have three children: Crown Princess Victoria (1977–), Prince Carl Philip (1979–) and Princess Madeleine (1982–).

Carle *See* **Vernet, Antoine Charles Horace**

Carle, Eric 1929– •*US picture book artist*• He was born in Germany. He has written and illustrated many children's books, using a distinctive collage technique, but he is best known for *The Very Hungry Caterpillar* (1970), in which the voracious creature burrows through the pages of the book in search of delicacies.

Carleton, Sir Guy, 1st Baron Dorchester 1724–1808 •*British soldier and governor of British North America*• He was born in Strabane, Ireland. As General **James Wolfe**'s quartermaster at the capture of Quebec in 1759, he realized that the American colonies were close to rebellion and that British imperial authority would require a base, which he set out to establish in Quebec. He refused to consider the English-speaking settlers' demands for *habeas corpus* and other aspects of English law, yet it was they who took up arms against the US rebels when they invaded (1775–76). Criticized for the slowness with which he pursued the rebels, he resigned. Sent out as Governor of Quebec again in 1786, he became Governor-General after the Constitutional Act of 1791. He resigned in 1794 and left the province in 1796.

Carlile, Wilson 1847–1942 •*English Anglican clergyman*• Born in Brixton, London, he founded the Church Army in 1882, and was made a prebendary of St Paul's in 1906.

Carling, Will(iam David Charles) 1965– •*English rugby union player*• Born in Bradford-on-Avon, he was England's most capped center (60) and also held the world record for the most international wins as captain (40 in 53 games). He made his senior debut for England in 1988 and at 22 was made England's captain. He played a vital role in England's three Grand Slam wins (1991, 1992, 1995) but was sacked in 1995 when he called Rugby Football Union administrators "old farts," only to be reinstated two days later. Press exposure over his friendship with Princess **Diana** coincided with the breakup of his marriage and he announced his retirement as captain of the England team later in 1995.

Carloman 751–71 •*Frankish prince*• The younger son of **Pepin the Short**, king of the Franks, and brother of **Charlemagne**, he ruled the eastern Franks from 768. At his death Charlemagne took over his lands.

Carlos, Don 1545–68 •*Spanish prince*• Born in Valladolid, son of King **Philip II** of Spain by his first wife, Maria of Portugal, he was sent to study at Alcalá de Henares, where he showed so little improvement that the king invited a nephew, Archduke Rudolf, to Spain, intending to make him his heir. Weak, irascible, and cruel, and with a hatred of the king's advisers, he was tried and found guilty of conspiring against the life of his father. The sentence was left for the king to pronounce. Philip declared that he could make no exception in favor of such an unworthy son, but a sentence of death was not formally recorded. When, shortly afterward, Don Carlos died, it was suspected that he had been poisoned or strangled but no evidence was found to support this.

Carlos, Don 1788–1855 •*Spanish pretender*• Born in Madrid, he was the second son of **Charles IV** of Spain. On the accession of his niece **Isabella II** (1833), he asserted his claim to the throne, and was supported by the Church, but he was defeated by the liberals in the first Carlist War (1834–39) and went into exile.

Carlson, Carolyn 1943– •*US dancer and choreographer*• Born in California, she studied at San Francisco Ballet School and with Alwin Nikolais (1910–93), in whose company she danced from 1966 to 1971. After freelancing in Europe, in 1973 she was invited to create a piece for the Paris Opera Ballet. Her dreamlike, ritualistic dance spectacles and independent working methods had a great impact on French and European modern/experimental dance. From 1980 she directed her own troupe at Venice's Teatro Fenice, but later returned to Paris.

Carlson, Chester Floyd 1906–68 •*US inventor*• Born in Seattle, Washington, he studied physics and then earned a law degree and worked as a patent lawyer in an electronics firm. On his own he began to experiment with copying processes using photoconductivity and by 1938 had discovered the basic principles of the electrostatic "xerography" process. Patented in 1940, it was subsequently developed and from 1959 marketed worldwide by the Xerox Corporation, making him a multimillionaire.

Carlsson, Ingvar Costa 1934– •*Swedish statesman*• Educated at Lund (Sweden) and Northwestern (US) Universities, he was secretary in the Prime Minister's office (1958–60) before entering active party politics. In 1964 he was elected to the Riksdag (parliament). After holding a number of junior posts (1967–76), he became Deputy Prime Minister to **Olof Palme** in 1982 and succeeded him as Prime Minister and SAP leader after Palme's assassination in 1986, serving from 1986 to 1991 and from 1994 to his retirement in 1996. In 1999 he led the inquiry into UN actions during the Rwanda genocide in 1994.

Carlucci, Frank Charles 1930– •*US diplomat and politician*• Born in Scranton, Pennsylvania, he was educated at Princeton and Harvard, and after fighting in the Korean War he served as a career diplomat in Africa and South America. He returned to the US in 1969 to work in the **Nixon** administration (1969–74) and then served, under Presidents **Gerald Ford** (1974–76) and **Jimmy Carter** (1977–81), as US ambassador to Portugal and, later, as Deputy Director of the CIA. In 1986 he replaced Rear Admiral **Poindexter** as National Security Adviser, and served as Secretary of Defense (1987–89), supporting Soviet-US arms reduction initiatives.

Carlyle, Jane (Baillie) Welsh, *née* **Welsh** 1801–66 •*Scottish diarist, the wife of Thomas Carlyle*• She was born in Haddington, East Lothian, and married **Thomas Carlyle** in 1826. She declined to become a writer despite Carlyle's promptings, and spent much of her life supporting her husband through his depressions and chronic ill health. She is, nevertheless, remembered for her vividly written letters and diaries, edited by Carlyle, which were eventually published after his death in 1883, and which show her to have been one of the best letter writers in the English language.

Carlyle, Robert 1961– •*Scottish actor*• He was born in Glasgow and studied at the Royal Scottish Academy of Music and Drama. As director of the Rain Dog Theatre Company he has acted in and produced numerous plays, and he has appeared widely on television. His role in *The Full Monty* (1996) earned him a British Academy of Film and Television Arts award for Best Actor, and he electrified audiences in the same year as the rabid Begbie in *Trainspotting*. Other films have included *Angela's Ashes* (1999) and *The Beach* (2000).

Carlyle, Thomas 1795–1881 •*Scottish historian and essayist*• Born in Ecclefechan, Dumfriesshire, the son of a stonemason, he was educated at Edinburgh University, and then became a teacher. Returning to Edinburgh in 1818 to study law, he immersed himself in the study of German literature, publishing a translation of **Goethe**'s *Wilhelm Meister* in 1824 which brought him entry into literary London. He married Jane Baillie Welsh (**Jane Carlyle**) in 1826, and from 1828 they lived on her estate of Craigenputtock, near Dumfries. There Carlyle wrote his first major work on social philosophy, *Sartor Resartus*, which was published in installments in *Fraser's Magazine* (1833–34) and as a book in the US (1836), with an introduction by **Ralph Waldo Emerson**. It was partly a satirical discourse on the value of clothes, and partly a semiautobiographical discussion of creeds and human values. In 1834 the couple moved to Chelsea, London, where Carlyle spent the rest of his life. Here he completed his romantic history of *The French Revolution* (3 vols, 1837), despite the accidental burning of the manuscript of most of the first volume by **John Stuart Mill**'s maidservant, and his six-volume work *History of … Frederick the Great* (1858–65), a compelling portrait of the practical autocrat as a heroic idealist. His *Reminiscences* were published in 1881.

“ ”

A mind that has seen, and suffered, and done, speaks to us of what it has tried and conquered.

*1824 **Goethe**, introduction to German Romance, volume 4.*

Carmen Sylva 1843–1916 •*Pen name of Elizabeth, Queen of Romania*• The daughter of Prince Hermann of Wied Neuwied, she married King (then Prince) **Carol I** of Romania in 1869. Her only child, a daughter, died in 1874, and in her grief she turned to writing. Two poems, printed privately at Leipzig (1880) under the name Carmen Sylva, were followed by *Stürme* (1881), *Leidens Erdengang* (1882, Eng trans *Pilgrim Sorrow* by H Zimmern, 1884), and other works.

Carmichael, Hoagy, *in full* **Hoagland Howard Carmichael** 1899–1981 •*US songwriter*• Born in Bloomington, Indiana, a self-taught pianist and musician, he studied law at Indiana University and became friends with jazz bandleader **Bix Beiderbecke**, who recorded his composition "Riverboat Shuffle" (1924). He went on to compose many popular songs, including "Georgia on My Mind" (1930) and "Lazy River" (1931). His song "Stardust" (first version 1927) is reputed to be the most frequently recorded popular composition of all time.

Carmichael, Ian 1920– •*English actor*• Born in Hull, he trained at the Royal Academy of Dramatic Art and made his stage debut in Karel Čapek's *R.U.R.* at the People's Palace, East London (1939). After wartime service as an army officer, he became Britain's top box-office comedy actor in **Boulting Brothers** films such as *Private's Progress* (1956), *Brothers in Law* (1956), *Lucky Jim* (1957) and *I'm All Right, Jack* (1959). Later, he found television fame as Bertie Wooster in *The World of Wooster* (1966–68), the title role in *Lord Peter Wimsey* (1972–75), and Lord Cumnor in *Wives and Daughters* (1999).

Carmichael, Stokely, *later known as* **Kwame Touré** 1941–98 •*US civil-rights activist*• He was born in Port-of-Spain, Trinidad, and educated in the US from 1952. Carmichael joined the Student Nonviolent Coordinating Committee in 1964, and became its president in 1966–67 after the murder of **Malcolm X**. He came to stand for "Black power" and was leader of the more militaristic Black Panthers from 1967 to 1969.

Carmona, Antonio 1869–1951 •*Portuguese general and politician*• He entered the army in 1888 and became a general in 1922. After a military coup in 1926 he was made Prime Minister and Minister of War, with dictatorial powers. In 1928 he was elected President for life by plebiscite. In 1932 he appointed **António Salazar** as Prime Minister and virtual dictator.

Carnap, Rudolf 1891–1970 •*US philosopher and logician*• Born in Wuppertal, Germany, he studied at the Universities of Jena and Freiburg im Breisgau and taught at Vienna (1926–31), Prague (1931–35), Chicago (1936–52) and California (1954–70). He was a leading member of the "Vienna Circle" of logical positivists, who dismissed most traditional metaphysics as a source of meaningless answers to pseudo-problems. His important work on the foundations of knowledge, scientific method, logic and semantics is represented in *Der logische Aufbau der Welt* (1928, "The Logical Construction of the World"), *Logische Syntax der Sprache* (1934, "Logical Syntax of Language"), *Meaning and Necessity* (1947) and especially in *The Logical Foundations of Probability* (1950).

Carnarvon, George Edward Stanhope Molyneux Herbert, 5th Earl of 1866–1923 •*English amateur Egyptologist*• Born at Highclere Castle, Berkshire, he was the son of the politician Henry Carnarvon (1831–90). From 1907 he sponsored **Howard Carter**'s excavations of the royal tombs at Thebes. He died shortly after the spectacular discovery of **Tutankhamun**'s tomb in the Valley of the Kings in 1922.

Carné, Marcel 1909–96 •*French film director*• Born in Paris, he worked in a bank, a grocery and an insurance company before securing the position of assistant to film director Jacques Feyder. As a director his long and profitable collaboration with poet and screenwriter **Jacques Prévert** resulted in such admired fatalistic dramas as *Quai des brumes* (1938, *Port of Shadows*) and *Le jour se lève* (1939, *Daybreak*). *Les enfants du paradis* (1944, "Children of Paradise"), made during the German occupation, evokes a romantic theatrical past with wit and sensitivity and is considered his masterpiece. The quality of his work declined in the postwar years and he was swept aside by the contempt of the "nouvelle vague" generation of filmmakers. Later films include *Thérèse Raquin* (1953), *Les tricheurs* (1958, "Youthful Sinners") and his last, the television documentary, *La Bible* (1977).

Carnegie, Andrew 1835–1919 •*US industrialist and philanthropist*• He was born in Dunfermline, Scotland, the son of a weaver who emigrated to Pittsburgh in 1848. After several jobs, he founded his first company in 1865, which grew into the largest iron and steel works in the US. He retired in 1901, a multimillionaire, to Skibo Castle in Sutherland, Scotland, and died in Lenox, Massachusetts. His benefactions funded public libraries throughout the US and Great Britain, Hero Funds, the Pittsburgh Carnegie Institute, the Washington Carnegie Institution, the Hague Peace Temple, and substantial gifts to Scottish and US universities. Besides an autobiography (1920), he wrote *Triumphant Democracy* (1886), *The Gospel of Wealth* (1889), and *Problems of Today* (1908).

Carnegie, Dale 1888–1955 •*US author and teacher of self-improvement techniques*• He was born in Maryville, Missouri, and during his childhood his family lived meagerly on a small farm. He worked first as a salesman and later as a teacher of public speaking, and in 1936 he published *How to Win Friends and Influence People*. In the wake of the book's enormous popularity, he founded hundreds of branches of the Dale Carnegie Institute for Effective Speaking and Human Relations, which enrolled 50,000 people a year at the time of his death.

Carner, Josep 1884–1970 •*Catalan poet and essayist*• He was born in Barcelona, and pursued a career as a diplomat until the advent of the **Franco** dictatorship, which he opposed. His masterpiece is the long narrative poem on the theme of Jonah and the whale, *Nabí*. Carner is regarded as being responsible for the remarkable revival of the Catalan language. He died in exile in Brussels.

Carnot, Lazare Nicolas Marguerite 1753–1823 •*French revolutionary and politician*• Born in Nolay, Burgundy, he was known as the "organizer of victory" during the French Revolutionary Wars. He entered the army as an engineer, in 1791 became a member of the Legislative Assembly. Elected to the Committee of Public Safety, he raised 14 armies, and drew up a plan by which the forces of the European reaction were repelled from the frontier. In 1797, as a member of the Directory, he opposed the extreme measures of **Paul Barras**, and was sentenced to deportation as a suspected royalist. Escaping to Germany, he wrote a defense which led to the overthrow of his colleagues in 1799. The coup d'état of 18th Brumaire (1799) brought him back to Paris, where in 1800, as Minister of War, he helped to organize the successful Italian and Rhenish campaigns. He retired when he understood the ambitious plans of **Napoleon I**, but later commanded at Antwerp (1814). During the Hundred Days he was Minister of the Interior, but after the second restoration (1815) he was banished, retiring first to Warsaw and then to Magdeburg.

Carnot, (Nicolas Léonard) Sadi 1796–1832 •*French physicist*• Born in Paris, he was the son of **Lazare Carnot**. From 1819, he concentrated on scientific research, and in his sole published work, *Réflexions sur la puissance motrice du feu* (1824, Eng trans *Reflections on the Motive Power of Fire*, 1890), he applied for the first time scientific principles to an analysis of the working cycle and efficiency of the steam engine, arriving at an early form of the second law of thermodynamics and the concept of reversibility in the form of the ideal Carnot cycle. His work became known through the reinterpretation of Bénoit Clapeyron (1799–1864), and was taken up by **Rudolf Clausius** and Lord **Kelvin** from the late 1840s.

Caro, Sir Anthony 1924– •*English sculptor*• Born in London, he studied engineering at Cambridge but turned to sculpture after World War II. In the early 1950s he made rugged bronze animal and human figures, but he soon developed his characteristic abstract style, typically large pieces of metal welded together and painted in primary colors, for example, *Early One Morning* (1962). In 1966 he won the David E Bright Prize at the Venice Biennale, and he has had major solo exhibitions worldwide. With **Norman Foster** he codesigned London's Millennium Bridge (2000). He was given the honorary title of Commander, Order of the British Empire, in 1969, knighted in 1987 and awarded the Order of Merit in 2000.

Carol I 1839–1914 •*King of Romania*• Born Prince Karl of Hohenzollern-Sigmaringen, he became Romania's first king (1881). He promoted urban industrial development and military expansion, but failed to deal with rural problems, and brutally crushed a peasant rebellion (1907). He married (1869) Princess Elizabeth of Wied, a prolific writer under the pseudonym **Carmen Sylva**. At the outset of World War I, King Carol declared Romanian neutrality, but his successor (his nephew King Ferdinand I) declared for the Allies (1916).

Carol II 1893–1953 •*King of Romania*• He was born in Sinaia, the eldest son of King Ferdinand I (reigned 1914–27) and great-nephew of **Carol I**. In 1917 he made a morganatic marriage to Zizi Lambrini, whom he divorced to marry Princess Helen of Greece (1921) and by whom he had a son, King **Michael**. In 1925 he renounced his right of succession to the throne, deserted his wife, and went into exile with his mistress Magda Lupescu. In 1930 he returned to Romania and became king in a coup that overthrew his son. He admired the authoritarian methods of **Mussolini** and, in an attempt to counter the pro-Nazi Iron Guard movement, he banned all political parties (1938) and created a Front of National Rebirth. In 1940 he was deposed in favor of his son, and fled into exile in Spain, where he married Lupescu (1947).

Caroline of Ansbach 1683–1737 •*Queen of Great Britain and Ireland*• Born in Ansbach, the daughter of the Margrave of Brandenburg-Ansbach, she married George, Electoral Prince of Hanover (1705), later **George II**, and went to England with him when his father became King **George I** (1714). As Princess of Wales she established a court of writers and politicians at Leicester House. Sensible, and avoiding abuse of the power she loved, she was a strong supporter of Sir **Robert Walpole**, and acted as regent during her husband's absences abroad. They had five children, including Frederick Louis (1707–51), Prince of Wales and father of **George III**, and William Augustus, Duke of **Cumberland**.

Caroline of Brunswick, Amelia Elizabeth 1768–1821 •*Queen of Great Britain and Ireland, and wife of George IV*• Born in Brunswick, she was the daughter of **George III**'s sister Augusta. She was married (1795) to the Prince of Wales (later **George IV**), her first cousin, and although she bore him a daughter, Princess **Charlotte**, he made her live by herself at Shooters Hill and Blackheath, and from 1814 she lived chiefly in Italy. When George came to the throne (1820), she refused an annuity of £50,000 to renounce the title of queen and live abroad. The government instituted proceedings against her for adultery, but they were dropped. She was turned away from Westminster Abbey at George IV's coronation a few days before she died.

Carothers, Wallace Hume 1896–1937 •*US industrial chemist and inventor*• Born in Burlington, Iowa, he studied at the University of Illinois and at Harvard, and taught at various universities before concentrating on research. Working for the Du Pont Company in Wilmington, Delaware, he produced the first successful synthetic rubber, neoprene, and followed this with nylon. He committed suicide, and the patent for nylon, awarded posthumously, was given to the Du Pont Company.

Carpenter, Harry Leonard 1925– •*English sports commentator*• Born in London, he worked on the *Greyhound Express* at the age of 16, and entered the Royal Navy at 18. After World War II he became a greyhound owner. He was with the BBC from 1949 to 1994 and has become known as the voice of boxing. He was given the honorary title Officer, Order of the British Empire, in 1991 and published his autobiography, *Where's Harry? My Story*, in 1992.

Carpenter, Mary Chapin 1959– •*US singer and songwriter*• Born in Princeton, New Jersey, she lived in Japan for a time before settling with her family in Washington DC. Her characteristic fusion of country with soft rock and folk on *Hometown Girl* (1987) was a success, and she has gone on to establish herself as a major commercial force. Her subsequent albums include *State of the Heart* (1989), *Stones in the Road* (1994) and *time*sex*love* (2001).

Carpentier, Alejo 1904–80 •*Cuban novelist*• Born in Havana to a French mother and a Russian father, he studied architecture as a young man, and later became a musicologist. After World War II he served in several official government posts, including cultural attaché in Paris to **Fidel Castro**. He also spent some years in the US and Venezuela. A widely admired writer, his numerous books include *El reino de este mundo* (1949, Eng trans *The Kingdom of This World*, 1957), *Los pasos perdidos* (1953, Eng trans *The Lost Steps*, 1956) and *El siglo de las luces* (1962, Eng trans *Explosion in a Cathedral*, 1963).

Carpocrates of Alexandria 2nd century AD •*Greek religious leader*• He founded the gnostic sect of Carpocratians. They sought through contemplation the union, or return, of the individual soul to God and claimed among their spiritual predecessors **Pythagoras**, **Plato**, **Aristotle** and **Jesus**.

Carrà, Carlo 1881–1966 •*Italian painter*• Born in Quargnento, Alexandria, he studied at the Brera Academy, Milan, aligning himself first (1909–14) with the Futurists, with paintings like *Funeral of the Anarchist Galli* (1911). He was one of the signatories of the Futurist Manifesto at the Exhibition in Paris in 1911. In 1915 he met **Giorgio de Chirico** and was influenced by his metaphysical painting movement.

Carracci, Agostino 1557–1602 •*Italian engraver*• Born in Bologna, he dabbled in poetry and literature, but made his reputation as a painter and engraver on copper. His brother **Annibale Carracci**'s jealousy is said to have driven him from Rome (where they did the frescoes in the Farnese Palace) to Parma, where he died. He was the cousin of **Ludovico Carracci**.

Carracci, Annibale 1540–1609 •*Italian artist*• Born in Bologna, he was the brother of **Agostino Carracci** and cousin of **Ludovico Carracci**, and leading member of a Bolognese dynasty. He was responsible for the revival of Italian painting after the vapid excesses of the later Mannerist period. He was a talented draftsman, and many of the family's drawings are in the British Royal Collection at Windsor. In his greatest work, the ceiling of the Palazzo Farnese in Rome (1597–1600), he combines the influence of the antique with those of the High Renaissance masters, **Michelangelo** and **Raphael**. He was also the father of the idealized landscape which reached perfection in the hands of **Claude** and **Nicolas Poussin**.

“ ”

Poets paint with words, painters speak with works.

Attributed rebuke to his brother Agostino.
Quoted in G P Bellori ***Vite*** *(1672).*

Carracci, Ludovico 1555–1619 •*Italian painter*• Born in Bologna, he studied art there and in Parma, Mantua and Venice, and became a distinguished teacher. With his cousins, **Agostino Carracci** and **Annibale Carracci** he established an "eclectic" school of painting in Bologna, the Accademia degli Incamminati. His own works include the *Madonna and Child Enthroned* and the *Transfiguration* (both still in Bologna).

Carranza, Venustiano 1859–1920 •*Mexican political leader*• Born into a landowning family in Cuatro Ciénegas, he became governor of his native state, Cohuila, which he led (1910) in the revolution against **Porfirio Díaz**. In 1913 he became the leader of the forces that overthrew General **Victoriano Huerta**. After he failed to enforce the progressive constitution of 1917, he was overthrown (1920) by a reform coalition. He fled on horseback into the mountains but was overtaken and killed.

Carr-Boyd, Ann Kirsten 1938– •*Australian composer, teacher and music historian*• She was born in Sydney and educated at Sydney University. A leading authority on Aboriginal and early Australian music, her many orchestral, chamber and instrumental compositions include *Symphony in Three Movements* (1964), *Three Songs of Love* (1975), *Australian Baroque* (1984) and *Suite Veronese* (1985).

Carré, John Le *See* **Le Carré, John**

Carrel, Alexis 1873–1944 •*US experimental surgeon, Nobel Prize winner*• Born in Lyons, France, he studied medicine at Lyons University, and early in his career discovered a method of suturing blood vessels which made it possible to replace arteries. Later, he experimented with transplantation of organs, such as kidneys, in animals, and much of the later progress in this field relied on his pioneering work. In 1906 he was appointed to the Rockefeller Institute for Medical Research in New York City, where he developed techniques for tissue culture. He was awarded the 1912 Nobel Prize for physiology or medicine for these experiments.

Carreras, José Maria 1946– •*Spanish tenor*• Born in Barcelona, he made his debut at the Liceo there in 1970. He first appeared at Covent Garden, London, and at the Metropolitan Opera in 1974, at La Scala in 1975 and at Salzburg in 1976. After severe illness in the mid-1980s, he returned to the stage. In 1990 he performed alongside **Placido Domingo** and **Luciano Pavarotti** in the acclaimed "Three Tenors" concert at the open-air Caracalla Theater in Rome, and the three have sung in concert together at several subsequent events.

Carrero Blanco, Luis 1903–73 •*Spanish politician and naval officer*• Director of Naval Operations in 1939, he later rose to the rank of admiral (1966). He became an under-secretary to the presidency in 1941, and for the next 32 years he was effectively General **Franco**'s right-hand man, becoming in 1973 the first Prime Minister other than Franco since 1939. His assassination by the Basque nationalist organization ETA was a grave blow to the regime.

Carriera, Rosalba Giovanna 1675–1757 •*Italian painter*• Born in Venice, she was famed for her flattering portraits and miniatures, some of them in pastel, especially on ivory, such as *Portrait of a Man* (National Gallery, London). She introduced the pastel technique to France, on a visit in 1720–21, and wrote an account of her visit, *Diario* ... (1865).

Carrington, Dora de Houghton, *known as* **Carrington**, *married name* **Partridge** 1893–1932 •*English painter*• Born in Hereford, she went to the Slade School of Art in 1910 and became a member of the Bloomsbury Group. She painted landscapes and portraits inspired by her many intense relationships, notably her deep love for **Lytton Strachey**, with whom she set up home in 1916. Several weeks after his death she committed suicide.

Carrington, Peter Alexander Rupert Carrington, 6th Baron (Ireland) 1919– •*English Conservative politician*• Born in London and educated at Eton and Sandhurst, after service in World War II, he held ministerial posts in the Conservative administrations of **Churchill** (1951–54), **Anthony Eden** (1954–56), **Harold Macmillan** (1957–63), Alec Douglas-Home (Baron **Home**) (1963–64), **Edward Heath** (1970–74) and **Margaret Thatcher** (1979–82). As Foreign Secretary (1979–82) he was instrumental in establishing independence for Zimbabwe (1980). He resigned in 1982, accepting responsibility for the Argentinian invasion of the Falkland Islands. He was Secretary-General of NATO (1984–88) and Chairman of the EC conference on Yugoslavia (1991–92).

Carroll, Charles 1737–1832 •*American Revolutionary leader*• Born in Annapolis, Maryland, into a powerful Irish Catholic family, he was the cousin of **John Carroll**, the first American Catholic bishop. He was barred, as a Roman Catholic, from taking part in colonial politics, but he became involved in the pamphlet wars of the mid-1770s on behalf of the colonies. He was a member of the Continental Congress (1776–78) and later became one of Maryland's first senators (1789–92). His politics were markedly conservative, but his adherence to the revolutionary cause was inspirational to other American Catholics. At his death he was the last surviving signer of the Declaration of Independence.

Carroll, James 1854–1907 •*US physician*• Born in Woolwich, England, he emigrated in childhood to Canada and then the US. Serving as a surgeon in the US Army, and in association with Walter Reed (1851–1902), he did valuable research on yellow fever, deliberately infecting himself with the disease in the process (1900). He and Reed were the first to implicate a virus in human disease.

Carroll, John 1735–1815 •*American prelate*• Born in Upper Marlbro, Maryland, he trained for the priesthood in France and then Belgium. He entered the Jesuit Order in 1753 and was ordained priest in 1769. The Maryland priests petitioned **Pius VI** for a bishop in America, and Carroll was appointed to the see of Baltimore in 1789, the first American Catholic bishop.

Carroll, Lewis, *pseudonym of* **Charles Lutwidge Dodgson** 1832–98 •*English children's writer and mathematician*• He was born in Daresbury, Cheshire, and educated at Christ Church, Oxford, where he lectured in mathematics after 1855 and took orders in 1861. His most famous book, *Alice's Adventures in Wonderland* (1865), had its origin in a boat trip which he made with Alice Liddell and her sisters, the daughters of the dean of his college, Henry George Liddell. A sequel, *Through the Looking-Glass and What Alice Found There*, appeared in December 1871 (dated 1872). They were illustrated by Sir **John Tenniel**, and have since appeared in innumerable translations and editions. Their success among children was doubtless due to their cast of fantastic characters (Tweedledum and Tweedledee, the White Rabbit and the March

Hare) and the fact that Carroll eschewed moralizing. His other works include *The Hunting of the Snark* (1876), *Rhyme? and Reason?* (1883) and *Sylvie and Bruno* (2 vols, 1889 and 1893). Of his mathematical works, *Euclid and His Modern Rivals* (1879) is still of interest. He was also a pioneer photographer, and took many portraits, particularly of young girls.

“ ”

"And what is the use of a book," thought Alice, "without pictures or conversations?"

1865 ***Alice's Adventures in Wonderland***, *chapter 1, "Down the Rabbit-Hole."*

Carson, Johnny (John William) 1925– •*US television host*• Born in Corning, Iowa, he studied journalism at the University of Nebraska and started his career as a radio comedy writer before working as a television announcer in Omaha, Nebraska, and Los Angeles. He soon had his own television comedy show, *Carson's Cellar* (1951), then became a writer for *The Red Skelton Show*, which led to *The Johnny Carson Show* (1955–56). He took over from Jack Paar as host of *The Tonight Show* in 1962, soon becoming the highest-paid star on television. He wrote *Happiness Is a Dry Martini* (1965) and formed his own company, Carson Productions, in 1980. He retired from *The Tonight Show* in 1992.

Carson, Kit (Christopher) 1809–68 •*US frontiersman*• Born in Madison County, Kentucky, he became a trapper and hunter in New Mexico in 1825, ranging as far afield as California and Montana and marrying a woman of the Arapahoe people in 1836. His knowledge of Native American customs and languages led to his becoming guide for **John C Frémont**'s explorations (1842–45), and Indian agent in New Mexico (1853). He took part in the conquest of California, and as a brigadier general of volunteers he fought Native American tribes that sided with the Confederacy in the Civil War.

Carson, Rachel Louise 1907–64 •*US naturalist and science writer*• Born in Springdale, Pennsylvania, she studied biology at Johns Hopkins University, taught at the University of Maryland (1931–36) and worked as a marine biologist for the US Fish and Wildlife Service (1936–49). She became well known with *The Sea Around Us* (1951), which warned of the increasing danger of large-scale marine pollution, and the hard-hitting *Silent Spring* (1962), which directed public concern to the problems caused by synthetic pesticides and their effect on food chains. The resulting controls on their use owe much to her work.

Carson, Willie (William Hunter Fisher) 1942– •*Scottish jockey*• Born in Stirling, in 1972 he became the first Scotsman to be a champion jockey and recorded his first Classic success on High Top in the 2000 Guineas. He recorded a notable royal double for Queen **Elizabeth II** in 1977 when winning the Oaks and the St Leger on Dunfermline. He had to wait until 1979 for his first Derby winner, Troy, but won again on Henbit in 1980, 1989 and 1994. A serious accident in the summer of 1996 led to his retirement the following year.

Carstares, William 1649–1715 •*Scottish clergyman*• Born in Cathcart, Glasgow, he studied at Edinburgh and Utrecht, Holland, and became friend and adviser to the Prince of Orange (**William III**). He was arrested as a spy in London (1675), and imprisoned in Edinburgh until 1679. In 1683 he was again arrested, and after an imprisonment of a year and a half, returned to Holland to be chaplain to the Prince of Orange. From 1693 to the death of the king in 1702 he had great influence in Scottish affairs, and was popularly called "Cardinal Carstares" by the Jacobites. His influence helped to pass the Treaty of Union (1707).

Cartan, Élie Joseph 1869–1951 •*French mathematician*• Born in Dolomieu, and one of the most original mathematicians of his time, he worked on **Lie** groups and differential geometry, and founded the subject of analysis on differentiable manifolds, essential to modern fundamental physical theories. Among his discoveries are the theory of spinors, the method of moving frames and the exterior differential calculus. He is now seen to be an important figure for much of the mathematics of the 20th century.

Carte, Richard D'Oyly 1844–1901 •*English impresario and manager*• He was born in London and after working in his father's musical instrument-making business, became a concert agent. From 1875 he produced the first operettas by **Gilbert** and **Sullivan**, with whom he formed a partnership. He built the Savoy Theatre in London in 1881. After his death the D'Oyly Carte company continued to perform Gilbert and Sullivan.

Carter, Angela Olive, *née* **Stalker** 1940–92 •*English novelist and short-story writer*• Born in London and educated at Bristol University, she taught creative writing in England, the US and Australia, and lived in Japan for two years, an experience recorded in *Nothing Sacred* (1982). Her fiction, characterized by imaginative use of fantasy, vibrant humor and psychological symbolism, includes the novels *The Magic Toyshop* (1967), *The Infernal Desire Machines of Dr Hoffman* (1972) and *Wise Children* (1991), and a number of short-story collections. *The Sadeian Woman* (1979) is a feminist reinterpretation of the Marquis **de Sade**. She also wrote poetry, children's stories, and radio plays and, with **Neil Jordan**, wrote the screenplay for his film from her stories, *The Company of Wolves* (1984).

“ ”

What is marriage but prostitution to one man instead of many?

1985 ***Nights at the Circus***, *"London 2."*

Carter, Benny (Bennet Lester) 1907–2003 •*US alto saxophonist, trumpeter and composer*• Born in New York City, he was largely self-taught as a musician, and played trumpet and clarinet in addition to his primary instrument, alto saxophone. His warm tone and elegant flowing lines were hugely influential on the style of the swing era, and he was among the most important writers of big band arrangements, composing for the **Benny Goodman** orchestra among others. He was one of the first African-American writers to work on film (and later television) soundtracks within the studio system in Hollywood. He continued playing into the 1990s in a sophisticated mainstream style that registered his awareness of post-swing developments.

Carter, Betty, *professional name of* **Lillie Mae Jones**, *also called* **Lorraine Carter** 1929–98 •*US jazz singer*• Born in Flint, Michigan, and raised in Detroit, she came of age in the bebop era, and sang with touring bebop musicians, including **Charlie Parker** and **Dizzy Gillespie**. Bandleader **Lionel Hampton**, who employed her from 1948, nicknamed her "Betty Bebop." A brilliant vocal improviser and a genuine jazz singer, she always resisted commercial alternatives, even when times were hard. After being "rediscovered" in 1975, she went on to reestablish herself as a major jazz name in the 1990s.

Carter, Elliott Cook, Jr 1908– •*US composer*• Born in New York City, he was befriended by **Charles Ives**, who introduced him to contemporary music. His first work to gain international recognition was a string quartet (1953), the first of four quartets, the second of which won a Pulitzer Prize in 1960. This and subsequent works display an intellectual yet emotionally charged style, with the serial element extended to great rhythmic and metrical complexity. His output includes symphonies, other orchestral music, several concertos, songs and chamber music.

Carter, Howard 1874–1939 •*English Egyptologist*• Born in London, he joined **Flinders Petrie**'s archaeological survey of Egypt as a draftsman in 1891. From 1907 he conducted his own research under the patronage of George Herbert, 5th Earl of **Carnarvon**. His discoveries included the tombs of Hatshepsut (1907), **Tuthmosis IV** and, most notably, in 1922 the virtually intact burial of the 18th-Dynasty king **Tutankhamun**. The work of emptying the chambers, photographing, conserving and dispatching the treasures to Cairo occupied him for the rest of his life, but he failed through ill health to produce a final, detailed report.

Carter, Jimmy (James Earl) 1924– •*39th President of the US*• Born in Plains, Georgia, he graduated from the US Naval Academy in 1946 and served in the US Navy until 1953, when he took over the family peanut business and other business enterprises. As governor of Georgia (1970–74) he expressed an enlightened policy toward the rights of African Americans and women. In 1976 he won the Democratic presidential nomination and went on to win a narrow victory over **Gerald Ford** for the presidency. On election, he promised to set up effective energy and health programs, to concern himself with civil and human rights issues and to try to restrict the making of nuclear weapons. His presidency (1977–81) was notable for the Panama Canal Treaty, which provided for the eventual transfer of the canal to Panamanian control, and the Camp David Accords (1978), which he brokered between Israel and Egypt against considerable odds. As an outsider in Washington he had little success in dealing with Congress, which refused to ratify his arms limitation treaty with the Soviet Union. High inflation, recession and the energy crisis irritated the US public and eroded Carter's popularity, which plummeted in 1979–80 as a result of the seizure of US embassy hostages by Islamic fundamentalists in Iran. He was defeated by the Republican **Ronald Reagan** in the 1980 election. A prolific human rights campaigner, he has worked as a leader of international observer teams (1989–90), hosted peace negotiations (Ethiopia, 1989) and has been highly active in his role as UN ambassador, taking part in talks with Rwanda in 1996. He was awarded the Nobel Peace Prize in 2002.

Carter, Rosalynn Smith, *née* **Smith** 1927– •*US humanitarian and First Lady*• Born in Plains, Georgia, she married **Jimmy Carter** in 1946. When her husband was governor of Georgia (1971–74), she began to devote herself to developing a national strategy for helping the mentally ill, a work that she continued as First Lady (1977–81). Since then she has served on numerous committees dedicated to helping the mentally ill, and promoting children's health and worldwide peace. She received the Volunteer of the Decade Award from the National Mental Health Association (1980) and the **Eleanor Roosevelt** Living World award for peace links (1992), and with her husband was jointly awarded the Presidential Medal of Freedom in 1999. Her books include *Helping Yourself Help Others: A Book for Caregivers* (1994).

Carter Family •*US country music artists*• The Carter Family, along with **Jimmie Rodgers**, were the first stars of country music. The original group in 1927 featured A(lvin) P(leasant Delaney) Carter (1891–1960); his wife, Sara Carter (1898–1979, *née* Dougherty); and her cousin, Maybelle Carter (1909–78, *née* Addington). Their recordings of 1928–35 established a new style of harmony singing that has been hugely influential in the development of modern country music. The original trio broke up in 1943, but Maybelle continued to perform with her daughters as the Carter Sisters. A P and Sara made a comeback in 1952, while Maybelle and Sara later reunited as The Original Carter Family in 1967. Several of their children were involved in the group, the best known of whom is singer June Carter Cash (1929–2003), who was married to **Johnny Cash**.

Cartier, Sir Georges Étienne 1814–73 •*Canadian politician*• He was born in St Antoine, Quebec, and trained as a lawyer. In 1837 he took part in the rebellion led by Louis Papineau (1789–1871). He was attorney general under **John Macdonald** in 1856 and then, as the leader of the *Bleu* bloc of Canada East, served with him as joint Conservative Prime Minister (1858–62). In 1858 the Macdonald-Cartier administration was defeated, but Cartier returned to government in the great coalition of 1864 that negotiated confederation.

Cartier-Bresson, Henri 1908–2004 •*French photographer and artist*• Born in Paris, he studied painting and literature before taking up photography after a trip to West Africa in 1930. His first photographs were published in 1933. In the later 1930s he visited Mexico and the US and worked as an assistant to film director **Jean Renoir**. After World War II, during which he escaped from imprisonment to join the Resistance, he cofounded the independent photographic agency, Magnum Photos. He worked only in black and white, concerned exclusively with the spontaneous capturing of moments illustrating contemporary life. His books include *Images à la sauvette* (1952, "The Decisive Moment") and *The World of Henri Cartier-Bresson* (1968).

Cartland, Dame (Mary) Barbara Hamilton 1901–2000 •*English popular romantic novelist*• She was born in Edgbaston, Birmingham. She published her first novel, *Jigsaw*, in 1923, and throughout her life produced well over 600 best-selling books, mostly novels of chaste romantic love designed for female readers, but also including biographies and books on food, health and beauty, and several volumes of autobiography. She earned a place in the *Guinness Book of Records* for writing 26 books in the year 1983.

Caruso, Enrico 1873–1921 •*Italian tenor*• He was born in Naples, the 18th of 20 children. He made his first professional appearance in *Faust* (1895), then went to London (1902) and New York (1903). The great power and musical purity of his voice, combined with his acting ability, won him recognition as one of the finest tenors of all time.

Carvalho e Mello, Marquês de Pombal *See* **Pombal, Marquês de**

Carver, George Washington c. 1860–1943 •*US botanist and scientist*• Born into slavery on a farm near Diamond Grove, Missouri, he worked his way through Iowa State College, obtaining an MA in agriculture in 1896. He was then invited by **Booker T Washington** to become director of agricultural research (1896–1943) at the Tuskegee Institute in Alabama. Hoping to improve the lives of disadvantaged African-American farmers and the economy of the South, he promoted sweet potatoes and peanuts as alternatives to soil-depleting cotton and developed numerous products that could be made from each of these crops. He lectured widely on his work and was influential in the crop diversification that occurred in the South in the early 20th century.

Carver, Raymond 1939–88 •*US poet and short-story writer*• Born in Clatskanie, Oregon, he married at 18 and struggled for many years with poverty and alcoholism. It was not until the publication of the collection *Will You Please Be Quiet, Please?* (1976) that his work began to reach a wider audience. Both his fiction and his poetry are remarkable for their spare narratives, focusing on the lower and middle classes and dealing with states of transition: couples breaking up, people between jobs. He wrote no novels. Other books include *Elephant and Other Stories* (1988), and the poetry collections *Where Water Comes Together with Other Water* (1985) and *Ultramarine* (1985, published in Great Britain as *In a Marine Light: Selected Poems*).

Cary, (Arthur) Joyce Lunel 1888–1957 •*English novelist*• Born in Londonderry, Northern Ireland, of English parents, he studied art in Edinburgh and Paris, graduating (1912) at Oxford. He served with the Red Cross in the Balkan War of 1912–13 and was decorated by the king of Montenegro. In 1913 he joined the Nigerian Political Service and fought in a Nigerian regiment in World War I. After the war he took up writing, drawing on his African experiences for several novels including *Mister Johnson* (1939). In 1941 he was awarded the James Tait Black Memorial Prize for *The House of Children*, and established himself with the trilogy, *Herself Surprised* (1940), *To Be a Pilgrim* (1942) and *The Horse's Mouth* (1944). Other books include *Prisoner of Grace* (1952) and *Not Honour More* (1955).

Casals, Pablo, *also known as* **Pau Casals** 1876–1973 •*Spanish cellist, conductor and composer*• Born in Vendrell, Tarragona, he studied at the Royal Conservatory, Madrid, and became Professor of Cello at the Conservatory in Barcelona (1896). In 1905 he formed, with Jacques Thibaud (1880–1953) and Alfred Cortot (1877–1962), a trio that became famous for its performance of classical works. He founded the Barcelona Orchestra (1919), which he conducted until he left Spain at the outbreak of the civil war (1936). In 1950 he founded an annual festival of classical chamber music in Prades, France. His own compositions consist of choral and chamber works.

“ ”

The most perfect technique is that which is not noticed at all.

Quoted in Julian Lloyd Webber ***The Song of the Birds*** *(1985).*

Casanova (de Seingalt), Giacomo Girolamo 1725–98 •*Italian adventurer*• Born in Venice, he was expelled from a seminary for scandalous conduct (1741), and by 1750 had been secretary to a cardinal, an ensign in the Venetian army, an abbé, a gambler, an alchemist and a violinist. In 1755 he was imprisoned in Venice for being a magician, but made a daring escape in 1756, and for the next 20 years wandered through Europe, meeting the great men and women of his time and indulging in romantic escapades. He was the director of state lotteries in Paris, was knighted in the Netherlands, visited Russia but fled after a duel, and worked as a spy for **Louis XV** and as a police informer for the Venetian Inquisition. His reputation rests on his *Mémoires de J. Casanova de Seingalt*, which were first published in edited form in Leipzig (12 vols, 1828–38). The complete edition, *Histoire de ma vie* (Eng trans *History of My Life*) was first published in 1960. Primarily, and memorably, an account of his numerous sexual adventures, they also give an intriguing portrait of his age.

Casement, Sir Roger David 1864–1916 •*Irish patriot and British consular official*• Born in Sandycove, County Dublin, he joined the British consular service and went to Africa where he condemned the treatment of native workers (1904). As consul general at Rio de Janeiro he exposed the exploitation of rubber workers in the Congo and Peru, for which he was knighted in 1911. He joined the Irish Volunteers in 1913, and at the outbreak of World War I went to Berlin to try to obtain German help for Irish independence, attempting to form an Irish Brigade of prisoners of war with which he intended to invade Ireland and end British rule. In 1916 he was arrested on landing in Ireland from a German submarine. He was tried in England for high treason and hanged. His controversial "Black Diaries," revealing, among other things, homosexual practices, were published in 1959.

Cash, Johnny (J R) 1932–2003 •*American country music singer, songwriter and guitarist*• Born in Kingsland, Arkansas, into a cotton-farming family, he was christened simply J R, and became Johnny by general usage. A complex and often deeply troubled personality, he became the best-known performer in country music in the 1960s, and helped spread it to a huge new audience. After discharge from the US Air Force, he signed with Sun records in 1955, where the success of "I Walk the Line" established his style, and brought him a contract with Columbia. He turned out a string of hits in the 1960s, and had his own television show from 1969 to 1971. Nicknamed "The Man in Black" (he had a 1971 hit of that name), he battled many personal problems, but bounced back as a member of the Highwaymen with **Willie Nelson**, Waylon Jennings (1937–2002) and Kris Kristofferson (1936–) from 1985, while his 1994 album, *American Recordings*, completed a remarkable renaissance. His daughter Roseanne Cash (1956–), is an important contemporary country artist.

Čáslavská, Věra 1942– •*Czech gymnast*• Born in Prague, she switched from ice skating to gymnastics as a 15-year-old, and went on to win 22 Olympic, World, and European titles (1959–68), and eight silver and three bronze medals. She won three Olympic gold medals in 1964, and four in 1968. She donated her medals (one each) to the four Czech leaders (**Alexander Dubček**, **Ludwik Svoboda**, Oldřich Černík and Smrkorsky) deposed following the Soviet invasion.

Caslon, William 1692–1766 •*English type founder*• Born in Cradley, Worcestershire, he worked as an apprentice to a gunlock and barrel engraver before he set up his own business as a gun engraver and toolmaker in London in 1716. He soon began cutting type for printers, and his graceful "old face" Caslon types have retained their popularity to the present day.

Cassander c. 358–297 BC •*King of Macedonia*• He assumed power over Macedonia after the death of his father, Antipater (319 BC), and became its king (305). An active figure in the power struggle after the death of **Alexander the Great** (323), he murdered Alexander's mother, widow and son, and contributed to the defeat of **Antigonus I Monophthalmos** at Ipsus (301). He married Thessalonica (Alexander's half-sister), for whom he built and named a city in Macedonia.

Cassatt, Mary 1844–1926 •*US Impressionist painter*• Born of French descent into a wealthy family in Allegheny (now part of Pittsburgh), Pennsylvania, she studied in Spain, Italy and Holland. From 1874 she worked mainly in France, where she was a friend and follower of **Edgar Degas**, who persuaded her to exhibit with the Impressionists (1879–81, 1886). From 1889 she produced the oils and pastels of mothers and children for which she is best known, for example, *Woman and Child Driving* (Philadelphia Museum). She also made a series of dry-point color prints influenced by Japanese wood blocks and prints, as in *The Tramway* (1891, Museum of Modern Art, New York).

Cassavetes, John 1929–89 •*US filmmaker*• Born in New York City, he studied at the American Academy of Dramatic Arts and acted in stock companies before making his film debut in *Fourteen Hours* (1951). Often cast as angry, alienated young men, he appeared in such films as *Crime in the Streets* (1956) and *Edge of the City* (1957) before finding popularity in the television series *Johnny Staccato* (1959–60). He made his directorial debut with the experimental cinema-vérité drama *Shadows* (1960). His subsequent films as an actor include *The Dirty Dozen* (1967) and *Rosemary's Baby* (1968). He earned great critical acclaim as a director of extemporized films of unflinching honesty that explore the darker side of human existence. Often starring his wife Gena Rowlands (1934–), these include *A Woman Under the Influence* (1974) and *Love Streams* (1984).

Cassell, John 1817–65 •*English publisher*• He was born in Manchester, the son of an innkeeper. After an apprenticeship as a carpenter, he went to London in 1836 as a temperance advocate. In 1850 he turned to writing and publishing educational books and magazines for the working classes, including *Cassell's Magazine* (1852).

Cassin, René 1887–1976 •*French jurist and politician, and Nobel Prize winner*• He was born in Bayonne and educated at Aix and Paris universities. He was Professor of International Law at Lille (1920–29) and at Paris (1929–60), combining this with membership in the French delegation to the League of Nations (1924–38). During World War II he joined General **de Gaulle** in London and, in the later years of the war, held important posts in the French government in exile in London and Algiers, and subsequently in the Council of State (of which he was president, 1944–60) in liberated France. He was the principal author of the Universal Declaration of the Rights of Man (1948) and played a leading part in the establishment of UNESCO. He was also a member of the European Court of Human Rights from 1959, and its president (1965–68). In 1968 he was awarded the Nobel Peace Prize.

Cassini, Giovanni Domenico 1625–1712 •*French astronomer*• Born in Perinaldo, near Nice, France (then in Italy), he was educated in Genoa. He became Professor of Astronomy at the University of Bologna (1650), where his determinations of the rotation periods of the planets and his tables of the motions of Jupiter's satellites (1668) brought him fame. In 1669 he became the first director of the new Paris Observatory, where he made a host of observations of Mars, Jupiter and Saturn, and discovered the division of Saturn's rings which still bears his name (1675). He also discovered four satellites of Saturn. One of Cassini's great achievements was his determination of the distance of the planet Mars, and thereby of the distance of the sun, from observations made simultaneously in Paris and in the French colony of Cayenne.

Cassiodorus, Flavius Magnus Aurelius c. 490–c. 580 •*Roman historian and statesman*• Born in Scylaceum (Squillace), Calabria, he was minister and counselor to **Theodoric the Great**, king of the Ostrogoths in Italy, and, after his death, chief minister to Queen Amalasontha. He retired c. 540 to devote himself to study and writing. He founded monasteries, and promoted the transcription of classical manuscripts, also compiling an encyclopedia on learning and the liberal arts for his monks, *Institutiones divinarum et saecularium litterarum*.

Cassirer, Ernst 1874–1945 •*German-Jewish neo-Kantian philosopher and historian of ideas*• Born in Wrocław, Poland, and educated at various German universities, he was appointed Professor of Philosophy (1919), then Rector (1930), at Hamburg, but resigned when **Hitler** came to power. He then taught at Oxford (1933–35), Göteborg (1935–41), Yale (1941–44) and Columbia (1944–45). His published works include *Substanzbegriff und Funktionsbegriff* (1910, *Substance and Function*, 1923) and *Die Philosophie der symbolischen Formen* (1923–29, "The Philosophy of Symbolic Forms"), which analyzes the symbolic functions underlying all human thought, language and culture.

Cassius, *in full* **Gaius Cassius Longinus** d. 42 BC •*Roman conspirator*• He was quaestor to **Marcus Licinius Crassus** in the Parthian War (54 BC), and in 49 supported **Pompey** during the civil war. He was pardoned by **Julius Caesar** after their defeat at the Battle of Pharsalia (48). Despite gaining political advancement through Caesar, he played a leading part in the conspiracy to murder him (44), having persuaded **Marcus Brutus** to join him. However, popular feeling turned against them, and they were defeated at Philippi (42) by **Mark Antony**. Cassius subsequently committed suicide.

Cassius, Dio *See* **Dio Cassius**

Cassivellaunus 1st century BC •*King of the Catuvellauni*• As a chief of the British tribe living in the area of modern Hertfordshire, he led the Catuvellauni in resistance to **Julius Caesar** on his second invasion (54 BC), and made peace after his principal base (probably situated at Wheathampstead) was stormed.

Casson, Sir Hugh Maxwell 1910–99 •*English architect*• Educated at Cambridge, he was Professor of Environmental Design at the Royal College of Art (1953–75), and was planning adviser to several authorities after World War II. Among his works are *Homes by the Million* (1947), *An Introduction to Victorian Architecture* (1948) and *Japan Observed* (1991). He was president of the Royal Academy from 1976 to 1984.

“ ”

Architecture cannot be understood without some knowledge of the society it serves.

1948 ***An Introduction to Victorian Architecture.***

Castagno, Andrea del, *properly* **Andrea di Bartolo de Simone** c. 1421–57 •*Italian painter*• Born in Castagno, Tuscany, he studied in Florence and became a painter of the Florentine school. His style shows the influence of **Masaccio** and **Donatello**. In about 1440 he painted some effigies of rebels hanged by their heels, which established his reputation as a painter of violent scenes. After a period in Venice he returned to Florence, where he designed a stained-glass window for the cathedral. Soon afterward he painted his celebrated *Last Supper* for Santa Apollonia (now in the Castagno Museum). His last dated work is the famous equestrian portrait *Niccolò da Tolentino*, which is in Florence Cathedral. He died of the plague.

Castelfranco, Giorgio Barbarelli *See* **Giorgione**

Castelnau, Noël Marie Joseph Edouard, Vicomte de Curières de 1851–1944 •*French soldier*• He was born in Aveyron of a military, royalist, Catholic family. Educated at St Cyr, he served on the Loire in the Franco-Prussian War (1870–71). He was a member of the Conseil de Guerre in 1913 and took command of the Army of Lorraine in 1914. As commander of all French armies in France, he directed the Champagne offensive (1915), and became General **Joffre**'s Chief of Staff.

Castelnuovo-Tedesco, Mario 1895–1968 •*US composer*• Born in Florence, Italy, he began composing as a boy. In addition to three operas he produced orchestral and instrumental works, but is probably best known for his songs, especially his complete series of the lyrics from **Shakespeare**'s plays, *33 Shakespeare Songs*. He emigrated to the US in 1939 and became a US citizen.

Castelo Branco, Camilo, Visconde de Correia Botelho 1825–90 •*Portuguese novelist*• Born in Lisbon, an illegitimate child, he was brought up by relatives in austere conditions. One of the most important of modern Portuguese novelists, with a deep understanding of the life of his people, his work ranges from romances like *Mysterios de Lisboa* (1958, "The Mysteries of Lisbon"), to closely observed, imaginative interpretations of the everyday Portuguese scene, such as *The Crime of Father Amara*. His best-known book is *Amor de perdição* (1862, "Fatal Love"). He was created viscount in 1885 for his services to literature. He committed suicide.

Castelo Branco, Humberto de Alencar 1900–67 •*Brazilian politician*• He was educated in Brazil, France and the US. He went on to fight with the Brazilian army in Italy, and coordinated the anti-Goulart military conspiracy of 1964. As President from 1964 to 1967, although the economy had been stabilized, the financial system reorganized and foreign debt renegotiated, his government failed to alter traditional patterns of authority and prevent the emergence of hard-line factions among the military, which established the "tutelary regime" which survived until 1985.

Castiglione, Baldassare, Count 1478–1529 •*Italian courtier and writer*• He was born near Mantua. In 1505 he was sent by the Duke of Urbino as envoy to **Henry VII** of England, who made him a knight, and he was later Mantuan ambassador at the papal court in Rome (1513–24). Thereafter he was papal nuncio for Pope **Clement VII** in Spain, from 1524. His chief work, *Il libro del cortegiano* (1528, "The Courtier"), is a manual for courtiers, in dialogue form, and was translated into English by Sir Thomas Hoby (as *The Courtyer*) in 1561.

Castle (of Blackburn), Barbara Anne Castle, Baroness, *née* **Betts** 1910–2002 •*English Labour politician*• Born in Bradford, and educated at St Hugh's College, Oxford, she worked in local government before World War II and entered parliament in 1945 as Member of Parliament for Blackburn. During the 1950s she was a convinced "**Bevan**ite," outspoken in her defense of radical causes. Chairman of the Labour Party (1958–59), after Labour came into power in 1964 she attained Cabinet rank, becoming Minister of Overseas Development (1964–65). She was a controversial Minister of Transport (1965–68), introducing a 70-mph speed limit and the "breathalyzer" test for suspected drunken drivers, in an effort to cut down road accidents, and then took over the newly created post of Secretary of State for Employment and Productivity (1968–70). From 1974 to 1976 she was Secretary of State for Social Services. As a Member of the European Parliament (1979–89), she served as vice chairman of the Socialist Group (1979–86). Two volumes of her diaries were published in 1980 and 1984 followed by her autobiography *Fighting All the Way* (1993). She was created a life peer in 1990.

Castlereagh, Robert Stewart, Viscount 1769–1822 •*British politician*• Born in Dublin, he was educated at Armagh and Cambridge (for one year) and entered the Irish Parliament in 1790 as Whig member for County Down. In 1795 he turned Tory, although he remained in favor of Catholic emancipation. As Irish Chief Secretary from 1797 he devoted himself to promoting **William Pitt** the Younger's measure of union, but, with Pitt, retired from office when Pitt's Catholic pledges were defeated. As War Minister (1806–07, 1807–09), he was made scapegoat for the failed Walcheren expedition, the dispute ending in a duel with **George Canning**. In 1812 he achieved recognition as Foreign Secretary under Lord **Liverpool**, as well as in the post of Leader of the House of Commons. After working at the heart of the coalition against **Napoleon I** (1813–14), Castlereagh also represented England at Chaumont and Vienna (1814–15), Paris (1815), and Aix-la-Chapelle (1818). Believing that he was being blackmailed for homosexuality, he committed suicide. Great Britain and Europe were indebted to him for the 40 years of peace that succeeded **Napoleon I**'s downfall, yet few politicians have been so disliked, and a shout of joy was given as his coffin was carried into Westminster Abbey.

Castro (Ruz), Fidel 1927– •*Cuban revolutionary*• Born near Birán, he was the son of a successful sugar planter. He studied law and practiced in Havana, fighting cases on behalf of the poor and against the official corruption and oppression which were rife under President **Fulgencio Batista**. In 1953, with his brother Raúl, also an ardent revolutionary, he led an unsuccessful uprising and was sentenced to 15 years' imprisonment, but, released under an amnesty within a year, he fled to the US and thence to Mexico, all the time organizing anti-Batista activities. In 1956 he landed in Cuba with a small band of insurgents, but he was betrayed and ambushed, barely escaping into the Sierra Maestra Mountains, from where he waged a relentless guerrilla campaign. The degeneration of Cuba into a police state brought many recruits to his cause, and in 1958 he mounted a full-scale attack and Batista was forced to flee. Castro, Prime Minister from February 1959, proclaimed a "Marxist-Leninist program" adapted to local requirements. He set about making far-reaching reforms in agriculture, industry, and education. His overthrow of US dominance in the economic sphere and routing of the US-connived émigré invasion at the Bay of Pigs (1961) was balanced by consequent dependence on Communist (mainly Russian) aid and the near-disaster of the 1962 missile crisis. Despite problems in sugar and tobacco production and two mass exoduses, Castro's popularity remained high. In 1979 he became president of the nonaligned countries movement despite Cuba's continuing substantial economic and political involvement with the Kremlin, but 1991 saw Cuba's worst economic crisis in its 32 years of Communist rule, caused mainly by flagging economic aid and a drastic fall in basic supplies from the economically compromised USSR. In 1994 Castro suffered great embarassment when his daughter fled Cuba and sought asylum in the US.

Catesby, Robert 1573–1605 •*English conspirator, leader of the Gunpowder Plot*• He was born in Lapworth, Warwickshire, into a wealthy Roman Catholic family. As a recusant he suffered fines and imprisonment under **Elizabeth I**. He was named as an accomplice in the 1603 plot against **James VI and I**, and in 1605 he was the chief instigator of the Gunpowder Plot. He was shot dead while resisting arrest.

Cather, Willa Sibert 1873–1947 •*US fiction writer, poet and journalist*• She was born on a farm near Winchester, Virginia, and her formative years were spent in Red Cloud, Nebraska. After attending college there (1891–95), she moved to New York as editor of *McClure's* magazine (1906–12), and her first novel, *Alexander's Bridge*, was published in 1912. She subsequently wrote three novels dealing with immigrants to the US: *O Pioneers!* (1913), *The Song of the Lark* (1915), and *My Ántonia* (1918). A lesbian who wrote primarily about independent women, she was a prolific writer, and other novels include *Death Comes for the Archbishop* (1927) and *One of Ours* (1922, Pulitzer Prize).

“ ”

The history of every country begins in the heart of a man or a woman.

1913 ***O Pioneers!****, part I, chapter 5.*

Catherine, St d. 307 AD •*Egyptian royal virgin*• Tradition maintains she was born in Alexandria. She is said to have publicly confessed the Gospel at a sacrificial feast appointed by Emperor Maximinus, and was consequently beheaded, after being tortured on a spiked wheel (later known as a "catherine" wheel). Her remains were miraculously transported to Mount Sinai, where her shrine is on display in St Catherine's monastery. Her feast day is November 25.

Catherine of Siena, St, *properly* **Caterina Benincasa** 1347–80 •*Italian mystic*• Born in Siena, she became a Dominican at the age of 16. She is their patron saint. Her enthusiasm converted many sinners, and she persuaded Pope **Gregory XI** to return the papacy from Avignon to Rome. The stigmata of Jesus were said to have been imprinted on her body in 1375. She wrote many devotional pieces, letters, and poems; her *Dialogue*, a work on mysticism, was translated in 1896. She was canonized in 1461. Her feast day is April 29.

Catherine I, *originally* **Martha** 1684–1727 •*Empress of Russia and wife of Peter the Great*• She was probably of Lithuanian peasant stock, and after her Swedish husband deserted her, she became mistress of **Peter I**'s Chief Minister, Prince **Aleksandr Menshikov**, and later of Peter himself, changing her name to Catherine and converting to Orthodoxy (1708). The czar married her (1712), and after his death (1725) Prince Menshikov ensured her succession to the throne. Illiterate and licentious, she allowed Menshikov to govern in her name. She was succeeded by Peter's grandson, **Peter II**.

Catherine II (the Great) 1729–96 •*Empress of Russia from 1762*• Born in Stettin in the Prussian province of Pomerania (now Szczecin in Poland), she was the daughter of the Prince of Anhalt-Zerbst. In 1745 she married Peter, Grand Duke and heir to the Russian throne, but the marriage was stormy and unhappy, with many quarrels. Catherine became notorious for her love affairs with Count Gregory Orlov (1734–83) and also with **Stanislas II Augustus Poniatowski**. After Peter's accession in 1762 (as **Peter III**), Catherine was compelled to live separately; later Peter was dethroned by a conspiracy in which Catherine was probably implicated, and Catherine herself was made empress despite a weak claim to the throne. A few days afterward Peter was murdered by Orlov and others. The government was carried on with great energy, and the dominions and power of Russia rapidly increased. When discontent was voiced, the young Prince Ivan, the hope of the disaffected, was murdered in the castle of Schlüsselburg. In 1774 Catherine suppressed a popular rebellion led by **Yemelyan Pugachev**, defeating his Cossack troops at the battle of Tsaritsyn the following year. She sought the support of the nobility in Russia, and promoted their cause by establishing them as a separate estate by charter in 1785. Under Catherine, internal politics consisted of court intrigues both for and against a succession of favorites, **Grigori Potemkin** being the best known. Three partitions (with Austria) of Poland in 1772, 1793 and 1795, and two Turkish wars (1774 and 1792) vastly increased the empire, as did a war with Sweden (1790) and the incorporation of the Baltic territory of Courland. Catherine was renowned for her intelligence and learning. She promoted French culture in Russia, and corresponded throughout her life with **Voltaire** and the Encyclopedists.

Catherine de Médicis, *Italian* **Caterina de' Medici** 1519–89 •*Queen and regent of France*• Born in Florence, the daughter of **Lorenzo de' Medici**, Duke of Urbino, she was to become the mother of three French kings. Married at 14 to Henry, Duke of Orléans (the future King **Henry II** of France), as Henry's queen (1547–59) she was constantly humiliated by his influential mistress, **Diane de Poitiers**. When her husband died (1559), Catherine acted as queen regent (1559–60) during the brief reign of her eldest son, **Francis II**, the first husband of **Mary Queen of Scots**, and again during the minority of her second son, **Charles IX**, whom she dominated throughout his reign (1560–74). She tried to pursue moderation, but she nursed dynastic ambitions and was drawn into political and religious intrigues. She was also implicated in the infamous St Bartholomew's Day Massacre (1572), together with Charles and her third son, Henry of Anjou, who succeeded to the throne (1574) as **Henry III**. Catherine's political influence waned during his troubled reign, but she survived long enough to ensure the succession of **Henry IV**, who married her daughter Margaret, and who restored royal authority.

Catherine de Valois 1401–37 •*Queen of England, wife of Henry V*• Born in Paris, she was the youngest daughter of King Charles VI (Charles the Foolish) of France, and married **Henry V** of England at Troyes (1420). In 1421 she gave birth to a son, the future **Henry VI** of England. After her husband's death (1422), she secretly married (c. 1431–32) Owen Tudor, a Welsh squire, despite parliamentary opposition. Their eldest son, Edmund, Earl of Richmond, was the father of **Henry VII**, the first of the Tudor kings of England.

Catherine Howard d. 1542 •*English queen*• She was the granddaughter of **Thomas Howard**, 2nd Duke of Norfolk, niece of **Thomas Howard**, 3rd Duke of Norfolk and cousin of **Anne Boleyn**. In 1540 she married **Henry VIII** as his fifth wife, immediately after his divorce from **Anne of Cleves**. In 1541 she was charged by **Thomas Cranmer** with sexual intercourse before her marriage with a musician (Henry Mannock), her secretary (Francis Dereham) and a kinsman (Thomas Culpepper), whom she had known before her marriage. The men were executed, and Catherine was attainted by parliament and beheaded.

Catherine of Aragon 1485–1536 •*English queen, the first wife of Henry VIII*• Born in Alcalá de Henares, Spain, the youngest daughter of **Ferdinand** and **Isabella** of Spain, she was first married (1501) to **Arthur**, Prince of Wales, the eldest son of **Henry VII**. Arthur died six months later, and in 1503 she was betrothed to his brother, the 11-year-old Prince Henry (later **Henry VIII**). They were married in 1509. Of their six children, only the Princess Mary (later **Mary I**) survived. In the years that followed, Henry's infidelities, and his anxiety for a son and heir, soured the marriage, and in 1527 he began proceedings for a divorce, in order to marry **Anne Boleyn**. Despite strong opposition from the pope, Henry and Anne were secretly married (1533), and the marriage to Catherine was annulled by Archbishop **Cranmer**. Catherine, who had offered a dignified, passive resistance throughout, was sent into retirement at Ampthill, Bedfordshire. In 1534 the pope pronounced her marriage valid, which provoked Henry's final break with Rome and began the Reformation in England. Catherine retired to lead an austerely religious life at Kimbolton, Cambridgeshire.

Catherine of Braganza 1638–1705 •*English queen, the wife of Charles II*• Born in Vila Viçosa, Portugal, the daughter of the Duke of Braganza (later King **John IV** of Portugal), she was a devout Roman Catholic. She married **Charles II** in 1662, bringing Tangier and Bombay as her dowry. She was forced to receive the king's mistress, **Barbara Villiers**, and their children, at court, and her own failure to bear children, and her parsimony, alienated her from the people. Charles resisted all pressure for a divorce, even defending her from malicious poisoning charges during the Popish Plot (1678–79), but forced her to live apart from him in retirement. In 1692 she went home to Portugal, where she became regent for her brother, Pedro II.

Catherine or **Katherine Parr** 1512–48 •*English queen*• The daughter of Sir Thomas Parr of Kendal, she married first Edward Borough, and next Lord Latimer, before becoming Queen of England by marrying **Henry VIII** as his sixth wife (1543). A learned, spirited and tactful woman, she managed Henry better than his other wives, persuaded him to restore the succession to his daughters Mary (**Mary I**) and Elizabeth (**Elizabeth I**) and showed them much kindness. Shortly after Henry's death (1547) she married a former suitor, **Thomas Seymour** of Sudeley, and died in childbirth the following year.

Catherine the Great *See* **Catherine II (the Great)**

Catilina, Lucius Sergius, *also called* **Catiline** c. 108–62 BC •*Roman conspirator*• An impoverished patrician, and adherent of **Lucius Sulla**, he was elected praetor in 68 BC, and next year Governor of Africa, but was disqualified from the consulship in 66 on charges of maladministration. Disappointed and crippled by debt, he entered into a conspiracy with other Roman nobles. In 63 he planned a complete revolution, and the assassination of **Cicero** and the hostile senators. Cicero discovered the plans and defeated the assassins; two days later, when Catilina appeared in the Senate, Cicero denounced him. He escaped from Rome, but some of the conspirators were arrested and executed. Insurrections in several parts of Italy were suppressed, and Catilina was defeated and killed by republican forces at Pistoria (now Pistoia).

Catiline *See* **Catilina, Lucius Sergius**

Catlin, George 1796–1872 •*US artist and author*• Born in Wilkes-Barre, Pennsylvania, during 1832–40 he studied the Native Americans of the Far West, painting 470 full-length portraits and other pictures illustrating their life and customs (now in the National Museum in Washington). He spent eight years in Europe with a Far West show, traveled in South and Central America (1852–57), and lived in Europe again until 1871. His works include *Manners of the North American Indians* (2 vols, 1841) and *Last Rambles in the Rocky Mountains* (1868).

Cato, Dionysius 4th century AD? •*Roman writer*• He was the supposed author of a volume of 164 moral precepts in Latin hexameters, known as *Dionysii Catonis disticha de moribus ad filium* ("Couplets on Morals, to His Son"), which was a great favorite during the Middle Ages.

Cato, Marcus Porcius the Elder, *also known as* **"the Censor"** 234–149 BC •*Roman statesman and orator*• He was born in Tusculum, of peasant stock. He distinguished himself in the Second Punic War (218–202 BC) and became successively quaestor, aedile, praetor, and consul (195). In Spain he crushed a formidable insurrection, and in 191, as legatus, he was instrumental in the defeat of **Antiochus III**. He advocated the simple, strict social life of ancient Roman tradition, and condemned Greek refinement and luxury. Elected censor (184), he introduced such rigorous legislative reforms that "Censor" became his permanent surname. He opposed good and bad innovations with equal intolerance. In 153 he was sent on a mission to Carthage, which so fueled his fear of Carthaginian power that he subsequently ended every speech in the Senate with the words "Carthage must be destroyed" (*Carthago delenda est*). He lived to see the start of the Third Punic War (149–146 BC). He wrote several works, including *De agri cultura* ("On Agriculture") and *Origines*, a summary of the Roman annals.

"

Rem tene, verba sequentur.
Stick to your subject, and words will follow.

Attributed advice to orators. Quoted in ***Caius Julius Victor Ars Rhetorica**, "De inventione."*

Cato, Marcus Porcius the Younger, *also called* **Uticensis** 95–46 BC •*Roman politician*• He served in the campaign against Spartacus (72 BC). Military tribune in 67, he brought back with him from Greece the Stoic philosopher Athenodorus. As tribune (63) he denounced **Julius Caesar** as an accomplice of **Catilina**, and his strenuous opposition to **Marcus Licinius Crassus**, **Pompey**, and Caesar, led to the formation of the first triumvirate. He later sided with Pompey, and after the Battle of Pharsalia (48) escaped into Africa, to defend Utica. When he heard of Caesar's decisive victory at Thapsus (46), he committed suicide. His great-grandfather was **Cato the Elder**.

Catt, Carrie Clinton Chapman, *née* **Lane** 1859–1947 •*US reformer and pacifist*• Born in Ripon, Wisconsin, and educated at Iowa State College, she joined the staff of the National American Woman Suffrage Association in 1890, and later became its president (1900–04, 1915–47), effecting dramatic changes in the organization and helping to bring about the 19th Amendment (1920), thus securing the vote for women. She organized the Women's Peace Party during World War I, helped establish the League of Women Voters (1919), and spent the later years of her life campaigning for world peace.

Cattell, Raymond B(ernard) 1905–98 •*English psychologist*• Born in Staffordshire, he was educated at London University. He taught at Harvard, Clark and Duke Universities before World War II, and after the war became research professor and director of the Laboratory of Personality Assessment at the University of Illinois. He later moved to the University of Hawaii. He applied the statistical techniques of factor analysis to the study of personality differences, and devised a lengthy questionnaire (the 16 PF scale) from which is derived a personality profile of 16 scores for the person tested.

Catullus, Gaius Valerius c. 84–c. 54 BC •*Roman lyric poet*• Born in Verona, he began to write verses at the age of 16. About 62 BC he settled in Rome where he met "Lesbia," a married woman whom he addresses in some of his most beautiful, and some of his most bitter poems. A fiery, unscrupulous partisan, he assailed his enemies, including **Julius Caesar**, with equal scurrility and wit. His extant works include love poems, satiric poems, mythological pieces (some of them adapted from the Greek), and "Attis." The text depends on a single manuscript discovered in the 14th century at Verona, inaccurately transcribed and subsequently lost. He exerted a wide influence on his successors and on English poetry.

Cauchy, Augustin Louis, Baron 1789–1857 •*French mathematician*• Born in Paris, he did important work on ordinary and partial differential equations, advocated the wave theory of light following **Augustin Fresnel**'s work, and gave a substantial impetus to the mathematical theory of elasticity. He is remembered as the founder of the theory of functions of a complex variable, which was to play a leading role in the development of mathematics during the rest of the 19th century. In algebra he gave a definitive account of the theory of determinants, and developed the ideas of permutation groups which had appeared in the work of **Joseph Luis de Lagrange** and **Évariste Galois**.

Cauer, Minna (Wilhelmine Theodore Marie), *née* **Schelle** 1841–1922 •*German feminist and suffragist*• She was born in Freyenstein (Ostprignitz) where her father was pastor. She held leading roles in the *Kaufmännischer Verband für weibliche Angestellete* and in the *Verein Frauenwohl* during the 1880s. In 1900 she founded with **Anita Augspurg** the important *Verband fortschrittlicher Frauenvereine* ("Federation of Women's Associations") and in 1902 was a founder, with Augspurg and **Lida Heymann**, of the

Deutscher Verband für Frauenstimmrecht, a women's suffrage organization. Later she was involved with Heymann and Augspurg in publishing the newspaper *Die Frau im Staat* (1919–33).

Causley, Charles 1917–2003 •*English poet and children's writer*• His close ties with his hometown of Launceston in Cornwall provided him with a unique, rooted point of view on the world, and his naval war experiences inspired his early verse, as in *Farewell, Aggie Weston* (1951). His *Collected Poems 1951–1975*, which combined verse intended for both adults and children, was published in 1975 and his *Collected Poems for Children* was published in 1995. *Collected Poems 1951–2000* was published in 2000.

Cavaco Silva, Anibal 1939– •*Portuguese politician*• Born in Loule, after studying economics in Great Britain and the US he became a university teacher and then a research director at the Bank of Portugal. Entering politics, he became Minister of Finance (1980–81). He then became leader of the Social Democratic Party (PSD) and Prime Minister (1985–95). Under his cautious, conservative leadership, Portugal joined the European Community (EC) in 1985.

Cavafy, Constantine, *pseudonym of* **Konstantínos Pétron Kaváfis** 1863–1933 •*Greek poet*• He was born in Alexandria, Egypt, of a Greek merchant family, and spent most of his life there working as a civil servant. His work tends to diverge into the erotic, in which he was one of the first modern writers to deal explicitly with gay themes, and the historical, in which he recreates the world of Greece and Alexandria in the Hellenistic period. His view of life is essentially tragic. His first book, containing 14 poems, was privately published when he was 41, and reissued five years later with an additional seven poems. He published no further work during his lifetime, but in recent years he has come to be regarded as one of the most influential modern Greek poets. His best-known poems are his earlier ones, such as *I polis* ("The City") and *Perimenondas tous varvarous* ("Waiting for the Barbarians").

Cavalcanti, Guido c. 1240–1300 •*Italian poet*• He was born in Florence. A friend of **Dante**, he married a Ghibelline, and was banished by the **Guelfs**. His works, which included ballads, sonnets and *canzoni*, were translated by **Dante Gabriel Rossetti** and **Ezra Pound**. He is said to have been studious and eccentric, and much of his poetry reflects his intellectualism, although he is also aware of the emotional depths of his usual subject, love.

Cavell, Edith Louisa 1865–1915 •*English nurse*• Born in Swardeston, Norfolk, she became a nurse in 1895, and in 1907 the first matron of the Berkendael Medical Institute in Brussels, which became a Red Cross hospital during World War I. In August 1915 she was arrested by the Germans and charged with having helped about 200 Allied soldiers to escape to the neutral Netherlands. Tried by court martial, she did not deny the charges and was executed.

“ ”

Standing, as I do, in view of God and eternity, I realize that patriotism is not enough. I must have no hatred or bitterness towards anyone.

1915 On the eve of her execution. Reported in ***The Times*** *(London), October 23.*

Cavendish, Henry 1731–1810 •*English natural philosopher and chemist*• Born in Nice, France, into an aristocratic family, he was educated at Peterhouse College, Cambridge (1749–53). Family wealth enabled him to devote an increasingly reclusive life entirely to scientific pursuits. He demonstrated chemical and physical methods for analyzing the distinct "factitious airs" of which normal atmospheric air was composed (1766). Among these were "fixed air" (carbon dioxide), and "inflammable air" (hydrogen), which Cavendish isolated. In 1784 he ascertained that hydrogen and oxygen, when caused to explode by an electric spark, combined to produce water, which could not therefore be an element. Similarly, in 1795 he showed nitric acid to be a combination of atmospheric gases. The famous "Cavendish experiment" (1798) employed a torsion balance apparatus devised by **John Michell** to estimate with great accuracy the mean density of the Earth and the universal gravitational constant. The Cavendish Laboratory (established 1871) in Cambridge was named in his honor.

Cavendish, Spencer Compton, Marquis of Hartington and **8th Duke of Devonshire** 1833–1908 •*English politician*• He was born at Holker Hall, Lancashire, the eldest son of William Cavendish, afterward 7th Duke of Devonshire. He was educated at Trinity College, Cambridge, and entered parliament in 1857, before becoming, on **W E Gladstone**'s temporary abdication, leader of the Liberal Opposition (1875). In 1880, on the fall of the **Disraeli** administration, he was invited by Queen **Victoria** to form a ministry. He declined the offer, choosing to serve under Gladstone as Secretary of State for India (1880–82) and as War Secretary (1882–85). He disapproved of Irish Home Rule and became head of the Liberal Unionists from 1886, serving in the Unionist government as Lord President of the Council (1895–1903).

Cavendish, Thomas c. 1555–c. 1592 •*English circumnavigator of the globe*• He was born in Trimley St Martin, near Ipswich, Suffolk, and after squandering his patrimony at court, shared in Sir **Richard Grenville**'s expedition to Virginia (1585). In 1586, he sailed with three ships for the Pacific Ocean, returning by the Cape of Good Hope in 1588 with a rich booty, but only his largest vessel, the *Desire*. Queen **Elizabeth I** knighted him. A second expedition, with **John Davis** (1591), ended in disaster, and Cavendish died off Ascension Island in the south Atlantic Ocean.

Cavendish, William, Duke of Newcastle 1592–1676 •*English soldier*• The nephew of the first Earl of Devonshire, he was created Knight of the Bath in 1610 and Earl of Newcastle in 1628 by **Charles I** after munificent entertainment at the family seat in Welbeck. His support for the king in the civil war was generous. As general of all the forces north of the Trent, he had power to issue declarations, confer knighthoods, coin money and raise men; the last function he executed with great zeal. After Marston Moor (1644) he lived on the Continent, at times in great poverty, till the Restoration. In 1665 he was created Duke of Newcastle. He was the author of two works on horsemanship and of several plays.

Cavendish, William, 1st Duke of Devonshire 1640–1707 •*English soldier and politician*• A steadfast Whig under **Charles II** and **James VII and II**, he was leader of the anticourt and anti-Romanist party in the House of Commons, and was a strong supporter of the "Glorious Revolution" of 1688 that brought **William III** to the throne. He was created Duke of Devonshire and Marquis of Hartington in 1694 in recognition of his services. He built Chatsworth House, Derbyshire.

Caventou, Joseph Bienaimé 1795–1877 •*French chemist*• Born in St Omer, Pas-de-Calais, he was educated in Paris and became professor at the École de Pharmacie there. In 1817, in collaboration with **Pierre Joseph Pelletier**, he isolated (and introduced the term) "chlorophyll." They also isolated strychnine and brucine from nux vomica (1819), and quinine and cinchonine from cinchona bark (1820). Cinchonine was particularly important for the treatment of fevers. Caventou also isolated veratrine (1818) and was one of the first to extract caffeine from coffee beans (1822).

Cavour, Camillo Benso, Conte di 1810–61 •*Italian statesman*• Abandoning his early military career, he spent most of the 1830s and 1840s concentrating on the scientific farming of his estates or traveling. His visits to England left him an admirer of the British liberal institutions, railways, industry and banking. He entered politics in 1849, and held various ministerial posts under **Massimo D'Azeglio** before replacing him as Prime Minister (1852); he was to remain premier until his death, except for a few months in 1859. Cavour's early policy was based on the economic development and modernization of the Kingdom of Sardinia-Piedmont. From 1855, however, he concentrated increasingly on foreign affairs, perhaps achieving his greatest success with the Plombières Agreement which laid the basis for the Piedmontese acquisition of Lombardy. In 1860 the Expedition of the Thousand to Sicily and **Garibaldi**'s subsequent victories in the Mezzogiorno made Cavour fear that the former Mazzinian might establish a republican government in the south or attempt to capture Rome, and Cavour sent Piedmontese troops through the Papal States (annexing Umbria and the Marche en route) to block Garibaldi's northward advance. Much to his relief, Garibaldi happily surrendered his conquests to **Victor Emmanuel II**.

Cawley, Evonne Fay, *née* **Goolagong** 1951– •*Australian tennis player*• Born in Barellan, New South Wales, she left for Sydney at the age of 10 to be coached in tennis. As a teenager she won 37 junior titles and in 1971 beat **Margaret Court** at Wimbledon, becoming the second-youngest woman to win, and the first Aboriginal to do so. During the 1970s, she won 92 major tennis tournaments, including the Australian Open four times, and was ranked second in the world. In 1980 she won her second Wimbledon title against **Chris Evert**.

Caxton, William c. 1422–c. 1491 •*English printer*• He was born in the Weald of Kent, possibly at Tenterden. In 1438 he was apprenticed to a London mercer, went to Bruges in 1446, and in 1471 attached himself to the household of Margaret, Duchess of Burgundy, **Edward IV**'s sister. In Bruges he joined with the Flemish calligrapher Colard Mansion to set up a press, and in 1474–75 he printed the first book in English, the *Recuyell of the Historyes of Troye*, which he himself had translated. *The Game and Playe of the Chesse* was another of his earliest publications. Late in 1476 he set up his wooden press in Westminster. The *Dictes or Sayengis of the Philosophres* (1477), translated from the French by the 2nd Earl **Rivers**, is the first book proved to have been printed in England. He began to use woodcut illustrations around 1480. Of about 100 books printed by him, over a third survive in unique copies or fragments only. Among the important books to come from his press were two editions of **Chaucer**'s *Canterbury Tales*, **John Gower**'s *Confessio amantis*, and Sir **Thomas Malory**'s *Morte d'Arthur*.

Cayley, Sir George 1773–1857 •*English amateur scientist and aviation pioneer*• Born in Scarborough, Yorkshire, in 1808 he constructed and flew a glider with a wing area of 300 square feet (27.9 square meters), probably the first practical heavier-than-air flying machine. Over the next 45 years he conducted thousands of model tests. He foresaw that the power to fly must come from a sufficiently light engine and an efficient airscrew. Such an engine was still half a century away when in 1853 he constructed the first successful manned glider, which carried his coachman safely a few hundred yards across a valley. He was also interested in railway engineering, allotment agriculture, and land reclamation methods, and invented a new type of telescope, artificial limbs, the caterpillar tractor and the tension wheel.

Ceadda, St *See* **Chad, St**

Ceauşescu, Nicolae 1918–89 •*Romanian politician*• Born in Scorniceşti into a peasant family and educated at the Academy of Economic Studies, Bucharest, he joined the Communist Party in 1936 and was imprisoned for antigovernment activities (1936–38). He became a member of the Central Committee of the Romanian Communist Party (RCP) in 1952 and of the politburo in 1955. In 1967 he became the RCP's first President. Under his leadership, Romania became increasingly independent of the USSR and pursued its own foreign policy, for which Ceauşescu was decorated by many Western governments. In internal affairs he instituted a strong personality cult and appointed family members to public office, manipulated Romanian nationalism and ruthlessly forced national minorities to adopt Romanian culture. His policy of "systematization" in the countryside, replacing traditional villages with collectives of concrete apartments, roused an international outcry in the late 1980s. In 1989 he was deposed when elements in the army joined a popular revolt. Following a trial by military tribunal, he and his wife, Elena, who had been second only to him in political influence, were shot.

Cech, Thomas 1947– •*US biochemist and Nobel Prize winner*• Born in Chicago, he trained at the Universities of California and Chicago, and taught at the University of Colorado, Boulder. He was the first to discover the ability of ribonucleic acid (RNA) to act as a biological catalyst, and in 1977 he studied the repair mechanisms of damaged DNA and identified regions sensitive to splitting. Subsequently he identified other catalytic RNA species that act without self-modification, called "ribozymes." For these pioneer discoveries Cech shared with **Sidney Altman** the 1989 Nobel Prize for chemistry. He has since extended this work to examine enzymes that use inbuilt RNA to add short repeat sections of DNA to chromosomal DNA.

Cecil, Lord (Edward Christian) David Gascoyne 1902–86 •*English literary critic*• Born in London, the younger son of James Edward Cecil, 4th Marquis of Salisbury (1861–1947), he was educated at Oxford. He was Professor of English Literature at Oxford from 1948 to 1970. Known chiefly as a literary biographer—**William Cowper** (in *The Stricken Deer*, 1929), *Sir Walter Scott* (1933), *Jane Austen* (1935), *Thomas Hardy* (1943) and **Max Beerbohm** (*Max*, 1964)—he also wrote an effective political biography of Lord **Melbourne**.

“ ”

It does not matter that Dickens's world is not life-like; it is alive.

1934 ***Early Victorian Novelists.***

Cecil, Robert, 1st Earl of Salisbury c. 1563–1612 •*English statesman*• Son of **William Cecil**, 1st Baron Burghley, he entered parliament in 1584. He became a Privy Councillor in 1591 and was appointed **Elizabeth I**'s Secretary of State in 1596. His control in the last years of the reign helped to smooth the succession of **James VI** of Scotland to the English throne as James I, and he was rewarded with an earldom in 1605. Lord Treasurer from 1608, he was an efficient administrator and financial manager who fought a losing battle against mounting royal debts.

Cecil, Robert Arthur James Gascoyne-, 5th Marquis of Salisbury 1893–1972 •*English Conservative statesman*• He was born at Hatfield House, Hertfordshire, the son of James Edward Cecil (1861–1947) and educated at Eton and Oxford. He became Member of Parliament for South Dorset in 1929, and in 1935 as Viscount Cranborne became Foreign Under-Secretary. He resigned with his chief, **Anthony Eden**, in 1938 over the "appeasement" of **Mussolini**. In the **Churchill** government of 1940 he became Paymaster General and was Dominions Secretary until 1941 when he was called to the Lords. As leader of the Opposition in the House of Lords (1945–51) he counseled acceptance by the Tory majority of most of the legislation of the political and economic revolution. In the Churchill government of 1951 he became Secretary of State for Commonwealth Relations and in 1952 Lord President of the Council (1952). In 1957 he resigned the lord presidency in protest of the government's action in releasing Archbishop **Makarios** of Cyprus from his exile.

Cecil, Robert Arthur Talbot Gascoyne-, 3rd Marquis of Salisbury 1830–1903 •*English Conservative statesman*• Born at Hatfield House, Hertfordshire, and educated at Eton and Christ Church, Oxford, he was elected Conservative Member of Parliament for Stamford (1853). In the **Derby** ministry (1866), he became Secretary for India, but resigned, along with others, when Lord Derby and **Disraeli** introduced a reform bill. In 1868 he succeeded his father as 3rd Marquis of Salisbury. A strong opponent of the disestablishment of the Irish Church, in 1870 he supported the Peace Preservation Bill, but disapproved of the Irish Land Act. In 1878 he succeeded Lord Derby as Foreign Secretary and accompanied Disraeli to the Berlin Congress. On the death of Disraeli (1881), he succeeded to the leadership of the Conservative Opposition and became Prime Minister and Secretary of State for Foreign Affairs in 1885. The contentious Irish Home Rule Bill defeated the Liberals, and Lord Salisbury, backed by Liberal Unionists, was Prime Minister again in 1886 and in 1895, when a succession of foreign complications brought the country several times to the verge of war. He resigned as Foreign Secretary in 1900 and, having remained at the head of the government during the Boer War (1889–1902), retired from public life in July 1902.

Cecil (of Chelwood), Robert Cecil, 1st Viscount 1864–1958 •*English Conservative politician and Nobel Prize winner*• Born in London, the son of **Robert Cecil** (3rd Marquis of Salisbury), he was educated at Eton and University College, Oxford. He was called to the bar in 1887, and entered parliament (1903). He was Minister of Blockade (1916–18), and as Under-Secretary for Foreign Affairs (1918) helped to draft the League of Nations Covenant and was British representative at various disarmament conferences. He was President of the League of Nations Union (1923–45). He resigned from the Cabinet in 1927 because he was unhappy with its attitude toward the League of Nations, and was awarded the Nobel Peace Prize in 1937.

Cecil, William, 1st Baron Burghley or **Burchleigh** 1520–98 •*English statesman*• He was born in Bourn, Lincolnshire. In 1547 **Henry VIII** appointed him "Custos Brevium" and in 1547, under the patronage of the Protector Somerset (**Edward Seymour**), he was made Master of Requests and his secretary in the following year. When Somerset fell from grace Cecil fell too, but in 1550 he returned to office as Secretary of State and in 1551 was knighted. During **Mary I**'s reign he adopted Catholicism but had already begun correspondence with Princess Elizabeth (later **Elizabeth I**) who, on her accession to the throne in 1558, appointed him Chief Secretary of State. For the next 40 years he was the main architect of the successful policies of the Elizabethan era. He was created Baron Burghley in 1571. He left lavish mansions which he had built or restored, and was the father of **Robert Cecil**, 1st Earl of Salisbury.

Cecilia, St c. 2nd century–c. 3rd century AD •*Roman Christian*• Born possibly in Rome, she was, according to a dubious tradition, compelled to marry a young pagan, Valerian, despite a vow of celibacy. She succeeded in persuading him to respect her vow, and converted him to Christianity. They were both put to death for their faith. According to legend she was a singer, and so became the patron saint of music. Her feast day is November 22.

Cela, Camilo José 1916–2002 •*Spanish novelist and Nobel Prize winner*• He was born in Iria Flavia, La Coruña, and attended Madrid University. He served in **Franco**'s forces, and his work is frequently interpreted as an eloquent, aggressive response to that error of judgment. His first novel, *La familia de Pascual Duarte* (1942, Eng trans *The Family of Pascual Duarte*, 1946) was banned, having stunned readers with its seemingly gratuitous violence. The range of his work is vast but he is best known for *La colmena* (1951, Eng trans *The Hive*, 1953), which recreates daily life in Madrid in the aftermath of the Spanish civil war with great feeling for the plight of ordinary people. Other notable titles are *San Camilo 1936* (1970) and *Mazurca para dos muertos* (1984, "Mazurka for Two Dead People"), which won Spain's national literature prize. He was awarded the Nobel Prize for literature in 1989.

Celestine •*Title assumed by five popes*• Celestine I (422–32); II (1143–44); III (1191–98); IV (1241); and V, Pietro di Morrone (1215–96). The last mentioned was born in Naples and, after a long life of ascetic severities, was reluctantly elected pope in 1294. He resigned his office after five months—"the great refusal"—for which **Dante** places him at the entrance of Hell. He was imprisoned by his successor, **Boniface VIII**. He founded the Celestine order, and was canonized in 1313.

Céline, Louis-Ferdinand, *pseudonym of* **L F Destouches** 1894–1961 •*French novelist*• He was born in Paris, the son of a poor clerk and a lace seamstress. In the first year of World War I he was wounded in the head and shell-shocked in an action for which he was decorated. The suffering, both mental and physical, caused by his wounds dogged him to the end of his days. He was invalided out of the military, took a medical degree, worked as a staff surgeon at the Ford plant in Detroit and later ministered to the poor of Paris. His first novel, *Voyage au bout de la nuit* (1932, "Journey to the End of Night"), brought international acclaim, which increased with his second novel, *Mort à crédit* (1936, "Death on the Installment Plan"). In the late 1930s he was a declared anti-Semite, and after the liberation of France (1944), fled to Denmark. He was tried and sentenced to death in absentia but this was later reversed and he spent his last years in France, with partial paralysis and tinnitus, and close to insanity. His final novels, *D'un château à l'autre* (1957) and *Nord* (1960), are ranked with his best.

Cellini, Benvenuto 1500–71 •*Italian goldsmith, sculptor and engraver*• He was born in Florence, from where he was banished after a duel. In Rome his skill as an artist in metalwork brought him fame, but he was imprisoned several times for murdering or maiming his rivals. His best work includes the gold salt-cellar of *Neptune and Triton* made for **Francis I** of France (now in Vienna), and his bronze *Perseus with the Head of Medusa*, which was made in Florence while he worked under the patronage of **Cosimo I de' Medici**. He is also remembered for his autobiography (1558–62).

Celsius, Anders 1701–44 •*Swedish astronomer*• Born in Uppsala, he taught mathematics and became Professor of Astronomy at the University of Uppsala (1730), where he later directed the observatory. Between 1732 and 1736 he traveled widely in Europe and, while in Nuremberg, published an aurora borealis compendium. (1733). The Celsius temperature scale originated with a mercury thermometer, described by him in 1742 before the Swedish Academy of Sciences. Two fixed points had been chosen: one (0 degrees) at the boiling point of water, the other (100 degrees) at the melting point of ice. A few years after his death, colleagues at Uppsala began to use the familiar inverted version of this centigrade scale.

Celsus 2nd century AD •*Roman philosopher*• He was a Platonist who published one of the first anti-Jewish and anti-Christian polemics in his *True Discourse* (c. 178 AD), refuted by **Origen** in his *Contra Celsum* (c. 248).

Celsus, Aulus Cornelius 1st century AD •*Roman writer and physician*• He compiled an encyclopedia on medicine, rhetoric, history, philosophy, war and agriculture. The only extant portion of the work is the *De medicina*, rediscovered by Pope Nicholas V (1397–1455) and one of the first medical works to be printed (1478).

Cenci, Beatrice 1577–99 •*Italian beauty*• She was the youngest daughter of a wealthy Roman nobleman, Count Francesco Cenci, who conceived an incestuous passion for her. With her stepmother and her brother, Giacomo, she hired two assassins to murder him (1598). The Cenci family were arrested and tortured, and all three were beheaded, by order of Pope Clement VIII. She was the central figure of a tragedy by **Shelley** (1819).

Centlivre, Susannah, *also known as* **Susannah Carroll**, *née* **Freeman** c. 1667–c. 1723 •*English playwright and actress*• She was born probably in Lincolnshire. According to some sources she was taught French by a tutor, and there is a story of her masquerading as a young man in order to gain entrance to Cambridge. In 1700 her first play, *The Perjured Husband*, a tragicomedy, was produced at Drury Lane, and she subsequently appeared on the stage in Bath in her own comedy, *Love at a Venture* (1706). Also in 1706, she married Joseph Centlivre, head cook to Queen **Anne** at Windsor. She wrote 19 plays, of which *The Busie Body* (1709), *A Bold Stroke for a Wife* (1717) and *The Wonder: A Woman Keeps a Secret* (1714) were enormously popular farcical comedies of intrigue. A great woman of the theater, she knew many actors, dramatists and writers, including **George Farquhar** and **Nicholas Rowe**.

Cerdic d. 534 •*Saxon leader*• He invaded Britain, landing in Hampshire with his son Cynric in AD 495. By c. 500 he had created the kingdom of Wessex for himself and founded the West Saxon royal dynasty.

Cernuda, Luis 1902–63 •*Spanish poet and critic*• He is often considered the greatest of all the famous "Generation of '27," which included **Federico García Lorca** and **Rafael Alberti**. His first teacher and mentor was Pedro Salinas (1891–1951) and his poetry is soaked in his Andalusian origins, and combines explicit homosexuality with all the sad and beautiful virtues of Mediterranean art. His militaristic father is present as a symbol of the unavoidable, unlovable hostility of reality in his work. His 11 collections were finally published as *La realidad y el deseo* (1964, "Reality and Desire").

Cervantes (Saavedra), Miguel de 1547–1616 •*Spanish writer, author of Don Quixote*• He was born in Alcalá de Henares, near Madrid, the son of a poor medical practitioner. In 1569 he published his first known work, a collection of pieces on the death of the queen. He then enlisted as a soldier, and after service against the Turks in Tunis, he was returning to Spain in 1575 when the galley he sailed in was captured by Algerian corsairs, and with his brother Rodrigo he was carried into Algiers, where he remained in captivity for five years, during which he made four daring attempts to escape. In 1580 he was ransomed through the efforts of Trinitarian monks, Algiers traders and his family. His first important work was the pastoral romance *La galatea* (1585, Eng trans 1867), and for some years he strove to gain a livelihood by writing plays; *La numancia* (1784, Eng trans 1870) and *El trato de Argel* (1798, Eng trans *The Commerce of Algiers*, 1870), have survived. In 1594 he was appointed collector of revenues for the kingdom of Granada, but in 1597, failing to make up the sum due to the treasury, he was sent to prison in Seville, released after three months, but not reinstated. Local tradition maintains that he wrote *Don Quixote*, the first part of which came out in Madrid in early 1605, in prison at Argamasilla in La Mancha. It was immediately popular, but instead of giving his readers the sequel they asked for, Cervantes busied himself with writing for the stage and composing short tales, also writing his *Viage al Parnaso* (1614), a poem of over 3,000 lines in *terza rima*, which reviews the poetry and poets of the day. In 1614 a pseudonymous writer brought out a spurious second part of *Don Quixote*, with an insulting preface, which spurred Cervantes to the completion of the genuine second part (1615). Though it is the most carelessly written of all great books, *Don Quixote* is widely regarded as the precursor of the modern novel, as well as a great comic epic in its own right.

" "

La mejor salsa del mundo es el hambre.
Hunger is the best sauce in the world.

1615 ***Don Quixote**, part 2, chapter 5.*

Césaire, Aimé Fernand 1913– •*West Indian poet and playwright*• He was born in Basse-Point, Martinique, and his reputation is based largely on two plays, *La tragédie du roi Christophe* (1963, Eng trans *The Tragedy of King Christophe*) and an original adaptation of **Shakespeare**'s *The Tempest*. He is also noted for the influential long poem, *Cahier d'un retour au pays natal* (1939, *Notebook of a Return to My Native Land*). A militant Marxist and anticolonialist, he played a large role in rallying decolonized Africans in the 1950s.

Cesalpino, Andrea, *Latin* **Caesalpinus** 1519–1603 •*Italian botanist, physician and physiologist*• Born in Arezzo, he became the most original and philosophical botanist since **Theophrastus**, whose work he revived. He was Professor of Medicine and director of the botanic garden in Pisa from 1553 to 1592, when he became physician to Pope Clement VIII. After he had taught at the university for 30 years he published *De plantis* (1583), in which he stated the basic principles of botany and made the first attempt at a scientific classification of plants. In medicine he was no less original, propounding a theory of blood circulation.

César, *full name* **César Baldaccini** 1921–1998 •*French sculptor*• Born in Marseilles, he trained at the École des Beaux-Arts there, then at the Institute des Beaux-Arts in Paris. He became known in the 1950s with works such as *Petit déjeuner sur l'herbe* (1957, "Breakfast Picnic"), consisting of a crushed metal tumbler and sardine can on a metal plate. He then won fame in the 1960s with his "compressions," or crushed cars. In 1985 he was commissioned by Peugeot to produce *The Champions*, a permanent memorial to four damaged and burned-out racing cars. From around 1990 he also compressed paper, glass and rags, and for the 1995 Venice Biennale he constructed a huge monument to scrap metal—a mountain of hundreds of crushed cars.

Céspedes, Carlos Manuel de 1819–73 •*Cuban nationalist*• He came from a wealthy plantation family and studied law in Spain before returning to Cuba. There he raised a revolt against the Spanish colonial government, instigating the Ten Years' War in Oriente. With 200 poorly armed men, he took Santiago and freed the slaves and in 1869 devised a constitution and was elected provisional president of the incipient republic. However, in 1873 he was deposed, captured by the Spanish and shot. He became known as "The Father of the Country."

Cessna, Clyde Vernon 1879–1954 •*US aviator and aircraft manufacturer*• He was born in Hawthorne, Louisiana. The flexible monoplane design of his aircraft, which incorporated his invention, the cantilever wing, made them suitable for bush flying and as forest and rescue planes. The Cessna Aircraft Company eventually mass-produced about 8,000 planes each year.

Cetewayo or **Cetshwayo** c. 1826–84 •*King of Zululand*• Born near Eshowe, the nephew of **Shaka**, he was king of Zululand from 1873 to 1883. He destroyed the garrison at Isandhlwana when the British invaded Zululand (1879), but was later defeated at Ulundi and taken prisoner. After captivity in the Cape of Good Hope and England, where his proud and dignified bearing impressed, he was restored by the British to part of his kingdom (1883), but was soon driven out by his subjects.

Cézanne, Paul 1839–1906 •*French painter*• He was born in Aix-en-Provence, the son of a self-made businessman, and seemed destined to follow in his footsteps. From 1859 to 1861 he studied law at Aix, and there formed a friendship with **Émile Zola**, who persuaded him in 1862 to go to Paris to study art at the Académie Suisse, with a small allowance from his disgruntled father. His passion was for the Romantics, in particular **Delacroix**, whom he admired all his life. In Paris he met the circle of painters centered on **Manet**, but his main influence was **Camille Pissarro**, who brought him into the realm of Impressionism. Cézanne turned to the study of nature, as in the famous *Maison du pendu* (1873, "The Suicide's House"), now in the Louvre, and began to use his characteristic glowing colors. In his later period after 1886, when he became financially independent of his father, he emphasized the underlying forms of nature ("the cylinder, the sphere, the cone") by constructing his pictures from a rhythmic series of colored planes, painting not light but plastic form, and thus becoming the forerunner of Cubism. In 1886 his friendship with Zola was ended by the publication of Zola's novel *L'œuvre*, in which the central figure, an unsuccessful and unbalanced Impressionist painter, is in many respects identifiable as Cézanne. Cézanne described his aim as being "to make Impressionism something solid and durable like the art of the old masters." He achieved recognition only in the last years of his life, and two exhibitions of his work were held by Vollard, in 1895 and 1899. Cézanne's most famous paintings are *The Card Players* (1890–92) in the Musée d'Orsay, Paris; *Le jardinier* (c. 1906, "The Gardener"), in the Tate Gallery, London; and *La vieille au chapelet* (c. 1897–98, "The Old Woman with Beads"), in the National Gallery, London.

" "

The Louvre is the book in which we learn to read.

1905 Letter to Emile Bernard.

Chabrol, Claude 1930– •*French film director*• He was born in Paris, and became a leading figure in the Nouvelle Vague (New Wave) movement with films such as *Beau serge* (1958, *Bitter Reunion*) and *Les biches* (1968, *The Girlfriends*). Other films include *Le boucher* (1970, *The Butcher*), *Les noces rouges* (1973, *Wedding in Blood*), *Masques* (1987), *Une affaire des femmes* (1989, *Story of Women*) and *Merci pour le chocolat* (2000, *Nightcap*). Many of his films are about murder and suspense, and were much influenced by **Alfred Hitchcock**.

Chad or **Ceadda, St** d. 672 •*Anglo-Saxon churchman*• Born in Northumbria, he was a pupil of St **Aidan** in Lindisfarne. He spent part of his youth in Ireland, and in 664 became abbot of Lastingham, and in 666 Bishop of York. Doubt was cast on the validity of his consecration, and he withdrew in 669, but was immediately made Bishop of Mercia, fixing the see at Lichfield.

Chadli Benjedid 1929– •*Algerian politician and soldier*• He was born in Sebaa. He joined the guerrillas who were fighting for independence as part of the National Liberation Front (FLN) in 1955. When **Houari Boumédienne** overthrew **Ahmed Ben Bella** in 1965 he joined the Revolutionary Council. He succeeded Boumédienne as Secretary-General of the FLN and President in 1979, a post he held until 1992.

Chadwick, Sir James 1891–1974 •*English physicist and Nobel Prize winner*• Born near Macclesfield, Cheshire, he studied at the Universities of Manchester, Berlin and Cambridge, and worked on radioactivity with **Ernest Rutherford**. In 1932 he proposed the existence of a neutral particle whose mass was close to that of the proton. He named the particle the neutron and was awarded the 1935 Nobel Prize for physics for this discovery. He built Great Britain's first cyclotron in 1935 at Liverpool University and during World War II worked on the Manhattan Project to develop the atomic bomb in the US. He was elected a Fellow of the Royal Society in 1927 and knighted in 1945.

Chadwick, Lynn Russell 1914–2003 •*English sculptor*• Born in London, he trained as an architect, but in 1945 turned to making constructions and mobiles. He was an artist whose work, although abstract, nevertheless carries suggestions of the human figure, as in *Winged Figures* (1955). In 1956 he won the International Sculpture prize at the Venice Biennale. He was represented in important collections around the world, and his first retrospective exhibition was in 1991 in Yorkshire.

Chadwick, Roy 1893–1947 •*English aeronautical engineer*• Born in Farnworth, Greater Manchester, the son of a mechanical engineer, he was educated at the Manchester College of Technology. During World War I he designed many famous airplanes including the Avro 504 trainer. Other designs were the Baby (a truly light aircraft), Avian, Anson (used for RAF coastal reconnaissance) and in World War II the Manchester and the famous Lancaster heavy bombers. Following the war he designed the Tudor and Ashton, both jet-propelled. He was killed in a test flight of the Tudor II prototype.

Chagall, Marc 1887–1985 •*French painter*• Born of Jewish parents in Vitebsk, Russia (now in Belarus), in 1914 he held a one-man show in Berlin, and for a short time was commissar of fine arts at Vitebsk, but in 1922 he left Russia and settled near Paris. He spent the years 1941–47 in the US. He is most famous for fanciful pictures, in which a visual potpourri of animals, objects, and people from his past life and dreams, and from Russian and Belarusian folklore, is presented in an arbitrary color scheme of blues, greens, yellows, and pinks, as in *Bouquet with Flying Lovers* (1947). The word *surrealist* is said to have been coined by **Guillaume Apollinaire** to describe his work. In 1945 he designed décors and costumes for **Igor Stravinsky**'s *Firebird*. He wrote his autobiography, *Ma vie*, in 1931.

Chain, Sir Ernst Boris 1906–79 •*British biochemist and Nobel Prize winner*• Born in Berlin of Russian-Jewish extraction, he studied physiology and chemistry at Berlin, then taught in the biochemistry department at Cambridge (1933–35), where he identified an enzyme in snake venom that caused paralysis of the nervous system. He then joined Sir **Howard Florey** at the Dunn School of Pathology in Oxford (1935–48) to characterize lysozyme and determine its mode of action on bacteria. He encountered Sir **Alexander Fleming**'s paper on penicillin (1929), discovered that penicillin was not an enzyme but a new small molecule, and greatly improved its purification. Fleming, Chain and Florey shared the 1945 Nobel Prize for physiology or medicine. He was knighted in 1969.

Chalayan, Hussein 1970– •*Turkish Cypriot fashion designer*• Born in Nicosia, he moved to London as a child and studied at St Martin's College of Art and Design. He established his own design label in 1993 and became known for his theatrical, sometimes shocking shows, on one occasion featuring models wearing Muslim headscarves and nothing else. He won the British Designer of the Year award in 1999 and 2000.

Chaliapin, Feodor Ivanovich, *also spelled* **Fyodor Ivanovich Shalyapin** 1873–1938 •*Russian bass*• Born in Kazan, he was a singer of great power. Also talented as an actor, he sang in opera at Tiflis, now Tbilisi (1892), Moscow (1896), and London (1913). He left Russia after the Revolution.

Chalmers, Alexander 1759–1834 •*Scottish journalist and biographer*• Born in Aberdeen, he studied medicine there, but about 1777 became an active writer in London. His reputation rests mainly on his vast *General Biographical Dictionary* (32 vols, 1812–17).

Chamberlain, Sir (Joseph) Austen 1863–1937 •*English politician and Nobel Prize winner*• The eldest son of **Joseph Chamberlain**, he was Chancellor of the Exchequer (1903–06, 1919–21), Secretary for India (1915–17), a member of **Lloyd-George**'s War Cabinet, Lord Privy Seal, Leader of the House and Unionist leader (1921–22). As Foreign Secretary (1924–29), he was made Knight of the Garter in 1925, and shared with **Charles G Dawes** the 1925 Nobel Peace Prize for negotiating the Locarno Pact.

Chamberlain, Joseph 1836–1914 •*English politician*• Born in London, he was educated at University College School, entered Nettlefold's Birmingham screw factory, and retired in 1874 with a fortune. A Radical politician, in 1868 he became a Birmingham town councilor, and mayor (1873–75). Returned unopposed for Birmingham in 1876, in 1880 he was appointed President of the Board of Trade, with a seat in the Cabinet. Regarded as the leader of the extreme Radical Party, he produced an "unauthorized" program during the general election of 1886, which included the readjustment of taxation, free schools, and the creation of allotments by compulsory purchase. He became the most strenuous opponent of **Gladstone**'s Home Rule Bill, and from 1889 he was leader of the Liberal Unionists, taking office as Secretary for the Colonies. In 1903 he resigned office to be free to advocate his program of tariff reform, giving preferential treatment to colonial imports and protection for native products. Subsequently, in 1919 and especially 1932, the program was carried out by his sons **Neville** and **Austen Chamberlain**. In 1906 he withdrew from public life after a stroke.

Chamberlain, (Arthur) Neville 1869–1940 •*English statesman*• He was born in Birmingham, the son of **Joseph Chamberlain** by his second marriage, and educated at Rugby and Birmingham University. He was Lord Mayor of Birmingham (1915–16) and a Conservative Member of Parliament from 1918. He was Chancellor of the Exchequer (1923–24, 1931–37), Minister for Health (1924–29) and became Prime Minister in 1937. For the sake of peace, and with the country unprepared for war, he chose initially to follow a policy of appeasement of Italy and Germany and signed the 1938 Munich Agreement, claiming to have found "peace in our time." Having meantime pressed on with rearmament, he declared war in 1939. Criticism of his war leadership accompanied initial military reverses, and in 1940 he yielded the premiership to **Churchill**, dying six months later. Subsequent reevaluations of Chamberlain's career have shown his policy of appeasement in a more favorable light.

Chamberlain, Owen 1920– •*US physicist and Nobel Prize winner*• Born in San Francisco, he was educated at Dartmouth College, England, and at the University of Chicago, where he received his doctorate in 1949. He became professor at the University of California (emeritus in 1989) after working on the Manhattan (atomic bomb) Project (1942–46) and at the Argonne National Laboratory (1947–48). The first antiparticle (the antielectron, or positron) had been discovered in 1932 by **Carl Anderson**, and in 1955, Chamberlain and **Emilio Segrè** set up an experiment to identify the antiproton. In 1959 Chamberlain and Segrè were awarded the Nobel Prize for physics for this discovery.

Chamberlain, Wilt(on Norman), *nicknamed* **Wilt the Stilt** 1936–99 •*US basketball player*• Born in Philadelphia, he was more than 7 ft tall. He began his professional career with the Harlem Globetrotters, and in 1959 he signed with the Philadelphia (later San Francisco) Warriors. At various times he played with the New York Knickerbockers, the Philadelphia Seventy-Sixers and the Los Angeles Lakers. He was on four occasions the NBA's Most Valuable Player (MVP).

Chambers, Ephraim c. 1680–1740 •*English encyclopedist*• He was born in Kendal, Cumbria, and while apprenticed to a globe-maker in London he conceived the idea of a *Cyclopaedia, or Universal Dictionary of Arts and Sciences* (2 folio vols, 1728). A French translation inspired **Denis Diderot**'s great French *Encyclopédie*.

Chambers, Robert 1802–71 •*Scottish writer and publisher*• Born in Peebles, he was the younger brother of **William Chambers**. He began as a bookseller with his brother in Edinburgh in 1819, and wrote in his spare time. In 1824 he produced *Traditions of Edinburgh*. The success of *Chambers's Edinburgh Journal*, started by his brother in 1832, was largely due to his essays and his literary insight. Later that year he and his brother formed the publishing house of W & R Chambers. In 1844 he published anonymously the pre-Darwinian *Vestiges of Creation*. A prolific writer of reference books, he edited the *Chambers Encyclopaedia* (1859–68) and *The Cyclopaedia of English Literature* (1842), and himself wrote *A Biographical Dictionary of Eminent Scotsmen* (1832–34) and *The Book of Days* (2 vols, 1863, an almanac of historical data), which broke his health. His other works include *Popular Rhymes of Scotland* (1826), a *History of the Rebellions in Scotland, Life of James I, Scottish Ballads and Songs* (1829), *The Life and Works of Robert Burns* (4 vols, 1851), and *Songs of Scotland Prior to Burns* (1862).

Chambers, Sir William 1726–96 •*Scottish architect*• Born of Scottish ancestry in Stockholm, and educated in Edinburgh and Ripon, Yorkshire, he studied in Italy and France and practiced in England. He designed Somerset House (1776) and the pagoda in Kew Gardens. In Edinburgh he designed Dundas House (1771, now the Royal Bank of Scotland) and Duddingston House, and in Dublin, Charlemont House (1763).

Chambers, William 1800–83 •*Scottish publisher*• Born in Peebles, he was the older brother of **Robert Chambers**. In 1814 he was apprenticed to a bookseller in Edinburgh, and in 1819 started in business for himself, first bookselling, then printing. Between 1825 and 1830 he wrote the *Book of Scotland* and, in conjunction with his brother Robert, a *Gazetteer of Scotland*. In 1832 he started *Chambers's Edinburgh Journal*, six weeks in advance of the *Penny Magazine*. He later joined Robert to found W & R Chambers. In 1859 he founded and endowed a museum, library and art gallery in Peebles. Lord Provost of Edinburgh from 1865 to 1869, he promoted a successful plan for improving the older part of the city, and carried out at his own cost a restoration of St Giles' Cathedral. He also wrote *Stories of Remarkable Persons*, *Stories of Old Families*, and a *Historical Sketch of St Giles' Cathedral* (1879).

Chambord, Henri Charles Dieudonné, Comte de 1820–83 •*French Bourbon pretender*• He was born in Paris and after the assassination of his father, the Duc de **Berry**, he was taken into exile with the remaining **Bourbon**s following the abdication in 1830 of King **Charles X**, whose grandson he claimed to be. On Charles' death in 1836, he was proclaimed king of France by the Legitimist Party. Another attempt was made after the fall of **Napoleon III** in 1870, but Chambord's refusal to accept the tricolor flag rendered this abortive.

Champaigne, Philippe de 1602–74 •*French painter*• Born in Brussels, Belgium, he trained as a landscape painter there, but moved to Paris (1621). A lifelong friend of **Nicholas Poussin**, he assisted him in decorating the Luxembourg Palace, and in 1628 was appointed painter to Marie de' **Medici** and was patronized by **Louis XIII** and Cardinal **Richelieu**.

Champlain, Samuel de 1567–1635 •*French explorer, "founder of Canada"*• Born in Brouage, Saintonge, he made his first voyage to Canada in 1603. From 1604 to 1607 he explored the coasts, and on his third voyage (1608) he founded Quebec. He was appointed Lieutenant of Canada in 1612. During the Anglo-French war, Quebec was seized by the English, and he successfully negotiated its return to French sovereignty. Lake Champlain is named after him.

Champollion, Jean François 1790–1832 •*French founder of Egyptology*• Born in Figeac, he was educated at Grenoble and became Professor of History there (1809–16). He is remembered for his use of the Rosetta stone to decipher Egyptian hieroglyphics (1822–24) and for promoting the study of early Egyptian history and culture. In 1828 he mounted a joint expedition with the Italian Ippolito Rosellini (1800–43) to record the monuments of the Nile as far south as Aswan; on his return a chair of Egyptology was founded for him at the Collège de France.

Chand, Dhyan 1905–79 •*Indian field hockey player*• Born in Allahabad, he captained India to three consecutive Olympic gold medals (1928, 1932, 1936), and is revered as hockey's most prolific goal scorer. Roop Singh (his brother) and Dhyan scored 18 goals against the US in the 1932 Olympics, to make the final score India-24, US-1. After World War II, he became captain and coach for the Indian national hockey team.

Chandler, Raymond 1888–1959 •*US novelist*• Born in Chicago, he was brought up in England from the age of seven, and educated at Dulwich College and in France and Germany. He worked as a freelance writer in London before going to California in 1912, and then served in the Canadian army in France, and in the RAF during World War I. During the depression he began to write short stories and novelettes. On such stories he based his subsequent full-length "private eye" novels, *The Big Sleep* (1939), *Farewell, My Lovely* (1940), *The High Window* (1942) and *The Lady in the Lake* (1943), all of which were successfully filmed. He did much to establish the conventions of his genre, particularly with his cynical but honest anti-hero, Philip Marlowe, who also appeared in such later works as *The Little Sister* (1949), *The Long Goodbye* (1953) and *Playback* (1958).

“ ”

A big hard-boiled city with no more personality than a paper cup.

*1949 Of Los Angeles. **The Little Sister**, chapter 26.*

Chandrasekhar, Subrahmanyan 1910–95 •*US astrophysicist and Nobel Prize winner*• Born in Lahore, India (now in Pakistan), nephew of Sir **Chandrasekhara Venkata Raman**, he was educated at the Presidency College, Madras, before going to Cambridge, where he studied under **Paul Dirac**. In 1936 he moved to the US. He studied the final stages of stellar evolution, showing that the fate of a star depends on its mass. He also concluded that stars with masses greater than about 1.4 solar masses will be unable to evolve into white dwarfs, and this limiting stellar mass, confirmed by observation, is known as the Chandrasekhar limit. He suggested that if the mass of a star is greater than this, it can become a white dwarf star only if it ejects its excess mass in a supernova explosion before collapse. He was awarded the 1983 Nobel Prize for physics, jointly with **William Fowler**.

Chanel, Coco (Gabrielle) 1883–1971 •*French couturier who designed the "little black dress"*• Orphaned at an early age, she worked with her sister as a milliner until 1912, when she opened a shop of her own, followed by a couture house in Deauville (1913). During World War I she served as a nurse. She opened her second couture house in the Rue Cambon in Paris (1924), and it was from here that she was to revolutionize women's fashions during the 1920s. For the first time in a century women were liberated from the restriction of corsets. In 1920 she designed her first "chemise" dress, and in 1925 the collarless cardigan jacket. The combination of simple elegance and comfort in her designs gave them immediate, widespread and lasting appeal, and many of the features she introduced, such as the vogue for costume jewelry, the evening scarf, and the "little black dress," have retained their popularity. At the height of her career she managed four businesses, including the manufacture of her world-famous perfume, Chanel No. 5, and her great wealth and dazzling social life attracted great public interest. She retired in 1938, but made a surprisingly successful comeback in 1954, when, following her original style, she regained her prominence in the fashion world.

Chaney, Lon, *originally* **Alonso Chaney** 1883–1930 •*US film and stage actor*• He was born in Colorado Springs, Colorado, and became known as "the man of a thousand faces" from his skill at make-up and miming. He made his film debut in 1913 and became famous for his portrayal of deformed villains and other spine-chilling parts, most notably in *The Miracle Man* (1919), *The Hunchback of Notre Dame* (1923) and *The Phantom of the Opera* (1925).

Channing, Carol Elaine 1921– •*US singer and actress*• Born in Seattle, Washington, she achieved star status as Lorelei Lee in *Gentlemen Prefer Blondes* (1949, 1951–53). Later stage work includes *Wonderful Town* (1954), *Show Girl* (1961) and *Hello Dolly!* (1964–67, Tony award). She received a special Tony in 1968, returned to her earlier role in *Lorelei* (1973–75) and continued to tour in various stage versions of *Hello Dolly!* Her rare film appearances include *The First Traveling Saleslady* (1956) and *Thoroughly Modern Millie* (1967), for which she received an Academy Award nomination.

Chao Tzu-yang *See* **Zhao Ziyang**

Chaplin, Charlie (Sir Charles Spencer) 1889–1977 •*English film actor and director*• He was born in Kennington, London, the son of music-hall performers. After a difficult early life, he joined Karno's vaudeville company and went to Hollywood in 1914, entering the motion picture business, then in its infancy. He made over 50 films between 1914 and 1916, including *The Pawn Shop* and *The Vagabond* (1916), and *Easy Street*, *The Immigrant* and *The Adventurer* (1917). In these early comedies he adopted the bowler hat, outturned feet, moustache and walking cane which became the hallmarks of his consummate buffoonery in films such as *The Kid* (1920), *The Gold Rush* (1924), *The Champion* (1915) and *Shoulder Arms* (1918). He achieved greater control of his work by forming United Artists with **Douglas Fairbanks, Sr** and director **D W**

Griffith. *The Circus* (1928) won him a special Oscar. His art was essentially suited to the silent film, and when sound arrived he experimented with new forms, as in *City Lights* (1931) and *Modern Times* (1936), part speech and part mime. Eventually he entered the orthodox sound film field with the satirical caricature of **Adolf Hitler** in *The Great Dictator* (1940), for which he received his only Oscar nomination as best actor. After a long absence, he took on a very different role, that of mass murderer in the black comedy *Monsieur Verdoux* (1947), which was not popular. He returned to more traditional methods in *Limelight* (1952), in which he acted, directed and composed the music and dances. His left-wing sympathies caused him to run afoul of the rabid anti-Communist factions of postwar America, and he emigrated to Switzerland. He made only two further films: *A King in New York* (1957) and *A Countess from Hong Kong* (1967). He was knighted in 1975.

“ ”

All I need to make a comedy is a park, a policeman and a pretty girl.

*1964 **My Autobiography**, chapter 10.*

Chapman, George c. 1559–1634 •*English dramatist*• Born near Hitchin, Hertfordshire, his earliest extant play, the popular comedy *The Blind Beggar of Alexandria*, was produced in 1595. His complete translation of *The Whole Works of Homer: Prince of Poets*, appeared in 1611, after which he set to work on the *Odyssey* (completed 1616). His *Homer* is known to many through **Keats**'s poem "On First Looking into Chapman's *Homer*." He joined **Ben Jonson** and **John Marston** in the composition of *Eastward Hoe* (1605), in which slighting references to the Scots earned the authors a jail sentence. Other plays include a graceful comedy, *The Gentleman Usher* (1606), *The Widow's Tears* (1612) and *Caesar and Pompey* (1631). Two posthumous tragedies (1654), *Alphonsus* and *Revenge for Honour*, bear his name, but it is doubtful that he wrote them. *The Ball*, a comedy, and *The Tragedie of Chabot* (1639) were the joint work of Chapman and **James Shirley**. Among his nondramatic works are the epic philosophical poem *Euthymiae & Raptus* (1609), *Petrarch's Seven Penitentiall Psalmes* (1612) and *The Georgicks of Hesiod* (1618).

Chapman, Mark David c. 1955– •*US murderer*• A security guard in Hawaii, he shot and killed former **Beatles** member **John Lennon** on December 8, 1980, outside Lennon's apartment in Manhattan. At the trial, his lawyer initially entered a plea of insanity, which Chapman later overturned with a plea of guilty. Chapman had been a fan of the Beatles, and had idolized Lennon to the extent that he often imagined that he was Lennon. He was also obsessed with and inspired by **J D Salinger**'s novel *The Catcher in the Rye*. He was sentenced to life imprisonment.

Chappell, Greg(ory Stephen) 1948– •*Australian cricket player*• He was born in Unley, South Australia, the younger brother of **Ian Chappell**. One of the most graceful of modern batsmen, he played 87 times for his country and scored 24 Test centuries, and succeeded his brother as captain. He played in England for Somerset for two years.

Chappell, Ian Michael 1943– •*Australian cricket player*• He was born in Unley, South Australia, the elder brother of **Greg Chappell**. A more combative character than his brother, he played 75 times for Australia, scoring over 5,000 runs and 14 Test centuries.

Charcot, Jean Martin 1825–93 •*French pathologist and neurologist*• Born and educated in Paris, he eventually became the most eminent French physician of his day, making important observations on multiple sclerosis, amyotrophic lateral sclerosis and familial muscular atrophy. During the last twenty years of his life, he began using hypnosis in the diagnosis and treatment of functional disorders. His lectures stimulated the young **Sigmund Freud**, who also translated some of Charcot's work into German.

Chardin, Jean Baptiste Siméon 1699–1779 •*French painter*• Born in Paris, he was the son of **Louis XIV**'s billiard-table maker. He was selected to assist in the restoration of the royal paintings at Fontainebleau, and, emerging as a genre painter, he produced many pictures of peasant life and domestic scenes. *Grace Before Meal* (1740, Louvre), perhaps his masterpiece in this vein, earned the praise of **Denis Diderot**. In 1755 he was appointed treasurer of the Académie Française, with an apartment in the Louvre.

Chargaff, Erwin 1905–2002 •*US biochemist*• Born in Czernowitz, Austria-Hungary (now Chernivsti, Ukraine), he studied in Vienna before spending two years at Yale (1928–30). He returned to Berlin (1930–33), where he extended his study of bacterial lipids, and briefly visited Paris before settling at Columbia University, New York, in 1935. After initial research on plant chromoproteins, he produced his best-known work on the base composition of DNA, which he found to be characteristic of a species and identical in different tissues of the same animal. His most significant finding was that the concentrations of the DNA bases were in pairs.

Charisse, Cyd, *originally* **Tula Ellice Finklea**, *also acting as* **Lily Norwood** 1921– •*US dancer*• Born in Amarillo, Texas, she trained as a ballet dancer from the age of 8, was signed to the Ballets Russes at 14, and toured in Europe and the US. Moving to Los Angeles, she played small film roles under the name of Lily Norwood before signing a contract with MGM in 1946. Described by **Fred Astaire** as "beautiful dynamite," she appeared in such classic musicals as *Singin' in the Rain* (1952), *Brigadoon* (1954) and *Silk Stockings* (1957), partnering with both Astaire and **Gene Kelly**. She married singer Tony Martin (1912–) in 1948.

Charlemagne ("Charles the Great"), *Latin* **Carolus Magnus** 747–814 •*King of the Franks and Christian emperor of the West*• He was the eldest son of **Pepin III (the Short)**. On Pepin's death in 768 the Frankish kingdom was divided between Charlemagne and his younger brother **Carloman**; three years later, on Carloman's death, he became sole ruler. The first years of his reign were spent in strenuous campaigns to subdue and Christianize neighboring kingdoms, particularly the Saxons to the northeast (772–77) and the Lombards of northern Italy (773), where he was crowned king of Lombardy, and the Moors in Spain (778). Between 780 and 800 Charlemagne added Bohemia to his empire; subdued the Avars (Turko-Finnish nomads) in the middle Danube basin (795–96) to create an eastern "March" to buttress his frontiers; created the "Spanish March" on the southern side of the Pyrenees (795); and entered Italy (800) to support Pope **Leo III** against the rebellious Romans. There on Christmas Day in St Peter's Church, the pope crowned him emperor of the Romans as "Carolus Augustus." The remaining years of his reign were spent in consolidating his vast empire, which reached from the Ebro in northern Spain to the Elbe. The emperor established his capital and principal court at Aachen (Aix-la-Chapelle), where he built a magnificent palace and founded an academy to which many of the greatest scholars of the age were invited. Charlemagne zealously promoted education, architecture, bookmaking and the arts, created stable administrations and good laws, and encouraged agriculture, industry and commerce. He also fostered good relations with the East. His reign was a noble attempt to consolidate order and Christian culture among the nations of the West, but his empire did not long survive his death, for his sons lacked both his vision and authority.

Charles I 1887–1922 •*Emperor of Austria as Karl I and king of Hungary as Károly IV, the last of the Habsburg emperors*• Born at Persenbeug Castle, the son of Archduke Otto and grandnephew of Emperor **Franz Joseph**, he became heir presumptive (1914) on the assassination at Sarajevo of his uncle, Archduke **Franz Ferdinand**. On his great-uncle's death (1916) he proclaimed himself emperor of Austria and king of Hungary. He made secret attempts (which failed) to withdraw Austria/Hungary from World War I. In 1918 he was deposed and exiled to Switzerland (1919). In 1921 he made two unsuccessful attempts to regain the Crown of Hungary, and was deported to Madeira, where he died.

Charles I 1600–49 •*King of Great Britain and Ireland*• Charles was born in Dunfermline, the son of **James VI** of Scotland (later James I of England) and **Anne of Denmark**. Having been baptized as the Duke of Albany, and made Duke of York at the age of five, he became Prince of Wales in 1616, four years after the death of his brother Prince Henry had left him heir to the throne. He failed in his attempt to marry the Infanta Maria of Spain (1623), marrying instead Princess **Henrietta Maria** of France. This received a hostile reception from the growing body of Puritans, because the marriage articles permitted her the free exercise of the Catholic religion. Charles was undeterred, and three months after succeeding his father James I to the throne in 1625, he welcomed his new bride at Dover. In the 12 years following the murder of the **Duke of Buckingham** in 1628, Henrietta Maria came to exercise growing influence over the affairs of state, and it was largely at her behest that Charles dissolved no fewer than three parliaments in the first four years of his reign, and then ruled without one for 12 years. With England now at peace with France and Spain, Charles addressed the task of refreshing his dwindling treasury with unpopular taxation of the inland counties, and of pulling Presbyterian Scotland into line with the imposition of a common prayer book. The hostility that both measures engendered forced Charles to recall parliament in 1640, and in 1641 he was compelled to allow the impeachment and execution of his loyal Lord Deputy for Ireland, the Earl of **Strafford**, after his secret plan to suppress the king's opponents in Ireland and England was exposed. The following year, his arrival in the chamber of the House of Commons to supervise the arrest of **John Pym** and four other MPs, which had been prompted by his fear that the queen would soon be impeached, made civil war inevitable; on August 22, 1642, the royal standard was raised at Nottingham, marking the start of more than three years of bitter fighting. The war effectively came to an end with the defeat of the Royalist forces in June 1645 at the Battle of Naseby, but the king spent another year trying to rally support from his refuge in Oxford before finally surrendering to the Scots at Newark on May 5, 1646. In January 1647 he was handed over to parliament and held at Holmby House near Northampton, where he exploited his comparative freedom to negotiate a treaty with the Scots and to foment a brief resurgence of civil war. In November 1647 he escaped to the Isle of Wight, but he and his family were soon recaptured and he was returned to stand trial at Westminster. His three refusals to plead were interpreted as a silent confession, and on January 30, 1649, Charles was beheaded on a scaffold erected outside the Guildhall in Whitehall. Two of Charles's three sons were eventually to take the throne, as **Charles II** and James II (see **James VII and II**), and he was also survived by three daughters.

“ ”

I tell you (and I pray God it be not laid to your charge) that I am the martyr of the people.

1649 Speech upon the scaffold.

Charles II, *called* **the Merry Monarch** 1630–85 •*King of Great Britain and Ireland*• He was the son of **Charles I** and **Henrietta Maria** and the years of his reign are known in English history as the Restoration Period. As Prince of Wales he sided with his father during the 1642–46 Civil War, and was then forced into exile in Sicily, Jersey (where his mistresss, Lucy Walter, bore him a son, James, Duke of Monmouth) and France. When his father was executed in 1649, Charles was proclaimed monarch by Scotland, and crowned at Scone on January 1, 1651. Leading poorly organized forces into England, he met disastrous defeat at the Battle of Worcester the following September. The next nine years were spent in exile until an impoverished England, in dread of a revival of military despotism, invited him back as king. In 1662 he married the Catholic **Catherine of Braganza**, and in 1663 he attempted to issue a Declaration of Indulgence (allowing religious toleration of the Roman Catholics and Nonconformists), but it was bitterly resented. His wars against the Dutch (1665–67) were unpopular, and the first of these led to the dismissal of his adviser, Edward Hyde, 1st Earl of **Clarendon**, who was replaced by a group of Ministers acting in concert, effectively forming the country's first Cabinet. The king negotiated subsidies from France in the secret Treaty of Dover (1670), by which he also promised **Louis XIV** of France to make England Catholic once more. His brother James (the future **James VII and II**) openly professed his allegiance to Catholicism, and in 1673 married a Catholic, **Mary of Modena**. Meanwhile, Charles's attempt to issue a second Declaration of Indulgence to annul the penal laws against the Catholics and dissenters was rejected by parliament, which instead passed the 1673 Test Act, which excluded Roman Catholics from sitting in parliament or holding government office. It was followed by repeated attempts to legislate against James's succession to the throne, or to drastically limit his powers if he did so. Catherine's failure to produce an heir compelled Charles to consent to the marriage in 1677 of his Protestant niece Mary (the future **Mary II**) to William of Orange (the future **William III**), and anti-Catholicism returned in the light of the fabricated account by **Titus Oates** of a popish plot to murder the king. The next three years saw the future of the Stuart dynasty hanging in the balance, and the emergence for the first time of party distinctions, with the Whigs favoring James's exclusion, and the Tories opposed to any tampering with the succession. The Tories and Charles won the day, and the king immediately legislated for changes to borough government that effectively excluded the Whigs from power. Despite the absence of parliamentary opposition after Charles seized total power in 1681, anti-Catholic sentiment grew, and reached a peak after the 1683 Rye House plot to murder Charles and James came to light. However, James's succession was now safe, and on his deathbed Charles finally publicly acknowledged his conversion to Roman Catholicism. He died without producing an heir, but through his affairs with Barbara Villiers, **Nell Gwyn**, Louise de Kéroualle, Duchess of **Portsmouth**, and many others, he fathered several children, most of whom were later ennobled.

Charles I, *called* **the Bald**, *also* **Charles II** 823–77 •*King of France and Holy Roman emperor*• The son of **Louis the Pious** and grandson of **Charlemagne**, he was king from 843 and emperor (as Charles II) of the West from 875. His reign was characterized by rivalries within the royal family, and aristocratic factionalism, but also saw the zenith of the Carolingian renaissance, mainly due to his patronage of arts and letters.

Charles II, *called* **the Fat** 839–88 •*King of France and Holy Roman emperor*• He became emperor in Germany (as Charles III) in 881 and king of France in 884, but, listless and incompetent, he was deposed from the imperial throne after making a humiliating treaty with the Vikings in Paris (887).

Charles III, *called* **the Simple** 879–929 •*King of France*• He ruled France from 893. He ceded Normandy to the Vikings under **Rollo**, and was deposed (922).

Charles IV, *called* **the Fair** 1294–1328 •*King of France and Navarre*• King from 1322, he was the last of the Capetian dynasty.

Charles V, *called* **the Wise** 1338–80 •*King of France*• He was born at Vincennes, and as dauphin he acted as regent during the long captivity of his father, **John II**, after the Battle of Poitiers (1356), and succeeded his father in 1364. He reorganized the army, established a navy and regained most of the territory lost to the English. A patron of the arts, he redecorated the Louvre to house his splendid library.

Charles VII, *called* **the Victorious** 1403–61 •*King of France*• Born in Paris, the son of Charles VI (the Foolish), he came to the throne in 1422, when Paris and the north of the country were in the hands of the English, who proclaimed **Henry VI** of England king of France, and appointed the Duke of **Bedford** regent. Charles was compelled to evacuate Champagne and Maine, but at Montargis (1426) the Comte de **Dunois** gained the first victory over the English, who laid siege to Orleans (1426). **Joan of Arc** incited the nobles and the people, leading to the end of the siege (1429). The English gradually lost nearly all they had gained in France, and Charles entered Paris (1436). Bayonne fell (1451), and with the death of Sir **John Talbot**, 1st Earl of Shrewsbury, under the walls of Castillon (1453), the whole south finally passed to France, and the Hundred Years War came to an end. Charles increased his solvency by obtaining the permanent right to tax without the permission of the Estates General, and enhanced his control of the French Church by the Pragmatic Sanction of Bourges (1438). His last years were embittered by the conduct of his son, the dauphin (later **Louis XI**).

Charles VIII, *called* **the Affable** 1470–98 •*King of France*• Born in Amboise, he succeeded his father, **Louis XI**, in 1483. Until 1492 the government was run by his sister, Anne de Beaujeu, and her husband. In 1494 he invaded Italy, but he failed in an attempt to secure the Kingdom of Naples (1495–96), which inaugurated a series of French expeditions to Italy that lasted until 1559.

Charles IX 1550–74 •*King of France*• Born in St Germain-en-Laye, the second son of **Henry II** and **Catherine de Médicis**, he succeeded his brother, **Francis II** (1560). His reign coincided with the Wars of Religion. He was dominated by his mother, whose counsels drove him to authorize the infamous slaughter of Huguenots known as the St Bartholomew's Day Massacre (1572).

Charles X 1757–1836 •*King of France*• Born at Versailles, the grandson of **Louis XV**, he received the title of Count of Artois. After a dissolute youth, he lived abroad during the French Revolution, returning to France in 1814 as lieutenant general of the kingdom. In 1824 he succeeded his brother **Louis XVIII** to become the last **Bourbon** king of France, but his repressive rule led to the July Revolution (1830), and his eventual abdication and exile.

Charles I of Spain *See* **Charles V**

Charles II 1661–1700 •*Last Habsburg king of Spain*• Born in Madrid, he was the younger son and successor in 1665 of **Philip IV**. In 1690 he joined the League of Augsburg and went to war against **Louis XIV** in the Grand Alliance (1688–97). The weak, indolent end-product of Habsburg inbreeding, he was childless despite two marriages, and bequeathed the Crown to Philip of Anjou (**Philip V**), grandson of Louis XIV. The prospect of a union of the Crowns of Spain and France under the House of **Bourbon** precipitated the War of the Spanish Succession (1701–13).

Charles III 1716–88 •*King of Spain, and King Charles IV of Naples and Sicily*• Born in Madrid, he was the younger son of **Philip V**, and succeeded his half brother Ferdinand VI. He became Duke of Parma (1732), and in the War of the Polish Succession (1734) he became King Charles IV of Naples and Sicily. When he succeeded to the throne of Spain (1759) he handed over Naples and Sicily to his third son, **Ferdinand I**. Frugal, informal, and disliking court ostentation, he chose effective ministers. At home he reformed the nation's economy, creating the conditions for industry to flourish. He strengthened the Crown's authority over the Church, ending the Inquisition (1767), and he expelled the Jesuits (1767). He was succeeded by his son, **Charles IV**.

Charles IV 1784–1819 •*King of Spain*• Born in Portici, Naples, the son and successor of **Charles III**, he was an ineffectual ruler (1788–1808), dominated by his wife, Maria Louisa of Parma, and her lover, **Manuel de Godoy**, whom he appointed Prime Minister (1792). During the Napoleonic wars the Spanish fleet was destroyed by Admiral **Nelson** off Cape Trafalgar (1805), France was invaded (1807) and Charles was forced to abdicate (1808) in favor of **Napoleon** I's brother, **Joseph Bonaparte**. He died in exile in Rome.

Charles IV 1316–78 •*Holy Roman emperor*• He became Margrave of Moravia (1334) and gradually assumed the government of the Czech lands during the frequent absences of his father, King John the Blind (1296–1346). After the latter's death (1346) he became king of Bohemia, was elected king of Germany (1347) and crowned Holy Roman emperor in Rome (1355), but unlike his predecessors tried to avoid being drawn into Italian conflicts. Instead, through shrewd diplomacy, he built up a dynastic empire based around his hereditary domains of Bohemia and Moravia, with his capital at Prague, where he founded the first university within the empire (1348). His *Golden Bull* of 1356 became the new constitutional framework for the empire; it established the procedure for the election of the monarch, excluded papal pretensions, and defined the rights of the seven electors, whose domains were declared indivisible. He was succeeded by his son as Wenceslas IV (1361–1419).

Charles V, *also* **Charles I of Spain** 1500–58 •*Holy Roman emperor*• He was born in Ghent, Belgium, the son of Philip the Handsome (briefly king of Spain as **Philip I**) and Joanna, the Infanta of Spain ("Juana the Mad" (1479–1555). Charles's father died in 1506, and his mother, who was regarded as insane, was kept in confinement in Spain. Charles and his sisters were brought up in Flanders by their aunt, the Archduchess **Margaret of Austria**. In 1516 his maternal grandfather, Ferdinand of Aragon, died, and Charles inherited from him Spain, Naples and Spanish America. In 1519 his paternal grandfather, Maximilian, died, and from him Charles inherited the Crown of Germany. In 1519 he was crowned Holy Roman Emperor at Aachen, having defeated **Francis I** of France for the election, and thereby became the most powerful monarch in Europe at the age of 19. The ensuing years were dominated by virtually continuous wars with France for possession of Italy, and by a series of fruitless attempts to achieve religious unity in Germany. The Treaty of Cambrai (1529) brought a temporary peace, and Charles made a triumphal procession through Italy and in 1530 was crowned by the pope in Bologna as emperor and king of Italy. In 1532 he defeated Sultan **Süleyman the Magnificent** at the Siege of Vienna. In 1521 he presided over the Imperial Diet of Worms, and he also called the Diets of Augsburg (1530) and Regensburg (1541) which, however, failed to reconcile the differences between Catholics and Lutherans. He was eventually forced to grant Protestantism legal recognition through the Treaty of Passau (1552) and the Peace of Augsburg (1555). Elsewhere, Charles extended Spanish dominions in the New World by the conquest of Mexico by **Hernán Cortés** (1519–21) and of Peru by **Francisco Pizarro** (1531–35). Toward the end of his long reign, his health broken by gout, Charles devoted himself to consolidating his vast dominions for the benefit of his heirs. In 1527 he had married Isabella of Portugal, by whom he had a son, Philip (the future **Philip II** of Spain). In 1555–56 he resigned his kingdoms to Philip and retired to live in seclusion in the monastery of San Geronimo de Yuste, in Estremadura.

Charles (Karl Ludwig Johann) 1771–1847 •*Archduke of Austria*• He was born in Florence, the son of Emperor **Leopold II** and brother of Emperor **Francis II**. He became Governor-General of the Austrian Netherlands (1793) and, as commander of the Austrian army on the Rhine (1796), defeated **Jean Victor Moreau** and Comte **Jean-Baptiste Jourdan** in several battles, drove the French over the Rhine, and took Kehl. He defeated Jourdan again in 1799, only to be defeated by **André Masséna**. After victory at Aspern, and defeat at Wagram, he retired (1809) and became Governor of Mainz (1815).

Charles, Prince of Wales, *in full* **Charles Philip Arthur George** 1948– •*British prince*• He is the eldest son of Queen **Elizabeth II** and Prince Philip, Duke of **Edinburgh**, and heir apparent to the British throne. He was given the title of Prince of Wales (1958), and invested at Caernarvon (1969). Educated at Cheam School, Berkshire, and Gordonstoun School in Scotland, he spent a term at Geelong Grammar School, Australia (1966), and studied at Trinity College, Cambridge (1967–70). He served in the RAF and Royal Navy (1971–76), and in 1981 married Lady **Diana** Frances, younger daughter of the 8th Earl Spencer. They announced their separation in 1992 and were divorced in 1996. Their children are Prince William (1982–), and Prince Harry (1984–). Since leaving the navy, he has taken a special interest in industry, the problems of the inner cities, and unemployed young people. He has expressed strong views on architecture, conservation, organic farming and education.

Charles d'Orléans *See* **Orléans, Charles, Duc d'**

Charles Martel c. 688–741 •*Ruler of the Franks, founder of the Carolingian dynasty*• He was the illegitimate son of **Pepin II (the Younger)** and in 719 became "Mayor of the Palace" of Austrasia and real ruler of all the Frankish kingdom. He earned his nickname of Martel "the Hammer" by his defeat of the Moors in a desperate battle at Tours, near Poitiers, in 732, which turned back the tide of Arab conquest in Europe, then drove the Saracens out of Burgundy and Languedoc (737). After his death the Frankish kingdom was divided between his sons Carloman and **Pepin III (the Short)**. His grandson was **Charlemagne**.

Charles of Anjou 1226–85 •*Angevin king of Naples and Sicily*• The posthumous son of Louis VIII of France, he was crowned king of Naples and Sicily (1265), and defeated his Hohenstaufen rivals **Manfred**, king of Sicily, in 1266 and Conradin of Swabia (1252–68) in 1268. He conquered much of mainland Greece, but his rule was unpopular, partly because he used French officials. He aimed to reestablish the Latin Empire in Constantinople (Istanbul), but when Peter III of Aragon seized Sicily after the revolt known as the Sicilian Vespers (1282), his plans failed and he was expelled.

Charles of Jesus, Brother *See* **Foucauld, Charles Eugène**

Charles of Valois 1270–1325 •*French nobleman*• The second son of **Philip III** of France and Isabelle of Aragon, he was put forward as French claimant to the Kingdom of Aragon, which he was unable to conquer (1283–89). He continued to figure in the diplomatic schemes of his brother **Philip IV** as unsuccessful candidate for the thrones of Constantinople (Istanbul) from 1301 to 1307 and the Holy Roman Empire in 1308, and achieved great influence during the short reigns of Philip's three sons, Louis X (1289–1316), Philip V (1293–1322) and **Charles IV**, commanding French armies in Guyenne and Flanders. Three years after his death, his only son, **Philip VI**, became the first of the Valois kings of France.

Charles Robert 1288–1342 •*First king of Hungary of the Angevin dynasty*• Born in Naples, he claimed the throne (through his mother) on the death of the last male member of the House of Árpád, Andrew III (1301), and after the defeat of rival claimants was crowned in 1310. He restored the royal authority in a struggle against the rebellious great magnates, whose lands he redistributed to the minor nobility, thus creating a new aristocracy loyal to him. He was pious and civilized, and his court was famous as a school of chivalry. In 1337 he obtained recognition of his son Louis, the future Louis I (the Great), as heir also to the Polish throne.

Charles the Bold 1433–77 •*Duke of Burgundy*• He was born in Dijon, and succeeded his father, **Philip the Good**, as duke (1467). Hasty and obstinate, though nominally a French vassal, he was continually at war with **Louis XI** of France, aiming to restore the old Kingdom of Burgundy. He gained power over Lorraine (1475) and invaded Switzerland, but was defeated at Granson and Morat (1476). He then laid siege to Nancy, but was killed in the battle. Under him Burgundy reached the zenith of its power, but it was a fragile achievement that then fell apart in the minority of his daughter.

Charles, Bob (Robert) 1936– •*New Zealand golfer*• Born in Carterton, New Zealand, he won the New Zealand Open championship in 1954 but did not turn professional until 1960. In 1963 he won five US Tour events and that same year also became the only left-handed player to triumph in the British Open championship (despite the fact that he was naturally right-handed), the greatest of his total of eight major European victories.

Charles, Dame (Mary) Eugenia 1919– •*Dominican politician*• Born in Pointe Michel, she qualified in London as a barrister, then returned to the West Indies to practice law in the Windward and Leeward Islands. She entered politics in 1968 and two years later became cofounder and first leader of the centrist Dominica Freedom Party (DFP). Two years after independence, the DFP won the 1980 general election and she became the Caribbean's first female Prime Minister, a position she maintained until 1995.

Charles, Ray, *originally* **Ray Charles Robinson** 1930–2004 •*US singer and pianist*• Born in Albany, Georgia, he was blind from the age of 5. Orphaned at the age of 15, he went to Seattle and, after writing arrangements for several pop groups, was contracted to Atlantic Records in 1952. With *I've Got a Woman* (1955) he established an influential new style of rhythm and blues which introduced elements of gospel music. He was awarded the National Medal of Arts in 1993.

Charlevoix, Pierre François Xavier de 1682–1761 •*French Jesuit explorer*• He was born in St Quentin, Picardy, and in 1720 was sent by the French regent to find a route to western Canada. For two and a half years he traveled by canoe up the St Lawrence River, across the Great Lakes, and down the Mississippi River to New Orleans, and was finally shipwrecked in the Gulf of Mexico. He became the only traveler of that time to describe the interior of North America, writing *Histoire et description de la Nouvelle France* (1774, "History and Description of New France").

Charlie, Bonnie Prince *See* **Stuart, Prince Charles Edward**

Charlotte (Augusta), Princess 1796–1817 •*Princess of Great Britain and Ireland*• Born at Carlton House, London, the only daughter of **George IV** and **Caroline of Brunswick**, who separated immediately after her birth, she was the heir to the British throne, and was brought up in strict seclusion. In 1816 she married Prince Leopold of Saxe-Coburg, the future **Leopold I** of Belgium and uncle of **Victoria**. She died in childbirth.

Charlotte Sophia 1744–1818 •*Queen of Great Britain and Ireland and wife of George III*• She married **George III** (1761), shortly after his accession to the throne, and bore him 15 children during their long and successful marriage. Their eldest son was the future **George IV**.

Charlton, Bobby (Sir Robert) 1937– •*English soccer player*• Born in Ashington, Northumberland, he made his full-team debut in 1956 and played with Manchester United throughout his career (1954–73). He survived the Munich air disaster (1958) which killed eight teammates, won three league championship medals (1956–57, 1964–65, 1966–67), a Football Association Cup winner's medal in 1963, and captained Manchester United to victory in the 1968 European Cup. He played 106 games for England between 1957 and 1973, scoring a record 49 goals, and was a member of the England team that won the World Cup in 1966. He turned to running highly successful coaching schools and also became a director of Manchester United. He was knighted in 1994. He is the younger brother of **Jack Charlton**.

Charlton, Jack (John) 1935– •*English soccer player*• Born in Ashington, Northumberland, he was a vital part of the great Leeds United team of 1965–75 under the management of Don Revie (1927–89). He was almost 30 before he was capped for England, but then retained his place for five years. His playing days over, he became manager of Middlesbrough (1973), Sheffield Wednesday (1977) and Newcastle United (1984). He was given the honorary title Officer, Order of the British Empire, in 1974. In 1986 he was unexpectedly appointed manager of the Republic of Ireland. He retired from international soccer, a national hero, in 1996 and published *Jack Charlton—The Autobiography* the same year. He is the elder brother of **Bobby Charlton**.

“ ”

Soccer is a man's game; not an outing for mamby-pambies.

1967 ***For Leeds and England.***

Charteris, Leslie, *pseudonym of* **Leslie Charles Bowyer Yin** 1907–93 •*US crime-story writer*• Born in Singapore, the son of an English mother and a Chinese father, he was educated at Cambridge. He was author of a series of books featuring a criminal hero, Simon Templar, "the Saint," starting with *Meet the Tiger* (1928) and *Enter the Saint* (1930). He moved to the US in 1932 and worked in Hollywood as a screenwriter. He was naturalized in 1941.

Chartier, Alain c. 1390–c. 1440 •*French writer and courtier*• Born in Bayeux, he went on diplomatic missions to Germany, Venice and Scotland (1425–28). His much-imitated poem, *La belle dame sans merci* (1424, "The Beautiful Woman with No Mercy"), is a piece of escapism in the midst of his preoccupation with the plight of France in the Hundred Years War. This forms the backdrop for his two best works, the *Livre des quatre dames* (1415–16, "Book of Four Women"), in which four ladies on the day after Agincourt weep for their lost lovers, and the prose *Quadrilogue invectif* (1422, A Debate Between Four People, Containing Invective).

Chase, James Hadley, *pseudonym of* **René Raymond** 1906–85 •*English novelist*• Born in London, he served in the RAF during World War II. As a writer of mystery stories he adopted the manner of the US "hard-boiled" school, and had an immediate success with his first novel, *No Orchids for Miss Blandish* (1939). He continued in a similar vein to write prolifically, employing a number of different detectives in various series, but his hallmark is always an intricate plot and a fast-moving, harshly realistic narrative.

Chastelain, John de *See* **de Chastelain, (Alfred) John (Gardyne Drummond)**

Chateaubriand, (François) René, Vicomte de 1768–1848 •*French writer and statesman*• Born of a noble Breton family in St Malo, he served for a short time as an ensign. From 1793 to 1800 he lived in London, teaching and translating. *Atala* (1801, Eng trans 1802), an unfinished Romantic epic of Native American life, established his literary reputation, and *Le génie du christianisme* (1802, Eng trans *The Beauties of Christianity*, 1813), a vindication of the

Church of Rome, made him prominent among French men of letters. He was appointed secretary to the embassy in Rome (1803) and was sent as envoy to the little republic of Valais (1804), but later refused to hold office under **Napoleon I**. He supported the Restoration monarchy from 1814 and was made a peer and minister, and in 1822–24 was ambassador extraordinary at the British court. Disappointed in his hope of becoming Prime Minister, he figured as a Liberal from 1824 to 1830, but on the downfall of **Charles X** he went back to the Royalists. His celebrated *Mémoires d'outre-tombe* ("Memoirs from Beyond the Grave") was translated as *Memoirs* in three volumes in 1848, but the whole work, in six volumes, did not appear until 1902.

Chatham, William Pitt, 1st Earl of, *known as* **Pitt the Elder** 1708–78 •*English statesman and orator*• He was born in Westminster, and educated at Eton and Trinity College, Oxford. In 1735 he entered parliament for the family borough, Old Sarum. He sided with **Frederick Louis**, Prince of Wales, against the king, and as leader of the young "Patriot" Whigs, offered a determined opposition to **Robert Walpole**. In 1756, on the outbreak of the Seven Years' War with France, Pitt became Secretary of State in a coalition government with Sir **Thomas Pelham-Holles**, 1st Duke of Newcastle. He immediately put into effect his plan of carrying on the war with France, raised the militia, and strengthened naval power. **George III**'s hostility and German predilections led him to resign in April 1757, only to be recalled in June, in response to popular demands. His vigorous war policy was widely successful against the French on land (in India, Africa, Canada, and on the Rhine) and at sea, but Pitt himself was compelled to resign (1761) when the majority of the cabinet refused to declare war with Spain. He formed a new ministry from 1766 to 1768, with a seat in the House of Lords as Viscount Pitt and Earl of Chatham. However, ill health prevented him from taking any active part in this ministry, and after his resignation (1768) he held no further office. He spoke strongly against the arbitrary and harsh policy toward the American colonies, and warmly urged an amicable settlement. However, when it was proposed to make peace on any terms, Chatham came down to the House of Lords (April 2, 1778), and in his final speech secured a majority against the motion. But the effort exhausted him and he collapsed into the arms of his friends. A few weeks later, he was dead. Chatham was honored with a public funeral and a statue in Westminster Abbey; the government voted £20,000 to pay his debts, and conferred a pension of £4,000 a year on his descendants. His second son was **William Pitt** the Younger.

Chatterjee, Bankim Chandra 1838–94 •*Indian writer and social critic*• He was born in Katalpura, Bengal, and became a district magistrate there. A contemporary of **Rabindranath Tagore**, he founded (1872) *Bangadarshan*, a Bengali newspaper which soon became a vehicle for expounding Hindu philosophy and culture. His novels include *Durgesanandini* (1864) and *Anandamath* (1882), a novel of the Sannyasi rebellion of 1772, from which the Nationalist song *Bande mataram* ("Hail to thee, Mother") was adopted. In his novels he was able to forge a sense of Indian nationality while at the same time pointing out the inequities institutionalized in Hindu society.

Chatterjee, Gadadhar *See* **Ramakrishna Paramahasa**

Chatterton, Thomas 1752–70 •*English poet*• Born in Bristol, he was a scholar of Colston's Bluecoat Hospital (1760–65), and then was apprenticed to an attorney. He wrote and published pseudoarchaic poems purporting to be the work of a 15th-century Bristol monk, Thomas Rowley, and in 1770 and went to London, where he worked on innumerable satires, essays and epistles, and a burlesque opera, *The Revenge*, but later that year he poisoned himself with arsenic. His "Rowley" poems, although soon exposed as forgeries, are considered to show genuine talent, and he became a romantic hero to later poets. His story was dramatized by **Alfred de Vigny** in 1835, and is the subject of the celebrated painting by Henry Wallis, *Chatterton* (1856, Tate Britain, London).

Chatwin, Bruce 1940–89 •*English writer and traveler*• He was born in Sheffield, educated at Marlborough College, and worked at Sotheby's until he temporarily went blind. To recuperate, he went to Africa and the Sudan. He was converted to a life of nomadic asceticism and began writing beguiling books which defy classification, combining fiction, anthropology, philosophy and travel. They include *In Patagonia* (1977), which won the Hawthornden prize and the **E M Forster** award of the American Academy of Letters, *The Viceroy of Ouidah* (1980), *On The Black Hill* (1982, winner of the Whitbread award for the best first novel), *The Songlines* (1987), and *Utz* (1988).

❝ ❞

Tyranny sets up its own echo-chamber.

1988 ***Utz.***

Chaucer, Geoffrey c. 1345–1400 •*English poet best known for The Canterbury Tales, the most influential English poetry of the Middle Ages*• He was born in London. In 1357 and 1358 Geoffrey was a page in the service of the wife of Lionel, Duke of Clarence; later he transferred to the household of **Edward III**. His first work as a poet was the *Book of the Duchess* (1369), on the death by plague of **John of Gaunt**'s first wife, Blanche. He traveled widely in the king's service and also held a number of posts at home, including Comptroller of the Petty Customs (1382). In 1386 he was appointed knight of the shire for Kent, and, influenced by **Boccaccio**, went on to write *Troilus and Cressida*. However, about the end of 1386 Chaucer lost his offices, and fell upon hard times. In 1389 he was appointed clerk of the King's Works, but this did not last and he fell into debt. In 1394 King **Richard II** granted him a pension of £20 for life; but the advances of payment he applied for, and the issue of letters of protection from arrest for debt, indicate his condition. On the accession in 1399 of **Henry IV**, he was granted a pension of 40 marks (£26 13s 4d), and his few remaining months were spent in comfort. Chaucer's greatest work, probably begun in the late 1380s and not completed, was *The Canterbury Tales*, some 17,000 lines of verse and prose recounting, with a prologue, the tales told by a group of pilgrims on their journey to Canterbury. The work shows a profound understanding of human nature, ranging from the urbane to the bawdy, and is written in a variety of meters, principally the rhyming couplet. Chaucer was the first great English poet, and he established the southern English dialect as the literary language of England.

Chauliac, Guy de c. 1300–68 •*French surgeon*• Born in Chauliac, Auvergne, he became the most famous surgeon of the Middle Ages. His *Chirurgia magna* (1363) was translated into French over a century later and used as a manual by generations of doctors.

Chavannes *See* **Puvis de Chavannes, Pierre**

Chávez, Carlos 1899–1978 •*Mexican composer*• Born in Mexico City, he formed the Mexican Symphony Orchestra in 1928, becoming director of the National Conservatory. A founder and director of the National Institute of Fine Arts (1947–52), Chávez's influence on every aspect of Mexican music was considerable. His works are less known outside his own country, partly owing to their large scale, but are influenced by Mexican folk music and include ballets, symphonies, concertos and an unusual *Toccata for Percussion* (1942).

Chávez, César Estrada 1927–93 •*US labor leader*• Born near Yuma, Arizona, the son of a family of Mexican-American migrants, he worked in the fields from early childhood and received little formal schooling. In 1962 he founded the National Farm Workers Association, which sought to unionize migrant workers. He used strikes, pickets, and marches in the struggle to win contracts from growers and himself undertook long fasts to publicize the movement. In 1968 he promoted a nationwide boycott of California grapes, which led to the table-grape growers recognition of the union in 1970. In 1972 the United Farm Workers (UFW), with Chávez as its president, became a member union of the AFL-CIO.

Chayefsky, Paddy, *originally* **Sidney Chayefsky** 1923–81 •*US stage and television playwright and screenwriter*• He was born in New York City, and studied at the City College of New York. His work includes *Marty* (1953, television), which won an Academy Award for Best Screenplay when filmed (1954), and *The Bachelor Party* (1954, screenplay). Other screenplays include *Paint Your Wagon* (1969), *The Hospital* (1971, Academy Award for Best Screenplay), and *Network* (1976, Academy Award for Best Screenplay).

Cheever, John William 1912–82 •*US short-story writer and novelist*• Born in Quincy, Massachusetts, he began telling stories when he was eight or nine. He sold his first story, "Expelled," to *The New Republic* after he was thrown out of Thayer Academy in South Braintree, Massachusetts, at the age of 17. By the time he was 22 the *New Yorker* was accepting his work, and for years he contributed a dozen stories a year to it. In 1951 a Guggenheim Fellowship allowed him to devote his attention to writing, and his first novel, *The Wapshot Chronicle* (1957), won the National Book award and its sequel, *The Wapshot Scandal* (1964), was awarded the Howell's Medal for Fiction. A steady stream of novels and stories followed, including *Bullet Park* (1969), *The World of Apples* (1973) and *The Stories of John Cheever*, winner of the Pulitzer Prize and the National Book Critics award in 1979.

Chekhov, Anton Pavlovich 1860–1904 •*Russian dramatist and short-story writer*• He was born in Taganrog, and studied medicine at Moscow University. In 1892 he settled on a farm estate at Melikhovo, near Moscow; five years later, suffering from tuberculosis, he moved to the Crimea. He then moved to Yalta in 1900 and spent the rest of his life there. As a student, he had written humorous stories, sketches and articles for various magazines, and his first book, *Pëstrye rasskazy* (1886, "Motley Stories"), was successful enough for him to think of writing as a profession. However, he continued to regard himself as a doctor rather than a writer, although he practiced very little except during the cholera epidemic of 1892–93. He developed an interest in the popular stage of vaudeville and French farce and, after the failure of his first full-length play, *Ivanov* (1887, Eng trans 1912), he wrote several one-act plays, such as *Medved* (1889, Eng trans *The Bear*, 1909) and *Predlozheniye* (1889, Eng trans *A Marriage Proposal*, 1914). His next full-length plays, *Leshy* (1889, Eng trans *The Wood Demon*, 1926) and *Chayka* (1896, Eng trans *The Seagull*, 1912), were also failures and he had decided to concentrate on his stories (which had introduced him to **Tolstoy** and **Maxim Gorky**) when Nemirovich-Danchenko persuaded him to let the Moscow Art Theater revive *Chayka* in 1898. The play was produced by **Stanislavsky** and its reception encouraged Chekhov to write his masterpieces for the same company: *Dyadya Vanya* (1896, Eng trans *Uncle Vanya*, 1912), *Tri sestry* (1901, Eng trans *The Three Sisters*, 1916) and *Vishnyovy sad* (1904, Eng trans *The Cherry Orchard*, 1908). Meanwhile he continued to write short stories. Chekhov is perhaps the most popular Russian author outside his own country. His stories have influenced many writers and his plays are firmly established in the classical repertoires of Europe.

" "

Brevity is the sister of talent.

1889 Letter to Alexander Chekhov, April 11.

Chemnitz or **Kemnitz, Martin** 1522–86 •*German Lutheran theologian*• Born in Treuenbrietzen, in Brandenburg, he studied at the University of Wittenberg (1545) under **Philip Melanchthon**. His skill in astrology led to his appointment as ducal librarian at Königsberg in 1549, where he devoted himself to theology. His works include *Examen Concilii Tridentini* (1565–73) and *De duabus naturis in Christo* (1571).

Cheney, Dick (Richard Bruce) 1941– •*US politician*• Born in Lincoln, Nebraska, he studied at the Universities of Wyoming and Wisconsin. He rose in successive Republican administrations to become Secretary of Defense under **George Bush** from 1989 to 1993, when he oversaw military operations in Panama and the Middle East. In January 2001, despite qualms about his health, he was sworn in as Vice President under **George W Bush**, and took an aggressive stance following the September 11 attacks on New York and Washington in 2001.

Chenier, Clifton 1925–87 •*US zydeco accordionist*• Born in Opelousas, Louisiana, he was a key figure in the development of zydeco, a distinctly African American variant on the Cajun two-step tradition, spiced up with borrowings from rhythm and blues. He sang in French patois, Creole and English, and after a string of regional hits during the 1950s, he succeeded in bringing this vibrant musical form to a wider audience in the 1960s and 1970s. He recorded for many different labels, and was twice nominated for Grammy awards (1979, 1986). His brother Cleveland Chenier played *frottoir* (a corrugated steel breastplate) in his band, while his son C J Chenier is also an accordionist.

Chénier, (Marie) André 1762–94 •*French poet*• Born in Constantinople (Istanbul), he studied at the Collège de Navarre, Paris. At 20 he joined the army, but returned to Paris to study, and wrote his famous idylls *Le mendiant* ("The Beggar") and *L'aveugle* ("The Blind Man"). He traveled in Switzerland, Italy and the Greek islands, returned to Paris in 1786 and began several poems, most of which remained fragments. In 1787 he went to England as secretary to the French ambassador, and in 1790 he returned again to Paris, at first supporting the revolution but later offending **Robespierre** by political pamphlets promoting liberal monarchism. He was thrown into prison, and six months later was guillotined. The appearance of his collected poems in 1819 made a notable impression on subsequent French poetry.

Chen Kaige 1954– •*Chinese film director*• Born in Beijing, he was educated at Beijing Cinema College. After working as a laborer on a rubber plantation and serving in the army, he made *Yellow Earth* (1984), the story of a Communist soldier who is sent to the countryside to collect folk songs for the Revolution. It won Best Film at the Berlin Film Festival, and was followed by such international successes as *Farewell My Concubine* (1993) and *The Assassin* (1999).

Chen Ning Yang *See* **Yang, Chen Ning**

Chen Shui-bian 1951– •*Taiwanese politician*• Born into a poor family in Tainan County, he won a scholarship to Taiwan University, and began his career in law. He later joined the opposition Democratic People's Party and ran successfully for Mayor of Taipei (1994–98) and later President of Taiwan (2000–). In office his hard-line proindependence policies softened somewhat and he sought rapprochement with Beijing.

Chen Yi (Ch'en I) 1901–72 •*Chinese Communist leader*• He studied in France, and joined the Communist Party on his return. He supported **Mao Zedong** in the struggle with the Guomindang (Kuomintang), and the Japanese (1934). He took various army commands from 1940, and prepared an amphibious operation against Taiwan, but failed to capture Jinmen (Quemoy) Island in 1949. Created Marshal of the People's Republic in 1955, he became Foreign Minister in 1958. He was dropped from the politburo during the Cultural Revolution in 1969.

Cheops 26th century BC •*Hellenic form of Khufu, King of Memphis in Egypt*• He was second of the Fourth Dynasty, and is famous as the builder of the Great Pyramid. An active ruler, he centralized the government and reduced priestly power. A son and successor, Chephren (Khafre), built the next largest pyramid.

Cher, *originally* **Cheryl Sarkisian La Pier** 1946– •*US pop singer and film actress*• Born in El Centro, California, of partly Cherokee parentage, she began her career as a backup vocalist, then teamed up with Salvatore "Sonny" Bono (1935–98). They married in 1964, and had their first major hit single, "I Got You Babe," in 1965. They divorced in 1975, and she began to gain fame as a solo singer, but also pursued an acting career. She won an Academy Award nomination for *Silkwood* (1983), a Cannes Best Actress Award in *Mask* (1985), and a Best Actress Academy Award for *Moonstruck* (1987). Other films include *Mermaids* (1990), *If These Walls Could Talk* (1996), which she also codirected, and *Tea with Mussolini* (1999).

Cherenkov, Pavel Alekseyevich 1904–90 •*Soviet physicist and Nobel Prize winner*• He was born in Voronezh in western Russia and educated at Voronezh University and the Soviet Academy of Sciences. In 1934 he observed the emission of blue light from water bombarded by gamma rays. This so-called Cherenkov effect was explained by **Igor Tamm** and **Ilya Frank** as being produced by particles traveling through a medium at velocities greater than the speed of light in that medium. The three shared the Nobel Prize for physics in 1958. Cherenkov also contributed to the development and construction of electron accelerators, and to the study of the interactions of photons with nuclei and mesons.

Chernenko, Konstantin Ustinovich 1911–85 •*Soviet politician*• Born of peasant stock in Bolshaya Tes in Central Siberia, he joined the Komsomol (Communist Youth League) in 1929 and the Communist Party (CPSU) in 1931. During the 1940s, he worked as a specialist in party propaganda, impressing **Leonid Brezhnev**, who adopted Chernenko as his personal assistant. He was inducted into the CPSU Central Committee in 1971, the secretariat in 1976 and into the politburo, as a full member, in December 1978. During his final years in power, Brezhnev sought to promote Chernenko as his heir apparent, but on Brezhnev's death in 1982 Chernenko was passed over in favor of **Yuri Andropov**. However, when Andropov died in 1984, Chernenko was selected as the CPSU's stopgap leader by cautious party colleagues. As Soviet leader he sought to promote a new era of détente, but from mid-1984, suffering from emphysema, he progressively retired from the public gaze. He was succeeded by **Mikhail Gorbachev**.

Chernomyrdin, Viktor Stepanovich 1938– •*Russian politician*• Born in Cherny-Otrog in the Orenburg district, he was educated at the Kuybyshev Polytechnic. He served in the army (1957–60) before entering the oil industry. Having entered politics in 1978, he became Minister for Gas (1985–89) and did much to exploit the USSR's natural gas and oil resources. Appointed Prime Minister of Russia in 1993, he assumed greater political authority when he was deputized for **Boris Yeltsin** during the Russian president's lengthy spell of illness.

Cherry, Don(ald Eugene) 1936–95 •*US jazz trumpet player*• Born in Oklahoma City, he was one of the most individual voices in contemporary jazz and world music. In an age of technically fearsome trumpet players, he preferred to emphasize expression and musical communication on his distinctive pocket trumpet. He first came to notice in the epochal **Ornette Coleman** Quartet in 1958, and was a crucial factor in that group. He recorded as a leader from the mid-1960s, and incorporated the ethnic musics and instruments of Africa, India and Asia into his work with groups like Codona and Multikulti from the early 1970s on. His devotion to Coleman's "harmolodic" teachings remained strong throughout his career, which also included collaborations with rock musicians.

Cheshire, (Geoffrey) Leonard Cheshire, Baron 1917–92 •*English philanthropist*• He was educated at Stowe School and Merton College, Oxford. A pilot in the RAF in World War II, he won the Victoria Cross in 1944 on completing a hundred bombing missions, often at low altitude, on heavily defended German targets. With **William Penney** he was the official British observer of the destruction caused by the atomic bomb over Nagasaki (1945). This experience, together with his newfound faith in Roman Catholicism, made him decide to devote the rest of his life to the relief of suffering. He founded the "Cheshire Foundation Homes" for the incurably sick in many countries. In 1959 he married Sue, Baroness **Ryder**, who founded the Sue Ryder Foundation for the sick and disabled of all age groups. He was created Baron Cheshire in 1991.

Chesnius *See* **Duchesne, André**

Chesnut, Mary Boykin Miller, *née* **Miller** 1823–86 •*US diarist*• Born in South Carolina and educated at private schools in Camden and Charleston, she married James Chesnut, a US senator from South Carolina (1859–60) in 1840. He resigned his position in order to assist in the formation of the Confederacy, and she accompanied him, keeping a diary of her experiences and observations on military and political leaders of the Confederacy from 1861 to 1865. It was published in 1905 as *A Diary from Dixie*.

Chessman, Caryl Whittier 1921–60 •*US convict and writer*• Born in St Joseph, Michigan, he was sentenced to death in 1948 on 17 charges of kidnapping, robbery and rape, but was granted eight stays of execution by the governor of California, amounting to a period of 12 years under sentence of death without a reprieve. While in prison he conducted a brilliant legal battle, learned four languages and wrote the best-selling autobiographical books against capital punishment *Cell 2455 Death Row* (1954), *Trial by Ordeal* (1955) and *The Face of Justice* (1958). His ultimate execution provoked worldwide criticism of US judicial methods.

Chesterfield, Philip Dormer Stanhope, 4th Earl of 1694–1773 •*English statesman and man of letters*• Born in London, he was a Member of Parliament from 1715 to c. 1723. In 1730 he was made Lord Steward of the household. He joined the **Pelham** ministry in 1744, became Irish Lord Lieutenant in 1745, and was in 1746 one of the principal secretaries of state. Intimate with **Jonathan Swift**, **Pope** and Viscount **Bolingbroke**, he drew from **Samuel Johnson** a famous indignant letter. Besides the *Letters to His Son* (a guide to manners and success), he also wrote *Letters to his Godson and Successor*. His *Letters to Lord Huntingdon* were published in 1923, his verse in 1927.

Chesterton, G(ilbert) K(eith) 1874–1936 •*English critic, novelist and poet*• Born in London, he was educated at St Paul's School and studied art at the Slade School. Much of his best work went into essays and articles, some of which appeared in his own *G.K's Weekly*, founded in 1925. He became a Roman Catholic in 1922. His early books include two collections of poetry, followed by *The Napoleon of Notting Hill* (1904), liberal and anti-Imperialist in outlook, brilliant literary studies of **Robert Browning** (1903), **Dickens** (1906) and **Robert Louis Stevenson** (1907), and the provocative *Heretics* (1908) and *Orthodoxy* (1908). The amiable detective-priest Father Brown, who brought Chesterton popularity with a wider public, first appeared in *The Innocence of Father Brown* (1911). He also wrote lives of St **Francis of Assisi** (1923), and St **Thomas Aquinas** (1933), *Collected Poems* (1933), and an *Autobiography* (published posthumously in 1936). An ebullient personality, quick-witted, with a robust humor, he was one of the most colorful and provocative writers of his day. He was married to Frances Blogg.

“ ”

Literature is a luxury; fiction is a necessity.

1901 ***The Defendant***, *"Defence of Penny Dreadfuls."*

Chevalier, Albert 1861–1923 •*English entertainer*• He acted at the Prince of Wales's Theatre, London, in 1877, and in 1891 became a music-hall singer. Writing, composing and singing barrow-boy ballads, he immortalized such songs as "My Old Dutch" and "Knocked 'em in the Old Kent Road." In 1901 he published *Before I Forget*.

Chevalier, Maurice 1888–1972 •*French film and vaudeville actor and entertainer*• Born in Paris, he began his career as a child, singing and dancing in small cafés, and became dancing partner to **Mistinguett** at the Folies Bergère (1909–13). A prisoner during World War I, he won the Croix de Guerre, and became a member of the Legion of Honor. He made his first Hollywood film, *The Innocents of Paris*, in 1929. Almost 30 years later his individual, straw-hatted, *bon-vivant* personality, with his distinctive French accent, was still much admired, as in the musical *Gigi* (1958). He received a Special Academy Award in 1959. His autobiography, *Ma route et mes chansons* (Eng trans *The Man in the Straw Hat*) was published in 1949.

Chevallier, Gabriel 1895–1969 •*French novelist*• Born in Lyons, after a series of less successful psychological novels he won wide acclaim with his *Clochemerle* (1934, Eng trans 1936), an earthy satire on petty bureaucracy in a small French town. Other books include *La peur* (1930, "Fear"), *Les héritiers Euffe* (1945, "The Euffe Inheritance"), *Le petit général* (1951, "The Little General") and *Clochemerle Babylone* (1954).

Chevrolet, Louis 1878–1941 •*US car designer and racecar driver*• Born in La Chaux-de-Fonds, Switzerland, he emigrated to the US in 1900 and became a racecar driver, setting records on every important racing circuit in the US. In 1911 with William Crapo Durant he founded the Chevrolet Motor Company, but had little confidence in it and sold his interest to Durant in 1915, who incorporated it with General Motors in 1916. Other cars designed by Chevrolet won important races, including the Indianapolis in 1920 and 1921. In 1936 he returned to work for General Motors in the Chevrolet Division as a minor employee.

Chiang Ch'ing *See* **Jiang Qing**

Chiang Ching-kuo 1910–88 •*Taiwanese politician*• The son of **Chiang Kai-shek**, he studied in the USSR during the early 1930s, returning to China with a Russian wife in 1937 at the time of the Japanese invasion. After the defeat of Japan in 1945 he held a number of government posts before fleeing with his father and the defeated Guomindang (Kuomintang, or Nationalist Party) forces to

Taiwan in 1949. He was Prime Minister from 1972 to 1978 and thereafter State President. Under his stewardship, Taiwan's postwar "economic miracle" continued, but in the political sphere there was repression. During the closing years of his life, he instituted a progressive program of political liberalization and democratization, which was continued by his successor, **Lee Teng-hui**.

Chiang Kai-shek (Jiang Jieshi) 1887–1975 •*Chinese general and politician*• Born in Fenghua, Zhejiang (Chekiang), he received his military training in Tokyo. In 1926 he commanded the army that aimed to unify China, a task which he completed by 1928. Meanwhile he opposed Communism and rid the Guomindang (Kuomintang, or Nationalist Party) of its influence. As President of the Republic (1928–31), he consolidated the nationalist regime, but dangerous left-wing splinter groups retained a foothold in several areas. Head of the executive from 1935 to 1945, he was also Commander in Chief of China united against Japanese aggression. In 1948 the Guomindang collapsed before the Communist advance and Chiang was forced to withdraw to Formosa (Taiwan). There the Chinese national government, "White China," trained new forces, aided by the US. He wrote *Summing up at Seventy* (1957). His second wife, Song Meiling (Mayling Soong, 1897–2003), was educated at American universities, and distinguished herself in social and educational work, and wrote a number of works on China.

Chiang Tse-min *See* **Jiang Zemin**

Chichele, Henry c. 1362–c. 1443 •*English prelate and diplomat*• Envoy to the Vatican (1405, 1407), he became Bishop of St David's (1408), and Archbishop of Canterbury (1414). He was the founder of two colleges at Oxford (1437): St John's and All Souls.

Chichester, Sir Francis Charles 1901–72 •*English adventurer and yachtsman*• Born in Barnstaple, Devon, and educated at Marlborough, he emigrated to New Zealand in 1919, and became a land agent. He took up flying, and made a solo flight to Australia in a Gipsy Moth plane. He was an air navigation instructor in Great Britain during World War II. In 1953 he took up yacht racing, and in 1960 won the first solo transatlantic yacht race with his boat *Gipsy Moth III*, sailing from Plymouth to New York in 40 days. He made a successful solo circumnavigation of the world (1966–67) in *Gipsy Moth IV.* He was knighted in 1967. He wrote *The Lonely Sea and the Sky* (1964) and *Gipsy Moth Circles the World* (1967).

The Chieftains •*Irish folk group*• Possibly the best-known folk group in the world, the original band met while members of **Seán Ó Riada**'s Ceoltóirí Cualann orchestra in the late 1950s. They have worked with many artists from other musical areas over the years, including Mike Oldfield, **Van Morrison** and **James Galway**, contributed to a number of film soundtracks, and remain a major concert attraction. Key players include Uillean piper Paddy Moloney, harpist Derek Bell, and flautist Matt Molloy.

Chifley, (Joseph) Ben(edict) 1885–1951 •*Australian politician*• He was born in Bathurst, New South Wales. Briefly a federal Labor Member of Parliament, he became Treasurer under **John Curtin** in 1941 and Prime Minister in 1945. His administration was marked by the Snowy Mountains hydroelectric project and unsuccessful attempts at a national health plan and nationalization of the airlines and the banks. He was defeated by **Robert Menzies** in 1949.

Child, Julia, *née* **McWilliams** 1912–2004 •*US author and chef*• Born in Pasadena, California, she served in the Office of Strategic Services in Ceylon during World War II, and from 1948 to 1954 she and her diplomat husband lived in Paris, where she studied cooking at the Cordon Bleu. In 1951 she and two French partners, Simone Beck and Louisette Bertholle, founded a cooking school, and in 1961 the three women published the classic cookbook *Mastering the Art of French Cooking*. Child wrote many other cookbooks and hosted a series of public television programs, notably *The French Chef* (1963–76), for which she won an Emmy award in 1966. She cofounded the American Institute of Food and Wine in 1982.

" "

The view of history that we get through the kitchen window is a more gentle view, not of war and politics, but of family and community and sharing.

*1993 In **Memory and Imagination**, PBS TV, August 15.*

Child, Lydia Maria 1802–80 •*US social campaigner, essayist and novelist*• Born in Watertown, Massachusetts, she was a committed campaigner for social and political reform, becoming editor of the *National Anti-Slavery Standard* and publishing many essays on political and social issues. Her book *The History of the Condition of Women in Various Ages and Nations* (1835) suggested women's equal capacity in the workplace, and *An Appeal in Favor of That Class of Americans Called Africans* (1833) was particularly influential for the abolitionist cause. She also published several novels including *Hobomok* (1824), describing the conflict between the Puritans and Native American tribes in the Massachusetts Bay Colony, and *A Romance of the Republic* (1867), a 19th-century antislavery story.

Childe, (Vere) Gordon 1892–1957 •*Australian archaeologist*• He was born in Sydney. Educated at Sydney University and Oxford, he established a reputation with his first book, *The Dawn of European Civilization* (1925), a brilliant and erudite work that charted the prehistoric development of Europe. With *The Most Ancient Near East* (1928) and *The Danube in Prehistory* (1929) it established him as the most influential archaeological theorist of his generation.

Childers, (Robert) Erskine 1870–1922 •*Anglo-Irish writer and nationalist*• Born in London and educated at Haileybury and Trinity College, Cambridge, he served as a volunteer in the Second Boer War (1899–1902). He wrote a popular spy novel about a German invasion of Britain, *The Riddle of the Sands* (1903) and several nonfiction works. In 1910 he devoted himself to working for Irish Home Rule, and used his yacht to bring German arms to the Irish volunteers in 1914. Nonetheless he served in the Royal Navy in World War I. In 1921 he became a Sinn Fein member of the Irish parliament for County Wicklow and Minister for Propaganda. He then joined the IRA, but was captured by the Free State authorities and executed in Dublin. One of his sons, Erskine Hamilton Childers (1905–74), became the fourth President of Ireland (1973–74).

Childs, Lucinda 1940– •*US dancer and choreographer*• Born in New York City, she studied dance at Sarah Lawrence College, and then later trained with **Merce Cunningham**. A founding member of the experimental Judson Dance Theater (1962–64), she developed a minimalist style of choreography, often incorporating dialogue. In 1976 she performed her own solo material in the **Robert Wilson** and **Philip Glass** opera *Einstein on the Beach. Dance 1–5* was set to a 90-minute score by Philip Glass and film by sculptor and painter Sol le Witt. Other works include *Relative Calm* (1981) and *Premier Orage* (1984), the year she put her choreography on *pointe* for the first time, as well as *Rhythm Plus* (1991) and *One and One* (1992). In 1995 she directed the opera *Zaïde*, and in 1999 worked on Verdi's *Macbeth* for the Scottish Opera.

Chinese Gordon *See* **Gordon, Charles George**

Chippendale, Thomas 1718–79 •*English furniture designer*• Born in Otley, Yorkshire, he set up a workshop in St Martin's Lane, London, in 1753. He earned a reputation for graceful neoclassical furniture, especially chairs, which he made mostly from mahogany, then newly introduced from South America. His book *The Gentleman and Cabinet Maker's Director* (1754), the first comprehensive trade catalog of its kind, had a widespread influence on later craftsmen like **George Hepplewhite** and **Thomas Sheraton**. His son Thomas (1749–1822) carried on his business until 1813.

Chirac, Jacques René 1932– •*French Conservative politician*• Born in Paris, he graduated from the École Nationale d'Administration. In 1967 he was elected to the National Assembly and during the presidency of **Georges Pompidou** (1969–74) served as a junior secretary in the finance ministry, then as Minister for Agriculture and later Minister for Industry. Between 1974 and 1976 he was Prime Minister to President **Valéry Giscard d'Estaing**, but the relationship was uneasy. On resigning as Prime Minister in August 1976, Chirac went on to establish the new neo-Gaullist Rassemblement (Rally) pour la République (RPR). He emerged as the National Assembly leader for the right coalition during the Socialist administration of 1981–86. Following the right coalition's victory in the 1986 National Assembly elections, Chirac was appointed Prime Minister by President **François Mitterrand** in a unique "cohabitation" experiment. However, he was subsequently defeated by Mitterrand in the presidential election of 1988. His third attempt to win the presidency at last succeeded in May 1995. During his period of administration he was harshly criticized for his decision to test nuclear weapons in the Pacific Ocean. From 1997 to 2002 he had to work with Socialist Prime Minister, **Lionel Jospin**, whom he had defeated in the presidential election in 1995. Jospin resigned when Chirac won a second term as President in 2002, having himself been knocked out of the presidential campaign.

Chirico, Giorgio de 1888–1978 •*Italian artist*• Born in Volo, Greece, of Sicilian parents, he worked in Paris and with **Carlo Carrà** in Italy, where he helped found the *Valori plastici* review in 1918. About 1910 he began to produce a series of dreamlike pictures of deserted squares, such as *Nostalgia of the Infinite* (1911, in the Museum of Modern Art, New York). These had considerable influence on the surrealists, with whom he exhibited in Paris in 1925. His work after 1915 included semiabstract geometric figures and stylized horses. In 1929 he wrote *Hebdomeros*, a dream novel, but in the 1930s he renounced all his previous work and reverted to an academic style and to a study of the techniques of the old masters. He published his autobiography, *Memorie della mia vita*, in 1945.

Chisholm, Caroline 1808–77 •*Australian social worker and philanthropist*• Born near Northampton, England, she married an officer in the army of the East India Company, based in Madras. In 1838 they settled in Windsor, New South Wales. Concerned at the plight of abandoned and impoverished immigrant women in the colony, Caroline Chisholm established an office to provide shelter for the new arrivals, and then set about finding them work. In the 1840s she cared for over 11,000 women and children, thereby helping to alleviate the overcrowding in Sydney. She persuaded the British government to grant free passage to families of convicts already transported, and established the Family Colonization Loan Society, to which in 1852 the New South Wales government voted £10,000 for her work.

Chissano, Joaquim Alberto 1939– •*Mozambique politician*• Born in Chibuto, he joined the National Front for the Liberation of Mozambique (Frelimo) during the campaign for independence in the early 1960s and became secretary to its leader, **Samora Machel**. When internal self-government was granted in 1974 he was appointed Prime Minister. He then served under Machel as Foreign Minister, and on Machel's death in 1986 he succeeded him as President. He then won the first presidential election in 1994 and was reelected in 1999.

Ch'iu Chin *See* **Qiu Jin**

Chlodwig *See* **Clovis**

Choiseul, Étienne François, Duc de 1719–85 •*French politician*• A minister of **Louis XV**, he served in the War of the Austrian Succession (1740–48), and became lieutenant general in 1748, and Duc de Choiseul in 1758. He arranged the alliance between France and Austria against **Frederick the Great** (1756), and obtained good terms for France at the end of the Seven Years' War (1763). He improved the army and navy and developed industry and trade, particularly with India. He had spies in every court, and **Catherine the Great** nicknamed him *Le Cocher de l'Europe* ("Europe's Coachman").

Chomsky, (Avram) Noam 1928– •*US linguist and political activist*• Born in Philadelphia, he studied under Zellig S Harris at the University of Pennsylvania, and then went to Harvard. In 1955 he began teaching modern languages and linguistics at MIT, becoming a full professor in 1961, Ferrari P Ward Professor of Foreign Languages and Linguistics in 1966, and Institute Professor in 1976. He is one of the founders of transformational generative grammar, and his book *Syntactic Structures* (1957) began a revolution in the field of linguistics. He views language and other facets of human cognitive behavior as being the result of innate cognitive structures built into the mind, and is strongly critical of empiricism. Among his other major works on linguistic theory are *Aspects of the Theory of Syntax* (1965), *Reflections on Language* (1975), *The Logical Structure of Linguistic Theory* (1975), *Language and Problems of Knowledge* (1987), and *The Minimalist Program* (1995). Politically radical, he was an outspoken opponent of American military involvement in Vietnam, and published *American Power and the New Mandarins* (1969) and *At War with Asia* (1970). He has continued his critiques of American policy in such works as *Deterring Democracy* (1991) and *Powers and Prospects* (1996), and has also written on the Israeli-Palestinian conflict in *The Fateful Triangle* (1983, updated 1999). In *Manufacturing Consent: The Political Economy of the Mass Media* (1988, with Edward S Herman) he outlines a theory of how the media functions to silence or marginalize dissident opinion.

Chopin, Frédéric François 1810–49 •*Polish composer and pianist*• Born in Zelazowa Wola, near Warsaw, where his father, a Frenchman, had settled, he first played in public at the age of 8, and published his first work, *Rondo in C minor*, at 15. From 1826 to 1829 he studied at the Warsaw Conservatory, then visited Vienna and Paris (1831). On a groundwork of Slavonic airs and rhythms, notably that of the mazurka, Chopin wrote clearly identifiable music, mainly for the piano. His compositions include 50 mazurkas, 27 études, 25 preludes, 19 nocturnes, 13 waltzes, 12 polonaises, 4 ballades, 3 impromptus, 3 sonatas, 2 piano concertos, and a funeral march. In 1836 he met **George Sand**, and lived with her from 1838 to 1847, when they became estranged. He died from tuberculosis.

Chopin, Katherine, *née* **O'Flaherty** 1851–1904 •*US novelist, short-story writer and poet*• Born in St Louis, Missouri, the daughter of an Irish immigrant and a French-Creole mother, she was well educated at the Sacred Heart convent, made her debut in society and married Oscar Chopin, a Creole cotton trader from Louisiana. After her husband died of swamp fever (1882) she returned with their six children to St Louis where she began to compose sketches of her life in "Old Natchitoches," such as *Bayou Folk* (1894) and *A Night in Acadie* (1897). This work gives no indication of the furor she was later to arouse with the publication of a realistic novel of sexual passion, *The Awakening* (1899), which was harshly condemned by the public. Interest in her work was revived by **Edmund Wilson**, and she has since been embraced by feminists as a fin de siècle iconoclast bravely articulating the plight of the "lost" woman.

“ ”

The past was nothing to her ... The future was a mystery which she never attempted to penetrate. The present alone was significant.

1899 ***The Awakening****, chapter 15.*

Chosroes or **Khosrow I**, *called* **Anushirvan ("Immortal Soul")** d. 579 •*Sassanid king of Persia*• He ruled Persia (Iran) from 531 and waged war against the Roman Emperor **Justinian I** for 20 years. At home he promoted agriculture, commerce and science.

Chosroes or **Khosrow II**, *called* **Parviz ("the Victorious")** d. 628 •*Sassanid king of Persia*• The grandson of **Chosroes I**, he became king in c. 588 and conquered Syria, Palestine, Egypt and parts of Asia Minor (613–19), and almost defeated the Byzantine Empire. However, the Emperor **Heraclius** led a recovery and penetrated Persia (Iran), defeating Chosroes at Nineveh (627), after which he was deposed and executed by his son, Kavadh.

Chou En-lai *See* **Zhou Enlai**

Chow, Elizabeth Kuanghu *See* **Han Suyin**

Chow Yun-Fat 1956– •*Chinese actor*• He was born on Lamma Island, Hong Kong. His first major film was *The Story of Woo Viet* (1981) and in 1986 he began a partnership with the action-film director **John Woo**, making hugely successful films for the Chinese market such as *The Killer* (1989) and *Hard Boiled* (1992). His Hollywood debut was *The Replacement Killers* (1998) and he went on to star with Michelle Yeoh in *Crouching Tiger, Hidden Dragon* (2000).

Chrétien, Jean Joseph Jacques 1934– •*Canadian politician*• A French Catholic, born in Shawinigan, Quebec, he studied law at Laval University, Quebec City, and was first elected to parliament in 1963, holding several ministerial positions in the next two decades. He opposed the Quebec separatist movement and was instrumental in securing the new Canadian constitution in 1982. A member of the Liberal Party, he was prime minister from 1993 to 2003. In 1995 he responded to renewed Quebec separatist sentiment by proposing to give the province greater autonomy within the Canadian federation.

Chrétien de Troyes d. c. 1183 •*French poet and troubadour*• Born in Troyes, he was author of the earliest romances dealing with the King **Arthur** legend. He was a member of the court of the Countess Marie de Champagne, daughter of **Louis VII**, to whom he dedicated his *Yvain et Lancelot*. His other romances were *Érec et Énide* (c. 1160), *Cligès* (c. 1164), and the unfinished *Perceval, ou le conte du Graal* (c. 1180, "Percival, or the Story of the Holy Grail").

Christensen, Harold 1904–89, **Lew** 1909–84 and **Willam** 1902–2001 •*US dancers*• Born to a family of music and dance teachers in Utah, all three toured as children in vaudeville, performing classical dance. In 1932 Willam opened a ballet school in Portland, Oregon, from which emerged the Portland Ballet. In 1938 he became ballet master and choreographer of the San Francisco Opera Ballet, choreographing the first full-length US productions of *Coppelia*, *Swan Lake* and *The Nutcracker*. In 1951 he established in Salt Lake City the first dance department at a US university and, in the following year, the Utah Ballet (since 1968, Ballet West). Harold, having danced for various companies on both coasts of the US, retired from the stage in 1946 and took charge of the San Francisco Ballet School until 1975. As a member of the American Ballet, Lew was cast as the first US Apollo in **George Balanchine**'s ballet of the same name. In the mid-1940s he was on the faculties of the School of American Ballet and New York City Ballet. In the 1950s he replaced Willam as director and choreographer of the San Francisco Opera Ballet.

Christian I 1426–81 •*King of Denmark, of Norway and of Sweden*• The founder of the Oldenburg royal line, he was the son of Dietrich, Count of Oldenburg, and Hedvig, heiress of Schleswig and Holstein. Improvident and spendthrift, he maintained a splendid court in Copenhagen, but was chronically short of money; to provide part of a dowry for the marriage of his daughter Margaret to **James III** of Scotland, he mortgaged Orkney and Shetland—a pledge that was never redeemed. In Denmark he founded the University of Copenhagen in 1478. He was succeeded by his son, Johan I (1455–1513).

Christian II 1481–1559 •*King of Denmark and Norway, and of Sweden*• Born in Nyborg, Denmark, he succeeded his father, Johan I, as king of Norway and Denmark from 1513. He overthrew **Sten Sture**, the regent of Sweden, and became king of Sweden (1520), but his treacherous massacre of the leading men of Sweden in the infamous Stockholm Bloodbath (1520) caused such hostility toward him that he was driven out by **Gustav I Vasa** (1523). He was also expelled from Denmark, largely because of his sweeping legal reforms. An attempt to regain his lost territories (1531) was defeated, and he spent his remaining years in prison. His death marked the end of the Kalmar Union (1397–1523) of Denmark, Norway and Sweden.

Christian III 1503–59 •*King of Denmark and Norway*• Born in Gottorp, Schleswig, the son and successor of **Frederik I**, he was an ardent Lutheran, imposed the Reformation on Denmark, Norway and Iceland, and established the Lutheran State Church. His reign began in 1534, during the civil war (1533–36) between the Catholic supporters of the ex-king, **Christian II**, and the Protestant son of Frederik. After the capitulation of Copenhagen (1536), Christian confiscated Church lands, made Denmark more aware of its national identity, and hugely strengthened the monarchy.

Christian IV 1577–1648 •*King of Denmark and Norway*• Born at Frederiksborg Castle, the son of **Frederik II**, he acceded in 1588 and ruled under regents until 1596. Blunt, dissolute and hard-drinking, he won the affection of his nation. He strengthened the Danish navy, encouraged industry, enhanced Copenhagen with magnificent new buildings, and founded new towns, including Christiania (now Oslo). Against his councilors' advice, he invaded Sweden (1611), but failed to capture Stockholm and made peace (1613) by the Treaty of Knäred. In the Thirty Years' War (1618–48) he joined the Protestant Union (1625) to protect Danish and Lutheran interests in North Germany, but was defeated at Lutter (1626). In a second war with Sweden (1643–45), he lost an eye and dominion of the Baltic. He was succeeded by his son, **Frederik III**.

Christian VII 1749–1808 •*King of Denmark and Norway*• Born in Copenhagen, the son and successor (1766) of Frederik V, he married his cousin Caroline Matilda, sister of King **George III** of Great Britain (1766), and toured Europe (1768), accompanied by his court physician, Count Johann Struensee (1737–72). Struensee became the queen's lover and seized effective power, but in 1772 he was charged with treason and executed, while the queen was divorced and exiled to Hanover. The king was judged insane in 1784, and relinquished control to his son, Crown Prince Frederik, who later succeeded as **Frederik VI**.

Christian VIII 1786–1848 •*King of Denmark*• Born in Copenhagen, the son and successor of **Frederik VI**, he was elected king of Norway (1814), but was ousted by **Karl XIV Johan** (Bernadotte) of Sweden. As king of Denmark (from 1839) he allowed freedom of trade with Iceland and revived the ancient Althing (parliament) of Iceland as an Icelandic consultative assembly (1843). He signed an order early in 1848 abolishing monarchical absolutism, which was implemented by his son and successor, **Frederik VII**.

Christian IX 1818–1906 •*King of Denmark*• A prince of Glücksburg, he was born in Gottorp, Schleswig. He became king in 1863 in succession to the childless **Frederik VII**, and was immediately obliged to sign the November Constitution incorporating Schleswig into the Danish kingdom, an act which led to war with Prussia and Austria and the loss of both Schleswig and Holstein (1864). In 1874, on the 1,000th anniversary of the settlement of Iceland, he paid the first royal visit by a reigning monarch, and granted Iceland's first constitution, of limited autonomy under a governor. In Denmark, he presided over the move to full parliamentary government. He was succeeded in 1906 by his elder son as **Frederik VIII**, while his younger son became King **George I** of Greece. His elder daughter, **Alexandra**, married the future King **Edward VII** of Great Britain, and his younger daughter, Mari Dagmar, married the future Czar **Alexander III** of Russia.

Christian X 1870–1947 •*King of Denmark, and of Iceland*• Born in Charlottenlund, the son of **Frederik VIII**, he was revered as a symbol of resistance during the German occupation in World War II. He signed a new constitution granting the vote to women (1915), and in 1918 signed the Act of Union with Iceland which granted Iceland full independence in personal union with the Danish sovereign (this ended in 1944). During World War II he elected to stay on in Denmark under house arrest (1943–45). He was succeeded by his son, **Frederik IX**.

Christian, Charlie (Charles) 1916–42 •*US jazz guitarist*• Remembered as the father of the modern jazz guitar, he was born in Dallas, Texas, and learned to play a homemade "cigar box" guitar as a child. His skill developed to the point where he was hired by bandleader **Benny Goodman** in 1939, playing mainly with the Goodman sextet rather than the big band. Christian pioneered the use of the amplified guitar as a solo instrument, freeing the guitar from a purely rhythmic role. He was one of the musicians who laid the basis of the bebop revolution.

Christian, Fletcher c. 1764–c. 1794 •*English seaman*• Born in Cockermouth, Cumberland, he joined the navy at the age of 18. He was selected by Captain **William Bligh** as first mate on the *Bounty* on a voyage to Tahiti to collect breadfruit plants for the West Indies, and was the ringleader of the mutiny against Bligh in 1789. After the mutiny Christian, along with eight other mutineers, including **John Adams**, took refuge on Pitcairn Island with some Tahitian men and women, where they founded a settlement. Christian was probably killed by the Tahitians, along with three other mutineers.

Christie •*Family of London auctioneers*• The founder of the firm, in 1766, was James (1730–1803), two of whose sons were James (1773–1831), antiquary and auctioneer, and Samuel Hunter (1784–1865), student of magnetism and Professor of Mathematics at Woolwich (1806–50). Samuel's son, Sir William Henry Mahoney (1845–1922), was Astronomer Royal (1881–1910).

Christie, Dame Agatha Mary Clarissa, *pen name also* **Mary Westmacott**, *née* **Miller** 1890–1976 •*English writer*• She was born in Torquay, Devon, and educated at home. Under the surname of her first husband (Colonel Christie, divorced 1928), she wrote more than 70 classic detective novels, including those featuring the popular characters Hercule Poirot, a Belgian detective, and Miss

Jane Marple, a village spinster. Between December 1953 and January 1954, she achieved three concurrent West End productions, *The Spider's Web*, *Witness for the Prosecution* and *The Mousetrap*, which continued its record-breaking run into the 21st century. Her best-known novels are *The Mysterious Affair at Styles* (1920), *The Murder of Roger Ackroyd* (1926), *Murder at the Vicarage* (1930), *Murder on the Orient Express* (1934), *Death on the Nile* (1937), and*And Then There Were None* (1941) and *Curtain* (1975), in which Poirot met his end. She also wrote under the pen name Mary Westmacott.

“ ”

He tapped his forehead. "These little grey cells. It is up to them—as you say over here."

1920 ***The Mysterious Affair at Styles***, *chapter 10.*

Christie, John Reginald Halliday 1898–1953 •*English murderer*• Born in Yorkshire, he was hanged for the murder of his wife, and confessed to the murder by strangulation of five other women. He also confessed to the murder of Mrs Evans, wife of Timothy John Evans, who had lived in the same house. Evans had been convicted and hanged for the murder of his infant daughter in 1950. He had been charged at the same time with the murder of his wife, but the case never came to court. After a special inquiry by the Home Office, and several debates in the House of Commons, no definite conclusion was reached, but there was an increasing body of opinion that Evans was technically innocent and that Christie had killed both Mrs Evans and the child. In 1966 Evans was granted a free pardon. The trial of Christie played an important part in altering legislation affecting the death penalty.

Christie, Julie Frances 1940– •*English actress*• Born in Chukua, Assam, India, she studied at the Central School of Music and Drama and worked in repertory before a television serial, *A for Andromeda* (1962), led to a small film role in *Crooks Anonymous* (1962). Her portrayal of a free spirit in *Billy Liar* (1963) brought further offers and in 1965 she won an Academy Award for *Darling*. Judged to typify "Swinging Sixties" London, she also enjoyed further success with *Dr Zhivago* (1965), *Far From the Madding Crowd* (1967) and *The Go-Between* (1971). Romantically linked with **Warren Beatty**, she costarred with him in *Shampoo* (1975) and *Heaven Can Wait* (1978). Other notable films include *Don't Look Now* (1973) and *Heat and Dust* (1982). Committed to a number of political causes, she has been an infrequent performer in recent years but returned to the stage in *Old Times* (1995) and to film in *Dragonheart* (1996) and *Afterglow* (1997), for which she won an Academy Award nomination.

Christie, Linford 1960– •*English athlete*• He was born in St Andrews, Jamaica, and his family moved to the UK when he was a child. He was educated at Wandsworth Technical College. He made his international debut for Great Britain in 1980 and has since made over 50 appearances, establishing himself as the fastest man outside the US in 1986, the year of his 100-meters victory in the European championships. In 1990 he won a gold medal at the Commonwealth Games. The pinnacle of his career came at the Barcelona Olympics of 1992, when he captained the British men's team and won the 100-meters gold medal. In 1993 he won the 100-meters gold medal in the world championships in Stuttgart.

Christine de Pisan c. 1364–1431 •*French poet*• She was born in Venice, Italy, the daughter of an Italian who was court astrologer to **Charles V**. She was brought up in Paris, and by 1389 was widowed with three children and no money. Obliged to call upon her literary talents, she produced between 1399 and 1415 a number of impressive works in both prose and verse, including a biography of **Charles V**, *Cité des dames* ("City of Women"), and *Livres des trois vertus* ("Books of the Three Virtues"), an educational and social compendium for women. She also wrote love poems. She is noteworthy for her defense of the female sex, hitherto a target for satirists. Saddened by the misfortunes of the Hundred Years War she withdrew to a nunnery about 1418 but wrote in celebration of **Joan of Arc**'s early successes in 1429.

Christo and **Jeanne-Claude**, *originally* **Christo Javacheff** 1935– and **Jeanne-Claude de Guillebon** 1935– •*US avant-garde artists*• Born in Gabrova, Bulgaria, Christo studied art first in Sofia (1951–56), then briefly in Vienna (1957), before moving to Paris in 1958, where he met Jeanne-Claude, his wife and artistic collaborator. In 1964 they moved permanently to New York. Their work typically consists of wrapping objects, buildings, and landscapes in fabric, or of creating "assemblages," for example, of stacked oil drums. Their *Surrounded Islands* (1980–83) transformed eleven small islands off Florida into water lilies using six million square feet of pink fabric. Between 1984 and 1991 they succeeded in linking Japan and the US by means of *The Umbrellas*, an event involving the simultaneous opening of innumerable blue and yellow umbrellas and which survives only in its documentation. Their *Wrapped Reichstag* in 1995 was the biggest piece of artwork of the year involving the covering of the German parliament building with over 1,000,000 square feet of silver fabric and nearly 10 miles of blue rope.

Christophe, Henri, *also known as* **Henri I** 1767–1820 •*Haitian ruler*• Born a slave on the island of Grenada, he joined the Black insurgents in Haiti against the French in 1790, and with his gigantic stature and courage proved an able lieutenant to their leader **Toussaint Louverture**. In 1802 he defended Cape Haiti against the French. In 1806 he assassinated the emperor Jean Jacques I (**Jean Jacques Dessalines**), whose cruelty and debauchery had alienated all his supporters, and in 1807 was appointed President. He was proclaimed king of Haiti as Henri I in 1811, and ruled with enthusiasm, but his own avarice and cruelty led to an insurrection, and he shot himself.

Christopher, St 3rd century AD •*Syrian Christian*• He was, according to tradition, a man some 11 ft 6 in (3.5 m) tall. His name in Greek (*Christophoros*) means "Christ-bearing," which gave rise to the legend that he had carried the Christchild (and all the weight of the world's sin) across a river. He is said to have suffered martyrdom under the emperor **Decius** (c. 250 AD). He is the patron saint of travelers, and his feast day is July 25.

Christopher, Warren Minor 1925– •*US diplomat*• Born in Scranton, North Dakota, he began his career as a lawyer, then entered public service and was deputy Secretary of State in the **Carter** administration (1977–81), helping to negotiate the release of the hostages from Iran in 1981. As Secretary of State (1993–96) under President **Bill Clinton**, he furthered Middle East peace talks and struggled to find a diplomatic solution to the fighting in Bosnia.

Christy, Edwin P(earce) 1815–62 •*US entertainer*• He was born in Philadelphia, and began his Christy Minstrels show in Buffalo (1842), steadily increasing the reputation of his troupe and the success of his "black-face" ministrelsy in New York and London. Many of his songs were commissioned from **Stephen Foster**. Credited with establishing the minstrel show's format, he retired in 1855. He threw himself out of a window during the Civil War.

Chrysippus c. 280–c. 206 BC •*Stoic philosopher*• Born in Soli, Cilicia, Asia Minor, he went to Athens as a youth and studied under **Cleänthes** to become the third and greatest head of the Stoa. Only fragments remain of over 700 works in which he developed the Stoic system into what became its definitive and orthodox form.

Chrysler, Walter Percy 1875–1940 •*US automobile manufacturer*• Born in Wamego, Kansas, he worked his way up to become plant manager with the American Locomotive Company, but left in 1912 to become works manager of Buick Motor Company at half the salary. By 1916 he had become president, but resigned (1919) to become a director of Willys-Overland and Maxwell Motor Company (1921). This became the Chrysler Corporation in 1925. He introduced the Plymouth motor car and designed the first high-compression engine.

Chrysostom, St John c. 347–407 AD •*Syrian churchman and one of the Doctors of the Church*• Born in Antioch, he was named from the Greek meaning "golden-mouthed," due to his eloquence. He spent six years as a monk in the mountains, but illness forced his return in AD 381 to Antioch, where he was ordained. In 398 he was made Archbishop of Constantinople, where he carried out many reforms, but his reproof of vices caused the empress Eudocia (wife of **Arcadius**) to have him deposed and banished (404). His works are *Homilies*, *Commentaries* on the whole Bible, *Epistles*, *Treatises* and *Liturgies*. His feast day is January 27.

Chubb, Charles 1772–1846 •*English locksmith*• Born in London, he patented improvements in "detector" locks, originally (1818) patented by his brother, Jeremiah, of Portsea. He was in the hardware business in Winchester and Portsea, before settling in London. Under his son, John Chubb (1816–72), further patents were taken out.

Chulalongkorn, Phra Paramindr Maha, *also called* **Rama V** 1853–1910 •*King of Siam (Thailand)*• Born in Bangkok, he was the son of King Mongkut, and the model for the best-selling novel *Anna and the King of Siam*, which was subsequently adapted for stage and screen as *The King and I*. He was educated by English teachers, after which he went, as traditionally prescribed, to a Buddhist monastery, where he remained until the age of 20, having ceremonially succeeded his father (1868). His ambitious structural reforms reduced arbitrary government and provincial autonomy, and he introduced conscription and compulsory primary education, abolished slavery, freed his subjects from approaching him on hands and knees, proclaimed liberty of conscience, built schools, hospitals, roads and railways, and followed his father in extending the armed forces. He sent his crown prince to study in Great Britain, visited Queen **Victoria**, and ultimately paid for his Westernization by being forced to accept treaties with France (weakening his power in Laos and Cambodia) and with Great Britain (removing his rule over four Malayan states).

Chung, Kyung-Wha 1948– •*US violinist*• Born in Seoul, South Korea, she moved to New York in 1960 and studied at the Juilliard School of Music until 1967, when she made her debut with the New York Philharmonic. Her London debut came three years later. Her sister Myung-Wha (1944–) is a distinguished cellist, and her brother Myung-Whun (1953–), a pianist and conductor who was appointed music director of the new Bastille Opera, Paris, in 1989.

Church, Sir Richard, *known as* **the Liberator of Greece** 1785–1873 •*Irish general*• Born in Cork, the son of a Quaker merchant, he ran away from school to join the British army. He served in the British and Neapolitan services in the Mediterranean (1808–09) and with Greek troops (1812–43). He took part in the Greek War of Independence (1821–32), and was appointed generalissimo of the Greek insurgent forces in 1827. He led the revolution in Greece in 1843, and was subsequently promoted to general.

Churchill, Arabella 1648–1730 •*English aristocrat*• She was the elder sister of John Churchill, 1st Duke of **Marlborough**. In 1665 she entered the service of the Duchess of York (**Mary of Modena**), wife of the future **James VII and II**, and soon became James's mistress. She was the mother by James of two daughters and two sons: James Fitzjames (Duke of **Berwick**), and Henry Fitzjames (Duke of Albemarle).

Churchill, Caryl 1938– •*English dramatist*• Born in London, she was educated in Montreal and at Lady Margaret Hall, Oxford, where she began writing plays. Her themes include history, the nature of the female spirit, and the effects upon the individual of living in a capitalist and sexist society. Her work includes *Cloud Nine* (1979), *Top Girls* (1982), *Fen* (1983), *Softcops* (1984), *Serious Money* and *The Skriker* (1993).

Churchill, Charles 1731–64 •*English satirical poet*• Born in Westminster, London, he was educated at St John's College, Cambridge, but ruined his academic career with a clandestine marriage at the age of 17. He was ordained a priest in 1756 but gave up the church in 1763. His *Rosciad* (1761) had already made him famous and *The Apology* (also 1761) was an onslaught on his critics, particularly **Tobias Smollett**. *The Ghost* (1762) ridiculed **Samuel Johnson** and others. For *The Epistle to Hogarth* (1763) the artist retaliated with a savage caricature. Other works include *The Candidate* (1764), *Independence* (1764) and *Dedication*.

Churchill, John *See* **Marlborough, 1st Duke of**

Churchill, Lord Randolph Henry Spencer 1849–95 •*English politician*• Born in Blenheim Palace, he was the third son of the 7th Duke of Marlborough. He entered parliament in 1874, became Secretary for India (1885–86), and for a short while Chancellor of the Exchequer and Leader of the House of Commons. His powers rapidly diminished by syphilis, he resigned after his first budget proved unacceptable, and thereafter devoted little time to politics. He was the father of **Winston Churchill**.

Churchill, Randolph Frederick Edward Spencer 1911–68 •*English journalist*• Born in London, the son of Sir **Winston Churchill**, he was educated at Eton and Christ Church, Oxford. He served in World War II in North Africa and Italy and in the Middle East as an intelligence officer on the general staff. He was Conservative Member of Parliament for Preston (1940–45). He published two volumes (1966, 1967) of a full-length biography of his father.

Churchill, Sarah, Duchess of Marlborough, *née* **Jennings** 1660–1744 •*English aristocrat*• In 1673 she entered the service of the Duke of York (the future **James VII and II**), and became a close friend of his younger daughter, Princess (the future Queen) **Anne**. After the Glorious Revolution of 1688, when **William III** supplanted James II on the throne, she and her husband, John Churchill, 1st Duke of **Marlborough**, tried to draw Anne into Jacobite intrigues for the restoration of her father. After Anne became queen, Sarah, who was beautiful, but fiery and headstrong, dominated her household and the Whig ministry. Queen Anne broke with the Marlboroughs in 1711, and Sarah was replaced by her cousin, Mrs **Abigail Masham**.

Churchill, Sir Winston Leonard Spencer 1874–1965 •*English statesman and Nobel Prize winner*• He was born at Blenheim Palace, Woodstock, the eldest son of Lord **Randolph Churchill**. Educated at Harrow and Sandhurst, he was commissioned in the 4th Queen's Own Hussars in 1895. He served in the 1897 Malakand and 1898 Nile campaigns and, as a London newspaper correspondent in the Boer War, was captured but escaped with a £25 reward offered for his recapture. In 1900 he entered parliament as a Conservative MP, but crossed the floor of the House to join the Liberal majority in 1904. He was appointed Colonial Under-Secretary, and as President of the Board of Trade (1908–10) he introduced labor exchanges. As Home Secretary (1910), he witnessed the famous Siege of Sidney Street, and as First Lord of the Admiralty from 1910 began strengthening Great Britain's army and navy in preparation for the war with Germany that he foresaw. He succeeded in rebuilding his reputation after the disastrous Dardanelles expedition of 1915, and **David Lloyd George** appointed him Minister of Munitions in 1917. He was Secretary of State for War and Air from 1919 to 1921, but then found himself out of favor and excluded from the Cabinet. His warnings of the rising Nazi threat in the mid-1930s and his criticisms of the national government's lack of preparedness for war went unheeded, but in 1940 **Neville Chamberlain** at last stepped down and Churchill began his "walk with destiny" as Prime Minister of the coalition that was to see the country through five of the most momentous years in its history. Churchill's compassion and his loathing of the scale of Allied casualties made him impatient for that victory, and in the course of four years he traveled thousands of miles, shaped the 1941 Atlantic Charter, drew an initially reluctant American people into the battle, masterminded the strategy adopted for the Battle of Britain, Alamein and the North African campaign, and, after the enemy had been defeated, contrived with **Franklin D Roosevelt** and **Joseph Stalin** the means of gutting Germany's historic status as an epicenter of territorial ambition. In the general election of 1945 Churchill was rejected by the British electorate; but by 1951, at the age of 77, he was Prime Minister again. He set about reconstructing a country economically and physically ravaged by war, and when in 1955 he finally relinquished the premiership to **Anthony Eden** at the age of 81, its postwar recovery was nearly complete. He achieved a world reputation not only as a great strategist and inspiring war leader, but as a classic orator with a supreme command of English, a talented painter, and a writer with a great breadth of mind and a profound sense of history. His published works include *Great Contemporaries* (1937), *History of the Second World War* (6 vols, 1948–54), and *A History of the English Speaking Peoples* (1956–58). In 1953 he was knighted and awarded the Nobel Prize for literature.

“ ”

You ask what is our aim. I can answer in one word—victory. Victory at all costs, victory in spite of all terror, victory, however long and hard the road may be.

1939 Radio broadcast, October 1.

Churriguera, Don José 1650–1725 •*Spanish architect*• Born in Salamanca, he was royal architect to **Charles II** and developed the extravagant style which has come down to us as Churrigueresque. He designed Salamanca Cathedral. His brothers Joaquin (1674–1720) and Alberto (1676–1750) were also architects.

Chu Teh *See* **Zhu De**

Chuter-Ede, Baron *See* **Ede (of Epsom), Baron Chuter**

Ciano, Galeazzo, Conte di Cortellazzo 1903–44 •*Italian politician and diplomat*• Born in Livorno, Tuscany, the son of an admiral, he took part in the march on Rome and had a successful diplomatic career from 1925 to 1930, when, after marrying **Mussolini**'s daughter, he was rapidly promoted, becoming Foreign Minister (1936). He negotiated the Axis Agreement with Germany and supported the Italian invasion of Albania (1939) and the Balkans (1940–41), but was unenthusiastic about the invasion of France. Dismissed as Foreign Minister (February 1943), Ciano was one of those who called for the Duce's resignation in July 1943. He fled to Germany after his father-in-law's arrest but was blamed by the Nazis for Mussolini's defeat and was executed.

Cibber, Mrs, *née* **Susannah Maria Arne** 1714–66 •*English actress and singer*• She was born in London, the sister of the composer **Thomas Arne**. An accomplished contralto, she made her stage debut in her brother's *Rosamund* (1733), and the following year married Theophilus Cibber (1703–58), the son of **Colley Cibber**. Thereafter she turned to drama and played opposite **David Garrick** at Drury Lane with enormous success.

Cibber, Colley 1671–1757 •*English actor and dramatist*• He was born in London and educated at Grantham School, Lincolnshire. In 1690 he joined the Theatre Royal in Drury Lane, and there, except for short intervals, spent his whole career. His first comedy, *Love's Last Shift* (1696), established his fame both as dramatist and actor. From 1711 he was joint manager of Drury Lane. In 1730 he was appointed poet laureate. *An Apology for the Life of Mr Colley Cibber, Comedian* (1740), his autobiography, gives a vivid picture of the theater of his time.

Cicero, Marcus Tullius 106–43 BC •*Roman orator, statesman and man of letters*• He was born at Arpinum in Latium into a wealthy equestrian family. At Rome he studied law and oratory, Greek philosophy, and Greek literature. He embarked on a political career and in 63 he held the consulship, and foiled the plot of **Catilina** after the elections of 62. The Senate voted the death penalty for the conspirators, and Cicero had the sentence carried out immediately. Cicero was, for a brief time, the great man of the day. His great political ambition, not achieved, was the "harmony of the orders" (*concordia ordinum*, i.e., of the senatorial and equestrian classes). Then the tide turned against him. In 59 Cicero had declined an invitation to join the triumvirate of Pompey, **Caesar** and **Crassus**. He was now without real support, and his enemies exploited the situation by accusing him of having violated the constitution, since a Roman citizen could not be put to death except by the sentence of the people in regular assembly. Cicero took refuge at Thessalonica (58), but in 57 the people, with Pompey's support, had almost unanimously voted his recall. In his subsequent speeches he tried to secure compensation for himself and his supporters, but he was no longer a power in politics; nervously sensitive to the fluctuations of public opinion, he could not decide between Pompey and the aristocracy and **Caesar** and the new democracy. He lived in retirement in Rome (46–44), where he wrote most of his chief works on rhetoric and philosophy and brooded over his disappointments. In 43, after Caesar's death, his famous speeches against **Marcus Antonius**, the *Philippics*, were delivered, and cost him his life. As soon as Antony, Octavian and **Lepidus** had formed a second triumvirate, they proscribed their enemies, and Cicero's name was high on the list. Old and feeble, he fled to his villa at Formiae, pursued by the soldiers of Antony, and was overtaken as he was being carried in a litter. With calm courage he put his head out of the litter and bade the murderers strike. As orator and pleader Cicero stands in the first rank; of his speeches the most famous are those against Verres and Catilina; equally fine is his speech in defense of Milo. As a politician, though in the end defeated, he was one of the outstanding figures of the late Republic. He is also remembered as an essayist and letter writer, especially for his essays *De senectute* ("On Old Age"), *De amicitia* ("On Friendship") and *De officiis* ("On Duty"). His extensive correspondence (notably with Atticus) is one of the principal sources of knowledge of the politics of his time (in some years we are told of events from day to day), and his prose style was a model for the orators of the next four centuries.

“ ”

O fortunatam natam me consule Romam!

O lucky Rome, born when I was consul!

His only extant line of poetry, quoted in Juvenal, ***Satires*** *10, l. 122.*

Cid, El, *properly* **Rodrigo** or **Ruy Díaz de Vivar** or **Bivar**, *also called* **El Campeador** c. 1043–99 •*Spanish hero*• He was born in Burgos and immortalized as "El Cid" (The Lord) or "El Campeador" (The Champion). Both soldier of fortune and patriot, he was constantly fighting. In 1081 he was banished and served both Spaniards and Moors. He besieged and captured Valencia from the Moors (1093–94) and became its ruler. He has inspired many legends, poems, and ballads, as well as **Corneille**'s *Le Cid* (1636).

Cidenas 4th century BC •*Babylonian astronomer*• The head of an astronomical school at Sippra, he discovered the precession of the equinoxes.

Cilento, Lady Phyllis Dorothy, *née* **McGlew** 1894–1987 •*Australian medical practitioner, author and broadcaster*• Born in Sydney, she was educated at Adelaide University and became lecturer in child rearing and obstetrical physical therapy at the University of Queensland. Her life's work, for which she was awarded the Member of the Order of Australia, was devoted to family planning, childbirth education, and nutrition, on which subjects she broadcast and wrote many books and newspaper columns.

Cimabué, Giovanni c. 1240–c. 1302 •*Italian painter*• Born in Florence, he is famous chiefly as the teacher of **Giotto**, and was the first artist to move away from the stylized and rigid conventions of Byzantine art. Early critics attribute the famous *Rucellai Madonna* to him, but this is now generally believed to be by **Duccio**. Cimabué is known to have been in Rome in 1272 and is documented as having worked on the mosaic figure of Saint John in the apse of Pisa Cathedral in 1302. He also executed several important works in the Lower Church of San Francesco at Assisi.

Cimon c. 507–c. 450 BC •*Athenian soldier and politician*• His father was **Miltiades** the Younger, the conqueror at Marathon. He fought at the Battle of Salamis (480 BC) and from 476 was in supreme command of the Delian League in the patriotic struggle against the Persians. He is most famous for his destruction of a Persian fleet and army at the River Eurymedon (c. 476). He led an unsuccessful expedition to support the Spartans during the Helot uprising in 462, and was dismissed and ostracized in 461, recalled in 454. He died at the siege of a town in Cyprus.

Cincinnatus, Lucius Quinctius fl. 460 BC •*Roman soldier*• He was a favorite hero of the old Roman republic. In 460 BC he was made consul, and two years later dictator. The story goes that when the messengers came to tell Cincinnatus of his new dignity they found him plowing his farm. He rescued the consul Minucius, who had been defeated and surrounded by the Aequi, and 16 days later he laid down his dictatorship and returned to his farm.

Cineas d. 270 BC •*Greek politician*• He was born in Thessaly. The friend and minister of **Pyrrhus**, the king of Epyrus, he was said to be the most eloquent man of his time.

Cione, Andrea del *See* **Verrocchio, Andrea del**

Citroën, André Gustave 1878–1935 •*French engineer and motor manufacturer*• Born in Paris, he was responsible for the mass production of armaments during World War I. After the war he applied these techniques to the manufacture of low-priced small cars. In 1934 he became bankrupt and lost control of the company which still bears his name.

Cixi (Tz'u Hsi), *known as* **the Old Buddha** 1835–1908 •*Dowager empress of China*• The daughter of a minor Manchu mandarin, she was presented as a concubine to the Manchu Emperor Xianfeng (Hsien-Feng) and on his death (1861) became regent, initially to her infant son, Tongzhi (T'ung-chih), and then, following his death (1874), to her nephew Guangxu (Kuang-hsü), despite a dynastic custom which forbade women to reign. A conservative force within the Chinese court and an inveterate intriguer, she remained dominant even after Guangxu (1871–1908) formally assumed imperial power (1889) and from 1898, after the emperor had attempted to promote far-reaching reform, she confined him to the palace. In 1900 she helped foment the antiforeigner Boxer agitation, and a day before her own death, some claim that she organized the murder of Guangxu.

Claiborne, Craig 1920–2000 •*US food critic and writer on cooking*• Born in Sunflower, Mississippi, he was food editor of the *New York Times* and published books on cooking such as *Craig Claiborne's Memorable Meals* (1985).

Claiborne, Liz 1929– •*US fashion designer*• Born in Brussels, Belgium, she studied fine art in Belgium and France before moving to the US and winning a *Harper's Bazaar* design competition. Turning to fashion design, she worked with Omar Kiam in New York City before founding her own company with her husband in 1976. Her medium-priced, ready-to-wear collections, targeted at working women, have made her company one of the largest and most successful womenswear firms in the world.

Clair, René, *pseudonym of* **René Lucien Chomette** 1898–1981 •*French film director*• Born in Paris, he established his reputation with avant-garde films like *Paris qui dort* (1923, *The Crazy Ray*) and *Entr'acte* (1924), and developed a gift for ironic, light comedy in a string of successful films made in France, and later in the US, including *La proie du vent* (1927, "Prey of the Wind"), *Un chapeau de paille d'Italie* (1927, *The Italian Straw Hat*), *Paris* (1930), *The Ghost Goes West* (1935) and *It Happened Tomorrow* (1944). He returned to France in 1946, and his final film was *Les fêtes galantes* (1965).

Clapton, Eric 1945– •*English rock and blues guitarist*• Born in London, he was once identified as "God" by worshipful fans, but is rarely comfortable with the limelight. He publicly concurred with **Enoch Powell**'s controversial views on immigration at a difficult point in his career, but he has been one of the most significant white exponents of Black music, particularly the blues. He began his recording career with The Yardbirds and John Mayall's Bluesbreakers, before forming the enormously influential power trio Cream, with Jack Bruce and Ginger Baker. After a number of lower-key ventures, he briefly retired, overcame heroin addiction, and returned with the laid-back *461 Ocean Boulevard* (1974), which established his subsequent middle-of-the-road style. In 1994, he returned to a straight blues idiom on his *From the Cradle* project, and later collaborated with **B B King** on *Riding with the King* (2000). He was given the honorary title Officer, Order of the British Empire, in 1995.

Clare, St 1194–1253 •*Italian Christian saint*• Born in Assisi, she became a follower of St **Francis of Assisi** at 18. With him and her younger sister she founded the order of Poor Ladies of San Damiano ("Poor Clares," formerly called "Minoresses"). She was canonized in 1255, and in 1958 she was designated patron saint of television by Pope **Pius XII** on the grounds that at Christmas 1252, when she was in her cell at San Damiano, she "saw and heard Mass being held in the Church of St Francis at Assisi. She was the elder sister of **St Agnes**. Her feast day is August 11.

Clare, Anthony Ward 1942– •*Irish psychiatrist and broadcaster*• Born in Dublin, he studied at Gonzaga and University Colleges, Dublin. He began his psychiatric career at Maudsley Hospital, London (1970–75), later undertaking a career in lecturing and research, and becoming Clinical Professor of Psychiatry at Trinity College, Dublin (1989–). His work for radio as a writer and broadcaster includes such long-running series as *In the Psychiatrist's Chair* (1982–) and *All in the Mind* (1988–). He has published widely.

Clare, John 1793–1864 •*English peasant poet*• Born in Helpston, Northamptonshire, he was almost without schooling, but studied **James Thomson**'s *Seasons*, and then began to write verse. After serving in the Northamptonshire militia (1812–14), he published *Poems Descriptive of Rural Life* (1820), which were well received. His other published works were *Village Minstrel* (1821), *The Shepherd's Calendar* (1827) and *Rural Muse* (1835). He lived in poverty, became insane, and died in an asylum.

“ ”

The present is the funeral of the past,
And man the living sepulchre of life.

1845 "The present is the funeral of the past."

Clarence, George, Duke of 1449–78 •*English nobleman*• Born in Dublin, Ireland, he was the third son of Richard, Duke of **York**, and brother of **Edward IV** and **Richard III**. He was created Duke of Clarence on Edward's accession (1461). He married Isabella, elder daughter of Richard Neville, Earl of **Warwick**, against Edward's wishes (1469), and supported Warwick against his brother in the brief restoration of **Henry VI** (1470), but deserted to his brother's side (1471). In 1478 he was impeached by his brothers for treason, and secretly executed. According to tradition, he was put to death in the Tower of London, drowned in a butt of malmsey wine. Despite his traditionally bad historical reputation, he had many of the good qualities of his time.

Clarendon, Edward Hyde, 1st Earl of 1609–74 •*English statesman*• Born in Dinton, near Salisbury, he sat in the Short Parliament of 1640 and the Long Parliament, where he criticized **Charles I**'s unconstitutional actions. In 1641 he broke with the revolutionaries and became a royal adviser. On the king's defeat in 1646 he joined Prince Charles (later **Charles II**) in Jersey, and in 1651 he became chief adviser to Charles II in exile. After the Restoration he was created Earl of Clarendon. He further increased his influence by marrying his daughter Anne to the Duke of York in 1660. He introduced the "Clarendon Code" to ensure the supremacy of the Church of England but his moderate policies were opposed by the extremists. He lost the confidence of Charles II when he criticized his private life, and the disasters of 1667, when the Dutch sailed up the Medway, confirmed his downfall. He was exiled to Rouen, where he died, but was buried in Westminster Abbey, London.

Clarendon, George William Frederick Villiers, 4th Earl of 1800–70 •*English politician*• Born in London, he studied at Cambridge. In 1833 he was appointed ambassador in Madrid, where he employed his great influence in helping Espartero to establish a constitutional government. In 1838 he succeeded his uncle as 4th Earl, and in 1840 was made Lord Privy Seal under Viscount **Melbourne**. When the Whigs fell (1841) he became an active member of the Opposition, but supported Sir **Robert Peel** and his own brother, **Charles Pelham Villiers**, in the abolition of the Corn Laws. He became president of the Board of Trade under Lord **John Russell** in 1846 and from 1847 to 1852 was Irish viceroy. Secretary of State for Foreign Affairs (1853), he incurred the responsibility for the Crimean War, and John Roebuck's resolution in 1855 cost him his office, which he resumed at Lord **Palmerston**'s request. He was Foreign Secretary again in 1865 and 1868.

Clark, Helen Elizabeth 1950– •*New Zealand politician*• She was born in Hamilton, and studied at Auckland University, initially choosing a career as a university lecturer (1973–81). She became a Labour Member of Parliament in 1981, and after holding several ministerial posts became deputy Prime Minister (1989–90), deputy Leader of the Opposition (1990–93), Leader of the Opposition (1993–99) and Prime Minister (1999–).

Clark, Jim (James) 1936–68 •*Scottish racecar driver*• Born in Berwickshire, and educated at Loretto School in Musselburgh, he won his first auto race in 1956, and became Scottish Speed Champion in 1958 and 1959. In 1960 he joined the Lotus team as a Formula One driver, and thereafter won the world championship in 1963 and 1965. Also in 1965 he became the first non-American since 1916 to win the Indianapolis 500. Of his 72 Grand Prix races, he won 25, breaking the record of 24 held by **Juan Fangio**. He was killed during a practice for a Formula Two race at Hockenheim, in Germany.

Clark, Joe (Charles Joseph) 1939– •*Canadian politician*• Born in High River, Alberta, he was educated at Alberta and Dalhousie universities. He was elected to the Federal Parliament in 1972 and four years later became leader of the Progressive Conservative Party (PCP). He defeated **Pierre Trudeau** in 1979 to become Canada's youngest Prime Minister, but was himself defeated a year later. In 1983 he was replaced as party leader by **Brian Mulroney** who, as Prime Minister in 1984, made Clark Secretary of State for External Affairs. In the last two years of the Mulroney administration he was Minister for Constitutional Affairs. Retiring from politics, from 1993 to 1996 he was the UN representative for Cyprus. In 1998 he returned as leader of the PCP, and was elected to the House of Commons in 2000.

Clark, Kenneth Mackenzie Clark, Baron 1903–83 •*English art historian*• Educated at Winchester and Trinity College, Oxford, he worked in Florence and became an authority on Italian Renaissance art, capping a distinguished teaching career as Professor of Art History at the Royal Academy (1977–83). A noted administrator, he was also chairman of the Arts Council (1953–60) and of the Independent Television Authority (1954–57). He wrote several books, including studies on **Leonardo da Vinci** (1935, 1939) and **Piero Della Francesca** (1951), and two surveys, *Landscape into Art* (1949) and *The Nude* (1955). He achieved fame with his pioneering television series, *Civilization* (1969), which stimulated widespread popular interest in art.

Clark, Mark Wayne 1896–1984 •*US soldier*• He was born in Maddison Barracks, New York, and graduated from West Point in 1917. He was deputy to General **Eisenhower** for the invasion of North Africa, and prior to the Allied landings in North Africa he was secretly landed in Algeria to make contact with friendly French officials, narrowly escaping capture by the Vichy Security Police. He commanded the 5th Army at the Salerno landing (1943) and Anzio, and the capture of Rome (1944), and was much criticized for choosing the latter instead of encircling the German forces. He commanded the US 6th Army in the Far East (1947–49), and relieved **Mathew B Ridgway** in command of UN forces in Korea (1952–53).

Clark, Michael 1962– •*Scottish dancer and choreographer*• Born near Aberdeen, he went to the Royal Ballet School in London at 13, going on to dance with the Royal Ballet and the Ballet Rambert, then with **Karole Armitage** in the US, starting his own company there in 1984. His original style incorporates punk, 1960s fantasy, nudity, video, platform shoes and giant hamburgers, but it is his keen, sculptural choreography which makes him one of the most inventive artists today. Major full-length productions include *No Fire Escape in Hell* (1986), *Because We Must* (1987) and *Mmm ... Modern Masterpiece* (1992). He appeared as Caliban in **Peter Greenaway**'s film *Prospero's Books* (1991). He retired from dance in the mid-1990s but returned in 1998 and later toured with *current/see*.

Clark, Petula, *originally* **Sally Owen** 1932– •*English singer and actress*• Born in Epsom, Surrey, she was a child singer, entertaining the troops during World War II, and had her own radio series, *Pet's Parlour* (1943). She made her film debut in *Medal for the General* (1944) and her many subsequent film appearances include *The Card* (1952) and *Goodbye, Mr Chips* (1969). She became one of Britain's most successful pop singers, earning 10 gold records, two Grammy awards and enjoying a string of international hits with such songs as "Downtown" in 1964 and "My Love" in 1966. Her stage work includes *The Sound of Music* (1981), *Someone Like You* (1987), which she cowrote, and *Sunset Boulevard* (1995), which opened in London and then toured the US (1998–2000). She was given the honorary title of Commander, Order of the British Empire, in 1998.

Clark, William 1770–1838 •*US explorer*• Born in Caroline County, Virginia, he joined the army in 1789, and was appointed joint leader with **Meriwether Lewis** of the successful transcontinental expedition to the Pacific coast and back (1804–06). He later became superintendent of Indian affairs in Louisiana Territory, and then governor of Missouri Territory.

Clarke, Sir Arthur C(harles) 1917– •*English science-fiction writer*• Born in Minehead, Somerset, he worked in scientific research before turning to fiction: he was a radar instructor in World War II, and originated the idea of satellite communication in a scientific article in 1945. A prolific writer, he focuses on themes of exploration—in both the near and distant future—and humanity's position in the universe, and is the author of some of science fiction's classic works, including *Rendezvous with Rama* (1973) and *The Fountains of Paradise* (1979). However, his name will always be associated first with *2001: A Space Odyssey* (1968), which, under the direction of **Stanley Kubrick**, became a highly successful film. He emigrated to Sri Lanka in the 1950s and since 1979 has been Chancellor of the country's Moratuwa University. He was knighted in 1998.

Clarke, Frank Wigglesworth 1847–1931 •*US geochemist*• Born in Boston and educated at Harvard, he became Professor of Chemistry and Physics, first at Howard University (1873–74) and then at the University of Cincinnati (1874–83). As chief chemist to the US Geological Survey (1883–1925), he undertook numerous analyses of rocks and minerals and compiled important lists of fundamental physical and chemical constants. He completed much work on the recalculation of atomic weights and he was the first to present a consistent theory of the chemical evolution of geological systems. His books include *Data of Geochemistry* (1908) and *The Composition of the Earth's Crust* (1924, with Henry Stephens Washington, 1867–1934). The new uranium mineral clarkeite was named in his honor.

Clarke, Sir Fred 1880–1952 •*Radical English educationist*• Born in Witney, Oxfordshire, he studied Modern History at Oxford. He became adviser (1935) and director (1936–45) of the Institute of Education, London, and wrote a number of books including *Foundations of History Teaching* (1929), but his really influential work was *Education and Social Change* (1940). Called "the **Beveridge** of education," he argued that after World War II the old class-divided education offered in Great Britain would be intolerable, especially at the secondary level, and his work was a forerunner of the thinking behind the Education Act of 1944.

Clarke, Gillian 1937– •*Welsh poet*• She was born in Cardiff and educated at the city's University College. Her earliest collections of poems, *Snow on the Mountain* (1971) and *Sundial* (1978), were followed by the more widely read *Letter from a Far Country* (1982). *Selected Poems* followed in 1985, then *Letting in the Rumour* (1989).

Clarke, Kenneth Harry 1940– •*English Conservative politician*• From Cambridge he was called to the bar in 1963. He entered parliament as Member of Parliament for Rushcliffe, Nottinghamshire, in 1970, and after junior posts in the **Heath** administration (1971–74) he joined **Margaret Thatcher**'s government in 1979. In 1988 he was appointed Secretary of State for Health, with the task of overseeing a major reform of the National Health Service, becoming Secretary of State for Education and Science (1990–92). Under **John Major** he was Home Secretary (1992–93), then succeeded **Norman Lamont** as Chancellor of the Exchequer (1993–97). After the Conservatives' defeat in the 1997 general election he entered the leadership contest but lost to **William Hague**, running again in 2001 but losing to **Iain Duncan Smith**.

Clarke, Marcus 1846–81 •*Australian novelist*• He was born and educated in London. Following the collapse of the family fortunes he was sent to Australia, where he contributed to the Melbourne press. As with many of his books, his first novel, *Long Odds* (1860), began life as a serial. He visited Tasmania to study its convict past, and the subsequent articles formed the basis for his best-known book, *His Natural Life* (1874, revised edition as *For the Term of His Natural Life*, 1882, under which title it was filmed and is now best known). He died destitute.

Clarke, Martha 1944– •*US dancer and choreographer*• Born in Baltimore, Maryland, she studied dance as a child and later trained at the American Dance Festival in Connecticut and at New York's Juilliard School of Music. She spent a few seasons in Anna

Sokolow's company before moving to Europe. On her return to the US she joined (1972) Pilobolus, a collectively run dance-theater ensemble. As the troupe achieved worldwide popularity, Clarke and dancers Robby Barnett and Felix Blaska formed the trio Crowsnest. Since the mid-1980s, she has concentrated on unclassifiable dance-theater productions such as *Garden of Earthly Delights* (1984), *Vienna: Lusthaus* (1986), and *An Uncertain Hour* (1993).

Clarke, Ronald William 1937– •*Australian athlete*• He was born in Melbourne. At one time he held the world records for three miles, five miles, 10 miles, 3,000, 5,000 and 10,000 meters. Although he had the reputation of being a better runner against the clock than against rivals, he lost only 25 of 500 races.

Clarke, Thomas James 1858–1916 •*Irish nationalist and revolutionary*• He was born in Hurst Castle, Isle of Wight. At the age of 21 he emigrated to the US, where he became involved in Clan-na-Gael, the clandestine US wing of the Irish Republican Brotherhood. Sent to England in 1883, he was arrested for taking part in the dynamite campaign against London civilians and was sentenced to be imprisoned for life. He served 15 years under the most severe conditions, and after his release (1898) he wrote *Glimpses of an Irish Felon's Prison Life*, and, once again in the US, became agent for the remilitarized **John Devoy**. Clarke returned to Ireland in 1907 and at his urging the Irish Republican Brotherhood set up a military council. Under Clarke's influence this brought about the Easter Rising of 1916. After the surrender he was court-martialed and shot.

Clarkson, Thomas 1760–1846 •*English antislavery campaigner*• Born in Wisbech, Cambridgeshire, and educated at St John's College, Cambridge, he gained a prize for a Latin essay in 1785 on the question "Is it right to make slaves of others against their will?" which in an English translation (1786) was widely read. In 1787, in association with **William Wilberforce** and **Granville Sharp**, he formed an antislavery society and after the passing of the British antislavery laws (1807) wrote *History of the Abolition of the African Slave Trade* (2 vols, 1808). He campaigned for the abolition of slavery in the colonies and saw it attained in 1833.

Claude, *in full* **Claude Le Lorrain**, *English* **Claude Lorrain**, *real name* **Claude Gelée** 1600–82 •*French landscape painter*• Born near Nancy, by tradition he is believed to have trained as a pastry cook, but by about 1613 he was in Italy, where he was apprenticed to Cavaliere d'Arpino and the landscapist Agostino Tassi. In 1625 he returned to Nancy, but in 1627 returned to Rome and soon achieved a distinguished reputation as a landscape painter. He is somewhat restricted in his subjects and natural effects and tends to be rather repetitive, but his color is always harmonious and mellow. He was a major influence on virtually every landscape painter from the 17th to the 19th centuries, including **Jean Antoine Watteau** and **J M W Turner**.

Claudel, Camille 1864–1943 •*French sculptor*• Born in La Fère-en-Tardenois, the daughter of a wealthy civil servant, and sister of the poet Paul Claudel (1868–1955), she decided to become a sculptor at an early age and in 1884 was introduced to **Auguste Rodin**. She became his student, model and mistress, and produced skillfully executed works which, while close to his, nonetheless show great individuality and vitality, such as *The Waltz* (1895, Musée Rodin, Paris, in bronze). After a fiery relationship, Claudel and Rodin parted company, but the break with Rodin affected her mental stability and from 1913 until her death she was confined to various institutions.

Claudian, *properly* **Claudius Claudianus** AD 340–410 •*Roman poet*• Born in Alexandria, Egypt, he was the last of the great Latin poets. He went to Rome in AD 395, and obtained patrician dignity by favor of **Flavius Stilicho**. A pagan, he wrote first in Greek, though he was of Roman extraction. Several epic poems by him, including *The Rape of Proserpine*, panegyrics on **Flavius Honorius**, Stilicho and others, invectives against Rufinus (c. 345–410) and Eutropius, occasional poems, and a Greek fragment, *Gigantomachia*, are still extant.

Claudius I, *full name* **Tiberius Claudius Drusus Nero Germanicus** 10 BC–AD 54 •*Fourth Roman emperor*• Born in Lyons, he was the younger son of the elder **Drusus** and nephew of the emperor **Tiberius**. His supposed imbecility saved him from execution by **Caligula**, but he was a great scholar. After Caligula's assassination (AD 41), Claudius was the only surviving adult male of the imperial family, and was proclaimed emperor by the army. His reign was marked by expansion of the Roman Empire: he created new provinces (Mauretania and Thrace), and inaugurated the conquest of Britain, taking part in the opening campaign in person (43). A hostile tradition portrays him as a weak personality, too influenced by his freedmen and his wives. His third wife, **Valeria Messalina**, was notorious, and when she went through a form of public marriage with a young lover, Claudius had her executed (48). He next married his niece, **Agrippina the Younger**, who persuaded him to adopt **Nero** her son by an earlier husband, although Claudius had a son of his own, **Britannicus**. Agrippina is believed to have poisoned Claudius with a dish of mushrooms to secure the succession of Nero.

Claudius, Appius (Caecus) fl. 312 BC •*Roman statesman and lawgiver*• He was regarded by the Romans as being the father of Latin prose and oratory. He was censor in c. 312–307 BC, and held several other important posts. He promoted many reforms giving privileges to the plebeians, and built the Aqua Appia aqueduct and the Via Appia highway (the Appian Way).

Clausewitz, Karl Marie von 1780–1831 •*Prussian soldier*• Born in Burg, he entered the Prussian army in 1792 and saw active service in the Revolutionary War (1793–94). He served as a Russian staff officer (1812), but returned to the Prussian service and in 1815 became **Gneisenau**'s Chief of Staff, taking part in the Waterloo campaign. His great treatise *Vom Kriege* (1833, "On War") has had a major impact on strategic studies.

Clausius, Rudolf Julius Emmanuel 1822–88 •*German physicist*• Born in Köslin, Prussia, he studied at the University of Berlin (1840–44), received a PhD (Halle, 1847), then taught physics at Berlin (1850), Zurich, Würzburg (1867) and Bonn (1869). In 1850, in order to validate **Sadi Carnot**'s theorem of perfect engines while rejecting the caloric theory, he postulated that heat cannot of itself pass from a colder body to a hotter one (the second law of thermodynamics). He later introduced the term "entropy" (1865) in such a way that dissipation was equivalent to entropy increase, thus enabling the two laws of thermodynamics to be stated succinctly. He studied electrolysis, calculated the mean speed of gas molecules, ignoring collisions (1857), and introduced the concepts of mean free path and effective radius (1858).

Clavell, James du Maresq 1924–94 •*US novelist, film producer and director*• Born in Sydney, Australia, he served during World War II and was a prisoner of war in Changi Jail, Singapore. The clash of East and West runs through his "Asian Saga," which covers three and a half centuries, beginning in the year 1600 with *Shogun* (1975), *Tai-Pan* (1966) and *Gai-Jin* (1983). *King Rat* (1962), *Noble House* (1980) and *Whirlwind* (1986) bring the story up to the year 1979. His work in film includes scripting the epic war movies *The Great Escape* (1960, from the book by **Paul Brickhill**) and *633 Squadron* (1963). He became a naturalized US citizen in 1963.

“ ”

These men too were criminals. Their crime was vast. They had lost a war. And they had lived.

1962 ***King Rat.***

Claverhouse, John Graham of *See* **Dundee, 1st Viscount**

Clay, Cassius Marcellus *See* **Ali, Muhammad**

Clay, Henry 1777–1852 •*US politician*• Born in Hanover County, Virginia, he entered the lower house of Congress in 1811, and was chosen as Speaker, a post he filled for many years. As leader of the "War Hawk" group he was active in bringing on the War of 1812 with Great Britain, and was one of the commissioners who arranged the Treaty of Ghent that ended it (1814). He was US Secretary of State (1825–29) and a US senator (1831–42). In 1832 and 1844 he was an unsuccessful candidate for the presidency. The compromise of 1850 between the opposing free-soil and proslavery interests, by which he attempted to avoid civil war, was largely Clay's work.

Clayton, John Middleton 1796–1856 •*US politician*• Born in Sussex County, Delaware, he practiced as a lawyer, then became a US senator in 1829. While Secretary of State from 1849 to 1850 he negotiated the Clayton-**Bulwer**Treaty with Great Britain.

Cleänthes c. 331–232 BC •*Greek Stoic philosopher*• Born in Assos, Troas, Asia Minor, he studied under **Zeno of Citium** in Athens for 19 years and succeeded him as head of the Stoa in 262 BC. His own contributions to Stoicism were especially in the areas of theology and cosmology, and the best known of his surviving works is the *Hymn to Zeus*.

Cleese, John Marwood 1939– •*English comic actor and writer*• Born in Weston-super-Mare, Avon, he studied at Cambridge, where he joined the Footlights Revue (1963). He appeared in the Broadway production of *Half a Sixpence* (1965) and returned to the UK to write and perform in such television series as *The Frost Report* (1966). With Graham Chapman (1941–89) he wrote scripts for television (*Doctor in the House*, 1968) and film (*The Rise and Rise of Michael Rimmer*, 1970). He then joined *Monty Python's Flying Circus* (1969–74), an anarchic series that changed the face of British television humor. The Monty Python team subsequently collaborated on such films as *Monty Python's Life of Brian* (1979) and *Monty Python's Meaning of Life* (1983). He had further success as the writer and star of the series *Fawlty Towers* (1975, 1979) and the films *A Fish Called Wanda* (1988) and *Fierce Creatures* (1996). His other film appearances include *Clockwise* (1985) and *Harry Potter and the Sorcerer's Stone* (2001).

Cleisthenes 6th century BC •*Athenian politician*• A member of the Alcmaeonid family, he was the founder of Athenian democracy. After the fall of the tyrant Hippias (see **Pisistratus**) in 510 BC, he completely reorganized the Athenian state. He divided the citizen body of Athens into 10 tribes (phylai), each comprising citizens from all regions of Attica: the city, coast and inland areas. Each tribe contributed 50 members annually to the democratic council of 500, which provided the organizational basis for the democracy as it developed in the 5th to 4th century BC.

Cleland, John 1709–89 •*English novelist*• He was born in London, and was educated at Westminster School. After a spell in the consular service and in the East India Company, he published a pornographic novel, *Memoirs of a Woman of Pleasure* (1748–49, later published in an expurgated abridged form, *Fanny Hill*, in 1750), a bestseller in its time which achieved a second succès de scandale on its prosecution under the Obscene Publications Act in 1963. He also wrote *Memoirs of a Coxcomb* (1751) and *The Surprises of Love* (1764).

Clemenceau, Georges Eugène Benjamin 1841–1929 •*French statesman*• Born in Mouillon-en-Pareds, he studied medicine. Elected to the National Assembly (1871), he resigned his seat in protest of the actions of the government that provoked the uprising in Paris known as the Paris Commune. Reelected in 1876, he became the leader of the radicals (on the extreme Left). Implication in the Panama Scandal led to his defeat in the 1893 elections. He was a leader of the campaign for the rehabilitation of **Alfred Dreyfus**, which allowed his return to parliament as a senator in 1903. As Prime Minister (1906–09, 1917–20), his determination spurred France to make the effort to pursue victory in World War I. He presided at the Paris Peace Conference (1919), where he sought unsuccessfully to obtain in the Treaty of Versailles a settlement that would preserve France from another German attack.

Clemens, Roger 1962– •*US baseball player*• Born in Dayton, Ohio, he became a pitcher for the Boston Red Sox in 1984 and won the **Cy Young** award in 1986, 1987, 1991, 1997, 1998 and 2001. He moved to the Toronto Blue Jays in 1997, the New York Yankees in 1999 and the Houston Astros in 2004. He is known for his extraordinary pitching control, his 95-mph (153-kph) fastball, and his quick temper. In 1986 he set the major-league record for the most strikeouts (20) in a single game, equaled by Kerry Wood in 1998.

Clemens, Titus Flavius *See* **Clement of Alexandria, St**

Clément V c. 1260–1314 •*French pope*• Born in Bordelais region, and formerly Archbishop of Bordeaux, he was pope from 1305. He suppressed the Knights Templars, and moved the seat of the papacy to Avignon (1309), a move disastrous to Italy.

Clement VII, *originally* **Giulio de' Medici** 1478–1534 •*Italian pope*• Born in Florence, he became pope from 1523 and allied himself with **Francis I** of France against the Holy Roman emperor **Charles V**, whose troops sacked Rome in 1527, and for a while became the prisoner of the Constable **Bourbon**. His indecisiveness, along with his refusal to sanction **Henry VIII**'s divorce from **Catherine of Aragon**, hastened the Reformation.

Clement IX, *originally* **Giulio Rospigliosi** 1600–69 •*Italian pope*• He was papal ambassador to Spain (1644–53) and secretary of state to **Alexander VII**. Becoming pope in 1667 he sought, through the so-called Clementine Peace (Jan 1669), to prevent **Louis XIV** of France from persecuting the Jansenists. The issue of Jansenism, however, took on a lesser significance than Louis's increasing insistence on Gallican rights to limit the authority of the papacy within France.

Clement XI, *originally* **Giovanni Francesco Albani** 1649–1721 •*Italian pope*• Born in Urbino, he was elected pope in 1700 at a difficult time for the papacy, with its political role in decline and its control of national churches increasingly threatened. Although Clement hoped to avoid conflict with either of the great ruling houses of Europe, he succeeded in antagonizing first the Austrian Habsburgs, by supporting the recognition of **Louis XIV**'s grandson, Philip of Anjou, as king of Spain (**Philip V**), and then the **Bourbon**s, when he agreed to the demands of Joseph I of Austria to recognize his brother, Charles, as the rightful pretender to the Spanish throne. By the Treaties of Utrecht (1713) and Rastatt (1714), Clement was forced to concede suzerainty over Naples, Sicily, Parma and Piacenza, while papal influence in France was increasingly marginalized by the growth of Gallicanism and the rise of Jansenism.

Clement XIII 1693–1769 •*Italian pope*• As pope from 1758, he faced considerable hostility from most of Europe's more powerful Catholic princes who, at the time, were seeking to exert greater control over their own national churches. The Portuguese and the **Bourbon** rulers of Spain, Naples and France were all engaged in anti-Jesuit campaigns, and the **Habsburg** Empire was witnessing a surge of Febronianism, the German equivalent of Gallicanism. Despite Clement's attempts to defend the Jesuits, they were expelled from Portugal (1759), France and its dominions (1764), the Spanish Empire (1767) and the Kingdom of Naples and Sicily (1768). Finally in 1769 the ambassadors of the three Bourbon powers demanded that the Society of Jesus be suppressed totally. Clement refused, but within a month had a stroke and died.

Clement XIV, *originally* **Vincenzo Antonio Ganganelli** 1705–74 •*Italian pope*• Born near Rimini, he was educated by the Jesuits, and made a cardinal by **Clement XIII** (1759), who hoped he would prove a useful ally in his struggle against the rulers of Portugal, Naples, Spain and France. Naples had proved determined to destroy the Society of Jesus, not least because it was seen as a symbol of papal interference in their domestic affairs. However, when elected pope on Clement XIII's death in 1769, he feared that open schism might emerge unless he placated the great **Bourbon** powers. In July 1773, therefore, he issued the *Dominus ac Redemptor* ("Lord and Savior") dissolving the society. The suppression lasted until 1814.

Clement of Alexandria, St, *also called* **Titus Flavius Clemens** c. 150–c. 215 AD •*Greek Church Father*• Born probably in Athens, he lived chiefly in Alexandria, Egypt. He became head of the Catechetical school (c. 180–201 AD) and together with his pupil **Origen** made it a celebrated center of learning, until forced to flee to Palestine during the persecutions of Emperor **Severus**. His chief surviving works are *Who Is the Rich Man That Is Saved* and the trilogy of *The Missionary, The Tutor* and *The Miscellanies*.

Clement, Clemens Romanus d. c. 101 AD •*Roman pope*• Born in Rome, he was pope (AD 88–89 or AD 92–101), and the first of the Apostolic Fathers. He is reckoned variously as the second or third successor of St **Peter** in the see of Rome. He may have been a freedman of Jewish parentage belonging to the imperial household. He was the author of an *Epistle to the Corinthian Church* (c. 95), which discusses social dissensions and the Resurrection. A tradition suggests that he was martyred.

Clemente, Roberto Walker 1934–72 •*Puerto Rican baseball* *player*• He was born in Carolina, Puerto Rico. An outstanding outfielder, he played for the Pittsburgh Pirates for 17 years (1955–72), led the National League in batting five times, and was in the World Series in 1971. In 1966 he was voted the Most Valuable Player (MVP). He was killed in an air crash while flying on a relief mission to the victims of the earthquake at Managua in Nicaragua. In 1973 he was elected to the National Baseball Hall of Fame without the usual five-year wait.

Cleopatra 69–30 BC •*Queen of Egypt, the last of the Macedonian dynasty of the Ptolemies*• She was the daughter of Ptolemy XII Auletes, who died in 51 BC. By the terms of his will he appointed her joint successor, as Cleopatra VII, with her younger brother as Ptolemy XIII (who was also her husband in name, in the Egyptian manner), but she was ousted by Ptolemy's guardians, and was about to assert her rights when **Julius Caesar** arrived in Egypt in pursuit of Pompey (48). After the Battle of Philippi (42), **Mark Antony** (Marcus Antonius) summoned her to Tarsus in Cilicia. They spent the following winter in Alexandria, but Antony then married **Octavia** (40), sister of Octavian (the future **Augustus**), and did not see Cleopatra again until 37, by which time he had become estranged from his wife. He acknowledged the paternity of the twins (a son and a daughter) Cleopatra had borne him in 40, and a third child was born in 36. From this time their personal and political careers were linked, although how far their aims coincided is not easy to determine. Cleopatra's ambition was most probably to achieve the restoration of Ptolemaic power. But Antony's position in the East and his relations with Cleopatra were ambiguous and susceptible to distortion for propaganda purposes, especially by Octavian, who was brilliantly successful in swaying Roman public opinion against his absent rival. War was declared against Cleopatra, who was presented as a threat to the power of Rome, and after the Battle of Actium (31), in which they were defeated, Antony and Cleopatra fled to Egypt. When Octavian appeared before Alexandria, Cleopatra opened negotiations with him to try to save her dynasty. Antony, misled by a false report of Cleopatra's death, committed suicide by falling on his sword. Finding that she could not move Octavian, and unwilling to bear the shame of being taken to Rome to be paraded in his triumph, she is said to have killed herself by causing an asp (the Egyptian symbol of royalty) to bite her breast.

Clerides, Glafcos John 1919– •*Cypriot politician*• Born in Nicosia, Cyprus, he was educated at the Pancyprian Gymnasium, Nicosia, and at King's College, London University, and served with the RAF during World War II. In 1960 he became a member of the Cypriot House of Representatives, having played a major role in the establishment of the Republic of Cyprus. He was President of the House of Representatives (1960–76) and was briefly acting President of Cyprus following the coup of July 1974. He founded the Democratic Rally Party in 1976 and was President of Cyprus from 1993 to 2003.

Clerk-Maxwell, James *See* **Maxwell, James Clerk**

Cleve, Cornelis 1520–67 •*Flemish painter*• Born in Antwerp, he was the son of **Joos van Cleve**. He specialized in portraits of the rich Flemish bourgeoisie, and in 1554 he went to England, hoping for the patronage of **Philip II** of Spain, who was there for his marriage to **Mary I** (Tudor). However, his arrival coincided with that of a collection of pictures by **Titian** and others from Italy, which ousted the Flemish school from royal favor. The disappointment mentally deranged Cornelis, who never entirely recovered, being known thereafter as "Sotte ('mad') Cleve."

Cleve, Joos van c. 1480–1540 •*Flemish painter*• He was born in Antwerp, and most of his work was done there, although he also worked in Cologne and was invited to Paris to paint portraits of **Francis I** and his family. He is best known for his religious pictures and is sometimes called "the Master of the Death of the Virgin" from two triptychs of that subject at Munich and Cologne.

Cleveland, (Stephen) Grover 1837–1908 •*US statesman and 22nd and 24th President*• Born in Caldwell, New Jersey, the son of a Presbyterian minister, he was admitted to the bar in 1859 and began to practice in Buffalo. As mayor of Buffalo (from 1882), he became known as a reformer independent of political posses, and after a year in office was elected Governor of New York (1882). He was nominated by the Democrats for the presidency (1884), and took his seat as President in 1885 after a campaign marked by energetic mudslinging on all sides. In his first term (1885–89) he advocated tariff reduction and Civil Service reform, but his stand on the tariff issue was unpopular, and he lost the 1888 election to the Republican candidate **Benjamin Harrison**. Four years later he defeated Harrison to win a second term as President (1893–97). The panic of 1893 prompted Cleveland to force the repeal of the Sherman Silver Purchase Act, thus angering free-silver advocates in the West, and his intervention on the side of the railroads in the **Pullman** strike of 1894 also aroused much protest. In foreign affairs he invoked the **Monroe** Doctrine to resolve Great Britain's boundary dispute with Venezuela, and he showed admirable integrity by refusing to recognize the Hawaiian government set up largely by US planters. By 1896 he had lost the support of his party, and the Democratic nomination went to **William Jennings Bryan**.

Cleves, Anne of *See* **Anne of Cleves**

Cliff, Clarice 1899–1972 •*English ceramic designer*• Born in Tunstall, Staffordshire, she attended local art schools there and at Burslem, and set up a design studio at Wilkinson's Newport Showroom where she developed a unique style using bold designs, stylized trees and abstract patterns in vivid colors. By 1929 the Newport Pottery was given over entirely to the decoration of her work, which was marketed under the name "Bizarre," a range which also included work by contemporary artists such as **Vanessa Bell** and **Laura Knight**.

Clift, (Edward) Montgomery 1920–66 •*US film and stage actor*• Born in Omaha, Nebraska, he worked in summer stock as a teenager, moved to New York and for 10 years acted exclusively on stage. He then appeared on film in *Red River* (1946) and was briefly considered the most promising of postwar actors. His performances in *The Search* (1948), *A Place in the Sun* (1951) and *From Here to Eternity* (1953) earned him Academy Award nominations. Broodingly handsome, his slight, intense figure was particularly adept at conveying the introspective turmoil of society's drifters and outsiders, but a car accident in 1957 left him permanently scarred. Troubled by his homosexuality and by poor health, his later career never fulfilled its early promise, although his sincerity remained evident, particularly in his last major role *Freud* (1962).

Cline, Patsy, *stage name of* **Virginia Petterson Hensley** 1932–63 •*US country singer*• Born in Winchester, Virginia, she was spotted on the television show *Talent Scout* (1957) and signed to the Decca label. Her powerful voice allowed her to cross over from country to a wider pop audience, and songs like "Crazy" (1961) and "She's Got You" (1962) made her extremely popular worldwide. She died in a plane crash in Tennessee.

Clinton, Bill (William Jefferson) 1946– •*US Democratic politician and 42nd President*• Born in Hope, Arkansas, he was educated at Georgetown University and Yale Law School, and at Oxford (Rhodes Scholar). He taught law at the University of Arkansas (1973–76), marrying **Hillary Clinton** in 1975, before he was elected state Attorney General (1976). Elected Governor of Arkansas in 1978, he served for five terms (1979–81, 1983–92). In 1992, on a platform of hope and change in a climate of economic recession and voter disillusionment, he defeated **George Bush** and was elected President, thus ending a 12-year Republican hold on the office. In the 1996 elections he became the first Democratic President to gain reelection since **Franklin D Roosevelt** in 1936. A popular and charismatic figure, his presidency saw peace and economic prosperity, with low inflation and unemployment, and a focus on promoting peace on the international stage in Northern Ireland and Israel. However, it was also marked by some scandal, most notably in 1998 when his initial denial of an affair with White House intern Monica Lewinsky was followed by charges of perjury and obstruction of justice. He was subsequently acquitted by the Senate.

" "

If something makes you cry, you have to do something about it. That's the difference between politics and guilt.

On what makes a liberal. Quoted in Meredith Oakley ***On the Make*** *(1994).*

Clinton, De Witt 1769–1828 •*US politician*• Admitted to the New York bar in 1788, he sat in the state legislature (1797) and the state senate (1798–1802), and in 1802 was elected to the US Senate, but resigned in the same year on being appointed Mayor of New York by his uncle. In this office he continued, except for two short intervals, until 1815; he was defeated by **James Madison** in the presidential contest of 1812. He pressed the Erie Canal project, was elected Governor of New York in 1817, and in 1825 opened the canal.

Clinton, Sir Henry c. 1738–95 •*British soldier*• He was born in Newfoundland, Canada. He was sent to America in 1775, where he fought at Bunker Hill, and in 1776 was repulsed in an attack on Charleston. In 1778, Clinton succeeded Admiral **Howe** as Commander in Chief. In 1780 he captured Charleston and the entire Southern army, but after Lord **Cornwallis**'s capitulation at Yorktown in 1781 he resigned and returned to England, where he published a *Narrative* of the campaign (1783). In 1794 he was appointed Governor of Gibraltar.

Clinton, Hillary Rodham, *née* **Rodham** 1947– •*US politician and lawyer*• Born in Chicago, Illinois, she was educated at Wellesley College and studied law at Yale. She then practiced law privately, specializing in family issues and children's rights. She married **Bill Clinton** in 1975 and campaigned vigorously for his political offices. Following his election as US President she served as chief presidential adviser and was appointed head of his Health Care Task Force. In 1996 she became the first wife of a President in office to appear before a grand jury in the so-called Whitewater affair, an inquiry concerning property deals in Arkansas in the 1980s. In 2001 she became senator for New York, the first First Lady to be elected to public office.

Clitherow, St Margaret, *known as* **the Pearl of York**, *née* **Middleton** c. 1556–86 •*English religious martyr*• She was born in York, married a butcher, and was converted to Catholicism in 1574. She harbored priests in her home during **Elizabeth I**'s reign, for which she was tried, condemned and pressed to death. She was canonized in 1970, and her feast day is March 25.

Clive (of Plassey), Robert Clive, Baron, *also called* **Clive of India** 1725–74 •*English general and colonial administrator*• He was born near Market Drayton, Shropshire. In 1743 he joined the East India Company in Madras, where he tried to commit suicide. In 1751 he held Arcot with a small force against a French-Indian army for 53 days before being relieved, and in 1753 returned to England in triumph. In 1755 he returned to India where he was called on to avenge the so-called Black Hole of Calcutta (1757). Calcutta was soon retaken, and Chandernagore, the French settlement, captured. At Plassey (1757) he defeated the Nawab of Bengal, **Suraja Dowlah**. For three years he was sole ruler in all but name of Bengal on behalf of the East India Company. In 1760 he again returned to England, to be hailed by Lord **Chatham** (Pitt the Elder) as "a heaven-born general." In 1761 he entered parliament, and in 1762 was made Baron Clive of Plassey. Clive was sent to India again in 1764 as Governor and Commander in Chief of Bengal. He established British supremancy throughout India, but on his return to England in 1767 he was faced with a parliamentary storm about his handling of the East India Company's affairs, and although ultimately vindicated in 1773, committed suicide soon afterward.

Clodion *See* **Michel, Claude**

Clooney, George 1961– •*US actor*• Born in Maysville, Kentucky, he studied at Northern Kentucky University. He began acting in television in the early 1980s, appearing in *E/R* in 1984–85, and playing parts in *Roseanne* (1988–89), *Sisters* (1992–94) and the hugely successful *ER* (1994–99). He has appeared in several feature films, including *Batman and Robin* (1997), *The Perfect Storm* (1999) and *Oceans Eleven* (2001).

Clopinel, Jean *See* **Meung, Jean de**

Close, Chuck (Charles Thomas) 1940– •*US artist*• Born in Monroe, Washington, he studied painting at Yale (1962–64), and has lived in New York since 1967. In 1967–68 he began copying portrait photographs, painstakingly reproducing every detail, and has since continued with this photorealist method. His works are often large scale and many are monochromatic. In the 1980s, he adopted the techniques of finger painting and collage to achieve the same hyper-detailed results.

Close, Glenn 1947– •*US film and stage actress*• Born in Greenwich, Connecticut, she was a student of anthropology and acting and made her Broadway debut in *Love for Love* (1974). Her theater work includes *The Singular Life of Albert Nobbs* (1982), for which she received an Obie award, and *The Real Thing* (1984–85), for which she received a Tony award. She made her television debut in *Too Far to Go* (1979) and received an Emmy nomination for *Something about Amelia* (1984). Other television roles include *Sarah Plain and Tall* (1991) and *Serving in Silence* (1995). Her film debut was in *The World According to Garp* (1982, Academy Award nomination). Later stage performances include *Death and the Maiden* (1992, Tony award), and *Sunset Boulevard*, (1993–95, Tony award) and her film appearances include *Dangerous Liaisons* (1988, Academy Award nomination), *101 Dalmations* (1996), *Air Force One* (1997) and *Cookie's Fortune* (1999).

Clotaire or **Chlotar I** 6th century •*King of all the Franks from 558*• The son of the Frankish king **Clovis**, he inherited the kingdom jointly with his three brothers (511), but gradually added to his holdings until, on the death of his brother Childebert I (558), he became ruler of all the Franks. Brutal and ruthless, he extended his rule into central Germany, but faced a serious rebellion by his son, Chram, whom he had burned to death.

Clotaire II 584–629 •*King of the Franks*• The grandson of **Clotaire I**, he assumed rule (613) after a period of regency, recovered lost territories and, by seizing Austrasia and Burgundy, extended rule over all the Franks.

Clotilda, St AD 474–545 •*Queen of the Franks*• The daughter of the Burgundian king Childeric, she married the Frankish king **Clovis** (AD 493) and converted him to Christianity. After his death (511) she lived a life of austerity and good works at the abbey of St Martin at Tours, where she died.

Clough, Anne Jemima 1820–92 •*English educationist*• Born in Liverpool, she was a vigorous proponent of higher education for women. She secured the admission of women to Manchester and Newcastle colleges, and in 1871 she became the first principal of the first hall for women students at Cambridge, Newnham Hall, later called Newnham College. She was the sister of **Arthur Hugh Clough**.

Clough, Arthur Hugh 1819–61 •*English poet*• Born in Liverpool, he was the son of a cotton merchant who emigrated to Charleston, West Virginia, US, in 1823. The boy was sent back to England in 1828 and entered Rugby, where he became a pupil of Dr **Thomas Arnold** and a friend of **Matthew Arnold**. He was elected a Fellow of Oriel College and there lived through the crisis which resulted in **John Henry Newman**'s conversion to Catholicism. His own difficulties with the Thirty-nine Articles led to his resignation in 1848. He enjoyed the friendship of **John Ruskin**, Arnold, and **Thomas Carlyle**, and at Oriel, as the leader of the members of the Decade group, he took reading parties to the Lake District and to Scotland. The latter resulted in *The Bothie of Tober-na-Vuolich* (1848). Arnold wrote the poem "Thyrsis" in Clough's memory in 1866. Clough's two-volume *Correspondence* was published in 1957.

Clough, Brian 1935– •*English soccer player and manager*• Born in Middlesbrough, Cleveland, he became a manager when injury terminated his playing career. He took Derby County and Nottingham Forest to league championship wins and, in the case of Nottingham Forest, two European Cup successes. He was given the honorary title Officer, Order of the British Empire, in 1991 and the freedom of the city of Nottingham in 1993, the year he retired.

“ ”

Say nowt, win it, then—talk your head off.

Summarizing his managerial style. Quoted in Colin Jarman ***The Guinness Dictionary of Sports Quotations*** *(1990).*

Clovis, *Old German* **Chlodwig** AD 465–511 •*Merovingian ruler of the Franks*• The grandson of **Merovech**, he succeeded his father, Childeric I (AD 481), as king of the Salian Franks. In 486 he overthrew the last Roman governor in Gaul, Syagrius, near Soissons, and took control of the whole country between the Somme and the Loire, making his capital at Soissons. He married **St Clotilda** of Burgundy (493), who converted him to Christianity, and he championed orthodox Christianity against the heretic Arians, defeating the Alemonni (496) and the Arian Visigoths under **Alaric II** (507). A heroic figure, he was the traditional founder of the historic French monarchy, and when he died his Frankish kingdom was divided among his four sons, who further enlarged the empire by conquest.

Clune, Frank (Francis Patrick) 1893–1971 •*Australian writer*• He was born in Woolloomooloo, Sydney, of Irish extraction, and his early life was one of travel and adventure at sea, in Europe and the US. He served in World War I and was wounded at Gallipoli. A vagabond life was followed by marriage, then a career in accountancy. At the age of 40 he published *Try Anything Once* (1933), the story of his early years. He went on to write over 60 books, often in collaboration with P R ("Inky") Stephensen, and became one of Australia's bestselling writers. His works include *Rolling Down the Lachlan* (1935), *Wild Colonial Boys* (1948) and *Ben Hall the Bushranger* (1947)

Cluverius or **Clüver, Phillip** 1580–1622 •*German geographer and antiquary*• Born in Danzig, he is regarded as the founder of historical geography. He studied law at Leiden, and visited Norway, England, Scotland, France and Italy. He wrote *Introductio in universam geographium* (1624, "Introduction to Universal Geography").

Clyde, Lord *See* **Campbell, Sir Colin**

Coanda, Henri 1885–1972 •*Romanian aeronautical engineer*• He built the first jet-propelled airplane, which used a ducted fan, not a turbojet. Because of a phenomenon not then understood, the hot exhaust gases set fire to the structure. He subsequently became an aircraft designer with the British & Colonial Aeroplane Company (later the Bristol Aircraft Company).

Coates, Anne V 1925– •*English film editor*• Born in Reigate, Surrey, she began her working life as a nurse, but moved into film editing in the early 1950s. Her early films include *The Pickwick Papers* (1952). She went on to become a leading film editor, working both in Great Britain and in Hollywood, and has been responsible for cutting a number of very important films, including the epic *Lawrence of Arabia* (1962), for which she received an Academy Award.

Coates, Eric 1886–1957 •*English composer*• Born in Hucknall, Nottinghamshire, he studied in Nottingham and at the Royal Academy of Music, working as violinist in chamber music groups. In 1912 he became leading violist in the Queen's Hall Orchestra under Sir **Henry Wood**. Success as a composer of attractive light music enabled him to devote himself to composition after 1918. Among his best-known compositions are the *London Suite* (1933), *The Three Bears* (1926), the suites *Four Centuries* (1941) and *The Three Elizabeths* (1944), and a number of popular waltzes and marches.

Coates, Wells Wintemute 1895–1958 •*English architect*• Born in Tokyo, he was one of the principal figures of the modern movement in architecture. He studied in Canada and London, and in 1933 formed the Modern Architectural Research Society group of architects. He was responsible for the design of BBC studios, the EKCO laboratories, and many other buildings in Great Britain and in Canada, and he also played an important part in the development of industrial design. His work in this field included furniture and an innovative bakelite circular radio for EKCO.

Cobain, Kurt (Donald) 1967–94 •*US singer and guitarist*• He was born in Aberdeen, Washington. He formed the band Nirvana, the chief catalyst in Seattle's grunge scene of the late 1980s. Their first album, *Bleach* (1989), established their characteristic sound, a dense compound of punk's ferocity with strong melodies. *Nevermind* (1991), and the single "Smells Like Teen Spirit" from it, were an international success. Cobain became increasingly disaffected with the publicity which success brought, which reached a frenzy after he married guitarist and singer Courtney Love in 1992. His mental state was also affected by his heroin addiction, and after recording a third album, *In Utero* (1993), he committed suicide at his home in Seattle.

Cobb, Ty(rus Raymond), *nicknamed* **the Georgia Peach** 1886–1961 •*US baseball player*• Born in Narrows, Georgia, he was considered the outstanding offensive player of all time. He played for the Detroit Tigers (1905–26) and the Philadelphia Athletics (1926–28), and until **Pete Rose** in 1985 was the only player with more than 4,000 hits in major-league baseball. His career batting average was an astonishing .367, meaning that he had a hit more than once every three times at bat.

Cobbett, William 1763–1835 •*English writer and champion of the poor*• Born in Farnham, Surrey, the son of a small farmer, he taught himself to read and write, and while serving as sergeant-major in New Brunswick (1785–91) studied rhetoric, geometry, logic and French. He bought his discharge in 1791, and the following year sailed for America. In Philadelphia he taught English to French refugees, opened a bookshop and published a paper, the *Porcupine's Gazette* (1797–99). In 1802, back in Britain, he started his weekly *Cobbett's Political Register*, which was Tory at first, but from 1804, he gradually became the most uncompromising champion of radicalism. He spent two years in Newgate Prison, London (1810–12), for his strictures on flogging in the army, and in 1817 financial problems and fear of further imprisonment drove him back to the US, where he farmed on Long Island. Returning to England in 1819, he started a seed farm at Kensington, defended himself against a charge of sedition (1831), and in 1832, after the First Reform Bill, became Member of Parliament for Oldham. His celebrated *Rural Rides* (1830), a delightful picture of a vanishing world, were reprinted from the *Register*. His 40 or more other works include a savage *History of the Reformation* (1824–27), *The Woodlands* (1825) and *Advice to Young Men* (1830).

Cobden, Richard, *known as* **the Apostle of Free Trade** 1804–65 •*English economist and politician*• He was born in Heyshott, near Midhurst, Sussex. After a childhood spent in poverty he set up an establishment for calico printing with two friends in Lancashire (1831), and settled in Manchester (1832). He visited the US (1835), and the Levant (1836–37), the result being two pamphlets, *England, Ireland, and America* (1835), and *Russia* (1836), the former preaching free trade and nonintervention, and the latter directed against "Russophobia." He failed to be elected to the parliament for Stockport on free-trade principles (1837). In 1838 seven Manchester merchants founded the Anti-Corn-Law League, its most prominent member being Cobden. His lectures all over the country and his speeches in parliament (to which Stockport had returned him in 1841) were characterized by clear, quiet persuasiveness. Sir **Robert Peel** acknowledged that Cobden had played a large part in abolition of the Corn Laws (1846). His public work had detracted from his business, but when he ended up a ruined man, a subscription of £80,000 was raised in recognition of his services. He was elected for both Stockport and the West Riding and he chose West Riding.

Cobham, Lord *See* **Oldcastle, Sir John**

Coborn, Charles, *stage name of* **Colin Whitton McCallum** 1852–1945 •*English comedian*• He made his stage debut in 1875 and immortalized the songs "Two Lovely Black Eyes" (1886) and "The Man Who Broke the Bank at Monte Carlo" (1890). In 1928 he published the autobiographical *The Man Who Broke the Bank*.

Cochba, Simon Bar *See* **Bar Kokhba, Simon**

Cochise d. 1874 •*Native American leader*• Born in Arizona, he became a chief of the Chiricahua band of the Apache, and in 1861 a decade of coexistence with the US government was broken when Cochise was falsely accused of having abducted a white child. His imprisonment and escape from an army post led to the execution of hostages on both sides, and he began a campaign of fierce resistance to white settlement, terrorizing Arizona settlers in the 1860s. He led raids from his base in the Dragoon Mountains until 1871, when he was forced to surrender to General **George Crook**. He retired to an Arizona reservation the following year.

Cochran, Jacqueline 1910–80 •*US aviator*• Born in Pensacola, Florida, she received her pilot's license in 1932, and in 1938 she secured the transcontinental record at 10 hours and 28 minutes. The International League of Aviators named her the world's outstanding woman pilot (1937–50, 1953). The first woman to pilot a bomber across the Atlantic Ocean in World War II, she became director of

Women Auxiliary Service Pilots in the US Air Force in 1943. In 1953 she became the first woman to fly faster than sound (in an F-86 Sabre fighter), and in 1964 flew faster than twice the speed of sound.

Cockcroft, Sir John Douglas 1897–1967 •*English nuclear physicist and Nobel Prize winner*• Born in Yorkshire and educated at the Universities of Manchester and Cambridge, he became Jacksonian Professor of Natural Philosophy at Cambridge (1939–46). In 1932, with **Ernest Walton**, he induced the disintegration of a lithium nucleus by proton bombardment in the first successful use of a particle accelerator. Cockcroft and Walton were awarded the 1951 Nobel Prize for physics for this work. Cockcroft later assisted in the design of some special experimental equipment for the Cavendish Laboratory, including the cyclotron. During World War II, he was director of Air Defence Research (1941–44) and of the Atomic Energy Division of the Canadian National Research Council (1944–46). He became the first director of the UK's Atomic Energy Research Establishment at Harwell in 1946. He was knighted in 1948.

Cockerell, Sir Christopher Sydney 1910–99 •*English radio engineer and inventor of the hovercraft*• Born in Cambridge and educated at Peterhouse, Cambridge, he worked on radar in World War II, and later on hydrodynamics. In 1955 he pioneered the amphibious hovercraft, which rides on a cushion of jet-generated air. A prototype of it, the SR-N1, made the Calais-Dover crossing of the English Channel in 1959.

Cocteau, (Clement Eugène) Jean 1889–1963 •*French poet, playwright and film director*• Born in Maisons-Lafitte, near Paris, success came early with *La lampe d'Aladin* (1909, "Aladdin's Lamp"), and he exploited it. He had astonishing success with whatever he touched, and figured as a sponsor of **Picasso**, **Stravinsky**, **Giorgio de Chirico** and the group of young French composers known as Les Six. As an actor, director, scenario writer, novelist, critic and artist, his work was marked by vivacity and a pyrotechnic brilliance. He was elected to the Académie Française in 1955. Significant works are his novels *Le grand écart* (1923, Eng trans *The Grand Escort*, 1925), *Thomas l'imposteur* (1923, Eng trans *Thomas the Imposter*, 1925) and plays: *Les mariés de la Tour Eiffel* (1921, Eng trans *The Eiffel Tower Wedding Party*, 1963), *Orphée* (1926, Eng trans *Orpheus*, 1933) and *L'aigle a deux têtes* (1946, Eng trans *The Eagle Has Two Heads*, 1948). His films include *Le sang d'un poète* (1930, *The Blood of a Poet*), *La belle et la bête* (1945, *Beauty and the Beast*), *Orphée* (adapted from his play, 1949) and *Le testament d'Orphée* (1960).

" "

Life is a horizontal fall.

1930 ***Opium.***

Cody, William F(rederick), *known as* **Buffalo Bill** 1846–1917 •*US showman*• Born in Scott County, Iowa, he became an army scout and pony express rider. He earned his nickname after killing nearly 5,000 buffalo for a contract to supply meat to the workers on the Kansas Pacific Railway (1867–68). He served as a scout in the Sioux wars, but from 1883 toured with his own Wild West Show. The town of Cody in Wyoming is situated on part of his ranch.

Coe, Sebastian Newbold Coe, Baron 1956– •*English athlete and Conservative politician*• Born in Chiswick, London, he won the 1,500-meters gold medal and the silver medal in the 800 meters at both the 1980 Moscow Olympics and at Los Angeles four years later. In 1981 he broke the world record for the 800 meters, 1,000 meters and the mile. Between September 1976 and June 1983 he did not lose the final of any race over 1,500 meters or a mile. Following the 1990 Commonwealth Games, he retired from athletics to pursue a career in politics. He was Conservative Member of Parliament for Falmouth and Cambourne from 1992 to 1997 and was made a life peer in 2000.

Coen, Ethan 1957– •*US film producer and screenwriter*• Born in St Louis Park, Minnesota, and educated at Princeton University, he established his reputation working in collaboration with his brother **Joel Coen**. Their films, admired for their innovative style and wit, include *Blood Simple*, *Raising Arizona* (1987), *Miller's Crossing* (1990), *Barton Fink* (1991), which won the Palme d'Or at the Cannes Festival, *The Hudsucker Proxy* (1994), *Fargo* (1996), *The Big Lebowski* (1998) and *O Brother, Where Art Thou?* (2000).

Coen, Joel 1954– •*US film director and screenwriter*• Born in St Louis Park, Minnesota, and educated at Simon's Rock College and at the University of New York, he has won acclaim as a director and screenwriter working in collaboration with his brother **Ethan Coen**. Their films include *Blood Simple* (1984), *Raising Arizona* (1987), *Miller's Crossing* (1990), *Barton Fink* (1991), *The Hudsucker Proxy* (1994), *Fargo* (1996), for which Joel won the Best Director award at the Cannes Film Festival, *The Big Lebowski* (1998) and *The Man Who Wasn't There* (2001).

Coetzee, J(ohn) M(ichael) 1940– •*South African novelist*• He was born in Cape Town. The political situation in his native country provided him with the base from which to launch his allegories and fables, attacking colonialism and demythologizing historical and contemporary myths of imperialism. His first work of fiction was *Dusklands* (1974), followed by *In the Heart of the Country* (1977), *Waiting for the Barbarians* (1980), *Life and Times of Michael K* (1983), for which he was awarded the Booker Prize, *Foe* (1986) and *The Master of Petersburg* (1994). He won the Booker Prize for the second time with *Disgrace* (1999).

Cœur de Lion *See* **Richard I**

Coggan, (Frederick) Donald Coggan, Baron 1909–2000 •*English prelate, Archbishop of Canterbury*• Born in London, he was educated at St John's College, Cambridge. He lectured widely in Semitic languages and theology before being made Bishop of Bradford (1956–61) and Archbishop of Canterbury (1974–80). He wrote several theological works, including *On Preaching* (1978), *Mission to the World* (1982), *God of Hope* (1991), *Voice from the Cross* (1993) and *The Servant Son* (1995).

Coggeshall, Ralph de d. c. 1227 •*English chronicler*• A native of Cambridgeshire, he was abbot from 1207 to 1218 of the Cistercian abbey of Coggeshall, Essex, and continued the Latin Chronicle (*Chronicon Anglicanum*) kept at the abbey, covering the period from 1187 to 1224.

Cohan, George M(ichael) 1878–1942 •*US showman and songwriter*• Born in Providence, Rhode Island, he spent his childhood acting in vaudeville with a family theatrical group, The Four Cohans. He grew up to write, produce, and perform in musicals and dramas, which were usually centered on flag-waving patriots and the allure of show business, such as *The Song and Dance Man* (1923). He wrote many songs that have remained favorites, including "Yankee Doodle Dandy" (1904), "Give My Regards to Broadway" (1904), and "Over There" (1917). In the film *Yankee Doodle Dandy* (1942), he was played with gusto by **James Cagney**.

Cohan, Robert 1925– •*British dancer, choreographer and director*• Born in Brooklyn, New York, he took British citizenship in 1989. After serving in World War II he dropped his career as a research naturalist to take up training with the **Martha Graham** Company in New York. From 1946 to 1957 he was Martha Graham's partner, and created his first role in her *Diversion of Angels* (1948). He became codirector in 1966. From 1967 to 1983 he was the founding artistic director of London Contemporary Dance Theatre. His many works include *Cell* (1969), *Stages* (1971), *Class* (1975) and *Video-Life* (1987).

Cohen, Leonard Norman 1934– •*Canadian poet, novelist and singer*• Though his background is Jewish, he was born and grew up in the predominantly Catholic city of Montreal, and the title of his first poetry collection, *Let Us Compare Mythologies* (1956), offers an indication of how he has moved between traditions. His novels include *The Favorite Game* (1963) and *Beautiful Losers* (1966). The first of his many albums as a singer-songwriter was *The Songs of Leonard Cohen*, which appeared in 1968, the same year as his *Selected Poems*.

Cohl, Emile, *originally* **Emile Courtet** 1857–1938 •*French cartoonist, inventor of the animated cartoon*• Born in Paris, his first cartoons were published in *Le rire* (1880), and he was given a position as comedy film writer and director at the **Gaumont** Studio. Using simple stick figures he produced the first frame-by-frame animated cartoon film, *Fantasmagorie* (1908), projecting it in negative so that it looked like chalk drawings on a blackboard.

Cohn, Ferdinand Julius 1828–98 •*German botanist and bacteriologist*• Born in Breslau, Germany (now Wrocław, Poland), he was barred as a Jew from taking the degree examinations at Breslau University, and so went to Berlin, where he obtained his doctorate in botany at the age of 19. Professor of Botany at Breslau from 1859 and founder of the Institute of Plant Physiology, he is regarded as the father of bacteriology. He did important research in plant pathology, and worked with **Robert Koch** on anthrax. His work was a major factor in the overthrow of the theory of spontaneous generation.

Coke, Sir Edward, *also called* **Lord Coke** or **Lord Cooke** 1552–1634 •*English judge and jurist*• Born in Mileham, Norfolk, he studied at Trinity College, Cambridge, and was called to the bar in 1578. He became Speaker of the House of Commons (1593), Attorney General (1594), Chief Justice of the Common Pleas (1606), Chief Justice of the King's Bench (1613), and Privy Councilor. He vigorously prosecuted the Earl of **Essex**, Sir **Walter Raleigh**, and the Gunpowder Plot conspirators, but after 1606 increasingly supported the idea of national liberties vested in parliament, against the royal prerogative. From 1620, he led the popular party in parliament, serving nine months in prison. The Petition of Right (1628) was largely of his making.

“ ”

We have a saying in the House of Commons; that old ways are the safest and surest ways.

1628 Speech, London, May 8.

Coke, Thomas William *See* **Leicester of Holkham**

Colbert, Claudette, *originally* **Lily Claudette Chauchoin** 1903–96 •*US film and stage actress*• Born in Paris and educated in New York, her first film, *For the Love of Mike* (1927), led to a long-term contract with Paramount. Petite, saucer-eyed and glamorous, with a deep-throated laugh, she played historical seductresses in *The Sign of the Cross* (1932) and *Cleopatra* (1934) and sparkled in spirited comedy roles in such films as *It Happened One Night* (1934, Academy Award), *Tovarich* (1937), *Midnight* (1939) and *The Palm Beach Story* (1942).

Colbert, Jean-Baptiste 1619–83 •*French statesman*• Born in Rheims, he entered the service of Cardinal **Mazarin** (1651), and became the chief financial minister of **Louis XIV** (1661). His series of successful financial reforms doubled the revenue in 10 years, and he also reorganized the colonies in Canada, Martinique and Santo Domingo, provided a strong fleet, improved the civil code, and introduced a marine code. The wars and the extravagance of the court undid all that he had accomplished, however, and he died bitterly disappointed, hated by the people as the cause of their oppressive taxes.

Cole, George 1925– •*English actor*• Born in South London and educated in Morden, he worked on stage and in film before finding fame in radio's *A Life of Bliss*. His best-remembered films are the farcical *The Belles of St Trinian's* (1954), three *St Trinian's* sequels and *Too Many Crooks* (1959), in all of which he played flashy and incompetent minor crooks. His many television roles include Arthur Daley in *Minder* (1979–94), Sir Giles Lynchwood in *Blott on the Landscape* (1985), Henry Root in *Root into Europe* (1992) and Peter Banks in *My Good Friend* (1995). He was given the honorary title Officer, Order of the British Empire, in 1992.

Cole, G(eorge) D(ouglas) H(oward) 1889–1958 •*English economist, historian and detective-story writer*• Born in London, he was educated at St Paul's School and Balliol College, Oxford, where he later taught. Historian, chairman (1939–46, 1948–50) and president of the Fabian Society from 1952, he wrote numerous books on socialism, including biographies of **William Cobbett** (1925) and **Robert Owen** (1925) and a history of the British working-class movements, 1789–1947 (1948), often in collaboration with his wife, **Margaret Isabel Cole** and her brother, Raymond Postgate. The Coles also collaborated in writing detective fiction.

Cole, Dame Margaret Isabel, *née* **Postgate** 1893–1980 •*English writer, historian and political analyst*• Born in Cambridge, she was educated at Roedean School and Girton College, Cambridge. A socialist and feminist, she taught for a time at St Paul's School, London, before becoming a researcher for the Fabian Society, where she met her husband, **G D H Cole**. They married in 1918 and together they wrote *An Intelligent Man's Review of Europe Today* (1933), *A Guide to Modern Politics* (1934) and 29 detective stories. In addition she wrote many distinguished works including *The Makers of the Labour Movement* (1948), and a highly acclaimed biography of **Beatrice Webb** (1945).

Cole, Nat "King," *originally* **Nathaniel Adams Coles** 1919–65 •*US singer and pianist*• Born in Montgomery, Alabama, the son of a Baptist minister, he was brought up in Chicago and played the organ in his father's church before embarking on a career as a jazz pianist in the 1930s. His King Cole Trio (1939–51) made its first hit record, "Straighten Up and Fly Right," in 1943. Remembered mainly as a vocalist, Cole's mellow, caressing voice and impeccable phrasing produced a series of hit ballads, including "Mona Lisa" (1950) and "Unforgettable" (1951). He began acting in films in 1943, and became the first African American to host his own television show in 1956, but was subject to racist harassment when he bought a house in the Beverly Hills area. His daughter, Natalie Maria Cole (1949–), is also a singer. Her albums include *Everlasting* (1987) and *Unforgettable* (1991).

Coleman, David 1926– •*English sports commentator and broadcaster*• Born in Alderley Edge, Cheshire, he began his sporting life as a middle-distance runner, winning the Manchester Mile in 1949. He entered journalism, working on the *Stockport Express* and other local newspapers, and joined the BBC in 1959. Noted for his reporting at the 1972 Munich Olympics when Israeli athletes were taken hostage, he built up a reputation for high-quality coverage, but also found fame for his inadvertently funny sayings. He has covered World Cup finals since 1958 and Olympic Games since 1960, and hosted the long-running television quiz program *A Question of Sport* from 1979 to 1997.

Coleman, Ornette 1930– •*American jazz musician and composer*• He was born in Fort Worth, Texas, where he began playing alto saxophone in rhythm and blues and jazz bands. He moved to Los Angeles, and began to experiment from the mid-1950s with free-form jazz and his own distinctive approach to melodic and harmonic organization, later dubbed Harmolodics. A series of important recordings in 1959–60 with sympathetic collaborators like **Don Cherry**, Charlie Haden and Ed Blackwell established him as a leading but controversial innovator, and he became the figurehead of the free jazz movement of the 1960s. He adopted electric instrumentation in the 1970s, and he has also written for chamber groups and symphony orchestras.

Coleridge, Samuel Taylor 1772–1834 •*English poet*• He was born in Ottery St Mary, Devon. The son of a vicar, and the youngest of a very large family, he had an unhappy childhood. He was educated at Christ's Hospital and Jesus College, Cambridge, where he studied for the Church. His university career was interrupted in 1793 by a runaway enlistment in the 15th Dragoons from which he was rescued by his family. In 1794 he met **Robert Southey**, and together they planned, but never created, a "Pantisocracy" or commune on the banks of the Susquehanna, in Pennsylvania. In 1795 he married Sarah Fricker, a friend of Southey's, who married her sister Edith. He became immersed in lecturing and journalism in Bristol, interspersed with itinerant preaching at Unitarian chapels. He published his first book of poems, *Poems on Various Subjects* (1796), which contained the "Ode to France." In 1797 the Coleridges moved to a cottage at Nether Stowey, Somerset, and later that year met **William** and **Dorothy Wordsworth**. It was a significant meeting for English poetry—their discussions produced a new poetry which represented a revulsion from neoclassic artificiality and, consequently, the renovation of the language of poetry. *Lyrical Ballads* (1798), which opened with Coleridge's "The Rime of the Ancient Mariner" and closed with Wordsworth's "Tintern Abbey," was thus in the nature of a manifesto. German philosophy and criticism influenced Coleridge greatly and he published translations of **Schiller**'s *Piccolomini* and *Wallenstein*. In 1800 he settled at Keswick and for a time, with the Wordsworths at Grasmere and Southey already resident at Keswick, it looked as if a fruitful career was opening out for him, but he was deeply unhappy at this time, due partly to his addiction to opium, and partly to an increasingly unhappy marriage. From then on his association with Wordsworth was strained; his relations with Dorothy continued only through her devotion to him. In 1809 he began a weekly paper, *The Friend*, which ran for 28 issues and was published as a book in 1818. In 1810 he finally broke with Wordsworth and settled in London, where he engaged in miscellaneous writing and lecturing, and in 1816 he published *Christabel and Other Poems*, which included "Christabel" and the fragment, "Kubla Khan," both written in his earlier period of inspiration. His critical writing in these middle years is important as the finest creative criticism in the language, collected in *Biographia Literaria* (1817), *Aids to Reflection* (1825), and *Anima Poetae* (edited from his *Notebooks*, 1895). He also wrote some moving late poems, including "Youth and Age" and "Constancy to an Ideal Object."

" "

"God save thee, ancient Mariner!
From the fiends that plague thee thus!
Why look'st thou so?"—With my cross-bow
I shot the Albatross.

1798 "The Rime of the Ancient Mariner," part 1.

Coleridge-Taylor, Samuel 1875–1912 •*English composer*• Born in London, the son of a West African doctor and an Englishwoman, he studied at the Royal College of Music. He composed *Hiawatha* (1898–1900), and other popular cantatas and orchestral works.

Colette, *properly* **Sidonie-Gabrielle Colette**, *also known as* **Colette Willy** 1873–1954 •*French novelist*• She was born in Saint-Sauveur-en-Puisaye, Burgundy. Her early novels, the *Claudine* series, were published by her first husband, Henri Gauthier-Villars, under his pen name "Willy." From 1904 (the end of their collaboration) to 1916 she wrote under the name "Colette Willy." After their divorce in 1906 she appeared in music halls in dance and mime, and out of this period came *L'envers du music-hall* (1913, Eng trans *Music-Hall Sidelights*, 1957). Keenly perceptive, she writes with an intense, sensual responsiveness to the world of nature and to her childhood. Her novels include *Chéri* (1920, Eng trans 1929), *La fin de Chéri* (1926, Eng trans *The Last of Chéri*, 1932), and *Gigi* (1944, Eng trans 1953).

Coligny, Gaspard II de, Seigneur de Châtillon 1519–72 •*French Huguenot leader*• Born in Châtillon-sur-Loing, he fought in the wars of **Francis I** and **Henry II** of France, and was made Admiral of France (1552). In 1557 he became a Protestant, and commanded the Huguenots during the second and third Wars of Religion. Disliking his influence over her son, **Charles IX**, **Catherine de' Médicis** made him one of the first victims in the St Bartholomew's Day Massacre in Paris (1572).

Collett, (Jacobine) Camilla, *née* **Wergeland** 1813–95 •*Norwegian novelist*• Born in Kristiansand, she had a strict upbringing and in her adult life became a passionate champion of women's rights. Her novel *Amtmandens døttre* (1855, "The Magistrate's Daughters") is notable for its sympathetic portrayal of young women trapped by stultifying convention. *I den lange naetter* (1862, "Through the Long Nights") is an insomniac's pillow book, reconstructing childhood scenes. Her brother was the writer Hendrik Arnold Wergeland (1808–45).

Collings, Jesse 1831–1920 •*English politician*• Born in Littleham-cum-Exmouth, Devon, he was elected Radical Member of Parliament for Ipswich in 1880. He was Member of Parliament for Bordesley as a Unionist (1886–1918), and was especially identified with the Agricultural Labourers' Union and measures for promoting allotments and smallholdings ("three acres and a cow").

Collingwood, Cuthbert Collingwood, Baron 1750–1810 •*English naval commander*• Born in Newcastle upon Tyne, from 1778 his career was closely connected with that of Lord **Nelson**. He played a prominent part in the naval victories of Lord **Howe** off Brest (1794), of Lord **Jervis** off Cape St Vincent (1797), and of Nelson off Cape Trafalgar (1805), where he held the second command. He died at sea, and was buried beside Nelson, in St Paul's Cathedral, London.

Collingwood, R(obin) G(eorge) 1889–1943 •*English philosopher, historian and archaeologist*• Born in Coniston, Cumbria, and educated at Rugby and Oxford, he taught at Oxford. He was an authority on the archaeology of Roman Britain, and much of his philosophical work was concerned with the relations of history and philosophy, viewing philosophy as always influenced by its own time and culture. His many books include: *Speculum Mentis* (1924), *Roman Britain and the English Settlements* (1936), *The Principles of Art* (1937), *Autobiography* (1939), *Essay on Metaphysics* (1940), *The New Leviathan* (1942), and two posthumous works, *The Idea of Nature* (1945) and *The Idea of History* (1946).

Collins, Albert 1932–93 •*US blues guitarist and singer*• Born in Leona, Texas, he was a cousin of **Lightnin' Hopkins**, and inherited the Texas blues guitar tradition of Hopkins and T-Bone Walker. He had a regional hit in 1958 with "The Freeze," and became known for an "icy," spare guitar sound. He recorded in a crossover blues-funk style in the late 1960s, and flourished in the blues revival of the 1980s. He joined Cray and Johnny Copeland on the best-selling *Showdown* (1985), one of several records for which he received Grammy award nominations.

Collins, Francis Sellers 1950– •*US genetic scientist*• Born in Staunton, Virginia, he was educated at the University of Virginia, Yale University, and the University of North Carolina. While working at the University of Michigan (1984–93), he led a team that identified the genes responsible for cystic fibrosis (1989), neurofibromatosis (1990) and Huntington's disease (1993). As director (from 1994) of the National Human Genome Research Institute he led their Human Genome Project to complete the successful sequencing of the human genome (completed in 2000 in conjunction with their commercial rivals Celera Genomics).

Collins, Jackie 1941– •*English author*• Born in London, she went with her sister **Joan Collins** to Hollywood hoping to become a film star but instead established herself as a best-selling author with *The World Is Full of Married Men* (1968). Subsequent novels typically dealt with the themes of love, lust and power in the film world. *The Stud* (1969) and *The Bitch* (1979) were both made into successful films starring Joan Collins, while *Hollywood Wives* (1983), *Lucky* (1985) and *Lady Boss* (1989) became television miniseries. Later books have included *Dangerous Kiss* (1999) and *Hollywood Wives: The New Generation* (2001).

Collins, Joan Henrietta 1933– •*English actress and writer*• Born in London, she made her film debut in *Lady Godiva Rides Again* (1951) and used her sultriness and headline-catching private life to build a career as an international celebrity. By the 1970s she was appearing in low-budget horror films such as *Tales from the Crypt* (1972), but her fortunes were revitalized with a leading role in the popular television soap opera *Dynasty* (1981–89). She has written the novels *Prime Time* (1988) and *Too Damn Famous* (1994), and her memoirs, *Second Act* (1996). Her sister is the best-selling novelist **Jackie Collins**.

Collins, Michael 1890–1922 •*Irish politician and Sinn Fein leader*• Born in County Cork, he became an active force in the Sinn Fein independence movement, and was imprisoned in England in 1916 for his part in the Easter Rebellion. On the declaration of independence, he raised funds for the movement and was subsequently responsible, with **Arthur Griffith**, for negotiating the 1921 treaty that created the Irish Free State (1922). But when **Eamon de Valera** and his supporters insisted on a fully independent republic, civil war between the two factions broke out. Collins became head of the provisional Free State Government in 1922, but only 10 days after taking office he was killed in an IRA ambush.

Collins, Michael 1930– •*US astronaut*• Born in Rome, Italy, he graduated from the US Military Academy, West Point, then became an experimental test pilot at the Air Force Flight Test Center, Edwards Air Force Base, California. He joined NASA as an astronaut in 1963 and went into orbit as copilot in Gemini 10, which was launched on July 18, 1966. On the historic Apollo 11 moon-landing mission in 1969 he was in the command module while **Neil Armstrong** and **Buzz Aldrin** set foot on the moon. His publications include the autobiographical *Carrying the Fire* (1974) and *Mission to Mars* (1990).

Collins, Phil(ip) 1951– •*English singer, drummer and songwriter*• Born in Hounslow, West London, he joined Genesis as drummer in 1970, and took over as lead vocalist when singer **Peter Gabriel** left the group (1985). As a solo artist his success was greater, with albums like *Face Value* (1981), *But Seriously* ... (1989) and *Both Sides* (1993), and won an Academy Award for the song "You'll Be in My Heart" from the soundtrack of the film *Tarzan* (1999). He has appeared on television, in *Miami Vice*, and starred in the films *Buster* (1987) and *Frauds* (1992).

Collins, Wilkie (William) 1824–89 •*English novelist*• Born in London, the elder son of the artist **William Collins**, he was educated partly at Highbury, but from 1836 to 1839 was with his parents in Italy. After his return he spent four years in business, and then was called to the bar, but gradually devoted himself to literature, writing the first full-length detective stories in English. His best work was written in the 1860s when he produced *The Woman in White* (1860), *No Name* (1862), *Armadale* (1866) and *The Moonstone* (1868). Perhaps because of his poor health and opium addiction, his later novels, often driven by pressing social issues, are more uneven in quality.

Collins, William 1788–1847 •*English landscape and figure painter*• Born in London, he studied at the Royal Academy. He is remembered for his subject pictures of country scenes, such as *Blackberry Gatherers* and *The Bird-Catchers* (1814). He was the father of **Wilkie Collins**.

Collins, William 1789–1853 •*Scottish publisher*• He was born in Eastwood, Renfrewshire. A weaver by trade, he opened a private school for the poor in Glasgow in 1813. A friend of the evangelist Thomas Chalmers (1780–1847), in 1819 he set up business in Glasgow as a bookseller and publisher with Chalmers's brother. The company became the largest independent publishing house in Britain, and remained under family control until 1979.

Collip, James Bertram 1892–1965 •*Canadian biochemist*• Born in Belleville, Ontario, and educated at the University of Toronto, he taught at the University of Alberta at Edmonton, McGill University and Western Ontario University. Early in 1921 he went to the Toronto laboratory of **John Macleod**, where he worked with Sir **Frederick Banting** and **Charles Best** on the isolation and identification of insulin. This research earned the team the 1923 Nobel Prize, with Banting sharing his half with Best and Macleod doing the same with Collip. In 1922 Collip returned to Edmonton to focus his career on biochemical aspects of endocrine function.

Collymore, Frank Appleton 1893–1980 •*Barbadian poet and story writer*• He was educated at Combermere School, where he taught from 1910 to 1958. As founder and editor of the long-running literary magazine *Bim* (1942–1975), he was a major force in the rise of modern West Indian literature. He published five books of poems, notable chiefly for their evocation of the sea and Caribbean landscape. His *Collected Poems* were published in 1959.

Colman, St d. 676 •*Irish monk*• He was a monk on the island of Iona and became Bishop of Lindisfarne in 661, but in 664 withdrew to Iona on the defeat of the Celtic party at the Council of Whitby.

Colman, Ronald 1891–1958 •*English film and stage actor*• Born in Richmond, Surrey, he moved to Hollywood, where he made his screen debut in 1919 in *The Live Wire*. His dashing good looks, mellifluous voice and gentlemanly manner made him a popular romantic leading man for three decades, and he was one of the few major Hollywood stars to survive the transition to the sound era. His films include *Raffles* (1930), *A Tale of Two Cities* (1935), *The Prisoner of Zenda* (1937) and *Random Harvest* (1942).

Colmcille *See* **Columba, St**

Colombine *See* **Burgos Seguí, Carmen de**

Colt, Samuel 1814–62 •*US inventor*• Born in Hartford, Connecticut, in 1836 he took out his first patent for a revolver, which after the Mexican War (1846–48) was adopted by the US Army. He financed an immense armory in Hartford, and also worked on submarine mines and a submarine telegraph.

Coltrane, John William 1926–67 •*US jazz saxophonist and composer*• Born in Hamlet, North Carolina, he emerged in the 1950s as one of the most influential jazz performers of the postbebop era. His early engagements included working with **Dizzy Gillespie** and **Bud Powell**, but his distinctive style coalesced with the **Miles Davis** Quintet from 1955, and then with pianist **Thelonious Monk** in 1957. His so-called sheets-of-sound style of harmonic exhaustiveness reached a logical culmination in *Giant Steps* (1959). The intensity of his attack and dense flow of notes influenced a generation of future saxophone players, as did his adoption of the soprano saxophone as a second instrument to the tenor. His post-1960 quartet with pianist McCoy Tyner and drummer Elvin Jones produced some of his most important recordings, notably *A Love Supreme* (1964). His music grew increasingly experimental toward the end of his life, when his collaborators (in both music and Eastern philosophy) included his wife, Alice Coltrane (*née* McLeod, 1937–), who went on to have a significant musical career in her own right. Their sons, Ravi and Omar, are also musicians.

“ ”

The main thing a musician would like to do is to give a picture to the listener of the many wonderful things he knows and senses in the universe.

1966 Quoted in sleeve-note to the reissue of ***Coltrane's Sound*** *(originally published 1961).*

Coltrane, Robbie, *originally* **Robin McMillan** 1950– •*Scottish actor*• Born in Rutherglen, near Glasgow, his early career included an involvement with writer **John Byrne** in *The Slab Boys* (1978) and its sequel *Cuttin' A Rug* (1980). A talented mimic and wit, he displayed his comic skills on television in a succession of satirical sketch shows and in a serious vein as police psychologist Fitz in *Cracker* (1993–96). His films include *Mona Lisa* (1986), *The Fruit Machine* (1987), *Henry V* (1989), in which he played Falstaff, *Nuns on the Run* (1990), *The Pope Must Die* (1991), *Golden Eye*, *Harry Potter and the Sorcerer's Stone* (2001) and *Harry Potter and the Chamber of Secrets* (2002).

Colum, Pádraic 1881–1972 •*Irish poet and playwright*• Born in County Longford, he became a leader of the Irish literary revival, and wrote plays for the Abbey Theatre, including *Broken Soil* (1903, later called *The Fiddler's House*), *The Land* (1905) and *Thomas Muskerry* (1910). He published his first collection of poems, *Wild Earth*, in 1907. In 1916 he was cofounder of the *Irish Review*. From 1914 he lived and taught in the US, where he wrote several further volumes of verse. His novel *The Flying Swans* (1957) was followed by the memoir *Our Friend James Joyce* (1958), written with his wife, Mary.

Columba, St, *also known as* **Colmcille ("Colm of the Churches")** 521–97 •*Irish missionary in Scotland*• He was born into the royal warrior aristocracy of Ireland at Gartan, County Donegal, and according to his 7th-century biographer, **Adomnan**, he studied under St Finnian at Clonard with St **Ciaran**. In 546 he founded the monastery of Derry. In 561 he was accused of having been involved in the bloody Battle of Cuildreimhne, for which he was excommunicated. In 563, accompanied by 12 disciples, he found haven on the Hebridean island of Iona, where he founded a monastery that became the mother church of Celtic Christianity in Scotland. He organized the monastery as a school for missionaries, founded numerous churches in the islands, and played a vigorous role in the politics of the country. Although he spent the last 34 years of his life in Scotland, he visited Ireland on occasion, and toward the end of his life he founded the monastery of Durrow in Ireland. He was renowned as a man of letters and revered as a warrior saint, and his supernatural aid was frequently invoked for victory in battle. His feast day is June 9.

Columban or **Columbanus, St**, *known as* **the younger Columba** 543–615 •*Irish missionary*• Born in Leinster, he studied under St **Comgall** at Bangor in County Down, and in c. 585 went to Gaul with 12 companions and founded the monasteries of Anegray,

Luxeuil and Fontaine in the Vosges. His adherence to the Celtic Easter involved him in controversy, and his vigorous criticism of the vices of the Burgundian court led to his expulsion in 610. After a year or two in Bregenz, on Lake Constance, he went to Lombardy, and in 612 founded the monastery of Bobbio, in the Appenines, where he died. His writings include sermons and a commentary on the Psalms (Eng trans, ed G S M Walker, 1957). His feast day is November 23.

Columbus, Christopher 1451–1506 •*Genoese explorer, and discoverer of the New World*• He was born in Genoa and went to sea at the age of 14. As early as 1474 he had conceived the design of reaching India by sailing westward, a design in which he was encouraged by Florentine astronomer Paolo Toscanelli; in 1477 he "sailed 100 leagues beyond Thule," probably to or beyond Iceland; and, having also visited the Cape Verde Islands and Sierra Leone, he began to seek a patron for his intended expedition. Finally, his plans were accepted by **Ferdinand** and **Isabella of Castile** in April 1492. On Friday August 3, Columbus set sail in command of 50 men on the small *Santa Maria*; they were attended by two little caravels, the *Pinta* and the *Niña*, the whole squadron comprising only 120 adventurers. He first made the Canary Islands, and new land was descried on Friday October 12, probably Watling's Island in the Bahamas. He then visited Cuba and Hispaniola (Haiti), planted a small colony, and set sail with his two caravels (for the flagship had been wrecked). After a difficult and stormy voyage, he reentered the port of Palos on March 15, 1493, and was received with the highest honors by the court. He set out on his second voyage on September 25 with 3 carracks and 17 small caravels, and on November 3 sighted Dominica in the West Indies. After a succession of wretched quarrels with his associates, and a long illness in Hispaniola, he returned to Spain much dejected in 1496. His third voyage, begun in 1498, resulted in the discovery of the South American mainland. In 1500 Columbus and his brother were sent home in irons by a newly appointed royal governor, but the king and queen repudiated this action and restored Columbus to favor. His last great voyage (1502–04), along the south side of the Gulf of Mexico, was accomplished in the midst of great hardships. He died at Valladolid in Spain.

Comaneci, Nadia 1961– •*Romanian gymnast*• Born in Onesti, Moldavia, at the 1976 Olympic Games at the age of 14, she won gold medals in the parallel bars and beam disciplines, becoming the first gymnast to obtain a perfect score of 10 for both events. She also won a gold medal in the beam at the 1978 world championships. She won both the beam and floor-exercise gold medals in the 1980 Olympics. Later she became an international judge, and coach to the Romanian national team. In 1989 she defected to the US via Hungary.

Combe, William 1741–1823 •*English writer and adventurer*• Born in Bristol, he was educated at Oxford, inherited a fortune in 1762 and led the life of an adventurer, spending much time in debtors' jails. He made his name with his three verse satires on popular travel books: *The Tour of Dr Syntax in Search of the Picturesque* (1809), *The Second Tour of Dr Syntax in Search of Consolation* (1820) and *The Third Tour of Dr Syntax in Search of a Wife* (1821). Illustrated with cartoons by **Thomas Rowlandson**, they recounted the travels of "Dr Syntax," a clergyman-schoolmaster. He also wrote the text for Rowlandson's *Dance of Death* (1815–16), *Dance of Life* (1816) and *Johnny Quae Genus* (1822).

Comgall, St c. 515–602 •*Irish abbot*• Born in Ulster, he founded, c. 558, the great Abbey of Bangor, in County Down. He is said to have lived on the Hebridean island of Tiree for a time, and accompanied St **Columba** on his journey to the north of Scotland.

Commodus, Lucius Aurelius AD 161–92 •*Roman emperor*• The son of **Marcus Aurelius**, he proved unable to live up to the example of his virtuous father, and his reign (from AD 186) degenerated into one of imperial despotism. After the discovery of his sister Lucilla's plot against his life (183), he became increasingly unbalanced, imagining that he was the god Hercules, and renamed Rome after himself. At length his mistress, Marcia, had him strangled by Narcissus, a famous athlete. His death brought to an end the dynasty of the Antonine emperors.

Comnenus 1057–1461 •*Byzantine rulers*• Originally Italian, many members of the family occupied the Byzantine throne (1057–1185), and that of Trebizond (1204–1461). See **Alexius I Comnenus**, **Isaac I** and **Anna Comnena**. David Comnenus, the last in Trebizond, was executed at Adrianople with all his family (1462), by **Mehmet II**.

Compaoré, Blaise 1940– •*Burkina Faso soldier and politician*• Educated locally and in military academies in Senegal and France, he joined the army in 1958, rising to command the Artillery Group (1975–76). In 1980 he was appointed Minister of Rural Development and from 1983 to 1987 was second in command to Thomas Sankara (1950–87). He overthrew Sankara and became Chairman of the Popular Front of Burkina Faso and Head of Government in 1987. In 1991 military rule in Burkina Faso ended and Compaoré became President in an election boycotted by the opposition. He was reelected in 1998.

Compton, Arthur Holly 1892–1962 •*US physicist and Nobel Prize winner*• Born in Wooster, Ohio, he studied at Princeton University and Cambridge, and held posts at Washington University in St Louis and at the University of Chicago. He developed a theory to describe the interaction of X-rays with matter, and confirmed the theory by measuring the wavelength of X-rays scattered by a target. For this important test of the particle nature of light, he shared the 1927 Nobel Prize for physics with **Charles Wilson**. He was involved in the Manhattan Project and built the first reactor with **Enrico Fermi** in Chicago (1942).

Compton, Denis Charles Scott 1918–97 •*English cricket player and journalist*• Born in Hendon, he first played for Middlesex in 1936, and was first capped for England the following year. He played in 78 Test matches, scoring 17 Test centuries. In his first-class career he scored over 38,000 runs, including 123 centuries; in 1947 he scored a record 18 centuries. He was also a talented soccer player, a member of the Cup-winning Arsenal team in 1950, and was capped for England in 1943.

Compton, John George Melvin 1926– •*St Lucian politician*• Born in Canouan in St Vincent and the Grenadines, he graduated from the London School of Economics. At independence in 1979 he was St Lucia's first Prime Minister.

Compton-Burnett, Dame Ivy 1884–1969 •*English novelist*• Born in London, she graduated in classics from the Royal Holloway College, London University, and published her first novel, *Dolores*, in 1911. Her rather stylized novels are often set in upper-class Victorian or Edwardian society, and the characters usually belong to a large family, spanning several generations. She was noted for her skillful use of dialogue. Her works include *Brothers and Sisters* (1929), *Parents and Children* (1941), *Mother and Son* (1955, James Tait Black Memorial Prize), *A Father and His Fate* (1957), *The Mighty and Their Fall* (1961) and *A God and His Gifts* (1963).

“ ”

As regards plots I find real life no help at all. Real life seems to have no plots.
1945 **Orion**, *no. 1, "A Conversation."*

Comstock, Anthony 1844–1915 •*US morals crusader*• He was born in New Canaan, Connecticut. As founder and secretary (1873–1915) of the New York Society for the Suppression of Vice, he lobbied to keep obscene materials from being sent through the mail and worked to prosecute not only quack doctors and fraudulent advertisers, but also many writers, poets, and painters. He brought legal proceedings against **George Bernard Shaw**'s play *Mrs. Warren's Profession* in 1905; Shaw had already coined the term *comstockery* to describe narrow-minded and puritanical crusading.

Comte, Auguste 1798–1857 •*French philosopher and social theorist*• Born in Montpellier, he was educated at the École Polytechnique in Paris (1814–16). In 1826 he began teaching philosophy, but suffered a breakdown, and was largely supported by **J S Mill** and other friends. His two major works were *Cours de philosophie positive* (6 vols, 1830–42) and *Système de politique positive* (4 vols, 1851–54, "System of Postive Philosophy"). His positivism sought to expound the laws of social evolution, to describe the organization and hierarchy of all branches of human knowledge, and to establish a true science of society as a basis for social planning and regeneration. He is generally regarded as the founder of sociology.

Condé, Louis I de Bourbon, Prince de 1530–69 •*French nobleman and Huguenot leader*• Born in Vendôme, he was the younger brother of Antony of Bourbon, king of Navarre. Although a hunchback, he fought in the wars between **Henry II** of France and Spain (1551–57), and joined the Huguenots on the accession of **Francis II** (1559). He led the Huguenots during the French Wars of Religion and was defeated at Dreux during the first civil war (1562). In the second war (1567–69) he was defeated at Jarnac, taken prisoner, and shot.

Condé, Louis II de Bourbon, 4th Prince de, *known as* **the Great Condé** 1621–86 •*French nobleman*• The great-grandson of Louis I de Bourbon (Prince de **Condé**), he was born in Paris. Proud, hot-tempered, aggressively atheist, during the Thirty Years' War he defeated Spain at Rocroi (1643) and Lens (1648). He was recalled (1649) to suppress the first French uprising (Fronde) against Cardinal **Mazarin** and the Regent **Anne of Austria**. In 1650 he rebelled and led the second Fronde, but fled to Spain, where he served for six years against France, until he was defeated at the Battle of the Dunes (1658). Pardoned in 1659, he became one of **Louis XIV**'s greatest generals; he defeated the Spanish in Franche-Comté (1668), and with the Vicomte de **Turenne** commanded the French armies in the Netherlands. After a last indecisive battle at Seneffe (1674) against **William III** of Orange, he retired, gout-ridden, to Chantilly.

Condorcet, Marie Jean Antoine Nicolas de Caritat, Marquis de 1743–94 •*French mathematician, politician and philosopher*• Born in Ribemont, he studied in Paris, and his *Essai sur le calcul intégral* (1765, "Essay on Integral Calculus") won him a seat in the Academy of Sciences. He wrote five volumes of obituaries of famous scientists, amounting to intellectual biographies, and contributed to **Denis Diderot**'s *Encyclopédie*. On the outbreak of the revolution he was sent by Paris to the Legislative Assembly (1791), and in 1792 he became president of the Assembly, siding usually with the Girondins. Condemned by the extremist Jacobins, he hid for eight months, but, forced to move, was recognized and imprisoned; he was found dead the next morning. In his *Progrès de l'esprit humain* (1794, "Progress of the Human Mind"), written in hiding, he insisted on the justice and necessity of establishing a perfect equality of civil and political rights between the sexes, and proclaimed the infinite perfectibility of the human race.

Cone, James Hal 1938– •*US theologian*• Born in Fordyce, Arkansas, he studied at Garrett Theological Seminary and Northwestern University, becoming Charles A Briggs Professor of Systematic Theology at Union Theological Seminary, New York (1977–87, Distinguished Professor from 1987). His angry criticisms of the presuppositions of White theology in *A Black Theology of Liberation* (1970) were followed by the more measured *God of the Oppressed* (1975), *For My People* (1984), *Speaking the Truth* (1986), the autobiographical *My Soul Looks Back* (1987) and *Martin and Malcolm and America* (1991).

Confucius, *Latin for* **Kongfuzi (K'ung-fu-tzu, "the Master K'ung")** 551–479 BC •*Chinese philosopher*• Confucius was born of an aristocratic but impoverished family in the state of Lu, part of the present province of Shandong (Shantung). He married at 19, and became a government official in Lu with a retinue of disciples, mostly young gentlemen whom he was preparing for government service. He was promoted to ministerial rank and enjoyed a successful and highly popular career, which eventually attracted jealousy and hostility and led to a breach with the ruler. In 497 BC he left Lu and for a dozen years became an itinerant sage, wandering from court to court seeking a sympathetic patron and attended by a company of his disciples. In about 485 he returned to Lu and spent his final years teaching and possibly writing. After his death his pupils compiled a volume of memorabilia, the *Analects*, which record Confucius's sayings and doings; most of the other works attributed to him are later compilations which, like the philosophy of "Confucianism" itself, are probably only loosely related to his own teachings. Confucius emerges as a great moral teacher who tried to replace the old religious observances with moral values as the basis of social and political order. In his Way (*dao*) he emphasized the practical virtues of benevolence (*ren*), reciprocity (*shu*), respect, and personal effort that were to be interpreted pragmatically with regard to individual circumstances and cases rather than any abstract system of imperatives.

" "

The people may be made to follow a course of action, but they may not be made to understand it.

c. 479 BC ***Analects***.

Congreve, William 1670–1729 •*English dramatist and poet*• Born in Bardsey near Leeds, he was educated at Trinity College, Dublin, where he was a fellow student of **Jonathan Swift**. In 1693 his first comedy, *The Old Bachelor*, produced under **John Dryden**'s auspices, with the celebrated **Mrs Bracegirdle** as heroine, achieved brilliant success. His second comedy, *The Double Dealer* (also 1693), was in every way stronger, but the satire on the heartless sexual morals of the time was aimed too directly at the theater's best customers, and it failed to please. His best-known play, *Love for Love* (1695), generally regarded as his masterpiece, is more vital than its predecessors, and has a more coherent plot and truer characterization. In 1697 his only tragedy, *The Mourning Bride*, appeared, best remembered for the quotations "music hath charms to soothe a savage breast" and "nor hell a fury like a woman scorned" (often misquoted as "hell hath no fury like a woman scorned"). His last play, *The Way of the World* (1700), was not a success. He died in a coach accident.

Conley, Rosemary 1946– •*British writer and dietitian*• She was a sickly child, and was told that she would not live past the age of 10. However, she survived an operation, became a committed Christian and lived to produce numerous books on diet, cooking and exercise, starting with *Rosemary Conley's Complete Hip and Thigh Diet* (1989). She also owns a nationwide exercise franchise business and produces fitness videos such as *Rosemary Conley's Flat Stomach Plan* (1995). Between 1988 and 1995 the British Top Ten Paperback list always featured one of her books.

Connaught, Prince Arthur, Duke of 1850–1942 •*British prince and soldier*• Born at Buckingham Palace, London, the third son of Queen **Victoria**, he trained at the Royal Military Academy, Woolwich, then served in Canada, Gibraltar, Egypt and India (1869–90). Thereafter he was Commander in Chief in Ireland (1900–04), Commander in Chief of the Mediterranean (1907–09) and Governor-General of Canada (1911–16). He was created Duke of Connaught and Strathearn (1874). In 1879 he married Princess Louise Margaret of Prussia (1860–1917). Of their children, Margaret (1882–1920) married the future King **Gustav VI** of Sweden (1905), and their son, Prince Arthur (1883–1938), was Governor-General of South Africa (1920–23).

Conner, Denis Walter 1942– •*US yachtsman*• He was born in San Diego, California. He won the 1974 America's Cup, as coskipper of *Courageous*, and was Star Class world champion twice. However, after 1983 he became the only US skipper to lose the America's Cup in 132 years, when *Liberty* was beaten by *Australia II* in a 4–3 victory. He regained the cup from the Australians in *Stars and Stripes* in Perth (1987). He put up a successful defense against New Zealand in 1988, but lost to them (captained by **Peter Blake**) in 1995.

Connery, Sir Sean Thomas 1930– •*Scottish film actor*• Born in Edinburgh, he had a succession of jobs, including milkman, lifeguard and coffin polisher. His powerful physique won him a position in the chorus line of the London stage production of *South Pacific* (1951–52). Sporadic film work followed, but it was as **Ian Fleming**'s secret agent James Bond in *Dr. No* (1962) that he became an international film star. He played the role on seven occasions until *Never Say Never Again* (1983). Other notable film roles include an army rebel in *The Hill* (1965), a 19th-century union leader in *The Molly Maguires* (1969), and a roistering adventurer in *The Man Who Would Be King* (1975). He won the British Academy of Film and Television Arts Best Actor Award for *The Name of the Rose* (1986) and an Academy Award for his portrayal of an aging Irish cop with true grit in *The Untouchables* (1987). Later films include *The Hunt for Red October* (1990) and *The League of Extraordinary Gentlemen* (2003). He was knighted in 2000.

Connolly, Billy 1942– •*Scottish comedian*• Born in Glasgow, he became a shipyard welder and entertained his workmates with caustic patter and tunes plucked out on a banjo. Affectionately known as the "Big Yin," he gained a loyal following as a stand-up comic and singer, and in 1975 he enjoyed a number-one hit with the single "D.I.V.O.R.C.E." His stage act was captured in the documentary film *Big Banana Feet* (1975). He has acted in such films as *Water* (1985), *The Big Man* (1990) and *The Debt Collector* (1999), and his other work includes a production of *Die Fledermaus* (1978) and such television dramas as *Androcles and the Lion* (1984) and *Dreaming* (1990). He starred in the US television sitcoms *Head of the Class* (1990–92) and *Billy* (1992), and has starred in British series following his comedy tours.

Connolly, Cyril Vernon 1903–74 •*English author and journalist*• He was born in Coventry, Warwickshire, and educated at Eton and Balliol College, Oxford. He contributed to the *New Statesman* and other periodicals and wrote regularly for the *Sunday Times*. He was founder-editor of *Horizon* (1939–50) with **Stephen Spender**. Among his works are *The Rock Pool* (1936), his only novel; *Enemies of Promise* (1938), critical essays with "A Georgian Boyhood" describing his own childhood; *The Unquiet Grave* (1944), under the pseudonym "Palinurus," containing miscellaneous aphorisms and reflections; and various collections of essays.

Connolly, Maureen Catherine, *known as* **Little Mo** 1934–69 •*US tennis player*• Born in San Diego, California, she made tennis history by becoming the first woman to win the so-called Grand Slam of the four major titles (British, US, French and Australian) in the same year (1953). She won the US title in three consecutive years (1951–53) and the Wimbledon singles in three consecutive years (1952–54).

Connors, Jimmy (James Scott) 1952– •*US tennis player*• He was born in East St Louis, Illinois. He was Wimbledon men's singles champion in 1974 and 1982, won the Australian Open in 1974, and the US Open in 1974, 1976, 1978, 1982, and 1983. He was World Championship Tennis champion in 1977 and 1980, Masters champion in 1978, and was a member of the US Davis Cup team in 1976 and 1981. A left-handed player, he was one of the first to use the double-fisted backhand.

Conrad I d. 918 •*King of Germany*• He was the son of the Count of Franconia, and nephew of the emperor Arnulf. Elected king on the extinction of the direct Carolingian line (911), he gradually reestablished imperial authority over most of the German princes, carried on an unsuccessful war with France, and at last fell mortally wounded at Quedlinburg in a battle with the Hungarians.

Conrad II c. 990–1039 •*King of Germany and Holy Roman Emperor*• The son of the Duke of Franconia and founder of the Salian dynasty (crowned king in Mainz, 1024), in 1026 he crushed a rebellion in Italy and was anointed Holy Roman emperor by the pope (1027). He was soon recalled to Germany to put down four revolts, which he achieved by 1033, when he was also crowned king of Burgundy. A fresh rebellion recalled him to Italy (1036); but this time he was forced to grant various privileges to his Italian subjects. Shortly after his return he died at Utrecht. He was succeeded by his son **Henry III**.

Conrad III 1093–1152 •*King of Germany and Holy Roman Emperor*• He was the first **Hohenstaufen** Holy Roman Emperor. His support of **Henry V** earned him the duchy of Franconia in 1115. On the death of Emperor Lothar III he was crowned at Aachen (1138). When St **Bernard of Clairvaux** preached a new crusade, Conrad set out for Palestine with a large army (1147). He designated his nephew, **Frederick I Barbarossa**, as his successor.

Conrad, Joseph, *originally* **Józef Teodor Konrad Nalecz Korzeniowski** 1857–1924 •*British novelist*• He was born of Polish parents in Berdichev, Poland (now Ukraine). His father was a revolutionary and writer who was exiled in 1862. In 1878 Joseph joined an English merchant ship, and he was naturalized in 1884 when he gained his certificate as a master. In the 10 years that followed, he sailed to Singapore, Borneo and the Belgian Congo, and his experiences at sea inspired much of his writing. In 1895 he married and soon afterward settled in Kent, England, where he devoted himself to writing. His first novel was *Almayer's Folly* (1894), followed by *An Outcast of the Islands* (1896), *The Nigger of the Narcissus* (1897), *Lord Jim* (1900), *Nostromo* (1904), *The Secret Agent* (1907) and *Under Western Eyes* (1911). Perhaps the short story was his true medium—*Tales of Unrest* (1898), *Heart of Darkness* (1902), *Youth* (1902) and *Twixt Land and Sea* (1912). His semiautobiographical *The Mirror of the Sea* (1906) and his *Personal Record* (1912) testify to his high artistic aims. His later work such as *The Arrow of Gold* (1919) owes its popularity largely to his earlier work. His unfinished novel *Suspense* was published in 1925.

Conran, Jasper 1959– •*English fashion designer*• He was born in London, the son of **Terence** and **Shirley Conran**. He trained at the Parsons School of Art and Design in New York, and produced his first collection of easy-to-wear, quality clothes in London in 1978. He has designed clothes for several stage productions such as *My Fair Lady* (1992) and the Scottish Ballet's *Sleeping Beauty* (1994).

Conran, Shirley Ida, *née* **Pearce** 1932– •*English designer, fashion editor and author*• Born in London and educated at St Paul's Girls' School and Portsmouth College of Art, she was married to **Terence Conran** from 1955 to 1962, and designed for and directed Conran Fabrics. Their sons **Jasper Conran** and Sebastian both became designers. In 1964 she turned to journalism and became woman's editor for the *Observer* magazine and editor of the *Daily Mail*. After a debilitating illness she wrote the best-selling *Superwoman* (1975), a book telling working women and mothers how to cope, which was followed by four more superwoman books. In 1979 she moved to Monaco, and published her first fiction book, *Lace* (1982).

Conran, Sir Terence Orby 1931– •*English designer and businessman*• Born in Esher, Surrey, and educated at Bryanston School, Dorset, he founded and ran the Habitat Company (1971), based on his own success as a furniture designer and the virtues of good design and marketing. He has since been involved in the management of several related businesses such as Richard Shops, Conran Stores and Habitat Mothercare, and several restaurants. He has published a variety of books about interior design, gardening and cooking including *Terence Conran's Kitchen Book* (1993) and *The Essential Home Book* (1994). He was married to **Shirley Conran** (1955–62) and is the father of **Jasper Conran**. He was knighted in 1983.

Constable, Archibald 1774–1827 •*Scottish publisher*• Born in Carnbee, Fife, he became a bookseller in 1795. He bought the *Scots Magazine* in 1801, and was chosen as publisher of the *Edinburgh Review* (1802). For his flair and respect for editorial independence he is regarded as the first modern publisher, and his quick appreciation of **Walter Scott** became the envy of the book trade. In 1812 he purchased the copyright to the *Encyclopaedia Britannica*, but in 1826 was financially ruined, heavily involving Scott in his bankruptcy.

Constable, John 1776–1837 •*English landscape painter*• Born in East Bergholt, Suffolk, he assisted his father for a year in the family mill (1794), but the landscape painter and art patron Sir George Beaumont (1753–1827) prevailed on his family to send him to London, where he studied at the Royal Academy Schools. In 1828, on the death of his father-in-law, an inheritance of £20,000 enabled him to devote himself exclusively to his landscape work, which expressed his profound love of the country, and his interest in the effects of changing light and the movement of clouds across the sky. In 1824 he had a success with *The Haywain* (1821) in the Paris Salon, and in 1825 at Lille with his *White Horse*. His later years were saddened by bereavements, ill health and depression, but he worked steadily, though his landscapes were frequently unsold. Some of his finest landscapes, including *The Cornfield* and *The Haywain*, are in the National Gallery, London. Other works include *View on the Stour* (1819) and *Salisbury Cathedral* (1823).

“ ”

When I set down to make a sketch from nature, the first thing I try to do is to forget that I have ever seen a picture.

Quoted in C R Leslie ***Memoirs of the Life of John Constable*** *(1843).*

Constans I, Flavius Julius c. 320–50 AD •*Roman emperor*• The youngest son of **Constantine I** (the Great), he received Illyricum, Italy and Africa as his share of the empire in AD 337. After defeating his brother Constantine at Aquileia (340), he became sole ruler of the West until his death at the hands of Magnentius.

Constans II, Flavius Heraclius 630–68 •*Byzantine emperor*• Born in Constantinople (Istanbul), he succeeded his father Constantine III in 641. His reign was marked by the loss of Egypt and much of the Middle East to the Arabs. His despotism and attempt at Church unity aroused antagonism, and he was murdered in his bath by a chamberlain five years after transferring his capital to Syracuse.

Constantine I, *known as* **Constantine the Great**, *properly* **Flavius Valerius Aurelius Constantinus** c. 274–337 AD •*Roman emperor*• He was born in Naissus, in Upper Moesia, the eldest son of **Constantius Chlorus** and **Helena**. Before Constantius died at York (306) he designated his son as his successor; the army proclaimed him Augustus. **Galerius** did not dare to quarrel with Constantine, yet he granted him the title of Caesar only, refusing that of Augustus. Political complications now increased, until in 308 there were actually no fewer than six emperors at once —Galerius, Licinius and Maximin in the East; and Maximian, Maxentius his son, and Constantine in the West. Maxentius drove his father from Rome, and after some intrigues Maximian committed suicide (309). Maxentius threatened Gaul with a large army. Constantine, crossing the Alps by Mont Cénis, defeated Maxentius on three occasions; Maxentius was drowned after the last great victory at the Milvian Bridge near Rome (312). Constantine was now sole emperor of the West and, with the death of Galerius in 311 and of Maximian in 313, Licinius became sole emperor of the East. After a war (314) between the two rulers, Licinius was forced to cede Illyricum, Pannonia and Greece. For the next nine years Constantine devoted himself vigorously to the correction of abuses and the strengthening of his frontiers. In 323 he again defeated Licinius, and put him to death, becoming sole ruler of the Roman world. He chose Byzantium (modern-day Istanbul) for his capital, and in 330 inaugurated it under the name of Constantinople ("City of Constantine"). Christianity became a state religion in 324, although paganism was not suppressed. In 325 the great Church Council of Nicaea was held, in which the court sided against the Arians and the Nicene Creed was adopted. Yet it was only shortly before his death that Constantine was baptized. His later years were vicious, seeing the execution of his eldest son Crispus (326) for treason and of his own second wife Fausta (327) on some similar charge. He proposed to divide the empire between the three sons he had by Fausta—**Constantius**, Constantine II and **Constans I**—but in 340 Constantine II lost his life in war with Constans.

Constantine I 1868–1923 •*King of Greece*• Born in Athens, he was the son and successor (1913) of **George I**. As a military commander he was unsuccessful in the Turkish War (1897), but led the Greeks to victory in the Balkan War (1912–13). Brother-in-law to Kaiser **Wilhelm II** of Germany, he insisted on Greek neutrality in World War I, but was forced to retire in favor of his son Alexander. In 1920 he was restored to the throne by plebiscite, but after a military revolt (1922), abdicated again in favor of his son **George II**.

Constantine II or **XII** 1940– •*King of Greece*• Born near Athens, he was the son and successor of **Paul I**. In 1967 the Colonels' Junta seized power in a military coup. The king made an abortive attempt to regain power, but fled into exile in Rome. He was formally deposed (1973), and the monarchy was abolished by national referendum (1974). He now lives in London. His heir is Crown Prince Paul (1967–).

Constantine IV d. 685 •*Byzantine emperor*• The son and successor (668) of **Constans II**, he gave up much territory to the Bulgarians, Serbs and Croats.

Constantine V Copronymus 718–75 •*Byzantine emperor*• The son of **Leo III**, he was crowned coemperor at the age of two. On the death of his father (741) he defeated a revolt by his brother-in-law, Artabasdus, and thereafter intensified Leo's iconoclastic policies. A well-managed Council of the Church (754) promulgated the destruction of icons, starting an era of persecution of the Orthodox party. Constantine directed numerous expeditions against the Bulgarians, whom he defeated (763, 773), and died on campaign.

Constantine XI Palaeologus Dragases 1404–53 •*Last Byzantine emperor*• Born in Constantinople (Istanbul), he was the fourth son of Manuel II and the Serbian princess Helen Dragaš. During the reign of his elder brother, John VIII, he and his other brothers jointly ruled the despotate of Morea, a Byzantine appanage in the Peloponnese, and on John's death (1448) Constantine succeeded to an empire consisting of little more than Constantinople and its environs, threatened by the vast Ottoman Empire which surrounded it. Powerless to prevent the inevitable Ottoman siege, Constantine died fighting in the final Turkish assault.

Constantine, Learie Nicholas Constantine, Baron 1901–71 •*West Indian cricket player and politician*• Born in Trinidad, he was an accomplished all-rounder and respected fast bowler. In 1928 he became the first West Indian cricket player to achieve 1,000 runs and 100 wickets in a single season. A barrister, he was appointed to defend the interests of West Indians working in Britain during World War II and subsequently became high commissioner in London for Trinidad and Tobago (1962–64) and a member of the British Race Relations Board (1966). He was knighted in 1962 and given a life peerage in 1969.

Constantine Nikolayevich, *Russian* **Konstantin Nikolayevich** 1827–92 •*Russian grand duke*• The son of Czar **Nicholas I**, he commanded the Russian fleet in the Crimean War (1854–56). He became president of the council in 1865 and 1878, but was dismissed in 1882 for revolutionary views.

Constantius AD 317–61 •*Roman emperor*• He was the third son of **Constantine I** (the Great). As Eastern Roman emperor from AD 337, he fought against the Persians, and after the death of his brother **Constans I** (350), he became sole emperor. He was a supporter of Arian Christianity and exiled Catholic bishops.

Constantius Chlorus c. 250–306 AD •*Roman emperor*• The father of **Constantine I** (the Great), he took the title Caesar (AD 292). After reestablishing Roman power in Britain and defeating the Alemanni, thus strengthening the Rhine frontier, he took the title of Augustus (305). He died in York.

Conté, Lansana c. 1945– •*Guinean soldier and politician*• Military commander of the Boke Region, he led a bloodless coup on the death of President **Ahmed Sékou Touré** (1984) and set up the Military Committee for National Recovery (CMRN) and became president himself. He relaxed the centralizing policies of Touré and successfully encouraged many exiles to return. In 1993 he was elected as a civilian president, and was reelected in 1998. In 2001 he announced a desire to change the constitution to allow him to stand for a third successive term in office.

Conti, Tom 1941– •*Scottish actor*• Born in Paisley, Strathclyde, of part-Italian extraction, he studied acting at the Royal Scottish Academy of Music and Drama. He was praised for his stage performance as the defiant paraplegic in *Whose Life Is It Anyway?* (1978), a role he later repeated on Broadway; other stage performances include *Jeffrey Bernard Is Unwell* (1990) and the world première of **Arthur Miller**'s *The Ride Down Mount Morgan* (1991). His films include *Galileo* (1973), *Reuben, Reuben* (1983, Academy Award nomination), *Heavenly Pursuits* (1986) and *Shirley Valentine* (1989).

Contucci, Andrea *See* **Sansovino**

Conyngham, Barry Ernest 1944– •*Australian composer, lecturer and performer*• Born in Sydney, he studied at Sydney University and the New South Wales Conservatorium. Influenced by jazz in his early years, he has also used computer-generated sound, which he actively promotes. Japanese influences are also strong in his work. His output includes the operas *Edward John Eyre* and *Ned* (about **Ned Kelly**), a cello concerto and a ballet, *Vast* (1989), as well as music for film and theater.

Cook, Beryl 1937– •*English painter*• Born in Plymouth, she started to paint in the early 1960s and was entirely self-taught. Her humorous paintings of the inhabitants and views of her hometown are often deemed "naive" and "primitive" but her acute character observation is both penetrating and flamboyant. Refusing to admit to any significant artistic influences, she claims that television, in particular "The Flintstones" cartoon characters, have influenced her work. She was given the honorary title Officer, Order of the British Empire, in 1996.

Cook, Frederick Albert 1865–1940 •*US explorer and physician*• Born in Calicoon Depot, New York, he studied medicine at the Universities of Columbia and New York. He was the surgeon on an Arctic expedition to Greenland in 1891 led by **Robert Peary**, and further expeditions to Greenland and the Antarctic followed in the mid-1890s. In 1906 he claimed to have made the first ascent of the highest mountain in North America, Mount McKinley, Alaska. On July 3, 1907, he sailed from Gloucester, Massachusetts, and crossed Ellesmere Island, reaching Axel Heilberg Island on March 17, 1908. From there he apparently reached the North Pole on April 21, 1908. Although he was treated as a hero on his return, his claim to the Pole was questioned by Peary. An investigative committee set up by Copenhagen University discredited both Cook's claim to be the first man to the North Pole and his ascent of Mount McKinley. He denied this vehemently in public statements and in his book *My Attainment of the Pole* (1911). His subsequent imprisonment for fraud in 1923 brought his character into further question, and although he was pardoned shortly before his death, the controversy continues.

Cook, James 1728–79 •*English navigator*• He was born in Marton, Yorkshire, the son of an agricultural laborer. He was apprenticed to Whitby shipowners, and spent several years in the coasting and Baltic trade, then joined the navy (1755), becoming master in 1759. He was engaged in surveying around the St Lawrence and the shores of Newfoundland, and commanded the *Endeavour*, for the Royal Society, to observe the transit of Venus across the sun (1768–71). On the return, New Zealand was circumnavigated and charted, the east coast of Australia was surveyed and claimed for Great Britain, the strait between Australia and New Guinea was sailed through. Made commander, he was given control of a second voyage of discovery on the *Resolution* and *Adventure* (1772–75) to discover how far the lands of the Antarctic stretched northward, and sailed round the edge of the ice, reaching 71° 10' S at longitude 106° 54' W. During the intervals between the Antarctic voyages, he visited Tahiti and the New Hebrides, and discovered New Caledonia and other groups. Owing to his precautions, there was only one death among his crews during all three years. His next and last voyage (1776–79) was to discover a passage around the north coast of America from the Pacific, which he surveyed from 45° N as far as Icy Cape in the Bering Strait, where he was forced to turn back, reaching Kailua Bay in Hawaii in January 1779. The inhabitants, at first friendly, changed their attitude, and on February 14, when he landed on Kealakekua Beach to recover a stolen boat, he was killed. Cook did more than any other navigator to add to our knowledge of the Pacific and the Southern Ocean.

Cook, Peter Edward 1937–95 •*English comedian and actor*• Born in Torquay, Devon, he had his first success while studying languages at Cambridge as one of the writers and performers of the revue *Beyond the Fringe* (1960, sequel *Behind the Fridge*, 1971–72). He invented the stage character E L Wistey, a forlorn figure perplexed by the complexities of life. He collaborated with **Dudley Moore** in the irreverent television program *Not Only … But Also* (1965–71) and made regular film appearances, notably as the devil in *The Wrong Box* (1966), and in *The Bed Sitting Room* (1969), *The Secret Policeman's Ball* (1979), *The Princess Bride* (1987) and *Without a Clue* (1988). He was cofounder of both The Establishment club in London and the satirical magazine *Private Eye*, and made many recordings with Moore under the names Derek and Clive.

Cook, Robin, *originally* **Robert Finlayson Cook** 1946– •*Scottish Labour politician*• Born in Bellshill, Lanarkshire, he was educated at Edinburgh University. He was a teacher and an adult education organizer before embarking on a political career with the Labour Party. An Edinburgh town councilor (1971–74), Member of Parliament for Edinburgh Central (1974–83) and then for Livingston (1983–), he became chief Opposition health spokesman in 1989. He became Trade and Industry spokesman in 1992, then Foreign and Commonwealth Affairs spokesman in 1994. Widely recognized as one of the most intellectually formidable parliamentarians of recent years, he entered **Tony Blair**'s Cabinet as Foreign Secretary after Labour won the general election in 1997. In 2001 he became Leader of the House of Commons, a position he resigned in 2003 over the invasion of Iraq.

Cook, Thomas 1808–92 •*English railway excursion and tourist pioneer*• Born in Melbourne, Derbyshire, he left school at the age of 10 and worked at various jobs before becoming a Baptist missionary. He established a travel agency in London and his first railway trip (a temperance one) was made from Leicester to Loughborough in 1841, and was the first public excursion train journey in England. In 1856 he introduced a railway tour of Europe, and in the early 1860s he began the travel firm Thomas Cook and Sons, which included tours of the US. His travel agency is now a worldwide organization.

Cooke, (Alfred) Alistair 1908–2004 •*US journalist and broadcaster*• Born in Salford, England, he was educated at Cambridge and at Yale and Harvard. He joined the BBC in 1934 as a film critic but then became a foreign correspondent and specialized in US affairs. He returned to the US in 1937 and became a US citizen in 1941. He has written numerous books, including *One Man's America* (1952) and *America Observed* (1988). He wrote and narrated the award-winning *America: A Personal History of the United States* (1971–72), and broadcast the radio program *Letter from America* from 1946 until 2004. He was was given the honorary title Knight Commander, Order of the British Empire, in 1973.

Cooke, Sam, *originally* **Sam Cook** 1931–64 •*US soul, gospel, and rhythm and blues singer*• Born in Clarksdale, Mississippi, he first sang in a gospel quartet with his siblings, and was a member of the innovative Soul Stirrers (1951–56). His mainstream hit, "You Send Me," sold 2 million copies, and a string of pop, soul and rhythm and blues hits followed, but his career ended when he was shot by the woman manager of a motel in Los Angeles over a dispute with a girl. The posthumously released classic "A Change Is Gonna Come" was a poignant reminder of the loss of this highly influential artist.

Cookson, Dame Catherine Ann 1906–98 •*English popular novelist*• She was born in East Jarrow, Tyneside, and her best-selling, mostly historical fiction is largely set in the northeast of England. She was the author of more than 70 books of tragedy and romance, including the Mallen trilogy and the Tilly Trotter series, and a 1988 survey revealed that almost a third of all fiction borrowed from British public libraries was by Cookson. She was given the honorary title of Dame Commander, Order of the British Empire, in 1993 for her generous donations to hospitals and charities in the northeast.

Cooley, Denton Arthur 1920– •*US cardiac surgeon*• Born in Houston, Texas, he received his MD from the Johns Hopkins University Medical School. With **Michael DeBakey** and others, he pioneered open-heart surgery as well as the surgical treatment of diseases of the arteries, especially the treatment of aortic aneurysms by graft replacement.

Coolidge, (John) Calvin 1872–1933 •*30th President of the US*• Born in Plymouth, Vermont, he became a lawyer and then Governor of Massachusetts (1919–20), where he achieved renown in decisively using the state militia to break the Boston police strike in 1919. Vice President from 1921 to 1923, he succeeded as President on **Warren G Harding**'s death (1923). A strong supporter of US business interests, he was triumphantly reelected by the Republicans in 1924. Known for his reserved demeanor and cautious temperament, he cut taxes and reduced regulations on business. He was not greatly interested in foreign policy, but his administration did see the signing of the **Dawes** Plan to reduce Germany's reparations and the **Kellogg-Briand** Pact outlawing war. He declined to run for reelection in 1928, thereby escaping the public acrimony that was visited on his successor, **Herbert Hoover**, made to appear responsible for his policies, later thought to have contributed to the stock market crash of 1929.

“ ”

Prosperity is only an instrument to be used, not a deity to be worshipped.
1928 Speech, Boston, June 11.

Coolidge, Susan, *pseudonym of* **Sarah Chauncy Woolsey** 1835–1905 •*US children's writer and literary critic*• Born in Cleveland, Ohio, she wrote the *Katy* books (*What Katy Did*, 1872, and its sequels) and other stories for girls. She also edited some correspondence by **Fanny Burney** and **Jane Austen**.

Cooney, Ray(mond George Alfred) 1932– •*English dramatist, director and producer*• Born in London, he made his debut as an actor in *Song of Norway* (1946), and appeared in several stage comedies and farces in the 1950s and 1960s, but is best known as an author and director. His first play, a farce, *One for the Pot*, appeared in 1961, and was followed by many others, including *Two into One* (1981), *Run for Your Wife* (1983), which had a record-breaking nine-year run, *Wife Begins at Forty* (1986), *Out of Order* (1990), *Funny Money* (1994) and *Caught in the Net* (2001). In 1983 he created the Theatre of Comedy, based at the ShaftesburyTheatre, London.

Cooper, Anthony Ashley *See* **Shaftesbury, 3rd Earl of**

Cooper, Sir Astley 1768–1841 •*English surgeon*• Born at Brooke Hall, Norfolk, he studied in London and Edinburgh, and then lectured on anatomy at St Thomas's Hospital (1789) and at the College of Surgeons (1793). In 1800 he became surgeon at Guy's Hospital, and in 1813 Professor of Comparative Anatomy at the College of Surgeons. In his work he raised surgery from its primitive state to a science, and was the first to tie the abdominal aorta in treating an aneurysm. In 1820 he removed a tumor from the head of King **George IV**, and was made a baronet, and in 1828 he was appointed Sergeant-Surgeon to the King.

Cooper, Eileen 1933– •*English artist*• Born in Glossop, Derbyshire, she studied at Goldsmiths College and at the Royal College of Art, London, and became a visiting lecturer at Central St Martins College of Art, also in London. Her works, which explore a wide range of emotions, often from a feminist viewpoint, are executed in a bold linear fashion and are often haunting in their simplicity.

Cooper, Gary Frank James 1901–61 •*US film actor*• Born in Helena, Montana, he was originally a cartoonist. He moved to Los Angeles and began working as an extra and stunt rider in Western films before his appearance as the laconic cowboy in *The Virginian* (1929) made him a star. He then starred as the archetypal hero of many Westerns, and also made light comedy and high adventure. His many film credits include *A Farewell to Arms* (1932), *The Lives of a Bengal Lancer* (1935), *For Whom the Bell Tolls* (1943) and *Friendly Persuasion* (1956). He was nominated for an Academy Award for his performance in *Mr Deeds Goes to Town* (1936) and won Best Actor Academy Awards for performances as the World War I Quaker hero *Sergeant York* (1941) and as the sheriff who stood alone in *High Noon* (1952). He also received a Special Academy Award in 1960.

Cooper, Sir Henry 1934– •*English boxer*• Born in London, he was Amateur Boxing Association light heavyweight champion in 1952 and 1953, then turned professional. In 1959 he beat Brian London to gain the British heavyweight title that he held, apart from a brief spell, until 1971. He floored **Muhammad Ali** (then known as Cassius Clay) in 1963, though he did not win the fight, and in 1966 he fought him for the world heavyweight title but was forced to retire in the sixth round on account of a bad cut. In 1971 he lost his British heavyweight title in a disputed contest against Joe Bugner, and announced his retirement. Since retiring from the ring he has appeared regularly as a guest on television. He was knighted in 2000.

Cooper, James Fenimore 1789–1851 •*US novelist*• He was born in Burlington, New Jersey. His family later moved to Cooperstown, New York, then in a wild frontier region of great natural beauty. He was educated at Yale, but was expelled during his third year, and joined the merchant marine (1806), and then the navy as a midshipman (1808). He rose to the rank of lieutenant, but in 1811 resigned his commission and settled down as a country gentleman. His best works are his stories of the sea and of Native Americans—*The Spy* (1821), *The Pilot* (1823), *The Last of the Mohicans* (1826), *The Red Rover* (1827), *The Pathfinder* (1840), *The Deerslayer* (1841) and *Satanstoe* (1845). His other writings include a scholarly *Naval History of the United States* (1839). After visiting England and France, he was US consul at Lyons (1826–29). His later years were much disturbed by literary and newspaper controversies and litigation.

“ ”

The tendency of democracies is, in all things, to mediocrity.
1838 ***The American Democrat***, *"On the Disadvantages of Democracy."*

Cooper, Jilly, *née* **Sallitt** 1937– •*English author*• Born in Hornchurch, Essex, she was educated at Godolphin School, Salisbury, and worked as a reporter, copywriter and typist before becoming a columnist. She began publishing her own brand of buoyant observations on life, sex and country pursuits in the late 1960s with books such as *How to Stay Married* (1969) and *Supercooper* (1980), later diversifying into racy and highly successful novels such as *Riders* (1985), *Polo* (1991), and *Score* (1999). She has also written several children's books.

Cooper, Leon N(eil) 1930– •*US physicist and Nobel Prize winner*• Born in New York City and educated at Columbia University, he moved to the University of Illinois to join **John Bardeen** and **John Schrieffer** in producing the BCS (Bardeen-Cooper-Schrieffer) theory of superconductivity. Cooper made a theoretical prediction that at low temperatures electrons in a conductor could act in bound pairs (Cooper pairs), making the effective electrical resistance of the material zero. This theory won Bardeen, Cooper and Schrieffer the 1972 Nobel Prize for physics.

Cooper, Tommy 1922–84 •*Welsh comic*• Born in Caerphilly, Glamorgan, he first became interested in magic when given a present of tricks as a child. A member of the Horse Guards (1939–46), he began performing with the Combined Services Entertainment in the Middle East, where he acquired his trademark headgear of a red fez. He later refined his act in clubs and music halls before achieving television renown in numerous variety shows and his own 1950s series *It's Magic*. His act thrived on his apparent ineptitude at performing elaborate tricks. He also made occasional appearances in films like *The Plank* (1967). He died during the transmission of the television show *Live from Her Majesty's*.

Coote, Sir Eyre 1726–83 •*Anglo-Irish soldier*• He was born in Ash Hill, County Limerick. He entered the army early and saw service in Scotland, and from 1756 to 1762 served in India. It was he who induced **Robert Clive** to risk the Battle of Plassey (1757). In 1760 he defeated Thomas, Comte de Lally (1702–66), at Wandiwash, and his capture of Pondicherry in 1761 completed the downfall of the French in India. In 1777 he became Commander in Chief in India.

Cope, Edward Drinker 1840–97 •*US paleontologist*• Born to a Quaker family in Philadelphia, he studied zoology and was a curator and professor at Haverford College, Pennsylvania, by the age of 24. From 1889 he was professor at the University of Pennsylvania. From 1868 he led a series of excavations in the American West which produced a wealth of dinosaur skeletons, especially from the Badlands of South Dakota and Como Bluff, Wyoming. A famous rivalry developed between him and **O C Marsh**, each descending to underhanded tactics in the race for important fossils. Cope dynamited fossil localities to prevent Marsh from excavating there, while Marsh's employees readdressed Cope's crates of fossils to his own laboratory. Cope wrote 1,400 books and articles on his fossil discoveries and also contributed to evolutionary theory, giving his name to two influential ideas: "Cope's rule"—that animals have a tendency to ever-increasing size during their evolution—and the Cope-Osborn theory on the origin of mammalian molars.

Cope, Wendy 1945– •*English poet*• Born in Erith, Kent, and educated at Oxford, she worked as a primary-school teacher in London for 15 years before becoming a professional writer in 1986, with a talent for parody and for light-hearted demolitions of male authors such as **Ted Hughes** or **Philip Larkin**. She is a little less cruel to **T S Eliot** in "Limericks on The Wasteland." The titles *Making Cocoa for Kingsley Amis* (1986) and *Men and Their Boring Arguments* (1988) are fair indications of her approach.

Copernicus, Nicolaus, *Latin name of* **Mikojaj Kopernik** 1473–1543 •*Polish astronomer*• He was born in Torún in Prussia (now in Poland). After studying mathematics at the University of Cracow (1491–94) he went to Italy (1496) where he studied canon law and heard lectures on astronomy at the University of Bologna, while at Padua he studied medicine (1501–05). He was made a Doctor of Canon Law by the University of Ferrara (1503), and though nominated a canon at the cathedral of Frombork (1497), he never took holy orders. He pondered deeply on what he considered the unsatisfactory description of the world by **Ptolemy**, which had the Earth as the stationary center of the universe, and became converted to the idea of a sun-centered universe. He set out to describe this mathematically in 1512. Copernicus hesitated to make his work public, having no wish to draw criticism from Aristotelian traditionalists or from theologians such as **Martin Luther**, who had ridiculed him, but was eventually persuaded by his disciple **Rheticus** to publish his complete work, *De revolutionibus orbium coelestium* (1543, "The Revolutions of the Celestial Spheres"), which he dedicated to Pope **Paul III**. In the new system, the Earth is merely one of the planets, revolving around the sun and rotating on its axis. Copernicus was already old and ill by the time his book was printed, and he was unaware that it carried an anonymous and unauthorized "Preface to the Reader," presenting the work as a hypothesis rather than a true physical reality, written by Andreas Osiander (1498–1552), a Lutheran pastor of Nuremberg who supervised the last stages of the printing. Osiander's misguided intention was to forestall criticism of the heliocentric theory. The first printed copy of Copernicus's treatise, a work that fundamentally altered humanity's vision of the universe, reached its author on his deathbed. It was later banned by the Catholic Church, and remained on the list of forbidden books until 1835.

Copland, Aaron 1900–90 •*US composer*• Born in New York City, he studied in New York, and in France, under **Nadia Boulanger**. After his return to the US (1924), he was awarded a Guggenheim Fellowship (1925)—the first to be awarded to a composer. A series of early works influenced by **Stravinsky**, neoclassical in outlook and employing jazz idioms, was followed by compositions which drew on US tradition and folk music, of which the ballets *Billy the Kid* (1938) and *Appalachian Spring* (1944), and *A Lincoln Portrait* (1942), for orator and orchestra, are typical. As well as ballets and impressive film scores, he composed two operas and three symphonies.

“ ”

The difference between Beethoven and Mahler is the difference between watching a great man walk down the street and watching a great actor act the part of a great man walking down the street.

Quoted in the ***Wall Street Journal****, June 9, 1995.*

Copley, Sir Godfrey d. 1709 •*English philanthropist*• Born in Yorkshire, he left a fund in trust to the Royal Society that has been applied since 1736 to the provision of the annual Copley Medal, awarded for philosophical research.

Copley, John Michael Harold 1933– •*English theatrical producer*• He was born in Birmingham and, after a brief career on the stage, became stage manager at Sadler's Wells, London, 1953, both for the ballet and the opera companies. He joined the Covent Garden Opera Company as deputy stage manager (1960), becoming resident producer in 1972. He has produced most of the standard operatic repertoire for opera houses and festivals in Europe, the US and Canada, and has had a long and successful connection with Australian Opera, with productions including *Die Zauberflöte* (1973), and the Australian premiere of **Leoš Janáček**'s *Jenůfa* (1984).

Copley, John Singleton 1738–1815 •*American portrait and historical painter*• Born in Boston, Massachusetts, of Anglo-Irish parents, he was executing portraits at the age of 16, and in 1755 **George Washington** sat for him. His vigorous and original portraits of colonial figures such as **Paul Revere**, **Samuel Adams** and **John Hancock** are now seen as his finest work. In 1774 he left for England, and was commissioned to paint the king and queen. *The Death of Chatham* (1779–80) and *The Death of Major Pierson* (1783) are both in Tate Britain, London. Other works include an enormous canvas of the Siege of Gibraltar painted for the City of London (1786–91) and a group of the royal princesses in Buckingham Palace.

Coppard, A(lfred) E(dgar) 1878–1957 •*English short-story writer and poet*• Born in Folkestone, Kent, he left school when he was nine, and became a professional writer in 1919. In 1921 he published *Adam and Eve and Pinch Me*, and soon became celebrated for his tales of country life and character. His prose is remarkable for its detailed observations and poetic quality. Other volumes of stories include *The Black Dog* (1923) and *Lucy in Her Pink Jacket* (1954). His *Collected Poems* appeared in 1928.

Coppin, Fanny Marion Jackson, *née* **Jackson** 1837–1913 •*US teacher*• She was born a slave in the District of Columbia, and her aunt bought her freedom for her for $125 when she was young. From 1851 to 1857 she worked for the author George Henry Calvert, who encouraged her education, and she went on to study at Oberlin College, Ohio (1860–65). She became principal of the girls' high school department of the Institute for Colored Youth, Philadelphia (1865), then became its head principal (1869–1902), the first African-American woman to hold such a position, and during her 37 years at the institute she extended its curriculum, raised academic qualifications and provided vocational training.

Coppola, Francis Ford 1939– •*US film director, screenwriter and producer*• Born in Detroit, Michigan, he graduated from UCLA and worked on low-budget productions before directing the horror film *Dementia 13* (1963), followed by the musical *Finian's Rainbow* (1967). An accomplished screenwriter, he won an Academy Award for *Patton* (1970). Among his outstanding films are *The Godfather* (1972; *Part II*, 1974; *Part III*, 1990) and his controversial study of the Vietnam War, *Apocalypse Now* (1979). Later films include works as diverse as the romance *One from the Heart* (1982), the existentialist *Rumble Fish* (1983), *The Cotton Club* (1984), *Peggy Sue Got Married* (1984) *Tucker* (1988), *Bram Stoker's Dracula* (1992) and *The Rainmaker* (1997). He has also been the producer of numerous films. His daughter Sofia Coppola (1971–) is a director, writer and actress.

Corbett, Harry H 1925–82 •*British actor*• Born in Rangoon, Burma, the son of an army officer, he served with the Royal Marines during World War II. On demobilization, he joined **Joan Littlewood**'s Theatre Workshop and acted in the West End. He played rag-and-bone man Harold Steptoe alongside Wilfrid Brambell as his father, Albert, first in *The Offer*, in the BBC's Comedy Playhouse series (1962), then in the long-running *Steptoe and Son* (1962–74). Fond of playing the classics on stage, he has also starred in the television sitcoms *Mr Aitch* (1967) and *Grundy* (1980).

Corbett, "Gentleman" Jim (James John) 1866–1933 •*US boxer*• Born in San Francisco, California, he won the world heavyweight championship in 1892 by knocking out John L Sullivan (1858–1918) in the 21st round, and lost it in 1897 to Bob Fitzsimmons (1862–1917) in the 14th round. He failed to regain his title in two fights with his former sparring partner, James J Jeffries (1875–1953), in 1900 and 1903. Corbett, who is said to have introduced "science" into the art of boxing, also made several appearances on stage and in films.

Corbett, Ronnie (Ronald Balfour) 1930– •*Scottish comedian and actor*• He was born in Edinburgh, and following national service in the RAF, he entered showbusiness. Spotted in Danny La Rue's nightclub by **David Frost**, he appeared on television in *The Frost Report* (1966–67) and *Frost on Sunday* (1968–69). His small stature, impish sense of fun and inimitably discursive delivery soon gained him national popularity, and his own television series have included *No—That's Me Over Here* (1967–70) and *Sorry!* (1981–88). A fruitful partnership with **Ronnie Barker** led to the long-running *The Two Ronnies* (1971–87). His film appearances include *Casino Royale* (1967) and *No Sex Please, We're British* (1973).

Corbière, Tristan, *pseudonym of* **Édouard Joachim Corbière**

1845–75 •*French poet*• He was born in Coat-Congar, Finistère. He was largely unknown until **Paul Verlaine** included him in his *Les poètes maudits* (1884, "The Accursed Poets"). Corbière's collection *Amours jaunes* (1873, "Yellow Loves") was an acknowledged influence on **T S Eliot**. His bitter early work reflected the landscape of Brittany, and represented a powerful reaction against the excesses of Romanticism, and his later, more ironic poetry reads as if it had been written at least 50 years after its time.

Corbin, Margaret, *née* **Cochran** 1751–1800 •*American Revolutionary War heroine*• Born in Franklin County, Pennsylvania, she was raised by her uncle from the age of five, when her father was killed fighting Native Americans and her mother had been taken prisoner. Her husband John Corbin enlisted in the Revolution, and when he was killed during the Battle of Harlem Heights (1776), she took over his artillery station and continued firing his cannon until she herself was shot. Her injuries resulted in the permanent loss of the use of one arm. In 1779 she became the first woman to receive a military pension from Congress, and a monument at West Point was erected in her honor in 1916.

Corday, Charlotte, *properly* **Marie Charlotte Corday d'Armont** 1768–93 •*French noblewoman*• She was born in St Saturnin. Despite her aristocratic background she welcomed the Revolution at first, but was then so horrified by the behavior of the Jacobins that she resolved to kill either **Robespierre** or **Jean Paul Marat**. After hearing of Marat's demand for 200,000 more victims, she entered his house in Paris. Marat was having a bath, and his heartless comment about the fugitive Girondins ("I will have them all guillotined at Paris") incited her to stab him to death. Unrepentant, she was brought before the Revolutionary Tribunal and guillotined four days later.

Corea, Chick (Armando Anthony) 1941– •*US jazz pianist, bandleader and composer*• Born in Chelsea, Massachusetts, he was brought up in a musical family, and cut his professional teeth in Latin bands. He first recorded as a leader in 1966, but came to prominence after joining **Miles Davis**'s early jazz-rock fusion bands, then forming his own group, Return to Forever, in that vein in 1971. He has written some works that are closer to a classical vein than jazz, but has continued to move between straight jazz and fusion settings with his clearly demarcated Akoustic and Elektric bands.

Corelli, Arcangelo, *nicknamed* **Il divino** 1653–1713 •*Italian composer*• He was born in Fusignano, near Bologna. His concerti grossi and his solo and trio sonatas for violin mark an epoch in chamber music, and greatly influenced **J S Bach** and contemporary string technique.

Corelli, Marie, *pseudonym of* **Mary Mackay** 1855–1924 •*English novelist*• She was born in London, educated by governesses, and trained as a pianist but from 1885 devoted herself to writing. *A Romance of Two Worlds* (1886) was a bestseller and marked the beginning of a prolific career. A sentimental, self-righteous moralist, she was the writer that critics loved to hate, but her admirers included **Gladstone** and **Oscar Wilde**, and her readership was immense. Her novels include *Barabbas* (1893), *The Devil's Motor* (1910), *Eyes of the Sea* (1917) and *The Secret Power* (1921).

Cori, Carl Ferdinand 1896–1984 •*US biochemist and Nobel Prize winner*• Born in Prague, he married and graduated in medicine there, and in 1922 emigrated with his wife **Gerty Cori**. Both became professors at Washington University in St Louis from 1931. In 1936 he studied an ester isolated from frog muscle and discovered that the enzyme involved in its formation existed in muscle, heart, brain and liver. He obtained it in crystalline form in 1942, and recognized that it had both inactive and active forms and required a prosthetic group, adenylic acid. He shared the 1947 Nobel Prize for physiology or medicine with his wife and the physiologist **Bernardo Houssay**.

Cori, Gerty Theresa Radnitz 1896–1957 •*US biochemist and Nobel Prize winner*• Born in Prague, she trained in medicine at the German University of Prague, and married her fellow student **Carl Cori**, later emigrating with him to the US. With her husband she conducted research into carbohydrate metabolism, analyzing the process whereby glycogen is enzymatically broken down to glucose, liberating energy in the process. They also studied the effects of many hormones including insulin, adrenaline and pituitary extracts, and examined glycogen and glucose metabolism in biochemically abnormal circumstances. The latter work led her to the first demonstration that glycogen storage disease could be caused by abnormalities or deficits in enzymes. Gerty and Carl shared the Nobel Prize for physiology or medicine with the physiologist **Bernardo Houssay** in 1947.

Coriolanus, Gaius, *also called* **Gnaeus Marcius** 5th century BC •*Roman folk hero*• Named after his capture of the Volscian town of Corioli, and the subject of **Shakespeare**'s play *Coriolanus*, he was banished by the Romans for tyrannical behavior during a famine (491 BC). He took refuge with the Volsci, and proceeded to lead them against Rome, but after entreaties from his mother and wife, he spared Rome, and was executed by the Volsci.

Coriolis, Gustave Gaspard 1792–1843 •*French physicist*• Born in Paris, he was educated at the École Polytechnique, where he became professor in 1816. Intrigued by the problem of motion above a spinning surface, he considered the problem from around 1835, and in this study identified the "Coriolis force." This apparent force acting on objects moving across the Earth's surface results from the Earth's rotation. In the Northern Hemisphere, the path of an object appears deflected to the right, in the Southern Hemisphere to the left. It is responsible for wind and ocean current patterns.

Cormack, Allan MacLeod 1924–98 •*US physicist and Nobel Prize winner*• Born in Johannesburg, South Africa, he studied physics and engineering at Cape Town University and did postgraduate work at Cambridge. He pioneered the development of computerized axial tomography (CAT) scanning, which enables the production of detailed X-ray pictures of the human body. He shared the 1979 Nobel Prize for physiology or medicine with Sir **Godfrey Hounsfield**, who had independently developed a similar device.

Corneille, Pierre 1606–84 •*French dramatist*• Born in Rouen, he was educated in a Jesuit school and studied law. He moved to Paris in 1629, where his comedy *Mélite* (1629, Eng trans *Melite*, 1776) proved highly successful. He became one of Cardinal **Richelieu**'s "cinq auteurs" (five authors), engaged to compose plays on lines laid down by the cardinal, and produced such plays as *L'aveugle de Smyrne* (1638, "The Blind Man of Smyrna") and *La grande pastorale* (1639, "The Great Pastoral"), but he was too independent to retain Richelieu's favor. *Médée* (1635, "Medea") showed a marked advance on his earlier works, and *Le Cid* (first produced in January 1637) took Paris by storm, and had a profound impact on French drama. Richelieu ordered his literary retainers to criticize it, but the general enthusiasm remained strong. Other major tragedies were *Cinna* (1640, Eng trans *Cinna's Conspiracy*, 1713) and *Polyeucte* (1642, Eng trans *Polyeuctes*, 1655). *Le menteur* (1643, Eng trans *The Mistaken Beau; or, The Liar*, 1685) entitles him to be called the father of French comedy as well as of French tragedy. He returned to the stage in 1659 with *Œdipe*, and in 1671 joined **Molière** and Quinault in writing the opera *Psyché*. His last works were *Pulchérie* (1672) and *Suréna* (1674, Eng trans *Surenas*, 1969). A master of the Alexandrine verse form, his plays deal with heroes, but he concerned himself with moral and mental conflict rather than physical action, exploring the tensions between duty and honor on one hand, and passion on the other, and exalting humankind's capacity for freedom, strength of will, and spiritual development.

Corneille, Thomas 1625–1709 •*French playwright*• He was born in Rouen, the brother of **Pierre Corneille**. His tragedies, including *Timocrate* (1656), *Bérénice* (1657), *Camma* (1661), *Laodice* (1668), *Ariane* (1672), *Pyrrhus* (1690) and *Bradamante* (1696), are, in general, superior to his comedies.

Cornelius Nepos *See* **Nepos, Cornelius**

Cornelius, Peter 1824–74 •*German composer*• Born in Mainz, he went to Weimar in 1852, becoming a devotee of **Franz Liszt**, **Richard Wagner** and the New German school. He produced his famous comic opera, *Der Barbier von Bagdad* ("The Barber of Baghdad") in 1858, and his grand opera, *Der Cid*, in 1865. He was the nephew of **Peter von Cornelius**.

Cornelius, Peter von 1783–1867 •*German painter*• Born in Düsseldorf, he joined the group of Philipp Veit (1793–1862) and

Johann Overbeck in Rome in 1811, and assisted in the decoration of the Casa Bartoldi. In 1819 he was called to Munich by Crown Prince Ludwig of Bavaria (later **Ludwig I**). Here he remained until 1841, and executed the large frescoes of Greek mythological scenes in the Glyptothek and the New Testament frescoes in the Ludwigskirche, which was built to give scope for his art. Among his productions in Berlin are the frescoes for the Campo Santo, or royal burial place, the finest of which is his *Four Riders of the Apocalypse*.

Cornell, Eric A(llin) 1961– •*US physicist and Nobel Prize winner*• He was born in Palo Alto, California, and studied at Stanford University and the Massachusetts Institute of Technology. He won the Nobel Prize for physics (2001; with **Wolfgang Ketterle** and **Carl E Wieman**) for the achievement of Bose-Einstein condensation in dilute gases at very low temperatures, effectively creating a new state of matter.

Cornell, Ezra 1807–74 •*US industrialist and philanthropist*• Born in Westchester Landing, New York, he became a carpenter and millwright, and in association with **Samuel Morse** devised insulation for telegraph wires on poles. He founded and organized telegraph companies, including the Western Union Telegraph in 1855. In 1865, in association with Andrew Dickson White (1832–1918), he founded and heavily endowed Cornell University, which opened in Ithaca, New York, in 1868.

Cornforth, Sir John Warcup 1917– •*Australian chemist and Nobel Prize winner*• Born in Sydney, he studied at the university there and at Oxford. He took part in the wartime effort to synthesize the new drug penicillin, and also studied the biosynthesis of cholesterol and other steroids. From 1962 he and George Popják studied in detail the stereochemistry of the interaction between an enzyme and its substrate and biological oxidation-reduction reactions. He also collaborated extensively with Hermann Eggerer on the stereochemistry of enzyme action. In 1975 he was awarded the Nobel Prize for chemistry, which he shared with **Vladimir Prelog**, for his work on the chemistry of enzyme action. He was knighted in 1977.

“ ”

In a world where it is so easy to neglect, deny, pervert and suppress the truth, the scientist may find his discipline severe. For him, truth is so seldom the sudden light that shows new order and beauty; more often, truth is the uncharted rock that sinks his ship in the dark.

1975 Nobel Prize speech.

Cornwallis, Charles Cornwallis, 1st Marquis 1738–1805 •*English soldier*• Born in London, he served as aide-de-camp to the Marquis of **Granby** during part of the Seven Years' War. In the American Revolution (1775–83), with an inferior force he defeated **Horatio Gates** at Camden, South Carolina, in 1780, but in 1781 he was besieged at Yorktown, Virginia, and forced to surrender—a disaster that proved the ruin of the British cause in America. From 1786 to 1793 he was Governor General of India and Commander in Chief, defeating **Tippoo Sultán**. As Lord Lieutenant of Ireland (1798–1801) he crushed the 1798 rebellion, and as plenipotentiary to France he negotiated the Peace of Amiens in 1802. He was reappointed Governor General of India in 1804.

Corot, (Jean Baptiste) Camille 1796–1875 •*French landscape painter*• Born in Paris, in 1822 he took up the study of art. His main sketching ground was at Barbizon, in the Forest of Fontainebleau, but he made two other visits to Italy in 1835 and 1843. It was not until about 1840 that he fully developed his style, characterized by breadth and delicacy, and sacrificing accuracy of detail to unity of impression and harmony of effect. The Universal Exhibition of 1855 established his fame. Among his masterpieces are *Danse de nymphes*, *Homère et les bergers*, *Orphée*, *Joueur de flûte* and *Le bûcheron*.

Correggio, Antonio Allegri da c.1494–1534 •*Italian painter*• He was born in Correggio, near Parma. He painted for the Franciscan convent a *Virgin Enthroned* in 1514, now in the Dresden Gallery, and began his great series of mythological frescoes for the convent of San Paolo at Padua in 1518. *The Ascension* in the cupola of the Benedictine church of San Giovanni dates from 1521–24, and the decoration of the cathedral of Parma was commissioned in 1522. He also painted easel pictures, including *Ecce Homo* (National Gallery, London) and his celebrated nativity scene *The Night* commissioned in 1522, now in the Dresden Gallery. Five years later he painted *Il giorno*, an exquisite picture of St **Jerome** (Parma Gallery). *Education of Cupid* (National Gallery, London), *Danae* (Borghese Gallery, Rome) and *Leda* (Berlin Museum) have been assigned to his later years. His only son, Pomponio (1521–c. 1593), was also a painter, and an altarpiece by him is in the Academy in Parma.

Corrigan(-Maguire), Mairead 1944– •*Northern Irish peace activist and Nobel Prize winner*• Born in Belfast, she was cofounder with **Betty Williams** of the Northern Ireland Peace Movement in 1976. She started organizing peace petitions in the face of the sectarian violence in Northern Ireland, and the initiative became a mass movement of Roman Catholic and Protestant women known as the Community of the Peace People. She shared with Betty Williams the 1976 Nobel Peace Prize.

Cortés or **Cortéz, Hernán** or **Hernando** 1485–1547 •*Spanish conquistador and conqueror of Mexico*• He was born into a family of low nobility in Medellin, Estremadura. In 1511 he accompanied **Diego Velázquez de Cuellar** in his successful expedition to conquer Cuba. Inspired by the discoveries of **Pedro de Alvarado** and others, in 1518 Velázquez fitted out a small expedition of 550 men with 17 horses and 10 cannons and gave the command to Cortés. He landed first in the Yucatán, and subjugated Tabasco. At San Juan de Ulua, messengers from **Montezuma II**, the Aztec king, reached him, bringing presents. He founded Vera Cruz, and marched to Tlaxcala, whose warlike inhabitants, subdued after hard fighting, became his faithful allies. After some delay, he started on his march to Mexico, with his Tlaxcalan allies. He escaped a dangerous ambush at Cholula, and on November 8, 1519, he reached the capital, Tenochtitlán. There he was well received by Montezuma, who was captured and forced to submit to a public act of vassalage to Spain. In 1520 Cortés marched to the coast, leaving Alvarado in command, to deal with a force sent by Velázquez to arrest him, and succeeded in winning them to his side. Meanwhile Alvarado's harshness had provoked the Mexicans to revolt, and Cortés was forced to evacuate Tenochtitlán with heavy losses (the "Night of Sorrows"). In retreat, Cortés overcame a huge Aztec army at Otumba, and eventually reached Tlaxcala. After rebuilding his forces he laid siege to Tenochtitlán in 1521, capturing it and razing it to the ground, building Mexico City in its place. In 1522 he was appointed Governor and Captain General of New Spain. In May 1528 he went back to Spain, and was received with honor by **Charles V**. He returned in 1530 as Captain General, but not as Civil Governor, of New Spain. Poor and broken in health, he returned to Spain in 1540, and died near Seville.

Cortona, Pietro Berrettini da 1596–1669 •*Italian painter and architect*• Born in Cortona, he ranks, with **Gian Lorenzo Bernini**, as one of the great figures of the Roman Baroque. With **Lanfranco** and **Guercino** he was the founder of the Roman High Baroque style in painting. He specialized in highly illusionistic ceiling painting in which paint is combined with stucco and gilt to create arresting effects. The greatest of these is his *Allegory of Divine Providence* and *Barberini Power* (1633–39) in the Barberini Palace in Rome. Although he once said that he regarded architecture as a pastime, his church of Santi Martina e Luca in Rome is of high quality. His easel painting is usually less impressive.

Corvo, Baron *See* **Rolfe, Frederick William**

Cory, Charles Barney 1857–1921 •*US naturalist and traveler*• Born in Boston, he developed an early interest in ornithology and traveled widely in the eastern US and the Caribbean. A founder-member of the American Ornithologists' Union, he published *The Birds of the Bahamas* (1878) and the monumental *Birds of the Americas* (4 vols, 1918–19). Cory's shearwater was named in his honor.

Cosby, Bill (William Henry) 1937– •*US comedian*• Born in North Philadelphia, he served in the US Navy (1956–60), and later studied at Temple University, Philadelphia. He began performing as a nightclub comic, and an appearance on *The Tonight Show* (1965) led to his being cast in the television series *I Spy* (1965–68) where his role won him three Emmy awards and broke new ground in the portrayal of African Americans on screen. Subsequent television series include *The Bill Cosby Show Kids* (1969–71), *The New Bill Cosby Show* (1972–73), *The Cosby Show* (1984–92) and *Cosby* (1996). He also hosted the quiz show *You Bet Your Life* (1992). A congenial figure, his wholesome humor is based on quirky observations of the world around him and offbeat anecdotes based on personal experience. He has appeared in films such as *Uptown Saturday Night* (1974), *Ghost Dad* (1990) and *Jack* (1996). He has recorded more than 20 albums, and his book *Fatherhood* (1986) was a bestseller.

Cosgrave, Liam 1920– •*Irish statesman*• Born in Templeogue, County Dublin, the son of **William Thomas Cosgrave**, he was educated at St Vincent's College, Castleknock, Dublin. He was called to the bar in 1943 and was a member of the Dáil (1943–81). He was Minister for External Affairs (1954–57), Leader of the Fine Gael Party (1965–77) and Prime Minister (1973–77).

Cosgrave, William Thomas 1880–1965 •*Irish statesman*• Born in Dublin, he joined the Sinn Fein movement at an early age, and took part in the Easter Rising (1916). He became a Sinn Fein Member of Parliament (1918–22), and after his years as first President of the Irish Free State (1922–32), was Leader of the Opposition (Fine Gael, 1932–44). He was the father of **Liam Cosgrave**.

Cosimo, Piero di *See* **Piero di Cosimo**

Cosmas, *called* **Indicopleustes ("Indian Traveler")** fl. 6th century •*Merchant of Alexandria*• He traveled much in Ethiopia and parts of Asia. He returned to Egypt about 550, and in monastic retirement wrote a Greek work on Christian topography to prove the authenticity of the biblical account of the world.

Costa, Lucio 1902–98 •*Brazilian architect*• Born in Toulouse, France, to Franco-Brazilian parents, he studied in Rio de Janeiro. Influenced by **Walter Gropius**, **Mies van der Rohe** and **Le Corbusier**, in 1957 his plan for the city of Brasilia was chosen by an international jury for its clarity and ability to integrate monumentality and daily life. He devoted much of his time to the Brazilian Society for Historical Preservation, and was an authority on the colonial architecture of Brazil. He is considered the father of modern Brazilian architecture.

Costa, Manuel Pinto da 1937– •*São Tomé politician*• Born in Agua Grande, he founded the Movement for the Liberation of São Tomé and Príncipe (MLSTP) in Gabon (1972) and in 1974, taking advantage of a military coup in Portugal, returned and persuaded the new government in Lisbon to recognize the MLSTP as the sole representative of the people and to grant independence a year later. He became President in 1975 and set his country on a politically nonaligned course, serving until 1991.

Costello, Elvis, *real name* **Declan Patrick McManus** 1955– •*English singer-songwriter*• The most important songwriter to emerge from the English new wave of the late 1970s and one of the finest pop chroniclers of Great Britain in the 1980s, he was born in Paddington, London, the son of big band singer Ross McManus. He started his own career with the unrecorded band Flip City and as a solo folk-club singer. Signed to Stiff Records in 1977, he established his reputation as an intense and vitriolic musician with his debut album *My Aim Is True*. For his second album, *This Year's Model* (1978), he was joined by the Attractions—a three-piece group consisting of Steve Nieve, Pete Thomas and Bruce Thomas who worked with Costello on most of his albums over the next eight years. His albums have included *Get Happy* (1980), *Almost Blue* (1981, a collection of country and western songs), *Imperial Bedroom* (1982), *Goodbye Cruel World* (1984) and *King of America* (1986). More recently he has collaborated with Burt Bacharach, producing the album *Painted from Memory* (1998).

Costello, John Aloysius 1891–1976 •*Irish politician*• Born in Dublin and educated at University College, Dublin, he was called to the bar in 1914 and became Attorney General (1926–32). In 1948 he became Prime Minister of a government of several parties dominated by his own Fine Gael Party. As, foremost, a constitutional lawyer, one of his first acts was to repeal the External Relations Act, which paved the way that year for the formal change from the State of Eire to the Republic of Ireland. He was Prime Minister again from 1954 to 1957.

Costello, Lou *See* **Abbott, Bud**

Coster, Charles de 1827–79 •*Belgian storyteller*• He was born in Munich, and studied at Brussels. His most famous work, the prose epic *La légende et les aventures héroiques, joyeuses et glorieuses d'Ulenspiegel* (1866, Eng trans *The Legend of the Glorious Adventures of Tyl Ulenspiegel*, 1918), took 10 years to write.

Costner, Kevin 1955– •*US film actor and director*• He was born in Los Angeles, California, and graduated from California State University with a BA in marketing. He worked as a stage manager for Raleigh Studios before turning to acting and making his film debut in the low-budget *Sizzle Beach US* (1981). He achieved leading-man status with roles in *Silverado* (1985), *The Untouchables* (1987) and *No Way Out* (1987), and subsequent films include *Bull Durham* (1988), *Field of Dreams* (1989), *Robin Hood: Prince of Thieves* (1991), the critical and commercial flop *Waterworld* (1995) and *Tin Cup* (1996). He won a Best Director Academy Award for the epic Western *Dances with Wolves* (1990) in which he also starred.

Cotman, John Sell 1782–1842 •*English landscape artist*• Born in Norwich, he made journeys all over Great Britain sketching architecture and the countryside. In 1806 he returned to his birthplace and became a leading member of the "Norwich School," but from 1811 to 1823 lived in Yarmouth. His work exhibits a variety of styles, the best being characterized by skillful arrangement of masses of light and shade, with a minimum of modeling, giving an effect reminiscent of a Japanese print or a modern poster, as in his famous *Chirk Aqueduct* and *Greta Bridge* (1805, in the British Museum, London).

" "

Three quarters of mankind, you know, mind more what is represented than how it is done.

*Quoted in William Vaughn **Romantic Art** (1978).*

Cottier, Daniel 1838–91 •*Scottish stained-glass artist, designer, interior decorator and art dealer*• He was born in Glasgow, and by 1862 he was working as chief designer for a firm in Leith, Edinburgh. In 1867 he established a studio in Glasgow, and began working with the famous Glasgow architect **Alexander "Greek" Thomson**. Cottier produced decorative works and stained-glass designs for at least two of Thomson's best-known commissions: painted paneling in the United Presbyterian Church, Queen's Park, Glasgow, and the interior decoration of the eastern section of Glasgow's Great Western Terrace. In 1870, he went into partnership with Bruce Talbert, William Wallace and J M Brydon in London, and in 1873 branches were opened in the US and Australia. While in the US, Cottier collaborated with John La Farge to produce designs for a window in Holy Trinity Parish Church, Copley Square, Boston. He was a major exponent of the "aesthetic movement."

Cotton, Sir (Thomas) Henry 1907–87 •*English golfer*• Born at Holmes Chapel, Cheshire, and educated at Alleyn's School, in the 1930s and 1940s he almost single-handedly defended the US challenge in the British Open championship, winning in 1934, 1937 and 1948. He won many other titles, and played in the Ryder Cup against the US four times between 1929 and 1953.

Cotton, John, *known as* **the Patriarch of New England** 1585–1652 •*English Puritan clergyman*• Born in Derby, Derbyshire, he was educated at Trinity College, Cambridge, became a tutor there, and from about 1612 was a vicar in Boston, Lincolnshire. Cited for his Puritan views before Archbishop **Laud**, in 1633 he emigrated to Boston, Massachusetts. He became the head of Congregationalism in the US.

Coty, René 1882–1962 •*French statesman*• Born in Le Havre, he became a barrister, and was elected a Left Republican deputy in 1923. He entered the Senate in 1935 and was Minister of Reconstruction in 1947, and in 1953 became the last President of the French Fourth Republic (1953–59). After the constitutional crisis precipitated by the generals in Algeria in 1958, he assisted the return to power of General **de Gaulle** and the consequent birth of the new constitution and Fifth Republic in 1959, with de Gaulle as his successor.

Coué, Émile 1857–1926 •*French pharmacist and hypnotist*• As a pharmacist in Troyes from 1882 he took up the study of psychotherapy, and in 1910 opened a free clinic in Nancy. His system became world-famous as "Couéism," expressed in the famous formula: "Every day, in every way, I am becoming better and better."

Coulomb, Charles Augustin de 1736–1806 •*French physicist*• Born in Angoulême, he completed his education in Paris at the École du Génie. At the outbreak of the Revolution, he was forced to leave Paris, but returned in 1795 and was appointed Inspector General of Public Instruction (1802–06). His experiments on mechanical resistance resulted in "Coulomb's law" concerning the relationship between friction and normal pressure (1779), and he became known for the torsion balance for measuring the force of magnetic and electrical attraction (1784–85). With "Coulomb's law" he observed that the force between two small charged spheres is related to the charges and the distance between them. The unit of quantity of charge is named after him.

Coulson, Charles Alfred 1910–74 •*English theoretical chemist*• Born in Dudley, Worcestershire, he was educated at Cambridge, where he studied mathematics and natural sciences. He worked at the Physical Chemistry Laboratory, Oxford (1945–47), was Professor of Theoretical Physics at King's College London (1947–52), and in 1952 was appointed Rouse Ball Professor of Mathematics at Oxford. He was chairman of Oxfam from 1965 to 1971, and in 1972 became Oxford's first Professor of Theoretical Chemistry; the chair of this subject at Oxford now bears his name. Coulson's research interests were almost entirely within theoretical chemistry; probably his most important contribution was his definition of fractional bond order and the relation of this to bond length. He extended quantum-mechanical methods to analyze giant molecules such as graphite and diamond, and his book *Valence* (1952) was highly influential.

Coulthard, David 1971– •*Scottish racecar driver*• Born in Twynholm, Kirkcudbrightshire, he raced in go-karts and in Formula 3 and Formula 3000 before graduating to Formula 1 in 1994 with the Williams team, taking the place left vacant by the death of **Ayrton Senna**. He won his first Grand Prix in Portugal in 1995. He switched to McLaren in 1996 and emerged as a consistently strong contender for the Formula 1 title, finishing third in 1997, 1998 and 2000, and second in 2001.

Couperin, François, *known as* **le Grand** 1668–1733 •*French organist and composer*• Born in Paris, he was taught by his father, Charles Couperin, whom he eventually followed as organist of Saint-Gervais in 1685. In 1693 he became organist to **Louis XIV**. In 1717 he was appointed composer-in-ordinary of chamber music to the king. Internationally famous as a harpsichord composer whose principles are contained in his textbook *L'art de toucher le clavecin* (1716, "The Art of Playing the Harpsichord"), he had a great influence on **J S Bach**. His other compositions include many chamber concertos as well as motets and other church music.

Courbet, Gustave 1819–77 •*French painter*• Born in Ornans, he had little formal art training and scorned the rigid classical outlook, preferring Flemish and Spanish models, especially **Velázquez**. The founder of Realism, in 1844 he began exhibiting pictures in which everyday scenes were portrayed with complete sincerity and no idealism, as in *Peasants of Flagzey* (1850, Musée des Beaux-Arts, Besançon) and *Burial at Ornans* (1850, Musée d'Orsay, Paris), both of which were condemned as "socialistic" though not painted with any political intent. Perhaps his most famous canvas is the large *Studio of the Painter: An Allegory of Realism* (1855), in the Louvre. He joined the Commune in 1871, and on its suppression was imprisoned and fined. On his release in 1873 he fled to Switzerland.

Cournand, André Frédéric 1895–1988 •*US physician and Nobel Prize winner*• Born in Paris, France, he was educated at the Sorbonne, and emigrated to the US in 1930, where he became a citizen in 1941. A specialist in cardiovascular physiology, he was awarded the Nobel Prize for physiology or medicine in 1956 jointly with **Werner Forssman** and **Dickinson Richards** for developing cardiac catheterization. The technique made it possible to study heart functions, and modifications of it are now important in treating heart disease.

Court, Margaret Jean Smith, *née* **Smith** 1942– •*Australian tennis player*• Born in Albury, New South Wales, she was the winner of more Grand Slam events (66) than any other player: 10 Wimbledon titles (including the singles—the first Australian to do so—in 1963, 1965, 1970), 22 US titles (singles in 1962, 1965, 1968–70, 1973), 13 French titles (singles 1962, 1964, 1969–70, 1973), and 21 Australian titles (singles 1960–66, 1969–71, 1973).

Courtauld, Samuel 1876–1947 •*English industrialist*• He was a descendant of Samuel Courtauld (1793–1881), the founder of the silk manufacturing company in 1816. As chairman of Courtaulds Limited he was a patron of art and music, built the Courtauld Institute of Art in Portman Square, London, and donated it with his art collection to London University.

Courtenay, Sir Tom (Thomas Daniel) 1937– •*English actor*• Born in Hull, Humberside, he made his professional debut as Konstantin in **Chekhov**'s *The Seagull* with the Old Vic company in Edinburgh in 1960. Other stage appearances include leading roles in *The Dresser* (1980), the title role in the musical *Andy Capp* (1982), Harpagon in a translation of **Molière**'s *Le misanthrope* (1991, "The Miser") and *Art* (1996). A distinguished film actor, he appeared in *The Loneliness of the Long-Distance Runner* (1962), *Billy Liar* (1963), *Dr Zhivago* (1965), *One Day in the Life of Ivan Denisovitch* (1971) and *Last Orders* (2001). He was knighted in 2001.

Courtneidge, Dame Cicely Esmerelda 1893–1980 •*English actress*• She was born in Sydney, Australia, and was an actress from the age of 8. She made her London debut at 14 in a musical version of *Tom Jones* and later became widely known as an actress in musicals, pantomime and revue, having a great success in *By-the-Way* (1935). She also appeared in several straight comedies, including her final West End stage appearance in *Move Over, Mrs Markham*, by **Ray Cooney** (1971). She published an autobiography, *Cicely*, in 1953.

Courtney, Dame Kathleen D'Olier 1878–1974 •*English suffragette and world peace activist*• Born in Gillingham, Kent, she studied at Oxford. A woman of independent means, she devoted her life to improving the position of women and to world peace. On the outbreak of World War I, like other constitutional suffragettes, she diverted her energies to international Quaker relief work. A founder of the Women's International League for Peace, she chaired the British section and was an executive member of the British League of Nations Union (1928–39). She took part in the drawing up of the UN Charter, and was vice chair, then chair of the UN Association in Great Britain (1949–51). She was given the honorary title of Dame Commander, Order of the British Empire, in 1952.

Courtois, Bernard 1777–1838 •*French chemist*• Born in Dijon, he studied pharmacy in Auxerre and chemistry in Paris, later working in the laboratory at the École Polytechnique and at the Thénard Laboratory. While investigating opium with Baron Louis Guyton de Morveau he isolated morphine, the first alkaloid known. In 1804 he took over the management of his father's factory, which made saltpeter from seaweed ash. In 1811 he accidentally added too much sulfuric acid to the ash and produced a violet gas which condensed into dark crystals; his discovery of iodine was announced at the Institut de France in 1813.

Cousins, Frank 1904–86 •*English trade union leader*• Born at Bulwell, Nottingham, a miner's son, he started work in the pits at the age of 14 and by 1938 was a full-time union organizer. In 1955 he was appointed General Secretary of the Transport and General Worker's Union. Defying the Trades Union Congress and the leaders of the Labour Party, he aligned his union behind a near-unilateral nuclear disarmament policy in 1958. In 1965 he was elected Member of Parliament for Nuneaton, having been appointed Minister of Technology (1964), a post he resigned from in 1966 because of the government's prices and incomes policy. He gave up his parliamentary seat the same year and resumed his former union post.

Cousteau, Jacques Yves 1910–97 •*French naval officer and underwater explorer*• Born in Saint André, Gironde, he was educated at Stanislas, Paris, and the Navy Academy, Brest. He served in the Resistance during World War II, for which he was made a Commander of the Legion of Honor and awarded the Croix de guerre with palm. As Lieutenant de Vaisseau (1939–43) he was partly responsible for the invention of the Aqua-Lung diving apparatus (1943). In 1946 he founded the French navy's undersea research group, and in 1950 became commander of the oceanographic research ship *Calypso*, from which he made the first underwater film. He was director of the Musée Océanographique de Monaco from 1957 to 1988. His other achievements include developing an underwater television and the bathyscaphe, and promoting the Conshelf program, which investigated the possibilities of undersea living (1962–65). He is best known for the popularization of marine biology with his many films, including *The Undersea World of Jacques Cousteau* (1968–76) and *Lilliput in Antarctica* (1990).

“ ”

The sea is the universal sewer.

1971 Testimony before the House Committee on Science and Astronautics, January 28.

Coustou, Guillaume 1678–1746 •*French sculptor*• Born in Lyons, he was the brother of **Nicolas Coustou**, and was trained by **Antoine Coysevox**. His many spectacular works include the *Chevaux de Marly* (1740–45) at the entrance of the Champs Elysées, Paris (originals in the Louvre). His style was vigorous in the manner of **Gian Bernini**, whose work he saw in Rome.

Coustou, Guillaume 1716–77 •*French sculptor*• Born in Paris, he was the son of **Guillaume Coustou** (1678–1746). His works include the bronze bas-relief *Visitation* at Versailles, and the mausoleum of the Dauphin (father of **Louis XVI**) in the cathedral at Sens (c. 1767).

Coustou, Nicolas 1658–1733 •*French sculptor*• Born in Lyons, he was the brother of **Guillaume Coustou** (1678–1746), and sculpted the *Descente de la Croix* at Notre Dame, Paris.

Cousy, Bob (Robert Joseph) 1928– •*US basketball player*• Born in New York City, he is considered to be one of the greatest players ever. He played professionally with the Boston Celtics (1950–63), and then went on to coach the Cincinnati Royals and the Kansas City–Omaha Kings. He later became a sports commentator.

Couthon, Georges 1756–94 •*French revolutionary*• He was born in Orcet, in Auvergne. An advocate at the outbreak of the Revolution, he was sent by Puy de Dôme to the National Convention, and in July 1793 he became a member of the Committee of Public Safety. He crushed the Lyons insurrection with merciless severity (1793), and helped usher in the Reign of Terror. **Robespierre**'s fall brought down Couthon also, and he was executed.

Coutts, Russell 1962– •*New Zealand yachtsman*• Coutts learned to sail as a child in New Zealand and in 1980 became the single-handed world youth sailing champion. An Olympic gold medal in the Finn class followed in 1984. Ranked the best match racer in the world in 1993, he led New Zealand to victory in the 1995 America's Cup (only the second time the US had lost the cup). He repeated his triumph in 2000 when he led New Zealand, in their yacht *Black Magic*, in their successful defense of the America's Cup against Italy.

Coutts, Thomas 1735–1822 •*Scottish banker*• He was born the son of the Edinburgh merchant and banker John Coutts (1699–1751), who was Lord Provost in 1742–44. He founded the London banking house of Coutts & Co. with his brother James, on whose death in 1778 he became sole manager. In 1815 he married the actress **Harriot Mellon**. His granddaughter was **Angela Burdett-Coutts**.

Coverdale, Miles 1488–1568 •*English Protestant reformer and biblical scholar*• Born in Yorkshire, he studied at Cambridge, was ordained priest at Norwich in 1514, and joined the Augustinian Friars at Cambridge, where he was converted to Protestantism. He lived abroad from 1528 to 1534 to escape persecution and in 1535 published in Zurich the first translation of the whole Bible into English, with a dedication to **Henry VIII**. Many of the finest phrases in the Authorized Version of 1611 are directly due to Coverdale. In 1539, Coverdale superintended the production of the "Great Bible," which was presented to Henry VIII by **Thomas Cromwell**. The second "Great Bible," known also as "Cranmer's Bible" (1540), was also edited by Coverdale, who on Cromwell's fall found it expedient to leave England. In March 1548 he returned to England, was well received through **Thomas Cranmer**'s influence, and in 1551 was made Bishop of Exeter. On **Mary I**'s accession he was deprived of his see, but was allowed to leave the country, at the earnest intercession of the King of Denmark, whose chaplain, Dr Macchabaeus (MacAlpine), was Coverdale's brother-in-law. Returning to England in 1559, he was granted a benefice at St Magnus, near London Bridge, by Edmund Grindal (1519–83); this he resigned due to growing Puritan scruples about the liturgy in 1566.

Cowan, Clyde Lorrain, Jr 1919–74 •*US physicist*• Born in Detroit, he was educated at the Universities of Missouri and Washington, and became a group leader at Los Alamos Scientific Laboratory (1949–57). He served as Professor of Physics at George Washington University (1947) and at the Catholic University of America (1948–74). Together with **Frederick Reines**, Cowan demonstrated the existence of nature's most elusive particle, the neutrino, the definitive experimental evidence being produced in 1956.

Coward, Sir Noël Peirce 1899–1973 •*English actor, playwright and composer*• He was born in Teddington, Middlesex. His first play, written with Esme Wynne, was produced in 1917, and he acted thereafter in other plays, including many of his own. His many successes as a playwright include *Hay Fever* (1925), *Private Lives* (1930), *Blithe Spirit* (1941), *This Happy Breed* (1943) and *Nude With Violin* (1956), all showing his strong satiric humor and unique gift for witty dialogue. He was a gifted singer and wrote the music for most of his works, including his operetta *Bitter Sweet* (1929) and his play *Cavalcade* (1931), and for a series of revues, including *Words and Music* (1932) with its "Mad Dogs and Englishmen" and *Sigh No More* (1945). He produced several films based on his own scripts, including *In Which We Serve* (1942), *Blithe Spirit* (1945) and *Brief Encounter* (1945). He published two autobiographies, *Present Indicative* (1937) and *Future Indefinite* (1954).

“ ”

Very flat, Norfolk.

1930 ***Private Lives****, act 1.*

Cowdrey, (Michael) Colin Cowdrey, Baron 1932–2000 •*English cricket player*• Born in India, he was educated at Brasenose College, Oxford. He played in a record 114 Tests for England (23 as captain), despite being dogged by injuries and illness, and made six tours of Australia, also a record. In his long first-class career (1951–75) he was captain of Kent from 1957 to 1971. He became International Cricket Council chairman between 1989 and 1993, overseeing the return of South Africa to international cricket and the agreement of the international code of conduct in 1991. Consequently the 1992 World Cup was the first in which every team could play every other team. He was knighted in 1992.

Cowley, Abraham 1618–67 •*English poet*• Born in London, he wrote verses at the age of 10, and at 15 published five poems. He went in 1637 to Trinity College, Cambridge, where he wrote a large portion of his epic the *Davideis*, which was published in 1656 with a reprint of his first book, *The Mistress*, and a number of other poems. During the British Civil War he was ejected from Cambridge (1644) but studied at Oxford for another two years. In 1646 he accompanied or followed the queen (**Henrietta Maria**) to Paris, was sent on Royalist missions, and carried on her correspondence in cipher with King **Charles I**. He returned to England in 1654 and in 1655 was arrested and released on bail. On **Cromwell**'s death he returned to Paris, but he went home to England at the Restoration.

Cowley, Hannah, *née* **Parkhouse**, *pseudonym* **Anna Matilda** 1743–1809 •*English playwright and poet*• She was born in Tiverton, Devon, the daughter of a bookseller. Her first play, *The Runaway* (1776), was written in a fortnight and produced by **David Garrick**

at Drury Lane Theatre, London. She rapidly produced 13 further works for the stage, the most successful being *The Belle's Stratagem* (1780), which was frequently revived. She also wrote long narrative verses (1780–94) and under her pseudonym carried on a sentimental, poetic correspondence in *The World*. The name Anna Matilda became a byword for sentimental fiction.

Cowper, William 1666–1709 •*English surgeon and anatomist*• Born in Petersfield, Sussex, he settled as a surgeon in London. He wrote *The Anatomy of Human Bodies* (1698), and discovered "Cowper's glands." Also called bulbourethral glands, these are glands near the prostate in mammals which produce mucus under sexual stimulation.

Cowper, William 1731–1800 •*English poet*• Born in Berkhamstead, Hertfordshire, he was educated at Westminster School. He was called to the bar in 1754, but made no attempt to practice. He showed signs of mental instability and in 1763 tried to commit suicide. With the clergyman **John Newton**, he wrote the *Olney Hymns* (1779), to which Cowper contributed some hymns which are still favorites. His other works include the ballad "John Gilpin" (1783), "The Castaway" (1799), *The Task* (1785), and translations, including **Milton**'s Latin poems. He is generally regarded as the poet of the evangelical revival and as the precursor of **Wordsworth** as a poet of nature.

Cox, Brian Dennis 1946– •*Scottish actor, teacher and director*• Born in Dundee, he made his London debut as Orlando in *As You Like It* in 1967, and went on to perform extensively on the London stage and with the Royal Shakespeare Company. His many television appearances include roles in *The Lost Language of Cranes* (1991), *The Cloning of Joanna May* (1992) and *Grushko* (1994). He has acted in films such as *Braveheart* (1995) and *Rushmore* (1998).

Cox, William 1764–1837 •*Australian road builder*• Born in Wimbourne Minster, Dorset, England, he arrived in Australia in 1800 as a lieutenant in the New South Wales Corps, and purchased land to farm. In 1814 Governor **Lachlan Macquarie** made him superintendent of works for a new road over the Blue Mountains. With 30 convict laborers, in just six months Cox constructed 101 miles (162 km) of road through rugged hills with precipitous gradients, building more than a dozen bridges to cross the mountain streams.

Coysevox, Antoine 1640–1720 •*French sculptor*• Born in Lyons, he became court sculptor to **Louis XIV** in 1666 and was responsible for much of the decoration at the Palace of Versailles. His vigorous and decorative Baroque style—ultimately derived from **Gian Bernini**—was appropriate for the flamboyance of the French court, though he also sculpted very fine portrait busts of, and memorials to, many important figures of the time.

Cozens, Alexander 1717–86 •*English watercolor painter*• Born in St Petersburg, Russia, he is believed to be one of the two illegitimate sons of **Peter the Great** by a woman from Deptford who accompanied the czar to Russia. After studying in Italy, he settled in England in 1746. In 1785 he published a treatise describing his method of using accidental inkblots as the basis for landscape compositions.

Cozens, John Robert 1752–c.1799 •*English watercolor landscape painter*• Born in London, he was the son of **Alexander Cozens**. In 1776 he visited Switzerland, and in 1783 he returned from Italy. In 1794 he became insane, and in his later days was befriended by Sir George Beaumont. His drawings were copied by **J M W Turner** and Thomas Girtin (1775–1802), and **John Constable** pronounced that he was "the greatest genius that ever touched landscape."

Cozzens, James Gould 1903–78 •*US writer*• Born in Chicago, he wrote his first novel, *Confusion* (1924), at the age of 19 while a student at Harvard. He fought with the US Air Force in World War II, and on his release from service wrote the Pulitzer Prize–winning *Guard of Honor* (1948). Among his other works are *Ask Me Tomorrow* (1940), *The Just and the Unjust* (1942), *By Love Possessed* (1958) and *Children and Others* (1965).

Crabbe, George 1754–1832 •*English poet*• Born in Aldeburgh, Suffolk, he set up as a surgeon there. Having already published *Inebriety, A Poem* in 1775 and *The Candidate*, he ventured into the literary world in London in 1780, but lived in poverty, until, as the guest of **Edmund Burke** at Beaconsfield, he met the noted men of the day, published *The Library* (1781), and patronage followed. In 1783 *The Village*, a harshly realistic poem about village life sponsored by Burke and **Samuel Johnson**, brought him fame, and he wrote nothing for 24 years. His narrative poems include *The Borough* (1810), a collection of 24 tales in letter form (which were later to form the basis of **Benjamin Britten**'s opera *Peter Grimes*); *Tales* (1812); and *Tales of the Hall* (1819).

Craddock, Charles Egbert, *pseudonym of* **Mary Noailles Murfree** 1850–1922 •*US writer*• She was born in Murfreesboro, Tennessee. Her short stories were published in the *Atlantic Monthly* from 1878, and collected as *In the Tennessee Mountains* (1884). She went on to become a prolific novelist of mountain backwoods life.

Cradock, Fanny, *originally* **Phyllis Primrose-Pechey** 1909–94 •*English television chef and author*• She became known from the mid-1950s as television's first celebrity chef, appearing on her programs with her long-suffering husband, Johnnie, both in immaculate evening dress. She wrote a number of cookbooks, including *The Sherlock Holmes Cookbook* (1976), and several regular cooking and restaurant columns, as well as publishing novels under the name Frances Dale.

Cragg, Tony (Anthony) Douglas 1949– •*English sculptor*• Born in Liverpool, he worked as a laboratory technician before attending art school in Cheltenham and London. He graduated from the Royal College of Art in 1977, and since then he has lived and worked in Wuppertal, Germany. He retrieves discarded materials such as plastic, glass, and masonry rubble, arranging them by color into wall mosaics, as in *Britain Seen from the North* (1981, Tate Britain, London). He has also produced freestanding forms, eg *Mother's Milk* (1988) and *On the Savannah* (1988). He won the Turner Prize in 1988.

Craig, Charles 1922– •*English tenor*• Born in London, he was "discovered" by Sir **Thomas Beecham**. His fine, powerful tenor voice, coupled with a pleasing stage personality, made him naturally suited to opera and he joined the Carla Rosa Company in 1952. Three years later, he was playing principal roles for Sadler's Wells Opera and giving guest performances in many of the world's leading opera houses. It was for his performances in roles like Otello and Sigmund that he was most celebrated, but his versatility was such that he scored a great success in a revival of **Franz Lehár**'s operetta *Land of Smiles*.

Craig, Christopher c. 1936– •*English murderer*• Born in south London, he was a young friend of **Derek Bentley**. On Sunday November 2, 1952, he and Bentley broke into a confectionery warehouse in Croydon. The police were alerted, and approached Bentley, who was carrying a knife and brass knuckles, and Craig, who was armed with a gun. Craig fired several shots, initially wounding one policeman and then killing another. Craig's defense claimed that his actions were provoked by the violent comics and films he favored. He and Bentley were both found guilty. Craig was sentenced to an indefinite period of detention, as he was too young to receive the death penalty, but Bentley was sentenced to be hanged. Despite vigorous attempts to gain a reprieve, Bentley was executed. Craig was released from prison in 1963.

Craigie, Sir William Alexander 1867–1957 •*Scottish philologist and lexicographer*• Born in Dundee, he was educated there and at St Andrews, and went to Balliol College, Oxford, for a year before going to Copenhagen to study Old Icelandic. In 1897 he joined Sir **James Murray** in the compilation of the *Oxford English Dictionary* (joint editor, 1901–33). In 1916 he was appointed Professor of Anglo-Saxon at Oxford, and in 1925–36 was Professor of English at the University of Chicago, where he compiled the *Historical Dictionary of American English* (4 vols, 1936–44). From 1936 to 1955 he was editor of the *Dictionary of the Older Scottish Tongue*. A scholar of encyclopedic knowledge, he also wrote *The Icelandic Sagas* (1913), *Easy Readings in Anglo-Saxon* (1923), and a monumental study of Icelandic *rímur* ("rhymes"), *Sýnisbók íslenkra rímna* (3 vols, 1952).

Cram, Donald James 1919–2001 •*US chemist and Nobel Prize winner*• Born in Chester, Vermont, he studied chemistry at Rollins College, Florida, and at the University of Nebraska, and at Harvard

(1945–47), and taught at UCLA. His most highly praised work began in 1972, when he described the synthesis of chiral crown ethers. He also introduced the informative description "host-guest chemistry," for which he shared the 1987 Nobel Prize for chemistry with **Jean-Marie Lehn** and **Charles Pedersen**.

Cram, Steve(n) 1960– •*English middle-distance runner*• Born in Jarrow, Tyne and Wear, as a young athlete he was inspired by the feats of another runner from the northeast of England, Brendan Foster, and emerged from the shadows of **Sebastian Coe** and **Steve Ovett**, who had dominated 800-meter and 1,500-meter running. He won the 1,500-meter titles in the world championships (1983), European championships (1982) and Commonwealth Games (1982), as well as the silver medal in the 1984 Olympics. In 1985 he broke three world records in just 19 days—at 1,500 meters, one mile and 2,000 meters. He now appears on television as a host and commentator.

Cranach, Lucas the Elder 1472–1553 •*German painter*• Born in Kronach, near Bamberg, he became court painter in Wittenberg of the elector Frederick the Wise of Saxony. In 1509 he accompanied an embassy to Emperor **Maximilian I**, and while in the Netherlands painted the future **Charles V**. His paintings include sacred and a few classical subjects, hunting scenes and portraits. He was closely associated with the German Reformers, including **Martin Luther** and **Philip Melanchthon**, who were painted by Cranach and his pupils. A *Crucifixion* in the Stadtkirche, Weimar, is his masterpiece. His wood engravings are numerous. Of three sons, all painters, the second, Lucas the Younger (1515–86), painted so like his father that their works are difficult to distinguish.

Crane, (Harold) Hart 1899–1932 •*US poet*• Born in Garrettsville, Ohio, he had little formal education, but worked as an advertising copywriter in New York before he found a patron who enabled him to travel and devote himself to poetry. A gay alcoholic, he placed a heavy burden on his friends' tolerance and wallets. He published two volumes—*White Buildings* (1926) and the long, symbolic *The Bridge* (1930). Crane is now recognized as a major US poet, having much in common with **Walt Whitman**. Returning to the US from Mexico, he drowned himself by leaping from a steamboat into the Caribbean.

Crane, Stephen 1871–1900 •*US writer and war correspondent*• He was born in New Jersey, and worked as a journalist in New York before publishing his first novel, *Maggie: A Girl of the Streets* (1893). His reputation, however, rests on *The Red Badge of Courage* (1895), which relates vividly the experiences of a soldier in the Civil War. He had no personal experience of the war, but *The Red Badge of Courage* was received with acclaim, in particular for its psychological realism. He never repeated its success but was lionized by literary London before succumbing to tuberculosis in Baden Baden.

Crane, Walter 1845–1915 •*English painter and illustrator*• Born in Liverpool, he came under the influence of the Pre-Raphaelites, and became a leader with **William Morris** in the Arts and Crafts Movement, and in early socialism. He was well known as an illustrator of children's books, but his main achievement was his illustrated edition of **Edmund Spenser**'s *Faerie Queen* (1894–96). In his paintings he was much influenced by **Botticelli**.

Cranko, John 1927–73 •*South African choreographer*• He was born in Rustenburg. In 1946 he moved to Great Britain to study, and joined Sadler's Wells Theatre Ballet (1946–61, becoming resident choreographer 1951–57). He made over 30 dances, including *Pineapple Poll* (1951) and his first full-length ballet, *Prince of the Pagodas*, with music by **Benjamin Britten** (1957). He also wrote the musical revue *Cranks* (1955). In 1961 he moved to Germany to become artistic director of the Stuttgart Ballet, which became, under his influence, an internationally famous company. A lover of drama and physical intensity, he choreographed ballets like *Romeo and Juliet* (1958), *Onegin* (1969) and *Carmen* (1971).

Cranmer, Thomas 1489–1556 •*English prelate and Archbishop of Canterbury*• He was born in Aslacton or Aslockton, Nottinghamshire, and educated at Jesus College, Cambridge, taking holy orders in 1523. Appointed Grand Penitentiary of England at Rome by Pope **Clement VII**, he was consecrated Archbishop of Canterbury in 1533, and took the oath of allegiance to the pope "for form's sake." In May, Cranmer pronounced **Henry VII**'s marriage to **Catherine of Aragon** null and void *ab initio* and the private marriage to **Anne Boleyn**, which had taken place four months earlier, valid; in September he was godfather to Anne's daughter **Elizabeth**. He later annulled Henry's marriage with Anne Boleyn (1536), divorced him from **Anne of Cleves** (1540), informed him of **Catherine Howard**'s premarital affairs, then strove to coax her into confessing them (1541). He promoted the translation of the Bible and a service book, and curtailed the number of holy days. In 1547 Henry died, and Cranmer sang a requiem mass for his soul. He had been slowly drifting into Protestantism, but now was quickly swept into great religious changes. In 1549 he compiled **Edward VI**'s first Book of Common Prayer (which converted the Mass into Communion), composed the 42 articles of religion (1553) later called the 39 Articles, and in 1552 rephrased the Book of Common Prayer. He still took little part in affairs of state, although he was one of the council of regency. However, he signed **Thomas Seymour**'s death warrant (1549), and reluctantly subscribed the instrument diverting the succession from the princess Mary (later **Mary I**) to Lady **Jane Grey** (1553). In this he was guilty of conscious perjury, yet when the 12-day reign was over he made no attempt to escape. On September 14 he was sent to the Tower, on November 13 was arraigned for treason, and, pleading guilty, was condemned to die. In rapid succession he signed seven increasingly submissive recantations, but when the time came for him to read these, he retracted all that he had written, and was burned alive.

" "

This hath offended! Oh this unworthy hand!

1556 Last words at the stake, referring to the hand which had signed the recantations.

Cranston, Kate (Catherine) 1850–1934 •*Scottish tea-room proprietress and patron of art*• Born in Glasgow, she opened a chain of highly successful tea rooms there (1884–1904), known for their distinctive "artistic" interiors. **Charles Rennie Mackintosh** redesigned the furniture and fittings in the Argyle Street tea rooms (1896), and later did the interior decoration for the Ingram Street branch (1900) and the Willow tea rooms in Sauchiehall Street (1911). She then commissioned **George Walton** to decorate the Buchanan Street tea rooms, opened in 1896.

Crashaw, Richard c. 1613–49 •*English religious poet*• Born in London, he was educated at Charterhouse and Pembroke Hall, Cambridge, and became a Fellow of Peterhouse College (c. 1636). In 1634 he published a volume of Latin poems, *Epigrammatum sacrocorum liber*. As his Catholic leanings prevented him from receiving Anglican orders, he lost his fellowship (1643) for refusing to take the Covenant. He went to Paris and became a Catholic, and in 1646 published his *Steps to the Temple*. He was introduced by John Cowley to Queen **Henrietta Maria**, who recommended him at Rome, and in April 1649 he became a subcanon at Loretto.

Crassus, Lucius Licinius 140–91 BC •*Roman orator*• In 95 BC he was elected consul, along with Quintus Scaevola, and during their consulship a rigorous law was enacted banishing from Rome all who had not the full rights of citizens. It was one of the chief causes of the Social War (90–88). Crassus is the chief speaker in **Cicero**'s *De oratore*, and represents the writer's own opinions.

Crassus, Marcus Licinius, *known as* **Dives ("the Rich")** c. 115–53 BC •*Roman politician*• He was a protégé and supporter of **Lucius Cornelius Sulla** in the civil war against **Gaius Marius** (88–82 BC). As praetor he defeated **Spartacus** at the Battle of Lucania (71), and in 70 he was made consul with **Pompey**. The richest of Roman citizens, he became a friend of **Julius Caesar** and formed the first triumvirate with him and Pompey (60). In 53, as Governor of Syria, he attacked the Parthians, but was routed and killed at the Battle of Carrhae.

Crates of Athens early 3rd century BC •*Greek philosopher*• He succeeded Potemo and preceded **Arcesilaus** as head of the Academy in Athens. He should not be confused with Crates of Tarsus, who was head of the Academy about 130 BC, or Crates of

Thebes, a disciple of **Diogenes of Sinope** in the 4th century BC. His main claims to fame were that he was teacher of **Zeno of Citium** and that he had sex in public to make a philosophical point about social conventions.

Cratinus c. 519–423 BC •*Greek comic poet*• Next to Eupolis and **Aristophanes**, he best represents the Old Attic comedy. He limited the number of actors to three, and was the first to add biting personal attack to comedy—even **Pericles** did not escape his pen. Of his 21 comedies, only some fragments are extant; they are collected in Meineke's *Fragmenta Comicorum Graecorum* (1840, Berlin).

Cratippus 1st century BC •*Greek peripatetic philosopher*• He was born in Mitylene, and was a contemporary of **Cicero**, whose son Marcus he taught at Athens in 44 BC. **Pompey** visited him after the Battle of Pharsalus, and **Marcus Brutus** traveled to Athens to hear him, even while making preparations to meet **Augustus** and **Marcus Antonius**. Nothing that he wrote has survived.

Crawford, Cheryl 1902–86 •*US actress, theater director and producer*• Born in Akron, Ohio, she was centrally involved in some of the most important US theatrical developments of her time, including the Group Theater (1931, with **Harold Clurman** and **Lee Strasberg**), the American Repertory Theater (1946, with **Eva Le Gallienne** and Margaret Webster (1905–72)) and the Actors Studio (1947). An important producer, she mounted productions ranging from the musical *Brigadoon* (1947) to **Bertolt Brecht**'s *Mother Courage* (1963).

Crawford, Cindy (Cynthia Ann) 1966– •*US supermodel, actress and television celebrity*• Born in DeKalb, Illinois, she had plans to become a chemical engineer before being discovered by photographer Victor Skrebenski in Chicago. Moving to New York, she became established as a top model and has produced exercise videos and calendars, appeared on television shows, and advertised many high-profile brands. She also starred in *Fair Game* (1995) and *Catwalk* (1995). She was married to **Richard Gere** from 1991 to 1994.

Crawford, Joan, *originally* **Lucille Le Sueur** 1906–77 •*US film actress*• Born in San Antonio, Texas, she arrived in Hollywood in 1924. During the 1920s and 1930s she developed into the archetypal glamorous Hollywood movie queen. Declared "box-office poison" in 1938, she returned as the wickedly witty husband stealer in *The Women* (1939). Later, she continued to suffer in jewels and ermine as the older woman beset by emotional problems, such as in *Mildred Pierce* (1945, Academy Award) and *Whatever Happened to Baby Jane?* (1962), and she retired after *Trog* (1970). She published an autobiography, *Portrait of Joan* (1962), and her adopted daughter Christina wrote a scathing attack on her in *Mommie Dearest* (1978).

Crawford, Michael, *originally* **Michael Patrick Smith** 1942– •*English actor and singer*• Born in Salisbury, Wiltshire, his performance in *No Sex, Please—We're British* (1971–72) established him as a gifted comedy actor. He went on to star in such musicals as *Billy* (1974–76) and *Barnum* (1981–83), and won awards for his role in *The Phantom of the Opera* (West End, Broadway and Los Angeles, 1986–90). The television series *Some Mothers Do 'Ave 'Em* (1974–78), in which he played the accident-prone Frank Spencer, made him a household name. His films include *The Knack … and How to Get It* (1965), *A Funny Thing Happened on the Way to the Forum* (1966) and *Condorman* (1980).

Craxi, Bettino 1934–2000 •*Italian politician*• He was born in Milan. After being active in the Socialist Youth movement he became a member of the Central Committee of the Italian Socialist Party in 1957 rising to become General Secretary in 1976. After the general election of 1983 he became Italy's first Socialist Prime Minister, successfully leading a broad-based coalition until 1987. In 1995 a warrant was issued for his arrest on charges of receiving bribes, but his self-imposed exile in Tunisia allowed his lawyers to argue that as a political refugee, he was protected under the extradition treaty between Tunisia and Italy.

Craxton, John 1922– •*English painter*• Born in London, he studied at Westminster Art School, the Central School of Art, and Goldsmiths College before settling in Hania on Crete in 1948. His style is linear, and early work is pastoral, influenced by **William Blake** and **Samuel Palmer**, for example, *Dreamers in a Landscape* (1942, Tate Britain, London). Later he was impressed by the color of Byzantine mosaics, as shown in *Sunlit Ravine* (1982–85, Christopher Hull Gallery, London).

Cray, Seymour R 1925–96 •*US computer designer*• Born in Chippewa Falls, Wisconsin, he was educated at Minnesota University. He established himself at the forefront of large-scale computer design and in 1972 he organized Cray Research Inc in Chippewa Falls to develop and market the most powerful computer systems available. These "supercomputers" are used in military, weather-forecasting and advanced engineering design applications. The Cray 1, delivered in 1976, was the world's fastest computer, and by the 1980s this machine and its later derivatives dominated the supercomputer market. The Cray 3 supercomputer materialized in 1993, but the end of the Cold War and cuts in government spending brought about the folding of his company in 1995.

Crazy Horse, *Sioux name* **Ta-Sunko-Witko** c. 1849–77 •*Oglala Sioux chief*• Born in South Dakota and regarded as the foremost Sioux military leader, he defeated General **Custer** at the Battle of Little Big Horn (1876) with a combined force of Sioux and Cheyennes. He and his followers surrendered the following year, and he died in custody at Fort Robinson, Nebraska.

Creasey, John 1908–73 •*English crime and espionage writer*• Born in Southfields, Surrey, he was educated in London, and wrote full-time from 1935, two years after the first Department Z thriller was published. An astonishingly prolific writer, he used no less than 25 pseudonyms (male and female), of which J J Marric was perhaps the best known. His characters include Inspector Roger West and the former jewel thief John Mannering (known as "The Baron"). He has more than 550 novels to his credit.

Credi, Lorenzo di 1459–1537 •*Italian painter*• Born in Florence, he was the fellow pupil, lifelong friend and executor of **Leonardo da Vinci**. He mainly painted Holy Families, examples of which may be seen in the National Gallery, London, and in the Louvre, Paris.

Creeley, Robert White 1926– •*US poet*• Born in Arlington, Massachusetts, he dropped out of Harvard and spent some years in Spain before being appointed by **Charles Olson** to the faculty of Black Mountain College in North Carolina in 1954. There he became linked with the Black Mountain school of poets and founded and edited the *Black Mountain Review*. His poems, characterized by dense syntax and abrupt endings, have appeared in numerous collections including *If You* (1956), *For Love: Poems 1950–60* (1962), *St Martin's* (1971), *Memory Gardens* (1986) and *Places* (1990). He has written one novel, *The Island* (1963), and more prose in *The Collected Prose of Robert Creeley: A Story* (1984).

Crespi, Giuseppe Maria, *called* **Lo Spagnuolo** 1665–1747 •*Italian painter of the Bolognese school*• Born in Bologna, he painted religious and mythological subjects showing the influence of the Eclectic school of the **Carracci**.

Cresson, Edith 1934– •*French politician*• She was born in Boulogne-sur-Seine and educated at the École des Hautes Études Commerciales. An active member of the Socialist Party, she was its youth organizer in 1975, became Mayor of Thuré in 1977 and was elected a member of the European parliament in 1979. A close friend of President **François Mitterrand** for more than 25 years, and having a reputation as a fiery socialist equivalent of **Margaret Thatcher**, she held various portfolios during the 1980s and after a brief return to industry in 1990 became her country's first woman Prime Minister in 1991, though she resigned the following year. She was a member of the European Commission from 1995 but was part of the mass resignation of the commission in 1999.

Crichton, James, *known as* **the Admirable Crichton** 1560–c. 1585 •*Scottish prodigy of the Scottish Enlightenment*• The son of the Scottish Lord Advocate, he was born in Cluny, Perthshire, and educated at St Andrews. After graduating in 1575, he earned a reputation on the Continent as a scholar, poet, linguist and swordsman. In Mantua in the service of the duke, he was killed by the duke's son in a nocturnal brawl. His popular reputation rests on the fantastic account of his exploits written by Sir **Thomas Urquhart** in his panegyric on the Scots nation, *The Discoveryie of a Most Exquisite Jewel* (1652). "Admirable Crichton" became synonymous with all-round talents, the ideal man; the phrase was used by **J M Barrie** for his play about a perfect butler, *The Admirable Crichton* (1902).

Crichton, (John) Michael 1942– •*US writer and filmmaker*• Born in Chicago, he graduated from Harvard Medical School in 1969. His many bestselling scientific and medical thrillers, among them *The Andromeda Strain* (1969), *Congo* (1980), *Jurassic Park* (1990) and *Timeline* (1999), have earned him the nickname "the father of the techno-thriller." He has also written several nonfiction books. Many of his novels have been made into films, which he has usually directed or coproduced, most notably *The Great Train Robbery* (1978) and *Jurassic Park* (1993). His one foray into television, the creation (1994) of the medical drama series *ER*, has garnered him Peabody (1995), Writer's Guild of America (1995) and Emmy (1996) awards. A species of armored dinosaur was named *Bienosaurus crichtoni* in his honor in 2000.

Crichton Smith, Iain *See* **Smith, Iain Crichton**

Crick, Francis Harry Compton 1916–2004 •*English molecular biologist and Nobel Prize winner*• Born near Northampton, Northamptonshire, he studied physics at University College London. In the early 1950s, in Cambridge, he met **James Watson** and together they worked on the structure of DNA, publishing in 1953 their model of a double-helical molecule, consisting of two chains of nucleotide bases wound round a common axis in opposite directions. This structure suggested a mechanism for the reproduction of the genetic code, which Crick continued to study for the next decade. He then worked in Cambridge and at the Salk Institute, California, carrying out research into the visual systems of mammals and the connections between brain and mind. With Watson and **Maurice Wilkins** he was awarded the Nobel Prize for physiology or medicine in 1962, and he received the Order of Merit in 1991. His publications include *The Astonishing Hypothesis: The Scientific Search for the Soul* (1994).

Crippen, Hawley Harvey 1862–1910 •*US murderer*• Born in Michigan, he studied medicine and dentistry there and in London. In 1896 he returned to London, settling there with his second wife, Cora Turner, an unsuccessful opera singer and music-hall performer. He fell in love with his secretary, Ethel le Neve, and poisoned his wife after a party at their home at Hilldrop Crescent, Holloway; he dissected the body, burned the bones, and buried the remains in the cellar. His wife's friends were told she had died while vacationing in the US. After the police had unsuccessfully investigated Cora's disappearance, Ethel took fright, and the pair fled to Antwerp, where they boarded an Atlantic liner as Mr and Master Robinson. The suspicious captain, who had read reports of the second and successful search at Hilldrop Crescent, contacted Scotland Yard by radiotelegraphy (the first use of radio for police purposes), and the couple was arrested and tried. Crippen was executed at Pentonville.

Cripps, Sir (Richard) Stafford 1889–1952 •*English Labour statesman, economist, chemist and patent lawyer*• Born in London, the son of the politician Charles Alfred Cripps (1852–1941), and of Theresa, sister of **Beatrice Webb**, he was educated at Winchester and won a scholarship to New College, Oxford. At 22 he was coauthor of a chemistry paper read before the Royal Society. He also pursued legal studies and was called to the bar in 1913, became the youngest barrister in the country in 1926, and made a fortune in patent and compensation cases. In 1930 he was appointed Solicitor General in the second Labour government, but refused to serve in **Ramsay MacDonald**'s coalition (1931–35). From then until the outbreak of World War II, Cripps was associated with a succession of extreme left-wing movements, at first pacific in character, but later, as the Nazi threat increased, concerned with rallying everyone, and not only socialists, to active opposition to **Neville Chamberlain**'s policy of appeasement. He sat as an independent Member of Parliament throughout the war. Appointed ambassador to Moscow (1940–42), under **Churchill**'s leadership, in 1942 he became Lord Privy Seal and Leader of the Commons, then in November succeeded **Max Beaverbrook** in the vital post of Minister of Aircraft Production; this he held for the remainder of the war. When Labour came to power in July 1945, Cripps was readmitted to the party and appointed President of the Board of Trade. In 1947 he became Chancellor of the Exchequer. His at first unpopular policy of austerity caught the public conscience, and the trade unions took the unprecedented step of imposing a voluntary wage freeze. Illness from overwork forced his resignation in 1950. Cripps firmly believed that politics was a proper sphere for the practice of Christianity, and he wrote *Towards a Christian Democracy* (1945).

Crispi, Francesco 1819–1901 •*Italian statesman*• Born at Ribera, Sicily, he was called to the bar and became a member of the provisional government established in Palermo after the insurrection of 1848. He was exiled from the Kingdom of the Two Sicilies in 1849 and settled in Turin; he organized the successful movement of 1859–60, and reentered Sicily with **Garibaldi**. In the restored kingdom of Italy he became Premier (1887–90, 1894). The Abyssinian disaster of the Battle of Adowa (1896) compelled his resignation.

Crispus, Gaius Sallustius *See* **Sallust**

Cristofori or **Cristofaloi, Bartolomeo** 1655–1731 •*Italian harpsichord maker and inventor of the pianoforte* • He was born in Padua and worked in Florence from about 1690. He is generally credited with inventing the pianoforte (c. 1709). The name refers to the instrument's ability to be played either softly or loudly, according to the amount of pressure put on the keys. Three of his pianos survive, dated 1720, 1722 and 1726.

Critias c. 460–403 BC •*Athenian orator and politician*• He was a pupil of **Socrates**. Implicated with **Alcibiades** in the mutilation of the Hermae on the eve of the Sicilian expedition (415 BC), he nonetheless escaped punishment. In 411 he took part in the oligarchical revolution that set up the government of Four Hundred. As a strong supporter of Sparta, he became one of the Thirty Tyrants set up by the Spartans after their defeat of Athens at the end of the Peloponnesian War (431–404). In the same year he was killed at Munychia. He had a high reputation as an orator, and wrote poetry and tragedies.

“ ”

Is not living at all not better than living badly?

Fragment, quoted in H Diels and W Kranz (eds) ***Die Fragmente der Vorsokratiker*** *(1952), vol 2, 385, no. 23.*

Crivelli, Carlo c. 1430–95 •*Italian painter of the Venetian school*• Trained probably by the **Vivarini** family in Venice, he spent most of his time working elsewhere in the Marches. His style is a highly individual combination of old-fashioned International Gothic opulence with a contemporary Renaissance setting of figures in architectural frameworks and against landscapes. His style of draftsmanship is similar to that of **Botticelli**. His *Annunciation* is in the National Gallery, London.

Croce, Benedetto 1866–1952 •*Italian philosopher, historian, literary critic and politician*• Born in Pescasseroli, Aquila, he was buried and lost his parents and sister in an earthquake on the island of Ischia in 1883. He studied at Rome, and in Naples devoted himself at first to literature and antiquarian studies. He developed a phenomenology of the mind in which the four principal activities of the mind, art and philosophy (theoretical), political economy and ethics (practical), do not oppose, as they do for **Hegel**, but complement each other. He founded the review, *La critica*, in 1903, and made major contributions to idealistic aesthetics in his *Estetica* (1902, "Aesthetic") and *La poesia* (1936, "Poetry"). In 1910 he became a senator, and was Minister of Education (1920–21) when, with the rise of **Mussolini**, he had to resign his professorship at Naples. With the fall of Mussolini (1943) he helped to resurrect liberal institutions in Italy. He became president of the Italian Liberal Party in 1947 and a member of the Constituent Assembly; he became a senator again in 1948. He also wrote literary studies of **Goethe**, **Dante**, **Ariosto** and **Corneille**.

Crockett, Davy (David) 1786–1836 •*US frontiersman*• Born near Greeneville, Tennessee, he grew up on the frontier, repeatedly moving westward with his family, and had little schooling. He distinguished himself against the Creek Indians in **Andrew Jackson**'s campaign of 1814, was elected to the Tennessee state legislature in 1821 and served in Congress (1827–31, 1833–35), where his colorful personality and humorous oratory drew much attention. Defeated in the 1835 election, he left his home state for Texas, and he died defending the Alamo during the Texas Revolution.

Croesus 6th century BC •*Last king of Lydia*• He succeeded his father, Alyattes, in c. 560 BC. He made the Greeks of Asia Minor his tributaries, and extended his kingdom eastward from the Aegean to the Halys. His conquests, his mines, and the golden sand of the Pactolus made his wealth proverbial. **Cyrus the Great** defeated and imprisoned him (546).

Crome, John, *known as* **Old Crome** 1768–1821 •*English landscape painter*• Born in Norwich, he was educated locally and taught himself to paint. He helped found the Norwich Society of Artists in 1803, and became its president (1808). He occasionally visited London, where he exhibited in the Academy and the British Institution, and a tour through Belgium and France in 1814 resulted in *The Fishmarket on the Beach, Boulogne* and *The Boulevard des Italiens, Paris*. However, he nearly always painted the scenery of his native county, which, though influenced by the Dutch landscapists, he treated in a direct and individual fashion. His son, John Berny Crome (1794–1842), known as Young Crome, was also a landscape painter.

Crompton, Richmal, *originally* **Richmal Lamburn** 1890–1969 •*English writer*• Born in Bury, Lancashire, she was educated in Lancashire and Derby and at Royal Holloway College, London. She published 50 adult titles thereafter but she is best known for her *Just William* books, 38 short-story collections (and one novel, *Just William's Luck*) about a perpetual schoolboy, the 11-year-old William Brown. Children love the judicious deliberation with which his escapades are described and their reduction of ordered adult life to chaos.

Crompton, Samuel 1753–1827 •*English inventor of the spinning mule*• Born in Firwood, Lancashire, the son of a farmer, he set out to invent a spinning machine that would improve on that of **James Hargreaves**. In 1779, after five years' work, he produced his spinning mule, so called because it was a cross between Hargeaves' spinning jenny and **Richard Arkwright**'s water frame. Too poor to apply for a patent, he sold the rights to a Bolton manufacturer for £67. In 1812 he was granted a reward of £5,000 by the House of Commons.

Cromwell, Oliver 1599–1658 •*English soldier and statesman*• He was born in Huntingdon and educated at Huntingdon Grammar School and Sydney Sussex College, Cambridge. He studied law in London, and developed a dislike for **Charles I** after first sitting in the House of Commons in 1628. When the king dissolved parliament the following year, he took up farming in Huntingdon and subsequently at St Ives and Ely. At the start of the English Civil War in 1642, he raised a troop of cavalry for the battles of Edgehill and Gainsborough, and in 1644 he brought the war nearer to an end with a cavalry charge against Royalist troops at Marston Moor. Back in parliament, he led the independent faction that rejected reconciliation with the king, and commanded the army that won a decisive victory over the king's forces at Naseby on June 14, 1645. Cromwell at first professed a willingness to negotiate terms by which the throne might be saved, but Charles's success in rallying the Scots from the Isle of Wight brought further fighting in 1648 and Cromwell resolved to rid himself of the king forever. Charles was taken to Westminster for trial, and Cromwell's signature was among those on the death warrant that brought the king's execution on January 30, 1649. The monarchy was abolished and Cromwell declared the establishment of a Commonwealth with himself as chairman of its Council of State. He brutally massacred the Catholic garrisons at Drogheda and Wexford, and between 1650 and 1651 defeated at Dunbar and at Worcester the supporters of **Charles II** who had declared him King of Scotland. Frustrated by the obstruction presented by the substantial body of Royalists remaining in the Commons, Cromwell dissolved the Long Parliament in 1653 and ruled briefly as head of the Puritan Convention and then, on the implementation of a new Constitution, as Lord Protector. He reorganized the Church of England and established Puritanism, brought prosperity to Scotland under his administration, and granted Irish representation in parliament. He dissolved parliament again in 1655 with a view to imposing regional rule under ten major generals in England, but the experiment failed, and after recalling the Commons in 1656 he was offered the Crown. He declined it, but instead won the right to name his son, **Richard Cromwell**, as Lord Protector. However, his relations with parliament worsened and brought another dissolution in 1658, and Cromwell continued to rule absolutely until his death later that year. His son took the promised title of Lord Protector, but failed to emulate his father's iron grip and surrendered the office a year later. On the Restoration in 1660, Oliver Cromwell's body was disinterred from the tomb of kings in Westminster Abbey, hung from Tyburn gallows and afterwards buried there.

“ ”

A few honest men are better than numbers.

1643 Letter to Sir William Spring, September. Quoted in Thomas Carlyle ***Letters and Speeches of Oliver Cromwell*** *(1845).*

Cromwell, Richard 1626–1712 •*English statesman*• The third son of **Oliver Cromwell**, he served in the parliamentary army, sat in parliament in 1654 and 1656, and was a member of the Council of State in 1657. In September 1658 he succeeded his father as Lord Protector, but he soon fell out with parliament, which he dissolved in 1659. He recalled the Rump Parliament of 1653, but proved incapable of ruling, and was forced to abdicate in May 1659. After the Restoration (1660) he lived abroad, in France and Geneva, under the alias "John Clarke," but returned to England in 1680, and spent the rest of his life at Cheshunt.

Cromwell, Thomas, Earl of Essex c. 1485–1540 •*English statesman*• Born in Putney, London, the son of a blacksmith and brewer, he lived from 1504 to 1512 on the Continent, where he may have served in the French army in Italy, and gained experience as a clerk and trader. He then became a wool-stapler and scrivener, practiced some law, and entered the service of Cardinal **Wolsey** in 1514, and parliament in 1523. In 1525 he acted as Wolsey's chief agent in the dissolution of the smaller monasteries, and as his general factotum. In 1530 he entered the service of **Henry VIII** and quickly became his principal adviser, as Privy Councilor (1531), Chancellor of the Exchequer (1533) and Secretary of State and Master of the Rolls (1534). The guiding hand behind the Reformation acts of 1532–39 which made the king head of the English Church, as vicar general from 1535, and as Lord Privy Seal and the king's deputy as the head of the Church (from 1536), he organized the dissolution of the monasteries (1536–39). Though appointed Lord Great Chamberlain in 1539 and ennobled as the Earl of Essex in 1540, he lost favor with the king after negotiating the disastrous marriage with **Anne of Cleves**. He was sent to the Tower, condemned by parliament under a bill of attainder, and executed.

Cronin, A(rchibald) J(oseph) 1896–1981 •*Scottish novelist*• Born in Cardross, Dunbartonshire, he graduated in medicine at Glasgow in 1919, but in 1930 abandoned his practice as a result of a breakdown in his health. He had an immediate success with his brooding and melodramatic autobiographical novel *Hatter's Castle* (1931). Subsequent works include *The Citadel* (1937), *The Keys of the Kingdom* (1941), *Beyond This Place* (1953), *Crusader's Tomb* (1956) and *A Song of Sixpence* (1964). The medical stories in his Scottish novels formed the basis of the popular radio and television series *Dr Finlay's Casebook* in the 1960s, and again in 1993.

Cronin, James Watson 1931– •*US physicist and Nobel Prize winner*• Born and educated in Chicago, he worked at the Brookhaven National Laboratory before teaching at Princeton University and the University of Chicago. In 1964, together with **Val Fitch**, J Christensen and R Turlay, Cronin made a study of neutral kaons and discovered that a combination of parity and charge conjugation was not conserved. Since it was known from the charge conjugation parity time reversal (CPT) theorem that a combination of parity, charge conjugation and time is conserved, this important result implied that the decay of kaons is not symmetrical with respect to time reversal. This is still not understood today, but the idea of CP violation has been used to explain the domination of matter over antimatter in the universe. Cronin and Fitch shared the 1980 Nobel Prize for physics for their work in particle physics.

Cronje, Hansie (Wessel Johannes) 1969–2002 •*South African cricket player*• Born in Bloemfontein, he established a reputation as a versatile right-handed batsman playing for Free State (as captain in 1990–96) and for Ireland and Leicestershire. He was appointed captain of South Africa in 1994 and led his country to five successive Test victories as well as to victory against England in 1995–96 and subsequently against the West Indies. He scored five Test centuries himself and proved particularly effective in one-day cricket but his career was halted in 2000 when he admitted to involvement in a bookmaking scandal and was banned for life from the game.

Cronkite, Walter Leland, Jr 1916– •*US journalist and broadcaster*• Born in St Joseph, Missouri, he was a student of political science, economics and journalism at Texas University (1933–35). Employed by the United Press (1939–48), he provided vivid eyewitness accounts of World War II in Europe, and remained to cover the Nuremberg trials and work as the bureau chief in Moscow (1946–48). At CBS from 1950, he hosted a number of shows and narrated *You Are There* (1953–56), but became best known for his informative, straightforward reporting on the *CBS Evening News* (1962–81). In 1981 he was awarded the Presidential Medal of Freedom.

Cronstedt, Axel Fredrik, Baron 1722–65 •*Swedish metallurgist and mineralogist*• Born in Turinge, he studied mathematics at Uppsala before embarking on a career in mining and metallurgy. He first isolated nickel (1751) and noted its magnetic properties. He is renowned for his *Essay Toward a System of Mineralogy* (1758), in which minerals and stones were distinguished for the first time and chemical composition was advocated as the primary method of classification of minerals.

Crookes, Sir William 1832–1919 •*English chemist and physicist*• Born in London, he superintended the meteorological department of the Radcliffe Observatory, Oxford, and from 1855 lectured on chemistry at the Science College, Chester. He discovered the metal thallium (1861), and the sodium amalgamation process (1865). He also improved vacuum tubes, promoted electric lighting and invented the radiometer and the spinthariscope.

Crosbie, Annette 1934– •*Scottish actress*• Born in Edinburgh, she trained at Bristol Old Vic Theatre School and won two British Academy of Film and Television Arts Best Actress awards for her performances on television as **Catherine of Aragon** in *The Six Wives of Henry VIII* (1970) and Queen **Victoria** in *Edward the Seventh* (1975). She later played Margaret Meldrew in the sitcom *One Foot in the Grave* (1990–2000) and Janet MacPherson in *Doctor Finlay* (1993–96). Her films include *The Slipper and the Rose* (1976) and *Leon the Pig Farmer* (1992).

Crosby, Bing, *originally* **Harry Lillis Crosby** 1904–77 •*US singer and film actor*• Born in Tacoma, Washington. From the 1930s on, his distinctive crooning style made him a top attraction on radio, and later on television. He was one of the greatest sellers of records of the 20th century, and his version of "White Christmas" sold over 30 million copies. Consistently among the most popular prewar film stars, his partnership with **Bob Hope** and Dorothy Lamour (1914–96) resulted in a series of *Road to ...* comedies and he won an Academy Award for *Going My Way* (1944). Later notable films include *The Bells of St Mary's* (1945), *Blue Skies* (1946), *White Christmas* (1954), *The Country Girl* (1954) and *High Society* (1956). A keen golfer, he continued to record and perform sold-out concerts until his death on a golf course in Spain.

Crosby, Fanny (Frances Jane), *later* **Mrs Van Alstyne** 1820–1915 •*US hymnwriter*• Born in Putnam County in southeastern New York, she was blind from infancy, and was both pupil and teacher in New York City's Institute for the Blind. She composed about 6,000 popular hymns, including "Safe in the Arms of Jesus" (played at President **Ulysses S Grant**'s funeral) and "Pass Me Not, O Gentle Savior" (reportedly a favorite of Queen **Victoria**). Dwight L Moody (1837–99) and Ira Sankey (1840–1908) acknowledged a great debt to her.

Crosland, Anthony (Charles Anthony Raven) 1918–77 •*English Labour politician*• He was born at St Leonards-on-Sea, Sussex, and educated at Oxford (president of the Union, 1946), where he also taught after serving in World War II. He was elected Member of Parliament for South Gloucester (1950–55) and for Grimsby from 1959. He held several government posts under **Harold Wilson**, and made an unsuccessful bid for the party leadership in 1976, but served **James Callaghan** as the Foreign and Commonwealth Secretary (1976–77) before dying suddenly at the age of 58. A strong supporter of **Hugh Gaitskell**, he was a key member of the revisionist wing of the Labour Party, aiming to modernize socialist ideology, and wrote one of its seminal texts, *The Future of Socialism* (1956).

Crossman, Richard Howard Stafford 1907–74 •*English Labour politician*• The son of a judge, he was educated at New College, Oxford, where he stayed on as a Fellow, and lay dean. He left the university in 1937 to lecture for the Workers' Educational Association and join the staff of the *New Statesman*. During World War II he worked in political and psychological warfare, and in 1945 became the Labour Member of Parliament for Coventry East. A Bevanite activist, his brilliant intellect, and also perhaps his prosperous middle-class background, alienated him from some sections of the party, and neither **Clement Attlee** nor **Hugh Gaitskell** appointed him to high government office. **Harold Wilson**, however, brought him into the Cabinet as Minister of Housing and Local Government (1964–66). His last office was Secretary of State for Social Services and head of the Department of Health, and in 1970, on the defeat of the government, he returned to the *New Statesman* as editor until 1972. He began a political diary in 1952 during the internal struggles of the party, and, published posthumously in four volumes (1975, 1976, 1977, 1981), they provide an invaluable insight into the Wilson administration.

Crowe, Russell 1964– •*Australian actor*• He was born in Auckland, New Zealand, and moved to Australia with his family at the age of four. His mainstream film acting career began in the late 1980s with appearances in *Romper Stomper* (1992), *Heaven's Burning* (1997) and *L A Confidential* (1997), but it was with *Gladiator* (2000) that he became an international star and heartthrob, and won an Academy Award for Best Actor.

Crowley, Aleister, *originally* **Edward Alexander Crowley** 1875–1947 •*English writer and magician*• He became interested in the occult while an undergraduate at Cambridge, and was for a time a member of the Order of the Golden Dawn, which **W B Yeats** also joined. Expelled for extreme practices, he founded his own order, the Silver Star, and traveled widely, settling for several years in Sicily. Rumors of drugs, orgies and magical ceremonies involving the sacrifice of babies culminated in his expulsion from Italy. In 1921 a series of newspaper articles brought him the notoriety he craved—he liked to be known as "the great beast" and "the wickedest man alive"—and certainly many who associated with him died tragically, including his wife and child.

“ ”

Do what thou wilt shall be the whole of the Law.

1909 ***Book of the Law.***

Crowley, Bob (Robert) 1954– •*English stage designer*• He has worked at the Bristol Old Vic, the Royal Exchange, Manchester, and, in London, at the Greenwich Theatre and the National Theatre, where he designed **Bill Bryden**'s revival of *A Midsummer Night's Dream* (1982) and **Howard Davies**'s production of **Ibsen**'s *Hedda Gabler* (1989). Other stage work includes **Richard Eyre**'s productions of **David Hare**'s *Murmuring Judges* (1991) and **Edward Bond**'s *The Sea*. He is considered to be one of the finest of contemporary stage designers.

Crowther, Samuel Adjai 1809–91 •*African missionary*• Born in Ochugu, West Africa, he was carried off as a slave in 1819, and sold more than once, but rescued by a British warship and put ashore at Sierra Leone in 1822. He was baptized in 1825, taking the name of a London vicar, ran a mission school at Regent's Town, and accompanied the Niger expeditions of 1841 and 1854. Ordained in London in 1842, he was consecrated Bishop of the Niger Territory in 1864. He translated the Bible into Yoruba.

Cruft, Charles 1852–1939 •*English dogshow organizer*• He was for many years the general manager of James Spratt, dog-biscuit manufacturers. He organized his first dog show in 1886, and the annual shows since then became world-famous.

Cruickshank, Andrew John Maxton 1907–88 •*Scottish actor*• Born in Aberdeen, he made his London debut in the celebrated **Paul Robeson** production of *Othello* (1930). His many stage performances included *Dial M for Murder* (1952), *The Master Builder* (1962, 1972), *The Wild Duck* (1980) and his last in *Beyond Reasonable Doubt* (1987). His films included *The Cruel Sea* (1953) and *Richard III* (1955), but he gained his greatest renown on television as the gruff but kindly Dr Cameron in *Dr Finlay's Casebook* (1962–71).

Cruikshank, George 1792–1878 •*English caricaturist and illustrator*• Born in London, he made his name as a political caricaturist with *The Scourge* (1811–16) and *The Meteor* (1813–14). He contributed colored etchings to the *Humorist* (1819–21) and *Points of Humour* (1823–24), and his book illustrations included the etchings for *Peter Schlemihl* (1823) and **Grimm**'s *German Popular Stories* (1824–26). He also illustrated **Dickens**'s *Sketches by Boz* (1836) and *Oliver Twist* (1838), and **Thackeray**'s *Legend of the Rhine*. He devoted much of his later work to temperance, with a series of plates entitled *The Bottle* (1847), *The Drunkard's Children* (1848), and his cartoon *Worship of Bacchus* (1862). He is buried at St Paul's Cathedral.

Cruise, Tom, *in full* **Tom Cruise Mapother IV** 1962– •*US film actor*• He was born in Syracuse, New York, and moved to New York City in 1980, making his film debut in *Endless Love* (1981). The success of the teen comedy *Risky Business* (1983) confirmed his stardom. A charismatic performer with a winning smile and great intensity, he has had many box-office successes including *Top Gun* (1986), *Rain Man* (1988), *A Few Good Men* (1992), *Jerry Maguire* (1996), and *Minority Report* (2002). He was married to actress **Nicole Kidman**, his costar in *Days of Thunder* (1990), *Far and Away* (1992) and *Eyes Wide Shut* (1999).

Crutzen, Paul Josef 1933– •*Dutch chemist and Nobel Prize winner*• Born in Amsterdam, he was educated there and at Stockholm University, where he joined the department of meteorology and helped to run barotropic weather prediction models. Having done pioneering work on the photochemistry of atmospheric ozone and conducted research into stratospheric chemistry, he shared the 1995 Nobel Prize for chemistry with **F Sherwood Rowland** and **Mario J Molina** for work on the role of CFCs (chlorofluorcarbons) in the catalytic destruction of atmospheric ozone.

Cruyff, Johan 1947– •*Dutch soccer player*• Born in Amsterdam, he became one of the great European forwards of his time. With Ajax Amsterdam he won three European Cup medals in succession and was European Footballer of the Year in 1973 and 1974. In 1974 he was captain of the Dutch team that lost to West Germany in the finals of the World Cup. He afterward moved to Barcelona.

Cruz, Juan de la *See* **John of the Cross, St**

Cruz, Sor Juana Inés de la 1648–95 •*Mexican feminist, poet and playwright*• Born in San Miguel Nepantle, Amecameca, she was invited to live at the court after receiving attention for her scholarship. At the age of 20 she joined the Hieronymite convent in Mexico City. When instructed by a bishop, an officer of the Inquisition, to give up learning as "unbefitting to a woman" she issued the stately *Respuesta* (1691, "Response"), a key document in the history of feminism. Her own parodic, mystical poetry is individualistic, especially the "Primer sueño" ("First Dream"). Her poems about male stupidity, in particular "Redondillas" ("Verses"), have hardly been forgiven, but have been translated. Among the greatest and least understood of all writers, she sold all her books, scientific equipment, and musical instruments in order to care for the poor, and died of the plague while ministering to them.

Čsokonai Vitéz, Mihály 1773–1805 •*Hungarian poet*• Born in Debrecen, he was Professor of Poetry at the university there until his political sympathies lost him the post. His fame persists chiefly through his lyrics, which are based on old Hungarian folk songs. Among his works are the drama *Tempefoi* (1793), the poems *Magyar-Musa* (1797) and *Dorottya* (1804), a mock-heroic poem.

Ctesias 5th century BC •*Greek historian and physician*• He was physician to **Artaxerxes II Mnemon** of Persia, and accompanied him in the expedition against his rebellious brother **Cyrus** the Younger (401 BC). He wrote a history of Persia in 23 books, *Persika*, of which only some fragments remain.

Ctesibius 2nd century BC •*Greek inventor*• Born in Alexandria to Greek parents, he invented the force pump and water organ, and improved the clepsydra, or water-clock. He was the teacher of **Hero of Alexandria**.

Cubitt, Sir William 1785–1861 •*English civil engineer*• Born in Dilham, Norfolk, he was a miller, a cabinetmaker and a millwright until 1812, and then chief engineer in **Robert Ransome**'s Orwell Works in Ipswich, in which he was a partner (1821–26). The Bute Docks at Cardiff, the Southeastern Railway and the Berlin waterworks were constructed by him. He also invented the treadmill and was associated with the construction of the Great Exhibition buildings (1851). He was Lord Mayor of London in 1860–61, and Cubitt Town on the Isle of Dogs is named after him.

Cudworth, Ralph 1617–88 •*English philosopher and theologian*• Born in Aller, Somerset, he was the leading member of the Cambridge Platonists, becoming Master of Christ's College, Cambridge (1654), where he lived until his death. His monumental work, *The True Intellectual System of the Universe* (1678), was a systematic but unwieldy and incomplete treatise which aimed to refute determinism and materialism and to establish the reality of a supreme divine Intelligence. An important work on ethics, directed against **Thomas Hobbes**, was published posthumously in 1731 as *Treatise Concerning Eternal and Immutable Morality.*

Cui, César Antonovich 1835–1918 •*Russian composer and engineer*• Born in Vilna (now Vilnius, Lithuania), he was virtually self-taught as a musician and composed *William Ratcliff* (1861) and other operas. He was also an expert on fortification, and became a lieutenant general of engineers.

Cuijp, Albert *See* **Cuyp, Albert**

Cukor, George D(ewey) 1899–1983 •*US film director*• He was born in New York City, and became involved with the theater from an early age. In Hollywood he made his directorial debut with *Grumpy* (1930). *A Bill of Divorcement* (1932) and *Little Women* (1933) began a 50-year association with **Katharine Hepburn** that resulted in a succession of polished entertainments including *The Philadelphia Story* (1940) and *Love Among the Ruins* (1975). Drawn to sophisticated comedies and literary subjects, he enjoyed a reputation for his sensitive handling of many major stars in films like *Camille* (1936, with **Greta Garbo**), *Gaslight* (1944, with **Ingrid Bergman**), *Born Yesterday* (1950, with Judy Holliday) and *A Star Is Born* (1954, with **Judy Garland**). He won an Academy Award for *My Fair Lady* (1964).

Culbertson, Ely 1891–1955 •*US bridge player and peace campaigner*• Born in Romania, he devised contract bridge's first successful bidding system and in the early 1930s was acknowledged the best player in the world. As a young man he was imprisoned in the Caucasus as an anarchist revolutionary and emigrated after the Russian Revolution. From 1938 he dedicated his life to the campaign for world peace, developing a peace plan that contributed to the foundation of the United Nations. His publications included the autobiography *The Strange Lives of One Man* (1940).

Culkin, Macaulay 1980– •*US film actor*• Born in New York City, he made his film debut in *Rocket Gibraltar* (1988) and became a successful child star. Among his subsequent films are *Jacob's Ladder* (1990), *Home Alone* (1990), *Home Alone 2* (1992) and *The Good Son* (1993).

Cullberg, Birgit Ragnhild 1908–99 •*Swedish dancer, choreographer and ballet director*• Born in Nyköping, she studied in England with **Kurt Jooss**, and later in New York with **Martha Graham**. In the mid-1940s she toured Europe with Svenska Dansteatern, a group she cofounded, and later worked with companies including the Royal Swedish Ballet, American Ballet Theater and Royal Danish Ballet. Her ballets are influenced by modern dance and characterized by their strong dramatic content, often of a psychological nature. Her best known work, *Miss Julie*, dates from 1950.

Cullen, Countee 1903–46 •*US poet*• Born in New York City, the son of a Methodist Episcopal minister, he studied at New York University and Harvard. He began his literary career with *Color* (1925), a book of poems in which classical models such as the sonnet are used with considerable effect, and he became a leading figure in the Harlem Renaissance. He published several subsequent volumes of verse, and a novel, *One Way to Heaven* (1932).

Cullmann, Oscar 1902–99 •*German biblical scholar and theologian*• He was born in Strassburg (now Strasbourg, France). As professor at Basel (from 1938) and Paris (from 1948), he was the chief representative in New Testament studies of the 1950s and 1960s "biblical theology" movement and an exponent of the concept of Salvation-history (*Heilsgeschichte*). His works include *Christ and Time* (1950), *Salvation in History* (1967), *The Christology of the New Testament* (1959) and several studies of early Church worship and practice.

Culpeper, Nicholas 1616–54 •*English physician*• Born in London, he studied at Cambridge, and in 1640 started to practice astrology and medicine in Spitalfields, London. In 1649 he published an English translation of the College of Physicians' Pharmacopoeia, *A Physical Directory*, renamed in 1654 *Pharmacopoeia Londinensis, or the London Dispensatory*. His *The English Physician Enlarged, or the Herbal* appeared in 1653. Both books had enormous sales, the latter forming the basis of herbalism in the English-speaking world.

Cumberland, William Augustus, Duke of, *known as* **the Butcher** 1721–65 •*English military commander*• The third son of **George II** and **Caroline of Ansbach**, he was created duke in 1726. He was defeated at Fontenoy by Marshal **Saxe** in 1745, but nevertheless was sent to crush the 1745 Jacobite Uprising in Scotland, which he achieved at Culloden (1746); his cruelties earned him the lasting title of "Butcher." In the latter stages of the War of the Austrian Succession he was defeated by Saxe at Langfeld (1747), and in the Seven Years' War he had to surrender at Kloster-Zeven (1757), after which he retired.

cummings, e e, *properly* **Edward Estlin Cummings** 1894–1962 •*US writer and painter*• Born in Cambridge, Massachusetts, he was educated at Harvard, and studied art in Paris. He is known for his verse, characterized by unusual typography and eccentric punctuations. His collections of poetry include *Tulips and Chimneys* (1923), and his best-known prose work, *The Enormous Room* (1922), describes his wartime internment—brought about by an error by the authorities—in France. He also wrote a travel diary, a morality play, *Santa Claus* (1946), and a collection of six "non-lectures" delivered at Harvard entitled *i* (1953).

“ ”

spring
when the world is puddle wonderful

1923 ***Tulips and Chimneys****, "Chanson Innocente."*

Cunard, Sir Samuel 1787–1865 •*Canadian shipowner*• Born in Halifax, Nova Scotia, he succeeded early as a merchant and shipowner and emigrated to Great Britain in 1838. For the new steam mail service between Great Britain and the US, he joined up with George Burns of Glasgow and David McIver of Liverpool to found (1839) the British and North American Royal Mail Steam Packet Company, later known as the Cunard Line.

Cunctator ("Delayer") *See* **Fabius, Quintus Fabius Maximus Verrucosus**

Cunliffe, Barry (Barrington Windsor) 1939– •*English archaeologist*• Born in Portsmouth, he was educated at St John's College, Cambridge, then taught at Bristol and Southampton and in 1972 became Professor of European Archaeology at Oxford. He established a reputation in his twenties with spectacular excavations at the Roman palace of Fishbourne near Chichester (1961–67). He has since worked at sites such as Roman Bath, and three sites in Wessex: the Roman fort of Portchester near Portsmouth, the Iron Age hillfort at Danebury near Stockbridge, and the late prehistoric trading settlement at Hengistbury Head near Christchurch.

Cunningham, Sir Alan Gordon 1887–1983 •*British general*• Educated at Cheltenham College and the Royal Military Academy, Woolwich, he served with distinction in World War II. In 1941 he struck through Italian Somaliland from Kenya and freed Abyssinia and British Somaliland from the Italians. He was High Commissioner for Palestine (1945–48). His brother was Admiral Lord **Cunningham**.

Cunningham, Allan 1791–1839 •*English botanist and explorer*• Born in Wimbledon, Surrey, he became plant collector for Sir **Joseph Banks**, first in Brazil and then, in 1816, in New South Wales, Australia. While searching for new specimens, Cunningham made many valuable explorations of the hinterland of New South Wales and Queensland, also visiting New Zealand and Norfolk Island. He became Colonial Botanist for New South Wales in 1837. Many indigenous Australian trees now bear his name.

Cunningham (of Hyndhope), Andrew Browne Cunningham, 1st Viscount 1883–1963 •*British naval commander*• The brother of Sir **Alan Cunningham**, he was educated at Stubbington and HMS *Britannia* at Dartmouth. He commanded a destroyer in World War I, and in World War II he was Commander in Chief of British naval forces in the Mediterranean (1939–43). He defeated the Italian navy at Taranto (1940) and Cape Matapan (1941), and was in command of Allied naval forces for the invasion of North Africa (1942), and Sicily and Italy (1942). Promoted to Admiral of the Fleet in 1943, he was First Sea Lord from 1943 to 1946.

Cunningham, E V *See* **Fast, Howard Melvin**

Cunningham, Imogen 1883–1976 •*US photographer*• Born in Portland, Oregon, she worked with **Edward Curtis** before opening her own portrait studio in Seattle in 1910. Her personal style was pictorial romanticism, particularly in still-life flower studies. In 1932 she met **Edward Weston** and became part of his Group f/64, which insisted on sharply defined images and precise tonal gradation. After the breakup of the group she worked at her portrait gallery for almost 40 years more, and was still teaching at the Art Institute in San Francisco in her nineties.

Cunningham, Jack (John) 1939– •*English Labour politician*• Born in Newcastle upon Tyne, he studied chemistry at the University of Durham and became Member of Parliament for Whitehaven, Cumbria, in 1970, subsequently representing Copeland from 1983. He served as Parliamentary Under-Secretary of State in the Department of Industry (1976–79) and was a senior opposition spokesman in the 1980s. Following Labour's landslide victory in 1997 he served as Minister of Agriculture, Fisheries and Food (1997–98) under **Tony Blair** prior to being appointed Minister for the Cabinet Office and Chancellor of the Duchy of Lancaster (1998–99).

Cunningham, Merce 1919– •*US choreographer, dancer, teacher and director*• Born in Centralia, Washington, he danced with the **Martha Graham** Dance Company (1939–45), began to choreograph in 1942, and gave his first solo concerts, with the composer **John Cage**, in 1944. His choreographic works include *Suite for Five* (1956), *Antic Meet* (1958), *Scramble* (1967), *Landrover* (1972), *Duets* (1980) and *Loosestrife* (1991). In 1953 he founded the Merce Cunningham Dance Company. He is credited with redefining modern dance and developing a new vocabulary for it. He was awarded the US National Medal of Arts in 1990.

Cunningham, Michael 1952– •*US author*• Born in Cincinnati, Ohio, he was educated at Stanford University. His early books included *Golden States* (1984) and *Flesh and Blood* (1995), but major recognition came with the Pulitzer Prize–winning novel *The Hours* (1998), a study of three women linked by **Virginia Woolf**'s book *Mrs Dalloway*.

Cunobelinus *See* **Cymbeline**

Cupitt, Don 1934– •*English theologian*• Born in Oldham and educated at Cambridge, he was ordained an Anglican priest in 1959. In 1962 he was appointed Vice Principal of Westcott House, Cambridge, and he was Dean of Emmanuel College (1966–91). He has been a prolific writer, often provoking controversial reaction to some of his more radical views. This was perhaps most notably illustrated by the response to *Sea of Faith* (1984), which was also a successful television series. Other works include *Christ and the Hiddenness of God* (1971), *Taking Leave of God* (1980), *The Long-Legged Fly* (1987), *The Time Being* (1992) and *The Last Philosophy* (1995).

Curie, Marie, *originally* **Maria**, *née* **Skłodowska** 1867–1934 •*Polish-born French physicist and Nobel Prize winner*• She was born in Warsaw and brought up in poor surroundings after her father, who had studied mathematics at the University of St Petersburg, was denied work for political reasons. After brilliant high school studies, she worked as a governess for eight years. In 1891 she went to Paris, where she graduated in physics from the Sorbonne (1893), taking first place. She then received an Alexandrovitch Scholarship from Poland which allowed her to study mathematics. She met **Pierre Curie** in 1894 and they married the following year. Together they worked on magnetism and radioactivity (a term she coined in 1898), and isolated radium and polonium, which she named after her native Poland. They were jointly awarded the Nobel Prize for physics in 1903, with **Antoine Henri Becquerel**. After her husband's death in 1906, she succeeded him as Professor of Physics at the Sorbonne. She isolated pure radium in 1910, and received the 1911 Nobel Prize for chemistry. During World War I she developed X-radiography and afterwards became director of the research department at the newly established Radium Institute in Paris (1918–34). She was also Honorary Professor of Radiology at Warsaw (1919–34). She died of leukemia, probably caused by her long exposure to radiation. Her elder daughter was the nuclear physicist **Irène Joliot-Curie**.

“ ”

In science, we must be interested in things, not in persons.

*Quoted in Eve Curie **Madame Curie** (1937), chapter 16 (translated by Vincent Sheean, 1943).*

Curie, Pierre 1859–1906 •*French physicist and Nobel Prize winner*• Born in Paris and educated at the Sorbonne, he was laboratory chief at the School of Industrial Physics and Chemistry until 1904, when he was appointed to a new chair in physics at the Sorbonne. With his brother Jacques, he discovered piezoelectricity in 1880 and used a piezoelectric crystal to construct an electrometer; this was later used by Pierre's wife, **Marie Curie**, in her investigations of radioactive minerals. In studies of magnetism, Pierre showed that a ferromagnetic material loses this property at a certain temperature—the "Curie point." Another of his important discoveries was "Curie's law," which relates the magnetic susceptibility of a paramagnetic material to the absolute temperature. From 1898 he worked with his wife on radioactivity, and showed that the rays emitted by radium contained electrically positive, negative and neutral particles. With his wife and **Antoine Henri Becquerel** he was awarded the Nobel Prize for physics in 1903.

Curl, Robert Floyd, Jr 1933– •*US chemist and Nobel Prize winner*• Born in Alice, Texas, he was educated at the William Marsh Rice University and the University of California at Berkeley. After working as a research fellow at Harvard (1957–58) he held posts at Rice University (1958–). His research at the university with **Harold Kroto** and **Richard Smalley** led to the discovery of the C_{60} molecules known as "buckminsterfullerene" (known as "buckyballs"). For this work Curl, with Kroto and Smalley, was awarded the 1996 Nobel Prize for chemistry.

Currie, Ken 1960– •*Scottish painter*• Born in North Shields, Tyne and Wear, he attended the Glasgow School of Art. He worked on two community-based films about Glasgow and the shipbuilding industry on the Clyde and is influenced by the social realist painters of the 19th century and by the 20th-century political realist art of Germany and Mexico. His most ambitious polemical work to date has been a series of murals for the People's Palace Museum in Glasgow, depicting the Socialist history of Glasgow.

Currier, Nathaniel 1813–88 •*US lithographer*• Born in Roxbury, Massachusetts, he founded a lithography house in New York City in 1835, and in 1857 he entered into a partnership with **James Merritt Ives** (1824–95). Ives contributed drawings of his own, oversaw a staff of other artists, and chose subjects ranging from current events to country scenes. From 1840 to 1890 the firm produced more than 7,000 hand-colored prints, now collectors' items, chronicling life in 19th-century America.

Curtin, John (Joseph Ambrose) 1885–1945 •*Australian Labor politician*• Born in Creswick, Victoria, he entered federal politics for Fremantle, Western Australia in 1928, and became leader of the Australian Labor Party in 1935. As Prime Minister (1941–45), he recognized Australia's vulnerable remoteness from Great Britain and placed it firmly under the control of the US forces during World War II, recalling Australian troops from the Middle East. He died in office and was succeeded first by his deputy Frank Forde, then by **Ben Chifley**.

Curtis, Edward Sheriff 1868–1952 •*US photographer and writer*• Born in Madison, Wisconsin, he was brought up in Seattle, Washington. He devoted almost the whole of his career from 1896 to recording the North American peoples and their way of life, which was to vanish almost completely during the 35 years of his study. With financial assistance from **J Pierpont Morgan**, he published the first of 20 volumes in 1907, combining evocative and detailed photographs with an equally informative text. In contrast to earlier US photographers who portrayed Native Americans as warriors, Curtis stressed their peaceful arts and culture, perhaps in idealized terms.

Curtis, Jamie Lee 1958– •*US actress*• Born in Los Angeles, the daughter of **Tony Curtis** and Janet Leigh (1927–), she studied at the University of the Pacific, California. She appeared in the *Halloween* series (from 1979), and later turned in energetic performances in films such as *Trading Places* (1983), *A Fish Called Wanda* (1988) and *True Lies* (1994). She has appeared widely on television and written several children's books. She married the actor and director Christopher Guest in 1984, becoming Lady Haden-Guest.

Curtis, Tony, *originally* **Bernard Schwartz** 1925– •*US actor and painter*• Born in New York, he served as a signalman during World War II. He made his film debut in *Criss Cross* (1948) and quickly gained popularity as the athletic star of exotic adventure stories like *The Prince Who Was a Thief* (1950) and *Son of Ali Baba* (1952). A deft, light comedian in films like *Some Like It Hot* (1959), he also proved himself a dramatic actor of merit in *The Defiant Ones* (1958), for which he received an Academy Award nomination, and *The Boston Strangler* (1968). He found further popularity in such television ventures as *The Persuaders* (1971–72) and *Mafia Princess* (1986). He is also an accomplished painter. Actress **Jamie Lee Curtis** is his daughter.

Curtis, Tony 1946– •*Welsh poet*• Born in Carmarthen, he was educated at University College, Swansea, and Goddard College, Vermont. He has published collections of verse, prose-poems, short stories, critical essays, and has edited several anthologies. He chaired The Welsh Academy from 1984 to 1987. In 1984 he won first prize in the National Poetry Competition.

Curtiss, Glenn Hammond 1878–1930 •*US aviation pioneer and inventor*• He was born in Hammondsport, New York. Originally a bicycle mechanic, in 1905 he set a world speed record of 137 mph (220 kph) on a motorcycle of his own design. He also designed motors for airships, and with **Alexander Graham Bell** formed the Aerial Experiment Association (1907). He gained the Scientific American award in 1908 for the first public flight of 0.62 miles (1 km) in the US, flying at 40 mph (64.4 kph). He won the James Gordon Bennett Cup in France in 1909 in his *Golden Arrow* at 46.65 mph (75.1 kph). In 1911 he invented the aileron, and also flew the first practical seaplane (Hydroplane), which he patented, as well as the flying boat. During World War I he produced military aircraft like the JN-4 (Jenny) and the Navy-Curtiss flying boat.

Curtiz, Michael, *originally* **Mihaly Kertész** 1888–1962 •*Hungarian film director*• Born in Budapest and educated at Markoszy University and the Budapest Royal Academy of Art and Theater, he first worked as a film actor and director in 1912. He directed about 60 films in Europe before moving to Hollywood (1926), where he made another 125 films, despite his notoriously uncertain grasp of the English language. His biggest successes included *Angels with Dirty Faces* (1938), *The Adventures of Robin Hood* (1938), *Yankee Doodle Dandy* (1942) and *Casablanca* (1943).

Curzon (of Kedleston), George Nathaniel Curzon, Marquis 1859–1925 •*English statesman*• Born in Kedleston Hall, Derbyshire, he was educated at Eton and Oxford. In 1886 he was elected Member of Parliament for Southport, and the following year began extensive travels, writing books on Asiatic Russia (1889), on Persia (1892) and on problems of the Far East (1894). In 1898, at only 39, he became Viceroy of India and was given an Irish barony, having been unwilling to accept an English peerage with its accompanying bar from the House of Commons. He introduced many reforms, both social and political, including the establishment of the Northwest Frontier Province and the partition of Bengal. After the arrival of Lord **Kitchener** as Commander in Chief in 1902, a difference of opinion arose which led to Curzon's resignation in 1905. He returned to politics as Lord Privy Seal in the Coalition of 1915, and became a member of **David Lloyd George**'s War Cabinet in 1916. From 1919 to 1924 he was Foreign Secretary. He was created a marquis in 1921.

Cusack, Cyril 1910–93 •*Irish actor, director and playwright*• Born in Durban, South Africa, he was a child actor. A member of the Abbey Theatre (1932–45), he appeared in over 65 plays including the major works of **Sean O'Casey**, **J M Synge** and **George Bernard Shaw**. He subsequently formed his own company, touring Ireland and the world, and received the International Critics award for his performance in **Samuel Beckett**'s *Krapp's Last Tape* (1960) in Paris. He was also known for telling cameo parts in films like *Odd Man Out* (1947), *Fahrenheit 451* (1966) and *Little Dorrit* (1988). Several members of his family have followed in his professional footsteps, including his daughter, actress Sinead Cusack (1948–).

Cusack, (Ellen) Dymphna 1902–81 •*Australian writer*• Born in Wyalong, New South Wales, she was educated at Sydney University, and trained as a teacher. The first of her 12 novels, *Jungfrau*, was published in 1936 and dealt frankly (for its time) with sexual issues. This was followed in 1939 by *Pioneers on Parade*, written jointly with **Miles Franklin**. In 1948 she won the (Sydney) *Daily Telegraph* novel competition with *Come in Spinner*, the story of the lives of a group of women in wartime Sydney, written in collaboration with the New Zealand writer Florence James (1902–93). Cusack wrote nine other novels and eight plays which illustrate her preoccupation with social and political disadvantage.

Cushing, Harvey Williams 1869–1939 •*US neurosurgeon*• Born in Cleveland, Ohio, he was educated at Yale and Harvard, became Professor of Surgery at Harvard (1912–32), served with the Army Medical Corps during World War I, and in 1933 became Sterling Professor of Neurology at Yale. A talented and innovative neurosurgeon, he depended for much of his success on the important new techniques and procedures he developed to control blood pressure and bleeding during surgery. He discovered a new operative approach to the pituitary gland, and made a detailed study of its activity. He was also interested in the history of medicine and won a Pulitzer Prize in 1926 for his biography of the Canadian physician, Sir **William Osler**.

Cushing, Peter 1913–94 •*English actor*• Born in Kenley, Surrey, he studied at the Guildhall School of Music and Drama. A trip to the US resulted in his Hollywood film debut in *The Man in the Iron Mask* (1939). After World War II he established himself as a classical actor with the Old Vic Company (1948–49) and worked in television. Lasting fame resulted from a long association with the gothic horror films produced by Hammer Films, in which his cadaverous figure and gentlemanly manner brought conviction to a succession of misguided scientists and vampire hunters in films like *The Curse of Frankenstein* (1956), *Dracula* (1958) and *The Mummy* (1959). Other films include *Dr Who and the Daleks* (1965) and *Tales from the Crypt* (1972). He also enjoyed a long screen association with the character of Sherlock Holmes that included a 1968 television series and the film *The Hound of the Baskervilles* (1959).

Custer, George Armstrong 1839–76 •*US soldier*• Born in New Rumley, Ohio, he trained at West Point and served with distinction throughout the Civil War (1861–65), becoming a brigadier general at the age of 23. From 1866 he commanded the 7th Cavalry against the Native American tribes of the Great Plains, and in 1874 he led an expedition that discovered gold in the Black Hills, which were sacred to the Cheyenne and the Sioux and protected by treaty. The gold rush that followed greatly escalated the conflict between Native Americans and whites, and in 1876 Custer was ordered to lead the 7th Cavalry as part of a three-pronged campaign against an alliance of Cheyenne and Sioux organized by **Sitting Bull**, **Crazy Horse** and other chiefs. When he discovered them in the valley of the Little Big Horn River (in present-day Montana), Custer attacked (June 25, 1876) without waiting for reinforcements, pitting his regiment of 647 men against an army of thousands of warriors. He and his central unit of some 260 soldiers were surrounded and killed to the last man, an event that became known as "Custer's Last Stand." His death made him a legend, but many critics have called the attack vainglorious and suicidal.

Cuthbert, St c.635–87 •*Anglo-Saxon bishop and missionary*• Born probably in Lauderdale, in the Scottish Borders, in 651 he entered the monastery of Old Melrose, and in 661 was elected prior. He traveled widely in the north of England as a missionary, and many miracles were reported. In 664 he left Melrose for the island monastery of Lindisfarne, but in 676 he left Lindisfarne for a hermit's cell built on Farne Island (Inner Farne). Shortly after 684 he became bishop of Lindisfarne, and after two years he returned to his cell, where he died. His body was elevated with a coffin reliquary in 689, and the magnificent Lindisfarne Gospels book was made for the occasion. After many wanderings his body was finally buried in 999, in Durham, where, enclosed in an elaborate shrine, and believed to work many miracles daily, it remained until the Reformation. The grave was opened in 1826; inside the triple coffin his skeleton was found still apparently entire, wrapped in five robes of embroidered silk. His feast day is March 20.

Cuthbert, Betty, *known as* **the Golden Girl** 1938– •*Australian sprinter*• She was born in the Merrylands district of Sydney. Shortly before the 1956 Olympic games, she broke the world record for the 200 meters, and went on to win Olympic gold medals for the 100-meters, 200-meters and 4 × 100-meters relay, setting three Olympic records and the world record for the relay. Over the next nine years she set 16 world records, 11 individual and 5 relay, culminating in a fourth gold medal (for the 400 meters) at the 1964 Olympics in Tokyo. In 1981 she was diagnosed as having multiple sclerosis; she has since worked to raise public awareness of the disease.

Cuvier, Georges Léopold Chrétien Frédéric Dagobert, Baron 1769–1832 •*French anatomist*• Born in Montbéliard, he studied for the ministry at Stuttgart but developed an interest in zoology. In 1795 he was appointed Assistant Professor of Comparative Anatomy in the Jardin des Plantes at the Museum of Natural History in Paris, and in 1789 he became Professor of Natural History at the Collège de France. After the Restoration he was made Chancellor of the University of Paris, and admitted into the Cabinet by **Louis XVIII**. His opposition to the royal measures restricting freedom of the press lost him the favor of **Charles X**, but under **Louis Philippe** he was made a peer of France in 1831, and Minister of the Interior in 1832. In his scientific work he originated the natural system of animal classification that anticipates the modern division of the animal kingdom into phyla. His studies of animal and fish fossils, through his reconstructions of the extinct giant vertebrates of the Paris basin, linked paleontology to comparative anatomy. He was a militant antievolutionist, and accounted for the fossil record by positing "catastrophism"—a series of extinctions due to periodic global floods after which new forms of life appeared. Cuvier's works include: *Leçons d'anatomie comparée* (1801–05, "Lessons of Comparative Anatomy"), *Les ossements fossiles des quadrupèdes* (1812, "The Fossilized Bones of Quadrupeds") and *Histoire naturelle des poissons* (1828–49, "The Natural History of Fish"). He is known as the father of comparative anatomy and paleontology.

Cuyp or **Cuijp, Albert** 1620–91 •*Dutch painter*• Born in Dordrecht, he traveled along his local rivers making sketches and studies from nature, but unlike many of his peers, he never went to Italy. Although he had little influence on the history of Dutch painting, he is widely regarded as one of the greatest Dutch landscapists. He excelled at depicting sunlight in scenes of munching cattle.

Cymbeline or **Cunobelinus** fl. c. 5–41 AD •*British chief of the Catevellauni tribe*• He is described by **Suetonius** as "rex Britannorum" ("King of Britain"). Several of his coins are extant. **Shakespeare**'s Cymbeline is loosely based on him, following his portrait in the chronicles of **Raphael Holinshed**.

Cynewulf c. 700–c. 800 •*Anglo-Saxon poet and scholar*• He came from Mercia or Northumberland. The works attributed to him are now restricted to four poems which have his name worked into their runic inscriptions: *The Ascension of Christ* and *Elene* in the *Exeter Book*, and *St Juliana* and *The Fates of the Apostles* in the *Vercelli Book*.

Cyprian, St, *properly* **Thascius Caecilius Cyprianus** c. 200–58 AD •*North African Christian and Father of the Church*• Born probably in Carthage, Tunisia, he taught rhetoric there, and became a Christian in c. 245 AD. He was made Bishop of Carthage in 248, and became unpopular because of his efforts to restore strict discipline. Excommunicated by Pope Stephen I (d. 257) for denying the validity of heretic baptism, at a synod in Carthage in 256 Cyprian maintained that the Roman bishop, in spite of **St Peter**'s primacy, could not claim judicial authority over other bishops. He was martyred during the reign of **Valerian**. He wrote a treatise on church unity called *De unitate ecclesiae*. His feast day is September 6.

Cypselus fl. c. 657–625 BC •*Tyrant of Corinth*• He was one of the earliest self-made rulers who arose in many Greek cities in the 7th and 6th centuries. He seized power from the Bacchiads who had ruled Corinth since the 8th century, and founded the Cypselid dynasty. The earliest account of his rule in **Herodotus** is unfavorable, yet there are indications that Cypselus's rule enjoyed some popular support. He was succeeded by his son **Periander**.

Cyrankiewicz, Jozef 1911–89 •*Polish statesman*• Born in Tarnow, he studied in Kraków, where he became Secretary of the Socialist Party in 1935. Taken prisoner by the Germans in 1939, he escaped and organized resistance in the Kraków Province, but was sent to Auschwitz in 1941. In 1945 he became Secretary-General of the Socialist Party and was Prime Minister from 1947 to 1952. He resumed the premiership from 1954 to 1970.

Cyrano de Bergerac, Savinien 1619–55 •*French writer and dramatist*• He was born in Paris. As a soldier in his youth, he fought more than a thousand duels, mostly on account of his monstrously large nose. His works, often crude, but full of invention, vigor, and wit, include a comedy, *Le pédant joué* (1654, "The Pedant Outwitted") and the satirical science fantasies *Histoire comique des états et empires de la lune et du soleil* (1656 and 1662, Eng trans, 1 vol *Voyages to the Moon and the Sun*, 1754). He was the subject of **Edmond Rostand**'s play, *Cyrano de Bergerac* (1897).

Cyril of Alexandria, St AD 376–444 •*Greek theologian and a Doctor of the Church*• Born in Alexandria, he succeeded his uncle, Theophilus, as Patriarch of Alexandria (AD 412), and vigorously implemented Orthodox Christian teaching. He expelled the Jews from the city (415), and relentlessly persecuted the Patriarch of Constantinople, **Nestorius** (d. 451), who was deposed at the Council of Ephesus (431). Pope **Leo XIII** declared him a Doctor of the Church in 1882. Among his extant works are a defense of Christianity, written against the emperor **Julian** in 433, and a series of homilies and treatises. His feast day is June 9 or 27.

Cyril of Jerusalem, St c. 315–86 AD •*Middle Eastern Christian ecclesiastic and Doctor of the Church*• Born in Jerusalem, he was ordained Bishop of Jerusalem in 351 AD. He was twice expelled from his see, in 358 and by a synod at Constantinople (Istanbul) in 360, but on the accession of **Julian** the Apostate in 361 he resumed his duties till 367, when, by order of Valens, he was again expelled. He returned again on the death of Valens in 378. He was the author of 23 *Katéchéseis* (instructions to catechumens). His feast day is March 18.

Cyril, St 827–69 and **Methodius, St** 826–85, *known as* **the Apostles of the Slavs** •*Greek Christian missionaries*• They were born in Thessalonica. Cyril, traditionally the inventor of the Cyrillic alphabet, first worked among the Tartar Khazars (c. 860), and Methodius among the Bulgarians of Thrace and Moesia (c. 863). In Moravia they made Slav translations of the Scriptures and chief liturgical books, for which they were summoned to Rome to explain. After Cyril's death, Methodius continued as Bishop of Moravia to evangelize the Slavs, and he gained the approval of Pope John VIII when he was called to Rome (879) to justify his celebration of the Mass in the native tongue. Their feast day is July 7.

Cyrrhestes *See* **Andronicus**

Cyrus the Great c. 600–529 BC •*Founder of the Persian Empire*• He was a cousin of **Darius I**. In c. 550 BC, he made Astyages, last king of Media, a prisoner, and took his capital, Ecbatana. By 548 BC he was king of Persia (Iran), and with the support of the tribes on "the Lower Sea," or Persian Gulf, he took Sippara (Sepharvaim) and Babylon itself (539 BC). Cyrus, a polytheist, at once began a policy of religious conciliation, restoring enslaved nations, including the Jews, to their native countries, and granting them religious freedom. The empire of Lydia had fallen to Cyrus (c. 546 BC), and by 539 BC he ruled Asia from the Mediterranean to the Hindu Kush. He extended his empire from the Arabian Desert and the Persian Gulf in the south, to the Black Sea, the Caucasus and the Caspian in the north. He became the epitome of the heroic conqueror: brave, magnanimous and tolerant. His son **Cambyses II** became King of Babylon. The *Cyropaedia* of **Xenophon** is a historical romance drawn from his life.

Cyrus the Younger 424–401 BC •*Persian prince and satrap*• He was the second son of the Achaemenid king **Darius II Ochus**. He was accused of conspiring against his brother, **Artaxerxes II Mnemon**, and was sentenced to death (404 BC), but was afterward pardoned and restored as satrap of Asia Minor. In 401 he led an army of Greek mercenaries (which included Xenophon) against his brother, but was killed at Cunaxa.

D

Dadd, Richard 1819–87 •*English painter*• Born in Chatham, Kent, he traveled extensively in Europe and the Middle East. In 1843 he suffered a mental breakdown and murdered his father. He was sent first to the asylum of Bethlem, where he spent 20 years, and subsequently to Broadmoor. He is best known for the fantastically detailed fairy paintings which made up the bulk of his output after his incarceration; *The Fairy-Feller's Master Stroke* (1855–64) is a typical example.

Dafoe, Willem 1955– •*US actor*• Born in Appleton, Wisconsin, he began his screen career in the late 1970s and is known for his powerful, haunted characterizations in films such as *Platoon* (1986), *The Last Temptation of Christ* (1988), *Born on the Fourth of July* (1990), *Body of Evidence* (1992), *Affliction* (1997) and *Shadow of the Vampire* (2000).

Dafydd ap Gruffydd d. 1283 •*Welsh prince*• The brother of Llywelyn ap Gruffydd, he opposed his brother's accession, but eventually supported him in his battles with the English. He succeeded his brother as Prince of Gwynedd in North Wales (1282), but was betrayed and executed (1283), the last native prince of Wales.

Dafydd ap Gwilym c. 1315–c. 1370 •*Welsh poet and bard*• Born near Aberystwyth, of noble birth, he introduced many elements of European writing into Welsh verse while managing to bring Welsh verse into the European mainstream. A poet in the wandering bard tradition, he wrote verse set in forests and peopled with birds and animals. Often hailed as the greatest of Welsh poets, he is sometimes credited with having invented the *cywydd* form of verse; he was certainly responsible for its becoming the dominant form in Welsh verse after his time.

da Gama, Vasco *See* **Gama, Vasco da**

Daguerre, Louis Jacques Mandé 1789–1851 •*French photographic pioneer and painter*• Born in Cormeilles, he became a scene painter for the opera in Paris. From 1826 on, and partly in conjunction with **Joseph Nicéphore Niepce**, he perfected his "daguerreotype" process, in which a photographic image is obtained on a copper plate coated with a layer of metallic silver sensitized to light by iodine vapor. This reduced the exposure time required to produce an image from around eight hours for Niepce's original method to around 25 minutes.

Dahl, Roald 1916–90 •*British children's author, short-story writer, playwright and versifier*• Dahl was born in Llandaff, Glamorgan, to Norwegian parents. His first short stories, collected as *Over to You* (1946), were based on his wartime experiences in the RAF. As his mature style developed he began to specialize in the macabre, and subsequent collections such as *Someone Like You* (1954) and *Kiss Kiss* (1960) achieved enormous success. His last major collection of adult stories was *Switch Bitch* (1974). Although he is among the most popular children's authors of all time, some parents, teachers and librarians have expressed disapproval of his anarchic rudeness and violence. *Charlie and the Chocolate Factory* (1964), the story of a poor boy who by his honesty becomes heir to Willy Wonka's extraordinary chocolate empire, is Dahl's best-known children's book, and was successfully filmed; its sequel was *Charlie and the Great Glass Elevator* (1972). Others include *James and the Giant Peach* (1961), *Fantastic Mr Fox* (1970), *The Enormous Crocodile* (1978), *The BFG* (1982), *Matilda* (1988) and *Esio Trot* (1990). *The Minpins* and *The Vicar of Nibbleswicke* were published posthumously in 1991. He also wrote the screenplays for *You Only Live Twice* (1967) and *Chitty Chitty Bang Bang* (1968). A number of his stories were adapted for television as *Tales of the Unexpected*, and his children's books have been successfully portrayed on film and on stage. His first wife was the actress **Patricia Neal**.

Dahlie, Bjørn 1967– •*Norwegian skier*• Born in Raholt, he first specialized in competitive Nordic skiing as a teenager and went on to achieve legendary status as a cross-country skier. Nicknamed "The Rocketman," he dominated international competition through the 1990s, winning numerous medals in the World Cup and world championship. He also shattered the record for medals won by an individual in the Winter Olympics, winning three gold medals and one silver at Albertville in 1992, two golds and two silvers at Lillehammer in 1994 and three golds and a silver at Nagano in 1998.

Dahmer, Jeffrey Lionel 1960–94 •*US serial killer*• Born in Milwaukee, Wisconsin, he began drinking heavily at the age of 14 and murdered his first victim shortly after leaving high school. He joined the US Army in January 1979 but by 1981 had been discharged for excessive drinking. He turned to killing again, murdering and dismembering young men and dissolving their bodies in acid. On capturing Dahmer in his apartment in 1991, the police discovered the remains of at least 11 people. He admitted to acts of dismemberment, necrophilia and cannibalism on 17 men and boys, and at his trial in 1992 he was given 15 life sentences. In 1994 he was beaten to death by a fellow prisoner.

Daiches, David 1912– •*Scottish critic*• Born in Sunderland, the son of a rabbi, he was brought up in Edinburgh, and educated at Edinburgh University. He served in the British embassy in Washington during World War II, then returned to academic life at Cornell University (1947–51), taught at Cambridge (1951–61), and was Professor of Literature at the University of Sussex (1961–77), before retiring to Edinburgh. He was then Director of the Institute for Advanced Studies in the Humanities at Edinburgh University (1980–86). He made many valuable contributions to literary criticism, especially in his insistence on the inclusion of modern literature within the academic syllabus. His works include a book on **Robert Burns** (1950, rev edn 1966) and a provocative study of the Scottish Enlightenment, *The Paradox of Scottish Culture* (1964).

Daimler, Gottlieb Wilhelm 1834–1900 •*German engineer and inventor*• He was born in Schorndorf, and studied engineering at the Stuttgart Polytechnic Institute. From 1872 he worked on improving the gas engine. In 1885 he built one of the earliest roadworthy motorcars, using a high-speed internal combustion engine, and he founded the Daimler-Motoren-Gesellschaft in Cannstatt in 1890.

Dakin, Henry Drysdale 1880–1952 •*English chemist*• Born in London, he was trained in Marburg before returning to work at the Lister Institute, where he independently synthesized adrenaline (1906). He carried out extensive research on the oxidation processes of the body (1908–12). After World War I, he emigrated to the US and joined the staff of the Rockefeller Institute, New York, where he made early contributions to the understanding of protein structure. His most enduring contribution came from his study of antiseptics. "Dakin's," or the "Carrel-Dakin," solution (a 0.5 percent solution of sodium hypochlorite) was widely used for treating wounds during the two world wars and is still used extensively as a safe, cheap sterilizing agent today. He was elected a Fellow of the Royal Society in 1917.

Daladier, Édouard 1884–1970 •*French politician*• He was born in Carpentras. He became leader of the radical Socialists in 1927, and in 1933 Minister of War and Prime Minister of a short-lived government. Again Minister of War, he was asked to form a Cabinet in 1934, but his government, embroiled in the **Stavisky** crisis, lasted only a few weeks. In 1936 he became War Minister in the Popular Front Cabinet, and in 1938 again took office as premier. Pacifist in outlook, he supported "appeasement" and was a signatory of the Munich Pact. In 1940 he resigned, became successively War Minister and Foreign Minister, and on the fall of France was arrested and interned until 1945.

Dalai Lama, *originally* **Tenzin Gyatso** 1935– •*Spiritual and temporal head of Tibet*• He was born into a peasant family in Taktser, Amdo province, and was designated the 14th incarnation of the Dalai Lama by the monks of Lhasa in 1937. He was enthroned in 1940, but his rights were exercised by a regency until 1950. He fled to Chumbi in southern Tibet after an abortive anti-Chinese uprising in 1950, but negotiated an autonomy agreement with the People's Republic the following year and for the next eight years served as nominal ruler of Tibet. After China's suppression of the Tibetan national uprising in 1959, he was forced into permanent exile and settled with other Tibetan refugees at Dharamsala in Punjab, India, where he established a democratically based alternative government and sought to preserve Tibetan culture. A revered figure in his homeland and highly respected internationally, the Dalai Lama has continually rejected Chinese overtures to return home as a figurehead, seeking instead full independence. In 1988 he modified this position, proposing the creation of a self-governing Tibet in association with China. The following year he was awarded the Congressional Human Rights award and the 1989 Nobel Peace Prize in recognition of his commitment to the nonviolent liberation of his homeland.

" "

Frankly speaking, it is difficult to trust the Chinese. Once bitten by a snake, you feel suspicious even when you see a piece of rope.

1981 Quoted in the ***Observer Colour Magazine****, April 5.*

Daldry, Stephen 1961– •*English theater director*• He studied at Sheffield University, then ran away with a circus to Italy. On his return he was an associate director of the Metro Theatre (1984–86) and of the Sheffield Crucible Theatre (1986–88), then artistic director of the Gate Theatre in Notting Hill, London (1989–92). His many successful productions include *An Inspector Calls* (1992), which won a Laurence Olivier award. He has also moved into film, receiving an Academy Award nomination for Best Director for the hugely successful *Billy Elliot* (2000).

d'Alembert, Jean le Rond *See* **Alembert, Jean le Rond d'**

Dalén, Nils Gustav 1869–1937 •*Swedish physicist, engineer and Nobel Prize winner*• Born in Stenstorp, he graduated as a mechanical engineer from the Chalmers Institute in Göteborg (1896), and began to experiment on hot-air turbines, compressors and air pumps. He invented lighthouses, and to conserve acetylene, he produced a sun valve that extinguished the flame during daylight hours. He was awarded the 1912 Nobel Prize for physics, but was unable to attend the award ceremony due to a serious accident, in which he lost his sight.

Dalglish, Kenny (Kenneth Mathieson) 1951– •*Scottish soccer player and manager*• Born in Glasgow, he is considered one of Scotland's greatest internationals. He joined Glasgow Celtic in 1967 and in ten years there won every honor in the Scottish game. Transferred to Liverpool in 1977 for a then-record fee between two British clubs of £440,000, he won every major English honor in addition to three European Cups. Unexpectedly invited to manage Liverpool (1985), he confounded the pundits by winning both cup and league in his first season. In 1991 he became manager of the Blackburn Rovers, then director (1995), and led the team to win the 1994–95 Premiership. He left Blackburn and succeeded **Kevin Keegan** as manager of Newcastle United in 1997, but was sacked in 1998. He later had a brief spell with Celtic, but has now retired.

Dalhousie, James Andrew Broun-Ramsay, Marquis of 1812–60 •*Scottish politician and administrator in India*• Born at Dalhousie Castle, Midlothian, and educated at Harrow and Christ Church, Oxford, he was the third son of the 9th Earl of Dalhousie. In 1837 he was elected Member of Parliament for Haddingtonshire and in 1838, on the death of his father, entered the House of Lords as Earl of Dalhousie. In 1845 he succeeded **Gladstone** as president of the Board of Trade. In 1847 he was appointed Governor-General of India—the youngest viceroy ever sent there. He conquered Pegu and the Punjab and annexed Nagpur, Oudh, Sattara, Jhansi and Berar, and meanwhile encouraged the development of roads, railways, irrigation networks and a telegraph system. He also energetically opposed suttee, thuggee, female infanticide and the slave trade. He organized the Legislative Council, improved Civil Service training, and encouraged the development of agriculture and industry. Broken in health, he left India in 1856.

Dalí, Salvador, *properly* **Salvador Felipe Jacinto Dalí y Domenech** 1904–89 •*Spanish artist*• He was born in Figueras, and after studying at the Academy of Fine Arts, Madrid, he moved to Paris. The theories of **Sigmund Freud** had an important influence on him at this time, particularly the concept of the unconscious mind, and he joined the surrealists in 1928, becoming one of the principal figures of the movement. He made a deep study of abnormal psychology and dream symbolism, and represented "paranoiac" objects with an almost academic realism in harsh sunburnt landscapes remembered from his Spanish boyhood. Notable paintings from this early period include *The Great Masturbator* (1929), *Soft Construction with Boiled Beans: Premonition of Civil War* (1936), *Swans Reflecting Elephants* (1937) and *Sleep* (1937). He collaborated with **Luis Buñuel** in producing the surrealist films *Un chien andalou* (1928) and *L'age d'or* (1930). In 1940 he settled in the US, and later became a Catholic, devoting his art to symbolic religious paintings under the influence of **Raphael** and **Leonardo da Vinci**, though continuing to stage outrageous acts of self-promotion. His best-known paintings are probably *The Persistence of Memory* (1931, also known as the *Limp Watches*), which is in the Museum of Modern Art, New York, and *Christ of St John of the Cross* (1951), which is in the St Mungo Museum of Religious Life and Art, Glasgow. His publications include *The Secret Life of Salvador Dalí* (1942) and the surrealist novel *Hidden Faces* (1944).

" "

At the age of six I wanted to be a cook. At seven I wanted to be Napoleon. And my ambition has been growing steadily ever since.

1942 ***The Secret Life of Salvador Dalí****, prologue.*

Dalton, John 1766–1844 •*English chemist and natural philosopher*• Born in Eaglesfield, Cumbria, he received his early education at a Quaker school there and began teaching at the age of 12. In 1793 he moved to Manchester and taught mathematics, but after about six years turned to private teaching and scientific research. In 1794 he described color blindness (Daltonism), exemplified partly by his own case. In his chemical and physical research Dalton was a crude experimentalist, but his results led him to his atomic theory, on which his fame rests. Of particular importance were his studies showing that in a mixture of gases each gas exerts the same pressure as it would if it were the only gas present in the given volume (Dalton's law). This led to the interpretation of chemical analyses in terms of the relative weights of the atoms of the elements involved and to the laws of chemical combination. His atomic theory recognized that all matter is made up of combinations of atoms, the atoms of each element being identical. He concluded that atoms could be neither created nor destroyed, and that chemical reactions take place through the rearrangement of atoms.

Daly, Mary 1928– •*US feminist and theological writer*• Born in Schenectady, New York, she studied theology at St Mary's College, Indiana, and Fribourg University, Switzerland, and taught at Fribourg (1959–66) and Boston College (1969–99). Having analyzed the effects of male bias in *The Church and the Second Sex* (1968), she gave up her attempts to reform official Roman Catholic attitudes and became a post-Christian radical feminist (*Beyond God the Father*, 1973). Later works include *Webster's First New Intergalactic Wickedary of the English Language* (1987), written with Jane Caputi, and her autobiography *Outercourse: The Be-dazzling Voyage: Containing Recollections from My Logbook of a Radical Feminist Philosopher (be-ing an account of my time/space travels and ideas—then, again, now, and how)* (1992).

Dalyell, Tam 1932– •*Scottish Labour politician*• Born into an ancient Scottish landed family, he was educated at Eton and Oxford, trained as a teacher at Moray House, Edinburgh, and taught at Bo'ness in West Lothian. A convert to the Labour Party, he was Member of Parliament for West Lothian (1962–83), then for Linlithgow (1983–). During the Conservative administration he established a reputation as the quintessential backbencher—ready to champion unpopular causes and to question ministers relentlessly on issues such as the sinking of the *Belgrano* during the Falklands War (1982) and the environmental consequences of the Gulf War (1991). As the longest-serving Member of Parliament, after the 2001 elections he became the Father of the House of Commons.

Dam, (Carl Peter) Henrik 1895–1976 •*Danish biochemist and Nobel Prize winner*• Born in Copenhagen, he taught there from 1923 until 1940, when he went to live and teach in the US. For his discovery of the coagulant agent vitamin K (1934) he shared the Nobel Prize for physiology or medicine in 1943 with the US biochemist **Edward Doisy**.

Damasus I, St c. 304–84 AD •*Roman deacon and pope*• He was possibly of Spanish descent. His election in AD 366 was violently contested, but confirmed by **Valentinian I**. He opposed Arianism, and condemned **Apollinaris** the Younger at the Council of Constantinople in 381. He commissioned **St Jerome**, his secretary, to revise the Bible, which resulted in the Vulgate version. His feast day is December 11.

d'Amboise, Jacques 1934– •*US dancer and choreographer*• Born in Dedham, Massachusetts, he trained at the School of American Ballet and joined the New York City Ballet in 1949. A powerful and acrobatic dancer, he performed in new ballets such as *Stars and Stripes* (1958) as well as classical works such as *Swan Lake*. He also choreographed his own ballets. In 1976 he founded the National Dance Institute to bring dance instruction into the public schools.

Damian, St Peter *See* **Damiani, Pietro**

Damiani, Pietro, *also called* **St Peter Damian** 1007–72 •*Italian ecclesiastic and Doctor of the Church*• Born in Ravenna, he herded swine as a boy, and in 1035 joined the hermitage at Fonte Avellana; he rose to be cardinal and Bishop of Ostia (1057). He labored strenuously to reform the clergy, which at the time was at a low ebb of immorality and indolence. His feast day is February 23.

Damien, Father, *originally* **Joseph de Veuster** 1840–89 •*Belgian Roman Catholic missionary*• Born in Tremelo, he is renowned for his work among the lepers of the Hawaiian island of Molokai, where he lived from 1873 until his death from the disease.

Damocles 4th century BC •*Greek courtier*• He was a member of the court of **Dionysius the Elder**. Having praised the happiness of royalty, he was invited to a royal feast; but on looking upwards he saw a sword suspended over his head by a single hair—the "Sword of Damocles"—symbolizing the precarious nature of happiness. The story is told by **Cicero**.

Damon and **Pythias** or **Phintias** 4th century BC •*Pythagorean philosophers of Syracuse*• Condemned to death by **Dionysius the Elder**, tyrant of Syracuse, Pythias begged to be allowed to go home to arrange his affairs, and Damon pledged his own life for his friend's. Pythias returned just in time to save Damon from death. Moved by so noble an example, Dionysius pardoned Pythias.

Damon, Matt(hew Paige) 1970– •*US actor and screenwriter*• Born in Cambridge, Massachusetts, he studied at Harvard, leaving to pursue a career in acting. He became a bankable star with *Good Will Hunting* (1997), which he cowrote with Ben Affleck, and which won numerous awards. Further high-profile appearances were in *Dogma* (1999) and *The Talented Mr Ripley* (1999).

Dampier, William 1652–1715 •*English navigator, pirate and travel writer*• He was born near Yeovil, Somerset. In 1679 he joined a band of buccaneers who crossed the Isthmus of Darién (in central America) and ravaged the coast as far south as the Juan Fernández Islands. In 1683 he reached the Philippines, China and Australia, a voyage recounted in *A New Voyage Round the World* (1697). After exploring the west coast of Australia (1699–1700), and the coasts of New Guinea and New Britain, he gave his name to the Dampier Archipelago and Strait, and published his findings in *A Voyage to New Holland* (1703–09). However, Dampier was apparently a better pilot than commander, and his cruelty to his lieutenant led to his being court-martialed. He was reappointed to the command of two privateers to the South Seas in 1703, but is again said to have been guilty of drunkenness and brutality. This is reputed to have been the voyage during which **Alexander Selkirk** (the model for **Daniel Defoe**'s Robinson Crusoe) was sent—by his own request—into arid exile on one of the Juan Fernández Islands. Dampier returned home in 1707, poor and broken, but sailed again in 1708 as pilot on **Woodes Rogers**'s ship, which rescued Selkirk.

Dana, Richard Henry, Jr 1815–82 •*US writer and lawyer*• Born in Cambridge, Massachusetts, he was obliged to suspend his studies at Harvard because of eyestrain, and he shipped out as a common sailor on a voyage around Cape Horn to California and back, which he described in *Two Years Before the Mast* (1840). After graduating in 1837 he was admitted to the Massachusetts bar in 1840. Among his works are *The Seaman's Friend* (1841) and *To Cuba and Back* (1859).

Dance, Charles 1946– •*English actor*• Born in Rednal, Worcestershire, he became an actor comparatively late in life after a career in industry. He joined the Royal Shakespeare Company in 1975 and began appearing on television from the early 1980s, notably in *The Jewel in the Crown* (1984; British Academy of Film and Television Arts award nomination for Best Actor). His film career has included roles in *Don't Go Breaking My Heart* (1999) and *Dark Blue World* (2000).

Dandridge, Dorothy 1920–65 •*US singer and actress*• Born in Cleveland, Ohio, she was a child star in films, but broke through to adult roles in *A Day at the Races* (1937). The most beautiful African-American actress of her generation, and one of the first ever to be acclaimed a star, Dandridge had her greatest successes in *Carmen Jones* (1954) and *Porgy and Bess* (1959). She died young, and an edited memoir, *Everything and Nothing: The Dorothy Dandridge Story*, appeared in 1970.

Dane, Clemence, *pseudonym of* **Winifred Ashton** 1888–1965 •*English novelist and playwright*• She was born in Blackheath, London, and educated in England and France. Her novels include *Regiment of Women* (1917), *Broome Stages* (1931) and *The Flower Girls* (1954), the last two dealing with theatrical families. Many of her plays achieved long runs, including *A Bill of Divorcement* (1921); the ingenious reconstruction of the poet's life in *Will Shakespeare* (1921); the stark tragedy of *Granite* (1926); and *Wild Decembers* (1932), about the **Brontës**.

Dangerfield, Thomas 1650–85 •*English thief and conspirator*• Born in Waltham, Essex, he was a thief, a soldier on the Continent, and a pseudoconvert to Catholicism. In 1679 he accused the Presbyterians of plotting to bring down the government. Imprisoned when this was shown to be a lie, he claimed he had been deceived by a Roman Catholic tale invented to screen a plot of their own against King **Charles II**. Papers proving this would, he alleged, be found in a meal tub in the house of a Mrs Cellier (who was tried and acquitted). He was whipped and pilloried, and on returning from Tyburn was killed by a blow in the eye from a bystander.

Daniel, *also called* **Belteshazzar** 6th century BC •*Judean exile and prophet*• Born of noble descent, he was taken from Jerusalem after the capture of King Jehoiakim of Judah to serve in the court of **Nebuchadnezzar**. He quickly gained a reputation for the interpreting of dreams, and had visions prophesying the coming of the Messiah's kingdom. In translating the writing on the walls of the banquet chamber, "Mene mene tekel u-pharsim," he predicted the downfall of King Belshazzar. Because of his wisdom he was appointed third in rank in the kingdom and went on to serve **Darius I**, king of the Medes, and **Cyrus**, king of the Persians.

Daniel, Arnaut fl. late 12th century •*Provençal poet*• Born at the Castle of Rebeyrac, Périgord, he became a member of the court of **Richard I** and was esteemed one of the best of the troubadours, particularly for his treatment of the theme of love. He introduced the sestina, the pattern of which was later adapted by **Dante** and **Petrarch**.

Daniel, Paul Wilson 1958– •*English conductor*• Born in Birmingham, he studied at King's College, Cambridge, and at the

Guildhall School of Music and Drama. He has conducted most of Britain's major orchestras as well as many orchestras abroad, and has been a notable musical director of the Opera Factory (1987–90), Opera North (1990–97) and the English National Opera (1997–). He was given the honorary title of Commander, Order of the British Empire, in 2000.

Danilova, Alexandra Dionysievna 1904–97 •*US dancer and teacher*• Born in Petergof (Petrodvorets), she trained at the Imperial Ballet School, Petrograd (now St Petersburg), before joining the MaryinskyTheater (now Kirov Ballet) in 1922. She defected on a tour to Europe in 1924 and that year became a member of **Sergei Diaghilev**'s Ballets Russes, leaving in 1929. She danced for Colonel **de Basil**'s Ballet Russe (1933–38) and its splinter group the Ballets Russes de Monte Carlo (until 1952) and also made guest appearances with many companies. She later formed her own group, Great Moments of Ballet (1954–56), staged many ballets, and earned an impressive reputation as a teacher.

Dankworth, John Philip William 1927– •*English jazz musician and composer*• Born in London, he studied at the Royal Academy of Music. He was a founder-member (on clarinet and alto saxophone) of the legendary Club 11 in 1948, before forming the first of his own influential groups in 1950. **Cleo Laine** sang with his big band from 1953, and went on to become a major artist in both jazz and musical theater. After they married in 1958, he acted as her musical director, and concentrated on composition and arrangement. Their son, Alec Dankworth, is a jazz bass player, and coleads the Dankworth Generation Band with his father.

d'Annunzio, Gabriele 1863–1938 •*Italian writer, adventurer and political leader*• Born in Pescara, he made his name as a poet in 1879 with the publication of *Primo vere* ("In Early Spring"). During the 1890s he wrote "Romances of the Rose" and a trilogy of novels with **Nietzsche** on heroes. He was elected a parliamentary deputy in 1897, and became notorious for his passionate affair with the actress Eleanora Duse, for whom he wrote the tragedies *La gioconda* (1899) and *Francesca da Rimini* (1901). His greatest play is considered to be *La figlia di Jorio* (1904, "The Daughter of Jorio"). An enthusiastic patriot, he urged Italian entry into World War I and served as a soldier, sailor and airman. In 1916 he lost an eye in aerial combat, and in 1918 carried out a sensational reconnaissance over Vienna. In 1919 he seized and held Fiume and ruled as dictator until he was removed by the Italian government (1920). He became a strong supporter of the Fascist Party under **Mussolini**. He is regarded as one of the most important Italian literary figures of the late 19th and early 20th centuries.

Dante Alighieri 1265–1321 •*Italian poet, author of the Divina Commedia ("Divine Comedy")*• Dante was born in Florence, the son of a lawyer of the noble **Guelf** family. He was baptized Durante, afterwards abbreviated to Dante. According to his own account, he first set eyes on his lifelong love, Beatrice Portinari (c. 1265–90), at the age of nine in 1274. There is no evidence that she returned his passion; she was married at an early age to one Simone de' Bardi, but neither this nor the poet's own subsequent marriage interfered with his pure and Platonic devotion to her, which intensified after her death. The story of his boyish but unquenchable passion is told in *La Vita Nuova* (c. 1292). Dante was banished from Florence in 1309 and sentenced to death in absentia. From then on he led a wandering life, eventually settling in Ravenna (1318), where for the most part he remained until his death. His most celebrated work is the *Divina Commedia*, begun around 1307, his spiritual testament, which narrates a journey through Hell and Purgatory, guided by **Virgil**, and finally to Paradise, guided by Beatrice. It gives an encyclopedic view of the highest culture and knowledge of the age, all expressed in the most exquisite poetry. The *Divina Commedia* (which Dante began in Latin) established Italian as a literary language.

“ ”

Lasciate ogni sperenza voi ch'entrate.
Abandon all hope you who enter.

c. 1307 Inscription above the gates of Hell.
***Divina Commedia**, "Inferno," canto 3, l. 9.*

Danton, Georges Jacques 1759–94 •*French revolutionary leader*• He was born of peasant stock, in Arcis-sur-Aube. At the outbreak of the French Revolution he was practicing as an advocate in Paris, where he had instituted the Revolutionists' Cordeliers' Club with **Jean Paul Marat** and **Camille Desmoulins**. In 1792 he became Minister of Justice in the new republic following the fall of the monarchy. Elected to the National Convention, he voted for the death of the king in January 1793 and was one of the nine original members of the Committee of Public Safety. He also contributed to the fall of the Girondins, or moderate party (October 1793), and to the subsequent supremacy of the extremist Jacobins. As president of the Jacobin Club he strove for domestic unity, government stability, and to abate the pitiless severity of the Revolutionary Tribunal (which he had himself set up), but he lost power to **Robespierre** in the Reign of Terror. In March 1794 he and his followers were arrested for conspiracy to overthrow the goverment. His audacious, satirical defense moved the people so greatly that the Revolutionary Tribunal concocted a decree to shut the mouths of men who had "insulted Justice," and on April 5 Danton was guillotined.

Darby, Abraham c. 1678–1717 •*English ironmaster*• Born near Dudley, Worcestershire, he founded the Bristol Iron Company (1708), and is generally acknowledged to have been the first man to use coke successfully in the smelting of iron (1709). This was important because charcoal had become increasingly scarce and was too soft to allow larger furnaces to be used, and coal itself was almost always contaminated with sulfur and other undesirable impurities.

Darby, Abraham 1711–63 •*English ironmaster*• The son of **Abraham Darby** (c. 1678–1717), he is reputed to have discovered how to produce wrought iron from coke-smelted ore; if he did, he kept the process such a close secret that no details of it are known. It is likely that the first man to achieve this on a commercial scale was **Henry Cort** in the 1780s with his puddling process. The Darby foundry at Coalbrookdale did, however, manufacture large numbers of cast-iron cylinders for **Thomas Newcomen**'s atmospheric steam engines, and later the first high-pressure steam boiler for **Richard Trevithick**.

Darby, John Nelson 1800–82 •*English churchman*• Born in London, he was educated at Westminster School and Trinity College, Dublin. For a short time an Anglican clergyman, he became the principal founder in 1830 of the Plymouth Brethren, and in 1840 founded an exclusive sect of it known as the "Darbyites." He wrote 30 works.

Dare, Virginia b. 1587 •*First child of English parents to be born in America*• She was born on Roanoke Island and disappeared along with the other members of Roanoke's "Lost Colony" (c. 1590).

Darío, Rubén, *pseudonym of* **Felix Rubén García Sarmiento** 1867–1916 •*Nicaraguan poet*• Born in Metapa, he wrote poetry from an early age and left Nicaragua in 1886 to work for newspapers in Chile and Argentina. He inaugurated the Spanish-American Modernist movement with his major works *Azul* (1888, "Blue") and *Prosas profanas* (1896, Eng trans *Prosas Profanas and Other Poems*, 1922), which combined exotic imagery and simple, direct language. A well-traveled man who held many diplomatic posts, he was plagued in later life by financial problems, heavy drinking and poor health. He wrote short stories, plays, travel books and literary criticism but is best known for his poetry, especially his collection *Cantos de vida y esperanza* (1905, "Songs of Life and Hope"). His work greatly influenced Spanish-language writers worldwide.

Darius I 548–486 BC •*King of Persia*• An Achaemenid, he ascended the Persian throne in 521 BC, after putting to death the Magian Gaumáta, who pretended to be **Cambyses II**'s brother. He reorganized the administration and finances of the Persian Empire, making Susa the capital, while achieving conquests as far as the Caucasus and the Indus. His expedition against the Scythians (c. 515) took him as far as the Volga, and enabled him to subdue Thrace and Macedonia. His expedition against the Athenians to punish them for supporting the Ionian revolt (499–94) was decisively defeated at Marathon (490). He died before the Egyptian revolt (487) had been quelled, and was succeeded by **Xerxes I**. Darius was a Persian by birth, and of the Zoroastrian faith, which under him became the state religion.

Darius II, *surnamed* **Ochus**, *surnamed in Greek* **Nothos ("Bastard")** d. 404 BC •*King of Persia*• The illegitimate son of **Artaxerxes I**, he seized power (c. 424 BC) after his father's death, but was the tool of his cruel half sister and spouse Parysatis. His reign was a long series of struggles and revolts ruthlessly suppressed. After the defeat of the Sicilian expedition of the Athenians (413), he resumed active Persian intervention in Greek affairs, and broke Athenian power (405). He was succeeded by his eldest son, **Artaxerxes II**.

Darius III, *surnamed* **Codommanus** c. 381–330 BC •*King of Persia*• The grandson of **Artaxerxes II**, he was king from 336 BC. He was defeated by **Alexander the Great** at the Granicus (334), at Issus (333) and at Gaugamela or Arbela (331), and was killed by a satrap, Bessus, on his retreat. He was the last king of the Achaemenid dynasty.

Dark, Eleanor, *née* **O'Reilly** 1901–85 •*Australian novelist*• Born in Sydney, she was the daughter of the writer Dowell O'Reilly (1865–1923). *Slow Dawning*, her first novel, was completed in 1923, but not published until 1932. A committed socialist and feminist, her other novels include *Prelude to Christopher* (1934), *The Little Company* (1945), *Lantana Lane* (1959) and a trilogy of novels (1941–53) charting the early years of European settlement of New South Wales.

Darling, Alistair Maclean 1953– •*Scottish Labour politician*• Born in London, he studied law at Aberdeen University and in due course qualified as an advocate. He was elected Member of Parliament for Edinburgh Central in 1987. He was shadow Chief Secretary to the Treasury (1996–97) and after Labour's landslide victory in 1997 was appointed Chief Secretary to the Treasury (1997–98) and Secretary of State for Social Security (1998–2001) and Transport Security (2002–).

Darling, Grace 1815–42 •*English heroine*• She was born in Bamburgh, Northumberland, and with her father, William Darling (1786–1865), was a lighthouse keeper on one of the Farne Islands. On September 7, 1838, she rescued the survivors of the *Forfarshire*.

Darnley, Henry Stewart, Lord 1545–67 •*Scottish nobleman*• Born in Temple Newsome, England, the eldest son and heir of Matthew, 4th Earl of Lennox, he was proposed as a husband for his cousin **Mary Queen of Scots**, upon the death of her first husband, **Francis II** of France. In 1565 he married Mary at Holyroodhouse in Edinburgh, having been proclaimed Henry, King of Scots, the previous day. A son was born (the future **James VI and I**), but the marriage was disastrous. Darnley's participation in the plot to murder **David Rizzio**, the queen's Italian secretary, finally estranged him from her. He was himself murdered in Edinburgh when the house in which he was sleeping was blown up at the instigation of his wife's new suitor, the Earl of **Bothwell**, who subsequently married the queen.

Darrow, Clarence Seward 1857–1938 •*US civil liberties lawyer*• Born in Kinsman, Ohio, he was admitted to the bar in 1878. In 1907 he successfully defended "Big Bill" **Haywood** and Charles Moyer of the Western Federation of Miners, who had been implicated in the murder of Frank Steunenberg, ex-governor of Idaho. In 1924, Darrow's defense of Richard Loeb and Nathan Leopold in a highly publicized murder trial saved them from the death penalty; and in the Scopes Monkey Trial of 1925, at Dayton, Tennessee, he defended the high school biology teacher John Scopes, who was charged under the Tennessee state law forbidding the teaching of **Darwin**'s theory of evolution. Although Scopes was found guilty and fined, Darrow dismantled the arguments of the prosecution. In 1934 he was appointed to investigate Senator Gerald Nye's charge that the codes introduced by the National Recovery Board were favoring monopolies. His report led to the abolition of price control.

Dart, Raymond A(rthur) 1893–1988 •*South African anatomist*• Born in Toowong, Australia, he graduated in medicine from Sydney University in 1917, and became Professor of Anatomy at Witwatersrand University, Johannesburg, in 1923. In 1925 he described an apelike infant partial skull found in Botswana, which he considered to be a human ancestor, *Australopithecus africanus*. Later work by Dart and others supports this view, and indicates that bipedalism preceded brain expansion, although whether the australopithecines were tool users and in the direct ancestral line to *Homo sapiens* remains uncertain.

Darusmont, Frances *See* **Wright, Frances**

Darwin, Charles Robert 1809–82 •*English naturalist, the originator (with Alfred Wallace) of the theory of evolution by natural selection*• Charles Darwin was born in Shrewsbury, Shropshire, the grandson of **Erasmus Darwin** and of **Josiah Wedgwood**. In 1828, he entered Christ's College, Cambridge, where his biological studies began in earnest. He was recommended to serve as naturalist on the HMS *Beagle*, which was about to undertake a scientific survey of South American waters (1831–36). Darwin visited Tenerife, the Cape Verde Islands, Brazil, Montevideo, Tierra del Fuego, Buenos Aires, Valparaiso, Chile, the Galápagos, Tahiti, New Zealand, Tasmania and the Keeling Islands; it was there that he started his seminal studies of coral reefs. By 1846 he had published several works on his geological and zoological discoveries. From 1842 he lived at Downe, Kent, where he addressed himself to the great work of his life—the problem of the origin of species. After five years of collecting the evidence, he "allowed himself to speculate" on the subject, and drew up in 1842 some short notes, enlarged in 1844 into a sketch of conclusions for his own use. These embodied in embryonic form the principle of natural selection, the germ of the Darwinian theory; but Darwin delayed publication of his hypothesis, which was only precipitated by accident. In 1858 **Alfred Wallace** sent him a memoir on the Malay Archipelago, which, to Darwin's alarm, contained in essence the main idea of his own theory of natural selection. **Charles Lyell** and **Joseph Dalton Hooker** persuaded Darwin to submit a paper of his own, based on his 1844 sketch, which was read simultaneously with Wallace's before the Linnaean Society on July 1, 1858. Though not the sole originator of the theory of evolution, Darwin was the first thinker to gain for the concept a wide acceptance among biological experts.

“ ”

A mathematician is a blind man in a dark room looking for a black cat which isn't there.

Quoted in John D Barrow ***Pie in the Sky, Counting, Thinking and Being*** *(1992).*

Darwin, Erasmus 1731–1802 •*English physician and poet*• Born near Newark, Nottinghamshire, he studied at Cambridge University and the University of Edinburgh. At Lichfield he became a popular physician and prominent figure on account of his ability, his radical and freethinking opinions, his poetry, his eight-acre botanical garden, and his imperious advocacy of temperance in drinking. After his second marriage in 1781, he settled in Derby. He was grandfather of **Charles Darwin** by his first wife, and of **Francis Galton** by his second. He anticipated **Jean-Baptiste Lamarck**'s views on evolution, and also those of his own grandson.

Das, Chitta Ranjan 1870–1925 •*Bengali patriot and politician*• Called to the bar in 1894, he soon acquired a reputation for skillfully representing nationalists accused of terrorism by the British government in India. He participated in the campaign against the partition of Bengal, chaired the Bengal Provincial Congress (1917) and the Indian National Congress (1918), and joined **Mahatma Gandhi**'s Non-Cooperation Movement (1920). Imprisoned in 1921, he emerged in 1922 to help form the Swaraj Party, popular with both Muslim and Hindu communities in Bengal, and came to an agreement with Gandhi which allowed both Swarajists and Gandhians to campaign from the Congress platform. Although he himself rejected violence, many of his followers were either involved in terrorism or openly advocated the use of violence to oppose colonial rule. Sadly, his achievements in forging unity between Hindus and Muslims in Bengal survived his death by only a few years: factionalism and violence led ultimately to the partition of the province on independence in 1947.

Dassault, Marcel, *originally* **Marcel Bloch** 1892–1986 •*French aviation pioneer, industrialist and politician*• Born in Paris, he saw one of the **Wright** brothers in flight while a schoolboy, and was inspired to study aeronautical design and electrical engineering. He joined Henri Potez in building aircraft during and after World War I. A Jew, he was imprisoned in Buchenwald concentration camp during World War II. Following the war he adopted the name Dassault and founded his own company, Général Aéronautique Marcel Dassault, building a series of highly successful craft in the 1950s, such as the Mystère and Mirage. He was Deputy in the National Assembly (1951–55), Deputy for the Oise (1957–58), and was elected to the National Assembly in 1986.

Daubié, Julie-Victoire 1824–74 •*French writer and feminist*• Born in eastern France, she had little formal education, but was taught Latin and Greek by her brother and became a governess. In 1858 she won an essay competition organized by the Académie de Lyons. Encouraged by one of the competition judges, she took the *baccalauréat* exam in 1861 despite government opposition, and became the first woman to obtain this qualification in 1862. She went on to pass the *license,* a more advanced exam, in 1871. Her writings include *L'émancipation de la femme* (1871, "Women's Emancipation").

Daubigny, Charles François 1817–78 •*French artist*• Born in Paris, he was a pupil of **Paul Delaroche**. A member of the Barbizon school, he painted landscapes, such as *The Banks of the Oise* (1872, Musée des Beaux-Arts). Daubigny painted moonlight and river scenes, a number of which are to be seen in the National Gallery in London.

Daudet, Alphonse 1840–97 •*French writer*• Born in Nîmes, he was educated at the Lyons Lycée. From 1862 he published a number of theatrical pieces, notably *L'Arlésienne* (1872, "A Woman from Arles"), with incidental music by **Bizet**. His best-known work is his series of sketches and short stories of Provençal life, originally written for the newspaper *Le Figaro*, especially *Lettres de mon moulin* (collected 1869, "Letters from My Mill") and the charming extravaganza of *Tartarin de Tarascon* (1872). *Le petit chose* (1868, "Young What's His Name") is full of pathos and of reminiscences of Daudet's own early struggles. Other works include his long naturalistic novels on the social conditions of the day, such as *Fromont jeune et Risler aîné* (1874, "Fromont Junior and Risler Senior") and *L'immortel* (1888, "The Immortal One"), in which Daudet's powers of ridicule are turned against the Académie Française.

Daumier, Honoré 1808–78 •*French caricaturist and painter*• Born in Marseilles, he was taken to Paris as a child. He made his name as a satirical caricaturist, and was imprisoned for six months for a caricature of **Louis Philippe** in 1832. He made more than 4,000 lithographs and 4,000 caricatures. Later he worked as a serious painter of realistic subject pictures, such as *Don Quixote* and *The Third Class Carriage*, and also as a sculptor. In his old age he became blind and was befriended by **Camille Corot**.

Daurat or **Dorat, Jean** c. 1510–88 •*French scholar and poet*• As president of the Collège de Coqueret he supervised the studies of **Pierre de Ronsard** and **Joachim du Bellay**, among others. These poets, with whom he was united in the famous Pléiade, he carefully trained for the task of reforming the vernacular and ennobling French literature by imitation of Greek and Latin models. He was appointed court poet by **Charles IX**.

Dausset, Jean 1916– •*French immunologist and Nobel Prize winner*• Born in Toulouse, he studied medicine in Paris. Service in a blood transfusion unit in World War II led to his special interest in transfusion responses and the way they can lead to antibody production. His results led to tissue typing, which greatly reduced rejection risks in organ transplant surgery. He shared the 1980 Nobel Prize for physiology or medicine with **George Snell** and **Baruj Benacerraf**.

D'Auvergne, Henri de la Tour *See* **Turenne, Henri de la Tour d'Auvergne, Vicomte de**

D'Avenant, Sir William 1606–68 •*English poet and playwright*• He was born in Oxford. His father kept a tavern at which **Shakespeare** used to stay, thereby giving rise to the rumor that D'Avenant was Shakespeare's illegitimate son. From 1628 he produced many plays, including *The Cruel Brother* (1630) and *The Wits* (1636), and in 1638 he was appointed poet laureate in succession to **Ben Jonson**. About the same time he lost his nose through an illness, a calamity which exposed him to public ridicule. Although knighted by King **Charles I** in 1643, he was later imprisoned in the Tower of London (1650–52), where he completed his epic, *Gondibert* (1651). He is considered to have been the founder of English opera with his *Siege of Rhodes* (1656), and he opened a theater, the Cockpit, in Drury Lane, London, in 1658.

Davenport, Lindsay 1976– •*US tennis player*• Born in Palos Verdes, California, her most important victories in the women's singles have included the European Open (1993), Olympic (1996), US Open (1998), Wimbledon (1999) and Australian Open (2000) titles. She also partnered with Corina Morariu to victory in the women's doubles at Wimbledon in 1999.

David, *Hebrew* **"beloved"** 11th century BC •*First king of the Judean dynasty of Israel*• He was the youngest son of Jesse of Bethlehem, and is traditionally the author of several of the psalms and the ancestor of **Jesus**. His success as a warrior against the Philistines, especially in killing Goliath, aroused King **Saul**'s jealousy, and he was forced to flee, but after Saul's death he became king over Judah in Hebron, and later was chosen king of all Israel. Jerusalem became the political and religious center of his kingdom, and he built a palace for himself on its highest hill, Zion (the "city of David"), and placed the Ark of the Covenant there under a tent. He united the many tribes of Israel, and extended his territory from Egypt to the Euphrates. The later part of his reign was troubled by attempted revolutions by his sons Absalom and Adonijah. He was succeeded by his son **Solomon**.

David or **Dewi, St** c. 520–601 •*Patron saint of Wales*• Born near St Bride's Bay, Pembrokeshire, he presided over two Welsh synods, at Brefi and the "Lucus Victoriae," or Synod of Victory. According to the *Annales Cambriae* (10th century) he died in 601 as Bishop of Moni Judeorum, or Menevia, afterward St David's. His feast day is March 1.

David I c. 1080–1153 •*King of Scotland*• He was the youngest of the six sons of **Malcolm Canmore** and St **Margaret**. In 1100 his sister Matilda married **Henry I** of England, and he accompanied her to the English court. When his brother **Alexander I** succeeded to the throne (1107), David became Prince of Cumbria, and, through marriage, became Earl of Huntingdon (1113). He was therefore loyal to England under Henry I's daughter, **Matilda**, Empress Maud, when he succeeded Alexander (1124), until **Stephen** took the English throne (1135). He invaded northern England in support of Matilda but made peace at the Treaty of Durham (1136), and when war broke out again (1138), he made a further treaty (1139). During his reign the authority of the monarch was consolidated, the first Scottish royal coinage issued, and a common law of Scotland produced. The Scottish Church was reformed and reorganized, and twenty monasteries were founded.

David II 1324–71 •*King of Scotland*• He was born in Dunfermline, the only surviving son of **Robert Bruce** (King Robert I), and married the daughter of **Edward II** of England, Joanna (1328). In 1329 he succeeded his father, and he and his child queen were crowned at Scone (1331). The success of the victory by **Edward de Balliol** and **Edward III** at Halidon Hill (1333) forced David's guardians to send him and his consort to France (1334). He returned in 1341 and, five years later, invaded England, but was defeated and captured (1346), and was kept prisoner for 11 years. His release (1357), on promise of a heavy ransom, brought 27 years of truce with England, but strains over payment of the ransom brought increased customs duties and direct taxation, and caused resentment when the hostages of 1357 were abandoned (1363) as a result of defaulting on payments. Yet David maintained a firm grip on his kingdom, with little sign of the tensions between king and nobles that afflicted later reigns. He left no children, and was succeeded by his sister's son, **Robert II**.

David, (Père) Armand 1826–1900 •*French naturalist and Lazarist missionary*• Born in Espelette in the Pyrenees, he was educated at the Grand Séminaire de Bayonne. He entered the Lazarist Order of St Vincent de Paul (1848) and went to Savona, Italy (1851–61), where he taught science and formed the foundation of the Savona

Natural History Museum. After ten years he was an expert in many fields and a brilliant all-round naturalist. He was then ordained and sent to China as a missionary. Between 1866 and 1874 he explored the Peking plain, Mongolia, Tibet and central China. He discovered the unique handkerchief tree named after him (*Davidia involucrata*) and Père David's deer (*Elaphurus davidianus*).

David, Elizabeth 1913–92 •*English cookbook writer*• Born in Sussex, she spent time in France, on a Greek island, and in Cairo before returning to a Great Britain beset by food rationing (1946). Her early books, such as *Mediterranean Cooking* (1950) and *Italian Food* (1954), are a reminder of a culinary world unrestricted by the lack of butter, cream, and imported delicacies. Her best-known work is her influential *French Provincial Cooking* (1960).

David, Jacques Louis 1748–1825 •*French painter*• Born in Paris, he won the Prix de Rome in 1774, and in Rome devoted himself to drawing from classical models. It is in his works of the 1780s, such as the *Death of Socrates* (1788) and *Brutus Condemning His Son* (1789), that the neoclassical style is first clearly discernible. David entered with enthusiasm into the Revolution, and in 1792 became a representative for Paris in the Convention. He voted for the death of **Louis XVI**, was a member of the Committee of Public Safety, and was the artistic director of the great national fêtes founded on classical customs. After **Robespierre**'s death he was twice imprisoned, and narrowly escaped with his life. Released in 1795, he produced his masterpiece, *The Rape of the Sabines* (1799), and in 1804 was appointed court painter by **Napoleon I**. After the **Bourbon** restoration he was banished in 1816 as a regicide.

David, Moses, *originally* **David Brandt Berg** 1919–94 •*US cult leader*• Born in California into a devoutly Christian home, he began a ministry with the Christian and Missionary Alliance Church, but involvement with the hippie lifestyle of 1960s California led to his adopting an increasingly independent style of ministry. In 1968 he founded the Children of God, which later became the Family of Love, and moved to London in 1971. This millenarian movement, based on the teachings of the Bible and David's own *Mo Letters*, followed a radical antimaterialist philosophy, but the increasing use of controversial methods of attracting converts led to strong criticism of the sect, and to some decline in its influence.

David-Néel, Alexandra 1868–1969 •*French Oriental scholar and traveler*• Born in Paris, she studied Sanskrit in Ceylon (Sri Lanka) and India, and toured internationally as an opera singer. In 1911 she returned to India, visiting the Dalai Lama in exile in Darjeeling and studying Tibetan Buddhism. Invited to Sikkim, she wintered in a high mountain cave with a religious hermit and her lifelong servant, Yongden. Having traveled illegally to Tashilhumpo in Tibet, she was expelled from India in 1916 and went to Burma, Japan and Korea with Yongden, arriving in Beijing (Peking) on October 8, 1917. Together they traveled 2,000 miles (3,220 km) to the Kumbum monastery near the Koko Nor and on to Chengdu through northern Tibet, Mongolia and across the Gobi Desert; she then donned the disguise of a Tibetan pilgrim, as described in *My Journey to Lhasa* (1927). They returned to Tibet in 1934 to work in Kanting until forced to leave by the Japanese advance of 1944, and retired to Digne in France, where she died at age 100.

Davidson, Eric Harris 1937– •*US molecular biologist*• Born in New York City, he studied at the University of Pennsylvania and Rockefeller University in New York. Since 1981 he has been Norman Chandler Professor of Cell Biology at the California Institute of Technology. He has written many publications on DNA sequence organization, gene expression during embryonic development, and gene regulation. Together with Roy Britten, he elucidated genome organization in higher animals, and showed that the genome has enormous stretches of "junk" DNA.

Davidson (of Lambeth), Randall Thomas Davidson, Baron 1848–1930 •*Scottish Anglican prelate and Archbishop of Canterbury*• Born in Edinburgh into a Presbyterian family, he studied at Harrow and Trinity College, Oxford, and became chaplain to Archbishop **Tait** (his father-in-law) and to Queen **Victoria**. He was also dean of Windsor and Bishop of Rochester (1891) and of Winchester (1895). As Archbishop of Canterbury (1903–28) he was not afraid to speak out on social and political issues.

Davie, Alan 1920– •*Scottish painter and jazz musician*• Born in Grangemouth, central Scotland, he studied at Edinburgh College of Art (1937–40). During wartime service with the Royal Artillery he concentrated on his other major pursuit—jazz. He played the saxophone and in 1971 produced his first record, which was followed by concerts and broadcasts (1973–75). His paintings of the 1950s had much in common with US abstract expressionism, as, for example, in *Birth of Venus* (1955). Other works testify to his interest in Zen and Oriental mysticism.

Davies, Arthur Bowen 1862–1928 •*US painter*• Born in Utica, New York, he studied at the Art Institute of Chicago and at the Art Students League in New York City. Known for idyllic pastoral scenes and allegorical paintings, he belonged to the group of US artists known as the Eight, or the Ashcan School, whose first exhibition he organized in New York in 1908. He was also the chief organizer of the Armory Show in 1913, which brought avant-garde European painters—Post-Impressionists, Cubists and Futurists—to New York for the first time.

Davies, Christian, *known as* **Mother Ross** 1667–1739 •*Irish woman soldier*• Born in Dublin, she served for many years in the army, masquerading as a man. She went to Flanders in search of her husband, Richard Welsh, who had been pressed into the Duke of **Marlborough**'s army. There she enlisted under the name of Christopher Welsh, fought in the Battle of Blenheim (1704), and eventually was reunited with her husband in 1706. When he was killed at the Battle of Malplaquet (1709) she married a grenadier, Hugh Jones, who was killed the following year. In England she was presented to Queen **Anne**, and returned to Dublin where she married another soldier.

Davies, (Stephen) Howard 1940– •*English stage director*• He was born in Reading, Berkshire, and after taking a director's course at Bristol University, became associate director of Bristol Old Vic. He joined the Royal Shakespeare Company (RSC) in 1975 and became an associate director to establish and run the Warehouse, the RSC's London studio theater (1977–82). His RSC work includes *Macbeth* (1982), *Henry VIII* (1983) and *Troilus and Cressida* (1985), which he set during the Crimean War. He became an associate director of the National Theatre in 1989. His first operatic production was *Idomeneo* (1991) for the Welsh National Opera.

Davies, Jonathan 1962– •*Welsh rugby union and league player*• Born in Carmarthenshire, he first played for Wales in 1985, won 27 caps and then left to join rugby league in 1988, and set a record of 13 drop goals. He made headlines with his transfer to Widnes in January 1989 and scored 1,000 points in 109 matches. He moved to Warrington in 1993, and led Wales in league games. He returned to rugby union at the end of 1995, playing for Cardiff until his retirement in 1997.

Davies, Laura 1963– •*English golfer*• Born in Coventry, Warwickshire, she turned professional in 1985. By 1994 she was ranked number one in the world and had achieved the distinction (unique in both the men's and women's game) of winning on five different tours. Her most significant victories include the British Women's Open (1986) and the US Women's Open (1987), and being a member of winning Curtis Cup and Solheim Cup teams. In 1997 she became the first player to win an LPGA (Ladies Professional Golf Association) tournament for a fourth consecutive time.

Davies, Peter Maxwell *See* **Maxwell Davies, Peter**

Davies, (William) Robertson 1913–95 •*Canadian novelist, playwright and essayist*• He was born in Thamesville, Ontario, and attended Balliol College, Oxford. A teacher, actor, and journalist, he was editor of the *Examiner* (Peterborough, Ontario) (1942–63), a professor of English at the University of Toronto (1960–81) and a writer. His first novel was *Tempest-Tost* (1951), the first of the "Salterton trilogy," but he is best known for the "Deptford trilogy"—*Fifth Business* (1970), *The Manticore* (1972) and *World of Wonders* (1975). This work evolved from his earlier books set in Salterton, an imagined Ontario city, patently Kingston, which is dominated by its old families, the Anglican Church, a military school, the university, and belief in the virtues of England and the English. Among his other novels are *What's Bred in the Bone* (1985), *The Lyre of Orpheus* (1988) and *The Cunning Man* (1995).

Davies, Sarah Emily 1830–1921 •*English feminist and education reformer*• She was born in Southampton, and was a vigorous campaigner for higher education for women. In 1869 she founded a small college for women students at Hitchin, which was transferred to Cambridge as Girton College in 1873. She was mistress of Girton (1873–1875), and honorary secretary (1882–1904). She also campaigned for London degrees for women, which were granted in 1874.

❝ ❞

If neither governesses or mothers *know*, how can they teach? So long as education is not provided *for* them, how can it be provided *by* them?

1868 Paper read at the Annual Meeting of the National Association for the Promotion of Social Sciences, published in ***Thoughts on Some Questions Relating to Women 1860–1908****.*

Davies, Siobhan, *originally* **Susan Davies** 1950– •*English choreographer and dancer*• Born in London, she studied with the London Contemporary Dance Theatre (LCDT). She became resident choreographer with LCDT in 1971, when she retired as a dancer. While still at LCDT, she also worked under commission for Ballet Rambert (1979, *Celebration*), ran Siobhan Davies and Dancers for a short period during 1981, and became a founding member of Second Stride in 1982. In 1988 she formed the Siobhan Davies Dance Company and in 1989 became associate choreographer for Ballet Rambert. Her work includes *Wyoming* (1988) and *Arctic Heart* (1991), both to music by John-Marc Gowans, *Different Trains* (1990) (with a score by **Steve Reich**), *Winnsboro Cotton Mill Blues* (1992) and *Of Oil and Water* (2000).

Davies, Terence 1945– •*British film director and screenwriter*• Born in Liverpool, he trained at Coventry Drama School and at the National Film School but worked as an accountant before establishing a career in cinema. His early films included *Madonna and Child* (1980) and *Death and Transfiguration* (1983). Subsequently he won particular acclaim for a grimly realistic series of films loosely based upon his own working-class childhood in postwar Liverpool, comprising *Distant Voices, Still Lives* (1988), which won the International Critics' prize at the Cannes Film Festival; *The Long Day Closes* (1992); and *The Neon Bible* (1995). *The House of Mirth* (2000), a film of **Edith Wharton**'s 1905 novel, was a completely new departure, and won critical acclaim.

Davies, William Henry 1871–1940 •*Welsh poet*• Born in Newport, Monmouthshire, he emigrated to the US at the age of 22. He lived partly as a tramp and partly as a casual workman until the loss of a leg while jumping a train caused him to return to England. There he began to write and worked as a peddler to obtain money to have his poems printed. In 1907 **George Bernard Shaw** arranged a publication of his first work, *A Soul's Destroyer*. The success of this book was consolidated by *The Autobiography of a Super-tramp* (1908). He also published poems and lyrics, two novels, and further volumes of autobiography.

da Vinci, Leonardo *See* **Leonardo da Vinci**

Daviot, Gordon *See* **Tey, Josephine**

Davis, Benjamin Oliver 1877–1970 •*US general*• Born in Washington DC, he began his career as a first lieutenant of volunteer troops in the Spanish-American War. Promoted to major during World War I and colonel in 1930, he taught military science at Wilberforce University and the Tuskegee Institute. Davis became the first African-American general (1940–48) in the US Army. His son, Benjamin Oliver Davis, Jr (1912–2002), was the first African-American general (1954–70) in the US Air Force.

Davis, Bette (Ruth Elizabeth) 1908–89 •*US film actress*• Born in Lowell, Massachusetts, she studied at the Robert Milton–John Murray Anderson School of the Theater, and made her film debut in *Bad Sister* (1931). Her first Hollywood success was in *The Man Who Played God* (1932), and her numerous leading roles included *Of Human Bondage* (1934) and *Dangerous* (1935, Academy Award). Highly dedicated, she brought an emotional honesty to the most unprepossessing of melodramas. She was nominated on ten occasions for an Academy Award, winning her second for *Jezebel* (1938). She received great critical acclaim for her role in *Whatever Happened to Baby Jane?* (1962); later film appearances also included *Death on the Nile* (1979). Married four times, she wrote several volumes of autobiography.

❝ ❞

Evil people ... you never forget them. And that's the aim of any actress—never to be forgotten.

1966 On her favorite character roles. In the New York State Theater program, June.

Davis, Sir Colin Rex 1927– •*English conductor*• Born in Weybridge, Surrey, he was educated at Christ's Hospital and the Royal College of Music. He has worked as conductor and musical director for numerous orchestras, including the BBC Symphony Orchestra (1967–71), Boston Symphony Orchestra (1972), London Symphony Orchestra (1974) and Bavarian Radio Symphony Orchestra (1983–92). At Covent Garden (1971–86) he gained a reputation as a **Wagner** conductor of international standing with the *Ring* cycle. He is also a noted interpreter of **Berlioz**. He is principal conductor of the London Symphony Orchestra (1996–) and principal guest conductor of the New York Philharmonic Orchestra (1998–). He was knighted in 1980 and was made a Companion of Honour in 2001.

Davis, David Michael 1948– •*English Conservative politician*• He was educated at Warwick University, the London Business School and at Harvard before going into business and in 1980 becoming managing director of Tate & Lyle. He became a Member of Parliament in 1987, and was an assistant government whip (1990–93), Europe Minister (1994–97) and chairman of the Commons Public Accounts Committee (1997–2001). In 2001, having run unsuccessfully for the leadership of the party, he became chairman of the Conservative Party under **Iain Duncan Smith**.

Davis, Dwight Filley 1879–1945 •*US public official*• He was born in St Louis, Missouri. In 1900 he donated an international challenge cup for tennis, competed for annually. The Davis Cup signifies the world team championship.

Davis, Fred 1913–98 •*English billiards and snooker champion*• He was born in Whittingham Moor, Derbyshire, the younger brother of **Joe Davis**. In 1948 he succeeded his brother as world snooker champion—the first of eight world-championship wins—and in 1980 won the World Billiards championship.

Davis, Geena 1957– •*US actress*• Born in Wareham, Massachusetts, she studied at Boston University. She began her career as a stage actress and model and moved to the screen as an offbeat character actress in films such as *The Accidental Tourist* (1988; Academy Award for Best Supporting Actress), *Beetlejuice* (1988), *Thelma and Louise* (1991) and *Stuart Little* (1999).

Davis, Jefferson 1808–89 •*US statesman, president of the Confederate States of the US*• Born in Christian County, Kentucky, he studied at West Point and served in several frontier campaigns, but resigned his commission in 1835. He entered Congress in 1845 for Mississippi, and served in the Mexican War as colonel of volunteers (1846–47). He was a senator from 1847 to 1851, and from 1853 to 1857 he was secretary of war, in which position he improved US military readiness. Returning to the Senate for a second term (1857–61), he carried in the Senate (1860) his seven resolutions asserting the inability of Congress or the legislatures of the territories to prohibit slavery. In January 1861 Mississippi seceded from the Union; a few weeks later Davis was chosen provisional president of the Confederate States, an appointment confirmed for six years in November. The history of his presidency is that of the Civil War (1861–65). He struggled to govern the Confederacy as a whole nation, and astutely allowed General **Robert E Lee** to determine much of the strategy of the war. Lee's final surrender at Appomattox in April 1865 was made without his agreement, and intending to continue the struggle he fled south, only to be captured a month later by Union cavalry in Georgia. He was imprisoned for two years in Fort Monroe, Virginia, and then released on bail. Though indicted for treason, he was never brought to trial.

Davis, Joe 1901–78 •*English billiards and snooker champion*• Born in Whitwell, near Chesterfield, Derbyshire, in 1927 he won the first world professional snooker championship and was never beaten until he retired from competitive snooker and billiards in 1946. In 1928 he won the billiards championship, which he held till 1933. A new event was introduced in 1934, and while Walter Lindrum (1898–1960) became the world champion, Davis continued to hold the UK championship. His younger brother **Fred Davis** followed the same career.

Davis or **Davys, John** c. 1550–1605 •*English navigator*• He was born in Sandridge, near Dartmouth, Devon, and between 1585 and 1587 undertook three Arctic voyages in search of the Northwest Passage. In the last voyage he sailed as far north as 73°. He also made two ill-fated voyages toward the South Seas and as pilot of a Dutch vessel to the East Indies. On his last voyage, he was killed by Japanese pirates off Singapore. He wrote *World's Hydrographical Description* (1595) and *The Seaman's Secrets* (1594), and invented the navigational instrument Davis's quadrant.

Davis, Judy 1955– •*Australian actress*• Born in Perth, Western Australia, she studied at the National Institute of Dramatic Arts in Sydney (1974–77). Her performance as the strong-willed, 19th-century heroine of the film *My Brilliant Career* (1979) earned her international attention. She has portrayed a range of forceful individuals in such films as *Winter of Our Dreams* (1981), *Heatwave* (1981) and *Husbands and Wives* (1992) while continuing a parallel stage career with *Piaf* (1980), *Lulu* (1981) and, in London, *Insignificance* (1982). She won an Emmy for her role in the television production *Life with Judy Garland: Me and My Shadows* (2001).

Davis, Miles Dewey, III 1926–91 •*US jazz trumpeter and bandleader*• Born into a middle-class African-American family in Alton, Illinois, and brought up in St Louis, in 1944 he began studies at the Juilliard School of Music, New York, but left to perform in the 52nd Street clubs where the new bebop style was emerging. At 19 he became a member of the foremost of these groups, the **Charlie Parker** Quintet. Although not then the most technically accomplished of jazz trumpeters, Davis played in an understated style that became highly influential, and he continued to be at the forefront of new stylistic departures. In 1948, working with pianist-arranger **Gil Evans**, he led a nonet that inspired the "cool jazz" school. In the late 1950s, his quartet featuring saxophonist **John Coltrane** introduced a "modal" approach which broke away from the harmonic principles previously accepted in jazz. Ten years later, his bands were featuring electronic instruments and synthesizers as well as rock-style rhythms. Davis retired from performing from 1975 to 1980, but he returned thereafter, further developing the use of electronics but using a commercial approach that did not find favor with all of his previous followers.

Davis, Sammy, Jr 1925–90 •*US entertainer*• Born in Harlem, New York, he began to receive star billing in the early 1950s, appearing in musicals such as *Mr Wonderful* (1956) and *Golden Boy* (1964), and in films such as *Porgy and Bess* (1959). He was associated with the glitzy world of the Las Vegas "rat-pack" performers **Frank Sinatra** and **Dean Martin**, and among his many recordings he had a number-one hit in the US charts with *Candy Man* (1972). His television appearances included *The Sammy Davis Junior Show* (1966).

“ ”

Being a star has made it possible for me to get insulted in places where the average Negro could never hope to go and get insulted.

1965 ***Yes I Can****, part 3, chapter 23.*

Davis, Steve 1957– •*English snooker player*• He was born in London. Between 1980 and 1985 he won three world titles, and of 96 major matches played, he won all but 11. Calm and imperturbable, he was distinguished by the maturity of his play even while very young. In 1985 he lost on the final black of the world championship to Dennis Taylor in a 35-frame match often considered the finest snooker match ever televised. For most of the 1980s, when he won the world championships six times, he was ranked as the world's leading player.

Davison, Emily 1872–1913 •*English suffragette*• Born in Blackheath, she was educated first at London University and then at Oxford. In 1906 she became a militant member of the Women's Social and Political Union (WSPU). Her activities included stone throwing, setting mailboxes on fire and attacking a Baptist minister whom she mistook for **Lloyd George**. Frequently imprisoned, she often went on hunger strikes, and was repeatedly force-fed. In the 1913 derby, wearing a WSPU banner, she tried to catch the reins of the king's horse, but she was trampled underfoot and died several days later.

Davisson, Clinton Joseph 1881–1958 •*US physicist and Nobel Prize winner*• Born in Bloomington, Illinois, he was educated at the University of Chicago and Princeton University. In 1927, with Lester Germer (1896–1971), Davisson was observing electron scattering from a block of nickel when their vacuum system broke down. When the experiment continued, the results were completely different, as they found the familiar peaks and troughs of a diffraction pattern, confirming **Louis de Broglie**'s theory of the wave nature of particles. This accidental discovery was crucial to the development of the quantum theory of matter. In 1937 he shared the Nobel Prize for physics with **George Paget Thomson**.

Davitt, Michael 1846–1906 •*Irish Nationalist politician and founder of the Irish Land League*• Born in Straid, County Mayo, he emigrated with his family to Haslingden in Lancashire, England (1851), where he lost his right arm in a machinery accident in a cotton factory in 1857. In 1866 he joined the Fenian movement, and was sentenced in 1870 to 15 years' penal servitude for sending guns to Ireland. He was released in 1877 and founded the Land League in 1879. Davitt was imprisoned in Portland for breaking his ticket-of-leave (1881–82), and during this time he was elected a Member of Parliament (1882) but was disqualified from taking his seat. He opposed **Charles Parnell** and was returned to parliament in 1892 as an anti-Parnellite, but was unseated on grounds of clerical intimidation (1893). In 1895 he was returned unopposed by South Mayo, but resigned in 1899.

Davout, Louis Nicolas 1770–1823 •*French general*• Born in Annoux, Burgundy, he was educated with **Napoleon I** at the military school of Brienne. As general he largely secured the victory at Aboukir (1799), and as a Marshal of the Empire (1804) he fought brilliantly at Austerlitz (1805) and Auerstädt (1806). At Eckmühl and Wagram (1809) he checked the Austrian attack. As Governor of Poland he ruled despotically, and in the Russian campaign of 1812–13 he won victories at Mohilev and Vitebsk. After the retreat from Moscow he became Governor-General of the Hanse towns, and at Hamburg maintained a regime of repression until the first Restoration (1814). In 1815 he was appointed Minister of War, and after Waterloo he received the command of the remnant of the French army under the walls of Paris. In 1819 he was made a peer of France.

Davy, Edward 1806–85 •*Australian physician and scientist*• Born in Ottery St Mary, Devon, England, he studied medicine, then in 1829 established the firm of Davy & Co, supplying scientific apparatus, including some of his own inventions, such as "Davy's blowpipe" for chemical analysis, and "Davy's diamond cement" for repairing broken china. He invented the electric relay and he deserves to stand alongside **Charles Wheatstone** and William Cooke (1806–79) as one of the inventors of wireless telegraphy. He later emigrated to Adelaide, South Australia (1838), where he continued his experiments.

Davy, Sir Humphry 1778–1829 •*English chemist and science promoter*• Born in Penzance, Cornwall, he was an assistant at the Pneumatic Institute in Bristol (1798), where he discovered the anesthetic effect of laughing gas (nitrous oxide). He also showed that heat can be transmitted through a vacuum and suggested that it is a form of motion. He became assistant lecturer in chemistry at the Royal Institution (1801), where his research into electrochemistry was organized by **Jöns Jacob Berzelius** into a coherent system. He isolated the metals sodium and potassium, as well as barium, strontium, calcium and magnesium. Following up on the work of **Bernard Courtois**, Davy showed that fluorine and chlorine are related to iodine, and his work also refuted **Antoine Lavoisier**'s theory that all acids contain oxygen. He also proved that diamond is a form of carbon. His *Elements of Agricultural Chemistry* (1813) was the first book to apply chemical principles systematically to farming.

From 1813 to 1815 he traveled on the Continent, taking the young **Michael Faraday** as chemical assistant and valet. He invented the safety lamp (1815, the "Davy lamp"), which enabled deeper, more gaseous seams to be mined with less risk of explosion. He was one of the founders of the Athenaeum Club and of the Zoological Society, which in its turn founded London Zoo. He was made a baronet in 1812.

Davys, John *See* **Davis, John**

Dawes, Charles G(ates) 1865–1951 •*US diplomat, politician and Nobel Prize winner*• Born in Marietta, Ohio, he studied at Cincinnati Law School and was admitted to the bar. He gained administrative experience as brigadier general in charge of military procurement for US forces in France in World War I and was head of the commission that drew up the Dawes Plan (1924) for reducing and reorganizing German reparation payments. He shared the 1925 Nobel Peace Prize with Sir **Austen Chamberlain** for negotiating the Locarno Pact. He served as Republican vice president (1925–29) under **Calvin Coolidge** and later became US ambassador to Great Britain.

Dawes, Sophia 1790–1840 •*English adventuress*• She was born in St Helens on the Isle of Wight. She later became an inmate in a workhouse, an officer's mistress, and a servant in a brothel. She was mistress to the Duc de **Bourbon**, and married his aide-de-camp, the Baron de Feuchères, in 1818. She is thought to have murdered the Duc (1830).

Dawkins, (Clinton) Richard 1941– •*British ethologist*• Born in Nairobi, Kenya, he was educated at Oxford and taught at the University of California at Berkeley before returning to Oxford (1970), where he is a Fellow of New College. In *The Selfish Gene* (1976), he shows how natural selection acts on individual genes rather than at the organismic or species level, and also describes how apparently altruistic behavior in animals is designed to increase the probability of survival of genes. The ways in which small genetic changes or mutations form the basis for evolution are set out in *The Blind Watchmaker* (1986). *The Extended Phenotype* (1982), a more advanced book, argues that genes can have effects outside the bodies that contain them. His later publications include *River out of Eden* (1995).

“ ”

However many ways there may be of being alive, it is certain that there are vastly more ways of being dead.

1986 ***The Blind Watchmaker****, chapter 1.*

Dawson, Charles 1864–1916 •*English solicitor and antiquary*• Born in Sussex, he became an amateur geologist. He was the victim (or possibly the perpetrator) of the celebrated "Piltdown skull" hoax, in which cranial fragments, found by him at Piltdown (1908–12), together with parts of a jawbone unearthed later, were accepted by anthropologists as the "missing link" in **Charles Darwin**'s theory of evolution, and as such one of the greatest discoveries of the age. It was not until 1953 that the skull was formally denounced as a fake, after scientific tests had established that the jawbone was that of a modern ape, colored to simulate age, that the cranium had also been stained to match the gravel deposits in which it was found, and that the fragments had clearly been "planted" on the site.

Dawson, Les 1934–93 •*English comedian*• Born in Collyhurst, Manchester, he began his career performing in working-men's clubs. He made his break into television in the late 1960s with shows such as *Sez Les* (1969–76), later hosting the frequently feeble game show *Blankety Blank* (1984–89). Known for his dourly delivered mother-in-law jokes, his deliberately atrocious piano playing and his moments of soaring poetic fancy, he also wrote several novels including *Well Fared, My Lovely* (1991).

Day, Doris, *originally* **Doris Kappelhoff** 1924– •*US singer and film actress*• Born in Cincinnati, Ohio, she was a vocalist with several big bands and a radio favorite before she made her film debut in *Romance on the High Seas* (1948). Her sunny personality, singing talent and girl-next-door image enlivened many standard Warner Brothers musicals of the 1950s. More satisfying material followed with *Calamity Jane* (1953), *Young at Heart* (1954) and *The Pajama Game* (1957). A top-selling recording artist, she was also able to show her dramatic talent in *Storm Warning* (1950) and *Love Me or Leave Me* (1955). The popularity of the comedy *Pillow Talk* (1959) earned her an Academy Award nomination and a further career as the perennial virgin in a series of frothy farces where she was often partnered with Rock Hudson (1925–85). Her television appearances include *The Doris Day Show* (1968–73).

Day, Dorothy 1897–1980 •*US writer and radical social reformer*• Born in Brooklyn, New York, she became a lifelong socialist, having worked in the New York slums as a probationary nurse. Converted to Catholicism in 1927, she cofounded the monthly *Catholic Worker* in 1933, drawing on her earlier experience as a reporter for Marxist publications like *Call* and *The Masses* in the Lower East Side of Manhattan. Under the influence of the French itinerant priest Peter Maurin (1877–1949), she founded the Catholic Worker Movement, which established "houses of hospitality" and farm communities for people hit by the Depression, as described in her *House of Hospitality* (1939). A pacifist, she helped turn her church's attention to peace and justice issues.

Day, John 1574–1640 •*English dramatist*• He was born in Norfolk, and studied at Gonville and Caius College, Cambridge. He collaborated freely with Henry Chettle (c. 1560–1607), **Thomas Dekker**, and others. His works, privately printed in 1881, include a graceful comedy, *Humour out of Breath*, and *The Parliament of Bees*, an allegorical masque.

Day, Sir Robin 1923–2000 •*English journalist and broadcaster*• Born in London, he served in the Royal Artillery (1943–47), studied law at St Edmund Hall, Oxford, and was called to the bar in 1952. He left for the British Council in Washington DC to become a freelance broadcaster in 1954, working at Independent Television News from 1955 to 1959. He then joined the BBC's *Panorama*, which he hosted from 1967 to 1972. He brought an acerbic freshness to interviewing techniques and proved a formidable inquisitor of political figures. His radio work included *It's Your Line* (1970–76) and *The World at One* (1979–88), while his television credits included *Question Time* (1979–89). He was knighted in 1981.

Dayan, Moshe 1915–81 •*Israeli soldier and politician*• Born in Palestine, he founded the Haganah underground militia. He was Chief of Staff of the Israeli army when Israel conquered Gaza and the Sinai in the Suez War of 1956. He was elected to the Knesset as a Labor member in 1959 and was made Minister of Agriculture (1959–64) by **David Ben-Gurion**. He left the Labor Party in 1966 to set up the Rafi Party with Ben-Gurion. In 1967, as a member of the opposition, he was appointed Defense Minister, and masterminded the Israeli victory in the Six-Day War. Dayan then cleared Jerusalem of Arab/Jewish barriers and mines, and declared it a free city. He was Defense Minister again from 1969 to 1974, but his reputation was tarnished by Israel's disastrous start to the 1973 (Yom Kippur) War, and he was dropped from the Cabinet. In 1977, as Foreign Minister, he helped secure the historic peace treaty with Egypt. In 1981 he launched a new center party, but died the same year.

Day-Lewis, Cecil, *pen name* **C Day Lewis**, *pseudonym* **Nicholas Blake** 1904–72 •*Irish poet, critic and detective-story writer*• Born in Ballintubbert, County Leix, he was educated at Wadham College, Oxford. He published his first verse, *Beechen Vigil and Other Poems*, in 1925. He made his name as a lyric poet with *Transitional Poems* (1929), and during the 1930s, with **W H Auden** and **Stephen Spender**, became associated with left-wing causes, and also wrote literary criticism in *A Hope for Poetry* (1934). During World War II he worked in the Ministry of Information, and then published his major critical work, *The Poetic Image* (1947). He became Professor of Poetry at Oxford (1951–56) and at Harvard (1964–65), and published his last critical work, *The Poetic Impulse*, in 1965. He made notable translations of **Virgil** and St Valery, and was appointed poet laureate in 1968. Under the pseudonym Nicholas Blake he wrote 20 sophisticated detective novels. He was the father of **Daniel Day-Lewis**.

Day-Lewis, Daniel 1958– •*English actor*• Born in London, the son of Poet Laureate **Cecil Day-Lewis**, he acquired extensive stage experience before winning recognition for his West End appearance in *Another Country* (1982–83). His screen versatility was established with contrasting roles as the gay punk in *My Beautiful Laundrette* and the prissy Edwardian suitor in *A Room with a View* (both 1985). His stage work with the National Theatre includes *The Futurists* (1986) and *Hamlet* (1989). Highly selective in his choice of film roles, he won a Best Actor Academy Award as the handicapped writer Christy Brown in *My Left Foot* (1989). More recent films include *The Last of the Mohicans* (1992, Academy Award nomination), *The Age of Innocence* (1994), and *Gangs of New York* (2002, Academy Award nomination).

Deacon, Richard 1949– •*British sculptor*• Born in Bangor, Wales, he trained in London at St Martins School of Art, the Royal College of Art, and Chelsea School of Art. His work is abstract and varied, ranging from sinuous forms to bulky objects that expose the nuts and bolts of fabrication. He plays on associations between language and aspects of reality, as with *Listening to Reason* (1986), *Double Talk* (1987) and *The Back of My Hand* (1987). Since winning the Turner prize in 1987 he has exhibited widely abroad and executed many public commissions.

Deakin, Alfred 1856–1919 •*Australian statesman*• Born in Collingwood, Victoria, he entered the Victorian Legislative Assembly in 1879 and went to Great Britain with **Edmund Barton**'s delegation to present the draft constitution to the British parliament in 1900. When Barton became the first Prime Minister of Australia's first federal government in 1901, Deakin was appointed Attorney General and was largely responsible for the immigration legislation that created the White Australia Policy. On Barton's retirement in 1903 he became Prime Minister until 1904 and was reelected twice (1905–08, 1909–10).

Dean (of Thornton-Le-Fylde), Brenda Dean, Baroness 1943– •*English trade union leader*• Born in Manchester, she left school in 1959 and became an employee of the printing trade union SOGAT. She was secretary of the Manchester branch (1976–83) before becoming president of the renamed and reconstituted SOGAT '82. From 1985 to 1991 she was general secretary and became a national figure during the printers' dispute with **Rupert Murdoch**'s News International. In 1993 she became chairman of the Independent Committee for Supervision of Standards of Telephone Information Services, and that same year was awarded a life peerage. She became Chairman of the Housing Corporation in 1998.

Dean, Christopher 1958– •*English ice skater*• Born in Nottingham, he was a policeman before taking up skating full time. He formed a skating partnership with **Jayne Torvill** in 1975. They were six times British champions (1978–83) and won the grand slam of World, Olympic and European ice-dance titles in 1984, with a haunting interpretation of **Ravel**'s "Bolero." After turning professional in 1985, he continued to tour the world with Torvill in their own ice show.

Dean, Dixie (William Ralph) 1907–80 •*English soccer player*• Born in Birkenhead, Merseyside, he voluntarily attended Borstal for part of his schooling because it had better soccer facilities. He turned professional with Tranmere Rovers at the age of 16, and scored 27 goals in 27 matches in the following season. He joined Everton in 1925, for whom he scored a record 349 goals in 399 games, despite a severe motorcycle accident in 1926 which fractured his skull.

Dean, James Byron 1931–55 •*US film actor*• Born in Marion, Indiana, he started acting at UCLA, and in 1952 he moved to New York City, where he joined the Actors Studio. After small parts in theater, films and television, he gained overnight success in the film *East of Eden* (1955). He starred in only two more films, *Rebel Without a Cause* (1955) and *Giant* (released 1956), before he was killed in a car crash. In just over a year he had become a cult figure, the personification of contemporary US youth, restless and without direction.

Dean, Laura 1945– •*US dancer, choreographer and teacher*• Born in Staten Island, New York, she studied at Manhattan's High School of Performing Arts and the School of American Ballet, danced in **Paul Taylor**'s company (1965–66), and worked with **Robert Wilson**. She began choreographing in 1967, developing a style based on her interest in simple, repetitive movement. Formed in 1976, Laura Dean Dancers and Musicians mainly features her own scores and those of composer **Steve Reich**.

Deane, Seamus 1940– •*Irish writer*• He was born in Derry, Northern Ireland, and educated in Belfast and at Cambridge. He taught in the US before returning to Ireland to become Professor of Modern English and American Literature at University College Dublin. In 1971 he became codirector of the Field Day Theatre Company, a post he held until 1993. His three-volume *Field Day Anthology of Irish Writing* was published in 1991. Of his own work, *Gradual Wars* (1972) was one of the first poetry collections to address the political unrest in Ireland since the late 1960s. He has also published a number of subsequent collections and several volumes of essays. His first novel, *Reading in the Dark*, was published in 1996.

DeBakey, Michael Ellis 1908– •*US cardiovascular surgeon*• He was born in Lake Charles, Louisiana, and received his medical training at Tulane University. He subsequently taught surgery there until 1948, when he moved to Baylor University College of Medicine in Houston, Texas, where he has held various appointments and has been director of the De Bakey Heart Center since 1985. DeBakey was particularly involved in the surgical treatment of aortic aneurysms and arterial occlusion through replacement with grafts, but also contributed to other aspects of surgery, including gastric.

de Balliol, Edward *See* **Balliol, Edward de**

de Balliol, John *See* **Balliol, John de**

de Bergerac, Cyrano *See* **Cyrano de Bergerac, Savinien**

de Bernières, Louis 1954– •*English author*• He spent his earliest years in the Middle East, was brought up in Surrey, and studied philosophy at Manchester University. In the early 1990s he published a trilogy of novels set in Latin America, but achieved international fame with *Captain Corelli's Mandolin* (1994), a love story set on a small island in Greece during World War II. A children's book, *Red Dog* (2001), followed the fortunes of a traveling dog in rural Australia.

de Bono, Edward Francis Charles Publius 1933– •*British psychologist and writer*• Born in Malta, he took a degree in medicine at the Royal University there, then went as a Rhodes Scholar to Christ Church, Oxford, where he studied psychology, physiology and medicine. From 1976 to 1983 he was a lecturer in medicine at Cambridge, and he is involved with a number of organizations to promote the skills of thinking, including the Cognitive Research Trust, Cambridge (director since 1971). His books include *The Use of Lateral Thinking* (1967), *Handbook for a Positive Revolution* (1990) and *Textbook of Wisdom* (1996).

De Bono, Emilio 1866–1944 •*Italian Fascist politician and general*• He was born in Cassano d'Adda. After an army career in World War I, he took part in **Mussolini**'s March on Rome (1922), became Governor of Tripolitania (1925), colonial secretary (1939) and commanded the Italian forces invading Abyssinia (1935) until he was replaced by **Pietro Badoglio**. He voted against Mussolini in the Fascist Supreme Council (1943) and was summarily tried and executed as a traitor by Fascists in Verona.

Debray, Regis 1941– •*French Marxist theorist*• Educated at the École Normale Supérieure, he gained international fame through his association with **Che Guevara** in Latin America during the 1960s and, in 1967, was sentenced to 30 years' imprisonment in Bolivia. He was released from jail in 1970, and from 1981 to 1984 he was appointed an adviser to President **François Mitterrand** on Third World affairs. His most influential writings have been *Strategy for Revolution* (1970) and *The Power of the Intellectual in France* (1979).

Debré, Michel Jean Pierre 1912–96 •*French politician*• He was born in Paris. After taking part in the Resistance, he was elected to parliament as a member of the Gaullist Party in 1948, and violently attacked the constitution of the Fourth Republic. In 1958 he was appointed Minister of Justice, and **Charles de Gaulle** charged him with the task of producing the new constitution of the Fifth Republic (adopted later that year); he was appointed its first

Prime Minister in 1959, but was displaced by **Georges Pompidou** in 1962. Between 1966 and 1973 he held various offices, and in 1979 became a Member of the European Parliament.

Debrett, John c. 1750–1822 •*English publisher and biographer*• Presumed to have been born in London, he took over in 1781 the publishing business of John Almon (1737–1805), editor of *The New Peerage* (first published 1769). This became *Debrett's Peerage of England, Scotland and Ireland* in 1802. His shop, opposite the Royal Academy in Piccadilly, became the meeting place of the Whig intelligentsia, and Debrett was the leading publisher of books on the new colony of Australia. *Debrett's Peerage*, under various titles, continues to be published.

De Broglie, Louis-Victor Pierre Raymond *See* **Broglie, Louis-Victor Pierre Raymond de**

De Bruijn, Inge 1973– •*Dutch swimmer*• Born in Barendrecht, she first swam competitively at the age of 12 and joined the top rank in 1991, when she won four medals at the European championships. At the 2000 Olympics she created a sensation by winning gold medals in the 100-meter butterfly, 100-meter freestyle and the 50-meter freestyle events, setting new world records in each. She also won a silver medal in the 4 × 100-meter freestyle relay.

Debs, Eugene V(ictor) 1855–1926 •*US politician and union leader*• Born in Terre Haute, Indiana, he organized an industrial union of railroad workers, the American Railway Union (ARU), in 1893. He pledged the ARU's participation in the Pullman strike of 1894, which was broken by federal authorities and brought Debs a six-month prison sentence. He helped to found the Socialist Party of America, standing unsuccessfully as its candidate in all the presidential elections between 1900 and 1920, except that of 1916. His pacifism during World War I and his denunciation of the Espionage Act led to his imprisonment (1918–21); he conducted his final presidential campaign from an Atlanta penitentiary, receiving nearly a million votes.

Debussy, (Achille-)Claude 1862–1918 •*French composer*• He was born in St Germain-en-Laye and educated at the Paris Conservatoire (1873–84), where he studied the piano and composition. In 1884 he won the Prix de Rome with his cantata *L'enfant prodigue*. His early work was influenced by **Richard Wagner**, for whom he had great admiration, but he developed a more experimental and individual vein in his first mature work, the *Prélude à l'après-midi d'un faune*, evoked by **Stéphane Mallarmé**'s poem, which first won him fame. He added to his reputation with his admired operatic setting of **Maurice Maeterlinck**'s *Pelléas et Mélisande*, begun in 1892 but not performed until 1902, and some outstanding piano pieces, *Images* and *Préludes*, in which he moved further from traditional formulas and experimented with novel techniques and effects, producing the pictures in sound which led to his work being described as "musical Impressionism." He extended this new idiom to orchestral music in *La Mer* (1905), the orchestrated *Images*, and other pieces, and later elaborated his piano style still further, as in the scintillating *Feux d'artifice* and the atmospheric *La cathédrale engloutie*. In his later period he composed much chamber music, including pieces for the flute and the harp, two instruments peculiarly suited to his type of music.

“ ”

A century of aeroplanes deserves its own music. As there are no precedents, I must create anew.

1913 Quoted in ***La Revue S.I.M.***

Debye, Peter Joseph Wilhelm, *originally* **Petrus Josephus Wilhelmus Debije** 1884–1966 •*US physicist, physical chemist and Nobel Prize winner*• Born in Maastricht, the Netherlands, he taught at various universities including Berlin (1934–40), where increasing political interference led him to leave for the US (1940). He was chairman of the Cornell University chemistry department from 1940 until his retirement in 1950. Debye's work included development of the theory of the specific heats of crystalline solids in 1911, followed by his work on dielectric constants and, in 1912, molecular dipole moments (now known as Debyes), which were used during the 1920s and 1930s to investigate the details of chemical bonding. In the Debye-**Hückel** theory of strong electrolytes (1923), their behavior was related quantitatively to electrostatic forces between ions. The Debye-Scherrer X-ray diffraction powder method was developed in 1916–20 and the theory of X-ray scattering by gaseous molecules in 1925. Experimental studies of X-ray diffraction by gases and liquids were made from 1929 to 1933, and for this work Debye was awarded the 1936 Nobel Prize for chemistry. Later he made important studies by means of electron diffraction (1938). He also provided the theoretical treatments for the electro-optical Kerr effect (1925), adiabatic demagnetization (1926) and thermal diffusion (1939). After his move to the US he worked on light scattering related to molecular and media structures (1944–66) and many aspects of polymer behavior (1945–66).

Decatur, Stephen 1779–1820 •*US naval commander*• Born in Sinepuxent, Maryland, of French descent, he served against the French, and in the war with Tripoli (1801–05) gained great distinction burning the captured *Philadelphia*, and escaping under the fire of 141 guns. Promoted to captain in 1804 and commodore in 1810, in the War of 1812 with Great Britain he captured the British frigate *Macedonian*, but in 1814 surrendered. He was killed in a duel.

de Chastelain, (Alfred) John (Gardyne Drummond) 1937– •*Canadian soldier and diplomat*• Born in Bucharest, Romania, he emigrated to Canada in 1955, became a Canadian citizen in 1962, and was educated in Edinburgh, Calgary, at the Royal Military College of Canada at Kingston and at the British Army Staff College, Camberley. He had a distinguished career in the Canadian army, reaching the rank of general and serving as Chief of the Defence Staff (1989–93, 1994–95). In 1995 he joined the Body on the Decommissioning of Arms in Northern Ireland, facilitating the Good Friday Agreement.

Decius, Caius Messius Quintus Trajanus c. 200–51 AD •*Roman emperor*• He was born in Lower Pannonia, and was sent (AD 249) by the emperor **Philip I** (the Arab), to reduce the rebellious army of Moesia. An able general and administrator, he was proclaimed emperor by the soldiers against his will, and he defeated and killed Philip near Verona. His brief reign was one of warring with the Goths and persecuting the Christians. He was killed near Abricium.

de Coster, Charles *See* **Coster, Charles de**

Dedekind, Julius Wilhelm Richard 1831–1916 •*German mathematician*• Born in Brunswick, he studied at the University of Göttingen under **Carl Gauss** and was influenced by **Lejeune Dirichlet**, who led Dedekind into number theory. Dedekind gave one of the first precise definitions of the real number system, and his important work in number theory led him to introduce many concepts that have become fundamental in all modern algebra. With his friend **Georg Cantor**, he did much to found mathematics on the naive concept of a set, and also made important contributions to the early history of lattice theory.

Dee, John 1527–1608 •*English alchemist, geographer and mathematician*• Born in London, he was educated in London, Chelmsford, and at St John's College, Cambridge. He earned the reputation of a sorcerer by using a mechanical beetle in a representation of **Aristophanes**'s *Peace*. He claimed to have found in the ruins of Glastonbury a quantity of the Elixir, and his assistant, Edward Kelley, professed to confer with angels by means of Dee's magic crystal, and talked him into consenting to a community of wives. As astrologer to Queen **Mary I (Tudor)**, he was imprisoned but acquitted on charges of plotting her death by magic (1555). For most of his life he was concerned with the search for the Northwest Passage to the Far East. He wrote numerous works on logic, mathematics, astrology, alchemy, navigation, geography and the calendar (1583), but died in poverty. His eldest son, Arthur Dee (1579–1651), was also an alchemist.

Deeping, (George) Warwick 1877–1950 •*English novelist*• Born in Southend-on-Sea, Essex, he qualified as a doctor, but turned to writing. It was not until after World War I, in which he served, that he gained recognition as an author with his bestseller, *Sorrell and Son* (1925), which was later filmed. Other novels include *Old Pybus* (1928) and *Roper's Row* (1929). In his sentimental stories, good breeding is represented as the cardinal virtue.

Deere, John 1804–86 •*US inventor and manufacturer*• Born in Rutland, Vermont, he was apprenticed to a blacksmith at the age of 17, and after establishing himself in the trade, he moved to Grand Detour, Illinois, in 1837. He discovered that the dense prairie soil was too tough for cast-iron plows, and in 1838 he designed a steel plow. His plow helped transform the prairie into a vast cropland, and the business which he founded to manufacture it (incorporated as Deere and Co in 1868) made his fortune.

de Fleury, André-Hercule *See* **Fleury, André-Hercule de**

Defoe, Daniel 1660–1731 •*English writer and adventurer*• Born in Stoke Newington, London, the son of a butcher, he set up in the hosiery trade there in 1683, then joined **William III**'s army in 1688 and up to 1704 strenuously supported the king's party. In Queen **Anne**'s reign he ran into trouble with his famous satire *The Shortest Way with the Dissenters* (1702), which eventually cost him a ruinous fine, the pillory and imprisonment in Newgate Prison. After his release, he founded a newspaper, *The Review* (1704–13), which included the feature the "Scandal Club," anticipating such magazines as *Tatler* and the *Spectator*. From 1704 he undertook various secret commissions for the Tory minister **Robert Harley**, including dubious dealings with the Scottish commissioners for Union in 1706–07. He turned to writing fiction after 1714, and in 1719–20, at the age of nearly 60, published his best-known book, *Robinson Crusoe*. His other major fictions include *Journal of the Plague Year* (1722), *Moll Flanders* (1722), his most vivid and still one of the best tales of low life, and *Roxana* (1724). A writer of astonishing versatility, he published more than 250 works in all, among them a three-volume travel book (*Tour Through the Whole Island of Great Britain*, 1724–27).

De Forest, Lee 1873–1961 •*US physicist and inventor*• Born in Council Bluffs, Iowa, he was educated at Yale and Chicago. He introduced the grid into the thermionic valve (1906), and invented the "audion" and the four-electrode valve. He also did much early work on sound reproduction and on television, and received his last patent at the age of 84 for an automatic dialing device. A pioneer of radio and wireless telegraphy, he patented more than 300 inventions in all and is known as the "father of radio" in the US.

Degas, (Hilaire Germain) Edgar 1834–1917 •*French artist*• Born in Paris, he studied at the École des Beaux-Arts, then went to Italy, where he was influenced by the art of the Renaissance painters. On his return to Paris he associated with the Impressionists and took part in most of their exhibitions from 1874 to 1886. He was also influenced by Japanese woodcuts and, in the seemingly casual composition of his paintings, by photography. He traveled in Spain and Italy and visited New Orleans in the US, in 1872–73, but most of his paintings and pastels of dancers and women at their toilet were produced in his Paris studio, often with the aid of wax and clay models. *Rehearsal of the Ballet* (c. 1874) is in the Louvre, Paris, *Dancer Lacing Her Shoe* (c. 1878) is in the Paris Museum of Impressionism, *Dancer at the Bar* is in the Metropolitan Museum, New York, and the well-known *Cotton-Brokers Office* (1873) is in Pau Museum. In later life, because of failing sight, he concentrated on sculpture.

“ ”

Everybody has talent at twenty-five. The difficult thing is to have it at fifty.
Quoted in R H Ives Gammell ***The Shop-Talk of Edgar Degas*** *(1961).*

De Gasperi, Alcide 1881–1954 •*Italian statesman*• He was born in Pieve Tesino in the Austrian province of Trentino, educated at Vienna University, and was elected to the Austrian parliament (1911–16, 1919). After Trentino was united with Italy, he became a member of the Italian Chamber of Deputies until 1925, when the Fascist regime of **Mussolini** banned political activity. He was arrested in 1926 but found refuge in the Vatican until Mussolini's overthrow in 1943. From 1945 he was a leading force in the creation of the Christian Democratic Party (DC), of which he remained Secretary-General until his death, and, as Prime Minister (1945–53), was Italy's most notable postwar politician.

de Gaulle, Charles André Joseph Marie 1890–1970 •*French general and first president of the Fifth Republic*• He was born in Lille. He served as an army officer in World War I, and in 1940 was promoted to general and junior War Secretary. Days before the signing of the French Armistice he sought refuge in England to found the Free French Army. Though largely ignored by both **Winston Churchill** and **Franklin D Roosevelt**, he served as a focus for the resistance movement, in which he played an active role during the rest of the war. He returned to Paris in 1944 with the first liberation forces. He was the country's natural first choice as postwar leader. He failed to form an all-party coalition and resigned in 1946 to found a new party, Rally of the French People, which took 40 percent of the votes in the 1947 election. He relinquished its leadership in 1953, and, in the wake of the failure of successive administrations to resolve the Algerian question, was free to accept office as first president of the Fifth Republic in 1958. In 1959–60 he granted self-government to all French African colonies (including Algeria, which finally achieved independence in 1962), and at home consolidated France's growing international importance by establishing its own nuclear deterrent, fostering better relations with West Germany, blocking Great Britain's attempts in 1962 and 1967 to enter the Common Market, and recognizing the Peking (Beijing) government in 1964. Despite his extensive use of the referendum, his autocratic presidential style and the growing popularity of the Left among the new young electorate created by the postwar baby boom, he won reelection in 1965 after a second vote, and recovered with an overwhelming victory in 1968 on seeking a mandate in the wake of violent student riots. However, he lost a referendum on constitutional reform in 1969, and resigned. His three-volume memoirs, *Mémoires de guerre*, were published between 1954 and 1959.

De Havilland, Sir Geoffrey 1882–1965 •*English aircraft designer*• Born near High Wycombe, Buckinghamshire, he was educated at Crystal Palace Engineering School. He built his first plane in 1908 and became director of the firm bearing his name, which produced many famous aircraft, including the Tiger Moth (1930), the Mosquito (1941, of revolutionary plywood construction) and the Comet jet airliner (1952). He established a height record for light aircraft in 1928, and won the King's Cup air race at the age of 51.

de Havilland, Olivia Mary 1916– •*US actress*• She was born in Tokyo, Japan, of British parentage, and was raised in California. Under contract to **Warner** Brothers, she proved an excellent foil to such stars as **Errol Flynn** in boisterous tales such as *Captain Blood* (1935) and *The Adventures of Robin Hood* (1938). She received an Academy Award nomination for her portrayal of Melanie in *Gone with the Wind* (1939), secured a further nomination for *Hold Back the Dawn* (1941) and won the award for both *To Each His Own* (1946) and *The Heiress* (1949). In 1942, her case against Warner Brothers resulted in a landmark decision limiting all film contracts to seven years. Her television work includes *Noon Wine* (1967) and *The Mystery of Anna* (1986).

Deighton, Len (Leonard Cyril) 1929– •*English thriller writer*• Born in London, he has been an art student, a railway plate layer and an air steward. His first novel, *The Ipcress File* (1962), was written when he was 33 and became a bestseller, as have almost all his books. Notable titles are *Funeral in Berlin* (1965), *Only When I Larf* (1968) and the *Game, Set and Match* trilogy: *Berlin Game* (1984), *Mexico Set* (1985) and *London Match* (1986). It was followed by another trilogy, *Spy Hook* (1988), *Spy Line* (1989) and *Spy Sinker* (1990). He also writes cookbooks.

Deisenhofer, Johann 1943– •*US molecular biologist and Nobel Prize winner*• Born in Zusamaltheim, Bavaria, Germany, he graduated in physics at the University of Munich (1971) and taught in Germany until 1988, when he moved to the US. From 1974 he studied pancreatic enzymes, and in 1976 he began a series of studies on immunoglobulin structure, identifying receptor and effector sites. He later collaborated with **Hartmut Michel** and **Robert Huber** to determine the structure of the reaction center of the bacterium *Rhodopseudomonas viridis*, work for which they shared the 1988 Nobel Prize for chemistry.

De Keersmaeker, Anne Teresa 1960– •*Belgian dancer and postmodern choreographer*• Born in Mechelen, she studied in Brussels and New York, and created a style which blends the abstract qualities of new US dance with the expressionist energies of Europeans like **Pina Bausch**. Her own company, Rosas, opened in 1983 with *Rosas Danst Rosas*. She has set her pieces to both minimalist and classical music and has used film and speech in her work. Well-known pieces include *Elena's Aria* (1984) and *Bartók/Aantekeningen* (1986).

Dekker, Thomas c. 1570–1632 •*English dramatist and pamphleteer*• He was born in London. Around 1598 he was employed by **Philip Henslowe** to write plays, and in 1600 published two comedies, *The Shoemaker's Holiday, or the Gentle Craft*, and *The Pleasant Comedy of Old Fortunatus*. His most powerful dramatic writing is seen in *The Honest Whore* (Part I, 1604, written with **Thomas Middleton**; Part II, written 1605, performed 1630). In 1607 he published three plays written in conjunction with **John Webster**, the *Famous History of Sir Thomas Wyat*, *Westward Ho!* and *Northward Ho!* These were followed by several other collaborative works. From 1613 to 1616 he was mostly in prison for debt. His pamphlets include *The Wonderful Year* (1603), which gives a tragic account of the plague, and *The Bellman of London* (1608), a lively account of London vagabonds.

de Klerk, F(rederik) W(illem) 1936– •*South African politician and Nobel Prize winner*• Born in Johannesburg, he graduated from Potchefstroom University, established a legal practice in Vereeniging and became active in the National Party. He entered the South African parliament in 1972, and then served in the Cabinets of **John Vorster** and **P W Botha** (1978–89). In 1989, he replaced Botha as National Party leader and acting State President. He began gradual reform of the apartheid system and improved diplomatic relations, and in 1989 he secured electoral victory for his party. In February 1990 he ended the 30-year-old ban on the African National Congress (ANC) Black opposition movement and sanctioned the release from imprisonment of its effective leader **Nelson Mandela**, with whom in 1993 he was jointly awarded the Nobel Peace Prize. By 1994 apartheid had been abolished and South Africa experienced its first democratic elections with de Klerk appointed vice president. He resigned his post as National Party leader in 1997.

de Kooning, Willem 1904–97 •*US painter*• Born in Rotterdam, the Netherlands, he emigrated to the US in 1926 and settled in New York City. By the 1950s he had emerged as a leader of the abstract expressionist movement (New York school), though he retained some figurative elements in his work and was preoccupied by the human form, which he represented most famously in his controversial series *Woman I–V* (1952–53). He began in the late 1950s to spend much of his time on Long Island, chronicling this shift from city to country in works such as *Montauk Highway* (1958) and *Pastorale* (1963). From his studio near the ocean he continued to produce vibrant abstract paintings that echoed nudes and landscapes into the late 1980s.

Delacroix, (Ferdinand Victor) Eugène 1798–1863 •*French painter*• He was born in Charenton, the son of Charles Delacroix (1741–1805), who had been Foreign Minister under the Directory, and prefect of Marseilles. In 1816 he entered the studio of Pierre Guérin (1774–1833), where his fellow pupil was **Theodore Géricault**. In 1822 he exhibited *Dante and Virgil in Hell* at the Salon, and in 1824 *The Massacre at Chios* (Louvre, Paris). These pictures, particularly the latter with its loose drawing and vivid coloring, shocked the devotees of the austere classical style and aroused a storm of criticism. Delacroix, however, moved even further away from traditional treatment with brilliant canvases of historical and dramatic scenes, often violent or macabre in subject, among them the famous *Liberty Guiding the People* (1831, Louvre). A journey to Morocco and Spain with a diplomatic mission in 1832 led to several pictures with an Oriental flavor, such as *Algerian Women* (1834), and he also turned to literary themes, notably from **Shakespeare** and **Torquato Tasso**. In 1838 he began work on a series of panels for the library of the Chamber of Deputies, choosing as his subject the history of ancient civilization. Perhaps the greatest figure in 19th-century French art, Delacroix was one of the most accomplished colorists of all time, and was responsible for a shift away from the meticulous but pallid techniques of **Jean Ingres** and **Jacques Louis David**. The daily journal that he kept from the age of 23 until his death records fascinating details of his life and work.

“ ”

Painters who are not colorists produce illumination and not painting.
*1852 **The Journal of Eugène Delacroix** (translated by W Pach, 1948).*

Delafield, E M, *pseudonym of* **Edmée Elizabeth Monica Dashwood**, *née* **de la Pasture** 1890–1943 •*English novelist*• Born in Llandogo, Monmouth, Wales, she worked first as a nurse and then at the Ministry of National Service in Bristol during World War I, and then became a civil servant, and served as a magistrate. She was the prolific author of novels which took a mildly but affectionately satirical look at the mores of genteel provincial life. Her best-known works are the series which began with *Diary of a Provincial Lady* (1930).

de la Hunty, Shirley Barbara, *née* **Strickland** 1925–2004 •*Australian athlete*• Born in Guildford, Western Australia, she won seven Olympic medals over the course of the three Games from 1948 to 1956, specializing in the 80-meter hurdles, 200-meter and 100-meter sprints. She also set world record times on successive days in the 80-meter hurdles at the Helsinki Olympics in 1952.

De La Madrid Hurtado, Miguel 1934– •*Mexican politician*• Born in Colima, Mexico, he studied law in Mexico City and public administration at Harvard. He entered government service in the Ministry of Finance, and as Minister of Planning and Budget under José López Portillo (1920–2004), he formulated an economic development plan that sought to use Mexico's oil wealth to promote economic growth. He was chosen as the candidate of the ruling Institutional Revolutionary Party in 1981 and was President of Mexico from 1982 to 1988.

de la Mare, Walter John 1873–1956 •*English poet and novelist*• Born in Charlton, Kent, of Huguenot descent, he was educated at St Paul's Choir School, London. His first book of verse, *Songs of Childhood* (1902), was published under the pseudonym of Walter Ramal. A popular writer with adults and children, he produced novels, poetry and short stories. His works include the prose romance *Henry Brocken* (1904), the children's story *The Three Mulla Mulgars* (1910), the novel of the occult *The Return* (1910), the collection of poetry *The Listeners* (1912), the fantasy novel *Memoirs of a Midget* (1921), and short stories in *On the Edge* (1930). A *Complete Poems* was issued in 1969.

de la Mettrie, Julien Offray *See* **La Mettrie, Julien Offroy de**

Delaney, Shelagh 1939– •*English playwright and screenwriter*• Born in Salford, Lancashire, she left school at the age of 16 and completed her first and best-known play a year later. *A Taste of Honey*, produced in London in 1958, is the story of a young white girl's abrasive home life and her pregnancy following a casual affair with a Black sailor. It was immediately seen as part of a young, "angry" movement dealing realistically with working-class, provincial life, and which included the playwrights **John Osborne** and **Arnold Wesker**. Among her later work is the screenplay for *Dance with a Stranger* (1985), a film depicting the fraught life of **Ruth Ellis**, the last woman to be hanged in England.

de la Renta, Oscar 1932– •*US fashion designer*• He was born in Santo Domingo, in the Dominican Republic. After studying art there and in Madrid, he worked at **Cristóbal Balenciaga**'s couture house in Madrid. He later worked for Lanvin-Castillo in Paris and **Elizabeth Arden** in New York. In 1965 he started his own company. He has a reputation for opulent, ornately trimmed clothes, particularly evening dresses, and he also designs daywear and accessories.

de la Roche, Mazo 1885–1961 •*Canadian novelist*• She was born in Newmarket, Ontario, and published *Jalna*, the first of a series of novels about the Whiteoak family, in 1927. *Whiteoaks* (1929) was dramatized with considerable success. She also wrote children's stories, history and travel books and an autobiography, *Ringing the Changes* (1957).

Delaroche, (Hippolyte-)Paul 1797–1856 •*French painter*• Born in Paris, he specialized in romantic historical subjects such as the *Death of Queen Elizabeth* (1827) and the *Execution of Lady Jane Grey* (1834). From this period until 1841 he was engaged on his largest work, the mural *Apotheosis of Art* in the École des Beaux-Arts, in which he was aided by **Edward Armitage** and other pupils.

de la Rochefoucauld, François *See* **La Rochefoucauld, François, 6th Duc de**

de la Rúa, Fernando 1937– •*Argentinean politician*• Born in Córdoba, he was educated at the National University in Córdoba and subsequently joined the staff of the Ministry of the Interior (1963–66). He lectured abroad during the period of Argentina's military dictatorship (1983–96). He served as mayor of Buenos Aires (1996–99) and, as leader of the Alianza coalition, became President of Argentina in 1999. He resigned in 2001 amidst economic crisis.

Delaunay, Robert 1885–1941 •*French painter*• Born in Paris, he abandoned stage design for painting in 1905 and his first works are painted in a colorful divisionist (pointillist) technique. Under the influence of **Cézanne** he subdued his palette, but later returned to high-key color in a series of pictures of Saint-Severin and the Eiffel Tower (c. 1910), by which he is best known. Later he started isolating areas of pure color in his pictures, a method he called Orphism. In 1912 he was visited by members of the Blaue Reiter group, upon whom he was to exert considerable influence, and by 1914 he had become recognized as the most significant painter in Paris.

Delaunay, Sonia Terk, *née* **Stern** 1885–1979 •*French painter and textile designer*• Born in Odessa, Russia (now in Ukraine), she was brought up in St Petersburg, and studied art at Karlsruhe and in Paris. In 1910 she married the French painter **Robert Delaunay** and together they founded the movement known as Orphism. In 1918 they designed sets and costumes for **Sergei Diaghilev**. She was a textile designer of international importance, and her work was included in the Exposition des Arts Décoratifs in 1925.

De la Warr, Thomas West, 3rd or **12th Baron** 1577–1618 •*English soldier and colonist*• After serving under Robert, 2nd Earl of **Essex**, he was appointed the first governor of Virginia in 1610. Returning to England in 1611, he wrote the *Relation* on Virginia. He died on a return voyage to Virginia. The state of Delaware is named after him.

Delbrück, Max 1906–81 •*German biophysicist and Nobel Prize winner*• Born in Berlin, he studied atomic physics at the University of Göttingen. He worked with **Niels Bohr** at Copenhagen University in 1932, moved to Berlin in 1935 to work with **Lise Meitner**, and in 1937 emigrated to the US, where he held appointments at the California Institute of Technology (Caltech). In the 1940s Delbrück began working on the genetics of the phage virus, a simple organism with a protein coat surrounding a coil of DNA. Independently of **A D Hershey**, he discovered in 1946 that viruses can exchange genetic material to create new types of virus, and together with **Salvador Luria** they set up the Phage Group, to encourage the use of phage as an experimental tool. The three were awarded the 1969 Nobel Prize for physiology or medicine for their work in viral genetics.

Deledda, Grazia 1875–1936 •*Italian writer and Nobel Prize winner*• Born on Sardinia, her early work focused on peasant stories of her native island. The lyricism and intensity of novels like *Cenere* (1904, "Ashes"), *L'edera* (1908, "Ivy"), *Marianna Sirca* (1915) and *La madre* (1920, "The Mother") won her a considerable reputation. Her later books left the Sardinian setting, but were similar in style. The posthumous *Cosima* (1937) is autobiographical. She won the 1926 Nobel Prize for literature.

De Leon, Daniel 1852–1914 •*US radical*• Born in Curaçao, in the Netherlands Antilles, the son of a Dutch Jewish surgeon on Dutch colonial military service, he studied in Hildesheim, Germany, and then in Amsterdam, emigrating to the US in 1874. He studied law at Columbia, afterward practicing in Texas, and then lecturing in Latin American diplomacy at Columbia (1883–89). He edited the Socialist Labor Party journal, *The People* (1890–1914), and founded the Socialist Trade and Labor Alliance in 1895. He assisted in the formation of the Industrial Workers of the World (1905), merging it with his Alliance, but broke away from them and founded a rival body, the Workers' International Industrial Union. De Leon wrote several Marxist treatises, including *The Socialist Reconstruction of Society*, and profoundly influenced **Lenin**'s theoretical writings.

de León, Juan Ponce *See* **Ponce de León, Juan**

Deleuze, Gilles 1925–95 •*French philosopher and critic*• Born in Paris, he studied at the Sorbonne and taught philosophy at the University of Vincennes (1969–87) and elsewhere. His work is wide-ranging, encompassing philosophy, literary and art criticism, and writings on the cinema and contemporary culture. His early works include *The Logic of Sense* (1969), and he wrote several collaborations with the philosopher Félix Guattari (1930–92), including *Anti-Oedipus* (1972) and *A Thousand Plateaus* (1980). He committed suicide at age 70.

Delfont (of Stepney), Bernard Delfont, Baron, *originally* **Boris Vinogradsky** 1909–94 •*British theater producer*• Born in Tokmak, Russia, the brother of **Lew Grade**, he moved with his family to Great Britain in 1912. He entered theatrical management in 1941, and during the next 20 years acquired many theatrical properties, notably the London Hippodrome. He acquired control of more than 30 companies, embracing theater, film, television, music and property interests. He also hosted the annual Royal Variety Performance (1958–78) and a record number of West End shows. He was made a life peer in 1976.

Delibes, (Clement Philibert) Léo 1836–91 •*French composer*• Born in St Germain du Val, Sarthe, he studied under **Adolphe Adam** at the Paris Conservatoire, where he was himself appointed Professor of Composition (1881). He enjoyed his greatest success as a composer of such light operas as *Le roi l'a dit* (1873) and *Lakmé* (1883) and with such ballets as *Coppélia* (1870), his most lastingly popular work, and *Sylvia* (1876).

Delilah •*Biblical character*• At the instigation of the Philistines she enticed **Samson** to reveal the secret of his great strength, which was his uncut hair, according to his Nazirite vow. She contrived to cut his hair to weaken him (Judges 16).

Delille, Jacques 1738–1813 •*French poet*• He was born near Aigueperse, Auvergne. His popular verse translation of **Virgil**'s *Georgics* (1769) was praised by **Voltaire**, though his own didactic poem *Les jardins* (1782, "The Gardens") was generally accepted as his masterpiece. The Revolution compelled Delille to leave France, and he traveled in Switzerland and Germany, then to London, where he translated *Paradise Lost*. After his return to France in 1802, he produced a translation of Virgil's *Aeneid* (1804) and several volumes of verse.

Delius, Frederick 1862–1934 •*British composer*• Born in Bradford, Yorkshire, of German-Scandinavian descent, he went to Florida in the US as an orange planter at the age of 20, but studied music in his spare time. He entered the Leipzig Conservatory (1886) where he became a friend of **Edvard Grieg**. After 1890 he lived mainly in France. A prolific composer, he wrote six operas, including *A Village Romeo and Juliet* (1901), and a variety of choral and orchestral works, such as *Appalachia* (1902) and *On Hearing the First Cuckoo in Spring* (1912). By 1924 he was paralyzed and blind from a syphilitic infection, but with the English musician Eric Fenby (1906–97) as his amanuensis from 1928, he produced a group of works, including the complex *A Song of Summer* (1930), *Songs of Farewell* (1930) and *Idyll* (1930–32).

“ ”

It is only that which cannot be expressed otherwise that is worth expressing in music.

1920 "At the Crossroads."

Della Robbia or **Robia, Luca** c. 1400–82 •*Italian sculptor*• He worked in Florence, and between 1431 and 1440 executed, in a warm natural style, ten panels of angels and dancing boys (the Cantoria) for the cathedral there. He also made (1448–67) a bronze door for the sacristy, with ten panels of figures in relief. From 1457 to 1458, he sculpted the marble tomb of the Bishop of Fiesole. He is equally famous for his figures in terra cotta, including medallions and reliefs, and he established a business producing glazed terra cottas.

Deller, Alfred George 1912–79 •*English countertenor*• He was born in Margate, Kent. In 1943, while a member of Canterbury Cathedral Choir, he was heard by **Michael Tippett**, who was looking for a countertenor to sing music by **Henry Purcell**, and arranged his first London concert. In 1947 he began a full-time musical career. He made many recordings of early English songs, notably those of **John Dowland** and Purcell, and in 1950 formed the Deller Consort, a small group of musicians devoted to the authentic performance of early music.

Delors, Jacques 1925– •*French Socialist politician*• Born in Paris, he served as social affairs adviser to Prime Minister Jacques Chaban-Delmas (1969–72). He joined the Socialist Party in 1973 and represented it in the European parliament from 1979, chairing the economic and monetary commission. He served as Minister of Economy and Finance in the **Mitterrand** administration (1981–84). He became President of the European Commission in 1985, a position he held until 1995, when **Jacques Santer** took over. As Commission President, he oversaw significant budgetary reforms and the move toward the removal of all internal barriers in the EC in 1992, with increased powers residing in Brussels. In 1994 he was appointed President of UNESCO's International Commission on Education for the Twenty-First Century.

de los Angeles, Victoria, *originally* **Victoria López Cima** 1923– •*Spanish soprano*• Born in Barcelona, she made her operatic debut at the Liceo Theater, Barcelona, in 1945. She then performed at the Paris Opera and La Scala, Milan (1949), Covent Garden, London (1950), the New York Metropolitan (1951) and subsequently at all the great houses and festivals throughout the world. She notably portrayed Carmen, Dido, **Puccini**'s heroines, **Mozart** roles, and Elisabeth in *Tannhäuser*, and was an exponent of Spanish songs. After retiring from the stage in 1969 she carried on giving recitals.

del Piombo, Sebastiano *See* **Sebastiano del Piombo**

del Sarto, Andrea *See* **Sarto, Andrea del**

Delvaux, Paul 1897–1994 •*Belgian surrealist painter*• Born in Antheit, he lived mainly in Brussels, where he exhibited mainly Neoimpressionist and Expressionist pictures until 1935. He was influenced by **Giorgio de Chirico** and **René Magritte**, and produced a series of paintings depicting nude and seminude girls in dreamlike settings (eg, *The Call of the Night*).

Demades c. 380–319 BC •*Athenian politician*• A bitter enemy of **Demosthenes**, he supported **Philip II** of Macedon, and after the Battle of Chaeronea (338 BC) secured an honorable peace. He also secured lenient treatment for Athens after the revolt of 335. In 332 Demades arranged the death of Demosthenes and his followers, but was himself executed by Cascander, the son of Antipater.

Demarco, Richard 1930– •*Scottish artist, broadcaster and teacher*• Born in Edinburgh, he studied there at the College of Art (1949–53). He has been a leading promoter of modern art in Scotland, including the work of such international figures as **Joseph Beuys**, especially at the Edinburgh Festival since 1967, and has presented annual programs of theater, music and dance. He was cofounder of the Traverse Theatre Club, director (1966–92) of the Richard Demarco Gallery, and since 1993 has been Professor of European Cultural Studies at Kingston University.

Demetrius *See* **Dmitri**

de Mille, Agnes George 1905–93 •*US dancer, choreographer and writer*• Born in New York City, she went to London and danced with **Marie Rambert**'s company in the original production of **Antony Tudor**'s *Dark Elegies* (1937). *Three Virgins and a Devil* (1941) marked her breakthrough into choreography and she went on to choreograph for such hit musicals as *Oklahoma!* (1943), *Carousel* (1945), *Brigadoon* (1947) and *Paint Your Wagon* (1951). She was also known for her wit and eloquent public speaking, and her contribution to television and film. She was the niece of the film director **Cecil B De Mille**.

De Mille, Cecil B(lount) 1881–1959 •*US film producer and director*• Born in Ashfield, Massachusetts, he acted on the stage and wrote unsuccessful plays before discovering Hollywood with **Samuel Goldwyn** (with whom he founded Paramount Films) as a suitable place for shooting the first US feature film, *The Squaw Man* (1914). With the **Gloria Swanson** comedy, *Male and Female* (1919), he became the most "advanced" of US film directors. His box-office spectacles included *The Ten Commandments* (1923), *The Sign of the Cross* (1932), *Reap the Wild Wind* (1942) and *The Greatest Show on Earth* (1952, Academy Award). A notable exception to the usual formula of a high moral theme enlivened by physical violence and sex was the filmed Passion Play, *King of Kings* (1927). He also organized the first commercial passenger airline service in the US in 1917.

Demirel, Suleyman 1924– •*Turkish politician*• Born in Islam Köy, he qualified as an engineer at Istanbul Technical University and worked on hydroelectric projects in the US and Turkey. In 1964 he became president of the centrist Justice Party (JP), now subsumed in the True Path Party (TPP). He served three terms as Prime Minister from 1965, until a military coup in 1980 resulted in a three-year ban on political activity. He was placed in detention and banned from participating in politics for ten years, but was released in 1983. However, Demirel was not prevented from forming the True Path Party, and when **Turgut Özal**'s party lost in the 1991 elections, Demirel became Prime Minister (1991–93), then President (1993–2000).

Demme, Jonathan 1944– •*US film director, producer and writer*• Born in Rockville Center, New York, he studied at the University of Florida. He began his career as a film critic and later worked as a screenwriter and producer on films such as *The Hot Box* (1974) and *Caged Heat* (1974). Subsequent films as a director included *Melvin and Howard* (1980), *The Silence of the Lambs* (1992), *Philadelphia* (1993) and *Beloved* (1998).

Democritus c. 460–c. 370 BC •*Greek philosopher*• Born in Abdera, Thrace, he was one of the most prolific of ancient authors, publishing many works on ethics, physics, mathematics, cosmology and music, but only fragments of his writings (on ethics) survive. He is best known for his physical speculations, and in particular for the atom theory he developed from **Leucippus**, whereby the world consists of an infinite number of everlasting atoms whose different characteristics and random combinations account for the different properties and qualities of everything in the world. Supposedly known as "the laughing philosopher" in the ancient world because of his wry amusement at human foibles, he was an important influence on **Epicurus** and **Lucretius**.

" "

Nothing exists except atoms and empty space; everything else is opinion.
Diogenes Laertius, *vol. 9.*

de Moivre, Abraham *See* **Moivre, Abraham de**

Demosthenes d. 413 BC •*Athenian soldier*• During the Peloponnesian War (431–404 BC) he captured Anacterium (425) and helped assist **Cleon** in capturing a body of Spartan troops on the island of Sphacteria, but failed to conquer Boeotia in 424. In 413, having been sent to Sicily to relieve **Nicias**, he was captured by the Syracusans during a brave rearguard action and was put to death.

Demosthenes 384–322 BC •*Athenian orator and statesman who opposed the Macedonians*• He was born in Athens and took up law as a profession. Up to the age of 30 he confined himself to speechwriting for others, and gained a reputation as a constitutional lawyer. He did not embark on his political career until 351 BC, around which time the Greek cities were under threat from **Philip II** of Macedon; Demosthenes from the outset advocated a policy of total resistance. Philip's attack on the northern state of Olynthus gave rise to the *Olynthiacs* (349), which, with the orations against Philip called the *Philippics* (351, 334 and 341), are Demosthenes' greatest speeches. When war broke out in 340 and ended in the fatal Battle of Chaeronea (338), in which Athens and her allies were totally defeated, the Macedonian Party in Athens seized on a proposal to present Demosthenes with a gold crown as a means of publicly discrediting him. The trial was held in 330, when in the famous speech *On the Crown* Demosthenes gloriously vindicated himself against his political opponent, **Aeschines**. Meanwhile, in

336 **Alexander the Great** had succeeded his father Philip to the Macedonian throne. In 324 Harpalus, Alexander's treasurer, absconded to Athens with an enormous sum of money. It was placed in the state treasury under the care of Demosthenes and others, and when Alexander demanded it, half was missing. Demosthenes was accused and condemned, but escaped from prison into exile. In 323 Alexander died, and Demosthenes was recalled to head a fruitless attempt to throw off the Macedonian yoke. The Battle of Crannon ended the revolt; sentenced to death, Demosthenes fled to the island of Calauria, where he took poison.

Dempsey, (William Harrison) Jack, *nicknamed* **the Manassa Mauler** 1895–1983 •*US boxer*• Born in Manassa, Colorado, he worked in copper mines before taking to the ring as "Kid Blackie" in 1914. In 1919 he defeated Jess Willard to win the world heavyweight title, which he lost to Gene Tunney in 1926. In a controversial rematch the following year, he knocked Tunney down but was himself too dazed to retire promptly to his corner, and so delayed the count; Tunney struggled to his feet and went on to win the fight on points. Dempsey retired from the ring, but briefly made a comeback in the early 1930s, and became a successful restaurateur on Broadway in New York.

Dench, Dame Judi(th Olivia) 1934– •*English actress*• She was born in York and studied at the Central School of Speech and Drama, London. She made her stage debut as Ophelia in *Hamlet* (1957) with the Old Vic Company, with whom she remained until 1961. She is one of Great Britain's most distinguished classical actresses, and her distinctive voice and versatility have brought warmth and emotional veracity to a kaleidoscope of characters from the sensual to the homely. Her television credits include many individual plays and the popular sitcom *A Fine Romance* (1981–84) in which she costarred with Michael Williams (1935–2001), her husband since 1971. She made her film debut in *The Third Secret* (1964) but has only recently become a regular film performer, with incisive character parts in *A Room With a View* (1985) and *Henry V* (1989). In 1999, she won the Best Supporting Actress Academy Award for her role as Elizabeth I in *Shakespeare in Love*. She has played "M" in James Bond films since 1995. Other film work includes *Mrs Brown* (1997), *Chocolat* (2001), and *Iris* (2001). She was given the honorary title of Dame Commander, Order of the British Empire, in 1988 and made her directorial debut in the same year with a production of *Much Ado About Nothing* for **Kenneth Branagh**'s Renaissance Theatre Company.

Deneuve, Catherine, *originally* **Catherine Dorléac** 1943– •*French actress*• Born in Paris, she made her film debut in *Les collégiennes* (1956), but her career only took off in 1964, with the unexpected popularity of the musical *Les parapluies de Cherbourg* (*The Umbrellas of Cherbourg*). Her image of exterior calm concealing passion or intrigue were seen to great effect as a psychopath in *Repulsion* (1965) and a bourgeois housewife turned prostitute in *Belle de jour* (1967, "Lady of the Day"). Her other successes include *Tristana* (1970), *La sauvage* (1975, *The Savage*) and *Le dernier métro* (1980, "The Last Metro"). She received a Best Actress Academy Award nomination for *Indochine* (1992). Recent films include *Les voleurs* (1996) and *Dancer in the Dark* (2000). She was married to the photographer **David Bailey** from 1965 to 1970, has a child by director Roger Vadim (1928–2000), born in 1963, and a daughter by actor **Marcello Mastroianni** called Chiara (1972–), who is also an actress.

Deng Xiaoping (Teng Hsiao-p'ing), *originally* **Deng Xixian** 1904–97 •*Chinese Communist politician*• Born in Sichuan (Szechuan) Province into a middle-class landlord family, he joined the Chinese Communist Party (CCP) in 1925 as a student in Paris, where he met a fellow student, **Zhou Enlai**, and adopted the name Xiaoping ("Little Peace"). He later studied in Moscow (1926) where he became associated with **Mao Zedong**. He took part in the Long March (1934–36) and served as a political commissar to the People's Liberation Army (PLA) during the civil war (1937–49). In 1954 he became Secretary-General of the CCP, but reacted strongly to the excesses of the Great Leap Forward (1958–59). During Mao's 1966–69 Cultural Revolution he was criticized and purged, but was rehabilitated by Zhou Enlai in 1974, becoming vice premier. After Zhou died in 1976, he became the dominant figure in Chinese politics. Working with his protégés **Hu Yaobang** and **Zhao Ziyang** he proceeded to introduce a pragmatic new economic modernization program. Despite retiring from the politburo in 1987, he remained influential. He attempted to create a "socialism with Chinese characteristics," but his reputation was tarnished by his sanctioning of the army's massacre of around 3,000 unarmed prodemocracy demonstrators in Tiananmen Square, Beijing (Peking), in June 1989.

Denham, Sir John 1615–69 •*Irish poet*• Born in Dublin, he was educated in London and at Trinity College, Oxford, and was called to the bar in 1639. At the outbreak of the English Civil War he immediately joined the king, and on the capture of Farnham Castle, Sir **William Waller** sent him as a prisoner to London, but he was soon freed and went to Oxford. In 1641 he produced *The Sophy*, a historical tragedy of the Turkish court, and in 1642 he published a long poem, *Cooper's Hill*, a description of the scenery around Egham, which **Pope** imitated in his *Windsor Forest*. Being discovered in secret services for **Charles I** in 1648, he fled to Holland and France, but returned several times for further secret missions. At the Restoration he was appointed Surveyor General of works, with **Christopher Wren** as his deputy, and in 1661 he was created a Knight of the Bath.

De Niro, Robert 1943– •*US film actor*• Born in New York City, he worked off-Broadway before attracting critical attention as the baseball player in the film *Bang the Drum Slowly* (1973), and winning an Academy Award for Best Supporting Actor for *The Godfather, Part II* (1974). He has become noted for his versatility and authenticity of characterization. His films made with **Martin Scorsese** include *Taxi Driver* (1976), *Raging Bull* (1980), for which he won a Best Actor Academy Award, and *Casino* (1995). Other films include *The Deer Hunter* (1978), *Awakenings* (1990), *Cape Fear* (1991), *Heat* (1995), *Meet the Parents* (2000) and *City by the Sea* (2002). He made his directorial debut with *The Bronx Tale* (1994).

Denis or **Denys, St**, *properly* **Dionysius** 3rd century AD •*Italian cleric and patron saint of France*• Born probably in Rome, he was sent from Rome about AD 250 to preach the Gospel to the Gauls, and became the first Bishop of Paris. Under the persecutions of the emperor **Valerian** (reigned 253–60) he was beheaded on Montmartre ("Martyrs' Hill"). Later his legend was confused with that of **Dionysius the Areopagite**, and he was supposed to have carried his own head to his burial place, the site of the abbey church of Saint-Denys. His feast day is October 9.

Denis, Maurice 1870–1943 •*French artist and art theorist*• Born in Grandville, he was one of the original group of Symbolist painters, and then of the Nabis ("prophets"), influenced by **Gauguin**. His comments on the aesthetics of the modern movement have obtained a wide currency. He wrote *Théories* (1912), *Nouvelles théories* (1921, "New Theories") and *Histoire de l'art religieux* (1939, "History of Religious Art"). In 1919 he helped found, with George-Olivier Desvallières (1861–1950), the Studios of Sacred Art, devoted to the revival of religious painting. His most famous picture is perhaps the *Hommage à Cézanne* (1900) in the Musée d'Art Moderne, Paris.

“ ”

Remember that a painting—before it is a battlehorse, a nude woman, or some anecdote—is essentially a flat surface covered with colors assembled in a certain order.

*1912 **Théories**.*

Denison, Edmund Beckett *See* **Grimthorpe, 1st Baron**

Denman, Lady Gertrude Mary, *née* **Pearson** 1884–1954 •*English founder of the National Federation of Women's Institutes*• Born in London and educated privately, she married Thomas, 3rd Baron Denman (1874–1954) in 1903, and accompanied him when he was appointed Governor-General of Australia in 1911. Following their return to Great Britain, she chaired a subcommittee of the Agricultural Organization Society (1915), which that year had founded the Women's Institutes. When the institutes were transferred to the Board of Agriculture in 1917, she insisted they should be self-governing, and the National Federation of Women's Institutes was formed, with herself as chairman until 1946. She was also involved in the foundation of the National Birth Control (later Family Planning) Association.

Dennett, Daniel Clement 1942– •*US philosopher and author*• Born in Boston, he was educated at Harvard and Oxford Universities. He taught at the University of California, Irvine (1965–71), and has since worked chiefly as a Professor of Philosophy and Director of the Center for Cognitive Studies at Tufts University. His influential writings on the mind have included the books *Brainstorms* (1978), *Consciousness Explained* (1991), *Darwin's Dangerous Idea* (1995) and *Brainchildren* (1998), a collection of essays.

Denning (of Whitchurch), Alfred Thompson Denning, Baron 1899–1999 •*English judge*• He was educated at Andover Grammar School and Magdalen College, Oxford. Called to the bar in 1923, he became a King's Counsel (1938), a judge of the High Court of Justice (1944), a Lord Justice of Appeal (1948), Lord-of-Appeal-in-Ordinary (1957) and Master of the Rolls (1962–82). In 1963 he held the inquiry into the circumstances of **John Profumo**'s resignation as Secretary of State for War and was responsible for many controversial decisions. Among his many legal publications are *The Road to Justice* (1955), *What Next in the Law* (1982), and several autobiographical books.

Denny, Robyn 1930– •*English painter*• Born in Abinger, Surrey, he studied in Paris and in London at St Martin's School of Art and the Royal College of Art. In 1959 he helped organize the exhibition *Place* in London's Institute of Contemporary Arts, and the following year he was responsible for two more "situation" exhibitions, aimed at bypassing dealers and promoting abstract art. Inspired by US abstract artists, his paintings are symmetrical and subtle in color; they include *Baby Is Three* (1960), *First Light* (1965–66) and *Garden* (1966–67), all owned by the Tate Collection, London.

Dent, Joseph Malaby 1849–1926 •*English publisher*• He worked as a bookbinder in London before opening his own bookbinding business in 1892. In 1888 he founded the publishing house of J M Dent & Sons, which brought out the pocket-sized *Temple Classics* from 1893, and also *Everyman's Library* from 1906.

Denys, St *See* **Denis, St**

Depardieu, Gérard 1948– •*French film actor*• Born in Châteauroux, he was an unruly child, and was encouraged to act as therapy. He made his film debut in *Le beatnik et le minet* (1965, "The Beatnik and the Pussy Cat"), and his imposing physique and peasant's looks were seen in an increasing variety of roles as he gained a reputation as one of the most versatile and skilled actors of his generation. Able to combine strength and gentleness, he has appeared in many films, including *Le dernier métro* (1980, "The Last Metro"), *Danton* (1982), *Le retour de Martin Guerre* (1982, *The Return of Martin Guerre*), *Jean De Florette* (1986), *Cyrano de Bergerac* (1990) and *Germinal* (1993). His first English-speaking role was in *Green Card* (1990). He also directed *Le Tartuffe* (1984). Later films include *Hamlet* (1996), *The Man in the Iron Mask* (1998), *Asterix et Obelix contre César* (1999) and *Le Placard* (2001, *The Closet*).

De Paul, St Vincent *See* **Vincent de Paul, St**

Depp, Johnny (John Christopher) 1963– •*US actor*• Born in Owensboro, Kentucky, he studied at the Loft Studio, Los Angeles, and played in a rock group, the Kids, before settling on a career in acting. His starring roles have tended toward the outlandish, in films such as *Edward Scissorhands* (1990), *What's Eating Gilbert Grape* (1993), and *Ed Wood* (1994), and he received an Academy Award nomination for Best Actor for *Pirates of the Caribbean* (2003). He wrote and directed *The Brave* (1997).

Depretis, Agostino 1813–87 •*Italian politician*• A friend of both **Garibaldi** and **Giuseppe Mazzini**, he broke with the latter after the abortive Milanese insurrection of 1853. He played a key part in the Expedition of the Thousand to Sicily in 1860, serving for a while as the island's "prodictator." Although he began his parliamentary career on the political left, he abandoned his earlier radicalism and achieved ministerial office in 1862 and 1866. He was to be Prime Minister for all but two years between 1876 and 1887 and became the archexponent of "trasformismo" (the practice of forming alliances in parliament, almost regardless of political ideology, in order to guarantee a government majority). He played a key part in steering Italy toward the Triple Alliance with Germany and Austria-Hungary (1882).

De Priest, Oscar Stanton 1871–1951 •*US politician*• Born in Alabama, he ran away from home to Chicago where he was the first African American to be elected to the city council (as a Republican in 1915). He became the first African-American congressman from the North in 1928. Holding office until 1934, when he was defeated by an African-American Democrat, he secured passage for a bill to reduce discrimination in the Civilian Conservation Corps.

De Quincey, Thomas 1785–1859 •*English critic and essayist*• Born in Manchester, he was educated at Manchester Grammar School, but in 1802 ran away and wandered in Wales, and then to London, where he lived with a young prostitute called Ann. He later described this experience in his *Confessions of an English Opium-Eater* (1822). He then spent a short time at Worcester College, Oxford, and it was here that he became addicted to opium. A visit to his mother in Bath brought him into contact with **Coleridge**, and through him with **Robert Southey** and **Wordsworth**. When these poets settled in the Lake District, De Quincey visited them there and went to stay in Grasmere in 1809. Except for *The Logic of Political Economy* (1841) and an unsuccessful novel, his whole literary output, including the *Confessions*, consisted of magazine articles. The *Confessions* appeared in 1821 as a serial in *The London Magazine*, and at once made him famous. In 1828 the lure of the Edinburgh literary scene drew him to the northern capital, where he lived and worked until his death. For 20 years he lent distinction to various periodicals with articles like *Murder Considered as One of the Fine Arts* (1827), *Lake Reminiscences* (1834–40) and *Vision of Sudden Death* (1849).

“ ”

A duller spectacle this earth of ours has not to show than a rainy Sunday in London.

1822 ***Confessions of an English Opium-Eater.***

Derain, André 1880–1954 •*French artist*• Born in Chatou, he is most famous for his Fauve pictures, executed from 1904 to 1908, when he was associated with **Maurice de Vlaminck** and **Henri Matisse**. Later landscape pictures show a romantic realism influenced by **Cézanne**. He also designed for the theater (notably the **Diaghilev** ballet) and illustrated several books.

Derby, Edward George Geoffrey Smith Stanley, 14th Earl of 1799–1869 •*English statesman*• Born at Knowsley Hall, Lancashire, he was educated at Eton and Christ Church, Oxford, and entered parliament for Stockbridge in 1820. In 1830 he became Chief Secretary for Ireland and in 1833 Colonial Secretary. In this capacity he carried the emancipation of West Indian slaves. In 1831 he seceded from the Whigs and maintained an independent position. In 1844 he resigned his seat in the House of Commons and went to the House of Lords as Baron Stanley of Bickerstaffe. When Peel attempted to repeal the Corn Laws, Stanley headed the Protectionists in the Upper House and was seen as Conservative leader. In 1851 he succeeded his father as Earl of Derby and briefly became Prime Minister. He returned as premier in 1858, but resigned the following year on a vote of no confidence. Returning to power in 1866, he passed the Reform Act of 1867 in conjunction with **Disraeli**, to whom he passed the premiership in 1868.

Derby, James Stanley, 7th Earl of, *known as* **the Great Earl of Derby** 1606–51 •*English soldier*• He fought on the Royalist side throughout the English Civil War. After the Battle of Worcester in 1651, he helped **Charles II** to escape but was captured by the Parliamentary forces and beheaded at Bolton. His wife, Countess Charlotte de la Trémouille (d. 1663), is famous for her heroic defense of Lathom House (1644) and of the Isle of Man (1651).

de Ribera, Jusepe *See* **Ribera, Jusepe de**

Deringer, Henry 1786–1868 •*US manufacturer of small arms*• Born in Easton, Philadelphia, he supplied rifles to the US Army, and in 1852 invented the pocket pistol known as a "der(r)inger."

Dern, Laura Elizabeth 1967– •*US actress*• Born in Santa Monica, California, the daughter of the actors Bruce Dern and Diane Ladd, she studied drama at the Lee Strasberg Institute and at the Royal Academy of Dramatic Art. Her early films included striking performances in *Blue Velvet* (1987) and *Wild at Heart* (1990); subsequent films include *Jurassic Park* (1993) and *Novocaine* (2001).

Dernesch, Helga 1939– •*Austrian soprano*• Born in Vienna, where she studied at the Conservatory, she made her debut in Bern in 1961 and at Covent Garden, London, in 1970. She has sung throughout Europe and the US, and is especially noted for her portrayals of **Wagner**, **Strauss** and the modern German repertory. Since 1979 she has sung mezzo-soprano roles.

de Rojas, Fernando *See* **Rojas, Fernando de**

Derrida, Jacques 1930– •*French philosopher*• Born in El Biar, Algeria, he studied in Paris and taught at the Sorbonne (1960–64) and at the École Normale Supérieure (1965–84). His work is highly original and has attracted great interest in the English-speaking world, spanning literary criticism, psychoanalysis and linguistics as well as philosophy. He stresses the primacy of the written over the spoken text ("there is nothing outside the text") and founded the school of criticism known as "deconstruction." Among his works are the influential *La voix et le phénomène* (1967, Eng trans *Speech and Phenomena*, 1967), *De la grammatologie* (1967, "Of Grammatology") and *L'écriture et la différence* (1967, "Writing and Difference"). His later publications include *La vérité en peinture* (1978, "Truth in Painting"), *La carte postale* (1980, "The Postcard") and *Aporias* (1994).

de Ruyter, Michiel Adriaanszoon *See* **Ruyter, Michiel Adriaanszoon de**

der Weyden, Rogier van *See* **Weyden, Rogier van der**

Derzhavin, Gavril Romanovich 1743–1816 •*Russian poet*• Born in Kazan, he joined the army as a private in 1762, but rose to officer rank, was transferred to the Civil Service, and later to governorships. In 1802 he became Minister of Justice. He published a variety of original and imaginative lyric poetry on many subjects, both personal and public, and is considered one of Russia's greatest poets.

Desai, Anita, *née* **Mazumbar** 1937– •*Indian novelist*• Born in Mussoorie, Uttar Pradesh, the daughter of a Bengali father and a German mother, she was educated at the University of Delhi. Her works include novels for adults and children, and short stories. *Clear Light of Day* (1980) and *In Custody* (1984) were both shortlisted for the Booker Prize and *The Village by the Sea* won the Guardian award for children's fiction in 1982. More recently she published *Journey to Ithaca* (1995), was again shortlisted for the Booker Prize with *Fasting, Feasting* (1999), and published *Diamond Dust and Other Stories* (2000).

Desai, Morarji Ranchhodji 1896–1995 •*Indian politician*• Born in Gujarat and educated at the University of Bombay, he was a civil servant for 12 years before embarking on a long and varied political career. He joined Congress in 1930, but was twice imprisoned as a supporter of **Mahatma Gandhi**'s Civil Disobedience Campaign before serving in the Bombay government (1937–39). He was again imprisoned (1941–45) for his part in the "Quit India" movement, before returning to government posts in Bombay. He then entered central government, and was a candidate for the premiership in 1964 and again in 1966, when he was defeated by **Indira Gandhi**. Deputy premier and Minister of Finance in her administration, Desai resigned in 1968 over differences with the premier. In 1974 he supported political agitation in Gujarat, and the following year began a fast in support of elections in the state, being detained when a state of emergency was proclaimed. After his release in 1977 he was appointed leader of the Janata Party, a coalition opposed to Mrs Gandhi's rule, and he finally became Prime Minister after the elections that same year. The Janata government was, however, characterized by much internal strife, and Desai was forced to resign in 1979.

Desalvo, Albert, *also known as* **the Boston Strangler** 1931–73 •*US sex offender*• Born in Chelsea, Massachusetts, he was arrested in late 1964 for sex attacks on women in their homes. He then confessed to a psychiatrist that he was the Boston Strangler, who had murdered and sexually assaulted 13 women between 1962 and 1964 in Boston. He was never tried for the murders, because under Massachusetts law a doctor who receives information from a suspect cannot use it as evidence. He was sentenced to life imprisonment for his other crimes. In 1973 he was found stabbed to death in his cell in Walpole (now Cedar Junction) Prison, Massachusetts.

Desani, Govindas Vishnoodas 1909–2000 •*US novelist*• Born in Nairobi, Kenya, he went to Great Britain in 1926 and from 1928 was a correspondent for the *Times of India*, Reuters, and Associated Press. He was a broadcaster during World War II. From 1952 to 1966 he visited Buddhist and Hindu monasteries, studying yoga and meditation. Throughout the 1960s he filed a provocative column with the *Illustrated Weekly for India*. He was a US citizen from 1979. His prose-poem *Hali* (1950) and some uncollected stories notwithstanding, his claim to posterity is dependent on *All About H Hatterr* (1948), now recognized as a modern classic.

Desargues, Gérard 1591–1661 •*French mathematician*• Born in Lyons, he was in Paris by 1626, and he took part as an engineer in the Siege of La Rochelle in 1628. He founded the use of projective methods in geometry, inspired by the theory of perspective in art, and introduced the idea that parallel lines "meet at a point at infinity." His style of writing and a reluctance to publicize his ideas greatly hindered their reception, and mostly they were independently rediscovered by others.

Descartes, René 1596–1650 •*French philosopher and mathematician*• He was born near Tours in a small town now called La-Haye-Descartes, and was educated from 1604 to 1614 at the Jesuit College at La Flèche. He remained a Catholic all his life, and he was careful to modify or even suppress some of his later scientific views, for example his sympathy with **Nicolaus Copernicus**, no doubt aware of **Galilei**'s condemnation by the Inquisition in 1634. He was in Germany with the army of the Duke of Bavaria one winter's day in 1619 when he had his famous intellectual vision in the "stove-heated room": he conceived a reconstruction of the whole of philosophy, and indeed of knowledge, into a unified system of certain truth modeled on mathematics and supported by a rigorous rationalism. Descartes's more popular works were published in French, the more scholarly ones first in Latin. The *Discours de la méthode* (1637, "Discourse on Method"), the *Meditationes de prima philosophia* (1641, "Mediations on First Philosophy") and the *Principia philosophiae* (1644, "Principles of Philosophy") set out the fundamental Cartesian doctrines: the method of systematic doubt; the first indubitably true proposition, *je pense, donc je suis* or *cogito ergo sum* ("I think, therefore I am"); the idea of God as the absolutely perfect Being; and the dualism of mind and matter. In 1649 he left Holland for Stockholm at the invitation of Queen **Kristina**, who wanted him to tutor her in philosophy. These lessons took place three times a week at 5 am and were especially taxing for Descartes, whose habit of a lifetime was to stay in bed meditating and reading until about 11 am. He contracted pneumonia and died. His last words were supposedly, *A mon âme, il faut partir* ("So my soul, a time for parting"). He was buried in Stockholm but his body was later removed to Paris and eventually transferred to Saint-Germain-des-Prés.

Deschamps, Eustache, *known as* **Morel** c. 1345–c. 1406 •*French poet*• He was born in Vertus, Champagne. A soldier, a magistrate, a court favorite, and a traveler, he held important posts in Champagne, but after his patron, **Charles V**, died, his possessions were ravaged by the English. He composed 1,175 lyrics, besides *Le miroir de mariage* ("The Mirror of Marriage," a long poem satirizing women), two dramatic works, and several poems deploring the miseries of the Hundred Years War. He is known to have influenced **Chaucer**.

" "

Rien ne se peut comparer à Paris.
Nothing can compare to Paris.

c. 1370 "Ballade de Paris," refrain.

De Sica, Vittorio 1902–74 •*Italian actor and film director*• Born in Sera, he graduated from the University of Rome and established himself as a romantic star of stage and screen in the 1930s before turning to direction (1940). In the immediate postwar years he was at the forefront of the neorealist movement, depicting the social problems of battle-ravaged Italy with compassion and sensitivity in films like *Sciuscia* (1946, *Shoeshine*), *Ladri di biciclette* (1948, *Bicycle Thieves*) and *Umberto D* (1952). Later films tended to be more lighthearted, although with *La ciociara* (1960, *Two Women*) and *Il giardino dei Finzi Contini* (1970, *The Garden of the Finzi Continis*) he returned to the subject of earlier triumphs.

De Sitter, Willem *See* **Sitter, Willem de**

Desmarets, Jean, Sieur de Saint-Sorlen 1596–1676 •*French writer*• Born in Paris, he was a protégé of Cardinal **Richelieu** and wrote many volumes of poetry and critical works, notably *Comparaison de la langue et la poésie française avec la grecque et la latine* (1670, "Comparison of French Language and Poetry with Greek and Latin"). His play *Les visionnaires* (1637, "The Visionaries") was a great success, and he also wrote two verse epics and a novel on biblical and classical themes. He was the first chancellor and a cofounder of the Académie Française.

Desmoulins, Camille 1760–94 •*French revolutionary and journalist*• Born in Guise, he studied law as a fellow student of **Robespierre**. He wrote on classical republicanism in his pamphlets, *La philosophie du peuple français* (1788) and *La France libre* (1789), and took part in the destruction of the Bastille. In November 1789 he began the witty, sarcastic *Révolutions de France et de Brabant* which appeared weekly until July 1792. Desmoulins had been a member of the Cordeliers' Club from its foundation, and was close to **Danton**. In the struggle between the Girondins and Danton he took an active part, but in late 1793 he published the *Vieux cordelier* ("Old Franciscan Friar"), an eloquent expression of his and Danton's longing for clemency. Robespierre took fright at its reception, and soon became actively hostile. On March 30, 1794, Desmoulins was arrested with Danton; on April 5 he was guillotined. A fortnight later his wife, Lucile Duplessis (1771–1794), was also executed.

de Soto, Hernando *See* **Soto, Hernando de**

Despard, Charlotte, *née* **French** 1844–1939 •*English social reformer*• A sister of **John French** (1st Earl of Ypres), she was an advocate of women's rights and Irish self-determination. Her politics seriously embarrassed her brother during his viceroyalty of Ireland.

Despenser, Hugh, Earl of Winchester 1262–1326 •*English baron*• He became chief adviser to **Edward II** after the death of Piers de Gaveston (c. 1284–1312), but was banished with his son, Hugh (1321). Recalled the next year by Edward II, he was created Earl of Winchester. After Queen **Isabella** of France's landing in England (1326), he was captured by the queen's party and hanged at Bristol; his son was hanged at Hereford.

Despréaux, Boileau *See* **Boileau, Nicolas**

Dessalines, Jean Jacques c. 1758–1806 •*Emperor of Haiti*• Born in Guinea, he was imported into the French West Indian colony of Saint-Domingue (Haiti) as a slave and was bought by a French planter, whose name he assumed. In the slave revolt of 1791 he was second only to **Toussaint Louverture**. He became governor of the southern part of the island, but after the arrest of Toussaint (1802), compelled the French to evacuate Saint-Domingue (1803). He was created governor in 1804, and in October of that year was crowned emperor of an independent Haiti as Jean Jacques I. However, his cruelty, especially against whites and mulattos, and his debauchery soon alienated even his firmest adherents, and while trying to repress a revolt he was cut down by **Henri Christophe**, who succeeded him.

Dessau, Paul 1894–1979 •*German composer and conductor*• Born in Hamburg, he studied in Berlin, after which he became an opera coach. He conducted opera at Cologne from 1919, Mainz from 1923 and the Berlin State Opera from 1925. During the Nazi era he moved to Paris (1933) and the US (1939). From 1942 he collaborated with **Bertolt Brecht**. He settled in 1948 in East Berlin, where he produced operas such as *Die Verurteilung des Lukullus* (1949, "The Trial of Lucullus," text by Brecht) and other compositions, which all show dramatic inventiveness and socialist commitment.

de Torres, Luis Vaez *See* **Torres, Luis Vaez de**

Dettori, Frankie (Lanfranco) 1970– •*Italian jockey*• Born in Milan, the son of a famous jockey, he had his first British win in 1987. A year later he became the first teenager since **Lester Piggott** to ride 100 winners in a season. He was Champion Jockey in 1994 and 1995 and the following year achieved the unparalleled feat of winning all seven races on the card at Ascot. His most notable victories have included The Oaks (1994 and 1995), the St Leger (1995 and 1996), the Prix de l'Arc de Triomphe (1995 and 2001), the One Thousand Guineas (1998) and the Two Thousand Guineas (1999). In 2000 he was given the honorary title Member, Order of the British Empire.

de Valera, Éamon 1882–1975 •*Irish statesman*• He was born in Brooklyn, New York, of Spanish-Irish parentage. He was brought up in Bruree, County Limerick, by a laborer uncle, and became a mathematics teacher. Taking up Irish, he joined the Gaelic League, and under the influence of **Thomas MacDonagh** he rose in the Irish Volunteers, leading his men into action in the Easter Rising of 1916. The sentence of execution imposed on him after his court-martial was commuted through the intervention of the US consul. After his release from jail (1917), he was elected Member of Parliament for East Clare, and became the focus of nationalist opposition to conscription (1918). He was again arrested, an act that helped his Sinn Fein Party achieve a massive electoral victory (1918). After a sensational escape, he toured the US as President of the Irish Republic (actually of Dáil Éireann, the secret assembly of Irish Members of Parliament refusing participation at Westminster), 1919–20. He drew in massive funds and moral support. Meanwhile, guerrilla warfare had exploded in Ireland without him, and on his return he was believed a more moderate influence than **Michael Collins**, but ultimately Collins signed the Anglo-Irish Treaty of 1921 and incurred de Valera's anger. Narrow victory for the treaty in the Dáil led de Valera to resign as President. He played only a symbolic part in the antitreaty effort during the civil war (1922–23), but was ultimately imprisoned (1923–24) and in 1926 formed a Republican Opposition party which entered the Irish Free State Dáil (1927), and which brought him to power there in 1932. He severed most of the remaining constitutional links with Great Britain and introduced a new constitution (1937) under which his prime ministerial title was altered to *taoiseach* (to which he was reelected until 1948, and then again in 1951 and 1957). In international affairs he pursued neutrality, all the more because of antidemocratic threats from Right and Left. In 1959 he resigned his position as taoiseach and was elected president (1959–1973).

“ ”

Why doesn't he use a spoon?

1921 On being told that David Lloyd George had said talking to him was like trying to pick up mercury with a fork.

DeVito, Danny 1944– •*US actor*• Born in Asbury Park, New Jersey, he worked as a hairdresser in his sister's beauty parlor before enrolling at the American Academy of Dramatic Arts in New York City. He played small roles in films like *One Flew Over the Cuckoo's Nest* (1975) before starring as a petty tyrant in the television show *Taxi* (1978–83). He made a return to film as a character actor and became a popular comic star in films like *Ruthless People* (1986), *Batman Returns* (1992), in which he played the Penguin, and *L A Confidential* (1997). He has also directed such films as *The War of the Roses* (1989) and *Hoffa* (1992). His company, Jersey Films, has been behind such films as *Pulp Fiction* (1994) and *Erin Brockovich* (2000), which earned an Academy Award nomination for Best Picture.

Devlin, Joseph 1871–1934 •*Irish nationalist*• Born in Belfast to working-class Catholic parents, he was educated by the Christian Brothers. With Irish nationalist politics in disarray following the **Parnell** divorce case, he established himself in the Irish Party under John Redmond and **John Dillon** and also made use of his presidency (1905–1934) of the Ancient Order of Hibernians to consolidate his leading role among Belfast nationalists. He was returned unopposed as Member of Parliament for North Kilkenny in 1902 and went on to win West Belfast in 1906. Although support had grown for Sinn Fein elsewhere in Ireland, in the 1918 election Ulster Catholics continued to support the Irish Party, and Devlin defeated **Éamon de Valera** to win the Falls division of Belfast, a seat he held until 1922. The Northern Ireland Settlement of 1920 resulted in a Protestant Unionist majority in Ulster politics. Devlin oscillated between ostracism of, and ineffectual opposition to, the new sub-state, but he remained the political and economic leader of Catholics within it, as was shown by his representation in the Stormont parliament at various times of Armagh, Tyrone, Fermanagh and Catholic Belfast.

Devoy, John 1842–1928 •*US journalist and Irish nationalist*• Born in Kill, County Kildare, Ireland, he became a member of the Irish Republican Brotherhood, and was responsible for recruiting nationalist support in the British Army in Ireland. Arrested for this in 1866, he was sentenced to fifteen years' imprisonment, but was amnestied after five years on the condition that he go into exile from the UK. He settled in the US where he worked as a journalist with the New York *Herald* and became a leading member of Clan na Gael, an organization supporting Irish freedom. Through **Thomas James Clarke** he helped tie the Easter uprising of 1916 to alliance with Germany in World War I, rousing US support for the victims of its repression. His hatred of **Woodrow Wilson** may have weakened the Irish cause. In any event, **Éamon de Valera**, President of Dáil Éireann, broke with Devoy and kept the Irish cause free from identification with any one US political faction, as Devoy now wished. He wrote *Recollections of an Irish Rebel* (published posthumously, 1929).

Devoy, Susan 1964– •*New Zealand squash player*• Born in Rotorua, she went to England in 1982, winning the British championship in 1984. Improving steadily throughout her career, she won the world championship in 1985 and went on to take the world title another four times. She won the British Open another seven times, and was the first New Zealand woman to win the world championships.

de Vries, Hugo Marie *See* **Vries, Hugo Marie de**

De Vries, Peter 1910–93 •*US novelist*• Born in Chicago to Dutch immigrant parents, he was the editor of a community newspaper in Chicago and associate editor of *Poetry*. In 1943 he lured **James Thurber** to Chicago to give a benefit lecture for *Poetry*, and Thurber subsequently encouraged him to write for the *New Yorker*. This he did, later joining the editorial staff. A satirist in his mentor's mold, he favored word play in the manner of **S J Perelman** and was an inveterate (and inventive) punster and epigrammatist. He wrote more than 20 novels such as *Reuben, Reuben* (1964), *The Glory of the Hummingbird* (1974) and *Parkham's Marbles* (1986), but none eclipsed the reception of his first, *The Tunnel of Love* (1954).

Dewar, Donald Campbell 1937–2000 •*Scottish Labour politician*• Born in Glasgow, and educated at Glasgow University, he qualified as a solicitor. He won Aberdeen South for the Labour Party in 1966, but lost his seat in 1970, and spent eight years out of parliament before returning in the Glasgow Garscadden by-election of 1978. He retained the seat with ease in the general elections. Following Labour's landslide win in 1997, he entered **Tony Blair**'s Cabinet as Secretary of State for Scotland (1997–99) and was First Minister of the Scottish Parliament (1999–2000).

Dewar, Sir James 1842–1923 •*Scottish chemist and physicist*• Born in Kincardine-on-Forth, Fife, and educated at Edinburgh University, he became the first director of the new Davy-Faraday Laboratory (from 1896) at the Royal Institution, London. He devised the structure for benzene known as the "Dewar formula," and with Sir Frederick Abel, discovered cordite (1889). He also accomplished the liquefaction of hydrogen (1898) and invented the vacuum flask. He was knighted in 1904.

de Wet, Christiaan Rudolf *See* **Wet, Christiaan Rudolf de**

Dewey, Melvil 1851–1931 •*US librarian*• Born in Adams Center, New York, he was the founder of the Dewey Decimal Classification system, which he designed for the Amherst College Library in 1876. He became chief librarian and Professor of Library Economy at Columbia (1883–88), and director of the New York State Library (1889–1906).

Dewi, St *See* **David, St**

de Witt, Jan *See* **Witt, Jan de**

Dexter, Colin 1930– •*English author*• Born in Stamford, Lincolnshire, he was educated at Christ's College, Cambridge, and worked as a teacher of the classics (1954–66) and later for the Oxford Delegacy of Local Examinations (1966–88). He began publishing crime fiction in the mid-1970s, introducing readers to his most famous character, the bitter-drinking crossword-solving Oxford detective Inspector Morse. Among the Morse canon are *The Wench Is Dead* (1989), *The Way Through the Woods* (1992) and *The Remorseful Day* (1999). Many of his stories have been the bases for hugely successful television adaptations starring **John Thaw**.

Dexter, John 1925–90 •*English stage director*• He began as an actor in repertory and television before becoming a director in 1957. During the next 20 years, he directed for the Royal Court Theatre, London, and became an associate of the National Theatre (1963–66). He has directed opera in London, New York, Paris and Hamburg. He cofounded the New Theatre Company in 1986.

d'Hérelle, Felix *See* **Hérelle, Felix d'**

Diaghilev, Sergei Pavlovich 1872–1929 •*Russian ballet impresario*• Born in Novgorod, in 1898 he became editor of *Mir Iskusstva* ("World of Art") and during the next few years arranged exhibitions and concerts of Russian art and music. He presented *Boris Godunov* in Paris (1908), and the next year brought a ballet company to the Châtelet. His permanent company, Ballets Russes de Diaghilev, was founded in 1911 (with headquarters in Monte Carlo) and remained in existence for 20 years, successfully touring Europe, despite constant financial anxiety. Most of the great dancers, composers and painters of this period—among them **Vaslav Nijinsky**, **George Balanchine**, **Picasso** and **Stravinsky**—contributed to the company's success. A temperamental tyrant who combined ruthlessness with charm, he seemed to activate the creation of works of art through his mere presence.

Diamond, I A L, *originally* **Itek Dommnici** 1920–88 •*US screenwriter*• Born in Romania, he emigrated to the US in 1929. After his graduation from Columbia University, New York, he secured a contract as a junior writer at Paramount Studios (1941–43). Success came during his 25-year collaboration with the writer-director **Billy Wilder**; together they created witty, incisive classics of contemporary US cinema, including the uproarious farce *Some Like It Hot* (1959) and bittersweet romantic comedies such as *The Apartment* (1960), for which he and Wilder won a joint Academy Award for Best Screenplay. He received the Writer's Guild Laurel award in 1979 and collaborated a final time with Wilder on *Buddy, Buddy* (1981).

Diana, Princess of Wales, *formerly* **Lady Diana Frances Spencer** 1961–97 •*British princess*• Born in Sandringham, Norfolk, the daughter of Viscount Althorp (1921–92), who became 8th Earl of Spencer in 1975, she left school at 16 with no formal qualifications. In 1979 she began work at a kindergarten in London, and in 1981 she married **Charles**, Prince of Wales. Within 11 months she provided him with an heir, Prince William Arthur Philip Louis (b. 1982). Prince Harry (Henry Charles Albert David) was born in 1984. Launched into an inescapable world of fame, she developed into a beautiful, glamorous celebrity who enjoyed international adoration. However, her external perfection stood in contrast to her domestic turmoil. The couple had little in common; they separated in 1992 and were divorced in 1996. Once released from many of the constraints of royal convention and denuded of her title HRH, she remained devoted to her sons and directed much time and effort, coupled with her immense media appeal, to supporting such charities and causes as the Red Cross, helping people with AIDS, and the campaign for an international ban on landmines. Her tragic death in a car crash in Paris shocked the world.

Diane de France 1538–1619 •*Duchess of Montmorency and Angoulême*• An illegitimate daughter of **Henry II** of France and of a

Piedmontese (according to some, of **Diane de Poitiers**), she was born in Paris. Formally legitimized, she was married to a son of the Duke of Parma, then to the eldest son of the 1st Duke of **Montmorency**. She enjoyed great influence at court under **Henry III** and **Henry IV**, and supervised the education of the future **Louis XIII**.

Diane de Poitiers 1499–1566 •*Mistress of Henri II of France*• Married at 13 and left a widow at 32, she attracted the attention of the young dauphin, Henry (later King **Henry II**), who was 20 years her junior and already married to **Catherine de Médicis**. On his accession in 1547 Diane, who was lively, cultivated, and the patron of poets, enjoyed great influence and was created Duchess of Valentinois. After his death (1559) she retired to her château at Anet.

Diaz or **Dias, Bartolomeu** c. 1450–1500 •*Portuguese navigator and explorer*• At the royal court of Aragon he met many scientists. In 1486 King John II gave him the command of two vessels to follow up the discoveries already made on the west coast of Africa. Diaz soon reached the limit that had been attained in South Atlantic navigation and, driven by a violent storm, he sailed around the southern extremity of Africa without immediately realizing the fact, so opening the route to India. He equipped **Vasco da Gama**'s expedition of 1497 and traveled with them as far as the Cape Verde Islands. He established a number of trading posts before joining the expedition of **Pedro Cabral**, the discoverer of Brazil, in 1500, but was lost in a storm after leaving Brazil.

Díaz, (José de la Cruz) Porfirio 1830–1915 •*Mexican soldier and statesman*• Born in Oaxaca City to a modest mestizo family, he studied for the priesthood and then for the law. As a student and follower of **Benito Juárez**, he opposed the dictatorship of **Antonio de Santa Anna**, joined the Oaxaca National Guard and rose to the rank of general. Hero of the War of Reform (1857–60) and the French Intervention (1861–67), in 1871 he rebelled against the unconstitutional fourth reelection of Juárez, rebelled again in 1876 in support of the principle of no reelection, and became President. When his term ended (1880) he relinquished office peacefully to Manuel González (1833–93), was elected again in 1884 and ruled without interruption until he was deposed in 1911. He pursued a program of "peace and progress," attracting foreign investment to modernize Mexico, which produced a remarkable growth in railroads and other material improvements. However, eventually the dictator's age and his neglect of political and social reforms led to the 1911 revolution of **Francisco Madero**. He died in poverty in Paris.

Díaz del Castillo, Bernal c. 1492–1581 •*Spanish soldier and historian*• He was one of the handful of conquistadors who accompanied **Hernán Cortés** in 1519. His *Historia de la conquista de la Nueva España* (1904, Eng trans 1908–16), written at the age of 84, is notable.

Dibdin, Charles 1745–1814 •*English songwriter*• Born in Southampton, he lived an unsettled life as an actor and composer of stage music, and in 1788 began a series of musical entertainments that became popular. He wrote nearly 100 sea songs—among the best "Poor Jack" and "Tom Bowling"—as well as nearly 70 dramatic pieces. Two of his sons, Charles (1768–1833) and Thomas John (1771–1841), wrote songs and dramas.

" "

For a soldier I listed, to grow great in fame,
And be shot at for sixpence a day.

1791 "Charity."

DiCaprio, Leonardo 1974– •*US actor*• He was born in Hollywood, California, and began working in television at the age of five. His first feature films included *What's Eating Gilbert Grape?* (1993; Academy Award nomination for Best Supporting Actor) and *William Shakespeare's Romeo and Juliet* (1996), but it was with *Titanic* (1997) that he earned worldwide female adulation. He subsequently starred in *Celebrity* (1998), *The Beach* (2000) and *Gangs of New York* (2002).

Dick, King *See* **Seddon, Richard John**

Dick, Philip K(indred) 1928–82 •*US science-fiction writer*• Born in Chicago, Illinois, from 1952 to 1955 he published a profusion of short stories, but in 1962 he turned to writing novels. Despite a penchant for modish titles, such as *Do Androids Dream of Electric Sheep?* (1968, later filmed as *Blade Runner* in 1982) and *Galactic Pot-Healer* (1969), the story of a master potter who has never thrown his own pots, he was not so much interested in technological gimmickry and space-age jargon as in his characters. A spare and humorous writer, he received the Hugo award in 1963.

Dicke, Robert Henry 1916–97 •*US physicist*• Born in St Louis, Missouri, he studied physics at Princeton University and the University of Rochester, and spent his career at Princeton as Professor of Physics from 1957. Independently of **Ralph Alpher** and **George Gamow**, he deduced in 1964 that a "big bang" origin of the universe should have left an observable remnant of microwave radiation. This radiation was later detected by **Arno Penzias** and **Robert Wilson**. In the 1960s he carried out important work on gravitation, proposing that the gravitational constant G slowly decreases with time (the Brans-Dicke theory, 1961). After a critical review of Roland von Eötvös's work on showing that inertial mass is equal to gravitational mass (**Einstein**'s equivalence principle), he verified this to one part in 10^{11}.

Dickens, Charles John Huffam 1812–70 •*English writer*• He was born in Landport, then a suburb of Portsmouth, and moved with his family to London in 1821. Hoping to become a journalist, he taught himself shorthand and visited the British Museum daily to supplement some of the shortcomings of his reading. In 1828 he became a reporter of debates at the House of Commons for the *Morning Chronicle*. In December 1833, the *Monthly Magazine* published a sketch, "Dinner at Poplar Walk," under the pen name "Boz," which was the nickname of Charles's younger brother. Eventually he made an arrangement to contribute papers and sketches regularly to the *Evening Chronicle*, continuing to work as a reporter for the *Morning Chronicle*, and received an increase in salary. The *Sketches by Boz* were collected and published early in 1836. Dickens received £150 for the copyright; he later bought it back for 11 times that amount. In the last week of March 1836 the first number of the *Pickwick Papers* appeared. Once he had become established, Dickens for the rest of his life allowed himself little respite. His prodigious output includes *Oliver Twist* (1837–39), *Nicholas Nickleby* (1838–39), *David Copperfield* (1849–50), *Bleak House* (1852–53), *Hard Times* (1854), *A Tale of Two Cities* (1859) and *Great Expectations* (1860–61). His last work was *The Mystery of Edwin Drood*, a story influenced by the work of his friend **Wilkie Collins**; it remained unfinished. Dickens is the most widely known English writer after **Shakespeare**, and no other novelist has managed to find both popular success and critical respect on such a lavish scale. His novels are a vivid portrayal of social life in Victorian England, much of it derived from his own experiences. The breadth, perception and sympathy of his writing, his abiding concern with social deprivation and injustice, his ability to conjure up memorable characters in a few paragraphs, and the comic genius which permeates even his most serious works, have all ensured that he continues to find a receptive audience, both for the books themselves and in film and stage adaptations of his work.

Dickey, James Lafayette 1923–97 •*US poet and novelist*• Born in Georgia, he wrote with an intense concern for the fragile harmony of nature and human enterprise in collections such as *Into the Stone* (1960). His wider fame depends on his one novel, *Deliverance* (1972), a Hemingwayesque rite of passage later filmed by **John Boorman**. Later poetry collections include *Head-Deep in Strange Sounds: Free Flight Improvisations from the UnEnglish* (1979).

Dickinson, Emily Elizabeth 1830–86 •*US poet*• Born in Amherst, Massachusetts, she was educated at Amherst Academy and Mount Holyoke Female Seminary in South Hadley. At the age of 23 she withdrew from most social contacts and lived a secluded life in Amherst, writing in secret over 1,700 poems, most in a period of creative ferment between 1858 and 1865. In later years she dressed in white and seldom consented to meet even family visitors, though she did correspond with a few friends and literary acquaintances such as **Thomas Wentworth Higginson**. Apart from several poems published anonymously, her work remained unknown and unpublished until after her death, when her sister Lavinia brought out three highly praised volumes (1890, 1891, 1896). Her lyrics, which show great originality both in thought and in form, have had considerable influence on modern poetry.

“ ”

Success is counted sweetest
By those who ne'er succeed.

c. 1859 ***Complete Poems***, *no. 67 (first published 1890).*

Diddley, Bo *See* **Bo Diddley**

Diderot, Denis 1713–84 •*French writer*• Born in Langres, he was trained by the Jesuits. He refused to become either a lawyer or a physician, and worked instead as a tutor and bookseller's hack (1734–44). His *Pensées philosophiques* (1796, Eng trans *Philosophical Thoughts*, 1916) was burned by the Parlement of Paris in 1746, and in 1749 he was imprisoned for his *Lettre sur les aveugles* (1749, Eng trans *An Essay on Blindness*, 1750). In 1748 he had published his first novel, *Les bijoux indiscrets* (Eng trans *The Indiscreet Toys*, 1749), and he was then invited to edit an expanded translation of **Ephraim Chambers**'s *Cyclopaedia* (1727) with **Jean d'Alembert**. In Diderot's hands the character of the work was transformed. He enlisted nearly all the important French writers of the time as contributors to his *Encyclopédie, ou Dictionnaire raisonné des sciences, des arts et des métiers* (35 vols, 1751–76, "Encyclopedia, or Critical Dictionary of Sciences, Arts and Trades"), and produced a major work of the Enlightenment. However, it was seen as propaganda for the Philosophe Party, and its sale was repeatedly prohibited. He was rescued from financial difficulties by **Catherine II** of Russia, to whom in 1773 he paid a five-month visit. His later works include novels such as *La religieuse* (1796, Eng trans *The Nun*, 1797), which exposed convent life, and plays such as *Est-il bon? Est-il méchant?* (1784, "Is He Good? Is He Bad?", not produced until 1913). His letters to Sophie Volland are the most interesting of his voluminous correspondence. As a critic he stood far in advance of his contemporaries and anticipated the Romanticists. His *Salons* (4 vols, 1957–67) are the earliest example of modern aesthetic criticism.

Didi, *professional name of* **Valdir Pereira** 1928–2001 •*Brazilian soccer player*• Born in Campos, he was the master strategist of the Brazil team that won the 1958 World Cup in Sweden, despite a slightly crippled right leg. He later managed the Peruvian national team, which reached the quarterfinals of the World Cup in Mexico in 1970.

Didion, Joan 1934– •*US writer*• She was born in Sacramento, California, and educated at the University of California at Berkeley (1952–56). From 1956 to 1963 she was associate feature editor of *Vogue* in New York and has worked and written for numerous magazines. Her essays have been published as *Slouching Towards Bethlehem* (1968), *The White Album* (1979), *After Henry* (1992) and *Political Fictions* (2001). Her novels portray contemporary social tensions in a laconic style that has aroused much admiration. *Run River* (1963) was her first, but she is best known for *A Book of Common Prayer* (1977). Her other works include the novels *Democracy* (1984) and *The Last Thing He Wanted* (1996), and nonfiction such as *Salvador* (1983). In 1996 she cowrote the film *Up Close and Personal*.

Didrickson, Babe *See* **Zaharias, Babe**

Diebenkorn, Richard 1922–93 •*US painter*• Born in Portland, Oregon, he enrolled in 1946 at the California School of Fine Arts, San Francisco, where he taught from 1947 to 1950. During the 1950s he developed a style close to abstract expressionism while retaining suggestions of the Californian landscape and of city motifs. The loose, gestural brushwork of the 1950s gave way to more geometrical compositions during the 1960s and 1970s. Diebenkorn evoked the dazzling Californian light by using bright, semi-translucent colors, particularly blues and yellows.

Diefenbaker, John G(eorge) 1895–1979 •*Canadian politician*• Born in Normanby Township, Ontario, and educated at the University of Saskatchewan, he was called to the bar in 1919. In 1940 he entered the Canadian Federal House of Commons, and was chosen as leader of the Progressive Conservatives in 1956. He became Prime Minister in 1957. His government extended the federal franchise to Canada's native peoples, but a recession eroded his party's support and he lost office in 1963.

Diels, Otto 1876–1954 •*German chemist and Nobel Prize winner*• Born in Hamburg, he studied chemistry at Berlin (1895–99) and in 1916 became professor at Kiel. He investigated a number of reactions, but is most famous for the discovery of the reaction of an activated olefin with a diene to give a cyclic structure with a predictable stereochemistry, a reaction of enormous synthetic value. It was discovered in collaboration with **Kurt Alder**, and they shared the 1950 Nobel Prize for chemistry for this work.

Diem, Ngo Dinh *See* **Ngo Dinh Diem**

Diesel, Rudolf Christian Karl 1858–1913 •*German engineer*• Born in Paris, France, to German parents, he studied at the Munich Polytechnic and trained as a refrigeration engineer, but in 1885 began work on internal-combustion engines. Subsidized by the Krupp Company, he set about constructing a "rational heat motor," demonstrating the first practical compression-ignition engine in 1897. The diesel engine achieved an efficiency about twice that of comparable steam engines. He spent most of his life at his factory at Augsburg, but in 1913 he vanished from the Antwerp-Harwich mail steamer and was presumed drowned.

Dietrich, Marlene, *originally* **Maria Magdalena Von Losch** 1901–92 •*US film actress and cabaret performer*• Born in Berlin, Germany, she made her film debut as a maid in *Der kleine Napoleon* (1922, "The Little Napoleon"), but it was her performance as the temptress Lola in Germany's first sound film *Der blaue Engel* (1930, *The Blue Angel*) that brought her international attention and a Hollywood contract. With the director **Josef von Sternberg**, she developed a sensual film personality, used to effect in a succession of exotic films like *Morocco* (1930), *Blonde Venus* (1932), *The Scarlet Empress* (1934) and *The Devil Is a Woman* (1935). Labeled "box-office poison" in 1937, she returned in triumph as the brawling saloon singer Frenchie in *Destry Rides Again* (1939). Later film work tended to exploit her legendary mystique, although she was effective in *Rancho Notorious* (1952) and *Judgment at Nuremberg* (1961). She made frequent tours to entertain US troops during World War II, and after the war pursued a career as an international chanteuse and cabaret star. Later she became increasingly reclusive.

Dietrich von Bern *See* **Theodoric the Great**

Dietzenhofer •*German family of architects*• The family consisted of five brothers. They were active over the period 1643 to 1726, and their work was of great importance in the development of the Late Baroque in central Europe. They were the successors of **Francesco Borromini** and **Guarino Guarini**, and the precursors of **Balthasar Neumann**. A good example of their work is Christoph's St Nicholas in the Lesser Town Prague (1703–11).

Dieudonné, Henri Charles *See* **Chambord, Henri Charles Dieudonné, Comte de**

Dilas, Milovan *See* **Djilas, Milovan**

Dill, Sir John Greer 1881–1944 •*Northern Irish field marshal*• Educated at Cheltenham College and trained at Sandhurst, he served in the Second Boer War (1899–1902) and World War I, in which he was decorated and promoted to brigadier general. In World War II he commanded the 1st Army Corps in France, and became Chief of the Imperial General Staff (1940–41) and field marshal (1941). His strategical insight and organizational ability made him head of the British Service Mission in Washington from 1941.

Dillenius, Johann Jacob 1687–1747 •*German botanist and botanical artist*• Born in Darmstadt, he went to England in 1721, and from 1734 was first Sherardian Professor of Botany at Oxford. He was the author and artist of *Hortus Elthamensis* (1732) and *Historia Muscorum* (1741), of fundamental importance in the study of mosses.

Dillinger, John 1903–34 •*US gangster*• Born in Indianapolis, Indiana, he was convicted of attempted robbery in 1923 and imprisoned for ten years. On his parole in 1933 he and his gang began a series of violent bank robberies. Designated "public enemy number one" by the FBI, he was held responsible for 16 killings. After escaping from Crown Point county jail, where he was being held on a murder charge, he was betrayed by his girfriend's landlady and shot dead by FBI agents as he left a theater in Chicago.

Dillon, John 1851–1927 •*Irish nationalist politician*• Born in Blackrock, County Dublin, the son of the nationalist John Blake Dillon (1816–66) and educated at the Catholic University medical school in Dublin, he became a committed supporter of **Charles Parnell** in the Land League and in 1880 was voted Member of Parliament for County Tipperary. In parliament he distinguished himself by the violence of his language, while speeches delivered by him in Ireland led to his imprisonment (1881, 1881–82, 1888). After the divorce case involving Parnell in 1890, he became leader of the anti-Parnellite group (1896–99), but resigned in favor of **John Redmond** (1900). In 1918 he became leader of the remnant of the Irish Nationalist Party, but was defeated in the election of 1919 by **Éamon de Valera**.

Dilthey, Wilhelm 1833–1911 •*German philosopher and historian of ideas*• Born in Biebrich, Hesse, he was a student of the great historian **Leopold von Ranke**. He taught at Basel, Kiel and Breslau (now Wrocław, Poland), and was Professor of Philosophy at Berlin (1882–1911). He was much influenced by **Kant** and is himself a key figure in the idealist tradition in modern social thought. One of his central themes is the radical distinction he made between the natural sciences (*Naturwissenschaften*) and the human sciences (*Geisteswissenschaften*), the former offering explanations of physical events through causal laws, the latter offering understanding (*Verstehen*) of events in terms of human intentions and meanings. He developed a typology of worldviews (*Weltanschauungen*) which would set out the different ways of conceiving our relation to the world. A further innovation was his theory of hermeneutics for the interpretation of historical texts.

DiMaggio, Joe (Joseph Paul), *nicknamed* **Joltin' Joe** and **the Yankee Clipper** 1914–99 •*US baseball player*• Born in Martinez, California, he was a powerful and elegant center fielder and hitter, and played his entire career (1936–51) with the New York Yankees. His greatest achievement was hitting safely (recording a hit) at least once in 56 consecutive games in the 1941 season. He won the batting championship twice (1939, 1940), and was voted the American League's Most Valuable Player (MVP) three times. During his career he hit 361 home runs and compiled a lifetime batting average of .325. In 1954 he married (briefly) the film actress **Marilyn Monroe**.

“ ”

There's no skill involved. Just go up there and swing at the ball.

Of baseball. Quoted in Colin Jarman ***The Guinness Dictionary of Sports Quotations*** *(1990).*

Dimbleby, David 1938– •*English broadcaster*• He was educated at Charterhouse and at Christ Church, Oxford, and has been with the BBC since 1960, when he was a reporter with BBC Bristol. He was a special correspondent with CBS News in 1966–68. After a period in children's programs (including *Top of the Form*, 1961–63), he became a host of *Panorama* for several series and of BBC election results programs from 1979, also producing several documentaries and reports. He has hosted *Question Time* since 1994.

Dimbleby, Jonathan 1944– •*English broadcaster*• He was educated at University College London and joined the BBC in 1969, when, like his brother **David**, he became a reporter with BBC Bristol. Now a freelance broadcaster and author in current affairs, he has written an authorized biography of **Charles, Prince of Wales**, about whom he also made a television documentary (1994). He has chaired BBC Radio 4's *Any Questions?* since 1987, *Any Answers?* since 1989, and hosted ITV's *Jonathan Dimbleby* since 1995.

Dimbleby, Richard 1913–65 •*English broadcaster*• He was educated at Mill Hill School and worked on the editorial staff of various newpapers before being appointed first news reporter of the BBC in 1936. In 1939 he became the BBC's first war correspondent and went with the British Expeditionary Force to France. He was the first radio reporter in Berlin and at Belsen. In 1946 he became a freelance broadcaster and gave commentaries on many major events, particularly royal occasions, and reported on royal tours abroad and on state visits in Great Britain (notably that of **Charles de Gaulle** in 1960), as well as on the funerals of US President **John F Kennedy** (1963) and **Winston Churchill** (1965). He took part in the first Eurovision relay in 1951 and in the first live television broadcast from the USSR in 1961. He was host of a number of current affairs programs, most famously of *Panorama* and *About Britain*, and was a member of the *Twenty Questions* radio team for 18 years. He is commemorated by the annual BBC Dimbleby Lectures on topical subjects. His sons, **David** and **Jonathan**, followed their father into broadcasting.

Dimitrov, Georgi Mikhailovich 1882–1949 •*Bulgarian Communist politician*• Born near Radomir, he was imprisoned in 1917 for antimilitarist agitation. He helped found the Bulgarian Communist Party in 1919, and after visiting Moscow, returned to Bulgaria and led an uprising that earned him a death sentence (1923). He fled to Yugoslavia, and then lived under an assumed name in Vienna and Berlin. In 1933 he was one of those accused of setting fire to the Reichstag. He then became a Russian citizen and served as Executive Secretary of the Comintern (1934–43). Returning to Bulgaria in 1945, he became Prime Minister (1946–49).

d'Indy, (Paul Marie Théodore) Vincent 1851–1931 •*French composer*• Born in Paris, he was a student, disciple and biographer of **César Franck**, and founded the Schola Cantorum in Paris in 1894. He published *Treatise of Composition* (1900) and composed operas, chamber music and, notably, *Symphonie sur un chant montagnard français* (1886, "Symphony on a French Mountain Song") in the spirit of French Romanticism.

Dine, Jim (James) 1935– •*US artist*• Born in Cincinnati, Ohio, he studied at the Boston Museum of Fine Arts School. In 1959 he exhibited his first series of ready-made objects as images, alongside **Claes Oldenburg**, with whom he also pioneered "happenings." His own happening, *The Car Crash* of 1960, was a classic of this type. One of the foremost US pop artists, he is essentially a collage painter, as in *Double Red Self-Portrait (Green Lines)* (1964, New York), where clothing is fastened to canvas against a freely painted background. During the late 1960s he also collaborated with **Eduardo Paolozzi** on collages. He has since turned to more traditional painting, such as *Cardinal* (1976, Pace Gallery, New York).

Ding Ling (Ting Ling), *pseudonym of* **Jiang Bingzhi (Chiang Ping-chih)** 1902–86 •*Chinese feminist writer and Communist Party activist*• Born in Linli County, Hunan Province, she went to Shanghai University (1923–24), where she started publishing stories of rebelliousness against traditional society, such as *The Diary of Miss Sophia* (1928), which dealt candidly with questions of female psychology and sexual desires. In 1932 she joined the Chinese Communist Party, and after a period of imprisonment by the Guomindang (Kuomintang) authorities (1933–36), she succeeded in escaping to the Communist base at Yenan, where she became a star attraction for Western journalists. In 1958 she was "purged" and sent to raise chickens in the Heilongjiang. She was imprisoned (1970–75) during the Cultural Revolution, but was rehabilitated by the party in 1979, and published a novel based on her labor camp experiences, *Comrade Du Wanxiang* (1979).

Dio Cassius c. 150–c. 235 AD •*Roman historian*• Born in Nicaea, Bithynia, he went to Rome (c. 180 AD), held high offices of state, and was twice consul. He became a close friend of **Alexander Severus**, who sent him as legate to Dalmatia and Pannonia. About 229 he retired to his native city. Of the 80 books of his *History of Rome*, from the landing of Aeneas in Italy until 229, only 19 (from the period 68 BC–AD 10) have survived complete.

Diocletian, *properly* **Gaius Aurelius Valerius Diocletianus** AD 245–313 •*Roman emperor*• He was born of humble parentage near Salona, Dalmatia. He served under Probus, **Aurelian** and Carus, and was proclaimed emperor by the army (AD 284). To aid him against barbarian attacks, he made Maximian his coemperor over the Western Empire (286), and also pronounced **Constantius Chlorus** and **Galerius** caesars (292). Britain, after maintaining independence under **Marcus Aurelius Carausius** and Allectus, was restored to the empire (296), the Persians were defeated (298), and the Marcomanni and other northern barbarians were driven beyond the Roman frontier. Diocletian's domestic reforms displayed his genius for administration. He strengthened the frontiers, increased the size of the army, revised legal codes and restored a sound coinage. A conservative, he also instituted severe persecution of the Christians (303). Diocletian and Maximian abdicated (305), and Diocletian retired to Salona (now Split) to philosophy and gardening.

Diodorus Siculus 1st century BC •*Greek historian*• Born in Agyrium, Sicily, he traveled in Asia and Europe, and lived in Rome. For 30 years he collected the material for his *Bibliotheke Historike*, a history of the world in 40 books, from the creation to the Gallic wars of **Gaius Julius Caesar**. Five of the books are extant entire, some are lost, and fragments of the rest remain.

Diogenes of Apollonia 5th century BC •*Greek philosopher*• He continued the pre-Socratic tradition of speculation about the primary constituent of the world, which he identified as air, operating as an active and intelligent lifeforce. He was caricatured along with **Socrates** in **Aristophanes**'s comedy *The Clouds* (423 BC).

Diogenes of Sinope c. 412–c. 323 BC •*Greek Cynic philosopher and moralist*• Born in Sinope, Pontus, Asia Minor, he moved to Athens as a young man and became a student of **Antisthenes**, with whom he founded the Cynic sect, preaching an austere asceticism and self-sufficiency. Legendary for his unconventional behavior and ostentatious disregard for domestic comforts, he was said to have lived in a tub "like a dog" (Greek *kyon*), the origin of the term "Cynic." When **Alexander the Great** visited him and asked what he could do for him he answered, "You could move away out of the sun and not cast a shadow on me." According to another story he would wander around Athens by day with a lamp "looking for an honest man." Later he was captured by pirates while on a sea voyage and was sold as a slave to Xeniades of Corinth. He was soon freed, was appointed tutor to Xeniades' children and remained in Corinth for the rest of his life.

Diogenes Läertius fl. 2nd century AD •*Greek writer*• He was born in Läerte, Cilicia. His best known work is a compilation, in ten books, giving a secondhand account of the principal Greek thinkers.

Dion 409–353 BC •*Syracusan magnate*• He was both brother-in-law and son-in-law of **Dionysius the Elder**. This connection with the tyrant brought him great wealth, but he fell out with **Dionysius the Younger**, who banished him in 366 BC. Thereupon he retired to Athens to study philosophy under **Plato**. A sudden attack upon Syracuse made him master of the city in 357, but his severity alienated the Syracusans, and he was murdered.

Dion or **Dio Chrysostom**, *literally* **"the golden-mouthed"** c. 40–c. 112 AD •*Greek orator and philosopher*• Born in Prusa, Bithynia, Asia Minor, he went to Rome under **Vespasian**, but was banished by **Domitian**. On **Marcus Cocceius Nerva**'s accession (AD 96) he returned to Rome, and lived in great honor under him and **Trajan**. Fragments of his work survive, as well as around 80 orations or treatises on politics, morals and philosophy.

Dion, Céline 1968– •*Canadian pop singer*• Born into a French-Canadian family in Charlemagne, Quebec, she achieved stardom in her native Quebec before attracting international attention after learning to sing in English. The best-selling album *Unison* (1990) produced several hit singles and was followed by *Celine Dion* (1992), from which came the single "Beauty and the Beast," and *The Color of My Love* (1993), from which came perhaps her greatest hit "The Power of Love." Subsequent releases include the albums *Let's Talk About Love* (1998), which includes the song "My Heart Will Go On" used in the film *Titanic*, and *All the Way* (1999).

Dionysius *See* **Denis, St**

Dionysius Exiguus d. 556 •*Scythian Christian scholar*• Abbot of a monastery in Rome, he was one of the most learned men of his time. He fixed the dating of the Christian era in his *Cyclus Paschalis* (525).

Dionysius of Alexandria, St, *called* **the Great** c. 200–64 AD •*Greek theologian*• Born in Alexandria, he was a pupil of **Origen**, and succeeded him as head of the Catechical school in Alexandria (AD 231). He became Bishop of Alexandria in 247. In the persecutions under **Caius Decius** he escaped to a refuge in the Libyan desert and was restored at the death of Decius in 251. He was banished again in 257, under **Valerian**, but returned in 261. Only fragments of his writings have survived. His feast day is November 17.

Dionysius of Halicarnassus 1st century BC •*Greek critic, historian and rhetorician*• From 30 BC he lived and worked in Rome. He wrote, in Greek, *Roman Antiquities*, a history of Rome down to 264 BC, a mine of information about the constitution, religion, history, laws and private life of the Romans. Of its 20 books, only the first nine are complete. He also wrote a number of valuable critical treatises on literature and rhetoric, particularly *On the Arrangement of Words*.

Dionysius the Areopagite fl. 1st century AD •*Greek or Syrian churchman*• Born in Athens, he was one of the few Athenians converted by the Apostle **Paul** (Acts 17:34). Tradition makes him the first Bishop of Athens and a martyr. The Greek writings bearing his name were written not by him, but probably by an unknown Alexandrian of the early 6th century. They include the treatises *On the Heavenly and Ecclesiastical Hierarchies*, *On Divine Names*, *On Mystical Theology*, and a series of ten *Epistles*, and had a great influence on the development of theology.

Dionysius the Elder 431–367 BC •*Tyrant of Syracuse*• He made himself absolute ruler of his native city in 405 BC. After ferociously suppressing several insurrections and conquering some of the Greek towns of Sicily, he warred with the Carthaginians (397–392) and concluded an advantageous peace. In 387 he captured Rhegium, gaining influence over the Greek cities of Lower Italy. From 383 until his death he tried to drive the Carthaginians from Sicily. He was a poet and patron of poets and philosophers, but a hostile tradition depicts him as the destroyer of Greek liberties.

Dionysius the Younger fl. 367–343 BC •*Tyrant of Syracuse*• The son of **Dionysius the Elder**, he succeeded him in 367 BC. Reportedly indolent and dissolute, he fell out with **Dion**, who had invited **Plato** to Syracuse. Dion was banished, but ten years afterward expelled Dionysius. He fled to Locri, and made himself master of the city, which he ruled despotically until dissensions in Syracuse (346) enabled him to return there. However, in 343 **Timoleon** went to free Sicily, and Dionysius was exiled to Corinth.

Dionysius Thrax fl. c. 100 BC •*Greek grammarian*• A native of Alexandria, he taught at Rhodes and at Rome. His *Tekhne grammatike* is the basis of all European works on grammar.

Diophantus fl. 3rd century AD •*Greek mathematician*• He lived in Alexandria, and his largest surviving work is the *Arithmetica*, which deals with the solution of algebraic equations. In contrast to earlier Greek works, it uses a rudimentary algebraic notation instead of a purely geometric one. In many problems there is no uniquely determined solution, and these have become known as Diophantine problems. The study of Diophantus's work inspired **Pierre de Fermat** to take up number theory in the 17th century with remarkable results.

Dior, Christian 1905–57 •*French couturier*• Born in Granville, Normandy, he first began to design clothes in 1935, and founded his own Paris house in 1947. He achieved worldwide fame with his long-skirted New Look in that year, followed by the A-line, the Holine trapeze look, and the Sack.

“ ”

In the world today *haute couture* is one of the last repositories of the marvelous, and the *couturiers* the last possessors of the wand of Cinderella's Fairy Godmother.

Dior by Dior *(translated by Antonia Fraser, 1957).*

Diori, Hamani 1916–89 •*Niger politician*• He was educated in Dahomey and then at the William Ponty School in Dakar. In 1956 he became Prime Minister of Niger and in 1960, at independence, its first President. Building on close relations with France, he ran one of the most stable countries in West Africa, being reelected in 1965 and 1970, but opposition within his party led to his overthrow in 1974 through a military coup led by army Chief of Staff Seyni Kountche. He was placed under house arrest for 13 years before he left for Morocco, where he died.

Dioscorides, Pedanius c. 40–c. 90 AD •*Greek physician*• Born in Anazarb, Cilicia, he wrote *De materia medica*, for many centuries the standard work on substances used in medicine and the science of their properties.

Diouf, Abdou 1935– •*Senegalese politician*• Born in Louga, northwest Senegal, he studied at the Universities of Dakar and Paris before graduating with a law degree and returning to Senegal to work as a civil servant. After holding a number of posts, including that of Secretary-General to President **Léopold Sédar Senghor**, he became Prime Minister in 1970 and succeeded Senghor on the latter's retirement (1981). He was reelected President of Senegal in 1983, 1988 and 1993, serving until his defeat by Abdoulaye Wade (1926–) in 2000.

Dirac, P(aul) A(drien) M(aurice) 1902–84 •*English mathematical physicist and Nobel Prize winner*• He was born in Bristol and educated at Bristol and Cambridge Universities. Using the matrix approach of **Max Born**, **Pascual Jordan** and **Werner Heisenberg**, in 1928 he produced his relativistic wave equation, which explained the electron spin discovered by George Uhlenbeck (1900–88) and **Samuel Goudsmit** in 1925. This equation had negative energy solutions that he later interpreted as antimatter states (1930). He predicted that a photon could produce an electron-positron pair, which was confirmed experimentally by **Carl Anderson** in 1932. In 1930 Dirac published the classic work *The Principles of Quantum Mechanics* and in the same year he was elected a Fellow of the Royal Society. Lucasian Professor of Mathematics at Cambridge (1932–69), he was awarded the Nobel Prize for physics in 1933 with **Erwin Schrödinger** for their work in quantum theory.

Dirichlet, (Peter Gustav) Lejeune 1805–59 •*German mathematician*• Born in Düren, he showed a precocious interest in mathematics and entered the Collège de France in Paris in 1822. After teaching privately, he became extraordinary professor at Berlin in 1828, and succeeded **Carl Friedrich Gauss** as professor at the University of Göttingen in 1855. His main work was in number theory, **Fourier** series, and boundary value problems in mathematical physics.

Disney, Walt(er Elias) 1901–66 •*US artist and film producer*• Born in Chicago, he worked as a commercial artist before setting up a small studio in which he produced animated cartoons, his most famous character being Mickey Mouse, who first appeared in *Plane Crazy* and *Steamboat Willie* in 1928. Among his early successes were the *Silly Symphonies* (from 1929) and the first full-length color cartoon film, *Snow White and the Seven Dwarfs* (1937). This was followed by *Pinocchio* (1940), *Dumbo* (1941), and *Fantasia* (1940), the first successful attempt to realize music in images. His other achievements include a series of color nature films (eg, *The Living Desert*, 1953) and several swashbuckling color films for young people, including *Robin Hood* (1952), *Treasure Island* (1959) and *The Swiss Family Robinson* (1960), as well as family films such as *Mary Poppins* (1964). He opened the family theme park, called Disneyland, in California in 1955; others have since been built in Florida (1971), in Tokyo (1983) and on the outskirts of Paris (1992).

Disraeli, Benjamin, 1st Earl of Beaconsfield 1804–81 •*English statesman and novelist*• He was born in London, the eldest son of the writer Isaac D'Israeli (1776–1848). In 1826 he became the talk of the town with his first novel, *Vivian Grey*. After four unsuccessful attempts at election, he entered parliament for Maidstone in 1837. His over-ornate maiden speech was drowned in shouts of laughter, except for the closing words, "ay and though I sit down now, the time will come when you will hear me." By 1842 he was head of the "Young England" group of young Tories. **Robert Peel** did not reward Disraeli's services with office and was fiercely attacked by him over the repeal of the Corn Laws (1846); this helped bring about Peel's political downfall. As Chancellor of the Exchequer and leader of the Lower House in the brief **Derby** administration of 1852, he coolly rejected protectionism, and came off on the whole with flying colors; but his budget was rejected. In opposition (1858–66), Disraeli displayed talent as a debater, and a spirit and persistency under defeat that won for him the admiration of his adversaries. As Chancellor of the Exchequer in the third Derby administration (1866), he introduced and carried a Reform Bill (1867). In February 1868 he succeeded Lord Derby as premier; but, in the face of a hostile majority, he resigned in December. Disraeli returned to power in 1874 and from this time his curious relationship with Queen **Victoria** began. After almost a decade of prosperity, the increase of taxation and loss of trade brought about a catastrophic defeat for the Tories at the polls in 1880, and Disraeli retired to writing. The most famous of his written works is the political trilogy *Coningsby* (1844), *Sybil* (1845) and *Tancred* (1847). He drew extensively on his travel experiences in his writing, notably in the trilogy *The Young Duke* (1831), *Contarini Fleming* (1832) and *Alroy* (1833), the last set in 12th-century Azerbaijan. *Henrietta Temple* and *Venetia* were love stories, published in 1837.

Di Stefano, Alfredo 1926– •*Argentine soccer player and coach*• Born in Buenos Aires of Italian descent, his lasting fame rests on his spell with Real Madrid, during which time he played in five European Cup successes. He did not like competition from clubmates and had **Didi** removed from the Real Madrid staff. With the Hungarian player **Ferenc Puskas** he formed a partnership of equals, however, and between them they scored all the goals in Real Madrid's 7–3 win over Eintracht Frankfurt at Hampden Park, Glasgow, in the European Cup Final of 1960. Later he became a coach and took Valencia to the Spanish League Championship in 1971.

Ditiatin, Aleksandr 1957– •*Russian gymnast*• Born in Leningrad (now St Petersburg), he was educated at the Leningrad Lesgraft Institute of Physical Culture and was the first person to win eight medals in one Olympic Games—in Moscow, 1980. He won three golds for overall, team and rings, four silvers for parallel bars, horizontal bar, pommel horse and vault, and one bronze for floor. He was also the first male gymnast to receive a 10 in an Olympic event, with the longhorse vault. He was overall world champion in 1979 and overall champion in the Soviet Summer Games in 1975 and 1979.

Dives *See* **Crassus, Marcus Licinius**

Divine, Father, *originally* **George Baker** 1877–1965 •*US religious leader*• An African American born near Savannah, Georgia, he became an itinerant preacher, and spent several years traveling through the South under the name of "the Messenger." In 1919 he founded the Peace Mission movement, which stressed communal living, celibacy, and complete racial equality. Most of his followers believed that he was God, and after his death the movement faltered.

Dix, Dorothea Lynde 1802–87 •*US humanitarian and reformer*• Born in Hampden, Maine, she established at the age of 19 her own school for girls in Boston (1821–35). In 1841 she visited a Massachusetts prison and was shocked to find inmates confined because of insanity and subject to chaining, flogging and other forms of abuse. She began a lifelong crusade for specialized treatment of the mentally ill, and her efforts led to the founding of numerous state mental hospitals in the US, Canada and Europe. She was also an advocate of prison reform. Throughout the Civil War she served as superintendent of women nurses in the army.

Dix, Otto 1891–1969 •*German Realist painter*• Born in Gera-Unternhaus, he is best known for his etchings and paintings of World War I casualties, portrayed with biting realism, and of Berlin prostitutes in the decadent postwar period. He was a brilliant and savage portraitist and social commentator; his work was regarded as unwholesome by the Nazis, who included it in the famous exhibition of Degenerate Art. After World War II he painted mostly religious subjects in isolation at Hemmenhofen.

Djerassi, Carl 1923– •*US chemist*• Born in Vienna, he studied at Kenyon College and at the University of Wisconsin and subsequently worked as a research chemist and professor at Wayne State and Stanford Universities. His work resulted in breakthroughs that led to the development of the contraceptive pill, antihistamines and anti-inflammatory agents.

Djilas or **Dilas, Milovan** 1911–95 •*Yugoslav politician and writer*• Born in Montenegro, he was active in the outlawed Yugoslav Communist Party in the 1930s and was subsequently imprisoned (1933–36). He was, with his friend **Tito**, a remarkable partisan leader during World War II. In the postwar government, he was vice president of Yugoslavia, but his criticisms of the Communist system practiced in Yugoslavia led to his expulsion from the party in 1954, and imprisonment (1956–61, 1962–66), though he was later released under amnesty. He was formally rehabilitated by the Yugoslav authorities in 1989. His books include *The New Class* (1957) and *Conversations with Stalin* (1962), as well as novels, short stories and political memoirs.

Dmitri or **Demetrius** 1583–91 •*Russian prince*• The youngest son of Czar **Ivan IV**, he was murdered by the regent **Boris Godunov**. In c. 1603 a runaway Moscow monk, Grigorii Otrepiev (the "false Demetrius"), impersonated him and was crowned czar by the army (1605) but was killed in a rebellion (1606). A second and a third "false Demetrius" appeared within the next few years, but their fate was no better.

Dobell, Sir William 1899–1970 •*Australian portrait painter*• Born in Newcastle, New South Wales, he studied at the Julian Ashton Art School, Sydney, and the Slade School of Art in London. His portrait of the artist Joshua Smith won the Archibald prize in 1944 and became the center of a bitter artistic storm. Dobell won the ensuing legal battle, but it resulted in permanent damage to his health. He was further vindicated in 1948 by not only winning the Archibald again, but also receiving the Wynne prize for landscape painting. In 1959 he won the Archibald for a third time. He left his estate to establish the art foundation that bears his name.

Döblin, Alfred 1878–1957 •*German-French novelist*• Born in Stettin, Germany (now Szczecin, Poland), he grew up in Berlin, studied medicine both there and in Freiburg, and practiced as a doctor and psychiatrist from 1911. He published stories before writing epic novels like *Die drei Sprünge des Wang-Lun* (1915, "The Three Leaps of Wan Lung") and the futuristic *Berge, Meere und Giganten* (1924, "Mountains, Seas and Giants"). *Berlin Alexanderplatz* (1929, Eng trans *Alexanderplatz Berlin*, 1931), the story of a reformed criminal in the dark underworld of Weimar Germany, is considered to be his masterpiece. He left for France in 1933, where he continued to write ambitious works like the trilogy *Amazonas-Trilogie* (1937–47, "The Amazon Trilogy"). His perilous 1940 flight to the US is described in *Shicksalreise* (1949, "Fateful Journey"). He returned to Germany in 1945 and cofounded the Academy of Science and Literature (1949).

Dobson, Frank 1888–1963 •*English sculptor*• Born in London, he was associated with the London Group (including **Eric Gill**, **Jacob Epstein** and **Roger Fry**) for many years, and was Professor of Sculpture at the Royal College of Art until 1953. His very individual style (with simplified contours and heavy limbs) is shown at its best in his female nudes, such as *Cornucopia* (1925–27, University of Hull). Among his best-known works are *The Man Child*, *Morning*, and a polished brass bust of **Osbert Sitwell** (1922).

Dobson, Rosemary de Brissac 1920–87 •*Australian poet*• Born in Sydney, her poems reflect her love of antiquity, manuscripts and fine printing, as seen in "The Missal." She first published *In a Convex Mirror* (1944), then *The Ship of Ice*, which won an award in 1948. Later books were *Child with a Cockatoo* (1955) and *Cock Crow* (1965). She also edited the feminist anthology *Sister Poets* (1979), and in the same year received the Robert Frost prize. In 1984 she won the Patrick White Literary award.

Dobzhansky, Theodosius 1900–75 •*US geneticist*• Born in Nemirov, Russia (now in Ukraine), he studied zoology at the University of Kiev and taught genetics in Leningrad (St Petersburg), before going to the US to join **Thomas Hunt Morgan** at Columbia University in 1927. He taught thereafter at the California Institute of Technology (Caltech, 1929–40), Columbia (1940–62) and Rockefeller University, New York (1962–71). He showed that the genetic variability in a population is large, conferring versatility when the population is exposed to environmental change, and set out his influential ideas in works such as *Genetics and the Evolutionary Process* (1970). His work linked **Darwin**ian evolutionary theory with **Gregor Mendel**'s laws of heredity, and he applied his ideas to the concept of race in man, defining races as Mendelian populations differing in gene frequencies.

" "

Nature's stern discipline enjoins mutual help at least as often as warfare. The fittest may also be the gentlest.

1962 ***Mankind Evolving.***

Doctorow, E(dgar) L(awrence) 1931– •*US novelist*• Born in New York City, he was educated at Kenyon College and Columbia University. From 1960 to 1964 he was editor of the New American Library, and he has held teaching posts in several colleges and universities. He is currently Gluckman Professor of American and English Letters at New York University (1987–). His novels include *Welcome to Hard Times* (1961), *The Book of Daniel* (1971), based on the story of the **Rosenberg**s, *Ragtime* (1975, filmed 1981), *Loon Lake* (1980), *Billy Bathgate* (1989, filmed 1991) and *City of God* (2000).

Dod, Lottie (Charlotte) 1871–1960 •*English sportswoman*• She was born in Cheshire and was tennis's first child protégé, winning her first Wimbledon title at the age of 15, becoming the youngest-ever champion. She then won another four singles titles. Turning her attention to hockey, she represented England in 1899 before taking up golf and going on to win the British Ladies Open Golf championships in 1904 at Troon. She then completed her career by winning a silver medal in archery at the 1908 Olympic Games in London. She is probably the greatest all-around athlete that Great Britain has ever produced.

Dodd, Ken (Kenneth Arthur) 1927– •*English stand-up comedian, singer and actor*• Born in Liverpool, he made his debut at the Empire Theatre, Nottingham, in 1954. He set a record at his London debut in 1965 by starring in his own 42-week season of *Doddy's Here* at the Palladium. He has since appeared regularly on stage in variety and pantomime, on radio and, often supported by the famous Diddymen, in television programs such as *The Ken Dodd Show* (1959–66) and *An Audience with Ken Dodd* (1994). He has also had hits with songs such as *Tears* and *Happiness*.

Dodds, Johnny (John M) 1892–1940 •*US jazz clarinettist*• Born in New Orleans, he was self-taught on the clarinet. His measured embroideries typified the role of his instrument in the early three-part ensemble style, and recordings in the 1920s with **King Oliver** and **Louis Armstrong** secured this reputation. Dodds's influence continues among clarinet players in the New Orleans style.

Dodge, Mary Elizabeth, *née* **Mapes** 1831–1905 •*US writer*• Born in New York City, she married William Dodge, a lawyer, in 1851, and after his death in 1858 turned to writing books for children, notably *Hans Brinker; or, The Silver Skates* (1865), which became a children's classic.

Dodgson, Charles Lutwidge *See* **Carroll, Lewis**

Dods, Meg *See* **Johnstone, (Christian) Isobel**

Dodsley, Robert 1704–64 •*English playwright*• He was born in Mansfield, Nottinghamshire. In 1735 his *Toy Shop*, a dramatic piece, was through **Pope**'s influence acted at Covent Garden with great success. With his profits, and £100 from Pope, he set up as a bookseller, publishing **Edward Young**, **Oliver Goldsmith** and the as-yet-unknown **Samuel Johnson**, among others. He founded the *Annual Register* with **Edmund Burke** in 1759. He is chiefly remembered for his *Select Collection of Old Plays* (12 vols, 1744–45) and his *Poems by Several Hands* (3 vols, 1748; 6 vols, 1758).

Doesburg, Theo van, *originally* **Christian Emil Marie Kupper** 1883–1931 •*Dutch painter, architect and writer*• Born in Utrecht, he became a poet, but took up painting and exhibited at The Hague in 1908. With **Piet Mondrian** he founded the avant-garde magazine *De Stijl* (1917–31), which propounded a severe form of geometrical abstraction known as Neo-Plasticism. By 1921 he was in touch with **Le Corbusier**, and with the leading figures of the Bauhaus design school. He later became increasingly involved in architectural projects.

Doherty, Peter Charles 1940– •*Australian immunologist and Nobel Prize winner*• Born in Brisbane, he studied at the University of Queensland and at Edinburgh University, and later became a research Fellow in the department of microbiology at the John Curtin School of Medical Research, Canberra. There in 1973 he and **Rolf M Zinkernagel** made a breakthrough in the understanding of the human immune system that led to their joint Nobel Prize for physiology or medicine in 1996.

Dohnanyi, Ernst (Erno) von 1877–1960 •*Hungarian composer and pianist*• Born in Pressburg, he achieved some success with his opera *The Tower of Voivod* (1922), but is perhaps best known for his piano compositions, especially *Variation on a Nursery Theme* (1913), for piano and orchestra.

Doig, Peter 1959– •*British painter*• Born in Edinburgh, he lived in Quebec and Ontario (1966–79) before moving to London and training at the Wimbledon, St Martin's, and Chelsea schools of art (1979–90). Since 1991 he has become known for his landscapes and snowscapes, which emerge out of layers, skeins and blots of paint. Drawn to the woodland setting of **Le Corbusier**'s Habitation, at Briey-en-Forêt, Doig became a resident, and exhibited six paintings of it in London in 1994.

Doisneau, Robert 1912–94 •*French photographer*• Born in Gentilly, Seine, he became assistant to the Modernist photographer André Vigneau. After World War II Doisneau worked for several picture magazines, including *Life* magazine. A master of humor who could capture life's absurdities on film, he created images that radiated a mixture of satire and warmth and paid homage to the ordinary. *The Kiss* (1950) is perhaps his best-known picture.

Doisy, Edward Adelbert 1893–1986 •*US biochemist and Nobel Prize winner*• Born in Hume, Illinois, he studied at Harvard. In collaboration with the US embryologist Edgar Allen (1892–1943), he studied the female sex hormones estrone (1929), estriol (1930) and estradiol (1935). In his Porter Lectures at the University of Kansas (1936), he delineated the four stages of endocrinology as recognition of gland, detection of the hormone, its extraction and purification, and finally structure and synthesis. In 1939 he isolated two forms of the coagulant agent Vitamin K (discovered earlier by **Henrik Dam**), and they shared the 1943 Nobel Prize for physiology or medicine.

Dolci, Carlo 1616–86 •*Italian painter*• He was born in Florence. His works, which are scattered across Europe, include many Madonnas, *St Cecilia* (Dresden), *Herodias with the Head of John the Baptist* (Dresden) and the *Magdalene*, in the Uffizi, Florence.

Dole, Bob (Robert) 1923– •*US Republican politician*• Born in Russell, Kansas, he served in the Kansas state legislature and the House of Representatives before he won a Senate seat in 1968. He was Senate Republican Leader from 1985 to 1996, and was an unsuccessful Republican nominee for the vice presidency in 1976. Having sought the Republican nomination for the presidency in 1980 and 1988, without success, he became a presidential candidate in 1996, but lost the election to **Bill Clinton**, and retired from elected office. He is married to **Elizabeth Dole**.

Dole, Elizabeth Hanford, *née* **Hanford** 1936– •*US politician and campaign organizer*• Born in Salisbury, North Carolina, she trained as a lawyer and in 1975 married **Robert Dole**, who had become US Senator for Kansas in 1969. She has held numerous posts in the US government, including two Cabinet-level positions. From 1990 to 2000 she was the president of the American Red Cross. She has also taken an active role in her husband's campaigns to be elected for the office of vice president of the US in 1976, and supported his bids for the presidency. She sought the Republican presidential nomination in 2000, although she withdrew for lack of funds. She was elected to the US Senate in North Carolina in 2002.

“ ”

Sometimes I think we're the only two lawyers in Washington who trust each other.

1987 On her marriage to Senator Robert Dole. In ***Newsweek****, August 3.*

Dolet, Étienne, *known as* **the Martyr of the Renaissance** 1509–46 •*French printer and humanist*• Born in Orléans, he studied at the University of Paris. Living in Lyons from 1534, he wrote *Dialogus de imitatione ciceroniana* (1535) against **Erasmus**, and came under strong suspicion of heresy. He killed a man in self-defense and fled to Paris, where friends intervened with the king (1537). In Lyons he set up a printing press, on which he printed translations of the classics, as well as Erasmus and **Rabelais**. In 1544 he was found guilty of heresy (on a charge mainly based on an alleged mistranslation of **Plato**, in which he was accused of denying the immortality of the soul) and was burned in Paris. His chief contribution to classical scholarship was his *Commentarii* (2 vols, 1536–38, "Commentaries on the Latin Language").

Dolin, Anton, *originally* **Patrick Healey-Kay** 1904–83 •*English dancer and choreographer*• Born in Slinfold, Sussex, he was a principal with **Sergei Diaghilev**'s Ballets Russes from 1924. He was a founding member of the Camargo Society and a principal with the Vic-Wells Ballet during the 1930s, cofounding the **Markova**-Dolin Ballet in 1935. The partnership became known particularly for its interpretation of *Giselle*. From 1950 to 1961 he served as London Festival Ballet's first artistic director, choreographing for the company. His list of works includes *Rhapsody in Blue* (1928), *Variations for Four* (1957) and *Pas de deux for Four* (1967).

D'Oliveira, Basil Lewis 1931– •*South African cricket player*• Born in Cape Town, he was prohibited from playing cricket in South Africa as a nonwhite and so moved to England, where he played league cricket in Lancashire before joining Worcestershire. He made his debut for England in 1966 and went on to win 44 caps and score five Test centuries. The South African government's refusal to admit him into the country with the English team in 1968–69 resulted in the tour being canceled and South Africa being banned from international cricket.

Dollfuss, Engelbert 1892–1934 •*Austrian politician*• Born in Texing, he studied at Vienna and Berlin. He became leader of the Christian Socialist Party, and as Chancellor (1932–34) he suspended parliamentary government, drove the Socialists into revolt and crushed them (February 1934). Purged of its Socialist majority, parliament then granted Dollfuss power to remodel the state, but in July 1934 a Nazi putsch in Vienna culminated in his assassination.

Dolmetsch, (Eugène) Arnold 1858–1940 •*British musical-instrument maker*• Born in Le Mans, France, he went to England to study at the Royal College of Music (1883). Interested in early music and original instruments, he became involved in their restoration and manufacture around 1890. From 1892 he gave concerts at the Century Guild, owned by **Arthur Heygate Mackmurdo**. He exhibited a harpsichord at the Arts and Crafts Exhibition in 1896, and his clavichord of 1897 was decorated by **Edward Burne-Jones**. In 1919 he made the first modern recorder and in 1928 the Dolmetsch Foundation was established to support his work.

Dolphy, Eric (Allan) 1928–64 •*US jazz saxophonist and clarinettist*• Born in Los Angeles, he began to play clarinet at school and developed into an important, iconoclastic jazz performer on several reed instruments, notably alto saxophone and bass clarinet. He moved to New York in 1959, where he worked with such seminal (and diverse) figures as **Charles Mingus**, **John Coltrane**, **Ornette Coleman** and **Max Roach** among many others. His own recordings, notably *Out to Lunch* (1964), are crucial works of the period.

Domagk, Gerhard Johannes Paul 1895–1964 •*German biochemist and Nobel Prize winner*• Born in Lagow (now in Poland), he earned a degree in medicine from the University of Kiel (1921), and taught at the Universities of Greifswald and Münster before becoming director of the I G Farbenindustrie laboratory for experimental pathology and bacteriology in 1927. Domagk particularly sought a treatment against streptococci infections; one dye became of potent benefit when added to a substance called prontosil, which only worked in the living animal, being converted to sulfanilamide in the body. This discovery led to a new wonder drug and ushered in a new age in chemotherapy. In 1939 Domagk's original acceptance of the Nobel Prize for physiology or medicine was canceled upon instruction from the German government, but he finally received the award in 1947.

Domenichino, *also called* **Domenico Zampieri** 1581–1641 •*Italian painter*• He was born in Bologna and he painted in the style of the Bolognese school. His masterpiece is the *Last Communion of St Jerome* (1614), in the Vatican.

Domenico Veneziano c. 1400–61 •*Italian painter*• Known for his altarpiece in the Uffizi in Florence, he is represented in the National Gallery, London, by a *Madonna and Child.*

Domenico Zampieri *See* **Domenichino**

Domingo, Placido 1941– •*Spanish tenor*• Born in Madrid, he moved to Mexico with his family and studied piano and conducting at the National Conservatory of Music, Mexico City. In 1959 he made his debut as a baritone, taking his first major tenor role, that of Alfredo in *La Traviata*, in 1960. From 1962 to 1965 he was a member of the Israeli National Opera. He first sang in New York in 1965; at La Scala, Milan, in 1969; and Covent Garden, London, in 1971. His controlled, intelligent vocal technique and skillful acting have made him one of the world's leading lyric-dramatic tenors, and among his successes have been **Puccini**'s *Tosca*, **Verdi**'s *Otello*, **Bizet**'s *Carmen*, and **Jacques Offenbach**'s *Les contes d'Hoffmann* ("The Tales of Hoffmann"). In 1990 he performed alongside **José Carreras** and **Luciano Pavarotti** in the acclaimed "Three Tenors" concert in Rome, and has performed with them on several subsequent occasions. In 1994 he became artistic director of the Washington Opera, and in 2000 took up the same role at the Los Angeles Opera.

Dominic, St, *also called* **Dominic de Guzman** c. 1170–1221 •*Spanish founder of the Order of Friars Preachers*• Born in Calaruega, Old Castile, he studied at Palencia. His life was focused on missionary work, but his memory is stained by his consent to the cruel crusade instigated by **Innocent I** against the Albigenses. By the time Dominic died, the Dominican order, which he had founded in 1216, based on the Augustine rule, occupied 60 houses and had spread as far as England, where, from their dress, the monks were called "Black Friars." He was canonized in 1234 by **Gregory IX** and his feast day is August 4.

Domino, Fats (Antoine) 1928– •*US rhythm and blues pianist and singer*• Born in New Orleans, he learned to play the piano as a youngster, and performed in local clubs while working in a factory. He had the first of many collaborative hits with "The Fat Man" in 1950. His light-toned singing and laid-back but infectious piano style, compounded from New Orleans's rich Creole, Cajun, Latin, blues and jazz heritage, made him one of the first stars of the rock and roll era with songs like "Ain't That a Shame" and "Blueberry Hill."

Domitian, *originally* **Titus Flavius Domitianus** AD 51–96 •*Roman emperor*• The son of **Vespasian**, he succeeded his elder brother **Titus** as emperor in AD 81. He ruled well at first, and was a zealous administrator and builder; he expanded Roman territory in Britain and tried to improve public morality. However, his autocratic manner and severity alienated the Roman upper classes, and his reign declined into violence and terror. He eventually fell victim to one of many conspiracies, and the Flavian dynasty came to an end with him.

Donat, Aelius *See* **Donatus Magnus**

Donat, Robert 1905–58 •*English film and stage actor*• He was born in Manchester, of Polish descent. His stage performances included parts in *Julius Caesar* (1921), *Knave and Queen* (1930), *Saint Joan* (1931) and *Precious Bane* (1932), which brought him a contract with **Alexander Korda**. One of the most popular stars of 1930s British cinema, he appeared in films like *The Private Life of Henry VIII* (1932), *The Thirty-Nine Steps* (1935) and *Goodbye, Mr Chips* (1939), which earned him an Academy Award (Best Actor). His later career was blighted by ill health, although he continued to give much-admired performances. He died shortly after completing a poignant performance as the Chinese mandarin in *Inn of the Sixth Happiness* (1958).

Donatello, *real name* **Donato di Niccolo** c. 1386–1466 •*Florentine sculptor*• One of the most important artists of early Renaissance Italy, he trained in the Florence Cathedral workshop under **Ghiberti** and received his first commission in 1408. He was the first sculptor since classical times to produce works that are fully rounded and independent in themselves and not mere adjuncts of their architectural settings. The evolution of his highly charged and emotional style can be traced in a series of figures of saints he executed for the exterior of Or San Michele and another series of prophets for the Campanile, in which his interest in classical antiquity is evident. In the 1420s, in partnership with **Michelozzi**, he produced the monument to the antipope **John XXIII** in the Baptistery, which influenced all subsequent tomb design. In 1443 he migrated to Padua, where he produced the bronze equestrian portrait of the military commander known as Gattemelata—the first life-size equestrian statue since antiquity. The celebrated bronze statue of **David** is a key work of the Renaissance, as is the multiple-viewpoint *Judith and Holofernes* in the Piazza della Signoria in Florence. The anguished, expressive statue of **Mary Magdalene** has no counterpart elsewhere in the 15th century.

Donatus, Aelius fl. 4th century AD •*Roman grammarian*• He taught grammar and rhetoric in Rome in about AD 360 to St **Jerome**, among others. His treatises form a course of Latin grammar (*Ars grammatica*) and in the Middle Ages were the only textbooks used in schools, so that "Donat" in western Europe came to mean a grammar book. He also wrote commentaries on **Terence** and **Virgil**.

Donatus Magnus, *also called* **Aelius Donat** d. c. 355 AD •*North African bishop*• He was a leader of the Donatists, a 4th-century puritan Christian sect in North Africa who objected to Roman influences. As Bishop of Carthage (AD 312–47), he was involved in the Donatist schism of the North African Church.

Don Carlos *See* **Carlos, Don**

Dönitz, Karl 1891–1980 •*German Nazi politician and naval commander*• Born in Grünau, near Berlin, he joined the submarine service of the Imperial German Navy in 1916, and became a staunch advocate and supporter of U-boat warfare. He planned **Hitler**'s U-boat fleet, was made its commander in 1936, and in 1943 succeeded **Erich Raeder** as Commander in Chief of the German navy. Becoming Führer on the death of Hitler, he was responsible for the final surrender to the Allies, and in 1946 was sentenced to ten years' imprisonment for war crimes.

Donizetti, (Domenico) Gaetano (Maria) 1797–1848 •*Italian composer*• Born in Bergamo, he studied music there and in Bologna. His first opera, *Enrico di Borgogna*, was successfully produced in Venice (1818), but his first internationally famous work was *Anna Bolena*, produced in Milan in 1830. *L'elisir d'amore* (1832, "The Elixir of Love") and *Lucrezia Borgia* (1833) also achieved lasting popularity, as did *Lucia di Lammermoor* (1835). In Paris (1840), he staged *La fille du régiment* ("The Daughter of the Regiment") and *La favorita* ("The Favorite"). The comic opera *Don Pasquale* (1843) was his last success, soon after which he became paralyzed and then insane.

Donleavy, J(ames) P(atrick) 1926– •*Irish author*• He was born in Brooklyn, New York, to Irish parents, and after serving in the US Navy during World War II, studied microbiology at Trinity College, Dublin, where he became a friend of **Brendan Behan**. While living on a farm in Wicklow, he wrote his first novel, *The Ginger Man*, published in 1955. Picaresque, bawdy, presenting an apparently totally irrational hero, it was hailed as a comic masterpiece. Further works include *The Beastly Beatitudes of Balthazar B* (1968), *The Onion Eaters* (1971), *Schultz* (1980), *Are You Listening, Rabbi Low?* (1987) and *That Darcy, That Dancer, That Gentleman* (1990), *The Lady Who Liked Clean Rest Rooms* (1995) and *Wrong Information Is Being Given Out at Princeton* (1998). His paintings have been exhibited in Dublin, New York, London and Belfast.

Donne, John c. 1572–1631 •*English poet*• He was born in London, the son of a prosperous ironmonger, and connected through his mother with Sir **Thomas More**. Although a Catholic, he was admitted to Hart Hall, Oxford, and later graduated at Cambridge. He decided to take up law and entered Lincoln's Inn in 1592. After taking part in the 2nd Earl of **Essex**'s two expeditions to Cádiz in 1597 and the Azores in 1598 (reflected in his poems "The Storm" and "The Calm"), he became (1598) secretary to Sir **Thomas Egerton**, keeper of the Great Seal. His daring works and strong personality indicated a career as notable as that of his contemporary, **Francis Bacon**, but he was dismissed and imprisoned after his secret marriage to Egerton's niece, Anne More. Having turned Protestant, he lived in Mitcham in Surrey, but still sought favor and employment at the court. He had already written his passionate and erotic poems, *Songs and Sonnets* and his six *Satires* and his *Elegies*, but published no verse until 1611 when his *Anniversarie* appeared, a commemorative poem for Elizabeth Drury, daughter of his benefactor, Sir Robert Drury. A second *Anniversarie* followed, which displayed his metaphysical genius at its best. His religious temper is seen in more lyrical form in the *Divine Poems*, some of which certainly date from before 1607. These, like most of his verse, were published posthumously, but his pieces circulated widely among learned and aristocratic friends. How difficult his journey to the Anglican faith was may be judged from the satirical "Progresse of the Soule" (1601). In his funeral poems, of which the first and second *Anniversaries* are the best, he also paid court to the great, and he flattered the distinguished ladies of the time in verse letters of labored but indigenous compliment. His prose works of this period include *Pseudo-Martyr* (1610), which is an acute polemic against the Jesuits. More interesting is his *Biothanatos*, which discussed the question of suicide, which he claimed to contemplate on occasion. King **James VI and I** encouraged him to go into the Church (1614), and promoted him to the deanship of St Paul's in 1621. Several of his sermons are still extant. In this middle period of his life he accompanied Sir Robert Drury to France and Spain. In 1619 and 1620 he was in Germany, where he preached one of his most noble sermons before the exiled Queen **Elizabeth** of Bohemia, King James's daughter. Donne's creative years fall into three periods: from 1590 to 1601, a time of action, passion and cynicism; from his marriage to his ordination in 1614, a period of anguished meditation and flattery of the great; and the period of his ministry, which includes two sonnet sequences, *La corona* and *Holy Sonnets*, the latter containing (no. xvii) an anguished tribute to his wife, who died in 1617. Also of this period are the fine "Hymne to God, the Father," "To God My God, in My Sicknesse" and "The Author's Last Going into Germany."

“ ”

The world is a great volume, and man the index of that book.

1626 "Sermon Preached at the Funeral of Sir William Cockayne," December 12.

Donnelly, Ignatius 1831–1901 •*US politician and writer*• Born in Philadelphia, he moved to Minnesota in 1856, becoming lieutenant governor and governor (1859–63) and later Radical Republican congressman (1863–69). As a prophet of reform his most enduring legacy is a horrific novel, *Caesar's Column* (1891), predicting tyranny and oppression. His *Atlantis, The Antediluvian World* (1882) was a highly popular development of the idea of a former continent drowned under the Atlantic Ocean. His *The Great Cryptogram* (1888) sought to prove **Francis Bacon** had written the plays usually attributed to **Shakespeare**.

Donoso (Yanez), José 1928–96 •*Chilean novelist*• Born in Santiago, he attended the University of Chile and Princeton in the US, and worked as a longshoreman, teacher, editor and journalist. In 1962 he received the William Faulkner Foundation prize for Chile for his novel *Coronación* (1957, Eng trans *Coronation*, 1965). His work reflects urban life with its madness, opulence and decay. Among his other novels are *El obsceno pájaro de la noche* (1970, Eng trans *The Obscene Bird of Night*, 1973), *Casa de campo* (1978, Eng trans *A House in the Country*, 1984), *La desesperanza* (1985, "Desperation") and *Conjecturas sobre la memoria de mi tribu* (1996, "Conjectures About the Memory of My Tribe").

Donovan, Terence Daniel 1936–96 •*English photographer*• Born in the East End of London, he left school at the age of 11 and later studied at the London School of Engraving and Lithography. By the age of 15 he had joined the studio of John French, a leading fashion photographer. He became famous for a style that juxtaposed the luxurious with the everyday, photographing models against harsh and bleak backgrounds. He published a collection of photographs, *Glances*, in 1983.

Doolittle, Hilda, *known as* **H D** 1886–1961 •*US Imagist poet*• Born in Bethlehem, Pennsylvania, she was educated at Gordon School, the Friends' Central School in Philadelphia, and Bryn Mawr College (1904–06). She lived in London from 1911 and married **Richard Aldington** in 1913. After their divorce in 1937, she settled near Lake Geneva. Her many volumes of poetry include *Sea Garden* (1916), *Flowering of the Rod* (1946) and *Helen in Egypt* (1961). She also wrote several novels, notably *Palimpsest* (1926), *Tribute to Freud* (1956) and *Bid Me to Live* (1960).

Doppler, Christian Johann 1803–53 •*Austrian physicist*• Born in Salzburg, he studied at the Polytechnic Institute in Vienna and in 1851 was appointed Professor of Physics at the Royal Imperial University of Vienna. "Doppler's principle," which he enunciated in a paper in 1842, explains the frequency variation observed when a vibrating source of waves and the observer approach or recede from one another. The Doppler effect applies to all forms of electromagnetic radiation and is used in astronomy, where the changing wavelengths of approaching or receding celestial bodies provide important evidence for the concept of an expanding universe.

Dorat, Jean *See* **Daurat, Jean**

Dorati, Antal 1906–88 •*US conductor and composer*• He was born in Budapest, Hungary, and studied at the Budapest Academy and University. After various opera and ballet posts in Europe, he went to the US in 1945 and became a US citizen two years later. There he directed the Minneapolis Symphony Orchestra (1949–60) and made a number of acclaimed recordings with them. He recorded all the symphonies of **Haydn** with the Philharmonia Hungarica. He also conducted 20th-century music, notably that of **Stravinsky** and Les Six, and of his compatriot **Bartók**. He was principal conductor of the BBC Symphony Orchestra (1963–67), and received an honorary knighthood in 1983.

Doré, Gustave 1832–83 •*French painter and book illustrator*• Born in Strasbourg, he first became known for his illustrations to **Rabelais**'s works (1854) and to *The Wandering Jew* and **Honoré de Balzac**'s *Contes drolatiques* (1865). Other works include illustrated editions of **Dante**'s *Inferno* (1861), the *Contes* of **Charles Perrault** and *Don Quixote* (1863), the *Purgatorio* and *Paradiso* of Dante (1868), the Bible (1865–66), *Paradise Lost* (1866), **Tennyson**'s *Idylls of the King* (1867–68), and **Jean de La Fontaine**'s *Fables* (1867).

Doren, Carl Clinton Van *See* **Van Doren, Carl Clinton**

Doren, Mark Albert Van *See* **Van Doren, Mark Albert**

Dorfman, Ariel 1942– •*Chilean playwright, novelist and short-story writer*• Born in Argentina, he was brought up in Chile but was forced into exile in 1973 and did not return until 1990. He gained international acclaim with his play *Death and the Maiden* (1991, Laurence Olivier award for Best Play, 1992), about a South American torture victim who takes revenge on her torturer. He also wrote the screenplay for the film of the same name by **Roman Polanski** (1995). Dorfman's other works include a book of essays, *Some Write to the Future* (1991), novels such as *Konfidenz* (1995) and *The Nanny and the Iceberg* (1999), and plays such as *The Reader* (1995).

Dorn, Friedrich Ernst 1848–1916 •*German chemist*• Born in Guttstadt, East Prussia, he was educated at Königsberg and taught physics at Darmstadt and Halle. In 1900 he noticed that radium apparently becomes less radioactive if swept with a current of gas. This led him to the discovery of a radioactive gas that is emitted by radium as part of its decay processes. He called it "niton," but it is now known as radon.

Dornberger, Walter Robert 1895–1980 •*US rocket engineer*• Born in Giessen Hesse, Germany, he was an engineer and officer in the German army. By 1934 he had designed a 3,300-pound-thrust rocket (1,497-kilogram) that reached a height of 1.5 miles (2.4 kilometers). In World War II the work was transferred to Peenemünde, where in 1942 a 46-foot (13.8-meter), 14-ton rocket was launched to the edge of the atmosphere. From 1944 to 1945, 1,500 of these V-2 rockets with explosive warheads were launched against Great Britain, and 2,000 into Antwerp, Belgium. After spending three years as a prisoner of war in England (1945–47), he went to the US and in 1950 joined the Bell Aircraft Corporation.

Dornier, Claudius 1884–1969 •*German aircraft designer*• Born in Kempten, he was educated at technical college in Munich. He designed the first all-metal aircraft in 1911 after entering the service of

Graf von Zeppelin, and in 1914 founded the Dornier works at Friedrichshafen on Lake Constance. He manufactured seaplanes and flying boats, including the famous 12-engine Do X (1929) and the Dornier twin-engine bomber, which was a standard Luftwaffe type in World War II.

Dorrell, Stephen James 1952– •*English Conservative politician*• Born in Worcester, he was educated at Uppingham and Oxford and became Member of Parliament for Loughborough in 1979. During **John Major**'s administration he rose to Financial Secretary to the Treasury (1992–94) and Secretary of State for National Heritage (1994–95). In 1995 he succeeded **Virginia Bottomley** as Secretary of State for Health, and was a key figure in the subsequent affair over the outbreak of bovine spongiform encephalopathy (BSE) in British beef. Following the Conservatives' election defeat in 1997, he lost the leadership contest to **William Hague**.

Dors, Diana, *originally* **Diana Fluck** 1931–84 •*English actress*• Born in Swindon, Wiltshire, she was a student at the Royal Academy of Dramatic Art. She signed a long-term contract with Rank who groomed her for stardom in their "Charm School." Promoted as a sex symbol, she was cast in various low-budget comedies, and despite an effective dramatic performance in *Yield to the Night* (1956) and highly publicized visits to Hollywood, she was soon typecast in blowsy supporting roles. Her accomplished stage work in *Three Months Gone* (1970) brought her a selection of good character parts in films like *Deep End* (1970) and *The Amazing Mr Blunden* (1972). Later roles were undistinguished, but her personal popularity never dimmed as she performed in cabarets and as a television advice columnist.

Dorsey, Thomas A(ndrew) 1899–1993 •*US gospel musician*• Born in Villa Rica, Georgia, the son of a revivalist preacher, he began his career as a blues pianist. He combined blues melodies and rhythms with Christian religious music in about 1,000 gospel songs, including "Take My Hand, Precious Lord" (1931). He founded the first gospel choir at Ebenezer Baptist Church in Chicago (1931) and established the National Convention of Gospel Choirs and Choruses (1933) to promote gospel music. He is known as "the father of gospel music."

Dorsey, Tommy (Thomas) 1905–56 •*US trombonist and bandleader*• Born in Shenandoah, Pennsylvania, the son of a bandleader, he formed big bands, sometimes co-led by his brother Jimmy (1904–57, alto saxophone, clarinet), that included many accomplished jazz soloists. They existed as the Dorsey Brothers Orchestra from 1932 to 1935, reforming again in 1953 until Tommy's death. Both brothers were in great demand as session musicians in the late 1920s with the expansion of radio in the US, and their fame was revived through a regular television show in the 1950s.

Dos Passos, John Roderigo 1896–1970 •*US novelist, playwright and journalist*• Born in Chicago, the grandson of a Portuguese immigrant, he was educated at Choate and Harvard. In 1916 he went to Spain to study architecture but was caught up in World War I and served in the US Medical Corps. Thereafter he lived in the US but traveled widely on journalistic assignments. He had a precocious start as an author, publishing *One Man's Initiation* in 1917 when he was 21. The fiercely antiwar *Three Soldiers* (1921) confirmed his talent, and in *Manhattan Transfer* (1925) his confidence and ambition grew, its rapid narrative transitions and collectivist approach foreshadowing the monumental *U.S.A.* trilogy: *The 42nd Parallel* (1930), *1919* (1932) and *The Big Money* (1936). A digressive, dynamic epic, it consists of a medley of newsreel footage, snatches of popular songs, brief but vivid sketches of public figures and prose-poetry. *The Best Times* (1966), his last book, was a reminiscence of his youth.

Dos Santos, Jose Eduardo 1942– •*Angolan politician and nationalist*• Born in Luanda, he joined the People's Movement for the Liberation of Angola (MPLA) in 1961 and was forced into exile in what is now the Democratic Republic of Congo while the struggle for independence developed into a civil war between the MPLA and the National Union for the Total Independence of Angola (UNITA). In Congo he founded the MPLA Youth and in 1963 was sent to Moscow to study petroleum engineering and telecommunications. He returned to Angola in 1970 and rejoined the war between the government (assisted by Cuba) and UNITA (supported by South Africa). He held key positions under President **Agostinho Neto**, and when Neto died in 1979, succeeded him. By 1989, with US help, he had negotiated the withdrawal of South African and Cuban forces, and a ceasefire between MPLA and UNITA. A peace agreement was signed in 1991, and a general election was held in 1992. An inconclusive result led to the resumption of the civil war, leaving Dos Santos in power.

Dosso Dossi, *properly* **Giovanni di Niccolò Lutero** 1479–1542 •*Italian religious painter*• Born near Mantua, he was a friend of **Ludovico Ariosto** and painted some pictures jointly with his brother Battista (c. 1497–1548).

Dostoevsky, Fyodor Mikhailovich, *also spelled* **Dostoyevsky** 1821–81 •*Russian novelist*• He was born in Moscow. His mother died in 1837 and his father was murdered a little over two years later. His first published short story was "Poor Folk," which gained him immediate recognition. In 1849 he was arrested and sentenced to death for participating in the socialist "Petrashevsky Circle," but during the preparations for his execution a commutation was announced and he was sent instead to Siberia, where he was confined in a prison at Omsk until 1854. There, among other works, he read **Dickens**'s *Pickwick Papers* and *David Copperfield*; and he experienced a religious crisis in which he rejected socialism for Russian Orthodoxy. *The House of the Dead* (1860) was a result of his experience at Omsk. In 1861 he began the review *Vremya* ("Time") with his brother Mikhail, and he spent the next two years traveling abroad, which confirmed his anti-European outlook. At this time he met Mlle Suslova, the model for many of his heroines, and succumbed to the gaming tables. He fell heavily into debt but was rescued by Anna Grigoryevna Smitkina, whom he married in 1867. They lived abroad for several years, but he returned to Russia in 1871 to edit *Grazhdanin*, to which he contributed his "Author's Diary." Like **Dickens**, Dostoevsky was both horrified and fascinated by the Industrial Revolution, and his fiction is dark with the suffering caused by poverty and appalling living conditions, crime and the exploitation of children. Second only to those of **Leo Tolstoy**, his novels *Crime and Punishment* (1866), *The Idiot* (1868), *The Devils* (1872) and *The Brothers Karamazov* (1880) have been profoundly influential, and their impact on **Robert Louis Stevenson**'s *Dr Jekyll and Mr Hyde* (1886), among many others, is conspicuous. Others have reacted with hostility to his work, including **Henry James**, **Joseph Conrad**, and **D H Lawrence**.

" "

Power is given only to him who dares to stoop and take it ... one must have the courage to dare.

1866 ***Crime and Punishment****, part 5, chapter 4 (translated by David Magarshak).*

Dou or **Douw, Gerard** 1612–75 •*Dutch painter*• Born in Leiden, he studied under **Rembrandt** (1628–31). At first he mainly occupied himself with portraiture, but soon turned to genre painting characterized by precisely painted scenes of everyday life. He is known as the founder of the Leiden school of *fijnschilders* ("fine painters"), and his 200 works include portraits of himself and his wife, *The Poulterer's Shop*, in the National Gallery, London, and his celebrated *Dropsical Woman* (1663), in the Louvre, Paris.

Doubleday, Abner 1819–93 •*US general and alleged inventor of baseball*• Born in Ballston Spa, New York, he served as a major general of volunteer Union troops in the Civil War. In 1907 a commission reported that Doubleday had invented baseball at Cooperstown, New York, in 1839. This report has been discredited, and it is now known that a game similar to baseball was played in the US and England long before Doubleday's time.

Douglas, Lord Alfred Bruce 1870–1945 •*English poet*• The son of the 8th Marquis of **Queensberry**, he wrote a number of impressive sonnets, collected in *In Excelsis* (1924), *Sonnets* (1935) and *Lyrics* (1935). He is remembered for his association with **Oscar Wilde**, to which his father objected, thereby provoking Wilde to bring the ill-advised libel action which led to his own arrest and imprisonment. He wrote two books on Oscar Wilde, and *The Autobiography of Lord Alfred Douglas* (1929).

Douglas, Bill 1934–91 •*Scottish film director*• Born in Newcraighall, near Edinburgh, the illegitimate son of a miner, he was brought up amid misery and penury, an experience that formed the basis of his famed autobiographical trilogy. After National Service he pursued a career as an actor and writer before making his directorial debut with *My Childhood* (1972). Together with *My Ain Folk* (1973) and *My Way Home* (1977), it formed an intense, dramatic interpretation of his childhood and adolescence. He made only one further feature film, *Comrades* (1986), an ambitious, epic account of the Tolpuddle Martyrs.

Douglas, David 1799–1834 •*Scottish botanist and plant collector*• Born in Scone, Perthshire, he went on many collecting trips with Sir **William Hooker**. In 1823 he became a plant collector for the Horticultural Society of London, and left on an expedition to North America, where he discovered many new species such as *Aster douglasii*, *Garrya elliptica* and *Paeonia brownii*. The most famous of the many plants Douglas introduced into cultivation was the Douglas fir (*Pseudotsuga taxifolia*), and the Douglas squirrel was also renamed after him. After some months in London, Douglas sailed again for western North America and explored southern California (1830–32), traveled up the Fraser and Simpson Rivers in western Canada, and sailed to Hawaii, where he was gored to death by a bull.

Douglas, Donald Wills 1892–1981 •*US aircraft designer and manufacturer*• Born in Brooklyn, New York, he attended the US Naval Academy and the Massachusetts Institute of Technology (MIT). He set up his own company (Davis-Douglas Co) in California in 1920, producing the all-metal low-wing Douglas DC-2 transport of 1934. The DC-3 (C-47, Dakota) followed in 1936, and the DC-4, -6 and -7 and the jet-engine transports DC-8, -9 and -10 appeared thereafter. During World War II he produced the B-19 bomber and other craft. He was chairman of his company, Douglas Aircraft, until it merged with McDonnell Aircraft as the McDonnell Douglas Corporation in 1967.

Douglas, Gawain or **Gavin** c. 1474–1522 •*Scottish poet and prelate*• Born in Tantallon Castle, East Lothian, he was educated at St Andrews, and possibly Paris, for the priesthood, and from 1501 to 1514 was dean or provost of the Collegiate Church of St Giles, Edinburgh. After the Battle of Flodden (1513), in which King **James IV** fell, Douglas's nephew, the 6th Earl of Angus, married the widowed Queen **Margaret Tudor**, and through her influence Douglas became Bishop of Dunkeld (1515). His works include *The Palice of Honour* (c. 1501) and a translation of **Virgil**'s *Aeneid*, with prologues (finished c. 1513), the first version of a Latin poet published in the vernacular.

Douglas, Kirk, *originally* **Issur Danielovich** 1916– •*US film actor*• Born in Amsterdam, New York, the son of poor Russian immigrants, he acted on Broadway and served in the US Navy before moving to Hollywood and making his film debut in *The Strange Love of Martha Ivers* (1946). An ambitious actor, noted for his intensity, he received Best Actor Academy Award nominations for *Champion* (1949), *The Bad and the Beautiful* (1952) and *Lust For Life* (1956), in which he played **Van Gogh**. His numerous films include *Paths of Glory* (1957), *Spartacus* (1960) and *Lonely Are the Brave* (1962). He has published an autobiography, *The Ragman's Son* (1988), and several novels. In 1996 he received a special Academy Award.

Douglas, Mary, *née* **Tew** 1921– •*English social anthropologist*• Born in Italy, she studied at Oxford, and carried out fieldwork among the Lele of the Belgian Congo in 1949–50 and 1953. From 1970 until 1978 she taught at University College London, and in 1977 she moved to the US where she held various professorships. She is especially known for her studies of systems of cultural classification and beliefs about purity and pollution, as in *Purity and Danger* (1966). She has contributed significantly to economic anthropology in *The World of Goods* (1979, with Baron Isherwood), and to the sociology of risk in *Risk and Blame* (1992).

Douglas, Michael (Kirk) 1944– •*US film actor and producer*• Born in New Brunswick, New Jersey, he gained experience of the film industry through his father, **Kirk Douglas**. Working as a producer, he shared the Best Picture Academy Award for *One Flew Over the Cuckoo's Nest* (1975). Among the films he has starred in are *Romancing the Stone* (1984), *Jewel of the Nile* (1985), *Fatal Attraction* (1987), *Wall Street* (1987), for which he won a Best Actor Academy Award, *Basic Instinct* (1992), *Disclosure* (1994) and *Traffic* (2000), in which he costarred with his wife, Catherine Zeta Jones (1969–).

Douglas-Home, Alec *See* **Home (of the Hirsel), Baron**

Douglass, Andrew Ellicott 1867–1962 •*US astronomer*• He was born in Windsor, Vermont, and became Professor of Physics and Astronomy at the University of Arizona (1906) and later director of the Stewart Observatory (1918–38). He investigated the relationship between sunspots and climate by examining and measuring the annual growth rings of long-lived Arizona pines and sequoias. He coined the term "dendrochronology" ("tree-dating") in his *Climatic Cycles and Tree Growth* (3 vols, 1919–36).

Douglass, Frederick, *originally* **Frederick Augustus Washington Bailey** 1817–95 •*US abolitionist*• Born a slave in Tuckahoe, Maryland, he learned to read and write in childhood as a household servant. He escaped from a Baltimore shipyard in 1838, and changed his name. He settled in New Bedford, Massachusetts, became an agent of the Massachusetts Anti-Slavery Society and wrote *Narrative of the Life of Frederick Douglas* (1845). He lectured on slavery (1845–47) in Great Britain, but returned to the US to buy his freedom, thus banishing his fear of recapture. In 1847 he started *The North Star* in Rochester, New York, an abolitionist journal that he edited for 16 years. He held various public offices and was US minister to Haiti (1889–91).

“ ”

The white man's happiness cannot be purchased by the black man's misery.

1849 "The Destiny of Colored Americans" in ***The North Star**, November 16.*

Doulton, Sir Henry 1820–97 •*English pottery manufacturer*• Born in Lambeth, London, he entered his father's pottery there and in 1846 introduced stoneware drain pipes instead of flat-bottomed brick drains. In 1848 he started works, later the largest in the world, near Dudley. He furthered the revival in artistic pottery.

Douw, Gerard or **Gerrit** *See* **Dou, Gerard**

Dove, Rita Frances 1952– •*US poet*• Born in Akron, Ohio, she is Commonwealth Professor of English at the University of Virginia. Her first book was *Ten Poems* (1977). *The Yellow House on the Corner* (1980) contained a sequence of poems told from the point of view of slaves, and historical figures have recurred throughout her work. She was awarded the Pulitzer Prize for poetry in 1987 for *Thomas and Beulah* (1986), in which she recreated the lives of her grandparents from courtship to death. *Fifth Sunday* (1985) is a collection of short stories. Later works include *Mother Love* (1995) and *On the Bus with Rosa Parks* (1999). From 1993 to 1995 she was US poet laureate.

Dowding, Hugh Caswall Tremenheere Dowding, 1st Baron 1882–1970 •*Scottish air force chief*• Born in Moffat, Dumfriesshire, and educated at Winchester and at the Royal Military Academy, Woolwich, he joined the air force in 1914 and was decorated for service in World War I. As Commander in Chief of Fighter Command (1936–40), he organized the air defense of Great Britain, and in August to September 1940 the German air force was defeated in the momentous Battle of Britain. Created a peer in 1943, he became interested in spiritualism, and his *Many Mansions* (1943) contained communications attributed to men killed in the war.

Dowell, Sir Anthony 1943– •*English dancer and director*• Born in London, he trained at Sadler's Wells and the Royal Ballet School. A skillful and elegant technician, he first performed with the Royal Ballet in 1961 and was chosen as partner to **Antoinette Sibley** in Sir **Frederick Ashton**'s *The Dream* (1964), a partnership which was to be highly successful. He was promoted to principal dancer in 1966 and since then has danced all the major roles in the classical repertoire as well as having many new roles created for him by major choreographers. He was principal dancer of the American Ballet Theater (1978–80), but returned to the Royal Ballet as artistic director (1986–2001). He was knighted in 1995.

Dowie, John Alexander 1847–1907 •*US religious leader*• Born in Edinburgh, Scotland, he emigrated to Australia in 1860 and in 1888 to the US, where he organized the Christian Catholic Church in Zion (1896). He became a faith healer, and in 1901 he founded near Chicago the prosperous industrial and banking community called "Zion City." He was deposed from his autocratic rule there in 1906 due to opposition to his fiscal irresponsibility (and alleged polygamy).

Dowland, John 1563–1626 •*English lutenist and songwriter*• Born possibly in Westminster, London, he earned a music degree at Oxford in 1588, later also graduating from Cambridge. He entered the service of the Duke of Brunswick in 1594, and his *First Books of Songes or Ayres of Foure Partes with Tableture for the Lute* appeared in 1597. In 1598 he became lutenist to **Christian IV** of Denmark. Back in London, he brought out his *Lachrymae* (1605), which contains some of the finest instrumental consort music of the period, and is dedicated to **Anne of Denmark**.

Dowson, Ernest Christopher 1867–1900 •*English poet*• Born in London and brought up mainly in France, he studied at Oxford. His friends included **Arthur Symons**, **Oscar Wilde** and **W B Yeats**. From 1894 writing became his livelihood, and *Verses* appeared in 1896 and *Decorations* in 1899. His two best-known poems, "Vitae summa brevis" (1896) and "Cynara" (1891), have contributed several stock phrases to English: "days of wine and roses," "gone with the wind" and "I have been faithful to thee, Cynara! in my fashion."

Doyle, Sir Arthur Conan 1859–1930 •*Scottish writer of detective stories and historical romances, creator of Sherlock Holmes*• Born of Irish parentage in Edinburgh, he was educated at Stonyhurst and in Germany, and studied medicine at Edinburgh. Initial poverty as a young practitioner in Southsea and as an oculist in London coaxed him into authorship. *A Study in Scarlet* introduced that prototype of the modern detective in fiction, Sherlock Holmes, and his good-natured friend Dr John Watson. *The Adventures of Sherlock Holmes* were serialized in the *Strand Magazine* (1891–93) and published as books under such titles as *The Sign of Four* (1890) and *The Hound of the Baskervilles* (1902). They became so popular that when Conan Doyle tried to kill off his hero, he was compelled in 1903 to revive him. However, his historical romances, *The White Company* (1890), *Brigadier Gerard* (1896) and *Sir Nigel* (1906), have more literary merit and are underrated, and *Rodney Stone* (1896) is one of his best novels. He served as a physician in the Second Boer War (1899–1902), and his pamphlet, *The War in South Africa* (1902), justifying Great Britain's action, earned him a knighthood (1902). He also wrote on spiritualism, to which he became a convert in later life.

Doyle, Roddy 1958– •*Irish novelist*• Born in Dublin, he worked for 14 years as a teacher in a community school in Kilbarrack (North Dublin), a deprived area which is the "Barrytown" of his novels. *The Commitments* (1987, filmed 1991), *The Snapper* (1990, filmed 1993) and *The Van* (1991, filmed 1996) spoke for communities denied a media voice, their comic style acting as a vehicle for Doyle's statement on the plight of the urban dispossessed. The Booker Prize–winning *Paddy Clarke Ha Ha Ha* (1993), narrated through the sense and senses of a 10-year-old boy, similarly exhibits the tragedy that underlies all comedy, as does *The Woman Who Walked into Doors* (1996). Other work includes *A Star Called Henry* (1999) and the screenplay *When Brendan Met Trudy* (filmed 2000).

Drabble, Margaret 1939– •*English novelist*• Born in Sheffield, Yorkshire, she was educated at the Mount School, York (the Quaker boarding school where her mother taught), and Newnham College, Cambridge. She acted for a short time, then turned to writing. Frequently mirroring her own life, her novels concentrate on the concerns of intelligent, often frustrated middle-class women. *A Summer Bird-Cage* (1963), *The Garrick Year* (1964), *Jersualem the Golden* (1967), *The Needle's Eye* (1972), *The Ice Age* (1977), *The Middle Ground* (1980), and the trilogy comprising *The Radiant Way* (1987), *A Natural Curiosity* (1989) and *The Gates of Ivory* (1991) are among her titles. She was the editor of the fifth and sixth editions of the *Oxford Companion to English Literature*, and has written biographies of **Arnold Bennett** (1974) and **Angus Wilson** (1995). Later works include *The Witch of Exmoor* (1996) and *The Peppered Moth* (2001). Her elder sister is the novelist **A S Byatt**.

“ ”

Sometimes it seems the only accomplishment my education ever bestowed on me was the ability to think in quotations.

*1963 **A Summer Bird-Cage**, chapter 1.*

Draco 7th century BC •*Athenian legislator*• His harsh codification of the law in 621 BC produced the word "draconian." The code was largely abolished by **Solon** (594), and only his law on homicide remained.

Drake, Sir Francis c. 1540–96 •*English navigator*• Born in Crowndale, near Tavistock, by 1565 was voyaging to Guinea and the Spanish Main. In 1567 he commanded the *Judith* in his kinsman Sir **John Hawkins**'s ill-fated expedition to the Gulf of Mexico and in 1570 and 1571 sailed to the West Indies to make good the losses he had then sustained from the Spaniards, gaining great popularity in England in the process. In 1572, with two small ships, the *Pasha* and *Swan*, and a privateer's license from Queen **Elizabeth I**, he plundered on the Isthmus of Panama and became the first Englishman to see the Pacific Ocean. In 1577 he set out with five ships to explore the Strait of Magellan, and on entering the Pacific Ocean, he encountered violent tempests for 52 days, during which the *Marigold* foundered with all hands and the *Elizabeth* returned home. Drake sailed north alone to Vancouver, but failing to find a Northwest Passage back into the Atlantic, he turned south and moved across the Pacific, and for 68 days did not sight land until he made the Pelew Islands. After refitting in Java, he headed for the Cape of Good Hope, and was knighted on his arrival home in September 1580, the first Englishman to circumnavigate the world. In the autumn of 1585 he sailed against the Spanish Indies, plundered Hispaniola, Cartagena and the coast of Florida, and brought home the 190 dispirited Virginian colonists, with tobacco and potatoes. Early in 1587 he pillaged Cádiz, and in 1588, as vice admiral under **Charles Howard**, took a leading part in harassing the Spanish Armada as it passed through the English Channel. He died while on an expedition with **Hawkins** to the West Indies.

Draper, Henry 1837–82 •*US astronomer and pioneer of astronomical photography*• Born in Prince Edward County, Virginia, he graduated in medicine from City University, New York, and taught there from 1860 to 1882. At the same time he applied himself to astronomical photography. In 1872 he obtained a photograph of the spectrum of the star Vega and in 1874 he directed the photographic section of the US commission that observed the transit of Venus. After his death his widow furthered his work, the result being the *Henry Draper Catalogue* of stellar spectra (9 vols, 1918–24).

Draper, John William 1811–82 •*US author and scientist*• Born in St Helens, Lancashire, England, he began medical studies in London in 1829. In 1831 he emigrated to Virginia, qualified in medicine in 1836, and subsequently taught chemistry at New York University. He was an early pioneer of photography, and in 1840 made what is probably the oldest surviving photographic portrait, a picture of his sister, which required an exposure of 65 seconds. In the same year, he photographed the moon, and later made early ultraviolet and infrared photographs of the sun, describing **Fraunhofer** lines in the solar spectrum. In 1850 he made the first photomicrographs, which served as illustrations of a book called *Physiology*. In 1841 he formulated Draper's law, the principle that only absorbed radiation can produce chemical change.

Drayton, Michael 1563–1631 •*English poet*• Born in Hartshill, near Atherstone, Warwickshire, he became a page in a wealthy household and spent the rest of his life in the households of patrons. His first major poem, *Mortimeriados* (1596, recast in 1603 as *The Barons' Wars*) was followed by *England's Heroical Epistles* (1597). *Poems, Lyric and Pastoral* (c. 1606) contains some of his most familiar poems, including the *Ballad of Agincourt*. The first 18 "songs" or books of his greatest work, the panoramic *Polyolbion*, were published in 1613, and the complete poem appeared in 1622.

Drechsler, Heike, *née* **Daute** 1964– •*German athlete*• Born in Gera, in 1983 she won the world championship, becoming the youngest-ever long jump world champion, and in 1985 added wins in the European and World Cup events. She consistently jumped over 23 ft (7 m), winning 27 successive competitions at long jump before 1987, when she was injured, and setting three world records before 1988. She was also a strong sprinter, picking up a variety of Olympic and world medals at 100 and 200 meters and equaling **Marita Koch**'s 200-meter world record. She won the Olympic gold medal for long jump in 1992 and again in 2000, and won the World Championship in 1993.

Dreiser, Theodore Herman Albert 1871–1945 •*US novelist*• Born in Terre Haute, Indiana, he was brought up on the breadline and left home for Chicago at the age of 15. He did odd jobs before becoming a successful journalist, and wrote *Sister Carrie* (1900), a powerful and frank treatment of a young working girl's climb toward worldly success. After suffering a nervous breakdown and abandoning serious literary work for a decade, he wrote *Jennie Gerhardt* (1911), on a similar theme, which established him as a novelist. He went on to write a trilogy about a power-hungry business tycoon: *The Financier* (1912), *The Titan* (1914) and *The Stoic* (published posthumously in 1947). *An American Tragedy* (1925), based on a real-life murder case, has survived as a classic, despite its leaden prose. A large, egocentric man with an excessive sexual appetite, he occupied himself increasingly with philosophical speculations and left-wing journalism.

Dressler, Marie, *originally* **Leila Marie Koerber** 1869–1934 •*Canadian actress*• Born in Coburg, Ontario, she made her first Broadway appearance in *Robber on the Rhine* (1892). A popular straight actress, vaudeville headliner and comedienne, she made her film debut in *Tillie's Punctured Romance* (1914), but her support for an actors' strike in 1917 adversely affected her career and she struggled for a decade before returning to the cinema in small supporting roles. Her effective dramatic performance opposite **Greta Garbo** in *Anna Christie* (1930) revived her fortunes and she was gainfully employed until her death. Her film appearances include *Min and Bill* (1930, Best Actress Academy Award), *Emma* (1932) and *Dinner at Eight* (1933).

Dreyer, Carl Theodor 1889–1968 •*Danish filmmaker*• Born in Copenhagen, his early career as a journalist brought him into contact with the developing film industry and he began writing scripts in 1912. Works like *Blade af Satans bog* (1920, *Leaves from Satan's Book*), *La passion de Jeanne d'Arc* (1928, "The Passion of Joan of Arc") and *Vampyr* (1932, *Castle of Doom*) combine technical experimentation with a desire to explore spiritual themes and the influence of evil through torment and martyrdom. An exacting perfectionist whose work rarely found commercial favor, he returned to journalism in the 1930s and subsequently concentrated on documentaries.

Dreyer, John Louis Emil 1852–1926 •*Danish astronomer*• Born in Copenhagen, he is remembered for his catalogue of nebulae and star clusters. His *New General Catalogue*, published in 1888, was so influential that many nebulae are still referred to by their NGC number. Dreyer's two great literary contributions to astronomy were his biography of **Tycho Brahe** (1890) and his *History of Planetary Systems from Thales to Kepler* (1906). Dreyer was awarded the Gold Medal of the Royal Astronomical Society in 1916.

Dreyfus, Alfred c.1859–1935 •*French soldier*• Born in Mülhausen, Alsace, he was the son of a rich Jewish manufacturer. He joined the army, but in 1893–94 he was unjustly accused of delivering documents connected with the national defense to a foreign government. He was transported for life to Devil's Island, but the efforts of his supporters to prove his innocence provoked **Émile Zola**'s *J'accuse* (1898), in which he denounced the government's militarism and anti-Semitism. In 1898 the then Chief of Military Intelligence, Major Hubert Joseph Henry (1846–98), confessed to forging the papers for the original trial with Major Marie Charles Esterhazy (1847–1923). Dreyfus was eventually found guilty but pardoned, but it was not until 1906 that the verdict was reversed by a civilian court. Dreyfus was restored to his rank of artillery captain, fought in World War I and was awarded the Legion of Honor.

Dreyfuss, Richard Stephan 1947– •*US actor*• Born in New York, he studied at San Fernando Valley State College. Among his important early films were *American Graffiti* (1972), *Jaws* (1975), *Close Encounters of the Third Kind* (1976) and *The Goodbye Girl* (1977), which won him an Academy Award for Best Actor. After a lull in his career in the early 1980s he returned in such films as *Mad Dog Time* (1996) and *The Crew* (2000).

Droeshout, Martin 17th century •*Flemish engraver*• Resident in London, he was widely known by his portrait of **Shakespeare**, prefixed to the folio edition of 1623.

Droste-Hülshoff, Annette Elisabeth, Baroness von 1797–1848 •*German poet*• Born in Westphalia, she is regarded as Germany's greatest woman writer. She led a reclusive life and from 1818 to 1820 wrote religious verses, published posthumously as *Geistliche Jahre* (1851). Her long narrative poems, notably *Das Hospiz auf dem Grossen Sankt Bernard* (1838, "The Hospice on the Great Saint Bernard") and *Die Schlacht im Loener Bruch* ("The Battle in the Loener Marsh"), were influenced by **Byron**. She also wrote a novella, *Die Judenbuche* (1841, "The Jew's Beech Tree").

Drucker, Peter Ferdinand 1909– •*US management consultant*• Born in Vienna, Austria, and educated in Austria and England, he became an economist with a London international bank before going to live in the US in 1937. He is well known as a management consultant and has written numerous successful textbooks on management, including *The Effective Executive* (1967), *Management: Tasks, Practices, Responsibilities* (1974), *The New Realities* (1989) and *Managing at a Time of Great Change* (1995). He has also written two novels.

Drummond, George 1687–1766 •*Scottish entrepreneur and philanthropist*• Born in Perthshire, he is known as the founder of the New Town in Edinburgh. An anti-Jacobite Whig, he fought at the Battle of Sheriffmuir (1715) and commanded a company in the 1745 uprising. He was Lord Provost of Edinburgh six times between 1725 and 1764 and was the driving force behind the building of the Royal Infirmary (1738) and the Royal Exchange (1760, now the City Chambers), the expansion of the University of Edinburgh, and the proposal to create a New Town to the north of Princes Street. He drained the Nor'Loch (1759), and in 1763 laid the foundation stone of the North Bridge.

Drummond (of Hawthornden), William 1585–1649 •*Scottish poet*• Born in Hawthornden, near Edinburgh, he was educated at the University of Edinburgh, studied law at Bourges and Paris, then became Laird of Hawthornden (1610), and devoted his life to poetry and mechanical experiments. His chief works are the pastoral lament *Tears on the Death of Moeliades* (ie, Prince Henry, 1613), *Poems, Amorous, Funereall, Divine, Pastorall in Sonnets, Songs, Sextains, Madrigals* (1614), *Forth Feasting* (1617), and *Flowers of Sion* (1623).

Drusus, Nero Claudius, *also known as* **Drusus Senior** 39–9 BC •*Roman soldier*• He was the son of Livia Drusilla, stepson of the emperor **Augustus**, and younger brother of the emperor **Tiberius**. His campaign against the Rhaeti and other Alpine tribes (15 BC) was celebrated by **Horace** in his *Odes*. Until his death he was engaged chiefly in establishing Roman supremacy in Germany, and received the title Germanicus. **Germanicus Caesar** was his son.

Dryden, John 1631–1700 •*English poet*• He was born at the vicarage of Aldwinkle All Saints, Northamptonshire, and educated at Trinity College, Cambridge, where he stayed until 1657. Going up to London in that year he attached himself to his cousin Sir Gilbert Pickering, **Cromwell**'s chamberlain, in hopes of employment, as both sides of his family were Parliamentarians. His *Heroic Stanzas*, on the death of Cromwell (1658), was soon followed by his *Astrea Redux* (1660), celebrating the Restoration. In 1663 he married Lady Elizabeth Howard, eldest daughter of the Earl of Berkshire. In 1667 he published *Annus Mirabilis: The Year of Wonders, 1666*, which established his reputation, and he was appointed poet laureate in 1668, and historiographer royal in 1670. Meanwhile he was writing a series of comedies for the stage, including *The Rival Ladies* (1664, in rhymed verse), and culminating with *Marriage à la Mode* (1672). He used blank verse for *All for Love* (1677), his best play and comparable to **Shakespeare**'s *Antony and Cleopatra*. He wrote a series of important critical essays as prefaces to his plays, including his charming *Essay of Dramatic Poesy* (1668).

In 1680 he began a series of satirical and didactic poems, starting with the most famous, "Absalom and Achitophel" (1681), and followed by "The Medal" (1682) and "MacFlecknoe" (1684), written some years before, which did much to turn the tide against the Whigs. At the Revolution of 1688 he lost the poet laureateship and took up translation to earn a living. His final work, published in 1699, was *Fables, Ancient and Modern*, which, with its paraphrases of **Chaucer**, **Ovid** and **Boccaccio**, has delighted generations of readers. These works are only the most outstanding of a lifetime's industry. Dryden is transitional between the Metaphysical poets of the school of **John Donne** and the neoclassic reaction which he did so much to create.

“ ”

An horrid stillness first invades the ear,
And in that silence we the tempest fear.

*1660 **Astraea Redux**, l. 7–8.*

dsh *See* **Houedard, Dom Sylvester**

Dubček, Alexander 1921–92 •*Czechoslovak statesman*• Born in Uhrovec, Czechoslovakia (now in Slovakia), he lived from 1925 to 1938 in the USSR, where his father was a member of a Czechoslovakian industrial cooperative. He returned home and joined the Communist Party in 1939, fought as a Slovak patriot against the Nazis (1944–45), and gradually rose in the party hierarchy until in 1968 he became First Secretary. He implemented a program of far-reaching economic and political reforms, including the abolition of censorship, increased freedom of speech, and suspension of ex-President **Antonín Novotný** and other former Stalinist party leaders. His policy of liberalization during the Prague Spring led in August 1968 to the occupation of Czechoslovakia by Warsaw Pact forces, and in 1969 he was replaced as First Secretary by **Gustav Husák**. He was elected president of the Federal Assembly for a few months in 1969, but was expelled from the Presidium in September and deprived of party membership in 1970. He spent the next 18 years working as a clerk in a Slovak lumberyard. Following the overthrow of the existing Communist regime in November 1989 in a bloodless "Velvet Revolution," he dramatically reemerged from retirement to be elected chairman of the Federal Assembly in December 1989 but lost his parliamentary seat in 1992. He was awarded the Sakharov Peace prize in 1989.

Dubois, Guillaume 1656–1723 •*French prelate*• Born in Brive-la-Gaillarde, he studied for the priesthood, then was appointed first tutor and later secretary to the Duc de Chartres, and became very influential when his employer (now Duc **d'Orléans**) became regent in 1715. He was appointed Foreign Minister and Archbishop of Cambrai (1720), a cardinal (1721), and Prime Minister of France (1722).

Dubois, Marie Eugène François Thomas 1858–1940 •*Dutch paleontologist*• Born in Eijsden, Limburg, he studied medicine in Amsterdam and taught there from 1899. His interest in the "missing link" between the apes and humans took him to Java in 1887, where in the 1890s he found the humanoid remains named as *Pithecanthropus erectus* (Java Man) and which he claimed to be the missing link. His view was contested and even ridiculed. When in the 1920s it eventually became widely accepted, Dubois began to insist that the fossil bones were those of a giant gibbon, and maintained this view until his death.

Du Bois, W(illiam) E(dward) B(urghardt) 1868–1963 •*US writer and editor*• Born in Great Barrington, Massachusetts, he studied at Fisk University, Tennessee, and at Harvard, from where he was the first African American to be awarded a PhD (1895), and was later Professor of Economics and History at Atlanta University (1897–1910). He was cofounder of the National Association for the Advancement of Colored People (1908), and wrote a number of important works on slavery and the "color problem," including *The Negro* (1915) and *Color and Democracy* (1945). He also wrote novels, such as *The Dark Princess* (1928) and *Worlds of Color* (1961). He was a passionate advocate of radical Black action and an early supporter of the suffragette movement, which he tried to link with the struggle for African-American rights. He joined the Communist Party in 1961, moved to Ghana at the age of 91, renounced his US citizenship and became a naturalized Ghanian just before he died.

Dubuffet, Jean 1901–85 •*French painter and printmaker*• Born in Le Havre, he enrolled at the Académie Julian in Paris in 1918, but never studied seriously, enjoying life as the son of a rich wine merchant whose business he took over in 1925. He began painting again during World War II, when he invented the concept of Art Brut and pioneered the use of rubbish such as discarded newspapers, broken glass, and rough plaster daubed and scratched like an old wall, to create "pictures." His artwork is regarded as presaging the pop art and Dada-like fashions of the 1960s.

Duccio di Buoninsegna c. 1260–c. 1320 •*Italian painter*• He founded the Sienese school, and in his work the Byzantine tradition in Italian art is seen in its most highly developed state. His masterpiece is the *Maestà* for the altar of Siena Cathedral (1311), and the *Rucellai Madonna* in Santa Maria Novella at Florence, long attributed to **Giovanni Cimabué**, is now generally considered to be his work. He is represented in the National Gallery, London, by the *Annunciation*, *Christ Healing the Blind Man* and the *Transfiguration*.

Duchamp, Marcel 1887–1968 •*US painter*• Born in Blainville, France, he moved to Paris to join his brother, **Raymond Duchamp-Villon**, and half brother, **Jacques Villon**, in 1904. Associated with several modern movements including Cubism and Futurism, he shocked his generation with such works as *Coffee-Mill* (1911) and *Nude Descending a Staircase* (1912, Philadelphia), and was one of the pioneers of Dadaism, the anti-art protest, which favored the presentation of energy and change above classical aesthetic values and fulminated against mechanization. In 1914 he introduced the first "ready-made" by inscribing a bottle rack and declaring it to be art. In 1915 he left Paris for New York City, where he worked for eight years on a 10-foot high composition in glass and metal, *The Bride Stripped Bare by Her Bachelors Even*, known as *The Large Glass*. He edited the US art magazine, *VVV* (1942–44), and became a US citizen in 1955.

Duchamp-Villon, Raymond 1876–1918 •*French sculptor*• Born in Damville, Normandy, the half brother of **Jacques Villon** and brother of **Marcel Duchamp**, he turned to sculpture in 1898. By 1914 he was one of the leading Cubist sculptors in Paris. His most striking work is the bronze *Horse* (1914, Peggy Guggenheim Collection, Venice), in which realism is rejected in favor of an abstract swirl of forms that captures the energetic movement of the animal.

Duchenne, Guillaume Benjamin Amand 1806–75 •*French physician*• Born in Boulogne-sur-Mer, he was educated at Douai and Paris. After 11 years as a general practitioner in Boulogne, he returned to Paris and devoted himself to the physiology and diseases of muscles. A pioneer of electrophysiology and electrotherapeutics, he did important work on poliomyelitis, locomotor ataxia and a common form of muscular ("Duchenne's") dystrophy. He also developed a method of taking small pieces of muscle (biopsy) from patients for microscopical examination.

Duchesne, André, *Latin* **Chesnius** or **Quercetanus** 1584–1640 •*French historian*• He was a royal historiographer, and is known as the "Father of French history." He wrote histories of England, Scotland and Ireland, of the popes up to **Paul V**, and of the House of Burgundy. He also made collections of the early Norman and French histories.

Duchesne, Père *See* **Hébert, Jacques René**

Duddell, William du Bois 1872–1917 •*English engineer*• He worked on radiotelegraphy and in 1897 invented an improved version of the oscillograph. He also designed a high-frequency generator. The Physical Society instituted the Duddell Medal in his honor.

Dudley, Lord Guildford d. 1554 •*English nobleman*• The fourth son of John Dudley, Earl of **Warwick** and Duke of Northumberland, he was persuaded by his father to marry the unwilling Lady **Jane Grey** (1553) as **Edward VI** lay dying, and then proclaimed her queen on July 9. After the accession of Edward's sister, **Mary I (Tudor)**, Dudley and his wife were imprisoned in the Tower of London and beheaded.

Dudley, William Stuart 1947– •*English stage designer*• He was born in London and educated at St Martin's School of Art and the Slade School of Art, London. He has designed many productions for the Royal Court, National Theatre and Royal Shakespeare Company. He has also worked extensively in opera in Great Britain and elsewhere, and designed **Peter Hall**'s production of *The Ring* at Bayreuth (1983), and **Bill Bryden**'s productions of *The Ship* (1990) and *The Big Picnic* (1994) in Glasgow.

Dufay, Charles François de Cisternay 1698–1739 •*French chemist*• Born in Paris, he was appointed chemist at the Academy of Sciences (1723), rising to the position of director in 1733. He reported his observations of natural magnetism and the effect of distance on the force between magnets, but his most important work concerned electrostatics, in which he defined the difference between positive and negative electricity and recognized that they exhibit repulsive as well as attractive forces.

Dufay, Guillaume c.1400–74 •*French composer*• Born probably in Cambrai, he was the most celebrated 15th-century composer. Almost 200 of his works are extant, including eight complete masses, many motets, and songs. His warmth of emotion, strong sense of melody and pioneering of the *cantus firmus* Mass greatly influenced Renaissance composers.

Duffy, Carol Ann 1955– •*Scottish poet*• Born in Glasgow, she is considered one of the leading woman poets of her generation. Much influenced by the dramatic monologues of **Robert Browning**, and by **Laura Riding**, she is striking in her use of a kind of toughened and good-natured whimsicality in her verse. Her collections include *Standing Female Nude* (1985), *The Other Country* (1990) and *Meeting Midnight* (1999), a collection for children. In 1993 she won the Whitbread award for poetry for her collection *Mean Time*.

Du Fu (Tu Fu) 712–70 •*Chinese poet of the Tang dynasty*• He was born in Xiangyang, and spent much of his youth traveling, during which time he soaked up impressions of his country's sharply juxtaposed cultural riches and social ills. One of the foremost lyricists in the language, his poems include "The Ballad of Beautiful Women," "The Newlyweds' Parting" and "The Chariots' Song." These last two reflect the violent uncertainties of life at the time, but they are also beautifully crafted and full of memorable imagery.

Dufy, Raoul 1877–1953 •*French artist and designer*• Born in Le Havre, he was much influenced by the brightness and color of Fauvism, which he did much to popularize. Later he abandoned it, but retained his singing blues and reds. From 1907 his medium was woodcuts, and he engraved many book illustrations, also producing woodcuts for making printed silk fabrics for dress designers. He also made pottery and tapestries, but in 1919 he returned to painting on the Riviera, where he produced a notable series of seascapes, bathers, sailing regattas and racecourse scenes.

Duhamel, Georges 1884–1966 •*French novelist and poet*• Born in Paris, he originally studied medicine and worked as an army surgeon in World War I. This provided the background for *La vie des martyrs* (1917, "Life of the Martyrs") and *Civilization* (1918, awarded the Prix **Goncourt**). Many of his 50 volumes of vigorous, skillful writing have been translated. They include *Salavin* (1920–32), *Le notaire du Havre* (1913, Eng trans *News from Le Havre*, 1934), and the first of the ten parts of *Chronique des Pasquier* (1933–44, Eng trans *The Pasquier Chronicles*, 1937–45).

Dukakis, Michael 1933– •*US politician*• Born in Boston, Massachusetts, the son of Greek immigrants, he studied law at Harvard and served in Korea (1955–57) before concentrating on a political career in his home state. Elected as a Democrat to the Massachusetts legislature in 1962, he became governor of that state in 1974. He was defeated in 1978, but returned in 1982, and his second term coincided with the state's emergence as a center of US high technology. Its newfound prosperity helped assure his reelection with an increased majority in 1986. He captured the Democratic Party's presidential nomination, defeating **Jesse Jackson** and presenting himself as a neoliberal, but was defeated by the Republican **George Bush** in 1988.

Dukas, Paul Abraham 1865–1935 •*French composer*• He was born in Paris. Some of his music was classical in approach, but he tended mainly toward musical Impressionism, and is noted for the symphonic poem *L'Apprenti sorcier* (1897, "The Sorcerer's Apprentice") and the opera *Ariane et Barbe-Bleu* (1907, "Ariadne and Bluebeard"). He also wrote several orchestral and piano pieces.

Dulbecco, Renato 1914– •*Italian virologist and Nobel Prize winner*• Born in Catanzaro, he studied medicine at the University of Turin, and in 1947 he emigrated to the US, securing various university appointments. In 1977 he became Research Professor at the Salk Institute, La Jolla, of which he is currently president emeritus (1993–). Dulbecco demonstrated how certain viruses can transform some cells into a cancerous state, such that those cells grow continuously, unlike normal cells. For this discovery he was awarded the 1975 Nobel Prize for physiology or medicine, jointly with his former students, **David Baltimore** and **Howard Temin**.

Dulles, Allen Welsh 1893–1969 •*US intelligence officer*• Born in Washington DC, he was educated at Princeton. He entered the US diplomatic service when his uncle, Robert Lansing (1864–1928), was secretary of state. When the **Truman** administration decided on the formation of the Central Intelligence Agency (CIA), Dulles was made deputy director (1951), becoming director in 1953 coincident with his brother, **John Foster Dulles**, becoming secretary of state. Under his direction the agency had some success in clandestine operations, but the 1961 disaster at the Bay of Pigs in Cuba was followed by his resignation. Two years later he served on the Warren Commission investigating **John F Kennedy**'s death.

Dulles, John Foster 1888–1959 •*US Republican politician*• Born in Washington DC, the brother of **Allen Welsh Dulles**, he was educated at Princeton and the Sorbonne. In 1953 he became US secretary of state. By the end of 1954 he had traveled nearly 180,000 miles and had visited more than 40 countries, signing treaties and agreements and drawing the attention of the Western nations more strongly to the threat of Communism. In 1954 he launched the concept of SEATO (Southeast Asia Treaty Organization) and backed the plan to bring West Germany into NATO. In 1956, after the nationalization of the Suez Canal by Egypt, he proposed the Suez Canal Users' Association, and later opposed the Anglo-French military intervention. Possibly the most powerful secretary of state ever seen in the US to that time, he was awarded the highest US civil decoration, the Medal of Freedom, shortly before his death from cancer. He published *War or Peace* (1950).

Dumas, Alexandre, *in full* **Alexandre Dumas Davy de la Pailleterie**, *known as* **Dumas père** 1802–70 •*French novelist and playwright*• Born in Villers-Cotterêts, he moved to Paris in 1823, where he worked as a clerk and took up writing. At the age of 27, he became famous for his play *Henri III et sa cour* (1829, "Henry III and His Court"), performed at the Théâtre Français, which revolutionized historical drama. In 1831 he did the same for domestic tragedy with *Antony*, and scored a tremendous success with *Richard Darlington*. In 1832 he carried the romantic "history" to its culmination in *La tour de Nesle* (in collaboration with Gaillardet). In that same year he fell ill with cholera, went to Switzerland to recuperate, and wrote for the *Revue des deux mondes* the first of his famous and delightful travelogues called *Impressions de voyage*. Dumas was a prodigious worker, and his output was enormous. It was as a storyteller on historical themes that he gained enduring success. He chronicled the history of France in a series of novels, but he is best known for works such as *Le Comte de Monte Cristo* (1844–45, *The Count of Monte Cristo*) and the three works *Les trois mousquetaires* (1844, *The Three Musketeers*), *Vingt ans après* (1845, "Twenty Years After") and *Dix ans plus tard, ou le Vicomte de Bragelonne* (1848–50, "Ten Years Later; or, The Vicomte de Bragelonne"), which are set in the reign of **Louis XIII** and follow the adventures of d'Artagnan, who joins the king's musketeers and shares in the adventures of Athos, Porthos and Aramis.

Dumas, Alexandre, *known as* **Dumas fils** 1824–95 •*French writer*• He was born in Paris, the illegitimate son of **Alexandre Dumas**, and at the age of 16, after a course of training at the Institution Goubaux and the Collège Bourbon, he joined the literary society to which his father belonged. "Dumas fils" began by writing fiction, then turned, with equal success, to drama and theoretical writings on art, morals, politics and even religion. His novels include *La dame aux camélias* (1848, Eng trans *The Lady with the Camellias*, 1856) and *L'affaire Clémenceau* (1864, Eng trans *Wife Murder; or, The Clémenceau Tragedy*, 1866), which was a great success in dramatic form (1852). Of his 16 plays, *Le demi-monde* (1855, Eng trans 1921), *Monsieur Alphonse* (1873, Eng trans 1874) and *Denise* (1885, Eng trans 1885) are masterpieces. Other famous dramas in which he had a share include *Le supplice d'une femme* (1865, "The Torture of a Woman"). He completed and produced his father's *Joseph Balsamo* (1878).

Dumas, Jean Baptiste André 1800–84 •*French chemist*• Born in Alais, he started his professional life as an apothecary there, but moved in 1816 to Geneva where he studied pharmacy, chemistry and botany. In 1823 he returned to teach in France. In 1840 he became the editor of *Annales de chimie et de physique*. His most important contribution to science was his attempts to classify organic compounds. He developed a simple method for the determination of vapor density, and thus relative molecular mass, but interpretation of the data was confused by the lack of distinction between an atom and a molecule. In 1834 he proposed that many organic compounds are formed by substitution for hydrogen by another element. This theory was developed further by Auguste Laurent (1807–53) and Charles Frédéric Gerhardt (1816–56).

du Maurier, Dame Daphne 1907–89 •*English novelist and short-story writer*• Born in London, the daughter of the actor-manager Sir **Gerald du Maurier**, she wrote a number of highly successful period romances and adventure stories. Many of them were inspired by Cornwall, where she lived, including *Jamaica Inn* (1936), *Rebecca* (1938) and *My Cousin Rachel* (1951). Several of these have been filmed, and her short story, "The Birds" (published in *The Apple Tree*, 1952) became a classic **Hitchcock** movie. Later books include *The House on the Strand* (1969), *The Winding Stair*, a study of **Francis Bacon** (1976), *The Rendezvous and Other Stories* (1980), and a volume of memoirs, *Vanishing Cornwall* (1967).

“ ”

Last night I dreamt I went to Manderley again.

*1938 **Rebecca**, opening words.*

---

du Maurier, George Louis Palmella Busson 1834–96 •*British artist, cartoonist and novelist*• Born in Paris, he was the grandson of émigrés who had originally fled to England during the revolution. He studied at Paris, Antwerp and Düsseldorf and, back in England, he made his name as an illustrator, with new editions of **Thackeray**'s *Esmond* and his ballads, **John Foxe**'s *Book of Martyrs*, and stories in periodicals like the *Cornhill Magazine*. He joined the staff of *Punch* (1864–96), and some of his illustrations were collected as *English Society at Home* (1880). He also wrote and illustrated three novels, *Peter Ibbetson* (1891), *The Martian* (1897) and the very successful *Trilby* (1894), the story of a young singer under the mesmeric influence of another musician, Svengali.

du Maurier, Sir Gerald Hubert Edward Busson 1873–1934 •*English actor-manager*• He was born in London and educated at Harrow, and left a business career for the stage. He played a small part in his father **George du Maurier**'s *Trilby* (1895), but became known for criminal roles, starting with a dramatization of *Raffles* (1906). He became joint manager of Wyndham's Theatre (1910–25), and was knighted in 1922 for his services to the stage. He was manager of the St James's Theatre from 1926 until his death.

Dumouriez, Charles François du Périer 1739–1823 •*French general*• He was born in Cambrai. In 1792 he defeated the Prussians at Valmy (1792), and overthrew the Austrians at Jemappes. At Neerwinden (1793) he sustained a severe defeat from the Austrians. His leanings toward constitutional monarchy aroused the suspicion of the Revolutionists, and soon he was denounced as a traitor and summoned to Paris. To save his head he went over to the Austrian camp. After wandering through Europe he finally settled in England.

Dunant, Jean Henri 1828–1910 •*Swiss philanthropist and Nobel Prize winner*• Born in Geneva, he inspired the foundation of the International Red Cross after seeing the plight of the wounded on the battlefield of Solferino (1859). His efforts brought about the conference at Geneva (1863) from which came the Geneva Convention (1864). In 1901 he shared the first Nobel Prize with French economist Frédéric Passy (1822–1912).

Dunaway, (Dorothy) Faye 1941– •*US actress*• Born in Bascom, Florida, she trained at the Boston University School of Fine and Applied Arts. She was signed to a personal contract with producer-director **Otto Preminger**, and first appeared in *The Happening* in 1966. She quickly acquired popularity, winning a Best Actress Academy Award nomination for her performance in *Bonnie and Clyde* (1967). She also appeared in *The Three Musketeers* (1973), *Chinatown* (1974) and *Network* (1976, Academy Award). Her television work includes *Cold Sassy Tree* (1989). Later films include *Mommie Dearest* (1981), *Barfly* (1987) and *Don Juan De Marco* (1995).

Dunbar, Paul Laurence 1872–1906 •*US poet*• Born in Dayton, Ohio, he was the son of escaped slaves. He gained a reputation with *Lyrics of Lowly Life* (1896), many of which were in dialect. He published several other volumes of verse and four novels. His *Complete Poems* appeared in 1913.

“ ”

We wear the mask that grins and lies,
It hides our cheeks and shades our eyes.

1895 "We Wear the Mask," stanza 1.

Dunbar, William c.1460–c.1520 •*Scottish poet*• Born probably in East Lothian, he seems to have studied at St Andrews University (1475–79). He then became secretary to some of **James IV**'s emissaries to foreign courts. In 1500 the king gave him a pension. The following year he visited England, and as a courtier of James IV he wrote poems, including *The Thrissil and the Rois* and the *Lament for the Makaris*. In 1508 Walter Chepman (c.1473–1538) printed seven of his poems—the earliest specimen of Scottish typography. Dunbar also wrote satires, such as *The Dance of the Sevin Deadly Synnis*. His name disappears from the records altogether after the Battle of Flodden (1513).

Duncan I c.1010–40 •*King of Scots*• He was the son of Bethoc and Crinan, Abbot of Dunkeld, and the grandson of **Malcolm II**. He succeeded to Strathclyde in 1034 and probably ruled over most of Scotland except the islands and the far north. He attempted southwards expansion, and a long and unsuccessful siege of Durham weakened his position. He was killed by **Macbeth** at Pitgaveney, near Elgin.

Duncan, Isadora, *originally* **Angela Duncan** 1877–1927 •*US dancer and choreographer*• Born in San Francisco, she traveled throughout Europe, performing her own choreography, and founded schools in Berlin, Salzburg and Vienna. A pioneer of modern dance, she based her work on Greek-derived notions of beauty and harmony, but also used running, skipping, and walking movements. In Moscow (1922) she married a young Russian poet, **Sergei Yesenin**, who later committed suicide. An influential and controversial figure, she held unconventional views for her time on marriage and women's liberation. She was accidentally strangled when her scarf caught in the wheel of her car.

Duncan, Robert Edward, *originally* **Edward Howard Duncan** 1919–88 •*US poet*• Born in Oakland, California, he was educated at the University of California, he was editor of *Experimental Review* (1938–40) and *Phoenix and Berkeley Miscellany* (1948–49). Aligned with the Black Mountain school of poets, he wrote in a style that emphasized natural forms and processes. His collections include *Heavenly City, Earthly City* (1947), *The Opening of the Field* (1960) and *The Years as Catches* (1966).

Duncan Smith, (George) Iain 1954– •*English Conservative politician*• Born in Edinburgh, he was educated at Dunchurch College of Management, at the Royal Military Academy, Sandhurst, at the University of Perugia, Italy, and at HMS Conway Cadet School, Anglesey. He served with the Scots Guards (1975–81) and worked for GEC (1981–88), Bellwinch PLC (1988–89) and Jane's Information Group (1989–92) before becoming Member of Parliament for Chingford in 1992. On the Eurosceptic right wing of the party, he served as shadow Social Security Secretary (1997–99) and shadow Defence Secretary (1999–2001), and in the wake of crushing electoral defeat in 2001 succeeded **William Hague** as leader of the Conservative Party.

Dundee, John Graham of Claverhouse, 1st Viscount, *known as* **Bonny Dundee** or **Bloody Claverse** c. 1649–89 •*Scottish soldier*• He served in both the French and Dutch armies as a professional soldier. In 1677 he returned to Scotland, and became lieutenant in a cavalry unit commanded by his kinsman, the Marquis of **Montrose**, against the Covenanters, commanding the cavalry at Bothwell Brig (1679). From 1682 to 1685 he was active in hunting down Covenanters in the southwest of Scotland. When William III landed in England in 1688 at the start of the "Glorious Revolution," Dundee marched into England in support of **James VII and II**. In Scotland, after leaving the Convention of 1689, he raised an army in the Highlands. He defeated the loyalist forces in a fierce encounter at Killiecrankie in July 1689, but in the process was mortally wounded.

Dunham, Katherine 1909– •*US dancer, choreographer and teacher*• Born in Chicago, she studied anthropology at the University of Chicago and researched dance in the West Indies before her appointment as dance director of the Federal Theater Project (1938). Her first New York concert in 1940 launched her career as a leading choreographer of African-American dances. She subsequently worked on Broadway and in Hollywood on *Stormy Weather* (1943) among other projects. Her Dunham School of Dance (1945–55) exerted considerable influence on the direction of US African-American dance.

Dunhill, Thomas Frederick 1877–1946 •*English composer and teacher*• Born in London, he studied at the Royal College of Music there, and taught at Eton (1899–1908). In 1907 he organized concerts to publicize the works of younger British composers. He made his name with chamber works, songs, and the light opera *Tantivy Towers* (1931) to words by **A P Herbert**.

Dunlop, Frank 1927– •*English stage director and administrator*• He was born in Leeds, and after founding and directing the Piccolo Theatre, Manchester (1954), he became an associate director of the Bristol Old Vic (1956). From 1961 to 1964 he was director of the Nottingham Playhouse, and directed Pop Theatre, a company he founded himself, in *The Winter's Tale* and **Euripides**' *The Trojan Women* at the Edinburgh Festival (1966). He became associate director at the National Theatre (1967–71), and also administrator (1968–71). He founded the Young Vic (1970), and was the company's director (until 1978, 1980–83). He was director of the Edinburgh Festival for eight years (1984–91).

Dunlop, Joey (William Joseph) 1952–2000 •*Northern Irish motorcyclist*• Born in Ballymoney, Londonderry, he was an outstanding rider at Isle of Man Tourist Trophy (TT) races, winning 26 races between 1977 and 2000, including the Senior Tourist Trophy in 1985, 1987–88 and 1995. He won the Formula One TT for the sixth successive season in 1988, and was Formula One World champion (1982–86). In 1988, he set the TT lap record at 118.54 mph (190.73 kmph).

Dunlop, John Boyd 1840–1921 •*Scottish inventor*• Born in Dreghorn, Ayrshire, he is generally credited with inventing the pneumatic tire, having in 1887 fitted his child's tricycle wheels with inflated rubber hoses instead of solid rubber tires. The principle had already been patented in 1845 by Scottish engineer **Robert William Thomson**, but in 1889 Dunlop formed the business that became the Dunlop Rubber Company Ltd, which produced commercially practical pneumatic tires for bicycles and, later, motor cars.

Dunn, Douglas 1942– •*US postmodern dancer and choreographer*• Born in Palo Alto, California, he studied dance while at Princeton, moving later to New York and the **Merce Cunningham** studio. While working there (1969–73), he met **Yvonne Rainer**. As well as performing in her works, he joined her as one of the founders of the experimental dance group Grand Union, with which he was associated for six years until 1976. During that time, he made a solo piece, *101*, which required him to lie motionless for four hours a day, six days a week for two months. In 1977 he founded his own company. His fun, original and loose-limbed choreography has been seen in later works such as *Landing* (1992) and *Caracole* (1995).

Dunn, Douglas Eaglesham 1942– •*Scottish poet*• Born in Inchinnan, Renfrewshire, he attended the Scottish School of Librarianship and Hull University, where he was employed in the library simultaneously with **Philip Larkin**, who became a friend and mentor. His first collection of poems, *Terry Street* (1969), articulates contempt and warmth in almost equal measure for the working-class suburb of Hull where he was then living. He returned to Scotland in 1984. *Elegies* (1985), written on the death of his first wife, is a moving valediction, emotionally raw but tightly controlled. It won the Whitbread prize. Other works include *Secret Villages* (1985), a collection of stories, *Selected Poems: 1964–1983* (1986), *Dante's Drum-Kit* (1993), another volume of stories, *Boyfriends and Girlfriends* (1994), *The Year's Afternoon* (2000) and *The Donkey's Ears* (2000). He has been Professor of English at St Andrews University since 1991.

Dunne, Irene, *originally* **Irene Marie Dunn** 1898–1990 •*US actress*• Born in Louisville, Kentucky, she trained at the Chicago Musical College, establishing herself as a musical comedy star on Broadway. Her Hollywood debut came with *Leathernecking* (1930), and she received the first of five Best Actress Academy Award nominations for the Western *Cimarron* (1931). An intelligent, versatile actress, she had many successes including *Love Affair* (1939) and *I Remember Mama* (1948). She retired in 1952 and served as an alternate delegate to the United Nations 12th General Assembly in 1957. An active charity worker, she was honored for her lifetime achievement at the Kennedy Arts Center in 1985.

Dunne, John William 1875–1949 •*English inventor and philosopher*• He designed the first British military airplane (1906–07) and wrote the best-selling speculative works *An Experiment with Time* (1927), *The Serial Universe* (1934), *The New Immortality* (1938) and *Nothing Dies* (1940).

Dunnett, Dorothy, *née* **Halliday** 1923–2001 •*Scottish novelist*• Born in Dunfermline, Fife, she began her career with the Civil Service as a press secretary in Edinburgh. In 1946 she married the journalist Alastair Dunnet (1908–98). A recognized portrait painter from 1950, she exhibited at the Royal Academy and was a member of the Scottish Society of Women Artists. She used her maiden name for a series of detective novels, but her best-known works comprise a series of historical novels, including *Game of Kings* (1961) and *Checkmate* (1975). In 1986 she embarked upon a second historical series, this time featuring the house of Charetty and Niccoló, which ran to eight books.

Duns Scotus, John, *Latin* **Joannes** c. 1265–1308 •*Scottish Franciscan philosopher and theologian*• His brief life is scantily documented. Born probably in Duns, Berwickshire, he became a Franciscan and was ordained priest in St Andrews Church, Northampton, in 1291. He studied and taught at Oxford and Paris, probably also in Cambridge, and finally at Cologne, where he died and was buried. His works, consisting mainly of commentaries on the Bible, **Aristotle** and the *Sentences* of **Peter Lombard**, many incomplete, were later collected and edited (not always very responsibly) by his associates. The main works are now taken to be the *Opus Parisiense* (the Parisian Lectures, as recorded by a student), the *Opus Oxoniense* (the Oxford lectures, also known as the *Ordinatio*, and probably revised by the author), the *Tractatus de primo principio* (Eng trans *A Treatise on God as First Principle*, 1966) and the *Quaestiones quodlibetales*. His philosophy represents a strong reaction against both Aristotle and St **Thomas Aquinas**. He propounded the primacy of the individual (in the dispute about universals), and the freedom of the individual will. He saw faith as the necessary foundation of Christian theology, but faith was for him exercised through an act of will and was practical. He also pioneered the doctrine of the Immaculate Conception. He rivaled Aquinas as the greatest theologian of the Middle Ages—the Franciscans followed Scotus as the Dominicans did Aquinas—and was known by contemporaries as "Doctor Subtilis" for his dialectical skill. In the 16th century the Scotists were ridiculed by the English Reformers and dubbed "Dunses" (hence "dunce") for their defense of the papacy against the divine right of kings.

Dunstan, St c. 909–88 •*Anglo-Saxon prelate*• Born near

Glastonbury, Somerset, he was educated at the abbey there and took monastic vows. Appointed abbot of Glastonbury in 945, he transformed Glastonbury into a center of religious teaching. An adviser of King **Edmund I**, he fled during Edwy's reign, but was recalled by King **Edgar**, who was now king of the country north of the Thames, and was created Bishop of Worcester (957) and of London (959), then Archbishop of Canterbury (959). Dunstan strove to make the clergy real teachers of the people in secular as well as religious matters. He made the payment of tithes by landowners obligatory and introduced the Benedictine rule into England. On Edgar's death he declared for **Edward** the Martyr, Edgar's elder son, and crowned him. On Edward's murder (978), **Ethelred** succeeded, whose hostility ended Dunstan's political career. His feast day is May 19.

Dunwoody, Richard 1964– •*Northern Irish National Hunt jockey*• Born in Ulster, the son of a jockey, he rode his first winner in 1983. His highly impressive career includes victories at the Grand National (1986), Gold Cup (1988) and the Champion Hurdle (1990). He retired in 1999. Since 1993 he has been vice president of the Jockey's Association. He is the coauthor of three books, *Hell for Leather* (1993), *Duel* (1994) and *Hands and Heels* (1997). In 2000 he published his autobiography, *Obsessed*.

Duplessis, Maurice le Noblet 1890–1959 •*French-Canadian politician*• He led the Union Nationale to power in Quebec in 1936, gaining power through a methodical exploitation of nationalism and fear of anglicization, yet he encouraged further encroachments by US corporations on Quebec's economic life. His attitude toward labor was expressed in the notorious Padlock Act of 1937 which crippled the socialist Cooperative Commonwealth Federation (CCF), but it was his antagonistic attitude toward federal government (which he claimed was invading provincial rights through the War Measures Act) which contributed most to his defeat in 1939. He regained power in 1944, but an alliance between labor, professionals, academics, and churchmen eventually succeeded in demonstrating the scale of corruption in his government, and although Duplessis himself died suddenly in 1959, the Union Nationale was defeated by the Liberals in 1960.

Dupond, Patrick 1959– •*French dancer*• Born in Paris, he was the youngest dancer ever accepted into the Paris Opera Ballet (at the age of 15), and at 17 won top honors at the Varna international competition. In 1980 he was made *étoile*, and he has since been a guest performer with various companies around the world. An unconventional and mercurial virtuoso, one of his most notable roles was that of **Vaslav Nijinsky** in **John Neumeier**'s tribute to the dancer (1979). From 1988 to 1990 he was artistic director of Ballet de Nancy, and from 1990 to 1995 he was artistic director of the Paris Opera Ballet.

du Pont, Pierre Samuel 1870–1954 •*US businessman*• Born in Wilmington, Delaware, he graduated from Massachusetts Institute of Technology (MIT) and joined the family gunpowder company. In 1902 he bought the company with his cousins, Thomas Coleman du Pont and Alfred Eugene du Pont. As president (1915–20) he introduced and developed many new industrial management techniques, including a systematic approach to strategic planning, control systems, and the pioneering of modern industrial accounting methods. He became president of General Motors (GM) in 1920 after the du Pont company had rescued it from near bankruptcy. He reorganized GM and appointed **Alfred Sloan, Jr**, as its chief executive officer.

du Pré, Jacqueline Mary 1945–87 •*English cellist*• Born in Oxford, she studied at the Guildhall School of Music, then with **Paul Tortelier** in Paris, **Pablo Casals** in Switzerland and **Mstislav Rostropovich** in Moscow. She made her concert debut at the Wigmore Hall at age 16, and subsequently toured internationally. In 1967 she married the pianist **Daniel Barenboim**. After developing multiple sclerosis in 1972 she pursued a teaching career, including master classes on television.

Durand, Marguerite 1864–1936 •*French feminist writer*• Born in Paris, she became an actress at the Comédie Française in 1881 but abandoned her acting career and married Georges Laguerre (1888), whom she later divorced. She became a feminist and was for a time vice president of *La ligue française pour le droit des femmes*. She established the first women's daily paper in the world, *La Fronde* ("The Insurrectionist"), and campaigned for better working conditions for women and for female suffrage.

Durante, Jimmy 1893–1980 •*US comedian*• Born in New York City, he played the piano and told jokes in saloons and nightclubs in the 1920s and performed on Broadway in the 1930s. A fixture in US show business for more than half a century, he appeared in many Hollywood films and had his own radio and television programs. Known for his battered hat, gravelly voice, and oversized nose (he was nicknamed "Da Schnozz"), he often mangled and invented words and repeated trademark lines such as his sign-off "Goodnight, Mrs. Calabash, wherever you are."

Duras, Marguerite, *pseudonym of* **Marguerite Donnadieu** 1914–96 •*French novelist*• Born in Gia Dinh, Indochina, she studied law and political science at the Sorbonne in Paris, and during World War II took part in the Resistance at great risk to herself as a Jew. Her novels include *Le vice-consul* (1966, Eng trans *The Vice Consul*, 1968) and *Détruire, dit-elle* (1969, Eng trans *Destroy, She Said*, 1970). She also wrote film scripts such as *Hiroshima mon amour* (1960, "Hiroshima My Love"), and a number of plays. The semiautobiographical *La douleur* was published in 1985 (Eng trans 1986), and *L'amant* (1984, Eng trans *The Lover*, 1985) won the Prix **Goncourt**. Her final novel *C'est tout* ("That's All") was published in 1995.

Durbin, Deanna, *originally* **Edna Mae Durbin** 1921– •*Canadian entertainer*• Born in Winnipeg, Manitoba, she and her family moved to California, where she first appeared in the short film *Every Sunday* (1936), and became an immediate star with *Three Smart Girls* (1936). Already popular on radio, she had box-office successes with *One Hundred Men and a Girl* (1937), *Mad About Music* (1938) and *Three Smart Girls Grow Up* (1939). Her flair for comedy was evident in *It Started with Eve* (1941), and she gave creditable dramatic performances in *Christmas Holiday* (1944) and *Lady on a Train* (1945).

Durcan, Paul 1944– •*Irish poet*• Born in Dublin, he graduated in history and archaeology from University College, Cork, in 1973. His poems, which have won the Patrick Kavanagh award for poetry (1974) and the Whitbread Poetry prize (1990), are direct statements of commitment to a relentless humanist standpoint. His publications include *O Westport in the Light of Asia Minor* (1975), *Teresa's Bar* (1976) and *Jesus and Angela* (1988). A more meditative and reflective tone is present in the autobiographical *Daddy, Daddy* (1990) and the politically informed *A Snail in My Prime* (1993).

Dürer, Albrecht 1471–1528 •*German painter and engraver*• He was born in Nuremberg. In 1486 he was apprenticed to Michael Wolgemut, the chief illustrator of the *Nuremberg Chronicle*, and in 1490 started on travels that lasted four years. In 1497 he set up on his own; he completed many paintings, among them the Dresden triptych, and the Baumgartner altarpiece in Munich. In 1498 he published his first great series of designs on wood, the illustrations of the *Apocalypse*. The copperplates of this period include *The Prodigal Son* (1500) and *Adam and Eve* (1504). From 1505 to 1506 he visited Venice, and there produced the *Feast of the Rosaries*, now the property of Strahow monastery, Prague. On or before his return he painted *Adam and Eve* (1507), now in Madrid; and the triptych *Assumption of the Virgin*, the center of which was destroyed by fire in Munich in 1674. It was followed in 1511 by the *Adoration of the Trinity*, now in Vienna. As an engraver on metal and a designer of woodcuts he ranks even higher than as a painter. His work is distinguished by an unerring perception of the capabilities of the material, his metalplates being executed with extreme finish and refinement, while his woodcuts are boldly drawn with a broad expressive line. His copperplates, over 100 in number, include: the *Little Passion* (16 plates, 1508–13); the *Knight, Death, and the Devil* (1513); *St Jerome in His Study*; and *Melancholia* (1514). He may also be regarded as the inventor of etching, as he produced several plates in which all the lines are bitten with acid. He completed around 200 woodcuts, including the *Greater Passion*, 12 subjects; the *Small Passion*, 37 subjects; and the *Apocalypse*, 16 subjects. He also wrote several treatises on measurement and human proportion.

" "

The art of painting cannot be truly judged save by such as are themselves good painters; from others verily it is hidden even as a strange tongue.

c. 1512 Quoted in William Martin Conway ***Literary Remains of Albrecht Dürer*** *(1889).*

Durkan, Mark 1960– •*Northern Irish politician*• Born in Derry, Northern Ireland, he was educated at St Columb's College, Derry, Queen's University, Belfast, and the University of Ulster. He became assistant to Social Democratic and Labour Party (SDLP) leader **John Hume** in 1984 and was himself SDLP chairperson (1990–95). He played a key role in the so-called Good Friday Agreement and was elected to the Northern Ireland Assembly in 1998, representing Foyle. He became Minister of Finance in 1999 and in 2001 succeeded Hume as SDLP leader and became Northern Ireland's deputy First Minister.

Durkheim, Émile 1858–1917 •*French sociologist*• Born in Épinal, he was educated at the École Normale Supérieure, Paris, and he taught at the University of Bordeaux (1887–1902) and at the Sorbonne (1902–16). He was appointed to the first chair of sociology in France in 1913. He believed that sociology should be rigorously objective and scientific, and he developed a systematic sociological methodology based on the view that what he called "social facts," that is, social phenomena, should be treated as "things" to be explained solely by reference to other social facts, not in terms of any individual person's actions. This approach is presented in his methodological writings, such as *Les règles de la méthode sociologique* (1894, "The Rules of Sociological Method") and is applied particularly in his study of suicide (1897). He is generally regarded as one of the founders of sociology.

Durrell, Gerald Malcolm 1925–95 •*English writer and naturalist*• He was born in Jamshedpur, India. His interest in zoology was sparked when his family moved to Corfu in the 1930s, an experience which he recorded in *My Family and Other Animals* (1956). He combined writing with zoology, published many popular books, including the autobiographical *Birds, Beasts and Relatives* (1969), and made many expeditions and wildlife films. He founded the Jersey Zoological Park in 1959. His discovery in Madagascar of an aye-aye (a lemur which was thought to have been extinct) is described in his book *The Aye-Aye and I* (1992). He was the brother of **Lawrence Durrell**.

Durrell, Lawrence George 1912–90 •*English novelist, poet, travel writer and playwright*• He was born in Jullundur, India, and sent to England to be educated at St Edmund's School, Canterbury. He took numerous odd jobs—in nightclubs, as an estate agent and in the Jamaica police—and once said he had been driven to writing "by sheer ineptitude." His family moved to Corfu until the outbreak of World War II, during and after which he traveled widely as a journalist and in the service of the Foreign Office. He made his name with the "Alexandria Quartet"—*Justine* (1957), *Balthazar* (1958), *Mountolive* (1958) and *Clea* (1960)—a complex, interlocking series set in Egypt, remarkable for its sensuous language. The *Avignon Quincunx—Monsieur* (1974), *Livia* (1978), *Constance* (1982), *Sebastian* (1983) and *Quinx* (1985)—is conceived on a similarly grand and elaborate scale. He also wrote travel books, *Prospero's Cell* (1945) and *Bitter Lemons* (1957), verse (*Collected Poems, 1931–1974*), comic sketches, criticism, plays and a children's novel, *White Eagles over Serbia* (1957).

Duse, Eleonora, *known as* **the Duse** 1859–1924 •*Italian actress*• Born near Venice, she rose to fame in Italy, then triumphed (1892–93) throughout the European capitals, mainly acting in plays by **Ibsen**, contemporary French dramatists, and the works of her lover, **Gabriele D'Annunzio**. She returned to the stage in 1921 after years of retirement. She ranks among the greatest actresses of all time.

Dutrochet, (René Joachim) Henri 1776–1847 •*French physiologist*• Born in Néon, he qualified in medicine at the University of Paris, becoming an army medical officer physician and serving as personal physician to **Joseph Bonaparte** of Spain. After the Peninsular War he conducted research in animal and particularly plant physiology. He isolated stomata, identified the role of chlorophyll in photosynthesis, and made wide-ranging studies of osmosis.

Dutton, Geoffrey Piers Henry 1922–98 •*Australian poet, novelist, critic and editor*• Born in Kapunda, South Australia, he began working in publishing after serving in World War II. His verse collections include *Night Flight and Sunrise* (1944), *Antipodes in Shoes* (1958) and *A Body of Words* (1977). Other works include the novels *The Mortal and the Marble* (1950) and *Queen Emma of the South Seas* (1976), and critical studies of **Patrick White** (1961) and **Walt Whitman** (1961). He also wrote three historical biographies of pioneering Australians, as well as art appreciation, short stories and books for children. His work as a scholarly and enthusiastic editor produced the acclaimed *The Literature of Australia* (1964, rev edn 1976).

Duvalier, François, *known as* **Papa Doc** 1907–71 •*Haitian politician*• Born in Port-au-Prince, he trained in medicine and became Minister of Health in 1949. After the military coup in 1950 he opposed the government, and in 1957 was overwhelmingly elected President of Haiti in army-supervised elections. His rule became increasingly autocratic and murderous, and saw the creation of the brutal civil militia of the so-called Tontons Macoutes. A professed believer in voodoo, he fought off invasions and threatened uprisings with US economic help. He was made President for life in 1964 and was succeeded by his son, **Jean-Claude (Baby Doc) Duvalier**.

Duvalier, Jean-Claude, *known as* **Baby Doc** 1951– •*Haitian politician*• He was born in Port-au-Prince, son of **François (Papa Doc) Duvalier**. After studying law at the University of Haiti he followed his father into politics. At the age of 20 he became President for life, ruling, as had his father, through a private army. In 1986 he was deposed in a military coup led by General Henri Namphrey and went into exile in Grasse, in the south of France.

Duvall, Robert 1931– •*US actor*• Born in San Diego, California, he studied at the Neighborhood Playhouse in New York. His career as a character actor took off in the late 1960s and 1970s with films including *True Grit* (1969), *M*A*S*H* (1970), *The Godfather* (1972) and *The Eagle Has Landed* (1977), and he played the psychopathic surf-loving Lieutenant Colonel Kilgore in *Apocalypse Now* (1979). He won an Academy Award for Best Actor in *Tender Mercies* (1983) and wrote, directed and starred in *The Apostle* (1997).

Dvořák, Antonín Leopold 1841–1904 •*Czech composer*• He was born near Prague, the son of a butcher. He worked in the business for a time, but showed such musical talent that he was sent to the organ school in Prague in 1857. In 1859 he began to earn his living playing the viola in an orchestra and giving lessons, but all the while he was composing in secret. It was not until 1873 that he attracted attention with his *Hymnus*, a nationalistic cantata based on Halek's poem *The Heroes of the White Mountain*. In 1873 he married, and from 1874 to 1877 was organist at St Adalbert's church in Prague, during which time he made a name for himself with several compositions which were promising enough to bring him to the notice of the authorities and secure him a state grant. In 1877 **Brahms** became a member of the committee which examined the compositions of grant holders. He recognized Dvořák's talent and introduced his music to Vienna by sponsoring the publication of the *Klänge aus Mähren*, which were followed by the *Slavonic Dances* (1878), a commissioned work. Brahms's friendship was a great influence and stimulus in the life of the young composer. His work, basically classical in structure but characterized by colorful Slavonic motifs, won increasing recognition, culminating in European acclaim for his *Stabat Mater* (1877), first performed in London in 1883. He had now written six symphonies and much chamber and piano music, and enjoyed a worldwide reputation. In 1891 he was offered the directorship of the New York Conservatory. It was in the US in 1893 that he wrote his Ninth Symphony, the ever-popular "From the New World," containing themes redolent of American folk music yet retaining a distinct Slavonic flavor. At this time he also wrote some of his best chamber music. He returned to Prague in 1895. The last period of his life was spent composing chiefly orchestral music.

“ ”

I have composed too much.

Letter to Sibelius.

Dvorák, Tomás 1972– •*Czech athlete*• Born in Zlín, Czechoslovakia (now in the Czech Republic), he became a specialist in the decathlon and won the bronze medal at the Olympic Games of 1996. He won the gold medal in the European Cup in 1995 and 1999, when he scored a world record of 8,994 points, and was also victorious in the world championships at Athens in 1997, at Seville in 1999 and at Edmonton in 2001.

Dworkin, Andrea 1946– •*US feminist and critic*• Born in Camden, New Jersey, and educated at Bennington College, she worked as a waitress, a receptionist and a factory employee before joining the contemporary women's movement. Her early publications include *Woman Hating* (1974) and *The New Women's Broken Heart* (1980). Her crusade against pornography is detailed in *Take Back the Night: Women on Pornography* (1980) and *Pornography: Men Possessing Women* (1981), where she identifies pornography as a cause rather than a symptom of a sexist culture. Her later works include *Letters from a War-Zone, 1976–1987* (1989) and *Mercy* (1990).

Dyck, Sir Anthony Van *See* **Van Dyck, Anthony**

Dyke, Dick Van *See* **Van Dyke, Dick**

Dylan, Bob, *originally* **Robert Allen Zimmerman** 1941– •*US singer and songwriter*• Born in Duluth, Minnesota, he was instrumental in the popular revival of the folk tradition in the early 1960s, when his work, with its overt social and political concerns, was greatly influenced by the pioneering folksinger and songwriter **Woody Guthrie**. His unconventional vocal style was immediately influential, and many of his songs, notably "Blowin' in the Wind" and "The Times They Are A-Changin'," were widely performed and imitated. Quickly tiring of his unsought role as spokesman for his generation, he turned in 1965 to rock and roll music. The use of amplified instruments alienated many of his early admirers. Dylan soon reached a much wider rock audience, however, and songs like "Mr Tambourine Man," "Desolation Row," "Subterranean Homesick Blues" and "Like a Rolling Stone" had a profound influence. There has been a slackening in his productivity since the 1980s, but he remains one of the seminal influences on popular songwriting. Major recordings include *Bringing It All Back Home* (1965), *Highway 61 Revisited* (1965), *Blonde On Blonde* (1966), *John Wesley Harding* (1968), *Nashville Skyline* (1969), *Blood on the Tracks* (1974) and *Slow Train Coming* (1979). He has issued records and toured at regular intervals into the mid-1990s, often reworking old songs in radical ways alongside new material on stage. He has also appeared in or directed a number of films, including the celebrated documentary *Don't Look Back* (1967), the concert film *Hard Rain* (1976), and the sprawling *Renaldo and Clara* (1978).

Dympna c. 9th century •*Irish princess*• She is said to have been killed by her pagan father in Gheel, Belgium, for resistance to his incestuous passion. She is the patron of the mentally ill.

Dyson, Freeman John 1923– •*US physicist and author*• Born in Crowthorne, England, he was educated at Cambridge and Cornell Universities and went on to carry out research into nuclear engineering while based at the Institute for Advanced Study, alongside **Robert Oppenheimer** and others. He became best known, however, as a writer on science, interpreting complex scientific topics for the general reader. His influential writings on a diverse range of subjects have included the autobiographical *Disturbing the Universe* (1979), *Weapons and Hope* (1984), in which he discusses nuclear disarmament, and *The Sun, the Genome, and the Internet* (1999).

Dyson, James 1947– •*English designer*• Born in Cromer, Norfolk, he studied at the Royal College of Art. He worked for the industrial equipment manufacturer Rotork from 1970 to 1973, developing the SeaTruck high-speed landing craft, then left to become a freelance inventor, producing the Ballbarrow wheelbarrow and the "bagless" Dyson Dual Cyclone vacuum cleaner, both of which enjoyed huge commercial success. He is founder and chairman of Dyson Research (1979–) and Dyson Appliances (1992–).

Dzerzhinsky, Felix Edmundovich 1877–1926 •*Russian revolutionary*• He was born in Dzerzhmovo, near Minsk, of Polish descent. In 1897 he was exiled to Siberia for political agitation, fought in the Russian Revolution of 1905, and in 1917, as one of the organizers of the coup d'état, became chairman of the secret police and a member of the Bolshevik Central Committee until his death. After 1921 he also reorganized the railway system, and was chairman of the Supreme Economic Council (1924–26), trying to combine industrialization with good relations with the peasantry.

Eadgar *See* **Edgar**

Eadmer d. c. 1124 •*English monk and historian*• He was the devoted friend of Archbishop **Anselm**, to whom he had been sent by Pope **Urban II**. In 1120 at **Alexander** I's request he became Bishop of St Andrews. He was the author of *Historia novorum in Anglia* (c. 1115) and a *Vita Anselmi* (c. 1125, "Life of Anselm").

Eads, James Buchanan 1820–87 •*US engineer and inventor*• Born in Lawrenceburg, Indiana, he invented a diving bell and founded a salvage company that made a fortune from sunken river steamboats. In 1861 he built in 100 days eight iron-clad Mississippi steamers for the government. He built the steel triple-arched Eads Bridge (1867–74) across the Mississippi at St Louis, with a central span of 520 feet (158.6 m), and his works for improving the Mississippi mouth were completed in 1875–79.

Eagleton, Terry (Terence Francis) 1943– •*British literary critic*• After a distinguished academic career he became Thomas Warton Professor of English Literature and Fellow of St Catherine's College, Oxford, in 1992. His works include *Criticism and Ideology* and *Marxism and Literary Criticism* (both 1976), *The Function of Criticism* (1984) and *The Crisis of Contemporary Culture* (1993).

Eakins, Thomas 1844–1916 •*US painter and photographer*• Born in Philadelphia, he was influenced by **Édouard Manet** and went on to become the leading US Realist painter. Fond of river scenes, he was a master of light effects. In the 1870s he allowed both sexes to draw from the nude model in his class at the Pennsylvania Academy, and as a result was forced to resign. His interest in photography led him to extend the advances made by **Eadweard Muybridge** in his studies of figures in motion, and his composite plates inspired **Marcel Duchamp**'s *Nude Descending the Staircase* (1912).

Eames, Charles 1907–78 and **Ray**, *née* **Kaiser** c. 1916–88 •*US designers and architects*• Charles Eames was born in St Louis, Missouri. In 1930 he set up an office as an architect and industrial designer and taught at Cranbrook Academy of Art from 1936. The furniture designs of this early period used new materials such as molded plywood, foam upholstery and steel rod frames with great versatility. He and Ray Kaiser were married in 1941 and they established an office in California. Their Santa Monica House (1949) is constructed entirely from standard building components, but the contrast between these components and the building's lighthearted feel made it a seminal building in postwar architecture. They are best known for their range of furniture designed in 1946, and for such pieces as the "Lounge Chair," originally designed for **Billy Wilder**. In 1979 the couple were awarded the RIBA (Royal Institute of British Architects) Gold Medal for their record of innovation and excellence in the fields of architecture, furniture design and, more recently, film, graphics and exhibition design.

Eardley, Joan 1921–63 •*English painter*• Born in Warnham, Sussex, she began her studies at Goldsmiths College of Art, London (1938) but moved to study at the Glasgow School of Art in 1940. After World War II she studied at Hospitalfield, Arbroath, and at Glasgow School of Art, winning various prizes and traveling to France and Italy on a **Carnegie** scholarship. In 1949 she took a studio in Cochrane Street, Glasgow, and began to paint poor children from the nearby tenements. In 1950 she first visited Catterline, the tiny fishing village on the northeast coast of Scotland that inspired her finest landscapes and seascapes. She lived and worked there until her death.

Earhart, Amelia Mary 1897–1937 •*US aviator*• Born in Atchison, Kansas, she became the first woman to fly across the Atlantic Ocean on June 17, 1928. Although merely a passenger on that initial flight, she later became the first woman to fly solo across the Atlantic (1932) and the first person to fly alone from Hawaii to California (1935). Her records made her a celebrity and a spokeswoman both for commercial aviation and for feminism. In 1937 she attempted an around-the-world flight, but her plane disappeared in the Pacific somewhere between New Guinea and Howland Island. Her autobiography, *Last Flight* (1938), was published posthumously.

Earp, Wyatt (Berry Stapp) 1848–1929 •*US lawman and gunfighter*• Born in Monmouth, Illinois, he served as assistant marshal in the Kansas cattle town of Dodge City, then moved (1878) to Tombstone, Arizona, where his brother Virgil served as marshal. His falling-out with the Clanton gang led to the famous shootout at the OK Corral (1881). Though they were represented later in the stories of the Old West as the champions of law and order, at the time Wyatt and his friends were seen by the townspeople of Tombstone as little more than criminals.

Eastaway, Edward *See* **Thomas, (Philip) Edward**

Eastman, Crystal 1881–1928 •*US suffragette*• She graduated from New York University with a law degree (1907), then spent a year in Pittsburgh researching *Work Accidents and the Law*. In 1909 she drafted New York's first worker compensation law, which was later used as a model nationwide, and in 1913 she founded the forerunner of the National Women's Party, which campaigned for the Equal Rights Amendment of 1923. She was also a founder of the Feminist Congress that convened in New York in 1919. After her second marriage she moved to England and became involved in the women's rights movement there.

Eastman, George 1854–1932 •*US inventor and philanthropist*• Born in Waterville, New York, and educated in Rochester, he turned from banking to photography, producing a successful roll film (1884) and the Kodak box camera (1888). He joined **Thomas Edison** in experiments which made the moving-picture industry possible. He formed the Eastman Kodak Co in 1892 and produced the Brownie camera in 1900. He was the founder of the Eastman School of Music in Rochester, New York.

Eastwood, Clint 1930– •*US actor and director*• Born in San Francisco, he found television fame in *Rawhide* (1958–65) and then became an international star with three Italian-made "spaghetti" Westerns as the laconic gunslinger, The Man with No Name, beginning with *Per un Pugno Di Dollari* (1964, *A Fistful of Dollars*). In the US his box-office status was confirmed in adventure films and as tough detective *Dirty Harry* (1971). He was actor-director for the first time in the thriller *Play Misty for Me* (1971). Later films include *Pale Rider* (1985), *Heartbreak Ridge* (1986), *Bird* (1988), *Unforgiven* (1992), for which he won a Best Director Academy Award, *In the Line of Fire* (1993), *The Bridges of Madison County* (1995) and *Mystic River* (2003). From 1986 to 1988 he was mayor of Carmel, California, where he now lives.

“ ”

You've got to ask yourself a question. Do I feel lucky? Well, do you punk?
*1971 as Harry Callahan in **Dirty Harry** (screenplay by Harry Julian Fink, Rita M Fink and Dean Riesner).*

Eberhart, Richard Ghormley 1904– •*US poet*• Born in Minnesota, he is the author of almost 30 collections, including *A Bravery of Earth* (1930), *The Quarry* (1960) and *Fields of Grace* (1972). With his *Selected Poems 1930–1965* he won a Pulitzer Prize in 1966, and with *Collected Poems 1930–1976* a National Book award in

1977. A traditional, lyrical, reflective writer, deliberating upon the natural world and the cycles of life and death, he writes in the Romantic tradition of **William Blake**, **William Wordsworth** and **Walt Whitman**. He is considered to be one of the most important of 20th-century US poets.

Eberst, Jakob *See* **Offenbach, Jacques**

Ebert, Friedrich 1871–1925 •*German statesman*• Born in Heidelberg, a tailor's son, he became a saddler there, then a Social Democratic journalist and Reichstag member (1912). Chairman of his party (1913), he was a leader in the Revolution of 1918–19. He was the first President of the German Republic (1919–25).

Eccles, Sir John Carew 1903–97 •*Australian neurophysiologist and Nobel Prize winner*• Born in Melbourne, he was educated at the University of Melbourne and Oxford University, where he collaborated with Sir **Charles Sherrington** on papers on neural inhibition, and later taught at Sydney University, Otago University, the Australian National University, and from 1968 the State University of New York at Buffalo. His significant contributions to the neurosciences include the recording of the depolarization of a postsynaptic muscle fiber in response to a neural stimulus, the identification of inhibitory neurons, and the demonstration of how inhibitory synapses control the flow of information within the nervous system. He was awarded the 1963 Nobel Prize for physiology or medicine, with Sir **Alan Hodgkin** and Sir **Andrew Huxley**, for discoveries concerning the functioning of nervous impulses. He was knighted in 1958.

Ecevit, Bülent 1925– •*Turkish writer and politician*• Born in Istanbul, he became a member of parliament for the center-left Republican People's Party in 1957. He became prime minister of a coalition government in 1974, during which he ordered the invasion of Cyprus. He resigned later that year over differences of opinion with the other coalition party. Briefly prime minister in 1977, he resumed the office in 1978 and imposed martial law on Turkey, but his government lasted for only 22 months. After the military coup of 1980, Ecevit was imprisoned twice for criticizing the military regime. A distinguished poet and writer, he was committed to maintaining Turkey's independence within NATO and to improving the country's traditionally poor relations with neighboring Greece. He was reelected to parliament in 1991 and in 1998 returned as prime minister, serving until 2002.

Echegaray y Eizaguirre, José 1833–1916 •*Spanish dramatist and Nobel Prize winner*• Born in Madrid, of Basque descent, he taught mathematics and held portfolios in various ministries (1868–74). His plays are usually on simple themes, but with elaborate plot twists and rhetorical passages, and some incorporate social comment, as in his masterpiece, *El gran Galeoto* (1881, "The Great Galeoto"). He was jointly awarded the Nobel Prize for literature (with Frédéric Mistral, 1830–1914) in 1904. The following year he returned to politics as Minister of Finance, and to science as Professor of Physics at Madrid University.

Eckart, Johannes *See* **Eckhart, Johannes**

Eckert, J(ohn) Presper 1919–95 •*US engineer and inventor*• Born in Philadelphia, he studied at the University of Pennsylvania, where he remained for a further five years as a research associate. From 1942 to 1946, with **John Mauchly**, he worked on the Electronic Numerical Integrator and Calculator (ENIAC), one of the first modern computers. It weighed several tons, used thousands of valves and resistors, and required 100 kW of electric power. He and Mauchly continued to develop improved versions of their computer, including UNIVAC I, which in 1951 became one of the first computers to be sold commercially.

Eckhart or **Eckart, Johannes**, *also called* **Meister Eckhart** c. 1260–1327 •*German theologian and mystic*• Born in Hochheim, near Gotha, he entered the Dominican order, studied and taught in Paris, and held posts including Dominican provincial in Saxony (1303–11) and vicar general of Bohemia (1307). Eckhart's teaching is a mystic pantheism, which influenced later religious mysticism and speculative philosophy. In 1325 he was accused of heresy by the Archbishop of Cologne, and two years after his death his writings were condemned by Pope **John XXII**. His extant works consist of Latin and German sermons and tractates.

Eco, Umberto 1932– •*Italian novelist and semiotician*• Born in Alessandria, Piedmont, he was a student of philosophy at the University of Turin and was awarded a doctorate for his thesis on St **Thomas Aquinas**. He taught at Turin (1956–67), and was appointed Professor of Semiotics at the University of Bologna in 1971. Imbued with a "taste and passion" for the Middle Ages, he undertook a prolonged study of the commentary of Beatus of Liébana, an 8th-century saint, on the Book of Revelation and of 11th-century illuminations, all of which bore fruit in *The Name of the Rose* (1980), a suspense story set in a medieval monastery, centering on the criminal investigation of Brother William of Baskerville, an English Franciscan. It was an international bestseller and was successfully translated to celluloid in a film of the same name. He has published two other novels, *Foucault's Pendulum* (1989) and *L'isola del giorno prima* (1995, Eng trans *The Island of the Day Before*).

Edberg, Stefan 1966– •*Swedish tennis player*• He was born in Vasternik. He won the men's singles title at Wimbledon in 1988 and 1990. Other wins include the Australian Open (1985, 1987) and the US Open (1991–92). He retired in 1996.

Eddery, Pat(rick James John) 1952– •*Irish jockey*• Born in Newbridge, Kildare, he was champion jockey 11 times between 1974 and 1996, and had several successes in the Classics, including Derby winners in 1975, 1982 and 1990. He also won the Oaks twice, as well as the St Leger. He had a particularly good record in France, winning the Prix de l'Arc de Triomphe in 1980, 1985, 1986 and 1987.

Eddington, Sir Arthur Stanley 1882–1944 •*English astronomer*• Born in Kendal, Westmorland (Cumbria), he studied at Manchester and Cambridge. He was appointed chief assistant at the Royal Observatory Greenwich (1906) and Plumian Professor of Astronomy and Experimental Philosophy at Cambridge (1913), and in the following year also became director of the university observatory. His first book, *Stellar Movements and the Structure of the Universe* (1914), dealt with the kinematics and dynamics of stars in the Milky Way. In 1916 he deduced a theoretical relationship between the mass of a star and its total output of radiation, and suggested that extreme values of density may exist in stars such as white dwarfs. He published these investigations in *Internal Constitution of the Stars* (1926). Concurrently, he published a nonmathematical account of the theory of relativity, *Space, Time and Gravitation* (1920), which he extended to his *Mathematical Theory of Relativity* (1923). He also wrote a series of scientific books for the layman. Eddington was knighted in 1930 and received the Order of Merit in 1938.

Eddington, Paul Clark 1927–95 •*English actor*• Born in London and trained at the Royal Academy of Dramatic Art, he joined Birmingham Repertory in 1945. After making his West End debut in *The Tenth Man* (1961), he rose to become one of Great Britain's most authoritative actors. Among his celebrated roles were George in *Who's Afraid of Virginia Woolf?* (1981) and the headmaster in *Forty Years On* (1984), George in *Jumpers* (1985), Orgon in *Tartuffe* (1991) and Spooner in *No Man's Land* (1992). On television, he played Jerry in *The Good Life* (1975–77) and Jim Hacker in *Yes, Minister* and *Yes, Prime Minister* (1980–87), as well as straight roles in *The Prisoner* (1967) and *King Henry IV* (1995).

Eddy, Mary (Morse), *née* **Baker** 1821–1910 •*US founder of the Christian Science Church*• She was born in Bow, New Hampshire. Frequently ill as a young woman, she later turned to faith healing. She developed the spiritual and metaphysical system she called Christian Science while recovering from a severe fall in 1866, and published her beliefs in *Science and Health with Key to the Scriptures* (1875), which proclaimed the illusory nature of disease. She married Asa G Eddy in 1877 (her third marriage), and in 1879 founded in Boston, Massachusetts, the Church of Christ, Scientist, which attracted great numbers of followers. She founded various publications, including the *Christian Science Journal* (1883) and the *Christian Science Monitor* (1908).

Ede (of Epsom), James Chuter Ede, Baron Chuter- 1882–1965 •*English politician*• Born in Epsom, Surrey, he was educated at Christ's College, Cambridge, and was elected Member of Parliament in 1923. As Minister of Education (1940–45) he helped to bring about the Education Act of 1944. He was Home Secretary from 1945 to 1951, during which time he introduced the Criminal Justice Act of 1948 and was involved in controversy on capital punishment.

Edel, (Joseph) Leon 1907–97 •*US scholar and biographer*• He was born in Pittsburgh, Pennsylvania. A professor at New York University from 1955, he edited the works of **Henry James** and won the Pulitzer Prize for parts of his five-volume biography (1953–72) of James. His other books include biographies of **James Joyce**, **Willa Cather**, and **Henry David Thoreau**. He examined the art of biography in his book *Writing Lives: Principia Biographia* (1984), asserting that biography is a literary form in its own right.

Edelman, Gerald Maurice 1929– •*US biochemist and Nobel Prize winner*• Born in New York City, he was educated at the University of Pennsylvania and at Rockefeller University. He purified the light chain from a human multiple myeloma, and reported the complete amino acid sequence (1969). He also analyzed the antibody structure and the nature of the subunit interactions, subsequently investigating the number of antibody forms in different vertebrates. This work, together with **Rodney Porter**'s studies in England, enabled a picture of a typical Y-shaped human immunoglobulin (IgG) antibody molecule to be established. For these discoveries they shared the 1972 Nobel Prize for physiology or medicine.

Eden, Sir (Robert) Anthony, 1st Earl of Avon 1897–1977 •*British statesman and Prime Minister*• Born at Windlestone Hall, Bishop Auckland, County Durham, he was educated at Eton and Christ Church, Oxford. He won the Military Cross in 1917, and became a Member of Parliament in 1923. In 1931 he became Foreign Under-Secretary, in 1934 Lord Privy Seal and in 1935 Foreign Secretary. He resigned in 1938 following differences with the Prime Minister, **Neville Chamberlain**, principally on the issue of the policy toward Fascist Italy. In 1940 he was **Churchill**'s Secretary of State for War, issuing the historic appeal that brought the Home Guard into being. In 1940 he was Foreign Secretary again. Strenuous wartime work culminated in his leadership of the British delegation to the 1945 San Francisco Conference that established the United Nations. He returned to the Foreign Office once more in 1951 in Churchill's government. He succeeded Churchill as Prime Minister in 1955, a year marked by the summit conference at Geneva with the heads of government of the US, France and the USSR. In 1956 he ordered British and French forces to occupy the Suez Canal Zone ahead of the invading Israeli army. His action was condemned by the UN and caused a bitter and prolonged controversy in Great Britain that did not subside when he ordered a withdrawal. In poor health, he abruptly resigned the premiership in 1957. He was created an earl in 1961. He wrote *Freedom and Order* and *Days for Decision* (1949), his memoirs (3 vols, 1960–65) and an account of his prepolitical life, *Another World* (1976).

Ederle, Gertrude Caroline 1906–2003 •*US swimmer*• She won a gold medal at the 1924 Olympic Games, as a member of the US 400-meter relay team, and two bronze medals. On August 6, 1926, she swam the English Channel from Cap Gris Nez to Kingsdown, the first woman to do so, in 14 hours 31 minutes, nearly 2 hours faster than the existing men's record.

Edgar or **Eadgar** 944–75 •*English King*• The younger son of King Edmund of Wessex, he was made king of Northumbria and Mercia (957) and succeeded to Wessex on his brother Eadwig's death (959), thus becoming ruler of a united England. He recalled St **Dunstan** from exile and made him his closest adviser and Archbishop of Canterbury. His reign was one of secure peace and prosperity, with the acceptance of the Danelaw as a separate but integral part of England, under his nominal authority. He is renowned for his legal codes, his coinage reform and his revival of the English Church. His two sons became **Edward** the Martyr and **Ethelred II** (the Unready).

Edgar the Ætheling c. 1050–c. 1125 •*English prince*• Born in Hungary, the son of **Edward the Ætheling**, he was the legitimate heir to the English throne on the death of his great-uncle **Edward the Confessor** (1066). He was passed over as king in favor of **Harold Godwinsson**, but after Harold's defeat and death at Hastings, some English nobles supported the Ætheling's claims against **William the Conqueror**, until he was compelled to submit to William (1067). In 1068 he fled to Scotland, where King **Malcolm III** (Canmore) welcomed him and where he married the Ætheling's sister, St **Margaret**. In 1074 the Ætheling made peace with William and led the Norman expedition that conquered Apulia (1086) and an expedition to Scotland (1097), which deposed the usurper Donald Bane and put Malcolm's son Edgar on the throne. He was captured by **Henry I** (1106) but was released and spent his last years in obscurity.

Edgar, David 1948– •*English dramatist*• Born in Birmingham, he studied drama at the University of Manchester and was a journalist in Bradford before deciding to write for the stage full time. *Destiny* (1976), a large-scale play looking at the roots of fascism in British society, was produced by the Royal Shakespeare Company (RSC). His eight-hour adaptation of **Dickens**'s *The Life and Adventures of Nicholas Nickleby* for the RSC (1980) brought his work to a massive audience. *Maydays* (1983), the first contemporary play to be presented by the RSC at the Barbican Theatre in London, was similarly ambitious. Other works include *Entertaining Strangers* (1985), a television documentary *Civil War* (1991), a radio play *A Movie Starring Me* (1991), many adaptations, and *Pentecost* (1994).

Edgeworth, Maria 1767–1849 •*Irish novelist*• Born in Blackbourton, Oxfordshire, the eldest daughter of the inventor and educationist Richard Lovell Edgeworth (1744–1817), she was educated in England, then returned to Edgeworthstown in County Longford, Ireland, in 1782 where she became her father's assistant and governess to his many other children. To illustrate her father's educational ideas, she wrote with him *The Parent's Assistant* (1796) and *Practical Education* (1798). In 1800 she published her first novel, *Castle Rackrent*, which was an immediate success, followed by *Belinda* in 1801. She was praised by Sir **Walter Scott** and was lionized on a visit to London and the Continent. The next of her social novels of Irish life was *The Absentee* (1809), followed by *Ormond* (1817). All her works were written under the influence of her father, which may have inhibited her natural story-telling talent. After her father's death (1817) she did little writing apart from a late novel, *Helen* (1834). She is also remembered for her children's stories.

Edinburgh, Prince Philip, Duke of 1921– •*Consort of Queen Elizabeth II*• The son of Prince Andrew of Greece and Princess Alice of Battenburg, grandson of **George I** of Greece and great-grandson of Queen **Victoria**, he was born in Corfu and educated at Cheam School, Gordonstoun and Dartmouth. He joined the Royal Navy (1939) as Lieutenant Philip Mountbatten. In 1941 he joined HMS *Valiant*, on which he fought in the Battle of Cape Matapan, subsequently serving in the Pacific on HMS *Whelp*. In 1947 he became a naturalized British subject, and on November 20, 1947, as the Duke of Edinburgh, he married his third cousin, Princess Elizabeth, the future Queen **Elizabeth II**. As a prince of Great Britain and Northern Ireland since 1957, he has shown a keen and occasionally outspoken interest in science and technology, as well as in youth adventure training, through the Duke of Edinburgh's awards, and world wildlife.

Edison, Thomas Alva 1847–1931 •*US inventor and physicist*• Born in Milan, Ohio, he lost much of his hearing as a boy and had little formal education. He worked as a railroad newsboy on the Grand Trunk Railway, and soon printed and published his own newspaper on the train, the *Grand Trunk Herald*. During the Civil War he worked as a telegraph operator in various cities and invented an electric vote-recording machine. In 1871 he invented the paper ticker-tape automatic repeater for stock exchange prices, which he then sold in order to establish an industrial research laboratory in Newark, New Jersey. In 1876 he moved the laboratory to Menlo Park, New Jersey, where he was able to give full scope to the astonishing inventive genius that won him the name "the Wizard of Menlo Park." He took out more than 1,000 patents in all, including the gramophone (1877), the incandescent light bulb (1879), and the carbon granule microphone as an improvement for **Alexander Graham Bell**'s telephone. To make possible the widespread use of electric light, he invented a system for generating and distributing electricity, and he designed the first power plant (1881–82). Among his other inventions were a megaphone, a storage battery, the electric valve (1883) and the kinetoscope (1891). He moved his laboratory to West Orange, New Jersey, in 1887, and in 1912 he produced the first talking motion pictures. He also discovered thermionic emission, formerly called the "Edison Effect."

" "

Genius is one percent inspiration, ninety-nine percent perspiration.
c. 1903 Quoted in ***Harper's Monthly Magazine****, September 1932.*

Edmonds, Noel 1948– •*English television host*• Born in Ilford, Essex, he joined Radio Luxembourg as a disk jockey in 1968 while still a student teacher, moved to BBC Radio 1 in 1969 and, later, to television. His first success was the children's show, *Multi-Coloured Swap Shop* (1976–81). Moving to prime time, he hosted *The Late Late Breakfast Show* (1982–86) and *Noel's House Party* (1991–99), as well as the long-running quiz show *Telly Addicts* (1985–98).

Edmund, St c. 841–70 •*King of East Anglia*• According to tradition, he was the son of a Frankish king and succeeded **Offa** of Mercia as his adopted heir. When the great Danish invasion of 865 entered East Anglia (870), Edmund met them at Hoxne, Suffolk, and was defeated and killed. Tradition also claims that he was taken captive, and when he refused to abjure his Christian faith, he was tied to a tree and shot to death with arrows by the pagan Danes. A miracle cult quickly sprang up and in 903 his remains were moved from Hoxne to Bury St Edmunds, which became a popular pilgrimage center.

Edmund, St, *originally* **Edmund Rich** 13th century •*English ecclesiastic and scholar*• Born in Abingdon, Oxfordshire, he studied and taught at Oxford and Paris and, acquiring fame as a preacher, was commissioned by Pope **Gregory IX** to preach the Sixth Crusade throughout England (c. 1227). In 1234 he was made Archbishop of Canterbury and became the spokesman of the national party against **Henry III**, even threatening him with excommunication if he did not dismiss foreign favorites. But his gentleness, generosity, austerity and purity led to the diminution of his authority and in 1240 he retired to France. The last Archbishop of Canterbury to be canonized, his feast day is November 16. St Edmund Hall, Oxford, was named in his honor.

Edmund I 921–46 •*King of the English*• The son of **Edward the Elder**, he succeeded his half brother, **Athelstan**, in 939. He reestablished English control of Mercia against the Norse Vikings of Northumbria, and reconquered from them the Five Boroughs of the Danelaw whose Danish settlers now regarded themselves as English citizens. He subdued the Norsemen in Cumbria and Strathclyde, which he entrusted to **Malcolm I** of Scotland as an ally. He was killed at Pucklechurch, Gloucestershire, by an outlawed robber. His reign saw the beginning of the 10th-century monastic revival.

Edmund II (Ironside) c. 990–1016 •*King of the English*• The son of **Ethelred II** (the Unready) and half brother of **Edward the Confessor**, he was lord of most of Mercia from 1015. When **Knut Sveinsson** (Canute) invaded England that summer, Edmund was elected king by the beleaguered defenders of London on his father's death (April 1016), while Knut was chosen king by the Witan (Council) in Southampton. Edmund raised an army, reconquered Wessex and rescued London, before being routed by Knut in a fierce battle at Ashingdon in Essex. He agreed to partition the country, but died a few weeks later, leaving Knut as sole ruler. Edmund's elder son, **Edward the Ætheling**, became the legitimate heir apparent to the throne of his uncle, Edward the Confessor.

Edward, St, *called* **Edward the Martyr** c. 963–78 •*Anglo-Saxon king of England*• The elder son of King **Edgar**, he succeeded to the throne at the age of 12 (975). His accession provoked rival claims on behalf of his younger half brother, **Ethelred II** (the Unready), and in 978 he was treacherously murdered by Ethelred's household at Corfe Castle in Dorset. He was canonized in 1001.

Edward the Confessor c. 1003–66 •*King of England and saint*• Born at Islip, Oxfordshire, he was the elder son of **Ethelred II** (the Unready) by his wife **Emma**, and half brother of **Edmund II (Ironside)**. In 1016 the English throne passed to **Knut Sveinsson** (Canute), who married Ethelred's widow and had a son by her, **Hardaknut Knutsson**. Edward meanwhile went to Normandy (1016–41) and became very religious, taking a vow of chastity. Hardaknut recalled him to England (1041) and Earl **Godwin** of Wessex helped him to the throne (1042). In 1045 he married Godwin's only daughter, Edith. His reign was marked by the conflict between the Norman party at court and the "National" party led by Godwin and his son, Harold Godwinsson, later **Harold II**. Although his legitimate heir was **Edgar the Ætheling** (the grandson of Edmund Ironside), on his deathbed he allegedly nominated Harold Godwinsson as his successor. He was buried in Westminster Abbey, which he founded shortly before his death, and became the subject of a cult that saw him canonized in 1161.

Edward I, *also known as* **Edward Longshanks** and **the Hammer of the Scots** 1239–1307 •*King of England*• Born in Westminster, London, the elder son of **Henry III** and **Eleanor of Provence**, he married **Eleanor of Castile** (1254) and later Margaret of France, the sister of **Philip IV** (1299). He initially supported **Simon de Montfort** in the Barons' War (1264–67), but rejoined Henry III and defeated de Montfort at Evesham (1265). He became king on his father's death (1272) while away on the Eighth (and last) Crusade to the Holy Land (1270), but was not crowned until his return (1274). He annexed north and west Wales (campaigns in 1276–77, 1282–83) and tried to unite England and Scotland through the marriage of his infant son Prince Edward (later **Edward II**) to **Margaret, Maid of Norway**, Queen of Scotland. When Margaret died, he chose **John de Balliol** as king (1292) in preference to **Robert de Bruce**. However, Balliol refused to recognize Edward and allied with France (1295), starting the Scottish Wars of Independence. Despite victories such as the defeat of **William Wallace** at Falkirk (1298), Edward could not subdue Scotland. **Robert de Bruce** (son of Robert de Bruce) had himself crowned King Robert I of Scotland at Scone (1306). Edward marched north, but died near Carlisle (1307). He made many legal reforms, with several statutes (1275–90) reorganizing the state both centrally and locally. He regularly summoned local representatives to central assemblies (such as the so-called Model Parliament of 1295), which voted him useful revenues and gave him national approval for his actions. He expelled the Jews from England (they were not readmitted until 1655).

Edward II, *called* **Edward of Caernarvon** 1284–1327 •*King of England*• Born in Caernarvon, Wales, the son of **Edward I** and **Eleanor of Castile**, he was created the first Prince of Wales in 1301. On his father's death (1307) he abandoned Edward I's plans to subdue the Scots and went to France (1308) to marry **Isabella**, daughter of **Philip IV**, leaving his foreign favorite, Piers Gaveston, Guardian of the Kingdom. Not an energetic ruler, Edward antagonized the barons, who wanted to regain their place in government and rid the country of such royal favorites. Edward invaded Scotland (1314), but was decisively defeated by **Robert de Bruce** at Bannockburn (1314). Bruce went on to capture Berwick (1318) and undid virtually every trace of the conquest of Edward I. Uprisings in Wales and Ireland followed. Edward's authority was challenged by Thomas, Earl of Lancaster, but with the aid of his new favorites, **Hugh Despenser** and his son, Edward, he overthrew Lancaster (1321), and put him to death (1322). He made a truce with Scotland for 13 years in 1323, but then **Charles IV** of France, brother of his wife, Isabella, seized Edward's French territories. Edward sent Isabella to negotiate with Charles, but she despised her husband and had fallen in love with Roger de Mortimer, one of the disaffected nobles. In 1326 she landed with a large body of malcontents on the coast of Suffolk. The Despensers—as Hugh Despenser's followers were called—were executed, and Edward was imprisoned in Kenilworth Castle and forced to abdicate (1327) in favor of his eldest son (**Edward III**). He was murdered at Berkeley Castle.

Edward III, *called* **Edward of Windsor** 1312–77 •*King of England*• Born in Windsor, he was the son of **Edward II**, who was forced to abdicate in his favor (1327). During his minority the country was governed by his mother, **Isabella**, sister of **Charles IV** of France, and her lover, Roger de Mortimer. Edward married **Philippa of Hainault** (1328), executed Mortimer, banished his mother and assumed full control of the government (1330). He successfully supported **Edward de Balliol** against **David II** of Scotland, and David sought refuge in France (1333–1341). Balliol failed to hold Scotland, and despite successive English invasions, the Scots rallied each time. Edward then claimed the French crown, declared war against **Philip VI** (1337), and started the Hundred Years' War. He raised money for the war by tallages, forced loans, and seizing wool, but progressively wrecked the country's public finances. He destroyed the French navy at Sluys (1340), and in 1346, with his son, **Edward the Black Prince**, conquered a large part of Normandy and defeated the French at Crécy. There were further successes, and Calais fell after a year's siege. Meanwhile the Scots had been defeated at Neville's Cross (1346), and David II was captured and imprisoned. In England, a third of the population died from the Black Death (1349). War in France was renewed (1355) with a great victory at Poitiers (1356), where King **John II** of France was taken prisoner. A three-year truce was concluded in 1374, but Edward had failed to win the French crown. His mistress, Alice Perrers, became increasingly influential, until his fourth (third surviving) son, **John of Gaunt**, took over the government.

Edward IV 1442–83 •*King of England*• Born in Rouen, France, he was the eldest son of **Richard**, Duke of York, and bore the title Earl of March. His father Richard claimed the throne as the lineal descendant of **Edward III**'s third and fifth sons (Lionel, Duke of Clarence, and Edmund, Duke of York), against the Lancastrian King **Henry VI** (the lineal descendant of Edward III's fourth son, **John of Gaunt**). Richard was killed at Wakefield (1460), but Edward entered London (1461) and was recognized as king when Henry VI was deposed (1461). With the support of his cousin, Richard Neville, Earl of **Warwick**, he defeated the Lancastrians at Towton (1461). He threw off his dependence on Warwick, and secretly married **Elizabeth Woodville** (1464), but Warwick forced him into exile in Holland (1470), and Henry VI regained the throne. Edward returned to England (March 1471), was restored to kingship (April), then defeated and killed Warwick at Barnet (April), and destroyed the remaining Lancastrian forces at Tewkesbury (May). Henry VI was murdered at the Tower of London soon afterward, and Edward remained secure for the rest of his reign. Direct, straightforward and intelligent, he ensured his court rivaled the splendid court of Burgundy. In his financial reforms he foreshadowed the Tudors, but his advancement of his wife's family was to have serious repercussions in the royal minority that followed his death.

Edward V 1470–83 •*King of England*• Born in Westminster, London, he was the son of **Edward IV** and **Elizabeth Woodville**. When his father died (1483), he and his younger brother, the Duke of York, were left to the guardianship of their paternal uncle, Richard, Duke of Gloucester (the future **Richard III**). The Woodvilles (headed by Edward V's uncle, Anthony Woodville, 2nd Earl **Rivers**) tried to gain influence over him, but Richard took Edward to London (May 1483), and the same month was appointed Protector. In June the Duke of York also reached London, and the two boys were placed in the Tower of London (then a royal residence as well as a prison). Parliament petitioned Richard to take over the throne the day after that originally set for Edward's coronation, and the "Princes in the Tower" made no more public appearances. From about October 1483 there were rumors that Richard had had them murdered, and in 1674 some bones were discovered and reinterred as theirs in Westminster Abbey. In recent years it has been suggested that **Henry VII** may equally have been responsible for their deaths.

Edward VI 1537–53 •*King of England and Ireland*• Born in London, the son of **Henry VIII** and his third wife, **Jane Seymour**, he was 10 years old at his accession (1547). The government was at first in the hands of his uncle, **Edward Seymour**, Duke of Somerset. The Western Rebellion against the publication of the conservative first *Book of Common Prayer* and **Robert Kett**'s rebellion in East Anglia (both 1549) helped cause Somerset's fall; his moderate religious policy pleased no one, while his cautious approach toward popular discontent worried those who advocated a harder line. He was executed (1552) and replaced by John Dudley, Earl of **Warwick**, who had achieved great influence over the young king. Edward was highly intelligent, with a mind of his own, but his religious views were intensely narrow. A revised prayer book was produced, confirmed by a second Act of Uniformity (1552), and the Forty-Two Articles (1553) were intended to give the English Church a definitive creed. As the English Reformation flourished, the king's health, never robust, deteriorated suddenly, and Warwick persuaded the dying boy to alter the succession in favor of his own daughter-in-law, Lady **Jane Grey**. Edward died of tuberculosis, and Lady Jane Grey was overthrown after only nine days on the throne by his Catholic half-sister, **Mary I**.

Edward VII 1841–1910 •*King of Great Britain and Ireland*• The eldest son (Albert Edward) of Queen **Victoria** and Prince **Albert**, he was born at Buckingham Palace, London. He served a 60-year apprenticeship as Prince of Wales during his mother's long reign. He was educated privately, and also at Edinburgh University, Christ Church, Oxford, and Trinity College, Cambridge. In 1860 he made the first tour of Canada and the US undertaken by a royal prince, and after his father's death (1861), took his seat in the House of Lords as Duke of Cornwall. In 1863 he married Princess **Alexandra**, eldest daughter of **Christian IX** of Denmark. Considered too frivolous for responsibility by his mother, he was devoted to social and leisure activities such as horse racing, theater going and yachting. He had several mistresses, and caused a scandal by being cited as a witness in a divorce suit (1870). He succeeded to the throne in 1901 and was crowned the following year. As king he restored vitality and flair to the monarchy, and endeavored to promote international friendship by visits to Continental capitals. He and Queen Alexandra had six children: Albert Victor, Duke of Clarence (1864–92); George, later King **George V**; Louise, Princess Royal (1867–1931); Victoria (1868–1935); Maud (1869–1938), who married King **Haakon VII** of Norway; and Alexander (born and died in 1871).

Edward VIII 1894–1972 •*King of Great Britain and Northern Ireland*• The eldest son of **George V**, he was born at White Lodge in Richmond, Surrey, and educated at Osborne, Dartmouth, and Magdalen College, Oxford. Invested as Prince of Wales (1911), he was in the navy and (in World War I) the army, traveled much, and achieved considerable popularity. He was forthright in his comments on poverty, especially in South Wales. He succeeded his father (January 20, 1936), but abdicated (December 11) on account of general disapprobation of his proposed marriage to Mrs **Wallis Simpson**. He was thereupon given the title of Duke of Windsor, and the marriage took place in June 1937. From 1940 to 1945 he was Governor of the Bahamas, as described in his *A King's Story* (1951). After 1945 he lived in Paris and was not invited back to England with his wife to an official public ceremony until 1967.

“ ”

I have found it impossible to carry the heavy burden of responsibility, and to discharge my duties as King as I would wish, without the help and support of the woman I love.

1936 Radio broadcast to the nation, December 11.

Edward, *called* **Edward the Elder** c. 870–c. 924 •*King of Wessex*• The son of **Alfred** the Great, he succeeded his father in 899. Tenacious and imaginative, he was the best Anglo-Saxon royal strategist. He brought back under English rule the whole of the Danelaw south of the Humber, building a series of fortresses to consolidate his rule. He took control of Mercia (918) after the death of his sister **Ethelflæd** (the "Lady of the Mercians"), and subdued the Scots, the Norsemen in Northumbria, and the Welsh Britons of Strathclyde.

Edward, Prince *See* **Wessex, Prince Edward, Earl of**

Edward the Black Prince 1330–76 •*English heir to the throne*• Born in Woodstock, Oxfordshire, the eldest son of **Edward III**, he was created Earl of Chester (1333), Duke of Cornwall (1337) and Prince of Wales (1343). While still a boy, he commanded the right wing at Crécy (1346), and is said to have won his popular title (first cited in the 16th century) from his black armor. He won several victories in the Hundred Years' War, including the great victory of Poitiers (1356). In 1361 he married his cousin, Joan, the "Fair Maid of Kent" (1328–85), who bore him two sons, Edward (1365–70) and the future **Richard II**. In 1362 his father created him Prince of Aquitaine, and he lived there until 1371, when a revolt forced him to return to England. In 1367 he espoused the cause of **Pedro** the Cruel of Castile and restored him to the throne, winning, at Najera, his third great victory and taking **Bertrand du Guesclin** prisoner. He mercilessly sacked Limoges (1370), after which, mortally ill, he returned to England and took no further part in public life. A chivalric legend in his own lifetime, brave and inspirational, he tended to live beyond his means, and it is doubtful if he had the pragmatic realism necessary for medieval kingship.

Edward the Ætheling, Prince d. 1057 •*English nobleman*• He was the son of **Edmund II (Ironside)** and nephew of the childless **Edward the Confessor**. After Edmund's death (1016), he was taken for safe keeping to Hungary, where he had a son, **Edgar the Ætheling**. Edward the Ætheling was recognized as the proper heir to Edward the Confessor's throne, but he died shortly after landing in England (1057).

Edwards, Gareth Owen 1947– •*Welsh rugby player*• Born in Gwaun-cae-Gurwen, near Swansea, he was first capped for Wales in 1967 at the age of 19, and became their youngest-ever captain a year later. With **Barry John** and Phil Bennett he created the most famous Welsh halfback partnerships, and he also played fullback or center. His 53 consecutive caps set a Welsh record.

Edwards, Jimmy (James Keith O'Neill) 1920–88 •*English comedian*• Born in London, he performed with Cambridge Footlights before serving during World War II in the RAF. His distinguishing feature was his huge handlebar mustache, worn to disguise the results of plastic surgery after his Dakota was shot down at Arnhem (1944). After the war he played Pa Glum in the hit radio series *Take It from Here* (1948–60), developing his bluff and blustering characterization, and headmaster "Professor" James Edwards in the television series *Whack-O!* (1956–60, 1971). His films included *Bottoms Up!* (1959), *The Plank* (1967), *The Bed Sitting Room* (1969) and *Rhubarb* (1970).

Edwards, Jonathan 1703–58 •*American philosopher and theologian*• Born in East Windsor, Connecticut, he was educated at Yale and succeeded his grandfather, Solomon Stoddard, as minister of the Congregationalist Church at Northampton, Massachusetts, in 1729. Renowned for his powerful preaching and hard-line **Calvin**ism, he helped inspire the revivalist movement known as the "Great Awakening." He was dismissed in 1750 for his zealous orthodoxy and became a missionary to the Housatonic people in Stockbridge, Massachusetts. In 1758, he became president of the College of New Jersey (now Princeton College). He is regarded as the greatest theologian of American Puritanism, his main doctrinal work being the *Careful and Strict Enquiry into the Modern Prevailing Notions of the Freedom of the Will* (1754).

Edwards, Jonathan 1966– •*English athlete*• Born in London, he gave up work as a genetics research officer to specialize in the triple jump. In 1995 he became the world champion, twice breaking his own world record to clear 18.29 meters. He won silver medals in the Olympic Games (1996), the world championships (1997 and 1999) and world indoor championships (2001) and further golds in the European championships (1998), the European indoor championships (1998), the Goodwill Games (1998 and 2001), the Olympic Games (2000), the world championships (2001), and the Commonwealth Games (2002). He published *A Time to Jump* in 2000.

Edwards, Jorge 1931– •*Chilean author and diplomat*• Born in Santiago and educated at the University of Chile and at Princeton University, his early career as a diplomat involved high-level posts in Cuba and France. His books include *Persona Non Grata* (1973), *The Imaginary Woman* (1985) and *The Whisky of the Poets* (2000). He was awarded the Cervantes prize for literature in 2000.

Edwards, Robert Geoffrey 1925– •*British physiologist*• He was educated at the Universities of Wales and Edinburgh, and his distinguished posts have included Ford Foundation Reader in Physiology (1969–85) and Professor of Human Reproduction (1985–89) at Cambridge University. In collaboration with **Patrick Steptoe** he contributed substantially to the successful development of the in vitro fertilization (test-tube babies) program. Edwards was able to analyze and then re-create the conditions necessary for the egg and sperm to survive outside the womb. He discovered the factors that would facilitate the ripening of immature eggs, and he provided the appropriate artificial conditions to ensure successful fertilization and subsequent maturation of the embryo. In July 1978 the first healthy test-tube baby was born as a result of their research. With Steptoe he established the Bourne Hallam Clinics, of which he became scientific director (1988–91).

Edwards, Shaun 1966– •*English rugby league player*• He signed with Wigan at the age of 17 for £35,000—then the world's biggest fee paid to a schoolboy. He went on to become the youngest player to appear in a Challenge Cup final and was the youngest international player when he played against France at the age of 18. He played in 43 consecutive winning Challenge Cup games, as Wigan won the trophy for a record eight successive seasons (1988–95). Considered to be one of the greatest rugby league players ever, he retired in 2000.

Edwin, St c. 585–633 •*King of Northumbria*• The son of Ælla, king of Deira, Edwin was kidnapped by Æthelfrith, king of Bernicia, when Ælla died (588). King Rædwald of East Anglia gave him sanctuary and with his support, Edwin killed Æthelfrith (616), creating a united Northumbrian kingdom. He extended the kingdom north to the Lothians in Scotland and west to Anglesey and the Isle of Man, and, when Rædwald died (c. 625), into East Anglia, soon becoming master of all England except Kent. He accepted Christianity in order to marry the daughter of **Ethelbert**, king of Kent, who had been converted by St **Augustine** of Canterbury. He was killed at Hatfield Chase, near Doncaster (633), defending Northumbria from invasion by **Cadwallon** of Wales and **Penda** of Mercia.

Egas Moniz, António Caetano de Abreu Freire 1874–1955 •*Portuguese neurosurgeon and Nobel Prize winner*• He was born in Avanca. Professor of Neurology at Coimbra (from 1902) and Lisbon (1911–44), he did important work on the use of dyes in the X-ray localization of brain tumors and developed prefrontal lobotomy for the control of schizophrenia and other mental disorders. In 1949 he shared the Nobel Prize for physiology or medicine with **Walter Hess**. The early promise which lobotomy seemed to some to show was not substantiated, and the operation has fallen into disrepute. Egas Moniz also had a successful political career.

Egbert d. 839 •*West Saxon king, and first ruler of all the English*• The son of Ealhmund of Kent, he was driven into exile by **Offa** of Mercia to **Charlemagne**'s court (789). In 802 he returned to England and was recognized as king of Wessex. He ended Mercian dominance at the Battle of Ellendun (Wroughton, Wiltshire), conquering Mercia itself (829), and the Northumbrians accepted his overlordship. He became *Bretwalda*, the (first) sole ruler of Britain, but by 830 he had lost Mercia again. His last years were dominated by Viking invasions, and in 839 he defeated an alliance of Cornish insurgents and Danish invaders at Hingston Down, near the River Tamar.

Egerton, Francis Henry, 8th Earl of Bridgewater 1756–1829 •*English clergyman and antiquary*• He was a prebendary of Durham, but lived in Paris for many years and kept his house and garden full of animals dressed up like manikins, because he was fond of shooting. He left £8,000 to be paid to the author of the best treatise on the subject of God manifested in Creation, which was eventually awarded to eight authors of the *Bridgewater Treatises*.

Egerton, Sir Thomas, Baron Ellesmere and **Viscount Brackley** 1540–1617 •*English lawyer and statesman*• Having been called to the bar in 1572, he acquired a large practice in Chancery. He became Solicitor General in 1581, a confidant of **Elizabeth I** and **James VI and I**, and a friend of **Francis Bacon** and Robert Devereux, Earl of **Essex**. He took part in the trial of **Mary Queen of Scots** (1586) and of Essex (1600–01), and became Lord Chancellor in 1603.

Egidius, St *See* **Giles, St**

Ehrlich, Paul 1854–1915 •*German bacteriologist and Nobel Prize winner*• He was born to a Jewish family in Strehlen, Silesia (now Strzelin, Poland). He trained in medicine at Leipzig. A pioneer in hematology and chemotherapy, he synthesized salvarsan as a treatment for syphilis, and propounded the side-chain theory in immunology. He was joint winner, with **Elie Metchnikoff**, of the 1908 Nobel Prize for physiology or medicine.

Eichmann, (Karl) Adolf 1906–62 •*Austrian Nazi war criminal*• Born in Solingen and a fanatical anti-Semite, he became a member of the SS and organized anti-Jewish activities, particularly the deportation of Jews to concentration camps. Captured by US forces in 1945, he escaped from prison some months later, having kept his identity hidden, and in 1950 reached Argentina. He was traced by Israeli agents and in 1960 taken to Israel, condemned for crimes against humanity and executed.

Eiffel, (Alexandre) Gustave 1832–1923 •*French engineer*• Born in Dijon, he was the designer of many notable bridges and viaducts. The Eiffel Tower, 985 feet (295.5 meters) high, was erected (1887–89) on the Champ-de-Mars in Paris at a cost of $1,500,000 for the World Exhibition of 1889, and was the highest building in the world until 1930. In 1893 he was condemned to two years' imprisonment and fined for breach of trust in connection with the abortive French Panama Canal project.

Eigen, Manfred 1917– •*German physical chemist and Nobel Prize winner*• Born in Bochum and educated in Göttingen, he was the director of the **Max Planck** Institute for Physical Chemistry there from 1964. He developed methods for the study of very fast chemical reactions, and for this work shared the Nobel Prize for chemistry in 1967 with **Ronald Norrish** and Sir **George Porter**.

Eijkman, Christiaan 1858–1930 •*Dutch physician, pathologist and Nobel Prize winner*• He was born in Nijkerk and studied medicine at the University of Amsterdam. He investigated the disease beriberi in the Dutch East Indies (Indonesia), and was the first to produce a dietary deficiency disease experimentally (in chickens) and to propose the concept of "essential food factors," later called vitamins. He showed that the substance (now known as thiamine, a B-complex vitamin) that protects against beriberi is contained in the husks of grains of rice, and carried out clinical studies on prisoners in Java to show that unpolished rice could cure the disease. He shared the 1929 Nobel Prize for physiology or medicine with Sir **Frederick Gowland Hopkins**.

Einstein, Albert 1879–1955 •*German-Swiss-US mathematical physicist*• He was born in Ulm, Bavaria, of Jewish parents, and educated in Munich, Aarau and Zurich. He took Swiss nationality in 1901, was appointed examiner at the Swiss Patent Office (1902–05), and began to publish original papers on the theoretical aspects of problems in physics. He achieved world fame with his special and general theories of relativity (1905 and 1916), and won the 1921 Nobel Prize for physics for his work. The special theory provided a new system of mechanics which accommodated **James Clerk Maxwell**'s electromagnetic field theory, as well as the hitherto inexplicable results of the **Michelson-Morley** experiments on the speed of light. He showed that in the case of rapid relative motion involving velocities approaching the speed of light, puzzling phenomena such as decreased size and mass are to be expected. His general theory accounted for the slow rotation of the elliptical path of the planet Mercury, which Newtonian gravitational theory had failed to do. After **Hitler**'s rise to power, Einstein left Germany and lectured at Princeton University in the US from 1934, becoming a US citizen and professor at Princeton in 1940. In September 1939 he wrote to President **Roosevelt** warning him of the possibility that Germany would try to make an atomic bomb, thus helping to initiate the Allied attempt to produce one (called the Manhattan Project). After World War II Einstein urged international control of atomic weapons and protested against the proceedings of the House un-American Activities Committee, which had arraigned many scientists. He spent the rest of his life trying, by means of his unified field theory (1950), to establish a merger between quantum theory and his general theory of relativity, but his attempt was unsuccessful. His works include *About Zionism: Speeches and Letters* (1930), *Why War* (1933, with **Sigmund Freud**), *The Evolution of Physics* (1938) and *Out of My Later Years* (1950).

“ ”

The whole of science is nothing more than a refinement of everyday thinking.

1950 ***Out of My Later Years.***

Einthoven, Willem 1860–1927 •*Dutch physiologist and Nobel Prize winner*• Born in Semarang, Dutch East Indies (Indonesia), he trained in medicine at Utrecht University before becoming Professor of Physiology at Leiden in 1886. In 1903 he invented the string galvanometer, prompting great advances in electrocardiography. He was awarded the 1924 Nobel Prize for physiology or medicine.

Eiríksson, Leifur heppni *See* **Leif the Lucky**

Eisenhower, Dwight D(avid), *nicknamed* **Ike** 1890–1969 •*US general and 34th President of the US*• He was born in Denison, Texas, of immigrant stock originating in the Rhineland. He graduated from the US Military Academy at West Point in 1915, took the war college course in 1928 and gained experience under the assistant secretary of war. By 1939 he had become chief military assistant to General **MacArthur** in the Philippines. In 1942 he assumed command of Allied forces mustered for the amphibious descent on French North Africa. His successful conduct of the North African operations, plus the preponderant American element in the forces earmarked for Operation Overlord, led to his selection as supreme commander for the 1944 cross-channel invasion of the Continental mainland, which he resolutely launched despite unnervingly capricious weather conditions. With the establishment of NATO in 1950 he was made supreme commander of the Allied forces, but in 1952 the popularity that he had gained as a war hero swept him to nomination in the presidential elections. Running as a Republican, he won by a large majority despite the even balance of parties in the House, and he was reelected in 1956. During his presidency the US government was preoccupied with foreign policy and the campaign against Communism, and undercurrents of extremism and excess of zeal often placed the President in an invidious position, but his political inexperience was balanced by sincerity, integrity and a flair for conciliation. More recently his presidency has been subject to a favorable reassessment, now seen as maintaining stability during a difficult period.

Eisenstaedt, Alfred 1898–1995 •*US photojournalist*• Born in Dirschau, Germany (now Tczew, Poland), he moved with his family to Berlin in 1906, and served in the German army in World War I. He started freelancing as a photojournalist in the 1920s and emigrated to the US in 1935, where he became one of the original photographers working on *Life* magazine (1936–72). His worldwide assignments and telling photo essays made him one of the most impressive practitioners of the 20th century. His publications include *Witness to Our Time* (1966), *The Eye of Eisenstaedt* (1969), *Photojournalism* (1971) and *Eisenstaedt Remembrances* (1990). He was awarded the National Medal of Arts in 1990.

Eisenstein, Sergei Mikhailovich 1898–1948 •*Russian film director*• Born in Riga, Russia (now Latvia), he served in the Red Army during the Russian Revolution (1916–18), and after training in theatrical scene painting was appointed to make propaganda films on the history of the revolution with *The Battleship Potemkin* (1925), on the 1905 mutiny, and *Ten Days That Shook The World* (1928), on the October Revolution. His substitution of the group or crowd for the traditional hero, and his consummate skill in cutting and recutting to achieve mounting impressionistic effects, especially in the macabre Odessa steps sequence of *The Battleship Potemkin*, greatly influenced film art. Later he made *Alexander Nevski* (1938), *The Magic Seed* (1941), *Ivan the Terrible* (1944), and *The Boyars Plot*, which was banned in the USSR for many years.

Eisner, Will (William Erwin) 1917– •*US comic book artist and writer*• Born in New York City, he studied at the Art Students League, then became staff artist on the *New York American*. In 1936 he submitted a strip, *The Flame*, to a new comic, *Wow*, and in 1937 he started mass-producing strips for *Wags*, in which he developed *The*

Flame into the long-running weekly serial *Hawks of the Seas*. In 1940 he produced the first comic insert for Sunday newspapers.

Ekelöf, (Bengt) Gunnar 1907–68 •*Swedish poet*• A leader of the postwar Modernists, he is considered one of the most significant Swedish poets of the 20th century. *En Mölna-elegi* (1960) was translated into English (*A Mölna Elegy*, 1979), as were his *Selected Poems* (1966) and *Guide to the Underworld* (1967).

Elagabalus *See* **Heliogabalus**

Elcano *See* **Cano, Juan Sebastian del**

Eldridge, Roy (David) 1911–89 •*US jazz trumpet player*• Born in Pittsburgh, Pennsylvania, he was sometimes known as "Little Jazz." His originality and technical facility made him a jazz virtuoso comparable to **Louis Armstrong** and **Dizzy Gillespie** (on whom he was an early influence). A passionate improviser, able to play with ease in the ultra-high register, he was in demand as a featured soloist with top bands of the 1930s, such as McKinney's Cotton Pickers and the Teddy Hill and **Fletcher Henderson** Orchestras. He adapted to the changing demands of the modern jazz era after the late 1940s, and continued to perform until suffering a stroke in 1980.

Eleanor of Aquitaine c. 1122–1204 •*Queen of France and of England*• She was the daughter of William, Duke of Aquitaine, whom she succeeded as duchess (1137) when she married Prince Louis, who became King **Louis VII** of France a month later. Beautiful and volatile, she led her own troops on the Second Crusade (1147–49), dressed as an Amazonian warrior. In 1152 the marriage was annulled, and she married Henry Plantagenet, who became **Henry II** of England (1154). As a result of Henry's infidelities she supported their sons, Richard and John, in a rebellion against him, and was imprisoned (1174–89). She acted as regent for her son **Richard I** during his crusading campaigns abroad (1189–94), and raised the ransom for his release. In 1200 she led the army that crushed a rebellion in Anjou against her second son, King **John**.

Eleanor of Castile c. 1245–90 •*Queen of England*• The daughter of **Ferdinand III** of Castile, she married the future **Edward I** of England in 1254. She accompanied him to the Crusades (1270–73), but the story that she saved his life by sucking the poison from a wound is probably apocryphal. She died in Harby, Nottinghamshire, and the Eleanor Crosses at Northampton, Geddington and Waltham Cross are survivors of the nine erected by Edward at the halting places of her cortège. The last stopping place was Charing Cross, where a replica now stands.

Eleanor of Provence 1223–91 •*Daughter of Raymond Berengar IV, Count of Provence*• In 1236 she married **Henry III** of England but alienated the barons by advancing her foreign uncles to high office. In the Barons' War (1264) she raised an army of mercenaries in France to support her husband, but her invasion fleet was wrecked. After the accession of her son, **Edward I**, she retired to a convent.

Eleonora of Arborea c. 1350–1404 •*Sardinian ruler and national heroine*• The daughter of a district chieftain (*giudice*), she defeated an incursion from Aragon (1383) and became regent of Arborea for her infant son, Frederick. In 1395 she introduced a humanitarian code of laws (*Carta di Logu*), which was far ahead of its time. Her statue stands in the Piazza Eleonora in Oristano. She gave special protection to hawks and falcons, and Eleonora's falcon is named after her.

Elgar, Sir Edward 1857–1934 •*English composer*• Born in Broadheath, Worcestershire, he was the son of an organist and music dealer, but musically was largely self-taught. In his youth, he worked as an orchestral violinist and became conductor of the Worcester Glee Club and the County Asylum Band, and organist of St George's Roman Catholic Church, Worcester, succeeding his father. Devoting himself to composition from 1891, he wrote the *Enigma Variations* (1899) and the oratorio *The Dream of Gerontius* (1900), both of which consolidated his position as the leading figure in English music. Other works include the oratorios *The Apostles* (1903) and *The Kingdom* (1906), two symphonies and concertos for violin and cello. In 1924 he became Master of the King's Musick. His command of the orchestra and of late 19th-century musical styles within his own personal idiom were very influential in reestablishing English music internationally. He was knighted in 1904.

“ ”

To my friends pictured within.

1899 Dedication to the ***Enigma Variations***.

Elgin, Thomas Bruce, 11th Earl of Kincardine and **7th Earl of** 1766–1841 •*British diplomat and art connoisseur*• While ambassador to the Ottoman sultan (1799–1803) he became interested in the decorated sculptures on the ruined Parthenon in Athens and, because they were in danger of damage and destruction, arranged for some of them to be transported to England. This action brought criticism and accusation of vandalism, but the earl was vindicated by a government committee, and the Elgin Marbles were purchased for the nation in 1816 and later placed in the British Museum, London.

El Greco *See* **Greco, El**

Eliade, Mircea 1907–86 •*Romanian historian and philosopher of comparative religion*• He was born in Bucharest and studied Indian philosophy and Sanskrit at Calcutta University (1928–31) before returning to Romania as a lecturer in the history of religion and metaphysics at Bucharest (1933–39). He served in the diplomatic service during World War II and later taught at the Sorbonne, Paris (1946–48), and the University of Chicago (1957–85). A pioneer in the systematic study of world religions, he published numerous books and papers, including *The Myth of the Eternal Return* (1949), *Patterns in Comparative Religion* (1958), *Yoga: Immortality and Freedom* (1958), *The Sacred and the Profane* (1959), *A History of Religious Ideas, I–III* (1978–85), and two volumes of autobiography (1982, 1988). He wrote a number of novels, including *The Forbidden Forest* (1955).

Eliezer, Israel ben *See* **Baal-Schem-Tov**

Elijah fl. c. 900 BC •*Hebrew prophet*• His story is told in 1 Kings 17–19, 21, and 2 Kings 1–2. His loyalty to God inspired him to oppose the worship of Baal in Israel under King **Ahab** and **Jezebel**, and was rewarded by his direct ascent into heaven in a whirlwind.

Elion, Gertrude Belle 1918–99 •*US biochemist and Nobel Prize winner*• Born in New York City, she studied at Hunter College and New York University, before joining Burroughs Wellcome in 1944 as a research associate of **George Hitchings**. She progressed through the company to become head of experimental therapy (1967–83). With Hitchings she worked extensively on drug development, synthesizing compounds that inhibited DNA synthesis, in the hope of preventing the rapid growth of cancer cells. Their work resulted in a variety of drugs, including ones that are active against leukemia and malaria, that are used in the treatment of gout and kidney stones, and that suppress the normal immune reactions of the body, which are vital in transplant surgery. In the 1970s they produced an antiviral compound active against the herpes virus. In 1988 Elion and Hitchings, with Sir **James Black**, shared the Nobel Prize for physiology or medicine.

Eliot, George, *pseudonym of* **Mary Ann** or **Marian Evans** 1819–80 •*English writer*• She was born on Arbury Farm in Astley, Warwickshire. She was taught German and Italian, and music, of which she was passionately fond throughout her life. In 1841 her father moved to Coventry, and there she met Charles Bray, a writer on the philosophy of necessity from the phrenological standpoint, and his brother-in-law, Charles Hennell, who had published a rationalistic *Inquiry Concerning the Origin of Christianity* (1838). Under their influence she rejected the evangelical Christianity of her upbringing. In 1844 she took on the laborious task of translating **David Strauss**'s *Leben Jesu* (published 1846). After her father's death in 1849 she traveled on the Continent. Returning to England in 1850 she began to write for the *Westminster Review*, and was also at the center of a literary circle, two of whose members were **Herbert Spencer** and **G H Lewes**. She translated **Ludwig Feuerbach**'s *Essence of Christianity* (1854), the only book that bore her real name. Her intimacy with Lewes grew, and in 1854 she formed a liaison with him which lasted until his death in 1878. Her first novel, *Adam Bede* (1859), had enormous success. *The Mill on the*

Floss (1860), *Silas Marner* (1861), *Romola* (1863) and *Felix Holt* (1866) appeared next. Her first poem, "The Spanish Gypsy" (1868), was followed by "Agatha" (1869), "The Legend of Jubal" (1870) and "Armgart" (1871), and in 1871–72 appeared *Middlemarch*, generally considered her greatest work. After that came *Daniel Deronda* (1876), her last great novel. Following the death of Lewes, she was coaxed out of her grief to write *Impressions of Theophrastus Such* (1879), a volume of miscellaneous essays. She fell in love with John Walter Cross (d. 1924), a friend of long standing whom she married in 1880. As a novelist, George Eliot will always stand among the greatest of the English school. Her pictures of farmers, tradesmen, and the lower middle class, generally of the Midlands, are not surpassed in English literature.

Eliot, John, *known as* **the Apostle to the Indians** 1604–90 •*English missionary*• Born in Widford, Hertfordshire, he graduated from Cambridge (1622), took holy orders, left England for America on religious grounds and settled in Roxbury, Massachusetts (1632). In 1646 he began to preach to the Native Americans at Nonantum, establishing his converts, who numbered 3,600 in 1674, in 14 self-governing settlements nearby. However, the numbers diminished after the war (1675) with King **Philip** (Metacomet), and at the hands of the English. He was the author of *A Primer or Catechism, in the Massachusetts Indian Language* (1653). Eliot also translated the Bible into Algonquin (1661–63), which was the first Bible printed in America.

Eliot, Sir Thomas *See* **Elyot, Sir Thomas**

Eliot, T(homas) S(tearns) 1888–1965 •*US-born British poet, critic and dramatist, one of the most important figures of 20th-century English literature*• Born in St Louis, Missouri, he attended Smith Academy in St Louis and Harvard University (1906–10). He had distinguished teachers, such as **Bertrand Russell**. A traveling scholarship from Harvard took him to Merton College, Oxford. In 1914 he met **Ezra Pound**, to whom he had shown his poems; Pound persuaded him to remain in England, where he lived from then on. After a period of teaching school, he worked for eight years in Lloyds Bank before becoming a director of the publishing firm Faber & Gwyer (later Faber & Faber). Pound's support led to the publication of Eliot's first volume of verse, *Prufrock and Other Observations* (1917). In the same year Eliot became assistant editor of *The Egoist*, to which he contributed criticism, and he wrote reviews for the *Times Literary Supplement* and *Athenaeum*. In 1922 he published *The Waste Land*, which received wide attention and helped to reinforce his reputation. However, *The Hollow Men* (1925) gave more reason for regarding Eliot at that point as a cynical defeatist. In 1939 Eliot published a collection of children's verse, *Old Possum's Book of Practical Cats*, which revealed another side of his character, influenced by **Edward Lear**. It has been one of his most popular works, and was adapted as a musical (*Cats*, 1981). Eliot's literary criticism includes *The Sacred Wood* (1920, on Jacobean dramatists), *Homage to Dryden* (1924), *The Use of Poetry and the Use of Criticism* (1933), and *On Poetry and Poets* (1957). In 1927, the year in which he became a British subject, Eliot was baptized and confirmed in the Anglican Church, having been raised as a Unitarian. Eliot's standing was greatly enhanced in 1948 when he received the Order of Merit and was awarded the Nobel Prize for literature.

Elis-Thomas, Dafydd, Baron 1946– •*Welsh nationalist leader*• He was born in Carmarthen, Wales. After an early career as a lecturer, writer and broadcaster, and as a self-proclaimed Marxist, in 1974 he was elected Plaid Cymru Member of Parliament and president of the party in 1984. He continued to lead the party until resigning in 1991 over growing criticism that he was moving to the right and ignoring the interests of traditional Welsh nationalists. He was created a life peer in 1992. Since 1999 he has been presiding officer of the Welsh National Assembly.

Elisha 9th century BC •*Hebrew prophet*• He succeeded **Elijah**, and his activities are portrayed in 1 Kings 19 and 2 Kings 2–9, 13. He was active in Israel under several kings, from **Ahab** to Jehoash, was credited with miraculous signs, counseled kings, and attempted to guide the nation against her external enemies, especially the Syrians.

Elizabeth I 1533–1603 •*Queen of England and Ireland*• She was the daughter of **Henry VIII** and his second wife, **Anne Boleyn**. When her father married his third wife, **Jane Seymour**, in 1536, Elizabeth and her elder half sister Mary Tudor (the future **Mary I**) were declared illegitimate by parliament in favor of Jane Seymour's son, the future **Edward VI**. Unlike her sister she was brought up in the Protestant faith. On Edward's death she sided with her half sister Mary against Lady **Jane Grey** and the Earl of **Warwick** (Northumberland), but her identification with Protestantism aroused the suspicions of her Catholic sister, and she was imprisoned in the Tower. Her accession to the throne in 1558 on Mary's death was greeted with general approval as an assurance of religious tolerance after the persecutions of the preceding reigns. Under the able guidance of Sir **William Cecil** (later Lord Burghley) as Secretary of State, Mary's Catholic legislation was repealed, and the Church of England was fully established (1559–63). Elizabeth made peace with France and Scotland, and strengthened her position by secretly helping Protestants in these countries. **Mary Queen of Scots** was forced to abdicate in 1567, and in 1568 escaped to England, where she was imprisoned, causing numerous conspiracies among English Catholics. After the **Babington** Plot was discovered (1586), Elizabeth was reluctantly persuaded to execute Mary in 1587; many other Catholics were persecuted in the 1580s and 1590s. Infuriated by this, and by Elizabeth's part in inciting the Netherlands against him, **Philip II** of Spain attacked England with his "invincible Armada" (1588), but England managed to repel the attack, though war continued her policy of strengthening Protestant allies and dividing her enemies. At Elizabeth's death in March 1603, the Tudor dynasty came to an end, and the throne passed peacefully to the Stuart **James VI** of Scotland as James I of England.

" "

I know that I have the body of a weak and feeble woman, but I have the heart and stomach of a king—and a king of England too.

1588 Address at Tilbury on the approach of the Spanish Armada.

Elizabeth II 1926– •*Queen of Great Britain and Northern Ireland, and Head of the Commonwealth*• Born in London, she was formerly known as Princess Elizabeth Alexandra Mary, being proclaimed Queen Elizabeth II on the death of her father, **George VI** (1952). Her coronation in 1953 was the first major royal event to be televised. The queen is accepted as Head of the Commonwealth. She is Queen of Great Britain and Northern Ireland, Canada, Australia, New Zealand, and of several other more recently independent countries. Her husband was created Duke of **Edinburgh** on the eve of their wedding (1947), and styled Prince Philip (1957). They have three sons, Prince **Charles**, Prince **Andrew** and Prince **Edward**, and a daughter, Princess **Anne**. The Queen has aimed to modernize the monarchy and make it more informal, instituting luncheon parties for distinguished individuals and pioneering royal walkabouts. She shows a strong personal commitment to the Commonwealth as a voluntary association of equal partners.

Elizabeth, *known as* **the Winter Queen** or **the Queen of Hearts** 1596–1662 •*Queen of Bohemia*• The eldest daughter of **James VI and I** of Scotland and England and **Anne of Denmark**, she married **Frederick V**, Elector Palatine, in 1613. Intelligent and cultured, she enlivened the court at Heidelberg by her presence and, with Frederick's championship of the Protestant cause and his brief, unhappy winter as king of Bohemia, she became a potent symbol of the Protestant cause in Europe. Driven from Prague and deprived of the palatinate by **Maximilian I** of Bavaria, the couple lived in exile in The Hague with their numerous children, continually beset by financial difficulties. Frederick died in 1632, Elizabeth outliving him by 30 years. Her son, Charles Louis, was restored to the palatinate in 1648, but his mother remained in Holland.

Elizabeth, *originally* **Lady Elizabeth Bowes-Lyon** 1900–2002 •*Queen Mother, and Queen Consort of Great Britain and Northern Ireland*• Born in London, the daughter of the future 14th Earl of Strathmore, she spent much of her childhood at Glamis Castle in Scotland, where she helped the nursing staff in World War I. In 1920 she met the Duke of York, second son of **George V**, and they were married in 1923. Princess Elizabeth (later **Elizabeth II**) was born in 1926 and Princess **Margaret** in 1930. The Duke of York came to the throne as King **George VI** in 1936. She was with the king when Buckingham Palace was bombed (1940), and traveled with him to visit heavily damaged towns throughout the war. After George VI's death (1952), the Queen Mother continued to perform public duties, becoming a widely loved figure. She never retired and, from 1953 onward, found a new interest in restoring the Castle of Mey, on the Pentland Firth, as her favorite Scottish home. She was an expert fisherwoman and had great enthusiasm for horse racing. In 2000 her 100th birthday was widely celebrated.

Elizabeth of Hungary, St 1207–31 •*Hungarian princess*• Born in Sáros, Patak, she was the daughter of Andreas II of Hungary. At the age of four she was betrothed to Louis IV, Landgrave of Thuringia. She was educated at his father's court, the Wartburg, near Eisenach. At 14 she was married, and had two children. Louis, who admired her for her long prayers and generous charity, died as a crusader at Otranto in 1227, and Elizabeth was exiled by her husband's brother. At length, she was received into the monastery of Kitzingen by the abbess, her aunt. She was canonized by Pope **Gregory IX** in 1235. Her feast day is November 17.

Elizabeth of Romania *See* **Carmen Sylva**

Elizabeth Petrovna 1709–62 •*Empress of Russia*• Born in Kolomenskaye, near Moscow, the daughter of **Peter I** (the Great), and **Catherine I**, she became empress on the deposition of Ivan VI in 1741. Her animosity toward Frederick II (the Great) (1712–86) led her to take part in the War of the Austrian Succession (1740–48) and the Seven Years' War (1756–63), which helped establish Russia as a European power. At home, she contributed considerably to the extension and entrenchment of serfdom. She founded Russia's first university (in Moscow) and built the Winter Palace (now the Hermitage Art Gallery) in St Petersburg. She was succeeded by her nephew, **Peter III**.

Ellesmere, Baron *See* **Egerton, Sir Thomas**

Ellington, Duke (Edward Kennedy) 1899–1974 •*US jazz pianist, composer and bandleader*• He was born in Washington DC into a middle-class African-American family. He received his only formal musical education as a child through elementary piano lessons, but he was influenced while young by church music and burlesque theater. He led his first regular group, the Washingtonians, in New York in 1925, and in 1927 he began a four-year residence at the Cotton Club in Harlem, which offered him a high-profile live engagement (albeit to segregated white-only audiences), regular access to radio airtime, and recording contracts. His music of this period was largely written and performed as the accompaniment for dance shows, but he began to emerge as one of the most important of jazz composers, producing around 2,000 works over the course of his career. He worked closely with his staff arranger, Billy Strayhorn (1915–67), who was an important composer in his own right, and wrote the tune which became the band's signature, "Take the A Train." He broke new ground in jazz by writing extended works and suites like *Black, Brown and Beige* (1943) and *The Perfume Suite* (1945), a style which remained a regular feature of his output until the end of his career. His use of instrumental colors and textures and innovative chord voicings make him a major figure in 20th-century music, irrespective of genre, although his real genius is arguably more accurately reflected in his shorter works and in individual segments of extended suites, rather than in his genuine long-form works. Many of his song-length pieces, such as "Mood Indigo" and "Sophisticated Lady," became part of the standard jazz repertoire. He also wrote and performed music for films such as *Anatomy of a Murder* (1959). His son, Mercer Ellington (1919–96), continued to run the orchestra after his father's death.

Elliott, Denholm 1922–92 •*English actor*• Born in London, he studied at the Royal Academy of Dramatic Art and served in the RAF during World War II, spending three years in a POW camp. *Venus Observed* (1950) won him the Clarence Derwent award, and his New York debut in *Ring Round the Moon* (1950) received the Donaldson award. Following his first film appearance in *Dear Mr Prohack* (1949) he played breezy juveniles and heroic servicemen in films like *The Cruel Sea* (1953) and *They Who Dare* (1954). *Nothing But the Best* (1964) launched a second career as a distinguished character actor, playing largely rogues, bounders and losers in films like *Alfie* (1966), *Scorchers* (1992) and *Noises Off* (1992). A prolific performer in all media, and an inveterate scene stealer, he won British Film awards for *Trading Places* (1983), *A Private Function* (1984) and *Defense of the Realm* (1985).

Ellis, (Henry) Havelock 1859–1939 •*English physician and writer*• Born in Croydon, Surrey, the son of a sea captain, he traveled widely in Australia and South America before studying medicine at St Thomas's Hospital, London. In 1891 he married Edith Lees and throughout his life had a number of female followers, notably **Olive Schreiner**. His interest in human biology and his own personal experiences led him to compile his controversial seven-volume *Studies in the Psychology of Sex* (1897–1928, rev edn 1936), which was banned in Great Britain. He also founded the "Mermaid" series on Elizabethan and Jacobean dramatists.

Ellis, Ruth, *née* **Neilson** 1926–55 •*Welsh murderer*• Born in Rhyl, Clwyd, she was a nightclub hostess. She shot dead her former lover, David Blakely, a racecar driver, outside a Hampstead pub in April 1955. The case achieved notoriety as a "crime of passion." Blakely was trying to extricate himself from their tempestuous, often violent relationship at the time of his murder. Ellis was the last woman to receive the death penalty in Great Britain, and was hanged on July 13, 1955.

Ellis, William Webb 1805–72 •*English sportsman*• According to a rather doubtful tradition, he was a pupil at Rugby School in 1823 when he broke the rules by picking up and running with the ball during a game of association soccer, thus inspiring the new game of rugby football.

Ellison, Ralph Waldo 1914–94 •*US novelist*• Born in Oklahoma City, he studied music at Tuskegee Institute and served during World War II in the US Merchant Marine. He met **Richard Wright** in 1937, through whom he gained a new perspective on social and racial injustice, and who encouraged him to write. His early work appeared in *New Challenge* magazine. *Invisible Man* (1952), his only completed novel, is the quest of a nameless African-American man, traveling from the South to the North, in search of a personal and racial identity. Allusive but highly original and ingenious, it had a seminal influence on other African-American writers and won the National Book award. He was Albert Schweitzer Professor in the Humanities at New York University (1970–79). He published two books of essays, *Shadow and the Act* (1964) and *Going to the Territory* (1986). A book-length manuscript of his long-awaited, unfinished second novel, *Juneteenth*, was published posthumously in 1999.

Ellmann, Richard 1918–87 •*US biographer and academic*• Born in Detroit, Michigan, he graduated from Yale, and after World War II lived in Dublin for a year, where he wrote his first book, *Yeats: The Man and the Mask* (1948). Some 10 years later came his masterful biography of **James Joyce**, now accepted as one of the great 20th-century biographies, as much for its elegant composition as its astute judgment and erudition. A professor at Northwestern University, Illinois, until 1968, he moved to Oxford in 1970 as Goldsmiths' Professor of English Literature, remaining there until his death. His biography of **Oscar Wilde** (1987) was published posthumously to wide acclaim.

Ellsworth, Lincoln 1880–1951 •*US explorer*• Born in Chicago, the son of a millionaire financier, he was the first person to fly over both the North Pole (in the airship *Norge* with **Umberto Nobile** and **Roald Amundsen** in 1926) and the South Pole (in 1935). In his Antarctic explorations (1935, 1939), he claimed thousands of square miles of territory for the US (Ellsworth Land).

Elman, Mischa 1891–1967 •*US violinist*• Born in Talnoye, Ukraine, he was a child prodigy. His debuts were in Berlin (1904), London (1905) and New York (1908), and they confirmed him as an exceptional violinist. He settled in the US in 1911 and became a US citizen in 1923.

Elms, Lauris Margaret 1931– •*Australian singer*• Born in Melbourne, Victoria, she studied in Paris and made her debut

(1957) at Covent Garden, London, becoming principal resident artist there. She toured Australia with **Joan Sutherland** in 1965, and appeared at the royal opening of the Sydney Opera House in 1973. She has appeared with all the leading Australian companies, and is renowned for her Azucena in Verdi's *Il trovatore* ("The Troubadour"). A frequent broadcaster, she gives regular lieder recitals with pianist Geoffrey Parsons. She has also made a number of successful recordings.

Els, Ernie 1969– •*South African golfer*• Born in Johannesburg, he established his reputation in 1992 by winning a hat trick of the South African Open, Professional Golfers' Association and Masters titles. In 1994 he became only the fourth foreign-born player since 1927 to win the US Open, a feat he repeated in 1997. His other achievements have included an unprecedented three successive World Match Play championship wins (1994–96) and victory in the British Open in 2002.

Elsheimer, Adam 1578–1610 •*German painter*• Born in Frankfurt, he worked in Venice after 1598 and in Rome after 1600. Basing his style on a close study of **Tintoretto** and other Italian masters, he excelled in the portrayal of atmosphere and effects of light, and exerted a profound influence on the development of German landscape painting.

Elton, Ben(jamin Charles) 1959– •*English comedian and writer*• Born in Catford, South London, he made his first professional appearance as a stand-up comedian at the Comic Strip Club in 1981. At the forefront of the alternative comedy movement, he has cowritten such popular television comedies as the anarchic *The Young Ones* (1982, 1984), the *Blackadder* series (1986–89), and *The Thin Blue Line* (1995–96). He has also written stage plays, best-selling novels, a musical and a film. His own television shows include *Ben Elton—The Man from Auntie* (1990, 1994).

Elton, Charles Sutherland 1900–91 •*English ecologist*• Born in Liverpool, he studied at New College, Oxford, and spent most of his career there (1936–67). His four Arctic expeditions in the 1920s and his use of trappers' records for fur-bearing animals led to his classic books on animal ecology. His talents were turned to reduction of food loss in World War II through his studies of rodent ecology. His work on animal communities led to the recognition of the ability of many animals to counter environmental disadvantage by change of habitats, and to the use of the concepts of "food chain" and "niche." His books include *Animal Ecology* (1927) and *The Pattern of Animal Communities* (1966). He founded and edited the *Journal of Animal Ecology*.

Éluard, Paul, *pseudonym of* **Eugène-Émile Paul Grindel** 1895–1952 •*French poet*• Born in Saint-Denis, he was founder with **André Breton** and **Louis Aragon** of the Surrealist movement, and was also involved with the Dada movement. He became France's leading 20th-century love poet. His chief Surrealist poetry is in *Les dessous d'une vie ou la pyramide humaine* (1926, "The Underbelly of Life or the Human Pyramid"). In 1938 he broke with the movement. During World War II he was active in the Resistance, joined the Communist Party in 1942, and circulated his poetry secretly (*Poésie et vérité*, 1942, and *Au rendez-vous allemand*, 1944). His postwar work was more lyrical and personal, especially his last volume, *Le Phénix*. English translations include *Thorns of Thunder* (1936), *Selected Writings* (1951) and *Last Love Poems* (1980).

“ ”

Le poète est celui qui inspire bien plus que celui qui est inspiré.
The poet is more the inspirer than the one who is inspired.

1936 ***L'Evidence poétique.***

Elvehjem, Conrad Arnold 1901–62 •*US biochemist*• Born in McFarland, Wisconsin, he studied and spent most of his career at the University of Wisconsin, ultimately becoming president (1958–62). Studying pellagra, a human dietary disease, Elvehjem showed in 1935 that liver extracts cured pellagra-like symptoms. In 1937 he confirmed and extended his original finding by curing the related disease, black tongue, in dogs. A year later, with collaborators, he showed that nicotinic acid also cured the canine disease, and they correctly anticipated its efficacy for curing pellagra in humans. Elvehjem also showed that certain elements are essential in animal nutrition in trace levels, including copper (necessary for the formation of hemoglobin), cobalt and zinc.

Elvström, Paul 1928– •*Danish yachtsman*• He is the only yachtsman to have won four individual Olympic gold medals: in the Firefly class in 1948 and the Finn class in 1952, 1956, and 1960. He was also the first to win the same event at four consecutive Olympics. He placed fourth in the Tornado class at the 1984 Olympics, his seventh Games, with his daughter, Trine.

Elyot or **Eliot, Sir Thomas** c. 1490–1546 •*English scholar and diplomat*• Born in Wiltshire, the son of a jurist, he was educated at Oxford and the Middle Temple, and in 1523 became clerk of the Privy Council. In 1531–32, as ambassador to Emperor **Charles V**, he visited the Low Countries and Germany, having orders to procure the arrest of **William Tyndale**. His chief work, *The Boke Named the Gouernour* (1531), is the earliest English treatise on moral philosophy. He also compiled the first English dictionary (1538).

Elytis, Odysseus, *pseudonym of* **Odysseus Alepoudelis** 1911–96 •*Greek poet and Nobel Prize winner*• Born in Heraklion, Crete, he was educated at the University of Athens and at the Sorbonne, Paris, and worked in broadcasting and as a critic of art and literature. His pseudonym is said to combine the three most prevalent themes in his work: Greece, hope and freedom. He was influenced by the Surrealists, both French and Greek. His early poems exude a love of Greece, sun and life, but after his war experience in Albania, violence and the imminence of death also figure in his work. His greatest achievement was *To axion esti* (1959, Eng trans *The Axion Esti*, 1974), a long, optimistic poem which took 14 years to write. His final poetic collection ("West of Sorrow") was published in Greek in 1995. In 1979 he was awarded the Nobel Prize for literature.

Emanuel I *See* **Manoel I**

Emecheta, (Florence Onye) Buchi 1944– •*British novelist*• Born near Lagos, Nigeria, she was educated at the Methodist Girls' High School, Lagos, and the University of London. She moved to England in 1962 and has since lived in London. She writes of marriage as a battle of the sexes, and her novels are powerful social documents, graphic in their depiction of man's inhumanity to woman. Her work includes *In the Ditch* (1972) and *Second-Class Citizen* (1974), which were published together as *Adah's Story* (1983), *The Joys of Motherhood* (1979), *The Rape of Shavi* (1983) and *Gwendolen* (1989). She has also written children's stories and television plays.

Emerson, Ralph Waldo 1803–82 •*US poet and essayist*• Born in Boston, Massachusetts, of a long line of ministers, he graduated from Harvard in 1821 and became pastor of the Second Church (Unitarian) in Boston (1829), but his controversial views resulted in his resignation. In 1833 he went to Europe and visited **Thomas Carlyle**, beginning their 38-year correspondence the next year. He moved to Concord, Massachusetts (1834), and in 1836 published a prose rhapsody entitled *Nature*, which was followed by "The American Scholar," an oration delivered at Harvard. His "address before the Divinity Class, Cambridge, 1838," produced a great sensation, especially among the Unitarians. He also published *Representative Men* (1850), *English Traits* (1856), *The Conduct of Life* (1860), *Society and Solitude* (1870) and *Letters and Social Aims* (1876). He was a Transcendentalist in philosophy, a rationalist in religion, and a firm advocate of individualism and spiritual independence.

Emerson, Roy Stanley 1936– •*Australian tennis player*• Born in Queensland, he holds the record for the most Grand Slam titles—28 (12 singles and 16 doubles)—and his record of 12 Grand Slam singles titles was only surpassed by **Pete Sampras** in 2000. These victories, however, were at a time when the majority of his rivals had turned professional and were ineligible for those championships. A classic all-court player, he is celebrated as the first man to play a serve-volley game for five sets.

Emin, Tracey 1964– •*English artist*• Born in London and brought up in Margate, she studied at Maidstone College of Art and the Royal College of Art. She gained widespread public attention with various "confessional" installation works such as *Everyone I Have*

Ever Slept With (1995), which featured a small tent with dozens of names embroidered inside, and the stained and detritus-littered *My Bed* (1998). Her major exhibitions include *Minky Manky* (1995), *Personal Effects* (1998) and *You Forgot to Kiss My Soul* (2001).

Emin Pasha, *originally* **Eduard Schnitzer** 1840–92 •*German doctor, explorer and linguist*• Born in Neisse, of Jewish parents, he studied medicine at Breslau and Berlin, and practiced at Scutari (Albania), where he adopted the Muslim faith. After 1876, as Emin Effendi, he was in the Egyptian service, becoming bey and pasha. General **Charles Gordon** appointed him Governor of the Equatorial Province in 1878. A skillful linguist, Emin Pasha added enormously to the knowledge of African languages, wrote valuable geographical papers, and sent to Europe rich collections of plants and animals. He was "rescued" by **Henry Morton Stanley**'s expedition in 1889, and, isolated by disaffection within his troops, he accompanied Stanley to Zanzibar, but immediately returned to extend the German sphere of influence around Lake Victoria. He never regained his old influence, and was marching for the west coast when he was murdered by Arabs in the Manyema country.

Emma d. 1052 •*Queen of England*• The daughter of Richard II, Duke of Normandy, she was a forceful, ambitious and unscrupulous survivor who played a leading part in English political life for 40 years. She married **Ethelred II** (the Unready) (1002), and had a son, **Edward the Confessor**. She fled to Normandy when **Svein Haraldsson**, (Fork-Beard), invaded England (1013), returning to England (1017) to marry Ethelred's successor, **Knut Sveinsson** (Canute). She tried to put their son, **Hardaknut Knutsson**, on the throne after Knut's death (1035), but was thwarted by **Harold I Knutsson**, (Harefoot), her stepson, and fled to the Flemish court of Baldwin the Pious. When Hardaknut was elected king (1040), Emma returned to England, but on his death (1042) his successor, her other son, Edward the Confessor, confiscated her property when she apparently favored his rival, **Magnus I** (the Good) of Norway.

Emmerich, Anna Katharina, *known as* **the Nun of Dülmen** 1774–1824 •*German visionary*• Born near Coesfeld, she entered the Augustinian Order in 1802, and from 1812 bore the stigmata of Christ's Passion. Her revelations were recorded by the poet **Clemens von Brentano**.

Empedocles fl. c. 450 BC •*Greek philosopher and poet*• He was born in Acragas (Agrigento), Sicily, and was by tradition a doctor, politician and soothsayer. He attracted various colorful but apocryphal anecdotes—such as the story that he jumped into Mount Etna's crater to support his own prediction that he would one day be taken up to heaven by the gods. We have only fragments of his writings from two long poems. *On Nature* describes a cosmic cycle in the which the basic elements, Earth, Air, Fire and Water, periodically combine and separate under the influence of dynamic forces akin to what we might call "love" and "strife." This notion was adopted by **Aristotle**, and the doctrine of four elements became central to Western thought for the following 2,000 years. *Purifications* has a Pythagorean strain and describes the Fall of Man and the transmigration and redemption of souls. Empedocles was the first to demonstrate that air has weight. He was also aware of the possibility of an evolutionary process.

Empson, Sir William 1906–84 •*English poet and critic*• Born in Howden, Yorkshire, he was educated at Winchester and Magdalene College, Cambridge, where he studied mathematics and literature. His first work of criticism was his university dissertation, published as *Seven Types of Ambiguity* (1930). From 1931 to 1934 he was Professor of English Literature in Tokyo, and at Peking (now Beijing, 1937–39, 1947–53), having been in the meantime with the BBC's Far Eastern Service. In 1953 he became Professor of English Literature at Sheffield University. His other critical works include *The Structure of Complex Words* (1951) and *Milton's God* (1961). *Collected Poems* was published in 1955.

Encke, Johann Franz 1791–1865 •*German astronomer*• Born in Hamburg, he was educated at the University of Göttingen. His principal work was concerned with facilitating computations of the movements of comets and asteroids, and included a method of calculating the gravitational influences of the planets on the motion of comets. On investigating the orbit of a comet discovered by Jean-Louis Pons in Marseilles (1818), he demonstrated that the same comet had been observed on previous returns and deduced that it moved around the sun in an elliptic orbit with a period of only 3.25 years. Encke's comet, as it is called, has the shortest known period of any comet.

Ender, Kornelia 1958– •*German swimmer*• Born in Bitterfeld, she won three Olympic silver medals in 1972 at age 13, and between 1973 and 1976 broke 23 world records (the most by a woman under modern conditions). At the 1973 and 1975 world championships she won 10 medals, including a record 8 golds. In 1976 she became the first woman to win 4 gold medals at one Olympic Games.

Enderby, Samuel fl. 1830–39 •*English entrepreneur*• The grandfather of General **Charles Gordon**, he was a member of a firm of London merchants who fitted out three Antarctic expeditions (1830–39). The name Enderby Land was given in 1831 to a tract of Antarctica by its discoverer, John Biscoe, a whaler employed by the company.

Enders, John Franklin 1897–1985 •*US bacteriologist and Nobel Prize winner*• Born in West Hartford, Connecticut, he studied literature at Harvard, but turned to science and received a PhD in bacteriology. He shared, with **Frederick Robbins** and **Thomas Weller**, the 1954 Nobel Prize for physiology or medicine for the cultivation of polioviruses in human tissue cells, thus greatly advancing virology and making possible the development of a polio vaccine by **Jonas Edward Salk**. In 1962 Enders developed an effective vaccine against measles.

Endo, Shusako Paul 1923–96 •*Japanese novelist and short-story writer*• He was born in Tokyo. He graduated with a degree in French literature from Keio University, then studied for several years in Lyons. He has gained wide recognition in the West and, although he is considered by some Japanese to be "un-Japanese," has won many literary awards. His books include *Chimmoku* (1966, Eng trans *Silence*), *Umi to dokuyaku* (1972, Eng trans *The Sea and the Poison*), *Obakasan* (1974, Eng trans *Wonderful Fool*), *Iesu no shogai* (1978, Eng trans *Life of Jesus*, Dag Hammarskjöld Prize) and *Samurai* (1982, Noma Literary Prize).

Enfield, Harry (Henry Richard) 1961– •*English comedian*• Born in London, he studied at York University. He made his television breakthrough in 1987 with the characters Loadsamoney and Stavros on *Saturday Live*, gaining his own series, *Harry Enfield's Television Programme* (1990, 1992) and *Harry Enfield and Chums* (1994, 1997), which introduced the characters Tim Nice-but-Dim, Wayne and Waynetta Slob, and Kevin and Perry the teenagers.

Engelbart, Douglas Carl 1925– •*US computer scientist*• Born on a farm near Portland, Oregon, he studied at Oregon State University, and, after war service in the navy, at the University of California. He subsequently took up a position at the Stanford Research Institute, where he became a pioneer of ARPANET, the forerunner of the Internet. The first public trials of Englebart's best-known invention, the computer mouse, took place in 1968, and he also helped develop many of the features that are now integral to modern computing, including e-mail.

Engels, Friedrich 1820–95 •*German philosopher and politician*• Born in Barmen, he lived mostly in England after 1842. Having gained experience from working in his father's cotton factory in Manchester and established contacts with the Chartist movement, he wrote *Condition of the Working Classes in England in 1844* (1845). He first met **Karl Marx** at Brussels in 1844 and collaborated with him on the *Communist Manifesto* (1848). He returned to Germany with his mentor in 1848 to work on the *Neue Rheinische Zeitung* and fight on the barricades at Baden during the unsuccessful revolution of that year. After Marx's death in 1883, Engels devoted the remaining years of his life to editing and translating Marx's writings.

“ ”

Der Staat wird nicht "abgeschafft," er stirbt ab.
The state is not "abolished"; it withers away.

1878 ***Anti-Dühring**, part 3, chapter 2.*

Ennius, Quintus c. 239–169 BC •*Roman poet*• Born in Rudiae, Calabria, probably of Greek extraction, he is said to have served in the Punic Wars, and returned from Sardinia to Rome with **Cato** the Elder. Having attained the status of Roman citizen, he introduced the Greek hexameter into Latin, using it in his *Annales*, which became the model for Latin epic poetry. In addition, he wrote satires, didactic verse, epigrams and numerous plays. Only fragments of his works survive.

Enoch •*Biblical character*• The son of Jared and father of Methuselah, he was depicted as extraordinarily devout, and therefore was translated directly into heaven without dying (Genesis 5:24). In the Greco-Roman era his name became attached to Jewish apocalyptic writings allegedly describing his visions and journeys through the heavens (the three apocryphal books of Enoch).

Enquist, Per Olov 1934– •*Swedish playwright and novelist*• Born in Hjoggböle, his best-known work for the theater is a collection of three plays published in 1981 under the collective title *Triptych*, comprising *Lesbian Night* (about **Strindberg** and his wife), *To Phaedra* and *The Life of the Slow-Worms* (about **Hans Christian Andersen**). His major novel is *The Legionaries* (1968), about the expulsion of Baltic refugees to Russia from Sweden after World War II.

Ensor, James Sidney Ensor, Baron 1860–1949 •*Belgian painter and engraver*• He was born in Ostend, of Anglo-Belgian parentage, and trained at the Brussels Academy. He rarely left Ostend and was neglected as an artist for much of his life, but is now regarded as a pioneer of Expressionism. He is best known for his macabre carnival paintings of fighting skeletons and masked revelers, such as his *Entry of Christ into Brussels* (1888), which owe a great deal to **Hieronymus Bosch**, **Pieter Brueghel** the Elder, and **Goya**.

Enver Pasha 1881–1922 •*Turkish soldier and politician*• A leader in the 1908 revolution of Young Turks, as the pro-German Minister of War he steered the Turkish government into a secret alliance with Germany directed against Russia in August 1914. After the Turkish surrender in 1918 at the end of World War I, he fled to Russia and was killed in an insurrection in Turkestan.

Eoin *See* **MacNeill, John**

Epaminondas c. 418–362 BC •*Theban general*• His victory at the Battle of Leuctra (371 BC) broke the military power of Sparta and made Thebes the most powerful state in Greece. Two years later, with **Pelopidas**, he marched into the Peloponnesus, and incited some of the allies to desert Sparta. In 368 war was renewed, and Epaminondas made a somewhat unsuccessful invasion into the Peloponnesus. To atone for this he advanced into Arcadia, and near Mantinea broke the Spartan phalanx, but was killed there.

Épée, Charles Michel, Abbé de l' 1712–89 •*French educationist*• Born in Versailles, he became a preacher and canon at Troyes, but was deprived as a Jansenist. In 1765 he began to educate two sisters who could not hear or speak, and invented a language of signs. He also pioneered the use of spatial aids to assist the memorizing of, for example, vocabulary by associating words with particular locations in space. His attempts succeeding, at his own expense he founded an institute for those who could neither hear nor speak.

Ephron, Nora 1941– •*US screenwriter and director*• Born in New York City, to parents who were both writers, she was educated at Wellesley College. Her debut screenplay collaboration *Silkwood* (1983) earned her an Academy Award nomination, and she went on to write two of the most successful romantic comedies of the period, *When Harry Met Sally* (1989) and *Sleepless in Seattle* (1993). Among other work, she has also written and directed *This Is My Life* (1992), and *You've Got Mail* (1998).

Epicharmus c. 540–450 BC •*Greek poet*• Born in Cos or Syracuse, he wrote 35 or more comedies performed in Syracuse. Only fragments of his works survive.

Epictetus 1st century AD •*Greek Stoic philosopher and moralist*• Born in Hierapolis, Phrygia, he was a slave in Rome. After he was freed he taught philosophy there until banished by the emperor **Domitian** along with other philosophers in AD 90 when he settled at Nikopolis in Epirus. His pupil, the historian **Arrian**, collected his sayings into a manual entitled the *Enchiridion* and into eight volumes of *Discourses*, of which four survive. He taught a gospel of inner freedom through self-abnegation, submission to providence and love of one's enemies.

Epicurus c. 341–270 BC •*Greek philosopher and founder of the Epicurean school*• Born on the island of Samos, he opened a school at Mitylene (310 BC) and taught there and at Lampsacus. At Athens he established (305) a school of philosophy known as the "Gardens," where he led a life of temperance and simplicity. The Gardens became the model for other Epicurean communities, or communes, where members could live peacefully in friendship. Only three letters and a few fragments of his 300 or so works survive. Most of our knowledge of his doctrines comes from **Cicero**, **Plutarch** and in particular, **Lucretius**. He believed that pleasure is the chief good and the only goal of morality, by which he meant freedom from pain and anxiety, not (as the term "epicure" has since come to mean) one who indulges sensual pleasures without stint. These ethical views are supported by a materialistic psychology and an atomistic physics (largely derived from **Democritus**) that demonstrate that the world operates on mechanical principles, that death is not to be feared, and that the gods do not intervene in the world or punish the guilty. Epicureanism and Stoicism were the two great philosophies of the Hellenic period, and both found many followers in Rome and endured for many centuries.

Epimenides fl. 7th century BC •*Semilegendary Greek poet and priest*• Born in Crete, he is said to have lived for 299 years, during 57 of which he received, while sleeping, the divine inspiration that determined his future career. **Goethe** wrote a poem on the subject, *Des Epimenides Erwachen*. Epimenides is said to have gone to Athens about 600 BC, where he stayed, and with **Solon** reformed the Athenian constitution. He was the "prophet" quoted by St **Paul** in Titus 1:12, but it is unlikely that he wrote the epic poems ascribed to him.

Epiphanes *See* **Antiochus IV**

Epiphanius, St c. 315–403 AD •*Palestinian Christian Church father*• Born in Palestine, he founded a monastery near Eleutheropolis in AD 335. He was Bishop of Constantia in Cyprus from 367 until his death. He showed intolerance to St **John Chrysostom** and proclaimed **Origen** a heretic in 394. He wrote several works against Arianism and various other heresies.

Episcopius or **Biscop, Simon** 1583–1643 •*Dutch theologian*• Born in Amsterdam, he studied at Leiden under **Jacobus Arminius** and **Francis Gomarus**, and succeeded to the latter's chair in 1612. He and 12 other Arminians were banished by the Synod of Dort (1618), and in the Spanish Netherlands he wrote his famous Arminian *Confessio* (1622). Permitted to return in 1626, he was a professor at the Arminian College at Amsterdam from 1634, where he produced his *Institutiones theologicae* and *Responsio*.

Epstein, Sir (Michael) Anthony 1921– •*English microbiologist*• Born in London, he was educated at Trinity College, Cambridge, worked at Middlesex Hospital Medical School and moved to the University of Bristol before moving in 1985 to Oxford. In 1964 he discovered a new human herpes virus, known as the Epstein-Barr virus, which has been implicated in some forms of human cancer, notably Burkitt's lymphoma. This was the first virus to be associated with cancer in humans, and its discovery stimulated the current vast research. He has received many awards, and was knighted in 1991.

Epstein, Sir Jacob 1880–1959 •*British sculptor*• He was born in New York City, a Russian-Polish Jew, and studied at the École des Beaux-Arts in Paris (1902). He became a British subject in 1907, and his early commissions included 18 nude figures for the façade of the British Medical Association building in the Strand, London (1907–08) and *Night and Day* (1929) for the London Transport Building. These and later primitivist sculptures, such as the marble *Genesis* (1930, Granada Television), the *Ecce Homo* (1934), and the alabaster *Adam* (1939), resulted in great controversy and accusations of indecency and blasphemy. He modeled many impressive bronze portrait heads (such as *Ester* [1944], his youngest daughter), and also executed two bronze *Madonna and Child* works (1927, Riverside Church, New York; 1950, Holy Child Jesus Convent,

London). In the 1950s his last two large commissioned works, the aluminum *Christ in Majesty* (Llandaff Cathedral) and *St Michael and the Devil* (Coventry Cathedral), won more immediate critical acclaim.

Erasistratus of Ceos fl. c. 250 BC •*Greek physician*• Born on the island of Ceos (Chios), he studied medicine in Athens and later founded a school of anatomy at Alexandria. His writings are known largely through **Galen**'s accounts. On the basis of vivisection and dissection of animals, accompanied by postmortems on humans, he built up an extensive grasp of human and comparative anatomy. He traced arteries and veins to the heart, and like **Herophilus**, clearly recognized the difference between sensory and motor nerves.

Erasmus, Desiderius c. 1466–1536 •*Dutch Humanist and scholar*• He was born in Rotterdam and educated by the Brethren of the Common Life at Deventer. He joined an Augustinian monastery at Steyn near Gouda in 1487, and was ordained a priest in 1492; but he was already reacting against scholasticism and was drawn to the Humanists. He studied and taught in Paris, and later in most of the cultural centers in Europe, including Oxford (1499) and Cambridge (1509–14), where he was Professor of Divinity and of Greek. He traveled widely, writing, teaching and meeting Europe's foremost intellectuals (including, in England, **Thomas More**). He published many popular, sometimes didactic works, including *Adagia* (*Adages*, 1500, 1508), *Enchiridion militis Christiani* (*Handbook of a Christian Soldier*, 1503), and the famous *Encomium moriae* (*In Praise of Folly*, 1509). He also published scholarly editions of classical authors and the Church Fathers, and edited the Greek New Testament (1516). He became strongly critical of the pedantries and abuses of the Catholic Church, and his *Colloquia familiaria* of 1518 helped prepare the way for **Martin Luther** and the Reformation; but he also came to oppose the dogmatic theology of the Reformers and specifically attacked Luther in *De libero arbitrio* (1523). Despite these controversies he enjoyed great fame and respect in his last years, which he spent in Basel.

“ ”

In regione caecorum rex est luscus.
In the country of the blind the one-eyed man is king.
*1500 **Adages**, book 3, century 4, no. 96.*

Erastus, Thomas, *originally* **Thomas Liebler** or **Lieber** or **Lüber** 1524–83 •*Swiss theologian and physician*• Born in Swiss Baden, he studied theology at Basel, philosophy and medicine in Italy, and was appointed physician to the counts of Henneberg. Professor of Medicine at Heidelberg and physician to the Elector Palatine (1558), he became Professor of Ethics at Basel in 1580. He was a vigorous writer against **Paracelsus** and witchcraft. In theology he followed **Huldreich Zwingli**, and in England the name of Erastians was applied to the party that arose in the 17th century, denying the right of autonomy to the Church, which was neither maintained nor denied by Erastus.

Eratosthenes c. 276–194 BC •*Greek mathematician, astronomer and geographer*• Born in Cyrene, he became the head of the great library at Alexandria and was the most versatile scholar of his time, known as "pentathlos," or "all-rounder." He measured the obliquity of the ecliptic and the circumference of the Earth with considerable accuracy. In mathematics he invented a method called the "sieve of Eratosthenes" for listing the prime numbers and a mechanical method of duplicating the cube. He also wrote on geography, chronology and literary criticism.

Ercilla y Zúñiga, Alonso de 1553–c. 1595 •*Spanish poet*• Born in Bermeo on the Bay of Biscay, he entered the service of **Philip II** and accompanied him in 1554 to England on the occasion of his marriage to Queen **Mary I (Tudor)**. Shortly after, he joined the expedition against the Araucanians in Chile, whose amazing heroism inspired his monumental epic poem, *La Araucana* (1569–89, Eng trans 1945). When an unfounded suspicion of his complicity in an insurrection nearly led to his execution, he returned to Spain, then made a tour through Europe, and became chamberlain to the emperor **Rudolf II**.

Erhard, Ludwig 1897–1977 •*German economist and politician*• Born in Fürth, North Bavaria, he studied economics at Nuremberg. His career was held back during the 1930s as a result of his refusal to join the Nazi Party. However, immediately after World War II, he became Professor of Economics at the University of Munich. In 1949 he was elected to the Bundestag (federal parliament) at Bonn and was appointed Finance Minister in the **Adenauer** Christian Democrat administration. He was the pioneer of the West German "economic miracle" of recovery from wartime devastation, and succeeded Adenauer as Chancellor (1963–66), but economic difficulties forced his resignation.

Ericsson, John 1803–89 •*US inventor*• Born in Långbanshyttan, Värmland, Sweden, he served as an officer of engineers in the Swedish army (1816–26), and in 1826 moved to England, where he established himself as an engineering consultant. He built (1829) a formidable rival to **George Stephenson**'s *Rocket*, and in 1836 he patented, six weeks after Sir **Francis Pettit Smith**, one of the first successful screw propellers. In 1839 he went to the US, where he designed the warship *Princeton*. He became a naturalized US citizen in 1848. In 1861, during the Civil War, he designed the ironclad *Monitor* (the first warship with an armored revolving turret), and in 1878 *The Destroyer*, which could launch submarine torpedoes. His inventions largely revolutionized navigation and the construction of warships.

Erigena, John Scotus, *also called* **Johannes Scotus Eriugena** or **John the Scot** c. 810–c. 877 •*Irish philosopher and theologian*• Born in "Scotia" (Ireland), he taught at the court of **Charles I** (the Bald) in France, then supported Hincmar, Archbishop of Rheims, in the predestination controversy with his *De praedestinatione* (851), which the Council of Valence condemned as *pultes Scotorum* ("Irishman's porridge") and "an invention of the devil." His major work, *De divisione naturae* (c. 865), tried to fuse Christian and Neo-Platonic doctrines and to reconcile faith and reason, but his writing was later condemned for its pantheistic tendencies and eventually placed on the Index by **Gregory XIII** in 1685. Tradition has it that, having become abbot of Malmesbury, he was stabbed to death by his scholars with their pens "for trying to make them think."

Erik VII, *also known as* **Erik of Pomerania** c. 1381–1459 •*King of Denmark, Sweden (Erik XIII) and Norway (Erik III)*• The son of Duke Wratislaw VII of Pomerania and Maria, niece of Queen **Margrethe I**, he was adopted as heir to the triple monarchy by his great-aunt (1389) and crowned at Kalmar, Sweden (1397), when the treaty of union between the three countries was formally sealed. It was not until 1412, however, on Queen Margrethe's death, that he gained actual power. Aggressive commercial and military policies against Holstein and the Hanseatic League that ultimately failed led to economic disasters that provoked rebellion, and he was deposed by all three countries one by one: Sweden and Denmark (1438) and Norway (1442).

Erik IX Jedvardsson, *called* **Erik the Saint** d. 1160 •*King and patron saint of Sweden*• King of Sweden from c. 1150, he is said to have led a Christian crusade for the conversion of Finland, and to have been murdered at Mass in Uppsala by a Danish pretender to his throne. He was married to Kristina and was the father of King Knut Eriksson (d. c. 1195).

Erik XIV 1533–77 •*King of Sweden*• Born in Stockholm, the eldest son and successor of **Gustav I Vasa**, he ruled from 1560 to 1568. Suspicious of others to the point of paranoia, he imprisoned his half brother, Johan, for treason (1563) and launched a war against Denmark for control of the Baltic ports, which ended inconclusively with the Peace of Stettin (1570). He had several of his courtiers butchered on suspicion of treason and, after various attempts to marry Queen **Elizabeth I** of England and **Mary Queen of Scots**, he married a soldier's daughter, Karin Månsdotter. Her coronation (1568) provided a pretext for rebellion. He was dethroned (1568) in favor of his brother **Johan III**, and spent the rest of his life in captivity.

Erik Haraldsson, *called* **Erik Blódøx ("Bloodaxe")** d. 954 •*King of Norway*• The eldest son of **Harald I Halfdanarson**, he succeeded to the throne of Norway (c. 942) when his father abdicated. His wife was Gunnlaug, sister of King **Harald Gormsson** of Denmark. His reign in Norway was violent, and Erik killed several of his half brothers who had rebelled against him. He was deposed by his youngest brother, Haakon I Haraldsson (947) and sought refuge in England, where he was accepted as king in York of the Norse realm in Northumbria (948, 952–54). He was eventually expelled (954) and killed in battle at Stainmore, Yorkshire.

Erik of Pomerania *See* **Erik VII**

Erik the Red, *properly* **Erik Thorvaldson** 10th century •*Norwegian sailor*• He explored the Greenland coast and founded the Norse colonies there (985). His son **Leif the Lucky** landed in "Vinland," often identified as America (1000). Both men are the subject of Icelandic sagas.

Eriugena, Johannes Scotus *See* **Erigena, John Scotus**

Erixson, Sven, *known as* **X-et** 1899–1970 •*Swedish artist*• Born in Tumba, he spent much time in the Mediterranean countries and took his motifs from there as well as from Sweden. His colorful paintings, with their mixture of folk art and naiveness, full of incidents from everyday life, made him much in demand for large-scale public commissions, such as his tapestry *Melodies on the Square* (1937–39) in the Concert Hall in Gothenburg.

Erlanger, Joseph 1874–1965 •*US physiologist and Nobel Prize winner*• Born in San Francisco and educated at Johns Hopkins Medical School, he was subsequently appointed Professor of Physiology at the University of Wisconsin (1906–10) and then at Washington University, St Louis (1910–46). His early career was devoted to studying the heart and the circulation, but during World War I he studied different problems, including the treatment of wound shock. In 1921 he began collaborating with **Herbert Gasser** in analyzing fundamental properties of the neural conduction of impulses, discovering that the velocity of the impulse was proportional to the diameter of the nerve fiber. For this research they shared the 1944 Nobel Prize for physiology or medicine.

Ernest Augustus 1771–1851 •*King of Hanover*• Born at Kew, the fifth son of **George III**, he was educated at the University of Göttingen. He then entered the Hanoverian army and was created Duke of Cumberland (1799). In 1837 he succeeded his brother **William IV** of Great Britain as Ernest I of Hanover. His policy was reactionary, but in 1848 he saved his throne by the unwilling concession of liberal reforms. He was succeeded by his son, George V (1819–78).

Ernst, Max 1891–1976 •*German painter and sculptor*• He was born in Brühl, near Cologne. After studying philosophy and psychiatry at Bonn, he turned to painting, and in 1918 founded at Cologne the German Dada group. Later, in Paris, with **Paul Éluard** and **André Breton**, he participated in the Surrealist movement. He invented the technique of frottage (pencil rubbings on canvas), and settled in the US in 1941, but returned to France in 1953.

" "

The artist is a spectator, indifferent or impassioned, at the birth of his work, and observes the phases of its development.

Quoted in Saranne Alexandrian ***Surrealist Art*** *(1970).*

Ershad, Hossain Mohammad 1930– •*Bangladeshi soldier and chief martial law administrator*• He was born in Rangpur in northern Bangladesh and joined the Pakistani army. He subsequently served in East Pakistan, rising to the rank of colonel during the 1971 civil war. Ershad assumed power in a military coup in 1982, became president in 1983 and proceeded to introduce a new rural-orientated economic program. He was reelected president in 1986 and lifted martial law, but he confronted continuing demands for a full return to civilian rule and resigned in 1990. In the early 1990s he faced a number of criminal charges and subsequently spent time in prison at intervals throughout the following decade.

Erskine, Thomas Erskine, 1st Baron 1750–1823 •*Scottish jurist*• Born in Edinburgh, he entered Lincoln's Inn (1775) and Trinity College, Cambridge (1776), and was called to the bar in 1778. In 1783 he became a King's Counsel and Member of Parliament for Portsmouth. Sympathy with the French Revolution led him to join the "Friends of the People," and to undertake the defense in many political prosecutions of 1793–94. His acceptance of a retainer from **Tom Paine** cost him the attorney generalship under the Prince of Wales (held since 1786). Erskine's speeches for Paine, the Scottish radical Thomas Hardy (1794), and the English radical John Tooke (1794) are fine examples of forensic skill, and his defense of Hadfield (1800), indicted for shooting at **George III**, dismantled the contemporary theory concerning the criminal responsibility of the mentally ill. In 1806 he was appointed Lord Chancellor, but resigned the following year.

Erving, Julius 1950– •*US basketball player*• Born in Hempstead, New York, he played for the American Basketball Association's Virginia Squires (1971–73) and New York Nets (1973–76) and the National Basketball Association's Philadelphia 76ers (1976–87). Nicknamed "Dr J," he won fame for his dazzling moves and soaring slam dunks. He was named most valuable player four times (ABA, 1974–76; NBA, 1981) and placed third on the all-time scoring list with a career total of 30,026 points (in the ABA and NBA combined).

Esaki, Leo 1925– •*Japanese physicist and Nobel Prize winner*• Born in Osaka, he was educated at Tokyo University, working for his doctorate on semiconductors. He later investigated conduction by quantum mechanical "tunneling" of electrons through the potential energy barrier of a germanium p-n diode. He used the effect to construct a device with diode-like properties, the tunnel (or Esaki) diode. Their very fast speeds of operation, small size, low noise and power consumption give these diodes widespread application in computers and microwave devices. He shared the Nobel Prize for physics in 1973 with **Brian Josephson** and **Ivar Giaever**.

Esarhaddon d. 669 BC •*King of Assyria*• He was the younger son of **Sennacherib**, whom he succeeded in 680 BC. He achieved the conquest of Egypt (675–671). A great builder, he established the city of Nineveh. He was succeeded by his son, **Ashurbanipal**.

Esau •*Biblical character*• The elder son of Isaac, he is depicted as his father's favorite son, but he was deprived of Isaac's blessing and his birthright by his cunning brother **Jacob** (Genesis 27). The story explains why Esau's descendants, the Edomites, were thereafter hostile to Jacob's descendants, the Israelites.

Eschenbach, Wolfram von *See* **Wolfram von Eschenbach**

Escher, Maurits Cornelius 1898–1972 •*Dutch artist*• Primarily a printmaker, he created whimsical visual fantasies in lithographs and woodcuts. He often used geometric distortions and tricks of perspective to deceive the eye.

Escoffier, Auguste c. 1847–1935 •*French chef*• Born in Villeneuve-Loubet, he served with a Russian Grand Duke, then became chef de cuisine to the general staff of the Rhine army in the Franco-Prussian War (1871) and of the Grand Hotel, Monte Carlo, before César Ritz persuaded him to go to the Savoy, London, and finally to the Carlton. He invented the *bombe Nero* of flaming ice and *pêche Melba*, among other dishes.

Eshkol, Levi 1895–1969 •*Israeli politician*• Born in Oratovo, Russia (now in Ukraine), into a pious Jewish family, he settled in Palestine as an agricultural worker in 1914. After Israeli independence in 1948, he supervised the founding of several hundred new villages to absorb immigrants. A member of the Mapai Party, he served as Prime Minister and Defense Minister (1963–69), transferring the latter post to **Moshe Dayan** during the Six-Day War of 1967. Eshkol established diplomatic relations with West Germany and was also the first Israeli leader to visit the US.

Es-Sa'id, Nuri, *officially* **Nouri Said Pasha** 1888–1958 •*Iraqi politician*• Born in Kirkuk and educated at the Istanbul Staff College for the Turkish Army, in World War I he fought against the Turks under King **Hussein Ibn Ali** of the Hejaz. In 1921 he became Iraq's first Chief of the General Staff and a year later Defense Minister. From 1930 he filled the office of Prime Minister many times until he was assassinated in 1958 after the coup d'état of Brigadier **Abdul Kassem**.

Essex, Robert Devereux, 2nd Earl of 1566/67–1601 •*Elizabethan soldier and courtier*• Born in Netherwood, Herefordshire, he served in the Netherlands (1585–86), distinguishing himself at

Zutphen. At court he quickly rose in the favor of Queen **Elizabeth I**, despite his clandestine marriage (1590) with Frances Walsingham, the daughter of Sir **Francis Walsingham** and widow of Sir **Philip Sidney**. In 1591 he commanded the forces sent to help **Henry IV** of France against the Catholic League. He took part in the capture of Cádiz (1596), but was largely responsible for the failure of an expedition to the Azores (1597). Following his quarrel with Elizabeth over his marriage, they were never reconciled, and he was imprisoned after his six months' lord lieutenancy of Ireland proved a failure. Essex aimed at the highest state office, despite being politically and administratively unskilled. He plotted to raise revolt in London and remove Elizabeth's councilors (1601), but was found guilty of high treason and beheaded.

Esterházy •*Hungarian noble dynasty*• A powerful Magyar family originally founded by Ferenc Zerhazy (1563–94), it developed along the Frankńo, Csesznek and Zólyom lines and produced diplomats, soldiers and art patrons into the 20th century. The Frankńo line was founded by Zerhazy's son Miklós Esterházy (1582–1645), whose goal was to free Hungary from Turkish dominance and whose son Pál Esterházy (1635–1713) was made a prince of the empire (1687) for his successes against the Turks, thus establishing the princely line. He also strongly supported the **Habsburg** monarchy, whose wealth the Esterházy dynasty exceeded, and helped to reduce the power held by the Magyar nobles. Prince Miklós Joseph (1714–90), a notable art patron, employed **Haydn** in his private orchestra for nearly 30 years. The fourth Prince Miklós (1765–1833) formed a splendid collection of pictures in Vienna, but his extravagance put his estates into sequestration. He raised an army to fight the French in the Napoleonic Wars and refused the honor of becoming king. Prince Pál Antal (1786–1866) represented Austria in London until 1842, and in 1848 was Hungarian Minister of Foreign Affairs. His extravagance caused the estates to be sequestrated again in 1860. Count Moritz (1807–90) too was a diplomat.

Estes, Richard 1932– •*US painter*• Born in Keewane, Illinois, he studied at the Art Institute of Chicago (1952–56) and moved to New York in 1959. In the late 1960s, he began painting precise copies of photographs, particularly of New York street scenes, and for three decades he has continued to produce meticulously detailed photorealist works which can easily be confused with photographs. His works include *The Candy Store* (1969), *Downtown* (1978) and *The Plaza* (1991).

Esther 5th century BC •*Biblical queen*• She was the foster daughter of the Jew **Mordecai**. According to the Book of Esther she was chosen by the Persian king Ahasuerus (**Xerxes I**) as his wife in place of the disgraced Queen Vashti, and brought about the deliverance of her people.

Estridsson *See* **Svein II Ulfsson**

Ethelbert or **Æthelbert** d. 616/618 •*King of Kent*• He was the first English king to adopt Christianity. During his reign, which historians now tend to date from c. 590, Kent achieved hegemony over England south of the Humber. **Bede** describes him as powerful, but cautious and superstitious. Ethelbert welcomed St **Augustine** in 596, allowing him to settle at Canterbury and set up further bishoprics at Rochester and London. He himself was baptized with his court, and Canterbury became the capital of Roman Christianity in Britain. He was also responsible for the first written code of English laws.

Etheldreda or **Æthelthryth** or **Audrey, St** c. 630–79 •*Anglo-Saxon princess and abbess*• She was the daughter of King Anna of East Anglia, and was widowed after three years of her first marriage, which was said never to have been consummated. In 660 she married Ecgfrith, future king of Northumbria, but refused to consummate the marriage. Instead she took the veil and withdrew to the double monastery at Coldingham. In 672 she founded a double monastery herself on the Isle of Ely, of which she was appointed abbess.

Ethelflæd or **Æthelflæd** c. 870–918 •*Anglo-Saxon ruler of Mercia*• She was the daughter of **Alfred** the Great and sister of **Edward** the Elder, of Wessex. She married Ethelred (Æthelred), the alderman of Mercia (c. 886), and fought alongside him to repel the Danish invaders, the battle culminating in a decisive victory near Tettenhall in 910. She succeeded her husband (911) and planned and led Mercian counterattacks on the Danes. In 917, with her brother Edward, she captured Derby, and took Leicester in 918. She also kept up Mercian pressure on the Welsh. She died when poised to invade Danish-held Northumbria.

Ethelred or **Æthelred I** d. 871 •*Anglo-Saxon King of Wessex*• One of the five sons of King Ethelwulf (Æthelwulf) and elder brother of **Alfred** the Great, he succeeded to the throne in 865. In that year a large Danish invasion army landed in East Anglia intent on permanent conquest, and captured York and Northumbria. Ethelred, with Alfred as his second-in-command, helped to defend Mercia against them. Early in 870 the Danes established a fortified camp at Reading in Wessex. Ethelred and Alfred defeated them at Ashdown in Berkshire, but Ethelred died soon afterward, to be succeeded by Alfred.

Ethelred or **Æthelred II**, *wrongly referred to as* **the Unready** c. 968–1016 •*King of England*• The son of King **Edgar**, he was ten when he succeeded to the throne (978) after the murder of his half brother **Edward the Martyr**. He at first attempted to buy off Viking invaders. This gave rise to his Anglo-Saxon nickname *Unrœd*, meaning "lack of counsel" (mistranslated as "Unready"), intended as a pun on his name Ethelred, which means "good counsel." However, in 1002, he ordered a savage massacre of all Danish settlers. In 1013, beleaguered by the invasion of **Svein I Haraldsson** of Denmark, he abandoned his throne and fled to Normandy but was recalled in 1014. Recent scholarship has seen his reign in a more positive light than did the hostile *Anglo-Saxon Chronicle*, and has emphasized its administrative reforms and literary achievements. By a first marriage he left a son, **Edmund II (Ironside)**, who succeeded him for a few months, and by his second wife, **Emma**, he was the father of **Edward the Confessor**.

Etherege, Sir George c. 1635–91 •*English dramatist*• Born probably in Maidenhead, Berkshire, he married a wealthy widow, and in 1685 was sent to be resident at the Imperial court at Ratisbon, where he drank, flirted with actresses, and engaged in correspondence with **Thomas Middleton**, **Dryden** and Thomas Betterton. He sought his inspiration in **Molière**, and out of him grew the legitimate comedy of manners and the work of **Richard Brinsley Sheridan** and **Oliver Goldsmith**. His three plays are *The Comical Revenge, or Love in a Tub* (1664), *She Would If She Could* (1668) and *The Man of Mode, or Sir Fopling Flutter* (1676).

Etheridge, Melissa 1962– •*US singer and songwriter*• Born in Leavenworth, Kansas, she gained her first Grammy nomination with her 1988 debut album, *Melissa Etheridge*. It was her more experimental album *Never Enough* (1992) that won her a Best Female Rock Perfomance Grammy for the single "Ain't It Heavy." In 1995 she won her second Grammy for Best Female Rock Performance. Other albums include *Yes I Am* (1993), *Breakdown* (1999) and *SKIN* (2001). She is also well known as an activist for gay rights and supporter of the fight against AIDS and breast cancer, among other causes.

Etty, William 1787–1849 •*English painter*• Born in York, the son of a baker, he went to London in 1806 and studied at the Royal Academy Schools. In 1822–23 he spent 18 months in Italy, half of them at Venice, where he was deeply influenced by the Venetian masters. Renowned for his nudes, he depicted historical and classical subjects, as in *The Combat* (1825, National Gallery of Scotland), but was at his best when working on a scale that was less ambitious.

Eucken, Rudolf Christoph 1846–1926 •*German philosopher and Nobel Prize winner*• Born in Aurich, Ostfriesland, he was educated at the University of Göttingen. He became professor at Basel (1871) and at Jena (1874), and won the Nobel Prize for literature in 1908 in recognition of his "earnest search for truth" and "idealistic philosophy of life." His works include *Philosophie der Geschichte* (1907), *Der Sinn und Wert des Lebens* (1908, Eng trans *The Meaning and Value of Life*, 1916) and *Mensch und Welt* (1918).

Eucleides of Megara fl. c. 390 BC •*Greek philosopher*• A disciple of **Socrates**, mentioned by **Plato** as one of those present during Socrates' last hours, he founded a school of Megarians, who were evidently influenced by **Parmenides** as well as by Socrates and are associated with various developments in logic like the "liar paradox" (attributed to one of their number, Eubulides). Nothing of their writings survives.

Euclid fl. 300 BC •*Greek mathematician*• He taught in Alexandria, where he appears to have founded a mathematical school. His *Elements* of geometry, in 13 books, is the earliest substantial Greek mathematical treatise to have survived. It is probably better known than any other mathematical book, and was still used as the basis of school textbooks in the early part of the 20th century. It covers the geometry of lines in the plane, among them **Pythagoras**'s theorem, and goes on to discuss circles, ratio, and the geometry of three dimensions. He wrote other works on geometry, including the theory of conics, and on astronomy, optics and music.

Eudoxus of Cnidus 408–353 BC •*Greek mathematician, astronomer and geographer*• Thought to have been a member of **Plato**'s Academy, he formed his own school in Cyzicus. He made many advances in geometry and it is possible that most of **Euclid**'s Book XII is largely his work. He drew up a map of the stars and compiled a map of the known areas of the world. He correctly recalculated the length of the solar year and his philosophical theories are thought to have had a great influence on **Aristotle**.

Eugène of Savoy, Prince, *properly* **François Eugène de Savoie Carignan** 1663–1736 •*Austrian soldier*• Born in Paris, he entered the service of the emperor **Leopold I** against the Turks. He distinguished himself in the war against Louis XIV in Italy, and his defeat of the Turks at Zenta (1697) put an end to their power in Hungary. The War of the Spanish Succession (1701) recalled him to Italy, but **Louis, Duc de Vendôme,** defeated him there (1702). In command of the imperial army, he helped the Duke of **Marlborough** at Blenheim (1704). Eugène defeated the French in Italy, but a series of his own defeats led to the Peace of Rastadt (1714). He continued to fight the Turks from 1716, and then the French in a war over the crown of Poland. After the peace he returned to Vienna.

Eugénie, Empress, *originally* **Eugénie de Montijo** 1826–1920 •*Spanish empress of France*• Born in Granada, she was a Spanish noblewoman renowned for her beauty and was consort of **Napoleon III** from 1853 until 1871. She used her political influence to oppose liberal and democratic ideas and to serve as an advocate of the Church. After Napoleon III's deposition during the Franco-Prussian War, she fled to England, where she was befriended by Queen **Victoria**.

Eugenius IV, *originally* **Gabriele Condulmer** 1383–1447 •*Italian pope*• Born in Venice, he was installed as pope in 1431, and quarreled with the reforming Council of Basel convoked by his predecessor Martin V, which sought to limit papal power. Driven from Rome in 1434 by the Colonnas, he excommunicated the bishops assembled at Basel, but they deposed him (1439) and elected **Amadeus VIII** of Savoy as Felix V. At the Council of Ferrara, John Palaeologus II, Emperor of Constantinople (Istanbul), appeared with 20 Greek bishops, and a union between the Greek and Latin Churches was effected for a short time in 1439. In 1444 Eugenius returned to Rome.

Euhemerus fl. c. 300 BC •*Greek philosopher and mythographer*• Born probably in Messene, Sicily, he wrote *Hiera anagraphe*, or *Sacred History*, which "Euhemerized" Greek mythology by explaining the gods as distorted representations of warriors and heroes from remote history.

Euler, Leonhard 1707–83 •*Swiss mathematician*• Born in Basel, he studied mathematics there and at St Petersburg, where he became Professor of Physics (1731) and then Professor of Mathematics (1733). In 1741 he moved to Berlin at the invitation of **Frederick II** (the Great), but he returned to St Petersburg in 1766 and remained in Russia until his death. He published many books and papers on every aspect of pure and applied mathematics, physics and astronomy. He studied infinite series and differential equations, introduced or established many new functions, including the gamma function and elliptic integrals, and created the calculus of variations. His *Introductio in analysin infinitorum* (1748) and later treatises on differential and integral calculus and algebra became standard textbooks, and his notations such as e and i (the square root of -1) have been used ever since. In mechanics Euler studied the motion of rigid bodies in three dimensions, the construction and control of ships, and celestial mechanics. For the princess of Anhalt-Dessau he wrote *Lettres à une princesse d'Allemagne* (1768–72), a nontechnical outline of the main physical theories of the time. His powerful memory enabled him to continue mathematical work though nearly blind.

Euler, Ulf Svante von 1905–83 •*Swedish pharmacologist and Nobel Prize winner*• Born in Stockholm, the son of Nobel laureate **Hans Euler-Chelpin**, he studied at the Karolinska Institute. In 1935 he isolated a group of lipids he called prostaglandins, and in the early 1940s isolated and characterized the principal transmitter of the sympathetic nervous system, noradrenaline. Appointed Professor of Physiology at the Karolinska (1939–71), he shared the 1970 Nobel Prize for physiology or medicine with **Julius Axelrod** and **Bernard Katz**.

Euler-Chelpin, Hans Karl August Simon von 1873–1964 •*Swedish biochemist and Nobel Prize winner*• Born in Augsburg, Germany, after studying in Berlin, Göttingen and Paris, he became a lecturer in physical chemistry at Stockholm University (1900), and then was appointed Professor of Chemistry and director of the Institute for the Biochemistry of Vitamins in 1929. His work was oriented toward elucidating the chemistry and kinetics of peptidases, zymase (yeast extract causing fermentation), and in particular, saccharase. He showed that zymase was markedly activated by vitamins A and B, and purified the system by alcohol fractionation and aluminum oxide adsorption. He also analyzed the properties and reactions of the saccharases. With Sir **Arthur Harden**, Euler-Chelpin was awarded the Nobel Prize for chemistry in 1929 for his research on enzymes and fermentation.

Eunomius d. c. 399 AD •*Cappadocian prelate*• Born in Cappadocia, Asia Minor, he was Bishop of Cyzicus (c. 360 AD) but was deposed for his Arian views. With **Flavius Aëtius** he became the leader of an extreme sect of Arians known as the Anomoeans or Eunomians.

Euphranor 4th century BC •*Greek painter and sculptor*• Born in Corinth, he was famed for his decoration of the Stoa Basileios at Athens.

Euphronios fl. late 6th century–5th century BC •*Greek potter and vase painter*• His name is inscribed, as either painter or potter, on 15 vessels that constitute some of the finest surviving examples of vessels painted in the "red figure" style.

Euripides 484 or 480–406 BC •*Greek tragic dramatist*• Born probably in Salamis, he did not take much part in public life. Of about 80 of his dramas whose titles are known, 18 survive complete. They include *Medea* (431 BC, Eng trans 1959), *Andromache* (425 BC, Eng trans 1957), *Supplices* (423 BC, Eng trans 1957), *Troades* (415 BC, Eng trans *The Women of Troy*, 1954), *Phoenissae* (410 BC, Eng trans *The Phoenician Women*, 1959) and *Orestes* (408 BC, Eng trans 1959). *The Bacchae* (405 BC, Eng trans 1954) and *Iphigenia Aulidensis* (405 BC, Eng trans *Iphigenia in Aulis*, 1959) were put on the Athenian stage only after the author's death. He brought a new style to tragedy and the treatment of traditional mythology, and is notable for highlighting unusual opinions and portraying socially marginal characters. **Sophocles**, who deemed him "the most tragic of poets," also commented that while he himself showed people as they ought to be, Euripides portrayed them as they are.

“ ”

Regard this day's life as yours, but all else as Fortune's.

Alcestis, *l.788–9 (translated by D Kovacs, 1994).*

Eusebio, *in full* **Silva Ferreira da Eusebio** 1942– •*Portuguese soccer player*• Born in Mozambique, he was one of the first great players to emerge from the African continent. He had a long and successful career with Benfica of Lisbon, with whom he won European Cup medals. He was nominated European Footballer of the Year in 1965 and in the Centenary Match, to mark the foundation of the Football Association, he played for the Rest of the World against England in 1963. In the World Cup of 1966 he was the top goal scorer.

Eusebius of Caesarea, *known as* **the Father of Church History** c. 264–340 AD •*Palestinian theologian and scholar*• Born probably in

Palestine, he became Bishop of Caesarea (c. 313 AD), and in the Council of Nicaea was the head of the Semi-Arian, or moderate, party, which was averse to discussing the nature of the Trinity. His *Chronicon*, a history of the world to 325, contains extracts from lost works. His *Praeparatio Evangelica* is a collection of such statements by heathen authors to support the evidence of Christianity, and its complement is the *Demonstratio Evangelica* in 20 books, 10 of which are extant, intended to convince the Jews of the truth of Christianity from their own scriptures. His most important work, the *Ecclesiastical History*, is a record of the chief events in the Christian Church down to 324.

Eusebius of Nicomedia d. 342 AD •*Syrian prelate*• Born probably in Syria, he was Bishop first of Beryta (Beirut) in Syria, and then of Nicomedia. He defended **Arius** at the Council of Nicaea (AD 325) and afterward became the head of the Arian party. Exiled to Gaul for his views, he came back in 328 and influenced the emperor **Constantine I (the Great)** to move toward Arianism, and baptized him in 337, just before Constantine died. He had also been responsible for the deposition of **Athanasius** in 335. In 339 he was appointed Patriarch of Constantinople, and enjoyed the patronage of the emperor **Constantius I**.

Eustachio, Bartolomeo 1520–74 •*Italian anatomist*• Born in San Severino (now Ancona), he studied medicine in Rome, and after serving as a personal physican taught at the Collegia della Sapienza there. He made considerable studies of the thoracic duct, larynx, adrenal glands, the teeth, and above all the kidneys. From 1552 he was involved in the production of a remarkable, but unpublished, series of anatomical illustrations. He is remembered for his precise account of the eustachian canal (auditory tube) of the ear, and also of the eustachian valve in the fetus. His most important work was the *Opuscula anatomica* (1564).

Euthymides fl. late 6th century–early 5th century BC •*Greek vase painter of the so-called red-figure style*• He was a contemporary of **Euphronios** and, seemingly, a rival, since among the six surviving signed vessels is one inscribed with the words "Euphronios never did anything like it."

Eutyches c. 384–c. 456 AD •*Greek religious Archimandrite at Constantinople*• He was the founder of "Eutychianism," holding that after the incarnation, human nature became merged in the divine, and that **Jesus** had therefore but one nature. He was condemned by a synod at Constantinople (Istanbul) in AD 448, but the Council of Ephesus (449) decided in his favor and restored him, deposing his opponents. The Council of Chalcedon (451) annulled this decision, and he died in exile. His sect was put down by penal laws.

Evans, Sir Arthur John 1851–1941 •*English archaeologist*• He was born in Nash Mills, Hertfordshire. A curator at the Ashmolean Museum, Oxford (1884–1908), he developed an interest in the ancient coins and seals of Crete. Between 1899 and 1935 he excavated the Bronze Age city of Knossos (modern Kephala), discovering the remains of the civilization that in 1904 he named "Minoan" after Minos, the Cretan king of Greek legend. He later rebuilt and repainted substantial parts of the Minoan palace in an effort to recreate its original appearance.

Evans, Bill (William John) 1929–80 •*US jazz pianist and composer*• Born in Plainfield, New Jersey, he took up music seriously after leaving the army in 1954. He studied in New York, then began to play professionally with clarinettist Tony Scott in 1956, and was a member of the **Miles Davis** group which recorded the hugely influential *Kind of Blue* album in 1958. He is among the most influential pianists in jazz, and developed his essentially bop-based style in lyrical, highly sophisticated directions.

Evans, Caradoc, *pseudonym of* **David Evans** 1878–1945 •*Welsh short-story writer and novelist*• Born in Llanfihangel-ar-Arth, Dyfed, he worked as a shop assistant in Carmarthen, Barry, Cardiff and finally London. While in London, he attended evening classes and eventually found employment as a journalist (1906). His collections of short stories, *My People* (1915), *Capel Sion* (1916) and *My Neighbours* (1919), savagely exposed the hypocrisies, lust and greed of the chapel-going people of his native West Wales. His play *Taffy* (1923) was in a similar vein, and in his own time he was vilified by the Welsh as a traitor for his assaults on many cherished aspects of Welsh culture.

Evans, Chris 1966– •*English broadcaster*• Born in Warrington, Cheshire, he left school at age 16 and took numerous casual jobs before becoming a broadcasting assistant at Piccadilly Radio, Manchester. He later presented popular shows such as BBC Radio 1's *Breakfast Show* (1995–97) and Channel 4 television's *The Big Breakfast* (1992–94) and *TFI Friday* (1996–2000). His company, Ginger Productions, took over Virgin Radio in 1997. He married the pop singer Billie Piper (1982–) in 2001.

Evans, Dame Edith Mary 1888–1976 •*English stage and film actress*• Born in London, she became known for her versatility in roles in **Shakespeare**, **Shaw** and others, but her most famous role was as Lady Bracknell in *The Importance of Being Earnest* (also on film, 1952). During World War II she entertained the troops at home and abroad, and in 1946 was given the honorary title of Dame Commander, Order of the British Empire. She played her first major film role in *The Queen of Spades* (1948) and continued to act until her eighties.

" "

People always ask me the most ridiculous questions. They want to know, "How do you approach a role?" Well, I don't know. I approach it by first saying yes, then getting on with the bloody thing.

Attributed.

Evans, Sir Geraint Llewellyn 1922–92 •*Welsh baritone*• He was born in Pontypridd, Mid Glamorgan. He studied singing in Hamburg and Geneva, and made his London debut with the newly formed Covent Garden Opera Company in 1948, singing the Nightwatchman in **Wagner**'s *Meistersinger*. He performed regularly at Covent Garden until 1984, establishing a reputation in many roles, notably Figaro and Leporello in **Mozart**, Don Pasquale in **Donizetti**, and Falstaff in **Verdi**.

Evans, Gil (Ian Ernest Gilmore Green) 1912–88 •*Canadian jazz pianist, composer and arranger*• Born in Toronto of Australian parents, he spent his childhood in Washington State and California, and was self-taught as a musician. His first influential work was done in the mid-1940s when, apart from three years' military service, he was principal arranger for the Claude Thornhill Orchestra. Starting in the late 1940s there followed a series of collaborations between Evans and **Miles Davis**, which led to the emergence of the "cool jazz" style. As an arranger and conductor, Evans continued to collaborate with Davis until 1960, covering a very influential period in the trumpeter's career. Evans went on to lead and write for a range of groups until his death, and was one of the first modern jazz arrangers to use electronics and rock influences successfully in combination with the swing and bebop idioms.

Evans, (Thomas) Godfrey 1920–99 •*English cricket player*• Born in Finchley, London, he was educated at Kent College, Canterbury, and joined the Kent county cricket staff at the age of 16. First capped for England in 1946, he played in 91 Test matches, and made many new records, including 218 Test dismissals (75 against Australia). He was the first wicket keeper to have dismissed more than 200 batsmen and scored 2,000 runs in Test cricket.

Evans, Harold Matthew 1928– •*English journalist*• Born in Manchester, he studied at Durham University and the University of Chicago. He worked on the *Manchester Evening News* and the *Northern Echo* before becoming editor of the *Sunday Times* (1967–81), and was a pioneer of investigative journalism during the thalidomide scandal. He went to New York and from 1990 to 1997 ran Random House, the book publishing division belonging to the same company as Condé-Nast.

Evans, Janet 1971– •*US swimmer*• Born in Fullerton, California, she won three gold medals at the 1988 Olympics (400-meter freestyle, 800-meter freestyle and 400-meter medley) and one at the 1992 Olympics (800-meter freestyle). She set the world records in the 400-meter freestyle, the 800-meter freestyle and the 1,500-meter freestyle, and was a Sullivan award winner in 1989.

Evans, Marian or **Mary Ann** *See* **Eliot, George**

Evans, Oliver 1755–1819 •*US inventor*• Born in Newport, Delaware, he was apprenticed to a wagonmaker. By 1777 he had invented a high-speed machine for assembling the wire-toothed combs used in carding textile fibers. He next devoted himself to improving the very primitive steam engines then coming into use. Most engineers at that time followed the lead of **James Watt** in rejecting the use of high-pressure steam because of the practical difficulties and the danger of explosion, but by 1802 Evans had successfully built a high-pressure steam engine, and his amphibious steam dredging machine of 1804 is considered to have been the first US steam-powered road vehicle.

Evans-Pritchard, Sir Edward Evan 1902–73 •*English social anthropologist*• Born in Crowbridge, Sussex, he studied history at Oxford and succeeded his teacher **Alfred Radcliffe-Brown** in the chair of social anthropology (1946–70). He carried out fieldwork in East Africa in the 1920s and 1930s among the Azande and the Nuer, resulting in a number of classic monographs. Though strongly influenced by the sociological theory of **Émile Durkheim**, he came to reject Radcliffe-Brown's view that social anthropology could be regarded as a natural science of society, choosing instead to emphasize its affinity with history, requiring interpretation and translation rather than scientific explanation.

Evatt, Elizabeth Andreas 1933– •*Australian lawyer*• Born in Sydney, the daughter of a barrister, she was the youngest student at Sydney University Law School and at Harvard, before becoming a barrister in New South Wales at the age of 21. In 1958 she was called to the English bar, and on returning to Australia she became the deputy president of the Arbitration Commission (1973–89). She chaired the Royal Commission of Human Relationships (1974–77) and the Family Law Council (1976–79) and was chief judge in the Family Court of Australia (1976–88). A member of the UN Committee on the Elimination of Discrimination Against Women from 1984 until 1992, she joined the UN Human Rights Committee in 1993.

Eve •*Biblical character*• According to Genesis, Eve was made by God from one of Adam's ribs, as a companion for him. Adam, the first man, named the first woman "Eve," meaning "the mother of all living." They tended the Garden of Eden together, until they were expelled for eating the fruit of the tree of knowledge. Although both knew that God had forbidden this, Adam blamed Eve for tempting him.

Evelyn, John 1620–1706 •*English diarist and writer*• Born in Wotton, near Dorking, Surrey, he was brought up in Lewes (1625–37), then entered Balliol College, Oxford, and in 1640 the Middle Temple. The Covenant being pressed on him, he traveled for four years on the Continent, and then settled in Deptford in 1652. From 1685 to 1687 he was one of the commissioners of the privy seal, and then, from 1695 to 1703, treasurer of Greenwich Hospital and a prominent Fellow of the Royal Society. He was active in church affairs and involved in the rebuilding of St Paul's Cathedral in London. His three dozen literary works include *Fumifuigim, or the Inconvenience of the Air and Smoke of London Dissipated* (1661); *Sculptura, or the Art of Engraving on Copper* (1662); *Sylva, or a Discourse of Forest-trees* (1664); and a *Diary* (discovered in an old clothes basket at his brother's home in Wotton in 1817).

Everest, Sir George 1790–1866 •*Welsh military engineer*• Born in Gwernvale, Brecknockshire, he was Surveyor General of India from 1830. He completed the trigonometrical survey of the Indian subcontinent in 1841. He was knighted in 1861 and Mount Everest was named after him in 1865.

Evert, Chris(tine) Marie 1954– •*US tennis player*• She was born in Fort Lauderdale, Florida. Renowned for her two-handed backhand, she was extremely cool on the courts and her success helped popularize women's tennis in the US and Europe. She won 157 professional titles including 18 singles Grand Slam titles. She was married for a time to the English tennis player, John Lloyd, and was coauthor with him of *Lloyd on Lloyd* (1985). She retired in 1989 after reaching the quarterfinals of the US Open to become a mother and a television commentator.

Evita *See* **Perón, Eva Duarte de**

Ewing, Juliana Horatia, *née* **Gatty** 1841–85 •*English children's writer*• Born in Ecclesfield, Yorkshire, she was the daughter of Margaret Gatty (1809–73), also a children's writer. Her numerous books included *A Flat Iron for a Farthing* (1870), *Lab-Lie-by-the-Fire* (1873) and *Daddy Darwin's Dovecot* (1881). Her *The Brownies and Other Tales* (1870) provided the name by which the junior section of the Girl Guide and Girl Scout organization movement is known.

Ewing, Winnie (Winifred Margaret) 1929– •*Scottish nationalist politician*• Born in Glasgow, she was educated at Queen's Park School, Glasgow, and Glasgow University. She was a lawyer and president of the Glasgow Bar Association, and her victory at the Hamilton by-election (1967) established the Scottish National Party (SNP) as a major political force. Although ousted there in 1970, she won the Moray and Nairn seat in 1974. After losing this position in 1979, she was elected to the European Parliament in the same year, representing the Highlands and Islands, and was reelected in 1984, 1989 and 1994. In 1999 she became a member of the Scottish Parliament representing the Highlands and Islands. She retired in 2003.

Exekias or **Execias** fl. late 6th century BC •*Greek potter and vase painter*• He worked in the "black figure" style. The most famous of his vessels—on which is inscribed "Exekias made and decorated me"—is in the Vatican Museum, Rome.

Eyadéma, (Etienne) Gnassingbé 1937– •*Togolese politician and general*• Born in Pya, Lama Kara district, he joined the French army in 1953 and served in Africa for several years. In 1965 he became army Chief of Staff in Togo. In 1967 he led a bloodless coup to oust President Nicolas Grunitzky, and as President of Togo he banned all political activity until 1969, when he founded the Assembly of the Togolese People (RPT) as the only legal party. Surviving several attempts to overthrow him, he was reelected in 1993 and 1998. In 2000 he became chairman of the Organization of African Unity.

Eyck, Jan van c. 1389–1441 •*Flemish painter*• He was born near Maastricht. He was successively in the service of John of Bavaria, Count of Holland, and **Philip the Good** of Burgundy, for whom he undertook diplomatic missions in Spain and Portugal. From 1431 he lived in Bruges. All the works that can be definitively attributed to him date from the last ten years of his life. During this period there is evidence of his increasing wealth and importance as court painter, diplomat and city official. His style is created from a meticulous attention to detail and accuracy in rendering textures and realistic light effects. There are three works by him in the National Gallery, London, including the *Man in a Red Turban* (1433), which some have thought to be a self-portrait, and the mysterious Arnolfini marriage portrait. By far his most famous work is the altarpiece *The Adoration of the Holy Lamb* (1432) in the church of Saint Bavon, Ghent, which consists of 24 panels. He is regarded as the greatest Flemish artist of the 15th century.

Eyre, Edward John 1815–1901 •*English explorer and colonist*• Born in Hornsea, Yorkshire, the son of a clergyman, he emigrated to Australia at the age of 17 and settled on the Lower Murray as a sheep farmer and magistrate. In 1840–41 he explored the region between South and Western Australia, and discovered Lake Eyre. In 1847 he became governor of New Zealand, in 1854 of St Vincent, and in 1862 of Jamaica. In 1865 he suppressed a native rebellion at Morant Bay using severe measures, and the alleged ringleader (a wealthy Baptist mulatto who was also a member of the Jamaica House of Assembly) was court-martialed and hanged. Eyre was recalled to England and prosecuted amid great public controversy, but was cleared.

Eyre, Sir Richard Charles Hastings 1943– •*English stage director*• He was born in Barnstaple, Devon, and was educated at Cambridge, beginning his career in 1965 at the Phoenix, Leicester. He became associate director of the Lyceum Theatre, Edinburgh (1967), and director of productions (1970–72). He was artistic director of the Nottingham Playhouse (1973–78), and afterward producer of the BBC Television *Play for Today* series (1978–81) as well as other television plays. He has made films, including *The Ploughman's Lunch* (1983). Among his aims have been opening up the National Theatre to young directors and increasing the performance of multicultural works and children's drama. He left in 1997, and was replaced by **Trevor Nunn**. He has been a governor of the BBC since 1995 and was knighted in 1997.

Eysenck, Hans Jürgen 1916–97 •*British psychologist*• Born in Berlin, he left Germany in 1934 and studied psychology at the University of London under Sir **Cyril Burt**. He began his career in the field of clinical psychology, which led to psychometric research into the normal variations of human personality and intelligence. He frequently championed the view that genetic factors play a large part in determining the psychological differences between people, and often held controversial views, particularly with his study of racial differences in intelligence in *Race, Intelligence and Education* (1971). From 1955 to 1983 he was Professor of Psychology at the Institute of Psychiatry, University of London, afterward emeritus. His other publications include *Uses and Abuses of Psychology* (1953) and *Know Your Own IQ* (1962).

Eyskens, Gaston 1905–88 •*Belgian economist and politician*• After studying in Leuven and the US, he became Professor of Economics at Leuven (1934–75). In 1939 he was elected Member of Parliament for the Christian People's Party (Belgium), and in 1965 became a senator in the Upper House. He was four times Prime Minister (1949–50, 1958–61, 1968–72, 1972–73). He led coalitions with both the left and right, and was one of the pivotal figures of postwar Belgian politics.

Ezekiel c. 6th century BC •*Old Testament prophet*• He was the successor of **Isaiah** and **Jeremiah**. According to the Book of Ezekiel, he was carried captive to Mesopotamia by **Nebuchadnezzar** in 597 BC. The prophecies were composed during the Babylonian captivity and looked forward to a new Jerusalem after the destruction of the old.

Ezra, the Scribe 4th century–5th century BC •*Old Testament reformer*• He was living in Babylon either during the reign of **Artaxerxes I** Longimanus (465–425 BC) or during that of **Artaxerxes II** (404–359). He was commissioned to lead a band of his fellow countrymen from Babylon to Jerusalem (458 or 397) to reorganize the returned Jews there. He is believed to have arranged the books of the Mosaic law (the Pentateuch) as they are now. The Book of Ezra records the return of the Jews after the Babylonian captivity in c. 537 BC.

Fabergé, Peter Carl, *properly* **Karl Gustavovich Fabergé** 1846–1920 •*Russian goldsmith and jeweler*• He was born in St Petersburg, of Huguenot descent, and educated in Germany, Italy, France and England. He inherited his father's establishment in 1870, and moved from the design and manufacture of conventional jewelry to the creation of more elaborate objects, such as the celebrated imperial Easter eggs, first commissioned by **Alexander III** for his czarina in 1884. He died in exile in Lausanne after his business had been destroyed during the Russian Revolution.

Fabius, Laurent 1946– •*French socialist statesman*• The son of a wealthy Jewish art dealer in Paris, he had a brilliant academic career there at the École Normale Supérieure and the École Nationale d'Administration. He joined the Council of State as an auditor in 1973 and became economic adviser to the Socialist Party (PS) leader, **François Mitterrand**, in 1976. Elected to the National Assembly in 1978, he was appointed Budget Minister when the PS gained power in 1981, and Minister for Research and Industry in 1983. In 1984 he was appointed Prime Minister at the age of 37. He resigned following his party's electoral defeat in 1986. He was president from 1988 to 1992, and again from 1993 to 2000. Since 2000 he has been Finance Minister.

Fabius, Quintus Fabius Maximus Verrucosus, *also called* **Cunctator ("Delayer")** d. 203 BC •*Roman soldier*• He was five times consul and twice censor. In the Second Punic War (218–202 BC) he was elected dictator (217), and became known by his defensive tactics as Cunctator ("Delayer"). Avoiding direct encounters, he carried on guerrilla warfare and allowed Rome to muster her forces. The derisive nickname took on an honorable connotation after the disastrous Roman defeat at Cannae (216), and the "Fabian" tactics were resumed. He recovered Tarentum in 209 and was made consul for the fifth time. He died just before the successful conclusion of the war.

Fabre, Jean Henri 1823–1915 •*French entomologist*• Born in St Léon, Aveyron, he taught in schools at Carpentras, Ajaccio and Avignon. He is remembered for his detailed and carefully observed accounts of insect behavior and natural history, which resulted in the *Souvenirs entomologiques* (10 vols, 1879–1907). These dealt with the activities of insects such as scarab beetles, ant lions and parasitic wasps. From his observations he deduced that much of the wasp's behavior is inherited and not learned.

Fabriano, Gentile da, *properly* **Niccolò di Giovanni di Massio** c. 1370–1427 •*Italian painter*• Born in Fabriano in the Marches, along with **Lorenzo Ghiberti** he was the major exponent in Italy of the international Gothic style. His greatest surviving work is the *Adoration of the Magi*, now in the Uffizi Gallery, Florence, showing all the facets of his opulent style: complex lighting effects, rich use of color and gilding, and careful attention to detail. The overall impression is intensely decorative. Gentile's style is often considered old-fashioned for the period, but in comparison with that of his contemporary **Masaccio**, his work was thought advanced in his own day.

Faggin, Federico 1941– •*Italian-American computer scientist*• Born in Vicenza, Italy, he studied at the University of Padua. He emigrated to the US in 1968, and in 1970 joined Intel Corporation, where he pioneered the design of the world's first microprocessor, the 4004, with **Ted Hoff** and **Stanley Mazor**. Faggin cofounded Zilog, Inc., in 1974 where he supervised the design of the Z80 microprocessor.

Fahd (ibn Abd al-Aziz al-Saud) 1923– •*King of Saudi Arabia*• Born in Riyadh, a son of **Ibn Saud**, he served as Minister of Education (1953) and Minister of the Interior (1962–75), before becoming First Deputy Prime Minister and effective ruler in 1975 on the assassination of his half-brother **Faisal**. He officially became king in 1982 on the death of his other half-brother **Khalid**. He has been a promoter of the modernization of his country.

Fahrenheit, (Gabriel) Daniel 1686–1736 •*German instrument-maker and physicist*• Born in Danzig (now Gdańsk, Poland), he was sent (1701) to Amsterdam, where he learned the trade of instrument maker. He produced high-quality meteorological instruments, devising an accurate alcohol thermometer (1709) and a commercially successful mercury thermometer (1714). Adopting the practice of taking thermometric fixed points as the temperatures of melting ice and of the human body, Fahrenheit eventually devised a temperature scale with these points calibrated at 32 and 96 degrees, and zero fixed at the freezing point of water and salt. He was the first to show that the boiling point of liquids varies at different atmospheric pressures, and suggested this as a principle for the construction of barometers.

Fairbairn, Sir William 1789–1874 •*Scottish engineer*• Born in Kelso, in the Scottish Borders, he was apprenticed in 1804 to an engine maker at North Shields, where he also studied mathematics and met **George Stephenson**. By 1817, however, he had established an engineering works in Manchester, and within a few years he had gained a reputation as one of the most capable engineers in the country. From 1830 onward he pioneered the building of iron boats, and his works at Millwall, London (1835–49), turned out hundreds of vessels. He developed the rectangular wrought-iron tubes for Stephenson's railway bridge over the Menai Strait (1850), the two main spans of which measured almost 460 feet (140 m) and were not surpassed for the next 25 years. He was made a baronet in 1869.

Fairbanks, Douglas Elton, Sr, *originally* **Julius Ullman** 1883–1939 •*US film actor*• Born in Denver, Colorado, he first appeared in stage plays (from 1901), but in 1915 went into films and specialized in swashbuckling hero parts, as in *Robin Hood* (1922) and *The Thief of Baghdad* (1924), in which he did all his own stunts. He was a founder of United Pictures. In 1920 he married **Mary Pickford** but was divorced in 1935. His son, **Douglas Fairbanks, Jr**, followed in his footsteps.

Fairbanks, Douglas Elton Ulman, Jr 1909–2000 •*US film actor*• He was born in New York City, the son of **Douglas Fairbanks, Sr**. In his youth he made Hollywood movies in his father's style, including *Catherine the Great* (1934), *The Prisoner of Zenda* (1937) and *Sinbad the Sailor* (1947), and also gained a reputation as a producer. He later became interested in international affairs, and made a name for himself as a diplomat. He published two volumes of autobiography, *The Salad Days* (1988) and *A Hell of a War* (1993).

Fairey, Sir (Charles) Richard 1887–1956 •*English aeronautical inventor and industrialist*• He was born in Hendon, London, and studied electrical engineering at Finsbury Technical College. He formed Fairey Aviation Company in 1915, and by 1925 half the aircraft in the RAF were of Fairey origin. Famous types from his factory include the Hendon, Fantome, Swordfish, Barracuda and Firefly. In 1927 he took up yachting, designing advanced hulls and winning many races.

Fairfax (of Cameron), Thomas Fairfax, 3rd Baron 1612–71 •*English general*• Born in Denton, Yorkshire, he was the son of Ferdinando, Lord Fairfax, and from 1629 he served in the Netherlands. In the English Civil War (from 1642) he was general of parliamentary cavalry. After distinguished action at Marston Moor (1644), he was appointed to succeed the 3rd Earl of **Essex** in the supreme command in 1645, and defeated **Charles I** at the decisive Battle of Naseby (1645). In 1650, on Fairfax's refusal to march against the Scots, who had proclaimed **Charles II** king, **Cromwell** was appointed Commander in Chief, and Fairfax withdrew into private life. After Cromwell's death he assisted **George Monk**, 1st Duke of Albermarle, against **John Lambert** and was head of the commission dispatched to The Hague in 1660 to arrange for the return of Charles II.

Fairweather, Ian 1891–1974 •*Australian painter*• Born in Bridge of Allan, Stirlingshire, Scotland, he served in the army in World War I. He attended the Slade School of Art, London, from 1920, where he developed an interest in Oriental art. From 1924 he traveled extensively. His *Bathing Scene, Bali* was acquired by the Tate Gallery, London, in 1934. In 1940 he served in the British army in India until, released from duty due to ill health in 1943, he returned to settle in Australia, where he later lived and worked in a hut he built on Bribie Island off the Queensland coast. He exercised considerable influence over the younger generation of artists in Sydney during the 1960s as his work became more abstract, as in *Monastery* (1961, Rudy Komon Gallery, Sydney).

Faisal, *in full* **Faisal ibn Abd al-Aziz** 1905–75 •*King of Saudi Arabia*• He was born in Riyadh, and was declared crown prince and foreign minister on the accession of his brother **Saud** in 1953. He was given full executive powers during the economic crisis of 1958, which he retained until 1960, and was made viceroy in 1964, succeeding to the throne when Saud abdicated later in the year. His foreign policy was cautious, although he joined the Arab states in the Arab-Israeli War of 1967. He was shot dead in the royal palace by his nephew.

Faisal I 1885–1933 •*King of the Hejaz*• Born in Ta'if, he was the son of **Hussein ibn Ali**. He played a prominent role in the Arab revolt against Turkey (1916–18) and became king of Iraq (1921). He negotiated with Great Britain a treaty (1930) that gave Iraq independence and League of Nations membership (1932).

Faisal II, *in full* **Faisal ibn Ghazi ibn Faisal el Hashim** 1935–58 •*King of Iraq*• Born in Baghdad, the great-grandson of **Hussein ibn Ali** and cousin of King **Hussein** of Jordan, he succeeded his father, King Ghazi, who was killed in an accident in 1939. After an education at Harrow he was installed (1953) as the third king of modern Iraq. Although, in the aftermath of the Suez intervention (1956), he formally declared that Iraq would continue to stand by Egypt, rivalry later grew between the two incipient Arab blocs. In 1958 he united with King Hussein of Jordan in opposition to Egypt and Syria. In July of that year, he was assassinated during a military coup d'état and Iraq became a republic.

Faithfull, Emily 1835–95 •*English publisher and feminist*• Born at Headley Rectory, Surrey, she founded in London a printing house with women compositors in 1860, and was appointed printer and publisher-in-ordinary to Queen **Victoria**. In 1863 she started *Victoria Magazine*, advocating the claims of women to remunerative employment. In 1865 she founded a penny weekly, *Women and Work*, and she published *Change Upon Change*, a novel, in 1868.

Faithfull, Marianne 1946– •*English singer, songwriter and film actress*• Born in Hampstead, London, she was "discovered" by the manager of the **Rolling Stones** and at the age of 18 had a hit with "As Tears Go By," followed by "Summer Nights" (1965) and others. As **Mick Jagger**'s girlfriend, she received headline attention when the Stones were arrested on drug charges. Her acting career began with *I'll Never Forget Whatshisname* (1967). Faithfull's singing career seemed to be over in the 1970s, but the extraordinary *Broken English* (1979) revived her fortunes. Subsequent records include *Dangerous Acquaintances* (1981) and *Strange Weather* (1987).

Falco, Louis 1942–93 •*US dancer and choreographer*• Born in New York City, he studied with **José Limón**, **Martha Graham**, and Charles Weidman (1901–75), joining the Limón company in 1960. In 1967 he formed his own company and began to choreograph. His works, popular with audiences, have since been included in the repertoires of many of the world's major contemporary dance companies.

Falconet, Étienne Maurice 1716–91 •*French sculptor*• He was born in Paris and was director of sculpture at the Sèvres Porcelain Factory from 1757 to 1766. **Catherine II** (the Great) invited him to Russia in 1766 to execute what is his most impressive work, a bronze equestrian monument to **Peter I** (the Great) in St Petersburg (1767–78). After suffering a stroke in 1783, he turned to writing art theory.

Faldo, Nick (Nicholas Alexander) 1957– •*English golfer*• He was born in Welwyn Garden City, Hertfordshire. Within seven years of turning professional he was the top European player. His early successes included winning the Professional Golfers' Association (PGA) championships in 1978, 1980 and 1981. He went on to win six more major victories: the Open championship (1987, 1990, 1996) and the Masters (1989, 1990, 1996). His greatest victory was perhaps the 1996 Masters when he overcame a six-stroke deficit to win the competition by five shots.

Falkenhayn, Erich von 1861–1922 •*German soldier*• Following a varied military career, he succeeded **Helmuth von Moltke** as chief of the German General Staff in 1914. He decided against a German retreat in the West, despite the French success at the first Battle of the Marne (1914) and in 1916 he launched the offensive at the Battle of Verdun. His failure led to his replacement by **Paul von Hindenburg** and **Erich Ludendorff** in 1917. He continued to serve successfully as a field commander in Romania, Palestine and Lithuania.

Falla, Manuel de 1876–1946 •*Spanish composer*• Born in Cádiz, after two years of studying under the composer Felipe Pedrell (1841–1922), he won prizes both for his piano playing and for his opera *La vida breve* ("Short Life") in 1905. After seven years in Paris he returned to Spain in 1914. His works include the ballet *El sombrero de tres picos* (1919, "The Three-Cornered Hat"), the opera *El retablo de Maese Pedro* (1919–22, "Master Peter's Puppet Show"), and the piano and orchestra suite *Noches en los jardines de España* (1909–16, "Nights in the Gardens of Spain"). With the outbreak of the Spanish Civil War, he settled in Argentina.

Fallopius, Gabriele, *Italian* **Gabriello Fallopio** or **Falloppia** 1523–62 •*Italian anatomist*• He was born in Modena, and became Professor of Anatomy at Pisa (1548) and Padua (1551). He particularly studied bones and the reproductive organs, and the Fallopian tube connecting the ovaries with the uterus is named after him.

Faludi, Susan 1960– •*US journalist and writer*• Born at Yorktown Heights, New York, and educated at Harvard University, she has worked for the *New York Times* and the *Wall Street Journal*. In 1991 she was awarded the Pulitzer Prize for her investigative journalism as well as the 1991 National Book Critics award for nonfiction for *Backlash* (1991), which argues that despite appearances, women are still controlled and repressed in contemporary society. In 2000 she published *Stiffed: The Betrayal of Modern Man*.

" "

The more women are paid, the less eager they are to marry.

*1992 **Backlash** (UK edition), chapter 2, "Man Shortages and Barren Wombs."*

Falwell, Jerry 1933– •*US evangelist*• Born in Lynchburg, Virginia, he studied engineering there, but after a religious conversion graduated from Baptist Bible College, Springfield, Missouri. In 1956 he founded and became pastor of Thomas Road Baptist Church, Lynchburg. There he inaugurated the television show "Old-Time Gospel Hour," and founded Liberty Baptist College. In 1979 he established Moral Majority, Inc., which formed a rallying point for conservative opinion in the 1980 and 1984 presidential election campaigns. He wrote *Listen, America!* (1980) and the autobiographical *Strength for the Journey* (1987).

Faneuil, Peter 1700–43 •*US merchant and philanthropist*• Born in New Rochelle, New York, he made a fortune in Boston and built Faneuil Hall there (1742), later to become known as "the cradle of American liberty," and presented it to the town.

Fangio, Juan Manuel 1911–95 •*Argentine racecar driver*• Born in Balcarce, of Italian descent, he first took part in European Grand Prix racing in 1949, and in 1951 won the first of his five world championships; he was world champion again for four consecutive years from 1954 to 1957. His record of 24 Grand Prix wins was only bettered 10 years later by **Jim Clark**. Fangio retired in 1958.

Fanshawe, Richard 1608–66 •*English poet, translator and diplomat*• Born at Ware Park, Hertfordshire, he attended Jesus College, Cambridge, and went abroad to study languages. In the English Civil War he fought for the Royalists, but in 1651 he was taken prisoner at Worcester. After the Restoration he was appointed ambassador at the courts of Portugal and Spain. He translated **Horace**, Giovanni Guarini's *Il Pastor Fido*, and the *Lusiads* (1655) by **Camoëns**. His wife Ann's *Memoirs* were published in 1829.

Fanthorpe, U(rsula) A(skham) 1929– •*English poet*• She was educated at Oxford and the University of London Institute of Education, where she obtained a teacher's diploma. Since the mid-1970s she has worked as an admissions clerk in a Bristol hospital. Her collections include *Side Effects* (1978), *Four Dogs* (1980), *Standing To* (1982) and *Voices Off* (1984). A major selection appeared in 1986.

Fantin-Latour, (Ignace) Henri Joseph Théodore 1836–1904 •*French painter and printmaker*• Born in Grenoble, he studied at the École des Beaux Arts under **Gustave Courbet** and was a regular exhibitor at the French Salon from 1861 to 1899. He became friendly with some of the most advanced painters of his day, and made several visits to London where he exhibited at the Royal Academy. His subject matter was varied: in France he was particularly admired for his portrait groups, in England for his still lifes, especially of flowers.

Fanu, Sheridan Le *See* **Le Fanu, (Joseph) Sheridan**

Farabi, Abu Nasr al-, *Latin* **Alfarabius** 878–c. 950 •*Islamic philosopher*• Born in Farab, he studied in Baghdad and published commentaries on **Aristotle** and **Porphyry**. He was much influenced by **Plato**'s *Republic* and can be regarded as the first Islamic Neo-Platonist. He also published a utopian political philosophy of his own, known under the title *The Perfect City*.

Faraday, Michael 1791–1867 •*English chemist and physicist, creator of classical field theory*• Born in Newington Butts near London, he was apprenticed to a bookbinder whose books sparked his interest in science. In 1813, after applying to **Humphry Davy** for a job, he was taken on as his temporary assistant, accompanying him on a European tour. In 1827 he succeeded to Davy's chair of chemistry at the Royal Institution, in that year publishing his *Chemical Manipulation*. His early publications on physical science include papers on the condensation of gases, limits of vaporization and optical deceptions. He was the first to isolate benzene, and he synthesized the first chlorocarbons. His great life's work, however, was the series *Experimental Researches on Electricity* published over 40 years in *Philosophical Transactions*, in which he described his many discoveries, including electromagnetic induction (1831), the laws of electrolysis (1833) and the rotation of polarized light by magnetism (1845). He received a pension in 1835 and in 1858 was given a house in Hampton Court. As adviser to the Trinity House in 1862 he advocated the use of electric lights in lighthouses. Greatly influential on later physics, he nevertheless had no pupils and worked with only one assistant. He is generally considered the greatest of all experimental physicists.

Farhi, Nicole 1946– •*British fashion designer*• Born in Nice, France, she worked there as a freelance designer before moving to London. Launching her own company in 1983, she has become known for her comfortable, uncomplicated clothes which feature soft structure, subtle coloring and fine quality fabrics. She won the British Classis award in 1989 and the British Fashion Award for British Contemporary Designer in 1995, 1996 and 1997.

Farjeon, Eleanor 1881–1965 •*English writer*• Born in Hampstead, London, she wrote fantasies and children's stories, beginning with her successful first novel, *Martin Pippin in the Apple Orchard* (1921). She collaborated with her brother Herbert in *Kings and Queens* (1932) and the play *The Glass Slipper* (1944). Her childhood is described in her autobiographical *A Nursery in the Nineties* (1935). There is an annual Eleanor Farjeon award for outstanding service to children's literature.

Farman, Henri 1874–1958 •*French pioneer aviator and aircraft manufacturer*• With his brother Maurice (1878–1964) he made the first flight in a Voisin biplane (1908) which they had built. In 1912 they established a factory at Boulogne-sur-Seine to manufacture the Farman biplane, and built the first long-distance passenger plane, the *Goliath*, in 1917.

Farmer, Fannie Merritt 1857–1915 •*US cooking expert*• Born in Boston, she suffered a stroke at the age of 16 and was unable to attend college, so she turned to cooking at home and then attended the Boston Cooking School. She later became a director there (1891–1902), during which time she edited the *Boston Cooking School Cook Book* (1896). In 1902 she opened Miss Farmer's School of Cookery in Boston. Her insistence on precise measurements in her recipes was innovatory.

Farnese, Alessandro 1546–92 •*Spanish soldier*• Born in Rome, he was the son of the 2nd Duke of Parma and the illegitimate daughter of the emperor **Charles V**, and nephew of **Philip II** of Spain. He distinguished himself under his uncle, **John of Austria**, at the naval battle of Lepanto (1571), and became one of the great land-force commanders of his era as well as a gifted diplomat. He joined his uncle in the Spanish Netherlands in 1577, then in 1578 defeated the rebellious Dutch at Gembloux and captured Maastricht. As governor-general himself he captured Antwerp in 1585. In 1590 he compelled **Henry IV** of France to raise the Siege of Paris.

Farouk I 1920–65 •*King of Egypt*• Born in Cairo, he was educated privately in England. On ascending the throne, he dismissed the premier, Nahas Pasha, and for a while devoted himself to programs of economic development and land reform. In 1942, with Axis troops threatening Egypt, Great Britain insisted on the reappointment of Nahas Pasha. After the war, his lifestyle became increasingly flamboyant, and he alienated the armed forces, especially after defeat by Israel (1948). General **Neguib**'s coup d'état (1952) forced Farouk to abdicate. He was exiled to Italy and in 1959 he became a citizen of Monaco.

Farquhar, George c. 1677–1707 •*Irish playwright*• He was born in Londonderry, possibly in 1677 (but he is said to have fought at the Battle of the Boyne in 1690). Educated at Trinity College, Dublin, he became an actor in a Dublin theater, but the accidental wounding of a fellow actor so shocked him that he quit the theater, and shortly after received a commission in a regiment stationed in Ireland. His first comedies, *Love and a Bottle* (1698) and *The Constant Couple* (1699), proved a success, and were followed by *The Inconstant* (1703), founded on **John Fletcher**'s *Wild Goose Chase*, and *The Recruiting Officer* (1706). He wrote the best of his plays, *The Beaux Stratagem*, during an illness in 1707, but died before he could enjoy its success.

" "

I hate all that don't love me, and slight all that do.

1699 ***The Constant Couple****, act 1, scene 2.*

Farragut, David Glasgow 1801–70 •*US naval commander*• Of Spanish origin, he was born near Knoxville, Tennessee. He joined the navy in 1810 and served against the British (1812), and against pirates (1820). In the Civil War he served with the Union forces and commanded the ships fitted out for the capture of New Orleans (1862). He took part in the siege and capture of Vicksburg (1863) and helped establish Union control of the Mississippi River. His most famous victory occurred at Mobile Bay (1864), into which he sailed his fleet despite floating mines, crying "Damn the torpedoes!".

Farrakhan, Louis, *originally* **Louis Eugene Wolcott**, *formerly known as* **Louis X** 1933– •*US leader of the Nation of Islam*• He was born in New York City and his tough upbringing led him to join **Elijah Muhammed**'s Black Muslim movement. The sect was plagued by factionalism, and in 1978 Farrakhan was excommunicated by the World Community of Islam and revived the Nation of Islam, which promotes self-reliance, healthy eating and abstinence from drugs. He has been widely criticized for his anti-Jewish rhetoric, but the growing influence among African-Americans of his message of self-respect was demonstrated in the 1995 Million Man March in Washington DC.

Farrar, Geraldine 1882–1967 •*US soprano*• Born in Melrose, Maine, she studied in Boston, Paris and Berlin, making her professional debut in **Charles Gounod**'s *Faust* in Germany. Her first role in the US came five years later, again in Gounod's work, as Juliet. She retired from the opera stage in 1922, but continued giving recitals until the early 1930s. Many of her finest roles, including Cio-Cio San and Carmen, were recorded.

Farrell, J(ames) G(ordon) 1935–79 •*British author*• Born in Liverpool, he worked as a teacher in Dublin and as a laborer and clerk in the Canadian Arctic before studying at Brasenose College, Oxford. He published six novels, among them *Troubles* (1970), set in 1920s Ireland; *The Siege of Krishnapur* (1973), the story of the Sepoy uprising of 1857, which won the Booker Prize; and *The Singapore Grip* (1978), an account of the surrender of British forces to the Japanese in World War II. He drowned in an accident in Ireland at age 44.

Farrell, James T(homas) 1904–79 •*US novelist, short-story writer, critic and essayist*• Born in Chicago, he paid for his own education at the University of Chicago (1925–29) and lived in Paris in the early 1930s. His first novel was *Young Lonigan* (1932), which began the *Studs Lonigan* trilogy about life on Chicago's South side, realistically and graphically portrayed. The other volumes were *The Young Manhood of Studs Lonigan* (1934) and *Judgment Day* (1935). This was followed by a five-novel sequence centered on Danny O'Neill (1936–53), and another trilogy, on Bernard Clare (1946–52). He published more than 50 novels in all.

Farrell, Suzanne 1945– •*US ballerina*• Born in Cincinnati, Ohio, she graduated from the School of American Ballet at the age of 16. From there, she went to the New York City Ballet (NYCB), where she became an inspiration to the choreographer and artistic director **George Balanchine**. She and her then husband, dancer Paul Majia, left the company to join **Maurice Béjart**'s Ballet of the 20th Century (1971–75). Upon her return to the NYCB in 1975, she formed a fruitful onstage partnership with dancer Peter Martins (1946–). Tall, strong and supple, with great musical sensitivity, she was the ideal Balanchine dancer. She retired as a dancer in 1989.

Farren-Price, Ronald William 1930– •*Australian pianist*• Born in Brisbane, Queensland, he was educated at the University of Melbourne, then studied in Germany and in London. From 1967 he toured extensively in the US, England and Europe, and was the first Australian pianist to tour the USSR. A regular broadcaster and recitalist, he performed as a soloist with many major orchestras, and has recorded widely. In 1955 he joined the Melbourne Conservatorium of Music (now the department of music at Melbourne University).

Farrow, Mia (Maria de Lourdes Villiers) 1945– •*US actress*• She was born in Los Angeles, the daughter of the film director John Farrow and the actress Maureen O'Sullivan. She made her Broadway debut in 1963 and first came to notice in *Peyton Place* on television in the 1960s. Her films include *Rosemary's Baby* (1968), *The Great Gatsby* (1974), and a number of **Woody Allen** films, notably *Hannah and Her Sisters* (1986). Her high-profile marriages to **Frank Sinatra** (1966–68) and **André Previn** (1970–79), and her subsequent relationship with Woody Allen, which ended in court in 1992, have attracted significant media attention.

Fasch, Johann Friedrich 1688–1758 •*German composer*• Born in Buttelstedt near Weimar, he was educated at the Thomasschule, Leipzig, and founded the *Collegium Musicum* there, the forerunner of the *Gewandhaus* concerts. In 1722 he was appointed Kapellmeister at Zerbst. He wrote overtures in the style of **Georg Telemann**, orchestral suites admired by **J S Bach**, three operas (since lost), and also several masses, a requiem, trios and sonatas.

Fassbinder, Rainer Werner 1946–82 •*German film director*• Born in Bad Wörishofen, he began his career as an actor in fringe theater in Munich, founding his own "anti-theater" company. Moving into film (1969), he was much influenced by **Jean-Luc Godard**, believing that films should have a social purpose. His first film to gain international recognition was *Warum läuft Herr R. amok?* (1970, *Why Does Herr R. Run Amok?*). He made over 40 films, usually politically committed criticisms of contemporary Germany, contrasting personal failure and frustration with the country's superficial economic success, and illustrating the misuse of power. Notable among these were *Die bitteren Tränen der Petra von Kant* (1972, *The Bitter Tears of Petra von Kant*), *Effi Briest* (1974, based on a classic novel of the 1890s by **Theodor Fontane**), and *Die Ehe der Maria Braun* (1979, *The Marriage of Maria Braun*), an allegory of postwar Germany, which won first prize at the 1979 Berlin Film Festival.

Fassett, Kaffe 1937– •*US designer*• Born in San Francisco, he was brought up in Big Sur, California, and the community there remains the biggest influence on his work, although his career has been made in the UK. Originally a painter, he learned to knit after moving to the UK in 1964. His colorful, highly individual designs and the sources of many of his ideas are seen in such books as *Glorious Knitting* (1985), *Glorious Needlepoint* (1987) and *Glorious Interiors* (1995).

Fast, Howard Melvin, *pseudonym* **E V Cunningham** 1914–2003 •*US novelist, playwright and political commentator*• Born in New York City, he came of age during the radical 1930s and wrote on this time in a sequence of historical novels. His allegiance to Popular Front Communism eventually led to his being imprisoned for "contempt of Congress" in 1947 and to his blacklisting by Hollywood, but he later recanted in a much-quoted account of writers' dealings with the Communist Party, called *The Naked God* (1957). A prolific writer, he wrote *Spartacus* (1951), which owed its success to the absence of ideological speeches and to a powerful Hollywood adaptation.

Fateh Singh, Sant 1911–72 •*Sikh religious leader*• Born in the Punjab, India, he was a campaigner for Sikh rights and founded many schools and colleges in Rajasthan. In 1942 he joined the Quit India Movement, and was imprisoned for his political activities. During the 1950s he agitated for a Punjabi-speaking state, which was achieved once Haryana was created as a separate state in 1966.

Fatima c. 605–33 •*Arab religious figure*• Born in Mecca, Arabia, she was the youngest daughter of **Muhammad**, and wife of the fourth Muslim Caliph, **'Ali**. Their descendants were the Fatimids, a radical Shiite group that ruled over Egypt and North Africa (909–1171), and later over Syria and Palestine.

Faulkner, William 1897–1962 •*US novelist and Nobel Prize winner*• Born near Oxford, Mississippi, he became a pilot in the Canadian Flying Corps in World War I, and later attended Mississippi University. While working in New Orleans, he met **Sherwood Anderson**, who offered to recommend his first novel, *Soldier's Pay* (1926), to a publisher on condition that he did not have to read it. In 1929 Faulkner took a job shoveling coal, and while on night duty at a local power station apparently wrote *As I Lay Dying* (1930) in just six weeks, working between midnight and 4 AM. *Sanctuary* (1931) was intended as a potboiler and was more successful commercially, but it had a profound impact on **Jean-Paul Sartre** and **Albert Camus**. However, it is the lyrical style of novels like *The Sound and the Fury* (1929), *Light in August* (1932), *Absalom, Absalom!* (1936) and *Intruder in the Dust* (1948) that account for his reputation as one of the modern masters of the novel. Other titles include *Sartoris* (1929), *The Town* (1957) and *The Mansion* (1959). He received the 1949 Nobel Prize for literature.

“ ”

Yes, he thought, between grief and nothing I will take grief.

*1939 Wilborne. **The Wild Palms**, "Wild Palms," no. 5.*

Faulks, Sebastian Charles 1953– •*English author and journalist*• Born in Newbury, Berkshire, he studied at Emmanuel College, Cambridge. He has worked extensively as a journalist and columnist, and became deputy editor and later associate editor of the *Independent on Sunday* (1989–91). His novels include *A Fool's Alphabet* (1992), *Birdsong* (1993) and *On Green Dolphin Street* (2001).

Faure, Edgar Jean 1908–88 •*French politician*• Born in Béziers, he trained as a lawyer in Paris, entered politics as a Radical Socialist, and was Minister of Finance and Economic Affairs (1950, 1951, 1954, 1958). He served as Prime Minister (1952, 1955–56), was president of the National Assembly (1973–78) and a member of the European Parliament from 1979. He also published several detective novels under the pseudonym Edgar Sanday.

Fauré, Gabriel Urbain 1845–1924 •*French composer*• Born in Pamiers, he became organist (1896) at La Madeleine, Paris, and director of the Conservatoire (1905–20). Though he is chiefly remembered for his songs, including "Après un rêve" (c. 1865, "After a Dream"), he also wrote operas and orchestral pieces, such as *Masques et bergamasques* (1919, "Masks and Bergamasks"), and a requiem (1887–90).

Faust, Frederick Schiller *See* **Brand, Max**

Favart, Charles Simon 1710–92 •*French dramatist*• He was born in Paris, and had his first success with the comic opera *Deux jumelles* (1734, "The Twin Girls"). He went on to direct the Opéra-Comique, and in 1745 married the actress Marie Justine Benoîte Duronceray (1727–72). At the end of 1745 the Favarts went to Flanders with a company of actors attached to Marshal de Saxe. The marshal attempted to make Madame Favart his mistress, and when she fled from him took out a *lettre de cachet* against her husband. Favart had to remain in hiding until the marshal's death in 1750. Among his best comic operas are *Les amours de Bastien et Bastienne* (cowritten with his wife, 1753, "The Loves of Bastien and Bastienne") and *Les trois sultanes* (1776, "The Three Sultans' Wives").

Fawcett, Dame Millicent, *née* **Garrett** 1847–1929 •*English suffragette and educational reformer*• Born in Aldeburgh, Suffolk, the younger sister of **Elizabeth Garrett Anderson**, she opposed the militancy of the Pankhursts, but campaigned for woman suffrage and higher education for women. She was a founder of Newnham College, Cambridge (1871), and was president of the National Union of Women's Suffrage Societies (1897–1919). Among her books is *The Women's Victory—and After* (1920).

Fawkes, Guy 1570–1606 •*English conspirator*• Born in York of Protestant parentage, he developed his fervent Catholicism while still a schoolboy, appalled by the persecution of his Catholic friends. In 1592, he fought with the Spanish in the Netherlands, and in 1603 rode to Spain in a fruitless attempt to persuade the king to raise an army against his Protestant homeland. The following year, Fawkes secretly returned to London to join the small group of conspirators, led by **Robert Catesby**, who devised a plan to blow up the House of Lords during the State Opening. The plot was supposedly discovered with only hours to spare, and Fawkes and seven other conspirators were beheaded. There is strong evidence, however, to suggest that they were merely pawns in an elaborate hoax, engineered by the state to discredit Rome.

“ ”

A desperate disease requires a dangerous remedy.

1605 When questioned after his arrest on November 5.

Fawkner, John Pascoe 1792–1869 •*Australian pioneer*• Born in Cripplegate, London, he moved with his family to the colony of Port Phillip in 1803, after his father was sentenced to transportation. He chartered a ship (1835) to explore Western Port and Port Phillip Bay on the mainland of Australia, and made camp at the mouth of the Yarra River, the future site of the city of Melbourne. He later became a member of the first legislative council for Victoria.

Fayed, Mohamed al- 1933– •*Egyptian businessman*• Born in Alexandria, he made a fortune there through his diverse shipping, property, oil and construction interests before settling in the UK in the 1970s. In 1979 he became owner of the Ritz Hotel, Paris, and in 1985 he became chairman of Harrods Limited in London. His desire to win British nationality has been unfulfilled and his name has frequently been associated with widely publicized court battles and political controversies. In 1997 he was once again in the public spotlight when his son Dodi al-Fayed was killed alongside **Diana, Princess of Wales**, in a car crash in Paris.

Fayette, Comtesse de la *See* **La Fayette, Marie Madeleine Pioche de Lavergne, Comtesse de**

Feather, Vic(tor Grayson Hardie Feather), Baron 1908–76 •*British trade union leader*• Educated at Hanson Grammar School, Bradford, he began work at the age of 14, and joined the Shopworkers' Union. Shop steward at 15 and chairman of his branch committee at 21, he was a stirring speaker and in 1937 joined the staff of the Trades Union Congress (TUC). He traveled widely as assistant secretary (1947–60), reorganizing trade unions in Europe, India and Pakistan. In 1969 he succeeded **George Woodcock** as General Secretary. Feather retired in 1973, becoming president of the European Trade Union until 1974, at which time he became a life peer.

Feininger, Lyonel Charles Adrian 1871–1956 •*US artist and cartoonist*• Born in New York City of German immigrant parents, he studied in New York, Berlin and Hamburg, and then worked as a newspaper cartoonist. From 1907 he devoted himself to painting, working in a style reminiscent of Cubism. After World War I he taught at the Bauhaus in Weimar (1919–24) and Dessau (1925–33). When the Nazis came to power he returned to the US where, with **Walter Gropius** and **Ludwig Mies van der Rohe**, he founded the Chicago Bauhaus.

Feinstein, Dianne, *née* **Goldman** 1933– •*US politician*• Born in San Francisco, California, and educated at Stanford University, she became mayor of San Francisco in 1978 following the assassination of George Mascone. She was elected mayor in 1979 and reelected in 1983, remaining in the office until 1988. She was elected to the Senate for two years in 1992, and was reelected in 1994 and 2000.

Feld, Eliot 1942– •*US dancer and choreographer*• Born in Brooklyn, New York, he trained in both the classical and modern idioms at the School of American Ballet. He appeared in the 1957 Broadway and 1961 Hollywood versions of *West Side Story* before joining the American Ballet Theater (ABT) in 1963, where he quickly rose to the status of soloist. He made his choreographic debut in 1967 with *Harbinger* and *At Midnight*. He formed Eliot Feld Ballet in 1974. His other works include *Papillon* (1979), *The Jig Is Up* (1984) and *Paper Tiger* (1996).

Felix *See* **Sulla, Lucius Cornelius**

Felix II d. 365 AD •*The first antipope*• He was consecrated when Liberius was banished (AD 355) for refusing to condemn **Athanasius**. When Liberius was restored in 357, Felix retired, but he was ultimately regarded as a saint and martyr.

Felix V *See* **Amadeus VIII**

Fell, Dame Honor Bridget 1900–86 •*British cell biologist*• Educated at the University of Edinburgh, her research included a long tenure as director of Strangeways Research Laboratory in Cambridge (1929–70). She greatly advanced biochemical study through her investigations using the organ culture method, which demonstrated that excess vitamin A could destroy intercellular material, and which led to the use of such organ cultures in studies of the physiological effects of vitamins and hormones. In later life she investigated the pathogenesis of arthritis. Elected a Fellow of the Royal Society in 1952, she was given the honorary title of Dame Commander, Order of the British Empire, in 1963.

Fell, John 1625–86 •*Anglican divine*• He was born in Longworth, Berkshire. With three others he contrived to maintain the Church of England services during the Commonwealth, and after the Restoration he was made dean of Christ Church, Oxford, royal chaplain and doctor of divinity. In 1676 he became Bishop of Oxford.

Feller, William 1906–70 •*US mathematician*• Born in Zagreb, Croatia, he studied at the Universities of Zurich and Göttingen, and left Germany in 1933 for Stockholm. In 1939 he emigrated to the US, holding chairs at various universities. His work in probability theory introduced new rigor without losing sight of practical applicability, and his textbook *Introduction to Probability Theory and Its Applications* (1950) is an influential classic.

Fellini, Federico 1920–93 •*Italian film director*• Born in Rimini, and educated at Bologna University, he started as a cartoonist, journalist and scriptwriter, before becoming an assistant film director (1942). His highly individual films, always from his own scripts, include *I Vitelloni* (1953, *The Young and the Passionate*), *La Strada* (1954, "The Road"), which won an Academy Award for Best Foreign Film (1957), *Le notte di Cabiria* (1957, *The Nights of Cabiria*) which also won an Academy Award (1958), *Satyricon* (1969), *Amarcord* (1974, "I Remember"), *Casanova* (1976), *Città delle donne*

(1980, "City of Women") and *Ginger and Fred* (1986). His most famous and controversial work, *La Dolce Vita* (1960, "The Sweet Life," Cannes Festival prize winner), was a cynical evocation of modern Roman high life. *Otto e mezzo* (1963, *8½*) is his most obviously autobiographical work. In 1943 he married the actress Giulietta Masina (1920–94), star of several of his films.

Fenley, Molissa 1954– •*US dancer and choreographer*• Born in Las Vegas, she studied dance at Mills College, California, before moving to New York. Although she created ensemble pieces for her own now-defunct group and other companies, her reputation rests on physically demanding, high-energy solos like *Eureka* (1982), *State of Darkness* (1988) and *Regions* (1995).

Fenton, James 1949– •*English poet*• Born in Lincoln, he is mainly a political and satirical rather than a "personal" poet, and makes a virtue out of reticence. His main collections are *Terminal Moraine* (1972), *The Memory of War* (1982), *Children in Exile: Poems 1968–84* (1984) and *Out of Danger* (1993). He was Professor of Poetry at Oxford from 1994 to 1999.

"

Oh let us not be condemned for what we are.
It is enough to account for what we do.

1983 "Children in Exile."

Fenton, Roger 1819–69 •*English photographer*• Born in Lancashire, he studied painting in Paris and exhibited at the Royal Academy, London (1849–51). He photographed in Russia in 1852 and was a founder and the first honorary secretary of the Photographic (later Royal) Society in 1853. Queen **Victoria** became its patron, and Fenton photographed the royal family at Balmoral and Windsor. In 1855 he went to the Crimea as the world's first accredited war photographer.

Ferber, Edna 1885–1968 •*US writer*• Born in Kalamazoo, Michigan, she became a journalist in Wisconsin at the age of 17. She was the author of numerous novels and short stories, including *Gigolo* (1922), *So Big* (1924, Pulitzer Prize) and *Saratoga Trunk* (1941). Her work gives a lively, though sometimes sentimental, account of 1920s and 1930s US life, and she is probably best remembered as the writer of *Show Boat* (1926), which inspired the musical of that name. She also wrote plays with **George Kaufman**, such as *Dinner at Eight* (1932).

Ferdinand I 1861–1948 •*Prince and first king of modern Bulgaria*• Born in Vienna, Austria, the youngest son of Prince Augustus I of Saxe-Coburg and Princess Clementine of Orléans, he served in the Austrian army. On the abdication of Prince Alexander of Battenberg, he accepted the crown, as prince (1887). Dominated at first by the premier, Stephan Stambolov, he later took increasing control of the government. After proclaiming Bulgaria independent of the Ottoman Empire (1908), he took the title of king. Territorially ambitious, he joined the Balkan League against Turkey (1912), and, allying himself with the Central Powers, invaded Serbia (1915). His armies routed, he abdicated in 1918, to be succeeded by his son, Boris III (1894–1943). He retired to live in Coburg.

Ferdinand I 1503–64 •*Holy Roman Emperor*• Born in Alcalá de Henares, Spain, he was the second son of **Philip I (the Handsome)** (briefly king of Castile), and younger brother (and successor) of Emperor **Charles V**. In 1521 Charles recognized Ferdinand as ruler of the family's hereditary possessions in Austria and in the same year Ferdinand married Anna, daughter of Ladislas II of Bohemia. He was elected king of Bohemia (1526), but failed to secure Hungary, where John Zapolya (1487–1540) was made king (1527). There ensued a 12-year struggle over Hungary, before the union between Austria, Bohemia and Hungary was secured. Ferdinand was principally responsible for the settlement at Augsburg (1555) that brought the religious wars to an end. He succeeded as Holy Roman Emperor in 1558.

Ferdinand II 1578–1637 •*King of Bohemia and of Hungary, and Holy Roman Emperor*• The grandson of **Ferdinand I**, he was born in Graz, Austria, and educated at the Jesuit University of Ingolstadt (1590–95). Privately genial and kind-hearted, he was ruthless in enforcing absolutism and religious orthodoxy as king of Bohemia (1617–27) and of Hungary (1618–26), and Holy Roman Emperor from 1619. He instigated the Thirty Years' War (1618–48) by compelling the Protestant subjects in his Austrian lands to choose between conversion and exile. Threatened by the election of the Protestant Elector Palatine, **Frederick V**, as king of Bohemia, and of the Protestant Prince of Transylvania, **Bethlen Gábor**, as king of Hungary, he assembled a formidable pan-Catholic force. Troops from Spain and Bavaria overran the Palatinate, while the forces of the Catholic League routed the Bohemian Protestants at the White Mountain, near Prague (1620), and Polish forces under **Sigismund III** forced Gábor to renounce his throne. The peace of Lübeck (1629) cemented the Catholic victory. The Protestants regrouped under **Gustav II Adolf** of Sweden, but although the Battle of Lützen (1632) was a Protestant victory, Gustav Adolf was killed and the Swedish army was defeated at Nördlingen (1634). The Edict of Restitution (1629) ordered the restoration within the empire of all Church lands, secularized by the Protestants since 1552, but Ferdinand failed to extirpate Protestantism. The compromise Peace of Prague (1635) was primarily effected by his son, the future **Ferdinand III**.

Ferdinand III 1608–57 •*King of Hungary and of Bohemia, and Holy Roman Emperor*• The son of Emperor **Ferdinand II**, he was born in Graz, Austria. Although scholarly, shy and artistic, he governed with vigor and skill as ruler of Hungary from 1626, of Bohemia from 1627, and Holy Roman Emperor from 1637. He conspired in the overthrow of **Albrecht von Wallenstein** and succeeded him as commander of the imperial armies. As emperor he continued the struggle against the Protestants but signed the Peace of Westphalia (1648) which ended the Thirty Years' War.

Ferdinand the Catholic, *also known as* **Ferdinand V of Castile** (from 1474), **Ferdinand II of Aragon and Sicily** (from 1479), and **Ferdinand III of Naples** (from 1503) 1452–1516 •*The first monarch of all Spain*• Born at Sos, Aragon, he was the son of John II of Navarre and Aragon, and married (1469) **Isabella of Castile**, sister of Henry IV of Castile, ruling Castile jointly with her after Henry's death (1474). When his own father died (1479), the crowns of Aragon and Castile were united to form the basis of modern Spain. During their reign Ferdinand and Isabella suppressed local bandits by forming a *santa hermandad* ("holy brotherhood") of militia police, and also introduced the Inquisition (1478). They completed the reconquest of Granada (1482–92) and expelled the Jews from Spain (1492). He and Isabella sponsored the voyage of **Columbus** to the New World (1492). In 1495 he formed a Holy League to help the pope drive the French from Naples, for which he gained the title "the Catholic," and Naples became a Spanish possession (1503). When Isabella died (1504), Ferdinand became regent in Castile for their insane daughter, the Infanta Juana (1479–1555). In 1505 he married Germaine de Foix, a niece of **Louis XIII** of France. He conquered Oran, North Africa (1509), and also Navarre (1512), thus becoming monarch of all Spain from the Pyrenees to Gibraltar. He was succeeded by his grandson, the Holy Roman Emperor **Charles V**.

Ferdinand I 1751–1825 •*King of the Two Sicilies*• He was born in Naples, the third son of **Charles III** of Spain. When Charles ascended the Spanish throne (1759) he succeeded him as Ferdinand IV of Naples (1759–99, 1799–1806, 1815–16) and as Ferdinand III of Sicily (1759–1816). After his marriage (1768) to Maria Carolina, daughter of **Maria Theresa**, he fell completely under her influence, and lost his popularity. He joined England and Austria against France (1793), but was forced to make a treaty with **Napoleon I** (1801). A violation of this treaty compelled him to take refuge in Sicily (1806). The French took possession of Naples, but Ferdinand was reinstated by the Congress of Vienna (1815), and in 1816 united his two states into the Kingdom of the Two Sicilies. Despite the demands for a constitutional government, he maintained a harsh absolutism. He was succeeded by his son, Francis I.

Ferdusi *See* **Firdausi**

Ferguson, Adam 1723–1816 •*Scottish philosopher and historian*• Born in Logierait, Perthshire, he studied at St Andrews University, and served as a Black Watch chaplain before settling in Edinburgh, where he became Professor of Natural Philosophy (1759) and then of Moral Philosophy (1764). He traveled to Philadelphia as secretary to the 1778–79 commission sent by Lord **North** to negotiate with the American colonists. A member of the Scottish "Common Sense" school of philosophy, his *Essay on the History of Civil Society* (1767) was a major contribution to political thought.

Ferguson, Sir Alex(ander) Chapman 1941– •*Scottish soccer manager*• Born in Govan, Glasgow, he played in international games as a schoolboy and began his managerial career at East Stirling in 1974. After three months he left to manage St Mirren, which he took to the Second Division in his first season with them. As manager of Aberdeen (1978–86), he won numerous championship titles, and with Manchester United his achievements included the Double (League Championship and Football Association Cup) in 1994 and 1996, and in 1999 the Treble (League Championship, Football Association Cup and European Championship).

Ferguson, Harry George 1884–1960 •*Irish engineer and inventor*• Born in Hillsborough, County Down, he started a garage business in Belfast at the age of 16, and built his own airplane, which made the first flight from Irish soil in 1909. Over many years he developed the famous Ferguson farm tractor, which played a large part in the mechanization of British agriculture during and after World War II.

Ferguson, Sarah *See* **York, Duchess of**

Fergusson, Robert 1750–74 •*Scottish poet*• Born in Edinburgh, he was educated at St Andrews University. He contributed poems to *Weekly Magazine* from 1771, which gained him local fame. A religious interest, inspired by the minister John Brown (1722–81), was followed by deep depression, and he eventually died in a public asylum. He was a major influence on **Robert Burns**, who placed a headstone on his grave in 1789. He left 33 poems in Scots, and 50 poems in English. Essentially an Edinburgh poet, he is most famous for *Auld Reekie* (1773), tracing a day in the life of the city.

Ferlinghetti, Lawrence 1919– •*US poet and publisher*• Born in Yonkers, New York, he studied at the University of North Carolina, Columbia University, and the Sorbonne, and served in the US Naval Reserve (1941–45). He moved to San Francisco in 1951, where he contributed to the so-called San Francisco Renaissance. He was cofounder of the City Lights Bookstore, which acted as a cultural forum and publishing house for radical poets. His work made a major contribution to Beat poetry and beyond, beginning with *Pictures of the Gone World* (1955) and *A Coney Island of the Mind* (1958). He has published over 40 books of poetry as well as two novels, and a number of plays.

“ ”

For even bad poetry has relevance
for what it does not say
for what it leaves out

1988 "Uses of Poetry."

Fermat, Pierre de 1601–65 •*French mathematician*• Born in Beaumont, he studied law at Toulouse University, where he became a councilor of parliament, but his passion was mathematics. His correspondence with **Blaise Pascal** marks the foundation of probability theory. He studied maximum and minimum values of functions before the invention of differential calculus, but is best known for his work in number theory, the proofs of many of his discoveries being first published by **Leonhard Euler** a hundred years later. His "last theorem" was the most famous unsolved problem in mathematics, stating that there are no positive integers x, y, and z such that $x^n+y^n = z^n$ if n is greater than 2. Its solution was finally published in 1995.

Fermi, Enrico 1901–54 •*US nuclear physicist and Nobel Prize winner*• Born in Rome, Italy, he studied at the University of Pisa, Göttingen University and the University of Leiden. He became Professor of Theoretical Physics at the University of Rome in 1927. Between 1927 and 1933 he expanded upon the work of **Wolfgang Pauli**, published his semiquantitative method of calculating atomic particles, and in 1934 he and his colleagues split the nuclei of uranium atoms by bombarding them with neutrons, thus producing artificial radioactive isotopes. This led to the discovery that slow neutrons are much more efficient than high-energy neutrons in initiating nuclear reactions, which proved an important step in the development of nuclear power and weapons. He was awarded the 1938 Nobel Prize for physics. Fearing for the safety of his Jewish wife in the light of Italy's anti-Semitic legislation, he went straight from the prize presentation in Stockholm to the US, where he became professor at Columbia University (1939). He constructed the first US nuclear reactor at the University of Chicago (1942), and produced the first controlled chain reaction. The element fermium is named after him.

Fermor, Patrick Michael Leigh 1915– •*English travel writer*• Expelled from King's School, Canterbury, he set out in 1933 on a leisurely walk from Rotterdam to Constantinople (Istanbul). *A Time of Gifts* (1977) recounted the journey as far as Hungary, and *Between the Woods and the Water* (1986) the remainder. Among his other books are *The Traveller's Tree*, about the West Indies, which won the Heinemann Foundation prize in 1950, *Mani* (1958, Duff Cooper Memorial prize) and *Three Letters from the Andes* (1991).

Fernandel, *pseudonym of* **Fernand Joseph Désiré Contandin** 1903–71 •*French film comedian*• Born in Marseilles, he made his stage debut in 1922. From 1930 he appeared in over 100 films, interrupted only by military service and Nazi occupation. He established himself internationally with his moving portrayal of the naive country priest in *The Little World of Don Camillo* (1953), and with his versatile handling of six separate roles in *The Sheep Has Five Legs* (1953), which gave full rein to his memorable facial mobility.

Fernández, Emilio 1904–86 •*Mexican film actor and director*• Born in Coahuila, Mexico, of a Native American mother, he was nicknamed "El Indio" and as a young man took part in Mexico's revolutionary struggles. While in exile in Hollywood in the 1920s and 1930s he started a career as a film actor and learned the basics of filmmaking before returning to Mexico in 1933. He was often typecast in both Mexican and US films as a villain, most famously in **Sam Peckinpah**'s *The Wild Bunch* (1969). He emerged as a leading director in the 1940s with such films as *Flor Silvestre* (1943), *Maria Candelaria* (1943) and *The Pearl* (1945), based on **John Steinbeck**'s novel.

Fernández, Juan c. 1536–c. 1604 •*Spanish navigator*• In 1563 he discovered the Pacific islands named after him. He also discovered San Felix and San Ambrosio Islands.

Ferranti, Sebastian Ziani de 1864–1930 •*English electrical engineer and inventor*• Born in Liverpool, he was educated in a Roman Catholic college at Ramsgate and at evening classes at University College London. From his early experiments with dynamos and alternators he conceived the idea of the large-scale generation and distribution of electricity at high voltages. In 1887 he was appointed chief electrician to the London Electric Supply Corporation that planned to provide power to the whole of London north of the Thames from a power station at Deptford. This scheme contained all the elements of the national electricity grid system that came into being some 40 years later. From 1882 to 1927 he took out 176 patents, and founded the firm of Ferranti Ltd in 1905.

Ferrari, Enzo 1898–1988 •*Italian car manufacturer*• Born in Modena, he became a racecar driver for Alfa Romeo in 1920 and in 1929 formed his own racing team. In 1939 he formed Ferrari SpA, remaining there as president until 1977. Ferrari's cars became known for their technological superiority and speed, winning numerous Formula One Grand Prix races and other championships from the 1950s. The luxury cars of the marque are likewise known for speed, elegance and precision.

Ferrier, Kathleen 1912–53 •*English contralto*• Born in Higher Walton, Lancashire, she was an accomplished amateur pianist. The range and richness of her voice, together with her technical control, rapidly won her great respect. In 1946 she sang Lucrezia in **Benjamin Britten**'s *The Rape of Lucrezia*, and Orpheus in **Gluck**'s *Orfeo* at Glyndebourne, and thereafter was in great demand throughout Europe and the US. Her greatest success, perhaps, was in **Mahler**'s *Das Lied von der Erde* ("The Song of the Earth"), at the first Edinburgh Festival (1947) and at Salzburg (1949).

" "

Now I'll have eine kleine pause.

1953 Last words. Quoted in Gerald Moore ***Am I Too Loud?*** *(1962).*

Fessenden, Reginald Aubrey 1866–1932 •*US radio engineer and inventor*• Born in East Bolton, Quebec, and educated in Canada, he became the chief chemist in **Thomas Edison**'s research laboratories in New Jersey. He was later Professor of Electrical Engineering at the University of Pittsburgh (1893–1900). Of his many patents (over 500), the one of most fundamental importance was his invention of amplitude modulation. On Christmas Eve, 1906, he used this to broadcast what was probably the first US radio program from the transmitter he had built at Brant Rock, Massachusetts. Another of his discoveries was the heterodyne effect, which soon developed into the superheterodyne circuit that rapidly became an integral part of the design of radio receivers.

Festinger, Leon 1919–89 •*US psychologist*• Born in New York City, he was educated at the University of Iowa. He went on to teach at various US universities. His contribution to postwar social psychology has centered on the introduction and development of the deceptively simple concept of "cognitive dissonance." According to the theory, people are unable to tolerate conflicting cognitions (beliefs, thoughts, perceptions) for any length of time, and have to resolve such internal conflicts by rejecting or devaluing one or more of the cognitions. The theory has proved useful in the understanding of a variety of psychological phenomena.

Fettes, Sir William 1750–1836 •*Scottish merchant and philanthropist*• He made a fortune from tea and wine, was twice Lord Provost of Edinburgh and left £166,000 to found Fettes College there (1870), designed by **David Bryce**.

Feuchtwanger, Lion 1884–1958 •*German writer*• Born in Munich, he studied there and in Berlin. He won a reputation in Europe with the 18th-century historical novel *Jud Süss* (1925, Eng trans *Jew Süss*, 1926), presenting an elaborately detailed picture of the lives, sufferings and weaknesses of central European Jewry. The 14th-century tale *Die hässliche Herzogin* (1923), translated as *The Ugly Duchess* (1927), was a great success in Great Britain.

Feuerbach, Ludwig Andreas 1804–72 •*German philosopher*• Born in Landshut, Bavaria, he was a pupil of **Hegel** at Berlin but reacted against his Idealism. His best-known work, *Das Wesen des Christentums* (1841), which was translated by Mary Ann Evans (**George Eliot**) as *The Essence of Christianity* (1854), claims that religion rises from one's alienation from oneself, and is "the dream of the human mind," projecting ideal qualities onto a fictitious supreme "other." His ideas strongly influenced **Karl Marx** and **Friedrich Engels**.

Feydeau, Georges Léon Jules Marie 1862–1921 •*French dramatist*• Born in Paris, the son of **Ernest Aimé Feydeau** and a prostitute, he wrote his first play, *Le tailleur pour dames* (1886, Eng trans *A Gown for His Mistress*, 1969), when he was 24 and subsequently maintained a prolific output. His name is synonymous with French bedroom farce. His characters are Parisian bourgeois couples seeking diversion from each other, and his farces rely on the twin themes of adultery and the chase. Among his plays are such enduring classics as *Le Dindon* (1896, Eng trans *Paying the Piper*, 1972) and *Une puce à l'oreille* (1907), produced as *A Flea in Her Ear* at the National Theatre, London, in 1965.

Feynman, Richard Phillips 1918–88 •*US physicist and Nobel Prize winner*• Born in New York City, he studied at the Massachusetts Institute of Technology (MIT) and Princeton. Overcoming moral doubts, he worked on the Manhattan atomic bomb project at Los Alamos and after World War II he was appointed professor at Cornell University. There he worked with **Hans Bethe** on quantum electrodynamics, the application of quantum theory to interactions between electromagnetic radiation and particles, which became the model on which other quantum field theories are based. He devised his own pictorial way of describing quantum processes, the "path integral approach," which has proved to be a very powerful theoretical tool. Using this he further developed quantum electrodynamics and introduced "Feynman diagrams," which provide a pictorial representation of particle interactions. For his work on quantum electrodynamics he was awarded the Nobel Prize for physics in 1965 together with **Sin-Itiro Tomonaga** and **Julian Schwinger**.

" "

For a successful technology, reality must take precedence over public relations, for nature cannot be fooled.

1988 ***What Do YOU Care What Other People Think?***

Fibonacci, Leonardo, *also called* **Leonardo of Pisa** c. 1170–c. 1250 •*Italian mathematician*• He popularized the modern Arabic system of numerals, which originated in India. His main work *Liber abaci* (1202, "The Book of Calculation") illustrated the virtues of the new numeric system, showing how it can be used to simplify highly complex calculations. The book also includes work on geometry, the theory of proportion and techniques for determining the roots of equations. His greatest work, the *Liber quadratorum* (1225, "The Book of Square Numbers"), contains remarkably advanced contributions to number theory. He discovered the "Fibonacci sequence" of integers in which each number is equal to the sum of the preceding two (1,1,2,3,5,8, ...).

Fichte, Johann Gottlieb 1762–1814 •*German philosopher*• Born in Rammenau, Saxony, he studied at the University of Jena and made a precarious living for some years as an itinerant tutor in philosophy, in the course of which he met **Kant** at Königsberg and became a devoted disciple. He was appointed Professor of Philosophy at Jena in 1794. His *Wissenschaftslehre* (1785, "The Science of Knowledge") modified Kant's doctrine of the "thing-in-itself" as the absolute reality, substituting the "ego," a more subjective reality, affirming itself in the act of consciousness and constructing the external world (the "non-ego") as its field of action. He went on to teach at Berlin (1799), after an accusation of atheism, and became Professor of Philosophy at Erlangen (1805), where he published *Grundzüge des gegenwärtigen Zeitalters* (1806, Eng trans *The Characteristics of the Present Age*, 1844) and *Anweisung zum seligen Leben und Religionslehre* (1806, Eng trans *The Way Towards the Blessed Life*, 1844). He delivered a famous series of patriotic lectures, *Reden an die Deutsche Nation* (1807–08, "Addresses to the German Nation"), in which he tried to foster German nationalism in resistance to **Napoleon I**.

Ficino, Marsilio 1433–99 •*Italian philosopher*• He was born in Figline, Florence. **Cosimo de' Medici** appointed him head of the Platonic Academy in Florence, and commissioned from him translations (into Latin) from and commentaries on **Plato**, **Plotinus** and the *Corpus Hermeticum*. He was ordained a priest in 1473, and became rector of two churches and canon of the cathedral in Florence. He was a major influence in the Renaissance revival of Platonism.

Fick, August 1833–1916 •*German philologist*• Born in Petershagen, he was a professor at Göttingen (1876) and Breslau (1887), and pioneered the comparative study of Indo-European vocabulary with his Indo-European dictionary (1870). He also wrote works on Greek personal names and on the original language of the *Iliad*.

Fiedler, Arthur 1894–1979 •*US conductor*• Born in Boston, he studied music in Berlin and joined the Boston Symphony Orchestra as a violinist. In 1930 he founded the Boston Pops Orchestra, which gave free outdoor concerts that blended both classical and popular music. He served as its director for nearly 50 years until his death.

Field, Cyrus West 1819–92 •*US merchant*• Born in Stockbridge, Massachusetts, the younger brother of **David Dudley Field**, he conceived the idea of a transatlantic telegraph cable. He organized companies in England and the US, and after repeated attempts he had a brief success (1858). During the three weeks before the cable failed, Queen **Victoria** used it to send a message to President **James Buchanan**. Field laid a new transatlantic cable in 1866, and later promoted other oceanic cables.

Field, David Dudley 1805–94 •*US jurist*• Born in Haddam, Connecticut, he was educated at Williams College, Williamstown, Massachusetts, and was admitted to the New York bar in 1828. He was appointed by the state in 1857 to prepare penal, political and civil codes, of which the first was adopted by New York, and all by other states. He made great contributions to international law and to law reform, and his *Outlines of an International Code* (1872) was translated into several languages. He was the brother of **Cyrus West Field**.

Field, Marshall 1834–1906 •*US merchant*• Born in Conway, Massachusetts, he worked as a clerk before moving to Chicago (1856), where he became founder of the Chicago department store known from 1881 as Marshall Field and Company, one of the world's largest and most progressive emporiums.

Field, Nathan 1587–c. 1620 •*English actor and dramatist*• He was born in London and educated there at St Paul's School. He became one of the comedians of the Queen's Revels (1604–13) and various other troupes. As a playwright he collaborated with **Francis Beaumont** and **John Fletcher**, and with **Philip Massinger** in the latter's *The Fatal Dowry* (1632). He also wrote two comedies, *A Woman Is a Weathercocke* (1612) and *Amends for Ladies* (1618).

Field, Sally 1946– •*US film actress*• Born in Pasadena, California, she studied at the Actors Studio in California and gained popularity as the star of lightweight television series like *The Flying Nun* (1966–70). She later proved her credentials as a dramatic actress, winning an Emmy for the miniseries *Sybill* (1976) and Academy Awards for *Norma Rae* (1979) and *Places in the Heart* (1984). Other notable films include *Steel Magnolias* (1989), *Mrs Doubtfire* (1993) and *Forrest Gump* (1994).

Fielding, Helen 1958– •*English author*• Born in Morley, Yorkshire, she studied at St Anne's College, Oxford, and achieved fame as the creator of *Bridget Jones's Diary.* This humorous newspaper column parodying contemporary cosmopolitan society through the confusions and neuroses of a discontented single young woman first appeared in the *Independent on Sunday* in 1995 and was later taken up by the *Daily Telegraph*. It was also published in book form as *Bridget Jones's Diary* (1999) and *Bridget Jones: The Edge of Reason* (2000), both of which were made into successful films (2001, 2004).

Fielding, Henry 1707–54 •*English novelist*• Born at Sharpham Park, near Glastonbury, Somerset, he was educated at Eton. Thereafter he studied at the University of Leiden (1728–29) before returning to London, and in the space of eight years he wrote 25 dramatic pieces: light comedies, adaptations of **Molière**, ballad operas, burlesques (including *Tom Thumb*), and a series of satires attacking Sir **Robert Walpole** and his government. This last prompted the introduction of the Theatrical Licensing Act of 1737 and effectively ended his career as a playwright and theater manager. He turned to the law and was called to the Bar in 1740, but was hampered by his disabling gout. Incensed by the publication of **Samuel Richardson**'s prudish *Pamela*, he ridiculed it in a pseudonymous parody, *An Apology for the Life of Mrs Shamela Andrews* (1741). In 1742 came *The Adventures of Joseph Andrews and His Friend, Mr Abraham Adams*. The three volumes of *Miscellanies* (including *The Life of Jonathan Wild the Great*) followed in 1743. In the interim he caused a scandal by marrying Mary Daniel, the maid of his first wife, Mary Craddock (d. 1744). He was made a justice of the peace for Westminster and Middlesex in 1748 and campaigned vigorously against legal corruption, helping his half-brother, Sir John Fielding (1721–80), to found the Bow Street Runners as an embryonic detective force. In 1749 *The History of Tom Jones, a Foundling* was published to public acclaim, though its reception by some literary luminaries was unenthusiastic. **Samuel Johnson** called it vicious and there were those who held it responsible for two earth tremors that shook London shortly after its publication. However, it has endured as one of the great comic and picaresque novels in the English language. He followed it with *Amelia* in 1751. In 1752 he was heavily involved with *The Covent Garden Journal*, which contains some of his most acerbic satire. During his last years, however, illness overtook him. He was still ardent in his fight against corruption but at the age of 45 he could not move without the help of crutches.

Fields, Dame Gracie, *originally* **Grace Stansfield** 1898–1979 •*English variety artist and singer*• Born in Rochdale, Lancashire, she first appeared on stage at the age of ten, making her London debut in 1915. Affectionately known as "Our Gracie," she had a chirpy, natural talent and was adept at both comic songs and sentimental ballads. Her long career spanned radio, recordings, television and films like *Sally in Our Alley* (1931), *Sing As We Go* (1934) and *Holy Matrimony* (1943). She was given the honorary title of Dame Commander, Order of the British Empire, in 1978.

Fields, W C, *originally* **William Claude Dukenfield** 1880–1946 •*US comedian*• Born in Philadelphia, he was a carnival juggler as a teenager. He moved on to vaudeville, appearing all over the US and Europe before becoming the star attraction at the *Ziegfeld Follies* (1915–21). He made his film debut in *Pool Sharks* (1915) and appeared in many short comedies during the silent era. A bulbous nose and gravelly voice enhanced his creation of a tippling, child-hating misanthrope. The writer and performer of several classic comedies like *The Bank Dick* (1940), *My Little Chickadee* (1940) and *Never Give a Sucker an Even Break* (1941), he also played Micawber in *David Copperfield* (1935). Illness and a reputation for being difficult restricted later creative opportunities, and his final appearance was as a guest artist in *Sensations of 1945*.

“ ”

Anybody who hates children and dogs can't be all bad.

Attributed.

Fiennes, Sir Ranulph Twisleton-Wykeham 1944– •*English explorer*• Born in Windsor, Berkshire, he was educated at Eton, served with the Royal Scots Greys and the Special Air Service, and fought with the Sultan of Oman's armed forces. He was the leader of six major expeditions between 1969 and 1986, including a journey up the White Nile by hovercraft, traveling 4,000 miles (6,440 km) up rivers in northern Canada and Alaska (1971), and over land toward the North Pole (1976–78). Between 1979 and 1982 he organized the Transglobe expedition, which traced the Greenwich Meridian crossing both poles. Since then he has made several attempts to reach the North Pole unsupported, achieving the record 88° 58' N in 1990. In 1993 he and Dr Michael Stroud successfully completed the first-ever unsupported crossing of the Antarctic on foot.

Fierstein, Harvey Forbes 1954– •*US playwright and actor*• Born in Brooklyn, New York, he studied art at the Pratt Institute, and made his dramatic debut as an asthmatic lesbian cleaning woman in the **Andy Warhol** play *Pork* (1971). In 1976 he wrote and acted in *The International Stud*, the first of three bittersweet, semiautobiographical plays covering the life of sardonic, incurably romantic New York drag queen Arnold Beckoff. Premiered on Broadway as *Torch Song Trilogy* (1982), it won Tony awards for Best Play and Best Actor; Fierstein also wrote and starred in the film adaptation (1988). He won a further Tony for the book of the long-running Broadway musical *La Cage aux Folles* (1983). Later plays include *Spookhouse* (1984) and *Legs Diamond* (1989).

Figes, Eva, *née* **Unger** 1932– •*British feminist writer*• Born in Berlin, she escaped from Nazi Germany and went to England in 1939, taking British nationality. She was educated at Queen Mary College, London University. Her first novel, *Equinox*, was published in 1966. Her other works include *Patriarchal Attitudes: Women in Society* (1970); a radio play *The True Tale of Margery Kempe* (1985); a highly acclaimed work written in 17th-century prose entitled *The Tree of Knowledge* (1990); *The Tenancy* (1993) and *The Knot* (1996).

Figo, Luis Filipe Madeira Caeiro 1972– •*Portuguese soccer player*• Born in Lisbon, he played for Sporting Lisbon (1990–96) before joining Barcelona (1996–2000). An outstanding winger in the mold of **Alfredo Di Stefano**, he won numerous honors at Barcelona, including (1996) the triple of the Spanish Cup, the Super Cup and the European Cup Winners' Cup as well as (as captain in 1998) the Spanish League, the cup double and the European Super Cup. He also emerged as a star player for Portugal, playing with distinction in the Euro 2000 Finals. He currently plays for Real Madrid (2000–).

Figuero, Ana 1908–70 •*Chilean feminist and political activist*• Born in Santiago, she studied at the University of Chile and became a teacher. During World War II she studied at Columbia University and Colorado State College. On returning to Chile, she campaigned for woman suffrage, directed the National School System, and headed the Woman's Bureau in the Ministry of Foreign Affairs. Having become Chile's special envoy to the United Nations in 1951, she went on to become the first woman head of a UN Committee of the General Assembly and the first woman member of the Security Committee.

Figueroa, Leonardo de c. 1650–1730 •*Spanish architect*• Born in Seville, he was an innovative exponent of Hispanic Baroque. He was interested in surface complexity and was the first to use exposed brickwork in Seville at the Hospital de los Venerables Sacerdotes (1687–97). In the Magdalena Church in Seville (1691–1709) he used the undulant cornice for the first time in Spain in this rebuilding of a Mudéjar building. His most influential and important work is the San Telmo doorway, Seville (1724–34).

Filarete, Antonio, *originally* **Antonio di Pietro Averlino** c. 1400–c. 1469 •*Florentine sculptor, architect and theorist*• Born possibly in Florence, he may have trained with **Lorenzo Ghiberti**. Banished from Rome for the alleged theft of a relic, he traveled north and in 1450 settled in Milan, where he worked for **Francesco Sforza** (1451–65). He is best known for his remarkable *Trattato d'architettura* (1460–64), which includes a plan for an ideal city built to a symmetrical plan, called Sforzinda.

Fillmore, Millard 1800–74 •*13th President of the US*• Born in Summer Hill, New York, the son of a farmer, he grew up in poverty but educated himself and became a lawyer. He entered New York state politics, then served in the US House of Representatives (1833–35, 1837–43), was elected vice president under **Zachary Taylor** in 1848 and became president (1850) on Taylor's death. A moderate on the slavery issue, he signed the Compromise of 1850 and tried to enforce the Fugitive Slave Act. His efforts to purge the Whig Party of radicalism alienated many in the party and led to his being passed over for the presidential nomination in 1852.

Finch, (Frederick George) Peter Ingle, 1916–77 •*British actor*• Born in London, of Australian parents, he moved to Australia permanently during the Depression when he worked in vaudeville, radio, theater and film. He was encouraged to move back to Great Britain by **Laurence Olivier**. Rugged and authoritative, with an offscreen reputation as a hellraiser, he gained international fame in a wide variety of film roles, including *The Nun's Story* (1959), *Far From the Madding Crowd* (1967), *Sunday, Bloody Sunday* (1971) and *Network* (1976), for which he received the first ever posthumous Academy Award.

Fine, Anne 1947– •*English novelist*• She was born in Leicester and educated at Warwick University. Primarily a writer for children and teenagers, she made her reputation with *Goggle Eyes* (1989, published in the US as *My War With Goggle Eyes*), a moving but witty account of a young girl coming to terms with her divorced mother's new boyfriend. This won the Carnegie Medal, as did *Flower Babies* (1993), while *Madame Doubtfire* (1987, published in the US as *Alias Madame Doubtfire*, 1988) was turned into a successful Hollywood movie (1994, *Mrs Doubtfire*). Fine has also written adult novels, including *The Killjoy* (1986), *Taking the Devil's Advice* (1990) and *In Cold Domain* (1994). She was named the second Children's Laureate in 2001.

Fini, Thommaso di Cristoforo *See* **Masolino da Panicale**

Finlay, Ian Hamilton 1925– •*Scottish artist, poet and writer*• Born in the Bahamas to Scottish parents who returned to Scotland when he was a child, he spent a brief period at the Glasgow School of Art before World War II. His writings of the early 1960s played a leading part in the foundation of the concrete poetry movement.

Finnbogadóttir, Vígdis 1930– •*Icelandic stateswoman*• She was born in Reykjavík, and studied French language and literature at the University of Grenoble and the Sorbonne, Paris (1949–53). She returned to Iceland to work for the National Theater, and for ten years (1962–72) she taught French, French drama and theater history. In 1980 she was persuaded to stand for the nonpolitical office of President of Iceland, winning a narrow victory against three male candidates and becoming the first woman in world history to be elected head of any state. She was returned unopposed in 1984, was reelected in 1988 and retired in 1996.

Finney, Albert 1936– •*English actor*• Born in Salford, Lancashire, and educated at the Royal Academy of Dramatic Art, his definitive portrayal of the working-class rebel in *Saturday Night and Sunday Morning* (1960) established him as a star. He later received Academy Award nominations for his appearances in *Tom Jones* (1963), *Murder on the Orient Express* (1974), *The Dresser* (1983) and *Under the Volcano* (1984). He continued to appear on stage, joining the National Theatre in 1965 and serving as associate artistic director of the Royal Court Theatre (1972–75). His television work includes the series *The Green Man* (1990) and the **Dennis Potter** plays *Karaoke* (1996) and *Cold Lazarus* (1996). Recent films include *Washington Square* (1997) and *Erin Brockovich* (2000).

Finney, Sir Tom (Thomas) 1922– •*English soccer player*• Born in Preston, Lancashire, he was regarded as one of the greatest wing-ers ever to play soccer. More direct than his contemporary, Sir **Stanley Matthews**, he gained 76 England caps. He played for Preston North End all his professional life, and so did not gain any major domestic honors in English soccer. He was knighted in 1998.

Finsch, Friedrich Hermann Otto 1839–1917 •*German naturalist and traveler*• Born in Silesia, he traveled all over the world and published accounts of the birds in every quarter of the globe, particularly East Africa and Polynesia, but is best remembered as an expert on the parrots of the world (*Die Papageien*, 1867). Finsch's wheatear was named in his honor.

Finsen, Niels Ryberg 1860–1904 •*Danish physician, scientist and Nobel Prize winner*• Born in the Faroe Islands, he studied medicine at the University of Copenhagen and became interested in the therapeutic uses of light. Founding the science of phototherapy, he showed that the light-induced inflammation of the skin occurring in patients with smallpox was caused by the blue and ultraviolet parts of the spectrum, but that red and infrared rays promoted healing. He was awarded the 1903 Nobel Prize for physiology or medicine.

Fiorelli, Giuseppe 1823–96 •*Italian archaeologist*• Born in Naples, he became Professor of Archaeology at the University of Naples and director of excavations from 1860 to 1875. His work at Pompeii helped preserve the ancient city. He made the first layer-by-layer excavation, working on a large scale to reveal complete buildings and blocks of the city, and devised a method for making plaster casts of the humans and animals that had been buried by the volcanic ash which covered Pompeii in AD 79.

Firbank, (Arthur Annesley) Ronald 1886–1926 •*English novelist*• Born in London, he was educated at Cambridge, where he converted to Roman Catholicism, but left university without earning a degree and traveled extensively in Spain, Italy, the Middle East and North Africa. He cultivated various eccentricities, such as growing a palm tree in his apartment and employing a gardener to water it twice a day. His novels, which include *Vainglory* (1915) and *Valmouth* (1919), are slight, but witty and innovative, anticipating **Evelyn Waugh**, **Anthony Powell** and **Ivy Compton-Burnett**, and he was championed by **Edith**, **Osbert** and **Sacheverell Sitwell**. His last complete work was *Concerning the Eccentricities of Cardinal Pirelli* (1926), in which the protagonist meets his end while in ardent pursuit of a choir boy.

“ ”

There was a pause—just long enough for an angel to pass, flying slowly.

1915 ***Vainglory****, chapter 6.*

Firdausi or **Firdousi**, *pseudonym of* **Abū Al-Qāsim Mansūr** c. 935–c. 1020 •*Persian poet*• Born near Tūs, Khorasan, he spent some years when he was about 60 at the court of **Mahmud of Ghazni**, where he wrote his masterpiece the *Shāhnāma* (1010, "Book of Kings"), based on actual events from the annals of Persia. He also wrote a number of shorter pieces, kasidas and ghazals.

Firestone, Harvey Samuel 1868–1938 •*US industrialist*• Born in Columbiana, Ohio, he started by selling solid rubber carriage tires in Chicago and in 1900 he founded the Firestone Tire and Rubber Company in Akron, Ohio. The company grew to be one of the biggest industrial corporations in the US. He pioneered the pneumatic tire for the Ford Model T, nonskid treads, and tires for farm tractors and motor trucks. To break the monopolistic power of rubber growers in Southeast Asia he started rubber plantations in Liberia in 1924.

Firth, Mark 1819–80 •*English industrialist and philanthropist*• He was born in Sheffield, and in 1849 with his father and brother he established there the great Norfolk steelworks. He was a munificent benefactor to Sheffield, his gifts including almshouses, a park and Firth College (1879), now part of the university.

Firth, Sir Raymond William 1901–2002 •*English social anthropologist*• Born and educated in Auckland, New Zealand, he studied at the London School of Economics (LSE) and carried out fieldwork (1928–29) on the island of Tikopia in the Solomon Islands. He spent two years at the University of Sydney before returning to England to teach at the LSE (1935–68). Among his monographs are *We, the Tikopia* (1936), *Primitive Polynesian Economy* (1939) and *Social Change in Tikopia* (1959). Other significant contributions include studies of Malay peasant fishermen, kinship in London, and a major work on symbolism entitled *Symbols: Public and Private* (1973). The later *Religion: A Humanist Interpretation* (1996) is a cross-cultural survey of religion as "art" and as a tool for economic and political manipulation.

Fischer, Bobby (Robert James) 1943– •*US chess player*• Born in Chicago, he became the first Western player to make a living solely by playing chess and was world champion from 1972 to 1975. Early in his career, he won both the US junior and senior chess titles (aged 14). His brilliance over the board led to his achieving the highest results rating (Elo 2,785) in the history of chess. In 1972 he won the world championship title in an acrimonious battle with **Boris Spassky** in Reykjavík, Iceland, and thereafter withdrew from competitive chess. For the next two decades Fischer lived in virtual seclusion, but in 1992 he beat Spassky in an exhibition match in Yugoslavia.

Fischer, Edmond Henri 1920– •*US biochemist and Nobel Prize winner*• Born in Shanghai, China, he was educated at the Universities of Geneva, Montpellier and Basel, and moved to the US in 1953, where he became professor at the University of Washington, Seattle (1961–). With **Edwin Krebs**, he showed in 1955 that conversions to and from compounds of phosphorus are involved in activating glycogen phosphorylase. This fundamental mechanism controls a wide variety of processes from muscle contraction to the expression of genes, and for this work they were jointly awarded the 1992 Nobel Prize for physiology or medicine.

Fischer, Emil Hermann 1852–1919 •*German chemist and Nobel Prize winner*• Born in Euskirchen, Prussia, he studied chemistry in Bonn. He worked with **Johann von Baeyer** in Strasbourg and Munich, and taught in Erlangen, Würzburg and Berlin. After his discovery of phenylhydrazine in 1875, he found that it reacted with aldehydes to give phenylhydrazones. By a series of related reactions, phenylhydrazine reacts with a simple sugar to give an osazone and this permits the interconversion of simple sugars. This, together with studies of optical activity, led to the elucidation of the structures of the 16 possible aldohexoses (which include glucose). Textbook diagrams of the 16 isomers are known as Fischer projections. It was for this work that he was awarded the Nobel Prize for chemistry in 1902.

Fischer, Ernst Otto 1918– •*German organic chemist and Nobel Prize winner*• Born in Munich, he was educated at the Munich Institute of Technology. In 1951, independently of Sir **Geoffrey Wilkinson** with whom he shared the Nobel Prize for chemistry in 1973, he deduced the structure of the synthetic compound ferrocene. Concluding that its molecule consists of a sandwich of two carbon rings with an iron atom centrally placed between them, he confirmed his theory by X-ray crystallography. Fischer himself synthesized compounds from aromatic hydrocarbons, olefins, carbenes and carbonyls.

Fischer, Hans 1881–1945 •*German chemist and Nobel Prize winner*• Born in Frankfurt am Main, he studied at the Universities of Marburg and Munich. Medical work in Munich was followed by chemical research in Berlin at **Emil Fischer**'s institute. From Berlin he moved to Innsbruck (1916) to become Professor of Medical Chemistry and then back to Munich as Professor of Organic Chemistry in 1921. His most important research concerned the structure of the naturally occurring pigments hemin and chlorophyll. He was awarded the Nobel Prize for chemistry in 1930 for the synthesis of hemin.

Fischer-Dieskau, Dietrich 1925– •*German baritone*• Born in Berlin, he made his professional debut in Freiburg in 1947 and then joined the Berlin Municipal Opera as a principal baritone, but he soon became one of the foremost interpreters of German lieder, particularly the song cycles of **Schubert**.

Fishbein, Morris 1889–1976 •*US physician, writer and editor*• He was born in St Louis, Missouri. Soon after receiving his medical degree from Rush Medical College, Chicago, he joined the staff of the *Journal of the American Medical Association* where as assistant editor (1913–24) and editor (1924–49) he gradually acquired enormous influence in US medical politics. For decades he was known as the "voice of the AMA," where he campaigned against government involvement in medical practice. He castigated unorthodox medical practitioners and sought to increase health consciousness among laypeople through his syndicated newspaper column and his many popular books.

Fisher, Andrew 1862–1928 •*Australian politician*• He was born in Crosshouse, Ayrshire, Scotland, where he was a coal miner from the age of 12, and emigrated to Queensland in 1885. He gradually moved into trade union activity and politics, entering the first federal parliament in 1901. He became leader of the Australian Labor Party in 1907 and then Prime Minister (1908–09, 1910–13, 1914–15). At the start of World War I he made the dramatic promise to support the war effort "to the last man and the last shilling."

Fisher, Bud, *originally* **Harry Conway** 1885–1954 •*US cartoonist*• Born in Chicago, he left college early to become staff cartoonist at the *San Francisco Chronicle* (1905). He introduced a regular strip, *A.Mutt*, illustrating the racing tips of a gambler named Mr A Mutt, and involving Mutt's family and cat (1907). Fisher moved to the *San Francisco Examiner*, where Jeff, Mutt's partner, was introduced in 1908, but the title did not change to *Mutt and Jeff* until 1915. He later set up an animation studio and produced a weekly *Mutt and Jeff* cartoon.

Fisher (of Lambeth), Geoffrey Francis Fisher, Baron 1887–1972 •*English prelate and Archbishop of Canterbury*• Born in Higham-on-the-Hill, near Nuneaton, Warwick, he was educated at Marlborough and Oxford. In 1912 he was ordained, and from 1914 to 1932 was headmaster of Repton School. He took up his first ecclesiastical appointment as Bishop of Chester in 1932. In 1939 he became Bishop of London. As Archbishop of Canterbury (1945–61) he crowned Queen **Elizabeth II** in Westminster Abbey in 1953. He was created a life peer in 1961.

Fisher, St John 1469–1535 •*English prelate and humanist*• Born in Beverley, Yorkshire, he was educated at Michaelhouse, Cambridge, of which he became Master (1497). In 1504 he became Chancellor of Cambridge University and Bishop of Rochester. He resisted the **Luther**an schism, and in 1527 firmly pronounced against **Henry VIII**'s divorce from **Catherine of Aragon**. In 1534 he was accused of treason and was sent with Sir **Thomas More** to the Tower of London. On June 17 he was tried for refusing to recognize Henry as head of the Church of England and on June 22 was beheaded on Tower Hill, London. He was canonized in 1935, and his feast day is July 9.

Fisher, M(ary) F(rances) K(ennedy), *née* **Kennedy** 1908–92 •*US cookbook writer*• Born in Albion, Michigan, she was educated in California and Illinois. Her first published book, *Serve It Forth*, appeared in 1937, published under her initials to conceal the fact that she was a woman (at the time only men wrote about food). She also translated *The Physiology of Taste* by **Anthelme Brillat-Savarin**, whose philosophy she admired. Her books include the wartime *How to Cook a Wolf* (1942), *The Art of Eating* (1976) and *With Bold Knife and Fork* (1979). She later became a Hollywood screenwriter and joined the civil rights movement.

Fisher, Sir Ronald Aylmer 1890–1962 •*English statistician and geneticist*• Born in East Finchley, London, he was educated at Harrow and Cambridge. In 1919 he became statistician at the Rothamsted Agricultural Research Institute, and produced his classic work *Statistical Methods for Research Workers* (1925), which had a major impact on medical and biological research. The leading figure in biological and agricultural statistics in the first half of the 20th century, he also worked on genetics and evolution, and studied the genetics of human blood groups, elucidating the Rh factor. He became Professor of Eugenics at University College, London (1933–43), and of Genetics at Cambridge (1943–57).

Fitch, Val Logsdon 1923– *•US physicist and Nobel Prize winner•* Born in Merriman, Nebraska, he was educated at McGill and Columbia Universities, and in 1954 moved to Princeton University where he became professor in 1960. Using the Nevis cyclotron, Fitch and **James Rainwater** studied muonic atoms. These are atoms in which an orbital electron is replaced by its heavier relative, the muon. From observations of one of the spectral lines (the K-line) they deduced that the nuclear radius was smaller than had previously been believed, which was later verified in the experiments of **Robert Hofstadter**. In 1964 together with **James Cronin** and others, Fitch observed the nonconservation of the combined symmetry of parity and charge conjugation in the weak decays of neutral kaons. For this work Fitch and Cronin shared the 1980 Nobel Prize for physics.

Fitton, Mary c.1578–1647 *•English courtier•* She became maid of honor to Queen **Elizabeth I**. She was the mistress of **William Herbert**, Earl of Pembroke in 1600, and has been identified by some as the "dark lady" of **Shakespeare**'s sonnets cxxvii–cliv.

Fitzgerald, Barry, *stage name of* **William Joseph Shields** 1888–1961 *•Irish actor•* Born in Dublin and educated at Merchant Taylor's School there, he joined the Irish Civil Service in 1911. He later became a full-time actor, toured the US and was acclaimed as Fluther Good and Captain Boyle in **Sean O'Casey**'s *The Plough and the Stars* and *Juno and the Paycock* respectively, both on stage and screen. He moved to Hollywood (1937) and made over 40 films, notably *The Long Voyage Home* (1940) and *And Then There Were None* (1945), as well as the phenomenally successful *Going My Way* (1944) and the police thriller *Naked City* (1948). Other films include *The Quiet Man* (1952) and *Happy Ever After* (1954).

FitzGerald, Edward 1809–83 *•English scholar and poet•* Born near Woodbridge, Suffolk, he was educated at Trinity College, Cambridge, where he developed close literary friendships with **Thackeray**, **Thomas Carlyle** and **Tennyson**. He wrote poetry, and in 1851 published *Euphranor: A Dialogue on Youth* (a comment on English education). After studying Spanish, he published blank-verse translations in 1853 of six plays by **Pedro Calderón de la Barca**, but he is best known for publishing (1859, anonymously at first) his free poetic translation of the *Rubáiyát of Omar Khayyám* (4th revision, 1879). He also translated **Aeschylus** and **Sophocles**.

“ ”

The moving finger writes; and, having writ,
Moves on: nor all thy piety nor wit
Shall lure it back to cancel half a line,
Nor all thy tears wash out a word of it.

1859 ***The Rubáiyát of Omar Khayyám****, stanza 51.*

Fitzgerald, Ella (Jane) 1917–96 *•US jazz and popular singer•* She was born in Newport News, Virginia, and raised in New York City. She participated in talent contests in Harlem, and then began her professional career with the Tiny Bradshaw Band, before moving to the Chick Webb Orchestra, where she recorded her first substantial body of songs. She made her first record in 1935 (and her last in 1992, giving her one of the longest recording histories of any artist), and had her first hit with the novelty song "A Tisket, a Tasket" in 1938. She became the nominal leader of the band after Webb's death in 1939, and continued in that capacity until 1942. She embarked on her solo career in earnest at that point, and worked with both swing-based musicians and the emerging bop generation in the 1940s. In 1948, her first husband, the bass player Ray Brown, persuaded her to come onstage at one of Norman Granz's famous Jazz at the Philharmonic concerts, and by 1950 she was a regular feature on the JATP bills. Granz, initially skeptical, became the major influence on her career, and added a more commercial facet to her mastery of jazz phrasing, rhythm and scat singing, notably in the series of *Songbook* recordings of great US songwriters, which began in 1956. She sang with orchestras in the later part of her career, initially at the invitation of Arthur Fiedler of the famous Boston Pops, but remained equally at home with a jazz trio, and worked with some of the finest piano accompanists in jazz, including Tommy Flanagan, Jimmy Rowles, and Hank Jones. She appeared in cameo roles in a handful of films, including *Pete Kelly's Blues* (1955). She remained a major influence on jazz and popular singing throughout her lengthy performing career, which was halted by declining health in 1992.

Fitzgerald, F(rancis) Scott (Key) 1896–1940 *•US novelist•* Born in St Paul, Minnesota, he was educated at Princeton. He enlisted in the US army in World War I but never left the US. He married Zelda Sayre (1900–47), and in 1920 published his first novel, *This Side of Paradise*, based on his experience at Princeton. He captured the spirit of the 1920s (the Jazz Age) in *The Great Gatsby* (1925), his best-known book. Other novels include *The Beautiful and Damned* (1922) and *Tender Is the Night* (1934). His short stories, in collections such as *All the Sad Young Men* (1926), were equally notable. In keeping with his fiction, which revealed both a fascination with the rich and a moral dismay at the aridity of their lives, he led the strenuous life of a playboy in Europe and the US, exhausting both his financial and emotional resources and exacerbating his wife's mental illness. He described his own problems—and those of his generation—in an influential essay, "The Crack Up" (1935). Driven by debts and alcoholism, he went to Hollywood in 1937 as a scriptwriter, where he wrote a final, unfinished novel, *The Last Tycoon* (1941).

FitzGerald, Dr Garret Michael 1926– *•Irish politician•* He was born in London into a political family and educated at University College and King's Inns, Dublin, became a barrister, lectured in political economy at University College, Dublin (1959–73), and was elected Fine Gael member of the Irish parliament for Dublin South-East in 1969. Minister for Foreign Affairs (1973–77), he then became leader of the Fine Gael Party (1977–87), and Prime Minister (1981–82, 1983–87). In 1985 he took part in the formulation and signing of the Anglo-Irish Agreement and since 1989 he has been European Deputy Chairman of the Trilateral Commission.

Fitzgerald, George Francis 1851–1901 *•Irish physicist•* He was born in Dublin and studied at Trinity College, Dublin. In 1881 he became Professor of Natural and Experimental Philosophy, a post that he held until his death. One of the first physicists to take **James Maxwell**'s electromagnetic theory seriously, he made important discoveries in this field and also in electrolysis and cathode rays, but his name is associated with the Fitzgerald-**Lorentz** contraction, suggested to account for the negative result of the **Michelson-Morley** experiment. It was one of the steps that eventually led to **Einstein**'s theory of relativity, which provided a new physical description of the contraction of bodies when moving at high speed relative to an observer.

Fitzherbert, Mrs Maria Anne, *née* **Smythe** 1756–1837 *•English wife of George IV•* Born into a Roman Catholic family in Hampshire, she was widowed for the second time in 1781 and secretly married the Prince of Wales, later **George IV** (1785). This marriage, contracted without King **George III**'s consent, was invalid under the Royal Marriage Act (1772), and the prince afterward denied that there had been a marriage at all. On his marriage to Princess **Caroline of Brunswick** (1795) the connection was interrupted, but it was later resumed with the pope's consent, and finally broken off in 1803.

Fitzjames, James *See* **Berwick, 1st Duke of**

Fitz-John *See* **Winthrop, John**

Fitzpatrick, Sean (Brian Thomas) 1963– *•New Zealand rugby union player•* Born in Auckland, he is New Zealand's most capped player. From 1986 he was a mainstay of the All Black front row, becoming the world's most capped hooker, and setting a further world record of 63 consecutive caps (1986–95). He first captained New Zealand in 1992 and went on to play a total of 33 caps as captain (1992–95).

Fitzroy, Robert 1805–65 *•English naval officer and meteorologist•* Born at Ampton Hall, Suffolk, he was educated at Royal Naval

College (1819–28), and as commander of the *Beagle* he surveyed the coasts of South America (1828–30). In 1831 he circumnavigated the globe in the *Beagle* accompanied by **Charles Darwin**, with whom he collaborated in publishing *Narrative of the Surveying Voyages of HMS Adventure and Beagle* (1839). He was made Governor of New Zealand (1843–45). In 1854 he was assigned to the meteorological department of the Board of Trade and became the first director of the Meteorological Office (1855). A pioneer in making weather charts, he began a system of gale warnings for shipping, and analyzed the famous Royal Charter storm of 1859. He also invented the "Fitzroy barometer."

Fitzwilliam (of Meryon), Richard, 7th Viscount 1745–1816 •*Irish peer*• He was founder by bequest of the Fitzwilliam Museum in Cambridge.

Flagstad, Kirsten 1895–1962 •*Norwegian soprano*• Born in Hamar, she studied in Stockholm and Oslo, where she made her operatic debut in 1913. She distinguished herself in **Wagner**ian roles such as Sieglinde at Bayreuth (1934) and Isolde in New York (1935), and was acclaimed in most of the world's major opera houses. In 1958 she was made director of the Norwegian State Opera.

Flaminius, Gaius d. 217 BC •*Roman general*• Consul in 223 BC, he was the first Roman commander to cross the Po when he defeated the Insubres at the Addua (223). He extended his road, the Via Flaminia, from Rome to Ariminum (Rimini) in 220, and built the Circus Flaminius (the biggest arena for chariot racing in Republican times). Consul again in 217, he tried to stem **Hannibal**'s invasion of Etruria but was defeated and killed at Lake Trasimene.

Flamsteed, John 1646–1719 •*English astronomer*• Born in Denby, near Derby, he was the only son of a malt maker. Following early astronomical studies pursued privately and a period at Cambridge (1671–74), he was appointed to a commission concerned with finding longitude at sea. The commission's report induced King **Charles II** to found a national observatory at Greenwich, which was built in 1675–76 with Flamsteed as director and first Astronomer Royal. In the 1680s he started an immense program of stellar positional observations. Aiming for the highest possible accuracy, he was slow in presenting his observations, much to the annoyance of **Isaac Newton** who claimed that he needed them for the perfection of his lunar theory. After much commotion, the *Historia Coelestis*, embodying the first Greenwich star catalog, was printed in 1712 under the editorship of **Edmond Halley**. Flamsteed, denouncing the production as surreptitious, burned 300 copies of it. He pressed for an adequate publication of his work, but died before its 1725 completion as the *Historia Coelestis Britannica*. Its three volumes were supplemented by the *Atlas Coelestis* in 1729.

Flanagan, Barry 1941– •*British sculptor*• Born in Prestatyn, North Wales, he trained at St Martin's School of Art. He at first reacted against the current vogue for steel, experimenting instead with stuffed burlap, as in *aaing j gni aa* (1965). After 1975, however, he returned to stone and gilded bronze carving. He was a prizewinner at the Venice Biennale in 1982. He demonstrated an impish humor and an affinity with animals in works like *A Nose in Repose* (Tate), his *Leaping Hare* series of the 1980s, and his *Field Day* horses of 1996.

Flanders, Michael 1922–75 •*English entertainer and writer*• Born in London, he was confined to a wheelchair by polio from 1943. He contributed words and lyrics to a number of London revues during the 1950s, and cotranslated **Stravinsky**'s *The Soldier's Tale* for the Edinburgh Festival (1954). In 1956 he wrote the words and lyrics and **Donald Swann** the music, for *At the Drop of a Hat*. It was followed by *At the Drop of Another Hat* (1963).

Flanner, Janet, *pseudonym* **Genêt** 1892–1978 •*US journalist and novelist*• Born in Indianapolis, Indiana, she settled in Paris in 1922, and for half a century (1925–75) she served as the Paris correspondent for the *New Yorker*, reporting on French life and culture. She was a leading member of the influential coterie of mostly lesbians that included **Djuna Barnes**. She wrote pieces from elsewhere in Europe as well as profiles of famous people, and her journalism is of lasting historical value, providing a social and political anatomy of her era enlivened by her insight into human character and her novelistic eye for detail.

Flather (of Windsor), Shreela Flather, Baroness 1938– •*British politician*• Born in Lahore, India (now in Pakistan), she attended University College London, and was called to the bar in 1962. She entered politics in 1976 as the first female member of an ethnic minority in Great Britain to be elected a councilor, and has since served on numerous advisory committees. She was a member of the Commission for Racial Equality from 1980 to 1986, in which year she was elected Mayor of Windsor and Maidenhead. In 1987, she was chosen as UK delegate to the European Community's economic and social committee. She became Britain's first Asian woman life peer in 1990.

Flaubert, Gustave 1821–80 •*French novelist*• Born in Rouen, the son of a doctor, he reluctantly studied law at Paris, where his friendship with **Victor Hugo**, the writer Maxime du Camp (1822–94) and the poet Louise Colet (1810–76)—his lover from 1846 to 1854—stimulated his talent for writing. As a young man he was afflicted by a nervous disease, which may to some extent account for the morbidity and pessimism which characterize much of his work. This, together with a violent contempt for bourgeois society, is revealed in his best-known novel, *Madame Bovary* (1857, Eng trans 1881). The book achieved a *succès de scandale* after it had been condemned as immoral and its author prosecuted (unsuccessfully), but it has held its place among the classics. His second work, *Salammbô* (1862, Eng trans 1886), was followed by *L'éducation sentimentale* (1869, Eng trans *Sentimental Education*, 1896) and *La tentation de St Antoine* (1874, Eng trans *The Temptation of St Anthony*, 1895). *Trois contes* (1877, Eng trans *Three Stories*, 1903) reveals his mastery of the short story and foreshadows the work of **Guy de Maupassant**. *Bouvard et Pécuchet* (1881, Eng trans *Bouvard and Pécuchet*, 1896) and his correspondence with **George Sand** (1884) were published posthumously.

“ ”

Axiome: la haine du bourgeois est le commencement de la vertu.

Axiom: Hatred of the bourgeois is the beginning of wisdom.

1867 Letter to George Sand, May 10.

Flavin, Dan 1933–96 •*US artist*• Born in New York City, he attended the US Air Force Meteorological Technician Training School, University of Maryland and the New York School of Social Research, but had no art education. In 1961 he began to make his "electric light icons," fluorescent tubes hung on walls or set up as freestanding "proposals" (he preferred this term to "sculptures"). His work has been described by some critics as luminism, and has obvious links with minimalism, as for example his *Monument for V Tatlin* (1966–69). In 1983 he established the Dan Flavin Art Institute in New York.

Flaxman, John 1755–1826 •*English sculptor and draftsman*• Born in York, he studied at the Royal Academy of Art, London. His style was Neoclassical, and he worked for 12 years, from 1775, as a designer for **Josiah Wedgwood**. He then directed the Wedgwood studio in Rome (1787–94), where he also executed several classical groups and began his drawings for the *Iliad* and *Odyssey* (published in 1793) and **Dante**'s *Divine Comedy* (1787). In 1810 he was appointed the first Professor of Sculpture at the Royal Academy. His sculptures include monuments to the poet **Thomas Chatterton** (St Mary Redcliffe, Bristol), to Lord **Nelson** (1808–18, St Paul's Cathedral, London) and to **Robert Burns** (1822, National Portrait Gallery, Edinburgh).

Flecknoe, Richard c. 1600–c. 1678 •*Irish poet*• After traveling (1640–50) in Europe, Asia, Africa and Brazil, he went to London, where he wrote five plays, and published his *Short Discourse on the English Stage* (1664). This provoked **Dryden** to caricature him as "MacFlecknoe" in his satire on **Thomas Shadwell**, and inspired a good-humored lampoon by **Andrew Marvell**.

Fleetwood Mac •*British-US pop group*• Originally an English cult blues group, Fleetwood Mac gradually transformed itself into a British-US rock band. Early lineups reflected the blues purism of

English founder-members drummer Mick Fleetwood (1942–) and the guitarist Peter Green (1946–). After "Man of the World" (1969), "Oh Well" (1969) and the proto-heavy-metal surrealism of "Green Manalishi (With the Two-Pronged Crown)" (1970), Green left and was replaced by vocalist Christine McVie (1945–). Various personnel changes took place and during the early 1970s the group became Americanized, hiring Lindsay Buckingham (1947–) and singer Stevie Nicks (1948–) who helped create the smooth, high-finish rock of *Rumours* (1976), which topped the charts in the UK and US. Legal, contractual and relationship problems abounded and the music became progressively tamer.

Flémalle, Master of *See* **Campin, Robert**

Fleming, Sir Alexander 1881–1955 •*Scottish bacteriologist and discoverer of penicillin*• He was born near Darvel, Ayrshire, and educated in Kilmarnock. He worked as a shipping clerk in London for five years before embarking on a brilliant medical studentship, qualifying as a specialist surgeon at St Mary's Hospital, Paddington (1909), where he spent the rest of his career. It was only by his expert marksmanship on the college rifle team, however, that he managed to find a place in Sir **Almroth Wright**'s bacteriological laboratory there. In his research he became the first to use antityphoid vaccines on human beings, and pioneered the use of salvarsan against syphilis (see **Paul Ehrlich**). During World War I he served as a medical officer in France and continued researching antibiotics. In 1922, while trying unsuccessfully to isolate the organism responsible for the common cold, he discovered lysozyme, an enzyme present in tears and mucus that kills some bacteria without harming normal tissues. While this was not an important antibiotic in itself as most of the bacteria killed were nonpathogenic, it inspired Fleming's search for other antibacterial substances. In 1928, by chance exposure to a culture of staphylococci, he noticed a curious mold, penicillin, which he found to have unsurpassed antibiotic powers. Unheeded by colleagues and without sufficient chemical knowledge, he had to wait 11 years before **Howard Florey** and **Ernst Chain**, with whom he shared the 1945 Nobel Prize for physiology or medicine, perfected a method of producing the volatile drug. Fleming was appointed Professor of Bacteriology at London in 1938 and knighted in 1944.

Fleming, Amalia, *née* **Coutsouris** 1909–86 •*Greek-British bacteriologist and politician*• Born in Constantinople (now Istanbul) to Greek parents, she studied medicine at Athens University. During World War II she joined the Resistance, was captured, sentenced to death, and rescued by the Allied advance. After the war she went to London, where she worked with Sir **Alexander Fleming**, whom she married in 1953. After his death, she continued her research as a bacteriologist. Returning to Greece in 1967, she protested against the military regime that had seized power. Arrested in 1971, she was deported to London. She returned to Greece in 1973, becoming a Member of Parliament, a European member of parliament, leader of the Greek committee of Amnesty International and a member of the European Human Rights Commission.

Fleming, Ian Lancaster 1908–64 •*English novelist*• Born in London, he was educated at Eton and Sandhurst, studied languages at the Universities of Munich and Geneva, then worked as a foreign correspondent with Reuters in Moscow (1929–33), and as a banker and stockbroker (1933–39). He was a senior naval intelligence officer during World War II, and then became the foreign manager of *The Sunday Times* (1945–59). His 12 novels and seven short stories featuring Commander James Bond, the archetypal, suave British Secret Service agent 007, starting with *Casino Royale* (1953), included *From Russia With Love* (1957), *Dr No* (1958), *Goldfinger* (1959) and *The Man With the Golden Gun* (1965). They sold millions of copies worldwide, and have been turned into highly successful films. He was the brother of **Peter Fleming**.

" "

I would like a medium Vodka dry Martini—with a slice of lemon. Shaken and not stirred, please. I would prefer Russian or Polish vodka.

1958 ***Dr No**, chapter 14.*

Fleming, Sir John Ambrose 1849–1945 •*English physicist and electrical engineer*• Born in Lancaster, he won an entrance exhibition to St John's College, Cambridge, where he studied under **James Clerk Maxwell**. During his tenure in the chair of electrical engineering at University College London (1885–1926), he invented in 1904 the thermionic rectifier, or "Fleming valve," which for half a century was a vital part of radio, television, and early computer circuitry, until superseded by the transistor diode in the early 1950s. He was also a pioneer in the application of electricity to lighting and heating on a large scale. He was knighted in 1929.

Fleming, (Robert) Peter 1907–71 •*English travel writer and journalist*• He was born in London. Educated at Eton and Christ Church, Oxford, he worked as an assistant literary editor on *The Spectator* before taking part in an expedition to explore rivers in Central Brazil and ascertain the fate of Percy Fawcett (b. 1867), who had disappeared without a trace in 1925. It provided the colorful copy which surfaced in *Brazilian Adventure* (1933), an immediate bestseller. In a similar vein are *One's Company* (1934) and *News from Tartary* (1936). He was the brother of **Ian Fleming**.

Fleming, Tom 1927– •*Scottish actor, director and poet*• Born in Edinburgh, he cofounded the Gateway Theatre, Edinburgh (1953), and until 1962 appeared in and directed many productions there. He joined the Royal Shakespeare Company in 1962. In 1965 he was appointed the first director of the Edinburgh Civic Theatre Trust, and founded a new company at the Royal Lyceum Theatre in the city. He revived **David Lyndsay**'s *Ane Satyre of the Thrie Estaitis* for the Edinburgh Festival (1984, 1991). His books of poetry include *Sax Roses for a Luve Frae Hame* (1961). He has also been a radio and television commentator since 1952, specializing in state and royal events.

Fleming, Williamina Paton, *née* **Stevens** 1857–1911 •*US astronomer*• Born in Dundee, Scotland, she emigrated to Boston, Massachusetts, and after her marriage failed, she took up domestic work for the director of the Harvard College Observatory, Edward Pickering (1846–1919). She joined the research team at the Observatory in 1881 and frequently collaborated with Pickering; some feel the discovery that Beta Lyrae is a double star has been wrongly accredited to Pickering rather than to Fleming. Her technique, known as the Pickering-Fleming technique, involved the study of many thousands of celestial photographs. She also discovered new stars and variables, investigated stellar spectra, including 10 of the 24 novae recorded up until 1911, and categorized 10,351 stars in the *Draper Catalogue of Stellar Spectra* (1890). In 1906 she became the first US woman to be elected to the Royal Astronomical Society.

Fletcher, John 1579–1625 •*English dramatist*• He was born in Rye, Sussex. All that we know of him, apart from his work for the theater, is that he entered Benet (now Corpus) College, Cambridge, and that he died of the plague in 1625. Much of his writing was achieved in collaboration with **Francis Beaumont**, **Philip Massinger**, **William Rowley** and **William Shakespeare**. The best of his own plays are *The Faithful Shepherdess*, *The Humorous Lieutenant* and *Rule a Wife and Have a Wife* (1624). The 10 or so plays on which he collaborated with Beaumont include the romantic comedy *Philaster* (1610), *A King and No King* (1611), and *The Maid's Tragedy* (1611), generally considered their best work. Collaboration with Shakespeare probably resulted in *Two Noble Kinsmen* (c. 1613), a melodramatic version of **Chaucer**'s *Knight's Tale*, and *Henry VIII* (or insertions therein).

Fleury or **Flory, André-Hercule de** 1653–1743 •*French prelate and politician*• He was born in Lodève. As a young priest, he entered court service (1679), became almoner (distributor of alms) to **Louis XIV** (1683), and Bishop of Fréjus (1698). Tutor to the future **Louis XV** from 1715, he became Chief Minister (1726) and was made a cardinal, effectively controlling the government of Louis XV until 1743. Through skillful diplomacy he limited the involvement of the French in the War of the Polish Succession (1733–38). His moderation gave France the stability her finances needed, and he carried out legal and economic reforms that stimulated trade.

Flexner, Simon 1863–1946 •*US microbiologist and medical administrator*• He was born in Louisville, Kentucky. He studied at

Johns Hopkins University, and joined the newly established Rockefeller Institute for Medical Research, New York City, as director of laboratories (1903–35). Among important contributions to bacteriology, virology and immunology he isolated the dysentery bacillus (1900), developed a serum for cerebrospinal meningitis (1907), and led the team that determined the cause of poliomyelitis. Equally important, he shaped the Rockefeller Institute into a powerful and productive center of medical research.

Flinders, Matthew 1774–1814 •*English explorer*• Born in Donington, Lincolnshire, he became a naval officer and hydrographer. From 1795 to 1800 he surveyed the coast of New South Wales and the strait between Australia and Tasmania with **George Bass**, and from 1801 to 1803 was commissioned to circumnavigate Australia. On the return voyage he was wrecked, and detained by the French Governor of Mauritius until 1810. The Flinders River in Queensland and the Flinders Ranges in South Australia are named after him.

Flo-Jo *See* **Griffith-Joyner, Florence**

Florey (of Adelaide and of Marston in the City of Oxford), Howard Walter Florey, Baron 1898–1968 •*Australian pathologist, developer of the antibiotic penicillin*• He was born in Adelaide. He went to Oxford in 1922 as a Rhodes scholar to study physiology, and later did postgraduate research in pathology at Cambridge and in the US, where he made contacts that in due course were to prove invaluable. Returning to Oxford as Professor of Pathology in 1935, he worked with the biochemist **Ernst Chain** in purifying the antibiotic penicillin, which had been discovered in 1928 by **Alexander Fleming**. Florey supervised clinical testing of the drug in the US where it was put into mass production; by 1943 it was readily available, and by the end of World War II, it had already saved many lives. Florey was knighted in 1944 and he, Chain and Fleming were jointly awarded the Nobel Prize for physiology or medicine in 1945. Florey became the first Australian president of the Royal Society in 1960, and was awarded a life peerage in 1965. He retired from his Chair in 1962 to become provost of Queen's College, Oxford, and was chancellor of the Australian National University, Canberra (1965–67).

Florio, John c.1533–1625 •*English lexicographer*• Born in London, of Italian Protestant parentage, he became a tutor in foreign languages at Oxford (c.1576), and in 1578 published his *First Fruits*, accompanied by *A Perfect Induction to the Italian and English Tongues*. His Italian and English dictionary, entitled *A World of Words*, was published in 1598. In 1603 Florio was appointed Reader in Italian to Queen **Anne** and in 1604 groom of the privy chamber. His famous translation of **Montaigne** (1603) has appeared in several modern editions.

“ ”

England is the paradise of women, the purgatory of men, and the hell of horses.

1591 ***Second Frutes****, chapter 12.*

Flory, André-Hercule de *See* **Fleury, André-Hercule de**

Flory, Paul John 1910–85 •*US physical chemist and Nobel Prize winner*• Born in Sterling, Illinois, he was educated at Ohio State University and in a distinguished career taught at Cornell and Stanford Universities. He was awarded the Nobel Prize for chemistry in 1974. His main research area was the physical chemistry of polymers. From the 1950s he also worked on liquid crystal behavior.

Floyd, Keith 1943– •*English chef and cookbook writer*• Born in Somerset and educated at Wellington, he began his career as a journalist and broadcaster. As a chef he is best known for the flamboyant style of his television programs, demystifying cooking from around the world, including Australia, Spain, Italy and Africa. He has produced numerous books and television series. His autobiography, *Out of the Frying Pan*, was published in 2000.

Fludd, Robert 1574–1637 •*English physician, mystic and pantheistic theosophist*• Born in Bearsted, Kent, he studied at St John's College, Oxford. Influenced by **Paracelsus**, he recognized three cosmic elements of God (archetypus), world (macrocosmos) and man (microcosmos). In 1616 he wrote a treatise in defense of the Rosicrucians.

Flynn, Errol, *originally* **Leslie Thomson Flynn** 1909–59 •*US film actor*• Born in Hobart, Tasmania, Australia, his early occupations included searching for gold in New Guinea. After his first film role as **Fletcher Christian** in the Australian film *In the Wake of the Bounty* (1933), he moved to England to gain acting experience with the Northampton Repertory Company. His first US film, *Captain Blood* (1935), established him as a hero of historical adventure films, and his good looks and athleticism confirmed him as the greatest Hollywood swashbuckler, in such films as *The Charge of the Light Brigade* (1936), *The Adventures of Robin Hood* (1938) and *The Sea Hawk* (1940). His legendary reputation for drinking, drug taking and womanizing eventually affected his career, which was briefly revived by his acclaimed performance as a drunken wastrel in *The Sun Also Rises* (1957).

“ ”

The public has always expected me to be a playboy and a decent chap never lets his public down.

Quoted in Gary Herman ***The Book of Hollywood Quotes*** *(1979).*

Fo, Dario 1926– •*Italian dramatist, actor and Nobel Prize winner*• Born in San Giano, Lombardy, he began his career as a stage designer and author of comic monologues, and from 1959 to 1968 ran a small theater company in Milan with his wife, the actress Franca Rame. His international fame rests primarily upon *Morte accidentale di un anarchico* (1970, Eng trans *Accidental Death of an Anarchist*, 1979), in which a political prisoner falls from a window while in police custody, and the frenetic *Non si paga, non si paga* (1974, Eng trans *Can't Pay, Won't Pay*, 1981), a protest against taxation which achieved popularity in Great Britain during the heated debate over the Poll Tax. Both use traditional techniques of farce in order to propound a socialist point of view. He was awarded the Nobel Prize for literature in 1997.

Foch, Ferdinand 1851–1929 •*French marshal*• He was born in Tarbes. He taught at the École de Guerre, proved himself a great strategist at the Battle of the Marne, Ypres (both 1914), and other World War I battles, and became Allied Commander in Chief in 1918. He quarreled with the French prime minister, **Georges Clemenceau**, about the peace settlement, regarding it as not providing adequately for French security. He wrote *Principles of War* (Eng trans 1919) and his *Memoirs* (1931).

Fokine, Michel, *originally* **Mikhail Mikhailovich Fokine** 1880–1942 •*US dancer and choreographer*• Born in St Petersburg, he trained at the Imperial Ballet there. He joined **Sergei Diaghilev**'s Ballets Russes in 1909 as a choreographer, and on leaving the company he worked in Europe, teaching and choreographing for both theater and ballet. He is credited with the creation of a more expressive approach to the ballet than the artificial, stylized mode prevalent at the turn of the century. He settled in New York in 1923.

Fokker, Anthony (Anton Herman Gerard) 1890–1939 •*US aircraft engineer*• Born in Kediri, Java, of Dutch parentage, he taught himself to fly and built his first plane in 1911. In 1913 he founded the Fokker aircraft factory at Schwerin in Germany, which made warplanes for the German air force in World War I. He also developed the apparatus allowing machine guns to shoot through revolving propeller blades. He emigrated to the US in 1922, where he became president of the Fokker Aircraft Corporation of America.

Fonda, Henry Jaynes 1905–82 •*US actor*• Born in Grand Island, Nebraska, he became involved with the Omaha Community Playhouse and enjoyed some success on Broadway, before moving to Hollywood (1935). His Hollywood debut in *A Farmer Takes a Wife* (1935) was followed by over 100 films, notably *Young Mr. Lincoln* (1939), *The Grapes of Wrath* (1940) and *The Oxbow Incident* (1943), which established him in the role of the honest US folk hero. Later films include *Twelve Angry Men* (1957) and *On Golden Pond* (1981), for which he won an Academy Award. He was also a frequent stage performer. He was married five times, and among his children are actors **Jane Fonda** and Peter (1939–).

Fonda, Jane Seymour 1937– •*US actress*• Born in New York City, she studied at the Actor's Studio and worked as a part-time model. She then moved to Europe and married director Roger Vadim (1928–2000), with whom she made *La Ronde* (1964) and *Barbarella* (1968). Later her "sex kitten" image receded and she became established as a versatile dramatic actress of considerable emotional depth and sensitivity in such films as *Klute* (1971, Academy Award), *Coming Home* (1978, Academy Award), *The China Syndrome* (1978), *On Golden Pond* (1981), *The Dollmaker* (1983, Emmy Award) and *Stanley and Iris* (1990). In the 1980s she also became involved with women's health and fitness through bestselling videos and books. She was married to **Ted Turner**, owner of CNN, from 1991 to 2001.

Fonseca, Manoel Deodoro da 1827–92 •*Brazilian politician*• He was born in Alagoas, and was the first president of Brazil (1889–91).

Fontaine, Jean de la *See* **La Fontaine, Jean de**

Fontana, Carlo 1634 or 1638–1714 •*Italian architect*• Born in Switzerland, he was a pupil of **Gian Bernini**. He worked as papal architect in Rome, where he designed many major works including the fountain in the Piazza di San Pietro, and the tombs of popes **Clement XI** and **Innocent XII** and of Queen **Christina** of Sweden, in St Peter's. He designed Loyola College in Spain and the Palazzo Durazzo at Genoa.

Fontana, Domenico 1543–1607 •*Italian architect*• He was born in Melide, near Lugano, Switzerland. He was papal architect in Rome, where he worked on the Lateran Palace and the Vatican Library. Afterward, he was royal architect in Naples.

Fontana, Lucio 1899–1968 •*Italian artist*• Born in Rosario, Argentina, his family returned to Italy when he was six. He signed the first Manifesto of Italian Abstract Artists in 1935. After World War II, he made his name as the inventor of *Spazialismo* (Spatialism) and as a pioneer of "environmental art." He is best known for his bare or monochrome canvases, holed or slashed to create what he called *Attese* (Waiting).

Fontane, Theodor 1819–98 •*German poet and novelist*• Born in Neuruppin, he worked in the family pharmacy business until in 1849 he turned to literature in Berlin. He was a war correspondent in 1866 and 1870–71, and became the secretary of the Prussian Royal Academy of Arts. He wrote his first novel, *Vor dem Sturm* (1878, "Before the Storm"), at the age of 56. *L'Adultera* (1882, Eng trans *The Woman Taken in Adultery*, 1979) and *Effi Briest* (1895, Eng trans 1967) focused on the position of women in German society, and he extended his appraisal of social mores into the realms of politics and power in *Die Poggenpuhls* (1896, Eng trans *The Poggenpuhl Family*, 1979) and *Der Stechlin* (1898). His novels influenced **Thomas Mann**.

Fonteyn, Dame Margot, *in full* **Margot Fonteyn de Arias**, *née* **Margaret Hookham** 1919–91 •*English ballerina*• Born in Reigate, Surrey, she studied dance in Hong Kong and in London under **Nikolai Legat** and **Ninette de Valois** among others, then joined the Vic-Wells Ballet, which later became Sadler's Wells Ballet and finally the Royal Ballet, with which she spent her entire career. She created many roles under the choreography of Ninette de Valois and Sir **Frederick Ashton**, and rose in the Royal Ballet to become one of the most impressive technicians of the 20th century. Her career was extended and enhanced in the 1960s by her acclaimed partnership with **Rudolph Nureyev**. She performed work by **Roland Petit** and **Kenneth MacMillan**, and also wrote and introduced a six-part television series, *The Magic of Dance* (1979).

Foot, Michael Mackintosh 1913– •*English Labour politician and journalist*• Born in Plymouth, Devon, he was educated at Oxford, where he was president of the Union (1933). He worked widely as a journalist and editor, particularly for the *Tribune* (1955–60), and became Labour Member of Parliament for Ebbw Vale (1960–83) and Blaenau Gwent (1983–92). In 1980 he became Leader of the Labour Party, replacing **James Callaghan**. A man of undoubted political integrity, he was known as a master of rhetoric in parliamentary debates, but proved no match for **Margaret Thatcher** in the media-dominated election of 1983, in which his party was heavily defeated. He was replaced that year by **Neil Kinnock**. A prominent figure on the left of the Labour Party and a pacifist, he has long been a supporter of the Campaign for Nuclear Disarmament (CND). His books include the influential *Guilty Men* (1940), written with colleagues, a two-volume biography of **Aneurin Bevan** (1962, 1973) and a biography of **H G Wells** (whom he had known) entitled *HG: The History of Mr Wells* (1995).

“ ”

Men of power have not time to read; yet men who do not read are unfit for power.

1980 ***Debts of Honour.***

Forbes, Bryan, *originally* **John Theobald Clarke** 1926– •*English actor and director*• He was born in London and studied at the Royal Academy of Dramatic Arts. After a number of years in acting, he founded Beaver Films with Sir **Richard Attenborough** in 1959. His film productions include *The Slipper and the Rose* (1976) and *International Velvet* (1978). In the theater he has directed *Macbeth* (1980) and *The Living Room* (1987). He has also produced drama for television. He married the actress Nanette Newman (1939–) in 1958.

Forbes, Malcolm Stevenson 1919–90 •*US publisher*• He was born in Brooklyn, New York City, where his father, a Scot, founded *Forbes* (1917), then the only business magazine in the US. Malcolm became its editor in chief and publisher in 1957. Despite the later existence of rivals such as *Fortune* and *Business Week*, circulation and profits escalated, making its owner the talk of gossip columns and a multimillionaire.

Forbes, (Joan) Rosita 1893–1967 •*English writer and traveler*• She was born in Swinderby, Lincolnshire. Having visited almost every country in the world and particularly Arabia and North Africa, she used her experiences as the raw material for exciting travel books, including *The Secret of the Sahara-Kufara* (1922), *From Red Sea to Blue Nile* (1928) and *Islands in the Sun* (1950).

Ford, Betty (Elizabeth), *née* **Bloomer** 1918– •*US health administrator and First Lady as the wife of President Gerald Ford*• Born in Chicago, Illinois, she was originally a dancer, and toured with the **Martha Graham** Concert Group. In 1948 she married **Gerald Ford**, who later became president of the US (1974–77). As First Lady, Betty Ford's public battle with breast cancer created awareness of health problems for women. Her struggle with substance abuse led her to found the Betty Ford Center, of which she is president of the board of directors.

Ford, Ford Madox, *originally* **Ford Hermann Hueffer** 1873–1939 •*English novelist, editor and poet*• He was born in Merton, Surrey, grandson of the Pre-Raphaelite painter **Ford Madox Brown**. In 1894 he eloped with and married Elsie Martindale, beginning a life of emotional upheaval. He met **Joseph Conrad** in 1898 and they coauthored various works including *The Inheritors* (1901) and *Romance* (1903). In 1908 he founded the *English Review*, which he edited for 15 months and in which he published **Thomas Hardy**, **H G Wells**, **D H Lawrence**, and **Wyndham Lewis**, among others. In 1924, while living in Paris, he was founding editor of the *Transatlantic Review*, which gave space to **James Joyce**, **Ezra Pound**, **Gertrude Stein** and **Ernest Hemingway**. He wrote almost 80 books in a hectic career but is best remembered for three novels: *The Fifth Queen* (1906), *The Good Soldier* (1915) and *Parade's End*, the title he gave to what is often known as the "Tietjens war" tetralogy (1924–28).

Ford, Gerald R(udolph) 1913– •*38th President of the US*• Born in Omaha, Nebraska, he attended the University of Michigan on a football scholarship, studied law at Yale and served in the US Navy during World War II. From 1949 to 1973 he was a Republican member of the House of Representatives. On the resignation of **Spiro Agnew** in 1973 he was appointed vice president, becoming president in 1974 when President **Richard Nixon** resigned as a result of the Watergate scandal. Ford assumed the presidency during a time of economic difficulties and was faced with a resurgent, Democrat-dominated Congress that firmly resisted his domestic and external policy initiatives. His relations with Congress were made worse by his controversial decision to grant a full pardon to former president Nixon in September 1974. In the 1976 presidential election he was defeated by **Jimmy Carter**. His publications include *Humor and the Presidency* (1987).

Ford, Harrison 1942– •*US film actor*• Born in Chicago, he appeared in summer stock theater before making small appearances in films and television. He achieved fame in *Star Wars* (1977) and its two sequels. Cast as resourceful, swashbuckling heroes, he found great popularity as an archaeologist adventurer in *Raiders of the Lost Ark* (1981) and its sequels *Indiana Jones and the Temple of Doom* (1984) and *Indiana Jones and the Last Crusade* (1989). Other successes include *Witness* (1985, Academy Award nomination), *The Mosquito Coast* (1986), *Presumed Innocent* (1990), *The Fugitive* (1993) and *What Lies Beneath* (2000).

Ford, Henry 1863–1947 •*US auto engineer and manufacturer*• Born near Dearborn, Michigan, he produced his first gasoline-driven motor car in 1893. In 1899 he became chief engineer of the Detroit Automobile Company and in 1903 founded the Ford Motor Company. He pioneered the modern assembly line mass-production techniques for his famous Model T (1908–09), 15 million of which were produced by 1928. He also branched out into aircraft and tractor manufacturing. An eccentric who once declared that "history is bunk," he espoused pacificism during World War I and tried to negotiate a European peace in 1915 by chartering a "Peace Ship" to Europe. He paid his employees far more than the standard rate, advancing the influential argument that decently paid industrial workers themselves provided a market for the product they were manufacturing.

Ford, John c. 1586–c. 1640 •*English dramatist*• Born in Ilsington, Devon, he studied for a year at Oxford and entered the Middle Temple in 1602. He was greatly influenced by **Robert Burton**, whose *Anatomy of Melancholy* (1621) turned Ford's dramatic gifts toward stage presentation of the melancholy, the unnatural and the horrible in *The Lover's Melancholy* (1629), *'Tis Pity She's a Whore* (1633), *The Lady's Trial* (1639) and others. He also wrote a masterful chronicle play, *Perkin Warbeck* (1634). Ford often collaborated with **Thomas Dekker**, **William Rowley** and **John Webster**.

Ford, John, *originally* **Sean Aloysius O'Fearna** 1895–1973 •*US film director*• Born in Cape Elizabeth, Maine, of Irish immigrant parents, he went to Hollywood in 1913, where he worked as a stuntman, actor and assistant director, before directing his first Western, *The Tornado* (1917). An affectionate chronicler of American history in films like *The Iron Horse* (1924), *Young Mr. Lincoln* (1939) and *My Darling Clementine* (1946), he enjoyed a long association with actor **John Wayne** which resulted in such classics as *Stagecoach* (1939), *The Searchers* (1956) and *The Man Who Shot Liberty Valance* (1962). He frequently explored his Irish roots, as in *The Informer* (1935, Academy Award). His other Academy Awards were for *The Grapes of Wrath* (1940), *How Green Was My Valley* (1941) and *The Quiet Man* (1952).

Foreman, George 1949– •*US boxer*• Born in Marshall, Texas, he grew up in troubled circumstances in Houston and won a gold medal at the 1968 Olympics in Mexico City after only 18 amateur fights. He turned professional in 1969, and defeated Joe Frazier to win the world heavyweight championship in 1973. In 1974 he lost the title to **Muhammad Ali** in one of the most famous fights of all time (the "Rumble in the Jungle"). Following a religious conversion in 1977, he was ordained and gave up boxing for 10 years. In 1987, short of funds for the youth and community center he founded in Houston, he decided to return to boxing. In 1994, aged 45, he knocked out reigning heavyweight champion Michael Moorer to regain the title.

Forest, Lee De *See* **De Forest, Lee**

Forester, C(ecil) S(cott) 1899–1966 •*British writer*• Born in Cairo, of British parents, he studied medicine at Guy's Hospital, London, but turned to writing full-time after the success of his first novel, *Payment Deferred* (1926). He also wrote *The African Queen* (1935, filmed 1951), *The General* (1936) and *The Ship* (1943). He is best known for his creation of Horatio Hornblower, a British naval officer in the Napoleonic era who appeared in a series of novels starting with *The Happy Return* (1937). He also wrote biographies and travel books and collaborated with C E Bechhofer Roberts on a play about **Edith Cavell**.

Forman, Miloš 1932– •*US film director*• Born in Caslav, Czechoslovakia (now in the Czech Republic), he received international recognition for the films, *Lásky jedné plavovlásky* (1965, "A Blonde in Love") and *Hoří, má panenko!* (1967, "The Fireman's Ball"), made in Prague. He moved to the US in 1970 and made his English-language debut with *Taking Off* (1971). He received Best Director Academy Awards for *One Flew Over the Cuckoo's Nest* (1975) and *Amadeus* (1984). Other films include *Ragtime* (1981) and *The People vs. Larry Flynt* (1996).

Formby, George 1904–61 •*English entertainer*• Born in Wigan, Greater Manchester, the son of a North Country comedian, he developed an act in music halls throughout England that was subsequently transferred to film. In a series of low-budget, slapstick comedies he portrayed a shy young man with an irrepressible grin and ever-ready ukulele to accompany his risqué songs. From *Boots Boots* (1934) to *George in Civvy Street* (1946) he was one of Great Britain's most popular film stars. Falling out of favor with postwar cinema audiences, he returned to the stage. Later dogged by ill health, he was long dominated by his formidable wife Beryl, who died in 1960.

Forrest, Edwin 1806–72 •*US actor*• He was born in Philadelphia, where he made his debut (1820). At the age of 20 he appeared as Othello in New York with great success. He had favorable seasons in London (1836–37), but in 1845 his Macbeth was booed by the audience. A resentment which prompted him to boo **William Macready**'s performance in Edinburgh destroyed his reputation in Great Britain. The booing of Macready's Macbeth by Forrest's sympathizers in New York in 1849 led to a riot which cost 22 lives.

Forrest (of Bunbury), John Forrest, 1st Baron 1847–1918 •*Australian explorer and politician*• He was born in Bunbury, Western Australia, and from 1864 was a colonial surveyor. In 1869 he penetrated inland from Perth as far east as 123°, and the next year reached South Australia from the west along the south coast. With his brother Alexander (1849–1901) he made an eastward journey in 1874. He was the first premier of Western Australia (1890–1901). He died at sea (off Sierra Leone) on his way to London, where he was due to receive a peerage, the first to an Australian.

Forssman, Werner 1904–79 •*German physician, surgeon and Nobel Prize winner*• Born in Berlin, he studied at the university there, served as an army doctor until 1945, then practiced urological surgery at various places including Bad Kreuznach and Düsseldorf. He became known for his pioneering work in the late 1920s on cardiac catheterization, in which he carried out dangerous experiments on himself. He abandoned them in the face of criticism, but was awarded the 1956 Nobel Prize for physiology or medicine jointly with **André Cournand** and **Dickinson Richards**, who had extended Forssman's original techniques and demonstrated their clinical and experimental usefulness.

Forster, E(dward) M(organ) 1879–1970 •*English novelist and critic*• Born in London, he was educated at King's College, Cambridge, where he reveled in the Bloomsbury circle of **G E Moore**, **G M Trevelyan** and Lowes Dickinson (1862–1932), with whom he founded the *Independent Review* in 1903. In his novels he examined with subtle insight the pre-1914 English middle-class ethos. Early titles include *Where Angels Fear to Tread* (1905), *The Longest Journey* (1907), *A Room With a View* (1908) and *Howards End* (1910). He became secretary to the Maharajah of Dewas Senior in India in 1921, and in 1924 published his masterpiece, *A Passage to India*, in which he puts English values and Indian susceptibilities under his finest scrutiny. It was awarded the James Tait Black Memorial and Femina Vie Heureuse prizes in 1925. He also wrote short stories, essays, and the Cambridge Clark lectures *Aspects of the Novel* (1927). In 1951 he collaborated with Eric Crozier on the libretto of **Benjamin Britten**'s opera, *Billy Budd*. He was elected a Fellow of King's College, Cambridge, in 1946. His gay-themed novel *Maurice* (written 1913–14) was published posthumously in 1971.

“ ”

The poor cannot always reach those whom they want to love, and they can hardly ever escape from those whom they no longer love.

1910 ***Howards End****, chapter 7.*

Forsyth, Bill (William David) 1946– •*Scottish filmmaker*• Born in Glasgow, he entered the film industry in 1963 and started making his own documentaries after the death of his employer. He dropped out of the National Film School after a year (1971), but his *That Sinking Feeling* ("a fairy tale for the workless"), a comedy using actors from the Glasgow Youth Theatre, was warmly received at the 1979 Edinburgh Film Festival. Later films include the adolescent romance *Gregory's Girl* (1980), *Local Hero* (1983), *Comfort and Joy* (1984), *Housekeeping* (1987), *Breaking In* (1989), *Being Human* (1994) and *Gregory's Two Girls* (1999).

Forsyth, Bruce, *originally* **Bruce Joseph Forsyth-Johnson** 1928– •*English entertainer*• Born in Edmonton, London, he trained as a dancer, making his debut as "Boy Bruce—The Mighty Atom" at the Theatre Royal, Bilston (1942). His vast show-business experience includes a spell as the resident comedian at the Windmill Theatre (1949–51) as well as innumerable appearances in cabarets and music halls. He gained national popularity as the compere of *Sunday Night at the London Palladium* (1958–60). With a jaunty manner, catchphrases and deftness at audience participation, he has won affection as the host of game shows like *The Generation Game* (1971–78, 1990–95), *Play Your Cards Right* (1980–87, 1994–2000) and the talk show *Bruce's Guest Night* (1992–93).

Forsyth, Frederick 1938– •*English writer*• Born in Ashford, Kent, he was educated at Tonbridge School, Kent. He served in the RAF and later became a journalist. His reputation rests on three taut suspense thrillers, *The Day of the Jackal* (1971), *The Odessa File* (1972) and *The Dogs of War* (1974), meticulously researched and precisely plotted. Others include *The Fourth Protocol* (1984, filmed 1987), *The Fist of God* (1993) and *Icon* (1996). He was given the honorary title of Commander, Order of the British Empire, in 1997.

Forte, Charles Forte, Baron 1908– •*Scottish catering and hotel magnate*• Born in Italy, he was educated there and at Alloa Academy and Dumfries College. He entered the catering trade via the family ice-cream business, and then became proprietor of the first ice-cream parlor in London (1933), later diversifying into hotels and other business interests. A merger created Trusthouse Forte in 1970, and he won a boardroom battle to be chief executive of the new company from 1971 to 1978. He was executive chairman until 1981, and became chairman in 1982. Ten years later the chairmanship passed to his son Rocco Forte (1945–) and Forte became life president. He was made a life peer in 1986.

Fosbury, Dick (Richard) 1947– •*US athlete*• He was born in Portland, Oregon. He pioneered a new technique in high jumping which revolutionized this event after he won the Olympic gold medal in Mexico City in 1968 with a jump of 2.24 meters (7 feet $4\frac{1}{4}$ inches), using what came to be known as the "Fosbury Flop." This cut across conventional athletics coaching in that the bar was jumped over headfirst and backward.

Foss, Lukas, *originally* **Lukas Fuchs** 1922– •*US composer*• Born in Berlin, Germany, he settled in the US in 1937. He first attracted attention with his cantata, *The Prairie* (1941). His numerous works include *A Parable of Death* (1953), for soloist, narrator, choir and orchestra, and the opera *The Jumping Frog of Calaveras County* (1950), as well as symphonies, concertos and chamber music. His later music includes radical reworkings of Renaissance Baroque music, for example in his *Renaissance Concerto* (1986).

Fosse, Bob (Robert Louis) 1927–87 •*US theater and film choreographer and director*• Born in Chicago, the son of a vaudeville entertainer, he made his Broadway debut in the revue *Dance Me a Song* (1950), but it was his contribution to the musical *The Pajama Game*, a witty number called "Steam Heat," which established him as a choreographer. During his long career he choreographed 11 Broadway shows, including *Damn Yankees* (1955), *Little Me* (1963), *Pippin* (1973) and *Dancin'* (1978), and won six Tony awards. Moving into film, he was both director and choreographer of *Cabaret* (1972, Best Director Academy Award), and continued his success with *All That Jazz* (1979), which he directed and choreographed, and for which he supplied the screenplay.

Fossey, Dian 1932–85 •*US zoologist*• She was born in San Francisco, and in 1963 went to Africa where she met the anthropologists **Louis** and **Mary Leakey**, and first encountered gorillas in the Virunga mountain range of central Africa. In 1966, encouraged by the Leakeys, she returned to Tanzania and set up the Karisoke Research Center in Rwanda in order to study the gorilla population. Her 18-year study is documented in her 1983 book *Gorillas in the Mist* (filmed 1988). Fossey advocated "active conservation," rallying international opposition to the threats posed to the gorillas by poaching and local farming methods. In 1985 she was murdered at the Center.

Foster, Jodie, *originally* **Alicia Christian Foster** 1962– •*US film actress*• She was born in Los Angeles, and started her career as a toddler in commercials. She made her film debut in *Napoleon and Samantha* (1972), and progressed to playing streetwise adolescent characters in films such as *Alice Doesn't Live Here Any More* (1974) and *Taxi Driver* (1976). Her adult roles include *The Accused* (1988), for which she won an Academy Award, *The Silence of the Lambs* (1991), *Contact* (1997) and *Panic Room* (2002). She made her directorial debut in 1991 with *Little Man Tate*. Other films she has directed include *Home for the Holidays* (1996).

Foster (of Thames Bank), Norman Robert Foster, Baron 1935– •*English architect*• He was born in Manchester, and trained there and at Yale. A major early influence was the US architect **Buckminster Fuller**, with whom he collaborated on a number of projects in the 1960s. Foster also founded, with **Richard Rogers** and their wives, the Team 4 practice before founding Foster Associates (later Foster and Partners) in 1967. Foster went on to explore the technological limits of steel-framed glass, producing notable early designs such as the Willis Faber Dumas Building, Ipswich (1975), and the Sainsbury Centre at the University of East Anglia (1978). His Hong Kong and Shanghai Bank, Hong Kong (1979–85), represented an important stylistic development, with its boldly expressive structure and immaculate detailing, and was also widely praised. Among numerous commissions in Japan, the Century Tower Tokyo was completed in 1991. Other 1991 commissions included a new terminal at Stansted Airport in England, a communications tower for the 1992 Barcelona Olympics, and the ITN headquarters and a remodeling of the Royal Academy in London. He designed the world's largest airport at Chek Lap Kok, Hong Kong, in 1998, and in 1999 won the Pritzker Architecture prize in Berlin, the city where he had redesigned the Reichstag, home of the German parliament. His initially troubled Millennium Bridge and his Great Court of the British Museum were both completed in London in 2000. He was created a life peer in 1999.

Foster, Stephen Collins 1826–64 •*US songwriter*• Born in Pittsburgh, he was a largely self-taught musician who began his career as a bookkeeper in Cincinnati and spent his spare time writing songs inspired by African-American life and the South. Himself a white Northerner, he published *Foster's Ethiopian Melodies* in 1849, the same year his song "O Susannah" became the popular favorite of the migrants to the California Gold Rush. Of his 125 compositions the best known are "Camptown Races," "Beautiful Dreamer," "Jeannie With the Light Brown Hair" and "Old Kentucky Home." The **Edwin P Christy** minstrel troupe helped make his work widely known, but by the time of his death in New York City he was in debt and living in poverty.

“ ”

Beautiful dreamer, wake unto me,
Starlight and dewdrop are waiting for thee.

1864 "Beautiful Dreamer."

Foucauld, Charles Eugène, Vicomte de, *known as* **Brother Charles of Jesus** 1858–1916 •*French soldier, explorer, monk and mystic*• Born in Strasbourg, he achieved fame through his exploration of Morocco (1883–84). He felt called to imitate **Jesus** in a life of personal poverty in small contemplative communities financed solely by the members' own manual labor. He spent time as a Trappist monk in France and Syria, a hermit in Nazareth, a garrison priest at Beni-Abbès, Algeria, and a nomadic hermit among the Tuareg around Tamanrasset. He was murdered, but his ideals survived in the foundation of the Little Brothers (1933) and Little Sisters (1939) of Jesus, now active worldwide.

Foucault, Jean Bernard Léon 1819–68 •*French physicist*• Born in Paris, he determined the velocity of light by the revolving mirror method originally proposed by François Arago (1786–1853), and proved that light travels more slowly in water than in air (1850), showing the inverse relation between the speeds in the two media and their refractive indices. This was convincing evidence of the wave nature of light and earned Foucault his doctorate. In 1851, by means of a freely suspended pendulum, he convincingly demonstrated the rotation of the Earth. In 1852 he constructed the first gyroscope, in 1857 the Foucault prism and in 1858 he improved the mirrors of reflecting telescopes.

Foucault, Michel 1926–84 •*French philosopher and historian of ideas*• Born in Poitiers, he became Professor at the Collège de France, Paris (1970). He wrote a series of very influential and provocative books including *Histoire de la folie* (1961, Eng trans *Madness and Civilization*, 1971), *Les mots et les choses* (1966, Eng trans *The Order of Things*, 1970), *L'archéologie du savoir* (1969, Eng trans *The Archaeology of Knowledge*, 1972) and *Histoire de la sexualité* (1976, Eng trans *The History of Sexuality*, 1984). An important thesis in these works was that prevailing social attitudes are manipulated by those in power, both to define such categories as insanity, illness, sexuality and criminality, and to use these in turn to identify and oppress the "deviants."

Fouché, Joseph, Duc d'Otrante 1763–1829 •*French revolutionary politician*• Born in Nantes, he was a member of a Catholic teaching order before 1789, was elected to the National Convention (1792), and then became an extreme revolutionary. He was noted for his zealous support of attacks on the Christian religion, and for his part in the bloody suppression of opposition at Lyons. He then turned against **Robespierre**, being one of the main organizers of the Thermidor coup. Appointed chief of police in 1799, he helped to bring **Napoleon I** to power, and he retained the post until 1815. The First Empire gave him his titles of nobility and great wealth. He was banished in 1816.

Fouquier-Tinville, Antoine Quentin 1747–95 •*French Revolutionary politician*• Born in Herouël, he was public prosecutor to the Revolutionary tribunal from 1793. He superintended all the political executions during the Reign of Terror until July 1794, when he sent his friends, among them **Robespierre**, **Danton** and **Hébert**, to execution. He himself was guillotined.

Fourcroy, Antoine François, Comte de 1755–1809 •*French chemist*• Born in Paris, he studied medicine, qualifying in 1780. He became professor at the Jardins des Plantes in 1784, and from 1786 onward promulgated the revolutionary chemical theories of **Antoine Lavoisier**. He discovered the double salts of ammonia and magnesia, studied the physiology of muscles, made extensive chemical investigations of animal organs and fluids, and with **Nicolas-Louis Vauquelin** discovered iridium. He also helped to develop a new system of chemical nomenclature.

Fourier, (François Marie) Charles 1772–1837 •*French social theorist*• Born in Besançon, he worked for some years as a commercial traveler but became repelled and obsessed by the abuses of civilization. After the Revolution (in which he was imprisoned, and only just escaped the guillotine) he published a number of Utopian socialist works, *Théorie des quatre mouvements et des destinées générales* (1808, Eng trans *The Social Destiny of Man*, 1857) and *Le nouveau monde industriel et sociétaire* (1829, "The Industrial New World"). In these he advocated a reorganization of society into self-sufficient units (*phalanstères*, "phalanxes"), in which conventional living arrangements, property ownership and marriage would all be radically redesigned.

Fourier, (Jean Baptiste) Joseph, Baron de 1768–1830 •*French mathematician*• Born in Auxerre, he joined the staff of the École Normale and then the École Polytechnique in Paris. Fourier introduced the expansion of functions in trigonometric series, now known as Fourier series, which proposed that almost any function of a real variable can be expressed as a sum of the sines and cosines of integral multiples of the variable. This method has become an essential tool in mathematical physics and a major theme of analysis. His *Théorie analytique de la chaleur* (1822, "Analytical Theory of Heat") applied the technique to the solution of partial differential equations to describe heat conduction in a solid body. He also discovered an important theorem on the roots of algebraic equations.

Fournier, Alain- *See* **Alain-Fournier**

Fournier, Henri-Alban *See* **Alain-Fournier**

Fowler, Henry Watson 1858–1933 •*English lexicographer*• Born in Tonbridge, Kent, he was educated at Rugby and Balliol College, Oxford. After the failure of his *Collected Essays*, published in 1903 at his own expense, he went to Guernsey where his brother Frank George Fowler (1871–1918) was a tomato grower. Together they produced *The King's English* (1906) and the *Concise Oxford Dictionary* (1911). After the death of his brother, Fowler produced the *Pocket Oxford Dictionary* (1924) and his immensely successful, if mannered, *Dictionary of Modern English Usage* (1926).

Fowler, Sir John 1817–98 •*English civil engineer*• Born in Wadsley Hall, Sheffield, he constructed railways from an early age. These included the London Metropolitan Railway, the original London Underground and Victoria Station, London. River improvement and dock construction also occupied his attention. He was consulting engineer to **Ismail Pasha**, the Khedive of Egypt (1871–79). He designed the Pimlico Railway Bridge (1860), and, with Sir **Benjamin Baker**, the Forth Railway Bridge (1882–90).

Fowler, William Alfred 1911–95 •*US physicist and Nobel Prize winner*• Born in Pittsburgh, Pennsylvania, he studied at Ohio State University and the California Institute of Technology, where he became professor (1946). He made detailed measurements of nuclear reactions at low energies and extrapolated to obtain a better idea of what occurs at higher stellar energies. Fowler established the existence of the excited helium state predicted by Sir **Fred Hoyle**, which proved a crucial link in the stellar evolution theory which he developed with Hoyle and **Geoffrey** and **Margaret Burbidge** to explain the synthesis of heavy elements in stellar cores. Fowler continued to work on the details of stellar nucleosynthesis, including solar neutrino flux calculations. For his work on stellar evolution and nucleosynthesis he shared the 1983 Nobel Prize for physics with **Subrahmanyan Chandrasekhar**.

Fowles, John Robert 1926– •*English novelist*• Born in Leigh-on-Sea, Essex, he was educated at Bedford School, Edinburgh University and New College, Oxford, where he studied French. He served in the Royal Marines (1945–46), and thereafter taught in schools in France, Greece (1951–52) and London. An allusive and richly descriptive writer, he wrote his first novel, and still perhaps his most sensational, *The Collector*, in 1963. However, *The Magus* (1965, rev edn 1977) is the book which made his name. Set in the 1960s on a remote Greek island, it is a disturbing and much-imitated tale about an English schoolteacher, his bizarre experiences, and his involvement with a master trickster. *The French Lieutenant's Woman* (1969), however, exceeded it in popularity, in large part due to the film version with **Meryl Streep** in the title role. Later books include *Daniel Martin* (1977), *Mantissa* (1982) and *A Maggot* (1985).

Fox, Charles James 1749–1806 •*English politician*• Born in London, he was the third son of the 1st Lord Holland. Educated at Eton and Hertford College, Oxford, he became the Member of Parliament for Midhurst at the age of 19. He later became a supporter of Lord **North** and a Lord of the Admiralty, but North dismissed him in 1775 after a quarrel. During the American War of Independence, Fox was the most formidable opponent of the coercive measures of government. After the downfall of North (1782), he was a Secretary of State. In 1783 the North and Fox coalition was formed, and Fox resumed his former office, but the rejection of his India Bill by the House of Lords led to the resignation of his government. When **William Pitt**, the Younger, came to power, the long contest between him and Fox began. The regency, the trial of **Warren Hastings** and the French Revolution afforded scope to his talents. After Pitt's death in 1806, Fox, recalled to office, set into motion negotiations for a peace with France. Although Fox was addicted to gambling and drinking, **Edmund Burke** called him "the greatest debater the world ever saw."

Fox, George 1624–91 •*English religious leader and founder of the*

Society of Friends• Born in Fenny Drayton, Leicestershire, he seems to have received little formal education and was apprenticed to a cobbler. A Puritan by upbringing, at the age of 19 he rebelled against the formalism of the established Church. He traveled around the country, attracting many followers and often interrupting services to expound his own teaching. In 1646 he had a divine revelation that inspired him to preach a gospel of brotherly love and call his society the "Friends of Truth." In 1656, the year after he and his followers refused to take the Oath of Abjuration, nearly 1,000 of them were in prison. He went to Barbados, Jamaica, America, Holland and Germany, later accompanied by **William Penn**, **Robert Barclay**, and other Quaker leaders. His preaching and writings were often turgid, incoherent and mystical, but as a writer he will be remembered for his *Journal* (published posthumously in 1694).

" "

Walk cheerfully over the world, answering that of God in everyone.

1694 ***Journal of George Fox.***

Fox, Henry Richard *See* **Holland, 3rd Baron**

Foxe, John 1516–87 •*English martyrologist*• Born in Boston, Lincolnshire, he entered Brasenose College, Oxford, at the age of 16. During the reign of **Mary I (Tudor)** he lived on the Continent, where he met **John Knox**. On **Elizabeth** I's accession he received a pension and a prebend of Salisbury (1563). His best known work is *History of the Acts and Monuments of the Church*, popularly called *Foxe's Book of Martyrs*, the first part of which was published in Latin in Strasbourg in 1554 (trans 1563).

Fox Quesada, Vicente 1942– •*Mexican politician*• Born in Guanajuato in central Mexico, he was educated at the Universidad Iberoamericana, Mexico City, and at Harvard. Having risen from salesman to president of the Mexican subsidiary of the Coca-Cola Group, he joined the center-right National Action Party and was elected a Federal Deputy in 1988. He became Governor of Guanajuato in 1995 and was elected President of Mexico in December 2000, ending 71 years of uninterrupted rule by the Institutional Revolutionary Party.

Foyt, A(nthony) J(oseph), Jr 1935– •*US racecar driver*• He was born in Houston, Texas, and became arguably America's most successful driver. He was the first to win the prestigious Indianapolis 500 four times (1961, 1964, 1967, 1977). He also won the equally famous Le Mans 24-hour race in 1967. He won seven national championships, and retired in 1993.

Fra Angelico *See* **Angelico, Fra**

Fra Bartolommeo *See* **Bartolommeo, Fra**

Fragonard, Jean Honoré 1732–1806 •*French painter and engraver*• Born in Grasse, he studied under **François Boucher** and **Jean Chardin** in Paris. With luscious coloring and a loose touch, Fragonard painted genre pictures of contemporary life, the amours of the French court, and landscapes foreshadowing Impressionism. His *Bacchante endormie* ("The Sleeping Bacchante"), *La chemise enlevée* ("The Shift Withdrawn") and other works are in the Louvre, Paris, and he is also represented in the Wallace Collection, London. The French Revolution ruined his career.

Frame, Janet Paterson 1924–2004 •*New Zealand novelist and short-story writer*• She was born in Dunedin, and educated at Otago University and Dunedin Teachers' Training College. She spent much time in psychiatric hospitals after severe mental breakdowns, and her novels describe an existence in which the looming threat of disorder both attracts and frightens. She was applauded in her homeland, but only belatedly received international recognition with her key books *Scented Gardens for the Blind* (1963), *A State of Siege* (1966), *Intensive Care* (1970) and *Living in the Maniototo* (1979). She also published short stories and verse. The background to her work is implicit in three volumes of autobiography, *To the Island* (1982), *An Angel at My Table* (1984, filmed, 1990) and *The Envoy From Mirror City* (1985). *An Autobiography* was published in 1990.

France, Anatole, *pseudonym of* **Anatole François Thibault** 1844–1924 •*French writer and Nobel Prize winner*• Born in Paris, he published his first volume of stories, *Jocaste et le chat maigre* ("Jocasta and the Thin Cat"), in 1879, followed by his first novel, *Le crime de Sylvestre Bonnard* (1881). Under the literary patronage of Madame de Caillavet, whose love affair with him brought about his divorce (1893), he poured out a number of graceful, lively novels, critical studies and the like, such as the Parnassian *Le livre de mon ami* (1885, "My Friend's Book"), a picture of childhood happiness, which stands in strong contrast to later satirical, solipsistic and skeptical works such as *Les opinions de Jérôme Coignard* (1893). The **Dreyfus** case (1896) drew him into politics as an opponent of Church and State and champion of internationalism. His *Île des pingouins* (1908, "Isle of Penguins"), in which the evolution of mankind is satirically treated, was followed by *Les dieux ont soif* (1912, "The Gods are Thirsty"), a fable about the Terror, and *La Révolte des anges* (1914, "The Angels' Revolt"), a satire on Christianity and theology. He was awarded the Nobel Prize for literature in 1921.

" "

Je tiens à mon imperfection comme à ma raison d'être.

I hold on to my imperfection as tightly as my reason for being.

1894 ***Le Jardin d'Epicure.***

Francesca, Maria *See* **Cabrini, St Francesca Xavier**

Francesca, Piero Della *See* **Piero Della Francesca**

Francesco di Paula, San *See* **Francis of Paola, St**

Francia, José Gaspar Rodriguez de 1756–1840 •*Dictator of Paraguay*• Born near Asunción, he studied theology, was a professor of divinity, and practiced law for 30 years with a high reputation. He assumed a prominent role in Paraguay's movement for independence and held absolute power from 1814 until his death, adopting a policy of isolating Paraguay from the outside world. Frugal and honest, but intensely cruel, he attempted national self-sufficiency through agricultural and industrial reform, and abolished noble privileges together with the Inquisition.

Francis I 1494–1547 •*King of France*• Born in Cognac, he was the son of Charles, Count of Angoulême, and nephew and son-in-law of **Louis XII**, whom he succeeded (1515). His military reputation was established when he gained control of Milan at Marignano (1515). On the death of Emperor **Maximilian I** (1519) he became a candidate for Holy Roman Emperor, but lost the election to Charles I of Spain (Emperor **Charles V**). In 1520 he met **Henry VIII** of England at the Field of the Cloth of Gold, near Calais, a costly and portentous occasion intended to woo England away from its alliance with Charles, and subsequently waged intermittent war against the emperor. A number of reverses followed, including Francis's capture at Pavia (1525), the price of his release (1526) being Flanders, Artois, Burgundy, and all his Italian possessions. In religious affairs he won control over the French Church through the Concordat of Bologna (1516) and was increasingly hostile to Protestants and heretics, becoming involved in the massacre of the Vaudois (Provençal peasants) in 1545.

Francis II 1544–60 •*King of France*• He was the eldest son of **Henry II** and **Catherine de Médicis**. As the Dauphin of France, in 1558 he married **Mary Queen of Scots**. He was a sickly boy, and his short reign (1559–60) was dominated by the Guise family in their struggle against the Protestants.

Francis I 1708–65 •*Holy Roman Emperor*• Born in Nancy, Lorraine, the eldest son of Leopold, Duke of Lorraine and Grand Duke of Tuscany, he married **Maria Theresa** of Austria in 1736 and became emperor in 1745. Capable but easygoing, he was overshadowed by his wife, and had little influence on government, except in economic matters.

Francis II of the Holy Roman Empire and **I of Austria** 1768–1835 •*Holy Roman Emperor, King of Hungary and of Bohemia*• Born in Florence, he succeeded his father, **Leopold II**, as Holy Roman Emperor (1792). In Austria's wars against France, she lost the Netherlands and Lombardy in return for Venice, Dalmatia and Istria (1797). After defeats at Ulm and Austerlitz and the capture of Vienna (1805), Francis renounced the title of Holy Roman Emperor, and retained that of Emperor of Austria (Francis I), which he had assumed in 1804. In 1809 Austria lost further territories, but after a short alliance with France, Francis allied with the Russians and Prussians, attacked **Napoleon I** and helped win the Battle of Leipzig (1813). Through the Treaty of Vienna (1815) he recovered, thanks to Prince **Clemens Metternich**, Lombardy, Venetia and Galicia. He was the king of Hungary until 1830, and of Bohemia until his death.

Francis II Rákóczi *See* **Rákóczi, Francis II**

Francis of Assisi, St, *baptized* **Giovanni** *originally* **Francesco di Pietro di Bernardone** c. 1181–1226 •*Italian founder of the Franciscan Order*• Born in Assisi, the son of a wealthy merchant, he was highly sociable and fond of good living. In c. 1205, however, he joined a military expedition, but then, halted by a dream, returned to live as a hermit and devote himself to the care of the poor and the sick. By 1210 he had a brotherhood of 11 for which he drew up a rule repudiating all property, originally approved by Pope **Innocent III**. In 1212 he also founded the Poor Clares, a Franciscan order for women. At the first General Assembly in 1219, 5,000 members were present. His works consist of letters, sermons, ascetic treatises, proverbs and hymns, including the well-known *Canticle of the Sun*. He was canonized by Pope **Gregory IX** in 1228. His feast day is October 4.

Francis of Paola, St, *Italian* **San Francesco di Paula** 1416–1507 •*Italian Franciscan monk*• He was born in Paola, Calabria. He went to live in a cave at the age of 14 and was soon joined by others. He founded his order of Minim friars in 1436. **Louis XI** of France summoned Francis to his deathbed, and **Charles VIII** and **Louis XII** built him convents at Plessis-les-Tours and Amboise. He died at Plessis on Good Friday, and was canonized in 1519. His feast day is April 2.

Francis of Sales, St 1567–1622 •*French Roman Catholic prelate and writer*• Born in Sales, Savoy, he was educated by the Jesuits in Paris. He studied civil law at Padua, took orders and became a distinguished preacher. He successfully converted the Calvinistic population of Chablais, and in 1599 was appointed Bishop of Nicopolis. In 1602 he became Bishop of Geneva. He established a congregation of nuns of the Order of the Visitation under the direction of Madame de Chantal. His *Introduction to a Devout Life* (1608) was the first manual of piety addressed to those living in society. In 1665 he was canonized by **Alexander VII**. He is the patron saint of writers and his feast day is January 24.

Francis, Connie, *originally* **Concetta Rosa Maria Franconero** 1938– •*US pop singer and film actress*• Born in Newark, New Jersey, she was discovered on a television talent show at age 11, and had her first hit with "Who's Sorry Now" (1957). In the late 1950s, she rivaled fellow-Newarkian **Frank Sinatra** for records sold, and capitalized on the new pop boom with songs like "Lipstick on Your Collar." Her first film appearance was in *Where the Boys Are* (1951), and she became known for appearances on military bases and for charity work.

Francis, Dick (Richard Stanley) 1920– •*English jockey and writer*• Born in Surrey, he became a professional jockey at the age of 28, and was on the point of winning the 1956 Grand National when his horse Devon Loch collapsed. He retired the following year and became a racing correspondent with the *Daily Express*. He also began writing popular thrillers with a racing background, and in 1980 he won the Golden Dagger Award of the American Crime Writers' Association. He has written over 30 novels, including *Second Wind* (1999) and *Shattered* (2000).

Francis, Sam 1923–94 •*US abstract painter*• Born in San Mateo, California, he began as a medical student but in 1945 turned to painting, studying at the California School of Fine Arts, San Francisco. His technique, applying thinned paint in small irregular blots which he allowed to trickle down the surface to create an all-over pattern, reflects both US action painting of the late 1940s and early 1950s, and traditional Oriental calligraphy, for example, *The Over Yellow* (1957–58, Stuttgart) and *In Lovely Blueness* (1957, Pompidou Centre).

Francis Xavier, St, *known as* **the Apostle of the Indies** 1506–52 •*Spanish missionary*• Born in Xavier near Sanguesa, in the Basque country, he was the youngest son of Juan de Jasso, Privy Councilor to the king of Navarre. He studied, then lectured, at Paris, becoming acquainted with **Ignatius Loyola** with whom he founded the Jesuit Society (1534). Ordained priest in 1537, he lived in Rome, and was sent in 1542 by John III of Portugal as a missionary to Goa, where he worked among both the native population and the Europeans. He visited Malacca, the Banda Islands, Amboyna, the Moluccas and Ceylon, where he converted the king of Kandy and many of his people. He was canonized in 1622, and his feast day is December 3.

Franck, César Auguste 1822–90 •*French composer*• Born in Liège, Belgium, of German parents, he studied at the Liège Conservatory, and later in Paris, where he acquired French nationality. Much of his considerable output was undistinguished, and his reputation rests on a few great works all written after the age of 50, the best known being his String Quartet (composed in the year of his death), Symphony in D minor (1886–88), Violin Sonata (1886), *Variations symphoniques* for piano and orchestra (1885) and tone poem *Le chasseur maudit* (1881–82, "The Accursed Hunter").

Franck, James 1882–1964 •*US physicist and Nobel Prize winner*• Born in Hamburg, Germany, he was educated in Heidelberg and Berlin, and became Professor of Physics at Göttingen University (1920). He left Germany in 1933 in protest against Nazi policies and eventually settled and taught in the US. He worked with **Gustav Hertz** in researching the laws governing energy transfer between molecules, for which they were jointly awarded the Nobel Prize for physics in 1925. They showed that atoms would only absorb a fixed amount of energy, thus demonstrating the quantized nature of the atom's electron energy levels. Franck was also one of the formulators of the Franck-Condon principle of vibrational transitions, and later worked on the development of the nuclear bomb in World War II at Los Alamos, although he headed the Franck Committee of scientists who urged that the bomb should not be used.

Franco, Francisco, *in full* **Francisco Paulino Hermenegildo Teódulo Franco Bahamonde** 1892–1975 •*Spanish general and dictator*• He was born in El Ferrol, Galicia, and graduated from Toledo military academy in 1910. He rose rapidly through the ranks in Spanish Morocco to become Europe's youngest general (1926). He oversaw the repression of the Asturias miners' revolt (1934), and during 1935 served as Chief of Staff. In 1936, at the last moment, he joined the conspiracy against the newly elected Popular Front government, which was launched on July 17–18; the rebellion led to the Spanish Civil War. Franco's leadership of the vital Army of Africa, and his close relations with the rebels' Italian and German allies, led to his becoming (September 1936) *generalísimo* of the rebel forces and chief of the Nationalist state. Between October 1936 and April 1939 he led the Nationalists to victory, and presided over the construction of an authoritarian regime. During World War II, he wanted to join Germany and Italy, but **Hitler** was not prepared to pay his price of France's northern African territories. Franco therefore kept Spain out of the war, but sent the Blue Division to fight in the USSR, and provided Germany with logistical and intelligence support. In 1947, Franco was declared head of state for life by the reconstituted parliament (Cortes). During the 1950s, his anti-communist stand made possible a rapprochement with the Western powers, the 1953 Bases Agreement with the US providing Franco with his breakthrough. The greatest paradox of Franco's rule was that it oversaw the modernization of the Spanish economy in the 1950s and 1960s that ultimately undermined the political foundations of the police state and prepared it for the transition to democracy. In 1969 Franco announced that on his death the monarchy would return in the person of **Juan Carlos I**, grandson of Spain's last ruling king. Franco died in Madrid, and within two years almost every vestige of his dictatorship had disappeared.

François II *See* **Francis II**

Francome, John 1952– •*English jockey, television commentator and author*• Born in Swindon, he first rode a winning horse in 1969. Between then and his retirement in 1985, he established a National Hunt record of 1,138 wins. He was champion jockey seven times.

Resourceful and adaptable, he has since continued his involvement with the sport as a trainer, commentator, and writer of several novels set in the racing world.

Frank, Anne 1929–45 •*German Jewish diarist*• Anne Frank was born in Frankfurt am Main, the second daughter of Otto Frank, a member of a banking family who took his family to Holland in 1933 to establish a pharmaceutical company in Amsterdam. After the Nazi occupation of Holland, Anne hid with her family and four others in a specially prepared hiding place in the two upper floors of an office building used by Frank's firm. There, supported with essential supplies by their friends (especially Miep Gies, who later wrote a memoir of her), they lived from July 1942 to August 1944, when they were betrayed. Anne was sent to Auschwitz and later Bergen-Belsen concentration camps, and died along with the other members of her family except for her father, who devoted the rest of his life to promoting the message of the lively, moving diary his daughter kept from June 14, 1942, and during her concealment. The diary was published in 1947 as *Het Achterhuis* and was translated into English as *The Diary of Anne Frank* in 1952. It has since been published in over 50 languages, as well as dramatized and filmed. In 1989 further entries from the diary, previously suppressed, were also published; these afford moving insights into Anne's repressed sexual feelings. A recent edition is *The Diary of a Young Girl: The Definitive Edition* (1997).

Frank, Hans 1900–46 •*German Nazi politician*• He was born in Karlsruhe and studied at the Universities of Munich, Vienna and Kiel. In 1939 he became Governor-General of Poland, where he established concentration camps and conducted a policy of persecution and extermination. He was condemned as a war criminal and hanged.

Frank, Ilya Mikhailovich 1908–90 •*Soviet physicist and Nobel Prize winner*• Born in Leningrad (now St Petersburg), he was educated at Moscow State University, and in 1944 was appointed Professor of Physics there. By 1937, working with **Pavel Cherenkov** and **Igor Tamm**, he and his colleagues were able to explain the Cherenkov effect, which arises when a charged particle traverses a medium when moving at a speed greater than the speed of light in that medium. The effect is dramatically visible in the blue glow in a uranium reactor core containing heavy water. Cherenkov, Frank and Tamm shared the Nobel Prize for physics in 1958.

Frank, Robert 1924– •*Swiss-US photographer and filmmaker*• He was born in Zurich and worked in fashion photography until 1948, then traveled in the US, South America and Europe. During the mid-1950s in the US he created a series of photographs that were to establish him as one of the most influential photographers of his time. Bold images of US culture capturing often shocking pictures of everyday trivia, they were published, with text by **Jack Kerouac**, as *The Americans* (1959) and exemplified Frank's eye for bold composition and his often ironical point of view. He subsequently made films, including *Pull My Daisy* (1959, screenplay by Kerouac) about the authors of the Beat generation.

Frankenthaler, Helen 1928– •*US abstract painter*• Born in New York, she studied at Bennington College, Vermont. Influenced by **Hans Hofmann**, with whom she studied briefly at the Art Students League in New York (1950), and **Jackson Pollock**, she developed a technique of applying very thin paint to unprimed canvas, allowing it to soak in and create atmospheric stains and blots on the surface. Her best-known picture is *Mountains and Sea* (1952). She was married to the artist **Robert Motherwell** from 1958 to 1971.

Frankland, Sir Edward 1825–99 •*English chemist*• Born in Churchtown, Lancashire, he studied under Lyon Playfair (1819–98) in London, **Robert Wilhelm Bunsen** in Marburg and **Justus von Liebig** in Giessen. He became the first Professor of Chemistry at the newly founded Owen's College, Manchester, and from 1863 to 1865 was Professor of Chemistry at the Royal Institution. In 1865 he joined the Royal School of Mines, where he remained for 20 years. His pioneering work in organometallic chemistry around 1850 led to his development of the theory of valences, which underlies all structural chemistry. With Sir **Norman Lockyer** he studied the solar spectrum and in 1868 they jointly discovered helium in the sun's atmosphere. In applied chemistry Frankland did important work on water supply and sanitation. He was knighted in 1897.

Franklin, Aretha 1942– •*US soul singer and pianist*• Born in Memphis, Tennessee, she had established her name on the gospel circuit before she signed a recording contracts with Columbia Records (1960) and Atlantic Records (1967). Producer Jerry Wexler capitalized on both her piano playing skills and her gospel roots, most notably on *I Never Loved a Man the Way I Love You* (1967) and *Lady Soul* (1968). In 1972 she returned to the church with her album *Amazing Grace*, a two-record set of gospel songs recorded live in Los Angeles. Subsequent recordings have included *With Everything I Feel in Me* (1974), *Almighty Fire* (1978), *Love All the Hurt Away* (1981), *Aretha* (1980), *Get It Right* (1983) and *Jazz to Soul* (1992). In 1987 she recorded *One Lord, One Faith, One Baptism* in her father's Detroit church. She has had more million-selling singles than any other female recording artist.

Franklin, Benjamin, *pseudonym* **Richard Saunders** 1706–90 •*US statesman, diplomat, printer, publisher, inventor and scientist*• He was born in Boston, the fifteenth of 17 children, and was apprenticed at the age of 12 to his brother James, a printer, who started a newspaper, the *New England Courant*, in 1721. During 1724–26 he worked for 18 months in London, before returning to Philadelphia to establish his own successful printing house, and in 1729 he purchased the *Pennsylvania Gazette*. In 1732 Franklin commenced the publication of *Poor Richard's Almanac*, which became popular for its witty aphorisms and attained an unprecedented circulation. He was an energetic citizen of Philadelphia, taking the lead in founding its first subscription library, paid police force, hospital, volunteer fire department, and academy (later the University of Pennsylvania). He was appointed Clerk of the Assembly (1736), postmaster of Philadelphia (1737), and then deputy postmaster general for the colonies (1753), being elected and reelected a member of the Assembly almost uninterruptedly until his first mission to England. His invention of the Franklin stove and its commercial success encouraged him to turn from printing to the natural sciences in the 1740s, and in 1746 he commenced his famous researches in electricity. He brought out fully the distinction between positive and negative electricity, proved that lightning and electricity are identical, and suggested that buildings could be protected by lightning conductors. In 1764 he was again sent to England to contest the pretensions of Parliament to tax the American colonies without representation. The differences, however, between the British government and the colonies became too grave to be reconciled by negotiation, and in 1775 Franklin returned to the colonies, where he helped draft the Declaration of Independence. To secure foreign assistance in the war Franklin was sent to Paris in 1776. His skill as a negotiator and his personal popularity, reinforced by the antipathy of the French and English, favored his mission, and in February 1778 a treaty of alliance was signed, while munitions of war and money were sent from France that made possible the American victory in the Revolutionary War. He helped negotiate the Treaty of Paris (1783), ending the war with Great Britain, and remained US ambassador in Paris till 1785, when he returned to Philadelphia. In 1787, frail and elderly, he was a delegate to the convention that framed the US Constitution. He retired from public life in 1788, but his mind remained active, and at the age of 83 he invented bifocal eyeglasses.

“ ”

We must indeed all hang together or, most assuredly, we shall all hang separately.

1776 On signing the Declaration of Independence, July 4.

Franklin, Frederic 1914– •*English dancer, ballet director and teacher*• He was born in Liverpool, and worked in cabarets and casinos in London and Paris, until **Anton Dolin** invited him to join the **Markova**-Dolin Ballet (1935–37). He consolidated his international status as a member of Ballets Russes de Monte Carlo (1938–49, 1954–56), and became company ballet master in 1944. Later he worked with various companies, including his own Slavenska-Franklin Ballet, the National Ballet of Washington, the Pittsburgh Ballet Theater and the Chicago Ballet.

Franklin, Sir John 1786–1847 •*English explorer*• Born in Spilsby, Lincolnshire, he joined the navy at the age of 14 and was present at the battles of Copenhagen (1801) and Trafalgar (1805). From 1818 he made extensive land journeys along the Coppermine River and the Canadian Arctic coast, including the Mackenzie River (1819–22, 1825–27). He was governor of Van Diemen's Land (Tasmania) from 1834 to 1845. In 1845 he commanded the *Erebus* and *Terror* in an attempt to discover the Northwest Passage. Leaving Baffin Bay via Lancaster Sound, the crews wintered at Beechey Island, then worked along the coast of the North American mainland, but were beleaguered by thick ice in the Victoria Strait (1846). Franklin died during the following year. The 105 survivors under Captain Crozier attempted to walk to Back's River, but died of starvation and scurvy. One of the numerous relief expeditions sent out found a record of the expedition to April 1848 with definite proof that Franklin had discovered the Northwest Passage.

Franklin, John Hope 1915– •*US historian*• Born in Rentiesville, Oklahoma, the son of an African-American attorney, he was educated at Fisk University and Harvard. He taught at several Black institutions, joining Howard University in 1947 when he published his survey of the African-American historical experience, *From Slavery to Freedom: A History of American Negroes* (1947). In 1956 he joined Brooklyn College and published *The Militant South*. Other books include *Reconstruction After the Civil War* (1961), which laid a judicious foundation for a reappraisal of the post–Civil War era from the African-American standpoint, and *The Emancipation Proclamation* (1963).

Franklin, (Stella Marian Sarah) Miles, *pseudonym* **Brent of Bin** 1879–1954 •*Australian novelist*• Born in Talbingo, near Tumut, New South Wales, she spent her first 10 years on a farm in the bush country, described in *Childhood at Brindabella* (1963). Later the family moved "downmarket" to the district fictionalized in *My Brilliant Career* (1901) as Possum Gully, and eventually settled in a Sydney suburb. In 1906 she emigrated to the US, where she worked as a secretary for the Women's Trade Union League. Moving to England in 1915, she helped with the war effort, serving with the Scottish Women's Hospital in Ostrovo, Macedonia. In 1932 she returned permanently to Australia, and began the "Brent of Bin" series, starting with *Up the Country* (1928). Her best work appeared under her own name, including the early autobiographical novel *All That Swagger* (1936) and a collection of essays on Australian literature, *Laughter, Not for a Cage* (1956). The Miles Franklin awards are among Australia's most prestigious literary prizes.

Franklin, Rosalind Elsie 1920–58 •*English X-ray crystallographer*• Born in London, she studied physical chemistry at Cambridge and held a research post at the British Coal Utilization Research Association (1942–46), where her work was important in establishing carbon fiber technology. At the Central Government Laboratory for Chemistry in Paris (1947–50), she became experienced in X-ray diffraction techniques. She returned to London in 1951 to work on DNA at King's College. She produced X-ray diffraction pictures of DNA which were published in the same issue of *Nature* (1953) in which **James Watson** and **Francis Crick** proposed their double-helical model of DNA. Finding it difficult to cooperate with **Maurice Wilkins**, who was also working on DNA at King's College, Franklin left to join **John Bernal**'s laboratory at Birkbeck College, London, to concentrate on the tobacco mosaic virus. She died four years before the 1962 Nobel Prize for physiology or medicine was awarded to Watson, Crick and Wilkins for the determination of the structure of DNA.

Franz Ferdinand 1863–1914 •*Archduke of Austria*• Born in Graz, he was the nephew and heir apparent (from 1896) of Emperor **Franz Joseph**. On a visit to Sarajevo (now in Bosnia and Herzegovina) in 1914, he and his wife Sophie were assassinated by a group of young Serbian nationalists led by **Gavrilo Princip**. Austria used the incident as a pretext for attacking Serbia, which precipitated World War I.

Franz Joseph, *properly* **Franz Joseph I** 1830–1916 •*Emperor of Austria and king of Hungary*• Born at the Schönbrunn Palace, Vienna, he was the son of the Archduke Francis (Emperor **Francis** I's son), and the nephew of Ferdinand I (1793–1875), whom he succeeded (1848). He reigned longer than any other European monarch. The aspirations of the various nationalities of the empire were rigorously suppressed, and a determined effort made to fuse them into one state. The emperor reasserted his claim to rule as an absolute sovereign and a close alliance was entered into with the Church to combat liberal progress. In 1859 Lombardy was wrested from Austria by Sardinia. Through the war with Prussia (1866) Austria was ostracized by Germany, and compelled to surrender Venetia to Sardinia, Prussia's ally. Hungary was granted autonomy in the Compromise of 1867, and Franz Joseph took the additional title of king of Hungary. The emperor then adopted a more conciliatory policy toward the various national groups within the empire. His annexation of Bosnia and Herzegovina (1908) agitated Europe and his attack on Serbia (1914) precipitated World War I. By the suicide at Mayerling of his son Rudolf (1858–89), and the murder in Sarajevo of his heir apparent, **Franz Ferdinand**, eldest son of the emperor's brother Charles Louis (1833–96), the crown passed to **Charles**.

Fraser, Lady Antonia, *née* **Pakenham** 1932– •*British writer*• She is the daughter of the 7th Earl of Longford. She was educated at Lady Margaret Hall, Oxford, and has written a series of historical biographies, including *Mary Queen of Scots* (1969, James Tait Black Memorial Prize), *King James VI and I* (1974), *King Charles II* (1979) and *Marie Antoinette* (2001). She has also written mystery stories, including *Quiet as a Nun* (1977) and *Have a Nice Death* (1983). She was married to Hugh Fraser (1956–77), and married **Harold Pinter** in 1980.

Fraser, Dawn 1937– •*Australian swimmer*• She was born in Balmain, Sydney. In her swimming career she broke 27 world records and won 29 Australian championships. Her outstanding achievement was in winning gold medals at three successive Olympic Games—Melbourne (1956), Rome (1960) and Tokyo (1964)—in each case setting a new Olympic record. At the Rome Olympic Games she broke three world records within one hour. In 1964 she became the first woman to break the "magic minute" for the 100 meters with a time of 58.9 seconds, a record that was to stand for 20 years.

Fraser, George MacDonald 1925– •*English historical novelist*• He grew up in Carlisle and Glasgow. He is best known for *Flashman* (1969) and subsequent novels, in which he turned the bully of **Thomas Hughes**'s *Tom Brown's Schooldays* into a representative figure of the English caste system and of imperial values. Other books include a parallel sequence of novels with the more down-to-earth hero, McAuslan, as in *McAuslan in the Rough* (1974). He also wrote the screenplays for the James Bond film *Octopussy* (1983) and a 1987 adaptation of the life of **Casanova**. His war experiences fueled the surprisingly lyrical and elegiac *Quartered Safe out Here* (1992).

Fraser, (John) Malcolm 1930– •*Australian politician*• Born in Melbourne, he was educated at Oxford. In 1955 he became the youngest Member of Parliament in the House of Representatives and succeeded Billy Snedden as leader of the Liberal Party in 1975. After the constitutional crisis of November 1975 he was asked to head a caretaker government until the elections in December, in which the Liberal-National Country coalition he was leading was returned to power. He remained Prime Minister until his party's defeat in the elections of 1983 by the Labor Party (for which it was only the second victory in 33 years). Soon after, he resigned his parliamentary seat. Since then he has worked as a member of the Commonwealth Group of Eminent Persons which advises on global trouble spots, and was briefly special envoy to Africa for the **Howard** Government (1996).

" "

Life is not meant to be easy.

1971 The Deakin Lecture, Melbourne, July 20.

Fraser, Peter 1884–1950 •*New Zealand politician*• He was born in Fearn, Ross and Cromarty, Scotland, emigrated to New Zealand (1910), and became involved in trade union organization. A founding member of the New Zealand Labour Party (1916), he was imprisoned during World War I for opposing conscription. He entered parliament in 1918 and was Prime Minister from 1940 to 1949.

Fraser Darling, Sir Frank 1903–79 •*English ecologist and conservationist*• Born in Chesterfield, Derbyshire, he attended the University of Edinburgh. From 1930 to 1934 he studied the ecology of the red deer, publishing *A Herd of Red Deer* (1937), and subsequently carried out research on sea birds, showing how to improve the breeding of colonial birds by stimulating other members of the species, a phenomenon now known as the Fraser Darling effect. He was one of the early champions of conservation and a senior lecturer in ecology and conservation at Edinburgh (1953–58) and vice president of the Conservation Foundation, Washington DC (1959–72).

Fraunhofer, Joseph von 1787–1826 •*German physicist*• Born in Straubing, Bavaria, in 1823 he was appointed director of the Physics Museum of the Bavarian Academy of Sciences. Fraunhofer advanced the design of achromatic doublet lenses, showing how to minimize their spherical aberration, and using these improved designs he developed the prism spectrometer to discover the dark lines in the sun's spectrum which now bear his name (1814–17). He invented the transmission diffraction grating in 1821, and subsequently the reflection grating. Diffraction phenomena observed at very large distances from the diffracting aperture are known as Fraunhofer diffraction.

Frayn, Michael 1933– •*English dramatist, journalist and humorist*• He was born in London. A journalist by training, he has published a number of comic novels, among them *The Tin Men* (1965) and *Towards the End of the Morning* (1967), about the newspaper business. His stage plays include *Noises Off* (1982), a frenetic farce about putting on a frenetic farce; *Benefactors* (1984), a piece about middle-class mores; and *Copenhagen* (1998). Arguably his finest play is *Make and Break* (1980), a satirical look at the lives of salesmen at a foreign trade fair. He also wrote the script for the film *Clockwise* (1986), and is a translator of **Chekhov**.

Frazer, Sir James George 1854–1941 •*Scottish social anthropologist, classicist and folklorist*• Born in Glasgow, he was educated at Larchfield Academy in Helensburgh, Glasgow University and Trinity College, Cambridge, where he became a Classics Fellow. His interest in anthropology, in combination with his classical studies, produced his major work, *The Golden Bough: A Study in Comparative Religion* (1890, rewritten in 12 vols, 1911–15). In addition to other anthropological works he published an edition of **Sallust** (1884), and a translation of **Pausanias**'s *Description of Greece* (1898).

Frazier, Joe (Joseph) 1944– •*US boxer*• Born in Beaufort, South Carolina, he left school at age 13 to work as a mule driver. After several years spent in the amateur ring, culminating in a gold medal at the Tokyo Summer Games of 1964, he turned professional, winning 19 straight fights by 1967 and defeating Buster Mathis to gain the world heavyweight title in 1968. In 1971 Frazier defeated **Muhammad Ali** in one of the most publicized boxing matches in history, but lost to **George Foreman** in 1973. Beaten twice by Ali and once by Foreman in subsequent matches, he retired in 1976.

Frears, Stephen Arthur 1941– •*English film director*• He was born in Leicester. After making his directorial debut with the 30-minute drama *Burning* in 1967, he directed the feature-length *Gumshoe* (1971) and worked extensively for television over the next decade with such feature-length plays as *Walter* (1982). He returned to the big screen with *The Hit* (1984) and went on to direct the films *My Beautiful Laundrette* (1985), *Prick Up Your Ears* (1987), *Sammy and Rosie Get Laid* (1987), *Dangerous Liaisons* (1988), *The Grifters* (1990), *The Van* (1996) and *High Fidelity* (2000).

Frece, Lady de *See* **Tilley, Vesta**

Fredegond, *also spelled* **Fredegund** or **Frédégonde** d. 598 •*Frankish queen*• She was first mistress, then wife, of Chilperic, king of Neustria. Monstrously cruel, she waged a relentless feud with her rival **Brunhilde**, wife of Sigebert, king of Austrasia, and sister of Chilperic of Neustria's first wife, a feud which was intensified by the rivalry between the two kingdoms.

Frederick I 1657–1713 •*King of Prussia and Elector of Brandenberg*• Born in Königsberg, Prussia (now Kaliningrad, Russia), the second son of **Frederick William**, the Great Elector, he married (1684) Sophia Charlotte (1668–1705), sister of **George I** of Great Britain, and succeeded his father as Frederick III, Elector of Brandenberg (1688). In return for military aid to Emperor **Leopold I** in the War of the Spanish Succession (1701–14), he was made the first king of Prussia (1701). He maintained a large court, and was a great patron of the arts and of learning (especially of **Gottfried Leibniz**) and encouraged the influx of Huguenots to create new industries. During his reign the Academy of Sciences at Berlin and the University of Halle were founded.

Frederick II, *known as* **Frederick the Great** 1712–86 •*King of Prussia*• He was born in Berlin, the son of **Frederick William I**, and of Sophia-Dorothea, daughter of **George I** of Great Britain. His early years were devoted to military training and a rigid system of education, against which he initially rebelled, to no avail. In 1733 he dutifully accepted as his bride the Princess Elizabeth of Brunswick-Wolfenbüttel (1715–97), and he was restored to favor. On May 31, 1740, Frederick became king; and in October the accession of **Maria Theresa** separated the crown of Austria from the imperial diadem. Frederick, in possession of a fine army and a well-filled treasury, seized the opportunity. He entered Silesia (December 1740), defeated the Austrians at Mollwitz (1741) and Chotusitz (1742), and, after concluding an alliance for 15 years with France, forced Maria Theresa to yield him Upper and Lower Silesia by the Treaty of Breslau (1742). The second Silesian War (1744–45) left Frederick with increased territories and a reputation as one of the best military commanders of the day. The next 11 years were years of peace but in 1756 the third Silesian War, the "Seven Years' War," began. Frederick anticipated the attack by taking the offensive, and displayed great courage and military genius. In 1772 he shared in the first partition of Poland, by which he acquired Polish Prussia and a portion of Great Poland. In 1778 he completed the acquisition of the Franconian duchies. One of his last political actions was the formation of the "Fürstenbund," which marked the emergence of Prussia as a rival to Austria for the lead in Germany. By the end of his reign the area of Prussia had doubled, and, despite a temporary eclipse under **Napoleon I**, the foundation of Prussia's greatness was laid. Frederick was essentially a just, if somewhat austere man, and the administration of justice under his rule was pure, the press enjoyed comparative freedom, and freedom of conscience was promoted.

“ ”

My people and I have come to an agreement that satisfies us both. They are to say what they please, and I am to do what I please.

Attributed.

Frederick I (Barbarossa) c. 1123–90 •*Holy Roman Emperor and king of Germany and Italy*• Of the **Hohenstaufen** family, he was the son of Frederick, Duke of Swabia. He succeeded his uncle **Conrad III** as Emperor in 1152. Earnest and distinguished, he channeled his intelligence and enthusiasm into establishing German predominance in western Europe. In 1162 his conquest of Milan subdued the rebellious Italian states, but his failure to defeat the pope led to revolt in Lombardy. After his defeat at Legnano (1176) he won Lombard support by more lenient rule, and in 1177 he acknowledged **Alexander III** as pope, and finally achieved peace (1183). In Germany, Frederick increased the authority of his strongest rebels and checked the weaker by supporting their municipal communities. He subdued **Henry the Lion** of Bavaria, and gained authority over Poland, Hungary, Denmark and Burgundy. In 1189 he led the Third Crusade against **Saladin**, defeating the Muslims at Philomelium and Iconium, but drowned at Cilicia. His son, **Henry VI**, succeeded him.

Frederick II 1194–1250 •*Holy Roman Emperor and king of Germany*• The last great ruler of the **Hohenstaufen**s, he was born in Jesi, near Ancona, the grandson of **Frederick I (Barbarossa)** and son of Emperor **Henry VI**. He inherited Sicily from his mother (1198). In 1212 he took the imperial crown from **Otto IV**, gaining Pope **Innocent III**'s sanction (1215) for his coronation in 1220. During his crusade (1228–29) he captured Bethlehem and Nazareth, and crowned himself king of Jerusalem, but when he returned to Italy he experienced difficulties with the papacy, and was temporarily deposed. In 1235 he married the daughter of King **John** of England and sister of **Henry III**. Frederick tolerated Jews and Muslims, encouraged free trade, recognized popular representation by parliaments, and anticipated the humanistic movement, but persecuted heretics and upheld absolute sovereignty. He wrote poetry and a book on falconry. A complex figure of sharp contradictions, he was referred to as *stupor mundi* ("the amazement of the world"). However, his claim of imperial preeminence coincided with the historical development of separate nation-states.

Frederick III 1415–93 •*Holy Roman Emperor and king of Germany*• Born in Innsbruck, Austria, the son of Duke Ernest of Austria, he was elected king of Germany as Frederick IV (1440) and crowned emperor (1452). His reign was one of anarchy, with wars raging on the frontiers of the empire and disorders within. During its course Frederick lost his hold upon Switzerland, Milan, Bohemia and Hungary, purchased peace from his brother Albert in Upper Austria, and failed to oppose two Turkish invasions (1469, 1475). Nevertheless, by the marriage (1477) of his son, **Maximilian I**, to Mary, daughter of **Charles the Bold** of Burgundy, he laid the foundation of the subsequent greatness of the **Habsburg** dynasty. Although he neglected government for alchemy, astrology and botany, he lost no opportunity to aggrandize his own family, and from his time the Holy Roman Empire was almost exclusively ruled by the House of Austria.

Frederick V, *known as* **the Winter King** 1596–1632 •*Elector Palatine and king of Bohemia*• The son of Elector Frederick IV, he was born in Amberg, Upper Palatinate, and educated at the Huguenot academy at Sedan. He became Elector Palatine (1610–23) and in 1613 married **Elizabeth**, daughter of **James VI and I** of Scotland and England. Their daughter **Sophia** became the mother of **George I** of Great Britain. Under the refined young couple, Heidelberg, the capital of the Palatinate, became known for its artistic and cultural life. During his father's reign, the Protestant Union had been formed under Palatine leadership (1608), and when in 1619 the crown of Bohemia was offered to Frederick his Calvinist ministers urged him to accept. His regal power lasted only one winter (1619–20), hence his nickname, and the Bohemian Protestants were routed by imperial forces at the White Mountain, near Prague (1620). His hereditary lands passed to his Catholic cousin, Maximilian I of Bavaria. His son, Charles Louis, recovered his electorate at the Peace of Westphalia (1648).

Frederick Augustus, Duke of York and Albany 1763–1827 •*English nobleman*• Born at St James's Palace, London, the second son of **George III** of Great Britain, he was a soldier by profession, but was unsuccessful both in the field in the Netherlands (1793–99) and as British Commander in Chief (1798–1809), and earned the nickname of the "grand old Duke of York" in the nursery rhyme. However, his painstaking reform of the army proved of lasting benefit, especially to the Duke of **Wellington**.

Frederick Charles, Prince, *called* **the Iron Prince** or **the Red Prince** 1828–85 •*Prussian field marshal*• Born in Berlin, he was the nephew of the emperor **Wilhelm I**. He commanded the right wing in the Danish War (1864), and in the Seven Weeks' War of 1866 against Austria helped to win the victory of Königgrätz. In the Franco-German War (1870–71) he commanded the second army, drove Marshal **Achille Bazaine** into Metz, which capitulated, and, promoted to field marshal, then captured Orléans, broke up the army of the Loire, and scattered Antoine Chanzy (1823–83) and his troops at Le Mans.

Frederick Louis 1707–51 •*Prince of Wales*• Born in Hanover, he was the eldest son of **George II** and his queen **Caroline of Ansbach**, and father of **George III**. He married Princess Augusta of Saxe-Gotha (1736). In 1737 he joined the parliamentary opposition, which was centered on his new home, Leicester House, and was banished from court.

Frederick William I 1688–1740 •*King of Prussia*• Born in Berlin, he succeeded his father, **Frederick I**, in 1713. Boorishly contemptuous of art and learning, but thrifty and practical, he had a passion for soldiering which secured him Swedish Pomerania, with Stettin. He laid the foundation of the future power of Prussia by establishing a centralized hierarchy of administrative offices and an efficient army that he increased to 80,000 men. He encouraged native industries, particularly wool (to clothe the army), introduced compulsory primary education, resettled his eastern provinces, and pursued a policy of religious toleration. He was succeeded by his son **Frederick II (the Great)**.

Frederick William II 1744–97 •*King of Prussia*• Born in Berlin, he was the nephew and successor in 1786 of **Frederick II (the Great)**. He soon lost the regard of his subjects by his predilection for unworthy favorites and his abrogation of the freedom of the press and religion (1788). He dissipated the fortune his uncle left in the treasury in a useless war with Holland. He acquired large areas of Polish Prussia and Silesia by the partitions of Poland (1793, 1795), and also Ansbach, Bayreuth and Danzig. He presided over a flourishing Berlin culture; he played the cello, and **Mozart** and **Beethoven** dedicated chamber music to him.

Frederick William III 1770–1840 •*King of Prussia*• Born in Potsdam, he succeeded his father, **Frederick William II** in 1797. At first he was neutral toward **Napoleon I** but eventually declared war against him in 1806. After defeat at Jena and Auerstädt, he fled into East Prussia, and by the Treaty of Tilsit (1807) lost all his territories west of the Elbe. Prussia was finally victorious at Leipzig (1813). The territories west of the Elbe were returned at the Treaty of Vienna (1815) and other territorial gains made. The latter part of his reign was one of reaction. The democratic movements of 1819 and 1830 were rigorously suppressed, and the freedom of the press curtailed. Nevertheless, provincial diets were established (1823), education was encouraged, and the *Zollverein*, or customs union, was established.

Frederick William IV 1795–1861 •*King of Prussia*• Born in Cölln, near Berlin, he succeeded his father, **Frederick William III**, in 1840, and began his reign by granting minor reforms and promising, but never fulfilling, radical changes. He was possessed by vague ideas of the divine right of kings, and by a mystic pietism. He refused the Imperial Crown offered to him by the liberal Frankfurt Diet (1849), and opposed the popular movement of 1848, but was forced to establish a representative parliament (1850). In 1857, having become insane, he resigned the administration to his brother, who from 1858 acted as regent until his accession as **Wilhelm I**.

Frederick William, *known as* **the Great Elector** 1620–88 •*Elector of Brandenburg*• He was born near Berlin. After his accession in 1640, he was responsible for rebuilding the war-ravaged and sparsely populated electorate, adding to the Hohenzollern territories, establishing an effective standing army, crushing the Estates, and reorganizing the privy council and civil service. He supported Sweden, then Poland, in the First Northern War (1655–60), switched from the anti-French alliance of 1674 to support for **Louis XIV** in 1679, and returned to his anti-French stance in the 1680s. Tolerant regarding religion, he granted asylum by the Edict of Potsdam (1685) to Huguenots expelled from France following Louis's revocation of the Edict of Nantes, recognizing their economic potential. He established the Royal Library and Art Gallery in Berlin, and founded the University of Duisburg.

Frederik I 1471–1533 •*King of Denmark and Norway*• The son of **Christian I** and uncle of **Christian II**, he was Duke of Holstein before being chosen king (1523) when Christian II, who had just lost Sweden to **Gustav I Vasa**, was dethroned by a rebellion in Denmark. An invasion of Norway (1531–32) by the ex-king failed. Frederik died soon afterward, and was succeeded by his son **Christian III**.

Frederik II 1534–88 •*King of Denmark and Norway*• Born in Hadenslev, he succeeded his father, **Christian III** (1559), and soon became involved in a seven-year war against Sweden and its deranged king, **Erik XIV**, which ended with the inconclusive Treaty of Stettin (1570). The remainder of his reign was a period of peace and prosperity. He built the magnificent Renaissance castle of Kronborg at Elsinore, to which he brought English musicians to provide entertainment, and was a patron of the astronomer **Tycho Brahe** and other scientists. He was succeeded by his young son, **Christian IV**. His daughter, **Anne of Denmark**, married King **James VI and I** of Scotland and England.

Frederik III 1609–70 •*King of Denmark and Norway*• The son and successor of **Christian IV**, he was born at Haderslev. The first half of his reign (1648–70) was taken up with costly wars against Sweden, but after the peace settlement of 1660 he established absolute hereditary monarchy over Denmark, Norway and Iceland, embodied in the Royal Law (*Kongelov*) of 1665. He founded the Royal Library in Copenhagen. Under him the bourgeoisie were able to increase its hold over the government and former crown lands.

Frederik VI 1768–1839 •*King of Denmark and Norway*• Born at Christiansborg Castle, the son of **Christian VII**, he was appointed regent (1784) when his father was declared insane, and became king of both Denmark and Norway in 1808. He abolished serfdom, amended the criminal code, prohibited the slave trade in Danish colonies, and promoted free trade and industrial development. During the Napoleonic Wars, the Danish fleet was destroyed off Copenhagen by **Nelson** (1801), and in 1807, despite Danish neutrality, Copenhagen was bombarded for three days. This forced Denmark into the arms of **Napoleon I**, and with the overthrow of Napoleon's empire (1814), Denmark lost Norway to Sweden. He granted a new constitution with four consultative provincial assemblies (1834), which was the start of parliamentary democracy in Denmark. He was succeeded by his son, **Christian VIII**.

Frederik VII 1808–63 •*King of Denmark*• Born at Amalienborg Castle, the son and successor (1848) of **Christian VIII**, he was the last of the Oldenburg line. In 1849 he promulgated a new and liberal constitution abolishing monarchical absolutism. He died childless, and was succeeded by **Christian IX**.

Frederik VIII 1843–1912 •*King of Denmark*• Born in Copenhagen, he was the son and successor (1906) of **Christian IX**, and brother of Queen **Alexandra** of Great Britain. In 1907 he made a state visit to Iceland to celebrate the granting of home rule there (1904). His second son, Prince Carl, became King **Haakon VII** of Norway. He was succeeded by his eldest son, **Christian X**.

Frederik IX 1899–1972 •*King of Denmark*• Born at Sorgenfri Castle, near Copenhagen, he was the son and successor (1947) of **Christian X**. In 1935 he married Ingrid, daughter of King **Gustav VI** of Sweden. During World War II he assisted his father in resistance to the German occupation, and was held under house arrest (1943–45). He was crowned in 1947 and was a popular monarch. He granted home rule to the Faroe Islands (1948), and in 1953 a new constitution provided for female succession to the throne. His eldest daughter became Crown Princess and succeeded him as Queen **Margrethe II** (1972). His youngest daughter, Anne-Marie, married ex-King **Constantine II** of Greece (1964).

Fredrik I 1676–1751 •*King of Sweden*• Born in Kassel, Germany, he fought for England in the War of the Spanish Succession (1701–13). As Prince Frederick of Hesse-Kassel, he married (1715) **Ulrika Eleonora**, the younger sister of King **Karl XII** and future Queen of Sweden. In 1720 his wife abdicated the throne in his favor. He spent most of his time on hunting and love affairs, leaving the government to his chancellor, Arvid Horn. He died childless, and was succeeded by Adolf Fredrik (1710–71).

Freeman, Cathy 1973– •*Australian athlete*• Born in Mackay, Queensland, she won a gold medal in the 4 × 100 meters relay at the 1990 Commonwealth Games and in 1992 became the first Australian Aboriginal to compete in the Olympic Games. She won gold medals in the 400-meter and 200-meter events at the 1994 Commonwealth Games. A controversial defender of Aboriginal rights, she was chosen to light the Olympic flame at the 2000 Sydney Olympics and went on to win the gold medal in the 400-meter event.

Freeman, Morgan 1937– •*US actor*• He was born in Memphis, Tennessee. After serving in the US Air Force, he acted in the theater, winning the Clarence Derwent award for *The Mighty Gents* (1978) and Obie awards for *Coriolanus* (1980), *Mother Courage* (1980) and *The Gospel at Colonus* (1984). He received an Academy Award nomination for his performance as a vicious pimp in *Street Smart* (1987). He was nominated again, re-creating his stage performance as the patient, compassionate chauffeur in *Driving Miss Daisy* (1989). He has subsequently established himself as a versatile character actor, bringing distinction to such popular films as *Robin Hood: Prince of Thieves* (1991), *Unforgiven* (1992) and *Seven* (1995). He received a further Academy Award nomination for *The Shawshank Redemption* (1994).

Frege, (Friedrich Ludwig) Gottlob 1848–1925 •*German logician, mathematician and philosopher*• Born in Wismar, he was educated at the University of Jena, where he spent his whole professional career, becoming professor in 1879. His particular contribution to logic was the theory of quantification. His main works are *Begriffschrift* (1879, "Concept Script"), *Die Grundlagen der Arithmetik* (1884, Eng trans *The Foundations of Arithmetic*, 1950), and *Die Grundgesetze der Arithmetik* (2 vols, 1893, 1903, "Basic Laws of Arithmetic"). He also wrote influential philosophical essays analyzing such basic logical concepts as meaning, sense and reference, and attempted to derive the whole of arithmetic from logic. He is now regarded as the founding father of modern mathematical logic and the philosophy of language.

Frei (Montalva), Eduardo 1911–82 •*Chilean politician*• He became one of the leaders of the Social-Christian Falange Party in the late 1930s, and of the new Christian Democratic Party after 1957. His presidency (1964–70) saw an ambitious program of social reform, which brought Chile substantial international support. By the time of his death, he was widely seen as the father of opposition to the dictatorship.

Frémont, John Charles 1813–90 •*US explorer and politician*• Born in Savannah, Georgia, he started surveying in 1838. In 1842 he crossed the Rocky Mountains (where a peak is named after him), and demonstrated the feasibility of an overland route across the continent. In 1843 he explored the Great Salt Lake, and in 1845 examined the continental watershed. After participating in the annexation of Upper California in 1847, he became a senator of California in 1850. He was the Republican and antislavery candidate for the presidency in 1856 but was defeated by **James Buchanan**.

French, Daniel Chester 1850–1931 •*US sculptor*• Born in Exeter, New Hampshire, he studied sculpture in New York and in 1873–74 produced *The Minuteman* monument to the American Revolution for the town of Concord, Massachusetts. Following a period in Florence, he studied at the École des Beaux-Arts in Paris from 1886 to 1888. He produced a 60-foot-high *Statue of the Republic* for the 1893 Chicago World's Fair and the seated figure of **Abraham Lincoln** for the Lincoln Memorial in Washington DC (1918–22).

French, Dawn 1957– •*English comedienne and actress*• Born in Holyhead, she trained at the Central School of Speech and Drama, where she met **Jennifer Saunders**. Starting at the Comedy Store in London, they created a double act that took them to the forefront of the "alternative" comedy of the time. After appearing in *The Comic Strip Presents ...* films on television (1982–93), the duo were given their own successful BBC series, *French and Saunders* (1987–). They also wrote and starred in *Girls on Top* (1985–86). Outside the partnership, French has appeared on television in *Murder Most Horrid* (1991–) and *The Vicar of Dibley* (1994–). She has also appeared widely on stage and in films such as *The Strike* (1988). She married comedian **Lenny Henry** in 1984.

French, Sir John Denton Pinkstone, 1st Earl of Ypres 1852–1925 •*English field marshal*• He was born in Ripple, Kent. He joined the navy in 1866, but transferred to the army in 1874. He was with the 19th Hussars in Sudan (1884–85), and was cavalry commander in South Africa in the Second Boer War (1899–1901). Chief of the Imperial General Staff from 1911–14, he was promoted to field marshal in 1913 and took command of the British Expeditionary Force in France in 1914. He was superseded by General **Haig** and became Commander in Chief of the home forces in 1915.

Freni, Mirella 1936– •*Italian soprano*• She was born in Modena, where her mother worked in the same cigarette factory as the mother of **Luciano Pavarotti**—later to be her operatic partner in many productions. By the age of 20 she had appeared with the Modena Opera as Micaela in *Carmen*. International success followed quickly with, among others, the Netherlands Opera (1959), Glyndebourne (1960), Covent Garden (1961) and La Scala (1962). In 1963 she played Mimi in **Herbert von Karajan**'s film of *La Bohème*.

Fresnel, Augustin Jean 1788–1827 •*French physicist*• Born in Broglie, he was head of the Department of Public Works in Paris. His intensive study of the problem of projecting well-defined beams of light led to the celebrated multifaceted lighthouse lens (the Fresnel lens). His investigations contributed greatly to the establishment of the wave theory of light. He also invented a special prism (Fresnel's rhomb) to produce circularly polarized light. His most brilliant papers were a series published in 1818–21 relating polarization phenomena to **Thomas Young**'s hypothesis of transverse waves, and his *Œuvres Complètes* ("Complete Works"), published in three volumes in the 1860s, contains practically everything that was known in optics up to the time of his death.

Freud, Anna 1895–1982 •*British psychoanalyst*• Born in Vienna, Austria, the youngest daughter of **Sigmund Freud**, she taught at the Cottage Lyceum there, and emigrated (1938) with her father to London, where she organized (1940–45) a residential war nursery for homeless children. A pioneer of child psychoanalysis, she founded the Hampstead Child Therapy Clinic. Her works include *The Ego and the Mechanism of Defence* (1937) and *Beyond the Best Interests of the Child* (1973).

Freud, Lucian 1922– •*British painter*• Born in Berlin, Germany, he is a grandson of **Sigmund Freud**. After moving to Great Britain in 1931, he studied at the Central School of Arts and Crafts in London (1938–39) and the East Anglian School of Painting and Drawing, Dedham (1939–42). In his early years he was one of the Neo-Romantic group of English painters, but since the mid-1940s he has developed a linear, realistic style. This is seen best in his acutely observed portraits and nude studies, such as *Girl With a White Dog* (1951–52, Tate, London). From c. 1958, he developed a freer style, painting his figures from disconcerting angles, shown in *Standing by the Rags* (1988–89, Tate Britain). Exhibitions of his work in 1974 (London) and 1987 (Washington DC) contributed to international interest in his traditional, representational style, which continued into the 1990s, with a major exhibition in 1996 in Kendal, Cumbria, attracting over 25,000 visitors. He became a British citizen in 1939, and was appointed to the Order of Merit in 1993.

Freud, Sigmund 1856–1939 •*Austrian neurologist, the founder of psychoanalysis*• He was born in Freiburg, Moravia. He studied medicine at Vienna and joined the staff of the Vienna General Hospital in 1882, specializing in neurology. He collaborated with the Austrian neurologist Joseph Breuer in the treatment of hysteria by the recall of painful experiences under hypnosis, then moved to Paris in 1885 to study under **Jean Martin Charcot**; it was there that he changed from neurology to psychopathology. Returning to Vienna, he developed the technique of conversational free association in place of hypnosis and refined psychoanalysis as a method of treatment. In 1895 he published, with Breuer, *Studien über Hysterie* (Eng trans *Studies on Hysteria*, 1955), but two years later their friendship ended as a result of Freud's controversial theories of infantile sexuality. In 1900 he published his seminal work, *Die Traumdeutung* (Eng trans *Interpretation of Dreams*, 1913), arguing that dreams, like neuroses, are disguised manifestations of repressed sexual desires. He was appointed Extraordinary Professor of Neuropathology at the University of Vienna in 1902; there he began to hold weekly seminars in his home with kindred minds like **Alfred Adler**. In 1908 these weekly meetings became those of the Vienna Psychoanalytical Society, and, in 1910, the International Psychoanalytical Association, with **Carl Jung** as its first president. Both Adler (1911) and Jung (1913) broke with Freud to develop their own theories. Undeterred, Freud produced *Totem und Tabu* (1913, Eng trans *Totem and Taboo*, 1918), *Jenseits des Lustprinzips* (1920, Eng trans *Beyond the Pleasure Principle*, 1922) and *Das Ich und das Es* (1923, Eng trans *The Ego and the Id*, 1927), elaborating his theories of the division of the unconscious mind into the id, the ego, and the superego. He was awarded the prestigious Goethe Prize in 1930, and in 1933 published *Warum Krieg?* (Eng trans *Why War?*, 1933), a correspondence between Freud and **Albert Einstein**. In 1938, after the annexation of Austria, Freud was extricated from Vienna and brought to London with his family. He made his home in Hampstead, but died of cancer the following year.

> I am actually not at all a man of science… I am by temperament nothing but a conquistador, an adventurer.
>
> *1900 Letter to Wilhelm Fliess, February.*

Freyberg, Bernard, 1st Baron Freyberg 1889–1963 •*New Zealand soldier*• Born in London, he was educated at Wellington College, New Zealand. At the outbreak of World War I he enlisted in England and served in Gallipoli and France, winning the Victoria Cross at Beaumont Hamel. In World War II he was given command of the New Zealand forces in the Middle East. He commanded Commonwealth forces in ill-fated operations in Greece and Crete (1941) and in the Sahara. He commanded the New Zealand Corps in Italy (1944–45), and was Governor-General of New Zealand (1946–52).

Freyre, Gilberto de Mello 1900–87 •*Brazilian writer and intellectual*• Born in Recife, he was educated in Rio de Janeiro and in Texas and New York City. A prolific author, he came to prominence with a large-scale historical work, *Casa-grande & senzala* (1933, Eng trans *The Masters and the Slaves*, 1946), which altered previous thinking about colonial Brazil and its relations with Europe. The book won him the Felipe d'Oliveira award (1934), the first of many prestigious prizes and honorary doctorates.

Freyssinet, Marie Eugène Léon 1879–1962 •*French civil engineer*• Born in Objat, Corrèze, he graduated from both the École Polytechnique and the École des Ponts et Chaussées in Paris. His intuitive rather than analytical approach to reinforced concrete design reached its height in his airship hangars at Orly (1916–24, destroyed 1944) where he used corrugated parabolic arches over 200 feet high yet only $3\frac{1}{2}$ inches thick. He succeeded in developing practical techniques for prestressing concrete by the use of stretched steel tendons, and from 1930 he was one of the leading exponents of this virtually new structural material.

Freytag, Gustav 1816–95 •*German novelist and playwright*• He was born in Kreuzburg, Silesia. A deputy to the North German Diet, he attended the Prussian crown prince in the Franco-German campaign (1870). His comedies and other plays, such as *Die Valentine* (1846), proved brilliant successes, but his greatest achievement is *Soll und Haben* (1855, Eng trans *Debit and Credit*, 1857), a realistic novel of German commercial life. It was followed by *Die Verlorene Handschrift* (1864, Eng trans *The Lost Manuscript*, 1865), and the series called *Die Ahnen* (1872–81, "The Ancestors").

Frick, Henry Clay 1849–1919 •*US industrialist and philanthropist*• Born in West Overton, Pennsylvania, he received little education, but capitalized on post–Civil War expansion by forming a company to supply the Pittsburgh steel mills with coke, and was a millionaire at age 30. **Andrew Carnegie** was associated with Frick from 1884, and invited him to become chairman of the Carnegie Steel Company in 1889. He was a hard and ruthless employer, unsuccessfully using 200 hired Pinkerton guards in pitched battle to dislodge strikers at the Carnegie steel plant at Homestead, Pennsylvania (1892), and, when the guards failed, called in the Pennsylvania National Guard. The strike was broken, but Frick was shot and stabbed, although he ultimately recovered. He later became director of **John Pierpont Morgan**'s United States Steel (1901). He built up the distinguished Frick Collection of fine art, now a museum in New York City. He also endowed hospitals, schools and a large park in Pittsburgh.

Frick, Wilhelm 1877–1946 •*German Nazi politician*• Born in Alsenz, he participated in **Hitler**'s Munich putsch (1923), led the Nazi faction in the Reichstag from 1924, and as Minister of the Interior from 1933 banned trade unionism and freedom of the press, and encouraged anti-Semitism. Ousted by **Heinrich Himmler** in 1943, he became "Protector" of Bohemia and Moravia. He was found guilty of war crimes at Nuremberg and executed.

Fricker, Peter Racine 1920–90 •*English composer*• Born in London, he studied at the Royal College of Music, was musical director of Morley College, London (1952–64), and then moved to the University of California, Santa Barbara (1964). The influence of **Béla Bartók** and **Arnold Schoenberg** is apparent in such works as the First Symphony (1948–49) and the Sonata for Violin and Piano

(1950). Later works include symphonies, a cello sonata, an oratorio, and other chamber, choral and keyboard pieces.

Friday, Nancy 1937– •*US feminist author*• She was born in Pittsburgh, Pennsylvania, the daughter of a financier, and was educated at Wellesley College. Her best-known work, *My Secret Garden* (1976), which exploded the myth surrounding women's sexual fantasies, sold over 1.5 million copies worldwide. In 1980 she published *Men in Love*, an exploration of men and their sexual fantasies. *Women on Top* (1991) reexamines modern women in the context of feminism and renewed sexual freedom, and documents the manner in which women appear to have incorporated male pornography into their own sexual fantasies. These issues are dealt with again in *Forbidden Flowers* (1994).

Fried, Alfred Hermann 1864–1921 •*Austrian pacifist and Nobel Prize winner*• He was born in Vienna, and founded the *Deutsche Friedensgesellschaft* (German Society for Peace) in Berlin in 1892. In World War I he lived in Switzerland, and on its conclusion he protested against the terms of the Treaty of Versailles, while maintaining his pacifist stance. He shared the Nobel Prize for peace with **Tobias Asser** in 1911.

Friedan, Betty (Elizabeth Naomi), *née* **Goldstein** 1921– •*US feminist and writer*• Born in Peoria, Illinois, she was educated at Smith College. She wrote a best-selling book, *The Feminine Mystique* (1963), which analyzed the role of women in US society and articulated their frustrations. She was founder and first president of the National Association for Women (1966), and headed the National Women's Strike for Equality (1970). In *The Second Stage* (1981), she emphasized the importance of both the new and the traditional female roles. She also wrote *The Fountain of Age* (1993), which explores the virtues and possibilities of old age.

Friedman, Herbert 1916–2000 •*US astrophysicist*• Born in New York City and educated at Brooklyn College and Johns Hopkins University, he spent his career at the US Naval Research Laboratory in Washington. From the 1940s he initiated the use of rockets carrying detectors to study X-rays from space. In 1949 he began investigations of the X-ray activity of the sun, producing the first X-ray and ultraviolet photographs of the sun in 1960. He also showed that an X-ray source in the constellation Taurus coincided with the remnant of a luminous supernova in the Crab Nebula (1964). After this early work, X-ray astronomy developed as an important area of astrophysics, as has the use of rockets to transport astronomical instruments above the absorbing layer of the earth's atmosphere.

Friedman, Milton 1912– •*US economist and Nobel Prize winner*• He was born in New York City and educated there and in Chicago. After eight years at the National Bureau of Economic Research (1937–45), he became Professor of Economics at the University of Chicago (1946–83), now emeritus, where he became the foremost exponent of monetarism. In such works as *A Monetary History of the United States, 1867–1960* (1963) and *Inflation: Causes and Consequences* (1963) he argued that a country's economy can be controlled through its money supply. He was awarded the 1976 Nobel Prize for economics, and was a policy adviser to the **Reagan** administration (1981–88). His ideas were applied in Great Britain by **Margaret Thatcher**.

“ ”

No major institution in the US has so poor a record of performance over so long a period as the Federal Reserve, yet so high a public reputation.

1988 "The Fed Has No Clothes," in the ***Wall Street Journal****, April 15.*

Friedrich, Caspar David 1774–1840 •*German painter*• Born in Pomerania, he studied at the Academy of Copenhagen from 1794 to 1798, then spent the rest of his life in Dresden. His work won the approval of **Goethe**, and in 1805 he won a Weimar Art Society prize. His paintings from c. 1808 were highly controversial in their treatment of landscape as vast and desolate expanses in which man—often a solitary figure—is depicted as a melancholy spectator of nature's awesome power. Such works helped establish the notion of the sublime as a central concern of the Romantic movement.

Friel, Brian 1929– •*Northern Irish playwright and short-story writer*• He was born in Omagh, County Tyrone, and studied for the priesthood in Maynooth, Ireland, choosing not to enter it upon graduation in 1948. He then taught for 10 years in Londonderry. His first major success was *Philadelphia, Here I Come!* (1964), a play about emigration and the relationship between a man and his son. Friel's writing often concentrates on the relation between people, language, custom and the land, which form the principal theme of the plays *Translations* (1980) and *Dancing at Lughnasa* (1990). With actor Stephen Rea, Friel cofounded the Field Day Theatre Company (1980). His short-story collections include *A Saucer of Larks* (1962).

Frink, Dame Elisabeth 1930–93 •*English sculptor*• Born in Thurlow, Suffolk, she entered Guildford Art School in 1947, then trained at Chelsea School of Art. She taught there for 10 years and at Central St Martins College of Art, London, and was a visiting lecturer at the Royal College. Her work displays a combination of sensuality, strength and vulnerability, seen particularly in her series of horse and rider sculptures. She undertook many major public commissions and worked in France (1967–73) before returning to live and work in Dorset. She was given the honorary title of Dame Commander, Order of the British Empire, in 1982.

Frisch, Karl von 1886–1982 •*Austrian ethologist, zoologist and Nobel Prize winner*• Born in Vienna, he studied zoology at the Universities of Munich and Trieste. After teaching at several universities he settled in Munich, where he established the Zoological Institute in 1932. He was a key figure in developing ethology using field observation of animals combined with ingenious experiments. He is mainly remembered for his later work on honeybees. He demonstrated that bees are able to distinguish odors, tastes and colors, and that the honeybee's visual spectrum allows it to see ultraviolet light, and described how hive bees communicate the location of a source of food by means of coded dances. In 1949 he further showed that bees can navigate even on cloudy days by making use of the pattern of polarized light in the sky. In 1973 he shared the Nobel Prize for physiology or medicine with other pioneers of ethology, **Konrad Lorenz** and **Nikolaas Tinbergen**. His books include *Aus dem Leben der Bienen* (1927, Eng trans *The Dancing Bees* 1954) and *Animal Architecture* (1974).

Frisch, Max Rudolph 1911–91 •*Swiss novelist and playwright*• Born in Zurich, his *Blätter aus dem Brotsack* (1940, Eng trans *Leaves From a Knapsack*, 1942), was published while he was serving with the Swiss frontier guard. As a novelist he is chiefly known outside German-speaking Europe for the novels *Stiller* (1954, Eng trans *I'm Not Stiller*, 1958), *Homo Faber* (1957, Eng trans 1959) and *Der Mensch erscheint im Holozän* (1979, Eng trans *Man in the Holocene*, 1980). As a playwright, he was a disciple of **Bertolt Brecht** in the 1940s, and his *Biedermann und die Brandstifter* (1953, Eng trans *The Fire Raisers*, 1962) and *Andorra* (1961, Eng trans 1962) have become modern stage classics.

“ ”

Ich kann nur berichten, was ich weiß.

I can only report on what I know.

1957 ***Homo Faber****, part 1.*

Frisch, Otto Robert 1904–79 •*British physicist*• Born in Vienna, Austria, and educated at Vienna University, he became assistant to **Otto Stern** in 1930 and worked with him and **Emilio Segrè** on diffraction experiments. In 1933, as a result of the Nazi racial laws, Frisch left Germany to work with **Patrick Blackett** at Imperial College, London, before moving to **Niels Bohr**'s institute in Copenhagen. In 1939, with **Lise Meitner** (his aunt), he confirmed that **Otto Hahn**'s observation of uranium splitting was due to nuclear fission. During World War II he worked at the University of Birmingham, where he and Sir **Rudolf Peierls** studied the possibility of nuclear chain reactions. This work led to his involvement in the British and US atom bomb projects, and he worked for a time at Los Alamos on the Manhattan Project. After the war he became head of the nuclear physics division of the Atomic Energy Research Establishment at Harwell, and later accepted a chair at Cambridge.

Frisch, Ragnar Anton Kittil 1895–1973 •*Norwegian economist and Nobel Prize winner*• Born in Oslo, he studied there, and was Professor of Economics at Oslo University from 1931 to 1965, and editor of *Econometrica* (1933–55). He was a pioneer of econometrics, the application of statistics to economic planning. He shared the first Nobel Prize for economics in 1969 with **Jan Tinbergen**.

Frith, William Powell 1819–1909 •*English painter*• Born in Aldfield, he became the wealthiest artist of his time by selling both paintings and their copyrights. The Pre-Raphaelites criticized the vulgarity of his historical and genre works, but he took a new direction with his huge canvases of Victorian scenes, *Ramsgate Sands* (1854, bought by Queen **Victoria** for Buckingham Palace), *Derby Day* (1858, Tate Britain, London) and *The Railway Station* (1862, Holloway College), which achieved huge popular success and were hailed by **John Ruskin** as the art of the future.

Fritsch, Elizabeth 1940– •*English potter*• Born in Shropshire, she studied harp and piano at the Royal Academy of Music before attending the Royal College of Art, London. One of the most talented contemporary potters of her generation, she uses coiling spires and geometric patterns in colored slips with a mat texture akin to ivory frescoes.

Frobenius, Ferdinand Georg 1849–1917 •*German mathematician*• Born in Berlin, he studied at the Universities of Göttingen and Berlin, and taught at Zurich and Berlin. After early work on the theory of differential equations, he founded the theory of group representations, using it both to clarify the notion of an abstract group and also to derive the properties of groups inaccessible by more direct methods. Representation theory later became essential in quantum mechanics and a major theme in the mathematics of the 20th century.

Frobisher, Sir Martin c.1535–94 •*English sailor*• Born in Altofts, near Wakefield, Yorkshire, he was sent to sea as a boy. In 1576, with the *Gabriel* and the *Michael*, he set off in search of a northwest passage to Cathay, reached Labrador and discovered Frobisher Bay. From two expeditions (1577, 1578) he brought back "black earth" which was supposed to be gold from Frobisher Bay. He commanded a vessel in 1585 in **Francis Drake**'s expedition to the West Indies, and was knighted for his services against the Armada. He was mortally wounded at the siege of Crozon, near Brest, France.

Fröding, Gustaf 1860–1911 •*Swedish poet*• Born in Alstern, near Karlstad, he studied at Uppsala, and became a schoolmaster and journalist, but suffered from mental illness. He is considered the greatest Swedish lyric poet, often compared to **Robert Burns**, combining dialect and folksong rhythm in his portrayal of local characters, as in *Guitarr och dragharmonika* (1891, "Guitar and Concertina") and *Räggler å paschaser* (1896, "Drops and Fragments").

Froebel, Friedrich Wilhelm August 1782–1852 •*German educationist and founder of the kindergarten system*• Born in Oberweissbach, he studied in Jena, Göttingen and Berlin, and in 1805 began teaching at Frankfurt am Main. In 1816 he put into practice his educational system at a school that he founded in Griesheim. He expounded its aim (to help the child's mind to grow naturally and spontaneously) in *Die Menschenerziehung* (1826, Eng trans *The Education of Man*, 1885). He opened his first kindergarten school at Blankenburg (1836).

Froissart, Jean c.1333–c.1404 •*French chronicler and poet*• Born in Valenciennes, Hainault, he served **Philippa of Hainault**, the wife of **Edward III** of England (1361–69), and traveled in Scotland, France and Italy. His *Chroniques* (Eng trans *Chronicles*, 1523–25) cover European history from 1325 to 1400. Mainly occupied with France, England, Scotland and Flanders during the Hundred Years' War (1337–1453), he also supplies valuable information about Germany, Italy and Spain. He wrote poems for noble patrons and became private chaplain to Guy of Châtillon.

Fromm, Erich 1900–80 •*US psychoanalyst and social philosopher*• Born in Frankfurt, Germany, he was educated at the Universities of Frankfurt, Heidelberg and Munich, and at the Psychoanalytic Institute of Berlin. He emigrated to the US in 1934, and after holding various university appointments became professor in New York (1962). He emphasized social, economic and cultural factors on human behavior. His works include *Man for Himself* (1947), *Psychoanalysis and Religion* (1951) and *The Heart of Man* (1964).

Frontenac, Louis de Buade, Comte de 1622–98 •*French-Canadian politician*• In 1672 he was appointed governor of the French possessions in North America. He extended the boundaries of New France down the Mississippi, launched attacks on New England villages, repulsed the British siege of Quebec (1690) and defeated the Iroquois.

Fronto, Marcus Cornelius c.100–c.176 AD •*Roman orator*• Born in Cirta, Numidia (North Africa), he was entrusted by **Antoninus Pius** with the education of **Marcus Aurelius** and Lucius Verus. In AD 143 he was consul with Herodes Atticus. Two series of his letters to Marcus Aurelius were discovered in Milan in 1815.

Frost, Sir David Paradine 1939– •*English broadcaster and businessman*• Born in Tenterden, Kent, and educated at Cambridge, he entered television in 1961. He hosted *That Was the Week That Was* (1962–63), an irreverent late-night revue show with topical satire. Shows in Great Britain and the US include *The Frost Report* (1966–67), *The David Frost Show* (1969–72) and *Breakfast with Frost* (1993–), and he has been a diligent interviewer of world leaders in *The Nixon Interviews* (1976–77) and *The Shah Speaks* (1980). A producer of films like *The Slipper and the Rose* (1976), he was also a cofounder and presenter of Britain's *TV-am* (1983–92). His many international honors include the Golden Rose of Montreux (1967). He was knighted in 1993.

Frost, Robert (Lee) 1874–1963 •*US lyric poet*• Born in San Francisco, he studied at Dartmouth and Harvard but did not graduate. As a teacher, cobbler and New Hampshire farmer he wrote poetry that he was unable to get published. From 1912 to 1915 he lived in Great Britain, where, encouraged by **Rupert Brooke** and others, he published *A Boy's Will* (1913) and *North of Boston* (1914), which brought him an international reputation. Returning in glory to the US, he became Professor of English at Amherst (1916), and continued to write lyric and narrative poetry that drew its characters, background and imagery from New England. His volumes of poetry include *West-Running Brook* (1928), *A Witness Tree* (1942), *Steeple Bush* (1947) and *In the Clearing* (1962). He was awarded the Pulitzer Prize in 1924, 1931, 1937 and 1943, and was Professor of Poetry at Harvard from 1939 to 1943 before returning to Amherst (1949–63). Recognized as a major US poet, he read his poem "The Gift Outright" at President **John F Kennedy**'s inauguration in 1961. His *Complete Poems* appeared in 1967.

“ ”

A sentence is a sound in itself on which sounds called words may be strung.

1914 Letter to John Bartlett, February 22.

Frost, Sir Terry (Terence Ernest Manitou) 1915–2003 •*English painter*• Born in Leamington Spa, Warwickshire, he was taken prisoner in Crete in 1941 and spent World War II in POW camps. After the war, he studied under **Victor Pasmore** (1947–50), then moved to St Ives, Cornwall, and later to nearby Newlyn. His first abstract paintings date from 1949 and typically consist of segments of color, as in *Green, Black and White Movement* (1951). Since 1952 he had over 30 solo shows in Great Britain, Europe and the US. He was knighted in 1998.

Froude, James Anthony 1818–94 •*English writer and historian*• Born in Dartington, Devon, he was educated at Westminster and Oriel College, Oxford. In 1842 he was elected a Fellow of Exeter College, Oxford. His early controversial novels, *Shadows of the Clouds* (1847) and *The Nemesis of Faith* (1848), cost him his fellowship. For the next few years he wrote for *Fraser's Magazine* (which he edited for a while) and the *Westminster Review*, and produced his *History of England From the Fall of Wolsey to the Spanish Armada* (12 vols, 1856–69). As literary executor of **Thomas Carlyle** he edited his *Reminiscences* (1881) and **Jane Welsh Carlyle**'s *Letters* (1882), and wrote Carlyle's biography (1882–84). Other works are *Oceana* (1886), *The English in the West Indies* (1888) and *The Spanish Story of the Armada* (1892). He later became Professor of Modern History at

Oxford (1892). He was the brother of **Richard Hurrell Froude** and **William Froude**.

Froude, Richard Hurrell 1803–36 •*English tractarian*• Born in Dartington, Devon, he became Fellow and tutor of Oriel College, Oxford, in 1827. With **John Henry Newman** and **John Keble** he helped to initiate the Oxford Movement, which favored the early and medieval church. His diaries, posthumously published as *Remains* (1838–39), encouraged the development of Anglo-Catholicism. He was the brother of **James Anthony Froude** and **William Froude**.

Froude, William 1810–79 •*English engineer and applied mathematician*• Born in Dartington, Devon, in 1827 he became an assistant to **Isambard Kingdom Brunel**. He was the brother of **James Anthony Froude** and **Richard Hurrell Froude**.

Fry, Christopher Harris 1907– •*English dramatist*• Born in Bristol, he was a schoolmaster before being appointed director of Tunbridge Wells Repertory Players (1932–36). After service in the Non-Combatant Corps during World War II, he began a series of outstanding plays in free verse, often with religious and mystic undertones, including *A Phoenix Too Frequent* (1946), *The Lady's Not for Burning* (1949), *Venus Observed* (1950), *The Dark Is Light Enough* (1954), *Curtmantle* (1962) and *A Yard of Sun* (1970). He has also produced highly successful translations of **Jean Anouilh** and **Jean Giraudoux**.

Fry, Elizabeth, *née* **Gurney** 1780–1845 •*English Quaker prison reformer*• Born in Norwich, Norfolk, she became a preacher for the Society of Friends in 1810. Visiting Newgate Prison for women in 1813 she found 300 women, with their children, in terrible conditions, and thereafter devoted her life to prison and asylum reform at home and abroad. She also founded hostels for the homeless, as well as charitable societies.

Fry, Joseph 1728–87 •*English Quaker businessman and type founder*• Born in Sutton Benger, Wiltshire, he settled in Bristol as a doctor but later went into a pottery enterprise. He founded the chocolate business that bears his name. From 1764 onward he became eminent as a type founder, founding types that were similar to those of **William Caslon**. He also brought out a five-volume version of the Bible (1774–76).

Fry, Roger Eliot 1866–1934 •*English artist and art critic*• He was born in London and was educated at Cambridge. A landscape painter himself, he became a champion of modern artists, particularly **Cézanne**, and organized the first London exhibition of Post-Impressionists in 1910. He wrote extensively on art and aesthetics, propounding a theory of "significant form" and color, rather than content, as the only criteria for great art. He founded the Omega Workshops in London (1913–21), in association with **Vanessa Bell** and **Duncan Grant** and others of the Bloomsbury Group, to design textiles, pottery and furniture. His writings include *Vision and Design* (1920), *Transformations* (1926), *French Art* (1932) and *Reflections on British Painting* (1934).

Fry, Stephen John 1957– •*English actor and writer*• Born in London, he studied at Queen's College, Cambridge, during which time he appeared in more than 30 plays. He later wrote the book for the long-running West End musical *Me and My Girl* (1984–). Frequently partnered by his Cambridge Footlights compatriot Hugh Laurie, he has appeared with him in *A Bit of Fry & Laurie* (1989–95), *Jeeves and Wooster* (1990–93) and the film *Peter's Friends* (1992). Other television work includes *Stalag Luft* (1993) and *Cold Comfort Farm* (1995), and other film work includes *A Handful of Dust* (1988), *A Fish Called Wanda* (1988), and *Wilde* (1996). His novels include *The Liar* (1991) and *Making History* (1996).

Frye, (Herman) Northrop 1912–91 •*Canadian literary critic*• Born in Sherbrooke, Quebec, he studied at the University of Toronto and at Oxford. He joined the faculty at Toronto in 1940 and remained at the university for half a century. Two early works established him as one of the most eminent literary critics of his generation: *Fearful Symmetry* (1947), a study of the writings of **William Blake**; and *Anatomy of Criticism* (1957), an examination of literary archetypes and of the social needs satisfied by myths and symbols. Subsequent writings include *The Educated Imagination* (1964), *Secular Scripture* (1976) and *The Great Code* (1982).

Fuad I 1868–1936 •*Egyptian ruler*• Born in Cairo, the son of Khedive **Ismail Pasha** and father of **Farouk I**, he was sultan of Egypt from 1917 and king from 1922, when the British protectorate was terminated. His reign was a period of uneasy relations with Egyptian nationalists, represented by the Wafd Party.

Fuchs, (Emil) Klaus (Julius) 1912–88 •*British spy and physicist*• Born in Rüsselsheim, Germany, he escaped from Nazi persecution to the UK in 1933, was interned during World War II, then naturalized in 1942. From 1943 he worked in the US on the atom bomb, and in 1946 became head of the theoretical physics division at Harwell, UK. He was sentenced in 1950 to 14 years' imprisonment for disclosing nuclear secrets to the Russians, but was released (1959) and worked in the nuclear research center of East Germany until 1979.

Fuchs, Sir Vivian Ernest 1908–99 •*English explorer and scientist*• Born in Freshwater, Isle of Wight, the son of a farmer of German origin, he was educated at Brighton College and St John's, Cambridge. After four geological expeditions in East Africa (1930–38), he served in West Africa and Germany during World War II. As director of the Falkland Islands Dependencies Survey (1947) he set up scientific bases on Graham Land peninsula, and while marooned there for a year, conceived the plan for an overland crossing of Antarctica, which materialized in 1955 when he was appointed leader of the Commonwealth expedition. On November 24, 1957, he and a party of 10 set out from Shackleton Base, Weddell Sea, reaching Scott Base, Victoria Land, on March 2, 1958.

Fuentes, Carlos 1928– •*Mexican novelist and playwright*• Born in Panama City, Panama, the son of a diplomat, he was educated at the National University of Mexico and the Institut des Hautes Études Internationales in Geneva, which led to a career in international affairs. A secretary of the Mexican delegation to the International Labor Organization, he eventually became Mexican ambassador to France (1975–77), and has held a variety of teaching posts. An energetic cultural promoter, writer of articles and reviewer, he has published prolifically since his first collection of fantastic, myth-inspired short stories, *Los días enmascarados* ("The Masked Days") in 1954. Many of his novels have been published in English, among them *Terra nostra* (1975, "Our Land"), regarded as his masterpiece. His novel *Gringo viejo* (1985, "The Old Gringo"), concerning the final days of US writer **Ambrose Bierce**, was filmed in 1989. Further publications include *Diana* (1997) and *The Years With Laura Diaz* (1999).

Fugard, Athol 1932– •*South African dramatist and theater director*• He was born in Middelburg, Cape Province, and educated at Cape Town University. Since 1965 he has been director of the Serpent Players in Port Elizabeth, and in 1972 he cofounded the Space Experimental Theatre, Cape Town. His plays are mostly set in South Africa, but his presentation of the bleakness and frustration of life for those especially on the fringes of society raises them to the level of universal human tragedy. His work met with official opposition: *The Blood Knot* (1960), about two Coloured brothers, one light- and one dark-skinned, was censored, and some of his work has only been published and produced abroad. His plays include *Statements After an Arrest Under the Immorality Act* (1972), *A Lesson From Aloes* (1979), *The Road to Mecca* (1984) and *A Place With the Pigs* (1987), which was inspired by a newspaper story about a Red Army deserter who hid in a pigsty for over 40 years. He has also written film scripts and a novel, *Tsotsi* (1980).

Fujimori, Alberto Kenyo 1939– •*Peruvian politician*• He was born in Lima. He founded and led the conservative Cambio '90 (Change '90) Party, and, promising reform, succeeded **Alan García Perez** to become president (1990–2000). Within two years he had dismantled the existing order in Peru by dismissing Congress (1992), sacking senior judges, imposing order through an "Emergency National Reconstruction Government," and changing the constitution. He resigned in 2000 amid allegations of corruption and went into exile in Japan.

Fukui, Kenichi 1918–98 •*Japanese chemist and Nobel Prize winner*• Born in Nara prefecture, he studied at Kyoto University, and worked

(1941–45) in the Army Fuel Laboratory. He was made Professor of Hydrocarbon Physical Chemistry in 1951. His main interest was in the way atomic structure affects the course of a chemical reaction. He published his conclusions in highly mathematical terms and it was not until **Robert Woodward** and **Roald Hoffmann** produced their rules for the conservation of orbital symmetry that the value of Fukui's approach was appreciated. His frontier orbital theory has been widely used in rationalizing organic reactivity and preceded sophisticated computer calculations. Fukui shared the Nobel Prize for chemistry with Hoffmann in 1981.

Fulbright, J(ames) William 1905–95 •*US politician*• Born in Sumner, Missouri, and educated at the University of Arkansas, George Washington University Law School, and Oxford, he taught law in Washington and Arkansas. He was elected to the US House of Representatives as a Democrat in 1942 where, in 1943, he introduced a resolution advocating the creation of the United Nations, and was elected to the Senate in 1944. He sponsored the Fulbright Act (1946), which established an exchange scholarship system for students and teachers between the US and other countries. He distinguished himself in 1954 by his opposition to **Joseph McCarthy**. As chairman of the Senate Foreign Relations Committee, he became a major critic of the escalation of the Vietnam War. He wrote *Old Myths and New Realities* (1965) and *The Arrogance of Power* (1967).

“ ”

We have the power to do any damn fool thing we want to do, and we seem to do it every 10 minutes.

*1952 In **Time**, February 4.*

Fuller, (Richard) Buckminster 1895–1983 •*US engineer and architect*• Born in Milton, Massachusetts, he studied at Harvard and the US Naval Academy, Annapolis, Maryland. In 1917 he discovered energetic/synergetic geometry, and he later devised a structural system known as Tensegrity Structures. He experimented with structural designs aimed at economical, efficient, trouble-free living (developed from systems of aircraft and chassis construction) intended for mass-production. Dymaxion House (1927) embodied these practical ideas. After 1945 he designed geodesic domes, great space-frame enclosures based on polyhedra. The largest design was realized at the Union Tank Car Repair Shop, Louisiana (1958), and the best-known design at the US Pavilion, Montreal Exhibition (1967).

Fuller, Charles H, Jr 1939– •*US playwright*• Born in Philadelphia, he is noted for his exploration of relationships, especially those between African Americans and whites, and between African Americans and a white-dominated bureaucracy. His successful plays include *The Brownsville Raid* (1976), based upon a true incident in 1906, in which an entire US Army regiment of African-American soldiers was dismissed following a riot in Brownsville, Texas. His Pulitzer Prize–winning *A Soldier's Play* (1981) deals with the murder of an unpopular sergeant and was made into the film *A Soldier's Story* in 1984.

Fuller, Loie, *originally* **Marie Louise Fuller** 1862–1928 •*US dancer, choreographer and producer*• Born in Fullersburg, Illinois, she was a pioneer in the field of performance art, and her exotic solo skirt-dance, using multidirectional colored lights on the yards of swirling silk she wore, created a sensation in 1891, especially in Europe. She founded a dance school in 1908, and was a model for **Toulouse-Lautrec**, **Auguste Rodin** and many other prominent artists.

Fuller, (Sarah) Margaret, Marchioness Ossoli 1810–50 •*US feminist, writer and revolutionary*• Born in Cambridgeport, Massachusetts, she assumed an important role in the transcendentalist circle that centered around **Ralph Waldo Emerson**. From 1840 to 1842 she was editor of *The Dial*, the transcendentalist journal, and in 1844 went to New York where she became literary critic for the *New York Tribune*. Moving to Italy in 1847, she met and married Marquis Giovanni Ossoli, an Italian nobleman and republican. After becoming involved in the unsuccessful Revolution of 1848, she sailed for New York with her husband and infant son, but the ship was wrecked off Fire Island and all aboard were drowned. Her publications include *Summer on the Lakes* (1844) and *Woman in the 19th Century* (1855), the earliest major piece of US feminist writing.

Fuller, Roy Broadbent 1912–91 •*English poet and novelist*• Born in Oldham, Lancashire, his first collection of poetry, *Poems* (1939), was strongly influenced by **W H Auden**. His experience of war in the Royal Navy (1941–45) prompted *The Middle of a War* (1942) and *A Lost Season* (1944). His traditionalist attitude kept him apart from the neo-Romantic revival initiated by **Dylan Thomas** after the war, but his *Brutus's Orchard* (1957) and *Collected Poems* (1962) established him as a major poet. His later poetic works include *Buff* (1965), *Retreads* (1979) and *Available for Dreams* (1989), and his novels include *Second Curtain* (1953), *The Ruined Boys* (1959), *The Carnal Island* (1970) and *Stares* (1990). He was Professor of Poetry at Oxford (1968–73).

Fulton, Rikki 1924–2004 •*Scottish actor and comedian*• Born in Glasgow, he began his broadcasting career there in drama, features, children's and religious programs for the BBC. He starred in the *Five past Eight* variety shows in Edinburgh and Glasgow, and since the 1950s has regularly appeared in pantomime. He also had a stage double act with Jack Milroy (1915–2001) in which they appeared as the amiable pair of Teddy boys (young British hoodlums affecting Edwardian dress) Francie and Josie. On television, he appeared in his own comedy sketch series, *Scotch and Wry* and played Macphall in *The Tales of Para Handy* (1994–95). In 1985 he adapted and starred in *A Wee Touch of Class*, a successful transposition of **Molière**'s *Le Bourgeois Gentilhomme* from 17th-century France to 19th-century Edinburgh.

Fulton, Robert 1765–1815 •*US engineer*• Born in Lancaster County, Pennsylvania, to Irish parents, in 1786 he went to London to study under the painter **Benjamin West**. However, he began to apply his energies wholly to mechanical engineering, and in 1794 patented a double inclined plane to supersede locks, and invented a mill for sawing and polishing marble. In 1797 he went to Paris, where he developed a submarine torpedo boat. He returned to the US in 1806, and the next year launched on the Hudson River a steam vessel, the *Clermont*. Although he was not the first person to apply steam to inland navigation, he was the first to do so successfully. He was employed by the US government in constructing (1814) the world's first steam warship, *Fulton the First*.

Funk, Casimir 1884–1967 •*US biochemist*• Born in Warsaw, Poland, he studied in Berlin and Bern, and worked as a research assistant at the Lister Institute, London (1910–13), where he attempted to isolate vitamin B_1. He suggested the general name "vitamine," later altered to "vitamin." Funk emigrated to the US in 1915, and later headed research institutes in Warsaw (1923–27) and Paris (1928–39). He achieved a crude extract of the male sex hormone androsterone from human urine in 1929.

Funk, Walther 1890–1960 •*German Nazi politician*• One of **Hitler**'s chief advisers, he became minister of economics and president of the Reichsbank, and played a leading part in planning the economic aspects of the attack on Russia, and in the exploitation of occupied territories. Captured in 1945, he was sentenced to life imprisonment as a war criminal, but was released in 1957 on account of illness.

Furnivall, Frederick James 1825–1910 •*English philologist*• The son of a doctor at Egham, he studied at London and Cambridge Universities. Influenced by **Frederick Denison Maurice** and Christian socialism, he helped to found the Working Men's College in London. It was, however, as a philologist and editor of English texts that he became famous, giving a great impulse to Early English scholarship. He founded the Early English Text Society, the **Chaucer**, Ballad, New **Shakespeare**, **John Wycliffe** and **Shelley** Societies, and edited many texts, including Chaucer, **Robert Mannyng**'s *Handlyng Synne*, **William Harrison**'s *Description of England* and Hoccleve (c. 1368–1426). He also edited the Philological Society's dictionary (from 1861) that later became the *Oxford English Dictionary*.

Furtwängler, (Gustav Heinrich Ernst Martin) Wilhelm 1886–1954 •*German conductor*• Born in Berlin, in 1922 he became conductor of the Gewandhaus Orchestra in Leipzig and of the Berlin Philharmonic. His reputation was established by international tours, though his highly subjective interpretations of the standard German repertoire aroused controversy. His apparently ambivalent attitude to the **Hitler** regime caused him some unpopularity outside Germany, but after World War II he quickly reestablished himself.

Fuseli, Henry, *originally* **Johann Heinrich Füssli** 1741–1825 •*British painter and art critic*• Born in Zurich, Switzerland, he studied theology at the Collegium Carolinum there. He settled in England in 1764, and was encouraged by Sir **Joshua Reynolds** to go to Italy (1770–78). He became Professor of Painting at the Royal Academy and Keeper in 1804. His 200 paintings include *The Nightmare* (1781) and two series to illustrate **Shakespeare**'s and **Milton**'s works. An edition of his literary works, with a biography, was published in 1831.

Fysh, Sir (Wilmot) Hudson 1895–1974 •*Australian civil aviation pioneer*• Born in Launceston, Tasmania, he was educated at Launceston Grammar and Geelong Grammar schools. He served with the Australian Imperial Forces at Gallipoli in World War I, and later, having transferred to the Australian Flying Corps, was awarded the Distinguished Flying Cross. In 1920 he established the Queensland and Northern Territory Aerial Services Limited, now known as QANTAS.

G

Gabin, Jean, *originally* **Jean Alexis Moncorgé** 1904–76 •*French actor*• Born in Paris, he made his film debut in *Chacun sa chance* (1930). In subsequent films, such as *La grande illusion* (1937, *Grand Illusion*) and *Le jour se lève* (1939, *Daybreak*), his world-weary antiheroes seemed to embody the pessimistic spirit of prewar France. He escaped to the US during World War II, later joining the Free French Navy. Returning to France, he made films including *Touchez pas au Grisbi* (1954, *Grisbi*) and *Le Chat* (1971, *The Cat*).

Gable, Christopher 1940–98 •*English dancer*• Born in London, he studied at the Royal Ballet School there, and was soon dancing solo roles as a principal and partner of **Lynn Seymour**. He retired as a dancer in 1967. He was the founder and artistic director (1982–98) of the Central School of Ballet, and in 1987 became director of the Northern Ballet Theatre. His innovative approach was evident in his staging of *Swan Lake* in 1992, which was set during a coup in 1870s Russia and ended in massacre. As an actor he had roles in films such as **Ken Russell**'s *The Boy Friend* (1972).

Gable, (William) Clark 1901–60 •*US film actor*• He was born in Cadiz, Ohio, and his assault on Hollywood stardom resulted in a role in *The Painted Desert* and 11 other film appearances in 1931. He won an Academy Award for *It Happened One Night* (1934), and was voted "King of Hollywood" in 1937. His sympathetic, ruggedly masculine and humorous persona made him the perfect Rhett Butler in *Gone with the Wind* (1939). He returned to the cinema after World War II army service and remained in demand, appearing as an aging cowboy in his last film, *The Misfits* (1961). Married five times, his third wife was the actress **Carole Lombard**.

Gabo, Naum, *originally* **Naum Neemia Pevsner** 1890–1977 •*US constructivist sculptor*• Born in Bryansk, Russia, he first studied medicine and engineering, then art in Munich (1911–12). With his brother, **Antoine Pevsner**, and **Vladimir Tatlin** and **Kasimir Malevich**, he was associated with the Moscow Suprematist Group (1913), and in 1920 he broke away with his brother and Tatlin to form the group of Russian Constructivists, who have had considerable influence on 20th-century architecture and design. In 1920 they published their *Realistic Manifesto*. As their theories did not coincide with those of Russian official art circles, he was forced into exile, and lived in Berlin (1923–33), Paris (1933–35) and England (1936–45), before going to the US in 1946. He was naturalized in 1952. There are several examples of his completely nonfigurative geometrical "constructions in space," mainly made in transparent plastics, in the Museum of Modern Art, New York.

Gabor, Dennis 1900–79 •*British physicist and Nobel Prize winner*• Born in Budapest, he studied in Berlin but left Germany in 1933. After writing the first book on the electron microscope, he was appointed to a readership at Imperial College, London (1948), and later became Professor of Applied Electron Physics (1958–67). He is best remembered for conceiving in 1947 the technique of (and the name) holography, a method of photographically recording and reproducing three-dimensional images, for which he was awarded the 1971 Nobel Prize for physics. In the late 1960s he developed an acute interest in the sociopolitical and environmental questions raised by the Club of Rome, and visited many countries to lecture on economic expansionism and the limitations imposed by the earth's finite resources.

Gabriel, Peter Brian 1950– •*English rock singer and songwriter*• Born in Woking, Surrey, he cofounded the rock band Genesis in 1966, recording such albums as *Trespass* (1970) and *The Lamb Lies Down on Broadway* (1974). He left Genesis in 1975 and released four untitled solo albums from which came such hit singles as "Games Without Frontiers" (1980), "Biko" (1980) and "Sledgehammer" (1986). More recent projects have included the multimedia live show *Ovo* that was the centerpiece of London's Millennium Dome in 2000. Since 1982 he has also organized the WOMAD (World of Music, Arts and Dance) concerts and recordings featuring artists from many countries.

Gabrieli, Andrea c.1533–86 •*Italian composer*• Born in Venice, he studied under Adrian Willaert (c. 1490–1562), and was later appointed organist of St Mark's Church. He wrote masses and other choral works, and his organ pieces include toccatas and ricercari, the latter foreshadowing the fugue.

Gabrieli, Giovanni c. 1555–1612 •*Italian composer*• Born in Venice, he composed choral and instrumental works in which he exploited the acoustics of St Mark's in Venice with unusual antiphonal and echo effects, using double choirs, double ensembles of wind instruments and other devices.

Gaddafi, Muammar *See* **Qaddafi, Muammar**

Gaddis, William 1922–98 •*US novelist*• Born in New York City and educated at Harvard, he wrote four novels: *The Recognitions* (1955), a densely allusive post-Christian epic about art, forgery, money and magic; followed by *J R* (1976), about an 11-year-old "ragged capitalist" operating from pay phones; *Carpenter's Gothic* (1985), in which a Vietnam War veteran works as a media consultant for a fundamentalist preacher; and *A Frolic of His Own* (1994), a story of litigiousness and greed in US society. An ambitious satirist, he was one of the US's most prominent contemporary novelists. He won the National Book Award in 1976 and 1994.

Gades, Antonio 1936– •*Spanish dancer, choreographer and teacher*• Born in Alicante, he made his debut in cabaret as a teenager. In the early 1960s he worked mainly in Italy, collaborating with **Anton Dolin** and staging dances at La Scala, Milan. The company he formed for the New York World's Fair of 1964 has since toured the world. He has appeared in various films, the most acclaimed being the flamenco trilogy directed by Carlos Saura: *Blood Wedding* (1981), *Carmen* (1983) and *El Amor Brujo* (1986).

Gagarin, Yuri Alekseyevich 1934–68 •*Soviet cosmonaut*• Born near Gzhatsk, he joined the Soviet air force in 1957, and in 1961 became the first man to travel in space, completing a circuit of the Earth in the *Vostok* satellite. Nominated a Hero of the Soviet Union, he shared the Galabert Astronautical prize with **John Glenn** in 1963. He was killed in a plane accident while training.

" "

I could have gone on flying through space forever.

1961 In the ***New York Times****, April 14.*

Gage, Matilda Joslyn, *née* **Joslyn** 1826–98 •*US feminist and women's rights activist*• Born in Cicero, New York, she developed a radical feminist perspective and incisive analysis of the nature of patriarchal society, working with the more conservative reformers **Susan B Anthony** and **Elizabeth Cady Stanton** to launch the first wave of the American suffrage movement. With them, she later compiled the four-volume *History of Woman Suffrage* (1881–1906). She joined the National Woman Suffrage Association (NWSA) and became its president, but withdrew in protest at the union of the NWSA and the conservative Women's Christian Temperance Union. Believing that church and state colluded to oppress women, she founded the Women's National Liberal Union (1890), and wrote *Woman, Church and State: the Original Exposé of Male Collaboration Against the Female Sex* (1893).

Gage, Thomas 1721–87 •*English soldier*• He was born in Firle, Sussex. He became military Governor of Montreal in 1760, Commander in Chief of the British forces in America (1763–72), and Governor of Massachusetts (1774). In April 1775 he sent a force to seize arms from the colonists at Concord, and the next day the skirmish at Lexington took place which began the American Revolution. After the Battle of Bunker Hill (June 1775) he was relieved by **William Howe**.

Gainsborough, Thomas 1727–88 •*English landscape and portrait painter*• Born in Sudbury, Suffolk, he copied Dutch landscapes in his youth and at the age of 14 was sent to London where he learned the art of rococo decoration. *The Charterhouse* (1748) marks the end of his apprenticeship, and he settled as a portrait painter at Ipswich in 1745. *Mr and Mrs Andrews* (1748) and several "chimney-piece" paintings belong to this, his Suffolk period. In 1760 he moved to Bath, where he established himself with his portrait of *Earl Nugent* (1760). His portraits combine the elegance of **Van Dyck** with his own characteristic informality, although in his later work he increasingly tends toward fashionable artificialities. Among his early masterpieces are *Lord and Lady Howe*, *Mrs Portman* (Tate, London) and *Blue Boy* (Huntington Collection, Pasadena), and the great landscapes *The Harvest Wagon* (1767, Barber Institute, Birmingham) and *The Watering Place* (1777, Tate) in which **Rubens**'s influence is discernible. He became a founding member of the Royal Academy in 1768, and moved to London in 1774. To this last period belong the character study *Mr Truman*, the luxuriant *Mrs Graham* (1777, Edinburgh), *George III* and *Queen Charlotte* (1781, Windsor Castle), and *Mrs Siddons* (1785). Landscapes include *The Morning Walk* (1780) and *Cattle Crossing a Bridge* (1781), the most rococo of all his work.

Gaiseric or **Genseric** c. 390–477 AD •*King of the Vandals and Alans*• The son of the Vandal leader Godigisel, he succeeded his half brother Gunderic in AD 427. Gaiseric entered Numidia (429), captured and sacked Hippo (430), and seized Carthage (439), establishing a formidable maritime power, ranging as far as the Peloponnese. An Arian, he ferociously persecuted Catholics. Eudoxia, the widow of Roman emperor Valentinian III, invited Gaiseric to Rome to destroy her husband's murderer Maximus. Gaiseric's fleet took and sacked the city (455), and one of Eudoxia's daughters married his son and successor, Huneric.

Gaisford, Thomas 1780–1855 •*English Greek scholar*• He became Regius Professor of Greek at Oxford in 1812 and in 1831 was made Dean of Christ Church. He produced editions of **Herodotus**, Hephaestion, Johannes Stobaeus and Suidas. The Gaisford prizes were founded in his memory.

Gaitskell, Hugh Todd Naylor 1906–63 •*English Labour politician*• Born in London, he was educated at Winchester and at New College, Oxford, becoming a socialist during the 1926 general strike. In 1938 he became Reader in Political Economy at the University of London. Elected Member of Parliament for Leeds South in 1945, he became Parliamentary Secretary to the Ministry of Fuel and Power in 1946, Minister in 1947, Minister of State for Economic Affairs in 1950, and Chancellor of the Exchequer that same year. His introduction of National Health Service charges led to the resignation of **Aneurin Bevan** as Minister of Health and to a long feud with Bevan and the hostile left wing of the Labour Party. However, his ascendancy in the party grew steadily and in 1955 he was elected Leader of the Opposition by a large majority over Bevan, succeeding **Clement Attlee**. He bitterly opposed **Anthony Eden**'s Suez action (1956), attempted to modify Labour policy from total nationalization to the development of a shareholder state, and refused to accept a narrow conference vote for unilateral disarmament (1960). This caused a crisis of leadership in which he retained the loyalty of most Labour Members of Parliament. Gaitskell was also a keen European, and in his final years in office strongly supported Great Britain's entry into the EEC.

“ ”

Let us not forget that we can never go farther than we can persuade at least half the people to go.

1961 Labour Party conference speech, October.

Gaius fl. 130–80 AD •*Roman jurist*• His *Institutes* (lost until 1816) formed the basis for those of **Justinian** and are the only substantial texts of Roman law that have survived. His other works were largely used in the compilation of the *Digest*.

Gajdusek, Daniel Carleton 1923– •*US virologist, pediatrician, and Nobel Prize winner*• Born in Yonkers, New York, he studied physics at Rochester and medicine at Harvard. He spent much time in Papua New Guinea, studying the origin and dissemination of a slowly developing lethal viral disease called kuru. He identified the causative agent as a "slow virus," now implicated in many other diseases, which may take years to induce symptoms. He shared the 1976 Nobel Prize for physiology or medicine with **Baruch Blumberg** for his work on slow-virus infections, which cause such diseases as Creutzfeld-Jakob disease.

Galba, Servius Sulpicius 3 BC–AD 69 •*Roman emperor*• He became consul (AD 33), and administered Aquitania, Germany, Africa and Hispania Tarraconensis with competence and integrity. In 68 the Gallic legions rose against **Nero** and proclaimed Galba emperor. However, he soon made himself unpopular by favoritism, ill-timed severity and avarice, and was assassinated by the praetorians in Rome.

Galbraith, J(ohn) K(enneth) 1908– •*US economist*• Born in Ontario, Canada, and educated at the Universities of Toronto and California and at Cambridge, he emigrated to the US in 1931. In 1939 he became Assistant Professor of Economics at Princeton and held various administrative posts before becoming Paul M Warburg Professor of Economics at Harvard from 1949 to 1975. He was US ambassador to India (1961–63). A Keynesian economist, he advocated government spending to stimulate the economy, and he criticized the US mania for consumer goods, arguing that a greater portion of wealth should be spent on infrastructure, education and other improvements shared by the public. His written works include *The Great Crash* (1955), *The Affluent Society* (1958), *The New Industrial State* (1967), *The Age of Uncertainty* (1977), which was made into a BBC television series, *The Anatomy of Power* (1983) and *The Good Society* (1996).

Galdós *See* **Pérez Galdós**

Gale, Zona 1874–1938 •*US novelist, story writer and dramatist*• Born in Portage, Wisconsin, she began writing sentimental romances. She was scorned and disliked for her increasing pacifism and feminism, but gained some recognition for her novel *Birth* (1918), which was dramatized in 1924 as *Mr Pitt*. However, she found fame with her novel *Miss Lulu Bett* (1920), and her dramatization of it won her a Pulitzer Prize (1921).

Galen, *properly* **Claudius Galenus** c. 130–c. 201 AD •*Greek physician*• Born in Pergamum in Mysia, Asia Minor, he studied medicine there and in Smyrna, Corinth and Alexandria. He was chief physician to the gladiators in Pergamum from AD 157, then moved to Rome and became friend and physician to the emperor **Marcus Aurelius**. He was also physician to emperors **Lucius Aurelius Commodus** and **Lucius Septimius Severus**. He was a voluminous writer on medical and philosophical subjects, and collated all the medical knowledge of his time, especially promoting the work of **Hippocrates**. An active experimentalist and dissector of animals, he elaborated a physiological system whereby the body's three principal organs—heart, liver and brain—were central to living processes, and he was the first to use the pulse as a diagnostic aid. He was long venerated as the standard authority on medical matters.

Galerius, *properly* **Gaius Galerius Valerius Maximianus** d. 311 AD •*Roman emperor*• Born near Serdica, Dacia, he rose to a high rank in the army. He was made Caesar by **Diocletian** (AD 293), and on Diocletian's abdication (305) became, with **Constantius Chlorus**, joint ruler of the Roman Empire, Galerius taking the eastern half. When Constantius died in York (306) the troops in Britain and Gaul transferred their allegiance to his son, **Constantine I (the Great)**, but Galerius retained the east until his death. Christian tradition presented him as a persecutor of their faith, though in his last year he granted full toleration throughout the empire.

Galgacus *See* **Calgacus**

Galileo, *properly* **Galileo Galilei** 1564–1642 •*Italian astronomer, mathematician and natural philosopher*• He was born in Pisa, the son of a musician. He matriculated at Pisa University (1581), where he accepted the chair of mathematics in 1589. From watching the movement of a lamp in the cathedral of Pisa, he discovered (1582) the principle of the isochronism of the pendulum (equality in time whatever the range of its swing), which indicated the value of the pendulum as a timekeeper. In his study of falling bodies, Galileo showed that, contrary to the Aristotelian belief that the rate at which a body falls is proportional to its weight, all bodies would fall at the same rate if air resistance were not present. He also showed that a body moving along an inclined plane has a constant acceleration, and demonstrated the parabolic trajectories of projectiles. In 1592 he moved to the University of Padua, where his lectures attracted pupils from all over Europe. He made his first contribution to astronomy in 1604 when he demonstrated that a bright new star which had appeared in the constellation Ophiuchus was more distant than the planets, confirming **Tycho Brahe**'s conclusion that changes take place in the celestial regions beyond the planets. In 1610 he perfected a refracting telescope, which he used in the course of many astounding astronomical revelations published in his *Sidereus nuncius* (1610, "Sidereal Messenger"). These included the mountains of the moon, the multitude of stars in the Milky Way, and the existence of four of Jupiter's satellites. Galileo was appointed Chief Mathematician and Philosopher by the Grand Duke of Tuscany. On a visit to Rome in 1611 he was elected a member of the Accademia dei Lincei and feted by the Jesuit mathematicians of the Roman College. Further discoveries included the phases of Venus, spots on the sun's disk, the sun's rotation, and Saturn's appendages (though not then recognized as a ring system). These brilliant researches led Galileo to affirm the truth of the **Copernican** system with the sun at its center, which he defended in his *Dialogue on the Two Principal Systems of the World* (1632). Its sale was prohibited by the ecclesiastical authorities; Galileo was brought before the Inquisition and, under threat of torture, recanted. He was finally allowed to live under house arrest in his own home at Arcetri, near Florence; there he continued his researches and completed his *Discourses on the Two New Sciences* (1638), in which he discussed at length the principles of mechanics. In 1637 he became blind, but he continued working until his death on January 8, 1642. The sentence passed on him by the Inquisition was formally retracted by Pope **John Paul II** on October 31, 1992.

Gall, Franz Joseph 1758–1828 •*German physician, founder of phrenology*• Born in Tiefenbrunn, Baden, he settled in Vienna as a physician in 1785. He gradually evolved theories by which he traced talents and other qualities to the functions of particular areas of the brain, and the shape of the skull. His lectures on phrenology were a popular success, but were suppressed in 1802 as being subversive of religion.

Gallagher, Liam *See* **Oasis**

Gallagher, Noel *See* **Oasis**

Galle, Johann Gottfried 1812–1910 •*German astronomer*• Born in Pabsthaus, near Wittenberg, and educated at the University of Berlin, he became director of the observatory at Breslau (now Wrocław, Poland, 1851–91). He took a special interest in comets, discovered three new ones and for many years computed ephemerides of comets and minor planets for the *Astronomisches Jahrbuch*. His most dramatic discovery, made in Berlin, was of the planet Neptune, whose existence had been theoretically predicted and whose expected position had been calculated by **Urbain Leverrier**. In 1872 he proposed the use of asteroids rather than regular planets for determinations of the solar parallax, a suggestion which bore fruit in a successful international campaign (1888–89).

Galliano, John, *originally* **Juan Carlos Galliano** 1961– •*British fashion designer*• Born in Gibraltar, he moved with his family to England when he was six years old. Trained at the Central St Martin's School of Art and Design, his designs are inspired by a range of historical and cultural references. He was Designer of the Year in 1987, and showed in Paris in 1990, the first British designer to show in the Louvre tent. In 1992 he set up a new workshop in Paris and in 1995, he replaced **Hubert de Givenchy** as designer in chief at his eponymous Paris fashion house. After only one year there Galliano left to become designer in chief at the House of **Dior** in 1996.

Gallienus, Publius Licinius c. 218–68 AD •*Roman emperor*• He ruled jointly with his father, **Valerian**, from AD 253 until 260. His authority was constantly challenged (for example, by Postumus in Gaul and Gothic raids into Greece), while the legions frequently proclaimed their commanders Caesars. He abandoned Valerian's persecution of Christians, and developed a formidable force of cavalry. In 268, while besieging one of his rivals in Milan, he was murdered by his own officers.

Gallup, George Horace 1901–84 •*US public opinion pollster*• Born in Jefferson, Iowa, he became Professor of Journalism at Drake University (1929–31) and also at Northwestern University (1931–32). He was then director of research for the Young & Rubicam advertising agency in New York (1932–47). In 1935 he founded the American Institute of Public Opinion, and evolved the Gallup Polls for testing the state of public opinion, which made its name by correctly predicting the outcome of the 1936 US presidential elections. He wrote *Public Opinion in a Democracy* (1939) and *Guide to Public Opinion Polls* (1944, 1948).

“ ”

I could prove God statistically.

Attributed.

Gallus, Gaius Cornelius c. 70–26 BC •*Roman poet*• Born in Forum Julii (now Fréjus) in Gaul, he lived in Rome and was a friend of **Virgil**. Appointed prefect of Egypt by **Augustus**, he was recalled and banished, and committed suicide. He was considered the founder of the Roman love elegy, from his four books of elegies upon his mistress "Lycoris" (in reality the actress Cytheris). Only part of one line of his verse survives.

Galois, Évariste 1811–32 •*French mathematician*• Born in Bourg-la-Reine, he entered the École Normale Supérieure in 1829, but was expelled in 1830 due to his extreme Republican sympathies. His mathematical reputation rests on fewer than 100 pages of work of original genius, which include a memoir on the solubility of equations by radicals, and a mathematical testament giving the essentials of his discoveries on the theory of algebraic equations and Abelian integrals. Some of his results had been independently obtained by **Niels Henrik Abel**, but Galois put them in a theoretical setting which proved to be very useful to later mathematicians. The brevity and obscurity of his writing delayed the understanding of his work, but it gradually came to be seen as a cornerstone of modern algebra.

Galsworthy, John 1867–1933 •*English novelist, playwright, and Nobel Prize winner*• Born in Coombe, Surrey, he was educated at Harrow and New College, Oxford, and was called to the bar in 1890, but chose to travel and become a writer. He met **Joseph Conrad** and they became lifelong friends. He published his first book, a collection of short stories, *From the Four Winds*, in 1897, under the pseudonym John Sinjohn. In 1906 he published *The Man of Property*, the first in his celebrated *Forsyte Saga* series—the others being *In Chancery* (1920) and *To Let* (1921). In these novels he describes both nostalgically and critically the life of the affluent middle class that ruled England before World War I. The second cycle of the saga, *A Modern Comedy* (1929), includes *The White Monkey* (1924), *The Silver Spoon* (1926) and *Swan Song* (1928), and examines the plight of the postwar generation. Among his other novels are *The Country House* (1907), *Fraternity* (1909) and *The Patrician* (1911). A prolific playwright, he produced more than 30 plays for the London stage. They best illustrate his reforming zeal and also his sentimentality, and while technically first-rate theater, they are marred, especially the later ones, by the parsimony of his dialogue. He won the Nobel Prize for literature in 1932.

Galt, John 1779–1839 •*Scottish novelist and pioneer in Canada*• Born in Irvine, Ayrshire, the son of a sea captain, he was educated at Greenock Grammar School. From 1809 to 1811 he traveled in the

Levant, where he met **Byron**. On his return he published *Letters from the Levant* and other accounts of his travels. He later started to write novels: *The Ayrshire Legatees* appeared in 1820, followed by *The Steam-Boat* in 1821. Its successor, *The Annals of the Parish* (1821), is his masterpiece. *Sir Andrew Wylie* (1822), *The Provost* (1822) and *The Entail* (1823) followed, then in 1826 he went to Canada, where he founded the town of Guelph, and played a prominent part in organizing immigration. He returned ruined in 1829, but wrote a new novel, *Lawrie Todd* (1830), followed by *The Member* (1832), on corruption in politics.

Galtieri, Leopoldo Fortunato 1926–2003 •*Argentine soldier and statesman*•He was born in Caseras, in the province of Buenos Aires. After training at the National Military College he progressed steadily to the rank of lieutenant general in 1979, when he joined the junta which had been in power since the military coup which ousted **Isabelita Perón** in 1976. In 1981 he became President. In 1982 Galtieri ordered the invasion of the long-disputed Malvinas (Falkland) Islands. Their recovery by Great Britain, after a brief and humiliating war, brought about his downfall. He was court-martialed in 1983 and sentenced to twelve years' imprisonment for negligence in starting and losing the Falklands War. He was released in 1989.

Galton, Sir Francis 1822–1911 •*English scientist*• Born in Birmingham, he studied medicine at Birmingham Hospital and King's College London and graduated from Trinity College, Cambridge. In 1850 he explored unknown territory in southern Africa, publishing *Narrative of an Explorer in Tropical South Africa* and *Art of Travel* (1853). His investigations in meteorology in *Meteorographica* (1863) were the basis for modern weather maps. He supported the evolutionary thinking of his cousin **Charles Darwin**, and devoted himself to heredity, founding the study of eugenics (the science of creating superior offspring), and publishing *Hereditary Genius* (1869), *English Men of Science: Their Nature and Nurture* (1874) and *Natural Inheritance* (1889). He also devised the system of fingerprint identification with *Finger Prints* (1892). His researches into color blindness and mental imagery were also of great value. He was knighted in 1909.

Galvani, Luigi 1737–98 •*Italian physiologist*• Born in Bologna, he became a lecturer in anatomy in 1768, and from 1782 was Professor of Obstetrics. He is famous for the discovery of animal electricity, inspired by his observation that dead frogs suffered convulsions when fixed to an iron fence to dry. He then showed that paroxysms followed if a frog was part of a circuit involving metals, wrongly believing the current source to be in the material of muscle and nerve. Galvani's name lives on in the word "galvanized," and in the galvanometer, used from 1820 to detect electric current.

Galway, James 1939– •*Northern Irish flautist and conductor*• Born in Belfast, he gained experience playing in flute bands in Northern Ireland before training at the Royal College and the Guildhall in London. He was an orchestral player, notably as part of the woodwind section of the Berlin Philharmonic Orchestra, before establishing himself as an internationally renowned soloist in his own right from 1975. His repertoire includes not only classical and contemporary music, but a great deal of popular music, which, along with frequent television exposure, helped him win a mass audience. He plays a 14-carat gold flute.

Gama, Vasco da c. 1469–1525 •*Portuguese navigator*• Born in Sines, Alentejo, he was selected by King **Manoel I** to discover a route to India around the Cape of Good Hope. The expedition left Lisbon in 1497, and after rounding the Cape, despite hurricanes and mutinies, reached Malindi (in East Africa) early in the following year. Here da Gama found a skillful Indian pilot, crossed the Indian Ocean, and arrived at Calicut in 1498, the first Westerner to sail around the Cape to Asia. The ruler of Calicut soon became actively hostile, and da Gama had to fight his way out of the harbor, but he arrived safely back in Lisbon in 1499 and was ennobled. However, 40 other Portuguese left behind were murdered, and to avenge them the king sent out a squadron of 20 ships under da Gama (1502), which founded the colonies of Mozambique and Sofala, bombarded Calicut, and returned to the Tagus with 13 richly laden vessels in 1503. In 1524 da Gama became Viceroy of India.

Gambon, Sir Michael John 1940– •*Irish actor*• Born in Dublin, he moved to England and joined the National Theatre, London (1963), becoming its leading actor with performances including the title role in **John Dexter**'s production of **Bertolt Brecht**'s *The Life of Galileo* (1980). He has also made many television appearances, notably as **Dennis Potter**'s *The Singing Detective* (1986), and as **Georges Simenon**'s *Maigret* (1992). His films include *The Cook, The Thief, His Wife and Her Lover* (1989), *The Wings of the Dove* (1997) and *Sleepy Hollow* (1999). He was knighted in 1998.

Gamow, George 1904–68 •*US physicist*•Born in Odessa, Ukraine, he was educated at Leningrad (now St Petersburg) University, where later he was Professor of Physics (1931–34). After research at the Universities of Göttingen and Copenhagen and Cambridge University, he moved to the US as Professor of Physics at George Washington University (1934–55) and at the University of Colorado (1956–68). In 1948, with **Ralph Alpher** and **Hans Bethe**, he suggested an explanation for the universal abundance of chemical elements based on thermonuclear processes in the early universe, and he was a major exponent of the big bang theory. In molecular biology he made a major contribution to the problem of how the order of nucleic acid bases in DNA chains governs the synthesis of proteins from amino acids. He realized that short sequences of the bases could form a code capable of carrying information directing the synthesis of proteins, a proposal shown by the mid-1950s to be correct.

Gance, Abel 1889–1981 •*French film director*•He was born in Paris, the illegitimate son of a wealthy doctor, and became involved in filmmaking in 1911. His five-hour-long *Napoleon* (1927) was a classic of silent film, but was largely forgotten until its resurrection in the early 1980s. Other films include *Lucrezia Borgia* (1935) and *The Battle of Austerlitz* (1960). He was a pioneer of color cinematography and wide-screen techniques.

Gandhi, Indira Priyad Arshini 1917–84 •*Indian politician*• Born in Allahabad, the daughter of **Jawaharlal Nehru**, she was educated at Visva-Bharati University (Bengal) and Somerville College, Oxford. She was deeply involved in the independence issue, and spent a year in prison. She married Feroze Gandhi (d. 1960) in 1942 and had two sons, **Rajiv Gandhi** and Sanjay (1946–80), who died in an airplane crash. She became a member of the central committee of the Indian Congress (1950), president of the Indian Congress Party (1959–60), and took over as Prime Minister in 1966. In 1975, after her conviction for election malpractices, she declared a state of emergency in India but lost the general election in 1977. Acquitted after her arrest on charges of corruption, she resigned in 1978 from the Congress Parliamentary Party, and became leader of the new Indian National Congress, returning to power as Prime Minister following the 1980 general election. She was recognized for her work as a leader of developing nations, but failed to suppress sectarian violence at home. She was assassinated in 1984 by members of her Sikh bodyguard, resentful of her employment of troops to storm the Golden Temple at Amritsar. This murder provoked a Hindu backlash in Delhi, involving the massacre of 3,000 Sikhs. She was succeeded by her elder son, Rajiv.

Gandhi, Mahatma ("Great Soul"), *properly* **Mohandās Karamchand Gandhi** 1869–1948 •*Indian leader*• He was born in Porbandar, Kathiawar, the son of a politician. He studied law in London, and in 1893 went to South Africa, where he spent over 20 years opposing discriminatory legislation against Indians. In 1914 he returned to India and supported the Home Rule movement (*Swaraj*). As leader of the the Indian National Congress he advocated a policy of nonviolent noncooperation to achieve independence. Following his first major noncooperation and civil disobedience campaign (1919–20), he was jailed for conspiracy. In 1930 he led a 200-mile (320-kilometer) march to the sea to collect salt in symbolic defiance of the government monopoly; this marked the beginning of the second major campaign of civil disobedience. On his release from prison (1931), he attended the London Round Table Conference on Indian constitutional reform. In 1946 he negotiated with the British Cabinet Mission that recommended the new constitutional structure. After independence (1947), he tried to stop the Hindu/Muslim conflict in Bengal, a policy that led to his assassination in Delhi by Nathuram Godse, a Hindu fanatic.

“ ”

Nonviolence is the first article of my faith. It is also the last article of my creed.

1922 Speech at Shahi Bag, March 18.

Gandhi, Rajiv 1944–91 •*Indian politician*•The eldest son of **Indira Gandhi** and the grandson of **Jawaharlal Nehru**, he was born in Bombay, into a Kashmiri-Brahmin family which had governed India for all but four years since 1947. He was educated at Doon School and Cambridge. He married an Italian, Sonia Maino, in 1968. Following the death of his brother Sanjay (1946–80)in an airplane crash, he inherited his brother's Amethi parliamentary seat in 1981 and was appointed a General Secretary of the Congress Party in 1983. After the assassination of Indira Gandhi in 1984 he became Prime Minister and secured a record majority in the parliamentary elections later that year. He attempted to cleanse and rejuvenate the Congress, inducting new technocrats and introducing a freer market economic program. Congress suffered heavy losses in the 1989 general election, and he resigned as premier after his party's defeat. He was assassinated during an election campaign.

Gao Xingjian 1940– •*Chinese author and Nobel Prize winner*• He was born in Ganzhou and began his career as a translator and a playwright for the People's Art Troupe. During the Cultural Revolution he spent five years undergoing "reeducation" and was unable to publish in China until 1979. He emigrated to France in 1988. His plays include *Bus Stop* (1983) and *The Other Shore* (1986), which show the influences of **Brecht** and **Beckett**. *Soul Mountain* (2000), a novel about the search for roots in a shattered Communist China, was his first major international success. He was awarded the Nobel Prize for literature in 2000.

Garbarek, Jan 1947– •*Norwegian saxophonist and composer*• He was born in Mysen. Self-taught at first, he was playing at European jazz festivals by 1966 and one year later joined the Scandinavian orchestra led by US avant-garde composer George Russell. He worked with experimental US musicians like **Keith Jarrett** and **Don Cherry** in the early 1970s, but his own projects have moved increasingly away from jazz in favor of an exploration of influences from Norwegian folk music, and also the ethnic music of India, Pakistan and South America, sometimes with musicians from those traditions. More recently he combined saxophone with medieval plainsong in his collaboration with the Hilliard Ensemble, producing the album *Officium*.

Garbo, Greta, *professional name of* **Greta Lovisa Gustafsson** 1905–90 •*Swedish-born US film actress, a glamorous star of 1930s films*•She was born in Stockholm. After working as a shop assistant and model, she won a bathing beauty competition at 16, then won a scholarship to the Royal Theatre Dramatic School in Stockholm. She was given a starring role in *Gösta Berling's Saga* (1924) by the Swedish director **Mauritz Stiller**; he also gave his star the name Garbo (chosen before he met her), trained her in acting technique, and insisted that she be given a contract at MGM in Hollywood when he moved there in 1925. He codirected her in *The Temptress* (1926). She was an actress of remarkable talent and legendary beauty, as her appearances in *Flesh and the Devil* (1927), *Love* (1927) and *A Woman of Affairs* (1928) showed. Her first talking role was in *Anna Christie* (1930), and this was followed by her greatest successes, *Queen Christina* (1933), *Anna Karenina* (1935), *Camille* (1936), *Conquest* (1937) and *Ninotchka* (1939). She retired from films in 1941, distressed by the scathing reviews of *Two-Faced Woman*. She became a US citizen in 1951 but lived in New York as a total recluse for the rest of her life. In 1955 she was awarded an honorary Academy Award for her unforgettable screen performances."

Garcia, Jerry (Jerome John) 1942–95 •*US rock and country guitarist and singer*• Born in San Francisco, he began playing in folk and bluegrass bands before drifting into San Francisco's Haight-Ashbury hippie scene of the mid-1960s, which led to the formation of The Grateful Dead in 1967. The band became an institution in US music, with Garcia, Bob Weir and Phil Lesh as its key members. They moved from psychedelia into a more blues- and country-oriented sound in the early 1970s, but remained famous for their long, improvised live performances, and retained a huge worldwide following—the "Deadheads." His health, exacerbated by drug addiction, grew fragile, and his death ended an era in US rock music.

García Gutiérrez, Antonio 1813–84 •*Spanish dramatist*• He was born in Chiclana de la Frontera. His first success, *El trovador* (1836, "The Troubadour"), provided **Verdi** with his opera *Il Trovatore* (1853), and he went on to write some 50 plays. His work at its best, as in *Juan Lorenzo* (1865), is exceedingly skillful, written in a clever combination of prose and verse, and presenting unusually acute portrayals of women.

García Lorca, Federico 1898–1936 •*Spanish poet and playwright*• Born in Fuente Vaqueros, he is best known for his powerful dramatic tragedies, which deal with elemental themes in a striking fashion. The best of these plays are *Bodas de Sangre* (1933, Eng trans *Blood Wedding*, 1947), *Yerma* (1934, Eng trans 1947) and *La Casa de Bernarda Alba* (first performed in 1945, Eng trans *The House of Bernarda Alba*, 1947). His gypsy songs, which include *Canciones* (1927, Eng trans 1976) and *Romancero Gitano* (1928, 1935, Eng trans *Gypsy Ballads*, 1963), reveal a classical control of imagery, rhythm and emotion. The elegiac poems in *Llanto por la muerte de Ignacio Sánchez Mejías* (1935, Eng trans *Lament for the Death of a Bullfighter and Other Poems*, 1937) have been seen as a foreshadowing of his own death. He was assassinated on the orders of the Nationalist Civil Governor early in the Spanish civil war in Granada.

García Márquez, Gabriel *See* **Márquez, Gabriel García**

García Robles, Alfonso 1911–91 •*Mexican diplomat and Nobel Prize winner*• After studying law at universities in Mexico and Paris and at the Academy of International Law in the Netherlands, he became a member of the Mexican Foreign Service. From 1964 to 1971 he was Undersecretary for Foreign Affairs. In this capacity he was instrumental in forming the Treaty of Tlateloco (1967), which aimed to abolish nuclear weapons in Latin America. He was awarded the 1982 Nobel Peace Prize, jointly with **Alva Myrdal**.

Garden, Mary 1874–1967 •*Scottish soprano*• Born in Aberdeen, she was taken to the US as a child, and studied singing in Chicago and then in Paris. In 1902 she created the role of Mélisande in **Debussy**'s *Pelléas et Mélisande* at the composer's request, and in 1903 she recorded songs with Debussy. **Jules Massenet** and Frédéric d'Erlanger also wrote leading roles for her. She sang at Covent Garden (1902–03), starring in roles such as Thaïs, Salomé, Carmen and Juliet (**Charles Gounod**). She made her US debut as Thaïs (1907), and in 1910 she began a 20-year association with Chicago Grand Opera.

Gardiner, Stephen c.1483–1555 •*English prelate*•Born in Bury St Edmunds, Suffolk, he studied at Cambridge (1520–21), and was made Master of Trinity Hall, Cambridge (1525–49, 1553–55). He became **Thomas Wolsey**'s secretary (1525), then Bishop of Winchester (1531), and was sent to Rome to further **Henry VIII**'s divorce from **Catherine of Aragon** (1527–33). He supported the royal supremacy, but opposed doctrinal reformation, and for this was imprisoned and deprived of his bishopric on **Edward VI**'s accession. Released and restored by **Mary I (Tudor)** (1553), he became a vigorous persecutor of Protestants.

Gardner, Ava, *originally* **Lucy Johnson** 1922–90 •*US film actress*• Born in North Carolina, she was signed on by MGM as a teenager, emerging from the ranks of decorative starlets with her portrayal of a femme fatale in *The Killers* (1946). A green-eyed brunette once voted the world's most beautiful woman, she remained a leading lady for two decades, portraying an earthy combination of sensuality and cynicism in films like *Mogambo* (1953), *The Barefoot Contessa* (1954) and *Night of the Iguana* (1964). She continued to work as a character actress in films and on television. She was married to **Mickey Rooney**, **Artie Shaw** and **Frank Sinatra**.

“ ”

What I'd really like to say about stardom is that it gave me everything I never wanted.

1990 ***Ava: My Story***.

Gardner, Erle Stanley 1889–1970 *•US crime novelist•* Born in Malden, Massachusetts, he was educated at Palo Alto High School, California, studied in law offices and was admitted to the California bar (1922–38). A hugely prolific writer, he dictated up to six or seven novels simultaneously to a team of secretaries and used a number of pseudonyms. His best-known creation is the lawyer-sleuth Perry Mason, hero of 82 courtroom dramas, who first appeared in *The Case of the Velvet Claws* (1933). With a little help from Della Street, his faithful secretary, and private eye Paul Drake, Mason frequently defied the rulebook in his quest to clear his client's name. With Raymond Burr (1917–93) playing Perry Mason, the books enjoyed enhanced popularity when they were made into a long-running television series.

Garfield, James Abram 1831–81 *•20th President of the US•* Born near Orange, Ohio, he was brought up in poverty but managed to graduate from Williams College in 1856. He became a lawyer and was elected to the state senate in 1859. On the outbreak of the Civil War he commanded a regiment of volunteers, seeing action at Shiloh and winning promotion to major general for gallantry at Chickamauga in 1863. That year he resigned his command to enter Congress as a representative from Ohio, and he kept his seat for 17 years, becoming leader of the Republicans. In 1880 he was elected President by a slim margin, and at once alienated the stalwart faction of the Republican Party by asserting the right of the President to make political appointments without regard to party patronage. On the morning of July 2 he was shot in the Washington railroad station. He died on September 19 and was succeeded by Vice President **Chester Arthur**.

Garfinkel, Harold 1917– *•US sociologist•* Born in Newark, New Jersey, he was educated at Harvard. He taught briefly at Ohio State University and then in the department of sociology at UCLA (1954–88). He is the founder of the sociological tradition of ethnomethodology, an approach to social science that focuses on the practical reasoning processes that ordinary people use in order to understand and act within the social world.

Garibaldi, Giuseppe 1807–82 *•Italian revolutionary, soldier and politician•* He was born in Nice, French Empire (now in France), the son of a sailor. The greatest figure of the Risorgimento, he was a member of Young Italy and took part in an abortive **Mazzini**an insurrection in Genoa in 1834. He subsequently fled to South America, where he fought in defense of the Rio Grande do Sul Republic against the Brazilian Empire and in Uruguay against the Argentine dictator **Juan Manuel de Rosas**. He returned to Italy (1848) and offered his services to King Charles Albert (1798–1849) against the Austrians. Rejected, he instead took part in the government and defense of the Roman Republic before attempting to relieve the Venetian republic of **Daniele Manin**. In 1856 he backed the Italian National Society and played a minor but brilliant part in the 1859 campaign against the Austrians. In 1860 he set sail from Genoa with 1,000 volunteers ("Red Shirts") to assist the anti-**Bourbon** rebellion which had broken out in Sicily. Having seized control of the island, he crossed to the mainland of the Kingdom of the Two Sicilies and overran much of the Mezzogiorno before handing it over to **Victor Emmanuel II**. Two attempts to march on Rome (1862, 1867) ended in failure. He fought with limited success against the Austrians in 1866, and in 1870 he offered his services to the French after the Battle of Sedan. In 1870 he was elected a Deputy at the Bordeaux Assembly. He spent his last years as a farmer on Caprera.

Garioch, Robert, *pseudonym of* **Robert Garioch Sutherland** 1909–81 *•Scottish poet•* Born in Edinburgh and educated at the University there, he made his literary debut in 1933 with the surrealistic verse play *The Masque of Edinburgh* (published in expanded form in 1954). His first publications, *Seventeen Poems for Sixpence* (1940), in which he collaborated with **Sorley Maclean**, and *Chuckies on the Cairn* (1949), were hand-printed. His later work included *The Big Music* (1971) and *Dr Faust in Rose Street* (1973). He wrote in the Scots language in various styles and moods, from the colloquial to the literary, and translated many other authors into Scots. His prose works include *Two Men and a Blanket* (1975), an account of his experience in POW camps during World War II.

Garland, (Hannibal) Hamlin 1860–1940 *•US writer•* Born in West Salem, Wisconsin, in 1884 he went to Boston to teach and finally to write. In short stories such as the collections *Main Travelled Roads* (1887) and *Prairie Folks* (1892), in verse and in novels, he vividly, often grimly, described the farming life of the Midwest. *Rose of Dutcher's Coolly* (1895) was an important forerunner of the 1920s "revolt from the village." *A Daughter of the Middle Border* (1921) won the Pulitzer Prize. *Crumbling Idols* (1894) was a collection of essays, setting out Garland's theories of "veritism."

Garland, Judy, *originally* **Frances Ethel Gumm** 1922–69 *•US actress and singer•* Born in Grand Rapids, Minnesota, she became a juvenile film star in *Broadway Melody of 1938* and appeared in several fine film musicals, among them *The Wizard of Oz* (1939), *Meet Me in St Louis* (1944) and *Easter Parade* (1948). Personal appearances confirmed the emotional power of her voice, and in *A Star Is Born* (1954) she gave an impressive dramatic performance. Despite emotional and medical difficulties and a reputation for unreliability, she achieved the status of a legendary performer and actress. She was married five times, once to director Vincente Minnelli, and her daughters **Liza Minnelli** and Lorna Luft (1952–) also became actresses.

Garner, Errol (Louis) 1921–77 *•US jazz pianist•* Born in Pittsburgh, Pennsylvania, he was playing professionally as a teenager. He moved to New York City in 1944, where he worked in both the jazz clubs and the cabaret and cocktail lounge circuit. He never learned to read music, but evolved a distinctive, fearsomely virtuosic piano style which is readily identifiable in almost any setting. His growing popularity, bolstered by successful records like *Concert by the Sea* (1955), saw him lean increasingly toward the lucrative cabaret circuit.

Garner, Helen 1942– *•Australian writer•* Born in Geelong, Victoria, she taught in Melbourne schools until being dismissed for answering pupils' questions on sex. Her adult fiction appeals strongly to adolescents because of its nonjudgmental approach to contemporary problems. *Monkey Grip* (1977), dealing with the subculture of drug addiction, won the National Book Council award that year and was filmed in 1981. Other works include two novellas, *Honour* and *Other People's Children* (both 1980), *The Children's Bach* (1984), and collections of short stories such as *Cosmo Cosmolino* (1993). *First Stone* (1995) drew upon a Melbourne academic *cause célèbre* and attracted strong criticism from parts of the feminist movement. She has also written screenplays.

Garnett, David, *nicknamed* **Bunny** 1892–1981 *•English novelist•* He was born in Brighton, and studied botany at the Royal College of Science, London. His first novel, *Lady into Fox* (1922), won both the Hawthornden and the James Tait Black Memorial prizes. *A Man in the Zoo* (1924) and *The Sailor's Return* (1925) and several others followed. Associated with the Bloomsbury Group of artists and writers, he was also a prominent literary adviser and editor. He joined the RAF in 1939, and used this experience for *War in the Air* (1941).

Garnett, Eve 1900–91 *•English children's author and illustrator•* Born in Worcestershire, she studied at the Royal Academy of Art. Her artistic career included a commission for murals at Children's House, Bow, London, and an exhibition at the Tate Gallery, London, in 1939. Her name as an author rests upon *The Family from One End Street* (1937, Carnegie Medal), one of the first attempts to present working-class family life sympathetically in children's fiction.

Garnett, Tony 1936– *•English television and film producer•* Born in Birmingham, Midlands, he studied at London University, became an actor, and joined the BBC drama department (1964) as a script editor working on the Wednesday Play series. As a producer, he enjoyed a long association with director **Ken Loach** on such influential television work as *Cathy Come Home* (1966) and *Days of Hope* (1975). His films, also in collaboration with Loach, include *Kes* (1969) and *Black Jack* (1979). He made his directorial debut with *Prostitute* (1980). Now residing in Los Angeles, he has directed *Handgun* (retitled *Deep in the Heart*, 1983), and returned to production with *Earth Girls Are Easy* (1989), *Beautiful Thing* (1996) and various television series.

Garnier, Robert 1534–90 *•French poet and playwright•* Born in Maine, France, he was the most distinguished of the predecessors of **Pierre Corneille**. His *Œuvres complètes* (2 vols, 1923, 1949, "Complete Works") include the tragedy *Antigone* (1580).

Garrett, Lesley 1955– •*English opera singer*• Born near Doncaster, Yorkshire, she studied at the Royal Academy of Music and in 1979 won the prestigious Decca–Kathleen Ferrier Competition. In 1984, after stints with the Wexford Festival, Welsh National Opera, Opera North, Buxton Festival and Glyndebourne, she joined the English National Opera and became the subject of much media attention after baring her backside in a production of *Die Fledermaus*. She subsequently emerged as contemporary opera's most provocative diva and a popular favorite. She has also hosted several television series.

Garrick, David 1717–79 •*English actor, theater manager and playwright*• He was born in Hereford and educated at Lichfield Grammar School. In 1736 he was sent to study Latin and Greek under **Samuel Johnson** at Edial, and in 1737 he set off for London to study law, but became a wine merchant and then turned to the stage. His first play was performed at Drury Lane in 1740 and in 1741 he made his successful debut as an actor at Ipswich. The same year he appeared in London at Goodman's Fields, where his success as Richard III was so great that within a few weeks the two patent theaters were deserted, and crowds flocked to the unfashionable East End playhouse. When Goodman's Fields closed, he played at both Drury Lane and Covent Garden, but ultimately settled at Drury Lane, of which he became joint manager (1747), and from where he dominated the English stage for 30 years. He was buried in Westminster Abbey.

" "

Comedy is a very serious thing.

Attributed.

Garrison, William Lloyd 1805–79 •*US journalist and antislavery campaigner*• He was born in Newburyport, Massachusetts. A printer by trade, he became editor of the *Newburyport Herald* (1824) and the *National Philanthropist* (1828). Encouraged by abolitionist Benjamin Lundy (1789–1839), he denounced slavery so vigorously that he was imprisoned. He was founding editor of *The Liberator* (1831–65), visited Great Britain on lecture tours, and in 1833 founded the American Anti-Slavery Society.

Garson, Greer 1903–96 •*British actress*• Born in County Down, Northern Ireland, and educated at the University of London, she made her professional stage debut in 1932 with the Birmingham Repertory Company. She made her film debut as Mrs Chipping in *Goodbye Mr Chips* (1939). She won a Best Actress Academy Award for her role as the English matriarch in *Mrs Miniver* (1942) and generally portrayed wholesome, independent women in romantic dramas like *Random Harvest* (1942) and *Mrs Parkington* (1944). She played **Eleanor Roosevelt** in *Sunrise at Campobello* (1960) and appeared on television as Aunt March in *Little Women* (1978).

Garvey, Marcus Moziah Aurelius 1887–1940 •*Jamaican leader and advocate of Black nationalism*• Born in St Ann's Bay, Jamaica, he founded the Universal Negro Improvement Association (UNIA) in 1914 to foster worldwide Black unity and pride and moved its headquarters from Jamaica to New York City two years later. Rejecting integration, he called for a "back to Africa" movement, in which people of African descent from the US and elsewhere would settle in Liberia and build a modern Black state. In 1924 the Liberian government rejected his plans for resettlement, fearing that he intended to rule the country. After the collapse of his Black Star Steamship Line, which had been financed by the sale of stock to UNIA members, he was convicted of mail fraud (1925) and deported to Jamaica (1927). He died in obscurity in London.

Gascoigne, Paul John, *known as* **Gazza** 1967– •*English soccer player*• Born in Gateshead, Tyne and Wear, an unpredictable, at times explosive, midfielder, he was voted England's Young Player of the Year in 1988 while still with his first club, Newcastle. Transferred to Tottenham that same year for a then record sum of £2 million, he soon established himself as the creative heart of the English international team. His performances during the 1990 World Cup in Italy brought him to the attention of the Roman club Lazio, for whom he eventually signed for £5.5 million in June 1992. In 1995 he moved from Lazio to the Glasgow Rangers, followed by moves to Middlesbrough (1998) and Everton (2000).

Gaskell, Mrs Elizabeth Cleghorn, *née* **Stevenson** 1810–65 •*English novelist*• She was born in Cheyne Row, Chelsea, London, and was brought up by an aunt in Knutsford—the Cranford of her stories. In 1832 she married William Gaskell (1805–84), a Unitarian minister in Manchester. There she studied working men and women, and made important contributions to what came to be known as the "Condition of England" novel. *Mary Barton* was published anonymously in 1848, followed by *The Moorland Cottage* (1850), *Cranford* (1853), *Ruth* (1853), *North and South* (1855), *Round the Sofa* (1859), *Right at Last* (1860), *Sylvia's Lovers* (1863), *Cousin Phillis* (1865) and *Wives and Daughters* (1865). She also wrote *The Life of Charlotte Brontë* (1857).

Gasperi, Alcide de *See* **De Gasperi, Alcide**

Gass, William H(oward) 1924– •*US novelist*• He was born in Fargo, North Dakota, and educated at Ohio Wesleyan University, Delaware, and Cornell University. His novels include *Omensetter's Luck* (1966) and *Willie Masters' Lonesome Wife* (1971), an essay-novella, and his stories are collected as *In the Heart of the Heart of the Country* (1968). A philosopher and literary critic as well as novelist, he is linked with the symbolists, New Critics and the structuralists. His massive autobiographical novel, *The Tunnel* (1995), was in progress for more than 20 years.

Gasser, Herbert Spencer 1888–1963 •*US physiologist and Nobel Prize winner*• Born in Plattville, Wisconsin, he graduated in medicine from Johns Hopkins University in 1915, and moved in 1916 to the department of physiology at Washington University in St Louis, to rejoin **Joseph Erlanger**, an instructor from his student years, thus beginning a fruitful collaboration in neurophysiology. Gasser and Erlanger used powerful new electrical equipment to dissect and analyze the nature and function of the nerve fibers, sharing the Nobel Prize for physiology or medicine in 1944.

Gasset, José Ortega y *See* **Ortega y Gasset, José**

Gates, Bill (William Henry) 1955– •*US computer scientist and businessman*• He was born in Seattle, Washington, and attended Harvard, but left without graduating. In 1975, at the age of 19, he founded Microsoft Corporation with Paul Allen, and in 1980 they licensed a computer operating system to International Business Machines (IBM) for use in the fledgling personal computer (PC) industry. Microsoft became phenomenally successful, Gates became a billionaire by 1986, and by the turn of the century was estimated to be the world's most wealthy private individual. In 2000 Gates stepped down as chief executive officer of Microsoft, taking on the title of Chief Software Architect. His hi-tech, ecologically friendly home on the shore of Lake Washington has been one of his few acts of conspicuous expenditure, though he has set up several charitable foundations, including the Bill & Melinda Foundation, often expressing his intention, like **Andrew Carnegie**, to give away the vast bulk of his wealth by the time of his death. His best-selling business books include *The Road Ahead* (1995) and *Business @ the Speed of Thought* (1999).

Gates, Henry Louis, Jr 1950– •*US historian*• Born in Keyser, West Virginia, he studied history at Yale and Cambridge. He won a Macarthur "genius" grant in 1981 and has held professorships at several US universities, including Harvard (1991–). Perhaps the most eminent African-American scholar since **W E B Du Bois**, he has written critical works on race and identity and brought to light neglected Black fiction and poetry as well as autobiographical texts such as early slave narratives. His works include *The Signifying Monkey* (1988), *Colored People: A Memoir* (1994) and *Wonders of the African World* (1999).

Gates, Horatio 1728–1806 •*American revolutionary general*• Born in Maldon, England, he entered the English army, served in America and, on the peace of 1763, purchased an estate in Virginia. In the American Revolution (1775–83) he sided with his adoptive country. In August 1777 he commanded the northern department, and compelled the surrender of the British army at

Saratoga in October. This success gained him a great reputation, and he sought to supplant **George Washington**, the Commander in Chief. In 1780 he commanded the army of the South, but was routed by **Charles Cornwallis** near Camden, South Carolina.

Gatling, Richard Jordan 1818–1903 *•US inventor•* He was born in Money's Neck, North Carolina. He studied medicine but never practiced, and is known for his invention (1861–62) of the rapid-fire "Gatling gun," a revolving battery gun with 10 parallel barrels, firing 1,200 shots a minute.

Gaudí (i Cornet), Antoni 1852–1926 *•Spanish architect•* Born in Riudoms, Catalonia, he studied architecture at the Escuela Superior de Arquitectura in Barcelona. He became the leading exponent of Catalan modernism, inspired by a nationalistic search for a romantic medieval past. Strikingly original and ingenious, he designed a number of highly individualistic and unconventional buildings, such as the Palacio Güell (1886–89) and Parque Güell (1900–14) for his chief patron (Don Basilio Güell), the Casa Batlló (1904–17) and the Casa Milá (1905–09). His most celebrated work, the ornate church of the Sagrada Familia in Barcelona, occupied him from 1884 until his death. It is still under construction.

Gaudier-Brzeska, Henri, *originally* **Henri Gaudier** 1891–1915 *•French sculptor•* He was born in St Jean de Braye, near Orléans. In Paris (1910) he met the Polish artist Sophie Brzeska and from 1911 they both used the hyphenated name. In 1911 they settled in London. He became a founding member of the London Group (incorporating groups of younger artists) in 1913, and the following year signed the Vorticist Manifesto. He drew inspiration from African tribal art, but rapidly developed a personal abstract style exemplified in both carvings and drawings, for example *Red Stone Dancer* (1913, Tate Collection, London), *Crouching Figure* (1913–14, Minneapolis), and *Two Men with a Bowl* (1914, bronze, National Museum of Wales, Cardiff). He was killed in action at Neuville-Saint-Vaast.

Gauguin, (Eugène Henri) Paul 1848–1903 *•French postimpressionist painter•* He was born in Paris, and went to sea at the age of 17, but settled down in Paris in 1871 and became a successful stockbroker with a fondness for painting and for collecting impressionist paintings. By 1883 he had already exhibited his own work with the help of **Camille Pissarro** and determined to devote himself entirely to art. He left his Danish wife and five children, and went to Pont Aven, Brittany, where he became the leader of a group of painters. He traveled to Martinique (1887–88), and gradually evolved his own style, *synthesism*, in accordance with his hatred of civilization and identification with the emotional directness of primitive peoples. He moved more permanently to Tahiti in 1891–1901, and from there to the Marquesas Islands. His output developed markedly from the earlier Brittany seascapes—the *Still Life with Three Puppies* (1888, Museum of Modern Art, New York), the stained-glass effects of *The Vision after the Sermon* (1888, National Gallery, Edinburgh) with its echoes of Romanesque, Japanese and Breton folk art, to the tapestry-like canvases, painted in purples, greens, dark-reds and browns, of native subjects on Tahiti and at Dominiha on the Marquesas Islands, such as *No Te Aha De Riri, Why Are You Angry?* (1896, Chicago) and *Faa Iheihe, Decorated with Ornaments* (1898, Tate, London), which echoes his great allegorical painting dashed off prior to an unsuccessful suicide attempt, *D'où venons-nous? Que sommes-nous? Où allons-nous?* ("Whence do we come? What are we? Where are we going?" 1898, Boston). Gauguin also excelled in wood carvings of pagan idols and wrote an autobiographical novel, *Noa-Noa* (1894–1900). He is remembered not only because of the tragic choices he made, and as the subject of many popular novels (particularly **Somerset Maugham**'s *The Moon and Sixpence*, 1919), but because he directed attention to primitive art as a valid field of aesthetic exploration and consequently influenced almost every school of 20th-century art.

" "

There are noble tones, ordinary ones, tranquil harmonies, consoling ones, others which excite by their vigor.

1885 Letter to Emile Schuffenecker.

Gaulle, Charles de *See* **de Gaulle, Charles**

Gaultier, Jean-Paul 1952– *•French fashion designer•* He was born in Paris. Since launching his first collection in 1978 with a Japanese colleague, he has earned international renown for his fashions for both women and men. He also designs for ballet and for film (for example *The Cook, The Thief, His Wife and Her Lover*, 1989), has coreleased a record, *How to Do That* (1989), and launched his own perfume in 1993.

Gaumont, Léon Ernest 1864–1946 *•French cinema inventor•* He synchronized a projected film with a phonograph in 1901 and was responsible for the first talking pictures, demonstrated at the Académie des Sciences in Paris in 1910. In 1912 he introduced an early form of colored cinema film, using a three-color separation method with special lenses and projectors.

Gaunt, John of *See* **John of Gaunt**

Gauss, (Johann) Carl Friedrich 1777–1855 *•German mathematician, astronomer and physicist•* Born in Brunswick to poor parents, he came to the notice of the Duke of Brunswick, who paid for his education at the Collegium Carolinum, Brunswick, and the University of Göttingen. A notebook kept in Latin by him as a youth and discovered in 1898 showed that, from the age of 15, he had conjectured and often proved many remarkable results, including the prime number theorem. In 1796 he announced that he had found a ruler and compass construction for the 17-sided polygon, and in 1801 published his *Disquisitiones arithmeticae*, containing wholly new advances in number theory. In 1807 he became director of the Göttingen Observatory, also studying celestial mechanics (on which he published a treatise in 1809) and statistics (he was the first to use the method of least squares). From 1818 to 1825 he directed the geodetic survey of Hanover, during which time he produced a study of the theory of errors of observation. He also worked on differential equations, the hypergeometric function, the curvature of surfaces, four different proofs of the fundamental theorem of algebra, six of quadratic reciprocity and much else in number theory. In physics he studied the earth's magnetism and developed the magnetometer in conjunction with Wilhelm Eduard Weber (1804–91), and gave a mathematical theory of the optical systems of lenses. Manuscripts unpublished until long after his death show that he had made many other discoveries, including the theory of elliptic functions that had been published independently by **Niels Henrik Abel** and **Carl Gustav Jacobi**, and had come to accept the possibility of a non-Euclidean geometry of space, first published by **János Bolyai** and **Nikolai Lobachevski** in the 1820s.

Gautama, *also known as* **Gotama** 1st century AD *•Indian philosopher•* Born in Bihar, he founded *Nyaya*, one of the six classical systems of Hindu philosophy. His *Nyaya Sutras* are principally concerned with ways of knowing and of reaching valid logical conclusions. They are thought to have been written in the 1st century AD, though tradition maintains Gautama lived in the 3rd century BC.

Gautama Siddhartha *See* **Buddha**

Gavaskar, Sunil Manohar, *nicknamed* **the Little Master** 1949– *•Indian cricket player•* Born in Bombay and educated at St Xavier's College and Bombay University, the perfection of his style as well as his short stature earned him his nickname. He played in 125 Test matches for India from 1971 to 1997, and scored 10,122 runs, including a record 34 Test centuries. He was the first player to score more than 10,000 Test runs.

Gawain Poet, The fl. c. 1370 *•Anonymous English poet•* He is the presumed author of *Cleanness*, *Patience*, *Pearl* and *Sir Gawain and the Green Knight*, the Arthurian masterpiece after which he is named. All four poems, written in the same northern England dialect, are found together in a single surviving manuscript. Each of the shorter poems has an explicitly religious theme. *Gawain* itself is a richer, longer, less overtly didactic work: the story of one of King **Arthur**'s knights and a threatening stranger who comes to Camelot, it can be read as a straightforward adventure or as a quest for spiritual knowledge. Either way it is one of the most remarkable works in the history of English poetry.

Gay, John 1685–1732 *•English poet•* Born in Barnstaple, Devon, he was apprenticed to a silk merchant in London, but soon returned home to write. In 1708 he published his first poem, *Wine*, and in 1711 a pamphlet on the *Present State of Wit*. Appointed secretary to the Duchess of Monmouth (1712), in 1713 he dedicated to **Pope** the georgic *Rural Sports*. In 1714 he published *The Fan* and *The Shepherd's Week*, and accompanied Lord Clarendon, envoy to Hanover, as secretary. With Pope and **John Arbuthnot**, he wrote the play *Three Hours after Marriage* (1717), and in 1727 he produced the first series of his popular *Fables*. His greatest success was *The Beggar's Opera* (1728), set to music by German composer Johann Pepusch (1667–1752), the outcome of a suggestion made by **Jonathan Swift** in 1716.

" "

Praising all alike, is praising none.

1714 "A Letter to a Lady," l. 114.

Gaye, Marvin 1939–84 •*US soul singer*• Born in Washington DC, the son of a clergyman, he started singing and playing the organ in church and at 15 joined the doo-wop group The Rainbows. Moving to Detroit, he signed a recording contract with the Tamla/Motown company in 1961. Most of his early recordings were in the beat ballad idiom, although there were notable exceptions including the dance-oriented "Hitch Hike," and the 12-bar blues of "Can I Get a Witness." "I Heard It Through the Grapevine" (1968) was his last standard Motown recording and from 1970, despite arguments with the company management, he adopted a more independent attitude. *What's Going On* (1971) was a concept album that showed a fluidity and intelligence far removed from his previous teen ballad hits. Subsequent albums included *In Our Lifetime* (1981) and *Midnight Love* (1982). He was killed by a gunshot during a quarrel with his father.

Gay-Lussac, Joseph Louis 1778–1850 •*French chemist and physicist*• Born in Saint-Léonard, Haute Vienne, he was educated at the École Polytechnique and the École des Ponts et Chaussées. He became assistant to **Claude Louis Berthollet** in 1800 and subsequently held teaching posts at the École Polytechnique (from 1809)and the Sorbonne (1809–32) and the National Museum of Natural History (from 1832), also overseeing production at the government gunpowder factory (from 1818) and the Mint (from 1829). He became an Academician (1806), member of the Chamber of Deputies (1831) and member of the Upper House (1839). His earliest research was on the expansion of gases with temperature increases, and he discovered independently the law which is commonly known as Charles's law. In 1804 he made balloon ascents to make magnetic and atmospheric observations, and he traveled with Baron **Alexander von Humboldt** (1805–06), making measurements of terrestrial magnetism. In 1808 he published his important law of gas volumes, based on work which he had begun with Humboldt in 1805. From around 1808 he collaborated with **Louis Jacques Thénard** on the isolation and investigation of sodium, potassium, boron and silicon, and the improvement of methods of organic analysis. His last great pure research was on hydrocyanic acid and cyanogen and their derivatives.

Gaynor, Janet, *originally* **Laura Gainor** 1906–84 •*US actress*• Born in Philadelphia, she was educated in San Francisco. After various small comedy roles, she went on to win the first ever Best Actress Academy Award for a trio of performances in *Sunrise* (1927), *Seventh Heaven* (1927) and *Street Angel* (1928). She became a major star in the 1930s, and her many successes include *State Fair* (1933) and *A Star Is Born* (1937). She occasionally performed on television and the stage, and her later theater work included *Harold and Maude* (1980) on Broadway.

Gazza *See* **Gascoigne, Paul John**

Geber 14th century •*Spanish alchemist*• Nothing is known about him except his name as the author of Latin works on chemical and alchemical theory and practice. He took the name "Geber" (Latin for "Jabir") from Abu Musa Jabir ibn Hayyan, a famous Islamic alchemist and physician of the 8th century. It was through Geber's works that the discoveries of the early Arab chemists, along with many basic laboratory techniques, were relayed to Europe.

Gebrselassie, Haile 1973– •*Ethiopian athlete*• Born in Arsi, he had to run 10 kilometers each day to and from school and attracted international attention in 1992 when he won the 5,000-meter and 10,000-meter events at the world junior championships. Subsequently he established himself as the greatest long-distance runner ever, including among his triumphs 15 track world records, four world titles in the 10,000 meters and gold medals in the same event at the Olympic Games of 1996 and 2000.

Geertz, Clifford James 1926– •*US cultural anthropologist*• Born in San Francisco, he studied at Antioch College and Harvard, and taught at the University of California, Berkeley (1958–60), and at the University of Chicago (1960–70) before becoming Professor of Social Science at Princeton's Institute of Advanced Study (1970). He carried out fieldwork in Java (1952–54) and Bali (1957–58), which resulted in *The Religion of Java* (1960) and *Person, Time and Conflict in Bali* (1966), and in the 1960s and 1970s made several field trips to Morocco, producing *Islam Observed* (1968). His eloquent theoretical essays on topics ranging from art and ideology to politics and nationalism, collected in *The Interpretation of Cultures* (1973) and *Local Knowledge* (1983), were particularly influential.

Gehrig, Lou (Henry Louis), *nicknamed* **the Iron Horse** 1903–41 •*US baseball player*• Born in New York City, he earned his nickname through his endurance. His record number of 2,130 consecutive major league games for the New York Yankees (1925–39) stood for 56 years before being beaten by **Cal Ripken Jr**, and he was voted Most Valuable Player four times. His career was cut short by amyotrophic lateral sclerosis (also called Lou Gehrig's disease). The story of his life was told in the film *Pride of the Yankees* (1942).

Gehring, Walter Jacob 1939– •*Swiss geneticist*• Born in Zurich, he was educated at the University of Zurich and Yale University, where he taught from 1969 to 1972. Since 1972 he has been Professor of Genetics and Developmental Biology at the University of Basel. His career has mainly been concerned with the genetics of the fruit fly, in the mid-1980s discovering the short DNA sequence, called the homeobox, which controls genetic mutation and development in the insect. It was later found that similar control sequences occur in mammals, thus encouraging new lines of research.

Geiger, Hans Wilhelm 1882–1945 •*German physicist*• Born in Neustadt-an-der-Haardt, he was educated at the University of Erlangen and worked under **Ernest Rutherford** at Manchester (1906–12). With Rutherford, he devised a means of detecting alpha particles (1908), and subsequently showed that two α-particles are emitted in the radioactive decay of uranium. With J M Nuttall he demonstrated the linear relationship between the logarithm of the range of α-particles and the radioactive time constant of the emitting nucleus, now called the Geiger-Nuttall rule. In 1925 he became professor at the University of Kiel. There, he and Walther Müller made improvements to the particle counter, resulting in the modern form of the Geiger-Müller counter (Geiger counter), which also detects electrons and ionizing radiation.

Geissler, Heinrich 1814–79 •*German inventor*• Born in Saxony, he became a glass blower and settled in Bonn in 1854. The "Geissler tube," by which the passage of electricity through rarefied gases can be seen, and the "Geissler mercury pump," are among his inventions.

Gelasius I, St 5th century–6th century •*African pope*• Born in Africa, he was pope from AD 492 to 496, and was one of the earliest bishops of Rome to assert the supremacy of the papal chair. He repressed Pelagianism, renewed the ban against the Eastern patriarch, drove out the Manichaeans from Rome, and wrote against the Eutychians and Nestorians.

Geldof, Bob 1954– •*Irish rock musician and philanthropist*• Born in Dublin and educated at Black Rock College, he was lead singer in the rock group the Boomtown Rats (1975–86). Moved by television pictures of famine-stricken Ethiopia, he established the pop charity "Bandaid" trust in 1984. This raised £8 million for African famine relief through the release of the record "Do They Know It's Christmas?" In 1985, simultaneous "Live Aid" charity concerts were held in London and Philadelphia, which, transmitted by satellite throughout the world, raised a further £48 million. Further charitable events followed, and Geldof was given the honorary title Knight Commander, Order of the British Empire, in 1986, as well as a variety of international honors. From 1986 to 1996 he was married to Paula Yates (1959–2000).

Gellhorn, Martha Ellis 1908–98 •*US journalist and writer*• Born in St Louis, Missouri, and educated at Bryn Mawr College, she became a foreign correspondent for *Collier's Weekly*, covering, among other things, the Spanish civil war. She almost certainly saw more violent action than her first husband, **Ernest Hemingway**. Her interest in human conflict remained undimmed and she continued to report on wars in Java (1946), Vietnam (1966), the Middle East (1967) and Central America (1983–85). Her earlier reportage was collected in *The Face of War* (1959). Her novels include *What Mad Pursuit* (1934), *Liana* (1943) and *The Wine of Astonishment* (1948). Her short stories, in collections such as *The Weather in Africa* (1978), are marked by acute observation, moral straightforwardness and sympathy for the weak or oppressed.

“ ”

It would be a bitter cosmic joke if we destroy ourselves due to atrophy of the imagination.

*1959 **The Face of War**, introduction.*

Gell-Mann, Murray 1929– •*US theoretical physicist and Nobel Prize winner*• Born in New York City, he went to Yale when he was 15 years old, and graduated in 1948. He earned his PhD from MIT, spent a year at the Institute of Advanced Studies in Princeton, then joined the Institute for Nuclear Studies at the University of Chicago, where he worked with **Enrico Fermi**. He later taught at the California Institute of Technology (1956–93, now emeritus). When he was 24 he made a major contribution to the theory of elementary particles by introducing the concept of strangeness, a new quantum number that must be conserved in any so-called strong nuclear interaction event. Gell-Mann and Yuval Ne'eman (independently) used strangeness to group mesons, nucleons (neutrons and protons) and hyperons, and thus they were able to form predictions in the same way that **Dmitri Mendeleev** had about chemical elements. The omega-minus particle was predicted by this theory and observed in 1964. Gell-Mann and George Zweig (1937–) introduced the concept of quarks which have one-third integral charge and baryon number. Six quarks have been predicted, named up, down, strange, charm, bottom and top. For this work he was awarded the Nobel Prize for physics in 1969. In 1994 he published *The Quark and the Jaguar*.

Gemayel, Amin 1942– •*Lebanese politician*• Son of **Pierre Gemayel** and brother of **Bachir Gemayel**, he studied law. He was Bachir's successor to the presidency in 1982. Politically more moderate, he initially proved no more successful in determining a peaceful settlement of the problems of Lebanese government. In 1988 his presidency came to an end and no obvious Christian successor, as required by the constitution, was apparent until the appointment of Rene Muawad and then **Elias Hrawi** in 1989.

Gemayel, Bashir 1947–82 •*Lebanese army officer and politician*• He was the brother of **Amin Gemayel** and his father was **Pierre Gemayel**. He was an active leader of the Christian militia in the 1975–76 civil war, and led the military forces of East Beirut. His evident distancing of his party from Israeli support and wish to expel all foreign influence from Lebanese affairs effected his election as president in 1982. Having twice escaped assassination, he was killed in a bomb explosion while still president-elect.

Gemayel, Sheikh Pierre 1905–84 •*Lebanese politician*• The father of **Amin Gemayel** and **Bachir Gemayel**, he was a member of the Maronite Christian community of Lebanon, and was educated in Beirut and Paris, where he trained as a pharmacist. In 1936 he founded the Kataeb, or Phalangist Party, modeled on the Spanish and German fascist organizations, and in 1937 became its leader. He was twice imprisoned, in 1937 and in 1943, the year in which he organized a general strike. He held various ministerial posts (1960–67), and led the Phalangist Militia in the 1975–76 civil war.

Gems, Pam (Iris Pamela), *née* **Price** 1925– •*English dramatist*• She was born in Bransgore, Hampshire. It was *Dusa, Stas, Fish and Vi*, staged in London in 1975, which brought her widespread recognition. A study of the lives of four contemporary women, it was a courageous piece of feminist drama. Other plays include *Piaf* (1978), *Camille* (1984), *The Danton Affair* (1986) and *Stanley* (1997), for which she won an Olivier Award.

Genet, Jean 1910–86 •*French author*• Born in Paris, he spent many years in reform schools and prisons, in France and abroad, for theft, male prostitution, and other crimes, and began to write in 1942 in Fresnes prison where he was serving a life sentence. His first novel, *Notre-Dame des fleurs* (1944, Eng trans *Our Lady of the Flowers*, 1949), portraying his world of homosexuals and criminals in a characteristically ceremonial and religious language, created a sensation. Later novels include *Miracle de la rose* (1946, Eng trans *Miracle of the Rose*, 1965) and *Pompes funèbres* (1947, Eng trans *Funeral Rites*, 1969). In 1948 he was granted a pardon by the president after a petition by French intellectuals, and **Jean-Paul Sartre**'s book *Saint Genet* (1952, Eng trans 1963) later spread his fame. On release from prison he was associated with revolutionary movements in many countries. Several plays, including *Les Bonnes* (1946, Eng trans *The Maids*, 1954), *Les Nègres* (1958, Eng trans *The Blacks*, 1960) and *Les Paravents* (1961, Eng trans *The Screens*, 1962), and poems such as "Les Condamnés à mort" (1942, "Those Condemned to Death") share the criminal underworld setting and profoundly pessimistic outlook of the novels. His autobiography, *Le Journal du voleur*, was published in 1949 (Eng trans *Thief's Journal*, 1954).

Genêt *See* **Flanner, Janet**

Geneviève, St c. 422–512 AD •*French patron saint of Paris*• Born at Nanterre, near Paris, she took the veil from St **Germanus**. She acquired a reputation for sanctity, increased by her assurance that **Attila** and his Huns would not touch Paris in AD 451, and by her expedition for the relief of the starving city during Childeric's Frankish invasion. In 460 she built a church over the tomb of St **Denis**, where she herself was buried. Her feast day is January 3.

Genghis Khan, *also spelled* **Jingis, Chingis, Chinghiz** or **Chingiz**, *originally* **Temujin** c. 1162–1227 •*Mongol warrior and ruler*• He was born in Deligun Bulduk on the River Onon, the son of a Mongol chief. He was called upon at age 13 to succeed his father, and faced a long and hard struggle against hostile tribes to establish his authority. Continued success stimulated his ambition, and he spent six years subjugating the Naimans between Lake Balkhash and the Irtysh, and conquering Tangut, south of the Gobi Desert. The Turkic Uigurs voluntarily submitted, and from them the Mongols derived their civilization, their alphabet and their laws. In 1206 he was able to change his name from Temujin to Genghis Khan, "Universal Ruler." In 1211 he overran the empire of North China, and in 1217 he conquered and annexed the Kara-Khitai Khanate empire from Lake Balkhash to Tibet. In 1218 he attacked the powerful empire of Khwarezm, bounded by the Syr Darya (Jaxartes), Indus, Persian Gulf and Caspian, took Bukhara, Samarkand, Khwarezm and other chief cities, and returned home in 1225. Two of Genghis's lieutenants penetrated northward from the southern shore of the Caspian through Georgia into southern Russia and the Crimea, everywhere routing and slaying, and returned by way of the Volga. Meanwhile in the far east another of his generals had completed the conquest of all northern China (1217–23) except Honan. After a few months' rest Genghis set out to punish the king of Tangut. He brought the country under control, but died on August 18, 1227. Genghis was not just a warrior and conqueror, but a skilful administrator and ruler. He conquered empires stretching from the Black Sea to the Pacific, and organized them into states of some permanence, on which his successors were able to build.

Gennaro, San *See* **Januarius, St**

Genseric *See* **Gaiseric**

Gentile da Fabriano *See* **Fabriano, Gentile da**

Gentile, Giovanni 1875–1944 •*Italian philosopher, educationist and politician*• He was born in Castelvetrano, Sicily. He was Professor of Philosophy successively at Naples (1898–1906), Palermo (1906–14), Pisa (1914–17) and Rome (1917–44), and collaborated with **Benedetto Croce** in editing the periodical *La Critica* (1903–22). Gentile proposed a theory of "actualism," in which nothing is real except the pure act of thought, and his main philosophical work was the *Theory of Mind as Pure Act* (1916). He also became an apologist for Fascism and became the Fascist Minister of Public Instruction (1922–24), presiding over two commissions on constitutional reform and over the Supreme Council for Public Education (1926–28). Possibly his most important achievement was to plan the new *Enciclopedia Italiana* (35 vols, 1929–36), which became the main cultural monument of the regime. He was assassinated by anti-Fascist partisans in Florence after Mussolini's overthrow.

Gentileschi, Artemisia, *properly* **Artemisia Lomi** c. 1597–c. 1652 •*Italian painter*• Born in Rome, she was the daughter of **Orazio Gentileschi**. She moved to Naples in 1630, and visited her father in England (1638–39), leaving a fine self-portrait at Hampton Court. She often depicted the decapitation of a man by a woman, and her chief work is a *Judith and Holophernes* in the Uffizi, Florence.

Gentileschi, Orazio, *properly* **Orazio Lomi** 1563–1647 •*Italian painter*• Born in Pisa, he settled in England in 1626, the first Italian painter called to England by **Charles I**, having been patronized by the Vatican and the **Medici**s in Genoa. He was responsible for the decoration of the Queen's House at Greenwich (partly transferred to Marlborough House), and painted *Discovery of Moses* (Prado, Madrid), *Flight into Egypt* (Louvre, Paris) and *Joseph and Potiphar's Wife* (Hampton Court, London).

Geoffrey of Monmouth, *Latin name* **Gaufridus Monemutensis** c. 1100–c. 1154 •*Welsh chronicler and ecclesiastic*• Thought to be the son of Breton parents, he studied at Oxford, was archdeacon of Llandaff or Monmouth (c. 1140) and was appointed Bishop of St Asaph (1152). He compiled a fictitious history of Great Britain, *Historia regum Britanniae* (c. 1136), which traced the descent of British kings back to the Trojans, and he claimed to have based it on old Welsh chronicles that he alone had seen. Composed before 1147, it introduced the legends of King **Arthur** to European literature.

George, St early 4th century AD •*English patron of chivalry and guardian saint of England and Portugal*• He may have been put to death by **Diocletian** at Nicomedia in AD 303, or died at Lydda in Palestine (c. 250), where his alleged tomb is exhibited. He has been confused by many writers with the Arian George of Cappadocia (d. 361). St George of the Eastern Church was no doubt a real person of an earlier date than George of Cappadocia, but beyond this nothing is known of him, and his name was early obscured by fable. The famous story of his fight with the dragon cannot be traced much earlier than the *Legenda Aurea* of Italian prelate and hagiologist Jacobus de Voragine (1230–98). The crusades gave a great impetus to his cult, many chivalrous orders assumed him as their patron, and he was adopted as guardian saint by England, Aragon and Portugal. In 1348 **Edward III** founded St George's Chapel, Windsor, and in 1344 the Order of the Garter was instituted. His feast day is April 23.

George I 1660–1727 •*King of Great Britain and Ireland and elector of Hanover*• He was born in Osnabrück, Hanover, the eldest son of Ernest August, Elector of Hanover, and **Sophia**, daughter of **Elizabeth** of Bohemia. Elector of Hanover himself from 1698, he was a great-grandson of **James VI and I** of Scotland and England, and succeeded to the British throne in 1714 on the death of Queen **Anne** in accordance with the Act of Settlement (1701). He was the first Hanoverian king of Great Britain and Ireland. As a young man he held a military command in the War of Succession against **Louis XIV** of France. He married his cousin, Sophia Dorothea of Zell (1666–1726), in 1682, but divorced her in 1694 for adultery and, although he lived openly with his own mistresses, kept her imprisoned in the castle of Ahlden until her death. The Hanoverian succession was unpopular in England, but Whig support for him was strengthened by the unsuccessful Jacobite uprising in 1715 to restore the exiled **Stuart**s, who were debarred from the throne on account of their Roman Catholicism. The uprising was exploited by the Whigs to discredit the Tories in light of their lukewarm support for the Hanoverian king, while George's own preference for the Whigs served to give them a monopoly of power which was to last for another 50 years. George never learned English, but although he preferred whenever possible to spend time in Hanover, he was no mere figurehead in the government of Great Britain. His reign saw an unprecedented dominance of the court party over parliament, intensified during the premiership of Sir **Robert Walpole**, from 1721 onward.

George II 1683–1760 •*King of Great Britain and Ireland and elector of Hanover*• He was born in Herrenhausen, Hanover, the son of **George I**, whom he succeeded in 1727. In 1705 he married **Caroline of Ansbach**. Despite the personal antipathy that had existed between father and son during most of George's adult life and his opposition to his father's government, he maintained his father's principal minister, Sir **Robert Walpole**, in power. Walpole's peace policy was breached by war with Spain in 1737 and British participation in the War of the Austrian Succession (1742–48). The king, the last British monarch to take part in a battle, took the field as commander of the British army at the Battle of Dettingen (1743), which he won. In 1745 a Jacobite uprising in Scotland under the Young Pretender, **Charles Edward Stuart**, was at first alarmingly successful, but without the hoped-for aid from France the Scots had little real chance against the British army and were savagely cut down at Culloden by George's second son, William Augustus, the Duke of **Cumberland**. British involvement (1756–57) in the Seven Years' War (1756–63) was largely undertaken in defense of Hanover, but, while Great Britain suffered reverses in Europe, this was more than offset by successes further afield. **Robert Clive**'s victory at Plassey in 1757 helped to lay the foundations of British India, and the capture of Quebec by **James Wolfe** in 1759 established British supremacy in North America.

George III, *in full* **George William Frederick** 1738–1820 •*King of Great Britain and Ireland and of Hanover*• He was born in London, the eldest son of **Frederick Louis**, Prince of Wales. In 1760 he succeeded his grandfather, **George II**, as king of Great Britain and Ireland and elector of Hanover (king of Hanover from 1815). Eager to govern as well as reign, he did not lack ability but was not politically adept and caused considerable friction. With Lord **North** he shared the blame for the loss of the American colonies, and popular feeling ran high against him for a time in the 1770s. In 1783 he called **William Pitt** the Younger to office, an important stage in reducing the political influence of a small group of established Whig families. In 1810 the Princess Amelia, George's favorite child, fell dangerously ill; this preyed on the king's mind, and hastened an attack of mental derangement, not the first he had had. He also lost his sight, and his ailment is now believed to have been caused by porphyria. In 1811 the Prince of Wales (later **George IV**) was appointed regent.

George IV 1762–1830 •*King of Great Britain and Ireland and of Hanover*• Born in London, he was the eldest son of **George III**, and owing to his father's insanity he became prince regent (1811), succeeding in 1820. Until the age of 19 he was kept under strict discipline, against which he sometimes rebelled. In 1785, he secretly married Mrs **Maria Fitzherbert**, a Roman Catholic, which was canonically valid, but not acceptable under English law. In 1795 he married Princess **Caroline of Brunswick**, but later tried to divorce her, causing a scandal in which the people sympathized with the queen. Though a professed Whig when Prince of Wales (out of antagonism to his father), as George IV he governed, as his father had done, with the aid of the Tories. He left the nation a valuable collection of books and paintings, and as a patron of the arts recognized the genius of **John Nash** and supported Wyatville's restoration of Windsor Castle.

George V 1865–1936 •*King of Great Britain and Northern Ireland*• Born at Marlborough House, London, he served in the navy and was made Prince of Wales in 1901. He succeeded his father, **Edward VII**, in 1910. His reign was marked by various important events, such as his visit to India for the Coronation Durbar (1911), World War I (1914–18), the adoption of the surname Windsor (1917), the Sinn Fein Rebellion (1916), the Irish Free State settlement (1922), the first Labour governments (1924, 1929–31), a general strike (1926), economic crisis and a National government (1931), the Statute of Westminster, defining Dominion status (1931), and the Government of India Act (1935). He originated the famous Christmas Day broadcasts to the nation in 1932. In 1893 he married **Mary of Teck**. Although he was without intellectual curiosity and suspicious of new ideas, he was responsible for the development of the monarchy as a symbol of national unity. He had five sons: **Edward VIII**, **George VI**, Prince Henry, Duke of **Gloucester**, Prince George, Duke of **Kent**, and Prince John (1905–19), and one daughter, Mary, Princess Royal (1897–1965), who married the 6th Earl of Harewood.

“ ”

Today 23 years ago, dear Grandmama died. I wonder what she would have thought of a Labour government.

1924 Of Queen Victoria. Diary entry, January 22.

George VI 1895–1952 •*King of Great Britain and Northern Ireland*• The second son of **George V**, and father of **Elizabeth II** and Princess **Margaret**, he was born at Sandringham House, Norfolk, and educated at Dartmouth and at Trinity College, Cambridge. He served in the Grand Fleet at the Battle of Jutland (1916), and later in the Royal Naval Air Service and the RAF (1917–19). Keenly interested in the human problems of industry, he became president of the Boys' Welfare Association and originated the summer camps for public school and working-class boys. In 1920 he was created Duke of York and he married **Elizabeth** (Lady Elizabeth Bowes-Lyon) in 1923. An outstanding tennis player, he played at Wimbledon in the All-England championships (1926). On the abdication of his elder brother, **Edward VIII**, he ascended the throne in 1936. During World War II he set a personal example over wartime restrictions, continued to reside in bomb-damaged Buckingham Palace, visited all the theaters of the war and delivered many broadcasts. His last great public occasion was the opening of the Festival of Britain (1951). He died in his sleep on February 6, 1952, and was succeeded by his daughter **Elizabeth II**.

George I 1845–1913 •*King of Greece*• The second son of King **Christian IX** of Denmark, he was born in Copenhagen. He served in the Danish navy, and on the deposition of King Otto of Greece (1832–62) he was elected king (1863) by the Greek national assembly. His reign was a formative period in Greece's emergence as a modern European state. It saw the consolidation of Greek territory in Thessaly and Epirus, and the suppression of a Cretan insurrection (1896–97). Involved in the Balkan War of 1912–13, he was assassinated at Thessaloniki, and succeeded by his son **Constantine I**.

George II 1890–1947 •*King of Greece*• The son of **Constantine I** and grandson of **George I**, he was born in Tatoë, near Athens, and succeeded to the throne on his father's second abdication (1922), but was deposed (1923) by a military junta. Restored to the throne by plebiscite (1935), he worked closely and controversially with his dictatorial prime minister, **Yanni Metaxas**. When Greece was overrun by the Germans (1941) after successfully resisting the Italian invasion of 1940–41, he withdrew to Crete and then to England. In 1946 he was restored to the throne, again by plebiscite. He was succeeded by his brother **Paul I**.

George, David Lloyd *See* **Lloyd-George (of Dwyfor), 1st Earl**

Gerald of Wales *See* **Giraldus Cambrensis**

Gérard, François Pascal Simon, Baron 1770–1837 •*French painter*• Born in Rome but brought up in Paris, he became a pupil of **Jacques Louis David** and a member of the Revolutionary Tribunal in 1793. His full-length portrait of the miniaturist **Jean Baptiste Isabey** (1796) and his *Cupid and Psyche* (1798), both in the Louvre, Paris, established his reputation, and leading men and women of the Empire and the Restoration sat for him. After the fall of **Napoleon I** in 1815 he became court painter to **Louis XVIII**.

Gere, Richard 1949– •*US film actor*• Born in Philadelphia, he studied at the University of Massachusetts before gaining extensive experience in the theater. He rose to stardom playing narcissistic loners and rebels in films like *Looking For Mr Goodbar* (1977), *American Gigolo* (1980) and *An Officer and a Gentleman* (1982). His popularity dimmed in the late 1980s, but he reasserted himself with a chilling performance as a corrupt policeman in *Internal Affairs* (1989) and showed a deft comic touch in the box-office hit *Pretty Woman* (1990). Subsequent films include *Sommersby* (1993), *The Day Of The Jackal* (1997) and *Chicago* (2003). A committed Buddhist and spokesman for various Tibetan causes, he was briefly married (1991–94) to **Cindy Crawford**.

Gerhard, Roberto 1896–1970 •*British composer*• Born in Valls, near Tarragona, Spain, of Swiss parentage, he studied piano with Enrique Granados y Campiña (1868–1916), and composition with Felipe Pedrell (1841–1922) starting in 1916, and with **Arnold Schoenberg**. After the Republican collapse in the civil war he left Barcelona to settle in England (1939), becoming a British subject in 1960. Most of his music was written in England and is characterized by orchestral, rhythmic and melodic inventiveness. He composed ballets, an opera, *The Duenna* (1945–47), five symphonies, concertos, chamber music and some electronic music.

Gerhardie or **Gerhardi, William Alexander** 1895–1977 •*English novelist*• He was born in St Petersburg, Russia, of English parents, and educated there. He then served in the British Embassy at Petrograd (again St Petersburg) from 1917 to 1918, and later with the military mission in Siberia, before going to Worcester College, Oxford, where he wrote *Futility: A Novel on Russian Themes* (1922), and a lively study of **Chekhov** (1923). In 1925 he published *The Polyglots*, his most celebrated novel. Other works include *Of Mortal Love* (1936) and *Memoirs of a Polyglot*, his autobiography.

Géricault, (Jean Louis André) Théodore 1791–1824 •*French painter*• Born in Rouen, he became a pupil (1810) of **Pierre Guérin**, in whose studio he met and befriended **Eugène Delacroix**. A great admirer of the 17th-century Dutch and Flemish schools, Géricault revolted against the current classicism, and his unorthodox approach and bold use of color incurred the disapproval of his teacher, who advised him to give up painting. His first important exhibition piece was *Officer of Light Horse* at the Salon of 1812, which was followed by other canvases noteworthy for their realism, including his masterpiece *The Raft of the Medusa* (1818–19, Louvre, Paris). Based on a shipwreck that had shortly before caused a sensation in France, it impressed Delacroix but was harshly criticized, and Géricault withdrew to England, where he did a number of paintings of racing scenes and landscapes.

Germain, Sophie 1776–1831 •*French mathematician*• Born in Paris, she was not admitted, as a woman, to the newly established École Polytechnique, but in the guise of a male student she submitted a paper which so impressed **Joseph de Lagrange** that he became her personal tutor. She gave a more generalized proof of **Pierre de Fermat**'s "last theorem" than had previously been available, developed a mathematical explanation of the figures of Ernst Chladni (1756–1827) and went on to derive a general mathematical description of the vibrations of curved as well as plane elastic surfaces.

Germanicus Caesar 15 BC–AD 19 •*Roman soldier*• Son of Nero Claudius **Drusus** and of Antonia, daughter of **Mark Antony**, he was adopted by the emperor **Tiberius**. In AD 13 he was appointed to command the eight legions on the Rhine, and two years later he marched to meet **Arminius**, whom he overthrew in two desperate battles. Tiberius, jealous of his popularity, sent him to the East in AD 17, appointing Calpurnius Piso as viceroy of Syria in order secretly to counteract him. Germanicus died at Epidaphnae, near Antioch, probably of poison. His wife, **Agrippina** the Elder, and two of her sons were eventually put to death, but the third son, **Caligula**, survived to become emperor. The notorious **Agrippina** the Younger was his daughter.

Germanus, St c. 378–448 AD •*French religious*• Born near Augustodunum, Gaul (now Autun, France), he was made Bishop of Auxerre. He was invited to Britain to combat Pelagianism in AD 429, and under him the Christian Britons won the bloodless "Alleluia Victory" over the Picts and Saxons at Maes Garmon ("Germanus's field") in Flintshire. His feast day is July 31.

Geronimo, *Apache name* **Goyathlay ("One Who Yawns")** 1829–1909 •*Apache leader*• Born in Arizona, he became a chief of the Chiricahua Apaches and warred against the Mexicans (who killed his mother, wife and children) as well as the US soldiers and settlers who arrived in the region after Mexico ceded it to the US in 1848. Confined to a series of reservations outside their ancestral lands, he and his followers escaped repeatedly and led raids against the settlers for more than a decade. On their final surrender in 1886, they were placed under military confinement. Geronimo later became a farmer in Oklahoma with his people and adopted Christianity. He dictated his autobiography, *Geronimo: His Own Story* (1906).

Gerry, Elbridge 1744–1814 •*US politician*• Born in Marblehead, Massachusetts, he graduated from Harvard in 1762, served in the Continental Congress (1776–81, 1783–85), and was a signer of the Declaration of Independence. Elected governor of Massachusetts in 1810, he signed a bill (1812) creating an oddly shaped electoral district favoring his own Republican Party. The district was caricatured as a salamander in the press and dubbed a "gerrymander." Gerry later became vice president of the US (1813–14) under **James Madison**.

Gershwin, George, *originally* **Jacob Gershvin** 1898–1937 •*US composer*• Born in Brooklyn, New York, the son of Russian Jewish immigrants, he studied piano as a boy, published his first popular song at the age of 14 and left high school to work for Tin Pan Alley. In 1920 he had his first hit with "Swanee," recorded by **Al Jolson**. In 1924 he wrote his first successful musical comedy, *Lady Be Good*, collaborating with his brother **Ira Gershwin**, a brilliant lyricist who was to be his partner in songwriting until his death. In the 1920s and early 1930s he scored a series of hit musicals, including *Of Thee I Sing* (1931), and in the process produced numerous classics of US popular song, such as "Someone to Watch Over Me," "Embraceable You" and "I Got Rhythm." He also wrote songs and scores for motion pictures, notably several screen musicals with **Fred Astaire** and **Ginger Rogers**. In 1924 he produced *Rhapsody in Blue*, a concert work combining Romantic emotionalism and the jazz idiom with unusual success, and this was followed by the *Concerto in F* (1925) and *An American in Paris* (1928), exploiting the same forces. His and Ira's Black opera, *Porgy and Bess* (1935) also won worldwide popularity. At the age of 38, at the height of his powers, he died of a brain tumor. Gershwin showed genius in his innovation of "symphonic jazz" and in his carefree dexterity with modern popular song and musical comedy, and he was influential in winning recognition of the legitimacy of US popular music.

“ ”

Not many composers have ideas. Far more of them know how to use strange instruments which do not require ideas.

1930 "The Composer in the Machine Age."

Gershwin, Ira, *originally* **Israel Gershvin** 1896–1983 •*US lyricist*• Born in Brooklyn, New York, he was the brother of **George Gershwin**, with whom he collaborated to produce more than 20 successful Broadway musicals. Ira first wrote under the pseudonym of Arthur Francis, and wrote the lyrics for Vincent Youmans's *Two Little Girls in Blue* (1921), which includes "Oh Me, Oh My." Later, under his own name, he wrote lyrics for the *Ziegfeld Follies* (1936), and, most importantly, *Lady in the Dark* (1941, composed by **Kurt Weill**), which contains "Jenny" and "This Is New."

Gesell, Arnold Lucius 1880–1961 •*US psychologist*• He was born in Alma, Wisconsin, and educated at Clark University and at Yale. He was Professor of Child Hygiene at the Yale School of Medicine (1915–48) and established and directed the Clinic of Child Development there. A pioneer in the study of child psychology, he devised standard scales for measuring infant development. His writings were supplemented by an original and extensive use of film as a medium for scientific and educational communication. His books include *The Child from Five to Ten* (1946) and *Child Development* (1949).

Gesner, Conrad, *Latin* **Conradus Gesnerus** 1516–65 •*Swiss naturalist and physician*• Born in Zurich, he was a professor at the Universities of Lausanne and Zurich. He published 72 works, and left 18 others in progress. His *Bibliotheca universalis* (1545–49) contained the titles of all the books then known in Hebrew, Greek and Latin, with criticisms and summaries of each. His *Historia animalium* (1551–58) attempted to describe all animals then known. He collected over 500 plants not recorded by the ancients, and his third major work contains beautiful and accurate engraved illustrations that were reprinted more recently in eight volumes between 1973 and 1980. He also wrote on medicine, mineralogy and philology. He was the first to allude to the concepts of genus and species, and stressed the significance of flowers, fruit and seed in identification and discrimination. He was one of the most versatile and industrious scholars of the 16th century.

Getty, Jean Paul 1892–1976 •*US oil executive, billionaire and art collector*• Born in Minneapolis, he studied at the University of California, Berkeley, and Oxford, and then entered the oil business in his early twenties, making $250,000 in his first two years. His father (also a successful oil man) died in 1930, leaving him about $500,000. He merged his father's interests with his own and went on to acquire and control more than 100 companies, becoming one of the richest men in the world. Over the years he acquired a huge and extremely valuable art collection. He was married and divorced five times, and developed a legendary reputation for miserliness, installing a pay telephone for guests in his English mansion. He wrote several books, including a history of the family oil business and two autobiographies.

Getz, Stan(ley) 1927–91 •*US jazz saxophonist*• He was born in Philadelphia, and educated in New York. While still a teenager he was working under such important bandleaders as **Stan Kenton** and **Benny Goodman**. With the **Woody Herman** Orchestra from 1947 to 1949, he was a member of the "Four Brothers" saxophone section which gave the band a unique ensemble sound. He later led his own small groups, and during the 1960s he helped to popularize the bossa nova jazz style. With his light tone and articulate phrasing, he was one of the most copied of tenor saxophone stylists.

Ghazali, al- 1058–1111 •*Islamic philosopher, theologian and jurist*• He was born in Tus, Persia (near the modern Meshed). In 1091 he was appointed to the prestigious position of Professor of Philosophy at Nizamiyah College, Baghdad, where he exercised great academic and political influence. Following a spiritual crisis, he abandoned his position for the ascetic life of a mendicant Sufi (mystic) and eventually retired to Tus to found a monastic community. His doctrines represent a reaction against Aristotelianism and an attempt to reconcile philosophy and Islamic dogma. He was a prolific author, and his main works include *The Intentions of the Philosophers*, *The Incoherence of the Philosophers* and the monumental *The Revival of the Religious Sciences*.

Gheorgiu-Dej, Gheorghe 1901–65 •*Romanian communist politician*• Born in Bîrlad, he became a railway worker, then joined the Romanian Communist Party (RCP) in 1930 and was imprisoned in 1933 for his role in the Grivita railway strike. On his release in 1944, he became secretary-general of the RCP and Minister of Communications (1944–46). In 1945 he was instrumental in the establishment of a Communist regime, becoming Prime Minister (1952–55), then state President in 1961. A Stalinist, he nonetheless retained the support of **Nikita Khrushchev**'s Moscow, while developing increasingly independent policies during the 1950s and 1960s.

Ghiberti, Lorenzo 1378–1455 •*Italian goldsmith, bronze caster and sculptor*• Born in Florence, he executed frescoes in the palace of Pandolfo Malatesta at Rimini in 1400, and in 1402 won the competition to make a pair of bronze doors for the Florence Baptistery. Much of Ghiberti's life was spent completing this set of doors, and as soon as they were finished in 1424 he was entrusted with the execution of another set (1425–52), made to emulate the first pair, and dubbed by **Michelangelo** the "Gates of Paradise." He also executed the three bronze figures of saints that adorn the exterior of Or San Michele. His large and flourishing workshop was a training ground for a distinguished generation of Florentine artists, including **Donatello**, **Michelozzo Michelozzi** and **Paolo Uccello**.

Ghirlandaio, Domenico, *properly* **Domenico di Tommaso Bigordi** 1449–94 •*Italian painter*• Born in Florence, he was a metal garland maker, or *ghirlandaio*, becoming a painter at 31. Among his frescoes in his native city are six subjects from the life of St **Francis** (1485) and an altarpiece, the *Adoration of the Shepherds* (Florentine Academy), for the church of Santa Trinità, and, in the choir of Santa Maria Novella, a series illustrating the lives of the Virgin and the Baptist (1490). Between 1482 and 1484 he painted for Pope **Sixtus IV**, in the Sistine Chapel, the fresco *Christ Calling Peter and Andrew*. His easel pictures include the *Adoration of the Magi* (1488), in the church of the Innocenti at Florence, and the *Visitation of the Virgin* (1491), in the Louvre, Paris. He also executed mosaics.

Giacometti, Alberto 1901–66 •*Swiss sculptor and painter*• Born in Stampa, he was the son of an artist. He studied at Geneva and worked mainly in Paris. He joined the Surrealists in 1930, producing many abstract constructions of a symbolic kind, arriving finally at the characteristic "thin man" bronzes—long spidery statuettes, rigid in posture yet trembling on the verge of movement, suggesting transience, change and decay, such as *Man Pointing* (1947).

Giaever, Ivar 1929– •*US physicist and Nobel Prize winner*• Born in Bergen, Norway, he studied electrical engineering in Trondheim, then emigrated to Canada in 1954. In 1956 he joined the General Electric Research and Development Center in Schenectady, New York, where he examined tunneling effects in superconductors. His field of work, of great value in microelectronics, had previously been the subject of related work by **Leo Esaki** and was later further developed by **Brian Josephson**, and all three men shared the Nobel Prize for physics in 1973 for their contributions. Giaever's research interests later shifted to immunology.

Giap, Vo Nguyen *See* **Vo Nguyen Giap**

Gibb, Sir Alexander 1872–1958 •*Scottish civil engineer*• Born near Dundee, he was the fifth generation in a line of civil engineers, begun by his great-great-grandfather William (1736–91). His great-grandfather John (1776–1850) became **Thomas Telford**'s deputy on bridges and harbor works in Scotland. His grandfather Alexander (1804–67) worked with **Robert Stevenson**, and built railways in Scotland and England. His father, Easton (1841–1916), built reservoirs, railways, and the bridge over the Thames at Kew. Alexander joined the firm of Easton Gibb & Son in 1900, and from 1909 to 1916 worked on the construction of Rosyth naval dockyard, then set up in practice as a consulting engineer. His firm became one of the world's largest, its work at home and abroad including hydroelectric works, bridges, docks and harbors.

Gibbon, Edward 1737–94 •*English historian*• Born in Putney, Surrey, he was educated at Westminster and Magdalen College, Oxford. His *Autobiography* contains a scathing attack on the Oxford of his time and also tells of his return to Protestantism and of his forbidden love for Suzanne Curchod, who afterward became Madame Necker and the mother of Madame de **Staël**. On a visit to Rome in 1764 he decided to write *The Decline and Fall of the Roman Empire* (6 vols, 1776–88), the work for which he remains best known. Acclaimed as literature as well as history, and markedly pessimistic in tone, the work has as its chief concept the continuity of the Roman Empire down to the fall of Constantinople (Istanbul). Gibbon entered Parliament in 1774 and was made Commissioner of Trade and Plantations.

“ ”

Corruption, the most infallible symptom of constitutional liberty.

1776–88 ***The Decline and Fall of the Roman Empire****, chapter 21.*

Gibbon, Lewis Grassic, *pseudonym of* **James Leslie Mitchell** 1901–35 •*Scottish novelist*• Born near Auchterless, Aberdeenshire, he was educated at the local school before attending Mackie Academy, Stonehaven, which he left after a year to become a newspaper reporter. Stirred by the promise of the Russian Revolution he became a member of the Communist Party. In 1919 he moved to Glasgow, where he was employed on the *Scottish Farmer*, but he was dismissed for falsifying expenses. He attempted suicide, then enlisted with the Royal Army Service Corps and subsequently the RAF as a clerk until 1929. His first published book was *Hanno, or the Future of Exploration* (1928), followed by *Stained Radiance* (1930) and *The Lost Trumpet* (1932). *Sunset Song*, his greatest achievement, was published in 1932. Written in less than two months, it was published under his mother's name as the first in a projected trilogy of novels, *A Scots Quair*. The second volume, *Cloud Howe*, appeared in 1933, and the third part, *Grey Granite*, in 1934.

Gibbons, Grinling 1648–1721 •*English sculptor and woodcarver*• He was born in Rotterdam, the Netherlands, and was employed to decorate the king's rooms at Windsor and the choir at St Paul's Cathedral, London. At Chatsworth, Burghley, Hampton Court, Blenheim, and other mansions, he carved, often in limewood and with controlled exuberance, the festoons of fruit and flowers and the cherubs' heads for which he is famous. A ceiling at Petworth House, Sussex, is a tour de force. He also produced several fine pieces in marble and bronze, including the statues of Charles II at the Chelsea Hospital, London, and **James VII and II** in Trafalgar Square.

Gibbons, Orlando 1583–1625 •*English composer*• Born in Oxford, he was appointed organist of the Chapel Royal, London, in c. 1615. He studied at Cambridge and Oxford, and in 1623 became organist of Westminster Abbey, London. His compositions include the anthems, "O Clap Your Hands," "God Is Gone Up," and "Almighty and Everlasting God," and the madrigals, "The Silver Swan," "O That the Learned Poets" and "Dainty, Fine Sweet Bird." Besides these he left hymns and instrumental works.

Gibbons, Stella Dorothea 1902–89 •*English writer*• Born in London, she was educated at University College London, where she studied journalism. She worked as a journalist and later began a series of successful novels. Her reputation rests on *Cold Comfort Farm* (1933), a lighthearted satire on the melodramatic rural novels, which won the Femina Vie Heureuse prize, and established itself as a classic of parody.

Gibbs, James 1682–1754 •*Scottish architect*• Born in Aberdeen, he studied in Holland and then in Italy under **Carlo Fontana**. A friend and disciple of **Christopher Wren**, he became (1713) one of the commissioners for building new churches in London, but was dismissed in 1715 for his Roman Catholicism. He designed St Mary-le-Strand (1717), St Peter's, Vere Street (1724), and St Martin-in-the-Fields (1726), the latter being perhaps his most influential and attractive work. He was also responsible for the circular Radcliffe Camera at Oxford (1737–47) and the Senate House at Cambridge (1730). His *Book of Architecture* (1728) helped to spread the Palladian style and influenced the design of many churches of the colonial period in America.

Gibran or **Jibran, Kahlil** 1883–1931 •*Syrian mystical writer, poet and artist*• He was born in Bisharri in the Lebanese mountains, but became a permanent resident of New York City from 1912. His influences included **William Blake** and **Nietzsche**, and among his earliest works is *Al-Ajnihah al-mutakassirah* (1911, Eng trans *Broken Wings*, 1922), in which he liberated Arabic from its archaic, classical roots and replaced it with the language of nature, allegory, metaphor and symbolism. He is best known for *The Prophet* (1923), which was written in English. His books have sold more than 20 million copies worldwide. Later works include *Jesus the Son of Man* (1928) and *The Garden of the Prophets* (1934).

Gibson, Sir Alexander Drummond 1926–95 •*Scottish conductor*• Born in Motherwell, near Glasgow, he studied in Glasgow, London, Salzburg and Siena, and joined Sadler's Wells Opera as a répétiteur (singing coach). From 1952 to 1954 he was associate conductor of the BBC Scottish Symphony Orchestra, then returned to Sadler's Wells in 1957 as the company's youngest musical director. In 1959 he moved to Scotland as the first native-born principal conductor and artistic director of the Scottish National Orchestra, bringing many new works to Scotland, often in advance of their London performances. In 1962 he helped to form Scottish Opera.

Gibson, Althea 1927–2003 •*US tennis player*• Born in Silver, South Carolina, she entered her first tournament in 1942 and won the first of ten consecutive US singles titles at Forest Hills in 1947. In 1951 she became the first African-American player to compete at Wimbledon, and in 1957 and 1958 won both at Wimbledon and Forest Hills. On retiring from amateur play in 1958 she developed a career as a professional golfer. She appeared subsequently as a film actor and recording artist.

Gibson, Bob (Robert) 1935– •*US baseball player*• Born in Omaha, Nebraska, he was a noted pitcher with the St Louis Cardinals from 1959. He was twice named best pitcher in the National League and in 1968 became Most Valuable Player in the league on the strength of his exceptionally low earned-run average of 1.12. He set a World Series record of strikeouts against the Detroit Tigers in 1968.

Gibson, Charles Dana 1867–1944 •*US illustrator and cartoonist*• Born in Roxbury, Massachusetts, he was an accomplished black-and-white artist who drew society cartoons for various periodicals such as *Life*, *Scribner's*, *Century* and *Harper's*. In his celebrated "Gibson Girl" drawings, he created the idealized prototype of the beautiful, well-bred US woman.

Gibson, Guy 1918–44 •*English airman*• As a wing commander in the RAF, he led the famous "dambusters" raid on the Möhne and Eder dams in 1943, for which he received the Victoria Cross. He was killed on a later mission. His experiences are described in *Enemy Coast Ahead* (1946).

Gibson, John 1790–1866 •*British sculptor*• Born in Gyffin, Gwynedd, Wales, the son of a market gardener, from 1817 he lived mainly in Rome, where he studied under **Antonio Canova** and Bertel Thorvaldsen (1770–1844). His best works, in a neoclassical style, are *Psyche Borne by Zephyrs*, *Hylas Surprised by Nymphs* and *Venus with the Turtle*. He defended the innovation of tinting his figures, as in his *Venus* (1851–56, Walker Art Gallery, Liverpool), by reference to Greek precedents. His public statuary includes those of Sir **Robert Peel** (1852, Westminster Abbey) and Queen **Victoria** (1856, House of Lords).

Gibson, Josh 1911–47 •*US baseball player*• He was born in Buena Vista, Georgia. He was barred from major-league baseball because he was African-American, and could play only in the Negro Leagues. Playing for the Pittsburgh Homestead Grays and the Pittsburgh Crawfords, he became a legendary hitter. It is estimated that he hit more than 950 home runs in his career. In 1972 he was elected to the National Baseball Hall of Fame.

Gibson, Mel 1956– •*US-Australian film actor*• Born in Peekskill, New York, he emigrated to Australia in 1968 and studied at the National Institute of Dramatic Arts. He showed promise as the mentally retarded young man in *Tim* (1978) and gained international recognition in *Mad Max* (1979) and its two sequels. His many films include *Lethal Weapon* (1987) and its three sequels (1989, 1992, 1998), *Maverick* (1994) and *Signs* (2002). He also acted in and directed *Braveheart* (1995), which won him Academy Awards for Best Director and Best Film. He subsequently directed *The Passion of the Christ*, filmed entirely in Aramaic, Latin, and Hebrew.

Gibson, Mike (Cameron Michael Henderson) 1947– •*Irish rugby player*• He was born in Belfast, Northern Ireland. A brilliant center-threequarter, he established a worldwide reputation while still at Cambridge, and became Ireland's most capped player with a total of 69 caps.

Gide, André Paul Guillaume 1869–1951 •*French novelist, writer, diarist, and Nobel Prize winner*• Born in Paris, he was educated in a Protestant secondary school in Paris, and privately. He embarked on his career by writing essays, then poetry, biography, fiction, drama, criticism, memoirs and translation, and eventually completed more than 50 books. By 1917 he had emerged as the prophet of French youth and his unorthodox views were the subject of much debate. Although he married his cousin in 1892, he was bisexual. His international reputation rests largely on his stylish novels in which there is a sharp conflict between the spiritual and the physical. They include *L'immoraliste* (1902, Eng trans *The Immoralist*, 1930), *La symphonie pastorale* (1919, Eng trans *Two Symphonies*, 1931) and *Les faux-monnayeurs* (1926, Eng trans *The Counterfeiters*, 1927, rev edn 1950, *The Coiners*). He was a founder of the magazine *La Nouvelle Revue Française*, and was a critic of French bureaucracy at home and in the African colonies. His *Journals*, covering the years from 1889 to 1949, are an essential supplement to his autobiography, *Si le grain ne meurt* (1920–21, Eng trans *If It Die...*, 1935). He was awarded the Nobel Prize for literature in 1947.

“ ”

Nous avons bâti sur le sable
Des cathédrales impérissables.
We have built immovable cathedrals
In the sand.

1895 ***Paludes***.

Gielgud, Sir (Arthur) John 1904–2000 •*English actor and producer*• He was born in London and made his debut there in 1921. He established his reputation in *The Constant Nymph* (1926), *Hamlet* (1929) and *The Good Companions* (1931), becoming a leading Shakespearean actor in the British theater and directing many of the Shakespeare Memorial Theatre productions, as well as **Chekhov's** *The Cherry Orchard* (1954) and Enid Bagnold's *The Chalk Garden* (1956) in London. He also appeared in many films, notably as Disraeli in *The Prime Minister* (1940) and as Cassius in *Julius Caesar* (1952). He played Othello at Stratford (1961) and Prospero at the National Theatre (1974). Like **Laurence Olivier**, he adapted to changing dramatic styles and to the new wave of plays popularized by the Royal Court Theatre, appearing during the 1960s and 1970s in plays by **David Storey**, **Edward Bond** and **Harold Pinter**. He went on to appear increasingly in cameo roles in films, although he won an Academy Award for Best Supporting Actor for *Arthur* (1981), and played the lead role and voiced all the others in **Peter Greenaway**'s *Prospero's Books* (1991). Later film appearances include *Shine* (1996) and *Portrait of a Lady* (1996). He also returned to the stage (1988), playing in Hugh Whitemore's *Sir Sydney Cockerell: The Best of Friends*. He was awarded the British Academy of Film and Television Arts fellowship award for his lifetime contribution to show business (1992). His first autobiography, *Early Stages*, was published as early as 1938 (rev edn 1976); other books include *Distinguished Company* (1972) and *Notes from the Gods* (1994). He was knighted in 1953 and was appointed to the Order of Merit in 1996.

Gierek, Edward 1913–2001 •*Polish politician*• Born in Porabka (Bedzin district), the son of a miner, he lived in France (1923–34) during the **Piłsudski** dictatorship, and joined the French Communist Party in 1931. He was deported to Poland in 1934, and lived in Belgium (1937–48), becoming a member of the Belgian Resistance. On his return to Poland in 1948, he joined the ruling Polish United Workers' Party (PUWP), becoming its leader in 1970. Head of the party's "technocrat faction," he embarked on an ambitious industrialization program. This plunged the country heavily into debt and, following a wave of strikes in Warsaw and Gdańsk, spearheaded by the "Solidarity" free trade union movement, he was forced to resign in 1980.

Giffard, Henri 1825–82 •*French engineer and inventor*• Born in Paris, he studied there at the Collège Bourbon and the École Centrale. In 1852 he built a light 3-horsepower steam engine, fitted it with a propeller and succeeded in piloting a balloon, steered by a rudder, over a distance of 17 miles (27.4 kilometers). This can be considered the first powered and controlled flight ever achieved, in a craft that was a primitive example of the dirigible or semirigid airship.

Gilbert of Sempringham, St c.1083–1189 •*English priest*• Born in Sempringham, Lincolnshire, he was educated in Paris. In 1148 he founded, at his birthplace, the Gilbertine Order for both monks and nuns, and lay sisters and brothers. It was dissolved at the Reformation. His feast day is February 4.

Gilbert, Sir Alfred 1854–1934 •*English sculptor*• Born in London, he studied in France and Italy, where he was influenced by the work of **Donatello**, and executed work of remarkable simplicity and grace, including his aluminum statue of *Eros* (1886–93, Piccadilly Circus, London) and his bronze *Icarus* (1884, National Museum of Wales, Cardiff).

Gilbert, Cass 1859–1934 •*US architect*• Born in Zanesville, Ohio, he was educated at MIT. He is remembered as the designer of the first skyscraper, the flamboyant 66-story Woolworth Building in New York (1912), then the tallest building in the world (not counting the Eiffel Tower). He designed many equally outstanding public buildings, including the US Customs House in New York City (1907) and the Supreme Court Building in Washington DC (1935).

Gilbert, Walter 1932– •*US molecular biologist and Nobel Prize winner*• Born in Boston, he studied physics and mathematics at Harvard and Cambridge. In 1978 he founded the genetic engineering company Biogen NV and served as its chairman for three years. During the 1960s he isolated the repressor molecule that **Jacques Monod** and **François Jacob** had suggested to be centrally involved in controlling gene action. Using methods developed by **Frederick Sanger**, he described the nucleotide sequence of DNA to which the repressor molecule binds. For this work he shared the 1980 Nobel Prize for chemistry with Sanger and **Paul Berg**.

Gilbert, William 1544–1603 •*English physician*• Born in Colchester, Essex, he was elected Fellow of St John's College, Cambridge (1561) and was appointed physician to Queen **Elizabeth I** (1601) and King **James VI and I** (1603). In his *De magnete* (1600) he established the magnetic nature of the earth and conjectured that terrestrial magnetism and electricity were two allied emanations of a single force. He was the first to use the terms electricity, electric force and electric attraction, and to point out that amber is not the only substance that attracts light objects when rubbed. The gilbert unit of magnetomotive power is named after him.

Gilbert, Sir W(illiam) S(chwenck) 1836–1911 •*English parodist and librettist*• Born in London, he studied at King's College London and became a clerk in the Privy Council Office (1857–62). Called to the bar in 1864, he failed to attract lucrative briefs and made his living from magazine contributions to *Punch* and *Fun*, for which he wrote much humorous verse under his boyhood nickname "Bab." This verse was collected in 1869 as the *Bab Ballads*. He also wrote a Christmas burlesque, *Dulcemara, or The Little Duck and the Great Quack* (1866) and *The Palace of Truth* (1870), which both made a hit on the stage, followed by *Pygmalion and Galatea* (1871). But it is as the librettist of Sir **Arthur Sullivan**'s light operas that he is best remembered. Their famous partnership, which began in 1871, scored its first success with *Trial by Jury* under **Richard D'Oyly Carte**'s able management at the Royalty Theatre, London, in 1875. Numerous light operas followed, from *The Sorcerer* (1877), *HMS Pinafore* (1878) and *The Pirates of Penzance* (1879) to *The Gondoliers* (1889) and *The Grand Duke* (1896). Their works were performed initially at the Opéra Comique and from 1881 in the new Savoy Theatre, which had been specifically built for them by D'Oyly Carte. After Sullivan's death, Edward German's efforts to fill the gap in *Fallen Fairies* (1909) proved unsuccessful.

Gilbert and **George**, *properly* **Gilbert Proesch** 1943– and **George Passmore** 1942– •*English avant-garde artists*• Born in Italy, Gilbert studied at the Academy of Art in Munich and then at St Martin's School of Art, London, where he met Plymouth-born George, who had studied at Dartington Hall and at the Oxford School of Art. They made their name in the late 1960s as performance artists (the "singing sculptures"), with faces and hands painted gold, holding their poses for hours at a time. They have also more recently concentrated on photopieces, assembled from a number of separately framed photographs which fit together to make a single whole, such as *Death Hope Life Fear* (1984, Tate Collection, London). They won the Turner Prize in 1986 and have exhibited at the Venice Biennale in 1978, 1979 and 1993 (in the "Art against AIDS" exhibition).

Gildas, St c. 493–570 •*Roman-British historian and monk*• Born in Strathclyde, he fled the strife that raged in his neighborhood and went to Wales. After his wife died, he became a monk. His famous treatise, *De excidio et conquestu Britanniae*, probably written between 516 and 547, is the only extant history of the Celts, and the only contemporary British version of events from the invasion of the Romans to his own time. His feast day is January 29.

Giles or **Aegidius** or **Egidius, St** d. c. 700 •*Greek hermit*• Born in Athens, traditionally of royal descent, he renounced his patrimony and retired to a hermitage, where he lived on herbs and the milk of a hind. A Frankish king, hunting the hind, discovered him and was so impressed with his holiness that he built a monastery on the spot and made him its abbot. He is the patron of lepers, beggars and cripples, and his feast day is September 1.

Giles, *properly* **Carl Ronald Giles** 1916–95 •*British cartoonist and animator*• Born in London, he was a self-taught artist, and became an animator of advertising films, then worked on the *Come On Steve* cartoons (1935). He joined *Reynolds News* in 1938 to draw weekly topical cartoons and a strip, *Young Ernie*, before transferring to the *Daily Express* and *Sunday Express* (1943), where he developed his "Giles Family" cartoons, dominated by Grandma.

Giles, (William) Ernest (Powell) 1835–97 •*Australian explorer*• Born in Bristol, England, he emigrated to Adelaide in 1850. Under the sponsorship of Sir Ferdinand Mueller (1825–96), he was sent to explore areas to the west of the Central Overland telegraph between Adelaide and Darwin, first in 1872, when he discovered Lake Amadeus, and again in 1874, when he penetrated the Gibson Desert, named after a companion of his who died there. He tried again (1875–76), and managed to cross from Port Augusta to Perth, a distance of 2,500 miles (4,025 km) in five months, and back again. This extraordinary feat of endurance is described in his *Australia Twice Traversed* (1889).

Gill, (Arthur) Eric (Rowton) 1882–1940 •*English sculptor, engraver, writer and typographer*• Born in Brighton, Sussex, he trained as an architect, but then took up letter cutting and masonry, and later engraving. In 1907 he settled in Ditchling, East Sussex, where he founded a utopian community. Through the influence of **Augustus John** he exhibited at the Chenil Galleries, Chelsea, in 1911 (the year he carved *Ecstasy*, in the Tate, London), and from then on maintained a steady output of engravings and sculpture. He also created type designs, such as Perpetua, Bunyan and Gill Sans-serif, subsequently adopted by Monotype and used all over the world. He wrote a stream of books dealing with his various crafts, his thoughts and religious beliefs, including *Art* (1934) and *Autobiography* (1940). His sculptures include the *Stations of the Cross* in Westminster Cathedral, London (1913), war memorials up and down Great Britain after World War I, the gigantic figure *Mankind* (1928, Tate) and *Prospero and Ariel* (1931, Broadcasting House, London).

Gillespie, Dizzy (John Birks) 1917–93 •*US jazz trumpeter, composer and bandleader*• He was born in Cheraw, South Carolina, and studied musical theory and harmony at Laurinburg Institute, North Carolina. He began his career in swing bands led by Teddy Hill (1909–78), **Cab Calloway**, **Benny Carter** and Charlie Barnet (1913–91). Along with **Charlie Parker**, **Thelonious Monk** and others, he was involved in informal jam session experiments in New York that produced the bop style in the 1940s. In 1945 Gillespie formed the first of his several big bands, and in 1956 he led an orchestra on two international tours as cultural missions for the US State Department. He is best known as a virtuoso who extended the working range of the trumpet.

Gillette, King Camp 1855–1932 •*US inventor and businessman*• He was born in Fond du Lac, Wisconsin, and educated in Chicago. After working for years as a traveling salesman, he invented a safety razor and disposable blade, which he started marketing in 1901. A utopian socialist, he set up a "World Corporation" in Arizona in 1910 to advocate a world planned economy. His books of social theory include *The People's Corporation* (1924).

“ ”

> To be successful in business, you should produce something cheap, habit-forming, and consumed by use.
>
> *Attributed.*

Gilliam, Terry Vance 1940– •*US film director, writer, animator and actor*• Born in Medicine Lake, Minnesota, he studied at Occidental College, California, and worked in advertising before producing the animated sequences for the Monty Python's Flying Circus television series and films, also cowriting, codirecting and acting in many of them. His films as sole director, often fabulous, eccentric and visually stunning, though not always successful at the box office, include *Time Bandits* (1981), *Brazil* (1985), *The Fisher King* (1991), *Twelve Monkeys* (1996) and *Fear and Loathing in Las Vegas* (1998).

Gilliatt, Penelope Ann Douglas 1932–93 •*English film and theater critic, novelist and screenwriter*• She was born in London. She wrote a number of novels, including *The Cutting Edge* (1978), which describes the relationship between two brothers, as well as six collections of short stories. She was nominated for an Academy Award for her screenplay for *Sunday Bloody Sunday* (1971), based on her novel *One By One* (1965). Her profiles of filmmakers, such as **Jean Renoir** and **Jacques Tati**, several of which appeared in the *New Yorker*, are considered among the best of their kind.

Gilligan, Carol 1936– •*US psychologist*• She was born in New York City. Her studies in gender differences in moral development, published in *A Different Voice* (1982), point out the biases in studies that establish male behavior as normal and female behavior as different or abnormal. In 1984 she was recognized by *Ms* magazine (founded by **Gloria Steinem**) as Woman of the Year, and in 1987 she founded the Harvard Project on Women's Psychology and the Development of Girls. Her other books include *Meeting at the Crossroads: Women's Psychology and Girls' Development* (with Lynn Mikel Brown, 1992).

Gillray, James 1757–1815 •*English caricaturist*• Born in Chelsea, London, the son of a Lanark trooper, he first became known as a successful engraver about 1784, and between 1779 and 1811 issued 1,500 caricatures. They are full of humor and satire aimed against the French, **Napoleon I**, **George III**, the leading politicians and the social follies of his day. For the last four years of his life he was thought insane.

Gilman, Charlotte (Anna) Perkins, *née* **Perkins**, *first married name* **Stetson** 1860–1935 •*US feminist and writer*• Born in Hartford, Connecticut, she was educated at the Rhode Island School of Design. Moving to California, she published her first stories, most memorably "The Yellow Wall-Paper" (1892), and a collection of poetry, *In This Our World* (1893). She was married to Charles Stetson from 1884 to 1894, and married George Gilman in 1900. She lectured on women's issues, as well as wider social concerns, and in 1898 wrote *Women and Economics*, now recognized as a feminist landmark. She also founded, edited and wrote for the journal *The Forerunner* (1909–16). She later wrote *The Man-made World* (1911) and *His Religion and Hers* (1923).

Gilmore, Dame Mary Jean 1865–1962 •*Australian poet and author*• She was born in Cotta Walla, near Goulburn, New South Wales. She became the first woman member of the Australian Workers' Union, and in 1896 she joined William Lane's Utopian "New Australia" settlement in Paraguay, South America. There she married a shearer, William Gilmore, and they returned to Australia (1902) and settled in Sydney (1912). She campaigned for the betterment of the sick and the helpless through the women's column, which she edited for over 20 years, in the Sydney *Worker* newspaper, but also in her poetry. *Marri'd and Other Verses* (1910) was followed by *The Wild Swans* (1930) and *Battlefields* (1939), and in her 89th year she published her last collection, *Fourteen Men* (1954). She was given the honorary title of Dame Commander, Order of the British Empire, in 1937.

Gilmour, John Scott Lennox 1906–86 •*English botanist*• Born in London and educated at Uppingham and Clare College, Cambridge, he became director of the Royal Horticultural Society's gardens at Wisley, then returned to Cambridge, where he was director of the botanic gardens (1951–73). One of the original proponents of the "deme" terminology, a flexible classification system, he was one of the founding members of the Classification Society (later the Systematics Association) in 1937. He published many papers on the theory and philosophy of systematics, chaired many committees on horticultural nomenclature, and was influential in the establishment of the International Code of Nomenclature of Cultivated Plants.

Gilpin, Laura 1891–1979 •*US photographer*• Born in Colorado, she made autochromes (the first true color photographic process to be widely available) in Colorado Springs from 1908. In 1916 she photographed in the Grand Canyon. Also that year, she studied at the Clarence H White School of Photography in New York. She opened a portrait studio in 1918, worked on commercial commissions from the 1920s, and held solo exhibitions from 1924. In 1945 she photographed the Rio Grande from source to mouth, documenting the lifestyle of the Navajo people. Her publications include *The Rio Grande: River of Destiny* (1949) and *The Enduring Navaho* (1968).

Gilruth, Robert Rowe 1913–2000 •*US engineer*• Born in Nashwauk, Minnesota, he graduated from the University of Minnesota in aeronautical engineering, and was associated from then on with the design and operation of high-speed and supersonic aircraft, guided missiles, and space vehicles. In 1958 he was appointed head of the NASA man-in-space program which put the first American, **John Glenn**, into earth orbit in 1962. The next objective, known as the Apollo lunar landing project, was achieved under his direction on July 20, 1969, when **Neil Armstrong** became the first man to set foot on the moon.

Gil Vicente *See* **Vicente, Gil**

Gingrich, Newt (Newton Leroy) 1943– •*US politician*• Born in Harrisburg, Pennsylvania, he was elected to Congress as a US representative from Georgia in 1978. He became a leader of conservative Republicans and became famous for his scathing attacks on House Democrats. He was appointed Speaker of the House in 1995, but his popularity dropped sharply in 1996 as the public tired of his stridency. He was fined $300,000 in 1997 for violating House rules and then misleading the Congressional committee investigating his case. He continued as Speaker of the House until 1999.

Ginsberg, Allen 1926–97 •*US poet*• Born in Newark, New Jersey, he was brought up in a Jewish community and educated at Columbia University. A gay drug experimentalist, he was associated with the Beat movement, coined the phrase "flower power" and was a friend of **Jack Kerouac**, **William S Burroughs** and others. *Howl and Other Poems* (1956), his first book, was a *succès de scandale*. Numerous other poetry collections were published, including *Kaddish and Other Poems* (1961) and *Cosmopolitan Greetings: Poems 1986–92* (1994). Despite his initial antiestablishment stance, Ginsberg gained many honors and awards. His prose *Journals* were published in 1977.

“ ”

America I've given you all and now I'm nothing.

*1956 **Howl and Other Poems**, "America."*

Ginsburg, Ruth Bader, *née* **Bader** 1933– •*US federal judge*• Born in Brooklyn, New York, she was educated at Cornell University, and at Harvard and Columbia law schools. She became professor at the Columbia University School of Law (1972–80), US circuit court judge with the US Court of Appeals (1980–93), then was nominated by President **Bill Clinton** to the Supreme Court. As well as being the second woman Supreme Court justice (**Sandra Day O'Connor** was the first), she was also the second Jewish justice.

Giolitti, Giovanni 1842–1928 •*Italian politician*• Born in Mondovi, he was an astute and unprincipled parliamentary manager. He entered parliament in 1882 as a Liberal and became Prime Minister from 1892 to 1893, but was brought down by a banking scandal. He returned to politics as Interior Minister under Roman Zanardelli in 1901, becoming Prime Minister again from 1903 to 1909, except for a brief spell out of office in 1905–06. As Prime Minister, he sought to combat leftist strikes, and in foreign policy he strengthened Italy's ties with Austria and Germany. During his fourth term as prime minister (1911–14), he brought Italy into the Tripolitanian War, gaining Libya, Rhodes and the Dodecanese. However, the war resulted in unpopular tax increases, and a general strike forced him from office in 1914. His fifth ministry (1920–21) failed to block **Mussolini**'s ascent to power.

Giordano, Luca 1632–1705 •*Italian painter*• Born in Naples, he was able to work with great speed (hence his nickname "Luca Fa Presto," "Luca works quickly") and to imitate the great masters. In Florence he painted the ceiling frescoes in the ballroom of the Palazzo Medici-Riccardi. From 1692 to 1702 he was in Madrid as court painter to **Charles II** of Spain, and embellished the Escorial.

Giorgione, *also called* **Giorgio Barbarelli** or **Giorgio del Castelfranco** c. 1478–1511 •*Italian painter*• Born near Castelfranco, he probably studied at Venice under **Giovanni Bellini**, and soon developed a freer and larger manner, characterized by intense poetic feeling and richness of coloring. In Venice he was extensively employed in fresco painting, but fragments in the Fondaco de' Tedeschi are all that now remain of this work. *The Tempest* at

Venice is attributed to him, while *The Family of Giorgione* in Venice, *The Three Philosophers* in Vienna and the *Sleeping Venus* in the Dresden Gallery are genuine. Many of his pictures were completed by other painters, including **Titian**.

Giotto (di Bondone) c. 1267–1337 •*Italian painter and architect*• Born near Florence, he was the most innovative artist of his time, and is generally regarded as the founder of the Florentine school. At the age of 10, he was supposedly found by **Giovanni Cimabué** tending sheep and drawing a lamb on a flat stone and was taken by him to study art in Florence. As a painter he worked in all the major artistic centers of Italy, but his most important works are the frescoes in the Arena Chapel, Padua, the Navicella mosaic in Saint Peter's, Rome, the cycle of frescoes depicting scenes from the life of Saint **Francis of Assisi**, frescoes in the Peruzzi Chapel in the church of Santa Croce, Florence, and the Ognissanti Madonna, now in the Uffizi, Florence. Stylistically he broke with the rigid conventions of Byzantine art, and composed simplified and moving dramatic narratives peopled by realistically observed and believable figures. In 1334 Giotto was appointed Master of Works for the cathedral and city of Florence. Aided by **Andrea Pisano**, he decorated the façade of the cathedral with statues and designed the campanile himself. It still bears his name, although it has been much altered.

Giovanni di Paolo, *also known as* **Giovanni dal Poggio** c. 1403–1482/83 •*Italian painter*• Born in Siena, he may have trained with Taddeo di Bartoli, and was certainly influenced by **Gentile da Fabriano**, who was in Siena from 1424 to 1426. Though little is known of his life, many works by him have survived. Like his contemporary Sassetta, he worked in a style that continued the tradition of Sienese Trecento masters.

Giraldi, Giambattista, *surnamed* **Cynthius, Cinthio, Centeo** or **Cinzio** 1504–73 •*Italian writer*• Born in Ferrara, he taught in Florence and Pavia. He is the author of nine plays in imitation of **Seneca** the Younger of which *Orbecche* (1541) is regarded as the first modern tragedy on classical lines to be performed in Italy. His *Ecatommiti* (1565) is a collection of tales that was translated into French and Spanish and gave **Shakespeare** his plots for *Measure for Measure* and *Othello*.

Giraldus Cambrensis, *also called* **Girald de Barri** or **Gerald of Wales** c. 1146–c. 1223 •*Norman-Welsh chronicler and ecclesiastic*• Born in Manorbier Castle, Pembrokeshire, he was educated at the abbey of St Peter, Gloucester, and later studied in Paris. He was appointed royal chaplain (1184–89), and in 1185 accompanied Prince (later King) **John** on a military expedition to Ireland. He wrote *Topographia Hibernica* (c. 1188, "The Geography of Ireland"), a record of the natural history, inhabitants and folktales of Ireland, and collected material for his *Expugnatio Hibernica* (c. 1189, "The Conquest of Ireland"), an account of the conquest of Ireland by Henry II. Among his other works is *Gemma ecclesiastica* ("A Clergyman's Treasury"), a handbook for the instruction of the clergy.

Girardelli, Marc 1963– •*Luxembourg skier*• Born in Laustenau, Austria, he has won the overall World Cup title a record five times (1985–86, 1989, 1991 and 1993). Regarded as a classic all-around skier, he skis all the disciplines—downhill, slalom, giant slalom and super G. He won the 44th victory of his long career at Kitzbühl, where he won the combined event of downhill and slalom. After a disagreement with his Austrian coaches, he adopted Luxembourgeois nationality to make a one-man team. He was forced to retire due to injury in 1997.

Giraudoux, (Hippolyte) Jean 1882–1944 •*French writer*• He was born in Bellac, Limousin. After a brilliant academic career at the École Normale Supérieure, Paris, he joined the diplomatic service and became head of the French Ministry of Information during World War II, until his affiliations became suspect. He pioneered an impressionistic technique in literature, exemplified particularly in *Provinciales* (1909), *Simon le Pathétique* (1918), and his reflection on his war experiences, *Retour d'Alsace, août 1914* (1916, "Return from Alsace in August 1914"). His plays are mainly fantasies based on Greek myths and biblical lore. They include *La guerre de Troie n'aura pas lieu* (1935) and *Pour Lucrèce* (1953). The last two were translated as *Tiger at the Gates* (1955) and *Duel of Angels* (1958) by **Christopher Fry**. Giraudoux also wrote literary criticism, some short stories, and two film scripts.

" "

Le plagiat est la base de toutes les littératures, excepté de la première, qui d'ailleurs est inconnue.

Plagiarism is the base of all literature except the first text, which, however, is unknown.

1922 ***Siegfried et le Limousin.***

Giscard d'Estaing, Valéry 1926– •*French Conservative statesman*• Born in Koblenz, Germany, he was educated in Paris. He was awarded the Croix de Guerre for his activities for the Resistance during World War II. After the war he worked in the Ministry of Finance, before being inducted into the private "Cabinet" of Prime Minister **Edgar Faure** in 1953. He entered the National Assembly in 1956 as an Independent Republican and became Finance Minister to President **De Gaulle** in 1962. Giscard had a falling-out with De Gaulle in 1966, but returned as Finance Minister during the **Pompidou** presidency (1969–74). Following Pompidou's death he was narrowly elected President in May 1974 and proceeded to introduce a series of liberalizing reforms. He was defeated in 1981 by his 1974 opponent **François Mitterrand**. Giscard was reelected to the National Assembly in 1984 and was the influential leader of the Union pour la Démocratie Française (Union for French Democracy), a center-right group that he formed in 1978, until 1996. In 1989 he resigned from the French National Assembly to play instead a leading role in the European parliament.

Gish, Lillian Diana, *originally* **Lillian de Guiche** 1893–1993 •*US actress*• Born in Springfield, Ohio, she acted in touring theater companies with her sister, with whom she made a joint film debut in *An Unseen Enemy* (1912). A long association with **D W Griffith** brought her leading roles in *Birth of a Nation* (1915), *Intolerance* (1916) and *Broken Blossoms* (1919) and she created a gallery of waiflike heroines with indomitable spirits. Unsuited to talking pictures, she returned to the stage in 1930, and continued to play supporting roles in television and on film, including *Duel in the Sun* (1946) and *The Night of the Hunter* (1955), returning to a major screen role in *The Whales of August* (1987). She received an honorary Academy Award in 1971.

Gissing, George Robert 1857–1903 •*English novelist*• Born in Wakefield, Yorkshire, he earned a scholarship to Owens College (now the University of Manchester), and from there won another scholarship to the University of London. However, before he could take it up he fell in love with Marianne ("Nell") Harrison, thought to have been a prostitute, from whom he contracted a venereal disease. Intent on setting her up as a seamstress, he stole money from his fellow students, for which he was sentenced to a month's hard labor and expelled from college. After spending time in Chicago he returned to England in 1877, started his first novel, *Workers in the Dawn* (1880), and married Nell in 1879. He was doggedly productive, feeding the circulating libraries with novels such as *The Nether World* (1889), but the couple struggled financially until Nell died in 1888. Now better off, Gissing traveled on the Continent, and went on to produce some of his finest fiction, notably *New Grub Street* (1891), a grim rebuke to all aspiring authors. He moved to the south of France for the sake of his lungs, and wrote several books in the last five years of his life, including *The Private Papers of Henry Ryecroft* (1902), a spoof autobiography that was instantly successful.

Giuliani, Rudy (Rudolph William) 1944– •*US lawyer and politician*• Born in Brooklyn, New York, he studied at New York University Law School. Following a successful career in the US Attorney's office and in private practice, he was elected mayor of New York City in 1994. Reelected in 1997, he focused on reducing crime and improving the quality of life of the people of New York. In 2001, shortly before he left office, the September 11 terrorist attack on the World Trade Center brought Giuliani to international prominence. For his commitment to supporting those affected by the tragedy and restoring a sense of normality to the city, he was named *Time* magazine's Person of the Year in 2001 and awarded an honorary knighthood.

Giulini, Carlo Maria 1914– •*Italian conductor*• He was born in Barletta and quickly showed musical gifts. After studying at the Santa Cecilia Academy in Rome, by 1946 he had become director of music for Italian Radio. Five years later he was conducting at La Scala, Milan, and between 1969 and 1984 he worked as principal conductor of the Chicago Symphony, Vienna Symphony, and Los Angeles Philharmonic orchestras and gave guest performances all over the world.

Giulio Romano, *properly* **Giulio Pippi de'Giannuzzi** c. 1492–1546 •*Italian painter and architect*• Born in Rome, he assisted **Raphael** in the execution of several of his finest works, and completed the *Transfiguration* in the Vatican. In 1524 he went to Mantua, where the drainage of the marshes and the protection of the city from the floods of the Po and Mincio rivers attest to his skill as an engineer.

Givenchy, Hubert James Marcel Taffin de 1927– •*French fashion designer*• Born in Beauvais, he attended the École des Beaux-Arts and the Faculté de Droit in Paris. He opened his own house in 1952. In the early 1950s he met **Cristóbal Balenciaga**, who influenced and encouraged him. His clothes are noted for their elegance and quality. He produces ready-to-wear clothes under his Nouvelle Boutique label. He retired in 1995 after 43 years as designer in chief at his eponymous Paris fashion house, and was replaced by **John Galliano**.

Gladstone, William Ewart 1809–98 •*English Liberal statesman*• He was born in Liverpool, the son of a merchant and MP. He was educated at Eton and Christ Church, Oxford. He entered Parliament in 1832 as a Conservative, working closely with **Robert Peel**. After several junior appointments, he was appointed President of the Board of Trade (1843–45). He was Chancellor of the Exchequer in Lord **Aberdeen**'s coalition (1852–55) and then again under Lord **Palmerston** and Lord **John Russell** (1859–66). In 1867 he became leader of the Liberal Party, and soon after served his first term as Premier (1868–74). In a ministry notable for administrative reform, he disestablished and disendowed the Irish Church, reformed the Civil Service and established a system of national elementary education (1870). Frequently in office (1880–85, 1886 and 1892–94) until his resignation in 1894, he succeeded in carrying out a plan of parliamentary reform, which went a long way toward universal male suffrage. In his last two ministries he introduced bills for Irish Home Rule, but both were defeated. He died at Hawarden, and was buried in Westminster Abbey.

Glaisher, James 1809–1903 •*English meteorologist*• Born in Rotherhithe, London, he was self-educated. After various surveying posts, in 1835 he went to Greenwich Observatory and in 1840 became superintendent of the magnetic and meteorological department. He was a founding member in 1850 of the British Meteorological Society (which later became the Royal Meteorological Society). He is best known for 29 balloon ascents between 1862 and 1866, which were carried out in every month of the year and in different weather conditions. The main aim was to measure temperature, dewpoint and wind at different heights, and the highest ascent is believed to have reached 30,000 feet.

Glanvill, Joseph 1636–80 •*English philosopher and clergyman*• Born in Plymouth, Devon, he studied at Oxford. He served as vicar of Frome (1662), rector of the Abbey Church in Bath (1666) and prebendary of Worcester (1678). A sympathizer with the Cambridge Platonists, he attacked scholastic philosophy in his famous work *The Vanity of Dogmatising* (2nd edn, 1665) and supported experimental science. After his death Henry More (1614–87) edited and published his *Sadducismus triumphatus* (1681) which, surprisingly perhaps, attacked the rationalizing skepticism of those who denied the existence of ghosts, witches and other apparitions of the spirit.

Glanvill, Ranulf de d. 1190 •*English jurist*• Born in Stratford St Andrew, near Saxmundham, Suffolk, he was Chief Justiciary of England (1180–89). An adviser to **Henry II**, he reputedly wrote the earliest treatise on the laws of England, the *Tractatus de legibus et consuetudinibus Angliae* (c. 1187).

Glanville-Hicks, Peggy 1912–90 •*Australian composer*• Born in Melbourne, Victoria, she studied at the Conservatorium of Music there, at the Royal College of Music, London, and with **Ralph Vaughan Williams**, **Nadia Boulanger**, Arthur Benjamin and Egon Wellesz. In 1959 she went to Greece where her opera *Nausicaa* (to a text by **Robert Graves**) was produced for the 1961 Athens Festival. Other major works include the operas *The Transposed Heads* (story by **Thomas Mann**) and *Sappho* (by **Lawrence Durrell**), *Etruscan Concerto, Letters from Morocco* and *Concerto Romantico*.

Glaser, Donald Arthur 1926– •*US physicist and Nobel Prize winner*• Born in Cleveland, Ohio, he was educated at the Case Institute of Technology, Cleveland, and at the California Institute of Technology (Caltech), then became a professor at the University of Michigan (1949–59) and at the University of California at Berkeley (1960–). He was awarded the 1960 Nobel Prize for physics for inventing the "bubble chamber" for observing the paths of elementary particles.

Glasgow, Ellen Anderson Gholson 1874–1945 •*US novelist*• Born in Richmond, Virginia, she spent most of her life there aside from various trips to Europe from 1896. She was best known for her stories of the South, including *The Descendant* (1897), *Virginia* (1913) and *In This Our Life* (1941, Pulitzer Prize). *Barren Ground* (1925) is a more optimistic and progressivist narrative.

" "

Women like to sit down with trouble as if it were knitting.

1932 ***The Sheltered Life****, part 3, section 3.*

Glashow, Sheldon Lee 1932– •*US physicist and Nobel Prize winner*• Born in New York City, he studied at Cornell, Harvard, and the Universities of Copenhagen and Geneva, before becoming Professor of Physics at Harvard from 1967. Glashow developed one of the first models to describe simultaneously two of the four forces of nature, the electromagnetic and weak forces, and subsequently developed the "electroweak" theory of **Steven Weinberg** and **Abdus Salam** by introducing a new particle property known as "charm." He was a major contributor to the theory of quantum chromodynamics, which assumes that strongly interacting particles such as the protons and neutrons that form the nucleus are made of quarks and that "gluons" bind the quarks together. He shared the 1979 Nobel Prize for physics with Salam and Weinberg for their contributions to the "standard model" of all particle interactions.

Glaspell, Susan 1882–1948 •*US writer*• She was born in Davenport, Iowa, and studied at Drake University in Des Moines, Iowa. She began by writing short stories, collected in *Lifted Masks* (1912). Her novels include *Fidelity* (1915), *Brook Evans* (1928) and *The Fugitive's Return* (1929). She also wrote plays, among them *Trifles* (1917) and *Alison's House* (1930), based on the life of **Emily Dickinson**, which won a Pulitzer Prize.

Glass, Philip 1937– •*US composer*• Born in Baltimore, Maryland, he studied with **Nadia Boulanger** (1964–66) and **Ravi Shankar**. He was much influenced by Far Eastern music with its static harmonies, by the melodic repetition found in North African music, and by rock music. The resulting "minimalist" style, often cast over long periods with unremitting rhythmic patterns and simple diatonic chords, gained him a considerable following, especially in such stage works as *Einstein on the Beach* (1976), *Satyagraha* (1980), *Akhnaton* (1984), *The Making of the Representative for Planet 8* (1988) and *The Voyage* (1992). His other compositions include several film scores and the operas *Orphee* (1993) and *Monsters of Grace* (1998).

Glauber, Johann Rudolph 1604–70 •*German physician*• He was born in Karlstadt, Bavaria, but settled in the Netherlands. In 1648 he discovered hydrochloric acid, and he was probably the first to produce nitric acid. He also discovered "Glauber's salt" (sodium sulfate), the therapeutic virtues of which he greatly exaggerated, and acetone, benzine and alkaloids.

Glen, Esther 1881–1940 •*New Zealand journalist and children's writer*• Her first novel for younger readers was *Six Little New Zealanders* (1917), followed by its sequel *Uncles Three at Kamahi* (1926). Although she only wrote four books—the others were

Twinkles on the Mountain (1920) and *Robin of Maoriland* (1929)—her influence on New Zealand children's writing was considerable, and in 1945 the New Zealand Library Association established the annual Esther Glen award for distinguished contributions to the genre.

Glendower, Owen, *properly* **Owain Glyndwr** c. 1350–c. 1416 •*Welsh rebel*• Born in Montgomeryshire, he quarreled with Lord Grey (1401) over some lands and, unable to obtain redress from **Henry IV**, carried on a guerrilla war against the English lords of the Marches which became a national war of independence. In 1402 he captured Lord Grey and Sir Edmund Mortimer, both of whom married Glendower's daughters and joined him in coalition with **Henry Percy** (Hotspur). That coalition ended in the Battle of Shrewsbury (1403), won by Henry IV. In 1404 Glendower entered into a treaty with Charles VI of France, who in 1405 sent a force to Wales. Glendower, though often defeated, kept fighting until his death.

Glenn, John Herschel 1921– •*US astronaut and politician*• Born in Cambridge, Ohio, he was educated at Maryland University. He joined the US Marine Corps in 1943, and served in the Pacific during World War II, and later in Korea. In 1957 he completed a record-breaking supersonic flight from Los Angeles to New York. He became an astronaut in 1959, and in 1962 became the first American to orbit the Earth in a three-orbit flight in the Friendship 7 space capsule. From 1975 to 1998 he served as Democratic senator for Ohio. He sought the Democratic nomination for the presidency unsuccessfully in 1984 and 1988.

Glennie, Evelyn 1965– •*Scottish percussion player*• Born in Aberdeen, she studied timpani and percussion from the age of 12, and trained at the Royal Academy of Music, London. Judged to be a percussionist of outstanding abilities, she is additionally remarkable in her achievements as she experienced a gradual but total loss of hearing in her early teens. She has received innumerable prizes and awards and is a Fellow of the Royal College of Music. Many leading composers have written specially for her.

Glinka, Mikhail Ivanovich 1804–57 •*Russian composer*• Born in Novopasskoi, Smolensk, he became a civil servant, but after a visit to Italy began to study music in Berlin. Returning to Russia, he produced his opera *A Life for the Tsar* (1836, known earlier as *Ivan Susanin*). His *Russlan and Ludmilla* (1842), based on a poem by **Alexander Pushkin**, pioneered the style of the Russian national school of composers.

Gloucester, Prince Henry, Duke of 1900–74 •*British prince*• The third son of **George V**, he was educated privately and at Eton. He became a captain in the 10th Hussars and was created Duke of Gloucester (1928). In 1935 he married Lady Alice Montagu-Douglas-Scott, and they had two children: Prince William (1941–72) and Prince **Richard**, who succeeded him.

Gloucester, Prince Humphrey, Earl of Pembroke and **Duke of**, *nicknamed* **Good Duke Humphrey** 1391–1447 •*English prince and literary patron*• The youngest son of King **Henry IV**, as Regent of England (1420–21) and Protector (1422–29) during the minority of **Henry VI**, he was overshadowed by his elder brother, the Duke of **Bedford**. In 1447 he was arrested for high treason by Suffolk, Beaufort's successor as First Minister, at Bury St Edmunds and five days later was found dead in bed (apparently from natural causes). He cultivated friendships with literary figures like **John Lydgate** and the Italian humanists, who supplied him with manuscript books. He later presented these to Oxford to form the nucleus of the Bodleian library.

Gloucester, Prince Richard, Duke of 1944– •*British prince*• The younger son of Prince Henry, Duke of **Gloucester** and grandson of **George V**, he trained as an architect. In 1972 he married Brigitte Eva van Deurs (1946–), the daughter of a Danish lawyer, and they have one son, Alexander, Earl of Ulster (1974–), and two daughters, Lady Davina Windsor (1977–) and Lady Rose Windsor (1980–).

Gloucester, Prince Robert, Earl of d. 1147 •*English prince*• An illegitimate son of **Henry I**, he was the principal supporter of his half sister **Matilda**, the Empress Maud, in her civil war against **Stephen**.

Gloucester, Gilbert de Clare, 8th Earl of, *known as* **the Red Earl** 1243–95 •*English nobleman*• He was born in Christchurch, Hampshire, the son of Richard de Clare, 7th Earl of Gloucester. He sided with **Simon de Montfort** and helped him win the Battle of Lewes (1264) against the king's forces, but after quarreling with de Montfort, he joined Prince Edward (later **Edward I**), and won the Battle of Evesham (1265). He married Joan, daughter of Edward I, and built Caerphilly Castle in south Wales.

Gloucester, Gilbert de Clare, 9th Earl of 1291–1314 •*English nobleman*• Also 10th Earl of Clare and 8th Earl of Hertford, he was the son of Gilbert de Clare, 8th Earl of **Gloucester**. His younger sister Margaret was married to Piers Gaveston, the favorite of **Edward II**, and after Gaveston's execution Gloucester acted as mediator for the barons with the king. He was killed in the English defeat by the Scots at Bannockburn (1314). Another sister, Lady Elizabeth de Clare (c. 1291–1360), endowed Clare College, Cambridge (1336).

Glover, Jane Alison 1949– •*English conductor and musicologist*• Born in Helmsley, Yorkshire, she was educated at St Hugh's College, Oxford, where she became a lecturer in music (1976). She joined the Open University faculty of music in 1979, and also became a television host of such BBC programs as *Orchestra* (1983). She made her conducting debut at the Wexford Festival (1975), and went on to conduct nearly all the top orchestras in the world. After joining the Glyndebourne Opera in 1979, she worked as chorus director (1980–84) and as musical director of the touring opera (1982–85). She was artistic director of the London Mozart Players (1984–91).

Glovichisch, Jurni *See* **Clovio, Giulio**

Gluck, Christoph Willibald 1714–87 •*German composer*• Born in Erasbach, Bavaria, he studied in Milan, and in collaboration with the librettist Ranieri Calzabigi, he produced such works as *Orfeo ed Euridice* (1762, "Orpheus and Eurydice") and *Alceste* (1767). In the late 1770s, Paris was divided into two—the Gluckists, who supported Gluck's French opera style, and the Piccinnists, who supported the traditional Italian style of **Niccola Piccinni**, but Gluck won great accolades with his *Iphigénie en Tauride* (1778), and retired honorably from Paris.

Glyn, Elinor, *née* **Sutherland** 1864–1943 •*British novelist*• Born in Jersey, Channel Islands, she found fame with *Three Weeks* (1907), a book which gained a reputation for being risqué. She kept her public enthralled with such books as *Man and Maid* (1922), *Did She?* (1934) and *The Third Eye* (1940). Her novels were nonsensical, faulty in construction and ungrammatical, but were nevertheless avidly read. From 1922 to 1927 she lived in Hollywood, where "it" (her version of sex appeal) was glamorized on the screen.

Gneisenau, August Wilhelm Anton, Graf Neithardt von 1760–1831 •*Prussian soldier*• Born in Schildau in Prussian Saxony, he accompanied the German auxiliaries of England to America in 1782, joined the Prussian army in 1786, and in 1806 fought against **Napoleon I** at Saalfeld and Jena. His defense of Colberg (1807) led to his appointment on the commission with **Gerhard von Scharnhorst** for the reorganization of the Prussian army. In the War of Liberation (1813–14) he served at Leipzig (1813). In the 1815 Waterloo campaign, as Chief of Staff under **Gebhard von Blücher**, he directed the strategy of the Prussian army.

Göbbels, (Paul) Joseph *See* **Goebbels, (Paul) Joseph**

Gobbi, Tito 1913–84 •*Italian baritone and opera producer*• Born in Bassano del Grappa, he studied law, but took up singing in Rome, and made his operatic debut in *Gubbio* (1935). A regular performer with the Rome Opera from 1938, he was an acclaimed actor and soon made an international reputation, especially in **Verdi**an roles. He also produced operas and appeared in films.

Gobind Singh 1666–1708 •*Last of the 10 Sikh gurus*• He completed the process by which the Sikhs developed from the quietist faith propagated by Guru **Nanak** to a militant creed. Gaining the leadership on the execution by the Moguls of his father, Guru Tegh Bahadur (1664–75), he was implacably hostile to them, and in the final years of the 17th century established a small Sikh state in the Punjab foothills by military means. At the Baisakhi festival in 1699 he instituted the Khalsa, the new Sikh brotherhood marked by a new code of discipline, the "Five Ks" (visible symbols, including the uncut hair and beard), and common adoption of the name Singh for males and Kaur for females. He died at the hands of Pathan assassins. Traditionally, Gobind Singh declared on his deathbed that guruship would henceforth reside in the Sikh scripture (*Guru Granth*) and the Sikh community (*Guru Panth*).

Gobineau, Joseph Arthur, Comte de 1816–82 •*French Orientalist and diplomat*• Born in Bordeaux, he was a member of the French diplomatic service and secretary to **Alexis de Tocqueville** (1849–77). He wrote several romances and a history of Persia, but is best known for his essay *The Inequality of Human Races*. He has been called the "intellectual parent" of **Nietzsche** and the real inventor of the "superman" and super-morality.

Godard, Jean-Luc 1930– •*French film director*• Born and educated in Paris, he began his career as a cinema critic (1950). His first feature film *A Bout de souffle* (1960, *Breathless*), established him as a leader of the *Nouvelle vague* (New Wave) cinema. His elliptical narrative style and original use of jump cuts, freeze frames, and so on gained him much critical attention, both enthusiastic and otherwise. He wrote his own filmscripts on contemporary themes, such as *Vivre sa vie* (1962, *My Life to Live*). Other work from the 1960s includes *Pierrot le fou* (1965), *Alphaville* (1965) and *Weekend* (1967). After an unsuccessful trip to the US, he submerged himself in "revolutionary anticapitalist" films, although he returned to more mainstream concerns in the 1980s. More recent feature films include *Sauve qui peut* (1980, "Slow Motion"), a highly idiosyncratic *King Lear* (1987) and *Hélas pour moi* (1993, "Woe Is Me").

" "

La photographie, c'est la vérité. Le cinéma: la vérité vingt-quatre fois par seconde.

Photography is truth. And cinema is truth twenty-four times a second.

1963 Line in ***Le Petit Soldat****.*

Godber, John Harry 1956– •*English playwright and film and theater director*• Born in Hemsworth, West Yorkshire, he was educated at the University of Leeds. He began his career as a schoolteacher (1979–83) and became artistic director for Hull Truck Theatre Company in 1984. During a prolific writing career he has produced over 30 plays for stage and television including *Bouncers* (1986), *Teechers* (1987), *Lucky Sods* (1995) and *Thick as a Brick* (1999). *Up 'N' Under* (1984) was made into a film in 1997.

Goddard, Robert Hutchings 1882–1945 •*US physicist, rocket engineer and inventor*• Born in Worcester, Massachusetts, he received a PhD in physics from Clark University, Worcester, in 1911, and subsequently taught physics there for almost 30 years. Fascinated by the idea of space travel, he published *A Method of Reaching Extreme Altitudes* (1919) and in 1926 his first liquid-fuel rocket was launched. By 1929 he had developed the first instrument-carrying rocket able to make observations in flight. In 1935 he launched rockets that exceeded the speed of sound. Only after his death was he given due recognition for his pioneering work, which led directly to NASA and the US space exploration program.

Godden, (Margaret) Rumer 1907–98 •*English novelist, poet and children's author*• Born in Eastbourne, Sussex, she lived for many years in India, a country and culture that provide the backdrop to much of her fiction. Her third novel and first major success, *Black Narcissus* (1939), describes the struggles of nuns attempting to found a mission in the Himalaya region. Her first book for children was *The Dolls' House* (1947). Her later books include *Coromandel Sea Change* (1991), a love story set in southern India, *Pippa Passes* (1994) and *Cromartie vs the God Shiva* (1998).

Gödel or **Goedel, Kurt** 1906–78 •*US logician and mathematician*• Born in Brünn, Moravia (now Brno, Czech Republic), he studied and taught in Vienna, then emigrated to the US in 1940 and joined the Institute for Advanced Study at Princeton University. He propounded one of the most important proofs in modern mathematics, namely Gödel's theorem, published in 1931, which demonstrated the existence of formally undecidable elements within any formal system of arithmetic. This result put an end to hopes of giving a truly rigorous foundation to all mathematics on essentially finite terms.

Godfrey of Bouillon c. 1060–1100 •*French crusader*• He became Count of Verdun and Lord of Bouillon in the Ardennes in 1076 as heir to his maternal uncle Godfrey (the Hunchback). He had to fight to maintain this inheritance against rival claimants and other local enemies, and in 1096 he sold or mortgaged all of his lands and joined the First Crusade. In 1099 he was elected ruler of Jerusalem, taking the title of "Advocate" or Defender of the Holy Sepulcher. He had begun to extend the territory held by the Christians when he died after a reign of only a year.

Godfrey, Bob (Robert) 1921– •*British animated cartoon producer and director*• He was born in New South Wales, Australia, and brought to England as a baby. After training in animation as a background artist, he went on to make his own animated cartoons: *Watch the Birdie* (1954), which brought a new bawdy humor to British cartoons, *Henry 9 till 5* (1965), *Kama Sutra Rides Again* (1971), and others. *Great*, on the life of **Isambard Kingdom Brunel**, won an Academy Award in 1975. He is also known for the classic children's cartoons *Roobarb and Custard* and *Henry's Cat*.

Godiva, Lady d. c. 1080 •*English noblewoman and religious benefactor*• She was the wife of Leofric, Earl of Chester (d. 1057). According to the 13th-century chronicler **Roger of Wendover**, she rode naked through the marketplace of Coventry in order to persuade her husband to reduce the taxes he had imposed. A later embellishment of the legend suggests that she requested the townspeople to remain indoors, which they all did except for "Peeping Tom," who was struck blind.

Godolphin, Sidney, 1st Earl of 1645–1712 •*English statesman*• Born in Helston, Cornwall, he became a royal page in 1662, entered Parliament in 1668, and in 1684 was made head of the Treasury and Baron Godolphin. On **William III**'s landing in 1688 he started negotiations with William on behalf of **James VII and II**, and, when James fled, he voted for a regency. However, in 1689 William reinstated him as first commissioner of the Treasury. Queen **Anne** on her accession made him her sole Lord High Treasurer (1702) and in 1706 he was made earl. In 1698 he married Henrietta, daughter of the Duke of **Marlborough**. His able management of the Treasury financed Marlborough's campaigns without increasing the public debt by more than one million annually. To prevent his own overthrow, he forced Anne to dismiss **Robert Harley** (1708). But the influence of **Abigail Masham** helped Harley to power, and in 1710 Godolphin was himself dismissed.

Godoy, Manuel de, Duke of Alcudia 1767–1851 •*Spanish politician*• Born in Badajoz, he was a member of **Charles IV**'s bodyguard and became the royal favorite. Having deposed the Count of Aranda, he achieved dictatorial power at the age of 25 through the favor of the queen, Maria Luisa, whose lover he was. In 1796 he allied with France against England—a disastrous move that turned Spain into a virtual French satellite, and greatly contributed to Spain's loss of its American empire. On the French invasion of 1808, the king was obliged to imprison Godoy to protect him from popular fury. He subsequently conspired with **Napoleon I** and spent the rest of his life in exile in Rome and Paris.

Godunov, Boris *See* **Boris Godunov**

Godwin d. 1053 •*Anglo-Saxon nobleman and warrior*• The father of King **Harold II**, he was made Earl of Wessex by King **Knut** (Canute) (1018), and in 1042 helped raise **Edward the Confessor** to the throne, marrying him to his daughter Edith (1045). He had ambitions for his five sons, all of whom received earldoms (1043–57), and collectively their wealth almost equaled that of the royal family. His struggle against the king's Norman favorites caused Edward to confine Edith to a monastery and banish Godwin (1051). However, in 1052 Godwin won the support of Edward's forces and subjects, so that Edward was forced to reinstate him. His son Harold was for a few months Edward's successor.

Godwin, Edward William 1833–86 •*English architect and designer*• Born in Bristol, he trained there and from 1854 practiced as an architect. His mainly domestic architecture included the White House (1877), a studio house in Chelsea for his friend

James McNeill Whistler. He was a central figure in the Aesthetic movement, and his furniture designs after 1875 were much influenced by the Japanese style that that movement made fashionable. He was also a theatrical designer, clothing reformer and journalist. He was the lover of **Ellen Terry**, and their son was the actor and stage designer Edward Gordon Craig (1872–1966).

Godwin, Fay Simmonds 1931– •*English photographer*• Born in Berlin, Germany, she was educated in numerous schools worldwide. She began by taking photographs of her two young sons but has become best known for her landscapes, including Welsh and Scottish scenes. They now often make a sociological or ecological statement by incorporating pollution, in order to alert people to the potential for environmental disaster. Her many publications include *Our Forbidden Land* (1990).

Godwin, Francis 1562–1633 •*English prelate and author*• Born in Hannington, Northamptonshire, the son of Bishop Thomas Godwin (1517–90), he was educated at Oxford. He is best known for his science-fiction romance, *Man in the Moon or a Voyage Thither, by Domingo Gonsales* (1638), used as a source by Bishop John Wilkins (1614–72), **Cyrano de Bergerac** and **Jonathan Swift**.

Godwin, Mary *See* **Wollstonecraft, Mary**

Godwin, William 1756–1836 •*English political writer and novelist*• Born in Wisbech, Cambridgeshire, he spent his childhood in Guestwick, Norfolk, and then attended Hoxton Presbyterian College (1773–78). During a five-year ministry at Ware, Stowmarket and Beaconsfield, he turned Socinian and republican, and by 1787 was a "complete unbeliever." His *Enquiry Concerning Political Justice* brought him fame, and captivated **Coleridge**, **Wordsworth**, **Robert Southey**, and later and above all **Shelley**, who became his disciple, son-in-law and subsidizer. It was calmly subversive of everything (law and "marriage, the worst of all laws"), but it deprecated violence, and its author escaped prosecution. His masterpiece, *The Adventures of Caleb Williams* (1794), was designed to give "a general review of the modes of domestic and unrecorded despotism." In 1797 he married **Mary Wollstonecraft**, who was pregnant by him, but she died soon after their daughter, **Mary Wollstonecraft Shelley**, was born.

Goebbels or **Göbbels, (Paul) Joseph** 1897–1945 •*German Nazi politician*• Born in Rheydt, he was educated at a Catholic school and the University of Heidelberg. With a clubfoot absolving him from military service in World War I, he won a number of scholarships and attended eight universities. He became **Hitler**'s enthusiastic supporter, and was appointed editor of the Nazi paper *Völkische Freiheit* and led the Nazi Party in Berlin in 1923. With the Führer's accession to power, he was made head of the Ministry of Public Enlightenment and Propaganda. A bitter anti-Semite, he had a gift for mob oratory which made him a powerful exponent of the more radical aspects of Nazi philosophy. In 1943, while Hitler was running the war, Goebbels was virtually running the country. He retained Hitler's confidence to the last, and in the Berlin bunker he and his wife committed suicide after they had taken the lives of their six children. His diaries now represent a major historical source.

Goedel, Kurt *See* **Gödel, Kurt**

Goeppert-Mayer, Maria, *née* **Goeppert** 1906–72 •*US physicist and Nobel Prize winner*• Born in Kattowitz, Germany (now Katowice, Poland), she graduated from the University of Göttingen in 1930, emigrated to the US and taught at Johns Hopkins University and the University of California, San Diego. Based on the fact that certain nuclei are very stable, having "magic numbers" of neutrons and or protons, she drew an analogy with atomic physics in which stable atoms have a closed shell of electrons and developed the shell model of the nucleus, resolving some initial problems by discussions with **Enrico Fermi**. A similar model was developed by **Hans Jensen** in Germany. Goeppert-Mayer shared the 1963 Nobel Prize for physics with **Eugene Wigner** and Jensen.

Goering or **Göring, Hermann Wilhelm** 1893–1946 •*German Nazi politician*• He was born in Rosenheim, Bavaria. One of the first infantry officers to fight on the Western Front in World War I, he transferred to the air force in 1915, became an ace pilot and later commanded the famous "Death Squadron." An anti-Semite, he joined the Nazi party in 1922 and next year commanded the **Hitler** storm troopers, the Brown Shirts (SA), but went into exile for five years after the failure of the November Munich putsch. In 1928 he became one of the 12 Nazi deputies to the Reichstag, and in 1932 he became President of the Reichstag. When Hitler assumed power (1933) Goering's several posts included that of Reich Air Minister and, in 1938, War Minister. He founded the Gestapo, set up the concentration camps for political, racial and religious suspects, and, in the great purge of June 30, 1934 ("night of the long knives"), had his comrades murdered. When the Munich Agreement was made in 1938, he announced a fivefold extension of the Luftwaffe. Early in 1940 he became economic dictator of Germany and in June reached the pinnacle of his power when Hitler made him Marshal of the Reich. However, the Battle of Britain, the failure of the 1941 Nazi bombing attacks to disrupt the British ports and cities, and the mounting Allied air attacks on Germany in 1942 and 1943 led to a decline in his prestige. By the time of the Allied liberation of Normandy in 1944 he was in disgrace. As the war drew to a close, he attempted a revolution. Hitler condemned him to death, but he escaped and was captured by US troops. In 1946 he was the principal defendant at the Nuremberg War Crimes Trial, but committed suicide by poison a few hours prior to his intended execution.

Goes, Hugo van der c. 1440–82 •*Flemish painter*• Born probably in Ghent, and dean of the painters' guild at Ghent (1473–75), he painted the magnificent Portineri Altarpiece containing *The Adoration of the Shepherds* (now in the Uffizi, Florence) for the Santa Maria Nuova Hospital in Florence, and many other notable works.

Goethe, Johann Wolfgang von 1749–1832 •*German poet, dramatist, scientist and court official*• He was born in Frankfurt am Main. He was educated privately and reluctantly studied law at Leipzig (1765–68); however, a love affair inspired him to write his first two plays, *Die Laune des Verliebten* (1767, "The Beloved's Whim") and *Die Mitschuldigen* (staged 1787, "The Accomplices"). He continued his law studies at Strasbourg from 1770, where he came under the influence of **Johann Herder**, the pioneer of German romanticism. In 1771 he graduated and returned to Frankfurt, where he captured the spirit of German nationalism in an early masterpiece of drama, *Götz von Berlichingen* (1773), which epitomized the man of genius at odds with society. Goethe followed up his first triumph with his self-revelatory cautionary novel, *Die Leiden des jungen Werthers* (1774, "The Sorrows of Young Werther"), which mirrored his own doomed affair with Charlotte Buff, the fiancée of a friend. A romance with Lili Schönemann inspired the love lyrics of 1775. In the autumn Goethe (perhaps surprisingly) accepted the post of court official and privy councilor (1776) to the young duke of Weimar. His 10-year relationship with a young widow, **Charlotte von Stein**, served as a psychological support, but did little to help his development as a creative writer. Goethe also took an interest in the life sciences. In 1782 he extended his researches to comparative anatomy, discovered the intermaxillary bone in humans (1784), and formulated a vertebral theory of the skull. He wrote a novel on theatrical life, *Wilhelm Meisters theatralische Sendung* ("Wilhelm Meister's Theatrical Mission," not discovered until 1910), which contains the enigmatic poetry of Mignon's songs, including the famous "Nur wer die Sehnsucht kennt" ("Only He Who Knows Longing"). His visits to Italy (1786–88, 1790) cured him of his emotional dependence on Charlotte von Stein and contributed to a greater preoccupation with poetical form, as in the severely classical verse version of his drama, *Iphigenie auf Tauris* (1787), and the more modern *Egmont* (1788) and *Torquato Tasso* (1790). His love for classical Italy, coupled with his passion for Christiane Vulpius, whom he married in 1806, found full expression in *Römische Elegien* (1795, "Roman Elegies"). From 1794 he formed a friendship with **Schiller**, with whom he conducted an interesting correspondence on aesthetics (1794–1805) and carried on a friendly contest in the writing of ballads which resulted in Schiller's part in *Das Lied von der Glocke* ("The Song of the Bell") and Goethe's in the epic idyll *Hermann und Dorothea* (1798). Goethe's last great period saw the prototype of the favorite German literary composition, the

Bildungsroman, in *Wilhelm Meisters Lehrjahre* (1796, "Wilhelm Meister's Apprenticeship") continued as *Wilhelm Meisters Wanderjahre* (1821–29, "Wilhelm Meister's Travels"). *Wilhelm Meister* was to become the idol of the German romantics, of whom Goethe increasingly disapproved. Goethe's masterpiece, however, is his version of **Christopher Marlowe**'s drama *Faust*, on which he worked for most of his life. Begun in 1775, the first part was published after much revision and Schiller's advice in 1808, and the second part in 1832.

" "

Grau, teurer Freund, ist alle Theorie.
Und grün des Lebens goldner Baum.
All theory, dear friend, is grey,
but the golden tree of actual life springs ever green.

*1808 **Faust**, part 1, "Studierzimmer."*

Goetz von Berlichingen *See* **Götz von Berlichingen**

Gogarty, Oliver St John 1878–1957 •*Irish poet and memoir writer*• He was born in Dublin. Also a playwright, politician and surgeon, he knew **James Joyce** and was the model for "stately, plump Buck Mulligan" in *Ulysses*. He was a senator of the Irish Free State from its foundation in 1922 until 1939, when he moved to the US. His garrulous, witty prose is at its best in *As I Was Going Down Sackville Street* (1937) and *Tumbling in the Hay* (1939).

Gogh, Vincent Van *See* **Van Gogh, Vincent Willem**

Gogol, Nikolai Vasilevich 1809–52 •*Russian novelist and dramatist*• Born in Sorochinstsi, Poltava, he settled in St Petersburg in 1829, and in 1831–32 published his first major work, *Vechera na khutore bliz Dikanki* ("Evenings on a Farm Near Dikanka"). This was followed by two short-story collections, *Mirgorod* (1835, Eng trans 1928) and *Arabesques* (1835, Eng trans 1982), which contained some of his finest stories, like "Shinel" ("The Overcoat") and "Zapiski symashedshego" ("The Diary of a Madman"), introducing a nightmarish world of his fantastic imagination, detailing his fears, frustrations and obsessions. In 1836 he brought out his play, *Revizor* (Eng trans *The Inspector-General*, 1892), the best of Russian comedies, a wild and boisterous satire exposing the corruption, ignorance and vanity of provincial officials. He left Russia for Italy in 1836, and in Rome wrote the first part of *Myortvye dushi* (1842, Eng trans *Dead Souls*, 1854), one of the great novels in world literature. It deals with an attempt by small landowners to swindle the government by the purchase of dead serfs whose names should have been struck off the register. His later work shows increasing obsession with his own "sinfulness" and he burned many of his remaining manuscripts, including the second part of *Myortvye dushi*. He returned to Russia in 1846.

Gokhale, Gopal Krishna 1866–1915 •*Indian politician and social reformer*• Born in Kotluk, Bombay, he became Professor of History at Fergusson College, Poona, resigning in 1904, when he was selected representative of the Bombay legislative council at the supreme council. He founded the Servants of India Society in 1905 to work for the relief of the underprivileged, and in the same year was elected president of the Indian National Congress. He was a leading protagonist of Indian self-government and influenced **Mahatma Gandhi**.

Gold, Thomas 1920– •*US astronomer*• Born in Vienna, Austria, he studied at Cambridge and worked in the UK before moving to the US in 1956. While in England he worked with **Hermann Bondi** and **Fred Hoyle** on the steady-state theory of the origin of the universe. In 1968 he suggested the currently accepted theory that pulsars (discovered by Jocelyn Bell Burnell and **Antony Hewish** in that year) are rapidly rotating neutron stars, dense collapsed stars that produce beams of radio waves from their poles that appear as radio pulses on earth. His unorthodox theory of the origin of petroleum and natural gas proposed that some deposits arise from gas trapped in the earth's interior at the time of the planet's formation. He was Professor of Astronomy at Cornell University from 1971 to 1986, then emeritus.

Goldberg, Reuben Lucius, *known as* **Rube** 1883–1970 •*US cartoonist*• Born in San Francisco, he studied engineering at the University of California, Berkeley, but soon after graduating in 1904 he embarked on a career as a newspaper cartoonist. Syndicated from 1915, his popular cartoons often mocked the pointless complications of modern life, and he was famous for his drawings of ridiculously elaborate machines designed to accomplish simple tasks. He won a Pulitzer Prize in 1948.

Goldberg, Whoopi, *originally* **Caryn Johnson** 1949– •*US actress*• Born in New York City, she appeared on stage from the age of eight, and gradually developed her talent as a mimic and stand-up comedienne, which culminated in her Broadway triumph *Whoopi Goldberg* (1984–85). She made her major film debut in *The Color Purple* (1985), for which she won a Best Actress Academy Award nomination. Determined not to be restricted by her color, sex or perceived image as a comic, she made the best of the choices offered to her but was rarely given first-rate material. Unsurprisingly, she turned to television in the series *Star Trek: The Next Generation* and in the short-lived sitcom *Bagdad Café*. She acquired further recognition for her performance in *Ghost* (1990), which brought her a Best Supporting Actress Academy Award, and for the commercially successful *Sister Act* (1992) and *Sister Act 2* (1993). Along with the comedians Billy Crystal and **Robin Williams**, she has organized a cable-television show, *Comic Relief*, for several years in order to raise money for the homeless in the US. More recent films include *Boys on the Side* (1995) and *How Stella Got Her Groove Back* (1998). She has hosted the Academy Awards, and in 2003 she began producing and starring in the sitcom *Whoopi*.

Goldblum, Jeff 1952– •*US actor*• Born in Pittsburgh, Pennsylvania, he studied at the Neighborhood Playhouse in New York. He is known for his portrayals of nervy outsiders or maverick scientists in films such as *Invasion of the Bodysnatchers* (1978), *The Fly* (1986), *Jurassic Park* (1993), *Independence Day* (1996) and *The Lost World* (1997).

Golding, Sir William Gerald 1911–93 •*English novelist and Nobel Prize winner*• Born in St Columb Minor, Cornwall, he was educated at Marlborough Grammar School and Brasenose College, Oxford. He spent the next five years working in small theater companies, and in 1958 he adapted the short story "Envoy Extraordinary" for the stage as *The Brass Butterfly*. He married in 1939, spent World War II in the Royal Navy, and from 1945 to 1961 was a teacher. He gained international celebrity with *The Lord of the Flies* (1954), a chronicle of the increasingly malevolent actions of a group of schoolboys shipwrecked on a desert island in the wake of a nuclear war. Golding said that this book arose from his five years of war service and ten years of teaching small boys. *The Inheritors* (1955) was his second novel and is similar in theme and tone. Next came *Pincher Martin* (1956), *Free Fall* (1959), *The Spire* (1964) and *The Pyramid* (1967) and *Darkness Visible* (1979). *Rites of Passage* (1980) won the Booker Prize and was the first in a trilogy about a 19th-century voyage from England to Australia including *Close Quarter* (1987) and *Fire Down Below* (1989). His only other novel was *The Paper Men* (1984). He was awarded the Nobel Prize for literature in 1983.

" "

Life should serve up its feast of experience in a series of courses.

*1987 **Close Quarters**.*

Goldoni, Carlo 1707–93 •*Italian dramatist*• Born in Venice, he studied law, but turned to writing for the stage. After several years in northern Italy, he settled in Venice in 1740, and over the next 20 years wrote no fewer than 250 plays in Italian, French and the Venetian dialect. He was greatly influenced by **Molière** and the "commedia dell' arte," although many of his subjects are derived from direct observation of daily life.

Goldschmidt, Richard Benedikt 1878–1958 •*German biologist*• Born in Frankfurt am Main, he was appointed biological director of the Kaiser Wilhelm Institute, Berlin (1921), and in 1935 went to the US, where he became Professor of Zoology at the University of California, Berkeley (1936–58). He proposed the idea that chromosomes themselves, and not the individual genes, are the units of heredity. One of his more important contributions was to show that much geographical variation is genetic and not environmental in origin. He also demonstrated that environmental effects could mimic some of the effects of genetic mutations.

Goldsmith, Oliver 1730–74 •*Irish playwright, novelist and poet*• Born in Pallasmore, County Longford, he was educated at Trinity College, Dublin. In 1752 he went to Edinburgh to study medicine, then set out to make the "grand tour" on foot, but returned penniless in 1756. He practiced as a poor physician in Southwark, and was proofreader to **Samuel Richardson**. An *Enquiry into the Present State of Polite Learning in Europe* (1759) attracted some notice. Goldsmith started and edited a weekly, *The Bee* (1759), and wrote essays for **Tobias Smollett**'s *British Magazine*. For **John Newbery**'s *Public Ledger* he wrote the *Chinese Letters* (1760–71, republished as *The Citizen of the World*). *The Vicar of Wakefield* (1766) secured his reputation as a novelist, *The Deserted Village* (1770) as a poet, and three years later he also achieved high regard as a playwright with *She Stoops to Conquer*.

Goldstein, Joseph Leonard 1940– •*US molecular geneticist and Nobel Prize winner*• Born in Sumter, South Carolina, he studied at the University of Texas, Dallas, where he later held distinguished posts. With **Michael Brown**, he has worked on cholesterol metabolism in the human body, particularly studying the low-density lipoproteins (LDLs) which carry cholesterol in the blood. In some diseases the liver cells cannot remove cholesterol from the bloodstream because they are missing a receptor site for the LDLs, but in 1984 Goldstein and Brown described several mutations in the LDL receptor gene, opening up possibilities for new drugs to combat these diseases. For this work, they were jointly awarded the 1985 Nobel Prize for physiology or medicine.

Goldstein, Vida 1869–1949 •*Australian feminist*• Born in Portland, Victoria, and educated at the University of Melbourne, she ran a school with her sister and became involved with the campaign for women's suffrage. She was a member of the first Australian suffrage group, the Woman's Suffrage Society, and later formed the Woman's Federal Political Association. She also founded the feminist publication *Australian Woman's Sphere* and stood as an independent candidate in Victoria five times (1903–17). She became the first woman in the British Empire to run in national parliamentary elections.

Goldsworthy, Andy (Andrew Charles) 1956– •*English sculptor*• Born in Cheshire, he studied at Bradford and Lancaster Art Colleges. An exponent of land art, he has created works in Britain and elsewhere featuring natural materials such as snow, ice, stone, wood and earth, the spirit of his creations encapsulated in the title of a 1989 book, *A Collaboration with Nature*. He has taught in Britain and the US.

Goldwater, Barry M(orris) 1909–98 •*US Republican politician and author*• Born in Phoenix, Arizona, the son of a Jewish father of Polish descent, he was educated at the University of Arizona and served as a ferry pilot during World War II. He worked at his family's department store before representing his home state in the US Senate (1952–64). He was a conservative Republican, supporting **Joseph McCarthy** and opposing President **Dwight D Eisenhower** and state intervention in economic affairs. He ran in the 1964 presidential election for the Republicans, but was heavily defeated by **Lyndon B Johnson**. Returning to the Senate in 1969, he chaired the Senate Armed Services Committee before retiring in 1987. He was one of the architects of the conservative revival within the Republican Party.

Goldwyn, Samuel, *originally* **Samuel Goldfish** 1882–1974 •*US film producer*• Born of Jewish parents in Warsaw, Poland, he was orphaned and, at the age of 11, ran away to relatives in England, and again, at 13, to the US. After working as a glove salesman, he founded a film company with a depressed playwright, **Cecil B de Mille**, as director and produced *The Squaw Man* (1913). In 1925 he founded the Metro-Goldwyn-Mayer Company, allying himself with United Artists from 1926. His "film-of-the-book" policy included such films as *Bulldog Drummond* (1929), *All Quiet on the Western Front* (1930), and *Wuthering Heights* (1939). He also produced *The Little Foxes* (1941), *The Best Years of Our Lives* (1946, Academy Award), *The Secret Life of Walter Mitty* (1947), *Guys and Dolls* (1955) and *Porgy and Bess* (1959). Examples of well-known "Goldwynisms" are "include me out," and "a verbal contract isn't worth the paper it's written on."

Golgi, Camillo 1843–1926 •*Italian cytologist and Nobel Prize winner*• He was born in Corteno, Lombardy. He began his career as a physician in Abbiategrasso, where he made the invaluable discovery of how to stain nerve tissue using silver nitrate (1873). As Professor of Pathology at Pavia (1876–1918), he discovered the "Golgi bodies" in animal cells which, because of their affinity for metallic salts, are readily visible under the microscope, and opened up a new field of research into the central nervous system, sense organs, muscles and glands. He shared with **Santiago Ramón y Cajal** the 1906 Nobel Prize for physiology or medicine.

Gollancz, Sir Victor 1893–1967 •*English publisher, author and philanthropist*• He was born in London and was educated at St Paul's School and New College, Oxford. He became a teacher, and founded his own publishing firm in 1928, becoming known for his innumerable campaigns and pressure group activities. In 1936 he founded the Left Book Club, which influenced the growth of the Labour Party, and during World War II he helped get Jewish refugees out of Germany. After the war he worked hard to relieve starvation in Germany and tried to oppose the belief in German collective guilt for Nazi crimes. He founded the Jewish Society for Human Service. He also launched national campaigns for the abolition of capital punishment and for nuclear disarmament.

Gompers, Samuel 1850–1924 •*US labor leader*• Born in London, England, he emigrated to the US in 1863. Self-educated, he studied and rejected Marxism and socialism, developing instead the US practice of nonpolitical trade unionism. He helped found (1886), and was long-time president of, the American Federation of Labor (AFL), and with the AFL's triumph as the main force in organized labor, he became a major public figure.

Gomułka, Władysław 1905–82 •*Polish Communist leader*• Born in Krosno, southeast Poland, he became a local trade union leader. He organized underground resistance to the Germans during World War II and took an active part in the defense of Warsaw. In 1943 he became secretary of the outlawed underground Communist Party. He became vice president of the first postwar Polish government, but from 1948 was gradually relieved of all his posts for "non-appreciation of the decisive role of the Soviet Union" and was arrested in 1951, serving three years in solitary confinement. He was rehabilitated in August 1956 and returned to power as party first secretary in October. Gomułka sought to put Poland on the road to a measure of freedom and independence, allowing freer discussion within a Marxist framework. He resigned office in 1971, following a political crisis.

Gonçalves, Nuno fl. 1450–72 •*Portuguese painter*• He is recorded, in 1463, as court painter to **Alfonso V**. He was virtually forgotten until the discovery of his only extant work, an altarpiece for the convent of St Vincent (the patron saint of Portugal) in 1882. This work was exhibited in Paris in 1931 and established him as the most important Portuguese painter of the 15th century.

Goncharov, Ivan Aleksandrovich 1812–91 •*Russian novelist*• Born in Simbirsk, he graduated from Moscow University (1834), and led an uneventful life in the Civil Service, punctuated by a trip to Japan, which he described in *Freget Pallada* (1858, Eng trans *The Frigate Pallas: Notes on a Journey*, 1965). He wrote three novels, the most important being *Oblomov* (1859, Eng trans 1915), one of the greatest and most typical works in the Russian Realist style.

“ ”

The trouble is that no devastating or redeeming fires have ever burnt in my life ... My life began by flickering out.

*1859 **Oblomov**, part 2, chapter 4 (translated by David Magarshak).*

Goncharova, Natalia Sergeyevna 1881–1962 •*French painter and designer*• Born in Ladyzhino, Tula province, Russia, she began as a science student but turned (c. 1898) to sculpture, studying at the Moscow Academy of Art. She began painting in 1904 and, like **Mikhail Larionov** (with whom she lived and whom she eventually married on her 74th birthday) and **Kasimir Malevich**, chose the flat colors and primitive forms of Russian folk art, combining these with the new influences of cubism and fauvism with an original flair. She moved to Paris in 1921, and took French citizenship in 1938.

Goncourt, Edmond de 1822–96 and **Jules de** 1830–70, *known as* **the Goncourt Brothers** •*French novelists*• Born in Nancy and Paris, respectively, they were primarily artists, but after collaborating in studies of history and art they turned to writing novels. Their subject was the manners of the 19th century, and the enormous influence of environment and habit on people. The first of their novels, *Les hommes de lettres* (1860, "The Men of Letters"; new edn as *Charles Demailly*, 1868), was followed by *Sœur Philomène* (1861, Eng trans *Sister Philomène*, 1890), *Manette Salomon* (1867) and *Madame Gervaisais* (1869), their greatest novel. After Jules's death, Edmond published the extraordinarily popular *La fille Élisa* (1878, Eng trans *Elisa*, 1959), *La Faustin* (1882, Eng trans 1902) and *Chérie* (1885, "Darling"). The interesting *Idées et sensations* (1866, "Ideas and Sensations") had already revealed their morbid acuteness of sensation, and *La maison d'un artiste* (1881, "An Artist's House") had shown their love for bric-à-brac. In the *Lettres de Jules de Goncourt* (1885) and in the *Journal des Goncourt* (9 vols, 1888–96), they revealed their methods and their conception of fiction. Edmond, in his will, founded the Académie Goncourt to foster fiction with the annual Prix Goncourt.

Góngora (y Argote), (Don) Luis de 1561–1627 •*Spanish lyric poet*• Born in Córdoba, he studied law, but in 1606 took orders and eventually became chaplain to **Philip III**. His earlier writings were sonnets, romances and satirical verses, but he is best known for his longer poems, such as *Soledades* (1613, Eng trans *The Solitudes*, 1931), written in an affected style which came to be called "gongorism," which his followers designated the *estilo culto*.

Gonne, Maud, *married name* **MacBride** 1865–1953 •*Irish nationalist and actress*• The daughter of an English colonel, she was an agitator for the cause of Irish independence and edited a nationalist newspaper, *L'Irlande libre*, in Paris. She met **W B Yeats** in the early 1890s and, though Yeats wished to marry her, she ultimately rejected him and married Major John MacBride, who fought against the British in the Boer War and was executed as a rebel in 1916. She was one of the founders of Sinn Fein. Her son **Seán MacBride** was Foreign Minister of the Irish Republic from 1948 to 1951.

Gonzaga, Luigi, *known as* **St Aloysius** 1568–91 •*Italian Jesuit*• Born near Brescia, the eldest son of the Marquis of Castiglione, he renounced his title to become a missionary and entered the Society of Jesus in 1585. When Rome had an epidemic of the plague in 1591 he devoted himself to the care of the sick, but was himself infected and died. He was canonized in 1726. His feast day is June 21.

Gonzalès, Eva 1849–83 •*French painter*• Born in Paris, she was noted for her great beauty at an early age. When she was 20, **Manet** requested her family's permission to paint her portrait, and she became both his model and his pupil. She was the only artist permitted by him to sign "pupil of Manet" on Salon entries, and her first entry to the Salon in 1870, *L'enfant de troupe* ("The Boy Soldier"), was purchased by the government.

González (Márquez), Felipe 1942– •*Spanish politician*• Born in Seville, he studied law and practiced as a lawyer, and in 1962 joined the Spanish Socialist Workers' Party (PSOE), at that time an illegal organization. The party regained legal status in 1977, three years after he became Secretary General. He persuaded the PSOE to adopt a more moderate, less overtly Marxist line, and in the general elections of 1982 they won a substantial overall majority, and González was made Prime Minister, remaining in power until 1996, when the conservative Popular Party, led by **José María Aznar López**, won the election.

Gooch, Graham 1953– •*English cricket player*• Born in Leytonstone, London, he made his debut for Essex in 1973, and was captain of the club (apart from 1988) from 1986 to 1994. First capped for England in 1975, he went on to play in over 100 Test matches. In July 1993 he resigned as captain of England after their eighth defeat in nine Test matches. He has published two volumes of autobiography, *Testing Times* (1991) and *Gooch: My Autobiography* (1995, cowritten with Frank Keating).

Goodall, Jane 1934– •*English primatologist and conservationist*• Born in London, she worked in Kenya with the anthropologist **Louis Leakey**, obtained her PhD from Cambridge in 1965, and subsequently set up the Gombe Stream Research Centre in Tanzania. She has held various academic posts and since 1967 has been scientific director of the Gombe Wildlife Research Institute. She has carried out a study of the behavior and ecology of chimpanzees that has transformed the understanding of primate behavior by demonstrating its complexity. She discovered that chimpanzees modify a variety of natural objects to use as tools and weapons, and showed that they hunt animals for meat. Her books include *In the Shadow of Man* (1971) and *The Chimpanzee: The Living Link between "Man" and "Beast"* (1992).

Goodman, Benny (Benjamin David) 1909–86 •*US clarinettist and bandleader*• Born in Chicago, he was a musical prodigy who was working in dance bands by the age of 13. He formed his own orchestra in New York in 1934 and became one of the best-known leaders of the era with the sobriquet "King of Swing." Hiring top African-American musicians such as pianist **Teddy Wilson** and vibraphone player **Lionel Hampton**, Goodman successfully defied racial taboos of the time. He led a succession of large and small bands for three decades, occasionally performing as a classical player, and was noted for his technical facility and clean tone.

Goodyear, Charles 1800–60 •*US inventor*• He was born in New Haven, Connecticut. Having failed as an iron manufacturer, he began research into the properties of rubber in 1834. Amid poverty and ridicule he pursued the experiments that culminated, in 1844, in the invention of vulcanized rubber, which led to the development of the rubber-manufacturing industry and the production of the well-known tires named after him.

Goolagong *See* **Cawley, Evonne**

Goossens, Sir Eugène 1893–1962 •*English composer and conductor*• Born in London, he studied in Bruges and London, and became associate conductor to Sir **Thomas Beecham** (1916–20) in his opera seasons. In 1921 he gave a successful series of orchestral concerts in which he brought out some of his own music. From 1923 to 1945 he worked as a conductor in the US, and from 1947 to 1956 in Australia, becoming a major influence on Australian music. His own music includes the operas *Judith* (1929) and *Don Juan de Mañara* (1937), a large-scale oratorio, *The Apocalypse* (1950–54), and two symphonies.

Goossens, Léon 1897–1988 •*English oboist*• Born in Liverpool, he studied at the Royal College of Music, London. After 1913, he held leading posts in most of the major London orchestras. He then retired from orchestral work to devote himself to solo playing and teaching. He was the brother of the composer and conductor Sir **Eugène Goossens**.

Gorbachev, Mikhail Sergeyevich 1931– •*Russian statesman and Nobel Prize winner*• He was born in Privolnoye in the North Caucasus. He went to Moscow University to study law in 1950, where he met and married a philosophy student, Raisa Titorenko (see **Raisa Gorbachev**), who was to play an important part in his later career. He joined the Communist Party (CPSU) in 1952. He held a variety of senior posts in the Stavropol city and district Komsomol and Party organizations (1956–70), and was elected a deputy to the USSR Supreme Soviet (1970) and a member of the Party Central Committee (1971). He became Central Committee Secretary for Agriculture (1979–85); candidate member of the Politburo (1979–80) and full member (1980–91) of the Central Committee. On the death of **Chernenko**, he became General Secretary of the Party (1985–91). In 1988 he also became Chairman of the Presidium of the Supreme Soviet (i.e., head of state) and in 1990 the first executive President of the USSR. On becoming General Secretary, he launched a radical program of reform and restructuring (*perestroika*) of the Soviet economy and political system. A greater degree of political participation, civil liberty, public debate, and journalistic and cultural freedom were allowed under the policy of *glasnost* (openness). In defense and foreign affairs he reduced military expenditures and pursued a policy of détente, disarmament and arms control with the West. He ended the Soviet military occupation of Afghanistan (1989) and accepted the breakup of COMECON and the Warsaw Pact, the withdrawal of Soviet troops from Eastern Europe and the reunification of Germany. Following the unsuccessful coup against him in August 1991, he lost power to **Boris Yeltsin** despite accepting the demise of the Communist Party. In December 1991 he resigned as the USSR itself disintegrated into 15 separate republics. His works include *Perestroika: New Thinking for Our Country and the World* (1987), *The August Coup: The Truth and the Lessons* (1992) and *Memoirs* (1996).

“ ”

The Soviet people want full-blooded and unconditional democracy.
1988 Speech, July.

Gorbachev, Raisa Maksimovna, *née* **Titorenko** 1932–99 •*Russian educationist*• Born in the Altai region, she graduated from Moscow University and pursued a career in sociological research and lecturing. She worked as a sociologist at Stavropol Teacher Training Institute (1957–61) and was a lecturer at Moscow University (1977–85). As the wife of **Mikhail Gorbachev**, the then general secretary of the Communist Party of the USSR, she accompanied him on special occasions and overseas tours. At the end of his presidency she continued as a member of the board of the Cultural Heritage Commission.

Gordimer, Nadine 1923– •*South African novelist and Nobel Prize winner*• Born in Springs, Transvaal, she was educated at a convent school, and at the University of the Witwatersrand, Johannesburg. Her first book was a collection of short stories, *Face to Face* (1949). In 1953 she published her first novel, *The Lying Days*, in which a white girl triumphs over the provincial narrowness and racial bigotry of her parents, though she, too, has to come to terms with the limitations of her social background. This recurrent theme dominates Gordimer's early books, such as *Occasion for Loving* (1963) and *The Late Bourgeois World* (1966). Apartheid, and her characters' reaction to it, is ever present in her fiction, most powerfully in *The Conservationist* (1974), joint winner of the Booker Prize. Other important titles are *A Guest of Honour* (1970), *July's People* (1981) and *A Sport of Nature* (1987). She was awarded the Nobel Prize for literature in 1991. Later publications include *Writing and Being* (1995).

Gordon, Adam Lindsay 1833–70 •*Australian poet*• Born in Fayal in the Azores, he completed his education in England but vanished to Australia after a series of reckless adventures. Much of his best work is collected in *Sea Spray and Smoke Drift* (1867, reissued 1876 with a preface by **Marcus Clarke**) and in *Bush Ballads and Galloping Rhymes* (1870). A succession of unfortunate incidents precipitated a mental breakdown and his suicide. He is the only Australian poet honored in the Poets' Corner of Westminster Abbey, London.

Gordon, Charles George, *known as* **Chinese Gordon** 1833–85 •*English general*• Born in Woolwich, London, he joined the Royal Engineers in 1852, and in 1855–56 fought in the Crimean War. In 1860 he went to China, where he crushed the Taiping Rebellion. In 1877 he was appointed governor of the Sudan. He resigned in poor health in 1880, but returned in 1884 to relieve Egyptian garrisons that lay in rebel territory. He was besieged at Khartoum for ten months by the troops of the Mahdi (**Muhammad Ahmed**) and killed there two days before a relief force arrived.

Gordon, David 1936– •*US dancer and choreographer*• Born in Brooklyn, New York, he was a founding member (1962) of the seminal Judson Dance Theater and, in the following decade, the improvisational dance–theater collective Grand Union. In 1974 he formed the Pick-Up Company. He became known for his often humorous experimentation, and several of his works are in the repertories of major US and British classical and modern dance companies.

Gordon, Lord George 1751–93 •*English anti-Catholic agitator*• Born in London, he became a Member of Parliament in 1774. With the aim of repealing the Catholic Relief Act of 1778, Lord George, as president of a Protestant association, led a mob of 50,000 to the House of Commons. For five days, serious rioting took place during which much Catholic property was destroyed. Five days later the troops were called out, and almost 300 of the rioters were killed, 21 being executed. Lord George was tried for high treason, but **Thomas Erskine**'s defense earned his acquittal. He subsequently converted to Judaism, and was known as Israel Abraham George Gordon. In 1787 he was convicted of libeling **Marie Antoinette**, and taken to Newgate Prison, where he died.

Gordon, Noele 1922–85 •*English actress*• Born in East Ham, London, she made her first stage appearance at the age of two. After studying at the Royal Academy of Dramatic Art she worked in repertory and pantomime and assisted **John Logie Baird** with his early experiments in color television. She later studied television techniques in the US, and returned to Great Britain as an adviser to ATV (Associated Television) and became a household name as the owner of the motel in the television soap opera *Crossroads* (1964–81). Unceremoniously dismissed from the series, she returned to the stage in barnstorming musicals like *Gypsy* (1981), *Call Me Madam* (1982–83) and *No, No, Nanette* (1983).

Gordy, Berry, Jr 1929– •*US record executive, producer and songwriter*• He was born in Detroit, Michigan. He became an independent producer in 1958, and launched Tamla Records the following year, the company which he built into Tamla Motown, one of the most famous labels in the history of US popular music. He oversaw the whole operation in the 1960s, when his artists like **Diana Ross** and The Supremes, **Stevie Wonder**, The Four Tops, **Marvin Gaye** and Smokey Robinson ruled the charts. He sold the company to MCA (Music Corporation of America) in 1988.

Gore, Al(bert Arnold), Jr 1948– •*US Democratic politician*• Born in Washington into a prominent political family, he was educated at Harvard and served as a US Army reporter in Vietnam (1969–71). He then studied theology at Vanderbilt University and worked for the *Nashville Tennessean* newspaper and as a farmer before entering the House of Representatives, representing Tennessee, in 1977. He was elected to the Senate in 1984 and made an unsuccessful bid for the Democratic nomination for president in 1988. In 1992 he was chosen as **Bill Clinton**'s running mate and went on to serve as his vice president (1992–2000), taking an active role in policymaking. In 2000 he ran for president in what turned out to be the closest contest in over 100 years. Although he won the popular vote, he lost to Republican **George W Bush** in the Electoral College by a narrow margin.

“ ”

You get all the French fries the President can't get to.
1994 On being vice president. In the ***New York Times****, April 8.*

Gore, Catherine Grace Frances, *née* **Moody** 1799–1861 •*English novelist*• Born in East Retford, Nottinghamshire, she was a prolific and immensely popular writer of novels, mainly of fashionable life in the manner of the "silver fork" school. They include *Mothers and Daughters* (1831), *Mrs Armytage* (1836) and *The Banker's Wife* (1843). She also wrote three plays and short stories.

Gore, Spencer Frederick 1878–1914 •*English painter*• Born in Epsom, Surrey, he joined the New English Art Club in 1909. He was a founding member and first president of the Camden Town Group (1911), and became a member of the London Group in 1913. He met **Walter Sickert** in Dieppe, France, in 1904 and was inspired to paint theater and music hall subjects. In 1912 he contributed to **Roger Fry**'s second postimpressionist exhibition.

Gorenko, Anna Andreyevna *See* **Akhmatova, Anna**

Gorgias c. 490–c. 385 BC •*Greek philosopher and rhetorician*• Born in Leontini, Sicily, he was one of the sophists who were professional itinerant teachers of oratory and political skills. He went to Athens as ambassador in 427 BC and quickly became a celebrity for his public performances. His philosophy was an extreme form of skepticism or nihilism: that nothing exists, that if it did it would be unknowable, that if it were knowable it would be incommunicable to others, and that we live in a world of opinion, manipulated by persuasion. He is memorably portrayed in **Plato**'s dialogue the *Gorgias*, where he and **Socrates** debate the morality implicit in his teachings and activities.

Göring, Hermann Wilhelm *See* **Goering, Hermann Wilhelm**

Gorky, Arshile, *originally* **Vosdanig Manoog Adoian** 1905–48 •*US painter*• Born in Khorkom Vari, in Turkish Armenia, he emigrated to the US in 1920 and studied at the Rhode Island School of Design and in Boston before moving to New York City in 1925. His art combined ideas from the European surrealists who had fled to New York in the early 1940s with the biomorphic abstraction of such artists as **Joán Miró**, and he played a key role in the emergence of the New York school of Action Painters in the 1940s.

Gorky, Maxim, *pseudonym of* **Aleksei Maksimovich Peshkov** 1868–1936 •*Russian novelist*• Born in Nizhny Novgorod, he was a peddler, dishwasher, gardener, dock hand, tramp and writer, leading a restless, nomadic life which he described brilliantly in his autobiographical trilogy, *Detstvo* (1913–14, Eng trans *My Childhood*, 1915), *Vlyudakh* (1915–16, Eng trans *In the World*, 1918) and *Moi universitety* (1922, Eng trans *My University Days*, 1923). He first achieved fame with his story *Chelkash* (1895), followed by others in a romantic vein, with vividly drawn characters, mostly tramps and down-and-outs. *Foma Gordeyev* (1899, Eng trans 1902) marks his transition from romanticism to realism. In 1902 he produced his best-known play, *Na dne* (Eng trans *A Night's Lodging*, 1905, better known as *The Lower Depths*, 1912). Involved in strikes and imprisoned in 1905, he lived abroad again on account of his health, but then returned, a wholehearted supporter of the Soviet regime. He sponsored "Social Realism" as the official school in Soviet literature and art.

Gormley, Antony Mark David 1950– •*English sculptor*• Born in London, he studied at Cambridge, and then went on to train at the Central School of Art and Design, Goldsmiths College, and the Slade School of Art, London. In 1981 he began to make molds from his own body in various poses, for example *Untitled (for Francis)* (1985). In 1982 and 1986 he exhibited at the Venice Biennale. After 1990 his bodies expanded into bulbous forms, such as *Still Running* (1990–93, Galerie Nordenhake). In 1993 his exhibition *Testing a World View* featured five identical figures, their bodies bent at right angles, "testing" themselves against walls, floor and ceiling. More recently, his *Field for the British Isles* (1993) toured Liverpool, Edinburgh and the Hayward Gallery, London (1996–97), and his *Angel of the North* (1997–98), a figure some 66 feet (20 meters) high with a wingspan of 177 feet (54 meters), was erected in Gateshead, northeast England.

Gort, John Standish Surtees Prendergast Vereker, 6th Viscount 1886–1946 •*English field marshal*• Educated at Harrow and the Royal Military College, Woolwich, he served with the Grenadier Guards in World War I and won the Victoria Cross in 1918. He was appointed Chief of the Imperial General Staff in 1938. In World War II he was Commander in Chief of the British forces overwhelmed in the initial German victories of 1940. Afterward he was Governor of Gibraltar (1941–42) and of Malta (1942–44), and was promoted to field marshal in 1943.

Gorton, Sir John Grey 1911–2002 •*Australian politician*• Educated at Geelong Grammar School and Brasenose College, Oxford, he joined the Royal Australian Air Force in 1940, serving in Europe, Malaya and Australia. Seriously wounded, he was discharged in 1944. He served in the governments of Sir **Robert Menzies** and **Harold Holt** and, when Holt died in 1967, succeeded him as Prime Minister. In 1971, following a vote of no confidence, he resigned in favor of **William McMahon**, becoming Deputy Leader of his party.

Gossaert, Jan *See* **Mabuse, Jan**

Gosse, Sir Edmund William 1849–1928 •*English poet and critic*• Born in London, he was educated privately. He initially regarded himself as a poet, and published several works, including the volumes *On Viol and Flute* (1873) and *Collected Poems* (1911). His *Studies in the Literature of Northern Europe* (1879) and other critical works first introduced **Ibsen** to English-speaking readers. His finest work is considered to be the autobiographical *Father and Son* (1907), in which he describes his puritanical father's domineering character and beliefs and his own escape into the literary world.

Gotama *See* **Gautama**

Gottfried von Strassburg fl. 1200 •*German poet*• He wrote the masterly German version of the legend of *Tristan and Isolde*, based on the Anglo-Norman poem by Thomas. He is also noteworthy as an early exponent of literary criticism.

Gottlieb, Adolph 1903–74 •*US painter*• Born in New York City, he attended the Art Students' League in New York, and from 1921 to 1923 studied in Paris. In 1935 he joined the New York avant-garde group The Ten, whose members included **Mark Rothko**. From 1941 he painted an unusual series of pictographs in which a grid system is drawn onto the canvas and a primitive symbol inserted in each space. After 1950 his paintings became radically simplified, consisting of gestural marks of bright color. He stands as one of the most original of the abstract expressionist school of painters.

Gottschalk, Laura Riding *See* **Riding, Laura**

Gottschalk, Louis Moreau 1829–69 •*US pianist and composer*• Born in New Orleans, he studied in Paris (1842–46), and impressed **Chopin** and **Berlioz**. After touring in France, Switzerland and Spain, he returned to the US (1853) and enjoyed success with his piano and piano-orchestral compositions, many of which explore Creole, African and Spanish idioms.

Gottwald, Klement 1896–1953 •*Czechoslovakian politician*• Born in Dedice, Moravia, he fought with the Austro-Hungarian army in World War I. He then joined the Communist Party, whose Secretary General he became in 1927. He opposed the Munich Agreement of 1938 and later went to Moscow, where he was trained for eventual office. In 1945 he became vice premier in the Czechoslovakian provisional government. Prime Minister in 1946, he carried out the Communist coup d'état that averted a defeat for his party at the polls in February 1948. In June he became President and established a Stalinist dictatorship in Czechoslovakia. He died of an illness contracted while he was attending Stalin's funeral.

Götz or **Goetz von Berlichingen** 1480–1562 •*German soldier*• He was born in Jaxthausen in Württemberg, and gained the nickname "Götz mit der eisernen Hand" ("Götz with the iron hand") because of a steel replacement for his right hand, lost in the Siege of Landshut (1505). From 1497 he was involved in continual feuds, in which he displayed both lawless daring and chivalrous magnanimity. In 1542 he fought in Hungary against the Turks, and in 1544 in France. He wrote an autobiography, published in 1731.

Goudge, Elizabeth 1900–84 •*English novelist*• Born in Wells, Somerset, she studied at the University of Reading and taught art and design. Her first major success was with the novel *Green Dolphin Country* (1944), set in 19th-century New Zealand and the Channel Islands, which was made into a film in 1947. Other important novels include *Gentian Hill* (1949) and *The Child from the Sea* (1970). *The Little White Horse* (1946), a book for children, won a Carnegie medal, and she wrote several books with a Christian theme.

Goudsmit, Samuel Abraham 1902–78 •*US physicist*• Born in The Hague, the Netherlands, he studied in Amsterdam and Leiden and emigrated in 1927 to the US, where he was professor at the University of Michigan (1932–46) and later worked at the Brookhaven National Laboratory, Long Island (1948–70). Aged 23, he and his fellow student George Uhlenbeck (1900–88) proposed the idea that electrons in atoms can have intrinsic spin angular momentum, a finding later confirmed by **P A M Dirac** in 1928.

Gough, Hugh Gough, 1st Viscount 1779–1869 •*Anglo-Irish soldier*• Born in Woodstown, County Limerick, he served in the West Indies (1797–1800) through the Peninsular War and in India, and in 1838 was made Commander in Chief of the forces sent against China during the first Opium War. After storming Canton, he compelled the Chinese to sign the Treaty of Nanking (1842), and in 1843 defeated the Marathas in India. In the Sikh War in 1845 and later in 1848, he won victories that resulted in the annexation of the Punjab.

Goujon, Jean c. 1510–c. 1568 •*French sculptor*• He was a Huguenot, but seems to have died before the St Bartholomew Massacre (1572). From 1555 to 1562 he worked in the Louvre, Paris, and some of his finest works can be seen there, such as *Diana Reclining by a Stag*, and the reliefs for the *Fountain of the Innocents* (1549). He also created the monument to the Duke of Brézé in Rouen Cathedral (1541–44).

Gould, Glenn 1932–82 •*Canadian pianist and composer*• Born in Toronto, he studied at the Royal Conservatory of Music there before making his debut, at 14, as a soloist with the Toronto Symphony Orchestra. He toured extensively in the US and Europe and made many recordings, particularly of works by **Bach** and **Beethoven**. His own work, *A String Quartet*, was premiered in 1956. In 1964 he retired from the concert platform, believing concerts were obsolescent, and devoted himself to recording and broadcasting.

Gould, Morton 1913–96 •*US composer*• He was born in New York City. His music is national in style and exploits the various aspects of popular music from both North and South America. He composed symphonies and a variety of works in more popular style, including a *Tap-Dance Concerto* (1952). He won a Pulitzer Prize for *Stringmusic* in 1995, written for and premiered by the National Symphony in Washington DC.

Gould, Shane Elizabeth 1956– •*Australian swimmer*• She was born in Brisbane, Queensland, and between 1971 and 1972 set world records in every freestyle event from the 100 meters to the 1,500 meters. Gould also became the first woman to win three individual swimming golds in world record times at the 1972 Olympics. As well as breaking or equaling 11 world records throughout her short career, she won numerous Australian individual championships, all before retiring at the age of 17.

Gould, Stephen Jay 1941–2002 •*US paleontologist*• Born in New York City and educated at Antioch College and the University of Ohio and Columbia University, he became Professor of Geology in 1973 and Alexander Agassiz Professor of Zoology there in 1982. In an influential paper published in 1972, he, together with the paleontologist Niles Eldredge, posited the theory of punctuated equilibrium. He also championed the idea of hierarchical evolution. He emphasized that many characteristics of organisms are not adaptive in the strict sense, popularizing his ideas in such books as *Ever Since Darwin* (1977), *The Panda's Thumb* (1980), *The Flamingo's Smile* (1985), *Bully for Brontosaurus* (1991) and *Eight Little Piggies* (1993). His books have won many awards, including the 1990 Science Book prize for *Wonderful Life* (1989), a reinterpretation of the Cambrian Burgess Shale fauna. Gould admitted to Marxist influence in his scientific work and was a forceful speaker against pseudoscientific racism and biological determinism; *The Mismeasure of Man* (1981) is a critique of intelligence testing. He was also a witness in a courtroom trial about the teaching of evolution in US public schools. His final work, *The Structure of Evolutionary Theory*, was published shortly before his death.

“ ”

A man does not attain the status of Galileo merely because he is persecuted, he must also be right.

1977 ***Ever Since Darwin.***

Gouled Aptidon, Hassan 1916– •*Djiboutian politician*• Born in the city of Djibouti, he joined the African People's League for Independence (LPAI) in 1967 and when independence was achieved in 1977, became the country's first President. Later the LPAI was amalgamated with other parties to become the People's Progress Party (RPP) and Djibouti's sole political party. He pursued a largely successful policy of amicable neutralism in a war-torn region and remained President until he stepped down in 1999.

Gounod, Charles François 1818–93 •*French composer*• Born in Paris, he studied at the Paris Conservatoire and in Rome. His major works include the comic opera *Le médecin malgré lui* (1858, "The Mock Doctor") and *Faust* (1859). He also published hymns, masses, and anthems, and was popular as a songwriter. He fled to England during the Franco-Prussian War (1870). He was made a commander of the French Legion of Honor in 1877.

Gourd, Emilie 1879–1946 •*Swiss feminist and writer*• She founded and edited the newspaper *Le mouvement féministe*, and continually lobbied the Swiss authorities at both the regional and the national level on behalf of the cause of women's suffrage. She was president of the Swiss Women's Association (1914–28), and was also secretary of the International Alliance of Women.

Gow, Niel 1727–1807 •*Scottish violinist and songwriter*• Born in Inver, near Dunkeld, Perthshire, he became Scotland's most famous fiddler and songwriter, known as "the father of Strathspey and Reel players." Patronized by the dukes of Atholl, he was much in demand as a player at important balls and parties. His compositions include Strathspeys, jigs, reels, and laments.

Gower, David Ivon 1957– •*English cricket player*• Born in Tunbridge Wells, Kent, he came to the fore quickly, chiefly because of the elegance of his left-handed stroke play. He was captain of England in the mid-1980s, though without particular success. He was recalled as captain in 1989, only to lose the captaincy and his place on the team after a crushing defeat in the Test series against Australia. He has become a cricket commentator on both radio and television and also regularly appears on the comedy sports quiz *They Think It's All Over* (1995–).

Gower, John c. 1325–1408 •*English medieval poet*• Born in Kent, he spent most of his life in London and had contacts with the court in the service of **Richard II** and **Henry IV**. A friend of **Chaucer**, he wrote *Speculum meditantis* ("The Mirror of Thought"), in French verse, which was discovered at Cambridge only in 1898, and 50 French ballads. Other works include the *Vox clamantis* ("The Voice of One Crying Out"), elegiacs in Latin (1382–84), describing the uprising under **Wat Tyler**, and the long English poem *Confessio amantis* (c. 1383, "A Lover's Confession"), consisting of over 100 stories taken from classical and medieval sources.

Gowers, Sir Ernest Arthur 1880–1966 •*English civil servant*• The son of the neurologist Sir William Richard Gowers (1845–1915), he was educated at Rugby and Clare College, Cambridge, and called to the bar in 1906. After a distinguished career in the civil service he emerged as the champion of *Plain Words* (1948) and *ABC of Plain Words* (1951), designed to maintain standards of clear English.

Gowing, Sir Lawrence Burnett 1918–91 •*English painter and writer on art*• Born in Stoke Newington, London, he studied at the Euston Road School under William Coldstream (1908–87), and his impressionist style is often applied to portraits, such as *Mrs Roberts* (1944). One of his best-known prewar paintings is *Mare Street, Hackney* (1937). His studies of **Renoir** (1947) and **Vermeer** (1952) initiated his reputation as an art historian.

Gowon, Yakubu 1934– •*Nigerian soldier and politician*• Born in Garam, Plateau state, he was a Christian in a Muslim area and was educated at a missionary school. After military training in Ghana and Great Britain (Sandhurst), he joined the Nigerian army (1956), becoming chief of staff in 1966. The ethnic conflicts in the country precipitated a coup in January 1966, led by Ibo officers, and Gowon headed a countercoup (July 1966). He then became head of the federal military government and Commander in Chief. Unable to prevent a civil war, with US and Soviet aid he successfully retained Biafra (the eastern region) within a single Nigeria, while acceding to ethnic concerns by increasing the number of states. However, his delayed return to democracy encouraged another military coup. He was deposed in 1975.

Goya y Lucientes, Francisco (José) de 1746–1828 •*Spanish artist*• Born in Fuendetodos, near Saragossa, he returned to Spain in 1775 after traveling in Italy to design for the Royal Tapestry Works. He worked quite conventionally at first, painting scenes of court pastorals strongly influenced by **Giovanni Tiepolo** and the Neapolitans, but soon began introducing scenes from everyday Spanish life, such as in *Blind Guitarist* (1778). At the same time he studied **Velázquez** in the Royal Collections, and this prompted him to begin painting the portraits for which he became famous. In 1786 he was appointed court painter to **Charles IV** (chief painter in 1799). The portraits, particularly those of the Spanish royal family, are painted in an unflattering style that makes one wonder how acceptable they were to their subjects. Other works include *Maja Nude* and *Maja Clothed* (c. 1797–1800, Prado, Madrid). In a series of 82 satirical etchings called *Los caprichos* issued in 1799, Goya castigated the follies of the court. After the Napoleonic occupation he produced an equally sardonic series entitled *The Disasters of War*. His religious paintings, particularly the frescoes (1798) for the church of San Antonio de la Florida, Madrid, are extremely freely painted. After 1792 he became increasingly deaf and in later life retired to the outskirts of Madrid, where he painted some extraordinary decorations for his own house (*House of the Deaf Man*, now in the Prado, Madrid). In 1824, on the accession of **Ferdinand VII**, he went into voluntary exile in France. His work has influenced virtually every major painter from **Eugène Delacroix** to **Picasso**.

Goytisolo, Juan 1931– •*Spanish novelist and critic*• Born in Barcelona, he was associated with progressive, anti-Franco writers in his early career, when he cofounded the group "Turia." Then in 1957 he left Spain for Paris, where he worked for the publisher Gallimard. His early novels, such as *Juegos de manos* (1954, Eng trans *The Young Assassins*, 1959), show the influence of both his bisexuality and the Arabic elements in Spanish literature. He became a determined and influential modernist and postmodernist, and later novels such as *Juan sin tierra* (1976, Eng trans *John the Landless* 1977), are essentially a "deconstruction" of Spain's official history (1939–64).

Gozzi, Count Carlo 1720–1806 •*Italian dramatist*• He was born in Venice and wrote the very popular comedy, *Fiaba dell' amore delle tre melarance* (1761, Eng trans *The Love of Three Oranges*, 1949). He also wrote several similar "dramatic fairy tales," of which the best-known, from **Schiller**'s translation of it, is *Turandot* (Eng trans *Turandot, Princess of China*, 1913).

Gozzoli, Benozzo, *properly* **Benozzo di Lese** c. 1420–97 •*Italian painter*• Born in Florence, he was a pupil of **Fra Angelico**. In Florence (1456–64) he adorned the Palazzo Medici-Riccardi with scriptural subjects, including his famous *Journey of the Magi*, in which Florentine councilors appear accompanied by members of the **Medici** family.

Graaff, Robert J(emison) Van de *See* **Van de Graaff, Robert J(emison)**

Grable, Betty (Elizabeth Ruth) 1916–73 •*US actress*• Born in St Louis, Missouri, she lived in Los Angeles from 1928 and studied dancing, subsequently making her film debut as a chorus girl in *Let's Go Places* (1930). She appeared in numerous small roles throughout the 1930s but began to build a following at Twentieth Century Fox, appearing in such popular films as *Down Argentine Way* (1940) and *Moon Over Miami* (1941). Her good looks and shapely legs made her a favorite pin-up girl of wartime troops. Her most successful films, usually musicals, include *The Dolly Sisters* (1945), *Mother Wore Tights* (1947) and *How to Marry a Millionaire* (1953). Her last film appearance was in *How to Be Very Very Popular* (1955), but she continued to work in cabaret and on stage in such productions as *Hello, Dolly!* (1965–67) and *Belle Starr* (1969).

Gracchus, Gaius Sempronius c. 159–121 BC •*Roman politician*• After the murder of his brother **Tiberius Sempronius Gracchus** he continued trying to solve major social and economic problems by enacting reforms. He was Tribune of the Plebs in 123 and 122 BC, and when he failed to achieve a third term he led a demonstration that turned into a riot. Many of his followers were killed and he committed suicide.

Gracchus, Tiberius Sempronius 168–133 BC •*Roman statesman*• In 137 BC he was quaestor in Spain, where his family's popularity enabled him to gain better terms from the Numantines for 20,000 conquered Roman soldiers. He was concerned by the poverty of thousands of the Roman citizens and, elected Tribune in 133, he requisitioned all land held in excess and distributed it in allotments to the poor. The authority of the Senate was threatened when he deposed Tribune Marcus Octavius, who had vetoed his proposal. He was accused of having violated the character of the tribuneship by the deposition of his colleague Caecina. The common people deserted him, and during the next election for the tribuneship he was murdered, along with 300 of his friends. He was the brother of **Gaius Sempronius Gracchus**.

Grace, W(illiam) G(ilbert) 1848–1915 •*English cricket player and doctor*• Born in Downend, near Bristol, he is considered the first genuinely great cricketer of modern times. He started playing first-class cricket for Gloucestershire in 1864, and was immediately picked for the Gentlemen Players match. He scored 2,739 runs in a season in 1871, and in 1876 he scored 344 runs in an innings for Marylebone Cricket Club. He took his medical degree in 1879 and opened a practice in Bristol, but devoted most of his time to cricket. He toured Canada and the US, and twice captained the Test team against Australia, in 1880 and 1882. By 1895 he had scored 100 first-class centuries, and by the end of his career in 1908 he was a national hero.

" "

They haven't come to see you umpiring, they have come to see me bat.
Attributed.

Gracian (y Morales), Baltasar 1601–58 •*Spanish philosopher and writer*• Born in Belmonte, Aragon, he entered the Jesuit order in 1619 and later became head of the college at Tarragona. His early works such as *Oráculo manual y arte de prudencia* (1647, Eng trans *The Courtier's Manual Oracle and the Art of Prudence*, 1685) are all heavily didactic guides to life. He is best known, however, for his three-part allegorical novel *El criticón* (1651, 1653, 1657, "The Critic"), in which civilization and society are portrayed through the eyes of a savage.

Grade (of Elstree), Lew Grade, Baron, *originally* **Louis Winogradsky** 1906–98 •*British theatrical impresario*• Born near Odessa, Russia, he was the eldest of three brothers who were to dominate British show business for over 40 years. He moved to Great Britain in 1912, with his parents and brothers Boris (later Bernard, Baron **Delfont** of Stepney) and Leslie. Lew and Boris became dancers (semiprofessional at first), winning competitions during the Charleston craze of the 1920s, but gave up dancing to become theatrical agents. Lew joined forces with his youngest brother, Leslie, and was joint managing director of their theatrical agency until 1955, helping to establish such stars as **Norman Wisdom** and **Morecambe and Wise**. He launched the independent television company Associated Television in 1956, and headed several large film entertainment and communications companies. He was made a life peer in 1976.

Grade, Michael Ian 1943– •*English television administrator*• Born in London, the son of Leslie Grade and nephew of **Lew Grade** and Baron **Delfont** of Stepney, he began his career as a journalist. He then became a theatrical agent for his family's Grade Organization. In 1973 he was appointed deputy controller of London Weekend Television, where he remained until 1977. He was the controller of BBC1 (1984–86), then became the BBC's director of programs (1986–88). In 1988 he sought a new challenge by becoming chief executive officer of Channel 4, but unexpectedly resigned in 1997.

Graf, Steffi 1969– •*German tennis player*• Born in Brühl, she first came to prominence in 1984 when she reached the last 16 at Wimbledon. In 1988 she won the Grand Slam of singles titles—the US, French, and Australian opens and Wimbledon—as well as the gold medal at the Seoul Olympics. Other singles wins include the French Open (1987, 1993, 1995–96, 1999), the Australian Open (1989–90, 1994), the US Open (1989, 1993, 1995–96), and the Wimbledon championship (1989, 1991–93, 1995–96). In 2001 she married **Andre Agassi**.

Graham, Billy (William Franklin) 1918– •*US evangelist*• He was born in Charlotte, North Carolina. After studying at the Florida Bible Institute (now Trinity College) from 1938 to 1940, he was ordained a minister of the Southern Baptist Church (1940). He has conducted preaching crusades on all continents, visiting the former USSR and other countries in eastern Europe during the Cold War, and drawn huge audiences. His books include *Peace with God* (1952), *World Aflame* (1965), *Angels* (1975), *Storm Warning* (1992) and his autobiography, *Just as I Am* (1997).

Graham, George 1944– •*Scottish soccer player and manager*• He was born in Bargeddie, North Lanarkshire. His career as a player started at Aston Villa in 1961, and he played for Chelsea, Arsenal, Manchester United, Portsmouth and Crystal Palace, as well as for California (1978), and was capped 12 times for Scotland. He was manager of Millwall (1982–86) and Arsenal (1986–95). Dismissed in February 1995 following proceedings relating to the receipt of a "bung," or cash gift, from a players' agent, he nevertheless returned to soccer as manager of Leeds (1996–98) and Tottenham Hotspur (1998–2001).

Graham, Martha 1894–1991 •*US dancer, teacher, choreographer and pioneer of modern dance*• She was born in Pittsburgh. She trained in Los Angeles with the Denishawn School and appeared on stage first in vaudeville and revue. In 1926 she made her independent debut in New York, and set up her School of Contemporary Dance the following year. She was much influenced by the composer Louis Horst, and her early work constitutes a major contribution to the American expressionist movement and to the development of modern dance. *Lamentation* (1930) and *Frontier* (1935) are among her better-known early works. In 1930 she founded the Dance Repertory Theater, and trained the company in her own method, which was to use every aspect of the body and mind to dramatic purpose, including movement, breathing and muscular control. One of her best-known ballets, *Appalachian Spring* (1958, music by **Aaron Copland**), was a product of her great interest in Native American life and mythology and the early American pioneer spirit, and much of her work was based on the reinterpretation of ancient myths and historical characters. Her method of dance training has been widely adopted in schools and colleges around the world.

Graham, Thomas 1805–69 •*Scottish chemist*• Born in Glasgow, he was educated at the Universities of Glasgow and Edinburgh. In 1830 he became Professor of Chemistry at Anderson's College and in 1837 moved to London as Professor of Chemistry at University College. His most famous research was on the diffusion of gases and related phenomena; Graham's law states that the rate of diffusion of a gas is inversely proportional to the square root of its density. He discovered the properties of colloids and their separation by dialysis. He was a founding member and first president of the Chemical Society (1841).

Grahame, Kenneth 1859–1932 •*Scottish children's writer*• Born in Edinburgh, the son of an advocate, he was educated at St Edward's School, Oxford, and in 1876 entered the Bank of England as a clerk. He became its secretary in 1898. His early work consisted of collected essays and country tales, such as *Pagan Papers* (1893) and *Dream Days* (1898). In 1908 he published his best-known work, *The Wind in the Willows*, originally written in the form of letters to his son Alastair, and featuring the quaint and unforgettable riverside characters Rat, Mole, Badger and Toad. It did not at first win acclaim, but within a few years of Grahame's death had become a children's classic.

“ ”

Believe me, my young friend, there is *nothing*—absolutely nothing—half so much worth doing as simply messing about in boats.

1908 ***The Wind in the Willows****, chapter 1.*

Grainger, (George) Percy Aldridge 1882–1961 •*Australian-US composer and pianist*• Born in Brighton, Victoria, as a child he toured as a concert pianist under the management of his mother. In 1914 he settled in the US after collecting folk tunes in the UK and Europe. He took US citizenship and served in the US Army as a bandsman. A friend and admirer of **Edvard Grieg**, he followed his example in championing the revival of English and Scandinavian folk music in such works as *Molly on the Shore* (1914) and *Shepherd's Hey* (1911), which make skillful use of traditional dance themes. He also experimented with "free-form" music and mechanical music machines, and wrote *The Warriors: Music to an Imaginary Ballet*.

Gram, Hans Christian Joachim 1853–1938 •*Danish bacteriologist*• Born in Copenhagen, he developed in 1884 the most important staining technique in microbiology, which divides bacteria into two groups, *gram-positive* and *gram-negative*, depending on the structure of their cell walls.

Grammaticus ("the Grammarian") *See* **Ælfric**

Gramme, Zénobe Théophile 1826–1901 •*Belgian electrical engineer*• He was born in Jehay-Bodegnée. In 1869 he built the first successful direct-current dynamo, incorporating a ring-wound armature (the "Gramme ring"), which after various improvements he manufactured from 1871. It was the first electric generator to be used commercially, for electroplating as well as electric lighting. In 1873 he showed that a dynamo could function in reverse as an electric motor.

Gramsci, Antonio 1891–1937 •*Italian journalist, politician and political thinker*• Born in Ales, Sardinia, into a poor family, he was educated at the University of Turin. A founding member of the PCI (Italian Communist Party) in 1921, he was Italian delegate at the Third International (an association of national communist parties) in Moscow (1922). In 1924 he became leader of the Communists in parliament. He was one of a number of outspoken Communist critics of the Fascist regime to be arrested in 1928 and was sentenced to 20 years' imprisonment; he spent the rest of his life in prison. His reputation rests primarily on his *Lettere del carcere* (1947, *Prison Notebooks*), which were a collection of thoughts and reflections written while in confinement and published posthumously. They are regarded as one of the most important political texts of the 20th century.

Gran, Ahmad *See* **Ahmad ibn Ibrahim al-Ghazi**

Granby, John Manners, Marquis of 1721–70 •*English soldier*• He was born in Scarborough, Yorkshire. Member of Parliament for Grantham in 1742, he served on the Duke of **Cumberland**'s staff. As colonel of "The Blues" and second-in-command of the British cavalry at Minden (1759), he witnessed the failure of Lord George Sackville (1716–85) to lead the cavalry into action, which earned his commander the contemptuous title of "The Great Incompetent." In 1760 Granby redeemed the cavalry's reputation with the spectacular victory of Warburg.

Grand, Sarah, *pseudonym of* **Frances Elizabeth Bellenden McFall**, *née* **Clarke** 1854–1943 •*British novelist*• She was born in Donaghadee, Ireland, of English parentage. In 1923 and from 1925 to 1929 she was Mayoress of Bath. Her reputation rests on *The Heavenly Twins* (1893) and *The Beth Book* (1898), in which she skillfully attacks immorality and marital hypocrisy. Her later works, including *The Winged Victory* (1916), are advocacies of women's emancipation.

Grandi, Dino, Count of Mordano 1895–1988 •*Italian politician and diplomat*• Born in Mordano, near Bologna, he studied law and joined the Fascist quadrumvirate during the 1922 March on Rome. He became **Mussolini**'s Foreign Minister (1929–32), then Italian ambassador in London (1932–39). He was created count in 1937. He was recalled in 1939 after the formation of the Berlin-Rome Axis, and appointed Minister of Justice. He became extremely concerned about Mussolini's regard for **Hitler**'s policies and in 1943 he moved the motion in the Fascist grand council that full constitutional powers be restored to **Victor Emmanuel III**. This brought about Mussolini's resignation. Grandi then fled to Portugal, later living in exile in Brazil, before returning to Italy in 1973.

Granger, Stewart, *originally* **James Stewart** 1913–93 •*English actor*• Born in London, he trained at the Webber-Douglas School of Dramatic Art. He progressed via repertory companies in Hull and Birmingham to the West End and a leading role in the film *So This Is London* (1939). After wartime service in the Black Watch, his handsome looks and virile manner made him a popular leading man in costume melodramas like *Caravan* (1946) and *Blanche Fury* (1948). He made his Hollywood debut in *King Solomon's Mines* (1950) and proved an adept swashbuckler and man of adventure. He later starred in a succession of "continental Westerns" and the television series *The Men from Shiloh* (1970).

Granit, Ragnar Arthur 1900–91 •*Swedish physiologist and Nobel Prize winner*• Born in Helsinki, Finland, he studied at the University of Helsinki, specializing in neurophysiology. He won a fellowship in 1929 in medical physics to work at the Johnson Foundation at the University of Pennsylvania, where he met both **George Wald** and **Haldan Hartline**, with whom he was to share the 1967 Nobel Prize for physiology or medicine. After two years he returned to Helsinki and became Professor of Physiology in 1937. After the Soviet invasion of Finland he escaped to Sweden, where he became Professor of Neurophysiology at the Karolinska Institute in Stockholm (1940–67). His analyses of retinal processing revealed that visual mechanisms were complex responses to light and dark, and he pioneered the recording of the mass response of the retina, the electroretinogram (ERG).

Grant, Alexander Marshall 1925– •*New Zealand dancer and director*• Born in Wellington, he won a scholarship to London and the Royal Ballet, Covent Garden, where he was to spend his entire dancing career. He was director of the Royal Ballet's offshoot, Ballet For All (1971–75), and from 1976 to 1983 he was director of the National Ballet of Canada. Guest artist at the Royal Ballet (1985–89) and Joffrey Ballet (1987–89), he was also senior principal at the London Festival Ballet (now English National Ballet) from 1989 to 1991.

Grant, Bernie (Bernard Alexander Montgomery) 1944–2000 •*British Labour politician*• Born in Georgetown, British Guiana (now Guyana), he was educated at St Stanislaus College, Georgetown, Tottenham Technical College, London, and at Heriot-Watt University in Edinburgh. He worked as an analyst in Guyana before moving to Great Britain in the early 1960s, where he found employment as a railway clerk and, from 1969 to 1978, as a telephone operator. An area officer with the National Union of Public Employees (1978–83), he entered local government service in London (1985–87) and was elected Member of Parliament for Tottenham in 1987. He was founder and chairman of the Parliamentary Black Caucus, which promotes greater parliamentary representation of ethnic minorities in Britain.

Grant, Cary, *originally* **Archibald Leach** 1904–86 •*US film actor*• Born in Bristol, England, he worked as an acrobat and juggler before moving (1920) to the US, where he stayed to pursue a stage career. He went to Hollywood in 1928. A suave, debonair performer, he played leads in sophisticated light comedy, displaying metronomic timing and a sense of the ridiculous in films like *Bringing Up Baby* (1938), *His Girl Friday* (1940) and *Arsenic and Old Lace* (1944). He was also notable in **Alfred Hitchcock**'s thrillers, including *Suspicion* (1941), *Notorious* (1946), *To Catch a Thief* (1955) and *North by Northwest* (1959). Married five times, he retired from the screen in 1966 and received a special Academy Award (1970) for his "unique mastery of the art of screen acting."

" "

Old Cary Grant fine. How you?

His response to a journalist's terse cable to his press agent, "How old Cary Grant?" Attributed.

Grant, Duncan James Corrowr 1885–1978 •*Scottish painter*• Born in Rothiemurchus, Inverness, he studied at the Westminster and Slade School of Art, London, and in Italy and Paris. He was associated with **Roger Fry**'s Omega Workshops, and later with the London Group. His works were mainly landscapes, portraits and still-lifes, but he also designed textiles and pottery. Through his cousin, **Lytton Strachey**, he became friends with many of the Bloomsbury Group. He collaborated on many projects with **Vanessa Bell**, with whom he lived for many years.

Grant, Hugh 1960– •*English actor*• Born in London, he studied at Oxford where he appeared on stage as part of the Dramatic Society and made his film debut in *Privileged* (1982). He worked at the Nottingham Playhouse and performed comedy revues with the Jockeys of Norfolk. A prolific actor in often forgettable films and television miniseries, the phenomenally popular *Four Weddings and a Funeral* (1994) revealed him as a polished light comedian with charm and wit, while the character of a bumbling, emotionally repressed Englishman endeared him to audiences worldwide. Subsequent films include *Sense and Sensibility* (1995), *Notting Hill* (1999) and *Bridget Jones's Diary* (2001).

Grant, James Augustus 1827–92 •*Scottish soldier and explorer*• Born in Nairn, in the Scottish Highlands, he was educated at Marischal College, Aberdeen. He joined the Indian army, eventually reaching the rank of colonel. With **John Hanning Speke** he explored the sources of the Nile (1860–63) and made important botanical collections. On Speke's death he took over as the main spokesman for the expedition, becoming a leading African specialist.

Grant, Richard E, *originally* **Richard Grant Esterhuysen** 1957– •*British actor*• He was born in Mbabane, Swaziland, and studied at the University of Cape Town before moving to London in the early 1980s. Among his earliest films was the one that made his reputation, *Withnail and I* (1986), where he played the rancorous failed thespian Withnail. Subsequent films include *How to Get Ahead in Advertising* (1989), *Keep the Aspidistra Flying* (1997) and *Gosford Park* (2001).

Grant, Ulysses S(impson), *originally* **Hiram Ulysses Grant** 1822–85 •*18th President of the US*• Born in Point Pleasant, Ohio, he graduated from West Point in 1843 and fought in the Mexican War (1846–48), gaining promotion to the rank of captain in 1853. He resigned from the army (1854) and settled on a farm near St Louis, Missouri. However, on the outbreak of the Civil War in 1861 he returned to the army, swiftly becoming a brigadier general, and in 1862 he captured Fort Henry and Fort Donelson in Tennessee, securing for the Union its first major victory. He was criticized for high Union casualties at Shiloh, but in 1863 he besieged Vicksburg, Mississippi, and forced its surrender, thus capturing the last major Confederate stronghold on the Mississippi River and cutting the Confederacy in half. Having driven the enemy out of Tennessee, he was made a lieutenant general and given command of the Union forces in 1864. With General **Sherman** moving toward Atlanta, Grant accompanied the army of the Potomac against Richmond. He encountered General **Robert E Lee** in the wilderness, and fought a desperate battle in which the enemy was driven within the lines of Richmond, culminating in Lee surrendering his entire army in April 1865. The fall of Richmond essentially ended the war. In July 1866 Grant was appointed a full general but relinquished the rank when in 1868 and 1872 he was elected President as the Republican candidate. Despite his military skill, he was politically naïve, and his administration (1869–77) was marked by corruption and incompetence. Most of the achievements of his presidency were traceable to his brilliant Secretary of State, Hamilton Fish (1808–93). The proposal of a third term of presidency not having been approved, Grant returned to private life but lost all he possessed when business partners defrauded him. In 1884 he developed cancer at the root of the tongue. The sympathies of the nation were aroused, and in March 1885 Congress restored him to his rank of general, thus qualifying his dependents for an army pension. His *Personal Memoirs* (2 vols, 1885–86) are a classic of US military history.

" "

I know no method to secure the repeal of bad or obnoxious laws so effective as their stringent execution.

1869 Inaugural address, March 4.

Grant, William 1839–1923 •*Scottish distiller*• He was born in Dufftown, Banffshire. Having bought secondhand equipment from a neighboring distiller he proceeded, with his six sons, to build the Glenfiddich distillery, where most of the whiskey would be sold for blending. This accomplished, production began in 1887, and it was so successful that a second distillery was opened at Balvenie in 1893. Grant then sent both his son and his son-in-law to Glasgow to set up the family's own blending business. From this time Glenfiddich became established as a popular five-year-old scotch, and William's eldest son, John, took over running the company.

Grant, William 1863–1946 •*Scottish lexicographer*• Born in Elgin, Grampian, he studied in France, Belgium and Germany, and became a lecturer in English, modern languages and phonetics at the University of Aberdeen. Until his death he was editor of the *Scottish National Dictionary*, and published various works on Scottish dialects.

Granville-Barker, Harley 1877–1946 •*English actor, playwright and producer*• He was born in London. His career as an actor was noted for his appearances in plays by **George Bernard Shaw**, who chose him to play Marchbanks in *Candida* (1900). In 1904 he became comanager of the Court Theatre, and staged the first performances in England of plays by Count **Maurice Maeterlinck**, **Gerhart Hauptmann**, **W B Yeats**, **John Galsworthy**, **John Masefield** and Shaw, in circumstances that set new standards of acting and design. He left the Court (1907) and continued his success with a series of **Shakespeare** plays at the Savoy. His plays include *The Marrying of Ann Leete* (1902), *The Voysey Inheritance* (1905) and *The Madras House* (1910). His prefaces to Shakespeare's plays (4 vols, 1927–45) are valuable for their original criticism and ideas on production.

Grappelli, Stephane 1908–97 •*French jazz violinist*• He was born in Paris and had a classical training in violin and other instruments. With the Belgian gypsy guitarist **Django Reinhardt** as co-leader, he was a founding member of the Quintette du Hot Club de France, which brought a European influence into jazz from the mid-1930s. He went on to perform prolifically throughout the world, usually leading a quartet and adhering to the bright swing-based style of which he was a recognized master.

Grass, Günter Wilhelm 1927– •*German novelist and Nobel Prize winner*• Born in Danzig (now Gdańsk, Poland), he was educated at the Academy of Art, Düsseldorf, and the State Academy of Fine Arts, Berlin. He served in World War II and was a prisoner of war, and after various jobs became a speechwriter for **Willy Brandt** when Brandt was Mayor of West Berlin. *Die Blechtrommel* (1959, Eng trans *The Tin Drum*, 1962) was the first of the novels that have made him Germany's greatest living novelist. Ostensibly the autobiography of Oskar Matzerath, detained in a mental hospital for a murder he did not commit, it caused a furor in Germany because of its depiction of the Nazis. Intellectual and experimental in form, theme and language, his books, including *Katz und Maus* (1961, Eng trans *Cat and Mouse*, 1963), *Hundejahre* (1963, Eng trans *Dog Years*, 1965), *Der Butt* (1977, Eng trans *The Flounder*, 1978), *Die Ratten* (1987, Eng trans *The Rats*, 1987) and *Unkenrufe* (1992, Eng trans *The Call of the Toad*, 1992), consistently challenge the status quo and question our reading of the past. In 1995 he published *Ein weites Feld* ("A Broad Field"), one of the first major novels to tackle the issue of German reunification. He has also written plays, poetry and essays. He was awarded the Nobel Prize for literature in 1999.

Grassic Gibbon, Lewis *See* **Gibbon, Lewis Grassic**

Grassmann, Hermann Günther 1809–77 •*German mathematician and philologist*• Born in Stettin, he studied theology and classics at the University of Berlin (1827–30). His book *Die lineale Ausdehnungslehre: Ein neuer Zweig der Mathematik* (1844, "The Theory of Linear Extension: A New Branch of Mathematics") set out a new theory of *n*-dimensional geometry. Despite its almost complete neglect by mathematicians of the time, its importance has gradually been recognized, as it anticipated much later studies in quaternions, vectors, tensors, matrices and differential forms. From 1849 he studied Sanskrit and other ancient Indo-European languages.

Gratian, *properly* **Flavius Augustus Gratianus** AD 359–83 •*Roman emperor*• The son of the emperor **Valentinian I**, he was born in Sirinium, Pannonia, and in AD 367 his father made him Augustus in Gaul. He and his half brother Valentinian II (371–92) succeeded their father on his death (375). Gaul, Spain and Britain fell to Gratian's share, but as his brother was only four years old, he virtually ruled the whole Western Empire, and in 378, on the death of his uncle Valens, he suddenly became sovereign also of the Eastern Empire. Thereupon he recalled **Theodosius I** (the Great) from Spain, and appointed him his colleague (379). He was much influenced by St **Ambrose**, and persecuted pagans and heretics. He was eventually overthrown by the usurper **Magnus Maximus**, and was murdered at Lyons.

Gratian, *Latin* **Franciscus Gratianus** 12th century •*Italian jurist and Camaldolese monk of Bologna*• Between 1139 and 1150 he compiled the collection of canon law known as the *Decretum Gratiani*, which was to become the basic text for all studies of canon law.

Grattan, Henry 1746–1820 •*Irish politician*• Born in Dublin and educated at Trinity College, Dublin, and at the Middle Temple, he became a fervent supporter of Henry Flood (1723–91), and entered the Irish parliament for Charlemont. When Flood, who had been leading the fight for Irish independence, accepted a government post, Grattan immediately took his place, attempting to secure the removal of the restrictions imposed on Irish trade. When the concessions he won were revoked in 1779, he began the struggle for legislative independence. He secured the abolition of all claims by the British parliament to legislate for Ireland in 1782, but was unable to prevent the Act of Union.

Gravelet, Jean François *See* **Blondin, Charles**

Graves, Michael 1934– •*US architect*• Born in Indianapolis, Indiana, he studied architecture in Cincinnati and at Harvard, and after spending two years as a Fellow at the American Academy in Rome, he began to teach at Princeton University in 1962. His designs in the 1960s, influenced by **Le Corbusier**, were in the sleek, functional style of orthodox Modernism, but in the late 1970s he began to incorporate into his work "quotations" from earlier architectural styles, including pyramids, columns, pilasters, and vaults. He has also designed furniture and housewares. Denounced by some as a maker of empty and arbitrary historical allusions and praised by others for the energy and inventiveness of his designs, Graves is one of the leading proponents of Postmodernism in architecture.

Graves, Robert Ranke 1895–1985 •*English poet, novelist, essayist and critic*• Born in London and educated at Charterhouse, he was Professor of English at Cairo and Professor of Poetry at Oxford (1961–66). His first poetry, such as *Over the Brazier* (1916) and *Fairies and Fusiliers* (1917), was published during World War I. In 1925 he met **Laura Riding**, with whom he went into exile to Majorca on the proceeds of his autobiography, *Goodbye to All That* (1929). He returned to England in 1939 for World War II, but settled permanently in Majorca in 1946. His best-known novels are *I, Claudius* (1934) and *Claudius the God* (1934), which were adapted for television in 1976. *The White Goddess* (1948) is his most significant nonfiction title, and his interest in myth prompted *Greek Myths* (1955) and *Hebrew Myths* (1963). He is generally regarded as the best love poet of his generation.

Gray, Alasdair James 1934– •*Scottish novelist, painter and playwright*• Born in Glasgow, he was educated at Glasgow School of Art. Painting was his first vocation and he came late to novel writing; *Lanark*, his first novel, was published in 1981. His novel *1982 Janine* (1984) is typically erotically charged and very funny. His other novels include *The Fall of Kelvin Walker* (1985), *Something Leather* (1990), *McGrotty and Ludmilla* (1990) and *A History Maker* (1994). He has also published volumes of short stories, a volume of poetry and the autobiographical *Saltire Self-Portrait No. 4* (1989). He was also editor of *The Book of Prefaces* (2000).

"

Art is the only work open to people who can't get along with others and still want to be special.

1981 ***Lanark****, book 3, chapter 1.*

Gray, Asa 1810–88 •*US botanist*• Born in Sauquoit, New York, he was educated there and in Clinton, Iowa, before going to Fairfield Academy, to whose medical school he transferred after a year. He practiced medicine briefly in Bridgewater, New York (1831–32), and began collecting plants. In 1836 he became Professor of Natural History at the University of Michigan, Ann Arbor (1838–42). Following a tour of European botanical institutes, he became Professor of Natural History at Harvard (1842–73). He eventually became the US's leading 19th-century plant taxonomist and was a dedicated Darwinian. His works include *Manual of Botany of the Northern United States* (1848, known as "Gray's Manual") and *A Free Examination of Darwin's Treatise* (1861).

Gray, Eileen 1878–1976 •*Irish architect and designer*• Born in Enniscorthy, County Wexford, she studied at the Slade School of Art, London (1898), then moved to Paris in 1902, studying at the Académie Colarossi and Académie Julian. She also worked with the Japanese craftsman Sugawara. Specializing in lacquering, she began to design furniture and started making carpets, lamps and wall hangings. In 1922 she opened her Galerie Jean Désert in the Rue du Fauborg Saint-Honoré, where she showed her famous lacquer screens. Self-taught as an architect, she worked in the modern movement with Jean Badovici. She later exhibited at the Paris 1937 Exhibition with **Le Corbusier**, and her furniture designs were reproduced in Italy, France and the UK.

Gray, Gordon Joseph 1910–93 •*Roman Catholic archbishop and cardinal*• Born in Leith, near Edinburgh, he was educated at Holy Cross Academy, Edinburgh, St Joseph's Seminary, Sussex, and St John's, Surrey, and was ordained as a priest in 1935. Following various appointments, in 1969 he was named cardinal by Pope **Paul VI**, the first such appointment in Scottish history (apart from exiled clerics in Rome). In 1982 he played a major part in bringing Pope **John Paul II** to Scotland. An ecumenist, he made possible the great improvement in the acceptability of Catholics in Scottish life.

Gray, Hanna Holborn, *née* **Holborn** 1930– •*US historian*• She was born in Heidelberg, Germany, the daughter of the historian Hajo Holborn, who fled the Nazis with his family in 1934 and settled in the US. As a Renaissance and Reformation scholar, she worked in various universities during the 1950s and 1960s. She was appointed Professor of History and provost of Yale in 1974, and became acting president (1977–78). Her appointment as president of the University of Chicago (1978–93) made her the first woman to head a major US university.

Gray, Simon James Holliday 1936– •*English dramatist, director and novelist*• Born on Hayling Island, Hampshire, he studied at Cambridge. He has written novels and several television plays, but is best known as a stage dramatist. His first play, *Wise Child*, was produced in 1967. Subsequent plays include *Otherwise Engaged* (1975), *Quartermaine's Terms* (1981), *Melon* (1987) and *Cell Mates* (1995), whose staging was the focus of much media attention following the walkout and disappearance of **Stephen Fry**. His television plays include *After Pilkington* (1987) and *They Never Slept* (1991).

Gray, Stephen 1666–1736 •*English physicist*• He was born in Canterbury, and his first scientific paper (1696) described a microscope made of a water droplet, similar to the simple glass bead microscopes made so famous by **Anton van Leeuwenhoek** in the following decade. He was one of the first experimenters in static electricity, using frictional methods to prove conduction; this work had a great influence on the electrical theory of **Charles Dufay**.

Gray, Thomas 1716–71 •*English poet*• Born in London, he was educated at Eton and Peterhouse, Cambridge. At Eton he met **Horace Walpole**, whom he accompanied (1739) on a two-and-a-half-year tour of France and Italy. Gray returned to England and in 1742 he wrote his "Ode on a Distant Prospect of Eton College" (1747), and began the "Elegy Written in a Country Churchyard" (1751) in Stoke Poges, Buckinghamshire. He then went back to Cambridge, where he wrote his *Pindaric Odes* (1757). He declined the laureateship in 1757. In 1768 he collected his poems in the first general edition, and became Professor of History and Modern Languages at Cambridge.

Graziani, Rodolfo, Marchese di Neghelli 1882–1955 •*Italian soldier*• He was born near Frosinone. He served in Libya in 1913 and on the Italian front during World War I. In 1936 he led the Italian forces on the Somalian front during the conquest of Abyssinia. He succeeded **Pietro Badoglio** as Viceroy of Ethiopia, and was placed in charge of the Italian forces in North Africa (1940–41) but was replaced after a series of defeats by the British. He was captured in 1945 and tried for war crimes, and in 1950 he was sentenced to 25 years in prison, but was released the same year. He was active in the Italian Social Movement until his death.

Greco, El, *properly* **Domenico Theotocopoulos** 1541–1614 •*Spanish painter*• Born in Candia, now Iráklion, Crete, of Greek descent, he studied in Italy, possibly as a pupil of **Titian**. Around 1570 he painted a *View of Mount Sinai and the Monastery of St Catherine* (Historical Museum of Crete, Heraklion). He is known to have settled in Toledo about 1577, when he was commissioned to execute the decorations for the new church of Santo Domingo el Antiguo, the centerpiece being the *Assumption of the Virgin* (1577, now at Chicago). He became a portrait painter whose reputation fluctuated because of the suspicion that greeted his characteristic distortions. His painting is a curious blend of Italian Mannerism and Baroque rhythm, with elongated flamelike figures, arbitrary lighting and color, and, in his later pictures, almost impressionist brushwork. The most famous of his paintings is probably the *Burial of Count Orgaz* (1586) in the Church of Santo Tomé, Toledo. Many of his works are to be seen in Toledo (Museo del Greco).

Greeley, Horace 1811–72 •*US editor and politician*• Born in Amherst, New Hampshire, he went to New York in 1831, started the weekly *New Yorker* in 1834 and in 1841 the daily *New York Tribune*, of which he was the leading editor until his death, exerting a strong influence on US opinion. He published in the *Tribune* his "Prayer of Twenty Millions," and within a month the Emancipation Proclamation was issued. After **Robert E Lee**'s surrender he advocated a universal amnesty, and his going to Richmond and signing the bailbond of **Jefferson Davis** awakened a storm of public indignation. He was an unsuccessful Liberal Republican candidate in 1872 for the presidency.

“ ”

Go West, young man, and grow up with the country.

1850 ***Hints Toward Reforms.***

Green, George 1793–1841 •*English mathematician and physicist*• Born in Sneinton, near Nottingham, he was largely self-taught and in 1828 published a pamphlet entitled *An Essay on the Application of Mathematical Analysis to the Theories of Electricity and Magnetism*, containing Green's theorem and Green's functions. Green's theorem relates integrals taken over a volume with those taken over the surface enclosing that volume, and has valuable implications for potential theory. His functions are a valuable technical tool for solving partial differential equations. He went to Caius College, Cambridge, in 1833, published several papers on wave motion and optics, and was elected a Fellow of the college in 1839.

Green, Henry, *pseudonym of* **Henry Vincent Yorke** 1905–73 •*English novelist*• Born in Tewkesbury, Gloucestershire, and educated at Oxford, he became managing director in his father's engineering company in Birmingham, but pursued a parallel career as a novelist. His first novel, *Blindness* (1926), was published while he was still an undergraduate. An elliptical and highly stylized writer, he was partial to terse and sophisticated titles, such as *Caught* (1943), *Loving* (1945), *Back* (1946), *Concluding* (1948), *Nothing* (1950) and *Doting* (1952). *Pack My Bag: A Self Portrait* (1940) is autobiographical.

Green, Lucinda, *née* **Prior-Palmer** 1953– •*British three-day-event player*• Born in London, she won the Badminton Horse Trials a record six times (1973, 1976–77, 1979, 1983–84), and the Burghley Horse Trials in 1977 and 1981. At the European championships she won an individual gold medal in 1975 and 1977, and a team gold in 1977, 1985, and 1987. She was the 1982 world champion on Regal Realm, when she also won a team gold medal.

Greenaway, Kate (Catherine) 1846–1901 •*English artist and book illustrator*• Born in London, she started publishing her popular portrayals of child life in 1879 with *Under the Window*, followed by *The Birthday Book* (1880) and *Mother Goose* (1881). The Greenaway Medal is awarded annually for the best British children's book artist.

Greenaway, Peter 1942– •*English filmmaker and painter*• Born in London, he trained as a painter. Employed at the Central Office of Information (1965–76), he worked as an editor and began making his own short films. *The Draughtsman's Contract* (1982) won him critical acclaim and a wider audience. He has subsequently pursued a prolific career utilizing ravishing visual composition, a painterly sense of color and the distinctive music of **Michael Nyman** to explore such preoccupations as sex, death, decay and gamesmanship in films like *The Belly of an Architect* (1987), *Drowning by Numbers* (1988), *The Cook, the Thief, His Wife and Her Lover* (1989), *Prospero's Books* (1991), *The Baby of Mâcon* (1993), *The Pillow Book* (1996) and *8 Women* (1999).

Greene, (Henry) Graham 1904–91 •*English writer*• Born in Berkhamsted, Hertfordshire, he was educated at Berkhamsted School where his father was headmaster. In *A Sort of Life* (1971), the first of two autobiographies (*Ways of Escape*, the second volume, appeared in 1980), he recounts how he played Russian roulette and of how, at age 13, he tried to cut open his leg with a penknife. He went to Balliol College, Oxford, became a Roman Catholic in 1926 and joined the staff of *The Times*. He married in

1927 and was later separated but not divorced. His first novels, *The Man Within* (1925), *The Name of Action* (1930) and *Rumour at Nightfall* (1932), made little impression, and he subsequently disowned them, though he later allowed the first to be included in the collected edition. *Stamboul Train* (1932) was his first fully successful novel, although he termed it an "entertainment." Like many of his subsequent novels it is somberly romantic, fusing tragedy and comedy in a peculiar no-man's land that critics christened "Greeneland." He was the film critic for *Night and Day*, and was partly responsible for its demise when the magazine was successfully sued after he had accused Twentieth Century Fox of "procuring" **Shirley Temple** "for immoral purposes." His career as a so-called Catholic novelist began with *Brighton Rock* (1938), a thriller which asserts that human justice is inadequate and irrelevant to the real struggle against evil, a theme also explored in *The Power and the Glory* (1940), *The Heart of the Matter* (1948) and *The Quiet American* (1955). Other notable novels include *The Third Man* (1950, filmed by **Carol Reed**), *The End of the Affair* (1951), *Our Man in Havana* (1958), *A Burnt-Out Case* (1961), *The Comedians* (1965), *Travels with My Aunt* (1969), *The Honorary Consul* (1973) and *The Human Factor* (1978). The multifarious settings reflect his wanderlust and his fascination with uncomfortable countries—Argentina, the Congo, Mexico, Vietnam—as well as his seeming disregard for his personal safety. He settled in Antibes in 1966, where he lived for the rest of his life. In 1982 he broke his relative seclusion by publishing an incendiary pamphlet, *J'accuse*, which brought him into conflict with the local authorities in Nice. He published travel books: *Journey Without Maps* (1936) and *The Lawless Roads* (1939). The *Collected Essays* appeared in 1969, the *Collected Stories* in 1972. His plays include *The Living Room* (1953), *The Potting Shed* (1957) and *The Complaisant Lover* (1959). Few modern writers have his range and power, critical acclaim and popular success.

Greene, Maurice 1974– •*US athlete*• Born in Kansas City, Missouri, he began training as a runner at eight and subsequently dominated the 100-meter event in international competition. He won his first gold medal in the 100 meters at the world championships in 1997 and was world champion again in 1999 and in 2001. In 2000 he added Olympic gold in the 100 meters, as well as winning in the 4 × 100 meters relay. He has held world records in the 100 meters, and in the 50-meter and 60-meter indoor dash.

Greene, Nathanael 1742–86 •*American soldier*• Born in Warwick, Rhode Island, he was a Quaker's son. At the Brandywine (September 1777) he commanded a division and saved the American army from complete destruction. In 1780 he succeeded **Horatio Gates** in command of the army of the South, which had just been defeated by **Charles Cornwallis**, and improved its condition. Although defeated by Cornwallis at Guilford Courthouse (March 1781), he conducted a masterly retreat into South Carolina which, with Georgia, was rapidly retaken, until at Eutaw Springs (September 1781) the war in the South was ended in what was virtually an American victory. A general second perhaps only to **George Washington**, he died at Mulberry Grove, Georgia.

Greene, Robert 1558–92 •*English dramatist*• Born in Norwich, Norfolk, and educated at Cambridge, he wrote plays and romances. The latter are often tedious and insipid, but they abound in beautiful poetry. One of them, *Pandosto* (1588), supplied **Shakespeare** with hints for the plot of *The Winter's Tale*. The most popular of his plays was *Friar Bacon and Friar Bungay* (c. 1591). As Greene helped to lay the foundations of the English drama, even his worst plays are valuable historically. His *Groatsworth of Wit Bought with a Million of Repentance* (1592) contains one of the few authentic contemporary allusions to Shakespeare.

Greenwood, Joan 1921–87 •*English actress*• Born in Chelsea, London, she studied at the Royal Academy of Dramatic Art. She toured with the Entertainment National Service Association (ENSA) during World War II and afterward joined **Donald Wolfit**'s company. She was a woman of distinctive style, and her husky tones, wit and sensuality were evident in both classical roles and contemporary femmes fatales. Her film credits include the influential and enduring Ealing comedies *Whisky Galore* (1948), *Kind Hearts and Coronets* (1949) and *The Man in the White Suit* (1951). Later stage successes include *Lysistrata* (1957), *Hedda Gabler* (1960) and *Oblomov* (1964). Later films were *Tom Jones* (1963) and *Little Dorrit* (1987).

Greenwood, Walter 1903–74 •*English writer*• He was born in Salford, Lancashire, of working-class parents, and educated at the local grammar school. His novel, *Love on the Dole* (1933), inspired by his experiences of unemployment and depression in the early 1930s, made a considerable impact as a document of the times and was subsequently dramatized. He also wrote other novels with a social slant, and several plays.

Greer, Germaine 1939– •*Australian feminist and author*• Born in Melbourne, she attended the Universities of Melbourne and Sydney, and Cambridge University, becoming a lecturer in English at Warwick University (1968–73). Her controversial and successful book *The Female Eunuch* (1970) portrayed marriage as a legalized form of slavery for women, and attacked the denial and misrepresentation of female sexuality by male-dominated society. A regular contributor to newspapers and periodicals, and a frequent television panelist, she became (1981) director of the Tulsa Center for the Study of Women's Literature. Her later works include *Sex and Destiny: The Politics of Human Fertility* (1984), *The Change* (1991) and *The Whole Woman* (1999). She has recently returned to Warwick University, where she is Professor of English and Comparative Studies (1998–).

“ ”

If women understand by emancipation the adoption of the masculine role then we are lost indeed.

*1970 **The Female Eunuch**, "Soul: Womanpower."*

Gregory, St, *known as* **the Illuminator** c. 240–332 AD •*Armenian Christian*• Born in Cappadocia, of Armenian parents, he is said to have been of the royal Persian race of the Arsacids. Known as "the Apostle of Armenia," he was kept a prisoner for 14 years by Tiridates III for refusing to condone idolatry but, after converting the king (AD 301), he was made patriarch of his country.

Gregory I, *known as* **Gregory the Great** c. 540–604 •*Pope (from 590) and saint, a Doctor of the Church*• He was born in Rome and, though appointed by Justin II as praetor of Rome, he relinquished this office, distributed his wealth among the poor and withdrew into a monastery in Rome. It was while he was there that he is said to have seen some Anglo-Saxon youths in the slave market, and to have been seized with a longing to convert their country to Christianity. He embarked on this but was called back, and Pelagius II sent Gregory as nuncio to Constantinople for aid against the Lombards. Gregory reluctantly agreed to become pope on the death of Pelagius. He proved to be a great administrator, and during his period of office the Roman Church underwent a complete overhaul of its public services and ritual and the systematization of its sacred chants, from which arose the Gregorian chant. He entrusted the mission to convert the English to **Augustine**, and the Gothic kingdom of Spain, long Arian, was reconciled with Rome. He left homilies on **Ezekiel**, **Job** and on the Gospels, the *Regulae pastoralis liber* ("Book of Rules for Pastors"), and the *Sacramentarium* and *Antiphonarium*. Gregory was tolerant toward heathens and Jews, and he used all his efforts to repress slave dealing and to mitigate slavery. He is buried in St Peter's Basilica, Rome, and his feast day is March 12.

Gregory III d. 741 •*Syrian pope*• Born in Syria, he became pope in 731, and excommunicated the Iconoclasts. The threat of the Lombards became so formidable that, the Eastern emperors being powerless to help, the Romans compelled Gregory to send a deputation to **Charles Martel**, asking for his help, and offering to make him a consul of Rome. This offer is of historical significance in that it failed to enlist the aid of Charles, but it was a step toward the independence of the West.

Gregory VII, St, *originally* **Hildebrand** c. 1020–85 •*Italian pope*• Born near Soana, Tuscany, he was educated at the monastery of Santa Maria, Rome. As pope (1073–85), he worked to change the secularized condition of the Church, which led to conflict with the Holy Roman Emperor **Henry IV**, who declared Gregory deposed in a diet at Worms (1076), but then yielded to him after excommunication. In 1080 Henry resumed hostilities, appointing an antipope (Clement III), and after a siege took possession of Rome (1084). Gregory was freed by Norman troops, but was forced to withdraw to Salerno. He was canonized in 1606, and his feast day is May 25.

Gregory IX, *originally* **Ugo** or **Ugolino de Segni** 1148/55–1241 •*Italian pope*• He was the nephew of Pope **Innocent III**. A strong supporter of the Franciscans and the Dominicans, he became pope in 1227 and constantly feuded with Emperor **Frederick II** of Germany, asserting the supremacy of papal power. A ferocious conflict broke out over Frederick's Constitutions of Melfi that subjected Sicily to his will. Rome itself was under siege when the pope died. He was responsible for ordering the first authoritative collection of papal decretals (1234), which were to remain the basic source of canon law in the Catholic Church until 1917.

Gregory XI, *originally* **Pierre Roger de Beaufort** 1329–78 •*French pope*• He became pope in 1370, and despite the opposition of France and his own family, he ended the Babylonian Captivity of the papacy, moving its seat from Avignon to its original place in Rome (1377). He was the last French pope, and the elections held after his death began the Great Schism.

Gregory XIII, *originally* **Ugo Buoncompagni** 1502–85 •*Italian pope*• Born in Bologna, he studied at the university there and became Professor of Law (1531–39). He became one of the theologians at the Council of Trent, then in 1565 a cardinal and legate to Spain. As pope (1572–85), he did much to promote education, and endowed many of the colleges in Rome. His pontificate is notable for the correction of the calendar and the introduction of the Gregorian Computation in 1582. Gregory published a valuable edition of the *Decretum Gratiani*.

Gregory XV, *originally* **Alessandro Ludovisi** 1554–1623 •*Italian pope*• Born in Bologna, he became pope in 1621. He established the still-used procedure for papal elections, set up the congregation of the Propagation of the Faith, regained Moravia and Bohemia to the Roman faith, and canonized **Francis Xavier**, **Ignatius Loyola** and **Teresa of Ávila**, among others.

Gregory of Nazianzus or **Nazianzen, St** c. 330–c. 389 AD •*Greek prelate and theologian*• Born of Greek parents in Cappadocia, he was educated in Caesarea, Alexandria and Athens. He became a close friend of **Basil the Great**, and was made Bishop of Sasima, but withdrew to a life of religious study at Nazianzus. He was made patriarch of Constantinople (Istanbul) in AD 380, but also resigned this in the following year. His theological works were largely concerned with upholding Nicene orthodoxy and include discourses, letters and hymns. His feast day in the West is January 2.

Gregory of Nyssa AD 331–95 •*Greek Christian theologian*• Born in Caesarea, Cappadocia, he was consecrated Bishop of Nyssa in Cappadocia (c. 371 AD) by his brother **Basil the Great**. He was present at the Council of Constantinople in 381, and was appointed to share in the overseeing of the diocese of Pontus. He traveled to Arabia and Jerusalem to set in order the churches there, and was again at a synod in Constantinople (Istanbul) in 394. His chief works are his *Twelve Books Against Eunomius*, a treatise on the Trinity, several ascetic treatises, many sermons, 23 epistles, and his great *Catechetical Oration*.

Gregory of Tours c. 538–94 •*Frankish prelate and historian*• Born in Arverna (now Clermont), into a distinguished Roman family of Gaul, he made a recovery from sickness following a pilgrimage to the grave of St **Martin** of Tours. This led Gregory to devote himself to the Church, and he was elected Bishop of Tours in 573. As a supporter of Sigbert of Austrasia and his wife **Brunhilde** against Chilperic and his wife **Fredegond**, he was relentlessly persecuted. His *Historia Francorum* ("History of the Franks") is the chief authority for the history of Gaul in the 6th century.

Gregory, Isabella Augusta, Lady, *née* **Persse** 1852–1932 •*Irish playwright*• She was born at Roxborough House near Coole, County Galway, the daughter of a wealthy family. In 1880 she married Sir William Henry Gregory (1817–92), who was Governor of Ceylon (1872–77). After her husband's death, Lady Gregory furthered her study of Irish mythology and folklore, an interest which led in 1896 to her meeting **W B Yeats**. She shared his vision of a resurgent Irish drama and, with Yeats and the writer Edward Martyn (1859–1923), cofounded the Abbey Theatre, Dublin, which opened in 1904. Lady Gregory wrote or translated about 40 short plays about the Irish rural peasantry, including the comedy *Spreading the News* (1904) and the patriotic *Cathleen ni Houlihan* (1902, with Yeats). *The Gaol Gate* (1906) is a tragedy, while *The White Cockade* (1905) and *The Deliverer* (1911) are history plays.

Gregory, James 1638–75 •*Scottish mathematician*• Born in Drumoak, Aberdeenshire, he graduated from the University of Aberdeen and went to London in 1662, and the following year published *Optica promota*, containing a description of the Gregorian reflecting telescope that he had invented in 1661. Much of his later work was concerned with infinite series, a term which he introduced into the language.

Gregory Thaumaturgus c. 213–c. 270 AD •*Roman Christian*• Born in Neocaesarea in Pontus, he became a disciple of **Origen**, and was consecrated Bishop of Neocaesarea. His *Ekthesis* ("Confession of Faith") is a summary of Origen's theology. His name means "wonder worker" in Greek.

Greig, John 1942– •*Scottish soccer player and manager*• Born in Edinburgh, he spent his entire senior career, from 1960 to 1978, with the Rangers, much of it as club captain. He won five league championships and six Scottish Cups while with the club, as well as the European Cup Winners' Cup in 1972. Winning 44 caps for Scotland, he was voted Scottish player of the year in 1966 and 1976. Retiring as a player in May 1978, he immediately became the Rangers' manager, holding the post until 1983.

Grenfell, Joyce 1910–79 •*English entertainer*• Born in London, she made her debut in *The Little Revue* in 1939. After touring hospitals with concert parties during World War II, she appeared in revue until the early 1950s, performing comic monologues. She later appeared in her own solo shows, such as *Joyce Grenfell Requests the Pleasure*. Her monologues gently mocked the habits and manners of the middle class, English schoolmistresses and aging spinster daughters.

“ ”

Stately as a galleon, I sail across the floor,
Doing the Military Two-step, as in the days of yore.

1978 "Stately as a Galleon" (song).

Grenville, George 1712–70 •*English politician*• He practiced as a lawyer and became a Member of Parliament in 1741, rising to Lord of the Admiralty (1744–47), Lord of the Treasury (1747–54) and Treasurer of the Navy (1754–55, 1756–62). He was briefly Secretary of State for the Northern Department (1762–63) and then became Prime Minister (1763–65). During his period in office, the closer supervision of revenue collection (1764–65) and the Stamp Act (1765), began to alienate the American colonies from British rule. His tactlessness and clumsy handling of arrangements to cover a possible regency during **George III**'s first serious illness (1765) led to his dismissal by the king, and he remained in opposition for the rest of his life.

Grenville, Sir Richard c. 1541–91 •*English naval commander*• Born in Buckland Abbey, Devon, he fought in Ireland (1566–69) and Hungary. He was knighted (c. 1577) and was a Member of Parliament for Cornwall (1571–84). In 1585 he commanded the seven ships carrying his cousin **Walter Raleigh**'s first colony to Virginia. He contributed three ships to the English fleet against the Spanish Armada (1588). In 1591, as commander of the *Revenge*, he fought alone against a large Spanish fleet off the Azores, dying of wounds on board a Spanish ship.

Grenville, William Wyndham Grenville, 1st Baron 1759–1834 •*English politician*• The son of **George Grenville**, he studied at Eton and Oxford, and became a Member of Parliament in 1782. In 1783 he was Paymaster General, in 1789 Speaker, and while Home Secretary (1790) was made baron. He became Foreign Secretary in 1791, and resigned, along with his cousin **William Pitt** the Younger, in 1801 on the refusal of **George III** to assent to Catholic emancipation. In 1806 he formed the government of "All the Talents" which, before its dissolution in 1807, abolished the slave trade. From 1809 to 1815 he acted along with Charles, 2nd Earl **Grey**.

Gresham, Sir Thomas 1519–79 •*English financier and philanthropist*• Born probably in London, the son of Sir Richard Gresham (c. 1485–1549), he founded the Royal Exchange, and became Lord Mayor of London (1537). From Cambridge in 1543 he passed into the Mercers' Company, and in 1551 was employed as "king's merchant" at Antwerp. In two years he paid off a heavy loan and restored the king's credit. As a Protestant he was dismissed by Queen **Mary I (Tudor)**, but was soon reinstated by Queen **Elizabeth I**, who made him ambassador to the Netherlands (1559–61). In 1569, on his advice, the state borrowed money from London merchants instead of from foreigners. He made the observation, known as "Gresham's Law," that of two coins of equal legal exchange value, that of the lower intrinsic value would tend to drive the other out of use. From 1566 to 1568 he devoted a portion of his great wealth to building an exchange, in imitation of that of Antwerp. He made provision for founding Gresham College, London, and he left money for eight almshouses.

Gresley, Sir (Herbert) Nigel 1876–1941 •*English locomotive engineer*• Born in Edinburgh, he was the foremost British locomotive designer for 30 years from 1911, designing such classic trains as the streamlined "Silver Jubilee" and "Coronation" in the mid-1930s. His A4-class Pacific 4-6-2 "Mallard" achieved a world record speed for a steam locomotive of 126 mph (201.5 kph) in July 1938 which has never been exceeded.

Gretzky, Wayne 1961– •*Canadian ice hockey player*• Born in Brantford, Ontario, he played for the Edmonton Oilers (1978–88), then joined the Los Angeles Kings (1988–96) and signed with the New York Rangers in 1996 after a brief stint with the St Louis Blues. He set numerous records, including most points scored in a National Hockey League career (2,857). He is nicknamed the "Great One" and considered the greatest player in the history of the game. He retired in 1999.

Greuze, Jean Baptiste 1725–1805 •*French genre and portrait painter*• Born in Tournus, near Mâcon, he painted Italian subjects after a visit to Italy (1755), but he is seen at his best in such studies of girls as *The Broken Pitcher* in the Louvre, Paris, and *Girl with Doves* in the Wallace Collection, London. He died in poverty.

Greville, Sir Fulke, 1st Baron Brooke 1554–1628 •*English poet and courtier*• Born in Beauchamp Court, Warwickshire, he was educated at Shrewsbury and Jesus College, Cambridge. A friend of Sir **Philip Sidney** and a favorite of **Elizabeth I**, he held many important offices and was made baron in 1620. He wrote several didactic poems, over a hundred sonnets and two tragedies, one of which was *The Tragedy of Mustapha* (1609), printed in 1633. His best-remembered work is his *Life of the Renowned Sir Philip Sidney* (published 1652) with its vivid pictures of contemporary figures. He was murdered by an old retainer who thought himself cut out of his master's will.

Grévy, François Paul Jules 1807–91 •*French politician*• The vice president of the Constituent Assembly of 1848, he opposed **Napoleon III**, and after the coup d'état retired from politics. In 1871 he was elected president of the National Assembly and in 1879 he became President of the Republic. Reelected in 1885, he resigned in 1887 after a financial scandal involving his son-in-law.

Grew, Nehemiah 1641–1712 •*English botanist and physician*• Born in Atherstone, Warwickshire, and educated at Cambridge and Leiden Universities, he practiced at the Universities of Coventry and London, and was author of *Comparative Anatomy of the Stomach and Guts* (1681) and of the pioneering *Anatomy of Plants* (1682). In this work he used the microscope to elucidate plant structure and gave the first complete account of plant anatomy, and it remained the most significant and authoritative work in this field for more than 150 years. As well as making enormous contributions to anatomy and physiology, his analytical studies presaged the development of phytochemistry.

Grey, Dame Beryl, *stage name of* **Mrs Beryl Svenson** 1927– •*English ballerina*• Born in London, she won a scholarship to Sadler's Wells Ballet School at the age of nine. The youngest Giselle ever at the age of 16, she was prima ballerina of the Sadler's Wells Ballet (1942–57), and also appeared with the Bolshoi Ballet in Russia (1957–58) and the Chinese Ballet in Peking (1964). She was artistic director (1968–79) of the London Festival Ballet (now English National Ballet). She was given the honorary title of Dame Commander, Order of the British Empire, in 1988.

Grey, Charles, 2nd Earl 1764–1845 •*English statesman*• He was born in Fallodon, Northumberland, and educated at Eton and King's College, Cambridge. He joined the Whig Opposition in Parliament in 1786, and wasted little time in attacking the government of **William Pitt** the Younger for its domestic and foreign policies and its union with Ireland in particular. On the Whigs' return to power in 1806, he became First Lord of the Admiralty, and later as Foreign Secretary managed the abolition of the African slave trade. After succeeding his father to the earldom in 1807, he withdrew from the Commons, but after the 1830 general election returned as Prime Minister of the new Whig administration. He introduced his first Reform Bill a year later, but it was defeated. When the second bill was passed by the Commons but rejected by the Lords, there were violent demonstrations, and Grey managed a third attempt that reached its second reading in the Lords but collapsed when ministers resigned over its disenfranchisement clauses. After the Duke of **Wellington** failed to form a government, Grey returned as Premier and persuaded **William IV** to create a sufficient number of new peers to guarantee the legislation's adoption in the Upper House. His bill finally received royal assent in 1832, and Grey continued to lead the reformed Parliament, extending his earlier antislavery measures to the colonies. However, a Cabinet split over reform of the Church of Ireland made Grey's position untenable, and he resigned in 1834.

Grey, Sir George 1799–1882 •*English politician*• Born in Gibraltar, the nephew of Charles, 2nd Earl **Grey**, he graduated from Oriel College, Oxford, and succeeded his father in the baronetcy in 1828. Member of Parliament for Devonport (1832–47), in 1839 he became judge-advocate, in 1841 Chancellor of the Duchy of Lancaster, and in 1846 Home Secretary. During the Chartist disturbances he discharged his duties with much vigor and discrimination. He passed the Crown and Government Security Bill, the Alien Bill, and a measure for the further suspension in Ireland of the Habeas Corpus Act (1849). In 1854 he became Colonial Secretary, and in 1855, under Viscount **Palmerston**, took his old post of Home Secretary. From 1859 he was Chancellor of the Duchy of Lancaster, and Home Secretary again from 1861 to 1866.

Grey, Sir George 1812–98 •*British explorer and administrator*• He was born in Lisbon, Portugal. He made two expeditions (1837, 1839) to the northwest of Western Australia, and was later appointed magistrate at King George Sound, where he produced a vocabulary of local Aboriginal dialects. In 1840 he was appointed Governor of South Australia, then was transferred to New Zealand as Lieutenant Governor in 1845. In 1854 he became Governor of Cape Colony and High Commissioner of South Africa, and in 1861 was sent back to New Zealand for a second term (1861–68) when he brought the Maori Wars to a close. He was a member of the New Zealand House of Representatives (1874–94) and Premier (1877–79) before retiring to England in 1894.

Grey, Henry, 3rd Earl 1802–94 •*English politician*• The son of Charles, 2nd Earl **Grey**, he entered parliament in 1826 as Lord Howick, became Undersecretary for the colonies in his father's ministry, retired in 1833, but was subsequently Undersecretary in the home department, and in 1835 Secretary for War. In 1845 he succeeded to the peerage, in 1846 became Colonial Secretary, and in 1852 published his *Defence of Lord John Russell's Colonial Policy*. He was an opposer of the Crimean War, and condemned **Disraeli**'s Eastern policy.

Grey, Lady Jane 1537–54 •*Queen of England for nine days*• Born in Bradgate, Leicestershire, she was the great-granddaughter of **Henry VII**, the great-niece of **Henry VIII**, and the eldest daughter of Henry Grey, Marquess of Dorset. During the final illness of **Edward VI**, she was married against her will to Lord **Guildford Dudley**, fourth son of John Dudley, Duke of Northumberland, as part of the latter's plot to make sure of a Protestant succession. Declared queen three days after Edward's death (July 9, 1553), she was forced to abdicate nine days later in favor of Edward's sister, **Mary I (Tudor)**, and imprisoned in the Tower of London. Following a rebellion in her favor under Sir Thomas Wyatt the Younger, in which her father (by then Duke of Suffolk) also participated, she was beheaded with her husband.

Grey, Maria Georgina, *née* **Shirreff** 1816–1906 •*English pioneer of women's education*• The sister of **Emily Shirreff**, she married her cousin William Thomas Grey in 1841. She helped found the National Union for Promoting the Higher Education of Women (1871), which created the Girls' Public Day School Company, later Trust, in 1872 to establish "good and cheap Day Schools for Girls of all classes above those attending the Public Elementary Schools," and eventually had some 38 schools which set new academic standards for girls' education.

Grey, Zane 1875–1939 •*US novelist*• Born in Zanesville, Ohio, he began his working life as a dentist, but after a trip out West in 1904 turned out "Westerns" with machinelike regularity, totaling 54 novels and overall sales estimated at around 12 million copies. His best known, *Riders of the Purple Sage*, sold nearly two million copies. His hobby of big-game fishing off the coasts of Australia and New Zealand was utilized in such books as *Tales of Fishing* (1919).

Grey-Thompson, Tanni 1969– •*Welsh paralympic athlete*• Born in Cardiff, Wales, she was confined to a wheelchair from the age of eight and emerged as a promising athlete while still at school. By 2002 she had amassed 13 paralympic medals, including four at Sydney in 2000 (in the 100 meters, 200 meters, 400 meters and 800 meters). Her other triumphs have included nine medals in the London marathon and numerous British and world records. She has received the honorary titles Member, Order of the British Empire (1993) and Officer, Order of the British Empire (2000) in recognition of her achievements.

Grieg, Edvard Hagerup 1843–1907 •*Norwegian composer*• Born in Bergen, of Scots descent, he studied at the Leipzig Conservatory. He made Copenhagen his main base between 1863 and 1867, and there was in close contact with Niels Gade, **Hans Christian Andersen** and the young Norwegian poet-composer Nordraak. With their encouragement, he evolved into a strongly national Norwegian composer with an intense awareness of his folk heritage. After some years teaching and conducting in Christiania (Oslo), the success of his incidental music for **Ibsen**'s *Peer Gynt* (1876), on top of the award of a state pension in 1874, enabled him to settle near Bergen. Apart from his Piano Concerto in A Minor, some orchestral suites, three violin sonatas and one quartet, his large-scale output was small, although he wrote many songs.

“ ”

I am sure my music has a taste of codfish in it.

1903 Speech. Quoted in Ian Crofton and Donald Fraser ***A Dictionary of Musical Quotations*** *(1985).*

Grieg, (Johan) Nordahl Brun 1902–43 •*Norwegian poet and dramatist*• Born in Bergen, he studied at Oslo and Oxford, and spent much of his youth traveling. His novel, *Skibet gaar videre* (1924, "The Ship Sails On"), about his experiences on a voyage to Australia as an ordinary seaman, was the model for **Malcolm Lowry**'s *Ultramarine*. A committed antifascist, he wrote dramas about national freedom, as in *Vår ære og vår makt* (1935, "Our Honor and Our Might") and *Nederlaget* (1937, "Defeat") about the Paris Commune of 1871. During World War II he joined the Resistance, escaped to London, and broadcast his patriotic verses to Norway. His plane was shot down over Berlin in 1943.

Griffin, Donald Redfield 1915– •*US zoologist*• Born in Southampton, New York, and educated at Harvard, he demonstrated for the first time that the ultrasound produced by bats is used in echolocation. During World War II he studied the effects of background noise on radio communication, and investigated night vision using infrared light. Continuing his prewar studies of birds' homing abilities, he showed in 1968, by the use of radar, that migrating birds are able to maintain their orientation while flying blind in clouds. He launched the study of cognitive ethology in 1981, an investigation of the way in which nonhumans think and feel.

Griffin, Walter Burley 1876–1937 •*US architect and town planner*• Born in Maywood, Illinois, he graduated from Illinois State University and was for some years an associate of **Frank Lloyd Wright** before establishing his own practice in 1905. In 1910 he married a colleague, Marion Mahony (1871–1961). In 1912 he won an international competition for the design of the new federal capital of Australia, Canberra, then went into private practice in Australia, designing a number of notable buildings and the eccentric Castlecrag estate in north Sydney. In 1935 he went to India following an invitation to design a library for Lucknow University.

Griffith, Arthur 1872–1922 •*Irish nationalist politician*• Born in Dublin, in 1905 he founded a new political party, Sinn Fein ("We Ourselves"), and a paper of that name in 1906. A supporter of the Irish Volunteers, he took no part in the Easter Rising of 1916, but was imprisoned as a nationalist. He became Vice President in **Éamon De Valera**'s provisional government (1919). During the Anglo-Irish War (1919–21) he was imprisoned again (1920–21), but signed the Anglo-Irish Treaty of 1921 that brought about the Irish Free State. He was a moderate President of Dáil Éireann (1922), but died suddenly as further fighting broke out between those who opposed and those who supported the 1921 Treaty.

Griffith, D(avid Lewelyn) W(ark) 1875–1948 •*US pioneer film director*• Born in Floydsfork, Kentucky, he began as an actor and short-story writer before turning to the film industry, learning his trade in hundreds of silent films. Using technical innovations such as close-ups, fade-outs, flashbacks and moving cameras, he did much to create the conventions of modern cinematic art. His first great film, *The Birth of a Nation* (1915), was both hailed as a masterpiece for its subtlety and dramatic force and bitterly criticized by African-American groups appalled by its racism. Subsequent films include his epic *Intolerance* (1916) and his war film *Hearts of the World* (1918), which incorporated battle scenes actually filmed at the front. He discovered many stars, including **Lillian Gish**.

Griffith, Nanci 1954– •*US folk and country music singer and songwriter*• Born near Austin, Texas, she recorded her first album in 1978, and began to attract attention both for her winsome vocal style, which encompasses both folk and country, and her sophisticated, acutely observant songs. A string of increasingly successful records followed, and she formed her backup band, The Blue Moon Orchestra, in 1986. She recorded an album of songs by her favorite songwriters, *Other Voices, Other Rooms*, in 1993, followed by the more introspective and personal material on *Flyer* (1994).

Griffith, Samuel Walker 1845–1920 •*Australian judge*• Born in Merthyr Tydfil, Glamorgan, Wales, he emigrated to Australia in 1854, and studied at Sydney University. From 1867 he practiced law in Queensland, and became Prime Minister of that state three times. As chairman of the Constitutional Committee of the National Australian Convention in 1891, he had a major role in drafting what became in 1900 the Australian Commonwealth Constitution. He was first Chief Justice of the High Court of Australia (1900–19).

Griffith-Joyner, Florence, *known as* **Flo-Jo** 1959–98 •*US track and field sprinter*• She was born in Los Angeles, California. At the 1988 Olympics she won three gold medals: for the 100 meters and 200 meters—setting world records of 10.54 seconds for the former and 21.34 seconds for the latter—and for the 4 × 400 meter relay. That year her awards included the Sullivan award as the top amateur athlete in the US and the Associated Press Female Athlete of the Year award. She died following a heart seizure, aged 38.

Griffiths, James 1890–1975 •*Welsh miners' leader and politician*• Born in Betws, near Ammanford, Carmarthenshire, he was elected Labour Member of Parliament for Llanelli (1936–70). In the Labour governments of 1945 to 1951, he was Minister of National Insurance and Secretary of State for the Colonies. A strong believer in a measure of devolution for Wales, he argued for a separate Welsh Office, and became the first Secretary of State for Wales (1964–66).

Griffiths, Richard 1947– •*English actor*• Born in Stockton-on-Tees, Cleveland, he studied at the University of Manchester. He was a member of the Royal Shakespeare Company for much of his early career, later appearing in films such as *Greystoke* (1984), *A Private Function* (1985), *Withnail and I* (1987), *Sleepy Hollow* (1999), *Harry Potter and the Philosopher's Stone* (2001) and *Harry Potter and the Chamber of Secrets* (2002). He is known to television audiences for roles including the generously proportioned detective-cum-restaurateur Henry Crabbe in *Pie in the Sky* (1994–95).

Griffiths, Trevor 1935– •*English dramatist*• He was born in Manchester, and his first plays, *The Wages of Thin* (1969) and *Occupations* (1970), were staged there. These were followed by plays such as *The Party* (1973), *Comedians* (1975), *The Gulf Between Us* (1992), *Hope in the Year Two* (1994) and *Thatcher's Children* (1994).

Grignard, (François Auguste) Victor 1871–1935 •*French chemist and Nobel Prize winner*• Born in Cherbourg, he joined the chemistry department in Lyons, where he became "Chef de travaux pratiques" (1898) and began his work on the use of organomagnesium compounds in organic synthesis. Since then such compounds (Grignard reagents) have proved to be among the most useful and versatile reagents available for the synthesis of complex molecules, giving many different types of molecules under mild conditions. He received the Nobel Prize for chemistry in 1912 for this work.

Grigorovich, Yuri Nikolayevich 1927– •*Russian dancer, artistic director, teacher and choreographer*• Born in Leningrad (now St Petersburg), he trained at the Leningrad Choreographic School before joining the Kirov Ballet as a soloist in 1946. His first major ballet, *The Stone Flower* (1957), marked a new stage for Soviet choreography, which he followed with *Legend of Love* (1961). In 1964 he switched allegiance from the Kirov to the Bolshoi Ballet, creating pieces such as *Spartacus* (1968), for which he was awarded the Lenin prize in 1970, and *Ivan the Terrible* (1975). He has also staged new versions of the classics. Named a People's Artist of the USSR in 1973, he is married to Bolshoi dancer **Natalia Bessmertnova**. His resignation from the Bolshoi in 1995 prompted a strike by the dancers, led by Bessmertnova, which caused a performance to be canceled for the first time in the company's 219-year history. The ringleaders of the strike were subsequently fined and fired.

Grigson, Geoffrey Edward Harvey 1905–85 •*English poet, critic and editor*• He was born in Pelynt, Cornwall, and was the founder of the influential magazine *New Verse* (1933–39). He published several volumes of precisely observed and tersely expressed verse, gathered in *Collected Poems, 1924–62* (1963). A later *Collected Poems* included his subsequent work of 1963 to 1982, and was followed by *Montaigne's Tree* (1984). As a literary critic he was often outspoken. He was married to the cookbook writer **Jane Grigson**.

Grigson, (Heather Mabel) Jane 1928–90 •*English writer on cooking*• After graduating from Newnham College, Cambridge, she worked as an editorial assistant (1953–55) and as a translator from Italian (1956–67) before writing her first book, *Charcuterie and French Pork Cookery* (1967), which acknowledged the influence of **Elizabeth David** on her work. She became cooking correspondent for *The Observer* magazine and continued to write books, much influenced by her country lifestyle, including the three now regarded as cooking classics: *English Food* (1974), *Jane Grigson's Vegetable Book* (1978) and *Jane Grigson's Fruit Book* (1982). Her husband was the poet **Geoffrey Grigson**.

Grillparzer, Franz 1791–1872 •*Austrian dramatic poet*• Born in Vienna, he first attracted notice in 1817 with a tragedy, *Die Ahnfrau* ("The Ancestress"), followed by *Sappho* (1818, Eng trans 1820), *Das goldene Vlies* (1820, Eng trans *Medea*, 1879), *Der Traum ein Leben* (1834, Eng trans *A Dream Is Life*, 1946), and others. He wrote lyric poetry and one notable prose novel entitled *Der arme Spielmann* (1848, "The Poor Musician"), the only one of his works set in the Vienna of his day.

" "

Ich süchste dich und habe mich gefunden.
I sought you and I found myself.

1818 ***Sappho****, act 5, scene 6.*

Grimald, Nicholas 1519–62 •*English poet and playwright*• Born of Genoese ancestry in Huntingdonshire, he went to Christ's College, Cambridge, and became **Nicholas Ridley**'s chaplain, but recanted under **Mary I (Tudor)**. He contributed 40 poems to **Richard Tottel**'s *Songes and Sonettes* (1557), known as *Tottel's Miscellany*, and translated **Virgil** and **Cicero**. He also wrote two Latin verse tragedies on religious subjects.

Grimaldi, Francesco Maria 1618–63 •*Italian physicist*• Born in Bologna, he was educated by the Jesuits at Parma, Ferrar and Bologna, where he became Professor of Mathematics (1648). Among many other contributions, he verified **Galileo**'s laws of falling bodies, produced a detailed lunar map, and, more notably, discovered diffraction of light, and investigated interference and prismatic dispersion.

Grimaldi, Joseph 1779–1837 •*English comic actor, singer and acrobat*• Born in London, he first appeared at Sadler's Wells, London, in 1781 as an infant dancer. He appeared as the pantomime clown ("Joey") there and at Drury Lane, and from 1806 to 1823 was engaged at Covent Garden. Many of his innovations became the character's distinctive characteristics. His memoirs were edited by **Dickens**.

Grimké, Angelina Emily 1805–79 •*US feminist and social reformer*• Born in Charleston, South Carolina, she joined her sister **Sarah Grimké** in 1829 in Philadelphia, where she vigorously appealed to the women of the US to support their fight against slavery in *Appeal to the Christian Women of the South* (1836) and *Appeal to Women of the Nominally Free States* (1837). They became public figures, and Angelina went on a speaking tour. In 1838 she married the abolitionist **Theodore Weld** and gave up public life, though continuing to work for reform. Their most significant work was *American Slavery As It Is: Testimony of a Thousand Witnesses* (1838).

Grimké, Sarah Moore 1792–1873 •*US feminist and social reformer*• Born in Charleston, South Carolina, the daughter of a slave-owning judge, she deplored slavery. Moving to Philadelphia in 1821, she became a Quaker, and was joined by her sister **Angelina Grimké** in 1829. Together they campaigned for the abolition of slavery, moving to New York City, where they lectured for the American Anti-Slavery Society (the first women to do so), and broadened their concern to include women's emancipation. Sarah's works include *Epistle to the Clergy of the Southern States* (1836) and *The Condition of Women* (1838).

Grimm, Jacob Ludwig Carl 1785–1863 and **Wilhelm Carl** 1786–1859 •*German folklorists and philologists*• Born in Hanau, Hesse-Kassel, they were brothers who both studied in Marburg. In 1808 Jacob became librarian to **Jérôme Bonaparte**, king of Westphalia, and published a work on the Meistersingers (1811). In 1812 the brothers published the first volume of the famous *Kinder- und Hausmärchen* (*Grimm's Fairy Tales*, first translated as *German Popular Stories*, 1823). This work formed a foundation for the science of comparative folklore. The second volume followed in 1815, the third in 1822. In 1841 the brothers received professorships in Berlin, where they began to compile the monumental *Deutsches Wörterbuch* (1854–1961, "German Dictionary"). As a philologist, Jacob Grimm published *Deutsche Grammatik* (1819, "German Grammar"), perhaps the greatest philological work of the age, and formulated "Grimm's Law" of consonant sound changes, an elaboration of earlier findings by Johan Ihre (1707–80) and **Rasmus Rask**, but an important contribution to the subject. Wilhelm's chief independent work was *Die deutsche Heldensage* (1829, "The German Heroic Myth").

Grimmelshausen, Hans Jacob Christoffel von c. 1622–76 •*German novelist*• Born in Gelnhausen, Hesse-Kassel, he served on the Imperial side in the Thirty Years' War (1618–48). In later life he produced a series of remarkable novels, the best of which are on the model of the Spanish picaresque romances. The sufferings of the German peasantry at the hands of lawless troopers who overran the country have seldom been more powerfully pictured than in his *Der abenteuerliche Simplicissimus Teutsch und Continuatio* (1669, Eng trans *Simplicissimus the Vagabond*, 1924). It was followed by *Trutz Simplex* (1669, Eng trans *Mother Courage*, 1965), *Das wunderbarliche Vogelnest* (1672, "The Amazing Bird's Nest") and others.

Grimond, Jo(seph) Grimond, Baron 1913–93 •*Scottish Liberal politician*• Born in St Andrews and educated at Eton and Balliol College, Oxford, he was called to the bar in 1937, and served during World War II with the Fife and Forfar Yeomanry. In 1945 he ran for the Orkney and Shetland seat, which he ultimately won in 1950. From 1956 to 1967 he was leader of the Liberal Party, during which time Liberal representation in Parliament was doubled. He served again as party leader for a short period following the resignation of Jeremy Thorpe (1976). He retired from Parliament in 1983, when he was made a life peer. He published his *A Personal Manifesto* the same year.

Grinnell, Henry 1799–1874 •*US shipping merchant*• Born in New Bedford, Massachusetts, he financed an Arctic expedition to search for Sir **John Franklin** in 1850, and another in 1853 under **Elisha Kent Kane**. Grinnell Land was named after him.

Gris, Juan, *pseudonym of* **José Victoriano González** 1887–1927 •*Spanish painter*• Born in Madrid, he went in 1906 to Paris, where he associated with **Picasso** and **Matisse** and became an exponent of synthetic Cubism. He exhibited with the Cubists in the Section d'Or exhibition in Paris (1912), and in 1920 at the Salon des Indépendants. He settled at Boulogne and in 1923 designed the décor for three productions by **Sergei Diaghilev**. He also worked as a book illustrator.

Grisham, John 1955– •*US author*• Born in Jonesboro, Arkansas, he studied law at the University of Mississippi and set up his own legal practice before establishing himself as a best-selling writer of suspenseful courtroom dramas. *A Time to Kill* (1988) was well received but was far outstripped by the enormously successful *The Firm* (1991), which like many of Grisham's most popular stories has also been filmed. Best-selling titles since then have included *The Pelican Brief* (1992) and *The Brethren* (2000).

Grivas, Georgeios Theodoros 1898–1974 •*Greek-Cypriot nationalist leader*• Born in Trikomo, Cyprus, he commanded a Greek Army division in the Albanian campaign of 1940–41 and was leader of a secret organization called "X" (Khi) during the German occupation of Greece. In 1945 he headed an extreme nationalist movement against the Communists. Some nine years later he became head of the underground campaign against British rule in Cyprus. Founder and leader of EOKA (Ethnikí Orgánosis Kipriakoú Agónos, or the National Organization of Cypriot Struggle), he had a price of £10,000 on his head. After the Cyprus settlement (February 1959), Grivas left Cyprus and, acclaimed as a national hero by the Greeks, was promoted to general in the Greek army. He returned secretly to Cyprus in 1971 and directed a terrorist campaign for *enosis* (union with Greece) until his death.

Grock, *stage name of* **Adrien Wettach** 1880–1959 •*Swiss clown*• Born in Reconvilier, he became world-famous for his virtuosity in both circus and theater. He wrote several books, including *Ich lebe gern* (1930) and *Grock, King of Clowns* (1956, trans Creighton).

Gromyko, Andrei Andreyevich 1909–89 •*Soviet politician and diplomat*• Born near Minsk into a peasant family, he became a research scientist at the Soviet Academy of Sciences. In 1939 he joined the staff of the Soviet embassy in Washington DC, becoming ambassador in 1943 and attending the famous "big three" conferences at Tehran, Yalta and Potsdam. In 1946 he became Deputy Foreign Minister and was made permanent delegate to the UN Security Council, achieving an unenviable reputation through his use of the power of veto no fewer than 25 times. For a few months (1952–53) he was ambassador to the United Kingdom. He became Foreign Minister in 1957, holding this post until 1985, and being responsible for conducting Soviet relations with the West during the Cold War, showing no relaxation of the austere and humorless demeanor for which he had become notorious. During the 1970s, however, he adapted to the new policy of détente. **Mikhail Gorbachev** promoted him to the largely ceremonial and mainly domestic post of President in 1985, but he retired from office in 1988.

“ ”

This man, Comrades, has a nice smile, but he has iron teeth.

1985 Speech to the Supreme Soviet on proposing Mikhail Gorbachev as the new party leader.

Groot, Huig de *See* **Grotius, Hugo**

Gropius, Walter Adolph 1883–1969 •*US architect*• Born in Berlin, Germany, he studied in Munich and worked in the office of **Peter Behrens** in Berlin. After World War I he was appointed director of the Grand Ducal group of schools in art in Weimar, which he amalgamated and reorganized to form the Bauhaus, which aimed at a new functional interpretation of the applied arts, utilizing glass, metals and textiles. His revolutionary methods and bold use of unusual building materials were condemned as "architectural socialism" in Weimar, and the Bauhaus was transferred (in 1925) to Dessau, housed in a building that Gropius had designed for it. When the Nazis came to power the Bauhaus became a Nazi training school and Gropius went (1934–37) to London. In 1937 he emigrated to the US, where he became Professor of Architecture at Harvard (1938–52), and designed the Harvard Graduate Center (1949) and the American Embassy in Athens (1960).

Gros, Antoine Jean, Baron 1771–1835 •*French historical painter*• Born in Paris, he studied under **Jacques Louis David**, and later traveled with **Napoleon I**'s armies and acquired celebrity by his depictions of battles (1797–1811). Works such as his *Charles V and Francis I* (1812) and *Embarcation of the Duchess of Angoulême* (1815) combine classicism and romanticism. He subsequently attempted a return to classicism, but found his work ignored and drowned himself in the Seine.

Gross, Michael, *also called* **the Albatross** 1964– •*German swimmer*• Born in Frankfurt, a butterfly and freestyle swimmer, he won 13 gold medals between 1981 and 1987 for West Germany at the European championships. He has won three Olympic gold medals: the 100-meter butterfly and 200-meter freestyle in 1984, and the 200-meter butterfly in 1988.

Grosseteste, Robert c. 1175–1253 •*English prelate*• Born in Stradbroke, Suffolk, he was educated at Lincoln, Oxford and Paris, and became Bishop of Lincoln in 1235. He undertook the reformation of abuses, including the granting by Pope **Innocent IV** of English benefices to priests who used the income of their offices but seldom appeared in their parishes. In the last year of his life he refused the pope's request to promote his nephew, an Italian, to a canonry. The pope is said to have excommunicated him, but his clergy continued to work with him regardless.

Grossmith, George 1847–1912 •*English humorist, actor and writer*• He was born in London. In 1870 he became a singer and entertainer, creating several leading roles in the premieres of operettas by **Gilbert** and **Sullivan**. He published his *Reminiscences of a Clown* in 1888, and *Piano and I* in 1910. He is best remembered, though, for his collaboration with his brother Weedon Grossmith (1854–1919) on *The Diary of a Nobody*, serialized first in *Punch* and published in book form in 1892. An imaginary journal of domestic life in Holloway, London, it records the doings of the amiable, pompous city clerk Mr Pooter, striving to better himself culturally and socially but who, unwittingly, becomes the butt of numerous jokes he fails to understand.

“ ”

I left the room with silent dignity, but caught my foot in the mat.

1892 ***The Diary of a Nobody****, chapter 7.*

Grosz, George 1893–1959 •*US artist*• Born in Berlin, Germany, he was associated with the Berlin Dadaists in 1917 and 1918. While in Germany he produced a series of bitter, ironic drawings attacking German militarism and the middle classes. He fled to the US in 1932 (becoming naturalized in 1938) and went on to produce many oil paintings of a symbolic nature. He returned to Berlin in 1959, where he died.

Grósz, Károly 1930–96 •*Hungarian politician*• Born in Miskolc, he began his career as a printer and then a newspaper editor. He joined the ruling Hungarian Socialist Workers' Party (HSWP) in

1945, served as Budapest party chief (1984–87), and was inducted into the HSWP politburo in 1985. He became Prime Minister in 1987 and succeeded **János Kádár** as HSWP leader in 1988, giving up his position as Prime Minister six months later. Following the lead given by **Mikhail Gorbachev** in Moscow, he became a reformer in both the economic and political spheres. However, when, in 1989, the HSWP reconstituted itself as the new Hungarian Socialist Party (HSP), he was replaced as party leader by Rezso Nyers, a radical social democrat.

Grotius, Hugo, *also called* **Huig de Groot** 1583–1645 •*Dutch jurist, politician, diplomat, poet and theologian*• Born in Delft, he studied in Leiden, practiced in The Hague, and in 1613 was appointed Pensionary of Rotterdam. He was a political champion of the Remonstrants, and was imprisoned in 1618. In 1621 he escaped in a trunk from Loevestein Castle to Paris. Recognized as one of the founders of international law, he published his great work on the subject, *De jura belli et pacis* ("On the Law of War and Peace") in 1625. He led diplomatic missions for Sweden from 1634 until his death. He also wrote Latin and Dutch verse. His tragedy, *Adamus exsul*, was one of **Milton**'s sources, and he wrote the famous *De veritate religionis Christianae* (1627) and annotated the Bible (1641–46). His most impressive historical work is *Annales de rebus Belgicis* (1657).

Grotowski, Jerzy 1933–99 •*Polish theater director, teacher and drama theorist*• Born in Rzeszów, he trained at the Kraków Theater School. He founded the Theater of 13 Rows in Opole (1959–64), which moved to Wrocław as the Theater Laboratory (1965–84). In 1968 the company visited the Edinburgh Festival, and went on to London and New York City. In 1976 he disbanded his Laboratory Theater and began working with actors and students on shows of his own devising to which no audiences were admitted. His work had a major impact on experimental theater and actor training in the West in the 1960s and 1970s.

Grouchy, Emmanuel, Marquis de 1766–1847 •*French soldier*• Born in Paris, he fought at Hohenlinden, Eylau, Friedland and Wagram, and in the 1812 Russian campaign, and after Leipzig covered the retreat of the French. On **Napoleon I**'s escape from Elba he destroyed the **Bourbon** opposition in the south of France, and helped to rout **Gebhard von Blücher** at Ligny. After Waterloo (1815), he was Commander in Chief of the broken armies of France and led them skillfully back toward the capital before retiring to the US. He returned in 1819, and was reinstated as marshal in 1831.

Grove, Sir George 1820–1900 •*English musicologist, biblical scholar and civil engineer*• Born in London, he trained as a civil engineer, erected lighthouses, and worked on the Britannia tubular bridge. He became secretary and director of the Crystal Palace Company in 1852. Editor of *Macmillan's Magazine* (1868–83), he was a major contributor to Sir William Smith's *Dictionary of the Bible*. His major work was as editor of the *Dictionary of Music and Musicians* (4 vols, 1878–89; 6th ed 1980). His *Beethoven and His Nine Symphonies* (1896; new ed 1956) remained a standard work for years. Knighted in 1883 on the opening of the Royal College of Music, he was its director until 1895.

Grove, Sir William Robert 1811–96 •*Welsh physicist and jurist*• Born in Swansea, he was educated at Oxford. He invented a new type of voltaic cell named after him (1839), and also a "gas battery," the first fuel cell. He also invented the earliest form of filament lamp intended for use in mines. As Professor of Physics at the London Institution (1841–64), he studied electrolytic decomposition and demonstrated the dissociation of water. Thereafter he returned to law and became a judge in the High Court of Justice (1875–87). He was knighted in 1872.

Groves, Sir Charles Barnard 1915–92 •*English conductor*• He was born in London and studied at the Royal College of Music. He was appointed conductor of the BBC Northern Symphony Orchestra (1944–51), the Bournemouth Symphony Orchestra (1951–61), the Royal Liverpool Philharmonic Orchestra (1963–77), and the Leeds Philharmonic Society (1988–92). He also conducted with the Welsh National Opera (1961–63) and English National Opera (1978–79). He was knighted in 1973, and established a wide reputation, especially for his work in the early Romantics and in English music.

Grumman, Leroy Randle 1895–1982 •*US engineer and aircraft pioneer*• Born in Huntington, New York, he studied engineering at Cornell University, served as a navy pilot in World War I, then formed the Grumman Aircraft Engineering Corporation in Bethpage, Long Island. He produced a series of successful navy aircraft—the Wildcat, Hellcat, Bearcat and Tiger Cat—which played vital roles in the naval wars in the Pacific and the Atlantic in World War II. These were followed by the Panther, Cougar and Tiger jet fighters, and several attack and search aircraft. Grumman built the Lunar Excursion Module (LEM) for the Apollo flights to the moon.

Grün, Anastasius *See* **Auersperg, Anton Alexander, Graf von**

Grünewald, Matthias, *originally perhaps* **Mathis Nithardt**, *otherwise* **Gothardt** c. 1475–1528 •*German artist, architect and engineer*• Born probably in Würzburg, Bavaria, very little is known of his life, but he was trained in Alsace in the style of **Martin Schongauer**, and became court painter to the Archbishop of Mainz (1508–14) and to Cardinal Albrecht of Brandenburg (1515–25), and he designed waterworks for Magdeburg (c. 1526). In 1516 he completed the great Isenheim altarpiece (Colmar Museum, Alsace), the nine paintings of which exhibit his rare livid colors and his use of distortion to portray passion and suffering. Toward 1524 he painted an even more dramatic *Crucifixion* (Karlsruhe, Kunsthalle) with its greenish, blood-spattered body of Christ.

Guardi, Francesco 1712–93 •*Italian painter*• Born in Pinzolo, he was a pupil of **Canaletto**, and was noted for his views of Venice, full of sparkling color, with an impressionist's eye for light effects. His *View of the Church and Piazza of San Marco* is in the National Gallery, London. His brothers, Giovanni Antonio (1669–1760) and Nicolò (1715–86), often collaborated with him.

Guardia, Fiorello H(enry) la *See* **La Guardia, Fiorello H(enry)**

Guare, John 1938– •*US dramatist*• Born in New York City, he studied at the Yale School of Drama. He won an Obie award for *The House of Blue Leaves* (1971), which investigated the grotesquely inappropriate ambitions of a family in the borough of Queens. In later plays, such as *Six Degrees of Separation* (1990) and *Four Baboons Adoring the Sun* (1992), he has written in a style more naturalistic but still highly inventive. His screenplays for *Atlantic City* (1981) and for the film version of *Six Degrees of Separation* (1991) were nominated for Academy Awards.

Guareschi, Giovanni 1908–68 •*Italian journalist and writer*• He was born in Parma, and became editor of the Milan magazine *Bertoldo*. After World War II, in which he was a prisoner, he wrote *Mondo piccolo "Don Camillo"* (1950, Eng trans *The Little World of Don Camillo*, 1951), which brought him fame. These stories of a village priest and a Communist mayor, with their broad humor and rich humanity, have been translated into many languages. They were followed by *Mondo piccolo "Don Camillo e il figliol prodigo"* (Eng trans *Don Camillo and the Prodigal Son*, 1952) and others.

Guarini, Guarino, *originally* **Camillo** 1624–83 •*Italian Baroque architect, philosopher and mathematician*• Born in Modena, he became a Theatine monk at the age of 15. A love of complexity and movement in all dimensions is the keynote of his work. He designed several churches in Turin—of which the only two survivors are San Lorenzo (1668–80) and the Capella della Sindone (1668)—and the Palazzo Carignano (1679), as well as palaces for Bavaria and Baden. He also published books on mathematics, astronomy and architecture. His influential *Architectura civile* (published posthumously in 1737), concerns the relationship of geometry and architecture.

Guarnieri or **Guarneri** •*Italian family of violin makers*• From Cremona, the most important were Andrea (fl. 1650–95), his sons Giuseppe (fl. 1690–1730) and Pietro (fl. 1690–1725), and Giuseppe's son Giuseppe (fl. 1725–45), the last commonly known as Giuseppe del Gesù (of Jesus) because he signed his violins with IHS (Iesu hominum salvator) after his name.

Guderian, Heinz (Wilhelm) 1888–1953 •*German general*• After serving in World War I, he stayed in the small army allowed to Germany by the Treaty of Versailles, and pioneered mechanized warfare. Created general of panzer (armored) troops in 1938, he advocated fast-moving *Blitzkrieg* warfare which he later put into brilliant effect, commanding forces in France and the USSR. He had a stormy relationship with **Hitler** and was dismissed and reinstated several times.

Guelf, *properly* **Welf** •*German dynasty*• The first known Welf was a Frankish noble with lands in Bavaria and Swabia (c. 825). The family was most powerful under **Henry the Lion**, Duke of Saxony and Bavaria, but **Frederick I (Barbarossa)** took both duchies, only allowing him the area of Braunschweig-Lüneburg, which became a duchy in 1235 for Henry's grandson Otto. They became electors (1692) and later kings (1814) of Hanover, and in 1714 the elector George Ludwig became **George I** of England. The death of **William IV** (1837) separated the British and Hanoverian crowns, when Salic law prevented **Victoria** from ruling Hanover. Her cousin, **George V** of Hanover, lost his throne to Prussia in 1866. In medieval Italy, the term Guelfs represented political factions supporting the papacy and the Angevin rulers of Naples. Their opponents were the imperialist Ghibellines, who were originally supporters of the **Hohenstaufen** dynasty.

Guercino, *literally* **"the Squint-Eyed,"** *properly* **Gian-Francesco Barbieri** 1590–1666 •*Italian painter of the Bolognese school*• Born in Cento, he painted the famous *Aurora* at the Villa Ludovisi in Rome for Pope **Gregory XV**. In 1642, after the death of **Guido Reni**, he became the dominant painter of Bologna, combining in his work the liveliness and movement of the **Carracci** with a warmer, more Venetian coloring.

Guericke, Otto von 1602–86 •*German engineer and physicist*• Born in Magdeburg, he studied law and mathematics, mechanics and the art of fortification. After devising a vacuum pump, he arranged a dramatic demonstration of the effect of atmospheric pressure on a near vacuum in 1654 at Regensburg before the emperor **Ferdinand III**. Two large metal hemispheres were placed together and the air within pumped out. They could not then be separated by two teams of eight horses, but fell apart when the air was allowed to re-enter. He showed that in a vacuum candles cannot remain alight and small animals die, and he devised several experiments that demonstrated the elasticity of air. He also carried out some experiments in electricity and magnetism.

Guerra, Tonino (Antonio) 1920– •*Italian screenwriter*• Born in Sant'Arcangelo, Emilia Romagna, he was a poet and novelist before writing for the cinema. He began a lengthy partnership with director **Michelangelo Antonioni**, and their most notable films include *La Notte* (1961, "The Night") and *Il deserto rosso* (1964, "The Red Desert"). He received Academy Award nominations for his contribution to the screenplays for *Casanova '70* (1965), *Blow-Up* (1966) and *Amarcord* (1973). Among his other scripts are *Cadaveri eccellenti* (1976, "Illustrious Corpses") for Francesco Rosi, *La notte di San Lorenzo* (1981, "The Night of San Lorenzo") for the Taviani brothers and *Stanno tutti bene* (1990, "Everybody's Doing Fine") for Guiseppe Tornatore.

Guerrouj, Hicham el- 1974– •*Moroccan athlete*• Born in Berkane, he won the world indoor title in the 1,500 meters in 1995 and went on to set six world records at various distances, becoming in 1999 the first athlete to hold world record times in the mile and the 1,500 meters, both indoors and outdoors. The dominant figure in middle-distance running, he won the 1,500 meters at the world championships in 1997, 1999 and 2001.

Guesclin, Bertrand du c. 1320–80 •*French soldier, Constable of France*• Born near Dinan, he displayed military skill against the English, particularly at Rennes (1356) and Dinan (1357), until he was taken prisoner at Auray and ransomed. He next supported Henry of Trastamare against Pedro, the Cruel, king of Castile, but was defeated and taken prisoner by **Edward the Black Prince** (1367). Again ransomed, he defeated Pedro in 1369, and crowned Henry of Trastamare, but was recalled by **Charles V** of France to be made Constable of France. In 1370 he opened his campaigns against the English, and soon nearly all their possessions were in the hands of the French. He died during the Siege of Châteauneuf de Randon.

Guevara, Che, *properly* **Ernesto Guevara de la Serna** 1928–67 •*Argentine Communist revolutionary leader*• Born in Rosario, he graduated in medicine from the University of Buenos Aires (1953), then joined **Fidel Castro**'s revolutionary movement in Mexico (1955), played an important part in the Cuban revolution (1956–59) and afterward held government posts under Castro. He left Cuba in 1965 to become a guerrilla leader in South America, and was captured and executed by government troops in Bolivia while trying to foment a revolt. He became an icon for left-wing youth in the 1960s. His writings include *Guerrilla Warfare* (1961).

Guggenheim, Meyer 1828–1905 •*US industrialist*• Born in Langnau, Switzerland, he emigrated to the US in 1847 and made a fortune in the copper industry. He had seven sons, including the famous philanthropists Simon Guggenheim (1867–1941), who established the Guggenheim Foundation (1925) to provide scholars, writers, and artists with grants for studying or working abroad, and Solomon Robert Guggenheim (1861–1949), who endowed the Solomon R Guggenheim Museum (1937) in New York City. His granddaughter, **Peggy Guggenheim**, was also an art patron.

Guggenheim, Peggy (Marguerite) 1898–1979 •*US art collector*• Born in New York City, she went to live in Paris (1930–1941), socializing with all the prominent artists of the time and purchasing many paintings by new (now famous) artists. During World War II she returned to the US with the artist **Max Ernst**, to whom she was married (1941–45), and opened a gallery called "Art of This Century" in New York. There the works of the European artists, as well as those of **Jackson Pollock**, **Mark Rothko** and **Hans Hofmann**, were exhibited, changing the course of US art. After the war, Guggenheim moved to Venice, where she lived on the Grand Canal in the Palazzo Venier dei Leoni, which now houses the famous Guggenheim Collection.

Guilhem or **Guillaume, 9th Duke of Aquitaine, 7th Count of Poitou** 1071–1126 •*The earliest known troubadour*• The establishment in his territory of the proto-Catharist mystical order of Fontrevrault offers the key to the understanding of a man who, on the one hand, sacrificed an army of 60,000 men in a pointless crusade (1101), and on the other possibly "invented" *amour courtois* (courtly love"). He left 11 poems whose high quality no one has doubted: five are capably and amusingly obscene, one is an exercise, and the rest are exquisitely cryptic.

Guillaume, Charles Édouard 1861–1938 •*Swiss physicist and Nobel Prize winner*• Born in Fleurier, he was educated at the University of Neuchâtel and at the Zurich Polytechnic, and became director of the Bureau of International Weights and Measures at Sèvres. In this post he redetermined the volume of the liter, and investigated the effect of thermal movement on standards of length. His search for a material with little or no thermal expansion or contraction led to the discovery of a nickel-steel alloy, christened "Invar," the use of which significantly improved the accuracy and stability of timekeeping devices, precision instruments and standards of measurement. For this discovery Guillaume was awarded the Nobel Prize for physics in 1920.

Guillemin, Roger (Charles Louis) 1924– •*US physiologist and Nobel Prize winner*• Born in Dijon, France, he studied at the Universities of Dijon and Lyons, and held posts at Baylor University School of Medicine in Houston (1953–70) and the Salk Institute, San Diego (1970–89). Guillemin and his colleagues isolated and identified the chemical structures of hypothalamic hormones, principally the hormone that stimulates the thyroid gland, and the hormones that release and inhibit the growth hormone. These discoveries have important applications, and potential uses for the treatment of various endocrinological diseases. Guillemin and **Andrew Schally** shared half of the 1977 Nobel Prize for physiology or medicine, with the other half awarded to **Rosalyn Yalow**.

Guillén, Jorge 1893–1984 •*Spanish poet*• He was born in Valladolid and began his career as an academic at the University of Seville. The first edition of his most important work, *Cántico* (1928), was a collection of poems consisting of what the author termed pure poetry—verse stripped of the prosaic, the explanatory or the merely functional. His other major work is *Homage* (1967). His critical works include *Language and Poetry* (1961).

Guillén, Nicolás 1902–89 •*Cuban poet*• He was born in Camagüey. His poetry is famous for its relating of Black to Latin-American themes. He was the first to recognize that the Black presence on his island was not merely exotic. He became Cuba's best-known poet, celebrated even by the illiterate. Much of his poetry is political, as was natural from a man who for many years was a leading member of the Communist Party of Cuba. Volumes of his poetry in translation include *Man-Making Words* (1972).

Guillotin, Joseph Ignace 1738–1814 •*French doctor and revolutionary*• He was born in Saintes. As a deputy in the Estates General in 1789, he proposed to the Constituent Assembly the use of a decapitating instrument, which was adopted in 1791 and was named after him, although similar instruments had been used earlier in Scotland, Germany and Italy.

Guimarães Rosa, João 1908–69 •*Brazilian novelist and short-story writer*• Born in Cordisburgo, Minas Gerais, he practiced as a doctor before becoming a diplomat in 1932. The chief area of his concern was that of Euclydes da Cunha, the backlands of Brazil. *Sagarana* (1946, rev edn 1958, Eng trans 1966) collects nine "parables of the sertão," some of them about animals. One of the most important Latin-American writers of the 20th century, he is best known for *Grande Sertão: Veredas* (1956, rev edn 1958), for which its translators chose the title *The Devil to Pay in the Backlands* (1968).

" "

Um está sempre no escuro, só no último derradeiro é que clareiam a sala.
One is always in the dark, and it is only at the last moment that they turn on the lights in the room.

1956 ***Grande Sertão: Veredas.***

Guimard, Hector Germain 1867–1942 •*French architect*• Born in Lyons, he was the most important Art Nouveau architect active in Paris between 1890 and World War I. For his impressive architectural plan, the *Castel Béranger* apartment block (1894–98), he designed every aspect of the building and its interiors. He is best known for the famous Paris Métro entrances of the early 1900s, many of which are still in place.

Guimerá, Ángel 1849–1924 •*Catalan poet and dramatist*• He was born in Santa Cruz, Tenerife. His work falls into three periods, of which the first and third—for the most part, historical plays—show the influence of the French Romantics. His middle period owes its preoccupation with contemporary life to **Ibsen**. He is regarded as the greatest Catalan dramatist. His best-known play is *Terra Baixa* (1896, "Lowlands"), on which Eugen d'Albert based his opera *Tiefland*.

Guin, Ursula K le *See* **Le Guin, Ursula K(roeber)**

Guinness, Sir Alec 1914–2000 •*English actor*• Born in London, he trained to become an actor at the Fay Compton Studio of Dramatic Art. He made his stage debut in *Libel* (1934), and joined the Old Vic in 1936 where he played *Hamlet* (1938). He rejoined the company in 1946 after serving in the Royal Navy throughout World War II. He made his film debut as an extra in *Evensong* (1934) but began his cinema career in earnest with the **Dickens** adaptations *Great Expectations* (1946) and *Oliver Twist* (1948). Long associated with Ealing Studios, his many comic triumphs include *Kind Hearts and Coronets* (1949), *The Lavender Hill Mob* (1951) and *The Ladykillers* (1955). He received a Best Actor Oscar for *The Bridge on the River Kwai* (1957). Other films include *Lawrence of Arabia* (1962), *Star Wars* (1977) and *Little Dorrit* (1988). Although infrequent, his many distinguished stage performances include *The Cocktail Party* (1949–50), *A Voyage Round My Father* (1971) and *A Walk in the Woods* (1989). His television work includes two appearances as inscrutable spycatcher George Smiley in *Tinker, Tailor, Soldier, Spy* (1979) and *Smiley's People* (1982). He was knighted in 1959.

Guinness, Sir Benjamin Lee 1798–1868 •*Irish brewer*• Born in Dublin, the grandson of Arthur Guinness (1725–1803), founder of Guinness's Brewery (1759), he joined the firm at an early age, and became sole owner at his father's death (1855). Under him the brand of stout became famous and the business grew into the largest of its kind in the world. He was the first Lord Mayor of Dublin in 1851 and a Member of Parliament from 1865 to 1868.

Guiscard, Robert c. 1015–85 •*Norman adventurer*• He was born near Coutances, and as the champion of Pope Nicholas II, he campaigned with his brother Roger I (1031–1101) of Sicily against the Byzantine Greeks in southern Italy and Sicily (1060–76). In 1059 the papacy recognized him as Duke of Apulia, Calabria, and Sicily. He defeated the Byzantine emperor **Alexius I Comnenus** in 1081 at Durazzo. He interrupted his march on Constantinople (Istanbul) to liberate Pope **Gregory VII** from the emperor Henri IV in Italy (1084), and died during his second attempt on Constantinople.

Guise, Charles of 1525–74 •*French prelate*• He was the son of Claude of Lorraine, 1st Duke of **Guise** and brother of **Mary of Guise** and Francis, 2nd Duke of Guise, with whom he became all-powerful in the reign of **Francis II**. Archbishop of Rheims, he was created Cardinal of Guise in 1547. He introduced the Inquisition into France and exerted a great influence at the Council of Trent (1562–64).

Guise, Claude of Lorraine, 1st Duke of 1496–1550 •*French nobleman and soldier*• Born at the Château of Condé, Lorraine, the fifth son of René II, Duke of Lorraine, he fought under **Francis I** at Marignano, Italy, in 1515, but subsequently remained at home to defend France against the English and Germans, and defeated the army of the Holy Roman emperor **Charles V** at Neufchâteau. He was regent during the captivity of Francis (1525–26). For suppressing a peasant revolt in Lorraine (1527) he was made Duke of Guise. His daughter, **Mary of Guise**, married **James V** of Scotland and was the mother of **Mary Queen of Scots**.

Guise, Francis, 2nd Duke of, *called* **Le Balafré ("the Scarred")** 1519–63 •*French soldier and politician*• The son of Claude of Lorraine, 1st Duke of **Guise**, he commanded the expedition against Naples in 1556, and took Calais (1558), bringing about the Treaty of Château Cambrésis (1559). He and his brother, Cardinal **Charles of Guise**, shared the main power in the state during the reign of **Francis II** (of France). They headed the Roman Catholic Party, sternly repressing Protestantism. With the Duc de Montmorency, he defeated the Huguenots at Dreux (1562), and was besieging Orleans when he was assassinated by a Huguenot.

Guise, Henri, 3rd Duc de 1550–88 •*French soldier and politician*• The son of Francis, 2nd Duke of **Guise**, he was one of the contrivers of the St Bartholomew's Day Massacre (1572) and was the head of the Holy League against the **Bourbon**s (1576).

Guise, Mary of *See* **Mary of Guise**

Gulbenkian, Calouste Sarkis 1869–1955 •*British financier, industrialist and diplomat*• Born in Scutari, Turkey, of Armenian descent, he entered his father's oil business in Baku in 1888. He became a naturalized British subject in 1902. In 1940 in Vichy France, the five-percent Iraq Petroleum Company interest was confiscated by Great Britain, and he was declared an "Enemy under the Act," whereupon he assumed Persian citizenship. From 1948 to 1954 he negotiated oil concessions between the US and Saudi Arabia. He left $70 million and vast art collections to finance an international Gulbenkian Foundation.

Gummer, John Selwyn 1939– •*English Conservative politician*• Born in Stockport, he was educated at Selwyn College, Cambridge, and worked in publishing. In 1970 he was elected Conservative Member of Parliament for Lewisham West. Although he was defeated in the 1974 general election, he returned to Parliament in 1979 as Conservative Member of Parliament for Eye (Suffolk Coastal from 1983). He was Secretary of State for Agriculture (1989–93) and Secretary of State for the Environment (1993–97). He retained his seat in the 1997 general election when Labour came to power.

Gunn, Neil M(iller) 1891–1973 •*Scottish novelist*• He was born in Dunbeath, Caithness, the son of a fisherman. Educated at the village school and privately in Galloway, he passed the civil service examination in 1907, and moved to London. He was in the civil service until 1937. After writing a number of short stories, he published his first novel, *Grey Coast* (1926), which was immediately acclaimed, following it with books such as *The Lost Glen* (serialized in 1928), *Morning Tide* (1931), *Highland River* (1937, James Tait Black Memorial Prize), *Wild Geese Overhead* (1939), *Bloodhunt* (1952) and *The Other Landscape* (1954).

Gunn, Thom(son) William 1929– •*English poet*• Born in Gravesend, Kent, he attended Trinity College, Cambridge, and moved to the US in 1954. From 1990 to 1999 he was a senior lecturer in English at the University of California, Berkeley. His first collection, *Fighting Terms* (1954), labeled him a "Movement" poet. Other volumes include the existentialist *The Sense of Movement* (1957), the contemplative *My Sad Captains* (1961), *The Passages of Joy* (1982) and *The Man with Night Sweats* (1992), which includes a series of elegies on men who died as a result of AIDS. *Boss Cupid* was published in 2000.

“ ”

At worst, one is in motion; and at best,
Reaching no absolute, in which to rest,
One is always nearer by not keeping still.

1957 "On the Move."

Gunnell, Sally (Jane Janet) 1966– •*English track and field athlete*• Born in Chigwell, Essex, she is the only female British athlete to have won world, Olympic, European and Commonwealth titles. She won a gold medal in the 100-meter hurdles at the Commonwealth Games in 1986, and golds at the Commonwealth Games in 1990 and the Olympic Games in 1992. She became world champion in 1993 in a record time of 52.74 seconds and set a new world record in the 400-meter hurdles in Stuttgart, also winning that event in the European Cup. She won the European and Commonwealth titles in 1994. She retired in 1997 and now works as a television commentator.

Gunter, Edmund 1581–1626 •*English mathematician and astronomer*• Born in Hertfordshire and educated at Christ Church, Oxford, in 1619 he became Professor of Astronomy at Gresham College, London. He invented many measuring instruments that bear his name: Gunter's chain, the 22-yard (20.1-meter) long 100-link chain used by surveyors; Gunter's line, the forerunner of the modern slide rule; Gunter's scale, a navigational rule; and the portable Gunter's quadrant. He made the first observation of the variation of the magnetic compass, and introduced the words "cosine" and "cotangent" into the language of trigonometry.

Gurdjieff, Georgei Ivanovich c. 1865–1949 •*Armenian thinker*• He was born in or near Kars. He practiced as a healer in St Petersburg (1910–17) and in 1914 met **Peter Ouspensky**, who became his disciple. He left Russia during the Revolution and in 1922 moved to Fontainebleau, France, where he set up the Institute for the Harmonious Development of Man. It was here that **Katherine Mansfield** died in 1923. A charismatic modern Christian gnostic, Gurdjieff synthesized an extraordinary and profound system that influenced many writers.

Guðjónsson, Halldór *See* **Laxness, Halldór Kiljan**

Gurdon, Sir John Bertrand 1933– •*English geneticist*• Born in Dippenhall, Hampshire, he was educated at Oxford. Since 1983 he has been John Humphrey Plummer Professor of Cell Biology at Cambridge, and since 1991, chairman of the Wellcome Cancer Research Campaign Institute. Gurdon solved one of the central questions in biology in the 20th century, investigating the mechanism by which one cell type (the fertilized egg) gives rise to all the different cell types in the adult animal. In 1968 he transplanted a nucleus derived from frog gut into a fertilized egg, and produced a normal tadpole. This demonstrated that fully differentiated animal cells retain the genetic information to become any cell type under the correct environmental stimuli. He was knighted in 1995.

Gurevich, Mikhail Iosifovich 1893–1976 •*Soviet aircraft designer*• Born in Rubanshchina, near Kursk, he graduated in 1925 from the aviation faculty of Kharkov Technological Institute. He was best known for the fighter aircraft produced by the design bureau he headed with **Artem Mikoyan**, the MiG (Mikoyan and Gurevich) series.

Gurney, Ivor 1890–1937 •*English composer and poet*• Born in Gloucester, he studied composition at the Royal College of Music, London, under **Charles Stanford**. Gassed and shell-shocked in 1917, he published two volumes of poems (the first while he was in the hospital): *Severn and Somme* (1917) and *War's Embers* (1919). He returned to the Royal College to study with **Ralph Vaughan Williams**, and published his first songs, *5 Elizabethan Songs* (1920), which are considered his best work. From 1922 he was confined in an asylum. Some 300 of his songs and 900 poems survive.

Gustav I Vasa 1496–1560 •*King of Sweden and founder of the Vasa dynasty*• He was born in Lindholmen, Uppland, into an aristocratic Swedish family. He was taken to Denmark (1518) as a hostage, on the orders of King **Christian II**, but managed to escape. After the death of his father in the infamous Stockholm Bloodbath (1520), he led an uprising against Christian, captured Stockholm (1523) and was elected king by the Diet, effectively ending the Kalmar Union. An orator of impressive presence and a hard worker, Gustav imposed order and peace on the demoralized kingdom. He introduced the Lutheran Reformation, made himself head of the Swedish Church, and confiscated Catholic Church properties, using the revenues to build up a well-organized standing army and navy. He was succeeded by his son **Erik XIV**. Ruthless in dealing with opponents, he crushed a series of revolts, and left the country united and stable.

Gustav II Adolf, *originally* **Gustavus Adolphus**, *known as* **the Lion of the North** 1594–1632 •*King of Sweden, a champion of Protestantism*• Born in Stockholm, he was the son and successor of **Charles IX** and grandson of **Gustav I Vasa**. When he came to the throne in 1611 he found the country immersed in wars and disorder, but he quickly appeased the nobility, reorganized the government, and revitalized the army. He made a favorable peace at Knäred (1613) with Denmark, defeated Russia (1613–17) and received a large part of Finland and Livonia from Poland through the Treaty of Stolbova (1617). He fought King **Sigismund III Vasa** of Poland (1621–29) for the Swedish throne, took Livonia and forced a favorable six-year truce with the Treaty of Altmark (1629). This left him free to intervene directly in the Thirty Years' War (1618–48) on behalf of the Protestants against the Catholic League of the Habsburg Holy Roman Emperor **Ferdinand II**. Leaving the government in the care of the chancellor, **Axel Oxenstjerna**, he crossed to Pomerania in 1630 with 15,000 men and took Stettin (now Szczecin, Poland). In 1631 he failed to prevent the massacre of Magdeburg by Count von **Tilly**, but in September of that year he decisively defeated Tilly at Breitenfeld, near Leipzig, and took the Palatinate and Mainz. In the spring of 1632 he advanced into Bavaria, defeated and killed Tilly and captured Augsburg and Munich. The emperor Ferdinand's forces, now under **Albrecht von Wallenstein**, met him in November 1632 at Lützen, near Leipzig, and although the Swedes won, Gustav Adolf was killed. A leader of impressive abilities, he left Sweden the strongest power in Europe and reformed the country's central and local administration.

Gustav III 1746–92 •*King of Sweden*• Born in Stockholm, he was the son of King **Adolf Fredrik**. A brilliant and captivating figure, when he ascended the throne in 1771 he was determined to break the power of the oligarchy of nobles. He arrested the council, declared a new form of government (1772), and encouraged agriculture, commerce and science. He granted religious toleration, but also created a secret police system and introduced censorship. His court became a northern Versailles, with the foundation of the Royal Opera House (1782), the Swedish Academy (1786) after the French pattern, and the Royal Dramatic Theater (1788). With poor harvests and a failing economy creating discontent, as a diversion he launched into a war against Russia (1788–90) that proved unpopular and inconclusive, and in 1789 he assumed new royal prerogatives as absolute monarch. At the beginning of the French Revolution he planned to use his army to help **Louis XVI**, but in 1792 he was shot by a former army officer, and later died. He was succeeded by his young son, **Gustav IV Adolf**.

Gustav IV Adolf 1778–1837 •*King of Sweden*• Born in Stockholm, he was the son and successor (1792) of **Gustav III**. In the first years of his reign as an absolute monarch he did much to improve

Swedish agriculture with a General Enclosure Act (1803). He abandoned Swedish neutrality to declare war on France (1805) and when Russia became an ally of **Napoleon I**, the Swedes lost their last German possessions. In 1808 Sweden was attacked by Denmark, and Finland was simultaneously invaded and then annexed by Russia. He was arrested in a military coup and forced to abdicate (1809). He was exiled with his family, and after divorcing his wife (1812) wandered alone in Europe for 25 years as Colonel Gustafsson until he died in Switzerland.

Gustav V 1858–1950 •*King of Sweden*• Born in Stockholm, the son and successor (1907) of **Oskar II**, he was shy and reserved by nature. He disliked pomp and spectacle and refused a coronation ceremony, thus becoming the first uncrowned king on the Swedish throne. On the outbreak of World War I, Sweden mobilized but remained neutral. Thereafter he reigned as a popular constitutional monarch, and in World War II came to symbolize the unity of the nation. He was the longest-reigning king in Swedish history. In 1881 he married Princess Viktoria, daughter of the Grand Duke of Baden and granddaughter of Sofia of Sweden (**Gustav IV Adolf**'s daughter), thus uniting the reigning Bernadotte dynasty with the former royal House of Vasa. His nephew was Count Folke **Bernadotte**. He was succeeded by his son, **Gustav VI**.

Gustav VI 1882–1973 •*King of Sweden*• He was born in Stockholm, the son and successor of **Gustav V**, and became a respected scholar and archaeologist and an authority on Chinese art. He married (1905) Princess Margaret (1882–1920), granddaughter of Queen **Victoria**, by whom he had four sons and a daughter, Ingrid, who married King **Frederik IX** of Denmark. In 1923 he married Lady Louise Mountbatten (1889–1965), sister of Earl **Mountbatten** of Burma. On Gustav's accession (1950) Lady Louise became the first British-born queen in Swedish history. The king worked to transform the Crown into a democratic monarchy, which helped to preserve it against political demands for a republic. As his eldest son, Gustav Adolf (1906–47), was killed in an air crash, he was succeeded by his grandson, **Carl XVI Gustaf**.

Gutenberg, Beno 1889–1960 •*US geophysicist*• Born in Darmstadt, Germany, he studied geophysics and mathematics at Darmstadt Technische Hochschule, and earned a PhD from the University of Göttingen. From 1913 to 1916 he was an assistant at the International Seismological Association in Strassburg (now Strasbourg, France). There he made the first correct determination of the depth to the Earth's core, which he concluded is liquid.

Gutenberg, Johannes Gensfleisch 1400–68 •*German printer, regarded as the inventor of printing*• He was born in Mainz, and between 1430 and 1444 he was in Strasbourg, probably working as a goldsmith, and it is there (by 1439) that he may have begun printing. Living in Mainz again by 1448, he entered into partnership (c. 1450) with Johann Fust, who financed a printing press. This partnership ended in 1455; Fust sued him for the debt when the loan was not repaid, and received the printing plant in lieu of payment. He carried on the concern with the assistance of his son-in-law Peter Schöffer and completed the famous Bible which Gutenberg had begun, while Gutenberg, aided by Konrad Humery, set up another printing press. Although Gutenberg is credited with the invention of printing, it is probable that rudimentary printing was practiced before his development of the art. Apart from his Forty-Two-Line Bible, Gutenberg is credited with the *Fragment of the Last Judgment* (c. 1445), and editions of **Aelius Donatus**'s school grammar.

Guthorm or **Guthrum** d. 890 •*Danish King of East Anglia*• An opponent of King **Alfred** the Great, he led a major Viking invasion of Anglo-Saxon England in 871 (the "Great Summer Army"), seized East Anglia, and conquered Northumbria and Mercia. He attacked Wessex (878) and drove Alfred into hiding in Somerset. Alfred recovered sufficiently to defeat the Danes at the crucial Battle of Edington, Wiltshire (878). In the ensuing treaty, Guthorm agreed to leave Wessex and accept baptism as a Christian, and he and his army settled down peacefully in East Anglia.

Guthrie, Janet 1938– •*US racecar driver*• Born in Iowa City, Iowa, she began building and racing cars in 1962. In 1976 she became the first woman to race in a NASCAR Winston Cup event, and the following year she became the first woman to compete in the Indianapolis 500, though she did not finish. Her 1978 Indianapolis 500 driver's suit and helmet are in the Smithsonian Institution in Washington DC, and she is in the International Women's Sports Hall of Fame.

Guthrie, Woody (Woodrow Wilson) 1912–67 •*US folksinger, songwriter and author*• He was born in Okemah, Oklahoma. A folk poet in the true sense, he traveled the length and breadth of the US and wrote hundreds of songs about his experiences, using mostly traditional country music and blues themes. His concern for the poor turned into active campaigning for trade unions and racial equality in the 1930s and 1940s, and, along with **Pete Seeger**, he formed the influential radical group the Almanac Singers. He wrote many much-loved songs for children, but it is for classic folksong statements like "This Land Is Your Land," "So Long It's Been Good to Know You," and "Pastures of Plenty" that he is best remembered. In the 1950s his career was prematurely ended by Huntington's chorea, an inherited degenerative disease. His son, Arlo Guthrie (1947–), became a popular figure on both the folk and rock scenes from the late 1960s.

" "

You can't write a good song about a whore-house unless you been in one.

*1964 Quoted in **Broadside**.*

Gutiérrez, Gustavo 1928– •*Peruvian theologian*• He was born in Lima. Abandoning medical studies for the Roman Catholic priesthood, he studied at Louvain (1951–55) and Lyons (1955–59) before ordination in Lima, becoming Professor of Theology at the Catholic University there in 1960. His seminal work, *A Theology of Liberation* (1971, Eng trans 1973), is dedicated to "doing" theology, based on responding to the needs of the poor and the oppressed rather than on imposing solutions from the outside. His arguments have challenged supporters of the status quo in Latin America and practitioners of academic theology elsewhere. His other works include *The Power of the Poor in History* (1984), *We Drink from Our Own Wells* (1984) and *On Job* (1987).

Gutiérrez Alea, Tomás 1928–96 •*Cuban film director*• He was born in Havana and trained in law before moving to Rome in the early 1950s to study film. On his return to Cuba in 1953 he began making films supporting the struggle against the **Batista** regime and after the revolution he helped found the national revolutionary film institute ICAIC (*Instituto del Arte y Industria Cinematográfica*), directing films such as *Stories of the Revolution* (1960) and *Memories of Underdevelopment* (1968). Later films include *The Last Supper* (1976) and *Strawberry and Chocolate* (1994), which featured a gay critic of the **Castro** regime and was nominated for an Academy Award.

Guy of Lusignan d. 1194 •*French crusader*• He became king of Jerusalem in 1186 as consort of Sibylla, daughter of Amalric I, but was defeated and captured at Hattin (1187) by **Saladin**, who overran most of the kingdom. On the death of his wife in 1190 the throne passed to Conrad of Montferrat (d. 1192), but Guy received Cyprus as compensation, where his family ruled until 1474.

Guy, Buddy (George) 1936– •*US blues guitarist and singer*• Born in Lettsworth, Louisiana, he began playing in his native Louisiana, but his mature style was not formed until he moved to Chicago in 1957, where he inherited the electric urban blues style of **Muddy Waters** and **B B King**. His frenetic style won him fans in the rock audience in the 1960s, helped by admiring endorsements from **Jimi Hendrix** and **Eric Clapton**.

Guy, Thomas c. 1644–1724 •*English bookseller and philanthropist*• Born in Horselydown, Southwark, he amassed a fortune by importing and printing bibles, and by selling out South Sea shares. He was Member of Parliament from 1695 to 1707. In 1707 he built and furnished three wards of St Thomas's Hospital, London, and in 1722 he founded the hospital in Southwark, Guy's Hospital, which bears his name. He also built and endowed almshouses.

Guyon, Jeanne Marie de la Mothe, *née* **Bouvier** 1648–1717 •*French mystic*• Born in Montargis, she became a widow at 28, and determined to devote her life to the poor and needy, and to the cultivation of spiritual perfection. To this end, she went to Geneva (1681), but three years later was forced to leave on the grounds that her Quietist doctrines were heretical. In Turin, Grenoble, Nice, Genoa, Vercelli and Paris, where she finally settled in 1686, she became the center of a movement for the promotion of "holy living." In 1688 she was arrested for heretical opinions, but released by the intervention of Madame de **Maintenon**. Imprisoned in 1695, she was not released from the Bastille until 1702. Her works include *Les Torrents spirituels, Moyen court de faire oraison* (1685, The Short and Very Easy Method of Prayer").

Guzman, Martín Luis 1887–1976 •*Mexican novelist, editor and journalist*• He was born in Chihuahua. Originally a lawyer, he became a supporter of **Francisco Madero**, and then, after the latter's assassination, private secretary to **Pancho Villa**. Guzmán was the most important novelist of the revolution, all the events of which he recorded in his fiction. His novels include *El águila y la serpiente* (1928, Eng trans *The Eagle and the Serpent*, 1930), *La sombra del caudillo* (1929, "In the Shadow of the Leader") and *Memorias de Pancho Villa* (1938–51, Eng trans *Memoirs of Pancho Villa*, 1965), the last of which is certainly a novel, but told in the authentic voice of the illiterate caudillo.

Guzmán Blanco, Antonio 1829–99 •*Venezuelan politician*• Born in Caracas and educated in Europe, he was violently anticlerical and a bitter opponent of **José Antonio Páez**. He was Vice President from 1863 to 1868, when he was driven from office. He then headed a revolution which restored him to power in 1870, and became dictator, holding the presidency on three occasions (1873–77, 1879–84, 1886–88). He died in exile.

Gwyn, Nell (Eleanor), *also spelled* **Gwynn** or **Gwynne** c.1650–87 •*English actress, and mistress of Charles II*• Born of humble parents, she lived precariously selling oranges before establishing herself as a comedienne at Drury Lane, London, especially in breeches parts. "Pretty, witty Nell's" first protector was Lord Buckhurst, but the transfer of her affections to **Charles II** was genuine. She had at least one son by the king—Charles Beauclerk, Duke of St Albans—and James Beauclerk is allegedly a second. She is said to have urged Charles to found Chelsea Hospital.

" "

Pray, good people, be civil; I am the Protestant whore.

1675 Attributed, when angry crowds pressed round her carriage in the belief that she was Charles II's unpopular Catholic mistress, Louise de Kérouaille.

Gwynne, Nell *See* **Gwyn, Nell**

Gwynne-Vaughan, Dame Helen Charlotte Isabella, *née* **Fraser** 1879–1967 •*English botanist and servicewoman*• Educated at Cheltenham Ladies' College and King's College London, she became head and later Professor of Botany at Birkbeck College, London (1909). She became an authority on fungi. In World War I she was organizer (1917) and later controller of the Women's Army Auxiliary Air Force in France, and commandant of the Women's Royal Auxiliary Air Force (1918–19). In World War II she was chief controller of the Women's Auxiliary Territorial Service (1939–41).

Gyatso, Geshe Kelsang 1931– •*Tibetan Buddhist teacher and monk*• He was born in western Tibet and spent 15 years at Sera Je monastery and a further 20 years in meditation in the Himalayas before moving to Great Britain in 1977. The founder of the modernizing New Kadampa tradition of Buddhism, he is the Spiritual Guide at the Manjushri Buddhist Center in Ulverston, Cumbria, and has founded numerous centers around the world. His books include *Introduction to Buddhism* (1992).

Gyges d. c. 648 BC •*King of Lydia*• He came to power in c. 685 BC, when he murdered his predecessor, Candaules, married his wife, and became king of Lydia. He also founded the Marmnad dynasty. Under him, Lydian power and wealth began to grow, and close relations developed with the Greeks. He initiated an aggressive policy toward the Greek cities of Asia Minor that his successors continued down to **Croesus**, also cultivating good relations with the Oracle of Apollo at Delphi, and with **Ashurbanipal** of Assyria. He died fighting an invasion of the Cimmerians.

H

Haakon VII 1872–1957 •*King of Norway*• Born in Charlottenlund, Denmark, he was the second son of King **Frederik VIII**, and was elected king of Norway (1905) when the country voted for independence from Sweden. In 1896 he married Princess Maud, youngest daughter of King **Edward VII** of Great Britain. When Germany invaded Norway (1940) he refused to abdicate, and carried on the resistance from Great Britain, returning in triumph in 1945. He was succeeded by his son, **Olav V**.

Haber, Fritz 1868–1934 •*German physical chemist and Nobel Prize winner*• Born in Breslau (Wrocław, Poland), he studied at the Universities of Berlin and Heidelberg, and at the Technische Hochschule, Charlottenberg. In 1904 he began to study the direct synthesis of ammonia from nitrogen and hydrogen gases, in association with **Carl Bosch**; this led to the large-scale production of ammonia. This was important in maintaining an explosives supply for the German war effort from 1914 to 1918. It also led to Haber receiving the Nobel Prize for chemistry in 1918. This occasioned some criticism because he had been involved in the organization of gas warfare. In 1911 he moved to Berlin to direct the Kaiser Wilhelm Institute for Physical Chemistry and Electrochemistry; however, he resigned in 1933 in protest of the anti-Jewish policies of the Nazi regime.

Habsburg or **Hapsburg** •*Royal dynasty of Austria-Hungary*• The first Count of Habsburg was Werner I (d. 1096). His descendant, Count Rudolf IV, was elected king of Germany (1273) as **Rudolf I**, de facto the first Habsburg emperor, although he was never anointed by the pope. The first recognized emperor was **Frederick III** of Germany, crowned in 1452. From that time, with one interruption from 1742 to 1745, the imperial crown was a family possession until the empire was dissolved in 1806. The zenith of Habsburg power was reached under the emperor **Charles V** (Charles I of Spain), who presided over an empire stretching from the Danube to the Caribbean. After his death the House of Habsburg divided into two lines; the Spanish line died with **Charles II** of Spain (1700), but the Austrian line continued until the abdication of **Charles** (1887–1922), the last Habsburg-Lorraine emperor of Austria and Hungary, in 1918.

Hácha, Emil 1872–1945 •*Czechoslovakian lawyer and politician*• Born in Trhové Sviny (now in the Czech Republic), he became president of Czechoslovakia in 1938 on **Eduard Beneš**'s resignation following the German annexation of the Sudetenland; under duress, he turned over the state to **Hitler** in 1939. He was puppet president of the subsequent German protectorate of Bohemia and Moravia. Arrested after liberation in 1945, he died in prison.

Häckel, Ernst Heinrich Philipp August *See* **Haeckel, Ernst Heinrich Philipp August**

Hackman, Gene (Eugene Alden) 1930– •*US actor*• Born in San Bernardino, California, he was a marine and had studied journalism before pursuing acting at the Pasadena Playhouse. Moving into film, he received Academy Award nominations for *Bonnie and Clyde* (1967) and *I Never Sang for My Father* (1970) before winning the award for his performance as the obsessive cop "Popeye" Doyle in *The French Connection* (1971). His star roles include *The Poseidon Adventure* (1972), *The Conversation* (1974), *Night Moves* (1975) and *Eureka* (1982). He received a further Academy Award nomination for *Mississippi Burning* (1988) and won the Best Supporting Actor award for *Unforgiven* (1992). Other films include *Twilight* (1998) and *Under Suspicion* (2000).

Hadamard, Jacques Salomon 1865–1963 •*French mathematician*• Born in Versailles and educated in Paris, he became lecturer in Bordeaux (1893–97), the Sorbonne (1897–1909), Paris, and then professor at the Collège de France and the École Polytechnique. He worked in complex function theory, differential geometry and partial differential equations, and in 1896 he and the Belgian mathematician Charles de la Vallée Poussin independently proved the definitive form of the prime number theorem.

Hadlee, Sir Richard John 1948– •*New Zealand cricket player*• He was born in Christchurch. He and his father, Walter, and brother Dayle represented New Zealand at Test level. He made his Test debut for New Zealand in 1973. In 1988 he became the first bowler to take more than 400 Test wickets, several times taking 10 or more wickets in a match. He set a new world record of 431 wickets in 1990, the year he retired, and still holds the New Zealand record for most wickets in a series.

Hadrian, *in full* **Publius Aelius Hadrianus** AD 76–138 •*Roman emperor*• Born probably in Rome, of Spanish origin, he was the ward and protégé of the emperor **Trajan**. He became prefect of Syria (AD 114), and after Trajan's death was proclaimed emperor by the army (117). He concluded a peace with the Parthians, and after appeasing the invaders of Moesia, he established his authority at Rome, and suppressed a conspiracy against his life (118). He spent little of his reign in Rome, and from c. 120 he visited Gaul, Germany, Britain (where he built the wall named after him from the Solway Firth to the Tyne), Spain, Mauretania, Egypt, Asia Minor and Greece. After crushing a major revolt in Judea (132–34), he returned to Italy, where he died. Although at times ruthless and tyrannical, he was an able administrator, and a patron of the arts and architecture.

Hadrian IV *See* **Adrian IV**

Haeckel or **Häckel, Ernst Heinrich Philipp August** 1834–1919 •*German naturalist*• Born in Potsdam, he gave up the study of medicine to study anatomy at the University of Jena, where he became Professor of Zoology (1862–1909). He made expeditions to the Mediterranean, Madeira, Canaries, Arabia, India and elsewhere. The first to attempt a genealogical tree of all animals, he postulated the idea that in its embryological development, each species illustrates its evolutionary history. Known as the "German Darwin," he was a charismatic and enthusiastic ambassador for evolution, and many of his books, including *The Evolution of Man* (1874) and *Welträtsel* (1899, "The Riddle of the Universe"), became bestsellers.

“ ”

God … a gaseous vertebrate.

1899 ***Welträtsel***.

Hafiz or **Hafez**, *pseudonym of* **Mohammad Shams od-Din Hafez** c. 1326–90 •*Persian lyric poet*• Born in Shiraz, he was named by his contemporaries Chagarlab (Sugar-lip) because of the sweetness of his poetry. His *ghazals* (short poems) are all on sensuous subjects—wine, flowers, beautiful damsels—but they also possess an esoteric significance. Like nearly all the great poets of Persia, he belonged to the sect of Sufi philosophers.

Hagen, Walter Charles, *nicknamed* **the Haig** 1892–1969 •*US golfer*• Born in Rochester, New York, he was the first US-born winner of the British Open championship, which he won four times (1922, 1924, 1928–29). He won the US Open twice (1914, 1919), the US Professional Golfers' Association championship five times (1921, 1924–27), a record since equaled by **Jack Nicklaus**, and captained the first six US Ryder Cup teams (1927–37).

Haggard, Sir H(enry) Rider 1856–1925 •*English novelist*• He was born in Bradenham Hall, Norfolk. Educated at Ipswich Grammar School, he went to Natal in 1875 as secretary to Sir Henry Bulwer, and next year accompanied Sir Theophilus Shepstone to the Transvaal. He returned to England in 1881, married, and settled down to a literary life. He wrote a number of books on South Africa, but is remembered for his 34 vivid and fast-paced adventure novels, especially *King Solomon's Mines* (1885). This was followed by *She* (1887), *Allan Quatermain* (1887), *Ayesha: The Return of She* (1905) and many other stories.

Haggard, Merle (Ronald) 1937– •*US country music singer and songwriter*• Born in Bakersfield, California, he is one of the most influential artists in the history of country music. His early experiences included serving prison sentences for various crimes, material which later surfaced in his music, as did his parents' experiences as migrants from the Oklahoma Dust Bowl in the 1930s. He made his first record in 1963, and went on to achieve stardom with a string of hits later in the decade. His tribute albums helped restore interest in pioneering figures **Jimmie Rodgers**, Bob Wills and Lefty Frizzell.

Hague, William Jefferson 1961– •*English Conservative politician*• Born in Wentworth, Yorkshire, he addressed the 1977 Tory conference and received a standing ovation. He was educated at Oxford, and entered Parliament as Member of Parliament for Richmond, Yorkshire, in 1989. He rose quickly to be Secretary of State for Wales (1995–97) and he became leader when **John Major** resigned following Labour's landslide win in the 1997 general election. He then resigned following defeat in the 2001 general election and was succeeded by **Iain Duncan Smith**.

Hahn, Otto 1879–1968 •*German radiochemist and Nobel Prize winner*• Born in Frankfurt am Main, he studied at the Universities of Marburg and Munich. From 1907 to 1938 much of his work was done in collaboration with the Austrian physicist **Lise Meitner**. Hahn was involved in the discovery of several new radioactive isotopes, among them thorium 228, thorium 227 and mesothorium, but his best-known research was on the irradiation of uranium and thorium with neutrons. This work led to the discovery of nuclear fission (1938), and for this Hahn received the Nobel Prize for chemistry in 1944. Greatly upset that his discovery led to the horror of Hiroshima and Nagasaki, he became a staunch opponent of nuclear weapons.

Hahnemann, (Christian Friedrich) Samuel 1755–1843 •*German physician and founder of homeopathy*• Born in Meissen, he studied in Leipzig, and for 10 years practiced medicine. After experiments on the curative power of cinchona bark (the source of quinine), he came to the conclusion that drugs produce a condition in healthy persons very similar to that which they relieve in the sick. This was the origin of his famous principle, *similia similibus curantur* (like cures like). His own infinitesimal doses of medicine provoked the apothecaries, who refused to dispense them. Accordingly, he illegally gave his medicines to his patients, free of charge, and was prosecuted in every town in which he tried to settle from 1798 until 1810. Many of his drugs were herbal in origin, and subsequent homeopathists have continued to emphasize natural remedies.

Haidar or **Hyder Ali** 1728–82 •*Indian soldier and Muslim ruler of Mysore*• He was born in Budikote, and by his bravery he attracted the notice of the maharajah of Mysore's prime minister, and soon rose to power, ousting both prime minister and rajah (c. 1761). He conquered Calicut, Bednor and Cannanore, and by 1766 his dominions included more than 84,000 square miles (218,000 sq km). Defeated by the Marathas (1772), he claimed British support, but when this was refused he became their enemy. Taking advantage of the war between Great Britain and the French (1778), he and his son **Tippoo Sahib** routed the British in the Carnatic, but were defeated in three battles by Sir **Eyre Coote**.

Haig, Alexander Meigs, Jr 1924– •*US soldier and public official*• Born in Philadelphia, and educated at West Point, the Naval War College and Georgetown University, he joined the US Army in 1947. He served in Korea (1950–51) and Vietnam (1966–67) and was made a general in 1973. During the **Nixon** presidency he was deputy to **Henry Kissinger** in the National Security Council, and became White House Chief of Staff (1973–74) at the height of the Watergate scandal. Returning to military duty in 1974 he became NATO's Supreme Allied Commander, Europe (1974–79). He was President **Reagan**'s secretary of state (1981–82), and unsuccessfully sought the Republican Party's presidential nomination in 1988.

Haig (of Bemersyde), Douglas Haig, 1st Earl 1861–1928 •*Scottish field marshal*• Born in Edinburgh, he was educated at Oxford and Sandhurst. Active service in Egypt and South Africa, followed by assignments in India, led to his appointment in 1911 as General Officer Commanding Aldershot. In August 1914 he took the 1st Corps of the British Expeditionary Force to France, and succeeded Sir **John French** as Commander in Chief in December 1915. Haig was forced to wage a costly and exhausting war of attrition, for which he was much criticized. However, under the overall command of Marshal **Foch**, Haig led the final successful offensive of August 1918. In the postwar years he organized the Royal British Legion. His earldom was awarded in 1919.

Haile Selassie I, *previously* **Prince Ras Tafari Makonnen** 1891–1975 •*Emperor of Ethiopia*• He was born near Harer. Son of Ras Makonnen, he led the revolution (1916) against Lij Yasu, and became regent and heir to the throne. In 1930 he became emperor of Ethiopia. A Coptic Christian, he westernized the institutions of his country. He settled in England after the Italian conquest of Abyssinia (1935–36), but in 1941 was restored after the liberation by British forces. In the early 1960s he played a crucial part in the establishment of the Organization of African Unity (OAU). The disastrous famine of 1973 led to economic chaos, industrial strikes and mutiny among the armed forces, and in 1974 he was deposed in favor of the crown prince, though he was allowed to return to his palace in Addis Ababa. Accusations of corruption leveled against him and his family have not destroyed the unique prestige and reverence in which he is held by certain groups, notably the Rastafarians.

Hailey, Arthur 1920– •*Canadian novelist*• He was born in Luton, Bedfordshire, England, and became a naturalized Canadian in 1947. He has written many bestselling blockbusters about disasters, several of which enjoyed a new lease of life when filmed. Titles include *Hotel* (1965), *Airport* (1968), *Wheels* (1971), *Strong Medicine* (1984), *The Evening News* (1990) and *Detective* (1997).

Hailsham, Quintin McGarel Hogg, 2nd Viscount 1907–2001 •*English jurist and politician*• He was born in London, the son of Douglas Hailsham. Educated at Eton College and Christ Church, Oxford (president of the Union, 1929), he became a Fellow of All Souls in 1931. In 1932 he was called to the bar and from 1938 to 1950 he was Member of Parliament for Oxford City. He became viscount in 1950, and, among several political posts, was First Lord of the Admiralty (1956–57), Minister of Education (1957), Lord President of the Council (1957–59, 1960–64), and chairman of the Conservative Party (1957–59). He was Minister for Science and Technology (1959–64), and Secretary of State for Education and Science (1964). In the Conservative leadership crisis of 1963, he renounced his peerage for life, and was reelected to the House of Commons in the St Marylebone by-election. In 1970 he was made a life peer (Baron Hailsham of Saint Marylebone) and became Lord Chancellor (1970–74, 1979–87).

Haitink, Bernard 1929– •*Dutch conductor*• Born in Amsterdam, in 1964 he became chief conductor with the Amsterdam Concertgebouw Orchestra. He was appointed principal conductor of the London Philharmonic Orchestra in 1967, and was its artistic director from 1969 to 1978. He was appointed music director of the Glyndebourne Festival (1977), and of the Royal Opera House, Covent Garden (1987). He has toured internationally and, in addition to opera, is an acclaimed interpreter of **Bruckner** and **Mahler**. He was given the honorary title Knight Commander, Order of the British Empire, in 1977.

Hakkinen, Mika 1968– •*Finnish racecar driver*• Born in Helsinki, he won the Formula Three world championship in 1990. A year later he made his debut in Formula One, driving for Lotus-Judd. He switched to McLaren in 1993 and won his first victory at the

European Grand Prix in 1997. He secured the Formula One championship in 1998, reclaimed it once more in 1999, and was runner-up, behind **Michael Schumacher**, in 2000.

Hakluyt, Richard c. 1552–1616 •*English geographer, cleric and historian*• Born in Hertfordshire, he was educated at Westminster School and Christ Church, Oxford. His works include *Principal Navigations, Voyages, and Discoveries of the English Nation* (1589, and enlarged in 3 vols, 1598–1600), which contained accounts of the voyages of the **Cabots**, Sir **Francis Drake**, Sir **Humphrey Gilbert**, Sir **Martin Frobisher** and many others. The Hakluyt Society was instituted in 1846 to promote an interest in geography and the maintainance of records of expeditions and geographical writings.

Halas, John, *originally* **John Halasz** 1912–95 •*British animated-cartoon producer*• Born in Budapest, Hungary, he moved to London, where he met and married **Joy Batchelor** and formed the Halas-Batchelor animation unit. The producers of more than 2,000 films between 1940 and 1980, they also made the world's first fully digitized film, *Dilemma*, in 1982.

Haldane, Elizabeth Sanderson 1862–1937 •*Scottish writer*• Born in Edinburgh, she was the sister of **John Scott Haldane** and **Richard Burdon Haldane**. She studied nursing, for a while managed the Royal Infirmary, Edinburgh, and became the first woman justice of the peace in Scotland (1920). She wrote a biography of **Descartes** (1905) and edited his philosophical works, translated **Hegel** and wrote commentaries on **George Eliot** (1927) and Mrs **Gaskell** (1930).

Haldane, J(ohn) B(urdon) S(anderson) 1892–1964 •*Indian biologist*• Born in Oxford, England, he was the son of physiologist **John Scott Haldane**, and the brother of **Naomi Mitchison**. He studied at Oxford and became Reader in Biochemistry at Cambridge (1922–32), then switched to population genetics and the mathematics of natural selection. He became Professor of Genetics at the University of London (1933–37), but again switched to the chair of biometry at University College London (1937–57), and studied underwater conditions and submarine safety. In 1957 he emigrated to India, adopted Indian nationality, and became professor at the Indian Statistical Institute in Calcutta, but resigned in 1961. His numerous popular works included *Animal Biology* (with **Julian Huxley**, 1927), *Possible Worlds* (1927), *Science and Ethics* (1928), *The Inequality of Man* (1932), *Fact and Faith* (1934), *Heredity and Politics* (1938), and *Science in Everyday Life* (1939).

Haldane, John Scott 1860–1936 •*Scottish physiologist*• Born in Edinburgh, he was the younger brother of Richard Burdon, 1st Viscount **Haldane**, and father of **J B S Haldane** and **Naomi Mitchison**. He graduated in medicine from the University of Edinburgh in 1884, became a demonstrator and Reader in Medicine at Oxford (1887–1913), and was elected a Fellow of New College, Oxford. He developed the famous Haldane gas analysis apparatus in 1898, but his best-known research was concerned with the chemical control of ventilation, and he was an authority on the effects of industrial occupations upon respiration.

Haldane, Richard Burdon Haldane, 1st Viscount 1856–1928 •*Scottish jurist, philosopher and Liberal politician*• Born in Edinburgh, he was educated at the Universities of Edinburgh and Göttingen, and was called to the bar in 1879. He entered Parliament in 1879 as a Liberal. He is remembered for his term as Secretary of State for War (1905–12), when he remodeled the army, founded the Territorial Army and made the plans by which British mobilization took place in 1914. He was Lord Chancellor from 1912 to 1915 and again in 1924 following his move to the Labour Party.

Hale, George Ellery 1868–1938 •*US astronomer*• Born in Chicago, he studied at MIT and established in 1891 the Kenwood Observatory in Chicago, a private institution which became well known through its work in solar spectroscopy. In that year, simultaneously with **Henri Deslandres** (1853–1948) in France but independently of him, he invented the spectroheliograph. He was appointed the first director of the Mount Wilson Observatory in California in 1905, and the next year he set up the first tower telescope for solar research there. He discovered and measured magnetic fields in sunspots.

Hale, Nathan 1755–76 •*American Revolutionary War hero*• He was born in Coventry, Connecticut. He joined the Continental Army in 1775 and was captured and hanged by the British as a spy. Revered as a national hero, he is also the "patron saint" of US espionage agencies, and his statue stands at the headquarters of the CIA in Langley, Virginia.

“ ”

I only regret that I have but one life to lose for my country.

1776 At his execution, September 22.

Hale, Sarah Josepha, *née* **Buell** 1788–1879 •*US writer*• Born in Newport, New Hampshire, she embarked on a literary career on the death of her husband in 1822, in order to support herself and her five young children. In 1828 she became the first female editor of the *Ladies' Magazine* in Boston. She wrote a novel, *Northwood* (1827), and a book of *Poems for Our Children* (1830), which contained "Mary Had a Little Lamb." From 1837 to 1877 she was editor of the popular and influential women's magazine the *Lady's Book*. She advocated the education of women and wrote *Woman's Record, or, Sketches of All Distinguished Women from "the Beginning" till* A.D. *1850* (1853, 1869, 1876).

Hales, Stephen 1677–1761 •*English botanist and chemist*• Born in Bekesbourne, Kent, he entered Corpus Christi College, Cambridge in 1696. In 1709 he became vicar of Teddington. He was one of the founding members of the Society for the Encouragement of Arts, Manufactures and Commerce, now the Royal Society of Arts. He was also chaplain to Prince George, later **George III**. Hales's *Vegetable Staticks* (1727) was the foundation of plant physiology, setting standards in the methodology of biological experimentation. His most important work was on the water balance of plants, and he was the first to measure root and leaf suction and root pressure.

Halévy, (Jacques François) Fromental (Élie), *originally* **Elias Lévy** 1799–1862 •*French composer*• Born in Paris, he had early success with the opera *Clari* (1828). His masterpiece, *La Juive* (1835, "The Jewess"), made him famous across Europe. The same year, he produced the comic opera, *L'éclair* ("The Lightning Flash"), and followed it with about a dozen other operatic works. His *éloges* were collected as *Souvenirs et portraits* (1861–63, "Souvenirs and Portraits"). His brother was the writer Léon Halévy (1802–83).

Halévy, Ludovic 1834–1908 •*French playwright and novelist*• He was born in Paris, the son of the writer Léon Halévy (1802–83). With Henri Meilhac (1831–97) he wrote libretti for the best-known operettas of **Offenbach**, and for **Bizet**'s *Carmen*, and produced vaudevilles and comedies. His *Madame et Monsieur Cardinal* (1873) and *Les petites Cardinal* (1880) are delightful sketches of Parisian theatrical life. Other works include *L'invasion* (1872), *Un grand mariage* (1883, "A Grand Marriage"), *Princesse* (1884) and *Mariette* (1893).

Haley, Alex Palmer 1921–92 •*US novelist and biographer*• Born in Ithaca, New York, and raised in North Carolina, he worked in the Coast Guard for 20 years from 1939. He turned to writing with the publication of *The Autobiography of Malcolm X* (coauthor, 1965). *Roots* (1976) was a phenomenal success, being adapted for television and winning a Pulitzer Prize the following year. Beginning with the life of Kunta Kinte, an African who was enslaved and taken to the US, it documented the history of African Americans.

Haley, Bill, *originally* **John Clifton Haley** 1925–81 •*US pioneer of rock 'n' roll*• Born in Highland Park, Michigan, he began his career as a country music singer. With his band The Comets he had an international hit with "Rock Around the Clock" (1955), which was featured in the film *The Blackboard Jungle* (1955), directed by Richard Brooks (1912–92). Since then Haley has become synonymous with the beginnings of rock and roll. Other songs include "Shake, Rattle and Roll" and "See You Later, Alligator."

Halifax, Charles Montagu, 1st Earl of 1661–1715 •*English statesman and poet*• He was born in Horton, Northamptonshire, and educated at Westminster and Trinity College, Cambridge. As a poet his most notable achievement was the parody of **Dryden**'s *The Hind and the Panther*, entitled *The Story of the Country Mouse and the City Mouse* (1687), jointly written with **Matthew Prior**. As a lord of the Treasury in 1692 he established the national debt with a loan of £1,000,000 sterling. In 1694 he originated the Bank of England, and was appointed Chancellor of the Exchequer, raising a tax on windows to pay for the recoinage in 1695, and introducing Exchequer bills. In 1697 he became prime minister, but he was unpopular, and when the Tories came into power in 1699 he retired from the Commons to the Exchequer. On **George I**'s arrival he became an earl and First Lord of the Treasury.

Halifax, Edward Frederick Lindley Wood, 1st Earl of (2nd creation) 1881–1959 •*English Conservative politician*• Born at Powderham Castle, Devon, he was the grandson of Sir Charles Wood, 1st Viscount Halifax (1800–85) and a descendant of Charles Montagu, 1st Earl of **Halifax** (1st creation). He became (as Baron Irwin, 1925) Viceroy of India (1926–31), Foreign Secretary (1938–40) under **Neville Chamberlain**, whose appeasement policy he implemented, and ambassador to the US (1941–46). He was made earl in 1944.

Halifax, George Savile, 1st Marquis of 1633–95 •*English statesman*• Born in Thornhill, Yorkshire, he was made viscount (1668) for his part in the Restoration, and in 1672 was made marquis and Lord Privy Seal. In 1675 he opposed Lord Danby's (see Duke of **Leeds**) Test Bill, and in 1679 by a display of extraordinary oratory he procured the rejection of the Exclusion Bill. On the accession of **James VII and II** in 1685, he became President of the Council, but was dismissed soon after for opposing the repeal of the Test and Habeas Corpus Acts. One of the three commissioners appointed by James II to negotiate with William of Orange (later **William III**) after he landed in England, on James's flight he gave allegiance to William and resumed the office of Lord Privy Seal, but joined the Opposition and resigned his post in 1689.

“ ”

Men are not hanged for stealing horses, but that horses may not be stolen.

c. 1687 ***Political Thoughts and Reflections***.

Hall, Ben(jamin) 1837–65 •*Australian bushranger*• Born in New South Wales, son of an English convict, at 16 he married the daughter of a wealthy cattleman and settled down to farming. In 1862 he was arrested for armed robbery but was acquitted and freed. On returning home he found that his wife had left him, taking their young son. In anger Hall joined a gang led by Frank Gardiner, and was soon rearrested, on suspicion of involvement with the Eugowra gold robbery. Again released, Hall committed to a life of outlawry and a series of audacious raids followed. He was betrayed by a companion and shot dead by the police at the age of 28.

Hall or **Halle, Edward** c. 1499–1547 •*English historian*• Born in London, he was educated at Eton and King's College, Cambridge, where he was elected Fellow, and at Gray's Inn (one of the four Inns of Court, the societies that have the exclusive right of calling people to the bar). His *Union of the Two Noble Illustre Famelies of Lancastre and Yorke* (1542, commonly called *Hall's Chronicle*) was completed only to 1532; the rest, to 1546, was completed by the editor, **Richard Grafton**.

Hall, G(ranville) Stanley 1844–1924 •*US psychologist and educationist*• He was born in Ashfield, Massachusetts. He studied at the University of Leipzig, then taught at Antioch College, Ohio, followed by posts at Harvard and at Johns Hopkins University, where in 1882 he introduced experimental psychology on a laboratory scale. In 1887 he founded the *American Journal of Psychology*. He exercised a profound influence on the development of educational psychology and child psychology in the US, and became the first president of Clark University (1889–1920). His works include *The Contents of Children's Minds* (1883) and *Life and Confessions of a Psychologist* (1923).

Hall, Joseph 1574–1656 •*English prelate and writer*• Born in Ashby-de-la-Zouch, Leicestershire, he studied at Cambridge from 1589, and became dean of Worcester (1617). In the same year he accompanied **James VI and I** to Scotland to help establish church government by bishops. As Bishop of Exeter (1627–41) he was suspected by Archbishop **Laud** of Puritanism. As Bishop of Norwich (1641–47) he protested with other prelates against the validity of laws passed during their enforced absence from Parliament, and was imprisoned for seven months in the Tower of London and deprived of his episcopal income. Among his works are *Mundus alter et idem* (c. 1605, "The World Different and the Same") and the poetical satires *Virgidemiarum* (1597–98).

Hall, Marshall 1790–1857 •*English physician and physiologist*• Born in Basford, Nottinghamshire, he studied medicine at the University of Edinburgh. After further study in Paris, Göttingen and Berlin, he returned to Nottingham in 1817, where he practiced medicine. In 1826 he moved to London, where he was elected a Fellow of the Royal College of Physicians. He wrote copiously on many aspects of medicine, including the circulation of the blood and respiration, developed a successful technique for resuscitating the drowned, and notably opposed the immoderate blood-lettings then considered an essential part of treatment.

Hall, Sir Peter Reginald Frederick 1930– •*English theater, opera and film director*• Born in Bury St Edmunds, Suffolk, he was educated at St Catherine's College, Cambridge. After working in repertory and for the Arts Council, he was artistic director of the Elizabethan Theatre Company (1953), assistant director of the London Arts Theatre (1954) and director in 1955–56, and he formed his own production company, The International Playwrights' Theatre. He became director of the Royal Shakespeare Company (RSC), and remained as managing director of the company's theaters in Stratford and London until 1968, making his name by giving many of the classics a social context. Among his many productions during this period were the *Wars of the Roses* trilogy (*Henry VI Parts 1, 2* and *3*, and *Richard III*, 1963), **Harold Pinter**'s *The Homecoming* (1965) and **Nikolai Gogol**'s *The Government Inspector* (1966). Continuing to direct for the RSC, he was also from 1969 to 1971 director of the Covent Garden Opera. His operatic productions there and at Glyndebourne include *The Magic Flute* (1966), *Tristan and Isolde* (1971) and *A Midsummer Night's Dream* (1981). In 1973 he succeeded **Laurence Olivier** as director of the National Theatre; his notable productions there include *No Man's Land* (1975), *Amadeus* (1979) and the *Oresteia* (1981). In 1983 he became artistic director of the Glyndebourne Festival. Among his films are *Perfect Friday* (1971) and *Akenfield* (1974). Hall left the National Theatre in 1988, and that year set up the Peter Hall Company. He was knighted in 1977.

Hall, (Marguerite) Radclyffe 1880–1943 •*English writer*• She was born in Bournemouth, Dorset, and educated at King's College London, and then in Germany. She began as a lyric poet with several volumes of verse, but turned to novel writing with *The Forge* and *The Unlit Lamp* (both 1924). Her *Adam's Breed* (1926) won the Femina Vie Heureuse and the Tait Black Memorial prizes, but *The Well of Loneliness* (1928), which deals openly with lesbianism, was prosecuted for obscenity, and was banned in Great Britain for many years. It was republished in 1949.

Hall, Willis 1929– •*English dramatist*• Born in Leeds, his first stage success was *The Long and the Short and the Tall* (1958), dealing with the members of a British military patrol lost in the Malayan jungle in 1942. He followed this with the short plays *Last Day in Dreamland* and *A Glimpse of the Sea* (both 1959). He has since collaborated extensively with **Keith Waterhouse**, notably on *Billy Liar* (1960), derived from the latter's novel. *Saturday, Sunday, Monday* (1973) and *Filumena* (1973), based on plays by the Italian dramatist Eduardo de Filippo, were both enormous successes.

Hallé, Sir Charles, *originally* **Carle Halle** 1819–95 •*British pianist and conductor*• Born in Hagen, Westphalia, he studied first in Darmstadt, and from 1840 in Paris. Driven to England by the Revolution of 1848, Hallé settled in Manchester, where in 1858 he founded his famous orchestra. This did much to raise the standard of musical taste by familiarizing the British public with the great classical masters, and he was knighted in 1888.

Halle, Edward *See* **Hall, Edward**

Halleck, Henry Wager 1815–72 •*US soldier*• Born in Westernville, New York, he served in the Mexican War (1846–48) and, having taken a leading part in organizing the State of California, in the Civil War was appointed commander of the Department of the Missouri (1861). In 1862 he captured Corinth and was made general in chief, but in 1864 he was superseded by General **Ulysses S Grant**. Chief of Staff until 1865, Halleck commanded the military division of the Pacific until 1869, and that of the South until his death.

Haller, (Viktor) Albrecht von 1708–77 •*Swiss anatomist, botanist, physiologist and poet*• Born in Bern, he studied anatomy and botany in Tübingen and Leiden, and started practicing in 1729. From 1736 he taught at the new University of Göttingen, and here he organized a botanical garden, an anatomical museum and theater, and an obstetrical school, helped found the Academy of Sciences, wrote anatomical and physiological works, and took an active part in the literary movement. His *Elementa physiologiae corporis humani* (8 vols, 1757, "Physiological Elements of the Human Body") was a major contribution to the understanding of the functioning of the body.

Halley, Edmond 1656–1742 •*English astronomer and mathematician*• Born in London, he was educated at St Paul's School and Queen's College, Oxford. He left for St Helena in 1676 to make the first catalogue of the stars in the Southern Hemisphere (*Catalogus stellarum australium*, 1679). In 1680 he was in Paris with **Giovanni Cassini**, observing comets, and his calculation of the orbits of 24 comets enabled him to predict correctly the return (in 1758, 1835 and 1910) of a comet that had been observed in 1583 (Halley's comet). He established the mathematical law connecting barometric pressure with heights above sea level (on the basis of **Boyle**'s Law). He published studies on magnetic variations (1683), trade winds and monsoons (1686), investigated diving and underwater activities, and voyaged in the Atlantic Ocean to test his theory of the magnetic variation of the compass, which he embodied in a magnetic sea chart (1701). He encouraged **Isaac Newton** to write his celebrated *Principia Mathematica* (1687) and paid for its publication himself. In 1703 he was appointed Savilian Professor of Geometry at Oxford, where he built an observatory on the roof of his house which survives today, and in 1720 he succeeded **John Flamsteed** as Astronomer Royal of England.

Hals, Frans, *sometimes known as* **Frans Hals the Elder** c. 1580–1666 •*Dutch portrait and genre painter*• Born probably in Antwerp, he studied under Karel van Mander (1548–1606) and settled permanently in Haarlem (c. 1603). He was twice married, led a ramshackle domestic life with many children and, despite many commissions, was constantly overshadowed by poverty. Among his early conventional portraits are those of *Jacob Pietersz Olycan* and *Aletta Hanemans* (1625), and the dignified, sumptuously costumed *Portrait of a Man* (1622). But it is his studies of every nuance of smile, from the vague, arrogant amusement of *The Laughing Cavalier* (Wallace Collection, London) to the broad grins and outright vulgar leers of the low-life sketches *Gypsy Girl* (c. 1628–30, Louvre, Paris), *Malle Babbe* (c. 1630–33, Berlin) that have won him his perennial popularity.

Halsey, William F(rederick), Jr, *known as* **Bull Halsey** 1884–1959 •*US naval officer*• Born in Elizabeth, New Jersey, he was educated at the US Naval Academy, Annapolis (1904). He held destroyer commands in World War I and until 1925. He distinguished himself throughout the war in the Pacific (1941–45), ultimately as commander of the Third Fleet in the battles for the Caroline and Philippine Islands, and for carrier attacks on the Japanese mainland. In October 1944 he defeated the Japanese navy at the Battle of Leyte Gulf. He retired as fleet admiral in 1949.

Hambling, Maggi (Margaret) 1945– •*English artist*• Born in Sudbury, Suffolk, she attended the Ipswich and Camberwell Schools of Art and the Slade, London, where she won a traveling scholarship to New York. She became artist in residence at the National Gallery in London, where she met **Max Wall**, and became best known for her powerful and expressive portraits of him. She paints in a wide range of other styles and has exhibited regularly since 1967.

Hamburger, Michael Peter Leopold 1924– •*British poet and translator*• Born in Berlin, Germany, into a German family which emigrated to England in 1933, he served in the Royal Army Education Corps during World War II, and then became a university teacher. He established an international reputation for his distinguished translations of poets, including **Friedrich Hölderlin**, **Günter Grass** and **Nelly Sachs**. Among his own collections of poetry are *Flowering Cactus* (1950) and *Ownerless Earth* (1973).

Hamer, Fannie Lou, *née* **Townsend** 1918–77 •*US civil rights leader*• Born in Montgomery County, Mississippi, the granddaughter of a slave, she worked as a plantation worker until 1962. Her growing commitment to the civil rights movement was affected by her own experiences: in 1961 she was sterilized without her consent, and was dismissed for attempting to register as a voter. Throughout the 1960s and 1970s she campaigned for voter registration and the desegregation of schooling in Mississippi and other states. In 1964, with her coworkers, she founded the Mississippi Freedom Democratic Party.

Hamilcar, *also called* **Hamilcar Barca ("Lightning")** c. 270–228 BC •*Carthaginian soldier*• He and his son **Hannibal** were the greatest of the Carthaginian miltary leaders. From 247 BC he fought in the First Punic War, seizing the Sicilian stronghold of Ercte with a small band of mercenaries, from which he waged war for three years against Rome. He occupied Mount Eryx (244–242) and defended it against a Roman army. At the end of the First Punic War (241), Sicily was surrendered to Rome and the Carthaginian mercenaries revolted; Hamilcar crushed the rebellion after a terrible struggle in 238. He entered Spain in 237, and conquered most of the south and east of the peninsula before his death.

Hamilton, Alexander 1757–1804 •*American politician*• Born on the island of Nevis in the West Indies, he studied at King's College (now Columbia University) in New York. In 1782 he was elected to the Continental Congress. In 1786 he played the leading role in the convention at Annapolis, which prepared the way for the great Constitutional Convention that met in Philadelphia in 1787. In the same year he conceived the series of essays arguing in favor of ratification afterward collected as *The Federalist*, and himself wrote 51 of the 85. On the establishment of the new government in 1789, he was appointed Secretary of the Treasury and restored the country's finances to a firm footing. His successful effort to thwart the ambition of his rival, **Aaron Burr**, prompted Burr to challenge him to a duel in Weekauken, New Jersey, in which Hamilton was mortally wounded after firing into the air.

“ ”

A national debt, if it is not excessive, will be to us a national blessing.

1781 Letter to Robert Morris, April 30.

Hamilton, Alice 1869–1970 •*US physician and social reformer*• Born in New York City, she received a medical degree from the University of Michigan. After further training in pathology and bacteriology in Europe, she was made Professor of Pathology at the Woman's Medical College of Northwestern University (1897). She combined medical practice with social concerns, particularly the links between environment and disease, and served on state and national advisory committees on occupational disease. In 1919 she became the first woman professor at Harvard.

Hamilton, Emma, Lady, *née* **Amy Lyon** c. 1761–1815 •*Englishwoman, mistress of Lord Nelson*• Born in Great Neston, Cheshire, into a poor family, her girlhood was passed at Hawarden. Known for her great beauty, she had had two children by a navy captain and a baronet when in 1782 she became the mistress of the Hon Charles Greville (1749–1809), and subsequently (1786) of his uncle, Sir William Hamilton (1730–1803). After five years in Naples, she married Hamilton (1791). Lord **Nelson** first met her in 1793; they became lovers, and she gave birth to a daughter, Horatia (1801–81). After Nelson's death she squandered her inheritance from her husband, was arrested for debt (1813) and died exiled and impoverished.

Hamilton, Hamish 1900–88 •*Scottish publisher*• Born in Indianapolis, Indiana, he spent his childhood in Scotland and was educated at Rugby School and Caius College, Cambridge, becoming an accomplished Olympic oarsman. He joined Harper & Brothers, the New York publishers, as London manager in 1926. In 1931 he founded his own firm, Hamish Hamilton Ltd, with the support of Harpers, who helped him build up a particularly strong list of US writers. In 1965 he sold his company to Thomson Publications Ltd, who later sold it to Viking-Penguin.

Hamilton, Iain Ellis 1922–2000 •*Scottish composer*• Born in Glasgow, he entered the Royal College of Music in 1947. In 1951 he won the Royal Philharmonic Society's prize for his Clarinet Concerto, and an award from the Koussevitsky Foundation for his Second Symphony, which was followed by the Symphonic Variations (1953). He moved to the US in 1962. He produced many orchestral and chamber works as well as operas, including *The Royal Hunt of the Sun* (1967–69) and *The Catiline Conspiracy* (1972–73). After moving back to London in 1981, he completed several large-scale choral works, the operas *Lancelot* (1982–83) and *Raleigh's Dream* (1983), and a wind octet, *Antigone* (1992).

Hamilton, James, 2nd Earl of Arran and **Duke of Châtelherault** c. 1515–75 •*Scottish nobleman and regent of Scotland*• The grandson of James, 1st Baron Hamilton (d. 1479) by the niece of Cardinal **Beaton**, he was a young man when the death of **James V** (1542) left only an infant, the future **Mary Queen of Scots**, between him and the throne. He was chosen regent and tutor to the young queen, and held these offices until 1554, when **Mary of Guise** became regent. His regency was characterized by indecision and attention to family interests.

Hamilton, James, 3rd Marquis and **1st Duke of** 1606–49 •*Scottish nobleman*• He led an unsuccessful army of 6,000 men to support King **Gustav II Adolf** of Sweden (1631–32), and later played a conspicuous part in the contest between **Charles I** and the Covenanters. Made duke in 1643, he led a Scottish army into England (1648) but was defeated by **Cromwell** at Preston, and beheaded.

Hamilton, James Douglas, 4th Duke of 1658–1712 •*Scottish nobleman*• He fought against the Duke of **Monmouth**, led Scottish opposition to the union, but discouraged bloodshed. He was made 1st Duke of Brandon (1711), a title challenged by the House of Lords. He helped to negotiate the Treaty of Utrecht (1713). As described in **Thackeray**'s *Henry Esmond*, he fought a duel with Lord Mohun in which both men were killed.

Hamilton, Patrick 1503–28 •*Scottish Lutheran theologian and martyr*• Born in Glasgow, the son of Catherine Stewart, the illegitimate daughter of the Duke of Albany, second son of **James II**, he was educated in Paris, then went to Louvain. He returned to Scotland and was in St Andrews in 1523, but was forced to leave in 1527 on account of his Lutheranism. Settling for some months in Marburg, he wrote (in Latin) a series of theological propositions known as "Patrick's Places." In 1528 he was summoned to St Andrews by Archbishop **James Beaton**, and on a renewed charge of heresy was burned in front of St Salvator's College.

Hamilton, (Anthony Walter) Patrick 1904–62 •*English novelist*• He was born in Hassock, Sussex. *Craven House* (1926) was his first novel, but it was with *Rope* (1929) and *Gaslight* (the former filmed by **Alfred Hitchcock** and the latter by **George Cukor** and Thorold Dickinson) that he became well known. Apart from *Hangover Square* (1940), his most substantial achievement was the "Gorse" trilogy: *The West Pier* (1951), *Mr Stimpson and Mr Gorse* (1953) and *Unknown Assailant* (1955).

Hamilton, Richard 1922– •*English painter*• Born in London, he studied painting at the Royal Academy Schools. During World War II, he was trained as an engineering draftsman. In 1948 he entered a further period of study, at the Slade School of Art, and subsequently taught at the Central School of Art and Crafts, London, and at Durham University. During the 1950s, he devised and participated in several influential exhibitions, notably "This Is Tomorrow" (1956, Whitechapel Art Gallery, London), with its entrance display, the collage picture *Just What Is It That Makes Today's Homes So Different, So Appealing?* This introduced the concept of Pop Art, of which Hamilton became a leading pioneer. Among his best-known works are *Hommage à Chrysler Corp* (1952), *Study of Hugh Gaitskell as a Famous Monster of Film Land* (1964) and his replica of **Marcel Duchamp**'s *The Bride Stripped Bare by Her Bachelors, Even (The Large Glass)* (1965). He was made Companion of Honour in 2000.

Hamilton, Thomas 1784–1858 •*Scottish architect*• Born in Glasgow, he was a leading figure in the international Greek Revival, together with his contemporary in Edinburgh, **William Henry Playfair**. In 1826 he was among the founders of the Royal Scottish Academy. His Grecian designs include the Burns Monument, Alloway (1820), the Royal High School, Edinburgh (1825–29), and the Royal College of Physicians, Edinburgh (1844–45).

Hamilton, Sir William Rowan 1805–65 •*Irish mathematician*• He was born in Dublin. At the age of nine he had a knowledge of 13 languages, and at 15 he read **Isaac Newton**'s *Principia* and began original investigations. In 1827, while still an undergraduate, he was appointed Professor of Astronomy at Trinity College, Dublin, and Irish Astronomer Royal. His first published work was on optics, and he then adopted a new approach to dynamics, later and independently proposed by **Carl Jacobi**, which became of considerable importance in the 20th-century development of quantum mechanics. In 1843 he introduced quaternions after realizing that a consistent algebra of four dimensions was possible. The discovery proved to be the seed of much modern algebra. He was knighted in 1835.

Hamilton and Brandon, Douglas Douglas-Hamilton, 14th Duke of 1903–73 •*Scottish aviator*• Educated at Eton and Balliol College, Oxford, he held many distinguished royal positions, such as hereditary keeper of Holyroodhouse and, from 1940 to 1964, lord steward of the royal household. He developed an interest in aviation during the 1920s and 1930s, first as a pilot, then as commander of the 602 Squadron of the Auxiliary Air Force (1927–36). In 1932 he was the chief pilot in the Houston Mount Everest Expedition, about which he wrote in *The Pilot's Book of Everest* (1936).

Hammarskjöld, Dag Hjalmar Agne Carl 1905–61 •*Swedish statesman and Nobel Prize winner*• He was born in Jönköping. After an academic career he became chairman (1941–48) of the Bank of Sweden, then Swedish Foreign Minister (1951–53), and a delegate to various UN bodies. He became Secretary-General of the UN in 1953. Hammarskjöld, who once described himself as "the curator of the secrets of 82 nations," played a leading part in the setting up of the UN Emergency Force in Sinai and Gaza in 1956, and worked for conciliation in the Middle East (1957–58). He was awarded the 1961 Nobel Peace Prize after his death in an air crash near Ndola in Zambia while he was engaged in negotiations over the Congo crisis.

Hammer, Armand 1899–1990 •*US business executive*• Born in New York City, he trained as a physician at Columbia, and served with the US Army medical corps (1918–19). In 1921 he went to the USSR to help with an influenza epidemic, but turned to business, dealing face-to-face with **Lenin** and subsequent Soviet leaders. He maintained strong trading and political connections with the USSR, acting as intermediary between it and the US government on a number of occasions, including the Soviet troop withdrawal from Afghanistan in 1987. In 1961 he bought the small Occidental Petroleum Corporation of California, and turned it into a giant. He founded Hammer Galleries Inc (New York) in 1930.

Hammerstein, Oscar, II 1895–1960 •*US lyricist and librettist*• Born in New York City, he graduated from Columbia College in 1916 and by the early 1920s was writing books and lyrics for Broadway musicals. Among his several collaborators were composers **Jerome Kern**, with whom he wrote *Showboat* (1927), and **Richard Rodgers**, with whom he formed a famous partnership in 1943. Together he and Rodgers produced such classic musicals as *Oklahoma!* (1943), *Carousel* (1945), *South Pacific* (1949, Pulitzer Prize), *The King and I* (1951) and *The Sound of Music* (1959).

Hammett, (Samuel) Dashiell 1894–1961 •*US crime writer*• Born in St Mary's County, Maryland, he grew up in Philadelphia and Baltimore and left school at age 14. After numerous jobs, including a stint as a Pinkerton detective, he began writing stories for magazines like *Black Mask*, and became the first US author of authentic "private eye" crime novels. Original, unsentimental and an acute social observer, his four best novels are *Red Harvest* (1929), *The Dain Curse* (1929), *The Maltese Falcon* (1930) and *The Glass Key* (1931). In New York he met **Lillian Hellman**, with whom he lived for the rest of his life. Already a chronic alcoholic, his subsequent work never equaled his first literary successes. *The Thin Man* (1934), written in a brief period of sobriety, was made into a popular film, as were all his novels. Politically a radical, he was anti-**McCarthy** and served a six-month jail sentence for his sympathies.

“ ”

I distrust a man that says when. If he's got to be careful not to drink too much it's because he's not to be trusted when he does.

*1930 **The Maltese Falcon**, "The Fat Man."*

Hammett, Louis Plack 1894–1987 •*US physical chemist*• Born in Wilmington, Delaware, he graduated from Harvard in 1916, worked for a year with **Hermann Staudinger** in Zurich, and after wartime research he joined the chemistry faculty of Columbia University, becoming full professor in 1935. He is regarded as a founder of physical organic chemistry, a field greatly influenced by his book *Physical Organic Chemistry* (1940).

Hammond, Eric Albert Barratt 1929– •*English trade union leader*• He became active in trade union affairs in his early twenties and rose to be general secretary of the Electrical, Electronics, Telecommunications and Plumbing Union (EETPU) in 1984. He was a long-time outspoken critic of what he considered old-fashioned unionism, and he concluded single-union, "no strike" agreements with employers in defiance of Trades Union Congress (TUC) policy. Criticism of him and his union came to a head in 1988 when the EETPU was dismissed from the TUC. He retired from the EETPU in 1992, the same year that the union merged with the TUC-affiliated Amalgamated Engineering Union to form the Amalgamated Engineering and Electrical Union.

Hammond, Dame Joan Hood 1912–96 •*Australian soprano*• Born in Christchurch, New Zealand, she studied at the Sydney Conservatorium of Music, originally as a violinist. When an arm injury forced her to give up the violin, she turned to singing, making her operatic debut in 1939 in Vienna. From 1945 she sang leading roles in some 30 operas, and made many recordings. She retired from singing in 1971 to become the artistic director of the Victoria Opera Company, and took up academic posts at the Victorian College of the Arts (1975–92) and elsewhere. She was given the honorary title of Dame Commander, Order of the British Empire, in 1974.

Hammurabi or **Hammurapi** d. c. 1750 BC •*Amorite king of Babylon*• He ruled from c. 1792 to 1750 BC, and is best known for his code of laws (a tablet inscribed with it is in the Louvre, Paris). He is also famous for his military conquests that made Babylon the greatest power in Mesopotamia.

Hamnett, Katharine 1952– •*English fashion designer*• She was born in Gravesend, Kent. Educated at Cheltenham Ladies College, she studied fashion at St Martin's School of Art in London, then worked as a freelance fashion designer, setting up a short-lived company (1969–74) and then her own business in 1979. She has drawn inspiration for designs from workwear, and from movements that she supports such as the peace movement. In 1991 she produced her first theatrical designs for a production of Japanese writer **Yukio Mishima**'s *Madame de Sade*.

Hampden, John 1594–1643 •*English parliamentarian*• He became a Member of Parliament in 1621, and in 1626 he helped prepare the charges against the Duke of **Buckingham**. The next year, having refused to pay his proportion of the general loan which **Charles I** attempted to raise on his own authority, he was imprisoned. He was prosecuted again (1637) when Charles levied a navy tax, and on his conviction became the most popular man in England. He was one of the five members whose attempted seizure by Charles in 1642 precipitated the English Civil War. When hostilities broke out he raised a regiment of infantry for the parliamentary army, and demonstrated bravery and generalship at the battles of Edgehill and Reading, but was killed at Thame. He was the most moderate, tactical, urbane and single-minded of the leaders of the Long Parliament.

Hampton, Christopher 1946– •*English dramatist*• He was born in the Azores, and educated at Oxford. His first play, *When Did You Last See My Mother?* (1964), led to his appointment as the first resident dramatist at the Royal Court Theatre, London. The Court produced all his earlier plays, including *Total Eclipse* (1968), *Savages* (1973) and *Treats* (1976). His finest play is considered to be *Tales from Hollywood* (1982), but the most commercially successful has been *Les liaisons dangereuses* (1985, filmed 1988), adapted from the novel by **Pierre Choderlos de Laclos**. He wrote and directed the film *Carrington* in 1995, based on the life of **Dora Carrington**.

Hampton, Lionel 1909–2002 •*US jazz musician and bandleader*• Born in Louisville, Kentucky, he began as a drummer but was given xylophone lessons while a young man in Chicago. He later introduced the vibraphone into jazz, recording with **Louis Armstrong** in 1930. He was a member of **Benny Goodman**'s small groups in the late 1930s. He first formed a permanent big band in 1940, continuing as a leader until the 1980s and making many overseas tours.

Hamsun, Knut, *pseudonym of* **Knut Pedersen** 1859–1952 •*Norwegian novelist and Nobel Prize winner*• Born in Lom, Gudbrandsdal, he had no formal education, and spent his boyhood with his uncle, a fisherman on the Lofoten Islands. He worked at various odd jobs, and twice visited the US (1882–84, 1886–88), where he worked as a streetcar attendant in Chicago and a farmhand in North Dakota. He sprang to fame with his novel *Sult* (1890, Eng trans *Hunger*, 1899). His masterpiece is considered *Markens grøde* (1917, Eng trans *Growth of the Soil*, 1920), which was instrumental in his receiving the 1920 Nobel Prize for literature. His last novel was the unfinished *Ringen slutlet* (1936, Eng trans *The Circle Is Closed*, 1937).

Hanbury-Brown, Robert 1916–2002 •*British radio astronomer*• Born in Aruvankadu, India, he studied engineering at Brighton Polytechnic before joining a radar research program during World War II. In 1949 he moved to Jodrell Bank (University of Manchester), and in 1962 took up the chair of astronomy at the University of Sydney, Australia. In 1951, with Cyril Hazard, he obtained the first radio map of an external galaxy, later improving it using a radio interferometer he constructed. In 1956 he demonstrated the "intensity interference" phenomenon at optical wavelengths, which proved to be one of the key discoveries in the development of quantum optics in the early 1960s.

Hanbury-Tenison, (Airling) Robin 1936– •*English explorer and author*• Brought up in Ireland and educated at Eton and Oxford, in 1958 he achieved the first land crossing of South America at its widest point. His concern for Indian tribes led to his being one of the founding members of the charity Survival International, of which he is now president. In 1971 he undertook a three-month expedition for the Brazilian government, visiting 33 tribes, and publishing a report on their plight. He took part in the British Trans-Americas expedition of 1972, crossing the Darién gap and writing a report on the impact of the road on the Cuna Indians, and led the Royal Geographical Society's Gunung Mulu (Sarawak) Expedition (1977–78), a multidisciplinary survey of a tropical forest ecosystem. In more recent years he has ridden on horseback from Cornwall to the Camargue, along the Great Wall of China (1986), and south to north through New Zealand (1986).

Hancock, Herbie (Herbert Jeffrey) 1940– •*US jazz pianist, bandleader and composer*• Born in Chicago, he studied classical music as a child, but began performing jazz as a student. He joined the seminal **Miles Davis** Quintet in 1963, where he confirmed his escalating reputation while continuing to make important records under his own name. He followed Davis's example in turning to electric jazz-funk with his Headhunters sextet, and has worked back and forth in both genres ever since, including signing to two different record companies in the 1990s, one for each form. He has exerted a wide-ranging influence in each field, and is also a successful composer of film music. He won an Academy Award for his music for the jazz film *Round Midnight* (1987), in which he also appeared.

Hancock, John 1737–93 •*American revolutionary and political leader*• Born in Quincy, Massachusetts, he graduated from Harvard and became a merchant in Boston. He opposed the Stamp Act (1765), and in 1768 his sloop *Liberty* was seized by the British for smuggling. As president (1775–77) of the Continental Congress, he was the first to sign the Declaration of Independence, writing his name in a bold hand.

Hancock, Sheila 1933– •*English actress*•Born in Blackgang, Isle of Wight, she was trained at the Royal Academy of Dramatic Art and made her name on television as shop treasurer Carole in the sitcom *The Rag Trade* (1961–62). She followed it with the roles of Thelma Teesdale in *Mr Digby, Darling* (1969) and Sarah Ryan in *Dangerous Lady* (1995). Her films include *Doctor in Love* (1960), and *3 Men and a Little Lady* (1990). On stage, she appeared in the West End in *The Anniversary* (1966) and on Broadway in *Entertaining Mr Sloane*. She was married to the actor **John Thaw**.

Hancock, Tony (Anthony John) 1924–68 •*English comedian*• Born in Birmingham, he tried his hand as a standup comic before making his professional stage debut in *Wings* (1946). Pantomimes, cabaret and radio appearances in *Educating Archie* (1951) contributed to his growing popularity and he made his film debut in *Orders Is Orders* (1954). The radio series *Hancock's Half Hour* (1954), written by Alan Simpson and Ray Galton, allowed him to refine his lugubrious comic persona as a pompous misfit whose changeable social ambitions and blinkered patriotism are frequently thwarted or belittled. The series transferred to television (1956–61), gaining large viewing figures. Dispensing with his regular costars and writers, he made ill-advised attempts at solo projects and serious "artistic" endeavors in films like *The Punch and Judy Man* (1963). A chronic alcoholic beset by self-doubt, he committed suicide.

Hancock, Winfield Scott 1824–86 •*US soldier*• Born in Montgomery County, Pennsylvania, he organized the Army of the Potomac in 1861, was prominent at South Mountain, Antietam and Fredericksburg, and in 1863 took command of the 2nd Corps. At Gettysburg he was in command until **George G Meade**'s arrival, and was severely wounded. In 1864 he was conspicuous in the battles of the Wilderness, Spottsylvania and Cold Harbor.

Handel, George Frideric, *German (until 1715)* **Georg Friedrich Händel** 1685–1759 •*German-English composer*• He was born in Halle, Saxony. He became organist of Halle Cathedral at the age of 17. After some experience playing in the Hamburg opera orchestra, and four years in Italy, he was appointed in 1710 to the court of the elector of Hanover. He took frequent leaves of absence to try his fortune in London, introducing himself with the opera *Rinaldo* (1711). These frequent absences displeased the elector, whose succession to the English throne as **George I** led at first to some awkwardness; the *Water Music*, composed for a river procession, is said to have been a peace offering. Between 1713 and 1720 Handel was attached to the households of the Earl of **Burlington** and the Duke of Chandos. Later he devoted himself to the promotion of opera at the King's Theatre, Haymarket, under the auspices of the newly founded Royal Academy of Music. Attempting to satisfy the fickle taste of the fashionable London world with Italian opera was difficult, and his success varied. The Royal Academy of Music came to an end in 1728, was resuscitated temporarily, but collapsed again, after which Handel went into partnership with John Rich at his theater in Covent Garden. Eventually he turned to a new form, the English oratorio, which proved to be enormously popular. In 1735 Handel conducted 15 oratorio concerts in London. Despite a stroke in 1737, in the next five years he produced the oratorios *Saul* (1739), *Israel in Egypt* (1739), and the *Messiah* (1742), which had been first performed in Dublin. *Samson* followed in 1743, succeeded by *Joseph and His Brethren* (1744), *Semele* (1744), *Judas Maccabaeus* (1747), *Solomon* (1749), and others; his last, *Jephtha*, appeared in 1751. His *Music for the Royal Fireworks* had appeared in 1749, only serving to enhance his reputation in the eyes of the British people. A sociable, cultivated, cosmopolitan figure, he was a very prolific composer, and his output included 46 operas, 32 oratorios, large numbers of cantatas, sacred music, concerti grossi and other orchestral, instrumental and vocal music. Regarded as the greatest composer of his day, Handel was buried in Westminster Abbey.

Handley, Tommy (Thomas Reginald) 1892–1949 •*English comedian*•Born in Liverpool, he worked in variety and concert parties during World War I, and in the early days of radio he became a regular broadcaster. In 1939 he achieved nationwide fame through his weekly program *ITMA* (*It's That Man Again*), which, with its endearing mixture of satire, parody, slapstick and wit, provided a major boost to wartime morale.

Hands, Terry (Terence David) 1941– •*English stage director*• Born in Aldershot, Hampshire, he was educated at Birmingham University, and cofounded the Everyman Theatre, Liverpool, in 1964. He joined the Royal Shakespeare Company (RSC) in 1966, rising to become artistic director and chief executive (1986–91), now director emeritus. He was consultant director of the Comédie Française (1975–77), and has directed **Shakespeare** at the Burgtheater in Vienna. In 1992, he returned to the RSC to direct an award-winning production of **Christopher Marlowe**'s *Tamburlaine the Great*, with **Antony Sher** in the lead role. More recent productions include *The Merry Wives of Windsor* (1995) with the Royal National Theatre and *The Importance of Being Earnest* (1995) with the Birmingham Repertory Theatre. He is currently director of the Clwyd Theatr Cymru (1997–).

Handy, Charles Brian 1932– •*Irish teacher and writer on management*• Born in Dublin and educated at Oxford, he was a manager at Shell Petroleum and an economist in London, and in 1977 was appointed Warden of St George's House, Windsor (the Church of England's staff college). His comparative study of managers in Great Britain, the US, Europe and Japan, *The Making of Managers*, published in 1988, has helped to shape current management education. Later publications include *Beyond Certainty* (1995) and *The New Alchemists* (1999).

“ ”

Words are the bugles of social change.

1991 ***The Age of Unreason***.

Handy, W(illiam) C(hristopher) 1873–1958 •*US musician and composer*• He was born in Florence, Alabama, and joined a minstrel show as a cornet player. In 1903 he formed his own band in Memphis, Tennessee, and drew on various genres of African-American music, including spirituals, folk ballads, work songs and early jazz, to develop the form of music known as the blues. His earliest known composition "The Memphis Blues" (1911), was followed by "St Louis Blues" (1914), "Beale Street Blues," "Yellow Dog Blues," "Careless Love" and many others. He was the first to introduce the blues style to printed music, and is known as the "father of the blues."

Hanks, Tom (Thomas J) 1956– •*US actor*• Born in Concord, California, he was praised for his performance in the television sitcom *Bosom Buddies* (1980–82) before the unexpected popularity of the film *Splash* (1984) boosted his career. Nominated for an Academy Award for his role as a young boy trapped in an adult world in *Big* (1988), he later won the award for his performance as a defiant AIDS sufferer in *Philadelphia* (1993) and as the title character in *Forrest Gump* (1994). His many popular successes include *Sleepless in Seattle* (1993), *Apollo 13* (1995), *Saving Private Ryan* (1998) and *Cast Away* (2000). He made his feature-length directorial debut with *That Thing You Do* (1995).

Hanley, Ellery 1961– •*English rugby league player*•Born in Leeds, he played for a Leeds amateur club and signed for Bradford Northern in 1978. He transferred to Wigan in 1985 for the record fee of £150,000 and transferred to Leeds in 1991 for £250,000. He was contemplating retirement when he was offered a job by the Australian Rugby League and signed as coach for a reputed £433,000 in May 1995.

Hanna-Barbera, *properly* **William Denby Hanna** 1910–2001 and **Joseph Roland Barbera** 1911– •*US animated cartoonists*• Born in New Mexico, Hanna became a structural engineer, then turned to cartooning. He was one of the first directors at the new MGM animation studio in Hollywood in 1937, making *Captain and the Kids*. There he teamed up with New York City–born Barbera, who had studied accounting before he too turned to animation. Together they made *Puss Gets the Boot* (1939), featuring a cat and mouse; developing the idea, they went on to make over 200 film shorts of the immortal duo, *Tom and Jerry*, for which they received seven Academy Awards between 1943 and 1953. In 1957 they formed Hanna-Barbera Productions and turned to television, creating dozens of popular series such as *Yogi Bear* and *The Flintstones*.

Hannibal, "my grace (is) Baal" 247–182 BC •*Carthaginian soldier*• He was the son of **Hamilcar** and at the age of nine his father made him swear eternal enmity toward Rome. He served in Spain under Hamilcar and his brother-in-law Hasdrubal, and was elected general after Hasdrubal's death. He won control of southern Spain up to the Ebro (221–219), and the fall of Saguntum in 218 sparked the Second Punic War with Rome. In 218 he surprised the Romans by marching from Spain through southern Gaul and crossing the Alps into Italy with an army that included elephants. He defeated the Taurini, forced Ligurian and Celtic tribes to serve in his army, and at the River Ticinus drove back the Romans under **Publius Cornelius Scipio** the Elder (218). In 217 he crossed the Apennines, devastating Etruria and marching toward Rome. He awaited the consul **Gaius Flaminius** by Lake Trasimene, where he inflicted on him a crushing defeat; the Roman army was annihilated. In 216 he utterly destroyed another Roman army under **Quintus Fabius** ("Cunctator") at Cannae, but after this the tide turned. Rome's allies remained loyal, and Hannibal received inadequate support from Carthage. Although he was not defeated, as his veterans were lost to him he had no means of filling their places, while the Romans could put army after army into the field. In 203 he was recalled to Africa and he was finally defeated by Scipio at Zama (202), leaving Carthage to the mercy of Rome. At the conclusion of peace, Hannibal devoted himself to political reform, but he aroused such strong opposition that he fled to the court of **Antiochus III** at Ephesus, and then to Bithynia. When the Romans demanded his surrender, he took poison.

Hanno 5th century BC •*Carthaginian navigator*• He undertook a voyage of exploration along the west coast of Africa. He founded colonies, and reached Cape Nun or the Bight of Benin. An account of his voyages, known as *Periplus of Hanno*, survives in a Greek translation.

Hansard, Luke 1752–1828 •*English printer*• He was born in Norwich, Norfolk. He and his descendants printed the parliamentary reports from 1774 to 1889, and the official reports of proceedings in Parliament are still called "Hansard" in his honor. **William Cobbett**'s *Parliamentary Debates* was continued from 1806 by Hansard's son, Thomas, and successors.

Hansberry, Lorraine 1930–65 •*US playwright*• She was born in Chicago, where her father was a successful real-estate broker, and his efforts to move the family into a segregated neighborhood in the late 1930s (their victory came only after he carried a lawsuit all the way to the Supreme Court) provided an early lesson in the explosive drama of race relations in the US. Her play *A Raisin in the Sun* (1959) became the first work by an African-American woman to be produced on Broadway and won the New York Drama Critics Circle Award. She also wrote *The Sign in Sidney Brustein's Window* (1964), staged shortly before her death from cancer at the age of 34. Selections of her writings and letters were assembled posthumously as a dramatic self-portrait in *To Be Young, Gifted and Black* (1969).

Hansford Johnson, Pamela 1912–81 •*English novelist, playwright and critic*• Born in London, she left school at age 18. For a short time in the early 1930s she was engaged to be married to **Dylan Thomas**. Her first novel, *This Bed Thy Centre* (1935), was set in working-class south London, and her many subsequent novels, such as the tragicomic *The Unspeakable Skipton* (1958), are observant of both the world of her youth and of society in the sixties and seventies. Her critical works include writings on **Thomas Wolfe** and **Marcel Proust**. In 1950 she married the novelist **C P Snow** and they collaborated on many literary projects.

Hansom, Joseph Aloysius 1803–82 •*English inventor and architect*• Born in York, he invented the "Patent Safety (Hansom) Cab" in 1834, and designed Birmingham Town Hall and the Roman Catholic cathedral in Plymouth.

Hanson, Duane 1925–96 •*US sculptor*• He was born in Alexandria, Minnesota, and studied at the Cranbrook Academy of Art in Bloomfield, Michigan, before going to Germany, where he lived from 1953 to 1961. He specialized in life-size figures made from polyester resin stiffened with fiberglass, then painted realistically and clothed. His earlier work was violent (for example, *Abortion*, 1966), but he later shifted to mildly satirical pieces like *Woman with Shopping Trolley* (1969).

Hanson, James Edward Hanson, Baron 1922– •*English business executive*• Born in Huddersfield, West Yorkshire, he was for a time engaged as a young man to the then-unknown actress **Audrey Hepburn**. He became chairman of Hanson Trust in 1965, building up a huge and diversified conglomerate of businesses under that umbrella. He was made a Life Peer in 1983.

Hanson-Dyer, Louise Berta Mosson 1884–1962 •*Australian music publisher and patron*• Born in Melbourne, she helped establish the British Music Society there in 1921, then went to Paris, where she established Éditions du Oiseau-Lyre, a music publisher. In 1933 she brought out a complete edition of the works of **Couperin**, followed by works of **Purcell** and John Blow (1649–1708). In the 1950s the press was among the first to issue on LP some of the works of **Monteverdi**, Purcell and **Handel**. She also published the works of leading Australian composers.

Hansson, Per Albin 1885–1946 •*Swedish politician*• He was elected to parliament in 1918, and served as Minister of Defense in Social Democrat administrations (1918–25) under **Karl Hjalmar Branting**, whom he succeeded as leader of the party (1925). He became prime minister of a minority Social Democrat government in 1932, and, apart from a brief period in 1936, was in office from then until his death. He presided over the foundation of the modern welfare state in Sweden and guided his country's successful policy of neutrality during World War II.

Han Suyin, *originally* **Elizabeth Kuanghu Chow** 1917– •*British novelist*• Born in Beijing, China, she studied medicine in Beijing, Brussels and London. She then practiced in Hong Kong, which provided the background for her first partly autobiographical novel, *A Many Splendoured Thing* (1952, filmed 1955). From 1952 she practiced in an antituberculosis clinic in Singapore. Her other novels include *And the Rain My Drink* (1954) and *Four Faces* (1963). She also wrote *China*, a semiautobiographical and historical work in six volumes, and two volumes of contemporary Chinese history (1972).

Hapsburg *See* **Habsburg**

Harald I Halfdanarson (Finehair or **Fairhair)** c. 860–c. 945 •*King of Norway*• He was the first ruler to claim sovereignty over all Norway. The son of Halfdan the Black (King of Vestfold), he achieved power and became king after the naval battle of Hafursfjord, off Stavanger (c. 890). His authoritarian rule caused many of the old aristocratic families to emigrate west to Orkney, Hebrides and Ireland, and to newly settled Iceland. In 942 he abdicated in favor of his eldest son, **Erik Haraldsson (Blood-Axe)**.

Harald II Eriksson, Greycloak d. c. 970 •*King of Norway*• The eldest son of **Erik Haraldsson (Blood-Axe)**, he retreated to Denmark with his mother, Gunnhild, the sister of King **Harald Gormsson (Blue-Tooth)** after his father's death in England (954). With Danish support he and his four brothers made several assaults on Norway from 960 against their uncle, King Haakon I Haraldsson (the Good), and eventually killed him in battle off Hardangerfjord (c. 961), and Harald became king. His reign was unpopular, especially when he tried to impose Christianity on his subjects, and he was killed fighting the Earl Haakon of Lade and Harald Blue-Tooth.

Harald III Sigurdsson, *also called* **Harald Hardraade (the Ruthless)** 1015–66 •*King of Norway*• The half brother of **Olaf II Haraldsson** (St Olaf), he retreated to Kiev with his nephew **Magnus I Olafsson** after St Olaf had been killed. He served as a Viking mercenary with the Varangian Guard in Constantinople (Istanbul), and returned to Norway (1045) to demand, and receive, a half-share in the kingdom from his nephew. He became sole king on his nephew's death (1047). He expanded Norway's possessions in Orkney, Shetland and the Hebrides, and invaded England (1066) to claim the throne after the death of **Edward the Confessor**, but was defeated and killed by **Harold II** at Stamford Bridge.

Harald V 1937– •*King of Norway*• Born in Oslo, like his father, **Olav V**, he was educated at the University of Oslo, at a military academy, and at Oxford. He served briefly in each of the country's three armed services, and in 1968 took the then unprecedented step of marrying a commoner, Sonja—a shopkeeper's daughter. As prince regent, he formally succeeded to the throne on Olav's death in January 1991.

Harald Gormsson (Blue-Tooth) c. 910–85 •*King of Denmark*• The son of Gorm the Old and father of **Svein I Haraldsson (Fork-Beard)**, he became king in c. 940 and was the first king to unite all the provinces of Denmark. He was converted to Christianity by a German missionary, Poppo (c. 960), and made Christianity the state religion of Denmark. He is thought to have built the fortified military barracks at Trelleborg and elsewhere in Denmark as well as the Jelling Stone, proclaiming his conversion. He was deposed by his son Svein (985), and died in exile soon afterward.

Harcourt, Dame Catherine Winifred, *known as* **Kate Harcourt** 1927– •*New Zealand actress*• Born in Amberley, North Canterbury, she studied music at Melbourne Conservatorium and in 1954 joined the Joan Cross Opera Studio at Sadler's Wells in London. She returned to New Zealand in 1956, and has since been active in theater, radio, film and television drama. In 1996 she was appointed the first Dame Commander of the New Zealand Order of Merit.

Hardaknut Knutsson or **Hardacanute** or **Hardicanute** 1018–42 •*King of Denmark and of England*• He was the son of **Knut Sveinsson** (Canute the Great) and **Emma** and was Knut's only legitimate heir. He inherited Denmark upon his father's death (1035), but the English elected his illegitimate half brother, **Harold I Knutsson (Harefoot)**, as regent, confirming Harold as king in 1037. Hardaknut prepared to invade England to claim the crown, but Harold died before he arrived. Hardaknut was made king (1040), and promptly punished the English by imposing a savage fleet tax to pay for his expedition. His reign was universally disliked, and he died of convulsions at a wedding party.

Harden, Sir Arthur 1865–1940 •*English chemist and Nobel Prize winner*• Born in Manchester, he worked in the Jenner (later Lister) Institute from 1897. Investigating the fermentation of sugars by bacteria, he made the crucial discovery that the first step in fermentation was the phosphorylation of the sugar to form an ester (1905), and he isolated fructose 1,6–bisphosphate. Later he isolated two other intermediates. Harden also showed that dialysis destroyed fermentation activity, thereby implicating a dialyzable cofactor in fermentation, and he recognized the presence of more than one enzyme. For this work he shared the 1929 Nobel Prize for chemistry with **Hans Euler-Chelpin**. He was knighted in 1936.

Hardenberg, Karl August, Fürst von 1750–1822 •*Prussian politician*• Born in Essenrode, near Hanover, he held appointments in Hanover, Brunswick, Ansbach and Bayreuth, and became a Prussian Minister upon Bayreuth's union with Prussia in 1791. In 1803 he was the Prussian Foreign Minister. In 1810 he was appointed Chancellor and completed the reforms begun by Baron von **Stein**. He played a prominent part in the war of liberation, and after the Treaty of Paris (June 1814) was made a prince.

Hardicanute *See* **Hardaknut Knutsson**

Hardie, Gwen 1962– •*Scottish painter*• Born in Newport-on-Tay, Fife, she studied at the Edinburgh College of Art, then moved to West Berlin where she studied under **Georg Baselitz**. She first received critical notice in her postgraduate diploma show at Edinburgh, in which she exhibited a number of large-scale paintings of close-ups of female heads and torsos. She has continued to explore the theme of the female form from a feminist viewpoint, sometimes opening the figure up to reveal internal organs. The importance of these works lies particularly in the intention to reinvent the female form in pictorial art.

Hardie, (James) Keir 1856–1915 •*Scottish Labour leader and politician*• Born near Holytown, Lanarkshire, he worked from the age of seven and was employed in a coal mine from the age of 10. Victimized as champion of the miners (whom he organized), he moved to Cumnock and became a journalist. The first of all Labour candidates, he stood as candidate for the Scottish Labour Party in Mid-Lanark (1888), but sat for West Ham, South (1892–95), and Merthyr Tydfil (1900–15), and inside and outside Parliament worked strenuously for socialism and the unemployed. In 1893 he founded the Independent Labour Party. He was chairman of the party until 1900 and again in 1913–14 (the party having been renamed the Labour Party). A pacifist, he opposed the Boer War, and lost his seat in 1915 after opposing Britain's involvement in World War I.

Hardie Boys, Sir Michael 1931– •*New Zealand governor-general*• Born in Wellington and educated at Victoria University, Wellington, he joined his father's legal practice and was a member of the Legal Aid Board, becoming chairman (1978) until his appointment as a judge of the New Zealand High Court (1980–89). He served on the Bench of the Court of Appeal from 1989 to 1996. In that year he was nominated to succeed Dame **Catherine Tizard** as Governor-General of New Zealand (1996–2001).

Harding (of Petherton), John Harding, 1st Baron 1896–1989 •*English field marshal*• He was born in South Petherton, Somerset. A subaltern in World War I, he rose to Chief of Staff of the Allied Army in Italy in 1944. From 1955 to 1957, as Governor-General of Cyprus during the political and terrorist campaign against Great Britain, he reorganized the security forces and the press to combat terrorism, and banished Archbishop **Makarios**. He was knighted in 1944 and made a peer in 1958.

Harding, Warren G(amaliel) 1865–1923 •*29th President of the US*• Born in Blooming Grove (now Corsica), Ohio, he was a journalist and newspaper owner (the *Marion Star*), then entered politics as a Republican. During his term in the US Senate (1915–20), he proved himself an unremarkable party loyalist, and perhaps because he was offensive to nobody, in 1920 he was the compromise choice as the Republican presidential candidate. He promised a "return to normalcy" after World War I, and his presidency (1921–23) saw the conclusion of peace treaties with Germany, Austria and Hungary. Politically naive, he had little notion of the real activities of his appointees and advisers until 1923, when he learned that the corrupt activities of several of his Cabinet members were about to be exposed. The investigations that followed brought to light the Teapot Dome scandal and revealed a level of corruption seldom matched in US presidential history.

Hardinge (of Lahore), Henry Hardinge, 1st Viscount 1785–1856 •*English soldier and administrator*• He was born in Wrotham, Kent. After **Napoleon**'s escape from Elba he was appointed commissioner at the Prussian headquarters. From 1820 to 1844 he was a Member of Parliament, Secretary of War under the Duke of **Wellington** (1828–30, 1841–44) and Chief Secretary for Ireland (1830, 1834–35). In 1844 he was appointed Governor-General of India. During the First Sikh War he was second in command to Lord **Gough** and negotiated the peace of Lahore (1845). Returning to England in 1848 he succeeded Wellington as Commander in Chief (1852), but was demoted to field marshal in 1855 following the disasters early in the Crimean War (1854–56).

Hardy, Bert 1913–95 •*English photojournalist*• Born in London, he was, in 1938, one of the first to use a Leica 35mm camera. He was on the staff of *Picture Post* until 1957, except for service as an army photographer from 1942 to 1945, during which period he recorded scenes in concentration camps. Later assignments took him to the Korean and Vietnam wars. In both war and peace his portrayal of ordinary people was of very high quality.

Hardy, Godfrey Harold 1877–1947 •*English mathematician*• Born in Cranleigh, Surrey, he was educated at Cambridge. In 1920 he became Savilian Professor at Oxford, but returned to Cambridge as Sadleirian Professor (1931–42). An internationally important figure in mathematical analysis, he was chiefly responsible for introducing English mathematicians to the great advances in function theory that had been made abroad. In his one venture into applied mathematics, he developed (concurrently with, but independent of, William Weinberg) the Hardy-Weinberg law, fundamental to population genetics.

" "

Beauty is the first test: there is no permanent place in the world for ugly mathematics.

1941 ***A Mathematician's Apology.***

Hardy, Oliver, *originally* **Norvell Hardy, Jr** 1892–1957 •*US comic actor*• Born near Atlanta, Georgia, he ran away from home at the age of eight to become a boy singer in a traveling minstrel show, but later returned home to enter films in 1913. He played the straight man to many comedians and the Tin Man in the 1925 version of *The Wizard of Oz*. By then, he had already teamed up with **Stan Laurel**, as Laurel and Hardy; they made their screen debut together in *A Lucky Dog* (1917). The partnership produced more than 100 films, including silent shorts such as *Leave 'Em Laughing* (1928) and *Big Business* (1929), the sound shorts *Men o' War* (1929), *Perfect Day* (1929) and *The Music Box* (1932), and the feature film *Way Out West* (1937). Hardy also made more than 200 films outside the partnership.

Hardy, Thomas 1840–1928 •*English novelist, poet and dramatist*• He was born in Upper Bockhampton, near Dorchester in Dorset, the son of a stonemason. He was educated in Dorchester and at the age of 16 was apprenticed to a local architect, returning home in 1867 to pursue his chosen profession. However, he had already begun his first novel, *The Poor Man and the Lady*, which was never published. There is speculation that around this time he met and fell in love with Tryphena Sparks, to whom he was related. The nature of their relationship is unclear, but in 1870 he was sent to St Juliot, Cornwall, where he met Emma Gifford, whom he married in 1874, after the success of his novel *Far from the Madding Crowd* (1874). This was his fourth published novel in as many years: *Desperate Remedies* (1871), *Under the Greenwood Tree* (1872) and *A Pair of Blue Eyes* (1873) had been less successful. His marriage to Emma was not without difficulties but, ironically, when she died in 1912, Hardy was inspired to write some of the most moving love poems in the language ("Poems of 1912–13," in *Satires of Circumstance*, 1914). A flood of novels continued to appear until 1895, with vibrant, brooding descriptive passages providing the backdrop to potent tragicomedies. Among the most durable are *The Return of the Native* (1878), *The Mayor of Casterbridge* (1886) and *Tess of the D'Urbervilles* (1891). Alhough Hardy was held in high esteem, critics carped at his seemingly inbred pessimism, and both *Tess* and *Jude the Obscure* (1895) were attacked virulently. Thereafter, Hardy turned his attention to poetry. His first collection, *Wessex Poems*, appeared in 1898; his last, *Winter Words*, posthumously in 1928, the year of his death. *The Dynasts*, a gargantuan drama in blank verse, occupied him for many years and was published in three installments (1904, 1906, 1908).

Hare, Sir David 1947– •*English dramatist, director and filmmaker*• Born in Bexhill, Sussex, he graduated from Cambridge and was active in fringe theater for many years. He succeeded **Christopher Hampton** as resident dramatist and literary manager of the Royal Court Theatre in London (1969–71), and at Nottingham Playhouse in 1973, before becoming associate director of the National Theatre, London (1984). The best of his early works is *Teeth 'n' Smiles* (1975), a commentary on the state of modern Britain. *Racing Demon* (1990) and *Murmuring Judges* (1991) were the first two parts of a trilogy about British institutions. His plays often have linked films, such as *The Secret Rapture* (1988) and the complementary political film *Paris by Night* (1988). His television films include *Dreams of Leaving* (1980) and the play *Heading Home* (1991). He wrote and directed his first feature film, *Wetherby*, in 1985. Later plays include *The Absence of War* (1993) and *The Judas Kiss* (1998). He was knighted in 1998.

Hare, William *See* **Burke, William**

Harewood, Sir George Henry Hubert Lascelles, 7th Earl of 1923– •*English nobleman and arts patron*• The elder son of Mary, Princess Royal, and cousin of Queen **Elizabeth II**, he was born in Harewood, near Leeds. Educated at Eton and King's College, Cambridge, he was a captain in the Grenadier Guards in World War II, and was a prisoner of war. Keenly interested in music and drama, he was artistic director of the Edinburgh International Festival (1960–65), and managing director of English Opera North (1978–81). From 1985 to 1996 he was president of the British Board of Film Classification.

Hargrave, Lawrence 1850–1915 •*Australian aeronautical pioneer*• Born in Greenwich, England, he arrived in Sydney in 1865. In 1893 he developed the box kite to produce a wing form used in early aircraft. In 1894, four tethered kites successfully lifted Hargraves five meters from the ground. His later work on curved wing surfaces foreshadowed the wing shape of the **Wright** brothers' airplane of 1903.

Hargreaves, James c. 1720–78 •*English inventor*• Born probably in Blackburn, Lancashire, he worked as a weaver and carpenter in Standhill. About 1764 he invented the spinning jenny, an early type of spinning machine with several spindles, but his fellow workers (fearing its effect on employment) broke into his house and destroyed his frame (1768).

Haring, Keith 1958–1990 •*US artist*• Born in Kutztown, Pennsylvania, he was involved in the New York graffiti movement in the 1980s, and came to public attention with his drawings of dancing children and animals and AIDS-inspired images, such as *Ignorance = Fear* (1989). He also designed stage sets, murals, record jackets and book covers, including *Painted Velum* (1986, Stedelijk Museum, Amsterdam).

Harington, Sir John 1561–1612 •*English courtier and writer*• He was born in Kelston, near Bath, and educated at Eton and King's College, Cambridge. From Cambridge he went to the court of his godmother, Queen **Elizabeth I**. His wit made him popular, but the freedom of his satires, as well as his *The Metamorphosis of Ajax* (1596), containing the earliest design for a water closet, brought a period of exile from the court. He is remembered as the metrical translator of **Ariosto**'s *Orlando Furioso* (1591).

Harlan, John Marshall 1833–1911 •*US judge and jurist*• Born in Boyle County, Kentucky, he was admitted to the bar in 1853 after studying law at Transylvania University. He supported the Union in the Civil War (1861–65), Kentucky having declared its neutrality, and commanded a volunteer Union regiment, resigning in 1863 to be elected as the attorney general of Kentucky. By 1867, he was a radical Republican, and was appointed to a commission to decide between rival state governments in Louisiana, and then to the Supreme Court. He served from 1877 to 1911, invariably and often the sole defender of the civil rights of African Americans.

Harland, Sir Edward James 1831–96 •*Northern Irish shipbuilder*• In Belfast in 1858 he founded the firm that later became Harland and Wolff, builders of many famous Atlantic liners and warships. Gustav William Wolff (1834–1913), his partner from 1860, was born in Hamburg, Germany, but learned engineering in Liverpool and Manchester.

Harland, Henry, *also known as* **Sidney Luska** 1861–1905 •*US novelist and short-story writer*• Born in New York, not, as he claimed, in St Petersburg, after briefly attending Harvard Divinity School, he turned to writing sentimental melodramatic novels about Jewish immigrants to the US under the pseudonym Sidney Luska. In 1890 he moved to London. He is best known as the founder and editor of the infamous quarterly *The Yellow Book* (1894–97) which became one of the leading influences on turn-of-the-century tastes and aesthetics. He also wrote popular fiction, including *The Cardinal's Snuff Box* (1900).

Harley, Robert, 1st Earl of Oxford and Mortimer 1661–1724 •*English statesman*• He was born in London. A Whig Member of Parliament from 1689, he became Secretary of State in 1704. He soon joined the Tories, however, and was Chief Minister to Queen **Anne** from 1711 to 1714. His administration included the Treaty of Utrecht (1713) but he was dismissed for alleged treasonable acts and imprisoned in the Tower of London for two years.

Harlow, Jean, *originally* **Harlean Carpentier** 1911–37 •*US actress*• Born in Kansas City, Missouri, she eloped with a business tycoon at the age of 16 and moved to Los Angeles, where she made her film debut in *Moran of the Marines* (1928) and worked as an extra before being signed to a contract by **Howard Hughes** and being featured in *Hell's Angels* (1930). Roles in *Platinum Blonde* (1931) and *Red Dust* (1932) established her screen image as a fast-talking, wisecracking blonde. With MGM (from 1932) she made the notorious *Red-Headed Woman* (1932), and developed into a deft comedienne in films like *Dinner at Eight* (1933) and *Bombshell* (1933). She died at the age of 26 from cerebral edema.

Harman, Harriet 1950– *•English Labour politician•* Born in London, she trained as a lawyer and became an outstanding legal officer for the National Council of Civil Liberties (1978–82), before becoming Member of Parliament for Peckham (1982). She was Opposition Chief Secretary to the Treasury (1992–94), a member of the Labour Party's National Executive Committee (1993–), and Opposition front bench spokesperson on employment (1994–95), on health (1995–96) and on social security (1996–97) before entering **Tony Blair**'s Cabinet as Secretary of State for Social Security (1997–98). She is currently Solicitor-General (2001–).

Harmodius d. 514 BC *•Athenian murderer•* With Aristogeiton in 514 BC, he murdered Hipparchus, son of **Pisistratus** and younger brother of the tyrant Hippias, and intended to kill Hippias also. Harmodius was killed, while Aristogeiton, who fled, was later captured and executed. Subsequently they were regarded as patriotic martyrs, and were revered in Athens as champions of liberty.

Harmsworth, Alfred Charles William, 1st Viscount Northcliffe 1865–1922 *•Irish journalist and newspaper magnate•* Born in Chapelizod, County Dublin, he was brought up in London and became one of the pioneers of mass-circulation journalism. He was editor of *Youth* and, with his brother **Harold Sydney Harmsworth**, started *Answers to Correspondents* (1888). He founded *Comic Cuts* (1890) and an imitation, *Chips*, to discourage competitors. In 1894 he took over the *London Evening News* and in 1896 revolutionized Fleet Street with his US-style *Daily Mail*. With Harold he bought the *Sunday Dispatch* and many provincial papers, founded the Amalgamated Press, and became proprietor of *The Times*.

Harmsworth, Harold Sydney, 1st Viscount Rothermere 1868–1940 *•Irish newspaper magnate•* Born and educated in London, he was closely associated with his brother **Alfred Harmsworth**, and founded the *Glasgow Daily Record*. In 1910 he established the King Edward chair of English literature at Cambridge and received a baronetcy. He dissociated himself from his brother in 1914 and concentrated on the *Daily Mirror*, which reached a circulation of three million by 1922.

Harold I Knutsson (Harefoot) d. 1040 *•King of England•* He was the younger son of **Knut Sveinsson** (Canute the Great) and his English mistress Ælfgifu of Northampton. On Knut's death the English elected Harold Harefoot regent for his half brother **Hardaknut**, king of Denmark, the legitimate heir to the throne, who could not leave Denmark to claim the Crown. In 1037 Harold was elected king, but died just as Hardaknut was poised to invade England.

Harold II c. 1022–66 *•Anglo-Saxon king of England•* He was the second son of Earl **Godwin**. By 1045 he was Earl of East Anglia. In 1053 he succeeded to his father's earldom of Essex and became the right hand of King **Edward the Confessor**. His brother Tostig became Earl of the Northumbrians in 1055. In 1063, provoked by the incursions of the Welsh King Gruffyd, he marched against him, defeated the enemy at every point, and gave the government to the dead king's brothers. In c. 1064 he made a celebrated visit to the court of **William**, Duke of Normandy, to whom he seems to have made some kind of oath and whom he helped in a war with the Bretons. In 1065 the Northumbrians rebelled against Tostig, and Harold acquiesced in his replacement by Morcar and Tostig's banishment. In January 1066 King Edward died, and Harold, his nominee, was chosen king, and crowned in Westminster Abbey. He defeated Tostig and **Harald III Sigurdsson**, king of Norway, at Stamford Bridge in September 1066, but four days later Duke William landed in the south of England at Pevensey. Harold marched southward and the two armies met at Senlac, about nine miles from Hastings. On October 14, 1066, the English fought stubbornly all day but were defeated. Harold, the last Anglo-Saxon king of England, was killed; he was supposedly pierced through the eye with an arrow.

Harold Godwinsson *See* **Harold II**

Harper, Edward James 1941– *•English composer•* Born in Taunton, Somerset, he studied at Oxford and at the Royal College of Music, and in Milan. He became a lecturer in music at the University of Edinburgh, and directs the New Music Group of Scotland. Early works owed much to serial and aleatoric styles (where chance influences the choice of notes), but with the orchestral *Bartók Games* (1972) and a one-act opera *Fanny Rodin* (1975) he evolved a more tonally based style. Other works include the opera *Hedda Gabler* (1985), a symphony, concertos, choral works, two string quartets and other chamber and vocal pieces.

Harper and Brothers *•New York publishers•* The firm consisted originally of James (1795–1869), John (1797–1875), Joseph Wesley (1801–70) and Fletcher (1806–77). James and John began publishing in 1818. The firm of Harper and Brothers, established in 1833, is carried on by descendants, and issues *Harper's Magazine* (monthly since 1850) and other publications.

Harriman, W(illiam) Averell 1891–1986 *•US politician and diplomat•* He was born in New York City and educated at Yale. A close friend of President **Franklin D Roosevelt**, he was Roosevelt's special war-aid representative in Britain. In 1943 he was appointed ambassador to the USSR and in 1946 to Britain. He was special assistant to President **Harry S Truman** (1950–51), helping to organize NATO, and was governor of New York (1955–58). Chief negotiator for the partial nuclear test–ban treaty between the US and USSR in 1963, he continued to visit the USSR on behalf of the government until the age of 91.

Harris, Sir Arthur Travers, *nicknamed* **Bomber Harris** 1892–1984 *•English air force officer•* Born in Cheltenham, Gloucestershire, he was educated at Allhallows School and emigrated to Rhodesia in 1910. He served with the 1st Rhodesian Regiment in South West Africa (1914–15) and with the Royal Flying Corps in France and in defense of London. On the formation of the Royal Air Force (April 1918) he received a permanent commission. He commanded No. 4 Group Bomber Command (1937–38), and RAF Palestine and Transjordan (1938–39). He was deputy chief of Air Staff (1940–41), and as Commander in Chief Bomber Command RAF (1942–45), he organized bombing raids on industrial targets in Germany, earning his nickname.

Harris, Barbara Clementine 1930– *•US Episcopal cleric•* Born in Philadelphia, she worked as a social activist in the 1960s, and a supporter of the ordination of people without regard to sex or sexual orientation in the 1970s. After attending Villanova University she was ordained in 1980, and consecrated suffragan (assistant) bishop of Massachusetts in 1989. Though not a diocesan bishop, she was the first female bishop in the Anglican Communion. Her consecration was ratified in 1990 when Penelope Jamieson (1942–) was consecrated the first female Anglican diocesan bishop in Dunedin, New Zealand.

Harris, Bomber *See* **Harris, Sir Arthur Travers**

Harris, Emmylou 1947– *•US country singer•* Born in Birmingham, Alabama, she began her career as a folk singer, but moved into country rock through her association with Gram Parsons (1946–73). She continued her explorations after his death in records like *Pieces of the Sky* (1975). Her Hot Band was one of the best groups in Nashville, and she experimented with more traditional country and bluegrass in *Roses in the Snow* (1980) and *Angel Band* (1987). She led a fine acoustic group, The Nash Ramblers, in the early 1990s, before making a surprise change of direction into the evocative, ambient country of *Wrecking Ball* (1995).

Harris, Frank, *properly* **James Thomas Harris** 1856–1931 *•Irish writer and journalist•* He was born, according to his autobiography, in Galway, but according to his own later statement, in Tenby, Dyfed. He ran away to New York at the age of 15 and, after various jobs, began studying law in 1874 at the University of Kansas. Returning to England about 1876, he became editor of the *Fortnightly Review*, *Saturday Review*, *Vanity Fair* and of the famously sensationalist *Evening News*. His best-known work is his boastful and unreliable autobiography *My Life and Loves* (4 vols, 1923–27), which was banned for pornography.

Harris, Joel Chandler 1848–1908 *•US writer•* Born in Eatonton, Georgia, he was in turn printer, lawyer, and journalist on the staff of the Atlanta *Constitution* (1876–1900). Having absorbed much Georgia African-American folklore and many sayings and stories, he began to publish his "Uncle Remus" tales in the *Constitution*. His

Uncle Remus: His Songs and Sayings (1880) made him internationally famous. A gifted storyteller, he also wrote *Nights with Uncle Remus* (1883).

“ ”

Watch out w'en you're gottin all you want.
Fatterin' hogs ain't in luck.

1880 ***Uncle Remus: His Songs and Sayings.***

Harris, Julie (Julia Ann) 1925– •*US actress*• Born in Grosse Point, Michigan, she made her New York debut in 1945 as a student at Yale School of Drama, and in 1946 won critical acclaim as a member of the Old Vic New York company. She established her reputation as a leading actress with her performance as Frankie Adams in **Carson McCullers**'s *The Member of the Wedding* in 1950 (later starring in the film version of 1952), following this with an appearance as Sally Bowles in *I Am a Camera* (1951). She is renowned for her solo performance as **Emily Dickinson** in *The Belle of Amherst* (1976).

Harris, Rolf 1930– •*Australian entertainer and artist*• Born in Bassendean, Perth, Western Australia, he won a radio “Amateur Hour” competition at the age of 18, and after graduating from the University of Western Australia went to London in 1952 where he studied art. He returned to Perth in 1960 to host a children's television program and then had commercial success with records such as *Tie Me Kangaroo Down, Sport* (1960) and the number one single “Two Little Boys” (1969). His many television shows have included *The Rolf Harris Show* (1967–72), *Rolf's Cartoon Club* (1989–93), *Animal Hospital* (1994–) and *Rolf on Art* (2001).

Harris, Roy Ellsworth 1898–1979 •*US composer*• Born in Lincoln County, Oklahoma and brought up on a farm in California, he had no specialized musical training until the age of 24, but studies in Los Angeles led to a Guggenheim Fellowship, which enabled him to study in Paris under **Nadia Boulanger**. Ruggedly American in character, his compositions are strongly rhythmic and melodic. He wrote some 15 symphonies, of which the best known are his *Third Symphony* (1938) and his *Folksong Symphony* (No. 4, 1940). Other works include the orchestral piece *When Johnny Comes Marching Home* (1935).

Harris, (Theodore) Wilson 1921– •*British novelist*• Born in New Amsterdam, British Guiana (now Guyana), he was educated at Queen's College, Georgetown, and worked as a surveyor. In 1959 he moved to London. His masterpiece is *The Guyana Quartet* (1960–63), which begins with a poetic exploration, and evolves into a composite picture of the various landscapes and racial communities of Guyana. Later works include *The Waiting Room* (1967), *Carnival* (1985), *The Four Banks of the River of Space* (1990) and *Resurrection at Sorrow Hill* (1993).

Harrison, Benjamin 1833–1901 •*23rd President of the US*• Born in North Bend, Ohio, the grandson of **William Henry Harrison**, he studied at Miami University in Ohio, and in 1854 settled as a lawyer in Indianapolis. He took an active part in **Ulysses S Grant**'s presidential campaigns of 1868 and 1872. He was senator for Indiana (1881–87) and in 1888 he was nominated for president against the Democrat **Grover Cleveland**. The contest turned on the issue of free trade, and Harrison's election was a triumph for protectionism. His administration (1889–93) saw the adoption in 1890 of the **McKinley** Tariff, which set the highest tariff rates in US history, as well as the passage of the Sherman Silver Purchase Act. He took an active interest in foreign affairs, pressing for the establishment of US military bases overseas and sponsoring the first Pan-American Conference (1889). In 1892 he failed to gain reelection against Cleveland, and returned to legal practice.

Harrison, George 1943–2001 •*English songwriter, vocalist and lead guitarist*• Born in Liverpool, he joined the Quarrymen (who adopted the name **The Beatles** in 1960) in 1958 and went solo after the group disbanded in 1970. “My Sweet Lord” (1970) reflected his continuing interest in spiritual matters, while other hit singles included “Bangla Desh” (1971) and “Give Me Love” (1973). Acclaimed solo albums included *All Things Must Pass* (1970), *Dark Horse* (1974) and *Cloud Nine* (1987). In 1971 he organized a charity concert in aid of Bangladesh and in 1988, with **Bob Dylan** and others, he formed a “supergroup” called the Traveling Wilburys. This aside, he recorded less after the 1970s, concentrating upon work as a successful film producer.

Harrison, John 1693–1776 •*English inventor and horologist*• He was born in Foulby, Yorkshire, and by 1726 had constructed a timekeeper with compensating apparatus for correcting errors due to variations of climate. In 1713 the British government had offered three prizes for the discovery of a method to determine longitude accurately. After long perseverance he developed a marine chronometer which, in a voyage to Jamaica (1761–62) determined the longitude within 18 geographical miles (or 29 km). After further trials, he was awarded the first prize (1765–73).

Harrison, Sir Rex, *originally* **Reginald Carey Harrison** 1908–90 •*English actor*• Born in Houghton, Lancashire, he joined the Liverpool Playhouse on leaving school and made his West End debut in *Getting Gertie Married* (1930) and his film debut in *The Great Game* (1930). His films include *Major Barbara* (1940), *Blithe Spirit* (1945), *Anna and the King of Siam* (1946), *Cleopatra* (1962) and *Dr Dolittle* (1967). His urbane and somewhat blasé style led to many leading comedy roles, including that of Professor Higgins in *My Fair Lady* (1956–58), which he was the first to play and which he repeated on film (1964, Academy Award). He married six times and published his autobiography, *Rex* (1974). He was knighted in 1989.

Harrison, Tony 1937– •*English poet*• He was born in Leeds, and educated at the University of Leeds. His working-class background and subsequent education in the classics create a social tension which has proved his most fruitful theme. The desire to give a poetic voice to those who have historically lacked one informs much of his work. He has gained international recognition for his verse translations and adaptations for the theater, notably of the York Mystery Plays and the Greek tragedies. He has also explored the possibilities of poetry on television with *V* (1985), a denunciatory journey through modern British life. His publications include *Earthworks* (1964), *The Gaze of the Gorgon* (1992, Whitbread Poetry Award) and *Laureate's Block and Other Poems* (2000).

Harrison, William Henry 1773–1841 •*9th President of the US*• Born in Charles City County, Virginia, he joined the troops Anthony Wayne (1745–96) led against the Native Americans, and distinguished himself at the Battle of Fallen Timbers in 1794. When Indiana Territory was formed in 1800 he was appointed governor. He represented Ohio in the US House (1816–19) and in the Senate (1825–28). Gaining the Whig presidential nomination in 1840, he joined with vice-presidential nominee **John Tyler** in waging an energetic and image-conscious campaign, emphasizing his log-cabin frontier days. Elected by an overwhelming majority, he caught pneumonia at his inauguration and died a month later (April 1841). He was the grandfather of **Benjamin Harrison**.

Harry, Blind fl. 1470–92 •*Scottish poet*• Blind from birth, he lived by telling tales, and from 1490 to 1492 was at the court of **James IV**, receiving occasional small gratuities. His major known work is *Wallace*, on the life of the Scottish patriot **William Wallace**, written in rhyming couplets. The poem transfers to its hero some of the achievements of **Robert the Bruce**, and contains many mistakes or misrepresentations, but much of the narrative can bear the test of historical criticism.

Harry, Deborah, *also known as* **Debbie Harry** 1945– •*US singer and actress*• Born in Miami, Florida, she worked as a beautician, waitress and Playboy Bunny. In 1973, with her partner Chris Stein, she formed the Stilettoes, which later became Blondie. People tended to believe that the name referred to her alone, and after a string of New Wave hits such as “Heart of Glass” and “Denise,” and the albums *Parallel Lines* (1978) and *Eat to the Beat* (1979), she went solo under her own name. Her first solo record was *Koo-Koo* (1981), followed by *Rockbird* (1986). She also turned to acting, with parts in *Atlantic City* (1980) and *Videodrome* (1982).

Hart, Gary, *originally* **Gary Hartpence** 1936– •*US Democratic politician*• He was born in Ottawa, Kansas, and educated at Yale University, where he became immersed in Democratic Party politics. He moved to Denver, Colorado, where he established a law practice and, after managing **George McGovern**'s presidential campaign between 1970 and 1972, entered the US Senate in 1974. He acquired a reputation for his advocacy of realistic liberal reforms, and ran for the Democratic presidential nomination in 1980, almost defeating the "party insider," **Walter Mondale**. He retired from the Senate in 1986 to concentrate on a bid for the presidency, but in 1987 he withdrew from the race when his wholesome, family image was thrown into question by newspaper reporting of his private life. He reentered the race in 1988 but withdrew shortly afterward.

Hart (of South Lanark), Dame Judith Constance Mary Hart, Baroness 1924–91 •*English Labour politician*• Born in Burnley, Lancashire, she was educated at the London School of Economics. She became a Labour Member of Parliament in 1959, and joined **Harold Wilson**'s government in 1964, reaching Cabinet rank as Paymaster-General in 1968. She then had three successful terms as Minister of Overseas Development (1969–70, 1974–75, 1977–79). She was a popular and influential left-winger, with a strong concern for the needs of Third World countries, and was given the honorary title of Dame Commander, Order of the British Empire, in 1979 and awarded a life peerage in 1988.

Hart, Lorenz Milton 1895–1943 •*US lyricist*• Born in New York City, he studied at Columbia University. He met the young composer **Richard Rodgers** in 1918, and over the next two decades they collaborated on 28 Broadway musicals, including *A Connecticut Yankee* (1927), *The Boys from Syracuse* (1938) and *Pal Joey* (1940). Hart's classic songs with Rodgers included "The Lady Is a Tramp," "Blue Moon" and "My Funny Valentine." Hart's alcoholism eventually forced Rodgers to seek another collaborator in **Oscar Hammerstein II**.

Hart, Moss 1904–61 •*US dramatist and director*• Born in the Bronx, New York, he began his career as an office boy, selling his first play, *The Beloved Bandit*, when still a teenager. With **George S Kaufman** he wrote several plays, the most popular being the wry comedies *Merrily We Roll Along* (1934), *You Can't Take It with You* (1936) and *The Man Who Came to Dinner* (1939), described by one reviewer as "a merciless cartoon" of the critic Alexander Woollcott (1887–1943).

Harte, (Francis) Bret(t) 1836–1902 •*US author*• Born in Albany, New York, he went to California in 1854. He was US consul in Crefeld, Germany (1878–80) and in Glasgow (1880–85), and then lived in London. His most famous poems, written in San Francisco, include "John Burns of Gettysburg" and "The Society upon the Stanislaus." His humorous verse includes "Plain Language from Truthful James" (1870), commonly referred to as "The Heathen Chinee." In 1868 he founded and edited the *Overland Monthly*, to which he contributed short stories, later collected in *The Luck of Roaring Camp and Other Sketches* (1870).

Hartington, Marquis of *See* **Cavendish, Spencer Compton**

Hartley, David 1705–57 •*English philosopher, physician and psychologist*• Born in Luddenden, Halifax, Yorkshire, and educated at Cambridge, he became a successful medical practitioner. His *Observations on Man, His Frame, His Duty and His Expectations* (1749) relates psychology closely to physiology, and develops a theory of the association of sensations with sets of ideas which forms part of an associationist tradition running from **David Hume** through to **John Stuart Mill** and **Herbert Spencer**.

Hartley, L(eslie) P(oles) 1895–1972 •*English writer*• He was born near Peterborough, Cambridgeshire, and educated at Harrow and at Balliol College, Oxford. Early short stories such as *The Killing Bottle* (1932) established his reputation as a master of the macabre. Later he transferred his Jamesian power of "turning the screw" to psychological relationships and made a new success with such novels as his Eustace and Hilda trilogy *The Shrimp and the Anemone* (1944), *The Sixth Heaven* (1946) and *Eustace and Hilda* (1947). Among his finest work is *The Boat* (1950), and his best-known novel *The Go-Between* (1953).

" "

The past is a foreign country: they do things differently there.

1953 ***The Go-Between****, prologue.*

Hartley, Marsden 1877–1943 •*US painter and writer*• Born in Lewiston, Maine, he visited France and Germany in 1912–15. Inspired by **Wassily Kandinsky** and **Franz Marc**, his work became abstract, and he exhibited with the Blaue Reiter group, but landscapes—especially mountains—always attracted him. He traveled widely in the 1920s and did not settle finally in Maine until 1934. He was one of the pioneers of US modern art.

Hartline, Haldan Keffer 1903–83 •*US physiologist and Nobel Prize winner*• Born in Bloomsburg, Pennsylvania, he received a medical degree from Johns Hopkins Medical School, and in 1931 he went to the Johnson Foundation of the University of Pennsylvania, where he remained until 1949. Inspired by the work of Detlev Bronk (1887–1975) and **Edgar Adrian**, Hartline carried out experiments in the optic nerve of the horseshoe crab and the visual system of the frog, analyzing the several physiological stages by which an eye distinguishes shapes. His work led directly to that of **David Hubel** and **Torsten Wiesel**, and he shared the 1967 Nobel Prize for physiology or medicine with **George Wald** and **Ragnar Granit**.

Hartnell, Sir Norman 1901–78 •*English couturier and court dressmaker*• Born in London, he was educated at Magdalene College, Cambridge. He started his own business in 1923, receiving the Royal Warrant in 1940. Costumes for leading actresses, wartime "utility" dresses, the Women's Royal Army Corps uniform and Princess **Elizabeth**'s wedding and coronation gowns all formed part of his work.

Hartree, Douglas Rayner 1897–1958 •*English mathematician and physicist*• He was born in Cambridge, where he graduated after working on the science of antiaircraft gunnery during World War I. From 1929 to 1945 he was Professor of Applied Mathematics and Theoretical Physics at the University of Manchester, returning to Cambridge as Professor of Mathematical Physics in 1946. His work ranged from atomic physics, where he invented the method of the self-consistent field in quantum mechanics, to the automated control of chemical plants. At Manchester he developed the differential analyzer, an analog computer, and was deeply involved in the early days of the electronic digital computer.

Hartung, Hans 1904–89 •*French artist*• Born in Leipzig, Germany, he studied in Basel, Leipzig, Dresden and Munich. Although in his earlier years he was influenced by the German impressionists and expressionists, from 1928 onward he produced mainly abstract work. During World War II he served in the French Foreign Legion and gained French citizenship in 1945. His later paintings, which have made him one of the most famous French abstract painters, show a free calligraphy resembling that of Chinese brushwork.

Hartwell, Lee, *in full* **Leland H(arrison)** 1939– •*US biologist and Nobel Prize winner*• Born in Los Angeles, he studied at the California Institute of Technology and at MIT. He was professor at the University of California, Irvine (1965–68) and University of Washington (1968–) before becoming president and director of the Fred Hutchinson Cancer Research Center, Seattle (1998–). In 2001 he shared the Nobel Prize for physiology or medicine with **Paul M Nurse** and **Tim Hunt** for their discoveries of key regulators of the cell cycle, allowing more accurate cancer diagnostics.

Harun al-Rashid, *in full* **Harun al-Rashid ibn Muhammad al-Mahdi ibn al-Manṣur al-'Abbasi** 766–809 •*Fifth 'Abbasid caliph*• His reign, and that of his son al-Mamun (786–833), marked the apogee of the 'Abbasid caliphate, which ruled an empire stretching from North Africa to Central Asia. Harun came to the throne upon the death of his brother al-Hadi (786) with the help of the influential Barmakid family, which he permitted to dominate his early reign but gradually removed from power. A great patron of the arts, enthusiastic in waging war against the Byzantines, he weakened the empire through his attempts to divide it among his three sons. He is the caliph who figures in many of the tales of the *Arabian Nights*.

Harvard, John 1607–38 •*American colonial clergyman*• Born in Southwark, London, he studied at Emmanuel College, Cambridge, and in 1637 went out to Charlestown, Massachusetts, where he preached. He bequeathed £800 and over 300 volumes to the newly founded college in Cambridge that was later named in his honor.

Harvey, William 1578–1657 •*English physician, discoverer of the circulation of the blood*• Born in Folkestone, Kent, he studied medicine at Caius College, Cambridge, then went to Padua to work under Hieronymus Fabricius (1537–1619). In 1602 he began practicing as a physician in London, and in 1615 he was Lumleian Lecturer at the College of Physicians. His celebrated treatise *Exercitatio anatomica de motu cordis et sanguinis in animalibus* ("An Anatomical Exercise on the Motion of the Heart and the Blood in Animals"), in which the circulation of the blood was first described, was published in 1628. He was successively physician to **James VI and I** (from 1618) and **Charles I** (from 1640). His *Exercitationes de generatione animalium* ("Essays on the Generation of Animals"), in which he confirmed the doctrine that every living being has its origin in an egg, appeared in 1651. The key claim of his earlier, distinguished work on the cardiovascular system was that the heart was a muscle functioning as a pump, and that it effected the movement of the blood through the body via the lungs by means of the arteries, the blood then returning through the veins to the heart. His views contradicted ideas central to medicine since **Galen**, and he was widely ridiculed by traditionalists, notably in France. He was not able to show how blood passed from the arterial to the venous system, there being no connections visible to the naked eye. However, he rightly supposed that the links existed but must be too minute to see, and **Marcello Malpighi** observed them with a microscope, shortly after Harvey's death.

Harvey-Jones, Sir John Henry 1924– •*English industrial executive*• Born in Kent, he was educated at Dartmouth Naval College and served in the navy until 1956, when he joined Imperial Chemical Industries. As its chairman (1982–87) he was largely responsible for reshaping the company, and from 1987 to 1996 he was chairman of Parallax Enterprises. His publications include *Getting It Together* (1991) and *All Together Now* (1994). On television he has appeared in *Troubleshooter* (1990) and later similar programs including *Troubleshooter Returns* (1995). He was knighted in 1985.

Harvie Anderson, Betty 1914–79 •*Scottish Conservative politician*• Born into a political family, she was elected Member of Parliament for Renfrewshire (East) in 1959, becoming a member of the 1922 Committee of Backbench Members of Parliament. In 1970 she became the first woman to take the Speaker's chair, keeping order during turbulent times, especially through the passage of the Industrial Relations Act (1970–71) and the Common Market debates.

Harwood, Gwen(doline Nessie), *née* **Foster** 1920–95 •*Australian poet and librettist*• Born in Taringa, a suburb of Brisbane, she did not publish her first book of verse, *Poems*, until 1963. Subsequent volumes include *The Lion's Bride* (1981), *Bone Scan* (1988) and *The Present Tense* (1995). She also wrote libretti for leading Australian composers, including **Larry Sitsky**, James Penberthy and Ian Cugley. She received the **Robert Frost** award in 1977, and the **Patrick White** Literary award in 1978, and won the Melbourne *Age* Book of the Year award for 1990 with *Blessed City*, a collection of letters from her Brisbane home of the 1940s to a friend in the navy.

Harwood, Sir Henry 1888–1959 •*English naval commander*• As commander of the South American division, he commanded the British ships at the Battle of the River Plate, in which the German battleship *Graf Spee* was trapped in Montevideo and later scuttled (December 1939). He was made Commander in Chief of the Mediterranean fleet in 1942.

Hasdrubal, *also called* **Hasdrubal Barca ("Lightning")** d. 207 BC •*Carthaginian general*• The son of **Hamilcar** and the brother of **Hannibal**, from 218 to 208 he fought successfully against the great Roman general **Scipio Africanus**, known as Scipio the Elder, and his son **Scipio Africanus**, known as Scipio the Younger. In 207 Hasdrubal marched across the Alps to Italy to support his brother, but was intercepted at the river Metaurus and killed.

Hašek, Jaroslav 1883–1923 •*Czech novelist and short-story writer*• Born in Prague, he is best known for the novel *Osudy dobrého vojáka Švejka* (1920–23, Eng trans *The Good Soldier Švejk*, 1930), a brilliantly incisive satire on military life. The character of Švejk, an irresponsible and undisciplined drunkard, liar, scrounger and philistine, is widely thought to be at least partly autobiographical in inspiration. In 1915 he deserted the Austrian army (Austria ruled Bohemia at the time) and crossed over to the Russian side. Characteristically, however, he managed to make satirical attacks on both regimes.

Hassan II 1929–99 •*King of Morocco*• He was born in Rabat, the eldest son of King Mohammed V. Educated in France at the University of Bordeaux, Crown Prince Hassan served his father as head of the army (1955) and, on his accession to the throne (1961), also became prime minister. After initially introducing a new constitution, with a popularly elected legislature, he suspended parliament and established a royal dictatorship in 1965, after riots in Casablanca. His forces occupied Spanish (Western) Sahara (1975), and he mobilized a large army to check the incursion of Polisario guerrillas across his western Saharan frontier (1976–88). Unrest in the larger towns led Hassan to appoint a coalition government of national unity under a civilian prime minister in 1984.

Hassel, Odd 1897–1981 •*Norwegian physical chemist and Nobel Prize winner*• Born in Oslo, he was educated at the Universities of Oslo, Munich and Berlin. From 1925 until his retirement in 1964 he was on the staff of the department of physical chemistry of the University of Oslo, and received the Nobel Prize for chemistry jointly with Sir **Derek Barton** in 1969. Hassel's most distinguished research was carried out in the 1930s and involved the application of X-ray and electron diffraction, and the measurement of dipole moments. He elucidated the details of the molecular structure of cyclohexane and related compounds, and thereby helped to establish the concepts and procedures of conformational analysis.

Hastings, Francis Rawdon-Hastings, 1st Marquis of 1754–1826 •*English soldier and administrator*• He was born in Dublin and educated at Harrow. He fought with distinction (1775–81) in the American Revolutionary War, and in 1794 he led reinforcements to **Frederick Augustus** at Malines. In 1813 he was made governor-general of India. Here he fought successfully against the Gurkhas (1814–16) and the Pindaris and Marathas (1817–18), encouraged Indian education and freedom of the press, reformed the law system, and elevated the civil service. In 1821, however, he resigned after apparently unfounded charges of corruption had been made against him, and from 1824 until his death was governor of Malta.

Hastings, (Andrew) Gavin 1962– •*Scottish rugby player*• Born in Edinburgh and educated at Cambridge, he made his debut for Scotland in 1986. A powerful attacking fullback, he played in the 1987, 1991 and 1995 World Cups, and was an indispensable member of the Scotland team which won the Grand Slam in 1990. He has also played three times for the British Lions and captained them in the 1993 tour of New Zealand. He became captain of the Scotland team for the first time in the 1992–93 season. Having broken **Andy Irvine**'s record number of points scored for Scotland in international matches, he stepped down after the 1995 World Cup in South Africa.

Hastings, Warren 1732–1818 •*English colonial administrator*• Born in Churchill, Oxfordshire, he was educated at Westminster School. In 1750 he went to Calcutta in the service of the East India Company, becoming a member of council at Calcutta. In 1772 he became Governor of Bengal and President of the Council, and a year later he was created governor-general. Hastings extended the power of the East India Company in India, improving the administration of justice, organizing the opium revenue, and waging vigorous war with the Marathas. He returned to England in 1785 and was charged with cruelty and corruption, and impeached at the Bar of the House of Lords. The trial began on February 13, 1788. Finally, in April 1795, Hastings was acquitted on all charges.

Hatshepsut c. 1540–c. 1481 BC •*Queen of Egypt of the 18th dynasty*• She was the daughter of Tuthmosis I, and married Tuthmosis II, his son by another wife. Tuthmosis II succeeded in 1516 BC, and was himself succeeded in 1503 by **Tuthmosis III**, his son by a minor wife, for whom Hatshepsut ruled as regent. She had herself crowned pharaoh with full powers and titles. She was represented in male attire, including an artificial beard. During her 20-year reign, she built her mortuary temple at Deir el Bahri, erected obelisks at Karnak and dispatched a trading expedition to Punt (now Eritrea/Somalia).

Hattersley, Roy Sydney George Hattersley, Baron 1932– •*English Labour politician*• Born in Sheffield, Yorkshire, and educated at Hull University, he was a journalist and Health Service executive as well as a member of Sheffield City Council before becoming a Labour Member of Parliament (1964–97). He was Minister of State at the Foreign Office for two years, then Secretary of State for Prices and Consumer Protection in the **Callaghan** government (1976–79). Regarded as being on the right wing of the party, he was elected deputy Leader of the Labour Party (1983–92), with **Neil Kinnock** as Leader. Though reelected in 1988, following the defeat of Labour in the 1992 general election they were replaced, Kinnock by **John Smith** and Hattersley by **Margaret Beckett**. He is a regular contributor to newspapers and periodicals and has written novels and his autobiography, *Who Goes Home? Scenes from a Political Life* (1995). He was made a life peer in 1997.

Haughey, Charles James 1925– •*Irish politician*• Born in Castlebar, County Mayo, and educated at University College, Dublin, he was called to the bar in 1949. A former chartered accountant, Haughey became a Fianna Fáil Member of Parliament in 1957, and from 1961 held posts in justice, agriculture and finance, until his dismissal after a political disagreement with the prime minister **Jack Lynch** (1970). He was subsequently tried and acquitted on a charge of conspiracy to import arms illegally. He succeeded Lynch as prime minister in 1979, and governed for two years. Premier again in 1982 and from 1987 to 1992, he was succeeded by **Albert Reynolds**.

Hauptman, Herbert Aaron 1917– •*US mathematical physicist and Nobel Prize winner*• Born in New York City, he was educated at the City College of New York, Columbia University and at the University of Maryland. While working at the US Naval Research Laboratories in Washington with **Jerome Karle** during the 1950s and 1960s, he helped develop a statistical technique that increased the speed of methods by which X-ray crystallography mapped structures of molecules. In 1985, 22 years after publishing the work, Hauptman and Karle were jointly awarded the Nobel Prize for chemistry.

Hauptmann, Gerhart Johann Robert 1862–1946 •*German dramatist and novelist, and Nobel Prize winner*• Born in Obersalzbrunn, Silesia, he studied sculpture in Breslau and Rome before settling in Berlin (1885). His first play, *Vor Sonnenaufgang* (1889, Eng trans *Before Dawn*, 1909), introduced the new social drama of **Ibsen**, **Émile Zola** and **August Strindberg** to Germany, but Hauptmann's naturalism was alleviated by a note of compassion. His works include *Die Weber* (1892, Eng trans *The Weavers*, 1899), *Florian Geyer* (1896, Eng trans 1894), *Die Versunkene Glocke* (1896, Eng trans *The Sunken Bell*, 1898), *Rose Bernd* (1903, Eng trans 1913) and the comedies *Der Biberpelz* (1893, Eng trans *The Beaver Coat*, 1912) and *Der rote Hahn* (1901, Eng trans *The Conflagration*, 1913). His novels include *Der Narr in Christo: Emanuel Quint* (1910, Eng trans *The Fool in Christ: Emanuel Quint*, 1911) and *Atlantis* (1912, Eng trans 1912). He was awarded the Nobel Prize for literature in 1912.

Hauteclocque, Vicomte de *See* **Leclerc, Jacques Philippe**

Haüy, René Just 1743–1822 •*French crystallographer and mineralogist*• Born in St Just, Picardy, he initially studied botany and embryology before developing his interests in mineralogy and crystallography. His *Traité de minéralogie* ("Treatise of Mineralogy") was published in 1801, the same year that he succeeded **Déodat de Dolomieu** as Professor of Mineralogy at the Museum of Natural History in Paris. He is widely regarded as the father of crystallography.

Havel, Václav 1936– •*Czech dramatist and statesman*• Born in Prague, where he was educated at the Academy of Dramatic Art, he began work as a stagehand at the Prague *Theater Na Zábradlí* (Theatre on the Balustrade), becoming resident writer there (1960–69). His work includes *Zahradní slavnost* (1963, Eng trans *The Garden Party*, 1969) and *Audience* (1976, Eng trans *Temptation*, 1976). He was one of the founders of Charter 77 in 1977. Deemed subversive, in 1979 he was imprisoned for four and a half years. He was again imprisoned in February 1989, but was released three months later. In December 1989, after the overthrow of the Czechoslovakian Communist Party during the so-called Velvet Revolution, he was elected president by direct popular vote. He oversaw the peaceful division of Czechoslovakia into the separate nations of the Czech Republic and Slovakia in 1992 and was president of the Czech Republic (1993–2003).

Havelock, Sir Henry 1795–1857 •*English soldier*• He was born in Bishop-Wearmouth, Sunderland. A lawyer by training, he entered the army and went to India in 1823. On the outbreak of the Indian Mutiny (1857–58), he organized a column of 1,000 Highlanders and others at Allahabad with which to relieve Cawnpore and Lucknow, and entered Cawnpore, having marched 125 miles and fought four actions in nine days, in the heat of July. Crossing the Ganges, he fought eight victorious battles, but, through cholera and dysentery in his army, had to retire to Cawnpore. In September General James Outram (1803–63) arrived with reinforcements, and Havelock again advanced, Outram waiving his superior rank and serving under Havelock as a volunteer. The relieving force fought their way to the Lucknow Residency, where they in turn were besieged by the determined rebel forces until November, when Sir **Colin Campbell** forced his way to their rescue. Four days later Havelock died of dysentery.

Havilland, Sir Geoffrey De *See* **De Havilland, Sir Geoffrey**

Havilland, Olivia Mary de *See* **de Havilland, Olivia Mary**

Haw-Haw, Lord *See* **Joyce, William**

Hawke, Bob (Robert James Lee) 1929– •*Australian trade union executive and politician*• Born in Bordertown, South Australia, he was educated at the University of Western Australia and University College, Oxford. He worked for the Australian Council of Trade Unions for over 20 years (president, 1970–80) before becoming a Member of Parliament in 1980. His Labor Party defeated the ruling Liberals in the 1983 general election only one month after adopting him as leader, and he became prime minister (1983–91). Frequently described as colorful, he is a skilled orator who won praise for his handling and settling of industrial disputes. In 1990, he became the first Labor prime minister to win a fourth term in office, but in 1991 he was replaced as prime minister by **Paul Keating**.

Hawke (of Towton), Edward Hawke, 1st Baron 1705–81 •*English admiral*• Born in London, he joined the navy in 1720. In the Seven Years' War (1756–63) he destroyed the French fleet in Quiberon Bay in November 1759, thus preventing an invasion of Great Britain. He became a Member of Parliament (1747), First Lord of the Admiralty (1766–71), Admiral of the Fleet (1768) and a baron (1776).

Hawkes, Jacquetta, *née* **Hopkins** 1910–96 •*English archaeologist and writer*• Born in Cambridge and educated at the Perse School and Newnham College, Cambridge, she was the first woman to study archaeology and anthropology to degree level. Her publications include *Early Britain* (1945) and *A Land* (1951). She also wrote on Egyptian topics, produced a biography of **Sir Mortimer Wheeler**, and wrote a book of poetry, *Symbols and Speculations* (1948). With her second husband, **J B Priestley**, she wrote *Journey Down the Rainbow* (1955), a jovial indictment of US life in letter form, as well as fictional works. She was a cofounder of the Campaign for Nuclear Disarmament in 1957.

Hawking, Stephen William 1942– •*English theoretical physicist*• Born in Oxford, he graduated from the University of Oxford and received his PhD from Cambridge. He was elected a Fellow of the Royal Society in 1974, and became Lucasian Professor of Mathematics at Cambridge in 1980. His early research on relativity led him to study gravitational singularities, such as the big bang, when the universe originated, and black holes, where space-time is curved due to enormous gravitational fields. The theory of black holes, which result when massive stars collapse under their own gravity at the end of their lives, owes much to his mathematical work. Since 1974 he has shown that a black hole could actually evaporate through loss of thermal radiation, and predicted that mass can escape entirely from its gravitational pull. This loss of mass is known as the Hawking process. His achievements are even more remarkable because from the 1960s he has suffered from a highly disabling and progressive neuromotor disease, amyotrophic lateral sclerosis (Lou Gehrig's disease). He has nevertheless continued to work and produce scientific papers as well as several best-selling popular science books, the first of which, *A Brief History of Time* (1988), is an account of modern cosmology. More recent publications have included *Black Holes and Baby Universes* (1993) and *The Universe in a Nutshell* (2001).

“ ”

If we find the answer to that, it would be the ultimate triumph of human reason—for then we would know the mind of God.

1988 Referring to the question of why we and the universe exist. ***A Brief History of Time****, chapter 11.*

Hawkins, Coleman 1904–69 •*US tenor saxophonist*• Born in St Joseph, Missouri, he received piano lessons as a child and studied music at Washburn College, Topeka. In 1923 he joined the **Fletcher Henderson** Orchestra, where he laid the foundations of the tenor saxophone's future preeminence as a jazz solo instrument. His 1939 recording of the ballad "Body and Soul" became a benchmark for jazz saxophonists in the swing style. Renowned for his full tone and well-constructed improvisations, Hawkins later embraced the bop movement and was also a member of the touring Jazz at the Philharmonic groups.

Hawkins, Jack (John Edward) 1910–73 •*English actor*• Born in Wood Green, London, he trained for the theater at the Italia Conti School of Acting. His adult debut was in *Young Woodley* (1929), and his first New York appearance was in *Journey's End* (1930). His first film, *Birds of Prey* (1930), began a prolific cinema career that ran parallel with a series of admired Shakespearean roles opposite **John Gielgud**. A colonel in the Royal Welsh Fusiliers (1940–46) during World War II, he often played heroes with stiff upper lips and authoritarian figures in such films as *The Cruel Sea* (1953), *The Bridge on the River Kwai* (1957) and *Lawrence of Arabia* (1962).

Hawkins or **Hawkyns, Sir John** 1532–95 •*English navigator and naval commander*• Born in Plymouth, he became the first Englishman to traffic in slaves (1562), taking slaves from West Africa to the Spanish West Indies. During his third voyage (1567), he and **Francis Drake** were intercepted and their fleet destroyed by the Spanish. He was knighted for his services against the Armada (1588), and in 1595, with his kinsman Drake, he commanded an expedition to the Spanish Main, but died in Puerto Rico.

Hawks, Howard Winchester 1896–1977 •*US film director*• Born in Goshen, Indiana, he graduated with a degree in mechanical engineering, served in the US Army Air Corps and wrote scripts for silent films before making his directorial debut with *The Road to Glory* (1926). He survived the transition to sound, establishing himself as one of the great American filmmakers, noted for his versatility, storytelling skills, love of dialogue, and focus on women who could be just as tough and sassy as their male counterparts. His many successful films include *Bringing Up Baby* (1938), *His Girl Friday* (1940), *To Have and Have Not* (1944), *The Big Sleep* (1946), *Red River* (1948) and *Rio Bravo* (1959). He received an honorary Oscar in 1975.

Hawksmoor, Nicholas 1661–1736 •*English architect*• Born in Nottinghamshire, he became a clerk for Sir **Christopher Wren** and also assisted Sir **John Vanbrugh** at Blenheim Palace and Castle Howard. His most individual contributions are the London churches St Mary Woolnoth, St George's, Bloomsbury, St Anne's, Limehouse and Christ Church, Spitalfields, as well as parts of Queen's College and All Souls, Oxford.

Hawn, Goldie Jeanne 1945– •*US film actress*• Born in Washington DC, she trained in ballet and tap and dropped out of college to form her own dancing school. Turning to television, she soon became popular as one of the ensemble troupe in *Rowan and Martin's Laugh-In* (1968–70). She won a Best Supporting Actress Academy Award for *Cactus Flower* (1969) and starred in many comedy roles throughout the 1970s. She was the executive producer and star of the popular film *Private Benjamin* (1980); other notable successes include *Bird on a Wire* (1990), *The First Wives Club* (1996) and *Everyone Says I Love You* (1996).

Haworth, Sir (Walter) Norman 1883–1950 •*English chemist and Nobel Prize winner*• Born in Chorley, Lancashire, he learned most of his early chemistry from working in his father's linoleum factory, and it was 1903 when he enrolled at the University of Manchester. He undertook further study at Göttingen, and after various research and teaching posts took up the chair of organic chemistry at the University of Birmingham in 1925. He shared the Nobel Prize for chemistry with **Paul Karrer** in 1937 for determining the structure of vitamin C. He was knighted in 1947.

Hawthorne, Nathaniel 1804–64 •*US novelist and short-story writer*• He was born in Salem, Massachusetts. He attended Bowdoin College, then returned to Salem and shut himself away for 12 years, writing tales and verses. Some of his short stories were favorably reviewed in the London *Athenaeum*, and were collected as *Twice-Told Tales* (1837), but his talent was not yet appreciated in his own country. In 1839 he was appointed weigher and gauger in the customhouse, a post he held until 1841. In that year he spent several months at the Brook Farm, an idyllic, semi-socialistic community near Boston. Moving to Concord, Massachusetts, in 1842, he issued *Biographical Stories* for children and brought out an enlarged edition of *Twice-Told Tales* (1842). His sketches and studies written for the *Democratic Review* were collected as *Mosses from an Old Manse* (1846). Having lost all his savings at Brook Farm, he was forced to accept a place in the customhouse again—this time as surveyor in Salem. In 1850 he published *The Scarlet Letter*, still the best known of his works. At Lenox, Massachusetts, he then entered upon a phase of remarkable productiveness, writing *The House of the Seven Gables* (1851), *Wonder Book* (1851), *The Snow Image* (1852) and *The Blithedale Romance* (1852), which drew upon his Brook Farm experience. He settled in Concord in 1852, and wrote a campaign biography of his old schoolfriend, President **Franklin Pierce**, and on Pierce's inauguration became consul in Liverpool (1853–57). He completed *Tanglewood Tales* in 1853, as a continuation of *Wonder Book*.

“ ”

Let men tremble to win the hand of woman, unless they win along with it the utmost passion of her heart!

1850 ***The Scarlet Letter****, chapter 15.*

Hawthorne, Sir Nigel Barnard 1929–2001 •*English actor*• Born in Coventry, he moved to South Africa with his parents as a child and made his stage debut there. Returning to Great Britain in 1951, he quickly conquered the London stage, and his long list of distinguished productions includes *Rosencrantz and Guildenstern Are Dead* (1971), *The Magistrate* (1986) and *Hapgood* (1988). He performed in *Shadowlands* in the West End (1989) and on Broadway (1990–92). He was best known on television as Sir Humphrey Appleby in *Yes Minister* (1980–92) and *Yes, Prime Minister* (1986–88). The film version of *The Madness of King George* (1994) earned him a Best Actor Academy Award nomination, and he subsequently starred in such films as *Twelfth Night* (1996) and *Amistad* (1997). He was knighted in 1999.

Hay, Will 1888–1949 •*English comic actor*• Born in Stockton-on-Tees, he was an apprentice engineer and entertained at charity shows before turning professional. He worked in music halls and radio prior to his film debut in *Know Your Apples* (1933). Appearing as seedy, disreputable figures of authority with delusions of grandeur in comedies like *Boys Will Be Boys* (1935) and *Oh, Mr Porter!* (1937), he was one of the country's top film attractions between 1937 and 1942. Also a respected amateur astronomer, he published *Through My Telescope* (1935).

Hayden, Bill (William George) 1933– •*Australian politician*• He was born in Brisbane. He served in the state civil and police services, joining the Australian Labor Party and entering the federal parliament in 1961. He served under **Gough Whitlam** and replaced him as party leader in 1977. In 1983 he surrendered the leadership to the more charismatic **Bob Hawke** and was Foreign Minister in his government (1983–88). From 1989 to 1996 he was Governor-General of Australia.

Haydn, (Franz) Joseph 1732–1809 •*Austrian composer*• Born in Rohrau, Lower Austria, he was educated at the Cathedral Choir School of St Stephen's, Vienna, earning his living to begin with by playing in street orchestras and teaching. He became musical director (1759–60) for Count von Morzin, who kept a small company of court musicians for whom he wrote his earliest symphonies. He then entered the service of Prince Pál Antal **Esterházy** (d. 1762) in 1761, and remained in his service and that of his successor, Prince Miklós Joseph, until 1790. As musical director of a princely establishment, his duties included the performance and composition of chamber and orchestral music, sacred music and opera for domestic consumption. These favorable conditions led to a vast output, notable, technically, for his near-standardization and development of the four-movement string quartet and the classical symphony, with sonata or "first movement" form as a basic structural ingredient. This was to influence the whole course of European music. Retiring in fact though not in name from Esterházy in 1790, he later paid two visits to London, sponsored by the violinist and impresario J P Salomon (1745–1815), during which he directed performances of the specially commissioned "Salomon" or "London" Symphonies (Nos. 93–104). He was made a Doctor of Music of Oxford in 1791. During the closing years of his life in Vienna, his main works were *The Creation* (1798), *The Seasons* (1801) and his final string quartets. He was the most famous composer of his day, but was quick to recognize the genius of the young **Mozart**, although slower to appreciate the turbulent, questing spirit of **Beethoven**, who was his pupil in 1792. His output includes 104 symphonies, about 50 concertos, 84 string quartets, 24 stage works, 12 masses, orchestral divertimenti, keyboard sonatas, and various chamber, choral, instrumental, and vocal pieces.

Hayek, Friedrich August von 1899–1992 •*British political economist and Nobel Prize winner*• He was born in Vienna and became director of the Austrian Institute for Economic Research (1927–31), later teaching at Vienna, London, Chicago and Freiburg. Books such as *Monetary Theory and the Trade Cycle* (1933) and *The Pure Theory of Capital* (1941) dealt with important problems arising out of industrial fluctuations. Strongly opposed to **Keynes**ianism, he showed an increasing concern for the problems posed for individual values by increased economic controls, and later broadened his interests to publish on theoretical psychology and the history of ideas. He was awarded the Nobel Prize in economic science in 1974, jointly with **Gunnar Myrdal**.

Hayes, Helen 1900–93 •*US actress*• Born in Washington DC, she made her Broadway debut in 1909 and went on to become one of the premier stage actresses of her generation. She appeared in a wide variety of stage productions, including *Victoria Regina* (1935–39), *The Wisteria Trees* (1951) and *A Touch of the Poet* (1958). She appeared in such films as *The Sin of Madelon Claudet* (1931, Academy Award, British title *The Lullaby*), *A Farewell to Arms* (1932), *Airport* (1970, Academy Award) and *Candleshoe* (1977).

Hayes, Rutherford B(irchard) 1822–93 •*19th President of the US*• Born in Delaware, Ohio, he graduated from Kenyon College, Ohio, and practiced law in Cincinnati (1849–61). He served in the Civil War with distinction, retiring as major general. He represented Ohio in Congress (1865–67) and was elected governor of Ohio three times (1867, 1869, 1875). In 1876 he was the Republican candidate for the presidency, the Democratic candidate being **Samuel J Tilden**. When the returns from four states were disputed, a Republican-dominated electoral commission awarded all the questionable votes to Hayes, securing him a majority of one in the electoral college. As president (1877–81) he withdrew the last remaining federal troops from the South, ending Reconstruction, and pursued a hard-money policy, bringing about the resumption of specie payments. He chose not to run for reelection in 1880.

Hays, Will(iam Harrison) 1879–1954 •*US politician and film censor*• Born in Sullivan, Indiana, he was a lawyer by training. As the first president of the Motion Picture Producers and Distributors of America (1922–45), he formulated the Production Code (1930) known as the Hays Code, which imposed a rigorous code of morality on US films, and which remained in force until 1966.

Hayward, Susan, *originally* **Edythe Marrenner** 1917–75 •*US film actress*• Born in Brooklyn, New York, she left her job as a cloth designer in a Manhattan handkerchief factory in 1936, and used her modest savings to enroll at the Feagin School of Dramatic Arts. Her abrasive personality combined successfully with her roles as crisis-ridden women and she received the first of five Best Actress Academy Award nominations for her performance as an alcoholic in *Smash-Up: The Story of a Woman* (1947). She went on to win this award for her role in *I Want to Live* (1958). She continued to act until the early 1970s and spent her last years battling brain tumors, making a final, typically defiant, public appearance as a hostess of the 1974 Academy Award ceremony.

Haywood, Eliza, *née* **Fowler** c. 1693–1756 •*English novelist*• She was born in London. After being deserted by her husband, she became an actress and wrote plays, as well as a number of scandalous society novels, in which the characters resembled living persons so closely as to be libelous. **Pope** denounced her in *The Dunciad*. She issued the periodicals *The Female Spectator* (1744–46) and *The Parrot* (1747). Her works include *Memoirs of a Certain Island Adjacent to Utopia* (1725) and *The History of Miss Betsy Thoughtless* (1751).

Haywood, William D(udley), *known as* **Big Bill** 1869–1928 •*US labor leader*• Born in Salt Lake City, Utah, he worked as a miner, homesteader, and cowboy, then joined the Western Federation of Miners (1896) and quickly became prominent. In 1905 he helped found the Industrial Workers of the World. An active socialist, he was convicted of sedition in 1917 for his opposition to World War I, then fled from the US (1921) and took refuge in the Soviet Union.

Hayworth, Rita, *originally* **Margarita Carmen Cansino** 1918–87 •*US film actress and dancer*• She was born into a showbusiness family in New York City, a cousin of **Ginger Rogers**. Nightclub appearances led to a succession of small roles in B movies. Blossoming into an international beauty, she appeared in many films, sometimes cast as an enigmatic temptress, as in *Blood and Sand* (1941) and *Gilda* (1946). She appeared in a number of musicals, and although her singing voice was dubbed, she was a skilled dancer, notably partnering **Gene Kelly** and **Fred Astaire**. Later roles were largely lackluster, although she was effective as the faded beauty in *Separate Tables* (1958). Her five husbands included **Orson Welles** and Prince Aly Khan. She suffered from Alzheimer's disease for many years prior to her death.

Hazlitt, William 1778–1830 •*English essayist*• He was born in Maidstone, Kent, and spent much of his childhood in Wem, Shropshire. At the age of 15 he was sent to Hackney College, London, to study for the ministry, but he had abandoned the notion by 1796 when he met **Coleridge**, who encouraged him to write *Principles of Human Action* (1805). He turned briefly to portrait painting, then published *Free Thoughts on Public Affairs* (1806), *Reply to Malthus* (1807), and in 1812 found employment in London. From 1814 to 1830 he wrote essays on literary criticism and other subjects for the *Edinburgh Review* and the *London Magazine*, and lectured at the Surrey Institute. A passion for Sarah Walker, the daughter of a tailor with whom he lodged, found expression in the frantic *Liber Amoris* (1823). His *Spirit of the Age, or Contemporary Portraits* appeared in 1825, and his *Life of Napoleon Bonaparte* between 1828 and 1830. Other essay collections include *Table Talk* (1821) and *Plain Speaker* (1826).

Hazzard, Shirley 1931– •*US novelist*• Born and educated in Sydney, Australia, she moved to the US in 1951 and spent a decade working for the United Nations. Her first book, *The Evening of the Holiday*, was published in 1966. Her second novel, *People in Glass Houses* (1967), satirized the UN, and she later published a factual exposé of that organization in *Defeat of an Ideal* (1973), followed by *Countenance of Truth* (1990). Other novels include *The Bay of Noon* (1970), and *The Transit of Venus* (1980), which explored the tension between romantic love and moral courage and established her as a major contemporary writer.

H D *See* **Doolittle, Hilda**

Head, Edith 1907–81 •*US costume designer*• Educated at UCLA and Stanford, she taught art and languages for a time before joining Paramount Studios in the late 1930s, later moving to Universal Studios in 1967. She designed opulent dresses for many of the major stars of the era, including **Barbara Stanwyck**, **Elizabeth Taylor**, **Audrey Hepburn** and **Bette Davis**, as well as the stylish suits worn by **Robert Redford** and **Paul Newman** in *The Sting* (1973), one of eight films for which she received an Academy Award for costume design.

Head, Sir Henry 1861–1940 •*English neurologist*• Born in Stamford Hill, London, he studied at Trinity College, Cambridge, and University College Hospital, London. He became a consulting physician at the London Hospital, and is best known for his neurological research. His famous observations on the sensory changes in his own arm, after cutting some nerve fibers, provided important information about the physiology of sensation, and reinforced his reputation as a leading scientifically inclined neurologist. He wrote widely on aphasia (disorders of speech), for example in *Aphasia and Kindred Disorders of Speech* (1926). He edited the influential neurological journal *Brain* (1905–21) and also published poetry. He was knighted in 1927.

Healey, Denis Winston Healey, Baron 1917– •*English politician*• Born in Keighley, Yorkshire, and educated at Oxford, he served with the Royal Engineers in North Africa and Italy (1940–45), attaining the rank of major. He became Member of Parliament for Leeds in 1952, and was a member of the Shadow Cabinet for five years before becoming Secretary of State for Defense in the **Wilson** government of 1964, a post which he held for six years. His five years (1974–79) as Chancellor of the Exchequer were a rather stormy period marked by a currency crisis and subsequent intervention by the International Monetary Fund. Healey unsuccessfully ran for the Labour Party leadership in 1976 and again in 1980, when he was somewhat unexpectedly defeated by **Michael Foot**. He was, however, elected Deputy Leader ahead of his left-wing opponent, **Tony Benn**. In 1987 he resigned from the Shadow Cabinet, and he became a life peer in 1992.

Healy, Timothy Michael 1855–1931 •*Irish Nationalist leader*• He was born in Bantry, County Cork. He sat in Parliament (1880–1918), headed the 1890 revolt against **Charles Stewart Parnell**, and became an Independent Nationalist. He was the first governor-general of the Irish Free State (1922–28).

Heaney, Seamus Justin 1939– •*Northern Irish poet, critic and Nobel Prize winner*• Born in Castledawson, County Derry, he was educated at St Columba's College, Londonderry, and at Queen's College, Belfast, where he later lectured (1966–72). He taught at Caryfort College, Dublin (1975–81), was Boylston Professor of Rhetoric and Oratory at Harvard (1985–97), and Professor of Poetry at Oxford (1989–94). Since 1998 he has been Ralph Waldo Emerson Poet in Residence at Harvard University. He made his debut as a poet with *Eleven Poems* (1965). Redolent of the rural Ireland in which he grew up, his work seems nurtured by the landscape—lush, peaty and, to an extent, menacing. One of the greatest modern poets writing in English, he is regarded as a worthy successor to **W B Yeats**. Significant collections include *Death of a Naturalist* (1966), *Wintering Out* (1972, much influenced by the outbreak of sectarian violence in Northern Ireland), *North* (1975), *Bog Poems* (1975), *Field Work* (1979), *Station Island* (1984), *The Haw Lantern* (1987) and *Seeing Things* (1991). *Selected Poems 1965–75* appeared in 1980, and *New Selected Poems 1966–87* in 1990. His first play, *The Cure at Troy* (1991), is a translation of **Sophocles**'s *Philoctetes* and was written for the Field Day Theatre Company in Dublin, and *Sweeney's Flight* (1992) is Heaney's version of the Irish odyssey of Mad Sweeney. A collection of essays, *Preoccupations*, was published in 1980. He was awarded the Nobel Prize for literature in 1995 and won the Whitbread prize in 1997 for his collection *The Spirit Level*. He won the Whitbread prize again for his translation of *Beowulf* (1999). A more recent collection is *Electric Light* (2001).

Hearne, Samuel 1745–92 •*English explorer*• Born in London, he joined the Hudson's Bay Company, which sent him to Canada in 1769. In 1770 he became the first European to travel overland to the Arctic Ocean by following the Coppermine River north of the Great Slave Lake. He gave detailed reports of the frozen wastes and the Inuit conflicts he observed. In 1774 he set up the first interior trading post for the company at Cumberland House, and then he became governor of Fort Prince of Wales (Churchill), where he was captured and taken to France in 1782. He returned to reestablish Churchill as a trading post in 1783. *A Journey from Prince of Wales' Fort ... to the Northern Ocean* was published in 1795.

Hearst, William Randolph 1863–1951 •*US newspaper publisher*• He was born in San Francisco, the son of a newspaper proprietor. After studying at Harvard he took over the *San Francisco Examiner* in 1887 from his father. Invading the territory of **Joseph Pulitzer**, he acquired the *New York Morning Journal* (1895), launching the *Evening Journal* a year later. He revolutionized journalism by the introduction of banner headlines, lavish illustrations and other sensational methods, and made himself the head of a national chain of newspapers and periodicals which included the *Chicago Examiner*, *Boston American*, *Cosmopolitan* and *Harper's Bazaar*. In 1897–98 he published exaggerated and fabricated reports on the Cuban struggle for independence, which helped bring about the Spanish-American War. He was a member of the US House of Representatives from 1903 to 1907. He built an impressive residence in San Simeon, California, furnished with some of the huge collection of antiquities and paintings that he compulsively acquired, on which he spent much of his vast wealth. It is now a museum. His career inspired the **Orson Welles** film *Citizen Kane* (1941).

Heath, Sir Edward Richard George, *also called* **Ted Heath** 1916– •*English Conservative politician*• Born in Broadstairs, Kent, he was a scholar of Balliol College, Oxford. After service in World War II he entered Parliament in 1950, one of **R A Butler**'s "One Nation" new Tory intellectuals. He was the chief negotiator for Great Britain's entry into the European Common Market, although the French attitude prevented the UK from joining. In the **Douglas-Home** administration (1963) he became Secretary of State for Industry and president of the Board of Trade (1963). Elected Leader of the Conservative Party in July 1965, he was Opposition leader until, on the Conservative victory in the 1970 general election, he became prime minister. After a long confrontation with the miners' union in 1973, the Conservatives narrowly lost the general election of February 1974, the loss being confirmed by another election in October 1974. In 1975 he was replaced as leader by **Margaret Thatcher**. From 1979 he became an increasingly outspoken critic of what he regarded as the extreme policies of "Thatcherism." He has resisted attempts to move him to the House of Lords, and retained his seat (Old Bexley and Sidcup) in the 1997 general election, stepping down in 2001 after more than 50 years in the House of Commons. He is an expert yachtsman, and, after winning the 1969 Hobart ocean race, captained the British crew for the Admiral's Cup races of 1971 and 1979. He is also an accomplished musician.

“ ”

If you want to see the acceptable face of capitalism, go out to an oil rig in the North Sea.

1974 Election campaign speech, February 18.

Heathcoat Amory, Derick *See* **Amory, Derick Heathcoat Amory, 1st Viscount**

Heaviside, Oliver 1850–1925 •*English physicist*• Born in London, a telegrapher by training, he spent much of his life living reclusively in Devon. There he made various important advances in the study of electrical communications, and in 1902, independently of Arthur Kennelly (1861–1939), he predicted the existence of an ionized gaseous layer capable of reflecting radio waves, the "Heaviside layer" (part of the ionosphere), which was verified 20 years later.

Hebb, Donald Olding 1904–85 •*Canadian psychologist*• Born in Chester, Nova Scotia, he was educated at Dalhousie, McGill and Harvard Universities, and was latterly chancellor at McGill. His best-remembered theoretical contributions to psychology were embodied in his book *The Organization of Behavior* (1949), in which he argued that long-term memories could be encoded in the brain by means of changes occurring at the synapse (the point at which one nerve cell can communicate chemically with another), and that repeated use would itself strengthen such a synapse. There is now good physiological evidence for such "Hebb synapses." He also introduced and developed the concept of the "cell assembly," a diffuse network of nerve cells which could be activated for relatively short periods and which would be the physical embodiment of transient thoughts and perceptions. His ideas have had a renaissance in the field of "computational neuroscience."

Hebbel, Friedrich 1813–63 •*German dramatist*• Born in Wesselburen, Dithmarschen (now part of Schleswig-Holstein), he studied in Hamburg from 1835 and later settled in Vienna (1846). He wrote several historical or biblical plays, such as *Herodes und Mariamne* (1849, Eng trans *Herod and Mariamne*, 1914) and his masterpiece, the *Nibelungen* trilogy (1855–60, Eng trans *The Nibelungs*, 1921).

Hébert, Jacques René, *also called* **Père Duchesne** 1757–94 •*French revolutionary*• He was born in Alençon. A servant in Paris, soon after the outbreak of the Revolution he became a prominent Jacobin. As a member of the Revolutionary Council, he was active in the September Massacres and was on the commission appointed to examine **Marie Antoinette**. After denouncing the Committee of Public Safety for its failure to help the poor, he tried to incite a popular uprising, but he incurred the suspicion of **Danton** and **Robespierre** and was guillotined with 17 of his followers (Hébertists).

Hecataeus of Miletus c. 550–476 BC •*Pioneering Greek historian and geographer*• He attempted to demythologize Greek history in his prose *Genealogies* (or *Histories*) by giving the poetic fables about the divine or heroic ancestries of leading Milesian families a pseudochronological framework. He traveled widely, and wrote a *Tour of the World* (of which only fragments remain) describing local customs and curiosities, and which he published with an improved version of the map made by **Anaximander** of Miletus.

Hecht, Ben 1894–1964 •*US writer*• Born in New York City, he worked as a journalist in Chicago from 1910 and wrote a series of novels. His initial efforts to write for the stage were unsuccessful, but in 1928 he teamed up with his fellow newspaperman Charles MacArthur (1895–1956) to write *The Front Page*, a fast-paced comedy about the moral ambiguities of the newspaper business. He scored a hit with this play and its subsequent film adaptation, and later wrote numerous screenplays, including *Wuthering Heights* (1939), *Spellbound* (1945) and *Notorious* (1946).

Hedley, William 1779–1843 •*English inventor*• He was born in Newburn, near Newcastle upon Tyne. A colliery superintendent and lessee, in 1813 he improved on **Richard Trevithick**'s locomotive, proving that loads could be moved by the traction of smooth wheels on smooth rails. His locomotive, known as *Puffing Billy*, was the first commercial steam locomotive.

Heeger, Alan J 1936– •*US physicist and Nobel Prize winner*• Born in Sioux City, Iowa, he was educated at the University of Nebraska and at the University of California, Berkeley. Following various posts in teaching, research and industry, in 1999 he became chief scientist at the University of Utah. In 2000 he shared the Nobel Prize for chemistry with **Alan G MacDiarmid** and **Hideki Shirakawa** for their discovery and development of conductive polymers (used, among other applications, to shield computer screens against electromagnetic radiation).

Heem, Jan Davidsz de c. 1606–84 •*Dutch still-life painter*• Born in Utrecht, he settled in Antwerp in 1636. His paintings of flowers and exquisitely laid tables are in most galleries in Europe and the US. He is arguably the greatest Dutch still-life painter. His son Cornelis (1631–95) was also a painter and a close follower of his father.

Heenan, John Carmel 1905–75 •*English Roman Catholic archbishop*• Born in Ilford, Essex, and educated in Ushaw and at the English College, Rome, he was ordained in 1930. He became a parish priest in the eastern part of London, and during World War II worked with the BBC, becoming well known as "the Radio Priest." He became Archbishop of Westminster in 1963. A convinced ecumenical, he supported the causes of religious liberty and reconciliation with the Jews at the Second Vatican Council, and was created cardinal in 1965.

Heffer, Eric Samuel 1922–91 •*English Labour politician*• Apprenticed as a carpenter-joiner at the age of 14, he worked in the trade, except for war service in the RAF, until he became a Member of Parliament in 1964. A traditional socialist, favoring public ownership and strongly unilateralist, he distrusted centrist tendencies and had a brief, uncomfortable period as a junior minister (1974–75). He unsuccessfully challenged **Roy Hattersley** for the deputy leadership in 1988.

Hefner, Hugh Marston 1926– •*US editor and publisher*• He was born in Chicago into a family of Methodists, and his upbringing was strict. He attended Southern Illinois University, did postgraduate work in psychology, and after working for *Esquire* magazine, published the first issue of *Playboy* in December 1953, with **Marilyn Monroe** posing nude. "Girly" photographs, practical advice on sexual problems, men's talk and articles of high literary standard combined to make him conspicuously wealthy and the magazine a notorious success. The *Playboy* empire extended into real estate, clubs (with "bunny-girl" hostesses) and sundry products.

Hegel, Georg Wilhelm Friedrich 1770–1831 •*German philosopher*• He was born in Stuttgart, the last and perhaps the most important of the great German idealist philosophers in the line from **Kant**, **Fichte** and **Schelling**. He studied theology in Tübingen, and taught in Bern (1793), Frankfurt am Main (1796) and Jena (1801), but his academic career was interrupted in 1806 by the closure of the university after **Napoleon I**'s victory at Jena. In 1807 he published his first great work, *Phänomenologie des Geistes* (Eng trans *The Phenomenology of Mind*, 1910), which describes how the human mind has progressed from mere consciousness through self-consciousness, reason, spirit and religion to absolute knowledge. This was followed by *Wissenschaft der Logik* (2 vols, 1812 and 1816, Eng trans *The Logic of Hegel*, 1874), in which he set out his famous dialectic, a triadic process whereby thesis generates antithesis and both are superseded by a higher synthesis which incorporates what is rational in them and rejects the irrational. His work gained him the chair at the University of Heidelberg in 1816, and he now resumed his university career and produced in 1817 a compendium of his entire system entitled *Encyclopädie der philosophischen Wissenschaften im Grundrisse* (Eng trans *Encyclopedia of the Philosophical Sciences in Outline*, 1959). In 1818 he succeeded **Fichte** as professor in Berlin and remained there until his death from cholera in 1831. Though Hegel's philosophy is difficult and obscure, it has been a great influence on later philosophies, including Marxism, positivism, and existentialism.

Hegley, John 1953– •*English poet*• Born in Islington, London, he studied literature and sociology at Bradford University before embarking on a career as a poet, becoming well known as a performer on stage, radio and television. His poems, which are characterized by his laconic and often poignant sense of humor, include works for both adults and children. Collections of his poetry include *Can I Come Down Now Dad?* (1991), *Five Sugars Please* (1993), *These Were Your Father's* (1994) and *Dog* (2001).

Heidegger, Martin 1889–1976 •*German philosopher*• Born in Messkirch, Baden, the son of a Catholic sexton, he joined the Jesuits as a novice and went on to teach philosophy at the University of Freiburg. He was Professor of Philosophy at the University of Marburg (1923–28) and then succeeded **Edmund Husserl** as Professor of Philosophy at Freiburg (1929–45), where he was appointed Rector in 1933. In a notorious inaugural address he declared his support for **Hitler**. He was officially retired in 1945 but continued to be an influential teacher and lecturer. He succeeded Husserl as a leading figure in the phenomenological movement, but was also much influenced by **Søren Kierkegaard**, and was a key influence on **Jean-Paul Sartre** through his writings on the nature and predicament of human existence. His major work is the original but almost unreadable *Sein und Zeit* (1927, "Being and Time"), which presents an exhaustive ontological classification of "being" and an examination of the distinctively human mode of existence (*Dasein*) characterized by participation and involvement in the world of objects.

Heidenstam, (Karl Gustav) Verner von 1859–1940 •*Swedish writer and Nobel Prize winner*• Born in Olshammer, he lived in southern Europe and the Middle East (1876–87). He published his impressions in a volume of poetry, *Vallfart och Vandringsår* (1888, "Pilgrimage and Years of Wandering") which, together with his programmatic work, *Renässans*, inspired a literary renaissance in Sweden. His other volumes of poetry included *Endymion* (1889), the epic *Hans Alienus* (1892) and *Ett folk* (1897–98, "One People"). Later he turned to historical fiction, as in *Karolinerna* (1897–98, "The Carlists"). He was once a friend of **Strindberg**, but they later became bitter rivals. He was awarded the 1916 Nobel Prize for literature.

Heifetz, Jascha 1901–87 •*US violinist*• Born in Vilnius, Lithuania, he began studying at the St Petersburg Conservatory in 1910, and toured Russia, Germany, and Scandinavia at the age of 12. After the Russian Revolution he settled in the US and took US citizenship (1925). **William Walton**'s Violin Concerto is among the works commissioned by him from leading composers.

Heine, (Christian Johann) Heinrich 1797–1856 •*German poet and essayist*• Born of Jewish parents in Düsseldorf, he studied banking in Frankfurt and law in Bonn, Berlin and Göttingen. In Berlin in 1821 he published *Gedichte* ("Poems"), which was an immediate success, followed by *Lyrisches Intermezzo* (1823, "Lyrical Intermezzo"), the first and second volumes of the prose *Reisebilder* (1826–27, "Pictures of Travel") and the well-known *Das Buch der Lieder* (1827, revised 1844, Eng trans *Book of Songs*, 1856). He went into voluntary exile in Paris after the 1830 revolution. Having written two more volumes of *Reisebilder* (1830–31, all four vols Eng trans *Pictures of Travel*, 1855), he turned to politics, becoming leader of the cosmopolitan democratic movement. From 1848, while confined to bed by spinal paralysis, his publications included *Neue Gedichte* (1844, revised 1851, Eng trans *New Poems*, 1910) and three volumes of *Vermischte Schriften* (1854, "Various Writings"). Many of his poems were set to music, most notably by **Franz Schubert** and **Robert Schumann**.

Heinemann, Gustav 1899–1976 •*German statesman*• Born in Schwelm, and educated at the Universities of Marburg and Münster, he lectured on law in Cologne (1933–39). After World War II he was a founder of the Christian Democratic Union (CDU), and was Minister of the Interior in **Adenauer**'s government (1949–50). A pacifist, he opposed Germany's rearmament. He formed his own neutralist party, but later joined the Social Democratic Party, was elected to the Bundestag (1957) and was Minister of Justice in **Kiesinger**'s Grand Coalition government from 1966. In 1969 he was elected president but resigned in 1974.

Heinemann, William 1863–1920 •*English publisher*• Born in Surbiton, London, he studied music in England and Germany, but turned to publishing instead. He founded his publishing house in London in 1890 and established its reputation with the works of **Robert Louis Stevenson**, **Rudyard Kipling**, **H G Wells**, **John Galsworthy**, **Somerset Maugham**, **J B Priestley**, and others.

Heinkel, Ernst Heinrich 1888–1958 •*German aircraft engineer*• Born in Grunbach, he was chief designer of the Albatros Aircraft Company in Berlin before World War I. He founded the Heinkel Flugzeugwerke at Warnemünde in 1922, making at first seaplanes, and later bombers and fighters that achieved fame in World War II. He built the first jet plane, the HE-178, in 1939, and also the first rocket-powered aircraft, the HE-176.

Heinz, H(enry) J(ohn) 1844–1919 •*US food manufacturer and packer*• He was born to German parents in Pittsburgh, Pennsylvania. In 1876 he became cofounder of F & J Heinz, a firm producing pickles and other prepared foods. The business was reorganized as the H J Heinz Company in 1888, and he was its president from 1905 to 1919. He invented the advertising slogan "57 Varieties" in 1896, promoted the pure food movement in the US, and was a pioneer in staff welfare work.

Heisenberg, Werner Karl 1901–76 •*German theoretical physicist and Nobel Prize winner*• Born in Würzburg, Bavaria, he was educated at the Universities of Munich and Göttingen, before becoming Professor of Physics at the University of Leipzig (1927–41). He then became professor at the University of Berlin and director of the Kaiser Wilhelm Institute (1941–45). From 1945 to 1958 he was director of the **Max Planck** Institute in Göttingen, which later moved to Munich. In 1925 he reinterpreted classical mechanics with a matrix-based quantum mechanics where phenomena must be describable both in terms of wave theory and quanta. For this theory and its applications he was awarded the Nobel Prize for physics in 1932. In his revolutionary principle of indeterminacy, or the uncertainty principle (1927), he showed that there is a fundamental limit to the accuracy to which certain pairs of variables (such as position and momentum) can be determined, a limit which may be interpreted as a result of disturbance to a system due to the act of measuring it. In 1958, he and **Wolfgang Pauli** announced the formulation of a unified field theory, which if established would remove the uncertainty principle and reinstate **Albert Einstein**.

Hekmatyar, Gulbuddin 1949– •*Afghan guerrilla leader*• Formerly an engineer, in the 1970s he opposed the Republican government of General Mohammad Daud Khan, and rose to prominence during the 1980s in the fight to oust the Soviet-installed Communist regime in Afghanistan. As leader of one of the two factions of the Hizb-i Islami (Islamic Party), he was seen as the most intransigently fundamentalist. He was injured in a car bomb attack in 1987, and in 1988 briefly served as president of the seven-party Mujahideen alliance. He was prime minister of Afghanistan from 1993 to 1994 and 1996 to 1997.

Helena, St c.255–330 AD •*Roman empress*• She was the wife of the emperor **Constantius Chlorus** and mother of **Constantine I (the Great)**. According to tradition she came from Bithynia, the daughter of an innkeeper. When Constantine was declared emperor by his army in York in 306, he made her dowager empress. In 312, when toleration was extended to Christianity, she was baptized. According to tradition, she visited Jerusalem (326), discovered the cross of Jesus, and founded the basilicas on the Mount of Olives and in Bethlehem. Her feast day is August 18 (May 21 in the East).

Heliodorus fl. 3rd and 4th century AD •*Greek writer and Sophist*• He was born in Emesa, Syria. One of the earliest Greek novelists, he was the author of *Aethiopica*, which narrates in poetic prose, at times with almost epic beauty and simplicity, the loves of Theagenes and Chariclea.

Heliogabalus or **Elagabalus**, *divine name of* **Caesar Marcus Aurelius Antonius Augustus**, *originally* **Varius Avitus Bassianus** AD 204–22 •*Roman emperor*• Born in Emesa, Syria, he was appointed high priest of the Syro-Phoenician sun god Elagabal, and assumed the name of that deity. In AD 218 he was proclaimed emperor by the army and defeated his rival Macrinus. His brief reign was marked by extravagant homosexual orgies and intolerant promotion of the god Elagabal (Baal). He was murdered by the praetorians in a palace revolution.

Heller, Joseph 1923–99 •*US novelist*• Born in Brooklyn, New York, he served in the US Army Air Force in World War II and drew on the experience for his black comedy, *Catch-22* (1961), which is based on the simple premise that men on dangerous missions must be considered insane, and may therefore ask to be excused from duty, but by making the request they prove that they are sane and fit to fly. It became an international bestseller and a byword for war's absurdity. Later books include *Something Happened* (1974), *Good as Gold* (1979), *God Knows* (1984) and *Picture This* (1988). During the later period his output was hampered by a neurological ailment, described in his autobiographical account *No Laughing Matter* (with Speed Vogel, 1986). He published a sequel to *Catch-22*, entitled *Closing Time*, in 1994.

“ ”

He was a self-made man who owed his lack of success to nobody.

*1961 Of Colonel Cargill, **Catch-22**, chapter 3.*

Hellman, Lillian Florence 1907–84 •*US playwright*• Born into a Jewish family in New Orleans, she was educated at New York and Columbia Universities, then worked for the New York *Herald Tribune* as a reviewer (1925–28) and for MGM in Hollywood as a reader of plays (1927–32). She lived for many years with the detective writer **Dashiell Hammett**, who encouraged her writing. Her first stage success, *The Children's Hour* (1934), ran on Broadway for 86 weeks. It was followed by *Days to Come* (1936) and *The Little Foxes* (1939). During World War II she wrote the antifascist plays *Watch on the Rhine* (1941, winner of the Critics Circle award) and *The Searching Wind* (1944). When she came before the House Un-American Activities Committee in 1952 during the **Joseph McCarthy** era, she coined the famous phrase "I can't cut my conscience to fit this year's fashions." This period was described in her controversial memoir *Scoundrel Time* (1976).

Helmholtz, Hermann von 1821–94 •*German physiologist and physicist*• Born in Potsdam, Brandenburg, he was successively Professor of Physiology at the Universities of Königsberg (1849), Bonn (1855), and Heidelberg (1858). In 1871 he became Professor of Physics in Berlin. He was equally distinguished in physiology, mathematics, and experimental and mathematical physics. His physiological works are principally connected with the eye, the ear, and the nervous system, with his work on vision regarded as fundamental to modern visual science. In 1850 he invented an ophthalmoscope independently of **Charles Babbage**. He is also important for his analysis of the spectrum, his explanation of vowel sounds, his papers on the conservation of energy with reference to muscular action and for research into the development of electric current within a galvanic battery.

Helmont, Johannes Baptista van 1579–1644 •*Flemish chemist, physiologist and physician*• Born in Brussels, he studied philosophy and theology at the University of Louvain, subsequently turning to science and medicine. He traveled and studied widely, and received an MD in 1609. His collected works were published after his death by his son under the title *Ortus medicinae vel Opera et opuscula omnia* (1648). Van Helmont occupies a position on the border of the old and the new learning, bridging the gap between alchemy and chemistry. He accepted traditional beliefs in alchemy and in the intervention of supernatural agencies, and he developed a two-element theory of matter (water and air). In a more modern approach, he was the first to take the melting point of ice and the boiling point of water as standards for temperature.

Helms, Jesse 1921– •*US politician*• Born in Monroe, North Carolina, he joined the US Navy in World War II and later became a radio-broadcasting executive, whose ultraconservative radio editorials in the 1960s launched his political career. He served in the US Senate as a Republican from North Carolina from 1973 to 2003 and was known for his dogged advocacy of school prayer and the death penalty, and for his vehement attacks on the National Endowment for the Arts. He was chair of the powerful Senate Foreign Relations Committee from 1995 until 2001.

Héloïse c. 1098–1164 •*French abbess*• She was the niece of canon Fulbert of Notre Dame, who arranged for her to be educated by the theologian **Peter Abelard**. Héloïse and Abelard fell in love but had to flee to Brittany when Fulbert discovered their affair. Secretly married, they had a son, but Héloïse's family was angered at this. She sought safety at the convent at Argenteuil but Abelard was attacked one night and castrated. He became a monk and persuaded his wife to take the veil at Argenteuil. Later he gave her the Benedictine convent, the Paraclete, that he had founded and she became abbess there, despite her self-confessed devotion to Abelard rather than God. Abelard's account of their tragic story, *Letters to a Friend*, and their famous correspondence form the basis for a plethora of literature on the subject.

Helpmann, Sir Robert Murray 1909–86 •*Australian dancer, actor and choreographer*• Born in Mount Gambier, South Australia, he studied with **Anna Pavlova**'s touring company (1929) and moved to Great Britain to study under **Ninette de Valois** (1931). He was the first dancer of the newly founded Sadler's Wells Ballet (1933–50) and became known for his dramatic roles in de Valois's works. A master of mime, he created the role of Master of Tregennis in the *Haunted Ballroom* (1934). His choreographic work includes *Hamlet* (1942), *Miracle in the Gorbals* (1944) and *Yugen* (1965). His acting roles were mainly in works by **Shakespeare** and **George Bernard Shaw**. He also danced in the ballet films *The Red Shoes* (1948) and *The Tales of Hoffmann* (1950).

Helvétius, Claude-Adrien 1715–71 •*French philosopher*• Born to Swiss parents in Paris, he became chamberlain to the queen's household, where he met philosophers such as **Diderot** and **Jean d'Alembert**, with whom he later collaborated on the *Encyclopédie*. His controversial work *De l'esprit* (1758, "On the Mind") advanced the view that sensation is the source of all intellectual activity and that self-interest is the motivating force of all human action. The book was denounced by the Sorbonne in Paris, and condemned by parliament to be publicly burned. As a result it was widely read, was translated into all the main European languages, and together with his posthumous *De l'homme* (1772, "On Man"), greatly influenced **Jeremy Bentham** and the British Utilitarians.

Hemans, Felicia Dorothea, *née* **Browne** 1793–1835 •*English poet*• Born in Liverpool, she published three volumes of poems between 1808 and 1812, and when her husband deserted her in 1818, she began writing for a living. She produced a large number of books of verse of all kinds—love lyrics, classical, mythological, sentimental—such as *The Siege of Valencia* (1823) and *Records of Women* (1828). She is perhaps best remembered for the poem *Casabianca*, better known as "The Boy Stood on the Burning Deck," and for "The Stately Homes of England."

Hemerken, Thomas *See* **Kempis, Thomas à**

Hemingway, Ernest Millar 1899–1961 •*US writer of novels and short stories, and Nobel Prize winner*• Hemingway was born in Oak Park, a respectable suburb of Chicago. He was educated at grammar school and the palatial Oak Park and River Forest Township High School, where he distinguished himself only in English. His mother wanted him to become a violinist but, modeling himself on **Ring Lardner**, he was determined to become a journalist and a writer and got a job on the *Kansas City Star* as a cub reporter. In April 1918 he resigned and joined the Red Cross, to be hurled into World War I as an ambulance driver on the Italian front, where he was badly wounded. Returning to the US he began to write features for the Toronto *Star Weekly* in 1919 and married Hadley Richardson, the first of four wives, in 1921. That same year he went to Europe as a traveling correspondent and covered several large conferences. In Paris he moved easily and conspicuously among other émigré artists and came into contact with **Gertrude Stein**, **Ezra Pound**, **James Joyce** and **F Scott Fitzgerald**. *A Moveable Feast* (1964) records this time. *Three Stories and Ten Poems* was given a limited circulation in Paris in 1923, and in 1924 he published *In Our Time*, which met with critical approval in the US a year later. *The Sun Also Rises* (1926) and a volume of short stories, *Men Without Women* (1927), confirmed his reputation, and in 1928, divorced from Richardson and remarried to Pauline Pfeiffer, he moved to Key West, Florida. Disentangling fact from myth in the years that followed is not easy. Drinking, brawling, posturing, big-game hunting, deep-sea fishing and bullfighting all competed with writing. Nevertheless the body of Hemingway's work is impressive, if uneven. In 1929 he published *A Farewell to Arms*, and in 1932 the bullfighting classic, *Death in the Afternoon*. *Green Hills in Africa* (1935) tells of tension-filled big-game hunts. Perhaps his most popular book is *For Whom the Bell Tolls*, published in 1940, about the civil war in Spain, to which he went as a journalist. He continued to work as a war correspondent during World War II, and in 1945 he settled in Cuba, where he wrote *Across the River and into the Trees* (1950) and *The Old Man and the Sea* (1952). He won the Pulitzer Prize in 1953 and the Nobel Prize for literature in 1954. Suffering from depression, he shot himself in the mouth at his home in Ketchum, Idaho.

Hench, Philip Showalter 1896–1965 •*US physician and Nobel Prize winner*• He was born in Pittsburgh, Pennsylvania, and took his medical degree there. Head of the department of rheumatics at the Mayo Clinic in Rochester from 1926, and Professor of Medicine at the University of Minnesota from 1947, he discovered cortisone, widely hailed as a miracle drug, and shared with **Edward Kendall** and **Tadeus Reichstein** the 1950 Nobel Prize for physiology or medicine. Several patients severely crippled by arthritis were demonstrated to have much greater freedom of movement and suffer much less pain. Unfortunately, the early improvement often did not last, and a variety of side effects from high doses of steroids began to manifest themselves. The early reports of dramatic cures of severe rheumatoid arthritis were thus premature, but steroids such as cortisone have played an important part in modern treatments.

Henderson, Arthur 1863–1935 •*Scottish Labour politician and Nobel Prize winner*• Born in Glasgow, he was brought up in Newcastle upon Tyne, where he worked in an iron foundry and became a lay preacher. Several times chairman of the Labour Party (1908–10, 1914–17, 1931–32), he was elected a Member of Parliament in 1903, and became Home Secretary (1924) and Foreign Secretary (1929–31) in the first Labour governments. He was president of the World Disarmament Conference (1932), won the 1934 Nobel Peace Prize, and also helped to establish the League of Nations.

Henderson, Fletcher 1897–1952 •*US pianist, arranger and bandleader*• Born in Cuthbert, Georgia, he graduated in chemistry from the all-Black Atlanta University, but upon moving to New York in 1920 to continue his studies, he became diverted into a musical career. In 1924 he put together a big band for what was supposed to be a temporary engagement, but stayed at the head of an orchestra until the mid-1930s, attracting the finest instrumentalists and arrangers of the time. His own orchestrations, and those of **Don Redman**, set the standard for the swing era.

Henderson, Hamish 1919–2002 •*Scottish folklorist, composer and poet*• He was born in Blairgowrie, Perthshire. One of his early poetic works, "Ninth Elegy for the Dead in Cyrenaica" (1948), won him the Somerset Maugham award, but his literary output was overshadowed by his impressive contributions to folk song. Through his research for the School of Scottish Studies, he was largely responsible for bringing to the fore great but little-known traditional singers, like **Jeannie Robertson**, and many of his own compositions have become part of the traditional singer's repertoire.

Henderson, Joe (Joseph) 1937–2001 •*US jazz saxophonist, bandleader and composer*• Born in Lima, Ohio, he studied music before going into the army (1960–62), but established his reputation as a sideman, notably with Horace Silver (1964–66) and **Herbie Hancock** (1969–70). He recorded under his own name for Blue Note from 1963. He played briefly with the rock group Blood, Sweat and Tears, and made a number of fusion-influenced recordings for Milestone. He concentrated on teaching for a time, but his acclaimed *State of the Tenor* (1985) effected a revival of interest in his work, and he became a highly creative force in the 1990s, making award-winning records for the jazz label Verve.

Henderson, Ricky Henley 1958– •*US baseball player*• Born in Chicago, Illinois, he played for the Oakland Athletics (1979–84, 1989–93, 1994, 1995, 1998) between bouts with the New York Yankees (1985–89), the Toronto Blue Jays (1993), the San Diego Padres (1996, 1997, 2001) and the Seattle Mariners (2000). Described as the best lead-off man of all time, he set numerous records, including those for most lead-off home runs (77) and for the most steals in a single season (130).

Hendrix, Jimi (James Marshall) 1942–70 •*US rock guitarist and singer*• One of rock music's most innovative and influential instrumentalists, he was born into a poor Black neighborhood of Seattle, Washington, and taught himself to play the guitar. After being released from the army in 1962 due to ill health, he moved to Nashville and played in numerous groups, then moved to Great Britain in 1966 and formed the Jimi Hendrix Experience (with Noel Redding and Mitch Mitchell). The band's first single, "Hey Joe," was an immediate British success and his adventurous first album, *Are You Experienced?*, made him famous worldwide. The two subsequent albums—*Axis: Bold As Love* and *Electric Ladyland*—helped make 1968 his most commercially successful year. However, the pressures of success also helped to destroy him both professionally and personally. The Jimi Hendrix Experience broke up in 1969 and a subsequent group, The Band of Gypsies, disbanded after recording only one album. He died after mixing barbiturates and alcohol.

Hendry, Stephen 1969– •*Scottish snooker player*• Born in Edinburgh, he started playing at the age of 12, and turned professional at age 16. He showed his exceptional talent by becoming the youngest-ever winner of a professional title with his 1987 victory in the Rothmans Grand Prix. In 1989 he won a host of titles, among them the British Open. The following year he became the youngest winner of the Embassy world championship, a title he has now won a record seven times (1990, 1992–96, 1999).

Hengist d. 488 AD and **Horsa** d. 455 AD •*Semilegendary Jutish brothers*• According to **Nennius** and the *Anglo-Saxon Chronicle*, they led the first Germanic invaders to Britain. They landed from Jutland at the Isle of Thanet in AD 449 to help King **Vortigern** against the Picts, and were rewarded with the gift of Thanet. Soon after they turned against Vortigern, but were defeated at Aylesford, where Horsa was killed. Hengist, however, is said to have conquered Kent. Their names mean "stallion" and "horse."

Henley, W(illiam) E(rnest) 1849–1903 •*English poet, playwright, critic and editor*• Born in Gloucester, he suffered from tuberculosis as a boy, had a leg amputated, and spent nearly two years in Edinburgh Infirmary (1873–75), where he wrote several of the poems in *A Book of Verses* (1888). In Edinburgh he became a close friend of **Robert Louis Stevenson**, with whom he collaborated on four plays, and whose character of Long John Silver he inspired. His verse was notable for its unusual rhymes and esoteric words, and several other volumes followed, including *In Hospital* (1903), which contains his best-known poem, "Invictus." A pungent critic, he successfully edited the *Magazine of Art* (1882–86) and the *Scots Observer* (from 1889), which became *The National Observer* in 1891. He was joint compiler of a dictionary of slang (7 vols, 1894–1904).

Henman, Tim(othy) 1974– •*English tennis player*• Born in Oxford, he emerged as the leading British player on the international tennis circuit in the mid-1990s. Having turned professional in 1993, he won the British National men's singles title in 1995 and 1996 and subsequently added a silver medal in the Olympic men's doubles in 1996, among other titles. He reached the quarterfinals at Wimbledon in 1996 and the semifinals in 1998, 1999 and 2001.

Henrietta Anne, Duchesse d'Orleans, *known as* **Minette** 1644–70 •*English princess*• The youngest daughter of **Charles I** of Great Britain and **Henrietta Maria**, and sister of **Charles II**, she was born in Exeter during the English civil wars. Brought up as a Roman Catholic by her mother in France, she married **Louis XIV**'s gay brother Philippe, Duc d'**Orléans**, but was also rumored to have been the mistress of the French king himself. She played an important part in negotiating the Secret Treaty of Dover (1670) between Charles and Louis.

Henrietta Maria 1609–69 •*French princess and queen of England*• Born at the Louvre, Paris, she was the youngest child of **Henry IV** of France. After his assassination (1610), she was brought up by her mother, **Marie de Médicis**. She was married in 1625 to **Charles I** of Great Britain, which became a true love match. Her French attendants and Roman Catholic beliefs made her unpopular, and in 1642, under the threat of impeachment, she fled to Holland and raised funds for the Royalist cause. A year later she returned and met Charles near Edgehill. In 1644 she gave birth to **Henrietta Anne**, but two weeks later she fled again to France, never seeing her husband again. She spent most of her remaining years in France.

Henry I c. 1008–60 •*King of France*• The son of Robert II, he ascended the throne in 1031. He was involved in struggles with Normandy and with Burgundy, which he had unwisely granted to his younger brother, Robert. Several of his conflicts were with William of Normandy (the future **William the Conqueror**).

Henry II 1519–59 •*King of France*• Born at St Germain-en-Laye, near Paris, he was the son of **Francis I**. In 1533, as Duke of Orléans, he married **Catherine de Médicis**, by whom he had seven surviving children, three of whom became kings of France (**Francis II**, **Charles IX** and **Henry III**). He became king in 1547. Dominated by his mistress, **Diane de Poitiers**, and by Anne de Montmorency, Constable of France, he introduced reforms to curb extravagance at court and regularize the country's disordered finances. Through the influence of the **Guise**s he formed an alliance with Scotland, declared war on England, and captured Boulogne (1550) and Calais (1558). He continued the war against the Holy Roman emperor, **Charles V**, in alliance with the German Protestant princes, gaining Metz, Toul and Verdun, but his ambitions in Italy and the

Low Countries were thwarted, including the annihilation of his army at St Quentin (1557). At home he began the persecution of Huguenots that would lead to the Wars of Religion (1562–98). He died of wounds received in a tournament, and was succeeded by his son as Francis II.

Henry III 1551–89 •*King of France*• Born in Fontainebleau, the third son of **Henry II** and **Catherine de Médicis**, in 1659 he won victories over the Huguenots and took an active part in the St Bartholomew's Day Massacre (1572). In 1573 he was elected king of Poland, but two years later succeeded his brother **Charles IX** on the French throne. His reign was marked throughout by civil war between the Huguenots and Catholics. In 1588 he engineered the assassination of Henry, Duke of **Guise**, enraging the Catholic League. He joined forces with the Huguenot Henry of Navarre (**Henry IV**), and while marching on Paris was assassinated by a fanatical priest. The last of the Valois line, he named Henry of Navarre as his successor.

Henry IV, *known as* **Henry of Navarre** 1553–1610 •*First Bourbon king of France*• He was born in Pau, southwest France, the third son of Antoine de **Bourbon** and Jeanne d'Albret, heiress of Henry d'Albret (**Henry II**) of Navarre. He led the Huguenot army at the Battle of Jarnac (1569) and became leader of the Protestant Party. Henry married **Margaret of Valois** in 1572, but this marriage was annulled in 1599, and in 1600 he married **Marie de Médicis** (their children included the future **Louis XIII** and **Henrietta Maria**, queen consort to **Charles I** of Great Britain). After the St Bartholomew's Day Massacre (1572), he was spared by professing himself a Catholic, and spent three years virtually a prisoner at the French court. In 1576 he escaped, revoked his conversion, and resumed command of the army in continuing opposition to the Guises and the Catholic Holy League. After the murder of Henry III, he succeeded to the throne. In 1593 he became a Catholic, thereby unifying the country, and by the Edict of Nantes (1598) protestants were granted liberty of conscience. His economic policies, implemented by his minister, the Duc de **Sully**, gradually brought new wealth to the country. He was assassinated in Paris by a Catholic religious fanatic.

Henry of Navarre *See* **Henry IV**

Henry I 1068–1135 •*King of England and duke of Normandy*• The youngest and only English-born son of **William the Conqueror**, he was supposedly born in Selby, Yorkshire. When war broke out between his brothers, **William II (Rufus)** and Robert Curthose, Henry helped the latter defend Normandy, yet in the treaty which followed in 1091 he was excluded from the succession. Immediately after William's death, Henry seized the royal treasure, and was elected king by the Witan (1100). He strengthened his position by a marriage with Eadgyth (Matilda), daughter of King **Malcolm III (Canmore)** of Scotland and Queen **Margaret**, who was descended from the old English royal house. Robert had been granted a pension to resign his claim to the English crown and concentrate his attentions on Normandy, but in 1105–06 Henry made war against his badly governed duchy. Robert was defeated at Tinchebrai (1106), and was kept a prisoner for life (28 years). To keep Normandy, Henry was obliged to wage nearly constant warfare. The first war ended in the favorable peace of Gisors (1113), and in 1114 Henry's daughter **Matilda** was married to the emperor Henry V of Germany. The second war (1116–20) was marked by the defeat of the French king at Noyon in 1119. In 1126 Matilda, now a widow, returned from Germany. In 1127 Henry nominated her as his heir, and in 1128 she was married to Geoffrey Plantagenet, son of the Count of Anjou. However, when Henry died the crown was seized by his sister Adela's son, **Stephen** of Blois. Henry I was able and crafty, consistent and passionless in his policy, but often guilty of acts of cold-blooded cruelty. His reign marks a milestone in the development of English governmental institutions such as the Exchequer and the itinerant justices.

Henry II 1133–89 •*King of England*• He was born in Le Mans, France, the son of **Matilda**, **Henry I**'s daughter, and her second husband, Geoffrey Plantagenet, count of Anjou. He was invested with the duchy of Normandy (1150) and became count of Anjou on the death of his father (1151). His marriage with **Eleanor of Aquitaine**, the divorced wife of **Louis VII**, added Poitou and Guienne to his dominions. In January 1153 he landed in England, and in November was declared the successor of **Stephen**, founding the Angevin or Plantagenet dynasty of English kings, and ruling England as part of a wider Angevin empire. He was crowned in 1154, and began repairing the chaos and disorder which had arisen during Stephen's reign. To help him in restricting the authority of the Church in England he appointed his Chancellor, **Thomas à Becket**, as Archbishop of Canterbury, and compelled Becket and the other prelates to agree to the Constitutions of Clarendon, but Becket resisted, and the struggle between them ended only with Becket's murder (1170). In 1174 Henry did penance at Becket's tomb. Meanwhile he organized an expedition to gain control over Ireland (1171–72), and during his stay there he broke the power of Richard de Clare, Earl of Pembroke (nicknamed Strongbow) and other nobles. By 1186, however, Prince John (the future King **John**), who had been given responsibility for the country, was driven out, and all was left in confusion. The eldest of Henry's sons had died in childhood, and the second, Henry (b. 1155), was crowned as his father's associate and successor in 1170. In 1173, encouraged by Queen Eleanor, John and his brother **Richard I (Cœur de Lion)** rebelled—ultimately unsuccessfully—against their father, backed by the kings of France and Scotland. During a second, more limited rebellion, Henry the Younger died (1183), and in 1185 Geoffrey, the next son, was killed in a tournament at Paris. In 1188 Richard joined the French king, and in 1189, Henry, having lost Le Mans and the chief castles of Maine, agreed to a peace recognizing Richard as his sole heir for the Angevin empire. Soon afterward Henry died and was succeeded by Richard. On the whole, Henry was an able and enlightened sovereign, a clear-headed, unprincipled politician, and an able general.

“ ”

Will no one rid me of this turbulent priest?

Of Thomas à Becket. Attributed.

Henry III 1207–72 •*King of England*• Born in Winchester, the elder son of King **John**, he became king in 1216. He declared an end to his minority in 1227, and in 1232 he removed his regent, **Hubert de Burgh**. A war with France cost him Poitou, but **Louis IX** allowed him the rest of his Continental possessions and he was granted the kingdom of Sicily in 1254. His arbitrary assertion of his royal rights antagonized many of his subjects, so that in 1258 he was forced to agree to the far-reaching reforms of the provisions of Oxford, transferring his power to a commission of barons. Louis IX supported him against the barons and **Simon de Montfort**, and the provisions were annulled (1263). De Montfort and his party rebelled and imprisoned the king at Lewes (1264), and forced him to the humiliating agreement called the Mise of Lewes. However, within a year Gilbert de Clare, 9th Earl of **Gloucester**, deserted de Montfort, and, with Prince Edward (later **Edward I**), defeated and killed him at Evesham (1265). Organized resistance ended in 1267, and the rest of his reign was stable. He was succeeded by his elder son, Edward I.

Henry IV, *originally* **Henry Bolingbroke** c. 1366–1413 •*First Lancastrian king of England*• The son of **John of Gaunt**, he was surnamed Bolingbroke from his birthplace in Lincolnshire. In 1397 he supported **Richard II** against the Duke of Gloucester, and was made Duke of Hereford, but in 1398 he was banished, and in 1399, when his father died, his estates were declared forfeit to Richard. Henry landed at Ravenspur in Yorkshire and then induced Richard to sign a renunciation of his claims. He had himself crowned king (1399), and four months later Richard died, possibly murdered. During Henry's reign rebellion and lawlessness were rife, and frequent descents were made upon the coast by expeditions from France. Under **Owen Glendower** the Welsh maintained a large degree of independence, and although he invaded Scotland in 1400, besieging Edinburgh Castle, he was compelled by famine to retire. In 1402, while the king was engaged against the Welsh, the Scots invaded Northumberland, but they encountered and were defeated by Henry Percy, Earl of Northumberland, and his son **Henry Percy** (Hotspur), where Archibald, 4th Earl of Douglas, was taken prisoner. The Percys shortly after allied with Douglas and Glendower against Henry, but the king met them at Shrewsbury (1403), where they were utterly defeated, Hotspur slain, and Douglas again taken prisoner. The civil wars in France gave Henry an opportunity to send two expeditions (1411–12) there, but in his later years his physical strength waned. He chose to be buried in Canterbury, and his second wife, **Joan of Navarre**, was later buried there with him.

Henry V 1387–1422 •*King of England*• Born in Monmouth, Wales, the eldest of the six children of **Henry IV** by Mary de Bohun, he became Prince of Wales in 1399. He fought against **Owen Glendower** and the Welsh rebels (1401–08), and became Constable of Dover (1409), and Captain of Calais (1410). He was crowned king in 1413, and began his reign by freeing the young Earl of March, the true heir to the throne, restoring lands and honors to his son, and arranging for **Richard II**'s body to be buried at Westminster. His reign was marked by his attempt to claim the French Crown (from 1414). He sailed (1415) with a great army and took Harfleur, and at Agincourt (1415) he won against very great odds. Two years later he again invaded France and regained Normandy (1418). By the "perpetual peace" of Troyes (1420) Henry became regent of France and was recognized as heir to the French throne. He married Charles VI's daughter, **Catherine de Valois**, and took his young queen to England to be crowned (1421), but a month later he was recalled to France by news of the defeat of his brother Thomas, Duke of Clarence. Henry became ill, and died in Vincennes, leaving his baby son, **Henry VI**, to succeed him. Vigorous, efficient and autocratic, he was also devout and just, but he mercilessly persecuted his enemies, notably the Lollards, who had become the first group of English heretics to represent a political threat.

Henry VI 1421–71 •*King of England*• Born in Windsor, Berkshire, he was the son of **Henry V** and **Catherine de Valois**, and became king on the death of his father in 1422. During his minority, his uncle John, Duke of **Bedford**, was regent in France, and another uncle, Humphrey, Duke of **Gloucester**, was Protector of England. English power in France declined steadily from 1429, and after Bedford's death (1435), the English were gradually expelled from all France, except Calais (1453). Henry was obsessively pious, and from 1453 experienced bouts of insanity. In 1445 he married the strong-minded **Margaret of Anjou**, who had Gloucester arrested for treason (1447). Five days later he was found dead in his bed, but there is no proof that he was murdered. **Jack Cade** obtained temporary possession of London, but was soon captured and executed (1450). As a descendant of Lionel, Duke of Clarence, **Edward III**'s third son, Richard, Duke of **York**, had a better claim to the crown than Henry, and in 1454, during one of Henry's mental lapses, York was appointed Protector, later taking Henry prisoner at St Albans (1455). This was the first of many battles between the Houses of York and Lancaster in the Wars of the Roses. A return of Henry's illness made York Protector again (1455–56), but York was killed at the Battle of Wakefield (1460). His heir, **Edward IV**, was proclaimed king (1461), and Henry was deposed (1461), imprisoned in the Tower of London, and then exiled. Richard Neville, Earl of **Warwick** restored him to the throne (1470), but six months later he was again in Edward's hands. At Tewkesbury (1471) his son, Edward, was killed and his wife, Margaret, who had headed the Lancastrian forces, was taken prisoner. Edward returned to London, and that night Henry was murdered in the Tower of London. Henry founded Eton and King's College, Cambridge. It was probably his inability to govern rather than the advent of bastard feudalism which was responsible for the so-called Wars of the Roses.

Henry VII 1457–1509 •*First Tudor king of England*• Born in Pembroke Castle, Wales, he was the son of Edmund Tudor, Earl of Richmond, and **Margaret Beaufort**, and the grandson of Owen Tudor, who married **Catherine de Valois**, widow of **Henry V**. His mother, a great-granddaughter of **John of Gaunt**, ranked as the lineal descendant of the House of Lancaster. After the Lancastrian defeat at Tewkesbury (1471), he was taken to Brittany. On August 1, 1485, Henry landed, unopposed, at Milford Haven and defeated **Richard III** on Bosworth Field. As king, his undeviating policy was to restore peace and prosperity to a warworn and impoverished land, an aim which his marriage of reconciliation with Elizabeth of York (eldest daughter of **Edward IV**) materially advanced. Minor Yorkist revolts were firmly dealt with, but Henry's policy in general was mercantilist and pacific, as was demonstrated by his readiness to conclude peace with France for a promised indemnity of £149,000. He also subsidized shipbuilding to expand his merchant marine while giving him first call on craft speedily convertible into warships. The marriage of Henry's heir, the future **Henry VIII**, to **Catherine of Aragon** cemented an alliance with Spain that largely nullified the soaring aspirations of France, while animosity with Scotland ended when **James IV** of Scotland married Henry's daughter **Margaret Tudor**. His personal fortune of over £1.5 million reflected the commercial prosperity his prudent policy had restored to the realm.

Henry VIII 1491–1547 •*King of England*• He was born in Greenwich, the second son of **Henry VII**. Soon after his accession to the throne in 1509 he married **Catherine of Aragon**, his brother Prince **Arthur**'s widow, a step of tremendous consequence. As a member of the Holy League formed by the pope and Spain against King **Louis XII** of France, in 1512 he invaded France, and next year won the so-called Battle of Spurs. During his absence an English army won a greater triumph over the Scots at Flodden (1513). It was in this French war that Cardinal **Wolsey** became prominent as the king's advisor. By 1514 he was, after the king, the first man in the country. In 1521 Henry published a defense of the sacraments in reply to **Martin Luther**, and received from Pope **Leo X** the title Defender of the Faith. From 1527 he determined to divorce Catherine. All her children, except Mary Tudor (later **Mary I**), had died in infancy, and Henry professed to see in this the judgment of heaven on an unnatural alliance. Henry had set his affections on **Anne Boleyn**, the niece of **Thomas Howard**, 3rd Duke of Norfolk. The pope, supported by the emperor, declined to support Henry. This proved the ruin of Wolsey, who now found himself without a friend at home or abroad. In 1529 he was stripped of his goods and honors, and dismissed in disgrace; the next year he was summoned to London on a charge of high treason, but died on the way. He was succeeded as Chancellor by Sir Thomas More. Henry remained determined about the divorce, and by humbling the clergy he thought he could bring the pope to terms. In 1531 the clergy was declared guilty of treason and only pardoned after payment of a large fine. The following year, the dues paid to the pope were canceled. Thomas More asked to be relieved of the Great Seal. Meanwhile Henry was privately married to Anne Boleyn (1533). In 1534 it was enacted that the king's marriage with Catherine was invalid and that the king was the sole supreme head of the Church of England. The suppression of the monasteries continued, with the support of the new Chancellor **Thomas Cromwell**. In 1536 Catherine died, and the same year Anne Boleyn herself was executed for infidelity. Henry then married **Jane Seymour**, who later died leaving a son (the future **Edward VI**). In 1540 **Anne of Cleves** became his fourth wife, in the hope of attaching the Protestant interest of Germany. Anne's personal appearance proved so little to Henry's taste that he consented to the marriage only on the condition that a divorce should follow speedily. He then married **Catherine Howard**, who two years later suffered the same fate as Anne Boleyn, on the same charge. In 1543 Henry married his sixth wife, **Catherine Parr**, widow of Lord Latimer, who survived him. His later years saw further war with France and Scotland, before peace was concluded with France in 1546. He was succeeded by his son, Edward VI.

Henry I, King of Germany *See* **Henry the Fowler**

Henry III 1017–56 •*King of Germany and Holy Roman Emperor*• The son of **Conrad II** and father of **Henry IV**, he became king of the Germans (1026), Duke of Bavaria (1027), Duke of Swabia (1038), and emperor (1039). One of the strongest German emperors in the Middle Ages, in 1046 he deposed all three rival popes and elected Clement II in their stead. He compelled the Duke of Bohemia to acknowledge himself a vassal of the empire (1042), established supremacy in Hungary (1044), and also extended his authority over the Norman conquerors of Apulia and Calabria. He promoted learning and the arts, founded numerous monastic schools, and built many churches.

Henry IV 1050–1106 •*King of Germany and Holy Roman Emperor*• Elected king of the Germans in 1053, he succeeded his father, **Henry III**, in 1056. In 1070, once free of his mother Agnes of Poitou's regency, he tried to break the power of the nobles, but his measures provoked an uprising of the Saxons. He defeated them at Hohenburg (1075), and then took action against the rebel princes. Pope **Gregory VII** took part in the dispute, and Henry declared him deposed (1076). Gregory then excommunicated Henry. Henry lost support and submitted, and the ban of excommunication was removed (1077). With Lombard support, he renewed the conflict and, having been excommunicated a second time, appointed a new pope, Clement III (the antipope), who crowned him emperor (1084). Henry defeated three rival German kings, but when he learned that his son Conrad had betrayed him and been crowned king at Monza, he retired to Lombardy. In 1097 he returned to Germany, and his second son, Henry, was elected king of the Germans, and Henry IV was compelled to abdicate. Taken prisoner, he escaped and died in Liège. While his opponents considered him a tyrannical supporter of heresy, his friends saw him as pious and intelligent, a lover of justice and scholarship. He was succeeded by Prince Henry as **Henry V**.

Henry V 1081–1125 •*King of Germany and Holy Roman Emperor*• In 1106 he allied himself with the nobility and dethroned his father, **Henry IV**. His reign was dominated by the issues involved in the Investiture Controversy and his power struggle with the princes. In 1111 he agreed with Pope Pascal II to give up his rights to invest bishops in return for coronation as emperor and the return of the royal insignia. This agreement was rejected by the German bishops and princes, whereupon Henry took the pope prisoner and forced him to concede both coronation and rights of investiture. This concession was later withdrawn and Henry was excommunicated. Finally, negotiations with Pope Calixtus II led to the end of the Investiture Controversy in the Concordat of Worms.

Henry VI 1165–97 •*King of Germany and Holy Roman Emperor*• The son of **Frederick I (Barbarossa)**, he was born in Nijmegen, the Netherlands, and married Constance, aunt and heiress of William II of Sicily (1186). He succeeded his father as king of Germany and emperor in 1190. He was opposed by the papacy, the **Guelfs**, **Richard I** of England and Constance's illegitimate brother **Tancred**, who had succeeded William in Sicily. This hostile coalition collapsed when Richard fell into the hands of Leopold V of Austria, who turned his captive over to Henry. When Tancred died (1194) Henry overran Sicily, where Constance bore him a son, **Frederick II**. Emperor (from 1191) and king of Sicily, Henry was extremely powerful, but failed to make the empire hereditary. He died young, of malaria, while preparing for a crusade.

Henry VII c. 1274–1313 •*King of Germany and Holy Roman Emperor*• Born in Valenciennes, Hainault, he was originally Count of Luxembourg, a French-speaking minor prince from the extreme west of the empire. He was elected emperor (1308) as an alternative candidate to **Charles of Valois**. His family soon rose to great power with the marriage in 1310 of his son John to Elizabeth, heiress of Bohemia. In the same year Henry led an army to Italy, but made little progress against the opposition of King Robert of Naples and the **Guelf** cities, and the imperialist cause collapsed when he died near Siena, probably of malaria.

Henry 1594–1612 •*Prince of Wales*• Born at Stirling Castle, he was the eldest son of **James VI and I** and **Anne of Denmark**, and was appointed Prince of Wales in 1610. Dignified and athletic, he won national popularity by his support for a Protestant and anti-Spanish foreign policy, and he became the focus for the hopes of those at court with Puritan sympathies. His death from typhoid (rumored to be a result of poison) led to the hopes of Protestants being centered increasingly upon Henry's sister, **Elizabeth** (the Winter Queen), and her husband, **Frederick V** of the Palatinate.

Henry of Blois 1101–71 •*English prelate*• He was Bishop of Winchester from 1129, and papal legate in England from 1139. He supported his younger brother, King **Stephen**, against the empress **Matilda** (Maud), and went to France after Stephen's death (1154).

Henry of Huntingdon c. 1084–1155 •*English chronicler*• He was archdeacon of Huntingdon from 1109. In 1139 he visited Rome. He compiled a *Historia Anglorum*, which covered the years up to 1154.

Henry the Fowler c. 876–936 •*King of Germany*• The founder of the Saxon dynasty, he was Duke of Saxony from 912. As Henry I (from 919), he brought Swabia and Bavaria into the German confederation, regained Lotharingia (925), defeated the Wends (928) and the Magyars in 933, and seized Schleswig from Denmark (934). He was about to claim the imperial crown (936) when he died. He was succeeded by his son, **Otto I (the Great)**. Another son was St **Bruno**.

Henry the Lion 1129–95 •*Duke of Saxony and Bavaria*• He was head of the **Guelf** family. After Bavaria was restored to him by **Frederick I (Barbarossa)** (1156), he became the most powerful prince in Germany, with domains stretching from the Baltic to the Adriatic. He expanded the frontiers of Saxony to the east against the Slavs, and did much to encourage the commerce of his lands, founding the city of Munich, but his ambitions and growing power aroused the opposition of a league of Saxon princes (1166) and of Frederick I, who defeated him and deprived him of his lands (1180). Henry went into exile at the court of **Henry II** of England, whose daughter Mathilda he had married (1168). He finally returned to Germany after 1190 and was reconciled to Emperor **Henry VI** in 1194.

Henry the Navigator 1394–1460 •*Portuguese prince*• The third son of John I, king of Portugal, and Philippa, daughter of **John of Gaunt**, he was born at Porto. He was made Governor of the Algarve (1419), and set up court at Sagres. He founded an observatory and school of scientific navigation at Cape St Vincent, and sponsored many voyages of exploration, resulting in the discovery of the Madeira Islands (1418), the Azores and the Cape Verde Islands (1456). His school used classical and Arabic learning to help produce the caravel, a vessel especially fitted for long voyages. His pupils also explored, and established trading posts on the west coast of Africa as far as Sierra Leone, thereby preparing the way for the discovery of the sea route to India.

Henry, Joseph 1797–1878 •*US physicist*• Born in Albany, New York, he studied at Albany Academy, and was appointed Professor of Mathematics there in 1826. In 1832 he became Professor of Natural Philosophy at Princeton University, and in 1846 first secretary of the Smithsonian Institution. He discovered electrical induction independently of **Michael Faraday**, constructed the first electromagnetic motor (1829) and also appreciated the effects of resistance on current, formulated precisely by **Georg Ohm** in 1827. He demonstrated the oscillatory nature of electric discharges (1842). The unit of inductance (the henry) is named after him.

Henry, Lenny 1958– •*English comic actor*• Born in Dudley, West Midlands, he made his television debut as a winning contestant on *New Faces* (1975) and went on to appear in such series as *Tiswas* (1979–82) and *Three of a Kind* (1981, 1983), showcasing an array of characters such as Delbert Wilkins and Theophilus P Wildebeest. He returned to television in 1992 with *Chef*, and has since appeared in *Hope and Glory* (1999). A leading figure in the charity Comic Relief, he is married to comedienne **Dawn French**.

Henry, O., *pseudonym of* **William Sydney Porter** 1862–1910 •*US short-story writer*• Born in Greensboro, North Carolina, he was brought up during the depression in the South, and settled in Austin, Texas, where he became a bank teller. In 1894 he "borrowed" money from the bank to help his consumptive wife and to start a literary magazine, the *Rolling Stone*. He fled at the height of the scandal, but returned in 1897, to his wife's deathbed, was found technically guilty of embezzlement, and spent three years in jail (1898–1901). There, he adopted his pseudonym and began to write short stories. From 1902, he roamed the back streets of New York, where he found ample material for his tales. His first of many collections was *Cabbages and Kings* (1904).

Henry, William 1774–1836 •*English physician and chemist*• Born in Manchester, he studied medicine at the University of Edinburgh, but ill health forced him to give up practicing medicine. Under the influence of his friend **John Dalton**, he turned to teaching and research in chemistry. His best-known work was the study of the influence of pressure and temperature on the solubility of gases in water, which resulted in the generalization that has become known as Henry's law, that the solubility of a gas at a given temperature is proportional to its pressure (1803). He committed suicide.

Hensen, Christian Andreas Viktor 1835–1924 •*German physiologist*• Born in Kiel, he studied medicine at the University of Würzburg then returned to the University of Kiel, where he graduated. He remained in Kiel, teaching anatomy and histology, becoming full Professor of Physiology in 1868. He studied the organs of hearing, describing what are now known as Hensen's duct and Hensen's supporting cells. In marine biology he investigated the marine fauna that he named plankton.

Henslowe, Philip c. 1550–1616 •*English theater manager*• Born in Lindfield, Sussex, he was originally a dyer and starch maker, but became lessee of the Rose Theatre on the Bankside, London, in 1584. From 1591 until his death he was in partnership with **Edward Alleyn**. Henslowe's business diary from 1593 to 1609, preserved at Dulwich College, was published in 1961 (eds R A Foakes and R T Rickert), and contains invaluable information about the stage of **Shakespeare**'s day.

Henson, Jim (James Maury) 1936–90 •*US puppeteer and fantasy filmmaker*• Born in Greenville, Mississippi, he worked in local television in Washington DC, later hosting his own show, *Sam and Friends* (1955–61). After he graduated from the University of Maryland, his endearing creations began to appear on national television, and in 1969 he launched *Sesame Street*, a series that entertained and educated preschool children. Many of his puppets, like Kermit the Frog and Miss Piggy, gained international popularity in the series *The Muppet Show* (1976–81). The characters subsequently appeared in a string of films as well as a Grammy award–winning album of the same title (1979). He continued to make innovative television programs combining live action and puppetry, including *Fraggle Rock* (1983–88), and received numerous Emmy awards. His special-effects adventure films include *The Dark Crystal* (1982) and *The Witches* (1989).

Henze, Hans Werner 1926– •*German composer*• Born in Gütersloh, he studied at Heidelberg, Darmstadt and Paris. After early absorption of serial techniques, Henze later reacted against the strictness and exclusiveness of the Darmstadt school. His political awareness was also stimulated, particularly by the Vietnam War and the student movements of 1967 to 1968, and his subsequent music reflects his commitment to socialist movements in Germany, Italy and Cuba. His stage works include thirteen full-length and three one-act operas, notably *Das Wundertheater* (1948, revised 1964, "The Wonder Theater"), *König Hirsch* (1955, "King Stag"), *Elegy for Young Lovers* (1961), *The Bassarids* (1965) and *The English Cat* (1983). He has also written full-length and chamber ballets, and other music-theater works. He has composed nine symphonies, string quartets, concertos, and other orchestral, chamber, vocal and piano music.

Hepburn, Audrey, *originally* **Edda Van Heemstra Hepburn-Ruston** 1929–93 •*Belgian actress*• Born in Brussels, she trained in ballet in Amsterdam and London. She first appeared on Broadway in *Gigi* (1951), and won a Best Actress Academy Award for *Roman Holiday* (1953). An enchanting, pencil-slim actress of coltish grace, she had many film successes, including *Funny Face* (1957), *Breakfast at Tiffany's* (1961), *My Fair Lady* (1964), *Two for the Road* (1967) and *Wait Until Dark* (1967). In her later years she traveled extensively as a goodwill ambassador for UNICEF. She made her final appearance in *Always* (1989).

Hepburn, James *See* **Bothwell, 4th Earl of**

Hepburn, Katharine Houghton 1907–2003 •*US film and stage actress*• She was born in Hartford, Connecticut, and educated at Bryn Mawr College. She made her professional stage debut in *The Czarina* (1928) in Baltimore and acted on Broadway, but from 1932 attained international fame as a film actress. Her many enduring films include *Bringing Up Baby* (1938), *The Philadelphia Story* (1940), *Woman of the Year* (1942), which saw the beginning of a 25-year professional and personal partnership with costar **Spencer Tracy**, *The African Queen* (1951) and *Long Day's Journey into Night* (1962). Noted for her distinctive New England diction, fine bone structure and versatile talent, she won Academy Awards for *Morning Glory* (1933), *Guess Who's Coming to Dinner?* (1967), *The Lion in Winter* (1968) and *On Golden Pond* (1981). On stage she enjoyed enormous success in the musical *Coco* (1970). She continued to act despite suffering from Parkinson's disease. Her television work included *The Glass Menagerie* (1973) and *Mrs Delafield Wants to Marry* (1986).

Hepplewhite, George d. 1786 •*English furniture designer*• He seems to have trained as a cabinetmaker with the Lancaster firm of Gillow, and then set up a workshop in London, but no extant furniture is attributable to him. His simple and elegant designs, characterized by the free use of inlaid ornament and the use of shield or heart shapes in chair backs, became famous only with the posthumous publication by his widow of his *Cabinet-Maker and Upholsterer's Guide* (1788), containing nearly 300 designs.

Hepworth, Dame (Jocelyn) Barbara 1903–75 •*English sculptor*• Born in Wakefield, she studied at the Leeds School of Art (with **Henry Moore**), the Royal College of Art, and in Italy. She married the sculptor John Skeaping (1901–80), and later the painter **Ben Nicholson**. In 1939 she went to live in St Ives, Cornwall. She was one of the foremost nonfigurative sculptors of her time, notable for the strength and formal discipline of her carving (as in the *Contrapuntal Forms*, exhibited at the Festival of Britain, 1951). Other works include *Pierced Form* (1931), *The Unknown Political Prisoner* (1953) and *Single Form* (1963). Until the early 1960s her works were mainly in wood, including *Forms in Echelon* (1938) and *Group II (People Waiting)* (1952). She then worked in stone, producing *Two Forms with White (Greek)* (wood and stone, 1963) and *Three Monoliths* (marble, 1964), and in metal, producing *Four Square (Walk Through)* (bronze, 1966). She was given the honorary title Dame Commander, Order of the British Empire, in 1965.

“ ”

There is an inside and an outside to every form.

1970 ***A Pictorial Biography.***

Heracleides of Pontus and Ekphantus c. 388–c. 315 BC •*Greek philosopher and astronomer*• Born in Heraklea, he moved to Athens to become a pupil of **Plato**. It is reported that he was the first to propose that the Earth spins. It is also suggested that he took the first steps toward describing a heliocentric solar system.

Heraclitus d. 460 BC •*Greek philosopher*• Born in Ephesus, Asia Minor, of an old aristocratic family, he was criticized by his contemporaries for his oracular style, and was known as "the obscure" and "the riddler." Only fragments remain of his book *On Nature*. He seems to have held that everything is in a state of flux ("you can never step into the same river twice") and that the apparent unity and stability of the world conceals a dynamic tension between opposites, which is somehow measured and controlled by reason (*Logos*) or its physical manifestation, fire. Fire is the ultimate constituent of the world, and the fire of the human soul is thus linked to the cosmic fire which virtuous souls eventually join.

Heraclius c. 575–641 •*Byzantine emperor*• Born in Cappadocia, he revolted against Phocas, killed him, and took his throne (610). The empire was threatened to the north by the Avars, and to the east by the Persians under **Chosroes II**, who overran Syria, Egypt and Asia Minor. After carrying out far-reaching reorganizations of the army, the provincial government, and the empire's finances, he defeated the Persians in a series of campaigns which restored the lost territories (628–33). However, he failed to resolve the differences between the orthodox and monophysite parties in the Church, and from 634 the recent gains in the East were almost completely lost to the followers of **Muhammad** under the caliph 'Umar.

Herbert, Sir A(lan) P(atrick) 1890–1971 •*English writer and politician*• Born in Elstead, Surrey, he studied law at Oxford, then served in the navy during World War I. He was called to the bar but never practiced, having established himself in his twenties as a witty writer of verses, joining *Punch* in 1924. His first theatrical success, with Nigel Playfair (1874–1934) in the revue *Riverside Nights* (1926), was followed by a series of brilliant libretti for comic operas, including *Tantivy Towers* (1930) and *Bless the Bride* (1947). He was also the author of several successful novels, notably *The Secret*

Battle (1919) and *Holy Deadlock* (1934). Independent Member of Parliament for Oxford University from 1935 to 1950, he did much to improve marriage and divorce law in England. He was knighted in 1945.

Herbert (of Cherbury), Edward Herbert, 1st Baron 1583–1648 •*English soldier, politician and philosopher*• Born in Eyton-on-Severn, Shropshire, he was made a Knight of the Bath (1603) and as a member of the Privy Council was sent as ambassador to France in 1619 to negotiate between **Louis XIII** and his Protestant subjects. In 1624 he was made a peer of Ireland, and in 1629 of England. When the English Civil War broke out, he at first sided half-heartedly with the Royalists, but in 1644 surrendered to the Parliamentarians. Considered one of the finest deistic writers, his works include *De veritate* (1624, "On Truth") and *De religione gentilium* (published posthumously in 1663, Eng trans *The Antient Religion of the Gentiles*, 1705). He also wrote poetry, contemporary histories and an autobiography. He was the brother of the poet **George Herbert**.

Herbert, Frank Patrick 1920–86 •*US science-fiction writer*• Born in Tacoma, Washington, he was a journalist before turning to full-time fiction writing. His first novel, *The Dragon in the Sea* (1956), is an acute psychological study set on a submarine. He is best known for his series of novels about the desert planet *Dune* (1965), one of the most complex and fully realized examples of an alternative world in science fiction. Persistent themes of his work include the development of higher or artificial intelligence in human and nonhuman species, genetic engineering, ecology and overpopulation. Important titles include *The Green Brain* (1966), *The Santaroga Barrier* (1968) and *Hellstrom's Hive* (1973).

Herbert, George 1593–1633 •*English metaphysical poet and clergyman*• He was the son of Lady Magdalen Herbert (to whom **John Donne** addressed his *Holy Sonnets*) and brother of **Edward Herbert** (of Cherbury). Educated at Westminster School and Trinity College, Cambridge, he was Member of Parliament for Montgomery (1624–25). His connection with the court, and particularly the favor of King **James VI and I**, seemed to point to a worldly career, but in 1630, under the influence of Archbishop **Laud**, he took orders and spent his last years as a parish priest of Bemerton, in Wiltshire. Herbert represents in both his life and works the counterchallenge of the Laudian party to the Puritans. He died of consumption at the age of 39. Practically all his religious lyrics are included in *The Temple, Sacred Poems and Private Ejaculations*, posthumously published in 1633. His chief prose work, *A Priest in the Temple*, containing guidance for the country parson, was published in his *Remains* (1652).

Herbert, Victor 1859–1924 •*US composer*• Born in Dublin, Ireland, he trained as a cellist. In 1893 he began his career as a bandleader and conductor, and composed his first successful operetta, *Prince Ananias* (1894), which was followed by a long series of similar works containing such popular songs as "Ah, Sweet Mystery of Life" and "Kiss Me Again." Immensely prolific and possessed of accurate theatrical instincts, he wrote more than 40 operas, operettas and musical comedies, of which the best known are *Babes in Toyland* (1903), *The Red Mill* (1906) and *Naughty Marietta* (1910).

Herbert, Sir Wally (Walter William) 1934– •*British explorer*• Brought up in South Africa and trained at the School of Military Survey, he spent two years in Egypt before joining the Falkland Islands Dependencies Survey in Antarctica (1955–57). This was followed by expeditions to Lapland, Svalbard and Greenland. He made the first surface crossing of the Arctic Ocean (1968–69), a 464-day journey of 3,800 miles (6,115 km) from Alaska to Spitsbergen via the Pole, the longest sustained sledge journey in history. He lived in the Arctic, filming the Inuit, and between 1978 and 1982 made several attempts to circumnavigate Greenland. He has written a number of books, and was knighted in 2000.

Herbert, William, 3rd Earl of Pembroke 1580–1630 •*English poet*• He was a patron of **Ben Jonson**, **Philip Massinger** and **Inigo Jones**, and a Lord Chamberlain of the Court (1615–30). He became Chancellor of Oxford in 1617 and had Pembroke College named after him. **Shakespeare**'s "W H," the "onlie begetter" of the *Sonnets*, has been taken by some to refer to him.

Herblock *See* **Block, Herbert Lawrence**

Herder, Johann Gottfried 1744–1803 •*German critic and poet*• Born in Mohrungen, East Prussia, he studied at Königsberg. In 1764 he became a schoolteacher and assistant pastor in a church in Riga. He met **Goethe** in Strasbourg (1769), was appointed court preacher at Bückeburg (1770), and first preacher in Weimar (1776). His belief that the truest poetry is the poetry of the people found expression in his collection of folksongs, *Stimmen der Völker in Liedern* (1778–79, "Voices of the Peoples in Songs"), *Vom Geist der ebräischen Poesie* (1782–83, Eng trans *The Spirit of Hebrew Poetry*, 1833), in his version of the *Cid* (1805), and other works. His *Ideen zur Geschichte der Menschheit* (1784–91, Eng trans *Outlines of a Philosophy of the History of Man*, 1800) is remarkable for its anticipation of evolutionary theories.

Hérelle, Felix d' 1873–1949 •*Canadian bacteriologist*• Born in Montreal, he studied there and worked in Central America, Europe and Egypt before holding a chair at Yale from 1926 to 1933. A competitor of Frederick Twort (1877–1950), he was independently the discoverer in 1915 of the bacteriophage, a type of virus that infects bacteria. However, phages later proved of great value in research, and along with Twort, Hérelle can be regarded as one of the founders of molecular biology.

Hereward, *known as* **Hereward the Wake** fl. 1070 •*Anglo-Saxon thane and rebel*• A Lincolnshire squire, he led a raid on Peterborough Abbey in 1070 as a protest against the appointment of a Norman abbot by **William the Conqueror**. He took refuge on the Isle of Ely with other rebels. When William succeeded in penetrating to the English camp in 1071, Hereward cut his way through to the swampy fens northward and escaped. He was the hero of **Charles Kingsley**'s romance, *Hereward the Wake* (1866).

Hergé, *pseudonym of* **Georges Rémi** 1907–83 •*Belgian cartoonist*• Born in Etterbeek, near Brussels, he drew his first strip, *Totor*, for a boy scouts' weekly in 1926. He created the *Tin-Tin* boy-detective strip for the children's supplement of the newspaper *Le Vingtième Siècle*, using the pen name Hergé, a phonetic version of his initials in reverse, RG. *Tintin in the Land of the Soviets* was quickly republished in album format (1930), as were all the adventures of the young detective (22 vols in all).

Heriot, George 1563–1624 •*Scottish goldsmith and philanthropist*• Born in Edinburgh, he started business in 1586, and in 1597 was appointed goldsmith to **Anne of Denmark**, and then to her husband, King **James VI**, in 1603. He followed King James to London, where, as court jeweler and banker, he amassed considerable wealth. He bequeathed £23,625 to found a hospital or school in Edinburgh for sons of poor burgesses, now an independent school known as George Heriot's.

Herman, Woody (Woodrow Charles) 1913–87 •*US bandleader, alto saxophonist and clarinettist*• He was born in Milwaukee, Wisconsin, and having learned to play saxophone at the age of nine, left home at 17 to begin his professional career. A member of the band led by Isham Jones, when this broke up in 1936, Herman formed his own band, which established itself by the mid-1940s as a stylistic leader, particularly in its saxophone voicings. The Herman Orchestra was one of the very few to survive intact beyond the 1950s, continuing to tour until the 1980s.

Hermandszoon, Jakob *See* **Arminius, Jacobus**

Hermannsson, Steingrímur 1928– •*Icelandic politician*• He trained as an electrical engineer in the US, returning to Iceland to work in industry. He was director of Iceland's National Research Council (1957–78) and then made the transition into politics, becoming chairman of the Progressive Party (PP) in 1979. He became a minister in 1978 and then prime minister, heading a PP–Independence Party (IP) coalition (1983–87). He became prime minister again in 1988, but was defeated in the 1991 elections.

Hernández, Miguel 1910–42 •*Spanish poet and playwright*• A goatherd's son, he was encouraged by **Juan Ramón Jiménez**, Antonio Machado (1875–1939) and members of the Generation of '27 (**Federico García Lorca** and others) to publish his *Gongorista* early poetry. He fought against Franco, and died in a prison hospital of cold, starvation and tuberculosis. His best work has been translated in *Songbook of Absences* (1972) and in *Miguel Hernández and Blas de Otero: Selected Poems* (1972).

Hero of Alexandria 1st century AD •*Greek mathematician*• He wrote on mechanics and invented many machines, including the aeolipile (the earliest known steam engine), a fire engine pump, and coin-operated devices. He also formulated an expression for the area of a triangle in terms of the lengths of its sides.

Herod, *known as* **Herod the Great** c. 74–4 BC •*Ruler of Palestine in Roman times*• The second son of the Idumaean chieftain Antipater, procurator of Judea, he owed his initial appointment as governor of Galilee (47 BC) to **Julius Caesar**, his elevation to the kingship of Judea (37 BC) to **Mark Antony**, and his retention in that post after Actium (31 BC) to **Augustus**. He was a loyal Roman client king who ruthlessly kept all his subjects in check, but he also did much to develop the economic potential of his kingdom. He had 10 wives and 14 children, and life at his court was marked by constant and bloody infighting between the members of his family. His undoubted cruelty is detailed in the Gospel account of the slaughter of the infants of Bethlehem (the Massacre of the Innocents).

Herod Agrippa I 10 BC–AD 44 •*Ruler of Judea*• The son of Aristobulus and Berenice, and grandson of **Herod** the Great, he was educated at the court of the emperor **Augustus** after his father was executed by Herod the Great, and lived there until his debts compelled him to take refuge in Idumaea. Having formed a friendship with **Caligula**, he received from him four tetrarchies, and, after the banishment of **Herod Antipas**, that of Galilee and Peraea. **Claudius** added to his dominions Judea and Samaria. He showed some skill in conciliating the Romans and Jews, but repressed the Christians, executing St **James** and imprisoning St **Peter**.

Herod Agrippa II AD 27–c. 100 •*Ruler of Palestine in Roman times*• The son of **Herod Agrippa I**, he was in Rome when his father died (AD 44). **Claudius** detained him, and changed the kingdom back into a Roman province. In 53 he received nearly all his paternal possessions, which were subsequently enlarged by **Nero** (54). When Jerusalem was taken by the Jews, he went with his sister to Rome, where he became praetor. It was before him that St **Paul** made his defense.

Herod Antipas 21 BC–AD 39 •*Ruler of Palestine in Roman times*• The son of **Herod** the Great, by whose will he was named tetrarch of Galilee and Peraea, he divorced his first wife in order to marry Herodias, the wife of his half brother Philip—a union against which **John the Baptist** remonstrated. It was when Herod Antipas was in Jerusalem for the Passover that **Jesus** was sent before him by **Pontius Pilate** for examination. In AD 39 he went to Rome in the hope of obtaining from **Caligula** the title of king; he not only failed, but, through the intrigues of his nephew **Herod Agrippa I**, he was banished to Lugdunum (now Lyons, France), where he died.

Herodian c. 170–c. 240 AD •*Greek historian*• Born in Syria, he lived in Rome, and wrote a history of the Roman emperors in eight books, from the death of **Marcus Aurelius** (AD 180) to the accession of Gordian III (AD 238).

Herodotus c. 485–425 BC •*Greek historian*• He was born in Halicarnassus, a Greek colony on the coast of Asia Minor. He traveled extensively in Asia Minor and the Middle East, and visited Sicily and Lower Italy. On his travels, he collected historical, geographical, ethnological, mythological and archaeological material for his great narrative history, which included a record of the wars between Greece and Asia. Beginning with the conquest of the Greek colonies in Asia Minor by the Lydian king **Croesus**, he gives a history of Lydia, Persia, Babylon and Egypt. He was the first to make the events of the past the subject of research and verification, and **Cicero** and others have called him "the father of history."

“ ”

In peace, children inter their parents; war violates the order of nature and causes parents to inter their children.

*c. 440 BC **The Histories of Herodotus**, book 1, chapter 87 (translated by Aubrey de Selincourt).*

Heron, Patrick 1920–99 •*English painter, critic and textile designer*• Born in Headingley, Leeds, he studied at the Slade School of Art, London (1937–39). A conscientious objector during World War II, he worked as a farm laborer. In St Ives (1944–45) he met **Ben Nicholson**, **Barbara Hepworth** and Adrian Stokes. He was art critic for the *New Statesman and Nation* (1947–50), and taught at the Central School of Art, London (1953–56). He traveled and lectured in Australia, Brazil and the US. His paintings show a preoccupation with color, and include *Scarlet, Lemon and Ultramarine* (1957) and *Cadmium with Violet, Scarlet, Emerald, Lemon and Venetian* (1969).

Herophilus c. 335–c. 280 BC •*Greek anatomist*• Born in Chalcedon, he was the founder of the Alexandria school of anatomy. He was the first to dissect the human body to compare it with that of other animals. He described the brain, liver, spleen, sexual organs and nervous system, dividing the latter into sensory and motor, and was the first to measure the pulse, for which he used a water clock.

Herrick, Robert 1591–1674 •*English poet*• Born in London, the son of a goldsmith, he was educated at Trinity Hall, Cambridge, ordained in 1623 and worked in Devon from 1629 until he was deprived of his position as Dean Prior in 1647 for being a Royalist. His writing is mainly collected in *Hesperides; or, the Works Both Humane and Divine of Robert Herrick Esq* (1648), with a separate section of religious verse entitled *Noble Numbers*. He was at his best when describing rural rites, as in *The Hock Cart* and *Twelfth Night*, and in well-known lyrics such as "Gather Ye Rosebuds While Ye May" and "Cherry Ripe." He resumed his position in his Devon parish in 1662 after the Restoration.

Herriot, Édouard 1872–1957 •*French radical-socialist statesman*• Born in Troyes, he became professor at the Lycée Ampère, Lyons, and was mayor there from 1905 until his death. He was minister of transport during World War I, premier (1924–25, 1926 [for two days], 1932) and several times president of the Chamber of Deputies, a post which he was holding in 1942 when he became a prisoner of Vichy and of the Nazis. After the liberation, he was president of the National Assembly (1947–53), and was then elected life president. A keen supporter of the League of Nations, he opposed German rearmament.

Herschel, Caroline Lucretia 1750–1848 •*British astronomer*• Born in Hanover, Germany, she was the sister of **William Herschel**. In 1772 her brother took her to England to assist with his musical activities, and she became his collaborator when he abandoned his first career for astronomy (1782). Between 1786 and 1797 she discovered eight comets. Among her other discoveries was the companion of the Andromeda nebula (1783). Her *Index to Flamsteed's Observations of the Fixed Stars* and a list of errata were published by the Royal Society (1798). Following her brother's death she returned at the age of 72 to Hanover, where she worked on the reorganization of his catalog of nebulae. She was elected (with **Mary Somerville**) an honorary member of the Royal Astronomical Society (1835).

Herschel, Sir John Frederick William 1792–1871 •*English astronomer*• The only child of Sir **William Herschel**, he was born in Slough, and educated at St John's College, Cambridge. His first award was the Copley Prize of the Royal Society for his mathematical research in 1821. In collaboration with Sir James South, he reexamined his father's double stars (1821–23) and produced a catalog which earned him the Lalande Prize (1825) and the gold medal of the Royal Astronomical Society (1826). He reviewed his father's great catalog of nebulae in Slough (1825–33), adding 525 new ones, for which he received the gold medals of the Royal Astronomical Society (1826) and the Royal Society (1836). To extend the survey to the entire sky, he went to South Africa and in four years there (1834–38) he completed a survey of nebulae and clusters in the southern skies, observing 1,708 of them, the majority previously unseen. His southern observations, published as *Cape Observations* (1847), earned him the Copley Medal of the Royal Society (1847). He was made a baronet at Queen **Victoria**'s coronation.

Herschel, Sir (Frederick) William, *originally* **Friedrich Wilhelm Herschel** 1738–1822 •*British astronomer*• Born in Hanover,

Germany, he was the son of a musician. William joined the Hanoverian Guards band as an oboist and moved in 1755 to England, where he built up a successful career in music, eventually settling in Bath in 1766, where his interest in astronomy began. He built his own telescopes, learning to cast his own metal disks for his mirrors. In 1781 he discovered the planet Uranus, which he named *Georgium Sidus* in honor of King **George III**, who a year later appointed him his private astronomer. At Slough, near Windsor, assisted by his sister **Caroline Herschel**, he continued his research and built ever-larger telescopes. Herschel's discoveries included two satellites of Uranus (1787) and two of Saturn (1789), but his epoch-making work lay in his studies of the stellar universe. He drew up his first catalog of double stars (1782), later demonstrating that such objects constitute bodies in orbit around each other (1802), and observed the sun's motion through space (1783). His famous paper, *On the Construction of the Heavens* (1784), produced a model of the Milky Way. Following the publication of **Charles Messier**'s catalog of nebulae and star clusters (1781), he began a systematic search for such objects, which revealed a total of 2,500, published in three catalogs (1786, 1789, 1802), and he distinguished different types of nebulae. He was knighted in 1816.

Hersey, John Richard 1914–93 •*US writer*• Born in Tianjin (Tientsin), China, to US missionary parents, he was educated at Yale University, and became correspondent in the Far East for *Time* magazine. He wrote the novel *A Bell for Adano* (1944, Pulitzer Prize winner; it was also dramatized and filmed), on the US occupation of Italy, and the nonfiction work *Hiroshima* (1946), the first on-the-spot description of the effects of a nuclear explosion. Later works included *The War Lover* (1959), *The Walnut Door* (1977) and *Antonietta* (1991).

Hershey, A(lfred) D(ay) 1908–97 •*US biologist and Nobel Prize winner*• Born in Owosso, Michigan, he studied at Michigan State College, and from 1950 to 1974 worked at the Carnegie Institution in Washington, where from 1962 he was director of the Genetics Research Unit. He became an expert on the viruses which infect bacteria (bacteriophages, or phages), and set up the Phage Group with **Salvador Luria** and **Max Delbrück** in the late 1940s to encourage the use of phages as an experimental tool. Working with Martha Chase in the early 1950s, Hershey provided firm evidence for the idea (suggested by **Oswald Avery** in 1944) that DNA was a genetic information-carrying mechanism. Hershey shared the 1969 Nobel Prize for physiology or medicine with Luria and Delbrück.

Hertz, Gustav Ludwig 1887–1975 •*German physicist and Nobel Prize winner*• He was born in Hamburg, the nephew of **Heinrich Hertz**, and educated at the University of Berlin. With **James Franck**, he showed that atoms would only absorb a fixed amount of energy, thus demonstrating the quantized nature of the atom's electron energy levels. For this work they shared the 1925 Nobel Prize for physics. The results provided data for **Niels Bohr** to develop his theory of atomic structure, and for **Max Planck** to develop his ideas on quantum theory. After World War II Hertz went to the USSR to become head of a research laboratory (1945–54), then returned to Germany to become director of the Physics Institute in Leipzig (1954–61).

Hertz, Heinrich Rudolf 1857–94 •*German physicist*• Born in Hamburg, he was educated at the Johanneum Gymnasium before moving to Berlin, where he studied under **Gustav Kirchhoff** and **Hermann von Helmholtz**, becoming the latter's assistant. In 1889 he became professor at the University of Bonn. In 1887 Hertz confirmed **James Clerk Maxwell**'s predictions by his fundamental discovery of Hertzian waves, now known as radio waves, which behave like light waves except in wavelength. Later he explored the general theoretical implications of Maxwell's electrodynamics, was widely honored for his work on electric waves, and in 1890 he was awarded the Rumford Medal of the Royal Society.

Hertzog, J(ames) B(arry) M(unnik) 1866–1942 •*South African statesman*• Born in Wellington, Cape Colony, he studied law at Stellenbosch and Amsterdam, became a Boer general (1899–1902), and in 1910 became Minister of Justice in the first Union government. In 1913 he founded the Nationalist Party, advocating complete South African independence from the British Empire, and in World War I opposed cooperation with Great Britain. As prime minister (1924–39), he pursued a program which destroyed the African franchise, created reservations for whites, and tightened land segregation. He renounced his earlier secessionism, but at the outbreak of World War II declared for neutrality, was defeated, lost office, and in 1940 retired.

Hertzsprung, Ejnar 1873–1967 •*Danish astronomer*• Born in Fredriksberg, Copenhagen, he graduated in chemical engineering from the Technical High School in Copenhagen and joined the staff of the university observatory in Copenhagen. He published in 1905 the principle of what was later to be called the Hertzsprung-**Russell** diagram, which became the key for the theory of stellar evolution. In 1909 he obtained a position under **Karl Schwarzschild** at the University of Göttingen, and then he moved with Schwarzschild to the Astrophysical Observatory in Potsdam. He was appointed director of the Leiden Observatory, where his enthusiasm and example were of great benefit to astronomy in the Netherlands.

Herzberg, Gerhard 1904–99 •*Canadian physical chemist and Nobel Prize winner*• Born in Hamburg, Germany, he was educated in Göttingen and Berlin, and taught in Darmstadt before emigrating to Canada in 1935, where he taught at the University of Saskatchewan (1935–45). From 1949 to 1969 he was director of the division of pure physics at the National Research Council in Ottawa. He developed spectroscopic methods for a variety of purposes, including the detailed study of energy levels in atoms and molecules and the detection of unusual molecules both in laboratory work and in interstellar space. He was awarded the Nobel Prize for chemistry in 1971.

Herzl, Theodor 1860–1904 •*Hungarian Zionist leader*• Born in Budapest, he moved to Vienna at the age of 18, where he studied law and pursued a career as a journalist and author. In Paris as a newspaper correspondent (1891–95), he covered the **Dreyfus** trial (1894). He became convinced that the only adequate Jewish response to anti-Semitism was a political one, and in 1895 published *Der Judenstaat* ("The Jewish State"), in which he argued that the Jews should have their own state. In 1897, in Basel, he convened the First Zionist Congress, which declared its goal to be the founding of a national Jewish home in Palestine, and established the World Zionist Organization to that end. His name is inseparable from the emergence of political Zionism in the modern period.

Herzog, Émile *See* **Maurois, André**

Herzog, Roman 1934– •*German Christian Democrat politician*• Born in Landshut, he was educated at the University of Munich and the Free University of Berlin. In 1973 he was elected the representative for Rhineland-Palatinate and was appointed Minister of the Interior in 1980. He was president of the Federal Constitutional Court from 1987 to 1994, then president of Germany from 1994 to 1999.

Herzog, Werner, *originally* **Werner Stipetic** 1942– •*German film director*• He was born in Munich and studied at the universities of Munich and Pittsburgh. His films are often set in remote regions or time periods, as in *Aguirre, Wrath of God* (1972), which deals with the exploits of a rebel soldier in **Pizarro**'s army in 16th-century Peru, or *Fitzcarraldo* (1982), the story of a misguided attempt to build an opera house in the Amazon jungle; both films starred Klaus Kinski. Other notable films include *Where the Green Ants Dream* (1984), *Cobra Verde* (1987) and *Lessons in Darkness* (1992). He has also staged several operas.

Heseltine, Michael Ray Dibdin 1933– •*English Conservative politician*• Born in Swansea, South Wales, and educated at Pembroke College, Oxford, after military service he established a successful publishing business, Haymarket Press, before becoming Member of Parliament for Tavistock in 1966, and, from 1974, Henley-on-Thames. After holding junior posts under **Edward Heath**, he joined **Margaret Thatcher**'s Cabinet in 1979 as secretary of state for the environment and was made defense secretary in 1983. He resigned dramatically in 1986, claiming that he had been calumnied over the Westland Affair, which involved the sale of the British helicopter manufacturer Westland to a US rather than a

European company. Always popular at party conferences, he has long been seen as a potential Conservative leader, but was unsuccessful in the leadership contest which led to Margaret Thatcher's resignation in 1990. He returned to the Cabinet under **John Major** and again became secretary of state for the environment (1990–92). As president of the Board of Trade (1992–95) he announced the closure of 31 coal mines in 1992. First secretary of state and deputy prime minister from 1995 to 1997, when the Conservatives were defeated in the general election, he declined to run in the ensuing leadership contest for health reasons. His publications include *The Challenge of Europe* (1989).

Hesiod c. 8th century BC •*Greek poet*• Born in Ascra, Boeotia, he is one of the earliest known Greek poets. He wrote in a didactic style and is best known for the epics *Works and Days*, which deals with the farmer's life and gives a realistic picture of a primitive peasant community, and *Theogony*, which teaches the origin of the universe and the history of the gods.

“ ”

The ill design is most ill for the designer.

Opera et dies, *266 (translated by M L West, 1988).*

Hess, Germain Henri 1802–50 •*Russian chemist*• Born in Geneva, Switzerland, he was taken to Russia in childhood. After studying medicine, chemistry and geology at the University of Dorpat (Tartu, Estonia), he took part in a geological expedition to the Urals and practiced medicine in Irkutsk, but from around 1830 devoted himself to chemistry. His earliest research was on mineral analysis and on the natural gas of Baku, but he then turned to thermochemistry. After extensive measurements of the heats of chemical reaction, he established the law of constant heat summation (1838–40), commonly called Hess's law, which states that the heat developed in a given chemical change is constant, independent of whether the change is carried out in one stage or in several stages.

Hess, Dame Myra 1890–1965 •*English pianist*• Born in London, she studied under **Tobias Matthay** at the Royal Academy of Music, and was an immediate success on her first public appearance in 1907. She worked as a chamber musician, recitalist and virtuoso, achieving fame in North America as well as Great Britain. During World War II she organized the lunchtime concerts in the National Gallery, London, for which she was given the honorary title of Dame Commander, Order of the British Empire, in 1941.

Hess, (Walter Richard) Rudolf 1894–1987 •*German Nazi politician*• Born in Alexandria, Egypt, and educated at Bad Godesberg, he fought in World War I, after which he studied at the University of Munich, where he fell under **Hitler**'s spell. He joined the Nazi Party in 1920, took part in the abortive Munich putsch (1923) and, having shared Hitler's imprisonment and, it is said, taken down from him *Mein Kampf*, became in 1934 his deputy as party leader and in 1939 his successor designate, after **Hermann Goering**, as Führer. In May 1941, on the eve of Germany's attack on Russia, he flew alone to Scotland (Eaglesham), supposedly to plead the cause of a negotiated Anglo-German peace. He was temporarily imprisoned in the Tower of London, then placed under psychiatric care near Aldershot. At the Nuremberg Trials (1946) he was sentenced to life imprisonment. He spent the rest of his life in Spandau jail, Berlin, where after 1966 he was the sole remaining prisoner.

Hess, Victor Francis 1883–1964 •*US physicist and Nobel Prize winner*• He was born in Waldstein, Austria, and while on the staff of the University of Vienna during 1911–12, he made a number of manned balloon flights carrying ionization chambers. He demonstrated that the radiation intensity in the atmosphere increased with height, and concluded that the high-energy cosmic radiation that was responsible must originate from outer space. He also helped to determine the number of alpha particles given off by a gram of radium (1918). For his work on cosmic radiation he was awarded the 1936 Nobel Prize for physics, jointly with **Carl Anderson**.

Hess, Walter Rudolf 1881–1973 •*Swiss physiologist and Nobel Prize winner*• Born in Frauenfeld, he studied medicine at the Universities of Lausanne, Bern, Zurich, Berlin and Kiel. As Professor of Physiology and director of the Physiology Institute of the University of Zurich (1917–51), he studied the regulation of blood pressure and heart rate, and their relationship to respiration, and from 1925 worked on the function of structures at the base of the brain. He developed methods of stimulating localized areas of the brain by means of fine-needle electrodes, and was able to show that stimulating different parts of the hypothalamus causes changes in body temperature, blood pressure, respiration, and also anger, sexual arousal, and sleep. He was awarded the 1949 Nobel Prize for physiology or medicine with **António Egas Moniz**.

Hesse, Eva 1936–70 •*US sculptor*• She was born in Hamburg, Germany, into a Jewish family which emigrated to the US in 1939 and settled in New York. There she attended the Pratt Institute (1952–53) and Cooper Union (1954–57). From 1965 she worked in a variety of materials, such as rubber, plastic, string and polyethylene, creating objects designed to rest on the floor or against a wall or to be suspended from the ceiling, as in *Hang-up* (1965–66). She exerted a strong influence on later conceptual artists.

Hesse, Hermann 1877–1962 •*Swiss novelist and poet, and Nobel Prize winner*• Born in Calw, Württemberg, Germany, he was a bookseller and antiquarian in Basel from 1895 to 1902, and published his first novel, *Peter Camenzind*, in 1904 (Eng trans 1961). From then on he devoted himself to writing, living in Switzerland from 1911 and becoming a naturalized citizen in 1923. Though he disclaimed any ruling purpose, the theme of his work might be stated as a musing on the difficulties put in the way of the individual in his efforts to build up an integrated, harmonious self. This is expressed in sensitive and sensuous language in such prose works as *Demian* (1919, Eng trans 1971), *Narziss und Goldmund* (1930, Eng trans *Death and the Lover*, 1932), *Steppenwolf* (1927, Eng trans 1929) and *Das Glasperlenspiel* (1943, Eng trans *The Glass Bead Game*, 1949). Hesse was awarded both the **Goethe** Prize and the Nobel Prize for literature in 1946. His poetry was collected in *Die Gedichte* in 1942 (a selection, Eng trans *Hours in the Garden and Other Poems*, 1979), and his letters, *Briefe*, appeared in 1951. His *Beschwörungen* (1955, "Affirmations") confirmed that his powers were not diminished by age.

Heston, Charlton, *originally* **Charles Carter** 1923– •*US film actor*• Born in Evanston, Illinois, he made his film debut in an amateur production of *Peer Gynt* (1941). After World War II service in the air force, he made his Broadway debut in *Antony and Cleopatra* (1947). His major early successes were the **Cecil B De Mille** films *The Greatest Show on Earth* (1952) and *The Ten Commandments* (1956). He also played the larger-than-life heroes for which his strapping physique suited him in *Ben Hur* (1959, Academy Award) and *El Cid* (1961). Other films include *Touch of Evil* (1958) and *The War Lord* (1965). He has frequently returned to the stage, and has also directed *Antony and Cleopatra* (1972) on film and, for television, *A Man for All Seasons* (1988). A staunchly conservative Republican, Heston has for several years been an outspoken member of the National Rifle Association (NRA), becoming its president in 1998. He stepped down from the leadership of the NRA in 2003 after announcing that he had symptoms consistent with Alzheimer's disease.

Heuss, Theodor 1884–1963 •*German statesman*• Born in Brackenheim, Württemberg, he was educated in Munich and Berlin and became editor of the political magazine *Hilfe* (1905–12), professor at the Berlin College of Political Science (1920–33), and Member of Parliament (1924–28, 1930–32). A prolific author and journalist, he wrote two books denouncing **Hitler**, and when the latter came to power in 1933, Heuss was dismissed from his professorship and his books were publicly burned. In 1946 he became founding member of the Free Democratic Party (FDP), and helped draft the new federal constitution. He was the first president of the Federal Republic of Germany (1949–59).

Hevelius, Johannes 1611–87 •*Polish astronomer*• Born in Gdańsk, he studied law at the University of Leiden. He constructed an observatory with a terrace for large quadrants and sextants, and high masts for the attachment of long telescopes in the 1640s. His *Selenographica* (1647) was a description of the moon with 133 copper plates of lunar features made by his own hand. He named many details on the moon after features on earth, and some of these names survive today. In the 1660s his interest turned to comets, resulting in his *Cometographia* (1668), a list of all comets observed up to that year. The first part of his major publication, *Machina Coelestis*, appeared in 1673, containing a detailed description of his observatory.

Hevesy, George Charles de 1885–1966 •*Hungarian chemist and Nobel Prize winner*• He was born in Budapest, studied at Freiburg and held posts at Zurich and Manchester, where he worked with **Ernest Rutherford**. He moved to Vienna in 1912, and after service in the Austro-Hungarian army during World War I, he moved to Copenhagen to join **Niels Bohr**. There he and **Dirk Coster** discovered hafnium in 1923. In 1935 he returned to Freiburg, and in World War II he fled to Sweden, where he became professor at Stockholm. His work on isotopes has been very influential, and from 1934 he pioneered the use of radioactive tracers to study chemical processes, particularly in living organisms. This work won him the Nobel Prize for chemistry in 1943.

Hewish, Antony 1924– •*English radio astronomer and Nobel Prize winner*• Born in Fowey, Cornwall, he studied at Cambridge and spent his career there, becoming Professor of Radio Astronomy (1971–89), then Emeritus Professor. In 1967 he and his student Jocelyn Bell Burnell (1943–) discovered the first astronomical radio sources emitting radio signals in regular pulses, now known as pulsars. He shared the Nobel Prize for physics in 1974 with his former teacher Sir **Martin Ryle**.

He Xiangning (Ho Hsiang-ning) 1880–1972 •*Chinese revolutionary and feminist*• Educated in Hong Kong and Japan, she married fellow revolutionary **Liao Zhongkai** in 1905 and was an active advocate of links with the communists and Russia. Her husband was assassinated in 1925, and when two years later **Chiang Kai-shek** broke with the communists, she returned to Hong Kong and was an outspoken critic of his leadership. She returned to Beijing (Peking) in 1949 as head of the overseas commission. She was one of the first Chinese women publicly to advocate nationalism, revolution and female emancipation.

Heydrich, Reinhard, *nicknamed* **the Hangman** 1904–42 •*German Nazi politician*• Born in Halle, as a youth he joined the violent anti-Weimar Freikorps (Volunteer Corps) (1918). He served in the navy (1922–31) but quit to join the Nazi Party, and entered the SS (*Schutzstaffel*, protective force), rising to be second-in-command of the Gestapo. He was charged with subduing **Hitler**'s occupied countries, during which he ordered numerous mass executions. He was killed by Czech assassins parachuted in from Great Britain. In the murderous reprisals, the village of Lidice was razed and all the men put to death.

Heyer, Georgette 1902–74 •*English historical and detective novelist*• Born in London, partly of South Slavic descent, she studied at Westminster College, London. She produced several well-researched historical novels from various periods, as well as fictional studies of **William the Conqueror**, **Charles II**, and the Battle of Waterloo. *Regency Buck* (1935) was the first of her novels on the Regency period. She also wrote modern comic detective novels such as *Behold, Here's Poison* (1936), and used detective and thriller plots with pace and irony in historical fiction such as *The Reluctant Widow* (1946) and *The Quiet Gentleman* (1951).

Heyerdahl, Thor 1914–2002 •*Norwegian anthropologist*• Born in Larvik and educated at the University of Oslo, he served with the free Norwegian military forces during World War II. In 1937 he had led his first expedition to Fatu Hiva in the Marquesas Islands of the Pacific and during his year there developed the theory that certain aspects of Polynesian culture owed their origins to settlers from the Americas, possibly the pre-Inca inhabitants of Peru. To prove this, in 1947 he and five colleagues sailed a balsa raft, *Kon-Tiki*, from Callao, Peru, to Tuamotu Island in the South Pacific, spending 101 days adrift. In 1970, to test the theory that ancient Mediterranean people could have crossed the Atlantic to Central America before **Christopher Columbus**, he sailed from Morocco to the West Indies in a papyrus-reed boat, *Ra II*, reaching Barbados in 57 days. His subsequent journey (1977–78) from Iraq to Djibouti in the reed-ship *Tigris* was to show that these craft could be maneuvered against the wind and so complete two-way journeys via the Persian Gulf and Arabian Sea. His books include *The Tigris Expedition* (1980), *The Maldive Mystery* (1986) and *Easter Island: The Mystery Solved* (1989).

Heymann, Lida Gustava 1867–1943 •*German feminist and political activist*• Born in Hamburg, she was financially independent and during the 1890s organized a number of projects for women, including a day nursery, a women's home and training for apprentices. In 1898, with Minna Cauer, she campaigned against legalized prostitution, and together with **Anita Augspurg** they founded the women's suffrage society *Deutscher Verband für Frauenstimmrecht* (1902). They joined the more radical *Deutscher Frauenstimmrechtsbund* in 1913. The three colleagues then started a newspaper, *Die Frau im Staat*, in 1918.

Heymans, Corneille Jean François 1892–1968 •*Belgian physiologist and Nobel Prize winner*• Born in Ghent, he studied medicine at the university there. After postgraduate work in Paris, Lausanne, Vienna, London and Cleveland, Ohio, he became director of the Institute of Pharmacology and Therapeutics in Ghent (1925). He developed the technique of cross circulation to demonstrate that the rate of respiration is controlled by nerves, and showed that structures in the arteries contain special cells sensitive to blood pressure and blood chemicals which monitor the nervous mechanism by which respiration is controlled. He received the 1938 Nobel Prize for physiology or medicine.

Heyrovský, Jaroslav 1890–1967 •*Czech physical and analytical chemist and Nobel Prize winner*• Born in Prague, he began to study chemistry, physics and mathematics at Charles University, but in 1910 he moved to University College London. He did war service as a dispensing chemist and radiologist in a military hospital and was able to continue his studies, obtaining his PhD in Prague in 1918. After the war he became an assistant at Charles University and became Professor of Physical Chemistry by 1926. He invented the polarograph (1922–25) and his scientific effort for the rest of his life was devoted to the improvement of the polarographic technique and extending its applications. He received the Nobel Prize for chemistry in 1959.

Heyse, Paul Johann von 1830–1914 •*German writer and Nobel Prize winner*• He was born in Berlin, and settled in Munich in 1854. He excelled as a short-story writer, his tales being marked by a graceful style, sly humor and frequent sensuality. They were collected in *Das Buch der Freundschaft* (1883–84, "The Book of Friendship") and other volumes. He also wrote novels, plays and epic poems, and translations of Italian poets. He was awarded the 1910 Nobel Prize for literature.

Heywood, John c. 1497–c. 1580 •*English epigrammatist, playwright and musician*• He was born probably in London and studied at Oxford. Introduced at court by Sir **Thomas More**, he made himself, by his wit and his skill in singing and playing on the virginal, a favorite with **Henry VIII** and with Queen **Mary I**. He was a devout Catholic, and after the accession of **Elizabeth I** went to Belgium. He wrote several short plays or interludes, but is remembered above all for his collections of proverbs and epigrams. He was the grandfather of **John Donne**.

Heywood, Thomas c. 1574–1641 •*English dramatist, poet and actor*• Born in Lincolnshire, he was educated at Cambridge, and in 1598 was engaged by **Philip Henslowe** as an actor with the Lord Admiral's Men. He contributed to the composition of 220 plays up to 1633, and he also wrote poetry, *Nine Bookes of Various History Concerning Women* (1624), a volume of rhymed translations from **Lucian**, **Erasmus**, and **Ovid**, various pageants, tracts and treatises, and *The Life of Ambrosius Merlin* (1641). Of the 24 of his plays that have survived, the best are *A Woman Kilde with Kindnesse* (acted 1603, printed 1607) and *The English Traveller* (1633).

“ ”

That Time could turn up his swift sandy glass,
To untell the days.

c. 1607 ***A Woman Kilde with Kindnesse**, scene 16.*

Hiawatha, *originally* **Haionhwat'ha ("He Makes Rivers")** c. 1570 •*Native American leader (perhaps legendary)*• A chieftain of the Mohawk or the Onondaga, he is said to have been a founder of the League of the Five Nations of the Iroquois (known as the Iroquois Confederacy), uniting the Mohawk, Oneida, Onondaga, Cayuga, and Seneca tribes. According to legend, he joined the Huron mystic Deganawida in a plan to end warfare among Native Americans in what is now New York State, traveling from tribe to tribe to negotiate the alliance and build a confederacy governed by elected representatives. **Henry Wadsworth Longfellow** used his name for the hero of his poem *The Song of Hiawatha* (1855).

Hibbert, Robert 1770–1849 •*British merchant and philanthropist*• Born in Jamaica, where he became a slave owner, he moved to England. In 1847 he founded the Hibbert Trust, whose funds, in 1878 applied to the Hibbert Lectures, also aided the *Hibbert Journal* (1920–70).

Hick, John Harwood 1922– •*English theologian and philosopher of religion*• He was born in Scarborough, Yorkshire. During a long teaching career in the US and Cambridge, followed by professorships in Birmingham and at Claremont Graduate School, California, he produced several standard textbooks and anthologies on the philosophy of religion. His concern with questions about the status of Christianity among the world religions is raised in *God and the Universe of Faiths* (1973) and *Problems of Religious Pluralism* (1985). Later works include *The Rainbow of Faiths* (1995).

Hickok, Wild Bill, *originally* **James Butler Hickok** 1837–76 •*US frontier marshal*• Born in Troy Grove, Illinois, he became a stagecoach driver, a fighter of Indians, and a Union Army scout during the Civil War. He gained fame as the gambling, ready-to-kill marshal of Hays (1869) and Abilene (1871), Kansas. After touring briefly with **William F Cody**'s Wild West Show (1872–73), and teaming up with **Calamity Jane**, in Deadwood, Dakota, he was shot dead during a poker game.

Hicks, Edward 1780–1849 •*US painter*• Born in Attleboro (now Langhorne), Pennsylvania, for a time he was an itinerant Quaker preacher, but fearing that he took excessive pride in his ability to sway congregations, he left preaching for easel painting. He created naive, vivid landscapes and historical and religious paintings, which were characterized by flattened figures and rich colors, as well as by delicate detail and an almost mystical aura of religious faith. He is the best-known US primitive painter of the 19th century.

Hicks, Elias 1748–1830 •*US clergyman*• Born in Hempstead, Long Island, he became a Quaker preacher in 1775, and was held responsible, because of his Unitarianism, for the split of the US Quakers into Orthodox and "Hicksite" Friends in 1827.

Hicks, Sir John Richard 1904–89 •*English economist and Nobel Prize winner*• Born in Leamington Spa, Warwickshire, he was educated at Balliol College, Oxford. He taught at the London School of Economics (1926–35), and was Professor of Political Economy at Manchester (1938–46) and Oxford (1952–65). He wrote a classic book on the conflict between business-cycle theory and equilibrium theory, *Value and Capital* (1939), and other works include *Causality in Economics* (1979). He shared the 1972 Nobel prize for economics with **Kenneth Arrow**.

" "

The best of all monopoly profits is a quiet life.

1935 ***Econometrica***, *"The Theory of Monopoly."*

Hidalgo (y Costilla), Miguel 1753–1811 •*Mexican priest and revolutionary*• Born in Guanajuato state, Mexico, he was a priest in the village of Dolores and a member of a secret society that favored independence from Spain. Threatened with arrest, he rang the bell of the village church on September 16, 1810 (now celebrated as Mexican independence day), and shouted the *grito de Dolores*—"Long live Our Lady of Guadalupe, death to bad government, death to the Spaniards!"—thus beginning the revolution. Although his untrained army initially was successful, it was later defeated by the Spanish in January 1811 and Hidalgo was captured and executed. Hidalgo is known as the father of Mexican independence.

Hideyoshi Toyotomi 1536–98 •*Japanese soldier*• He became the second of the three great historical unifiers of Japan, the others being Nobunaga and Ieyasu **Tokugawa**. Unusually, he was an ordinary soldier who rose to become Nobunaga's foremost general. His law forbade all except samurai to carry swords (1588), and he banned Christianity for political reasons (1597).

Hieronymus, Eusebius *See* **Jerome, St**

Hieronymus Cardanus *See* **Cardano, Girolamo**

Higden, Ralph or **Ranulf** d. 1364 •*English chronicler*• A Benedictine monk of St Werburgh's monastery in Chester, he wrote a Latin *Polychronicon*, or general history from the creation to about 1342, which was continued by others to 1377. An English translation by John of Trevisa was printed by **William Caxton** in 1482.

Higgins, Jack, *pseudonym of* **Harry Patterson** 1929– •*English thriller writer*• Born in Newcastle upon Tyne, he was educated at the London School of Economics. He was a teacher and college lecturer before becoming a best-selling author with the success of *The Eagle Has Landed* (1975, filmed 1976), set during World War II, in which the Germans plot to kidnap **Winston Churchill**. Higgins also writes as Martin Fallon, Hugh Marlowe and James Graham.

Higgins, Rosalyn, *née* **Inberg** 1937– •*English lawyer*• Educated at Cambridge and Yale, she developed an interest in United Nations law and was staff specialist in international law at the Royal Institute of International Affairs (1963–74). After an appointment as Professor of International Law at the University of Kent at Canterbury (1978), she moved to the chair at the London School of Economics (1981–95). She became the UK representative on the United Nations Committee on Human Rights in 1985 and was appointed Queen's Counsel the following year. In 1995 she became a judge in the International Court of Justice, the first woman to be so honored.

Higginson, Thomas Wentworth Storrow 1823–1911 •*US writer*• Born in Cambridge, Massachusetts, he graduated from Harvard Divinity School and became a Unitarian minister, preaching forcefully in favor of women's rights and abolitionism. He retired from the ministry in 1858, and during the Civil War he commanded (1862–64) the first Black regiment in the Union army, the 1st South Carolina Volunteers, which was raised from among former slaves. In 1880–81 he was a member of the Massachusetts legislature. His numerous books include *Army Life in a Black Regiment* (1870) and *Common-Sense about Women* (1881). He corresponded for 20 years with **Emily Dickinson**.

Higgs, Peter Ware 1929– •*British theoretical physicist*• Born in Newcastle upon Tyne, he was educated at King's College London and appointed to a lectureship in mathematical physics at Edinburgh in 1960. Building on **Chen Yang**'s simple gauge theories, which described interactions through the exchange of gauge bosons without mass, Higgs developed a field theory in which the gauge bosons could have mass. This was later used by **Steven Weinberg** and **Abdus Salam** to develop the electroweak theory of particle interactions. The so-called Higgs mechanism, which allows massive-gauge bosons, does so by introducing another family of particles, the Higgs bosons.

Highsmith, Patricia 1921–95 •*US novelist*• Born in Fort Worth, Texas, she wrote 20 novels and seven collections of stories. She specialized in crime fiction and thrillers, and her first novel, *Strangers on a Train* (1950), was filmed by Alfred Hitchcock in 1951. Her best novels are generally thought to be the five describing the criminal adventures of her amoral psychotic antihero, Tom Ripley. These include *The Talented Mr Ripley* (1956, filmed as *Plein Soleil*, 1960 and as *The Talented Mr Ripley*, 1999).

Hilarion, St c. 291–371 AD •*Palestinian hermit*• Born in Tabatha, Palestine, he was educated at Alexandria, where he became a Christian. He lived as a hermit in the desert between Gaza and Egypt from AD 306, and was founder of the first monastery in Palestine (329). His feast day is October 21.

Hilary, St c. 315–68 AD •*French prelate, and one of the Doctors of the Church*• Born of pagan parents in Limonum (modern Poitiers), he was converted to Christianity quite late in life. He was elected Bishop of Poitiers c. 350 AD, and became a major opponent of

Arianism. His principal work is that on the Trinity. His feast day is January 13, which also marks the beginning of a term at the universities of Oxford and Durham, and English law sittings, to which his name is applied.

Hilary of Arles, St c.403–49 AD •*French prelate*• Born probably in Northern Gaul, he was educated in Lerins, and became Bishop of Arles in AD 429. He presided at several synods, especially that of Orange in 441, whose proceedings involved him in a serious controversy with Pope **Leo I**. His feast day is May 5.

Hilbert, David 1862–1943 •*German mathematician*• Born in Königsberg, Prussia (now Kaliningrad, Russia), he studied and taught at the university there until he became professor at the University of Göttingen (1895–1930). His definitive work on invariant theory, published in 1890, removed the need for further work on a subject that had occupied so many 19th-century mathematicians, at the same time laying the foundations for modern algebraic geometry. In 1897 he published a report on algebraic number theory which was the basis of much later work. In 1899 he was the first to give abstract axiomatic foundations of geometry which made no attempt to define the meaning of the basic terms but only to prescribe how they could be used.

Hilda, St 614–80 •*Anglo-Saxon abbess*• Born in Northumbria, she was baptized at age 13 by **Paulinus**. In 649 she became abbess of Hartlepool and in 657 founded the monastery at Streaneshalch or Whitby, a double house for nuns and monks, over which she ruled wisely for 22 years. It became an important religious center and housed the Synod of Whitby in 664. Her feast day is November 17.

Hildebrand *See* **Gregory VII, St**

Hildegard of Bingen 1098–1179 •*German Benedictine abbess, mystical philosopher, healer and musician*• She was born to a noble family in Böckelheim. At age 15 she entered the convent at Diessenberg, where she succeeded Jutta as abbess in 1136. The community later moved to Rubertsberg, near Bingen, and she undertook missions throughout the German states under the protection of **Frederick I Barbarossa**. In her youth, she experienced apocalyptic visions, 26 of which were collected in the *Scivias* (1141–52). Visions also prompted her *Liber vitae meritorum* (1158–63) and *Liber divinorum operum* (1163–74). Her spiritual advice was widely sought, and she also wrote a body of religious music. In parts of Germany she is treated as a saint.

Hill, Alfred Francis 1870–1960 •*Australian composer*• Born in Melbourne, he moved with his family to Wellington, New Zealand. He became conductor of the Wellington Orchestral Society, and collected and recorded much Maori music. Returning to Australia in 1897, he worked in Sydney, and for 20 years from 1915 he was Professor of Composition and Harmony at the New South Wales Conservatorium of Music. His work includes 13 symphonies, many of which are orchestrations of his earlier string quartets, 10 operas, a *Maori Rhapsody*, five concertos, and a considerable body of chamber music, keyboard and vocal music.

Hill, A(rchibald) V(ivian) 1886–1977 •*English physiologist and Nobel Prize winner*• Born in Bristol, he was educated at Cambridge. He became professor at Manchester (1920), University College London (1923), and from 1926 to 1951 was Foulerton Research Professor of the Royal Society. He shared the 1922 Nobel Prize for physiology or medicine with **Otto Meyerhof** for his researches into heat production in muscle contraction. He organized air defense in World War II and was Member of Parliament for Cambridge (1940–45).

Hill, Benny, *originally* **Alfred Hawthorne Hill** 1924–92 •*English comedian*• Born in Southampton, he was a milkman, drummer and driver before getting a job as an assistant stage manager. During World War II he appeared in *Stars in Battledress* and later followed the traditional comic's route of working men's clubs, revues and end-of-the-pier shows. An early convert to the potential of television, he was named TV Personality of the Year in 1954. He gained national, and eventually international popularity with the saucy *The Benny Hill Show* (1955–89). His few film appearances include *Those Magnificent Men in Their Flying Machines* (1965), *Chitty Chitty Bang Bang* (1968) and *The Italian Job* (1969). He enjoyed a hit record with "Ernie (The Fastest Milkman in the West)" (1971).

Hill, Sir (Austin) Bradford 1897–1991 •*English medical statistician*• Educated at University College London, he became Professor of Epidemiology and Medical Statistics at the London School of Hygiene and Tropical Medicine, then dean from 1955 to 1957. He studied occupational hazards, the value of immunization against whooping cough and poliomyelitis, and the effects of smoking. Together with Richard Doll (1912–) he designed a case control study of patients with lung cancer (1950) which enabled him to conclude that smoking was one important cause of the disease.

Hill, Damon 1960– •*English racecar driver*• Born in London, the son of **Graham Hill**, he worked as a motorcycle dispatch rider to fund his racing career (1982–85). He became test driver for Williams's Grand Prix team in 1991, and joined **Alain Prost** in Williams Grand Prix team in 1993. He finished third overall in his first full season and partnered **Ayrton Senna** in 1994, finishing second to **Michael Schumacher** in 1994 and 1995. His last race for Williams was the Japan Grand Prix, which he won; his 67th race of his Formula One career, it was his 21st win and made him world champion.

Hill, David Octavius 1802–70 •*Scottish photographer and painter*• Born in Perth, he studied art in Edinburgh. In 1821 he issued probably the first set of lithographs published in Scotland, *Sketches of Scenery in Perthshire*. *The Land of Burns*, published in 1840, was illustrated by Hill, with text by Professor John Wilson (1785–1854). In 1843 he was commissioned to portray the founders of the Free Church of Scotland and, with the help of the Edinburgh chemist Robert Adamson (1821–48), did so using the calotype process of **William Henry Fox Talbot**.

Hill, Geoffrey William 1932– •*English poet*• Born in Bromsgrove, Worcestershire, he was educated at Keble College, Oxford, and taught at the University of Leeds and at Cambridge and Boston Universities. Brooding on death, sex and religion, his first collection of *Poems* was published in 1952. He also wrote *King Log* (1968), *Mercian Hymns* (1971), *Somewhere Is Such a Kingdom: 1952–1971* (1975), *Tenebrae* (1978) and *The Mystery of the Charity of Charles Péguy* (1983), which all won prestigious literary prizes, and a book of literary criticism, *The Enemy's Country* (1991).

Hill, (Norman) Graham 1929–75 •*English racecar driver*• Born in London, he won the world championship in 1962 in a BRM (British Racing Motor), and was runner-up twice in the following three years. In 1967 he rejoined Lotus and won the world championship for a second time (1968). He won the Monaco Grand Prix five times (1963–65, 1968–69). In 1975 he started his own racing team, Embassy Racing, but was killed when the plane he was piloting crashed near London. His son **Damon Hill** also became a racing driver.

Hill, Octavia 1838–1912 •*English reformer*• She was born in Wisbech, Cambridgeshire. Influenced by the Christian socialism of **F D Maurice**, and tutored in art by **John Ruskin**, she became an active promoter of improved housing conditions for the poor in London. From 1864, with Ruskin's financial help, she bought slum houses for improvement projects. With Maurice she founded the Charity Organization Society (1869). A leader of the open-space movement, she was a cofounder in 1895 of the National Trust for Places of Historic Interest or Natural Beauty.

Hill, Sir Rowland 1795–1879 •*English originator of penny postage*• He was born in Kidderminster, Worcestershire, and until 1833 was a teacher, noted for his system of school self-discipline. In his *Post-Office Reform* (1837) he advocated a low and uniform rate of postage, to be prepaid by stamps, between places in the British Isles, and in January 1840 a uniform penny rate was introduced. In 1846 the Liberals made him Secretary to the Postmaster General and in 1854 Secretary to the Post Office.

Hill, Susan Elizabeth 1942– •*English novelist, critic and broadcaster*• Born in Scarborough, North Yorkshire, and educated at King's College London, she published her first novel, *The Enclosure* (1961), while still a student there. Her novels, which tend to be formally structured deliberations on the nature of loss and grief, deal with a wide range of themes, such as old age in *Gentleman and Ladies* (1969) and the bereavement of a young wife in *In the Springtime of the Year* (1974). Other novels include *Strange Meeting* (1971) and *The Woman in Black* (1983), which was adapted into a long-running West End stage play. She also writes plays and short stories, and her books for children include *The Glass Angels* (1991). A more recent publication is *Mrs de Winter* (1993) a sequel to **Daphne du Maurier**'s *Rebecca*.

Hillary, Sir Edmund Percival 1919– •*New Zealand mountaineer and explorer, the first person to conquer Mount Everest*• He was born in Auckland. An apiarist by profession and climber by inclination, active in both New Zealand and the Himalayas, he joined the 1953 British Everest Expedition, led by **John Hunt**, and with the sherpa **Tenzing Norgay** reached the summit of Mt Everest (at 8,850 m or 29,028 ft) on May 29, 1953. He was knighted for this achievement. During the International Geophysical Year (1957–58), Hillary was deputy leader under **Vivian Ernest Fuchs** of the British Commonwealth Antarctic Expedition, and made the first overland trip to the South Pole using tracked vehicles. He made further expeditions to the Everest area in 1960–61 and 1963–66, and led a geological expedition to Antarctica in 1967, during which he made the first ascent of Mt Herschel (3,335 m or 10,941 ft). His publications include *High Adventure* (1955) and *Nothing Venture, Nothing Win* (autobiography, 1975).

Hillel I, *also called* **Hillel Hazaken (the Elder)**, or **Hillel Hababli (the Babylonian)** 1st century BC–1st century AD •*Jewish teacher*• He was born probably in Babylonia, and went to Palestine at about age 40. He founded a school of followers bearing his name which was frequently in debate with the contemporary followers of **Shammai**. Noted for his use of seven rules in expounding Scripture, he was one of the most respected teachers of his time, and influential on later rabbinic Judaism.

Hiller, Dame Wendy 1912–2003 •*English actress*• Born in Bramhall, Cheshire, she joined the Manchester Repertory Theatre in 1930. At the 1936 Malvern Festival she played both Saint Joan and Eliza Doolittle, a role she also played in the film of *Pygmalion* (1938) at the invitation of **George Bernard Shaw**. She was noted for her clear diction and spirited personality. Her sporadic but distinguished film performances included *Major Barbara* (1940), *Sons and Lovers* (1960), *A Man for All Seasons* (1966), *Separate Tables* (1958, Academy Award) and *The Lonely Passion of Judith Hearne* (1987). She was given the honorary title of Dame Commander, Order of the British Empire, in 1975.

Hillery, Patrick (John) 1923– •*Irish politician*• Following his election as a Member of Parliament (1951), he held ministerial posts in Education (1959–65), then Industry and Commerce (1965–66) and Labour (1966–69), then became Foreign Minister (1969–72). He served as the EEC Commissioner for Social Affairs (1973–76), and became president of the Irish Republic (1976–90).

Hilliard, Nicholas c. 1547–1619 •*English court goldsmith and miniaturist*• Born in Exeter, the son of a goldsmith, he worked for Queen **Elizabeth I** and **James VI and I** and founded the English school of miniature painting.

Hillier, James 1915– •*US physicist*• Born in Brantford, Ontario, Canada, he was educated at the University of Toronto. While at Toronto, Hillier developed one of the first high-resolution electron microscopes produced. Later he moved to the US (1940) and made his career with RCA (the Radio Corporation of America), giving him the resources to develop the electron microscope further, whose commercial availability after World War II revolutionized biology.

Hilton, Conrad Nicholson 1887–1979 •*US hotelier*• Born in San Antonio, New Mexico, he helped his father turn their house into an inn. He became a cashier in the New Mexico State Bank in 1913, and was president and partner in A H Hilton and Son, General Store by 1915. He took over the family inn on the death of his father in 1918, and bought his first hotel, the Mobley Hotel in Cisco, Texas, in 1919, building up a chain of hotels in the major cities of the US. He continued to expand the company until his son, Barron Hilton, took over as president in 1966.

Hilton, James 1900–54 •*English novelist*• Born in Leigh, Lancashire, he was educated at Cambridge before working as a freelance journalist. He quickly established himself as a writer, his first novel, *Catherine Herself*, being published in 1920. Many of his novels were filmed—*Lost Horizon* (1933, awarded the Hawthornden Prize in 1934), *Goodbye Mr Chips* (1934) and *Random Harvest* (1941). He went to Hollywood during the 1940s to work as a scriptwriter.

Hilton, Roger 1911–75 •*English painter*• Born in Northwood, Middlesex, he studied at the Slade School of Art, London (1929–31). After spending some time in Paris in the 1930s, he was captured at Dieppe in 1942 and was a prisoner of war until 1945. He produced his first abstract paintings, suggestive of landscape, in 1950, and from 1954 to 1956 taught at the Central School of Art, London. From 1961 the female figure often appears in his work, as in *Oi yoi yoi* (1963). From 1965 he settled permanently in Cornwall, working with the St Ives group.

Himes, Chester Bomar 1909–84 •*US novelist*• Born in Jefferson City, Missouri, and educated in Ohio, he spent nearly nine years in prison for armed robbery. His first novel, *If He Hollers Let Him Go* (1945), was an account of racial prejudice in the California shipyards and factories, while *Cast the First Stone* (1952) exorcized his prison experiences. He emigrated soon after to Europe, where his tough detective stories were welcomed as serious existential fiction. *For Love of Imabelle* (1957) was originally a story called "La reine des pommes" and was republished (and subsequently filmed) as *A Rage in Harlem*. His subsequent Harlem thrillers, featuring two black detectives, Grave Digger Johnson and Coffin Ed Jones, were very popular.

Himmler, Heinrich 1900–45 •*German Nazi leader and chief of police*• Born in Munich and educated at the Landshut High School, he joined the army. In 1919 he studied at the Munich Technical College. He joined the Nazi Party in 1925. In 1929 **Hitler** made him head of the SS (*Schutzstaffel*, protective force), which he developed from Hitler's personal bodyguard into a powerful party weapon. With **Reinhard Heydrich**, he used it to carry out the assassination of **Ernst Röhm** (1934) and other Nazis opposed to Hitler. Inside Germany and later in Nazi war-occupied countries, he unleashed through his Gestapo (secret police) an unmatched political and anti-Semitic terror of espionage, wholesale detention, mass deportation, torture, execution and massacre. His systematic liquidation of whole national and racial groups initiated the barbarous crime of genocide. In 1943 he was given the post of Minister of the Interior to curb any defeatism. After the attempt on Hitler's life by the army in July 1944, he was made Commander in Chief of the home forces. His offer of unconditional surrender to the Allies (but excluding Russia) having failed, he disappeared but was captured by the British near Bremen. He committed suicide at Lüneburg by swallowing a cyanide vial concealed in his mouth.

Hinault, Bernard, *known as* **Le Blaireau ("the badger")** 1954– •*French cyclist*• Born in Yffiniac, he won the Tour de France five times (1978–79, 1981–82, 1985), one of five people to do so. He has also won the Tour of Italy three times and the Tour of Spain twice. In 1985 he won his last Tour despite a fall midway through in which he broke his nose. He retired on his 32nd birthday and became technical adviser to the Tour de France.

Hindemith, Paul 1895–1963 •*German composer*• Born in Hanau, near Frankfurt am Main, he ran away from home at age 11 because of his parents' opposition to a musical career, and earned a living by playing in cafés, cinemas and dance halls. He studied at Hoch's Conservatory in Frankfurt, and from 1915 to 1923 was leader of the Frankfurt Opera Orchestra, which he often conducted. In 1927 he was appointed a professor at the Berlin High School for music. He pioneered *Gebrauchsmusik*, pieces written with specific utilitarian aims such as children's entertainment, newsreels and community singing, but the Nazis banned his politically pointed *Mathis der Maler* (1934, symphony, 1938, opera "Matthias the Painter"). After a short time in the UK, where he composed the *Trauermusik* ("Mourning Music") for viola and strings (1936) on **George V**'s death, he moved to the US (1939). His later, mellower compositions include a requiem based on **Walt Whitman**'s commemorative *For*

Those We Love (1944). In 1947 he was appointed a professor at Yale and in 1953 at Zurich, where he composed his opera on **Johannes Kepler**'s life, *Die Harmonie der Welt* (1957, "The Harmony of the World").

" "

Tonality is a natural force, like gravity.

*1937 **The Craft of Musical Composition**.*

Hindenburg, Paul Ludwig Hans Anton von Beneckendorff und von 1847–1934 •*German soldier and statesman*• Born in Posen of a Prussian Junker family, he was educated at the cadet schools at Wahlstatt and Berlin, fought at the battle of Königgrätz (1866), and in the Franco-Prussian War (1870–71) rose to the rank of general (1903), retiring in 1911. Recalled at the outbreak of World War I, he and General **Ludendorff** won decisive victories over the Russians at Tannenberg (1914) and at the Masurian Lakes (1915). His successes against the Russians were not, however, repeated on the Western Front, and in the summer of 1918 he was obliged to supervise the retreat of the German armies (to the "Hindenburg line"). A national hero and father figure, he was the second president of the German Republic (1925–34).

Hindley, Myra 1942–2002 •*English murderer*• Born in Gorton, near Manchester, she met **Ian Brady** while working as a typist. They became lovers and soon carried out a series of shocking murders. The couple lured children back to their house in Manchester and tortured them before killing them. David Smith, Hindley's brother-in-law, contacted the police on October 7, 1965, about the murders. Hindley and Brady were arrested, the body of 17-year-old Edward Evans was found at their house. The graves and remains of 10-year-old Lesley Ann Downey and 12-year-old John Kilbride were found on Saddleworth Moor, and Hindley and Brady therefore became known as the "Moors Murderers." Hindley was convicted on two counts of murder and was sentenced to life imprisonment. She made a private confession to two other murders in 1986.

Hindmarsh, Sir John c. 1782–1860 •*English naval officer and administrator*• Born probably in Chatham, Kent, he was the son of a naval gunner. He joined the HMS *Bellerophon* at the age of 14 and fought with the Channel fleet under Admiral **Howe**, and later in the Mediterranean under Lord **Nelson** at the Battle of the Nile (1798) and at Trafalgar (1805). In 1836 he was appointed the first governor of South Australia.

Hine, Lewis Wickes 1874–1940 •*US photographer*• Born in Oshkosh, Wisconsin, he studied sociology in Chicago and New York (1900–07), making a photographic study of Ellis Island immigrants. A similar record of child labor took him all over the US (1908–15), and during World War I he recorded refugees for the US Red Cross. He photographed the construction of the Empire State Building in a survey entitled *Men at Work* (1932) and in the later 1930s registered the effects of the depression for a US government project. This work left a detailed picture of the social life of industrial US which spanned some three decades.

Hines, (Melvin) Barry 1939– •*English novelist*• Born in Barnsley, Yorkshire, he worked as a physical education teacher before turning to writing. His novels are all set in his native Yorkshire, and deal with working-class life. He is best known for *A Kestrel for a Knave* (1968), also known as *Kes* following a successful film adaptation from his own screenplay (1969), one of a number of collaborations with the filmmaker **Ken Loach**. His television scripts include *Born Kicking* (1992) and other novels include *The Blinder* (1966), *The Gamekeeper* (1975), *Unfinished Business* (1983) and *The Heart of It* (1994).

Hines, Earl Kenneth, *also called* **Fatha** 1903–83 •*US jazz pianist and bandleader*• Born in Duquesne, Pennsylvania, he began to play professionally as a teenager. Moving to Chicago in 1923, he met **Louis Armstrong**, and his 1928 recording of "Weather Bird" with Armstrong was a highly influential duet performance. He improvised single-note lines in the treble clef and punctuated them with internal rhythms in the bass, a style later known as "trumpet piano" which began a significant development among jazz pianists. In 1928 Hines formed his own band, expanding it to a large orchestra, and found fame as one of the masters of the swing era.

Hinkler, Bert (Herbert John Louis) 1892–1933 •*Australian pioneer aviator*• Born in Bundaberg, Queensland, he went to England in 1913 and enlisted in the Royal Naval Air Service in World War I. In 1921 he flew 700 miles nonstop to Bundaberg, and in 1928 he created a new England-Australia record, arriving in Darwin, Northern Territory, 16 days after leaving England. In 1933 he crashed in the Italian Alps on a solo flight from England to Australia.

Hinshelwood, Sir Cyril Norman 1897–1967 •*English physical chemist and Nobel Prize winner*• Born in London, his education was interrupted by World War I, during which he served as a chemist at an explosives factory. In 1919 he went to Oxford, where he later became Dr Lee's Professor of Chemistry (1937), and retired (1964) to become a Senior Research Fellow of Imperial College, London. His research work was largely in chemical kinetics. In the 1920s he carried out pioneering work in gas reactions and their interpretation in terms of the kinetic theory. He also studied heterogeneous catalysis and solution kinetics, but from 1936 onward he was increasingly interested in the kinetics of bacterial growth. In 1956 he was awarded the Nobel Prize for chemistry, jointly with **Nikolai Semenov**, for his contributions to chemical kinetics. He was knighted in 1948 and admitted to the Order of Merit in 1960.

Hipparchos or **Hipparchus** c. 190–120 BC •*Greek astronomer and mathematician*• Born in Nicaea, Bithynia, he made his observations from Rhodes, and may also have lived in Alexandria. He compiled a catalog of 850 stars (completed in 129 BC), giving their positions in celestial latitude and longitude, the first such catalog ever to exist, and this remained of primary importance up to the time of **Edmond Halley**. He discovered the precession of the equinoxes, observed the annual motion of the sun, and made similar observations of the moon's more complex motion. He also estimated the relative distances of the sun and moon, and improved calculations for the prediction of eclipses.

Hipper, Franz von 1863–1932 •*German naval officer*• He commanded the German scouting groups at the battles of Dogger Bank (1915) and Jutland (1916). He succeeded as Commander in Chief of the German High Seas fleet in 1918.

Hippias of Elis 5th century BC •*Greek Sophist*• A contemporary of **Socrates**, he was vividly portrayed in **Plato**'s dialogues as a virtuoso performer as teacher, orator, memory-man and polymath.

Hippocrates c. 460–377/359 BC •*Greek physician*• Known as the "father of medicine," and associated with the medical profession's Hippocratic oath, this most celebrated physician of antiquity was born and practiced on the island of Cos, but little is known of him except that he taught for money. Skilled in diagnosis and prognosis, he gathered together all the work of his predecessors which he believed to be sound, and laid the early foundations of scientific medicine. His followers developed the theories that the four fluids, or humors (blood, phlegm, yellow bile and black bile), of the body are the primary seats of disease. The Hippocratic oath has been seen as the foundation of Western medical ethics, and is still occasionally used in a Christianized version. Of Hippocrates' works, *Airs, Waters, Places* contained shrewd observations about the geography of disease and the role of the environment in shaping the health of a community; *Epidemics III* examined epidemics in a population and offered case histories of patients with acute diseases; *The Sacred Disease* elaborated a rigorous defense of the naturalistic causes of diseases; and *Aphorisms* consisted of a series of short pithy statements.

Hippolyte *See* **Delaroche, Paul**

Hippolytus, St AD 170–235 •*Christian leader and antipope in Rome*• He defended the doctrine of the *Logos* and attacked the Gnostics. He was with **Irenaeus** in Gaul in AD 194, and in 218 was elected antipope in opposition to the heretical (Monarchian) **Calixtus I**. In 235, both Hippolytus and Calixtus were deported to work in the Roman mines in Sardinia, where they died as martyrs. Hippolytus is generally believed to be the author of a *Refutation of All Heresies* in 10 books, discovered in 1842. His feast day is August 13 in the West, and January 30 in the East.

Hird, Dame Thora 1911–2003 •*English actress*• Born of theatrical parents in Morecambe, Lancashire, she was "discovered" in repertory theater at the age of 16 and given a film contract, making her screen debut in *Spellbound* (1940) and following it with 60 films, including *A Kind of Loving* (1962) and *Rattle of a Simple Man* (1964). On television, she starred in *Meet the Wife* (1964–66), *In Loving Memory* (1979–86) and *Last of the Summer Wine* (1973–), as well as the **Alan Bennett** *Talking Heads* monologue *A Cream Cracker Under the Settee* (1988, British Academy of Film and Television Arts Best Television Actress Award) and plays such as *Wide Eyed and Legless* (1993). She also hosted religious series such as *Praise Be!* She was given the honorary title of Dame Commander, Order of the British Empire, in 1993.

Hirohito 1901–89 •*Emperor of Japan*• He was born in Tokyo, the eldest son of Crown Prince Yoroshito (Emperor Taisho 1912–26) and the 124th emperor in direct lineage. His reign was marked by rapid militarization and aggressive wars against China (1931–32, 1937–45) and Great Britain and the US (1941–45), which ended after the two atomic bombs were dropped on Hiroshima and Nagasaki. Under US occupation, Hirohito in 1946 renounced his legendary divinity and became a democratic constitutional monarch. He was a notable marine biologist.

Hiroshige, Ando, *originally* **Ando Tokutaro** 1797–1858 •*Japanese Ukiyo-e painter and wood engraver*• He was born in Edo (now Tokyo). He is celebrated for his impressive landscape color prints, executed in a freer, less austere manner than those of his greater contemporary **Hokusai**. His *Fifty-Three Stages of the Tokaido* (1832) had a great influence on Western impressionist painters, but heralded the decline of Ukiyo-e (wood block print design, "pictures of the floating world" art). His masterpieces are striking compositions of snow or rain and mist.

Hirst, Damien, *originally* **Damien Steven David Brennan** 1965– •*English painter and installation artist*• Born in Bristol and brought up in Leeds, Yorkshire, he studied at Goldsmiths College, London University (1986–89). From 1988 he produced "spot" paintings, or grids of colored circles on white canvas, deliberately mechanistic and devoid of emotion. In his installations he employs controversial materials, such as blood, maggots, dying butterflies, dead animals, and fish in tanks, claiming to "access people's worst fears." In 1991 he began to enclose objects in Plexiglas and steel chambers, such as the tiger shark in *The Physical Impossibility of Death in the Mind of Someone Living* (1991, Saatchi Collection, London). In 1993 Hirst caused a sensation at the Venice Biennale with his *Mother and Child, Divided*, where a cow and a calf, both sliced in half, expressed the severing of the closest of bonds. The following year he organized a touring exhibition featuring a white lamb in formaldehyde, entitled *Away from the Flock*; this was vandalized with black ink by an intruder at the Serpentine Gallery in London. For this exhibition, and other work, Hirst was awarded the 1995 Turner Prize.

His, Wilhelm 1831–1904 •*German anatomist and embryologist*• Born in Basel, Switzerland, he studied medicine at the Universities of Basel, Bern, Berlin and Würzburg, qualifying in 1855. He became Professor of Anatomy in Basel (1857–72) and later, from 1872, at Leipzig. He pursued valuable studies on the lymphatic system, and made investigations into developmental processes and embryonic growth. One of his most important contributions lay in the development of the microtome (1866) for cutting very thin serial sections for microscopical purposes. He also used photography for anatomical purposes, and furnished the first accurate description of the human embryo.

Hislop, Ian David 1960– •*English editor, writer and broadcaster*• Born in Mumbles, Wales, he studied at Magdalen College, Oxford. He joined the satirical magazine *Private Eye* in 1981, becoming its editor from 1986. He began a career in television from the mid-1980s, writing scripts for series such as *Spitting Image* (1984–89) and **Harry Enfield**'s *Television Programme* (1990–92), later appearing as a panelist on *Have I Got News for You* (1990–) and presenting documentary series such as *School Rules* (1997). His radio work has included *The News Quiz* (1985–90).

Hispalensis, Isidorus *See* **Isidore of Seville, St**

Hiss, Alger 1904–96 •*US state department official*• Born in Baltimore, Maryland, and educated at Johns Hopkins University and Harvard Law School, he began his career as secretary to Supreme Court Justice **Oliver Wendell Holmes** and joined the state department in 1936. He was actively involved in organizing the United Nations, attending the Dumbarton Oaks conference and advising President **Franklin D Roosevelt** at the Yalta Conference (1945). From 1946 to 1949 he served as president of the Carnegie Endowment for International Peace. He stood trial twice (1949, 1950) on a charge of perjury, having denied before the House Committee on Un-American Activities that he had passed secret state documents to *Time* magazine editor and communist spy Whittaker Chambers in 1938. He was convicted at his second trial and sentenced to five years' imprisonment. On the collapse of the USSR, doubts were cast on the conviction after examination of KGB files.

Hitchcock, Sir Alfred Joseph 1899–1980 •*English filmmaker*• Born in Leytonstone, London, he began as a film technician in 1920, and directed his first film in 1925. His early films were made in Britain, and included *The Man Who Knew Too Much* (1934), *The Thirty-Nine Steps* (1935), *Sabotage* (1936) and *The Lady Vanishes* (1938). By the time he moved to Hollywood in 1939 his work was settled firmly in the area of the suspense thriller, and his first Hollywood film, *Rebecca* (1940), won an Academy Award for Best Picture. Subsequent films starred many of the industry's most celebrated actors and actresses, among them **James Stewart**, **James Mason**, **Cary Grant**, **Carole Lombard**, **Grace Kelly** and Janet Leigh, and included *Spellbound* (1945), *Notorious* (1946), *Rope* (1948), *Dial M for Murder* (1954), *Rear Window* (1955), *Psycho* (1960), *The Birds* (1963) and *Frenzy* (1972). He appeared briefly and wordlessly in many of his films, which were internationally recognized for their unequalled mastery of suspense and innovative camerawork, with common themes including murder, deception and mistaken identity, all shot through with subtle touches of ghoulish humor. He produced and occasionally directed a number of US television series in the 1950s and 1960s. He received the American Institute's Life Achievement award in 1979, and was knighted in 1980.

“ ”

Television has brought back murder into the home—where it belongs.
1965 In ***The Observer**, December 19.*

Hitchens, Ivon 1893–1979 •*English painter*• Born in London, he studied at St John's Wood School of Art and at the Royal Academy, London. Painting in a semiabstract style with obvious roots in Cubism, he always retained a strongly expressive feeling for natural forms, especially in the wide, horizontal landscapes which he painted from 1936. His work for the Festival of Britain in 1951, *Aquarian Nativity*, won an Arts Council award.

Hitchings, George Herbert 1905–98 •*US biochemist and Nobel Prize winner*• Born in Hoquiam, Washington, he studied and worked at the University of Washington (1926–28) and at Harvard (1928–39), and among various distinguished posts became director (1968–77) at Burroughs Wellcome, North Carolina (later emeritus). His early research involved the preparation and testing of RNA and DNA bases and amino acids as growth factors. In 1948 these investigations revealed the folic acid antagonist which paved the way for the discovery of drugs to alleviate gout and to combat cancer and malaria. In 1954 his team synthesized the very successful antileukemia drug 6-mercaptopurine, followed by azathioprine (or Imuran®), which suppresses the body's immune system to enable organ transplantation from an unrelated donor. His laboratory also produced the antiviral acyclovir (Zovirax®), active against herpes, and the anti-AIDS drug zidovudine (Retrovir®). Hitchings shared with **Gertrude Elion** and **James Black** the 1988 Nobel Prize for physiology or medicine for these achievements.

Hite, Shere, *originally* **Shirley Diana Gregory** 1943– •*US feminist writer*• Born in St Joseph, Missouri, she studied history at the University of Florida and Columbia University and worked as a model before entering the feminist arena. She directed the feminist sexuality project at the National Organization for Women in New

York (1972–78), and lectured at Harvard, McGill University and Columbia. In 1976 she published *The Hite Report: A Nationwide Study of Female Sexuality,* which caused an uproar, exploding traditional attitudes about sex. It was followed by such works as *The Hite Report on Male Sexuality* (1981), *The Hite Report on Women* (1987) and *Good Guys, Bad Guys* (1989).

Hitler, Adolf, *known as* **Der Führer ("The Leader")** 1889–1945 •*German dictator*• The son of a minor customs official, he was educated at the secondary schools of Linz and Steyr, attended art school in Munich, but failed to pass into the Vienna Academy. He lived by his wits in Vienna (1904–13), inhabiting hostels and doing odd jobs. In 1913 he emigrated to Munich, where he found work as a draftsman. In 1914 he volunteered for war service in a Bavarian regiment, where he rose to the rank of corporal, was decorated, and was wounded at the end of World War I. In 1919 he joined a small political party which in 1920 he renamed the *Nationalsozialistische Deutsche Arbeiterpartei* (National Socialist German Workers' Party). In 1923, with other right-wing factions, he attempted to overthrow the Bavarian government as a prelude to a "March on Berlin" in imitation of **Mussolini**'s "March on Rome," but was imprisoned for nine months in Landsberg prison, during which time he dictated his autobiography and political testament, *Mein Kampf* (1925, "My Struggle," Eng trans 1939). He expanded his party greatly in the late 1920s, enjoyed important parliamentary elections in 1930 and 1932, and though he was unsuccessful in the presidential elections of 1932 against **Paul von Hindenburg**, he was made chancellor in January 1933. He then suspended the constitution, silenced all opposition, exploited successfully the burning of the Reichstag (February 1933), and brought the Nazi Party to power, having dozens of his opponents within his own party and the SA (Storm Division) murdered by his bodyguard, the SS, in the Night of the Long Knives (1934). He openly rearmed the country (1935), established the Rome-Berlin axis with Mussolini's Italy (1936) and pursued an aggressive foreign policy that culminated in World War II (September 3, 1939). His domestic policy traded off social and economic improvements for political dictatorship enforced by the Secret State Police (*Geheime Staatspolizei*, or Gestapo). His government established concentration camps for political opponents and Jews, over 6 million of whom were murdered throughout World War II. He wantonly extended the war with his long-desired invasion of the USSR in 1941. The tide turned in 1942 after the defeats at El Alamein and Stalingrad. He miraculously survived the explosion of the bomb placed at his feet by Colonel **Stauffenberg** (July 1944), and purged his army of all suspects. When Germany was invaded, he retired to his bunker, an air-raid shelter under the Chancellory building in Berlin. The available evidence suggests that Hitler and his wife, **Eva Braun**, committed suicide and had their bodies cremated on April 30, 1945.

Hoagland, Mahlon Bush 1921– •*US biochemist*• Born in Boston, he studied medicine at Harvard, and was a visiting researcher at the University of Copenhagen and at Cambridge before returning to Harvard (1952–67). His major scientific contribution was his confirmation that in protein synthesis the carrier for each amino acid is identified by an RNA transcript. Hoagland went on to illustrate the role played by amino acids in protein synthesis and the formation of ester links.

Hoare, Sir Samuel John Gurney, 1st Viscount Templewood of Chelsea 1880–1959 •*English Conservative politician*• Born in London and educated at Harrow and New College, Oxford, he became a Member of Parliament in 1910, and held Colonial Office appointments in Russia and Italy as well as other distinguished posts. As Foreign Secretary in 1935, he made a memorable speech to the League of Nations on collective security, but was criticized for his part in the Hoare-**Laval** Pact, by which large parts of Abyssinia were ceded to Italy, and resigned the following year. He was made First Lord of the Admiralty in 1936, and during World War II was Lord Privy Seal, Secretary of State for Air, and ambassador to Spain. His strong opposition to capital punishment was argued in *The Shadow of the Gallows* (1952).

Hoban, James c. 1762–1831 •*US architect*• Born in County Kilkenny, Ireland, he emigrated to the US after the American Revolution and worked as an architect in Philadelphia. After he designed the capitol of South Carolina, he won the design competition for the White House in Washington DC, supervising its construction as well as that of the US Capitol. He rebuilt the White House after it was burned in the War of 1812.

Hoban, Russell Conwell 1925– •*US writer*• Born in Lansdale, Pennsylvania, he began by writing successful children's books, beginning with *Bedtime for Frances* (1960), the first of several picture books about a young badger. He moved to England in 1969 and turned to adult writing. Much of his subsequent work has a fantasy or science-fictional strand to it, and includes *Riddley Walker* (1980, stage adaption 1986) and *The Medusa Frequency* (1987).

Hobbema, Meindert 1638–1709 •*Dutch landscape painter*• Born probably in Amsterdam, he studied under **Jacob van Ruïsdael**, but lacked his master's brilliance and range, contenting himself with florid, placid and charming watermill scenes. Nevertheless his masterpiece, *The Avenue, Middelharnis* (1689), in the National Gallery, London, is a striking exception and has greatly influenced modern landscape artists.

Hobbes, Thomas 1588–1679 •*English political philosopher*• He was born in Malmesbury, Wiltshire, brought up by an uncle, and educated at Magdalen Hall, Oxford (1603–08). He had numerous notable patrons, in particular the Cavendish family, the Earls of Devonshire, with whom he traveled widely as family tutor, thereby making the acquaintance of many leading intellectual figures of his day: **Francis Bacon**, **John Selden** and **Ben Jonson** in England, **Galileo** in Florence, and the circle of **Marin Mersenne** in Paris, including **René Descartes**. His interest in political theory had already been indicated in his first published work, a translation of **Thucydides**'s *History* (1629), and, becoming increasingly concerned with the civil disorders of the time, he wrote the *Elements of Law Natural and Politic* (completed in 1640 but not properly published until 1650), in which he attempted to set out in mathematical fashion the rules of a political science, and went on to argue in favor of monarchical government. When the Long Parliament assembled (1640) he quickly departed for France, to be followed by other Royalists, who helped him to the position of tutor (1646) in mathematics to the exiled Prince of Wales (the future **Charles II**) in Paris. By then he had completed a set of "Objections" (1641) to Descartes's *Meditations*, which Mersenne had commissioned from him (as from other scholars), and the *De Cive* (1642), a fuller statement of his new science of the state or "civil philosophy." His next work was his masterpiece, *Leviathan* (1651), which presented and connected his mature thoughts on metaphysics, psychology and political philosophy. He was a thoroughgoing materialist, seeing the world as a mechanical system and humans as wholly selfish. Enlightened self-interest explains the nature and function of the sovereign state: we are forced to establish a social contract in which we surrender the right of aggression to an absolute ruler, whose commands are the law. The *Leviathan* offended the royal exiles in Paris and the French government by its hostility to Church power and religious obedience, and in 1652 Hobbes returned to England, made his peace with **Cromwell** and the Parliamentary regime, and settled in London. He continued to write and to arouse controversy. *De Corpore* appeared in 1655, *De Homine* in 1658. At the Restoration Charles II gave his old tutor a pension. He was banned from publishing in England in 1666 and his later books were published in the Netherlands first.

Hobbs, Jack, *properly* **Sir John Berry Hobbs** 1882–1963 •*English cricket player*• Born in Cambridge, he became one of England's greatest batsmen. He first played first-class cricket for Cambridgeshire in 1904, but joined Surrey the following year and played for them for 30 years (1905–35). He played in 61 Test matches between 1907 and 1930, when he and **Herbert Sutcliffe** established themselves as an unrivaled pair of opening batsmen, and he captained England in 1926. In his first-class career he made 197 centuries, and scored 61,237 runs (including the highest score at Lord's with 316 in 1926). He also made the highest-ever score in the Gentlemen v. Players match, 266 not out. He was knighted in 1953.

Hobson, Thomas c. 1544–1631 •*English livery-stable keeper and innkeeper*• He kept a stable of horses to rent out to students at Cambridge, and required each customer to take the horse nearest the stable door, whatever its quality. From this comes the expression "Hobson's choice," meaning no choice at all.

Hochhuth, Rolf 1931– •*German dramatist*• Born in Eschwege, he studied history and philosophy in Munich and Heidelberg. His controversial play *Der Stellvertreter* (1963, Eng trans *The Representative*, 1963) accused Pope **Pius XII** of not intervening to stop the Nazi persecution of the Jews. It caused a furor, as did the implication in his second play, *Soldaten* (1967, Eng trans *Soldiers*, 1968), that **Winston Churchill** was involved in the assassination of the Polish wartime leader, General **Sikorski**. He also wrote a novel, *Eine Liebe in Deutschland* (1978, "German Love Story"), about Nazi atrocities.

Ho Chi Minh, *originally* **Nguyen That Thanh** 1890–1969 •*Vietnamese statesman*• Born in the region of Annam, from 1912 he worked in London and the US, and in France from 1918, where he was a founding member of the French Communist Party. From 1922 until 1930 he was often in Moscow. He founded the Viet Minh Independence League in 1941, and between 1946 and 1954 directed the successful military operations against the French, becoming prime minister (1954–55) and president (1954) of North Vietnam. Reelected in 1960, with Chinese assistance he was a leading force in the war between North and South. Despite huge US military intervention in support of South Vietnam between 1963 and 1975, Ho Chi Minh's Viet Cong forced a ceasefire in 1973, four years after his death. The civil war continued until 1975, when Saigon fell and was renamed Ho Chi Minh City.

Hockney, David 1937– •*English artist*• He was born in Bradford, Yorkshire. His paintings began to attract interest while he was studying at the Royal College of Art. Associated with the Pop Art movement, his early paintings are a juxtaposition of artistic styles and fashions, with graffiti-like figures and words, as in *We 2 Boys Together Clinging* (1961, Arts Council, London), and a technique ranging from the broad use of heavy color to a minute delicacy of line. A visit to the US inspired his series of etchings, *The Rake's Progress* (1963), based on his adventures in New York, and while he was in California (1963–67) he began to develop his celebrated "swimming-pool" paintings, such as *The Sunbather* (1966, Museum Ludwig, Cologne). His later work, often double portraits, is more representational, such as *Mr and Mrs Clark and Percy* (1970–71). He also made designs for several operas. In 1982 he began a series of photo-collages (*Cameraworks*), composed from myriad separate shots. He has also experimented with computer technology and digital inkjet printings, as in *The Studio March 28th 1995*, and has transmitted huge murals to exhibitions by fax. He was made a Royal Academician in 1991.

“ ”

It's a myth that if you're liked by only four people it must be good. It might also be very bad: they might be your mother, your brother, your uncle and your aunt.

1978 ***David Hockney***.

Hodgkin, Sir Alan Lloyd 1914–98 •*English physiologist and Nobel Prize winner*• Born in Banbury, Oxfordshire, he studied natural sciences at Trinity College, Cambridge, and spent almost his entire career in Cambridge. During World War II he worked on airborne radar research, and then on the conduction of nerve impulses. With **Andrew Huxley**, he described in physico-chemical and mathematical terms the mechanisms by which nerves conduct electrical impulses by the movement of electrically charged particles across the nerve membrane. The techniques they developed have enabled scientists to study and understand many different kinds of excitable membranes. The two men shared the 1963 Nobel Prize for physiology or medicine with Sir **John Eccles**.

Hodgkin, Dorothy Mary, *née* **Crowfoot** 1910–94 •*British crystallographer and Nobel Prize winner*• Born in Cairo, Egypt, she studied chemistry at Somerville College, Oxford, moved to Cambridge to study for her PhD and became a tutor and Fellow at Somerville (1935–77). After various appointments within the university, she became the first Royal Society Wolfson Research Professor at Oxford (1960–77). In X-ray crystallography studies at Cambridge, Irish crystallographer John Bernal (1901–71) introduced her to the complex and demanding study of biologically interesting molecules. With him she began work on sterols, which she continued after her return to Oxford. Her detailed X-ray analysis of cholesterol was a milestone in crystallography, but an even greater achievement was the determination of the structure of penicillin (1942–45). After World War II, computational facilities increased and Hodgkin was the first to apply them to the analysis of complex chemical structures; even so, the determination of the structure of vitamin B_{12e} (used to fight pernicious anemia), which was her real triumph, occupied eight years (1948–56). Among her many honors she was elected a Fellow of the Royal Society (1947), and in 1964, "for her determination by X-ray techniques of the structures of biologically important molecules," she was awarded the Nobel Prize for chemistry.

Hodgkin, Sir Howard 1932– •*English painter*• Born in London, he studied at the Bath Academy of Art and taught at the Chelsea School of Art. His highly personal style has not followed any of the major art movements of recent decades. Although apparently abstract, his paintings are in fact representational, capturing a particular moment in time, as in *Rain* (1959). He won the Turner Prize for contemporary British art in 1985.

Hodgkin, Thomas 1798–1866 •*English physician and pathologist*• Born in Tottenham, Middlesex, he was educated at Edinburgh, and held various posts at Guy's Hospital, London. He described what came to be known as Hodgkin's disease, a disease marked by proliferation of cells arising from the lymph nodes and bone marrow; enlargement of the lymph nodes, spleen, and liver; fever; and anemia.

Hodgkins, Frances Mary 1869–1947 •*New Zealand artist*• Born and educated in Dunedin, she traveled extensively in Europe, with long visits to Paris and England. Her paintings, examples of which are in the Tate Collection and the Victoria and Albert Museum, London, are characterized by a harmonious use of flat color reminiscent of **Matisse**.

Hodler, Ferdinand 1853–1918 •*Swiss painter*• Born in Bern, he developed a highly decorative style of landscape, historical and genre painting with strong coloring and outline, sometimes using parallel motifs for effect. His works, in a Symbolist style influenced by the Rosicrucians in Paris, include *The Return from Marignano* (1896), *William Tell*, *Night* (1890) and *Day*.

Hodja, Enver *See* **Hoxha, Enver**

Hoey, Kate (Catharine Letitia) 1946– •*British Labour politician*• Born in Northern Ireland and educated in Belfast and at the City of London College, she worked as a lecturer and as educational adviser to London Football Clubs (1985–89) before entering Parliament in 1989. After Labour came to power in 1997, she served as a Parliamentary Private Secretary in the Department of Social Security (1997), as Parliamentary Under-Secretary of State in the Home Office (1998–99) and as Minister for Sport (1999–2001).

Hofer, Andreas 1767–1810 •*Austrian political leader*• Born in St Leonhard, in 1808 he called the Tyrolese to arms to expel the French and Bavarians, and defeated the Bavarians at the Battle of Iusel Berg (1809). He retook Innsbruck from the French, and for the next two months was ruler of his native land. Subsequently, however, he was forced to disband his followers and take refuge in the mountains. Two months later he was betrayed, captured, tried and shot.

Hoff, Jacobus Henricus van't 1852–1911 •*Dutch physical chemist and Nobel Prize winner*• Born in Rotterdam, he was educated at the Universities of Leiden, Bonn, Paris and Utrecht, and became a professor at Amsterdam (1878), and Berlin (1896). His first work was in organic chemistry, but from 1877 he began to devote himself to physical chemistry, developing the principles of chemical kinetics and applying thermodynamics to chemical equilibria. The equation for the effect of temperature on equilibria is commonly called the Van't Hoff equation. His important work on osmotic pressure was published in 1886, and was further developed in the next decade. He was awarded the first Nobel Prize for chemistry in 1901. He is regarded as one of the founders of physical chemistry.

Hoff, Ted (Marcian Edward) 1937– •*US computer scientist*• Born in Rochester, New York, he studied at Rensselaer Polytechnic Institute, New York, and Stanford University. In 1969 he joined Intel Corporation, where he worked on the specifications of the early Intel microprocessors. Further refinements in design by **Federico Faggin** and **Stanley Mazor** led to the development of the 4004 microprocessor in 1971, the first "computer on a chip." In 1995 he became chief technologist for FTI Teklicon.

Hoffa, Jimmy (James Riddle) 1913–75 •*US labor leader*• He was born in Brazil, Indiana. He was a grocery warehouseman when he joined the International Brotherhood of Teamsters, Chauffeurs, Warehousemen and Helpers of America (the Teamsters' Union) in 1931. He proceeded to reorganize it, and was elected president in 1957. In the same year the Teamsters were expelled from the American Federation of Labor and Congress of Industrial Organizations (AFL-CIO) for repudiating its ethics code. Following corruption investigations by the attorney general, **Robert F Kennedy**, Hoffa was imprisoned in 1967 for attempted bribery of a federal court jury. He was given parole in 1971, on condition that he resign as the Teamster's leader. In 1975 he disappeared and is thought to have been murdered.

Hoffman, Dustin 1937– •*US actor*•Born in Los Angeles, he studied music at the Santa Monica City College, and acting at the Pasadena Playhouse (1956–58), before beginning a career on stage and television in New York, interspersed with a variety of odd jobs. Following a modest film debut in *The Tiger Makes Out* (1967), he received an Academy Award nomination for his first leading role in *The Graduate* (1967). Similar antihero roles followed in *Midnight Cowboy* (1969), *Little Big Man* (1970) and *Marathon Man* (1976). A notorious perfectionist, he has displayed his versatility in such films as *All the President's Men* (1976), *Kramer vs Kramer* (1979, Academy Award), *Tootsie* (1982) and *Rain Man* (1988, Academy Award). Later films include *Accidental Hero* (1993), *American Buffalo* (1995) and *Sleepers* (1996).

Hoffman, Malvina 1887–1966 •*US sculptor*• Born in New York City, she trained under **Rodin** in Paris. She created busts and full figures of artistic and literary figures such as **Anna Pavlova**. In 1929, she was commissioned by the Field Museum of Natural History in Chicago to sculpt figures of ethnic types observed all over the world. She duly produced the series of over 100 bronze figures (1930–33) for which she remains best known.

Hoffmann, E(rnst) T(heodor) W(ilhelm), *known as* **Amadeus** 1776–1822 •*German writer, music critic and caricaturist*• Born in Königsberg, Prussia (now Kaliningrad, Russia), he trained as a lawyer and in 1816 attained a high position in the Supreme Court in Berlin. His shorter tales were mostly published in the collections *Fantasiestücke* (1814, "Fantasies"), *Nachtstücke* (1817, "Nighttime Tales") and *Die Serapionsbrüder* (1819–21, Eng trans *The Serapion Brothers*, 1886–92). His longer works include *Elixiere des Teufels* (1816, Eng trans *The Devil's Elixirs*, 1824), and the partly autobiographical *Lebensansichten des Katers Murr* (1821–22, "Opinions of the Tomcat Murr"). Three of his stories provided the basis for **Jacques Offenbach**'s opera, *Les Contes d'Hoffmann* (1880, Eng trans *Tales of Hoffmann*, 1881), and another for **Léo Delibes**'s *Coppelia* (1870). As a composer his most important opera was *Undine* (1816). He also composed vocal, chamber, orchestral and piano works.

Hoffmann, Josef 1870–1956 •*Austrian architect*• Born in Pirnitz, he was a leader of the Vienna "Secession" group, and in 1903 founded the *Wiener Werkstätte* (Vienna Workshops), devoted to arts and crafts. He himself designed metalwork, glass and furniture. His main architectural achievements were the white-stuccoed Purkersdorf Sanatorium (1903–05) and Stociet House (1905–11) in Brussels.

Hoffmann, Roald 1937– •*US chemist and Nobel Prize winner*• Born in Złoczów, Poland (now Zoločiv, Ukraine), he arrived in New York City in 1949. In 1955 he went to Columbia and Harvard, also spending nine months at Moscow State University. In 1964 he began a collaboration with **Robert Woodward**, in which factors controlling the way in which cyclization reactions occur when bonds are made and broken simultaneously were established. The results of these considerations became known as the Woodward-Hoffmann rules for the conservation of orbital symmetry. It was for this work that, along with **Kenichi Fukui**, he received the 1981 Nobel Prize for chemistry. In 1965 Hoffmann moved to Cornell University.

Hoffnung, Gerard 1925–59 •*British cartoonist and musician*• Born in Berlin, he was taken to England as a boy. After studying art at Highgate School of Arts, he became art master at Stamford School (1945) and Harrow (1948). He was staff cartoonist on the London *Evening News* (1947) and freelanced for *Punch* and others. His interest in music led to his creation of the Hoffnung Music Festivals at the Royal Festival Hall in which his caricatures came to life and sound. They were also animated by **Halas-Batchelor** in the television series *Tales from Hoffnung* (1965).

Hofmann, August Wilhelm von 1818–92 •*German chemist*• He was born in Giessen, and his most successful post was as professor at the College of Chemistry in London. He and his students had considerable success in extracting from coal tar some of its most valuable constituents (such as aniline) in pure form and in exploring the chemistry of these compounds, thus preparing the way for the development of the dye industry. He described the ammonia type and developed the process of exhaustive methylation for the conversion of amines into the corresponding olefin. In 1865 he became professor in Berlin, where he continued to exercise a profound influence over European chemistry.

Hofmannsthal, Hugo von 1874–1929 •*Austrian poet and dramatist*• He was born in Vienna into a banking family of Austro-Jewish-Italian origin, and while still at school attracted attention by his lyrical dramas such as *Gestern* (1896, "Yesterday"). An emotional and intellectual crisis precipitated *Ein Brief des Lord Chandos* (1901, "A Letter from Lord Chandos"), in which he conveys his reasons for abandoning poetry. Thenceforth he devoted himself to drama in works such as *Das gerettete Venedig* (1905, translated from **Thomas Otway**'s *Venice Preserved*), the morality play *Jedermann* (1911, Eng trans *The Salzburg Everyman*, 1930) and the comedy *Der Schwierige* (1921, Eng trans *The Difficult Man*, 1963). He also wrote the libretti for *Der Rosenkavalier* (1911, "Knight of the Rose"), *Ariadne auf Naxos* (1912), and other works.

Hofmeister, Wilhelm Friedrich Benedikt 1824–77 •*German botanist*• Born and educated in Leipzig, he combined botanical research with a full-time career in music publishing. He became an authority on embryology and was one of the first to observe chromosomes, although he did not appreciate their significance. His most epoch-making discovery was of the alternation of generations in plants (in which a generation that reproduces sexually alternates with one that reproduces asexually).

Hofstadter, Robert 1915–90 •*US physicist and Nobel Prize winner*• Born in New York City, he was educated at City College, New York, and Princeton University. He then worked at the Norden Laboratory Corporation (1943–46) and at Princeton, before moving to Stanford, where he became professor in 1954. In 1948 he developed a scintillation counter for X-ray detection. Later at Stanford, he used the linear accelerator to probe nuclear structure, investigating nuclear charge distribution and revealing that protons and neutrons also contain inner structure (now known to be due to quarks). For this work, he shared the 1961 Nobel Prize for physics with **Rudolf Mössbauer**.

Hogan, Ben (William Benjamin) 1912–97 •*US golfer*• Born in Dublin, Texas, in 1948 he became the first man in 26 years to win all three US major titles. Despite a bad car accident in 1949, he returned to win three of the four major golf titles in 1953 (US Open, US Masters, and British Open). He won the US Open four times (1948, 1950–51, 1953) before retiring in 1970.

Hogarth, William 1697–1764 •*English painter and engraver*• He was born in Smithfield, London. Early apprenticed to a silverplate engraver, he studied painting under Sir **James Thornhill**, whose daughter he married, after eloping with her, in 1729. By 1720 he already had his own engraving business, also painting conversation pieces and portraits, including that of *Sarah Malcolm*, the triple murderess (1732–33). Tiring of conventional art forms, he resurrected the "pictured morality" of medieval art by his "modern moral subjects," depicted with an unerring eye for human foibles, and often comprising several pictures in a series. The first of these was *A Harlot's Progress* (1730–31), destroyed by fire (1755). Single works such as *Southwark Fair* and the successfully captured atmosphere of a stag party entitled *A Midnight Modern Conversation* (both 1733) precede his eight pictures of *A Rake's Progress* (1733–35, Soane Museum, London). In 1735 he opened his own academy in St Martin's Lane. He later returned to moral narrative, of which his masterpiece is the *Marriage à la mode* series (1743–45, National Gallery, London), and then extended his social commentaries to "men of the lowest rank" by drawing attention to their typical vices in prints such as the *Industry and Idleness* series (1747), *Gin Lane*, and *Beer Street* (1751). He later ventured into politics with a cartoon of John Wilkes (1727–97), the Earl of **Chatham** and Richard Grenville, 1st Earl Temple (1711–79) as warmongers (1762). He explained his artistic theories in *The Analysis of Beauty* (1753).

“ ”

Simplicity, without variety, is wholly insipid.

1753 ***The Analysis of Beauty.***

Hogg, Douglas Martin 1945– •*English Conservative politician*• Born in London, the son of the distinguished Conservative politician Lord **Hailsham**, he was educated at Eton and at Christ Church, Oxford. He trained as a barrister and was appointed Queen's Counsel in 1990. He entered Parliament in 1979. His ministerial appointments include Trade and Industry (1989–90) and the Foreign and Commonwealth Office (1990–95). As Minister for Agriculture, Fisheries and Food (1995–97), he was given the difficult task of directing Britain's agricultural policy in Europe following a crisis over the safety of British beef in 1996. He is currently Member of Parliament for Sleaford and North Hykeham (1997–).

Hogg, James, *also called* **the Ettrick Shepherd** 1770–1835 •*Scottish poet and novelist*• He was born on Ettrickhall Farm in the Ettrick Forest, Selkirkshire. He inherited a rich store of oral ballads from his mother. He published *The Mountain Bard* in 1803, and a further volume of poems, *The Queen's Wake* (1813), which gained him cordial recognition. A regular contributor to *Blackwood's Magazine*, and the "Ettrick Shepherd" of John Wilson's *Noctes Ambrosianae*, he described himself as "the King of the Mountain and Fairy School." Of Hogg's prose works, the most remarkable is *Private Memoirs and Confessions of a Justified Sinner* (1824), a macabre novel which anticipates **Robert Louis Stevenson**'s *Dr Jekyll and Mr Hyde*.

Hogg, Quintin McGarel *See* **Hailsham, 2nd Viscount**

Hohenstaufen •*German royal dynasty*• Named after the castle of Staufen in northeast Swabia, dukes of Swabia from 1079, its members were Holy Roman emperors from 1138 to 1254, starting with **Conrad III** and ending with Conrad IV, and including **Frederick I (Barbarossa)** and **Frederick II**. They were also kings of Germany and of Sicily. The Hohenstaufen period is associated with a flowering of German courtly culture.

Hohenzollern •*German dynasty*• They ruled in Brandenburg-Prussia from 1415 to 1918. In 1415 a member of the family was made Elector of Brandenburg by Emperor **Sigismund**, thus founding the Prussian dynasty. The last elector, Frederick III (1688–1713), became the first king of Prussia as **Frederick I** (1701). The kings of Prussia were German emperors from 1872 to 1918 (**Wilhelm I**, Frederick III and **Wilhelm II**). Another branch of the family produced kings of Romania from 1881 to 1947 (**Carol I**, Ferdinand I and **Carol II**). World War I ruined Hohenzollern militarism, and forced the abdication of the last emperor, Wilhelm II (1918).

Ho Hsiang-ning *See* **He Xiangning**

Hokusai, Katsushika 1760–1849 •*Japanese artist and wood engraver*• Born in Edo (modern Tokyo), he was apprenticed to a wood engraver. He soon abandoned the traditional styles of engraving for the colored woodcut designs of the Ukiyo-e ("pictures of the floating world") school, which treated commonplace subjects in an expressionist manner, and of which he became the acknowledged master. His best-known works are his landscapes, an innovation to the Ukiyo-e movement; they include his *36 Views of Mount Fuji* (c. 1826–33). His work greatly influenced the French impressionists.

Holbein, Hans, the Younger 1497–1543 •*German painter*• Born in Augsburg, he was the son of Hans Holbein the Elder (c. 1460–1524), who was also a painter of merit. He studied under his father, and was influenced by the work of **Hans Burgkmair**. He worked in Basel in about 1516, but did not settle there till 1520. During this interval he was painting portraits at Zurich and Lucerne, including those of **Erasmus** and **Philip Melanchthon**. In 1519, he painted his *Noli Me Tangere* (c. 1522, Royal Collection), but he largely concentrated on designs for woodcuts, including illustrations for various editions of **Martin Luther**'s Old and New Testaments (1522 and 1523). His most important woodcuts, however—the *Dance of Death* series and the *Old Testament* cuts—were not issued till 1538. He visited England at the end of 1526, where he began his great series of portraits of eminent Englishmen of the time, such as *Sir Thomas More* (1527, Frick Collection, New York). On his return to Basel (1529) he painted the group of his wife and two children, now in the museum there. In 1532 he again visited London, where he painted several portraits for the German merchants of the Hanseatic League, including the exquisite *Derick Born* (1533, Royal Collection) and the portrait group, *The Ambassadors* (1533, National Gallery, London). In 1536 he was appointed painter to **Henry VIII**, and executed miniatures of outstanding quality, such as *Mrs Pemberton* (1536, Victoria and Albert Museum, London). He also painted **Anne of Cleves** at Cleves in 1539 (miniature in the Victoria and Albert Museum, London). He died of the plague in London.

Holcroft, M(ontague) H(arry) 1902–93 •*New Zealand writer, critic and historian*• Born in Rangiora, Canterbury, he was editor of the influential periodical *The Listener* from 1949 to 1967. From this, he drew *The Eye of the Lizard* (1960) and *Graceless Islanders* (1970). His novels include *The Deepening Stream* (1940), which won first prize in the New Zealand Centenary literary competition.

Holcroft, Thomas 1745–1809 •*English playwright and novelist*• Born in London, he was servant-secretary to **Granville Sharp**, before in 1770 becoming a traveling actor. He then settled in London (1778), where he became a friend of **William Godwin**, **Thomas Paine** and **Charles Lamb**, and took to writing. *Alwyn, or the Gentleman Comedian* (1780) was the first of four novels. He also wrote nearly 30 plays, mostly melodramas. His entertaining memoirs were continued by **William Hazlitt** in 1816.

Hölderlin, (Johann Christian) Friedrich 1770–1843 •*German poet*• Born in Lauffen, north of Stuttgart, he studied theology in Tübingen, and philosophy with **Schelling** and **Hegel** under **Johann Fichte** in Jena. As family tutor in Frankfurt am Main (1796–98) he found the wife of his employer, Susette Gontard (the "Diotima" of his works), the feminine embodiment of all he venerated in Hellenism. His early poetry owed much to **Friedrich Klopstock** and to **Schiller**; he also wrote a philosophical novel, *Hyperion* (1797–99, Eng trans 1965). He went on to write elegiac odes and the elegy "Menon's Laments for Diotima," which examines the discrepancy between the actual and the ideally possible. After tutoring in Switzerland (1801), he wrote "Brot und Wein" ("Bread and Wine") and "Der Rhein" ("The Rhine"), but not long after was suffering from schizophrenia, aggravated by the news of "Diotima's" death, and spent a period in an asylum (1806–07).

Holiday, Billie, *originally* **Eleanora Fagan** 1915–59 •*US jazz singer*• Born in Baltimore, Maryland, she was one of the most influential singers in jazz. She had an insecure childhood and was jailed for prostitution while a teenager, and insecurity and exploitation in personal relationships became a recurring theme in her life. In the early 1930s, she was working as a singer in New York clubs, and her wistful voice and remarkable jazz interpretation of popular songs led to work with **Benny Goodman** and recording sessions with such leading soloists as **Teddy Wilson** and **Lester Young**, who bestowed her familiar nickname, Lady Day. Her memorable ballads include "Easy Living" (1937), "Yesterdays" (1939) and "God Bless the Child" (1941). In the late 1930s she worked with the big bands of **Count Basie** and **Artie Shaw**. During the 1940s she appeared in several films (including *New Orleans*, with **Louis Armstrong**), but by the end of that decade she was falling victim to drug addiction; nevertheless she continued to make absorbing recordings until late in her career. Her self-serving autobiography, *Lady Sings the Blues* (1956, actually written by William Dufty), was turned into a spurious film in 1972.

Holinshed, Raphael d. c. 1580 •*English chronicler*• Born apparently into a Cheshire family, he went to London early in **Elizabeth I**'s reign, and became a translator in a printing office. He compiled *The Chronicles of England, Scotland, and Ireland* (2 vols, 1577), which together with its predecessor, **Edward Hall**'s *Chronicle*, was the source for many of the plays of **Shakespeare**.

Holland, Agnieszka 1948– •*Polish film director*• Born in Warsaw, she graduated from the Polish Film School in 1971, and worked as assistant director on Zanussi's *Illuminations* in 1973. Her directing debut came with *Evening at Abdan's* the following year, and she became a leading figure in the Polish New Wave during the 1970s, her film *Provincial Actors* tying for the International Critics Prize at Cannes in 1980. She also worked as a screenwriter for the leading Polish director **Andrzej Wajda**. Later films include *The Secret Garden* (1993), *Washington Square* (1997) and *The Third Miracle* (1999).

Holland, Henry Richard Fox, 3rd Baron 1773–1840 •*English Liberal politician*• Born at Winterslow House, Wiltshire, the nephew of **Charles James Fox**, he succeeded to the title when he was a year old. Educated at Eton and Christ Church, Oxford, he was Lord Privy Seal in the **Grenville** ministry (1806–07). He worked for reform of the criminal code, attacked the slave trade, although he was himself a West Indian planter, and was involved in the Corn Law struggle. He was chancellor of the Duchy of Lancaster from 1830 to 1834. He also wrote a biography of **Lope de Vega**, translated Spanish comedies and prepared a biography of his uncle, among other works.

Holland, John Philip 1840–1914 •*US inventor*• Born in Liscannor, County Clare, Ireland, and educated in Limerick, he was a school teacher in Ireland (1852–72) and, after emigrating to the US in 1873, in Paterson, New Jersey. He offered a submarine design to the US Navy which was rejected in 1875 as impracticable, but he continued his experiments and in 1898 he launched the *Holland VI* and successfully demonstrated it on and under the Potomac River. It had almost all the features of a modern nonnuclear submarine, and convinced the navies of the world that the submarine must be taken seriously as a weapon of war.

Holland, Jools (Julian) 1958– •*English pop musician and television host*• Born in London, he played with the successful band Squeeze from 1974 to 1980. He formed The Millionaires, then went solo in 1983. He rejoined Squeeze (1985–90), and formed his Rhythm and Blues Orchestra in 1994. His piano style is rooted in the New Orleans boogie-woogie tradition, and he is a fine exponent of it. His high profile owes much to his success as a host of music programs on television, including *The Tube*, *Juke Box Jury* and *Later*.

Holland, Sir Sidney George 1893–1961 •*New Zealand politician*• Born in Greendale, Canterbury, he was managing director of an engineering company before taking up politics. Entering parliament as a member of the National Party in 1935, he was Leader of the Opposition (1940–49) and then premier (1949–1957), resigning to become Minister without Portfolio.

Hollerith, Herman 1860–1929 •*US inventor and computer scientist*• Born in Buffalo, New York, he graduated in 1879 from the School of Mines at Columbia University, and worked as a statistician. Realizing the need for automation in the recording and processing of such a mass of data, he devised a system based initially on cards with holes punched in them, using electrical contacts made through the holes in his cards to actuate electromechanical counters. He established his own company in 1896, and later merged with two others to become the International Business Machines Corporation (IBM) in 1924.

Holley, Robert William 1922–93 •*US biochemist and Nobel Prize winner*• Born in Urbana, Illinois, he worked mainly at Cornell Medical School. He was a member of the team which first synthesized penicillin in the 1940s. In 1962 he identified two distinct transfer RNAs, and later secured the first pure transfer RNA (t-RNA) sample. In 1965 he published the full molecular structure of this nucleic acid—**Crick**'s "adapter molecule," which plays a central role in the cellular synthesis of proteins. He shared the 1968 Nobel Prize for physiology or medicine with **Har Gobind Khorana** and **Marshall Nirenberg**.

Holliday, Judy, *originally* **Judith Tuvim** 1922–65 •*US comic actress*• Born in New York, an engagement in Los Angeles earned her a contract with Twentieth Century Fox and some minor film roles. As an understudy for *Born Yesterday* (1946), she replaced the original star and enjoyed a long-running Broadway triumph in the role of Billie Dawn, a dumb blonde with a heart of gold. The 1950 film version earned her the Best Actress Academy Award. She made a scene-stealing appearance in *Adam's Rib* (1949) and starred in such comedy classics as *It Should Happen to You* (1954) and *The Solid Gold Cadillac* (1956). *Bells Are Ringing* (1956) became her final film role in 1960.

Hollis, Sir Roger Henry 1905–73 •*English civil servant*• Educated at Clifton and Worcester College, Oxford, he traveled extensively in China before joining the British counterintelligence service MI5 in the late 1930s, and he was appointed director general (1956–65). In his memoirs, *Spycatcher* (1987), **Peter Wright** argued that Hollis, with **Anthony Blunt**, **Guy Burgess**, **Donald Maclean** and **Kim Philby**, was a Soviet spy.

Holloway, Stanley 1890–1982 •*English entertainer*• Born in London, he was a World War I army lieutenant. Popular on radio and in pantomime, he created the monologue characters of Sam Small and the Ramsbottom family, while his hearty, down-to-earth manner and booming tones made him a genial comedy actor in Ealing film classics like *Passport to Pimlico* (1948), *The Lavender Hill Mob* (1951) and *The Titfield Thunderbolt* (1952). He made his New York debut in *A Midsummer Night's Dream* (1954) and created the role of Alfred Doolittle in *My Fair Lady* on Broadway (1956–58) and later in film (1964). He also had his own television series *Our Man Higgins* (1962) and published an autobiography, *Wiv a Little Bit of Luck* (1969).

Holly, Buddy, *originally* **Charles Hardin** 1936–59 •*US rock singer, songwriter and guitarist*• He was born in Lubbock, Texas. Despite the fact that his recording career lasted less than two years, he was one of the most influential pioneers of rock 'n' roll, and was the first to add drums and a rhythm-and-blues beat to the basic country style. With his band The Crickets, he was the first to use what was to become the standard rock 'n' roll line-up of two guitars, bass and drums, and the first to use double tracking and overdubbing on his recordings. Leaving The Crickets in 1958, he died when a plane carrying him between concerts crashed. After his death he became a cult figure and much of his material was released posthumously. His most popular songs include "That'll Be the Day," "Not Fade Away," "Peggy Sue" and "Oh Boy."

Holm, Sir Ian, *originally* **Ian Holm Cuthbert** 1931– •*English actor*• Born in Goodmayes, Essex, he was a member of the Shakespeare Memorial Theatre company at Stratford-upon-Avon (1954–55) and toured Europe with **Laurence Olivier** in *Titus Andronicus* (1955). His subsequent Royal Shakespeare Company roles included the title roles in *Richard III* (1963–64) and *Romeo and Juliet* (1967). He has also acted in **Harold Pinter**'s *The Homecoming* (1965), **Edward Bond**'s *The Sea* (1973), and in 1993 gave a highly acclaimed performance in Pinter's *Moonlight*. His film appearances include *Chariots of Fire* (1981), *The Fifth Element* (1997) and *Lord of the Rings: The Fellowship of the Ring* (2001). On television, his many roles include **F R Leavis** in *The Last Romantics* (1992). He was knighted in 1998.

Holmes, Arthur 1890–1965 •*English geologist*• Born in Hebburn-on-Tyne, Tyne and Wear, he studied at Imperial College, London under Lord **Rayleigh**, who encouraged Holmes to develop the uranium-lead dating method. A pioneer of geochronology, he determined the ages of rocks by measuring their radioactive constituents and played a large part in gathering age data for the Precambrian. He was an early scientific supporter of **Alfred Wegener**'s continental drift theory, and his predictions of the amount of heat generated by radioactive decay in the Earth revealed a mechanism for continental plate movement. His distinguished teaching posts included that of Regius Professor of Geology at Edinburgh (1943–56).

Holmes, Larry, *nicknamed* **the Easton Assassin** 1949– •*US boxer*• Born in Cuthbert, Georgia, he beat Ken Norton for the World Boxing Council heavyweight title in 1978, and held it until 1985, when he lost to Michael Spinks. He lost the return contest with Spinks, and in 1988 challenged **Mike Tyson** for the title, but was defeated in four rounds. Holmes staged a comeback in 1995, but after his defeat by Anthony Willis in 1996, his 23-year career came to an end.

Holmes, Oliver Wendell 1809–94 •*US physician and writer*• Born in Cambridge, Massachusetts, he studied law and graduated from Harvard College in 1829, then studied medicine, receiving his degree from Harvard in 1836. He was Professor of Anatomy and Physiology at Dartmouth College (1839–40), and in 1842 discovered that puerperal fever was contagious. From 1847 to 1882 he was Professor of Anatomy at Harvard. Although he began writing verse while an undergraduate, it was 20 years later that *The Autocrat of the Breakfast Table* (1857–58) made him famous. This was followed by *The Professor at the Breakfast Table* (1858–59) and *The Poet at the Breakfast Table* (1872). *Elsie Venner* (1859–60) was the first of three novels.

“ ”

Put not your trust in money, but put money in your trust.

1857–58 ***The Autocrat of the Breakfast Table.***

Holmes, Oliver Wendell, *nicknamed* **the Great Dissenter** 1841–1935 •*US jurist*• Born in Boston, he was educated at Harvard Law School and served in the Union Army during the Civil War (1861–65). He practiced law in Boston starting in 1867, and became Weld Professor of Law at Harvard (1882). He made his reputation with a fundamental book on *The Common Law* (1881). Associate Justice (1882–99) and Chief Justice (1899–1902) of the Massachusetts Supreme Court, he became Associate Justice of the US Supreme Court (1902–32). He earned his nickname, “the Great Dissenter,” because he frequently dissented from his conservative colleagues' majority opinions, especially as the Court moved to dismantle social legislation. He was the son of the writer **Oliver Wendell Holmes**.

Holmes, William Henry 1846–1933 •*US archaeologist and museum director*• Born near Cadiz, Ohio, he trained as an artist, and became interested in archaeology in 1875 when exploring ancient cliff dwellings in the Southwest with the US Geological Survey. A visit to the Yucatán stimulated a major contribution to Mesoamerican archaeology, his magnificently illustrated *Archaeological Studies Among the Ancient Cities of Mexico* (1895–97). He worked at the Smithsonian Institution, Washington DC, for much of his career.

Holroyd, Michael de Courcy Fraser 1935– •*English biographer*• He was born in London, and studied sciences at Eton, and literature at Maidenhead Public Library. His first book was *Hugh Kingsmill: A Critical Biography* (1964). His two-volume life of **Lytton Strachey**, *The Unknown Years* (1967) and *The Year of Achievement* (1968), is recognized as a landmark in biographical writing. He is the official biographer of **George Bernard Shaw**, with *The Search for Love* (1988), *The Pursuit of Power* (1989), *The Lure of Fantasy* (1991), *The Last Laugh* (1992) and *The Shaw Companion* (1992). He is married to **Margaret Drabble**.

Holst, Gustav Theodore, *originally* **Gustav Theodore von Holst** 1874–1934 •*English composer*• Born in Cheltenham, Gloucestershire, of Swedish origin, he studied at the Royal College of Music. He taught music at St Paul's School, Hammersmith (1905–34), and also became musical director at Morley College (1907) and at Reading College (1919). His interest in the English folksong tradition inspired his *St Paul's Suite for Strings* (1913) and many charming arrangements of songs. He emerged as a major composer with the seven-movement suite *The Planets* (1914–16). Among his other major works are *The Hymn of Jesus* (1917), his comic operas *The Perfect Fool* (1922) and *At the Boar's Head* (1924), and his orchestral tone poem *Egdon Heath* (1927), inspired by **Thomas Hardy**'s *Return of the Native*. His daughter Imogen (1907–84), like him, was a musical educationist, conductor and composer of folksong arrangements, and was associated with **Benjamin Britten** in the Aldeburgh Festivals.

Holt, Harold Edward 1908–67 •*Australian politician*• Born in Sydney, he studied law at the University of Melbourne, joined the United Australia Party, which was to be replaced by the Liberal Party of Australia, and entered the House of Representatives in 1935. He became leader of his party and prime minister when Sir **Robert Menzies** retired in 1966. During the Vietnam War he strongly supported the US with the slogan “all the way with LBJ.” He died in office, lost at sea while swimming at Portsea.

Holtby, Winifred 1898–1935 •*English novelist and feminist*• Born in Rudston, Yorkshire, she was educated at Oxford, and served in France with the Women's Auxiliary Army Corps. She was a prolific journalist, and was a director from 1926 of *Time and Tide*. She wrote a number of novels with strong-willed women as her heroines, including *The Land of Green Ginger* (1927), but is chiefly remembered for her last and most successful, *South Riding* (1935).

Holub, Miroslav 1923–98 •*Czech poet and scientist*• Born in Plzeň, he studied immunology and had a distinguished career in medicine. He published several collections, many of which have been translated into English. His *Selected Poems* were published in 1967; other collections include *Sagittal Section* (1980) and *On the Contrary* (1982). He published a collection of essays, *The Dimension of the Present Moment*, in 1990. *Immunology of Nude Mice* (1989) is one of his scientific publications.

Holyfield, Evander 1962– •*US boxer*• Born in Alabama, he was described by his trainer, Don Turner, as “rich enough to air-condition hell.” His earnings exceed $100 million. His three fights against **Riddick Bowe** are considered to be the fiercest and best of modern heavyweight boxing, and in 1996 he beat **Mike Tyson** to regain the heavyweight title. He defended his title against Tyson in 1997 when Tyson was disqualified for biting off a piece of Holyfield's ear. He eventually lost to **Lennox Lewis** in 1999.

Holyoake, Sir Keith Jacka 1904–83 •*New Zealand politician*• The son of a shopkeeper and farmer, he worked on the family farm at Scarborough, near Pahiatua, on North Island. He joined the Reform Party, which was to be superseded by the New Zealand National Party, and entered the House of Representatives (1932–38). Reelected in 1943, he became deputy leader of the National Party in 1946, deputy prime minister in 1949, and party leader and prime minister, on the retirement of Sir **Sydney Holland**, in 1957. He was prime minister again from 1960 to 1972, and later served as governor-general of New Zealand (1977–80).

Hom, Ken(neth) 1949– •*US chef and cookery writer*• Born of Cantonese parents, he has become an international popularizer of Chinese cooking, earning renown as a food consultant. His television series include BBC's *Hot Wok*, for which he produced the book *Hot Wok* (1996).

Home (of the Hirsel), Alec (Alexander Frederick) Douglas-Home, 14th Earl of Home, Baron 1903–95 •*English Conservative politician and Prime Minister*• Born in London, heir to the Scottish earldom of Home, he was educated at Eton and Christ Church, Oxford, entered Parliament in 1931 and was **Neville Chamberlain**'s secretary during the latter's abortive negotiations with Hitler and Mussolini (1937–39). He succeeded to the peerage as 14th Earl in 1951, was Commonwealth-Relations Secretary (1955–60), Leader of the House of Lords and Lord President of the Council (1957–60), and Foreign Secretary (1960–63). After **Harold Macmillan**'s resignation, he was his party's surprise choice as leader (1963). He made history by renouncing his peerage and fighting a by-election at Kinross, during which, although prime minister, he was technically a member of neither House. Although a man of enormous political integrity and ability, his rather distant manner and aristocratic image did not serve him well in comparison with the streetwise and charismatic Labour leader, **Harold Wilson**, and the Conservatives lost the 1964 election by only 20 seats. The following year, he was replaced as party leader by **Edward Heath**. He was foreign secretary in Heath's government (1970–74), and in 1974 he was made a life peer and retired from active politics.

> " "
> When I read economic documents, I have to have a box of matches and start moving them into position, to illustrate and simplify the points to myself.
>
> *1965* ***The Making of a Prime Minister.***

Home, Henry *See* **Kames, Henry Home, Lord**

Home, John 1722–1808 •*Scottish clergyman and dramatist*• Born in Leith, Edinburgh, he graduated from the University of Edinburgh, fought on the government side in the 1745 Jacobite Rising, and in 1747 became minister of Athelstaneford. His play *Douglas* (1754), produced in the Canongate Theatre, Edinburgh, in 1756, met with brilliant success, and evoked the oft-quoted and possibly apocryphal "whaur's yer Wullie Shakespeare noo?" from an overenthusiastic member of the audience. However, it gave such offense to the Edinburgh Presbytery that Home resigned his ministry (1757), and became tutor to the Prince of Wales (later **George III**).

Homer, *Greek* **Homeros** c. 8th century BC •*Greek epic poet, a major figure of Ancient Greek literature*• He was regarded in Greek and Roman antiquity as the author of the *Iliad* (dealing with episodes in the Trojan War) and the *Odyssey* (dealing with Odysseus's adventures on his return from Troy). He was thought to be a blind poet, and was traditionally associated with Ionia, directly across the Aegean from mainland Greece, where four city-states had claims to be his birthplace: the mainland cities of Smyrna, Colophon and Ephesus, and the island of Chios. Little is known for certain of these epics, but some believe that they were developed from orally transmitted poems, which were much modified and extended over many generations.

Homer, Winslow 1836–1910 •*US painter*• Born in Boston, he began his career as an illustrator for magazines, and specialized in watercolors of outdoor life painted in a naturalistic style which, in their clear outline and firm structure, were opposed to contemporary French impressionism. He spent most of his later life at Prouts Neck, an isolated fishing village on the coast of Maine.

Honda, Soichiro 1906–91 •*Japanese motorcycle and car manufacturer*• Born in Iwata Gun, he started as a garage apprentice in 1922 and opened his own garage in 1928. He began producing motorcycles in 1948, and became president of Honda Corporation in the same year, until 1973. He stayed on as a director, and was appointed "supreme adviser" in 1983.

Honecker, Erich 1912–94 •*German politician*• Born in Neunkirchen in the Saarland, he joined the German Communist Party in 1929 and was imprisoned for anti-Fascist activity between 1935 and 1945. After World War II, he was elected to the East German parliament (Volkskammer) in 1949. In 1958 Honecker became a full member of the Socialist Unity Party (SED) politburo and secretariat, and in 1961 oversaw the building of the Berlin Wall. He was appointed head (first secretary) of the SED in 1971. Following **Walter Ulbricht**'s death in 1973, Honecker became the country's effective leader. He proceeded to govern in an outwardly austere and efficient manner and closely followed the lead given by the USSR. Following a wave of pro-democracy demonstrations, he was replaced in 1989 by Egon Krenz (1937–) who himself was forced to resign two months later. Honecker was arrested in 1990 and faced trial on charges of treason, corruption, and abuse of power, but in 1993 he was judged too ill to attend trial and he retired to Chile.

Honegger, Arthur 1892–1955 •*French composer*• Born in Le Havre, of Swiss parentage, he studied in Zurich and at the Paris Conservatory, and after World War I became one of the group of Parisian composers known as Les Six. His dramatic oratorio *Le Roi David* (1921, "King David") established his reputation, and among his subsequent works, *Pacific 231* (1923), a musical picture of a locomotive, won considerable popularity. He also composed five symphonies.

Hongwu (Hung-wu), *originally* **Zhu Yuanzhang (Chu Yuan-chang)** 1328–98 •*Emperor of China and founder of the Ming dynasty*• The son of a peasant, he became a leader of the Red Turbans, one of a number of Buddhist- and Daoist-inspired millenarian sects that rose in revolt against the Mongol Yuan dynasty during the 1340s. In 1356 he captured Nanjing and during the next few years established his own dynasty, the Ming. His reign (1368–98) was marked by the consolidation of imperial power. He also introduced low land taxes, reforestation, and the resettlement of abandoned land, and intimidated the landed and scholarly elites, a reflection of his peasant origins.

Honorius I d. 638 •*Italian pope*• Born in Roman Campania (Italy), he was pope from 625 to 638. He was involved with the paschal controversy in Ireland and with the Anglo-Saxon Church. In the Monothelite controversy he abstained from condemning the new doctrines, and for so doing was stigmatized as a heretic at the Council of Constantinople (680). The three other popes of that name, all Italians, were Honorius II (1124–30, an antipope), **Honorius III**, and IV (1285–87).

Honorius III, *original name* **Cencio Savelli** d. 1227 •*Italian pope*• Unanimously elected in 1216 as successor to **Innocent III**, his pontificate was at first dominated by the need to involve Emperor **Frederick II** in crusade. Concessions to achieve this aim were exploited by the emperor for his own ends. Honorius then devoted his energies to the suppression of heresy within the boundaries of Christendom and the extension of those boundaries into the Baltic and Spain.

Honorius, Flavius AD 384–423 •*Western Roman emperor*• He was the second son of **Theodosius I (the Great)**, at whose death (AD 395) the empire was divided between his sons **Arcadius** and Honorius, the latter (only 10 years old) receiving the western half. **Stilicho** was the de facto ruler of the western empire until 408, and after his death **Alaric I** overran Italy, and took Rome (410). Honorius died at Ravenna, which he had made his capital in 403.

Hooch or **Hoogh, Pieter de** c. 1629–84 •*Dutch genre painter*• Born in Rotterdam, by 1654 he was living in Delft and probably came under the influence of Carel Fabritius (1622–54) and the latter's pupil, **Jan Vermeer**. His *Interior of a Dutch House* (National Gallery, London) and the *Card Players* in the Royal Collection are among the outstanding examples of the Dutch School of the 17th century, with their characteristically serene domestic interior or courtyard scenes, warm coloring and delicate light effects.

Hood, Alexander, 1st Viscount Bridport 1727–1814 •*English naval commander*• The brother of **Samuel, 1st Viscount Hood**, he joined the navy in 1741. In 1761 he recaptured from the French the *Warwick*, a 60-gun ship, and during the French Revolutionary Wars he served under **Richard, 1st Earl Howe**. He took part in the defeat of the French off Ushant, at the Battle of the Glorious First of June (1794) and later became Commander in Chief of the Channel fleet from 1797 to 1800.

Hood, John B(ell) 1831–79 •*US Confederate soldier*• Born in Owingsville, Kentucky, he graduated from West Point in 1853. He commanded the Texas Brigade in the Confederate army, leading his troops into action at Gaines's Mill, Manassas, and Antietam, and winning praise for his tenacity and courage. He was severely wounded at Gettysburg and again at Chickamauga, after which his right leg was amputated. In 1864 he was sent to assist **Joseph Johnston** in command of the army of Tennessee. Besieged for five weeks in Atlanta, he was forced to evacuate the city in September. He afterward pushed as far north as Nashville but, defeated by **George H Thomas**, was relieved of command in January 1865 at his own request. He later went into business in New Orleans.

Hood (of Whitley), Samuel Hood, 1st Viscount 1724–1816 •*English naval commander*• The brother of **Alexander Hood**, he was born in Thorncombe, Dorset. He joined the navy in 1741, and, in command of the frigate *Vestal*, he took the French frigate *Bellona* (1759). In 1780, promoted to flag rank, he was sent to reinforce Admiral **George Rodney** on the North American and West Indian stations, and took part in the battle in Chesapeake Bay (1781). In the West Indies in 1782 he defeated the French off St Kitts, and played a part in the decisive victory off Dominica for which he was made a baron in the Irish peerage. In 1784 he was elected to parliament, and in 1788 he became a Lord of the Admiralty. In the

French Revolutionary Wars he captured Toulon (1793) and Corsica (1794). He was created a viscount in 1796.

Hood, Thomas 1799–1845 •*English poet and humorist*• Born in London, the son of a bookseller, he was sent in 1815 to Dundee, where he wrote for local newspapers and magazines. In 1818 he returned to London, and in 1821 was appointed assistant editor of the *London Magazine*, and met **Thomas De Quincey**, **William Hazlitt**, **Charles Lamb** and other literary men. Encouraged by John Hamilton Reynolds, he began to write poetry, publishing such poems as "Lycus the Centaur" and "Two Peacocks of Bedfont" in the *London Magazine*. In 1825 he published (anonymously, with J H Reynolds) a volume of *Odes and Addresses to Great People* which was an instant success. He produced the *Comic Annuals* yearly and single-handedly from 1830 to 1839. In 1834 the failure of a publisher plunged Hood into serious difficulties. From 1835 he spent five years in Koblenz and Ostend, and on his return to England he became editor of the *New Monthly Magazine* (1841) and started *Hood's Monthly Magazine* in 1844.

" "

I saw old Autumn in the misty morn
Stand shadowless like silence, listening
To silence

1823 "Ode: Autumn."

Hoogh, Pieter de *See* **Hooch, Pieter de**

Hooke, Robert 1635–1703 •*English experimental philosopher and architect*• He was born in Freshwater, Isle of Wight, educated at Christ Church, Oxford, and worked as an assistant to John Wilkins (1614–72) on flying machines and **Robert Boyle** on the construction of his air pump. In 1662 he was appointed the first curator of experiments at the newly founded Royal Society of London, and in 1665 he became Professor of Physics at Gresham College, London. In that year he published his *Micrographia*, an impressive account of his microscopic investigations. One of the most brilliant and versatile scientists of his day, he was also an argumentative individual who became involved in a number of controversies, including several priority disputes with **Isaac Newton**. He anticipated the development of the steam engine, discovered the relationship between the stress and strain in elastic bodies known as "Hooke's law," and formulated the simplest theory of the arch, the balance spring of watches, and the anchor escapement of clocks. He also anticipated Newton's law of the inverse square in gravitation (1678), constructed the first Gregorian or reflecting telescope, and materially improved or invented the compound microscope, the quadrant, a marine barometer, and the universal joint. After the Great Fire of London (1666) he was appointed city surveyor, and designed the new Bethlehem Hospital (Moorfields) and Montague House.

Hooker, John Lee 1920–2001 •*US blues singer and guitarist*• Born in Clarksdale, Mississippi, he learned blues guitar as a child, and worked as a street musician in the South before moving to Detroit in 1943, where he established himself as a leading blues artist. Unlike the slicker Chicago school, he drew on the raw emotion of early blues styles for his inspiration. His music was very influential on the UK blues boom of the 1960s, but went into relative decline in the 1980s. He bounced back in the 1990s with successful recordings and live performances.

Hooker, Joseph, *nicknamed* **Fighting Joe** 1814–79 •*US Union soldier*• Born in Hadley, Massachusetts, during the Civil War he commanded a division of the 3rd Corps in the Peninsular Campaign of 1862, and fought at Manassas and Antietam. In January 1863 he succeeded General **Burnside** in the command of the Army of the Potomac, but was defeated at the Battle of Chancellorsville and was superseded by **George G Meade** in June. In November he captured Lookout Mountain, and took part in the attack on Missionary Ridge. He accompanied General **Sherman** in his invasion of Georgia, and served until the fall of Atlanta in 1864.

Hooker, Sir Joseph Dalton 1817–1911 •*English botanist*• Born in Halesworth, Suffolk, he was the second child of Sir **William Jackson Hooker**, and was educated at the University of Glasgow, where he studied medicine. His first post was as assistant surgeon and naturalist on HMS *Erebus* in the Southern Ocean, and led to the six-volume *The Botany of the Antarctic Voyage*. Between 1848 and 1851 he explored Sikkim, Darjeeling, eastern Nepal and Assam, introducing many species to cultivation. His monumental *Genera Plantarum* (3 vols, 1862–83) formed the basis of a new classification system still used, with modifications, at Kew and elsewhere. His *Flora of British India* (7 vols, 1872–97) remains the standard flora for the whole Indian subcontinent. On becoming director of Kew in 1865, Hooker instigated the compilation of a list of all scientific names of flowering plants, *Index Kewensis* (1892), which continues to be compiled today. President of the Royal Society from 1872 to 1877, he was knighted in 1877 and received the Order of Merit in 1907.

Hooker, Sir Stanley George 1907–84 •*English aircraft engine designer*• Born on the Isle of Sheppey, Kent, he studied at Imperial College, London, and at Oxford. He joined Rolls-Royce in 1938, leading the company into the production of the jet engine in 1943, and as chief engineer produced the Welland, Nene, Derwent, Avon and Trent engines. In 1949 he moved to the aircraft engine division of the Bristol Aeroplane Company, working on Proteus, Olympus (for Concorde), Orpheus, and Pegasus (Harrier) jet engines. He returned from retirement in 1970 to Rolls-Royce to resolve the problems of the RB-211.

Hooker, Thomas c.1586–1647 •*English Nonconformist clergyman*• Born in Markfield, Leicestershire, he was a Puritan, and became a Fellow of Emmanuel College, Cambridge. In 1631 his Nonconformist views forced him to flee to Holland, and in 1633 he sailed for Massachusetts, and became a pastor in Cambridge, Massachusetts. In 1636 he moved with his congregation to Connecticut, and founded the town of Hartford. He was the author of the Fundamental Orders of Connecticut (1638), the first political constitution in North America, which was the forerunner of the US Constitution and the reason for Connecticut being called the "Constitution State."

Hooker, Sir William Jackson 1785–1865 •*English botanist*• Born in Norwich, Norfolk, he collected specimens in Scotland in 1806, and later in Iceland. His first five botanical works dealt mostly with mosses, but his *British Jungermanniae* (22 parts, 1812–16) established hepaticology (the study of liverworts) as an independent discipline. In 1820 he became Regius Professor of Botany at Glasgow and in 1841 became first director of the Royal Botanic Gardens, Kew. While at Kew he published several still standard works on ferns. He was knighted in 1836.

Hooks, Benjamin Lawson 1925– •*US civil rights leader*• Born in Memphis, Tennessee, he became a lawyer, banker, and minister. He was appointed by President **Richard Nixon** to the Federal Communications Commission (1972) and was its first African-American member. From 1977 to 1993 he served as executive director of the National Association for the Advancement of Colored People (NAACP).

Hoon, Geoff(rey William) 1953– •*English Labour politician*• Born in Derby, he studied law at Jesus College, Cambridge, and subsequently lectured in law at the University of Leeds (1976–82) and at the University of Louisville in Louisville, Kentucky (1979–80). He was a barrister in Nottingham (1982–84) before being elected Member of the European Parliament for Derbyshire (1984–94) and then Member of Parliament for Ashfield (1992). After Labour's victory in 1997, he was appointed a Parliamentary Secretary in the Lord Chancellor's department. He became a Minister of State in the Foreign Office in 1998 and in 1999 was made Secretary of State for Defense.

Hoover, Herbert Clark 1874–1964 •*31st President of the US*• Born of Quaker parentage in West Branch, Iowa, and orphaned at the age of 9, he was trained in mining engineering at Stanford University. He worked in this field in the US, Australia, and China (during the Boxer Rebellion) and founded his own successful mining firm in 1908. He became involved in relief activities in Europe during World War I, supervising the evacuation of stranded Americans, raising private funds to aid war-devastated Belgium, and directing voluntary rationing in the US. His skillful administration of these ambitious projects made him a popular public figure and opened the way to a political career. As Secretary of Commerce (1921–29) under **Warren Harding** and **Calvin Coolidge**, he helped initiate such engineering projects as the St Lawrence Seaway and the Boulder (later Hoover) Dam. He defeated Democratic candidate Al Smith (1873–1944) to win the presidency. His administration (1929–33) was overshadowed by the Great Depression, beginning with the stock market crash in October 1929. His popularity plummeted, and the shantytowns that sprang up around the country were called Hoovervilles after him. Though he did initiate some public relief efforts later enlarged in **Franklin D Roosevelt**'s New Deal, notably the Reconstruction Finance Corporation, he was defeated in his reelection bid by Roosevelt in 1932. He retired to private life until World War II, when he organized civilian relief operations in Europe. He later headed the Hoover Commissions (1947–49, 1953–55), which suggested many administrative and policy reforms later adopted.

Hoover, J(ohn) Edgar 1895–1972 •*US law enforcement official*• Born in Washington DC, he supported his family after the premature death of his father, earning a law degree from George Washington University in 1917. He then entered the Justice Department, becoming special assistant to the attorney general in 1919 and assistant director of the FBI in 1921. He became FBI director in 1924 and remained in charge of the Bureau until his death, remodeling it to make it more efficient and adding such improvements as a national fingerprint file and a crime laboratory. He campaigned against city gangster rackets in the interwar years and communist sympathizers in the postwar period, but in his later years in office he was criticized for abusing his power by persecuting liberal and civil-rights activists, notably **Martin Luther King**. His 48-year term as head of the FBI has been interpreted both as a tribute to his national importance in the fight against crime and as a recognition that he had learned too much about the politicians.

Hoover, William Henry 1849–1932 •*US industrialist*• He was born in Ohio. He ran a tannery business (1870–1907), then bought the patent of an electric cleaning machine from a janitor, James Murray Spangler, and formed the Electric Suction Sweeper Co in 1908 to manufacture and market it throughout the world. The company was renamed Hoover in 1910.

Hope, A(lec) D(erwent) 1907–2000 •*Australian poet and critic*• Born in Cooma, New South Wales, he graduated from the University of Sydney and took up a scholarship at Oxford. He returned to Australia in 1931 and became a distinguished academic, teaching English at several Australian colleges. Preeminent among his contemporaries, he received many Australian awards since the appearance of his first collection, *The Wandering Isles*, in 1955. Subsequent volumes of new and collected poems include *A Late Picking* (1975), *A Book of Answers* (1978), *The Tragical History of Dr Faustus* (1982) and *Orpheus* (1991). He talked humorously on literature as "Anthony Inkwell" in a long-running 1940s radio program for children.

Hope, Anthony, *pseudonym of* **Sir Anthony Hope Hawkins** 1863–1933 •*English novelist*• Born in London, the son of a clergyman, he was educated at Balliol College, Oxford, and was called to the bar in 1887. He wrote several plays and novels in his spare time, but is chiefly remembered for his "Ruritanian" romances, *The Prisoner of Zenda* (1894; dramatized 1896) and its sequel, *Rupert of Hentzau* (1898).

Hope, Bob (Leslie Townes) 1903–2003 •*US comedian*• Born in Eltham, London, and raised in Ohio from 1907, he became a US citizen in 1920. He made his Broadway debut in *The Sidewalks of New York* (1927), and his first film appearances in a string of shorts, beginning with *Going Spanish* (1934). He had a string of hit films, including *The Cat and the Canary* (1939), *The Princess and the Pirate* (1944) and *Paleface* (1948). In partnership with **Bing Crosby** and Dorothy Lamour (1914–96), he appeared in the seven highly successful *Road to* … comedies (1940–61). During World War II and the Korean and Vietnam Wars he spent much time entertaining the troops in the field. He received a Special Academy Award on five occasions.

" "

I don't know what people have got against Jimmy Carter. He's done nothing.

1980 Campaign speech for Ronald Reagan, November 2.

Hope, Thomas Charles 1766–1844 •*Scottish chemist*• Born in Edinburgh, he studied medicine there, and afterward taught chemistry in Glasgow and from 1795 in Edinburgh, where he worked with, and then succeeded, **Joseph Black**. Hope confirmed the earlier but neglected observations that water has a maximum density close to 4°C, an important result in biology, climatology and physics. He recognized and described a new mineral from Strontian in Scotland (1793); he even described the characteristic red flame color of the new element present in it (strontium) that was isolated by Sir **Humphry Davy** in 1808.

Hopkins, Anthony 1937– •*Welsh-born US film and stage actor*• He was born in Port Talbot, Wales, and after graduating from the Royal Academy of Dramatic Art, made his stage debut in *The Quare Fellow* (1960) at Manchester. Very successful on stage, his appearances include *Equus* (1974) and three triumphant National Theatre performances, in *Pravda* (1985), *King Lear* (1986) and *Antony and Cleopatra* (1987). Film appearances include *The Elephant Man* (1980), *The Silence of the Lambs* (1991, Best Actor Academy Award), *Howards End* (1992), *Shadowlands* (1993), *The Remains of the Day* (1993), *Nixon* (1995), *Surviving Picasso* (1996) and *The Mask of Zorro* (1998). Television work includes *War and Peace* (1972, British Academy of Film and Television Arts award) and *The Bunker* (1981, Emmy). Knighted in 1993, he renounced his title in 2000 following his decision to become a US citizen. He made his directorial debut with the film *August* (1995).

Hopkins, Sir Frederick Gowland 1861–1947 •*English biochemist and Nobel Prize winner*• Born in Eastbourne, Sussex, he learned chemistry in a pharmaceutical firm before beginning a brilliant career at Guy's Hospital, where he qualified in medicine. Following his publication on estimating uric acid in urine, he became the first lecturer in chemical biology at Cambridge (1897). He was appointed professor there in 1914 and served as Sir William Dunn Professor from 1921 until his retirement in 1943. He discovered accessory food factors, now called vitamins, associated lactate production in muscle with muscle contraction (1907), and discovered glutathione (1921). He became the Royal Society's president (1931). Knighted in 1925, he shared with **Christiaan Eijkman** the 1929 Nobel Prize for physiology or medicine.

Hopkins, Gerard Manley 1844–89 •*English poet*• Born in London, he was educated at Highgate School and Balliol College, Oxford, where he was a pupil of **Benjamin Jowett** and **Walter Pater** and a disciple of **Edward Pusey**. He also met his lifelong friend **Robert Bridges** there. Having joined the Roman Catholic Church in 1866, he was ordained a Jesuit priest in 1877. He taught at Stoneyhurst (1882–84) and became Professor of Greek at University College, Dublin (1884). None of his poems was published in his lifetime, but his friend Bridges brought out a full edition in 1918. His best-known poems include "The Wreck of the Deutschland" (1876), "The Windhover" and "Pied Beauty," in which he used what he called "sprung rhythm."

Hopkins, Johns 1795–1873 •*US businessman*• He was born in Anne Arundel County, Maryland. He set up a grocery business in 1819 in Baltimore, and retired in 1847 with a large fortune. Besides a public park for Baltimore, he endowed an orphanage for black children, a free hospital, and gave over $3 million to found Johns Hopkins University.

Hopkins, Lightnin' (Sam) 1912–82 •*US blues singer and guitarist*• Born in Centerville, Texas, he began to perform blues as a child. He cut his first record in 1946, and is thought to be the most recorded of all blues artists, although his use of pseudonyms to avoid contractual problems has made an accurate count difficult. He was "rediscovered" singing in clubs in 1959, and his acoustic country-blues style won favor with the folk revival audiences of the early 1960s. He was one of the most important artists to have worked in the country-blues tradition.

Hopkins, Matthew d. 1647 •*English "witchfinder-general"*• He is said to have been a lawyer in Ipswich. Appointed witchfinder in

1644, he caused the deaths of scores of victims, and discharged his duties so conscientiously that he himself became suspect, and, being found guilty by his own test in that he floated in water while bound, was hanged. His *The Discovery of Witches* was published in 1647.

Hopper, Dennis 1936– •*US film actor and director*• Born in Dodge City, Kansas, he first appeared in *Johnny Guitar* (1954), though *Rebel Without a Cause* (1955) is more often cited as his film debut. He played several hotheaded young malcontents and petulant weaklings during the late 1950s, and was the villain in Westerns such as *True Grit* (1969), before making his directorial debut with the highly successful *Easy Rider* (1969, with Peter Fonda). During the 1980s he emerged as a hard-working character actor and was a notable villain in *Blue Velvet* (1986). He also continues to direct (eg, *Colors*, 1988).

Hopper, Edward 1882–1967 •*US painter*• Born in Nyack, New York, he studied under Robert Henri (1865–1929). His paintings of commonplace urban scenes are characterized by a sense of stillness and isolation, as in *Early Sunday Morning* (1930, Whitney Museum, New York), and figures are anonymous and uncommunicative, as in *Nighthawks* (1942, Art Institute of Chicago). He gave up painting for a time (1913–23) to work as a commercial illustrator, but he received official recognition with a retrospective exhibition at New York's Museum of Modern Art in 1933, and is regarded as a master of 20th-century US figurative art.

Hopper, Grace Murray 1906–92 •*US computer programmer*• Born in New York City, she was educated at Vassar College, where she taught in the mathematics department between 1931 and 1944. She then joined the Naval Reserve and was drafted to join **Howard Aiken**'s team at Harvard as a coder for the Mark I. She gradually developed a set of built-in routines and was eventually able to use the machine to solve complex partial differential equations. In 1951 she conceived of a new type of internal computer program called a compiler, which was designed to scan a programmer's instructions and produce (compile) a set of binary instructions that carried out the programmer's commands. Hopper's ideas spread and were influential in setting standards for software developments, such as for COBOL.

Hopwood, Sir David Alan 1933– •*English geneticist*• Born in Kinver, Staffordshire, he was educated at Cambridge, and later moved to a lectureship at the University of Glasgow (1961). From 1968 to 1998 he was the first John Innes Professor of Genetics at the University of East Anglia and head of the genetics department at the John Innes Institute (now emeritus). His major contribution has been in understanding the genetics of the bacteria which produce most of the antibiotics used in human and veterinary medicine. His work has led to the ability to manipulate genes for antibiotic production. He was knighted in 1994.

Horace, *in full* **Quintus Horatius Flaccus** 65–8 BC •*Roman poet and satirist*• Born near Venusia, southern Italy, the son of a freed slave, he was educated in Rome and Athens, and was still there when the murder of **Julius Caesar** (44 BC) rekindled civil war. The same year he joined **Brutus**'s army and fought (and, he says, ran away) at the Battle of Philippi (42), then went back to Italy and began writing. Some of his first lyrical pieces made him known to **Virgil**, who around 38 BC introduced him to **Maecenas**, a generous patron who gave Horace a farm in the Sabine Hills. His first book of *Satires* (35 BC) was followed by a second and a small collection of lyrics, the *Epodes* (c. 30 BC). In 23 BC he produced his greatest work, three books of *Odes*, and in about 20 BC his *Epistles*. These, together with other works, including *Ars Poetica*, had a profound influence on poetry and literary criticism in the 17th and 18th centuries.

“ ”

Nunc est biberdum!
Now is the time to drink!

***Odes**, book 1, no. 32, l. 1.*

Hordern, Sir Michael Murray 1911–95 •*English actor*• He was born in Berkhamsted, Hertfordshire, and studied at Brighton College. He made his first professional appearance as Lodovico in *Othello* (1937), and following World War II, he joined the Stratford Memorial Theatre company (1952), and then the Old Vic (1953–54), giving a much-acclaimed Malvolio in *Twelfth Night*. Other notable roles include the philosopher in **Tom Stoppard**'s *Jumpers* (1972) and the judge in **Howard Barker**'s *Stripwell* (1975), and made numerous film and television appearances. A formidable classical actor, he also cornered the market in amiable, elderly eccentrics.

Hore-Belisha, Leslie Hore-Belisha, 1st Baron 1893–1957 •*English barrister and politician*• Born in Devonport and educated at Oxford, he became a London journalist after service in World War I, and in 1923, the year he was called to the bar, Liberal Member of Parliament for Devonport. In 1931 he became first Chairman of the National Liberal Party. In 1934, as Minister of Transport, he gave his name to the "Belisha" beacons at pedestrian crossings, drafted a new highway code and inaugurated driving tests for motorists. As Secretary of State for War (1937–40) he carried out several far-ranging and controversial army reforms. He was Minister of National Insurance in the 1945 caretaker government.

Horkheimer, Max 1895–1973 •*German philosopher and social theorist*• Born in Stuttgart, he studied in Frankfurt, and became a leading figure (together with **Theodor Adorno** and **Herbert Marcuse**) at the Frankfurt School as well as director of the Institut für Sozialforschung there (1930). He moved with the school to New York City when the Nazis came to power (1933), returning in 1950. He published a series of influential articles in the 1930s, later collected in two volumes under the title *Kritische Theorie* (1968, "Critical Theory"), which expound the basic principles of the school in their critique of industrial civilization and epistemology and the key tenets of their critical theory.

Hornby, A(lbert) S(idney) 1898–1978 •*English teacher, grammarian and lexicographer*• Born in Chester, he went to Japan in 1923 to teach English. In the 1930s he became involved in the preparation of an English dictionary for Japanese students of English, published in Japan in 1942, and printed in 1948 by Oxford University Press as *A Learner's Dictionary of Current English* (retitled in 1952 *The Advanced Learner's Dictionary of Current English*). Although he wrote many other books—including textbooks, grammars and dictionaries—it is for this dictionary that he is best known.

Hornby, Frank 1863–1936 •*English inventor of toys*• Born in Liverpool, in 1901 he opened a small factory for making the perforated constructional strips known originally as "Mechanics Made Easy" and patented in 1907 as Meccano. He began producing Hornby Trains in 1920 and in 1934 introduced a construction toy for younger children, the Dinky Builder, which evolved into the model car line Dinky Toys.

Hornby, Nick 1957– •*English author*• Born in London, he studied at Jesus College, Cambridge. He worked as an English teacher and journalist before his first major publishing success, *Fever Pitch* (1992), which explored the obsessive world of the (mostly male) football fan. Subsequent bestsellers included *High Fidelity* (1995) and *About a Boy* (1998), also exploring aspects of masculinity. His 2001 novel *How to Be Good* has a first-person female narrator.

Horne, Lena Calhoun 1917– •*US singer and actress*• Born in Brooklyn, New York, she made her debut at the legendary Cotton Club at age 16, but gradually switched from dancing to band singing. In 1942, she became the first African-American singer to win a contract from a major Hollywood company (MGM), appearing in *Cabin in the Sky* (1943) and *Stormy Weather* (1943). "Stormy Weather" became her signature song. She has bravely confronted racism throughout her career and describes its impact in her two memoirs, *In Person* (1950) and *Lena* (1965).

Horne, Marilyn Bernice 1934– •*US mezzo-soprano*• Born in Bradford, Pennsylvania, she made her debut in Los Angeles in **Bedřich Smetana**'s *The Bartered Bride* (1954), at Covent Garden, London, as Marie in *Wozzeck* (1964), and at the New York Metropolitan Opera as Adalgisa in *Norma* (1970). She is also a noted recitalist.

Horniman, Annie Elizabeth Fredericka 1860–1937 •*English theater manager and patron*• She was born in Forest Hill, London, the daughter of a wealthy Quaker tea merchant. She studied at the Slade School of Art, and traveled widely, especially in Germany. She went to Ireland in 1903 and financed the first staging of **W B Yeats**'s *The Land of Heart's Desire* and **George Bernard Shaw**'s *Arms and the Man*. She sponsored the building of the Abbey Theatre in Dublin (1904). In 1908 she purchased the Gaiety Theatre in Manchester, which she called "the first theater with a catholic repertoire in England," and her company put on over 100 new plays by the so-called Manchester School. In Great Britain, the Repertory Theatre movement and the reputations of many playwrights and actors are her legacy; in Ireland, perhaps Irish national theater itself.

Hornung, E(rnest) W(illiam) 1866–1921 •*English novelist*• He was born in Middlesbrough, Cleveland, and was educated at Uppingham. He was the brother-in-law of Sir **Arthur Conan Doyle**. He is best remembered as the creator of "Raffles," the gentleman burglar, hero of *The Amateur Cracksman* (1899), *Mr Justice Raffles* (1909) and many other adventure stories.

Horowitz, Vladimir, *originally* **Vladimir Gorowicz** 1904–89 •*US pianist*• Born in Kiev, Ukraine, he studied at the conservatory there. He settled in the US in 1940, and became a US citizen in 1944. He retired from public playing for long periods, but played in Russia again in 1986. One of the most skillful players of the century, his technique and interpretation were highly accomplished in music ranging from **Scarlatti** to **Liszt**, **Scriabin**, and **Prokofiev**.

Horrocks, Jane 1964– •*English actress*• She was born in Rawtenstall, Lancashire, and studied at the Royal Academy of Dramatic Art. Her films, often in comic or quirky roles, include *The Dressmaker* (1989), *Life is Sweet* (1991; Best Supporting Actress, L A Critics award 1992), *Little Voice* (1998) and *Born Romantic* (2001). She has appeared widely on television, notably in the comedy series *Absolutely Fabulous* (1992–95, 2001).

Horrocks, Jeremiah 1619–41 •*English astronomer*• Born in Toxteth, Liverpool, he went to Emmanuel College, Cambridge, in 1632 and in 1639 became curate of Hoole, Lancashire, where he made the first observation of the transit of Venus (November 24, 1639, according to the Julian calendar), deduced the solar parallax, corrected the solar diameter, made tidal observations and noticed irregularities in the motion of Jupiter and Saturn. Erroneously, Horrocks believed that comets were blown out of the sun, their velocities decreasing as they receded, but increasing again when they started to fall back.

Horta, Victor, Baron 1861–1947 •*Belgian architect*• Born in Ghent, he was influenced by the 1878 Paris World's Fair, and wanted to create a true modern Western architecture. His works in Brussels include the Hôtel Tassel (1892–93), which was at the same time individual and contemporary but conscious of tradition, and the Hôtel Solvay (1894–1900), a luxurious design full of light and movement. He also designed the first department store, l'Innovation (1901), in Brussels. His popularity declined after 1900 but he is now recognized as a master, and regarded as one of the earliest and most original exponents of Art Nouveau.

Horthy (de Nagybánya), Miklós 1868–1957 •*Regent of Hungary*• Born in Kenderes, after his victory at Otranto (1917) he became Commander in Chief of the Austro-Hungarian fleet (1918). He was Minister of War in the counterrevolutionary "white" government (1919), opposing **Béla Kun**'s Communist regime in Budapest and suppressing it with Romanian help (1920). His aim of restoring the **Habsburg** monarchy proved unpopular and so he allowed himself to be proclaimed regent. During the 1930s he ruled virtually as a dictator, but allowed some parliamentary forms. He backed Germany's invasion of Yugoslavia and Russia until Hungary itself was overrun (March 1944), but in October 1944 Horthy defied Hitler in broadcasting an appeal to the Allied powers for an armistice, and was imprisoned in the castle of Weilheim, Bavaria, where he fell into US hands (1945). He died in Estoril, Portugal, where he had lived since 1949.

Hoskins, Bob (Robert William) 1942– •*English actor*• Born in Bury St Edmunds, Suffolk, he made his debut in *Romeo and Juliet* (1969) at Stoke-on-Trent. Notable stage performances include *Richard III* (1971), *King Lear* (1971), *The Iceman Cometh* (1976) and *Guys and Dolls* (1981). His ebullient personality and stocky build lend themselves to exuberant comedy or hard-hitting drama, and he achieved widespread public recognition with the television series *Pennies From Heaven* (1978) and as the menacing hoodlum in the film *The Long Good Friday* (1980). After several busy years as a reliable supporting actor in films, he acquired international stardom with performances in *Mona Lisa* (1986) and *Who Framed Roger Rabbit?* (1988).

Hotspur *See* **Percy, Sir Henry**

Houdin, (Jean Eugène) Robert 1805–71 •*French magician*• Born in Blois, he worked in Paris for several years making mechanical toys and automata, and gave magical soirées at the Palais Royal (1845–55). In 1856 he was sent by the government to Algiers to destroy the influence of the dervishes by exposing their pretended miracles. He is considered the father of modern conjuring.

Houdini, Harry, *originally* **Erich Weiss** 1874–1926 •*US magician and escape artist*• He was born in Budapest, Hungary, and after his family emigrated to the US he became a trapeze performer. He later gained an international reputation as an escape artist, freeing himself from handcuffs, shackles, and other devices, even while imprisoned in a box underwater or hanging upside-down in mid-air. He was a vigorous campaigner against fraudulent mediums. He died from peritonitis following a stomach injury incurred when he was punched, unprepared, by a member of the public who wanted to test his famous ability to withstand any blow.

Houdon, Jean Antoine 1741–1828 •*French sculptor*• Born in Versailles, he won the Prix de Rome in 1761, then spent several years in Rome, where he executed the huge classical sculpture of *St Bruno* in Santa Maria degli Angeli. In 1785 he visited the US to execute a monument to **George Washington** (Virginia). His most famous busts are those of **Diderot** (1771), **Voltaire** (foyer of the Théâtre Français, Paris, and the Victoria and Albert Museum, London), **Napoleon** and **Jean Jacques Rousseau** (Louvre, Paris). He was appointed professor at the École des Beaux-Arts in 1805.

Houedard, Dom Sylvester, *pseudonym* **dsh** 1924–92 •*British poet, priest, Benedictine monk and scholar*• Born in Guernsey, he was the literary editor for the *New Testament Jerusalem Bible* (1967), and founded, with Bob Cobbing, *The Association of Little Presses* (1965). Under the pseudonym "dsh" he published over 1,000 "typetracts" during the 1960s and 1970s. These include *12 Nahuatl Dancepoems from the Cosmic Typewriter* (1969) and *Begin Again: A Book of Reflections & Reversals* (1975). Notorious for his appearance in *The Times* (1967) advertisement for the legalization of cannabis and his attacks on anti-lesbian and -gay legislation throughout the 1980s, he is justly famous for his work in both concrete and sound poetry.

Houellebecq, Michel 1958– •*French author*• Born on the island of Réunion in the Indian Ocean, he studied for a degree in agricultural engineering. His first novel, *Whatever* (1994), was followed by the worldwide bestseller *The Elementary Particles* (1998), which explores the nightmarish lives of two half brothers. In 2000 he released his first album, *Presence humaine*, in which he "sang" a number of his poems. Houellebecq has also published a collection of essays and a compendium of prose and photographs, *Lanzarote* (2000).

Houghton, 1st Baron *See* **Milnes, Richard Monckton, 1st Baron Houghton**

Hounsfield, Sir Godfrey Newbold 1919– •*English electrical engineer and Nobel Prize winner*• Born in Newark, Nottinghamshire, he studied at the City and Guilds and Faraday House colleges in London. He worked as a radar lecturer in the RAF during World War II, joined Thorn/EMI in 1951 and became head of medical systems research in 1972. He headed the team which, independently of **Allan MacLeod Cormack**, developed the technique of computer-assisted tomography (CAT scanning), which enables detailed X-ray pictures of cross sections of the human body to be produced. Hounsfield shared the 1979 Nobel Prize for physiology or medicine with Cormack, and was knighted in 1981.

Houphouët-Boigny, Felix 1905–93 •*Côte d'Ivoire (Ivory Coast) politician*• Born in Yamoussoukro, he studied medicine in Dakar, Senegal, and practiced as a doctor (1925–40). He then entered politics, sitting in the French Constitutional Assembly (1945–46) and the National Assembly (1946–59). When Côte d'Ivoire achieved full independence in 1960, he became its first president. His paternalistic rule saw Côte d'Ivoire initially develop more successfully than most other West African countries, but economic decline and profligacy, especially the building of a palace and cathedral at Yamoussoukro, reduced his popularity.

Houshiary, Shirazeh 1955– •*British sculptor*• Born in Shiraz, Iran, she went to London in 1975 and trained at the Chelsea School of Art. Her work shows the influence of Sufi poetry, especially that of **Jalal ad-din Rumi**, the 13th-century mystic, as in *The Earth Is an Angel* (1987). Later work is more austere, focusing on geometric shapes, as in *The Enclosure of Sanctity* (1993). In 1994 she was shortlisted for the Turner Prize for her exhibitions in Newcastle, London, Canada and the US.

Housman, A(lfred) E(dward) 1859–1936 •*English scholar and poet*• Born in Fockbury, Worcestershire, he was the older brother of **Laurence Housman**. Educated at Bromsgrove School and St John's College, Oxford, he failed his degree, but became a distinguished classical scholar, and was appointed Professor of Latin at University College London (1892), and at Cambridge (1911). He published critical editions of the Roman poet Marcus Manilius (1903–30), **Juvenal** (1905) and **Lucan** (1926). He is known primarily for his own poetry, notably *A Shropshire Lad* (1896), *Last Poems* (1922) and *More Poems*, published posthumously in 1936.

“ ”

I tell the tale that I heard told.
Mithridates, he died old.

*1896 **A Shropshire Lad**, no. 62.*

Housman, Laurence 1865–1959 •*English novelist and dramatist*• He was born in Bromsgrove, Worcestershire, the younger brother of **A E Housman**. He studied art at Lambeth and South Kensington, and is best known for his *Little Plays of St Francis* (1922) and his Victorian biographical "chamber plays," notably *Angels and Ministers* (1921) and *Victoria Regina* (1937). His novels included *Trimblerigg* (1924), a satire on **Lloyd George**, and he also published books of verse.

Houssay, Bernardo Alberto 1887–1971 •*Argentine physiologist and Nobel Prize winner*• Born in Buenos Aires, he graduated from the school of pharmacy of the University of Buenos Aires at age 17. He was Professor of Physiology at the medical school from 1919. Houssay studied interactions between the pituitary gland and insulin, showing that the gland produces a hormone with the opposite effect of insulin, and that removing the gland from a diabetic animal reduces the severity of the diabetes. This work produced fundamental insights into the working of the endocrine system. He shared the 1947 Nobel Prize for physiology or medicine with **Carl** and **Gerty Cori**.

Houston, Sam(uel) 1793–1863 •*US soldier and politician*• Born near Lexington, Virginia, he lived for three years among the Cherokee as a teenager. He was elected a member of Congress in 1823 and 1825 as a Democrat from Tennessee. In 1829 he returned to the Cherokee, being adopted into their nation and operating a trading post in their territory until 1832, when President Jackson sent him to negotiate with tribes in Texas. Caught up in the Texan struggle for independence, he led the force that overwhelmed the Mexican army under **Santa Anna** at San Jacinto (1836), and achieved Texan independence. He was elected the first president of the Republic of Texas (1836–38), was reelected in 1841, and upon the annexation of Texas in 1845 returned to the US Senate (1846–59) and was elected governor of Texas in 1859. Houston, Texas, is named after him.

Houston, Whitney 1963– •*US pop and soul singer*• She was born in Newark, New Jersey, the daughter of singer Cissy Houston, and cousin of **Dionne Warwick**. In 1988 she had her seventh US number-one hit with "Where Do Broken Hearts Go," thus breaking the **Beatles**' record of six. "I Will Always Love You" (1990), written by **Dolly Parton**, is her biggest success to date, boosted by her role in *The Bodyguard*, the film featuring the song.

Howard, Catherine *See* **Catherine Howard**

Howard, Charles, 1st Earl of Nottingham and **2nd Baron Howard of Effingham** 1536–1624 •*English admiral*• The son of Sir William Howard (c. 1510–73), he succeeded to his father's title in 1573 and became Lord High Admiral in 1585. A cousin of Queen **Elizabeth I**, he was Commander in Chief of the English fleet against the Spanish Armada (1588). In 1596 he led the expedition (with Robert Devereux, 2nd Earl of **Essex**) that sacked Cádiz. In 1601 he quelled Essex's rebellion.

Howard, Henry *See* **Surrey, Henry Howard, Earl of**

Howard, Sir John, 1st Duke of Norfolk, *known as* **Jack of Norfolk** c. 1430–85 •*English nobleman*• **Edward IV** made him Constable of Norwich Castle (1462), Sheriff of Norfolk and Suffolk, Treasurer of the Royal Household, and Lord Howard (1470). He was made Duke of Norfolk, Earl Marshal of England (a distinction still borne by his descendants), and Lord Admiral of England, Ireland and Aquitaine by **Richard III** (1483). He was killed at the Battle of Bosworth and his honors were attainted.

Howard, John 1726–90 •*English philanthropist and reformer*• Born in Hackney, London, in 1773, as High Sheriff of Bedfordshire, he was appalled by conditions in the Bedford jail and undertook a tour of British prisons that led to two acts of Parliament in 1774, one enforcing standards of cleanliness, and the other replacing prisoners' fees for jailers with official salaries. He traveled widely, and wrote *The State of Prisons in England and Wales, with an Account of Some Foreign Prisons* (1777), and *An Account of the Principal Lazarettos in Europe* (1780). He died of typhus contracted while visiting a Russian military hospital at Kherson in the Crimea. The Howard League for Penal Reform, founded in 1866, was named after him.

Howard, John Winston 1939– •*Australian Liberal politician*• Born in Sydney, he was educated at the University of Sydney. After graduating he worked as a lawyer, and in 1974 he entered politics as Liberal Member of Parliament for Bennelong, New South Wales. When in 1983 the Liberals lost power, he became deputy leader of the Opposition and then its leader (1985–89, 1995–96). In 1996 he became prime minister of Australia, leading the Liberal-National coalition government. He was reelected in 1998 and 2001.

Howard, Leslie, *originally* **Leslie Howard Stainer** 1893–1943 •*English actor*• Born in London, of Hungarian origin, he made his film debut in *The Heroine of Mons* (1914). Sent home because of illness during World War I, he concentrated on theater work over the next decade. From 1930 he turned to films, often portraying scholarly and archetypically tweedy Englishmen. His many film successes include *Pygmalion* (1938), which he codirected, and his best-known performance as Ashley Wilkes in *Gone with the Wind* (1939). Returning from Lisbon in 1943, his plane was shot down by the Nazis, who had believed **Winston Churchill** to be on board. Both his son, Ronald Howard (1918–96), and nephew Alan Howard (1937–) also became actors.

Howard, Michael 1941– •*British Conservative politician*• Born in Gorseinon, South Wales, he was educated at Llanelli Grammar School and Peterhouse, Cambridge. After graduating he trained as a barrister and was appointed Queen's Counsel in 1982. In 1983 he was elected Conservative Member of Parliament for Folkestone and Hythe. He became Secretary of State for Employment in 1990 and Secretary of State for the Environment in 1992. As Home Secretary (1993–97), he promoted controversial policies for stricter sentencing of offenders and the privatization of prison facilities.

Howard, Oliver Otis 1830–1909 •*US Union soldier*• Born in Leeds, Maine, he graduated from West Point in 1854. In 1864 he commanded the army of Tennessee. He was commissioner of the Freedmen's Bureau (1865–74), and also first president of Howard University in Washington DC, which was named after him (1869–74). Later he returned to military service, and conducted two campaigns against the Indians (1877–78).

Howard, Thomas, 2nd Duke of Norfolk and **1st Earl of Surrey** 1443–1524 •*English nobleman, soldier and politician*• Born in Stoke-by-Nayland, Suffolk, the son of **John Howard**, 1st Duke of Norfolk, he fought for **Richard III** and was wounded and captured at Bosworth (1485), but after three years' imprisonment in the Tower of London, he was released and restored to his estates. He put down a serious revolt in Yorkshire (1489) and, as Lieutenant General of the North for **Henry VIII**, he decisively defeated the Scots at Flodden (1513) and was made Duke of Norfolk (1514).

Howard, Thomas, 3rd Duke of Norfolk 1473–1554 •*English nobleman and politician*• The son of **Thomas Howard**, 2nd Duke of Norfolk, he married (1495) Anne (d. 1512), daughter of **Edward IV** and sister-in-law of **Henry VII**. He held several high offices, including Lord High Admiral (1513), and Lord Lieutenant of Ireland (1520). As Lord Steward he presided over the trial for adultery of the queen, his niece **Anne Boleyn** (1536). He also put down the Pilgrimage of Grace (1536) and opposed **Thomas Cromwell**. He lost influence at court when another niece, **Catherine Howard**, Henry VIII's fifth wife, was also beheaded for adultery (1542). He was saved from death for treason by Henry VIII's own death (1547), but throughout the reign of **Edward VI** he was kept in prison; his eldest son, Henry Howard, Earl of Surrey, was executed by Henry VIII (1547).

Howard, Thomas, 4th Duke of Norfolk 1536–72 •*English nobleman*• The son of Henry Howard, Earl of Surrey, he succeeded his grandfather, the 3rd Duke, as duke and Earl Marshal (1554). After the death of successive wives, as a commissioner appointed to inquire into Scottish affairs, he was imprisoned (1569–70) for attempting to marry **Mary Queen of Scots**. He was also involved in the Ridolfi plot with **Philip II** of Spain to free Mary, and was executed.

Howard, Trevor Wallace 1916–88 •*English actor*• Born in Cliftonville, Kent, he studied at the Royal Academy of Dramatic Art. Exclusively a theater performer until World War II, he was dismissed from the Royal Artillery due to illness, and made his film debut in *The Way Ahead* (1944). His performance in *Brief Encounter* (1945) made him one of the most popular British actors, a position he held for some years. A dependable leading man, he was occasionally asked to portray cynicism or weakness, as in *The Third Man* (1949). Developing into a character actor of international stature, he was nominated for an Academy Award in *Sons and Lovers* (1960), but spent his later years largely in cameo roles. He reminded audiences of his underused talents in television work such as *Staying On* (1980), in which he starred with **Celia Johnson**, his costar in *Brief Encounter.*

Howe (of Aberavon), (Richard Edward) Geoffrey Howe, Baron 1926– •*British Conservative politician*• Born in Port Talbot, Glamorgan, he was educated at Cambridge. He was called to the bar in 1952 and first elected to Parliament as a Conservative Member of Parliament in 1964. Knighted in 1970, he was Solicitor General (1970–72), Chancellor of the Exchequer (1979–83) and Foreign Secretary (1983–89). In a major Cabinet reshuffle, he was moved from the Foreign Office in 1989 to the leadership of the House of Commons (with the title of Deputy Prime Minister) following policy disagreements with **Margaret Thatcher** over European monetary union. A year later, he resigned in protest at her continuing intransigence, and his highly critical speech to the House in October 1990 heightened the party split that contributed to Thatcher's downfall and replacement by **John Major**. He was made a life peer in 1992.

Howe, Gordie (Gordon) 1928– •*Canadian ice-hockey player*• He was born in Floral, Saskatchewan. He began playing with the Detroit Red Wings (1946–71), then joined the World Hockey Association Houston Aeros (1973–77) and then the New England (then Hartford, NHL) Whalers (1977–80). During his career in the National Hockey League (NHL), he set records for scoring the most goals (801) and most points (1,850), and playing the most seasons (26) and most games (1,767). He was the first player to score 1,000 career major league goals.

Howe, Julia Ward, *née* **Ward** 1819–1910 •*US feminist, reformer and writer*• Born in New York, a wealthy banker's daughter, she became a prominent suffragist and abolitionist, and founded the New England Woman Suffrage Association (1868) and the New England Women's Club (1868). She published several volumes of poetry, as well as travel books and a play. She also wrote the "Battle Hymn of the Republic" (1862, published in *Atlantic Monthly*). In 1908 she became the first woman to be elected to the American Academy of Arts and Letters. She was married to **Samuel Gridley Howe**.

Howe, Richard Howe, 1st Earl 1726–99 •*English admiral*• Born in London, the brother of **William, 5th Viscount Howe**, he distinguished himself in the Seven Years' War (1756–63). He became First Lord of the Admiralty (1783), and earl (1788). In 1776 he was appointed commander of the British fleet during the American Revolution and, in 1778, defended the North American coast against a superior French force. On the outbreak of war with France (1793), he took command of the Channel fleet, defeating the French off Ushant at the Battle of the Glorious First of June (1794).

Howe, Samuel Gridley 1801–76 •*US reformer and philanthropist*• He was born in Boston. During the Greek revolution (1821–31) he organized the medical staff of the Greek army (1824–27) and formed a colony on the Isthmus of Corinth. Swamp fever drove him from the country in 1830. In 1831 he went to Paris to study the methods of educating the blind, and, becoming involved in the Polish insurrection, spent six weeks in a Prussian prison. On his return to Boston he established the Perkins School for the Blind, and taught **Laura Bridgman**, among others. Also concerned with the education of the mentally ill, he was a prison reformer and an abolitionist. He was the husband of **Julia Ward Howe**.

Howe, William Howe, 5th Viscount 1729–1814 •*English soldier*• Brother of **Richard, 1st Earl Howe**, he served under **James Wolfe** at Louisburg (1758) and at Quebec (1759), where he led the famous advance to the Heights of Abraham. In the American Revolution (1776–83) he won the victory at Bunker Hill (1775) and became Commander in Chief. Supported from the sea by his sailor-brother, in 1776 he captured Brooklyn, New York, and, the following year defeated the Americans at Brandywine Creek. He was replaced by Sir **Henry Clinton** in 1778 after failure at Valley Forge.

Howells, William Dean 1837–1920 •*US novelist and critic*• Born in Martin's Ferry, Ohio, he worked as a compositor for the *Ohio State Journal* (1856–61) and began to write poetry, some of which was published in the *Atlantic Monthly*, of which he later became editor (1871–81). His biography of **Abraham Lincoln** (1860) procured for him the post of US consul in Venice (1861–65) and his editorship at *Harper's Magazine* (1886–91) made him the king of critics in the US. A champion of realism in US literature, he wrote numerous novels, of which the best remembered are *A Modern Instance* (1882), *The Rise of Silas Lapham* (1885) and *A Hazard of New Fortunes* (1890). His theories of fiction were expounded in *Criticism and Fiction* (1891).

Howerd, Frankie, *originally* **Francis Alex Howard** 1917–92 •*English comedian and actor*• Born in London, he made his debut at the Stage Door Canteen, Piccadilly, London, in 1946, and appeared in revues in London during the 1950s. He occasionally acted in plays and gave a notable performance in **Stephen Sondheim**'s musical, *A Funny Thing Happened on the Way to the Forum* (1963). He appeared in the radio show *Variety Bandbox* (1946–47) and on television in *Frankie Howerd* (1964–65), *The Frankie Howerd Show* (1969) and, most memorably, as the Roman slave Lurcio in *Up Pompeii!* (1969–70), which spawned three film spinoffs. His other films included *The Mouse on the Moon* (1963), *Carry On Doctor* (1967) and *The House in Nightmare Park* (1973).

Howlin' Wolf, *stage name of* **Chester Arthur Burnett** 1910–76 •*US blues singer, guitarist and harmonica player*• Born in West Point, Mississippi, he began playing blues as a child, and was able to amalgamate several strains of country and urban blues into a distinctive, individual style. He settled in Chicago in 1953, where he was a giant (physically as well as metaphorically) of the emerging electric blues scene. He recorded a number of classics of the genre, many of which were later covered by rock bands like **The Rolling Stones** and The Doors in the 1960s.

How-Martyn, Edith, *née* **How** c. 1875–1954 •*English suffragist*• Born in Cheltenham, she was educated at University College, Aberystwyth, and the University of London. She was the secretary of the Women's Social and Political Union (1906–07), but left to co-found the Women's Freedom League with **Charlotte Despard** and **Teresa Billington-Greig**. As founder of the Birth Control International Information Centre (1929) she traveled widely, lecturing on women's issues.

Hoxha or **Hodja, Enver** 1908–85 •*Albanian politician*• Born in Gjirokastër and educated in France, he founded and led the Albanian Communist Party (1941) in the fight for national independence when the country was overrun by Germans and Italians during World War II. In 1946 he deposed King **Zog** (who had fled in 1939) and became effective head of state. From 1954, Hoxha controlled the political scene through his position as First Secretary of the Albanian Party of Labor (Communist Party), and instituted a rigid Stalinist program of thorough nationalization and collectivization which left Albania with the lowest per capita income in Europe on his death.

Ho Xuan Huong fl. c. 1780–c.1820 •*Vietnamese poet*• Her precise identity is unknown; we know from her work that Ho is her real family name, but Xuan Huong is a pseudonym. An educated, cultured woman, she produced some of the most sensuous, witty and readable verse to come out of Asia in the 19th century. Typically, a poem by Ho will pretend to be about a harmless domestic activity (weaving or making rice cakes), which will make it seem innocent, but there is a second level of meaning, usually sexual. She argues in her verse that the sexes should be more equal, and often comes out against marriage.

Hoyland, John 1934– •*English painter*• Born in Sheffield, he studied at the Art College there (1951–56) and at the Royal Academy Schools in London (1956–60), and has held numerous teaching posts, including principal lecturer at the Chelsea School of Art. In the mid-1960s he turned to hard-edged abstraction, using broad, freely painted rectangles of rich flat color, often untitled, but dated, such as *28.5.66* (1966) and *17.7.69* (1969, Waddington Galleries, London). From the late 1970s he explored the physical nature of paint, employing heavy impasto to create a three-dimensional canvas with geometric shapes, as for example in *Billy's Blues, 6.7.79* (private collection).

Hoyle, Sir Fred 1915–2001 •*English astronomer and mathematician*• Born in Bingley, Yorkshire, he was educated at Emmanuel College, Cambridge. He taught mathematics (1945–58) and astronomy (1958–72) at Cambridge, and was the Honorary Research Professor at both Manchester University (1972–2001) and University College, Cardiff (1975–2001). In 1948, with **Hermann Bondi** and **Thomas Gold**, he propounded the influential but now discredited steady-state theory of the universe, which proposed that the universe is uniform in space and unchanging in time. He also suggested the currently accepted scenario of the origin of supernovae, whereby a chain of nuclear reactions in a star is followed by a massive explosion, the ejected matter later forming second-generation stars. His books include *Nature of the Universe* (1952) and *Frontiers of Astronomy* (1955). He also wrote science fiction, including *A Is for Andromeda* (1962, with J Elliot), and *The Molecule Men* (1971, with his son Geoffrey Hoyle), as well as stories for children and two volumes of autobiography.

Hoyte, (Hugh) Desmond 1929– •*Guyanese politician*• Born in Georgetown, he studied at the University of London and the Middle Temple and practiced as a lawyer in Guyana. He joined the socialist People's National Congress Party (PNC) and in 1968, two years after Guyana achieved full independence, was elected to the National Assembly. He held a number of ministerial posts before becoming prime minister under **Forbes Burnham**. On Burnham's death, in 1985, he succeeded him as president, remaining in office until 1992.

Hrawi, Elias 1930– •*Lebanese statesman*• A Maronite Christian, he was born in Zahle in the Bekaa Valley. He became a businessman and a deputy of the National Assembly, until in 1989 he succeeded Rene Mouawad as president of Lebanon. Mouawad had been assassinated after only 17 days in office. In 1995 the term of the presidency (six years) was extended by a further three years to allow Hrawi to continue in office until 1998.

Hsiao-p'ing, Teng *See* **Deng Xiaoping**

Hsüan Tsang *See* **Xuan Zang**

Hua Guofeng (Hua Kuo-feng) 1920– •*Chinese politician*• Born in Hunan province into a poor peasant family, he fought under **Zhu De** during the liberation war of 1937–49, before later rising through the official ranks of the Communist Party (CCP) during the 1950s and 1960s in **Mao Zedong**'s home province of Hunan, eventually becoming local first secretary in 1970. Viewed as an orthodox and loyal Maoist, Hua, despite his relative inexperience, succeeded Mao as party leader on the latter's death in September 1976. From 1978, however, he was gradually eclipsed by the reformist **Deng Xiaoping**, being replaced as prime minister and CCP chairman by the latter's protégés, **Zhao Ziyang** and **Hu Yaobang**, in 1980 and 1981 respectively.

Huang-Ti *See* **Shih Huang Ti**

Hubbard, L(afayette) Ron(ald) 1911–86 •*US science-fiction writer and founder of the Church of Scientology*• He was born in Tilden, Nebraska, and from the age of 16 traveled extensively in the Far East before completing his education at George Washington University. He became a professional writer of adventure stories, turning to science fiction in 1938, with such classics as *Slaves of Sleep* (1939) and *Typewriter in the Sky* (1940). He served in the US Navy during World War II, and in 1950 published *Dianetics: The Modern Science of Mental Health*, which formed the basis of the Scientology philosophy. The first Church of Scientology was founded by a group of adherents in Los Angeles in 1954 and Hubbard became the executive director of the Founding Church, Washington (1955–66). From 1959 to 1966 his base was in East Grinstead, England. He resigned his position as executive director of the church in 1966. In 1982 he returned to science fiction with an epic bestseller, *Battlefield Earth: A Saga of the Year 3000*.

Hubble, Edwin Powell 1889–1953 •*US astronomer*• Born in Marshfield, Missouri, he studied mathematics and astronomy at the University of Chicago and law as a Rhodes scholar at Oxford (1910–13). Following military service during World War I, he moved in 1919 to the Carnegie Institution's Mount Wilson Observatory, where he began his fundamental investigations of the realm of the nebulae. He found that spiral nebulae are independent stellar systems and that the Andromeda nebula in particular is very similar to our own Milky Way galaxy. In 1929 he announced his discovery that galaxies recede from us with speeds which increase with their distance. This was the phenomenon of the expansion of the universe, the observational basis of modern cosmology. The linear relation between speed of recession and distance is known as Hubble's law. The 2.4-meter-aperture Hubble Space Telescope, launched in 1990, was named in his honor.

“ ”

We measure shadows, and we search among ghostly errors of measurement for landmarks that are scarcely more substantial.

Quoted in Dennis Overbye, ***Lonely Hearts of the Cosmos*** *(1991).*

Hubel, David Hunter 1926– •*US neurophysiologist and Nobel Prize winner*• Born in Windsor, Ontario, in Canada, he studied medicine at McGill University in Montreal, and moved to the US in 1954. After holding positions at Johns Hopkins Medical School (where he met **Torsten Wiesel**), he worked at the Walter Reed Army Research Institute in Washington DC, examining the electrical activity of the brain (1955–58). In 1959 he went to Harvard, where with Wiesel he investigated the mechanisms of visual perception, and they shared the 1981 Nobel Prize for physiology or medicine with **Roger Sperry**. Working on anesthetized animals, Hubel and Wiesel implanted electrodes into their brains and then analyzed individual cell responses to different types of visual stimulation.

Huber, Robert 1937– •*German biophysicist and Nobel Prize winner*• He was born and received his early training in Munich, remaining at the University of Munich as a lecturer (1968–76) and associate professor from 1976. Since 1972 he has been director of the **Max Planck** Institute for Biochemistry in Martinsried. A specialist in the high-resolution X-ray crystallography of biological macromolecules, he demonstrated that enzyme activation is not associated with a marked structural change (1972), and in 1974 helped elucidate the antibody structure proposed by **Rodney Porter**. Since 1979 he has studied the enzyme glutathione peroxidase, and contributed to the understanding of protein-DNA interactions. He has also collaborated with **Hartmut Michel** and **Johann Deisenhofer** (from 1982) to determine the structure of the reaction center of the purple bacterium *Rhodopseudomonas viridis*, work for which they shared the 1988 Nobel Prize for chemistry.

Huch, Ricarda 1864–1947 •*German novelist, historian and feminist*• Born in Brunswick, she studied history in Zurich and taught at a girls' school there, then traveled extensively in Italy, married (unhappily) twice, and finally settled in Munich in 1910. A neo-Romantic, she rejected naturalism, and wrote novels including the semiautobiographical *Erinnerungen von Ludolf Ursleu dem Jüngeren* (1893, "Memoirs of Ludolf Ursleu the Younger") and *Aus der Triumphgasse* (1902, "Out of Triumph Lane"). Her criticism includes *Die Blütezeit, Ausbreitung und Verfall der Romantik* (1899–1902, "The Blossoming, Spread and Decline of Romanticism"), and she wrote social and political works, such as *Der grosse Krieg in Deutschland* (1912–14, "The Great War in Germany"). She also wrote on religious themes. The first woman to be admitted to the Prussian Academy of Literature in 1931, she resigned in 1933 over the expulsion of Jewish writers. She lived in Jena during World War II.

Hückel, Erich 1896–1980 •*German physicist and theoretical chemist*• Born in Berlin-Charlottenburg, he studied physics and mathematics at the University of Göttingen before becoming assistant to **Peter Debye** in Zurich. He taught at Stuttgart and then at Marburg, becoming Professor of Theoretical Physics there (1937–61). Hückel's research interests were almost entirely in chemical physics. After work on strong electrolytes and interionic forces (resulting in the **Debye**-Hückel theory, 1923), his interests moved to the quantum-mechanical treatment of organic molecules. In 1937 he developed a procedure for calculating electron distribution and other characteristics of unsaturated compounds, Hückel molecular orbital (HMO) theory.

Hudd, Roy 1936– •*English actor and comedian*• Born in Croydon, Surrey, he grew up on music-hall entertainment, played banjo and sang in clubs, before becoming a holiday-camp entertainer. Fame came as half of the comedy duo Hudd and Kay. After turning solo, he became a regular on the radio show *Workers' Playtime* and has had a long career in radio with programs such as *The News Huddlines* (1976–). He has also fronted television series such as *Hudd*, and played character roles in the **Dennis Potter** serials *Lipstick on Your Collar* (1993) and *Karaoke* (1996).

Huddleston, (Ernest Urban) Trevor 1913–98 •*English Anglican missionary*• Educated at Christ Church, Oxford, and ordained in 1937, he entered the Community of the Resurrection and in 1943 went to Johannesburg, where he ultimately became provincial of the order (1949–55). From 1960 to 1968 he was Bishop of Masasi, Tanzania, then Bishop Suffragan of Stepney (until 1978), and Bishop of Mauritius and Archbishop of the Indian Ocean (1978–83). After his retirement he became chairman of the Anti-Apartheid movement (1981–94) and chairman of the International Defense and Aid Fund for Southern Africa (1983–98). He was distinguished by a passionate belief that the doctrine of the universal brotherhood of men in Christ should be universally applied. His book, *Naught for Your Comfort* (1956), reflects this conviction in the light of his experiences in South Africa and its racial problems and policies.

Hudson, Henry c.1550–1611 •*English navigator*• In 1607 he set sail in the *Hopewell*, on his first voyage for the English Muscovy Company, to seek a northeast passage across the North Pole to China and the Far East. He reached Spitsbergen and (probably) Jan Mayen Island. On his second voyage (1608) he reached Novaya Zemlya. He undertook a third voyage in 1609 for the Dutch East India Company, on the *Half Moon*, discovered the Hudson River, and followed it for 150 miles (241.5 km) to Albany. In April 1610 he set out on the *Discovery* with a crew of 20 and his 12-year-old son, and reached Greenland in June, arriving at the waters now named after him, Hudson Strait and Hudson Bay. He was accused of distributing food unfairly, and when the ice began to break up, the men mutinied. On June 23, Hudson and his son, with seven others, were cast adrift in an open boat, and never seen again.

Huerta, Victoriano 1854–1916 •*Mexican dictator*• Born in Colotlán, Jalisco state, he was a Huichol Indian who joined the Mexican army and advanced to the rank of general during the dictatorship of **Porfirio Díaz**. After Díaz went into exile, Huerta became an ally of liberal president **Francisco Madero**. In 1913, however, he overthrew Madero's regime and declared himself president of Mexico, violently suppressing all opposition. When the US government withdrew its support, and revolutionaries such as **Emiliano Zapata**, **Venustiano Carranza** and **Pancho Villa** joined together to fight him, Huerta was forced into exile (1914).

Hugensz, Lucas *See* **Lucas van Leyden**

Huggins, Charles B(renton) 1901–97 •*US surgeon and Nobel Prize winner*• Born in Halifax, Nova Scotia, Canada, he worked at the University of Chicago from 1927, where he became Professor of Surgery in 1936 and was head of the Ben May Laboratory for Cancer Research from 1951 to 1969. He was a pioneer in the investigation of the physiology and biochemistry of the male urogenital tract, including the prostate gland, and investigated the use of hormones in treating prostate cancer. He also worked on the use of hormones in treating breast cancer in women. He shared the 1966 Nobel Prize for physiology or medicine with **Peyton Rous**.

Huggins, Sir William 1824–1910 •*English astronomer*• Born in London, he went into the textile business, while in his spare time studying the sciences. He later devoted himself entirely to astronomy, erecting an observatory (1856) in the garden of his house in the suburbs of London. In collaboration with William Allen Miller (1817–70), Professor of Chemistry at King's College London, Huggins began observations of the spectra of stars (1864). His pioneering work included spectroscopy of comets, and observations of the **Doppler** shift in the spectra of stars as a means of measuring their radial motion. Huggins twice received the gold medal of the Royal Astronomical Society (1867, 1885) and was awarded the Royal (1866), Rumford (1880) and Copley (1898) medals of the Royal Society. He was knighted in 1897 and was among the 12 first recipients of the Order of Merit when it was instituted in 1902.

Hugh of Avalon, St, *also called* **St Hugh of Lincoln** c.1135–1200 •*English prelate*• He was born into a French noble family at Avalon in Burgundy. A priest at the Grande Chartreuse (1160–70), he was called to England by **Henry II** to found a Carthusian monastery at Witham in Somerset (1178). He became Bishop of Lincoln (1186), when he spoke against the draconian forestry laws in the royal forests and defended the Jews against rioting mobs. He refused to pay taxes to finance French wars (money grant). He was canonized in 1220 and his feast day is November 17.

Hugh of Lincoln, St *See* **Hugh of Avalon, St**

Hughes, Arthur 1830–1915 •*English painter*• Born in London, he entered the Royal Academy Schools in 1847, and, by 1852, had become associated with the Pre-Raphaelite Brotherhood and its principal members, **Holman Hunt**, **J E Millais** and **Dante Gabriel Rossetti**. Although he never formally joined the Brotherhood, he produced several paintings during the 1850s that rank as some of the finest of works executed in its typically precise and richly colored style, such as *April Love* (1855, Tate Britain, London). He also, from around 1855, pursued a successful career as an illustrator of the works of, among others, **Christina Rossetti**. He visited Italy in 1862 and the same year completed *Home from Sea* (Ashmolean, Oxford).

Hughes, Howard Robard 1905–76 •*US millionaire businessman, film producer, director, and aviator*• Born in Houston, Texas, he inherited his father's oil-drilling equipment company at the age of 18, and in 1926 began to involve himself and his profits in Hollywood films. During the next six years he made several films, including *Hell's Angels* (1930) and *Scarface* (1932). Already considered eccentric, he then turned his entire attention to designing, building and flying aircraft. He broke most of the world's air speed records (1935–38) before returning to filmmaking, producing and directing his most controversial film, *The Outlaw* (1943), starring **Jane Russell**. He continued his involvement in aviation by designing and building an oversized wooden seaplane, the "Spruce Goose," that was completed in 1947, flew only once, but yielded valuable technical knowledge to the aviation industry. Severely injured in an air crash in 1946, his eccentricity increased, and he eventually became a recluse, living in complete seclusion by 1966 while still controlling his vast business interests from sealed-off hotel suites, and giving rise to endless rumor and speculation.

Hughes, (James Mercer) Langston 1902–67 •*US poet, fiction writer and dramatist*• Born in Joplin, Missouri, he published his first poems while still in high school, and during his early adulthood spent several years drifting, traveling to Africa and Europe as a messman on a freighter. While working as a busboy in a Washington hotel he showed his poems to **Vachel Lindsay**, who championed his work, and he was awarded a scholarship to Lincoln University in Pennsylvania. Though initially rejected by Black critics who saw his use of African-American idioms and speech patterns as a betrayal of their efforts to elevate the race, he was eventually recognized as a major figure in the Harlem Renaissance of the 1920s. *Weary Blues* (1926) was his first of several collections of verse. His memorable character "Jesse B Simple" first appeared in racy newspaper sketches and thereafter appeared in several volumes. Hughes's lyrical verse, resonant of his vast knowledge of folk culture, jazz and the blues, had a profound influence on the development of African-American literature and later poets of the Beat generation.

Hughes, Richard Arthur Warren 1900–76 •*English novelist*• Born in Weybridge, Surrey, of Welsh descent, he was educated at Oriel College, Oxford. After publishing verse, drama and other works, and traveling widely in Europe, the US and the West Indies, he settled in Wales. He is best known for *A High Wind in Jamaica* (1929, US title *The Innocent Voyage*), a superior adventure story about a family of children captured by pirates while sailing to England. His later work includes *The Fox in the Attic* (1961), and *The Wooden Shepherdess* (1973).

" "

Do your bit to save humanity from lapsing back into barbarity by reading all the novels you can.

1975 Speech at Foyle's Literary Luncheon, London, in honor of his 75th birthday.

Hughes, Robert Studley Forest 1938– •*US-Australian art critic*• Born in Sydney, Australia, he studied art and architecture at the University of Sydney, then became a freelance writer. After traveling and living in Europe, he settled in New York City, and since 1970 has been art reviewer at *Time* magazine, becoming known for his irascible critical persona and his lucid, elegant prose. He has also written and narrated art documentaries for television, winning the Richard Dimbleby award for the series *American Visions* (1997). His books include *The Shock of the New* (1980), *The Fatal Shore* (1987) and *The Culture of Complaint* (1993).

Hughes, Shirley 1919– •*English children's writer and illustrator*• Born in Lancashire, she began as an illustrator of other people's works, but by 1960 she was writing her own books for young children, including *Lucy and Tom's Day*, *Alfie's Feet* (1982), *Here Comes Charlie Moon* (1980), *Bouncing* (1993), *Chatting* (1994) and *Hiding* (1994). She was given the honorary title Officer, Order of the British Empire, in 1999.

Hughes, Ted (Edward James) 1930–98 •*English poet, poet laureate from 1984*• Born in Mytholmroyd, a mill town in West Yorkshire, his family moved to Mexborough, Yorkshire, when he was seven. At Mexborough Grammar School he began to write poetry, usually bloodcurdling verses about Zulus and cowboys. He won a scholarship to Pembroke College, Cambridge, where he read English literature, but switched to archaeology and anthropology. After graduating he had a number of colorful jobs, including zookeeper, gardener and nightwatchman, and occasionally published poems in university poetry magazines. He married the US writer **Sylvia Plath** in 1956 and after two years in the US they settled in Cambridge, where Hughes taught while Plath studied. That same year he won an American poetry competition, judged by **W H Auden**, Sir **Stephen Spender** and **Marianne Moore**, with the poems that were to form *The Hawk in the Rain* (1957); they displayed a striking treatment of animal subjects and a vivid sense of nature. For the next few years he lived again in America, where he taught and was supported by a Guggenheim Foundation grant. *Lupercal* (1960), his second collection, won the **Somerset Maugham** award and the Hawthornden prize. In 1963 Sylvia Plath committed suicide and for the next few years Hughes published no new adult poetry, although he did complete books of prose and poetry for children. *Wodwo* (1967) was his next major work, and among later volumes are *Crow* (1970), *Cave Birds* (1975), *Season Songs* (1976), *Gaudete* (a long prose poem on the theme of fertility rites, 1977), *Moortown* (1979, revised edition 1989), *Remains of Elmet* (1979), on which he collaborated with the photographer **Fay Godwin**, *River* (1983), *Wolf Watching* (1989) and *Tales from Ovid* (1997). The retrospective volume *New Selected Poems: 1957–1994* was published in 1995. He edited Plath's collected poems in 1981 and in 1998 published *Birthday Letters*, poems about his relationship with her. Of his books for children, the most remarkable is *The Iron Man* (1968, published in the US as *The Iron Giant*), a fantasy story about a huge iron man who comes from nowhere and eats machines. His verse for children includes *Meet My Folks* (1961), *Season Songs* (1975), and *Ffangs the Vampire Bat and the Kiss of Truth* (1986). He also wrote plays for children, including the collection *The Coming of the King* (1970). Much acclaimed and imitated, he was appointed poet laureate in 1984. He was appointed to the Order of Merit in 1998.

Hughes, Thomas 1822–96 •*English reformer and novelist*• Born in Uffington, Berkshire, he was educated at Rugby and Oriel College, Oxford, before being called to the bar in 1848, and becoming a county court judge in 1882. He was a Liberal Member of Parliament (1865–74), was closely associated with the Christian Socialists, supported trade unionism, and helped found the Working Men's College and a model settlement in Tennessee. He is primarily remembered as the author of the semiautobiographical public school classic, *Tom Brown's Schooldays* (1857), based on his school experiences at Rugby under the headmastership of Dr **Thomas Arnold**. He also wrote a number of biographies and social studies.

Hughes, William Morris 1862–1952 •*Australian statesman*• He was born in Pimlico, London. He emigrated to Australia in 1884 and settled in Sydney in 1886. He entered politics in the New South Wales Legislative Assembly in 1894, rising to be a minister in 1904, attorney general (1908–09, 1910–13, 1914–15), and deputy prime minister (1910), and in 1915 replaced **Andrew Fisher** as prime minister and Labor leader. His attempts to introduce conscription were defeated but he survived at the head of various coalitions until 1922, when he was forced to retire in favor of **S M Bruce**. A strong figure in the Allied war councils during World War I, he secured an Australian mandate over the neighboring German colony of New Guinea (later incorporated in Papua New Guinea). He engineered the overthrow of the Bruce-Page government in 1929, for which he was expelled from the Nationalist Party, and in the **Menzies** administration of 1939 was minister for the Navy (1940–41).

Hugo, Victor Marie 1802–85 •*French poet and writer, a leading figure of the French Romantic movement*• Born in Besançon, the son of one of **Napoleon I**'s generals, he was educated in Paris at the Feuillantines, in Madrid, and at the École Polytechnique. He wrote a tragedy at the age of 14, and at 20, when he published his first set of *Odes et ballades* (1822), he had been victor three times at the Floral Games of Toulouse. In the 1820s and 1830s he produced further poetry and drama, establishing his place in the forefront of the Romantic movement, in particular with *Hernani* in 1830, the first of the five-act lyrics which are especially associated with him. In 1831 he produced one of his best-known novels, *Notre Dame de Paris*, an outstanding historical romance, later filmed as *The Hunchback of Notre Dame* (1924). During the 1840s Hugo became an adherent of republicanism, and he was elected to the Constituent Assembly in 1848. After the coup d'état of Louis Napoleon (**Napoleon III**) he was sent into exile to Guernsey in the Channel Islands (1851–70), where he issued his satirical *Napoléon le petit* (1852). His greatest novel, *Les Misérables*, a panoramic piece of social history, appeared in 1862. He returned to Paris in 1870 and stayed through the Commune, but then departed for Brussels, protesting publicly against the action of the Belgian government with respect to the beaten Communists, in consequence of which he was again expelled. In 1872 he published *L'année terrible*, a series of pictures of the war, and in 1874 his last romance in prose appeared, *Quatre-vingt-treize*. In 1876 he was made a senator. He was buried as a national hero in the Panthéon.

" "

Respirer Paris, cela conserve l'âme.
To inhale Paris preserves the soul.
*1862 **Les Misérables**, volume 3, book 1, chapter 6.*

Huidobro, Vicente 1893–1948 •*Chilean poet*• Born in Santiago, he once stood for the presidency of Chile. He resolutely lived out his private life in public, and when he met Ximena Amuntágui, a high school student, in 1925, he announced his intention to leave his wife and children in the nation's leading newspaper. One of the most influential figures in Latin-American literature, he is remembered mainly as a lyric poet, especially for the prose poems *Temblor de cielo* (1928, "Quivering Sky") and *Altazor* (1931, Eng trans 1988). There are many translations, including *The Poet Is a Little God* (1990).

Hull, Cordell 1871–1955 •*US politician and Nobel Prize winner*• Born in Overton, Tennessee, he was educated at Cumberland University, Tennessee. Under **Franklin D Roosevelt**, he became Secretary of State in 1933 and served for the longest term in that office until he retired in 1944, having attended most of the great wartime conferences. One of the architects of bipartisanship, he also helped organize the United Nations, for which he received the Nobel Peace Prize in 1944.

Hulme, Keri Ann Ruhi 1947– •*New Zealand writer*• Born in Otautahi, Christchurch, of mixed Maori, Orkney and English descent, she came to international notice by winning the Booker Prize with her first novel, *The Bone People* (1983), a spellbinding mixing of Maori myth and Christian symbolism. After another novel, *Lost Possessions* (1985), she published a collection of short stories, *Te Kaihau: The Windeater* (1986). Some of her verse in Maori and English is collected in *The Silences Between* (1982). Later works include *Bait* (1992).

Hulme, T(homas) E(rnest) 1883–1917 •*English critic, poet and philosopher*• Born in Endon, Staffordshire, he was expelled from St John's College, Cambridge, for fighting. After a stay in Canada he taught in Brussels and developed an interest in philosophy. He joined **Ezra Pound**, **Wyndham Lewis** and **Jacob Epstein** as a champion of modern abstract art, of the poetic movement known as Imagism and of the antiliberal political writings of **Georges Sorel**, which he translated. Killed in action in France, he left a massive collection of notes, edited by his friend **Herbert Read** under the titles *Speculation* (1924) and *More Speculation* (1956). Most of his poetry appeared in *The New Age* in 1912. He was described by **T S Eliot** as "classical, reactionary and revolutionary."

Humboldt, (Friedrich Heinrich) Alexander, Baron von 1769–1859 •*German naturalist*• Born in Berlin, he was the brother of **Wilhelm von Humboldt**. He studied at the Universities of Frankfurt an der Oder, Berlin, Göttingen, and under **Abraham Werner** in the Mining Academy at Freiburg. For five years (1799–1804) he and Aimé Bonpland (1773–1804) explored unknown territory in South America, which led to his monumental *Voyage de Humboldt et Bonpland aux regions équinoxiales* (23 vols, 1805–34, Eng trans *Personal Narrative of Travels to the Equinoctial Regions*, 7 vols, 1814–29). In 1829, he explored Central Asia with Christian Ehrenberg (1795–1876), and their various scientific observations are described in Humboldt's *Asie Centrale* (1843). Later works include *Géographie du nouveau continent* (1835–38) and the popular science book *Kosmos* (1845–62), which gave a comprehensive physical description of the universe.

Humboldt, (Karl) Wilhelm von 1767–1835 •*German politician and philologist*• He was born in Potsdam, the elder brother of **Alexander von Humboldt**. He traveled in Europe, then became a diplomat, but without official employment. A friend of **Schiller**, for some time he devoted himself to literature. In 1801 he became Prussian Minister at Rome, and was a patron of young artists and scientists. He returned to Prussia (1808) to become First Minister of Education, and founded the Friedrich Wilhelm (now Humboldt) University of Berlin. He was the first to study the Basque language scientifically, and he also worked on the languages of the East and of the South Sea Islands.

Hume, (George) Basil 1923–99 •*English Benedictine monk and cardinal*• Born in Newcastle upon Tyne, and educated at Ampleforth College, St Benet's Hall, Oxford, and Fribourg University, Switzerland, he was ordained as a priest in 1950, and returned to Ampleforth College as senior modern languages master in 1952. From 1957 to 1963 he was Magister Scholarum of the English Benedictine Congregation, and in 1963 he became abbot of Ampleforth, where he remained until he was made Archbishop of Westminster and a cardinal in 1976. His books include *To Be a Pilgrim* (1984) and *Remaking Europe* (1994).

Hume, David 1711–76 •*Scottish philosopher and historian*• He was born in Edinburgh. His early years were unsettled: he studied at but did not graduate from the University of Edinburgh. In 1734 he went to La Flèche in Anjou, where he studied for three years and worked on his first, and most important, work, *A Treatise of Human Nature*, which he had published anonymously in London (1739–40) when he returned to Scotland. The subtitle is "An attempt to introduce the experimental method of reasoning into moral subjects" and the book is in many ways a consolidation and extension of the empiricist legacy of **John Locke** and **George Berkeley** with major, and still influential, discussions of perception, causation, personal identity and what became known as "the naturalistic fallacy" in ethics. In political theory he argued for the "artificiality" of the principles of justice and political obligation, and challenged the rationalistic "natural law" and "social contract" theories of **Thomas Hobbes**, Richard Hooker (1554–1600), Locke and **Jean Jacques Rousseau**. Bitterly disappointed at the initial reception of the *Treatise*, he produced the more popular *Essays Moral and Political* (1741, 1742), which were immediately successful, and through which his views became more widely known. These essays heralded the new school of classical economics, of which his friend **Adam Smith** was to be the leader, advocating free trade and clearly stating the relationship between international specie flows, domestic prices and the balance of payments. Hume's atheism thwarted his applications for the professorships of moral philosophy at Edinburgh (1744) and logic at Glasgow (1751). He became tutor for a year (1745) to an insane nobleman, the Marquis of Annandale, then became secretary to General St Clair on an expedition to France (1746) and secret missions to Vienna and Turin (1748). In 1748 he published a simplified version of the *Treatise* entitled *Enquiry Concerning Human Understanding*. Its translation was said to wake **Immanuel Kant** from his "dogmatic slumbers." The brilliant *Dialogues Concerning Natural Religion* was written in 1750 but prudently left unpublished, and appeared posthumously in 1779. He achieved real fame and international recognition with his *Political Discourses* (1752) and his monumental *History of England* (5 vols, 1754–62). From 1763 to 1765 he acted as secretary to the ambassador in Paris, and returned to London in 1766 and became Under-Secretary of State for the Northern Department in 1767. He returned to Scotland in 1768 to settle in Edinburgh, where he died. He was a dominant influence on empiricist philosophers of the 20th century.

Hume, John 1937– •*Northern Ireland politician and Nobel Prize winner*• Born in Londonderry and educated at the National University of Ireland, he was a founding member of the Credit Union Party, which was a forerunner of the Social Democratic and Labour Party (SDLP). He sat in the Northern Ireland parliament (1969–72) and the Northern Ireland assembly (1972–73) and became widely respected as a moderate, nonviolent member of the Catholic community. He became SDLP leader in 1979 and in the same year was elected to the European Parliament. He has represented Foyle in the House of Commons since 1983. In the 1990s he took part in the Northern Ireland peace talks and in 1998 he shared the Nobel Peace Prize with **David Trimble**.

Humperdinck, Engelbert 1854–1921 •*German composer*• Born in Siegburg, near Bonn, he studied music in Cologne, Frankfurt am Main, Munich and Berlin, and traveled in France, Spain and Italy. He taught in Barcelona, Cologne, Frankfurt and Berlin, and became famous as the composer of the musical fairy play *Hänsel und Gretel* (1893), which was highly successful. *Schneewittchen* ("Snow White"), *Königskinder* (1897, "The King's Children"), *The Miracle* (1912) and others followed.

Humphrey, Doris 1895–1958 •*US dancer, choreographer and teacher*• Born in Oak Park, Illinois, she was one of the founders of modern dance. With her partner Charles Weidman (1901–75), she founded a company in New York (1928), which thrived until the early 1940s. She started the Juilliard Dance Theater (1935), and ran the Bennington College Summer School of Dance (1934–42). She choreographed highly original work often concerned with form and based on musical structures, including the trilogy *New Dance* (1935), *Theatre Piece* (1935) and *Day on Earth* (1947), building the foundations for the future vocabulary and philosophy of modern dance. Disabled by arthritis, she gave up dancing in 1944 but became artistic director (1946–58) for the company set up by one of her most talented students, **José Limón**. She also wrote *The Art of Making Dances* (1959), a key text on dance composition in modern dance.

Humphrey, Hubert H(oratio) 1911–78 •*US Democratic politician*• He was born in Wallace, South Dakota, and educated at the University of Minnesota and Louisiana State University. He entered politics as mayor of Minneapolis in 1945, and was elected Democratic senator in 1948. He built up a strong reputation as a liberal, particularly on the civil rights issue, but, as vice president from 1964 under the **Johnson** administration, alienated many by his apparent support for the continuation of the increasingly unpopular war in Vietnam. Although he won the Democratic presidential nomination in 1968 on the first ballot, a substantial minority of Democrats opposed him, and the general mood of disillusionment with Democratic policies and a compromise candidate led to **Richard Nixon**'s election victory.

“ ”

There are not enough jails, not enough policemen, not enough courts to enforce a law not supported by the people.

1965 Speech, May 1.

Humphries, (John) Barry 1934– •*Australian comedian and writer*• Born in Camberwell, Melbourne, he studied at the University of Melbourne. In Great Britain from 1959, he made his London debut in *The Demon Barber* (1959) and subsequently appeared in *Oliver!* (1960, 1963, 1968). He created the Barry McKenzie comic strip in *Private Eye* (1964–73), and wrote the screenplay for *The Adventures of Barry McKenzie* (1972), in which he appeared as Dame Edna Everage. His many stage shows include *An Evening's Intercourse with the Widely Liked Barry Humphries* (1981–82) and *Back with a Vengeance* (1987–89). His characters, including the repellent cultural attaché Sir Les Patterson and the acid-tongued superstar housewife Dame Edna Everage, have appeared in television shows such as *Dame Edna's Neighbourhood Watch* (1992–93) and *The Dame Edna Christmas Experience!* (1995). His straight roles on television have included playing **Rupert Murdoch** in *Selling Hitler* (1991). He has been in the films *The Getting of Wisdom* (1977) and *Les Patterson Saves the World* (1987).

Humphrys, John 1943– •*Welsh broadcaster*• Born in Cardiff, he studied at Cardiff High School. He worked as a BBC television correspondent from the early 1970s and later as a newsreader on the BBC Nine O'Clock News (1981–87), moving to radio in 1987 as the tenacious host of BBC Radio 4's *Today* program, and later *The John Humphrys Interview* (1995–). His political interview slot *On the Record* began on BBC television in 1993.

Hun Sen 1952– •*Cambodian politician*• Born in Kompang-Cham province, Cambodia, he was educated at a Buddhist monastery in Phnom Penh and joined the Khmer Rouge movement in 1970. Having risen to the post of Commandant of the Khmer Rouge, he went into exile (1977–79) in Vietnam during **Pol Pot**'s regime but, following the Vietnam-backed takeover of Cambodia in 1979, returned, ultimately becoming prime minister (1985–93). When the rival Funcinpec Party of Prince Norodom Ranariddh won more votes than his Cambodian People's Party in 1993, Hun Sen refused to cede power but agreed to serve as second prime minister alongside Prince Ranariddh, thus ending two decades of civil war. The coalition broke down in 1997, however, when Hun Sen ordered troops to attack Ranariddh's stronghold and forced him to flee the country. After disputed elections in 1998 Hun Sen reclaimed control as sole prime minister.

Hung-wu *See* **Hongwu**

Hunt, Geoff(rey) 1947– •*Australian squash rackets player*• Born in Victoria, he was the Australian amateur champion at the age of 17, the world amateur champion in 1967, 1969, and 1971, and the world Open champion in 1976–77 and 1979–80.

Hunt, (William) Holman 1827–1910 •*English painter*• Born in London, he became a student of the Royal Academy in 1845. He shared a studio with **Dante Gabriel Rossetti**, and the pair, along with **John Everett Millais** and four others, inaugurated the Pre-Raphaelite Brotherhood. The first of his Pre-Raphaelite works was *Rienze* (1849); others include *The Hireling Shepherd* (1852), *Claudio and Isabella* (1853), *Strayed Sheep* (1853) and *The Light of the World* (1854, Keble College, Oxford). The result of several visits to the East appeared in *The Scapegoat* (1856, Port Sunlight) and *The Finding of Christ in the Temple* (1860). Among his most famous canvases are *Isabella and the Pot of Basil* (1867) and *May Morning on Magdalen Tower* (1891).

Hunt, James (Simon Wallis) 1947–93 •*English racecar driver*• Born in London, and educated at Wellington College, he drove with the Hesketh and McLaren teams (1973–79), and was world motor racing Grand Prix champion in 1976. He retired in 1979 and was a BBC television broadcaster from 1980 until his death.

Hunt (of Lanfair Waterdine), (Henry Cecil) John Hunt, Baron 1910–98 •*English mountaineer and social reformer*• He was born in India, and educated at Marlborough College and at Sandhurst. After a distinguished military career in India and Europe, he led the first successful expedition to climb Mount Everest (see Sir **Edmund Hillary**), and was knighted. He also led the British party in the British-Soviet Caucasian mountaineering expedition (1958), and was involved in mountaineering expeditions in western Europe, the Middle East, the Himalayas, Greenland, Russia, Greece and Poland. From its inception in 1956, he was director of the Duke of **Edinburgh**'s Award (a program of personal development activities for young people) and was created a life peer for services to youth on his retirement in 1966. He later worked in penal reform. He became a Knight of the Garter in 1979.

Hunt, (James Henry) Leigh 1784–1859 •*English poet and essayist*• Born in Southgate, Middlesex, the son of an immigrant American preacher, he was educated at Christ's Hospital. His first collection of poetry was privately printed as *Juvenilia* in 1801. With his brother, a printer, he edited (1808–21) *The Examiner*, which became a focus of liberal opinion and attracted leading men of letters, including **Byron**, **Thomas Moore**, **Shelley** and **Charles Lamb**. He was imprisoned with his brother for two years (1813–15) for libeling the Prince Regent (the future **George IV**). Hunt published his own romance, *The Story of Rimini* in 1816. He also founded and edited *The Indicator* (1819–21).

“ ”

If you are ever at a loss to support a flagging conversation, introduce the subject of eating.

*1851 **Table-Talk**, "Eating."*

Hunt, (Richard) Tim(othy) 1943– •*English biologist and Nobel Prize winner*• He was born in Neston, Cheshire, and studied at Clare College, Cambridge. In 1991 he became principal scientist at the Imperial Cancer Research Fund's Clare Hall Laboratories, Hertfordshire, and in 2001 shared the Nobel Prize for physiology or medicine with **Lee Hartwell** and **Paul M Nurse** for their discoveries of key regulators of the cell cycle, allowing more accurate cancer diagnostics.

Hunter, Evan, *originally* **Salvatore A Lambino**, *pseudonym* **Ed McBain** 1926– •*US novelist*• Born and educated in New York City, he served in the US Navy and taught before concentrating on his career as a novelist. Writing under his pseudonym Ed McBain, he is renowned for his "87th Precinct" thrillers. As Evan Hunter he is best known for *The Blackboard Jungle* (1954), which was acclaimed for its realism and topicality. Later publications include *Criminal Conversation* (1994, written as Hunter) and *Romance* (1995, written as McBain).

Hunter, Holly 1958– •*US actress*• Born in Conyers, Georgia, she studied at Carnegie Mellon University, Pittsburgh, and established herself on screen with the comedies *Raising Arizona* (1987) and *Broadcast News* (1987). A diminutive figure, she won Best Actress Emmy awards for her roles as an unwed mother in *Roe vs Wade* (1989) and an obsessive Houston housewife in *The Positively True Adventures of the Alleged Texas Cheerleader-Murdering Mom* (1993), and received a Best Actress Academy Award for her performance in *The Piano* (1993). Other films include *The Firm* (1993), the controversial *Crash* (1996) and *O Brother, Where Art Thou?* (2000).

Hunter, John 1728–93 •*Scottish physiologist and surgeon*• He was born in Long Calderwood, East Kilbride, and from 1748 to 1759 assisted at the London anatomy school run by his elder brother, **William Hunter**. He then studied surgery at St George's and St Bartholomew's Hospitals, London, and in 1760 entered the army as staff surgeon. In 1776 he became surgeon extraordinary to King **George III**, and in 1790 surgeon general to the army. An indefatigable researcher, he built up huge collections of plant and animal specimens. His museum grew to contain an astonishing 13,600 preparations, and on his death it was bought by the government and subsequently administered by the Royal College of Surgeons in London. In the field of human pathology, Hunter investigated a wide range of subjects, from venereal disease and embryology to blood and inflammation. He developed new methods of treating aneurysm, and succeeded in grafting animal tissues. His *Natural History of Human Teeth* (1771–78) revolutionized dentistry. His biological studies included work on the habits of bees and silkworms and the electrical discharges of fish. He trained many of the leading doctors and natural historians of the next generation, including **Edward Jenner**, and is considered the founder of scientific surgery.

Hunter, William 1718–83 •*Scottish anatomist and obstetrician*• Born in Long Calderwood, East Kilbride, he studied divinity for five years at the University of Glasgow, but in 1737 took up medicine, and was trained in anatomy at St George's Hospital, London. In 1764 he was appointed physician extraordinary to Queen **Charlotte Sophia**, and in 1768 he became the first Professor of Anatomy to the Royal Academy. In 1770 he built a house with an amphitheater for lectures, a dissecting room, and a museum. His Hunterian museum was bequeathed finally to the University of Glasgow. His massive contributions to anatomy and obstetrics included his chief work, *The Anatomy of the Human Gravid Uterus* (1774). He was the brother of **John Hunter**.

Huntington, Collis Potter 1821–1900 •*US railway pioneer*• Born in Harwinton, Connecticut, he was a peddler and shopkeeper. He went to California in 1849 and pioneered the Central Pacific Railway, which was completed in 1869, as well as the Southern Pacific (1881). His nephew, Henry Edwards Huntington (1850–1927), also a railroad executive, acquired an immense art collection and library, which he presented to the nation in 1922, together with his estate at Pasadena, California.

Hunty, Shirley Barbara de la *See* **de la Hunty, Shirley Barbara**

Hunyady, János Corvinus or **John** c. 1387–1456 •*Hungarian warrior and statesman*• Born apparently in Wallachia (modern Romania), the Holy Roman Emperor **Sigismund** granted him Hunyad in Transylvania in 1409. He spent most of his life crusading against the Turks, whom he expelled from Transylvania (1442). Despite defeats at Varna (1444) and Kosovo (1448), in 1456 he routed the Turkish armies besieging Belgrade, thus securing a 70-year peace and becoming a national hero. During the reign of Ladislaus V (1446–53), he acted as governor of the kingdom. He left two sons, Ladislaus, who was beheaded on a charge of conspiracy, and Matthias Corvinus, who became king of Hungary as Matthias I.

Huppert, Isabelle 1955– •*French film actress*• Born in Paris, she studied acting at the Conservatoire National d'Art Dramatique in Paris, and made her film debut in *Faustine et le bel été* (1971, UK title *Faustine*). She won international acclaim for her performance in *La Dentellière* (1977, UK title *The Lacemaker*), which she followed by winning the Best Actress prize at the Cannes Film Festival for *Violette Nozière* (1978). Other films include *Coup de foudre* (1983, *At First Sight*), *Une affaire de femmes* (1988, *Story of Women*), *La vengeance d'une femme* (1990, *A Woman's Revenge*), *Madame Bovary* (1991), *Amateur* (1994) and *La Cérémonie* (1995). She made her British debut in *Mary Stewart* (1996).

Hurd (of Westwell), Douglas Richard Hurd, Baron 1930– •*English Conservative politician*• He was born in Marlborough, Wiltshire, the son of Baron Hurd, and educated at Eton and Trinity College, Cambridge, before joining the diplomatic service in 1952. After posts in Beijing (Peking), New York and Rome, he moved into active politics, becoming political secretary to **Edward Heath** (1968–74). As Member of Parliament for Mid-Oxon (1974–83) and then Witney (1983–97), he held junior posts in **Margaret Thatcher**'s government, including Northern Ireland Secretary (1984–85), Home Secretary in 1985 and, unexpectedly, Foreign Secretary (1989–95). He was unsuccessful in the leadership contest following Thatcher's resignation (1990). After leaving the Cabinet he turned to writing political thrillers and was awarded a life peerage in 1997.

Hurst, Sir Geoff(rey) Charles 1941– •*English soccer player*• Born in Ashton-under-Lyne, Lancashire, he became famous as the only player ever to score three goals in a World Cup Final, against West Germany at Wembley in 1966. This achievement resulted in the commentator Kenneth Wolstenholme's remark: "There are people on the pitch ... they think it's all over ... it is now!" Hurst scored 24 goals for England in 49 appearances. Most of his career was spent with West Ham United before he moved on to Stoke City. He was knighted in 1998.

Hurston, Zora Neale c. 1901–60 •*US novelist*• She was born in Eatonville, Florida, and described her early life as "a series of wanderings." She studied at Howard University, Washington DC, where she began to write and later studied cultural anthropology at Barnard College and Columbia University, and became a prominent figure in the Harlem Renaissance. Her best-known novel is *Their Eyes Were Watching God* (1937). Other works include *Jonah's Gourd Vine* (1934) and *Seraph on the Suwanee* (1948). Her last years were plagued by ill health and she died in poverty. **Alice Walker**'s collection of her writings, *I Love Myself When I Am Laughing*, was published in 1979.

Hurt, John 1940– •*English actor*• Born in Chesterfield, Derbyshire, he won a scholarship to study at the Royal Academy of Dramatic Art. An incisive character actor, drawn to roles on the fringes of mainstream society, his notable film work includes *A Man for All Seasons* (1966), *Midnight Express* (1978), *Alien* (1979), *The Elephant Man* (1980), *Scandal* (1989) and *Rob Roy* (1995). His stage performances include *The Dwarfs* (1963) and *Travesties* (1974). He portrayed Quentin Crisp in the television play *The Naked Civil Servant* (1974) and **Caligula** in the television series *I, Claudius* (1977).

Hurt, William 1950– •*US actor*• Born in Washington DC, he studied at the Juilliard School in New York. Describing himself as a "character actor in a leading man's body," he built a substantial reputation in the theater, winning an Obie award for *My Life* (1977) before making his film debut in *Altered States* (1980). Testing himself with often unpredictable choices, he appeared in such films as *Body Heat* (1981) and *The Big Chill* (1983) and won an Academy Award as a gay prisoner in *Kiss of the Spiderwoman* (1985). He received further nominations for *Children of a Lesser God* (1986) and *Broadcast News* (1987). Frequently returning to the stage, he received a Tony nomination for his supporting performance as a drug addict in *Hurlyburly* (1984–85). More recent films include *Smoke* (1995) and *Artificial Intelligence: AI* (2001).

Hurtado, Miguel De La Madrid *See* **De La Madrid Hurtado, Miguel**

Hus, Jan *See* **Huss, John**

Husain, Saddam *See* **Hussein, Saddam**

Husák, Gustáv 1913–91 •*Czechoslovakian politician*• Born in Bratislava, he trained as a lawyer and was a member of the Resistance movement during World War II. After the war he worked for the Slovak Communist Party (SCP) before being imprisoned on political grounds in 1951. Rehabilitated in 1960, he became First Secretary of the SCP and deputy premier in 1968. After the Soviet invasion of 1968, he replaced **Alexander Dubček** as leader of the Communist Party of Czechoslovakia (CCP) in 1969. He became state president in 1975 and, pursuing a policy of cautious **Brezhnev**ite reform, remained the dominant figure in Czechoslovakia until his retirement in 1987. He was replaced as state president by **Vaclav Havel** in 1989.

Huss, John, *also called* **Jan Hus** c. 1369–1415 •*Bohemian religious reformer*• Born in Husinetz (now Husinec, Czech Republic), from which his name derives, he studied at the University of Prague. In 1398 he began to lecture on theology at Prague. In 1408 he defied a papal bull which alleged heretical teaching by continuing to preach, and was excommunicated in 1411. After writing his main work, *De Ecclesia* (1413, "On the Church"), he was called before a general council at Constance, but he refused to recant and was burned at the stake. The anger of his followers in Bohemia (Hussites) led to the Hussite Wars, which lasted until the mid-15th century.

Hussein or **Husain, Saddam** 1937– •*Iraqi dictator*• Born in Tikrit, near Baghdad, into a peasant family, and educated in Baghdad, he joined the Arab Ba'ath Socialist Party in 1957. In 1959 he escaped to Syria and Egypt after being sentenced to death for the attempted assassination of the head of state, General **Kassem**. He returned to Iraq in 1963 after the downfall of Kassem, but in 1964 he was imprisoned for plotting to overthrow the new regime. After his release (1966) he took a leading part in the 1968 revolution that ousted the civilian government and established a Revolutionary Command Council (RCC), of which he became vice president. In 1979 he became RCC Chairman and state president. Ruthless in the pursuit of his objectives, he fought a bitter war against his neighbor, Iran (1980–88), to gain control of the Strait of Hormuz, and dealt harshly with Kurdish rebels seeking a degree of autonomy. In July 1990 his army invaded Kuwait, bringing about UN sanctions against Iraq and later the Gulf War, in which he was opposed by a UN-backed Allied force, involving US, European and Arab troops. Hussein's troops surrendered in February 1991 following Operation Desert Storm. He was immediately confronted with a civil war as his army retreated through southern Iraq, but managed to contain the uprising there. In accordance with the terms of the peace treaty agreed to at the end of the Gulf War, a special UN delegation was sent to inspect chemical, biological and nuclear sites. Initially Iraq refused to disclose all its nuclear sites, but when a resumed air offensive was threatened by the allies, the Iraqis supplied the necessary information. Hussein later defied UN ceasefire resolutions and made further raids on Iran in 1993. UN inspectors were sent to Iraq again in 2002, but were withdrawn in March 2003 when a US-led coalition began military action and Hussein was overthrown and later captured.

Hussein ibn 'Ali 1856–1931 •*King of the Hejaz, and founder of the modern Arab Hashemite dynasty*• He was born in Constantinople (Istanbul) and was emir of Mecca (1908–16). After first siding with the Turks and Germany in World War I, on the advice of **T E Lawrence** he went over to the side of the Allies, declaring his support for Arab independence (1916), and was chosen first king of the Hejaz. He refused to recognize the mandatory regimes imposed on Syria, Palestine and Iraq by the Allies (1919). He was defeated by the Wahhabi leader, **Ibn Saud**, was forced to abdicate (1924), and was exiled in Cyprus. He was the father of King **Faisal I** and great-grandfather of King **Hussein** of Jordan.

Hussein (ibn Talal) 1935–99 •*King of Jordan*• He was born in Amman, the great-grandson of **Hussein ibn Ali** and cousin of King **Faisal II** of Iraq. He was educated at Victoria College, Alexandria, and in Great Britain at Harrow and Sandhurst. In 1952 he succeeded his father, King Talal, who was deposed because of mental illness. His marriage (1955) to Princess Dina was later dissolved, and in 1961 he married an English girl, Antoinette Gardiner, given the title Princess Muna, who in 1962 gave birth to an heir, Abdullah. In 1972 he divorced Princess Muna and married Alia Baha Eddin Toukan, who was killed in an air accident in 1977. The following year he married Lisa Halaby. The young king maintained a vigorous and highly personal rule in the face of the political upheavals inside and outside his exposed country, on the one side favoring the Western powers, particularly Great Britain, on the other pacifying Arab nationalism. He lost the West Bank to Israel (1967) and had problems coping with Palestine Liberation Organization (PLO) guerrillas based in Jordan, who wanted a firmer anti-Israeli policy. From 1979 he was reconciled with **Yasser Arafat**, renounced Jordan's claim to the West Bank (1988) and attempted to prevent the outbreak of the Gulf War (1990). After the war he distanced himself from **Saddam Hussein**, and signed a peace treaty with Israel in Washington in 1994. He was succeeded by his son Abdullah.

Husserl, Edmund Gustav Albrecht 1859–1938 •*German philosopher and founder of the school of phenomenology*• Born of Jewish parents in Prossnitz in the Austrian empire, he studied mathematics in Berlin, psychology in Vienna and taught at the Universities of Halle (1887), Göttingen (1901) and Freiburg (1916). While at Göttingen he developed phenomenology (a philosophy concerned with describing personal experiences without seeking to arrive at metaphysical explanations of them). His works include *Ideen zu einer reinen Phänomenologie und phänomenologischen Philosophie* (1913, Eng trans *Ideas: General Introduction to Pure Phenomenology*, 1913). His approach greatly influenced philosophers in the US and in Germany, particularly **Martin Heidegger**, and helped give rise to Gestalt psychology.

Hussey (of North Bradley), Marmaduke James Hussey, Baron 1923– •*English manager and administrator*• Educated at Rugby and Trinity College, Oxford, his Oxford career was interrupted by World War II, when he served as platoon commander in the Grenadier Guards. He was wounded at Anzio and had his leg amputated at a German field hospital. After his recovery he completed his degree at Oxford and in 1949 joined Associated Newspapers as a management trainee. He went to Times Newspapers in 1971 and presided over the confrontation with the print union that led to the year's closure of *The Times* and the *Sunday Times* (1978). In 1986 he became chairman of the BBC. He was awarded a life peerage in 1996.

Huston, Anjelica 1951– •*US film actress*• Born in Los Angeles, California, the daughter of director **John Huston** and granddaughter of actor Walter Huston (1884–1950), she was brought up in County Galway, Ireland, and educated in London. Her film debut was in her father's *A Walk with Love and Death* (1969). She gained critical acclaim by winning a Best Supporting Actress Academy Award for her part in *Prizzi's Honor* (1985). Her films include *The Dead* (1987), *Crimes and Misdemeanors* (1989), *The Grifters* (1990), *The Addams Family* (1991) and *The Royal Tenenbaums* (2001). She has also moved behind the camera to direct *Bastard Out of Carolina* (1996) and *Agnes Browne* (1999).

Huston, John Marcellus 1906–87 •*US film director*• Born in Nevada, Missouri, son of the actor Walter Huston (1884–1950), his early career involved stints as a boxer in California, a competitive horseman in Mexico and a journalist in New York. He moved to Hollywood in 1930, where he acted and wrote or cowrote screenplays including *Murders in the Rue Morgue* (1932), *Juarez* (1939) and *High Sierra* (1941). His first film as director, *The Maltese Falcon* (1941), was followed by wartime documentaries and a series of successful films, including *The Treasure of the Sierra Madre* (1947; Best Director and Best Screenplay Academy Awards), *Key Largo* (1948), *The African Queen* (1951), *Moulin Rouge* (1952), *The Misfits* (1960), *The Man Who Would Be King* (1975) and *The Dead* (1987). Particularly adept at high adventure and film noir, he showed a consistent interest in quests that proved fruitless, or in men beset by delusions of grandeur. In later life a prolific actor, he displayed reptilian patriarchal menace in *Chinatown* (1974). He married five times and his children Danny, Tony and **Anjelica** have followed in his footsteps.

“ ”

A work of art doesn't dare you to realize it. It germinates and gestates by itself.

1982 Reply to a tribute from the Directors Guild of America. Reported in ***Variety****, April 26.*

Hutchins, William *See* **Tyndale, William**

Hutchinson, Anne, *née* **Marbury** c.1590–1643 •*New England colonist and religious leader*• Born in Lincolnshire, England, the daughter of a dissenting clergyman, she became a follower of **John Cotton**, and in 1634 she emigrated with her husband and family to Boston, Massachusetts. By 1636 she was holding religious meetings in her home, but the leaders of the Massachusetts Bay Colony saw Hutchinson's emphasis on the passivity of the soul before the visitation of the Holy Spirit as heretical. Tried and convicted by the General Court and banished from the colony, she set up a democracy with friends and family on the island of Aguidneck. After her husband's death (1642) she moved to a new settlement in what is now Pelham Bay in New York State, where she and all but one of her family of 15 were murdered by Indians.

Hutton, James 1726–97 •*Scottish geologist*• Born in Edinburgh, he studied medicine in Edinburgh, Paris and Leiden before becoming interested in geology. He returned to Edinburgh in 1768 and joined an active intellectual group which included **Joseph Black** and **Adam Ferguson**. Hutton developed his theories about the earth over a number of years as a result of many journeys into Scotland, England and Wales, and finally presented his ideas before the Royal Society of Edinburgh in *A Theory of the Earth* (1785; expanded, vols 1 and 2 1795, vol 3 1799). In this he demonstrated that the internal heat of the earth caused intrusions of molten rock into the crust and that granite was the product of the cooling of molten rock and not the earliest chemical precipitate of the primeval ocean as advocated by **Abraham Werner** and others. This “Plutonist” versus “Neptunist” debate raged on for a considerable time after Hutton's death. His system of the earth recognized that most rocks were detrital in origin, having been produced by erosion from the continents, deposited on the sea floor, lithified by heat from below and then uplifted to form new continents. These uniformitarian ideas attracted strong opposition from **William Buckland** and associates from the English School of geology. Nevertheless, Hutton's ideas held firm to form the basis of modern geology.

Hutton, Sir Leonard, *known as* **Len Hutton** 1916–90 •*English cricket player*• Born in Fulneck, Yorkshire, he was a Yorkshire player throughout his career. He first played for England in 1937, and in the Oval Test against Australia in 1938, he scored a world record of 364 runs, which stood for 20 years. Renowned for the perfection of his batting technique, he made 129 centuries in his first-class career. After World War II he captained England in 23 Test matches. Under his captaincy England regained the Ashes from Australia in the Test series of 1953, and retained them during the Australian tour of 1954–55, thus ending 20 years of Australian supremacy. He retired in 1956 and was knighted that year.

Huxley, Aldous Leonard 1894–1963 •*English novelist and essayist*• Born in Godalming, Surrey, the grandson of **T H Huxley**, he was educated at Eton and Balliol College, Oxford, where he studied English, not biology as he intended, because of an eye disease which made him nearly blind. It later compelled him to settle in the warmer climate of California (1937). His first novels were *Crome Yellow* (1921) and *Antic Hay* (1923), satires on postwar Great Britain. *Those Barren Leaves* (1925) and *Point Counter Point* (1928) were written in Italy. In 1932, in his most famous novel, *Brave New World*, Huxley warned of the dangers of moral anarchy in a scientific age by depicting a repulsive Utopia, achieved by scientifically breeding and conditioning a society of human robots. Despite the wit and satire, Huxley was in deadly earnest, as his essay *Brave New World Revisited* (1959) shows. From such pessimism Huxley took refuge in the exploration of mysticism. *Eyeless in Gaza* (1936) and *After Many a Summer* (1939, James Tait Black Memorial Prize) pointed the way to *Time Must Have a Stop* (1944), in which he attempted to describe a person's state of mind at the moment of, and just after, death. *The Doors of Perception* (1954) and *Heaven and Hell* (1956) explore a controversial shortcut to mysticism, the drug mescalin. *Island* (1962) is a more optimistic Utopian novel. He also wrote numerous essays on related topics, biographies, and a famous study in sexual hysteria, *The Devils of Loudun* (1952).

Huxley, Sir Andrew Fielding 1917– •*English physiologist and Nobel Prize winner*• A grandson of **T H Huxley** and the half brother of **Aldous** and **Julian Huxley**, he was born in London and studied natural sciences at Trinity College and at the Physiological Laboratory at Cambridge. Among numerous teaching and research posts he became Joddrell Professor of Physiology (1960–69) and Royal Society Research Professor (1969–83) at University College London. With **Alan Hodgkin** he provided a physicochemical explanation for the conduction of impulses in nerve fibers, and (1950) changed direction to study muscle physiology, devising a special microscope with which to study the contraction and relaxation of muscle fibers. He served as president of the Royal Society (1980–85), was knighted in 1974 and was awarded the Order of Merit in 1983. In 1963 he shared the Nobel Prize for physiology or medicine with Hodgkin and Sir **John Eccles**.

Huxley, Elspeth Josceline, *née* **Grant** 1907–97 •*English novelist*• She was born in Kenya, and wrote many novels and essays on her native land, its history, and its problems. Her best-known novel is *The Flame Trees of Thika* (1959), which deals with her childhood, as do *The Mottled Lizard* (1962) and *Death of an Aryan* (1986, also known as *The African Poison Murders*). She published a biography of Sir **Peter Scott** in 1993 entitled *Peter Scott: Painter and Naturalist*. Her husband, Gervas Huxley (1894–1971), was a grandson of **T H Huxley**.

Huxley, Hugh Esmor 1924– •*English biophysicist*• Born in Birkenhead, Merseyside, he studied natural sciences at Christ's College, Cambridge, graduating in 1943. In 1948 he joined the Molecular Biology Unit of the Medical Research Council (MRC) at Cambridge, and after a number of distinguished appointments returned to the MRC to become deputy director in 1977. From the 1950s he was a central figure in developing the model of muscle action in which muscle filaments slide past each other to produce contraction. He defined the detailed structure of the muscle cell, and analyzed the cellular location of the major proteins involved in contraction. He was Professor of Biology at Brandeis University from 1987 to 1997 (now emeritus) and director of the Rosenstiel Basic Medical Sciences Research Center there from 1988 to 1994.

Huxley, Sir Julian Sorell 1887–1975 •*English biologist and humanist*• The grandson of **T H Huxley** and brother of **Aldous Huxley**, he was educated at Eton and Balliol College, Oxford, was professor at the Rice Institute, Texas (1913–16), and after World War I became Professor of Zoology at King's College, London (1925–27), Fullerian professor at the Royal Institution (1926–29), and secretary to the Zoological Society of London (1935–42). His writings include *Essays of a Biologist* (1923), *Religion Without Revelation* (1927), *The Science of Life* (with **H G Wells**, 1931), *Evolutionary Ethics* (1943) and *Towards a New Humanism* (1957). He extended the application of his scientific knowledge to political and social problems, formulating a pragmatic ethical theory of “evolutionary humanism,” based on the principle of natural selection. He was the first director general of UNESCO (1946–48).

Huxley, T(homas) H(enry) 1825–95 •*English biologist*• He was born in Ealing, Middlesex, the son of a schoolmaster. He studied medicine at Charing Cross Hospital, and entered the Royal Navy medical service. As assistant surgeon on HMS *Rattlesnake* on a surveying expedition to the South Seas (1846–50), he collected and studied specimens of marine animals, particularly plankton. From 1854 to 1885 he was Professor of Natural History at the Royal School of Mines in London, and made significant contributions to paleontology and comparative anatomy. He was best known as the foremost scientific supporter of **Charles Darwin**'s theory of evolution by natural selection during the heated debates which followed its publication, tackling Bishop **Samuel Wilberforce** in a celebrated exchange at the British Association meeting in Oxford (1860), when he declared that he would rather be descended from an ape than a bishop. He influenced the teaching of biology and science in schools as a member of the London Schools Board. Later he turned to theology and philosophy, and coined the term "agnostic" for his views. He wrote *Lay Sermons* (1870), *Evolution and Ethics* (1893) and *Science and Education* (published posthumously in 1899).

Hu Yaobang (Hu Yao-pang) 1915–89 •*Chinese politician*• Born into a poor peasant family in Hunan province, he joined the Red Army in 1929 and took part in the Long March (1934–36). He held a number of posts under **Deng Xiaoping** before becoming head of the Communist Youth League (1952–67). During the Cultural Revolution (1966–69) he was purged, and did not return to high office until 1978, when he joined the Communist Party's politburo. He was promoted to party leader in 1981, but dismissed in 1987 for his relaxed handling of a wave of student unrest. Popularly revered as a liberal reformer, his death triggered an unprecedented wave of prodemocracy demonstrations.

Huygens, Christiaan 1629–93 •*Dutch physicist*• He was born in The Hague, the second son of the poet Constantyn Huygens (1596–1687). He studied at Leiden and Breda Universities, and his mathematical *Theoremata* was published in 1651. In 1655 he discovered the rings and fourth satellite of Saturn, using a refracting telescope he constructed with his brother. He later constructed the pendulum clock, based on the suggestion of **Galileo** (1657), and developed the latter's doctrine of accelerated motion under gravity. He discovered the laws of collision of elastic bodies at the same time as John Wallis (1616–1703) and Sir **Christopher Wren**, and improved the air pump. In optics he first propounded the wave theory of light, and discovered polarization. The principle of Huygens is a part of the wave theory. He was, after **Isaac Newton**, the greatest scientist of the second half of the 17th century.

Huysmans, J(oris) K(arl) 1848–1907 •*French novelist*• He was born in Paris of Dutch descent, and his works reflect many aspects of the spiritual and intellectual life of late 19th-century France. His early ultrarealism is reflected in such works as *Les Sœurs Vatard* (1879, "The Vatard Sisters"). His best-known work, *À rebours* (1884, Eng trans *Against Nature*, 1959), deals with a decadent, aesthetic hero who turns his back on the real world and constructs his own world of extreme artifice; it was much admired by **Oscar Wilde** and his circle, and established Huysmans as a leading light in the Decadent movement of the period. Later works include *Là-bas* (1891, "Down There") and *En Route* (1892).

Huysum, Jan van 1682–1749 •*Dutch painter*• Born in Amsterdam, the son of the painter Justus van Huysum (1659–1716), he painted conventional landscapes. His fruit and flower pieces, however, are distinguished for exquisite finish and are represented in the Louvre, Paris, and Vienna. A brother, Jacob (1680–1740), also a painter, worked in London.

Hyde, Edward *See* **Clarendon, 1st Earl of**

Hyder, Ali *See* **Haidar Ali**

Hyman, Libbie Henrietta 1888–1969 •*US zoologist*• Born in Des Moines, Iowa, she studied zoology at the University of Chicago (1906–10) and remained there as a research assistant until 1931. She wrote *A Laboratory Manual for Elementary Zoology* (1919) and *A Laboratory Manual for Comparative Vertebrate Anatomy* (1929), later editions of which are still in use. Her magnum opus was a series of comprehensive volumes on the invertebrates (*The Invertebrates*, 6 vols, 1940–68) which dealt with the protozoa, coelenterates, flatworms, nematodes, echinoderms and molluscs.

Hypatia c. 370–415 AD •*Greek philosopher*• The first notable female astronomer and mathematician, she taught in Alexandria and became head of the Neo-Platonist school there. She was the daughter of Theon, a writer and commentator on mathematics, with whom she collaborated, and was herself the author of commentaries on mathematics and astronomy, though none of these survives. She drew pupils from all parts of the Greek world, Christian as well as pagan. **Cyril**, Archbishop of Alexandria, resented her influence and she was murdered by a Christian mob he may have incited to riot.

Hyperides or **Hypereides** 389–322 BC •*Athenian orator and statesman*• He became a professional speechwriter, and earned large sums. He opposed peace with **Philip II** of Macedonia, and so supported **Demosthenes** until after the death of Philip and during the early portion of **Alexander the Great**'s career. He promoted the Lamian War against Macedonia (323–322 BC) after the death of Alexander, for which he was executed by the Macedonian general Antipater (398–319 BC). Although Hyperides was admired and studied in Roman times, it was not until 1847 that papyri containing four of his speeches were discovered. In these Hyperides is clear, fascinating, witty and ironic.

Hyrcanus I, John c. 134–104 BC •*High priest of Israel and possibly Syrian subject king*• He was the son of the high priest Simon Maccabaeus (see **Maccabees**), and in the line of Hasmonean priestly rulers. Hyrcanus consolidated his own hold over Israel, destroyed the Samaritan temple on Mount Gerizim, and forced the Idumeans to adopt Judaism. Eventually he supported the Sadduceans against the Pharisees. He was a just and enlightened ruler, and of his five sons, Aristobulus and Alexander became king.

Hyrcanus II d. 30 BC •*High priest of Israel*• He was the grandson of **Hyrcanus I** and son of Alexander. On the death of his father (76 BC) he was appointed high priest by his mother, Alexandra, who ruled Judea till her death (67). He then warred for power with his younger brother Aristobulus, with varying fortune until Aristobulus was poisoned in 49. In 47 **Julius Caesar** made **Antipater** of Idumaea Procurator of Judea with supreme power, and a son of Aristobulus, with Parthian help, captured Hyrcanus, and took him to Seleucia. But when **Herod** the Great, son of Antipater, came to power, the aged Hyrcanus was invited home to Jerusalem, where he lived in peace until, suspected of intriguing against Herod, he was put to death.

Iacocca, Lee (Lido Anthony) 1924– •*US businessman*• Born in Allentown, Pennsylvania, he studied engineering at Lehigh and Princeton Universities, and worked for the Ford Motor Company (1946–78), rising to become president in 1970. He then joined the troubled Chrysler Corporation in 1978, steering the company back to profitability and health. He published a best-selling autobiography (with William Kovak), *Iacocca* (1985), and a sequel, *Talking Straight* (1989).

Ibáñez, Vicente Blasco 1867–1928 •*Spanish novelist*• He was born in Valencia and studied law at the University of Madrid, and his works deal in realistic fashion with provincial life and social revolution. Notable among them are *La barraca* (1899, Eng trans *The Cabin*, 1919), *Sangre y arena* (1908, Eng trans *Blood and Sand*, 1913), and *Los cuatro jinetes del Apocalipsis* (1916, Eng trans *The Four Horsemen of the Apocalypse*, 1918), which vividly portrays World War I and earned him international fame.

Ibarruri (Gómez), (Isidora) Dolores, *known as* **La Pasionaria** 1895–1989 •*Spanish writer, Communist orator and politician*• Born in Gallarta, in Vizcaya province, she joined the Socialist Party in 1917 and worked as a journalist using the pseudonym La Pasionaria (the passion flower). She helped to found the Spanish Communist Party in 1920 and was a member of the Central Committee from 1930. She was Spanish delegate to the Third International (1933, 1935), founded the Anti-Fascist Women's League in 1934 and was elected to the Cortes (the legislative assembly) in 1936. During the Spanish Civil War (1936–39) she became legendary for her passionate exhortations to the Spanish people to fight against the Fascist forces, declaring that "It is better to die on your feet than to live on your knees." When **Franco** came to power in 1939 she took refuge in the USSR, returning to Spain in 1977 after his death. As Communist deputy for Asturias she reentered the National Assembly at the age of 81.

Ibn al-'Arabi 1165–1240 •*Arab mystic poet*• Born in Murcia, Spain, he was known as the "sultan of the Gnostics." Moving to Seville as a child, he studied there under Andalusian spiritual masters. Serious illness, in which he encountered visions, made him abandon ordinary life and his wife, and on his recovery he took to pilgrimage, traveling to Jerusalem and Mecca. In Mecca he wrote *The Interpreter of Longings*, poetry dedicated to a Persian sheikh's daughter. A great influence on Sufi philosophy, his unorthodoxy was viewed by some with suspicion. His many writings include a commentary on the Koran, *Kitab al-futuhat al-Makkiyya* ("Meccan Revelations"), and *Kitab fusus al-hikam* (1229, "The Wisdom of the Prophets").

Ibn Battutah or **Batuta** 1304–68 •*Arab traveler and geographer*• Born in Tangiers, North Africa, he spent 30 years (1325–54) traveling. He covered all the Muslim countries, visiting Mecca, Persia, Mesopotamia, Asia Minor, Bukhoro, India, China, Sumatra, southern Spain and Timbuktu. He then settled in Fez, and dictated the entertaining history of his journeys, the *Rihlah* ("Travels"), published with a French translation in 1855–59.

Ibn Daud, Abraham c. 1100–c. 1180 •*Spanish-Jewish philosopher*• Born in Toledo, he was the first to draw systematically on **Aristotle**. His *Al-aqida al Rafia* (1160, "The Exalted Faith") argues the essential harmony of philosophy and the Torah, and his *Sefer hak-kabbalah* (1161, "Book of Tradition") was an influential history demonstrating the tradition of Rabbinic authority from **Moses** to his own day.

Ibn Gabirol *See* **Avicebrón**

Ibn Khaldun 1332–1406 •*Arab philosopher, historian and politician*• Born in Tunis, he was widely involved in political intrigues before he turned to history, eventually becoming a college president and judge in Cairo. He wrote a monumental history of the Arabs, best known by its *Muqaddima*, or introduction, in which he explains the rise and fall of states by the waxing and waning of the spirit of *asabiya* ("solidarity").

Ibn Rushd *See* **Averroës**

Ibn Saud, *in full* **Ibn Abd al-Rahman al-Saud** 1880–1953 •*First king of Saudi Arabia*• Born in Riyadh, he followed his family into exile (1890) and was brought up in Kuwait. In 1901 he succeeded his father and with a small band of followers set out to reconquer the family domains from the Rashidi rulers, an aim which he achieved with British recognition (1927). He officially became the king of Saudi Arabia in 1932. The economic boom produced by oil undermined the traditional spartan Wahhabi lifestyle of the royal family, much to his regret. He sired 45 sons and over 200 daughters. His son Saud succeeded his father in 1953, only to be deposed by his brother Faisal in 1964.

Ibn Sīnā *See* **Avicenna**

Ibn Zohr *See* **Avenzoar**

Ibrahim, Abdullah, *formerly* **Dollar Brand** 1934– •*South African jazz pianist*• Born in Cape Town to Bushman and Basotho parents, he formed the Jazz Epistles group which recorded the country's first Black jazz album in 1960. He moved to Switzerland for political reasons and was heard there by **Duke Ellington** (1962), who invited him to work in the US. Since then, he has worked as a soloist and leader in the US and Europe, notably in the 1980s with his septet Ekaya (Home). Ibrahim, who also plays cello, soprano saxophone and flute, adopted his Muslim name in the 1970s. He is remarkable for his jazz interpretations of the melodies and rhythms of his African childhood.

Ibsen, Henrik 1828–1906 •*Norwegian dramatist generally regarded as the founder of modern prose drama*• He was born in Skien. He took his first job as a chemist's assistant in Grimstad (1844–50), with the intention of studying medicine, and during this time he wrote his first play, *Catilina* (1850, Eng trans *Catiline*), which was, however, rejected by the Christiania Theater. He worked briefly on a student journal in Christiania (Oslo), then was given a post as stage director and resident playwright at Ole Bull's Theatre, Bergen (1851), for which he wrote five conventional romantic dramas. In 1857 he was appointed director of the Norwegian Theater in Christiania, having just begun work on what would be his first play of significance, *Kongsemnerne* (1863, Eng trans *The Pretenders*), based on a historical Norwegian theme, in the manner of **Schiller**. In 1862 he wrote *Kjaerlighedens Komedie* (Eng trans *Love's Comedy*), on a satirical theme of marriage as a millstone to idealism. The theater went bankrupt the following year and, disillusioned with his homeland, Ibsen went into voluntary exile for 27 years, to Rome, Dresden and Munich (1864–91), where he wrote the bulk of his dramas. He published the dramatic poem *Brand* in 1866, which gave him his first major success, as well as the award of a government pension. The existentialist *Peer Gynt* (also in rhyming couplets) followed in 1867, and a third historical drama, *Kejser og Galilaer* (Eng trans *Emperor and Galilean*), in 1873. He then produced his realistic plays, concerned with social and political issues, which revolutionized European drama and on which his towering reputation rests: *Samfundets støtter* (1877, Eng trans *Pillars of Society*); *Et dukkehjem* (1879, Eng trans *A Doll's House*); *Gengangere* (1881, Eng trans *Ghosts*); *En folkefiende* (1882, Eng trans *An Enemy of the People*); *Vildanden* (1884, Eng trans *The Wild Duck*), *Rosmersholm* (1886), *Fruen fra havet* (1888, Eng trans *The Lady from the Sea*) and *Hedda Gabler* (1890). These plays caused a major stir among critics and audiences: Ibsen refused to provide happy endings and was often controversial in his subject matter (eg, his study of venereal, moral and societal disease in *Ghosts*). He returned to Norway in 1891, where he wrote his last plays. These are characterized by a strong emphasis on symbolism and the unconscious, as in *Bygmester Solness* (1892, Eng trans *The Master Builder*), *Lille Eyolf* (1894, Eng trans *Little Eyolf*), *John Gabriel Borkman* (1896) and *Naar vi døde vaagner* (1899, Eng trans *When We Dead Awaken*). In 1900 he suffered a stroke that ended his literary career.

“ ”

Luftslotter,—de er så nemme at ty ind i, de. Og nemme at bygge også.
Castles in the air—they are so easy to take refuge in. And so easy to build, too.
*1892 **The Master Builder**, act 3.*

Ichikawa, Fusaye 1893–1981 •*Japanese feminist and politician*• Starting her working life as a teacher, she moved to Tokyo as a young woman and became involved in politics and feminism. She helped to found the New Women's Association (c. 1920), which successfully fought for the right of women to attend political meetings. During her time in the US (1921–24) she was impressed by the suffrage movement, and in 1924 formed the Women's Suffrage League in Japan. Following World War II she became head of the New Japan Women's League, which secured the vote for women in 1945. She campaigned against legalized prostitution and served in the Japanese Diet (1952–71). After her defeat in 1971 she was voted back into parliament in 1975 and 1980.

Iglesias, Pablo 1850–1925 •*Spanish politician and trade union leader*• He was the founder and father figure of both the Spanish Socialist Party (PSOE) and its trade union movement, the UGT. Moralistic, austere and cautious, he preached revolutionary ideas while practicing a pragmatic reformism. He became the Socialists' first deputy to the Cortes through the alliance with the Republicans in 1910, though the PSOE never surpassed seven seats before his death in 1925.

Ignatius of Antioch, St c. 35–c. 107 AD •*Syrian Christian prelate*• He was one of the apostolic Fathers, reputedly a disciple of **St John**, the second Bishop of Antioch. According to **Eusebius**, he died a martyr in Rome under **Trajan**. The *Ignatian Epistles*, whose authenticity was long controversial, were written on his way to Rome after his arrest. They provide valuable information on the nature of the early Church. His feast day is February 1.

Ignatius Loyola, St, *properly* **Iñigo López de Recalde** 1491–1556 •*Spanish soldier and founder of the Society of Jesus*• He was born at his ancestral castle of Loyola in the Basque province of Guipúzcoa. He became a soldier but was severely wounded in the leg. During his long convalescence, he read the lives of **Jesus** and the saints, which inspired him with an intense spiritual enthusiasm. He renounced military life, and in 1522 set out on an arduous pilgrimage to the Holy Land. He returned to Venice and Barcelona in 1524. He then resolved to prepare himself for the work of religious teaching. In 1534, with St **Francis Xavier** and four other associates, he founded the Society of Jesus. Loyola went to Rome in 1539, and submitted his proposed rule to Pope **Paul III**. The rule was approved in 1540, and next year the association elected Loyola its first general. From this point on he resided in Rome. He sent out missionaries to Japan, India and Brazil, and founded schools for training the young. He was beatified in 1609, and canonized in 1622. His feast day is July 31.

Ihimaera, Witi Tame 1944– •*New Zealand author*• Born in Gisborne, he became the first published Maori writer in English with his collection of short stories *Pounamu, Pounamu* (1972). In his following collections, *The New Net Goes Fishing* (1977) and *Dear Miss Mansfield: A Tribute to Kathleen Mansfield Beauchamp* (1989), he alludes to the Paheka (white settler) fantasy *The Wizard of Oz* in his exploration of Maori identity. He also wrote an epic novel, *The Matriarch* (1986). More recent works include *Nights in the Gardens of Spain* (1995).

Iliescu, Ion 1930– •*Romanian politician*• Born in Oltenita, Ilfov, and educated at Bucharest Polytechnic and in Moscow, he joined the Communist Party in 1953, and from 1949 to 1960 served on its central committee. In 1965 he began a three-year term as Head of Party Propaganda, and as a member of the central committee again from 1968 held office as First Secretary and Youth Minister (1967–71) and First Secretary of Jassy County (1974–79). In the wake of the 1989 revolution and the execution of **Nicolae Ceauşescu**, he became president of the National Salvation Front later that year, and of its successor, the Provisional Council for National Unity. He was president from 1990 to 1996, and was re-elected in 2000.

Illingworth, Ray(mond) 1932– •*English cricket player*• Born in Pudsey, West Yorkshire, he established a reputation as a batsman and spin bowler playing for Yorkshire, Leicestershire and England. He captained both Yorkshire and Leicestershire to the county championship and won a total of 66 Test caps (36 as England captain). After retiring as a player he served as team manager of Yorkshire (1979–84) and subsequently served (1994–97) as England manager and chairman of selectors.

Ilyushin, Sergei Vladimirovich 1894–1977 •*Soviet aircraft designer*• Born in the region of Vologda, he began flight training in 1917. He graduated from the Northeast Zhukovsky Air Force Academy in 1926, leading to his appointment in 1931 as director of the aircraft construction section of the Scientific and Technical Committee, Main Air Force Board. His first successful design, the TSKB-30 (1936), gained several records and was extensively used as a bomber in World War II. His other designs included the IL-2 Shturmovik dive-bomber (1939), the IL-28 jet bomber (1948), the IL-18 Moskva turboprop airliner (1957), the 182-passenger IL-62 jet of 1957 and its wide-bodied successor, the IL-86 airbus (350 passengers).

Imhotep 27th century BC •*Egyptian physician*• He was adviser to King Zoser (3rd dynasty), and probably the architect of the so-called Step Pyramid at Sakkara, near Cairo. In time he came to be revered as a sage, and during the Saite period (500 BC) he was worshiped as the life-giving son of Ptah, god of Memphis. The Greeks identified him with their own god of healing, Asclepius, because of his reputed knowledge of medicine. Many bronze figures of him have been discovered.

Imran Khan 1952– •*Pakistani cricket player*• He was born in Lahore and educated in England at Oxford. He played county cricket for Worcestershire and Sussex, and made his Test debut in 1971. He captained Pakistan on several occasions (1982–83, 1985–87, 1988–92), and led them to victory in the World Cup in 1992. He scored over 3,000 Test runs and took over 325 wickets in Test matches before announcing his retirement from cricket in 1992. His high-profile marriage to Jemima Goldsmith thrust him into the eyes of the media again in 1995, the year he entered Pakistani politics.

Inchbald, Elizabeth, *née* **Simpson** 1753–1821 •*English novelist, playwright and actress*• Born in Bury St Edmunds, the daughter of a farmer, she ran away to go on the stage and in 1772 married John Inchbald (d. 1779), an actor in London. From 1789 she made her name as a playwright. She was the author of 19 sentimental comedies, including *The Wedding Day* (1794) and *Lovers' Vows* (1798), the play which the Bertram children act in **Jane Austen**'s *Mansfield Park*. She also wrote the novels *A Simple Story* (1791) and *Nature and Art* (1796), and edited the 24-volume *The British Theatre* (1806–09).

Indiana, Robert, *originally* **Robert Clarke** 1928– •*US painter and graphic designer*• Born in New Castle, Indiana, he studied art in Indianapolis (1945–46), in Ithaca, New York, and at the Art Institute of Chicago before traveling to Great Britain in 1953. Settling in New York in 1956, he began making hard-edged abstract pictures and stenciled wooden constructions, which fall into the early Pop Art movement. His best-known images are based on the letters LOVE, as featured in his first one-man show in New York (1962). His other word-paintings have included HUG, ERR, DIE, and the 20-foot *EAT Sign* (1964, New York World Fair).

Indurain, Miguel 1964– •*Spanish cyclist*• Born in Villava, Navarre, he is the fourth of five cyclists who have won the Tour de France (1991–95) five times. His second win of the Giro d'Italia in 1993 ranks him among only six other cyclists ever to have won both events in the same year. As the leader of the Banesto team, he became the richest man in cycle racing and a national hero in Spain. He announced his retirement in 1997.

Inge, William Motter 1913–73 •*US playwright and novelist*• Born in Independence, Kansas, he was educated at the University of Kansas and George Peabody College forTeachers, and taught and wrote art criticism for the St Louis *Star-Times*. Outside the mainstream of US theater, he is nevertheless important for his plays *Come Back, Little Sheba* (1950), *Picnic* (1953, Pulitzer Prize), *Bus Stop* (1955) and *The Dark at the Top of the Stairs* (first produced as *Farther off from Heaven* in 1947 and revised in 1957).

Inge, William Ralph, *also known as* **Dean Inge** 1860–1954 •*English prelate and theologian*• Born in Crayke, Yorkshire, and educated at Eton and King's College, Cambridge, from 1911 to 1934 he was dean of St Paul's, earning for himself the sobriquet of "the Gloomy Dean" from his pessimism in sermons and newspaper articles. His popular books included *Outspoken Essays* (1919, 1922) and *Lay Thoughts of a Dean* (1926, 1931); his more serious works examined, among other things, Neo-Platonism and Christian mysticism.

" "

A man may build himself a throne of bayonets, but he cannot sit on it.
1923 ***Philosophy of Plotinus**, volume 2, lecture 22.*

Ingersoll, Robert Green 1833–99 •*US lawyer and orator*• He was born in Dresden, New York. In the Civil War he was colonel of a Union cavalry regiment, and in 1867 became attorney general of Illinois. A successful Republican orator, he was also noted for his agnostic lectures attacking Christian beliefs, and wrote numerous books, including *The Gods, and Other Lectures* (1876) and *Why I Am an Agnostic* (1896).

Inglis, Elsie Maud 1864–1917 •*Scottish surgeon and reformer*• Born in Naini Tal, India, she was one of the first women medical students at Edinburgh and Glasgow. In 1901, appalled at the lack of maternity facilities, she founded a maternity hospital in Edinburgh, completely staffed by women. In 1906 she founded the Scottish Women's Suffragette Federation, which sent two women ambulance units to France and Serbia in 1915. She set up three military hospitals in Serbia (1916), fell into Austrian hands, was repatriated, but in 1917 returned to Russia with a voluntary corps, which was withdrawn after the revolution.

Ingold, Sir Christopher Kelk 1893–1970 •*English chemist*• Born in London, he studied at the University of London and chemistry at Hartley University College, Southampton, and was appointed professor at the University of Leeds (1924) and University College London. He classified organic reactions according to the transition state (the energy level which the molecules have to reach in order to react), which provided a convincing model for organic reactions and explained many experimental observations. During the 1930s and 1940s he undertook a massive study of the mechanism of aromatic nitration. A notable aspect of his work was his use of physical techniques not then normally employed by organic chemists (isotope effects, molecular spectroscopy). His monumental work *Structure and Mechanism in Organic Chemistry* (1953) influenced chemists worldwide. He was knighted in 1958.

Ingrams, Richard Reid 1937– •*English journalist*• Born in Westcliffe-on-Sea, Essex, he was educated at Shrewsbury School and University College, Oxford, where he met many of his future colleagues. In 1962 he founded with **Peter Cook**, **Willie Rushton** and other new-wave satirists, the satirical magazine *Private Eye*, which he edited until 1986. He was television critic for the *Spectator* (1979–84), and has been a columnist for the *Observer* (1988–90, 1992–), and in 1992 he founded and became editor of *The Oldie*. He is the author or coauthor of numerous books, including *Dear Bill: The Collected Letters of Denis Thatcher* (1980), *You Might As Well Be Dead* (1986), and a biography of **Malcolm Muggeridge** (1995).

Ingres, Jean Auguste Dominique 1780–1867 •*French painter*• Born in Montauban, he studied at Toulouse Academy, and then he went to Paris in 1796 to study under **Jacques Louis David**. In 1801 he won the Prix de Rome with *Achilles Receiving the Ambassadors of Agamemnon* (École des Beaux-Arts), but quarreled with David and from 1806 to 1820 lived in Rome, where he began many of his famous nudes, including *La grande odalisque* (1814), *The Valpinçon Bather* (1808) and *La Source* (begun in 1807 but not completed until 1856), all in the Louvre, Paris. Many of the paintings he sent to Paris from Rome attracted vehement criticism, especially from **Eugène Delacroix**, whose work Ingres detested. The leading exponent of the classical tradition in France in the 19th century, Ingres painted with superb draftsmanship, but little interest in facial characteristics or color. He also painted historical subjects such as *The Oath to Louis XIII* for Montauban Cathedral. He returned to Paris in 1826 and was appointed professor at the Academy, but again suffered criticism for his paintings such as *The Martyrdom of St Symphorian* (1834, Autun Cathedral), and went off again to Italy (1834–41), becoming director of the Académie Française in Rome. *Vierge à l'hostie* (Louvre) and *Odalisque à l'esclave* reestablished him in Paris and he returned in triumph, was awarded the Legion of Honor (1855) and made a senator (1862).

Innes, (Ralph) Hammond 1913–98 •*English author and traveler*• Born in Horsham, Sussex, he worked as a journalist on the *Financial Times* (1934–40), then served with the Royal Artillery for the next six years, during which time he began writing adventure novels. The first, *Wreckers Must Breathe* (1940), was followed by over 30 books, many with exotic locations and a maritime theme, and several have been made into successful films. Among the most popular are *The Lonely Skier* (1947), *The Mary Deare* (1956) and *The Strode Adventurer* (1965). Other publications include *Target Antarctica* (1993) and *Delta Connection* (1996).

Inness, George 1825–94 •*US landscape artist*• Born near Newburgh, New York, he visited Italy and France and came under the influence of the Barbizon school. Among his best-known paintings are *Delaware Valley* (1865), *Peace and Plenty* (1865) and *Evening at Medfield, Massachusetts*, in the Metropolitan Museum of Art in New York, and *Rainbow after a Storm* in the Chicago Art Institute. His late style is typified by *Sunrise* (1887, Metropolitan Museum).

Innocent I, St AD 360–417 •*Italian pope*• He was born in Albano. His pontificate (AD 402–417), next to that of **Leo I** (the Great), is the most important for the relations of Rome to the other churches. He enforced the celibacy of the clergy, he maintained the right of the Bishop of Rome to judge appeals from other churches, and his letters contain many assertions of universal jurisdiction. During his reign, Rome was sacked (410) by **Alaric I**. His feast day is July 28.

Innocent III, *original name* **Lotario de' Conti di Segni** 1160–1216 •*Italian pope*• Born at Agnagni, he studied in Paris and Bologna. He succeeded Pope **Celestine** III, and his pontificate (from 1198) is regarded as the culminating point of the supremacy of the Roman see. He judged between rival emperors in Germany and had **Otto IV** deposed. He put England under an interdict and excommunicated King **John** for refusing to recognize **Stephen Langton** as Archbishop of Canterbury. In his time the Latin conquest of Constantinople (Istanbul) in the Fourth Crusade destroyed the pretensions of his Eastern rivals. He zealously repressed simony (the buying and selling of ecclesiastical benefices) and other abuses of the time. Under him the famous Fourth Lateran Council was held in 1215

Innocent IV, *original name* **Sinibaldo Fieschi** d. 1254 •*Italian pope*• Born in Genoa and trained in Bologna, he was unscrupulous in using patronage to construct his own power network, and his pontificate (from 1243) brought the struggle between the papacy and Emperor **Frederick II** to its climax. At Frederick's death (1250), Innocent sought to establish papal overlordship in Sicily. This was acknowledged by Frederick's illegitimate son **Manfred** who nevertheless led a revolt in 1254. Innocent also put the Inquisition on a permanent basis in Italy.

Innocent XI, *original name* **Benedetto Odescalchi** 1611–89 •*Italian pope*• Born in Como, he studied law at the University of Naples. Elected pope in 1676 despite the opposition of **Louis XIV** of France, he embarked on a policy of retrenchment and tried, with some success, to end the practice of nepotism, also seeking financial aid from Catholic princes. The consequence of these reforms was that he was able to put papal finances on a sufficiently sound footing to aid **John III Sobieski** of Poland and the Holy Roman Emperor, **Leopold I**, to break the Turkish siege of Vienna (1683). His relations with Louis XIV, however, were poor. Louis summoned a French synod, which affirmed the limitations of papal authority within France, and in retaliation, Innocent refused to confirm the promotion of any French clergy involved in the synod. In 1685 he further angered Louis by condemning his treatment of the Huguenots and, in 1688, by opposing his candidate for the archbishopric of Cologne. Louis's response was to occupy the papal enclave of Avignon.

Innocent XII, *original name* **Antonio Pignatelli** 1615–1700 •*Italian pope*• He was educated by Jesuits and was papal ambassador before becoming a cardinal in 1681. He became pope in 1691. He brought an end to the poor relations between **Louis XIV** of France and the papacy by persuading the latter to withdraw the Gallican Articles of 1682 and to relinquish the occupied papal enclave of Avignon. In return, Innocent championed the candidacy of Philippe of Anjou (Louis XIV's grandson, later **Philip V** of Spain) as the heir to the Spanish throne and acknowledged the French monarch's right to administer vacant sees. He condemned both Jansenism (1696) and Quietism (1699), and worked to combat nepotism, notably in the bull *Romanum decet pontificem* (1692).

Innocent XIII, *original name* **Michelangelo dei Conti** 1655–1724 •*Italian pope*• A former papal ambassador to Switzerland and Portugal and a cardinal from 1706, he became pope in 1721. He invested the Holy Roman Emperor Charles VI with sovereignty over Naples (1721), and recognized **James Edward Stuart** (the Old Pretender) as king of England. Although he was hostile toward the Jansenists, he was also distrustful of the Jesuits, taking particular issue with modified "Chinese rites," which they employed with some success to attract converts in Asia.

Inönü, Ismet, *originally* **Ismet Paza** 1884–1973 •*Turkish soldier and politician*• He was born in Smyrna (now Izmir), Asia Minor. After a distinguished army career in World War I he became **Kemal Atatürk**'s Chief of Staff in the war against the Greeks (1919–22), defeating them twice at the village of Inönü, which he adopted as his last name. As the first Prime Minister of the new republic (1923–37), he signed the Treaty of Lausanne (1923), introduced many political reforms transforming Turkey into a modern state, and was unanimously elected president in 1938 on Atatürk's death. From 1950 he was Leader of the Opposition. He became Prime Minister again in 1961, but resigned in 1965 after failing to govern effectively with minority support.

Ionesco, Eugène 1912–94 •*French playwright*• Born in Slatina, Romania, he was educated in Bucharest and Paris, where he settled in 1940. He pioneered a new style of drama that came to be called the Theater of the Absurd, in which the absurdity of man's condition was mirrored in a dramatic form of unreal situations without traditional narrative continuity or meaningful and coherent dialogue. Many of his plays are in one act: they include *La cantatrice chauve* (1950, Eng trans *The Bald Soprano*, 1958) and *Les Chaises* (1952, Eng trans *The Chairs*, 1957). Other plays include *Amédée* (1954, Eng trans 1955), *Le Tableau* (1955, Eng trans *The Picture*, 1968) and *Rhinocéros* (1959, Eng trans 1960). His later plays received less attention outside France. He also wrote essays, children's stories and a novel *Le Solitaire* (1973, Eng trans *The Hermit*, 1974).

Iorga, Nicolae 1871–1940 •*Romanian politician and historian*• He was elected to the Romanian parliament (1907) and founded the National Democrat Party. As Prime Minister and Minister of Education (1931–32), he supported King **Carol II** of Romania. With the establishment of the **Antonescu** regime, Iorga was one of several leading figures in Romanian political and cultural life who were murdered in 1940 and 1941.

Iqbal, Sir Muhammad 1875–1938 •*Indian poet and philosopher*• Born in Sialkot, India (now in Pakistan), he was educated in Lahore, Cambridge (where he read law and philosophy) and Munich. On his return to India, he practiced law, but achieved fame through his poetry, where his mysticism and nationalism caused him to be regarded almost as a prophet throughout the Muslim world. President of the Muslim League in 1930, his efforts to establish a separate Muslim state eventually led to the formation of Pakistan. He was knighted in 1923, and his works include *Reconstruction of Religious Thought in Islam* (1934).

Ireland, John Nicholson 1879–1962 •*English composer*• Born in Bowdon, Cheshire, he studied at the Royal College of Music, London. His poetic feelings, inspired by ancient traditions and places, are in evidence in such works as the orchestral prelude *The Forgotten Rite* (1913), and the rhapsody *Mai-dun* (1921). He established his reputation with his Violin Sonata in A (1917), and between the wars was a prominent member of the English musical renaissance. The piano concerto (1930) and *These Things Shall Be* (1937) for chorus and orchestra feature strongly among his later works, which include song settings of poems by **Thomas Hardy**, **John Masefield**, **A E Housman** and others.

Ireland, William Henry 1777–1835 •*English literary forger*• He was born in London, the son of a dealer in rare books. Tempted by his father's enthusiasm for **Shakespeare**, he forged the poet's signature on a carefully copied old lease, and went on to fabricate private letters and annotated books. **James Boswell** was among the many who were duped, but **Edmund Malone** and others saw through the forgery and denounced it. Ireland then produced a deed of Shakespeare's bequest of his books and papers to a William-Henrye Irelaunde, an assumed ancestor. Next a new historical play, *Vortigern and Rowena*, was announced, and produced by **Richard Brinsley Sheridan** at Drury Lane (1796). It was damned at once, and Ireland, finally suspected by his father, was forced to confess. He published a statement in 1796, and expanded it in his *Confessions* (1805).

Irenaeus, St c. 130–c. 200 AD •*Greek theologian, and one of the Christian fathers of the Greek church*• Born of Greek parents in Asia Minor, he was a pupil of **Polycarp**, and became a priest and then bishop (AD 177) of the Graeco-Gaulish church of Lyons. **Gregory of Tours** says that Irenaeus met his death in the persecution under **Severus** in 202, but this has never been substantiated. Irenaeus was a successful missionary bishop, but he is chiefly remembered for his opposition to Gnosticism (especially the Valentinians), against which he wrote his invaluable work *Against Heresies*. He was a key figure in the maintenance of contact between Eastern and Western sections of the church. His feast day is July 3.

Irene c. 752–803 •*Byzantine empress*• She was a poor orphan of Athens, and her beauty and talents led the Emperor Leo IV to marry her (769). After his death (780) she ruled as regent for her son, Constantine VI. Powerful and resolute, she imprisoned and blinded him and her husband's five brothers, and ruled in her own right from 797, but in 802 she was banished to Lesbos. For her part in patronizing monasteries and restoring icon veneration she was recognized as a saint by the Greek Orthodox Church.

Ireton, Henry 1611–51 •*English soldier*• He was born in Attenborough, Nottinghamshire. At the outbreak of the English Civil War (1642–51) he offered his services to Parliament, fighting at Edgehill (1642), Naseby (1645) and the siege of Bristol. In 1646 he married **Oliver Cromwell**'s daughter Bridget. In 1647 he proposed a solution to the conflict in the form of a constitutional monarchy, but the proposals proved unacceptable, and he later signed the warrant for the king's execution (1649). He accompanied Cromwell to Ireland, and in 1650 became Lord-Deputy. He died of the plague and was buried in Westminster Abbey, but at the Restoration (1660), his remains, along with those of Cromwell and others, were ceremonially hanged and buried under the gallows at Tyburn.

Irigoyen or **Yrigoyen, Hipólito** 1850–1933 •*Argentine politician*• Born in Buenos Aires, he became leader of the Radical Civic Union Party in 1896 and worked for electoral reform, which, when it came in 1912, brought him to power as the first Radical president (1916–22). He was reelected in 1928, but deposed by a military coup in 1930.

Irons, Jeremy 1948– •*English actor*• Born in Cowes on the Isle of Wight, he was educated at the Bristol Old Vic Theatre School where he made his first professional appearance in 1971. He appeared in many productions before winning the Clarence Derwent award for *The Rear Column* (1977) and making his film debut in *Nijinsky* (1980).

Widespread public recognition followed his performances in the television series *Brideshead Revisited* (1981) and the film *The French Lieutenant's Woman* (1981). His films include *The Mission* (1986), *Reversal of Fortune* (1990, Best Actor Academy Award), *Damage* (1993), *Stealing Beauty* (1996) and *The Man in the Iron Mask* (1998). Stage work includes *The Real Thing* (1984–85), for which he received a Tony award. He is married to the actress Sinead Cusack.

Ironside, William Edmund Ironside, 1st Baron 1880–1959 •*Scottish field marshal*• He was born in Ironside, Aberdeenshire. He served as a secret agent in the Second Boer War (1899–1902) and held several staff appointments in World War I. He commanded the Archangel expedition against the Bolsheviks (1918) and the Allied contingent in North Persia (1920). He was Chief of the Imperial General Staff at the outbreak of World War II, was promoted to field marshal (1940) and placed in command of the home defense forces (1940). The "Ironsides," fast, light-armored vehicles, were named after him.

Irvine (of Lairg), Alexander Andrew Mackay, Baron 1940– •*Scottish judge*• He was educated at the University of Glasgow and Christ's College, Cambridge. Called to the bar in 1967, he became a Queen's Counsel (1978), a deputy High Court Judge (1987), shadow Lord Chancellor (1992) and ultimately Lord Chancellor (1997). As Lord Chancellor he has introduced many reforms in the way the courts and the judiciary are administered.

Irvine, Andy (Andrew Robertson) 1951– •*Scottish rugby player*• Born in Edinburgh, he attended George Heriot's School and took up rugby. A fullback, he played club rugby for Heriot's Former Pupils, and played for Scotland 51 times. His running talent and attacking style made him one of the most exciting players Scotland has ever produced. He toured with the British Lions in 1974, 1977 and 1980, and during his international career he scored a world record total of 301 points for Scotland and the Lions, a record that he held until it was broken by **Gavin Hastings**.

Irving, Sir Henry, *originally* **John Henry Brodribb** 1838–1905 •*English actor*• He was born in Keinton-Mandeville, Somerset, and made his first appearance at the Sunderland Theatre in 1856. In 1866 he made his London debut at St James's Theatre, transferring to the Lyceum in 1871. His *Hamlet* (1874), *Macbeth* (1875) and *Othello* (1876) gained him his reputation as the greatest English actor of his time, although his striking presence and flair for interpreting the subtler emotions made him more successful in parts such as Shylock and Malvolio than in the great tragic roles of King Lear or Hamlet. In 1878 he began his famous theatrical partnership with **Ellen Terry** at the Lyceum (where he became actor-manager-lessee), when she played Ophelia to his Hamlet. The association lasted until 1902, and among their successes was **William Wills**'s version of **Goethe**'s *Faust* (1885), in which Ellen Terry played Marguerite to Irving's Mephistopheles. They gave a command performance of *The Bells* for Queen **Victoria** at Sandringham (1889), and produced **Tennyson**'s play *Becket* in 1893. Irving toured the US with his company eight times. In 1895 he became the first actor to receive a knighthood. His ashes were buried in Westminster Abbey. His publications include *The Drama* (1893). Of his sons, Laurence (1871–1914) was a novelist and playwright who was drowned in the sinking of the *Empress of Ireland*, and Henry Brodribb ("H B"; 1870–1919) was an actor.

Irving, Washington 1783–1859 •*US writer*• Born in New York City, he studied law, visited Rome, Paris, the Netherlands and London, and on his return in 1806 was admitted to the bar. *Salmagundi* (1808), a series of satirical essays, was followed by a characteristically boisterous work, *Diedrich Knickerbocker's A History of New York* (1809). He served as an officer in the War of 1812 and from 1815–32 lived largely in Europe. Under the pseudonym Geoffrey Crayon he wrote *The Sketch Book* (1819–20), a miscellany including the tales "Rip Van Winkle" and "The Legend of Sleepy Hollow." Another miscellany, *Tales of a Traveller*, was published in 1824, and his stay in Spain (1826–29) prompted such studies as *The History of the Life and Voyages of Christopher Columbus* (1828). Work produced after his return to New York in 1932 includes *A Tour on the Prairie* (1835) and *The Adventures of Captain Bonneville, USA* (1837). From 1842 to 1846 he was US ambassador to Spain.

Isaacs, Sir Jeremy Israel 1932– •*Scottish television executive and arts administrator*• Born in Glasgow, he was educated at Merton College, Oxford. He became a producer with Granada Television in 1958, and later worked on the BBC's *Panorama* (1965) and at Thames Television (1968–78), where he produced the documentary *The World at War* (1975). His later programs include *Ireland: A Television History* (1981) and the brutal drama *A Sense of Freedom* (1981). He served as the first chief executive of Channel 4 (1981–87), and from 1988 to 1997 was general director of the Royal Opera House in Covent Garden. He was knighted in 1996.

Isaacs, Susan Brierley, *née* **Fairhurst** 1885–1948 •*English educationist*• Born in Bromley Cross, Lancashire, she studied at Manchester and Cambridge, and lectured in Manchester and London. A disciple of **Sigmund Freud**, she ran an experimental progressive school, Malting House, in Cambridge (1924–27), which aimed at letting children find out for themselves rather than by direct instruction, and at allowing them free emotional expression. From 1933 to 1944 she was the influential head of the department of child development at the Institute of Education, London. She wrote *Intellectual Growth in Young Children* (1930) and *Social Development of Young Children* (1933), and challenged the theories of **Jean Piaget** before it was acceptable to question his work.

Isabella I of Castile, *also known as* **Isabella the Catholic** 1451–1504 •*Queen of Spain*• The daughter of King John II of Castile and Leon, she succeeded her brother, Henry IV of Castile (1474). In 1469 she had married **Ferdinand the Catholic** of Aragon, and when he succeeded to the Crown of Aragon (1479), they became joint sovereigns (as Isabella I and Ferdinand V of Aragon and Castile). Together they strengthened royal administration, and curbed the privileges of the nobility and military orders. Also during their reign the reconquest of Granada was completed (1482–92). Isabella backed the Inquisition (introduced 1478) and was the main force behind the expulsion of the Jews (1492). She and Ferdinand sponsored the voyage of **Christopher Columbus** to the New World (1492). She was succeeded by her daughter **Juana the Mad**.

Isabella II 1830–1904 •*Queen of Spain*• Born in Madrid, she succeeded to the throne on the death of her father, **Ferdinand VII** (1833), with her mother, Queen María Cristina (1806–78), acting as regent. She attained her majority (1843), and in 1846 married her cousin, Francisco de Asis de **Bourbon**. Although popular with the Spanish people, her scandalous private life made her the tool of rival factions and in 1868 she was deposed and exiled to France, where in 1870 she abdicated in favor of her son, **Alfonso XII**.

Isabella of Angoulême c. 1188–1246 •*Queen of England*• She was the consort of King **John**, whom she married in 1200. In 1214 she was imprisoned by John at Gloucester, and after his death (1216) she returned to France, where she married (1220) Hugh of Lusignan, Comte de la Marche, the son of a former fiancé. She retired to Fontevrault Abbey (1243). She was the mother of **Henry III**; her daughter by John, Isabella (1214–41), married the Emperor **Frederick II**.

Isabella of France 1292–1358 •*Queen of England*• The daughter of **Philip IV** of France, she married **Edward II** at Boulogne (1308), but was treated badly by him, and returned to France (1325) when her brother, **Charles IV**, seized Edward's territories in France. She became the mistress of Roger de Mortimer (later Earl of March), with whom she invaded England (1326) and overthrew Edward, forcing him to abdicate in favor of her young son, **Edward III**, with herself and Mortimer as regents. They plundered the treasury and had Edward II murdered at Berkeley Castle (1327). However, three years later, Edward III asserted his authority. Mortimer was hanged, drawn and quartered, while Isabella was sent into retirement at Castle Rising, near King's Lynn, Norfolk, for the rest of her life.

Isaiah, *Hebrew* **Jeshaiah** 8th century BC •*Old Testament prophet*• Born in Jerusalem, he was the son of Amoz. He began to prophesy in c. 747 BC, and wielded much influence in the kingdom of Judah until the Assyrian invasion of 701. According to tradition, he was martyred.

Isherwood, Christopher William Bradshaw 1904–86 •*US*

novelist• Born in Disley, Cheshire, England, he was educated at Repton and Corpus Christi College, Cambridge, and studied medicine at King's College London (1928–29), but gave it up to teach English in Germany (1930–33). His best-known works, *Mr Norris Changes Trains* (1935) and *Goodbye to Berlin* (1939), were based on his experiences in the decadence of post-depression, pre-**Hitler** Berlin. In collaboration with **W H Auden**, he wrote three prose-verse plays with political overtones: *The Dog Beneath the Skin* (1935), *The Ascent of F6* (1937) and *On the Frontier* (1938). He traveled in China with Auden in 1938 and wrote *Journey to a War* (1939). In 1939 he emigrated to California to be a scriptwriter for MGM and in 1946 took US citizenship. The Broadway hit *I Am a Camera* (1951) and the musical *Cabaret* (1968) were based on his earlier Berlin stories, especially *Sally Bowles* (1937). Later novels include *Meeting by the River* (1967).

Ishiguro, Kazuo 1954– •*British novelist*• Born in Nagasaki, Japan, he settled in Great Britain and attracted attention as a student in a creative-writing course at the University of East Anglia. After working as a community worker in Glasgow in the late 1970s, he published the delicate *A Pale View of Hill* (1982), which represented a highly personal approach to modern Japanese history and society. *An Artist of the Floating World* (1988) was much more mannered, and so too, in the most positive sense, was *The Remains of the Day* (1989), which shifted the setting to England for the first time. An elegiac study of a vanishing class told through the eyes of a butler, it won Ishiguro the Booker Prize and was made into an award-winning film (1993). A more recent work is *When We Were Orphans* (2000).

Ishmael •*Biblical character*• He was the son of **Abraham** by **Hagar**, Abraham's second wife. He was expelled into the desert with his mother from Abraham's household after the birth of Isaac. He is purported to have fathered 12 princes, and is considered the ancestor of the Bedouin tribes of the Palestinian deserts (the Ishmaelites). **Muhammad** considered Ishmael and Abraham as ancestors of the Arabs, and therefore associated with the construction of the Kaba in Mecca.

Isidore of Seville, St, *also called* **Isidorus Hispalensis** c. 560–636 •*Spanish prelate, Doctor of the Church, and the last of the Latin Fathers of the Church*• Born in Seville or Cartagena, he was Archbishop of Seville in c. 600, and his episcopate included the Councils at Seville (618 or 619) and Toledo (633). A voluminous writer, he is best known for his weighty encyclopedia of knowledge, *Etymologiae* or *Origines*, which was a standard work for scholars throughout the Middle Ages. He also wrote an introduction to the Old and New Testaments, a defense of Christianity against the Jews, and a history of the Goths, Vandals and Suebi. He was canonized in 1598 and his feast day is April 4.

Isla, José Francisco de 1703–81 •*Spanish satirist*• Born in Vidanes, he joined the Jesuits and became a preacher, but is best known as a humorous and satirical writer. His novel *Fray Gerundio* (1758–70, "Friar Gerundio"), which ridiculed the vulgar buffooneries of the popular preachers, is a good example of his style. It was well received by all except the friars, but the Inquisition stopped the publication of the book. In 1767 he shared the fate of the Jesuits in their expulsion from Spain, and went to Bologna.

Islam, Kazi Nazrul, *known as* **the Rebel Poet of Bengal** and **the National Poet of Bangladesh** 1899–1976 •*Bengali poet*• Born in the West Bengali village of Churulia into extreme poverty, he rose to fame in the 1920s as a poet and leader of the anti-British movement in India with his poem *The Rebel*, and he spent 40 days on a hunger strike in jail. In the 1930s he concentrated more on composing music and songs—over 4,000 songs and lyrics in all—and became well known as an actor and radio personality. In 1942, brain disease left him bereft of his faculties, including his speech. After Partition, which he had always opposed, he lived in penury until he was brought home in honor to the newly independent state of Bangladesh and installed as the national poet. A Muslim, he married a Hindu and was a lifelong advocate of Muslim-Hindu unity, and wrote more than 500 devotional Hindu songs.

Ismail Pasha 1830–95 •*Khedive of Egypt*• The second son of Ibrahim Pasha (1789–1848) and grandson of **Mehemet 'Ali**, he was born in Cairo and educated at St Cyr, France. He succeeded Sa'id Pasha (1822–63) as viceroy (1863), and assumed the hereditary title of khedive (1866). In 1872 the Ottoman sultan granted him the right (withdrawn in 1879) of concluding treaties and maintaining an army, which virtually gave him sovereign powers. He began a series of vast internal reforms: he built roads, railways and docks, reclaimed land, expanded cotton exports and hugely increased the number of schools. He annexed Darfur (1874), and endeavored to suppress the slave trade. Although he tried to lead the opposition of the army, the landowners and the religious leaders against foreign domination, he was deposed by the sultan (1879), and Prince **Tewfik**, his eldest son, was proclaimed khedive.

Ismay (of Wormington), Hastings Lionel Ismay, 1st Baron, *nicknamed* **Pug** 1887–1965 •*English soldier*• Born in Naini Tal, India, and educated at Charterhouse and Sandhurst, he served on India's Northwest Frontier in 1908 and in Somaliland in World War I. His appointment in 1926 as assistant secretary to the Committee of Imperial Defence led to his service as Chief of Staff to **Winston Churchill**. He later became Secretary of State for Commonwealth Relations (1951–52), and then Secretary-General to NATO (1952–1957).

Isocrates 436–338 BC •*Greek orator and prose writer*• He was born in Athens, and after studying under **Gorgias** and **Socrates** he worked briefly and unsuccessfully as a lawyer. He then turned to speechwriting, and became an influential teacher of oratory (c. 390 BC), presenting rhetoric as an essential foundation of education. Many of his writings, like the *Symmachicus* and the *Panathenaicus*, were meant to serve as model speeches, but were widely circulated as instructional or argumentative constitutional texts, thus becoming the first-ever political pamphlets. His style employs complex sentence structure and the frequent use of antithesis, and it influenced **Demosthenes** and **Cicero**, through whom Isocrates's example was passed on to European literature.

Issigonis, Sir Alec (Alexander Arnold Constantine) 1906–88 •*British automobile designer*• Born in Smyrna (Izmir) in Turkey, he settled in Great Britain in 1923 and studied at Battersea Polytechnic. A period as an enthusiastic sports driver in the 1930s and 1940s familiarized him with all aspects of car design. His greatest successes during a long association with Morris (later British Motor Company) were the Morris Minor, launched in 1948 and produced until 1971, and the revolutionary Mini launched in 1959. A version of the Mini is still in production, and more than five million have been manufactured. He was knighted in 1969.

Ito, Hirobumi 1838–1909 •*Japanese statesman*• He was born in Choshu province. As Prime Minister (1885–88, 1892–96, 1898, 1900–01), he visited Europe and the US on several occasions, drafted the Meiji constitution (1889), and played a major role in abolishing Japanese feudalism and building up the modern state. He was assassinated in Harbin by a supporter of Korean independence.

Itten, Johannes 1888–1967 •*Swiss painter and teacher*• Born in Sudern-Linden, he studied art in Stuttgart (1913–16) before moving to Vienna where he started his own art school. A leading theorist at the Bauhaus (1919–23), he wrote on the theory of color (*Kunst der Farbe*, 1961) and developed the idea of a compulsory "preliminary course" based on research into natural forms and the laws of basic design.

Iturbide, Agustín de, *also known as* **Agustin I** 1783–1824 •*Mexican soldier and politician*• Born in Valladolid (now Morelia), he fought for the Crown in opposing the social revolution of the independence movement of **Miguel Hidalgo** and **José María Morelos**. He defeated Morelos's army at Valladolid (1810) and was given command of the royalist army but, dissatisfied with the imposition of a constitutional monarchy in Spain, he betrayed the royalists and joined with the Liberals to issue the Plan de Iguala declaring Mexico independent (1821). Then, betraying that movement, he crowned himself Emperor Agustín I. He was unable to govern and his popularity plummeted, forcing him to abdicate (1823). He went into exile in Europe but returned the following year and was captured and executed.

Ivan I, *also called* **Ivan Kalita ("Moneybag")** c. 1304–41 •*Grand Prince of Moscow*• He was a careful, financially shrewd administrator and skillful diplomat and reformer, who expanded Moscow's territory by purchase rather than conquest. He made Moscow the capital of Russia by transferring the metropolitan cathedral from Kiev (1326). He became Grand Prince of Moscow in 1328. His two sons, Simeon the Proud (reigned 1341–53) and Ivan II (reigned 1353–59), succeeded him.

Ivan III Vasilyevich, *called* **Ivan the Great** 1440–1505 •*Grand Prince of Moscow and Grand Duke of Russia*• Born in Moscow, he ruled from 1462, and ended his city's subjection to the Tatars. He gained control over a number of Russian principalities, including Novgorod, and after he married (1472) Sophia, a niece of **Constantine XI Palaeologus**, he assumed the title Sovereign of all Russia. He was the first Russian prince to establish contact with the West and laid the administrative basis of a centralized Russian state.

Ivan IV, *known as* **Ivan the Terrible** 1530–84 •*Czar of Russia from 1533*• He was the grandson of **Ivan III Vasilyevich** (Ivan the Great), and was only three years old at the death of his father, Grand Prince Vasili. Following a period when authority was in the hands first of his mother Elena, and then, following her murder in 1537, in the hands of the Russian boyars, Ivan assumed power in 1547, becoming the first ruler of Russia to adopt the title of "czar." He proceeded steadily to reduce the power of the upper nobility (princes and boyars) in favor of the minor gentry. He summoned a legislative assembly in 1549, inaugurating a period of reform in both State and Church that continued for the next decade, establishing a new code of law and a system of local self-government. In 1552 he wrested Kazan from the Tartars and in 1554 captured Astrakhan. In 1558 he invaded Livonia, capturing the important Baltic port of Narva. In 1565, suspecting that a boyar rebellion was imminent, he offered to abdicate, but he was brought back by popular demand with sweeping powers to take drastic measures against those who had opposed him. This led to a prolonged spate of arrests and executions. In 1570 he ravaged the free city of Novgorod. In 1571 the Crimean Tartars invaded Russia and Moscow, but Ivan was able to inflict a punishing defeat upon them the following year. In the last years of his reign, he rehabilitated posthumously many of the victims of his middle years, but in a fit of anger in 1581 accidentally killed his own eldest son, so that the throne passed on his death to his sickly and feeble-minded second son, Fyodor, who ruled from 1584 to 1598.

Ivan the Great *See* **Ivan III Vasilyevich**

Ivan the Terrible *See* **Ivan IV**

Ivanisevic, Goran 1971– •*Croatian tennis player*• Born in Split, he won the US Open Junior doubles title in 1987 and turned professional the following year. His notoriously mercurial temperament on the court sometimes disrupted his game, but he went on to play in the Yugoslavian Davis Cup squad and was runner-up in the men's singles at Wimbledon in 1992, 1994 and 1998 as well as a semifinalist in the ATP (Association of Tennis Professionals) world championship (1992). The left-handed Ivanisevic finally captured the Wimbledon title in 2001.

Ives, Burl 1909–95 •*US folk singer*• Born in Hunt, Illinois, he became a leader of the US folk movement, and during his career as a ballad singer and banjo player, his songs "Blue Tail Fly" and "Foggy Dew" were as well known as his radio show signature ballad "Wayfarin' Stranger." He also performed in dramas and musicals on the Broadway stage and in films (*The Big Country*, 1958, Academy Award). He won Grammy awards for his recordings "A Little Bitty Tear" (1961), "Funny Way of Laughin' " (1962), "Chim Chim Cheree" (1964), and "America Sings" (1974).

Ives, Charles Edward 1874–1954 •*US composer*• Born in Danbury, Connecticut, he studied music at Yale. His music is firmly based in the US tradition, but at the same time he experimented with dissonances, polytonal harmonies, and conflicting rhythms, anticipating modern European trends. He composed five symphonies, chamber music (including the well-known 2nd Piano Sonata, the "Concord" Sonata), and many songs. In 1947 he was awarded the Pulitzer Prize for his 3rd Symphony (*The Camp Meeting*, composed 1904–11).

“ ”

Please don't try to make things nice! All the wrong notes are *right* ... I want it that way.

*c. 1914 Note to the copyist of **The Fourth of July**.*

Ives, James Merritt 1824–95 •*US lithographer*• Born in New York City, he was technical director and a partner of **Nathaniel Currier** in the Currier & Ives firm. He directed the artists who produced popular hand-colored engravings depicting scenes of 19th-century US life. Between 1840 and 1890 the firm issued over 7,000 different prints, which became prized by collectors.

Ivory, James 1928– •*US film director*• He was born in Berkeley, California. He formed Merchant-Ivory Productions with producer **Ismail Merchant** and, frequently in collaboration with screenwriter and novelist **Ruth Prawer Jhabvala**, made several highly successful films. These are characterized by a literate, precise script, ironic humor, scrupulous attention to period detail and design, and impeccable performances and include *Shakespeare Wallah* (1965), *Heat and Dust* (1982), *The Bostonians* (1984), *A Room With a View* (1985), *Maurice* (1987), *Howards End* (1992), *Remains of the Day* (1993) and *Surviving Picasso* (1997).

Iwasa Matabei, *originally* **Araki** c. 1578–1650 •*Japanese painter*• A master of the Tosa school, he is credited with founding the Ukiyo-e school.

Izetbegovich, Alija 1925–2003 •*Bosnia and Herzogovinian politician*• Born in Bosanski Samac, he was educated at the University of Sarajevo. In 1945, following the creation of the Yugoslav Federation, he was imprisoned for three years for promoting Bosnian nationalist policies. In 1988 he became leader of the Party of Democratic Action. With the breakup of Yugoslavia he became president of Bosnia-Herzegovina (1990) and the inspirational leader of the Bosnian Muslims in the civil war that followed. He was co-president from 1996 to 2000 when he stepped down.

J

Jack the Ripper 19th century •*Unidentified murderer*• Between August and November 1888, six prostitutes were found murdered and mutilated in the East End of London. The murderer was never discovered. The affair aroused much public alarm, provoking a violent press campaign against the Criminal Investigation Department and the Home Secretary. Jack the Ripper has been the subject of many novels and films, and speculation about his identity continues.

Jacklin, Tony (Anthony) 1944– •*English golf player*• Born in Scunthorpe, Humberside, he became in 1969 the first Briton since 1951 to win the Open championship. Within 11 months he became the first Briton since Harry Vardon (who was Open champion in 1899 and 1900 US Open champion) to have held the Open and the US Open titles in the same 12 months. His US Open victory by seven strokes was the biggest winning margin since that of Jim Barnes in 1921. In 1985 he led the European team to its first Ryder Cup victory in 28 years, and in 1987 the team had its first victory on US soil.

Jackson, Andrew, *nicknamed* **Old Hickory** 1767–1845 •*Seventh President of the US*• Born into an Irish immigrant family in Waxhaw, South Carolina, he was raised on the frontier and fought in the Revolution at age 13, losing almost all of his immediate family in the war. After studying law and heading west he became public prosecutor in Nashville in 1788. He helped to frame the constitution of Tennessee, and became its representative in Congress in 1796, a senator in 1797 and a judge of the Tennessee Supreme Court (1798–1804). When war was declared against Great Britain in 1812, as major general of the state militia he took the field against the Creek Indians (allies of the British) in Alabama, achieving a decisive victory at Horseshoe Bend in 1814. Appointed to the command of the South, "Old Hickory" invaded Spanish soil, stormed Pensacola (a British base), and successfully defended New Orleans in 1815. The victory at New Orleans made him a national hero. In 1818 Jackson again invaded Florida, defeated the Seminoles and became the state's first governor. He soon resigned, and in 1823 was reelected to the US Senate. In 1824 as a Democratic candidate for the presidency, he lost narrowly to **John Quincy Adams**, but was elected in 1828. He relied heavily on a set of informal advisers (his "Kitchen Cabinet") and he quarreled with his vice president, **John C Calhoun**, on the issue of states' rights, with Calhoun resigning over the issue in 1832. He favored extended suffrage and sought to limit the power of the monied elite, and so is said to have ushered in the era of "Jacksonian Democracy," though paradoxically he had little respect for the checks and balances of the democratic system and was highhanded in his use of executive power. He vetoed legislation much more freely than any of his predecessors and was particularly vehement in opposing the effort to recharter the Bank of the United States, which he saw as the malignant agent of centralized money power. On this issue he was reelected president by an overwhelming majority in 1832, and in his second term he pursued hard-money policies. Throughout his presidency he pressed for Indian removal in order to free new lands for settlement on the frontier, and his most shameful act was his deliberate refusal to enforce the 1832 Supreme Court decision invalidating Georgia's effort to annex the territory of the Cherokee. As a plainspoken champion of the common man, however, he won enormous and enduring popularity.

Jackson (of Lodsworth), Dame Barbara Mary Ward, Baroness 1914–81 •*English economist, journalist and conservationist*• Born in Sussex and educated in Paris, Jugenheim and at Somerville College, Oxford, she became foreign editor of *The Economist* in 1939. After World War II she lectured in the US. She was president of the International Institute for Environment and Development from 1973 to 1980, and was made a life peer in 1976. She was a prolific and popular writer on politics, economics and ecology, and her books include *The International Share Out* (1936), *The Rich Nations and the Poor Nations* (1962), *Spaceship Earth* (1966) and *Only One Earth—the Care and Maintenance of a Small Planet* (1972).

Jackson, Glenda 1936– •*English actress and Labour politician*• She was born in Birkenhead, Cheshire, and became a student at the Royal Academy of Dramatic Art. She made her film debut in *This Sporting Life* (1963) but remained primarily a stage actress in such productions as *Alfie* (1963), *Hamlet* (1965) and *Marat/Sade* (1965). Her films include *Women in Love* (1969, Academy Award), *A Touch of Class* (1973, Academy Award), *Sunday, Bloody Sunday* (1971), *Hedda* (1975), *Stevie* (1978) and *Business as Usual* (1987). Among her stage performances are *Hedda Gabler* (1975), *Strange Interlude* (1984), *The House of Bernarda Alba* (1986), *Macbeth* (1988), and *Mother Courage* (1990). On television, she played the title role in the series *Elizabeth R* (1971) and appeared in the film *The Patricia Neal Story* (1981). Later turning to a career in politics, she was elected as Labour Member of Parliament for Hampstead and Highgate, London (1992).

Jackson, Helen Maria Hunt, *née* **Fiske** 1830–85 •*US writer*• Born in Amherst, Massachusetts, she was a friend of **Emily Dickinson** and a writer of poems (*Verses*, 1870) and popular prose works. After settling in Colorado Springs in 1875, she won public attention with *A Century of Dishonor*, an indictment of the US government for its shameful record of broken treaties and barbarous treatment of Native Americans. The book resulted in her government appointment in 1882 to investigate conditions among California Mission Indians. Her most popular novel, *Ramona* (1884), was a sentimental romance on Native American themes, written in the style of *Uncle Tom's Cabin*.

Jackson, Jesse Louis 1941– •*US politician and clergyman*• Born in Greenville, North Carolina, the adopted son of a janitor, he won a football scholarship to the University of Illinois. He was ordained as a Baptist minister in 1968, and as a charismatic preacher and African-American activist politician he worked with **Martin Luther King, Jr**. He was a candidate for the Democratic 1984 presidential nomination, being the first African American to mount a serious campaign for the office and constructing a "Rainbow Coalition" of liberal and minority groups, and won a fifth of the delegates' votes. He lost the nomination to **Walter Mondale**. In 1986 he successfully campaigned for US divestiture from South Africa. He came in second to **Michael Dukakis** in the 1988 Democratic presidential nomination contest, doubling his 1984 vote share.

" "

My constituency is the desperate, the damned, the disinherited, the disrespected, and the despised.

1984 Speech at the Democratic National Convention, San Francisco, July 17.

Jackson, John Hughlings 1835–1911 •*English neurologist*• Born in Providence Green, Green Hammerton, Yorkshire, he graduated in medicine from St Bartholomew's Hospital, and became a lecturer in pathology at the London Hospital, rising to consulting physician (1894–1911). Simultaneously he was assistant (1862–67) and full physician (1867–1906) at the National Hospital for the Paralysed and Epileptic, Queen Square. Jackson contributed extensively to the development of neurology, suggesting that function could be localized in specific regions of the cerebral cortex, investigating unilateral epileptiform seizures and the physiology of speech, and he also postulated that the evolution of the nervous system proceeded from the simplest centers to the most complex.

Jackson, Joseph Jefferson, *known as* **"Shoeless Joe"** 1889–1951 •*US baseball player*• Born in Pickens County, South Carolina, he joined the Philadelphia Athletics in 1908. He gained his nickname when a new pair of baseball shoes raised blisters and he played in his stocking feet. Signed to the Cleveland Naps (later Cleveland Indians) in 1911, he moved to the Chicago White Sox in 1915, helping them win the World Series in 1917. In 1921 he was convicted of taking bribes to throw the 1919 World Series (a still-controversial verdict) and was barred from baseball for life. The phrase "Say it ain't so, Joe" derives from a remark made to him by a young fan. His career batting average of .356 is the third highest in history.

Jackson, Laura Riding *See* **Riding, Laura**

Jackson, Mahalia 1911–62 •*US gospel singer*• Born in New Orleans, Louisiana, she grew up in a strict Baptist environment, but was attracted to the blues of **Bessie Smith**. She then moved north and sang in the choir of the Great Salem Baptist Church, Chicago (1927), and, from 1932, with the Johnson Gospel Singers. She collaborated with the hymn writer **Thomas A Dorsey** and scored chart successes with "Move on up a Little Higher" and other blues-inflected gospel themes. Despite commercial success, she refused all secular engagements, but did, however, sing at **John F Kennedy**'s inauguration, her emotional and fervid delivery underlining the social imperatives of Kennedy's groundbreaking proposals in social legislation.

Jackson, Michael 1958– •*US pop singer*• He was born in Gary, Indiana. He formed part of The Jackson Five with his brothers, Jackie, Tito, Marlon and Jermaine, from about 1965, when the group began to win local talent competitions. His distinctive vocals attracted particular attention, and the band was eventually signed by Tamla Motown records. The Jackson Five delivered four consecutive number-one hits for the label in 1969–70, when Michael was only 11. Between 1972 and 1975 he also had six solo hits on the label, while the group racked up 16 chart hits in all. They moved to the Epic label in 1976 and changed their name to The Jacksons; Michael left the group to pursue a solo career and was replaced by his cousin Randy. Michael's collaboration with producer Quincy Jones on *Off the Wall* produced four hit singles in 1979, and he consolidated his career with the album, single, and extended horror film–style video for *Thriller* (1982), which has sold over 45 million copies. In 1987 he had huge success with the album *Bad*. Having been a celebrity since childhood, he developed a reclusive lifestyle as an adult, and is usually portrayed in the media as an eccentric introvert. Bizarre plastic surgery, an onstage accident in which his hair caught fire, and an unlikely and short-lived "showbiz dynasty" marriage to Lisa Marie Presley did nothing to ease such speculation. His grip on his creativity was also called into question in the grandiose *HIStory* (1995). More recently he released the album *Invincible* (2001).

Jackson, Milt(on), *nicknamed* **Bags** 1923–99 •*US vibraphone player*• Born in Detroit, he learned the guitar and piano while at school, taking up xylophone and vibraphone in his teens. His discovery by **Dizzy Gillespie** in 1945 led to his emergence as the most important vibraphone player of the bop era. In 1952 he was a founding member of the Modern Jazz Quartet, which existed, with a change of drummer, until 1974, and formed again in the 1980s.

Jackson, Reggie (Reginald Martinez), *nicknamed* **Mr October** 1946– •*US baseball player*• Born in Wyncote, Pennsylvania, he equaled **Babe Ruth**'s 51-year-old record for hitting three home runs in one game in the 1977 World Series. He started his major-league career in 1967 with the Kansas City Athletics, then played for Oakland, and also played for the Baltimore Orioles, the New York Yankees, and the California Angels (1982-86) before returning to Oakland again in 1987.

Jackson, Samuel L(eroy) 1948– •*US actor*• Born in Washington DC, he studied drama at Morehouse College, later founding the Just Us theater company. He began his film career in the early 1970s and became well known for his roles in a number of **Spike Lee** films, including *Jungle Fever* (1991; Best Actor, Cannes Film Festival). He was later associated with the director **Quentin Tarantino** in films such as *Pulp Fiction* (1994) and *Jackie Brown* (1997), and starred in the remake of *Shaft* (2000).

Jackson, Thomas Jonathan, *known as* **Stonewall Jackson** 1824–63 •*US Confederate soldier*• Born in Clarksburg, West Virginia, in 1851 he became general professor at the Virginia Military Institute. At the outbreak of war in 1861 he took command of the Confederate troops at Harpers Ferry on the secession of Virginia, and led a brigade at Bull Run, where his firm stand earned him his nickname. In the campaign of the Shenandoah Valley (1862) he out-generaled **Nathaniel Banks** and **John C Frémont**, and drove them back to the Lower Shenandoah. He turned the scale at Gaines's Mills (June 27), and returned to defeat Banks at Cedar Run in August. He then seized General **John Pope**'s depot at Manassas. On September 15 he captured Harpers Ferry with 13,000 prisoners, and on the next day arrived at Sharpsburg, where his presence at the Battle of Antietam saved General **Robert E Lee** from disaster. At Chancellorsville (May 1, 1863) he repulsed General **Joseph Hooker**. The next night he fell on the right of the Union army and drove it back on Chancellorsville, but was accidentally killed by his own troops.

Jackson, Sir William Godfrey Fothergill 1917–99 •*English soldier and historian*• Educated at Shrewsbury School, the Royal Military Academy, Woolwich, and King's College, Cambridge, he was commissioned in the Royal Engineers (1937). He served during World War II in Norway (1940), North Africa, Sicily and Italy (1942–43) and the Far East (1945). Assistant Chief of General Staff (1968–70), he was Commander in Chief Northern Command (1970–72), and Quartermaster General at the Ministry of Defence (1973–76). He was Governor and Commander in Chief, Gibraltar (1978–82). His publications on military, historical and strategic subjects include *Seven Roads to Moscow* (1957), *Overlord: Normandy 1944* (1978) and *Salvador* (1995).

Jacob •*Biblical character*• The son of Isaac, he is the patriarch of the nation Israel. He supplanted his elder brother **Esau**, obtaining his father's special blessing and thus being seen as the inheritor of God's promises. He was renamed Israel (meaning "God has striven" or "he who strives with God") after his struggle with a divine being. By his wives Leah and Rachel and their maids he fathered 12 sons, to whom the 12 tribes of Israel are traced by tradition.

Jacob, François 1920– •*French biochemist and Nobel Prize winner*• Born in Nancy, he was educated at the University of Paris and the Sorbonne, and worked at the Pasteur Institute in Paris from 1950, later becoming Professor of Cellular Genetics at the Collège de France (1964–91). During the 1950s while working on the bacterium *Escherichia coli*, he suggested that genes are controlled by a system of other genes which regulate certain enzymes. He formulated the "operon system," in which a regulator gene controls structural genes by manipulating sections of DNA. With **André Lwoff** and **Jacques Monod**, Jacob was awarded the 1965 Nobel Prize for physiology or medicine for research in cell physiology and the structure of genes.

Jacobi, Carl Gustav Jacob 1804–51 •*German mathematician*• Born in Potsdam, he was educated at the University of Berlin, and became a professor at the University of Königsberg from 1827. His *Fundamenta nova* (1829) was the first definitive book on elliptic functions, which he and **Niels Henrik Abel** had independently ascertained. He also discovered many remarkable infinite series connected to elliptic functions, and he made important advances in the study of differential equations, the theory of numbers, and determinants.

Jacobi, Sir Derek George 1938– •*English actor*• Born in London, he had acted while a student at Cambridge and with the National Youth Theatre before he made his professional debut in N F Simpson's *One Way Pendulum* at Birmingham Repertory Theatre (1961). Since then, he has become one of Great Britain's most notable classical actors. He joined the National Theatre's inaugural 1963 company, making his London debut that year as Laertes in *Hamlet*. In 1972 he joined the Prospect Theatre Company and in

1982 the Royal Shakespeare Company. He made his debut as director in 1988, with *Hamlet* for the Renaissance Theatre Company. He has made several film and television appearances, notably the title role in the television adaptation of *I, Claudius* (1977). He was knighted in 1994.

Jacobs, Aletta 1851–1929 •*Dutch doctor and birth control pioneer*• The daughter of a doctor, after training as a pharmacist, she petitioned the prime minister of the Netherlands for the right to study medicine and was granted a place at the University of Groningen. In 1882 she established the world's first birth control clinic for women in Amsterdam and campaigned for improvements in health education, changes in marriage and prostitution laws, and female suffrage.

Jacobsen, Arne 1902–71 •*Danish architect and designer*• Born in Copenhagen, he was educated at the Royal Danish Academy. He won a House of the Future competition in 1929 and became a leading exponent of modernism. His theory was "economy plus function equals style." In 1956 he became Professor of Architecture at the Royal Danish Academy. He designed many private houses, and his main public buildings were the SAS skyscraper in Copenhagen (1959) and St Catherine's College, Oxford (1964). He also designed cutlery, textiles and classic furniture, especially the "Egg" and "Swan" chairs for his Royal Hotel in Copenhagen.

Jacobsz, Lucas *See* **Lucas van Leyden**

Jacquard, Joseph Marie 1752–1834 •*French silk weaver*• He was born in Lyons. His invention (1801–08) of the Jacquard loom, which used perforated cards for controlling the movement of the warp threads, enabled an ordinary worker to produce beautiful patterns in a style previously accomplished only with patience, skill and labor. But though **Napoleon I** rewarded him with a small pension and the Legion of Honor, the silk weavers themselves were so violently opposed to his machine that on one occasion, he narrowly escaped with his life. At his death his machine was in almost universal use.

Jacques, Hattie, *originally* **Josephine Edwina Jacques** 1924–80 •*English comic actress*• Born in Sandgate, Kent, she was a factory worker and Red Cross nurse during World War II, and she made her stage debut in 1944. Frequently called on to play bossy figures of authority, she was also a highly respected foil to many comedians, notably in *ITMA* (1948–50) and *Educating Archie* (1950–54) on radio, and on television with **Eric Sykes**. Later stage work included *Twenty Minutes South* (1955), which she directed, and *Hatful of Sykes* (1979). She also appeared in 14 of the *Carry On* ... films.

Jacuzzi, Candido 1903–86 •*US inventor*• Born in Italy, he was an engineer whose infant son suffered from arthritis, and in an attempt to relieve the pain by hydrotherapy, Jacuzzi devised a pump that produced a whirlpool effect in a bath. After his invention became generally available, it was known as a "jacuzzi."

Jaffrey, Madhur 1933– •*US cookbook writer and actress*• Born and educated in Delhi, India, she went to London to study at the Royal Academy of Dramatic Art, then married and moved to the US. There she collected the recipes sent in letters from her mother in India and published them. Her authentic and interesting recipes have encouraged the appreciation of the richness of Indian cooking, which she also promotes through television and radio appearances. Her film work includes roles in *Heat and Dust* (1982) and *Vanya on 42nd Street* (1994), as well as directing. She also writes children's books.

Jagan, Cheddi Berrat 1918–97 •*Guyanese Socialist statesman and writer*• He was born at Port Mourant, and in 1936 went to the US where he studied dentistry at Northwestern University, Chicago. He returned to British Guiana (renamed Guyana in 1966 upon becoming independent) in 1943. With **Forbes Burnham**, he led the nationalist People's Progressive Party (PPP) in demanding self-government in the early 1950s. The Jagan-Burnham alliance won the 1953 election, but the governor, accusing Jagan of "communist" policies, suspended the constitution, dismissed Jagan and his cabinet and called in British troops. Jagan came to power with the PPP again in 1957, but an austerity budget and his desire to hasten the end of imperial rule led to racial rioting, and a long general strike in Georgetown only ended with further British military intervention (1961–64). In the 1964 election Burnham's People's National Congress was victorious; Jagan was Leader of the Opposition for 28 years until he was elected president in 1992.

Jagger, Sir Mick (Michael Philip) 1943– •*English rock singer and songwriter*• He was born in Dartford, Kent, and is best known as the lead singer of the **Rolling Stones**. He reinvented himself from a rather shy middle-class student to a strutting rock hero and leading antiestablishment figure in the British pop music scene of the 1960s. His songwriting partnership with his Dartford contemporary, the Rolling Stones's guitarist Keith Richards (1943–), is one of the most celebrated in rock music. He has also acted in a number of films. He was knighted in 2002.

Jahangir, *originally* **Salim** 1569–1627 •*Mughal emperor*• Born in Fatehpur Sikri, India, he was the son of **Akbar the Great** and took the title of Jahangir on his accession in 1605. He was a shrewd judge of men and tolerant in religion, with a dilettantish interest in Christianity. His early reign saw peace and great prosperity for the empire and a flowering of the arts under royal patronage. Later there were continual rebellions against his rule, principally on behalf of his sons, especially Khurram (who succeeded him as **Shah Jahan**), and he was only able to survive through the vigor of Empress **Nur Jahan**.

Jahn, Helmut 1940– •*US architect*• Born in Allersberg, near Nuremberg, Germany, he moved to the US in 1966 and studied at the Illinois Institute of Technology (IIT) in Chicago. As chief executive officer of Murphy/Jahn Associates from 1983, he was appointed Chevalier, Ordre des Arts et des Lettres, Paris, in 1988, and won the IIT award for Outstanding Contribution to the Built Environment in 1992. An established architect of office buildings, civic structures and corporate office towers, he has undertaken international commissions in Berlin, Frankfurt, Amsterdam and Singapore, and has also moved toward planning work (Munich Airport Centre, 1996).

Jakeš, Miloš 1922– •*Czechoslovakian politician*• He was born in České Chalupy, he joined the Communist Party of Czechoslovakia (CCP) in 1945 and studied in Moscow (1955–58). He supported the Soviet invasion of Czechoslovakia in 1968 and later, as the leader of the CCP's central control commission, oversaw the purge of reformist personnel. He entered the CCP secretariat in 1977 and the politburo in 1981, and in 1987 he replaced **Gustáv Husak** as Party leader. Although enjoying close personal relations with the Soviet leader **Mikhail Gorbachev**, he emerged as a cautious reformer. He was forced to step down as CCP leader in 1989, following a series of pro-democracy rallies.

Jakobovits (of Regent's Park), Immanuel Jakobovits, Baron 1921–99 •*British rabbi*• He was born in Königsberg, Prussia (now Kaliningrad, Russia), but moved with his family to Great Britain and was educated at Jews College, London, and the University of London. He served as a rabbi in synagogues in London before being appointed Chief Rabbi of Ireland in 1949. He was rabbi of Fifth Avenue Synagogue, New York, from 1958 to 1967 before returning to Britain as Chief Rabbi of the United Hebrew Congregations of the British Commonwealth. He received a life peerage in 1987, and retired in 1991. His writings include *If Only My People—Zionism in My Life* (1985).

Jalal ad-Din ar-Rumi, *also called* **Mawlana** 1207–73 •*Persian lyric poet and mystic*• Born in Balkh (in modern Afghanistan), he settled at Iconium (now Konya) in 1226 and founded a sect. After his death his disciples became a group referred to in the West as the Whirling Dervishes. He wrote much lyrical poetry, including a long epic, *Masnavi y ma'navi*, on the Sufi mystical doctrine.

James, St, the Great *See* **James, son of Zebedee**

James, St, *also known as* **St James the Just** 1st century AD •*Early Christian*• He is listed with **Joseph**, Simon, and **Judas** (Matthew 13:55) as a "brother" of **Jesus** of Nazareth, and identified as the foremost leader of the Christian community in Jerusalem (Galatians 1:19, 2:9; Acts 15:13). He is not included in lists of the disciples of Jesus, and should not be confused with **James**, son of Alphaeus, or **James**, son of Zebedee. He showed Jewish sympathies over the question of whether Christians must adhere to the Jewish law. Most theologians consider him the author of the Epistle of James, although it has been ascribed to both of the other Jameses. The first of the Catholic Epistles, it was finally declared canonical by the third Council of Carthage (AD 397). According to **Josephus**, James was martyred by stoning (c. 62). His feast day is May 1.

James, son of Alphaeus, *also known as* **St James the Less** 1st century AD •*One of the 12 Apostles of Jesus*• He was possibly the James whose mother Mary is referred to at the crucifixion of **Jesus**. His feast day is May 1.

James, son of Zebedee, *also known as* **St James the Great** 1st century AD •*One of the 12 Apostles of Jesus*• Born in Galilee, Palestine, he is often listed with **John** (his brother) and **Peter** in the group closest to **Jesus**, who were among the first to be called, and who were with him at the Transfiguration and at Gethsemane. James and John were called *Boanerges* ("sons of thunder"). According to Acts 12:2, James was martyred under **Herod Agrippa I** (c. AD 44). His feast day is July 25.

James I 1394–1437 •*King of Scotland*• Born in Dunfermline, Fife, he was the second son of **Robert III**. After his elder brother David, Duke of Rothesay, was murdered at Falkland (1402), allegedly by his uncle, the Duke of **Albany**, James was sent for safety to France, but was captured at sea by the English in 1406 and imprisoned for 18 years. Albany meanwhile ruled Scotland as governor until his death (1420), when his son, Murdoch, assumed the regency and the country rapidly fell into disorder. Negotiations for the return of James were completed with the Treaty of London (1423) and James resumed his reign in 1424, marrying in that year Joan Beaufort (d. 1445), niece of **Richard II**. Murdoch, his two sons and the 80-year-old Earl of Lennox were all beheaded at Stirling, the first state executions since 1320, and others were dealt with almost as severely. By such methods he was able to triple the royal estates. The series of parliaments called after 1424 was dominated by the king's need for increased taxation, partly to pay off the ransom extracted for his release, and partly to meet increased expenditure on his court, artillery and building work at Linlithgow. He was the nominal founder and benefactor of the University of St Andrews. In foreign affairs, he attempted to increase trade by renewing a commercial treaty with the Netherlands, and also concluded treaties with Denmark, Norway and Sweden. His relations with the Church were abrasive and his criticisms of monastic orders pointed. His murder in the Dominican friary at Perth, the first assassination of a Scottish king for 400 years, was the work of a group of dissidents led by descendants of **Robert II**'s second marriage. James left one surviving son (James, the future **James II**), and six daughters; the eldest, Margaret (1424–45), who married the Dauphin, later **Louis XI** of France, was a gifted poet, as was James himself, who wrote the tender, passionate collection of poems, *The Kingis Quair* (c. 1423–24, the "king's quire," or book) to celebrate his romance with Joan Beaufort.

James I of England and VI of Scotland *See* **James VI and I**

James II 1430–60 •*King of Scotland*• The son of **James I** and known as James "of the fiery face" because of a birth mark, he was born at Holyrood, and was six years old when his father was murdered (1437). He took shelter in Edinburgh Castle with his mother, and was put under her charge and that of Sir Alexander Livingston. The liaison with Livingston lasted until 1444 when the Livingstons began to monopolize offices, power and access to the king. In 1449 James took control of the government and the Livingstons were dismissed from office. He also had to curb the rising power of the **Douglas** family. In a quarrel (in 1452) James killed William, the 8th Earl of Douglas, at Stirling Castle, but was allowed to get away with murder and eventually completely defeated the Douglases of Arkinholm, Dumfriesshire (1455). This smoothed the way for a series of grants of earldoms and lands to families such as the **Campbells**, Gordons and Hamiltons. A growing stability in domestic politics was vitiated by his reckless involvement in the English struggles between the houses of York and Lancaster. In 1460 he marched for England with a powerful army and laid siege to Roxburgh Castle, which had been held by the English for over a hundred years, but was killed by the bursting of a cannon.

James III 1452–88 •*King of Scotland*• The eldest son of **James II**, whom he succeeded at the age of eight (1460), he was brought up under the guardianship of Bishop Kennedy (c. 1408–65) of St Andrews, while the Earl of Angus was made lieutenant general. James's tutor was the leading humanist scholar Archibald Whitelaw, who inspired him with a love of culture and a sincere piety. The beginnings of the flowering of vernacular literature that marked **James IV**'s court began in this reign. His minority, although (from 1466) marked by the rise of the Boyds at the expense of others, did not see the degree of disturbance that had marked previous reigns. By 1469, when parliament condemned the Boyds and James was married to Margaret, daughter of **Christian I** of Denmark, bringing Orkney and Shetland in pledge as part of her dowry, the king was firmly in control, but he was unable to restore strong central government. Various aspects of his rule, however, created resentment: money was short, successive parliaments reluctant to grant taxes, and in the 1480s James resorted to debasement of the coinage, stigmatized as "black money." In 1479 he confiscated the estates of his brothers, the Duke of Albany and the Earl of Mar, the latter dying suspiciously. The breakdown of relations with England brought war (1480), and the threat of English invasion resulted in a calculated political demonstration by his nobles, who hanged Robert Cochrane and other unpopular royal favorites at Lauder Bridge (1482). Continued rebellion brought about his downfall and death at Sauchieburn (1488). His eldest son, who had fought against him, succeeded as **James IV**.

James IV 1473–1513 •*King of Scotland*• He became king at the age of 15 after the murder of his father **James III** (1488), and was soon active in government. Much of the early 1490s was taken up with securing recognition for the new regime. As a result his council was composed of a far broader and more stable coalition than under his three predecessors. Athletic, warlike and pious, James has been called an ideal medieval king; his reign was probably the epitome and climax of Scottish medieval kingship rather than of new monarchy (he was the last Scottish king to speak Gaelic). His rising status, as a king popular at home and respected abroad, was confirmed by his marriage (1503) to **Margaret Tudor**, eldest daughter of **Henry VII**—an alliance which ultimately led to the union of Scotland and England (1603). In his brilliant Renaissance court he encouraged musicians such as **Robert Carver** and poets such as **William Dunbar**. Despite his new alliance with England, he adhered to his old French alliance when **Henry VIII** invaded France (1513). He invaded England and was killed at Flodden (1513), when his army of 20,000 men, probably the largest ever in Scotland, was crushed.

James V 1512–42 •*King of Scotland*• Born in Linlithgow, the son of **James IV**, he was less than two years old when his father's death (1513) gave him the crown, leaving him to grow up among the quarreling pro-French and pro-English factions, during which time Scotland was reduced to a state of anarchy. Imprisoned (1525–28) by his former stepfather, the Earl of Angus, he eventually made his escape, and as an independent sovereign began trying to increase the revenues of his all-but-bankrupt kingdom. He raised taxes from the Scottish Church to finance his College of Justice (1532), and the pope, anxious to prevent the spread of the Reformation in Scotland, allowed the king the right to make ecclesiastical appointments. James later used this to appoint five of his six illegitimate sons to high ecclesiastical office. In 1536 he visited France and married first Madeleine, the daughter of **Francis I** (1537), and after her death, **Mary of Guise** (1538). Both wives brought a substantial dowry and confirmed the Franco-Scottish alliance. Relations with England, which had been deteriorating from 1536, burst into open war after he failed to attend a conference with **Henry VIII** at York (1541). By 1542 the countries were at war and England invaded. After James's army was defeated at Solway Moss (1542), he retired to Falkland Palace and died, less because of illness than a lack of will to live, only a few days after the birth of his daughter, **Mary Queen of Scots**. Sometimes seen as the most unpleasant of all **Stuart** kings, he was also a highly talented Renaissance monarch. The monuments to his reign are the literary works produced at his glittering court, such as the poems and plays of Sir **David Lyndsay**, and the ambitious, costly architectural transformation of Stirling Castle and the palaces of Holyrood, Falkland and Linlithgow.

James VI and I 1566–1625 •*King of Scotland from 1567 and of England from 1603*• James was born in Edinburgh Castle, the son of **Mary Queen of Scots**, and Lord **Darnley**. On his mother's forced abdication in 1567 he was proclaimed king as James VI. During his infancy, power was exercised through a sequence of regents. The execution of Mary Queen of Scots in 1587 drew a token protest from her son, but it was not allowed to disturb the agreement recently concluded with England by the Treaty of Berwick (1586). In 1589 James visited Denmark, and there married Princess **Anne of Denmark**, who was crowned queen in May 1590. During the early 1590s there took place a careful playing-off of Roman Catholic and ultra-Protestant factions against each other, and by 1596 a new stability resulted. On the death of **Elizabeth I** of England (1603), James succeeded to the throne of England as great-grandson of **James IV**'s English wife, **Margaret Tudor**. Although he promised to visit Scotland once every three years, he did not return until 1617. A joint monarchy became for Scotland an absentee monarchy, although the king's political skill and knowledge allowed him to govern Scotland "by his pen." In England, he was at first well received by his English subjects. After the failure of the Gunpowder Plot (1605), severe laws were brought to bear against Roman Catholics. Eventually, growing dislike of the joint rule of two kingdoms, Puritan resentment of his high-church stance, his use of court favorites, and his friendship with Spain all embittered the fragile relations between the Crown and Parliament, especially after 1621. The death of the king's eldest son, Henry, Prince of Wales (1612), caused the succession to pass to his second son, the future **Charles I**, who became closely attached to the king's new favorite, George Villiers, 1st Duke of **Buckingham**. James's achievements as King of England are still a matter of dispute, but he is widely recognized as one of the most successful kings of Scotland, in whose long reign politics and society were transformed.

James VII and II 1633–1701 •*King of Scotland as James VII, and then of England and Ireland as James II*• The second son of **Charles I** and brother of **Charles II**, he was born at St James's Palace, London, and was made Duke of York. Nine months before his father's execution in 1649 he escaped to the Netherlands, served under the Vicomte de **Turenne** (1652–55), and in 1657 took Spanish service in Flanders. At the Restoration (1660) James became Lord High Admiral of England, twice commanding the English fleet in the Dutch wars. In 1659 he had entered into a private marriage contract with Anne Hyde, daughter of the Earl of **Clarendon** and a professed Catholic, and the year after her death in 1671, he himself became a convert to Catholicism. In 1673 Parliament passed the Test Act, and he was obliged to resign the office of Lord High Admiral. Shortly after, he married **Mary of Modena**, daughter of the Duke of Modena. The national unrest caused by the Popish Plot (1678) became so formidable that he had to retire to the Continent. He returned at the close of 1679, and was sent to Scotland to manage its affairs. After defeat of the bill the exiled James returned to England, and in direct violation of the law took his seat in the council, and resumed the direction of naval affairs. When Charles II died in 1685, James ascended the throne, and immediately proceeded to levy, on his own warrant, the customs and excise duties which had been granted to Charles only for life. He sent a mission to Rome, heard mass in public, and became, like his brother, the pensioner of the French king. In Scotland, parliament remained loyal, despite renewed persecution of the Covenanters, but in England the futile rebellion of the Duke of **Monmouth** was followed by the "Bloody Assizes." The suspension of the Test Act by the king's authority, his prosecution of the Seven Bishops on a charge of seditious libel, his conferring ecclesiastical benefices on Roman Catholics, and numerous other arbitrary acts showed his fixed determination to overthrow the constitution and the Church. The indignation of the people was at length aroused, and the interposition of William, Prince of Orange, James's son-in-law and nephew (the future **William III**), was formally solicited by seven leading politicians. William landed at Torbay on November 4, 1688, with a powerful army, and marched toward London. He was hailed as a deliverer, while James was deserted not only by his ministers and troops, but even by his daughter, Princess Anne (later Queen **Anne**). At the first sign of danger, James had sent his wife and infant son to France, and escaped and joined them at St Germain. In 1689, aided by a small body of French troops, he invaded Ireland and made an unsuccessful attempt to regain his throne. He was defeated at the Battle of the Boyne (1690), and returned to St Germain, where he resided until his death. He left two daughters—**Mary II**, married to William III, and Anne, afterward queen—and one son, **James Francis Edward Stuart**, the "Old Pretender," by his second wife. He had several illegitimate children, one of them James Fitzjames, Marshal **Berwick**.

James, Clive Vivian Leopold 1939– •*Australian broadcaster and writer*• Born in Sydney, he studied at the universities of Sydney and Cambridge, and began his career as a television critic with the British newspaper the *Observer* (1972–82), later publishing some of his work and writing other nonfiction, fiction, and verse, and three volumes of autobiography. Known as a perceptive cultural commentator, he has appeared on such TV shows as *The Late Clive James* (1983–87), *Saturday Night Clive* and *Sunday Night Clive* (1989–94) and *The Clive James Show* (1995–).

James, C(yril) L(ionel) R(obert) 1901–89 •*Trinidadian writer, lecturer, political activist and cricket enthusiast*• He was born in Tunapuna, Trinidad, and won a scholarship to Queens Royal College, Trinidad. An autodidact and a skillful cricket player, he was urged to leave Trinidad for England by **Learie Constantine** and it was there that *The Life of Captain Cipriani* was published in 1929 at Constantine's expense. James repaid the kindness by acting as his mentor's amanuensis for his newspaper column and five books. An advocate for the freedom of the Black races through Marxism and revolution, James was deported from the US for his political activities, and while in Trinidad his former pupil, **Eric Williams**, the prime minister, put him under house arrest. Perhaps his most influential book was *The Black Jacobins: Toussaint L'Ouverture and the San Domingo Revolution* (1938). He wrote only one novel, *Minty Alley* (1936).

“ ”

Body-line was not an incident, it was not an accident, it was not a temporary aberration. It was the violence and ferocity of our age expressing itself in cricket.

*1963 **Beyond the Boundary**.*

James, Elmore, *originally* **Elmore Brooks** 1918–63 •*US blues guitarist and singer*• Born in Richmond, Mississippi, he taught himself to play on a homemade guitar, and was profoundly influenced by meeting **Robert Johnson** in 1937. He began performing with Sonny Boy Williamson (originally Rice Miller, 1910–65), and went on to establish the most important slide guitar style in modern blues. He made his first recording in 1952, and had an immediate hit with his adaptation of a Robert Johnson song, "Dust My Broom." He moved to Chicago, but always remained in touch with his roots in the Mississippi Delta.

James, Henry 1843–1916 •*US novelist*• He was born in New York City, of Irish and Scottish stock. His father, Henry James (1811–82), was a well-known theological writer and lecturer. After a roving youth in the US and Europe (where he met **Ivan Turgenev** and **Gustave Flaubert**) and desultory law studies at Harvard, he began in 1865 to produce brilliant literary reviews and short stories. His work as a novelist falls into three periods. To the first, in which he is mainly concerned with the impact of US life on the older European civilizations, belong *Roderick Hudson* (1875), *The American* (1877), *Daisy Miller* (1879), *Washington Square* (1880), *Portrait of a Lady* (1881), and *The Bostonians* (1886). From 1876 he made his home in England, chiefly in London and at Lamb House in Rye, Sussex, where he struck up an oddly contrasted friendship with **H G Wells**, one that lasted until the latter's savage attack on the Jamesian ethos in the novel *Boon* (1915). His second period, devoted to purely English subjects, comprises *The Tragic Muse* (1890), *The Spoils of Poynton* (1897), *What Maisie Knew* (1897) and *The Awkward Age* (1899). James returns to the theme of the international situation in his last period, which includes *The Wings of the Dove* (1902), *The Ambassadors* (1903) (possibly his masterpiece),

The Golden Bowl (1904) and two unfinished novels. Collections of his characteristic "long short stories" include *Terminations* (1895), *The Two Magics* (1898) and *The Altar of the Dead* (1909). His well-known ghost story, *The Turn of the Screw*, was published in 1898. The acknowledged master of the psychological novel, which profoundly influenced the 20th-century literary scene, he sacrifices plot in the interests of minute delineation of character. Many seemingly insignificant incidents, however, subtly contribute allegorically or metaphorically to the author's intentions. He became a British subject (1915) and shortly before his death was appointed to the Order of Merit. He also wrote critical studies, travel sketches and three volumes of memoirs. He was the brother of the philosopher and psychologist **William James**.

James, Jesse Woodson 1847–82 •*US outlaw*• Born in Clay County, Missouri, as a teenager he joined a band of pro-Confederate guerrillas, and at the war's end he and his brother Frank (1843–1915) turned to robbery, leading a gang of outlaws from 1866. They carried out numerous bank and train robberies over a period of 15 years, until a large price was put on Jesse's head and he was shot by Robert Ford, a member of his own gang seeking the reward. Frank gave himself up and after his release lived the rest of his life on the family farm. Jesse became a legendary figure, celebrated in ballads, dimestore novels and later in Hollywood films.

James, M(ontague) R(hodes) 1862–1936 •*English writer and scholar*• Born in Goodnestone, Kent, and educated at Eton and Cambridge, he had a distinguished career as an archaeologist, medievalist and paleographer, becoming Provost of King's College, Cambridge (1905–18), director of the Fitzwilliam Museum (1894–1908) and then Provost of Eton (1918). He also wrote *Ghost Stories of an Antiquary* (1904), which was followed by three more collections, in which erudite scholarly details add an air of veracity and evil manifestations tend to be hinted at rather than explicitly described. Among his best stories are "Oh, Whistle, and I'll Come to You, My Lad" (1904) and "Casting the Runes" (1911). He was appointed to the Order of Merit in 1930.

James, P(hyllis) D(orothy), Baroness James of Holland Park, *née* **White** 1920– •*English detective story writer*• Born in Oxford, she was educated at Cambridge Girls' High School. After the war she was employed in the Home Office, first in the police department, where she was involved with the forensic science service, thereafter in the criminal law department. *Cover Her Face*, published in 1962, was her first novel, a well-crafted but slight detective story. She has written steadily since, many of her works featuring the superior detective (and minor poet) Adam Dalgleish. *A Taste for Death* (1986), a macabre, elegant and substantial story, was an international hit and was followed by *Devices and Desires* (1989). *The Skull Beneath the Skin* (1982) featured a female private detective, Cordelia Gray. She was awarded the Crime Writers Association Diamond Dagger in 1987 and made a life peer in 1991. Later works include *The Children of Men* (1992) and *A Certain Justice* (1997).

“ ”

Murder is a unique crime for which we can never make reparation.

1991 "Series Detectives," collected in Brown and Munro (eds) ***Writers Writing*** *(1993).*

James, Sid 1913–76 •*British comedy actor*• He was born in Johannesburg, South Africa, the son of Jewish music-hall artists. After work in an entertainments unit, then in an antitank regiment during World War II, he moved to London in 1946. His early film roles included appearances in *The Lavender Hill Mob* (1951) and *The Titfield Thunderbolt* (1952). He was **Tony Hancock**'s foil in *Hancock's Half Hour* (radio 1954–59, television 1956–60) and starred in the television sitcoms *Citizen James* (1960–62) and *Bless This House* (1971–76). He is best remembered for his performances in 19 *Carry On* ... films.

James, William 1842–1910 •*US philosopher and psychologist*• Born in New York City, he received a medical degree from Harvard, where he taught comparative anatomy from 1872, then philosophy from 1882. Professor from 1885, he changed his professorial title in 1889 from philosophy to psychology. In his *Principles of Psychology* (1890) he places psychology firmly on a physiological basis and represents the mind as an instrument for coping with the world. He described himself as a "radical empiricist," maintaining that metaphysical disputes can be resolved or dissolved by examining the practical consequences of competing theories. He expounded these ideas most famously in *The Will to Believe* (1907) and *Pragmatism* (1907), and he treated ethics and religion in the same practical, nondogmatic way, as in *The Varieties of Religious Experience* (1902) in which he encouraged his readers, in an age of loss of faith, not to be afraid of religious and mystical experiences. James and **Henri Bergson** were responsible for the formulation of the concept of stream of consciousness, a term which James himself coined. He exercised a great influence both on politicians and on writers, such as his pupil **Gertrude Stein**. He also helped to found the American Society for Psychical Research. He was the elder brother of **Henry James**.

Jameson, Sir Leander Starr Jameson, 1st Baronet 1853–1917 •*South African politician*• Born in Edinburgh, he studied medicine there and in London, and began to practice in Kimberley in 1878. Through **Cecil Rhodes**, "Dr Jim," as he was called, was in 1891 made administrator for the South Africa Company at Fort Salisbury. During the troubles at Johannesburg between the Uitlanders and the Boer government, Jameson started with 500 troops to support the Uitlanders (The Jameson Raid, December 29, 1895). At Krugersdorp they were overpowered by an overwhelming force of Boers and compelled to surrender (January 2, 1896). Handed over to the British authorities, Dr Jameson was in July condemned in London to 15 months' imprisonment, but was released in December. In 1900 he was elected to the Cape Legislative Assembly, and in 1904–08 was (Progressive) premier of Cape Colony.

Jameson, (Margaret) Storm 1891–1986 •*English novelist*• She was born in Whitby, North Yorkshire, and studied at the University of Leeds. Her first success was *The Lovely Ship* (1927), which was followed by more than 30 books that maintained her reputation as a storyteller and stylist. These include *The Voyage Home* (1930), *The Black Laurel* (1948), *A Cup of Tea for Mr Thorgill* (1957) and *The White Crow* (1968). She also wrote poems, essays, criticism and biography, and several volumes of autobiography.

Jamison, Judith 1943– •*US dancer and choreographer*• Born in Philadelphia, she studied at the Judimar School there. She joined **Alvin Ailey**'s American Dance Theater in 1965, becoming one of his top soloists. He choreographed the solo *Cry* for her in 1971, a showcase for her statuesque physique, musical sensitivity and dramatic stage presence. As director of the Alvin Ailey Dance Theater since 1989, she has choreographed such works as *Sweet Release* (with music by **Wynton Marsalis**), staged at the New York State Theater in 1996.

Janáček, Leoš 1854–1928 •*Czech composer*• Born in Hukvaldy, Moravia (now in the Czech Republic), at the age of 16 he was choirmaster in Brno, where he settled after studying in Prague and Leipzig, and became Professor of Composition (1919). He matured late as a composer, and of his operas, *Jenůfa* (1904, first performed 1912) and *Osul* (1904) are among his most original in terms of rhythm and subtle melodic dependence upon language. His other works include *The Excursions of Mr Brouček* (1908–17, *Výletypana Broučka*), *Kátja Kabanová* (1921), *The Cunning Little Vixen* (1924, *Příhody lišky Bystroušky*) and *The Makropulos Case* (1925, *Věc Makropulos*), the *Glagolitic Mass* (1926, *Glagolská mše*), two string quartets (1923, 1928), *Sinfonietta* (1926) and *The Diary of One Who Disappeared* (1919–24, *Zápisník Zmizeleho*). Janáček's scientific study of the melodic shapes and rhythmic patterns of speech, enhanced by bold, idiosyncratic orchestration, his deep sense of nationalism and intimate choice of subject matter are easily distinguishable features of his work.

Jane Seymour c. 1509–37 •*English queen*• The daughter of Sir John Seymour, and sister of **Edward Seymour**, Protector Somerset, she was lady in waiting to both of **Henry VIII**'s former wives, **Catherine of Aragon** and **Anne Boleyn**. She became his third wife 11 days after Anne Boleyn's execution (1536), and gave birth to a son, Edward (the future **Edward VI**), but died 12 days later. Her portrait was painted by **Hans Holbein** the Younger.

Jane, Frederick Thomas 1870–1916 •*British naval author, journalist and artist*• Born in Upottery, Devon, he worked first as an artist, then as a naval correspondent on various periodicals. He founded and edited *Jane's Fighting Ships* (1898) and *All the World's Aircraft* (1909), the annuals by which his name is still best known. Inventor of the naval war game, his nonfiction works include *Heresies of Sea Power* (1906) and *The World's Warships* (1915). Among his novels are *A Royal Bluejacket* (1908).

Jansen, Cornelius Otto 1585–1638 •*Dutch Roman Catholic theologian, and founder of the Jansenist reform movement*• Born in Acquoi, near Leerdam, he studied in Utrecht, Louvain and Paris and became Professor of Theology at the University of Bayonne and in 1630 at the University of Louvain. In 1636 he was made Bishop of Ypres. He died just as he had completed his great work, the *Augustinus*, which tried to prove that the teaching of St **Augustine** against the Pelagians and Semi-Pelagians was directly opposed to the teaching of the Jesuit schools. On its publication in 1640 the *Augustinus* caused an outcry, especially among the Jesuits, and it was prohibited by a decree of the Inquisition in 1641. In the following year it was condemned by **Urban VIII** in the bull *In Eminenti*. Jansen's adherents included **Antoine Arnauld**, **Blaise Pascal** and the Port-Royalists. The controversy raged in France for nearly a century, when a large number of Jansenists emigrated to the Netherlands.

Jansky, Karl Guthe 1905–50 •*US radio engineer*• Born in Norman, Oklahoma, he studied at the University of Wisconsin, and joined the Bell Telephone Laboratories in 1928. Detecting a weak source of static on short-wave radio telephone transmissions, he concluded that it had a stellar origin, and by 1932 he had pinpointed it as emanating from the center of the Milky Way. His findings allowed the development of radio astronomy during the 1950s. In 1973 the unit of radio emission strength, the jansky, was named after him.

Janssen, Cornelis, *originally* **Cornelius Johnson** 1593–c. 1664 •*Dutch portrait painter*• Born in London, England, he moved to Amsterdam in 1643. His portraits show the influence of **Van Dyck**, with whom he worked at the court of **Charles I**. He is represented in the National Gallery, London, and at Chatsworth, Derbyshire.

Jansson, Tove 1914–2001 •*Finnish writer and artist*• She was born in Helsinki. Her "Moomintroll" books for children (written in Swedish), including *Comet in Moominland* (1946) and the *Finn Family Moomintroll* (1948), are as much appreciated by adults. Set in the fantastic yet real world of the Moomins, the books emphasize the security of family life, and reached an international audience. She was the recipient of many literary prizes. She later wrote a number of books for adults, including the psychological thriller *Den ärliga bedragaren* (1982, "The Honest Deceiver").

Januarius, St, *Italian* **San Gennaro** d. c. 305 AD •*Italian prelate, patron saint of Naples*• He was Bishop of Benevento. According to tradition, he was martyred in Pozzuoli in AD 305, during the persecutions of **Diocletian**. His body is preserved in Naples Cathedral, with two vials supposed to contain his dried blood, believed to liquefy on September 19, his feast day, and other occasions.

Jarman, Derek 1942–94 •*English painter and filmmaker*• Born in Northwood, Middlesex, he studied painting at the Slade School, London (1963–67), before moving into costume and set design for the Royal Ballet. He first worked in the cinema as a production designer for **Ken Russell**'s *The Devils* (1970). He directed his first feature film, *Sebastiane*, in 1976 and transferred his painterly instincts to the cinema in a succession of often controversial works exploring the decline of modern Britain, his gay sensibilities and artistic idols. His films include *Jubilee* (1977), *Caravaggio* (1985), *The Garden* (1991), *Edward II* (1991), an adaptation of **Christopher Marlowe**'s 1594 play, *Wittgenstein* (1993) and *Blue* (1994). He also directed pop videos and made stage designs for opera and ballet. His writings include *Modern Nature* (1991).

Jarrell, Randall 1914–65 •*US poet and critic*• Born in Nashville, Tennessee, he graduated from Vanderbilt University and served in the air force in World War II. Many of his early poems draw on his war experience, and his later work continues to focus on alienation and loss. He published several volumes of poetry, ranging from *Blood for a Stranger* (1942) to *The Lost World*, published posthumously in 1966. His *Complete Poems* appeared in 1969. A merciless reviewer of bad verse, he also wrote lucid and eloquent essays on writers he admired, and children's books, notably *The Animal Family* (1965), illustrated by **Maurice Sendak**. He taught English at a series of colleges and universities, satirizing a stint at Bennington College in his novel *Pictures from an Institution* (1954). Near the end of his life he was hospitalized for depression, and soon after being released he was hit by a car, probably a suicide.

Jarrett, Keith 1945– •*US jazz and classical musician and composer*• Born in Allentown, Pennsylvania, he gave his first recital at the age of seven. He played professionally while in school, and spent a year at Berklee College of Music in Boston. He moved to New York in 1965, played briefly with **Art Blakey**, then spent three years with saxophonist Charles Lloyd, and two with **Miles Davis**. He began performing lengthy solo concerts from 1972. He has recorded jazz with groups of various sizes, but most often with his Standards trio featuring Gary Peacock and Jack DeJohnette, and plays drums and soprano saxophone as well as piano. A brilliant improviser, he has also recorded works by **Bach** and **Dmitri Shostakovich**, and has composed music for classical settings.

Jarry, Alfred 1873–1907 •*French writer*• He was born in Laval, Mayenne, and was educated in Rennes. His satirical farce, *Ubu roi* was first written when he was 15 and performed as a puppet. He later revised it and it was produced in 1896 (Eng trans 1951). In a crude parody of **Shakespeare**'s *Macbeth*, le père Ubu, the grotesque hero, symbolizes the bourgeoisie pushed to absurd lengths by lust for power. He wrote two sequels, *Ubu enchaîné* (1900, Eng trans *Ubu Enslaved*, 1953) and *Ubu cocu* (1944, Eng trans *Ubu Cuckolded*, 1965), and a two-act musical version of *Ubu roi* for marionettes (1901), as well as short stories and poems and other plays. His belief that the writer should empty the mind of intelligence in order to open it to the possibilities of hallucination anticipates surrealism. He also invented a logic of the absurd, which he called "pataphysique," and his work is considered a precursor of the Theater of the Absurd. Almost as eccentric as his creation, Ubu, he lived a life of excess and died an alcoholic.

“ ”

La mort n'est que pour les médiocres.
Death is only for the mediocre.

1898 ***Gestes et opinions du Docteur Faustroll Pataphysicien****, volume 8, part 37.*

Jaruzelski, Wojciech Witold 1923– •*Polish soldier and politician*• He was born near Lublin. After a long and distinguished military career, he became a member of the politburo in 1971 and was appointed prime minister (1981–85) and Communist Party leader in 1981. Later that year, in an attempt to ease the country's crippling economic problems and to counteract the increasing political influence of the free trade union Solidarność (Solidarity), Jaruzelski declared a state of martial law. Solidarity was declared an illegal organization and its leaders were detained and put on trial. Martial law was lifted in July of 1983, and in 1985 Jaruzelski became state president, overseeing a transition to a new form of "socialist pluralist" democracy in 1989. He was president of the Polish Republic until December 1991, when he was succeeded by **Lech Wałęsa**.

Jason, David, *originally* **David John White** 1940– •*English actor*• Born in London, he acted in amateur theater while working as an electrician. One of his earliest television roles was in *Crossroads*, before playing Captain Fantastic in *Do Not Adjust Your Set* (1967–69). Teaming up with **Ronnie Barker**, he played Dithers in *Hark at Barker* (1969–70), Blanco in *Porridge* (1974–77) and Granville in *Open All Hours* (1976–85). Later roles included Derek Trotter in *Only Fools and Horses* (1981–91, and occasional "specials"), Skullion in *Porterhouse Blue* (1987, British Academy of Film and Television Arts Best Actor award 1988), Pop Larkin in *The Darling Buds of May* (1991–93) and Detective Inspector Jack Frost in *A Touch of Frost* (1992–).

Jaspers, Karl Theodor 1883–1969 •*German existentialist philosopher*• Born in Oldenburg, he studied medicine in Berlin, Göttingen and Heidelberg, where he was Professor of Psychology from 1916 to 1920. From 1921 he was Professor of Philosophy at the University of Heidelberg until dismissed by the Nazis in 1937. His work was banned but he stayed in Germany and was awarded the Goethe prize in 1947 for his uncompromising stand. In 1948 he settled in Basel as a Swiss citizen, and was appointed professor. The most important of his many works is considered to be *Philosophie* (3 vols, 1932). In this he developed his own brand of existentialism whereby *Existenz* (Being) necessarily transcends and eludes ordinary objective thought: at the limits of the intellect the "authentic self" must make a leap of apprehension of a different kind.

Jaurès, (Auguste Marie Joseph) Jean 1859–1914 •*French Socialist leader, writer and orator*• Born in Castres, Tarn, he was a deputy from 1885 to 1889, lectured on philosophy in Toulouse and became a deputy again in 1893. He founded the French Socialist Party, and in 1904 cofounded the Socialist paper *L'Humanité*, which he edited until his death. An advocate of Franco-German rapprochement in the crisis that followed the assassination of Archduke **Franz Ferdinand**, Jaurès was himself assassinated in July 1914 by a fanatical French patriot.

Jawara, Sir Dawda Kairaba 1924– •*Gambian politician*• He was born in Barajally. After graduating from the University of Glasgow, he returned to Gambia and entered politics in 1960. Progressing rapidly, he became minister of education and then premier (1962–65). When full independence was achieved in 1965, he became prime minister, and when republican status was attained in 1970, president. He was reelected in 1972, 1977, 1982 and 1987, despite an abortive coup against him in 1981. The coup was thwarted by Senegalese troops and brought the two countries closer together into the confederation of Senegambia. His presidency ended in 1994.

Jawlensky, Alexei von 1864–1941 •*Russian painter*• Born in Kuslovo, he began as an officer in the Imperial Guards but turned to painting in 1889, studying at the St Petersburg Academy. In 1896 he went to Munich where he met **Wassily Kandinsky**, and in 1905 to France where he was strongly influenced by the work of **Van Gogh**, **Gauguin** and **Matisse**, developing a personal style which combined traditional Russian icons and peasant art with the new Fauvist techniques. A founding member of the *Neue Künstlervereinigung* ("New Artists' Association," known as the NKV) in Munich in 1909, in 1924 he also founded with Kandinsky, **Paul Klee** and **Lyonel Feininger** the short-lived *Der blaue Vier* (Blue Four association).

Jay, John 1745–1829 •*American jurist and politician*• Born in New York City, he was admitted to the bar in 1768 and elected to the Continental Congress (1774–77). He drafted the constitution of the state of New York in 1777, and was appointed Chief Justice of that state. He was elected president of Congress in 1778, and in 1779 was sent as ambassador to Spain. From 1782 he was one of the most influential of the commissioners negotiating peace with Great Britain. He was Secretary for Foreign Affairs (1784–89), then became Chief Justice of the Supreme Court (1789–95). In 1794 he concluded with Lord **Grenville** the convention known as Jay's Treaty, which, though favorable to the US, was denounced by the Democrats as a betrayal of France. He was governor of New York from 1795 to 1801, when he retired.

Jayawardene, Junius Richard 1906–96 •*Sri Lankan politician*• Born in Colombo, he studied law at the University of Colombo before he entered the House of Representatives in 1947 as a representative of the Liberal-Conservative United National Party (UNP). He held a number of ministerial posts (1953–70) before becoming Leader of the UNP, and of the Opposition, in 1970. He so revitalized it that it returned to power in 1977. He introduced a new constitution in 1978, creating a republic, and became the country's first president (1978). He was confronted with mounting unrest between Tamil separatists and the indigenous Sinhalese, forcing the imposition of a state of emergency in 1983, and in 1989 he stepped down as president and was succeeded by **Ranasinghe Premadasa**.

Jean de Meung *See* **Meung, Jean de**

Jeanne d'Arc *See* **Joan of Arc**

Jeans, Sir James Hopwood 1877–1946 •*English physicist, astronomer and writer*• Born in Ormskirk, near Southport, he taught at Princeton University and at Cambridge before becoming a research associate at Mt Wilson Observatory in Pasadena. One of his first important findings was the development of a formula to describe the distribution of energy of enclosed radiation at long wavelength, now known as the Rayleigh-Jeans law. He also carried out important work on the kinetic theory of gases. He made significant advances in astrophysics, including studies of the formation of binary stars, stellar evolution, the nature of spiral nebulae and the origin of stellar energy, which he believed to be associated with radioactivity. He was renowned as a popularizer of physical and astronomical theories and their philosophical underpinnings in works such as *The Universe Around Us* (1929) and *The New Background of Science* (1933). He was knighted in 1928.

Jeb *See* **Stuart, James Ewell Brown**

Jebb, Eglantyne 1876–1928 •*English philanthropist*• Born in Ellesmere, Shropshire, she graduated from St Margaret Hall, Oxford, and then did some teaching and social work before going to Macedonia to administer the relief fund for the victims of the Balkan wars. After the end of World War I, the plight of the 4 to 5 million children starving in Europe prompted her to set up the Save the Children Fund (1919).

Jefferson, Blind Lemon 1897–1929 •*US blues guitarist and singer*• Born in Couchman, Texas, he was blind from birth. He performed locally in and around Worthman, Texas, and then moved to Dallas in 1917, where he played on the streets for small change. His recorded legacy comprises almost 100 songs (including some gospel and spiritual material using the pseudonym Deacon L J Bates). He was the first blues singer to establish a repertoire of his own songs, rather than buying from commercial songwriters, and his performing style, notably his intricate, improvisational guitar playing, was enormously influential in the development of the music.

Jefferson, Thomas 1743–1826 •*Third President of the US*• Born on his father's plantation, Shadwell, in Albemarle County, Virginia, he graduated from the College of William and Mary and was admitted to the bar in 1767. Two years later he was elected to the Virginia House of Burgesses, where he joined the Revolutionary Party. He played a prominent part in the calling of the first Continental Congress in 1774, to which he was sent as a delegate, drafting the Declaration of Independence. He helped to form the Virginia state constitution, and became governor of Virginia (1779–81). He was sent to France in 1784 with **Benjamin Franklin** and **Samuel Adams** as plenipotentiary, and succeeded Franklin as ambassador in 1785. In 1789 **George Washington** appointed him secretary of state. As leader of the Democratic-Republican Party, he advocated limited government and envisioned the USA as a republic of independent farmers, and he clashed repeatedly with **Alexander Hamilton** and the Federalist Party. After running second in the presidential election of 1796, he then became vice president (1797–1801) under **John Adams**. He was elected president in 1800, narrowly defeating **Aaron Burr**, and was reelected by a large majority for the next presidential term. Among the chief events of his first term were the war with Tripoli, which subdued the Barbary pirates, and the Louisiana Purchase of 1803, which Jefferson sponsored. He also planned the **Lewis** and **Clark** expedition to explore the lands to the west of the Mississippi. His second term saw the firing on the *Chesapeake* by the *Leopard*, the Embargo Act of 1807, the trial of Aaron Burr for treason, and the prohibition of the slave import trade (1808). In 1809 he retired to his Virginia estate, Monticello, and devoted much time to founding the University of Virginia and designing its campus. A man of letters as well as a gifted architect, he published several books, of which the most valuable is his *Notes on the State of Virginia* (1785). He and his former political rival John Adams both died on July 4, 1826, the 50th anniversary of the Declaration of Independence.

" "

I have seen enough of one war never to wish to see another.

1794 Letter to John Adams, 25 April.

Jeffreys, Sir Alec John 1950– •*English molecular biologist*• Born in Oxford, he graduated from Oxford University. After work at the University of Amsterdam (1975–77), he moved to the department of genetics at the University of Leicester, where he has remained throughout his career, becoming Professor of Genetics in 1987. He was elected a Fellow of the Royal Society in 1986 and became Wolfson Research Professor of the Royal Society in 1991. He developed the technique of "DNA fingerprinting," in which samples of blood or semen can conclusively identify an individual in much the same way as a fingerprint. He was knighted in 1994.

Jeffreys (of Wem), George Jeffreys, 1st Baron 1648–89 •*English judge*• Born in Acton, Clwyd, Wales, he was called to the bar in 1668. He rose rapidly, was knighted (1677), and became Recorder of London (1678). He was active in the Popish Plot prosecutions, became Chief Justice of Chester (1680), baronet (1681), and Chief Justice of the King's Bench (1683). In every state trial he proved a willing tool of the Crown, and was raised to the peerage by **James VII and II** (1685). Among his earliest trials were those of **Titus Oates** and **Richard Baxter**. His period in the West Country to try the followers of the Duke of **Monmouth** earned the name of the "Bloody Assizes" for its severity. He was Lord Chancellor (1685–88), but on James's flight into exile was imprisoned in the Tower of London, where he died.

Jeffreys, Sir Harold 1891–1989 •*English mathematician, geophysicist and astronomer*• Born in Fatfield, Durham, he was educated at St John's College, Cambridge. After working in dynamical astronomy he joined the Meteorological Office as an assistant to the director. Returning to Cambridge in 1922, he held various teaching appointments and later became Plumian Professor of Astronomy and Experimental Philosophy (1946–58). He discovered the discontinuity between the earth's upper and lower mantle, found evidence for the fluid nature of the core and did much pioneering theoretical work on the shape and strength of the earth. His analysis of seismic travel times was published as the *Jeffreys-Bullen Tables* (1940, see also **Keith Bullen**), which remains a standard reference work. This work led him to a Bayesian theory of probability applicable to a wide range of sciences. He was elected a Fellow of the Royal Society in 1925, and knighted in 1953.

Jeffries, Lionel 1926– •*English actor and director*• Born in London, he trained at the Royal Academy of Dramatic Art and became known as a comic performer in films such as *Blue Murder at St Trinian's* (1957), *Two Way Stretch* (1960), *The Wrong Arm of the Law* (1962) and *Chitty Chitty Bang Bang* (1968). As a director, he had great success with *The Railway Children* (1970), *The Amazing Mr Blunden* (1972) and *The Water Babies* (1978). On television, he acted in parts including the title role in the sitcom *Father Charlie* (1982).

Jehu 842–815 BC •*Hebrew general and king of Israel*• He had been military commander under King **Ahab**, but after Ahab's death he led a military coup and slaughtered the royal family, including Ahab's wife **Jezebel**. Having seized the throne for himself, he founded a dynasty that saw a decline in the fortunes of Israel, which was forced to pay tribute to Assyria.

Jekyll, Gertrude 1843–1932 •*English horticulturist and garden designer*• Born in London, she was trained as an artist but was forced by failing eyesight to abandon painting. Instead, she took up landscape design at her garden at Munstead Wood, Surrey. In association with the architect **Edwin Lutyens**, she designed more than 300 gardens for his buildings that had a great influence on promoting color design in garden planning. Her books include *Home and Garden* (1900), *Wall and Water Gardens* (1901) and *Garden Ornament* (1918).

Jellicoe, John Rushworth Jellicoe, 1st Earl 1859–1935 •*English admiral*• Born in Southampton, he served in the Egyptian war of 1882, and was one of the survivors of the collision between HMS *Victoria* and HMS *Camperdown* in 1893. He was Chief of Staff on an international overland expedition to relieve the legations in Peking (Beijing) during the Boxer Rebellion (1900), where he was severely wounded. At the outbreak of World War I he was appointed Commander in Chief of the Grand Fleet, and his main engagement was the inconclusive Battle of Jutland (1916), for which he was much criticized. He later became First Sea Lord (1916–17) and Admiral of the Fleet (1919), and was appointed governor of New Zealand (1920–24). He was made an earl in 1925.

Jenkins, David Edward 1925– •*English theologian and prelate*• Born in Bromley, Kent, to devout Methodist parents, he was a lecturer at the University of Birmingham and at Oxford and later became Professor of Theology at Leeds (1979–84). He became Bishop of Durham in 1984 amid controversy over his interpretation of the Virgin Birth and the Resurrection. His books include *A Guide to the Debate About God* (1966), *The Contradiction of Christianity* (1976), *God, Politics and the Furute* (1988), *God, Jesus and Life in the Spirit* (1988) and *Free to Believe* (1991). He retired as Bishop of Durham in 1994 and has since served as assistant bishop in the diocese of Ripon.

" "

Christians are not called to win battles, but to find ways of being in battles.

1988 ***Spirituality for Conflict.***

Jenkins, Robert fl. 1731–48 •*English merchant captain*• He was engaged in trading in the West Indies. In 1731 he alleged that his sloop had been boarded by a Spanish coast guard, and that, though there was no proof of smuggling, he had been tortured and had his ear torn off. He produced the alleged ear in 1738 in the House of Commons and so helped to force **Robert Walpole** into the War of Jenkins' Ear against Spain in 1739, which merged into the War of the Austrian Succession (1740–48). Jenkins served with the East India Company, and for a time as governor of St Helena.

Jenkins (of Hillhead), Roy Harris Jenkins, Baron 1920–2003 •*Welsh Labour politician and author*• Born in Abersychan, Monmouthshire, he studied at Balliol College, Oxford. Elected Member of Parliament for Central Southwark in 1948, he was the youngest member of the House. He was Member of Parliament for the Stetchford division of Birmingham from 1950 to 1976. He introduced the controversial Obscene Publications Bill, strengthening the position of authors, publishers and printers vis-à-vis prosecutions for obscenity. After a successful period as Minister of Aviation (1964–65) he was made Home Secretary. In 1967 he changed posts with **James Callaghan** to become Chancellor of the Exchequer, and was again appointed Home Secretary on Labour's return to power in 1974. He resigned as a Member of Parliament in 1976, and became president of the European Commission (1977–81). He was a founding member of the joint leadership of the Social Democratic Party (1981–82), became its first leader in 1982, but stepped down after the 1983 election in favor of Dr **David Owen**. He returned to represent Glasgow (Hillhead) from 1982 until he was defeated in 1987, when he was made a life peer, and also elected Chancellor of Oxford. He was appointed to the Order of Merit in 1993. A successful journalist and author, his published works include *Mr Balfour's Poodle* (1954), *Asquith* (1964), *W E Gladstone* (1995), which won the Whitbread Biography award, and *Churchill* (2001).

Jenkinson, Robert *See* **Liverpool, 2nd Earl of**

Jenner, Edward 1749–1823 •*English physician, the pioneer of vaccination*• Born in Berkeley vicarage, Gloucestershire, he was apprenticed to a surgeon at Sodbury, near Bristol, and in 1770 went to London to study under **John Hunter**. In 1773 he settled in Berkeley, where he acquired a large practice. He began to examine the truth of the traditions respecting cowpox (1775), and became convinced that it was efficacious as a protection against smallpox. In 1796 he vaccinated James Phipps, an eight-year-old boy, with cowpox matter from the hands of Sarah Nelmes, a milkmaid, and soon afterward inoculated him with smallpox, demonstrating that the boy was protected. The practice of vaccination met with brief opposition, until over 70 principal physicians and surgeons in London signed a declaration of their entire confidence in it, and within five years vaccination was being practiced in many parts of the world. Jenner devoted the remainder of his life to advocating vaccination. Parliament rewarded him with two large grants and **Napoleon I** had a medal struck in his honor.

Jennings, Elizabeth 1926–2001 •*English poet and critic*• Born in Boston, Lincolnshire, she was educated at St Anne's College,

Oxford. She published over 30 collections including *Song for a Birth or a Death* (1961), *Growing-Points* (1975) and *Praises* (1998). Her poetry deals with major themes such as love and bereavement but is often understated and cautious in the style of other "Movement" poets, with skillful use of traditional verse patterns. She wrote several volumes of poetry for children.

Jennings, Pat(rick) 1945– •*Northern Irish soccer player*• Born in Newry, County Down, he started his career with Newry Town and then played for Watford, Tottenham Hotspur and Arsenal, making a total of 747 Football League appearances and winning several cup-winner's medals. He gained 119 caps for Northern Ireland and retired in 1986.

Jennings, Waylon 1937–2002 •*US country music singer and songwriter*• Born in Littlefield, Texas, he was a radio disk jockey by the age of 12, and joined **Buddy Holly**'s band The Crickets in 1958, narrowly missing the fatal plane crash which killed his boss after giving up his seat to J P Richardson, The Big Bopper (1930–59). **Chet Atkins** signed him on to RCA in 1965, where his fight for greater artistic control produced the classic *Honky Tonk Heroes* (1972). He enjoyed great commercial success into the early 1980s and formed The Highwaymen with **Willie Nelson**, **Johnny Cash** and Kris Kristofferson (1936–) in 1985. He turned his autobiographical album *A Man Called Hoss* (1987) into a successful one-man show. Later albums include *Too Dumb for New York, Too Ugly for LA* (1992) and *Waymore's Blues Part II* (1994).

Jensen, (Johannes) Hans Daniel 1907–73 •*German physicist and Nobel Prize winner*• Born in Hamburg, he studied physics, mathematics and philosophy at the University of Hamburg. He was appointed professor at Hamburg (1936) and Heidelberg (1949) Universities. From the large amounts of data available on nuclei it had emerged that stable nuclides had a "magic number" of neutrons and/or protons, similar to the pattern observed in atoms where a filled shell of electrons corresponds to a stable element. Jensen used this similarity to apply the ideas of atomic physics to nuclei, leading to the nuclear shell model. This was done independently by **Maria Goeppert-Mayer** in Chicago, and for this work Jensen, Goeppert-Mayer and **Eugene Wigner** shared the 1963 Nobel Prize for physics.

Jensen, Johannes V(ilhelm) 1873–1950 •*Danish novelist, essayist and poet, and Nobel Prize winner*• He was born in Farsø, Jutland, and his native land and its people are described in his *Himmerlandshistorier* (1898–1910). Many of his other works are based on his extensive travels in the Far East and the US. However, the journey traced in *Den lange rejse* (1908–22, *The Long Journey*, 1922–24) is that of man through the ages, the three constituent novels being an expression of Jensen's **Darwin**ism. His psychological study of **Christian II** of Denmark, *Kongens Fald* (1933, "The Fall of the King"), his short prose works, and his lyric poetry (1901–41) all contribute to his high place in modern Scandinavian literature. He was awarded the Nobel Prize for literature in 1944.

Jeremiah 7th century BC •*Old Testament prophet*• Born in Anathoth, near Jerusalem, he was the son of the priest Hilkiah. In Jerusalem during the siege by **Nebuchadnezzar**, he is later said to have been martyred at Tahpanhes in Egypt. The Book of Jeremiah warned of the impending fall of Jerusalem to Nebuchadnezzar and the Babylonian exile, and foretold the coming of a Messiah.

Jerne, Niels Kai 1911–94 •*English immunologist and Nobel Prize winner*• Born in London to Danish parents, he studied physics at the University of Leicester and the University of Copenhagen. Among various distinguished medical posts that he held, he was founding director of the Basel Institute of Immunology (1969–80). Jerne's research into the immune system examined the creation of antibodies, explained the development of T-lymphocytes, and formulated the network theory, which views the immune system as a network of interacting lymphocytes and antibodies. He shared the 1984 Nobel Prize for physiology or medicine with **Cesar Milstein** and **Georges Köhler**.

Jeroboam I 10th century BC •*First king of the divided kingdom of Israel*• **Solomon** made him superintendent of the labors and taxes exacted from his tribe of Ephraim at the construction of the fortifications of Zion. The growing disaffection toward Solomon fostered his ambition, but he was obliged to flee to Egypt. After Solomon's death he headed the successful revolt of the northern tribes against Rehoboam, and, as their king, established idol shrines at Dan and Bethel to wean away his people from the pilgrimages to Jerusalem. He reigned for 22 years.

Jerome, St, *originally* **Eusebius Hieronymus** c. 342–420 AD •*Christian ascetic and scholar, one of the four Latin Doctors of the Church*• Born in Stridon, near Aquileia, Dalmatia, he studied at Rome, where he was also baptized. In AD 370 he settled in Aquileia with his friend the theologian Rufinus (c. 345–410), but then became a hermit (374–78) in the desert of Chalcis. Ordained as a priest at Antioch in 379, he became secretary to Pope **Damasus** (reigned 366–84), in Rome, where he enjoyed great influence. In 385 he led a pilgrimage to the Holy Land, and settled in Bethlehem in 386, where he wrote the first Latin translation of the Bible from the Hebrew (which became known as the Vulgate). He also wrote biblical commentaries, and vehement criticisms of Jovinian, Vigilantius and the Pelagians, and even of Rufinus and St **Augustine**. St Jerome was the most learned and eloquent of the four Latin Doctors. His feast day is September 30.

Jérôme Bonaparte *See* **Bonaparte, Jérôme**

Jerome, Jerome K(lapka) 1859–1927 •*English humorous writer, novelist and playwright*• He was born in Walsall, Staffordshire, and brought up in London. Leaving school at the age of 14, he was successively a clerk, schoolmaster, reporter, actor and journalist. He became joint editor of *The Idler* in 1892 and started his own twopenny weekly, *To-Day*. His magnificently ridiculous *Three Men in a Boat* (1889), the account of a boat trip up the Thames from Kingston to Oxford, established itself as a humorous classic. Other books include *The Idle Thoughts of an Idle Fellow* (1889), *Three Men on the Bummel* (1900), and his autobiography, *My Life and Times* (1926).

" "

It is impossible to enjoy idling thoroughly unless one has plenty of work to do.

1889 ***The Idle Thoughts of an Idle Fellow***, *"On Being Idle."*

Jespersen, (Jens) Otto Harry 1860–1943 •*Danish philologist*• Born in Randers, he became Professor of English Language and Literature at the University of Copenhagen (1893–1925), and revolutionized the teaching of languages. In 1904 his *Sprogundervisning* was published in English as *How to Teach a Foreign Language*. His other books include *Growth and Structure of the English Language* (1905), *A Modern English Grammar on Historical Principles* (1909), and *Philosophy of Grammar* (1924). He also invented an international language, "Novial," with its own grammar and lexicon.

Jesse, F(riniwyd) Tennyson 1888–1958 •*English novelist and dramatist*• She was born in Chislehurst, Kent, a grandniece of Alfred, Lord **Tennyson**. During World War I she took up journalism as one of the few female war correspondents, and afterward served on **Herbert Hoover**'s Relief Commission for Europe. In 1918 she married the dramatist **H M Harwood**, and with him collaborated on a number of light plays and a series of wartime letters. However, she is best known for her novels set in Cornwall, such as *The White Riband* (1921) and *Moonraker* (1927), as well as *The Lacquer Lady* (1929), set in Burma and regarded by many as her best novel, and *A Pin to See a Peepshow* (1934), based on the **Thompson-Bywaters** murder case. She also published poetry and edited several volumes of the *Notable British Trials* series.

Jesus c. 6 BC–c. 30 AD •*The central figure of the Christian faith*• Our knowledge of the life of Jesus Christ comes almost exclusively from the Gospel accounts and from other early Christian writing, including the Acts of the Apostles and the letters of St **Paul**. There are two aspects to a life of Christ: the establishing of historical facts, and the identification of parts of his ministry that are the basis for the development of the Christian faith. This article, as a biography, concentrates necessarily on Jesus as a historical figure. According to the accounts in Matthew and Luke, Jesus was the first-born child of **Mary** who at that time was engaged to be married to **Joseph**, a carpenter. According to Matthew, the child was born shortly before the death of **Herod the Great** (4 BC), although the Roman census referred to by Luke did not take place before AD 6. Little is known of the early life of Jesus. He is believed to have followed Joseph's trade of carpentry and after nearly 18 years of obscurity, he was baptized in the River Jordan by his cousin **John the Baptist**. His baptism marks the beginning of his public life. He gathered around him 12 disciples (called apostles) and undertook two missionary journeys through Galilee, culminating in the miraculous feeding of the five thousand (Mark 6:30–52). Jesus's association with "sinners," his apparent flouting of traditional religious practices, the performance of miracles on the Sabbath, the driving of the moneylenders from the temple and the whole tenor of his revolutionary Sermon on the Mount (Matthew 5–8), emphasizing love, humility, meekness and charity, alarmed the Pharisees. He sought refuge for a while in the Gentile territories of Tyre and Sidon. According to Mark, he returned to Jerusalem in triumph, a week before the Passover feast. After the famous Last Supper with his disciples, he was betrayed by **Judas Iscariot** and was condemned to death. The necessary confirmation of the sentence came from **Pontius Pilate**, the Roman prefect. Jesus was crucified early on the Passover or the preceding day (the "preparation of the Passover"). The year is thought to be AD 30 or 33. He was buried on the same day. The following Sunday, **Mary Magdalene**, possibly accompanied by other women, visited the tomb and found it empty. Jesus himself appeared to her, and she told the disciples of her experiences. Jesus also appeared to groups of his disciples after his death, according to stories that are thought to be late insertions into the Gospel accounts. The story that Jesus ascended into heaven is described explicitly only twice, in Acts (1:9) and at the end of Mark (thought to be a 2nd-century insertion). The cross, the instrument of the crucifixion, became the symbol of Christianity. The history of the church begins after the Resurrection with the Acts of the Apostles in the New Testament. The apostolic succession claimed by the Church begins with Jesus's public declaration to Peter (Matthew 16:17–19) that on him and on his declaration of faith he would build his Church.

Jewel, John 1522–71 •*English prelate*• Born in Berrynarbor, Devon, he was educated in Merton and Corpus Christi Colleges, Oxford. He absorbed Reformed doctrines early in his career, and therefore, on **Mary I**'s accession, went abroad. He was appointed Bishop of Salisbury by **Elizabeth I**, however, in 1559. Considered to be a father of English Protestantism, his ability as a controversialist soon made him one of the foremost churchmen of his age, demonstrated in his *Apologia Ecclesiae Anglicanae* (1562, "Defense of the Anglican Church") against Rome.

Jex-Blake, Sophia Louisa 1840–1912 •*English physician and pioneer of medical education for women*• Born in Hastings, Sussex, she studied at Queen's College for Women, London, and became a tutor in mathematics there (1859–61). From 1865 she studied medicine in New York under **Elizabeth Blackwell**, but since English medical schools were closed to women she could not continue her studies on her return. She matriculated at University of Edinburgh but the decision was reversed in 1873, and she then waged a public campaign in London, opened the London School of Medicine for Women in 1874 and in 1876 won her campaign when medical examiners were permitted by law to test women students. In 1886 she founded a medical school in Edinburgh, where women were finally allowed to graduate in medicine from 1894.

Jezebel d. 842 BC •*Phoenician princess*• She was the daughter of Ethbaal, king of Tyre and Sidon, and the wife of King **Ahab** of Israel. She introduced Phoenician habits and the worship of Baal and Ashera to the capital, Samaria, thus earning the undying hatred of the prophet **Elijah** and his successors. After Ahab's death, Jezebel was the power behind the throne of her sons until the usurper **Jehu** seized power in an army coup. He had Jezebel thrown from a window, and trampled her to death under his chariot. She has become the archetype of female wickedness.

Jhabvala, Ruth Prawer 1927– •*British novelist, and short-story and screenplay writer*• She was born in Cologne, Germany, of Polish parents, who emigrated to Great Britain in 1939. She graduated from Queen Mary College, University of London, married a visiting Indian architect, and lived in Delhi (1951–75). Most of her fiction relates to India, including *Esmond in India* (1958), *The Householder* (1960), and *Heat and Dust* (1975), which won the Booker Prize. In association with the filmmakers **James Ivory** and **Ismail Merchant**, she has written several accomplished screenplays, among them *Shakespeare Wallah* (1965), *A Room With a View* (1985, Academy Award for best adapted screenplay) and *Howards End* (1992).

Jiang Jieshi *See* **Chiang Kai-shek**

Jiang Qing (Chiang Ch'ing) 1914–91 •*Chinese politician*• Born in Zhucheng, Shandong (Shantung) Province, the daughter of a carpenter, she trained in drama before studying literature at Qingdao University, and became a stage and film actress in Shanghai. In 1936 she went to the Chinese Communist Party headquarters at Yenan to study Marxist-Leninist theory, and met the Communist leader, **Mao Zedong**, becoming his third wife in 1939. It was in the 1960s that she began her attacks on bourgeois influences in the arts and literature, and she became one of the leaders of the 1966–69 Cultural Revolution. In 1969 she was elected to the politburo, but after Mao's death in 1976 she was arrested with three others—the hated Gang of Four—after having attempted to seize power. She was imprisoned, expelled from the Communist Party, and tried in 1980 for subverting the government and wrongly arresting, detaining and torturing numbers of innocent people. She was sentenced to death, though the sentence was commuted to life imprisonment in 1983. The notice issued by the government after her death reported that she had committed suicide. It also stated that she had been out of custody and undergoing medical treatment since May 1984.

Jiang Zemin (Chiang Tse-min) 1926– •*Chinese politician*• Born in Yangzhou, in Jiangsu (Kiangsu) province, the son-in-law of former President **Li Xiannian**, he was Commercial Counselor at the Chinese Embassy in Moscow (1950–56) and during the 1960s and 1970s held a number of posts in the Heavy and Power Industry Ministries. Elected to the Chinese Communist Party (CCP)'s Central Committee in 1982, he was appointed mayor of Shanghai in 1985. He was inducted into the CCP's politburo in 1987 and in June 1989, following the Tiananmen Square massacre and the dismissal of **Zhao Ziyang**, was elected party leader. He was president from 1993 to 2003. Fluent in English and Russian, Jiang, as a compromise figure, pledged to maintain China's open door economic strategy.

Jibran, Kahlil *See* **Gibran, Kahlil**

Jiménez, Juan Ramón 1881–1958 •*Spanish lyric poet and Nobel Prize winner*• He was born in Moguer, Huelva, which he made famous by his story of the young poet and his donkey, *Platero y yo* (1914, Eng trans *Platero and I*, 1956), one of the classics of modern Spanish literature. His early poetry, which echoed that of **Paul Verlaine**, includes *Almas de Violeta* (1900, "Violet Souls") and *Jardines lejanos* (1905, "Far-Off Gardens"). He also wrote *Sonetos espirituales* (1916, "Spiritual Sonnets") and *El silencio de oro* (1922, "The Silence of Gold"). In 1936 he left Spain because of the Civil War and settled in Florida. He was awarded the Nobel Prize for literature in 1956.

Jiménez de Cisneros, Francisco *See* **Ximenes de Cisneros, Francisco**

Jinnah, Muhammad Ali 1876–1948 •*Pakistani statesman*• Born in Karachi, he studied in Bombay and at Lincoln's Inn, London, and was called to the bar in 1897. He ran a successful practice in Bombay, and in 1910 was elected to the viceroy's legislative council. Already a member of the Indian National Congress, in 1913 he joined the Indian Muslim League and as its president brought about peaceful coexistence between it and the Congress Party through the Lucknow Pact (1916). Although Jinnah supported the efforts of Congress to boycott the Simon Commission (1928), he opposed **Mahatma Gandhi**'s civil disobedience policy and resigned from the Congress Party, which he believed to be exclusively fostering Hindu interests. By 1940 he was strongly advocating separate statehood for Muslims and he resisted all British efforts, such as the mission by Sir **Stafford Cripps** (1942), to retain Indian unity. On August 15, 1947, the Dominion of Pakistan came into existence and Jinnah, *Quaid-i-Azam* (Great Leader), became its first governor-general.

Joad, C(yril) E(dwin) M(itchinson) 1891–1953 •*English philosopher and controversialist*• Born in Durham, and educated at Blundell's School and Balliol College, Oxford, he was a civil servant (1914–30), then became head of the philosophy department at Birkbeck College, London. He wrote 47 books in all, notably a *Guide to Philosophy* (1936) and a *Guide to the Philosophy of Morals and Politics* (1938). He was best known for his appearances on the BBC radio program *The Brains Trust* and for his catchphrase "It all depends what you mean by ..."

Joan of Arc, St, *French* **Jeanne d'Arc**, *known as* **the Maid of Orleans** c. 1412–31 •*French patriot and martyr*• She was born into a peasant family in Domrémy, on the border of Lorraine and Champagne. At the age of 13 she thought she heard the voices of St Michael, St **Catherine** and St **Margaret** bidding her rescue Paris from English domination in the Hundred Years' War; English soldiers had overrun the area in 1421 and withdrawn in 1424. She was taken across territory occupied by the English to the dauphin (the future **Charles VII**) at Chinon. She is said to have identified the dauphin, who was standing in disguise in a group of courtiers, an act which was interpreted as divine confirmation of his previously doubted legitimacy and claims to the throne. She was later allowed to join the army assembled at Blois for the relief of Orléans. Clad in a suit of white armor and flying her own standard, she entered Orléans (1429) and forced the English to retire from the principal strongholds on the Loire. To put further heart into the French resistance, she took the dauphin with an army of 12,000 through English-held territory to be crowned Charles VII in Reims Cathedral. She set out on her own to relieve Compiègne from the Burgundians, was captured in a sortie (1430) and sold to the English by John of Luxembourg for 10,000 crowns. She was put on trial (1431) for heresy and sorcery by an ecclesiastical court of the Inquisition. She was found guilty, taken out to the churchyard of St Ouen on May 24 to be burned, but at the last moment broke down and made a wild recantation. This she later abjured and she suffered her martyrdom at the stake in the marketplace of Rouen on May 30, faithful to her "voices." She was canonized in 1920. Her feast day is May 30.

" "

Si je ny y suis, Dieu m'y veuille mettre; et si je y suis, Dieu m'y veuille tenir.
If I am not in grace, may God set me there; and if I am, may God keep me there.
1431 Quoted in the record of her trial at Rouen, February 24.

Joan of Navarre, *also called* **Joanna of Navarre** c. 1370–1437 •*Queen of England*• She married first John, Duke of Brittany (1386), by whom she had eight children. After his death (1399), she married **Henry IV** (1402) and became stepmother of **Henry V**. After Henry's death (1413), she was imprisoned for three years (1419) on specious allegations of witchcraft.

Job Date unknown •*Biblical character, a wealthy landowner*• There is no objective evidence as to the authorship or date of the text describing this man who is referred to as "the greatest man in all the East" in wealth, and blameless, upright and god-fearing in character. His writings, possibly translated from Aramaic, are regarded as great Hebrew poetry and placed among the masterpieces of world literature. The subject matter of his writing is timeless, dealing with the probability of undeserved suffering, the question of why God allows suffering, the need to fight suffering, and God's vindication and forgiveness of his righteous servant.

Jobs, Steve(n) 1955– •*US computer inventor and entrepreneur*• Born in San Francisco, he was educated at Reed College, Portland, before becoming a computer hobbyist. Together with **Steve Wozniak** he set up the Apple Computer Company, in a garage, in 1976. Their brainchild, the Apple II computer (1977), helped launch the personal computer and made their company the fastest-growing in US history. In 1985 he left Apple and founded a new company, NeXT Inc, of which he was president (1985–97). He returned to Apple in 1997.

Jodl, Alfred 1890–1946 •*German general*• He was born in Aachen. He served in World War I and became a general of artillery in 1940. For the remainder of World War II he was the planning genius of the German High Command and **Hitler**'s chief adviser. He counseled the terror bombing of English cities and signed orders to shoot commandos and prisoners of war. He was found guilty of war crimes at Nuremberg (1946) and executed. A Munich denazification court posthumously exonerated him on charges of being a "major offender" in 1953.

Joffre, Joseph Jacques Césaire 1852–1931 •*French soldier*• Born in Rivesaltes, he entered the army in 1870, rose to be French Chief of Staff (1914), and planned the victory in the Battle of the Marne (1914). Silent, patient, mathematical, he carried out a policy of attrition against the Germans. He was Commander in Chief of the French armies from 1915 to 1916, but resigned after the French failure at Verdun (1916), and was made a Marshal of France. In 1917 he became president of the Allied War Council.

Joffrey, Robert, *originally* **Abdullah Jaffa Anver Bey Kahn** 1930–88 •*US dancer, choreographer, teacher and ballet director*• Born in Seattle, Washington, of Afghan descent, he studied at the School of American Ballet and New York's High School of Performing Arts. He choreographed his first ballet in 1952 and by 1954 had formed his own school and company, which began touring the US. Working closely with dancer-choreographer Gerald Arpino, he created a young and energetic image for his company, helping to usher in the US ballet revival of the 1960s that used topical themes, rock music and multimedia techniques alongside contemporary classics.

Johann Strauss II *See* **Strauss, Johann, the Younger**

Johannsen, Wilhelm Ludwig 1857–1927 •*Danish botanist and geneticist*• Born in Copenhagen, through his apprenticeship to a pharmacist he developed a knowledge of chemistry, and later learned botany. In 1905 he became Professor of Plant Physiology at the University of Copenhagen. He postulated the pure line theory of genetics, which states that "pure lines" are genetically identical, and that variation within them is due entirely to environmental forces. He introduced the term "gene" for the unit of heredity, and defined the genotype and the phenotype.

Johanson, Donald Carl 1943– •*US paleoanthropologist*• Born in Chicago of Swedish immigrant parents, he graduated from the University of Chicago and worked at the Cleveland Museum of Natural History from 1972. His spectacular finds of fossil hominids 3–4 million years old at Hadar in the Afar Triangle of Ethiopia (1972–77) generated worldwide interest. They include "Lucy," a unique female specimen that is half complete, and the so-called first family, a scattered group containing the remains of 13 individuals. He suggested that these remains belong to a species, which he named *Australopithecus afarensis* ("southern ape of Afar"). In 1981 Johanson founded the Institute of Human Origins in Berkeley, California (from 1997 part of Arizona State University), and became president there. His publications include *Lucy: The Beginnings of Humankind* (with Maitland Edey, 1981) and *Ancestors: In Search of Human Origins* (1994, with Lenora Johanson and Blake Edgar).

John, St, *also called* **John the Evangelist** 1st century AD •*One of the 12 Apostles of Jesus*• Born probably in Bethsaida, Galilee, he was the son of Zebedee and the younger brother of **James**. Formerly a fisherman, he was one of those closest to **Jesus**, and was with him at the Transfiguration and at Gethsemane. In Acts and Galatians he is described as one of the pillars of the early Jerusalem Church. He may have spent his closing years at Ephesus. He wrote the Revelation, the Gospel, and the three Epistles that bear his name (although his authorship of these works has been disputed by modern scholars). His feast day is December 27.

John, King, *surnamed* **Lackland** 1167–1216 •*King of England from 1199*• He was born in Oxford, the youngest son of **Henry II** and became one of the least favorite monarchs in English history. He tried to seize the crown during his brother **Richard** I's captivity in Germany (1193–94), but was forgiven and nominated as successor by Richard. John was crowned at Westminster (May 27, 1199), despite the claims of his nephew **Arthur**, supported by **Philip II** of France, whom John temporarily bought off. In the same year he obtained a divorce from his cousin Isabella of Gloucester, and married **Isabella of Angoulême**. In the war in France Arthur was taken prisoner, and before Easter 1203 was murdered. Philip at once marched against John until by March 1204 John had only Aquitaine and a few other small areas left. In 1206 John refused to accept **Stephen Langton** as Archbishop of Canterbury, and in 1208 his kingdom was placed under papal interdict. He was then excommunicated (1209), and finally conceded (1213). His oppressive government, and failure to recover Normandy, provoked baronial opposition, which led to demands for constitutional reform. The barons met the king at Runnymede, and forced him to seal the Great Charter (Magna Carta, June 1215), the basis of the English constitution. In August the pope annulled the charter, and war broke out again. The first successes were all on the side of John, until the barons called over the French dauphin (the future **Louis VIII**) to be their leader. Louis landed in May 1216, and John's fortunes had reached a desperate state when he died at Newark on October 19.

John II, *known as* **John the Good** 1319–64 •*King of France*• Born near Le Mans, the son of **Philip VI** of Valois, he succeeded his father in 1350. He was taken prisoner by **Edward** the Black Prince at Poitiers (1356) and taken to England. After the Treaty of Brétigny (1360), which surrendered most of southwest France to **Edward III**, he returned home, leaving his second son, the Duke of Anjou, as a hostage. When the duke broke his parole and escaped (1363), John chivalrously returned to London, where he died.

John IV 1604–56 •*King of Portugal and Duke of Braganza*• Born in Vila Viçosa, he was the great-grandson of **Manoel I** and the leading aristocrat and greatest landowner in Portugal. When the country bloodlessly freed itself from Spanish rule (1640), the duke became king of the newly independent Portugal. His daughter, **Catherine of Braganza**, married **Charles II** of England.

John II Comnenus 1088–1143 •*Byzantine emperor*• He succeeded his father **Alexius I Comnenus** in 1118. Apart from an abortive attempt to curtail the trading privileges of the Venetians, his energetic rule was distinguished by military and diplomatic success. In the Balkans his victory over the Patzinaks (1122) effectively ended a long-standing threat to the empire, and in the east he recovered territory in Cilicia and asserted Byzantine overlordship over the Normans of Antioch (1137). He was killed in a hunting accident while on a campaign.

John XXII, *originally* **Jacques Duèse** c. 1245–1334 •*French pope*• Born in Cahors, he studied in Paris and Orleans, and was the second pope of Avignon (1316–34). He intervened in the contest for the crown of the Holy Roman Empire between **Louis the Bavarian** and Frederick of Austria, in support of the latter. A long conflict ensued both in Germany and Italy between the **Guelf** (papal) Party and the Ghibelline (imperial) Party. In 1327 Louis entered Italy, was crowned emperor at Rome, deposed John, and set up an antipope, Nicholas V (1328).

John XXIII, *originally* **Angelo Giuseppe Roncalli** 1881–1963 •*Italian pope*• He was born in Sotto il Monte, near Bergamo in northern Italy, the son of a peasant. Ordained in 1904, he served as sergeant in the medical corps and as chaplain in World War I, and subsequently as apostolic delegate to Bulgaria, Turkey and Greece. Patriarch of Venice in 1953, he was elected pope in October 1958 on the twelfth ballot, and at once began attempts to modernize and reinvigorate the Roman Catholic Church. He convened the second Vatican Council in 1962. In 1963 he issued the celebrated encyclical *Pacem in Terris* ("Peace on Earth"), advocating reconciliation between East and West.

John Chrysostom, St *See* **Chrysostom, St John**

John of Austria, Don, *Spanish* **Don Juan** 1547–78 •*Spanish soldier*• The illegitimate son of Emperor **Charles V**, he defeated the Moors in Granada (1570) and the Turks at the Battle of Lepanto (1571). In 1573 he took Tunis, and was then sent to Milan and, in 1576, to the Spanish Netherlands as viceroy. He planned to marry **Mary Queen of Scots**, but died of typhoid at Namur.

John of Beverley, St d. 721 •*English prelate*• Born in Harpham, Humberside, he was educated at Canterbury, and became a monk at **St Hilda**'s double monastery (for nuns and monks) at Whitby in Yorkshire. In 687 he became Bishop of Hexham and in 705 was consecrated Bishop of York. During his ministry he took a special interest in the poor and disabled. In 717 he retired to the Monastery of Beverley, which he had founded while Bishop of York. His feast day is May 7.

John of Capistrano, St, *properly* **Giovanni da Capistrano** 1386–1456 •*Italian prelate*• Born in Capistrano in the Abruzzi, he entered the Franciscan Order at the age of 30, having been governor of Perugia from 1412, and was employed as a legate by several popes, acting as inquisitor against the Fraticelli. In 1450 he preached a crusade in Germany against Turks and heretics, and opposed the **Huss**ites in Moravia. His fanaticism led to many cruelties, such as the racking and burning of forty Jews in Breslau. He died of the plague after leading an army against **Mehmet II**, who had besieged Belgrade in 1456. He was canonized in 1690. His feast day is March 28.

John of Damascus, St c. 676–c. 754 •*Greek theologian and hymn writer of the Eastern Church*• Born in Damascus to Greek parents, he was educated by the Italian monk Cosmas. He vigorously defended image worship against the iconoclastic Emporer **Leo III**. His later years were spent in the monastery of Mar Saba near Jerusalem. There, ordained as a priest, he wrote his hymns, an encyclopedia of Christian theology, treatises against superstitions and Jacobite and Monophysite heretics, homilies, and *Barlaam and Joasaph*, now known to be a disguised version of the life of **Buddha**. His feast day is December 4.

John of Gaunt, Duke of Lancaster 1340–99 •*English prince*• Born in Ghent, Flanders, the fourth (but third surviving) son of **Edward III**, he married his cousin, Blanche of Lancaster (1359), and was made duke (1362). His son by Blanche became **Henry IV**. After Blanche died (1369), he married (1372) Constance, daughter of **Pedro the Cruel** of Castile, and assumed the title of king of Castile, though he failed in his expeditions to oust his rival, Henry of Trastamare. Reserved, haughty and conventional, he opposed the clergy and protected **John Wycliffe**, and was largely responsible for crushing the Peasants' Revolt (1381). Edward's successor, **Richard II**, distrusting him, sent him abroad (1386), and after his return to England (1389) he became an influential peacemaker, was made Duke of Aquitaine by Richard (1394), and went on several embassies to France. On his second wife's death (1394) he married his mistress, Catherine Swynford (1396), by whom he had three sons, legitimized in 1397, from the eldest of whom **Henry VII** of England was descended.

John of Leyden, *originally* **Jan Beuckelson** or **Bockhold** 1509–36 •*Dutch Anabaptist*• Born in Leiden, he worked as an itinerant tailor, then settled in his native city as a merchant and innkeeper, and became noted as an orator. Turning Anabaptist, he went to Münster in 1534, and led a Protestant rebellion, setting up a "kingdom of Zion" with polygamy and community of goods. In 1535 the city was taken by the Bishop of Münster, and John and his followers were executed.

John of Nepomuk, St c. 1345–93 •*Bohemian cleric and patron saint of Bohemia*• Born in Pomuk, near Pilsen (now Plzeň, Czech Republic), he studied at the University of Prague, and became vicar general to the Archbishop of Prague. For refusing to betray the confession of Queen Sophia to her husband Wenceslas IV, he was tortured and drowned in the Moldau. He was canonized in 1729 as part of the **Habsburg** and Jesuit campaign to ensure that there was an appropriate Catholic martyr to set against popular support for the Reformist martyr, **Jan Huss**. His feast day is May 16.

John of Salisbury c. 1115–80 •*English prelate and scholar*• Born in Salisbury, he studied at Paris, under **Abelard**. He was a clerk to Pope **Eugenius III** and to Archbishop **Theobald** at Canterbury, but fell into disfavor with **Henry II** and retired to Rheims. He returned to England and witnessed **Thomas à Becket**'s murder at Canterbury (1170). In 1176 he became Bishop of Chartres. A learned classical writer, he wrote biographies of Becket and **Anselm**, as well as works on diplomacy, logic and Aristotelian philosophy.

John of the Cross, St, *also called* **Juan de la Cruz**, *originally* **Juan de Yepes y Álvarez** 1542–91 •*Spanish mystic, poet and Doctor of the*

Church• Born in Fontiveros, Ávila, he was a Carmelite monk. He founded the ascetic order of Discalced Carmelites with St **Teresa of Ávila** in 1568, who later appointed him to a convent in Ávila. Arrested there in 1577, he was imprisoned in Toledo, where he wrote some of his finest poetry. After escaping in 1578, he became Vicar Provincial of Andalusia (1585–87). His surviving poetry is some of the greatest in the Spanish language. It includes the lyrical and mystical *Cántico espiritual* (1577, "Spiritual Canticle") and *Noche oscura del alma* (1577, "Dark Night of the Soul"). He was canonized in 1726, and declared a Doctor of the Church in 1926. His feast day is December 14.

John Paul I, *originally* **Albino Luciani** 1912–78 •*Italian pope for 33 days*• Born near Belluno, the son of a laborer, he was educated at the Gregorian University in Rome. Ordained in 1935, he became a parish priest and teacher in Belluno, vicar general of the diocese of Vittorio Veneto (1954), a bishop (1958), patriarch of Venice (1969) and a cardinal (1973). He was elected pope in August 1978 on the death of **Paul VI**, but died only 33 days later, being succeeded by **John Paul II**. The first pope to use a double name (from his two immediate predecessors, **John XXIII** and Paul VI), his was the shortest pontificate of modern times.

John Paul II, *originally* **Karol Jozef Wojtyła** 1920– •*Polish pope*• Born in Wadowice, he was educated in Poland, ordained in 1946, and became Professor of Moral Theology at Lublin and Kraków. Archbishop and Metropolitan of Kraków (1964–78), he was created cardinal in 1967 and pope in 1978, the first non-Italian pope in 450 years. His pontificate has seen many foreign visits, in which he has preached to huge audiences. In 1981 he survived an assassination attempt by a Turkish national, Mehmet Ali Agca. A champion of economic justice and an outspoken defender of the Church in communist countries, he has been uncompromising on moral issues. In the 1980s his visits to Poland and his meetings with **Mikhail Gorbachev** were of great assistance to Solidarity in promoting Polish independence, achieved in 1989. In 1995 he participated in historic meetings aimed at discussing relations between the Orthodox and Roman Catholic Churches and other concerns. He has written a play and several books, including *The Freedom of Renewal* (1972) and *The Future of the Church* (1979), and his *Collected Poems* appeared in 1982.

“ ”

Commitment to the poor is based on the Gospel: it does not have to rely on some political manifesto.

1979 Speech at the Third Conference of Latin American Bishops, Puebla.

John the Baptist, *also called* **St John** 1st century AD •*Jewish prophet and ascetic*• Born in Judaea, he was the son of the priest Zechariah. His mother was Elizabeth, cousin of **Mary**, the mother of **Jesus**. He baptized many, including Jesus, at the River Jordan, and preached repentance and forgiveness of sins and about the coming of the Lord. He was executed by **Herod Antipas**. In the New Testament, he is portrayed as Jesus's forerunner, and sometimes as a returned Elijah (Matthew 11:13–14). His feast day is June 24.

John the Good *See* **John II**

John the Scot *See* **Erigena, John Scotus**

John, Augustus Edwin 1878–1961 •*Welsh painter*• Born in Tenby, Pembrokeshire, he studied at the Slade School in London (1896–99) with his sister **Gwen John**, and in Paris, and made an early reputation for himself by his etchings (1900–14). In his portraits of women, including many of his wife Dorelia, he is concerned more with unique items of individual beauty or dignity than with portrayal of character, as shown in the beautifully caught posture of the scarlet-gowned cellist *Madame Suggia* (1923). However, he could portray character, as shown in the studies of **George Bernard Shaw** (c. 1914), **Thomas Hardy** (1923) and **Dylan Thomas**.

John, Sir Elton Hercules, *originally* **Reginald Kenneth Dwight** 1947– •*English pop singer, songwriter and pianist*• He was born in Pinner, Middlesex. One of the most successful pop-rock stars of the 1970s, he began his career as pianist with the group Bluesology, which he left after their 1967 hit "Let the Heartaches Begin." Teaming up with lyricist Bernie Taupin, his album *Elton John* (1970), which included the single "Your Song," brought his first solo success. In a prolific career his albums have included *Tumbleweed Connection* (1970), *Don't Shoot Me I'm Only the Piano Player* (1973), *Too Low for Zero* (1983) and *Sleeping with the Past* (1989). In the mid-1970s he developed a highly flamboyant stage image and an extravagant piano style. He formed his own record label, Rocket Records, and in 1979 became the first Western rock star to play in Moscow. In 1976 he became owner and chairman of Watford Football Club, but sold most of his shares in 1990. He returned as director until 1993, when he became life president. He was knighted in 1998.

John, Gwen 1876–1939 •*Welsh painter*• Born in Haverfordwest, Pembrokeshire, she was the elder sister of **Augustus John**, and studied at the Slade School of Art (1895–98). On moving to Paris in 1904, she worked as an artist's model, becoming **Auguste Rodin**'s mistress in c. 1906. After converting to Roman Catholicism in 1913 she lived in Meudon, where she became increasingly religious and reclusive. She painted some landscapes, but most of her paintings are of single female figures, nuns or young girls, and cats and interiors.

Johns, Jasper 1930– •*US painter, sculptor and printmaker*• Born in Allendale, South Carolina, he studied for a year at the University of South Carolina in Columbia (1947–48). In the mid-1950s, after meeting **Robert Rauschenberg**, he began to create bold pictorial images such as flags, targets and numbers, using heavily textured wax-based paint in a manner derived from the abstract expressionists and often incorporating plaster casts. This work became an important source for the development of pop art in the US. In the 1960s and 1970s he produced increasingly complex paintings, frequently with objects like brushes and rulers attached, and in recent years he has continued to create semiabstract works. From 1960 he worked extensively with lithography. His sculptures are of banal items, executed with detailed realism.

Johns, W(illiam) E(arl) 1893–1968 •*English aviator and children's author*• He was born in Hertford, Hertfordshire. He served in the Norfolk Yeomanry and when commissioned in 1916, transferred to the Royal Flying Corps where he served with some distinction before being shot down by **Ernst Udet** and sent to a prison camp. He retired from the Royal Air Force in 1930, edited *Popular Flying* and *Flying* in the 1930s, and served in the Ministry of Information (1939–45). His stories are strikingly good flying yarns, mostly based on his experiences in World War I. The "Biggles" series reflects unspoken anger at the expendability of airmen in bureaucratic thinking, while his World War II female pilot, "Worrals," is savagely contemptuous of male self-satisfaction and chauvinism toward women. He later tried his hand, less successfully, at space exploration stories.

Johns Hopkins *See* **Hopkins, Johns**

Johnson, Amy 1903–41 •*English aviator*• Born in Hull, Humberside, she became a pilot in 1929. In 1930 she flew solo from England to Australia (the first woman to do so) in her aircraft *Jason*, winning £10,000 from the London *Daily Mail*. In 1931 she flew to Japan via Moscow and back, and in 1932 made a record solo flight to Cape Town and back. In 1936 she set a new record for a solo flight from London to Cape Town. She joined the Air Transport Auxiliary as a pilot in World War II, and was lost after bailing out over the Thames estuary.

Johnson, Andrew 1808–75 •*17th President of the US*• Born in Raleigh, North Carolina, he worked as a journeyman tailor, and in 1826 emigrated to Greenville, Tennessee. In 1841 he was elected to the state senate, and in 1843 to Congress. In 1853 and 1855 he was governor of Tennessee, and in 1857 US senator. A moderate **Jackson**ian Democrat, Johnson was alone among Southern senators in standing by the Union during the Civil War and was made military governor of Tennessee (1862) and elected to the vice-presidency (March 1865). With the assassination of **Abraham Lincoln** on April 14, 1865, he became president. He sought to carry out the conciliatory policy of his predecessor, urging the readmission of Southern representatives, but the Radical Republican majority insisted that the Southern states should be kept for a period under military government. His removal of Secretary **Stanton** from the war department precipitated a crisis. Charged with violation of the "Tenure of Office Act," he was impeached and brought to trial, and acquitted by a single vote. He retired from office in 1869, and was elected to the Senate in 1875.

Johnson, Ben 1961– •*Canadian track athlete*• He was born in Falmouth, Jamaica. In the mid-1980s he was the world's fastest sprinter with **Carl Lewis**. He was unbeaten in 21 consecutive starts over 100 meters and at the 1988 Seoul Olympics set a new world 100 meters record. Later he had his medal withdrawn, was stripped of his world record, and was suspended after allegations that he had used steroids. His life ban from the Canadian team was lifted in 1990, but in March 1993 he was banned for life by the IAAF (International Amateur Athletic Federation) after he failed a drug test in Montreal.

Johnson, Dame Celia 1908–82 •*English actress*• Born in Richmond, Surrey, she was a student at the Royal Academy of Dramatic Art. She was often cast as a well-bred English lady, and her career ranged from exquisitely modulated portraits of quiet despair to sophisticated high comedy. Her many theatrical successes included *The Three Sisters* (1951), *The Reluctant Debutante* (1955), *Hay Fever* (1965), and *The Kingfisher* (1977). *Dirty Work* (1934) was the first of her rare screen appearances, although she had leading roles in **Noël Coward**'s films *In Which We Serve* (1942) and *This Happy Breed* (1944), and created an unforgettable impression as the sad suburban housewife in *Brief Encounter* (1945). She won a British Film award for *The Prime of Miss Jean Brodie* (1969) and continued in the theater and on television until her death.

Johnson, Eyvind Olof Verner 1900–76 •*Swedish novelist, short-story writer and Nobel Prize winner*• He was born to working-class parents in Svartbjörnsbyn, near Boden, and after a number of years in mainly manual occupations he spent most of the 1920s in Paris and Berlin. His four-part *Romanen om Olof* (1934–37, "The Story of Olof") is the finest of the many working-class autobiographical novels written in Sweden in the 1930s. Much involved in anti-Nazi causes, he produced a number of novels castigating totalitarianism. The same humanitarian values are evident in his later historical novels, such as *Hans nådes tid* (1960, "The Days of His Grace"). He shared the 1974 Nobel Prize for literature with fellow Swede **Harry Martinson**.

Johnson, James P(rice) 1894–1955 •*US pianist and composer*• Born in New Brunswick, New Jersey, while still at school, Johnson participated in informal after-hours sessions with other pianists, mainly ragtime performers. In 1912 he began a series of piano-playing jobs in movie houses, cabarets and dancehalls, gradually becoming the most accomplished player in the post-ragtime stride piano style. A prolific performer in the 1920s and during the traditional jazz revival of the 1940s, he wrote more than 200 songs (including "The Charleston") as well as several stage shows, and was a strong influence on such later pianists as **Fats Waller** and **Art Tatum**.

Johnson, James Weldon 1871–1938 •*US writer*• Born in Jacksonville, Florida, he practiced at the bar there (1897–1901), and later served as US consul in Puerto Cabello, Venezuela (from 1906), and in Corinto, Nicaragua (1909–12). He was secretary of the National Association for the Advancement of Colored People (1916–30), and from 1930 he was Professor of Creative Literature at Fisk University. His numerous works include his novel *The Autobiography of an Ex-Colored Man* (1912) and his collection of free-verse folk sermons, *God's Trombones* (1927).

Johnson, Linton Kwesi 1952– •*Jamaican reggae poet and performer*• He has lived in Great Britain since the age of nine, and studied sociology at the University of London. His verdict on British culture was most succinctly expressed in the title of a 1980 book and recording, *Inglan Is a Bitch*. He writes powerful, committed verse that follows the cadences of Caribbean speech and the rhythmic values of reggae and dub. He wrote *Voices of the Living and the Dead* (1974) and became part of a revived poetry/performance movement in Britain, adopted by the Anti-Nazi League in its crusade against British racism. His most powerful work is the somber rumble of *Dread Beat an' Blood* (1975).

Johnson, Lyndon B(aines), *known as* **L B J** 1908–73 •*36th President of the US*• Born near Stonewall, Texas, into a Baptist family, he was a high school teacher, then a congressman's secretary before being elected a strong "New Deal" Democrat representative in 1937. He joined the US Navy immediately after Pearl Harbor, and was decorated. He was elected senator in 1948, became majority leader in the Senate in 1955, and was vice president under **John F Kennedy** in 1960. After Kennedy's assassination in Dallas, Texas, in 1963, he became president and was reelected in the 1964 election with a huge majority. Under his administration the Civil Rights Act (1964), introduced by Kennedy the previous year, and the Voting Rights Act (1965) were passed, making effective, if limited, improvements to the position of African Americans. He also introduced, under the slogan the "Great Society," a series of important economic and social welfare reforms, including a Medicare program for the elderly. However, the ever-increasing escalation of the war in Vietnam led to active protest and growing personal unpopularity for Johnson, and in 1968 he announced his decision to retire from active politics.

Johnson, Magic, *real name* **Earvin Johnson** 1959– •*US basketball player*• Born in Lansing, Michigan, he began his career in college basketball at Michigan State University, then played with the Los Angeles Lakers (1979–91, 1996) and was a member of the gold medal–winning US Olympic basketball team ("Dream Team") in 1992. He was a member of the National Basketball Association (NBA) All-Star team (1980, 1982–92), and was named NBA Most Valuable Player in 1987, 1989 and 1990. He retired in 1992 after revealing that he had been diagnosed HIV-positive, and had a brief comeback the following year and in 1996. His publications include *Magic* (1983) and *What You Can Do to Avoid AIDS* (1992).

Johnson, Michael 1967– •*US track athlete*• Born in Dallas, he attended Baylor University in Waco, Texas. He won world championship races in the 200 meters in 1991 and 1995 and in the 400 meters in 1993 and 1995. At the 1996 Olympics in Atlanta, he tempted fate by wearing gold running shoes but nevertheless winning gold medals in both the 200-meter and 400-meter events, the first man ever to do so. At the same time he set a new world record in the 200 meters, breaking the world record he himself set at the Olympic trials. He became the Olympic champion in the 400 meters again in Sydney in 2000.

Johnson, Pamela Hansford *See* **Hansford Johnson, Pamela**

Johnson, Philip Cortelyou 1906– •*US architect and theorist*• Born in Cleveland, Ohio, he graduated from Harvard in 1927. He came late to architecture after working as a critic, author and director of the department of architecture at the Museum of Modern Art, New York (1930–36, 1946–54). He became renowned for his publication *The International Style* (1932, with Henry-Russell Hitchcock), which coined the popular term and helped promote architecture in the US. He designed his own home, the Glass House, New Canaan, Connecticut (1949–50), on principles of space unification derived from **Ludwig Mies van der Rohe**, with whom he collaborated on the Seagram Building, New York City (1956–58). Further works include the New York State Theater, Lincoln Center (1964). In mid-career he began to move away from the sleek simplicity of modernism, and he was eventually recognized as one of the most prominent architects of the postmodern movement. In 1978–84 he designed the granite American Telephone and Telegraph Building in New York City, following the structure and classical form of early skyscrapers.

Johnson, Randy (Randall David) 1963– •*US baseball player*• Born in Walnut Creek, California, he studied at the University of Southern California. He established himself as a pitcher with the Seattle Mariners (1989–1998) and later played for the Houston Astros (1998–99) and Arizona Diamondbacks (1999–), winners of the World Series title in 2001. In 2001 he also won his third Cy Young Award as the best pitcher in the American League. In 2004, he became the oldest pitcher to pitch a perfect game.

Johnson, Robert 1911–38 •*US blues singer and guitarist*• Born in Hazelhurst, Mississippi, he is perhaps the most famous name in blues, and his story has attained a semilegendary status in the mythology of the music. He was a virtuoso self-taught guitarist, and although he recorded only 29 songs, their impact on the development of blues has been incalculable. Little is known of his life, but the legend that he acquired his skills by selling his soul to the Devil has taken root in blues mythology. The passionate, haunted intensity of his singing and playing has ensured that most of his surviving songs, recorded in only two sessions in 1936 and 1937, have acquired classic status.

Johnson, Samuel, *known as* **Dr Johnson** 1709–84 •*English writer, critic and lexicographer*• He was born in Lichfield, Staffordshire. He was educated at Lichfield Grammar School and Pembroke College, Oxford, but left in 1731 without taking a degree. He taught briefly, and then moved to Birmingham where he turned to writing. In 1735 he married Elizabeth ("Tetty") Porter, and they opened a school at Edial, near Lichfield; one of the pupils was the future actor **David Garrick**. The school failed, and in 1737, accompanied by the young Garrick, the Johnsons moved to London where he finished writing a tragedy, *Irene* (not staged for 12 years), and earned a living writing parliamentary reports for *The Gentleman's Magazine*. In it he published (anonymously) his first poem, *London: A Poem in Imitation of the Third Satire of Juvenal*. In 1744 he produced a topical and successful *Life* of his friend **Richard Savage**. In 1747 he issued a prospectus of a *Dictionary of the English Language*, which was to take him eight years to complete. During this time he published a long didactic poem, *The Vanity of Human Wishes* (1749), based on another of **Juvenal**'s satires. Garrick fulfilled a boyhood promise by producing his *Irene* at Drury Lane Theatre (1749), and Johnson himself wrote and edited, practically single-handedly, a biweekly periodical, *The Rambler*, which ran for 208 issues (1750–52). In 1752 his wife died, plunging him into lasting depression. His great Dictionary appeared in 1755. Johnson was awarded an honorary degree at Oxford, but he had to continue literary hackwork to earn a living, contributing reviews to the *Literary Magazine* and *The Idler* series of papers in *The Universal Chronicle* (1758–60). During this time his mother died, and he wrote his moral fable, *Rasselas: The Prince of Abyssinia* (1759), in a week to defray the funeral expenses. With the accession of **George III** in 1760, Johnson was granted a pension of £300 for life, which brought him financial security for the first time. In 1763 he met the young Scot, **James Boswell**, who would become his biographer, and with whom he would share a delightful tour of the Hebrides in 1773 (*A Journey to the Western Isles of Scotland*, 1775). In 1764 he founded the Literary Club with a circle of friends, including **Joshua Reynolds**, **Edmund Burke** and **Oliver Goldsmith**; later members were Boswell, Garrick and **Charles James Fox**. In 1765 he published his critical edition of **Shakespeare**'s plays (8 vols), and then set to work on his monumental *Lives of the Most Eminent English Poets* (10 vols, 1779–81). He died in 1784, and was buried in Westminster Abbey.

“ ”

A man may write at any time, if he will set himself doggedly to it.

1750 Comment, March. Quoted in James Boswell ***The Life of Samuel Johnson*** *(1791), volume 1.*

Johnson, Virginia E(shelman) 1925– •*US psychologist and sexologist*• She was born in Springfield, Missouri. Educated at the University of Missouri, she joined the research group led by **William Masters** in 1957, and achieved fame through their investigations of the physiology of sexual intercourse, using volunteer subjects under laboratory conditions at their Reproductive Biology Research Foundation in St Louis (established 1970). She and Masters (who were married from 1971 to 1993) coauthored *Human Sexual Response* (1966), which became an international bestseller. Their other works include *On Sex and Human Loving* (1986).

Johnston, Albert Sidney 1803–62 •*US general*• Born in Washington, Kentucky, he graduated from West Point in 1826 and served in the US Army until 1834. He then enlisted as a private in the army of Texas (1836), rising to the rank of general within a year and assuming command of the army in 1837. He served in the Mexican War (1846–48) under General **Zachary Taylor**. From 1857 to 1859 he was sent to "pacify" the Mormons in Utah; in 1861 he resigned his commission to become a Confederate general in the Civil War (1861–65). Appointed to the command of Kentucky and Tennessee, he held the Union army in check until February 1862, when he retreated to Nashville and later to Corinth, Mississippi. Here he attacked **Ulysses S Grant** at Shiloh in 1862 where the advantage lay with the Confederates until Johnston was mortally wounded.

Johnston, Brian Alexander 1912–94 •*English commentator and broadcaster*• Educated at Eton and New College, Oxford, he served in the army during World War II, then joined the BBC in 1945 and remained there for 27 years, becoming a specialist in cricket commentary. He was also commentator for many significant royal occasions, such as the coronation of Queen **Elizabeth II** (1953). After retiring from the BBC, he continued in radio broadcasting and won various awards, including *Daily Mail* Radio Sports Commentator of the Year in 1988. His books include *Views From the Boundary* (1990) and *Someone Who Was* (1992).

Johnston, Joseph Eggleston 1807–91 •*US general*• Born near Farmville, Virginia, he fought in the Seminole War, served in the war with Mexico, and in 1860 was quartermaster general. At the outbreak of the Civil War (1861–65) he entered the Confederate service, and as brigadier general took command of the army of the Shenandoah. He supported **P G T Beauregard** at the first Battle of Bull Run, and in 1864 stubbornly fought General **Sherman**'s progress toward Atlanta, but he was forced to surrender to Sherman on April 26, 1865. He was elected to Congress in 1877 and was a US commissioner of railroads.

Johnstone, (Christian) Isobel, *pseudonym* **Meg** or **Margaret Dods** 1781–1857 •*Scottish cookbook writer, novelist and journalist*• Born in Fife, she married her second husband, John Johnstone, in 1812, writing for the *Inverness Courier* when he was its owner and editor, and producing historical novels which enjoyed considerable popularity. She made her name, however, with *The Cook and Housewife's Manual*, by Mistress Margaret Dods (1826), popularly known as *Meg Dod's Cookery*. Using characters from Sir **Walter Scott**'s *St Ronan's Well*, it was purportedly written by the landlady of the Cleikum Inn, St Ronan's.

Joliot-Curie, Frédéric, *originally* **Jean-Frédéric Joliot** 1900–58 •*French physicist and Nobel Prize winner*• Born in Paris, he studied under **Paul Langevin** at the Sorbonne, and in 1925 he joined the Radium Institute under **Marie Curie**. He married Marie's daughter **Irène Joliot-Curie** in 1926, and in 1935 he shared with his wife the Nobel Prize for chemistry for making the first artificial radioisotope. Professor at the Collège de France (1937), he became a strong supporter of the Resistance movement during World War II, and a member of the Communist Party. After the liberation he became director of scientific research and (1946–50) High Commissioner for atomic energy, a position from which he was dismissed for his political activities. He succeeded his wife as head of the Radium Institute, and was awarded the Stalin Peace Prize (1951). Commander of the Legion of Honor, he was given a state funeral by the Gaullist government after his death, caused by lifelong exposure to radioactivity.

Joliot-Curie, Irène, *née* **Curie** 1897–1956 •*French physicist and Nobel Prize winner*• She was born in Paris, the daughter of **Pierre** and **Marie Curie**, and in 1918 she joined her mother at the Radium Institute in Paris, beginning her scientific research in 1921. In 1926 she married **Frédéric Joliot-Curie**, and they collaborated in studies of radioactivity from 1931. In 1933–34 the Joliot-Curies made the first artificial radioisotope, and it was for this work that they were jointly awarded the Nobel Prize for chemistry in 1935. Similar methods led them to make a range of radioisotopes, some of which have proved indispensable in medicine, scientific research and industry. Irène Joliot-Curie became director of the Radium Institute in 1946 and a director of the French Atomic Energy Commission. She died from leukemia due to long periods of exposure to radioactivity.

Jolley, (Monica) Elizabeth 1923– •*Australian writer*• Born in Birmingham, England, she settled in Western Australia in 1959. Her first publication, *Five Acre Virgin* (1976), received immediate critical praise and was followed by *The Travelling Entertainer* (1979). Often using lesbianism as a major theme, she also wrote *Palomino* (1980) and *Mr Scobie's Riddle* (which won the Melbourne *Age* Book of the Year award in 1982). Her later books include a semiautobiographical trilogy set in postwar England, a number of plays, and the novels *The Sugar Mother* (1988, as *Tombe du Ciel*), *Lovesong* (1997) and *An Accommodating Spouse* (1999).

Jolliet or **Joliet, Louis** 1645–1700 •*French explorer*• Born in Quebec, Canada, he entered the fur trade in 1667. He first met Father **Jacques Marquette** at a Seneca village on the shore of Lake Ontario, and in 1673 the two men were commissioned to investigate Indian accounts of a great river called the Mississippi, which the French believed to empty into the Pacific. With five companions they traveled by canoe westward on the Fox and Wisconsin rivers and then down the Mississippi to the mouth of the Arkansas River. Suspecting that the river would empty into the Gulf of Mexico, and fearing to encroach on Spanish territory, Jolliet and Marquette turned back, ascending the Illinois River and on to the site of present-day Chicago on Lake Michigan. For his role in the expedition—the first European exploration of the Mississippi—he was rewarded with the island of Anticosti.

Jolson, Al, *originally* **Asa Yoelson** 1886–1950 •*US actor and singer*• Born in Srednike, Lithuania, the son of a rabbi, he emigrated to the US in 1893, lived in Washington DC and New York City, and toured with circus and minstrel shows. His sentimental songs such as "Mammy" (1909) and "Sonny Boy" moved vaudeville audiences in the 1920s but he is best known as the star of the first talking picture *The Jazz Singer* (1927). His recorded voice featured in the commemorative films *The Jolson Story* (1946) and *Jolson Sings Again* (1949).

Joly, John 1857–1933 •*Irish geologist and physicist*• Born in Offaly, King's County, he was educated at Trinity College, Dublin, where he became Professor of Geology and Mineralogy in 1897. He invented several pieces of scientific apparatus, including the meldometer, a hydrostatic balance, a steam calorimeter and a photometer. He was the first geologist to recognize the significance of radioactive atoms in maintaining the heat of the sun and in directly molding the history of the earth (1903), and in first realizing that pleochroic halos in some minerals were the product of radioactivity and could be used for dating (1907–14). In 1914, at his suggestion, the Radium Institute was founded in Dublin; there Joly became involved in developing groundbreaking methods in radiotherapy, including the radium treatment of cancer. He was also a pioneer of color photography.

Jones, Bob (Robert Reynolds) 1883–1968 •*US evangelist*• Born in Dale County, Alabama, he conducted revival meetings from the age of 13, and was licensed by the Methodist Church to preach at the age of 15. Educated at Southern University, Greensboro, South Carolina, he began full-time evangelistic work in 1902. In 1939 he left the Methodist Church, which he charged with theological liberalism. In 1927 he founded Bob Jones University, which in 1947 moved to Greenville, South Carolina. The school is known for its biblical theology, its puritanical code, and its tendency toward right-wing politics. He once drew unwelcome attention to himself with a pamphlet entitled "Is Segregation Scriptural?", to which he answered yes. His son, Bob Jones, Jr (1911–97), succeeded him as president of Bob Jones University.

Jones, Bobby (Robert Tyre) 1902–71 •*US amateur golfer*• Born in Atlanta, Georgia, he studied law. He won the US Open four times (1923, 1926, 1929, 1930), the British Open three times (1926, 1927, 1930), the US Amateur championship five times and the British Amateur championship once. In 1930 he achieved the staggering feat of winning the Grand Slam of the US and British Open and Amateur championships in the same year. He retired at 28, regarded as one of the greatest golfers in the history of the game. He was responsible for the founding of the US Masters in Augusta.

Jones, Chuck (Charles) 1912–2002 •*US animated cartoon director*• Born in Spokane, Washington, he became an animator in the 1930s and joined Warner Brothers. His early work included fast-paced duels between Wile E Coyote and the Road Runner, and he won his first Academy Award with *For Scentimental Reasons* (1951), featuring Pepe le Pew, the amorous skunk. His Bugs Bunny cartoons include the classic *What's Opera Doc* (1957) and the stereoscopic *Lumber Jack Rabbit* (1954). He won another Academy Award with *The Dot and the Line* (1965). For television he created many specials, among them *How the Grinch Stole Christmas*. He codirected the live-action/animated feature *The Phantom Tollbooth* (1969) and contributed to feature films such as *Gremlins 2* (1990). In 1996 he received a Special Academy Award for his contribution to the film industry.

Jones, Sir Harold Spencer 1890–1960 •*English astronomer*• Born in Kensington, London, he studied at Jesus College, Cambridge (1908). He was chief assistant at the Royal Observatory, Greenwich (1913–23), and His Majesty's Astronomer at the Royal Observatory at the Cape of Good Hope (1923–33), before he returned to Greenwich as the tenth Astronomer Royal (1933–55). At the Cape he organized an international project to improve the measurement of the distance between the Earth and the sun by utilizing the close approach of the asteroid Eros, which took 10 years. At Greenwich, following his analysis of the motions of the sun, moon and planets, he discovered long-term and irregular variations in the rate of the Earth's rotation (1939). This led to the concept of ephemeris time (1950), an independent system of measuring time that was adopted in the universal system of units in 1956. He was knighted in 1943.

Jones, Inigo 1573–1652 •*English architect and stage designer*• Born in London, he studied landscape painting in Italy, where he became a lifelong admirer of **Andrea Palladio**, and from Venice introduced the Palladian style into England. He introduced the proscenium arch and movable scenery to the English stage. From 1613 to 1614 he revisited Italy and on his return in 1615 was appointed surveyor general of the royal buildings. In 1616 he designed the Queen's House at Greenwich, completed in the 1630s. Other commissions included the rebuilding of the Banqueting House at Whitehall (1619–22), the nave and transepts and a large Corinthian portico of old St Paul's, Marlborough Chapel, the Double Cube room at Wilton (1649–52), and possibly the York Water Gate. He laid out Covent Garden and Lincoln's Inn Fields. He is regarded as the founder of classical English architecture.

Jones, James 1921–77 •*US novelist*• He was born in Robinson, Illinois, and educated at the University of Hawaii. He served in the US Army as a sergeant (1939–44), boxed as a welterweight in Golden Gloves tournaments, and was awarded a Purple Heart. His wartime experience in Hawaii led to *From Here to Eternity* (1951), a classic novel dealing with the period before Pearl Harbor, for which he received a National Book award. Later work included *The Thin Red Line* (1962, filmed 1998).

Jones, James Earl 1931– •*US actor*• Born in Arkabutla, Mississippi, he was raised by his grandparents on a farm in Michigan, and overcame a severe stammer to study acting at the University of Michigan and later with **Lee Strasberg** in New York. He made his Broadway debut in *Sunrise at Campobello* (1958) and won a Tony award for his performance as the African-American boxer Jack Jefferson in *The Great White Hope* (1968). He acted with the New York Shakespeare Festival in roles such as Othello and Caliban, starred in new plays by **Athol Fugard**, including *A Lesson from Aloes* (1980) and appeared in **August Wilson**'s *Fences* (1985). Noted for his resonant bass voice and commanding physical presence, he has starred in numerous films and provided the voice of the villain Darth Vader in *Star Wars* (1977) and its sequels.

Jones, John Paul, *originally* **John Paul** 1747–92 •*American naval officer*• Born in Kirkbean, Kirkcudbrightshire, Scotland, he was apprenticed as a sailor boy, made several voyages to America, and in 1773 he inherited a piece of property in Fredericksburg, Virginia. At about the same date he assumed the name Jones. At the outbreak of the American Revolution in 1775 he joined the navy. In 1778 in the *Ranger* he made a daring descent on the Solway Firth, Scotland. As commodore of a small French squadron displaying American colors, he threatened Leith (1779) and won an engagement on the *Bon Homme Richard* against the British Frigate *Serapis*. In 1788 he entered the Russian service and, as rear admiral of the Black Sea fleet, fought in the Russo-Turkish war of 1788–89.

Jones, Loïs Mailou 1905–98 •*US painter*• Born in Boston, she won a scholarship to the School of the Museum of Fine Arts in 1923, then worked as a textile designer and took advanced courses at Harvard, Howard and Columbia Universities and the Académie Julian, Paris. She began to paint works like *Mob Victim* (1944), dealing explicitly with her own background as an African American. Inspired by several trips to Africa, her later work became more abstract, as in *Moon Masque* and *Magic of Nigeria*. She was Professor of Art at Howard University in Washington DC for 45 years and a Fellow of the Royal Society of Arts in London.

Jones, Marion 1975– •*US athlete*• Born in Los Angeles in 1975, she was competing internationally by the age of 12. She won the 100 meters at the world championships in 1997, setting a new world record of 10.83 seconds. A year later she became the first US female athlete to be ranked number one in three track-and-field events at the same time (the 100 meters, the 200 meters and the long jump). At the 2000 Olympics she won three golds (for the 100 meters, 200 meters and 4 × 400 meters relay) and two bronzes (for the long jump and the 4 × 100 meters relay), becoming the first female athlete to win five track-and-field medals at a single Olympics.

Jones, Mary Harris, *known as* **Mother Jones**, *née* **Harris** 1830–1930 •*US labor activist*• Born in County Cork, Ireland, she migrated to the US via Canada, and lost her family to an epidemic in 1867, and her home to the Chicago fire of 1871. Thereafter, she devoted herself to the cause of labor, especially in the coal industry, and was imprisoned in West Virginia at the age of 82 on a charge of conspiracy to murder in 1912. Freed by a new governor, she returned to labor activism. She wrote *The Autobiography of Mother Jones* (1925).

Jones, Tom, *originally* **Thomas Jones Woodward** 1940– •*Welsh pop singer*• Born in Pontypridd, Wales, he worked as a bricklayer and door-to-door salesman before winning his first recording contract in 1964. His second single, "It's Not Unusual" (1964), established him as an international star and was followed by such hits as "Green Green Grass of Home" (1966), "I'll Never Fall in Love Again" (1967) and "Delilah" (1968). His career declined in the early 1980s but revived in 1987 with "A Boy from Nowhere" and again in 1999 with the album *Reload*, from which came such hits as "Burning Down the House" and "Sex Bomb."

Jonson, Ben(jamin) 1572–1637 •*English dramatist*• He was born in Westminster, London, probably of Border descent, and educated at Westminster School. After working for a while with his stepfather, a bricklayer, he volunteered for military service in Flanders before joining **Philip Henslowe**'s company of players. He killed a fellow player in a duel, became a Catholic in prison, but later returned to Anglicanism. His *Every Man in His Humour*, with **Shakespeare** in the cast, was performed at the Curtain in 1598, to be followed not so successfully by *Every Man out of His Humour* in 1599. The equally unpopular *Cynthia's Revels* (1600), largely allegorical, was succeeded by *The Poetaster* (1600–01), whose popularity was helped by a personal attack on **Thomas Dekker** and **John Marston**. He then tried Roman tragedy, but his *Sejanus* (1603) and his later venture, *Catiline* (1611), are so padded with classical references as to be merely closet plays and poor imitations of Roman tragedy. His larger intent of discarding romantic comedy and writing realistically helped to produce his four masterpieces—*Volpone* (1606), *The Silent Woman* (1609), *The Alchemist* (1610) and *Bartholomew Fair* (1614). *Volpone* is an unpleasant satire on senile sensuality and greedy legacy hunters. *The Silent Woman* is farcical comedy involving a heartless hoax. **John Dryden** praised it for its construction, but *The Alchemist* is tighter, with its single plot and strict adherence to the unities. *Bartholomew Fair* is livelier, salted by his anti-Puritan prejudices, though the plot is lost in the motley of eccentrics. After the much poorer *The Devil Is an Ass* (1616), Jonson turned again to the masques, until 1625 when **James VI and I**'s death terminated his period of court favor. His renewed attempt to attract theater audiences left him in the angry mood of the ode "Come Leave the Loathed Stage" (1632). Only his unfinished pastoral play *The Sad Shepherd* survives from his declining years. His lyric genius was second only to Shakespeare's.

" "

Calumnies are answered best with silence.

1606 ***Volpone****, act 2, scene 2.*

Jónsson, Einar 1874–1954 •*Icelandic sculptor*• Born on the farm of Galtafell, he went to Copenhagen to study art, and after exhibiting his powerful realistic work *Outlaws* (1901, now in Reykjavík), was given a grant by the Icelandic government to study in Rome. In 1905 he settled in Copenhagen, in 1909 he offered all his works to the Icelandic nation, and in 1914 he returned to Iceland, hailed as its national sculptor. He spent two years in the US making a statue of the first European settler in North America, Thorfinn Karlsefni, for a new sculpture park in Philadelphia. Thereafter he lived in increasing isolation in Reykjavík, producing works replete with allegory and symbolism, like *Evolution* and *New Life*.

Jooss, Kurt 1901–79 •*German dancer, choreographer, teacher and director*• Born in Wasseralfingen, he was a student at the Stuttgart Academy of Music. While working as a ballet master in Münster, he cofounded the Neue Tanzbühne (New Dance Stage), for which he choreographed his first works. In 1927 he was appointed director of the dance department at the Essen Folkwang School. Here he founded the Folkwang Tanztheater in 1928, which eventually became the Folkwang Tanzbühne. *Le Bal* (1930), *The Prodigal Son* (1931), *Pulcinella* (1932), *The Green Table* (1932) and *The Big City* (1932) were made during this productive period. He left Germany during the Nazi years and toured the world, returning to Essen in 1949, and was ballet master of Düsseldorf Opera from 1954 to 1956. He was one of the first choreographers to blend classical technique with modern theatrical ideas to create dance for "the common man."

Joplin, Janis 1943–70 •*US rhythm and blues singer*• Born in Port Arthur, Texas, she developed a powerful blues voice and sang in clubs in the mid-1960s in Houston, before joining Big Brother and the Holding Company in San Francisco, with which she recorded two albums (1967–68). She became a national star after a sensational appearance at the epochal Monterey Pop Festival in 1967. She formed the Kozmic Blues Band (1969), and then the Full Tilt Boogie Band, with which she recorded the unfinished *Pearl* (released 1971), which included the earlier "Ball and Chain" and "Piece of My Heart" in addition to her famous version of Kris Kristofferson's "Me and Bobby McGee." Always given to excess, she died of an apparently accidental drug overdose.

Joplin, Scott 1868–1917 •*US pianist and composer*• One of the originators of ragtime music and one of its foremost exponents, he was born in Texas and was largely self-taught. He became a professional musician in his teens, but later studied music at George Smith College, Sedalia, Missouri. His first major published work, the "Maple Leaf Rag," proved to be the turning point in his career, and the resulting prosperity enabled him to concentrate on composing and teaching rather than playing. Although he was responsible for several famous and popular tunes, he was disheartened by the lack of commercial success of his two operas. When ragtime experienced a revival in the 1970s, due in part to the film *The Sting* (1973), his music became more widely known.

Jordan, Barbara C(harline) 1936–96 •*US politician, lawyer, and educator*• Born in Houston, Texas, she was educated at Texas Southern and Boston Universities, becoming the first African-American student at Boston University Law School. Admitted to the bars of Massachusetts and Texas in 1959, she later served in the Texas Senate (1966–72) as the only woman and the only African American, and in Congress (1972–78). At the University of Texas, she was a **Lyndon Johnson** public services professor (1979–82), then was appointed to the Lyndon Johnson Centennial Chair in National Policy. She became a member of the House Judiciary Committee and in 1991 was appointed special counsel on ethics by the governor of Texas. She received numerous awards and honors, including induction into the Texas Women's Hall of Fame (1984), the National Women's Hall of Fame (1990) and the African-American Hall of Fame (1993). Her autobiography, *Barbara Jordan: A Self-Portrait*, was published in 1979.

Jordan, (Marie-Ennemond) Camille 1838–1922 •*French mathematician*• Born in Lyons, he was professor at the École Polytechnique and at the Collège de France, and as the leading group theorist of his day did much to establish the central ideas on the subject. His *Traité de substitutions* (1870, "Treatise on

Substitutions") remained a standard work for many years. He applied group theory to geometry and linear differential equations, and in the 1890s his *Cours d'analyse* was an influential textbook for the French school of analysts.

Jordan, Dorothy or **Dorothea**, *née* **Bland** 1762–1816 •*Irish actress*• She was born near Waterford, Ireland, and made her debut in Dublin (1777). She soon became popular, and was engaged by Tate Wilkinson in Leeds, England (1782). Moving to London, she appeared with great success at Drury Lane in *The Country Girl* in 1785 and was well known for playing mainly comic tomboy roles for nearly 30 years. From 1790 to 1811 she had a relationship with the Duke of Clarence (the future **William IV**), by whom she had 10 of her 15 children. In 1831 King William made their eldest son Earl of Munster.

Jordan, Michael Jeffrey 1963– •*US basketball player*• Born in Brooklyn, New York, he began his career in college basketball at the University of North Carolina, then joined the Chicago Bulls (1984–93, 1995–98). Perhaps the finest all-around player in the history of the game, he set numerous records. He was a member of the US Olympic gold medal–winning basketball teams in 1984 and 1992. A member of the NBA All-Star team (1985–93, 1996–98), he was named the NBA Most Valuable Player (MVP) in 1988, 1991, 1992, 1996 and 1998. He retired in 1993, but rejoined the Bulls in the 1994–95 season and led them to three NBA championships (1996–98) in a reprise of their 1991–93 wins. Having retired again in 1999, he came out of retirement for a second time in 2001 and joined the Washington Wizards.

Jordan, Neil 1950– •*Irish filmmaker and writer*• Born in Sligo, Ireland, he studied history and literature at University College, Dublin, and worked at various jobs in London before returning to Ireland and helping to form the Irish Writers Co-operative (1974). His first collection of stories, *Night in Tunisia* (1976), earned the Guardian Fiction prize and was followed by the acclaimed novels *The Past* (1980) and *The Dreams of the Beast* (1983). He made his directorial debut with the thriller *Angel* (1982) and has boldly emphasized the fairy-tale and fantasy elements of such challenging works as *The Company of Wolves* (1984) and *Mona Lisa* (1986). *The Crying Game* (1992) won an Academy Award for Best Original Screenplay. His subsequent films include *Interview With the Vampire* (1994), *Michael Collins* (1996), *The Butcher Boy* (1997) and *The End of the Affair* (1999).

Jordan, (Ernst) Pascual 1902–80 •*German theoretical physicist*• Born in Hanover, he was educated there and in Göttingen before obtaining a post at the University of Rostock. He was subsequently appointed Professor of Physics at the Universities of Berlin (1944–52) and Hamburg (1951–70). He worked with **Max Born** and **Werner Heisenberg**, and helped to formulate the theory of quantum mechanics in the matrix representation, showing how light could be interpreted as being composed of discrete quanta of energy.

Jorn, Asger Oluf, *original surname* **Jørgensen** 1914–73 •*Danish painter*• Born in Vejrum, West Jutland, he studied art in Paris from 1936 with **Fernand Léger** and **Le Corbusier**, and in 1948–50 founded the "Cobra" group (Co[penhagen], Br[ussels], A[msterdam]), which aimed to exploit fantastic imagery derived from the unconscious.

Joseph, St 1st century BC–1st century AD •*Biblical character*• He was a carpenter in Nazareth, and the husband of the Virgin **Mary**. He last appears in the Gospel history when **Jesus** is 12 years old. He is never mentioned during Jesus's ministry, and must be assumed to have already died. His feast day is March 19.

Joseph •*Old Testament character*• He was the 11th son of **Jacob**, and the first by his wife Rachel. He is depicted as Jacob's favorite son (marked by the gift of a multicolored coat), but was sold into slavery by his jealous brothers. The stories (Genesis 37–50) show him using his wisdom and God's help to rise to high office in Pharaoh's court, and he was reconciled with his brothers when they arrived in Egypt seeking food during a famine. His sons, Ephraim and Manasseh, were blessed by Jacob, and became ancestors of two of the tribes of Israel.

Joseph I 1678–1711 •*Holy Roman Emperor*• Born in Vienna, he was the eldest son of **Leopold I** and became emperor in 1705. Musically talented and worldly, he helped reorganize Austrian finances. He defeated the Hungarian rebels under **Francis II Rákóczi** (1711), while Prince **Eugène** of Savoy led the Imperial army in alliance with the British forces under the Duke of **Marlborough** in the continuing struggle against **Louis XIV** of France.

Joseph II 1741–90 •*Holy Roman Emperor*• Born in Vienna, the son of **Francis I** and **Maria Theresa**, he was elected king of the Romans in 1764, and after his father's death (1765) Holy Roman Emperor. Although he failed to add Bavaria to the Austrian dominions, he acquired Galicia, Lodomeria and Zips at the first partition of Poland (1772), and he appropriated a great part of Passau and Salzburg (1780). He declared himself independent of the pope, suppressed 700 monasteries, prohibited papal dispensations on marriage, and published an Edict of Toleration for Protestants and Greeks in 1781. He also abolished serfdom, freed the press and the theater, emancipated the Jews, reorganized taxation, and curtailed the feudal privileges of the nobles. In 1788 he engaged in an unsuccessful war with Turkey, and in the same year there were outbreaks of insurrection within his non-German territories, Hungary and the Austrian Netherlands. Although intellectually gifted and well read, he was unworldly, short-tempered and autocratic, and naïve in his idea of a monarch's capacity for wholesale change.

“ ”

Here lies a prince whose intentions were pure, but who had the misfortune to see all his plans collapse.

Epitaph for himself. Quoted in T C W Blanning ***Joseph II*** *(1994), page 1.*

Joseph of Arimathea, St 1st century AD •*New Testament councilor*• Born in Arimathea, Samaria, he was a wealthy Samaritan who went to **Pontius Pilate** and asked for the body of **Jesus** after the Crucifixion, and buried it in his own tomb. According to later Christian literature he visited England after the Crucifixion, with the Holy Grail, and built a church at Glastonbury. His feast day is March 17 (Western churches) or July 31 (Eastern churches).

Joseph, Père, *also called* **Eminence Grise ("Grey Eminence")**, *originally* **François Joseph le Clerc du Tremblay** 1577–1638 •*French diplomat and mystic*• Born in Paris, he became a Capuchin in 1599, and secretary to Cardinal **Richelieu** in 1611. His by-name derives from his contact with Richelieu (the "Eminence Rouge"), for whom he became adviser and agent, undertaking many diplomatic missions, notably during the Thirty Years' War.

Josephson, Brian David 1940– •*Welsh physicist and Nobel Prize winner*• Born in Cardiff, he studied at Cambridge, where he received his PhD in 1964, and has spent his career there as Professor of Physics since 1974. In 1962 he deduced theoretically the possibility of the Josephson effect on electric currents in superconductors separated by a very thin insulator. He demonstrated that a current can flow between the superconductors with no applied voltage, and that an applied DC voltage produces an AC current of a proportional frequency. The effect was soon observed experimentally by **Philip W Anderson**, and Josephson junctions have since been much used in research, in fast switches for computers and in SQUIDs (superconducting quantum interference devices) used in geophysical measurements. The AC Josephson effect has been used to determine the constant e/h and led to a quantum standard of voltage. Josephson shared the 1973 Nobel Prize for physics with **Leo Esaki** and **Ivar Giaever**. He coedited *Consciousness and the Physical World* in 1980.

Josephus, Flavius, *originally* **Joseph ben Matthias** AD 37–c. 100 •*Jewish historian and general*• Governor of Galilee, he took part in the Jewish revolt against the Romans (AD 66) and, under the patronage of **Vespasian** and then **Titus**, he went to Rome after the fall of Jerusalem. His works (in Greek) include *History of the Jewish War*, *Antiquities of the Jews*, a history of the Jews to 66, and *Against Apion*.

Joshua, *Hebrew* **Yehoshua** •*Biblical character*• The son of Nun, of the tribe of Ephraim, he was successor to **Moses** as leader of the Israelites. He was one of the 12 spies sent to collect information about the Canaanites, and during the 40-year wandering acted as minister or personal attendant of Moses. After "the Lord was angry with Moses," Joshua, a charismatic warrior, was expressly designated to lead the people into Canaan. The Book of Joshua is a narrative of the conquest and settlement of Canaan under his leadership.

Josiah 649–609 BC *•King of Judah•* He succeeded his father Amon (641 BC) at the age of eight. He reestablished the worship of Jehovah, and instituted the rites in the newly discovered Book of the Law. He is credited with destroying pagan cults and attempting to centralize worship in Jerusalem and the Temple. He died in battle against the Egyptians at Megiddo.

Jospin, Lionel Robert 1937– *•French socialist politician•* Born in Meudon, Hauts-de-Seine, he entered the École Nationale d'Administration and subsequently joined the Foreign Ministry. He studied in the US in the late 1960s before teaching economics at the University Institute of Technology of Paris-Sceaux (1970–81). He entered parliament as a member of the Socialist Party in 1977 and became a close confidant of party leader **François Mitterrand**. When Mitterrand became president, Jospin took over as Socialist leader and subsequently served as minister of education. In 1995 he was selected as the party's candidate for the presidency, but was defeated by **Jacques Chirac**. He was elected prime minister in 1997 and quickly won respect for his pragmatic style of leadership, his policies including fiscal restraint and a more cautious attitude toward the European Union. He ran for president again, but was knocked out in the first round by **Jean-Marie Le Pen** and resigned as prime minister.

Joubert, Piet (Petrus Jacobus) 1834–1900 *•Afrikaner soldier and politician•* Born in Cango, Cape Colony, he was elected to parliament in 1860, becoming Attorney-General in 1870 and acting president in 1875. In the First Boer War (1880–81) he commanded the Transvaal's forces, and defeated Colley in 1881. He negotiated the Pretoria Convention (1881), became vice president in 1883. In the Second Boer War (1899–1902) he held command at the outset, but resigned due to ill health and died soon afterward.

Joule, James Prescott 1818–89 *•English natural philosopher•* Born in Salford, Greater Manchester, he was educated by private tutors, notably the chemist **John Dalton**, and became famous for his experiments on heat. The Joule effect (1840) asserted that the heat produced in a wire by an electric current was proportional to the resistance and to the square of the current. In a series of notable researches (1843–78), he showed experimentally that heat is a form of energy, determined quantitatively the amount of mechanical (and later electrical) energy to be expended in the propagation of heat energy and established the mechanical equivalent of heat. Between 1853 and 1862 he collaborated with Lord **Kelvin**, showing that when a gas expands without doing external work, its temperature falls (the Joule-Thomson effect). He was also the first to describe the phenomenon of magnetostriction. During the 1850s his ideas were recast in terms of the principle of the conservation of energy. The joule, a unit of work or energy, is named after him.

Jourdan, Jean-Baptiste, Comte 1762–1833 *•French soldier•* Born in Limoges, he joined the Revolutionary army and defeated the Austrians at Wattignies (1793), won the victory of Fleurus (1794), and then drove the Austrians across the Rhine, took Luxembourg, and besieged Mainz. But in 1795 he was defeated at Höchst, and then by the archduke **Charles** of Austria. **Napoleon I** employed him in 1800 in Piedmont; in 1804 he was made marshal, and in 1806 Governor of Naples. In 1813 he was defeated by the Duke of **Wellington** at Vitoria. **Louis XVIII** made him a count.

Jowett, Benjamin 1817–93 *•English scholar•* Born in Camberwell, London, and educated at St Paul's School and Balliol College, Oxford, he was elected a Fellow there in 1838, and tutor from 1840. He was elected Master of Balliol in 1870, Regius Professor of Greek from 1855, and from 1882 to 1886 he was Vice Chancellor of Oxford. Jowett belonged to the Broad Church party. For his article "On the Interpretation of Scripture" in *Essays and Reviews* (1860), he was tried but acquitted by the Vice Chancellor's court. He is best known for his fine translations of the *Dialogues* of **Plato** (1871), **Thucydides** (1881), the *Politics* of **Aristotle** (1885), and Plato's *Republic* (1894).

Joyce, Eileen Alannah 1912–91 *•Australian pianist•* Born in Zeehan, Tasmania, she was discovered by **Percy Grainger** when she was a child and was sent at the age of 15 to study at the Leipzig Conservatory. In 1930 she was introduced to Sir **Henry Wood**, who arranged her debut at one of his Promenade Concerts. She became a prolific broadcaster and during World War II frequently visited the blitzed towns of Great Britain with **Malcolm Sargent** and the London Philharmonic. She also toured internationally. She is particularly known for her work on film soundtracks, especially of *Brief Encounter* and *The Seventh Veil*, and the film of her childhood, *Wherever She Goes*.

Joyce, James Augustine Aloysius 1882–1941 *•Irish writer and poet•* He was born in Dublin, which despite his long exile provides the setting for most of his work. He was educated by Jesuits at Clongowes Wood College and Belvedere College, and then at University College, Dublin, where he studied modern languages. He rejected Catholicism, and in 1902 went to Paris for a year, living in poverty and writing poetry. His mother's death prompted his return to Ireland, when he stayed briefly in the Martello Tower, which features in the early part of *Ulysses*; he then left Ireland with Nora Barnacle (1884–1951), who was to be his companion for the rest of his life. He taught English for a while in Trieste and Rome. He had two children and had to scrounge to make ends meet. After a war spent mainly in Switzerland, the couple settled in Paris. By now Joyce was the author of two books: *Chamber Music* (1907) and *Dubliners* (1914), a collection of short stories that includes, among other celebrated stories, "The Dead." The collection was greeted enthusiastically, and Joyce was championed by **Ezra Pound** and by Harriet Shaw Weaver, editor of *The Egoist*, in which the autobiographical *A Portrait of the Artist as a Young Man* appeared in installments (1914–15). The support of friends, and of his brother Stanislaus, also did much to mitigate the difficulties of these years. Petitioned by Yeats and Pound on his behalf, the Royal Literary Fund in 1915 made him a grant and shortly afterward he received a grant voted for by Parliament. But his health was failing, his eyesight deteriorating and he was deeply disturbed by his daughter Lucia's mental illness. In 1922 his seminal novel *Ulysses* was published in Paris on February 2. Its explicit stream-of-consciousness description of the thoughts and happenings of everyday life immediately provoked violent reactions, and it was banned in the US until 1933. But the story of Leopold Bloom's day-long perambulation through Dublin is now regarded as a major advance for fiction. Meanwhile Joyce and Nora Barnacle were married during a trip to London in 1931. Lucia was diagnosed with schizophrenia the following year. Although troubled by worsening glaucoma, Joyce supervised the publication of *Finnegans Wake*, which moved on from the consciousness of *Ulysses* to the semiconsciousness of a dream world, in 1939. On the outbreak of World War II he returned to Zurich, where he underwent an operation for a duodenal ulcer, but he failed to recover. Joyce exercised a major influence on his contemporaries, especially **Virginia Woolf** and **Samuel Beckett**, and on later generations of writers, among whom **Saul Bellow**, **Thomas Pynchon**, **John Updike** and **Anthony Burgess** have acknowledged their debt.

“ ”

All moanday, tearsday, wailsday, thumpsday, frightday, shatterday till the fear of the Law.

*1939 **Finnegans Wake**.*

Joyce, William, *also known as* **Lord Haw-Haw** 1906–46 *•British traitor•* Born in Brooklyn, New York, of Irish parentage, he lived in Ireland as a child and in 1922 emigrated to England with his family. In 1933 he joined Sir **Oswald Mosley**'s British Union of Fascists and secured a British passport by falsely claiming to have been born in Galway. He founded his own fanatical British National Socialist league and fled to Germany before World War II broke out. From September 1939 to April 1945, he broadcast propaganda against Great Britain from Radio Hamburg, gaining his nickname from his pretentious drawling accent. He was captured by the British at

Flensburg, tried at the Old Bailey in 1945, and executed. His defense was his US birth, but his British passport, valid until July 1940, established nine months of treason.

Joyner-Kersee, Jackie (Jacqueline), *née* **Kersee** 1962– •*US athlete*• Born in East St Louis, Illinois, she is a track-and-field competitor who has won five Olympic medals, including gold medals for the heptathlon (1988, 1992) and the long jump (1988). She was world champion of the long jump in 1991 and 1993 and of the heptathlon in 1993. She holds the world record for the heptathlon. Participating in the 1996 Olympics, she won the bronze medal in the long jump.

Juan Carlos I 1938– •*King of Spain*• Born in Rome, Italy, the grandson of **Alfonso XIII**, he spent his childhood in Rome and Spain. In 1954 Don Juan de Borbón (his father and third son of Alfonso) and General **Franco** agreed that Juan Carlos should take precedence over his father as pretender. He became king on Franco's death (1975), and has presided over a gradual return to democracy, despite internal political difficulties reflected in two attempted coups. In 1962 he married Sofia (1938–), elder daughter of King **Paul** of Greece. They have two daughters, Elena (1963–) and Cristina (1965–), and a son, Felipe (1968–), Prince of Asturias.

Juan de La Cruz *See* **John of the Cross, St**

Juárez, Benito (Pablo) 1806–72 •*Mexican national hero and statesman*• A Zapotec Indian, he became governor of Oaxaca (1847–52). Exiled by Conservatives under **Santa Anna** (1853–55), he returned to join the new Liberal government. Proposing fundamental change, he abolished the fueros (the set of legal privileges and immunities attached to the clergy and the military), seized control of Church lands, and passed the anticlerical and Liberal constitution of 1857. He was elected president on the Liberal victory (1861), a post he held until his death. The French invasion under **Maximilian** forced him to the far north; from there he directed resistance until Maximilian's defeat in 1867. He then restored republican rule, creating the basis for the regime of **Porfírio Díaz**.

Judah •*Old Testament figure*• The fourth son of **Jacob** and Leah, he founded the greatest of the 12 tribes of Israel.

Judas or **Thaddeus, St** 1st century AD •*One of the 12 Apostles*• Judas (not Iscariot) is mentioned in the book of the Acts of the Apostles. He is referred to as "Judas Son of James." Also called Thaddeus, he may have come from a party of zealots, a Jewish nationalist movement from before 70 AD. He is often paired with **Simon the Zealot**, for tradition holds that they were missionaries, first in Egypt and later in Persia where they were finally martyred. His role as the patron saint of desperate causes originated in the 18th century in France and Germany. His feast day is October 28 (Western churches) or August 21 (Greek Orthodox).

Judas Iscariot 1st century AD •*One of the 12 Apostles*• Born probably in Kerioth, in the tribe of Judah, he is identified as the one who betrayed **Jesus** for 30 pieces of silver by helping to arrange for his arrest at Gethsemane by the Jewish authorities (Mark 14:43–46). Other traditions indicate his role as treasurer (John 13:29) and his later repentance and suicide (Matthew 27:3–5). The meaning of Iscariot is uncertain: it may mean "man of Keriot," "assassin" or "man of falsehood." He was replaced by Matthias (Acts 1:26).

Jude, St 1st century AD •*Early Christian*• He was probably the Judas who was listed as one of the brothers of **Jesus** (Matthew 13:55, Mark 6:3), and perhaps a brother of St **James** the Just. A New Testament letter bears his name, but its authorship is disputed. It is said to be directed against the Gnostics of the 2nd century. According to tradition he was martyred in Persia with St **Simon**, who shares his feast day of October 28 (Western churches) and June 19 or (Eastern churches) August 21.

Judith •*Old Testament Jewish heroine*• In the Apocryphal Book of Judith, she is portrayed as a widow who went to the tent of Holofernes, general of **Nebuchadnezzar**, cut off his head, and so saved her native town of Bethulia.

Jugnauth, Sir Anerood 1930– •*Mauritian politician*• After qualifying as a barrister in London in 1954, he returned to Mauritius and was elected to the legislative council in the period before full independence in 1968. In 1970 he cofounded the socialist Mauritius Militant Movement (MMM), from which he later broke away to form his own Mauritius Socialist Party (PSM). In 1982 he became prime minister at the head of a PSM-MMM alliance. In 1983 his party was reconstituted as the Mauritius Socialist Movement (MSM), and he retained his control of an MSM-led coalition in elections in 1983, 1987, and 1991. In 1995 he was succeeded as prime minister by Navin Ramgoolam.

Jugurtha d. 104 BC •*King of Numidia*• By the murder of his cousin, Hiempsal, he secured a part of the kingdom of his grandfather **Masinissa**. He soon invaded his surviving cousin Adherbal's part of the kingdom, besieged him in Cirta (112), and put him, and the Romans who were with him, to death. Thus began the Jugurthine War, in which the Romans twice attempted to defeat him, until finally, in 106, Jugurtha had to flee to the king of Mauretania, who delivered him to **Sulla**. He was left to die in prison in Rome.

Julia 39 BC–AD 14 •*Roman noblewoman*• The daughter of the Emperor **Augustus** and Scribonia, she was married at the age of 14 to her cousin **Marcellus**, a nephew of Augustus. After his death (23 BC) she married (21) **Marcus Vipsanius Agrippa**, to whom she bore three sons and two daughters. He died (12), whereupon Julia was married to **Tiberius** (11). The marriage was unhappy, and in 2, when her father learned of her adulteries, she was banished to the isle of Pandataria, and from there to Reggio, where she died of starvation. Her mother shared her exile.

Julian, *in full* **Flavius Claudius Julianus**, *also known as* **Julian the Apostate** c. 331–63 AD •*Roman emperor*• Born in Constantinople (Istanbul), he was the youngest son of **Constantius**, and half-brother of **Constantine I (the Great)**. Only Julian and his elder half-brother Gallus survived a massacre of the Flavians on Constantine's death (AD 337). Julian subsequently rejected Christianity, by then an established religion. In 355 he became caesar, and served in the army, endearing himself to the soldiers by his personal courage, his success in war, and the severe simplicity of his life. In 360 the jealous emperor ordered him to serve against the Persians, but his soldiers protested and proclaimed him Augustus. He took his army to Constantinople, and declared himself a pagan. His cousin died in 361 and as emperor, Julian embarked on public reform, tolerating Christians and Jews while restoring the old religion. In 363 he invaded Persia (Iran), but was forced to retreat and was killed. His extant writings are a series of *Epistles*, nine *Orations*, *Caesares*, satires on past Caesars, and the *Misopogon*, a satire on the people of Antioch. His chief work, *Kata Christianon*, is lost.

Julian of Norwich c. 1342–c. 1413 •*English mystic*• Born probably in Norwich, Norfolk, she is thought to have lived in isolation outside St Julian's Church, Norwich. She had a series of visions in May 1373, and her account of these and meditations on their significance, published in modern versions as the *Showings* or *Revelations of Divine Love*, have had lasting influence on theologians stressing the power of the love of God.

Juliana, *in full* **Juliana Louise Emma Marie Wilhelmina** 1909–2004 •*Queen of the Netherlands*• She was born in The Hague and was educated at Leiden University where she took a law degree. She married (1937) Prince **Bernhard Leopold** of Lippe-Biesterfeld, and they had four daughters: Queen **Beatrix**, Princess Irene (1939–), Princess Margriet (1943–), and Princess Marijke (1947–). On the German invasion of Holland (1940) Juliana escaped to Great Britain and later resided in Canada. She returned to Holland (1945), and in 1948, on the abdication of her mother Queen **Wilhelmina**, became queen of the Netherlands. She herself abdicated (1980) in favor of her eldest daughter, Beatrix.

Julius II, *originally* **Giuliano della Rovere** 1443–1513 •*Italian pope*• Born in Albizula, Genoa, he became pope in 1503. His public career was mainly devoted to political and military enterprises for the reestablishment of papal sovereignty in its ancient territory, and for the ending of foreign domination in Italy. He is best remembered as a patron of the arts. He employed **Donato Bramante** for the design of St Peter's, begun in 1506, had **Raphael** brought to Rome to decorate his private apartments and commissioned **Michelangelo** for the frescoes on the ceiling of the Sistine Chapel and for his own tomb. His military exploits inspired **Erasmus**'s satire *Julius Exclusus*.

Jumblat, Kemal 1919–77 •*Lebanese socialist politician and hereditary Druze chieftain*• He was born in the Chouf Mountains. He founded the Progressive Socialist Party (1949) and held several cabinet posts (1961–70). The increasing power of his authority in partnership with the Palestinians resulted in the Syrian intervention on the side of the Christians (1976). He was assassinated near Baaklu in the Chouf Mountains, after which his son Walid became leader of the Druze.

Jung, Carl Gustav 1875–1961 •*Swiss psychiatrist*• Born in Kesswil, he studied medicine there and worked under **Eugen Bleuler** at the Burghölzli mental clinic in Zurich (1900–09). His early publications led to his meeting **Sigmund Freud** in Vienna in 1907. He became Freud's leading collaborator and was elected president of the International Psychoanalytical Association (1910). His independent researches, which made him increasingly critical of Freud's insistence on the psychosexual origins of the neuroses, were published in *The Psychology of the Unconscious* (1911–12), and caused a rift between them in 1913. From then onward he developed his own school of analytical psychology. He coined the term "complex," introduced the concepts of introvert and extrovert personalities, and developed the theory of the collective unconscious with its archetypes of man's basic psychic nature. He held professorships in Zurich (1933–41) and Basel (1944–61). His other main works include: *Psychology and Religion* (1937), *Psychology and Alchemy* (1944), *Aion* (1951), *The Undiscovered Self* (1957) and his autobiographical *Memories, Dreams, Reflections* (1962). He was seen by many as the founder of a new humanism.

Junkers, Hugo 1859–1935 •*German aircraft engineer*• Born in Rheydt, he became Professor of Mechanical Engineering at Aachen (1897–1912). After World War I he founded aircraft factories in Dessau, Magdeburg and Stassfurt, which produced many famous planes, both civil and military, including the Ju 87 Stuka dive bomber used in World War II.

Juppé, Alain Marie 1945– •*French politician*• Born in Mont-de-Marsan, Landes, he was educated in Paris at the Lycee Louis-le-Grand and the Institute for Political Studies. His first political appointment was in the office of the prime minister **Jacques Chirac** in 1976, but he made his reputation in local politics in Paris. Between 1984 and 1986 he was a member of the European Parliament. In 1995 he won the general election during a period of trade union unrest following cutbacks in public spending, and he became the country's prime minister (1995–97).

Justin, St, *known as* **the Martyr** c. 100–c. 165 AD •*Greek theologian, and one of the Fathers of the Church*• Born of Greek parents in Sichem, Samaria, after his conversion to Christianity in Ephesus (c. 130 AD) he traveled about on foot defending its truths. At Rome between 150 and 160 he wrote the *Apologia* of Christianity addressed to the Emperor **Marcus Aurelius**, followed by a second one, and a *Dialogue with Trypho*, defending Christianity against Judaism. He is said to have been martyred. His feast day is April 14.

Justinian I, *called* **the Great**, *in full* **Flavius Petrus Sabbatius Justinianus** c. 482–565 AD •*Emperor of the Eastern Roman Empire*• He was born in Tauresium in Illyria, the son of a Slavic peasant and the nephew of **Justin I**. Educated in Constantinople (Istanbul), he was named consul in 521, and in 527 was proclaimed by Justin his colleague in the empire. Justin died the same year, and Justinian, proclaimed sole emperor, was crowned along with his wife **Theodora**. His reign is the most brilliant in the history of the late empire. He selected the ablest generals, and under **Narses** and **Belisarius** his reign may be said to have largely restored the Roman Empire to its ancient limits, and to have reunited the East and the West. His first war—that with Persia—ended in a favorable treaty. The Vandal kingdom of Africa was reannexed to the empire, the imperial authority was restored in Rome, northern Italy and Spain, and Justinian constructed or renewed a vast line of fortifications along the eastern and southeastern frontier of his empire. It was as a legislator that Justinian gained his most enduring renown. He collected and codified the principal imperial *constitutiones* or statutes in force at his accession, and the *Codex*, by which all previous imperial enactments were repealed, was published in 529. The writings of the jurists or commentators on Roman law were streamlined and published under the title *Digesta* or *Pandectae* in 533. The direction of this work was entrusted to a committee of professors and advocates, who also prepared a systematic and elementary treatise on the law—the *Institutiones* (533), based on the *Institutiones* of **Gaius**. During the subsequent years of his reign, Justinian promulgated many new laws or constitutions, known as *Novellae*. The Institutes, Digest, Code and Novels together make up what is known as the *Corpus Juris Civilis*, a work which was immensely influential on the laws of nearly all European countries down to modern times.

Juvenal, *in full* **Decimus Junius Juvenalis** c. 55–c. 140 AD •*Roman lawyer and satirist*• He was probably born in Aquinum in the Volscian country. Almost nothing is known of his life except that he lived in Rome, was poor and was a friend of **Martial**. His 16 brilliant verse satires of Roman life and society (c. 100–c. 128), written from the viewpoint of an angry Stoic moralist, range from savage attacks on the vices and the extravagance of the ruling classes and the precarious makeshift life of their hangers-on, to his hatred of Jews, foreigners and society women. **Dryden**'s versions of five of Juvenal's satires are among the best of his work, and Dr **Johnson** imitated two in his *London* and *Vanity of Human Wishes*.

" "

Orandum ut sit mens sana in corpore sano.
One should pray to have a sound mind in a sound body.

***Satirae**, no. 10, l. 356.*

Kabila, Joseph 1970– •*Congolese soldier and politician*• The son of **Laurent Kabila**, he received his early military training in China before being appointed army chief by his father. On the assassination of his father in 2001, he succeeded to the posts of president and defense minister.

Kabila, Laurent-Désiré 1939–2001 •*Congolese politician*• Born in Jadotville, Belgian Congo (now Likasi, Democratic Republic of the Congo), he studied philosophy in France and subsequently led the opposition that after 30 years of fighting eventually forced the dictator **Mobutu Sese Seko** into exile, assuming the office of president himself in 1997. Having promised to free the people of poverty and corruption, he only succeeded in changing the country's name from Zaire to the Democratic Republic of the Congo, and started new conflicts with Uganda and Rwanda in which he lost half the country to rebel forces. On his assassination in 2001, apparently at the hands of one of his own bodyguards, his son **Joseph Kabila** succeeded to the offices of president and defense minister.

Kádár, János 1912–89 •*Hungarian politician*• Born in Kapoly in southwest Hungary, he was a member of the central committee of the underground party during World War II, escaping from capture by the Gestapo. He emerged after the war as First Party Secretary and as one of the leading figures of the Communist regime. In 1950, as Minister of the Interior, he was arrested for "**Tito**-ist" sympathies. He was freed in 1953, was rehabilitated in 1954 and became secretary of the party committee for Budapest in 1955. When the Hungarian anti-Soviet revolution broke out in October 1956, he was a member of the "national" anti-Stalinist government of **Imre Nagy**. On November 1 he declared that the Communist Party had been dissolved, but as Soviet tanks crushed the revolution, he formed a puppet government that, in the closing months of 1956, held Hungary in a ruthless reign of terror. The majority of his countrymen regarded him as a traitor, although a few saw him as a victim of forces beyond his control. He resigned in 1958, but became Premier and First Secretary of the Central Committee in 1961. In 1965 he lost the premiership, but remained First Secretary. He proceeded to introduce a series of "market socialist" economic reforms, while continuing to retain cordial political relations with the Soviet Union. In 1988 he stepped down as Communist Party leader, and was removed from the Communist Party's central committee in 1989, shortly before his death.

Kael, Pauline 1919–2001 •*US film critic*• Born in Petaluma, California, she was educated at the University of California at Berkeley. A waspish, insightful reviewer, she was movie critic of the *New Yorker* from 1968 to 1991. She published several anthologies of her articles: *Kiss Kiss Bang Bang* (1968), *When the Lights Go Down* (1980), *5001 Nights at the Movies* (1982) and *Movie Love* (1991).

Kafka, Franz 1883–1924 •*Austrian novelist*• Born to German-Jewish parents in Prague, he studied law there, and although overwhelmed by a desire to write, found employment (1907–23) as an official in the accident prevention department of the government-sponsored Workers' Accident Insurance Institution. A hypersensitive, introspective person who felt emasculated by his domineering father, he eventually moved to Berlin to live with Dora Dymant in 1923, his only brief spell of happiness before succumbing to a lung disease. He published several short stories and essays, including, "Der Heizer" (1913, "The Boilerman"), "Betrachtungen" (1913, "Meditations") and "Die Verwandlung" (1916, Eng trans "The Transformation," 1933; more widely known as "Metamorphosis"). His three unfinished novels, *Der Prozess* (1925, Eng trans *The Trial*, 1937), *Das Schloss* (1926, Eng trans *The Castle*, 1937) and *Amerika* (1927, Eng trans *America*, 1938), were published posthumously, through his friend **Max Brod**, and translated by **Edwin Muir** and **Willa Muir**. Literary critics have interpreted *Das Schloss* variously as a modern *Pilgrim's Progress* (however, there is literally no progress), as a literary exercise in Kierkegaardian existentialist theology, as an allegory of the Jew in a Gentile world, or psychoanalytically as a monstrous expression of Kafka's Oedipus complex, but his solipsism primarily portrays society as a pointless and irrational organization into which the bewildered individual has strayed (from which the term "Kafkaesque" derives). He has exerted a tremendous influence on Western literature, not least on such writers as **Albert Camus** and **Samuel Beckett**. A number of his other writings have been published posthumously, including *Briefe an Milena* (1952, Eng trans *Letters to Milena*, 1967) and *Briefe an Felice* (1967, Eng trans *Letters to Felice*, 1974), and his diary and other correspondence.

" "

Es ist oft besser, in Ketten als frei zu sein.
It is often safer to be in chains than to be free.

1925 ***Der Prozess***.

Kaganovich, Lazar Moiseyevich 1893–1991 •*Soviet politician*• He joined the Communist Party in 1911 and, after participating in the 1917 Russian Revolution, became First Secretary of the Ukrainian Party in 1925. In 1930, he became a full member of the politburo, as well as serving as First Secretary of the Moscow Party. He played a prominent role in the brutal, forced collectivization program in the early 1930s, and in the great purges of 1936–38. A close ally of **Stalin**, he survived the latter's death in 1953 but, having fallen afoul of **Nikita Khrushchev** and participated in the Anti-Party Plot, was dismissed in 1957 and relegated to a managerial position in a Siberian cement works.

Kahlo, Frida 1907–54 •*Mexican artist*• Born in Coyoicoán, Mexico City, she was the daughter of a Jewish-German immigrant photographer and a Catholic Mexican mother. A serious road accident at the age of 15 destroyed her dreams of a career as a doctor, but during her convalescence she started painting, and sent her work to the painter **Diego Rivera**, whom she married in 1928; it was a colorful but tortured marriage. They divorced, but ultimately remarried. Characterized by vivid imagery, many of her pictures were striking self-portraits. Pain, which dogged her all her life, and the suffering of women are recurring themes in her surrealistic and often shocking pictures. The surrealist poet and essayist **André Breton** likened her paintings to "a ribbon around a bomb" (1938). The Frida Kahlo Museum was opened in her house in Coyoicoán in 1958.

Kaiser, Georg 1878–1945 •*German expressionist dramatist, poet and novelist*• He was born in Magdeburg. He wrote 78 plays, and was thus the most prolific, as well as the most influential and gifted, of the expressionist playwrights. His own life had more than an expressionist tinge (it included a six-month stint in jail for stealing and pawning a landlord's furniture: his defense—supposed to annoy the judges, which it did—was that he needed the money to maintain the high standards of his youth and to satisfy his artistic requirement for luxuries and immunity from bourgeois pseudo-morality). His plays include *Von morgens bis mitternachts* (1916, Eng trans *From Morn to Midnight*, 1920), *Gas I* (1918) and *Gas II* (1920). His work was banned by the Nazis, and he left Germany in 1938. Later he wrote romantic dramas, and, finally, a *Hellenic Trilogy* (published posthumously in 1948). He wrote two libretti for **Kurt Weill**, and a now neglected novel, *Es ist genug* (1932, "It Is Enough"), about incest.

Kalashnikov, Mikhail Timofeyevich 1919– •*Russian military designer*• Born of peasant stock in the Altai area, he joined the army in 1938. Seriously wounded in 1941, he began experimenting with what was to be the famous AK-47 assault rifle taken into Soviet service in 1949. The rifle has also been extensively used by foreign armies and international terrorists, a fact deplored by Kalashnikov in later life. He was a Deputy of the USSR Supreme Soviet for a number of years.

Kalidasa fl. 450 AD •*Indian dramatist*• He is best known for his drama *Sakuntala* (Eng trans by Sir **William Jones**, 1789), and is considered India's greatest dramatist.

Kalinin, Mikhail Ivanovich 1875–1946 •*Soviet politician*• Born in Tver (which was renamed Kalinin after him from 1932 to 1991), he became head of the Soviet state after the 1917 revolution and during the years of **Stalin**'s dictatorship (1919–46). He entered politics as a champion of the poor classes, and won great popularity, becoming president of the Soviet Central Executive Committee (1919–38), and of the Presidium of the Supreme Soviet (1938–46). Upon his death Königsberg, East Prussia, was renamed Kaliningrad in his honor.

Kaltenbrunner, Ernst 1902–46 •*Austrian Nazi leader*• Born in Reid im Innkreis, Austria, he was head of the SS at the time of the Anschluss. After **Reinhard Heydrich**'s assassination, he became head of the security police in 1943, sent millions of Jews and political suspects to the concentration camps, and was responsible for orders sanctioning the murder of prisoners of war. He was condemned by the Nuremberg Tribunal and hanged.

Kamen, Martin David 1913– •*US biochemist*• Born in Toronto, Canada, he studied in Chicago and held positions in several US universities. In 1960 he was appointed Professor of Biochemistry at the University of California, San Diego, where he was the first to isolate the carbon isotope C-14. Studying photosynthesis, he confirmed that the oxygen released comes from water and not from carbon dioxide, determined the initial fate of the "fixed" carbon dioxide, and demonstrated that illumination increases the phosphorus turnover. Kamen also studied nitrogen fixation and bacterial ferridoxins.

Kamenev, Lev Borisovich, *originally* **Lev Borisovich Rosenfeld** 1883–1936 •*Russian revolutionary and politician*• Born of Jewish parentage in Moscow, he was an active revolutionary throughout Russia and abroad from 1901 onward, associating with **Lenin**, **Trotsky** and **Stalin**, and was exiled to Siberia in 1915. Liberated after the February Revolution, he was active as a Bolshevik throughout 1917, and subsequently held various party, government, and diplomatic appointments. Expelled from the party as a Trotskyist in 1927, he was readmitted the next year but again expelled in 1932. The same happened in 1933–34. He was finally executed for allegedly conspiring with Trotsky and **Grigori Zinoviev** against Stalin. Like many others falsely accused, he was posthumously rehabilitated in 1988 during the **Gorbachev** years.

Kamerlingh Onnes, Heike 1853–1926 •*Dutch physicist and Nobel Prize winner*• Born in Groningen, he studied physics and mathematics at the university there, and continued his studies at the University of Heidelberg. He later became Professor of Physics at the University of Leiden (1882–1923). He tested the ideas of **Johannes van der Waals**, studying liquids and gases over a wide range of temperatures and pressures. His most noteworthy achievements were the first liquefaction (1908) and later solidification of helium, and his discovery (1911) that the electrical resistance of metals cooled to near absolute zero disappears, a phenomenon later called superconductivity. In 1913 he was awarded the Nobel Prize for physics.

Kames, Henry Home, Lord 1696–1782 •*Scottish judge, legal historian and philosopher*• Born in Kames, Berwickshire, he was called to the bar in 1723 and was raised to the bench as Lord Kames in 1752. A leading figure in the Scottish Enlightenment, his publications include *Historical Law Tracts* (1759), *Principles of Equity* (1760), *An Introduction to the Art of Thinking* (1761), and his best-known book, *Elements of Criticism* (1762).

Kammerer, Paul 1880–1926 •*Austrian zoologist*• Born in Vienna, he was educated at the University of Vienna and later joined the Institute of Experimental Biology there. His work appeared to support the view of **Jean-Baptiste Lamarck** that characteristics acquired during life can be transmitted through subsequent generations. The best known of these results concerned the apparent acquisition of nuptial pads on the forefeet of midwife toads. However, in 1926 G K Noble and H Przibram examined material preserved from Kammerer's work in Vienna and showed that the dark swellings, which Kammerer claimed to be nuptial pads, were due to injections of ink. Kammerer shot himself a few months later.

Kandinsky, Wassily, *Russian* **Vasili Vasilyevich Kandinsky** 1866–1944 •*French painter*• Born in Moscow, Russia, he was the originator of abstract painting. After studying law in Moscow, he went to Munich to study art, and at the age of 30 he began painting. A watercolor he produced in 1910 is considered to be the first abstract work of art, but all representational elements were not banished from his work until the 1920s. In Paris he absorbed the influence of the Nabis and the Fauves, but Russian icon painting and folk art were equal influences on him. In 1912 he published his famous book *Über das Geistige in der Kunst* (Eng trans *On the Spiritual in Art*, 1947) and in the same year was a cofounder with **Franz Marc** and **Paul Klee** of the Blaue Reiter Group. He returned to Russia to teach in 1914, and after the Russian Revolution became head of the Museum of Modern Art (1919) and founded the Russian Academy of Artistic Sciences (1921). In 1922 he left Russia and was eventually put in charge of the Weimar Bauhaus School. From 1920 his paintings are predominantly geometric, in line with the Suprematist and Constructivist work he had left behind in Moscow, which was eventually to fall out of favor there. In 1933 he moved to France and became a naturalized citizen in 1939. As a painter and theoretician he has exerted considerable influence.

“ ”

We should never make a god out of form. We should struggle for form only as long as it serves as a means of expression for the inner sound.

1912 "On the Question of Form," in ***Blaue Reiter Almanac.***

Kane, Bob, *originally* **Robert Kahn** 1915–98 •*US cartoonist and animator, creator of Batman*• Born in New York, he studied art at Cooper Union, joined the **Max Fleischer** Studio as a trainee animator in 1934, and entered the comic-book field with *Hiram Hick* in *Wow* (1936). His early strips were humorous, but working to scripts by his partner, Bill Finger (1917–74), he created *The Batman* for No. 27 of *Detective Comics* (May 1939), which caught on rapidly. Kane then returned to animation to create *Courageous Cat* (1958) and *Cool McCool* (1969) for television.

Kane, Martin *See* **Ó Cadhain, Máirtín**

Kano Motonobu 1476–1559 •*Japanese painter*• Born in Kyoto, he was the son of the painter Kano Masanobu (1434–1530), who had introduced the Kano style of painting. Motonobu achieved a synthesis of Kanga (ink painting in the Chinese style) with the lively colors of Yamato-e (the Japanese style), arriving at a dynamic style of decorative art. Under him the Kano school established itself, both artistically as well as socially. His most famous works, originally in various sanctuaries and monasteries in Kyoto, now preserved in its National Museum, show the decorative treatment of nature, which became standard for the Kano school.

Kant, Immanuel 1724–1804 •*German philosopher*• Immanuel Kant was born in Königsberg, Prussia (now Kaliningrad, Russia), and stayed there all his life. He studied and then taught at the university, becoming Professor of Logic and Metaphysics in 1770. He lived a quiet, orderly life and local people were said to set their watches by the time of his daily walk. His early publications were in the natural sciences, particularly geophysics and astronomy, and in an essay on Newtonian cosmology (*Allgemeine Naturgeschichte und Theorie des Himmels*, 1755, "Universal Natural History and Theory of the Heavens"), he anticipated the nebular theory of **Pierre Laplace** and predicted the existence of the planet Uranus before its actual discovery by **William Herschel** in 1781. Kant published extensively, but his most important works were produced relatively late in his life: the *Kritik der reinen Vernunft* (1781, "Critique of Pure Reason"), *Kritik der praktischen Vernunft*

(1788, "Critique of Practical Reason") and *Kritik der Urteilskraft* (1790, "Critique of Judgment"). The first of these is a philosophical classic, albeit very difficult, which he himself described as "dry, obscure, contrary to all ordinary ideas, and prolix to boot." In it he responds to **David Hume**'s empiricism and argues that the immediate objects of perception depend not only on our sensations but also on our perceptual equipment, which orders and structures those sensations into intelligible unities. He likened his conclusions to a Copernican revolution in philosophy, whereby some of the properties we observe in objects are due to the nature of the observer, rather than the objects themselves. There exist basic concepts (or categories), like cause and effect, which are not learned from experience but constitute our basic conceptual apparatus for making sense of experience and the world. The second *Critique* deals with ethics, and his views are developed in the *Grundlagen zur Metaphysik der Sitten* (1785, "Groundwork to the Metaphysic of Morals") in which he presents the famous categorical imperative, "Act only on that maxim which you can at the same time will to become a universal law." The third *Critique* deals with aesthetics or judgments of taste, for which he tries to provide an objective basis and which he connects with our ability to recognize purposiveness in nature. He also wrote on political topics, and his *Perpetual Peace* (1795) advocates a world system of free states. Kant described his philosophy as transcendental or critical idealism, and he exerted an enormous influence on subsequent philosophy, especially the idealism of **Hegel**, **Johann Fichte** and **Friedrich von Schelling**. He is regarded as one of the great figures in the history of Western thought.

" "

Eben darin Philosophie besteht, seine Grenzen zu kennen.
It is precisely in knowing its limits that philosophy consists.
*1781 Kritik der reinen Vernunft (**Critique of Pure Reason**, translated by N Kemp Smith).*

Kantorovich, Leonid Vitalevich 1912–86 •*Soviet economist, mathematician and Nobel Prize winner*• Born and educated in St Petersburg, he was a professor at Leningrad (now St Petersburg) State University (1934–60) and later was director of the mathematical economics laboratory at the Moscow Institute of National Economic Management (1971–76) and the Institute of System Studies at the Moscow Academy of Sciences (from 1976). He shared the 1975 Nobel Prize for economics with **Tjalling Koopmans**.

Kapila 7th century BC •*Indian founder of the Samkhya school of Hindu philosophy*• An almost legendary figure, said to have spent the latter half of his life on Sagar Island at the mouth of the Ganges, he is held to be the originator of the philosophical system presently expounded in the commentary of Iśvarakrishna (3rd–5th century AD) and the *Samkhya Sutra* (c. 1400 AD). It is notable for parallels with Buddhist thought and a theory of evolution, or constant "becoming" of the world.

Kapil Dev, (Nihanj) 1959– •*Indian cricket player*• Born in Chandigarh, Punjab, an all-around player, he made his first-class debut for Haryana at the age of 16, and played county cricket in England for Northamptonshire and Worcestershire. He led India to victory in the 1983 World Cup. In 1994 he retired from the game, having set a world record of 434 Test wickets, surpassing the record (431 wickets) held by Sir **Richard Hadlee**. This record stood until 2000 when it was beaten by **Courtney Walsh**.

Kapitza, Peter, *Russian* **Pyotr Leonidovich Kapitsa** 1894–1984 •*Soviet physicist and Nobel Prize winner*• Born in Kronstadt, he studied at Petrograd (now St Petersburg) and under **Ernest Rutherford** at Cambridge, where he became assistant director of magnetic research at the Cavendish Laboratory (1924–32). He returned to the USSR in 1934, and was appointed director of the Institute of Physical Problems. He was dismissed in 1946 for refusing to work on the atomic bomb, but was reinstated in 1955. He is known for his work on high-intensity magnetism, on low temperature, and on the liquefaction of hydrogen and helium, and was awarded the Nobel Prize for physics, jointly with **Robert Wilson** and **Arno Penzias**, in 1978. In the 1970s he defended dissident physicist **Andrei Sakharov** from expulsion from the Soviet Academy of Sciences.

Kaplan, Mordecai Menahem 1881–1983 •*US rabbi and philosopher*• Born in Svencionys, Lithuania, he emigrated to the US with his family in 1889 and studied theology at various institutions before being ordained as a rabbi in 1902. He was the founder of the Jewish Center in New York City (1916) and the Society for the Advancement of Judaism (1922), and he originated the Reconstructionist movement in Judaism, which celebrated the richness of Jewish culture but questioned some of its religious traditions, notably the belief that the Jews are a chosen people. Though controversial, his views greatly influenced contemporary Reform Judaism, which answered his call for a more equal role for women in Jewish life.

Kapoor, Anish 1954– •*British sculptor*• Born in Bombay of Jewish-Indian parentage, he moved to Britain in 1972 and was trained at Hornsey College of Art and Chelsea School of Art. His early work was often brightly colored, consisting of disembodied shapes covered in powdered pigment that often spilled over onto the floor and around the form. He exhibited at the Venice Biennale in 1990, when he won the Premio Duemila for young artists, with his "voids," including a *Madonna* clothed in pigment of an intense blue shade. His later work features heavy materials, often stone or polished metal, as in *Turning the World Inside Out* (1995). He was awarded the Turner Prize in 1991.

Karadžić or **Karadjic, Radovan** 1945– •*Bosnian-Serb politician*• Born in Montenegro, he came to Sarajevo as a teenager after World War II. Formerly a psychiatrist and poet, he became prominent in politics in 1990 on the creation of the Serbian Democratic Party (SDS), the main Serbian party in Bosnia. As the self-styled president of Serb-controlled Bosnia from 1992 to 1996, he signed the **Vance-Owen** Peace Plan in May 1993, and the Dayton Peace Agreement in December 1995. However, with the aim of uniting all the Serbs in the former Yugoslavia into one Greater Serbia, his militias drove more than one million Muslims from their homes, killing many thousands. He was indicted by the UN war crimes tribunal in 1996.

Karajan, Herbert von 1908–89 •*Austrian conductor*• Born in Salzburg, he studied there and in Vienna, and his fame grew when he was conductor at the Berlin Staatsoper (1938–42). He joined the Nazi Party in 1933 and after World War II was not permitted to work until 1947, but in 1955 was made principal conductor of the Berlin Philharmonic Orchestra. He also frequently conducted at the Vienna State Opera, at many major festivals, and was artistic director of the Salzburg Festival (1956–60) and of the Salzburg Easter Festival (from 1967). His passion for the theater and for acoustical research was evident in his production of operas, his idiosyncratic casting, the refined, impressive (often controversial) quality of his recordings, and in the films he directed and conducted.

Karamanlis or **Caramanlis, Konstantinos** 1907–98 •*Greek politician*• He was born in Próti, Macedonia. A former lawyer, he held several government posts before being called upon by King **Paul I** to form a government in 1955. He remained prime minister almost continuously for eight years, during which time Greece signed a treaty of alliance with Cyprus and Turkey. He formed the National Radical Union Party. He became prime minister again in 1974, supervising the restoration of civilian rule after the collapse of the military government. He then served as president (1980–85, 1990–95).

Karan, Donna, *née* **Faske** 1948– •*US designer*• Born in Forest Hills, New York, she dropped out of Parson's School of Design to work for **Anne Klein**, becoming her successor in 1974. In 1984 she launched her own company, featuring luxurious, user-friendly clothes that appealed to successful working women. She launched the cheaper DKNY label in 1988.

Karl Ludwig Johann (of Austria) *See* **Charles**

Karle, Jerome 1918– •*US physicist and Nobel Prize winner*• Born in New York City, he studied at the City College of New York (CCNY), Harvard and the University of Michigan. After working briefly on the Manhattan Project to develop the atomic bomb in the 1940s, he spent his career at the US Naval Research Laboratories in Washington, specializing in diffraction methods for studying the fine structure of crystalline matter. He shared the 1985 Nobel Prize for chemistry with **Herbert Hauptman** for the development of the "direct method" for interpreting raw data from X-ray crystallography measurements. He later investigated the use of high-speed computers to produce real-time images of crystals and complex biomolecules.

Karloff, Boris, *originally* **William Henry Pratt** 1887–1969 •*English actor*• Born in Dulwich, London, he was educated at Uppingham and Merchant Taylors' schools. He emigrated to Canada in 1909 and became involved in acting. He spent 10 years in repertory companies, then went to Hollywood, and after several silent films made his name as the monster in *Frankenstein* (1931). His career was mostly spent in popular horror films, such as *The Body Snatcher* (1945), though his performances frequently transcended the crudity of the genre. He continued to appear in films and on television and the stage until his death.

“ ”

The monster was indeed the best friend I could ever have.

1991 On his success as Frankenstein's monster. Posthumous quotation in ***Connoisseur****, January.*

Karmal, Babrak 1929–96 •*Afghan politician*• The son of an army officer, he was educated at Kabul University, where he studied law and political science. He was imprisoned for anti-government activity during the early 1950s. In 1965 he formed the Khalq (masses) Party and, in 1967, the breakaway Parcham (banner) Party. These two groups merged in 1977 to form the banned People's Democratic Party of Afghanistan (PDPA). After briefly holding office as president and prime minister in 1978, he was forced into exile in eastern Europe, returning in 1979, after the Soviet military invasion, to become head of state. Karmal's rule was fiercely opposed by the mujahideen guerrillas and in 1986 he was replaced as president and PDPA leader by **Sayid Mohammad Najibullah**.

Karpov, Anatoli Yevgenevich 1951– •*Russian chess player*• Born in Zlatoust, in the Urals, he won the 1969 world junior championship. After **Bobby Fischer** refused to defend his title, he became world champion by default in 1975, defending his title successfully against Viktor Korchnoi in 1978 and 1982. His 1984–85 defense against **Garry Kasparov** was controversially halted by FIDE (Fédération Internationale des Échecs) when he led but showed signs of cracking under the physical and psychological pressure. Kasparov won the title when the match was resumed from scratch in 1985. Karpov made at least two attempts to regain his title, eventually succeeding in 1993. In 1994 two chess world championships were held. Karpov played and won the FIDE title. Kasparov elected to play, and eventually won, the Professional Chess Association (PCA) version. Karpov won the FIDE title again in 1996 and 1998.

Karrer, Paul 1889–1971 •*Swiss chemist and Nobel Prize winner*• Born in Moscow, Russia, he was educated in Switzerland and studied chemistry at the University of Zurich. In 1919 he became professor there. During the 1920s he developed an interest in plant pigments and elucidated the structure of carotene, which then led to important discoveries concerning vitamin A. He also elucidated the structures of vitamins E, K and B_2 (riboflavin). For these achievements and for important studies of the chemistry of vitamin C and biotin, he shared the 1937 Nobel Prize for chemistry with **Norman Haworth**. Karrer's later studies included important work on the coenzyme nicotinamide adenine dinucleotide, carotenoids and the curare-like alkaloids.

Käsebier, Gertrude, *née* **Stanton** 1852–1934 •*US photographer*• Born in Fort Des Moines (now Des Moines), Iowa, and raised in Golden, Colorado Territory, and later in Brooklyn, she began photographing her family in the late 1880s. Opening her own portrait studio in Manhattan (1897–98), she built up a successful business, and went on to become one of the first women members of the Linked Ring group in 1900 and a founding member of Photo-Secession in 1902. She was represented in **Frances Benjamin Johnston**'s exhibition of US women photographers (1900–01), and **Alfred Stieglitz** devoted the first issue of his influential magazine *Camera Work* to her in 1903.

Kasparov, Garry Kimovich, *originally* **Garry Weinstein** 1963– •*Russian chess player*• Born in Baku, Azerbaijan, his surname was changed by the authorities after his father died in a road accident. He became world junior champion at 16. His 1984–85 match with **Anatoli Karpov** for the world title was the longest in the history of chess—after 48 games, played over six months in Moscow, he had recovered from 0–5 to 3–5, with Karpov requiring only one more win, but showing signs of cracking under the physical and psychological pressure. The match was abandoned by FIDE (Fédération Internationale des Échecs), and the players were given six months to recuperate. On resumption from scratch Kasparov won the title, which he defended successfully in 1986, 1987 and 1990. Long-term friction between him and FIDE resulted in his establishing the Grandmasters' Association in 1987, and then the Professional Chess Association (PCA), a rival to FIDE, in 1993. In 1994, two chess world championships were held. Kasparov won the PCA one, but Karpov won the FIDE title. Kasparov retained his PCA title until defeated by **Vladimir Kramnik** in 2000, ending his 15-year domination of the game.

Kassem, Abdul Karim 1914–63 •*Iraqi soldier and revolutionary*• He was born in Baghdad. He joined the army and in 1958 he led the coup which resulted in the overthrow of the monarchy and the deaths of King **Faisal II**, his uncle Prince Abdul Ilah, and the pro-Western prime minister General **Nuri Es-Sa'id**. Kassem attempted to suspend the constitution and established a left-wing military regime with himself as prime minister and head of state, but soon found himself increasingly isolated in the Arab world. He failed to crush a Kurdish rebellion (1961–63) and was killed in a coup led by Colonel Salem Aref, who reinstated constitutional government.

Kastler, Alfred 1902–84 •*French scientist and Nobel Prize winner*• Born in Guebwiller (then in Germany), he taught physics at lycées in Mulhouse, Colmar and Bordeaux, before leaving to join the University of Bordeaux in 1931, where he later became Professor of Physics. He moved to the École Normale Supérieure in Paris in 1941 where he became professor in 1952. He obtained precise information about atomic structures by using visible light and radio waves to excite electrons in atoms, which then emitted radiation. He also used optical techniques to develop "optical pumping," which laid the foundations for the subsequent development of masers and lasers, and for which he was awarded the 1966 Nobel Prize for physics.

Kästner, Erich 1899–1974 •*German writer*• He was born in Dresden, and his writing career began with two volumes of verse, both cleverly satirical. In 1933 his books were publicly burned by the Nazis, but he continued to live in Germany. His novels include *Fabian: Die Geschichte eines Moralisten* (1931, Eng trans *Fabian: The Story of a Moralist*, 1932) and *Drei Männer im Schnee* (1934, Eng trans *Three Men in the Snow*, 1935). However, he is best known for his delightful children's books, among them *Emil und die Detektive* (1928, Eng trans *Emil and the Detectives*, 1930), *Annaluise und Anton* (1929, Eng trans 1932) and *Das fliegende Klassenzimmer* (1933, Eng trans *The Flying Classroom*, 1934), which gained him worldwide fame.

Kasyanov, Mikhail Mikhailovich 1957– •*Russian politician*• Born in Soltsevo, Moscow, he served in the Soviet army before pursuing a career as an engineer. He established a reputation as a leading economist in the 1980s, in due course joining the department of the Ministry of Economy of the Russian Federation. Having risen to the posts of Deputy Minister of Finance (1995–99) and Finance Minister (1999–2000), he became the country's prime minister in 2000.

Katherine Parr *See* **Catherine Parr**

Katz, Alex 1927– •*US painter*• Born in New York, he studied painting at Cooper Union there (1946–49) and at Skowhegan School, Maine (1949–50). From 1959 he began making portraits of his friends in a deliberately gauche, naïve style, simplifying forms and using a limited palette, as in *The Red Smile* (1963, Cologne). In later years he has also painted landscapes, rendered in a style that is reminiscent of Japanese art and characterized by an air of unreality.

Katz, Sir Bernard 1911–2003 •*British biophysicist and Nobel Prize winner*• Born and educated in Leipzig, Germany, he left Nazi Germany in 1935, and began physiological research at University College London. After work at the Kanematsu Institute in Sydney, Australia, with Sir **John Eccles**, in 1946 he returned to Britain. For the next three decades he focused on the mechanisms of neural transmission, showing that chemical neurotransmitters are stored in nerve terminals and released in specific portions called quanta when stimulated by the arrival of the neural impulse. For this work he shared the 1970 Nobel Prize for physiology or medicine with **Julius Axelrod** and **Ulf von Euler**. He was knighted in 1969.

Kauffmann, (Maria Anna Catharina) Angelica 1741–1807 •*Swiss painter*• Born in Chur in the Grisons, Switzerland, and trained in Italy, she was painting portraits of notables in Italy at the age of 11 and in 1766 went to London. There she became famous for her wit and intellect, as well as a painter of classical and mythological pictures and of portraits. She was also a founding member of the Royal Academy. In the 1770s she executed decorative paintings for houses, such as the ceiling depicting *Painting* (c. 1780) now in Burlington House, London. Her self-portrait (c. 1770–75) is in the National Gallery, London. Following her marriage to the Venetian painter **Antonio Zucchi**, with whom she worked closely in England, she returned to Italy in 1781.

Kaufman, George S(imon) 1889–1961 •*US playwright and director*• Born in Pittsburgh, Pennsylvania, he turned to writing comedies for the stage in the early 1920s. With **Moss Hart** he wrote such plays as *You Can't Take It With You* (1936, Pulitzer Prize) and *The Man Who Came to Dinner* (1939). Other well-known works include *Of Thee I Sing* (1931, Pulitzer Prize) with **Morrie Ryskind** and **Ira Gershwin**, as well as *Dinner at Eight* (1932) with **Edna Ferber**. He also worked on two **Marx Brothers** vehicles, *Cocoanut* (1925) and *Animal Crackers* (1928), which were later made into films. Another notable collaboration was with Howard Teichmann on *The Solid Gold Cadillac* (1953).

“ ”

Am sitting in the last row. Wish you were here.

*1932 Telegram sent during a performance of **Of Thee I Sing** to the actor William Gaxton, who was taking various liberties with Kaufman's lines while playing the leading role.*

Kaunda, Kenneth David 1924– •*Zambian statesman*• Born in Lubwa, he became a teacher and then entered politics and founded the Zambian African National Congress (1958). Subsequently he was imprisoned and the movement banned. In 1960 he was elected president of the United National Independent Party (UNIP) and played a leading part in his country's independence negotiations. After the breakup of the Federation of Rhodesia and Nyasaland, he was elected prime minister of Northern Rhodesia (Zambia) in January 1964, and then president when the country obtained independence in October of that year. He was reelected six times before being defeated in 1991 in the first multiparty election in 19 years.

Kaunitz(-Rietberg), Wenzel Anton, Prince von 1711–94 •*Austrian statesman*• He was born in Vienna. He distinguished himself at the Congress of Aix-la-Chapelle (1748), and as ambassador at the French court (1750–52). As Chancellor (1753–92), he instigated the Diplomatic Revolution and directed Austrian politics for almost 40 years under **Maria Theresa** and **Joseph II**.

Kaurismäki, Aki 1957– •*Finnish film director*• He was born in Orimattila, and worked in a series of menial jobs before forming a film production company, Villealfa, with his older brother and directorial collaborator Mika Kaurismäki (1955–). Many of his films are parodies of existing genres and blend Finnish melancholy with surreal comedy and rock-'n'-roll music, for example, the road movie *Leningrad Cowboys Go America* (1989). Other films include *Drifting Clouds* (1996) and *Juha* (1999).

Kavanagh, Patrick Joseph 1905–67 •*Irish poet and novelist*• He was born near Inniskeen, County Monaghan, and farmed before leaving for Dublin in 1939 to pursue a career as a writer and journalist. Perhaps his greatest achievement is *The Great Hunger* (1942), a passionate poem about the harsh reality of life for a frustrated Irish farmer and his elderly mother. Other works include the autobiographical novel *Tarry Flynn* (1948). His unorthodox, antisocial lifestyle in Dublin led to a savage anonymous profile (by the poet Valentin Iremonger). In his libel action, *Kavanagh v. The Leader* (1953), Kavanagh was the victim of a brutal cross-examination, from which he never recovered.

Kawabata, Yasunari 1899–1972 •*Japanese writer and Nobel Prize winner*• Born in Osaka, he was educated at Tokyo University (1920–24), studying English and then Japanese literature. His first novel, *Izu no odoriko* (Eng trans *The Izu Dancer*, 1955), was published in 1925. He experimented with various Western novel forms, but by the mid-1930s had returned to traditional Japanese forms. Later novels, which are typically melancholy, include *Yukiguni* (1935–47, Eng trans *Snow Country*, 1957) and *Sembazuru* (1949, Eng trans *Thousand Cranes*, 1959). He won the 1968 Nobel Prize for literature, the first Japanese writer to win the award. He committed suicide.

Kawakubo, Rei 1942– •*Japanese fashion designer*• Born in Tokyo and educated at Keio University in 1964, she became a fashion stylist and designed her own clothes, founding her company, Commes des Garçons, in 1969. The label, meaning "like boys," emphasizes her conviction that her clothes are for modern women "who do not need to assure their happiness by looking sexy to man, by emphasizing their figures." Her controversial 1980s "ripped" sweater is now in the clothing collection at the Victoria and Albert Museum, London.

Kaye, Danny, *professional name of* **David Daniel Kominski** 1913–87 •*US stage, radio and film actor*• Born in Brooklyn, New York, he toured as a singer and dancer in the 1930s, and made his first feature film, *Up in Arms*, in 1943. *Wonder Man* (1944) made his reputation as a film comedian and was followed by international success in *The Secret Life of Walter Mitty* (1947). Other films include *The Inspector General* (1950), *Hans Christian Andersen* (1952) and *The Court Jester* (1956). He received a Special Academy Award in 1955, and in later years worked for international children's charities, especially UNICEF.

Kaye, Nora, *originally* **Nora Koreff** 1920–87 •*US dancer*• Born in New York, she studied at the School of American Ballet and the New York Metropolitan Opera Ballet School. She joined American Ballet Theater (ABT) at its inception in 1939 and soon became one of the most acclaimed dramatic ballerinas of her generation, creating the role of Hagar in **Antony Tudor**'s *Pillar of Fire* (1942), and appearing in other modern ballets as well as in the classics. She was a member of the New York City Ballet (1951–54), and then returned to ABT until her retirement in 1961. In 1961 she cofounded Ballet of Two Worlds with her film director and choreographer husband Herbert Ross (1927–2001).

Kazan, Elia, *originally* **Elia Kazanjoglou** 1909–2003 •*US stage and film director*• Born in Constantinople (Istanbul), Turkey, he emigrated to the US in 1913. He studied at Williams College and Yale, then acted in minor roles on Broadway and in Hollywood before becoming a theater director. He was cofounder of the Actors Studio (1947) in New York, and his Broadway productions include the works of **Arthur Miller** and **Tennessee Williams**. He began as a film director in 1944, and many of his films show his social or political commitment, such as *Gentleman's Agreement* (1948, Academy Award), on anti-Semitism; *Pinky* (1949), on racism; *On the Waterfront* (1954, Academy Award); and *A Face in the Crowd* (1957). Other notable films include Tennessee Williams's *A Streetcar Named Desire* (1951), **John Steinbeck**'s *East of Eden* (1954), and **William Inge**'s *Splendor in the Grass*. He also wrote novels and published an autobiography, *My Life* (1988).

Kazantzakis, Nikos 1883–1957 •*Greek novelist, poet and dramatist*• He was born in Iráklion, Crete, and studied law at the University of Athens. He published his first novel, *Toda Raba*, in French in 1929 (Eng trans 1964), but is best known for the novel *Vios kai politeia tou Alexi Zorba* (1946, Eng trans *Zorba the Greek*, 1952) and the epic autobiographical narrative poem, *Odyseia* (1938, Eng trans *The Odyssey, a Modern Sequel*, 1958). He wrote several other novels, including *O Christos xanastavronetai* (1954, Eng trans *Christ Recrucified*, 1954), *O Kapetan Michalis* (1953, Eng trans *Freedom or Death*, 1955) and *O teleftaios peirasmos* (1955, Eng trans *The Last Temptation of Christ*, 1960), and translated many literary classics into modern Greek. He spent his last decade living in Antibes, France.

Kean, Edmund c.1789–1833 •*English actor*• Born in London, it is likely he was the illegitimate son of Anne Carey, an actress and entertainer, and granddaughter of **Henry Carey**. He was said to have been taught singing, dancing, fencing and elocution, and by the age of eight had made several appearances on the Drury Lane stage. Around 1804 he became an itinerant player. He finally appeared at Drury Lane in a major role in 1814, playing Shylock in *The Merchant of Venice*. A delighted audience acclaimed his unconventional interpretation of a dark, desperate, bitter rogue brandishing a cleaver. Villainous parts suited him best, and he excelled as Richard III and Iago. His debauched and profligate life finally lost him public approval when he was successfully sued for adultery in 1825. After his US tour of 1825 he returned to England, but he was visibly failing. His last performance was with his son Charles Kean (1811–68) at Drury Lane on March 25, 1833, where he collapsed while playing Othello. He died a few weeks later.

Keane, Molly, *originally* **Mary Nesta Skrine**, *pseudonym* **M J Farrell** 1904–96 •*Irish novelist*• She was born in County Kildare, into "a rather serious Hunting and Fishing and Church-going family," and when young wrote only to supplement the allowance she was given for clothing, adopting the pseudonym "M J Farrell." *The Knight of the Cheerful Countenance*, her first book, was written when she was 17. Between 1928 and 1952 she wrote 10 novels, including *The Rising Tide* (1937), *Two Days in Aragon* (1941) and *Loving Without Tears* (1951), drawing her material from the foibles of her own class. She also wrote spirited plays. When her husband died at age 36, she stopped writing for many years, but *Good Behaviour* (1981), shortlisted for the Booker Prize, led to the reprinting of many of her books and a revival of critical appreciation. *Loving and Giving* (1988) is a bleak comedy, describing the breakup of a marriage through the eyes of the couple's eight-year-old daughter.

Kearny, Philip 1814–62 •*US general*• Born in New York City, he began his military career as a second lieutenant of cavalry on the Western frontier under the command of his uncle, Colonel **Stephen Watts Kearny**. He later fought in the Mexican War, losing an arm, and in 1859 he went to France to serve with **Napoleon III**. He returned to the US at the outbreak of the Civil War and became a brigadier general of Union forces. A popular commander, he played an important role in the Peninsular Campaign, earning him promotion to major general. He was killed during a reconnoitering mission in Virginia.

Keating, Paul John 1944– •*Australian Labor politician*• Born in Sydney, he was educated at De La Salle College and entered politics in 1969 as Labor Member of Parliament. A committed republican, he opposed Australia's continuing links with the British royal family and made it his party's policy to end them. In 1991 he was elected Prime Minister and produced proposals which would turn Australia into a republic by the end of the 20th century. Although the policy attracted wide support, he was defeated in the 1996 general election and announced that he was leaving politics.

Keating, Tom (Thomas Patrick) 1917–84 •*English art restorer and forger*• He was born in London. Dismissed from the navy due to illness in 1947, he took a course at Goldsmiths College in London, where failing his exams left him with a lifelong grudge against what he saw as an elitist art world. He took up work restoring, and then faking, paintings, with the aim of exposing the fallibility of art experts. The scandal broke in 1976, when Keating admitted that a series of nine pictures, bearing imitations of Samuel Palmer's signature, were in fact drawn by him. He estimated that there were some 2,500 of his fakes in circulation. In 1979 he was put on trial at the Old Bailey for forgery, but charges were eventually dropped because of his deteriorating health. In 1982 Keating was given his own award-winning television art show and in 1983 sold paintings under his own name.

Keaton, Buster (Joseph Francis) 1895–1966 •*US film comedian*• Born in Piqua, Kansas, he joined his parents in vaudeville ("The Three Keatons") at the age of three, developing great acrobatic skill. His Hollywood film debut was in *The Butcher Boy* (1917), the start of a prolific career. Famous for his deadpan expression in all circumstances, he starred in and directed such classics as *The Navigator* (1924) and *The General* (1926). His reputation declined with the advent of talking films until the 1950s and 1960s, when many of his silent masterpieces were rereleased, and he began to appear in character roles in films like *Sunset Boulevard* (1950) and *Limelight* (1952). He received a Special Academy Award in 1959.

Keaton, Diane, *originally* **Diane Hall** 1946– •*US actress*• Born in Los Angeles, she won a scholarship to study at The Neighborhood Playhouse in New York City and began her association with **Woody Allen** with her Broadway appearance in *Play It Again, Sam* (1969–70), later appearing in Allen's *Annie Hall* (1977), which won her a Best Actress Academy Award, *Manhattan* (1979), and *Manhattan Murder Mystery* (1993) among others. She made further notable appearances in *Looking for Mister Goodbar* and *Reds* (1981), but has also made more commercially popular comedies such as *Father of the Bride* (1991) and *The First Wives Club* (1996). One of her best dramatic roles was as Kay in all three parts of *The Godfather* (1972, 1974, 1990). A noted photographer, she has also directed television programs, pop videos and such films as *Hanging Up* (2000).

Keats, Ezra Jack 1916–83 •*US illustrator and children's writer*• Born in Brooklyn, New York, his books often explored the emotional lives of young children in city apartment blocks. *My Dog Is Lost* (1960) was his first book, but *The Snowy Day* (1962)—about a small African-American boy's adventure in the snow—is the one for which he is best known. Later books include *Peter's Chair* (1967) and *Apt. 13* (1971).

Keats, John 1795–1821 •*English poet*• He was born in London, the son of a livery-stable keeper, and went to school in Enfield. In 1811 he was apprenticed to a surgeon at Edmonton, and later (1815–17) was a medical student in the London hospitals, but took to writing poetry. **Leigh Hunt**, his neighbor in Hampstead, introduced him to other young Romantics, including **Percy Bysshe Shelley**, and published his first sonnets in *The Examiner* (1816). His first volume of poems appeared in 1817, and his long mythological poem *Endymion* in 1818. He returned from a walking tour in Scotland (1818), which exhausted him, to find the savage reviews of *Endymion* in *Blackwood's Magazine*, by **John Gibson Lockhart**, and in the *Quarterly*. In addition, his younger brother Tom was dying of consumption, and his own love affair with Fanny Brawne seems to have brought him more pain than comfort. It was under these circumstances that he published the volume of 1820, *Lamia and Other Poems*, a landmark in English poetry. Except for the romantic poem "Isabella or The Pot of Basil," based on a story in **Boccaccio**'s *Decameron*, and the first version of his epic poem, "Hyperion," all the significant verse in this famous volume is the work of 1819, such as the two romances "The Eve of St Agnes" and "Lamia" and the odes—"On a Grecian Urn," "To a Nightingale," "To Autumn," "On Melancholy" and "To Psyche." In particular, "The Eve of St Agnes" displays a wealth of sensuous imagery almost unequaled in English poetry. In "Lamia," the best told of the tales, he turns from stanza form to the couplet as used by **Dryden** in his romantic *Fables*. Keats's letters are also greatly admired. It is clear that he was both attracted and repelled by the notion of the poet as teacher or prophet. Having prepared the 1820 volume for the press, Keats, now seriously ill with consumption, sailed for Italy in September 1820, reached Rome and died there.

" "

Morality
Weighs heavily on me like unwilling sleep.

1817 "On Seeing the Elgin Marbles."

Keble, John 1792–1866 •*English Anglican churchman and poet*• Born in Fairford, Gloucestershire, he studied at Corpus Christi College, Oxford. Ordained in 1816, he became a college tutor (1818–23). In 1827 his book of poems *The Christian Year* was widely circulated, and as Oxford Professor of Poetry (1831–41), he delivered his theory of poetry. The Oxford Movement was inspired by his sermon on "National apostasy" (1833), which encouraged a return to High Church ideals, and his circle (which originated the Tractarian movement) issued the 90 *Tracts for the Times* (ending in 1841). Other works include the *Lyra Innocentium* (1846) and a poetic translation of the Psalter (1839). Keble College, Oxford, was founded in his memory (1870).

Keegan, Kevin Joseph 1951– •*English soccer player and manager*• He was born in Armthorpe, Yorkshire. He played for several English teams, notably for Liverpool (1971–77) and Newcastle (1982–84), and also for Hamburg (1977–80). He played many times for England (1972–82, as captain 1976–82). He was appointed manager of Newcastle United in 1992. He enjoyed much success; but despite great popularity he resigned unexpectedly in 1997. He was appointed coach of the England national team in 1999, but resigned in 2000 and later became manager of Manchester City.

Keeler, Christine 1942– •*English model and showgirl*• After an unhappy childhood spent mainly in the Thames Valley, at Wraysbury, she left home at 16 and went to London, where she worked at Murray's Cabaret Club. Here she met **Mandy Rice-Davies**, who was to become a close friend. **Stephen Ward**, an osteopath, was a frequent visitor to the club and he and Keeler formed a relationship. Ward introduced her and Rice-Davies into his circle of influential friends, including the Conservative Cabinet minister, **John Profumo**, with whom Keeler had an affair, while being involved at the same time with a Soviet diplomat. This led to Profumo's resignation from politics (1963), the prosecution of Ward for living on immoral earnings, and Ward's eventual suicide. Keeler herself served a prison sentence for related offenses. In the late 1980s, her autobiography and the film *Scandal* (1988) revived interest in the events and raised doubts about the validity of the charges made against her and Ward.

Keersmaeker, Anne Teresa de *See* **De Keersmaeker, Anne Teresa**

Kefauver, (Carey) Estes 1903–63 •*US political leader*• Born near Madisonville, Tennessee, he was elected by his home state to the House of Representatives (1939–49) and the US Senate (1949–63). A Democrat, he supported the New Deal and fought monopolies. He was noted for conducting televised Senate hearings concerned with the investigation of organized crime (1950–51).

Keillor, Garrison (Gary Edward) 1942– •*US humorous writer and radio performer*• He was born in Anoka, Minnesota, and graduated from the University of Minnesota in 1966, already writing for the *New Yorker*. He hosts the live radio show, *A Prairie Home Companion* (1974–87, 1993–), delivering a weekly monologue set in the quiet, fictional Midwestern town of Lake Wobegon. His books include *Happy to Be Here* (1981), *Lake Wobegon Days* (1985), *Leaving Home* (1987), *We Are Still Married* (1989), *WLT: A Radio Romance* (1991), *Wobegon Boy* (1997) and *Me* (1999).

Keitel, Harvey 1941– •*US actor*• Born in Brooklyn, New York, he joined the Marine Corps straight out of school and later studied at the Actor's Studio and performed off-Broadway before making his film debut in *Who's That Knocking at My Door?* (1968), which began a long association with director **Martin Scorsese**. An intense performer who has illuminated all shades of human agony and ecstasy, he has appeared in such films as *Mean Streets* (1973), *Taxi Driver* (1976), *Bad Timing* (1980), *Bugsy* (1991), *Thelma and Louise* (1991), *Reservoir Dogs* (1992), *Bad Lieutenant* (1992), *The Piano* (1993), *Smoke* (1995) and *Holy Smoke* (1999).

Keitel, Wilhelm 1882–1946 •*German soldier*• He joined the army in 1901 and served in World War I. In the 1930s he became an ardent Nazi, and was appointed Chief of the Supreme Command of the armed forces (1938). In 1940 he signed the Compiègne armistice with France and was **Hitler**'s chief military adviser throughout the war. In May 1945, he was one of the German signatories of unconditional surrender to Russia and the Allies in Berlin. He was executed in October 1946 for war crimes.

Keith, Penelope, *originally* **Penelope Hatfield** 1940– •*English actress*• Born in Sutton, Surrey, she trained at the Webber Douglas Academy. Her West End plays include *The Norman Conquests* (1974), *The Apple Cart* (1977), *The Millionairess* (1978), *Moving* (1983) and *Hobson's Choice* (1983). She starred on television as Margo Leadbetter in *The Good Life* (1975–78), Audrey Fforbes-Hamilton in *To the Manor Born* (1979–81), Phillippa Troy in *Law and Disorder* (1994) and Maggie Prentice in *Next of Kin* (1995–97).

Kekkonen, Urho Kaleva 1900–86 •*Finnish statesman*• Born in Pielavesi, after studying law at the University of Helsinki and fighting against the Bolsheviks in 1918, he entered the Finnish parliament as an Agrarian Party deputy, holding ministerial office from 1936 to 1939 and in 1944. He was prime minister four times in the early 1950s before being elected president in 1956—a position he retained for 25 years—in succession to **Juo Paasikivi**. Although Kekkonen had always been hostile to Stalinist Russia, as president he encouraged a policy of cautious friendship with the USSR. At the same time his strict neutrality ensured that he retained the confidence of his Scandinavian neighbors. He resigned because of ill health in 1981.

Kekule von Stradonitz, (Friedrich) August, *originally surnamed* **Kekulé** 1829–96 •*German chemist*• Born in Darmstadt, he was educated there and at the University of Giessen. He began his teaching career in Heidelberg (1856), then became professor at the University of Ghent (1858). During this time, he solved the apparent irreconcilability of his views on the tetravalency of carbon with the known formula of benzene (C_6H_6)—the cyclic nature of the benzene molecule. In 1867 he moved to Bonn, where he proposed delocalized rather than fixed double bonds. Despite his ill health from 1875, his work in 1890 on the structure of pyridine (a compound analogous to benzene) is an important landmark in the development of structural organic chemistry.

Keller, Helen Adams 1880–1968 •*US writer*• Born in Tuscumbia, Alabama, she became deaf and blind at 19 months, and was unable to communicate through language until the age of 7, when she was put under the tutelage of Anne M Sullivan (later Mrs **Macy**), who taught her to associate words with objects and to read and spell through touch. She later learned to use sign language and to speak, and she graduated from Radcliffe College in 1904. She became a famous lecturer and crusader for the handicapped and published several books based on her experiences, notably *The Story of My Life* (1902).

Kelley, Florence 1859–1932 •*US feminist and social reformer*• Born in Philadelphia, she was educated at Cornell University and at the University of Zurich, where she became a socialist. From 1891 to 1899 she worked at **Jane Addams**'s Hull House Settlement and subsequently became the first woman factory inspector in Illinois, successfully fighting to reduce working hours and improve methods and conditions of production. She became general secretary of the National Consumers' League, was one of the founders of the National Association for the Advancement of Colored People, and in 1919 she helped establish the Women's International League for Peace and Freedom. Her works include *Some Ethical Gains Through Legislation* (1905) and a translation of **Friedrich Engels**'s *Condition of the Working Classes in England in 1844* (1887).

Kellogg, Frank B(illings) 1856–1937 •*US jurist, statesman and Nobel Prize winner*• He was born in Potsdam, New York, practiced law in Minnesota, became senator (1917–23), ambassador in London (1923–25), and Secretary of State (1925–29). With **Aristide Briand** he drew up the Kellogg-Briand Pact (1928) outlawing war as an instrument for national policy, which became the legal basis for the Nuremberg Trials (1945–46). He was a judge of the Permanent Court of Justice at the Hague (1930–35), and was awarded the 1929 Nobel Peace Prize.

Kellogg, John Harvey 1852–1943 and **W(ill) K(eith)** 1860–1951 •*US inventors*• Brothers, they were born in Tyrone and Battle Creek, Michigan. John Kellogg graduated from Bellevue Hospital Medical College in 1875. They joined forces, as physician and industrialist respectively, at Battle Creek Sanitarium to develop a process of cooking, rolling and toasting wheat and corn into crisp flakes that made a nourishing breakfast cereal for their patients. Soon their corn flakes were being sold through the mail, and in 1906 the W K Kellogg Company was founded. The result was a revolution in the breakfast eating habits of North Americans, and before long the rest of the Western world. In 1930 the W K Kellogg

Foundation took its place as one of the leading philanthropic institutions in the US.

Kelly, Emmett 1898–1979 •*US clown*• He was born in Sedan, Kansas, and began his career as a professional cartoonist, then drifted into circus jobs. Portraying the clown Weary Willie, a sad-faced tramp with a ragged suit and bulbous nose, he performed in the Ringling Brothers–Barnum & Bailey Circus and in the film *The Greatest Show on Earth* (1952).

Kelly, Gene (Eugene Curran) 1912–96 •*US actor, dancer, choreographer and film director*• Born in Pittsburgh, Pennsylvania, he graduated in economics from the University of Pittsburgh before turning to a career as a dancer, and it was his lead performance in *Pal Joey* (1939) that led to his film debut in *For Me and My Gal* (1942). An athletic, muscular dancer and choreographer, he revolutionized the screen musical in films like *On the Town* (1949), *An American in Paris* (1951), and *Singin' in the Rain* (1952). He received a Special Academy Award in 1951. With the demise of the original screen musical, he turned to dramatic acting in films such as *Inherit the Wind* (1960), and directed a number of films, including *Hello, Dolly!* (1969). He was the 1985 recipient of the American Film Institute Life Achievement award.

Kelly, Grace Patricia, *married name* **Grimaldi, Princess Grace of Monaco** 1929–82 •*US film actress and princess*• Born in Philadelphia, Pennsylvania, she acted on television and Broadway, before making her film debut in *Fourteen Hours* (1951). Her short but highly successful film career as a coolly elegant beauty included leading roles in *High Noon* (1952), *Dial M for Murder* (1954), *Rear Window* (1954), *The Country Girl* (1954, Academy Award), *To Catch a Thief* (1955), and *High Society* (1956). In 1956 she married Prince **Rainier III** of Monaco, and retired from the screen. She was killed in a car accident.

Kelly, Ned (Edward) 1855–80 •*Australian bushranger*• Born in Wallan, Victoria, he was the son of an Irish convict father. After minor brushes with the law, he was imprisoned briefly in 1870 before taking up livestock stealing. In 1878 he and his gang ambushed a group of policemen; Kelly shot three. Two bank robberies followed; a reward of £8,000 was offered for their capture and Aboriginal trackers were brought in to help. The failed holdup of a train at Glenrowan in Victoria led to the death of three gang members and the capture of Kelly, dressed in his homemade suit of armor. He was hanged in November 1880 and became a folk hero.

Kelly, Petra, *originally* **Petra Karin Lehmann** 1947–92 •*German politician*• Born in Günzburg, Bavaria, she moved with her mother to the US at the age of 13. After studying at American University in Washington DC, she worked for the EEC in Brussels. In 1979 she cofounded the Green Party (Die Grünen) and in 1983 the party entered the Bundestag with 28 seats. However, in the unification election of 1990, the party lost all its parliamentary seats and was dogged by internal divisions. She died in an apparent suicide pact along with her partner, Gert Bastian, but subsequent reports have cast a shadow on this finding, by linking his name with the *Stasi*, the secret police of the former East Germany.

Kelly, Walt(er Crawford) 1913–73 •*US animator and strip cartoonist*• Born in Philadelphia, Pennsylvania, he joined the **Walt Disney** studio in Hollywood as an animator in 1935. He moved to comics in 1941, creating his most famous characters, Albert Alligator and Pogo Possum of Okefenokee Swamp. He became art editor of the *New York Star* (1948), and introduced *Pogo* as a daily strip.

Kelly, William 1811–88 •*US inventor*• Born in Pittsburgh, Pennsylvania, he became involved in the manufacture of wrought-iron articles. He soon discovered that an air blast directed onto, or blown through, molten cast iron can remove much of the carbon in it, so that the resulting metal becomes a mild steel. He built seven of his converters between 1851 and 1856, when he heard that **Henry Bessemer** had been granted a US patent for the same process. He convinced the Patent Office of his prior claim, but was almost immediately bankrupted in the 1857 financial panic. Although he continued to improve his process and made it in every way as effective as Bessemer's, he never achieved commercial success, and his invention has come to be known as the Bessemer converter.

Kelman, James 1946– •*Scottish novelist, short-story writer and playwright*• Born in Glasgow, he left school at age 15 to become an apprentice compositor. His first publication, *Not Not While the Giro*, a collection of laconic stories, was published in 1983, and was followed by *The Busconductor Hines* (1984), *A Chancer* (1985), and *Greyhound for Breakfast* (1987), which evoked comparisons with **Chekhov** and **Beckett**. *A Disaffection*, his third novel, found a wide audience through its shortlisting for the Booker Prize in 1989. He has carved a niche as the spokesman for the downtrodden and the disfranchised. His fourth novel, *How Late It Was, How Late* (1994), won the Booker Prize. Further works include *Hardie and Baird & Other Plays* (1991) and *Translated Accounts* (2001).

Kelvin (of Largs), William Thomson, 1st Baron 1824–1907 •*Scottish physicist and mathematician*• He was born in Belfast and brought to Glasgow in 1832 when his father was appointed Professor of Mathematics there. He entered the University of Glasgow at the age of 10, went to Cambridge at 16, and after graduating was elected a Fellow of Peterhouse. He went to Paris to study under **Henri Victor Regnault**, and at the age of 22 was appointed Professor of Mathematics and Natural Philosophy (1846–99), and turned his mind to physics. In a career of astonishing versatility, he brilliantly combined pure and applied science. In an early paper (1842) he solved important problems in electrostatics. He proposed the absolute, or Kelvin, temperature scale in 1848. Simultaneously with **Rudolf Clausius** he established the second law of thermodynamics. He investigated geomagnetism and hydrodynamics (particularly wave motion and vortex motion). He was chief consultant on the laying of the first submarine Atlantic cable (1857–58), and became wealthy by patenting a mirror galvanometer for speeding telegraphic transmission. He improved ships' compasses, and invented innumerable electrical instruments (his house in Glasgow was the first to be lit by electric light); these instruments were manufactured by his own company, Kelvin & White. He was made 1st Baron Kelvin of Largs in 1892. He is buried in Westminster Abbey, beside Sir **Isaac Newton**.

Kemal Atatürk, Mustafa *See* **Atatürk, Mustapha Kemal**

Kemble, Fanny (Frances Anne) 1809–93 •*English actress*• She was born in London, the daughter of **Charles Kemble**. She made her debut at Covent Garden in 1829, when her Juliet created a great sensation. For three years she played leading parts in London, and went with her father to the US (1832), where she married Pierce Butler (1834), a Southern planter. They were divorced in 1848 and later she returned to London. Resuming her maiden name, she gave Shakespearean readings for 20 years. She published dramas, poems, and also an autobiography.

Kemble, John Philip 1757–1823 •*English actor*• He was born in Prescot, Lancashire. A member of a large acting family, he was the brother of **Sarah Siddons**, **Charles Kemble** and **Stephen Kemble**, and the eldest son of **Roger Kemble**. His father intended him for the Catholic priesthood, but the life of a priest did not appeal to him and he became an actor. The success of his sister gave him the opportunity to come to London, and in 1783 he made his London debut, as Hamlet at Drury Lane. He continued to play leading tragic characters at Drury Lane for many years, and in 1788 became **Richard Brinsley Sheridan**'s manager. He bought a share in Covent Garden Theatre (1802), became manager, but in 1808 the theater was burned. On the opening of the new building (1809) the notorious OP (Old Price) Riots broke out. Kemble retired in 1817, and afterward settled in Lausanne, Switzerland.

Kemnitz, Martin *See* **Chemnitz, Martin**

Kemp, Jack French 1935– •*US politician*• Born in Los Angeles, he graduated from Occidental College with a degree in physical education in 1957 and was a professional football quarterback until 1969, most notably with the Buffalo Bills in New York. Elected as a US representative from New York in 1970, he remained in Congress until 1989, becoming known as a conservative who championed supply-side economics and tax cuts and argued for deregulation. As Secretary of Housing and Urban Development (1989–93) under President **George Bush**, he advocated urban enterprise zones to stimulate inner-city neighborhoods but failed to secure sufficient funding for his plans. He ran unsuccessfully for vice president on the Republican ticket with **Bob Dole** in 1996.

Kemp, Lindsay 1939– •*Scottish mime artist, actor, dancer, teacher and director*• He was born on the Isle of Lewis. He grew up in Bradford, England, and began his dance training with Ballet Rambert. His colorful career was launched at the 1964 Edinburgh Festival, and he has had his own company in various forms since the early 1960s. Since then, he has created his own work in an extravagant, camp style, including *Cruel Garden* (1977, in collaboration with **Christopher Bruce**), *Flowers* (based on the writings of **Jean Genet**, 1973), and *The Big Parade* and *Onnagata* (1991) for his own company. He taught rock star **David Bowie** mime and appeared in films such as **Derek Jarman**'s *Sebastiane* (1975) and *Jubilee* (1977). More recent film appearances include *Travelling Light* (1993).

Kempe, Margery, *née* **Brunham** c. 1373–c. 1440 •*English mystic*• Born in Lynn, Norfolk, she married a burgess there and had 14 children. Following a period of insanity, she experienced a conversion and undertook numerous pilgrimages. Between 1432 and 1436 she dictated her spiritual autobiography, *The Book of Margery Kempe*. It recounts her persecution by devils and men, repeated accusations of Lollardism (following the teaching of **John Wycliffe**), and her journeys to Jerusalem and to Germany, and is regarded as a classic.

Kempe, Will(iam) c. 1550–c. 1603 •*English comedian*• A leading member of **Shakespeare**'s company, he left the stage when the Chamberlain's Men moved to the Globe Theatre, London. In 1600, he performed in a nine-day Morris dance from London to Norwich. He wrote *Nine Daies Wonder* (ed by Dyce, Camden Society).

Kempis, Thomas à, *also called* **Thomas Hemerken** or **Hämmerlein** 1379–1471 •*German religious writer*• He was named after his birthplace, Kempen, near Cologne. In 1400 he entered the Augustinian convent of Agnietenberg near Zwolle in the Netherlands, took holy orders in 1413, was chosen subprior in 1429, and died as Superior. He wrote sermons, ascetical treatises, pious biographies, letters and hymns, and in particular the influential devotional work *De Imitatione Christi* (c. 1415–24, *The Imitation of Christ*).

“ ”

Vere magnus est, qui magnam habet charitatem.
He is truly great who has great charity.
c. 1415–24 ***De Imitatione Christi****, book 1, chapter 4, section 6.*

Kendal, Felicity Anne 1946– •*English actress*• Born into a theatrical family in Olton, Warwickshire, she made her London debut in 1967 and has since played many leading roles, notably in the **Tom Stoppard** plays *The Real Thing* (1982), *Jumpers* (1985), *Hapgood* (1988) and *Arcadia* (1993). On television, she played Barbara Good in *The Good Life* (1975–78), Helena Cuthbertson in *The Camomile Lawn* (1992) and Nancy Belasco in *Honey for Tea* (1994).

Kendall, Edward Calvin 1886–1972 •*US chemist and Nobel Prize winner*• Born in South Norwalk, Connecticut, he trained in Canada and after various appointments joined the Mayo Foundation, Rochester (1914), where he was made professor and head of biochemistry. In 1914 he isolated thyroxine. Its structure was elucidated partly by Kendall and partly by Sir **Charles Robert Harington**. In collaboration, Kendall isolated cortisone and 29 related steroids from the adrenal cortex. He prepared synthetic corticosterone in 1944 and cortisone (active against Addison's disease) in 1947. With **Philip Hench**, he found that cortisone was effective against rheumatic fever and that cortisone plus adrenocorticotropic hormone was effective against rheumatoid arthritis. Kendall, Hench and **Tadeus Reichstein** shared the 1950 Nobel Prize for physiology or medicine.

Kendrew, Sir John Cowdery 1917–97 •*English molecular biologist and Nobel Prize winner*• Born in Oxford, he was educated at Clifton College, Bristol, and Trinity College, Cambridge, and was a cofounder (with **Max Perutz**) of the Medical Research Council Unit for Molecular Biology at Cambridge (1946–75). He carried out researches in the chemistry of the blood and determined by X-ray crystallography the structure of the muscle protein myoglobin. Awarded the 1962 Nobel Prize for chemistry jointly with Perutz, he was knighted in 1974.

Keneally, Thomas Michael 1935– •*Australian novelist*• Born in Sydney, New South Wales, he studied for the priesthood and the law, served in the Australian Citizens' Military Forces, and has taught and lectured in drama. His early novels include *Three Cheers for a Paraclete* (1968) and *The Survivor* (1969), character studies in the English tradition, but it was the publication of *The Chant of Jimmy Blacksmith* (1972), based on the slaughter of a white family by an Aboriginal employee, that marked the beginning of his mature fiction. His reputation grew steadily until he published *Schindler's Ark* (1982), which tells how a German industrialist helped over 1,000 Jews survive the Nazis. A controversial winner of the Booker Prize because the book blurred the boundary between fact and fiction, it was memorably filmed, as *Schindler's List*, in 1994. Recent books include *The Playmaker* (1987), *Flying Hero Class* (1991), *Woman of the Inner Sea* (1992) and *A River Town* (1995). His writings include travel and political commentary, but recent novels have been criticized for supposedly careless writing.

Kennan, George F(rost) 1904– •*US diplomat and historian*• Born in Milwaukee, Wisconsin, he graduated from Princeton in 1925 and joined the US Foreign Service. During World War II he served in the US legations in Berlin, Lisbon and Moscow, and in 1947 was appointed director of policy planning by Secretary of State **George C Marshall**. He advocated the policy of containment of the USSR, a strategy which was adopted by Secretary of State **Dean Acheson** and **John Foster Dulles**. Kennan subsequently served as US ambassador in Moscow (1952–53) and Yugoslavia (1961–63). He later revised his strategic views and called for US disengagement from Europe. His books include *Realities of American Foreign Policy* (1954), *The Nuclear Delusion* (1982) and *Around the Cragged Hill* (1993).

Kennedy, Charles Peter 1959– •*Scottish politician*• Born in Inverness, he studied at the University of Glasgow and became a Social Democratic Member of Parliament for Ross, Cromarty and Skye in 1983. After the party's split in 1987 he joined the Liberal Democrats and was a spokesperson on issues that included health and Europe. In 1999 he succeeded **Paddy Ashdown** as the party's leader.

Kennedy, Edward (Ted) M(oore) 1932– •*US politician*• Born in Brookline, Massachusetts, the youngest son of **Joseph Kennedy** and brother of **John F** and **Robert F Kennedy**, he was educated at Harvard and Virginia University Law School and admitted to the Massachusetts bar in 1959. He was elected as a Democratic senator in 1962. In 1969 his involvement in a car accident on Chappaquiddick Island in which a young campaign worker, Mary Jo Kopechne, was drowned dogged his subsequent political career, and was still a major liability during his unsuccessful campaign to win the Democratic presidential nomination in 1980. Despite the apparent disorder of his personal life, he has been one of the most influential members of the Senate for more than three decades, focusing on issues such as health care and serving as an advocate for the working class and middle class.

Kennedy, Helena Kennedy, Baroness 1950– •*Scottish barrister, broadcaster and writer*• Born in Glasgow into a working-class family, she studied law in London. Renowned for her persuasive charm in court, she has represented clients as diverse as anarchists, a member of the Guildford Four and **Myra Hindley**. Overtly left-wing and feminist, she has hastened changes in attitudes within the English legal profession. In 1991 she was made a Queen's Counsel and was appointed to the Bar Council. She was created a life peer in 1997. In 2000 she became the chairman of the Human Genetics Commission. Her publications include *Eve Was Framed* (1992).

Kennedy, Jackie *See* **Onassis, Jackie Kennedy**

Kennedy, John F(itzgerald) 1917–63 •*35th President of the US*• He was born in Brookline, Massachusetts, a son of **Joseph P Kennedy**. He graduated from Harvard in 1940 and the same year published *Why England Slept*, a bestselling analysis of Great Britain's unpreparedness for war. He served as a torpedo boat commander in the Pacific during World War II and was decorated for his courageous conduct when the boat was hit and sunk. Elected to the US House of Representatives as a Democrat from Massachussetts in 1946, he won a Senate seat in 1952, and the next year married Jacqueline Lee Bouvier (see **Jackie Kennedy Onassis**). While convalescing from spinal operations he wrote *Profiles in Courage* (1956), which won a Pulitzer Prize. Though he failed in his effort to gain the Democratic vice-presidential nomination in 1956, he won his party's presidential nomination in 1960, defeating Republican **Richard Nixon** by a narrow margin in the popular vote and becoming the first Catholic and, at the age of 43, the youngest person to be elected President. He introduced a legislative program, the "New Frontier," which aimed to extend civil rights and to provide funding for education, medical care for the elderly and the space program, but much of it stalled in Congress. Through his brother **Robert F Kennedy** he supported federal desegregation policy in schools and universities. He faced a series of foreign policy crises, including the unsuccessful invasion of **Fidel Castro**'s Cuba at the Bay of Pigs (April 1961), the building of the Berlin Wall (August 1961) and the Cuban Missile Crisis (October 1962). At the risk of nuclear war, he induced the Soviet Union to withdraw its missiles from Cuba, and he achieved a partial nuclear test ban treaty with the USSR in 1963. He also founded the Peace Corps and increased the US military involvement in Vietnam. On November 22, 1963, he was assassinated by rifle fire while being driven in an open car through Dallas, Texas. The alleged assassin, **Lee Harvey Oswald**, was himself shot and killed at point-blank range by Jack Ruby two days later.

" "

Mankind must put an end to war or war will put an end to mankind.

1961 Address to the United Nations, September 25.

Kennedy, Joseph P(atrick) 1888–1969 •*US businessman and diplomat*• Born in Boston, grandson of an Irish Catholic immigrant and the son of a Boston publican, he was educated at Harvard. He married Rose Fitzgerald in 1914, daughter of a local politician. They had nine children, including **John F**, **Robert F** and **Edward Kennedy**. He made a large fortune in the 1920s and during the 1930s was a strong supporter of **Franklin D Roosevelt**, being rewarded with minor administrative posts and the ambassadorship to Britain (1938–40). After World War II he concentrated on fulfilling his ambitions of a political dynasty through his sons and placed his large fortune at their disposal for that purpose. His eldest son, Joseph Patrick (1915–44), was killed in a flying accident while in naval service in World War II, but the others achieved international fame.

Kennedy, Sir Ludovic Henry Coverley 1919– •*Scottish broadcaster and writer*• Born in Edinburgh, and educated at Christ Church, Oxford, he served in the Royal Navy (1939–46) before becoming a librarian, lecturer and later editor of the BBC's *First Reading* (1953–54). On television, he introduced *Profile* (1955–56); was an Independent Television News newscaster (1956–58), the host of *This Week* (1958–60) and a contributor to the BBC's *Panorama* (1960–63); and has devoted himself to setting the record straight on the falsely accused and wrongly convicted. His many notable series include *Your Witness* (1967–70) and *A Life With Crime* (1979). He hosted *Tonight* (1976–78) and *Did You See?* (1980–88), among many others. His books include *Ten Rillington Place* (1961), *A Presumption of Innocence: The Amazing Case of Patrick Meehan* (1975), *Euthanasia: The Good Death* (1990), two volumes of autobiography and his collected writings. He was knighted in 1994.

Kennedy, Nigel Paul 1956– •*English violinist*• Born in Brighton, he trained at the **Yehudi Menuhin** School, London, and the Juilliard School of Performing Arts, New York, and was the subject of a five-year BBC television documentary on the development of soloists after his debut in 1977. He won international acclaim for his concerts and recordings, notably his award-winning performance of the **Elgar** *Violin Concerto* (1985) and his bestselling disk of **Vivaldi**'s *The Four Seasons*. His insistence that classical music should not be exclusive, together with his punk image and attitude, seemed increasingly at odds with the classical establishment. In 1992 he supposedly retired, but returned to the concert stage in 1997. He published an autobiography, *Always Playing*, in 1991, and the first album of his own music, *Kafka*, appeared in 1996.

Kennedy, Robert F(rancis) 1925–68 •*US politician*• Born in Brookline, Massachusetts, the third son of **Joseph Kennedy**, he was educated at Harvard and University of Virginia Law School and was admitted to the Massachusetts bar in 1951. As Chief Counsel of the Senate Select Committee on Improper Activities (1957–59), he prosecuted David Bech and **Jimmy Hoffa** of the Teamsters' Union, who were charged with corruption. He was an efficient manager of his brother **John F Kennedy**'s presidential campaign, and was an energetic Attorney General (1961–64) under the latter's administration, notable in his efforts to promote civil rights. He resigned after President Kennedy's assassination, and was elected Senator from New York in 1965. He declared his candidacy for the Democratic presidential nomination in 1968, quickly winning as an idealist reformer. On June 5, 1968, he was shot by a Jordanian immigrant, **Sirhan Sirhan**, and died the following day.

Kennedy, William Joseph 1928– •*US novelist and screenwriter*• Born in Albany, New York, he was educated at Siena College, New York, and served in the US Army (1950–52) before becoming a journalist and eventually a full-time writer. *The Ink Truck* (1969) is distinct from subsequent novels in that it does not use the locale of his hometown as a backdrop. *Legs* (1975), which combines fact and fiction to retell the story of Legs Diamond, the notorious gangster, is the first of the "Albany novels," which also include *Very Old Bones* and *Roscoe* (2002). *Ironweed* (1983), his best-known novel, describes the homecoming of a fallen baseball star, now down-and-out, drunk and maudlin. The book won a Pulitzer Prize and was filmed (1987).

Kenneth I, *called* **Kenneth MacAlpin** d. 858 •*King of the Scots*• He seems to have succeeded his father Alpin as king (841), and to have won acceptance by the Picts by 843. His reign marked a decisive step in the making of a united kingdom north of the rivers Forth and Clyde, and also saw the shift of the center of the Church from Iona to the court at Dunkeld.

Kenney, Annie 1879–1953 •*English suffragette*• Born in Springhead, near Oldham, she was a full-time worker from the age of 13. She started a union, then began a correspondence course at Ruskin College, Oxford. When she met **Christabel Pankhurst**, she became involved in the struggle for women's suffrage, the only working-class woman in the leadership. She was arrested with Pankhurst in 1905 and again in 1906. She took over the leadership during Pankhurst's exile in Paris, crossing the Channel every week to receive instructions. She withdrew from public life in 1926.

Kenny, Elizabeth, *known as* **Sister Kenny** 1886–1952 •*Australian nurse*• She began practicing as a nurse in the bush country in Australia (1912), and then joined the Australian army nursing corps (1915–19). She developed a new technique for treating poliomyelitis by muscle therapy rather than immobilization with casts and splints. She established clinics in Australia (1933), Great Britain (1937) and the US (Minneapolis, 1940), and traveled widely in order to demonstrate her methods.

Kent, Bruce 1929– •*British cleric and peace campaigner*• He was born in London, and after education in Canada and at Oxford, he was ordained in 1958. He was subsequently secretary in the Archbishop's House, Westminster, Catholic chaplain for the University of London and a parish priest. He grew increasingly involved in the Campaign for Nuclear Disarmament (CND), becoming its chairman from 1987 to 1990. He resigned his ministry in 1987 and stood unsuccessfully as Labour Party candidate for Oxford West and Abingdon in 1992. He became chairman of the National Peace Council in 1999.

" "

Preparing for suicide is not a very intelligent means of defense.

1989 Speech.

Kent, Prince George, Duke of, *in full* **George Edward Alexander Edmund** 1902–42 •*English duke*• The son of King

George V and Queen **Mary of Teck**, he was born at Sandringham. He passed out of Dartmouth (1920), but because of delicate health served in the Foreign Office and inspected factories for the Home Office. In 1934 he was made Duke of Kent, and married Princess Marina of Greece and Denmark (1906–68). Appointed Governor-General of Australia (1938), he was prevented from taking up the post by the outbreak of World War II. He was killed in active service, as chief welfare officer of RAF Home Command, when, on its way to Iceland, his Sunderland flying boat crashed into a mountain in the north of Scotland. His three children are Edward, Duke of **Kent**, Princess **Alexandra** and Prince Michael of Kent (1942–), who married (1978) Baroness Marie-Christine von Reibnitz, and whose children are Lord Frederick Michael George David Louis Windsor (1979–) and Lady Gabriella Marina Alexandra Ophelia, or "Ella," Windsor (1981–).

Kent, Edward, Duke of 1767–1820 •*British nobleman*• The fourth son of **George III**, he was born at Buckingham Palace, London. At Gibraltar, first as colonel (1790–91) and then as governor (1802), his martinet discipline caused continual mutinies, ending in bloodshed and his recall. In 1818 he married Victoria Mary Louisa (1786–1861), widow of the Prince of Leiningen. For the sake of economy they lived in Leiningen, and went to England (1819) for the birth of their child, the Princess **Victoria**. His three elder brothers, **George IV**, the Duke of York, and **William IV**, died leaving no children and Princess Victoria succeeded to the throne (1837).

Kent, Edward, Duke of, *in full* **Edward George Nicholas Paul Patrick** 1935– •*English duke*• The son of George, Duke of **Kent**, he was born in London and commissioned in the army in 1955. In 1961 he married Katharine Worsley (1933–), and they have three children, George Philip Nicholas Windsor, Earl of St Andrews (1962–), Lady Helen Marina Lucy (1964–), who married Timothy Verner Taylor in 1992, becoming Lady Helen Taylor, and Lord Nicholas Charles Edward Jonathan Windsor (1970–). He retired from the army in 1976.

Kent, William 1684–1748 •*English architect and landscape designer*• Born in Bridlington, Yorkshire, he studied painting in Rome (1709–19), and played a leading part in introducing the Palladian style of architecture into Great Britain. He designed many public buildings in London, including the Royal Mews in Trafalgar Square, the Treasury buildings and the Horse Guards block in Whitehall. As an interior designer he decorated Burlington House and Chiswick House in London. As a landscape designer he introduced romantic settings. A versatile artist, he also designed the Gothic screens in Westminster Hall and Gloucester Cathedral.

Kentigern, St, *also called* **St Mungo**, *known as* **the Apostle of Cumbria** c. 518–603 AD •*Celtic churchman*• Born in Culross, Fife, Scotland, he was, according to legend, the son of a Princess Thenew. Mother and child were baptized by St **Serf**, who educated the boy in his monastery, where he was so beloved that his name Kentigern (chief lord) was often exchanged for Mungo (dear friend). He founded a monastery at Cathures (now Glasgow), and in 543 was consecrated Bishop of Cumbria. In 553 he was driven to seek refuge in Wales, where he visited St **David**, and where he founded another monastery and a bishopric, which still bears the name of his disciple, St Asaph. In about 584 he was visited by **Columba**. He was buried in Glasgow Cathedral, which is named after him as St Mungo's. His feast day is January 13.

Kenton, Stan(ley Newcomb) 1912–79 •*US pianist, composer and bandleader*• Born in Wichita, Kansas, and brought up in Los Angeles, he studied piano privately before beginning his professional career in 1934 with a succession of lesser-known big bands. He first formed his own orchestra in 1941, but is more immediately associated with the big-band progressive jazz style of the 1950s, using dissonant ensemble writing. His innovations, employing adventurous arrangers and outstanding soloists, have stood the test of time.

Kenyatta, Jomo, *originally* **Kamau Ngengi** c. 1889–1978 •*Kenyan nationalist and political leader*• Born in Mitumi, orphaned, and educated at a Scots mission school, he worked as a herd boy. He joined the Kikuyu Central Association (1922), and became its president. He visited Britain (1929, 1931–44) to lobby the government, and studied for a year at the University of London. He visited Russia three times, and was president of the Pan African Federation with **Kwame Nkrumah** as secretary. He worked on the land during the war and married an Englishwoman in 1942. On returning to Kenya in 1946 he was elected president of the Kenyan African Union, and at the outbreak of the Mau Mau uprising, he was sentenced to seven years' hard labor in 1952, then released into internal exile in 1958. He was chosen in absentia to be president of the republic of Kenya in December 1964. A remarkable mixture of Kikuyu nationalist, pragmatic politician and father figure, he surprised observers by leading Kenya into a period of economic growth and unexpected tribal harmony.

Kenyon, Dame Kathleen Mary 1906–78 •*English archaeologist*• Born in London, she was educated at Somerville College, Oxford. She was lecturer in Palestinian archaeology at the University of London (1948–62), Principal of St Hugh's College, Oxford (1962–73), and director of the British School of Archaeology in Jerusalem from 1951 to 1966. Her most notable books are *Digging Up Jericho* (1957), *Archaeology in the Holy Land* (1965), and *Digging Up Jerusalem* (1974).

Kenzo, *in full* **Kenzo Takada** 1940– •*Japanese fashion designer*• He was born in Kyoto. After studying art in Japan, he moved to Paris and produced freelance collections from 1964. He creates clothes with both Asian and Western influences and is a trendsetter in the field of knitwear.

Keokuk 1788–c. 1848 •*Sauk leader*• Born near Rock Island, Illinois, he became a war chief of the Sauk, and a rival of **Black Hawk** for tribal leadership. Known for his accommodation to the US government, in contrast to Black Hawk, he aligned with the US cause and did not fight during the Black Hawk War (1832), in which the Illinois Sauks were defeated by US forces and sent to a reservation in Iowa. After speaking in Washington for peace between the Sauks and Sioux (1837), he was named chief of the united Sauk clans. He continued to support the US government, which moved the tribe farther west into Kansas.

Kepler, Johannes 1571–1630 •*German astronomer*• Born in Weilderstadt, Württemberg, he was educated at the University of Tübingen, where he obtained a master's degree in theology in 1591. He became Professor of Mathematics at the University of Graz in 1594. Among his duties at Graz was the publication of almanacs to forecast the weather and to predict favorable days for various undertakings. He recorded in his first major publication, the *Mysterium cosmographium* (1596), that the distances from the sun of the six planets including the Earth could be related to the five regular solids of geometry. He sent copies of his book to **Galileo** and **Tycho Brahe**, the greatest astronomers of the day, who responded favorably. When Kepler was later in difficulties in Graz, Brahe invited him to come to Prague, and when Brahe died in 1601 Kepler was appointed to succeed him as imperial mathematician. His chief interest was the study of the planet Mars. He found that its movement could not be explained in terms of the customary cycles and epicycles. In this he broke with the tradition of more than 2,000 years by demonstrating that the planets do not move uniformly in circles, but in ellipses with the sun at one focus and with the radius vector of each planet describing equal areas of the ellipse in equal times (Kepler's first and second laws). He completed his research in dynamical astronomy 10 years later by formulating his third law, which connects the periods of revolution of the planets with their mean distances from the sun. In 1627 he published the *Tabulae Rudolphinae*, which contained the ephemerides of the planets according to the new laws, and also an extended catalog of 1,005 stars based on Tycho's observations.

Kérékou, Mathieu Ahmed 1933– •*Benin soldier and politician*• Born in Natitingou, he was trained in France and served in the French army before joining the army of what was then Dahomey. He took part in the 1967 coup which removed the civilian government, and in 1972 he led the coup which deposed Justin Ahomadegbe, and established a National Council of the Revolution (CNR). He renamed the country Benin; gradually social and economic stability returned, the CNR was dissolved and a civilian administration installed. Kérékou was elected president in 1980 and reelected in 1984. He resigned from the army in 1987 as a gesture of his commitment to genuine democracy. Defeated in the elections of 1991, he handed over power to a national conference but was reelected president in 1996 and 2001.

Kerensky, Aleksandr Fyodorovich 1881–1970 •*Russian revolutionary leader*• Born in Simbirsk, he was the son of a high-school principal. He studied law in St Petersburg and made a name for himself as counsel for the defense in several leading political trials. In the 1917 Revolution he became Minister of Justice in March, Minister of War in May, and Prime Minister in July in the provisional government. Though crushing the military revolt of **Lavr Georgevich Kornilov** in August, he found it increasingly difficult to put through moderate reforms, and in October was swept away by the Bolsheviks, and fled to France. In 1940 he went to Australia and in 1946 to the US where he taught at Stanford University from 1956. His writings include *The Prelude to Bolshevism* (1919), *The Road to Tragedy* (1935), and *The Kerensky Memoirs* (1966). He died in New York City.

Kerguélen-Trémarec, Yves Joseph de 1745–97 •*French aristocrat and naval officer*• He was born in Quimper, Brittany. On an unsuccessful voyage of exploration seeking Terra Australis, he discovered a group of islands in the South Indian Ocean to which he gave the name Kerguélen's Islands (1772).

Kern, Jerome David 1885–1945 •*US composer*• Born in New York City, he studied music there and in Heidelberg, Germany. He spent the years of his theatrical apprenticeship in New York and London, writing songs that were interpolated into musicals by other composers. His inaugural complete score for a musical play was *The Red Petticoat* (1912), which first brought a Western setting to Broadway, followed by numerous successful Broadway shows. *Show Boat* (1928, book and lyrics by **Oscar Hammerstein II**) is considered his greatest musical. He also wrote songs for films, winning Academy Awards for "The Way You Look Tonight" and "The Last Time I Saw Paris."

Kerouac, Jack (John Louis) 1922–69 •*US novelist*• He was born in Lowell, Massachusetts. His parents, devout Roman Catholics, came from rural communities in the French-speaking part of Quebec, and he did not learn to speak English until he was six. He was educated at Lowell High School before accepting a football scholarship at Columbia University, but he turned his back on both and spent the early years of World War II working as a mechanic in Hartford before returning to Lowell, where he worked as a sports journalist. His energies were spent on an autobiographical novel that was never published. In 1942 he went to Washington DC, where he joined the US Merchant Marine, subsequently enlisting in the US Navy (1943). After only a month he was discharged and branded an "indifferent character." His friends included **Allen Ginsberg**, **Gary Snyder** and Neal Cassady, whom Kerouac portrayed as Dean Moriarty in his most famous novel, *On the Road* (1957). He was identified as leader and spokesman of the Beat Generation, a label he coined but then came to regret and repudiate. *On the Road*, his second novel after *The Town and the City*, is apparently structureless and episodic, and follows two friends as they weave their way across the US. It has been much imitated (on film as well as in fiction) and made Kerouac a cult hero. In later books, such as *The Dharma Bums* (1958) and *Big Sur* (1962), he flirted with Zen Buddhism.

Kerr, Deborah, *originally* **Deborah Jane Kerr Trimmer**, *married name* **Viertel** 1921– •*Scottish actress*• Born in Helensburgh, Strathclyde, she was trained as a dancer before deciding to take up acting. Work on stage was followed by roles in British films such as *The Life and Death of Colonel Blimp* (1943) and *Black Narcissus* (1947). Moving to Hollywood, she played numerous governesses and nuns, sensationally straying from her established image to play a nymphomaniac in *From Here to Eternity* (1953) for which she garnered an Academy Award nomination. She received further nominations for *Edward My Son* (1949), *The King and I* (1956), *Heaven Knows Mr Allison* (1957), *Separate Tables* (1958) and *The Sundowners* (1960). She retired from the screen in 1969 but continued to appear on the stage and on television, and made a return to the cinema in *The Assam Garden* (1985). In 1994 she received a special Academy Award and in 1998 was given the honorary title Commander, Order of the British Empire.

Kerr, Graham Victor 1934– •*New Zealand cookbook writer*• He was born in London, England, and became a successful sportsman (Uffa Fox Trophy Cup, 1950; British Army épée champion, 1955). After working as catering adviser to the British Army (1952–56) and to the Royal New Zealand Air Force (1958–63), he launched his highly popular television show *The Galloping Gourmet*, which was screened internationally. From this series came a number of books including *Galloping Gourmets* (1969).

Kerr, John 1824–1907 •*Scottish physicist*• Born in Ardrossan, Ayrshire, he was educated at the University of Glasgow in theology and became a lecturer in mathematics. He was one of the first research students of Lord **Kelvin**. In 1876 he discovered the magneto-optic effect named after him in which a beam of plane polarized light will become elliptically polarized when reflected from an electromagnet. The theoretical implications were later elucidated by **George Fitzgerald**.

Kerr, Sir John Robert 1914–91 •*Australian administrator*• Born in Sydney, the son of a boilermaker, he graduated from Sydney University and was admitted to the New South Wales bar in 1938. Following war service, he became a Queen's Counsel in 1953 and after a number of senior legal, judicial, and political appointments was sworn in as Governor-General of the Commonwealth of Australia in 1974. The next year he made Australian constitutional history when he exercised his vice-regal "reserve powers" and dismissed the Prime Minister, **Gough Whitlam**, asking the leader of the Opposition, **Malcolm Fraser**, to form a caretaker government and to call an immediate election. The voters elected a new coalition government, led by Fraser. He stepped down as Governor-General in 1977.

Kerry, John Forbes 1943– •*US politician*• Born in Denver, Colorado, he studied at Yale before joining the Navy in 1966. As a swift boat officer during the Vietnam War, he served two tours of duty and was awarded a Silver Star, the Bronze Star and three Purple Hearts for his service in combat. Returning home a military hero in 1970, he became an antiwar activist as a spokesperson for the Vietnam Veterans Against the War and cofounder of the Vietnam Veterans of America. After an unsuccessful bid for Congress in 1972, he attended Boston College Law School and received his degree in 1976. He thereafter worked as an assistant county prosecutor and as a private practitioner until 1982 when he was elected Lieutenant Governor of Massachusetts. He entered the US Senate as a Democrat in 1984 and was reelected in 1990, 1996 and 2002. In 1995 he married Teresa Heinz, heiress to the **Heinz** ketchup fortune. He won the Democratic Party's presidential nomination in 2004.

Kesey, Ken Elton 1935–2001 •*US writer*• He was born in La Junta, Colorado. Associated with the 1950s Beat movement, he also worked as a ward attendant in a mental hospital, an experience he used to telling effect in *One Flew Over the Cuckoo's Nest* (1962). Filmed in 1975 by **Miloš Forman**, it won five Academy Awards, including that for Best Film. *Sometimes a Great Notion* (1966) was a complete failure and he relinquished "literature" for "life." He served a prison sentence for marijuana possession and formed the "Merry Pranksters," whose exploits are described at length in *The Electric Kool-Aid Acid Test* (1967) by **Tom Wolfe**. Later works included *Demon Box* (1987), a collection of stories and pieces, and *Sailor Sorg* (1990).

> "" But it's the truth even if it didn't happen.
>
> *1962* ***One Flew Over the Cuckoo's Nest***, *part 1.*

Kesselring, Albert 1885–1960 •*German air commander and field marshal*• Born in Markstedt, Bavaria, he led the Luftwaffe attacks on France and (unsuccessfully) on Britain. He was made Commander in Chief in Italy (1941), and in the West (1945). Condemned to death as a war criminal in 1947, he had his sentence commuted to life imprisonment, but was released in 1952.

Ketch, Jack d. 1686 •*English executioner*• A hangman and headsman from about 1663, he was notorious for his barbarity and bungling, particularly at the executions of William, Lord **Russell** (1683), and the Duke of **Monmouth** (1685). His name became synonymous with the hangman's job.

Kettering, Charles Franklin 1876–1958 •*US engineer*• Born near Loudonville, Ohio, he studied mechanical and electrical engineering at Ohio State University. Among his inventions were the electric self-starter for automobiles and the high-compression automobile engine. He also worked on fast-drying lacquer finishes, engine-oil coolers, leaded gasoline and high-octane fuels, and variable-speed transmissions. He was a cofounder of the **Sloan**-Kettering Institute for Cancer Research, New York City.

Ketterle, Wolfgang 1957– •*German physicist and Nobel Prize winner*• He was born in Heidelberg and educated at the University of Munich and the Institute for Quantum Optics, Garching. In 1990 he moved to MIT. He won the Nobel Prize for physics (2001; with **Eric A Cornell** and **Carl E Wieman**) for the achievement of Bose-Einstein condensation in dilute gases at very low temperatures, effectively creating a new state of matter.

Key, Ellen Karolina Sophia 1849–1926 •*Swedish reformer and educationist*• Born in Sundsholm, Småland, she became a teacher in Stockholm (1880–99) when her father lost his fortune. She made her name as a writer on the feminist movement, child welfare, sex, love, and marriage, in *Barnets århundrade* (1900, Eng trans *The Century of the Child*, 1909) and *Lifslinjer* (1903–06, "Lifelines"). Although her radical and liberal values were controversial, her writings were influential and widely translated.

Key, Francis Scott 1780–1843 •*US lawyer and poet*• Born in Carroll County, Maryland, he practiced law in Washington DC. During the British bombardment of Fort McHenry, Baltimore, in September 1814, he wrote a poem about the lone US flag seen flying over the fort as dawn broke. It was published as *The Defense of Fort McHenry*, and later set to a tune by the English composer, **John Stafford Smith** (*To Anacreon in Heaven*). In 1931 it was adopted as the US national anthem and named "The Star-Spangled Banner."

Keyes (of Zeebrugge and of Dover), Roger John Brownlow Keyes, 1st Baron 1872–1945 •*English naval commander*• He joined the navy in 1885, and served at Witu (1890) and in the Boxer Rebellion (1900). In World War I he was Chief of Staff Eastern Mediterranean (1915–16) and in 1918 commanded the Dover Patrol, leading the raids on German U-boat bases at Zeebrugge and Ostend (1918). He was Commander in Chief Mediterranean (1925–29) and commander Portsmouth (1929–31). He was Member of Parliament for Portsmouth (1934–43), and was recalled in 1940 as director of combined operations (1940–41). His son, Lieutenant Colonel Geoffrey Keyes, Military Cross and posthumous Victoria Cross, was killed in the historic commando raid on Rommel's headquarters in 1941.

Keynes (of Tilton), John Maynard Keynes, 1st Baron 1883–1946 •*English economist, pioneer of the theory of full employment*• Born in Cambridge, he was educated at Eton and King's College, Cambridge, where he lectured in economics and became one of the Bloomsbury group. In both world wars he was an adviser to the Treasury. The unemployment crisis inspired his two great works, *A Treatise on Money* (1930) and the revolutionary *General Theory of Employment, Interest and Money* (1936). He argued that full employment was not an automatic condition, expounded a new theory of the rate of interest, and set out the principles underlying the flows of income and expenditure. He also fought the Treasury view that unemployment was incurable. His views on a planned economy influenced **Franklin D Roosevelt**'s New Deal administration. In 1943 he proposed the international clearing union, and in 1944–46 he played a leading part in the formulation of the Bretton Woods agreements, the establishment of the International Monetary Fund, and the troublesome, abortive negotiations for a continuation of American Lend-Lease. He died just prior to being appointed to the Order of Merit.

Khalid, *in full* **Khalid ibn 'Abd al-'Aziz ibn 'Abd ar-Rahman al-Sa'ud** 1913–82 •*King of Saudi Arabia*• Born in Riyadh, he was the fourth son of **Ibn Saud**, the founder of the Saudi dynasty, and ascended the throne after the assassination of his brother King **Faisal** (1975). Khalid's caution and moderation served as a stabilizing factor in the volatile Middle East and won international respect. His personal influence was evident at the halting of the Lebanese civil war (1975–76) and in Saudi Arabia's disagreement with the other members of the Organization of Petroleum Exporting Countries (OPEC) over oil price increases.

Khama, Sir Seretse 1921–80 •*African politician*• Born at Serowe, Bechuanaland (now Botswana), he was the nephew of Tshekedi Khama (1905–59), who was chief regent of the Bamangwato from 1925. Seretse was educated in Africa and Balliol College, Oxford. While a student at the Inner Temple in 1948 he married an Englishwoman, Ruth Williams, and in 1950, with his uncle, was banned from the chieftainship and the territory of the Bamangwato. Allowed to return in 1956, he became active in politics, and was restored to the chieftainship in 1963. He became first prime minister of Bechuanaland (1965) and first president of Botswana (1966–80).

Khan, Imran *See* **Imran Khan**

Khan, Jahangir 1963– •*Pakistani squash player*• Born in Karachi, he won three world amateur titles (1979, 1983, 1985), a record six World Open titles (1981–85, 1988), and 10 consecutive British Open titles (1982–91). He was undefeated from April 1981 to November 1986, when he lost to Ross Norman of New Zealand in the World Open final. He has mastered both soft and hardball squash.

Khan, Jinghit *See* **Genghis Khan**

Khatami, (Hojatoleslam Sayed) Mohammad 1943– •*Iranian politician*• Born in Ardakan in the province of Yazd, the son of a close associate of **Ayatollah Khomeini**, he was educated at the Qom and Isfahan seminaries and at the University of Tehran. He helped to organize the political opposition to the Shah of Iran in the 1970s and after the 1979 revolution joined the new parliament. He was appointed Minister of Culture and Islamic Guidance in 1982 and subsequently became cultural adviser to President **Rafsanjani**. He became president of Iran in May 1997.

Khatchaturian, Aram Ilyich 1903–78 •*Russian composer*• Born near Tbilisi, Georgia, he was a student of folk song, and an authority on Eastern music. His compositions include symphonies, concertos, ballets, and instrumental and film music.

Khayyám, Omar *See* **Omar Khayyám**

Khazini, al- fl. c. 1115–30 •*Arab mathematician*• Born in Merv, Iran (now Mary, Turkmenistan), he was a Byzantine slave (possibly a castrato) who was well educated in mathematics by his owner and became a notable maker of scientific instruments. He also devised astronomical tables and wrote on mechanics, especially on specific gravity and its use in analysis.

Khomeini, Ayatollah Ruhollah, *originally* **Ruholla Hendi** 1900–89 •*Iranian religious and political leader*• He was born in Khomeyn, became a religious scholar and was recognized as an ayatollah. A Shiite Muslim who was bitterly opposed to the pro-Western regime of Shah **Muhammad Reza Pahlavi**, Khomeini was exiled to Turkey, Iraq and France from 1964. He returned to Iran amid great popular acclaim in 1979 after the collapse of the Shah's government, and became head of state. Under his leadership, Iran underwent a turbulent Islamic Revolution in which a return was made to the strict observance of Muslim principles and traditions. His denunciation of US influences led to the storming of the US embassy in Tehran and the holding of 53 US hostages. In 1989 he provoked international controversy by publicly commanding the killing of **Salman Rushdie**, author of the novel *The Satanic Verses*.

Khorana, Har Gobind 1922– •*US molecular chemist and Nobel Prize winner*• Born in Raipur, India (now in Pakistan), he studied at Punjab University and the University of Liverpool, and was a Research Fellow at Cambridge. After a series of academic posts, in 1970 he became Professor of Biology and Chemistry at MIT. He determined the sequence of the nucleic acids, also known as bases, for each of the 20 amino acids in the human body. His work on nucleotide synthesis at Wisconsin was a major contribution to the elucidation of the genetic code. In the early 1970s he was one of the first to artificially synthesize a gene, initially from yeast, then later from the bacterium *Escherichia coli*. He shared the 1968 Nobel Prize for physiology or medicine with **Marshall Nirenberg** and **Robert Holley**.

Khosrow *See* **Chosroes**

Khrushchev, Nikita Sergeyevich 1894–1971 •*Soviet politician*• Born in Kalinovka, near Kursk, he was a shepherd boy and a locksmith and is said to have been almost illiterate until the age of 25. Joining the Bolshevik Party in 1918, he fought in the Civil War and rose rapidly in the party organization. In World War II he organized guerrilla warfare in Ukraine against the invading Germans and took charge of the reconstruction of devastated territory. In 1949 he launched a drastic reorganization of Soviet agriculture. In 1953, on the death of **Stalin**, he became First Secretary of the All Union Party. Three years later, at the 20th congress of the Communist Party, in a speech that had far-reaching results, he denounced Stalinism and the personality cult. In 1957 he went on to demote **Vyacheslav Molotov**, **Lazar Kaganovich** and **Georgi Malenkov**—all possible rivals. Among the events of his administration were the Hungarian uprising, which he crushed, and the failed attempt to install missiles in Cuba (1962). Khrushchev, who did much to enhance the ambitions and status of the USSR abroad, was nevertheless deposed in 1964 and forced into retirement, being replaced by **Leonid Brezhnev** and **Aleksei Kosygin**. He died in retirement in Moscow.

“ ”

Politicians are the same all over. They promise to build a bridge even where there is no river.

1960 Press conference, New York, October.

Khwarizmi, Muhammad ibn Musa al c. 800–c. 850 •*Arab mathematician*• He wrote in Baghdad on astronomy, geography and mathematics, and produced an early Arabic treatise on the solution of quadratic equations. His writings in Latin translation were so influential in transmitting Indian and Arab mathematics to medieval Europe that the methods of arithmetic based on the Hindu (or so-called Arabic) system of numeration became known in medieval Latin (by corruption of his name) as "algorismus," from which comes the English "algorithm." The word "algebra" is derived from the word *al-jabr* in the title of his book on the subject.

Kiarostami, Abbas 1940– •*Iranian film director*• Born in Tehran, Kiarostami started filmmaking in the 1970s, but his work only began to reach an international audience with *Where Is My Friend's House?* (1987), which tells the story of a young schoolboy's desperate quest to return a classmate's homework. After the remote mountain region where it was filmed was devastated by a 1990 earthquake, Kiarostami returned to make *And Life Goes On ...* (1991) and *Through the Olive Trees* (1994). His *Taste of Cherry* won the Palme d'Or at Cannes in 1997.

Kidd, Captain *See* **Kidd, William**

Kidd, Carol 1944– •*Scottish jazz singer*• Born in Glasgow, she began to sing with traditional jazz bands while still in school. In the late 1970s she became known in London clubs and later appeared on radio and television, as a singer and presenter, and began her recording career. During the late 1980s she gave performances with specially assembled larger orchestras, and won various awards.

Kidd, Dame Margaret Henderson 1900–88 •*Scottish pioneering lawyer*• The daughter of a Linlithgow solicitor, she determined to go to the bar and became the first woman member of the Scottish bar (1923), the first woman Queen's Counsel (1948) and the first woman (part-time) sheriff of a county (Dumfries, 1960–66; Perth, 1966–74). She was given the honorary title of Dame Commander, Order of the British Empire, in 1975.

Kidd, William, *known as* **Captain Kidd** c. 1645–1701 •*Scottish merchant and privateer*• Born in Greenock, Strathclyde, he worked as a successful sea captain with a small fleet of trading vessels, based in New York, in the 1680s. During the War of the League of Augsburg against France (1688–97) he fought as a privateer to protect Anglo-American trade routes in the West Indies. In 1695 he went to London and was given command of an expedition against pirates in the Indian Ocean, but instead of attacking pirates began to sanction attacks on merchant ships. He sailed to Boston, where he surrendered on promise of a pardon (1699), but was sent as a prisoner to London, where he was convicted of piracy and hanged.

Kidman, Nicole 1967– •*Australian actress*• Born in Honolulu, Hawaii, she moved with her family to Australia at an early age, appearing on screen from the age of 14 in films such as *BMX Bandits* (1984). She married **Tom Cruise** in 1990 and appeared in *Days of Thunder* with him in the same year. Her career as a leading actress took off from the mid-1990s with films including *To Die For* (1995), *Eyes Wide Shut* (1998) and *Moulin Rouge* (2001). In 2003 she won an Academy Award for her portrayal of Virginia Woolf in *The Hours*. Kidman and Cruise divorced in 2001.

Kiefer, Anselm 1945– •*German artist*• Born in Donaueschingen, Baden, he held his first solo show in Karlsruhe, in 1969. A pupil of **Joseph Beuys** in Düsseldorf (1970–72), he then lived and worked in Hornbach, producing expressionist paintings steeped in German myths reworked to comment on Germany's Fascist past, as in *Parsifal III* (1973, painted in oil and blood). From the late 1980s he was concerned with the disintegration of the planet, as in his cityscapes, such as *Lilith* (1989). Since the early 1990s he has lived in France.

Kierkegaard, Søren Aabye 1813–55 •*Danish philosopher and theologian*• He was born in Copenhagen and studied theology at the university there. He suffered anguish and emotional disturbances which his later writings sometimes reflect, and was particularly oppressed by his father's death (1838). He became engaged after leaving the university (1840), but broke it off. His philosophy represents a strong reaction against the dominant German traditions of the day, and in particular against **Hegel**. Kierkegaard attempted to reinstate the central importance of the individual and of the choices we each make in forming our future selves. His philosophical works tend to be unorthodox and entertaining in a literary and determinedly unacademic style: *Enten-Eller* (1843, "Either-Or") and *Afsluttende uvidenskabelig efterskrift* (1846, "Concluding Unscientific Postscript"). He was also opposed to much in organized Christianity, again stressing the need for individual choice against prescribed dogma and ritual in such works as *Frygt og baeven* (1843, Eng trans *Fear and Trembling*, 1939), *Christelige tales* (1848, Eng trans *Christian Discourses*) and *Sygdommen til döden* (1849, Eng trans *The Sickness Unto Death*, 1941). Regarded as one of the founders of existentialism, he achieved real recognition only in the 20th century and was a great influence on such thinkers as **Karl Barth**, **Martin Heidegger**, **Karl Jaspers** and **Martin Buber**.

“ ”

The thing is to find a truth *for me*, to find *the idea for which I can live and die*.

1835 Journal entry (translated by Alexander Dru, 1938).

Kiesinger, Kurt Georg 1904–88 •*West German politician*• Born in Ebingen, he practiced as a lawyer (1935–40). Having joined the Nazi Party in 1933, he served during World War II at the Foreign Office, broadcasting radio propaganda. Interned after the war until 1947, he was exonerated by a German court in 1948. The next year he became a member of the Bundestag until 1958, when he became a Minister-President of his native Baden-Württemberg until 1966. He was president of the Bundesrat from 1962 to 1963, and in 1966 succeeded **Ludwig Erhard** as Chancellor. Long a convinced supporter of **Konrad Adenauer**'s plans for European unity, he formed with **Willy Brandt** a grand coalition government which combinined the Christian Democratic Union and the Social Democrats, until in 1969 he was succeeded as Chancellor by Brandt. He remained in the Bundestag until 1980.

Kieślowski, Krzysztof 1941–96 •*Polish film director*• Born in Warsaw, he studied at the School of Cinema and Theatre in Łódź. He worked extensively in television, before moving to such cinema features as *Amator* (1979, *Camera Buff*) and *Bez konka* (1984, *No End*). His international reputation was enhanced with *Dekalog*

(1988–89, *The Ten Commandments*), a series of films for Polish television. Released to cinemas, *Krotki film o zabijaniu* (1988, *A Short Film About Killing*) earned an Academy Award as Best Foreign Film. Hailed as one of the most trenchant and humanistic of European auteurs, he subsequently directed *La double vie de Véronique* (1991, *The Double Life of Veronique*) and *Trois Couleurs: Blue* (1993), *Blanc* (1993), *Rouge* (1994) (*Three Colors: Blue, White* and *Red*)—a triptych inspired by the French Revolution ideals of liberty, equality and fraternity—that proved to be the crowning glory of his career.

Kilby, Jack S(t Clair) 1923– •*US electrical engineer and Nobel Prize winner*• Born in Jefferson City, Missouri, he was educated at the University of Illinois and the University of Wisconsin and joined Texas Instruments in Dallas (1958–70), where he invented the first microchip (1958). In 2000 he shared the Nobel Prize for physics with **Zhores I Alferov** and **Herbert Kroemer** in recognition of his invention of the microchip, which formed the basis of modern computer technology.

Killigrew, Thomas 1612–83 •*English playwright and theater manager*• He was born in London, the brother of the dramatist Sir William Killigrew (1606–95). In 1664 he published a collection of nine plays, the most popular of which was *The Parson's Wedding*, later described by **Samuel Pepys** as "an obscene, loose play." Killigrew did much to revive the energy of the English theater after the Restoration and introduced actresses into the theater. In 1663 he founded the Theatre Royal, Bridges Street (later Drury Lane), and also established one of the first training schools for actors, at the Barbican, London.

Killy, Jean-Claude 1944– •*French ski racer*• Born in St-Cloud and brought up in Val d'Isère, he won the downhill and combined gold medals at the world championship in Chile in 1966. In 1968, when the Winter Olympics were held almost on his own ground at Grenoble, he won three gold medals for slalom, giant slalom and downhill. He turned professional immediately afterward. Killy became a member of the International Olympic Committee in 1995.

Kilmer, (Alfred) Joyce 1886–1918 •*US poet*• Born in New Brunswick, New Jersey, he became a writer and poetry editor of the *Literary Digest* and *Current Literature* in New York City. He is best known for his poem "Trees," in *Trees and Other Poems* (1914), inexplicably chosen for immortality by popular taste ("I think that I will never see/A poem lovely as a tree"). He joined the US Army in World War I and was killed in France.

Kim Dae-Jung 1925– •*South Korean politician and Nobel Prize winner*• Born in Hugwang-ri, he studied at Kyunghee University, Seoul. He followed a tortuous early career as a businessman, newspaper editor and soldier, and was a prisoner of war in the troubled early 1950s. He became a member of the Central Committee of the opposition Democratic Party in 1957 and was elected to the National Assembly in 1961. During much of the 1970s he was either in prison or under house arrest, but emerged to reenter mainstream Korean politics in the late 1980s, and was president of the Republic of Korea from 1997 to 2002. In recognition of his commitment to human rights and democracy, he was awarded the Nobel Peace Prize in 2000.

Kim Chong-Il *See* **Kim Jong Il**

Kim-Il Sung, *originally* **Kim Song-ju** 1912–94 •*North Korean soldier and political leader*• He was born near Pyongyang. He founded the Korean People's Revolutionary Army in 1932 and led a long struggle against the Japanese. He proclaimed the Republic in 1948, three years after founding the Workers' Party of Korea, and remained as effective head of state until his death, first as premier until 1972, then as president. He established a unique personality cult welded to an isolationist, Stalinist political-economic system, and was succeeded by his son, **Kim Jong Il**. In 1998 Kim-Il Sung was posthumously proclaimed "Eternal President."

Kim Jong Il (Kim Chong-il) 1942– •*North Korean politician*• The eldest son and chosen heir of the North Korean communist leader **Kim-Il Sung**, he was born in a secret camp on Mount Paekdu in the USSR. Kim Jong Il played a leading part in ideological and propaganda work, helping to create the cult that surrounded his father. He held a number of political posts in his father's administration and effectively took over as leader upon his father's death in 1994, but reportedly had already been running the nation's day-to-day operations for some time. After a three-year mourning period, Kim Jong Il became the official leader of the Korean Worker's Party in 1997. He was then reelected as Chairman of the National Defense Commission, a post he had held since 1993 but which became the highest position of the state. In later years North Korea grew marginally less secretive, holding talks with South Korea's **Kim Dae-Jung**, improving international relations and allowing some reunions of families split by the north-south partition.

Kim Young Sam 1927– •*South Korean politician*• Born in Geoje District, in South Kyongsang province, and educated at Seoul National University, after election to the National Assembly in 1954 he was a founding member of the opposition New Democratic Party (NDP), becoming its president in 1974. His opposition to the **Park Chung-Hee** regime resulted in his being banned from all political activity until 1985. In that year he helped form the New Korea Democratic Party (NKDP) and in 1987, the centrist Reunification Democratic Party (RDP). In 1990 he merged the RDP with the ruling party to form the new Democratic Liberal Party (DLP). He was elected President in 1993, but his popularity suffered, and in the historic election of 1995 the DLP won only five of the top 15 posts. He was succeeded in 1998 by **Kim Dae-Jung**.

Kincaid, Jamaica, *originally* **Elaine Potter Richardson** 1949– •*US novelist and journalist*• Born in St John's, Antigua, she is known for her novels *At the Bottom of the River* (1983) and the semiautobiographical *Lucy* (1991), the tale of a young West Indian girl who, having fled to New York, grows more eager to return to her own land. She has also published a nonfictional account of her home island, *A Small Place*. She was a staff writer for the *New Yorker* from 1976 to 1995.

Kindi, al- c. 800–c. 870 •*Arab philosopher*• Born in Kufa, he became tutor at the court in Baghdad and was a prolific author. He was one of the first to spread Greek thought (particularly that of **Aristotle**) into the Arab world and to synthesize it with Islamic doctrine. He was known as "the philosopher of the Arabs."

King, B B, *originally* **Riley B King** 1925– •*US blues singer and guitarist*• He was born into an African-American sharecropping family in Itta Bena, Mississippi. One of the best-known blues performers, he has had a considerable influence on rock as well as blues players with his economical guitar style. As a disc jockey on the radio station WDIA in the 1940s he became known as the "Beale Street Blues Boy," later shortened to B B. He had a string of rhythm-and-blues hits from 1950 onward, and his reputation grew considerably in the late 1960s as the blues influence on rock music came to be acknowledged by white audiences. In the late 1970s he became the first blues artist to tour the USSR. Albums released during his prolific recording career have included *Live at the Regal* (1965), *Confessin' the Blues* (1966), the Grammy award–winning *There Must Be a Better World Somewhere* (1981), *There Is Always One More Time* (1991) and *Blues on the Bayou* (1998). The retrospective *King of the Blues* (1992) covers 40 years of his work.

King, Billie Jean, *née* **Moffitt** 1943– •*US tennis player*• She was born in Long Beach, California. She won the ladies' doubles title at Wimbledon in 1961 (with Karen Hantze) at her first attempt, and between 1961 and 1979 won a record 20 Wimbledon titles, including the singles in 1966–68, 1972–73, and 1975, and four mixed doubles. She also won 13 US titles, four French titles, and two Australian titles. Toward the end of her playing career she became involved in the administration of tennis, and as president of the Women's Tennis Association (1980–81), she played a prominent role in working for the improvement of remuneration and playing conditions for women in professional tennis. In 1973 she challenged the male player Bobby Riggs in the Houston Astrodome, watched by a crowd of 30,472, the biggest to date for a tennis match; a further 50 million television viewers witnessed her 6–4, 6–3, 6–3 victory.

King, Carole, *née* **Klein** 1942– •*US composer and singer*• Born in Brooklyn, New York, she cowrote numerous songs with her future husband Gerry Goffin, including "Will You Still Love Me Tomorrow." Her other songs include "Natural Woman," "The Locomotion," "Up on the Roof" and "It's Too Late." In 1971 her solo album *Tapestry* won four Grammy awards, including Album of the Year. In 1994 she appeared on Broadway in *Blood Brothers*.

King, Coretta Scott, *née* **Scott** 1927– •*US singer, civil rights campaigner and writer*• Born in Marion, Alabama, and trained in music at the New England Conservatory, she made her concert debut in 1948. She married **Martin Luther King, Jr**, in 1953. After her husband's assassination in 1968, King continued his legacy of nonviolent resistance by fighting (successfully) for a national holiday in his honor and by establishing the Martin Luther King, Jr, Center for Nonviolent Social Change. She served as its president until 1995.

King, Don 1932– •*US boxing promoter*• He was born in Cleveland, Ohio, and his colorful and contentious style, clothes, hair and monologues fascinate the sports world. Now so powerful that he is considered by some to have personal control of the boxing world, his clients have included **Muhammad Ali**, **Sugar Ray Leonard** and **Mike Tyson**. He has enjoyed great success despite a notorious past, which includes a prison sentence in the 1970s for homicide.

King, Ernest Joseph 1878–1956 •*US naval officer*• Born in Lorain, Ohio, of British parents, he was a graduate of the US Naval Academy, Annapolis. During World War I he served on the staff of Commander in Chief US Atlantic Fleet (1916–19). He was Commander in Chief of the Atlantic Fleet (January–December 1941), and Commander in Chief of the US Fleet (December 1941). From 1942 to 1945 he was chief of Naval Operations and masterminded the carrier-bases campaign against the Japanese.

King, John 1838–72 •*Australian traveler*• Born in Moy, County Tyrone, Ireland, he was a member of **Robert Burke** and **William Wills**'s expedition which set out from Melbourne in 1860 to cross Australia. King, Burke, Wills and another man reached the tidal marshes of the Flinders River at the edge of the Gulf of Carpentaria, but on the return journey all except King died of starvation. He was helped by the Aborigines and was found emaciated but alive by a relief party six months later. He was thus the first Australian of European descent to cross the continent from south to north and survive.

King, (William Lyon) Mackenzie 1874–1950 •*Canadian Liberal politician*• Born in Kitchener, Ontario, he studied law at Toronto, and won a fellowship in political science at the University of Ontario. He entered politics and became Minister of Labour (1909–14), then Liberal leader (1919) and was several times Prime Minister (1921–26, 1926–30, 1935–48). His view that the dominions should be autonomous communities within the British empire materialized in the Statute of Westminster (1931). He opposed conscription during World War II, except eventually for overseas service, signed agreements with **Franklin D Roosevelt** (1940–41) integrating the economies of the two countries, and represented Canada at the London and San Francisco foundation conferences of the United Nations (1945).

King, Martin Luther, Jr 1929–68 •*US clergyman, civil rights leader and Nobel Prize winner*• He was born in Atlanta, Georgia, the son of an African-American Baptist pastor. He studied at Morehouse College in Atlanta and Crozier Theological Seminary in Chester, Pennsylvania, and earned a PhD from Boston University in 1955. Shortly after he had become pastor of the Dexter Avenue Baptist Church in Montgomery, Alabama, the arrest of **Rosa Parks** sparked the Montgomery bus boycott (1955–56), and King came to national prominence as its eloquent and courageous leader. In 1957 he founded the Southern Christian Leadership Conference, which organized civil rights activities throughout the country. A brilliant orator, he galvanized the movement and in 1963 led the famous march on Washington, where he delivered his memorable "I have a dream" speech. Inspired by the example of **Mahatma Gandhi**, he espoused a philosophy of nonviolence and passive resistance, which proved effective when the spectacle of unarmed African-American demonstrators being harassed and attacked by white segregationists and police exposed the moral shabbiness of the opposing side. King's efforts were instrumental in securing passage of the Civil Rights Act of 1964 and the Voting Rights Act of 1965, and in 1964 he received an honorary doctorate from Yale, the Kennedy Peace Prize, and the Nobel Peace Prize. He was assassinated in Memphis, Tennessee, while on a civil rights mission. His assassin, James Earl Ray, was apprehended in London, and in 1969 was sentenced in Memphis to 99 years. King's widow **Coretta Scott King** has carried on his work. The third Monday in January is celebrated as Martin Luther King Day in the US.

“ ”

He who passively accepts evil is as much involved in it as he who helps to perpetuate it.

1958 ***Strides Towards Freedom.***

King, Phillip 1934– •*British sculptor*• Born in Kheredine, near Carthage, in Tunisia, he went to England in 1946, and studied at Christ's College, Cambridge. He then studied under **Anthony Caro** at St Martin's School of Art and became a teacher there in 1959. He worked as an assistant to **Henry Moore** in 1959–60 before traveling to Greece. In 1962 he began using fiberglass, with color an essential component, as in *And the Birds Began to Sing* (1964), one of a series of works exploring the cone. In 1969 he set up a studio for making large-scale steel sculpture for international commissions. He became president of the Royal Academy in 1999.

King, Rufus 1755–1827 •*US political leader*• Born in Scarboro, Maine (then part of Massachusetts), he graduated from Harvard in 1777 and was a delegate to the Continental Congress (1784–87), where he argued for the prohibition of slavery in the Northwest Territory, and to the Constitutional Convention (1787), where he argued influentially for a strong central government. He was elected to the US Senate from New York (1789–96, 1813–25). He also served as ambassador to Great Britain (1796–1803, 1825–27). He is regarded as a founding father of the US.

King, Stephen Edwin, *pseudonym* **Richard Bachman** 1947– •*US author*• Born in Portland, Maine, he studied at the University of Maine. In the mid-1970s he produced a series of highly suspenseful horror novels, often with a supernatural twist, which have since become classics: *Carrie* (1974), *Salem's Lot* (1975), *The Shining* (1976) and *The Stand* (1978). Later books include *Misery* (1988) and *Bag of Bones* (1998). Many of his books have been filmed, often from his own screenplays. He also writes widely under the pseudonym Richard Bachman.

Kingsford Smith, Sir Charles Edward 1897–1935 •*Australian pioneer aviator*• Born in Hamilton, Queensland, he enlisted on his 18th birthday in the Australian Imperial Force, later transferring to the Royal Flying Corps with whom he won the Military Cross in 1918. In 1927 he made a record-breaking flight around Australia with **Charles Ulm**. In the US they bought a Fokker Tri-motor, which they named *Southern Cross*, and flew it to Australia in 10 days, making the first air crossing of the Pacific Ocean. They also completed the first aerial circumnavigation of the globe (1929–30). In November 1935 his plane went missing over the Bay of Bengal.

Kingsley, Ben, *originally* **Krishna Bhanji** 1943– •*English actor*• Born in Snaiton, near Scarborough, Yorkshire, he was originally a laboratory research assistant, but after joining an amateur dramatic group, turned professional in 1964. He joined the Royal Shakespeare Company from 1967, gaining acclaim for his *Hamlet* (1975–76). Associated with the work of South African dramatist and director **Athol Fugard**, he appeared on stage in *Baal* (1979), *Nicholas Nickleby* (1979) and *Edmund Kean* (1981 and 1983), a one-man tour de force. He had made one previous film appearance in *Fear Is the Key* (1972) prior to starring in *Gandhi* (1982), a film that earned him a Best Actor Academy Award and which established his international reputation. Subsequent films include *Betrayal* (1983), *Bugsy* (1991), *Schindler's List* (1993), *Death and the Maiden* (1994), *Species* (1996), *Sexy Beast* (1999), and *House of Sand and Fog* (2003).

Kingsley, Charles 1819–75 •*English writer*• Born at Holne vicarage, Dartmoor, he studied at Magdalene College, Cambridge. As curate and then rector (1844) he spent the rest of his life at Eversley in Hampshire. In addition to his early social novels *Alton Locke* (1850) and *Yeast* (1851), brilliant novels which had enormous influence at the time, and "Parson Lot," he published an immense number of articles on current topics, especially in the *Christian Socialist* and *Politics for the People*. *Hypatia* (1853) concerns early Christianity in conflict with Greek philosophy in Alexandria, and *Westward Ho!* (1855) presents a realistic picture of Elizabethan England and the Spanish Main. He also wrote a number of popular songs and ballads, including "The Sands of Dee." He was appointed Professor of Modern History at Cambridge in 1860, but he resigned in 1869 and was appointed canon of Westminster and chaplain to Queen **Victoria**. The collected works of this combative, enthusiastic and sympathetic apostle fill 28 volumes (1879–81), and include *The Heroes* (1856), his children's classic *The Water Babies* (1863) and *Prose Idylls* (1873).

Kingsley, Mary Henrietta 1862–1900 •*English traveler and writer*• Born in Islington, London, she was a voracious reader in her father's scientific library. After her parents died, in 1893 she made the first of two remarkable journeys to West Africa, where she lived among the indigenous peoples. Returning from her second journey in 1895, she wrote *Travels in West Africa* (1899) and *West African Studies* (both 1899). She was subsequently consulted by colonial administrators for her wide understanding of African culture. Serving as a nurse in the Second Boer War, she died of typhoid fever. She was the niece of the author **Charles Kingsley**.

Kingsmill, Hugh, *originally* **Hugh Kingsmill Lunn** 1889–1949 •*English biographer and anthologist*• He was educated at Oxford and Dublin. After the failure of his *Matthew Arnold* (1928), he recovered himself with the satirical fantasy *The Return of William Shakespeare* (1929), *Frank Harris* (1932) and elegant essays such as *The Progress of a Biographer* (1949). He produced several anthologies, including *Johnson Without Boswell* (1940), and with **Hesketh Pearson** he published conversational literary journeys such as *Talking of Dick Whittington* (1947).

King-Smith, Dick 1922– •*English author*• Born in Bitton, Gloucestershire, his first book, published when he was 54, was *The Fox Busters* (1978). He followed it with more than 100 titles, including *The Sheep-Pig* (1986), the refreshingly unsentimental story of a pig who discovers it can herd sheep, which was filmed as *Babe* (1995) and became a huge international success.

Kinnock, Neil Gordon 1942– •*Welsh Labour politician*• Born in Tredegar, Monmouthshire, and educated at University College Cardiff, he became Labour Member of Parliament for Bedwellty in 1970, and leader of the British Labour Party in 1983. He was a member of the Labour Party's National Executive Committee from 1978 and chief Opposition spokesman on education from 1979. A skillful orator, Kinnock was the left's obvious choice in the Labour leadership contest of 1983, being regarded by many as the favored candidate of the outgoing leader, **Michael Foot**. He was elected party leader by a large majority and reelected in 1988. He succeeded in isolating the extreme elements within the party and persuaded it to adopt more moderate policies, better attuned to contemporary conditions. Nevertheless, the party was unsuccessful in the 1992 general election, following which Kinnock resigned and was replaced by **John Smith**. He was Member of Parliament for Islwyn from 1983 until 1995, and a member of the European Commission in 1995, becoming a Vice President of the Commission in 1999. His publications include *Making Our Way* (1986) and *Thorns and Roses* (1992).

Kinsey, Alfred Charles 1894–1956 •*US sexologist and zoologist*• Born in Hoboken, New Jersey, he studied at Bowdoin College and at Harvard. He was Professor of Zoology at Indiana University from 1920, and in 1942 was the founder and director of the Institute for Sex Research there. He published *Sexual Behavior in the Human Male* in 1948, known as the Kinsey Report, which was based upon 18,500 interviews and attracted much public attention. It appeared to show a greater variety of sexual behavior than had previously been suspected, although the report was much criticized for the interviewing techniques used. *Sexual Behavior in the Human Female* followed in 1953.

Kipketer, Wilson 1970– •*Kenyan athlete*• Born in Kapchemoiywo, he became a specialist in the 800-meter event, representing Kenya and then Denmark, where he settled in 1990. Having won gold medals in the 800 meters at the world championships in 1995 and 1997 and in the world indoor championships in 1997, he set a new world record of one minute 41.11 seconds in the event in 1997.

Kipling, (Joseph) Rudyard 1865–1936 •*English writer and Nobel Prize winner*• Born in Bombay, India, he was the son of John Lockwood Kipling (1837–1911), Principal of the School of Art in Lahore. He was educated at the United Services College, Westward Ho!, in Devon, England, but returned in 1880 to India, where he worked as a journalist. His mildly satirical verses *Departmental Ditties* (1886), and the short stories *Plain Tales From the Hills* (1888) and *Soldiers Three* (1889), won him a reputation in England. He returned in 1889 and settled in London, where *The Light That Failed* (1890), his first attempt at a full-length novel, was not altogether successful. Two collections of verse, *Barrack Room Ballads* (1892) and *The Seven Seas* (1896), proved much more popular, and he published further short stories in *Many Inventions* (1893) and *The Day's Work* (1899). The two *Jungle Books* (1894–95) have gained a place among the classic animal stories, and *Stalky and Co* (1899) presents semiautobiographical but delightfully uninhibited episodes based on his schooldays. *Kim* appeared in 1901, and the children's classic *Just So Stories* in 1902. The verse collection *The Five Nations* (1903) included the highly successful "Recessional," written for Queen **Victoria**'s Diamond Jubilee in 1897. Later works include *Puck of Pook's Hill* (1906), *Rewards and Fairies* (1910), *Debits and Credits* (1926), and the autobiographical *Something of Myself* (1937). Kipling's real merit as a writer has tended to become obscured in recent years and he has been accused of imperialism and jingoism, but this ignores not only the great body of his work which was far removed from this sphere, but also his own criticisms and satire on some of the less admirable aspects of colonialism. He was awarded the Nobel Prize for literature in 1907.

" "

Take my word for it, the silliest woman can manage a clever man; but it takes a very clever woman to manage a fool.

1888 ***Plain Tales From the Hills**, "Three and—an Extra."*

Kirchhoff, Gustav Robert 1824–87 •*German physicist*• He was born in Königsberg, Prussia (now Kaliningrad, Russia), and while still a student, he devised Kirchhoff's laws for electrical circuits. Professor at the Universities of Heidelberg (1854–75) and Berlin (1875–86), he distinguished himself in electricity, heat, optics and especially (with **Robert Bunsen**) spectrum analysis, which led to the discovery of cesium and rubidium (1859). More importantly, it resulted in his explanation of the **Fraunhofer** lines in the solar spectrum as the absorption of the corresponding spectral wavelengths in the sun's atmosphere. His law of radiation was later developed by **Max Planck** into the concept of the quantum. His electromagnetic theory of diffraction is still the most commonly used in optics.

Kirchner, Ernst Ludwig 1880–1938 •*German artist*• Born in Aschaffenburg, he studied architecture at Dresden, but became the leading spirit in the formation in Dresden, with **Erich Heckel** and **Karl Schmidt-Rottluff**, of Die Brücke (1905–13), the first group of German expressionists, whose work was much influenced by primitive German woodcuts. His work was characterized by erotic, vibrant colors and angular outlines. He moved to Switzerland in 1914. Many of his works were confiscated as degenerate by the Nazis in 1937, and he committed suicide in 1938.

Kirk, Norman Eric 1923–74 •*New Zealand politician*• Born on South Island at Waimate, Canterbury, he began his career as a driver of stationary engines. He joined the Labour Party and became involved in local, then national politics, becoming president of the party in 1964. He entered parliament in 1957, was Leader of the Opposition (1965–72) and became Prime Minister in 1972. He sought a more independent regional role for New Zealand, opposed French nuclear testing in the Pacific and sent ships into the test area. He died in office in 1974 and was succeeded by the Finance Minister **Wallace Rowling**.

Kirkland, Gelsey 1952– •*US dancer*• Born in Bethlehem, Pennsylvania, she studied at the School of American Ballet, and joined New York City Ballet in 1968, becoming a principal in 1972.

In 1975 she moved to the American Ballet Theater, where she began a highly successful partnership with **Mikhail Baryshnikov**. A troubled personal life hampered her career in the early 1980s, but she achieved a successful comeback in *Swan Lake* with the Royal Ballet in London. Her controversial autobiographies, *Dancing on My Grave* (1986) and *The Shape of Love* (1990), document her career.

Kirkpatrick, Jeane Duane Jordan 1926– •*US academic and diplomat*• Born in Duncan, Oklahoma, she was educated at Columbia University and the University of Paris, and pursued a career as a research analyst and academic. Noted for her hawkish, anticommunist defense stance and advocacy of a new Latin-American and Pacific-oriented diplomatic strategy, in 1981 she was made Permanent Representative to the United Nations by President **Ronald Reagan**, remaining there until 1985. She returned to teaching at Georgetown in 1986.

Kirkup, James 1918– •*English poet*• He was born in Sunderland and educated in South Shields, and at the University of Durham. His collections include *A Correct Compassion* (1952) and *Zen Contemplations* (1978). His poem "The Love That Dares to Speak Its Name" was the subject of a prosecution for blasphemous libel in 1977, the first in more than 50 years. He has also published plays, fiction, translations, and five volumes of autobiography.

Kissinger, Henry Alfred 1923– •*US political scientist, diplomat and Nobel Prize winner*• Born in Fürth, Germany, his family emigrated to the US in 1938 to escape Nazi persecution of the Jews. After war service he worked for a number of public agencies before he joined the Harvard faculty as Professor of Government (1962–71). He became President **Richard Nixon**'s adviser on national security affairs (1969), was the main US figure in the negotiations to end the Vietnam War, for which he shared the 1973 Nobel Peace Prize with the Vietnamese statesman **Le Duc Tho**, and the same year became Secretary of State. He played a major role in the improvement of relations (détente) with both China and the USSR during the early 1970s and in the peace negotiations between the Arabs and Israelis (1973–75), emerging as the arch exponent of shuttle diplomacy. He ceased to be Secretary of State in 1977, but was appointed by President **Reagan** to head a bipartisan commission on Central America.

“ ”

The statesman's duty is to bridge the gap between his nation's experience and his vision.

1982 ***Years of Upheaval.***

Kitaj, R(onald) B(rooks) 1932– •*US painter*• Born in Cleveland, Ohio, of Russian-Jewish descent, he was a sailor from 1951 to 1955 and traveled extensively. Following army service, he studied art at Oxford, and then entered the Royal College of Art, London (1960). His oil paintings and pastels demonstrate a mastery of figure drawing, while his economic use of line and flattened color recall East Asian art, as in *If Not, Not* (1976, National Gallery of Scotland, Edinburgh). There was a retrospective of his work at the Tate Gallery in 1994. Its hostile reception by the critics, followed by the sudden death of his second wife, the American painter Sandra Fisher (1947–94), had a profound and lasting effect on him and was the subject of his sole contribution to the Royal Academy Summer Exhibition of 1996, *The Critic Kills*. The following year he left London for Los Angeles. In 2001 the National Gallery put on the first exhibition of his work in London since the 1994 retrospective.

Kitasato, Baron Shibasaburo 1852–1931 •*Japanese bacteriologist*• Born in Oguni, after graduating from the Imperial University of Tokyo (1883), he moved to Berlin, and later founded in Japan an institute for infectious diseases. Kitasato succeeded in isolating the first pure culture of tetanus (1889), and he made the invaluable discovery of antitoxic immunity (1890), which led to the development of treatments and immunization for both tetanus and diphtheria. He also discovered the bacillus of bubonic plague (1894) and isolated the bacilli of symptomatic anthrax (1889) and dysentery (1898).

Kitchener (of Khartoum and of Broome), Horatio Herbert Kitchener, 1st Earl 1850–1916 •*British soldier and statesman*• Born near Ballylongford, County Kerry, Ireland, he was educated in Switzerland and the Royal Military Academy, Woolwich. He entered the Royal Engineers in 1871 and served in Palestine and Cyprus and in the Sudan campaign (1883–85). In 1898 he won back the Sudan for Egypt by the final rout of the Khalifa at Omdurman, and was made a peer. Successively Chief of Staff and Commander in Chief in South Africa (1900–02), he brought the Second Boer War to an end. He was then made Commander in Chief in India (1902–09), and agent and consul general in Egypt (1911). He was appointed field marshal and Secretary for War on August 7, 1914. He was lost with HMS *Hampshire* (mined off Orkney) on June 5, 1916.

Kitt, Eartha Mae c.1928– •*US entertainer*• Born in North, South Carolina, she graduated from the New York School of the Performing Arts. Her theatrical credits include *New Faces of 1952*, *Shinbone Alley* (1957) and *The Owl and the Pussycat* (1965–66). Since her debut in *Casbah* (1948), her film appearances included *New Faces* (1954), *St Louis Blues* (1957), *Anna Lucasta* (1958), the documentary *All by Myself* (1982), and *Erik the Viking* (1989). On television from 1953, she received the Golden Rose of Montreux for *Kaskade* (1962) and was appropriately cast as Catwoman in the series *Batman* (1966).

Kitzinger, Sheila Helen Elizabeth, *née* **Webster** 1929– •*British childbirth educationist*• Educated at Ruskin and St Hugh's colleges, Oxford, she conducted research into social anthropology from 1952 to 1953, and has worked with the Open University and the National Childbirth Trust. She has long been a campaigner for more natural childbirth procedures and her 1980 book *Pregnancy and Childbirth* sold over one million copies. Her other books, which cover all aspects of pregnancy and childbirth, include *The Good Birth Guide* (1979), *Homebirth* (1991), *Ourselves as Mothers* (1992), *Becoming a Grandmother* (1997) and *Rediscovering Birth* (2000).

Kivi, Aleksis, *pseudonym of* **Aleksis Stenvall** 1834–72 •*Finnish playwright and novelist*• Born in Nurmijärvi or Palojoki, he was the son of a poor tailor. He wrote in Finnish rather than Swedish, establishing the western dialect as the modern literary language of Finland, and is considered the father of the Finnish theater and novel. He wrote the first Finnish novel, *Seitsemän veljestä* (1870, Eng trans *Seven Brothers*, 1929), and a collection of Finnish poems, *Kanervala* (1866). As a dramatist he wrote rural comedies like *Nummisuutarit* (1864, "The Cobblers on the Heath"), and a tragedy, *Kullervo* (1864).

Kjarval, Jóhannes Sveinsson 1885–1972 •*Icelandic Symbolist painter*• Born on the remote farm of Efri-Ey, he was one of the pioneers of modern Icelandic art. He worked as a farm laborer and a deckhand for some years, and eventually realized his dream of becoming a professional painter when his friends held a lottery to raise funds for his schooling abroad. He went to London in 1911, then to Copenhagen where he studied at the Royal Academy (1912–18). From 1918 he lived in Iceland but traveled widely. Essentially an eccentric Romantic with strong mystical and Symbolist tendencies, he had a powerful sense of historical nationalism, and often featured the "hidden people" of Icelandic folklore. Long before his death he had become the best-loved painter in Iceland.

Klaproth, Martin Heinrich 1743–1817 •*German analytical chemist*• He was born in Wernigerode and grew up in poverty. He trained as an apothecary. He moved to Berlin in 1768 and married the niece of **Andreas Sigismund Marggraf**, who brought him some scientific connections and enough money for him to set up his own shop. From 1792 he held various lectureships, becoming Germany's leading chemist. Between 1789 and 1803 Klaproth discovered six new elements. His analytical techniques were as important as his discoveries: he found ways of treating particularly insoluble compounds, and made adjustments to overcome contamination from his apparatus. He was also one of the first scientists outside France to propagate the revolutionary ideas of **Antoine Lavoisier**.

Klee, Paul 1879–1940 •*Swiss artist*• Born in Münchenbuchsee near Bern, he studied at Munich and settled there (1906), and was associated with **Franz Marc** and **Wassily Kandinsky** in the Blaue

Reiter group (1911–12). From 1920 to 1931 he taught at the Bauhaus in Weimar and Dessau, with his *Pädagogisches Skizzenbuch* being published in 1925, and then taught in Düsseldorf (1931–33). After he had returned to Bern in 1933, many of his works were confiscated by the Nazis and 17 of them were included in the 1937 "Degenerate Art" exhibition in Munich. In his fantastic, small-scale, mainly abstract pictures he created, with supreme technical skill in many media, a very personal world of free fancy, for example the well-known *Twittering Machine* in the Museum of Modern Art, New York.

Klein, Anne Hannah, *née* **Hannah Golofski** c. 1921–74 •*US fashion designer*• She was born in New York City and in 1938 started as a sketcher on Seventh Avenue there. In 1948, Junior Sophisticates was launched, and Anne Klein & Co was established in 1968. She was a noted leader in designing sophisticated, practical sportswear for young women. She recognized early a need for blazers, trousers, and separates, and her designs were popular in the US.

Klein, Calvin Richard 1942– •*US fashion designer*• Born in New York City, he graduated from New York's Fashion Institute of Technology in 1962, and set up his own firm in 1968. He quickly achieved recognition, becoming known for understatement and the simple but sophisticated style of his clothes, including designer jeans and fashionable casual wear. Klein later diversified into perfume and underwear.

" "

You have to take things to an extreme and then bring them back to reality.

1988 On the fluctuating length of hemlines.
*In the **New York Times**, March 9.*

Klein, (Christian) Felix 1849–1925 •*German mathematician*• Born in Düsseldorf, he studied at the University of Bonn (1865–68), and became Professor of Mathematics at the University of Erlangen (1872–75). He later accepted professorships at the Universities of Leipzig (1880–86) and Göttingen (1886–1913). His "Erlanger Programm" (published 1872) showed how different geometries could be classified in terms of group theory. His subsequent work on geometry included studies of non-Euclidean geometry, function theory and elliptic modular and automorphic functions. He organized the *Encyklopädie der mathematischen Wissenschaften* (23 vols, 1890–1930).

Klein, Melanie 1882–1960 •*British psychoanalyst*• Born in Vienna, Austria, she trained with Sandor Ferenczi in his children's clinic. She studied under Karl Abraham in Berlin, then moved to London in 1926. She pioneered the now widely used techniques of play therapy and was the first to apply psychoanalysis to small children. Her belief that neuroses are fixed in the earliest months of life was always controversial and caused dissent among her colleagues. Her books include *The Psychoanalysis of Children* (1932).

Klein, Yves 1928–62 •*French artist*• Born in Nice, he was a judo expert (he lived in Japan from 1952 to 1953), musician and leader of the postwar European neo-Dada movement. His monochrome (usually blue) canvases date from 1946. His *Anthropométries* involved girls covered with blue paint being dragged across canvases to the accompaniment of his *Symphonie monotone* (one-note symphony, composed in 1947).

Klemperer, Otto 1885–1973 •*German conductor*• Born in Breslau (now Wrocław, Poland), he studied at the Hoch Conservatory in Frankfurt am Main and in Berlin and first appeared as a conductor in 1907. He made a name as a champion of modern music and was appointed director of the Kroll Opera in Berlin (1927), which was closed down in 1931. Nazism drove him to the US in 1933, where he became director of the Los Angeles Symphony Orchestra until 1939. In spite of continuing ill health, he was musical director of the Budapest Opera (1947–50). In his later years he was particularly known for his interpretation of **Beethoven**. His compositions included a mass and several lieder.

Klerk, F W de *See* **de Klerk, F(rederik) W(illem)**

Klestil, Thomas 1932–2004 •*Austrian politician*• Born in Vienna, he was educated at the University of Economics and Business Administration there. He worked in various civil posts and at the Austrian Embassy in Washington before becoming private secretary to Federal Chancellor Josef Klaus (1966–69). Among the senior diplomatic posts that followed were Austrian representative to the UN (1978–82) and Austrian ambassador to the US (1982–87). He was Austria's secretary-general for foreign affairs (1987–92) and became president of Austria in 1992 (reelected in 1998).

Klima, Viktor 1947– •*Austrian politician*• Born in Vienna, he was educated at Vienna's Technical University and at the University of Vienna. He established a reputation as a business executive before entering politics and in 1997 he succeeded **Franz Vranitzky** as leader of the center-left Social Democratic Party and as Chancellor of Austria. He later returned to business.

Klimt, Gustav 1862–1918 •*Austrian painter and designer*• Born in Vienna, from 1883 to 1892 he worked in collaboration with his brother and another artist as a painter of grandiose decorative schemes. He became a founder and the first president (1898–1903) of the Vienna Secession. His murals for the University of Vienna (1900–03) were considered pornographic and aroused official condemnation. He produced a number of portraits, mainly of women, as well as large allegorical and mythological paintings; typically, these combine a naturalistic though highly mannered delineation of the figure with an elaborately patterned, richly decorative treatment of the background or clothing, creating a luxuriant, languidly decadent effect.

Kline, Franz Joseph 1910–62 •*US artist*• Born in Wilkes-Barre, Pennsylvania, he studied in Boston and London. Throughout the 1940s he worked in a traditional style, painting urban scenery, but after c. 1950 his art became abstract, employing black, irregular shapes on white canvases, and becoming a leader of the action painting of the Abstract Expressionists. He added color to later works, such as *Orange and Black Wall* (1939). Much of his life was spent in New York City, where he taught at the Pratt Institute and Cooper Union.

Klitzing, Klaus Von *See* **Von Klitzing, Klaus**

Kluckhohn, Clyde Kay Maben 1905–60 •*US cultural anthropologist*• Born in Le Mars, Iowa, he studied at Princeton, Wisconsin, Vienna and Oxford, and was appointed to the faculty of Harvard in 1935. His abiding research interest was in the culture of the Navaho, and his classic monograph *Navaho Witchcraft* (1944) was outstanding for its combination of social-structural and psychoanalytic approaches. He was a major contributor to culture theory, in which he collaborated closely with **A L Kroeber**. He set out his views on culture patterns and value systems in the popular work *Mirror for Man* (1949).

Klug, Sir Aaron 1926– •*English biophysicist and Nobel Prize winner*• Born in Zelva, Poland (now in Belarus), he moved to South Africa as a young child and studied physics at the universities of Witwatersrand and Cape Town. He held numerous research posts, working with **John Bernal** and **Rosalind Franklin** and becoming director of the Medical Research Council's Laboratory of Molecular Biology (1986–91). His studies employed a wide variety of techniques to elucidate the structure of viruses. From the 1970s he applied these methods to the study of chromosomes and other biological macromolecules such as muscle filaments. He was the president of the Royal Society from 1995 to 2000. He was elected a Fellow of the Royal Society in 1969, awarded the Nobel Prize for chemistry in 1982, knighted in 1988 and appointed to the Order of Merit in 1995.

Kluge, (Hans) Günther von 1882–1944 •*German soldier*• He was born in Poznań, Poland. In 1939 he carried out the Nazi occupation of the Polish Corridor, commanded the German armies on the central Russian front (1942) and in July 1944 replaced **Karl von Rundstedt** as Commander in Chief of the Nazi armies in France confronting the Allied invasion, but was himself replaced after the Falaise gap débâcle. He committed suicide after being implicated in the failed plot to kill **Hitler**.

Kneller, Sir Godfrey, *originally* **Kniller** 1646–1723 •*German portrait painter*• Born in Lübeck, he studied in Holland and Italy. In 1676 he went to London, and in 1680 was appointed court painter.

In 1691 **William III** knighted him, and in 1715 **George I** made him a baronet. His best-known works are the *Beauties of Hampton Court* (painted for William III), and his 48 portraits of the "Kit-Cat Club" and of 10 reigning monarchs. His brother, John Zacharias (1644–1702), architectural and portrait painter, also settled in England.

Knight, Gladys 1944– •*US soul and rhythm-and-blues singer*• Born in Atlanta, Georgia, she began singing in the gospel choirs. At the age of eight, she won a television talent competition, and the same year formed a close-harmony group called the Pips with her brother and two cousins. They began to record in 1958 and in 1966 switched to the Tamla Motown label where a string of hits followed. In 1972 she scored a huge hit with "Help Me Make It Through the Night." She had further success with "Midnight Train to Georgia" and "The Way We Were."

Knight, Dame Laura, *née* **Johnson** 1877–1970 •*English artist*• Born in Long Eaton, she traveled widely. She produced a long series of oil paintings of the ballet, the circus and gypsy life in a lively and forceful style, and also executed a number of watercolor landscapes.

Knopfler, Mark 1949– •*British rock singer and guitarist*• Born in Glasgow, he worked as a journalist and teacher before forming the phenomenally successful rock band Dire Straits in London in 1976; his brother, David Knopfler (1952–), was also a founding member. The success of "Sultans of Swing" put the band onto the world stage, and the album *Brothers in Arms* (1985) confirmed their commercial standing. He has worked with **Bob Dylan**, **Chet Atkins**, **Eric Clapton**, Randy Newman (1943–) and **Tina Turner**, and issued his first official solo album, *Golden Heart*, in 1996. He has written several film soundtracks.

Knott, Alan Philip Eric 1946– •*English cricket player*• He was born in Belvedere, Greater London. One of a trio of noted Kent wicketkeepers (with **Leslie Ames** and **Godfrey Evans**), he played in 95 Test matches and claimed 269 dismissals. He was a genuine wicketkeeper-batsman whose 4,389 runs included five centuries. He kept wicket for England in 65 consecutive Test matches.

Knox, John c. 1513–72 •*Scottish Protestant reformer, founder of the Church of Scotland*• John Knox was born in or near Haddington, East Lothian. He was educated there and probably at the University of St Andrews. A Catholic priest, he acted as notary in Haddington (1540–43), and in 1544 he was influenced by **George Wishart** to work for the Lutheran reformation. After Wishart was burned (1546), Knox joined the reformers defending the castle of St. Andrews, and became a minister. After the castle fell to the French, he was kept a prisoner until 1549, then became a chaplain to Edward VI, and consulted over the Second Book of Common Prayer. On the accession of **Mary I**, he fled to the Continent, where he was much influenced by **John Calvin**. He returned to Scotland in 1555 to preach, and then again in 1559, when he won a strong party in favor of reform, and founded the Church of Scotland (1560). He played a lasting part in the composition of *The Scotts Confession*, *The First Book of Discipline*, and *The Book of Common Order*. His *History of the Reformation in Scotland* was published 1586. He died in Edinborough and was buried in the churchyard then attached to St Giles.

" "

Un homme avec Dieu est toujours dans la majorité.
One man with God is always a majority.
Inscription on the Reformation Monument, Geneva, attributed to Knox.

Knox, Robert 1791–1862 •*Scottish anatomist*• Born in Edinburgh, he studied medicine at the University of Edinburgh, in London, and later in Paris, prior to setting up an extramural anatomy school in Edinburgh. His need for a substantial supply of cadavers for dissection was met through the services of the disreputable **William Burke** and William Hare, who, unknown to Knox, obtained their corpses not by grave-robbing but by murder. Given the cold shoulder by the medical establishment, late in life Knox succeeded in gaining employment as pathologist to the London Cancer Hospital.

Knox-Johnston, Sir Robin (William Robert Patrick) 1939– •*English yachtsman*• He was the first person to sail nonstop and solo around the world in *Suhaili*—in 312 days from June 14, 1968, to April 22, 1969. The holder of the 1986 British Sailing Trans Atlantic Record (10 days, 14 hours and 9 minutes), he has since competed in many international races, and has won the Round Britain Race in both the two-man and crewed sections. In 1994, with coskipper **Peter Blake**, he achieved the world's fastest circumnavigation under sail—in 74 days, 22 hours, 17 minutes and 22 seconds. He has written several books and was knighted in 1995.

Knussen, (Stuart) Oliver 1952– •*English composer and conductor*• Born in Glasgow, of English parents, he showed early flair for composition, conducting the London Symphony Orchestra in his first symphony in 1968. He has since composed symphonies, a concerto, numerous orchestral, chamber and vocal works, and operas (including, 1979–83, *Where the Wild Things Are*). He was codirector of the Aldeburgh Festival from 1983 to 1998, when he became Music Director of the London Sinfonietta.

Knut Sveinsson, *also known as* **Canute** or **Cnut the Great** c. 995–1035 •*King of England, Denmark and Norway*• The son of **Svein I Haraldsson**, "Fork-Beard," he accompanied his father on his attempted conquest of England (1013–14), but on his father's death withdrew to Denmark where his elder brother Harald had inherited the throne. In 1015 Knut challenged **Ethelred II**, the Unready, and gained all of England except London. When Ethelred died in 1016, Knut challenged his son and successor **Edmund Ironside**, and became undisputed king of all England. He discarded his English mistress, Ælgifu of Northampton, and summoned Ethelred's widow, **Emma**, from Normandy to be his wife (their son was **Hardaknut**, king of Denmark and also, briefly, of England). He inherited the throne of Denmark from his brother (1018) and went there the following year to consolidate his power. Later he helped to overthrow **Olaf II Haraldsson** (St Olaf) of Norway, and seized the throne there in 1030, installing his son Svein (by Ælgifu) as a puppet ruler. As king of England he brought firm government, justice and security from external threat, and showed reverence and generosity to the Church and its native saints. The story of his apparent attempt to turn back the tide has been totally misconstrued in folklore: in fact, he was trying to demonstrate to his courtiers that only God could control the tide, not man. When he died, his Anglo-Scandinavian empire quickly disintegrated. He was succeeded in England by **Harold I Knutsson** (Harefoot), his younger son by Ælgifu, and then by Hardaknut, and in Norway Svein was immediately deposed by **Magnus I Olafsson**, who also inherited Denmark on the death of Hardaknut. Knut is regarded as one of the most effective early kings of England.

Knutsson, Karl *See* **Karl VIII**

Koch, C(hristopher) J(ohn) 1932– •*Australian novelist*• Born in Hobart, Tasmania, he published his first novel, *Boys in the Island*, in 1958 (rev edn 1974). It was followed by *Across the Sea Wall* (1965, rev edn 1982) and the exotic thriller *The Year of Living Dangerously* (1978), set in Indonesia just before the downfall of Sukarno in the 1960s, became immensely popular through **Peter Weir**'s 1982 film. *Crossing the Gap: A Novelist's Essays* appeared in 1993, and in the novel *Highways to a War* (1995) Koch returns to the theme of the journalist in a conflict.

Koch, Ed(ward) 1924– •*US politician*• Born in New York City, he practiced law and became a member of the City Council (1967). Elected to Congress as a Democrat in 1969, he became mayor of New York in 1978, and in the 1980s was a widely known political figure in the US.

Koch, Marita 1957– •*German athlete*• She was born in Wismar and studied pediatric medicine. Competing for East Germany, she won the Olympic 400 meters title in 1980 and the European title three times, remaining undefeated over 400 meters between 1977 and 1981. In the 200-meter race, she won three indoor European championship titles and a world Student Games title. Dominating these two events for over a decade, she set a total of 16 world records. She retired in 1986.

Koch, (Heinrich Hermann) Robert 1843–1910 •*German physician, pioneer bacteriologist and Nobel Prize winner*• Born in

Klausthal in the Harz, he entered the University of Göttingen, and practiced medicine at Hanover and elsewhere. Koch proved that the anthrax bacillus was the sole cause of the disease, and discovered in 1882 the tubercle bacillus. In 1883 he led a German expedition to Egypt and India, where he discovered the cholera bacillus, and in 1890 he produced a drug named tuberculin to prevent the development of tuberculosis. It proved to be ineffective as a cure, but useful in diagnosis. He became professor in Berlin and director of the Institute of Hygiene in 1885, and first director of the Berlin Institute for Infectious Diseases in 1891. He was awarded the Nobel Prize for physiology or medicine in 1905 for his work on tuberculosis. His formulation of essential scientific principles, known as Koch's postulates, established clinical bacteriology as a medical science in the 1890s.

Köchel, Ludwig Ritter von 1800–77 •*Austrian musicologist*• Born in Stein, he compiled the famous catalog of **Mozart**'s works, arranging them in chronological order, and giving them the "K" numbers now commonly used to identify them.

Kocher, Emil Theodor 1841–1917 •*Swiss surgeon and Nobel Prize winner*• He was born and educated in Bern, where he became a professor (1871). He developed general surgical treatment of disorders of the thyroid gland, including goiter and thyroid tumors. His observations of patients suffering the long-term consequences of removing the thyroid gland helped elucidate some of its normal functions, and by the 1890s the isolation of one of the active thyroid hormones made replacement therapy possible. He also pioneered operations of the brain and spinal cord, and during World War I did experimental work on the trauma caused by gunshot wounds. He was the first surgeon to be awarded the Nobel Prize for physiology or medicine (1909).

Kodály, Zoltán 1882–1967 •*Hungarian composer*• Born in Kecskemét, he studied at the Budapest Conservatory where he became a professor. Among his best-known works are his *Háry János* suite (1926, "John Háry"), *Dances of Galanta* (1933), and his many choral compositions, especially his *Psalmus Hungaricus* (1923, "Hungarian Psalm") and *Te Deum* (1936). He carried out important reforms in the field of musical education and developed an evolutionary system of training and sight-singing.

Koestler, Arthur 1905–83 •*British writer and journalist, political refugee and prisoner*• Born in Budapest, he studied at Vienna, then became a political correspondent and later a scientific editor for a German newspaper group. Dismissed as a Communist, he traveled in Russia (1932–33), but became disillusioned, breaking with the party finally in 1938, as described in *The God That Failed* (1950). He reported the Spanish Civil War (1936–37), was imprisoned under sentence of death by General **Franco**, as retold in *Spanish Testament* (1938) and *Dialogue With Death* (1942), and again by the French (1940). He escaped from German-occupied France via the French Foreign Legion and eventually joined the Pioneer Corps. These experiences provided the background for his first novel in English, *Arrival and Departure* (1943). He portrayed the degeneration of revolutionary idealism in Roman times under **Spartacus** in *The Gladiators* (1939), which was followed by the striking modern equivalent, *Darkness at Noon* (1940), Koestler's masterpiece. *The Act of Creation* (1964), *The Case of the Midwife Toad* (1971) and *Bricks to Babel* (1980) were among his later writings. He and his wife committed suicide together when he became terminally ill. Under the terms of his will, the Koestler Chair of Parapsychology was established at the University of Edinburgh (1985).

Koetsu, Honnami 1558–1637 •*Japanese calligrapher and decorative artist*• Born in Kyoto, he started his career as a teamaster, but his numerous interests made him one of the most creative figures in the history of Japanese art. He collaborated with the master of the later decorative style, Nonomura Sotatsu (1576–1643), founding the Kōrin school of Japanese painters. In 1615 he founded Takagamine, a community of artists and craftsmen in northern Kyoto. He was considered one of the three best calligraphists of his day, and invented a new kind of poem scroll.

Koffka, Kurt 1886–1941 •*German psychologist, cofounder of the Gestalt school of psychology*• He was born in Berlin. At the University of Giessen he took part in experiments in perception with **Wolfgang Köhler**, conducted by **Max Wertheimer**, and founded with them the Gestalt school of psychology, based on the concept that the organized whole is something more than the sum of the parts into which it can be logically analyzed. He later taught at Oxford, England, and at Smith College in the US.

Kohl, Helmut 1930– •*German statesman*• He was born in Ludwigshafen am Rhein and attended the Universities of Frankfurt and Heidelberg. He joined the Christian Democrats after World War II, and became chairman for the Rhineland-Palatinate in 1956, and minister-president of the state in 1969. He became a member of the federal parliament (1976) and was chosen to run as Christian Democrat and Christian Social Union candidate for the chancellorship. Although **Helmut Schmidt** retained power through his coalition with the Free Democratic Party (FDP), Kohl made the CDU/CSU the largest party in parliament. The sudden collapse of his coalition in 1982 led to Kohl's installation as interim Chancellor, and in the elections of 1983 the CDU/CSU increased its number of seats and formed a government. Very conservative, yet not in favor of an economy uncontrolled by state intervention, and anti-Soviet though by no means unquestioningly pro-USA, Kohl maintained an essentially central course between political extremes. From 1984 to 1986 Kohl was implicated in the Flick bribes scandal, but he was cleared of all charges of perjury and deception in 1986 and was reelected as Chancellor in the 1987 Bundestag elections and again in 1990 and 1994. He played a decisive part in the integration of the former East Germany into the Federal Republic. In 1991, six weeks after united Germany's first national elections, he announced a coalition government that, while maintaining CDU/CSU dominance in the key defense and Labor and Social Affairs Ministries, reflected the strength of the vote for the Free Democrats, with the FDP's **Hans-Dietrich Genscher** remaining as Foreign Secretary. The Kohl era ended in 1998 with the election victory of the Social Democrats, led by **Gerhard Schröder**.

Köhler, Georges Jean Franz 1946–95 •*German immunochemist and Nobel Prize winner*• Born in Munich, he studied at the University of Freiburg and joined **Cesar Milstein** at the Medical Research Council Laboratory in Cambridge, where they discovered how to produce hybridomas—hybrid cells created by fusing an antibody—generating cell with a cancer cell. Hybridomas possess infinite life and are used to produce a single type of antibody against a specific antigen (foreign body). Their use opened the way to a precise examination of antibody structure. He also studied the pattern of inheritance of hybridoma cells, and demonstrated that structural mutants of immunoglobulins could be formed by hybridomas (1980). Commercially produced monoclonal antibodies, derived from Köhler's hybridoma research, now provide an unambiguous and sensitive way of identifying and quantifying a wide range of substances, and are used in pregnancy and drug testing, and in the diagnosis and treatment of cancer and other diseases. For this work, Köhler shared with Milstein and **Niels Jerne** the 1984 Nobel Prize for physiology or medicine.

Köhler, Wolfgang 1887–1967 •*German psychologist, cofounder of the Gestalt school of psychology*• Born in Estonia, he was director of the anthropoid research station in the Canary Islands (1913–20), where he became an authority on problem solving in animals. He later held chairs of psychology at the University of Berlin, and at Swarthmore and Dartmouth Colleges in the USA. He was the cofounder with **Kurt Koffka** of Gestalt psychology.

Kohn, Walter 1923– •*US physicist and Nobel Prize winner*• Born in Vienna, Austria, he was educated at the University of Toronto and at Harvard and served in the Canadian Army (1944–45) before joining the staff at Harvard as an instructor (1948–50). He worked at the Carnegie Mellon Institute of Technology (1950–60) and while at the University of California, San Diego (1960–79), he devised the density functional theory, which simplified the mathematical description of the bonding between atoms in molecules. He founded the Institute of Theoretical Physics at the University of California, Santa Barbara, and served as its director (1979–84). In 1998 he shared the Nobel Prize for chemistry with **John A Pople** for his development of the density-functional theory.

Koizumi, Junichiro 1942– *•Japanese politician•* Born in Yokosuka, Japan, he studied economics at Keio University and was first elected to the House of Representatives in 1972. He became State Secretary for Finance in 1979 and included among his subsequent posts Minister of Health and Welfare (1988, 1996–98) and Minister of Posts and Telecommunications (1992–93). In 2001 he became president of the Liberal Democratic Party and prime minister of Japan.

Kokoschka, Oskar 1886–1980 *•British artist and writer•* Born in Pöchlarn, Austria, of Czech and Austrian parentage, he studied from 1904 to 1908 in Vienna. In Berlin he painted portraits and made striking posters and lithographs. Seriously wounded in World War I, he afterward taught at the Dresden Academy of Art (1919–24); thereafter he traveled widely, and painted many expressionist landscapes in Spain, France and England. In 1938 he fled to England for political reasons, becoming naturalized in 1947, and painted a number of politically symbolic works, as well as portraits and landscapes. In the 1920s he also wrote expressionist dramas, including *Orpheus und Eurydike*. He lived in Switzerland from 1953.

Kolchak, Aleksandr Vasilevich 1874–1920 *•Russian naval commander•* In World War I he was in command of the Black Sea fleet. After the Russian Revolution of 1917, he became war minister in the anti-Bolshevik government, and cleared Siberia, as leader of the White Army. In 1919 he was betrayed and shot.

Kolingba, André Birth date unavailable *•Central African Republic general and politician•* As chief of the armed forces of the Central African Republic, Kolingba became president of Central Africa following the overthrow of President **David Dacko** in a coup in 1981; he also held the posts of Minister of Defense and of War Veterans (1981–83, 1984–91), and of Prime Minister (1981–91). In 1985 the Cabinet became largely civilian and in 1986 Kolingba created and was first leader of the Central African Democratic rally (RDC). Constitutional change in 1992 allowed multiparty elections, and his presidency ended in 1993 when he lost in the presidential elections.

Kollontai, Aleksandra Mikhailovna, *née* **Domontovich** 1872–1952 *•Russian feminist and revolutionary•* Born in St Petersburg into an upper-class family, she rejected her privileged upbringing and became interested in socialism, and for her revolutionary behavior was exiled to Germany in 1908. In 1915 she traveled widely in the US, begging the nation not to join World War I, and in 1917, following the Revolution, returned to Russia, becoming Commissar for Public Welfare. In this post she was an activist for domestic and social reforms, including collective child care and easier divorce proceedings. Although her private liaisons shocked the party, she was appointed minister to Norway (1923–25, 1927–30), Mexico (1926–27) and Sweden (1930–45), becoming ambassador in 1943, the world's first woman ambassador. She played a vital part in negotiating the end of the Soviet-Finnish war (1944). Her writings, such as the collection of short stories *Love of Worker Bees* (1923), aroused much controversy because of their open discussion of sexuality and women's place in society. Her autobiography, written in 1926, was not published in Russia.

Kollwitz, Käthe, *née* **Schmidt** 1867–1945 *•German graphic artist and sculptor•* Born in Königsberg, East Prussia (now Kaliningrad, Russia), she was educated in Königsberg and in Berlin, where she studied drawing. Although she has been called an expressionist, she was uninterested in the fashions of modern art, and chose serious, tragic subjects, with strong social or political content such as her early etchings, the *Weavers' Revolt* (1897–98) and the *Peasants' War* (1902–08). From c. 1910 she preferred lithography, and after being expelled by the Nazis in 1933 from the Prussian Academy (of which she was the first woman member) she made a moving series of eight prints titled *Death* (1934–35). Her sculpture also shows compassion for suffering, as in *The Complaint* (1938, Munich, in bronze). In 1932 she executed the bronze war memorial at Dixmuiden, Flanders.

“ ”

I have never done any work cold … I have always worked with my blood, so to speak.

1917 Letter to her son Hans, April 16.

Kolmogorov, Andrei Nikolayevich 1903–87 *•Soviet mathematician•* Born in Tambov, he studied at Moscow State University and remained there throughout his career. He worked on a wide range of topics in mathematics, including the theory of functions of a real variable, functional analysis, mathematical logic, and topology. He is particularly remembered for his creation of the axiomatic theory of probability. His work with **Aleksandr Khinchin** on **Markov** processes, in which he formulated the partial differential equations which bear his name, was of lasting significance. He also worked in applied mathematics, on the theory of turbulence, on celestial mechanics, on information theory, and in cybernetics.

Konev, Ivan Stepanovich 1897–1973 *•Soviet military commander•* Born in Lodeyno, he was drafted into the Czarist army in 1916, and joined the Red Army and the Communist Party in 1918. He held various commands before the USSR was drawn into World War II, during which he commanded several different fronts against the Germans, then became Commander in Chief, Ground Forces (1946–50), first Deputy Minister of Defense, and Commander in Chief of the Warsaw Pact forces (1956–60).

Konstantin Nikolayevich *See* **Constantine Nikolayevich**

Koopmans, Tjalling Charles 1910–85 *•US economist and Nobel Prize winner•* Born in 's-Graveland in the Netherlands, and educated at Utrecht and Leiden Universities, he emigrated to the US in 1940, and worked for a shipping firm. He was Professor of Economics at the University of Chicago (1948–55) and at Yale (1955–81). He shared the 1975 Nobel Prize for economics (with **Leonid Kantorovich**) for his contributions to the theory of optimal allocation of resources.

Koppel, Herman D(avid) 1908–98 *•Danish composer and pianist•* Born in Copenhagen, he was educated at the Royal Danish Academy of Music, and became a professor there in 1955. He made his debut as a composer in 1929 and as a pianist in 1930. His many compositions include seven symphonies, four piano concertos, six string quartets, an opera (1970, *Macbeth*), a ballet, and music for theater, film and radio. His son, Thomas Herman Koppel (1944–), is also a composer.

Korbut, Olga Valentinovna 1956– *•Belarusian gymnast•* Born in Grodno, Belarus, she captivated the world at the 1972 Olympics at Munich with her supple grace, and gave gymnastics a new lease on life as a sport. She won a gold medal as a member of the winning Soviet team, as well as individual golds in the beam and floor exercises and silver for the parallel bars. After retiring, she became a coach.

Korda, Sir Alexander, *originally* **Sándor Laszlo Kellner** 1893–1956 *•Hungarian-British film producer•* He was born in Pusztatúrpáztó, Hungary, and began his career as a newspaperman in Budapest. He became a film producer there, then in Vienna, Berlin and Hollywood, where he directed for First National, before moving to the UK where he founded London Film Productions and Denham studios (1932). His many films as producer include *The Private Life of Henry VIII* (1932), which he also directed, *The Thief of Baghdad* (1940), *The Third Man* (1949), *The Red Shoes* (1948) and *Richard III* (1956). He was knighted in 1942.

“ ”

One can be unhappy before eating caviar, even after, but at least not during.

*1979 In **Newsweek**, November 26.*

Koresh, David, *originally* **Vernon Howell** 1959–93 *•US cult leader•* Born in western Texas, he founded the Branch Davidian sect, a breakaway from the Seventh Day Adventist Church. A self-proclaimed Messiah, he attracted a following of people to his compound at Mount Carmel. His apocalyptic pronouncements led to growing concern and the authorities laid siege to the heavily armed compound, the affair ending tragically with the deaths of many cult members, including Koresh himself.

Kornberg, Arthur 1918– *•US biochemist and Nobel Prize winner•* Born in Brooklyn, New York, he graduated in medicine from the University of Rochester, and after holding various distinguished posts he became professor at Stanford University in 1959. In studies of *Escherichia coli*, Kornberg discovered DNA polymerase, the enzyme that synthesizes new DNA. For this work he was awarded the 1959 Nobel Prize for physiology or medicine jointly with **Severo Ochoa**. Kornberg became the first to synthesize viral DNA (1967) and wrote *DNA Replication* (1980).

Korngold, Erich Wolfgang 1897–1957 •*US composer*• Born in Brno, Moravia (now in the Czech Republic), his teachers included **Alexander von Zemlinsky** in Vienna. From the age of 12, he achieved success there and throughout Germany as a composer of chamber, orchestral and stage works in the late Romantic vein. His most distinguished operas were *Violanta* (1916) and *Die tote Stadt* (1920, "The Dead City"). A professor at the Vienna State Academy of Music from 1930, he emigrated to Hollywood in 1934 (becoming a US citizen in 1943), and composed a series of film scores, two of which received Academy Awards. He was the son of the eminent music critic Julius Korngold (1860–1945).

Kornilov, Lavr Georgiyevich 1870–1918 •*Russian general*• Born in western Siberia, he was a Cossack. He was a divisional commander in World War I, tried to turn the tide against the Germans by an offensive in June 1917 and in August 1917 marched on Petrograd (now St Petersburg), in an attempt to set up a military directorate. He was forced to surrender by **Aleksandr Kerensky**, but subsequently escaped. Kornilov then organized a Cossack force against the Bolsheviks, but fell in battle.

Korolev, Sergei Pavlovich 1907–66 •*Soviet aircraft engineer and rocket designer*• Born in Zhitomir, Ukraine, he graduated from the Moscow Higher Technical School in 1929. He became a pilot and aircraft designer, and in 1931 he formed the group which launched the USSR's first liquid-propelled rocket in 1933. During World War II he worked on aircraft jet-assisted take-off systems. As chief designer of Soviet spacecraft he directed the USSR's space program with historic firsts such as the first orbiting Sputniks in 1957 and the first manned space flight (**Yuri Gagarin**) in 1961, the *Vostok* and *Voskhod* manned spacecraft, and the *Cosmos* series of satellites.

Kościuszko, Tadeusz Andrzej Bonawentura 1746–1817 •*US-Polish soldier and patriot*• Born near Slonim, Lithuania (now in Belarus) he was trained in the military academies in Warsaw and Paris. In 1776 he went to North America, where he fought for the colonists in the American Revolution (1775–83) and became a US citizen. He returned to Poland in 1784, and when Russia attacked in 1792 held Dubienka for five days, with 4,000 men against 18,000. In 1794, he took charge of a national uprising in Kraków, being appointed dictator and commander in chief. Despite defeating a greatly superior force of Russians at Racławice, he had to withdraw to Warsaw, and was later taken prisoner. Emperor Paul of Russia freed him in 1796. He went first to England, then to the US, and in 1798 to France. He settled in Switzerland in 1816.

Kosinski, Jerzy Nikodem 1933–91 •*US novelist*• Born in Łódź, Poland, into a Jewish family, he escaped becoming a victim of the Holocaust. He studied and taught at Łódź University before emigrating to the US (1957). His novels espouse a belief in survival at all costs, his characters machinating to make the most of a given situation. He wrote two polemical books, *The Future Is Ours, Comrade* (1960) and *No Third Path* (1962), under the pseudonym Joseph Novak. The trauma of war had rendered him (literally) speechless and his novels, particularly the quasiautobiographical *The Painted Bird* (1965), is a classic of Holocaust literature. Later works include *Being There* (1971), *Blind Date* (1977) and *Passion Play* (1979). He committed suicide in 1991.

Kossel, Albrecht 1853–1927 •*German physiological chemist and Nobel Prize winner*• Born in Rostock, Germany, he studied medicine at the University of Strasbourg and among other appointments became professor at the University of Heidelberg (1901–23). He investigated the chemistry of cells and proteins. He was able to explain that in a blood leukemia, the "guanide" found in the blood in large amounts derived from decomposed young nucleated erythrocytes. He also discovered histidine in spermatozoa (1896). In 1910 he was awarded the Nobel Prize for physiology or medicine.

Kossoff, Leon 1926– •*English painter*• Born in London, he studied at St Martin's School of Art, at the Borough Polytechnic, under **David Bomberg** (1949–53), and at the Royal College of Art (1953–56). Painting figures in interiors and views of London from the age of 12, he follows Bomberg and **Chaim Soutine** in his expressive style, using very thick impasto to portray bomb sites, building sites, railways, churches, schools, and even swimming pools. He often repeats subjects, such as *Christ Church, Spitalfields*, and his brother *Chaim*.

Kostunica, Vojislav 1944– •*Serbian politician*• Born in Belgrade, he was educated at Belgrade State University and lectured in law there until his expulsion in 1974. A Serbian nationalist and democrat, he emerged as a leading member of the opposition movement in the 1980s and was a founding member of the Democratic Party, but left in 1992 to form the Democratic Party of Serbia. A critic of President **Slobodan Milošević** and of NATO and US involvement in Yugoslavia, he was nominated to stand against Milošević for the presidency of Yugoslavia and became president.

Kosuth, Joseph 1945– •*US artist*• Born in Toledo, Ohio, he was trained in Toledo, Cleveland, and New York. Around 1965 he conceived the series which included *One and Three Chairs* (Museum of Modern Art, New York), where an object, a photograph of an object, and its dictionary definition were juxtaposed, the first of many such installations. From the early 1980s he focused on the writings of **Ludwig Wittgenstein** and **Sigmund Freud**. In 1991 he exhibited *The Play of the Unmentionable* (Brooklyn Museum), on the subject of censorship, followed in 1993 by *A Grammatical Remark* in Stuttgart.

Kosygin, Aleksei Nikolayevich 1904–80 •*Soviet politician*• He was born and educated in St Petersburg. A textile worker by training, he owed his advancement in the 1930s to the vacancies resulting from **Stalin**'s purges. Elected to the Supreme Soviet (1938), he held a variety of political industrial posts, and became a member of the politburo in 1948. He had a checkered career in the post–World War II period, falling in and out with both Stalin and **Nikita Khrushchev**. It was only when, in 1964, he succeeded the latter as Chairman of the Council of Ministers (or Prime Minister) that he could attempt serious, if decentralizing, reforms. However, he was blocked in the late 1960s by the party machine and the caution of **Leonid Brezhnev** and resigned in 1980.

Kotzebue, August Friedrich Ferdinand von 1761–1819 •*German dramatist*• Born in Weimar, he held various offices in the service of Russia, as well as writing plays, tales, satires and historical works. He quarreled with **Goethe** and satirized the leaders of the Romantic school. Among his 200 lively poetic dramas are *Menschenhass und Reue* (1788, Eng trans *The Stranger*, 1798), *Die Hussiten vor Naumburg* (1801, Eng trans *The Patriot Father*, 1830) and *Die beiden Klingsberge* (1799, Eng trans *Father and Son*, 1814). He was stabbed to death by a Jena student while on a mission from Emperor **Alexander I** to report on Western politics.

Koufax, Sandy (Sanford) 1935– •*US baseball player*• Born in Brooklyn, New York, he played for the Dodgers there, and then in Los Angeles. His short career (1955–66) reached its peak in the 1960s, and in 1963 he was named Most Valuable Player (MVP) when the Dodgers beat the New York Yankees in the World Series. In 1965 he again helped the Dodgers to a World Series victory over Minnesota. During his career he pitched four no-hitters, including a perfect game, and won the **Cy Young** award three times (1963, 1965, 1966). In 1966, aged only 31, he had to retire from baseball because of arthritis in his left elbow. He is considered one of the greatest pitchers in the history of the game.

Koussevitzky, Serge, *originally* **Sergei Alexandrovich Koussevitsky** 1874–1951 •*US conductor, composer and double-bass player*• Born in Vishny-Volotchok, Russia, after the Revolution he was director of the State Symphony Orchestra in Leningrad (now St Petersburg). He left the Soviet Union in 1920, and settled in 1924 in Boston, where he was the conductor of its symphony orchestra for 25 years. Throughout his life he championed new music. In Russia he performed and published **Prokofiev**, **Rachmaninov**, **Scriabin**, and **Stravinsky**, among others; in the US he commissioned and premiered many works which became 20th-century classics. He established the Berkshire Symphonic Festival (1934) and the Berkshire Music Center (1940) at Tanglewood, Massachusetts.

Krafft-Ebing, Richard, Freiherr von 1840–1902 •*German psychiatrist*• Born in Mannheim, he was professor at the Universities of Strasbourg and Vienna. Much of his work was on forensic psychiatry and sexual pathology (*Psychopathia Sexualis*, 1876).

Kramer, Dame Leonie Judith 1924– •*Australian academic, writer and administrator*•She was born in Melbourne and educated at the University of Melbourne and at St Hugh's College, Oxford. In 1968 she was appointed Professor of Australian Literature (now emerita) at Sydney University. She was the university's first female professor. As a scholar and critic she has held positions on a number of influential bodies, and she has been chairman of *Quadrant* magazine since 1988. She edited the *Oxford History of Australian Literature* (1981), coedited the companion *Oxford Anthology of Australian Literature* (1985), and edited volumes of poetry by David Campbell and **James McAuley**. She was Chancellor of the University of Sydney from 1991 to 2001 and was given the honorary title of Dame Commander, Order of the British Empire, in 1983.

Kramnik, Vladimir Borisovich 1975– •*Russian chess player*• Born in Tuapse, Krasnodar Territory, he started playing chess at the age of four and became world champion for the 16–18 age group in 1991, the year in which he was acclaimed a Grand Master. Winner of many major tournaments in the 1990s, he was ranked number one in the world by 1996 and in 2000 defeated **Garry Kasparov** in the world championship.

Kray, Ronnie (Ronald) 1933–95 and **Reggie (Reginald)** 1933–2000 •*English murderers and gang leaders*• Twin brothers, they were born in the East End of London, where they ran a criminal Mafia-style operation in the 1960s. Their gang or "firm" collected protection money, organized illegal gambling and drinking clubs and participated in gang warfare. Ronnie Kray, nicknamed "Colonel," was the dominant twin, who modeled himself on Chicago gangsters. In the late 1960s, Ronnie Kray shot dead a member of a rival gang and Reggie stabbed another to death. The twins were tried at the Old Bailey in 1969, found guilty and sentenced to imprisonment of not less than 30 years. Ronnie Kray died in prison; Reggie died two months after his release from prison on compassionate parole, following a diagnosis of terminal cancer.

Krebs, Sir Edwin Gerhard 1918– •*US biochemist and Nobel Prize winner*• Born in Lansing, Iowa, he joined the Howard Hughes Medical Institute (1977) and department of pharmacology at the University of Washington School of Medicine (1983), where he and **Edmond Fischer** built on **Carl Cori**'s work on the activation of glycogen enzymes to show that conversions to and from phosphorus compounds are involved, catalyzed by two enzymes. These initial findings led to the discovery of the cascade of enzymes that switches on glycogen phosphorylase and other enzymes under the influence of hormones such as glucagon and adrenaline (epinephrine). Similar systems controlled by other activators were also subsequently discovered. His later work covered the structure of the kinases and the properties of the phosphatases. With Fischer, Krebs was awarded the 1992 Nobel Prize for physiology or medicine. He was knighted in 1958.

Krebs, Sir Hans Adolf 1900–81 •*British biochemist and Nobel Prize winner*• Born in Hildesheim, Germany, he worked first in Berlin, before emigrating to Great Britain in 1934, where he worked with **Frederick Gowland Hopkins** on redox reactions. In 1932 he described the urea cycle whereby carbon dioxide and ammonia form urea in the presence of liver slices. Building on his earlier work, he elucidated the citric acid cycle (Krebs cycle) of energy production (c. 1943). He also carried out studies on acid oxidase, L-glutamine synthetase, purine synthesis in birds, and ketone bodies. In 1953 he shared with **Fritz Lipmann** the Nobel Prize for physiology or medicine for his discovery of the citric acid cycle.

Kreisky, Bruno 1911–90 •*Austrian politician*• Born in Vienna and educated at Vienna University, he joined the Social Democratic Party of Austria (SPO) as a young man and was imprisoned for his political activities from 1935 until he escaped to Sweden in 1938. He then returned to Austria and served in the Foreign Service (1946–51) and the Prime Minister's office (1951–53). In 1970, he became Prime Minister in a minority SPO government. After refusing to serve in a coalition in 1983, he resigned.

Kreisler, Fritz 1875–1962 •*US violinist*• Born in Vienna, Austria, he studied medicine and became an Uhlan officer. One of the most successful violin virtuosos of his time, he also composed violin pieces, a string quartet and an operetta, *Apple Blossoms* (1919), which was a Broadway success. He became a US citizen in 1943.

Kretzer, Max 1854–1941 •*German novelist*• He was born in Posen (now Poznań, Poland), and went to work in a factory at the age of 13. Wholly self-taught, his books include *Die Betrogenen* (1882, "The Duped"), which concerns poverty and prostitution, *Meister Timpe* (1888) and *Das Gesicht Christi* (1897, "The Face of Christ"). Essentially a writer on social problems and working people, he has, on account of his naturalism, been called the German **Zola**.

Kripke, Saul 1940– •*US philosopher and logician* • Born in Bay Shore, New York, he was educated at Harvard and has taught at Rockefeller University (1968–76) and Princeton University (from 1976, now emeritus). As a youthful prodigy he made remarkable technical advances in modal logic, whose wider philosophical implications were later explored in such famous papers as "Naming and Necessity" (1972).

Kristeva, Julia 1941– •*French theorist and critic*• Born in Bulgaria, she became a practicing psychoanalyst and began to question Western claims concerning philosophy, literary criticism, linguistics and politics. Her work focuses on language, literature and cultural history. *Desire in Language* (1977, Eng trans 1980) applies semiotics to literature and art. *Revolution in Poetic Language* (1974, Eng trans 1984) paved the way for a sociology of literature based on language. Her books *About Chinese Women* (1975, Eng trans 1976) and *Polylogue* (1977, Eng trans 1980) have brought her work to the forefront of feminist criticism.

Kristiansen, Ingrid, *née* **Ingrid Christensen** 1956– •*Norwegian athlete*• A former cross-country skiing champion, and then a long-distance runner, in 1985–86 she ran world best times for the 5,000 meters, 10,000 meters, and marathon. In 1986 she knocked 45.68 seconds off the world 10,000-meter record, and won the European title. She has won most of the world's major marathons, including London (1984–85, 1987–88), and was the world cross-country champion in 1988.

Kroeber, Alfred Louis 1876–1960 •*US cultural anthropologist*• Born in Hoboken, New Jersey, he studied at Columbia University, and went on to build up the anthropology department at the University of California at Berkeley (1901–46, professor from 1919). His primary influence lies in his concept of cultures as patterned wholes, each with its own "configuration" or "style," which undergo a process of growth or development analogous to that of an organism. His works include the highly influential *Anthropology* (1923) as well as *Cultural and Natural Areas of Native North America* (1939) and *Configurations of Natural Growth* (1944).

Kroemer, Herbert 1928– •*German physicist and Nobel Prize winner*• Born in Weimar, Germany, he was educated at the University of Göttingen. As Professor of Electrical and Computer Engineering at the University of California, Santa Barbara, he did pioneering work in semiconductor research. In 2000 he shared the Nobel Prize for physics with **Zhores I Alferov** and **Jack S Kilby** in recognition of his contribution to the development of fast transistors.

Krogh, (Schack) August (Steenberg) 1874–1949 •*Danish physiologist and Nobel Prize winner*• Born in Grenaa, he graduated with a PhD from the University of Copenhagen and worked there for the rest of his career on problems of respiration, then on the capillary system. He showed that blood flow through capillaries is determined by the activity of the surrounding muscle, rather than simply by blood pressure. He won the Nobel Prize for physiology or medicine in 1920 for this discovery, and later showed that the capillaries are under nervous and hormonal control.

Kronecker, Leopold 1823–91 •*German mathematician*• Born in Liegnitz, he obtained his doctorate at the University of Berlin (1845). He worked in algebraic number theory, elliptic functions and the foundations of analysis, and lectured widely. He was involved in a controversy with **Karl Weierstrass** and **Georg Cantor** over the use of the infinite in mathematics, as he believed that mathematics should be essentially based on the arithmetic of whole numbers.

“ ”

God made the integers, man made the rest.

Quoted in F Cajori ***A History of Mathematics*** *(1919).*

Kropotkin, Prince Peter, *Russian* **Knyaz Pyotr Alekseyevich Kropotkin** 1842–1921 •*Russian geographer and revolutionary*• Born in Moscow, he was educated at the Corps of Pages, St Petersburg (1857). After five years of service and exploration in Siberia, he returned to Moscow to study mathematics, while he also worked as secretary to the Geographical Society. In 1872, critical of the limited nature of reform in Russia, he became involved with extremist politics. Arrested and imprisoned in 1874 in Russia, he escaped to England in 1876 and then to Switzerland and France. He was condemned in Lyons in 1883 to five years' imprisonment for anarchism, but, released in 1886, he settled in England and then returned to Russia in 1917. Well known for his *Memoirs of a Revolutionist* (1900), he wrote widely on anarchism, social justice, and many topics in biology, literature and history.

Kroto, Sir Harold Walter 1939– •*English chemist and Nobel Prize winner*• Born in Wisbech, Cambridgeshire, and educated at the University of Sheffield, he held positions as the National Research Council, Ottawa, and at the Bell Telephone Laboratories, New Jersey. Kroto is noted for his work in detecting unstable molecules through the use of methods such as microwave and photoelectron spectroscopy. In 1985, together with his coworkers **Robert Curl** and **Richard Smalley** at Rice University, Texas, he discovered the third allotrope of carbon C_{60}, known as buckminsterfullerene (familiarly buckyballs), because its football shape resembles the buildings designed by the architect **Buckminster Fuller**. Kroto became Royal Society Research Professor at the University of Sussex in 1991, having been appointed Professor of Chemistry there in 1985. In 1996 he was joint recipient, with Curl and Smalley, of the Nobel Prize for chemistry, and was awarded a knighthood.

Kruger, Paul, *in full* **Stephanus Johannes Paulus Kruger** 1825–1904 •*South African politician*• Born in Colesberg in Cape Colony, he was a Boer. He trekked to Natal, the Orange Free State, and the Transvaal, and in the First Boer War (1880–81) he was appointed head of the provisional government. He was elected president of the Transvaal, or South African Republic, in 1883, and again in 1888, 1893 and 1898. “Oom Paul” (Uncle Paul) governed the Second Boer War of 1899–1902, but after the tide had turned against the Boers, went to Europe to seek (in vain) alliances against Great Britain. He made his headquarters in Utrecht, and published *The Memoirs of Paul Kruger, Told by Himself* (1902).

Krupp, Alfred 1812–87 •*German arms manufacturer*• Born in Essen, at the age of 14 he succeeded his father Friedrich (1787–1826), who had founded a small iron forge there in 1810, and began manufacturing arms in 1837. At the Great Exhibition in London (1851) he showcased a solid flawless ingot of cast steel weighing 4,000 kg. He established the first **Bessemer** steel plant and became the foremost arms supplier not only to Germany but to any country in the world, his first steel gun being manufactured in 1847.

Krupp (von Bohlen und Halbach), Alfried Alwin Felix 1907–67 •*German industrialist*• Born in Essen, he graduated from Aachen Technical College, became an honorary member of **Hitler**'s SS, and in 1943 succeeded his father, **Gustav Krupp**, to the Krupp empire. He was arrested (1945) and convicted (1947) with 11 fellow directors by a US military tribunal for plunder in Nazi-occupied territories and for employing slave labor under inhuman concentration camp conditions. He was sentenced to 12 years' imprisonment and his property was to be confiscated. By an amnesty (1951) he was released and his property restored, and he went on to play a prominent part in the West German economic miracle, building factories in Turkey, Pakistan, India and the Soviet Union. In 1959 he belatedly agreed to pay some compensation to former victims of forced labor. His son Arndt succeeded him.

Krupp, Gustav, *originally* **Gustav von Bohlen und Halbach** 1870–1950 •*German industrialist and arms manufacturer*• He was born in The Hague. In 1906 he married Bertha Krupp (1886–1957), daughter of Friedrich Alfred Krupp (1854–1902) and granddaughter of **Alfred Krupp**, and by special imperial edict he was allowed to adopt the name “Krupp” (inserted before the “von”). He took over the firm, gained the monopoly of German arms manufacture during World War I and manufactured the long-range siege gun nicknamed “Big Bertha.” He supported **Hitler** financially and connived in secret rearmament, contrary to the Versailles Treaty, after Hitler's rise to power in 1933. After World War II he was too senile to stand trial as a war criminal at Nuremberg.

Krupskaya, Nadezhda Konstantinova 1869–1939 •*Russian revolutionary*• A Marxist activist, she met **Lenin** in 1894. She was sentenced to exile about the same time as he was and allowed to join him in Siberia in 1898 on condition that they get married. Thereafter they were inseparable, and she acted as his agent and organizer. Following the Bolshevik Revolution, she was mainly active in promoting education and the status of women. As Lenin's widow, she at first opposed **Stalin** but later supported some of his policies, and was accordingly exploited. She left a rather brief *Reminiscences of Lenin*.

Kubelik, Rafael (Jeronym) 1914–96 •*Swiss conductor*• Born in Bychory (now in the Czech Republic), he was the son of the violin virtuoso Jan Kubelik (1880–1940). He studied at the Prague Conservatory, and first conducted the Czech Philharmonic Orchestra before he was 20. He was later conductor of the Chicago Symphony Orchestra (1950–53), at Covent Garden (1955–58) and from 1961 with the Bavarian Radio Orchestra. He composed two operas, symphonies, concertos, and other works.

Kubitschek (de Oliveira), Juscelino 1902–76 •*Brazilian politician*• He was born in Diamantina, Minas Gerais, the grandson of a Czech immigrant. He studied medicine in Belo Horizonte, Minas Gerais, and went on to become mayor of the city (1940–45). He was elected to Congress by the Social Democratic Party (PSD) in 1945 and was governor of Minas Gerais in 1951–55. As president (1956–61), his ambitious program emphasized transportation, energy, manufacturing and the building of a new capital, Brasília, rather than social measures, and was the blueprint for subsequent programs during military rule. The political necessity for high gross domestic product (GDP) growth rates hampered any effective counterinflationary policies, leaving massive problems for the subsequent governments.

Kublai Khan, *also spelt* **Kubla** 1214–94 •*Great Khan of the Mongols from 1260 and emperor of China from 1271*• Kublai Khan was the grandson of **Genghis Khan**. He was an energetic ruler, and completed his grandfather's conquest of northern China. He suppressed his rivals, adopted the Chinese mode of civilization, encouraged men of letters, and made Buddhism the state religion. An attempt to invade Japan ended in disaster. He established himself at Cambaluc (modern Beijing), the first foreigner ever to rule in China. His dominions extended from the Arctic Ocean to the Straits of Malacca, and from Korea to Asia Minor and the confines of Hungary. The splendor of his court inspired the graphic pages of **Marco Polo**, who spent 17 years in the service of Kublai, and at a later date fired the imagination of **Samuel Taylor Coleridge**.

Kubrick, Stanley 1928–99 •*US screenwriter, film producer and director*• Born in the Bronx, New York, he made his directorial debut with the documentary *Day of the Fight* (1950), and established his reputation with the thriller *The Killing* (1956) and the antiwar drama *Paths of Glory* (1958). He tackled a wide variety of subjects, painstakingly preparing each new film and shrouding his work in secrecy. Noted for his mastery of technique and visual composition, he was often criticized for an increasingly extravagant approach to his material. Resident in England from 1961, notable films include *Lolita* (1962), *Dr. Strangelove* (1963), *2001: A Space Odyssey* (1968), *A Clockwork Orange* (1971), *Barry Lyndon* (1975), *The Shining* (1980) and *Full Metal Jacket* (1987). After a 12-year absence, he returned to films with *Eyes Wide Shut* (1999).

Kučan, Milan 1941– •*Slovenian politician*• He was born in Krizevci and educated at Ljubljana University. During the late

1980s, as the communist President of Slovenia, he allowed the emergence of opposition parties in his republic. In 1990, after the Slovenes held the first free elections anywhere in Yugoslavia since World War II, he was reelected as nonparty president of Slovenia. He declared Slovenia's secession from the Yugoslav Federation in July 1991. With the backing of Serbia's President, **Slobodan Milošević**, Yugoslav Federal army units attacked Slovenia, but Milošević was obliged to withdraw and to accept Slovenia's independence. He was reelected in 1992 and 1998.

Kuhn, Richard 1900–67 •*German chemist and Nobel Prize winner*• Born in Vienna-Döbling, Austria, he studied at the University of Vienna and Munich. In 1926 he moved to Zurich, and in 1929 to the Kaiser Wilhelm Institute for Medical Research in Heidelberg. His early work on enzymes led to an interest in problems of stereochemistry and his research on conjugated polyenes led to important studies on carotenoids and vitamin A. Later work on vitamins B_2 and B_6 and on 4-aminobenzoic acid earned him the 1938 Nobel Prize for chemistry. He was forbidden by the Nazi government to accept the award, but it was presented to him after World War II.

Kuiper, Gerard Peter 1905–73 •*US astronomer*• Born in Harenkarspel, the Netherlands, and educated in Leiden, he moved to the US in 1933. After appointments at a number of major observatories, from 1960 he worked at the Lunar and Planetary Laboratory of the University of Arizona. In 1941 Kuiper pioneered the study of contact binary stars and he also suggested a system of spectroscopic classification of white dwarf stars. He discovered two new satellites: Miranda, the fifth satellite of Uranus; and Nereid, the second satellite of Neptune (1948–49). In 1951 he proposed that there is a flattened belt of some thousand million comets (now known as the Kuiper belt) just beyond the orbit of Pluto. In 1944 he detected methane on Titan and became the first to confirm that a planetary satellite had an atmosphere. A Lockheed C-141 jet aircraft fitted with an infrared telescope has been named the Kuiper Airborne Observatory and his name has also been given to the 7,500-angstrom bands in the spectrum of Neptune and Uranus. He was involved with the early US space flights, including the *Ranger* and *Mariner* missions.

Kumaratunga, Chandrika Bandaranaike 1945– •*Sri Lankan politician*• Born in Colombo, she was educated at the University of Paris. In 1974 she was elected to the Women's League of the Sri Lankan Freedom Party. In 1986 she became leader of the People's Party and was elected president of Sri Lanka in 1994. Although she was able to institute a number of land reforms, her period of office was marred by the bitter civil war fought by Tamil separatists in the north. She was reelected in 1999, surviving an assassination attempt during the election campaign.

Kummer, Ernst Eduard 1810–93 •*German mathematician*• Born in Sorau, he studied at the University of Halle, and then taught at the gymnasium in Liegnitz (1832–42). Following important work on the hypergeometric series, he was elected a member of the Berlin Academy of Sciences in 1839, and was later appointed Professor of Mathematics at the University of Breslau (1842–55) and subsequently at the University of Berlin (from 1855). He worked in number theory, where he gained a significant insight into **Pierre de Fermat**'s last theorem, proving it rigorously for many new cases, and in the process introduced the "ideal numbers." He also worked on differential equations and in geometry, where he discovered the quartic surface now named after him.

Kun, Béla 1886–c. 1937 •*Hungarian political leader and revolutionary*• Born in Szlágycseh, Transylvania, he was a journalist, soldier and prisoner in Russia, and in 1918 founded the Hungarian Communist Party. In March 1919 he organized a Communist revolution in Budapest and set up a Soviet republic which succeeded **Karolyi**'s government. It failed to gain popular support, and he was forced to flee for his life in August of that year. After escaping to Vienna he returned to Russia. He is believed to have been killed in a Stalinist purge.

Kundera, Milan 1929– •*Czech-born French novelist*• Born in Brno (now in the Czech Republic), he was educated in Prague at Charles University and the Academy of Music and Dramatic Arts Film Faculty, and worked as a laborer and a jazz musician before devoting himself to literature. For several years he was a professor at the Prague Institute for Advanced Cinematographic Studies. *Žert* (Eng trans, *The Joke*, 1969), his first novel, was published in 1967. After the Russian invasion in 1968 he lost his post and his books were proscribed. In 1975 he settled in France and took French citizenship. The publication in 1979 of *Kniha smichu a zapomnění* (Eng trans *The Book of Laughter and Forgetting*, 1980) prompted the revocation of his Czech citizenship, but in exile he has emerged as one of the major European writers of the late 20th century. Other novels include *Nesnesitelná lehkost bytí* (1984, Eng trans *The Unbearable Lightness of Being*, 1984), *Immortality* (1991), and *L'Identité* (1998, Eng trans *Identity*). He has also published a critical work, *Umění romanu* (1960, Eng trans *The Art of the Novel*, 1988).

Küng, Hans 1928– •*Swiss Roman Catholic theologian*• Born in Sursee, Lucerne, he became a professor in Tübingen in 1960, and has written extensively for fellow theologians and for lay people. His questioning of received interpretations of Catholic doctrine, as in *Unfehlbar?* (1971, Eng trans *Infallible?*), and his presentations of the Christian faith, as in *Christ sein* (1977, Eng trans *On Being a Christian*) aroused controversy both in Germany and with the Vatican authorities, who withdrew his license to teach as a Catholic theologian in 1979. He defended himself in *Why I Am Still a Christian* (1987).

Kunitz, Stanley Jasspon 1905– •*US poet*• Born in Worcester, Massachusetts, he was educated at Harvard University. A literature academic, he taught poetry at the New School for Social Research in New York City (1950–57) and Columbia University (1963–85). His first collection of verse was *Intellectual Things* (1930). *Selected Poems 1928–1958* was awarded a Pulitzer Prize in 1959. Subsequent books include *The Testing-Tree* (1971) and *Passing Through* (1995). He has also published literary reference books and translated several volumes of Russian poetry. In 2000 he became the US Poet Laureate.

Kupka, Frank (Frantisek) 1871–1957 •*Czech painter*• Born in Opocno (now in the Czech Republic), he entered the Academy of Prague in 1889. Moving to Paris in 1895, he worked as an illustrator and pursued his interest in theosophy and the occult, before meeting the Cubists. With **Wassily Kandinsky**, he was one of the pioneers of pure abstraction, a style called Orphism.

Kurchatov, Igor Vasilevich 1903–60 •*Soviet physicist*• Born in Sim, Russia, and educated at the University of Crimea, he became interested around 1932 in the study of the atomic nucleus in work at the Leningrad Physical-Technical Institute, where he supervised the construction of a cyclotron. He carried out important studies of neutron reactions and was the leading figure in the building of the USSR's first nuclear fission (1949) and hydrogen bombs (1953), and the world's first industrial nuclear power plant (1954). He became a member of the Supreme Soviet in 1949.

Kureishi, Hanif 1954– •*English author*• Born in London, he was educated at the University of London, and won widespread recognition for his screenplay *My Beautiful Laundrette* (1986). It was followed by successes such as the screenplay *Sammy and Rosie Get Laid* (1988) and the television play *The Buddha of Suburbia* (1993), originally written as a novel (1990). Among his other novels is *Gabriel's Gift* (2001). He has also written short stories, criticism and reviews.

Kurosawa, Akira 1910–98 •*Japanese film director*• Born in Tokyo, his first feature film was *Sanshiro Sugata* (1943, *Judo Saga*). He often adapted the techniques of the Noh theater to filmmaking, such as in *Rashomon* (1950), which won the Venice Film Festival prize, and *The Seven Samurai* (1954), an uncompromisingly savage view of the samurai code. Also characteristic are his literary adaptations, such as *The Throne of Blood* (1957, from **Shakespeare**'s *Macbeth*). His Siberian epic *Dersu Uzala* (1975) won an Academy Award as Best Foreign Film. Later films include *Kagemushi* (1980, "Shadow Warrior"), *Ran* (1985, "Chaos"), and *Rhapsody in August* (1991).

" "

Like a steak spread with butter and topped with good, rich, broiled eels.

1965 His concept of a great film. In ***Japan Quarterly****, volume 12.*

Kusch, Polykarp 1911–93 •*US physicist and Nobel Prize winner*• Born in Blankenburg, Germany, he became a naturalized US citizen in 1922, and studied at the Case Institute of Technology, Cleveland, and University of Illinois. Later he became Professor of Physics at Columbia University (1937–72) and at the University of Texas (1972–82). With **Isidor Rabi**, Kusch investigated **Samuel Goudsmit** and **George Uhlenbeck**'s theory that the electron has a magnetic moment. With the experimental results of **Willis Lamb**, this led to the reformulation of quantum electrodynamics by **Richard Feynman**, **Julian Schwinger** and **Sin-Itiro Tomonaga**. Kusch shared with Lamb the 1955 Nobel Prize for physics for his precise determination of the electron's magnetic moment. He retired in 1982.

Kushner, Tony 1956– •*US playwright*• Born in New York City and raised in Lake Charles, Louisiana, he was educated at Columbia University and New York University. His plays are highly political and are informed by an acute sense of historical awareness. *Yes, Yes, No, No* (1985) was followed by several more plays before the appearance of his epic *Angels in America*, which tells of the catastrophic effects of AIDS in New York, and was awarded the 1993 Pulitzer Prize for drama. Its two parts, running to almost seven hours, are *Millennium Approaches* (1991) and *Perestroika* (1992). Subsequent works include *Slavs!* (1995) and *Henry Box Brown* (1997).

Kutuzov, Mikhail Harionovich, Prince of Smolensk 1745–1813 •*Russian soldier*• He fought in Poland and in the Turkish wars, and from 1805 to 1812 was in command against the French. In 1812, as Commander in Chief he fought **Napoleon I** at Borodino, and later obtained a great victory over **Davout** and **Ney** at Smolensk. His army pursued the retreating French out of Russia into Prussia.

Kuyper, Abraham 1837–1920 •*Dutch theologian and politician*• Born in Maassluis, he was a pastor and founder of the Free University of Amsterdam (1880). He became a member of the Dutch parliament and prime minister (1900–05). He founded two newspapers and wrote numerous books, few of which have been translated into English, apart from *Lectures on Calvinism* (1898), *Principles of Sacred Theology* (1898), and *The Work of the Holy Spirit* (1900). His theology offered a Calvinistic version of Christian socialism. In the Netherlands he is remembered as the emancipator of the orthodox Calvinists and also as the founder of the Antirevolutionary Party.

Kuznets, Simon Smith 1901–85 •*US economic statistician and Nobel Prize winner*• Born in Pinsk, Ukraine, he emigrated to the US in 1922, studied at Columbia, and examined business cycles for the National Bureau of Economic Research from 1927. He was Professor of Economics at the University of Pennsylvania (1930–54), Johns Hopkins (1954–60) and Harvard (1960–71). His ideas on economic growth and social change include the 20-year Kuznets cycle of economic growth. He was awarded the Nobel Prize for economics in 1971.

Kwan, Michelle, *originally* **Kwan Shan Wing** 1980– •*US ice skater*• Born in Torrance, California, she began skating at age five and in 1992, at age 13, was a reserve for the US Olympic team. Having finished fourth in the world figure-skating championships in 1993, she became world champion in 1996, 1998, and 2000. Her autobiography, *Michelle Kwan, Heart of a Champion*, appeared in 1997.

Kyd, Thomas 1558–94 •*English dramatist*• Born in London, he was probably educated at Merchant Taylors' School, and was most likely brought up as a scrivener under his father. He wrote tragedies, which brought him a reputation early, especially *The Spanish Tragedy* (c. 1587), and he perhaps also produced *Solyman and Perseda* (1592) and *Arden of Faversham*. He has been credited with a share in other plays, and some claim he wrote the lost original *Hamlet*. Imprisoned in 1593 on a charge of atheism, which he tried to shift onto **Christopher Marlowe**'s shoulders, **Ben Jonson**'s "sporting Kyd" died in poverty.

Kylian, Jiří 1947– •*Czech dancer and choreographer*• Born in Prague, he was trained at the Prague Conservatory, and was given a scholarship (1967) to study in London at the Royal Ballet School. He began his prolific choreographic career in 1970, becoming artistic director at the Netherlands Dance Theater (NDT) from 1975 to 1999 and later its resident choreographer and adviser. His works include *Sinfonietta* with music by **Janáček** (1979), the all-male *Soldiers' Mass* (1980), *Return to the Strange Land* (1975), *Kaguya-Hine* (1988) and, based on Aboriginal culture, *Nomads* (1981) and *Dreamtime* (1983).

Kyprianou, Spyros 1932–2002 •*Cypriot politician*• Born in Limassol, where he attended the Greek Gymnasium, he continued his education at the City of London College, and was called to the bar in 1954. During that period he founded the Cypriot Students' Union and became its first president. He was secretary to Archbishop **Makarios** in London in 1952, and returned with him to Cyprus in 1959. He was foreign minister (1961–72), and in 1976 founded the Democratic Front (DIKO). On Makarios's death in 1977 he became acting president, and then president. He was re-elected in 1978 and 1983, but was defeated by **Georgios Vassilou** in 1988.

Laban, Rudolf von 1879–1958 •*Hungarian dancer, choreographer and dance theoretician*• Born in Pozsony (now Bratislava, Slovakia), he studied ballet, acting and painting in Paris and later danced in Vienna and all over Germany, and toured Europe and Northern Africa. In 1910 he founded a school in Munich, and went on to work as a choreographer and teacher throughout Germany. He started many European schools, theaters and institutions as well as heading an organization of amateur "movement choirs" throughout Germany. As early as 1920 he published the first of several volumes of his influential system of dance notation, now known as Labanotation.

Lacaille, Nicolas Louis de 1713–62 •*French astronomer*• Born in Rumigny, he became a deacon before taking up astronomy. At the age of 26 he became Professor of Mathematics at the Collège Mazarin (now the Institut de France, Paris). He worked on the problem of the Earth's shape, and from 1750 to 1754 he visited the Cape of Good Hope, where he was the first to measure a South African arc of the meridian. He charted 14 new constellations and compiled the first list of 42 "nebulous stars." His *Coelum australe stelliferum* ("Star Catalog of the Southern Sky") was published in 1763.

Lacan, Jacques 1901–81 •*French psychoanalyst*• Born in Paris, he studied forensic psychiatry at the Faculté de Médecine de Paris and spent much of his life as a practicing psychiatrist. Through his many writings and the École Freudienne in Paris that he founded in 1964, Lacan was largely responsible for introducing Freudian practices to France. His explorations of structural linguistics proved highly influential and emphasized the importance of language as the central means of investigating the unconscious, particularly in relation to childhood development.

Lackland, John *See* **John, King**

Laclos, Pierre Ambroise François Choderlos de 1741–1803 •*French novelist and politician*• Born in Amiens, he spent nearly all his life in the army but saw no active service until he was 60 and ended his career as a general. He is remembered by his one masterpiece, *Les liaisons dangereuses* (1782, Eng trans *Dangerous Connections*, 1784). This epistolary novel reveals the influence of **Jean Jacques Rousseau** and **Samuel Richardson** and is a cynical, detached analysis of personal and sexual relationships, influenced by his own profound feminism. He also wrote *De l'éducation des femmes* (1785, "On the Education of Women").

Lacroix, Christian 1951– •*French couturier*• He was born in Arles, Provence, the son of an engineer who sketched women and their clothes. He started sketching as a child and studied Classics in Montpellier, specializing in French and Italian painting and the history of costume. In 1981 he joined **Jean Patou**, who showed his first collection in 1982, but in 1987 he left to open The House of Lacroix in Paris. Lacroix made his name with ornate and frivolous clothes. In 1991 he was made Chevalier, L'Ordre des Arts et des Lettres, and in 1992 he published his autobiography, *Pieces of a Pattern*.

Lactantius, Lucius Caelius, *also called* **Firmianus Caecilius** 4th century AD •*North African Christian apologist*• Born and raised in North Africa, he was a teacher of rhetoric in Nicomedia in Bithynia, where he was converted to Christianity. About AD 313 he was invited to Gaul by **Constantine I** to act as tutor to his son Crispus. His principal work is his *Divinarum institutionum libri vii* ("Seven Books of Divine Institutions"), a systematic account of Christian attitudes to life.

Ladislas *See* **Władysław IV**

Laestadius, Lars Levi 1800–61 •*Swedish priest and botanist*• Born in Arjeplog, he became in 1826 the parson in Karesuando, where he continued his botanical work. After a profound spiritual crisis in the early 1840s he began the ecstatic revivalist preaching that had great influence among the Sami (Lapps). Today there are some 300,000 Laestadians in Finland and 20,000 in Sweden.

Lafayette, Marie Joseph Paul Yves Roch Gilbert du Motier, Marquis de 1757–1834 •*French soldier and revolutionary*• Born in Chavagnac into an ancient noble family, he spent a period at court before going to America, where he fought against the British during the American Revolution (1777–79 and 1780–82) and became a hero and a friend of **George Washington**. A liberal aristocrat, in the National Assembly of 1789 he presented a draft of a Declaration of the Rights of Man, based on the US Declaration of Independence. During the Restoration he sat in the Chamber of Deputies (1818–24), became a radical Leader of the Opposition (1825–30), and commanded the National Guard in the 1830 July Revolution.

La Fayette, Marie Madeleine Pioche de Lavergne, Comtesse de, *known as* **Madame de La Fayette** 1634–93 •*French novelist and reformer of French romance writing*• She was born in Paris. Having married the Comte de La Fayette in 1655, and in her 33rd year formed a liaison with **François La Rochefoucauld**, she played a leading part at the French court, as was proved by her *Lettres inédites* (1880, "Unabridged Letters"); prior to their publication, it was believed that her last years were given to religious devotion. Her masterpiece is *La Princesse de Clèves* (1678, Eng trans *The Princess of Clèves*, 1679), a study in conflict between love and marriage in the court life of her day, which led a reaction against the long-winded romances of, for example, **Madeleine de Scudéry**.

La Fontaine, Jean de 1621–95 •*French poet*• Born in Château-Thierry, Champagne, he devoted himself to studying the old writers and to writing verse. In 1654 he published a verse translation of the *Eunuchus* of **Terence**. He is best known for *Contes et nouvelles en vers* (1665–74, "Stories and Tales in Verse") and *Fables choisies mises en vers* (1668–93, Eng trans *Fables*, 1804). In 1684 he presented *Discours en vers* ("An Oration in Verse") on his reception by the Academy.

“ ”

Un auteur gâte tout quand il veut trop bien faire.
An author spoils everything when he wants too much to do good.
1668 ***Fables****, part 5, no. 1, "Le bûcheron et Mercure."*

Lafontaine, Oskar 1943– •*German Social Democrat politician*• Born in Saarlouis and educated at the University of Bonn, he was chairman (1977–96) of the Saarland regional branch of the Social Democratic Party (SPD) and served as mayor of Saarbrücken (1976–85). He gained a reputation for radicalism and was variously dubbed "Red Oskar" and the "Ayatollah of the Saarland." He began to mellow, however, after his election as prime minister of the Saarland regional parliament (1985–98), and was later leader of the SPD (1995–99) and president of the SPD-controlled Bundesrat, or upper chamber (1995–96). He was also Germany's finance minister (1998–99).

Lagerfeld, Karl-Otto 1938– •*German fashion designer*• Born in Hamburg, he attended art school there before becoming a fashion apprentice with Balmain and Patou from 1959. He joined Chloe in the early sixties and then moved to Chanel as director of collections and ready-to-wear in 1983. His own-name label was founded the same year. His reputation rests on his meticulous cut and use of furs, knitwear and bright colors.

Lagerkvist, Pär Fabian 1891–1974 •*Swedish novelist, poet, playwright and Nobel Prize winner*•He was born in Växjö, and educated in Uppsala. He began his literary career first as a prose writer and then as an Expressionist poet with *Ångest* (1916, "Angst") and *Kaos* (1918, "Chaos"), in which he emphasizes the catastrophe of war. Later, in the face of extremist creeds and slogans, he adopted a critical humanism with the (later dramatized) novel *Bödeln* (1933, "The Hangman") and *Dvärgen* (1944, "The Dwarf"). Man's search for God was also explored in the play *Mannen utan själ* (1936, "The Man Without a Soul"), and *Lät människan leva* (1949, "Let Man Live"), was a study of political terrorism in which Jesus, **Socrates**, **Bruno**, **Joan of Arc** and an African American appear as victims. He was awarded the Nobel Prize for literature in 1951.

Lagerlöf, Selma Ottiliaa Lovisa 1858–1940 •*Swedish novelist, the first woman winner of the Nobel Prize for literature*• Born in Värmland, she taught at Landskrona (1885–95), and first sprang to fame with her novel *Gösta Berlings saga* (1891, "The Story of Gösta Berling"), which was based on the traditions and legends of her native countryside, as were many of her later books, such as her trilogy on the Löwensköld family (1925–28, Eng trans *The Rings of the Lowenskolds*, 1931). She also wrote the children's classic *Nils Holgerssons underbara resa genom Sverige* (1906–07, "The Wonderful Adventures of Nils"). Although she was a member of the Neo-Romantic generation of the 1890s, her work is characterized by a social and moral seriousness, as in *Antikrists Mirakler* (1897, "The Miracles of Anti-Christ") and *Bannlyst* (1918, "The Outcast"). She was awarded the 1909 Nobel Prize for literature.

Lagrange, Joseph Louis de, Comte 1736–1813 •*French mathematician*• Born in Turin, Italy, he succeeded **Leonhard Euler** (1766) as director of the mathematical section of the Berlin Academy, having gained a European reputation by his research into the calculus of variations, celestial mechanics and the nature of sound. He returned to Paris in 1787 at the invitation of **Louis XVI**. Under **Napoleon I** he became a senator and a count and taught at the École Normale and the École Polytechnique. In 1788 he published *Traité de mécanique analytique*, one of his most important works, in which mechanics is based entirely on variational principles, giving it a high degree of elegance. His work on the theory of algebraic equations was one of the major steps in the early development of group theory, considering permutations of the roots of an equation.

La Guardia, Fiorello H(enry) 1882–1947 •*US lawyer and politician*• Born in New York City of Italian-Jewish origin, he became deputy attorney-general of New York (1915–17), served with the US Air Force in Italy and sat in the House of Representatives (1917–21, 1923–33) as a Republican. A popular Mayor of New York (reelected three times, 1933–45), he was one of the early opponents of **Hitler**'s anti-Semitic policies—he had his ears boxed in public by enraged US Fascists—and was civil administrator of Allied-occupied Italy. In 1946 he was appointed director general of the United Nations Relief and Rehabilitation Agency. One of New York City's airports is named after him.

Lahiri, Jhumpa 1967– •*US author*• She was born in London of Bengali parents, moved to the US at an early age, and studied at Boston University. Her first short stories were widely praised and received several awards, but her reputation was made by *The Interpreter of Maladies* (1999), a collection of stories set in India and New England, which won the Pulitzer Prize in 2000.

Laine, Dame Cleo, *originally* **Clementina Dinah Campbell** 1927– •*English jazz musician and actress*• Born in Southall, Middlesex, she began by singing with the big band of her husband-to-be **John Dankworth**, who was a founding member of the legendary Club 11 (1948). She became a highly successful singer, also winning roles in musical theater and in straight acting. Dankworth later acted as her musical director and assumed a less prominent public role, concentrating on composition and arrangement. She was given the honorary title of Dame Commander, Order of the British Empire, in 1997.

Laing, R(onald) D(avid) 1927–89 •*Scottish psychiatrist*• Born in Glasgow, he graduated in medicine from Glasgow University (1951), and then practiced as a psychiatrist in the city (1953–56). He joined the Tavistock Clinic, London, in 1957 and the Tavistock Institute for Human Relations in 1960, and was chairman of the Philadelphia Association (1964–82). He sprang to prominence with his revolutionary ideas about mental disorder with the publication of *The Divided Self* (1960). His principal thesis was that psychiatrists should not attempt to cure or ameliorate the symptoms of mental illness (a term which he repudiated) but rather should encourage patients to view themselves as going through an enriching experience. His writings extended from psychiatry into existential philosophy, and later into poetry. His other books include *The Politics of Experience* (1967), *Knots* (1970), *The Politics of the Family* (1976), *Sonnets* (1980) and *The Voice of Experience* (1982).

Lajpat Rai, Lala 1865–1928 •*Indian politician and writer*•He was a follower of the militant Hindu sect the Arya Samaj (Society of Nobles) and when, in 1893, it split, he and Hans Raj led the moderate "college faction" which concentrated on building up a chain of "Dayanand Anglo-Vedic colleges." Arguing that Congress should openly and boldly base itself on the Hindus alone, he led a wave of nationalism in Punjab (1904–07). The Congress split in the Surat session in 1907 and he formed the famous "extremist" trio of Lal, Pal and Bal, with **B G Tilak** and **Bipin Chandra Pal**. Deported on charges of inciting the peasants, he led the Non-Cooperation Movement in Punjab in 1921.

Laker, Sir Freddie (Frederick Alfred) 1922– •*English business executive*• Born in Kent and educated at Simon Langton School, Canterbury, he was a member of the Air Transport Auxiliary (1941–46) and a manager with British United Airways (1960–65). He was chairman and managing director of Laker Airways Ltd (1966–82), then chairman of Laker Airways (Bahamas) Ltd (1992–). His career suffered due to the failure of the Skytrain project in 1982, but in 1995 he founded Laker Airways Inc, which by 1997 ran a daily transatlantic flight (Gatwick-Miami).

Lalique, René 1860–1945 •*French jeweler and designer*•Born in Ay, he established a jewelry firm (1885) in Paris, producing Art Nouveau styles. He was also an artist-craftsman in glass, which he decorated with relief figures, animals and flowers.

Lam, Wilfredo 1902–82 •*Cuban painter*•Born in Sagua la Grande, he held his first solo show in Madrid in 1928. In 1938, in Paris, he met **Picasso**, who became his friend, and in 1940 the surrealist **André Breton**. Lam fused Latin-American, African and Oceanic elements with the forms and conventions of the European modern movement, as in *The Jungle* (1943). He won the Guggenheim International award in 1964.

Lamarck, Jean-Baptiste Pierre Antoine de Monet Chevalier de 1744–1829 •*French naturalist and evolutionist*• He was born in Bazentin. He became interested in Mediterranean flora, and while holding a post in a Paris bank began to study medicine and botany. In 1774 he became keeper of the royal garden (afterward the nucleus of the Jardin des Plantes), and from 1794 he was keeper of invertebrates at the newly formed Natural History Museum. He lectured on zoology, originating the taxonomic distinction between vertebrates and invertebrates. About 1801 he had begun to think about the relations between and origin of species, expressing his conclusions in his famous *Philosophie zoologique* (2 vols, 1809, Eng trans *Zoological Philosophy*, 1963) in which he postulated that acquired characteristics can be inherited by later generations. Lamarck broke with the old notion of immutable species, recognizing that species needed to adapt to survive environmental changes, and thus he prepared the way for the now accepted theory of evolution.

Lamartine, Alphonse Marie Louis de 1790–1869 •*French poet, politician and historian*•Born in Mâcon, he was brought up on ultraroyalist principles, spent much of his youth in Italy, and on the fall of **Napoleon I** joined the garde royale. His first, and probably his best-known and most successful volume of poems, the *Méditations*, was published in 1820. In 1829 he declined the post of Foreign Secretary in the **Bourbon** ministry of the Prince de Polignac and, with another series of poems, *Harmonies poétiques et religieuses* (1829, "Poetical and Religious Harmonies"), achieved his unanimous election to the Academy. Lamartine, still a royalist, disapproved of the revolution of 1830. A tour to the East produced his *Souvenirs d'Orient* (1841, Eng trans *Recollections of a Pilgrimage to the Holy Land*, 1850). Recalled to France in 1833, he became deputy for Mâcon. Between 1834 and 1848 he published his poems, *Jocelyn* (1836, Eng trans 1837) and *La chute d'un ange* (1838, "The Fall of an Angel"), and the celebrated *Histoire des Girondins* (1846, Eng trans *History of the Girondins*, 1847–48). He did not support the Orléanist regime and became a member of the Provisional Government (1848) and, as Minister of Foreign Affairs, its ruling spirit. On the accession to power of **Napoleon III**, Lamartine devoted himself to literature.

Lamb, Lady Caroline 1785–1828 •*English writer*• She was the daughter of Frederick Ponsonby, 3rd Earl of Bessborough, and spent her early childhood in Italy. She married William Lamb (later Viscount **Melbourne**) in 1805, and had a passionate affair with **Byron** (1812–13), of whom she famously wrote that he was "mad, bad, and dangerous to know." The affair is reflected in her Gothic novel *Glenarvon*, published anonymously in 1816, which contains a caricature portrait of Byron. Increasingly mentally unstable, she was separated from her husband in 1825.

Lamb, Charles 1775–1834 •*English essayist and poet*• Born in the Temple, London, the son of a clerk, he was educated at Christ's Hospital (1782–89), where he formed a lasting friendship with **Coleridge**. In 1792 he took a post at India House, where he remained for more than 30 years. In 1796 his sister Mary (1764–1847), in a fit of madness, stabbed their invalid mother to death. Her brother's guardianship was accepted by the authorities and to this trust Charles devoted his life. His early attempts at writing included poetry, a prose romance and other pieces, but it was only with the joint publication with Mary of *Tales from Shakespeare* (1807), for **William Godwin**'s "Juvenile Library" series, that he achieved success. They went on to write several more books for children. Then, in 1818 Charles collected his scattered verse and prose into two volumes as the *Works of Charles Lamb*, and was invited to join the staff of the new *London Magazine*. His first essay, in August 1820, "Recollections of the Old South Sea House," was signed "Elia," the name of a foreigner who had been a fellow clerk. Collected as the *Essays of Elia* (1823–33), these became his best-known works. In 1825 he resigned his post in the India House due to poor health, and with Mary eventually moved to Edmonton.

“ ”

Gone before
To that unknown and silent shore.

1803 "Hester," stanza 7.

Lamb, William *See* **Melbourne, 2nd Viscount**

Lamb, Willis Eugene 1913– •*US physicist and Nobel Prize winner*• Born in Los Angeles and educated at the University of California, Berkeley, he later became professor at Columbia University (1938–51), before being appointed to similar posts at Stanford (1951–56), Oxford (1956–62), Yale (1962–74) and the University of Arizona (1974–). His studies of the structure of the hydrogen spectrum found the two possible hydrogen energy states to differ in energy by a very small amount. This "Lamb shift" led to a revision of the theory of interaction of the electron with electromagnetic radiation, and ultimately to the theory of quantum electrodynamics. Lamb shared with **Polykarp Kusch** the 1955 Nobel Prize for physics for this research.

Lambert, John 1619–84 •*English general*• He was born in Calton, near Settle, Yorkshire, and studied law before joining the parliamentary army in the English Civil War, commanding **Thomas Fairfax**'s cavalry at Marston Moor in 1641 and participating in several victories. He headed the cabal which overthrew **Richard Cromwell** in 1659, suppressed the Royalist insurrection in Cheshire in August 1659, and virtually governed the country with his officers as the "committee of safety." He was sent to the Tower, tried in 1662, and kept prisoner on Drake's Island, Plymouth, until his death.

La Mettrie, Julien Offroy de 1709–51 •*French philosopher and physician*• Born in St-Malo, he first studied theology, then switched to medicine. His materialistic philosophy held that all psychical phenomena were to be explained as the effects of organic changes in the brain and nervous system. His first exposition of this in *L'histoire naturelle de l'âme* (1745, "Natural History of the Soul") provoked such hostility that the book was publicly burned and he was forced to flee to Leiden, Holland, then Berlin under the protection of **Frederick II (the Great)** of Prussia. He worked out the ethical implications of his materialism in such works as *Discours sur le bonheur* (1748, "Discourse on Happiness"), *Le petit homme à longue queue* (1751, "The Small Man in a Long Queue") and *L'art de jouir* (1751) where he argued that the only real pleasures are those of the senses, that pleasure is the only goal of life, that virtue is just enlightened self-interest and that the soul perishes with the body. He seems to have lived a life of carefree hedonism according to these precepts, and died of food poisoning.

Lamming, George Eric 1927– •*Barbadian novelist*• Born in Carrington Village, he was a teacher in Trinidad and Venezuela before going to England in 1950, where he worked as a factory laborer and hosted a book program for the BBC West Indian Service. Beginning with *In the Castle of My Skin* (1953), his first novels were written in an argot unfamiliar to many readers and so received a lukewarm reception. *Season of Adventure* (1960) articulates his own dilemma as an artist, and *Natives of My Person* (1972), with its archaic vocabulary and mythic roots, is perhaps his tour de force.

Lamont, Norman Stewart Hughson Lamont, Baron 1942– •*Scottish Conservative politician*• He was born in Lerwick, Shetland. He entered Parliament in 1972 as Member of Parliament for Kingston-upon-Thames. In the **Thatcher** administrations he rose to be Under-Secretary of State for Energy (1979–81) and Trade and Industry Minister (1981–85), before he entered the Treasury, and was appointed Chancellor (1990–93) under **John Major**. With the economy increasingly troubled, he withdrew Great Britain from the European Exchange Rate Mechanism (September 1992), which led to the effective devaluation of the pound. He resigned in 1993, and was replaced by **Kenneth Clarke**. When his seat was abolished in boundary changes, he was accepted in 1996 as candidate for the apparently "safe" seat of Harrogate and Knaresborough, but failed to be elected in 1997. He was created a life peer in 1998.

L'Amour, Louis 1908–88 •*US novelist*• Born in Jamestown, North Dakota, he earned his living as a prizefighter, tugboat deckhand, lumberjack, gold prospector and deputy sheriff. The first of his crude but effective novels about the Wild West, *Hondo* (1953), was an instant success. He followed it with another 80 titles, including *Hopalong Cassidy and the Riders of High Rock* (1951), *High Lonesome* (1962) and *The Iron Marshall* (1979). He received the 1984 Presidential Medal of Freedom.

Lampedusa, Giuseppe Tomasi di 1896–1957 •*Italian novelist*• He was born in Palermo, Sicily, the son of the Duke of Parma and grandson of the Prince of Lampedusa. His family had once been rich, but indolence, divided inheritance and apathy had reduced its circumstances. His only book, *Il Gattopardo* (1958, Eng trans *The Leopard*, 1960), is a violent, decadent and nostalgic historical novel, set in Sicily in the latter half of the 19th century. It has subsequently come to be regarded as one of the greatest Italian novels of the 20th century.

Lancaster, Duke of *See* **John of Gaunt**

Lancaster, Burt, *originally* **Stephen Burton Lancaster** 1913–94 •*US film actor*• Born in New York City, he was a circus acrobat, and made his film debut in *The Killers* (1946). Tall and muscular, he was cast in a succession of swashbuckling tough-guy roles. One of the first actors to form his own production company, he increasingly sought opportunities to test his dramatic abilities, winning an Academy Award for his performance in the title role in *Elmer Gantry* (1960), as well as earning Academy Award nominations for *From Here to Eternity* (1953), *Birdman of Alcatraz* (1962) and *Atlantic City* (1980).

Lancaster, Joseph 1778–1838 •*English educationist and Quaker*• In 1798 he opened a school in London based on a monitorial system which was taken up by the Nonconformists, while **Andrew Bell** and his rival system were supported by the Church of England. The Lancasterian schools were nondenominational, and the Bible formed a large part of the teaching. The Royal Lancasterian Society, afterward known as the British and Foreign School Society, was formed in 1808.

Lancaster, Sir Osbert 1908–86 •*English cartoonist and writer*• Born in London, he studied art at Byam Shaw and the Slade School of Art, and worked on *Architectural Review* (1934–39), writing and illustrating humorous articles. In 1939 he joined the *Daily Express* for a long series of front-page *Pocket Cartoons*, witty comments for which he created Lady Maudie Littlehampton and friends. He also designed sets and costumes for ballet and opera and wrote many books.

Lanchester, Frederick William 1868–1946 •*English engineer, inventor and designer*• Born in Lewisham, London, he won a scholarship to what is now Imperial College, London, and in 1893 set up his own workshop. He built the first experimental motor car in Great Britain (1895) and founded the Lanchester Engine Company in 1899, which produced the first Lanchester car in 1901. Over the next four years almost 400 of his cars were sold. Turning his attention to aeronautics, he laid the theoretical foundations of aircraft design in *Aerial Flight* (2 vols, 1907–08), which was ahead of its time in describing boundary layers, induced drag and the dynamics of flight.

Lander, Harald, *originally* **Alfred Bernhardt Stevnsborg** 1905–71 •*French dancer, choreographer and teacher*• Born in Copenhagen, Denmark, he trained at the Royal Danish Ballet School (RDBS) and then joined the company (1923) to become a distinguished character soloist. He studied and danced in the US, South America and the USSR (1926–29), returning to the RDBS as ballet master and, in 1932, director. He preserved the works of Danish choreographer August Bournonville (1805–79) while developing a new repertoire (some 30 ballets of his own, including his most famous, *Études*, 1948) of contemporary European works. He moved to Paris in the early 1950s, where he became ballet master and director of the Opera's school. He assumed French citizenship in 1956.

Landor, Walter Savage 1775–1864 •*English writer*• Born in Warwick, he was expelled from Rugby and Trinity College, Oxford, and spent a large part of his life in France and Italy. *Gebir* (1798), a poem showing the influence of **Milton** and **Pindar**, was the occasion of his lifelong friendship with **Robert Southey**, but the work was a failure. His best-known work is *Imaginary Conversations* (2 vols, 1824–29), a collection of prose dialogues. Other works include *Examination of Shakespeare* (1834), *Pericles and Aspasia* (1836), *Pentameron* (1837), *Hellenics* (1847) and *Poemata et Inscriptiones* (1847). In 1858 an unhappy scandal (see his *Dry Sticks Fagoted by Landor*, 1858), involving a libel action, drove him back to Italy.

“ ”

I strove with none; for none was worth my strife;
Nature I loved, and, next to Nature, Art.

1853 "Dying Speech of an Old Philosopher."

Landowska, Wanda 1879–1959 •*Polish pianist, harpsichordist, and musical scholar*• Born in Warsaw, she went to Paris in 1900, and in 1912 became Professor of the Harpsichord at the Berlin Hochschule. After World War I, when she was detained in Germany, she toured extensively, and in 1927 established her École de Musique Ancienne at Saint-Leu-la-Forêt, near Paris. In 1941 she moved to the US. A distinguished interpreter of **J S Bach** and **Handel**, she renewed interest in the harpsichord, and **Manuel de Falla** wrote his harpsichord concerto for her.

Landseer, Sir Edwin Henry 1802–73 •*English animal painter*• Born in London, he was trained by his father, the engraver John Landseer (1769–1852), to sketch animals from life, and he began exhibiting at the Royal Academy when only 13 years old. His animal pieces were generally made subservient to some sentiment or idea, but did not lose their correctness and force of draftsmanship. The scene of several fine pictures is laid in the Scottish Highlands, which he first visited in 1824. His *Monarch of the Glen* was exhibited in 1851, and the bronze lions at the foot of **Nelson**'s Monument in Trafalgar Square were modeled by him (1859–66).

Landsteiner, Karl 1868–1943 •*US pathologist, the discoverer of blood groups, and Nobel Prize winner*• Born in Vienna, Austria, he was a research assistant at the Pathological Institute there, and Professor of Pathological Anatomy from 1909. He later went to the US to work in the Rockefeller Institute for Medical Research, New York City (1922–39). He won the 1930 Nobel Prize for physiology or medicine, especially for his valuable 1901 discovery of the four major human blood groups (A, B, AB, O) and his 1927 discovery of the M and N groups. In 1940 he also discovered the Rhesus (Rh) factor.

Lane, Sir Allen, *originally* **Allen Lane Williams** 1902–70 •*English publisher and pioneer of paperback books*• Born and educated in Bristol, he was apprenticed in 1919 to the Bodley Head publishing house. He resigned as managing director in 1935 in order to form Penguin Books Ltd, a revolutionary step in the publishing trade. He began by reprinting novels in paper covers at sixpence each, expanding to other series such as nonfictional Pelicans and children's Puffins.

Lane, Dame Elizabeth, *née* **Coulbourn** 1905–88 •*English lawyer*• Educated privately and at Malvern Girls College, she became a barrister in 1940. In 1960 she was the third woman to be appointed Queen's Counsel, and she became a Master of the Bench in 1965. She was assistant Recorder of Birmingham (1953–61) before becoming Recorder of Derby and Commissioner of the Crown Court at Manchester (1961–62). She was then the first woman circuit court judge until 1965, when she became the first woman to be appointed a High Court judge, working in the Family Division. She was given the honorary title of Dame Commander, Order of the British Empire, in 1965.

Lane (of St Ippollitts), Geoffrey Dawson, Lord 1918– •*English judge*• Appointed a judge in 1966, he became a Lord Justice of Appeal (1974–79) then Lord-of-Appeal-in-Ordinary (1979–80) and Lord Chief Justice of England (1980–92), in which capacity he proved a vigorous leader of the courts. He was made a life peer in 1979.

Lanfranc c.1005–89 •*Italian prelate*• Born in Pavia, he studied law, and founded a school at Avranches c. 1039. In 1041 he became a Benedictine at Bec, and in 1046 was chosen prior. He contended against **Berengar of Tours** in the controversy over transubstantiation. In 1062 William of Normandy (**William I**) made him prior of St Stephen's Abbey at Caen, and in 1070 Archbishop of Canterbury. His chief writings are commentaries on the Epistles of St Paul, a treatise against Berengar's *De corpore et sanguine Domini* (1079), and sermons.

Lanfranco, Giovanni c.1581–1647 •*Italian religious painter*• Born in Parma, he was one of the first Italian Baroque painters. His work, the best of which can be seen on the dome of San Andrea della Valle in Rome and in his paintings for the cathedral at Naples, was widely copied by later painters.

Lang, Fritz 1890–1976 •*US film director*• Born in Vienna, Austria, he was educated there at the College of Technical Sciences and the Academy of Graphic Arts, intending to become a painter. Instead he joined the Decla Film Company (1919). In Berlin he directed two *Dr Mabuse* films (1926), and, also in 1926, his most famous film, *Metropolis*, a nightmare vision of the future where a large section of the population is reduced to slavery. When **Hitler** came to power in 1933, **Goebbels** offered Lang the post of head of the German film industry, but he refused and the same night fled to Paris and later to the US. Among his many films of this period, *Fury* (1936) was acclaimed as a masterpiece for its portrayal of mob rule. His many other films include *M* (1931), *You Only Live Once* (1937), *The Return of Frank James* (1940), *Hangmen Also Die* (1943), *The House by the River* (1949), *Human Desire* (1954) and *Beyond a Reasonable Doubt* (1956). Back in Germany in 1960 he directed a third *Dr Mabuse* film.

Lang, Helmut 1956– •*Austrian fashion designer*• Born in Vienna, he originally trained for a career in finance but began making men's clothes when he found himself unable to buy designs he liked. He established his own studio in 1977, opened his made-to-measure boutique in Vienna in 1979 and showcased his first range of ready-to-wear clothes in 1984.

lang, k.d., *properly* **Kathy Dawn Lang** 1962– •*Canadian singer and lesbian icon*• Born in Consort, Alberta, she attended drama college in Vancouver. She formed her group "the reclines" (in memory of **Patsy Cline**) by the age of 21, and made a big impact with her magnificent voice and raw, unrestrained take on country music. She recorded *Shadowland* in 1988, but after the successful *Absolute Torch and Twang* (1989), turned to sophisticated pop on the brilliant *Ingenue* (1992) and the less convincing *All You Can Eat* (1995). Later albums include *Drag* (1997) and *Invincible Summer* (2000).

Lange, David Russell 1942– •*New Zealand politician*• After studying law at the University of Auckland and qualifying as a solicitor and barrister, he worked as a crusading lawyer for the underprivileged in Auckland. In 1977 he was elected to the House of Representatives and rose rapidly to become Leader of the Labour Party in 1983. He won a decisive victory in the 1984 general election on a nonnuclear defense policy, which he immediately put into effect. He and his party were reelected in 1987, but, following bouts of ill health and disagreements within his party, he resigned the premiership in 1989. He was then Attorney-General and Minister of State until 1990.

Lange, Dorothea, *originally* **Dorothea Nutzhorn** 1895–1965 •*US photographer*• Born in Hoboken, New Jersey, she studied at Columbia University. She is best known for her social records of migrant workers, sharecroppers and tenant farmers throughout the South and West in the Depression years, and especially for her celebrated study, "Migrant Mother" (1936). With her husband, economist Paul Taylor, she collaborated on a book, *An American Exodus: A Record of Human Erosion* (1939). After World War II she worked as a freelance photo-reporter in Asia, South America and the Middle East (1958–63).

Lange, Jessica 1949– •*US film actress*• Born in Minnesota, she traveled across the US and Europe, settling for a time in Paris to study at the Opéra Comique before returning to New York. Her film debut was in the 1976 remake of *King Kong*, and she later won critical acclaim for her performances in *The Postman Always Rings Twice* (1981), *Frances* (1982), and *Tootsie* (1982, Best Supporting Actress Academy Award). Drawn to parts that reflect some of her political and environmental concerns, she has played diverse roles in such films as *Sweet Dreams* (1985), *Cape Fear* (1991), *Blue Sky* (1994, Best Actress Academy Award), *Rob Roy* (1995) and *Titus* (1999). She made her Broadway debut in *A Streetcar Named Desire* (1992) and won acclaim for her performance as Mary Tyrone in the West End production of *Long Day's Journey into Night* (2000).

Langer, Bernhard 1957– •*German golfer*• Born in Anhausen, he turned professional at the age of 15, won the US Masters twice and by 2001 had amassed 39 victories on the PGA (Professional Golfers' Association) European Tour. Regarded as the professional's professional, he recorded 68 tournaments without missing a cut, and in 2001 was selected for his tenth Ryder Cup team.

Langer, Susanne K(nauth) 1895–1985 •*US philosopher*• Born in New York City, she studied at Radcliffe College, where she taught (1927–42), later holding positions at the University of Delaware, Columbia University and Connecticut College. She was greatly influenced by **Ernst Cassirer**, and published important works in aesthetics and linguistic analysis, including *Philosophy in a New Key* (1942), *Problems of Art* (1957) and *Mind: An Essay on Human Feeling* (3 vols, 1967–82).

Langevin, Paul 1872–1946 •*French physicist*• Born in Paris, he was educated at the École Normale Supérieure, and spent a year in Cambridge. He returned to Paris to take his doctorate and study with **Pierre Curie**. In 1909 he was appointed Professor of Physics at the Sorbonne. Studying magnetic phenomena, he related the paramagnetic movement of molecules to their absolute temperature (1905), and predicted the paramagnetic saturation discovered by **Heike Kamerlingh Onnes** in 1914. He worked on the molecular structure of gases, and during World War I applied sonar techniques to the detection of submarines. Imprisoned by the Nazis, he managed to escape to Switzerland, and after the liberation returned to Paris.

Langland or **Langley, William** c. 1332–c. 1400 •*English poet*• Born possibly in Ledbury, Herefordshire, he is thought to have been the illegitimate son of the rector of Shipton-under-Wychwood in Oxfordshire. Educated at the Benedictine school at Malvern, he became a clerk. In 1362 he began his famous *Vision of William Concerning Piers the Plowman*, a medieval alliterative poem on spiritual pilgrimage.

“ ”

"Counseilleth me, Kynde," quod I, "what craft be best to lerne?"
"Lerne to love," quod Kynde, "and leef alle othere."

c. 1377 ***Vision of William Concerning Piers the Plowman*** *(B text), "Passus 20," l.207–08.*

Langley, Samuel Pierpont 1834–1906 •*US astronomer and aeronautical pioneer*• Born in Roxbury, Massachusetts, he first trained and practiced as an engineer and architect. At the age of 30 he began his astronomical career as an assistant at the Harvard College Observatory (1865–66). His chosen field was solar physics: he was the inventor of the bolometer (1880), an instrument which recorded the infrared radiation of the sun. A celebrated pioneer of heavier-than-air mechanically propelled flying machines, in 1896 he built a steam-driven pilotless airplane which flew a distance of 42,000 feet (12,802 m) over the Potomac River.

Langley, William *See* **Langland, William**

Langmuir, Irving 1881–1957 •*US physical chemist and Nobel Prize winner*• Born in Brooklyn, New York, he studied at Columbia University and worked on chemical research with **Walther Nernst** at Göttingen. From 1906 to 1909 he taught chemistry at Stevens Institute of Technology in Hoboken, New Jersey, and then joined the General Electric Company (GEC) laboratories at Schenectady, New York, from which he retired as associate director in 1950. His first work at GEC was on extending the life of the tungsten filament in the electric light bulb. The mathematical formulation of adsorption which he devised, now known as the Langmuir isotherm, is still of importance in the study of catalysis by surfaces. He also invented atomic hydrogen welding and contributed to the further development of the electronic theory of the atom and of chemical bonding. Langmuir investigated films on liquid surfaces and devised a useful piece of apparatus which became known as the Langmuir trough; he also invented the Langmuir pump for high vacuum work. He received the Nobel Prize for chemistry in 1932.

Langton, Stephen c. 1150–1228 •*English prelate*• He was educated at the University of Paris. In 1206 his friend and fellow student, Pope **Innocent III**, gave him a post in his household and made him a cardinal. On the disputed election to the see of Canterbury in 1205–07, Langton was recommended by the pope and, having been elected, was consecrated by Innocent at Viterbo in 1207. His appointment was resisted by King **John**, and Langton was kept out of the see until 1213. He sided with the barons against John and his name is the first of the subscribing witnesses of the Magna Carta.

Langtry, Lillie (Emilie Charlotte), *née* **Le Breton**, *nicknamed* **the Jersey Lily** 1853–1929 •*English actress*• She was born in Jersey, Channel Islands, the daughter of the dean of the island. She married Edward Langtry in 1874, and made her first major stage appearance in 1881. Her nickname originated in the title of Sir **John Millais**'s portrait of her. Her beauty brought her to the attention of the Prince of Wales, later **Edward VII**, and she became his mistress. Widowed in 1897, she married Hugo Gerald de Bathe in 1899, and became well known as a racehorse owner. She wrote her reminiscences, *The Days I Knew* (1925).

Lankester, Sir Edwin Ray 1847–1929 •*English zoologist*• Born in London, he was a tutor at, and Fellow of, Exeter College, Oxford, professor at the University of London and at Oxford, and from 1898 to 1907 director of the British Museum (Natural History). His research embraced a wide range of interests including comparative anatomy, protozoology, embryology and anthropology. A parasite related to the causative agent of malaria is named *Lankesterella* after him, and his work led to an understanding of this disease. His anthropological studies included the discovery of flint implements, and thus the presence of early humans, in the Pliocene sediments from Suffolk. Largely responsible for the founding of the Marine Biological Association in 1884, he became its president in 1892. He was knighted in 1907.

Lansbury, Angela 1925– *•US actress•* Born in London, she was evacuated to the US in 1940. Signed to a contract with MGM, she made her film debut in *Gaslight* (1944), for which she received a Best Supporting Actress Academy Award nomination. A versatile and talented performer, she subsequently appeared in such films as *National Velvet* (1944), *The Picture of Dorian Gray* (1945) and *State of the Union* (1948). She made her Broadway debut in *Hotel Paradiso* (1957) and later emerged as a leading stage star in the musical *Mame* (1966, Tony award). Her subsequent stage work includes *Dear World* (1969, Tony), *Gypsy* (1974, Tony) and *Sweeney Todd* (1979, Tony). On film, she became a scene-stealing character in the likes of *The Manchurian Candidate* (1962), *Death on the Nile* (1978) and *The Company of Wolves* (1984). She found her greatest popularity on television as the star of the mystery series *Murder She Wrote* (1984–96).

Lansbury, George 1859–1940 *•English politician•* Born near Lowestoft, Suffolk, he worked for the reform of the conditions of the poor for many years before entering Parliament. He was first elected Labour Member of Parliament for Bow and Bromley in 1910, and founded the *Daily Herald*, which he edited until 1922, when it became the official paper of the Labour Party. From 1931 to 1935 he was Leader of the Labour Party. The actress **Angela Lansbury** is his granddaughter.

Lansdowne, Henry Petty-Fitzmaurice, 3rd Marquis of 1780–1863 *•English politician•* He graduated from Cambridge in 1801, and became Member of Parliament for Calne the next year. He succeeded **William Pitt** as member for Cambridge University in 1806 and as Chancellor of the Exchequer in the **Grenville** administration. In 1809 he became marquis. A cautious Liberal, in 1826 he entered the **Canning** Cabinet, and in the Frederick Goderich administration (1827–28) was president of the Council, in which post he helped to pass the Reform Bill of 1832. Requested to form an administration in 1852, he preferred to serve without office in the **Aberdeen** coalition and in 1855 again declined the premiership.

Lansing, Sherry 1944– *•US film executive•* Born in Chicago, she became an actress in 1970. Her real ambitions lay behind the camera, and she rose from script reader to vice president in charge of production at Columbia. She was appointed president of Twentieth Century Fox in 1980, becoming the first woman ever to head a Hollywood studio, and remained there until 1982. She then formed her own production company with Stanley R Jaffe; their highly successful films include *Fatal Attraction* (1987), *The Accused* (1988) and *Indecent Proposal* (1993). She was appointed Chairman of Paramount Pictures in 1992.

Lantz, Walter 1900–94 *•US cartoonist and film animator•* Born in New Rochelle, New York, he worked as an office boy on the *New York American* (1914), studied cartooning by correspondence course and joined **William Randolph Hearst**'s animation studio in 1916. He became writer/director and "star" of his own *Dinky Doodle* cartoons, then went to Hollywood and joined Universal Pictures, where he remained for over 50 years. The most popular of his many characters is Woody Woodpecker, who first appeared on the screen in *Knock Knock* (1940), and whose characteristic laugh was supplied by Lantz's wife, the actress Grace Stafford (1904–92).

Lanza, Mario, *originally* **Alfredo Arnold Coccozza** 1921–59 *•US tenor and actor•* Born in Philadelphia, he studied singing under Enrico Rosati and took part in opera and recitals before appearing in such films as *The Toast of New Orleans* (1950), which includes the song "Be My Love," and *The Great Caruso* (1951).

Laozi (Lao Tzu), *literally* **the old master** 6th century BC *•Chinese philosopher and sage, traditional founder of Taoism•* He is probably a legendary figure and is represented as the older contemporary of **Confucius**, against whom most of his teaching is directed. The *Dao De Jing* (*Tao-Te-Ching*, "The Book of the Way and Its Power"), one of the principal works of Taoism, compiled some 300 years after his death, is attributed to him. It teaches self-sufficiency, simplicity and detachment.

La Pasionaria *See* **Ibarruri (Gómez), Dolores**

Laplace, Pierre Simon, Marquis de 1749–1827 *•French mathematician and astronomer•* Born in Beaumont-en-Auge, Normandy, he studied at Caen, went to Paris and became Professor of Mathematics at the École Militaire. In 1799 he entered the Senate, becoming its vice president in 1803. He was made marquis by **Louis XVIII** in 1817. His astronomical work culminated in the publication of the five monumental volumes of *Mécanique céleste* (1799–1825), the greatest work on celestial mechanics since **Isaac Newton**'s *Principia*. His *Système du monde* (1796, Eng trans in 2 vols, *The System of the World*, 1830) is a nonmathematical exposition of all his astronomical theories, and his famous nebular hypothesis of planetary origin occurs as a note in later editions. In his study of the gravitational attraction of spheroids, he formulated the fundamental differential equation in physics that bears his name. He also made important contributions to the theory of probability.

La Plante, Lynda 1946– *•English actress and writer•* Born in Formby, Lancashire, she began her acting career in 1972, working in both theater and television. She switched to writing, and her television successes have included *Widows* (1982), the award-winning *Prime Suspect* (1991–96), *Civvies* (1992), *Framed* (1992), *Comics* (1993), *The Governor* (1995–96), *Trial and Retribution* (1997–2000) and *Mind Games* (2000). She has also written a feature film, *The Profiler* (1996), starring **Sean Connery**. Her novels include *Bella Mafia*, which was adapted for television (1996).

Lara, Brian Charles 1969– *•West Indies cricket player•* Born in Santa Cruz, Trinidad, he was one of 11 children. He made 375 runs for the West Indies against England in the fifth Test in Antigua in 1994, the highest individual score in 117 years of Test cricket. Seven weeks later he recorded 501 for Warwickshire against Durham at Edgbaston, overtaking **Mohammed Hanif** to hold the record for the highest individual score in first-class cricket.

Lardner, Ring(gold Wilmer) 1885–1933 *•US short-story writer and journalist•* Born in Michigan, he was a successful sports writer and newspaper columnist in Chicago, St Louis and New York, and drew on his sporting background in his first collection of stories *You Know Me Al: A Busher's Letters* (1916). His cynical humor identifies him as a distinctive voice, and his story collections include *Gullible's Travels* (1917), *Treat 'Em Rough* (1918) and *First and Last* (1934). He also wrote one novel, *The Big Town* (1921), satirical verse, a satirical pseudo-autobiography, *The Story of a Wonder Man* (1927), and a musical comedy, *June Moon* (1929).

Larionov, Mikhail Fyodorovich 1881–1964 *•Russian painter•* Born in Tiraspol, Ukraine, he studied architecture and sculpture at the Moscow Institute of Painting until 1908. Beginning as a Russian postimpressionist, and influenced by **Pierre Bonnard** and the Fauves, he gradually took to a more "primitive" approach based on Russian folk art. He worked closely with his future wife, **Natalia Goncharova**, and together they developed Rayonism (1912–14), a style akin to Italian Futurism.

Larkin, Philip Arthur 1922–85 *•English poet, librarian and jazz critic•* Born in Coventry, Warwickshire, he was educated at St John's College, Oxford, and in 1955 became librarian at the University of Hull. His early poems appeared in the anthology *Poetry from Oxford in Wartime* (1944) and in *The North Ship* (1945). Other collections of poems include *The Less Deceived* (1955), *The Whitsun Weddings* (1964) and *High Windows* (1974). His *Collected Poems* was published posthumously in 1988 and was a best-seller. He wrote two novels, *Jill* (1946) and *A Girl in Winter* (1947), and his articles on jazz were collected in *All What Jazz?* (1970), and his essays in *Required Writing* (1983). Larkin also edited *The Oxford Book of Twentieth Century English Verse* (1973). He was a friend and correspondent of **Kingsley Amis**.

Laroche, Guy 1923–89 *•French fashion designer•* He was born in La Rochelle, near Bordeaux, into a cattle-farming family. In 1957 he started his own business and showed a small collection. By 1961 he was producing both couture and ready-to-wear clothes, achieving a reputation for skillful cutting. From 1966 his designs included menswear.

La Rochefoucauld, François, 6th Duc de 1613–80 *•French writer•* He was born in Paris. Having devoted himself to the cause of the queen, **Marie de Médicis**, in opposition to Cardinal **Ri-**

chelieu, he became entangled in a series of amorous and political intrigues and was forced to live in exile from 1639 to 1642. On Cardinal **Mazarin**'s death in 1661 he returned to the court of **Louis XIV**. A surreptitious edition of his *Mémoires* (1664), written in retirement, was published in 1662, but as it was considered offensive by many, he denied its authorship. *Réflexions, ou sentences et maximes morales* (1665) demonstrates his brevity and clarity, and his remorseless analysis of character.

Larousse, Pierre Athanase 1817–75 •*French publisher, lexicographer and encyclopedist*• Born in Toucy in Yonne, he was educated in Versailles. He founded a publishing house and bookshop in Paris in 1852 and issued educational textbooks, several grammars and dictionaries. His major work was his *Grand dictionnaire universel du XIXe siècle* (17 vols, 1866–76), a combined dictionary and encyclopedia.

Larsen, Henning 1925– •*Danish architect*• Educated at the Royal Danish Academy, Copenhagen, the Architectural Association, London, and MIT, he became a lecturer at the Royal Danish Academy in 1959 and has been Professor of Architecture since 1968. His buildings include the University of Trondheim (Norway), houses at Milton Keynes (England), and the Foreign Ministry and the Danish Embassy in Riyadh (Saudi Arabia). The Foreign Ministry in Riyadh has been described as one of the first buildings successfully to combine Eastern and Western architectural traditions.

Larwood, Harold 1904–95 •*English cricket player*• He was born in Nuncargate. His career was comparatively brief and he played in only 21 Test matches. He was employed by **Douglas Robert Jardine** to bowl body-line (hard and fast toward the body of the batter) in the controversial 1932–33 tour of Australia, when several of the home batsmen were seriously hurt and diplomatic relations between the two countries were imperiled. On his return, feeling that he had not been supported in official quarters, he retired from Test cricket and in later life settled happily in Australia.

“ ”

A cricket tour in Australia would be a most delightful period in one's life if one was deaf.

1933 ***Body-line***.

La Salle, René Robert Cavelier, Sieur de 1643–87 •*French explorer and pioneer of Canada*• Born in Rouen, he later settled as a trader near Montreal, Canada, and descended the Ohio and Mississippi to the sea (1682), claiming lands for France which he named Louisiane (Louisiana) after **Louis XIV**. After spending two years in fruitless journeys searching for the Mississippi Delta, his followers mutinied, and he was murdered.

Las Casas, Bartolomé de, *known as* **the Apostle of the Indians** 1474–1566 •*Spanish Dominican missionary*• He was born in Seville. He sailed in the third voyage of **Christopher Columbus** (1498), ordained to the priesthood in 1510, and in 1511 accompanied **Diego Velázquez** to Cuba. After missionary travels in Mexico, Nicaragua, Peru and Guatemala, he returned to devote four years to the cause of the Indians. Appointed Bishop of Chiapa, he was received (1544) with hostility by the colonialists, returned to Spain, and resigned his see (1547). He contended with the authorities in favor of the Indians until his death in Madrid, writing his *Veynte Razones* and *Brevísima relación de la destrucción de las Indias* (1552, "A Brief Report on the Destruction of the Indians"). His most important work is the unfinished *Historia de las Indias* (1875–76, "History of the Indians").

Lasdun, Sir Denys Louis 1914–2001 •*English architect*• Born in London, he was educated at Rugby School and was trained at the Architectural Association School. In 1960 he began the Denys Lasdun partnership. He was professor at Leeds from 1962 to 1963. His architecture follows the modern tradition, with horizontal emphasis, forceful articulation of mass and respect for urban context, and the occasional reference to the works of **Le Corbusier** is apparent. He is renowned particularly for the Royal College of Physicians (1958–64) in London, the University of East Anglia, Norwich (1962–68), the National Theatre, London (1965–76), and the European Investment Bank, Luxembourg (1975). He was awarded the Royal Gold Medal of the Royal Institute of British Architects in 1977. He was knighted in 1976.

Lashley, Karl Spencer 1890–1958 •*US psychologist*• Born in Davis, Virginia, he was professor at the Universities of Minnesota (1920–26) and Chicago (1929–35), and Research Professor of Neuropsychology at Harvard (1935–55). In 1942 he also became director of the Yerkes Laboratory for primate biology at Orange Park, Florida. He made valuable contributions to the study of localization of brain function, and is regarded as the father of neuropsychology.

Lasker, Emanuel 1868–1941 •*German chess player*• Born in Berlinchen (Barliner), Brandenburg, he gained a doctorate in mathematics from the University of Erlangen, and his theorem of vector spaces is still known by his name. He defeated **Wilhelm Steinitz** in 1894 for the world title before he reached his chess prime. Consequently, his tournament record as champion was greater than any other until **Anatoli Karpov**, and his reign was the longest in the history of chess. He lost the championship in 1921 to **José Raúl Capablanca**. He was driven out of Germany and had his property confiscated in 1933 because of his Jewish birth, and lived the remainder of his life in England, the USSR and the US.

Laski, Harold Joseph 1893–1950 •*English political scientist and socialist*• Born in Manchester, he was educated at Manchester Grammar School and New College, Oxford, and lectured widely in the US before joining the staff of the London School of Economics, becoming Professor of Political Science there in 1926. He was chairman of the Labour Party in 1945–46. A brilliant speaker, his political philosophy was a modified **Marx**ism. He had a strong belief in individual freedom, but the downfall of the Labour government in 1931 forced him to feel that some revolution in Great Britain was necessary. His works include *Liberty in the Modern State* (1930) and *The American Presidency* (1940).

Laski, Marghanita 1915–88 •*English novelist and journalist*• Born in Manchester, the niece of **Harold Joseph Laski**, she was educated at Oxford, and her first novel, *Love on the Supertax*, appeared in 1944. She wrote extensively for newspapers and reviews. Her later novels include *Little Boy Lost* (1949) and *The Victorian Chaise-longue* (1953). She also wrote various studies and critical works.

Lassalle, Ferdinand 1825–64 •*German revolutionary and political writer*• Born in Breslau (now Wrocław, Poland), the son of a rich Jewish merchant, he was a disciple of **Hegel**. He wrote a work on **Heraclitus** (1858), and in Paris made the acquaintance of **Heinrich Heine**. He took part in the revolution of 1848, during which he met **Karl Marx**, and for an inflammatory speech got six months in prison. At Leipzig he founded the Universal German Workingmen's Association (the forerunner of the Social Democratic Party) to agitate for universal suffrage. He died shortly after a duel with Count Racowitza of Wallachia over the hand of Helene von Domiges.

Lassus, Orlandus or **Orlando di Lasso** c. 1532–94 •*Netherlandish musician and composer*• Born in Mons (now in Belgium), he was a highly distinguished composer of early music, writing many masses, motets and other works. In 1570 he was knighted by **Maximilian II**. Unlike his contemporary, **Palestrina**, he wrote not only church music but also a large number of secular works.

Lathrop, Julia Clifford 1858–1932 •*US social reformer*• Born in Rockford, Illinois, and educated at Vassar College, she joined **Jane Addams**'s Hull House Settlement in Chicago in 1880. She was active in promoting welfare for children and the mentally ill. One of the founders of the Chicago Institute of Social Science (1903–04), she was first head of the Federal Children's Bureau (1912) and a member of the Child Welfare Committee of the League of Nations from 1925 to 1931.

Latimer, Hugh c. 1485–1555 •*English Protestant reformer*• Born in Thurcaston, Leicestershire, he was sent to Cambridge. A Roman Catholic, he was elected a Fellow of Clare College in 1510, and in 1522 was appointed a university preacher. Converted to Protestantism, he was one of the divines selected to examine the lawfulness of **Henry VIII**'s marriage to **Catherine of Aragon**. He judged in favor of the king, and was made chaplain to **Anne**

Boleyn and in 1535 Bishop of Worcester. He opposed Henry's Six Articles, for which he was imprisoned in 1536, 1546 and 1553. Under **Mary I** he was found guilty of heresy, with **Nicholas Ridley** and **Thomas Cranmer**, and on October 16, 1555, was burned with Ridley opposite Balliol College.

La Tour, Georges de 1593–1652 •*French artist*• Born in Vic-sur-Seille, Lorraine, the Duke of Lorraine became his patron and later King **Louis XIII** himself accepted a painting by him, liking it so much he had all works by other masters removed from his chambers. La Tour was entirely forgotten until his rediscovery in 1915, and in the meantime works by him were attributed to others. He specialized in candlelit scenes, using a palette of warm, glowing reds and browns to obtain eerie effects. Of the 40 works by him which have been positively identified, most are of religious subjects, such as *St Joseph the Carpenter* (Louvre, Paris).

La Tour, Maurice Quentin de 1704–88 •*French pastellist and portrait painter*• Born in St Quentin, he settled in Paris, where he became immensely popular. His best works include portraits of Madame de **Pompadour**, **Voltaire** and **Jean Jacques Rousseau**.

La Tour d'Auvergne, Henri de *See* **Turenne, Henri de La Tour d'Auvergne, Vicomte de**

Latrobe, Benjamin Henry 1764–1820 •*US civil engineer*• Born in Fulneck, Yorkshire, England, he was the son of a Moravian minister. He was trained as an architect and a civil engineer before emigrating to the US in 1796. He introduced the Greek Revival style to the US and was surveyor of public buildings in Washington DC (1803–17), his work including parts of the Capitol and the White House. As an engineer he designed waterworks for the city of Philadelphia (1801) and joined with **Robert Fulton** in a scheme to build steamboats (1813–15). When this project failed he was ruined financially. In 1817 his son Henry died of yellow fever while building the New Orleans waterworks. Latrobe went there in 1820 to complete the works but soon died of the same cause.

Lattimore, Owen 1900–89 •*US Sinologist and defender of civil liberties*• Born in Washington DC, the son of a US trader in China, he spent his early childhood in China, was educated in England and Lausanne, and worked in China in business and journalism in the 1920s. He traveled in Mongolia and Manchuria, and returned to the US to study at Harvard. He published outstanding narratives of his journeys and observations in central Asia such as *High Tartary* (1930), *Mongol Journeys* (1941), and his masterpiece, *Inner Asian Frontiers of China* (1940). He was made political adviser to **Chiang Kai-shek** by President **Franklin D Roosevelt** in 1941–42, and held major academic posts at Johns Hopkins University and in Leeds. While on a UN mission to Afghanistan in 1950, he was named as the top Russian agent in the US by Senator **Joseph McCarthy**. The five-year struggle to clear his name of this utterly baseless charge was carried out with great courage by himself and his wife Eleanor (1895–1970). He settled in England, and later in Paris, playing a major part in the development of Chinese studies in Europe.

Lattimore, Richmond (Alexander) 1906–84 •*US classicist and poet*• He was born in Paotingfu, China, to Protestant missionary parents, and educated at Dartmouth. A Rhodes scholar at Christ Church, Oxford, he then received his PhD from the University of Illinois. Professor of Greek at Bryn Mawr from 1935 until 1971, he achieved renown for his translations of classical Greek poetry, including the odes of **Pindar** (1947), the *Iliad* (1951, still widely regarded as the authoritative English translation), the works of **Hesiod** (1959), and the *Odyssey* (1967). With David Grene he coedited *The Complete Greek Tragedies* (1967–68), containing his critically acclaimed translations of Aeschylus and Euripides. In 1979 he published his own translation of the Gospels and Revelation. He also wrote poetry and criticism. For his translation of **Aristophanes**'s *Frogs* he was given the Bollingen Translation Prize in 1962.

Lattre de Tassigny, Jean de 1889–1952 •*French soldier*• He was born in Mouilleron-en-Pareds. He served during World War I and World War II, and was then sent by the Vichy government to command in Tunisia. He was recalled for sympathizing with the Allies and arrested in 1942 for resisting the Germans. He escaped to London in 1943, to become commander of the French 1st Army and take part in the Allied liberation of France (1944–45), signing the German surrender. He reorganized the French Army and was appointed Commander in Chief of Western Union Land Forces under **Montgomery** in 1948. In 1950, as Commander in Chief in French Indo-China, for a time he turned the tide against the Vietminh rebels.

Latynina, Larissa Semyonovna, *née* **Diril** 1935– •*Ukrainian gymnast*• Born in Kharsan, she collected 18 Olympic medals for the USSR in 1956 and 1964, a record for any sport, winning nine golds. During her 13-year career she earned 24 Olympic, world and European titles, including that of individual world champion in 1958 and 1962. She retired in 1966.

Laud, William 1573–1645 •*English prelate*• He was born in Reading, Berkshire and ordained in 1601. His learning and industry won him many friends and patrons, and he rapidly received preferment, becoming King's Chaplain (1611), Bishop of St Davids (1621), Bishop of Bath and Wells, and Archbishop of Canterbury (1633). He was also offered two cardinalships. With **Thomas Strafford** and **Charles I**, he worked for absolutism in Church and State. In Scotland, his attempt (1635–37) to anglicize the Church led to the "Bishops' Wars." In 1640 the Long Parliament impeached him. He was found guilty, and was beheaded on Tower Hill.

Lauda, Niki (Andreas Nikolas) 1949– •*Austrian racecar driver*• He was born in Vienna. World-champion racecar driver in 1975, he suffered horrific burns and injuries in the German Grand Prix (1976). After a series of operations he returned and won again in 1977. He crowned his comeback with McLaren by winning his third and last Grand Prix championship in 1984. He retired in 1985, and became the proprietor of Lauda-Air until he resigned in 2000.

Lauder, Estée, *née* **Mentzer** 1908–2004 •*US entrepreneur and beautician*• Born in New York City, the daughter of poor Hungarian immigrants, she worked her way up in the cosmetics industry by selling a face cream made by her uncle. She founded Estée Lauder Inc in 1946 and later multiplied the profits from Estée Lauder products by introducing deliberately competing lines, for example Aramis and Clinique. She published her autobiography, *Estée: A Success Story*, in 1985.

Lauder, Sir Harry (Henry) 1870–1950 •*Scottish comic singer*• He was born in Portobello, Edinburgh, and made his name as a singer of Scottish songs, many of which he wrote himself, such as "Roamin' in the Gloamin'." He was knighted in 1919 for his work in organizing entertainments for the troops during World War I. His popularity abroad was immense, especially in the US and the Commonwealth countries, which he toured almost annually after 1907.

Lauderdale, John Maitland, Duke of 1616–82 •*Scottish statesman*• Born in Lethington (now Lennoxlove), East Lothian, he ardently supported the Covenanters (1638), and in 1643 became a Scottish Commissioner at Westminster. He was taken prisoner at Worcester in 1651, and spent nine years in the Tower, at Windsor and at Portland. At the Restoration he became Scottish Secretary of State, and aimed to bring about the absolute power of the Crown in church and state. A member of the Privy Council, he had a seat in the so-called Cabal ministry and was made a duke in 1672.

Laue, Max Theodor Felix von 1879–1960 •*German physicist and Nobel Prize winner*• Born near Koblenz, he held various university and research positions and at the age of 71 he was appointed director of the former Kaiser Wilhelm Institute for Chemistry and Electrochemistry in Berlin-Dahlem (1951). He applied the concept of entropy to optics, and demonstrated that the formula for the velocity of light in flowing water followed from **Albert Einstein**'s theory of special relativity. In 1912 he discovered how X-rays are diffracted by the atoms in crystals, for which he was awarded the 1914 Nobel Prize for physics.

Laughton, Charles 1899–1962 •*English actor*• Born in Scarborough, Yorkshire, he worked in his family's hotel business before turning to the stage (1926), playing in and producing works by **George Bernard Shaw** and giving many renowned Shakespearean performances. He began to act in films in 1932, playing memorable roles as **Henry VIII** in *The Private Life of Henry VIII* (1933, Academy Award), Captain **Bligh** in *Mutiny on the Bounty* (1935) and Quasimodo in *The Hunchback of Notre Dame* (1939). He was married to the actress Elsa Lanchester (1902–86), and became a US citizen in 1950.

“ ”

But they can't censor the gleam in my eye.

1934 Of his role of Mr Barrett in ***The Barretts of Wimpole Street****.*

Laurel, Stan, *originally* **Arthur Stanley Jefferson** 1890–1965 *•US comic actor•* Born in Ulverston, Lancashire, England, he was a teenage member of Fred Karno's touring company and first went to the US in 1910. After gaining his first film part in 1917, he appeared in many of the early silent comedies and had tried producing and directing before his partnership with **Oliver Hardy** began in 1926. They made many full-length feature films, including *Bonnie Scotland* (1935) and *Way Out West* (1937), but their best efforts are generally reckoned to be their early (1927–32) shorts, one of which, *The Music Box* (1932), won an Academy Award. They survived the advent of the talkies better than many others, though their style was basically silent. Ollie—fat, pretentious and blustering—fiddled with his tie and appealed to the camera for help, while Stan—thin, bullied and confused—scratched his head, looked blank and dissolved into tears. Their contrasting personalities, their general clumsiness and stupidity, and their disaster-packed predicaments made them a universally popular comedy duo.

Lauren, Ralph, *originally* **Ralph Lipschitz** 1939– *•US fashion designer•* Born in the Bronx, New York, he attended night school for business studies and worked as a salesman in Bloomingdales. In 1967 he joined Beau Brummel Neckwear and created the Polo line for men, later including women's wear. He is famous for his US styles, such as the prairie look, frontier fashions and his preppy casualwear.

Laurence, (Jean) Margaret, *née* **Wemyss** 1926–87 *•Canadian novelist•* She was born in the prairie town of Neepawa, Manitoba, of Scots-Irish descent, and educated at United College (now the University of Winnipeg), from which she graduated in 1947, the same year she married John Laurence, a civil engineer. His job took them to England, Somaliland and, in 1952, to Ghana, where they spent five years. *A Tree for Poverty* (1954), a collection of translated Somali poetry and folk tales, and the travel book *The Prophet's Camel Bell* (1963), resulted from her East African experience. *This Side Jordan* (1960), her first novel, was set in Ghana. In 1962 she moved to England, where she wrote her famous "Manawaka series" based on her hometown: *The Stone Angel* (1964), *A Jest of God* (1966), *The Fire-Dwellers* (1969), *A Bird in the House* (1970) and *The Diviners* (1974).

Laurier, Sir Wilfrid 1841–1919 *•Canadian statesman•* He was born in St Lin, Quebec. He was a highly successful barrister and journalist, and became a member of the Quebec Legislative Assembly. He entered federal politics in 1874, becoming minister of inland revenue (1877). In 1887 he was leader of the Liberal Party and then prime minister in 1896. He was the first French-Canadian and also the first Roman Catholic to be premier of Canada. In 1911 his government was defeated, but he remained Liberal leader. Though he had a strong feeling for Empire, Laurier was a firm supporter of self-government for Canada. During World War I he was against conscription though entirely in agreement with Canada's entering the war. In his home policy he was an advocate of free trade, passing many reforms to benefit the working classes.

Lautréamont, Comte de, *pseudonym of* **Isidore Lucien Ducasse** 1846–70 *•French prose poet•* Born in Montevideo, Uruguay, the son of a consular officer, he went to France for his education. In 1868, the first installment of his lyrical prose poem *Les chants de Maldoror* ("The Songs of Maldoror") was published under his pseudonym of Lautréamont, borrowed from the title of a novel by **Eugène Sue**; it seems, however, that the printer refused to distribute the pamphlets. The work first appeared in Belgium and Switzerland. The author believed he would find there a more sympathetic audience for his "poetry of revolt," which combines nightmarish blasphemy and sexual obscenity with a profusion of lyrical and hallucinatory imagery. His writing caused the Surrealists to claim him as their precursor, and he exercised an enormous influence on **André Breton**, **Alfred Jarry**, and other writers.

Laval, Pierre 1883–1945 *•French politician•* He was born in Châteldon, Puy-de-Dôme. He became a lawyer, deputy (1914), senator (1926) and premier (1931–32, 1935–36). At first a Socialist, he moved to the Right during the late 1930s, and in the Vichy government was **Philippe Pétain**'s deputy (1940), rival and prime minister (1942–44). After the liberation he fled from France to Germany and Spain, but was brought back, charged with treason and executed.

La Vallière, Louise Françoise de la Baume le Blanc, Duchesse de 1644–1710 *•French aristocrat•* Born in Tours, she was brought to court by her mother. She became **Louis XIV**'s mistress (1661–67) and bore him four children. When the Marquise de **Montespan** superseded her she retired to a Carmelite nunnery in Paris (1674). *Réflexions sur la miséricorde de Dieu par une dame pénitente* (1680, "Reflections on God's Mercy by a Penitent Woman") is attributed to her.

Laver, Rod (Rodney George) 1938– *•Australian tennis player•* He was born in Rockhampton, Queensland. He first won the Wimbledon title in 1961, and again in 1962 in the course of a Grand Slam of all the major titles (British, US, French and Australian). He turned professional in 1962 and won the professional world singles title five times between 1964 and 1970. When Wimbledon allowed professionals to participate in 1968, he won it in that year, and again in the course of another Grand Slam the following year.

Laveran, Charles Louis Alphonse 1845–1922 *•French physician, parasitologist and Nobel Prize winner•* Born and educated in Paris, he became Professor of Military Medicine and Epidemic Diseases at the military college of Val de Grâce (1874–78, 1884–94). He studied malaria in Algeria (1878–83), discovering in 1880 the blood parasite which causes the disease. He suggested that the parasite was spread through mosquito bites, but the experimental demonstration of this was not provided until the late 1890s, by **Ronald Ross** and other investigators. Laveran also did important work on other tropical diseases, and from 1896 until his death he worked at the Pasteur Institute in Paris. He was awarded the 1907 Nobel Prize for physiology or medicine for his discovery of the malaria parasite, and donated half his money to equip a laboratory for tropical medicine at the Pasteur Institute.

Lavin, Mary 1912–96 *•Irish short-story writer and novelist•* She was born in East Walpole, Massachusetts, but returned to Ireland with her parents when she was nine, studied English at University College, Dublin, and thereafter lived in County Meath. "Miss Holland," her first short story, was published in the *Dublin Magazine* where it was admired by Lord Dunsany (1878–1957), who encouraged her and later wrote an introduction to her first collection, *Tales from Bective Bridge* (1942), which was awarded the James Tait Black Memorial Prize. Apart from two early novels—*The House in Clewe Street* (1945) and *Mary O'Grady* (1950)—she concentrated on the short story. Her many collections include *The Shrine and Other Stories* (1977) and *A Family Likeness* (1985). She was awarded the **Katherine Mansfield** prize (1961), two Guggenheim awards and the Gregory Medal.

Lavoisier, Antoine Laurent 1743–94 *•French chemist•* Born in Paris, he accepted the office of farmer-general of taxes (1768) to finance his investigations. As director of the government powder mills (1776), he greatly improved gunpowder, its supply and manufacture, and successfully applied chemistry to agriculture. He discovered oxygen, by rightly interpreting **Joseph Priestley**'s facts, its importance in respiration and combustion and as a compound with metals. His *Traité élémentaire de chimie* (1789, "Treaty of Elementary Chemistry") was a masterpiece. Politically liberal, he saw the great necessity for reform in France but was against revolutionary methods. Despite a lifetime of work for the state, inquiring into the problems of taxation, hospitals and prisons, he was guillotined.

Law, (Andrew) Bonar 1858–1923 •*Scottish statesman*• Born in Rexton, New Brunswick, Canada, of Scottish descent, he became a Unionist Member of Parliament from 1900. In 1911 he succeeded **Arthur Balfour** as Unionist leader in the House of Commons. He was colonial secretary (1915–16), then a member of the War Cabinet, chancellor of the exchequer (1916–18), Lord Privy Seal (1919), and from 1916 leader of the House of Commons. He retired in March 1921, but was recalled to serve as prime minister (1922–23), when the Conservatives withdrew from the coalition, forcing **David Lloyd George** to resign. Law resigned seven months later from ill health and died the same year.

Law, Denis 1940– •*Scottish soccer player*• He was born in Aberdeen. One of the greatest of Scottish soccer players, he never played at senior level in his own country. He made his international debut when only 18 years old and shortly afterward moved to Manchester City. After the Italian failure with Turin, he returned to Manchester United, the club with which he is indelibly associated. With them he won every major domestic honor, although injury excluded him from the European Cup success of 1968. Law shares with **Kenny Dalglish** the record of 30 goals scored for Scotland.

Law, William 1686–1761 •*English churchman and writer*• Born in Kingscliffe, Northamptonshire, he studied at Emmanuel College, Cambridge. About 1727 he became tutor to the father of **Edward Gibbon**. By around 1733 he had begun to study **Jakob Böhme**, and most of his later books are expositions of his mysticism. Law won his first triumphs against controversy with his *Three Letters* (1717). His *Remarks on Mandeville's Fable of the Bees* (1723) is a work of great caustic wit. His most famous work remains *A Serious Call to a Devout and Holy Life* (1729), which greatly influenced Dr **Johnson** and the **Wesley**s.

" "

If, therefore, a man will so live as to show that he feels and believes the most fundamental doctrines of Christianity, he must live above the world.

1729 ***A Serious Call to a Devout and Holy Life.***

Lawes, Sir John Bennet 1814–1900 •*English agriculturist*• Born in Rothamstead, near St Albans, he was educated at Oxford. In 1834 he inherited the estate of Rothamstead. Noticing that rock phosphate was only effective as a fertilizer on acid soils, he found that it was insoluble in alkaline soils and that by treating it with acid it became useful on all types of land. In 1843 he began to manufacture this "superphosphate" at Deptford Creek. The same year he founded the first agricultural research station in the world at Rothamstead, and asked agricultural chemist Henry Gilbert (1817–1901) to take charge of his laboratory. Lawes and Gilbert worked together for 50 years and earned Rothamstead an international reputation. Lawes was elected a Fellow of the Royal Society in 1854 and made a baronet in 1882. Rothamstead Experimental Station remains at the forefront of agricultural research.

Lawler, Ray(mond Evenor) 1921– •*Australian playwright*• Born in Melbourne, he began writing plays in his teens while working as a factory hand, but it was not until his ninth play, *The Summer of the Seventeenth Doll* (1955), that he achieved success. The play was filmed in 1960 and Lawler followed it with two prequels, *Kid Stakes* (1975) and *Other Times* (1976). In 1996 *Seventeenth Doll* was adapted successfully to the operatic stage with music by Australian composer Richard Mills (1949–).

Lawrence, D(avid) H(erbert) 1885–1930 •*English novelist, poet and essayist*• He was born in Eastwood, Nottinghamshire, the son of a miner. With his mother's encouragement, he became a schoolmaster and began to write, and, in 1911, after the success of his first novel, *The White Peacock*, he decided to write full-time. In 1912 he eloped with Frieda Weekley (*née* von Richthofen), a cousin of the German war ace Baron **Manfred von Richthofen** and wife of Ernest Weekley, and a professor at Nottingham University. They traveled in Europe for a year, and married in 1914 after her divorce. Lawrence had made his reputation with the semiautobiographical *Sons and Lovers* (1913). They returned to England at the outbreak of World War I. In 1915 he published *The Rainbow*, an exploration of marital and sexual relations, and he was horrified when prosecuted for obscenity. He left England in 1919, and after three years' residence in Italy, where he produced another exploration of sex and marriage, *Women in Love* (1921), he went to the US, settling in New Mexico until the tuberculosis from which he suffered drove him back to Italy, where his last years were spent. He was again shocked by further prosecutions for obscenity over the private publication in Florence of *Lady Chatterley's Lover* in 1928 and over an exhibition of his paintings in London in 1929. *Lady Chatterley's Lover* was not published in the UK in unexpurgated form until after a sensational obscenity trial in 1961. Lawrence attempted to explore human emotion on a deeper level of consciousness than that handled by his contemporaries, which provoked either sharp criticism or an almost idolatrous respect. His descriptive passages are sometimes superb, but he had little humor, and this occasionally produced unintentionally comic effects. His finest writing occurs in his poems, where all but essentials have been pared away, but most of his novels have an enduring strength. His other major novels include *Aaron's Rod* (1922), *Kangaroo* (1923, reflecting a visit to Australia) and *The Plumed Serpent* (1926, set in Mexico). His collected poems were published in 1928, and his *Complete Poems* in 1957. An edition of *Complete Plays* appeared in 1965, and his other writings include vivid travel narratives, essays, works of literary criticism and two studies of the unconscious. Over 5,000 of his letters have been published (7 vols, 1979).

Lawrence, Ernest Orlando 1901–58 •*US physicist and Nobel Prize winner*• Born in Canton, South Dakota, he studied at the Universities of South Dakota and Minnesota and at Yale, and in 1929 he constructed the first cyclotron for the production of artificial radioactivity, fundamental to the development of the atomic bomb. He was professor at the University of California at Berkeley from 1930, and in 1936 was appointed first director of the radiation laboratory there. He was awarded the Nobel Prize for physics in 1939.

Lawrence, Geoffrey, 3rd Baron Trevithin and **1st Baron Oaksey** 1880–1971 •*English lawyer*• He graduated from Oxford and was called to the bar in 1906. He became a judge of the High Court of Justice (King's Bench Division) in 1932, a Lord Justice of Appeal in 1944, and a Lord-of-Appeal-in-Ordinary (1947–57). As president of the international tribunal for the trial of war criminals at Nuremberg in 1945, he was distinguished for his fair and impartial conduct of the proceedings. Made Baron Oaksey in 1947, he succeeded his brother in the title of Trevithin in 1959.

Lawrence, Jacob 1917–2000 •*US painter*• Born in Atlantic City, New Jersey, the son of a railroad cook, he moved to New York City in 1930 and studied at the Harlem Art Workshop and the American Artists School. Influenced by Social Realism, Cubism and by primitive art, he began to paint scenes from African-American life in a bold, angular style. He often executed a series of works on a single theme, notably *Frederick Douglass* (1938–39), *Harriet Tubman* (1939–40) and *The Migration of the Negro* (1940–41). He taught at numerous institutions, notably the Art Students League and the New School for Social Research in New York City, and from 1970 was Professor of Art at the University of Washington in Seattle (emeritus from 1983).

Lawrence, Marjorie Florence 1908–79 •*Australian soprano*• Born in Deans Marsh, Victoria, she made her debut in 1932 with the Monte Carlo Opera, and the following year appeared in Paris. In 1935 she became a member of the Metropolitan Opera, New York, where for four years she was a leading Wagnerian soprano. In 1941, while touring in Mexico, she contracted poliomyelitis. Returning to the US she was treated by Sister **Elizabeth Kenny**, and by the end of the following year was making guest appearances at the Met in a wheelchair. During World War II she traveled extensively to entertain the troops, including visits to the Pacific and to Europe. Her autobiography, *Interrupted Melody* (1949), was filmed in 1955.

Lawrence, T(homas) E(dward), *known as* **Lawrence of Arabia** 1888–1935 •*Anglo-Irish soldier and writer*• Born in Tremadoc, Caernarvonshire, North Wales, he was raised in Oxford. He joined the archaeological team under Sir **Flinders Petrie** at Carchemish, on the Euphrates (1911–14), where he first met the Bedouins. In

World War I he worked for army intelligence in North Africa (1914–16). In 1916 he was British liaison officer to the Arab revolt against the Turks led by **Faisal I**. He cooperated with General **Allenby**'s triumphal advance and entered Damascus in October 1918. He was an adviser to Faisal at the Paris Peace Conference and a member of the Middle East Department at the Colonial Office (1921). His account of the Arab Revolt, *Seven Pillars of Wisdom*, became one of the classics of war literature. Lawrence enlisted in the ranks of the RAF (1922) as J H Ross, in the Royal Tank Corps (1923) as T E Shaw, and again in the RAF in 1925. He retired in 1935, and was killed that year in a motorcycling accident in Dorset.

“ ”

Many men would take the death sentence without a whimper to escape the life-sentence which fate carries in her other hand.

*1936 **The Mint**, part 1, chapter 4.*

Lawrence of Arabia *See* **Lawrence, T E**

Lawson, Henry Hertzberg 1867–1922 •*Australian poet and short-story writer*• He was born near Grenfell, New South Wales, the son of a Norwegian sailor and gold miner, and **Louisa Lawson**, a founder of the movement for women's suffrage in New South Wales. From his mother and her friends Henry acquired the radical opinions which colored his own writing, and his first collection, *Short Stories in Prose and Verse* (1894), was published by his mother. It was followed by the volume of verse *In the Days When the World Was Wide* (1896) and the short-story collection *While the Billy Boils* (1896). He then moved with his wife and son to London, where he prepared a collection of his earlier stories for *Blackwood's Magazine*. His later years were marred by ill health and alcoholism.

Lawson, Louisa, *née* **Albury** 1848–1920 •*Australian writer, social reformer and suffragist*• She was born in Guntawang, near Mudgee, New South Wales, and in 1866 married a Norwegian, Niels Hertzberg Larsen. The family name was anglicized to Lawson after the birth of their son, the later famous **Henry Lawson**. Louisa left her husband in 1883 and took her five children to Sydney, where she worked as a seamstress. Soon involved in radical and feminist politics and social reform, she bought the *Republican* in 1887, editing it with Henry until 1888, then founded the journal *Dawn*, which she edited for 17 years, offering household advice, stories and reports on women around the world. In 1889 she founded the Dawn Club, a feminist activist group. In 1900 she was thrown from a train and suffered physical and psychological injuries from which she never fully recovered. She lived the rest of her life in poverty. Australian women were given the vote in 1902.

Lawson, Nigel Lawson, Baron 1932– •*English Conservative politician*• Educated at Westminster and Christ Church, Oxford, he embarked on a career as a journalist after Royal Navy national service (1954–56). From *The Financial Times* he moved to the *Sunday Telegraph*, where he was city editor, then gradually entered politics, becoming Member of Parliament for Blaby, Leicestershire, in 1974. **Margaret Thatcher** appointed him Energy Secretary (1981–83) and Chancellor of the Exchequer in 1983. From this post he dramatically resigned in 1989, being replaced by **John Major**. Though at first one of Margaret Thatcher's closest Cabinet colleagues, by the late 1980s they had become increasingly estranged over Lawson's advocacy of lower interest rates to cure industrial stagnation and of Great Britain's full membership in the European monetary system. His resignation marked the beginning of a party split that widened during the following year and saw Thatcher dropped as party leader in November 1990. He resigned from the House of Commons in 1992 and was awarded a life peerage the same year. Following his dramatic weight loss, he published *The Nigel Lawson Diet Book* in 1996. He is the father of chef and author **Nigella Lawson** and the newspaper editor Dominic Lawson (1956–).

Lawson, Nigella 1960– •*English television chef and author*• The daughter of the former Chancellor **Nigel Lawson** and sister of the newspaper editor Dominic Lawson (1956–), she was born in London and studied at Lady Margaret Hall, Oxford. She began a restaurant column for the *Spectator* magazine in 1985 and in the following year became deputy literary editor of the *Sunday Times*. As well as her work as a journalist and columnist she is the author of the best-selling cookbooks *How to Eat* (1998), *How to Be a Domestic Goddess* (2000) and *Nigella Bites* (2001), the last of which she presented as a television series.

Laxness, Halldór Kiljan, *pseudonym of* **Halldór Guðjónsson** 1902–98 •*Icelandic novelist and Nobel Prize winner*• He was born in Reykjavík, and raised on a farm near there. After World War I he steeped himself in expressionism in Germany, Catholicism in a monastery in Luxembourg, and surrealism in France, before going to Canada and the US (1927–30), where he was converted to socialism. In his fiction he explored the reality of Iceland, past and present, and rejuvenated Icelandic prose in a series of incomparable epic novels like *Salka Valka* (1931–32) and *Íslandsklukkan* (1943–46, "Iceland's Bell"). After World War II he continued to turn out a stream of brilliantly executed novels on Icelandic life: *Atómstöðin* (1948, Eng trans *The Atom Station*, 1961), *Gerpla* (1952, Eng trans *The Happy Warriors*, 1958), *Brekkukotsannáll* (1957, Eng trans *The Fish Can Sing*, 1966) and *Kristnihald undir Jökli* (1968, Eng trans *Christianity at Glacier*, 1972) which was filmed in 1989. He also wrote a number of plays and seven volumes of autobiography (1963–87).

Layamon fl. early 13th century •*English poet and priest*• He lived at Ernley (Areley), Worcestershire. In c. 1200 he wrote an alliterative verse chronicle on the history of England, the *Brut*. It is the first poem written in Middle English.

Lazarus, Emma 1849–87 •*US poet and essayist*• Born in New York, she published volumes of poems and translations, including *Songs of a Semite* (1882) and *By the Waters of Babylon* (1887). She also wrote a prose romance, *Alide: An Episode of Goethe's Life* (1874), and a verse tragedy. A champion of oppressed Jewry, she is best known for her sonnet, "The New Colossus" (1883), inscribed on the Statue of Liberty in New York harbor.

Leach, Bernard Howell 1887–1979 •*English potter*• Born in Hong Kong, he studied at the Slade School of Art, London, and went to Japan at the age of 21 to teach and study pottery. He returned to England with his family in 1920 and, together with Shoji Hamada (1894–1978), established the pottery at St Ives, Cornwall. He produced stoneware and rakuware using local materials and also turned to the 17th century as inspiration to produce English slipware. One of his aims was to provide sound handmade pots sufficiently inexpensive for people of moderate means to use daily. He began teaching at Dartington Hall, Devon, in 1932, and his written works include *A Potter's Book* (1940).

Leach, Sir Edmund Ronald 1910–89 •*English social anthropologist*• Born in Sidmouth, Devon, he studied mathematics and engineering at Clare College, Cambridge, then under **Bronisław Malinowski** at the London School of Economics. Soon after he left to carry out fieldwork among the Kachin of Burma, World War II broke out. He spent the war serving in Burma, then took a post in anthropology at the London School of Economics (1947–53), and in 1954 published his first major monograph, *Political Systems of Highland Burma*. This overturned orthodox notions of social structural equilibrium, demonstrating the complex and fluctuating relationship between ideal models and political conduct. He became Reader in Social Anthropology at Cambridge (1957–72), and Professor (1972–78), and provost of King's College (1966–79). In later years his major interest shifted to structuralism, and the analysis of myth and ritual, as in *Genesis as Myth and Other Essays* (1969). His other publications include *Lévi-Strauss* (1970) and *Social Anthropology* (1982).

Leacock, Stephen Butler 1869–1944 •*Canadian humorist and economist*• He was born in Swanmore, Hampshire, England, and raised and educated in Canada. He studied at the University of Toronto, and became first a teacher, then a lecturer at McGill University, and in 1908 head of the economics department there. He wrote several books on his subject, but it is as a humorist that he became widely known. Among his popular short stories, essays and parodies are *Nonsense Novels* (1911), *Winsome Winnie* (1920) and *The Garden of Folly* (1924). He also wrote biographies of **Mark Twain** (1932) and **Dickens** (1933). *The Boy I Left Behind Me*, an autobiography, appeared in 1946.

Leadbelly or **Lead Belly**, *originally* **Huddie William Ledbetter** 1888–1949 •*US folk and blues singer and guitarist*• He was born in Mooringsport, Louisiana. He was twice sentenced to long prison terms, for murder in 1917 and intent to murder in 1930, but received an early pardon on each occasion. While serving the second sentence, he was heard by folk researcher Alan Lomax (see **John Avery Lomax**), who helped secure his release. He moved to New York, where he became an important figure in the burgeoning folk scene, alongside **Woody Guthrie** and **Pete Seeger**. His rough-hewn vocals and blues-soaked 12-string guitar style were hugely influential into the rock era.

Leakey, Louis S(eymour) B(azett) 1903–72 •*British archaeologist and physical anthropologist*• He was born of British missionary parents in Kabete, Kenya, where he grew up with the Kikuyu tribe. Educated at St John's College, Cambridge, he took part in several archaeological expeditions in East Africa, made a study of the Kikuyu and wrote widely on African anthropology. He was curator of the Coryndon Memorial Museum at Nairobi (1945–61). His great discoveries of early hominid fossils took place at Olduvai Gorge in East Africa, where in 1959, together with his wife **Mary Leakey**, he unearthed the skull of *Zinjanthropus*, subsequently reclassified as a form of *Australopithecus* and now thought to be about 1.75 million years old. In 1960–63 at Olduvai Gorge he found remains of *Homo habilis*, a smaller species some 2 million years old, which led him to postulate the simultaneous evolution of two different species, of which *Homo habilis* was the true ancestor of modern humanity, while *Australopithecus* became extinct. In 1967 he discovered *Kenyapithecus africanus*, fossilized remains of a Miocene ape, c. 14 million years old.

Leakey, Mary Douglas, *née* **Nicol** 1913–96 •*English archaeologist*•She was born in London. She met **Louis Leakey** while preparing drawings for his book *Adam's Ancestors* (1934), became his second wife in 1936, and moved soon afterward to Kenya where she undertook pioneering archaeological research. In 1948, at Rusinga Island, in Lake Victoria, she discovered *Proconsul africanus*, a 1.7-million-year-old dryopithecine (primitive ape) that brought the Leakeys international attention. From 1951 she worked at Olduvai Gorge in Tanzania, initially on a modest scale, but more extensively from 1959 when her discovery of the 1.75-million-year-old hominid *Zinjanthropus* (later reclassified as a form of *Australopithecus*), filmed as it happened, captured the public imagination and drew vastly increased funding. *Homo habilis*, a new species contemporary with, but more advanced than, *Zinjanthropus* was found in 1960–63. Perhaps most remarkable of all was her excavation in 1976 at Laetoli, 30 miles (48.3 km) south of Olduvai, of three trails of fossilized hominid footprints which demonstrated unequivocally that our ancestors already walked upright 3.6 million years ago.

Leakey, Richard Erskine Frere 1944– •*Kenyan paleoanthropologist and politician*• He was born in Nairobi, the second son of British archaeologists **Louis** and **Mary Leakey**, and from an early age worked in the field with his parents. He left school at 16 and trapped animals for zoos, collected animal skeletons for zoologists, and ran a safari company before organizing his first research expedition, to Peninj on Lake Natron (1964), Lake Baringo (1966), and the Omo Valley in Ethiopia (1967). From 1969 to 1975 he worked on the eastern shores of Lake Turkana, and discovered well-preserved hominid remains that drew worldwide publicity. Of particular note are crania of *Australopithecus boisei* (found 1969), of *Homo habilis* dated to 1.9 million years (found 1972), and of *Homo erectus* dated to 1.5 million years (found 1975). He was appointed administrative director of the National Museum of Kenya in 1968 (director 1974–89) and then in 1989 became chairman, then director (1993–94, 1998–99), of the Kenya Wildlife Service, where he organized a high-profile anti–ivory poaching campaign. In 1995 he cofounded and became secretary general of the Safina Party and then a Member of Parliament in 1998. He was appointed permanent secretary, secretary to the Cabinet and head of the Kenyan civil service in 1999, but resigned unexpectedly in 2001.

Lean, Sir David 1908–91 •*English film director*• Born in Croydon, London, he began in the film industry as a clapperboard boy. His codirection, with **Noël Coward**, of *In Which We Serve* (1942) and *Blithe Spirit* (1945) led to a full-scale directorial career in which his craftsmanship and compositional acumen were combined with a strong sense of narrative in films like *Brief Encounter* (1945), *Great Expectations* (1946) and *Oliver Twist* (1948). Increasingly drawn toward works of an epic and grandiose scale, he won Academy Awards for *Bridge on the River Kwai* (1957) and *Lawrence of Arabia* (1962). *Dr Zhivago* (1965) was followed by *Ryan's Daughter* (1970) and his last film, after a gap of 14 years, *A Passage to India* (1984). His sparse output has been attributed to exacting artistic standards.

Lear, Edward 1812–88 •*English artist, humorist and traveler*• He was born in London, the youngest of 20 children, and was educated at home, mainly by his sister, Anne. In 1832 he was engaged by the 13th Earl of Derby to make colored drawings of the rare birds and animals in the menagerie at Knowsley Hall (Merseyside). Under the Earl's patronage he traveled widely in Italy and Greece, making landscape sketches and oil paintings which he published in several travel books. He became a friend of his patron's grandchildren, whom he entertained with nonsense limericks and other verse which he illustrated with his own sketches and first published (anonymously) as *A Book of Nonsense* in 1846. Later he published *Nonsense Songs, Stories, Botany, and Alphabets* (1871), *More Nonsense Rhymes* (1871) and *Laughable Lyrics* (1876). He spent most of his latter years in Italy.

“ ”

And what can we expect if we haven't any dinner,
But to lose our teeth and eyelashes and keep on growing thinner?

1871 ***Nonsense Songs, Stories, Botany, and Alphabets***, *"The Two Old Bachelors."*

Lear, William Powell 1902–78 •*US inventor and electronic engineer*• Born in Hannibal, Missouri, he joined the US Navy at age 16 and studied radio and electronics. His 150 or more patents in the fields of radio, electronics, aviation and automobile engineering included the first practical car radio, the first commercial radio compass for aircraft, and an automatic pilot for jet aircraft. In 1962 he founded Lear Jet Corp, which became the largest manufacturer of small private jet planes. Lear Motors Corp (1967) tried unsuccessfully to introduce steam-powered cars and buses.

Leavis, F(rank) R(aymond) 1895–1978 •*English literary critic*• Born in Cambridge and educated at the university there, he fought against literary dilettantism in the quarterly *Scrutiny* (1932–53), which he founded and edited, as well as in his *New Bearings in English Poetry* (1932). From 1936 to 1962 he was a Fellow of Downing College, Cambridge. He developed **I A Richards**'s ideas about practical and close criticism into a kind of crusade against industrialization and mass culture, and his sociological study, *Culture and Environment* (1933, with D Thomson), deploring the separation of culture and environment in modern times and emphasizing the importance of impressing critical standards upon the young, has become a classic. Other works include *Revaluation* (1936), *The Great Tradition* (1948), *The Common Pursuit* (1952), *D H Lawrence* (1955) and *Dickens the Novelist* (1970). The oft-repeated judgment that he was "the most important English-speaking critic of his time" is debatable, chiefly because of his unwillingness to see the virtues of those poets and novelists he disliked.

Leavitt, Henrietta Swan 1868–1921 •*US astronomer*• Born in Lancaster, Massachusetts, she attended Radcliffe College, and joined the staff at Harvard College Observatory in 1902, quickly becoming head of the department of photographic photometry. While studying Cepheid variable stars, she noticed that the brighter they were the longer their period of light variation. By 1912 she had succeeded in showing that the apparent magnitude decreased linearly with the logarithm of the period. This simple relationship proved invaluable as the basis for a method of measuring the distance of stars.

Lebesgue, Henri Léon 1875–1941 •*French mathematician*• Born in Beauvais, he studied at the École Normale Supérieure, and taught at Rennes, Poitiers, the Sorbonne and the Collège de

France. Following the work of Émile Borel (1871–1956) and René Baire (1874–1932), he developed the theory of measure and integration which bears his name, and applied it to many problems of analysis, in particular to the theory of **Fourier** series. Overcoming the defects of the **Riemann** integral, this theory has proved indispensable in all subsequent modern analysis.

Lebrun, Albert 1871–1950 •*French politician*• He was born in Mercy-le-Haut, Meurthe-et-Moselle. He became a Left Republican deputy in 1900, and was minister for the Colonies (1911–14), for Blockade and Liberated Regions (1917–19), senator (1920), and president of the Senate (1931). The last president of the Third Republic, he surrendered his powers to **Philippe Pétain** in 1940, and went into retirement from which he did not reemerge. His health was affected by a period of internment after arrest by the Gestapo in 1943.

Le Brun, Charles 1619–90 •*French historical painter*• Born in Paris, he studied under **Nicolas Poussin**, and for nearly 40 years (1647–83) exercised a despotic influence over French art and artists. He helped to found the Academy of Painting and Sculpture in 1648 and was the first director of the Gobelins tapestry works (1662). From 1668 to 1683 he was employed by **Louis XIV** in the decoration of Versailles.

Le Carré, John, *pseudonym of* **David John Moore Cornwell** 1931– •*English novelist*• Born in Poole, Dorset, he was educated at Sherborne School, the University of Bern, and, after military service in Austria, at Oxford. He went into the British Foreign Service as Second Secretary in Bonn and consul in Hamburg, from which post he resigned in 1964 to become a full-time writer. His novels present the unglamorous side of diplomacy and espionage, a world of boredom, squalor and shabby deceit, and he questions the morality of present-day diplomacy and traditional patriotic attitudes. His first published novel, *Call for The Dead* (1961), introduced his antihero George Smiley, who appears in most of his stories. *A Murder of Quality* was published in 1962, followed the next year by the very successful *The Spy Who Came In From the Cold*. After *The Looking-Glass War* (1965) and *A Small Town in Germany* (1968), *The Naive and Sentimental Lover* (1971), a departure from his usual subject and style, was not well received. He returned to his former world with *Tinker, Tailor, Soldier, Spy* (1974), *The Honourable Schoolboy* (1977), *Smiley's People* (1980), *The Little Drummer Girl* (1983), *The Russia House* (1989) and *The Secret Pilgrim* (1992), in which Smiley takes his final bow. Many of his books have been successfully filmed or televised.

Leclerc or **Le Clerc (de Hauteclocque), Jacques Philippe**, *properly* **Philippe Marie, Vicomte de Hauteclocque** 1902–47 •*French soldier*• Born in Belloy-Saint-Léonard, he had a prestigious military training. In World War II he served with the French army in France (1939–40), was captured and escaped twice during the German invasion, and joined the Free French forces under **Charles de Gaulle** in England. He became Military Commander in French Equatorial Africa, and led a force across the desert to join the British 8th Army, in 1942. He commanded the French 2nd Armored Division in Normandy, and liberated Paris in 1944.

Leconte de Lisle, Charles Marie René 1818–94 •*French poet*• Born in Saint-Paul, Réunion, he traveled for some years, then settled in Paris. He influenced all the younger poets, headed the school called *Parnassiens*, and succeeded to **Victor Hugo**'s chair at the Academy in 1886. His early poems appeared as *Poésies complètes* (1858), and other volumes include *Poèmes barbares* (1862) and *Poèmes tragiques* (1884).

Lecoq, Jacques 1921–98 •*French mime artist, teacher and director*• Born in Paris, in 1948 he joined the Padua University Theater, Italy, as a teacher and director, where he produced his first pantomimes. He became a member of the Piccolo Theater in Milan (1951), returned to Paris (1956) and established his own school, the École Internationale de Mime et de Théâtre. He formed his own company (1959), and began his research into the various theatrical disciplines of the clown, the buffoon, commedia dell'arte, tragedy and melodrama.

Le Corbusier, *pseudonym of* **Charles Édouard Jeanneret** 1887–1965 •*French architect*• Born in La Chaux-de-Fonds, Switzerland, he worked in Paris with the architect Auguste Perret (1874–1954), then associated with **Peter Behrens** in Germany (1910–11). In 1918 he published in Paris (with **Amédée Ozenfant**) the Purist manifesto, *Après Le Cubisme*, and began to work on his theory of the interrelation between modern machine forms and the techniques of contemporary architecture. His books have had worldwide influence on town planning and building design. His first building, based on the technique of the Modulor (a system using standard-sized units, the proportions of which are calculated according to those of the human figure), was the *Unité d'habitation*, Marseilles (1945–50), which was conceived as one of a number of tall buildings which, when the overall scheme ("la Ville radieuse") had been completed, would form a pattern projecting from the "carpet" of low buildings and open spaces. This was his favorite type of town planning concept, used again in designing Chandigarh, the new capital of the Punjab. In the 1920s, in collaboration with Charlotte Perriand (1903–99), he designed furniture, especially chairs, which used tubular metal in their construction.

Ledbetter, Huddie William *See* **Leadbelly**

Lederberg, Joshua 1925– •*US biologist, geneticist and Nobel Prize winner*• Born in Montclair, New Jersey, he studied biology at Columbia University, and became professor at the University of Wisconsin (1947–59) and at Stanford (1959–78), then president of Rockefeller University (1978–90), University Professor (1990–95, now emeritus) and Sackler Scholar from 1995. With **Edward Tatum**, he showed that bacteria can reproduce by a sexual process known as conjunction, and made a further fundamental contribution with his description of "transduction" in bacteria, whereby the bacterial virus transfers part of its DNA into the host bacterium. In 1958 he was awarded the Nobel Prize for physiology or medicine, jointly with Tatum and **George Beadle**, and in 1989 won a US National Medal of Science.

Lederman, Leon Max 1922– •*US physicist and Nobel Prize winner*• Born in New York City, he was educated at Columbia University, and since 1992 has been Pritzker Professor of Science at the Illinois Institute of Technology. It was suspected that the muon was composed of two subparticles, the electron charge being carried by the electron neutrino and the muon charge being carried by the muon neutrino. After an experiment performed at Brookhaven by Lederman, **Melvin Schwartz** and **Jack Steinberger**, they announced in 1962 that they had observed 20 muon events confirming the existence of the two distinct neutrino types. This was the basis for the idea that fundamental particles come in generations, with the electron, the muon and the tau lepton all having associated neutrinos. Lederman went on to discover the long-lived neutral kaon and the bottom quark. In 1988 he was awarded the Nobel Prize for physics together with Schwartz and Steinberger. His publications include *The God Particle* (1992).

Ledoux, Claude Nicolas 1736–1806 •*French architect*• Born in Dormans-sur-Marne, he was one of the great artists of neoclassicism, and was architect to **Louis XVI**. His major works include the Château at Louveciennes for Madame **du Barry** (1771–73), acclaimed by **Jean Fragonard**. The saltworks at Arc-et-Senans (1775–80) expressed his **Jean Jacques Rousseau**-inspired philosophy that human happiness is found in the rational exploitation of nature and the healthy organization of labor. The theater at Besançon (1771–73) is another of his works. In 1785 he was employed by the Fermes-Général to erect 60 tax buildings around Paris; of the few that were built, La Villette—a rotunda—is the best.

Led Zeppelin •*English hard rock band*• Singer Robert Plant (1948–) and guitarist Jimmy Page (1944–) were the key members of the band, although bassist and organist John Paul Jones (originally John Baldwin, 1946–) and the aggressive drumming of John Bonham (1948–80) were integral to their sound. Despite a reputation as the founding fathers of hard rock, there was an undoubtedly respectful blues side and an increasingly folksy, semimystical aspect to their music. The group split up after Bonham's death, but the three surviving members reunited for a single concert in 1988. Plant and Page then toured and recorded their *Unledded* project in 1994.

Lee, Ang 1954– •*Taiwanese film director*• He was born in Taipei and moved to the US in 1978 to study at the universities of Illinois and New York. His early films, such as *Eat Drink Man Woman* (1994), examine conflicts within Chinese families, but his directorial versatility was shown in films such as the **Jane Austen** adaptation *Sense and Sensibility* (1995) and the war picture *The Berlin Diaries* (1998). *Crouching Tiger, Hidden Dragon* (2000), a new take on the traditional Chinese martial arts picture, received four Academy Awards in 2001.

Lee, Ann, *known as* **Mother Ann** 1736–84 •*American mystic and religious leader*• Born in Manchester, England, she was the illiterate daughter of a blacksmith. In 1758 she had joined the "Shaking Quakers," or "Shakers," and married Abraham Stanley, also a blacksmith, in 1762. She gave birth to four children, all of whom died in infancy, and in c. 1770 she experienced a spiritual crisis, rejected marriage and sexual relationships as sinful and asserted Christ was to appear in the Second Coming as a woman, a prophecy that the Shakers came to believe was realized in her. She emigrated with a handful of followers to America in 1774, and in 1776 founded the parent Shaker settlement at Niskayuna, 7 miles (11 km) northwest of Albany, New York. Her preaching and the peaceable communal life she helped to establish had attracted thousands of converts to the Shakers by the time of her death.

Lee, Christopher Frank Carandini 1922– •*English actor*• Born in London, he turned to acting in 1947 after distinguished service as an RAF flight lieutenant. His role as the monster in *The Curse of Frankenstein* (1956) began a long and profitable association with Hammer Films, and his portrayal of *Dracula* (1958) as an elegant and chilling sexual predator established him at the forefront of fantasy filmmaking. He quickly became one of the cinema's most prolific if less discriminating actors. His notable films include *Rasputin—The Mad Monk* (1965), *The Devil Rides Out* (1968), *The Creeping Flesh* (1972) and *The Wicker Man* (1973). A concerted attempt to widen his range resulted in a succession of character parts and star villains in such films as *The Private Life of Sherlock Holmes* (1970), *The Three Musketeers* (1973), *The Man With the Golden Gun* (1974) and *Serial* (1980). More recent work includes the part of Saruman in the *Lord of the Rings* trilogy (starting with *The Fellowship of the Ring*, 2001).

Lee, Gypsy Rose, *stage name of* **Rose Louise Hovick** 1914–70 •*US burlesque dancer and actress*• Born in Seattle, Washington, by the age of 17 she had joined the striptease troupe at Minsky's Burlesque in New York. She developed a sophisticated song style to accompany her suggestive, teasing dancing, and became the first burlesque artist to achieve widespread fame. She was the author of plays and stories, and her autobiography, *Gypsy* (1957), was adapted for the stage as a musical.

Lee, (Nelle) Harper 1926– •*US writer*• Born in Monroeville, Alabama, the daughter of a lawyer, she was a descendant of **Robert E Lee** and a childhood friend of **Truman Capote**. She won a Pulitzer Prize for fiction (1961) for her only novel, *To Kill a Mockingbird* (1960), which deals with racial injustice in a small Southern town through the eyes of a young girl.

Lee, James Paris 1831–1904 •*US inventor*• Born in Hawick, Scotland, he emigrated with his parents to Canada, later moving to Hartford, Connecticut. The "Lee-Enfield" and "Lee-**Metford**" rifles are based in part on his designs.

Lee (of Asheridge), Jennie Lee, Baroness 1904–88 •*Scottish Labour politician*• Born in Lochgelly, Fife, the daughter of a miner, she graduated from the University of Edinburgh, and at the age of 24, as a Labour Member of Parliament for North Lanark, became the youngest member of the House of Commons. In 1934 she married **Aneurin Bevan** and, despite her feminist principles, consciously stepped to one side as he rose within the Labour Party. Appointed Great Britain's first Arts Minister in 1964, she doubled government funding for the arts and was instrumental in setting up the Open University. She retired from the House of Commons in 1970 and was made a life peer.

Lee, Laurie 1914–97 •*English poet and writer*• He was born in Slad, Gloucestershire, and educated locally. He was a nature poet of great simplicity, whose works include *The Sun My Monument* (1944), *The Bloom of Candles* (1947) and *My Many-Coated Man* (1955). *A Rose For Winter* (1955) describes his travels in Spain, and his autobiographical books, *Cider With Rosie* (1959), *As I Walked Out One Midsummer Morning* (1969) and *I Can't Stay Long* (1975) are widely acclaimed for their evocation of a rural childhood, and of life in the numerous countries he visited. *A Moment of War* (1991, reprinted in 1992 as *Red Sky at Sunset*) takes up from the end of *As I Walked Out*, and recounts his experiences in Spain during the Civil War.

Lee, Nathaniel c. 1649/53–92 •*English playwright and actor*• Born possibly in London, he attended Westminster School, then went to Trinity College, Cambridge. When nervousness caused him to abandon an acting career, he turned to writing and produced about ten tragedies between 1674 and 1682. His finest, *The Rival Queens; or, The Death of Alexander the Great* (1677), is written in blank verse, and is representative not only of Lee's gift for dramatic rhetoric, but also of his grasp of character and political psychology. He collaborated with **John Dryden** on *The Duke of Guise* (1682). His plays were both popular and wildly sensational, containing many killings and several scenes of madness. Lee himself was not altogether a stable personality and was known to be one of the dissolute circle surrounding the notorious Earl of **Rochester**. His health subsequently broke down to the extent that he was confined in Bedlam from 1684 to 1689.

Lee, Richard Henry 1732–94 •*American Revolutionary leader*• Born in Westmoreland County, Virginia, he served in the Virginia House of Burgesses (1758–75), led the Patriot cause in Virginia with **Patrick Henry** and **Thomas Jefferson**, and coordinated several colonies' efforts toward independence. He was a member of the Continental Congress (1774–79, 1784–89) and signed the Declaration of Independence, although he opposed the new Constitution. He was also a US senator (1789–92).

Lee, Robert E(dward) 1807–70 •*US soldier, one of the greatest of the Confederate generals in the Civil War*• He was born in Westmoreland County, Virginia, and educated at the US Military Academy at West Point. He received a commission in the Engineer Corps, fought in the Mexican War (1846–48), and later became Superintendent of West Point. He commanded the US troops that captured **John Brown** at Harpers Ferry. When the Southern states seceded from the Union, he resigned from the US Army so he would be free to serve his native state of Virginia, and in 1861 he accepted the position of Commander in Chief of the Confederate Army of Virginia. Lee's achievements are central to the history of the Civil War. He was in charge of the defenses at Richmond, and halted Union forces in the Seven Days' Battles (1862). His forces were victorious in the second Battle of Bull Run (1862). At the Battle of Antietam (1862) his first northern invasion was stopped, but his troops repulsed the Union side in the Battle of Fredericksburg (1862) and were victorious at the Battle of Chancellorsville (1863). However, his second northern invasion ended in defeat at the Battle of Gettysburg (1863), and in the Wilderness Campaign (1864) Lee's forces were badly battered. In February 1865 Lee became Commander in Chief of all of the Southern armies, but the Confederate cause was hopeless at that point. Two months later he surrendered his army to General **Ulysses S Grant** at Appomattox Court House, Virginia. After the war, Lee became president of Washington College at Lexington.

“ ”

It is well that war is so terrible. We should grow too fond of it.

1862 Attributed, after the Battle of Fredericksburg, December.

Lee, Spike, *originally* **Shelton Jackson Lee** 1957– •*US filmmaker*• Born in Atlanta, Georgia, he grew up in Brooklyn, New York. He developed an interest in Super-8 filmmaking while at Morehouse College (1975–79), and at New York University's Institute of Film and Television he gained artistic recognition and a student Academy Award for his graduation film *Joe's Bed-Stuy Barbershop: We Cut Heads* (1982). Struggling to support himself, he sank his energies into the low-budget independent feature *She's Gotta Have It* (1986), which established him internationally. Determined to explode Hollywood's racial clichés and to express the texture and variety of African-American life, he sparked controversy with *School Daze* (1988) and *Do the Right Thing* (1989), a blistering assault on racism. An engaging actor in his own productions, his later films include *Mo' Better Blues* (1990), *Jungle Fever* (1991), *Malcolm X* (1992), *Crooklyn* (1994), *Girl 6* (1996), *He Got Game* (1998), *Summer of Sam* (1999) and *Bamboozled* (2000).

Lee, Tsung-Dao 1926– •*Chinese-US physicist and Nobel Prize winner*• He was born in Shanghai, China, and was educated at Jiangxi and at Zhejiang Universities. He won a scholarship to the University of Chicago in 1946, and from 1956 was professor at Columbia University, as well as a member of the Institute for Advanced Study (1960–63). With **Chen Ning Yang** he disproved the parity principle, till then considered a fundamental physical law, and they were awarded the Nobel Prize for physics in 1957.

Lee, Vernon, *pseudonym of* **Violet Paget** 1856–1935 •*English aesthetic philosopher, critic and novelist*• Born to English parents in Boulogne, France, she settled in Florence. Studies of Italian and Renaissance art were followed by her philosophical study, *The Beautiful* (1913), one of the best expositions of the empathy theory of art. She also wrote two novels and a dramatic trilogy, *Satan the Waster* (1920), giving full rein to her pacifism.

Leeds, Thomas Osborne, 1st Earl of Danby and **Duke of** 1631–1712 •*English statesman*• He became Member of Parliament for York in 1665. After opposition to the Earl of **Clarendon**, he was appointed Treasurer of the Navy (1668) and Privy Councillor (1673). He became Lord Treasurer in 1673, succeeding Thomas Clifford (1630–73) as King **Charles II**'s Chief Minister until his fall during the Exclusion Crisis (1679). He arranged for the marriage of Princess Mary (**Mary II**), daughter of James, Duke of York, to William of Orange (**William III**) (1677), but was impeached on charges of secret financial dealings with **Louis XIV** of France on Charles's behalf, and imprisoned in the Tower (1684). During **James VII and II**'s reign, he opposed the king's Catholic policies, and negotiated William of Orange's assumption of the Crown (1688). He was rewarded with the marquisate of Carmarthen and the presidency of the Council (1689–99) and made Duke of Leeds (1694), but further impeachment proceedings, for taking a bribe to secure a charter for the new East India Company (1695), ended his career as Chief Minister.

Lee Kuan Yew 1923– •*Singaporean statesman*• Born in Singapore into a wealthy Chinese family, he studied law at Cambridge and qualified as a barrister in London before returning to Singapore in 1951 to practice. He founded the moderate, anti-communist People's Action Party (PAP) in 1954 and became the country's first prime minister in 1959, overseeing the implementation of a successful program of economic development. He remained in power until November 1990, when his deputy Goh Chok Tong (1941–) took over. However, he still wields considerable influence as a senior minister in the Cabinet.

Lee Teng-Hui 1923– •*Taiwanese politician*• Born in Tamsui, Taiwan, and educated at universities in the US and Japan, he taught economics at the National Taiwan University before becoming mayor of Taipei in 1979. A member of the ruling Guomindang (Kuomintang) Party and a protégé of **Chiang Ching-Kuo**, he became vice president of Taiwan in 1984 and state president and Guomindang leader on Chiang's death in 1988. The country's first island-born leader, he was a reforming technocrat who significantly accelerated the pace of liberalization and "Taiwanization." His reelection in 1996 made him Taiwan's first democratically elected president. He stepped down at the 2000 elections, and then resigned as leader of the Guomindang party.

Leeuwenhoek, Anton van or **Antoni van** 1632–1723 •*Dutch amateur scientist*• Born in Delft, he was educated as a businessman, and became skilled in grinding and polishing lenses to inspect cloth fibers. With his microscopes, each made for a specific investigation, he discovered the existence of protozoa in water everywhere (1674) and bacteria in the tartar of teeth (1676). Independently, he discovered blood corpuscles (1674), blood capillaries (1683), striations in skeletal muscle (1682), the structure of nerves (1717) and plant microstructures, among numerous other observations.

Le Fanu, (Joseph) Sheridan 1814–73 •*Irish novelist and journalist*• Born in Dublin, he was a grandnephew of **Richard Sheridan**. Called to the bar in 1839, he soon abandoned law for journalism, and later bought three Dublin newspapers. His novels include *The House by the Churchyard* (1863) and *Uncle Silas* (1864), many of his short stories are collected in *In a Glass Darkly* (1872), and he wrote 14 other works, remarkable for their preoccupation with the supernatural. His *Poems* were published in 1896.

Legat, Nikolai Gustavovich 1869–1937 •*Russian dancer, teacher, ballet master and choreographer*• Born in St Petersburg, he joined the Maryinsky Theatre, where he spent 20 years as a principal. He took over the directorship of the company in 1905, dropping choreography for teaching. His pupils there included **Tamara Karsavina**, **Michel Fokine** and **Nijinsky**. In 1923 he moved to the US to become Ballet Master of **Sergei Diaghilev**'s company, but finally settled in London where he opened his own school and taught **Alexandra Danilova**, **Margot Fonteyn**, **Ninette de Valois**, **Anton Dolin** and **Serge Lifar**.

Legendre, Adrien-Marie 1752–1833 •*French mathematician*• Born in Paris, he studied at the Collège Mazarin, and became Professor of Mathematics at the École Militaire and a member of the French Academy of Sciences (1783). He proposed the method of least squares in 1806 (independently of **Carl Gauss**), and his classic work, *Essai sur la théorie des nombres* (1798, "Essay on the Theory of Numbers"), includes his discovery of the law of quadratic reciprocity. His *Traité des fonctions elliptiques* (1825, "Treatise on Elliptical Functions") became the definitive account of elliptic integrals prior to the work of **Niels Henrik Abel** and **Carl Jacobi**, and his *Éléments de géométrie* (1794), translated into English by **Thomas Carlyle**, reintroduced rigor to the teaching of elementary geometry in France.

Léger, Fernand 1881–1955 •*French painter*• Born in Argentan, he was a major force in the Cubist movement. Between 1903 and 1907 he studied at various Paris studios and initially painted in a diffuse Neo-Impressionist manner. He then discovered **Paul Cézanne** and began "constructing" his pictures with volumetric shapes. His pictures differ from those of his fellow members of the avant-garde in being more "tubist" than Cubist. By 1912, in pictures like *La femme en bleu* ("Woman in Blue"), Léger was nearing pure abstraction, but after World War I he returned to primarily figurative work in which the working man is combined with machinery in monumental patterns made up of heavy black outlines and primary color infill. He collaborated on the first "art-film," *Le ballet mécanique*, in 1923.

Legros, Alphonse 1837–1911 •*British painter*• Born in Dijon, France, he adopted England as his home. On the advice of **James McNeill Whistler**, he went to London in 1863 and by 1875 was in charge of the etching class at the Royal College. Appointed Slade Professor to University College in 1875–76, he exercised a strong traditional influence. His landscape and figure studies particularly mark him as an influential figure in the British etching movement.

Le Guin, Ursula K(roeber), *née* **Kroeber** 1929– •*US science-fiction writer*• She was born in Berkeley, California, the daughter of the anthropologist **Alfred Louis Kroeber**, and educated at Radcliffe College and Columbia University. Much of her work focuses on subjective views of a universe incorporating numerous habitable worlds, some spawned by beings from the "Hain." The Hain trilogy consists of *Rocannon's World* (1966), *Planet of Exile* (1966) and *City of Illusions* (1967). Other novels include *The Left Hand of Darkness* (1969), *The Word for World Is Forest* (1976) and *Dancing at the Edge of the World* (1989). In a prodigious work for children, known as the "Earthsea" trilogy, she depicts a magical but threatening world, in which every village has its small-time sorcerer and the forces of evil are uncomfortably close. She continued this trilogy in an overtly feminist vein with *Tehanu* (1990). Later works include *Searoad* (1991) and *The Telling* (2000).

" "

My imagination makes me human and makes me a fool; it gives me all the world and exiles me from it.

1990 "Winged Creatures on My Mind," in ***Harper's***, *August.*

Lehár, Franz 1870–1948 •*Hungarian composer*• Born in Komárom, he became a military band conductor in Vienna. He wrote a violin concerto but is best known for his operettas which include his most popular *The Merry Widow* (1905, *Die lustige Witwe*), *The Count of Luxembourg* (1909, *Der Graf von Luxemburg*), *Frederica* (1928, *Friederike*) and *The Land of Smiles* (1929, *Das Land des Lächelns*).

Lehmann, Beatrix 1903–79 •*English actress*• She was born in Bourne End, Buckinghamshire, the sister of **John** and **Rosamond Lehmann**. She first appeared on the stage in 1924 at the Lyric, Hammersmith, and subsequently appeared in many successful plays, including *Family Reunion*, **Peter Ustinov**'s *No Sign of the Dove*, and *Waltz of the Toreadors*. She also appeared in films and wrote two novels and several short stories.

Lehmann, John Frederick 1907–87 •*English writer and publisher*• He was born in Bourne End, Buckinghamshire, and educated at Trinity College, Cambridge. He founded the periodical in book format, *New Writing* (1936–41), was managing director of the Hogarth Press with **Leonard** and **Virginia Woolf** (1938–46), and ran his own firm, John Lehmann Ltd, with his sister, **Rosamond Lehmann**, as codirector from 1946 to 1953. In 1954 he inaugurated *The London Magazine*, which he edited until 1961. His first publications were volumes of poetry. He also wrote a novel, *Evil Was Abroad* (1938), and the studies *Edith Sitwell* (1952), *Virginia Woolf and Her World* (1975) and *Rupert Brooke* (1980). He wrote a three-volume autobiography.

Lehmann, Lotte 1888–1976 •*US soprano*• Born in Perleberg, Germany, she studied in Berlin, made her debut in Hamburg (1910), and sang at the Vienna Staatsoper (1914–38). She also appeared frequently at Covent Garden, London (1924–38), and at the New York Metropolitan Opera (1934–45). She was noted for her performances of **Schumann**'s songs and her roles in **Richard Strauss**'s operas. She became a US citizen, and retired to teach in Santa Barbara, California, in 1951.

Lehmann, Rosamond Nina 1901–90 •*English novelist*• She was born in High Wycombe, Buckinghamshire, the sister of **Beatrix** and **John Lehmann**, and studied at Girton College, Cambridge. Among her novels are *Dusty Answer* (1927), *An Invitation to the Waltz* (1932), *The Weather in the Streets* (1936), *The Echoing Grove* (1953) and *A Sea-Grape Tree* (1970), her last novel. She also wrote a play, *No More Music* (1939), and a volume of short stories, *The Gypsy's Baby* (1946), and in 1967 published the autobiographical *The Swan in the Evening*. She later became president of the College of Psychic Studies.

Lehn, Jean-Marie 1939– •*French chemist and Nobel Prize winner*• Born in Rosheim, Bas-Rhin, he studied at the University of Strasbourg, then collaborated with **Robert Woodward** at Harvard on vitamin B_{12} synthesis. He later joined the University of Strasbourg, becoming professor in 1970 and then professor at the Collège de France from 1979. Studying the mechanism of transport of metal ions across cell membranes, he built on **Charles Pedersen**'s work to show that metal ions can exist in a nonpolar environment if contained within the cavity of a large organic molecule. Such structures are known as cryptates, and similar compounds play an important role in the transport of metal ions across biological membranes. His research has initiated a new branch of organic chemistry—supramolecular chemistry—and earned him, along with Pedersen and **Donald Cram**, the Nobel Prize for chemistry in 1987.

Leibniz or **Leibnitz, Gottfried Wilhelm** 1646–1716 •*German philosopher and mathematician*• He was born in Leipzig, the son of a professor of moral philosophy. In 1667 he obtained a position at the court of the Elector of Mainz. There he codified laws, drafted schemes for the unification of the churches, and studied the work of **René Descartes**, **Isaac Newton**, **Blaise Pascal**, **Robert Boyle** and others. In London he came into contact with mathematicians of Newton's circle, causing a dispute later as to whether he or Newton was the inventor of the infinitesimal calculus; both had published systems in the 1680s. The Royal Society formally voted in favor of Newton in 1711, but the matter was never fully settled. In 1676 Leibniz became librarian to the Duke of Brunswick at Hanover. Here he continued to elaborate his mathematical and philosophical theories, without publishing them, and maintained a huge learned correspondence. In 1700 he persuaded **Frederick I** of Prussia to found the Prussian Academy of Sciences in Berlin, of which he became the first president. He was disliked by George of Hanover and was left behind in 1714 when the Elector moved the court to London to become king of Great Britain (as **George I**). Leibniz died in Hanover two years later, without real recognition and with almost all his work unpublished. Remarkable for his encyclopedic knowledge and diverse accomplishments outside the fields of philosophy and mathematics, he was perhaps the last universal genius, spanning the whole of contemporary knowledge. His best-known doctrine is that the world is composed of an infinity of simple, indivisible, immaterial, mutually isolated monads which form a hierarchy, the highest of which is God; the monads do not interact causally but constitute a synchronized harmony with material phenomena. Leibniz is recognized as one of the great rationalist philosophers, but he had perhaps his greatest influence (for example, on **Bertrand Russell**) as a mathematician and a pioneer of modern symbolic logic. He made original contributions to optics, mechanics, statistics, logic and probability theory; he conceived the idea of calculating machines, and of a universal language; he wrote on history, law and political theory; and his philosophy was the foundation of 18th-century rationalism. His *Essais de théodicée sur la Bonté de Dieu, la liberté de l'homme et l'origine du mal* (the *Theodicy*, 1710), was a relatively popular work in theology, which **Voltaire** satirized brilliantly in *Candide* ("all is for the best in this best of all possible worlds").

Leibovitz, Annie 1949– •*US photographer*• Born in Westbury, Connecticut, she was trained at the San Francisco Art Institute and established her reputation as a celebrity photographer working for *Rolling Stone* magazine in the 1970s. She worked for *Vanity Fair* from 1983 and founded the Anne Leibovitz Studio in New York in the early 1990s. Her most famous portraits include a wide variety of politicians, musicians and athletes, among them the last portrait ever taken of **John Lennon**. She published *Photographs 1970–90* in 1992 and (with **Susan Sontag**) *Women* in 2000.

Leicester, Robert Dudley, Earl of c. 1533–88 •*English nobleman*• He was the son of John Dudley, Earl of **Warwick**, who was executed for his support of Lady **Jane Grey**. Robert Dudley himself was sentenced to death, but, pardoned (1554), became a favorite of Queen **Elizabeth I**, who made him Earl of Leicester (1564). He was unpopular at court, and Elizabeth suggested him as a husband for **Mary Queen of Scots** (1563). He made a secret marriage to the Dowager Lady Sheffield, but he remained popular with Elizabeth, who was magnificently entertained by him at his castle of Kenilworth (1575). She was only temporarily offended when he bigamously married (1578) the widow of Walter Devereux, Earl of **Essex**. Sent in 1585 to command the expedition to the Low Countries in which Sir **Philip Sidney**, his nephew, died at Zutphen, he was recalled for incompetence in 1587, and his arrogance and touchiness were counterproductive, but he was nonetheless appointed as leader of the forces assembled at Tilbury to defend England against the Spanish Armada (1588). He died suddenly at Cornbury, in Oxfordshire, probably of malaria, but some alleged he had taken poison originally intended for his wife.

Leicester (of Holkham), Thomas William Coke, Earl of 1752–1842 •*English agriculturist*• One of the first agriculturists of England, by his efforts northwest Norfolk was converted from a rye-growing into a wheat-growing district, and animal husbandry generally improved. He represented Norfolk as a Whig Member of Parliament for periods during 1776–1833, and in 1837 was made Earl of Leicester of Holkham. He was a descendant of Sir **Edward Coke**.

Leif the Lucky, *real name* **Leifur heppni Eiríksson** fl. 1000 •*Icelandic explorer*• He was the son of **Erik the Red**. Just before the year 1000 he set sail from Greenland to explore lands to the west, reaching Baffin Land, Labrador, and an area he called "Vínland" (Wineland) because of the wild grapes he found growing there. The location of Vínland has defied precise identification, but incontrovertible remains of a Norse settlement have been found on Newfoundland. Two Icelandic sagas, *Eiríks saga rauða* ("Saga of

Eric") and *Grœnlendinga saga* ("Tale of the Greenlanders"), tell the story of the Norse discovery and attempted colonization of North America, 500 years before **Christopher Columbus** discovered the New World.

Leigh, Mike 1943– *•English film and theater director•* Born in Salford, Greater Manchester, he trained as an actor at the Royal Academy of Dramatic Art in London and subsequently studied at the Camberwell Art School, the Central School of Arts and Crafts, and the London Film School. An assistant director with the Royal Shakespeare Company from 1966, he began to develop his own style of reflecting the bittersweet ironies of everyday lives through pieces improvised in collaboration with handpicked actors. He made his film debut with *Bleak Moments* (1971) and created acutely observed social comedies for television including *Nuts in May* (1976) and *Abigail's Party* (1977). His stage work includes *Goose Pimples* (1981) and *Smelling a Rat* (1988). He returned to the cinema with *High Hopes* (1988), *Life Is Sweet* (1990), *Naked* (1993), *Secrets and Lies* (1996)—which gained the Palme d'Or at the Cannes Film Festival, five Academy Award nominations and three British Academy of Film and Television Arts awards—*Career Girls* (1997) and *Topsy-Turvy* (1999).

Leigh, Vivien, *originally* **Vivian Mary Hartley** 1913–67 *•British actress•* She was born in Darjeeling, India, and after training at the Royal Academy of Dramatic Art, her first film role was in *Fire Over England* (1936) with **Laurence Olivier**, whom she later married (1940–60). In Hollywood she played her best-known part, Scarlett O'Hara in *Gone With the Wind* (1939), which won her an Academy Award. Other major film roles were in *Anna Karenina* (1948) and *A Streetcar Named Desire* (1951), which gained her another Academy Award.

Leigh-Mallory, Sir Trafford 1892–1944 *•English air force officer•* Born in Cheshire, he was educated at Magdalen College, Oxford. He served with the Royal Flying Corps in World War I, and in World War II he commanded Groups in Fighter Command in the Battle of Britain. He was Commander in Chief of Fighter Command (1942–44) and of Allied Expeditionary Air Forces for the Normandy landings (1944). Appointed Commander in Chief of Allied Air Forces in Southeast Asia, he was killed in an air crash during the journey there.

Leighton (of Stretton), Frederic Leighton, Baron 1830–96 *•English painter•* Born in Scarborough, Yorkshire, he studied and traveled extensively in Europe and had immediate success with *Cimabue's Madonna Carried in Procession Through Florence* (1855)—a picture purchased by Queen **Victoria**. Also from his early period is his masterpiece *Songs Without Words* (1860–61, Tate Britain, London). Among his later works were *Paolo and Francesca* (1861), *The Daphnephoria* (1876) and *The Bath of Psyche* (1890). An aesthete and idealist, he was also a distinguished sculptor, and in 1877 his *Athlete Struggling With a Python* was purchased out of the **Chantrey** Bequest. A president of the Royal Academy, London, his final words are said to have been "Give my love to the Academy."

Leighton, Margaret 1922–76 *•English actress•* Born near Birmingham, she became one of the best-known actresses of her era. She joined the Old Vic under **Laurence Olivier** and **Ralph Richardson** in the 1940s, and made her Broadway debut in 1946. Her major plays include **Terence Rattigan**'s *Separate Tables* (1956) and **Tennessee Williams**'s *The Night of the Iguana* (1961). She was nominated for an Academy Award for the film *The Go-Between* (1971).

Leino, Eino, *pseudonym of* **Armas Eino Leopold Lönnbohm** 1878–1926 *•Finnish poet and novelist•* He published his first poetry collection, *Maaliskuun lauluja* (1896, "Spring Songs"), at age 18. He developed the meter of the *Kalevala*, or national epic, into a distinctive, somberly lyrical style of his own, best exemplified in the two volumes of *Helkavirsiä* (1903, 1916, "Whitsongs"), the second of which is overshadowed by his reaction to World War I. He also wrote novels, and various translations.

Leishman, Sir William Boog 1865–1926 *•Scottish bacteriologist•* Born in Glasgow, he obtained his MD from the University of Glasgow in 1886, and later became director-general of the Army Medical Service (1923). In 1900 he discovered the protozoan parasite (named after him as *Leishmania*) responsible for the disease known variously as kala-azar and dumdum fever. He went on to develop the widely used Leishman's stain for the detection of parasites in the blood. He also made major contributions to the development of various vaccines, particularly those used against typhoid fever, and it was as a result of his work that mass vaccination was introduced in 1914 for the British army. He was knighted in 1909.

Leland, John c.1506–52 *•English antiquarian•* Born in London, he was educated at Christ's College, Cambridge, and All Souls College, Oxford. After a stay in Paris he became chaplain to **Henry VIII**, who in 1533 made him "king's antiquary." His church preferments were the rectories of Peuplingues, near Calais, and Haseley in Oxfordshire, a canonry of King's College (now Christ Church), Oxford, and a prebend of Salisbury. Most of his papers are in the Bodleian and British Museums. Besides his *Commentarii de scriptoribus Britannicis*, his chief works are *The Itinerary* and *De rebus Britannicis collectanea*.

Leloir, Luis Frederico 1906–87 *•Argentine biochemist and Nobel Prize winner•* Born in Paris, France, and educated in Buenos Aires and at Cambridge, he worked mainly in Argentina where he set up his own research institute in 1947. He discovered a number of glucose enzymes and studied their reactions. In the 1950s Leloir linked these reactions to the formation of the energy storage material glycogen in the body. For this work, complementing that of **Carl Cori**, he was awarded the Nobel Prize for chemistry in 1970.

Lely, Sir Peter, *originally* **Pieter van der Faes** 1618–80 *•British painter•* Born probably in Soest, Westphalia, he settled in London in 1641 as a portrait painter. He was patronized by **Charles I** and **Oliver Cromwell**, and in 1661 was appointed court painter to **Charles II**, for whom he changed his style of painting. His *Windsor Beauties* series is collected at Hampton Court. The 13 Greenwich portraits titled *Admirals* are outstanding for their depth and sincerity of characterization, and present a marked contrast to his very popular and often highly sensuous court portraits, which sometimes have a hasty, superficial appearance.

Lemaître, Georges Henri 1894–1966 *•Belgian astrophysicist and cosmologist•* He was born in Charleroi, and studied engineering at the University of Louvain. After voluntary service in World War I, he turned to mathematical and physical sciences and obtained his doctorate in 1920. Three years later he was ordained as a Catholic priest and obtained a traveling scholarship from the Belgian government, which took him to Cambridge, Harvard and MIT. In Cambridge he came under the strong influence of Sir **Arthur Eddington**. In 1927 he published his first major paper on the model of an expanding universe and its relation to the observed red shifts in the spectra of galaxies. In the 1930s he developed his ideas on cosmology, and from 1945 on he put forward the notion of the "primeval atom" that is unstable and explodes, starting what is now called the big bang, the beginning of the expanding universe.

Le Mesurier, John, *originally* **John Elton Halliley** 1912–83 *•English actor•* Born in Bedford, he started working life as a solicitor's apprenticed clerk before training as an actor and touring in shows until World War II. After the war, he found success in British comedy films such as *I'm All Right, Jack* (1959), *The Punch and Judy Man* (1960) and *The Pink Panther* (1963). He was also a regular on television with Tony Hancock in *Hancock's Half Hour* (1956–61) and followed that with the sitcom *George and the Dragon* (1966–68), before finding fame as Sergeant Wilson in the long-running *Dad's Army* (1968–77).

Lemmon, Jack (John Uhler) 1925–2001 *•US film and stage actor•* Born in Boston, he graduated from Harvard and served in the navy in World War II. An appearance on the Broadway stage (1953) brought him to the attention of Hollywood, where he soon became established as one of the screen's most skilled comedy performers. *Some Like It Hot* (1959) began a successful seven-film collaboration with director **Billy Wilder**. Other acclaimed performances are *Days of Wine and Roses* (1962) and *The China Syndrome* (1979). His long association with **Walter Matthau** included *The Odd Couple* (1968) and many others. He directed one film, *Kotch* (1971). Nominated eight times for an Academy Award, he won Best

Supporting Actor for *Mister Roberts* (1955) and Best Actor for *Save the Tiger* (1973). Among his later films were *Glengarry Glen Ross* (1992) and *Hamlet* (1996).

LeMond, Greg(ory James) 1961– •*US cyclist*• Born in Lakewood, California, in 1986 he became the first American to win the Tour de France, winning it again in 1989 and 1990. His 1989 victory captivated the sporting world. After 23 days and 1,400 miles (2,253 km), LeMond rode the race's fastest-ever time-trial to beat French favorite Laurent Fignon (1960–) by just eight seconds. He retired after contracting a rare muscular wasting disease.

Lenard, Philipp Eduard Anton 1862–1947 •*German physicist and Nobel Prize winner*• Born in Pozsony, Hungary (now Bratislava, Slovakia), and educated at the University of Heidelberg, he was a researcher at the Universities of Bonn and Breslau before returning to Heidelberg as professor (1896–98). He then moved on to the University of Kiel (1898–1907) before returning to the University of Heidelberg until his retirement in 1931. His observations of the photoelectric effect were explained by **Albert Einstein** in 1905, and his studies of the magnetic deflection of cathode rays and their electrostatic properties led him to suggest that atoms contain units of both positive and negative charge. For these studies he was awarded the Nobel Prize for physics in 1905.

Lenbach, Franz 1836–1904 •*German portrait painter*• Born in Schrobenhausen, Bavaria, he worked mostly in Munich. For some time he copied the great masters, including **Titian**, **Rubens** and **Velázquez**, before becoming one of the greatest 19th-century German portrait painters. His portraits of **Bismarck** are particularly famous.

Lenclos, Anne, *known as* **Ninon de Lenclos** 1620–1705 •*French courtesan, poet and feminist*• Born of a good family in Paris, she started her long career at the age of 16, founding a salon which favored Jansenists. Among her lovers were two marquises, two marshals, the great **Condé**, and the Dukes of **La Rochefoucauld** and Sévigné. Her behavior cost her a spell in a convent in 1656 at the behest of **Anne of Austria**, but her popularity ensured a swift release, and afterward she wrote *La Coquette vengée* (1659, "The Coquette Avenged") in her own defense. She was celebrated almost as much for her manners and taste as for her beauty. She had two sons, one of whom, not realizing who she was, fell in love with her. Informed of their relationship, he killed himself.

Lenclos, Ninon de *See* **Lenclos, Anne**

Lendl, Ivan 1960– •*US tennis player*• He was born in Ostrava (now in the Czech Republic). He won the singles title at the US Open (1985–87), French Open (1984, 1986–87), and Australian Open (1989), and was the Masters champion (1986–87) and the World Championship Tennis champion (1982, 1985). He was runner-up at Wimbledon in 1986–87. He became the first official world champion in 1987. He became a US citizen in 1992 and retired from tennis in 1994.

Leng, Virginia, *née* **Holgate** 1955– •*British three-day-event athlete*• Born in Malta, she was the European junior champion in 1973. She then won the team gold at the senior championship in 1981, 1985 and 1987, and individual titles in 1985, 1987 and 1989. She won the world championship team gold in 1982 and 1986, and the individual title in 1986 on Priceless. She has also won at Badminton (1985, 1989, 1993) and at Burghley (1983–86, 1989).

L'Engle, Madeleine 1918– •*US novelist*• Born in New York City, she was educated at Smith College and at the New School for Social Research in New York. A prolific writer for children as well as adults, she imbues her work with explicitly Christian ideas and morals. Her most popular titles include *A Wrinkle in Time* (1962, Newbery Medal), *The Arm of the Starfish* (1965), and *The Young Unicorns* (1968), all of which combine elements of fantasy with tough ethical concerns.

Lenglen, Suzanne 1899–1938 •*French tennis player*• Born in Compiègne, she was trained by her father, and became famous in 1914 by winning the women's world hard-court singles championship at Paris at the age of 15. She was the woman champion of France (1919–23, 1925–26), and her Wimbledon championships were the women's singles and doubles (1919–23, 1925), and the mixed doubles (1920, 1922, 1925). She won the singles and doubles gold medals at the 1920 Olympic Games.

Lenin, Vladimir Ilyich, *originally surnamed* **Ulyanov** 1870–1924 •*Russian revolutionary*• He was born into a middle-class family in Simbirsk, and educated at the Universities of Kazan and St Petersburg, where he graduated in law. From 1895 to 1897 he was in prison and from 1897 to 1900 he was exiled to Siberia for participating in underground revolutionary activities; there he used his time to study and write extensively about **Marx**ism. At the Second Congress of the Russian Social Democratic Party (1903), he caused the split between what came to be called the Bolshevik and Menshevik factions. Apart from the frustrating period of the Russian Revolution of 1905, he spent from then until 1917 abroad, developing and publicizing his political views. Following the February Revolution in 1917, he returned to Petrograd from Zurich, and urged the seizure of power by the proletariat under the slogan "All Power to the Soviets." In October 1917 he initiated the Bolshevik revolution and became head of the first Soviet government. He made peace with Germany at Brest-Litovsk in order to concentrate on defeating the White Army in the ensuing Russian Civil War (1918–21), and then changed tactics again by switching from a ruthless centralized policy of "war communism" to the New Economic Policy, which his critics in the Communist Party saw as a "compromise with capitalism" and a retreat from strictly socialist planning. On his death, his body was embalmed and placed in a mausoleum in front of the Moscow Kremlin, where it still lies. In 1924 Petrograd (formerly St Petersburg) was renamed in his honor. Much was subsequently done in his name by **Stalin** and others, some of which he would not have approved of. But the nature of the USSR and the reasons for its final collapse in 1991 owed much to him; and it was not altogether surprising that the citizens of Leningrad eventually voted for their city to resume the name of St Petersburg.

Lenk, Timur *See* **Timur**

Lennon, John (Winston) 1940–80 •*English songwriter, vocalist and rhythm guitarist*• Born in Liverpool, he first found fame as a member of the **Beatles**, and pursued a solo career after the group disbanded in 1970. His marriage to Japanese conceptual artist **Yoko Ono** sharpened his social conscience and refocused the surreal wit that was part of his Lancashire Catholic inheritance. Their work together produced songs of mild protest such as "Give Peace a Chance" (1969), "Cold Turkey" (1969) and "Working Class Hero" (1970), a rare balance of the personal and political. His most successful albums were *Imagine* (1971) and *Mind Games* (1973). He was shot dead in New York.

" "

We're more popular than Jesus Christ now. I don't know which will go first, rock 'n' roll or Christianity.

*1966 In the **Evening Standard**.*

Lennox, Annie 1954– •*Scottish pop singer*• Born in Aberdeen, she was working as a waitress in Hampstead, London, when she met musician and composer Dave Stewart (1952–) in 1977. They formed The Tourists, and recorded three albums before disbanding in 1980 and forming The Eurythmics. The combination of his intricate pop hooks and her strong, soulful vocals made them one of the most successful pop bands of the decade, but each decided to pursue solo careers. She took a break from music in 1990, but returned in 1992 to launch her lavish solo album *Diva*. In 1999 she and Stewart briefly returned as The Eurythmics and produced the album *Peace*.

Leno, Dan, *originally* **George Galvin** 1860–1904 •*English comedian*• He began his career at the age of four, singing and dancing in public houses, and by 18 had become a champion clog-dancer. Ten years later he joined the Augustus Harris management at Drury Lane, where he appeared for many years as a "dame" in the annual pantomime. Leno was a slight man and his foil was the bulky Herbert Campbell (1844–1904). When Campbell had a fatal accident in 1904, Leno grieved and died six months later.

Leno, Jay (James Douglas Muir) 1950– •*US comedian and television host*• Born in New Rochelle, New York, and raised in Andover, Massachusetts, he was already performing stand-up comedy in nightclubs while studying speech therapy at Emerson College in Boston. After moving to Los Angeles in 1973 he started to write for and appear in comedy and variety shows on television, including *The Tonight Show* and *Late Night with David Letterman*. Since 1992 he has been host of *The Tonight Show*, for which he won an Emmy Award in 1995.

Lenya, Lotte, *originally* **Karoline Wilhelmine Blamauer** 1898–1981 •*Austrian actress and cabaret singer*• Born in Hitzing, Vienna, she studied dancing in Zurich (1914–20) and moved to Berlin (1920), where she took up acting and married **Kurt Weill** (1926). Her international reputation was made by her roles in his works, notably as Jenny in *Die Dreigroschenoper* (1928, *The Threepenny Opera*, a collaboration with **Brecht**). In 1933 the couple fled Germany to Paris and then settled in the US (1935), where she continued to act on stage and in film. After Weill's death she became the public custodian of his legacy, and supreme interpreter of his work.

Lenz, Heinrich Friedrich Emil 1804–65 •*German physicist*• Born in Dorpat, Russia (now Tartu, Estonia), he first studied theology, but became Professor of Physics at St Petersburg (1836) and a member of the Russian Academy of Sciences. He was the first to state Lenz's law governing induced current, and is credited with discovering the dependence of electrical resistance on temperature (**Joule**'s law).

Leo I, St, *known as* **the Great** c. 390–461 AD •*Italian pope*• Born possibly in Tuscany, he was one of only two popes (the other being **Gregory I**) to take the title "the Great." Pope from AD 440 to 461, he was one of the most eminent of the Latin Fathers. He summoned the Council of Chalcedon (451), which accepted his doctrine of the Incarnation, and made treaties with **Attila** the Hun (452) and with the Vandals (455) in defense of Rome.

Leo III, *called* **the Isaurian** c. 680–741 •*Byzantine emperor*• Born in northern Syria, near Isauria, he raised the Byzantine Empire from a very low condition after seizing the crown from Theodosius III (717). He reorganized the army and financial system, produced a new legal code, and repelled a formidable attack by the Saracens (718). In 726 he prohibited the use of images in public worship, and the subsequent controversy split the empire for over a century. In 728 Ravenna was lost, and the eastern provinces became the prey of the Saracens, over whom, however, Leo won a great victory at Phrygia.

Leo III c. 750–816 •*Byzantine pope*• During his pontificate (795–816), he saw the formal establishment of the Empire of the West. In the 8th century the popes, through the practical withdrawal of the Eastern emperors, had exercised a temporal supremacy in Rome, under the protectorate of the Frankish sovereigns. Leo was obliged to flee to Spoleto in 799, from which he went to Paderborn to confer with **Charlemagne**. On his return to Rome he was received with honor. In 800 Charlemagne, having come to Rome, was crowned emperor by Leo, and the temporal sovereignty of the pope over the Roman city and state was formally established, under the suzerainty of the emperor.

Leo X, *originally* **Giovanni de' Medici** 1475–1521 •*Italian pope*• He was born in Florence. The second son of **Lorenzo de' Medici**, the Magnificent, and the brother of **Piero de' Medici**, he was made a cardinal at age 13. Elected pope in 1513, he is best remembered as a patron of learning and the arts. He founded a Greek college in Rome and established a Greek press. His project for the rebuilding of St Peter's made it necessary to preach an indulgence in order to raise funds to do so and this provoked **Martin Luther**'s 95 theses. Leo's failure to respond either promptly or effectively helped to increase the Reformation's early momentum.

Leo Africanus, *properly* **Alhassan ibn Mohammed Alwazzan** c. 1494–c. 1552 •*Arab traveler and geographer*• He was born in the kingdom of Granada, and from c. 1512 traveled in northern Africa and Asia Minor. Falling into the hands of Venetian corsairs, he was sent to Pope **Leo X** in Rome, where he lived for 20 years, and accepted Christianity. He wrote *Descrittione dell'Africa* (1550, Eng trans *A Geographical Historie of Africa*, 1660), an account of his African travels in Italian and for a long time the chief source of information about the Sudan.

Leon, Daniel de *See* **De Leon, Daniel**

León, Ernesto Zedillo Ponce de *See* **Zedillo Ponce de León, Ernesto**

León, Juan Ponce de *See* **Ponce de León, Juan**

Leonard, Elmore John 1925– •*US thriller writer*• He was born in New Orleans, served in the US Navy during World War II, and afterward studied English literature at the University of Detroit. Throughout the 1950s he worked in advertising as a copywriter, but since 1967 he has concentrated on screenplays and novels, remarkable for their relentless pace and vivid dialogue. His numerous books include *Gold Coast* (1980), *Stick* (1983), *La Brava* (1983) and *Pronto* (1993). In later years he has reached a new audience through high-profile cinematic adaptations of his novels *Get Shorty* (1990, filmed 1995), *Rum Punch* (1992, filmed as *Jackie Brown* 1997 by **Quentin Tarantino**) and *Out of Sight* (1996, filmed 1998).

Leonard, Sugar Ray 1956– •*US boxer*• Born in South Carolina, he won an Olympic gold in Montreal in 1976, starting a professional career in which he fought 12 world title fights at various weights and won world titles in each weight. In 35 fights between 1977 and 1987, he was beaten only once, by Roberto Duran, who took the welterweight title from him on points in 1980. Leonard became the undisputed world welterweight champion in 1981 when he beat Tommy Hearns and earned a record fee of more than $10 million. He retired permanently in 1997.

Leonardo da Vinci 1452–1519 •*Italian painter, sculptor, architect and engineer*• He was born in Vinci, between Pisa and Florence. He showed unusual gifts at an early age, and around 1470 he was sent to study in the studio of **Andrea del Verrocchio**, where **Botticelli** and **Perugino** were also pupils. To this period belong the *Baptism of Christ* and the unfinished *Adoration of the Magi*, now in the Uffizi Gallery in Florence. In 1482 he settled in Milan in the service of Duke **Ludovico Sforza**. His famous tempera painting *Last Supper* (1498) was painted on a wall of the refectory of the convent of Santa Maria delle Grazie. Among other paintings in Milan were portraits of two mistresses of the duke, one of them perhaps *La belle ferronnière* of the Louvre. He also devised a system of hydraulic irrigation of the plains of Lombardy and directed the court pageants. After the fall of Duke Ludovico in 1500, Leonardo retired to Florence, and entered the service of **Cesare Borgia**, then Duke of Romagna, as architect and engineer. In 1503 he returned to Florence, and began work on a *Madonna and Child With St Anne*, of which only the cartoon now in the Royal Academy, London, was completed. About 1504 he completed his most celebrated easel picture, *Mona Lisa*. Another work portrayed the celebrated beauty Ginevra Benci; and Pacioli's *De divina proportione* (1509) contained 60 geometrical figures from Leonardo's hand. In 1506 he was employed by **Louis XII** of France. **Francis I** bestowed on him in 1516 a yearly allowance, and assigned to his use the Château Cloux, near Amboise, where he lived until his death. Among his later works are *The Virgin of the Rocks*, now in the National Gallery, London, a figure of *St John the Baptist*, and *Saint Anne*. Leonardo occupies a supreme place as an artist, but so few of his works have survived that he may be most fully studied in his drawings, of which there are rich collections in Milan, Paris, Florence and Vienna, as well as in England in the British Museum and at Windsor Castle. His celebrated *Trattato della pittura* was published in 1651; but a more complete manuscript, discovered by Manzi in the Vatican, was published in 1817. Voluminous manuscripts by him in Milan (*Codice Atlantico*), Paris, Windsor, and elsewhere have been reproduced in facsimile. Leonardo was the outstanding all-around genius of the Renaissance. He had a wide knowledge and understanding far beyond his times of most of the sciences, including biology, anatomy, physiology, hydrodynamics, mechanics and aeronautics, and his notebooks, written in mirror writing, contain original remarks on all of these.

“ ”

To devise is the work of the master, to execute the act of the servant.

Treatise on Painting *(published 1651, translated by A P McMahon, 1956).*

Leonardo of Pisa *See* **Fibonacci, Leonardo**

Leoncavallo, Ruggiero 1858–1919 •*Italian composer*• Born in Naples, he studied at the Naples Conservatorio. He produced *I Pagliacci* (1892, "Clowns"), traditionally staged with **Pietro Mascagni**'s *Cavalleria Rusticana* (1890, "Rustic Chivalry"). He followed this with other less successful operas, including a *La Bohème* (1897, "Bohemian life") which failed where **Puccini**'s (1896), on the same theme, was a success.

Leoni, Leone 1509–90 •*Italian goldsmith, medalist and sculptor*• Born in Arezzo, he worked in Milan, Genoa, Brussels and Madrid, and was the rival of **Benvenuto Cellini** in talent, vice and violence. His fine medals often depicted well-known artists, such as **Titian** and **Michelangelo**, and his sculpture, which was mostly in bronze, included busts of **Charles V** and **Philip II of Spain**, both of whom he served for some time.

Leonidas d. c. 480 BC •*King of Sparta*• He succeeded his half-brother, Cleomenes I (491 BC). When the Persian king **Xerxes I** approached with a large army, Leonidas opposed him at the narrow pass of Thermopylae (480) with his 300 Spartans and 700 Thespians, and there all of them died heroically.

Leonov, Aleksei Arkhipovich 1934– •*Russian astronaut*• Born in Listvyanka, in 1955 he went to the Chuguyev Air Force Flying School in Ukraine, thereafter serving with air force units. He specialized in parachute training and joined the astronaut corps in 1959. On March 18, 1965, he performed the first extravehicular activity from the spacecraft *Voskhod 2* in orbit around the Earth, walking in space for 10 minutes. In 1975 he took part in the joint US-USSR Apollo-Soyuz space mission.

Leontief, Wassily 1906–99 •*US economist and Nobel Prize winner*• Born in St Petersburg, Russia, and educated at Leningrad (now St Petersburg) State University and the University of Berlin, he went to the US in 1930. He taught at Harvard from 1931 to 1975 (professor from 1946), and from 1975 to 1985 was director of the Institute of Economic Analysis at New York University. His most important work was an analysis of US industry, *The Structure of the American Economy, 1919–29* (1941). He was awarded the 1973 Nobel Prize for economics for developing the input-output method of economic analysis, used in more than 50 industrialized countries for planning and forecasting.

Leopardi, Giacomo 1798–1837 •*Italian poet*• Born in Recanati, by the age of 16 he had read all the Latin and Greek classics, could write French, Spanish, English and Hebrew, and had written a commentary on **Plotinus**. He devoted himself to literature; although an invalid, he traveled widely. His works, which show his pessimistic views on life, include lyrics, collected under the title *I Canti* (1831, Eng trans *The Poems*, 1893), dialogues and essays classed as *Operette Morali* (1827, translated in a bilingual edition under the original title, 1983), *Pensieri* (7 vols, 1898–1900, "Thoughts") and letters.

Leopold I 1790–1865 •*King of Belgium*• Born in Coburg, he was the son of Francis, Duke of Saxe-Coburg, and uncle of Queen **Victoria**. A general in the Russian army, he served at Lützen, Bautzen and Leipzig (1813). He married (1816) Princess **Charlotte** of Great Britain (d. 1817). In 1831 he was elected king of the Belgians and married Marie-Louise, daughter of **Louis Philippe**, in 1832. By his moderate policies he did much to prevent Belgium becoming too involved in the revolutions which were raging in other European countries in 1848.

Leopold II 1835–1909 •*King of Belgium*• The son of **Leopold I**, he was born in Brussels. Energetic and well traveled, his chief interest was the expansion of Belgium abroad. In 1885 he became king of the independent state of the Congo, but the exposure of atrocities to natives working in rubber production (1904) led to its being annexed to Belgium (1908). At home he strengthened his country by military reforms and established a system of fortifications. He was not popular as a king, but under him Belgium flourished, developing commercially and industrially. He was succeeded by his nephew, **Albert I**.

Leopold III 1901–83 •*King of Belgium*• Born in Brussels, he was the son of King **Albert I** and became king in 1934. On his own authority he ordered the capitulation of his army to the Nazis (1940), and remained a prisoner in his own palace at Laeken and in Austria. After the war, 58.1 percent of voters favored his return in a plebiscite (1950), but continued unrest persuaded him to abdicate in favor of his son **Baudouin I** in 1951.

Leopold I 1640–1705 •*Holy Roman Emperor*• Born in Vienna, he was the second son of Emperor **Ferdinand III** and the Infanta Maria Anna of Spain (daughter of **Philip III**). He became king of Hungary (1655) and Bohemia (1656), and was elected emperor (1658) in succession to his father. For most of his reign he was at war either with the Ottoman Turks over Hungary, or with **Louis XIV** of France. The first war with Turkey (1661–64) ended in victory at St Gotthard. The second war (1682–99) involved the siege of Vienna (1683), relieved by John III Sobieski of Poland, and ended with the Treaty of Karlowitz, giving Leopold control of virtually all of Hungary. In 1686 he had combined with England and the Dutch Stadtholder William of Orange (later **William III** of Great Britain) to resist French expansionism in Europe, culminating in the War of the Spanish Succession (1701–14), which attempted to prevent the succession of the **Bourbon** House in Spain. Under him the Baroque flourished, and Vienna became renowned as a cultural center. In 1703 his refusal to respect the traditional rights of the Hungarian nobles led to an uprising under **Francis II Rákóczi**. By his third wife, Eleanora of Neuburg, he had two sons who both succeeded him as emperor, **Joseph I** and Charles VI.

Leopold II 1747–92 •*Holy Roman Emperor*• Born in Vienna, the third son of **Francis I** and **Maria Theresa**, he succeeded his father as Grand Duke of Tuscany (1765), and his brother, **Joseph II**, as emperor (1790). He pacified the Netherlands and Hungary, and after the downfall of his sister, **Marie Antoinette**, he formed an alliance with Prussia against France, but died before war broke out.

Le Pen, Jean-Marie 1928– •*French politician*• The son of a Breton fisherman, he graduated in law at Paris before serving in the 1950s as a paratrooper in Indo-China and Algeria, where he lost an eye during a violent street battle. In 1956 he won a National Assembly seat as a right-wing Poujadist. He formed the National Front in 1972, which, with its extreme right-wing policies, emerged as a new "fifth force" in French politics, winning 10 percent of the national vote in the 1986 Assembly elections. A controversial figure and noted demagogue, he was barred from public office for two years in 1998 due to his riotous behavior during the 1997 general election campaign. This was reduced to a year on appeal, and Le Pen was eventually allowed to retain his seat in the European Parliament, which he had held since 1984.

Lepidus, Marcus Aemilius d. 13 BC •*Roman politician*• He supported **Julius Caesar** against **Pompey** during the civil war (49–31 BC), and became Caesar's deputy at Rome (46). He supported **Mark Antony**, and became one of the triumvirate with him and Octavian (Emperor **Augustus**). Outmaneuvered by Octavian in the power struggle of the 30s BC, he retired from active politics, but remained head of state religion (Pontifex Maximus) until his death.

Lepsius, (Karl) Richard 1810–84 •*German Egyptologist*• He was born in Naumburg. His first work on paleography as an instrument of philology (1834) won the Volney prize of the French Institute, and in 1836 at Rome he studied Egyptology, Nubian, Etruscan and Oscan. From 1842 to 1845 he headed an antiquarian expedition sent to Egypt by **Frederick William IV** of Prussia, and in 1846 he was appointed professor in Berlin. His *Denkmäler aus Aegypten und Aethiopien* (12 vols, 1849–60, "Egyptian and Ethiopian Monuments") remains an important work, and his *Chronologie der Aegypter* (1849, "Egyptian Chronology") laid the foundation for a scientific treatment of early Egyptian history. Other works include the *Todtenbuch* (1867)—the Egyptian Book of the Dead—and writings on Chinese, Arabic and Assyrian philology.

Lermontov, Mikhail Yuriyevich 1814–41 •*Russian poet*• Born of Scottish parents in Moscow, he attended Moscow University and then the military cavalry school of St Petersburg, where he received a commission in the guards. A poem written in 1837 on the death of **Alexander Pushkin** caused his arrest and he was sent to the Caucasus. Reinstated, he was again banished following a duel with the son of the French ambassador. Another duel was the cause of his death in 1841. He wrote from an early age, but much of his work was not published until his last years and his fame was posthumous. He is best known for his novel *Geroy nashego vremeni* (1839, Eng trans *A Hero of Our Times*, 1854).

Lerner, Alan Jay 1918–86 •*US librettist, lyricist and playwright*• Born in New York City, he worked with **Frederick Loewe**, whom he met in 1942, and they collaborated to produce several successful Broadway musicals, including *Brigadoon* (1947), *Paint Your Wagon* (1951), and *My Fair Lady* (1956), and the film *Gigi* (1958). Lerner also wrote the script for the film *An American in Paris* (1951), and (with composer Burton Lane [1912–97]) produced the musical *On a Clear Day You Can See Forever* (1965, filmed 1970).

“ ”

Oozing charm from every pore
He oiled his way around the floor.

*1956 "You Did It," from **My Fair Lady** (music by Frederick Loewe).*

Lesage or **Le Sage, Alain René** 1668–1747 •*French novelist and dramatist*• He was born in Sarzeau, Brittany, and in 1692 went to Paris to study law. In 1707 *Don César Ursin*, from **Pedro Calderón de la Barca**, was played with success at court, and the following year the Théâtre Français showed interest in the play which later became his famous *Turcaret*. As a novelist his reputation rests on *Gil Blas* (4 vols, 1715–35). Later works include *Bachelier de Salamanque* (1736–38, "The Bachelor of Salamanque") and a volume of letters, *La valise trouvée* (1740, "A Suitcase Discovered"). The death of his son (1743), a promising actor, and his own increasing infirmities, made him abandon Paris and literary life, and he retreated to Boulogne, where he lived until his death. Some critics deny originality to one who borrowed ideas, incidents and tales from others as Lesage did, but he was a great raconteur and the first to perceive the capabilities of the picaresque novel.

Lescot, Pierre c. 1510–1578 •*French Renaissance architect*• Born in Paris, he was one of the greatest architects of his time. Among his works are the screen of St Germain l'Auxerrois, the Fontaine des Innocents and the Hôtel de Ligneris, all in Paris. His masterpiece was the Louvre, one wing of which he completely rebuilt.

Lese, Benozzo di *See* **Gozzoli, Benozzo**

L'Esperance, Elise, *née* **Strang** 1878–1959 •*US physician and founder of women's cancer clinics*• Born in Yorktown, New York, she studied at the Women's Medical College in New York. She worked in pediatrics for some years, then in 1910 she moved to the department of pathology at Cornell University, remaining there until 1932, and becoming the first woman assistant professor there in 1920. Her research on cancer stimulated her to found the Kate Depew Strang clinics in memory of her mother. Important work carried out at the Strang Clinics included the development by Dr **George Papanicolaou** of the "Pap" smear to detect cervical cancer.

Lesseps, Ferdinand, Vicomte de 1805–94 •*French diplomat and entrepreneur*• Born in Versailles, he was a cousin of the Empress **Eugénie**, wife of **Napoleon III**. From 1825 he held diplomatic posts in Lisbon, Tunis, Cairo, and other cities. In 1854 he began his campaign for the construction of the Suez Canal, and in 1856 obtained a concession from the viceroy. The works were begun in 1860 and completed in 1869. In 1881 work began on his overambitious scheme for a sea-level Panama Canal, but had to be abandoned in 1888. In 1892–93 the management was charged with breach of trust, and sentenced to five years' imprisonment for embezzlement, but the sentence was reversed.

Lessing, Doris May, *née* **Tayler** 1919– •*Rhodesian writer*• She was born in Kermanshah (Bakhtaran), Iran, the daughter of a British army captain, and her family moved to Southern Rhodesia (Zimbabwe) in 1924. From 1937 to 1949 she lived in Salisbury, where she became involved in politics and helped to start a nonracist left-wing party. She went to London in 1949, and her experiences of working-class life there are described in *In Pursuit of the English* (1960). Her first published novel was *The Grass Is Singing* (1950), a study of the sterility of white civilization in Africa. In 1952 *Martha Quest* appeared, the first novel in her sequence *The Children of Violence*. The other novels are *A Proper Marriage*, 1954, *A Ripple From the Storm*, 1958, *Landlocked*, 1965, and *The Four-Gated City*, 1969. Partly autobiographical, the sequence tells the life story of Martha, discussing contemporary social and psychological problems, particularly the unattainable ideal of a city where there is no violence. Other works include *The Golden Notebook* (1962) and *Briefing for a Descent Into Hell* (1971), both fictional studies of so-called mental breakdown. More recently, she has also attempted science fiction, but her commitment to exploring political and social undercurrents in contemporary society has never wavered and can be seen to potent effect in *The Good Terrorist* (1985). More recent publications include the autobiographical *Under My Skin* (1994) and *Walking in the Shade* (1997).

“ ”

There is only one real sin, and that is to persuade oneself that the second-best is anything but the second-best.

*1962 **The Golden Notebook**, "The Blue Notebook"*

Lessing, Gotthold Ephraim 1729–81 •*German writer*• Born in Kamenz, Saxony, he studied theology at Leipzig (1746). In 1751 he went to Wittenberg, took his master's degree, and produced a series of *Vindications* of unjustly maligned or forgotten writers. In 1755 he produced his classic tragedy *Miss Sara Sampson* (1755). It was based on English rather than French models, and in his contributions to a new critical Berlin journal, *Briefe, die neueste Literatur betreffend* (1758, "Letters Concerning the Latest Literature"), he protested against the dictatorship of French taste, and extolled **Shakespeare**. His famous critical treatise defining the limits of poetry and the plastic arts, *Laokoon; oder, Über die Grenzen der Malerei und Poesie* (1766, Eng trans *Laocoon; or, The Limits of Poetry and Painting*, 1853), was written while he was secretary to the governor of Breslau (now Wrocław, Poland). In 1769 he was appointed Wolfenbüttel librarian by the Duke of Brunswick, and between 1774 and 1778 he published the *Wolfenbüttelsche Fragmente eines Ungenannten* ("Anonymous Fragments From Wolfenbüttel"), a rationalist attack on orthodox Christianity from the pen of the theologian Hermann Reimarus (1694–1768) which, universally attributed to Lessing, provoked a storm of refutations. The best of Lessing's counterattacks were *Anti-Goeze* (1778) and the fine dramatic poem, *Nathan der Weise* (1779, Eng trans *Nathan the Wise*, 1868), a noble plea for toleration.

Lethaby, William Richard 1857–1931 •*English architect, designer and teacher*• Born in Barnstaple, Devon, he trained as an architect, then worked (1877–87) in London. He was a founder of the Art Workers' Guild (1884) and the Arts and Crafts Exhibition Society (c. 1886). He was associated with Ernest Gimsonin Kenton & Co during the period when he designed his most important building, Avon Tyrrell, near Salisbury, with Gimson plaster ceilings and Kenton furniture. The Central School of Arts and Crafts, London, was founded in 1896 with Lethaby and the sculptor, Sir George Frampton (1860–1928), as joint principals. Lethaby was sole principal from 1900 to 1912. The emphasis he placed on workshop practice at the Central School set a precedent for design education, including that at the Bauhaus in Germany.

Letterman, David 1947– •*US comedian and television host*• He was born in Indianapolis. After studying radio and television at Ball State University, Muncie, Indiana, he hosted various local television shows in Indianapolis before moving to Los Angeles in 1975. He became a regular guest host on *The Tonight Show* in 1978, and in 1981 began his own show, *Late Night with David Letterman*. Its hugely successful blend of traditional talk-show format with Letterman's own irreverent and oddball humor and comic stunts has won him several Emmy Awards.

Leucippus 5th century BC •*Greek philosopher*• Born in Miletus, Asia Minor (or in Elea, Lucania), he was the originator of the atomistic cosmology which **Democritus** later developed and which is most fully expounded in **Lucretius**'s great poem *De rerum natura*. Leucippus is thought to have written two books, *The Great World System* and *On the Mind*, but his theories and writings are not reliably separable from those of Democritus.

Le Vau or **Levau, Louis** 1612–70 •*French architect*• He was born in Paris, and headed a large studio of artists and craftsmen, producing outstanding Baroque designs for the aristocracy. Among his early works, the Hôtel Lambert, Paris, stands out particularly for the ingenious use of location. His masterful design of Vaux-le-Vicomte (1657–61), with formal landscape by **André Lenôtre**, constituted an influential milestone in French architecture, leading to his Baroque masterpiece of Versailles (from 1661, again with Lenôtre), designed on a palatial scale for court and government.

Levene, Phoebus Aaron Theodor, *originally* **Fishel Aaronovich Lenin** 1869–1940 •*US biochemist*• Born in Sasar, Russia, he received a medical degree from St Petersburg University in 1891 and emigrated to New York in 1892. His interest soon shifted to chemistry, and in 1905 he became a founding member of the Rockefeller Institute in New York, applying chemistry to biological problems, and spent his career there. The most important of his many biochemical studies is his pioneer research on the nucleic acids. His work established the nature of the sugar component which defines the two types of nucleic acid (RNA, ribonucleic acid; and DNA, deoxyribonucleic acid). Levene also published extensively on the chemistry of the sugar phosphates and the optical isomerism of organic substances.

Lever, Charles James 1806–72 •*Irish novelist*• Born in Dublin, of English parentage, he graduated from Trinity College, Dublin, in 1827, and then went to Göttingen to study medicine. His most popular work, *Charles O'Malley* (1841), is a description of his own college life in Dublin. About 1829 he spent some time in the backwoods of Canada and North America, and he later related his experiences in *Arthur O'Leary* (1844) and *Con Cregan* (1849). After practicing medicine in Ireland and Brussels, and publishing *Jack Hinton* (1843), he was again in Europe, where he wrote such novels as *Roland Cashel* (1850), *The Daltons* (1852) and the *Fortunes of Glencore* (1857). He was appointed British vice consul in Spezia in 1858, and in 1867 he was promoted to the consulship in Trieste. He wrote brilliant, rollicking sketches of a phase of Irish life which was passing away, but no doubt his caricatures created a false idea of Irish society and character.

Leverhulme, William Hesketh Lever, 1st Viscount 1851–1925 •*English soapmaker and philanthropist*• Born in Bolton, Greater Manchester, he worked in his father's grocery business. Later he opened new shops and, in 1886 with his brother, James, started the manufacture of soap from vegetable oils instead of tallow. He also founded the model industrial new town of Port Sunlight. Among his many benefactions, he endowed at the University of Liverpool a school of tropical medicine and gave Lancaster House to the UK.

Levertov, Denise 1923–97 •*US poet*• Born in Essex, England, to a Welsh mother and a Russian-Jewish father who became an Anglican clergyman, she was educated privately, and emigrated to the US in 1948. She was appointed poetry editor of *The Nation* in 1961. *The Double Image* (1946) was her first collection of verse and others appeared regularly. She was outspoken on many issues (including the Vietnam War and feminism), and her poetry was similarly questioning. Her *New and Selected Essays* were published in 1992.

Lévesque, René 1922–88 •*Canadian statesman*• Born in New Carlisle, Quebec, he became a journalist and television commentator and was elected to the Quebec National Assembly in 1960. In 1967 he helped found the separatist group called Mouvement Souveraineté-Association, which became the Parti Québecois. As president of the party, then Premier of Quebec (1976), he advocated establishment of a French country which would be independent from English-speaking Canada. Although the people of Quebec rejected Lévesque's plan in a popular referendum vote in 1980, he was reelected Premier the following year. He resigned in 1985 due to failing health.

Levi, Primo 1919–87 •*Italian writer and chemist*• He was born to Jewish parents in Turin and studied chemistry at the University of Turin. During World War II he fled into the mountains and tried to help set up a small guerrilla force, but this "deluge of outcasts" was accidentally discovered and in December 1943 Levi was arrested, turned over to the SS, and shipped off to Auschwitz. He was one of the few to survive, partly, after it was discovered he was Jewish, because he contracted scarlet fever as the Russians approached, causing the Germans to leave him behind when they evacuated the camp. Those 10 months in Auschwitz haunted him for the rest of his life and may have prompted his suicide. His first book, *Se questo è un uomo* (Eng trans *If This Is a Man*, 1959), was completed soon after his return to Turin and was published in 1947. A graphic account of life in a concentration camp, it is written with a chemist's detached sensibility, making it all the more powerful. His best-known book is *Il sistemo periodico* (1975, Eng trans *The Periodic Table*, 1984), a volume of memoirs and autobiographical reflections. His other titles include *La chiave a stella* (1978, Eng trans *The Wrench*, 1987) and *Se non ora, quando?* (1982, Eng trans *If Not Now, When?*, 1985).

Levi-Montalcini, Rita 1909– •*Italian neuroscientist and Nobel Prize winner*• She was born and educated in Turin, where she studied medicine, but from 1939 on she was prevented, as a Jew, from holding an academic position. In 1947 she was invited by Viktor Hamburger to Washington University in St Louis, where she was professor from 1958 until her retirement in 1977. Primarily studying chemical factors that control the growth and development of cells, she isolated a substance now called nerve growth factor, revealing that it had many diverse sources, that it was chemically a protein, and that cells are most responsive to its effects during the early stages of differentiation. This work has provided powerful new insights into the processes of some neurological diseases and possible repair therapies, as well as into tissue regeneration and cancer mechanisms. In 1986 she shared the Nobel Prize for physiology or medicine with **Stanley Cohen**.

Levine, James 1943– •*US pianist and conductor*• Born in Cincinnati, Ohio, he was a child prodigy who made his piano debut with the Cincinnati Symphony Orchestra at age 10, and he studied at the Juilliard School of Music in New York. He became apprentice conductor at the Cleveland Symphony Orchestra in 1964 and was soon appointed assistant conductor. In 1971 he made his debut at the Metropolitan Opera in New York, conducting **Puccini**'s *Tosca* and he was named the Met's principal conductor the following year. In 2004 he became the Music Director for the Boston Symphony Orchestra.

Lévi-Strauss, Claude 1908– •*French social anthropologist and philosopher*• Born in Brussels, Belgium, he was a graduate in law and philosophy, and became interested in anthropology while lecturing (1934–39) at the University of São Paulo, Brazil. He subsequently became director of studies at the École Pratique des Hautes Études in Paris (1950–74). Since the publication of *Les structures élémentaires de la parenté* (1949, Eng trans *The Elementary Structures of Kinship*, 1969), he has exerted a considerable influence on contemporary anthropology. In his extensive four-volume study *Mythologiques* (1964–72, "Mythologies"), he reveals the systematic ordering behind codes of expression in different cultures, and argues that myths are not "justifications" but are instead attempts to overcome "contradictions." *Anthropologie structurale* (vol 1, 1958, Eng trans *Structural Anthropology*, 1963) shows the influence of the structural linguistics of **Ferdinand de Saussure**, Roman Jakobson (1896–1982) and others on Lévi-Strauss's work, and confirms his outstanding contribution to the philosophy of structuralism. Later publications include *La potière jalouse* (1985, Eng trans *The Jealous Potter*, 1988) and *Regarder, écouter, lire* (1993, "Look, Listen, Read").

Levitt, Helen 1913– •*US photographer*• Born in Brooklyn, New York, she worked for a portrait photographer in the Bronx in 1931, then studied at the Art Students League in New York (1956–57). She was strongly influenced by photographer **Henri Cartier-Bresson**. She began small-camera street photography in 1936, and in 1938 she assisted the photographer Walker Evans with his exhibition "American Photographs" at the Museum of Modern Art, New York. She has also worked in film, as assistant film cutter with director **Luis Buñuel**, and with **James Agee** and painter and art historian Janice Loeb, she made the films *In the Street* (1945–46) and *The Quiet One* (1946–47).

Lévy-Bruhl, Lucien 1857–1939 •*French philosopher and anthropologist*• Born in Paris, he studied at the École Normale Supérieure in Paris and was appointed to a chair in the history of modern philosophy at the Sorbonne in 1904. His early work was in moral philosophy, and he went on to develop a theory of what he termed primitive mentality in *La mentalité primitive* (1922, Eng trans *Primitive Mentality*, 1923) and several later books. He believed that the mentality of primitive people was essentially mystical and prelogical, differing in kind from the rational and logical thought of the modern West. This view drew him into a sharp exchange with **Émile Durkheim**, and has few adherents today.

Lewes, G(eorge) H(enry) 1817–78 •*English writer*• Born in London, and educated in Greenwich, Jersey and Brittany, he went to Germany in 1838, and spent nearly two years there. On his return to London he became a contributor to numerous journals, reviews and magazines, as well as an editor of the *Leader* (1851–54) and of the *Fortnightly* (1865–66), which he founded. He was unhappily married, with a family, when in 1854 he began his lifelong affair with **George Eliot**. His other works include two novels, *Ranthorpe* (1847) and *Rose, Blanche and Violet* (1848), and 10 plays, but he is best known for his writings on biography, theater, and later the sciences, and in particular his *Life and Works of Goethe* (1855).

Lewis, Alun 1915–44 •*Welsh soldier-poet and short-story writer*• He was born in Cwmaman, near Aberdare, educated at the University College of Wales, Aberystwyth, and at the University of Manchester. His first work, a volume of short stories about army life, was *The Last Inspection* (1942), followed by a volume of poetry, *Raiders' Dawn*, in the same year. He died of gunshot wounds at Chittagong during the Burma campaign. Another volume of verse, ironically entitled *Ha! Ha! Among the Trumpets*, was published posthumously in 1945, followed by a collection of short stories and letters, *In the Green Tree* (1948).

Lewis, Sir (William) Arthur 1915–91 •*British economist and Nobel Prize winner*• Born in St Lucia, the West Indies, he was Professor of Economics at the University of Manchester from 1948 to 1958, then became first president of the University of the West Indies (1959–63). From 1963 until his retirement in 1983, he held a chair in economics at Princeton. In 1979 he was awarded the Nobel Prize for economics, with **Theodore Schultz**, for work on economic development in the Third World.

Lewis, Carl (Frederick Carlton) 1961– •*US track-and-field athlete*• Born in Birmingham, Alabama, he was a brilliant all-around athlete at the University of Houston (1979–82). He won four gold medals at the 1984 Los Angeles Olympics (100 m, 200 m, 4×100 m relay and long jump). At the 1988 Seoul Olympics he won a gold medal in the long jump and was awarded the 100-meter gold medal after **Ben Johnson** was stripped of the title. In 1992 at the Barcelona Olympics he acquired two more golds in the long jump and the 4×100 meters relay, and in the 1996 Atlanta Olympics he earned the ninth and final gold medal of his career in the long jump, only the fourth Olympian to win as many.

Lewis, C Day *See* **Day-Lewis, Cecil**

Lewis, C(live) S(taples) 1898–1963 •*British novelist, literary scholar and religious writer*• Born in Belfast, he won a scholarship to Oxford in 1916, but served in World War I before entering University College in 1918. His first book of poems, *Spirits in Bondage*, was published in that year. In 1925 he was made a Fellow of Magdalen College, where he headed an informal group of writers known as "The Inklings," which included **J R R Tolkien**. He became a distinguished teacher, and was appointed to the newly created chair of Medieval and Renaissance English at Cambridge in 1954. He won a wide popular audience during World War II for his radio talks (collected as *Mere Christianity*, 1952) and his books on religious subjects, notably *The Screwtape Letters* (1942). His most important adult novels are the science-fiction trilogy *Out of the Silent Planet* (1938), *Perelandra* (1939) and *That Hideous Strength* (1945). His enduring series of seven books for children, *The Chronicles of Narnia*, which began with *The Lion, the Witch and the Wardrobe* (1950) and ended with *The Last Battle* (1956, Carnegie Medal), is similarly suffused with Christian allegory and ethics.

" "

Gratitude looks to the past and love to the present: fear, avarice, lust and ambition look ahead.

1942 ***The Screwtape Letters***, no. 15.

Lewis, Daniel Day- *See* **Day-Lewis, Daniel**

Lewis, Denise 1972– •*English athlete*• Born in West Bromwich, West Midlands, she specialized in the heptathlon and won gold medals in the Commonwealth Games (1994) and the European Cup (1995), European and Commonwealth championships (1998), and Olympic Games (2000). She set new Commonwealth records in the heptathlon in 1997 and 2000. She was given the honorary title Member, Order of the British Empire, in 1999.

Lewis, Hywel David 1910–92 •*Welsh philosopher of religion*• Born in Llandudno, Gwynedd, he succeeded **Charles Arthur Campbell** as Professor of Philosophy at University College, Bangor, from 1947 to 1955. Professor of the History and Philosophy of Religion at King's College London (1955–77), he was president of Mind and other learned societies, founding editor of *Religious Studies* (1965–84), and author of many works, including *Our Experience of God* (1959), *The Self and Immortality* (1973), *Persons and Life After Death* (1978), and a trilogy based on his Gifford Lectures. He also published several books in Welsh, including a volume of poems.

Lewis, Ida 1842–1911 •*US lighthouse keeper*• She was born in Newport, Rhode Island, the daughter of a sea captain who was the lighthouse keeper on Lime Rock in Newport Harbor. She took over her father's duties when he suffered a stroke and she manned the lighthouse for 50 years, performing many rescues that began in 1858 when she saved four men whose boat had capsized. Lewis won public recognition in 1869 and **Susan B Anthony** reported her exploits in her suffrage journal *The Revolution*. She was awarded a gold medal by Congress and a pension by the Carnegie Hero Fund.

Lewis, Jerry, *originally* **Joseph Levitch** 1926– •*US entertainer*• He was born in Newark, New Jersey, and worked in a nightclub act before forming a partnership with singer and straight man **Dean Martin**. They made their film debut in *My Friend Irma* (1949) and became the US's favorite double act of the 1950s. A solo performer from 1956, Lewis wrote, produced and often directed a series of anarchic comedies that indulged his love of visual humor and crude slapstick, among them *The Bellboy* (1960) and *The Nutty Professor* (1963). A tireless fundraiser for muscular dystrophy, he gave a strong dramatic performance in *The King of Comedy* (1982), and starred in a record-breaking tour of the musical *Damn Yankees* (1995–96).

Lewis, Jerry Lee 1935– •*US rock and country singer and pianist*• He was born in Ferriday, Louisiana. His powerful, energized style and driven personality quickly established him as one of the great originals of rock and roll, and brought him the nickname "The Killer." His 1957 recordings "Whole Lotta Shakin'" and "Great Balls of Fire" became classics of rock and roll, and in 1958 he had further success with "Breathless" and "High School Confidential" (the title track to a film in which he appeared). After he married his 14-year-old (some sources say 13-year-old) cousin Myra in 1958, he was effectively boycotted by television and the pop radio stations. In the late 1960s he returned to country music, where he had begun, and was a huge success, but his personal behavior continued to be erratic, and he had problems compounded by personal tragedies, including the deaths of his son, Jerry Lee, Jr, and two of his wives. Undaunted, he has continued to tour and record.

Lewis, Lennox 1965– •*British boxer*• Born in London, he won a gold medal at the 1988 Olympics for Canada, his home country since boyhood. Having turned professional in 1989, he went back to Great Britain and became the European heavyweight champion in 1990. In 1991, he took the British heavyweight title from Gary Mason, and in December 1992 was awarded the World Boxing Council (WBC) title by default (thus becoming Britain's first world heavyweight champion of the century), when Riddick Bowe, then champion, refused to fight him. He retained his title three times before a defeat in 1994. He regained the title in 1997 and in 1999 was the undisputed world heavyweight champion, although he was later stripped of his World Boxing Association (WBA) title. He defended his WBC and International Boxing Federation (IBF) titles successfully in 2000, lost both briefly to Hasim Rahman in early 2001, but regained them both later that year.

Lewis, Meriwether 1774–1809 •*US explorer*• Born near Charlottesville, Virginia, in 1801 he became personal secretary to President **Thomas Jefferson**, and was invited with his long-time friend **William Clark** to lead an expedition (1804–06) to explore the vast unknown lands to the west of the Mississippi. It was to become the first overland journey across North America to the Pacific coast, and one of the longest transcontinental journeys ever undertaken. Considered a triumph for the young nation, the Lewis and Clark expedition strengthened US claims to the Oregon Territory and spurred settlement of the West. Lewis was appointed governor of the Louisiana Territory in 1806, but only three years later, while traveling to Washington, he died in a shooting incident in a cabin in Tennessee.

Lewis, (Harry) Sinclair 1885–1951 •*US novelist and Nobel Prize winner*• He was born in Sauk Center, Minnesota, the son of a doctor. Educated at Yale University, he became a journalist and wrote several minor works before *Main Street* (1920), the first of a series of best-selling novels satirizing the arid materialism and intolerance of US small-town life. *Babbitt* (1922) still lends its title as a synonym for American middle-class philistinism. Other titles of this period are *Martin Arrowsmith* (1925) and *Elmer Gantry* (1927). From then on he tended to exonerate the ideologies and self-sufficiency he had previously pilloried, but the shift of attitude did nothing to diminish his popularity. His later novels include *Cass Timberlane* (1945) and *Kingsblood Royal* (1947). He was awarded the Nobel Prize for literature in 1930, becoming its first US laureate.

Lewis, Sir Thomas 1881–1945 •*Welsh cardiologist and clinical scientist*• Born in Cardiff, he received his preclinical training at University College, Cardiff. In 1902 he went to University College Hospital, in London, where he remained as student, teacher and consultant until his death. He was the first to master completely the use of the electrocardiogram. Using animals in experiments, he was able to correlate the various electrical waves recorded by an electrocardiograph with the sequence of events during a contraction of the heart. This enabled him to use the instrument as a diagnostic aid when the heart had disturbances in its rhythm, damage to its valves, changes due to high blood pressure, and other conditions. He was knighted in 1921.

Lewis, (Percy) Wyndham 1882–1957 •*English novelist, painter and critic*• He was born on a yacht off Amehurst, Nova Scotia, to an American father and an English mother, and he was educated at the Slade School of Art, London. With **Ezra Pound** he instituted the Vorticist movement and founded *Blast* (1914–15), the magazine which expounded their theories. From 1916 to 1918 he served on the Western Front as a bombardier, then as a war artist. In the early 1930s, his right-wing sympathies were out of vogue. He emigrated to Canada at the beginning of World War II, returning to London in 1945. In 1951 he went blind. His novels, *Tarr* (1918), *The Childermass* (1928), and *The Apes of God* (1930), are powerful, vivid satires. Other important novels are *The Revenge for Love* (1937) and *Self Condemned* (1954), which is partly autobiographical. *The Human Age* (1955), a trilogy, was modeled in part on **Dante** and **Milton**. He also wrote political and critical essays, short stories, and an autobiography. As a writer he has been ranked by some critics alongside **James Joyce** and, as a painter, he was one of the foremost experimentalists of his time in British art, and a highly skilled portraitist.

“ ”

"Dying for an idea," again, sounds well enough, but why not let the idea die instead of you?

*1925 **The Art of Being Ruled**, part 1, chapter 1.*

Liao Zhongkai (Liao Chung-k'ai) 1878–1925 •*Chinese politician*• Born into a Chinese family in the US, he became the leading financial expert of the Guomindang (Kuomintang) after 1912. Associated with its left wing, he supported the United Front with the communists in 1923, advocating a planned economy along socialist lines. In 1924 he played an important role in setting up both the workers and peasant departments under Guomindang auspices as part of its new strategy of mass mobilization. He also laid the basis for the political commissar system that was to be used throughout the National Revolutionary Army. Right-wing members of the Guomindang may have been involved in his assassination.

Libau or **Libavius, Andreas** c. 1560–1616 •*German alchemist*• Born in Halle, Saxony, he studied at the University of Jena, taught history and poetry there, and in the 1590s moved to Rothenburg ob der Tauber, where he began to teach and write (voluminously) on alchemy. His main work was *Alchemia* (1597), a richly illustrated book which is possibly the first chemistry textbook; it gives accounts of a range of chemical methods and substances, and vigorously attacks the ideas of **Paracelsus**. However, his philosophical, diffuse and mystical style limited its influence.

Libavius, Andreas *See* **Libau, Andreas**

Libby, Willard Frank 1908–80 •*US chemist and Nobel Prize winner*• Born in Grand Valley, Colorado, he studied and lectured at the University of California at Berkeley. He carried out atom-bomb research (1941–45) on the separation of the isotopes of uranium at Columbia, and from 1945 to 1954 was Professor of Chemistry at Chicago. From 1954 to 1959 he served on the US Atomic Energy Commission. He was awarded the 1960 Nobel Prize for chemistry for his part in the invention of the carbon-14 method of determining the age of an object. He was Professor of Chemistry at UCLA from 1959 to 1976.

Liberace, *properly* **Wladziu Valentino Liberace** 1919–87 •*US entertainer*• Born in West Allis, a suburb of Milwaukee, Wisconsin, he was playing piano by ear at the age of four. He appeared as a soloist with the Chicago Symphony Orchestra at age 14 and earned a living in nightclubs and at student dances using the stage name Walter Busterkeys. He gradually developed an enduringly successful act of popular piano classics, which he performed with lavish showmanship. He made his film debut in *East of Java* (1949), but his one starring role in *Yours Sincerely* (1955) was not well received. *The Liberace Show* (1952–57), his television series, won him an Emmy as Best Male Personality. He broke all box-office records at Radio City Music Hall in New York in 1985.

Li Bo (Li Po), *also known as* **Li Tai Bo (Li T'ai-po)** 701–762 •*Chinese poet*• Born in Sichuan (Szechuan) Province, he led a dissipated life at the emperor's court and later became one of a wandering band calling themselves "The Eight Immortals of the Wine Cup." Regarded as the greatest poet of China, he wrote colorful verse about wine, women and nature. It is believed that he was drowned while attempting to grasp the moon's reflection.

Lichfield, (Thomas) Patrick John Anson, 5th Earl of 1939– •*English photographer*• Educated at Harrow and Sandhurst, he served in the Grenadier Guards from 1959 to 1962, when he decided to become a professional photographer. After working as an assistant for many years, he opened his own studio, and since 1981 has achieved success in travel and publicity photography as well as with his many royal portraits. His publications include *The Most Beautiful Women* (1981) and *Elizabeth R: A Photographic Celebration of 40 Years* (1991).

Lichtenstein, Roy 1923–97 •*US painter*• Born in New York City, he studied painting at the Art Students' League in New York, and at Ohio State University, Columbus (1940–43). He served in the US Army from 1943 to 1946 before returning to Ohio, where he taught (1946–51). In the mid-1950s he worked in an Abstract Expressionist style, but by 1961, influenced by **Claes Oldenburg**, he was painting enlarged versions of popular magazine advertisements and violent cartoon strips, duplicating their dot patterns. Regarded as one of the major figures of the Pop Art Movement, his works include *Whaam!* (1963, Tate, London), *As I Opened Fire* (1964, Stedelijk, Amsterdam) and *Little Big Painting* (1965, Whitney Museum of American Art, New York). As a sculptor, he created works such as *Dinnerware Objects* of the 1960s and bronze *Sculptures* of the 1970s.

Li Dazhao (Li Ta-chao) 1888–1927 •*Chinese revolutionary*• He was one of the founders of the Chinese Communist Party, and his interpretation of Marxism as applied to China had a profound influence on **Mao Zedong**. Appointed head librarian of Beijing (Peking) University in 1918 and Professor of History in 1920, he had the young Mao as a library assistant, and founded one of the first of the Communist study circles which in 1921 were to form the Communist Party.

Liddell, Eric Henry, *known as* **the Flying Scotsman** 1902–45 •*Scottish athlete and missionary*• Born in Tianjin (Tientsin), China, to Scottish missionary parents, he was educated at Eltham College, London, and at the University of Edinburgh. At the 1924 Olympics in Paris he would have been the favorite to win the 100 meters had he not refused to take part on religious grounds because the heats were to be run on a Sunday. Instead, he won the bronze medal in the 200 meters, and then caused a sensation by winning the gold medal in the 400 meters (at which he was comparatively inexperienced) in a then world-record time of 47.6 seconds. In 1925, he went to China to work as a Scottish Congregational Church missionary. During World War II he was interned by the Japanese at Weixian (Weihsien) camp, and there, not long before the war ended, he died of a brain tumor. The story of his athletic triumphs was told in the film *Chariots of Fire* (1981).

Liddell, Helen 1950– •*Scottish Labour politician*• Born in Monklands, Lanarkshire, she studied economics at the University of Strathclyde. A former General Secretary of the Labour Party in Scotland (1977–88), she entered Parliament in 1994 and became an opposition spokeswoman on Scotland (1995–97), Economic Secretary to the Treasury (1997–98), Minister of State in the Scottish Office (1998–99), Minister of Transport (1999), Minister for Energy and Competitiveness in Europe (1999–2001) and Secretary of State for Scotland (from 2001).

Liddell Hart, Sir Basil Henry 1895–1970 •*English military journalist and historian*• Born in Paris, he was educated at St Paul's and Cambridge, and served in World War I, retiring from the army in 1927. He was responsible for various tactical developments during the war, and wrote the postwar official manual of Infantry Training (1920). In 1937 he relinquished his position as personal adviser to the Minister of War to publicize the need for immediate development of air power and mechanized warfare. He wrote more than 30 books on warfare, as well as biographies of **Ferdinand Foch**, **T E Lawrence** and others. He was knighted in 1966.

Lidman, Sara 1923– •*Swedish writer*• She was born in Missenträsk, in the far north of the country, and that area was the setting for her early novels such as *Tjärdalen* (1953, "The Tar Still") and *Hjortronlandet* (1955, "Cloudberry Land"). The support for the underdog visible in these novels became more overt as her politics developed in the 1960s after visits to South Africa, Kenya and Vietnam. In the highly acclaimed series of novels beginning with *Din tjänare hör* (1977, "Thy Servant Heareth"), she returns to her roots and takes as her theme the building of the railways in the north. She has experimented with documentary forms of writing and has also written plays.

Lie, Jonas Lauritz Idemil 1833–1908 •*Norwegian novelist and poet*• He was born in Eker, near Drammen, and trained as a lawyer. His novels, which present realistic portrayals of fishing communities in Norway, include *Den fremsynte* (1870, "The Visionary"), *Lodsen og hans hustru* (1874, "Lodsen and His Wife"), *Livsslaven* (1883, "One of Life's Slaves") and *Kommandørens Døtre* (1886, "The Commander's Daughters"). He also wrote fairy tales like *Trold* (1891–92, "Trolls"), and some poetry and plays. He was enormously popular and influential in Scandinavia.

Lie, Marius Sophus 1842–99 •*Norwegian mathematician*• Born in Nordfjordeide, he studied at the University of Oslo University, where a chair of mathematics was created for him. In 1886 he succeeded **Felix Klein** at the University of Leipzig, but returned to Oslo in 1898. His study of contact transformations arising from partial differential equations led him to develop an extensive theory of continuous groups of transformations, now known as Lie groups. This theory became a central part of 20th-century mathematics and has important applications in quantum theory.

Lie, Trygve Halvdan 1896–1968 •*Norwegian politician*• He was born in Oslo. He was a Labor member of the Norwegian parliament and held several posts, including Minister of Justice and Minister of Supply and Shipping, before fleeing with the government to Great Britain (1940), where he acted as its Foreign Minister until 1945. He was elected first Secretary-General of the UN in 1946, but resigned in 1952 over Soviet opposition to his policy of intervention in the Korean War.

Liebermann, Max 1847–1935 •*German painter and etcher*• Born in Berlin, he studied at Weimar and in Paris, where he first won fame. In Germany from 1878 he painted open-air studies and scenes of humble life which were often sentimental. Later, however, his work became more colorful and romantic, and, influenced by the French Impressionists, he became the leading painter of that school in his own country.

Liebig, Justus von 1803–73 •*German chemist*• Born in Darmstadt, he studied in Bonn, Erlangen and Paris. In 1824 he was appointed Extraordinary Professor at the University of Giessen, where he set up an institute for training chemists. During this period he studied the phenomenon of isomerism and he and **Friedrich Wöhler** became close friends. He developed improved procedures for the elemental analyses of organic compounds. In his book *Die organische Chemie in Anwendung auf Agricultur und Physiologie* (1840, Eng trans *Organic Chemistry in Its Applications to Agriculture and Physiology*, 1840), he described the process we now know as photosynthesis and considered the value of fertilizers, which led to a number of improvements in agricultural practice. In 1852 he left Giessen for Munich, where he remained until his retirement.

Liebknecht, Karl 1871–1919 •*German politician and revolutionary*• He was a member of the Reichstag from 1912 to 1916. In World War I he was imprisoned as an independent, antimilitarist social democrat. He was a founding member with **Rosa Luxemburg** of the German Communist Party (KPD) in 1918 and led an unsuccessful revolt in Berlin, the "Spartacus Uprising," in January 1919, during which he and Rosa Luxemburg were killed by army officers.

Lifar, Serge 1905–86 •*French dancer and choreographer*• Born in Kiev, Ukraine, he became a student and friend of **Sergei Diaghilev**, whose Ballets Russes he joined in 1923. Following his first important appearance in *La boutique fantasque*, he danced with **Anna Pavlova**, Tamara Karsavina and Spessirtzeva, and was critically acclaimed for his roles in works by, among others, **Léonide Massine** (1928) and **George Balanchine**. He scored his first triumph as a choreographer in Paris with *Créatures de Promethée* in 1929, the year he became artistic director of the Paris Opera.

Ligachev, Yegor Kuzmich 1920– •*Russian politician*• He was born in Novosibirsk. After graduating as an engineer, he joined the Communist Party in 1944. As party chief (1957) of the new "science city" of Akademgorodok, he gained a reputation as an austere opponent of corruption. He was brought to Moscow by **Nikita Khrushchev** in 1961 but, after the latter was ousted in 1964, he was sent to Tomsk, where he was regional party boss for 18 years. However, he became a full member of the Central Committee in 1976, and in 1983 he was promoted to the Secretariat by **Yuri Andropov**, becoming Ideology Secretary in 1984. With the accession to power of **Mikhail Gorbachev** in 1985, he was brought into the politburo. He initially served as Gorbachev's deputy, but they became estranged over the issue of reform, and in 1990 he was expelled from the Central Committee as well as the politburo.

Ligeti, György Sándor 1923– •*Austrian composer*• Born in Dicsöszentmárton, Hungary, he studied and later taught at the Budapest Academy of Music (from 1950). He researched Hungarian folk music and wrote some folk-song arrangements, but not until he left Hungary in 1956 did he become seriously interested in composition. His first large orchestral work, *Apparitions* (1958–59), made his name widely known. *Atmosphères* followed in 1961, demonstrating his technique of chromatic complexes, and in *Aventures* (1962) and *Nouvelles Aventures* (1962–65) he used his own invented language of speech sounds. Other works are the choral *Requiem* (1963–65) and *Lux Aeterna* (1966), the orchestral *Lontano* (1967), the Double Concerto for flute, oboe and orchestra (1972), the "music theater" *Le grand macabre* (1978) and *The San Francisco Polyphony* (1996). He has held academic posts in Stockholm, California and Hamburg. He became an Austrian citizen in 1967.

Liguori, St Alfonso Maria de 1696–1787 •*Italian prelate*• Born in Naples, he founded the order of Liguorians, or Redemptorists, with 12 companions in 1732. Bishop of Sant' Agata de' Goti from 1762, he resigned in 1775, and returned to his order. He was canonized in 1839, and declared a Doctor of the Church in 1871. His voluminous writings embrace divinity, casuistry, exegesis, history, canon law, hagiography and poetry.

Li Hsien-nien *See* **Li Xiannian**

Lilburne, John c. 1614–57 •*English revolutionary*• He was born in Greenwich, London. Imprisoned by the Star Chamber in 1638 for importing Puritan literature, he rose in the Parliamentary army, but resigned in 1645 over the Covenant. He became an indefatigable agitator for the Levellers during the English Civil Wars, regarding **Cromwell**'s republic as too aristocratic. He was repeatedly imprisoned for his treasonable pamphlets.

Lilienthal, Otto 1849–96 •*German aeronautical inventor, pioneer of gliders*• Born in Anklam, he was educated at the trade school at Potsdam and the Berlin Trade Academy. He studied bird flight in order to build heavier-than-air flying machines resembling the birdman designs of **Leonardo da Vinci**. He made hundreds of short flights in his gliders, but in his last crashed to his death near Berlin.

Lillee, Dennis Keith 1949– •*Australian cricket player*• Born in Perth, Western Australia, he epitomized the move toward the more combative approach to international cricket. An automatic choice for his country when fit, he took 355 wickets in 70 Tests. His attempts to introduce a metal bat (illegal) into Test matches led to well-publicized clashes with the Australian cricketing authorities. He retired in 1984.

Lilley, Peter 1943– •*English Conservative politician*• He was born in Kent and educated at Dulwich College and Clare College, Cambridge. After graduating he worked as an economic consultant in industry and was elected Conservative Member of Parliament for St Albans in 1983. A right-winger, he came to prominence in 1990 when he was appointed Secretary of State for Trade and Industry. In 1992–97 he was Secretary of State for Social Security and introduced controversial proposals for ending the "dependency culture" of state aid for the unemployed. He was Shadow Chancellor (1997–98) and then Deputy Leader of the Conservatives from 1998 to 1999.

Lillie, Beatrice Gladys, *by marriage* **Lady Peel** 1894–1989 •*Canadian comic actress*• She was born in Toronto and educated in Ontario. She began as a serious singer of drawing-room ballads but turned to comedy, encouraged by André Charlot, and from 1914 she was renowned in music halls and in the new vogue of "intimate revue." She entertained the troops on leave in World War I, worked with **Noël Coward** in London, and made her debut in the US in 1932. During World War II she entertained the troops and was decorated by General **Charles de Gaulle**. During the 1950s she developed her own television series in the US. She also appeared in films, such as *Thoroughly Modern Millie* (1967).

Lily, John *See* **Lyly, John**

Limón, José 1908–72 •*US dancer, choreographer and teacher*• Born in Culiacan, Mexico, he went to New York, where he decided to become a dancer. Studies with **Doris Humphrey** and Charles Weidman (1901–75) led to his joining their company as a dancer (1930–40). He formed his own group in 1946, appointing his mentor, Doris Humphrey, as artistic director. In 1950 the José Limón Company was the first US modern dance group to tour Europe, and went on to tour the world. His choreography includes *La Malinche* (1949), *The Moor's Pavanne* (1949, one of his most well-known works), *The Traitor* (1954), *There Is a Time* (1956), *Missa Brevis* (1958), the all-male *The Unsung* (1970) and *Carlotta* (1972). His company survived after his death and is still based in New York.

Lin, Maya Ying 1959– •*US architect*• Born in Athens, Ohio, into a family of artists and intellectuals who had immigrated from China, she studied architecture at Yale. While still a student she entered and won the design competition for the Vietnam Veterans Memorial in Washington DC. Her design consisted of two black granite walls inscribed with the names of the dead, built into the earth and joining in a shallow V. Dedicated in 1982, it became a place of pilgrimage where mourners who leave tokens and messages are reflected in the polished stone. Her design for the Civil Rights Memorial (1989) in Montgomery, Alabama, uses flowing water to illustrate **Martin Luther King**'s biblical invocation: "justice rolls down like waters and righteousness like a mighty stream."

Linacre, Thomas c. 1460–1524 •*English humanist and physician*• Born in Canterbury, he studied at Oxford, and in Italy, taking his MD at Padua. Around 1500 **Henry VII** made him tutor to Prince **Arthur**. As king's physician to Henry VII and **Henry VIII** he practiced in London. In 1518 he founded the Royal College of Physicians, of which he became the first president. Late in life he took holy orders. He translated several of **Galen**'s works into Latin, and wrote grammatical treatises.

Lin Biao (Lin Piao) 1908–71 •*Chinese soldier and politician*• Born in Wuhan, Hubei (Hupeh) Province, in 1926 he joined the Communists to fight the Guomindang (Kuomintang), becoming Commander of the Northeast People's Liberation Army in 1945. He became Defense Minister in 1959 and emerged from the Cultural Revolution of 1966 as second-in-command to **Mao Zedong**, being designated as Mao's heir and successor at the congress of 1969. However, in 1971, Lin formulated "Project 571," designed to assassinate Chairman Mao and seize power in a military coup. This plot was uncovered and Lin was killed in 1971 in a plane crash while attempting to flee to the Soviet Union.

Lincoln, Abraham 1809–65 •*16th President of the US*• He was born in a log cabin near Hodgenville, Kentucky, the son of a restless pioneer. The family eventually settled in southwest Indiana in 1816. In 1830 the Lincolns moved on to Illinois and Abraham went to work as a clerk in a store at New Salem. He already had political ambitions, and saw the need to study law and grammar. Elected to the Illinois legislature in 1834, he became a lawyer in 1836. At Springfield, in 1842, he married **Mary Todd**. In 1846 he was elected to a single term in Congress, where he spoke against the extension of slavery, and in 1860 was elected president as the Republican Party's candidate on a platform of hostility to slavery's expansion. When the Civil War began (1861), he defined the issue in terms of national integrity, not antislavery, a theme he restated in the Gettysburg Address (1863). Nonetheless, in his Emancipation Proclamation that same year, he announced his intention of freeing all slaves in areas of rebellion. He was reelected in 1864; after the final Northern victory he proposed to reunite the nation on the most generous terms, but on April 14, 1865, he was shot at Ford's Theater, in Washington DC, by an actor, **John Wilkes Booth**, and died the next morning. Lincoln was fair and direct in speech and action, steadfast in principle, sympathetic and charitable, a man of strict morality, abstemious and familiar with the Bible—though not a professed member of any church—and he is regarded as one of the finest symbols of US democracy.

Lind, James 1716–94 •*Scottish physician*• Born in Edinburgh, he served in the navy as a surgeon's mate, then, after receiving a medical degree from the University of Edinburgh, became physician at the Royal Naval Hospital at Haslar. In 1747 he conducted a classic therapeutic trial, dividing 12 patients suffering from scurvy into six groups of two, treating each group with a different remedy. The two sailors given two oranges and a lemon each day responded most dramatically. His work on the cure and prevention of scurvy helped induce the Admiralty in 1795 at last to issue the order that the navy should be supplied with lemon juice, and during the Napoleonic Wars, the British navy suffered far less scurvy than the French. He also wrote major treatises on fevers and tropical diseases.

Lind, Jenny, *originally* **Johanna Maria Lind** 1820–87 •*Swedish soprano*• Born in Stockholm, she went to the court theater school of singing at the age of nine. After lessons in Paris, she made her debut in Stockholm (1838) and attained international popularity. Known as the "Swedish nightingale," she founded and endowed musical scholarships and charities in Sweden and in England, where she lived from 1856, and became Professor of Singing at the Royal College of Music (1883–86).

Lindbergh, Charles Augustus 1902–74 •*US aviator*• Born in Detroit, he worked as an airmail pilot on the St Louis–Chicago run. In May 1927 he made the first nonstop solo transatlantic flight from New York to Paris in a Ryan monoplane named *Spirit of St Louis* in 33½ hours, for which he was awarded the Congressional Medal of Honor. During World War II he advocated US neutrality. His autobiography, *The Spirit of St Louis* (1953), won the Pulitzer Prize in 1954. His wife, Anne Morrow Lindbergh (1906–2001), wrote *North to the Orient* (1935), *Gift From the Sea* (1955), *Earthshine* (1970) and others.

Lindgren, Astrid 1907–2002 •*Swedish children's novelist*• She was born in Vimmerby, and established her reputation with *Pippi Långstrump* (1945, Eng trans *Pippi Longstocking*, 1954). She wrote about 80 more books, including *Mästerdetektiven Blomkvist* (1946, Eng trans *Bill Bergson Master Detective*, 1951), but none has eclipsed *Pippi Longstocking*'s popularity. *Samuel August från Seudstorp och Hanna: Hult* (1975) portrays her parents.

Lindsay, Sir David *See* **Lyndsay, David**

Lindsay, (Nicholas) Vachel 1879–1931 •*US poet*• Born in Springfield, Illinois, into an evangelical family, he studied painting in Chicago and New York, and from 1906 traveled the US like a troubadour, reciting his poems in exchange for hospitality. He won fame during the World War I era and began to attract large audiences to his readings. Highly rhythmic and influenced by ragtime, band music and the cadences of evangelical preaching, his best work appears in *General William Booth Enters Into Heaven* (1913) and *The Congo* (1914).

Lindwall, Ray(mond Russell) 1921–96 •*Australian cricket player*• He was born in Sydney. A classic fast bowler, with Keith Miller (1919–) he formed an invincible Australian opening attack in the five years after World War II. He took 228 wickets in 61 Tests, and also scored more than 1,500 runs, including two Test centuries.

Lineker, Gary Winston 1960– •*English soccer player and commentator*• Born in Leicester, he turned professional with Leicester City in 1978. He made his debut for England in 1984, moved to Everton the following year, and then, the next year, to Barcelona. In 1989 he returned to the UK when he signed for Tottenham Hotspur, and then made the last move of his playing career with his transfer to Grampus Eight of Nagoya, Japan, in 1993. In 1992 he was voted Footballer of the Year by the Football Writers Association and regularly appears on television, presenting BBC sports programs, and on the comedy sports quiz *They Think It's All Over* (1995–).

Linh, Nguyen Van *See* **Nguyen Van Linh**

Linklater, Eric 1899–1974 •*Scottish novelist*• He was born in Penarth, Wales. His paternal ancestors were Orcadian and he spent much of his childhood on the islands, returning there in later life. He was educated at the grammar school and university in Aberdeen, and served in World War I as a private in the Black Watch. A Commonwealth fellowship took him to the US from 1928 to 1930, after which he had a varied career as a broadcaster and a prolific writer of novels, popular histories, books for children (*The Wind on the Moon* was awarded the Carnegie Medal in 1944), plays and memoirs. *Juan in America* (1931), a picaresque classic, is his most enduring novel. Other novels include *Magnus Merriman* (1934), *Juan in China* (1937), *Private Angelo* (1946) and *The Voyage of the Challenger* (1972). *The Man on My Back* (1941), *A Year of Space* (1953) and *Fanfare for a Tin Hat* (1970) are autobiographical.

Linnaeus, Carolus, *originally* **Carl von Linné** 1707–78 •*Swedish naturalist and physician*• Born in Råshult, he studied botany at the University of Uppsala, where he was appointed lecturer in 1730. He explored Swedish Lapland (1732), publishing the results in *Flora Lapponica* (1737), then went to Holland to study medicine (1735). In Holland he published his system of botanical nomenclature, *Systema naturae* (1735), followed by *Fundamenta botanica* (1736), *Genera plantarum* (1737) and *Critica botanica* (1737), in which he used his "sexual system" of classification based on the number of flower parts, long the dominant system. He returned to Sweden in 1738 and practiced as a physician in Stockholm, and in 1741 became Professor of Medicine and Botany at Uppsala. His other important publications included *Flora Suecica* and *Fauna Suecica* (1745), *Philosophia botanica* (1750), and *Species plantarum* (1753). His manuscripts and collections are kept at the Linnaean Society in London, established in his honor in 1788.

" "

Nature does not make jumps.

1750 ***Philosophia botanica**, no. 77.*

Linney, Romulus 1930– •*US playwright*• Born in Philadelphia and raised in the South, he was educated at Oberlin College and trained at the Yale School of Drama. He has taught at numerous institutions, including the University of Pennsylvania, Princeton and Columbia. He has written a series of historical plays such as *The Sorrows of Frederick* (1966), *Childe Byron* (1977) and *2* (1990), which paint real and immediate portraits of **Frederick William II** of Prussia, Lord **Byron** and **Hermann Goering** respectively. Other plays, notably *Holy Ghosts* (1977) and *Heathen Valley* (1988), focus on life in Appalachia. He has won two Obie awards, the first in 1980 for his play *Tennessee* and the second in 1992 for sustained excellence in playwriting.

Lin Piao *See* **Lin Biao**

Lionheart, Richard the *See* **Richard I**

Liouville, Joseph 1809–82 •*French mathematician*• Born in St Omer, he was educated at the École Polytechnique and the École des Ponts et Chaussées, where he trained as an engineer. He taught at the École Polytechnique (1831–51), and then at the Collège de France and the University of Paris. In 1836 he founded the *Journal de Mathématiques* His work in analysis continued the study of algebraic function theory begun by **Niels Abel** and **Carl Jacobi**, and he studied the theory of differential equations, mathematical physics and celestial mechanics. In number theory he introduced new methods of investigating transcendental numbers.

Lipchitz, Jacques 1891–1973 •*French sculptor*• He was born in Druskieniki, Lithuania, of Polish Jewish parents, and studied engineering before moving to Paris (1909), where he started producing Cubist sculpture in 1914. In the 1920s he experimented with abstract forms he called "transparent sculptures," such as *Reclining Nude With Guitar* (1928, New York). Later he developed a more dynamic style which he applied with telling effect to bronze figure and animal compositions in works like *Benediction* (1942, private collection, New York). From 1941 he lived in the US. He worked on the *Hagar* theme (Art Gallery of Toronto) from 1948 and on the *Spirit of Enterprise* (Philadelphia, bronze sketch in the Tate Modern, London) during the 1950s.

Li Peng (Li P'eng) 1928– •*Chinese politician*• Born in Chengdu, Sichuan (Szechuan) Province, he was adopted by **Zhou Enlai** on his mother's death in 1939. He trained as a hydroelectric engineer and was appointed minister with responsibility for the power industry in 1981. He became a vice premier in 1983, was elevated to the politburo in 1985 and made prime minister in 1987, serving until 1998. As a cautious, orthodox reformer, he favored improved relations with the Soviet Union. In 1989, he imposed martial law to counter widespread student agitation triggered by the failure of the leadership to honor promises made by party chief **Zhao Ziyang**. His refusal to make any concessions prompted the peaceful student occupation of Tiananmen Square, and Li Peng's action in using army units to bring the demonstration violently to an end, with the loss of about 3,000 lives, earned him international condemnation. In 1998 he became the chairman of the National People's Congress, and he remains a powerful political force in China.

Lipman, Maureen Diane 1946– •*English actress and writer*• Born in Hull, East Yorkshire, she first appeared in London's West End in *Candida* (1976), won a Laurence Olivier award for her role as Miss Skillen in *See How They Run* (1984) and enjoyed success as Joyce Grenfell in her solo show *Re: Joyce* (1988–91, 1993–94), among many other stage roles. Her films include *Up the Junction* (1967), *Educating Rita* (1983) and *Carry On Columbus* (1992). On television, she appeared in her writer husband **Jack Rosenthal**'s plays *The Knowledge* (1979) and *Eskimo Day* (1996).

Lipmann, Fritz Albert 1899–1986 •*US biochemist and Nobel Prize winner*• Born in Königsberg, Prussia (now Kaliningrad, Russia), he studied at the University of Berlin, and worked in Copenhagen (1932–39), before emigrating to the US, where he became professor at Harvard Medical School (1949–57), and at Rockefeller University, New York, from 1957. He studied the role of phosphorus compounds in providing the energy for respiration, and identified the relationship with electron transfer potential. He demonstrated in 1950 the formation of citric acid from oxaloacetate and acetate (the first step in the **[Hans] Krebs** cycle) and found that a previously unidentified thiol cofactor is required, coenzyme A. He then isolated and partially elucidated the molecular structure of coenzyme A, for which he shared the 1953 Nobel Prize for physiology or medicine with Hans Krebs.

Li Po *See* **Li Bo**

Lippi, Filippino c. 1458–1504 •*Italian painter*• Born in Prato, Florence, he was the son of **Fra Filippo Lippi**, and was apprenticed to **Botticelli**, who almost certainly was a pupil of his father. In c. 1484 he completed the frescoes in the Brancacci Chapel in Carmine, Florence. Other celebrated series of frescoes were painted by him between 1487 and 1502, one in the Strozzi Chapel in Santa Maria Novella and one in the Caraffa Chapel, Santa Maria sopra Minerva, in Rome. His easel pictures include *The Virgin and Saints* (c. 1485, National Gallery, London) and *The Adoration of the Magi* (1495, Uffizi, Florence).

Lippi, Fra Filippo, *called* **Lippo** c. 1406–69 •*Italian religious painter*• He was born in Florence. An orphan, he became a Carmelite monk. In 1424 he became a pupil of **Masaccio**, who was painting the frescoes in the Brancacci Chapel there. The *Tarquinia Madonna* (1437), his first dated painting, shows Flemish influence. His greatest work, on the choir walls of Prato Cathedral, was begun in 1452. Between 1452 and 1464 he abducted a nun and was released from his monastic vows by Pope **Pius II** in order to marry her. She was the model for many of his Madonnas and the mother of his son, **Filippino Lippi**. His later works are deeply religious and include the series *Nativities*. He was immortalized in **Robert Browning**'s poem "Fra Lippo Lippi" in *Men and Women* (1855).

Lippincott, Joshua Ballinger 1813–86 •*US publisher*• He was born in Juliustown, New Jersey, had a bookseller's business in Philadelphia (1834–36), and then established his well-known publishing firm. He founded *Lippincott's Magazine* in 1868.

Lippmann, Gabriel Jonas 1845–1921 •*French physicist and Nobel Prize winner*• Born in Hollerich, Luxembourg, he held various teaching positions in France. His research in electro-capillarity in the laboratory of **Gustav Kirchhoff** led to his invention of a very sensitive mercury capillary electrometer. His many contributions to instrument design include an astatic galvanometer, the coelostat, with which a region of the sky can be photographed for an extended period without apparent movement, and a new form of seismograph. For his technique of color photography based on the interference phenomenon, subsequently also used by Lord **Rayleigh**, he was awarded the 1908 Nobel Prize for physics.

Lippmann, Walter 1889–1974 •*US journalist*• Born in New York, he was educated at Harvard, and was on the editorial staff of the *New York World* until 1931, then became a special writer for the New York *Herald Tribune*. His daily columns became internationally famous and he won many awards, including the Pulitzer Prize for international reporting (1962).

" "

The present crisis of Western democracy is a crisis in journalism.
1920 ***Liberty and the News***, *"Journalism and the Higher Law."*

Lippo *See* **Lippi, Fra Filippo**

Lipscomb, William Nunn 1919– •*US inorganic chemist and Nobel Prize winner*• Born in Cleveland, Ohio, he studied at Kentucky and the California Institute of Technology, and was appointed Professor of Chemistry at Harvard in 1959. He deduced the molecular structures of a curious group of boron compounds by X-ray crystal diffraction analysis in the 1950s and then went on to develop novel theories for chemical bonding in these compounds, as well as developing ingenious experimental and theoretical methods. He received the 1976 Nobel Prize for chemistry.

Li Shih-chen *See* **Li Shizen**

Li Shizen (Li Shih-chen) 1518–93 •*Chinese pharmaceutical naturalist and biologist*• A talented physician, he was appointed to the Imperial Medical Academy, and produced an encyclopedia of pharmaceutical natural history, the *Ben Cao Gang Mu* ("Great Pharmacopoeia"), completed in 1578 and published in 1596. It gives an exhaustive description of 1,000 plants and 1,000 animals, and includes more than 11,000 prescriptions. It is much more than a pharmacopoeia, however, as it treats mineralogy, metallurgy, physiology, botany and zoology as sciences in their own right. By categorizing diseases, it also forms a system of medicine. He recorded many instances of the sophistication of Chinese medicine, and adopted a system of priority in naming plants and animals, assigning the first name as the standard term, and treating later names as synonyms.

Lissitzky, El(iezer Markovich) 1890–1941 •*Russian painter and designer*• Born in Smolensk, he studied engineering and architecture. In 1919 **Marc Chagall** appointed him Professor of Architecture and Graphic Art at the Art School in Vitebsk, where he came under the influence of his colleague **Kasimir Malevich**. Lissitzky produced a remarkable series of abstract works, called collectively *Proun*, in which he combined flat rectilinear forms with dramatic architectonic elements. Later he helped transmit Russian ideas to the West, especially through contact with **László Moholy-Nagy**.

Lister, Joseph Lister, 1st Baron 1827–1912 •*English surgeon, the "father of antiseptic surgery"*• He was born in Upton, Essex, the son of the microscopist Joseph Jackson Lister. After graduating from the University of London in arts (1847) and medicine (1852), he became house surgeon at Edinburgh Royal Infirmary. After holding chairs at the Universities of Glasgow, Edinburgh and London, he was elected president of the Royal Society (1895–1900). In addition to important observations on the coagulation of the blood and the microscopical investigation of inflammation, his great contribution was the introduction of his antiseptic system (1867), which revolutionized modern surgery. His system was a development of the work of **Louis Pasteur**. Lister began soaking his instruments and surgical gauzes in carbolic acid, a well-known disinfectant. His early antiseptic work was primarily concerned with the treatment by surgery of compound fractures and tuberculous joints; both conditions would previously have been dealt with by amputation. The procedures Lister developed made it possible for surgeons to open the abdominal, thoracic and cranial cavities without fatal infections resulting. He concentrated later in his life on the causes of wound infection and was an ardent advocate of the value of experimental science for medical and surgical practice. He was the first medical man to be elevated to the peerage.

Lister (of Masham), Samuel Cunliffe Lister, 1st Baron 1815–1906 •*English inventor*• Born in Bradford, in 1837 he and his brother were put in charge of a worsted mill built by their father at Manningham. Samuel applied himself to the improvement of textile machinery, inventing in 1845 a wool comber, which made him a fortune. Later he spent a quarter of a million pounds developing a machine to spin waste silk, and was nearly bankrupt by the time it was commercially successful, making him a second fortune. Among his 150 other inventions were a swivel shuttle, a velvet loom, and in 1848, anticipating the patent of **George Westinghouse** by 21 years, a compressed air brake for railways. He was also a generous benefactor, presenting Bradford with, among other gifts, Lister Park.

Liszt, Franz 1811–86 •*Hungarian composer and pianist*• Born in Raiding, he studied and played in Vienna and Paris, touring widely in Europe as a virtuoso pianist. In the late 1830s he lived with the Comtesse **d'Agoult**, by whom he had three children (his daughter Cosima married **Richard Wagner**), and in 1847 met Princess Carolyne zu Sayn-Wittgenstein with whom he lived until his death. In 1848 he went to Weimar, where he directed opera and concerts, composed, and taught, making it the musical center of Germany. He later received minor orders in the Catholic Church (1865) and was known as Abbé. His works include 12 symphonic poems, masses, two symphonies, and a large number of piano pieces. All his original compositions have a very distinct, sometimes strange, individuality. The vocal and piano works of his last years were experimental and prophetic of 20th-century developments. His literary works on music include monographs on his friends **Frédéric Chopin** and Robert Franz (1815–92).

Li Ta-chao *See* **Li Dazhao**

Lithgow, Sir James 1883–1952 •*Scottish shipbuilder*• Born in Port Glasgow, Strathclyde, he was educated locally, then at Glasgow Academy and in Paris. Both he and his brother Henry chose to enter the family engineering firm in Port Glasgow. By 1920 they had forged a diversified and integrated empire with interests in coal, iron and steel, marine engineering and shipowning, as well as shipbuilding. Their shipyards on the lower Clyde remained, however, the fulcrum.

Little Richard, *real name* **Richard Wayne Penniman** 1935– •*US rock-and-roll singer and pianist*• He was born in Macon, Georgia. His early recordings epitomized the hedonistic, sexually potent facets of rock and roll, and his wild piano style and manic songs were a model for many later performers. Raised as a Seventh-day Adventist, he sang in church choirs throughout his childhood, and screams and yells derived from gospel music were to become an important part of his recorded sound. He began his recording career with "Every Hour" (1952), but it was "Tutti Frutti" (1955) that really launched his career. Most of his recordings from 1958 to 1964 were of gospel songs. In the mid-1960s he recorded with a succession of labels and "Whole Lot of Shaking Goin' On" and "Lawdy Miss Clawdy" are among the better songs from this period. His real comeback came in 1970 with the release of *The Rill Thing* album, which was followed by several more strong releases.

Littlewood, Joan Maud 1914–2002 •*English theater director*• Having been trained at the Royal Academy of Dramatic Art, she cofounded Theatre Union with **Ewan MacColl**. An experimental company in Manchester (1935), it became the Theatre Workshop (1945), and opened at the Theatre Royal in Stratford East, London, with *Twelfth Night* (1953). The group quickly won acclaim and was invited to represent Great Britain at the Théâtre des Nations in Paris (1955, 1956), and played at the Moscow Art Theatre. Littlewood also directed the first British production of Brecht's *Mother Courage* in Barnstaple (1955), in which she played the title role. The ideology of the Theatre Workshop company was aggressively left-wing, and its artistic policy revolved around a fresh, political approach to established plays and the staging of new, working-class plays, notably **Brendan Behan**'s *The Quare Fellow* (1956), **Shelagh Delaney**'s *A Taste of Honey* (1958), and *Fings Ain't Wot They Used t'Be* (1959). In 1963 she directed the musical *Oh! What a Lovely War*.

Littré, Maximilien Paul Émile 1801–81 •*French lexicographer and philosopher*• Born in Paris, he became a doctor but abandoned medicine for philology. An ardent democrat, he fought on the barricades in 1830, was one of the principal editors of the *National* until 1851, and an enthusiastic supporter of **Auguste Comte**, after whose death in 1857 he became the leader of the positivist school. In 1854 he assumed the editorship of the *Journal des savants*. His splendid *Dictionnaire de la langue française* (1863–72, "Dictionary of the French Language") did not prevent the Academy from rejecting its author (1863), whom Bishop Félix Dupanloup (1802–78) denounced as holding impious doctrines. In 1871 he became Professor of History and Geography at the École Polytechnique. He was chosen representative of the Seine department in the National Assembly, and in December 1871 the Academy at last admitted him.

Litvinov, Maksim Maksimovich 1876–1951 •*Soviet politician and diplomat*• Born a Polish Jew in Bielostok, Russian Poland, in 1903 he joined in revolutionary activities with **Lenin**. He was exiled to Siberia, but escaped. At the Revolution he was appointed Bolshevik ambassador in London (1917–18). He became deputy People's Commissar for Foreign Affairs in 1921 and Commissar (1930–39), achieving US recognition of Soviet Russia in 1934. As ambassador to the US (1941–43) and Vice Minister of Foreign Affairs (1943–46), he strongly advocated cooperation between the USSR and the West and world disarmament.

Liu Shaoqi (Liu Shao-ch'i) 1898–1969? •*Chinese political leader*• Born in Yinshan, Hunan Province, into a land-owning family, he went to school with the future leader, **Mao Zedong**. Educated at Changsha and Shanghai, he went to Moscow to study (1921–22), joined the Chinese Communist Party, and returned to China to become a party labor organizer in Shanghai. He was elected to the politburo in 1934, and became its foremost expert on the theory and practice of organization and party structure, and wrote *How to Be a Good Communist* (1939, originally a series of lectures). In 1943 he became Secretary-General of the Party, Vice Chairman (1949), and Chairman of the People's Republic of China in 1958, second only to Mao Zedong. He advocated a freer market economy and financial incentives, but during the Cultural Revolution (1966–69) he was denounced as a bourgeois renegade and banished to Henan (Honan) Province, while **Lin Biao** emerged as Mao's heir-apparent. He reportedly died in detention. He was posthumously rehabilitated in 1980.

Lively, Penelope 1933– •*English novelist and children's author*• She was born in Cairo, Egypt, and read history at Oxford. A preoccupation with the relation of the present and the past, and a vivid sense of time and place, form the central thread of much of her writing, notably in her children's books *The Ghost of Thomas Kempe* (1973) and *A Stitch in Time* (1976). Novels written for adults include *Judgement Day* (1980), *Moon Tiger* (1987, Booker Prize), *Cleopatra's Sister* (1993) and *Spiderweb* (1998). Her short stories were collected in *Pack of Cards* (1986). She has also written *Oleander, Jacaranda* (1994), an autobiography of her early years in Egypt, and *A House Unlocked* (2001), a reflection on her family's house in Somerset.

" "

All habits are geared towards the linear, the sequential, but memory refuses such orderliness.

1994 ***Oleander, Jacaranda.***

Liverpool, Robert Banks Jenkinson, 2nd Earl of 1770–1828 •*English politician*• Born in London, he was the son of the 1st Earl (1727–1808). Educated at Charterhouse and Christ Church, Oxford, he entered Parliament in 1790. A Tory with Liberal ideas on trade and finance, in 1801 as Foreign Secretary he negotiated the unpopular Treaty of Amiens. In 1803 he was made Lord Hawkesbury, and on **William Pitt**'s return to power he went to the Home Office (1804–06). In 1807 he again took the Home Office, and the next year succeeded his father as Earl of Liverpool. In **Perceval**'s ministry of 1809 he was Secretary for War and the Colonies. In 1812 he formed an administration, regarded as reactionary, which lasted for nearly 15 years. He was a Free Trader, and ultimately sought to liberalize the tariff. He united the old and the new Tories at a critical period.

Livia, Drusilla, *later called* **Julia Augusta** 58 BC–AD 29 •*Roman empress*• She was the third wife of Emperor **Augustus**, whom she married in 38 BC after divorcing her first husband Tiberius Claudius Nero. From her first marriage she had two children, **Tiberius** the future emperor (who succeeded Augustus), and Nero Claudius **Drusus**, but none from her marriage with Augustus. She was believed to have influence over Augustus, cunningly promoting the interests of her sons at the expense of Augustus's kinsmen by fair or foul means. She was adopted into the Julian family by Augustus at his death in AD 14, and changed her name to Julia Augusta. Relations with her son Tiberius after his accession became strained. She was deified (AD 42) by her grandson **Claudius I**.

Livingstone, David 1813–73 •*Scottish missionary and traveler*• He was born in Blantyre, Lanarkshire, and from 10 until he was 24 he worked in a cotton factory there. After studying medicine in London he was attracted to Africa by Scottish missionary Robert Moffat (1795–1883), whose daughter Mary he married in 1844. He was ordained in the London Missionary Society in 1840, and for several years worked in Bechuanaland (now Botswana). Repulsed by the Boers for trying to plant native missionaries in the Transvaal, he traveled northward, discovered Lake Ngami, and gathered a vast amount of valuable information about the country, its products and the native tribes. He discovered the Victoria Falls of the Zambezi. He was welcomed home with extraordinary enthusiasm, and published his *Missionary Travels* (1857). In 1858 he was appointed chief of a government expedition for exploring the Zambezi and explored the Zambezi, Shiré and Rovuma, discovered Lakes Shirwa and Nyasa, and concluded that Lake Nyasa and its neighborhood was the best field for commercial and missionary operations, though he was hampered by the Portuguese authorities, as well as by the realization that the slave trade was spreading in the district. The expedition was recalled in 1863. His second book, *The Zambesi and Its Tributaries* (1865), was designed to expose the Portuguese slave traders, and to find means of establishing a settlement for missions and commerce near the head of the Rovuma. The Royal Geographical Society asked him to return to Africa to settle a disputed question regarding the watershed of central Africa and the sources of the Nile. In 1866 he started from Zanzibar, pressed westward amid innumerable hardships, and in 1867–68 discovered Lakes Mweru and Bangweulu. Obliged to return for rest to Ujiji, he headed westward again as far as the River Lualaba. On his return after severe illness to Ujiji, Livingstone was found there by **Henry Morton Stanley**, sent to look for him by the *New York Herald*. Determined to solve the problem, he returned to Bangweulu, but died in Old Chitambo (now in Zambia). His body was taken to England and buried in Westminster Abbey.

Livingstone, Ken(neth) 1945– •*English politician*• He was born in London and educated at Phillipa Fawcett College of Education. He worked as a scientific research technician from 1962 until devoting himself to a political career. After joining the Labour Party in 1969, he worked as a London regional executive (1974–86) and served as a Lambeth and Camden local councilor (1971–78). In 1973, he was elected to the Greater London Council (GLC), becoming leader in 1980. He transformed the GLC from being a significant but largely administrative element in the capital's political infrastructure into an instrument of left-wing policies and a key weapon in the Labour Party's criticism of national Conservative policies. The government in 1986 introduced legislation to dismantle the highest tier of Great Britain's regional political administration. The following year, Livingstone won election to Parliament as Member of Parliament for Brent East. He took the newly created post of Mayor of London in 2000.

Livius Andronicus fl. 3rd century BC •*Roman writer*• He was probably a Greek by birth, from Tarentum. He was taken prisoner at the Roman capture of the city and sold as a slave in Rome in 272 BC, but later freed by his master. He translated the *Odyssey* into Latin Saturnian verse, and wrote tragedies, comedies and hymns based on Greek models. Only fragments are extant. He is regarded as the father of Roman dramatic and epic poetry.

Livy, *properly* **Titus Livius** 59 BC–AD 17 •*Roman historian*• Born in Patavium (Padua), he settled in Rome in about 29 BC and was admitted to the court of **Augustus**. His history of Rome from its foundation to the death of Nero Claudius **Drusus** (9 BC) comprised 142 books, of which 35 have survived. Livy can be placed in the forefront of Latin writers, and his work was a major influence on subsequent historical writing.

Li Xiannian (Li Hsien-nien) 1905–92 •*Chinese politician*• Born into a poor peasant family in Hubei (Hupeh) Province, he worked as a carpenter before serving with the Nationalist Guomindang (Kuomintang) forces in 1926–27. After joining the Communist Party (CCP) in 1927, he established the Oyuwan Soviet (People's Republic) in Hubei, participated in the Long March (1934–36) and was a military commander in the war against Japan and in the civil war. He was inducted into the CCP politburo and secretariat in 1956 and 1958, but fell out of favor during the 1966–69 Cultural Revolution. He was rehabilitated, as Finance Minister, by **Zhou Enlai** in 1973, and later served as state president under **Deng Xiaoping** (1983–88).

Llosa, Mario Vargas *See* **Vargas Llosa, Mario**

Lloyd, Clive Hubert 1944– •*West Indian cricket player*• Born in Georgetown, Guyana, his first West Indies Test cap was in 1966. He then went to England to play for Haslingden in the Lancashire League before joining Lancashire (1968–86). A magnificent batsman and fielder, he played in 110 Test matches (captain 1974–85), scoring 7,515 runs and making 19 centuries. He captained the West Indies in 18 Test matches, losing only two, which made him the most successful Test captain. He also captained the West Indies teams that won the World Cup in 1975 and 1979. He later became a British citizen.

Lloyd, Edward d. c.1730 •*English coffee-house keeper*• From 1688 until 1726 he owned a coffee house in Lombard St, London, after which is named "Lloyd's," the London society of underwriters. His coffee house became a haunt of merchants and ship owners, and for them Lloyd started his *Lloyd's News*, later to become *Lloyd's List*.

Lloyd, Harold Clayton 1893–1971 •*US film comedian*• Born in Burchard, Nebraska, he was stage-struck from an early age and worked extensively as an extra from 1913. Gradually, he created his own character of the shy, sincere, bespectacled boy next door, developing a reputation for highly demanding stunts in works like *High and Dizzy* (1920) and, most famously, *Safety Last* (1923). He enjoyed a run of hits such as *Why Worry?* (1923) and *Speedy* (1928), but was less successful in the sound era and retired after *Mad Wednesday* in 1947. He received an honorary Academy Award in 1952.

Lloyd, Henry Demarest 1847–1903 •*US journalist and reformer*• Born in New York City, he was a graduate of Columbia University. He became a school lecturer in economics, studied law and was admitted to the bar in 1869. From 1872 he worked on the Chicago *Tribune* as a reporter and on the editorial staff. He became dedicated to exposure of capitalist abuses and his masterpiece, *Wealth Against Commonwealth* (1894), was a searing indictment of how **John D Rockefeller** built up Standard Oil. A strong advocate of cooperative methods, he visited New Zealand, reporting on it in *A Country Without Strikes* (1900), and supported the Populist Party, denouncing its fusion with the Democrats and the free silver movement under **William Jennings Bryan**.

Lloyd, Marie, *originally* **Matilda Alice Victoria Wood** 1870–1922 •*English music-hall entertainer*• Born in London, she had her first success with the song "The Boy I Love Sits up in the Gallery." She went on to become one of the most popular music-hall performers of all time, specializing in witty portrayals of working-class Londoners. She appeared in music halls throughout the country, and in the US, South Africa and Australia. Among her most famous songs were "Oh, Mr Porter" and "My Old Man Said Follow the Van."

Lloyd, Selwyn Brooke *See* **Selwyn-Lloyd, Baron**

Lloyd-George (of Dwyfor), David Lloyd George, 1st Earl 1863–1945 •*Welsh Liberal statesman*• He was born in Manchester of Welsh parentage. Aged two when his father died, his family was taken to Llanystumdwy, near Criccieth, Wales, the home of his uncle Richard Lloyd, who recognized the latent brilliance in the young Lloyd George and took responsibility for his education. Lloyd George thus acquired his religion, industry, vivid oratory, radical views and Welsh nationalism. He became a solicitor and in 1890 was elected as an advanced Liberal for Caernarvon Boroughs. From 1905 to 1908 he was president of the Board of Trade and was responsible for the passing of three important Acts—the Merchant Shipping Act and the Census Production Act in 1906, and the Patents Act in 1907. As chancellor of the exchequer from 1908 to 1915, he reached the heights as a social reformer with his Old Age Pensions Act (1908), the National Insurance Act (1911), and the momentous "people's budget" of 1909–10, whose rejection by the House of Lords led to constitutional crisis and the Parliament Act of 1911, which removed the Lords' power of veto. Although a pacifist, he strongly believed in the national rights of a smaller country and saw the parallel between the Welsh and the Boers. His condemnation of the Boer War had been loud but the threat of invasion of Belgium by Germany in 1914 dispelled all pacifist tendencies. In 1915 he was appointed minister of munitions, and in 1916 became war secretary and superseded **H H Asquith** as coalition prime minister (1916–22). By his forceful policy he was, as **Hitler** later said of him, "the man who won the war." He was one of the "big three" at the peace negotiations. At home there was a split in the Liberal Party which never completely healed. In 1921 he negotiated with Sinn Fein and conceded the Irish Free State. This was very unpopular with the Conservatives in the government and led to his downfall and the downfall of the Liberals as a party in the 1922 election. Following the 1931 general election he resigned as leader of the Liberal Party and led a group of Independent Liberal Members of Parliament. He retained his seat until the year of his death, in which year he was made an earl.

“ ”

You cannot feed the hungry on statistics.

1904 Speech advocating tariff reform.

Lloyd-Webber, Andrew Lloyd Webber, Baron 1948– •*English popular composer*• Born in London, he was educated at Westminster School and Magdalen College, Oxford, and at the Royal College of Music, London. He met **Tim Rice** in 1965, and together they wrote *Joseph and the Amazing Technicolor Dreamcoat* (1968), which was extended and staged in 1973 and revived in 1991. Their greatest success was the rock opera *Jesus Christ Superstar* (staged 1970, filmed 1973, revived 1996), the long-playing record of which achieved record-breaking sales. He composed the music for *Evita* (1978), which was the basis for the 1996 **Alan Parker** film of the same name (for which Lloyd-Webber and Rice shared an Academy Award for best song), *Tell Me on a Sunday* (1980), *Starlight Express* (1984) and *Cats* (1981). His later successes include *The Phantom of the Opera* (1986), based on the 1911 novel by Gaston Leroux (1868–1927), *Aspects of Love* (1989) and *Sunset Boulevard* (1993). He also composed the music for *Whistle Down the Wind* (1996) and *The Beautiful Game* (2000). He was knighted in 1992 and made a life peer in 1997. His brother Julian (1951–) is a cellist.

Llywelyn Ap Iorwerth, *called* **the Great** 1173–1240 •*Prince of Gwynedd*• He seized power from his uncle David (1194), and soon had most of northern Wales under his control. In 1205 he married Joan (d. 1237), the illegitimate daughter of King **John** of England. Welsh poetry and culture flourished under him, and there was harmony between him and the Church. He successfully maintained his independence from King John and **Henry III**. He was probably the ablest of all the medieval Welsh princes.

Loach, Ken(neth) 1936– •*English filmmaker*• Born in Nuneaton, Warwickshire, he acted before becoming a television director, and made his name in the Wednesday Play series, with productions such as *Cathy Come Home* (1966). His first feature film, *Poor Cow* (1967), was followed by the popular *Kes* (1969) and *Family Life* (1971). He has continued to explore social issues in such television work as *Days of Hope* (1975) and *The Price of Coal* (1977), and the film *Looks and Smiles* (1981). Subsequent films have included *Raining Stones* (1993), *Land and Freedom* (1995), *Carla's Song* (1997) and *Bread and Roses* (2000).

Lobachevski, Nikolai Ivanovich 1792–1856 •*Russian mathematician*• Born in Nizhny Novgorod, he became professor at Kazan University in 1814, where he spent the rest of his life. From the 1820s he developed a theory of non-Euclidean geometry in which **Euclid**'s parallel postulate (that there is only one straight line which passes through a given point and is parallel to another given line) did not hold. A similar theory was discovered almost simultaneously and independently by **János Bolyai**. He also wrote on algebra and the theory of functions.

Lochhead, Liz 1947– •*Scottish poet and dramatist*• Born in Motherwell, Lanarkshire, she studied at Glasgow School of Art and worked as an art teacher before becoming a full-time writer in 1979. A frank and witty poet, she has published several collections. Her most powerful work has been written for the stage, and includes *Mary Queen of Scots Got Her Head Chopped Off* (1987), a version of **Bram Stoker**'s *Dracula* (1985), which restored the serious intent of the original, and a highly acclaimed reworking of **Euripides**'s *Medea* (2000). She translated **Molière**'s *Tartuffe* (1985) into colloquial Glaswegian, and has written for radio and television. She wrote the text for the epic music theater production *Jock Tamson's Bairns* in Glasgow in 1990.

Lochner, Stefan c. 1400–51 •*German painter*• Born in Meersburg on Lake Constance, he was the principal master of the Cologne school, marking the transition from the Gothic style to naturalism. The influence of Netherlandish art, particularly **Jan van Eyck**, shows in his work, as in the *Madonna With the Violet* (c. 1443, Cologne). His best-known work is the triptych in Cologne Cathedral.

Locke, Alain Leroy 1886–1954 •*US educationist and critic*• Born in Philadelphia, he graduated from Harvard and became the first African-American Rhodes scholar at Oxford (1907–10). Professor of Philosophy at Howard University from 1917, he published numerous works that explored African-American culture in the US and its African antecedents. He was a leading figure in the Harlem Renaissance.

Locke, Bessie 1865–1952 •*US pioneer of kindergarten education*• Born in West Cambridge (Arlington), Massachusetts, she is said to have been deflected from business to education by her observation of a friend's kindergarten in a slum area of New York City. She founded the National Association for the Promotion of Kindergarten Education (National Kindergarten Association) in 1909, and was head of the kindergarten division of the US Bureau of Education (1913–19), working to improve kindergarten teacher training. From 1917 she published home education articles for parents, which became very influential. She helped open over 3,000 kindergartens, serving more than 1.5 million children.

Locke, Bobby, *properly* **Arthur D'Arcy Locke** 1917–87 •*South African golf player*• He was born in Germiston. A slow, methodical player, he won four British Open championships (1949, 1950, 1952, 1957), and between 1947 and 1950 won 11 events on the US tour circuit.

Locke, John 1632–1704 •*English empiricist philosopher*• He was born in Wrington, Somerset, and educated at Westminster School and Christ Church, Oxford. He reacted against the prevailing scholasticism at Oxford and involved himself instead in experimental studies of medicine and science. In 1667 he joined the household of Anthony Ashley Cooper, later 3rd Earl of **Shaftesbury**, as his personal physician and became his adviser in scientific and political matters generally. Through Ashley he made contact with the leading intellectual figures in London and was elected a Fellow of the Royal Society (1668). When Ashley became Earl of Shaftesbury and Chancellor (1672), Locke became secretary to the Council of Trade and Plantations, but retired to France (1675–79), partly for health reasons and perhaps partly from political prudence. After Shaftesbury's fall and death in 1683, Locke felt threatened and fled to the Netherlands. His *Two Treatises of Government*, published anonymously in 1690, constitute his reply to the patriarchal, divine right theory of Sir Robert Filmer (c. 1590–1653) and also to the absolutism of **Thomas Hobbes**. The *Treatises* present a theory of the social contract which embodies a defense of natural rights and a justification for constitutional law, the liberty of the individual and the rule of the majority. If the ruling body offends against natural law it must be deposed, and this sanctioning of rebellion had a powerful influence on the American and the French revolutions. His major philosophical work was the *Essay Concerning Human Understanding*, published in 1690 though developed over 20 years. The work is regarded as the first and probably the most important statement of an empiricist theory of knowledge in the British tradition which led from Locke to **George Berkeley** and **David Hume**. His other main works were *A Letter Concerning Toleration* (1689), *Some Thoughts Concerning Education* (1693) and *The Reasonableness of Christianity* (1695), and they are all characterized by the same tolerance, moderation and common sense.

Lockhart, John Gibson 1794–1854 •*Scottish biographer, novelist and critic*• Born in Cambusnethan, Lanarkshire, the son of a Church of Scotland minister, he spent his boyhood in Glasgow, and at 13 won a Snell exhibition to Balliol College, Oxford. In 1813 he graduated with top marks in classics. He then studied law at Edinburgh, and in 1816 was called to the bar. From 1817 he turned increasingly to writing, and with **John Wilson** ("Christopher North") became the chief mainstay of *Blackwood's Magazine*. There he exhibited the criticism and caustic wit that made him the terror of his Whig opponents. He went on to write four novels—*Valerius* (1821), *Adam Blair* (1822), *Reginald Dalton* (1823) and *Matthew Wald* (1824). His other works include biographies of **Robert Burns** (1828) and **Napoleon I** (1829), and his masterpiece, *The Life of Sir Walter Scott* (7 vols, 1837–38). In 1825 he moved to London to become editor until 1853 of the *Quarterly Review*. He also was auditor of the Duchy of Cornwall (1843). His closing years were clouded by illness and deep depression. He visited Italy for the sake of his health, but, like Scott, came back to Abbotsford in Scotland to die.

Lockwood, Belva Ann, *née* **Bennett** 1830–1917 •*US lawyer and reformer*• Born in Royalton, Niagara County, New York, and educated at Genesee College, she graduated from the National University Law School in Washington (1873) and was admitted to the bar. In 1868 she married Ezekiel Lockwood, her second husband (her first died in 1853). A skilled and vigorous supporter of women's rights, she became the first woman to argue before the Supreme Court, and helped to promote various reforms, such as the Equal Pay Act for female civil servants (1872). In 1884 and 1888, as a member of the National Equal Rights Party, she was nominated for the presidency.

Lockwood, Margaret 1911–90 •*English actress*• Born in Karachi, India, she studied at the Royal Academy of Dramatic Art before making her film debut in *Lorna Doone* (1934). Gaining a long-term contract with British Lion, she made a spirited young heroine in films like *Midshipman Easy* (1935) before achieving stardom in *The Lady Vanishes* (1938) and *Bank Holiday* (1938). She was briefly in Hollywood before World War II, then returned to Great Britain and starred in costume melodramas like *The Man in Grey* (1943) and *The Wicked Lady* (1945). Subsequent role choices failed to sustain her stardom and she played her last leading role in *Cast a Dark Shadow* (1955). She returned to the cinema for a final appearance as the wicked stepmother in *The Slipper and the Rose* (1976).

Lockyer, Sir (Joseph) Norman 1836–1920 •*English astronomer*• Born in Rugby, Warwickshire, he became a clerk at the British War Office to which he remained technically attached (1857–75), devoting as much time as he could spare to science. In 1868 he designed a spectroscope for observing solar prominences outside a total eclipse and succeeded in doing this independently of Pierre Jules César Janssen (1824–1907), who had used the same principle a few months earlier. In the same year he postulated the existence of an unknown element which he named helium (the "Sun element"), an element not found on earth until 1895 by **William Ramsay**. He also discovered and named the solar chromosphere. His research gave rise to unconventional ideas such as his theory of dissociation, whereby atoms were believed to be capable of further subdivision. Among other activities, he took part in eclipse expeditions and made surveys of ancient temples for the purpose of dating them by astronomical methods. The founder (1869) and first editor of the scientific periodical *Nature*, he was knighted in 1897. His solar physics observatory at South Kensington was transferred to Cambridge University in 1911.

Lodge, David John 1935– •*English novelist and literary critic*• Born in Dulwich, Greater London, he was educated at University College London, and at the University of Birmingham, where he was Professor of Modern English Literature (1976–87), becoming Honorary Professor in 1987. His critical and theoretical writing (most of which is concerned with contemporary fiction) has been influential, notably *Language of Fiction* (1966), *Working With Structuralism* (1981) and *The Art of Fiction* (1992). Several of his novels have an academic setting, including the best-known of them, *Changing Places* (1975) and its sequel, *Small World* (1984). He moved away from the academic into the industrial world with *Nice Work* (1988, adapted for television 1989). Later works include *Paradise News* (1991), *Therapy* (1995) and *Thinks* (2001).

“ ”

As to our universities, I've come to the conclusion that they are élitist where they should be egalitarian, and egalitarian where they should be élitist.

*1988 **Nice Work**, part 5, chapter 4.*

Lodge, Henry Cabot 1850–1924 •*US politician, historian and biographer*• Born in Boston, he studied at Harvard, and while serving in the US House of Representatives (1887–93) as a Republican, he also pursued a scholarly career, publishing historical studies and biographies of US statesmen. He was a US senator from 1893 until his death and is best remembered for leading Senate opposition to the League of Nations.

Lodge, Henry Cabot, Jr 1902–85 •*US politician and statesman*• Born in Nahant, Massachusetts, the grandson of **Henry Cabot Lodge**, he began a political career in the Massachusetts legislature (1932–36) and served as US Republican senator (1937–44, 1947–53). He was appointed US ambassador to the United Nations (1953–60), and was chosen by President Kennedy to be ambassador to South Vietnam (1963), returning to this post under President **Lyndon B Johnson** (1965–67). Ambassador to West Germany (1968), he resigned to become chief US negotiator (1969) at the Vietnam peace talks in Paris.

Lodge, Sir Oliver Joseph 1851–1940 •*English physicist*• Born in Penkhull, Staffordshire, he studied at the Royal College of Science and at University College London, and in 1881 became Professor of Physics at the University of Liverpool. In 1900 he was appointed first principal of the new university at Birmingham. He discredited the ether theory in 1893, thus preparing the way for the theory of relativity. Especially distinguished in electricity, he was a pioneer of wireless telegraphy. He gave much time to research into psychic phenomena, and on this subject wrote *Raymond* (1916) and *My Philosophy* (1933). He was knighted in 1902.

Lodge, Thomas c. 1558–1625 •*English dramatist, romance writer and poet*• Born in West Ham, London, he went to Trinity College, Oxford, and then to Lincoln's Inn (1578). He published a *Defence of Poetry* anonymously in 1580, and an attack on abuses by moneylenders, *An Alarum Against Usurers*, in 1584, along with his first romance, *The Delectable Historie of Forbonius and Priscilla*. This was followed by *Scillaes Metamorphosis* in 1589. About 1588 he took part in a buccaneering expedition to the Canary Islands, and wrote another romance, *Rosalynde* (1590), his best-known work, which supplied **Shakespeare** with many of the chief incidents in *As You Like It*. *The Wounds of the Civil War* and *A Looking-Glass for London and England* (with **Robert Greene**) appeared in 1594. Among his remaining writings are a collection of poems, *Phillis* (1593), *A Fig for Momus* (1595), and translations of **Josephus** (1602) and **Seneca** (1614).

Loeb, James 1867–1933 •*US banker*• Born in New York City, he founded the Institute of Musical Art in New York (1905) and a mental clinic in Munich. A classical scholar, in 1910 he provided funds for the publication of the famous Loeb Classical Library of Latin and Greek texts with English translations.

Loesser, Frank Henry 1910–69 •*US songwriter and composer*• Born in New York City, he published his first lyrics in 1931, and in 1937 went to Hollywood as a contract writer. With a succession of collaborators he turned out several hit songs, including *See What the Boys in the Backroom Will Have* and *Baby, It's Cold Outside*. He branched out into writing his own music with *Where's Charley*, a musical version of *Charley's Aunt* (1948), but he is best known for writing the music and lyrics for *Guys and Dolls* (1950). His other musicals include *The Most Happy Fella* (1956), and *How to Succeed in Business Without Really Trying* (1961), for which he shared the Pulitzer Prize for drama in 1962.

Loewe, Frederick 1904–88 •*US composer*• Born in Berlin, he went to the US in 1924, and worked as a composer on a number of Broadway musicals. Those he wrote in collaboration with **Alan Jay Lerner** were particularly successful, including *Brigadoon* (1947), *My Fair Lady* (1956) and the film score for *Gigi* (1958).

Loewi, Otto 1873–1961 •*German pharmacologist and Nobel Prize winner*• Born in Frankfurt am Main and educated in Strasbourg and Munich, he was appointed Professor of Pharmacology at the University of Graz (1909–38). Forced to leave Nazi Germany in 1938, he became research professor at New York University College of Medicine in 1940. From 1901 he worked for a time alongside physiologist Sir Henry Dale (1875–1968) at University College London, on nerve impulses and their chemical transmission. He subsequently identified several possible transmitter substances and distinguished acetylcholine. He shared with Dale the 1936 Nobel Prize for physiology or medicine for investigations on the chemical transmission of nerve impulses.

Lofting, Hugh John 1886–1947 •*English children's novelist*• He was born in Maidenhead, Berkshire. The "Dr Dolittle" books (1920–53) for which he is famous had their origins in the trench warfare of World War I, of which he had firsthand experience. The idea of the doctor who learns animal languages came to him from his reflections on the part that horses were playing in the war. Although he tired of his eponymous hero—on one occasion attempting to abandon him on the moon—his popularity with readers kept him alive. From 1912 Lofting resided mainly in the US.

Logan, James, *also called* **Tah-gah-jute** c. 1725–80 •*Native American leader*• Born in Shamokin (now Sunbury), Pennsylvania, he was a prominent member of the Mingo, of the Ohio and Scioto rivers. He was friendly toward whites until his family was slaughtered at the Yellow Creek massacre, an event that resulted in Lord Dunmore's War (1774). He refused to participate in a peace treaty meeting, sending instead an eloquent speech expressing anger at his undeserved loss, and he spent the rest of his life seeking revenge by killing white settlers.

Lollobrigida, Gina 1927– •*Italian actress*• Born in Subiaco, she studied to become a commercial artist and made a living as a model before entering the film industry in 1946. Her curvaceous figure and ability to attract publicity made her a popular sex symbol in the glamour-starved Europe of the immediate postwar years. An actress of limited range, she enjoyed a prolific career in such Italian films as *Pane, amore e fantasia* (1953, *Bread, Love and Dreams*). Under contract to **Howard Hughes** from 1949, she appeared in US films including *Beat the Devil* (1954), *Trapeze* (1956) and *Never So Few* (1959). She directed the documentary *Portrait of Fidel Castro* (1975) and has enjoyed some success as a photographer.

Lomax, Alan *See* **Lomax, John Avery**

Lomax, John Avery 1867–1948 •*US folklorist and musicologist*• Born in Goodman, Mississippi, he was raised in Texas and studied at Harvard, but turned to field research on cowboy songs. He worked in teaching and banking for 15 years, then returned to fieldwork, this time in African-American folksongs, blues, spirituals and work chants. He and his son, Alan Lomax (1915–2002), toured the South with basic recording equipment in the early 1930s, amassing a collection of some 10,000 invaluable recordings for the Library of Congress (where John was curator of American Folksong), and discovering the singer **Leadbelly** along the way. Alan continued his father's work, and made a series of important recordings with jazz pioneer **Jelly Roll Morton** in 1938, and **Muddy Waters** in 1942.

Lombard, Carole, *originally* **Jane Alice Peters** 1908–42 •*US actress*• Born in Fort Wayne, Indiana, she moved to California, where her blond beauty made her a decorative addition to many **Mack Sennett** comedies. She signed a long-term contract with Paramount in 1930, saw her roles gradually improve and revealed her comic flair in *Twentieth Century* (1934). Glamorous, sophisticated and effervescent, she was the perfect heroine of screwball comedies like *My Man Godfrey* (1936), *Nothing Sacred* (1937) and *To Be or Not to Be* (1942), while her dramatic potential was glimpsed in *They Knew What They Wanted* (1940). Married to **Clark Gable** (1939), she was one of Hollywood's most popular stars at the time of her death in a plane crash.

Lombard, Peter c. 1100–60 •*Italian theologian*• Born near Novara, Lombardy, he studied at the Universities of Bologna, Rheims, and (under **Abelard**) at Paris. After holding a chair of theology there, he became Bishop of Paris in 1159. He was generally styled *Magister Sententiarum* (the "Master of Sentences") from his collection of sentences from **Augustine of Hippo** and other church fathers on points of Christian doctrine, with objections and replies. The theological doctors of Paris in 1300 denounced some of his teachings as heretical, but his work was the standard textbook of Catholic theology down to the Reformation.

Lombardi, Vince(nt Thomas) 1913–70 •*US football coach*• Born in Brooklyn, New York, he was a noted defensive guard in his playing days with Fordham University, although he was better known as a coach. His best work was done with the Green Bay Packers from Wisconsin (1959–69). With this comparatively small-town team he earned five league titles and took them successfully to two Super Bowls (1967–68).

Lombardo, Pietro c. 1433–1515 •*Italian sculptor and architect*• Born in Corona, Milan, he worked in Padua, and probably Florence, then settled with his family in Venice c. 1467 and became the head of the major sculpture workshop of the day. With the assistance of his sons, Tullio (c. 1455–1532) and Antonio (c. 1458–1516), he was responsible for both the architecture and sculptural decoration of Santa Maria dei Miracoli (1481–89) in Venice. Among the many monuments he designed was the tomb of **Dante** in Ravenna.

Lomonosov, Mikhail Vasilevich 1711–65 •*Russian scientist and writer*• Born in Kholmogory, near Archangel, he ran away to Moscow in search of an education and later studied in St Petersburg, in Marburg in Germany under the philosopher **Christian von Wolff**, and finally in Freiburg, where he turned to metallurgy and glassmaking. He became Professor of Chemistry at the St Petersburg Academy of Sciences in 1745 and set up Russia's first chemical laboratory there. He also made important contributions to Russian literature. He advocated popular education and freedom for the serfs, and came to be revered by many people in his own day, but his papers were confiscated by **Catherine II (the Great)** after his death.

Lomu, Jonah 1975– •*New Zealand rugby union player*• Born in Mangere, he became the youngest-ever capped All Black. He made his international debut for New Zealand against France in 1994. He scored four tries against England in the semifinals of the 1995 Rugby World Cup, becoming a household name worldwide. Diagnosed with a serious kidney disorder in 1996, he fought his way back to fitness and won a gold medal in the rugby sevens at the 1998 Commonwealth Games. A superstar in international rugby union, he has remained there despite lucrative offers from rugby league.

London, Fritz Wolfgang 1900–54 •*US physicist*• He was born in Breslau, Germany (now Wrocław, Poland), brother of **Heinz London**. He studied classics at the Universities of Frankfurt and Munich and did research in philosophy leading to a doctorate at Bonn. Later he was attracted to theoretical physics and published on the quantum theory of the chemical bond with Walter Heitler. In 1930 he calculated the nonpolar component of forces between molecules, now called **van der Waals** forces. He and his brother fled Germany in 1933 to Oxford where they joined Sir **Francis Simon**'s group at the Clarendon Laboratory. Together they published major papers on conductivity giving the London equations (1935). Fritz moved to Duke University in the US (1939–54) and continued to work on superconductivity, and on superfluidity.

London, Heinz 1907–70 •*British physicist*• He was born in Bonn, Germany, the younger brother of **Fritz London**, and was educated at the Universities of Bonn, Berlin, Munich and Breslau, where he worked on his PhD with Sir **Francis Simon**. He fled Germany in 1933 with Fritz, and they joined Simon's group at the Clarendon Laboratory, Oxford, working together on conductivity. Heinz introduced a theory for the confinement of currents in a superconductor to a surface layer, and with his brother he published the London equations describing the electromagnetic behavior of superconductors (1935). He later worked on the development of the British atomic bomb, and at the Atomic Energy Research Establishment at Harwell (1946).

London, Jack, *pseudonym of* **John Griffith Chaney** 1876–1916 •*US writer*• Born in San Francisco with the double handicap of illegitimacy and poverty, he was successively sailor, tramp and gold miner before he began his career as a writer. He used his knowledge of the Klondike in his highly successful novels *The Call of the Wild* (1903), *The Sea-Wolf* (1904) and *White Fang* (1905), all of them reflecting his preoccupation with the struggle for survival. Among his later works are novels inspired by his socialist political beliefs, and his autobiographical tale of alcoholism, *John Barleycorn* (1913). With his health undermined by illness, accidents and heavy drinking, he died at the age of 40.

Long, Huey Pierce, *known as* **the Kingfish** 1893–1935 •*US politician*• Born near Winnfield, Louisiana, he was admitted to the bar in 1915 and headed the state's Public Service Commission. Styling himself as an advocate for the poor and rural folk of Louisiana, he became governor (1928–31) and proceeded to build one of the most effective political machines in the history of US politics. His program of extensive public spending not only reformed and developed Louisiana's public services, but also reduced the impact of the Depression on the state. In 1931 he became a Democratic US senator. Notorious for corruption and demagoguery, he secured the support of the poor by his intensive "Share the Wealth" social services and public works programs, but also squandered public funds on extravagant personal projects, including the construction of a marble and bronze statehouse at Baton Rouge. At first a supporter of the New Deal and President **Franklin D Roosevelt**, he became a critic of Roosevelt and planned to run against him in 1936, but Long was assassinated in the state capitol in Baton Rouge.

Long, Richard 1945– •*English land artist*• Born in Bristol, he trained at St Martin's School of Art, London. He takes country walks which he considers works of art in themselves, sometimes marking a place with a simple "sculpture," such as a circle of stones or a shallow trench. Afterward he exhibits these or, more often, photographs, maps and texts to document his actions, as with *A Hundred Mile Walk* (1971–72). He has made works on every continent except Antarctica. He won the 1989 Turner prize.

Longfellow, Henry Wadsworth 1807–82 •*US poet*• Born in Portland, Maine, he graduated from Bowdoin College in Brunswick, Maine, where one of his classmates was **Nathaniel Hawthorne**. He spent three years in Europe (1826–29) before becoming Professor of Foreign Languages at Bowdoin (1829–35), then Professor of Modern Languages and Literature at Harvard (1836–54). *Voices of the Night* (1839), his first book of verse, made a favorable impression, as did *Ballads* (1841), which included "The Wreck of the Hesperus" and "The Village Blacksmith." His most popular works are *Evangeline* (1847), a tale (in hexameters) of the French exiles of Acadia, and *The Song of Hiawatha* (1855), which is based on the legends of Native Americans. His gift of simple, romantic storytelling in verse brought him enduring popularity as a poet.

“ ”

If you would hit the mark, you must aim a little above it;
Every arrow that flies feels the attraction of earth.

1881 ***Elegiac Verse**, stanza 9.*

Longhi, Pietro, *originally* **Pietro Falca** 1702–85 •*Italian painter*• Born in Venice, he was a pupil of Antonio Balestra (1666–1740), and excelled in small-scale satiric pictures of Venetian life. Most of his work is in Venetian public collections, but the National Gallery, London, has three, of which the best known is *Rhinoceros in an Arena* (1751). His son Alessandro (1733–1813) was also a painter, and some of his portraits are now attributed to his father.

Longimanus *See* **Artaxerxes I**

Longinus probably 1st century AD •*Greek literary critic*• Nothing certain is known of his life, but he is author of *On the Sublime* (about two-thirds of which survives), which analyzes the qualities of great literature and has been enormously influential, particularly among Romantic critics.

Longman, Thomas 1699–1755 •*English publisher and founder of the Longman firm*• He was born in Bristol, the son of a merchant. He bought a bookselling business in Paternoster Row, London, in 1724, and shared in publishing Robert Ainsworth's *Latin Dictionary*, **Ephraim Chambers**'s *Cyclopaedia*, and **Samuel Johnson**'s *Dictionary*.

Longo, Jeannie 1958– •*French cyclist*• She was born in Annecy. Her numerous wins include the Women's Tour de France three times, the Colorado equivalent four times and the world title 13 times. Her numerous French Women's Champion wins include 11 consecutive titles between 1979 and 1989 and she has set world records indoors and out. Widely considered the best female road cyclist of all time, she is married to her coach Patrice Ciprelli, who was a former Alpine skiing internationalist.

Longus c. 3rd century AD •*Greek writer*• He was a native probably of Lesbos and was the author of the pastoral romance *Daphnis and Chloë*.

Lönnbohm, Armas Eino Leopold *See* **Leino, Eino**

Lönnrot, Elias 1802–84 •*Finnish philologist and folklorist*• Born in Sammatti, Nyland, he studied medicine, and was district medical officer for 20 years in Kajana. As a result of his folklore researches, he was appointed Professor of Finnish at Helsingfors (Helsinki) (1853–62). His major achievement was the collection of oral popular lays, which he organized into a long epic poem of ancient life in the far north, the *Kalevala*. Having standardized the national epic, he compiled a great Finnish-Swedish dictionary (1866–80), which helped establish a literary Finnish language.

Lonsdale, Hugh Cecil Lowther, 5th Earl of 1857–1944 •*English sportsman*• A landowner in Cumberland, he was a noted huntsman, steeplechaser, yachtsman and boxer. As president of the National Sporting Club he founded and presented the Lonsdale belts for boxing.

Lonsdale, Dame Kathleen, *née* **Yardley** 1903–71 •*Irish crystallographer*• Born in Newbridge, County Kildare, she studied at Bedford College, London. On graduating in 1922 she was invited by **William Bragg** to join his crystallography research team, first at University College London (UCL) and then at the Royal Institution, where she remained until 1946, apart from a short period when she worked at the University of Leeds (1929–31). She was one of the first two women to be elected a Fellow of the Royal Society, and was awarded the society's Davy Medal in 1957. She became Professor of Chemistry at UCL in 1949. She was given the honorary title of Dame Commander, Order of the British Empire, in 1956. Of her many contributions to crystallography, the most celebrated was her X-ray analysis of hexamethylbenzene and hexachlorobenzene in 1929, which showed that the carbon atoms in the benzene ring are coplanar and hexagonally arranged. She also made important contributions to space-group theory and to the study of anisotropy and disorder in crystals. She became a Quaker in 1935 and later worked tirelessly for various causes, including peace, penal reform and the social responsibility of science.

Loos, Adolf 1870–1933 •*Austrian architect and writer on design*• Born in Brno, Moravia (now in Czech Republic), he studied architecture in Dresden, spent three years in the US, then settled in Vienna in 1896. One of the major architects of the modern movement, he is particularly important for articulating the view that ornament is "wasteful," "decadent" and against modern "civilized" design. His buildings and other designs—such as furniture, glass and metalwork—reflect this view, but possess an elegance and visual interest which is derived from their functional form.

Loos, Anita 1893–1981 •*US writer*• Born in Sisson (now Mount Shasta), California, she began writing screenplays for **D W Griffith** in 1912. Her comic novel about Hollywood, *Gentlemen Prefer Blondes* (1925), with its naïve, gold-digging heroine Lorelei Lee, was enormously popular and was made into both a movie and a musical, though readers failed to recognize it as a satire. A prolific and successful screenwriter, Loos also adapted **Colette**'s *Gigi* for the stage (1952).

Lopez, Nancy 1957– •*US golf player*• Born in Torrance, California, she competed as an amateur in high school and college, winning the national championships of the Association for Intercollegiate Athletics for Women in 1976. Two years later she joined the professional tour and by 1997 had won 48 LPGA (Ladies Professional Golf Association) victories. She was selected by the Associated Press as Female Athlete of the Year (1978, 1985), and she has been the LPGA Player of the year four times—in 1978, 1979, 1985 and 1988.

Lopukhov, Fyodor Vasilevich 1886–1973 •*Russian dancer, choreographer and teacher*• Born in St Petersburg, he studied at the Imperial Ballet Academy there before joining the Maryinsky Theatre, where he established himself as a character dancer. He started choreographing in 1916, becoming one of the leading ballet experimentalists of his generation. His most influential ballet was *Dance Symphony* (1923). He was artistic director of the Kirov (1923–30, and in the mid-1940s and 1950s), and of the Maly Theatre and Bolshoi Ballet companies (both in the mid-1930s).

Lorca, Federico García *See* **García Lorca, Federico**

Loren, Sophia, *originally* **Sofia Scicolone** 1934– •*Italian film actress*• Born in Rome, and brought up in poverty near Naples, she was a teenage beauty queen and model before entering films as an extra in *Cuori sul mare* (1950). As the protégée of the producer Carlo Ponti (1913–), later her husband, she played the lead in *The Pride and the Passion* (1957) and other US productions. An international career followed and she won an Academy Award for her performance in De Sica's *La Ciociara* (1960, *Two Women*). Very beautiful, with a talent for earthy drama and vivacious comedy, among her many films are *The Millionairess* (1961), *Matrimonia all' Italiana* (1964, *Marriage Italian Style*) and *Una giornata speciale* (1977, *A Special Day*). Her career continued with television films like *Aurora* (1984) and *Courage* (1986). She received a Special Academy Award in 1991. Later films include *Prêt-à-Porter* (1994) and *Grumpier Old Men* (1995).

Lorentz, Hendrik Antoon 1853–1928 •*Dutch physicist and Nobel Prize winner*• Born in Arnhem, he studied at the University of Leiden and at the age of 25 was offered (1878) the first chair of theoretical physics at Leiden, which had been created for **Johannes van der Waals**. He remained there until 1912, when he was appointed director of Teyler's Institute in Haarlem. His major contribution to theoretical physics was his electron theory. His derivation in 1904 of a mathematical transformation, the **Fitzgerald**-Lorentz contraction, explained the apparent absence of relative motion between the Earth and the (supposed) ether, and prepared the way for **Albert Einstein**'s theories of relativity. In 1902 he was awarded, with **Pieter Zeeman**, the Nobel Prize for physics.

Lorenz, Konrad Zacharias 1903–89 •*Austrian zoologist, ethologist and Nobel Prize winner*• Born in Vienna, he studied there and founded, with **Nikolaas Tinbergen** in the late 1930s, the science of ethology (the study of animal behavior under natural conditions). Lorenz and his colleagues mainly studied birds, fish and some insects whose behaviors contain a relatively high proportion of stereotyped elements, or "fixed action patterns," and made comparisons between species. His studies have led to a deeper understanding of behavior patterns. In 1935 he published his observations on imprinting in young birds (the discovery for which he is chiefly known), by which hatchlings "learn" to recognize substitute parents at the earliest stages in life. In his book *On Aggression* (1963) he argued that, while aggressive behavior in man is inborn, it may be modified or channeled into other forms of activity, whereas in other animals it is purely survival motivated. He shared the 1973 Nobel Prize for physiology or medicine with Nikolaas Tinbergen and **Karl von Frisch**.

“ ”

Man appears to be the missing link between anthropoid apes and human beings.

*1965 In the **New York Times**, April 11.*

Lorenzo, Piero di *See* **Piero di Cosimo**

Lorimer, Sir Robert Stodart 1864–1929 •*Scottish architect*• He was born in Edinburgh, and educated at The Edinburgh Academy and the University of Edinburgh. He left without a degree and was apprenticed to an architect's office. He set up on his own in Edinburgh in 1892, working on Scottish country houses and creating a distinctive Scottish form of the Arts and Crafts tradition of his English contemporary **Edwin Lutyens**.

Lorrain, Claude *See* **Claude**

Lorre, Peter, *originally* **Laszlo Löwenstein** 1904–64 •*Hungarian actor*• Born in Rosenberg, he studied in Vienna, where he acted in repertory theater and gave one-man performances and readings. A diffident, sad-eyed figure with a whispering, wheedling voice, he was generally typecast as smilingly sinister villains and outcasts. He moved to Hollywood (1934), where his many successes included *Casablanca* (1942) and *The Beast With Five Fingers* (1946). A rare excursion to the right side of the law saw him cast as **John P Marquand**'s Japanese detective Mr Moto in eight films, and he also formed an unholy alliance with Sydney Greenstreet (1879–1954) that was seen to particular advantage in *The Maltese Falcon* (1941) and *The Mask of Dimitrios* (1944). He wrote and directed one film in Europe, *Der Verlorene* (1951, *The Lost One*).

Lorris, Guillaume de fl. 13th century •*French poet*• He wrote, before 1260, the first part (c. 4,000 lines) of the *Roman de la Rose* (completed c. 1280, Eng trans *The Romaunt of the Rose* by **Chaucer**, c. 1370), which was later continued by **Jean de Meung**. Nothing certain is known of his life.

Losey, Joseph (Walton) 1909–84 •*US film director*• He was born in La Crosse, Wisconsin, studied English literature at Harvard and wrote arts reviews and directed for the New York stage. His short film *A Gun in His Hand* (1945) received an Academy Award nomination. He directed *Galileo* (1947) in Los Angeles and New York before turning to film full-time with *The Boy With Green Hair* (1945) and *The Prowler* (1951). Falling afoul of the **McCarthy** witchhunts, he moved to the UK in 1951 and gained lasting acclaim for his collaborations with **Harold Pinter** on such films as *The Servant* (1963) and *Accident* (1967). *The Go-Between* (1971) won the Palme d'Or at the Cannes Film Festival. His later films include *Don Giovanni* (1979) and *Steaming* (1984).

Lo Spagnoletto *See* **Ribera, Jusepe de**

Lotto, Lorenzo c. 1480–1556 •*Italian religious painter*• Born in Venice, he was a brilliant portrait painter whose subjects are vivid and full of character. He worked in Treviso, Bergamo, Venice and Rome, finally becoming a lay brother in the Loreto monastery.

Lou, Miss *See* **Bennett, Louise Simone**

Louganis, Greg 1960– •*US diver*• Born in El Cajon, California, of Samoan and Swedish ancestry, he earned a BA in drama from the University of California, Irvine. He won the gold medal in both the springboard and platform diving competitions at the 1984 Los Angeles Olympics, and the world championship at both events in 1986. At the Seoul Olympics in 1988 he won gold medals in the same two categories despite receiving a head injury during the competition.

Louis I, *known as* **Louis the Pious** 778–840 •*King of Aquitaine, king of the Franks and emperor of the Western or Carolingian Empire*• He was born near Poitiers, and was the sole surviving son of **Charlemagne**. He was king of Aquitaine from 781 to 814, and Carolingian Emperor from 814 until his death. In 817 he attempted to secure his succession by dividing his territories between his three sons, Lothair (d. 855), Pepin (d. 838) and Louis "the German" (d. 876), with Lothair designated as emperor. In 829 a further share was given to a fourth son, Charles the Bald (**Charles I** of France). Louis I collaborated with St Benedict of Aniane to reform the Church, was a distinguished patron of scholarship, and defended the northwest from the raids of the Norsemen. It is greatly debated how far the proliferation of hereditary countships and of the institutions of vassalage, often thought to result from these raids, caused a general decline in imperial authority. After his death the empire disintegrated as his sons fought for supremacy.

Louis V, le Fainéant 967–87 •*King of France*• The son of Lothair IV, he was associated with Lothair's kingship (978). He ruled France from 986, but died heirless and was thus the last Carolingian ruler of France. The throne passed to **Hugo Capet**, the first of the Capetian line.

Louis VI, *known as* **Louis the Fat** 1081–1137 •*King of France*• He succeeded his father **Philip I** in 1108. For most of his reign he campaigned incessantly against the turbulent and unruly nobility of the Île-de-France and eventually reestablished his royal authority. Despite an inclination to gluttony and corpulence which left him unable to mount a horse after the age of 46, he was one of the most active of the House of **Capet**, and greatly increased the power and prestige of the monarchy.

Louis VII c. 1120–80 •*King of France*• The second son of **Louis VI**, he was originally educated for a Church career, but became heir on the death of his brother Philip (1131). In 1137 he was crowned king, married **Eleanor of Aquitaine**, and continued the consolidation of royal authority begun by his father. He participated in the Second Crusade (1147), and had his marriage annulled (1152), whereupon Eleanor married Henry Plantagenet, Count of Anjou, who became king of England in 1154 as **Henry II**.

Louis IX, *also called* **St Louis** 1214–70 •*King of France*• In 1226 he succeeded his father, Louis VIII (1187–1226); his mother, the pious Blanche of Castile, was his regent until 1234. Making Blanche regent again, he joined the Seventh Crusade (1248–54), but was defeated and captured, and ransomed for one million marks in 1250. He remained in Palestine, fortifying Christian strongholds, until his mother's death (1252). His long and peaceful reign strengthened the Capetian dynasty. He determined by the Pragmatic Sanction the relations between the French Church and the Pope, countenanced the Sorbonne, set up royal courts of justice or parliaments in the provinces, and authorized a new code of laws. By the Treaty of Paris (1259) he made peace with England, recognizing **Henry III** as Duke of Aquitaine in exchange for French suzerainty elsewhere. He was canonized by Pope **Boniface VIII** in 1297, and his feast day is August 25.

Louis XI 1423–83 •*King of France*• The son of **Charles VII** and Mary of Anjou, he was born in Bourges, and as Dauphin of France he married Margaret of Scotland (daughter of King **James I**) in 1436. He made two unsuccessful attempts to depose his father, but eventually succeeded to the throne on his father's death (1461). Though able and intelligent, his craftiness and treachery earned him the title "spider-king." He survived a coalition against him (1465) and broke the power of the nobility, led by **Charles the Bold** of Burgundy, who was killed in 1477. By 1483 Louis had succeeded in uniting most of France under one crown (with the exception of Brittany), and laid the foundations for absolute monarchy in France.

Louis XII, *known as* **the Father of the People** 1462–1515 •*King of France*• Born in Blois, the son of Charles, Duc d'**Orléans**, he succeeded his cousin **Charles VIII** (the Affable) in 1498, and married his widow **Anne of Brittany** (he had previously been married to a daughter of **Louis XI**). His military ambitions failed when his forces were driven from Italy (1512), and he was also defeated at the Battle of the Spurs by **Henry VIII** (1513). To guarantee peace, Louis married Mary Tudor, sister of Henry VIII, in 1514.

Louis XIII 1601–43 •*King of France*• The eldest son of **Henry IV** of France and his second wife **Marie de Médicis**, he was born at Fontainebleau, and was only nine years old when his father was assassinated. In 1615 his mother, as regent, arranged his marriage to **Anne of Austria** (daughter of **Philip III** of Spain). Their eldest son, not born until 1638, succeeded him as **Louis XIV**. In 1617 he overthrew the regency of his mother, exiling her to the provinces, and assumed power. In 1624 he appointed as his Chief Minister Cardinal **Richelieu**, who became the dominating influence of his reign. Richelieu subdued Huguenot resistance with the capture of La Rochelle (1628), while he supported the Protestants in Germany to prevent Habsburg domination of Europe. In 1629 Louis led a campaign in Italy to prevent Spanish expansion there. Although Richelieu was largely responsible for the centralization of administration and systematic patronage of the arts, the king was no cipher, and defended his minister against various plots, especially on the Day of Dupes (1630). On the death of Richelieu (1642), he turned to Cardinal **Mazarin**, who became his widow's favorite during her regency for Louis XIV.

Louis XIV, *known as* **Le Roi Soleil ("The Sun King")** 1638–1715 •*King of France from 1643*• He was born in St Germain-en-Laye, the son of **Louis XIII** and **Anne of Austria**, and came to the throne at the age of five. During his minority (1643–51), the government was carried on by his mother and her Chief Minister and lover, Cardinal **Jules Mazarin**. In 1660 Louis married the Infanta Maria Theresa (1638–83), daughter of **Philip IV** of Spain, through whom he was later to claim the Spanish succession for his second grandson. In 1661 he assumed sole responsibility for governing, advised by numerous royal councils. His obsession with France's greatness led him into aggressive foreign and commercial policies, especially against the Dutch. His patronage of the Catholic Stuarts also led to the hostility of England after 1689, but his major political rivals were the Austrian Habsburgs, particularly **Leopold I**. From 1665, Louis laid claim to part of the Spanish Netherlands, but later became obsessed with the acquisition of the whole Spanish inheritance. His attempt to create a Franco-Spanish Bourbon bloc led to the formation of the Grand Alliance of England, the United Provinces and the Habsburg Empire, and resulted in the War of the Spanish Succession. In his later years Louis was beset by other problems. His determination to preserve the unity of the French state and the independence of the French Church led him into conflict with the **Jansen**ists, the Huguenots and the papacy, with damaging repercussions. His old age was overshadowed by military disaster and the financial ravages of prolonged warfare. Yet Louis was the greatest monarch of his age, establishing the parameters of successful absolutism. In addition, his long reign marked the cultural ascendancy of France within Europe, symbolized by the Palace of Versailles, where he died, to be succeeded by his great-grandson, **Louis XV**.

" "

L'État, c'est moi.
I am the State.
1655 Address to the Parlement of Paris, April 13 (probably apocryphal).

Louis XV, *known as* **le Bien-Aimé ("the Well-Beloved")** 1710–74 •*King of France*• Born in Versailles, he succeeded, at age five, his great-grandfather, **Louis XIV**, in 1715. Until he came of age (1723), he was guided by the Regent, Philippe, Duc d'**Orléans**, and then by the Duc de **Bourbon**, who negotiated a marriage alliance with Maria, daughter of **Stanisłas I Leszczyński**, the deposed king of Poland. In 1726 the king's former tutor, the elderly Cardinal de **Fleury**, replaced Bourbon, and governed France well until his death (1744). Thereafter, Louis vowed to rule without a first minister, but allowed the government to drift into the control of ministerial factions, while indulging in secret diplomatic activity, distinct from official policy, through his own network of agents. This system (*le secret du roi*) brought confusion to French foreign policy in the years preceding the Diplomatic Revolution (1748–56), and obscured the country's interests overseas. Instead, France was drawn into a trio of continental wars during Louis's reign, which culminated in the loss of the French colonies in America and India (1763). Among innumerable mistresses, the two most famous and influential were Madame du **Barry** and Madame de **Pompadour**. In 1771 Louis tried to introduce reforms, but these came too late to staunch the decline in royal authority. He was succeeded by his grandson, **Louis XVI**.

Louis XVI 1754–93 •*King of France*• He was the third son of the Dauphin Louis and Maria Josepha of Saxony, and the grandson of **Louis XV**, whom he succeeded in 1774. He was married in 1770 to the Archduchess **Marie Antoinette**, daughter of the Habsburg Empress **Maria Theresa**, to strengthen the Franco-Austrian alliance. He failed to give support to ministers who tried to reform the outmoded financial and social structures of the country, such as **Jacques Necker** (1776–81). He allowed France to become involved in the American Revolution (1778–81), which exacerbated the national debt. To avert the deepening social and economic crisis, he agreed in 1789 to summon the Estates General. However, encouraged by the queen, he resisted demands from the National Assembly for sweeping reforms, and in October was brought with his family from Versailles to Paris as hostages to the revolutionary movement. Their attempted flight to Varennes (June 1791) branded the royal pair as traitors. Louis reluctantly approved the new consitution (September 1791), but his moral authority had collapsed. In August an insurrection suspended Louis's constitutional position, and in September the monarchy was abolished. He was tried before the National Convention for conspiracy with foreign powers. On January 21, 1793, he was guillotined in the Place de la Révolution, ending 1,025 years of monarchy.

Louis XVII 1785–95 •*Titular King of France*• Born Louis Charles at Versailles, the second son of **Louis XVI**, he became Dauphin on the death of his brother (1789). He became king (but only in name) in prison on the execution of his father (1793). He died, probably of tuberculosis, but possibly was poisoned. Many persons subsequently claimed to be the Dauphin.

Louis XVIII, *in full* **Louis Stanislas Xavier, Comte de Provence** 1755–1824 •*King of France*• Born at Versailles, he was the younger brother of **Louis XVI**. He fled from Paris to Belgium (1791), and eventually took refuge in England (1807). He declared himself king in 1795, following the death of his nephew, the Dauphin **Louis XVII**, and became the focal point for the Royalist cause. On **Napoleon I**'s downfall (1814) he reentered Paris, and promised a Constitutional

Charter. His restoration to the throne was interrupted by Napoleon's return from Elba until after Waterloo (1815). His reign was marked by the introduction of parliamentary government with a limited franchise.

Louis IV, *known as* **Louis the Bavarian** c. 1283–1347 •*Holy Roman Emperor*• The son of Louis, Duke of Upper Bavaria, he was born in Munich, and was elected king of Germany (1314) in opposition to Frederick II, Duke of Austria, whom he eventually defeated at Mühldorf (1322). In 1328 he received the imperial crown from the people of Rome, but was forced to leave Italy the next year. Thereafter Louis remained mostly in Germany. He waged a war of propaganda against the papacy with the help of Marsilius of Padua, William of **Ockham**, and the Spiritual Franciscans; he invaded Italy (1327–30), captured Rome and set up an antipope, Nicholas V (1328–30), in opposition to Pope John. His energetic policy of family aggrandizement, however, cost him his alliance with the House of Luxembourg, who raised up a rival emperor, **Charles IV**, a year before Louis met his death while hunting.

Louis Philippe, *known as* **the Citizen King** 1773–1850 •*King of the French*• Born in Paris, he was the eldest son of the Duc d'**Orléans**. He joined the National Guard, and, like his father, renounced his titles and assumed the surname "Égalité." He fought in the wars of the republic, but deserted to the Austrians. For a time he lived in exile, mainly in Twickenham, London (1800–09). In 1809 he married Marie Amélie, daughter of **Ferdinand I** of the Two Sicilies and on the Restoration he recovered his estates. After the Revolution of 1830 he was appointed lieutenant general and then elected king. Louis Philippe took a middle course between the extreme right-wing Legitimists and socialists and republicans. Numerous rebellions and assassination attempts led him to more repressive actions like muzzling newspapers and tampering with trial by jury. Agricultural and industrial depression (1846) caused widespread discontent, and when the Paris mob rose (February 1848), he was forced to abdicate, and escaped to England as "Mr Smith." He died in Claremont, Surrey.

Louis the Bavarian *See* **Louis IV**

Louis, Joe, *professional name of* **Joseph Louis Barrow** 1914–81 •*US boxer*• Born in Lexington, Alabama, he won the US amateur light-heavyweight title in 1934 and turned professional. He won the world championship by beating James J Braddock in 1937, and held it for a record 12 years, defending his title 25 times. He retired in 1949, but later made unsuccessful comebacks against Ezzard Charles in 1950 and **Rocky Marciano** in 1951. A boxer of legendary swiftness, power and grace, he won 68 of his 71 professional fights.

Louisa 1776–1810 •*Queen of Prussia*• She was born in Hanover, where her father, Duke Karl of Mecklenburg-Strelitz, was commandant. Married to the Crown Prince of Prussia (afterward **Frederick William III**) in 1793, she was the mother of **Frederick William IV** and **Wilhelm I**. She endeared herself to her people by her spirit and energy during the period of national calamity that followed the Battle of Jena (1806), and especially by her efforts to obtain concessions at Tilsit (1807) from **Napoleon I**.

L'Ouverture *See* **Toussaint Louverture**

Lovecraft, H(oward) P(hillips) 1890–1937 •*US science-fiction writer and poet*• He was born in Providence, Rhode Island, and as a young man supported himself by ghost writing and text revising. From 1923 he was a regular contributor to *Weird Tales*, and his cult following can be traced to the 60 or so stories first published in that magazine. He created what has come to be known as the "Cthulhu Mythos," which holds that the Earth was originally inhabited by fishlike beings called the "Old Ones" who worshiped the gelatinous Cthulhu. Among his various collections are *The Shadow Over Innsmouth* (1936), *The Outsider and Others* (1939), *Dreams and Fancies* (1962) and *Dagon and Other Macabre Tales* (1965). His novellas include *The Case of Charles Dexter Ward* (1928) and *At the Mountains of Madness* (1931).

Lovejoy, Arthur Oncken 1873–1963 •*US philosopher and historian of ideas*• Born in Berlin, Germany, he studied in the US at Berkeley and Harvard and in France at the Sorbonne, Paris. After holding various teaching positions in the US he became Professor of Philosophy at Johns Hopkins University (1910–38). He was cofounder (1938) and first editor of the *Journal of the History of Ideas* and effectively invented the discipline under that title. His works include *The Great Chain of Being: A Study of the History of an Idea* (1936) and *Essays in the History of Ideas* (1948).

Lovelace, (Augusta) Ada, Countess of, *née* **Byron** 1815–52 •*English writer and mathematician*• The daughter of Lord **Byron**, she taught herself geometry, and was educated in astronomy and mathematics. Acquainted with many leading figures of the Victorian era, she owes much of her recent fame to her friendship with **Charles Babbage**, the computer pioneer. She translated and annotated an article on his Analytical Engine written by an Italian mathematician, L F Menabrea, adding many explanatory notes of her own. The high-level universal computer programming language, ADA, was named in her honor, and is said to realize several of her insights into the working of a computer system.

Lovelace, Richard 1618–57 •*English Cavalier poet*• Born in Woolwich, near London, or perhaps in Holland, he was educated at Charterhouse and Gloucester Hall, Oxford. He entered the court and went on the Scottish expedition in 1639. He spent his estate in the king's cause, assisted the French in 1646 to capture Dunkirk from the Spaniards, and was sent to jail on returning to England (1648). There he revised his poems, including "To Althea, From Prison," and in 1649 published the collection *Lucasta*. He was freed at the end of 1649. In 1659 his brother published a second collection of his poems, *Lucasta: Posthume Poems*.

" "

I could not love thee, Dear, so much,
Loved I not honour more.

*1649 **Lucasta**, "To Lucasta, Going to the Wars."*

Lovell, Sir (Alfred Charles) Bernard 1913– •*English astronomer*• Born in Oldham Common, Gloucestershire, he graduated from the University of Bristol and then became a physics lecturer at the University of Manchester. During World War II he worked for the Air Ministry Research Establishment, where he developed airborne radar for blind bombing and submarine defense. In 1951 he became Professor of Radio Astronomy at the University of Manchester and director of Jodrell Bank Experimental Station (now the Nuffield Radio Astronomy Laboratories). Lovell was a pioneer in the use of radar to detect meteors and day-time meteor showers. In 1950 he discovered that the rapid oscillations in the detected intensity (or "scintillations") of signals from galactic radio sources were produced by the Earth's ionosphere. He was the energetic instigator of the funding, construction and use of the radio telescope at Jodrell Bank, Cheshire. From 1958 Lovell collaborated with **Fred Whipple** in the study of flare stars. He has written several books on radio astronomy and its relevance to life and civilization today. Elected a Fellow of the Royal Society in 1955, he was knighted in 1961.

Lovelock, James Ephraim 1919– •*English chemist*• Born in Letchworth, Hertfordshire, he was educated at the Universities of Manchester and London before he joined the National Institute for Medical Research in London (1941–61). He then held various positions in the US, and since 1964 has pursued a career as an independent scientist. Since 1994 he has been Visiting Fellow at Green College, Oxford. He invented the electron capture detector (1958), a high-sensitivity device which was used in the first and many later measurements of the accumulation of CFCs (or chlorofluorocarbons) in the atmosphere. In 1972 he put forward his controversial Gaia hypothesis, which proposes that the Earth's climate is constantly regulated by plants and animals to maintain a life-sustaining balance of organic substances in the atmosphere.

Lovett, Lyle 1956– •*US country music singer, guitarist and songwriter*• Born in Klein, Texas, he began performing while a student, and was encouraged by **Nanci Griffith**. He became a leading figure in the new country movement of the late 1980s with the release of his eponymous debut album in 1986, and consolidated his reputation as a huge talent with the blues-inflected *Pontiac* (1987), followed by the jazzier *And His Large Band* (1989), *Joshua Judges Ruth*

(1992) and *I Love Everybody* (1994). While clearly rooted in country, his original musical conception is not limited by generic boundaries. He married the actress **Julia Roberts** in 1993; their subsequent breakup is reflected in *The Road to Ensenada* (1996). Later albums include *Step Inside This House* (1998) and *Live in Texas* (1999). He has also worked as a film actor.

Low, Sir David Alexander Cecil 1891–1963 •*British political cartoonist*• Born in Dunedin, New Zealand, he worked for several newspapers in New Zealand and for the *Bulletin of Sydney*, then joined the *Star* in London (1919). In 1927 he started to work for the *Evening Standard*, for which he drew some of his most successful cartoons. His art ridiculed all political parties, and some of his creations will never die, notably Colonel Blimp, who has been incorporated into the English language. From 1950 he worked for the *Daily Herald*, and from 1953 with *The (Manchester) Guardian*. He produced many volumes of collected cartoons.

Lowe, Arthur 1914–82 •*English actor*• Born in Hayfield, Derbyshire, he became an actor while serving in the armed forces during World War II, appearing with the army entertainments division. It was television that brought him his greatest popularity, notably as the irascible Mr Swindley in *Coronation Street* (1960–65), and as the pompous patriot Captain Mainwaring in *Dad's Army* (1968–77). His later stage work included *Inadmissible Evidence* (1964), *The Tempest* (1974) and *Bingo* (1974). He appeared in films in supporting roles from 1948, and he had more substantial film roles in *The Ruling Class* (1972) and *O Lucky Man* (1973).

Löwe, Karl *See* **Loewe, (Johann) Karl Gottfried**

Lowell, Abbott Lawrence 1856–1943 •*US political scientist*• Born in Boston into distinguished Massachusetts industrial and cultural dynasties, he was the brother of **Percival Lowell** and **Amy Lowell**. He graduated from Harvard in 1877, received a law degree in 1880, and practiced law in Boston from 1880 to 1897, after which he lectured in law at Harvard and was made Professor of Government there in 1900. He was president of Harvard from 1909 to 1933. His publications include *Essays on Government* (1889), *The Government of England* (1908), *Public Opinion and Popular Government* (1913), *Conflicts of Principle* (1932) and *What a College President Has Learned* (1938).

Lowell, Amy 1874–1925 •*US Imagist poet*• Born in Brookline, Massachusetts, she was the sister of **Abbott Lowell** and **Percival Lowell**. She wrote volumes of *vers libre*, which she named "unrhymed cadence," starting with the conventional *A Dome of Many-Coloured Glass* (1912) and *Sword Blades and Poppy Seeds* (1914). She also wrote "polyphonic prose." Her other works include *Six French Poets* (1915), *Tendencies in Modern American Poetry* (1917) and a biography of **Keats** (1925). She was posthumously awarded the Pulitzer Prize in 1926 for *What's O'Clock* (1925).

Lowell, James Russell 1819–91 •*US poet, essayist and diplomat*• Born in Cambridge, Massachusetts, Lowell graduated from Harvard in 1838. In 1843 he helped to edit *The Pioneer*, with **Nathaniel Hawthorne**, **Edgar Allan Poe** and **John Whittier** as contributors. At the outbreak of war with Mexico (1846), he wrote a satiric poem in the Yankee dialect, out of which grew the *Biglow Papers* (1848). In 1855 he was appointed Professor of Modern Languages and Literature at Harvard. He edited the *Atlantic Monthly* from 1857, and with **Charles Eliot Norton** the *North American Review* (1863–67). His prose writings include *Among My Books* (1870) and *My Study Windows* (1871). The second series of *Biglow Papers* appeared in 1867. An ardent abolitionist, he was appointed US Minister to Spain in 1877, and was transferred in 1880 to Great Britain.

Lowell, Percival 1855–1916 •*US astronomer*• Born into a prominent Boston family, the brother of **Abbott** and **Amy Lowell**, he was educated at Harvard and established the Flagstaff (Lowell) Observatory in Arizona (1894). He is best known for his observations of Mars, which resulted in a series of maps showing linear features crossing the surface. In 1907 he led an expedition to the Chilean Andes which produced the first high-quality photographs of Mars. He popularized his ideas in a series of books including *Mars and Its Canals* (1906) and *Mars as the Abode of Life* (1910). He is known for his prediction of the brightness and position of a planet (which he called planet X) that was supposedly responsible for the orbital perturbation of Neptune and Uranus. In 1930, 14 years after his death, Pluto was found (discovered by **Clyde William Tombaugh**).

Lowell, Robert Traill Spence, Jr 1917–77 •*US poet*• Born in Boston, the great-grandnephew of **James Russell Lowell**, he studied poetry, criticism and classics under **John Crowe Ransom**, then attended Louisiana State University. During World War II he was a conscientious objector and was imprisoned for six months (1944). His first collection, *Land of Unlikeness* (1944), contained biographical poems, and his widely acclaimed second volume, *Lord Weary's Castle* (1946), won him the Pulitzer Prize in 1947. *Life Studies* (1959), *For the Union Dead* (1964) and *Near the Ocean* (1967) were also confessional. During the Vietnam War years, he wrote *Notebook* (1968), and in *The Dolphin* (1973) he made public personal letters and anxieties.

"

I often sigh still
for the dark downward and vegetating kingdom
of the fish and reptile.

1964 "For the Union Dead."

Lower, Richard 1631–91 •*English physician and physiologist*• Born in Tremeer, near Bodmin, he studied at Oxford. Earning his MD in 1665, Lower set up in medical practice and joined the Royal Society. He carried out early experiments on blood transfusion between dogs, and his *Tractatus de corde* (1669, "Treatise on the Heart") provides a fine account of contemporary knowledge in pulmonary and cardiovascular anatomy and physiology. Following **William Harvey**, Lower recognized that the heart acts as a muscular pump. He went on to investigate the color change between dark venous blood and red arterial blood, and with **Robert Hooke** deduced that the red color resulted from the mixing of dark blood with inspired air in the lungs. Lower thus established that the function of respiration lay in adding something to the blood.

Lowry, L(aurence) S(tephen) 1887–1976 •*English painter*• Born in Manchester, he worked as a clerk until 1952, but trained at the Manchester College of Art in the evenings (1905–15). From 1915 to 1925 he attended the Salford School of Art, and from 1918 the life class at the Manchester Academy of Fine Arts. He produced numerous pictures of the Lancashire industrial scene, often filled with uncommunicative matchstick antlike men and women. He lived at home nursing his mother until her death in 1939. Their claustrophobic relationship is the subject of a ballet. His work is represented in many major collections with the largest public collection at The Lowry in Salford Quays.

Lowry, (Clarence) Malcolm 1909–57 •*English novelist*• Born in New Brighton, Merseyside, he left public school to become a deckhand on a ship bound for China, but returned to take a degree at St Catherine's College, Cambridge. He wrote about the voyage in his first novel, *Ultramarine* (1933), but completed only one more book, *Under the Volcano* (1947), for which he is best known. In later life a wanderer and alcoholic, he lived in Mexico, then in British Columbia, returning to England where he died "by misadventure," choking in his sleep. Posthumous publications include stories, poems, letters, and three more novels.

Lowther, Hugh Cecil *See* **Lonsdale, 5th Earl of**

Loy, Myrna, *originally* **Katerina Myrna Adele Williams** 1905–93 •*US film actress and comedienne*• Born in Radersburg, Montana, of Welsh ancestry, she moved with her family to Los Angeles in 1919. She made her debut in *Pretty Ladies* (1925) and then appeared in scores of silent features. After her role as the sadistic daughter in *The Mask of Fu Manchu* (1932), she moved to comedy and made her first of 13 appearances opposite William Powell (1892–1984) in *The Thin Man* (1934) as husband-and-wife detectives. She was successful also in *Test Pilot* (1938), *The Rains Came* (1939) and *The Best Years of Our Lives* (1946). She later became a character actress and made a belated Broadway debut in 1974. She ended her acting career opposite **Henry Fonda** in the television film *Summer Solstice* (1981).

Loyola, St Ignatius *See* **Ignatius Loyola, St**

Lü d. 180 BC •*Empress of China*• The wife of Liu Bang (Liu Pang), or Gaozu (Kao Tsu), the founder of the Han dynasty, she was virtual regent for 15 years after his death in 195 BC, first for her son Hui Ti and then, after his death (188), for two other infants. By the time of her death, she had firmly established the authority of the ruling Liu family, although Chinese historiography condemns her for her resort to nepotism and employment of eunuchs at court.

Lubbers, Ruud (Rudolphus) Franz Marie 1939– •*Dutch politician*• After graduating from Erasmus University, Rotterdam, he joined the family engineering business of Lubbers Hollandia. He made rapid progress after entering politics, becoming minister of economic affairs (1973) and, at the age of 43, prime minister (1982–94), leading a Christian Democratic Appeal (CDA) coalition. In 2000 he became the United Nations high commisioner for refugees.

Lubitsch, Ernst 1892–1947 •*German film director*• Born in Berlin, he was a teenage actor in **Max Reinhardt**'s theater company, and began his directorial career with *Fräulein Seifenschaum* (1914). A specialist in comedies and costume epics like *Madame Dubarry* (1919), he was invited to Hollywood by **Mary Pickford**, whom he directed in *Rosita* (1923). He stayed to become an acknowledged master of sophisticated light comedies graced with "the Lubitsch touch": a mixture of wit, urbanity and visual elegance. His many films include *The Love Parade* (1929), *Trouble in Paradise* (1932), *Ninotchka* (1939) and *Heaven Can Wait* (1943). He became a US citizen in 1936, and received a Special Academy Award in 1947.

Luca Della Robbia *See* **Della Robbia, Luca**

Lucan, *in full* **Marcus Annaeus Lucanus** AD 39–65 •*Roman poet*• Born in Corduba (Córdoba), Spain, he was the nephew of the philosopher **Seneca** the Younger. He studied in Rome and in Athens, and became proficient in rhetoric and philosophy. He was recalled to Rome by the Emperor **Nero**, who made him quaestor and augur. In AD 62 he published the first three books of his epic *Bellum Civile* (*Pharsalia*) on the civil war between **Pompey** and **Julius Caesar**. In 65 Lucan joined the conspiracy of Piso against Nero, but was betrayed and compelled to commit suicide. He was a precociously fluent writer in silver age Latin, but *Pharsalia* is all that has survived of his work.

Lucan, George Charles Bingham, 3rd Earl of 1800–88 •*English field marshal*• He was born in London. As commander of cavalry in the Crimean War (1854–56), he passed on the disastrous and ambiguous order from Lord **Raglan** which resulted in the Charge of the Light Brigade at Balaclava (1854). He later fought at Inkermann and was promoted to field marshal in 1887.

Lucaris or **Lukaris, Cyril** or **Cyrillus** 1572–1638 •*Greek Orthodox prelate and theologian*• Born in Crete, he studied in Venice, Padua and Geneva, where he was influenced by **Calvin**ism. He rose by 1621 to be patriarch of Constantinople (Istanbul), and opened negotiations with the Calvinists of England and Holland with a view to union and the reform of the Greek Church. He corresponded with **Gustav II Adolf** of Sweden, and Archbishops Abbot and **Laud**, and he presented the Alexandrian Codex to **Charles I**. The Jesuits five times engineered his deposition, and are supposed by the Greeks to have instigated his murder by the Turks.

Lucas, Colin Anderson 1906–1984 •*English architect*• Born in London, he studied at Cambridge. In 1930 he designed a house at Bourne End, Buckinghamshire, which was the first English example of the domestic use of monolithic reinforced concrete. Subsequent designs (1933–39), often in partnership with Amyas Connell and Basil Ward, played an important part in the development in England of the ideas of the European modern movement in architecture. He was a founding member of the Modern Architectural Research Society.

Lucas, Edward Verrall 1868–1938 •*English essayist and biographer*• Born in Eltham, Kent, he became a bookseller's assistant, reporter, contributor to and assistant editor of *Punch*, and finally publisher. He compiled anthologies, and was the author of novels (the best of which is probably *Over Bemerton's*, 1908), books of travel and about 30 volumes of light essays.

Lucas, George 1944– •*US filmmaker*• Born in Modesto, California, he studied film at the University of Southern California. A protégé of **Francis Ford Coppola**, he received Best Director Academy Award nominations for both *American Graffiti* (1973) and *Star Wars* (1977); the latter became one of the most commercially successful films ever made. Lucas subsequently produced but did not direct a succession of big-budget adventure films, including the *Star Wars* sequels *The Empire Strikes Back* (1980) and *Return of the Jedi* (1983), and the *Indiana Jones* series. He has also extended the boundaries of cinematic special effects through his company Industrial Light and Magic (ILM) and developed the THX Sound System. In 1999 he wrote and directed the first of the planned trilogy of *Star Wars* prequels, *Episode 1: The Phantom Menace*; *Episode 2: Attack of the Clones* appeared in 2002.

Lucas Van Leyden, *also known as* **Lucas Jacobsz** or **Hugensz** 1494–1533 •*Dutch painter and engraver*• Born in Leiden, he practiced almost every branch of painting, and his most notable works include the triptych *The Last Judgment* (1526) and *Blind Man of Jericho Healed by Christ* (1531). As an engraver he is believed to have been the first to etch on copper, rather than iron. He was much influenced by **Albrecht Dürer**.

Luce, Henry R(obinson) 1898–1967 •*US magazine publisher and editor*• He was born in Shando Province, China, to a missionary family and was educated at a boarding school in Chefoo (Yantai), northern China, before going to the US to study at Yale. He founded *Time* (1923), *Fortune* (1930) and *Life* (1936) magazines. He also inaugurated the radio program "March of Time" in the 1930s, which became a film feature.

Lucian c. 117–c. 180 AD •*Greek satirist, rhetorician and writer*• Born in Samosata, Syria, he practiced as an advocate in Antioch, and wrote and recited show speeches for a living, traveling through Asia Minor, Greece, Italy and Gaul. Having made his name and fortune, he settled in Athens, and there produced a new form of literature, the humorous dialogue. The old faiths, philosophy and literature were all changing, and Lucian found many targets for his satire. The absurdity of retaining the old deities without the old belief is brought out in such works as the *Deorum dialogi* ("Dialogues of the Gods"), *Mortuorum dialogi* ("Dialogues of the Dead") and *Charon*.

Luciani, Sebastiano *See* **Sebastiano del Piombo**

Luciano, Lucky, *properly* **Charles Luciano** 1897–1962 •*US gangster*• Born in Sicily, Italy, he emigrated with his family to the US in 1907. Luciano, who earned his nickname by avoiding imprisonment and prosecution for many years, was a Mafia "godfather" who operated successfully and profitably in the 1920s and 1930s. His business included peddling narcotics, extortion, prostitution and networks of vice dens. When three prostitutes finally agreed to give evidence against him, he was arrested (1936) and found guilty of compelling women to become prostitutes. Even from prison, he retained control of his "family," setting up the Crime Syndicate of Mafia Families. In 1946 he was released and then deported to Italy as an undesirable alien.

Lucilius, Gaius c. 180–c. 102 BC •*Roman satirist*• Born in Suessa Aurunca, Campania, he wrote 30 books of *Satires*, of which only fragments remain. These *saturae* (or medleys), written in hexameters, are on a mixture of miscellaneous subjects: everyday life, politics, literature, travel. Their occasionally mocking and critical tone gave the word "satire" its modern meaning.

Lucretia 6th century BC •*Roman matron*• She was the wife of Lucius Tarquinius Collatinus. According to legend she was raped by Sextus Tarquinius, then summoned her husband and friends, and, making them take an oath to drive out the Tarquins, plunged a knife into her heart. The tale has formed the basis of several works, for example **Shakespeare**'s *Rape of Lucrece* (1594) and the opera *The Rape of Lucretia* by **Benjamin Britten**. The Tarquins were later expelled by **Lucius Junius Brutus**.

Lucretius, *in full* **Titus Lucretius Carus** c. 99–55 BC •*Roman poet and philosopher*• Little is known of his life, though he is said to have gone mad and committed suicide after drinking a love potion given to him by his wife Lucilia. His great work is the didactic poem *De* *rerum natura* ("On the Nature of Things"), in six volumes of hexameters, in which he sets out the theories of **Democritus** and **Epicurus** on the origin of the universe, and attempts to eradicate superstition and religious belief. Freedom from fear and a calm and tranquil mind were his goals, the way to them being through a materialistic philosophy. His poem abounds in strikingly picturesque phrases, and in episodes of exquisite pathos and vivid description rarely equaled in Latin poetry.

" "

Nil posse creari
De nilo.
Nothing can be created from nothing.

***De rerum natura**, book I, line 155.*

Lucullus, Lucius Licinius c. 110–57 BC •*Roman soldier*• His origins were humble, but after service with **Sulla** he commanded the fleet in the First Mithridatic War (88 BC). As consul he defeated **Mithridates** in the Third Mithridatic War (74), and introduced reforms into Asia Minor. He twice defeated Tigranes of Armenia (69 and 68), but his legions became mutinous, and he was superseded by **Pompey** (66). He became very wealthy and spent the rest of his life in such luxury that the term "Lucullan" has been used as an epithet for extravagant food. He was a notable patron of writers and artists.

Ludd, Ned fl. 1779 •*English farm laborer*• He worked in Leicestershire. About 1782 he destroyed some stocking frames, and it is from him that the "Luddite" rioters (1812–18) took their name.

Ludendorff, Erich 1865–1937 •*German soldier*• He was born near Posen (now Poznań, Poland). In 1914 he was appointed Chief of Staff in East Prussia, and masterminded the annihilation of the Russians at Tannenberg (August 1914). On the Western Front in 1918 he planned the major offensive that nearly won the war for Germany. In 1923 he was a leader in the **Hitler** putsch at Munich, but he was acquitted of treason. He was a Nazi member of the Reichstag from 1924 to 1928, but as a candidate for the presidency of the Reich in 1925 he polled few votes. Strongly opposed to Jews, Jesuits and Freemasons, he later became a pacifist.

Ludmilla, St d. 921 •*Bohemian religious and patron saint of Bohemia*• Born near Melník, Bohemia, the wife of Bohemia's first Christian duke, she was murdered by her heathen daughter-in-law, Drahomira.

Ludwig I 1786–1868 •*King of Bavaria*• Born in Strasbourg, the eldest son of Maximilian I, he was king from 1825 to 1848. By his lavish expenditure on pictures, public buildings and favorites, and by taxes and reactionary policy, he provoked active discontent in 1830 and 1848, and abdicated in favor of his son, Maximilian II.

Ludwig II, *also known as* **Mad King Ludwig** 1845–86 •*King of Bavaria*• The son of Maximilian II, he was born at Nymphenburg Palace. He succeeded in 1864 and devoted himself to the patronage of **Richard Wagner** and his music. In 1870 he threw Bavaria on the side of Prussia, and offered the imperial crown to **Wilhelm I**, though he took no part in the war, and lived the life of a morbid recluse. He was almost constantly at odds with his ministers and family, mainly on account of his vast outlays on superfluous palaces, like the fairy-tale Neuschwanstein, and was declared insane (1886). A few days later he was found drowned, with his physician, in the Starnberger Lake, near his castle at Berg.

Ludwig, Karl Friedrich Wilhelm 1816–95 •*German physiologist*• Born in Witzenhausen, he became a medical student in Marburg in 1834. In 1840 he returned to Marburg and was teaching there by 1846, later also teaching in Zurich, Vienna and Leipzig, where in 1865 he helped establish the famous Institute of Physiology. Ludwig's work proved fundamental to modern physiology. He devised many medical instruments, notably the kymograph (1846), which he used to study circulation and respiration, and the mercurial blood pump (1859), which allowed examination of blood gases and respiratory exchange. His research focused on the operation of the heart and kidneys, on the lymphatic system, and on salivary secretion. He also studied the circulation of the blood, and investigated the relationship of blood pressure to heart activity.

Lugosi, Bela, *originally* **Bela Ferenc Denzso Blasko** 1882–1956 •*US actor*• Born in Lugos, Hungary (now in Romania), he studied in Budapest, and appeared on stage (from 1902) and on film (from 1917), before moving to the US in 1921. He enjoyed his greatest success in film as *Dracula* (1931). With his heavy accent, he made a memorably menacing, aristocratic vampire but soon found himself typecast. His films include *Murders in the Rue Morgue* (1932), *Son of Frankenstein* (1939) and *Abbott and Costello Meet Frankenstein* (1948). After successfully undergoing treatment for drug addiction, he died during the production of *Plan 9 From Outer Space* (1956), frequently voted the worst film ever made.

Luhrmann, Baz(mark) Anthony 1962– •*Australian film director*• He was born in Sydney, where he studied at the National Institute of Dramatic Arts, making his acting debut in *The Winter of Our Dreams* (1982). In 1986 he wrote and directed the stage play *Strictly Ballroom*, about the Australian ballroom dance community, and he turned it into a hit film in 1992. Other films include *Romeo and Juliet* (1996), an update of the Shakespeare play set in the world of Latino gangsters, and *Moulin Rouge* (2001).

Lukács, Georg, *properly* **György Szegedy von Lukács** 1885–1971 •*Hungarian Marxist philosopher and critic*• Born in Budapest into a wealthy Jewish family, he studied in Budapest, Berlin and Heidelberg. He published two important early works on literary criticism, *Soul and Form* (1910) and *The Theory of the Novel* (1916). In 1918 he joined the Hungarian Communist Party, but after the defeat of the uprising in 1919 he lived abroad in Vienna (1919–29) and Moscow (1930–44). He returned to Hungary after World War II as professor at Budapest and joined **Imre Nagy**'s short-lived revolutionary government in 1956 as Minister of Culture. After the Russian suppression he was briefly deported to Romania and interned but returned to Budapest in 1957. He was a prolific writer on literature and aesthetics. His major book on Marxism, *History and Class Consciousness* (1923, Eng trans 1971), was repudiated as heretical by the Russian Communist Party and later, in abject public confession, by Lukacs himself.

" "

Nature is a social category.

*1923 **History and Class Consciousness**.*

Lukaris, Cyril *See* **Lucaris, Cyril**

Luke, St 1st century AD •*New Testament evangelist*• Born possibly in Antioch, Syria, he may have been the "beloved physician" and companion of **St Paul** (Colossians 4:14, Philippians 24). It is said that he was martyred. He was first named as author of the third Gospel in the 2nd century, and tradition has since ascribed to him both that work and the Acts of the Apostles. He is the patron saint of doctors and artists, and his feast day is October 18.

Lula, *properly* **Luis Inácio Lula da Silva** 1945– •*Brazilian politician*• Born in a small village, he grew up in Santos. He rose to national prominence as the leader of the Metalworker's Union of São Bernardo. He led strikes in the Saab-Scania plant in 1978 and 1979, which involved 500,000 workers and forced the employers to concede higher wages through direct negotiations rather than via government-led labor courts. In October 1979 Lula founded the PT (Partido dos Trabalhadores) to achieve representation for workers in Congress. Elected to Congress in 1986, he lost to **Fernando Cardoso** in presidential elections in 1994 and 1998, and beat Cardoso to win the election in 2002, taking office on January 1, 2003.

Lully, Jean Baptiste, *originally* **Giovanni Battista Lulli** 1632–87 •*French composer*• Born in Florence of Italian parents, he was made operatic director by **Louis XIV** (1672). With Philippe Quinault as librettist, he composed many operas, in which he made the ballet an essential part. Most popular were *Thésée* (1675), *Armide et Rénaud* (1686), *Phaéton* (1683) and *Acis et Galatée* (1686). He also wrote church music, dance music and pastorals.

Lully or **Lull, Raymond** or **Ramón**, *known as* **the Enlightened Doctor** c. 1232–1315 •*Spanish theologian and mystic*• Born in

Palma, Majorca, he served as a soldier and led a dissolute life, writing lyrical troubadour poetry, but from 1266 became an ascetic and resolved on a spiritual crusade for the conversion of the Muslims. To this end, after some years of study, he produced his *Ars Magna*, in which he explicated the Lullian method, intended to solve all possible problems by a systematic manipulation of certain fundamental notions (such as the Aristotelian categories). He also wrote a book against the principles of **Averroës**, and in 1291 went to Tunis to convert the Muslims, but was imprisoned and banished. After visiting Naples, Rome, Majorca, Cyprus and Armenia, he again sailed (1305) for Bugia (Bougie) in Algeria, and was again banished. He lectured in Paris and, returning to Bugia, was stoned and died a few days afterward. He was the first to use a vernacular language for religious and philosophical writings.

Lulu, *real name* **Marie McDonald McLaughlin Lawrie** 1948– •*Scottish singer and actress*• Born in Lennoxtown, near Glasgow, she had the first Scottish hit of the Beat era with a cover of the Isley Brothers' "Shout" in 1964 and subsequently had a hit in the US with the title song from the film *To Sir With Love* (1967), in which she had also acted. She was joint winner of the 1969 Eurovision Song Contest with *Boom Bang-a-Bang*. During the 1970s she became better known as an entertainer and television personality than as a pop singer, and she had her own BBC series *It's Lulu*. On television, she acted the part of Adrian's mother Pauline in *The Growing Pains of Adrian Mole* (1987). In 1993 she had her first number-one hit with the pop group Take That on "Relight My Fire."

Lumière, Auguste Marie Louis Nicolas 1862–1954 and **Louis Jean** 1865–1948 •*French industrial and physiological chemists, pioneers of motion photography*• The Lumière brothers were born in Besançon, the sons of a photographer and manufacturer of photographic materials. Auguste was educated at the University of Bern, Switzerland, and Louis at the École Technique, La Martinière. At the age of 17 Louis invented a dry-plate process which transformed the fortunes of the family business Lumière and Jougla. In 1894, after seeing a demonstration of **Thomas Alva Edison**'s kinetoscope, which recorded movement, Louis determined to invent a method by which moving pictures could be projected; together the brothers invented the *cinématographe* (cinematograph), the first machine to project images on a screen, in 1895. The same year they built the first cinema, in Lyons, and produced the first film newsreels and the first motion picture in history, *La sortie des ouvriers de l'usine Lumière* (Eng trans *Workers Leaving the Lumière Factory*). On December 28, 1895, which has since been regarded as the birthday of world cinema, the first film was projected to a paying public at the Grand Café on the Boulevard des Capucines in Paris. During the next five years the Lumières amassed a huge catalog of newsreel shot all over the world by their team of skilled photographers, and Louis directed 60 and produced about 2,000 films, including dramatizations of *Faust* and *The Life and Passion of Jesus Christ*. After 1900 they worked to improve color photography, inventing the Autochrome screen plate for color photography in 1903, and they studied colloidal substances in living organisms. Auguste also carried out research into cancer, vitamins, and oral vaccination. Both were elected to the French Academy of Sciences.

Lumley, Joanna 1946– •*English actress*• Born in Srinagar, Kashmir, of British parents, she worked as a model before switching to acting. She was a Bond girl in the film *On Her Majesty's Secret Service* (1969) and acted in *The Trail of the Pink Panther* (1982), *Curse of the Pink Panther* (1983) and *Shirley Valentine* (1989). She made her name on television, playing Purdey in *The New Avengers* (1976–77), for which she received a British Academy of Film and Television Arts Special Award in 2000; Sapphire in *Sapphire and Steel* (1979–82); Victoria Cavero in *Lovejoy* (1992); Patsy in *Absolutely Fabulous* (1992–95, winning her an Emmy award, and 2001); and Kate Swift in *Class Act* (1994–95). She has also made documentaries such as *Girl Friday* (1994). On stage, she has starred in *Noel and Gertie* (1983) and *The Revengers' Comedies* (1991).

Lumumba, Patrice (Hemery) 1925–61 •*Congolese politician*• Born in Katako Kombe and educated at mission schools, both Catholic and Protestant, he helped form the *Mouvement National Congolais* in 1958 to challenge Belgian rule and, when the Congo became an independent republic, he was made its first prime minister (1960). A major symbolic figure in the African history of the period, he sought a unified Congo and opposed the secession of Katanga under Moise Tshombe. He was arrested by his own army in 1960, handed over to the Katangese and murdered. His name, however, remains significant as the opponent of balkanization manipulated by ex-colonial countries and their allies.

Lunt, Alfred 1892–1977 •*US actor*• He was born in Milwaukee, Wisconsin, and educated at Carroll College, Waukesha. He made his stage debut with the Castle Square Theater Company in Boston (1912), and had his first major success in *Clarence* (1919–21). In 1922 he married actress Lynn Fontanne (1887–1983) and the couple seldom performed separately thereafter. He appeared in such plays as *The Guardsman* (1924), *Design for Living* (1933), *Idiot's Delight* (1936) and *The Seagull* (1938). He made his film debut in *Backbone* (1923) and also re-created *The Guardsman* (1931), but the couple appeared primarily on stage. Their last performance in New York and London in *The Visit* (1958–60) was an unqualified success. Broadway's Lunt Fontanne Theatre, opened in 1958, was named in their honor.

Lupino, Ida 1918–95 •*English film actress and director*• Born in London, the daughter of popular comedian Stanley Lupino (1893–1942), she trained at the Royal Academy of Dramatic Art and was still a teenager when she made her leading role debut in *Her First Affaire* (1932). Moving to Hollywood in 1933, she rose to stardom as the adulterous murderess in *They Drive by Night* (1940). Under contract to Warner Brothers, she appeared in musicals and comedies, but was most successful in roles expressing inner torment, repression and malevolence. Her films include *High Sierra* (1941), *The Hard Way* (1943) and *Road House* (1948). She left Warner Brothers in 1947 to form her own company, producing, cowriting and directing *Not Wanted* (1949). She continued to act, but focused increasingly on direction with *Outrage* (1950) and *The Bigamist* (1953). With the formation of Four Star Productions, she worked extensively for television.

Luria, Aleksandr Romanovich 1902–77 •*Soviet psychologist*• Born in Kazan, he began his studies at the Moscow Medical Institute under **Lev Semyonovich Vygotsky**. From 1945 he taught at Moscow State University, and carried out extensive researches into the effects of brain injuries that had been sustained by people during World War II. He established, and became head of, the neuropsychology section of the department of psychology at the university in 1967. His contributions to the field of neuropsychology have been both empirical and theoretical, his influence being particularly felt by researchers concerned with understanding the effects of damage to the frontal lobes and to those regions of the left hemisphere of the brain concerned with language. His books include *The Man With a Shattered World* (Eng trans 1972).

Luria, Salvador Edward 1912–91 •*US biologist and Nobel Prize winner*• Born in Turin, Italy, he earned a medical degree from the University of Turin in 1935, and went on to the Radium Institute in Paris to study medical physics, radiation and techniques of working with phage, the bacterial virus. Later he emigrated to the US. With **Max Delbrück**, he showed that bacteria and phage genes can mutate, and that different strains of phage can exchange and recombine genes. With **A D Hershey** and Delbrück, Luria founded the Phage Group, committed to using phages to investigate genetics. In 1969 he was awarded the Nobel Prize for physiology or medicine, jointly with Delbrück and Hershey, for discoveries related to the role of DNA in bacterial viruses.

Lurie, Alison 1926– •*US novelist*• She was born in Chicago and educated at Radcliffe College. Since 1968 she has taught at Cornell University, from 1976 as Professor of English (now emerita). Academic life forms the backdrop of her first books, the ironically titled *Love and Friendship* (1962), *The Nowhere City* (1965) and *Foreign Affairs* (1984)—the last of which won her the Pulitzer Prize. She has increasingly turned to nonfictional commentary, brilliantly in *The Language of Clothes* (1981), often contentiously in *Don't Tell the Grown-Ups: Children's Literature* (1990).

Lusignan, Guy of *See* **Guy of Lusignan**

Luska, Sidney *See* **Harland, Henry**

Luther, Martin 1483–1546 •*German religious reformer, and founder of the Reformation*• He was born in Eisleben, and educated at Magdeburg and Eisenach, and went to the University of Erfurt, taking his degree in 1505. He was also interested in the study of the Scriptures, and spent three years in the Augustinian monastery at Erfurt. In 1507 he was ordained as a priest, and in 1508 went to lecture and preach at the University of Wittenberg. On a mission to Rome in 1510–11 he was appalled by the corrupt practices he found there, in particular the sale of indulgences by the Dominican Johann Tetzel and others to raise funds for building and other purposes. From this experience, Luther's career as a Reformer began. In 1517 he drew up a list of 95 theses on indulgences, denying to the pope all right to forgive sins, and nailed them on the church door at Wittenberg. Tetzel published a set of countertheses and burned Luther's, and the Wittenberg students retaliated by burning Tetzel's. In 1518 Luther was joined by **Philip Melanchthon**. The pope, **Leo X**, at first took little notice of the disturbance, but in 1518 summoned Luther to Rome to answer for his theses. His university and the elector interfered, and ineffective negotiations were undertaken by Cardinal Cajetan and by Miltitz, envoy of the pope to the Saxon court. Catholic theologian Johann von Eck (1486–1543) and Luther held a memorable disputation at Leipzig (1519). Luther meanwhile attacked the papal system as a whole more boldly. **Erasmus** now joined in the conflict. In 1520 Luther published his famous address to the *Christian Nobles of Germany*, followed by a treatise *On the Babylonian Captivity of the Church of God*, which works also attacked the doctrinal system of the Church of Rome. A papal bull containing 41 theses was issued against him, and he burned it before a crowd of scholars, students and citizens in Wittenberg. Germany was convulsed with excitement; Luther was summoned to appear before the first Diet at Worms, which **Charles V** had convened in 1521. Finally he was put under the ban of the empire; on his return from Worms he was seized, at the instigation of the Elector of Saxony, and lodged (mostly for his own protection) in the Wartburg. During the year he spent there he translated the Bible and composed various treatises. His Bible translation and its subsequent revisions, written in a straightforward style, were hugely successful, and their form of German became the basis of the modern literary standard. Civil unrest called Luther back to Wittenberg in 1522; he rebuked the unruly elements, and made a stand against lawlessness on the one hand and tyranny on the other. In this year he published his acrimonious reply to **Henry VIII** on the seven sacraments. Estrangement had gradually sprung up between Erasmus and Luther, and there was an open breach in 1525, when Erasmus published *De libero arbitrio*, and Luther followed with *De servo arbitrio*. In that year Luther married Katherine von Bora (1499–1552), one of nine nuns who had withdrawn from convent life. In 1529 he engaged in his famous conference at Marburg with **Zwingli** and other Swiss theologians. The drawing up of the Augsburg Confession, with Melanchthon representing Luther, marks the culmination of the German Reformation in 1530. Luther died in Eisleben, and was buried at Wittenberg.

Luthuli or **Lutuli, Albert John Mvumbi** 1898–1967 •*South African Black resistance leader and Nobel Prize winner*• Born in Rhodesia, the son of a Zulu Christian missionary, and educated at a US mission school near Durban, he spent 15 years as a teacher before being elected tribal chief of Groutville, Natal. Deposed for anti-apartheid activities, he became president general of the African National Congress (1952–60), in which capacity he dedicated himself to a campaign of nonviolent resistance and was a defendant in the notorious Johannesburg treason trial (1956–57). He was awarded the 1960 Nobel Peace Prize for his unswerving opposition to racial violence in the face of repressive measures by the South African government and impatience from extremist Africans. In 1962 he published *Let My People Go*.

Lutyens, Sir Edwin Landseer 1869–1944 •*English architect*• He was born in London. His designs ranged from the picturesque of his early country houses, including Marsh Court, Stockbridge, and the restoration of Lindisfarne Castle, which owed much to the Arts and Crafts Movement, to those in the Renaissance style such as Heathcote, Ilkley and Salutation, Sandwich. He finally evolved a classical style exhibited in the Cenotaph, Whitehall, and which reached its height in his design for Liverpool Roman Catholic Cathedral. Other prominent works were his magnificent Viceroy's House, New Delhi, a masterpiece in classical design, and the British Embassy in Washington.

Lutyens, (Agnes) Elizabeth 1906–83 •*English composer*• Born in London, the daughter of Sir **Edwin Lutyens**, she studied in Paris and at the Royal College of Music. She was one of the first British composers to adopt the twelve-note technique, and the Chamber Concerto No. 1 (1939), composed in her own interpretation of this style, was a highly original work. Her compositions were, in general, not immediately well received, but she was later accepted as a leading British composer. Her work includes *O Saisons, O châteaux* (1946), the chamber opera *The Pit* (1947), *Concertante* (1950), *Quincunx* (1959), *The Country of the Stars* (1963), *Vision of Youth* (1970) and *Echoi* (1979). She published her autobiography, *A Goldfish Bowl*, in 1972.

Luxembourg, François Henri de Montmorency-Bouteville, Duc de 1628–95 •*French soldier*• Born in Paris, he was brought up by his aunt, mother of the Great **Condé**. **Louis XIV** made him Duc de Luxembourg (1661). In 1667 he served under Condé in Franche-Comté. In 1672 he himself successfully invaded the Netherlands although he was driven back in 1673. During the war he stormed Valenciennes and twice defeated the Prince of Orange. Made a marshal in 1675, in 1690 he commanded in Flanders and defeated the Allies at Fleurus, and later he twice more routed his old opponent, now King **William III** of Great Britain, at Steinkirk (1692) and Neerwinden (1693).

Luxemburg, Rosa 1871–1919 •*German left-wing revolutionary*• She was born in Zamość in Russian Poland. Converted to Communism in 1890, she took part in underground activities in Poland and founded the Polish Social Democratic Party (later the Polish Communist Party). A German citizen from 1895, she emigrated to Zurich in 1898, then to Berlin, and became a leader of the left-wing movement, writing tracts such as *Sozialreform oder Revolution*. At the outbreak of World War I she formed, with **Karl Liebknecht**, the Spartakusbund (Spartacus League), later the core of the German Communist Party (KPD), and spent most of the war in prison. After her release in 1919 she took part in an abortive uprising, and was murdered with Liebknecht in Berlin.

Lvov, Prince Georgi Yevgeniyevich 1861–1925 •*Russian politician*• Born in Popovka, he was head of the first and second provisional governments after the February Revolution of 1917, but his moderate policies and popular opposition to Russia's war effort led to the collapse of his government. He was succeeded by **Aleksandr Kerensky**, and arrested by the Bolsheviks, but escaped to Paris.

Lwoff, André Michel 1902–94 •*French microbiologist and Nobel Prize winner*• Born in Ainy-le-Château, of Russian-Polish extraction, he worked at the Pasteur Institute in Paris from 1921, becoming departmental head there in 1938. From 1959 to 1968 he was Professor of Microbiology at the Sorbonne. He researched the genetics of bacterial viruses (phages) and showed that, when a phage enters a bacterial cell, it becomes part of the bacterial chromosome and divides with it (lysogeny), in which form it protects the bacterium against further invasion by the same type of virus. These findings have had important implications for the development of drug resistance and for cancer research. In 1965 Lwoff was awarded the Nobel Prize for physiology or medicine jointly with **François Jacob** and **Jacques Monod**, for their discoveries concerning genetic control of enzyme and virus synthesis.

Lycurgus •*Traditional, possibly legendary, lawgiver of Sparta*• He is said to have instigated the Spartan ideals of harsh military discipline.

Lydgate, John c. 1370–c. 1451 •*English monk and poet*• He was born in Lydgate, Suffolk, and became a Benedictine monk. He may have studied at Oxford and Cambridge. He traveled in France and perhaps Italy, and became prior of Hatfield Broadoak, Essex, in 1423. A court poet, he wrote *The Troy Book* (1412–20), based on Colonna's Latin prose *Historia Trojana*, *The Siege of Thebes* (1420–22), represented as a new Canterbury tale, and the *Fall of*

Princes (1431–38), based on **Boccaccio**. Other works include the *Daunce of Machabre*, from the French, and *London Lickpenny*, on London.

“ ”

Woord is but wynd; leff woord and tak the dede.

***Secrets of Old Philosophers**, l. 224.*

Lyell, Sir Charles 1797–1875 •*Scottish geologist*• Born in Kinnordy, Forfarshire, he was educated at Ringwood, Salisbury and Midhurst, studied law at Exeter College, Oxford, and was called to the bar. He decided to give up law during an excursion to France in 1828 with **Roderick Murchison**, and on his return he completed the first volume of his *Principles of Geology* (1830). He had been appointed Professor of Geology at King's College London, by 1832. His authoritative *Principles of Geology* (1830–33) was very influential, as was his memoir *Consolidation of Lava Upon Steep Slopes of Etna*, in which he refuted the elevation crater theory of **Leopold von Buch**. His uniformitarian principle taught that the greatest geological changes might have been produced by the forces in operation now, given sufficient time. His interest was primarily in the biological side of geology, and his work had as great a contemporary influence as **Charles Darwin**'s *Origin of Species*. Lyell's other publications include *The Elements of Geology* (1838) and *The Geological Evidence of the Antiquity of Man* (1863), which startled the public by its unbiased attitude toward Darwin. He was knighted in 1848.

Lyle, Sandy, *properly* **Alexander Walter Barr Lyle** 1958– •*Scottish golfer*• Born in Shrewsbury, Shropshire, England, of Scottish parents, he started his golfing career by representing England at boys, youth and full international levels. His major championship successes have been the European Open in 1979, the French Open in 1981, the British Open in 1985 and the US Masters Championship in 1988. An extremely long hitter with an admirably phlegmatic temperament, with **Nick Faldo** he was largely responsible for the revival of British professional golf at world level.

Lyly or **Lily, John** c. 1554–1606 •*English dramatist and novelist, "the Euphuist"*• Born in the Weald of Kent, he earned his BA from Magdalen College, Oxford, in 1573, and studied also at Cambridge. Having in 1589 taken part in the Marprelate controversy, he became Member of Parliament for Aylesbury and Appleby (1597–1601). His *Euphues*, a romance in two parts, was received with great applause. From this work derived the term "euphuism," referring to an artificial and extremely elegant language, with much use made of complex similes and antitheses. His other works include the comedy *The Woman in the Moon*, produced in or before 1583, *Campaspe* and *Sapho and Phao* (both 1584), *Endimion* (1591), *Gallathea* and *Midas* (both 1592), *Mother Bombie* (1594) and *Love's Metamorphosis* (1601).

Lynagh, Michael Patrick 1963– •*Australian rugby union player*• Born in Queensland, he held the record for the most points scored in international rugby (911), and set a record for the most conversions (140 points) in his 72 international matches (1984–95). He had 72 caps and, with 177 points, he set a record for the most penalty goals in international rugby. He retired from the competitive international scene as Australia's captain after the 1995 World Cup.

Lynch, David 1946– •*US film director*• He was born in Missoula, Montana. His first full-length feature film, *Eraserhead* (1976), about a sensitive daydreamer who hurls his offspring against a wall, testified to Lynch's dark originality. It was followed by *The Elephant Man* (1980), a bleak, if more conventional, narrative about carnival freak Joseph Merrick, which earned Lynch a Best Director Academy Award nomination, as did the surrealistic thriller *Blue Velvet* (1986). He then masterminded the cult television series *Twin Peaks* (1990) before returning to the cinema with the sensational love story *Wild at Heart* (1990), which won the Palme d'Or at Cannes. He was nominated for the same award for subsequent films *Twin Peaks: Fire Walk With Me* (1992), *The Straight Story* (1999) and *Mulholland Drive* (2001), for which he won Best Director at Cannes.

Lynch, Jack (John) 1917–99 •*Irish statesman*• Educated at Cork and Dublin, he was called to the bar in 1945. He then entered politics and represented Cork for Fianna Fáil (1948–81). He served in education, industry and commerce, and finance before he assumed the Fianna Fáil leadership and became taoiseach (prime minister) in 1966. He was replaced by the Fine Gael leader, **Liam Cosgrave**, in 1973 but was reelected in 1977. He resigned in 1979, to be succeeded by **Charles Haughey**, and he retired from politics in 1981.

Lyndsay or **Lindsay, Sir David** c. 1486–1555 •*Scottish poet*• Born probably at The Mount, near Cupar, Fife, or at Garmylton (Garleton), near Haddington, East Lothian, in 1512 he was appointed usher, or tutor, to the newborn prince who became **James V**. He went on embassies to the Netherlands, France, England and Denmark, and he (or another David Lyndsay) represented Cupar in Parliament (1540–46). The earliest and most poetic of his writings is the allegorical *The Dreme* (1528), followed by *The Complaynt of the King* (1529) and *The Testament and Complaynt of Our Soverane Lordis Papyngo* (1530). His most remarkable work, *Ane Satyre of the Thrie Estaitis*, was performed at Linlithgow in 1540 and revived at the Edinburgh Festival.

Lynen, Feodor Felix Konrad 1911–79 •*German biochemist and Nobel Prize winner*• Born and educated in Munich, his appointments included director of the **Max Planck** Institute for Cell Chemistry and Biochemistry (1954–79). In 1951 he isolated coenzyme A and showed that it formed acetyl-S-CoA, an important intermediate in lipid metabolism. In 1953, with **Severo Ochoa**, he substituted compounds of ethanolamine for the full coenzyme A molecule in the study of the pathway of fatty acid degradation. At the same time as **Konrad Bloch**, Lynen contributed evidence toward elucidating the biosynthesis of cholesterol, for which he shared the Nobel Prize for physiology or medicine in 1964 jointly with Bloch.

Lynn, Loretta, *née* **Webb** 1935– •*US country singer*• She was born into rural poverty in Butcher's Hollow, Kentucky, married at the age of 14 and had four children by 18. Her first single, "Honky-Tonk Girl," was a success, and she matured into a major country singer and songwriter with a string of hits, including a celebrated series of duets with Conway Twitty (1933–93) in the 1970s. She composes both the melodies and lyrics of her songs, which often focus on the troubles of rural women and feature defiant parentheses such as "Don't Come Home A-Drinkin' (With Lovin' on Your Mind)" and "You Ain't Woman Enough (to Take My Man)." Her collaboration with **Tammy Wynette** and **Dolly Parton** on *Honky Tonk Angels* (1993) was a success, and in 2000 she released *Still Country*, her first solo album of new material since 1988. Her autobiography *Coal Miner's Daughter* (1976) became a best-seller, and was filmed in 1979. Her sister, Crystal Gayle (1951–), is a well-known country-pop singer.

Lynn, Dame Vera, *originally* **Vera Margaret Welch** 1917– •*English singer*• Born in the East End of London, she joined a singing troupe at the age of 11 and and at 15 became a vocalist with Howard Baker's orchestra. She began broadcasting and singing with ensembles such as the Joe Loss Orchestra in the late 1930s, and had her own radio show, *Sincerely Yours*, from 1941 to 1947. Her performances to the troops during World War II earned her the title "The Forces' Sweetheart," with songs including *We'll Meet Again* (1939) and *White Cliffs of Dover* (1942), and among her many honors is the honorary title of Dame Commander, Order of the British Empire (1975).

Lyon, Mary Mason 1797–1849 •*US educator*• Born in Buckland, Massachusetts, she was an early advocate of higher education for all women and founded Mount Holyoke Female Seminary in South Hadley, Massachusetts. She served as its president for 12 years, and her students included **Emily Dickinson** in 1848. The seminary later became Mount Holyoke College, the first women's college in the US.

Lyons, Dame Enid Muriel *See* **Lyons, Joseph Aloysius**

Lyons, Sir Joseph 1848–1917 •*English businessman*• Born in London, he first studied art and invented a stereoscope before joining with three friends to establish what was to become J Lyons and Co Ltd. Starting in Piccadilly with a teashop, he became head of one of the largest catering businesses in Great Britain.

Lyons, Joseph Aloysius 1879–1939 •*Australian statesman*• Born in Stanley, Tasmania, and educated at the University of Tasmania, he was a teacher before entering politics in 1909 as a Labour Member of Parliament in the Tasmanian House of Assembly. He held the post of minister of education and railways (1914–16) and was premier (1923–29). He held several positions in the federal parliament but in 1931 he broke away as a protest against the government's financial policy, he himself being in favor of reduced public expenditure, and founded and led an opposition party, the United Australian Party. He became prime minister (1932–39) after the 1931 election. His wife, Dame Enid Muriel Lyons (1897–1981), was born in Leesville, Tasmania, and was very active in her husband's career. In 1943, after his death, she won the Federal seat of Darwin, Tasmania, becoming the first woman member of the House of Representatives and later the first woman member of the Federal Cabinet.

Lyot, Bernard Ferdinand 1897–1952 •*French astronomer and inventor*• Born in Paris and trained as an engineer at the École Supérieure d'Électricité, he joined the staff of the Paris Observatory at Meudon (1920), where his early researches were concerned with the measurement of polarization of light from the moon and planets. In 1931 he succeeded in observing the solar corona from the summit of the Pic du Midi using his new coronagraph, an instrument in which scattered light was reduced to an absolute minimum. Previously such observations had only been possible during a total solar eclipse. Two years later he started photographing the sun through monochromatic polarizing filters: his pioneer cinematographic films of the movements of solar prominences taken in the light of the red hydrogen Ha line created a sensation.

Lysander d. 395 BC •*Spartan naval commander*• He commanded the fleet which defeated the Athenians at the Battle of Aegospotami in 405 BC, and in 404 took Athens, thus ending the Peloponnesian War. He died while unsuccessfully besieging Haliartus in Boeotia.

Lysenko, Trofim Denisovich 1898–1976 •*Soviet geneticist and agronomist*• Born in Karlovka, Ukraine, he graduated from Uman School of Horticulture (1921) and the Kiev Agricultural Institute (1925). During the famines of the early 1930s, he promoted vernalization, suggesting that plant growth could be accelerated by short exposures to low temperatures, a technique that seemed to offer a solution to food shortages, and gained him political support. In 1935 he developed a theory of genetics which suggested that environment can alter the hereditary material. As director of the Institute of Genetics of the Soviet Academy of Sciences (1940–65), he pronounced the **Mendel**ian theory of heredity to be wrong, ruthlessly silencing scientists who opposed him. After **Stalin**'s death in 1956, Lysenko increasingly lost support and was forced to resign in 1965.

Lysias c. 458–c. 380 BC •*Greek orator*• The son of a rich Syracusan, he was educated at Thurii in Italy, and settled in Athens about 440 BC. In 404 the Thirty Tyrants stripped him and his brother Polemarchus of their wealth, and killed Polemarchus. The first use to which Lysias put his eloquence was on the fall of the Thirty (403), to prosecute Eratosthenes, the tyrant chiefly to blame for his brother's murder. From his surviving speeches Lysias emerges as delightfully lucid in thought and expression. The family home in Athens is portrayed in **Plato**'s *Republic*.

Lysimachus d. 281 BC •*Macedonian general, King in Thrace*• He served **Alexander the Great** until he became king in Thrace, to which he later added northwest Asia Minor and Macedonia. He was defeated and killed at Koroupedion by **Seleucus I Nicator**.

Lysippus of Sicyon 4th century BC •*Greek sculptor*• He was a prolific worker, said to have made more than 1,500 bronzes, and introduced a new naturalism, reducing the size of the head and making the limbs more slender. There is a Roman marble copy of his bronze *Apoxyomenos* (*Man Using a Strigil*), which shows an awareness of space as part of sculpture, in the Vatican Museum, Rome (c. 330 BC). He made several portrait busts of **Alexander the Great**.

Lyttelton, Humphrey (Richard Adeane) 1921– •*English jazz trumpeter and bandleader*• He was born in Eton, Berkshire. He taught himself to play the cornet while at Eton (where his father was a housemaster), and after attending Camberwell School of Art and serving throughout World War II in the Grenadier Guards, he played trumpet with George Webb's Dixielanders before forming his own band in 1948. He was one of the first "trad" bandleaders to move toward mainstream jazz, replacing the banjo with a guitar and introducing an alto saxophone into the lineup. He founded his own record label, Calligraph, in 1984. He is also well known as a jazz broadcaster and writer, and as the host of the comedy radio panel show *I'm Sorry I Haven't a Clue* (1972–).

Lytton, Bulwer, *pseudonym of* **Edward George Earle Bulwer-Lytton, 1st Baron Lytton (of Knebworth)** 1803–73 •*English novelist, playwright, essayist, poet and politician*• He was born in London, the youngest son of General Earle Bulwer (1776–1807) by Elizabeth Barbara Lytton (1773–1843), the heiress of Knebworth in Hertfordshire, and educated at Trinity Hall, Cambridge (1822–25). His enormous output, vastly popular during his lifetime, but now mostly forgotten, includes *Eugene Aram* (1832), *The Last Days of Pompeii* (1834) and *Harold* (1843). Among his plays are *The Lady of Lyons* (1838), *Richelieu* (1839) and *Money* (1840), and his poetry includes an epic, *King Arthur* (1848–49). Member of Parliament for St Ives (1831–41), he was made a baronet in 1838, and in 1843 he succeeded to the Knebworth estate and assumed the surname of Lytton. He reentered Parliament as Member of Parliament for Hertfordshire in 1852, and in the **Derby** government (1858–59) was Colonial Secretary. He was raised to the peerage in 1866.

Lytton, (Edward) Robert Bulwer-Lytton, 1st Earl of, *pseudonym* **Owen Meredith** 1831–91 •*English poet, diplomat and politician*• Born in London, he was educated at Harrow school and in Bonn. In 1849 he went to Washington DC as attaché and private secretary to his uncle, **Henry Bulwer**, and subsequently was appointed attaché, secretary of legation, consul or chargé d'affaires at a number of European capitals. In 1873 he succeeded his father, **Bulwer Lytton**, as 2nd Baron Lytton, and in 1874 became Minister at Lisbon. From 1876 to 1880 he was Viceroy of India, where he effected reform but failed to prevent the Second Afghan War (1878), and in 1880 he was made Earl of Lytton; in 1887 he was sent as ambassador to Paris. His works, published mainly under his pseudonym, include novels, poems (such as the epic *King Poppy*, 1892), and translations from Serbian.

Ma, Yo-Yo 1955– •*US cellist*• Born in Paris, the son of Chinese immigrants who were professionals in classical music, he was a prodigy on the cello, an instrument he took up because his older sister already played the violin. After studying at the Juilliard School of Music and graduating from Harvard in 1976, he achieved international fame as a cello virtuoso, playing both as a soloist and in chamber music ensembles around the world. He has won 14 Grammy awards for his recordings. He also played on the musical score of the film *Crouching Tiger, Hidden Dragon* (2000).

Mabon *See* **Abraham, William**

Mabuse, Jan, *real name* **Gossaert** c. 1470–1532 •*Flemish painter*• Born in Maubeuge (Mabuse), he was influenced by **Quentin Matsys** and **Hans Memlinc**. In 1508–09 he accompanied Philip of Burgundy to Italy, where he adopted the High Renaissance style, which he introduced to Holland. He later lived in Middelburg.

Macalpin *See* **Kenneth I**

Macapagal-Arroyo, Gloria 1948– •*Philippine politician*• Born in Lubao, Pampanga, the daughter of Diosdado Macapagal (1910–1997), president (1961–65), she was educated at Assumption College, Georgetown University, the Ateneo de Manila University and at the University of the Philippines. She joined the Philippine government in 1986, became a senator in 1992, and having been secretary at the department of Social Welfare and Development, she became vice president of the Philippines in 1998 and president in 2001.

MacArthur, Douglas 1880–1964 •*US soldier*• He was born in Little Rock, Arkansas, and educated at West Point. In World War I he commanded the 42nd (Rainbow) Division in France and served with distinction. In 1930 he was made a general and chief of staff of the US Army. In 1935 he became head of the US military mission to the Philippines. In World War II he was appointed commanding general of the US armed forces in the Far East in 1941. In March 1942, after a skillful but unsuccessful defense of the Bataan Peninsula, he was ordered to evacuate from the Philippines to Australia, where he set up headquarters as supreme commander of the Southwest Pacific Area. As the war developed he carried out a brilliant "leap-frogging" strategy that enabled him to recapture the Philippine Archipelago from the Japanese. He completed the liberation of the Philippines in July 1945, and in September 1945, as supreme commander of the Allied powers, he formally accepted the surrender of Japan on board the *Missouri*. He then exercised almost unlimited authority in the occupied Empire, giving Japan a new constitution and carrying out a program of sweeping reform. When war broke out in Korea in June 1950, President **Truman** ordered MacArthur to support the South Koreans in accordance with the appeal of the UN Security Council. In July he became commander in chief of the UN forces. After initial setbacks he pressed the war far into North Korea, but after the Chinese entered the war in November, MacArthur demanded powers to blockade the Chinese coast, bomb Manchurian bases and to use Chinese nationalist troops from Formosa against the communists. This led to acute differences with the US Democratic administration, and in April 1951 President Truman relieved him of his commands. A brilliant military leader and a ruler of Japan imbued with a deep moral sense, MacArthur became a legend in his lifetime. Equally, he inspired criticism for his imperious belief in his own mission and his self-dramatization.

" "

In war, indeed, there can be no substitute for victory.

1951 Address to Congress, April 19. In the ***Congressional Record****, volume 97, part 3, p. 4125.*

Macarthur, Elizabeth, *née* **Veale** 1766–1850 •*Australian pioneer*• Born in Bridgerule, Devon, England, in 1788 she married **John Macarthur** and sailed with him and their son to New South Wales in 1789. In 1793 John received a grant of land near Parramatta, New South Wales, which he named Elizabeth Farm. During her husband's prolonged absences from the colony, she was left, with their seven surviving children, to manage Macarthur's involved business ventures, and succeeded in introducing the merino sheep onto her landholdings, effectively establishing the Australian wool industry.

MacArthur, Ellen 1977– •*English yachtswoman*• Born in Derbyshire, at the age of 18 she sailed single-handed around Britain. Following success in the Route de Rhum transatlantic race in 1998, she was named Yachtsman of the Year. In 2000 she faced the greatest challenge of her career when she took part in the Vendee Globe round-the-world event, finishing second and in the process becoming the youngest woman to sail single-handed around the globe and only the second person to complete a solo circumnavigation in less than 100 days.

Macarthur, John 1767–1834 •*Australian pioneer and wool merchant*• Born in England, he became a lieutenant in the New South Wales Water Corps, and emigrated to Australia with his wife, **Elizabeth Macarthur**, becoming leader of the settlers in New South Wales. He inspired the Rum Rebellion (1808–10), in which the British soldiers mutinied and imprisoned the governor, **William Bligh** of *Bounty* fame. Macarthur was banished to England in 1810, but returned in 1816 and made a fortune in the wool trade.

Macaulay, Dame (Emilie) Rose 1881–1958 •*English novelist and essayist*• She was born in Rugby, Warwickshire, and educated at Somerville College, Oxford. Her first novel was *Abbots Verney* (1906), followed by *Views and Vagabonds* (1912) and *The Lee Shore* (1920), winner of a £1,000 publisher's prize. Her later novels include *Dangerous Ages* (1921), which won the Femina Vie Heureuse prize, *Crewe Train* (1926), *They Were Defeated* (1932) and *And No Man's Wit* (1940). After World War II she wrote two further novels, *The World My Wilderness* (1950) and *The Towers of Trebizond* (1956), which won the James Tait Black Memorial Prize. She also wrote travel books and collections of essays. She was given the honorary title of Dame Commander, Order of the British Empire, in 1958.

Macaulay (of Rothley), Thomas Babington Macaulay, 1st Baron 1800–59 •*English writer and politician*• Born in Rothley Temple, Leicestershire, and educated at Trinity College, Cambridge, he was called to the bar in 1826, and then combined his legal career with writing, notably for the *Edinburgh Review*. He became Member of Parliament for the borough of Calne in 1830, and took part in the Reform Bill debates. He was legal adviser to the Supreme Council of India (1834–38) and on his return in 1839 became Member of Parliament for Edinburgh, and later Secretary of War under Lord **Melbourne**. He received a peerage in 1857. His *History of England from the Accession of James II* (5 vols, 1848–61) enjoyed unprecedented popularity for a work of its kind. He has been found guilty of historical inaccuracy, but as a picturesque narrator he has few rivals.

Macbeth c. 1005–57 •*King of Scotland*• He was Mórmaer (chief) of Moray (c. 1031) and married Gruoch, granddaughter of Kenneth III. He became king in 1040 when he defeated and killed King **Duncan I**

and drove Duncan's sons, Malcolm and Donald Bán, into exile. He seems to have represented a Celtic reaction against English influence and he ruled for over a decade. **Malcolm III**, Duncan's son, ultimately defeated and killed him at Lumphanan. The conventional, Shakespearean view of Macbeth as a villainous usurper has little historical basis. His usurpation was a normal feature of Celtic succession struggles, his reign was a period of plenty, he was a friend to the Church and went on a pilgrimage to Rome.

MacBride, Maud *See* **Gonne, Maud**

MacBride, Seán 1904–88 •*Irish statesman and Nobel Prize winner*• The son of **Maud Gonne** and Major John MacBride, he carried on his parents' commitment to Irish nationalism and served in the Irish Republican Army before entering the government of independent Ireland. He became involved in international human rights and was chairman of Amnesty International (1961–75). In 1974 he shared the Nobel Peace Prize with **Sato Eisaku**.

MacCaig, Norman Alexander 1910–96 •*Scottish poet*• Born in Edinburgh, he was educated at the university there. He was a primary school teacher for almost 40 years, became the first Fellow in creative writing at the University of Edinburgh (1967–69), then lectured in English Studies at the University of Stirling (1970–79). His *Collected Poems* was first published in 1985, and other collections include *Riding Lights* (1955), *The Sinai Sort* (1957), *A Round of Applause* (1962), *Rings on a Tree* (1968), *The White Bird* (1973), *The Equal Skies* (1980) and *Voice-Over* (1988).

MacColl, Ewan, *originally* **James Miller** 1915–89 •*Scottish folk-singer, composer, collector, author, playwright and socialist*• He was born in Auchterarder, Perthshire, and raised in industrial Lancashire. As a playwright, he collaborated with **Joan Littlewood** in forming the experimental Theatre Workshop in the 1940s. By the turn of the 1950s, however, his musical interests were prominent, and his series of "Radio Ballads," begun in 1957 and recorded with his third wife Peggy Seeger, combined contemporary social comment with traditional musical forms and had a powerful influence on songwriting and performing in subsequent decades. He founded the Ballads and Blues Club, subsequently known as the Singers Club, a bastion of his purist (but never reactionary or nostalgic) belief that folk music was a direct expression of everyday life, not high art and never mere "entertainment." He was one of the most influential pioneers of the British folk-music revival, and his best-known songs include "Dirty Old Town" (1946) and "The First Time Ever I Saw Your Face" (1958, hauntingly recorded by Roberta Flack in 1972).

MacDiarmid, Alan G 1927– •*US chemist and Nobel Prize winner*• Born in New Zealand, he was educated at the Universities of New Zealand and Wisconsin and at Cambridge University. He joined the staff of the University of Pennsylvania in 1955, where he went on to do pioneering work into conductive polymers. In 2000 he shared the Nobel Prize for chemistry with **Alan J Heeger** and **Hideki Shirakawa**.

MacDiarmid, Hugh, *pseudonym of* **Christopher Murray Grieve** 1892–1978 •*Scottish poet*• Born in Langholm, Dumfriesshire, he was educated at Langholm Academy. He served with the Royal Army Medical Corps in Greece and France during World War I, and was a munitions worker in World War II. A founding member of the National Party of Scotland (which became the Scottish National Party) in 1928, and intermittently an active Communist, he ran as a Communist candidate in 1964. He became the leader of the Scottish Renaissance and dedicated his life to the regeneration of Scots as a literary language. As a journalist in Montrose, he edited anthologies of contemporary Scottish writing. His early lyrical verse appeared in *Sangschaw* (1925) and *Penny Wheep* (1926), but he is best known for *A Drunk Man Looks at the Thistle* (1926). Other publications include *To Circumjack Cencrastus* (1930), the three *Hymns to Lenin* (1931, 1932, 1957), *Scots Unbound* (1932), *Stony Limits* (1934), *A Kist o' Whistles* (1947) and *In Memoriam James Joyce* (1955).

“ ”

The thistle yet'll unite
Man and the Infinite!

1926 ***A Drunk Man Looks at the Thistle**, l. 481–82.*

MacDonagh, Thomas 1878–1916 •*Irish poet, critic and nationalist*• He was born in Cloughjordan, County Tipperary, and later lived in Dublin, where he helped **Patrick Pearse** found St Enda's College (1908), and published several volumes of delicate and sardonic poems, original works and translations from the Irish. In 1914 he founded the Irish Theatre with Joseph Plunkett and Edward Martyn (1859–1923). He was also an outstanding critic of English literature, and his aspirations for Irish literature derived from his deep love of English and his recognition of comparable possibilities, as may be seen by his *Literature in Ireland* (posthumous, 1916) and *Thomas Campion* (1913). An Irish Volunteer, he was very belatedly drawn into preparations for the Easter Rising of 1916, commanded at Jacob's Factory in the fighting, and was executed. **W B Yeats** wrote his epitaph in "Easter 1916."

Macdonald, Flora 1722–90 •*Scottish Jacobite heroine*• Born in South Uist in the Hebrides, she was adopted by Lady Clanranald. After the Battle of Culloden (1746), which finally broke the 1745 Jacobite rebellion, she took the Young Pretender, **Charles Edward Stuart**, disguised as her maid "Betty Burke," from Benbecula to Portree. In 1750 she married the son of Macdonald of Kingsburgh, and in 1774 she emigrated to North Carolina with her husband, who fought in the American Revolution. She returned to Scotland in 1779, followed by her husband two years later.

MacDonald, Frances 1873–1921 •*Scottish painter and designer*• Born in Glasgow, the sister of **Margaret MacDonald**, she became the wife of Herbert MacNair (1868–1955). These three, together with **Charles Rennie Mackintosh**, comprised the Glasgow "Group of Four," the prime exponents of Art Nouveau in Scotland. Frances MacDonald's paintings and decorations are generally strongly poetic, incorporating insubstantial figures in symbolic settings.

Macdonald, Sir John Alexander 1815–91 •*Canadian statesman*• Born in Glasgow, Scotland, he emigrated with his parents in 1820. He was called to the bar in 1836 and appointed a Queen's Counsel. Entering politics he became leader of the Conservatives and premier in 1856, and in 1867 formed the first government for the new Dominion. He was again in power from 1878 until his death. He was instrumental in bringing about the confederation of Canada and in securing the construction of the intercolonial and Pacific railways.

MacDonald, Margaret, *married name* **Mackintosh** 1865–1933 •*Scottish artist*• Born in Staffordshire, the sister of **Frances MacDonald**, she studied at the Glasgow College of Art, and in 1900 married **Charles Rennie Mackintosh**. Best known for her work in watercolors and stained glass, she exhibited widely on the Continent. She collaborated with her husband in much of his work.

MacDonald, (James) Ramsay 1866–1937 •*Scottish Labour statesman*• He was born in Lossiemouth, Morayshire, and educated at a boarding school. He joined the Independent Labour Party in 1894 and was its secretary (1900–11) and Leader (1911–14, 1922–31). A member of Parliament from 1906, he became Leader of the Opposition in 1922, and from January to November 1924 was prime minister and foreign secretary of the first Labour government in Britain—a minority government at the mercy of the Liberals. He was prime minister again from 1929 to 1931. He met the financial crisis of 1931 by forming a predominantly Conservative "National" government (opposed by most of his party), which he rebuilt and led (1931–35) after a general election. In 1935 **Stanley Baldwin** took over the premiership and MacDonald became lord president.

MacGill, Patrick 1890–1963 •*Irish laborer, novelist and poet*• Born in the Glenties, County Donegal, and sold into servitude by his farming parents, he escaped to Scotland, working as a farm laborer and a construction worker. His early verses attracted the attention of patrons, and he was adopted as secretary by Canon John Dalton (1839–1931) of Windsor. His brilliantly naturalistic novel of migrant construction-worker life, *Children of the Dead End*, was published in 1914, followed a year later by a powerful feminist parallel narrative of the forcing of female Irish labor into prostitution, *The Rat-Pit*. He volunteered when war broke out, and wrote *The Amateur Army* (1915), then *The Red Horizon* (1916) and *The Great Push* (1916), describing action in France in which he was wounded. Later works include *Moleskin Joe* (1923), and *Black Bonar* (1928). He went to the US in 1930, where he declined into poverty and developed multiple sclerosis.

MacGregor, Robert *See* **Rob Roy**

MacGregor, Sue (Susan Katriona) 1941– •*English radio host*• She was born in Oxford and educated mainly in South Africa. Her first job was as an announcer and producer with the state-run South African Broadcasting Corporation (1962–67). Moving to London in 1967, she joined the BBC as a reporter (1967–72), working on *World at One*, *World This Weekend* and *PM*, before beginning her 15-year position as host of *Woman's Hour* for Radio 4 (1972–87). Among various other jobs on radio and television she presented BBC Radio 4's *Today* program from 1984 to 2002. She was given the honorary title Officer, Order of the British Empire, in 1992.

Mach, David 1956– •*Scottish sculptor*• Born in Methil, Fife, he studied at Duncan of Jordanstone College of Art, Dundee, and the Royal College of Art, London. He has attracted both critical and popular attention through his choice of materials and his working methods. Working to a time limit, often in public view, he has created monumental structures from society's surplus materials, which include a military tank constructed from car tires and enormous classical columns from magazines. He was elected to the Royal Academy in 1998 and became Professor of Sculpture there in 2000.

Mach, Ernst 1838–1916 •*Austrian physicist and philosopher*• Born in Turas, Moravia, he studied at the University of Vienna, and became Professor of Mathematics at the University of Graz in 1864, of Physics at the University of Prague in 1867, and of Physics again at Vienna in 1895. He carried out much experimental work on supersonic projectiles and on the flow of gases, obtaining some remarkable early photographs of shock waves and gas jets. His findings have proved of great importance in aeronautical design and the science of projectiles, and his name has been given to the ratio of the speed of flow of a gas to the speed of sound (Mach number) and to the angle of a shock wave to the direction of motion (Mach angle). In the field of epistemology he was determined to abolish idle metaphysical speculation. His writings greatly influenced **Albert Einstein** and laid the foundations of logical positivism.

Machel, Samora Moises 1933–86 •*Mozambique nationalist leader and politician*• He trained as a medical assistant before joining FRELIMO (Front for the Liberation of Mozambique) in 1963, soon becoming active in the guerrilla war against the Portuguese colonial power. Commander in chief in 1966, he succeeded Eduardo Mondlane after the latter's assassination in 1969 and was president of Mozambique from its independence in 1975 until his own death in a plane crash. An avowed Marxist, after the flight of white Portuguese in 1974 and the economic failure of his policies, he became more pragmatic, turning to the West for assistance, advising **Robert Mugabe** to temper principle with prudence, and establishing more harmonious relations with South Africa.

Machiavelli, Niccolò 1469–1527 •*Italian statesman, writer and political philosopher*• He was born in Florence, but little is known of his early life. He was among those who rapidly rose to power in 1498, despite his lack of political experience, when **Savonarola**'s regime in Florence was overthrown. He was appointed head of the Second Chancery and secretary to the Council of Ten (the main foreign relations committee in the republic). He served on a variety of diplomatic missions over the next 14 years and met many important political leaders including **Louis XII** of France, **Cesare Borgia**, Pope **Julius II** and Emperor **Maximilian I**. In 1512, when the **Medici** family, in exile since 1494, returned to run the city and the republic was dissolved, Machiavelli was dismissed from his post (for reasons that are unclear) and the following year was arrested on a charge of conspiracy against the new regime. He was tortured, and although soon released and pardoned, was obliged to withdraw from public life and devote himself to writing. He studied ancient history, pondered the lessons to be learned from his experiences in government service, and drafted "a little book" on the subject. That was his masterpiece, *The Prince*, which was written in 1513 and circulated in manuscript form before being published in 1532. It was intended to be a handbook for rulers, advising them what to do and what to say to achieve political success, and its main theme is that rulers must always be prepared to do evil if they judge that good will come of it. Machiavelli's admirers have praised him as a political realist; his critics have denounced him as a dangerous cynic and amoralist. He dedicated the book to the Medici, hoping to secure their sympathetic attention, but he was never offered any further political offices and he spent his last 15 years as a man of letters. Other works include a treatise on *The Art of War* (published 1521).

" "

It never or rarely happens that a republic or monarchy is well constituted, or its old institutions entirely reformed, unless it is only done by one individual.

1513–17 ***Discourses on the First Ten Books of Livy.***

MacIndoe, Sir Archibald 1900–60 •*New Zealand plastic surgeon*• He was born in Dunedin. Educated at the University of Otago, at the Mayo Clinic in the US, and at St Bartholomew's Hospital, London, he was the most eminent pupil of Sir Harold Gillies (1882–1960). He won fame during World War II as surgeon-in-charge at the Queen Victoria Hospital, East Grinstead, where the faces and limbs of injured airmen ("MacIndoe's guinea-pigs") were remodeled with unsurpassed skill.

Macintosh, Charles 1766–1843 •*Scottish industrial chemist and inventor*• He was born in Glasgow and studied at the university there and in Edinburgh. By 1786 he had started a chemical works, and in 1799 he and Charles Tennant (1768–1838) developed bleaching powder, which was used industrially to bleach cloth and paper until the 1920s. In 1823 Macintosh succeeded in bonding two pieces of woolen cloth together with a solution of dissolved rubber, and thus produced the first waterproof cloth. He patented the process that year and, joining forces with English inventor and manufacturer Thomas Hancock (1786–1865), began making waterproof garments at a factory in Manchester.

Mack, Connie, *originally* **Cornelius Alexander McGillicuddy** 1862–1956 •*US baseball player and manager*• Born in East Brookfield, Massachusetts, he was closely involved in the early days of US baseball. He was catcher with various teams from 1886 to 1916, and began his managerial career as player/manager in Pittsburgh (1894–96). He moved on to Philadelphia in 1901 and stayed for 50 years. He holds the record for most years managing (53), most games won (3,776), and most games lost (4,025), and won world championships in 1910–11, 1913 and 1929–30.

Mackay (of Clashfern), James Peter Hymers Mackay, Baron 1927– •*Scottish judge and jurist*• Born in Scourie, Sutherland, the son of a railway signalman, he was educated at George Heriot's School and the University of Edinburgh. After teaching mathematics at the University of St Andrews he switched to law, and was called to the bar in 1955. As a Queen's Counsel, specializing in tax law, he was unexpectedly made Lord Advocate for Scotland and a life peer by **Margaret Thatcher** in 1979. As Lord High Chancellor of Great Britain in succession to Lord Havers (1987–97), he created consternation proposing radical reform. He was succeeded in 1997 by **Lord Irvine of Lairg**, and was made a Knight of the Order of the Thistle the same year. He became Chancellor of Heriot-Watt University in Edinburgh in 1991.

Mackay, Mary *See* **Corelli, Marie**

Mackay, Robert, *English name of* **Rob Donn MacAoidh** 1714–78 •*Scottish Gaelic poet*• Born in Strathmore, Sutherland, he became a herdsman for the Mackay chief, Lord Reay. He became known as "Rob Donn," an oral bard who described rural life in his area and the disintegration of clan society in Strathnaver and Strathmore after the 1745 Jacobite rebellion. His poetry was later collected and written down by local ministers, and a first edition appeared in 1828.

Macke, August 1887–1914 •*German painter*• Born in Meschede in the Rhineland, he studied at Düsseldorf and designed stage scenery. Profoundly influenced by **Henri Matisse**, whose work he saw in Munich in 1910, he founded the Blaue Reiter group with **Franz Marc**. He was a sensitive colorist, and remained attached to the kind of subject matter favored by the Impressionists: figures in a park, street scenes, children and animals (as in *The Zoo*, 1912). He was killed fighting in World War I.

Mackendrick, Alexander 1912–93 •*US film director*• Born in Boston, Massachusetts, of Scottish origin, he was educated at the Glasgow School of Art, then worked as an animator and commercial artist before joining the script department at Pinewood Studios. During World War II he made documentaries, newsreels and propaganda films for the Ministry of Information, and after the war joined Ealing Studios, making his directorial debut on *Whisky Galore* (1948). A master of the Ealing comedy and a gifted children's director, he had success with *The Man in the White Suit* (1951), *Mandy* (1952) and *The Maggie* (1954). Embarking on international projects, he created a memorable portrait of greed in *Sweet Smell of Success* (1957).

Mackenzie, Sir Alexander 1764–1820 •*Scottish explorer and fur trader*• Born in Stornoway, Isle of Lewis, he joined the Northwest Fur Company in 1779, and in 1788 established Fort Chipewayan on Lake Athabasca, in Canada. From there he discovered the Mackenzie River (1789), followed it to the sea, and in 1792–93 became the first European to cross the Rocky Mountains to the Pacific Ocean.

Mackenzie, Sir (Edward Montague) Compton 1883–1972 •*English writer*• Born in West Hartlepool, Cleveland, he was educated at St Paul's School and Magdalen College, Oxford. His first novel, *The Passionate Elopement*, was published in 1911. There followed his successful story of theater life, *Carnival* (1912), and the autobiographical *Sinister Street* (2 vols, 1913–14) and *Guy and Pauline* (1915). In World War I he served in the Dardanelles, and in 1917 became director of the Aegean Intelligence Service in Syria, an experience described in his book on the Secret Service, *Extremes Meet* (1928). In 1923 he founded *The Gramophone* (now *Gramophone*), the oldest surviving record magazine in the world. His considerable output includes *Poor Relations* (1919), *Rich Relatives* (1921), *The Four Winds of Love* (4 vols, 1937–45), *Aegean Memories* (1940), *Whisky Galore* (1947) and *Rockets Galore* (1957).

“ ”

You are offered a piece of bread and butter that feels like a damp handkerchief and sometimes, when cucumber is added to it, like a wet one.

*1927 **Vestal Fire**, book 1, chapter 3.*

Mackenzie, William Lyon 1795–1861 •*Canadian politician*• Born in Dundee, Scotland, he emigrated to Canada in 1820. In 1828 he was elected to the provincial parliament for York, but was expelled in 1830 for libel on the assembly. He was mayor of Toronto in 1834. In 1837 he published in his paper a declaration of independence for Toronto, headed a band of 800 insurgents and attacked the city (December 5). Repulsed, he fled across the border, and on December 13 seized Navy Island in the Niagara River, where he declared a provisional government. Defeated by a Canadian force, he fled to New York (1838), where he was sentenced by the US authorities to 12 months' imprisonment. He returned to Canada in 1849, and became a Member of Parliament (1850–58). He was the grandfather of **Mackenzie King**.

Mackerras, Sir (Alan) Charles (MacLaurin) 1925– •*Australian conductor*• Born in Schenectady, New York, to Australian parents, he played the oboe with the Sydney Symphony Orchestra (1943–46), was a staff conductor at Sadler's Wells Opera (1949–53), and returned there as musical director (1970–77), gaining an international reputation. Subsequent conducting posts have included the BBC Symphony Orchestra, Sydney Symphony Orchestra, Royal Liverpool Philharmonic Orchestra and Welsh National Opera (musical director 1987–92) and he has been principal guest conductor of numerous orchestras. He is a noted scholar of the music of **Leoš Janáček** and was knighted in 1979.

MacKillop, Mary Helen, *known as* **Mother Mary of the Cross** 1842–1909 •*Australian nun, the country's first saint*• She was born in the Fitzroy district of Melbourne, Victoria, of Scottish parents. With Father Tenison-Woods she founded the Society of the Sisters of St Joseph of the Sacred Heart in Penola, South Australia, in 1866. Although the Society quickly grew, establishing 170 schools and 160 Josephite convents, diocesan rivalry caused Mother Mary to be excommunicated in 1871; however, she was reinstated two years later by Pope **Pius IX**, who approved the sisterhood in the same year. She was beatified (the first step toward canonization) in 1995.

MacKinnon, Catherine 1946– •*US feminist writer and legal scholar*• Born in Minneapolis, Minnesota, she studied for a PhD in political science at Yale. Her first publication arose from an extended student essay, *Sexual Harassment of Working Women: A Case of Sex Discrimination* (1979). In 1986 her fight for equality in the workplace bore fruit when the Supreme Court decreed that sexual harassment was sex discrimination. With feminist writer **Andrea Dworkin**, she formulated an ordinance which classified pornography as a human rights violation; it was, however, rejected in the courts. Her publications include *Only Words* (1994).

Mackintosh, Charles Rennie 1868–1928 •*Scottish architect, designer and watercolorist*• Born in Glasgow, he attended Allan Glen's School before starting his architectural apprenticeship and in 1900 marrying **Margaret MacDonald**. His architectural output, though not large, exercised very considerable influence on European design and he was both a leader of the Glasgow Style, a movement related to Art Nouveau, and the outstanding exponent of Art Nouveau in Scotland. His works include the Glasgow School of Art (1897–1909), the Cranston tearooms, and houses like Hill House in Helensburgh (1903–04). His style contrasted strong rectilinear structures and elements with subtle curved motifs, and in his houses there are deliberate references to traditional Scottish architecture. He also produced detailed interior design, textiles, furniture and metalwork. In 1914 he left Scotland and did no further major architectural work. In his later years he turned to painting, and produced a series of exquisite watercolors, chiefly in France (1923–27).

Mackintosh, Elizabeth *See* **Tey, Josephine**

Mackmurdo, Arthur Heygate 1851–1942 •*English architect and designer*• Born in London, he studied architecture, then came under the influence of his friends **John Ruskin** and **William Morris**, and became a central but very individual member of the Arts and Crafts Movement. In 1875 he set up in architectural practice and in 1882 was a founder of the Century Guild, a group which designed for all aspects of interiors. He himself designed furniture, textiles, metalwork and for print. The title page of his book *Wren's City Churches* (1883) is often seen as a forerunner of Art Nouveau.

MacLaine, Shirley, *originally* **Shirley MacLean Beaty** 1934– •*US actress*• Born in Richmond, Virginia, she made her film debut in **Alfred Hitchcock**'s black comedy *The Trouble with Harry* (1955). Adept at light comedy, she had an impish good humor and waiflike appearance that made her an unconventional leading lady, and Hollywood struggled at first to showcase her talent. She won the first of five Best Actress Academy Award nominations for her role opposite **Frank Sinatra** in *Some Came Running* (1958), and a second for her heart-rending performance in **Billy Wilder**'s *The Apartment* (1960). She was acclaimed in the musical *Sweet Charity* (1968), and has starred in such successful films as *Being There* (1979), *Terms of Endearment* (1983), for which she finally won her coveted Best Actress Academy Award, *Steel Magnolias* (1989), *Postcards from the Edge* (1990) and *The Evening Star* (1996). She is the sister of the actor **Warren Beatty**.

Maclaurin, Colin 1698–1746 •*Scottish mathematician*• Born in Kilmodan, Argyll, he graduated from the University of Glasgow (1713), and became professor at the University of Aberdeen (1717). In 1725 he was appointed to the chair of mathematics at the University of Edinburgh on **Isaac Newton**'s recommendation. His best-known work, *Treatise on Fluxions* (1742), gave a systematic account of Newton's approach to the calculus, taking a geometric, rather than analytical, point of view. This is often thought to have contributed to the neglect of analysis in 18th-century Great Britain.

MacLean, Alistair 1922–87 •*Scottish author*• Born in Glasgow, he was educated at the University of Glasgow and served in the Royal Navy (1941–46). In 1954, while a schoolteacher, he won a short-story competition held by the *Glasgow Herald*, contributing a tale of adventure at sea, then produced a full-length novel, *HMS*

Ulysses, which became an immediate bestseller. He followed it with *The Guns of Navarone* (1957), and turned to full-time writing. His settings are worldwide, including the China Seas (*South by Java Head*, 1958), Florida (*Fear Is the Key*, 1961), the Scottish islands (*When Eight Bells Toll*, 1966), a polar scientific station (*Ice Station Zebra*, 1963) and the Camargue (*Caravan to Vaccares*, 1970). As well as two secret-service thrillers (written as "Ian Stuart"), he wrote a Western (*Breakheart Pass*, 1974) and biographies of **T E Lawrence** and Captain **Cook**. Other titles include *Where Eagles Dare* (1967), *Force Ten From Navarone* (1968) and *Athabasca* (1980).

Maclean, Donald Duart 1913–83 •*English double agent*• Born in London, the son of Liberal cabinet minister Sir Donald Maclean, he was educated at Gresham's School and studied at Trinity College, Cambridge, at the same time as **Anthony Blunt**, **Guy Burgess** and **Kim Philby**. Similarly influenced by communism, he joined the diplomatic service in 1935, and from 1944 was a Soviet agent. After a nervous breakdown in 1950, he became head of the American department of the Foreign Office, but by 1951 was a suspected traitor, and in May of that year, after Philby's warning, disappeared with Burgess to the USSR. He was joined in 1953 by his wife, Melinda (b. 1916) and children, but she left him to marry Philby in 1966. Maclean became a respected Soviet citizen, working for the Foreign Ministry and at the Institute of World Economic and International Relations.

MacLean, Sorley, *Gaelic* **Somhairle MacGill-Eain** 1911–96 •*Scottish Gaelic poet*• Born on the island of Raasay, off Skye, he attended school there and on Skye before studying English at the University of Edinburgh. He began writing as a student, and by the end of the 1930s he was an established Scottish literary figure. In 1940 he published *Seventeen Poems for Sixpence*, which he produced with **Robert Garioch**, and in 1943, after his recovery from wounds sustained during active service at El Alamein, came *Dàin do Eimhir* ("Poems to Eimhir"), which contained many of his love lyrics addressed to the legendary Eimhir of the early Irish sagas. Influenced by the metaphysical poets as well as the ancient and later Celtic literature and traditional Gaelic songs, he reinvigorated the Gaelic literary language and tradition, much as his friend **Hugh MacDiarmid** was reinstating Scots as a serious literary language. A teacher and headmaster until his retirement in 1972, he produced his major collection of poems, *Reothairt is contraigh* ("Spring Tide and Neap Tide"), in 1977.

“ ”

Tha tìm, am fiadh, an coille Hallaig.
Time, the deer, is in the wood of Hallaig.

1970 "Hallaig," epitaph.

Maclehose, Agnes, *née* **Craig** 1759–1841 •*Scottish literary figure*• She was born in Edinburgh, the daughter of a surgeon. In 1776 she married a Glasgow lawyer, from whom she separated in 1780. She met **Robert Burns** at a party in Edinburgh in 1787, and subsequently, under the name "Clarinda," carried on a remarkable correspondence with him. A number of Burns's poems and songs were dedicated to her.

MacLeish, Archibald 1892–1982 •*US poet and librarian*• Born in Glencoe, Illinois, and educated at Yale and the Harvard Law School, he taught constitutional law briefly at Harvard College, but moved to Europe in 1923 to concentrate on writing. He was Librarian of Congress (1939–44), assistant secretary of state (1944–45), cofounder of UNESCO, and Boylston Professor of Rhetoric and Oratory at Harvard University (1949–62). His many works include *The Happy Marriage* (1923), *The Pot of Earth* (1925) and *The Hamlet of A. MacLeish* (1928). For *Conquistador* (1932) he was awarded the 1932 Pulitzer Prize for poetry; for *Collected Poems 1917–1952* he was awarded a second Pulitzer Prize, the Bollingen prize and a National Book award in 1953 and for *J.B.*, a verse play, he won the Pulitzer Prize in drama and a Tony award for best play in 1959.

Maclennan, Robert Adam Ross, Baron 1936– •*Scottish politician*• Born in Glasgow, he attended the Glasgow Academy, Balliol College, Oxford, Trinity College, Cambridge, and Columbia University, New York, before being called to the bar in 1962. He became a Member of Parliament in 1966. Originally a Labour supporter, he held junior posts in the governments of **Harold Wilson** and **James Callaghan** and was a founding member of the Social Democratic Party (SDP) in 1981. He came to prominence in 1987 when, after **David Owen** had resigned the SDP leadership, Maclennan became a "caretaker" leader until the terms of the merger had been agreed. He then became a leading member of the new party, the Liberal Democrats, under **Paddy Ashdown**, and president from 1994 to 1998. He stepped down as a Member of Parliament in 2001 and was created a life peer.

Macleod, Iain Norman 1913–70 •*British politician*• Born in Skipton, Yorkshire, and educated at Gonville and Caius College, Cambridge, he fought in France during World War II, and became a Member of Parliament in 1950. He was Minister of Health (1952–55) and of Labour (1955–59), before being appointed Secretary of State for the Colonies in 1959, in which office he oversaw the granting of independence to many British territories in Africa. He was Chancellor of the Duchy of Lancaster and Leader of the House of Commons and party chairman (1961–63), then edited the *Spectator* for two years. When **Edward Heath** became leader, MacLeod was appointed Chancellor for the Opposition (1965–70), and after the Conservative victory in 1970, he became Chancellor of the Exchequer until his death a month later. One of the most popular figures in his party, and a gifted orator, he had been considered a leading contender for the premiership.

Macleod, John James Rickard 1876–1935 •*Scottish physiologist and Nobel Prize winner*• Born in Cluny, Fife, he studied at Aberdeen, Leipzig and Cambridge, and became Professor of Physiology at Western Reserve University, Cleveland (1903), and at Toronto University (1918). His fame rests upon his involvement with the discovery of insulin. In 1921 he accepted **Frederick Grant Banting** into his department for research on the pancreas with **Charles Best**, and they succeeded in purifying a pancreatic extract which lowered blood sugar levels. The extract was insulin, and insulin therapy soon became the main treatment for diabetes. In 1923 Macleod and Banting were awarded the Nobel Prize for physiology or medicine.

Mac Liammóir, Mícheál, *originally* **Alfred Wilmore** 1899–1978 •*Irish actor, painter and writer*• Born in Cork, Ireland, he moved with his family to London, and became a child actor. After studying art at the Slade School, he cofounded the Gate Theatre Company in Dublin (1928), having toured Ireland with the Shakespearean company of Anew McMaster (1894–1962). His company's work made the most of dramatic possibilities of Irish writing, drew on much European drama using his translations, adaptations, design and lighting, and offered bold productions of classical material. He wrote fiction, plays and memoirs in Irish and in English, and in the 1960s his one-man shows brought him an international reputation. His film performances include Iago in **Orson Welles**'s *Othello* (1949) and the narrator in *Tom Jones* (1963).

MacMahon, Marie Edmé Patrice Maurice de 1808–93 •*French soldier and statesman*• Born in Sully near Autun, he was descended from an Irish Jacobite family. For his services in the Italian campaign (1859) he was made marshal and Duke of Magenta. He became governor-general of Algeria in 1864. In the Franco-Prussian War (1870–71) he commanded the 1st Army Corps, but was defeated at Wörth, and captured at Sedan. After the war, as commander of the army of Versailles, he suppressed the Commune (1871). In 1873 he was elected president of the Republic for seven years, and was suspected of reactionary and monarchical leanings. He resigned in 1879.

Macmillan, Daniel 1813–57 •*Scottish bookseller and publisher*• He was born in Upper Corrie, Arran, and was apprenticed to a bookseller in Irvine at the age of ten. In 1843 he and his brother Alexander opened a bookshop in London, then moved to Cambridge. By 1844 he had branched out into publishing, first educational and religious works, and, by 1855, English classics. In 1858, the year of his death, the firm opened a branch in London and by 1893 had become a limited liability company with Daniel's son, Frederick (1851–1936), as chairman. His other son, Maurice, father of **Harold Macmillan**, was also a partner.

Macmillan, (Maurice) Harold, 1st Earl of Stockton 1894–1986 •*English Conservative statesman*• Born in London, he was educated at Eton and Balliol College, Oxford, his studies having been interrupted by service with the Grenadier Guards during World War I, in which he was seriously wounded. Afterward he partnered his brother Daniel in the family publishing firm, but preserved his interest in politics and ran successfully as Conservative Member of Parliament for Stockton-on-Tees in 1924; he was defeated in 1929, but reelected in 1931. Not always willing to conform to the party line, he remained a backbencher until 1940, when **Churchill** made him parliamentary secretary to the ministry of supply. After a brief spell as colonial undersecretary, in 1942 he was sent to North Africa to fill the new cabinet post of minister resident at Allied Headquarters, where he showed great acumen and proved his ability as a mediator. He was minister of housing (1951–54), then minister of defense 1954–55, and thereafter foreign minister to the end of 1955, when he was appointed chancellor of the exchequer. On **Anthony Eden**'s resignation in 1957 he emerged, in **R A Butler**'s words, as "the best prime minister we have," his appointment being received without enthusiasm, for as an intellectual and a dyed-in-the-wool aristocrat he was regarded with suspicion by many. Nevertheless, his economic expansionism at home, his resolution in foreign affairs, his integrity, and his infectious optimism inspired confidence, and his popularity soared. Having told the people in 1957 that most "have never had it so good," he embarked on a new term as prime minister in 1959. His "wind of change" speech in Cape Town (1960) acknowledged the inevitability of African independence. In 1962, after some electoral setbacks, he carried out a drastic "purge" of his government, involving seven cabinet ministers. Further setbacks followed, such as the **Profumo** scandal (1963), and ill health brought about his reluctant resignation in 1963. An earldom was bestowed upon him on his 90th birthday in 1984, and he took the title Earl of Stockton. He wrote *Winds of Change* (1966), *Tides of Fortune* (1969), *Pointing the Way* and *At the End of the Day* (both 1972).

“ ”

We have not overthrown the divine right of kings to fall down for the divine right of experts.

1950 Speech, Strasbourg, August 16.

Macmillan, Sir Kenneth 1929–92 •*Scottish ballet dancer and choreographer*• Born in Dunfermline, Fife, he was one of the original members of the Sadler's Wells Theatre Ballet (1946–48). In 1953 he began to choreograph with the Royal Ballet, and, after three years as director at the Berlin Opera (1966–69), returned to the Royal Ballet in 1970 as artistic director and then principal choreographer. His works include *Romeo and Juliet* (1965), *Élite Syncopations* and *Manon* (both 1974), *Mayerling* (1978) and *The Judas Tree* (1992). As well as creating ballets for many of the world's foremost companies, he worked on theater, television, and musical shows.

Macnamara, Dame (Annie) Jean 1899–1968 •*Australian physician*• Born in Beechworth, Victoria, and educated at the University of Melbourne, she worked in local hospitals where she developed an interest in infantile paralysis. During the polio (poliomyelitis) epidemic of 1925, she tested the use of immune serum and, convinced of its efficacy, visited England, the US and Canada. With **Macfarlane Burnet**, she found that there was more than one strain of poliovirus, a discovery which led to the development of the Salk vaccine (named after US virologist **Jonas Salk**). She also supported the experimental treatment developed by **Elizabeth Kenny**, and introduced the first artificial respirator (iron lung) into Australia. She was given the honorary title of Dame Commander, Order of the British Empire, in 1935, and later became involved in the controversial introduction of the disease myxomatosis as a means of controlling the rabbit population of Australia.

MacNeice, (Frederick) Louis 1907–63 •*Northern Irish poet*• Born in Belfast, he was educated at Marlborough and at Merton College, Oxford, and became a lecturer in classics at the University of Birmingham (1930–36) and in Greek at Bedford College, University of London (1936–40). He was closely associated with the British left-wing poets of the 1930s, especially **W H Auden**, with whom he wrote *Letters from Iceland* (1937). Among his volumes of poetry are *Blind Fireworks* (1929), *Autumn Journal* (1938), *Autumn Sequel* (1954) and *Eighty-Five Poems* and *Solstices* (both 1961). He was the author of a novel, *Round about Way* (1932), and several verse plays for radio, notably *The Dark Tower* (1947), as well as various translations and volumes of literary criticism. A volume of autobiography, *The Strings Are False*, appeared posthumously in 1965.

“ ”

World is crazier and more of it than we think,
Incorrigibly plural.

*1935 **Poems**, "Snow."*

MacNeill, John, *pen name* **Eoin** 1867–1945 •*Irish historian and nationalist*• Born in Glenarm, County Antrim, and educated at St Malachy's College, Belfast, he made himself an authority on Old Irish, and ultimately became Professor of Early Irish history at University College, Dublin (1908–45). In 1913 he inspired and led the Irish Volunteers. His organization was taken over by **John Redmond**, who persuaded most of its members to support the Allied cause in 1914 after the outbreak of World War I. Irish Republican Brotherhood manipulation steered MacNeill's Volunteers toward insurrection in 1916 without his knowledge. After the Dublin Rising, MacNeill was interned, and played a part in organizing the new Sinn Fein Party and its abstentionist body Dáil Éireann, where, as Member of Parliament for Derry, he was given cabinet status. He supported the Anglo-Irish Treaty and was Minister for Education in the first Irish Free State government. He was delegate for his government to the Boundary Commission that shattered Irish nationalist hopes of a revision of Irish partition in the Catholics' favor; he resigned rather than accept its verdict, and the boundary was left unchanged.

Maconchy, Dame Elizabeth Violet 1907–94 •*English composer*• Born in Broxbourne, Hertfordshire, of Irish parentage, she studied under **Ralph Vaughan Williams** at the Royal College of Music and in 1929 went to Prague, where her first major work, a piano concerto, was performed (1930). Her suite, *The Land*, was performed at the London Proms the same year. Her most characteristic work is in the field of chamber music, and among her best-known compositions are her *Symphony* (1953) and overture *Proud Thames*, also written in Coronation Year; a carol cantata, *A Christmas Morning* (1962); a choral and orchestral work, *Samson and the Gates of Gaza* (1963); an opera for children, *The King of the Golden River* (1975); *Heloise and Abelard* (1978) and *My Dark Heart* (1981). She was given the honorary title of Dame Commander, Order of the British Empire, in 1987. Her daughter, Nicola Frances LeFanu (1947–), is also a composer.

Macphail, Agnes Campbell, *née* **Campbell** 1890–1954 •*Canadian suffragist and politician*• She was born in Grey County, Ontario, and became a schoolteacher. She became involved with the women's suffrage movement and was elected Canada's first woman Member of Parliament for the United Farmers of Ontario (1921–40). She was a leader of the Cooperative Commonwealth Federation of Canada, which had been formed in 1933 and represented Canada in the Assembly of the League of Nations.

Macpherson, James 1736–96 •*Scottish poet and "translator" of Ossian*• Born in Ruthven, Inverness-shire, he was educated at King's College and Marischal College, Aberdeen, and studied for the ministry, but in 1756 became a village schoolmaster in Ruthven. In 1758 he published some fragments of Gaelic oral poetry, *Fragments of Ancient Poetry Collected in the Highlands of Scotland* (1870). The introduction (by Hugh Blair) suggested that a poetic epic relating to the legendary hero Fingal, as told by his son **Ossian**, was still extant. In 1760 Macpherson claimed to have discovered this material, which he published in 1762 as *Fingal: An Ancient Epic Poem in Six Books*; it was followed by *Temora, an Epic Poem, in Eight Books* (1763). They were received with huge acclaim, but their authenticity was soon questioned, and Macpherson was unable to produce the originals. He seems, in fact, to have used some original Gaelic poetry, greatly amended, and invented the rest. He was Member of Parliament for Camelford from 1780 and was buried, at his own request and expense, in Westminster Abbey.

Macquarie, Lachlan, *known as* **the Father of Australia** 1761–1824 •*Scottish soldier and colonial administrator*• Born on the island of Ulva, off Mull, he joined the Black Watch in 1777, and after service in North America, India and Egypt was appointed governor of New South Wales following the deposition of Captain **William Bligh**. The colony, depressed and demoralized, populated largely by convicts and exploited by influential land-grabbers and monopolists, was raised by his energetic administration and firm rule to prosperity: its population trebled, extensive surveys were carried out, and many roads were built. He gave his name to the Lachlan and Macquarie rivers, and to Macquarie Island.

Macready, William Charles 1793–1873 •*English actor and theater manager*• He was born in London. After making his debut at Birmingham in 1810, he appeared at Covent Garden in London (1816), but it was not until 1837 that he became known as the leading English actor of his day. In that year he became manager of Covent Garden, where he produced **Shakespeare**. After two seasons he moved to Drury Lane (1841–43), then played in the provinces, Paris and the US. His last visit to the US was marked by riots (May 10, 1849), in which 22 people died, following the booing of his Macbeth by supporters of US actor **Edwin Forrest**.

Macrobius, Ambrosius Theodosius 5th century •*Roman writer and Neo-Platonist philosopher*• Born probably in Africa, he wrote a commentary on **Cicero**'s *Somnium Scipionis* ("The Dream of Scipio"), and *Saturnaliorum conviviorum libri septem*, a series of historical, mythological and critical dialogues.

MacThómais, Ruaraidh *See* **Thomson, Derick**

Macy, Anne Mansfield Sullivan, *née* **Sullivan** 1866–1936 •*US educator*• Born in Feeding Hills, Massachusetts, she lost most of her sight in childhood due to an infection and attended the Perkins Institute for the Blind in Boston. She regained some of her sight through surgery. In 1887 she was chosen to teach **Helen Keller**, a girl who could not see, hear or speak. Using the manual alphabet and a method of touch-teaching in which she allowed the child to hold objects rather than have their properties explained, she was dramatically successful in instructing her. She later accompanied Keller to Radcliffe College and on worldwide lecture tours.

Mademoiselle, La Grande *See* **Montpensier, Anne Marie Louise d'Orléans, Duchesse de**

Maderna, Bruno 1920–73 •*Italian composer and conductor*• Born in Venice, he appeared from the age of seven as an infant prodigy violinist and conductor, and studied composition and conducting. Early in his musical career he composed for films and radio, and taught at the Venice Conservatorio. In 1955 he began to research the techniques and possibilities of electronic music, founding, with **Luciano Berio**, the Studio di Fonologia Musicale of Milan Radio in Italy (1955). His compositions are intellectual, based on a mathematical calculation of form rather than an emotional or inspirational approach, but much of the resulting music is surprisingly lyrical. He wrote pieces for combinations of live and taped music, and a number of compositions for electronic music, such as *Dimensions II* (1960). His opera *Satyricon* appeared in 1973.

Maderna or **Maderno, Carlo** 1556–1629 •*Italian architect*• Born in Capalago, he had moved to Rome by 1588, where he became assistant to his uncle, **Domenico Fontana**. He was the leading exponent of the early Baroque in Rome, producing bold and vigorous designs, divorced from the Mannerist style of the preceding generation. In 1603 he was appointed architect to St Peter's, where he lengthened the nave and added a massive façade (1606–12).

Madhva 14th century •*Kanarese Brahmin philosopher*• Born near Mangalore, South India, he studied in Trivandrum, Benares and elsewhere, settled in Udipi and is traditionally held to have vanished in mid-lecture in 1317 and retired to the Himalayas. Taking **Ramanuja**'s side against **Śankara**, he promoted *dvaita*, or dualistic *Vedanta*, allowing for the separate existence of the Divine, human souls, and matter. His belief that some souls were eternally damned suggests a Christian influence on his thinking.

Madison, James 1751–1836 •*Fourth President of the US*• Born in Port Conway, Virginia, he graduated from the College of New Jersey (now Princeton) and quickly became involved in Revolutionary politics. In 1776 he was a member of the Virginia Convention, and he served in the Continental Congress (1780–83, 1787) and the Virginia legislature (1784–86). He was one of the most active delegates to the Constitutional Convention of 1787, and his capable management of the proceedings and ability to engineer compromises won him the title "master builder of the constitution." He suggested the compromise by which, for taxation, representation, and so forth, slaves were regarded as population and not chattel, five being counted as three persons, thus securing the adoption of the Constitution by South Carolina and the other slave-holding states. He joined **Alexander Hamilton** and **John Jay** in writing the *Federalist Papers* (1787–88). As a congressman from Virginia (1789–97) he was an advocate of the Bill of Rights and was anxious to limit the powers of the central government. He was a leader of the Jeffersonian Republicans, drawing up the Virginia Resolves, and when **Thomas Jefferson** was elected president in 1800, Madison was made secretary of state. In 1809 he succeeded Jefferson as president. His administration was dominated by concerns about the European wars of the period and the damage done to US commerce, and by the War of 1812, an unpopular conflict with Great Britain in which the US gained none of its objectives. In 1817, at the close of his second term, Madison retired to Virginia.

“ ”

What is government itself but the greatest of all reflections on human nature?

*1788 **The Federalist**, January.*

Madoc, *properly* **Madog ab Owain Gwynedd** fl. 1150–80 •*Welsh prince*• Probably legendary, he was long believed by his countrymen to have discovered America in 1170. The story is in **Richard Hakluyt**'s *Voyages* (1582) and Lloyd and Powell's *Cambria* (1584). An essay by Thomas Stephens, written in 1858 for the Eisteddfod (published 1893), proved it to be without foundation, but it provided the basis for **Robert Southey**'s poem *Madoc* (1805).

Madonna, *full name* **Madonna Louise Veronica Ciccone** 1958– •*US pop singer and actress*• Born in Bay City, Michigan, she trained as a dancer at the University of Michigan before moving to New York, where she began her professional career as a singer. In 1983 she produced her first hit, *Holiday*. Highly ambitious and commercially astute, she made her debut album in the same year, which delivered four more US hit singles. Her brash, overtly sexual stage persona and striking fashions made her an influential role model for teenagers from the 1980s onward, and her success has been greatly enhanced by clever promotion and imagemaking. Her major recordings include *Like a Virgin* (1984), *True Blue* (1986), *Like a Prayer* (1989), *Erotica* (1992), *Bedtime Stories* (1994), *In the Beginning* (1998), *Ray of Light* (1998) and *Music* (2000). In 1993 she published her enormously successful photobook *Sex*, which featured her posed in a number of sexual attitudes. She has appeared in a number of films, including *Desperately Seeking Susan* (1985), *In Bed with Madonna* (1991) and *Evita* (1996), the massively successful film musical of the life of **Eva Perón**. She heads the recording company Maverick, and has been married to Sean Penn (1985–89) and Guy Ritchie (2000–).

Maddux, Greg (Gregory Alan) 1966– •*US baseball player*• Born in San Angelo, Texas, he distinguished himself as a right-handed pitcher with the Chicago Cubs (1986–92) and the Atlanta Braves (from 1993). Admired as one of the most consistently accurate pitchers of the 1990s, capable of placing the ball exactly where he wants it, he was the first man to receive four consecutive **Cy Young** Awards (1992–95). He has also attracted praise as a fielder, winning 10 consecutive Gold Glove Awards (1990–99).

Maecenas, Gaius Cilnius d. 8 BC •*Roman statesman*• He was the trusted counselor of **Augustus**, and his name has become a synonym for a patron of letters.

Maedoc, St Maol *See* **Malachy, St**

Maes, Nicolaes 1634–93 •*Dutch painter*• Born in Dordrecht, from c. 1648 he was a pupil of **Rembrandt** in Amsterdam. Painting in a style close to his master's he specialized in painting genre scenes, especially of single figures praying or sleeping. He traveled to Antwerp (c. 1665) and there became influenced by Flemish art, especially that of **Van Dyck**.

Maeterlinck, Maurice, Count 1862–1949 •*Belgian dramatist and Nobel Prize winner*• Born in Ghent, he studied law there, but became a disciple of the Symbolist movement, and in 1889 produced his first volume of poetry, *Les serres chaudes* ("The Greenhouses"). In the same year came his prose play, *La Princesse Maleine* (Eng trans *The Princess Maleine*, 1890), and in 1892 *Pelléas et Mélisande* (Eng trans *Pelleas and Melisande*, 1894), on which **Claude Debussy** based his opera. *La vie des abeilles* (1901, Eng trans *The Life of the Bee*, 1901) is one of his many popular expositions of scientific subjects, and he also wrote several philosophical works. He was awarded the Nobel Prize for literature in 1911.

Magellan, Ferdinand c. 1480–1521 •*Portuguese navigator*• He was born near Villa Real in Tras os Montes, served in the East Indies and Morocco, then laid before **Charles V** a scheme for reaching the Moluccas by sailing to the west. Sailing from Seville on August 10, 1519, with five ships and 270 men, he coasted Patagonia, passing through the strait which bears his name (October 21 to November 28), and reached the ocean which he named the Pacific. He was later killed by local people in the Philippine Islands, but his ship, the *Victoria*, was taken safely back to Spain by the Spanish captain, **Juan Sebastian del Cano**, on September 6, 1522, to complete the first circumnavigation of the world. The four other ships had been lost, and of the 270 men who had set out three years earlier, fewer than 20 returned.

Magendie, François 1783–1855 •*French physiologist*• Born in Bordeaux, he graduated in medicine at Paris in 1808. A pioneer of scientific pharmacology, he used vivisection to conduct trials on plant poisons, and through such research he introduced into medicine the range of plant-derived compounds now known as alkaloids, many of which possess outstanding pharmacological properties. He investigated the role of proteins in the human diet, was interested in olfaction and inquired into the white blood cells. He worked extensively on the nerves of the skull and the paths of the spinal nerves. He became the president of the French Academy of Sciences in 1837, and is often regarded as the founder of experimental physiology.

Magician, Simon the *See* **Simon Magus**

Maginot, André Louis René 1877–1932 •*French politician*• Born in Paris, he was first elected to the Chamber of Deputies in 1910. As Minister of War (1922–24, 1926–31) he pursued a policy of military preparedness, and ordered the construction on the Franco-German border of the famous Maginot line of fortifications, comprising concealed weapons, underground stores and living quarters. However, in World War II, the German strategy of invading through Belgium made the scheme redundant.

Magnus I Olafsson, *called* **the Good** 1024–47 •*King of Norway and of Denmark*• The illegitimate son of King **Olaf II Haraldsson** (St Olaf), after his father's death at the Battle of Stiklestad (1030), the boy went to Prince Jaroslav the Wise in Kiev. In 1035 he assumed the Norwegian throne by popular acclaim. He inherited the Danish throne in 1042, and won a notable victory over the Wends in 1043 at Lürschau Heath in southern Jutland. In 1045 he agreed to share the throne of Norway with his uncle **Harald III Sigurdsson**, and died two years later during a campaign in Denmark.

Magnus III Olafsson, *called* **Barfot ("Barefoot")** c. 1074–1103 •*King of Norway*• One of the last of the Norse Viking sea kings bent on strengthening Norway's hold over her North Sea territories, he was the son of King **Olaf III Haraldsson**. He became king in 1093 and attacked the Hebrides, Orkney and Shetland (1098–99) and later Scotland and Ireland (1102–03). He took Dublin, and built new fortifications on the Isle of Man, but was killed in an ambush in Ulster. He earned his nickname because he abandoned Norse trousers in favor of the Scottish kilt.

Magnus V Erlingsson 1156–84 •*King of Norway*• The son of Earl Erling the Crooked, he became king in 1162 and was raised to the throne, under his father's regency, as a child. In 1164 he was crowned by Archbishop Eystein at a church ceremony in Bergen, the first religious coronation in Norway. After his father's death (1179) he was engaged in a long war against a rival claimant to the throne, the Faroese-born usurper **Sverrir Sigurdsson** and was forced to flee to Denmark for safety. He died in a naval battle in an attempt to regain his kingdom.

Magnus Maximus d. 388 AD •*Roman emperor*• He was a Roman army commander in Britain who, after being proclaimed emperor by his troops in AD 383, crossed to Gaul and overthrew the emperor of the West, **Gratian**. Recognized as emperor by the emperor of the East, **Theodosius I (the Great)**, who was then preoccupied with problems nearer home, Maximus proceeded to rule over Gaul, Spain and Britain. His attempts to add Italy to his empire backfired, as Theodosius defeated him in battle and had him executed.

Magnusson, Magnus 1929– •*Scottish journalist and broadcaster*• Born in Reykjavík, Iceland, he was raised in Edinburgh and educated at Oxford. He became a journalist and broadcaster, and his wide historical and cultural interests have informed such television series as *Chronicle* (1966–80), *BC: The Archaeology of the Bible Lands* (1977) and *Vikings!* (1980), although he remains best known as quizmaster of the long-running *Mastermind* (1972–97). His numerous publications and translations include *Introducing Archaeology* (1972) and *Scotland: The Story of a Nation* (2000). He was editor of the fifth edition of *Chambers Biographical Dictionary* (1990). In 1989 he was awarded an honorary knighthood.

Magoun, Horace Winchell 1907–91 •*US neuroscientist*• Born in Philadelphia, he studied at Rhode Island College and Northwestern University Medical School, where he later taught (1937–50). In 1950 he moved to the School of Medicine at UCLA as Professor of Anatomy. He demonstrated the important role of the hypothalamus, and was a pioneer in the development of the field of neuroendocrinology. He collaborated on many neurological and psychopharmacological projects and was one of the leaders in the creation of neuroscience, the multidisciplinary approach to the study of the nervous system.

Magritte, René François Ghislain 1898–1967 •*Belgian surrealist painter*• Born in Lessines, Hainault, he moved in 1913 to Charleroi after his mother committed suicide. He was educated at the Académie Royale des Beaux-Arts (1916–18) in Brussels. He became a wallpaper designer and commercial artist and in 1924 a leading member of the newly formed Belgian surrealist group. He made his name with *The Menaced Assassin* (1926, Museum of Modern Art, New York), but after a badly received one-man show in Brussels (1927), he lived in Paris until 1930 and became associated with **André Breton** and others there. Apart from a brief impressionist phase in the 1940s, Magritte remained faithful to surrealism, using Freudian symbols and recurring motifs of dreamlike incongruity, as in *Rape*, in which he substitutes a torso for a face. His best-known paintings include *Man with a Newspaper* and *The Reckless Sleeper* (1928), *The Red Model* (1935, Pompidou Centre, Paris), *The Wind and the Song* (1928–29) and *The Human Condition* (1, 1934; 2, 1935). He was acclaimed in the US as an early innovator of the pop art of the 1960s.

Maharishi Mahesh Yogi, *originally* **Mahesh Prasad Varma** 1911– •*Indian cult leader*• He was born in Jabalpur and abandoned his scientific studies to become a follower of the guru Dev. He first introduced his meditation technique, based on a literalist interpretation of yogic concepts and the use of mantras, to the West in 1958, and became one of the first Eastern gurus to attract a Western following, notably **The Beatles**, who traveled to meditate with him in 1968. He went on to found the Spiritual Regeneration movement, aimed at saving the world through meditation. This concept developed into a worldwide network of meditation centers.

Mahathir bin Mohamad, Datuk Seri 1925– •*Malaysian politician*• Born in Alur Setar, in Kedah state, he practiced as a doctor (1957–64) before being elected to the House of Representatives as a United Malays' National Organisation (UMNO) candidate. He won the support of UMNO's radical youth wing through his advocacy of affirmative action in favor of bumiputras (ethnic Malays) and a more Islamic social policy. He was appointed UMNO leader and prime minister in 1981, immediately launching a new "look east" economic policy, which sought to emulate Japanese industrialization. Despite internal ethnic conflicts, he was reelected in 1982, 1986, 1990, 1995 and 2000.

Mahdi, al- *See* **Muhammad Ahmed**

Mahfouz or **Mahfuz, Naguib** 1911– •*Egyptian novelist and Nobel Prize winner*• Born in the al-Gamaliyya old quarter of Cairo, the youngest son of a merchant, he studied philosophy at King Fuad I (now Cairo) University. He worked in university administration, then for the government's Ministry of Waqfs (religious foundations), and in journalism. By 1939 he had already written three novels, among them *Kifah Tiba* (1944, "The Struggle of Thebes"). However, his early work was overshadowed by the notoriety surrounding *Awlad Haratina* (1967, Eng trans *The Children of Gebelawi*, 1981), serialized in the magazine *al-Ahram*. An allegorical work which shows his disillusionment with religion, it depicts average Egyptians living the lives of **Cain** and **Abel**, **Moses**, **Jesus** and **Muhammad**, and portrays the decline of five communities toward futility and nihilism. It was banned throughout the Arab world, except in Lebanon. He subsequently became more interested in the plight of the individual, as in *Al-liss wa-l-kilab* (1961, "The Thief and the Dogs"), *Al-shahhadh* (1965, "The Beggar") and *Miramar* (1967, Eng trans 1978). He won the Nobel Prize for literature in 1988, the first Arab to receive the award. Later works include *Asda al-sira al dhatiyya* (1996, "Echoes of an Autobiography").

Mahler, Gustav 1860–1911 •*Bohemian-born Austrian composer*• He was born in Kalist in Bohemia (now the Czech Republic). He began to learn the piano at an early age, and in 1875 he went to the Vienna Conservatory, where he studied composition and conducting. He became a follower of **Anton Bruckner**, although he was not his pupil. He wrote the cantata *Das klagende Lied* for the Beethoven Prize in 1881, but was unsuccessful. He then turned to conducting, rapidly reaching important positions in Prague, Leipzig, Budapest and Hamburg, where in 1891 he became chief conductor of Hamburg Opera. There he introduced several new works and took the company on tour. In 1897 he became conductor and artistic director at the Vienna State Opera House. In 1902 Mahler married Alma Schindler (1879–1964), who played an important part in his life and published his letters and other documents and reminiscences after his death. Mahler detested the intrigues of theatrical life and was much affected by the frequent personal attacks upon him for his Jewish birth, despite (or perhaps because of) his conversion to Roman Catholicism, and he resigned after ten years to devote himself to composition and the concert platform. From 1908 to 1911 he was conductor of the New York Philharmonic Society, spending his summers composing in Austria. His mature works consist entirely of songs and symphonies. He wrote nine numbered symphonies plus the song-symphony *Das Lied von der Erde*, which he did not include in the nine for superstitious reasons (**Beethoven**, **Schubert** and Bruckner having all died after completing nine); in the end he too left a tenth symphony unfinished. He also wrote songs with orchestral accompaniment, notably *Kindertotenlieder* (1901–04, "Songs on the Death of Children"), based on poems by the German poet and scholar Friedrich Rückert (1788–1866). In his lifetime and for many years after, Mahler was known principally as a conductor; more recently, his compositions have gained enormous popularity in Europe and the US.

“ ”

He is young and perhaps he is right. Maybe my ear is not sensitive enough.
Of Schoenberg's music. Quoted in Lebrecht, ***Discord*** *(1982).*

Mahmud II 1785–1839 •*Ottoman Sultan of Turkey*• Born in Constantinople (Istanbul), he succeeded his brother Mustafa IV in 1808. His reign saw the loss to Russia of Bessarabia; the independence of Greece and Serbia; and the autonomy of Egypt under **Mehemet 'Ali**. At home he curbed the power of the religious leaders (ulama) and set up European-type schools. He suppressed the corps of janissaries, replacing it with a new regular army on the European model.

Mahmud of Ghazni 971–1030 •*Muslim Afghan conqueror of India*• The son of Sebüktigin, a Turkish slave who became ruler of Ghazni (modern Afghanistan), he succeeded to the throne in 997. He invaded India 17 times (1001–1026), and created an empire that included the Punjab and much of Persia. A great patron of the arts, he made Ghazni a remarkable cultural center.

Mahon, Derek 1941– •*Northern Irish poet*• Born in Belfast, he was educated at Belfast Institute and Trinity College, Dublin, and he taught before turning to journalism and other writing. He was associated with the Northern Poets in Belfast in the 1960s, with **Seamus Heaney** and Michael Longley (1939–). A poet drawn to squalid landscapes and desperate situations, his works include *Twelve Poems* (1965), *Night-Crossing* (1968), *The Snow Party* (1975), *The Hunt by Night* (1982), *A Kensington Notebook* (1984) and *Antarctica* (1985). He has also published translations and screenplays.

Maier, Hermann 1972– •*Austrian skier*• Born in Flachau, he worked as a bricklayer before winning a place with the Austrian national ski team. He rose rapidly to the top of the sport, winning his first World Cup race in 1997 and two gold medals in the slalom at the Winter Olympics at Nagano in 1998, and going on to capture the overall World Cup title that year. Further World Cup titles followed in 1998, 2000 and 2001.

Mailer, Norman Kingsley 1923– •*US novelist and journalist*• Born in Long Branch, New Jersey, he was raised in Brooklyn, educated at Harvard University, and during World War II served in the Pacific. His first novel, *The Naked and the Dead* (1948), an antiwar blast and social satire, became a bestseller, establishing him as a leading novelist of his generation. He maintained his antagonism toward contemporary society in *Barbary Shore* (1951) and *The Deer Park* (1955), but the writing of the period documents his gradual ideological shift from liberal socialism to a kind of anarchistic libertarianism. A proponent of the "New Journalism," and one who helped define that solipsistic genre, he has created a vast body of work, impressive for its energy and its self-obsession. *Advertisements for Myself* (1959) is generally regarded as one of his more successful books. As a polemicist, campaigner and protester he was prominent throughout the 1960s, publishing *An American Dream* (1965), *Why Are We in Vietnam?* (1967) and *Armies of the Night* (1968, winner of a National Book award and the Pulitzer Prize). Subsequent books include *The Executioner's Song* (1979, Pulitzer Prize) and *Harlot's Ghost* (1991), an account of the CIA from the end of World War II to the assassination of **John F Kennedy**. He published two biographical works in 1995, *Oswald's Tale*—a study of the life of **Lee Harvey Oswald**—and *Portrait of Picasso as a Young Man*. He has also been active as a screenwriter, film director and actor.

Maillol, Aristide Joseph Bonaventure 1861–1944 •*French sculptor*• Born in Banyuls-sur-mer, he studied at the École des Beaux-Arts in Paris, and spent some years designing tapestries. The latter half of his life was devoted to sculpting female nudes, such as the *Three Graces*, *Mediterranean*, *Crouching Woman* (c. 1901, Museum of Modern Art, New York) and *The Mountain* (1937), in a style of monumental simplicity and classical serenity.

Maiman, Theodore Harold 1927– •*US physicist who constructed the first working laser*• He was born in Los Angeles, and after military service in the US Navy, studied at the University of Colorado and Stanford. The maser (producing coherent microwave radiation) had been devised and constructed in 1953 by **Charles Townes** (and independently by **Nikolai Basov** and **Aleksandr Prokhorov** in the USSR in 1955). Maiman turned to the possibility of an optical maser, or laser (Light Amplification by Simulated Emission of Radiation), and constructed the first working laser in the Hughes laboratories in 1960. Lasers have found use in a variety of applications, including spectroscopy, surgical work (such as repair of retinal detachment in the eye), and in compact disk players. Maiman founded the Korad Corporation (1962) to build high-powered lasers and was a cofounder of the Laser Video Corporation (1972) to develop large-screen video displays.

Maimonides, Moses, *originally* **Moses ben Maimon** 1135–1204 •*Jewish philosopher*• Born in Córdoba, Spain (then ruled by the Moors), he studied Greek medicine and Aristotelian philosophy.

He settled in Cairo about 1165 and became physician to **Saladin**. The foremost figure of medieval Judaism, he wrote an important commentary in Hebrew on the Mishna (Jewish code of law), but his other main writings are in Arabic. His greatest work is the *Guide to the Perplexed* (1190), which argued for the reconciliation of Greek philosophy and Judaism. He had an enormous influence on a range of philosophers and traditions, Jewish, Muslim and Christian.

Mainbocher, *originally* **Main Rousseau Bocher** c. 1890–1976 •*US fashion designer*• He was born in Chicago, where he studied and worked. After World War I, he stayed on in Paris, eventually becoming a fashion artist with *Harper's Bazaar* and, later, editor of French *Vogue*. He started his couture house in Paris in 1930. One of his creations was the wedding dress of Mrs **Wallis Simpson**, the Duchess of Windsor (1937). He opened a salon for ready-to-wear clothes in New York in 1940, but returned to Europe in 1971.

Maintenon, Françoise d'Aubigné, Marquise de, *known as* **Madame de Maintenon** 1635–1719 •*French queen*• The second wife of **Louis XIV** and granddaughter of the Huguenot Théodore Agrippa d'Aubigné (1552–1630), she was born in Niort, Poitou. In 1652 she married the crippled poet **Paul Scarron**, whose death (1660) left her penniless. In 1669 she was appointed governess of the two illegitimate sons of her friend the Marquise de **Montespan** by Louis XIV, and she became the king's mistress. In 1674, with his help, she bought the estate and marquisate of Maintenon. After the death of Queen Maria Theresa in 1683, Louis secretly married Madame de Maintenon, and she was accused of influencing him, particularly over the persecution of Protestants after the revocation of the Edict of Nantes (1685). After Louis's death (1715), she retired to a home for poor noblewomen at Saint-Cyr.

Maitland, William, *known as* **Secretary Lethington** c. 1528–73 •*Scottish politician*• The son of Scottish lawyer and poet Sir Richard Maitland, in 1558 he became secretary of state to the queen-regent, **Mary of Guise**. He represented **Mary Queen of Scots** at the court of **Elizabeth I**, but aroused her hostility by his connivance in **David Rizzio**'s murder in 1566. He was also privy to the assassination of Lord **Darnley**. Accused of plotting against his colleagues, he was jailed in Edinburgh Castle and died in prison at Leith.

Major, John 1943– •*English Conservative statesman*• He was born in Merton, southwest London, the son of a trapeze performer, and educated at Rutlish Grammar School. He started a career in banking but his interest in politics grew and he eventually won a Commons seat, as Conservative Member of Parliament for Huntingdonshire, in 1979. He entered **Margaret Thatcher**'s government as a junior minister in 1981 and rose to become treasury chief secretary, under Chancellor **Nigel Lawson**, in 1987. Thereafter, having caught the eye of the prime minister, his progress was spectacular. In the summer of 1989 he became foreign secretary, and in the autumn of the same year chancellor of the exchequer when Lawson dramatically resigned. He remained loyal to Thatcher in the first round of the 1990 Conservative Party leadership election. When she stepped down, he ran successfully against **Michael Heseltine** and **Douglas Hurd** to become prime minister. Despite the country's deepening recession and Labour's improving showing in the opinion polls, he remained in power after the 1992 general election. However, when his party succumbed to the Labour landslide victory of 1997, Major immediately resigned the leadership. He published his autobiography in 1999 and stepped down as a Member of Parliament at the 2001 general election.

Makarios III, *originally* **Mihail Christodoulou Mouskos** 1913–77 •*Cypriot Orthodox archbishop and statesman*• Born in Pano Panayia, he was ordained as a priest in 1946, elected Bishop of Kition in 1948, and became archbishop and primate in 1950. Suspected of collaborating with anti-British (EOKA) guerrilla forces, he was exiled to the Seychelles by the colonial government, later lived in Athens, but returned after a 1959 agreement that gave Cyprus independence and made Makarios head of state as the first president of the Republic of Cyprus. He had to cope with a restive Turkish Muslim minority, fellow bishops who criticized his dual role, and a small but active Communist presence, which Makarios was not above using for his own ends. A short-lived coup removed him briefly from leadership in 1974. On his death the posts of archbishop and head of state were separated.

Makarova, Natalia 1940– •*Russian dancer*• Born in Leningrad (now St Petersburg), she studied there, joining the Kirov in 1959 and becoming one of their star dancers. She defected to the West in 1970, and established herself with American Ballet Theater in New York and often guested with the Royal Ballet, Covent Garden and other international companies. While specializing in the classics, she also created roles for contemporary choreographers like **Antony Tudor**, **Glen Tetley** and **George Balanchine**. Her work as producer includes *La Bayadère* (1980) for American Ballet Theater, and *The Kingdom of the Shades* (1985) and *Swan Lake* (1988), both for London Festival Ballet.

Makeba, Miriam 1932– •*US singer*• She was born in Johannesburg, South Africa, but was exiled because of her political views. After settling in the US she became widely known in the 1960s as "the empress of African song," and played a vital role in introducing the sounds and rhythms of traditional African song to the West. Her marriage to the militant black leader **Stokely Carmichael** in the late 1960s effectively ended her career in the US, as she was declared persona non grata; she moved to Guinea and virtually disappeared from the international concert arena, emerging only to take part in special, politically oriented events. Her marriage ended and she reemerged in the 1980s as awareness of the political situation in South Africa grew. In 1990 she returned to South Africa after 30 years in exile and resumed her recording career.

Makhmalbaf, Mohsen 1957– •*Iranian film director*• Born in Tehran, as a young man he was a militant Islamic opponent of the Shah, and was imprisoned and tortured for stabbing a policeman—an incident recreated in *A Moment of Innocence* (1996) (which features both Makhmalbaf and the policeman himself). *Once Upon a Time, Cinema* (1992) is a phantasmagoric history of Iranian film, while *Gabbeh* (1996) creates its own legendary world to celebrate the skills and traditions of carpet weavers. *Kandahar* (2001) is a sumptuously shot indictment of the repressive policies of the Taliban regime in Afghanistan.

Malachy, St, *also called* **St Maol Maedoc** c. 1094–1148 •*Irish prelate and reformer*• Born in Armagh, he became abbot of Bangor (1121), Bishop of Connor (1125) and, in 1134, Archbishop of Armagh. He substituted Roman for Celtic liturgy, and renewed the use of the sacraments. In 1139 he went to Rome, visiting St **Bernard** at Clairvaux. On his return (1142), he introduced the Cistercian Order into Ireland. In 1148 he once more went to France, and died at Clairvaux in St Bernard's arms. He was canonized in 1190—the first papal canonization of an Irishman. His feast day is November 3.

Malamud, Bernard 1914–86 •*US novelist*• He was born in Brooklyn, New York, and educated at Columbia University, then taught at Oregon State University (1949–61) and Bennington College (1961–86). One of the leading US writers of the latter half of the 20th century, he wrote fiction that mingled mysticism, pessimism and gentle humor, and drew on the idiom of Jewish America. *The Natural* (1952), his first novel, used baseball as an extended metaphor for life, following the fading career of a once-promising big-hitter. *The Assistant* (1957) was darker in mood, but had a warm critical reception. In *A New Life* (1961) he abandoned the close urban setting of his previous novels for the mountainous western US, where Seymour Levin arrives at a small college to teach and analyze happiness. *The Fixer* (1966), set in czarist Russia, is Malamud's bleakest and most potent book. Later novels include *Dubin's Lives* (1979) and *God's Grace* (1982). He was also an accomplished short-story writer. He won the National Book award twice, in 1959 and 1967, and the Pulitzer Prize in 1967.

“ ”

There comes a time in a man's life when to get where he has to go—if there are no doors or windows he walks through a wall.

1973 ***Rembrandt's Hat***, *"Man in the Drawer."*

Malan, Daniel F(rançois) 1874–1959 •*South African politician*• Born in Riebeek West, Cape Province, he was educated at the

University of Utrecht. On his return to South Africa in 1905, he became a predikant of the Dutch Reformed Church, but after 10 years abandoned his clerical career to become a newspaper editor. He became a member of parliament in 1918, and in 1924 in the **Hertzog** Nationalist-Labour government he was minister of the interior, of education and of public health. He introduced measures strengthening the Nationalist position—in particular, that of making Afrikaans an official language. He was leader of the Opposition (1934–39, 1940–48), and on becoming prime minister and minister for external affairs in 1948, embarked on the hotly controversial policies of apartheid, dividing the country into white, black and colored zones. The apartheid legislation, which involved strongly contested constitutional changes, was met by nonviolent civil disobedience at home and vigorous criticism abroad. Malan resigned from the premiership in 1954.

Malatesta, Enrico 1853–1932 •*Italian anarchist*• Born in Campania into a wealthy family, he studied medicine at the University of Naples but was expelled for encouraging student unrest. To demonstrate his beliefs, he gave away his personal wealth and worked as an electrician in cities around Europe, at the same time preaching anarchism and spending numerous periods in prison. He settled in London in 1900, advocating peaceful opposition to authority. He returned to Italy in 1913 and died peacefully 19 years later.

Malaurie, Jean 1922– •*French explorer and anthropogeographer*• Born in Mainz, Germany, he studied in Paris and began his career as a research fellow and later Professor in Arctic Geomorphology and Anthropogeography at the École des Hautes Études en Sciences Sociales, Paris, where he founded the Centre for Arctic Studies (1957–). He has led over 30 scientific expeditions to the Arctic, made several documentary films on the Inuit, and became the first European to reach the geomagnetic North Pole (1951).

Malcolm I d. 954 •*King of Scotland*• He was the son of Donald II, and succeeded his cousin, Constantine II, in 943. He annexed Moray, but lost Northumbria, and was killed near Dunnottar.

Malcolm II c. 954–1034 •*King of Scotland*• He was the son of Kenneth II, and became king in 1005 after his slaughter of Kenneth III. He won a great victory over the Northumbrians at Carham (1018) and secured Strathclyde, but had to submit to the English king **Knut Sveinsson** (Canute) in 1032. He was succeeded by his grandson **Duncan I**.

Malcolm III, *called* **Canmore**, *from Gaelic* **Ceann-mor ("Great Head")** c. 1031–93 •*King of Scotland*• He was a child when his father, King **Duncan I**, was killed by **Macbeth** (1040). In 1057, after Macbeth was killed, Malcolm became king of all Scotland. In 1069 he married **Margaret**, sister of **Edgar the Ætheling**. He invaded England five times (1061–1093), and was killed at Alnwick. He left five sons, of whom four succeeded him, Duncan, Edgar, **Alexander** and **David**.

Malcolm IV, *called* **the Maiden** c. 1141–65 •*King of Scotland*• He was the grandson and successor (1153) of **David I**. Compelled to restore the northern English counties to **Henry II** in return for the earldom and honor of Huntingdon (1157), he served on Henry's expedition to Toulouse (1159), and was then knighted. Malcolm continued to implement David I's Normanizing policies, despite native opposition. His byname was coined in the 15th century, in recognition of his well-attested reputation for chastity.

Malcolm X, *originally* **Malcolm Little**, *Muslim name* **el-Hajj Malik el-Shabazz** 1925–65 •*US Black Nationalist leader*• Born in Omaha, Nebraska, the son of a radical Baptist minister, he was raised in Lansing, Michigan, and Boston. After an adolescence of violence, narcotics and petty crime, he came under the influence of **Elijah Muhammad** while in prison for burglary, changed his name, and after his release in 1952 became Muhammad's chief disciple within the Black Muslims; he greatly expanded the organization's following and became the most effective spokesman for Black Power. In 1963 Malcolm was suspended from the Nation of Islam after disagreements with Muhammad, and founded the Organization for Afro-American Unity, dedicated to the alliance of American Blacks and other nonwhite peoples. In the last year of his life, following a pilgrimage to Mecca, Malcolm announced his conversion to orthodox Islam and put forward the belief in the possible brotherhood between Blacks and whites. In 1965 Malcolm was killed in Harlem by Black Muslim assassins who retaliated against the man they viewed as a traitor.

Malebranche, Nicolas 1638–1715 •*French philosopher*• Born in Paris, he studied theology and joined the Catholic community of Oratorians (1660), but became interested in philosophy, particularly the work of **René Descartes**. His own major work, *De la recherche de la vérité* (1674, Eng trans *Search for the Truth*), draws on Descartes's dualism of mind and body but explains all causal interaction between them by a theory of "occasionalism" (divine intervention, governing our bodily movements and all physical events), and argues as a corollary that "we see all things in God" since external objects cannot act directly upon us.

Malenkov, Giorgi Maksimilianovich 1901–79 •*Soviet politician*• Born in Orenburg in Central Russia, he joined the Communist Party in 1920, began working for the Central Committee in Moscow in 1925 and was quickly selected by **Stalin** to serve as his personal secretary. He was involved in the collectivization of agriculture and Stalin's purges of the 1930s. He was appointed deputy prime minister in 1946 and made a full member of the politburo, and on Stalin's death in 1953 took over as de facto party leader. This post, however, was soon assumed by **Nikita Khrushchev** and a power struggle ensued. In 1955 Malenkov was forced to resign as prime minister. He was succeeded by Marshal **Nikolai Bulganin**.

Malesherbes, Chrétien (Guillaume de Lamoignon) de 1721–94 •*French statesman*• He was born in Paris. In 1744 he became a counsellor of the Parlement of Paris, and in 1750 he was made chief censor of the press. On **Louis XVI**'s accession (1774) he was made secretary of state for the royal household. He brought about prison and legal reforms alongside **Anne Robert Jacques Turgot**'s economic improvements, but resigned on Turgot's dismissal (1776). Under the Convention he went to Paris to conduct the king's defense. Despite his integrity and reforming zeal, he was mistrusted as an aristocrat during the Revolution, arrested as a Royalist in 1794, and guillotined.

Malevich, Kasimir Severinovich 1878–1935 •*Russian painter and designer*• Born and trained near Kiev, he worked in Moscow from c. 1904. Around 1910 his work began to show Cubist and Futurist influences; however, he was above all interested in developing a totally nonobjective art, and in Moscow c. 1913 he launched Suprematism, a movement dedicated to the expression in painting of the absolute purity of geometrical forms. The austerity of the earliest Suprematist works had given way by 1917 to less rigid compositions, with a greater color range and a suggestion of three-dimensional space; in 1918–19, however, he returned to his early ideals with the *White on White* series.

Malherbe, François de 1555–1628 •*French poet*• Born in Caen, he ingratiated himself with **Henry IV**, and received a pension. He founded a literary tradition, "Enfin Malherbe vint," and led his countrymen to disdain the richly colored verses of **Pierre de Ronsard**, and to adopt a clear, refined, but prosaic style.

Malinovsky, Rodion Yakovlevich 1898–1967 •*Russian soldier*• He was born in Odessa. He fought in World War I and joined the Red Army after the Revolution (1917). A major general at the time of the Nazi invasion in 1941, he commanded the forces which liberated Rostov, Kharkov and the Dnieper basin and led the Russian advance on Budapest and into Austria (1944–45). He took a leading part in the Manchurian campaign against Japan. In October 1957 he succeeded Marshal **Georgi Zhukov** as **Nikita Khrushchev**'s Minister of Defense.

Malinowski, Bronisław (Kasper) 1884–1942 •*British anthropologist, a founder of modern social anthropology*• Born in Kraków, Poland, he studied physics and mathematics at the Jagellonian University, and went on to study psychology under **Wilhelm Max Wundt** at Leipzig, and sociology under **Edvard Westermarck** in London. In 1914 he left on a research assignment to Australia, but with the outbreak of war was partially confined to the Trobriand Islands, off the eastern tip of New Guinea. Returning to London in 1920, he was appointed in 1927 to the first chair in social anthropology at the London School of Economics. In 1938 he moved to the

US, where he taught at Yale and undertook field research in Mexico. He was the pioneer of "participant observation" as a method of fieldwork, and his works on the Trobriand Islanders, including *Crime and Custom in Savage Society* (1926) and *Sex and Repression in Savage Society* (1927), set new standards for ethnographic description. A major proponent of functionalism in anthropology, he set out his views in *A Scientific Theory of Culture* (1944).

Malkovich, John Gavin 1953– •*US actor and director*• Born in Christopher, Illinois, he studied at Eastern Illinois and Illinois State Universities, and cofounded the Steppenwolf Theater Company, Chicago, in 1976. He received an Academy Award nomination for Best Supporting Actor for *Places in the Heart* (1984), and went on to star in films such as *Empire of the Sun* (1987), *Dangerous Liaisons* (1989) and *Shadow of the Vampire* (2000). The surreal comedy *Being John Malkovich* (1999), about Malkovich's mind in the grip of an unemployed puppeteer, was a hit for the director Spike Jonze. Malkovich directed *The Dancer Upstairs* in 2000.

Mallarmé, Stéphane 1842–98 •*French Symbolist poet*• Born in Paris, he taught English in various schools in Paris and elsewhere, and visited England on several occasions. In prose and verse he was a leader of the Symbolist school. *L'Après-midi d'un faune* ("A Faun's Afternoon"), which inspired the prelude by **Debussy**, is one of his best-known poems. His *Les Dieux antiques* (1880, "The Ancient Gods"), *Poésies* (1899) and *Vers et prose* (1893) were other works admired by the "decadents." In the second half of the 20th century he was much admired by the structuralists.

" "

Il n'y que la Beauté—et elle n'a qu'une expression parfaite, la Poésie.
There is only beauty—and it has only one perfect expression, poetry.
1867 Letter to Cazalis.

Malle, Louis 1932–95 •*French film director*• Born in Thumières to a wealthy sugar-producing family, he attended the Institut des Hautes Études Cinématographiques and began his career working as an assistant of the explorer **Jacques Cousteau**; they shared an Academy Award for the underwater documentary *Le monde du silence* (1956, *The Silent World*). Malle made his directorial debut with the thriller *L'ascenseur pour l'échafaud* (1957, *Frantic*) and was associated with the nouvelle vague through innovative features like *Les Amants* (1958, *The Lovers*) and *Zazie dans le métro* (1960, *Zazie in the Underground*). Interested in social issues, world affairs and the problems of adolescence, he pursued his personal vision of cinema with equal success on both sides of the Atlantic. His later films include *Le souffle au cœur* (1971, *Murmur of the Heart*) and *Au revoir les enfants* (1987, "Goodbye Children"). He was married to US actress **Candice Bergen** from 1980 until his death.

Mallowan, Sir Max Edgar Lucien 1904–78 •*English archaeologist*• Born in London, he studied classics at New College, Oxford (1921–25). His apprenticeship in field archaeology was served with **Leonard Woolley** at Ur in Mesopotamia (1925–31), and it was at Ur that he met the novelist **Agatha Christie**, whom he married in 1930. He made excavations for the British Museum, London, at Arpachiyah near Nineveh (1932–33), and in Syria at Chagar Bazar (1935–36) and Tell Brak (1937–38). His later excavations were principally at Nimrud, the ancient capital of Assyria (1949–60), described in *Nimrud and Its Remains* (1970).

Malmesbury, William of *See* **William of Malmesbury**

Malone, Edmund 1741–1812 •*Irish editor of Shakespeare*• Born in Dublin, he graduated from Trinity College and was called to the Irish bar in 1767, but from 1777 devoted himself to literary work in London. His 11-volume edition of Shakespeare (1790) was warmly received. He had been one of the first to express his disbelief in **Thomas Chatterton**'s Rowley poems, and in 1796 he denounced the Shakespeare forgeries of **William Henry Ireland**. He left behind a large mass of materials for "The Variorum Shakespeare," edited in 1821 by James Boswell the younger.

Malone, Karl 1963– •*US basketball player*• Born in Summerfield, Louisiana, he was selected for the Utah Jazz in 1985 and quickly emerged as one of the best power forwards of all time. Nicknamed "The Mailman," by the end of the 2003–04 season he was ranked the NBA leader in free throws made (9,619), second in career points (36,374) and second in field goals made (13,335). He was a member of both the 1992 and 1996 Olympic teams and was twice named the NBA's Most Valuable Player (1997 and 1999). In 1996 the NBA selected him as one of the 50 Greatest Players in NBA History.

Malone, Moses 1955– •*US basketball player*• Born in Petersburg, Virginia, he began his 19-year professional career as a center with the Utah Stars. Subsequently he played for the St Louis Spirit (1975–76), the Buffalo Braves (1976–77), the Houston Rockets (1976–82), the Philadelphia 76ers (1982–86 and 1993–94), the Washington Bullets (1986–88), the Atlanta Hawks (1988–91), the Milwaukee Bucks (1991–93) and the San Antonio Spurs (1994–95). He was named Most Valuable Player in the NBA three times (1979 and 1982–83) and led the NBA in rebounding six times. His other achievements included making a record 8,531 free throws (broken by **Karl Malone** in 2001) and holding a single-game record of 15 offensive rebounds in playoffs (1977).

Malory, Sir Thomas d. 1471 •*English writer*• In **William Caxton**'s preface to Malory's masterpiece, *Le morte d'Arthur*, it states that Malory was a knight, that he finished his work in the ninth year of the reign of **Edward IV** (1469–70), and that he "reduced" it from some French book. It is probable that he was the Sir Thomas Malory of Newbold Revel, Warwickshire, whose quarrels with a neighboring priory and (probably) Lancastrian politics caused his imprisonment. Of Caxton's black-letter folio only two copies now exist. An independent manuscript was discovered at Winchester in 1934. *Le morte d'Arthur* is a prose romance, which gives epic unity to the whole mass of French Arthurian romance. **Tennyson** and many others took their inspiration from it.

Malouf, David 1934– •*Australian novelist and librettist*• He was born in Brisbane. A full-time writer since 1978, he has written some verse and short stories, but is best known for his novels, beginning with *Johnno* (1975). His second novel, *An Imaginary Life*, received wide acclaim and went on to win the 1979 New South Wales Premier's Literary award. Other novels are *Harland's Half Acre* (1984), *Great World* (1991) and *Remembering Babylon* (1993, Dublin Literary award). He is interested in opera as a vehicle of expression, and has written librettos for **Richard Meale**'s *Voss* (1982), from **Patrick White**'s novel loosely based on Australian explorer Leichhardt, and the same composer's *Mer de glace*. A later collaboration was with composer **Michael Berkeley** in *Baa Baa Black Sheep* (1993). Later works include *Untold Tales* (1999) and a collection of stories, *Dream Stuff* (2000).

Malpighi, Marcello 1628–94 •*Italian anatomist and microscopist*• Born near Bologna, where he studied philosophy and medicine, he later became professor at the Universities of Pisa, Messina and Bologna (1666), and from 1691 served as chief physician to Pope **Innocent XII**. He conducted a remarkable series of microscopic studies of the structure of the liver, lungs, skin, spleen, glands and brain, gave the first full account of an insect, the silkworm moth, and investigated muscular cells.

Malraux, André 1901–76 •*French writer*• Born in Paris, he studied Asian languages and spent much time in China, where he worked for the Guomindang (Kuomintang) and was active in the 1927 revolution. He also fought as a pilot with the Republican forces in the Spanish Civil War, and in World War II he escaped from a prisoner-of-war camp to join the French Resistance movement. He later served in a number of postwar ministerial positions. He is best known for his novels, which are a dramatic meditation on human destiny and are highly colored by his personal experience of war, revolution and resistance to tyranny. Among them are *Les Conquérants* (1928, Eng trans *The Conquerors*, 1929), *La condition humaine* (1933, Eng trans *Man's Fate*, 1934, winner of the Prix Goncourt) and *L'Espoir* (1937, Eng trans *Man's Hope*, 1938). He also wrote books on art and museums.

Malthus, Thomas Robert 1766–1834 •*English economist and clergyman*• Born near Dorking, Surrey, he was educated at Jesus College, Cambridge, of which he was elected a Fellow in 1793, and in 1797 he was appointed curate at Albury, Surrey. In 1798 he published anonymously his *Essay on the Principle of Population*, with a greatly enlarged and altered edition in 1807. In it he maintained that the optimistic hopes of **William Godwin** and **Jean Jacques Rousseau** are rendered baseless by the natural tendency of population to increase faster than the means of subsistence. (Malthus gives no sanction to the theories and practices currently known as Malthusianism.) The problem had been handled by many writers, but Malthus crystallized their viewss, and presented them in systematic form with elaborate proofs derived from history, and called for positive action to cut the birth rate. His other works included *An Inquiry into the Nature and Progress of Rent* (1815), largely anticipating **David Ricardo**, and *Principles of Political Economy* (1820). **Charles Darwin** read Malthus in 1838, and was greatly influenced by him.

" "

The perpetual struggle for room and food.

1798 ***An Essay on the Principle of Population****, chapter 3.*

Malus, Étienne Louis 1775–1812 •*French physicist*• Born in Paris, he carried out research in optics, discovering the polarization of light by reflection in 1808. This phenomenon provided a convincing demonstration of the transverse nature of light. Also in 1808 he discovered a fundamental theorem in geometrical optics, which generalizes **Christiaan Huygens**'s construction to determine the position of a wavefront after light originating from a point source has been reflected or refracted.

Malvern, 1st Viscount *See* **Huggins, Godfrey Martin**

Mamet, David Alan 1947– •*US dramatist, screenwriter and director*• Born in Chicago, he graduated from Goddard College, Vermont, and studied acting in New York. His best-known plays, including *American Buffalo* (1975), *Glengarry Glen Ross* (1983, Pulitzer Prize, filmed 1992), *Speed-the-Plow* (1988) and *Oleanna* (1992), address the psychological and ethical issues that confront modern urban society. Other plays include *Sexual Perversity in Chicago*, (1978), *A Life in the Theater* (1978), *Edmond* (1982), and *The Shawl* (1985). He has translated works by **Chekhov**, and his screenplays include a new adaptation of *The Postman Always Rings Twice* (1981), *Vanya on 42nd Street* (1994), based on Chekhov's *Uncle Vanya*, and *Wag the Dog* (1997). He wrote and directed *House of Games* (1987), a look at seedy professional gambling, and published essay collections such as *Writing in Restaurants* (1986). He won his third Obie award for *The Cryptogram* (1994).

Mamluks •*Egyptian sultans*• They are commonly divided into the two lines of Kipchak (Bahris, 1250–1382) and Circassian (Burjis, 1382–1517) origin. Their name derives from that originally applied to the group from which they were drawn, a privileged caste of military slaves recruited from various non-Muslim peoples (especially Turks and Caucasians) and who, as converts, served in the armies of most Islamic powers from the 9th century onward. In 1250 the Ayyubid sultan of Egypt, Turan-Shah, was murdered by a group of Turkish Kipchak mamluks belonging to his military household, who later enthroned one of their number, thus inaugurating the *dawlat al-Atrak* ("state of the Turks"). The Mamluks defeated the Mongol invaders of Syria at 'Ayn Jalut and Hims (1260) and in 1291 captured Acre, crushing the crusaders' kingdom. In the 15th century the Mamluks were decisively defeated by **Selim I**, who incorporated Egypt into the Ottoman Empire (1516–17), although the Mamluk class retained a privileged status under Ottoman rule until it was finally suppressed by **Mehemet 'Ali** in 1812.

Manasseh Ben Israel 1604–57 •*Dutch Jewish scholar*• Born in Lisbon, Portugal, he was taken early to Amsterdam. He became chief rabbi there at the age of 18, and set up the first printing press in Holland (1626). From 1655 to 1657 he was in England, securing from **Cromwell** the readmission of the Jews to Great Britain. He wrote important works in Hebrew, Spanish and Latin, and in English a *Humble Address* to Cromwell, *A Declaration*, and *Vindiciae Judaeorum* (1656, "Vindication of the Jews").

Manchester, William Raymond 1922–2004 •*US novelist and contemporary historian*• Born in Attleboro, Massachusetts, he began his career as a reporter and correspondent in the Middle East, India and Southeast Asia. His book *The Death of a President* (1967), written at the behest of the Kennedy family, was a landmark in reportage and sold millions but has subsequently been superseded as new evidence on the assassination of President **John F Kennedy** has emerged. Among his other major works are *The Arms of Krupp* (1968) and the biographies *American Caesar: Douglas MacArthur, 1880–1964* (1978) and *The Last Lion: Winston Spencer Churchill* (2 vols, 1983–87).

Mandela, Nelson Rolihlahla 1918– •*South African lawyer, statesman and Nobel Prize winner*• He was born in Umtata. Educated at Ft Hare College (1938–40), he practiced law in Johannesburg before joining the African National Congress (ANC) in 1944 and founding the Congress Youth League. For the next 20 years he was at the forefront of Black opposition to apartheid, being "banned" (1956–61) and sentenced to life imprisonment for his leadership of the ANC. From his prison cell on Robben Island, Mandela became a symbol of Black resistance to apartheid, acquiring a charisma that was enhanced by his refusal to enter into any kind of deal with the authorities. During the 1970s and 1980s, Mandela grew into an international figure and the focus of an increasingly powerful international campaign for his release, in which his second wife, **Winnie Mandela** (married to him in 1958), played a leading part. The liberalizing measures of **F W de Klerk** (president from 1989) began the process of dismantling apartheid; within months of his election, de Klerk visited Mandela in prison, and finally ordered his release in February 1990, after lifting the ban on the ANC. In 1991 Mandela was elected president of the ANC (his friend **Oliver Tambo** was elected chairman), and entered into talks with de Klerk about the country's future. In 1993 he was awarded the Nobel Peace Prize jointly with de Klerk for their work in the process of reform. On May 10, 1994, he was inaugurated as South Africa's first Black president. Mandela's marriage to Winnie came under increasing strain as a result of her controversial activities and associations, and they were separated in 1992 and divorced in 1996. His term as president ended in 1999 and he was succeeded as party leader and president by **Thabo Mbeki**. His autobiography, *Long Walk to Freedom*, was published in 1994.

" "

We are not a political party. We have not changed at all. On the contrary, the ANC is a Government in waiting.

1991 Interviewed for BBC TV, February.

Mandela, (Nomzano) Winnie (Winifred), *Xhosa surname* **Madikizela** 1934– •*South African civil rights activist*• Born in Bizana, she married **Nelson Mandela** in 1958, and became active in his work for the African National Congress (ANC). When he was put in prison by the South African government (1964–90), she too was banned, imprisoned (1969–70), and forced into internal exile (1977–85). In 1985 she returned to Soweto and became involved in the militant politics of the township. Throughout Nelson Mandela's incarceration (1964–90), she campaigned ceaselessly for Black rights on his behalf and for his release. Her popularity declined in 1988–89 when her bodyguards were implicated in the kidnapping, beating and murder of a Black youth. She was convicted of the kidnapping alone but her six-year sentence was commuted to a £9,000 fine. Separated in 1992 and divorced in 1996, she retained her position as president of the ANC Women's League, winning reelection in 1997.

Mandelson, Peter Benjamin 1953– •*English politician*• Born in London, and educated at St Catherine's College, Oxford, he was the Labour Party's director of campaigns and communications in 1985–90 and became Member of Parliament for Hartlepool in 1992. He was one of the chief strategists behind the New Labour victory in the general election of 1997 and subsequently served as secretary of state for trade and industry (1998) and for Northern Ireland (1999–2001). He resigned from both posts in circumstances of political scandal, the first involving alleged financial irregularities and the second accusations of cronyism in the issuing of British passports. In both instances Mandelson denied improper behavior on his part.

Mandelstam, Osip Yemilevich 1891–1938 •*Russian poet, critic and translator*• Born of Jewish parents in Warsaw, he grew up in St

Petersburg and attended the University of Heidelberg. A classicist whose Russian "sounds like Latin," he had a great love of Greek poetry. Three books of poems appeared during his lifetime—*Kamen* (1913, Eng trans *Stone*, 1981), *Tristia* (1922) and *Stikhotvoreniya* (1928, "Poems"). He is regarded by some as the greatest Russian poet of the century. Arrested, exiled and rearrested, he died on his way to one of **Stalin**'s camps.

Mandeville, Bernard 1670–1733 *•British satirist•* Born in Dort, the Netherlands, he received his MD at Leiden in 1691, then practiced medicine in London. He is known as the author of the satirical verse, *The Fable of the Bees* (1723, originally *The Grumbling Hive*, 1705). In it he argued that "private vices are public benefits," and that every species of virtue is basically some form of gross selfishness. The book was widely attacked. He also wrote several works arguing for an improvement in the status of women, including *A Modest Defence of Public Stews* (1724), on the condition of brothels.

Mandeville, Sir Jehan de or **John**, *also spelled* **Maundeville** or **Maundevylle** 14th century *•Unknown compiler of a travel book•* This writer compiled a famous book of travels, *The Voyage and Travels of Sir John Mandeville, Knight*. The book was published apparently in 1366, and was soon translated from the French into all European languages. It may have been written by a physician, Jehan de Bourgogne, otherwise Jehan à la Barbe, who died in Liège in 1372; some, however, attribute it to Jean d'Outremeuse, a Frenchman. "Mandeville" claims to have traveled through Turkey, Persia, Syria, Arabia, North Africa and India, but much of the book is a compilation from various literary sources.

Manet, Édouard 1832–83 *•French painter•* Born in Paris, he was originally intended for a legal career. Nevertheless, between 1850 and 1856 he studied under Thomas Couture (1815–79), and his *Spanish Guitar Player* was awarded an honorable mention at the 1861 Salon. Pursuing official recognition, he entered his *Déjeuner sur l'herbe* for the Salon of 1863, but it scandalized the jury with its portrayal of a nude female with clothed male companions, and was rejected. This was followed by the acceptance of his *Olympia* in 1865, but, being a stark depiction of a woman obviously modeled by a prostitute, it elicited a similar outcry from the public. Manet was influenced by conventional artists: *Olympia* owes a great deal to the nudes of **Giorgione**, **Titian** and **Raphael**, but his adherence to the advice of **Gustave Courbet** in always selecting subjects from contemporary life marked him out from the older Salon artists. In the 1870s he came under the influence of the impressionists and, in particular, of **Monet** while painting at Argenteuil, and his technique became more spontaneous. He never exhibited with the group, but became a father figure to them because of his stand against the conventions of the Salon. His last major work was *Un bar aux Folies-Bergère* (1881–82). In that year, official recognition finally arrived—he was appointed Chevalier of the Legion of Honor—but he died an embittered man.

Manetho 3rd century BC *•Egyptian historian•* He was high priest of Heliopolis. He wrote in Greek a history of the 30 dynasties from mythical times to 323 BC, of which only portions have been preserved in the works of Julius Africanus (AD 300), **Eusebius of Caesarea**, and George Syncellus (AD 800).

Manichaeus or **Mani** c. 215–76 AD *•Persian religious leader•* Born in Ecbatana, he was the founder of the heretical sect of Manichaeism. About AD 245 he began to proclaim his new religion at the court of the Persian king Sapor (Shahpur) I. He traveled widely, but eventually King Bahram I abandoned him to his Zoroastrian enemies, who crucified him.

Mankiewicz, Herman Jacob 1897–1953 *•US screenwriter•* He was born in New York. A member of the US Marine Corps, he later worked in Europe for the Red Cross Press Service, as **Isadora Duncan**'s publicity manager and as Berlin correspondent for the *Chicago Tribune*. Returning to the US in 1922, he was assistant drama editor for the *New York Times* (1922–26) and wrote his first screenplay for *The Road to Mandalay* (1926). He also became the producer of a number of films, including the **Marx Brothers**' comedies *Horse Feathers* (1932) and *Duck Soup* (1933). His most significant contribution to the cinema came as the cowriter of **Orson Welles**'s *Citizen Kane* (1941), for which he received an Academy Award. He was the brother of **Joseph L Mankiewicz**.

Mankiewicz, Joseph Leo 1909–93 *•US filmmaker•* Born in Wilkes-Barre, Pennsylvania, he was a reporter before joining Paramount Pictures as a junior writer in 1929. As a screenwriter, he collaborated on such films as *If I Had a Million* (1932) and *Manhattan Melodrama* (1934). Under contract to MGM from 1933, he produced sophisticated comedies like *The Philadelphia Story* (1940) and *Woman of the Year* (1942). He made his directorial debut with *Dragonwyck* (1946) and won Academy Awards for Direction and Screenwriting on both *A Letter to Three Wives* (1949) and *All About Eve* (1950).

Mankowitz, (Cyril) Wolf 1924–98 *•English author, playwright and antique dealer•* He was born in Bethnal Green, London, and studied at Cambridge. An authority on **Josiah Wedgwood**, he published several books on pottery and porcelain. Other publications include the novels *Make Me an Offer* (1952), *A Kid for Two Farthings* (1953) and *A Night With Casanova* (1991), and a collection of short stories, *The Mendelman Fire* (1957). Among his plays is *The Bespoke Overcoat* (1954), and his films, *The Millionairess* (1960), *The Long, the Short, and the Tall* (1961), *Casino Royale* (1967) and *The Hebrew Lesson* (1972), as well as his documentary on Yiddish cinema, *Almonds and Raisins* (1984).

Manley, Michael Norman 1924–97 *•Jamaican politician•* Born in Kingston, the son of **Norman Manley**, he served in the Royal Canadian Air Force in World War II, and then studied at the London School of Economics (1945–49). He spent some time in journalism in Britain before returning to Jamaica. He became a leader of the National Workers' Union in the 1950s, sat in the Senate (1962–67) and was then elected to the House of Representatives. He became leader of the People's National Party (PNP) in 1969 and prime minister in 1972. He embarked on a radical, socialist program, cooling relations with the US, and despite rising unemployment was reelected in 1976. He was decisively defeated in 1980 and 1983 but returned to power in 1989, with a much more moderate policy stance. Poor health forced him to resign in 1992.

Manley, Norman Washington 1893–1969 *•Jamaican politician•* He was born in Kingston. He studied law, was called to the bar and in 1938 won fame by successfully defending his cousin, and political opponent, **Alexander Bustamante**, who was then an active trade unionist, on a charge of sedition. In the same year Manley founded the People's National Party (PNP) and in 1955, seven years before Jamaica achieved full independence, became prime minister. He handed over leadership of the PNP to his son **Michael Manley** in 1969.

Mann, Heinrich 1871–1950 *•German novelist•* He was born in Lübeck, the brother of **Thomas Mann**. He began to be described as the German **Zola** for his ruthless exposure of pre-1914 German society in *Im Schlaraffenland* (1901, Eng trans *Berlin, the Land of Cockaigne*, 1925), and the trilogy describing the three classes of Kaiser **Wilhelm II**'s empire, *Die Armen* (1917, "The Poor"), *Der Untertan* (1918, "The Subject") and *Der Kopf* (1929, "The Head"). He is best known for the macabre, expressionist novel, *Professor Unrat* (1905, "Professor Garbage"), describing the moral degradation of a once outwardly respectable schoolmaster, which was translated and filmed as *The Blue Angel* (1932). He lived in France (1933–40) and then escaped to the US. Other works include a remarkable autobiography, *Ein Zeitalter wird besichtigt* (1945–46, "Exposition of an Era").

Mann, Horace 1796–1859 *•US educationist•* Born in Franklin, Massachusetts, he entered the Massachusetts legislature in 1827, and was president of the state senate (1827–37). As secretary of the Massachusetts Board of Education (1837–48), he improved and reorganized the public school system and established the basis for universal, nonsectarian public education. His call for free public education as a bulwark of democracy had a national influence. He became a member of the House of Representatives (1848–53), and president of Antioch College, Ohio (1852–59). He is regarded as the "father of American public education."

Mann, Thomas 1875–1955 *•German novelist and Nobel Prize winner•* He was born in Lübeck. His older brother was **Heinrich**

Mann, also a novelist, and his mother was a talented musician. At the age of 19, without completing school, he settled with his mother in Munich, and after a spell at the university joined his brother in Italy, where he wrote his early masterpiece, *Buddenbrooks: Verfall einer Familie* (1901, Eng trans *Buddenbrooks: The Decline of a Family,* 1924), the saga of a family like his own, tracing its decline through four generations as business acumen gives way to artistic sensibilities. On his return to Munich he became a reader for the satirical literary magazine *Simplicissimus*, which published many of his early, remarkable short stories. The novelettes *Tonio Kröger* (1902), *Tristan* (1903) and *Der Tod in Venedig* (1913, Eng trans *Death in Venice*, 1925) deal with the problem of the artist's salvation; in the last of these, the subject of an opera by **Benjamin Britten** (1973) and a film by **Luchino Visconti** (1971), a successful writer dies on the brink of perverted eroticism. World War I precipitated a quarrel between the two novelist brothers, with Thomas's *Betrachtungen eines Unpolitischen* (1918, Eng trans *Reflections of a Nonpolitical Man*, 1983) revealing his militant German patriotism, already a feature of his essay on **Frederick the Great**, and a distrust of political ideologies, including the radicalism of his brother. *Der Zauberberg* (1924, Eng trans *The Magic Mountain*, 1927), won him the Nobel Prize for literature in 1929, and in the same year, Mann delivered a speech against the rising Nazis and in 1930 exposed Italian fascism in *Mario und der Zauberer* (1930, Eng trans *Mario and the Magician*, 1930). He left Germany for Switzerland after 1933 and in 1936 delivered an address for **Freud**'s eightieth birthday. He settled in the US in 1936 and wrote a novel on a visit to **Goethe** by an old love, Charlotte Buff, *Lotte in Weimar* (1939). During World War II, he delivered anti-**Hitler** broadcasts to Germany, which were collected at the end of the war. In 1947 he returned to Switzerland. His greatest work, a modern version of the medieval legend *Doktor Faustus* (1947), combines art and politics in the simultaneous treatment of the life and catastrophic end of a composer, Adrian Leverkühn, and German disintegration in two world wars. His last unfinished work, hailed as Germany's greatest comic novel, was *Bekenntnisse des Hochstaplers Felix Krull*, Part I (1922; 1953, Eng trans *Confessions of Felix Krull, Confidence Man*, 1955).

“ ”

Und wenn man sich für das Leben interessiert, so interessiert man sich namentlich für den Tod.

If a person concerns himself with life, he also concerns himself with death.

1924 ***Der Zauberberg****, volume 2.*

Mannerheim, Carl Gustav Emil, Baron 1867–1951 •*Finnish soldier and politician*• He was born in Villnäs, but fought in the Russian army during the Russo-Japanese War (1904–05) and World War I. When Finland declared its independence (1918), he became supreme commander and regent. Defeated in the presidential election of 1919, he retired into private life, but returned as commander in chief against the Russians in the Russo-Finnish War of 1939–40. He continued to command the Finnish forces until 1944, when he became president of the Finnish Republic, remaining in office until 1946.

Manning, Olivia 1908–80 •*English novelist*• She was born in Portsmouth, but spent much of her youth in Ireland, and had "the usual Anglo-Irish sense of belonging to nowhere." She trained at art school, and then went to London, and in 1937 published her first novel, *The Wind Changes*. She married in 1939 and went abroad that year with her husband, a British Council lecturer in Bucharest. Her experiences there formed the basis of her "Balkan trilogy," comprising *The Great Fortune* (1960), *The Spoilt City* (1962) and *Friends and Heroes* (1965). Her prolific output includes *Artist Among the Missing* (1949), *A Different Face* (1953), and her "Levant trilogy," comprising *The Danger Tree* (1977), *The Battle Lost and Won* (1978) and *The Sum of Things* (1980). The Balkan trilogy and the Levant trilogy form a single narrative entitled *Fortunes of War*.

Mannyng, Robert, *also known as* **Robert of Brunne** d. c. 1338 •*English chronicler and poet*• Born in Bourne, Lincolnshire, he entered the nearby Gilbertine monastery of Sempringham in 1288. His chief work is *Handlynge Synne* (c. 1303), a free and amplified translation into English rhyming couplets of the *Manuel des Pechiez* of William of Wadington. It is a landmark in the transition from early to later Middle English, and a colorful picture of contemporary life.

Manoel I, *also spelled* **Manuel** or **Emanuel I**, *called* **the Fortunate** or **the Great** 1469–1521 •*King of Portugal*• Born in Alcocheta, he was the grandson of John I, and succeeded John II (1495). His reign, marred by persecution of the Jews, consolidated royal power, and marked a golden age for Portugal: he prepared the code of laws which bears his name, and made his court a center of chivalry and the arts. He also sponsored the voyages of **Vasco da Gama**, **Pedro Cabral**, **Albuquerque** and others, opened up sea trade with India, discovered Brazil and consolidated Portuguese presence in the East.

Manrique, César 1919–92 •*Spanish artist and ecologist*• Born in Arrecife, Lanzarote, Canary Islands, he fought in the Spanish Civil War in Catalonia in 1937. In 1945 he went to Madrid to study at the San Fernando Fine Art School, and in 1953 he defied General **Franco** by painting abstracts. Exhibitions in Europe, Japan, the US, and at the 28th Venice Biennale brought him international recognition, and he became the arbiter of artistic taste on his island. By prohibiting high-rise buildings he prevented some of the worst excesses of mass tourism. He left as lasting monuments to his sense of design a unique cactus garden, a house containing his paintings (the Fundacion César Manrique) and public sculptures all over Lanzarote.

Mansard or **Mansart, François** 1598–1666 •*French architect*• Born in Paris, he was apprenticed to the architect Salomon de Brosse (1565–1626). Considered to embody French 17th-century classicism, his mastery is evident in his first major work, the north wing of the Château de Blois, which featured the double-angled high-pitched roof which bears his name. Other projects include the Hôtel de la Vrillière and the Château de Maisons.

Mansard or **Mansart, Jules Hardouin** 1645–1708 •*French architect*• Born in Paris, he became chief architect to **Louis XIV** and designed many notable buildings, especially part of the Palace of Versailles, including the Grand Trianon. He was the grand-nephew by marriage of **François Mansard**.

Mansell, Nigel Ernest James 1953– •*English racecar driver*• Born in Solihull, West Midlands, he made his Grand Prix debut in 1980, and had his first win in 1985, with the Williams team. Following a stint with Ferrari, he returned to Williams in 1991, and in 1992 won the world championship. He did not defend his title, preferring to drive in the Indycar circuit in the United States, and in 1993 became the first man to win the Indycar world series championship in his rookie year. He made a brief return to Formula One racing in 1995 but retired later that year.

Mansfield, Katherine, *pen name of* **Kathleen Mansfield Beauchamp** 1888–1923 •*New Zealand short-story writer*• Born in Wellington, she was educated at Queen's College, London, returned briefly to New Zealand to study music, then left again for London in 1908, determined to pursue a literary career. Finding herself pregnant, she was installed by her mother in a hotel in Bavaria, but miscarried. The experience bore fruit in the stories collected as *In a German Pension* in 1911. That same year she met **John Middleton Murry**, and thereafter her work began to surface in Murry's *Rhythm*. From 1912 the couple lived together (they married in 1918), mingling with the literati, particularly **D H Lawrence**, who portrayed them as Gudrun and Gerald in *Women in Love* (1921). Her first major work was *Prelude* (1917), a recreation of the New Zealand of her childhood. *Bliss, and Other Stories* (1920) confirmed her standing as an original and innovative writer. The only other collection published before her premature death from tuberculosis was *The Garden Party, and Other Stories* (1922). *The Letters of Katherine Mansfield*, edited by Murry, appeared in 1928, and *Katherine Mansfield's Letters to John Middleton Murry 1913–1922*, detailing the couple's stormy but tender relationship, appeared in 1951. Vincent O'Sullivan edited *Poems of Katherine Mansfield* (1988), and her work for the theater was collected in *Katherine Mansfield: Dramatic Sketches* (1988).

" "

Looking back, I imagine I was always writing. Twaddle it was, too. But better far write twaddle or anything, anything, than nothing at all.

1922 Journal entry.

Mansfield, William Murray, 1st Earl of 1705–93 •*English judge*• Born in Perth, Scotland, the fourth son of Viscount Stormont, he was educated at Westminster and Christ Church, Oxford. He was called to the bar in 1730, entered the House of Commons as Member of Parliament for Boroughbridge, and became chief justice of the King's Bench (1756). His judgments were influential, particularly by developing the law of maritime contracts, insurance and bills. He also made important contributions to international law. He was impartial as a judge, but his opinions were unpopular. "Junius" (Sir Philip Francis, 1740–1818) bitterly attacked him, and during the Gordon riots of 1780 his house was burned. Made Earl in 1776, he resigned office in 1788.

Manship, Paul Howard 1885–1966 •*US sculptor*• Born in St Paul, Minnesota, he studied in New York and Philadelphia, and attended the American Academy in Rome from 1908 to 1912. Returning to New York, he became renowned for his bronze figurative sculptures, which drew heavily on Roman and Greek sources, treated in the stylized, decorative manner of the Art Deco period. From 1921 to 1927 he worked in Paris. His many important commissions include the gilded *Prometheus Fountain* (1934) for the Rockefeller Center, New York.

Manson, Charles 1934– •*US hippie cult leader, and murderer*• Born in Kentucky, the son of a prostitute, he committed armed robbery at the age of 13 and rape at 17. In 1960 he was imprisoned for a variety of offenses including procuring, fraud and theft. On his release in 1967 he set up a hippy commune in California whose members were known as "the Family," and which became a base for various criminal activities. He had enormous power over his followers and began drawing up a death list of "Pigs"—people to be killed starting on a day code-named Helter Skelter. He ordered his followers to carry out the killings. In 1979 he was found guilty of nine murders and sentenced to life imprisonment.

Manson, Sir Patrick, *known as* **Mosquito Manson** 1844–1922 •*Scottish physician*• Born in Old Meldrum, Aberdeen, he studied medicine in Aberdeen and then practiced in China (from 1871) and Hong Kong (from 1883). In China, he studied elephantiasis and showed that it is caused by a parasite spread through mosquito bites. This was the first disease to be shown to be transmitted by an insect carrier. In 1890 Manson set up practice in London, where he became the leading consultant on tropical diseases, and in 1899 he helped to found the London School of Tropical Medicine. He was the first to argue that the mosquito is host to the malaria parasite (1877).

Manstein, Fritz Erich von 1887–1973 •*German soldier*• At the outset of World War II he became chief of staff to **Karl von Rundstedt** in the Polish campaign and later in France, where he was the architect of **Hitler**'s Blitzkrieg invasion plan. After the disaster of Stalingrad, he successfully staged a counterattack at Kharkov, though he failed to relieve **Friedrich Paulus**'s 6th Army. After being captured in 1945 he was imprisoned as a war criminal but released in 1953.

Mantegna, Andrea 1431–1506 •*Italian painter*• Born near Vicenza, he was apprenticed to the tailor-painter Francesco Squarcione (1396–c. 1468) in Padua. In 1459 he was persuaded by Ludovico Gonzaga, Duke of Mantua, to work for him, and remained in Mantua in his service for the rest of his life, with the exception of a two-year stay in Rome (1488–90). His style is very sculptural and ostentatious in its use of foreshortening. At Mantua his most important works were nine tempera pictures of *The Triumph of Caesar* (c. 1486) which were later acquired by the English king **Charles I** and are now at Hampton Court Palace, and his decoration of the ceiling of the Camera degli Sposi. The latter is an illusionistic tour-de-force in which the ceiling is opened up to the heavens and putti look down from the painted balustrade. The other chief feature of his art was his incorporation of classical motifs into his compositions.

Mantell, Gideon Algernon 1790–1852 •*English paleontologist*• Born in Lewes, Sussex, he studied medicine in London and returned to Lewes as a practicing surgeon. Busy and successful, he also took time to study the local geology and collected many fossils, which were put on show to the public. He wrote *The Fossils of the South Downs* in 1822, moved to Brighton in 1833 and was able to complete his *Geology of the South-East of England* by 1837. His collection was sold to the British Museum in 1838 and he followed it to London in 1844. He discovered several dinosaur types, including the first to be fully described; noting the similarity between the fossil teeth and those of the living iguana, he named it *Iguanodon* (1825).

Mantle, Micky (Charles) 1931–95 •*US baseball player*• Born in Spavinaw, Oklahoma, he achieved legendary status as a star with the New York Yankees. Highlights of his career included a record-setting 565-foot home run, seven World Series titles and, in 1956, his winning of a Triple Crown in batting, home runs and runs batted in. Admired as a hitter, base runner and center fielder without equal, he won three Most Valuable Player awards and was elected to the Baseball Hall of Fame in 1974.

Manutius, Aldus *See* **Aldus Manutius**

Manzoni, Alessandro 1785–1873 •*Italian novelist and poet*• Born in Milan, of a noble family, he lived in Paris from 1805 to 1807, and published his first poems in 1806. The work which earned him European fame is his historical novel, *I promessi sposi* (1827, Eng trans *The Betrothed Lovers*, 1828), a Milanese story of the 17th century, and one of the most notable novels in Italian literature. Despite his Catholic devoutness, he was a strong advocate of a united Italy, and became a senator of the kingdom in 1860.

Manzú, Giacomo 1908–91 •*Italian sculptor*• He was born in Bergamo, and was apprenticed to various craftsmen before studying at the Fantoni Trade School. In 1930 he was commissioned to make religious reliefs and saints for the Catholic University of Milan. He held his first one-man exhibition in Rome in 1937, and subsequently taught sculpture in Milan (1940) and Turin (c. 1940–45). He revived classical techniques of relief sculpture in bronze, and is particularly known for the bronze doors of St Peter's in Rome (1950) and of Salzburg Cathedral, Austria (1955).

Mao Dun (Mao Tun), *pseudonym of* **Shen Yanbing (Shen Yenping)** 1896–1981 •*Chinese writer*• He was born in Wuzhen, Zhejiang (Chekiang) province, educated at the University of Beijing (Peking), and worked as a magazine editor. Moving to Shanghai, he taught a course of fiction at Shanghai College and worked as a newspaper editor, but in 1926 he had to go underground because of his Communist sympathies. He wrote a trilogy of novellas, published as *Shi* (1930, "Eclipse"), as well as a best-selling novel, *Ziye* (1932, "Midnight"). In 1930 he helped organize the influential League of Left-Wing Writers. After the Communists came to power in 1949, he was China's first Minister of Culture (1949–65) and was founding editor of the literary journal *People's Literature* (1949–53). During the Cultural Revolution he was kept under house arrest in Beijing (1966–78).

Mao Zedong (Mao Tse-tung) 1893–1976 •*Chinese Communist leader and first chairman of the People's Republic*• He was born in Shaoshan in Hunan province. Educated in Changsha, in 1918 he went to the University of Beijing (Peking), where as a library assistant he studied the works of **Marx** and others and helped found the Chinese Communist Party (CCP) in 1921. Seeing the need to adapt communism to Chinese conditions, and seeking a rural- rather than urban-based revolution, he set up a communist people's republic (soviet) at Jiangxi (Kiangsi) in southeast China between 1931 and 1934. The soviet defied the attacks of **Chiang Kai-shek**'s forces until 1934, when Mao and his followers were obliged to uproot themselves and undertake an arduous and circuitous Long March (1934–36) to Shaanxi (Shensi) Province in northwest China. During the Long March, Mao was elected CCP chairman. At the new headquarters of Yan'an, he set about formulating a unique communist philosophy that stressed the importance of ideology, reeducation and "rectification." Mao's communists successfully resisted the Japanese between 1937 and 1945, and on their collapse issued forth to shatter the nationalist regime of

Chiang Kai-shek and proclaim the People's Republic of China in Beijing in 1949, with Mao as chairman. Mao resigned the chairmanship of the Republic in 1959, but remained chairman of the CCP's politburo until his death. During the early 1960s, an ideological rift developed between Mao and **Khrushchev**, with Mao opposing the latter's policy of peaceful coexistence with the West and the USSR's volte-face during the Cuban missile crisis (1962). This developed into a formal split in 1962 when the Soviet Union supplied fighter aircraft to India during the brief Sino-Indian border war of that year. In China, Mao's influence waned during the early 1960s as a result of the failure of the 1958–60 Great Leap Forward experiment of rapid agricultural and industrial advance through the establishment of massive communes. However, Mao reestablished his dominance by implementing the 1966–69 Cultural Revolution, a campaign of rectification directed against liberal, revisionist forces. Following this, Mao, working closely with **Zhou Enlai**, oversaw a period of reconstruction from 1970. During his final years, he was beset by deteriorating health, and his political grip weakened. Mao's writings and thoughts, set out in *New Democracy* (1940) and, most popularly, in his *Little Red Book*, dominated the functioning of the People's Republic between 1949 and 1976. On his death at the age of 83, there followed a power struggle that was briefly won by the Gang of Four, who included Mao's widow, Jiang Qing. After 1978, the new Chinese leadership of **Deng Xiaoping** began to reinterpret Maoism and criticized its policy excesses. However, many of Mao's ideas remain influential in contemporary China.

Mar, John Erskine, 6th or **11th Earl of** 1675–1732 •*Scottish Jacobite*• He was born in Alloa, Clackmannanshire. He began public life as a Whig, but his frequent changes of side earned him the nickname of "Bobbing John." He headed the Jacobite rebellion of 1715, was defeated at Sheriffmuir, and died in exile at Aix-la-Chapelle. His *Legacy* was published by the Scottish History Society in 1896.

Maradona, Diego 1960– •*Argentine soccer player*• Born in Lanús, he played in the 1982 World Cup in Spain, and joined Barcelona. He captained the Argentine team to World Cup victory in Mexico in 1986, earning fame for fisting his first goal against England, an action which he subsequently attributed to "the hand of God." He moved to Naples, playing for the team from 1984 and helping them (1987) to their first-ever Italian championship. With his speed, phenomenal strength and balance, he is one of the greatest players of his generation, but in recent years his career has been marred by repeated suspensions for drug use. He left Naples in 1991 after being suspended for 15 months following a drug test, and in 1993 he returned to Argentina. He was again suspended after failing a drug test at the 1994 World Cup, and in later years has played only intermittently.

Marat, Jean Paul 1743–93 •*French revolutionary, physician and journalist*• Born in Boudry near Neuchâtel, Switzerland, he studied medicine and practiced in London and Paris. He was brevet-physician to the guards of the Comte d'Artois (afterward **Charles X**) until 1786, and during that time worked in optics and electricity, and produced several scientific works. In 1789 he established the radical paper, *L'Ami du Peuple*, inciting the "sans-culottes" to violence. The hatred he inspired forced him into hiding several times, once in the sewers of Paris, and his denunciations influenced the September Massacres. In 1792 he was elected to the Convention, and with **Robespierre** and **Danton** he overthrew the Girondins. A skin disease contracted in the sewers meant he could only write sitting in his bath, and on the evening of July 13 he was assassinated there by **Charlotte Corday**, a member of the Girondins.

Maravich, Peter Press, *nicknamed* **Pistol Pete** 1947–88 •*US basketball player*• Born in Aliquippa, Pennsylvania, he is widely considered the greatest creative offensive player of all time. He joined the Atlanta Hawks in 1970 and subsequently played for the New Orleans Jazz (1974–79), the Utah Jazz (1979–80) and the Boston Celtics (1979–80). He proved completely unpredictable on court and shattered numerous scoring records. As a college player he scored a record 3,667 points; as a professional he led the NBA in scoring in 1977 and notched up a career total of 15,948 points in 658 games. He collapsed and died of a heart attack following a three-on-three pickup game at the age of 40.

Marc, Franz 1880–1916 •*German artist*• Born in Munich, with **Wassily Kandinsky** he founded the Blaue Reiter Expressionist group in Munich in 1911. Most of his paintings were of animals (for example, *Tower of the Blue Horses*, 1911, and *The Fate of the Animals*, 1913), portrayed in forceful colors, with a well-defined pictorial rhythm. He was killed in World War I at Verdun.

“ ”

Traditions are lovely things—to create traditions, that is, not to live off them.

1914–15 ***Aphorisms***.

Marcantonio, *in full* **Marcantonio Raimondi** c. 1488–1534 •*Italian engraver*• Born in Bologna, he began as a goldsmith, but moved to Rome in 1510 and became an engraver of other artists' works, especially those of **Raphael** and **Michelangelo**. The capture of Rome by **Charles Bourbon** in 1527 drove him back to Bologna.

Marceau, Marcel 1923– •*French mime artist*• He was born in Strasbourg, and studied at the École des Beaux-Arts in Paris. In 1948 he founded and directed (1948–64) the Compagnie de Mime Marcel Marceau, specializing in and developing the art of mime, of which he has become the leading exponent. His white-faced character "Bip" became famous worldwide. Among the many original performances he has devised are the mime-drama *Don Juan* (1964) and the ballet *Candide* (1971). He became head of the École Mimodrame Marcel Marceau in 1978.

Marcel, Gabriel Honoré 1889–1973 •*French existentialist philosopher and dramatist*• Born in Paris, he was a Red Cross worker in World War I but made his living thereafter as a freelance writer, teacher, editor and critic. In 1929 he became a Catholic and came reluctantly to accept the label "Christian Existentialist," partly in order to contrast his views with those of **Jean-Paul Sartre**. He emphasized the importance and possibility of "communication" between individuals, as well as between the individual and God, but was suspicious of all philosophical abstractions and generalizations. He was not himself a system builder, and his philosophical works tend to have a personal, meditative character, as in *Journal métaphysique* (1927, Eng trans *Metaphysical Journal*, 1952), *Le mystère de l'être* (1951, Eng trans *The Mystery of Being*, 1951) and *L'homme problématique* (1955, Eng trans *Problematic Man*, 1967). His plays include *Un homme de Dieu* (1925, "A Man of God") and *La dimension Florestan* (1956, "The Florestan Dimension").

Marcellus, Marcus Claudius, *known as* **the Sword of Rome** c. 268–208 BC •*Roman general*• His main exploits were the defeat of the Insubrian Gauls (222 BC) and the capture of Syracuse (212). During the Second Punic War (218–201) he stopped **Hannibal** at Nola (216).

Marcellus, Marcus Claudius 42–23 BC •*Roman nobleman*• He was a son of **Octavia**, the sister of the emperor **Augustus**, and married his 14-year-old cousin **Julia** in 25 BC. That same year Augustus adopted Marcellus, who served under him in Spain, and named him his first successor; his early death was widely regarded as a national calamity and was lamented by **Virgil** in the *Aeneid* (vi. 861–87).

March, Fredric, *originally* **Frederick Ernest McIntyre Bickel** 1897–1975 •*US actor*• Born in Racine, Wisconsin, he served as an artillery lieutenant in World War I. He turned to acting in 1920, and proved a versatile and subtle screen performer whose work ranged from costume drama to screwball comedies. He won Best Actor Academy Awards for *Dr Jekyll and Mr Hyde* (1931) and as the homecoming veteran in *The Best Years of Our Lives* (1946). Other films in a long and distinguished career included *A Star Is Born* (1937), *Death of a Salesman* (1952) and *The Iceman Cometh* (1973). He was married to actress Florence Eldridge (1901–88) from 1927.

Marciano, Rocky, *originally* **Rocco Francis Marchegiano** 1923–69 •*US boxer*• Born in Brockton, Massachusetts, he first took up boxing as a serviceman in Great Britain during World War II, and turned professional in 1947. He made his name in 1951 when he defeated the former world champion **Joe Louis**, who had been knocked out only once. He won the world title the following year, and when he retired in 1956 was undefeated as world champion with a professional record of 49 bouts and 49 victories. He died in a plane crash.

Marcion c. 100–c. 165 AD •*Italian Christian Gnostic*• A wealthy shipowner of Sinope in Pontus, in about AD 140 he went to Rome and founded the quasi-Gnostic Marcionites (144), which soon had churches in many eastern countries.

Marconi, Guglielmo, Marchese 1874–1937 •*Italian physicist, inventor and Nobel Prize winner*• He was born in Bologna into a wealthy family. He was educated for a short time at the Technical Institute of Livorno, but mainly by private tutors, and started experimenting with a device to convert electromagnetic waves (recently discovered by **Heinrich Hertz**) into electricity. His first successful experiments in wireless telegraphy were made at Bologna in 1895, and in 1898 he transmitted signals across the English Channel. In 1899 he erected a wireless station at La Spezia, but failed to win the support of the Italian government and decided to establish the Marconi Telegraph Co in London. In 1901 he succeeded in sending signals in Morse code across the Atlantic, from Cornwall, England, to St John's, Newfoundland, and the following year he patented the magnetic detector. He later developed short-wave radio equipment, and established a worldwide radiotelegraph network for the British government. From 1921 he lived on his yacht, the *Elettra*, and in the 1930s he was a strong supporter of the Italian Fascist leader **Mussolini**. Marconi shared the 1909 Nobel Prize for physics with **Ferdinand Braun**.

Marco Polo *See* **Polo, Marco**

Marcos, Ferdinand Edralin 1917–89 •*Philippine politician*• He was born in Ilocos Norte, and educated at the University of the Philippines. He was accused, in 1939, while a law student, of murdering a political opponent of his father, but secured his own acquittal. During World War II he served in a Philippines army unit (but his claims of being a resistance fighter against the Japanese were later proved to be false). After the war he sat in the Philippines' House of Representatives (1949–59) and Senate (1959–66), and, promising a new program of industrial development, was elected president. His regime as president (1965–86) was marked by increasing repression, misuse of foreign financial aid and political murders, such as that of **Benigno Aquino** (1983). With a declining economy, and faced with a growing Communist insurgency, he declared martial law in 1972 and began to rule by decree. He was eventually overthrown in 1986 by a popular People's Power front led by **Cory Aquino**. The ailing Marcos and his influential wife, **Imelda Marcos**, fled into exile in Hawaii.

Marcos, Imelda Romualdez c. 1930– •*Philippine politician*• She was born in Manila, and after her businessman father went bankrupt, she was raised in conditions of extreme poverty. In 1954 she married a young politician, **Ferdinand Marcos**, who became president in 1965. Known to her fellow countrymen as the Iron Butterfly, she used her husband's power and position to build an extravagant financial empire, and served as governor of Metropolitan Manila (1975–86) and minister of Human Settlements and Ecology (1979–86). To maintain his rule Marcos turned his country into a dictatorship, but in 1986 he was deposed and fled with his wife into exile in Hawaii. In 1988 they were indicted in New York on corruption charges, but she was acquitted in 1990. In 1989 Marcos died and she returned to the Philippines, where in 1992 she was an unsuccessful presidential candidate.

Marcus Aurelius, *surnamed* **Antoninus**, *originally* **Marcus Annius Verus** AD 121–80 •*Roman emperor and philosopher*• He was born in Rome. At the age of 17 he was adopted by **Antoninus Pius**, who had in turn been adopted by **Hadrian**; Marcus Aurelius married Antoninus's daughter Faustina in 145. From 140, when he was made consul, until the death of Antoninus in 161, he discharged his public duties conscientiously, and maintained good relations with the emperor. At the same time he devoted himself to the study of law and philosophy, especially Stoicism; one of his teachers was the Stoic Apollonius of Chalcedon. On his accession, he voluntarily shared the throne with his brother by adoption, Lucius Aurelius Verus, who in 161 was sent to take command against the Parthians. The generals were victorious, but the army brought back from the East a plague that ravaged the empire. Peaceful by temperament, Marcus Aurelius was nevertheless destined to suffer from constant wars throughout his reign, and although in Asia, Britain, and on the Rhine the invaders were checked, permanent peace was never secured. Rome was suffering from pestilence, earthquakes and inundations when the imperial colleagues led the Roman armies against the northern barbarians on the Danube. Verus died in 169; the Marcomanni were subdued in 168 and 173; and the Quadi in 174. Marcus Aurelius was next called to the East by a rebellion of the governor, Avidius Cassius (175), who was assassinated before Aurelius arrived. On his way home, he visited lower Egypt and Greece. At Athens he founded chairs of philosophy for each of the chief schools: Platonic, Stoic, Peripatetic, and Epicurean. Toward the end of 176 he reached Italy, and the following autumn he departed for Germany, where fresh disturbances had broken out. He was victorious once more, but died in 180 in Pannonia. Marcus Aurelius wrote 12 books of *Meditationes*, which record his innermost thoughts and form a unique document. They show his loneliness, but also that he did not allow himself to be embittered by his experiences in life. They were published unedited only after his death. He was retrospectively idealized as the model of the perfect emperor, whose reign and style of rule contrasted with the disastrous period that began with the accession of his son **Commodus**.

Marcus Cocceius Nerva *See* **Nerva, Marcus Cocceius**

Marcuse, Herbert 1898–1979 •*US Marxist philosopher*• Born in Berlin, Germany, and educated at the Universities of Berlin and Freiburg, he became an influential figure in the Frankfurt Institute of Social Research (the so-called Frankfurt School) along with **Theodor Adorno** and **Max Horkheimer**. After the Nazis closed the Institute (1933), he fled to Geneva and thence to the US (1934), later becoming a naturalized citizen, and taking a series of teaching posts. He had published *Eros and Civilization* in 1955, offering a Freudian analysis of the repressions imposed by the unconscious mind, but became a celebrity at the age of 66 with the publication of *One Dimensional Man* (1964), condemning the "repressive tolerance" of modern industrial society, which both stimulated and satisfied the superficial material desires of the masses at the cost of more fundamental needs and freedoms. He expressed an equal hostility to bureaucratic communism in his *Soviet Marxism* (1958).

Marden, Brice 1938– •*US painter*• Born in Bronxville, New York, he studied at Boston University and Yale before settling in New York in 1963. By 1965 he was producing minimalist uniformly colored canvases of horizontal and vertical formats. His paintings of the 1980s moved away from minimalism, and involved crossing diagonal and vertical lines, and the use of bright color, as in *Thira* (1980, Pompidou Center, Paris), with its explicit reference to ancient architecture.

Mare, Walter de la *See* **de la Mare, Walter**

Margaret, St c. 1046–93 •*Queen of Scotland*• Born in Hungary, where her father, **Edward the Ætheling**, was in exile, she later went to England, but fled to Scotland after the Norman Conquest with her brother, **Edgar the Ætheling**. The Scottish king, **Malcolm III Canmore**, married her at Dunfermline (c. 1070). Much of her reputation comes from her confessor and biographer, Turgot. She refined and anglicized the court, brought Benedictine monks to Dunfermline, and stimulated change in usages in the Celtic Church. Canonized by **Innocent IV** (1251), her feast day is November 16.

Margaret, Maid of Norway 1283–90 •*Queen of Scotland*• The granddaughter of **Alexander III** of Scotland, she was the only child of King Erik II of Norway. When Alexander III died (1286), she was the only direct survivor of the Scottish royal line. In 1289 she was betrothed to the infant Prince Edward (the future **Edward II** of England), son of **Edward I**, but she died at sea in Orkney the following year on her way from Norway to England.

Margaret (Rose), Princess 1930–2002 •*British princess*• She was born at Glamis Castle, Scotland, the younger daughter of King **George VI** and only sister of Queen **Elizabeth II**. In 1955 she rejected a possible marriage to Group Captain Peter Townsend, on advice from the Church and the establishment, because his previous marriage had been dissolved. In 1960 she married Antony Armstrong-Jones, a photographer, who was made Earl of

Snowdon in 1961. Their children are David, Viscount Linley (1961–), and Lady Sarah Armstrong-Jones (1964–). The marriage was dissolved in 1978.

Margaret (Marguerite) of Angoulême, *also known as* **Margaret of Navarre** 1492–1549 •*Queen of Navarre, and writer*• The sister of **Francis I** of France, she married first the Duke of Alençon (d. 1525) and then (1527) Henry d'Albret (titular king of Navarre), to whom she bore Jeanne d'Albret (1528–72), mother of **Henry IV** of France. With a strong interest in Renaissance learning, Margaret also became influenced by **Erasmus** and the religious reformers of the Meaux circle, who looked to her for patronage and protection. One of the most brilliant women of her age, she encouraged agriculture, learning and the arts, and her court was the most intellectual in Europe. The patron of men of letters, including the heretical poet Clément Marot (c. 1497–1544), and **Rabelais**, she herself was a prolific writer. Her most celebrated work was *Heptaméron*, a collection of stories on the theme of love, modeled on the *Decameron* of **Boccaccio**, and published posthumously in 1558.

“ ”

L'amour n'est pas un feu que l'on tient dans la main.
Love is not a flame that one holds in the hand.

1558 ***Heptaméron****, 47.*

Margaret of Anjou 1430–82 •*Queen of England*• The daughter of René of Anjou, she was married to **Henry VI** of England in 1445, but because of his madness she became involved in government, acting as virtual sovereign, and was held responsible for the war of 1449, in which Normandy was lost. During the Wars of the Roses, Margaret was a leading Lancastrian, and after a brave struggle of nearly 20 years was finally defeated at Tewkesbury (1471). She was imprisoned in the Tower of London for four years, until she was ransomed by **Louis XI**. She then retired to France.

Margaret of Austria 1480–1530 •*Duchess of Savoy and regent of the Netherlands*• The daughter of Emperor **Maximilian I** and Mary of Burgundy, she was born in Brussels, and married first (1497) the Infante Juan of Spain, who died within a few months, then (1501) Philibert II, Duke of Savoy (d. 1504). Her father appointed her regent of the Netherlands (1507–15) and guardian of her nephew, the future emperor **Charles V**. In 1519 she was again appointed regent by Charles V (until 1530), and proved herself a wise and capable stateswoman.

Margaret of Navarre *See* **Margaret of Angoulême**

Margaret of Parma 1522–86 •*Regent of the Netherlands*• She was born in Oudenarde, the illegitimate daughter of Emperor **Charles V**. She married first (1536) Alessandro de' Medici and second (1538) Ottavio Farnese, later Duke of Parma, to whom she bore **Alessandro Farnese** (also later Duke of Parma) in 1546. As regent of the Netherlands (1559–67), she proved herself masterful, able, and a staunch Catholic. In 1567 she was replaced by the Duke of **Alva**. When her son Alessandro became governor of the Netherlands (1578–86), ruling as regent for **Philip II** of Spain, Margaret returned with him as head of the civil administration for a time, finally retiring to Italy in 1583.

Margaret of Valois 1553–1615 •*Queen of Navarre*• Born at St Germain-en-Laye, she was the daughter of **Henry II** of France and **Catherine de Médicis**, and sister of **Francis II**, **Charles IX** and **Henry III**. Noted for her beauty, learning and licentiousness, in 1572 she married Henri of Navarre (later **Henry IV**). The marriage was childless, and was dissolved by the pope (1599) in order to allow Henry to marry **Marie de Médicis**. She became famous for her *Mémoires*, published in 1628.

Margaret Tudor 1489–1541 •*Queen of Scotland*• Born in London, the eldest daughter of **Henry VII** of England, she married **James IV** of Scotland (1503), Archibald Douglas, the 6th Earl of Angus (1514), and, having divorced him, Henry Stewart, later Lord Methven (1527). She had a significant, enigmatic role in the conflict between pro-French and pro-English factions during the minority of her son, **James V** of Scotland, for whom she acted as regent. Her great-grandson, **James VI** of Scotland, inherited the English throne (1603).

Margolyes, Miriam 1941– •*English actress*• Born in Oxford, she studied at Newnham College, Cambridge, and the Guildhall School of Music and Drama. She often appears in comic roles as a fussy matriarch, and her film work has included *Yentl* (1983), *The Age of Innocence* (1993; British Academy of Film and Television Arts award for Best Supporting Actress), *William Shakespeare's Romeo and Juliet* (1996) and *Cold Comfort Farm* (1997). Her television appearances have included *Blackadder* (1983) and *Vanity Fair* (1998), and she has performed widely on radio.

Margrethe I, *also called* **Margareta** or **Margaret** 1353–1412 •*Queen of Denmark, Norway and Sweden*• Born in Søborg, Denmark, she was married to King Haakon VI of Norway (1363) at the age of 10. She became queen of Denmark (1375) on the death of her father, Valdemar IV Atterdag, holding the Crown in trust for her five-year-old son, Olav. By Haakon's death (1380), she also became regent of Norway for Olav, who died suddenly (1387), leaving her sole ruler of Denmark-Norway. In 1389, after disaffected Swedish nobles offered her the Swedish crown, she became queen of Sweden. She had her seven-year-old great-nephew, **Erik VII**, adopted as her successor to the three Scandinavian kingdoms, and his coronation (1397) as king of all three kingdoms effected the Union of Kalmar, whereby the kingdoms should remain forever under one ruler, each retaining its separate laws.

Margrethe II 1940– •*Queen of Denmark*• Born in Copenhagen, she was the daughter of **Frederik IX**, whom she succeeded in 1972, and she became the first reigning queen in Denmark for nearly 600 years. Previously she had studied at a number of European universities and become an archaeologist. In 1967 she married a French diplomat, Count Henri de Laborde de Monpezat, now Prince Henrik of Denmark. Their children are the heir apparent, Crown Prince Frederik (1968–) and Prince Joachim (1969–).

Margulis, Lynn, *née* **Alexander** 1938– •*US biologist*• Born in Chicago, she was educated at the Universities of Chicago and Wisconsin and at the University of California, Berkeley, then lectured in biology at Brandeis University (1963–65) and Boston University (1966–88), and later at the University of Massachusetts, Amherst (1988–). Her most important work deals with the origin of eukaryotic cells (cells with nuclei) and the role of symbiosis in cell evolution, and she has written numerous popular science books on the origin of life, the development of sex, and global ecology, many with her son Dorion Sagan (her son from her marriage to **Carl Sagan**). She collaborated with **James Lovelock** on the Gaia hypothesis.

Maria Theresa 1717–80 •*Holy Roman Empress, archduchess of Austria, and queen of Hungary and Bohemia*• The daughter of the emperor Charles VI, in 1736 she married the future **Francis I**, and in 1740 succeeded her father in the hereditary **Habsburg** lands. Her claim, however, led to the War of the Austrian Succession (1740–48), during which she lost Silesia to Prussia. In 1741 she received the Hungarian crown, and in 1745 her husband was elected Holy Roman emperor. Although her foreign minister, Prince von **Kaunitz-Rietberg**, tried to isolate Prussia by diplomatic means, military conflict was renewed in the Seven Years' War, and by 1763 she was finally forced to recognize the status quo of 1756. In her later years she strove to maintain international peace, and reluctantly accepted the partition of Poland (1772). Of her ten surviving children, the eldest son, **Joseph II**, succeeded her; Leopold, Grand Duke of Tuscany, succeeded him as **Leopold II**; Ferdinand became Duke of Modena; and **Marie Antoinette** married **Louis XVI** of France.

Marichal (Sánchez), Juan Antonio 1937– •*US baseball player*• Born in Laguna Verde in the Dominican Republic, he established a reputation as a formidable right-handed pitcher with the San Francisco Giants (1960–74). Nicknamed the "Dominican Dandy," his achievements include winning 21 or more games in no fewer than 6 seasons and a career total of 52 shutouts. During his 16-year career at the top level, he won 243 games and lost just 142, and twice led the National League in complete games and shutouts. After retiring as a player, he became minister of sports for the Dominican Republic.

Marie Antoinette, *in full* **Josèphe Jeanne Marie Antoinette** 1755–93 •*Queen of France*• Born in Vienna, Austria, she was the fourth daughter of the empress **Maria Theresa** and the emperor **Francis I**, and in 1770 was married to the Dauphin of France, afterward **Louis XVI** (from 1774). Young and inexperienced, she aroused criticism by her frivolity, extravagance and disregard for conventions, her devotion to the interests of Austria, and her opposition to all the measures devised by **Turgot** and **Necker** for relieving the financial distress of the country. She had an instinctive abhorrence of the liberal nobles such as the Marquis de **Lafayette** and the Comte de **Mirabeau**, and although she finally reached agreement with Mirabeau (July 1790), she was too independent to follow his advice, and his death in April 1791 removed the last hope of saving the monarchy. She and Louis tried to escape to the frontier, but were intercepted at Varennes. The storming of the Tuileries and slaughter of the Swiss guards, and the trial and execution of Louis (January 21, 1793) quickly followed, and soon she herself was sent to the Conciergerie (August 2, 1793). After eight weeks the "Widow Capet" was herself arraigned before the Revolutionary Tribunal, and guillotined on October 16, 1793.

Marie de France fl. c. 1160–c. 1190 •*French poet*• Born in Normandy, she spent much of her life in England. The *Lais* (sometime before 1167), her most important work, are dedicated to "a noble king," probably **Henry II** of England, and comprise 14 romantic narratives in octosyllabic verse based on Celtic material. A landmark in French literature, they influenced a number of later writers. She also wrote *Fables* (sometime after 1170).

Marie de Médicis, *Italian* **Maria de' Medici** 1573–1642 •*Queen of France*• Born in Florence, she was the daughter of **Francis I**, second wife of **Henry IV** from 1600, and mother of **Louis XIII**. After Henry's assassination (1610), she became regent (1610–17) for her nine-year-old son. Squandering state revenues and adopting a pro-Spanish foreign policy, she dismissed her husband's minister, the Duc de **Sully**, and relied on a circle of unscrupulous favorites, especially her Italian lover, Concini, and his wife. At the Estates General (1614), she received support from the young **Richelieu**, Bishop of Luçon, who was in charge of foreign affairs from 1616. In 1615 she had arranged a marriage for her son Louis with the Infanta **Anne of Austria** (daughter of **Philip III** of Spain), and for her eldest daughter, Elizabeth, to the heir to the Spanish throne (the future **Philip IV**), thus bringing an end to the war with the **Habsburg**s. In 1617 Louis assumed royal power, arranged for the assassination of Concini, and exiled his mother to the provinces. With Richelieu's mediation, she was reconciled to her son (1620), was readmitted to the council (1622), and persuaded Louis to make Richelieu his chief minister. Richelieu himself then broke her power on the Day of Dupes (1630), and she went into exile in Brussels.

Marie Louise 1791–1847 •*Empress of France*• Born in Vienna, Austria, she was the daughter of Francis I of Austria. She married **Napoleon I** in 1810 (after his divorce from **Joséphine**), and bore him a son (1811), who was made king of Rome and became **Napoleon II**. On Napoleon's abdication (1814), she returned to Austria and was awarded the duchy of Parma. In 1822 she contracted a morganatic marriage with Count von Neipperg (d. c. 1829) and another with the Count of Bombelles (1834).

Marillac, Ste Louise de 1591–1660 •*French Catholic cofounder of the Sisters of Charity*• Born in Ferrières-en-Brie, near Meaux, she lost both of her parents by the age of 15, and after marrying Antony Le Gras, was widowed in 1625. She took **Vincent de Paul** as her spiritual director, who saw her as the right person to train girls and widows to help the sick and the poor. In 1633 four girls started work in her Paris home. From this modest beginning sprang the Sisters of Charity, who ministered in hospitals, orphanages and schools in Paris and beyond. She was canonized in 1934, and her feast day is March 15.

Marin, Maguy 1951– •*French dancer and choreographer*• Born in Toulouse, she first worked with the Strasbourg Opera Ballet before continuing to study at the Mudra school in Brussels. This led to her joining **Maurice Béjart**'s Ballet of the 20th Century in the mid-1970s. In 1978 she won first prize at the Bagnolet international choreographic competition and that same year founded her own troupe, which in 1981 became the resident company of Créteil, a Paris suburb. She has choreographed for many major European companies including a notable 1985 version of *Cinderella* for Lyons Opera Ballet.

Marinetti, Emilio Filippo Tommaso 1876–1944 •*Italian writer*• He was born in Alexandria, Egypt, and studied in Paris and Genoa. One of the founders of futurism, he published the original futurist manifesto in *Figaro* in 1909. In his writings he glorified war, the machine age, speed and "dynamism," and in 1919 he became a fascist. His publications include *Le Futurisme* (1911) and *Teatro sintetico futuristo* (1916, "The Synthetic Futurist Theater"). He condemned all traditional forms of literature and art, and his ideas were applied to painting by **Umberto Boccioni**, **Giacomo Balla** and others.

Marini, Marino 1901–80 •*Italian sculptor and painter*• Born in Pistoia, he studied in Florence, and from 1929 to 1940 taught at the Scuola d'Arte di Villa Reale, Monza, before moving to Milan, where he was professor at Brera Academy (1940–70). Never part of any modern movement, his work was figurative and his best-known theme the horse and rider. He executed portraits of **Igor Stravinsky**, **Marc Chagall**, **Henry Miller** and others, and won many prizes, including the Venice Biennale (1952).

Marino, Dan 1961– •*US football player*• Born in Pittsburgh, he played as quarterback with the Miami Dolphins, and in the 1984 season he gained 5,084 yards passing to create a National Football League record. He completed a record 29 passes in the 1985 Super Bowl, and in 1986 established a record for the most passes completed in a season (378). He also set a record of 61,361 total passing yards, and another record of 420 touchdown passes. He retired in 2000.

Marion, Frances, *originally* **Frances Marion Owens** 1887–1973 •*US screenwriter and novelist*• She was born in San Francisco. She worked as a reporter, commercial artist and model before arriving in Hollywood in 1913 as the protégée of director Lois Weber. A prolific screenwriter during the silent era, she was associated with actress **Mary Pickford** on such films as *Rebecca of Sunnybrook Farm* (1918) and *Pollyanna* (1920). She was also one of the first female war correspondents during World War I. She later wrote star vehicles for the likes of **Greta Garbo** and **Jean Harlow** and received Academy Awards for *The Big House* (1930) and *The Champ* (1931). She subsequently wrote novels, including *The Powder Keg* (1954).

Marion, Francis, *known as* **the Swamp Fox** c. 1732–95 •*American Revolutionary general*• Born in Winyah, South Carolina, he first saw action against the Cherokee in 1759, and joined the Revolutionary army in 1776. After American forces were defeated, Marion gathered a rough militia (1780) and led a series of guerrilla attacks on British troops. His nickname referred to his skill in retreating to seemingly impassable swamps where the British could not follow. He was promoted to brigadier general in 1781, and in September of that year he won an important victory at Eutaw Springs.

Mariotte, Edmé c. 1620–84 •*French physicist and physiologist*• Born probably in Chazeuil, Burgundy, he attracted attention as a physiologist, studied pendulums and falling bodies (1667–68), and published an exposition of the laws of elastic and inelastic collisions (1673). In 1679 he restated the law bearing his name in France (elsewhere attributed to **Robert Boyle**) and used it to estimate the height of the atmosphere. He also discussed scientific methodology, hydrology, optics (including the rainbow), astronomy and the strength of materials.

Maris, Roger 1934–85 •*US baseball player*• Born in Hibbing, Minnesota, he spent the best part of his career with the New York Yankees (1960–67), although he also played for the Cleveland Indians (1957–58), the Kansas City Athletics (1958–59) and the St Louis Cardinals (1967–68). He was highly effective with the bat and in 1961 passed the single-season record of 60 home runs set by **Babe Ruth** in 1927 (it was not until 1998 that his own record of 61 was surpassed). He was named Most Valuable Player in the American League two years in succession (1960–61) and by the time of his retirement after 12 years at the top level had notched up a total of 275 home runs.

Marius, Gaius 157–86 BC •*Roman general and politician*• He was born in Arpinum, and was consul seven times. He reformed the Roman army and had victories over enemies including **Jugurtha** of Numidia (105 BC) in Africa. His final years were dominated by rivalry with the Roman dictator **Sulla** over the command against Mithridates. Civil war followed, and Marius was forced to flee to Africa. He returned to capture Rome for the Roman politician **Cinna** from the forces backing Sulla (87), but died soon after.

Marius, Simon, *German surname* **Mayr** 1570–1624 •*German astronomer*• A pupil of **Tycho Brahe**, in 1609 he claimed to have discovered the four satellites of Jupiter independently of **Galileo**. He named them Io, Europa, Ganymede and Callisto.

Marivaux, Pierre Carlet de Chamblain de 1688–1763 •*French playwright and novelist*• Born in Paris, he published *L'Homère travesti* ("Homer Burlesqued"), a burlesque of the *Iliad*, in 1716, and from then on wrote several comedies, of which his best is *Le jeu de l'amour et du hasard* (1730, Eng trans *Love in Livery*, 1907). His best-known novel, *La vie de Marianne* (1731–41, Eng trans *The Life of Marianne*, 1736–42), was never finished. It is marked by an affected, "precious" style ("Marivaudage").

“ ”

L'âme se raffine à mesure qu'elle se gâte.

The soul refines itself in proportion to how it spoils itself.

1741 ***Le Paysan parvenu****, chapter 4.*

Mark, St, *also called* **John Mark** 1st century AD •*New Testament evangelist*• Born probably in Jerusalem, he is described as "John whose surname was Mark" (Acts 12:12, 25), and is commended in Colossians 4:10 and 2 Timothy 4:11. He helped the Apostles Barnabas and **Paul** during their first missionary journey, but caused a split between them over the question of his loyalty. Traditionally the author of the second Gospel, he was also described as the "disciple and interpreter" of Peter in Rome. In medieval art, Mark is symbolized by the lion. His feast day is April 25.

Markham, Beryl 1902–86 •*English-African aviator*• Born in England, she moved with her father to East Africa in 1906, and she grew up learning Masai and Swahili. She apprenticed with her father as a horse trainer and breeder, until he left Africa for Peru in 1919. She decided to remain in her adopted homeland and later turned to aviation. From 1931 to 1936 she carried mail, passengers and supplies in her small plane to remote corners of Africa, including the Sudan, Tanganyika, Kenya and Rhodesia. In 1936 she became the first person to fly solo across the Atlantic from east to west, taking off in England and crashlanding in Nova Scotia 21 hours and 25 minutes later.

Markievicz, Constance Georgine, Countess, *née* **Gore-Booth** 1868–1927 •*Irish nationalist and first British woman member of Parliament*• Born in London, daughter of Sir Henry Gore-Booth of County Sligo, she was a society beauty who studied art at the Slade School in London and in Paris, where she met and married (1900) Count Casimir Markievicz. They settled in Dublin in 1903, and in 1908 she joined Sinn Fein and became a friend of **Maud Gonne**. Her husband left in 1913 for Ukraine and never returned. She fought in the Easter Rising in Dublin (1916) and was sentenced to death, but was reprieved in the general amnesty of 1917. In 1918 she was elected Sinn Fein Member of Parliament for the St Patrick's division of Dublin—the first British woman member of Parliament—but refused to take her seat. She was elected to the first Dáil Éireann in 1919 and became Minister for Labour, but was imprisoned twice. After the Irish Civil War she was a member of the Dáil from 1923.

Markov, Andrei Andreyevich 1856–1922 •*Russian mathematician*• Born in Ryazan, he studied at the University of St Petersburg, where he was professor from 1893 to 1905. He worked on number theory, continued fractions, the moment problem, and the law of large numbers in probability theory, but his name is best known for the concept of Markov chain, a series of events in which the probability of a given event occurring depends only on the immediately previous event.

Markova, Dame Alicia, *stage name of* **Lilian Alicia Marks** 1910– •*English ballerina*• Born in London, she joined **Sergei Diaghilev**'s Ballets Russes (1924–29), then returned to Britain to the Vic-Wells (later Sadler's Wells and Royal) Ballet. A period of partnership with **Anton Dolin** led to their establishment of The Markova-Dolin Company in 1935, and the pair was famed for their interpretations of *Giselle*. Their touring group developed into the London Festival Ballet (1949), which became English National Ballet in 1988. She was given the honorary title of Dame Commander, Order of the British Empire, in 1963, was a director of the Metropolitan Opera Ballet (1963–69), and has been a governor of the Royal Ballet since 1973 and president of the London Festival (now English National) Ballet since 1986.

Marks (of Broughton), Simon Marks, Baron 1888–1964 •*English businessman*• Born in Leeds, he was educated at Manchester Grammar School. In 1907 he inherited the 60 Marks and Spencer "penny bazaars," which his father, Michael Marks, and Thomas Spencer had built up from 1884. In collaboration with **Israel** (later Lord) **Sieff**, his schoolfriend and brother-in-law, Marks expanded Marks and Spencer from a company with the policy of "Don't ask the price—it's a penny" to a major retail chain.

Marlborough, Duchess of *See* **Churchill, Sarah**

Marlborough, John Churchill, 1st Duke of 1650–1722 •*English soldier*• Born in Ashe, Devon, he was the son of Sir Winston Churchill, an impoverished Devonshire Royalist. His first post was as page to the Duke of York (the future **James VII and II**). The patronage of Barbara Villiers (Duchess of Cleveland) enriched him, and brought him an ensigncy in the Guards (1667). Service in Tangier and the Netherlands, combined with the influence of his sister Arabella, mistress of the Duke of York, brought him promotion to colonel. His prospects were further enhanced by his secret marriage in 1677 to Sarah Jennings (see **Sarah Churchill**), an attendant to, and close friend of, the Princess, later Queen **Anne**. In 1678 his discreet handling of a confidential mission to William of Orange (**William III**) led to his ennoblement as Baron Churchill of Eyemouth (1682). In 1685 he crushed the rebellion led by the Duke of **Monmouth**. When William landed, Churchill pledged his support to his cause, and the value of his defection was recognized by his elevation to the earldom of Marlborough. After service in William's Irish campaign, Marlborough was given supreme command of the British and Dutch forces in the War of the Spanish Succession (1701–14). His march to the Danube brought him the vital cooperation of Prince **Eugène of Savoy**, and ended in the victory of Donauworth and the costly but unequivocal triumph of Blenheim (1704), which earned him a palatial residence at Woodstock. He defeated **Louis XIV** in the campaign of 1706 at Ramillies and foiled the Duc de **Vendôme**'s 1708 attempt to recover Flanders, which led to the surrender of Lille and Ghent. The French recovered from their failure of 1709 at Malplaquet; however in 1711 Marlborough displayed his military flair when he forced the Duc de **Villars**'s "impregnable" lines and went on to capture Bouchain. The Treaty of Utrecht (1713) sacrificed virtually everything for which the war had been fought and Marlborough fell from favor, while Queen Anne had transferred her friendship from Sarah to **Abigail Masham**. In 1711 Marlborough, charged with embezzlement, was dismissed, although he was later restored to his honors by **George I** (1714).

Marley, Bob (Robert Nesta) 1945–81 •*Jamaican singer, guitarist and composer of reggae music*• He was born in the rural parish of St Ann. He moved to Kingston at the age of 14, made his first record at 19, and in 1965, with Peter Tosh (originally Winston Hubert MacIntosh) and Bunny Wailer (originally Neville O'Reilly Livingston), formed the vocal trio The Wailers. Together they became the first reggae artists to gain international success; Marley continued to build on this through a series of world tours after the departure of his original collaborators. By the 1970s, both through his music and his religious and political views (which made him, at one point, the victim of an assassination attempt), he became a national hero, and in 1978 he staged the famous "One Love" concert to try to broker a deal between Jamaica's warring political parties. In 1980, as the international voice of political and cultural emancipation, he performed at the ceremonies marking independence for Zimbabwe. A devout Rastafarian, Marley made reggae popular with white audiences through his warm, expressive voice, his willingness to embrace rock styles and techniques, and his memorable compositions—from the lyrical "No Woman, No Cry" to the fiercely political "Exodus" and "I Shot the Sheriff" (covered by **Eric Clapton** in 1974). Although he suffered from cancer in his last years, his output was undiminished and he remained a major force in popular music. His albums include *Catch a Fire* (1972), *Exodus* (1977) and *Uprising* (1980).

Marlowe, Christopher 1564–93 •*English dramatist*• He was born in Canterbury, Kent, a shoemaker's son, and educated at King's School and Benet (Corpus Christi) College, Cambridge. His *Tamburlaine the Great*, in two parts, was first printed in 1590, and probably produced in 1587. In spite of its bombast and violence, it was infinitely superior to any tragedy that had yet appeared on the English stage. *The Tragical History of Dr Faustus* was probably produced soon after *Tamburlaine*; the earliest edition is dated 1604. *Faustus* is rather a series of detached scenes than a finished drama, and some of the scenes are evidently not by Marlowe. *The Jew of Malta*, produced after 1588 and first published in 1633, is very uneven. *Edward II*, produced about 1590, is the most mature of his plays. It does not have the impressive poetry of *Faustus* and the first two acts of *The Jew of Malta*, but it is planned and executed with more firmness and solidity. *The Massacre at Paris*, his weakest play, survives in a mutilated state, and *The Tragedy of Dido* (1594), left probably in a fragmentary state by Marlowe and finished by **Thomas Nashe**, is also of slight value. Marlowe doubtless contributed to the three parts of **Shakespeare**'s *Henry VI*, and probably to *Titus Andronicus*. A wild, shapeless tragedy, *Lust's Dominion* (1657) may have been adapted from one of Marlowe's lost plays. The unfinished poem, *Hero and Leander*, composed in heroic couplets, was first published in 1598; a second edition, with Chapman's continuation, followed the same year. Marlowe's translations of **Ovid**'s *Amores* and of the first book of **Lucan**'s *Pharsalia* add nothing to his fame. The pastoral ditty, "Come, Live with Me and Be My Love," to which Sir **Walter Raleigh** wrote an Answer, was imitated, but not equaled, by **Robert Herrick**, **John Donne** and others, and was first printed in *The Passionate Pilgrim* (1599). Marlowe led an irregular life, kept dubious company, and was on the point of being arrested when he was fatally stabbed in a tavern brawl. In tragedy he prepared the way for Shakespeare, on whose early work his influence is evident.

" "

Accurst be he that first invented war.

1587 ***Tamburlaine the Great*** *(printed 1590), part I, act 2, scene 4.*

Marquand, John P(hillips) 1893–1960 •*US novelist*• Born in Wilmingon, Delaware, he was educated at Harvard University. He served with the military, was a war correspondent and wrote advertising copy. He started as a writer of popular stories for magazines, featuring the Japanese detective Mr Moto, and went on to produce a series of notable novels gently satirizing affluent middle-class US life. Key titles are *The Late George Apley* (1937), *Wickford Point* (1939) and *Point of No Return* (1949).

Marquet, (Pierre) Albert 1875–1947 •*French artist*• Born in Bordeaux, he studied under **Gustave Moreau** and was one of the original Fauves. After initial hardships he became primarily an impressionist landscape painter and traveled widely, painting many pictures of the Seine (such as *Pont neuf*), Le Havre and Algiers in a cool restrained style.

Márquez, Gabriel García 1928– •*Colombian novelist and Nobel Prize winner*• Born in Aracataca, he studied law and journalism at the National University of Colombia, Bogotá. He worked as a journalist from 1950 to 1965, when he devoted himself to fiction writing. One of Latin America's most formidable writers, he is a master of "magic realism," the practice of representing possible events as if they were wonders and impossible events as if they were commonplace. His best-known work is *Cien años de soledad* (1967, Eng trans *One Hundred Years of Solitude*, 1970), a vast, referential "total" novel charting the history of a family, a house and a town, from edenic, mythic genesis through the history of wars, politics, and economic exploitation to annihilation at a moment of apocalyptic revelation. It is regarded as one of the great novels of the 20th century. Many of his other novels have been translated, including *El otoño del patriarca* (1975, Eng trans *The Autumn of the Patriarch*, 1976), *Crónica de una muerte anunciada* (1981, Eng trans *Chronicle of a Death Foretold*, 1982), *El amor en los tiempos del colera* (1985, Eng trans *Love in the Time of Cholera*, 1988) and *Doce cuentos peregrinos* (1992, Eng trans *Strange Pilgrims*, 1993). He was awarded the Nobel Prize for literature in 1982.

Marquis, Don(ald Robert Perry) 1878–1937 •*US novelist, playwright and poet*• Born in Walnut, Illinois, he abandoned formal education at age 15 and had a varied career as a journalist, but became a celebrity as a comic writer with *The Old Soak's History of the World* (1924). *archy and mehitabel* (1927) and *archys life of mehitabel* (1933) follow the fortunes of Archy the cockroach, who cannot reach the typewriter's shift key (hence the lowercase titles), and Mehitabel, an alley cat.

Marriner, Sir Neville 1924– •*English conductor and violinist*• He was born in Lincoln, and studied at the Royal College of Music. He was a violinist in the Philharmonia Orchestra and the London Symphony Orchestra (1956–68), and in 1958 founded his own chamber orchestra, the Academy of St Martin-in-the-Fields, which he directed until 1978. Although principally associated with baroque and rococo music for small orchestra, he has also performed 20th-century music and opera. He was knighted in 1985.

Marryat, Frederick, *known as* **Captain Marryat** 1792–1848 •*English naval officer and novelist*• Born in London, he sailed as midshipman under Lord **Cochrane** in 1806, and after service in the West Indies took command of a sloop cruising off St Helena to guard against the escape of **Napoleon I**. On his return to England (1826) he was given the command of the *Ariadne* (1828), but he resigned in 1830 to lead the life of a writer. He was the author of a series of novels on sea life, including *Frank Mildmay* (1829), *Peter Simple* (1833), *Mr Midshipman Easy* (1834) and *The Phantom Ship* (1839). Retiring to his small farm of Langham, Norfolk, in 1843, he wrote the stories for children for which he is best remembered, including *Children of the New Forest* (1847).

Marsalis, Wynton 1961– •*US trumpeter and composer*• He was born in New Orleans. His father, Ellis Marsalis, is a distinguished jazz pianist and teacher, and his brothers, Branford, Delfayeo and Jason, all became musicians. He learned to play from the age of eight, and is unusual in his dual achievement in both classical and jazz music. He played with **Art Blakey**'s Jazz Messengers (along with Branford Marsalis, tenor and soprano saxophones) from 1980–82, before forming the first of many ensembles under his own leadership. He became the figurehead of the neo-bop jazz renaissance of the 1980s, and went on to absorb wider aspects of the jazz tradition, including the early New Orleans, blues and gospel styles, within modern treatments in a range of recordings and performance projects. In 1983 he released *Think of One* (jazz) and *Trumpet Concertos* (classical), becoming the first musician to win (or even be nominated for) Grammy awards in both categories. In 1997 he was awarded the Pulitzer Prize for Music for *Blood on the Fields*.

Marsh, Dame (Edith) Ngaio 1899–1982 •*New Zealand detective novelist and theater director*• Born in Christchurch, she had brief careers on stage and as an interior decorator, then introduced her detective/hero Roderick Alleyn in her first novel *A Man Lay Dead* (1934), which was followed by 30 more stories ending with *Light Thickens* (1982). In theater, she toured with the Wilkie company during the early 1920s, and during the 1940s and 1950s devoted much time to theatrical production in New Zealand, founding the Little Theatre in Christchurch. She also wrote on art, theater, and crime fiction. She was given the honorary title of Dame Commander, Order of the British Empire, in 1948.

Marsh, O(thniel) C(harles) 1831–99 •*US paleontologist*• Born in Lockport, New York, and wealthy by inheritance, he studied at Yale and in Germany, and became first Professor of Paleontology at Yale in 1866, without a salary or classes to teach. From 1870 to 1873 he led a series of expeditions through the western territories making spectacular discoveries of vertebrate fossils; this led him into bitter clashes with **Edward Drinker Cope**, who organized rival dinosaur collecting expeditions. Marsh discovered (mainly in the Rocky Mountains) over a thousand species of extinct American vertebrates, including dinosaurs and mammals. By 1874 he was able to establish an evolutionary lineage for horses using the fossil remains which he had assembled, and he also contributed to the documentation of evolutionary changes with his discovery of Cretaceous birds with teeth.

Marsh, Rodney William 1947– •*Australian cricket player*• Born in Armadale, Perth, Western Australia, he established his reputation as a wicket-keeper playing for Western Australia, often in close collaboration with legendary fast bowler **Dennis Lillee**. He made his debut as wicket-keeper for Australia in 1970 and continued in the role for 14 years, making a record total of 355 dismissals. He was also highly effective as a batsman.

Marshal, William, 1st Earl of Pembroke and Strigul c. 1146–1219 •*English nobleman, regent of England*• The nephew of the Earl of Salisbury, he supported **Henry II** against **Richard I**, Cœur de Lion. Pardoned by Richard, he became a marshal of England and after Richard died supported the new king, **John**. He advised John in his conflicts with the pope and his barons, and brought peace and prosperity to Ireland (1207–13). After John's death he was appointed regent (1216–19) for the nine-year-old **Henry III**, and concluded a peace treaty with the French.

Marshall, George Catlett 1880–1959 •*US soldier, politician, and Nobel Prize winner*• He was born in Uniontown, Pennsylvania. He was commissioned in 1901, and as chief of staff (1939–45) he directed the US Army throughout World War II. After two years in China as special representative of the president, he became secretary of state (1947–49) and originated the Marshall Aid plan for the postwar reconstruction of Europe (ERP). In 1950 he was made secretary of defense by President **Truman**. He was awarded the Nobel Peace Prize in 1953.

Marshall, John 1755–1835 •*US jurist*• Born near Germantown, Virginia, he served (1775–79) in the Continental army during the American Revolution and afterward studied law and became active in Virginia state politics. President **John Adams** appointed him chief justice of the Supreme Court in 1801. During his 34-year tenure, he established the power and independence of the Supreme Court as well as the fundamental principles of constitutional law. He ended the practice by which each justice wrote a separate opinion, instead producing a single majority opinion that stood as the verdict of the Court. His most important decision was in the case of *Marbury* v. *Madison* (1803), which established the principle of judicial review, asserting the Court's authority to determine the constitutionality of legislation. He is the single most influential figure in US legal history.

Marshall, Sir John Hubert 1876–1958 •*English archaeologist and administrator*• Born in Chester, he studied classics at Cambridge and excavated in Greece before being appointed director general of archaeology in India (1902–31). He reorganized the Indian Archaeological Survey, recruiting Indians for the first time, established an ambitious program for the listing and preservation of monuments, expanded museum services, and excavated widely on early historic sites. Prehistoric research was established on an equal footing in the 1920s with extensive excavation at Mohenjo Daro and Harappa, the chief cities of the Indus civilization which flourished in the northwest of the subcontinent c. 2300–1750 BC.

Marshall, Paule, *originally* **Valenza Pauline Burke** 1929– •*US writer*• She was born in Brooklyn, New York, to parents who had emigrated from Barbados during World War I. She grew up during the Depression, graduated from Brooklyn College and worked for *Our World Magazine*. *Brown Girl, Brownstones* (1959), her first novel, is regarded as a classic of African-American literature, telling the story of the coming of age of Seling Boyce, the daughter of Barbadian immigrants living through the Depression and World War I. Her subsequent novels are *The Chosen Place, the Timeless People* (1969), *Praisesong for the Widow* (1983), *Daughters* (1992) and *The Fisher King* (2000).

Marshall, Penny, *originally* **Penny Marscharelli** 1942– •*US film director and comedienne*• Born in Brooklyn, New York, she established her reputation as a comedy actress in television shows like *The Odd Couple* (1971–75) and *Laverne and Shirley* (1976–83). She made her debut as a film director with *Jumpin' Jack Flash* (1986) and scored a box office success with *Big* (1988). Her other films include *Awakenings* (1990), *A League of Their Own* (1992), *The Preacher's Wife* (1996) and *Riding in Cars with Boys* (2001).

Marshall, Thurgood 1908–93 •*US jurist*• Born in Baltimore, Maryland, and educated at Lincoln and Howard universities, he joined the legal staff of the National Association for the Advancement of Colored People, and argued many important civil rights cases. He served as a judge of the US Court of Appeals (1961–65) and as Solicitor-General of the United States (1965–67) before becoming the first African-American justice of the US Supreme Court (1967–91).

“ ”

If the United States is indeed the great melting pot, the negro either didn't get in the pot or he didn't get melted down.

*1987 In the **New York Times**, September 9.*

Marston, John 1576–1634 •*English dramatist and satirist*• Born in Wardington, Oxfordshire, he attended Brasenose College, Oxford, and then studied law at the Middle Temple. He began to write for the theater in 1599, and in 1602 published *Antonio and Mellida* and *Antonio's Revenge*, two gloomy and ill-constructed tragedies, partially redeemed by some strikingly powerful passages. A comedy, *The Malcontent* (1604), more skillfully constructed, was dedicated to **Ben Jonson**, with whom he had many quarrels and reconciliations, and with Jonson and **George Chapman** he wrote the comedy *Eastward Ho* (1605), for which, due to some reflections on the Scots, the authors were imprisoned. Other plays include *The Dutch Courtesan* (1605, a comedy), *Parasitaster, or the Fawn* (1606), *Sophonisba* (1606, a tragedy) and *What You Will* (1607). He gave up playwriting, and took orders in 1609, and was a clergyman at Christchurch, Hampshire (1616–31).

Martel, Charles *See* **Charles Martel**

Martens, Wilfried 1936– •*Belgian statesman*• Educated at the University of Louvain, he became minister for community problems in 1968. He was president of the Dutch-speaking Social Christian Party (CVP) from 1972 to 1979, when he became prime minister at the head of a coalition. He continued in office until 1992, apart from a brief break in 1981, heading no fewer than six coalition governments. Since 1992 he has been minister of state.

Martial, *properly* **Marcus Valerius Martialis** c. 40–c. 104 AD •*Roman poet and epigrammatist*• Born in Bilbilis, Spain, he went to Rome in AD 64 and became a client of the influential Spanish house of the **Seneca**s, through which he found a patron in Calpurnius Piso. The failure of the Pisonian plot to assassinate **Cicero** lost Martial his closest friends—**Lucan** and Seneca. When the emperor **Titus** dedicated the Colosseum in 80, Martial's epigrams in *Liber Spectaculorum* ("Book of Spectacles") brought him equestrian rank. In 86 appeared the first 12 books of the *Epigrams*, satirical comments on contemporary events and society.

“ ”

Non est vivere, sed valere vita est.
Life's not just being alive, but being well.

***Epigrams**, book 6, no. 70.*

Martin, St c. 316–c. 400 AD •*French churchman and a patron saint of France*• Born in Savaria, Pannonia, he was educated at Pavia, serving in the army under **Constantine I (the Great)**, and **Julian**. He became a disciple of **St Hilary** of Poitiers, and went to Gaul, where he founded a monastery at Ligugé near Poitiers (c. 360), the first in France. In 371–72 he was made Bishop of Tours. The fame of his good works and his reputation as a worker of miracles attracted crowds of visitors. To avoid distraction he established the monastery of Marmoutier near Tours, in which he himself lived. His military cloak, which he gave to a beggar, has become the symbol of charity.

Martin, Agnes 1912– •*Canadian painter*• Born in Maklin, Saskatchewan, she studied at Columbia University in the 1940s, and began painting in a style called biomorphic abstraction. She lived in New Mexico from 1956 to 1957, and in 1959 began painting the barely visible grids of vertical and horizontal lines on pale monochrome backgrounds which characterize her work, and demand quiet concentration from the viewer. In 1967 she left New York and settled permanently in New Mexico.

Martin, Archer John Porter 1910–2002 •*English biochemist and Nobel Prize winner*• Born in London, he trained at Cambridge and then at the Lister Institute, where he studied the vitamin deficiency disease pellagra (1937–38) and the significance of B vitamins. Martin then moved to the Wool Industry Research Association in Leeds (1938–46) where, with **Richard Synge**, he developed the technique of partition chromatography (the use of silica gel to separate amino acid derivatives from protein compounds) in the analysis of protein structure. Their technique revolutionized analytical biochemistry, and it earned him the 1952 Nobel Prize for chemistry, shared with Synge.

Martin, Dean, *originally* **Dino Paul Crocetti** 1917–95 •*US entertainer*• Born in Steubenville, Ohio, he worked in a steel mill and boxed as a welterweight before starting to earn a living as a nightclub crooner. Teamed with comedian **Jerry Lewis** in 1945, he enjoyed spectacular success as a nightclub attraction and in such films as *The Stooge* (1953) and *Hollywood or Bust* (1956), and, going solo from 1956, displayed his dramatic abilities and comic touch in films like *The Young Lions* (1958) and *Kiss Me Stupid* (1964). He found enduring popularity as a booze-loving, mellow-voiced singer whose casual, lighthearted manner belied his consummate professionalism. Part of the **Frank Sinatra** Rat Pack, he starred in the long-running television series *The Dean Martin Show* (1965–74).

Martin, Glenn Luther 1886–1955 •*US aircraft manufacturer*• He was born in Macksburg, Iowa, and educated at Kansas Wesleyan University in Salina. Influenced as a boy by the flights of the **Wright** brothers, he built his first glider in California in 1905, and by 1909 had built and flown his first powered aircraft. He invented a bomb sight and a free-fall parachute in 1913 and produced his MB-1 bomber at a factory in Cleveland in 1918. In 1929 he moved to Baltimore, producing such famous aircraft as the B-10 bomber and the China Clipper flying boat. In World War II his factory created the B-26 Marauder, Mariner and Mars flying boats.

Martin, Homer Dodge 1836–97 •*US painter*• He was born in Albany, New York, and his early work was in the style of the Hudson River school, emphasizing the grandeur of the landscape. Despite failing eyesight, his later years were a time of creative flowering, and the contemplative, often melancholy paintings he made in the late 1880s and 1890s, including *Westchester Hills*, *The Sun Worshippers*, and *Adirondack Scenery*, are his finest work.

Martin, Michael John 1945– •*Scottish Labour politician*• Born in poverty in Glasgow, he was a sheet metal worker and trades union official before entering local government. He became member of Parliament for Glasgow, Springburn, in 1979, and in 2000 he was elected Speaker of the House of Commons, becoming the first Roman Catholic to hold the office since the Reformation.

Martin, Richard 1754–1834 •*Irish lawyer and humanitarian*• Born in Dublin, he was dubbed "Humanity Martin" by **George IV**, who was his friend. He was educated at Harrow and Trinity College, Cambridge. As Member of Parliament for Galway (1801–26) he sponsored a bill in 1822 to make the cruel treatment of cattle illegal, the first legislation of its kind. Through his efforts the Royal Society for the Prevention of Cruelty to Animals was formed.

Martin, Steve 1945– •*US film actor and writer*• Born in Waco, Texas, he began performing standup comedy as a student, when audiences of 20,000 witnessed the verbal dexterity and manic inventiveness that would eventually make him a star. As a comedy writer, he won an Emmy award for *The Smothers Brothers Comedy Hour* (1968) for television, and he was awarded Grammys for his best-selling albums *Let's Get Small* (1977) and *Wild and Crazy* (1978). He made his big screen debut in the short *The Absent-Minded Waiter* (1977) and took the title role in the juvenile comedy *The Jerk* (1979). His numerous films include the dramatic musical *Pennies from Heaven* (1981), *Dead Men Don't Wear Plaid* (1982), *The Man with Two Brains* (1983), *Little Shop of Horrors* (1986), *Roxanne* (1987), *Parenthood* (1989), *L.A. Story* (1991), *Novocaine* (2001), and *Cheaper by the Dozen* (2003).

Martin du Gard, Roger 1881–1958 •*French novelist and Nobel Prize winner*• He was born in Neuilly-sur-Seine. After studying history, he qualified as an archivist before turning to writing, publishing his first novel, *Devenir* ("Becoming"), in 1909. After serving in World War I he lived as a recluse and devoted himself to writing in various forms. His novels include *Jean Barois* (1913, Eng trans 1949), which deals, among other matters, with the **Dreyfus** affair, and *Vieille France* (1933, Eng trans *The Postman*, 1954), a study of a less-than-idyllic rural life. He is best known, however, for his eight-novel series *Les Thibault* (1922–40, Eng trans *The Thibaults*, 1939–41), dealing with family life during the first decades of the 20th century. He was awarded the Nobel Prize for literature in 1937.

Martineau, Harriet 1802–76 •*English writer*• She was born in Norwich, Norfolk. Her first publications included *Devotional Exercises for the Use of Young Persons* and *Addresses for the Use of Families* (both 1826), and she became a successful author through her *Illustrations of Political Economy* and *Poor Laws and Paupers Illustrated* (1833–34), and settled in London. After a visit to the US (1834–36) she published *Society in America* and the novels *Deerbrook* (1839) and *The Hour and the Man* (1840), the latter about **Toussaint Louverture**. From 1839 to 1844 she was an invalid, suffering from heart disease and lack of hearing at Tynemouth, but she recovered after mesmerism (a type of hypnotism), her subsequent belief in which alienated many friends. She visited Egypt and Palestine, and wrote *Eastern Life* (1848). In 1851, in conjunction with H G Atkinson, she published *Letters on the Laws of Man's Social Nature*, which was so agnostic that it gave much offense, and in 1853 she translated and condensed **Auguste Comte**'s *Philosophie positive*. She also wrote much for the daily and weekly press and the larger reviews.

Martinet, Jean d. 1672 •*French army officer*• He won renown as a military engineer and tactician, devising forms of battle maneuver, pontoon bridges, and a type of copper assault boat used in **Louis XIV**'s Dutch campaign. He also achieved notoriety for his stringent and brutal forms of discipline, and was "accidentally" killed by his troops at the siege of Duisburg.

Martini or **Memmi, Simone** c. 1284–1344 •*Italian painter*• Born in Siena, he was a pupil of **Duccio di Buoninsegna**. He was one of the major artists of the 14th-century Sienese school, notable for his grace of line and exquisite color. He worked in Assisi from 1333 to 1339 and at the papal court at Avignon from 1339 to 1344. His works include the *Annunciation* (1333, Uffizi, Florence), and *Christ Reproved by his Parents* (1342, Walker Art Gallery, Liverpool).

Martinson, Harry Edmund 1904–78 •*Swedish poet, novelist and Nobel Prize winner*• He was born in Jäshög, Blekinge, and after a harsh childhood as a parish orphan he went to sea as a stoker (1919). He made his poetic debut in 1929, and soon found an individual voice, particularly as a nature poet. His masterpiece, the poetic space epic *Aniara* (1956), questions whether humanity possesses sufficient ethical maturity to control its own technological inventions, and was set to music as an opera by Karl-Birger Blomdahl (1916–68). He shared the 1974 Nobel Prize for literature with the Swedish novelist **Eyvind Johnson**.

Martinů, Bohuslav 1890–1959 •*Czech composer*• Born in Policka, in 1906 he was sent to the Prague Conservatory, where disciplinary regulations and the routine course of studies irritated him. Expelled from there, he played the violin in the Czech Philharmonic Orchestra, and in 1920 attracted attention with his ballet *Ishtar*. Readmitted to the Conservatory, he studied under **Joseph Suk**, then worked in Paris. In 1941 he escaped from Occupied France to the US, where he produced a number of important works, including his First Symphony (1942). A prolific composer, he ranges from orchestral works in 18th-century style, including a harpsichord concerto, to modern program pieces evoked by unusual stimuli such as football (*Half Time*, 1925) or airplanes (*Thunderbolt P.47*). His operas include the miniature *Comedy on a Bridge* (1935).

Marvell, Andrew 1621–78 •*English metaphysical poet*• Born in Winestead, Yorkshire, he was educated at Hull Grammar School and Trinity College, Cambridge. He traveled (1642–46) in Holland, France, Italy and Spain. After a period as tutor to Lord **Fairfax**'s daughter, when he wrote his pastoral and garden poems, he was appointed tutor to **Cromwell**'s ward, William Dutton. In 1657 he became **Milton**'s assistant and two years later, Member of Parliament for Hull. In 1663–65 he accompanied Lord Carlisle as secretary to the embassy to Muscovy, Sweden and Denmark, but the rest of his life was devoted to his parliamentary duties. Marvell's works are divided by the Restoration into two very distinct groups. As a poet, he belongs to the pre-Restoration period, although most of his poetry was not published until 1681 as *Miscellaneous Poetry.* A subsequent volume was entitled *Poems on Affairs of State* (1689–97). After 1660 he concentrated on politics, writing *The Rehearsal Transpos'd* (1672–73), against religious intolerance, and in 1677 his most important tract, the *Account of the Growth of Popery and Arbitrary Government*, which was published anonymously.

Marx, Karl 1818–83 •*German social, political and economic theorist*• He was born in Trier and brought up in a Jewish family that converted to Protestantism in order to escape anti-Semitism. He studied at the Universities of Bonn (1835–36) and Berlin (1836–41), but took up history, **Hegel**ian philosophy and **Feuerbach**'s materialism. In 1842 he edited the liberal Cologne paper *Rheinische Zeitung*, and after it was suppressed moved to Paris (1843) and Brussels (1845). There, with **Friedrich Engels** as his closest collaborator and disciple, he reorganized the Communist League, which met in London in 1847. In 1848 he finalized the famous *Communist Manifesto*, which attacked the state as the instrument of oppression, and religion and culture as ideologies of the capitalist class. He was expelled from Brussels, and in 1849 settled in London, where he studied economics, and wrote the first volume of his major work *Das Kapital* (Vol 1 1867, Vols 2 & 3 posthumously 1884, 1894), one of the most influential works of the 19th century, in which Marx developed his mature doctrines of the theory of surplus value, class conflict and the exploitation of the working class, and predicted the victory of socialism over capitalism and the ultimate withering away of the state as the classless society of communism was achieved. He died with this work unfinished. Despite the apparent failure of Marxist principles as practiced in communist Europe, his theories still exert an enormous influence on social science. He died in 1883 and was buried in Highgate cemetery.

“ ”

In manufacture and in handicrafts, the worker uses a tool; in the factory, he serves a machine.

1867 ***Das Kapital.***

Marx Brothers •*US family of film comedians*• They were born in New York City, the sons of German immigrants, and were called Julius Henry (Groucho, 1890–1977), Leonard (Chico, 1887–1961), Adolph Arthur (Harpo, 1888–1964) and Herbert (Zeppo, 1901–1979). They began their stage career in vaudeville in a team called the Six Musical Mascots that included their mother, Minnie (d. 1929), and an aunt; another brother, Milton (Gummo, 1894–1977), left the act early on. As the Marx Brothers, their main reputation was made in films such as *Animal Crackers, Monkey Business* (both 1932), *Horse Feathers* and *Duck Soup* (both 1933). Herbert retired from films in 1935, but the others scored further successes in *A Night at the Opera* (1935), *A Day at the Races* (1937), *A Day at the Circus* (1939), *Go West* (1940) and *The Big Store* (1941). *Love Happy* (1950) was the team's last. Each had a well-defined role: Groucho with his oversized mustache and wisecracks, Chico, the pianist with an individual technique, and Harpo, the mute clown and harp maestro.

Mary, Mother of Jesus, *also entitled* **the Blessed Virgin Mary** d. c. 63 AD •*Mother of Jesus*• The New Testament records the Annunciation, the conception of **Jesus** by the Holy Spirit (Matthew 1:18), her betrothal to **Joseph**, and the birth of Jesus. She only occasionally appears in the ministry of Jesus, but in John 19:25 she is at the Cross. The belief that her body ascended into heaven is celebrated in the festival of the Assumption, defined as Roman Catholic dogma in 1950. The Immaculate Conception has been a dogma since 1854. Belief in the appearances of the Virgin in such places as Lourdes, Fatima, and Medjugorje attracts many thousands of pilgrims each year. In Roman Catholic and Orthodox Christianity, she holds a special place as an intermediary between God and humanity.

Mary Magdalene, St, *also called* **Mary of Magdala** 1st century BC–1st century AD •*Early follower of Jesus*• Mary Magdalene was born probably in Magdala on the west coast of the sea of Galilee, hence her name. Luke 8:2 reports that **Jesus** exorcized seven evil spirits from her, and throughout the Church's history she has epitomized the archetypal repentant sinner. She features also in the narratives of Jesus's passion and resurrection as, seemingly with other women, she was present at the Cross and later at the empty tomb. Her feast day is July 22.

Mary I (Tudor) 1516–58 •*Queen of England and Ireland*• She was born in Greenwich, near London, the daughter of **Henry VIII** and his first wife, **Catherine of Aragon**. She was well educated, a good linguist, fond of music and devoted to her mother and the Catholic Church. After her mother's divorce, Henry forced her to sign a declaration that her mother's marriage had been unlawful. During the reign of her half brother **Edward VI**, she lived in retirement, refusing to conform to the new religion. On his death (1553) she became queen. She upset the Duke of Northumberland's (Sir Thomas **Percy**) conspiracy to set Henry's will aside in favor of his daughter-in-law Lady **Jane Grey**, and, with the support of the whole country, entered London in triumph. Northumberland and two others were executed, but Lady Jane and her husband were, for the present, spared. Mary proceeded very cautiously to bring back Catholicism, reinstated the Catholic bishops and imprisoned some of the leading reformers, but dared not restore the pope's supremacy. In spite of national protests, she determined to marry **Philip II**, king of Spain. The unpopularity of the proposal brought about Sir Thomas Wyatt's rebellion (1554), quelled mainly through Mary's courage and coolness. Lady Jane, her husband and father were executed, and the Princess Elizabeth (later **Elizabeth I**), suspected of complicity, was committed to the Tower of London. In 1554 Philip was married to Mary; parliament petitioned for reconciliation to the Holy See, and the realm was absolved from the papal censures. Soon after, the persecution of Protestant opposition which gave Mary the name of "Bloody Mary" began. In 1555 **Nicholas Ridley** and **Hugh Latimer** were brought to the stake, and **Thomas Cranmer** followed the next year. To what extent Mary herself was responsible for the cruelties practiced is unknown, but during the last three years of her reign 300 victims were burned. She died childless.

Mary II 1662–94 •*Stuart queen of Great Britain and Ireland*• Born at St James's Palace, London, she was the daughter of the Catholic Duke of York (later **James VII and II**) and his first wife, Anne Hyde (1638–71), but was brought up a Protestant. She was married (1677) to her first cousin, William of Orange, Stadtholder of the Netherlands, who in 1688 landed in Torbay with an Anglo-Dutch army in response to an invitation from seven Whig peers hostile to the arbitrary rule of James II. When James fled to France, Mary went to London from Holland and was proclaimed queen (1689), sharing the throne with her husband, who became King **William III**. Mary left executive authority with William (except when regent during his frequent absences abroad), but she was largely responsible for raising the moral standard of court life, and she took great interest in church appointments. Naturally kind, gracious and sincere, she died, childless, of smallpox.

Mary Queen of Scots 1542–87 •*Queen of Scotland 1542–67*• The daughter of **James V** of Scotland by his second wife, **Mary of Guise**, she was born at Linlithgow. She became queen when she was a week old. Promised in marriage to Prince **Edward** of England, son of **Henry VIII**, the Scottish parliament declared the promise null, precipitating war with England. After the Scots' defeat at Pinkie (1547), she was sent to the French court and married (1558) the Dauphin (later **Francis II**), but was widowed at 18 (1560) and returned to Scotland (1561). A Catholic with a clear dynastic claim, she was ambitious for the English throne, and in 1565 she married her cousin, Henry Stuart, Lord **Darnley**, who was a son of Lady Margaret Dougles, a granddaughter of **Henry VII**, but disgusted by his debauchery, was soon alienated from him. The vicious murder of **David Rizzio**, her Italian secretary, by Darnley and a group of Protestant nobles in her presence (1566) confirmed her insecurity. The birth of a son (the future **James VI and I**) failed to bring a reconciliation. When Darnley was found strangled after an explosion at his residence (1567), the chief suspect was the Earl of **Bothwell**, who underwent a mock trial and was acquitted. Mary's involvement is unclear, but she consented to marry Bothwell, a divorcé with whom she had become infatuated. The Protestant nobles rose against her; she surrendered at Carberry Hill, was imprisoned at Loch Leven and compelled to abdicate. After escaping she raised an army, but was defeated again by the confederate lords at Langside (1568). Placing herself under the protection of Queen **Elizabeth I**, she found herself instead a permanent prisoner in a succession of strongholds, ending up at Fotheringay. Her presence in England stimulated numerous plots to depose Elizabeth. Finally, in 1586, the queen's secretary of state, **Francis Walsingham**, got wind of a plot by **Anthony Babington**, and contrived to implicate Mary. Letters apparently from her and seeming to approve of Elizabeth's death passed along a postal route to which Walsingham himself had access. Mary was brought to trial in 1586 and sentenced to death, although it was not until February 1587 that Elizabeth signed the warrant of execution. It was carried out a few days later, and Mary was buried at Peterborough. In 1612 her body was moved to Henry VII's chapel at Westminster, where it still lies.

Mary of Guise, *also called* **Mary of Lorraine** 1515–60 •*French noblewoman and Scottish queen*• The daughter of Claude of Lorraine, 1st Duke of **Guise**, she married Louis d'Orléans, Duke of Longueville (1534), and **James V** of Scotland (1538), at whose death (1542) she was left with one child, **Mary Queen of Scots**. During the troubled years that followed, she acted with wisdom and moderation, but after she was made regent of Scotland (1554) she campaigned against Protestantism and allowed the Guises so much influence that the Protestant nobles raised a rebellion (1559), which continued until her death at Edinburgh Castle.

Mary of Hungary 1505–58 •*Queen of Hungary and Bohemia*• The daughter of **Philip I** (the Handsome) of Castile and **Juana** the Mad, she married Louis II of Hungary and Bohemia (ruled 1516–26) in 1522. Their life of debauchery soon disqualified the king from affairs of state, and after his death (supposedly while fleeing from battle) Hungary was divided between the Turks and the Austrian Habsburgs. In 1531 Mary's brother, Emperor **Charles V**, asked her to act as regent in his Low Countries possessions, which she did from 1531 to 1555. Mary's rule subjugated the interests of the Netherlands provinces to those of Spain and the empire, which helped lay the ground for the Eighty Years' War (1568–1648) by the Low Countries against Habsburg rule.

Mary of Lorraine *See* **Mary of Guise**

Mary of Magdala *See* **Mary Magdalene, St**

Mary of Modena, *née* **d'Este** 1658–1718 •*Queen of Great Britain and Ireland*• Born in Modena, the only daughter of Alfonso IV, Duke of Modena, she married James, Duke of York (1672), later **James VII and II**. After losing five children in infancy, she gave birth in 1688 to **James Francis Edward Stuart** (the future Old Pretender). This was received with skepticism, and the "warming pan" legend was born. When William of Orange (the future **William III**) landed in England later that year, she escaped to France with her infant son, to be joined there later by her deposed husband. She spent the rest of her life at St Germain.

Mary of Teck 1867–1953 •*Queen of Great Britain and Northern Ireland*• Born at Kensington Palace, London, she was the only daughter of Francis, Duke of Teck, and Princess Mary Adelaide of Cambridge, and a granddaughter of **George III**. She accepted a marriage proposal (1891) from the eldest son of the Prince of Wales, the Duke of Clarence, who within six weeks died from pneumonia. She then became engaged to his brother, the Duke of York, marrying him in 1893. After his accession (as **George V**) in 1910, Queen Mary accompanied him to Delhi as empress of India for the historically unique Coronation Durbar (1911). Mary was more sympathetic to changing habits than her husband, whom she helped to mold into a "people's king." After the abdication of her eldest son, **Edward VIII**, the throne was taken by her second son, **George VI**, whom she survived by 13 months. She died at Marlborough House, London, less than three months before the coronation of her granddaughter, **Elizabeth II**.

Masaccio, *real name* **Tommaso de Giovanni di Simone Guidi** 1401–1428? •*Italian painter of the Florentine school*• In his short life he brought about a revolution in the dramatic and realistic representation of biblical events which was recognized by his contemporaries and had a great influence on **Michelangelo** and, through him, on the entire 16th century. In many ways Masaccio began where **Giotto** left off. He stripped away all the decorative affectations of the International Gothic style and concentrated on the drama of the situation. His greatest work is the fresco cycle in the Brancacci Chapel of the church of Santa Maria del Carmine in Florence (1424–27). **Masolino da Panicale**, an inferior painter with whom Masaccio is associated, also worked there, as did **Filippino Lippi**.

Masaoka Shiki 1867–1902 •*Japanese poet*• He came from Ehime but lived in Tokyo. He worked with the traditional poetic forms, especially *waka* and *haiku*, refining them and devising new ways of seeing them, to the extent that there is good reason to think of him as the originator of the modern haiku. Some of his most beautiful and poignant verse was written in the final stages of his drawn-out and agonizing death from spinal tuberculosis.

Masaryk, Jan 1886–1948 •*Czechoslovakian diplomat and politician*• Born in Prague, the son of **Tomáš Masaryk**, he entered the diplomatic service in 1918, and from 1925 to 1938 was Czechoslovak ambassador in London. There, his fluent English and personal charm won him many friends, but proved inadequate to prevent **Neville Chamberlain** from imposing the Munich Agreement on his country. He became a popular broadcaster to his home country during World War II. In July 1941 he was appointed foreign minister of the Czechoslovakian government-in-exile, returning with President **Eduard Beneš** to Prague in 1945 and remaining in office in the hope of bridging the growing gap between East and West in the developing Cold War. On March 10, 1948, following the Communist takeover of power in Czechoslovakia, his body was found beneath the open window of the foreign ministry in Prague, and it was assumed that he killed himself in protest at the Stalinization of his homeland.

Masaryk, Tomáš Garrigue 1850–1937 •*Czechoslovakian statesman*• Born in Hodonín in Moravia, the son of a coachman, half Czech and half Slovak, he studied in Vienna and Leipzig, and became Professor of Philosophy at the University of Prague in 1882. Entering politics in the nationalistic atmosphere of the 1880s and 1890s, he made his name as an independent of courage and common sense. A deputy in the Czech and Austrian Imperial parliaments off and on after 1891, he was variously a "realist" and a "progressive," but his main political contribution came after 1914 when he traveled abroad to France, Britain, Russia and the US to win support and recognition for an independent state, first Czech, then Czechoslovak. He became its first president in 1918 and was regularly reelected until he retired in 1935 in favor of **Eduard Beneš**.

Mascagni, Pietro 1863–1945 •*Italian composer*• Born in Livorno, he produced the highly successful one-act opera *Cavalleria Rusticana* ("Rustic Chivalry") in 1890, now frequently performed with **Leoncavallo**'s *I Pagliacci* (1892). His many later operas failed to repeat this success, though arias and intermezzi from them are still performed.

Mascall, Eric Lionel 1905–93 •*English Anglo-Catholic theologian, and author*• He read mathematics for four years at Cambridge, but his interest in philosophy led him to theology, and he was ordained in 1932. After a few years in parish work he was appointed assistant warden of Lincoln Theological College, where he remained for eight years. He then taught philosophy of religion at Christ Church, Oxford (1946–62), and was Professor of Historical Theology at the University of London (1962–73). His books *He Who Is* (1943) and *Existence and Analogy* (1949) have become standard texts on natural theology. His other works include *Christian*

Theology and Natural Science (Oxford Bampton Lectures, 1956), the ecumenical *The Recovery of Unity* (1958) and *The Triune God* (1986).

Masefield, John Edward 1878–1967 •*English poet and novelist*• Born in Ledbury, Herefordshire, and educated at the King's School, Warwickshire, he joined the merchant marine, but ill health drove him ashore, and he worked as a journalist and writer. His sea poetry includes *Salt Water Ballads* (1902) and *Dauber* (1913), and his best-known narrative poem is *Reynard the Fox* (1919). Other works are *The Everlasting Mercy* (1911), *The Widow in the Bye-Street* (1912), *Shakespeare* (1911) and *Gallipoli* (1916). He also wrote novels such as *Odtaa* (1926) and *The Hawbucks* (1929), and plays including *The Trial of Jesus* (1925) and *The Coming of Christ* (1928). He became poet laureate in 1930 and his final work was *Grace Before Ploughing* (1966).

“ ”

I must down to the seas again, for the call of the running tide
Is a wild call and a clear call that may not be denied.

1902 "Sea Fever."

Masham, Lady Abigail, *née* **Hill** d. 1734 •*English courtier*• She was a cousin of **Sarah Churchill**, Duchess of Marlborough, through whose influence she entered the household of Queen **Anne**. In 1707 she married Samuel (later Baron) Masham. A Tory and a subtle intriguer, she gradually turned the queen against the Marlboroughs, and superseded her cousin (1710) as the queen's confidante and the power behind the throne. On Anne's death (1714) she withdrew into obscurity.

Masire, Quett Ketumile Joni 1925– •*Botswana statesman*• He began a journalistic career before entering politics. In 1962, with **Seretse Khama**, he was a founding member of the Botswana Democratic Party (BDP) and in 1965 became deputy prime minister. When Bechuanaland became the Republic of Botswana within the Commonwealth and full independence was achieved in 1966, Masire became vice president and, on Seretse Khama's death in 1980, president. He continued his predecessor's policy of nonalignment and helped Botswana become one of the most politically stable nations in Africa. Reelected several times, he served until his retirement in 1998.

Maskell, Dan(iel) 1908–92 •*English tennis player and commentator*• Born in London, he began his tennis career as a ball boy at the Queen's Club, London. He captained Britain's Davis Cup, and was one of the leading professional players of the 1930s, winning 16 titles. He was also a coach, before becoming a television commentator on the sport in 1950. Working until 1991, he became one of Britain's best-loved broadcasters.

Maskelyne, Nevil 1732–1811 •*English astronomer*• Born in London, he studied divinity at Trinity College, Cambridge, and joined the Royal Greenwich Observatory in 1755. In 1763 he produced the *British Mariner's Guide* and in 1765 he was appointed Astronomer Royal. He improved methods and instruments of observation and invented the prismatic micrometer. He went to St Helena to observe the transit of Venus, the aim being to make better estimates of the earth-sun distance, and in 1767 he founded the *Nautical Almanac*. He also measured the earth's density from the deflection of a plumb line, obtaining a value between 4.56 and 4.87 times that of water.

Maskelyne, (John) Nevil 1839–1917 •*English magician*• Born in Wiltshire, he became a watchmaker and built magic boxes and automata which he used in his entertainments. He joined forces with George Cooke (d. 1904) and they appeared together, first at Cheltenham and then at the Crystal Palace, London, in 1865. After Cooke's death Maskelyne moved his "Home of Magic" to the St George's Hall in 1905 with David Devant as his partner. He devoted much energy to exposing spiritualistic frauds.

Masolino da Panicale, *properly* **Thommaso di Cristoforo Fini** c. 1383–1447 •*Florentine painter*• He is usually associated with **Masaccio** because of his work with him in the Brancacci Chapel of the church of Santa Maria del Carmine in Florence. Masolino was, however, a much older artist, trained in the International Gothic style in the **Ghiberti** and Starnina workshops. The strongest early influence on him was **Gentile da Fabriano**. Masolino's greatest work is the fresco cycle in the Baptistery and Collegiata of Castiglione d'Olona near Como (1430s).

Mason, Charles 1730–87 •*English astronomer*• As an assistant at Greenwich Observatory with the English surveyor Jeremiah Dixon, he observed the transit of Venus at the Cape of Good Hope in 1761. From 1763 to 1767 Mason and Dixon were engaged to survey the boundary between Maryland and Pennsylvania. They reached a point 224 miles west of the Delaware River, but were prevented from further work by Native Americans. The survey was completed by others, but the boundary was called the Mason-Dixon Line.

Mason, James 1909–84 •*English actor*• Born in Huddersfield, West Yorkshire, he appeared at the Old Vic, London, and with the Gate Company in Dublin before making his film debut in *Late Extra* (1935). He attained stardom with his suave, saturnine villainy in costume dramas like *The Man in Grey* (1943) and *The Seventh Veil* (1945). Moving to Hollywood (1947), he became one of the most prolific, distinguished and reliable of cinema actors. He was nominated for an Academy Award for *A Star Is Born* (1954), *Georgy Girl* (1966) and *The Verdict* (1982). Other respected performances from more than 100 films include *Odd Man Out* (1946), *Lolita* (1962) and *The Shooting Party* (1984).

Masséna, André 1758–1817 •*French general*• The greatest of **Napoleon I**'s marshals, he fought in the campaigns in Upper Italy, defeating Count **Suvorov**'s Russians at Zurich (1799), and became Marshal of the Empire in 1804. In Italy he kept the Archduke Charles in check, crushed him at Caldiero, and overran Naples. In 1807 he was made Duke of Rivoli, and in the campaign of 1809 against Austria he earned the title of Prince of Essling. However, forced to retreat on the Iberian peninsula by Wellington's forces, he was relieved of his command in 1810.

Massenet, Jules Emile Frédéric 1842–1912 •*French composer*• Born near St Étienne, he studied at the Paris Conservatoire, where he became a professor (1878–96). He made his name with the comic opera *Don César de Bazan* (1872). Other operas are *Hérodiade* (1884), *Manon* (1884), *Le Cid* (1885), *Werther* (1892) and *Thaïs* (1894), and among his other works are oratorios, orchestral suites, music for piano, and songs.

Massey, William Ferguson 1856–1925 •*New Zealand statesman*• Born in Ireland, he emigrated to New Zealand, where he became a farmer. Elected to the House of Representatives (1894), he became leader of the opposition (1903) and, in 1912, prime minister, which office he held until his death. During World War I, he formed a coalition government (1915–19) with Sir **Joseph Ward**.

Massie, Allan 1938– •*Scottish novelist, critic and journalist*• Born in Singapore and raised in Aberdeenshire, he was educated at Cambridge, then taught in a private school before going to Italy, where he taught English as a foreign language. His first two novels, *Change and Decay in All Around I See* (1978) and *The Last Peacock* (1980), can be compared to the work of **Evelyn Waugh**. In both *The Death of Men* (1981) and *Augustus* (1986) he turned to Italy, while *Tiberius* (1990) and *Caesar* (1993) draw on his knowledge of the ancient world. Other novels include *A Question of Loyalties* (1989), *The Ragged Lion* (1994), *Shadows of Empire* (1997) and *Nero's Heirs* (1999).

Massine, Léonide, *originally* **Leonid Fyodorovich Myassin** 1896–1979 •*Russian dancer and choreographer*• Born in Moscow, he studied with the Imperial Ballet School at St Petersburg, becoming principal dancer and choreographer with **Sergei Diaghilev** (1914–21, 1925–28) and developing his interests in choreography with ballets like *Parade* (1917). He choreographed some controversial "symphonic ballets," such as *Choreartium* (1933), which was danced to Brahms's Fourth Symphony, and became principal dancer and choreographer for the Ballets Russes de Monte Carlo (1938–43). Though he worked periodically in the US, Massine settled in Europe, working freelance for companies like Sadler's Wells and Ballets des Champs Elysées. He appeared in the ballet films *The Red Shoes* (1948) and *The Tales of Hoffmann* (1950).

Massinger, Philip 1583–1640 •*English dramatist*• He was born in Salisbury, Wiltshire. After leaving Oxford without a degree, he became a playwright and was associated with **Philip Henslowe**. In later years he wrote many plays on his own, but much of his work was done in collaboration with others, particularly **John Fletcher**. The first in order of publication is *The Virgin Martyr* (1622), partly written by **Thomas Dekker**. In 1623 *The Duke of Milan* was published, a fine tragedy, but too rhetorical. Other plays include *The Great Duke of Florence* (1627) and *The Emperor of the East* (1631). **Nathan Field** joined Massinger in writing *The Fatal Dowry* (1632). *The City Madam* (licensed 1632) and *A New Way to Pay Old Debts* (1633) are Massinger's most masterly comedies—brilliant satirical studies, although without warmth or geniality.

" "

He that would govern others, first should be
The master of himself.

1623 ***The Bondman**, act 1, scene 3.*

Massio, Niccolò di Giovanni di *See* **Fabriano, Gentile da**

Massys *See* **Matsys**

Master of Flémalle *See* **Campin, Robert**

Masters, Edgar Lee 1869–1950 •*US writer*• Born in Garnett, Kansas, he was a successful lawyer in Chicago, then turned to writing poetry. He became famous with the satirical *Spoon River Anthology* (1915), a book of epitaphs in free verse about lives of people in Illinois. He published several more collections and some novels, and returned to his first success with *The New Spoon River* (1924), attacking the new style of urban life. *Across Spoon River* (1936) is an autobiography.

Masters, William Howell 1915–2001 •*US gynecologist and sexologist*• Born in Cleveland, Ohio, he received his MD from the University of Rochester in 1943. He joined the faculty of the Washington University School of Medicine (St Louis) in 1947, where his studies in the psychology and physiology of sexual intercourse were carried out using volunteer subjects under laboratory conditions. Much of his research was done in collaboration with **Virginia Johnson**, whom he married in 1971, and with whom he published *Human Sexual Response* in 1966, which became an international bestseller. They also wrote *On Sex and Human Loving* (1986). They were divorced in 1993.

Mastroianni, Marcello 1923–96 •*Italian actor*• Born in Fontana Liri, Italy, he trained as a draftsman, survived a wartime Nazi labor camp, and became a cashier in postwar Rome, pursuing amateur dramatics as a hobby. From 1948 he was employed by **Luchino Visconti**'s theatrical troupe. *Peccato che sia una canaglia* (1955, *Too Bad She's Bad*) began an enduring film partnership with **Sophia Loren**, while his performances in Visconti's *Le notte bianchi* (1957, *White Nights*) and **Federico Fellini**'s *La Dolce Vita* (1960, *The Sweet Life*) established him as an international star. Stereotypically perceived as a "Latin lover," in his prolific career he encompassed a variety of roles and worked with some of the most distinguished European film directors. He received Academy Award nominations for *Divorzio all'Italiano* (1961, *Divorce Italian Style*), *Una Giornata Particolare* (1977, *A Special Day*) and *Oci ciornie* (1987, *Dark Eyes*). Other films include Fellini's $8\frac{1}{2}$ (1962), *Città delle donne* (1979, *City of Women*) and *Intervista* (1987, *Interview*). He made a belated American debut in *Used People* (1992).

Masur, Kurt 1927– •*German conductor*• He gained international fame in 1970 as the conductor of the Leipzig Gewandhaus Orchestra. He was a leader in public protests in Leipzig that helped bring down the Communist government of East Germany in 1989. In 1991 he became musical director of the New York Philharmonic Orchestra, and in 2000 also became principal conductor of the London Philharmonic Orchestra.

Mata Hari, *stage name of* **Margaretha Gertruida MacLeod**, *née* **Zelle** 1876–1917 •*Alleged Dutch spy*• Born in Leeuwarden, she married a Scottish officer in the Dutch army in 1895 and traveled with him before they separated in 1905 and she became a dancer in France. She was a beautiful woman with apparently few qualms about near-nudity on stage, and had many lovers, several in high military and governmental positions (on both sides before and during World War I). Found guilty of espionage for the Germans, she was shot in Paris.

Mather, Cotton 1662–1728 •*American clergyman*• Born in Boston, the son of **Increase Mather**, he studied at Harvard, and became the most prominent Puritan minister of his time in New England. A polymath, he wrote on history and botany, but his reputation was irrevocably harmed by his involvement in the Salem witchcraft trials of 1692. He published 382 books, including *Memorable Providences Relating to Witchcraft and Possessions* (1685) and *Christian Philosopher* (1721). He supported smallpox inoculation and other progressive ideas.

Mather, Increase 1639–1723 •*American theologian*• Born in Dorchester, Massachusetts, he studied at Harvard and Trinity College, Dublin. His first charge was Great Torrington in Devon, but in 1661, finding it impossible to conform, he returned to the US, and from 1664 till his death was pastor of the Second Church, Boston. From 1685 to 1701 he was also president of Harvard. Sent to England in 1689 to lay colonial grievances before the king, he obtained a new charter from **William III**. He published 136 works, including a *History of the War with the Indians* (1676), and his *Cases of Conscience Concerning Evil Spirits* (1693) helped to calm the atmosphere during the witchhunts of 1692.

Matilda, *called* **the Empress Maud** 1102–67 •*English princess*• The only daughter of **Henry I**, she was born in London and married (1114) Emperor **Henry V**. She returned to England as Empress Maud after his death (1125) and was acknowledged as the heir to the English throne. In 1128 she married Geoffrey Plantagenet of Anjou, by whom she had a son, Henry "FitzEmpress," the future **Henry II** of England. When Henry I died (1135), his nephew **Stephen** of Blois seized the throne and Matilda invaded England from Anjou (1139) with her half brother, Robert, Earl of **Gloucester**. Initially successful, she captured Stephen, but lost potential allies, especially the city of London, through her financial impositions. Stephen regained control, while Matilda left England (1148) and returned to her son in Normandy, where she exerted influence over his continental territories.

Matilda, Anna *See* **Cowley, Hannah**

Matisse, Henri (Emile Benoît) 1869–1954 •*French painter*• Born in Le Cateau, he studied law in Paris and then worked as a lawyer's clerk. In 1892 he began studying art seriously in Paris, first at the Académie Julian and then at the École des Beaux-Arts, where he met **Georges Rouault**. Between 1899 and 1900 he was working at the Académie Carrière, where he met **André Derain**. In the 1890s he came under the influence of Impressionism and Neo-Impressionism and, in particular, of the Divisionism developed by **Georges Seurat** and **Paul Signac**, but this was eclipsed for a time by his admiration for **Cézanne**. In 1904 he returned to his Divisionist technique while working in the brilliant light of St Tropez and started using high-pitched color, as in his celebrated *Woman with the Hat* (1905). From this departure grew the movement irreverently dubbed the Fauves (Wild Beasts) by critics. Matisse was the leader of this group, which also included Derain, **Maurice Vlaminck**, **Raoul Dufy** and Rouault. His most characteristic paintings display a bold use of luminous areas of primary color, organized within a two-dimensional rhythmic design. The purity of his line drawing is seen in his many sketchbooks and book illustrations. Resident in Nice from 1914, he designed some ballet sets for **Sergei Diaghilev**. The art of Matisse owes a great deal to Asian influences, and his sensuous art has been as influential in the 20th century as more cerebral movements such as Cubism. In his later years he began working with large paper cutouts, creating designs such as *L'Escargot* (1953). He also designed the stained glass for the Dominican Chapelle du Rosaire at Vence, Alpes-Maritimes. His sculptural works include the bronze *The Back I–IV* (1909–30).

" "

What I dream of is an art of balance, of purity and serenity ... a soothing, calming influence on the mind, rather like a good armchair which provides relaxation from physical fatigue.

1908 "Notes d'un peintre," in ***La Grande Revue**.*

Matsys or **Massys, Quentin** c. 1466–c. 1531 •*Flemish painter*• Born in Louvain, according to legend he was a blacksmith. In 1491 he joined the painters' guild of St Luke in Antwerp. His paintings are mostly religious and genre pictures, treated with a reverent spirit, but with decided touches of realism (as in *The Banker and His Wife*) and exquisite finish. He also ranks high as a portrait painter, notably for his portrait of **Erasmus**.

Matthau, Walter, *originally surnamed* **Matuschanskavasky** 1920–2000 •*US actor*• Born in New York City, he was a radioman-gunner on army airforce bombers before studying at the New School's Dramatic Workshop. He made his Broadway debut in *Anne of a Thousand Days* (1948) and appeared in such productions as *Will Success Spoil Rock Hunter?* (1955) and *A Shot in the Dark* (1961–62) before winning a Tony award for his role as the slob Oscar in *The Odd Couple* (1964–65), a part he recreated on film in 1968. He made his film debut in *The Kentuckian* (1955) and won an Academy Award for *The Fortune Cookie* (1966), which began a long association with costar **Jack Lemmon**. They subsequently appeared together in films like *The Front Page* (1974) and on stage in *Juno and the Paycock* (1974), and Lemmon directed him in the film *Kotch* (1971). An unlikely star with a lugubrious manner and a sure comic touch, he enjoyed renewed popularity in the 1990s, acting on television in *The Incident* (1990) and its two sequels, and in such cinema films as *I.Q.* (1994) and *I'm Not Rappaport* (1996).

Matthew, St 1st century AD •*One of the 12 Apostles of Jesus*• He was a tax collector before his conversion, and he is called Levi (his name may have been Matthew the Levite) in Mark 2:14 and Luke 5:27. According to tradition, he was the author of the first Gospel, was a missionary to the Hebrews, and was martyred. His feast day is September 21 (West) or November 16 (East).

Matthews, Sir Stanley 1915–2000 •*English soccer player*• Born in Hanley, he was the son of a notable featherweight boxer, Jack Matthews. He started his sporting career as a sprinter, but soon switched to soccer, and joined Stoke City as a winger in 1931. First picked for England at the age of 20, he won 54 international caps, spread over 22 years. He played for Blackpool from 1947 to 1961, winning a Football Association Cup Winner's medal in 1953 at the age of 38. He returned to Stoke in 1961, and continued to play First Division soccer until after the age of 50. He was twice the Footballer of the Year (1948, 1963), and was the inaugural winner of the European Footballer of the Year award in 1956. He was knighted in 1965. He later managed Port Vale, and became president of Stoke City Football Club in 1990.

Matthias 1557–1619 •*King of Bohemia and of Hungary, and Holy Roman Emperor*• Born in Vienna, the third son of Emperor **Maximilian II**, he was tolerant in religious matters, favoring a policy of moderation toward German Protestants, although as governor of Austria he suppressed uprisings of Protestant peasants (1595–97). He ruled Bohemia (1611–17) and Hungary (1608–18), and after being elected emperor on the death of his brother **Rudolf II** (1612), he continued to pursue a conciliatory policy which aroused the antagonism of other Catholic princes, including his nephew and heir, Ferdinand (later **Ferdinand II**). An asthmatic, he increasingly withdrew from public life.

Matthiessen, Peter 1927– •*US novelist, travel writer, naturalist and explorer*• Born in New York City, he studied at the Sorbonne and at the University of Paris. He has made anthropological and natural history expeditions to Alaska, the Canadian Northwest Territories, Peru, New Guinea, Africa, Nicaragua and Nepal, out of which have come a number of eloquent ecological and natural history studies which reflect the concerns of his cultish novel *At Play in the Fields of the Lord* (1965). He won the National Book Award with the best-selling *The Snow Leopard* (1978), one man's inner story of a mystical trek across the Tibetan plateau. Other novels include *Race Rock* (1954), *Far Tortuga* (1975), *Killing Mister Watson* (1990) and *African Silences* (1991).

Mauchly, John W(illiam) 1907–80 •*US physicist and inventor*• He was born in Cincinnati, Ohio, and graduated in physics from Johns Hopkins University. He joined **John Eckert** in 1943 at the University of Pennsylvania, where they developed the ENIAC (Electronic Numerical Integrator and Computer). This giant military calculator led to the pair's major contribution to computing: the design of a stored-program machine, the EDVAC (Electronic Discrete Variable Computer), which played a large part in launching the computer revolution in the second half of the 20th century. Following EDVAC, they built UNIVAC, the Universal Automatic Computer, first used in 1951 by the US Census Bureau. Although Mauchly and Eckert relied to a certain extent on the work of others, notably **John Vincent Atanasoff** (who later was awarded priority by the courts for inventing the computer) and **John von Neumann**, it was their conviction that computers had a commercial market that launched the modern data-processing industry in the US.

Maud, Empress *See* **Matilda**

Maude, Francis Anthony Aylmer 1953– •*English politician*• Born in Oxford, he studied at Corpus Christi College, Cambridge, and became Conservative Member of Parliament for Warwickshire North (1983–92) and later Horsham (1997–). He held several senior offices in the 1980s, including minister of state at the foreign and commonwealth office (1989–90) and financial secretary to the treasury (1990–92). He was also shadow chancellor (1998–2000) and shadow foreign secretary (2000–01).

Mauger, Ivan Gerald 1939– •*New Zealand speedway rider*• Born in Christchurch, he rode for Wimbledon, Rye House, Eastbourne, Newcastle, Belle Vue, Exeter, and Hull between 1957 and 1982, and won the world individual title a record six times (1968–70, 1972, 1977, 1979). He also won two pairs world titles, four team titles, and the world long-track title twice.

Maugham, W(illiam) Somerset 1874–1965 •*British writer*• Born in Paris, France, of Irish origin, he was educated at King's School, Canterbury, and studied philosophy and literature at the University of Heidelberg in Germany. He graduated as a surgeon from St Thomas's Hospital, London, and a year's medical practice in the London slums gave him the material for his first novel, the lurid *Liza of Lambeth* (1897), and the magnificent autobiographical novel, *Of Human Bondage*, eventually published in 1915. In 1914 he served first with a Red Cross unit in France, then as a secret agent in Geneva and finally in Petrograd (St Petersburg), attempting to prevent the outbreak of the Russian Revolution. *Ashenden* (1928) is based on these experiences. He also visited Tahiti and the Far East, which inspired *The Moon and Sixpence* (1919) and such plays as *East of Suez* (1922). In 1928 he settled in the south of France, where he wrote his astringent, satirical masterpiece, *Cakes and Ale* (1930). A British agent again in World War II, he fled to the US (1940–46), where he ventured into mysticism with *The Razor's Edge* (1945). He is best known for his short stories, several of which were filmed, including *Quartet* (1949). Other works include essays on **Goethe**, **Chekhov**, **Henry James** and **Katherine Mansfield**.

“ ”

At a dinner party one should eat wisely but not too well, and talk well but not too wisely.

1896 ***A Writer's Notebook*** *(published 1949).*

Maundeville, Jehan de *See* **Mandeville, Jehan de**

Maung, Shu *See* **Ne Win, U**

Maupassant, Guy de 1850–93 •*French novelist*• Born in the Norman château of Miromesnil, near Dieppe, he was educated at Rouen and spent his life in Normandy. After a short spell as a soldier in the Franco-Prussian war, and later a government clerk, he took to writing and mingled with **Zola** and other disciples of naturalism. Free from sentimentality or idealism, his stories lay bare with minute and merciless observation the pretentiousness and vulgarity of the middle class of the period and the cunning and traditional meanness of the Norman peasant. He first achieved success with *Boule de suif* (1880, "Ball of Tallow"), which exposes the hypocrisy, prudery and ingratitude of the bourgeois in the face of a heroic gesture by a prostitute, and went on to write nearly 300 short stories. *Le Horla* (1887, Eng trans 1890) and *La Peur* (posthumous 1925, "The Fear") describe madness and fear with a horrifying accuracy, foreshadowing the insanity which beset Maupassant in 1892 and finally precipitated his death. He also wrote several full-length novels, including *Une Vie* (1883, Eng trans *A Woman's Life*, 1888) and *Bel-Ami* (1885, Eng trans 1891).

Maura, Carmen 1945– •*Spanish actress*• Born in Madrid, her family was very conservative, and her decision to give up teaching in favor of acting caused a serious rift. Her career took off internationally in the 1980s through her collaboration with the controversial Spanish director **Pedro Almodóvar**, winning the Best Actress Award at the European Film Awards in 1988 for her performance in his *Women on the Verge of a Nervous Breakdown*. Subsequent films include *¡Ay, Carmela!* (1990), *Le Bonheur (est dans le pré)* (1995) and *La Comunidad* (2000).

Mauriac, François 1885–1970 •*French novelist and Nobel Prize winner*• Born in Bordeaux, he was educated at the University of Bordeaux, then the École Nationale des Chartes in Paris in 1906, but left to become a poet, publishing his first volume of verse in 1909. He was of Roman Catholic parentage, and came to be regarded as the leading novelist of that faith, exploring the themes of temptation, sin and redemption, set in the brooding Bordeaux countryside. Major titles are *Le baiser au lépreux* (1922, Eng trans *The Kiss to the Leper*, 1923), *Génitrix* (1923, Eng trans 1930) and *Le nœud de vipères* (1932, Eng trans *Vipers' Tangle*, 1933). Also important is his play *Asmodée* (1938, Eng trans 1939). He was awarded the 1952 Nobel Prize for literature.

Maurice 1567–1625 •*Count of Nassau, Prince of Orange*• Born in Dillenburg, Nassau, the second son of **William I (the Silent)**, he was appointed stadtholder by the States General of the United Provinces on his father's murder (1584), and took command of the republic's army in its struggle for independence from Spain. A master of siege warfare, with English aid he inflicted a series of defeats on the Spanish in the 1590s, leading to the Twelve Years' Truce (1609). His military reforms made the Dutch army the most advanced in Europe. He became Prince of Orange in 1618 on the death of his elder brother William, and established a virtually monarchical authority over the state. He died unmarried and was succeeded by his brother, Frederick Henry.

Maurice, (John) Frederick Denison 1805–72 •*English theologian and writer*• He was born in Normanston, Suffolk, and attended Trinity College and Trinity Hall, Cambridge, but as a Dissenter, left in 1827 without a degree, and began a literary career in London. Influenced by **Coleridge**, he took orders in the Church of England, and became chaplain to Guy's Hospital (1837) and to Lincoln's Inn (1841–60). In 1840 he became Professor of Literature at King's College London, where he was also Professor of Theology (1846–53), and from 1866 he was Professor of Moral Philosophy at Cambridge. The publication in 1853 of his *Theological Essays*, dealing with atonement and eternal life, lost him his professorship of theology. With **Thomas Hughes** and **Charles Kingsley** he founded the Christian socialism movement (1848). He also was the founder and first principal of the Working Man's College (1854) and of the Queen's College for Women.

Maurier, Daphne du *See* **du Maurier, Dame Daphne**

Maurier, George du *See* **du Maurier, George**

Maurier, Sir Gerald du *See* **du Maurier, Sir Gerald**

Maurois, André, *pseudonym of* **Émile Herzog** 1885–1967 •*French novelist and biographer*• He was born in Elbeuf into a family of Jewish industrialists. During World War I he was a liaison officer with the British army, and he began his literary career with two books of shrewd and affectionate observation of British character, *Les Silences du Colonel Bramble* (1918, "The Silences of Colonel Bramble") and *Les Discours du Docteur O'Grady* (1920, "The Speeches of Dr O'Grady"). His large output includes such distinguished biographies as *Ariel* (1923, on **Shelley**), *Disraeli* (1927), *Voltaire* (1935) and *À la recherche de Marcel Proust* (1949, "In Search of Marcel Proust"). He also wrote several novels, tales for children, and critical and philosophical essays.

Mauroy, Pierre 1928– •*French statesman*• He was a teacher before becoming involved with trade unionism and socialist politics. He was prominent in the creation of a new French Socialist Party in 1971 and in the subsequent unification of the left. He became Mayor of Lille in 1973, the same year that he was first elected to the National Assembly. President **François Mitterrand** made him prime minister in 1981. He oversaw the introduction of a radical, but unsuccessful, reflationary program and was replaced as prime minister by **Laurent Fabius** in 1984.

Mauser, Peter Paul von 1838–1914 •*German firearm inventor*• He was born in Oberndorf, Neckar. With his brother Wilhelm (1834–82) he was responsible for the improved needle gun (adopted by the German army in 1871) and for the improved breech-loading cannon. He produced the "Mauser" magazine rifle in 1897.

Mauss, Marcel 1872–1950 •*French sociologist and anthropologist*• Born in Épinal, he studied philosophy under his uncle **Émile Durkheim** at Bordeaux, and the history of religion at Paris. Before World War I, he collaborated closely with Durkheim and other members of the *Année sociologique* school on studies of sacrifice, magic, collective representations and social morphology. After World War I, he edited the work of the *Année* school and produced his best-known work, *Essai sur le don* (1925), in which he demonstrated the importance of gift exchange in primitive social organization.

Mawhinney, Sir Brian Stanley 1940– •*English Conservative politician*• Born in Belfast, he was educated at Queen's University there, and at the Universities of Michigan and London, and became Assistant Professor of Radiation Research at the University of Iowa (1968–70). He lectured at the Royal Free Hospital School of Medicine from 1970 to 1984, and was elected Member of Parliament in 1979. His government posts included Minister of State in the Northern Ireland Office (1990–92) and Secretary of State for Transport (1994–95) before he became the blunt, no-nonsense Chairman of the Conservative Party (1995–97).

Mawlana *See* **Jalal ad-Din ar-Rumi**

Mawson, Sir Douglas 1882–1958 •*Australian explorer and geologist*• Born in Bradford, Yorkshire, England, he was educated at the University of Sydney. In 1907 he joined the scientific staff of **Ernest Shackleton**'s Antarctic expedition and discovered the South Magnetic Pole. From 1911 to 1914 he was leader of the Australasian Antarctic expedition, and was knighted on his return. In 1929–31 he led the Australian-British-New Zealand expedition to the Antarctic.

Max, Adolphe 1869–1939 •*Belgian politician and patriot*• Born in Brussels, he was first a journalist and then an accountant. He became burgomaster of Brussels in 1909, and when German troops approached Brussels in August 1914, he boldly drove to meet them and opened negotiations. He defended the rights of the Belgian population against the invaders, and was imprisoned by the Germans. In November 1918 he returned to Belgium, was elected to the House of Representatives, and became a Minister of State.

Maxim, Sir Hiram Stevens 1840–1916 •*British inventor and engineer*• Born in Sangersville, Maine, from 1867 he took out patents for gas apparatus and electric lamps, among other devices. He emigrated to England in 1881, where he perfected his "Maxim" machine gun in 1883. He also invented a pneumatic gun, a smokeless powder, a mousetrap, carbon filaments for light bulbs, and a flying machine (1894). He became a naturalized British citizen in 1900, and was knighted in 1901.

Maximilian I 1459–1519 •*Holy Roman Emperor*• He was born Archduke of Austria in Weiner Neustadt, the eldest son of **Frederick III of Germany** and Eleanor of Portugal, and by his marriage with Mary, heiress of **Charles the Bold** (1477), he acquired Burgundy and Flanders. This involved him in war with **Louis XI** of France, and he was forced to give Artois and Burgundy to Louis (1482). Elected king of the Romans (1486), he drove out the Hungarians (1490), who, under **Matthias I Hunyadi** (Corvinus), had seized much of Austria. At Villach (1492) he defeated the Turks, and in 1493 he became Holy Roman emperor. He next turned his ambition toward Italy, but after years of war he had to cede Milan to **Louis XII** (1504), and despite the League of Cambrai (1508) he was defeated by the Venetians, and the Swiss broke away from the German Empire. The peaceful acquisition of the Tyrol, however, increased his territory, and the marriage of his son Philip to the Infanta Juana ("Juana the Mad") united the Houses of Spain and Habsburg, Philip becoming **Philip I (the Handsome)** of Spain. The marriage of his grandson Ferdinand to the daughter of Ladislas of Hungary and Bohemia brought both these kingdoms to Austria. He was genial, energetic and popular; he improved the administration of justice and greatly encouraged the arts and learning. He left his extended empire to his grandson **Charles V**.

Maximilian II 1527–76 •*Holy Roman Emperor*• Born in Vienna, the eldest son of Emperor **Ferdinand I** and Anne of Bohemia and Hungary, he became king of Bohemia (1548), king of Hungary (1563) and Holy Roman emperor (1564). An intelligent, tolerant and cultivated man who considered himself "neither Catholic nor Protestant but a Christian," as emperor he secured considerable religious freedom for Austrian Lutherans. Abroad, he fought unsuccessfully against the Turks, and continued to pay them tribute. A patron of the arts and sciences, he set out to make Vienna a center of European intellectual life.

Maximilian, Ferdinand Joseph 1832–67 •*Emperor of Mexico and Archduke of Austria*• He was born in Vienna, the younger brother of Emperor Francis Joseph I. He accepted the offer of the crown of Mexico (1863), supported by France, and was crowned emperor (1864). He attempted liberal reforms, largely in the interest of the Indian peasants, but when **Napoleon III** withdrew his troops, he refused to abdicate, made a brave defense at Querétaro against **Benito Juárez**, and was betrayed and executed.

Maxton, James 1885–1946 •*Scottish politician*• Born in Glasgow, he was educated at the university there and became a teacher in the east end of the city, where the poverty he witnessed converted him to socialism. He suffered imprisonment for attempting to foment a strike of shipyard workers during World War I, in which he was a conscientious objector. A Member of Parliament from 1922, and one of the most turbulent "Red Clydesiders," he was expelled from the House of Commons in 1923 for calling a minister a murderer. As chairman of the Independent Labour Party (1926–40), he led its secession from the Labour Party in 1932, and became increasingly isolated from mainstream Labour politics.

" "

In the interests of economy they condemned hundreds of children to death and I call it murder.

1923 Speech against the withdrawal of child benefits, including the supply of milk, in Scotland. In ***Hansard****, June 27.*

Maxwell, James Clerk, *surname also* **Clerk-Maxwell** 1831–79 •*Scottish physicist*• Born in Edinburgh, at the age of 15 he devised a method for drawing oval curves which was published by the Royal Society of Edinburgh. He studied at the University of Edinburgh and at Cambridge, and was appointed Professor of Natural Philosophy at Marischal College, University of Aberdeen (1856) and King's College London (1860). In 1871 he was appointed the first Cavendish Professor of Experimental Physics at Cambridge, where he organized the Cavendish Laboratory. He published papers on the kinetic theory of gases, theoretically established the nature of Saturn's rings (1857), investigated color perception and demonstrated color photography with a picture of tartan ribbon (1861). He worked on the theory of electromagnetic radiation, and his *Treatise on Electricity and Magnetism* (1873) treated mathematically **Michael Faraday**'s theory of electrical and magnetic forces and provided the first conclusive evidence that light consisted of electromagnetic waves. He suggested that electromagnetic waves could be generated in a laboratory, as **Heinrich Hertz** was to demonstrate in 1887. He was one of the greatest theoretical physicists the world has known.

Maxwell, (Ian) Robert, *originally* **Jan Ludvik Hoch** 1923–91 •*British publisher and politician*• Born in Czechoslovakia and self-educated, he served in World War II (1940–45) before founding the Pergamon Press, a publishing company specializing in scientific journals. A former Labour Member of Parliament (1964–70), Maxwell, who had many business interests, rescued the large British Printing Corporation from financial collapse in 1980, it transformed into the successful Maxwell Communication Corporation in 1985 and then became its joint managing director in 1988. Despite a 1973 declaration by the Department of Trade and Industry that Maxwell was unreliable in handling money, by 1991 he was head of a considerable empire. However, he was later revealed to have been involved in questionable transactions, using money taken from the pension funds of some of his companies to buy shares in others to prop them up. The cause of his mysterious death while at sea on his luxury yacht has never quite been ascertained.

Maxwell Davies, Sir Peter 1934– •*English composer*• Born in Manchester, he studied in Manchester and Rome. After three years as director of music at Cirencester Grammar School, he went to Princeton University in 1962 for further study. He has lectured in Europe, Australia and New Zealand, and was composer-in-residence at the University of Adelaide in 1966. The Fires of London, a group founded by him (1970), is particularly associated with his work. He has a keen interest in early English music, in particular the 16th-century composer **John Taverner**, the subject of his opera *Taverner* (1972), and has always experimented with different orchestral combinations. In later works he introduced stereo tape and electronic sounds. His works include *Prolation* (1959), *Revelation and Fall* (1965), two *Fantasias on an In Nomine of John Taverner* (1962, 1964), *Eight Songs for a Mad King* (1969), and a number of symphonies, operas and ballets. Since 1970 Maxwell Davies has done most of his work in Orkney, frequently using Orcadian or Scottish subject matter. He directed the St Magnus Festival (1977–86), and in 1988 received a commission of ten concertos for the Scottish Chamber Orchestra, for which he was associate conductor and composer from 1985 to 1994, and then composer laureate (1994–). He worked as composer with the BBC Philharmonic Orchestra from 1992 to 2000, and also works with the Royal Philharmonic Orchestra.

May, Elaine, *originally* **Elaine Berlin** 1932– •*US screenwriter and film director*• Born in Philadelphia, she was a child actress, then met Mike Nicols while studying at the University of Chicago. They developed a successful writing partnership for the stage until their breakup in 1961. She continued to write for both stage and film, and shared an Academy Award nomination for Best Screenplay with **Warren Beatty** for *Heaven Can Wait* (1978). Later screenplays include *The Birdcage* (1996) and *Primary Colors* (1998), for which she received an Academy Award nomination. Her work as a film director includes *A New Leaf* (1971) and the notorious failure *Ishtar* (1987).

May, Sir Robert McCredie 1936– •*Australian physicist and ecologist*• Born in Sydney, he studied physics at the university there, taught mathematics at Harvard (1959–61) and theoretical physics at the University of Sydney (1961–73). He was Professor of Biology at Princeton University from 1973 to 1988 and subsequently Royal Society Research Professor at Oxford. His realization of the widespread relevance of deterministic chaos has opened up fruitful areas of research. His investigations into the abundance and diversity of species have covered parasite-host relationships and the role of infectious diseases in controlling populations. He was chief scientific adviser to the government and head of the Office of Science and Technology from 1995 to 2000. Elected a Fellow of the Royal Society in 1979, he became president of the Royal Society in 2000. He was knighted in 1996.

Mayakovsky, Vladimir Vladimirovich 1894–1930 •*Russian poet and playwright*• Born in Bagdadi (Mayakovsky), Georgia, he was involved in the Social Democratic movement during his youth, and was repeatedly imprisoned. He was an enthusiastic supporter of the 1917 Revolution, and both his play *Misteriya-Buff* (1918, Eng trans *Mystery-Bouffe*, 1968) and the long poem *150,000,000* (1919–20) are well-known works of the period. The advent of the new conservative leaders in 1921 led him to write *Pro eto* (1923, "About This"), poems pre-Revolution in sentiment, and satirical plays like *Klop* (1929, Eng trans *The Bedbug*, 1960) and *Banya* (1930, Eng trans *The Bath-House*, 1968). *Vladimir Ilyich Lenin* (1924), *Khorosho!* (1927, "Good!") and the unfinished *Vo ves golos* (1929–30, translated into Scots by **Edwin Morgan**, 1972) made him famous in the former USSR. Toward the end of his life he was severely castigated by more orthodox Soviet writers and critics, and he committed suicide.

Mayall, Rik (Richard Michael) 1958– •*English comedian, actor and writer*• Born in Harlow, Essex, he studied at the University of Manchester. He became well known as a television comedy actor with series such as *The Young Ones* (1982–84), *Bottom* (1990–94) and *The New Statesman* (1987–94; British Academy of Film and Television Arts Best New Comedy 1990). He has worked widely in theater and standup comedy, and made film appearances, including *Kevin of the North* (2001).

Mayer, Louis B(urt), *originally* **Eliezer Mayer** 1885–1957 •*US film producer*• Born in Minsk, Russia, his family emigrated to Canada when he was three. In 1907 he bought a house in Haverhill in Massachusetts, refurbished it as a nickelodeon, and opened one of the earliest custom-designed cinemas. He subsequently acquired a chain of movie theaters in New England and bought the regional rights to such popular attractions as *Birth of a Nation* (1915). He set up a film production company in Los Angeles in 1919, and in 1924 became vice president of the newly merged group, Loew's Metro-Goldwyn-Mayer. He was instrumental in the creation of Hollywood as a dream factory, wielding enormous power for more than two decades, and oversaw such successes as *Ben Hur* (1926), *Grand Hotel* (1932), *Ninotchka* (1939) and countless others. He was also involved in setting up the Academy of Motion Picture Arts and Sciences (1927), from which he received an honorary Academy Award in 1950 before he retired in 1951.

Mayhew, Henry 1812–87 •*English writer*• Born in London, he ran away from Westminster School and collaborated with his brother Augustus (1826–75) in writing numerous successful novels such as *The Good Genius That Turns Everything to Gold* (1847) and *Whom to Marry* (1848). Of his other works, the best-known is the classic social survey, *London Labour and the London Poor* (1851–62). He was a cofounder and first joint editor of *Punch* (1841), with **Mark Lemon**.

Mayhew (of Twysden), Patrick Barnabas Burke Mayhew, Baron 1929– •*English Conservative politician*• He was born in Cookham, Berkshire, and educated at Tonbridge School and Balliol College, Oxford. After National Service in the 4th/7th Royal Dragoon Guards, he trained as a barrister and was appointed Queen's Counsel in 1972. He became a Conservative Member of Parliament (1974–97), and, knighted in 1983, he served as solicitor-general (1983–87), then attorney-general (1987–92) and secretary of state for Northern Ireland (1992–97); it was a time of hope for a peaceful solution to the province's political troubles. He proved to be a firm and resolute leader, capable of balancing the opposing unionist and nationalist interests, and was awarded a life peerage in 1997.

Mayling Soong *See* **Chiang Kai-shek**

Maynard Smith, John 1920– •*English geneticist and evolutionary biologist*• He was born in London, and educated at Eton and Cambridge, where he graduated as an aeronautical engineer (1941), and at University College London. He taught at University College London (1951–65) and the University of Sussex (1965–85, now emeritus). After early work in collaboration with **J B S Haldane**, he went on to develop a new phase of the mathematical understanding of evolutionary processes, in particular the application of game theory to behavioral ecology. Later research has focused on mutations and recombination in human mitochondrial DNA. His popular book, the *Theory of Evolution* (1958), was widely influential. He was elected a Fellow of the Royal Society in 1977.

Mayo, Charles Horace 1865–1939 •*US surgeon*• Born in Rochester, Minnesota, he studied medicine at Chicago Medical College and joined with his father, William Worrall Mayo (1819–1911), and his brother **William James Mayo** to establish the clinic in St Mary's Hospital, Rochester, which was to become the Mayo Clinic in 1905. A specialist in the treatment of goiter, he cofounded the Mayo Foundation for Medical Education and Research in 1915.

Mayo, Katherine 1868–1940 •*US journalist*• Born in Ridgeway, Pennsylvania, she is remembered for her books exposing social evils, especially *Isles of Fear* (1925), condemning US administration of the Philippines, and *Mother India* (1927), a forthright indictment of child marriage and other customs.

Mayo, William James 1861–1939 •*US surgeon*• He was born in Le Sueur, Minnesota. A specialist in stomach surgery, with his brother **Charles Horace Mayo** and his father, William Worrall Mayo (1819–1911), he established the clinic in St Mary's Hospital, Rochester, Minnesota, which was to become the Mayo Clinic in 1905. He also helped Charles in 1915 to set up the Mayo Foundation for Medical Education and Research.

Mayr, Ernst Walter 1904– •*US zoologist*• Born in Kempten, Germany, he studied at the University of Berlin and emigrated to the US in 1932, serving as Professor of Zoology at Harvard from 1953 to 1975. His early work was on the ornithology of the Pacific Ocean, and in his later career he became one of the most important proponents of Neo-**Darwin**ism. Mayr was first to propose the founder effect, describing the genetic bottleneck of a population "founded" by a few individuals. The author of one of the key works on synthesis, *Systematics and the Origin of Species* (1942), he also wrote an influential history of biology, *The Growth of Biological Thought* (1982).

Mayr, Simon *See* **Marius, Simon**

Mays, Willie Howard, Jr 1931– •*US baseball player*• Born in Fairfield, Alabama, he played for the New York Giants (1951–57), who moved to San Francisco (1958–72), and the New York Mets (1972–73). A magnificent fielder, batter and base runner, only he and **Hank Aaron** have performed the baseball double of more than 3,000 hits and 600 home runs. He was voted Most Valuable Player in 1954 and 1965, and was voted the Baseball Player of the Decade (1960–69).

Mazarin, Jules, *originally* **Giulio Mazarini** 1602–61 •*French cleric, diplomat and politician*• Born in Pescina, Italy, he studied under the Jesuits in Rome, and at Alcala in Spain. He was papal nuncio to the French court (1634–36) and entered the service of **Louis XIII** in 1639, having become a naturalized Frenchman. Through the influence of Cardinal **Richelieu** he was elevated to cardinal, succeeding him as chief minister in 1642. After Louis's death (1643), he retained his authority under the queen regent, **Anne of Austria**, to whom it is said he was married. Blamed by many for the civil disturbances of the Frondes, he twice fled France. His foreign policy was more fruitful: he gained the alliance of **Cromwell** at the price of Dunkirk, concluded the Peace of Westphalia (1648), and negotiated the Treaty of the Pyrenees (1659). His impressive library was bequeathed to the Collège Mazarin, and his name is borne by the rare Mazarin Bible.

“ ”

The French are nice people. I allow them to sing and to write, and they allow me to do whatever I like.

Attributed by the Duchess of Orléans in a letter dated October 25, 1715.

Mazor, Stanley 1941– •*US computer scientist*• Born in Chicago, Illinois, he studied mathematics at San Francisco State College. He joined Intel Corporation in 1969, where with **Ted Hoff** and **Federico Faggin** he pioneered the design of the world's first microprocessor, the 4004, which had processing power equal to the 1940s room-sized ENIAC (Electronic Numerical Integrator and Calculator) computer.

Mazzini, Giuseppe 1805–72 •*Italian patriot and political leader*• Born in Genoa, he was initiated into the Carbonari as a young man. He was arrested by the Piedmontese police and exiled to France, where in 1833 he founded his own movement, Young Italy. Expelled from France, he traveled widely in Europe, calling for republican insurrection. During the Revolution of 1848 he took part first in the Lombard revolt against Austrian rule and, subsequently, in the governing triumvirate of the Roman Republic established after **Pius IX** fled the city. A number of abortive Mazzinian insurrections during the 1850s largely discredited him. In the final decade of his life he continued to preach republicanism and women's emancipation and played a small part in the establishment of the First International, but never managed to reconcile his ideas to those of socialism.

Mazzola, Girolamo Francesco Maria *See* **Parmigiano**

Mbeki, Thabo Mvuyelwa 1942– •*South African politician*• He was born in Idutywa. After serving as a youth organizer for the

African National Congress (ANC), he was briefly imprisoned and subsequently left South Africa to live and campaign in London (1967–70). He received military training in the Soviet Union (1970) and began representing the ANC at a high level abroad. In 1989 he was the head of the ANC delegation in talks with the South African government that led to the unbanning of the ANC and the release of prisoners, including **Nelson Mandela**, and in 1993 he was elected chair of the ANC. He succeeded Nelson Mandela as president of South Africa in 1999.

Mbiti, John Samuel 1931– •*Kenyan theologian*• He was born in Kenya, and taught theology and comparative religion at Makere University College, Uganda, before becoming director of the World Council of Churches Ecumenical Institute, Bossey, Switzerland (1972–80). He then taught at the University of Bern and was a pastor in Burgdorf, Switzerland. His books, which include *African Religions and Philosophy* (1969) and *Bible and Theology in African Christianity* (1987), maintain that Africans are naturally religious and that the Christian message should be seen as a fulfillment of traditional African beliefs rather than a rejection of them.

Mboya, Tom (Thomas Joseph) 1930–69 •*Kenyan trade unionist and politician*• Born on a sisal estate in the white highlands of Kenya, he was educated at Holy Ghost College, Mangu, and Ruskin College, Oxford. He was elected secretary-general of the Kenyan Federation of Labor in 1955 and a member of the Legislative Council in 1957. He was a founding member and secretary-general (1960–69) of the Kenyan African National Union (KANU). His reformist instincts brought him into conflict with his fellow Luo, **Oginga Odinga**, but he eventually won out, forcing Odinga out of KANU after the party's conference at Limuru (1966), thus binding himself closer to **Jomo Kenyatta**. He held several ministerial posts and was Minister for Economic Planning and Development (1964–69) when he established the "free enterprise with state regulation" economic system which Kenya epitomizes. He was assassinated in 1969.

McAdam, John Loudon 1756–1836 •*Scottish inventor and engineer*• Born in Ayr, he went to New York in 1770, where he made a fortune in his uncle's countinghouse. On his return to Scotland in 1783, he bought the estate of Sauchrie in Ayrshire, and started experimenting with a revolutionary method of road construction. In 1816 he was appointed surveyor to the Bristol Turnpike Trust, and remade the roads there with crushed stone bound with gravel, raising them to improve drainage—the "macadamized" system.

McAleese, Mary Patricia, *née* **Leneghan** 1951– •*Irish politician*• Born in Belfast, she was educated at Queen's University, Belfast. She began her career in law and was appointed Reid Professor of Criminal Law at Trinity College, Dublin (1975–79 and 1981–87). In 1994 she became Pro-Vice Chancellor of Queen's University, Belfast. She has held several directorships, and was a founding member of the Irish Commission for Prisoners Overseas. She was elected president of Ireland in 1997.

McAliskey, (Josephine) Bernadette, *née* **Devlin** 1947– •*Irish political activist*• Born into a poor Catholic family, she was brought up in Dungannon, County Tyrone, and educated at Queen's University, Belfast. While a student she became the youngest Member of Parliament in the House of Commons since **William Pitt** the Younger, when she was elected as an Independent Unity candidate in 1969 at the age of 21. Her aggressive political style led to her arrest while leading Catholic rioters in the Bogside, Belfast, and she was sentenced to nine months' imprisonment. In 1971 she lost Catholic support when she gave birth to an illegitimate child. She was a cofounder of the Irish Republican Socialist Party in 1975. In 1981 she actively supported the IRA hunger strikers, making a dramatic appearance in Spain after her recovery from an attempted assassination in which she and her husband were shot.

McAlpine, Sir Robert 1847–1934 •*Scottish building contractor*• Born in Newarthill, Lanarkshire, he left school at the age of 10 to work in the mines, after which he was apprenticed as a bricklayer. In 1868 he set up a building business in the Hamilton area and began to win contracts nationally. A rapid expansion followed in which McAlpine made use of new building materials and techniques, such as concrete, and labor-saving machinery.

McAnally, Ray(mond) 1926–89 •*Irish actor*• Born in Buncrana, Donegal, he made his professional debut in *A Strange House* (1942). A member of Dublin's Abbey Theatre from 1947, he had appeared in some 150 productions there by 1963. After moving to work in London he frequently returned to the Abbey Theatre to direct and teach. Active in the cinema from 1957, his many films include *The Mission* (1986, British Academy of Film and Television Arts award) and *My Left Foot* (1989). A veteran of over 500 television productions after 1959, he also won British Academy of Film and Television Arts awards for *A Perfect Spy* (1988) and *A Very British Coup* (1989).

McAuley, Catherine Elizabeth 1787–1841 •*Irish religious*• Born in Dublin, she was left money by her adoptive parents to buy a site for a school for poor children and a residence for working women, to be called House of Our Blessed Lady of Mercy. In 1831 she founded the order of the Sisters of Mercy.

McBean, Angus Rowland 1904–89 •*Welsh stage photographer*• Born in Newbridge, Monmouth, he started as a full-time theatrical photographer in 1934. He became noted for his individual approach to portraiture (where he often used elaborate settings designed for the individual sitter) and for his use of photographic montage, collage and double exposure to achieve a surreal effect. In later years he worked in the field of pop music, but withdrew from professional photography after 1969.

McBride, Willie (William) John 1940– •*Northern Irish rugby player*• Born in Toomebridge, County Antrim, he played mostly with the Ballymena team from 1962. A lock forward, he won 45 caps and went on four British Lions tours in 10 years. He made a record 17 appearances for the British Lions on five tours, and played for Ireland 63 times.

McCabe, Patrick 1955– •*Irish writer*• He was born in Clones and originally worked as a teacher of disabled children. His books include *Mondo Desperado* (1998) and *Emerald Gems of Ireland* (2001). *The Butcher Boy* (1992), the dark and hilarious tale of a young killer in small-town Ireland, was shortlisted for the Booker Prize and made into a film in 1997.

McCarthy, Cormac 1933– •*US author*• Born in Providence, Rhode Island, he studied at the University of Tennessee, but left without graduating to work in an auto-parts store, publishing his first novel, *The Orchard Keeper*, in 1965. Acclaimed as an exemplar of "Southern Gothic," this was followed by novels such as *Outer Dark* (1968) and *Suttree* (1979). His Western-inspired "Border Trilogy" comprised *All the Pretty Horses* (1992), *The Crossing* (1994) and *Cities of the Plain* (1998), and won him a wide international readership.

McCarthy, John 1957– •*English journalist*• Born in Barnet, London, and educated at the University of Hull, he became a freelance journalist. Having worked for Worldwide Television News since 1981, he went to Lebanon as acting bureau chief. After only 32 days there, on April 17, 1986, he was abducted by the revolutionary fundamentalist group Islamic Jihad. He was held as a hostage for 1,943 days until his release on August 8, 1991. He wrote *Some Other Rainbow* (1993) with Jill Morrell about the experience.

McCarthy, Joseph Raymond 1909–57 •*US politician*• Born in Grand Chute, Wisconsin, he studied at Marquette University, Milwaukee, became a circuit judge in 1939, and after war service was elected senator in 1946. In 1953 he became chairman of the House Committee on Un-American Activities. By hectoring cross-examination and damaging innuendo, he arraigned many innocent citizens and officials, overreaching himself when he came into direct conflict with the army. This kind of anticommunist witchhunt became known as "McCarthyism." His power diminished after he was formally censured for his methods by the Senate in 1954.

McCarthy, Mary Thérèse 1912–89 •*US novelist and critic*• She was born in Seattle, Washington. Educated at Vassar College, New York, she became a book reviewer, theater critic and editor, as well as a writer of articles and novels. Her voice has often been described as scathing, yet although she brought little emotional warmth to her work, she was a highly intelligent, observant novelist. Her best-known fiction includes *The Groves of Academe* (1952) and *The Group* (1963). She also wrote the documentary denunciations of US involvement in the Vietnam War, *Vietnam* (1967) and *Hanoi* (1968). Other works include *A Charmed Life* (1955), *Sights and Spectacles* (1956), the autobiographical *Memories of a Catholic Childhood* (1957) and *Cannibals and Missionaries* (1979).

" "

The happy ending is our national belief.

1947 "America the Beautiful," in ***Commentary****, September.*

McCartney, Sir (James) Paul 1942– •*English songwriter, vocalist and bass guitarist*• Liverpool-born and a former member of the **Beatles**, he is one of the most distinctive lyricists in popular music. Following his first solo album, *McCartney* (1970), and a second, *Ram* (1971), recorded with his wife, Linda Eastman (1941–98), he recruited guitarist Denny Laine (1944–) to form Wings in 1971. His albums *Band on the Run* (1973) and *Venus & Mars* (1975) were highly successful, and "Mull of Kintyre" (1977) was a huge hit. Wings disbanded in 1981. His autobiographical film, *Give My Regards to Broad Street*, appeared in 1984. Subsequent albums include *Tripping the Light Fantastic* (1990), *Off the Ground* (1992) and *Driving Rain* (2001). He cocomposed his *Liverpool Oratorio* with Carl Davis in 1991, and wrote a symphony, *Standing Stone*, in 1997. In recent years he has also exhibited his paintings and has continued to campaign for a number of charitable and environmental causes. He was knighted in 1997.

McCartney, Stella 1972– •*English fashion designer*• The daughter of Linda and **Paul McCartney**, she was born in London and worked with **Christian Lacroix** and **Betty Jackson** before taking a degree at St Martin's College of Art and Design. Shortly after graduating she set up her own design company. In 1997 she became chief designer for Chloe, Paris, reviving the company's fortunes, and in 2001 launched her own fashion house in partnership with Gucci, the first show having a Cockney theme.

McCauley, Mary Ludwig Hays, *known as* **Molly Pitcher** 1754–1832 •*American Revolutionary war heroine*• Born near Trenton, New Jersey, she earned her nickname by carrying water to her husband, John Hays (or Heis), and the other men of the 7th Pennsylvania Regiment during the Battle of Monmouth on June 28, 1778. When her husband collapsed from the heat, like (or perhaps confused with) **Margaret Corbin**, she took his place at his cannon for the remainder of the battle. For this act of bravery she was rewarded with a government pension in 1822.

McClellan, George Brinton 1826–85 •*US general*• He was born in Philadelphia. In the Civil War in 1861, as major general in the Union army, he drove the enemy out of West Virginia, and was called to Washington to reorganize the Army of the Potomac. He advanced near to Richmond, but was compelled to retreat, fighting the Seven Days Battles (June 25 to July 1, 1862). After the disastrous second Battle of Bull Run (August 29–30), followed by a Confederate invasion of Maryland, he reorganized the army at Washington, marched north, met **Robert E Lee** at Antietam, and compelled him to recross the Potomac. He followed the Confederates into Virginia, too slowly for **Abraham Lincoln**, who replaced him with **Ambrose E Burnside**. In 1864, as Democratic candidate for the presidency, he was defeated by Lincoln, and in 1878 was elected governor of New Jersey.

McClintock, Barbara 1902–92 •*US geneticist and Nobel Prize winner*• Born in Hartford, Connecticut, she received a PhD in botany from Cornell University, where she worked from 1927 to 1935. Later she held positions at the University of Missouri (1936–41) and Cold Spring Harbor (1941–92). Her work on the chromosomes of maize provided the ultimate proof of the chromosome theory of heredity. In the 1940s she showed how genes can control other genes and can be copied from chromosome to chromosome. In 1983 she was awarded the Nobel Prize for physiology or medicine.

McColgan, Liz (Elizabeth) 1964– •*Scottish athlete*• Born in Dundee, she studied at the University of Alabama. She won the 10,000 meters gold medal in the 1986 Commonwealth Games, then won the silver medal at the Seoul Olympics of 1988. She retained her Commonwealth title in Auckland in 1990. Not long after the birth of her daughter, she won the 1991 New York Marathon in 2 hours, 27 minutes, the fastest female marathon debut. Also that year she won the 10,000 meters at the world championship in Tokyo. In 1993 she had two knee operations and was advised to give up racing, but returned to racing in 1995, coming in fifth in the London Marathon and fourth in the 10,000 meters in the European Cup. Her other marathon successes include the Tokyo Marathon (1992) and the London Marathon (1996). She retired in 2001.

McCollum, Elmer Verner 1879–1967 •*US biochemist*• Born in Fort Scott, Kansas, he studied at Yale and the Universities of Cincinnati and Manitoba, and became Professor of Biochemistry at Johns Hopkins University (1917–44). In 1913 he published the first description of a vitamin, and distinguished between vitamins A (fat-soluble) and B (water-soluble). In 1922 he discovered the "rickets-preventative factor," vitamin D. He was a prolific writer, and his works include the popular *The Newer Knowledge of Nutrition* (1918) and *A History of Nutrition* (1957).

McConnell, Jack 1960– •*Scottish Labour politician*• Born in Irvine and brought up on the island of Arran, he was educated at the University of Stirling and entered politics as Member of Parliament representing Motherwell and Wishaw. He served as General Secretary of the Scottish Labour Party (1992–98) and went on to become Scotland's Minister for Finance, Minister for Education, Europe and External Affairs and ultimately, in 2001, First Minister in succession to **Henry McLeish**.

McCormick, Cyrus Hall 1809–84 •*US inventor and industrialist*• Born in Rockbridge, Virginia, and educated locally, he was the son of Robert McCormick (1780–1846), who patented several agricultural implements but had in 1831 abandoned an attempt to build a mechanical reaper. Cyrus took up the challenge successfully, but did not patent his machine until 1834, the year after the reaper invented by **Obed Hussey** had been patented. US agriculture had entered a period of rapid expansion, and there was intense competition between the two men and with other manufacturers, but in the end the McCormick Harvesting Machine Company emerged as the leader. In 1902 it became the International Harvester Company.

McCourt, Frank 1931– •*US author*• Born in Brooklyn, New York, he moved with his family to Limerick, Ireland, at the age of four and did not return to the US until he was 19, when he became a teacher in New York. After retiring from teaching he teamed up with his brother Malachy to perform the two-man musical show *A Couple of Blackguards*, which drew on their youth in Ireland. McCourt's childhood experience of hardship and poverty in Ireland also provided the material for the best-selling memoir *Angela's Ashes* (1996) and its sequel, *'Tis: A Memoir.*

McCubbin, Frederick 1855–1917 •*Australian landscape painter*• Born in Melbourne, Victoria, where he lived and worked for most of his life, he taught drawing at the National Gallery of Victoria's Art School from 1886 until his death. The previous year, with other painters, including **Tom Roberts**, he had established the first of the artist camps which grew into the Heidelberg school of Australian painting. Although principally known for his landscapes, he also executed many successful portraits.

McCullers, (Lula) Carson, *née* **Smith** 1917–67 •*US novelist*• She was born in Columbus, Georgia, and attended classes at Columbia University, New York, and New York University. *The Heart Is a Lonely Hunter*, her first book, about a character who could neither hear nor speak, appeared in 1940, distinguishing her immediately as a novelist of note. She wrote the best and the bulk of her work in a six-year spell during World War II. Along with **William Faulkner**, **Tennessee Williams** and **Truman Capote**, she is credited with fashioning a type of fiction labeled by critics as Southern Gothic. Her books include *Reflections in a Golden Eye* (1941), *The Member of the Wedding* (1946), *The Ballad of the Sad Cafe* (1951) and *Clock Without Hands* (1961), a last ironic look at the South.

McCullough, Colleen 1937– •*Australian novelist*• Born in Wellington, New South Wales, she is best known for her novel *The Thorn Birds* (1977), a saga of sex, religion and disaster, later produced as a television series. Her earlier book *Tim* (1974) was also filmed, as was *An Indecent Obsession* (1981). A delicate novella, *The Ladies of Missalonghi* (1987), showed that she is capable of some fine writing, and her recent books, including a series of six novels set in ancient Rome, demonstrate a concern for historical detail. Later publications include *The Song of Troy* (1998) and *Morgan's Run* (2000).

McDonald, Sir Trevor 1939– •*Trinidadian television newscaster*• Born in San Fernando, Trinidad, he began his career reporting for local radio stations. He joined Trinidad Television in 1962, where he presented the news and interviewed for current affairs programs. Moving to London seven years later, he joined the BBC World Service and, in 1973, Independent Television News. After various assignments as a reporter and correspondent, he became the main anchor of *News at Ten*, where he remained until scheduling changes saw the end of the program in 1999. He then anchored ITV's *The Evening News* until returning as anchor of *News at Ten* after its reinstatement in early 2001. He also hosts the current affairs program *Tonight with Trevor McDonald* (1999–), and has published several books and an autobiography. The recipient of numerous broadcasting awards, he was knighted in 1999.

McDonnell, James Smith 1899–1980 •*US aircraft manufacturer and pioneer in space technology*• Born in Denver, Colorado, he graduated from Princeton before taking a master's degree in aeronautical engineering from MIT in 1925. He set up his own company in 1928. By 1938 he had organized the McDonnell Aircraft Corporation and embarked on a series of successful military and naval aircraft, including the Banshee, Demon, Voodoo, and the famous F-4 Phantom, of which over 5,000 were built. He took his company into space technology and constructed the Mercury and Gemini manned satellite capsules.

McDormand, Frances 1957– •*US actress*• Born in Illinois to a family of traveling preachers, she studied at the Yale University School of Drama. Her films have included *Blood Simple* (1984), *Raising Arizona* (1987), *Mississippi Burning* (1988) and *Miller's Crossing* (1990), and she won an Academy Award for Best Actress as the tenacious policewoman Marge Gunderson in **Joel** and **Ethan Coen**'s *Fargo* (1996). She has appeared widely on television and on stage.

McEnroe, John Patrick 1959– •*US tennis player*• He was born in Wiesbaden, Germany. He reached the semifinals at Wimbledon as a prequalifier in 1977, turned professional in 1978, and was runner-up to **Björn Borg** in the 1980 Wimbledon final. He won the Wimbledon title three times (1981, 1983–84), the US Open singles four times (1979–81, 1984), and eight Grand Slam doubles events. He was Grand Prix winner in 1979 and 1984–85, and world championship winner in 1979, 1981 and 1983–84. Throughout his professional career, his outbursts on court resulted in much adverse publicity. More recently he has become a popular commentator and television host.

“ ”

You cannot be serious!

1981 In protest at an umpire's decision at Wimbledon.

McEwan, Ian Russell 1948– •*English writer of novels, short stories and screenplays*• He was born in Aldershot, Hampshire, and educated at the Universities of Sussex and East Anglia. His first collections of stories, *First Love, Last Rites* (1975) and *In Between the Sheets* (1978), attracted notoriety for their preoccupation with the erotic and the macabre. Less obtrusive but equally consistent is the nature of romantic love, a theme explored in the novels *The Comfort of Strangers* (1981) and *The Innocent* (1990), and the screenplay *The Ploughman's Lunch* (1985). McEwan's 1987 novel, *The Child in Time*, won the Whitbread award. Later publications include *Black Dogs* (1992), *The Daydreamer* (1994), *The Short Stories* (1995), *Amsterdam* (1998), which won the Booker Prize, and *Atonement* (2001).

McGeechan, Ian 1946– •*Scottish rugby player and coach*• Having moved to Yorkshire as a teenager, he played club rugby for Headingley, and made his international debut in 1972. He played 32 times for Scotland between then and 1979 and also played eight times for the British Lions. Scotland's assistant coach in the inaugural World Cup of 1987, he took over as head coach the following year, and was also coach of the British Lions in 1989. In 1990, his crucial role in Scotland's Grand Slam win heightened his reputation as one of the best coaches in world rugby. He also coached the Lions in 1993 and 1997, but stepped down as Scotland coach after five years in 1993. He was then director of rugby at Northampton Saints before returning as Scotland coach in 2000.

McGill, Donald, *originally* **Fraser Gould** 1875–1962 •*English comic-postcard artist*• Born in Blackheath, West Midlands, in 1905 he drew his first comic card for Asher's Pictorial Postcards, for whom one popular card sold two million copies. Famous for his outsize women in bathing costumes paddling alongside gawky henpecked husbands, and for the double meanings in his captions, McGill did not receive critical attention until **George Orwell**'s *Horizon* article (1941). He is estimated to have drawn 500 cards a year for 50 years.

McGill, James 1744–1813 •*Canadian entrepreneur and philanthropist*• Born in Glasgow, Scotland, he emigrated to Canada in the 1770s, and made a fortune in the northwest fur trade and in Montreal. He bequeathed land and money to found McGill College, Montreal, which became McGill University in 1821.

McGough, Roger 1937– •*English poet, playwright and performer*• Born in Liverpool, Merseyside, and educated at the University of Hull, he worked as a schoolteacher and art college lecturer. He became associated forever with the "Mersey Sound," a title used for the hugely successful *Penguin Modern Poets No. 10* (1967, 1974, 1983), which he shared with the other "Liverpool Poets," **Adrian Henri** and **Brian Patten**. He enjoyed brief, bizarre pop success with the perfoming group The Scaffold. Much more of a "street" poet than either Henri or Patten, he uses the rhythms of speech in a curiously subversive way. This was evident in the novel-plus-poems *Frinck, A Life in the Day of*, and *Summer with Monika* (1967), and it saw service again in collections like *Gig* (1973), *In the Glassroom* (1976) and the acclaimed *Waving at Trains* (1982). McGough has written many plays, the novel *Defying Gravity* (1992) and a number of children's books.

McGovern, George Stanley 1922– •*US politician*• Born in Avon, South Dakota, the son of a Methodist minister, he served in the US Air Force during World War II, and became a Professor of History and Government at Dakota Wesleyan University. He served as a Democratic congressman (1956–61) and senator (1963–81) from South Dakota and was an early opponent of the Vietnam War. In July 1972, following a campaign expounding his new radicalism, he was chosen as Democratic candidate to oppose **Richard Nixon** in the presidential election but was heavily defeated, largely due to his wholly unsuccessful attempts to negotiate with Hanoi. His autobiography, *Grassroots*, was published in 1978. He was awarded the Presidential Medal of Freedom in 2000.

McGregor, Ewan 1971– •*Scottish actor*• Born in Perth, he studied at the Guildhall School of Music and Drama. He came to notice with two films by the director **Danny Boyle**, *Shallow Grave* (1994) and *Trainspotting* (1996), the latter of which propelled him to stardom. Later roles have included parts in *Star Wars Episode 1: The Phantom Menace* (1999), *Moulin Rouge* (2001) and *Star Wars Episode 2: Attack of the Clones* (2002).

McGregor, Sir Ian Kinloch 1912–98 •*US business executive*• He was born in Kinlochleven, Scotland, and educated at the University of Glasgow and the Royal College of Science and Technology (now the University of Strathclyde). He went to the US in 1940, when he was transferred to work with the US Army. In 1977 he returned to the UK as deputy chairman of British Leyland. In 1980 he was appointed chairman of the British Steel Corporation, and then became chairman of the National Coal Board (1983–86). Both industries required drastic cutbacks to survive and he faced strong trade union opposition, particularly from the miners in 1984–85. He was knighted in 1986.

McGuffey, William Holmes 1800–73 •*US educator*• Born near Claysville, Pennsylvania, he was a Presbyterian minister and university professor who is remembered for compiling four of the six

Eclectic Readers, known as *McGuffey's Readers*. His first two readers, published in 1836, extolled religion and patriotism and constituted a guide to social and moral conduct; his second pair, issued the following year, contained lessons on elocution as well as literary selections in which virtue was rewarded and vice was punished. The books were used as standard texts for nearly a century in the Midwest, and through them McGuffey helped shape the American character.

McGwire, Mark David 1963– •*US baseball player*• Born in Pomona, California, he began as a pitcher before realizing his potential with the bat. He joined the Oakland Athletics in 1984 and was a member of the US Olympic baseball team that year. He was soon breaking records with his powerful swing and played a major role in Oakland's victory in the 1989 World Series. In 1996 he became only the thirteenth player to hit 50 home runs in a single season. He joined the St Louis Cardinals the following year and in 1998 achieved a record-breaking 70 home runs in a single season.

McIlvanney, William Angus 1936– •*Scottish novelist and poet*• Born in Kilmarnock, Ayrshire, he was educated at Kilmarnock Academy and the University of Glasgow and taught from 1960 to 1975, when he took up writing full-time. His first novel was *Remedy Is None* (1966), a paean to working-class values, and it was followed in 1968 by *A Gift from Nessus*. Other novels include *Docherty* (1975), about an Ayrshire miner, which won the Whitbread award, *The Big Man* (1985) and *The Kiln* (1996). His thrillers featuring the Glasgow detective Jack Laidlaw evoke comparisons with **Raymond Chandler**. His volumes of poetry include *The Longships in Harbour* (1970) and *These Words* (1984).

McKay, Claude, *originally* **Festus Claudius** 1890–1948 •*US writer*• Born in the mountains of central Jamaica, he published two books of verse in dialect before emigrating to the US in 1912. Radicalized by his experiences of racial hatred in America, he wrote poems such as his sonnet "If We Must Die," urging African Americans to fight for their freedom and dignity. A leading figure in the Harlem Renaissance, he became the first best-selling African-American author with his novel *Home to Harlem* (1928), and although the vogue for African-American literature ended with the coming of the Depression, he continued to write fiction, including *Gingertown* (1932) and *Banana Bottom* (1933). His autobiography is entitled *A Long Way from Home* (1937).

McKay, Heather Pamela, *née* **Blundell** 1941– •*Australian squash player*• Born in Queanbeyan, New South Wales, she played hockey for Australia as a schoolgirl, then at the age of 18 was Queanbeyan tennis champion. Having taken up squash at 17 to keep fit for hockey, she won 14 Australian titles (1960–73), won the British Open in 16 successive years (1962–77), and was world champion in 1976 and 1979. She was unbeaten between 1962 and 1980. In 1975 she moved to Canada, where she became Canadian racketball champion.

McKellen, Sir Ian Murray 1939– •*English actor*• Born in Burnley, Lancashire, he made his London debut in *A Scent of Flowers* (1964) and, with the actor Edward Petherbridge, founded the Actors Company (1972). His many plays for the Royal Shakespeare Company include the title roles in *Faustus* (1974), *Romeo and Juliet* (1976), *Macbeth* (1976–77) and *Richard III* (1990), and he has also worked with the Royal National Theatre and with the West Yorkshire Playhouse. On television, he has acted the title role in *Walter* (1982), Iago in *Othello* (1989) and Amos Starkadder in *Cold Comfort Farm* (1995). His films include *Scandal* (1989), *Gods and Monsters* (1998) and the *Lord of the Rings* trilogy (2001, 2002, 2003). In 1996 he directed and starred in the leading role in the film of *Richard III*. He is an active campaigner for gay rights in the UK.

McKern, Leo, *originally* **Reginald McKern** 1920–2002 •*Australian actor*• Born in Sydney, Australia, he worked as a commercial artist before making his stage debut in *Uncle Harry* there (1944) and moving to London in 1946, where he made his debut with the Old Vic Company in *Love's Labour's Lost* (1949). On television, he played Number Two in *The Prisoner* (1967–68) and, most famously, the eccentric barrister Horace Rumpole in **John Mortimer**'s *Rumpole of the Bailey*. He also appeared in *Reilly—Ace of Spies* (1983) and *Monsignor Quixote* (1985).

McKim, Charles Follen 1847–1909 •*US architect*• Born in Chester County, Pennsylvania, he studied architecture at the École des Beaux-Arts in Paris, returning to the US in 1870 and working in the office of **H H Richardson**. In 1879 he and William Rutherford Mead (1846–1928) joined with **Stanford White** to found McKim, Mead, & White, which became the nation's leading architectural firm and remained so for decades. Working cooperatively, McKim and his partners designed buildings influenced by classical and Renaissance models, helping establish the neoclassical revival in the US. The firm's best-known buildings include the Boston Public Library (1887–95) and, in New York City, the old Madison Square Garden (1891), the Morgan Library (1903) and Pennsylvania Station (1904–10).

McKinley, William 1843–1901 •*25th President of the US*• Born in Niles, Ohio, he served in the Civil War, retiring with the rank of major in 1865 and later practicing law in Canton, Ohio. He was elected to Congress as a Republican in 1876, and repeatedly reelected. In 1891, with business community support, he was made Governor of Ohio, his name being identified with the high protective tariff passed in the McKinley Tariff Act of 1890. Chosen Republican candidate for the presidency in 1896 and 1900, he conducted exciting debates with **W J Bryan**, who advocated the cause of free silver, denounced trusts, high tariffs, and imperialism, and was understood to favor labor at the expense of capital. McKinley's administration (1897–1901) saw the adoption of the highest tariff rate in US history and the rise of US imperialism. In McKinley's first term the Spanish-American War (1898) brought the US possession of Puerto Rico, Guam and the Philippines, and its colonial empire was further increased by the annexation of Hawaii. The domain of US trade was likewise protected and extended by the proclamation of the Open Door Policy in China. Less than a year into his second term, McKinley was shot by an anarchist, Leon F Czolgosz, in Buffalo, New York, and died eight days later.

McLachlin, Beverley Marian, *née* **Gietz** 1943– •*Canadian judge*• Born in Pincher Creek, Alberta, she studied at the University of Alberta. She was called to the bar of Alberta in 1969, and after serving in a number of British Columbian courts joined the Supreme Court of Canada in 1989. She became Canada's first female chief justice of the Supreme Court in 2000.

McLaren, Bill 1923– •*Scottish rugby broadcaster and writer*• Born in Hawick, Roxburghshire, he was a wing-forward for Hawick, and was selected for a Scottish trial, but injury prevented him from playing. After retiring from the game he combined a career as a physical education teacher with journalism, and later became the BBC's chief rugby union commentator. His love and knowledge of the game have given him an unrivaled reputation as a sports broadcaster of warmth, intelligence and integrity.

McLaughlin, John 1942– •*English jazz guitarist and composer*• He was born in Doncaster. He played with British blues, rock and free jazz groups in the 1960s, and recorded two classic records, *Extrapolation* (1969) and *My Goal's Beyond* (1970). He played on **Miles Davis**'s important jazz-fusion albums *In a Silent Way* (1969) and *Bitches Brew* (1970) before forming his own fusion group, The Mahavishnu Orchestra, in 1971. His interest in Indian music and culture was manifest both in that band and more overtly in Shakti, a collaboration with Indian musicians. He has also written classical works, including a guitar concerto. He returned directly to jazz roots with imaginative tributes to **John Coltrane** and **Bill Evans** in the mid-1990s.

McLeish, Henry 1948– •*Scottish Labour politician*• Born in Methil, Fife, he was educated at Heriot-Watt University and worked as a planning officer in local government before entering Parliament. As Member of Parliament for Central Fife (1987–2000) he held several senior posts, and became First Minister of Scotland on the sudden death of **Donald Dewar** in 2000, but resigned unexpectedly in November 2001 following a controversy about undeclared rents on parliamentary offices.

McLuhan, (Herbert) Marshall 1911–80 •*Canadian writer*• Born in Edmonton, he studied at the University of Manitoba and at Cambridge, and in 1946 became a professor at St Michael's College, Toronto. In 1963, he was appointed director of the

University of Toronto's Centre for Culture and Technology. He held the controversial view that the invention of printing, with its emphasis on the eye rather than the ear, can lead to the destruction of a cohesive, interdependent society, since it encourages humans to be more introspective, individualistic and self-centered. His publications include *The Gutenberg Galaxy* (1962), *The Medium Is the Message* (with Q Fiore, 1967) and *Counter-Blast* (1970).

“ ”

The new electronic independence recreates the world in the image of a global village.

1962 ***The Gutenberg Galaxy.***

McMahon, Sir William 1908–88 •*Australian politician*• Born in Sydney, he studied at the university there and then qualified and practiced as a solicitor. After service in World War II he became active in the Liberal Party and was elected to the House of Representatives in 1949. Under **Harold Holt** he became treasurer and deputy leader. Precluded from the leadership on Holt's death by the veto of the Liberals' coalition partner, the Country Party, he became prime minister after **John Gorton**'s resignation in 1971, but was defeated at the 1972 election.

McMillan, Edwin Mattison 1907–91 •*US atomic scientist and Nobel Prize winner*• Born in Redondo Beach, California, he was educated at the California Institute of Technology (Caltech) and at Princeton University. He joined the staff of the University of California at Berkeley, moving to the Lawrence Radiation Laboratory in 1934. In 1940, following up the work of **Enrico Fermi**, McMillan and **Philip Hauge Abelson** synthesized an element heavier than uranium by bombarding uranium with neutrons in the Berkeley cyclotron. They called this first transuranic element "neptunium." The following year **Glenn Theodore Seaborg**, also working at Berkeley, synthesized plutonium, leading to the development of the atomic bomb. McMillan spent the rest of World War II working on radar and sonar, and on the atomic bomb at Los Alamos. He was awarded the Nobel Prize for chemistry, jointly with Seaborg, in 1951.

McMurtry, Larry Jeff 1936– •*US novelist*• Born in Wichita Falls, Texas, and educated at North Texas State College, Denton, and Rice University, Houston, he helped to establish the Western as a serious contemporary genre through his vision of the history of Texas. Hollywood's interest in his work consolidated his reputation: *Horseman, Pass By* (1961) was successfully filmed as *Hud* (1963). McMurtry also wrote the screenplay for Peter Bogdanovich's prize-winning movie of his third novel, *The Last Picture Show* (1966). Later books include *Terms of Endearment* (1975), the basis of a third successful film, and *Cadillac Jack* (1982), *Lonesome Dove* (1985), *Buffalo Girls* (1990) and *Comanche Moon* (1997).

McNamara, Robert Strange 1916– •*US Democratic politician and businessman*• Born in San Francisco, he served in the US Air Force (1943–46), then worked his way up in the Ford Motor Company to be president by 1960. In 1961 he joined the **Kennedy** administration as secretary of defense, in which post he was an early influential advocate of the escalation of the Vietnam War. By 1967 he was convinced that the war was unwinnable, but his pleas to seek a diplomatic solution went unheeded, and he resigned to become president of the World Bank (1968–81). In the 1980s he emerged as a critic of the nuclear arms race. He reawakened the Vietnam controversy with his 1995 memoir *In Retrospect: The Tragedy and Lessons of Vietnam*, which examined the blunders of the US government and expressed regret for his role.

McNeill, Billy (William), *known as* **Caesar** 1940– •*Scottish soccer player and manager*• Born in Bellshill, Lanarkshire, he was the backbone of the highly successful Glasgow Celtic team between 1965 and 1975. He received the European Cup after Celtic's victory at Lisbon in 1967, and had nine championship and seven Scottish Cup medals. He was capped 29 times. Appointed to succeed **Jock Stein** as manager of his old club in 1978, he left after a quarrel with the board, but returned in 1987. In his first season he guided Celtic to league and cup victories. They also won the 1989 Scottish Cup before McNeill was forced to leave the club in 1991.

McPherson, Aimee Semple, *née* **Kennedy** 1890–1944 •*US Pentecostal evangelist*• She was born near Ingersoll, Ontario, Canada, into a Salvation Army family. She became a Pentecostalist and married a preacher, Robert Semple. They went to China as missionaries, but on his death in 1910, she returned to North America and subsequently embarked on a hugely successful evangelistic career. In 1918 she founded the Foursquare Gospel movement in Los Angeles, and for nearly two decades she conducted a preaching and healing ministry in the Angelus Temple, Los Angeles, which cost her followers $1.5 million to construct.

McQueen, Alexander 1970– •*English fashion designer*• He was born in London and studied at St Martin's School of Art. His final collection there in 1992 established his presence on the fashion scene and he became notorious in the tabloids soon after with his low-cut "bumsters." He became chief designer for Givenchy in 1996, moving to the same position at Gucci in 2000. He won the London Fashion Awards Designer of the Year prize in 1996 and 2000 (with **John Galliano**).

McQueen, (Terence) Steve(n) 1930–80 •*US actor*• Born in Indianapolis, Indiana, after a delinquent youth he took up acting on stage and television, and by 1955 was a film star with a reputation as a tough, unconventional rebel, both on and off the screen. He costarred in *The Magnificent Seven* (1960), a role which helped create his image as a laconic loner, and became the archetypal 1960s cinema hero/rebel with his performances in *The Great Escape* (1963), *The Cincinnati Kid* (1965) and *Bullitt* (1968). He was married to actress Ali McGraw (1973–78), and died after a long struggle with cancer.

McQueen, Steve(n) 1969– •*English artist*• Born in London, he studied at the Chelsea School of Art, Goldsmiths College, London, and the Tisch School of the Arts, New York. He is known particularly for his video art pieces such as *Deadpan* (1997) and *Drumroll* (1999). Among his international prizes are the ICA Futures award (1996) and the Turner Prize (1999).

McRae, Colin 1968– •*Scottish rally driver*• Born in Lanark, he made his debut in 1986 and soon earned the nickname "The Flying Scotsman." Driving for Subaru (1991–98) and subsequently (from 1999) for Ford, he won the British rally championship in 1991, 1992 and 1998 and the world rally championship in 1995, becoming the youngest driver ever to win the title.

Mead, Margaret 1901–78 •*US anthropologist*• Born in Philadelphia, she studied with **Franz Boas** and **Ruth Benedict** at the graduate school of Columbia University. She was appointed assistant curator of ethnology at the American Museum of Natural History, New York City, in 1926, and curator from 1964. After expeditions to Samoa and New Guinea, where she studied sexual behavior and the rites of adolescence, she wrote *Coming of Age in Samoa* (1928) and *Growing Up in New Guinea* (1930). In later books she argued that personality characteristics, especially as they differ between men and women, are shaped by cultural conditioning rather than heredity. Her writings proved very popular and made anthropology accessible to a wide public.

Meade, George Gordon 1815–72 •*US soldier*• Born in Cádiz, Spain, he trained at West Point. In the Civil War he fought at the Second Battle of Bull Run and Antietam, after which he was promoted to major general of volunteers. He led troops at Fredericksburg and at Chancellorsville, and in 1863 he was given command of the Army of the Potomac. He defeated **Robert E Lee** at Gettysburg but was criticized for failing to press his advantage.

Meade, James Edward 1907–95 •*English economist and Nobel Prize winner*• Born in Swanage, Dorset, he worked for the League of Nations in the 1930s, and among subsequent positions was Professor of Political Economics at Cambridge (1957–68), where he remained a resident Fellow until 1974. A prolific writer, his principal contributions have been in the area of international trade, including *The Theory of International Economic Policy* (2 vols, 1951–55), *Principles of Political Economy* (4 vols, 1965–76) and *The Intelligent Radical's Guide to Economic Policy* (1975). He shared the 1977 Nobel Prize for economics with **Bertil Ohlin**.

Meade, Richard (John Hannay) 1938– •*British three-day-event athlete*• Born in Chepstow, Gwent, Wales, he won three Olympic gold medals: the Three Day Event team golds in 1968 and 1972, and the individual title in 1972, on Laurieston. He also won at Burghley (1964) and Badminton (1970, 1982), and won world championship team gold medals (1970, 1982) and European championship team gold medals (1967, 1971, 1981).

Meale, Richard Graham 1932– •*Australian composer, conductor and teacher*• Born in Sydney, he studied at the New South Wales State Conservatorium for Music, and later at the University of California in Los Angeles (1960). Returning to Australia, he made an immediate impact with his compositions *Los Alboradas* (1963) and *Homage to Garcia Lorca* (1964). The influence of Japanese music on him is apparent in *Images: Nagauta* (1966) and *Clouds Now and Then* (1969). Later works reflect the music of **Debussy**. His first opera, *Voss* (1982, with a libretto by **David Malouf** based on the novel by **Patrick White**), demonstrates the strength of his orchestral and vocal writing.

Meany, George 1894–1980 •*US labor leader*• Born in New York City, he followed his father into the plumbing trade and rose through union ranks to become head of the American Federation of Labor in 1952. He worked to heal the breach with the Congress of Industrial Organizations, and, when the two groups merged, he served as the first president (1955–79) of the new federation (the AFL-CIO). Under his leadership the AFL-CIO made an alliance with the Democratic Party, and Meany became an influential figure on the national political scene, supporting civil rights and the Great Society legislation, as well as, to the dismay of liberals, the Vietnam War. He was notable for his efforts to end corruption among member unions, which led to the expulsion of the Teamsters in 1957.

Mears, Rick 1951– •*US racecar driver*• Born in Wichita, Kansas, he is four times winner of the Indianapolis 500 (1979, 1984, 1988, 1991), and winner of the Indy Car national championship three times (1979, 1981, 1982). In the 1984 Indy 500 he set a record average speed of 163.612mph (263.301 kph). He retired in 1992 with almost 30 Indy car victories and career earnings in excess of $11 million.

Mechnikov, Ilya Ilyich or **Elie** *See* **Metchnikoff, Elie**

Medawar, Sir Peter Brian 1915–87 •*British zoologist, pioneering immunologist and Nobel Prize winner*• Born in Rio de Janeiro of English-Lebanese parents, he was educated in zoology at Magdalen College, Oxford. During World War II he studied skin grafting for burn victims, where he realized that rejection of a graft occurred by the same immunological mechanism as the response to foreign bodies. He was appointed Professor of Zoology at the University of Birmingham (1947–51), Jodrell Professor of Comparative Anatomy at University College London (1951–62), and director of the National Institute for Medical Research at Mill Hill from 1962. He investigated the problems of tissue rejection in transplant operations. In 1960 he shared the Nobel Prize for physiology or medicine with Sir **Macfarlane Burnet** for research into immunological tolerance. They showed that prenatal injection of tissues from one individual to another resulted in the acceptance of the donor's tissues. He was elected a Fellow of the Royal Society in 1949 and knighted in 1965.

“ ”

I cannot give any scientist of any age better advice than this: the intensity of a conviction that a hypothesis is true has no bearing over whether it is true or not.

1979 Advice to a young scientist, attributed.

Medici, Caterina de' *See* **Catherine de Médicis**

Medici, Cosimo de' 1389–1464 •*Florentine financier, statesman and philanthropist*• His father, Giovanni de' Bicci Medici, appears to have created the Medici wealth, and Cosimo was to use it to fuel the machine of his own power in Florence. He was exiled by the ascendant Albizzi faction in 1433, having opposed the imposition of taxes for what proved a disastrous war. He returned in 1434 and stifled family faction while maintaining the façade of republican government with a mixture of ruthlessness and urbanity. He employed some of his wealth in patronage of the arts, including Europe's first public library, and made the city the center of the new learning. He was posthumously commemorated as “Pater Patriae.”

Medici, Cosimo I de', *called* **the Great** 1519–74 •*Florentine politician*• Duke of Florence from 1537 and Grand Duke of Tuscany from 1569, he possessed the astuteness of his greater predecessors, but was cruel and relentless, though one of the ablest rulers of his century. A skilled soldier, he annexed the republic of Siena in 1555 and doubled the territory of Tuscany during his rule. He devoted his energies to developing the trade, agriculture and economic infrastructure of Tuscany, and to building up its armed forces. At the same time, he was a notable patron of artists and a great collector of Etruscan antiquities.

Medici, Giovanni Angelo de' *See* **Pius IV**

Medici, Lorenzo de', *called* **the Magnificent** 1449–92 •*Florentine ruler*• The son of Piero I de' Medici and grandson of **Cosimo de' Medici**, he succeeded as head of the family on the death of his father (1469), and was an able, if autocratic, ruler who made Florence the leading state in Italy. In 1478 he showed courage and judgment in thwarting an attempt by the malcontent Pazzi, rival bankers, to overthrow the Medici, with the encouragement of Pope **Sixtus IV**, although the uprising led to the assassination of Lorenzo's brother, Giuliano (1453–78). Lorenzo was a distinguished lyric poet as well as being, in the words of **Machiavelli**, “the greatest patron of literature and art that any prince has ever been.” He aroused the criticism of **Savonarola** for his secular tastes during his later years.

Medici, Maria de' *See* **Marie de Médicis**

Medici, Piero de', *called* **the Unfortunate** 1471–1503 •*Florentine ruler*• The eldest son of **Lorenzo de' Medici**, he succeeded his father (1492), but his disregard of republican ways made him unpopular. With the invasion of Italy by **Charles VIII** of France (1494), Piero was obliged to surrender key Florentine forces to the aggressor, a step strongly resented by the civic authorities, who banished the Medici from the state, placed a price on Piero's head and permitted the plundering of the Medici palace. Piero died fighting against the French.

Medina-Sidonia, Alonzo Pérez de Gusmàn, Duque de 1550–1619 •*Spanish seaman*• Captain general of Andalusia and one of the wealthiest and most influential men in Spain, he was involved in the conquest of Portugal as well as being an important administrator. Appointed to command the Great Armada in the Enterprise of England on the death of the Marquis of Santa Cruz (1588), he led the Armada successfully up the English Channel to rendezvous with Parma off the Dutch coast, but was thwarted by the latter's failure to break out, by the action of the English fleet, as well as by adverse weather.

Medlicott, William Norton 1900–87 •*English diplomatic historian*• Born in Wandsworth, London, he was known especially for his studies of the **Bismarck** period in international relations, and British diplomacy in the 20th century. Educated at University College London, he was Professor (later Principal) of History at the University of Exeter (1939–53) and Stevenson Professor of International History at the London School of Economics (1953–67). The Norton Medlicott Medal, awarded by The Historical Association, was instituted in his honor (1984).

Mee, Margaret Ursula 1909–89 •*English botanical artist and traveler*• Born in Chesham, Buckinghamshire, she trained at the Camberwell School of Art, London, and first visited the Amazon forests when she was 47. Ten years later, having settled in Brazil, she began her impressive career as a botanical artist. She was well known for her outspoken anger at the destruction of the Amazon, which she called “a valley of death.” The Margaret Mee Amazon trust was set up in 1988 to draw attention to the area's ecological crisis.

Meegeren, Han or **Henricus van** 1889–1947 •*Dutch artist and forger*• Born in Deventer, in 1945 he was accused of selling art treasures to the Germans. To clear himself he confessed to having forged the pictures, and also the famous *Supper at Emmaus*, “discovered" in 1937 and accepted by the majority of experts as by **Jan Vermeer**. His fakes were subjected to a detailed scientific examination, and in 1947 their maker was sentenced to 12 months' imprisonment for forgery. He died a few weeks later, a popular hero.

Meer, Simon van der *See* **van der Meer, Simon**

Megasthenes fl. 300 BC •*Greek historian*• He was ambassador (306–298 BC) at the Indian court of Sandrakottos or **Chandragupta**, where he gathered materials for his *Indica*, from which **Arrian**, **Strabo** and others borrowed.

Mehemet 'Ali, *also known as* **Muhammad 'Ali** c. 1769–1849 •*Viceroy of Egypt*• An Albanian military officer, he was sent to Egypt (1801) with a Turkish-Albanian force to counter the French invasion. After the departure of the French, he supported the Egyptian rulers in their struggles with the Mamluks and had himself proclaimed viceroy by his Albanians (1805). He formed a regular army, improved irrigation, and introduced elements of European civilization. He conquered part of Arabia (1816), annexed Nubia and part of the Sudan (1820), and occupied various points in the Morea and Crete (1821–28) to aid the Turks in their war with the Greeks. His fleet was defeated at Navarino (1827), but in 1831 the conquest of Syria was begun, and the Ottoman army was defeated at Konya (1832), after which he was given Syria on condition of tribute. The victory at Nezib (1839) might have elevated him to the throne of Constantinople (Istanbul); but the Quadruple Alliance (1840), the fall of Acre to the British, and the consequent evacuation of Syria compelled him to limit his ambitions to Egypt.

Mehmet I c. 1387–1421 •*Sultan of Turkey*• The youngest son of **Bayezit I**, his short reign (from 1413) marks the beginning of the recovery from the devastating effects of the conquests of **Timur**. He made gains in Albania, reestablished control over western Anatolia, and put down a religious revolt. He was the father of Sultan Murad II.

Mehmet II (the Conqueror), *also called* **Mohammed** 1432–81 •*Sultan of Turkey and founder of the Ottoman Empire*• Born in Adrianople (Edirne), he succeeded his father, Murad II, in 1451, and took Constantinople (1453), rebuilding it into a prosperous Ottoman capital, popularly known as Istanbul, and thus extinguishing the Byzantine Empire and giving the Turks their commanding position on the Bosporus. Checked by **János Hunyadi** at Belgrade (1456), he nevertheless annexed most of Serbia, all of Greece, and most of the Aegean Islands, threatened Venetian territory, was repelled from Rhodes by the Knights of St John (1479), took Otranto (1480) and died in a campaign against Persia (Iran).

Mehmet III 1566–1603 •*Sultan of Turkey*• The son of Murad III, he was born in Manisa, and on his succession in 1595 he invoked the law of fratricide by which the sultan could have his brothers put to death. All 19, of whom the eldest was aged 11, were executed by strangulation. His reign involved wars with Austria and Russia, and revolts in Anatolia.

Mehmet IV 1642–93 •*Sultan of Turkey*• Born in Constantinople (Istanbul), he succeeded his deposed father, Ibrahim I, as a child in 1648. The Turks were defeated by the Austrians under Count Montecucculi at the Battle of St Gotthard (1664), and in a war with Poland (1672–76) they were twice defeated by King **John III Sobieski**, but gained Polish Ukraine, which they lost to Russia (1681). In 1683 under the Grand Vizier Kara Mustafa, they besieged Vienna, which was relieved by John Sobieski. After defeat at the second Battle of Mohacs (1687), Mehmet was deposed, and replaced by **Süleyman II**.

Mehmet VI 1861–1926 •*Sultan of Turkey*• The brother of Mehmet V, he was the last Ottoman sultan (1918–22). Although clever and perceptive, he was unsuccessful in suppressing the nationalists led by Mustafa Kemal (**Kemal Atatürk**), who abolished the sultanate (1922). Mehmet fled to Malta, and after abortive attempts to become ruler in the Hejaz, he died in exile.

Mehta, Ved Parkash 1934– •*US writer*• He was born in Lahore. Blind from the age of eight, he went to the US for his education when he was 15 and attended the Arkansas School for the Blind in Little Rock and Pomona College, before going on to Oxford and Harvard. While at Pomona he published his first book, the autobiography *Face to Face* (1957). He has had a distinguished career as a journalist and has written biographies, stories, essays and portraits of India. His enduring achievement, however, is *Continents of Exile*, an acclaimed series of autobiographical books: *Daddyji* (1972), *Mamaji* (1979), *Vedi* (1982), *The Ledge Between the Streams* (1984), *Sound-Shadows of the New World* (1986), *The Stolen Light* (1989) and *Up at Oxford* (1993). He became a naturalized US citizen in 1975.

Mehta, Zubin 1936– •*US conductor*• Born into a Parsi family in Bombay, he was taught music by his father, a violinist and conductor of modest pretensions, and later studied at the Vienna Academy of Music, graduating in 1957. After conducting in Liverpool and Montreal, he became musical director of the Los Angeles Philharmonic (1962–78) and the New York Philharmonic (1978–91). Since 1968 he has also served as music director of the Israel Philharmonic, and in 1981 he was named its music director for life. In 1998 he also became general music director of the Bavarian State Opera. He specializes in late Romantic and early modern music and is known for his flamboyant style.

Meier, Richard Alan 1934– •*US architect*• Born in Newark, New Jersey, he was educated at Cornell University and founded his own practice in 1963. A prominent figure of the "New York Five" group that attracted attention in the 1970s, his most important works include the High Museum of Art in Atlanta, Georgia (1983), the Museum of Contemporary Art in Barcelona (1995), the City Hall and Central Library in The Hague (1996) and the J Paul Getty Center in Los Angeles (1997).

Meighen, Arthur 1874–1960 •*Canadian politician*• Born in Anderson, Ontario, he became a lawyer and sat in the Canadian House of Commons as a liberal Conservative (1908–26). In 1913 he became solicitor general in **Robert Borden**'s Union government and was the architect of much of its strategy during World War I. He later orchestrated the government's draconian response to the Winnipeg General Strike (1919), amending the Immigration Act and the criminal code so that strike leaders would face either deportation or long prison sentences. In 1920 Meighen succeeded Borden as prime minister. He became prime minister again in 1925, but when the Progressives deserted him, the governor-general allowed him to dissolve Parliament, a mechanism which had not been afforded to **Mackenzie King** in a similar situation. King won the election by promising to prevent such imperial intervention. Meighen then resigned as Conservative leader a few months later, and was replaced by Richard Bennett (1870–1947).

Meinhof, Ulrike Marie 1934–76 •*West German terrorist*• Born in Oldenburg, the daughter of a museum director, she campaigned for the creation of a neutral, nuclear-free "Greater Germany" while studying at the University of Marburg, and subsequently became a respected left-wing journalist. After an interview with the imprisoned arsonist, **Andreas Baader**, she became committed to the use of violence to secure radical social change. In May 1970, she helped free Baader and they both then headed an underground urban guerrilla organization, the Red Army Faction, which conducted brutal terrorist attacks against the postwar West German "materialist order." As the Faction's chief ideologist, she was arrested in 1972, and in 1974 was sentenced to eight years' imprisonment. She committed suicide in Stammheim high-security prison.

Meir, Golda, *née* **Goldie Mabovich**, *later* **Goldie Myerson** 1898–1978 •*Israeli politician*• She was born in Kiev and settled in Palestine in 1921, where she took up social work and became a leading figure in the Labor movement. She was Israeli ambassador to the Soviet Union (1948–49), minister of labor (1949–56), and foreign minister (1956–66). She was elected prime minister in 1969, but her efforts for peace in the Middle East were halted by the fourth Arab-Israeli War (1973) and she resigned in 1974.

Meitner, Lise 1878–1968 •*Austrian physicist*• Born in Vienna and educated at the University of Vienna, she became professor at the University of Berlin (1926–38) and a member of the Kaiser Wilhelm Institute for Chemistry (1907–38), where she set up a nuclear physics laboratory with **Otto Hahn**, with whom she had discovered the radioactive element protactinium in 1917. In 1938 she fled to

Sweden to escape the Nazis, and shortly afterward Hahn wrote to Meitner concerning his discovery of radioactive barium. With her nephew **Otto Frisch**, she proposed that the production of barium was the result of nuclear fission, later verified by Frisch. The element meitnerium (atomic number 109) was named after her.

Melanchthon, Philipp, *Greek surname for original name* **Schwartzerd ("Black Earth")** 1497–1560 •*German Protestant reformer*• Born in Bretten in the Palatinate, he studied at the Universities of Heidelberg (1509–11) and Tübingen (1512–14). Appointed Professor of Greek at the University of Wittenberg in 1516, he became **Martin Luther**'s fellow worker. The Augsburg Confession (1530) was composed by him. After Luther's death he succeeded to the leadership of the German Reformation movement but lost the confidence of some Protestants by concessions to the Catholics. His conditional consent to the introduction of the stringent Augsburg Interim (1549) in Saxony led to painful controversies. His *Loci Communes* (1521) is the first great Protestant work on dogmatic theology.

Melba, Dame Nellie, *née* **Helen Porter Mitchell** 1861–1931 •*Australian operatic soprano and pioneer recording artist*• Born in Richmond, a suburb of Melbourne, Victoria, she studied singing and piano under Madame Ellen Christian, a pupil of Manuel García. After her mother's death the family moved to Queensland, where she met and married Captain Charles Armstrong, the younger son of a baronet. A boy was born, but Helen grew bored with provincial domesticity, and in 1884 she returned to Melbourne to study under Pietro Cecchi (c. 1831–97), making her professional debut at Melbourne Town Hall in May of that year. After a visit to London, she had an audition in Paris with Madame Mathilde Marchesi (1826–1913), the leading vocal teacher of her time, and took her stage name from her native city. Marchesi added the polish to the fine instrument Cecchi had trained, and tutored Melba in the social graces—although Melba retained her forthrightness and earthy speech. She made her operatic debut at the Théâtre Royal de la Monnaie in Brussels in October 1887 as Gilda in **Verdi**'s *Rigoletto*. Her Covent Garden debut was in May 1888, in the title role of **Donizetti**'s *Lucia di Lammermoor*, but her first appearance in London left the critics indifferent. Her return to Covent Garden the following year was a different story. Covent Garden was in its heyday and Melba sang alongside other great singers such as the Italian tenor **Enrico Caruso**. With Caruso, she was one of the artists who made the recording industry, and who were made by it. She recorded on some early cylinders, but her first standard (78 rpm) records were issued in 1904 on a special purple label at the price of 21 shillings. She made her last recordings, in the new electrical process, at her Covent Garden farewell in 1926.

" "

The first rule in opera is the first rule in life: see to everything yourself.

1925 ***Melodies and Memories.***

Melbourne, William Lamb, 2nd Viscount 1779–1848 •*English statesman*• Born in London and educated at Trinity College, Cambridge, and Glasgow, he became Whig Member of Parliament for Leominster in 1805, but in 1827 accepted the chief-secretaryship of Ireland in **George Canning**'s government, and retained it under Viscount Goderich (1782–1859) and **Wellington**. Succeeding as second viscount (1828), he returned to the Whigs, became Home Secretary (1830) and then premier (1834, 1835–1841). His wife (1785–1828), a daughter of the Earl of Bessborough, wrote novels as Lady Caroline Lamb.

Melchett, 1st Baron *See* **Mond, Alfred Moritz**

Melchior, Lauritz Lebrecht Hommel 1890–1973 •*US tenor*• Born in Copenhagen, Denmark, his career began as a baritone in *Pagliacci* ("Clowns") in 1913. From 1918 he appeared as a tenor, making his Covent Garden, London, debut in 1924. One of the foremost Wagnerian singers of the century, he sang at Bayreuth (1924–31) and regularly at the New York Metropolitan (1926–50). He became a US citizen in 1947.

Meleager c. 140–c. 70 BC •*Greek poet and epigrammatist*• From Gadara, Syria, he was the author of 128 exquisite short poems and epigrams included in his *Stephanos* ("Garland"), the first large anthology of epigrams.

Melissus 5th century BC •*Greek philosopher and politician*• He commanded the Samian fleet which defeated the Athenians under **Pericles** in a battle in 441 BC. He was probably a pupil of **Parmenides of Elea** and wrote a book entitled *On Nature* which elaborated Parmenides' views on the properties of reality and which most influenced the atomists **Democritus** and **Leucippus**.

Mellon, Andrew W(illiam) 1855–1937 •*US financier, philanthropist and politician*• Born in Pittsburgh, Pennsylvania, he trained as a lawyer and entered his father's banking house in 1874. He took over in 1882, soon establishing himself as a banker and industrial magnate. Entering politics, he was secretary of the treasury from 1921 to 1932 and made controversial fiscal reforms, drastically reducing taxation of the wealthy. He was ambassador to the UK from 1932 to 1933. He endowed the National Gallery of Art in Washington DC.

Melly, (Alan) George (Heywood) 1926– •*English jazz singer*• Born in Liverpool, he was educated at Stowe School and served in the Royal Navy before singing with the Mick Mulligan jazz band (1951–62) and also working as a journalist and comic strip cartoonist. Subsequently he established a lasting relationship as singer with John Chilton's Feetwarmers. He became a familiar face on British television, becoming well known for his flamboyant dress and skills as a raconteur, and also appearing as an art critic. His publications include *Owning Up* (1965), *Rum, Bum and Concertina* (1977) and *Mellymobile* (1982).

Melville, Andrew, *nicknamed* **the Blast** 1545–c. 1622 •*Scottish Presbyterian reformer*• Born in Baldowie, Angus, he was educated at St Andrews and Paris. In 1568 he became Professor of Humanity at Geneva. On his return to Scotland he was appointed principal of the University of Glasgow (1574–80), and did much to reorganize university education. In 1582 he preached boldly against absolute authority before the General Assembly and advocated a presbyterial system of church government, and in 1584, to escape imprisonment, he went to London. He was repeatedly Moderator of the General Assembly of the Church of Scotland. In 1596 he headed a deputation to "remonstrate" with King James VI (**James VI and I**), and in 1606, with seven other ministers, was called to England to confer with him. Having ridiculed the service in the Chapel Royal in a Latin epigram, he was summoned before the English Privy Council and sent to the Tower, but released in 1611. His nickname stems from his religious fervor.

Melville, Herman 1819–91 •*US novelist, short-story writer and poet*• Born in New York City, he became a bank clerk but, in search of adventure, joined a whaling ship bound for the South Seas. His adventures in the Marquesas and Tahiti inspired his first two books, *Typee* (1846) and *Omoo* (1847). *White Jacket* (1850) drew on his experiences as a seaman on the man-of-war which eventually brought him home. He married in 1847, and after three years in New York acquired a farm near Pittsfield, Massachusetts, where **Nathaniel Hawthorne** was his neighbor and friend. It was during this period that he wrote his masterpiece, *Moby-Dick* (1851), a novel of the whaling industry, of extraordinary vigor and color. Later novels include *Pierre* (1852) and *The Confidence Man* (1857). Melville also wrote short stories, most notably "Benito Cereno" and "Bartleby the Scrivener," which were collected, with others, in *The Piazza Tales* (1856). Now regarded as one of the US's greatest novelists, he was not so successful during his life. Exhausted and disillusioned, from 1866 he was obliged to work as a New York customs official. Near the end of his life he returned tentatively to fiction with *Billy Budd*, an unfinished but brilliant novella published posthumously in 1924.

Memlinc or **Memling, Hans** c. 1440–94 •*Flemish religious painter*• Born in Seligenstadt, Germany, to Dutch parents, he lived mostly in Bruges. A pupil of **Rogier van der Weyden**, he repeated the types of his master. The triptych of the *Madonna Enthroned* at Chatsworth (1468), the *Marriage of St Catherine* (1479) and the *Shrine of St Ursula* (1489), both at Bruges, are among his best works. He was also an original and creative portrait painter.

Memmi, Simone *See* **Martini, Simone**

Menander c. 343–c. 291 BC *•Greek comic dramatist and poet•* He was born in Athens. His comedies were more successful with cultured than with popular audiences, but **Quintilian** praised him, and **Terence** imitated him closely. The greatest writer of Attic New Comedy, he wrote more than a hundred plays, but only a few fragments of his work were known until 1906, when a papyrus was discovered in Egypt containing 1,328 lines from four different plays. In 1957, however, the complete text of the comedy *Dyskolos* (Eng trans 1960) was brought to light in Geneva.

Menchú, Rigoberta Tum 1959– *•Guatemalan activist and Nobel Prize winner•* Born near San Marcos, she has worked as a domestic servant and as a cotton-field laborer. Her campaign for human rights began when she was a teenager, and later she had to flee to Mexico when her brother and parents were killed by security forces in 1980. In 1983 her book *I Rigoberta Menchú* was published and her cause was taken up by Madame Danielle Mitterrand, wife of President **Mitterrand** of France. In 1986 Menchú narrated the film *When the Mountains Tremble*, which portrays the difficulties experienced by the native Quiché people. A tireless worker for the rights of indigenous people, in 1992 she was awarded the Nobel Peace Prize. She has been a Goodwill Ambassador for UNESCO since 1996.

Mencius, *properly* **Mengzi** or **Meng-tzu** c. 372–c. 289 BC *•Chinese philosopher and sage•* Born in Shandong (Shantung), he helped to develop and popularize Confucian ideas and founded a school to promote their study. For over 20 years he traveled China searching for a princely ruler who would put into practice his system of social and political reform. The search was unsuccessful, but his conversations with rulers, disciples and others are recorded in a book of sayings which his pupils compiled after his death as the *Book of Mengzi*. His ethical system was based on the belief that humans were innately and instinctively good but required the proper conditions and support for moral growth.

“ ”

If the king loves music, there is little wrong in the land.

Discourses.

Mencken, H(enry) L(ouis) 1880–1956 *•US journalist, editor, critic and historian of language•* Born in Baltimore, Maryland, he became editor of the *Baltimore Herald*, then joined the *Sunpapers* in 1906. From 1908 to 1923 he worked with the *Smart Set*, and in 1924 he and **George Jean Nathan** founded the *American Mercury*. He attacked what he called the "boo-joy" (bourgeois), became a major influence on the US literary scene of the 1920s and supported many writers such as **Theodore Dreiser**. His main work is *The American Language* (1919). *The Vintage Mencken*, edited by **Alistair Cooke**, appeared in 1955.

Mendel, Gregor Johann 1822–84 *•Austrian botanist•* Born near Udrau, he was ordained as a priest in 1847, and after studying science at the University of Vienna (1851–53), he became an abbot in 1868. In the experimental garden of the monastery, he crossed species that produced tall and short plants, and the resulting numbers of tall and short plants in subsequent generations led him to suggest that each plant received one character from each of its parents, tallness being "dominant," and shortness being "recessive" or hidden. His experiments led to the formulation of Mendel's law of segregation and Mendel's law of independent assortment. His concepts have become the basis of modern genetics.

Mendeleev or **Mendeleyev, Dmitri Ivanovich** 1834–1907 *•Russian chemist•* He was born in Tobolsk, Siberia, and studied in St Petersburg and Heidelberg, Germany, where he collaborated briefly with **Robert Wilhelm Bunsen** and investigated the behavior of gases, formulating the idea of critical temperature. He was appointed professor at the St Petersburg Technical Institute in 1863 and at the St Petersburg University in 1866. In 1869 he tabulated the elements in ascending order of their atomic weight and found that chemically similar elements tended to fall into the same columns. Mendeleev's great achievement was to realize that certain elements still had to be discovered and to leave gaps in the table where he predicted they would fall. At first the periodic table was largely rejected by the scientific world, but as each new element that was subsequently discovered fit into it perfectly, skepticism turned to enthusiasm. The transuranic element mendelevium (atomic number 101) is named in his honor.

Mendelssohn(-Bartholdy), (Jakob Ludwig) Felix 1809–47 *•German composer•* Born in Hamburg, the grandson of **Moses Mendelssohn**, at a very early age he made the acquaintance of **Goethe** and **Carl Weber** and composed his Symphony in C minor (1824) and the B minor Quartet (1824–25). His *Midsummer Night's Dream* overture (1826) was a success, and a tour of Scotland in the summer of 1829 inspired the *Hebrides* overture (1830) and the "Scotch" Symphony. He settled in Berlin in 1841 when the king of Prussia asked him to cofound an Academy of Arts, and in 1843 his new music school at Leipzig was opened, with **Schumann** and the violinist Ferdinand David among his associates. He produced his *Elijah* in Birmingham in 1846. His sister's death in 1847 affected him profoundly, and he never recovered.

Mendelssohn, Moses 1729–86 *•German Jewish philosopher and biblical scholar•* Born in Dessau, he studied in Berlin. He is an important figure in the history of Jewish philosophy and in the Enlightenment. His most important works include *Phädon* (1767), an argument for the immortality of the soul, based on **Plato**'s *Phaedo*; *Jerusalem* (1783), which advocates Judaism as the religion of reason; and *Morgenstunden* (1785, "Morning Hours"), which argues for the rationality of belief in the existence of God. He was a friend of **Gotthold Lessing** and the prototype of his *Nathan*. He was the grandfather of **Felix Mendelssohn**.

Menderes, Adnan 1899–1961 *•Turkish statesman•* He was born near Aydin. Though trained as a lawyer, he became a farmer, then entered politics in 1932, at first in opposition, then with the party in power under **Kemal Atatürk**. In 1945 he became one of the leaders of the new Democratic Party and was made prime minister when it came to power in 1950. Reelected in 1954 and 1957, in 1960 he was deposed following an army coup, and was tried and hanged.

Mendes, Sam(uel) Alexander 1965– *•English theater and film director•* Born in Reading, Berkshire, he studied at Peterhouse, Cambridge. He began his career as artistic director at the Minerva Studio Theatre, Chichester (1989–92), and later at the Donmar Warehouse, London (1992–). During the 1990s he also worked as a freelance director for the Royal Shakespeare Company and Royal National Theatre. In 1999 he made his debut film *American Beauty*, an engaging take on US suburban ennui, which won an Academy Award for Best Director.

Menem, Carlos Saúl 1935– *•Argentine statesman•* Born in Anillaco, Argentina, the son of Syrian immigrants, he earned a law degree from the University of Córdoba in 1958. A follower of **Juan Perón**, he was a provincial governor from 1973, and was imprisoned for five years after the military coup in 1976. Elected president in 1989, he stabilized the economy and reduced inflation, and was reelected in 1995, serving until 1999.

Mengistu, Haile Mariam 1941– *•Ethiopian soldier and politician•* He was born in Addis Ababa and trained at Guenet Military Academy. He was one of the leaders of the bloody coup that successfully deposed emperor **Haile Selassie** in 1974 and later abolished the monarchy. He became undisputed leader and head of state in 1977. Allying himself with the USSR and modeling himself upon Cuba's **Fidel Castro**, he sought to create a Socialist state in Ethiopia. Civilian rule was formally established in 1987, when he became Ethiopia's first president, but mismanagement, drought and internal war weakened his hold on the country, and in 1991 he was overthrown by the Ethiopian People's Revolutionary Democratic Front. He resigned and fled to Zimbabwe, where he was offered political asylum and now has permanent residency. In 1994 he was tried in absentia in Ethiopia and found guilty of genocide and war crimes.

Mengzi *See* **Mencius**

Menno Simons 1496–1561 *•Dutch Anabaptist leader and founder of the Mennonite sect•* Born in Friesland, and ordained as a Catholic priest (1524), he left the Church after being influenced by the ideas of **Martin Luther** (1536). He organized Anabaptist groups in northern Europe that were persecuted by Catholics and Protestants alike. Mainly resident in the US, the evangelical Mennonite sect named after him practices adult baptism, close adherence to the New Testament, restriction of marriage to members of the group, excommunication, and refusal to hold civic office.

Menotti, Gian-Carlo 1911– •*US composer*• Born in Milan, Italy, he settled in the US at the age of 17, achieving international fame with a series of operas that began with *Amelia Goes to the Ball* (1937). He wrote his own libretti, and his other works, including *The Medium* (1946), *The Consul* (1950, Pulitzer Prize), *Amahl and the Night Visitors* (1951), composed for television performance, *The Saint of Bleecker Street* (1954, Pulitzer Prize), *Maria Golovin* (1958) and *The Most Important Man* (1971) had great theatrical effectiveness. In 1958 he founded the Festival of Two Worlds in Spoleto, Italy.

Menuhin, Yehudi Menuhin, Baron 1916–99 •*British violinist*• Born in New York in the US, he appeared as a soloist with the San Francisco Symphony Orchestra at the age of seven. In 1932 he recorded **Elgar**'s Violin Concerto, conducted by the composer, and subsequently appeared all over the world. During World War II he gave concerts to the troops, and after the war settled in England, beginning to conduct in 1957. In the same year, he set up the Gstaad Festival, and in 1963 he founded the Yehudi Menuhin School of Music for musically talented children. Noted also for raising the profile of Indian music in the West, he was given the honorary title Knight Commander, Order of the British Empire, in 1965 and Order of Merit in 1987. He took British citizenship in 1985 and was made a life peer in 1993.

Menzies, John Ross 1852–1935 •*Scottish wholesale publisher and distributor*• Born in Edinburgh, he joined his father's business in Princes Street, Edinburgh, and with his brother pushed the firm westward, opening a branch in Glasgow in 1868. This was followed by establishing bookstalls in almost all towns of significance. He also directed the creation of a huge network of railway station bookstalls.

Menzies, Sir Robert Gordon 1894–1978 •*Australian statesman*• Born in Jeparit, Victoria, he practiced as a barrister before entering politics, becoming a member of the Victoria parliament in 1928. He went to the Federal House of Representatives in 1934. A powerful orator and declared Anglophile, he was Commonwealth attorney general (1935–39), prime minister (1939–41), and leader of the Opposition (1943–49), when he again took office as premier of the coalition government. He continued as prime minister, exploiting the factionalism of his Labor opponents, and held office for a record 16 years, during which time Australia's economy grew and prospered. His final years were marked by Australia's entry into the Vietnam War.

“ ”

What Great Britain calls the Far East is to us the near north.

*1939 Quoted in the **Sydney Morning Herald**, April 27.*

Mercator, Gerardus, *originally* **Gerhard Kremer** 1512–94 •*Flemish geographer and mapmaker*• Born in Rupelmonde, Flanders, he graduated from Louvain in philosophy and theology. He studied mathematics, astronomy and engraving, and produced a terrestrial globe (1536) and a map of the Holy Land (1537). In 1544 he was imprisoned for heresy, but released for lack of evidence. In 1552 he settled at Duisburg in Germany, becoming cosmographer to the Duke of Cleves, and produced maps of many parts of Europe, including Great Britain. To aid navigators, in 1569 he introduced a map projection (Mercator's map projection), in which the path of a ship steering on a constant bearing is represented by a straight line on the map; it has been used for nautical charts ever since. In 1585 he published the first part of an "atlas" of Europe, said to be the first use of the word to describe a book of maps. On the cover was a drawing of Atlas holding a globe on his shoulders, hence "atlas" became applied to any book of maps.

Merchant, Ismail 1936– •*Indian film producer*• Born in Bombay, he studied at St Xavier's College and New York University. In 1961 he teamed with director **James Ivory** to make a series of feature films reflecting aspects of Indian culture and the legacy of colonial rule, including *Shakespeare Wallah* (1965) and *Bombay Talkie* (1970). One of the most successful and enduring independent production units, Merchant-Ivory has become synonymous with sensitive literary adaptations and costume dramas like *A Room with a View* (1985), *Howards End* (1992) and *The Remains of the Day* (1993). He has also collaborated with **Ruth Prawer Jhabvala** on these and other films, including more recent works such as *Jefferson in Paris* (1995) and *The Golden Bowl* (2000). Merchant has also published cookbooks and directed feature films, including *In Custody* (1993) and *The Proprietor* (1996).

Merckx, Eddy, *known as* **the Cannibal** 1945– •*Belgian racing cyclist*• He was born in Woluwe St Pierre, near Brussels. In the 1969 Tour de France he won the major prizes in all three sections: overall, points classification and King of the Mountains. He won the Tour de France five times (1969–72, and 1974). He also won the Tour of Italy five times, and all the major classics, including the Milan–San Remo race seven times. He was the world professional road race champion three times. He won more races (445) and more classics than any other rider before retiring in 1978.

Mercouri, Melina, *originally* **Anna Amalia Mercouri** 1923–94 •*Greek film actress and politician*• Born in Athens, she began her film career in 1955, and found fame in 1960 with *Never on Sunday*. Always politically involved, she was exiled from Greece (1967–74), so she played in British and US productions. She returned to be elected to parliament in 1977, and was Minister of Culture and Sciences (1981–85) and of Culture, Youth, and Sports (1985–90).

Mercury, Freddie, *originally* **Frederick Bulsara** 1946–92 •*British pop singer*• Born in Zanzibar, he became a naturalized British citizen. With guitarist Brian May (1947–), bassist John Deacon (1951–) and drummer Roger Taylor (originally Roger Meadows-Taylor, 1949–), he formed the group Queen. A darling of the fans yet seldom of the critics, Mercury developed an increasingly campy stage presence. Initial hits with "Seven Seas of Rhye" and "Killer Queen" (1974) were eclipsed by "Bohemian Rhapsody" (1975), a bizarre six-minute epic embracing opera, heavy metal and four-part harmony that has a permanent place in rock history and started the pop video boom. Later work includes "We Are the Champions" (1977) and "Radio Gaga" (1984). Mercury disappeared from view in the early 1990s, eventually succumbing to AIDS.

Meredith, George 1828–1909 •*English novelist*• Born in Portsmouth, Hampshire, he was educated privately in Germany. In London, after being articled to a solicitor, he turned to journalism and letters, and in 1849 he married Mary Ellen Nicolls, daughter of **Thomas Love Peacock**. This disastrous marriage gave him an insight into relations between the sexes, which appear as largely in his work as his other great interest, natural selection as Nature's way of perfecting humans. His prose works started with a burlesque Oriental fantasy, *The Shaving of Shagpat* (1855), followed in 1859 by *The Ordeal of Richard Feverel*, but he did not achieve general popularity as a novelist until *Diana of the Crossways* appeared in 1885. Other popular titles include *Evan Harrington* (1860), *Harry Richmond* (1871), and best of all, *Beauchamp's Career* (1875), which poses the question of class and party and is well constructed and clearly written. This cannot be said of his later major novels, *The Egoist* (1879), a study of refined selfishness, and *The Amazing Marriage* (1895). These two powerful works are marred by the artificiality and forced wit which occurs in so much of his poetry. His main poetic work is *Modern Love* (1862), based partly on his first marriage.

“ ”

I expect that Woman will be the last thing civilized by Man.

*1859 **The Ordeal of Richard Feverel**, chapter 1.*

Meredith, Owen *See* **Lytton, (Edward) Robert Bulwer-Lytton, 1st Earl of**

Merleau-Ponty, Maurice 1908–61 •*French phenomenological philosopher*• Born in Rochefort-sur-mer, Charente-Maritime, he studied in Paris, taught in various lycées, served as an army officer in World War II, and then held professorships at Lyons (1948) and the Sorbonne, Paris (from 1949). With **Jean-Paul Sartre** and **Simone de Beauvoir** he helped found the journal *Les Temps modernes* (1945). His philosophical works include *La Structure du comportement* (1942, "The Structure of Behavior") and *Phénoménologie de la perception* (1945, "The Phenomenology of Perception").

Merman, Ethel Agnes, *née* **Zimmerman** 1909–84 •*US actress and singer*• Born in Astoria, New York, she had no formal musical training, but her powerful, brassy voice and energy as a performer won her immediate success when she made her Broadway debut in **George Gershwin**'s *Girl Crazy* in 1930. She appeared in several **Cole Porter** shows, including *Anything Goes* (1934), and *Du Barry Was a Lady* (1939). She also starred in *Annie Get Your Gun* (1946), introducing the song "There's No Business Like Show Business," which became her trademark, and won praise as the indomitable stage mother in *Gypsy* (1959).

Merovech or **Merovius** 5th century AD •*Frankish ruler*• The grandfather of **Clovis**, he fought against **Attila** the Hun and gave his name to the Merovingian dynasty.

Merovius *See* **Merovech**

Merrick, Joseph Carey 1862–90 •*Englishman known as "the Elephant Man"*• Born in Leicester, he began at the age of five to develop the disease now thought to be the very rare Proteus syndrome, which caused irregular skin growths on much of his body, bone deformation and grotesque enlargement of the head. He entered a workhouse at age 17 and in 1883 joined a freak show, from which he was rescued by the surgeon Sir Frederick Treves and given a place at the London Hospital. He died of accidental suffocation at age 27. The film *The Elephant Man*, based on his life, appeared in 1980.

Merrifield, (Robert) Bruce 1921– •*US chemist and Nobel Prize winner*• Born in Fort Worth, Texas, he studied at UCLA. He joined the Rockefeller Institute for Medical Research in 1949 and Rockefeller University in New York City in 1957. He devised (1959–62) the important solid-phase method for synthesizing peptides and proteins from amino acids. This process has since been automated and computer controlled, allowing the ready synthesis of small quantities of quite large proteins. He was awarded the Nobel Prize for chemistry for this work in 1984.

Merrill, James Ingram 1926–95 •*US poet*• Born into the upper class in New York City, he was raised in Greenwich Village and attended Amherst College. Though he wrote two plays and two novels, he is best known for his poetry—metrically inventive meditations on memory and lost time, in which his own urbane and witty voice can be distinctly heard. His later work reflects his sometimes playful, sometimes genuine interest in the occult, which led him to use a Ouija board to communicate with the poets of the past. His collections include *Nights and Days* (1966), *Divine Comedies* (1976, Pulitzer Prize), and *The Changing Light at Sandover* (1982, revised 1992).

Mersenne, Marin 1588–1648 •*French mathematician and scientist*• Born in Oize, France, he became a Minim Friar in 1611, and lived in Paris. Devoting himself to science, he corresponded with all the leading scientists of his day including **Descartes**, **Pierre de Fermat**, **Pascal** and **Thomas Hobbes**. He experimented with the pendulum and found the law relating its length and period of oscillation, studied the acoustics of vibrating strings and organ pipes and measured the speed of sound. He also wrote on music, mathematics, optics and philosophy. A type of prime number, the Mersenne numbers, are named after him.

Merton, Walter de d. 1277 •*English prelate*• Born probably in Surrey, he founded Merton College, Oxford (1264), the prototype of the collegiate system in English universities. He was Bishop of Rochester from 1274.

Mesić, Stipe (Stjepan) 1934– •*Croatian politician*• Born in Orahovica, Yugoslavia, he studied law at the University of Zagreb before returning to his hometown and becoming mayor. He was imprisoned in 1971 as a counterrevolutionary and was a political outcast until 1989, when he became secretary of the nationalist Croatian Democratic Union (HDZ). He served as the last president of the Yugoslav Federation (1990–91) and on the creation of independent Croatia became president of the parliament, but subsequently left the HDZ and joined the Croatian National Party (HNS) in 1997. In 1999 the HNS defeated the HDZ, and Mesić became president of Croatia.

Mesmer, Franz Anton 1734–1815 •*Austrian physician and founder of mesmerism*• Born near Constance, he studied medicine at Vienna, and about 1772 claimed that there exists a power, which he called magnetism, that could be used to cure diseases. His treatment aimed to facilitate the flow of an invisible fluid around the body; known as mesmerism, it was the forerunner of hypnotism. In 1778 he was accused of fraud and went to Paris, where he created a sensation. However, in 1785 a learned commission appointed by King **Louis XVI** reported unfavorably, and he retired into obscurity in Switzerland.

Messalina, Valeria c. 25–c. 48 AD •*Roman matron*• She was the third wife of the emperor **Claudius I**, whom she married at the age of 14. She bore him two children, Octavia (the wife of **Nero**) and **Britannicus**. Her name became a byword for avarice, lust and cruelty, to which only Claudius was blind. In the emperor's absence she publicly married one of her favorites, the consul-designate Silius, and the emperor had her executed.

Messerschmitt, Willy (Wilhelm) 1898–1978 •*German aviation designer and engineer*• Born in Frankfurt am Main, he studied at the Munich Institute of Technology, and in 1923 established the Messerschmitt aircraft manufacturing plant. His ME-109 set a world speed record in 1939, and during World War II he supplied the Luftwaffe with its foremost types of combat aircraft. In 1944 he produced the ME-262 fighter, the first jet plane flown in combat. From 1955 he continued his activities with the revived Lufthansa and later also entered the car industry.

Messiaen, Olivier Eugène Prosper Charles 1908–92 •*French composer and organist*• Born in Avignon, he studied under Marcel Dupré (1886–1971) and **Paul Dukas**, and taught at the Schola Cantorum (from 1936). In 1941 he became Professor of Harmony at the Paris Conservatoire. He composed extensively for organ, orchestra, voice and piano, and made frequent use of new instruments. He is best known outside France for the two-and-a-half-hour piano work, *Vingt regards sur l'enfant Jésus* (1944, "20 Looks at the Child Jesus"), and the *Turangalila* Symphony (1946–48), which makes use of Indian themes and rhythms. His interest in birdsong provided the stimulus for several pieces, and other works include an oratorio, *La transfiguration de Notre Seigneur Jésus-Christ* (1965–69), and an opera, *St François d'Assise* (1975–83).

Messier, Charles 1730–1817 •*French astronomer*• Born in Badonville, Lorraine, he began his life as an astronomer in 1751 in Paris. He observed the return of Halley's comet in 1759 and later discovered 13 other comets. He mapped the faint unmoving nebulous objects in the sky which he could discard in comet searching, and drew up a catalog of 103 entries (1781) by which his name is perpetuated in astronomy. Messier's objects, known by the prefix M and their catalog number, comprise nebulae, galaxies and star clusters. The "ferret of comets," as he was nicknamed by **Louis XV**, was elected to the Royal Society (1764) and the Paris Academy of Sciences (1770).

Messner, Reinhold 1944– •*Austrian mountaineer*• Born in the South Tyrol, he became one of the world's foremost solo climbers. He pursued the goal of becoming the first person to climb all the world's 14 peaks over 8,000 meters, and realized his dream in 1986, but not without cost, when his brother died in an avalanche during a shared expedition. In 1978 Messner and his partner Peter Habelar became the first people to climb Everest without bottled oxygen, and Messner later climbed Everest alone by the North Col route without oxygen or support. He also made the first crossing of Antarctica on foot since Sir **Ernest Shackleton**. He has published several books, and since 1999 has been a member of the European Parliament.

Mesurier, John Le *See* **Le Mesurier, John**

Metaxas, Yanni 1870–1941 •*Greek politician*• He was born in Ithaka. He fought in the Thessalian campaign against the Turks in 1897, and helped reorganize the Greek army before the 1912–13

Balkan Wars, when he became Chief of the General Staff. A Royalist rival of the Republican **Eleutherios Venizelos**, he opposed Greek intervention in World War I. In 1923 he founded the Party of Free Opinion. In 1936 he became prime minister, establishing an authoritarian government with a cabinet of specialist and retired service officers. His work of reorganizing Greece economically and militarily bore fruit in the tenacious Greek resistance to the Italian invasion of 1940–41.

Metchnikoff, Elie, *Russian* **Ilya Ilyich Mechnikov** 1845–1916 •*Russian embryologist, immunologist and Nobel Prize winner*• Born in Ivanovka, Ukraine, he graduated from Kharkov University in 1864, and studied invertebrate and fish embryology at several European centers. After periods of teaching and research at St Petersburg and Odessa Universities, he took a research post at the University of Messina, Italy, where he began his immunological studies. Studying how mobile cells in starfish larvae attack foreign bodies, he called these cells phagocytes, and hypothesized that their role in vertebrate blood is to fight invasion by bacteria. He was awarded the 1908 Nobel Prize for physiology or medicine jointly with **Paul Ehrlich**.

Metford, William Ellis 1824–99 •*English engineer and inventor*• He was born in Taunton, Somerset. Having invented an explosive rifle bullet that was outlawed by the St Petersburg Convention of 1869, he turned to the design of a breech-loading rifle (1871). It was adapted by **James Paris Lee** as the Lee-Metford rifle, and adopted by the British War Office in 1888.

Methuen, Sir Algernon Methuen Marshall, *originally* **Algernon Stedman** 1856–1924 •*English publisher*• He was born in London. A teacher of classics and French (1880–95), he began publishing on the side with Methuen & Co in 1889 to market his own textbooks. His first publishing success was **Rudyard Kipling**'s *Barrack-Room Ballads* (1892), and, among others, he published works of **Hilaire Belloc**, **G K Chesterton**, **Joseph Conrad**, **John Masefield**, **Robert Louis Stevenson** and **Oscar Wilde**.

Metternich, Prince Clemens Lothar Wenzel 1773–1859 •*Austrian politician*• Born in Koblenz, Germany, he studied in Strasbourg and Mainz, was attached to the Austrian embassy in The Hague, and at age 28 was Austrian minister in Dresden, two years later in Berlin, and in 1805 (after Austerlitz) in Paris. In 1807 he concluded the Treaty of Fontainebleau. In 1809 he was appointed Austrian foreign minister, and as such negotiated the marriage between **Napoleon I** and **Marie Louise**. In 1812–13 he maintained a temporizing policy at first, but at last declared war against France. The Grand Alliance was signed at Teplitz, and he was made a Prince of the Empire. He took a prominent part at the Congress of Vienna, rearranging a German confederation and guarding Austria's interests in Italy. As the main supporter of autocracy and police despotism at home and abroad, he was largely responsible for the tension that led to the upheaval of 1848, and when the French Revolution of that year was felt in Vienna, he fled to England, later retiring to his castle on the Rhine.

“ ”

When Paris sneezes, Europe catches cold.

1830 Letter, January 26.

Mettrie, Julien Offray de la *See* **La Mettrie, Julien Offroy de**

Meung, Jean de, *also called* **Jean Clopinel** c. 1250–1305 •*French poet and satirist*• He flourished in Paris under **Philip IV (the Fair)**. He translated many books into French, and left a witty *Testament*. His major work is his lengthy continuation (18,000 lines) of the *Roman de la Rose* by **Guillaume de Lorris**.

Meyer, Adolf 1866–1950 •*US psychiatrist*• He was born in Niederweingen, Switzerland. After medical and psychiatric training in Zurich and elsewhere, he emigrated to the US in 1892, where he held positions in a number of universities and psychiatric hospitals, especially Johns Hopkins Medical School (1910–41). He was an eclectic at a time when psychoanalytic concepts dominated US psychiatry. Through his notion of psychobiology he sought to integrate psychiatry and medicine, seeing mental disorder as the consequence of unsuccessful adjustment patterns.

Meyer, Julius Lothar von 1830–95 •*German chemist*• Born in Varel, Oldenburg, he earned his medical degree in Zurich and subsequently studied and taught at several German universities. He studied the physiology of respiration and by 1857 had recognized that oxygen combines chemically with hemoglobin in the blood. Independently of **Dmitri Mendeleev**, he examined the relationship between the chemical reactivities of the elements and their atomic weights. In 1864 he showed that atomic volume is a function of atomic weight.

Meyer, Viktor 1848–97 •*German chemist*• Born in Berlin, he studied under **Robert Bunsen** and was professor successively in Zurich, Göttingen and Heidelberg. He discovered a method for determining vapor densities, and the apparatus he designed became standard laboratory equipment. He developed a method of synthesizing aromatic acids and investigated the nitroparaffins and their derivatives. He also discovered several new types of organic nitrogen compounds. He discovered oximes, studied their isomerism and introduced the term "stereochemistry" for the study of molecular shapes.

Meyerbeer, Giacomo, *originally* **Jakob Liebmann Meyer Beer** 1791–1864 •*German composer of operas*• Born in Berlin, he played **Mozart**'s D-minor Piano Concerto in public at age seven. After three years' study in Italy, he produced operas in the new (**Rossini**'s) style, which were immediately well received. After a careful study of French opera, he wrote the popular *Robert le Diable* (1831, libretto by **Eugène Scribe**), and followed it in 1836 with the even more successful *Huguenots*. He was severely condemned by **Schumann** and **Richard Wagner** on the grounds that he made everything subsidiary to theatrical effect.

Meyerhof, Otto Fritz 1884–1951 •*US biochemist and Nobel Prize winner*• Born in Hanover, Germany, and trained in medicine at the University of Heidelberg, he was appointed to a position in clinical psychiatry at the Heidelberg Clinic in 1910, where **Otto Warburg**'s work on chemical reactions in living cells inspired Meyerhof to change direction and study biochemical mechanisms. He then held posts in the physiology departments at the University of Kiel, the Kaiser Wilhelm Institute for Biology in Berlin and, from 1929, at the Kaiser Wilhelm Institute for Medical Research in Heidelberg. His biochemical research was primarily on muscle contraction and its related metabolic pathways, and he shared the 1922 Nobel Prize for physiology or medicine with **A V Hill** for this work. In 1938 he left Nazi Germany, and in 1940 he reached the US, where he was professor at the University of Pennsylvania.

Meyerhold, Vsevolod Yemilevich 1874–c. 1940 •*Russian actor and director*• Born in Penza, he joined the Moscow Art Theater when it opened in 1898. From 1902 to 1905 he toured Russia with his own company, the Society of New Drama, both acting and directing, and was appointed by **Stanislavsky** as the director of the new Studio on Povarskaya Street (1905). Later he founded his own studio in Moscow. He became an ardent Bolshevik, and directed the first Soviet play, **Vladimir Mayakovsky**'s *Mystery-Bouffe* (1918). In 1920 he was provided with the former Sohn Theater in Moscow in which to work and directed several new and revolutionary works, including two more Mayakovsky plays, *The Bedbug* (1929) and *The Bath House* (1930). During the 1930s, when socialist realism was decreed the official art form, he fell from favor. His theater was closed in 1938, and he was arrested and disappeared in prison.

Meynell, Alice Christiana Gertrude, *née* **Thompson** 1847–1922 •*English essayist and poet*• Born in Barnes, London, she spent her childhood on the Continent, and converted to Catholicism. Her volumes of essays include *The Rhythm of Life* (1893), *The Colour of Life* (1896) and *Hearts of Controversy* (1917). She published several collections of her own poems, starting in 1875 with *Preludes*, and anthologies of **Coventry Patmore**, of lyric poetry, and of poems for children.

Miandad, Javed 1957– •*Pakistani cricket player*• Born in Karachi, he is considered the finest batsman ever produced by Pakistan. As well as playing for Karachi, Sindh, Sussex and Glamorgan, he excelled as a Test player, making his debut for Pakistan in 1975 and going on to amass 8,832 runs in Tests and 7,381 runs in one-day internationals (often as captain). He took part in six Cricket World Cups, winning the title with Pakistan in 1992 and becoming the first man to score 1,000 runs in World Cup matches. He later became coach of the Pakistan team.

Micah 735–665 BC •*Old Testament minor prophet*• He was born in Moresheth Gath, in southwest Judah. He prophesied during the reigns of Jotham, Ahaz and Hezekiah, being a younger contemporary of **Isaiah**, **Hosea** and **Amos**.

Michael 1921– •*King of Romania*• The son of the future **Carol II**, he was born in Sinaira, and first succeeded to the throne (1927) on the death of his grandfather Ferdinand I, his father having renounced his own claims (1925). In 1930 he was supplanted by Carol, but was again made king (1940) when the Germans gained control of Romania. In 1944 he played a considerable part in the overthrow of the dictatorship of **Ion Antonescu**. He announced the acceptance of the Allied peace terms, and declared war on Germany. His attempts after the war to establish a broader system of government were foiled by the progressive Communization of Romania. In 1947 he was forced to abdicate and lived in exile, finally in Switzerland. Although deported from Romania when he first attempted to return in 1990, he regained his Romanian citizenship in 1997 and has since made several visits and reclaimed some property there.

Michael VIII Palaeologus c. 1224–1282 •*Byzantine emperor*• He was born into the Greek nobility and became a general in the empire of Nicaea. In 1258 he became regent and coruler with the eight-year-old emperor John IV Lascaris, whom he later had blinded and imprisoned. Resourceful and a master of intrigue, he conquered Constantinople (Istanbul) in 1261, extinguishing the empire of **Baldwin II**, and was crowned sole emperor, thus founding the Palaeologan dynasty. The papacy and **Charles of Anjou**, who aimed to reestablish the Latin Empire, opposed Michael, and Byzantium survived only by his diplomatic skill. Although his concentration on Europe tended to ignore the Ottoman threat to the east, he helped prolong Byzantine independence for another two centuries.

Michael Romanov 1596–1645 •*Czar of Russia*• The grandnephew of **Ivan IV** (the Terrible), he was the founder of the Romanov dynasty, which ruled Russia until the Revolution of 1917. He was elected czar (1613–45) by the boyars after a successful revolt against the Poles, when Russia was threatened with invasion from Sweden, and he brought an end to the Time of Troubles (1605–13). He concluded peace with Sweden (1617) and Poland (1618). He left domestic affairs to his father, the patriarch Filaret. Michael was succeeded by his son Alexis.

Michael, George, *originally* **Georgios Kyriacos Panayiotou** 1963– •*English pop singer and songwriter*• Born in Finchley, London, he became a teen idol alongside Andrew Ridgeley as the pop duo Wham! Such soul-influenced singles as "Young Guns (Go for It)" (1982), "Club Tropicana" (1983) and "Wake Me Up Before You Go-Go" (1984) did well on both sides of the Atlantic. In 1984 Michael enjoyed his first solo success with "Careless Whisper" and also sang on a Band Aid charity single. After Wham! split up in 1986, Michael continued as a solo artist with such albums as *Faith* (1987) and *Songs from the Last Century* (2000), from which came further chart-topping singles.

Michel, Claude, *pseudonym* **Clodion** 1738–1814 •*French sculptor*• He was born at Nancy. Perhaps the greatest sculptor of the Napoleonic era, he is famous for his small terracotta figures of classical subjects such as fauns, satyrs and nymphs. A fine example of his work is a vase in the Wallace Collection, London, of white marble carved with relief.

Michel, Hartmut 1948– •*German biochemist and Nobel Prize winner*• Born in Ludwigsburg, Germany, he studied at the Universities of Tübingen, Würzburg and Munich, and at the **Max Planck** Institute of Biochemistry, and was appointed director of the Max Planck Institute of Biophysics in Frankfurt in 1987. In 1981 he produced a crystal of the membrane-bound, photosynthetic reaction center of the bacterium *Rhodopseudomonas viridis*, and collaborated with **Robert Huber** and **Johann Deisenhofer** to determine its structure by X-ray crystallography. By 1985 they were able to report the complete structure, which confirmed and elaborated predictions about how the energy transfer process in photosynthesis operates. For this discovery Michel shared the 1988 Nobel Prize for chemistry with Huber and Deisenhofer.

Michelangeli, Arturo Benedetti 1920–95 •*Italian pianist*• Born in Brescia, he studied there and in Milan, and won the Geneva International Music Competition in 1939. After war service in the Italian air force, he acquired a considerable reputation as a virtuoso, which was enhanced by the rarity of his public performances. He became a noted teacher and founded and directed the International Pianists Academy in Brescia (1964–69).

Michelangelo, *in full* **Michelangelo di Lodovico Buonarroti** 1475–1564 •*Italian sculptor, painter and poet*• Born in Caprese in Tuscany, he was brought up in Florence. In 1488, against his father's wishes, he was apprenticed for three years to **Domenico Ghirlandaio**. He was recommended by Ghirlandaio to **Lorenzo de' Medici**, and entered the school for which Lorenzo had gathered together a priceless collection of antiques (1490–92). To this period belong two interesting reliefs, the *Battle of the Centaurs* and the *Madonna of the Steps*. After Lorenzo's death in 1492, **Piero de' Medici**, his son and successor, is said to have treated the artist with scant courtesy; Michelangelo fled to Bologna for three years, returning to Florence in 1495. During this time he made a marble *Cupid*, which was bought by Cardinal San Giorgio who recognized the talent of the sculptor and summoned him to Rome in 1496. The influence of Rome and the antique is easily discernible in the *Bacchus*, now in the National Museum in Florence. The *Pietà* (1497), now in St Peter's, shows a realism wholly at variance with the antique ideal. For four years the sculptor remained in Rome and then, returning to Florence, fashioned his *David* out of a colossal block of marble. During the same period he painted the *Holy Family of the Tribune* and the *Madonna* now in the National Gallery in London. In 1503 the new pope, **Julius II**, summoned Michelangelo back to Rome. The pope commissioned the sculptor to design his tomb, and for 40 years Michelangelo clung to the hope that he would yet complete the great monument; but other demands were continually made upon him. Instead of being allowed to devote himself to the monument, he was instructed, despite Michelangelo's urgings to consider **Raphael**, to decorate the ceiling of the Sistine Chapel with paintings (1508–12). In the event, Michelangelo achieved a masterpiece of decorative design, depicting the Creation, the Fall and the Flood. No sooner had he finished his work in the Sistine Chapel than he returned with eagerness to the tomb. But in 1513 Pope Julius II died, and the cardinals, his executors, demanded a more modest design. Then Pope **Leo X**, of the Medici family, commissioned Michelangelo to rebuild the façade of the church of San Lorenzo in Florence and enrich it with sculptured figures. He reluctantly complied, and set out for Carrara to quarry marble; from 1514 to 1522 his artistic record is a blank, as the elaborate project was ultimately given up, although Michelangelo remained in Florence. In 1528–29 he devoted his energies to improving the fortifications of Florence, now under siege. After the surrender he completed the monuments to Giuliano and Lorenzo de' Medici, which are considered to be among the greatest of his works. In 1537 he began to paint *The Last Judgment*. In 1547 he was appointed architect of St Peter's, and devoted himself to the work with loyalty until his death. Michelangelo is by far the most brilliant representative of the Italian Renaissance. He was not only supreme in the arts of sculpture and painting, in which grandeur and sublimity rather than beauty was his aim, but was versed in all the learning of his age, and wrote copious poetry.

“ ”

I've finished that chapel I was painting. The Pope is quite satisfied.

Letter written to his father after 18 months of painting the vault of the Sistine Chapel, quoted in Robert J Clements (ed) ***Michelangelo: A Self-Portrait*** *(1968).*

Michelet, Jules 1798–1874 •*French historian*• Born in Paris, he lectured on history at the École Normale, assisted François Guizot at the Sorbonne, and was appointed Professor of History at the Collège de France (1838–51). The greatest of his many historical works are his monumental *Histoire de France* (24 vols, 1833–67) and his *Histoire de la Révolution* (7 vols, 1847–53). By refusing to swear allegiance to **Louis Napoleon**, he lost his appointments.

Michelin, André 1853–1931 •*French tire manufacturer*• Born in Paris, he established the Michelin tire company in 1888 with his younger brother Edouard (1859–1940). They were the first to use demountable pneumatic tires on motor cars, and became known for their road maps and Michelin guides. The guides were introduced by André Michelin to promote tourism by car, and the first Red Guide, showing restaurant ratings, was published in 1900.

Michell, John 1724–93 •*English geologist and astronomer*• Born in Nottinghamshire, he was a Fellow of Queen's College, Cambridge, and Professor of Geology (1762–64), and became rector of Thornhill, Yorkshire (1767). He published an important work on artificial magnets (1750), but is best known as the founder of seismology. He invented a torsion balance, a device to measure the strength of small forces, and with it intended to measure the value of the gravitational constant. However, he died before he had the opportunity—it was **Henry Cavendish** who finally carried this out. Michell also made important contributions to astronomy.

Michelozzi, Michelozzo di Bartolommeo 1396–1472 •*Italian architect and sculptor*• Born in Florence, he was associated with **Lorenzo Ghiberti** on his famous bronze doors for the baptistery there, and collaborated with **Donatello** in several major sculpture groups. He was court architect to **Cosimo de' Medici**, with whom he was in exile in Venice, where he designed a number of buildings. One of his finest works is the Ricardi Palace in Florence.

Michelson, Albert Abraham 1852–1931 •*US physicist and Nobel Prize winner*• Born in Strzelno, Poland, he emigrated with his family to the US and graduated from the US Naval Academy in 1873. After various teaching positions, he became Professor of Physics at the University of Chicago in 1892. He is chiefly remembered for the Michelson-**Morley** experiment to determine ether drift, the negative result of which set **Albert Einstein** on the road to the theory of relativity. The interferometer which he invented for this experiment was developed subsequently for spectroscopic studies, and he also developed a stellar interferometer for measuring the sizes and separations of celestial bodies. In 1898 he invented the echelon grating, an ultra-high-resolution device for the study and measurement of hyperfine spectra. Michelson became the first US scientist to win a Nobel Prize when he was awarded the Nobel Prize for physics in 1907.

Michener, James A(lbert) 1907–97 •*US author*• He was born in New York City and educated at Swarthmore College, Pennsylvania. His short-story collection *Tales of the South Pacific* (1947) won the Pulitzer Prize and was adapted to make the Rodgers and Hammerstein musical *South Pacific* (1948). His later novels often have a panoramic historical or geographical perspective and include *Hawaii* (1959), *Centennial* (1974), *Chesapeake* (1980), *Texas* (1985), *Caribbean* (1989) and *Recessional* (1994).

Michie, Donald 1923– •*British specialist in artificial intelligence*• He was born in Rangoon, Burma (Myanmar), and educated at Balliol College, Oxford. His work during World War II on the Colossus code-breaking project acquainted him with computer pioneers such as **Alan Turing**. After a career in experimental genetics, he developed the study of machine intelligence at the University of Edinburgh as director of experimental programming (1963–66) and Professor of Machine Intelligence (1967–84, now emeritus). He is editor in chief of the *Machine Intelligence* series, and was chief scientist at the Turing Institute from 1986 to 1992, which he founded in Glasgow in 1984. In his publications he has argued that computer systems are able to generate new knowledge. His research contributions have primarily been in the field of machine learning.

Mickiewicz, Adam Bernard 1798–1855 •*Polish poet*• Born in Lithuania, he was educated in Vilnius and published his first poems in 1822. He was arrested and exiled for his revolutionary activities, and after the failure of the Polish revolt (1830–31), he fled to the West, where he wrote his epic *Pan Tadeusz* (1834, Eng trans *Thaddeus*, 1886), about Lithuania. Generally he tried to keep the Polish spirit alive through his writings, and in 1852 **Louis Napoleon** appointed him librarian in the Paris Arsenal. He is considered the national poet of Poland.

Middleton, Thomas c. 1580–1627 •*English dramatist*• Born in Newington Butts, Surrey, the son of a bricklayer, he is first mentioned in **Philip Henslowe**'s *Diary* in 1602. *Father Hubbard's Tale* and *The Black Book*, exposing London rogues, were published in 1604, to which year belongs the first part of *The Honest Whore* (mainly written by **Thomas Dekker**, partly by Middleton). Other early works include *A Mad World, My Masters* (1608), from which **Aphra Behn** pilfered freely in *The City Heiress*. *The Roaring Girl* (1611, written with Dekker) idealizes the character of a noted cutpurse and virago. Middleton was repeatedly employed to write the Lord Mayor's pageant. *A Chaste Maid in Cheapside* was probably produced in 1613, as was *No Wit, No Help Like a Woman's*. *A Fair Quarrel* (1617) and *The World Lost at Tennis* (1620) were written in conjunction with **William Rowley**. *A Game of Chess*, a curious and skillful play, was acted in 1624. Three posthumously published plays, *The Changeling*, *The Spanish Gypsy* and *Women Beware Women*, include some of his best writing. *The Widow*, published in 1652, was mainly by Middleton, and he was also concerned in the authorship of some of the plays included in the works of **Francis Beaumont** and **John Fletcher**.

Midler, Bette 1945– •*US comedienne, actress and singer*• Born in Honolulu, Hawaii, she studied drama at the University of Hawaii, then was hired as an extra in the film *Hawaii* (1966). Moving to New York, she made her stage debut in *Miss Nefertiti Regrets* (1966). She then developed a popular but bawdy nightclub act. Her album *The Divine Miss M* (1974) won her a Grammy award as Best New Artist, and in the same year she received a Tony award for her record-breaking Broadway show. Midler's performance in the film *The Rose* (1979) earned her an Academy Award nomination, and she has continued to enjoy commercial success in a series of film farces including *Down and Out in Beverly Hills* (1986), *Ruthless People* (1986) and *The First Wives Club* (1996). As a singer, her hit singles include "The Rose" and "Wind Beneath My Wings."

Mies van der Rohe, Ludwig 1886–1969 •*US architect*• Born in Aachen, Germany, he studied design under **Peter Behrens** and became a pioneer of glass skyscrapers. In prewar Berlin he designed high-rise flats and also tubular-steel furniture, particularly the "Barcelona chair." He was director of the Bauhaus in Dessau (1930–33), and emigrated to the US in 1937, where he became Professor of Architecture at the Armour (now Illinois) Institute of Technology in Chicago. He designed two glass apartment towers on Lake Shore Drive in Chicago and collaborated with **Philip Johnson** on the Seagram Building in New York (1956–58). His other works include the Public Library in Washington DC (1967), and two art galleries in Berlin (1968). He was a major figure in 20th-century architecture and a founder of the modern style.

Miguel, *properly* **Miguel Maria Evaristo de Bragança** 1802–66 •*King of Portugal*• Born in Lisbon, the third son of King John VI, he plotted (1824) to overthrow the constitutional government established by his father, but was banished with his mother, his chief abettor. His elder brother, **Pedro I**, resigned the throne to his daughter Maria, making him regent; but in 1828 he summoned a Cortes (or parliament), which proclaimed him king. In 1832 Oporto and Lisbon were captured, and **Charles Napier** destroyed his fleet off Cape St Vincent (1833). Maria was restored in 1834, and he withdrew to Italy.

Mihailovich, Draza 1893–1946 •*Serbian soldier*• After distinguished service in World War I, he rose to the rank of colonel in the Yugoslav army, and following the German occupation in 1941, headed the Chetnik mountain guerrilla movement. In exile from 1943, he was appointed minister of war, but when **Tito**'s Communist Partisans' resistance developed, Mihailovich allied himself with the Germans and then with the Italians in order to fight the communists. After the war he was captured and executed by the Tito government.

Mikoyan, Anastas Ivanovich 1895–1978 •*Soviet politician*• Born in Sanain, Armenia, of poor parents, the brother of **Artem Mikoyan**, he studied theology and became a fanatical revolutionary. Taken prisoner in the fighting at Baku, he escaped and made his way to Moscow, where he met **Lenin** and **Stalin**. A member of the Central Committee in 1922, he supported Stalin against **Trotsky**, and in 1926 became Minister of Trade, in which capacity he did much to improve Soviet standards of living. Mikoyan's genius for survival enabled him to become a first vice chairman of the Council of Ministers (1955–64), and president of the Presidium of the Supreme Soviet from 1964.

Mikoyan, Artem Ivanovich 1905–70 •*Soviet aircraft designer*• Born in Sanain, Armenia, he served in the Red Army before graduating from the NE Zhukovsky Air Force Academy (1936). He was best known for the fighter aircraft produced by the design bureau he headed with **Mikhail Gurevich**, the MiG (Mikoyan and Gurevich) series. The most notable of this series include: the MiG-1 (1940) and the MiG-3 (1941), both used in World War II, the MiG-9 (1946), one of the Soviet Union's first jet fighters, the MiG-15 and the MiG-17, which were deployed in the Korean War, the MiG-21 (1967), on which design the world's first supersonic passenger aircraft, the Tu-144, was based, and the MiG-25 (1971). He was the brother of **Anastas Mikoyan**.

Milburn, Alan 1958– •*English politician*• He was born in Birmingham and educated at the University of Lancaster, becoming Labour Member of Parliament for Darlington in 1992. In the New Labour government of 1997 he was appointed Minister of State for Health and subsequently Chief Secretary to the Treasury, and in 1999 became Secretary of State for Health.

Miles, Bernard James Miles, Baron 1907–91 •*English actor, stage director and founder of the Mermaid Theatre*• Born in Uxbridge, Middlesex, he made his London debut as an actor in 1930, and worked in several repertory theaters as a designer, scene painter, carpenter, property manager and character actor. He later went onto the music-hall stage. Wanting to rid the theater of snobbery and class distinctions, he founded the Mermaid Theatre (1951) as a small private theater on the grounds of his home in St John's Wood, London. In 1953 the Mermaid was rebuilt in the City of London, and in 1959 a permanent, professional Mermaid Theatre, financed by public subscription, was built at Puddle Dock, Blackfriars; it was seen as the model of many theaters during the next two decades.

Milhaud, Darius 1892–1974 •*French composer*• Born in Aix-en-Provence, he studied under **Vincent d'Indy**. He frequently collaborated with the playwright Paul Claudel (1868–1955), as on the opera *Christopher Columbus* (1928). For a time he was a member of the group of young French composers known as Les Six. From 1940 to 1947 he taught in the US. He was one of the most prolific of modern composers; his work includes several operas, much incidental music for plays, ballets (including the jazz ballet *La création du monde*, 1923, "The Creation of the World"), symphonies and orchestral, choral and chamber works.

Milk, Harvey 1931–78 •*US politician and gay rights activist*• Born in Woodmere, New York, he settled in California and became an outspoken advocate of gay rights in an era when homosexuality was rarely acknowledged in public. After being elected to the San Francisco Board of Supervisors in 1977, he was assassinated (along with Mayor George Moscone) by a former city supervisor.

Mill, James 1773–1836 •*Scottish philosopher, historian and economist*• Born in Northwater Bridge, Logiepert, Tayside, he studied for the ministry in Edinburgh and was ordained in 1798. He then moved to London (1802) and supported himself through journalism and editorial work. He became a disciple and friend of **Jeremy Bentham**, an enthusiastic proponent of utilitarianism, and a prominent member of the circle of "Philosophical Radicals" which included **David Ricardo**, **John Austin** and in due course his eldest son, **John Stuart Mill**. The group was active in social and educational causes, and James Mill took a leading part in the founding of University College London (1825). His first major publication was the *History of British India* (1817–18), on which he had worked for 11 years and which led to a permanent position with the East India Company. Further important books include *Elements of Political Economy* (1821), which derived from Ricardo and was an important influence on **Karl Marx**, and *Analysis of the Phenomenon of the Human Mind* (1829), his main philosophical work.

Mill, John Stuart 1806–73 •*English philosopher and social reformer*• He was born in London, the son of the Scottish philosopher **James Mill**, who taught him Greek at the age of three, Latin and arithmetic at eight, logic at 12, and political economy at 13. After a visit to France in 1820, he broadened his studies into history, law and philosophy, and in 1823 began a career under his father at the India Office. This forced education gave him an advantage, as he put it, of a quarter of a century over his contemporaries, and he began enthusiastically to fulfill the ambitions his father had for him to become the leader and prophet of the Benthamite utilitarian movement. He began publishing in the newspaper *The Traveller* in 1822; he helped form the Utilitarian Society, which met for reading and discussion in **Jeremy Bentham**'s house (1823–26), and with Bentham he helped found University College London in 1825; he was a major contributor to the *Westminster Review* and a regular performer in the London Debating Society; and he corresponded with **Thomas Carlyle** and met **Frederick Maurice**. He espoused **Malthus**ian doctrines, and was arrested in 1824 for distributing birth control literature to the poor in London. In 1826 he suffered a mental crisis that he describes in his autobiography. For a while he was in "a dull state of nerves," but the depression passed and he recovered, with his sympathies broadened and his intellectual position importantly modified, as his reviews of **Tennyson** (1835), **Carlyle** (1837), **Bentham** (1838) and **Coleridge** (1840) indicate. He effectively humanized utilitarianism by his recognition of the differences in the quality as well as the quantity of pleasures, thereby restoring the importance of cultural and idealistic values. In 1830 he had met Harriet Taylor, the bluestocking wife of a wealthy London merchant, and after a long, intense but apparently chaste romance, he married her in 1851, two years after her husband's death. She took an active interest in his writing and contributed significantly to his essay *On Liberty* (1859), the most popular of all his works, which eloquently defines and defends the freedoms of the individual against social and political control. Her views on marriage and the status of women helped inspire *The Subjection of Women* (1869), which provoked great antagonism. Remaining politically active in later life, he was elected to Parliament in 1865. He campaigned for women's suffrage and generally supported the Advanced Liberals. In 1872 he became godfather, "in a secular sense," to Lord Amberley's second son, **Bertrand Russell**. His last years were spent in France, and he died in Avignon. Mill's major work, *A System of Logic* (1843), ran through many editions, establishing his philosophical reputation and greatly influencing **John Venn**, John Neville Keynes, **Gottlob Frege** and **Bertrand Russell**, particularly in its treatment of induction. His other works include *Principles of Political Economy* (1848), *Considerations on Representative Government* (1861), *Utilitarianism* (1863), *Examination of Sir William Hamilton's Philosophy* (1865), *Auguste Comte and Positivism* (1873) and *Three Essays on Religion* (1874). His *Autobiography* was published in 1873.

“ ”

The worth of the State, in the long run, is the worth of the individuals composing it.

1861 ***Considerations on Representative Government***.

Millais, Sir John Everett 1829–96 •*English painter*• Born in Southampton, he became the youngest-ever student at the Royal Academy in 1840, and in 1846 exhibited his *Pizarro Seizing the Inca of Peru*. Along with **Dante Gabriel Rossetti** and **Holman Hunt**, he was a founding member of the Pre-Raphaelite Brotherhood, and was markedly influenced by them and by **John Ruskin**. His first Pre-Raphaelite picture, the banquet scene from *Isabella* by **Keats**, figured in the Academy in 1849, where it was followed in 1850 by *Christ in the House of His Parents*, which met the full force of the anti-Pre-Raphaelite reaction. The exquisite *Gambler's Wife* (1869) and *The Boyhood of Raleigh* (1870) mark the transition of his art into its final phase, displaying brilliant and effective coloring, effortless power of brushwork and delicacy of flesh painting. A late painting, *Bubbles* (1886), achieved huge popularity. Millais executed a few etchings, and his illustrations in *Good Words*, *Once a Week*, *The Cornhill*, and elsewhere (1857–64) place him in the first rank of woodcut designers.

Millan, Bruce 1927– •*Scottish Labour politician*• Born in Dundee and educated at the Harris Academy, he was certified as a chartered accountant. Member of Parliament from 1959, he held junior ministerial appointments (1964–70, 1974–76), then was appointed Secretary of State for Scotland (1976–79), in which position he proved a competent administrator in a period dominated by devolution legislation, sharply rising unemployment, and a weakening Scottish economy. He left Parliament to become European Community Commissioner (1989–95), with responsibility for regional development.

Milland, Ray, *originally* **Reginald Truscott-Jones** 1905–86 •*Welsh actor*• Born in Neath, Glamorganshire, he was a member of the Household Cavalry before turning to acting. Venturing to Hollywood, he built a substantial career as a leading man in light comedies and adventure yarns like *Easy Living* (1937), *Beau Geste* (1939) and *Reap the Wild Wind* (1942). Cast against type as the chronic alcoholic in *The Lost Weekend* (1945), he won a Best Actor Academy Award and explored the darker side of his character further in *Alias Nick Beal* (1949) and *Dial M for Murder* (1954). He also proved an able director of offbeat subjects like *Panic in Year Zero* (1962). He made a further career as cantankerous older figures after playing the role of the father in *Love Story* (1970).

Millay, Edna St Vincent 1892–1950 •*US poet*• Born in Rockland, Maine, she published her first volume of poetry, *Renaissance and Other Poems*, on graduating from Vassar College in 1917. It was followed by *A Few Figs from Thistles* (1920), which celebrated Bohemian life, and *The Harp Weaver and Other Poems*, for which she was awarded the 1923 Pulitzer Prize. The popularity she enjoyed during her own time waned after her death, and she was dismissed as petulant and artificial, but the admiration of writers like **Maya Angelou** has caused her to be reevaluated.

Mille, Agnes de *See* **De Mille, Agnes**

Mille, Cecil B de *See* **De Mille, Cecil B(lount)**

Miller, Arthur 1915– •*US playwright*• Born in New York City, he graduated from the University of Michigan in 1938. His first successful play, *All My Sons* (1947), focused on the family of an arms manufacturer and reflected the preoccupation with moral issues that was to characterize his work. His tragedy, *Death of a Salesman* (1949), won the Pulitzer Prize and brought him international recognition. *The Crucible* (1953) is probably, to date, his most lasting work, since its theme, the persecution of the Salem witches equated with contemporary political persecution, stands out of time. Other works include *A View from the Bridge* (1955), the film script of *The Misfits* (1960), *After the Fall* (1963), *The Creation of the World and Other Business* (1972), *Playing for Time* (1981), *The Ride Down Mount Morgan* (1991), *The Last Yankee* (1992) and *Mr Peter's Connections* (1998). His marriage to **Marilyn Monroe**, from whom he was divorced in 1961, and his brush with the authorities over early communist sympathies brought him considerable publicity.

“ ”

A small man can be just as exhausted as a great man.

1949 Linda. ***Death of a Salesman**, act I.*

Miller, Cheryl 1964– •*US basketball player*• Born in Riverside, California, she is noted as the first woman to dunk a basketball in regulation play. She set California Interscholastic Federation records for the most career points and the most points scored in one season. At the University of Southern California, she won nearly every major basketball award, including the Naismith Trophy (1984, 1985, 1986), the Broderick award as college player of the year (1984, 1985), and the Women's Basketball Coaches' Association Player of the Year (1985, 1986). Her number was retired by the university in 1986, marking the first time a basketball player had been so honored.

Miller, (Alton) Glenn 1904–44 •*US trombonist and bandleader*• He was born in Clarinda, Iowa, and went to the University of Colorado, but before completing his studies he joined the Ben Pollack Band (1924), moving to New York in 1928 and working as a freelance musician and arranger. From 1937 he led a succession of popular dance orchestras and joined the US Army Air Force in 1942, forming another orchestra—the Glenn Miller Army Air Force Band—to entertain the troops. While they were stationed in Europe, Miller was a passenger in a small aircraft lost without a trace over the English Channel.

Miller, Henry Valentine 1891–1980 •*US writer*• He was born in New York, to German-American parents, and brought up in Brooklyn. With money from his father intended to finance him through Cornell University, he traveled in the Southwest and Alaska. He then went to work in his father's tailor shop, left after trying to unionize the workforce, and held several jobs before moving to France, during which time he published *Tropic of Cancer* (1934) and *Tropic of Capricorn* (1938), as well as *Black Spring* (1936). He returned to the US in 1940 but traveled extensively both at home and abroad before settling in Big Sur, California. Much of his fiction is autobiographical and explicitly sexual, and he had to overcome many impecunious years and rebuffs from state censors. (US editions of the *Tropics* were not published until 1961 and 1962, respectively.) In his time, however, he became one of the most read US authors. Important books are *The Colossus of Maroussi* (1941), a dithyrambic travel book, *The Air-Conditioned Nightmare* (1945), a bleak essay on the contemporary US, and *The Rosy Crucifixion* trilogy of novels: *Sexus* (1949), *Plexus* (1953) and *Nexus* (1960).

Miller, Jonathan Wolfe 1934– •*English theater director and author*• Born in London, he qualified as a doctor at Cambridge, and coauthored and performed in the revue *Beyond the Fringe* at the 1960 Edinburgh Festival. He made his directorial debut with *Under Plain Cover* (1962), a play by **John Osborne**, at the Royal Court Theatre, and was editor and host of the BBC Television arts program *Monitor* (1964–65). He has been responsible for many memorable productions, and from 1974 has also specialized in opera productions for the English National Opera and other major companies. He has written and hosted two BBC television series related to the world of medicine, *The Body in Question* (1977) and *States of Mind* (1982). In 1985 he became Research Fellow in Neuropsychology at Sussex University. One of the most original of directors, he was artistic director of the Old Vic from 1988 to 1990 and in his first season staged **Racine**'s *Andromache* and an "anti-colonialist" version of *The Tempest* with **Max von Sydow** playing Prospero, and produced *King Lear* the following year. Later projects include the television series *Opera Works* (1997) and a production of *As You Like It* in Dublin in 2000.

Miller, Max, *originally* **Thomas Henry Sargent** 1895–1963 •*English music hall comedian*• Born in Brighton, he worked with the original Billy Smart's Circus and army concert parties during World War I. He subsequently pursued a solo career as a standup comedian, and by 1926 he was top of the bill at the Holborn Empire, a position he maintained for three decades. Traditionally attired in white trilby, two-tone shoes, kipper tie and rainbow-colored plus-four suit, he turned innuendo into an art form, earning the nickname the "Cheeky Chappie." He made his film debut in *The Good Companions* (1933), appearing in a host of modest British comedies during the next 10 years, but remained at his best as a live performer.

Miller, Stanley Lloyd 1930– •*US chemist*• Born in Oakland, California, he studied at the University of California, San Diego, and taught there from 1960. His best-known work was carried out in Chicago in 1953 and concerned the possible origins of life on Earth. Inspired by the theories of **Aleksandr Oparin** and **J B S Haldane**, with **Harold Clayton Urey**, he passed electric discharges (simulating thunderstorms) through mixtures containing reducing gases (hydrogen, methane, ammonia and water) which Haldane had suggested were likely to have formed the early planetary atmosphere. The formation of the Oparin-Haldane "primeval soup" is now accepted as the most plausible theory for the generation of complex organic molecules on Earth.

Miller, William 1782–1849 •*US religious leader*• Born in Pittsfield, Massachusetts, he became a farmer and, believing that the Second Coming of Christ was imminent, he began preaching in 1831 and founded the religious sect of Second Adventists, or Millerites. He attracted tens of thousands of converts, many of whom fell away when the event did not occur as predicted in 1843 or 1844. His remaining followers continued to meet and organized the Seventh-day Adventist Church in 1863.

Millet, Jean François 1814–75 •*French painter*• Born in Grouchy near Gréville, he worked on the farm with his father, a peasant, but, showing a talent for art, he was placed under a painter at Cherbourg in 1832. In 1837 he went to Paris and worked under **Paul Delaroche**. The 1848 Revolution and poverty drove him from Paris, and he settled with his wife and children at Barbizon, near the forest of Fontainebleau, painting the rustic life of France with sympathetic power. His famous *Sower* was completed in 1850. His *Peasants Grafting* (1855) was followed by *The Gleaners* (1857), *The Angelus* (1859) and other masterpieces. He also produced many charcoal drawings of high quality, and etched a few plates. Following the Great Exhibition of 1867 at Paris, in which nine of his best works were on show, he was awarded the Legion of Honor.

Millett, Kate (Katherine) Murray 1934– •*US feminist, writer and sculptor*• Born in St Paul, she was educated at the University of Minnesota, St Hilda's College, Oxford, and at Columbia University, NewYork. Her PhD thesis became the bestseller and feminist classic, *Sexual Politics* (1970). Early in her career as a sculptor she spent some time in Tokyo (1961–63), and has exhibited internationally. She also founded the Women's Art Colony at Poughkeepsie, New York. Her other publications include *The Prostitution Papers* (1973), the autobiographical *Flying* (1974), *Going to Iran* (1982) and *The Loony Bin Trip* (1990).

Milligan, Spike (Terence Alan) 1918–2002 •*Irish humorist*• Born in Ahmadnagar, India, he was a singer and trumpeter before doing war service. He made his radio debut in *Opportunity Knocks* (1949) and, along with **Peter Sellers**, **Harry Secombe** and **Michael Bentine**, cowrote and performed in the *Goon Show* (1951–60). His sense of the ridiculous and the surreal has had a great influence on British humor. On stage, he appeared in *Treasure Island* (1961, 1973, 1974, 1975) and *The Bed-Sitting Room* (1963, 1967), which he also cowrote. His many television programs include *Paging You* (1947), *Idiot Weekly, Price 2d* (1956), *A Show Called Fred* (1956), *The World of Beachcomber* (1968–69) and the *Q* series (1969–80). He appeared in films such as *The Bed Sitting Room* (1969) and *Digby—The Biggest Dog in the World* (1973). He published a variety of children's books, poetry, autobiography and comic novels including *Puckoon* (1963), *Adolf Hitler, My Part in His Downfall* (1971) and *Peacework* (1991). He was awarded an honorary knighthood in 2000.

Millikan, Robert Andrews 1868–1953 •*US physicist and Nobel Prize winner*• He was born in Illinois, and studied at Oberlin College and Columbia University. After working at the Universities of Berlin and Göttingen, he became **Albert Michelson**'s assistant at the University of Chicago, where he was appointed professor in 1910. In 1921 he moved to the California Institute of Technology (Caltech). At Chicago he refined **J J Thomson**'s oil-drop technique, and was able to show that the charge on each droplet was always a multiple of the same basic unit—the charge on the electron. In studies of the photoelectric effect, he confirmed **Albert Einstein**'s theoretical equations and gave an accurate value for **Planck**'s constant. For all these achievements he was awarded the 1923 Nobel Prize for physics. He also investigated cosmic rays, a term that he coined in 1925.

Mills, Sir John Lewis Ernest Watts 1908– •*English actor*• Born in Felixstowe, Suffolk, he took an early interest in amateur dramatics, which led to his London stage debut as a chorus boy in *The Five O'Clock Revue* (1927). More prestigious theater work followed before his film debut in *The Midshipmaid* (1932). He established himself as one of the hardest-working mainstays of the British film industry, portraying typically English roles in such films as *In Which We Serve* (1942), *Scott of the Antarctic* (1948) and *The Colditz Story* (1954). As a character actor his many credits include *Great Expectations* (1946) and *The History of Mr Polly* (1949). Later films include *Ryan's Daughter* (1970, Academy Award) and *A Woman of Substance* (1986). Active in the theater and on television, he also directed the film *Sky West and Crooked* (1965). He was knighted in 1977. Married to the playwright Mary Hayley Bell since 1941, both his daughters, Juliet (1941–) and Hayley (1946–), are actresses.

Milne, A(lan) A(lexander) 1882–1956 •*English writer*• Born in St John's Wood, London, he was educated at Westminster and Trinity College, Cambridge. He joined the staff of *Punch* as assistant editor, and became well known for his light essays and his comedies. In 1924 he achieved world fame with his book of children's verse, *When We Were Very Young*, written for his own son, Christopher Robin (1920–96). Further children's classics include the enchantingly whimsical *Winnie-the-Pooh* (1926), *Now We Are Six* (1927) and *The House at Pooh Corner* (1928), memorably illustrated by **E H Shepard**. He wrote an autobiography, *It's Too Late Now* (1939).

“ ”

I am a Bear of Very Little Brain, and long words Bother me.

*1926 **Winnie-the-Pooh**, chapter 4.*

Milner (of St James's and Cape Town), Alfred Milner, 1st Viscount 1854–1925 •*English politician and colonial administrator*• Born in Bonn, Germany, and educated at Oxford, he established his reputation in Egypt and was appointed governor of the Cape and high commissioner in South Africa (1897). There he became convinced that the British position was endangered by the South African Republic (Transvaal), and set about the political rationalization of the region through the Boer Wars. He additionally became governor of the Transvaal and Orange River Colony in 1901, but was forced to resign in 1905 as a result of irregularities over Chinese labor he had introduced for the Rand gold mines. He was secretary for war (1916–19) and colonial secretary (1919–21).

Milner, Brenda Atkinson, *née* **Langford** 1918– •*Canadian psychologist*• She studied at Cambridge and at McGill University, Montreal, then worked at the Ministry of Supply in England (1941–44) before emigrating to Canada. She has taught at the University of Montreal (1944–1952), McGill University, and the Neuropsychology Research Unit at the Montreal Neurological Institute (1970–91). Her contributions to neuropsychology have been mainly empirical, the best-known being a series of investigations of a man rendered profoundly amnesic following a radical brain operation for the relief of epilepsy. Other important research by Milner has concerned the asymmetrical activities of the two sides of the brain, particularly in relation to the temporal and the frontal lobes, and has been used in the development of the surgical treatment of temporal-lobe epilepsy.

Milnes, Richard Monckton, 1st Baron Houghton 1809–85 •*English politician and writer*• Born in London, he was a member of the Apostles Club at Cambridge along with **Tennyson** and **Thackeray**. He was Member of Parliament for Pontefract from 1837 until he entered the House of Lords in 1863. A patron of young writers, he befriended **David Gray**, was one of the first to recognize **Algernon Charles Swinburne**'s genius, and secured the poet laureateship for Tennyson (1850). He was the "Mr Vavasour" of **Disraeli**'s novel *Tancred*. He was the first publishing Englishman who gained access to the harems of the East, and championed oppressed peoples and the rights of women, and also carried a bill for establishing reformatories (1846). In addition to his poetry and essays, he published *Life, Letters and Remains of Keats* (1848).

Milo of Croton 6th century BC •*Semilegendary Greek wrestler*• From the Greek colony of Croton in southern Italy, he was the best-known Greek athlete of ancient times, and won the wrestling contest at five successive Olympic Games. A man of huge stature, it is said that he carried a live ox on his shoulders through the stadium at Olympia and then ate it all in a single day. He played a leading part in the military defeat of Sybaris in 511 BC. Tradition has it that in his old age he tried to split a tree which closed upon his hands and held him fast until he was devoured by wolves.

Milošević, Slobodan 1941– •*Serbian politician*• He was born in Pozarevac and educated at the University of Belgrade. He joined the Communist League in 1959, was active in student affairs, and entered government service as an economic adviser to the mayor of Belgrade in 1966. From 1969 to 1983 he held senior posts in the state gas and banking industries. He became president of the Serbian League of Communists in 1984, and president of Serbia in 1988. As a hard-line party leader in the pre-perestroika mold, he won immediate popularity by disenfranchising the Albanian majority in Kosovo province, and survived the republic's 1990 multiparty elections that removed the communist leadership in Croatia and Slovenia. However, his continued efforts to dominate the affairs of the more liberal republics prompted Croatia and Slovenia to declare their independence in 1991. Bitterly opposed to the breakup of Yugoslavia, he agitated for the Yugoslav federal army to be sent into Slovenia and Croatia and later (1992) into Bosnia-Herzegovina. An unrepentant champion of a "Greater Serbia," he did nothing to prevent the fighting in Bosnia led by avowedly "independent" Serbian militias bent on eliminating all non-Serb residents through "ethnic cleansing." In 1995 he played a key role in the release of UN hostages who had been captured by Bosnian Serbs. Later that year he took part in the peace talks in Dayton, Ohio, negotiating on behalf of the Bosnian Serbs. A treaty was signed and US sanctions against the country were lifted. In 1996 Milošević was reelected amid furious accusations of electoral rigging, and from 1998 onward oversaw Serb military incursions into the province of Kosovo, which was demanding autonomy from the Belgrade government. This led to NATO air strikes and the establishment of a NATO-led peacekeeping force in the province, forcing a Serb withdrawal. The loss of Kosovo was a severe political blow to Milošević, and he was defeated at the polls in 2000 by opposition candidate **Vojislav Kostunica**. He was subsequently indicted for crimes against humanity by the International Criminal Tribunal in the Hague and arrested in 2001 to face trial.

Milosz, Czesław 1911–2004 •*US poet, novelist and essayist, and Nobel Prize winner*• He was born in Šeteiniai, Lithuania. His parents settled in what was then Poland, and he later worked for the Resistance in Warsaw during World War II, and eventually became Professor of Slavic Languages and Literature at Berkeley in California (1961–78). He established a reputation with his first two volumes of poetry, *Poem on Time Frozen* (1933) and *Trzy zimy* (1936, "Three Winters"). In 1945 he published *Ocadenie* ("Rescue"), a collection primarily of war poems. He spent nearly 35 years in exile, first in Paris, then in California, and his works were banned in Poland for many years as a result. Later volumes include *Hymn of the Pearl* (1982), *Provinces* (1991), *A Year of the Hunter* (1994) and *Facing the River* (1995), and his *Collected Poems* were published in 1988. He was awarded the Nobel Prize for literature in 1980. He became a US citizen in 1970.

Milstein, Cesar 1927–2002 •*British molecular biologist, immunologist and Nobel Prize winner*• Born in Bahía Blanca, Argentina, he graduated in chemistry from the University of Buenos Aires in 1945, and worked on enzymes at Cambridge (1958–61), where he obtained a PhD in 1960. After work in Argentina (1961–63), he returned to Cambridge, where he joined the staff of the Medical Research Council at the Laboratory of Molecular Biology (1963–95) and was Fellow of Darwin College (1981–95). He conducted important research into antibodies, developing the technique of producing monoclonal antibodies by fusing together different cells to maintain antibody production. This technique became widely used in the commercial development of new drugs and diagnostic tests, and in 1984 it won Milstein the Nobel Prize for physiology or medicine, shared with **Georges Köhler** and **Niels Jerne**.

Miltiades (the Younger) c. 550–489 BC •*Athenian general and politician*• He became a vassal of **Darius I** of Persia and accompanied him on his Scythian expedition (c. 514 BC). He returned to Athens in 493, and was the chief strategist in the Greek victory against the Persians at Marathon (490). The following year he attacked the island of Paros, but failed and was impeached, and died in prison. He was the father of **Cimon**, also an Athenian hero.

Milton, John 1608–74 •*English poet*• Born in Bread Street, Cheapside, he was educated at St Paul's School and Christ's College, Cambridge. In 1635 his father moved to Horton in Buckinghamshire; there Milton wrote *L'Allegro* and *Il Penseroso*, *Comus* and the pastoral elegy *Lycidas* (1637). For the next two years Milton visited Italy (1638–39). The fame of his Latin poems had preceded him, and he was received in the academies with distinction. His Italian tour was interrupted by news of the imminent outbreak of civil war in England. During the years after his return to London in 1639, he devoted himself to the cause of the revolution with political activity and a series of pamphlets defending civil and religious liberties. These included five pamphlets against episcopacy, including *Apology for Smectymnuus* (1642). In 1642 Milton married Mary Powell, the daughter of a Royalist; when she failed to return to him after a visit to her parents in Oxford, Milton published *The Doctrine and Discipline of Divorce* (1643), followed by three supplementary pamphlets against the opponents of his views. *Areopagitica, A Speech for the Liberty of Unlicensed Printing* (1644) was the famous vindication which is still quoted when the press finds itself in danger. Meanwhile, in 1645 his wife returned to him, accompanied by her whole family as refugees after the Battle of Naseby, and two years later Milton inherited sufficient money to give up his schoolteaching. His wife died in 1652, leaving three daughters, and he now married Catherine Woodcock, whose death two years later is the theme of his beautiful sonnet "Methought I saw my late espoused Saint." Although blind from 1652 onward, he retained his Latin secretaryship until the Restoration (1660), which he roused himself to resist in a last despairing effort as pamphleteer. But the fire had gone out of him, and *The Readie and Easie Way*, which pointed to dictatorship, became the target of the Royalist wits. After the Restoration, Milton went into hiding for a short period, and then after the Act of Oblivion (August 1660), he devoted himself wholly to poetry, with the exception of his prose *De doctrina Christiana* (which did not appear until 1823). He married his third wife, Elizabeth Minshull, in 1662. This was the period of his most famous works, beginning with *Paradise Lost* (completed 1665, published 1667), the theme of which had been in Milton's mind since 1641. It was originally to be a sacred drama; but when in 1658 his official duties were lightened so as to allow him to write, he chose the epic form. The first three books reflect the triumph of the godly, so soon to be reversed; the last books, written in 1663, are tinged with despair. In *Paradise Regained* (1671), the tone is more of resignation, and the theme is the triumph of reason over passion. *Samson Agonistes*, published with it in 1671, shows the reviving spirit of rebellion, due perhaps to the rise of Whig opposition about 1670. The parallel of his own fortunes, both in the private and the public sphere, with those of **Samson** made Milton pour out his spirit into this Greek play, which also formed the libretto of **Handel**'s oratorio. His last years were spent in sociable comfort in Cripplegate, where he was buried next to his father in St Giles' Churchyard.

Mindszenty, József 1892–1975 •*Hungarian Roman Catholic primate*• Born in Mindszent, Vas, he became a priest in 1915, Archbishop of Esztergom and primate in 1945, and cardinal in 1946. He then acquired international fame in 1948 when he was charged with treason by the Communist government in Budapest. He was sentenced to life imprisonment the following year, but in 1955 was released on condition that he not leave Hungary. At the end of the Hungarian Uprising in 1956 he was granted asylum in the US legation, where he remained as a voluntary prisoner until 1971. He spent his last years in a Hungarian religious community in Vienna.

Minette *See* **Henrietta Anne, Duchesse d'Orléans**

Minghella, Anthony 1947– •*English director and playwright*• Born in Ryde, Isle of Wight, he studied at the University of Hull and taught drama there from 1976 to 1981. He began writing and directing for the theater in the early 1980s, later working as a television scriptwriter and director with various episodes of *Inspector Morse* and films such as *Truly, Madly, Deeply* (1991; British Academy of Film and Television Arts Award for Best Original Screenplay). His work for cinema includes *The English Patient* (1997; Academy Award for Best Director) and *The Talented Mr Ripley* (2000). He has also written widely for radio.

Mingus, Charles 1922–79 •*US jazz bassist, composer and bandleader*• He was born in Nogales, Arizona, and raised in Los Angeles. He was taught to play the cello at school, eventually performing with the LA Junior Philharmonic, but contact with jazz musicians led him to take up the double bass. He worked with big bands led by **Louis Armstrong** and **Lionel Hampton** in the 1940s, before moving to New York, where he played in smaller groups, notably with vibraphonist Red Norvo (1908–99). He was recognized as a leading figure on his instrument, but his ambitions lay in composition. He launched a record label, Debut, in 1953, and became involved with the experimental Jazz Composers Workshop before forming his own Jazz Workshop in 1955. Recordings like *Pithecanthropus Erectus* (1956) and *The Black Saint and the Sinner Lady* (1964) attempted to stretch and redefine the boundaries of jazz and the relationship of composition to improvisation within it, and his huge musical legacy is among the most important in jazz. His massive work *Epitaph,* for 31 instruments, was performed in complete form for the first time in 1989.

Minnelli, Liza May 1946– •*US singer and actress*• Born in Los Angeles, the daughter of director Vincente Minnelli (1910–86) and **Judy Garland**, she first appeared on screen in her mother's film *In the Good Old Summertime* (1949). She made her off-Broadway debut in *Best Foot Forward* (1963) and became the youngest actress to win a Tony award, for *Flora, the Red Menace* (1965). Roles in films like *Charlie Bubbles* (1967), *The Sterile Cuckoo* (1969) and *Tell Me That You Love Me, Junie Moon* (1970) revealed her dramatic skills. She won an Academy Award for *Cabaret* (1972), and a television special, *Liza with a Z* (1972), confirmed her versatility. Subsequent dramatic appearances include *New York, New York* (1977), the television film *A Time to Live* (1985) and *Victor-Victoria* on Broadway in 1997. Her private life has often seemed as volatile as her mother's, but she remains a potent attraction as a recording artist and concert performer.

Minogue, Kylie Ann 1968– •*Australian pop singer and actress*• Born in Melbourne, she achieved international stardom as Charlene in the soap opera *Neighbours* from 1986. She released her debut single, "Locomotion," in 1988 and subsequently concentrated on pop music. Such singles as "I Should Be So Lucky" (1988) and "Hand on Your Heart" (1989) established her as a favorite in pop charts across the world. In the 1990s she exchanged her wholesome pop image for a more mature sexually alluring persona and enjoyed renewed success with such releases as *Kylie Minogue* (1994) and *Light Years* (2000) as well as with the chart-topping single "Can't Get You Out of My Head" (2001). Her sister Danni (1971–) is also a pop singer and actress.

Minot, George Richards 1885–1950 •*US physician and Nobel Prize winner*• He was born in Boston, and educated at Harvard College and Medical School, with which he was associated for most of his working life. Using special staining techniques on blood smears, he studied anemia, and from 1925, working with **William Murphy**, he examined clinically **George Whipple**'s observation that dogs made anemic through repeated bleedings improved significantly when fed liver. Minot and Murphy established the importance of a liver diet for patients suffering from pernicious anemia, at that time a fatal disease, and shared with Whipple the 1934 Nobel Prize for physiology or medicine.

Mintoff, Dom(inic) 1916– •*Maltese Labour statesman*• Born in Cospicua, he was educated at Malta and Oxford Universities. In the first Malta Labour government (1947) he became minister of works and deputy prime minister. He became prime minister in 1955, and in 1956–57 undertook negotiations with Britain to integrate Malta more closely with the former. These broke down in 1958, and Malta's constitution was suspended in January 1959. Having resigned in 1958 to lead the Malta Liberation Movement, he became leader of the opposition in 1962. The country was granted full independence two years later, and Mintoff became prime minister in 1971. Three years later Malta became a republic within the Commonwealth. He continued as prime minister until 1984.

Minton, Thomas 1765–1836 •*English pottery and china manufacturer*• Born in Shrewsbury, Shropshire, he originally was trained as a transfer-print engraver, working for **Josiah Spode** for a time, but in 1789 he set up the firm which bears his name in Stoke-on-Trent, producing copperplates for transfer printing in blue underglaze. He is reputed to have invented the willow pattern. In 1793 he built a pottery works at Stoke, where he very soon produced a fine bone china. Much of it was tableware, decorated with finely painted flowers and fruit.

Mirabeau, Honoré Gabriel Riqueti, Comte de 1749–91 •*French revolutionary politician and orator*• Born in Bignon, he was dismissed from the cavalry for his disorderly behavior, and wrote *Essai sur le despotisme* in hiding in Amsterdam, having eloped with a young married woman. In May 1777 he was imprisoned for three and a half years, during which he wrote *Erotica biblion, Ma conversion*, and his famous *Essai sur les lettres de cachet* (2 vols, 1782). In 1786 he produced *Sur la monarchie prussienne sous Frédéric le Grand* (4 vols, 1787). In 1789 he was elected to the States General by the Third Estate, and later became a great force in the National Assembly. He advocated a constitutional monarchy on the English model but was distrusted both by the court and the extremists. Nonetheless he was elected president of the Assembly in January 1791, but died soon afterward.

“ ”

We will only leave our places by the force of the bayonet!

1789 Speech at the Séance Royale.
Quoted in Webster ***The French Revolution*** *(1919), page 50.*

Miralles, Enric 1955–2000 •*Spanish architect*• Born in Barcelona, he studied architecture at the School of Architecture there. He won awards working with the Piñon-Viaplana group (1973–85) and formed his own practice in partnership with Benedetta Tagliabue in 1992. His most important projects include the "Icaria Pergolas" street sunshades in Barcelona (1992), the entrance to the railway station in Takaoka, Japan (1993), the Park-Cemetery in Igualada, Barcelona (1995), considered his greatest achievement, and designs for the new Scottish Parliament in Edinburgh.

Miranda, Carmen, *professional name of* **Maria do Carmo Miranda Da Cunha**, *also known as* **the Brazilian Bombshell** 1909–55 •*Brazilian singer and actress*• Born near Lisbon and raised in Rio de Janeiro, she became a film and radio personality before going to the US in 1939. She became known as the "Brazilian Bombshell," and made fun of her diminutive stature by wearing platform shoes and towering hats of fruits and flowers. Her US debut was in the Broadway show *The Streets of Paris* (1939) with **George Abbott** and Tom Costello. She went on to star in *Down Argentine Way* (1941) and *The Gang's All Here* (1943).

Mirandola, Giovanni *See* **Pico Della Mirandola, Comte**

Miró, Joán 1893–1983 •*Spanish artist*• Born in Montroig, he studied in Paris and Barcelona. Before World War I he painted in Cézannesque and Fauve styles, but in 1920 he settled in Paris and came into contact with **Picasso** and **Juan Gris**. Seduced by surrealism, he invented a manner of painting using curvilinear, fantastical forms: eventually, these pictures became almost entirely abstract and had a great influence on American Abstract Expressionist artists such as **Arshile Gorky** in the late 1940s and 1950s. His works include *Catalan Landscape* (1923–24, New York) and *Maternity* (1924). He also designed ballet sets, sculptures, murals, and tapestries.

Mirren, Helen, *originally* **Helen Lydia Mironoff** 1945– •*English actress*• Born in Hammersmith, West London, she joined the Royal Shakespeare Company in 1967, where her performances included Ophelia in *Hamlet* (1970), the title role in *Miss Julie* (1971) and Lady Macbeth in *Macbeth* (1974–75). She made her film debut in *Herostratus* (1967) and won acclaim for her roles in *The Long Good Friday* (1979) and *Cal* (1984). Her subsequent pictures include *The Mosquito Coast* (1986), *The Cook, the Thief, His Wife & Her Lover* (1989), *Where Angels Fear to Tread* (1991), *The Madness of King George* (1994) and *Some Mother's Son* (1996). On television, she is best known as policewoman Jane Tennison in *Prime Suspect* (1991–96). She has continued to work widely on stage.

Mishima Yukio, *pseudonym of* **Hiraoka Kimitake** 1925–70 •*Japanese writer*• Born in Tokyo, he attended the University of Tokyo before becoming a civil servant and embarking on a prolific writing career, which produced 40 novels as well as poetry, essays and modern Kabuki and Nō drama. His first major work was *Kamen no kokuhaku* (1949, Eng trans *Confessions of a Mask*, 1958), which dealt with his realization that he was gay and the ways in which he attempted to conceal it. His great tetralogy, *Hojo no umi*

(1965–70, Eng trans *The Sea of Fertility*, 1972–74), has a central theme of reincarnation, and spans Japanese life and events in the 20th century. He became an expert in martial arts, and in 1968 founded the Shield Society, a group of 100 youths dedicated to a revival of *Bushido*, the Samurai knightly code of honor. In 1970 he committed suicide by performing *seppuku* following a carefully staged token attempt to rouse the nation to a return to prewar nationalist ideals.

Mistinguett, *stage name of* **Jeanne Marie Bourgeois** 1874–1956 •*French dancer and actress*• Born in a suburb of Paris, she was given her stage name by friends who thought that "Miss" characterized her "English" looks. She made her debut in 1895 and reached the height of her success with **Maurice Chevalier** at the Folies Bergère. A highly popular music-hall artiste for the next 30 years, she had a vivacious stage personality and made up for her weak voice by her remarkable versatility and originality in comedy. She also distinguished herself as a straight actress in *Madame Sans-Gène* and *Les Misérables*. Among her most famous songs are "Mon Homme" and "J'en ai marre."

Mistral, Gabriela, *pseudonym of* **Lucila Godoy de Alcayaga** 1889–1957 •*Chilean poet, diplomat and teacher, and Nobel Prize winner*• Born in Vicuña, she taught at Columbia, Vassar and in Puerto Rico, and was formerly consul at Madrid and elsewhere. The cost of publication of her first book, *Desolación* (1922, "Desolation"), was paid by the teachers of New York. Her work is inspired by religious sentiments and a preoccupation with sorrow and death. Her career as a teacher led her to write for children, notably the songs in *Ternura* (1924); much of her children's writing is translated in *Crickets and Frogs* (1972). She was awarded the Nobel Prize for literature in 1945.

Mitchell, Arthur 1934– •*US dancer, choreographer and director*• Born in New York City, he studied at the High School for Performing Arts and the School of American Ballet. In 1956 he joined New York City Ballet, the first African-American principal dancer to join that company, and his dream, following the assassination of **Martin Luther King** in 1968, was to found his own group in order to develop opportunities for fellow Black dancers. Dance Theater of Harlem made its highly successful debut in New York in 1971, and it has become a company of international standing.

Mitchell, George 1933– •*US Democratic politician*• Born in Waterville, Maine, he was called to the bar in 1960. In 1962 he became a special adviser to Senator **Edmund Muskie** and began his own political career. In 1980 he was elected a senator from Maine in succession to Muskie. In 1995, with the Democrats in power, he was appointed special adviser to President **Clinton** for Economic Initiatives in Ireland. The son of an Irishman, Mitchell had an interest in the country that led to his appointment as chairman of the Northern Ireland peace talks (1995–98). In 1999 he became chancellor of Queen's University, Belfast. In 2001 he produced the Mitchell Report on the Israeli-Palestinian conflict.

Mitchell, Sir James Fitzallen 1931– •*St Vincent and the Grenadines statesman*• He trained and worked as an agronomist (1958–65) and later became a hotelier. He entered politics through the St Vincent Labour Party (SVLP), and in the pre-independence period served as minister of trade (1967–72). He was then premier (1972–74), heading the People's Political Party (PPP). In 1975 he founded the New Democratic Party (NDP) and, as its leader, became prime minister in 1984, winning a historic fourth term in 1998. He resigned in 2000. He received a knighthood in 1995.

Mitchell, John Newton 1913–88 •*US attorney general*• Born in Detroit, he managed Nixon's successful presidential campaign in 1968. As attorney general (1969–72), he ordered wiretaps without court authorization and prosecuted antiwar protesters. He resigned when the Watergate break-in was exposed, and in 1975 he was convicted of conspiracy, obstruction of justice, and perjury. After serving 19 months in prison he was released in 1979.

Mitchell, Joni (Roberta Joan), *née* **Anderson** 1943– •*Canadian singer and songwriter*• Born in McLeod, Alberta, she studied commercial art for a time, then turned to folk music as a teenager. A short-lived marriage to folk singer Chuck Mitchell in 1965 took her to the US, where she made her first album, *Song of a Seagull* (1967). The original imagery of her songs established her as an important bridge between folk and pop, and she cut several highly regarded, and often highly confessional, albums. Her music became increasingly complex and jazz-influenced on later recordings like *The Hissing of Summer Lawns* (1975), culminating in her misjudged but sincere tribute *Mingus* (1979). She has continued to paint and make intelligent pop music.

Mitchell, Margaret 1900–49 •*US novelist*• Born in Atlanta, Georgia, she studied at Smith College, Northampton, Massachusetts, for a medical career, but turned to journalism. After her marriage in 1925, she began the 10-year task of writing her only novel, *Gone with the Wind* (1936), which won the Pulitzer Prize and was the subject of a celebrated film in 1939.

Mitchell, Warren, *originally* **Warren Misell** 1926– •*English actor*• Born in London, he studied at Oxford and the Royal Academy of Dramatic Art and made his first appearance at the Finsbury Park Open Air Theatre (1950). His interpretation of Willy Loman in **Arthur Miller**'s *Death of a Salesman* at the National Theatre (1979) was highly praised. He is best known for playing the character of Alf Garnett, a garrulous, foul-mouthed, right-wing Cockney in the television series *Till Death Us Do Part* (1966–78). The character returned in two films, a stage show, and a further television series, *In Sickness and in Health* (1985–92). Mitchell has also appeared in the series *So You Think You've Got Troubles* (1991) and the miniseries *Jackaroo* (1993). His many films include *Help!* (1965) and **Jack Rosenthal**'s *The Chain* (1985).

Mitchison, Naomi Margaret, *née* **Haldane** 1897–1999 •*Scottish writer*• Born in Edinburgh, the daughter of the physiologist **John Scott Haldane**, and educated at the Dragon School, Oxford, she won instant attention with her brilliant and personal evocations of Greece and Sparta in a series of novels including *The Conquered* (1923), *Cloud Cuckoo Land* (1925) and *Black Sparta* (1928). The erudite *The Corn King and the Spring Queen* (1931) brought to life the civilizations of ancient Egypt, Scythia and the Middle East. She traveled widely, and in 1963 was made tribal adviser and "mother" to the Bakgatla of Botswana. She wrote more than 70 books, and from 1937 lived in Carradale on the Mull of Kintyre, Scotland.

Mitchum, Robert 1917–97 •*US film actor*• Born in Bridgeport, Connecticut, a youth spent as a traveling laborer, vagrant and professional boxer took him to Hollywood, where he became a prolific leading man, especially noted for his association with the postwar film noir thriller. His laconic, heavy-lidded manner was deceptively casual, disguising a potent screen presence and thorough professionalism that enlivened many routine assignments. His many notable films include *The Night of the Hunter* (1955), *The Sundowners* (1960), *Ryan's Daughter* (1970), *The Friends of Eddie Coyle* (1973) and *Farewell My Lovely* (1975). His television performances include the epic miniseries *The Winds of War* (1983) and its sequel *War and Remembrance* (1989).

Mitford, Jessica Lucy 1917–96 •*English writer*• She was born in Burford, Oxfordshire, the fifth of the six daughters of the 2nd Baron Redesdale, and sister of Diana Mitford (1910–2003), **Nancy Mitford** and **Unity Mitford**. She went to the US in 1939 and joined the US Communist Party, her experiences of which were the subject for *A Fine Old Conflict* (1977), and also wrote the best-selling *The American Way of Death* (1963), an exposé of the funeral industry's unethical practices. *The Trial of Dr Spock* (1970), based on the trials of anti–Vietnam War activists, was inspired by her interest in civil-rights cases. Other works include *Hons and Rebels* (1960) and *The Making of a Muckraker* (1979).

Mitford, Mary Russell 1786–1855 •*English novelist and dramatist*• Born in Alresford, Hampshire, she won £20,000 in a lottery at the age of ten and attended school in Chelsea. However, her father was a spendthrift, and as the family became more and more impoverished, she had to write to earn money. She produced several plays, but her gift was for sketches of country manners, scenery and character, which after appearing in magazines were collected as *Our Village* (5 vols, 1824–32). In 1852 she published her *Recollections of a Literary Life*.

Mitford, Nancy Freeman 1904–73 •*English writer*• Born in London, daughter of the 2nd Baron Redesdale, and educated at home, she established a reputation with her witty novels such as *The Pursuit of Love* (1945) and *Love in a Cold Climate* (1949). After World War II she settled in France and wrote her major biographies *Madame de Pompadour* (1953), *Voltaire in Love* (1957), *The Sun King* (1966) and *Frederick the Great* (1970). As one of the essayists in *Noblesse Oblige*, edited by herself (1956), she helped to originate the famous "U," or upper-class, and "non-U" classification of linguistic usage and behavior. She was the elder sister of **Unity Mitford** and **Jessica Mitford**.

" "

I have only ever read one book in my life, and that is *White Fang*. It's so frightfully good I've never bothered to read another.

1945 ***The Pursuit of Love****, chapter 9.*

Mitford, Unity Valkyrie 1914–48 •*English socialite*• The daughter of the 2nd Baron Redesdale and sister of Diana Mitford, **Jessica Mitford** and **Nancy Mitford**, she was notorious for her attempted suicide on the outbreak of World War II and for her associations with leading Nazis in Germany, including **Hitler**. However she returned to Great Britain in 1940, suffering from a gunshot wound.

Mithridates VI, *surnamed* **Eupator**, *called* **the Great** c.132–63 BC •*King of Pontus*• He succeeded to the throne (c.120 BC) as a boy, but soon subdued the tribes who bordered on the Euxine as far as the Crimea, and made an incursion into Cappadocia and Bithynia, then Roman. In the First Mithridatic War (88), Mithridates, initially successful, was compelled to make peace with **Sulla** (85), relinquishing all his conquests in Asia. The aggressions of the Roman legate led to the Second Mithridatic War (83–81), which Mithridates won. In the Third Mithridatic War (74) he prospered with some Roman support until defeated by **Lucullus** (68). In 66 **Pompey** defeated Mithridates on the Euphrates, and his son's rebellion caused him to kill himself. He was cruel and sensual but energetic and determined, and his political skill enabled him to pose a serious threat to Rome.

Mitterrand, François Maurice Marie 1916–96 •*French statesman*• Born in Jarnac in southwest France, he attended the University of Paris during the mid-1930s. During World War II he served with the French forces (1939–40), was wounded and captured, but escaped (on the third attempt) in December 1941 from a prison camp in Germany and became a network commander in the French Resistance. He was awarded the Legion of Honor, the Croix de Guerre and the Rosette de la Résistance. He was a Deputy in the French National Assembly almost continuously from 1946, representing the constituency of Nièvre (near Dijon), and held ministerial posts in 11 centrist governments between 1947 and 1958. A firm believer in the democratic traditions of Republican France, he opposed **Charles de Gaulle**'s creation of the Fifth Republic in 1953 and, as a result, lost his Assembly seat in the 1958 election. He became radicalized, left the Catholic Church during the early 1960s, and began building up a strong new left-of-center anti-Gaullist alliance, the "Federation of the Left." After returning to the National Assembly in 1962, in 1971 he became leader of the new Socialist Party (PS). He embarked on a successful strategy of electoral union with the (then important) Communist Party, bringing major gains for the Socialists, establishing them as the single most popular party in France by 1978, and in 1981 was elected president. As president, Mitterrand initially introduced a series of radical economic and political reforms, including programs of nationalization and decentralization. However, deteriorating economic conditions after 1983 forced a policy U-turn, and in the 1986 election the Socialists lost their National Assembly majority, compelling him to work with a prime minister, **Jacques Chirac**, from the opposition "right coalition." Despite being forced to concede considerable executive authority to Chirac in this unique "cohabitation" experiment, Mitterrand, nicknamed "the fox," outmaneuvered his younger rival, and comfortably defeated him in the presidential election of 1988. **Michel Rocard** was subsequently appointed prime minister in a new left-of-center administration. In 1992 the Socialist Party suffered a crushing defeat, with the right-wing parties winning 484 seats to the left's 92. In 1995 Mitterrand lost the presidency to Jacques Chirac.

Miyake, Issey 1938– •*Japanese fashion designer*• He was born in Hiroshima, studied at Tama Art University in Tokyo, and spent six years in Paris and New York fashion houses. Although he showed his first collection in Tokyo in 1963, he founded his studio there only in 1971. His first subsequent show was in New York the same year, followed by a show in Paris in 1973. His distinctive style combines Eastern and Western influences in garments which have an almost theatrical quality.

Mizoguchi, Kenji 1898–1956 •*Japanese film director*• Born in Tokyo into a poor family, he left school at age 13 and worked in a number of jobs before becoming an actor in 1918. He made his debut as screen director two years later, and in a career lasting 34 years made more than 80 films, many exploring the place of women in Japanese society. Among his masterpieces are *The Life of Oharu* (1952) and *Ugetsu* (1953).

Mnemon *See* **Artaxerxes II**

Mnouchkine, Ariane 1938– •*French stage director, dramatist and founder of Théâtre du Soleil*• She studied at Paris and London universities, and set up the Association Théâtrale des Étudiants de Paris with fellow students of the Sorbonne (1959), putting on plays and organizing workshops and lectures. In 1962 she traveled to Cambodia and Japan, and on her return founded the Théâtre du Soleil as a theater cooperative (1963). The early productions were influenced by the teachings of **Stanislavsky**, and their first major success came with a production of **Arnold Wesker**'s *The Kitchen* (1967). One of the company's best-known works is *1789*, first produced in 1970.

Möbius, August Ferdinand 1790–1868 •*German mathematician*• Born in Schulpforta, he was professor at the University of Leipzig, where he worked on analytical geometry, statics, topology and theoretical astronomy. He extended Cartesian coordinate methods to projective geometry, and gave a straightforward algebraic account of statics, using vectorial quantities before vectors as such entered mathematics. In topology he investigated which surfaces can exist, and became one of the discoverers of the "Möbius strip" (a one-sided surface formed by giving a rectangular strip a half-twist and then joining the ends together). He also examined in detail the possible types of three-dimensional spaces that can be created by gluing similar constructions.

Mobutu Sese Seko Kuku Ngbendu Wa Za Banga, *originally* **Joseph-Désiré Mobutu** 1930–97 •*Zairean soldier and politician*• Born into a poor family in Lisala, he undertook army training and a period of study in Brussels before joining the Force Publique in 1949. He joined **Patrice Lumumba**'s Mouvement National Congolais in 1958 and was Chief of Staff in 1960 at the time of independence. After the 1963–65 civil war, he took over the government, renamed the country Zaire in place of the Belgian Congo and imposed a degree of stability which had hitherto been unknown. Backed by US money and the power of the army, his regime became increasingly unpopular. By 1993 Zaire (now renamed the Democratic Republic of Congo) was in a state of financial collapse; meanwhile, Mobutu lived in splendor, having amassed a fortune into the billions from his country's resources. He was forced to abandon democratic elections and ruled through a military council. In May 1997, **Laurent Kabila**'s army forced him into exile and brought his dictatorship to an end.

Model, Lisette, *née* **Elise Amelie Felicie Stern** 1901–83 •*US photographer*• Born in Vienna of Austrian-Italian and French parentage, she studied music with composer **Arnold Schoenberg** (1918–20), and in Paris (1922). She began to paint in 1932 and to photograph in 1937, both for pleasure and in the hope of finding employment as a darkroom technician. Moving to New York in 1938, she worked as a freelance photographer for *Harper's Bazaar* and other publications (1941–57). She also taught photography at the New School for Social Research, New York (1951–82), where **Diane Arbus** was among her students.

Modigliani, Amedeo 1884–1920 •*Italian painter and sculptor*• He was born in Livorno, Tuscany. His early work was influenced by the painters of the Italian Renaissance, particularly the primitives, and in 1906 he moved to Paris, where he was further influenced by **Toulouse-Lautrec** and the Fauves. In 1909 he took to sculpture and produced a number of elongated stone heads in African style. He continued to use this style when he later resumed painting, with a series of richly colored, elongated portraits. In 1918 in Paris he held one of his first solo shows, which included some very frank nudes; the exhibition was closed for indecency on the first day. It was only after his death from tuberculosis that he gained recognition and the prices of his paintings soared.

Mogae, Festus Gontebanye 1939– •*Botswanan politician*• He was born in Serowe and educated in Botswana and England at Oxford University and Sussex. His early career was in development planning and finance, and he became finance minister from 1989 to 1998, vice president of Botswana in 1992 and president in 1998.

Mohammad 'Ali *See* **Mehemet 'Ali**

Mohammad Reza Pahlavi *See* **Pahlavi, Muhammad Reza**

Mohammed (Prophet) *See* **Muhammad**

Mohammed *See* **Mehmet II (the Conqueror)**

Mohammed Nadir Shah c. 1880–1933 •*King of Afghanistan*• The brother of Dost Mohammed, as Commander in Chief to **Amanullah Khan** (ruler and later king of Afghanistan from 1926), he played a prominent role in the 1919 Afghan War against Great Britain, which secured the country's full independence (1922). He subsequently fell into disfavor and was forced to live in exile in France. In 1929, with British diplomatic support, he returned to Kabul and seized the throne, immediately embarking on a program of economic and social modernization. These reforms, however, alienated the Muslim clergy, and in 1933 he was assassinated.

Moholy-Nagy, László 1895–1946 •*US artist and photographer*• Born in Bucsborsod, Hungary, he trained in law in Budapest, and painted with Dada and constructivist groups in Vienna and Berlin (1919–23). He produced his first "photograms" (nonrepresentational photographic images made directly without a camera) in 1923 and joined the Bauhaus under **Walter Gropius** in 1925. There he began to use a camera and was quickly recognized as a leading avant-garde artist in the New Photographers movement in Europe (1925–35). He left Germany in 1935 and, after working as a designer in Amsterdam and London, was invited to the US in 1937 to head the new Bauhaus school in Chicago, later the Institute of Design. He taught photography there, and became a US citizen shortly before his death.

Mohs, Friedrich 1773–1839 •*German mineralogist*• Born in Gernrode, Sachsen-Anhalt, and educated at the University of Halle, he became professor at the Universities of Graz (1812), Freiburg (1818, succeeding **Abraham Werner**), and Vienna (1826). He developed a mineralogical classification system based on a variety of mineral characters, rather than adopting the traditional purely chemical system. The Mohs scale of hardness which he introduced is still in use. Around 1820, he arrived at the concept of the six crystal systems; this mineral classification system was based on the different orientation of crystallographic axes.

Moi, Daniel arap 1924– •*Kenyan statesman*• Born in Rift Valley Province, the son of a poor farmer, he was educated at the Mission School, Kabartonjo, and at the Government African School in Kapsabet. After entering the House of Representatives in 1963, in 1967 he was appointed vice president by **Jomo Kenyatta** as his nominated successor. He was provincial president of the Kenyan African National Union from 1966, and after becoming KANU president and head of state on Kenyatta's death in 1978, he purged the army, launched an ambitious plan to develop Kenya's economy and infrastructure, and preempted political opposition by proclaiming KANU as the country's only legal party. In 1992 he held multiparty elections and won amid controversy about the conduct of the elections, winning reelection again in 1997. He retired in 2002.

Moiseyev, Igor Aleksandrovich 1906– •*Russian dancer*• He studied privately and at the Bolshoi Ballet School, where he remained as character soloist and choreographer until 1939. Always interested in folk dance, he accepted an appointment in 1936 as director of the new Dance Department of the Moscow Theater for Folk Art. He formed a professional folk dance company the following year, developing simple steps and primitive patterns into full theatrical expression. This ensemble has toured the world, meanwhile gathering a substantial repertoire of dances from other nations. In 1967 he founded the State Ensemble of Classical Ballet.

Moivre, Abraham de 1667–1754 •*French mathematician*• Born in Vitry, Champagne, he left France for religious reasons and went to England around 1686. Elected a Fellow of the Royal Society in 1697, he helped the Royal Society decide the famous contest between Newton and **Gottfried Leibniz** on the origins of the calculus. His principal work was *The Doctrine of Chances* (1718) on probability theory, but he is best remembered for the fundamental formula on complex numbers, known as de Moivre's theorem, that relates the exponential and trigonometric functions.

Mokanna, al-, *properly* **Hakim ben Atta** c. 778 •*Arab prophet*• He was the founder of a sect in the Persian province of Khorasan. Ostensibly to protect onlookers from being dazzled by his divine countenance, but actually to conceal the loss of an eye, he wore a veil ("al-Mokanna" means "the Veiled One"). Claiming he was a reincarnation of God, he gathered enough followers to seize several fortified places, but the caliph Almahdi eventually took his stronghold of Kash, when Mokanna took poison.

Molière, *pseudonym of* **Jean Baptiste Poquelin** 1622–73 •*French playwright*• Born in Paris, he studied with the Jesuits at the Collège de Clermont, and may have been called to the bar. His mother died when he was young, and when he came of age he inherited some of her fortune. Instead of following his father's business, he embarked on a theatrical venture (1643) under the title of L'Illustre Théâtre, which lasted for over three years in Paris. The company then moved to the provinces from Lyons to Rouen, and had sufficient success to keep going from 1646 to 1658, eventually obtaining the patronage of the king's brother, **Philippe d'Orléans**. In 1658 he played before the king, and organized a regular theater, first in the Petit Bourbon, and later in the Palais Royal. As a theater manager he had to perform tragedy as well as comedy, but he had little success with either **Corneille**'s *Nicomède* or with the works of **Racine**, despite their personal friendship. Molière soon realized his own considerable resources as a comic writer. *Les précieuses ridicules* was published in November 1659, and every year until his death he produced at least one of his comic masterpieces, including *Tartuffe* in 1664, *Le Misanthrope* in 1666, *Amphitryon* in 1668, and *Le bourgeois gentilhomme* in 1671. In August 1665 the king adopted Molière's troupe as his own servants. In 1667 symptoms of lung disease were apparent. He died in his home in the Rue de Richelieu the night after having acted as the *Malade* in the seventh performance of his last play, *Le malade imaginaire*.

“ ”

On ne meurt qu'une fois et c'est pour si longtemps!
We only die once; and it's for such a long time!
1656 ***Le Dépit amoureux**, act 5, scene 3.*

Molina, Luis de 1535–1600 •*Spanish Jesuit theologian*• Born in Cuenca, he studied at Coimbra, and was Professor of Theology at Evora for 20 years. His views on predestination were seen as a revival of Pelagianism, provoking the dispute between Molinists and Thomists. His principal writings are a commentary on the *Summa* of **Thomas Aquinas** (1593); a treatise, *De justitia et jure* (1592, "On Law and Justice"); and the celebrated treatise on grace and free will, *Concordia liberi arbitrii cum Gratiae donis* (1588, "The Harmony of Free Will with Gifts of Grace").

Molina, Mario José 1943– •*Mexican scientist and Nobel Prize winner*• Born in Mexico City, he studied at the Universities of Mexico and Freiburg and at the University of California, Berkeley. Following work at the University of California, Irvine, he became senior research scientist at the Jet Propulsion Laboratory, California (1983–89), and Professor of Earth, Atmospheric and Planetary Sciences and Chemistry at MIT (1989–). His many honors and awards include the **Max Planck** research award (1994–96) and the Nobel Prize for chemistry (1995; with **Paul J Crutzen** and **Frank Sherwood Rowland**) for work on the role of CFCs in the catalytic destruction of atmospheric ozone.

Mollet, Guy Alcide 1905–75 •*French socialist politician*• Born in Flers, Normandy, to working-class parents, in World War II he was a captain in the secret Resistance army. In 1946 he became mayor of Arras, a member of Parliament, secretary-general of the Socialist Party and a cabinet minister in the **Blum** government. A keen supporter of a Western European Federation, he was a delegate to the Consultative Assembly of the Council of Europe (1949) and was its president in 1955. He became prime minister in 1956. He survived the international crisis over the Anglo-French intervention in Suez later that year, but lost office in 1957 after staying in power longer than any French premier since the war.

Mollison, James Allan 1905–59 •*Scottish aviator*• Born in Glasgow, he became a consultant-engineer. He was commissioned into the RAF in 1923, and won fame for his record flight, Australia–England in 1931 in 8 days 19 hours and 28 minutes. He made the first solo east-west crossing of the North Atlantic in 1932, and in February 1933 the first England–South America flight. With his wife, **Amy Johnson**, he made the first flight across the Atlantic to the US in 1933, and to India in 1934.

Molnár, Ferenc, *originally* **Ferenc Neumann** 1878–1952 •*Hungarian playwright and novelist*• He was born in Budapest, and changed his name to Molnár in 1896. He wrote 36 plays, mainly fantasies and romantic comedies, and there is probably no other Hungarian playwright more translated and performed outside his own country. *Liliom* (1909) later became the basis for the **Rodgers** and **Hammerstein** musical *Carousel* (1945). Subsequent plays include *A fehlér felho* (1916, "The White Cloud") and *A hattyú* (1920, "The Swan"). *Jétêk a Kastélyban* (1926), a sophisticated social comedy, was translated by **P G Wodehouse** as *The Play's the Thing* and by **Tom Stoppard** as *Rough Crossing*. *Olimpia* (1928, "Olympia") is a similarly well-made play, peopled by amiable, well-to-do hedonists. Molnár emigrated to the US in 1940, later becoming a US citizen.

Molotov, Vyacheslav Mikhailovich, *originally* **Vyacheslav Mikhailovich Skriabin** 1890–1986 •*Soviet politician*• Born in Kukaida, Vyatka, he was educated at Kazan High School and Polytechnic. In the 1905 revolution he joined the Bolshevik section of **Lenin**'s Social Democratic Workers' Party and in 1912 became the staunch disciple of **Stalin**. During the March 1917 revolution he was a member of the military revolutionary committee which directed the coup against **Aleksandr Kerensky**. In 1921 he became secretary of the Central Committee of the Russian Communist Party and the youngest candidate-member of the politburo. In 1928 his appointment to the key position of secretary of the Moscow committee of the All-Union Party marked the launching of the first Five-Year Plan. As chairman of the Council of People's Commissars (1930–41), he became an international figure in 1939 when he took on the extra post of Commissar for Foreign Affairs, shaping the policy which led to the nonaggression pact with Nazi Germany. He was Stalin's chief adviser at Tehran and Yalta and represented the Soviet Union at the 1945 founding conference of the United Nations at San Francisco and at the Potsdam Conference. After the war, Molotov, who negotiated the pacts binding the satellite states to the Soviet Union, emerged as the uncompromising champion of world Sovietism. His "*nyet*" at meetings of the United Nations and in the councils of foreign ministers became a byword. He resigned as Foreign Minister in 1956 and was appointed Minister of State Control. In 1957 **Nikita Khrushchev** called him a "saboteur of peace," accused him of policy failures and appointed him ambassador to Outer Mongolia until 1960. He was expelled from the Communist Party in 1962 but reinstated in 1984.

Moltke, Helmuth 1848–1916 •*German soldier*• He was a nephew of Count **Helmuth von Moltke**. Like his uncle, he rose to be Chief of the General Staff (1906), but in World War I, after losing the Battle of the Marne in September 1914, was superseded by **Erich von Falkenhayn**.

Moltke, Helmuth, Count von, *known as* **the Silent** 1800–91 •*Prussian soldier*• In 1819 he became lieutenant in a Danish regiment, but in 1822 entered Prussian service. From 1858 to 1888 he was Chief of the General Staff in Berlin and reorganized the Prussian army. His strategical skill was displayed in the successful wars with Denmark in 1863–64, with Austria in 1866, and with France in 1870–71.

“ ”

What our sword has won in half a year, our sword must guard for half a century.

1891 ***The Franco-Prussian War of 1870–71.***

Moltmann, Jürgen 1926– •*German Reformed theologian*• He was born in Hamburg. A professor in Wuppertal (1958–63), Bonn (1963–67) and Tübingen (1967–94, now emeritus), he is best known for his influential trilogies, *Theology of Hope* (1967), *The Crucified God* (1974) and *The Church in the Power of the Spirit* (1977), for *The Trinity and the Kingdom of God* (1981), and for the Gifford lectures *God in Creation* (1985) and *The Way of Jesus Christ* (1990). Probably the most significant Protestant theologian of the 20th century since **Karl Barth**, he espoused a theology of hope which marked a reaction against the individualistic existential approach of **Rudolf Bultmann**, and a revival in Protestant theology of concern for the social nature of Christian faith.

Mommsen, (Christian Matthias) Theodor 1817–1903 •*German historian and Nobel Prize winner*• Born in Garding, Schleswig-Holstein, he studied at Kiel for three years, and in 1848 was appointed to a chair of law at Leipzig, of which he was deprived two years later for the part he took in politics. In 1852 he became Professor of Roman Law at the University of Zurich, and in 1854 at the University of Breslau, and in 1858 Professor of Ancient History at the University of Berlin. He edited the monumental *Corpus Inscriptionum Latinarum*, helped to edit the *Monumenta Germaniae Historica*, and from 1873 to 1895 was permanent secretary of the Academy. His greatest works include *Römische Geschichte* (3 vols, 1854–55, Eng trans *The History of Rome*). He abandoned the fourth volume, but the fifth was translated as *The Provinces of the Roman Empire* (1885). He was awarded the Nobel Prize for literature in 1902.

Momoh, Joseph Saidu 1937– •*Sierra Leone soldier and statesman*• Born in Binkolo, in the Northern Province, he was trained at military schools in Ghana, Great Britain and Nigeria before being commissioned in the Sierra Leone army in 1963. In 1985 President **Siaka Stevens** announced his retirement, and Momoh was endorsed by Sierra Leone's only political party, the All-People's Congress (APC), as the sole presidential candidate. After taking office he pledged to fight corruption and improve the economy, but he was deposed in 1992.

Monash, Sir John 1865–1931 •*Australian soldier*• He was born in Melbourne of German parentage. He commanded the 4th Australian Brigade at Gallipoli (1914–15), the 3rd Australian Division in France (1916), and the Australian Corps as Lieutenant-General (1918). Recognized as one of the outstanding generals of World War I, he was noted for the meticulous preparation and planning of his operations. He retired in 1930 with the rank of general.

Monck, George *See* **Monk, George**

Mond, Alfred Moritz, 1st Baron Melchett 1868–1930 •*British industrialist and politician*• Born in Farnworth, Cheshire, the son of **Ludwig Mond**, after some years in industry and as chairman of the Mond Nickel Co, he became a Liberal Member of Parliament (1906–28). He was the first Commissioner of Works (1916–21) and was Minister of Health (1922). In 1926 he helped to form ICI (Imperial Chemical Industries Ltd), of which he became chairman.

Mond, Ludwig 1839–1909 •*British chemist*• Born in Kassel, Germany, he studied chemistry in Marburg and then under **Robert Wilhelm Bunsen** in Heidelberg. He settled in Great Britain in 1862, and developed a process to retrieve sulfur from the waste products of the Leblanc process. In 1873 he joined John Brunner in setting up a factory at Winnington, Cheshire, to manufacture soda by the new ammonia process invented by Ernest Solvay. Brunner-Mond & Co eventually grew to be the largest soda plant in the world. Mond also developed a new fuel, producer gas. He is perhaps best known for the process he invented for purifying nickel (the Mond process).

Mondale, Walter F(rederick) 1928– •*US politician and lawyer*• Born in the small town of Ceylon, Minnesota, he was the son of a Methodist preacher of Norwegian descent. After graduating from the University of Minnesota Law School, he made his reputation as a local Democratic machine politician before serving in the US Senate between 1964 and 1976. He served as **Jimmy Carter**'s vice president between 1977 and 1980. In 1984 he was the Democratic presidential nominee, but was crushingly defeated by the Republican candidate, **Ronald Reagan**.

Mondrian, Piet, *properly* **Pieter Cornelis Mondriaan** 1872–1944 •*Dutch artist*• Born in Amersfoort, he was associated with **Theo van Doesburg** in founding the De Stijl movement in architecture and painting. After moving to Paris in 1909 he came under the influence of **Henri Matisse** and Cubism. He then began painting still lifes—his early work included a series of abstracts, *Trees*—which are analyzed in terms of the relationship between the outlines and the planes. During World War I he discarded the subject altogether and concentrated on constructing grids of simple black lines filled in with primary colors. These rectilinear compositions depend for their beauty on the simple relationships between the colored areas. He was a great theoretician and published the pamphlet *Neo-Plasticism* in 1920, which inspired the Dutch philosopher Mathieu Schoenmaekers. He went to London in 1938, and from 1940 lived in New York City. Later works include more colorful abstracts (such as *Broadway Boogie-Woogie*, 1942–43, New York). His work has been a major influence on all purely abstract painters.

Monet, Claude 1840–1926 •*French Impressionist painter*• Born in Paris, he spent his youth in Le Havre, where he met the painter Eugène Boudin (1824–98), who encouraged him to work in the open air, then an uncommon artistic practice. After military service in Algeria he moved to Paris, associating with **Pierre Auguste Renoir**, **Camille Pissarro** and **Alfred Sisley**, and developing his plein-air style under the influence of Japanese prints, with their flat colors and casual notation of objects. The 1860s were financially precarious years during which he sold very little, although he had work accepted by the salons; in the early 1870s, however, he was introduced, with Pissarro, to the dealer Paul Durand-Ruel, who was instrumental in turning his fortunes around. In 1874 he exhibited at the first Impressionist Exhibition, and one of his works at this exhibition, *Impression: soleil levant*, gave its name to the movement. Later he worked much at Argenteuil. Along with Pissarro, Monet is recognized as one of the creators of Impressionism, and he was one of its most consistent exponents. He visited and painted extensively in England, Holland and Venice, and spent his career in an attempt to capture the most subtle nuances of color, atmosphere and light in landscape. Apart from many sea and river scenes, he also executed several series of paintings of subjects under different aspects of light, such as *Haystacks* (1890–91) and *Rouen Cathedral* (1892–95). In 1883 he and his mistress, Alice Hoschedé, as well as her children and Monet's own sons, Jean and Michel, bought a farmhouse in the hamlet of Giverny, 40 miles outside Paris. He lived and painted there as a comparative recluse until his death, and it was there that he produced his *Waterlilies* series (1899–1906).

Monge, Gaspard 1746–1818 •*French mathematician and physicist*• Born in Beaune, Burgundy, he became Professor of Mathematics at Mézières in 1768, and in 1780 Professor of Hydraulics at the Lycée in Paris. In 1783, independently of **James Watt** or **Henry Cavendish**, he discovered that water resulted from an electrical explosion of oxygen and hydrogen. He helped to found (1794) the École Polytechnique, and became Professor of Mathematics there. His work includes *Leçons de géométrie descriptive* (1795). In 1805 he was made a senator and Count of Pelusium, but lost both dignities upon the restoration of the **Bourbons**.

Moniz, António Egas *See* **Egas Moniz, António**

Monk or **Monck, George, 1st Duke of Albemarle** 1608–70 •*English soldier*• The second son of a Devonshire baronet of Loyalist sympathies, he was a volunteer in the *Île de Rhé* expedition of 1628, and campaigned in the Low Countries (1629–38). In the English Civil War (1642–51), he was at first a Royalist and fought in Ireland (1642–43), but he was captured at the Battle of Nantwich (1644), imprisoned, and thereafter supported the Commonwealth cause. His successful activities in Ireland brought him to the notice of **Cromwell**. He defeated the Scots at Dunbar in 1650, and was successful in pacifying Scotland. In the First Dutch War he played a major part in the 1653 victory over **Maarten Tromp**. Instrumental in bringing about the restoration of **Charles II**, he was rewarded with the duchy of Albermarle, and was appointed lieutenant general of the forces. He played a conspicuous and useful part in the Second Dutch War, and in 1667, with **Michiel de Ruyter** raiding the Medway virtually unopposed, Monk took command of the defenses. Thereafter he retired more and more into private life.

Monk, Thelonious Sphere 1917–82 •*US jazz pianist and composer*• He was born in Rocky Mount, North Carolina, and brought up in New York. After childhood piano lessons, he began to perform at "rent parties" in Harlem and to play in church. While in his twenties, he worked as a freelance musician and studied briefly at the Juilliard School of Music. Between 1939 and 1945 he worked under a succession of leaders in New York, and first recorded while with the **Coleman Hawkins** Sextet in 1944. During this period the bebop style was causing a ferment among young jazz musicians in New York, and Monk was a key figure in these experiments. He joined **Dizzy Gillespie**'s first big band in 1946, formed specifically to perform bop-style arrangements. Monk formed his own small group in 1947, later working with a quartet using such tenor saxophone players as **John Coltrane**, Johnny Griffin and (for 11 years) Charlie Rouse. World tours from the 1960s brought wide recognition for Monk's percussive and harmonically iconoclastic style. He played little after the mid-1970s, but many of his compositions, such as "Round Midnight" and "Straight No Chaser," are frequently performed.

Monmouth, James Scott, Duke of 1649–85 •*English claimant to the throne*• Born in The Hague (or Rotterdam), the illegitimate son of **Charles II** and **Lucy Walter**, in 1662 he went to England and was made Duke of Monmouth (1663), and became captain general (1670). Handsome, athletic, but a brainless libertine, he was popular because of his humanity toward the Scottish Covenanters at Bothwell Brig (1679), the Popish Plot and the Exclusion Bill, and his two semiroyal progresses (1680–82). The first Earl of **Shaftesbury** pitted the Protestant Duke against the popish heir-presumptive (later **James VII and II**), and involved him in the Rye House Plot (1683), after which Monmouth fled to the Low Countries. At Charles's death, he landed at Lyme Regis, quickly raised 4,000 troops, branded James a popish usurper, and asserted his own right to the Crown. He attempted to surprise the king's forces at Sedgemoor, but was defeated, captured and beheaded. His followers were persecuted in the "Bloody Assizes" of Judge **Jeffreys**.

Monod, Jacques Lucien 1910–76 •*French biochemist and Nobel Prize winner*• Born in Paris, he graduated from the university there, and then left to work at Columbia University before returning for further study at the Sorbonne. After World War II he began work at the Pasteur Institute in Paris, becoming head of the cellular biochemistry department in 1954 and director in 1971. From 1967, he was also Professor of Molecular Biology at the Collège de France. Monod worked closely with **François Jacob** on genetic control mechanisms, developing the theory of the operon system, whereby a regulator gene controls other genes by binding to a specific section of the DNA strand. In 1965 Monod and Jacob shared the Nobel Prize for physiology or medicine with **André Lwoff**.

Monophthalmos *See* **Antigonus**

Monroe, Harriet 1860–1936 •*US poet and critic*• Born in Chicago, she founded (1912) the magazine *Poetry*, which was influential in publicizing the work of **T S Eliot**, **Vachel Lindsay**, **Ezra Pound** and **Robert Frost**, among others. In 1917 she edited the influential free-verse anthology, *The New Poetry*. Her own work was collected in *Chosen Poems* (1935).

Monroe, James 1758–1831 •*5th President of the US*• Born in Westmoreland County, Virginia, he served in the American Revolution, and was elected to the assembly of Virginia and in 1783 to Congress, where he sat for three years. As a member of the US Senate (1790–94), he opposed **Washington** and the

Federalists; the government recalled him in 1796 from the post of minister to France. He was governor of Virginia (1799–1802), and in 1803 helped to negotiate the Louisiana Purchase. In 1811 he was again governor of Virginia, from 1811 to 1817 secretary of state, and from 1814 to 1815 also secretary of war. In 1816 he was elected president, and in 1820 was reelected overwhelmingly. His administration (1817–25) was a time of peaceful prosperity that became known as the "era of good feeling." He signed the Missouri Compromise of 1820, recognized the Spanish American republics and promulgated in a message to Congress (1823) the Monroe Doctrine, embodying the principle that "the American continents ... are henceforth not to be considered as subjects for future colonization by any European power," though existing colonies were not to be interfered with.

Monroe, Marilyn, *originally* **Norma Jean Mortenson** 1926–62 •*US film actress*• Born in Los Angeles, she had a disturbed childhood spent largely in foster homes on account of the mental illness suffered by her mother, Gladys Pearl Baker (*née* Monroe). She was married for the first time at the age of 16, and went on to have two more husbands: the baseball star **Joe DiMaggio** and the playwright **Arthur Miller**. She became a photographer's model in 1946, and after several small film parts and a very high-powered studio publicity campaign, she starred as a sexy, beautiful dumb blonde in *How to Marry a Millionaire* and *Gentlemen Prefer Blondes* (both in 1953). She developed her flair for light comedy in **Billy Wilder**'s *The Seven Year Itch* (1955) and *Some Like It Hot* (1959). Wanting more serious roles, she studied at **Lee Strasberg**'s Actors' Studio and appeared to critical acclaim in *Bus Stop* (1956) and *The Misfits* (1961), her last film, written for her by Arthur Miller. She came to London to make *The Prince and the Showgirl* (1957) with Sir **Laurence Olivier**, returning after two years to Hollywood. She was divorced from Arthur Miller in 1961, and the following year died of an overdose of sleeping pills. She had a close relationship with **John F Kennedy** and **Robert F Kennedy**, and famously sang "Happy Birthday Mr President" in 1961. Since her death, she has become a symbol of Hollywood's ruthless exploitation of beauty and youth. Some accounts maintain that she was murdered, possibly for political motives, but these views remain unsubstantiated.

“ ”

He's the only person I know who's in worse shape than I am.

1961 On Montgomery Clift, her costar in ***The Misfits.***

Monsarrat, Nicholas John Turney 1910–79 •*English novelist*• Born in Liverpool, and educated at Trinity College, Cambridge, he abandoned law for literature and wrote three quite successful novels and a play, *The Visitors*, which reached the London stage. During World War II he served in the navy, and out of his experiences emerged his best-selling novel *The Cruel Sea* (1951), which was subsequently filmed. *The Story of Esther Costello* (1953) repeated that success, followed by *The Tribe That Lost Its Head* (1956) and *The Pillow Fight* (1965).

Montagnier, Luc 1932– •*French molecular biologist*• He was educated at the Universities of Poitiers and Paris, became laboratory head of the Radium Institute (1965–71) in Paris, and from 1972 worked at the Pasteur Institute. In 1974 he also became director of research at the National Center for Scientific Research, and since 1997 he has been director of the Center for Molecular and Cellular Biology at Queen's College, City University of New York. Montagnier has published widely in molecular biology and virology, and is now credited with the discovery of the HIV virus in 1983.

Montagu, Ashley, *originally* **Israel Ehrenberg** 1905–99 •*US anthropologist*• Born in London, England, he studied at the Universities of London and Florence and at Columbia University. Throughout his work on human biosocial evolution, he argued strongly against the view that cultural phenomena are genetically determined. His many influential publications, both scholarly and popular, include *Coming into Being Among the Australian Aborigines* (1937), *The Natural Superiority of Women* (1953), *Man's Most Dangerous Myth: The Fallacy of Race* (1964), *The Nature of Human Aggression* (1976) and *The Peace of the World* (1986). He held posts at numerous universities, including Princeton University.

Montagu, Elizabeth, *née* **Robinson** 1720–1800 •*English writer and society leader*• In 1742 she married Edward Montagu, grandson of the 1st Earl of Sandwich and cousin of Edward Wortley Montagu (husband of Lady **Mary Wortley Montagu**). The first of the bluestockings, with £10,000 a year, she established a salon in Mayfair which became the heart of London social and literary life for people like **Samuel Johnson**, **David Garrick**, **Joshua Reynolds** and many others. She wrote an essay on **Shakespeare** (1768).

Montagu, Lady Mary Wortley 1689–1762 •*English writer*• A colorful, eccentric feminist, the eldest daughter of the 5th Earl (later Duke) of Kingston, she was a well-known society hostess, who had a celebrated quarrel with **Alexander Pope**. From 1716 to 1718 her husband was ambassador in Constantinople (Istanbul) and her letters from there and from Vienna were the basis of her contemporary reputation.

Montaigne, Michel Eyquem de 1533–92 •*French essayist*• He was born at the Château de Montaigne, Périgord, the third son of the Seigneur de Montaigne. As an experiment in humanist upbringing, his parents exposed him to no language but Latin until he was six. He then spent seven years at the Collège de Guienne in Bordeaux, studied law, and for 13 years was a city counselor. A translation (1569) of the *Natural Theology* of a 15th-century professor at Toulouse supplied the text for his *Apologie de Raymon Sebond* ("Apologia for Raymond Sebond"), in which he exhibited the full scope of his own skeptical philosophy. In 1571 he succeeded to the family estate at Château de Montaigne, and adopted the life of a country gentleman. He also began his *Essais* (1572–80 and 1588, Eng trans *Essays*, 1603) on the ideas and personalities of the time, which introduced a new literary genre and provided a major contribution to literary history.

Montale, Eugenio 1896–1981 •*Italian poet and Nobel Prize winner*• Born in Genoa, he worked as a journalist and critic, and was an early opponent of Fascism. World War I left him with a pessimism which permeates his writing. He was the leading poet of the modern Italian "Hermetic" school, and his primary concern was with language and meaning. His works include *Ossi di seppia* (1925, "The Cuttlefish Bones"), *Le occasioni* (1939, "Opportunities"), *Finisterre* (1943, "Finistère"), *Satura* (1962, Eng trans *Satura: Five Poems*, 1969) and *Xenia* (1966, Eng trans 1970). He was awarded the Nobel Prize for literature in 1975.

Montalembert, Charles René Forbes de, Comte de 1810–70 •*French historian and politician*• Born in London, the eldest son of a noble French émigré and his English wife, he was educated at Fulham and the Collège Ste Barbe. In 1830 he eagerly joined the Abbé Lamennais and Henri Lacordaire in *L'Avenir*, a Catholic liberal newspaper. His great speech (1848) on Switzerland is a famous protest against tyranny. After the February Revolution (1848) he was elected a member of the National Assembly, and supported Louis Napoleon (**Napoleon III**) until the confiscation of the Orléans property, when he became a determined opponent of the imperial regime. He wrote *De l'avenir politique de l'Angleterre* (1856, "The Political Future of England") and other works attempting to reconcile Catholicism and liberalism.

Montana, Joe 1956– •*US football player*• Born in New Eagle, Pennsylvania, he joined the San Francisco 49ers in 1979, and played on their winning Super Bowl teams in 1982, 1985, 1989, and 1990. He won the Super Bowl Most Valuable Player award in 1982, 1985, and 1990. He played for the Kansas City Chiefs in 1993 to 1995.

Montand, Yves, *originally* **Ivo Livi** 1921–91 •*French actor and singer*• Born in Monsummano in Tuscany, Italy, he worked at a variety of jobs before performing as a singer and impressionist in Marseilles and Paris. He was a star attraction with his one-man show, and his film career temporarily blossomed with *Le salaire de la peur* (1953, *The Wages of Fear*). His acting reputation was enhanced by an association with the director Costa-Gavras and films such as *Z* (1968) and *L'Aveu* (1970, *The Confession*), which also reflected his sympathy for a variety of left-wing causes. Married to actress Simone Signoret (1921–1985) from 1951, he became a distinguished elder statesman of the French film industry, in productions including *Jean de Florette* (1986), *Manon des Sources* (1986) and *IP5* (1991).

Montano *See* **Arias, Benito**

Montcalm, Louis Joseph, Marquis de Montcalm Gezan de Saint Véran 1712–59 •*French soldier*• He was born near Nîmes. A soldier at 15, in the Seven Years' War (1756–63) he commanded the French troops in North America in 1756. In 1758 he successfully defended Ticonderoga with a small force, won Louisburg and Fort Duquesne, and moved to defend Quebec against a British attack. In 1759 General **Wolfe** ascended the St Lawrence, and finally, in a battle on the Plains of Abraham, drove the French in retreat from the city. Montcalm tried to rally his force, but was mortally wounded.

Montespan, Françoise Athénaïs, Marquise de, *known as* **Madame de Montespan** 1641–1707 •*French courtier*• Born in Tonnay-Charente, the daughter of the Duc de Mortemart, she married the Marquis de Montespan (1663). In c. 1668 she became the mistress of **Louis XIV**. The marquis was exiled to Guyenne, and his marriage was annulled (1676). The Marquise de Montespan reigned supreme until 1682, and bore the king seven children, who were legitimized, but she was then replaced by Madame **de Maintenon**, the governess of her children. In 1691 she left the court, and retired to a convent.

Montesquieu, Charles-Louis de Secondat, Baron de la Brède et de 1689–1755 •*French philosopher and jurist*• Born at the Château de la Brède, near Bordeaux, he became counselor of the *parlement* of Bordeaux (1714) and its president (1716). He discharged the duties of his office faithfully, but until his poor eyesight hindered him, preferred scientific research. His first great literary success was the *Lettres persanes* (1721, "Persian Letters"), a satirical description of French society. Weary of routine work, he sold his office (1726) and moved to Paris. For three years he traveled extensively in order to study political and social institutions. His best-known work, the monumental *De l'esprit des lois* (1748, Eng trans *The Spirit of Laws*, 1750), a dialogue on despotism, was published anonymously and put on the index of prohibited books, but went through 22 editions in less than two years. A comparative study of legal and political issues, it had an immense influence.

“ ”

Les lois inutiles affaiblissent les lois nécessaires.
Useless laws weaken the necessary ones.
1748 ***De l'esprit des lois****, volume 29, chapter 16.*

Montessori, Maria 1870–1952 •*Italian physician and educator*• Born in Rome, the first woman in Italy to receive a medical degree (1894), she founded a school for children with learning disabilities (1899–1901), and developed a system of education for children of three to six based on spontaneity of expression and freedom from restraint. The system was later worked out for older children, and applied in Montessori schools throughout the world. She opened the first Montessori school for children in the slums of Rome in 1907.

Monteux, Pierre 1875–1964 •*US conductor*• Born in Paris and trained at the Paris Conservatoire, he was one of the 20th-century's leading conductors. From 1911 to 1914, and in 1917, he conducted **Sergei Diaghilev**'s Ballets Russes in Paris, leading the world premières of **Igor Stravinsky**'s *Petrushka* (1911) and *The Rite of Spring* (1913, *Vesna Svyashchennaya*) and **Maurice Ravel**'s *Daphnis and Chloé* (1912). After serving in the army in World War I, he went to the US, where he conducted in New York and Boston before returning to Europe in 1924. After founding and directing the Orchestre Symphonique de Paris between 1929 and 1938, he took over the newly organized San Francisco Symphony Orchestra in 1936, and in 1941 established a summer school for student conductors at Hanover, New Hampshire. He became a US citizen in 1942. From 1960 until his death he was principal conductor of the London Symphony Orchestra.

Monteverdi, Claudio 1567–1643 •*Italian composer*• Born in Cremona, he became a proficient violist and learned the art of composition. In about 1590 he was appointed court musician to the Duke of Mantua, who appointed him maestro di capella in 1602. In 1613 he took a similar post at St Mark's, Venice, where he remained until his death. Monteverdi left no purely instrumental compositions. His eight books of madrigals (1587–1638) contain some boldly experimental harmonies which brought criticism from academic quarters but showcased the composer's originality. His first opera, *Orfeo* (1607), with its programmatic use of orchestral sonorities, its dramatic continuity and the obbligato character of the accompaniment, marked a considerable advance in the evolution of the genre. The two surviving operas of his later period, *Il ritorno d'Ulisse in patria* (1641, "Ulysses's Return to His Native Land") and *L'Incoronazione di Poppea* (1642, "The Coronation of Poppea"), both written when he was in his seventies, show further development toward the baroque style and foreshadow the use of the leitmotif. His greatest contribution to church music is the *Mass* and *Vespers* of the Virgin (1610), another innovative work. Other new features which he introduced were the orchestral ritornello, and the use of tremolo and pizzicato.

Montez, Lola, *originally* **Maria Délores Gilbert** 1818–61 •*US dancer*• Born in Limerick, Ireland, she became a dancer in London in 1843. While touring Europe, she went to Munich (1846), where she had an affair with the eccentric artist-king, **Ludwig I** of Bavaria, a great boost to her career as a dancer. After a tour of the US (1848) she decided to settle in California.

Montezuma or **Moctezuma II** 1466–1520 •*Aztec emperor*• The ninth Aztec emperor to rule Mexico before the Spanish invasion, and a distinguished warrior and legislator, he succeeded to the title (1502) and became absolute monarch of a vast empire. When the Spanish conquistadors arrived under the leadership of **Hernán Cortés**, he gave them rich gifts in the belief that they might be incarnations of the white god Quetzalcoatl and reluctantly received them in his palace at Tenochtitlán. They, in turn, imprisoned him and made themselves rulers instead. He died before their conquest of Mexico was complete.

Montfort, Simon IV de, Earl of Leicester c. 1160–1218 •*Norman crusader*• He took part in the Fourth Crusade (1202–04); he also undertook a crusade against the Albingenses (1208) and fell at the Siege of Toulouse.

Montfort, Simon V de, Earl of Leicester c. 1208–65 •*English soldier and politician*• He married (1238) **Henry III** of England's youngest sister, Eleanor. In 1248, as King's Deputy in Gascony, he suppressed disaffection with a heavy hand. In 1253 he returned to England, where famine and taxation had exhausted the country. Prince Edward (the future **Edward I**) plotted with the subtenants, and the barons quarreled among themselves until de Montfort became their leader against the king in 1261. After varying success, he defeated the king's army at Lewes (1264). De Montfort, the Earl of **Gloucester**, and the bishop of Hereford were appointed to preside over a parliament in 1265. This, the Model Parliament, held the germ of modern parliaments. But the barons soon grew dissatisfied with the rule of "Simon the Righteous," and Prince Edward combined with Gloucester to defeat Simon at Evesham, where he was killed. His father was **Simon IV de Montfort**.

Montgolfier, Joseph Michel 1740–1810 and **Jacques Étienne** 1745–99 •*French aeronautical inventors*• Brothers, they were born in Annonay, near Lyons, the sons of a paper manufacturer. Joseph developed an early interest in science, while his younger brother became a successful architect before joining the family firm. After some preliminary model experiments, they constructed a balloon (1782) whose bag was lifted by lighting a cauldron of paper beneath it. The world's first manned balloon flight, of $7\frac{1}{2}$ miles (12.1 km) in less than half an hour, at a height of 3,000 feet (915 m), carrying Pilatre de Rozier and the Marquis d'Arlandes, took place in November 1783. Their achievement created great public interest, and many other inventors attempted to follow their example, not always with equal success. Joseph later became interested in other applications of science, inventing a type of parachute, a calorimeter and the widely used hydraulic ram, a device for raising small quantities of water to a considerable height. He was subsequently elected to the French Academy of Sciences and was created a Chevalier of the Legion of Honor by **Napoleon I**.

Montgomerie, Colin Stuart 1963– •*Scottish golfer*• Born in Glasgow, he turned professional in 1988 after an amateur career that included two Walker Cup appearances (1985, 1987) and victories in the 1985 Scottish Strokeplay Championship and the 1987 Scottish Amateur Championship. He was Europe's top golfer from 1993 to 1999 inclusive and has won numerous tournaments, including the PGA Championships (1998–2000). He also played in the Ryder Cup teams of 1991, 1993, 1995, 1997 and 1999 and was selected again for the (postponed) 2001 tournament.

Montgomery (of Alamein), Bernard Law Montgomery, 1st Viscount 1887–1976 •*English soldier*• He was born in London, the son of Bishop Montgomery, and was educated at St Paul's School and the Royal Military College, Sandhurst. He served with the Royal Warwickshire Regiment in World War I. In World War II he commanded the 3rd Division, with which he shared the retreat to Dunkirk. In North Africa in 1941 he commanded the 8th Army, restoring their bruised confidence and the will to win. Conforming to General **Harold Alexander**'s strategic plans, he defeated **Erwin Rommel** at the Battle of El Alamein (October 1942). This was followed up by a series of victories that eventually drove the Axis forces back to Tunis. His subsequent activities in Sicily and Italy were solid, if somewhat pedestrian. Appointed Commander for the Ground Forces for the Normandy invasion in 1944, he deliberately attracted the main weight of the German counteroffensive to the British flank, thus freeing the US armored formations to inaugurate the joint drive across France and Belgium. His attempt to roll up the German right flank by way of Arnhem (September 1944) ended in disaster, but his timely intervention helped materially to frustrate **Karl von Rundstedt**'s surprise offensive of December 1944. He accepted the German capitulation on Lüneburg Heath, and was commander of the British occupied zone in Germany (1945–46) and Chief of the Imperial General Staff (CIGS) in 1946–48. He was deputy Supreme Commander of NATO forces (1951–58).

Montgomery, L(ucy) M(aud) 1874–1942 •*Canadian novelist*• She was born in Clifton, Prince Edward Island, and graduated as a schoolteacher from Prince of Wales College, Charlottetown. After studying at Dalhousie University, Halifax, Nova Scotia, she returned to Cavendish to spend the next 13 years caring for her grandmother. Her first book was the phenomenally successful *Anne of Green Gables* (1908), the story of an orphan girl adopted in error for a boy by an elderly brother and sister. She followed it with several sequels. Her works are sometimes highly satirical, and at her best she captures memorably the mysteries and terrors of early childhood.

Montherlant, Henri Millon de 1896–1972 •*French novelist and playwright*• Born in Neuilly-sur-Seine, he was severely wounded in World War I, after which he traveled in Spain, Africa and Italy. A man of athletic interests, he advocates, in both his plays and novels, the overcoming of the conflicts of life by vigorous action, and disdains the consolation of bourgeois sentiment. His stylish novels include the largely autobiographical *La relève du matin* (1920, "The Morning Relief"). Among his plays are *Malatesta* (1946), *Don Juan* (1958) and *Le Cardinal d'Espagne* (1960, "The Cardinal of Spain").

Montpensier, Anne Marie Louise d'Orléans, Duchesse de, *known as* **La Grande Mademoiselle** 1627–93 •*French noblewoman*• The niece of **Louis XIII**, she was born in Paris, and supported her father and the Prince de **Condé** in the second Fronde (1651–52), where she commanded an army that occupied Orleans and later the Bastille. She wrote two novels and some literary portraits.

Montrose, James Graham, Marquis of 1612–50 •*Scottish general*• After traveling in Italy, France and the Low Countries, he returned in the year of the "Service-book tumults" (1637) in Edinburgh (see **Jenny Geddes**), and was one of the four noblemen who drew up the National Covenant in support of Presbyterianism. He served in the Covenanter army in 1640, but transferred his allegiance to **Charles I**, and led the Royalist army to victory at Tippermuir (1644). After the Royalist defeat at Naseby (1645), his army became disaffected, and his remaining force was defeated at Philiphaugh. He fled to Europe, returning to Scotland after Charles's execution to avenge his death, but his army was largely lost by shipwreck, and the remnant defeated at Invercharron (1650). He was captured and taken to Edinburgh, where he was hanged in the High Street.

Moon, Sun Myung 1920– •*South Korean religious leader*• In 1954 he founded the Unification Church, an amalgam of Christianity and the teachings of its self-declared prophet, Moon. In 1973 he moved its headquarters from South Korea to the US and the organization now has branches and properties worldwide. Known for holding mass weddings, he and his followers have been accused of brainwashing converts and of financial misdealings, and in 1984 Moon was convicted of tax evasion under US law and was sentenced to 18 months in prison.

Moorcock, Michael 1939– •*English novelist*• Born in Mitcham, Surrey, he became, at 17, editor of *Tarzan Adventures* and was a regular contributor to the *Sexton Blake Library*. From the mid-1960s onward, he was editor (1964–71), then publisher, of the influential science fiction series *New Worlds*. Much of his fiction has been organized in cycles. Perhaps his best-known sequence, starring the morally and sexually ambiguous "Jerry Cornelius," started with *The Final Programme* (1968). He introduced "Karl Glogauer" in *Behold the Man* (1969), a controversial reworking of the Crucifixion. A further enormous mythic cycle began with *The Eternal Champion* in 1970 and another with *Byzantium Endures* (1981). He has also written in non-sci-fi mode, such as *Mother London* (1988).

Moore, Archie, *originally* **Archibald Lee Wright** 1913–98 •*US boxer*• Born in Benoit, Wisconsin, he became a professional boxer in 1936, and eventually, in 1952, won the world light-heavyweight title by defeating Joey Maxim. He held the title for 10 years (1952–62), when he retired at the age of 49. He also challenged for the heavyweight title, despite a lack of weight and height, and in 1955 gave **Rocky Marciano** a hard fight before being knocked out. He also fought Floyd Patterson for the title in 1956. Of his 229 fights, he won more than half inside the distance, and ranks high in any list of the world's greatest-ever fighters.

Moore, Bobby (Robert) 1941–93 •*English soccer player*• Born in Barking, Essex, in a long career with West Ham (1958–74) and later Fulham (1974–77), he played 1,000 matches at senior level, winning a Football Association Cup-winner's medal in 1964 and a European Cup-winner's medal in 1965. He was capped 108 times (107 in succession), 90 of them as captain. He played in the World Cup finals in Chile in 1962, captained the victorious England team in the 1966 World Cup, and led the team with some success in Mexico in 1970. He was sports editor for the *Sunday Sport* from 1986 to 1990, when he became a commentator.

Moore, Brian 1921–99 •*Canadian novelist*• He was born in Belfast, Northern Ireland, and served with the British Ministry of War Transport during the latter stages of World War II. After the war he worked for the United Nations in Europe before emigrating to Canada in 1948, where he became a journalist and adopted Canadian citizenship. He spent time in New York before moving to California. Though he wrote thrillers under the pseudonym Michael Bryan, he is best known for novels like *The Feast of Lupercal* (1957) and *The Temptation of Eileen Hughes* (1981). Particularly admired for his portrayal of women, he won the Author's Club First Novel award with *The Lonely Passion of Judith Hearne* (1955). *The Great Victorian Collection* (1975) was awarded the James Tait Black Memorial Prize, and both *The Doctor's Wife* (1976) and *Black Robe* (1985, filmed 1991) were shortlisted for the Booker Prize. Later works include *The Statement* (1996).

Moore, Christy 1945– •*Irish folk singer*• Born in Dublin, he began as a solo singer, working the folk clubs and pubs between bouts of manual laboring in both Ireland and England. He was a cofounder of Planxty in 1971, and then Moving Hearts in 1981, two of the most influential groups in Irish music. He has taken a high-profile campaigning stance on controversial issues like nuclear power and the political situation in Northern Ireland (and elsewhere) in his music, mixed with a great deal of sometimes surreal humor.

Moore, Demi, *originally surnamed* **Guynes** 1962– •*US actress*• Born in Roswell, New Mexico, she started her career in modeling and small television roles. Her screen career began in the early 1980s, but it was with blockbusters such as *Ghost* (1990), *Indecent Proposal* (1993) and *Disclosure* (1994) that she achieved international stardom, becoming Hollywood's then highest-paid actress in 1996 with her $12-million role in *Striptease*.

Moore, Dudley Stuart John 1935–2002 •*English actor*• Born in Dagenham, Essex, he studied music at Oxford. In 1960, he joined fellow Oxbridge graduates in *Beyond the Fringe* at the Edinburgh Festival, then in London and on Broadway. He formed a satirical comedy partnership with **Peter Cook** that flourished on television in *Not Only ... But Also* (1965–71) and in such films as *The Wrong Box* (1966). He eventually went his own way and enjoyed belated Hollywood success as the middle-aged hero of comedies such as *10* (1979) and *Arthur* (1980). An acclaimed pianist and jazz performer, he also composed the music score for a number of films and presented the series *Concerto!* (1993). His career was curtailed in later years after he was diagnosed with the degenerative disease progressive supranuclear palsy.

Moore, Francis 1657–1715 •*English astrologer*• Born in Bridgnorth, Shropshire, he practiced medicine in London, and in 1700 started "Old Moore's" astrological almanac.

Moore, George Augustus 1852–1933 •*Irish writer*• Born in Ballyglass, County Mayo, the son of a landed gentleman, he was educated at Oscott College, Birmingham, and intended for the army, but soon became an agnostic, abandoned a military career and lived a bohemian life in London and Paris, until **Zola**'s example revealed to him his true métier as a novelist of the Realist school. Moore has been credited with introducing this type of fiction into Great Britain with novels of low life such as *A Modern Lover* (1883). During the Boer War he sought exile in Ireland, where he wrote *Evelyn Innes* (1898) and *Sister Teresa* (1901), which reflect his increasing interest in love, theology and the arts, and the stories in *An Untilled Field* (1903), which mark a move away from his earlier "sordid" realism. He returned to England early in the century and published his confessions, *Memoirs of My Dead Life* (1906), and the trilogy *Hail and Farewell*, in which he wrote about his friends and his associates in setting up the Abbey Theatre in Dublin, particularly **W B Yeats**.

Moore, G(eorge) E(dward) 1873–1958 •*English empiricist philosopher*• Born in London, he was educated at Trinity College, Cambridge, where a fellow student, **Bertrand Russell**, helped persuade him to switch from classics to philosophy. After some years of private study in Edinburgh and London, he returned to Cambridge to teach philosophy (1911) and became Professor of Mental Philosophy and Logic (1925–39). After a brief, early infatuation with the prevailing Hegelian idealism of **John M'Taggart** and others, in 1903 he published an article, "The Refutation of Idealism," and a book, the celebrated *Principia Ethica* ("Ethical Principles"). These marked an important change of direction and the effective revival, in a new form, of a British empiricist philosophical tradition, emphasizing in particular the intellectual virtues of clarity and precision, and the analysis of ordinary concepts and arguments. *Principia Ethica* analyzed the moral concept of goodness and commended the value of friendship and aesthetic experience; it was a major influence on the Bloomsbury Group. Other works include *Ethics* (1916), *Philosophical Studies* (1922), *Some Main Problems of Philosophy* (1953) and *Philosophical Papers* (1959).

Moore, Henry Spencer 1898–1986 •*English sculptor*• He was born in Castleford, Yorkshire, the son of a coal miner. He studied at Leeds and at the Royal College of Art, London, where he taught sculpture (1924–31); from 1931 to 1939 he taught at the Chelsea School of Art. He traveled in France, Italy, Spain, the US and Greece, and was an official war artist from 1940 to 1942. During this time he produced a famous series of drawings of air-raid shelter scenes. In 1948 he won the International Sculpture prize at the Venice biennale. He is recognized as one of the most original and powerful modern sculptors, producing figures and groups in a semiabstract style based on the organic forms and undulating rhythms found in landscape and natural rocks, and influenced by African and Mexican art. His interest lay in the spatial, three-dimensional quality of sculpture, an effect he achieved by the piercing of his figures. His principal commissions included the *Madonna and Child* in St Matthew's Church, Northampton (1943–44), the decorative frieze (1952) on the Time-Life building in London, and the massive reclining figures for the UNESCO building in Paris (1958) and the Lincoln Center in New York (1965).

“ ”

Sculpture in stone should look honestly like stone ... to make it look like flesh and blood, hair and dimples is coming down to the level of the stage conjuror.

1930 In the ***Architectural Association Journal***.

Moore, Sir (John) Jeremy 1928– •*English soldier*• He joined the Royal Marines (RM) at the age of 19 and saw service in Great Britain, Brunei and Australia in a variety of roles, including that of commandant of the RM School of Music. He had reached the rank of major general in the commando forces by 1979, and in 1982, when the decision was made to recapture the Falkland Islands from Argentina, he was made Commander of Land Forces. His success in the brief campaign brought him unexpected fame as well as a knighthood.

Moore, Sir John 1761–1809 •*Scottish soldier*• Born in Glasgow, he served in the American Revolution from 1779 to 1783, the Revolutionary War in France, the West Indies (1796), Ireland (1798) and Holland (1799). He was in Egypt in 1801, and in 1802 served in Sicily and Sweden. He is remembered for his command of the English army in Spain (1808–09) during the Peninsular War, where he was forced to retreat to Corunna (La Coruña). There he defeated a French attack, but Moore himself was mortally wounded in the moment of victory. His burial was immortalized in the poem "The Burial of Sir John Moore" by Charles Wolfe (1791–1823).

Moore, Julianne, *originally* **Julie Anne Smith** 1961– •*US actress*• Born in Fayetteville, North Carolina, she studied at Boston University. She began her career on the stage in the late 1980s and moved to film in the early 1990s, appearing in such films as *The Hand That Rocks the Cradle* (1992) and *Surviving Picasso* (1996). She has received Oscar nominations for Best Actress in a supporting role for *Boogie Nights* (1997) and *The Hours* (2002), as well as for Best Actress in a leading role for *The End of the Affair* (1999) and *Far from Heaven* (2002).

Moore, Marianne Craig 1887–1972 •*US poet*• Born in St Louis, Missouri, she was educated at Bryn Mawr College and Carlisle Commercial College in Pennsylvania. She taught commercial studies at Carlisle and was a branch librarian in New York (1921–25). She contributed to the Imagist magazine, *The Egoist*, from 1915, and edited *The Dial* from 1926. She was acquainted with important modernists like **Ezra Pound** and **T S Eliot**, but New York was her milieu, not Paris, and she associated with the Greenwich Village group including **William Carlos Williams** and **Wallace Stevens**. Idiosyncratic and a consummate stylist, she ranks high among the US poets of the 20th century. Editions of her work include *Collected Poems* (1951, Pulitzer Prize) and *The Complete Poems* (1967).

Moore, Mary Tyler 1936– •*US actress*• Born in Brooklyn, New York, she trained as a dancer. Small acting roles followed, and she was seen in the series *The Dick Van Dyke Show* (1961–66), which won her Emmy awards in 1964 and 1965. She starred on Broadway in *Breakfast at Tiffany's* (1966) but returned to television with the long-running *The Mary Tyler Moore Show* (1970–77; Emmy awards 1973, 1974, 1976). She went on to win an Emmy for *First, You Cry* (1978), a Tony Award for *Whose Life Is It Anyway?* (1980) and an Academy Award nomination for the film *Ordinary People* (1980). She had a rare chance to display her comic gifts on the large screen in *Flirting with Disaster* (1996).

Moore, Sir Patrick Alfred Caldwell 1923– •*English astronomer, author and broadcaster*• Born in Pinner, Middlesex, and educated privately owing to illness, he served in the RAF during World War II as a navigator in Bomber Command (1940–45). He began his perennially popular television series, *The Sky at Night*, in 1957, and it has continued since that time. He was director of Armagh Planetarium (1965–68) and has written more than 60 books, including *Atlas of the Universe* (1970, revised 1995) and *The Wondering Astronomer* (2000). He was made an Honorary Fellow of the Royal Society and was knighted in 2001.

Moore, Roger George 1927– •*English actor*• Born in London, he studied painting before making his film debut as an extra in *Perfect Strangers* (1945). He appeared in small roles on stage and in films prior to national service in the army. Subsequently performing in the US, he appeared in the Hollywood film *The Last Time I Saw Paris* (1954). On television his boyish good looks, smooth manner and athletic prowess won him stardom as the action-man hero of such series as *The Persuaders* (1971–72) and, most especially, *The Saint* (1962–68). His own wittiest critic, he brought a lightweight insouciance to the role of James Bond in seven films between *Live and Let Die* (1973) and *A View to a Kill* (1985). Now a goodwill ambassador for UNICEF, his more recent films include *The Quest* (1996).

Moore, Stanford 1913–82 •*US biochemist and Nobel Prize winner*• Born in Chicago, he studied chemistry at Vanderbilt University and the University of Wisconsin, and spent his career at the Rockefeller Institute (1939–82). He is best known for inventing, with **William Stein**, a chromatographic method for the identification and quantification of amino acids in mixtures of proteins or from physiological tissues (1950). By 1958 they had also developed an ingenious automated analyzer to carry out all the steps of the analysis of the structure of RNA on a small sample, and, in a study of streptococcus, Moore and Stein found the first example of convergent evolution at the molecular level—two enzymes of similar function arising by different evolutionary paths. They also complemented the structural studies of **Christian Anfinsen** (1954–56), and all three shared the Nobel Prize for chemistry in 1972.

Moore, Thomas 1779–1852 •*Irish poet and composer*• Born in Dublin, he was educated at Trinity College, Dublin, and became a lawyer. His translation of **Anacreon** (1800) proved a great success, and was followed by *Poems* (1801), the earlier of the *Irish Melodies* (1807–34), *The Twopenny Postbag* (1812) and, in 1817, *Lalla Rookh*. In 1819, to avoid arrest, Moore went to Italy and then to Paris. He returned in 1822 to Wiltshire and published *The Loves of the Angels* (1823) and a novel, *The Epicurean* (1827), and wrote biographies of **Richard Brinsley Sheridan** and **Byron**.

Morata, Olympia 1526–55 •*Italian humanist scholar and poet*• She was the daughter of the poet and scholar Pellegrino Morato. She gave public lectures at age 15, but, having married a German physician, Andreas Grundler, in 1548, she followed him to Germany, became a Protestant, and died penniless, leaving numerous Latin and Greek poems, a treatise on **Cicero**, dialogues and letters.

Moravia, Alberto, *pseudonym of* **Alberto Pincherle** 1907–90 •*Italian novelist and short-story writer*• He was born in Rome. Before the outbreak of World War II, he traveled extensively and lived for a time in the US when out of favor with the Fascist government. His first novel, *Gli indifferenti* (1929, Eng trans *The Indifferent Ones*, 1932), which achieved popular success, contains many of the ingredients of his later novels and short stories, and portrays the decadent bourgeois society of Rome, its preoccupation with sex and money, and the total incapability of action of even the intellectuals. *La romana* (1947, Eng trans *The Woman of Rome*, 1949) also encompasses socioeconomic problems of the working class, and in *Raconti romani* (1954, Eng trans *Roman Tales*, 1956) he turns his critical eye to the corruption of the lower middle class. His later works include *L'attenzione* (1965, Eng trans *The Lie*, 1966) and *L'uomo che guarda* (1985, Eng trans *The Voyeur*, 1986).

Moray, James Stewart, 1st Earl of 1531–70 •*Regent of Scotland*• The second illegitimate son of **James V** of Scotland and Lady Margaret Douglas, he was made prior *in commendam* of St Andrews (1538), and was educated at the university there. He emerged as one of the leaders of the Protestant Lords of the Congregation whose revolt produced the Scottish Reformation of 1560. In 1561 he visited his half sister, **Mary Queen of Scots**, in France, and after she returned to Scotland he defended her right to attend mass in her private chapel, and fended off the protests of **John Knox**. He was granted the earldoms of Mar and Moray (1562), which resulted in the revolt of the Catholic dissident the 4th Earl of Huntly. He remained the queen's chief adviser until her marriage to Lord **Darnley** (1565), which triggered an abortive coup by him and the **Hamilton**s and his flight to England. He returned to Edinburgh on the day after **David Rizzio**'s murder (1566) and was rehabilitated. His foreknowledge of the plot to murder Darnley (1567) induced another diplomatic absence, and he was in France when Mary was overthrown and imprisoned at Lochleven. He returned to become regent for Mary's infant son, **James VI**. He was shot as he rode through Linlithgow by James Hamilton of Bothwellhaugh, and died of his wounds soon after.

Mordecai c. 5th century BC •*Biblical character*• He is described in the Book of Esther as a Jew in exile in Persia (Iran) who cared for his orphaned cousin Esther and gained the favor of King **Xerxes I** after uncovering a plot against him. He used his subsequent influence to protect Jews from an edict issued against them, an event commemorated by the annual Jewish feast of Purim.

More, Kenneth Gilbert 1914–82 •*English actor*• Born in Gerrards Cross, Buckinghamshire, he turned to performing after working as a stagehand at the Windmill Theatre, London. A naval lieutenant during World War II, he appeared in the West End in *Power Without Glory* (1947) and gained extensive television and film experience as a reliable supporting performer. He later became one of the most popular British film stars of the 1950s, appearing in films such as *Genevieve* (1953), *Doctor in the House* (1954) and *Reach for the Sky* (1956). His career suffered with the decline of the British film industry, but he performed on television in *The Forsyte Saga* (1967–68) and *Father Brown* (1974) and had success on stage.

More, Sir Thomas, St 1478–1535 •*English politician and scholar*• He was born in London, the son of a judge. Educated at Oxford under John Colet (c. 1467–1519) and **Thomas Linacre**, he completed his legal studies at New Inn and Lincoln's Inn, was reader for three years in Furnival's Inn, and spent the next four years in the Charterhouse in "devotion and prayer." During the last years of **Henry VII** he became Under-Sheriff of London and a member of parliament. Introduced to **Henry VIII** through **Thomas Wolsey**, he rose to become Chancellor of the Duchy of Lancaster (1525). He was Speaker of the House of Commons, and was sent on missions to the French courts of **Francis I** and **Charles V**. On the fall of Wolsey in 1529, More, against his own strongest wish, was appointed Lord Chancellor. He executed his office with a primitive virtue and simplicity, but displayed particular harshness in his sentences for religious opinions. He sympathized with John Colet and **Erasmus** in their desire for a more rational theology and for radical reform in the manners of the clergy, but like them he felt no promptings to break with the historic Church. He saw with displeasure the successive steps which led Henry to the final schism from Rome. In 1532 he resigned the chancellorship. In 1534 Henry was declared head of the English Church, and More's steadfast refusal to recognize any other head of the Church than the pope led to his sentence for high treason after a harsh imprisonment of over a year. Still refusing to recant, he was beheaded. By his Latin *Utopia* (1516, Eng trans 1556), More takes his place with the most eminent humanists of the Renaissance. He was canonized in 1935. His feast day is July 9.

“ ”

Two evils—greed and faction—are the destruction of all justice.

1516 (English translation 1556) ***Utopia****, book 2.*

Moreau, Gustave 1826–98 •*French painter and teacher*• Born in Paris, he studied at the École des Beaux-Arts, Paris. An eccentric Symbolist, he painted colorful but usually rather sinister scenes from ancient mythology and the Bible (such as *Salome*, 1876). In 1892 he was appointed Professor of Painting at the École des Beaux-Arts; his pupils included **Georges Rouault** and **Henri Matisse**.

Moreau, Jean Victor 1761–1813 •*French general*• Born in Morlaix, he studied law, but at the Revolution in 1789 commanded the volunteers from Rennes, and in 1794 was made a general of division. He took part, under Charles Pichegru, in reducing Belgium and the Netherlands. He drove the Austrians back to the Danube, but was forced to retreat and was later deprived of his command (1797). In 1798 he took command in Italy and skillfully conducted the defeated troops to France. The party of the Abbé **Sieyès** offered him the dictatorship, but he declined it, instead assisting **Napoleon I** in the coup d'état of the 18th Brumaire. Subsequently, he commanded the army of the Rhine and won the decisive Battle of Hohenlinden. Napoleon, grown jealous of Moreau, accused him of sharing in the plot of Georges Cadoudal against Napoleon, and he was banished, settling in New Jersey. In 1813 he joined the Russian service and was fatally wounded by a French cannonball at Dresden.

Moreau, Jeanne 1928– •*French actress and director*• Born in Paris, she studied at the Conservatoire National D'Art Dramatique. An association with the directors of the French Nouvelle Vague (New Wave) brought her recognition as an intense, hypnotic film actress, capable of immersing her own personality in a succession of generally world-weary, sensual characterizations. Her most famous films include *Les Amants* (1958, *The Lovers*), *Jules et Jim* (1961, "Jules and Jim"), *Le Journal d'une Femme de Chambre* (1964, *Diary of a Chambermaid*) and *Viva Maria* (1965). Occasional English-language ventures met with little acclaim, but she proved herself a formidable director with *Lumière* (1976) and *L'Adolescente* (1978, "The Adolescent").

Morecambe and Wise, *properly* **Eric Morecambe**, *originally* **John Eric Bartholomew** 1926–84 and **Ernie Wise**, *originally* **Ernest Wiseman** 1925–99 •*English comedians*• Eric was born in Morecambe and, having appeared in workingmen's clubs since the age of 11, teamed up in 1941 with fellow entertainer Ernie in the touring stage "discovery" show *Youth Takes a Bow*. They made their West End debut in the revue *Strike a New Note* in 1943. In 1947 they teamed up again and, as Morecambe and Wise, worked in music halls, summer shows, pantomimes, radio, films and television. They were the most successful double act in the history of British television, known primarily for *The Morecambe and Wise Show* (1961–83) and hugely popular Christmas specials. Their films were not successful. Despite Eric's death in 1984, Ernie acted in the West End stage shows *The Mystery of Edwin Drood* and *Run for Your Wife*, and the US television comedy series *Too Close for Comfort*.

Morel *See* **Deschamps, Eustache**

Morelos (y Pavón), José María 1765–1815 •*Mexican revolutionary*• Born in Michoacán, New Spain, he was a mestizo and spent his early life as a muleteer before entering the priesthood. He then joined **Miguel Hidalgo** in the struggle for Mexican independence, becoming the leader in the south and reorganizing the insurgents (1810–13). In opposition to the Spanish Constitution of Cádiz, he convened a "sovereign congress" at Chilpancingo which declared independence at Apatzingán (October 1814). This first Mexican constitution was republican, and abolished the fuero and slavery. Isolated and trapped by royalist forces under viceroy Felix Calleja, he was captured and executed in Mexico City. He was one of the founders of the radical liberal tradition of Mexican politics.

Moresby, John 1830–1922 •*English naval commander and explorer*• He was born in Allerton, Somerset. He conducted exploration and survey work in New Guinea, where he discovered the natural harbor now fronted by Port Moresby, which was named after him.

Morgagni, Giovanni Battista 1682–1771 •*Italian physician*• Born in Forli, he graduated in Bologna, and taught anatomy there and later in Padua. His great work *De sedibus et causis morborum per anatomen indagatis* (1761, "The Seats and Causes of Diseases Investigated by Anatomy") was not published until he was 80. Case by case, Morgagni described the clinical aspects of illness during the patient's life, then detailed the postmortem findings, and his book may be seen as a crucial stimulus to the rise of morbid anatomy. Furthermore, Morgagni was the first to delineate syphilitic tumors of the brain and tuberculosis of the kidney. He grasped that where only one side of the body is stricken with paralysis, the lesion lies on the opposite side of the brain. His explorations of the female genitals, of the glands of the trachea, and of the male urethra also broke new ground.

Morgan, Barbara Brooks, *née* **Johnson** 1900–92 •*US photographer and writer*• Born in Buffalo, Kansas, she studied art at UCLA. She then painted and taught art in San Fernando (1923–24) and at UCLA (1925–30). From 1935 she worked mainly in photography, setting up a studio in Scarsdale, New York, in 1941. She was co-owner of the publishing company Morgan and Morgan. She is best known for vibrant black-and-white photographs of dancers, especially **Martha Graham** and **Merce Cunningham** (1935–40), for experimental photomontages and light abstractions, and for portraits and photographs of children.

Morgan, Edwin George 1920– •*Scottish poet and critic*• Born in Glasgow, he was educated at the University of Glasgow, where he later taught, and served in the Royal Army Medical Corps during World War II, an option he chose as a conscientious objector. He published his first volume of poems, *The Vision of Cathkin Braes*, and a translation of *Beowulf*, in 1952. His verse from the 1950s is introspective and rather gloomy, but his later work contains optimism, and by the time of *A Second Life* (1968), he had embraced his homosexuality. A collection of his influential essays and critical writings, *Crossing The Border* (1990), was published in 1990. A skilled translator, he collected his translations of various writers, such as **Boris Pasternak**, **Alexander Pushkin** and **Federico García Lorca**, in *Rites of Passage* (1976). His adaptation of **Edmond Rostand**'s *Cyrano de Bergerac* into colloquial Glaswegian in 1992 was highly acclaimed, as was his translation of **Racine**'s *Phèdre* into Scots as *Phaedra* in 2000.

“ ”

Deplore what is to be deplored,
and then find out the rest.

1968 "King Billy."

Morgan, Sir Henry c. 1635–88 •*Welsh buccaneer*• Born in Llanrhymney, Glamorgan, he was kidnapped as a child and shipped to Barbados, where he joined the buccaneers. His many raids against the Spanish and Dutch in the West Indies and Central America included the famous capture of Porto Bello and Panama (1671). Transported to London under arrest to placate the Spanish (1672), he was subsequently knighted (1674) on the renewal of hostilities, and died a wealthy planter and deputy governor of Jamaica.

Morgan, John Hunt 1825–64 •*US Civil War general*• Born in Huntsville, Alabama, he grew up in Kentucky, fought in the Mexican War, and joined the Confederate army in 1861. He became famous for his daring cavalry raids behind Union lines in Tennessee and Kentucky, during which he avoided direct combat and focused on destroying telegraph and railroad lines, burning supplies, and taking prisoners. In 1863 he raided as far north as Ohio, where he was captured and briefly imprisoned. He was killed by Union troops in Tennessee while attempting a final raid in 1864.

Morgan, J(ohn) Pierpont 1837–1913 •*US banker, financier and art collector*• He was born in Hartford, Connecticut, the son of the financier John Spencer Morgan (1813–90), and built his father's firm into the most powerful private banking house in the US. His house financed the Federal Reserve system in the depression of 1895, and he acquired a controlling interest in many of the country's principal railroads. In 1901 he bought out **Andrew Carnegie** and formed the US Steel Corporation, the world's largest corporation, and in the public mind he came to represent the manipulative forces of the money trust. He compiled one of the greatest private art collections of his day, which he bequeathed to the Metropolitan Museum of Art in New York. He was also noted for his extensive philanthropic benefactions. His son, John Pierpont Morgan, Jr (1867–1943), endowed the Pierpont Morgan Library in New York.

Morgan, (Hywel) Rhodri 1939– •*Welsh politician*• He was born in Cardiff and educated at St John's College, Oxford, and Harvard University. He became Labour Member of Parliament for Cardiff West in 1987 and was a candidate for the post of First Minister of the Welsh Assembly in 1999. A disagreement arose with the Labour leadership in Westminster, whose favored candidate was Alun Michael, but Michael was forced out in a vote of no confidence and Morgan took over the post in 2000. He resigned as a Member of Parliament after the 2001 general election.

Morgan, Thomas Hunt 1866–1945 •*US geneticist, biologist and Nobel Prize winner*• Born in Lexington, Kentucky, he studied at Kentucky State College and Johns Hopkins University. He became Professor of Experimental Zoology at Columbia University (1904–28) and then at the California Institute of Technology (Caltech, 1928–45). In work on *Drosophila*, the fruit fly, he found that certain traits are linked, but that the traits are not always inherited together. This suggested that certain traits are carried on the X chromosome, that traits can cross over to other chromosomes, and that the rate of crossing over could be used as a measure of distance along the chromosome. Among many other works, he wrote (with C B Bridges) *The Mechanism of Mendelian Heredity* (1915), which established the chromosome theory of inheritance in confirmation of **Mendel**'s work. He was awarded the 1933 Nobel Prize for physiology or medicine.

Morganwg, Iolo *See* **Williams, Edward**

Morisot, Berthe Marie Pauline 1841–95 •*French painter*• The granddaughter of **Jean Fragonard**, she painted mainly women and children, and was the leading female exponent of Impressionism. Her early work shows the influence of **Camille Corot**, who was her friend and mentor, but her later style owes more to **Renoir**. She herself exercised an influence on **Édouard Manet**, whose brother she married.

Morita, Akio 1921–99 •*Japanese businessman*• Born in Nagoya, he was educated at Osaka Imperial University. After World War II he founded, with Masaru Ibuka (1908–97), the electronics firm which since 1958 has been known as Sony. Among Sony's most important products have been early tape recorders for the domestic market (c. 1950), advanced television equipment and (one of the best examples of miniaturization) the Walkman range of radios and cassette players, first produced in 1980.

Morley, Edward Williams 1838–1923 •*US chemist and physicist*• Born in Newark, New Jersey, he was educated at Williams College in Williamstown, Massachusetts, and at Andover Theological Seminary. He later became pastor of the Congregational Church at Twinsburg, Ohio (1868), and Professor of Chemistry and Natural History at Adalbert College of Western Reserve University, an appointment he held until his retirement in 1906. Morley had a passionate concern for precise measurement. He analyzed the oxygen content of the atmosphere with a precision of 0.0025 percent, and endeavored to correlate the results for samples taken at different times and places with meteorological records. His later research interests involved collaborative studies with physicists, notably with **Albert Abraham Michelson** on the velocity of light and the "ether drift" problem.

Morley, John Morley, 1st Viscount 1838–1923 •*English journalist, biographer, philosophical critic and statesman*• Born in Blackburn, Lancashire, the son of a doctor, and educated at Oxford, he was called to the bar, but chose literature as a profession. From 1867 to 1882 he edited the *Fortnightly Review*, and from 1880 to 1883 the *Pall Mall Gazette*. He was Member of Parliament from 1883 until his elevation to the peerage in 1908, and his articles and speeches in favor of Home Rule made him **Gladstone**'s most conspicuous supporter. In 1886 he was a successful Irish secretary, and again from 1892 to 1895. He was secretary for India (1905–10) until the outbreak of World War I. His writings include lives of Gladstone (4 vols, 1903) and **Edmund Burke**.

Morley, Malcolm, *formerly* **Malcolm Evans** 1931– •*English painter*• Born in Highgate, London, he worked at sea and spent four years in Borstal and prison, where he took a correspondence course in art. He trained at Camberwell before emigrating to the US in 1958. Working as a waiter, he met **Barnet Newman** and began painting in horizontal bands, using a pastry gun. In the mid-1960s he painted in a superrealist style, later incorporating "accidents," as in *Los Angeles Yellow Pages* (1971), where the image is ripped through. By the 1980s he was painting landscapes, animals, and mythological motifs, for example *Arizonac* (1981, Saatchi Collection, London). Morley was the first winner of the Turner Prize (1984).

Morley, Robert 1908–92 •*English actor*• Born in Semley, Wiltshire, he studied at the Royal Academy of Dramatic Art. He toured throughout Great Britain, establishing his own summer theater in Cornwall, before a succession of London stage successes in *Oscar Wilde* (1936), *The Great Romancer* (1937) and *Pygmalion* (1937). His first film was the lavish Hollywood drama *Marie Antoinette* (1938) for which he received a Best Supporting Actor Academy Award nomination. He remained committed to the theater, appearing in *Edward, My Son* (1947), which he cowrote, and *The Little Hut* (1950). His films include *The African Queen* (1951), *Oscar Wilde* (1960) and *Someone Is Killing the Great Chefs of Europe* (1978). An entertaining wit and raconteur, he published numerous collections of droll observations.

" "

Anyone who works is a fool. I don't work: I merely inflict myself on the public.

Attributed.

Moro, Aldo 1916–78 •*Italian politician*• A leading figure of the Christian Democrats (DC), he served twice as prime minister (1963–68, 1974–76) and was foreign minister (1970–72). During the 1970s he was one of the DC moderates who sought to cooperate with **Enrico Berlinguer**. He was one of several important figures to die at the hands of the Red Brigades.

Morpurgo, Michael Andrew Bridge 1943– •*English author*• Born in St Albans, Hertfordshire, he studied at King's College London. He began work as a primary school teacher (1967–75) and in 1976 founded Farms for City Children with his wife Clare. His more than 60 books for children include *The Wreck of the Zanzibar* (1995; Whitbread award), *The Butterfly Lion* (1996; Smarties prize) and *Black Queen* (2000).

Morricone, Ennio 1928– •*Italian composer of film scores*• Born in Rome, he studied at the Academy of Santa Cecilia, Rome, and established his reputation with haunting scores for more than 400 films and television programs. He achieved international recognition with the vibrant score for Sergio Leone's "spaghetti Western" *A Fistful of Dollars* (1964), which was followed by a further six collaborations with Leone, including *The Good, the Bad, and the Ugly* (1966). Among his most memorable scores since then have been those for Roland Joffe's *The Mission* (1986) and for Brian De Palma's *The Untouchables* (1987).

Morris, Desmond John 1928– •*English ethologist and writer*• Born in Wiltshire, he was educated at the University of Birmingham and at Oxford. He was head of Granada TV and the film unit at the Zoological Society of London (1956–59), and subsequently curator of mammals at the Zoological Society (1959–67). He then became the director of the Institute of Contemporary Arts, London (1967–68), and later a Research Fellow at Wolfson College, Oxford (1973–81). He carried out important research on the ethology of several animals, but it was his interest in primate behavior which led to his best-known work, the popular *The Naked Ape* (1967). In this he described the behavior of humans using the approach and techniques of ethology. He used the same formula in several further books, such as *Manwatching: A Field Guide to Human Behaviour* (1977) and *The Human Animal* (1994), which was made into a television series.

Morris, Estelle 1952– •*English Labour politician*• Born into a political family from Manchester, she worked as a teacher (1974–92) before being elected Member of Parliament in 1992. She was appointed Opposition spokesperson on education in 1995, and after the landslide Labour victory became Schools Minister (1997), Schools Standards Minister (1998) and Secretary of State for Education (2001), succeeding **David Blunkett**, a position she resigned in 2002.

Morris, Mark William 1956– •*US dancer and choreographer*• Born in Seattle, Washington, he danced for several important modern choreographers (**Eliot Feld**, **Laura Dean**, and **Twyla Tharp**) before making an informal New York debut with his own company, The Mark Morris Dance Company, in 1981. He has devised over 100 dances for his own and other companies, and for opera. From 1988 to 1991 he was director of dance for the Théâtre de la Monnaie in Brussels, and in 1990 Morris founded the White Oak Dance Project with **Mikhail Baryshnikov**. Utterly original and profoundly unconventional, his works include *L'allegro, Dido and Aeneas* (1989), and an irreverent version of *The Nutcracker* entitled *The Hard Nut* (1991). Recent work includes directing and choreographing *Four Saints in Three Acts* for the English National Opera in 2000.

Morris, William 1834–96 •*English craftsman, poet and socialist*• He was born in Walthamstow, near London, and educated at

Marlborough School and Exeter College, Oxford. He studied for holy orders, but renounced the Church and studied architecture with his friends and fellow members of the Pre-Raphaelite Brotherhood, particularly the painter **Edward Burne-Jones**. He studied architecture under **George Edmund Street**, but on the advice of **Dante Gabriel Rossetti** became a professional painter (1857–62). In 1859 he married a model, Jane Burden, and moved into the Red House at Bexley Heath, which he designed and furnished with the architect **Philip Webb**. From the ideas expressed there, and with the help of his Pre-Raphaelite associates, in 1861 he founded the firm of Morris, Marshall, Faulkner and Company, which soon revolutionized the art of house decoration and furniture in England. His literary career began with a volume of poetry and longer narrative poems including *The Earthly Paradise* (1868–70), a collection of 24 classical and medieval tales. He developed a passionate interest in the heroic literature of Iceland, and worked with Eiríkur Magnússon (1833–1913) on a series of saga translations. He visited Iceland twice, in 1871 and 1873, and was inspired to write *Three Northern Love Songs* (1875) and a four-volume epic, *The Story of Sigurd the Volsung and the Fall of the Nibelungs* (1876), regarded as his greatest literary work. He founded the Society for the Protection of Ancient Buildings in 1877. His experience as a master craftsman, and his devotion to the Gothic, persuaded him that the excellence of medieval arts and crafts sprang from the joy of free craftsmen, which was destroyed by Victorian mass production and capitalism. He joined the Social Democratic Federation in 1883; his Utopian ideals did much to develop the philosophy of socialism, and when the Social Democratic Federation suffered disruption in 1884, he formed the breakaway Socialist League. In 1890, in a further rejection of Victorian values, he founded a publishing house, the Kelmscott Press at Hammersmith, for which he designed clear typefaces and wide ornamental borders; it produced a stream of his own works as well as reprints of English classics.

Morrison (of Lambeth), Herbert Stanley Morrison, Baron 1888–1965 •*English politician*• Born in Lambeth, London, he was educated at an elementary school and by intensive private reading. After being an errand boy and a shop assistant, he helped found the London Labour Party and became its secretary in 1915. Mayor of Hackney (1920–21), he entered the London County Council (1922), becoming its leader (1934). He grouped together London's passenger transport system, and much of the credit for the "Green Belt" was due to him. He was Member of Parliament for South Hackney three times between 1923 and 1945, when he was elected for East Lewisham. In **Churchill**'s war cabinet he was home secretary and minister of home security. He was a powerful figure in the postwar social revolution, uniting the positions of deputy prime minister, lord president of the Council, and leader of a House of Commons which enacted the most formidable body of legislation ever entrusted to it.

Morrison, Jim (James Douglas), *nicknamed* **the Lizard King** 1943–71 •*US rock singer and poet*• He was born in Melbourne, Florida. He was the lead singer of The Doors, an important Los Angeles–based rock band of the late 1960s which also included Ray Manzarek (1939–), Robbie Krieger (1946–) and John Densmore (1945–). He combined a poetic intensity with rebellious nonconformity, but his attempts to push beyond conventional behavior and states of consciousness brought him into conflict with the authorities, mainly over drugs, but also for outspoken political songs like "When the Music's Over" or "Five to One." He died in Paris in slightly mysterious circumstances, adding fuel to a familiar rock legend, and his grave there became a shrine for fans.

Morrison, Toni, *pen name of* **Chloe Anthony Morrison**, *née* **Wofford** 1931– •*US novelist, winner of the Nobel Prize for literature*• She was born in Lorain, Ohio, and educated at Howard and Cornell Universities, later teaching at Texas Southern University (1955–57) and at Howard (1957–64). She moved to New York in 1965 to work in publishing as a senior editor at Random House while becoming established as a fiction writer. Labeled a new James Joyce or **William Faulkner**, she explores in rich vocabulary and cold-blooded detail the story of African Americans in a white-dominated culture. *The Bluest Eye* (1970) focuses on an 11-year-old Black girl who feels a sense of inferiority at not having blue eyes, and suffers an incestuous rape; *Sula* (1974) again confronts a generation gap, but between a grandmother and the eponymous scapegoat; and *Song of Solomon* (1977) is a merciless study of genteel African Americans. Further novels, formidable in their mastery of technique and courageous in their subject matter, have included *Tar Baby* (1981), a story of race conflict on a Caribbean island; *Beloved* (1987), a Pulitzer Prize–winning account of a runaway slave woman who kills her baby daughter to prevent her becoming a slave; *Jazz* (1992), set in 1920s Harlem; and *Paradise* (1998), an account of an African-American utopian experiment. *Playing in the Dark: Whiteness and the Literary Imagination*, a study of African Americans in literature, was published in 1992. Morrison taught writing at the State University of New York at Albany from 1984, and moved to Princeton University in 1989. She was awarded the Nobel Prize for literature in 1993.

“ ”

In this country American means white. Everybody else has to hyphenate.

1992 In ***The Guardian****, January 29.*

Morrison, Van (George Ivan) 1945– •*Northern Irish rock singer and songwriter*• Born in Belfast, he first came to attention as the lead singer with the Irish band Them, remembered for their epic pop hit "Gloria" (1967). Following his first solo hit, "Brown Eyed Girl" in 1967, he moved onto a different plane of achievement with the haunting *Astral Weeks* (1968), the prelude to a classic period of his work in the early 1970s which includes *Moondance* (1970), *Saint Dominic's Preview* (1972), and the electrifying live recording *It's Too Late to Stop Now* (1974). His highly original fusion of soul, rhythm and blues, jazz and folk influences has continued to confound conventional expectations, and he remains one of the most original and powerful performers and writers in rock music.

Morse, Samuel Finley Breese 1791–1872 •*US artist and inventor*• Born in Charlestown, Massachusetts, he graduated from Yale in 1810 and went to England to study painting. On his return he was a founder and first president of the National Academy of Design in New York (1826) and became a professor at New York University (1832). In 1832 he conceived the idea of a magnetic telegraph, which he exhibited to Congress in 1837; in 1843 Congress granted him $30,000 for an experimental telegraph line between Washington and Baltimore, built by **Ezra Cornell**, over which he sent the historic message, "What hath God wrought?" on May 24, 1844. His system, widely adopted, at last brought him honors and rewards. The Morse code (originally called the Morse alphabet) was evolved by him for use with his telegraph.

Morshead, Sir Leslie James 1889–1959 •*Australian soldier*• He was born in Ballarat, Victoria. He commanded a company at Gallipoli, and later a batallion on the Western Front. In World War II he commanded the 18th Brigade in the Middle East and led the 9th Division at Tobruk during the siege of 1941 and at the battles of El Alamein. He returned to Australia to lead the New Guinea Force and to become general officer commanding of the First Australian Corps, ending the war in 1945 as commander of the Australian and US Task Force in Borneo.

Mortara, Edgar 1852–1940 •*Italian monk*• Born into a Jewish family, he became the unwitting principal in the celebrated "Mortara" case. In 1858 he was carried off from his parents by the Archbishop of Bologna, on the grounds that he had been secretly baptized by a Catholic maid servant when he was a gravely ill infant. The refusal of the authorities to give him up to his parents excited much indignation in Great Britain. Eventually he was discovered in Rome in 1870, but he chose to retain his Christian faith, and became an Augustinian monk.

Mortimer, Sir John Clifford 1923– •*English dramatist, novelist and barrister*• Born in London, he was called to the bar in 1948, participated in several celebrated civil cases, and was a constant defender of liberal values. His series of novels featuring Horace Rumpole, an amiable, late-middle-aged defense barrister and frequenter of Pomeroy's bar, has been adapted for television as *Rumpole of the Bailey*. His other novels, including *Paradise*

Postponed (1985) and *Summer's Lease* (1988), are highly popular, evoking, often savagely, what Mortimer perceives as the moral decline of the English middle class. His many plays and adaptations for the stage include *The Wrong Side of the Park* (1960) and an autobiographical play, *A Voyage Round My Father* (broadcast 1963, staged 1970), which was filmed for television in 1982. He has published three autobiographical volumes and some notable translations, especially of **Georges Feydeau**. His TV screenplays include *Brideshead Revisited* (1981), from the novel by **Evelyn Waugh**, *The Ebony Tower* (1984) from the story by **John Fowles**, and his own *Paradise Postponed* (1986). He also wrote the screenplay for the film *Tea with Mussolini* (1999). His first wife was the novelist Penelope Mortimer (1918–99). He was knighted in 1998.

Morton, James Douglas, 4th Earl of c. 1516–81 •*Regent of Scotland*• The younger son of Sir George Douglas of Pittendreich, near Edinburgh, he became Earl of Morton (1553), and, although a Protestant, was made chancellor by **Mary Queen of Scots** (1563). Involved in the murders of both **David Rizzio** (1566) and Lord **Darnley** (1567), he joined the Protestant nobles who defeated the Earl of **Bothwell** and Mary Queen of Scots at Carberry Hill (1567), "discovered" the "Casket Letters," led the forces at Langside (1568) and, after the brief regencies of **Moray**, Lennox and Mar, took over himself as regent for **James VI** (1572). After the end of the civil war in Scotland (1573), he increased links with England, but his high-handed attempts to control ecclesiastical appointments and to bring the Church into conformity with England brought him into sharp conflict with the radical ministers, led by **Andrew Melville**. His regency brought a welcome restoration of law and order, but it was achieved at the cost of a monopoly of many offices by the Douglas family, which caused intense resentment. His fall was engineered by Captain James Stewart, nominally for his part in Darnley's murder, and he was beheaded by the "Maiden," a device he had himself introduced to Scotland, in Edinburgh's Grassmarket.

Morton, Jelly Roll, *originally* **Ferdinand Joseph La Menthe** or **Lamothe** 1890–1941 •*US jazz pianist, composer and bandleader*• Born into a Creole family in New Orleans, he worked as a gambler and pimp as well as a piano entertainer in "sporting houses." His status as a jazz pioneer comes from his recordings (1923–27) while living in Chicago, and his unaccompanied piano solos made best-sellers of such tunes as "King Porter Stomp," "Wolverine Blues" and "Jelly Roll Blues." In 1926 he formed the recording band the Red Hot Peppers, a collection of some of the finest New Orleans sidemen of the day, and probably the first in jazz to combine arranged ensemble passages with collective improvisation and improvised solos.

Morton, John c. 1420–1500 •*English prelate and statesman*• Born probably in Milborne St Andrew, Dorset, he trained as a lawyer. Faithful to **Henry VI** until after the Lancastrian defeat at the Battle of Tewkesbury (1471), he made his peace with **Edward IV**, and became Master of the Rolls (1473) and Bishop of Ely (1479). After the accession of **Henry VII** he was made Archbishop of Canterbury (1486), Chancellor (1487) and a cardinal (1493).

Mosaddeq, Mohammad 1880–1967 •*Iranian statesman*• Born in Tehran, he held office in Iran in the 1920s, and returned to politics in 1944. By his Oil Nationalization Act of 1951 (in which year he became prime minister), he claimed to have expropriated the Anglo-Iranian Oil Co. His government was overthrown by a royalist uprising in 1953, and he was imprisoned. He was released in 1956.

Moseley, Harry (Henry Gwyn Jeffreys) 1887–1915 •*English physicist*• He was born in Weymouth, Dorset, and educated at Oxford, where he graduated in 1910. He then joined **Ernest Rutherford** in Manchester before returning to work at Oxford in 1913. He measured the X-ray spectra of over 30 different metals, and suggested that the regular variance from element to element was related to the nuclear charge, allowing the atomic numbers of elements to be calculated. Discontinuities in the spectral series made it clear that a number of elements were missing from the periodic table and allowed prediction of their properties; these elements were sought and soon discovered. Moseley's work was an important step in advancing knowledge of the nature of the atom, firmly establishing that the properties of the elements are determined by atomic number rather than atomic weight. He was killed in action at Gallipoli.

Moser-Pröll, Annemarie, *née* **Pröll** 1953– •*Austrian alpine skier*• Born in Kleinarl, she won a women's record 62 World Cup races (1970–79), and was overall champion (1979), downhill champion (1978, 1979), Olympic downhill champion (1980), world combined champion (1972, 1978), and world downhill champion (1974, 1978, 1980). She retired after the 1980 Olympics.

Moses, *Hebrew* **Môsheh** 15th–13th century BC •*Old Testament Hebrew prophet and lawgiver*• Moses is the principal figure dominating the Old Testament books from Exodus to Deuteronomy. The sequence begins with his birth and ends with his death, and describes him as the leader of the Israelites in their Exodus from captivity in Egypt and as receiver of the Divine Law. He was the younger son of a Levite couple and was hidden in a basket to avoid death at the hands of the Egyptians. He was discovered by a daughter of Pharaoh and raised as her son. After killing an Egyptian who was beating a Hebrew, Moses fled to Midian, and there married Zipporah, the daughter of a Midianite priest. According to the biblical account, God appeared to Moses in a burning bush, and ordered him to lead his people out of Egypt. He returned to Egypt with his brother **Aaron**, and eventually persuaded Pharaoh to release the Hebrews by producing signs and visiting plagues on the country. Moses led the Hebrews out of Egypt, pursued by Pharaoh's army, which was engulfed by the waters of the Red Sea after they had parted to allow the Hebrews through. After a long period in the wilderness, Moses took the people to Sinai, where he received the commandments from God in the mountain. On his return from the mountain, he interceded with God not to punish the Hebrews for adoring the golden calf. For 39 years Moses led his people in the wilderness, where they were fed with manna and quail. After failing to enter Canaan from the south, Moses settled the people in land north of Moab. After delivering a series of addresses, Moses died in the fortieth year after the Exodus, according to Deuteronomy (1:3). Moses represents the ideal leader and wise judge of his people, but it is difficult to separate legend from history in the biblical accounts that have come down to us.

Moses, Anna Mary, *known as* **Grandma Moses** 1860–1961 •*US primitive artist*• Born in Washington County, New York, she was a farmer's wife in Staunton, Virginia, and in New York State, and did embroideries of country scenes. She began to paint at about the age of 75, mainly country scenes remembered from her childhood—"old, timey things ... all from memory." From her first show in New York in 1940, she had great popular success in the United States.

“ ”

Paintin's not important. What's important is keepin' busy.

1954 In news summaries, January 2.

Moses, Ed(win Corley) 1955– •*US track athlete*• He was born in Dayton, Ohio. The greatest 400-meter hurdler ever, he was unbeaten in any race in this event from August 1977 to June 1987, and as Olympic champion in 1976 and 1984 and four times world record holder, he dominated this discipline for over a decade. He would have been the favorite for the gold medal in the 1980 Moscow Olympics as well, but missed them because of the US boycott.

Moses, Grandma *See* **Moses, Anna Mary**

Môsheh *See* **Moses**

Moshoeshoe II, Constantine Bereng Seeiso 1938–96 •*King of Lesotho*• Educated at Oxford, England, he was proclaimed king of Lesotho when the country became independent (1966). His desire for political involvement led to his being twice placed under house arrest, and in 1970 an eight-month exile in Holland ended when he agreed to take no further part in the country's politics. After a military coup in 1990, he was deposed and sent into exile in Britain (1990–92), and his eldest son, Letsie III, was put on his throne. Regional leaders led by **Nelson Mandela** later negotiated the restoration of constitutional rule, and Moshoeshoe was returned to power in 1995. He died in an automobile accident.

Mosimann, Anton 1947– •*Swiss chef and restaurateur*• Born in Solothurn, he studied at a private school in Switzerland and became a cuisinier at a number of hotels and restaurants worldwide, later becoming maître chef des cuisines at the Dorchester Hotel, London (1976–88). Among his numerous television series are *Cooking with Mosimann* (1989) and *Anton Mosimann Naturally* (1991). He is the owner of Mosimann's, formerly the Belfry Club (1988–), and is principal of the Mosimann Academy, London (1996–).

Mosley, Sir Oswald Ernald Mosley, 6th Baronet 1896–1980 •*English politician*• Successively a Conservative, Independent and Labour Member of Parliament, he was a member of the 1929 Labour government. He later resigned and became founder of the New Party (1931). After a visit to Italy he became founder and leader of the British Union of Fascists (1932), whose followers, the Blackshirts, provoked violent demonstrations by staging anti-Semitic marches through the traditionally Jewish east end of London. Detained under the Defence Regulations during World War II, he founded a new Union Movement in 1948. He married Cynthia, 2nd daughter of Earl **Curzon** of Kedleston, in 1920. His second wife, Diana Mitford (1910–2003), whom he married in 1936, was the sister of **Jessica**, **Nancy** and **Unity Mitford**.

Moss, Sir Stirling 1929– •*English racecar driver*• Born in London, he won many major races in the 1950s, including the British Grand Prix (1955, 1957), the Mille Miglia, and the Targa Florio. Between 1951 and 1961, he won 16 races in 66 starts. He retired in 1962 after a crash at Goodwood. He then became a journalist and broadcaster, and returned to saloon car racing in 1980. He was knighted in 2000.

“ ”

It is necessary to relax your muscles when you can. Relaxing your brain is fatal.

*1955 In **Newsweek**, May 16.*

Mössbauer, Rudolf Ludwig 1929– •*German physicist and Nobel Prize winner*• Born in Munich, he was educated at the Technical University in Munich, where he later taught, and the **Max Planck** Institute for Medical Research in Heidelberg. Before completing his PhD, he observed what is known as the Mössbauer effect, the narrow resonance in the energy spectrum produced when the whole of the nuclear lattice, rather than just one nucleus, recoils from gamma radiation. The effect has been used to test **Albert Einstein**'s theory of general relativity, to study the properties of nuclei and as an analytical tool in chemistry and biology. Mössbauer shared the 1961 Nobel Prize for physics with **Robert Hofstadter** for research into atomic structure.

Mota, Rosa 1958– •*Portuguese athlete*• She was born in Foz do Douro, and competed in her first marathon in Athens in 1982, when she won the European title. She possesses surprising reserves of stamina, which helped her to win 10 of her first 13 marathons. She had victories in Tokyo, Boston, Chicago, Rotterdam, London and Osaka, as well as two further European titles, and the world championship title in 1987. In 1988, she won an Olympic gold medal, making her the first Portuguese woman to do so.

Mother Mary of the Cross *See* **McKillop, St Mary Helen**

Motherwell, Robert Burns 1915–91 •*US painter and writer*• Born in Aberdeen, Washington, he briefly attended the California School of Fine Arts in San Francisco and studied philosophy at Stanford, Harvard, Grenoble and, later, Columbia. He wrote a good deal on the theory of modern art and helped found the abstract expressionist group in New York in the 1940s. His images often resemble semiautomatic doodles of a kind that the surrealists had explored, but enlarged to fill huge canvases. He is best known for *Elegy to the Spanish Republic*, a series of more than a hundred paintings. He was married to the artist **Helen Frankenthaler** from 1958 to 1971.

Motion, Andrew 1952– •*English biographer and poet laureate*• Born in London, he studied at University College Oxford, and lectured in English at the University of Hull (1977–81). After working as an editor for *Poetry Review* (1981–83) and the publishers Chatto and Windus (1983–87), he became Professor of Creative Writing at the University of East Anglia (1995–). Among his collections of poetry are *The Pleasure Steamers* (1978) and *Salt Water* (1997). He was appointed poet laureate in 1999. His biographies include those of **Philip Larkin** (1993) and **John Keats** (1997). He has published two novels.

Mott, John Raleigh 1865–1955 •*US religious leader, social worker and Nobel Prize winner*• He was born in Livingston Manor, New York. A Methodist layman, he became known the world over by his work for the Student Volunteer Movement (1888–1920), the Young Men's Christian Association (1915–31) and the World Missionary Council (1941–42). He shared the 1946 Nobel Peace Prize with **Emily Balch**.

Mott, Lucretia, *née* **Coffin** 1793–1880 •*US abolitionist and feminist*• Born in Nantucket, Massachusetts, she was educated near Poughkeepsie, New York, where she later became a teacher. She first rose to prominence in 1817 as a speaker at Quaker meetings, and became an active campaigner for temperance, peace, women's rights and the abolition of slavery. She helped organize the American Anti-Slavery Society (1833) and took an active part in the Anti-Slavery Convention of American Women (1837). She was strongly supported by her husband, James Mott, and under her influence he left his commission business because of its connection with slave-produced cotton, in which he had dealt throughout the 1820s. She and **Elizabeth Cady Stanton** organized the first Woman's Rights Convention in 1848.

Mott, Sir Nevill Francis 1905–96 •*English physicist and Nobel Prize winner*• Born in Leeds, he studied mathematics at Cambridge, where he became a lecturer and Fellow, working with **Ernest Rutherford**. He later became Professor of Theoretical Physics at Bristol University, where he studied the electronic behavior of "Mott transitions" between metals and insulators, and in 1954 was appointed Cavendish Professor of Physics at Cambridge. In 1965 he retired and returned to full-time research to work on the new area of noncrystalline semiconductors. He shared the 1977 Nobel Prize for physics (with **Philip Anderson** and **John van Vleck**) for his work on the electronic properties of disordered materials. Mott has been one of the major theoretical physicists of the 20th century, opening new and difficult areas of solid-state physics and materials science. He was knighted in 1962.

Mottelson, Ben(jamin) Roy 1926– •*Danish physicist and Nobel Prize winner*• Born in Chicago, in the US, he was educated at Purdue University and Harvard. From Harvard he moved to Copenhagen, where he worked with **Aage Bohr** on the problem of combining the two models of the atomic nuclei. They secured experimental evidence in support of **James Rainwater**'s collective model of the atomic nuclei, and Bohr, Mottelson and Rainwater shared the 1975 Nobel Prize for physics. From 1953 to 1957 Mottelson held a research position with CERN (Conseil Européen pour la Recherche Nucléaire) before returning to Copenhagen, where he became professor at Nordita (Nordic Institute for Theoretical Atomic Physics). He adopted Danish nationality in 1971.

Moulins, Master of c.1460–c.1529 •*French artist*• He is so called from his principal work, the triptych in Moulins Cathedral of the *Virgin and Child*. He is regarded as the most accomplished French artist of his time. The influence of **Hugo van der Goes** can be seen in his vividly colored and realistic paintings, and some authorities identify him with Jean Perreal or Jean de Paris, court painter of **Charles VIII**.

Mountbatten, Edwina Cynthia Annette, *née* **Ashley, Countess** 1901–60 •*English philanthropist*• The wife of **Louis, Earl Mountbatten of Burma**, whom she married in 1922, she rendered distinguished service during the London Blitz (1940–42) to the Red Cross and St John Ambulance Brigade, of which she became superintendent in chief in 1942. As vicereine of India (1947), her work in social welfare brought her the friendship of **Mahatma Gandhi** and **Jawaharlal Nehru**.

Mountbatten, *originally* **Battenberg, Prince Louis Alexander, 1st Marquess of Milford Haven** 1854–1921 •*British naval commander*• Born in Austria, the son of Prince Alexander of Hesse, he became a naturalized British subject and joined the Royal Navy in 1868. He served with distinction as a commodore in the Mediterranean fleet, as director of naval intelligence and senior sea commands.

He was First Sea Lord at the outbreak of World War I, but was forced to resign because of anti-German prejudice. He changed the family name from Battenberg to Mountbatten 1917, and was made Marquess of Milford Haven. He was promoted to admiral in 1919.

Mountbatten (of Burma), Louis Francis Albert Victor Nicholas Mounbatten, 1st Earl 1900–79 •*English naval commander and statesman*• Born near Windsor, Berkshire, the younger son of Prince **Louis Mountbatten** and great-grandson of Queen **Victoria**, he was known as Prince Louis Francis of Battenberg until 1917. Educated at Osborne and Dartmouth Royal Naval Colleges (1913–16), he served at sea in World War I. In World War II he commanded the 5th destroyer flotilla (1939–41), and became chief of Combined Operations Command (1941–43). He was Supreme Allied Commander Southeast Asia from 1943 to 1945, and was then appointed the last viceroy of India (1947) to oversee the rapid transfer of power. He returned to service at sea as Fourth Sea Lord and commander of the Mediterranean fleet (1952–55), and was appointed First Sea Lord (1955–59) and Chief of Defense Staff (1959–65). He was murdered by an IRA bomb while sailing near his holiday home in County Sligo, Ireland.

Mountford, Charles Pearcy 1890–1976 •*Australian ethnologist, writer and film director*• He was born in Hallett, South Australia. During his early years as a mechanic for the post office, he was brought into contact with the Aboriginals and became an expert on their way of life. In 1937 he led an expedition in search of the lost explorer Ludwig Leichhardt, and between 1938 and 1960 he led ten expeditions into central Australia. In 1948 he was leader of expeditions into Arnhem Land and to Melville Island. Beginning with *Brown Men and Red Sand* (1948), he wrote a series of books, illustrated with his own photographs, about the Aboriginals and their culture. He went on to direct feature films on Aboriginal life from 1950.

Mountjoy, Lord *See* **Blount, Charles**

Moussorgsky, Modest Petrovich *See* **Mussorgsky, Modest Petrovich**

Mowlam, Mo (Marjorie) 1949– •*English Labour politician*• Educated in Coventry, and at Durham University and the University of Iowa, she lectured at Florida State University (1977–78) before moving to Newcastle upon Tyne (1979–83). In 1987 she was elected Member of Parliament for Redcar. Within a year she was an assistant front bench spokesperson on Northern Ireland (1988–89), then became deputy coordinator for Labour's successful European parliament campaign in 1989. Rising through the Labour Party ranks, she was the spokesperson for national heritage (1993–94) and for Northern Ireland (1994–97) before entering **Tony Blair**'s cabinet as Secretary of State for Northern Ireland after Labour's landslide win in the 1997 general election. She became Minister for the Cabinet Office and Chancellor of the Duchy of Lancaster in 1999. She retired from politics at the 2001 general election.

Moynihan, Daniel Patrick 1927–2003 •*US politician*• Educated at the City College of New York and Tufts University, he taught at Syracuse, Harvard, and MIT. He served in the administrations of Presidents **Lyndon B Johnson** and **Richard Nixon**, acquiring notoriety as the author of *The Negro Family: The Case for National Action* (1965). He became ambassador to India (1973–74), and won a seat in the US Senate as a Democrat from New York in 1976, serving until 2001. He also wrote *Pandemonium: Ethnicity in International Politics* (1993).

Mozart, (Johann Chrysostom) Wolfgang Amadeus 1756–91 •*Austrian composer*• He was the son of Leopold Mozart, and displayed early musical gifts, playing the keyboard confidently at the age of four, composing his first pieces for it at five, and soon mastering the violin. Leopold was keen to exhibit his son's extraordinary talents along with those of his pianist-daughter, Maria-Anna, or "Nannerl" (1751–1829), and he undertook a series of tours of the European courts with them. On returning to Salzburg, Mozart was appointed honorary Konzertmeister to the court. There followed three extended visits by father and son to Italy (1770–72). His musical experiences on these tours helped mold his style, especially in dramatic music, although he was prolific also in writing sacred vocal pieces and instrumental works: by 1772 he had written about 25 symphonies (of which some are lost) and his first quartets. Further quartets and symphonies followed during and after a visit to Vienna in 1772, where Mozart came into contact with the music of **Haydn**. The years 1775–76 saw two stage works, *La finta giardiniera* ("The Feigned Gardener Girl,") and *Il rè pastore* ("The Shepherd King," K. 208), five violin concertos, the *Haffner* Serenade (K. 250), and masses for the Salzburg Court Chapel. Unhappy with the austere and unmusical Archbishop Colloredo of Salzburg, Mozart left his service in 1777 and, traveling with his mother, sought employment elsewhere. They stayed in Mannheim and he wrote a number of piano concertos and flute quartets, and fell in love with a singer, Aloysia Weber. Then in Paris, where his mother died in July, Mozart wrote the *Paris* Symphony. His father persuaded him to return to Salzburg, and he reluctantly accepted the post of court organist. At this time he composed the symphonies nos. 32 and 33, the *Coronation Mass*, and the *Sinfonia Concertante* for violin and viola. In 1780 he received an important commission from the elector of Bavaria for the opera seria *Idomeneo, rè di Creta* ("Idomeneo, king of Crete,"), produced in Munich in January 1781. In 1781 Archbishop Colloredo summoned Mozart to Vienna for the coronation of Emperor **Joseph II**. Again, after a stormy scene, he soon left the Archbishop's service but remained in Vienna, which became home for the rest of his short, crowded life. Here his reputation as composer and pianist was to reach its peak within a few years. Aloysia Weber had married a court actor, and Mozart turned his attentions to her sister Constanze, whom he married in 1782. Married life was happy, but insecure financially (they had six children, of whom two survived), and Mozart increased his meager income by teaching. In 1784, the year he became a Freemason, he produced six piano concertos; in 1785, another three; in 1786, three more. This was the rich flowering of his maturity, along with six string quartets dedicated to Haydn (who had declared Mozart to be the greatest composer known to him), the *Linz* and *Prague* symphonies and the three Italian comic masterpieces composed to libretti by Lorenzo Da Ponte (1749–1838): *Le nozze di Figaro* (1786, *The Marriage of Figaro*, after **Beaumarchais**), *Don Giovanni* (first performed in Prague, 1787), and *Così fan tutte* (1790, "Women Are All Like That"). Productions of his operas were usually more successful in Prague than in Vienna. The string quintets in C major and G minor (1787), the last three symphonies (1788), the quartets for the king of Prussia, the serenade *Eine kleine Nachtmusik* and the Clarinet Quintet mark the peak of his output of orchestral and chamber music. In 1787, Mozart's father, Leopold, died in Salzburg. In his final years Mozart suffered countless anxieties about finance or health. His last works were the opera *Die Zauberflöte* (*The Magic Flute*), based on a fairy tale with a libretto by Emanuel Schikaneder, and an opera seria, *La clemenza di Tito* (also 1791), a Clarinet Concerto and a Requiem. The last was unfinished when he died on December 5.

M'Taggart, John M'Taggart Ellis 1866–1925 •*English philosopher*• Born in London, he was educated at Clifton College and at Trinity College, Cambridge, where he later taught (1897–1923). His early works were commentaries on **Hegel**'s philosophy and were effectively preliminaries to his own systematic metaphysics set out in *The Nature of Existence* (2 vols, 1921, and posthumously, 1927). He is regarded as the most important of the Anglo-Hegelian or Idealistic philosophers who dominated British and US thought in the late 19th and early 20th centuries.

Mu'Awiyah c. 602–680 •*First Umayyad caliph*• He opposed the prophet **Muhammad** until the conquest of Mecca (630), then became his secretary. Under **Omar**, he took part in the conquest of Syria and was made governor (640). He rebelled against **Ali** for the murder of his kinsman, **'Uthman**, and fought him at the indecisive Battle of Siffin (657). With the help of **Amr ibn al-'As**, he gained control of Egypt, and after the assassination of Ali (661) took over the caliphate, thus founding the Umayyad dynasty, and moved the capital to Damascus. He extended the caliphate through conquests in North Africa and Afghanistan.

Mubarak, (Mohammed) Hosni Said 1928– •*Egyptian statesman*• Born in al-Minufiyah, he rose to become commander of the Egyptian Air Force. He was vice president under **Anwar Sadat** from 1975 until the latter's assassination in 1981. Mubarak was declared president and pledged to continue Sadat's domestic and international policies, including firm treatment of Muslim extremists, and the peace process with Israel. During the 1991 Gulf War, he was the Arab leader most critical of **Saddam Hussein**. In 1995 he survived an assassination attempt by Islamic fundamentalists and was involved in the events leading to the signing of a peace accord between the Palestinian Liberation Organization (PLO) and Israel. Reelected for a fourth term in 1999, he continues to be a key figure in both the complex politics of the Middle East and on the world stage.

Mucha, Alphonse, *originally* **Alfons Maria Mucha** 1860–1939 •*Czech graphic artist, painter and designer*• Born in Ivancise, he studied in Munich, Vienna, and at the Académie Julian and the Académie Colarossi, Paris. He designed jewelery, wallpaper and furniture, but his best-known works are his posters for **Sarah Bernhardt**, in the rich curvilinear art nouveau style of the 1890s. He devoted himself mainly to painting from c. 1903. He returned to Prague in 1914, where he painted a series of 20 monumental pictures, *The Slav Epic*.

Muddy Waters *See* **Waters, Muddy**

Mugabe, Robert Gabriel 1924– •*Zimbabwean nationalist leader and statesman*• Born in Kutama, Southern Rhodesia, and educated in Catholic mission schools and Fort Hare College, he was a teacher successively in Southern Rhodesia (Zimbabwe), Northern Rhodesia (Zambia) and Ghana before returning to Southern Rhodesia in 1960 as publicity secretary of the National Democratic Party. He was deputy secretary-general of the Zimbabwe African People's Union (ZAPU) in 1961 before being detained and then imprisoned, but escaped to cofound the Zimbabwe African National Union (ZANU) in 1963. He was detained again (1964–74), during which period he replaced **Ndabaningi Sithole** as president of ZANU and qualified as a lawyer. Released in 1974, he went to Mozambique to oversee the guerrilla war against the white regime. United uncomfortably with **Joshua Nkomo**'s ZAPU in the Patriotic Front to press for Black majority rule, Mugabe essentially retained his independence and, to the surprise of many, led ZANU (PF), as the combined party was called, to a decisive victory in 1980; hence, he became prime minister in the first government of independent Zimbabwe. In 1987 he became the country's first executive president. He was reelected in the 1996 presidential election after each of his challengers had withdrawn from the running. He has led an antihomosexual crusade for several years. Recent years have been marked by Mugabe's promotion of forcible land reclamation and redistribution from white farmers to his own supporters, increasing civil violence, and electoral intimidation and irregularity as ZANU (PF) faces a growing challenge from Morgan Tsvangirai's Movement for Democratic Change party.

Muggeridge, (Thomas) Malcolm 1903–90 •*English journalist and sage*• Born in Croydon, London, he lectured at the Egyptian University in Cairo (1927–30), then joined the *Manchester Guardian* (1930–33), serving as their Moscow correspondent. He was also assistant editor of the *Calcutta Statesman* (1934–35) and on the editorial staff of the *Evening Standard*. Serving with the Intelligence Corps during World War II, he received the Legion of Honor and the Croix de Guerre with Palm. He worked with *The Daily Telegraph* (1946–52), and was editor of *Punch* (1953–57) and also a television reporter and interviewer, making regular contributions to *Panorama* (1953–60). In his own series, *Appointment with …* (1960–61) and *Let Me Speak* (1964–65), he quizzed the great figures of the day and challenged minorities to defend their beliefs. In 1982 he became a Roman Catholic. Among his many books are *The Earnest Atheist* (1936), *Tread Softly for You Tread on My Jokes* (1966) and *Conversion: A Spiritual Journey* (1988).

“ ”

It's very nearly impossible to tell the truth in television.

1976 ***Christ and the Media***, *"Questions following the 3rd lecture."*

Muggleton, Lodowick 1609–98 •*English Puritan*• Born in London, he founded the sect of Muggletonians (1652) with his cousin, John Reeve (1608–58). They held that the Devil became incarnate in **Eve**, and denied the Holy Trinity. He was imprisoned and later fined for blasphemy, and published a *Spiritual Transcendental Treatise* (1652).

Muhammad or **Mohammed** c. 570–c. 632 •*Arab prophet and founder of Islam*• Muhammad was the son of Abdallāh, a poor merchant of the powerful tribe of Quaraysh, hereditary guardians of the shrine in Mecca. He was orphaned at six and brought up by his grandfather and uncle, Abu Tālib, who trained him to be a merchant. At 24 he entered the service of a rich widow, Khadija (c. 595–619), whom he eventually married. They had six children, including their daughters **Fatima** and Umm Kulthum, who married **'Uthman**, the third caliph. While continuing as a trader, Muhammad became increasingly drawn to religious contemplation. Soon after 600 (the traditional date is c. 610) he began to receive revelations from the angel Jibra'il (Gabriel) of the word of Allah, the one and only God. This Qur'an (Koran), or "reading," commanded that the numerous idols of the shrine should be destroyed and that the rich should give to the poor. This simple message attracted some support but provoked a great deal of hostility from those who felt their interests threatened. When his wife and uncle died, Muhammad was reduced to poverty, but he began making a few converts among pilgrims to Mecca from the town of Yathrib, an agricultural community to the north. By 622 Muhammad and his small band of devoted followers could no longer remain in Mecca; they were saved by an invitation from the people of Yathrib, who wanted Muhammad to come and arbitrate in the feuds that racked their community. He migrated there, and this migration, the Hegira, marks the beginning of the Muslim era. The name of the town was changed to Medina, "the city of the prophet." The most important act in the first year of the Hegira was Muhammad's granting permission to go to war with the enemies of Islam—especially the Meccans—in the name of God. In December 623 his Muslims defeated a Meccan force, but he was severely wounded in a battle at Ohod (January 625). In 627 he repelled a Meccan siege of Medina. By 629 he was able to take control of Mecca, which recognized him as chief and prophet. By 630 he had control over all Arabia. In March 632 he undertook his last pilgrimage to Mecca, and there on Mount Arafat fixed for all time the ceremonies of the pilgrimage. He fell ill soon after his return and died on June 8 in the home of the favorite of his nine wives, **Aïshah**, the daughter of one of his first followers, **Abu Bakr**. His tomb in the mosque at Medina is venerated throughout Islam.

Muhammad, Abu Abdallah *See* **Boabdil**

Muhammad, Elijah, *originally* **Elijah Poole** 1897–1975 •*US religious leader*• Born near Sandersville, Georgia, he left home at 16, married in 1919 and four years later took his family to Detroit, where he worked in a car factory and endured hard times, living on relief from 1929 to 1931. In 1931 he became an assistant to Wali Farad, the founder of the Nation of Islam (known as the Black Muslims), a sect that favored Black separatism and rejected Christianity as a tool of oppressive whites. Abandoning his "slave name" in favor of the name of the prophet, Elijah Muhammad embraced Farad's militant doctrines, seeking to win converts and to promote the movement's goal of African-American economic self-sufficiency. On Farad's disappearance in 1934, Elijah Muhammad became the leader of the movement, which grew rapidly even during his six-year imprisonment for opposing military conscription in World War II. During the late 1950s and 1960s he was critical of the integrationist agenda and nonviolent philosophy of the civil rights movement, but he benefited from the raising of African-American consciousness that accompanied it, and by 1962 there were an estimated 250,000 Black Muslims. A schism occurred in the Nation of Islam when his disciple **Malcolm X** broke away in 1965, and Malcolm's assassination was allegedly carried out by Black Muslims loyal to Elijah Muhammad. When Muhammad himself died in 1975, he was succeeded by his son Wallace D Muhammad (1933–), who moved the Black Muslims closer to orthodox Islam.

Muhammad Ahmed, *known as* **al-Mahdi ("Divinely Guided One")** 1844–85 •*Arab ascetic and rebel*• Born in Dongola, Sudan, the son of a shipbuilder, he was educated within a religious order, and was for a time in the Egyptian Civil Service and a slave trader before beginning his relentless and successful campaign against Egyptian rule in eastern Sudan. He was motivated by a conviction that, due to their apparent desertion of the Islamic faith, the ruling class were unfit to govern Muslims. He declared himself "al-Mahdi" in 1881 and gathered together a group of virtually unarmed disciples as his *ansar* ("helpers"). By 1883 he had proclaimed El Obeid (now al-Ubayyid) his capital and had united the nation's diverse and discontented citizens into an army strong enough to defeat any army Egypt could muster. On January 26, 1885, al-Mahdi took Khartoum in the action in which (against al-Mahdi's orders) General **Charles Gordon** was killed. Following these successes he consolidated his religious empire, establishing a new capital at Omdurman, but was taken ill and died a few months later, probably of typhus. The Mahdists were defeated by British forces led by **Horatio Herbert Kitchener** at the Battle of Omdurman (1898).

Muhammed, Shams ed-Dín *See* **Háfiz**

Muir, Edwin 1887–1959 •*Scottish poet*• Born in Deerness, Orkney, he migrated with his family to Glasgow at the age of 14, where he suffered the period of drab existence described in *The Story and the Fable* (1940), revised as *An Autobiography* in 1954. He became interested in left-wing politics, married the novelist Willa Anderson (1890–1970) in 1919, and traveled on the Continent (1921–24), where they collaborated on translations of **Franz Kafka** and Lion Feuchtwanger (1884–1958) and he wrote novels, notably *The Marionette* (1927). He spent most of the 1930s in Sussex and St Andrews. He also worked for the British Institute in Prague and Rome, and was appointed warden of Newbattle Abbey, near Edinburgh, in 1950. After a year as Eliot Norton Professor of Poetry at Harvard (1955–56), he retired near Cambridge. His poems appeared in eight slim volumes, including *First Poems* (1925), *The Voyage* (1946) and *The Labyrinth* (1949). Muir's critical work includes a controversial study of **John Knox** and *Scott and Scotland* (1936).

Muir, Frank 1920–98 •*English writer and broadcaster*• Born in Ramsgate, Kent, he was educated at Chatham House, Ramsgate, and Leyton County High School. Following service in the RAF during World War II, he began a fruitful professional partnership with **Denis Norden** in 1947, which lasted until 1964. Together they wrote the radio comedy series *Take It from Here* (1947–58) and *Whack-O!* (1958–60). He was also a well-known television personality, and his appearances include the long-running game show series *Call My Bluff*. His many publications include the best-selling *Oxford Book of Humorous Prose* (1989).

Muir, Jean Elizabeth 1928–95 •*English fashion designer*•She was born in London and educated at Dame Harper School, Bedford. She started as a salesgirl with Liberty's in London in 1950, then moved to Jaeger in 1956. In 1961 she started on her own as Jane & Jane. In 1966 she established her own company, Jean Muir. Her clothes are noted for their classic shapes and their softness and fluidity.

Muir, John 1838–1914 •*US naturalist*• Born in Dunbar, Scotland, he emigrated to the US in 1849 and studied at the University of Wisconsin. He concentrated his interest in natural history, exploring the western US, especially the Yosemite area. He farmed very successfully in California, and also campaigned for a national park there. It needed a decade of Muir's vigorous oratory and article writing, and President **Theodore Roosevelt**'s support, before the idea of wildlife conservation became widely accepted. The John Muir Trust to acquire wild land in Great Britain was established in 1984. He is regarded as the father of the modern environmental movement.

Mujibur Rahman, *known as* **Sheikh Mujib** 1920–75 •*Bangladesh statesman*• Born in Tungipana, into a landowning family, he was educated in Calcutta and at Dhaka University, from which he was expelled for political activities. He cofounded (1949) the Awami (People's) League, campaigning for autonomy for East Pakistan (Bangladesh), became its leader in 1953, and led it to electoral victory in 1970. In 1972, after the civil war between East and West Pakistan, he became prime minister of newly independent Bangladesh. Increasingly intolerant of opposition, he established a one-party state. In August 1975 he and his wife were assassinated in a military coup.

Muldoon, Paul Benedict 1951– •*Northern Irish poet*• Born in Portadown, he studied at Queen's University, Belfast. His collections of poetry include *New Weather* (1973), *Meeting the British* (1987) and *Hay* (1999). He has taught widely in Britain and the US, and was appointed Professor of Poetry at Oxford in 1999. His many honors and awards include the T S Eliot prize in 1995 for *The Annals of Chile*.

Muldoon, Sir Robert David 1921–92 •*New Zealand statesman*• Born in Auckland, he served as an infantryman in World War II before becoming an accountant. He was first elected to parliament (as a National Party MP) in 1960, and after five years as minister of finance became deputy prime minister. He became party leader and leader of the Opposition in 1974 and led the National Party to victory in the 1975 elections. He was prime minister from 1974 to 1984, when he gave up leadership of the National Party. He resigned from parliament in 1991.

Müller, (Karl) Alex(ander) 1927– •*Swiss physicist and Nobel Prize winner*• Born in Basel, he was educated at the Swiss Federal Institute of Technology, Zurich, where he received his PhD in 1958. After five years at the Battelle Institute in Geneva (1958–63) he joined the IBM Zurich Research Laboratory, working in the area of solid-state physics. For the discovery of new low-temperature superconductors, Müller shared the 1987 Nobel Prize for physics with **Georg Bednorz**.

Müller, Gerd 1945– •*German soccer player*• He is the highest-scoring player in World Cup finals. He scored 14 goals for West Germany between 1966 and 1974, and scored against every country West Germany met in the competition. He scored twice in the 1972 final and secured the World Cup title for West Germany in 1974 with his goal against Holland. At club level he played for Bayern Munich.

Müller, Hermann Joseph 1890–1967 •*US geneticist and Nobel Prize winner*• Born in New York City, he studied at Columbia University and spent the 1920s at the University of Texas at Austin, the Institute of Genetics at Leningrad (St Petersburg) and the University of Indiana. His major work was on the use of X-rays to cause genetic mutations, for which he was awarded the Nobel Prize for physiology or medicine in 1946. Concerned about the possible dangers of radiation-induced mutations, he campaigned for safety measures in hospitals and against nuclear bomb tests.

Müller, Johannes Peter 1801–58 •*German physiologist*• Born in Koblenz, he studied at the University of Bonn, was appointed to the chair of physiology there in 1826, and in 1833 moved to the University of Berlin. He won fame for his precocious research in embryology, and also showed early interest in the eye and vision. His later work was wide-ranging, covering electrophysiology, the glandular system, the human embryo and the nervous system. He worked on zoological classification. In 1840 he proposed the law of specific nerve energies, that is, the claim that each sensory system will respond in the same way to a stimulus whether this is mechanical, chemical, thermal or electrical. Müller was probably the most significant life scientist and medical theorist in Germany in the first half of the 19th century.

Müller, Paul Hermann 1899–1965 •*Swiss chemist and Nobel Prize winner*• He was born in Olten and educated at the University of Basel. From 1925 onward he worked at the experimental laboratory of the J R Geigy company. He is known for his work on insecticides, particularly for discovering and developing DDT (dichlorodiphenyltrichloroethane), which was first marketed in 1942. DDT is extremely toxic to a wide variety of disease carriers and plant pests, and was used in tropical areas during World War II and after the war in many parts of the world. However, in the 1960s it became clear that many species quickly became resistant to it, and that its cumulative effects in the food chain are very destructive, so its use was discontinued. For the discovery of DDT, Müller was awarded the 1948 Nobel Prize for physiology or medicine.

Mulligan, Gerry (Gerald Joseph) 1927–96 •*US jazz saxophonist, bandleader and composer*• Born in New York City, he learned piano as a child before specializing in the baritone saxophone. He began his career in jazz as an arranger for big bands. He moved to New York, and became involved in the **Miles Davis** sessions later known as *The Birth of the Cool* (1948–50). Moving to Los Angeles, he led a series of very popular small groups without the customary piano or guitar from 1952, in the cool West Coast style. His Concert Jazz Band transferred his ideas to a larger soundscape from 1960. He played with **Dave Brubeck** for a time (1968–1972), and continued to lead bands of various sizes into the 1990s.

Mulliken, Robert Sanderson 1896–1986 •*US chemical physicist and Nobel Prize winner*• Born in Newburyport, Massachusetts, he was educated at MIT and at the University of Chicago. After holding fellowships at Chicago and Harvard between 1921 and 1925, he became assistant Professor of Physics at Washington Square College of New York University (1926–28) and then joined the faculty of the University of Chicago. During World War II he worked on the development of the atomic bomb. His earliest work was on the isotope effect in the band spectra of diatomic molecules, but he is best known for his share in the creation of molecular orbital theory in the 1930s. Mulliken also made important contributions to the development of the concept of hyperconjugation and a scale of electronegativity of the elements, and studied donor-acceptor interactions and charge transfer spectra. He was awarded the Nobel Prize for chemistry in 1966.

Mullis, Kary Banks 1944– •*US biochemist and Nobel Prize winner*• Born in Lenoir, North Carolina, he was educated at Georgia Institute of Technology and the University of California. In the early 1980s he discovered a technique known as the polymerase chain reaction, which allows tiny quantities of DNA to be copied millions of times to make analysis practical. It is now used in a multitude of applications, including tests for the HIV virus and the bacteria which cause tuberculosis, forensic science, and evolutionary studies of the genetic material in fossils. For this work Mullis was awarded the 1993 Nobel Prize for chemistry (with **Michael Smith**).

Mulroney, (Martin) Brian 1939– •*Canadian statesman*• Born in Baie Comeau, Quebec province, the son of an Irish immigrant, he attended St Francis Xavier University in Nova Scotia and studied law at Laval University, Quebec City. He practiced as a labor lawyer in Montreal while becoming increasingly active in the Progressive Conservative Party. In 1983 he became party leader and in 1984 prime minister. He initiated a number of radical measures, including the Meech Lake Accords, which aimed at settling disputes between the provinces and the center, but which later collapsed. He was decisively reelected in 1988, and his efforts to bring about the free trade agreement with the US were crowned with success in 1993. In the same year, Mulroney resigned from office, returning to Montreal to practice law.

Mumford, Lewis 1895–1990 •*US author, editor and critic*• Born in Flushing, New York, he grew up in New York City and studied at several universities there, developing the fascination with urban society and architecture that was to characterize much of his work. *The Culture of Cities* (1938) and *The City in History* (1961) are perhaps the best known of his numerous writings. In studying civilizations, his object was always to determine how they reflected the values of the societies that created them, and he argued eloquently against the domination of modern urban environments by technology. His works include *The Story of Utopias* (1922), *The Myth of the Machine* (1967) and *The Pentagon of Power* (1971).

“ ”

Every generation revolts against its fathers and makes friends with its grandfathers.

1931 ***The Brown Decades**, page 3.*

Munch, Edvard 1863–1944 •*Norwegian painter*• Born in Löten, he studied in Oslo, traveled in Europe and finally settled in Norway in 1908. In Paris he came under the influence of **Paul Gauguin**. He began working in a distinctly Expressionist style around the turn of the century, and his work was widely published in periodicals. His use of primary colors and tortuously curved designs were a great influence on German Expressionists in particular. He became obsessed by subjects such as death and love, and his most characteristic work is *The Scream* (1893), depicting an anonymous figure on a bridge screaming, the swirling lines of color contributing to the mood of desperation. Other works include many self-portraits and various woodcuts and engravings. There is a Munch museum in Oslo.

Münchhausen, Karl Friedrich Hieronymus, Baron von 1720–97 •*German soldier and raconteur*• Born in Bodenwerder, he was a member of an ancient Hanoverian house. He was the narrator of ridiculously exaggerated exploits, and served in Russian campaigns against the Turks. A collection of stories attributed to him was first published in English as *Baron Munchausen's Narrative of His Marvellous Travels and Campaigns in Russia* (1785) by Rudolf Erich Raspe. *Munchausen* is based partly on 16th-century German jokes, partly as a satire on **James Bruce** and other travelers.

Munefusa, Matsuo *See* **Basho, Matsuo**

Mungo, St *See* **Kentigern, St**

Munnings, Sir Alfred 1878–1959 •*English painter*• Born in Suffolk, a specialist in the painting of horses and sporting pictures, he became president of the Royal Academy (1944–49). His work is in many public galleries, and he was well known for his forthright criticism of modern art.

Munro, Alice, *originally* **Alice Anne Laidlaw** 1931– •*Canadian short-story writer and novelist*• She was born and brought up in Wingham, Ontario, and attended the University of Western Ontario. She wrote short stories from an early age, waiting until she was “ready” to write a great novel. Her only novel to date, *Lives of Girls and Women* (1971), accomplished though it is, cannot claim to be that. Her stories, however, published for many years without being collected, are recognized as among the finest of the day. Her many collections of stories include *Dance of the Happy Shades* (1968), *Something I've Been Meaning to Tell You* (1974), *The Progress of Love* (1987), *Selected Stories* (1996) and *Hateship, Friendship, Courtship, Loveship, Marriage* (2001).

Munro, Hector Hugh, *pseudonym* **Saki** 1870–1916 •*British novelist and short-story writer*• He was born in Burma, the son of a police inspector. Educated in England at Bedford Grammar School, he returned to Burma and joined the police force in 1893, but went to London in 1896 and took up journalism. From 1902 he was the Balkans correspondent for the *Morning Post*. He is best known for his short stories, humorous and macabre, which are highly individual and full of eccentric wit and unconventional situations. Collections of his stories are *Reginald* (1904), *The Chronicles of Clovis* (1911) and *Beasts and Superbeasts* (1914). His novels *The Unbearable Bassington* (1912) and *When William Came* (1913) show his gifts as a social satirist of the upper-class Edwardian world. He was killed on the Western Front during World War I.

Munro, Sir Hugh Thomas 1856–1919 •*Scottish mountaineer*• Born in London, he inherited the family estate near Kirriemuir. A founding member of the Scottish Mountaineering Club in 1889, he served as its president from 1894 to 1897. He compiled the first authoritative list of what have come to be known as “Munros” when he published his *Tables of Heights over 3000 Feet* in the first issue of the *SMC Journal* in 1891. While “Munro-bagging” has become a commonplace pastime, Munro himself never achieved the distinction of climbing all the peaks he listed, remaining two short at his death.

Munro, Neil 1864–1930 •*Scottish novelist and journalist*• Born in Inveraray, Argyll, he worked in a law office before taking up journalism in Glasgow. He wrote romantic Celtic tales such as *The Lost Pibroch* (1896) and historical Highland novels, *Doom Castle* (1901) and *The New Road* (1914). However, he is best known for his humorous tales about the captain and crew of a small cargo boat, published as *The Vital Spark* (1906) and collected as *Para Handy and Other Tales* (1931).

Müntzer or **Münzer, Thomas** c. 1488–1525 •*German religious reformer and Anabaptist*• Born in Stolberg, he studied theology, and in 1520 began to preach at Zwickau, but his socialism and mystical doctrines led to conflict with the authorities. In 1525 he was elected pastor of the Anabaptists of Mülhausen, where his communistic ideas soon aroused the whole country. He joined the Peasants' Revolt of 1524–25, but was defeated at Frankenhausen and executed.

Muqaddasi 945–88 •*Arab geographer and pioneer of fieldwork*• Born in Jerusalem, he traveled widely and described Muslim lands in a geographical compendium (985).

Murad IV 1612–40 •*Ottoman sultan*• Born in Constantinople (Istanbul), he succeeded in 1623. A savage disciplinarian, he crushed a serious revolt among the janissaries (1632) and eliminated corruption in administration and justice. In 1638 he led an expedition against Persia (Iran), recapturing Baghdad, which had been taken by **Abbas I (the Great)** in 1624.

Murakami Haruki 1949– •*Japanese novelist*• He was born in Kobe and educated in classics at Waseda University. He started his career in writing as a translator, and his own highly original novels are remarkable for being more influenced by the Americans than by his Japanese predecessors. Wild, surreal, mystical and often extremely funny, he is a best-selling author in Japan. Of his works available in English, *A Wild Sheep Chase* (1982) is one of the best, and is a sort of detective novel in which a psychic detective searches for a war criminal, a woman with beautiful ears, and a supernatural sheep with a star on its back. He published a trilogy entitled *Nejimaki-dori kuronikura* (Eng trans *The Wind-up Bird Chronicle*) in 1995.

Murasaki Shikibu c. 970–c. 1015 •*Japanese writer*• She was a member of the Fujiwara family, one of the most powerful aristocratic dynasties in Japan, but her real name is unknown: "Shikibu Murasaki" is a later fictive construction. She was responsible for the *Genji Monogatari* (Eng trans *The Tale of Genji*, 1925–35), the first great work in Japanese. Complex, delicate and often sublimely beautiful, it far surpasses anything produced elsewhere in its day.

Murat, Joachim 1767–1815 •*French soldier and king of Naples*• He was born at La Bastide-Murat, Lot, the son of an innkeeper. He enlisted in the cavalry on the eve of the Revolution, and was promoted to general during **Napoleon I**'s Egyptian campaign (1799). He helped Napoleon become first consul, married his sister, and replaced his brother, **Joseph Bonaparte**, as king of Naples (1808). He commanded Napoleon's cavalry during the 1812 invasion of Russia, but resigned his commission (1812) to try to rescue Naples. He supported Napoleon after his defeat (1813), but, defeated by the Austrians at Tolentino (1815), he was eventually captured and executed by the troops of **Ferdinand I**.

Murchison, Sir Roderick Impey 1792–1871 •*Scottish geologist*• Born in Tarradale, Ross-shire, he devoted himself to geology after leaving the army in 1816. He established the Silurian system (1835) and, with **Adam Sedgwick**, the Devonian system. From 1840 to 1845, with others, he carried out a geological survey of the Russian empire. Murchison Falls (Uganda) and Murchison River (Western Australia) are named after him. In 1855 he was made director general of the Geological Survey and director of the Royal School of Mines. His principal works were *The Silurian System* (1839) and *The Geology of Russia in Europe and the Urals* (1845).

Murdoch, Dame (Jean) Iris 1919–99 •*Irish novelist, playwright and philosopher*• Born in Dublin, she was educated at Badminton School, Bristol, and Oxford, where she was a Fellow and tutor in philosophy at St Anne's College (1948–63). She married the literary critic John Bayley (1925–) in 1956, and was given the honorary title of Dame Commander, Order of the British Empire, in 1987. Her life and relationship with Bayley was portrayed in the film *Iris* (2001). She published a study of **Jean-Paul Sartre** in 1953 and two important but unfashionable philosophical works, much influenced by **Plato**, *The Fire and the Sun* (1977) and *The Sovereignty of Good* (1970). A later philosophical work is *Metaphysics as a Guide to Morals* (1992). Her fiction, which was at first a secondary activity, is mostly concerned with the preoccupations of middle-class intellectuals and deals with the conflict of good and evil in the context of involved personal relationships, often attended by strange situations and incidents. The popularity of her work derives largely from her narrative skill in controlling tangled and shifting patterns of relationships, the ironic or even startling circumstances in which the characters find themselves, and the pervasive blend of realism and symbolism. Her first novel, *Under the Net*, framed around a male narrator, appeared in 1954 and was followed by 26 more titles in the next 45 years, including *The Sandcastle* (1957), about a schoolmaster's relationship with a young artist; *The Bell* (1958), about the consecration of a bell by a lay community; *A Severed Head* (1961), a black comedy; *An Unofficial Rose* (1962); *The Red and the Green* (1965); *The Nice and the Good* (1968); *The Black Prince* (1973); *The Sea, the Sea* (1978), about an obsession with a childhood sweetheart, which won the Booker Prize; *Nuns and Soldiers* (1980); *The Good Apprentice* (1985); *The Book and the Brotherhood* (1987), about a group of Oxford intellectuals; *The Message to the Planet* (1989); and *The Green Knight* (1993). She also wrote several plays and a book of poetry, *The Year of the Birds* (1978). One of the finest writers of her generation, she spent her final years suffering from Alzheimer's disease.

" "

What can one do with the past?
Forgive it. Let it enter into you in peace.

1968 ***The Nice and the Good.***

Murdoch, (Keith) Rupert 1931– •*US newspaper publisher*• He was born in Melbourne, Australia, and educated at Geelong Grammar School and Oxford, where he was active in Labour politics. His father was a celebrated World War I correspondent who later became chief executive of the Melbourne *Herald* newspaper group. When his father died in 1952, Murdoch inherited the Adelaide *News*, and in the space of a decade he became Australia's second largest publisher and began to set his sights on expansion abroad. First he acquired the *News of the World* in London in 1969, and then, at the end of the same year, bought the *Sun*. Denounced for its puerile taste, including the introduction of daily "page 3" girls, the *Sun* defied its critics and maintained its lead in the circulation war. In 1981 he struck at the heart of the English Establishment when his British subsidiary company, News International, acquired *The Times* and *The Sunday Times* after a bitter struggle. In 1989 he bought the book publishers Collins and inaugurated Sky Television (now BSkyB), a satellite television network. He moved into the US market in 1976 with the purchase of the New York *Post*, and then acquired numerous other US publications as well as 20th Century Fox film studios. He created a successful television network, the Fox Network, and in 1996 bought New World Communications, becoming the owner of television stations that reached up to 40 percent of US viewership. His company, News Corporation, continues to expand into new markets, notably China. He has been a US citizen since 1985.

Murillo, Bartolomé Esteban 1618–82 •*Spanish painter*• He was born in Seville and spent most of his life there. He painted 11 remarkable pictures for the convent of San Francisco in 1645, which made his name. In 1660 he founded the Academy of Seville, of which he became first president. In 1681 he fell from a scaffold when painting an altarpiece at Cádiz, and died soon afterward. His pictures naturally fall into two groups—scenes from low life, such as gypsies and beggar children (mostly executed early in his life), and religious works.

Murnau, F W, *originally* **Friedrich Wilhelm Plumpe** 1888–1931 •*German film director*• Born in Bielefeld, Germany, he studied in Berlin and Heidelberg, and was briefly an actor before World War I. A combat pilot, he crash-landed in Switzerland during 1917. Returning to Germany two years later, he founded the Murnau Veidt Filmgesellschaft. Experimenting with the mobility of the camera, his expressive use of light and shade heightened the menace in such macabre works as *Der Januskopf* (1920, *Janus-Faced*, a version of *Dr Jekyll and Mr Hyde*), and *Nosferatu* (1922, a chilling and faithful rendition of the Dracula story). After a successful trio of films with actor Emil Jannings (1885–1950), he moved to the US and made *Sunrise* (1927), a tale of a young rural couple whose love is threatened by the sophistication of the big city, which won three of the first-ever Academy Awards. He had just completed the much-praised South Seas documentary *Tabu* (1931) before his death in a car crash.

Murphy, Dervla 1931– •*Irish travel writer*• Born in Cappoquin, County Waterford, she attended the Ursuline Convent, Waterford. She cycled to India to work with Tibetan refugees, and her first two books, *Full Tilt* (1965) and *Tibetan Foothold* (1966), financed further journeys to Nepal and Ethiopia. With her daughter Rachel (1968–) she subsequently made several long journeys in southern India, trekking through the Karakoram Mountains and 1,300 miles along the Andes. She has won several literary awards and has also written books on subjects closer to home, including Northern Ireland, racial conflict and the nuclear controversy.

Murphy, Eddie (Edward Regan) 1961– •*US comedian and film actor*• Born in the Bushwick section of Brooklyn, New York, he became a standup nightclub comic on Long Island. He first came to national prominence on the television show *Saturday Night Live* (1980–84). His debut in the film *48 Hrs* (1982) was followed by several box-office hits, including *Trading Places* (1983) and *Beverly Hills Cop* (1984). Subsequent films include *Coming to America* (1988), *Harlem Nights* (1989), which he also directed, *Boomerang* (1992), *The Nutty Professor* (1996), *Doctor Doolittle* (1998) and *Bowfinger* (1999). He voiced the part of Donkey in *Shrek* (2001).

Murphy, Graeme Lloyd 1950– •*Australian dancer, choreographer and ballet director*• Born in Melbourne, he trained at the Australian Ballet School, the youngest boy ever to enter, and subsequently joined the company. He worked as a freelance choreographer in 1975 before rejoining Australian Ballet as a dancer and resident choreographer. Appointed artistic director of Sydney Dance Company in 1976, he brought the ensemble international status. He also choreographed **Benjamin Britten**'s *Death in Venice* for the Canadian Ballet in 1984. He created *Vast*, an Australian bicentennial performance featuring the Australian Dance Theatre, Queensland Ballet, West Australian Ballet and his own troupe in 1988, and has led the company on over 20 international tours.

Murphy, Paul Peter 1948– •*Welsh Labour politician*• Born in Usk, Gwent, he was educated at Oxford University and worked as a lecturer in government and history before entering parliament as Member of Parliament for Torfaen in 1987. He served as Opposition front-bench spokesman for Wales (1988–94), on Northern Ireland (1994–95), on Foreign Affairs (1995) and on Defence (1995–97), and then became Minister of State in the Northern Ireland Office (1997–99). He was appointed Secretary of State for Wales in 1999 and Secretary of State for Northern Ireland in 2002.

Murphy, William Parry 1892–1987 •*US physician and Nobel Prize winner*• He was born in Stoughton, Wisconsin, and educated at the University of Oregon and Harvard Medical School. Although postgraduate training encouraged his interest in clinical research, Murphy entered private practice, working part-time at Harvard with **George Richards Minot** (from 1925) in their investigation of the effect of raw liver in the diets of patients diagnosed as suffering from pernicious anemia. He was awarded the 1934 Nobel Prize for physiology or medicine jointly with Minot and **George Whipple**.

Murphy-O'Connor, Cormac 1932– •*English prelate and cardinal*• Born in Reading, Berkshire, he was educated at Prior Park College, Bath, and at the Venerable English College and Gregorian University in Rome. He was ordained a priest in 1956, serving parishes in Portsmouth and Fareham, and became rector at the Venerable English College in Rome (1971), Bishop of Arundel and Brighton (1977) and ultimately Archbishop of Westminster (2000). He has been criticized by some for his handling of allegations of sex abuse against members of the clergy, but remains a highly regarded figure in the church.

Murray, Sir James Augustus Henry 1837–1915 •*Scottish philologist and lexicographer*• Born in Denholm in the Scottish Borders, he was for many years a schoolmaster at Mill Hill school. The great work of his life, the editing of the Philological Society's *New English Dictionary* (later called the *Oxford English Dictionary*), was begun at Mill Hill (1879), and completed (1928) at Oxford. Murray himself edited about half the work, and he created the organization and the inspiration for completing it.

Murray, Joseph Edward 1919– •*US surgeon and Nobel Prize winner*• He was born in Milford, Massachusetts, and educated at Harvard Medical School. He then joined the Peter Bent Brigham Hospital in Boston, where he became chief plastic surgeon (1951–86). In 1954 Murray and his colleagues first successfully transplanted a kidney between identical twins, and after testing the use of X-rays and drugs in attempts to suppress the immunological reactions, performed successful transplants between non-identical twin brothers, later using an unrelated kidney. By 1962 the use of X-ray and drug techniques were shown to be successful, and soon kidney transplants became common, with systems established for finding donors. He was also chief plastic surgeon at the Children's Hospital Medical Center in Boston (1972–85) and became Professor of Surgery at Harvard Medical School in 1970 (now emeritus). He was awarded the 1990 Nobel Prize for physiology or medicine with **Donnall Thomas**.

Murray (of Epping Forest), Len (Lionel) Murray, Baron 1922– •*English trade union leader*• Born in Shropshire, he studied at the University of London, but his studies were interrupted by World War II and were completed at New College, Oxford, in 1947, after which he joined the staff of the Trades Union Congress (TUC). He progressed to become Assistant General Secretary (1969–73) and then General Secretary (1973–84). He played a major role in the "social contract" partnership between the TUC and the Labour governments of **Harold Wilson** and **James Callaghan** (1974–78), but, from 1979, had an unhappy relationship with the new Conservative administration of **Margaret Thatcher**. He was made a life peer in 1985.

Murray, Les(lie Allan) 1938– •*Australian poet, critic and editor*• Born in Nabiac, New South Wales, he grew up on a dairy farm, then attended the University of Sydney, but left without graduating. He has worked as a translator and a freelance writer, and his poetry, which has made him one of Australia's leading literary figures, is revered for its perceptive evocation of rural life. His verse includes *The Ilex Tree* (1965, with Geoffrey Lehmann), *The Weatherboard Cathedral* (1969), *Poems Against Economics* (1972), a verse novel in 140 sonnets called the *Boys Who Stole the Funeral* (1980), and *The People's Otherworld* (1983), which won the 1984 Australian Literary Society's Gold Medal. In 1993 he received his fifth National Book Council poetry prize for *Translations from the Natural World* (1992). His later verse includes *Subhuman Redneck Poems* (1996), which won Murray the **T S Eliot** prize for poetry in 1997, and *Conscious and Verbal* (1999). He was the editor of the *New Oxford Book of Australian Verse* from 1985 to 1997.

Murrow, Edward R, *originally* **Egbert Roscoe Murrow** 1908–65 •*US journalist and broadcaster*• Born in Pole Creek, North Carolina, he joined CBS in 1935, worked widely in Europe, and reported on wartime Great Britain. In the postwar US he became a producer of and announcer on current affairs programs such as *Person to Person* (1953–60). His courageous questioning of Senator **Joseph McCarthy** in 1954 contributed to the latter's fall from grace, and he received five Emmy awards between 1953 and 1958. He later became director of the US Information Agency (1961–64). The recipient of numerous international distinctions, he was given the honorary title Knight Commander, Order of the British Empire, in 1964.

Murry, John Middleton 1889–1957 •*British writer and critic*• Born in Peckham, London, he was educated at Christ's Hospital and at Brasenose College, Oxford. He wrote some poetry and many volumes of essays and criticism that had a strong influence on the young intellectuals of the 1920s. In 1911 he met **Katherine Mansfield**, whom he married in 1918, and he introduced her work in *The Adelphi*, of which he was founder and editor from 1923 to 1948. He also produced posthumous selections from her letters and diaries, and a biography in 1932. He became a pacifist and was editor of *Peace News* from 1940 to 1946. His major works include critical studies on *Keats and Shakespeare* (1925), his friend *D H Lawrence* (1931), *William Blake* (1933) and *Swift* (1954). He also wrote religious works, including *The Life of Jesus* (1926).

Musaeus 5th-6th century •*Greek epic poet*• He was the author of *Hero and Leander*, which has been translated into many languages.

Museveni, Yoweri Kaguta 1944– •*Ugandan soldier and politician*• After graduating from the University of Dar-es-Salaam, he worked for President **Milton Obote** until his overthrow in 1971 by **Idi Amin**. From exile in Tanzania he formed the Front for National Salvation and, fighting with the Tanzanian army, took part in the defeat and expulsion of Amin in 1979. Obote returned to power in 1980, but only retained it with the help of Tanzanian troops; when these withdrew in 1982, a virtual civil war ensued and reasonable normalcy did not return until 1986 when Museveni became president, pledging himself to follow a policy of national reconciliation. In 1996 he restored limited powers to tribal leaders. Later that year he was reelected president, and was reelected again in 2001.

Musgrave, Thea 1928– •*Scottish composer*• Born in Edinburgh, she studied at the University of Edinburgh, the Paris Conservatoire, and with **Nadia Boulanger**. Her early work was largely Scottish in inspiration: her *Suite o' Bairnsangs* (1953) and the ballet *A Tale for Thieves* (1953) were followed by works such as her *Scottish Dance Suite* (1959). In the late 1950s her work became more abstract, and she began to use serial and aleatory devices. Her music includes two choral and orchestral works, *The Phoenix and the Turtle* (1962) and *The Five Ages of Man* (1963); a full-length ballet, *Beauty and the Beast* (1968); the operas *The Decision* (1964–65), *Mary, Queen of Scots* (1977) and *Simón Bolívar* (1993); the orchestral works *The Seasons* (1988) and *Rainbow* (1990); works for instruments and prerecorded tapes; and chamber operas. Later works include *Helios* (1995), the orchestral work *Phoenix Rising* (1997) and *Lamenting with Ariadne* (2000).

Musharraf, Pervaiz 1943– •*Pakistani soldier and politician*• Born in New Delhi, India, he moved with his family to Karachi, Pakistan, in 1947. He joined the Pakistani army in 1964 and fought with distinction against India in 1965 and again, as a commando, in 1971. He was appointed commander in chief of the army in 1998, and after leading a military coup in 1999 assumed power as president of Pakistan, adopting a relatively moderate, reformist stance. In 2001, after some hesitation, he aligned the country with the West in the campaign against Muslim terrorists based in neighboring Afghanistan.

Musial, Stanley Frank, *known as* **Stan the Man** 1920– •*US baseball player*• Born in Donora, Pennsylvania, he was a talented left-handed hitter and played a record number of major league games (3,026) with the St Louis Cardinals (1941–63). He won the batting championship seven times and was voted the Most Valuable Player (MVP) three times.

Musil, Robert 1880–1942 •*Austrian novelist*• He was born in Klagenfurt and trained as a scientist (he invented a chromatometer) and as a philosopher. During World War I he was an officer, and he drew on this experience for *Die Verwirrungen des Zöglings Törless* (1906, Eng trans *Young Törless*, 1955), a terrifying, sadistic story of life inside a military academy. Memorable though it is, it is eclipsed by *Der Mann ohne Eigenschaften* (1930–43, Eng trans *The Man Without Qualities*, 1953–60), his unfinished tour de force, which portrays a society on the brink through the eyes of Ulrich, the man who has dispensed with conventional qualities. It is widely acknowledged as one of the great novels of the 20th century.

Muskie, Edmund Sixtus 1914–96 •*US politician and lawyer*• Born in Rumford, Maine, he trained as a lawyer at Cornell Law School in Ithaca, New York, and was admitted to the bar in 1939. A former member of the Maine House of Representatives (1947–51) and governor of Maine (1955–59), he represented his home state in the Senate (1959–80), and was the Democratic vice presidential nominee in 1968. He served as secretary of state in 1980–81 under President **Jimmy Carter**.

Musset, (Louis Charles) Alfred de 1810–57 •*French poet and dramatist*• Born in Paris, he found, after tentative study of law and medicine, that he had a talent for writing, and at 18 published a translation of **Thomas De Quincey**'s *Confessions of an English Opium Eater* (*L'anglais mangeur d'opium*, 1828). His first collection of poems, *Contes d'Espagne et d'Italie* (1830, "Tales of Spain and Italy"), won the approval of **Victor Hugo**, though his first play, *La nuit vénitienne* ("A Night in Venice"), failed in 1830, and from then on he conceived an "armchair theater" with plays intended for reading only. When several of his "armchair" plays were staged successfully more than ten years later, he wrote *On ne saurait penser à tout* (1849, "You Can Never Think of Everything"), and other plays for actual performance. Musset had a stormy love affair with **George Sand**, which is traced in his four volumes of *Nuits* (1835–37). Other works include the autobiographical poem *Confessions d'un enfant du siècle* (1835, Eng trans *The Confessions of a Child of the Century*, 1892) and *L'espoir en Dieu* (1838, "Hoping in God").

Mussolini, Benito Amilcare Andrea 1883–1945 •*Italian dictator 1925–43*• Born in Predappio, near Forli, Romagna, he first worked as a teacher and a journalist. In 1902 he traveled to Switzerland, where he developed revolutionary beliefs, and in 1904 he returned to Italy. After a brief period of imprisonment for his political activities, he edited a socialist publication from Trento (which was then in Austria) and in 1912 became editor of the influential nationalist newspaper *Avanti*. He broke with the socialists when he refused to support their neutral stance in World War I, and founded *Il popolo d'Italia* to publicize his belief that only by supporting the Allies could Italy retrieve the disputed Austrian territories. He fought in World War I and was injured. In 1919 he founded the *Fasci di Combattimento* (Fascist Movement), ostensibly to serve the interests of neglected ex-servicemen, but in reality to promote the extreme form of nationalism to which he was now committed. The groups of Fascist Black Shirts whose creation he encouraged were turned to his advantage against the Communists, and in 1921 he exploited his growing personal popularity to win election to the Chamber of Deputies; the following year his Black Shirts marched on Rome. He presented himself as the only man capable of restoring order to a country that seemed to be slipping ever more rapidly into political chaos. In October 1922 he was asked by **Victor Emmanuel III** to form a government. In 1925 he took the title *Il Duce* ("the leader"). Using a mixture of intimidation, patronage and propaganda, he was able to turn Italy into a totalitarian state by 1929. Despite his early aggression over Corfu and his fierce nationalism, his foreign policy was not marked by overt expansionism or aggression until the mid-1930s. However, in 1935 he launched the conquest of Abyssinia, which was followed by large-scale intervention in the Spanish civil war on the side of General **Franco**. During this period he moved increasingly toward cooperation with **Hitler**, which culminated in the 1939 politico-military Pact of Steel (signed by **Galeazzo Ciano** and **Joachim von Ribbentrop**) and eventually in the invasion of France in 1940. In 1939 Mussolini annexed Albania, but the following year he failed to seize Greece. The arrival of German troops to assist in the conquest of Greece signaled the beginning of his dependence on Hitler, and from then on his actions were dictated largely by the needs of Berlin. Dissatisfaction with this policy and a realization of the likely victory of the Allies persuaded many of his supporters to oppose him. After the Allied landings in Sicily in 1942, even Mussolini's own Fascist Council turned on him, and he had to be rescued by German paratroops and taken to northern Italy in a doomed attempt to reestablish his authority. When that failed, he tried to flee the country with his mistress disguised as a German soldier, but was caught and unmasked by a member of the Italian resistance and summarily executed. His corpse was mutilated by the people after it was hung upside down in a public square in Como.

“ ”

If I advance, follow me. If I retreat, kill me. If I die, avenge me.

1926 Said to senior officials after an attempt on his life, April 6.

Mussorgsky, Modest Petrovich, *also spelled* **Moussorgsky** or **Musorgsky** 1835–81 •*Russian composer*• Born in Karevo (Pskov), he was educated for the army but resigned his commission in 1858 after the onset of a nervous disorder, and began the serious study of music under **Mili Balakirev**. A member of the **Glinka**-inspired nationalist group in St Petersburg, which included **Rimsky-Korsakov**, he first made a name with his songs, among them the well-known setting of **Goethe**'s satirical "Song of the Flea" (1879). His most impressive work is the opera *Boris Godunov*, first performed in St Petersburg in 1874, and his piano suite *Pictures at an*

Exhibition (1874, *Kartinki s vystavki*, orchestrated by **Ravel** in 1922) has also maintained its standing in the concert repertoire. Other operas and large-scale works remained uncompleted as the composer sank into the chronic alcoholism which hastened his early death. Rimsky-Korsakov arranged or completed many of these unfinished works.

Mustafa Kemal Atatürk *See* **Atatürk, Mustapha Kemal**

Mutsuhito 1852–1912 •*Emperor of Japan*• He was born in Kyoto, the son of the titular emperor Komei, whom he succeeded in 1867. Within a year he had recovered the full powers of the emperors when, after a brief civil war, he overthrew the last of the shoguns, who had exercised dictatorial authority in Japan for 700 years. He was intelligent and energetic, and his long reign saw the rapid political and military westernization of Japan, under the initiative of the emperor himself. Military success against China (1894–95) was followed by Japan's victories in the Russo-Japanese War (1904–05) and by the economic penetration of Korea and Manchuria. When Mutsuhito died, he was succeeded by his only son, Crown Prince **Yoshihito**. Assigned a posthumous title, in accordance with Japanese custom, Mutsuhito was styled Meiji Tenno.

Muybridge, Eadweard, *originally* **Edward James Muggeridge** 1830–1904 •*US photographer and inventor*• Born in Kingston upon Thames, England, he emigrated to California in 1852 and became a professional photographer, and eventually chief photographer for the US government. He invented a shutter that allowed an exposure of 1/500 seconds, and was able in 1877 to show that a trotting horse had all of its feet off the ground at times. In 1880 he devised the zoopraxiscope, a precursor of cinematography, in which the photographs were printed on a rotating glass disk, and with it went on tour in the US and Europe. In 1884–85 he carried out an extensive survey of the movements of animals and humans for the University of Pennsylvania, publishing the results as *Animal Locomotion* (1887).

Muzorewa, Abel (Tendekayi) 1925– •*Zimbabwean cleric and politician*• Born in Umtali, Southern Rhodesia (Zimbabwe), and educated in Methodist schools in Southern Rhodesia and at a theological college in the US, he was ordained in 1963 and became a bishop of the United Methodist Church in Southern Rhodesia in 1968. Founder-president of the African National Council (ANC) in 1971, he chose the path of an "internal settlement" rather than guerrilla war. After the ANC won the first universal suffrage election in 1979, he was prime minister of "Zimbabwe-Rhodesia" for a few months before the 1980 election swept **Robert Mugabe** into power. He was detained between 1983 and 1984, and then fled to the US in 1985, returning to Zimbabwe a year later. Since 1994 he has led the United Parties political opposition.

Mwalimu *See* **Nyerere, Julius Kambarage**

Mwinyi, Ndugu Ali Hassan 1925– •*Tanzanian politician*• Born in Zanzibar and educated at Zanzibar Teacher Training College and Durham University, England, he worked as a teacher and head teacher. He then joined the Ministry of Education and entered the government of **Julius Nyerere**, holding posts including minister for Home Affairs (1975–77), ambassador to Egypt (1977–81), and minister for Natural Resources and Tourism (1982–83). In 1985 he succeeded Nyerere as president of the United Republic of Tanzania, serving until 1995.

Myerson, Goldie *See* **Meir, Golda**

Myrdal, Alva, *née* **Reimer** 1902–86 •*Swedish sociologist, politician and peace reformer, and Nobel Prize winner*• Born in Uppsala, she was educated at Uppsala and Stockholm Universities and at the University of Geneva. In 1924 she married **Gunnar Myrdal**. A proponent of child welfare and equal rights for women, she was director of the United Nations Department of Social Sciences (1950–56). Appointed Swedish ambassador to India, Burma and Ceylon from 1955 to 1961, she was elected to the Swedish parliament in 1962, and was on the UN Disarmament Committee (1962–1973). As minister for Disarmament and Church Affairs (1966–73) she played a prominent part in the international peace movement. In 1982 she received the Nobel Prize for Peace, jointly with **Alfonso García Robles**.

Myrdal, (Karl) Gunnar 1898–1987 •*Swedish economist and politician, and Nobel Prize winner*• He studied at Stockholm, and taught economics at Stockholm from 1927 to 1950 and from 1960 to 1967. He wrote a classic study of race relations in the US (*An American Dilemma*, 1944), then was minister of Trade and Commerce in Sweden (1945–47), and then executive secretary of the UN Economic Commission for Europe (1947–57). His later works include *The Challenge of Affluence* (1963). He was awarded the Nobel Prize in economics in 1974 (jointly with **Friedrich August von Hayek**), principally for his work on the critical application of economic theory to Third World countries.

Myron 5th century BC •*Greek sculptor*• He was born in Eleutherae and lived in Athens. A contemporary of **Phidias**, he worked in bronze and is best known for the celebrated *Discobolos* (c. 450 BC, Roman marble copy from bronze original, Museo della Terme, Rome) and *Maryas*.

N

Nabokov, Vladimir 1899–1977 •*US novelist*• Born in St Petersburg, Russia, to aristocratic parents, he was educated at the relatively progressive Tenishev School. In 1919, following the Bolshevik Revolution, his family became émigrés, and he and his brother went to England to study, on scholarships to Cambridge. He then rejoined his family in Berlin (1922), where he lived for more than 15 years and published his first novels, among them *Korol', Dama, Valet* (1928, "King, Queen, Knave") and *Otchayanie* (1936, "Despair"). All were written in Russian, under the pseudonym V Sirin, the author himself later collaborating on English translations. From 1937 to 1940 he was in Paris, and he then emigrated to the US where he took citizenship in 1945. He began to write in English and published many short stories and novels, including *Bend Sinister* (1947) and *Pale Fire* (1962). *Lolita* (1955) was a succès de scandale and allowed him to abandon teaching and devote himself to writing full-time. From 1959 he lived in Montreux in Switzerland. Among 20th-century novelists he is regarded for his linguistic ingenuity and dazzling intellect.

Nadelman, Elie 1882–1946 •*US sculptor*• He was born in Warsaw and studied there at the Academy of Fine Arts, but left Poland to settle in Paris (c. 1902). His drawings and sculptures after 1906 reveal a simplification of forms and stylization close to Cubism,as in *Wounded Bull* (1915, New York) but also show an affinity with antique sculpture. In 1914 he moved to the US and began to produce a number of primitive painted figure sculptures in wood. He became a US citizen in 1927. From the 1930s he worked extensively in ceramics. Many of his sculptures were accidentally destroyed.

Nader, Ralph 1934– •*US lawyer and consumer activist*• He was born in Winsted, Connecticut, and educated at Princeton and Harvard Law School. Admitted to the Connecticut bar in 1959, he campaigned for improved consumer rights and protection, encouraging the establishment of powerful civic interest lobbies of which the US Congress, state legislatures and corporate executives were forced to take note. His bestseller about the automobile industry, *Unsafe at Any Speed* (1965), led to the passage of improved car safety regulations in 1966. In 1996 and 2000 he was nominated by the Green Party as a protest candidate for US president, and he ran as an independent in 2004.

Nadir Shah 1688–1747 •*King of Persia*• Born in Khurasan, of Turkish origin, he was king from 1736. A brigand leader who expelled the Afghan rulers of Persia (Iran), he forced Russia to hand over her Caspian provinces, defeated the Turks (1731), conquered Bahrain, Oman and Afghanistan, and ravaged northwest India, taking Delhi (1739) and capturing the Peacock Throne and the Koh-i-noor diamond. His domestic policy led to revolts, especially on religious matters, his harsh taxes ruined the economy, and he was assassinated at Fathabad.

Nagano, Osami 1880–1947 •*Japanese naval officer*• Educated at the Japanese Imperial Naval Academy, Etajima, he studied law at Harvard and served as naval attaché in Washington (1920–23). Promoted to rear admiral in 1928, as head of the Japanese delegation to the second London Naval Conference (1935–36), he advocated the expansion of Japanese naval power. He was Chief of Naval General Staff (1941–44), and planned and ordered the Japanese attack on Pearl Harbor in December 1941. He died while on trial for war crimes.

Nāgārjuna c. 150–c. 250 AD •*Indian Buddhist monk-philosopher*• He was the founder of the Madhyamika or Middle Path school of Buddhism.

Nagy, Imre 1895–1958 •*Hungarian politician*• Born in Kaposvar, he was captured while serving in the Austrian army in World War I, and was sent to Siberia. At the revolution he escaped, joined the Bolshevik forces, and became a Soviet citizen in 1918. Back in Hungary in 1919, he had a minor government post, but later fled to Russia, where he remained throughout World War II. Returning with the Red Army (1944), he became minister of agriculture in the provisional government, enforcing Communist land reforms. In 1947 he became speaker of the Hungarian parliament, and in 1953 prime minister, introducing a "new course" of milder political and economic control. When the Hungarian uprising broke out (October 1956), he promised free elections and a Russian military withdrawal. When, in November, Soviet forces began to suppress the revolution, he appealed to the world for help, but was displaced by the Soviet puppet **János Kádár** and later executed. In 1989, following the overthrow of the Communists, he was given a hero's reburial in Budapest.

Nahayan, Sheikh Zayed bin Sultan al 1918– •*Emir of Abu Dhabi*• He was governor of the eastern province of Abu Dhabi, one of the seven Trucial States on the southern shores of the Persian Gulf and the Gulf of Oman, which were under British protection, until he deposed his brother, Sheikh Shakhbut (1969), and became emir. When the states decided to federate as the United Arab Emirates (1971), he became president of its supreme council. He was unanimously reelected in 1986. Under his rule the UAE ceased to be a collection of medieval emirates and emerged as an efficient modern state with one of the highest per capita incomes in the world.

Nahum 7th century BC •*Old Testament minor prophet*• Born probably in either Israel or Judah, he may have been a captive in Nineveh. He prophesied the destruction of Nineveh by the Medes in 612 BC.

Naidu, Sarojini, *née* **Chattopadhyay**, *known as* **the Nightingale of India** 1879–1949 •*Indian feminist and poet*• Born in Hyderabad, she was educated at Madras, London and Cambridge, and published three volumes of lyric verse between 1905 and 1915. She organized flood relief in Hyderabad (1908) and lectured and campaigned on feminism, in particular the abolition of purdah. Associated with **Mahatma Gandhi**, she was the first Indian woman to be president of the Indian National Congress (1925). She was imprisoned several times for civil disobedience incidents, and took part in the negotiations leading to independence. In 1947 she was appointed governor of United Provinces (Uttar Pradesh).

Naipaul, Sir V(idiadhar) S(urajprasad) 1932– •*Trinidadian novelist and Nobel Prize winner*• Born in Chaguanas, he was educated at Queen's Royal College, Port of Spain, and at Oxford. The editor of "Caribbean Voices" for the BBC, he dabbled in journalism before his first novel, *The Mystic Masseur* (1957), was published. The book which made his name was *A House for Mr Biswas* (1961), a spicy satire spanning three Trinidadian generations but focusing on its eponymous six-fingered sign writer. Thereafter the Caribbean figured less prominently in his work, which grew steadily darker and more complex. *In a Free State* (1971) won the Booker Prize, and in 1979 he published *A Bend in the River*, a masterly re-creation of what it is like to live under an African dictatorship. In addition to novels, he has written several trenchant travel books, including *Among the Believers: An Islamic Journey* (1981). *Finding the Center* (1984) is autobiographical. Later works include *The Enigma of Arrival* (1987) and *A Way in the World* (1994). He was knighted in 1990 and awarded the Nobel Prize for literature in 2001.

“ ”

I do not regard the knighthood as a social accomplishment.

1993 Quoted in "Kingdom of Naipaul" by Zoë Heller in the ***Independent on Sunday*** *Review, March 28.*

Nairne, Lady Carolina, *née* **Oliphant** 1766–1845 •*Scottish songwriter*• She was born in Gask, Perthshire, the daughter of a Jacobite laird, and in 1806 married a cousin, Major Nairne (1757–1830), who became Lord Nairne in 1824. She collected traditional airs and wrote songs to them under the pseudonym "Mrs Bogan of Bogan"; these were published in *The Scottish Minstrel* (1821–24), and posthumously as *Lays from Strathearn.* They include the lament for Prince **Charles Edward Stuart**, "Will Ye No' Come Back Again," "The Land o' the Leal," "Caller Herrin," "The Laird o' Cockpen," "The Rowan Tree," and "The Auld Hoose."

Naismith, James 1861–1939 •*Canadian educator*• Born in Almonte, Ontario, he is regarded as being the originator of basketball in 1891 at the International YMCA Training School (now Springfield College) in Springfield, Massachusetts, using peach baskets on a gym wall. The game was originally designed merely to bridge the gap between the baseball and football seasons, but it soon became popular in its own right. Naismith attended the Berlin Olympics in 1936, at which basketball was elevated to the status of an Olympic sport.

Najibullah, Sayid Mohammad 1947–96 •*Afghan politician*• Born in Paktia province and educated at Habibia Lycée and Kabul University, he became active in the Moscow-inspired People's Democratic Party of Afghanistan (PDPA) in the mid-1960s, and was twice imprisoned for his political activities. After King **Mohammed Zahir Shah** was deposed in a military coup (1973), Najibullah rose rapidly in the party hierarchy, and played a key role in the negotiations that led to the 1978 treaty of friendship with the USSR. The treaty served as a pretext for the Russian invasion the following year, when he was made information minister. He was admitted to the Afghan politburo in 1981, and became president in 1987. Strong guerrilla resistance by the members of the National Islamic Front weakened his regime, however, and in 1991 the United Nations renewed its call for elections in Mujahideen-controlled territories with a view to establishing a democratically elected government. Najibullah finally resigned, handing over power to a coalition of Mujahideen leaders in May 1992, and took refuge in a UN compound until his death.

Nakasone, Yasuhiro 1917– •*Japanese politician*• Born in Takasaki and educated at Tokyo Imperial University (now the University of Tokyo), he served in the Japanese navy in World War II, and afterward entered politics as a member of the conservative Liberal Democratic Party (LDP), holding a number of ministerial posts from 1967 to 1982. He was elected secretary-general (1974–76), chairman (1977–80) and, in 1982, LDP president, and thus prime minister. His program combined greater economic liberalism at home with a more assertive posture abroad, and he became Japan's most forceful and popular political leader for decades. He stepped down as prime minister in 1987 and nominated **Noboru Takeshita** as his successor. Since 1988 he has been chairman and president of the Institute for International Policy Studies (formerly the International Institute for Global Peace).

Namath, Joe Willie (Joseph William), *known as* **Broadway Joe** 1943– •*US football player*• Born in Beaver Halls, Pennsylvania, he was noted for his high living off the field. An outstanding quarterback on the University of Alabama's unbeaten team of 1964, he joined the New York Jets in 1965. In a phenomenally successful career, he played for a total of 23 seasons, passing for a total of 27,663 yards and scoring 173 touchdowns. In 1967 he passed for a record 4,007 yards, and in 1969 inspired the Jets to an upset victory over the Baltimore Colts in the Superbowl. Following his retirement (1978) he remained in the public eye with appearances in films and on television.

Nanak, *also known as* **Guru Nanak** 1469–1539 •*Indian religious leader and founder of Sikhism*• Born near Lahore (now in Pakistan), he was a Hindu by birth and belief, but taught in both Hindu and Muslim centers. He settled in Kartarpur, in the Punjab, where he attracted many followers. His doctrine, set out later in the *Adi-Granth*, sought a fusion of Brahmanism and Islam on the grounds that both were monotheistic, although his own ideas leaned rather toward pantheism.

Nana Sahib, *properly* **Brahmin Dundhu Panth** c. 1820–59 •*Indian rebel*• The adopted son of the ex-peshwa (head) of the Marathas, he became the leader of the Sepoys in Cawnpore at the outbreak of the Indian Mutiny (1857), and was held responsible for the massacre of the British residents. After the collapse of the rebellion he escaped into Nepal.

Nansen, Fridtjof 1861–1930 •*Norwegian explorer, biologist and oceanographer, and Nobel Prize winner*• Born in Store-Frøen, he studied at Christiana University (now the University of Oslo) and later at Naples. His great achievement was the partial accomplishment of his plan for reaching the North Pole by letting his ship become frozen into the ice north of Siberia and drift with a current setting toward Greenland. He started in the *Fram*, built for the purpose, in August 1893, reached the New Siberian Islands in September, made fast to an ice floe, and drifted north to 84°4' in March 1895. There he left the *Fram* and pushed across the ice, reaching the highest latitude till then attained, 86°14' N, on April 7, and overwintering in Franz Josef Land. Professor of Zoology (1897) and of Oceanography (1908) at Oslo, he furthered the cause of Norwegian independence from Sweden, and was the first Norwegian ambassador in London (1906–08). In 1922 he was awarded the Nobel Peace Prize for Russian relief work, and he did much for the League of Nations.

Napier, Sir Charles 1786–1860 •*Scottish naval commander*• Born at Merchiston Hall near Falkirk, he went to sea at the age of 13, received his first command in 1808, then served as a volunteer in the Peninsular army. In the American War of 1812 he led the ascent of the Potomac River, and took part in the operations against Baltimore. In command of the loyalist Portuguese fleet (1831–33), he defeated the fleet of the pretender, **Maria Evaristo Miguel**, and restored Queen Maria II to the throne. Returning to the British navy in 1839, he stormed Sidon in the war between the Porte and **Mehemet 'Ali**, defeated Ibrahim Pasha in Lebanon, attacked Acre, blockaded Alexandria, and concluded a convention with 'Ali. He commanded the Baltic fleet in the Crimean War (1854–55). He twice sat in parliament.

Napier, John 1550–1617 •*Scottish mathematician, inventor of logarithms*• Born at Merchiston Castle, Edinburgh, he went to the University of St Andrews at the age of 13 but never graduated, traveled on the Continent, then settled down to a life of literary and scientific study. He described his famous invention of logarithms in *Mirifici logarithmorum canonis descriptio* (1614, "Description of the Marvelous Canon of Logarithms"). Formulated to simplify computation, his system used the natural logarithm base *e*, but was modified soon after by Henry Briggs (1561–1630) to use the base 10. Napier also devised a calculating machine, using a set of rods called "Napier's bones," which he described in his *Rabdologiae* (1617, Eng trans *Study of Divining Rods*, 1667).

Napoleon I, *originally* **Napoléon Bonaparte** 1769–1821 •*Emperor of France*• Born in Ajaccio in Corsica, he was the second son of **Charles Bonaparte**, a Corsican lawyer. He entered the military schools at Brienne (1779) and Paris (1784), and in 1793 was given command of the artillery at the Siege of Toulon, where he served with distinction and was promoted to brigadier general. He was appointed commander of the army of Italy (1796), in which role he was able to demonstrate his great military genius. Two days before his departure for Italy he married **Joséphine**, widow of General Vicomte de **Beauharnais**. He skillfully defeated the Piedmontese and the Austrians, and in October 1797 Austria signed the Treaty of Campo Formio, by which France made significant gains. Intending to damage British trade by conquering Egypt, he captured Malta (1798), entered Cairo, defeating the Turks, but the French fleet was destroyed by **Nelson** at the Battle of the Nile. Hearing of French reverses in Italy and on the Rhine, he embarked from France and took part in the revolution of 18th Brumaire (November 9, 1799), becoming first consul. Needing to improve the poor state of the French treasury to fund new military campaigns, he drew up plans with the Bank of France, sought to stabilize the franc and regulated the collection of taxes. Victory at Marengo (1800) led to the signing of the Treaty of Luneville (February 1801), consolidating the French gains of Campo Formio. France's power in Europe was further strengthened by a concordat with Rome, and by the Peace of Amiens with England (1802). In 1802 Napoleon was made first consul for life, and in May 1804 he assumed the hereditary title of emperor. Hostilities had resumed between England and France, and in 1805 he also faced a coalition of Russia and Austria. England's naval supremacy precluded any idea of invasion, and the French fleet was destroyed by Nelson at Trafalgar. Instead Napoleon defeated the Austrians at Ulm and then inflicted a disastrous defeat on the Russians and Austrians at Austerlitz. The Holy Roman Empire came to an end, the Confederation of the Rhine was formed under French protection, and Napoleon then entered into negotiations for peace with Russia and England. He crushed a Prussian army in October 1806, and defeated Russia in June 1807. By the Peace of Tilsit, Prussia lost half her territory and Napoleon became the arbiter of Europe, now master of an empire that extended from France to Italy and from the Pyrenees to the Dalmatian coast. The principal threat to his power remained the naval supremacy of England. Knowing England's reliance on trade, he tried to cripple her by ordering the European states under his control to boycott British goods. To enforce the blockade, he sent armies to occupy Spain and Portugal, precipitating the Peninsular War, which was to occupy a large part of the French army from 1808 until 1813, when **Wellington** routed them. In December 1809 Napoleon divorced the childless Joséphine and married the archduchess **Marie Louise** of Austria, with a desired heir (the future **Napoleon II**) born in 1811. Napoleon, suspecting Russia of seeking an alliance with England, invaded and defeated the Russians at Borodino (September 7, 1812), and occupied the city of Moscow. But his lines of communication were overstretched, his army was tired and hungry, and the Russian winter harsh, and he was forced to retreat. After initial successes, he was significantly defeated by the allies at the Battle of the Nations near Leipzig. The allies invaded France and attacked Paris (1814), which capitulated. Napoleon was forced to abdicate, and by the Treaty of Fontainebleau he was given the sovereignty of Elba. The return was unpopular. Napoleon hoped to take advantage of the situation and on March 20 entered Paris at the start of the "Hundred Days." Europe declared war against him and he was defeated by the combined armies of Wellington and **Blücher** at Waterloo in Belgium. Napoleon fled to Paris, abdicated on June 22, and surrendered to the British. He was banished by the British government to St Helena, where he died of a stomach illness on May 5, 1821.

“ ”

The English conquered us; but they are far from being our equals.

1815 Letter to Gaspar Gourgaud from St Helena, after the Battle of Waterloo.

Napoleon II, *originally* **François Charles Joseph Bonaparte** 1811–32 •*French nobleman and titular king of Rome*• Born in Paris, the son of **Napoleon I** and **Marie Louise**, he was styled king of Rome upon his birth at the Tuileries. From 1814 until his death he lived at the Austrian court and was created Duke of Reichstadt (1818) by his grandfather, **Francis I**. Loyal Bonapartists proclaimed him Napoleon II in Paris in 1815, but he was formally deposed five days later. He spent the rest of his life in Vienna.

Napoleon III, *originally* **Charles Louis Napoléon Bonaparte** 1808–73 •*President of the second French Republic and emperor of France*• Born in Paris, he was the third son of **Louis Bonaparte**, and a nephew of **Napoleon I**. His mother, Hortense de Beauharnais, was the daughter of Napoleon's first wife, **Joséphine**. Brought up in Switzerland, he assisted the Romagna in Italy in its revolt against pontifical rule in 1831. On the death of the Duke of Reichstadt (**Napoleon II**) in 1832, he considered himself the head of the Napoleonic dynasty. Between 1832 and 1836 he published his *Rêveries politiques, Projet de constitution*, and *Considérations politiques et militaires sur la Suisse*. Following an unsuccessful action against the French at Strasbourg in 1836, he went to the US, returning to Europe after his mother's death (1837), and at the insistence of the French government, he settled in London. In 1838 he published his *Idées napoléoniennes*. In 1840 he made a second and equally abortive attempt on the throne of France at Boulogne, and was sentenced to be imprisoned for life in the fortress of Ham, near Amiens. He escaped to England in 1846. The revolution of February 1848 was a victory for the workers, and he hurried back to France. He was elected deputy for Paris and three other departments, he took his seat in the Constituent Assembly on June 13, 1848. Two days later he resigned and left France. His quintuple election recalled him in September, and he won a huge victory over General Louis Cavaignac (1802–57), his genuinely republican competitor. On December 20 he took the oath of allegiance to the Republic as president, but at the beginning of 1849 a struggle emerged between the president and the majority of the Assembly. On December 2, 1851, he dissolved the Constitution and imprisoned or deported those who rebelled. France appeared to acquiesce, for when the vote was taken in December, he was reelected for ten years. He assumed the title Emperor of France in 1852. Political parties were either demoralized or broken, he gagged the press, awed the bourgeoisie, and courted the clergy to win the peasantry. In 1853 he married Eugénie de Montijo (1826–1920), a Spanish countess. The emperor now proclaimed the right of peoples to choose their own masters, helping his own cause with the annexation of Savoy and Nice to France (1860), his Mexican intervention through **Maximilian** of Austria, and in his handling of the Italian question. He regulated the price of bread, encouraged public works, and prompted the complete remodeling of Paris. He unwisely declared war against Prussia in July 1870 and suffered humiliating defeat, surrendering on September 2. On September 4 the Second Empire was ended. In 1871 he joined the ex-empress at Chislehurst, Kent, and resided there in exile until his death.

Narayan, Rasipuram Krishnaswamy 1906–2001 •*Indian novelist*• Born in Madras, in southern India, he was educated there and at Maharajah's College in Mysore. His first novel, *Swami and Friends* (1935), and its successor, *The Bachelor of Arts* (1937), are set in the enchanting fictional territory of Malgudi. Other Malgudi novels include *The Dark Room* (1938), *The English Teacher* (1945)—a thinly veiled account of his own marriage and the event that most matured and shaped his character, the early death of his beloved wife—*The Man-Eater of Malgudi* (1961), *The Painter of Signs* (1977), *A Tiger for Malgudi* (1983) and *The World of Nagaraj* (1990). His novel *The Guide* (1958) won him the National Prize of the Indian Literary Academy. He also published stories, travel books, books for children and essays, as well as *My Days: A Memoir* (1974).

Narayanan, Shri Kocheril Raman 1920– •*Indian politician*• Born in Ozhavoor, Kerala, he was educated at Travancore University and at the London School of Economics and initially took up a career as a lecturer and newspaper correspondent. Having entered India's Foreign Service in 1949, he served in Indian embassies worldwide, worked in the Ministry of External Affairs and was ambassador to Thailand (1967–69), Turkey (1973–75), China (1976–78) and the US (1980–83). He entered parliament as a Member of Parliament (1985–92) and held various senior posts before becoming vice president of India (1992–97) and ultimately president (from 1997).

Narses c. 478–573 •*Byzantine general*• He was born in Armenia and served **Justinian I** in Constantinople (Istanbul). In 552 he succeeded **Belisarius** in Italy, took possession of Rome, and completely extinguished the Gothic power in Italy. Justinian appointed him prefect of Italy in 554, and he administered its affairs with vigor and ability. He was charged with greed, and on Justinian's death the Romans complained to **Justin II**, who deprived him of his office in 567.

Narváez, Ramón María 1800–68 •*Spanish soldier and senator*• Born in Loja, a supporter of **Isabella II**, he defeated the Carlists in 1836, then took part in an unsuccessful insurrection against Espartero in 1840 and fled to France. In 1843 he led a republican insurrection in Madrid that drove Espartero from power, and became virtual dictator. He lost power temporarily in 1851, but from 1856 he was premier again several times.

Nash, John 1752–1835 •*English architect*• Born in London or Cardigan, Wales, he trained as an architect, but after coming into a legacy, retired to Wales. Having lost heavily on business speculations in 1792, he resumed practice in London and gained a reputation with his country-house designs. He came to the notice of the Prince of Wales (later **George IV**), and was engaged (1811–25) to plan the layout of the new Regent's Park and its environs of curved terraces. He laid out Regent Street (1825) to link the park with Westminster. He built Carlton House Terrace, and laid out Trafalgar Square and St James's Park. He re-created Buckingham Palace from old Buckingham House, designed the Marble Arch which originally stood in front of it (moved to its present site in 1851), and rebuilt Brighton Pavilion in Oriental style. The skillful use of terrain and landscape featured in his layouts marks him as one of the greatest town planners.

Nash, John F(orbes), Jr 1928– •*US economist and Nobel Prize winner*• Born in Bluefield, West Virginia, he was educated at Carnegie Mellon and Princeton Universities and subsequently worked at MIT and (from 1959) Princeton. He shared the 1994 Nobel Prize for economics with John C Harsanyi (1920–2000) and Reinhard Selten (1930–) for their pioneering work on game theory. His decades-long battle with schizophrenia was portrayed in the film *A Beautiful Mind* (2001).

Nash, (Frederic) Ogden 1902–71 •*US writer of light verse*• Born in Rye, New York, he was educated at Harvard and worked in teaching, editing, selling bonds and writing copy, before devoting himself to verse. He soon became a popular writer and frequently produced witty verse for the *New Yorker*. He used puns, parody, pastiche and alliteration to amuse as well as shock. He published many collections, including *Free Wheeling* (1931), *Parents Keep Out: Elderly Poems for Youngerly Readers* (1951), *The Private Dining Room and Other New Verses* (1953) and *Boy Is a Boy* (1960).

“ ”

The cow is of the bovine ilk;
One end is moo, the other, milk.

1931 ***Free Wheeling****, "The Cow."*

Nash, Paul 1889–1946 •*English painter*• Born in London, he became an official war artist in 1917 (remembered particularly for his poignant *Menin Road*, 1919). Developing a style which reduced form to bare essentials without losing the identity of the subject, he won renown as a landscape painter and also practiced scene painting, commercial design and book illustration. For a while he taught at the Royal College of Art. Experiments in a near-abstract manner were followed by a phase of surrealism until, in 1939, he again filled the role of war artist, producing such pictures as *Totes Meer*. Shortly before his death, he turned to a very individual style of flower painting.

Nashe, Thomas 1567–1601 •*English dramatist and satirist*• Born in Lowestoft, Suffolk, he studied at St John's College, Cambridge. His first work was the *Anatomie of Absurditie* (1589), perhaps written at Cambridge. He plunged into the Marprelate controversy, showing a talent for vituperation which he expressed in such works as *Pierce Penilesse, His Supplication to the Divell* (1592), against Richard Harvey, who had criticized Nashe's preface to **Robert Greene**'s *Menaphon*. In 1599 the controversy was suppressed by the Archbishop of Canterbury. Nashe's satirical masque *Summer's Last Will and Testament* (1592) contains the song "Spring the sweet Spring is the year's pleasant king." *The Unfortunate Traveller* (1594) is a picaresque tale, one of the earliest of its kind. After **Christopher Marlowe**'s death, Nashe prepared his unfinished tragedy *Dido* (1596) for the stage. His own play *The Isle of Dogs* (1597), now lost, drew such attention to abuses in the state that it was suppressed, the theater closed, and the writer himself thrown into the Fleet prison.

Nasser, Gamal Abd al- 1918–70 •*Egyptian statesman*• He was born in Alexandria. As an army officer, he became dissatisfied with the inefficiency and corruption of the **Farouk** regime, and was involved in the military coup of 1952. He became prime minister (1954–56) and then president (1956–70), deposing his fellow officer, General **Mohammed Neguib**. During his term in office, Nasser nationalized the Suez Canal, which led to Israel's invasion of the Sinai and the intervention of Anglo-French forces. His aim was to build an Arab empire stretching across North Africa, and in 1958 created the United Arab Republic, a federation with Syria from which Syria withdrew in 1961. After the six-day Arab-Israeli War (1967), heavy losses on the Arab side led to Nasser's resignation, but he was persuaded to stay on, and he died in office, one year before the completion of one of his greatest projects, the Aswan High Dam.

Nathans, Daniel 1928–99 •*US microbiologist and Nobel Prize winner*• Born in Wilmington, Delaware, of Russian-Jewish extraction, he studied at the University of Delaware and Washington University School of Medicine, St. Louis. After a disgruntled career in teaching and research, in 1962 he became a professor at Johns Hopkins University, where he pioneered the use of restriction enzymes to fragment DNA molecules, enabling him to make the first genetic map and to identify the location of specific genes on the DNA. For this work he shared the 1978 Nobel Prize for physiology or medicine with **Hamilton Smith** and **Werner Arber**.

Nation, Carry Amelia, *née* **Moore** 1846–1911 •*US temperance crusader*• She was born in Garrard County, Kentucky. As the widow of an alcoholic, she was adamantly opposed to the use of liquor, and conducted a series of raids on saloons in Kansas and other states (1899–1909), breaking bottles and destroying furniture with a hatchet. Her frequent arrests focused public attention on the cause of Prohibition, and she often appeared as a temperance lecturer.

Naughtie, (Alexander) James 1951– •*Scottish journalist and broadcaster*• Born in Aberdeen, he studied at the University of Aberdeen and Syracuse University, and worked for *The Scotsman* (1977–84) and *The Guardian* (1984–88), becoming the latter's chief political correspondent. He hosted BBC Radio 4's *The World at One* from 1988 to 1994, subsequently joining the *Today* program (1994–), and also hosts Radio 4's *Book Club* (1998–) and the annual Proms concerts (1991–) on radio and television.

Nauman, Bruce 1941– •*US sculptor*• Born in Fort Wayne, Indiana, he studied mathematics and art at the University of Wisconsin. In the 1960s he became a leading exponent of conceptual art, using neon lights and holograms in addition to producing minimalist sculptures from more conventional materials, as in *Six Inches of My Knee Extended to Six Feet* (1967). From 1970 he worked principally with wood and fiberglass, exploring the relationship between sculpture and the gallery space, producing installations such as *Room with My Soul Left Out/Room That Does Not Care* (1984). More recent works include *Raw Material* (1990), a series of video works.

Navratilova, Martina 1956– •*US tennis player*• Born in Prague, in 1975 she defected to the US (US citizen 1981) and immediately turned professional. Her rivalry with **Chris Evert** was one of the great features of the game from 1975. She won a record nine singles titles at Wimbledon (1978–79, 1982–87, 1990) and the US Open four times (1983–84, 1986–87) and recorded more than one hundred tournament successes. Her impressive number of wins makes her second only to **Margaret Smith Court**.

Nazarbaev, Nursultan Abishevich 1940– •*Kazakh politician*• Originally a metal worker, he turned to party duties in 1969 and rose dramatically in the 1980s. He was made first secretary of the Kazakh Communist Party in 1989. In 1990 he was chosen for the Soviet politburo and became president of the Kazakh Supreme Soviet. As elected president of Kazakhstan in 1991 he took his republic out of the USSR but kept it in the new Commonwealth of Independent States (CIS). He was reelected in 1999.

Nazianzus, Gregory of *See* **Gregory of Nazianzus, St**

Nazrul Islam, Kazi *See* **Islam, Kazi Nazrul**

N'Dour, Youssou 1959– •*Senegalese singer, musician and composer*• Born in Dakar, Senegal, into a musical family of griots, he developed a style based on the traditional music of the Wolof tribe of Senegal, but with added influences from Cuban, jazz, and later rock music. His Étoile de Dakar band became African superstars, and his magnificent singing voice brought him to the attention of **Peter Gabriel** and **Paul Simon**. His initial Western albums were not a success, and many felt he had left too much of Senegal behind him, but he remains one of the major artists bringing African music to a wider global audience.

Neagle, Dame Anna, *originally* **Marjorie Robertson** 1904–86 •*English actress*• Born in London, she studied and taught dance and was a chorus girl before graduating to leading roles, making her film debut in 1930. She emerged as a major star of historical film dramas, offering genteel portraits of inspiring heroines such as *Victoria the Great* (1937) and *The Lady with the Lamp* (1951). A series of musicals made her Great Britain's top box-office attraction, but later attempts to tackle contemporary subjects were ill judged, and she retired from the screen in 1958. She retained the affection of British audiences, later stage appearances including *Charlie Girl* (1965–71) and *My Fair Lady* (1978–79). Given the honorary title of Dame Commander, Order of the British Empire, in 1969, she wrote two autobiographies.

Neal, Patricia (Patsy Louise) 1926– •*US actress*• Born in Packard, Virginia, she studied drama at Northwestern University in Evanston, Illinois, and worked as a model before making her Broadway debut in *The Voice of the Turtle* (1946). Joining the New York Actors Studio, she won a Tony award for *Another Part of the Forest* (1946) and made her film debut in *John Loves Mary* (1949), later appearing in films such as *A Face in the Crowd* (1957), *Breakfast at Tiffany's* (1961) and *Hud* (1963, Best Actress Academy Award). Her brave fight to regain her health after several massive strokes was rewarded with the Heart of the Year award from President **Lyndon B Johnson** and a further Academy Award nomination for *The Subject Was Roses* (1968). She later appeared in a number of television productions and more recently in the film *Cookie's Fortune* (1999). She was married (1953–83) to the writer **Roald Dahl** and has written an autobiography *As I Am* (1988).

Nearchus 4th century BC •*Macedonian general*• Born in Crete, he settled in Amphipolis during the reign of **Philip II** of Macedon, and became the companion of the young **Alexander the Great**. In 329 BC he joined Alexander in Bacria with a body of Greek mercenaries and took part in the Indian campaigns. Having built a fleet on the Hydaspes (Jhelum), Alexander gave Nearchus the command. He left the Indus in 325, and, skirting the coast, reached Susa in 324. His narrative is preserved in the *Indica* of **Arrian**.

Neave, Airey 1916–79 •*British Army intelligence officer and politician*• Born in London, he was educated at Eton and at Merton College, Oxford. In World War II he was wounded at Calais (1940) and taken prisoner. He escaped from a Polish POW camp but was recaptured and sent to the maximum security prison at Colditz Castle, from which he was the first British officer ever to escape (1942). He was awarded many medals for his war service, including the croix de guerre. In 1943 he was called to the bar, and as a lieutenant colonel served charges on many of the war criminals who stood trial at Nuremberg. He entered parliament for the Conservatives at his third attempt, in 1951. He was prominent in the group that deposed **Edward Heath** as party leader (1975) and replaced him with **Margaret Thatcher**, who later rewarded Neave by appointing him secretary of state for Northern Ireland (1979). As an opponent of power sharing and of the withdrawal of British forces from the Province, Neave was killed by an INLA car bomb outside the House of Commons.

Nebuchadnezzar or **Nebuchadrezzar II** d. 562 BC •*King of Babylon*• He succeeded his father, Nabopolassar, and founded the New Babylonian Empire. He rebuilt Babylon and restored almost every temple in the land. He extended the Babylonian Empire as far as the Mediterranean, defeating the Egyptians at Carchemish (605 BC) and gaining control of Syria. He captured Jerusalem in 597 and 586, when he destroyed the city and deported the Jews into exile in Babylonia.

Necker, Anne Louise Germaine *See* **Staël, Madame de**

Necker, Jacques 1732–1804 •*French politician and financier*• Born in Geneva, he went to Paris as a banker's clerk when he was 15, and in 1762 established the London and Paris bank of Thellusson and Necker. In 1776 he was made the director of the treasury, and next year director general of finance. Some of his remedial measures assisted France, but his most ambitious scheme—the establishment of provincial assemblies with the power to gather taxes—proved a disastrous failure. His retrenchments were hateful to the queen, and he was dismissed. He was recalled in 1788, when he won popularity by recommending the summoning of the Estates General, but his proposals for reform displeased the king and he was dismissed once more. His dismissal contributed to the public mood that culminated in the storming of the Bastille. He was the father of Madame de **Staël**.

Neeson, Liam, *originally* **William John Neeson** 1952– •*Northern Irish actor*• Born in Ballymena, he was a boxer, architect's clerk and had studied to become a teacher before turning to acting and making his stage debut in *The Risen* (1976). He made his film debut in *Excalibur* (1981). Tall and physically imposing but capable of great sensitivity, he appeared in such films as *The Bounty* (1984), *The Mission* (1986), *Suspect* (1987), *The Good Mother* (1988) and *Husbands and Wives* (1992). He received an Academy Award nomination for his powerful performance as the philanthropic industrialist in *Schindler's List* (1993). Subsequent films include *Nell* (1994), *Michael Collins* (1996) and *Star Wars Episode 1: The Phantom Menace* (1999). He made his Broadway debut in *Anna Christie* (1993) opposite actress Natasha Richardson (1963–), whom he married in 1994.

Nefertiti (Neferneferuaten) *See* **Akhenaten**

Negri, Ada 1870–1945 •*Italian poet*• Born in Lodi, she became a teacher in a small primary school and made her literary debut with *Fatalità* (1892, "Destiny"), a derivative and idealistic collection of humanitarian poems. Her subsequent works, nine more volumes of verse and a number of prose works, refined the political, feminist and mystical basis of her work.

Neguib, Mohammed 1901–84 •*Egyptian leader*• As general of an army division, he carried out a coup d'état in Cairo (1952) which banished King **Farouk I** and initiated the "Egyptian Revolution." Taking first the offices of commander in chief and prime minister, he abolished the monarchy in 1953 and became president of the republic. He was deposed in 1954 and succeeded by Colonel **Gamal Abd al-Nasser**.

Negus, Arthur George 1903–85 •*English broadcaster and antiques expert*• Born in Reading, Berkshire, the son of a cabinetmaker, he took over the family shop in 1920 and spent 20 years as an antiques dealer. In 1946 he joined the Gloucester firm of fine art auctioneers, Bruton, Knowles & Co. Asked to expound on the merits and value of antiques, he became a regular panel member on the television series *Going for a Song* (1966–76), and his wry humor and expertise made him a popular broadcaster in such series as *Arthur Negus Enjoys* (1982) and *The Antiques Roadshow* (1982–83). His books include *A Life Among Antiques* (1982).

Nehemiah 5th century BC •*Old Testament prophet*• He was cupbearer for **Artaxerxes I**, who in 444 BC made him governor of Judea. He had the walls of Jerusalem rebuilt, and repopulated the city by drafts from the surrounding districts. In 432 BC he revisited Jerusalem, and either initiated or renewed and completed certain reforms which were among the most characteristic features of post-exilic Judaism. The canonical book of Nehemiah originally formed the closing chapters of the undivided work Chronicles-Ezra-Nehemiah.

Nehru, Jawaharlal, *known as* **Pandit ("teacher")** 1889–1964 •*Indian statesman*• Born in Allahabad, the son of **Motilal Nehru**, he was educated at Harrow and Trinity College, Cambridge. He studied for the bar, returned home and served in the High Court of Allahabad. He joined the Indian Congress Committee in 1918, became an admirer, if sometimes a critic of **Gandhi**, and was imprisoned several times by the British. In 1929 he was elected president of the Indian National Congress. From 1947 to 1964 Nehru was India's first prime minister and minister of external affairs, following a policy of neutralism during the Cold War. He committed India to a policy of industrialization and to a reorganization of its states on a linguistic basis, and acted with restraint over Kashmir. His daughter **Indira Gandhi** was later prime minister.

Nehru, Motilal 1861–1931 •*Indian nationalist leader, lawyer and journalist*• He became a follower of **Gandhi** in 1919, founded the *Independent* of Allahabad and became the first president of the reconstructed Indian National Congress. In the 1920s he coheaded the Swaraj Party (with **Chitta Ranjan Das**), and wrote a report as a basis for Indian constitutional development and to solve the political differences between Hindus and Muslims. The report was not, however, acceptable to the followers of **Muhammad Ali Jinnah**. He was the father of **Jawaharlal Nehru**.

Neil, Andrew Ferguson 1949– •*Scottish journalist*• Born in Paisley, Strathclyde, and educated at the University of Glasgow, he worked briefly in the Conservative Party's research department before joining *The Economist* magazine (1973–83), becoming UK editor. He was appointed editor of the *Sunday Times* in 1983, and with the encouragement of its proprietor, **Rupert Murdoch**, changed the paper's soft-left bias and strongly supported most of the key policies of **Margaret Thatcher**'s government. Neil left the *Sunday Times* in 1994, becoming a freelance writer and broadcaster, fronting his own discussion television program, *The Midnight Hour*. In 1996 he became editor in chief, then in 1999 publisher, of Press Holdings, owners of *The Scotsman, Scotland on Sunday, Edinburgh Evening News, The European* and *Sunday Business*.

Neill, A(lexander) S(utherland) 1883–1973 •*Scottish educator and author*• Born in Kingsmuir, Tayside, the son of a village schoolmaster, he became a pupil-teacher there (1899–1903), and assistant master at schools in Fife (1903–08), before studying English at the University of Edinburgh. He is best known as the founder of a community school at Hellerau, near Salzburg, which eventually settled at Leiston, Suffolk, in 1927 as Summerhill School. Summerhill was an attempt to provide an education free even of the authoritarian overtones of other progressive schools. Many pupils were "difficult," and Neill spent a lot of time in psychotherapy, at first called "Private Lessons." He was the most extreme and radical of British progressive schoolmasters and published over 20 books.

Neilson, Donald, *originally* **Donald Nappey** 1936– •*English murderer and kidnapper*• Born near Bradford, he was convicted of four murders. Three murders were committed during burglaries early in 1974. Soon after, 17-year-old heiress Lesley Whittle was abducted from her home, and a ransom demand of £50,000 was accompanied by a death threat. Whittle's body was found at the foot of a ventilation shaft two months later. Neilson evaded the police until late 1975, when a security guard he had shot and wounded was able to provide a description. He received life sentences for the murders and 21 years for kidnapping.

Nelson, (John) Byron, Jr 1912– •*US golfer*• Born in Fort Worth, Texas, he became one of the US's most outstanding players, winning the US Open in 1939, the US Masters twice (1937, 1942), and the PGA (Professional Golfers' Association) title twice (1940, 1945). In 1945 he won a remarkable 11 consecutive US Tour events—an all-time record. He played in two Ryder Cup matches, and retired in 1955 to become a broadcaster and coach.

Nelson, Horatio Nelson, Viscount 1758–1805 •*English admiral*• He was born in Burnham Thorpe rectory, Norfolk, and entered the navy in 1770. In 1780 he commanded the naval force in the expedition against San Juan, and in 1781 he commissioned the *Albemarle* and joined the squadron under Samuel, 1st Viscount **Hood** in the US. In 1784 he was appointed to the frigate *Boreas* for service in the West Indies, and here married a widow, Mrs Frances Nisbet (1761–1831). At the outbreak of the French Revolution (1792–1802), he commanded the *Agamemnon* and accompanied Lord Hood to the Mediterranean. When Toulon was given up to the Allies, Nelson was ordered to Naples, where he first met **Emma Hamilton**, the wife of the British ambassador. In 1794 he commanded the naval brigade in defeating Bastia and Calvi, where he lost his right eye. In 1796 he inflicted a signal defeat with John Jervis (Lord **Saint Vincent**) on the Spanish fleet off Cape St Vincent. Promoted to rear admiral, he was sent with an inadequate squadron to seize a richly laden Spanish ship at Santa Cruz, where he lost his right arm. In 1798, commanding the *Vanguard*, he defeated the French fleet by his victory at the Battle of the Nile, off Aboukir Bay. He returned in triumph to Naples and to a hero's welcome from Emma Hamilton, who became his mistress. Nelson was raised to the peerage as Baron Nelson of the Nile, parliament voted him a pension of £2,000 a year, the East India Company awarded him £10,000 and the king of Naples conferred on him the title of Duke of Bronte, in Sicily. He resigned his command and went back to England with the Hamiltons, where Emma gave birth to a daughter, Horatia, and Nelson separated from his wife. In 1801 he was promoted to vice admiral, and appointed second in command of the expedition to the Baltic, under Sir Hyde Parker (1739–1807). In the face of Parker's irresolution, Nelson disregarded orders and engaged in the Battle of Copenhagen, which he won decisively. In 1805 he won his greatest victory against the French and Spanish fleets at Trafalgar. He directed the engagement from the *Victory*, but was mortally wounded. His body was brought home and buried in St Paul's Cathedral.

Nelson, Willie (Hugh) 1933– •*US country singer and songwriter*• Born in Abbott, Texas, he began performing at the age of ten, and was a disc jockey for a time, but his initial success came as a songwriter in Nashville in the early 1960s. He continued to write and record throughout the decade, and upon returning to Texas in 1970 he became a major star, moving out from country to embrace both rock and jazz standards. He launched his annual Farm Aid concerts in 1985, and continued to record and tour prolifically.

Nemerov, Howard 1920– •*US poet, novelist and playwright*• Born in New York City, he was based in England while serving with the Royal Canadian Air Force during World War II. He has written several novels, but has won greater acclaim as a poet. His relatively accessible verse, in which, as he has said, he "writes of history from the point of view of the loser," includes *The Image and the Law* (1947) and *The Next Room of the Dream* (1962). His *Collected Poems* (1977) won the National Book Award.

“ ”

Children, to be illustrious is sad.

*1958 **Mirrors and Windows**, "The Statues in the Public Gardens."*

Nenni, Pietro 1891–1980 •*Italian socialist politician*• Born in Faenza, Romagna, he became an agitator at the age of 17. As editor of the socialist paper *Avanti!* he was exiled by the Fascists in 1926, and served as a political commissar for the International Brigade during the Spanish civil war. He became Secretary-General of the Italian Socialist Party (PSI) in 1944, vice premier (1945–46) and foreign minister (1946–47). From 1963 to 1968 he once again served as vice premier in the coalition headed by **Aldo Moro**. In 1968 he accepted the post of foreign minister but resigned in 1969.

Nennius fl. 769 •*Welsh writer*• He is reputedly author of the early Latin compilation known as the *Historia Britonum*, which gives an account of the origins of the Britons, the Roman occupation, the settlement of the Saxons, and King **Arthur**'s 12 victories. It contains much material of doubtful historical significance, and its real value lies in its preservation of material needed for the study of early Celtic literature in general, and the Arthurian legend in particular.

Nepomuk, St John of *See* **John of Nepomuk, St**

Nepos, Cornelius c. 99–c. 24 BC •*Roman historian*• A native of Pavia or Hostilia, northern Italy, he was the contemporary and close friend of **Cicero**, and **Catullus** dedicated his poems to him. His *De viris illustribus* ("Lives of Famous Men"), of which only some 25 (mainly on Greek warriors and statesmen) survive, are written in a clear, straightforward style.

Neri, St Philip 1515–95 •*Italian mystic*• Born in Venice, he went to Rome at the age of 18, and spent many years in charitable works and teaching and praying. In 1551 he became a priest, and later, with his followers, formed the Congregation of the Oratory (1564). The community was finally established at Vallicella, where Philip built a new church (Chiesa Nuova) on the site of Santa Maria. He was canonized with **Ignatius Loyola** and others in 1622, and his feast day is May 26.

Nernst, Walther Hermann 1864–1941 •*German physical chemist and Nobel Prize winner*• Born in Briesen, West Prussia, he studied physics at the Universities of Zurich, Berlin, Graz and Würzburg, and in 1887 he became the assistant of **Wilhelm Ostwald** at Leipzig. In 1891 he moved to Göttingen, then Berlin in 1905. During World War I he engaged in military activities, including gas warfare. He retired in 1933, being out of favor with the Nazi regime. Nernst is regarded as one of the cofounders of physical chemistry. His earliest research was in electrochemistry, and his development of the theory of electrode potential and the concept of solubility product were particularly important. He devised experimental methods for measuring dielectric constant, pH, and other physicochemical quantities. The electrochemical work led to a special interest in thermodynamics, and in 1906 he enunciated his heat theorem, which has come to be regarded as a statement of the third law of thermodynamics. He received the Nobel Prize for chemistry in 1920.

Nero AD 37–68 •*Roman emperor AD 54–68*• Born in Antium, he was the son of Cnaeus Domitius Ahenobarbus and of **Agrippina** the Younger. His mother became the wife of the emperor **Claudius**, who adopted him in AD 50. After the death of Claudius (54), the Praetorian Guard declared Nero emperor. His reign began well, but the influence of his mother and his own moral weakness and sensuality soon plunged him into debauchery, extravagance and tyranny. He caused **Britannicus**, the son of Claudius, to be poisoned, and afterwards murdered his mother and his wife Octavia. After this, **Seneca** the Younger was the main power behind the throne. In July 64 two-thirds of Rome was destroyed by fire. Nero is said to have been responsible, but this is doubtful, as is the story that he admired the spectacle from a distance while reciting his own verses. He rebuilt the city with great magnificence, but in order to provide for his expenditure, Italy and the provinces were plundered. A conspiracy against him in 65 failed, and Seneca and the poet **Lucan** fell victims to his vengeance. In a fit of passion he murdered his second wife, Poppaea Sabina. He then offered his hand to Antonia, daughter of Claudius, but was refused; whereupon he had her executed, and married Statilia Messallina after murdering her husband. He also executed or banished many eminent persons. In 68 the Gallic and Spanish legions, and after them the Praetorian Guards, rose against him to make **Galba** emperor. Nero fled Rome, and saved himself from execution by suicide.

Neruda, Jan 1834–91 •*Czech writer*• Born in Prague, he was brought up in poverty, an experience reflected in some of his work, notably *Povídky malostranské* (1878, Eng trans *Tales of the Little Quarter*, 1957), and became a teacher and journalist. He was a disciple of Romanticism but developed into the foremost classical poet in modern Czech literature. He is also known for some prose and drama.

Neruda, Pablo, *originally* **Ricardo Eliecer Neftalí Reyes** 1904–73 •*Chilean poet and Nobel Prize winner*• Born in Parral and educated at Santiago, he made his name with *Veinte poemas de amor y una canción desesperada* (1924, Eng trans *Twenty Love Poems and a Song of Despair*, 1969). From 1927 he held diplomatic posts in East Asia and Europe and Mexico. On his way back to Chile from Mexico (1943), he visited the Incan city of Macchu Picchu, which was the inspiration for one of his best-known poems. Once settled in Chile again, he joined the Communist Party and was elected to the Senate in 1945. He traveled in Russia and China (1948–52), was awarded the Stalin Prize in 1953, and was later the Chilean ambassador in Paris (1970–72). His works include *Residencia en la tierra I, II* and *III* (1933, 1935, 1947, "Residence on Earth"), *Alturas de Macchu Picchu* (1945, Eng trans *The Heights of Macchu Picchu*, 1966), which later became part of *Canto General* (1950, Eng trans in part as *Poems from Canto General*, 1966), and *Odas elementales* (1954, Eng trans *Elementary Odes*, 1961). In 1971 he was awarded the Nobel Prize for literature.

Nerva, Marcus Cocceius c. 32–98 AD •*Roman emperor*• He was elected (AD 96) by the Senate after the assassination of **Domitian**. He introduced liberal reforms after Domitian's tyranny, but lacked military support, and had to adopt **Trajan** as his successor.

Nerval, Gérard de, *properly* **Gérard Labrunie** 1808–55 •*French writer*• Born in Paris, he was greatly influenced by reading his uncle's collection of occult books as a youth, and at the age of 20 published a translation of **Goethe**'s *Faust*, expanded as *Faust, et le second Faust* (1840). He wrote in prose and verse, but his travels, criticism, plays and poems are less interesting than his fantastic short tales, the *Contes et facéties* (1852, "Stories and Jests"), the partly autobiographical series *Filles du feu* (1854, Eng trans *Daughters of Fire*, 1923), and *La Bohème galante* (1855, "Gallant Bohemian Life"). He is often seen as a precursor of both the Symbolist and surrealist movements.

Nervi, Pier Luigi 1891–1979 •*Italian architect and engineer*• Born in Sondrio, he graduated as an engineer, then set up as a building contractor. His many works include the Berta Stadium in Florence (1930–32) and a complex of exhibition halls in Turin (1948–50). He achieved an international reputation with his designs for the two Olympic stadiums in Rome (1960), in which bold and imaginative use is made of concrete for roofing in the large areas. He also designed St Mary's Cathedral in San Francisco (1970). He was professor at Rome from 1947 to 1961.

Nesbit, Edith 1858–1924 •*English writer*• Born in London, she was educated at a French convent and began her literary career by writing poetry, having met the **Rossetti**s and their friends. In 1880 she married the Fabian journalist Hubert Bland, and to help with the family finances, turned to popular fiction and children's stories, including *The Story of the Treasure Seekers* (1899), *The Would-Be-Goods* (1901), *Five Children and It* (1902) and *The Railway Children* (1906). She also wrote ghost stories and a number of other novels, the last of which was *The Lark* (1922).

“ ”

They were not railway children to begin with. I don't suppose they had ever thought about railways except as a means of getting to Maskelyne and Cook's, the Pantomime, Zoological Gardens, and Madame Tussaud's.

1906 ***The Railway Children*** *opening lines.*

Nesle, Blondel de *See* **Blondel**

Nestorius d. 451 AD •*Syrian ecclesiastic*• Born in Germanicia, he became a priest. Well known for his zeal, ascetic life, and eloquence, he was selected as patriarch of Constantinople (Istanbul) in AD 428. He defended the presbyter Anastasius in denying that the Virgin **Mary** could be truly called the Mother of God, and so emphasized the distinction of the divine and human natures that antagonists accused him—falsely—of holding that there were two persons in **Jesus**. A controversy ensued, and Nestorius was deposed by a general council in Ephesus (431). He was confined in a monastery near Constantinople, was banished to Petra in Arabia, and died after imprisonment in the Greater Oasis in Upper Egypt.

Netanyahu, Benjamin 1949– •*Israeli Likud politician*• He was born in Israel and educated at MIT in the US. Between 1967 and 1972 he served as a soldier in the Israeli Defense Forces and in 1976 became a director of the Jonathan Institute, a foundation which studies counterterrorism. In 1982 he was appointed Israel's ambassador to the United Nations and in 1988 was elected to the Knesset as a member of the right-wing Likud Party. Having served as deputy foreign minister (1988–91) and deputy prime minister (1991–92), he was elected prime minister (1996). He was defeated by **Ehud Barak** in 1999.

Neto, (Antonio) Agostinho 1922–79 •*Angolan nationalist and politician*• The son of a Methodist missionary, he was educated in a Methodist school in Luanda before studying medicine in Portugal. He returned to Angola to work in the colonial medical service and joined the MPLA. He was imprisoned several times (1952–62) but escaped to Zaire (now the Democratic Republic of Congo), where he soon became president of the MPLA and its leader in the guerrilla war against Portuguese colonialism. With both Cuban and Soviet backing, he prevailed in the civil war that followed the Portuguese retreat from Angola. He became the first president of Angola in 1974, holding the post until his death.

Neuberger, Julia Babette Sarah, *née* **Schwab** 1950– •*British rabbi, writer and broadcaster*• Born in London and educated at Cambridge, she took a rabbinical diploma at Leo Baeck College, where she later returned as lecturer in 1979. She became rabbi of the South London Liberal Synagogue (1977–89), the first female rabbi in Britain, and was picked to host *Choices* on BBC1 (1986–87). Noted for her liberal and reasonable approach, she has often been involved in religious and secular advisory committees on such topics as health and human rights. She was chancellor of the University of Ulster from 1993 to 2000. Since 1997 she has been chief executive of the King's Fund.

Neugebauer, Gerald 1932– •*US astronomer*• Born in Göttingen, Germany, he was educated at Cornell University and the California Institute of Technology (Caltech). After working at Mount Wilson and Palomar Observatories, he became Professor of Physics at Caltech (1970) and director of Palomar Observatory in 1981. He produced the first extensive infrared map of the heavens in the 1960s. Many new infrared sources were discovered, and new and curious objects were revealed. Working with E E Becklin, Neugebauer discovered a strange infrared source radiating intensely in the Orion Nebula, which is now known as the "Becklin-Neugebauer object" and is thought to be a young massive star blowing gases outwards at high speed.

Neumann, (Johann) Balthasar 1687–1753 •*German architect*• Born in Eger, he was at first a military engineer in the service of the Archbishop of Würzburg, but soon found his true métier, and after visiting Paris and absorbing new ideas, he became Professor of Architecture at Würzburg. Many outstanding examples of the Baroque style were designed by him, the finest being probably Würzburg Palace and Schloss Bruchsal.

Neumann, St John Nepomucene 1811–60 •*US Roman Catholic bishop and saint*• Born in Prachatice, Bohemia, he settled in the US in 1836, entered the Redemptorist order, and was appointed Bishop of Philadelphia in 1852. He was responsible for building 80 churches and nearly 100 parochial schools, and he founded US branches of several orders of teaching nuns. Miracles were said to have occurred at his tomb, and in 1977 he became the first US male to be canonized.

Neumann, John Von *See* **Von Neumann, John (Johann)**

Neurath, Otto 1882–1945 •*Austrian philosopher and social theorist*• Born in Vienna, he was a member of the influential Vienna Circle, which also included **Moritz Schlick**, **Kurt Gödel** and **Rudolf Carnap**. The group were logical positivists, generally hostile to metaphysics and theology and respectful of empirical science. Neurath is particularly associated with the radical version of positivism called physicalism, which aimed to establish an entirely materialist basis of knowledge. His best philosophical work was published in the group's journal *Erkenntnis*, but he also wrote books on sociology, education and social policy, and was active in public affairs as an independent Marxist.

Neville, Richard *See* **Warwick, Earl of**

Newbery, John 1713–67 •*English publisher and bookseller*• Born in Berkshire, a farmer's son, he settled in London around 1744 as a seller of books and patent medicines. He was the first to publish small books for children, and he was—perhaps with **Oliver Goldsmith**—part author of some of the best ones, notably *Goody Two-Shoes*. Since 1922 the Newbery medal has been awarded annually for the best US children's book.

Newbolt, Sir Henry John 1862–1938 •*English poet*• Born in Bilston, Staffordshire, he studied at Clifton School and Oxford, and became a barrister. He is best known for his sea songs—*Admirals All* (1897), which contained "Drake's Drum," *The Island Race* (1898), *Songs of the Sea*, and others. In World War I he was controller of telecommunications and an official war historian, and in 1920 he published *The Naval History of the Great War*.

Newby, Eric 1919– •*English travel writer*• Born in London, he worked briefly in advertising before joining a Finnish four-masted bark in 1938, an adventure described in *The Last Grain Race* (1956). In 1942 he was captured off Sicily while trying to rejoin the submarine from which he had landed to attack a German airfield. For some years he worked in the clothing industry, which he eagerly left to take *A Short Walk in the Hindu Kush* (1958). In 1963 he made a 1,200-mile (1,931-kilometer) descent of the Ganges, described with typical aplomb and wit in *Slowly Down the Ganges* (1966). Later he became travel editor of the *Observer*. Other significant books are *The Big Red Train Ride* (1978), the story of a journey from Moscow to the Pacific on the Trans-Siberian Railway; his autobiography, *A Traveler's Life* (1982); and *Round Ireland in Low Gear* (1987), about a mountain-bike journey. Later works include *Departures and Arrivals* (1999).

Newcomb, Simon 1833–1909 •*US astronomer*• Born in Wallace, Nova Scotia, Canada, he earned a degree in science from Harvard in 1858. He became Professor of Mathematics in the US Navy (1861–97) and was in charge of the naval observatory in Washington. From 1877 he edited the *American Nautical Almanac*, and also held academic posts. Newcomb's major work, begun in 1879, was the recalculation of the constants required for the preparation of ephemerides and the drawing up of immense tables of the motions of the planets. He was responsible for the worldwide adoption of a standard system of constants by almanac makers, which served until the middle of the 20th century.

Newcomen, Thomas 1663–1729 •*English inventor*• He was born in Dartmouth, Devon. A blacksmith by trade, in 1698 he teamed up with **Thomas Savery**, who had just patented an atmospheric steam engine for pumping water from mines, and by 1712 he had constructed a practical working engine that was widely used in collieries.

Newdigate, Sir Roger 1719–1806 •*English antiquary*• Born in Arbury, Warwickshire, he was Member of Parliament for 36 years for Middlesex (1741–47) and Oxford University (1750–80). He built up a famous collection of antiquities and endowed the Newdigate prize for English verse at Oxford, winners of which have included **John Ruskin**, **Matthew Arnold**, **Laurence Binyon** and **John Buchan**.

Ne Win, U, *also known as* **Shu Maung** 1911–2002 •*Burmese politician*• Educated at Rangoon University, he was an active anti-British nationalist in the 1930s. In World War II he became chief of staff in the collaborationist army after the Japanese invasion of Burma, but joined the Allied forces later in the war. He held senior military and cabinet posts after Burma's independence (1948), and became caretaker prime minister (1958–60). In 1962, following a military coup, he ruled the country as chairman of the revolutionary council and became state president in 1974. After leaving this office in 1981, he continued to dominate political affairs as chairman of the ruling Burma Socialist Program Party (BSPP), and followed a unique program blending Marxism, Buddhism and Burmese nationalism and isolationism. In 1988, with economic conditions rapidly deteriorating and riots in Rangoon, he was forced to step down as BSPP leader, although he remained a formidably powerful political figure.

Newlands, John Alexander Reina 1837–98 •*English chemist*• Born in London, he spent a year at the Royal College of Chemistry, and from 1868 to 1888 worked as an industrial chemist, and later as an independent analyst and consultant. By 1863 he had begun to build on earlier observations by Johann Döbereiner (1780–1849) and others that there was a relationship between the chemical properties of elements and their atomic weight. In 1865 he drew up a table of 62 elements arranged in eight groups in ascending order of atomic weight to illustrate what he described as the "law of octaves." **Dmitri Ivanovich Mendeleev** made the critical leap forward when he realized that spaces should be left for undiscovered elements. After Mendeleev published his periodic table, Newlands claimed priority.

Newman, Barnett 1905–70 •*US painter*• He was born in New York City. Until c. 1948 his art was biomorphic in style, and he was always interested in the primitive and in the psychiatrist **Carl Jung**'s primordial archetypes. In 1948, with **William Baziotes**, **Robert Motherwell** and **Mark Rothko**, he founded the Subject of the Artist school and produced *Onement I*, the first of his stripe paintings, which consist of vertical bands of color and look forward to his minimalist works of the 1960s, such as *Station of the Cross* (1966).

Newman, John Henry 1801–90 •*English autobiographer, poet and religious writer*• Born in London, he was appointed vicar of St Mary's, Oxford. He became celebrated as a preacher and leader of the Tractarian (or Oxford) Movement, but in the early 1840s drew closer to Roman Catholicism. Converted in 1845, he became a Catholic priest and established the Birmingham Oratory. He is famous chiefly for the *Apologia pro Vita Sua* (1864), in which he set out the history of his religious views. This unusual autobiography established him as one of the great stylists in the history of English prose. His poem "The Dream of Gerontius" (1865) provided the text of **Elgar**'s oratorio, and his hymn "Lead, kindly light" illustrates his gift for a memorable turn of phrase. He was made a cardinal in 1879.

Newman, Paul Leonard 1925– •*US film actor and philanthropist*• Born in Cleveland, Ohio, he studied at the Yale School of Drama and the Actors Studio in New York City. Starting in stage repertory and television, he became one of the major film actors of his generation, combining blue-eyed masculinity with a rebellious streak in films like *Cat on a Hot Tin Roof* (1958), *The Hustler* (1961) and *Cool Hand Luke* (1967). Later films include *Butch Cassidy and the Sundance Kid* (1969), *The Sting* (1973), *The Verdict* (1982), *The Color of Money* (1986), for which he won an Academy Award, *Mr and Mrs Bridge* (1990, with his wife, **Joanne Woodward**) and *Twilight* (1998). He also directed *Rachel, Rachel* (1968) and *The Glass Menagerie* (1987), among others, and has been active politically in liberal causes. He was given an Honorary Academy Award in 1986 and another in 1994 for his philanthropic donation of the profits from his food products to charity.

Newton, Helmut 1920–2004 •*Australian photographer*• Born in Berlin, Germany, he was educated there at the Heinrich von Treitschke Realgymnasium and at the American School, and emigrated to Australia in 1940 and set up as a freelance photographer in Melbourne. He moved subsequently to Paris and had fashion photographs published in such magazines as *Elle*, *Nova*, *Marie-Claire* and *Vogue*. His publications include *White Women* (1976), *Private Property* (1984) and *Naked and Dressed in Hollywood* (1992).

Newton, Sir Isaac 1642–1727 •*English scientist and mathematician*• Born in Woolsthorpe, Lincolnshire, and educated at Grantham Grammar School and Trinity College, Cambridge, he began his research at an early date. In 1665 or 1666 he contemplated the fall of an apple in his garden, which led him to begin formulating the law of gravitation. He was also concerned with the nature of light and the construction of telescopes, of a type that was later developed further by **William Herschel** and the Earl of Rosse (1800–67). Newton became a Fellow of Trinity College, Cambridge in 1667, and was appointed Lucasian Professor of Mathematics in 1669. By 1684 he had demonstrated the whole gravitation theory, which he expounded first in *De motu corporum* (1684). Newton showed that the force of gravity between two bodies, such as the sun and the earth, is directly proportional to the product of the masses of the bodies and inversely proportional to the square of the distance between them. He described this more completely in *Philosophiae naturalis principia mathematica* (1687, "The Mathematical Principles of Natural Philosophy"), his greatest work, edited and financed by **Edmond Halley**, who had encouraged him to develop his theories. In the *Principia* Newton stated his three laws of motion: (1) that a body in a state of rest or uniform motion will remain in that state until a force acts on it; (2) that an applied force is directly proportional to the acceleration it induces, the constant of proportionality being the body's mass ($F = ma$); and (3) that for every action force which one body exerts on another, there is an equal and opposite reaction force exerted by the second body on the first. Newton was involved throughout his life in controversies with other scientists, in particular with **John Flamsteed** and **Robert Hooke**, who claimed priority of discovery for some of Newton's work on the attraction of lunar bodies. The controversy between Newton and **Gottfried Leibniz** over the discovery of the differential calculus and the method of fluxions is still disputed. Throughout his life he also devoted much time to the study of alchemy and theology. In the political domain, Newton sat in parliament (1689–90), was appointed Warden of the Mint from 1696, and was Master of the Mint from 1699. He again sat in parliament in 1701. Knighted by Queen **Anne** in 1705, he is buried in Westminster Abbey.

“ ”

In the absence of any other proof, the thumb alone would convince me of God's existence.

Attributed.

Ney, Michel 1769–1815 •*French general*• Born in Saarlouis, he rose to be adjutant general (1794), general of brigade (1796) and general of division (1799), and under the empire he was made marshal. He fought at Jena and Eylau and Friedland, gaining the grand eagle of the Légion d'honneur. Serving in Spain, he quarreled with **André Masséna** and returned to France. In command of the Third Corps (1813), he fought at Smolensk and Borodino, received the title of Prince of the Moskwa, and led the rear guard in the disastrous retreat. In 1813 he was present at Lützen and Bautzen, but was defeated at Dennewitz. He fought at Leipzig, but submitted to **Louis XVIII**. Ney was sent against **Napoleon I** on his return from Elba, but went over to his old master's side and led the center at Waterloo (1815). On Louis XVIII's second restoration he was condemned for high treason and shot.

Ngata, Sir Apirana Turupa 1874–1950 •*New Zealand Maori lawyer and politician*• Born at Te Araroa, East Cape, he was the first Maori graduate—from the University of Canterbury in 1893—and was admitted to the bar in 1897. He was elected to parliament in 1905 and remained for 38 years, becoming Minister for Native Affairs three times. He wrote widely on Maori history.

Ngo Dinh Diem 1901–63 •*Vietnamese statesman*• Born in Annam, the son of a mandarin and himself a Roman Catholic, he worked as a civil servant before becoming minister of the interior in 1933. Refusing to support **Ho Chi Minh** and **Bao Dai**, he was forced into exile in 1950, but returned to South Vietnam as prime minister in 1954, masterminded Bao's fall from power, and succeeded him as president in 1955. Although almost wholly dependent on US support for his country's economic survival and with hostilities with the North mounting, he refused to be counseled by the US on his handling of the war and was murdered by dissident army officers.

Nguyen Van Linh 1914–98 •*Vietnamese politician*• Born in northern Vietnam, he joined the anticolonial Thanh Nien, a forerunner of the Communist Party of Vietnam (CPV), in Haiphong in 1929, and spent much of his subsequent party career in the south, gaining a reputation as a pragmatic reformer. He became CPV leader from 1986 to 1991. His leadership brought a new phase of economic liberalization and improved relations with the West, typified by his phased withdrawal of Vietnamese forces from Kampuchea (Cambodia) and Laos.

Nguyen Van Thieu 1923–2001 •*Vietnamese soldier and political leader*• Born in Ninh Thuan, he was educated at the National Military Academy in Hue. His military career began in the late 1940s, and by 1963 he was Chief of Staff of the Armed Forces of the Republic of Vietnam (South Vietnam). That year he was a leader in the coup against **Ngo Dinh Diem**. In 1967, as the war against the Vietcong escalated, he became president of the Republic of Vietnam, and in early 1973 was a signatory to the peace treaty that formally ended hostilities. However, fighting between North and South continued until the Communist victory in 1975 with the fall of Saigon (now Ho Chi Minh City), when Thieu escaped abroad, finally to the US.

Nicholas, St 4th century AD •*Christian prelate and patron saint of Greece and Russia*• He was born, according to legend, in the ancient Lycian seaport city of Patara. Allegedly the Bishop of Myra in Lycia (Turkey), he was imprisoned under **Diocletian** and released under **Constantine I (the Great)**. In legend he gave gifts of gold to three poor girls for their dowries, which gave rise to the custom of giving gifts on his feast day, still followed in the Netherlands and Germany. Elsewhere this has been transferred to December 25 (Christmas Day). His identification with Father Christmas began in Europe and spread to the US, where the name became Santa Claus. He is also the patron saint of children, scholars, merchants, sailors, travelers and thieves. His feast day is December 6.

Nicholas I, St, *called* **the Great** c. 820–867 •*Italian pope*• Born in Rome, he was pope from 858 to 867. He asserted the supremacy of the Church against secular rulers such as Lothair, king of Lorraine (whose divorce he forbade) and church leaders like Hincmar, Archbishop of Rheims. He had problems with the Eastern Church, however, particularly with **Photius**, whom he tried to depose as patriarch of Constantinople, leading to the Photian Schism. His feast day is November 13.

Nicholas I 1796–1855 •*Emperor of Russia*• The third son of **Paul I**, he married the daughter of **Frederick William III** of Prussia (1817) and became czar on the death of his elder brother **Alexander I** in 1825. He suppressed the Decembrist Rebellion that year, and began a reign characterized by despotism and militarism. Wars with Persia (now Iran) and Turkey gained Russia territory, and he crushed a Polish uprising (1830). He also attempted to Russianize all the inhabitants of the empire, and to convert Roman Catholics and Protestants to the Russian Orthodox Church. During the political storm of 1848–49 he assisted the emperor of Austria in quelling the Hungarian insurrection, and tightened the alliance with Prussia. The reestablishment of the French Empire confirmed these alliances, but the opposition of Great Britain and France to his plans to dominate Turkey brought on the Crimean War, during which he died.

Nicholas II 1868–1918 •*Emperor of Russia*• The eldest son of **Alexander III**, he succeeded his father in 1894. He married **Alexandra Fyodorovna**, a princess of Hesse, who dominated him. Diffident and easily swayed, he lacked the strength of will to fulfill his self-appointed autocratic role. His reign was marked by alliance with France, entente with Great Britain, a disastrous war with Japan (1904–05), and the establishment (1906) of the Duma (parliament). He took command of the Russian armies against the Central Powers (1915). Forced to abdicate (1917) at the revolution, he was shot with his entire family at Yekaterinburg by the Red Guards in 1918.

Nicholas of Cusa 1401–64 •*German philosopher, scientist and churchman*• Born in Kues, Treves, he studied at Heidelberg (1416) and Padua (1417–23) and was ordained about 1430. He was active in 1432 at the Council of Basel, supporting in his *De concordantia catholica* (1433, "On Catholic Concordance") the conciliarists, who advocated the supremacy of Church councils against the pope. He later switched allegiance to the papal party and was created cardinal in 1448. His best-known philosophical work is *De docta ignorantia* (1440, "On Learned Ignorance"), which emphasizes the limitations of human knowledge but at the same time argues that faith, science, theology and philosophy all pursue convergent though different paths toward the ultimately unattainable goal of absolute reality. He also wrote on mathematics and cosmology and anticipated **Copernicus** in his nongeocentric theories.

Nicholas, Grand-Duke 1856–1929 •*Russian soldier*• In World War I he was Russian Commander in Chief against Germany and Austria, and Commander in Chief in the Caucasus (1915–17). After 1919 he lived quietly in France. He was the nephew of **Alexander II**.

Nicholls, Sir Douglas Ralph 1906–88 •*Australian clergyman, activist and administrator*• Born at Cummeragunja Aboriginal station, southern New South Wales, he grew up on a mission station, then moved to Melbourne where, in 1935, he became the first Aborigine to represent his state in soccer. As pastor, he established a mission for Aborigines at Fitzroy in 1943 and worked actively for Aboriginal advancement. In 1972 he became the first Aborigine to be knighted.

Nichols, Mike, *originally* **Michael Igor Peschkowsky** 1931– •*US film and theater director*• Born in Berlin, Germany, he emigrated to the US with his family in 1938 and was naturalized in 1944. He studied acting with **Lee Strasberg** and also became popular on radio, records and stage performing satirical duologues with **Elaine May** (1957–61). The partnership culminated in a year-long Broadway engagement, after which he turned to direction, showing a flair for comedy and a liking for literate scripts. He has received seven Tony Awards for his theater work, which includes *Barefoot in the Park* (1963), *The Odd Couple* (1965) and *Death and the Maiden* (1992). He also coproduced the hit musical *Annie* (1977). He directed his first film, *Who's Afraid of Virginia Woolf?*, in 1966 and received an Academy Award for *The Graduate* (1967). His films offer sardonic portraits of US life, social mores and sexual politics, and include *Catch 22* (1970), *Silkwood* (1983), *Postcards from the Edge* (1990) and *Primary Colors* (1998).

Nicholson, Ben 1894–1982 •*English artist*• Born in Denham, London, the son of Sir William Nicholson (1872–1949), he exhibited with the Paris Abstraction-Création group from 1933 to 1934. He gained an international reputation as an abstract artist and won the first Guggenheim Award in 1957. Although he produced a number of purely geometrical paintings and reliefs, he generally used conventional still-life objects as a starting point for his finely drawn and subtly balanced variations. His second wife was **Barbara Hepworth**.

Nicholson, Jack 1937– •*US film actor*• Born in Neptune, New Jersey, he began his career as an office boy at MGM, and after studying and working with the Players Ring Theater, made his film debut in *Cry Baby Killer* (1958). He spent the next decade in a succession of low-budget exploitation films before his first major success in *Easy Rider* (1969). He won praise for his portrayals of explosive nonconformists in *Five Easy Pieces* (1970) and *The Last Detail* (1973). His charisma and acute sense of humor have illuminated a wide range of characters in such diverse films as *Chinatown* (1974), *The Shining* (1980), *Prizzi's Honor* (1985) and *Ironweed* (1987). He won Academy Awards for *One Flew over the Cuckoo's Nest* (1975), *Terms of Endearment* (1984) and *As Good As It Gets* (1997) and has appeared in *Batman* (1989), *A Few Good Men* (1993) and *About Schmidt* (2002). He has also written scripts, and he occasionally directs.

“ ”

She's like a delicate fawn, crossed with a Buick.

1984 Of actress Jessica Lange. In ***Vanity Fair****, October.*

Nicias d. 413 BC •*Athenian soldier and politician*• A member of the aristocratic party, he opposed Cleon and **Alcibiades**. In 427–426 BC he defeated the Spartans and the Corinthians. In 424 he ravaged Laconia, but in 421 made a short-lived peace between Sparta and Athens (the Peace of Nicias). He laid siege to Syracuse (415) and was at first successful, but subsequently experienced a series of disasters; his troops were forced to surrender, and he was put to death.

Nicklaus, Jack (William), *known as* **the Golden Bear** 1940– •*US golfer*• Born in Columbus, Ohio, he won the US Amateur championships twice while still a student at Ohio State University and played in the Walker Cup twice before turning professional in 1962. His first professional victory was the US Open (1962), a tournament he won another three times (1967, 1972, 1980). Of the other Majors, he won the Masters a record six times (1963, 1965–66, 1972, 1975, 1986); the Open championship three times (1966, 1970, 1978); and the US PGA (Professional Golfers' Association) a record-equaling five times (1963, 1971, 1973, 1975, 1980). His total of 20 Majors victories (including his two US Amateurs) is also a record, and he is arguably the greatest golfer in history.

Nicolini, Adelina *See* **Patti, Adelina**

Nicolle, Charles Jules Henri 1866–1936 •*French physician, microbiologist and Nobel Prize winner*• Born in Rouen, he was educated there and in Paris. He became director of the Pasteur Institute in Tunis (1902–32), which he and his colleagues turned into a leading research center, working on the mode of spread, prevention and treatment of a number of diseases, including leishmaniasis, toxoplasmosis, Malta fever and typhus. His discovery that typhus is spread by lice (1909) had important implications during World War I and led to his award, in 1928, of the Nobel Prize for physiology or medicine.

Nicolson, Sir Harold George 1886–1968 •*English diplomat, writer and critic*• He was born in Tehran, where his father was British chargé d'affaires, and was educated at Oxford. He had a distinguished career as a diplomat, entering the service in 1909 and holding posts in Madrid, Constantinople (Istanbul), Tehran and Berlin until his resignation in 1929, when he turned to journalism. From 1935 to 1945 he was National Labour Member of Parliament for West Leicester. He wrote several biographies, for example those of **Tennyson** and **George V**, as well as books on history, politics and, in *Good Behavior* (1955), manners. He was highly regarded as a literary critic. He was married to **Victoria Sackville-West**.

Niebuhr, Helmut Richard 1894–1962 •*US theologian*• Born in Wright City, Missouri, he taught at Yale from 1931, becoming Professor of Theology and Christian Ethics and director of graduate studies. Like his brother, **Reinhold Niebuhr**, he had enormous influence on generations of students. His classic study *The Meaning of Revelation* (1941) was followed by *Christ and Culture* (1951), *Radical Monotheism and Western Culture* (1960) and *The Responsible Self* (1963): a series of books advocating critical reflection on the relation between faith and moral action and a quest for a Christian transformation of society.

Niebuhr, Reinhold 1892–1971 •*US theologian*• Born in Wright City, Missouri, he was educated at Elmhurst (Illinois) College, Eden Theological Seminary and Yale Divinity School. He became an evangelical pastor in working-class Detroit (1915–28) and was Professor of Christian Ethics at the Union Theological Seminary, New York (1928–60). His early liberalism and social idealism eventually gave way to a more pessimistic theology known as Christian realism, which recognized man's sinfulness and propensity to abuse power and asserted that such a recognition was necessary if the struggle for social justice was to have any measure of success. He wrote *Moral Man and Immoral Society* (1932), *The Nature and Destiny of Man* (2 vols, 1941–43), *Structure of Nations and Empires* (1959), and many other books. He was the brother of **Helmut Richard Niebuhr**.

Nielsen, Carl August 1865–1931 •*Danish composer*• Born in Nörre-Lyndelse, near Odense, in 1883 he entered the Copenhagen Conservatory. His compositions from this period—including the G minor quartet and oboe fantasias—are not revolutionary, but with his First Symphony (1894) his progressive tonality and rhythmic boldness become apparent. His Second Symphony (1901–02, "The Four Temperaments") shows the first use in Danish music of polytonality, along with the contrapuntal style which was to become characteristic of him. His other works include four other symphonies (1912, 1916, 1922, 1925), the tragic opera *Saul and David* (1902), the comic opera *Masquerade* (1906), chamber music, concertos for flute, and a huge organ work, *Commotio* (1931). In 1915 he was appointed director of Copenhagen Conservatory. He tried to rid Danish music of its prevalent Romanticism, and exerted a great influence on the musical development of Denmark. He was also a distinguished conductor.

“ ”

Music is life, and, like it, inextinguishable.

1916 Symphony No. 4, motto.

Niemeyer, Oscar 1907– •*Brazilian architect*• Born in Rio de Janeiro, he studied at the National School of Fine Arts in Brazil and began work in the office of **Lucio Costa** (1935). From 1936 to 1943 he joined Costa and others to design the Ministry of Education and Public Health, Rio (1937–42). He became architectural adviser to Nova Cap, serving as its chief architect (1957–59), and coordinating the development of Brasilia. His expressionist powers are well displayed in a group at Pampúlha, including the Church of São Francisco (1942–44), where parabolic sections indicate the organic, antirationalist principles underlying his work. Further major works are the Exhibition Hall, São Paulo (1953), and the President's Palace, Law Courts and Cathedrals, Brasilia.

Niemöller, Martin 1892–1984 •*German theologian and resistance figure*• Born in Lippstadt, Westphalia, he served as a U-boat commander in World War I, then entered the Lutheran Church and held various positions. He was a prominent member of the anti-Nazi Confessing Church, for which he was arrested in 1937 and sent to Sachsenhausen and Dachau concentration camps. Freed in 1945, he resumed his church career and adopted outspoken views on current affairs, most notably on German reunification and nuclear disarmament. In 1961 he became president of the World Council of Churches. Collections of his sermons include *Six Dachau Sermons* (1946, Eng trans 1959).

Niepce, (Joseph) Nicéphore 1765–1833 •*French chemist and photography pioneer*• Born in Chalon-sur-Saône, Burgundy, he served under **Napoleon I** and in 1795 became administrator of Nice. With enough inherited wealth to support himself, he was able to devote himself to research in chemistry from 1801 on. He experimented with the new technique of lithography, using a camera obscura to project an image onto a wall, then tracing around the image in the time-honored fashion. Being a poor draftsman, he decided to look for ways of fixing the image automatically. In 1822, using silver chloride paper and a camera, he achieved a temporary image of the view outside his workroom window, but could not fix it. In 1826 he succeeded in making a permanent image using a pewter plate coated with bitumen of Judea, an asphalt which hardens on exposure to light. This historic negative, which Niepce termed a "heliograph," is now preserved at the University of Texas. From 1829 Niepce collaborated with **Louis Daguerre** in the search for materials which would reduce the exposure time, but he died before any progress was made.

Nietzsche, Friedrich Wilhelm 1844–1900 •*German philosopher, scholar and writer*• Born in Röcken, Saxony, the son of a Lutheran pastor, he proved himself a brilliant classical student at the Universities of Bonn and Leipzig. He was appointed Professor of Classical Philology at the University of Basel at the age of 24 and became a Swiss citizen, serving briefly as a medical orderly in 1870 in the Franco-Prussian War, but returning to the university in poor health. His first book, *Die Geburt der Tragödie* (1872, Eng trans *The Birth of Tragedy*, 1909), with its celebrated comparison between "Dionysian" and "Apollonian" values, was dedicated to **Richard Wagner**, who had become a friend. However, he broke violently with Wagner in 1876, nominally at least because he thought the Christian convictions expressed in *Parsifal* were "mere playacting." In 1878 he was forced to resign his university position after worsening bouts of his psychosomatic illnesses, and he spent most of the next 10 years at various resorts. In 1889 he had a complete mental and physical breakdown, probably syphilitic in origin, and he was nursed for the next 12 years, first by his mother at Naumberg, then by his sister Elizabeth at Weimar. He never recovered his sanity. In the 16 years from 1872 he had produced a stream of brilliant, unconventional works, often aphoristic or poetical in form, which have secured him an enormous, if sometimes cultish, influence in modern intellectual history. The best-known writings are: *Unzeitgemässe Betrachtungen* (1873–76, Eng trans *Thoughts Out of Season*, 1909), *Die Fröhliche Wissenschaft* (1882, Eng trans *The Joyful Wisdom*, 1910), *Also sprach Zarathustra* (1883–92, "Thus Spake Zarathustra"), *Jenseits von Gut und Böse* (1886, Eng trans *Beyond Good and Evil*, 1907) and *Ecce Homo* (his autobiography, completed in 1888 but not published till 1908). The characteristic themes of these often highly wrought literary works are the vehement repudiation of Christian and liberal ethics, the detestation of democratic ideals, the celebration of the *Übermensch* (superman), the death of God, and the life-affirming "will to power." His reputation suffered when his views were taken up in a simple-minded and perverted form by the German Nazis, but he is now regarded as a major influence on many strands of later thought, including existentialism and psychoanalysis, and on figures as various as **Martin Heidegger**, **Thomas Mann**, **W B Yeats** and **Michel Foucault**.

Nightingale, Florence 1820–1910 •*English nurse and hospital reformer*• Named after the place of her birth in Italy, she trained as a nurse at Kaiserswerth (1851) and Paris and in 1853 became superintendent of a hospital for invalid women in London. In the Crimean War she volunteered for duty and took 38 nurses to Scutari in 1854. She organized the barracks hospital after the Battle of Inkerman (November 5), and by imposing strict discipline and standards of sanitation, reduced the hospital mortality rate drastically. She returned to England in 1856 and a fund of £50,000 was allocated to enable her to form an institution for the training of nurses at St Thomas's and at King's College Hospital. She devoted many years to the question of army sanitary reform, to the improvement of nursing and to public health in India. Her main work, *Notes on Nursing* (1859), went through many editions.

Nijinska, Bronislava or **Bronisława** 1891–1972 •*Russian ballet dancer and choreographer*• She was born in Minsk, the sister of

Vaslav Nijinsky. Her parents were professional dancers, and she, like her brother, studied at the Imperial Ballet School in St Petersburg, graduating in 1908 and going on to become a soloist with the Maryinsky company. She danced with **Sergei Diaghilev**'s Ballets Russes in Paris and London before returning to Russia during World War I, when she started a school in Kiev, but went back to Diaghilev in 1921, following **Léonide Massine** as principal choreographer. Among the ballets she created for the company were her masterpieces *Les noces* (1923, "The Wedding") and *Les biches* (1924, "The Does"). After working in Buenos Aires and for Ida Rubinstein's company in Paris, she briefly formed her own company in 1932. From 1935 she choreographed for many companies in Europe and the US, but lived mainly in the US and started a ballet school in Los Angeles (1938). She was persuaded to stage a revival of *Les noces* and *Les biches* at Covent Garden in 1964.

Nijinsky, Vaslav 1890–1950 •*Russian dancer and choreographer*• Nijinsky was born in Kiev into a family of dancers who had their own dance company. Considered to be the greatest male dancer of the 20th century, he, like his sister **Bronislava Nijinska**, trained at the Imperial School of Ballet in St Petersburg, and first appeared in ballet at the Maryinski Theater. As the leading dancer in **Sergei Diaghilev**'s Ballets Russes, which performed in Paris in 1909, he became enormously popular, and in 1911 he appeared in the title role as Petrushka in the first perfomance of **Igor Stravinsky**'s ballet. His choreographic repertoire was small but had two exceptional high points, in **Claude Debussy**'s *L'après-midi d'un faune* (1912, "Prelude to the Afternoon of a Faun") and in Stravinsky's *Sacre du printemps* (1913, "The Rite of Spring"). He married in 1913 and was interned in Hungary during the early part of World War I. He rejoined Diaghilev for a world tour, but was diagnosed a paranoid schizophrenic in 1917. Even before his death Nijinsky had become a legendary figure.

Nilsen, Dennis 1945– •*Scottish convicted murderer*• He was born in Fraserburgh, Aberdeenshire, and after a period in the army and a year as a probationary policeman, he became a civil servant in 1974. While living in two rented apartments in London, he invited a series of young men home, strangling, or attempting to strangle, several of them. He dissected the dead victims, disposing of some of the remains by flushing them down the toilet. When, in 1983, the drains became blocked, he was discovered and arrested. He has admitted to 15 murders. Throughout the four years during which he committed his crimes, he had sustained his employment, gained promotion and was an active trade unionist.

Nilsson, (Märta) Birgit 1918– •*Swedish soprano*• Born near Karup, Kristianstadslaen, she studied at the Stockholm Royal Academy of Music. Following her debut in 1946, she sang with the Stockholm Royal Opera (1947–51), and at the Bayreuth Festival from 1953 to 1970. She was the leading **Wagner**ian soprano of that period, having a voice of great power, stamina and intense personality. Well known in most of the great houses and festivals of the world, her repertoire included works by **Verdi**, **Puccini** and **Richard Strauss**.

Nimitz, Chester William 1885–1966 •*US naval commander*• Born in Fredericksburg, Texas, he graduated from the US Naval Academy, Annapolis, in 1905, served mainly in submarines, and by 1938 was rear admiral. From 1941 to 1945 he commanded the US Pacific Fleet and Pacific Ocean areas, contributing largely to the defeat of Japan. Made Fleet Admiral in 1944, he signed the Japanese surrender documents for the US on the USS *Missouri* in Tokyo Bay (1945). He became chief of Naval Operations from 1945 to 1947 and led the UN mediation commission in the Kashmir dispute in 1949.

Nin, Anaïs 1903–77 •*US writer*• Born in Paris to parents of mixed Spanish-Cuban descent, she moved to the US at the age of 11. Ten years later, she returned to Paris, where she studied psychoanalysis under **Otto Rank**, became acquainted with many well-known writers and artists and began to write herself. Her first novel, *House of Incest*, was published in 1936 and was followed by volumes of criticism, among them *The Novel of the Future* (1968) and a series of novels including *A Spy in the House of Love* (1954) and *Collages* (1964). She also published an early collection of short stories, *Under a Glass Bell* (1944). Ultimately, however, her reputation as an artist and seminal figure in the new feminism of the 1970s rests on her seven *Journals* (1966–83). Spanning the years 1931–74 they are an engrossing record of an era and some of its most intriguing and avant-garde players, as well as a passionate, explicit and candid account of one woman's voyage of self-discovery.

" "

I stopped loving my father a long time ago. What remained was the slavery to a pattern.

1944 ***Under a Glass Bell**, "Birth."*

Ninian, St, *also known as* **Nynia** or **Ringan** fl. 390 AD •*Scottish bishop, the earliest known Christian leader in Scotland*• Born Ailred of Rievaulx, near the Solway Firth, according to his 12th-century biographer, he was also alleged to be the son of a Christian king. According to **Bede**, writing about 730, he was a bishop of the Old Welsh British, and studied in Rome. He was consecrated bishop by the pope (AD 394) and sent as an apostle to the western parts of Great Britain. He selected Wigtownshire for the site of a monastery and church, which was built around 400 (and named Candida Casa, or "White House," according to Bede). Successful in converting the southern Picts, he died at Whithorn and was buried there, although other sources suggest he may have withdrawn to Ireland.

Ninoy *See* **Aquino, Benigno**

Nirenberg, Marshall Warren 1927– •*US biochemist and Nobel Prize winner*• Born in New York City, he was educated at the Universities of Florida and Michigan, and worked from 1957 at the National Institutes of Health in Bethesda, Maryland. It had been proposed that there are different combinations of three nucleotide bases (triplets, or codons) in nucleic acid chains in DNA and RNA, with each triplet coded for a different amino acid in the biological synthesis of proteins, the fundamental process in the chemical transfer of inherited characteristics. The precise nature of the code, however, remained unknown. Nirenberg attacked the problem of the "code dictionary" by synthesizing a nucleic acid with a known base sequence, and then finding which amino acid it converted to protein. With his success, **Har Gobind Khorana** and others soon completed the task of deciphering the full code. In 1968 Nirenberg, Khorana and **Robery Holley** shared the Nobel Prize for physiology or medicine for this work.

Niro, Robert De *See* **De Niro, Robert**

Niven, David, *originally* **James David Graham Nevins** 1910–83 •*English actor*• Born in London, he was a graduate of the Royal Military College at Sandhurst, and took a variety of jobs before he arrived in Hollywood, where he joined the social set led by **Errol Flynn** and **Clark Gable**. Signed by **Samuel Goldwyn**, he developed into a polished light comedian and gallant hero in films like *Dodsworth*, *The Charge of the Light Brigade* (both 1936) and *Bachelor Mother* (1939). After service as an army officer in World War II, he spent 30 years as an urbane English-style leading man, perfectly cast as the gentlemanly voyager Phileas Fogg in *Around the World in 80 Days* (1956), and winning an Academy Award for *Separate Tables* (1958). An inimitable raconteur, he published two volumes of lighthearted autobiography, *The Moon's a Balloon* (1972) and *Bring on the Empty Horses* (1975).

Nixon, Richard Milhous 1913–94 •*37th President of the US*• Born in Yorba Linda, California, he was educated at Whittier College and Duke University. After five years' practice as a lawyer, he served in the US Navy (1942–46), then ran for Congress as a Republican in California in 1946, defeating his Democratic opponent by painting him as a Communist sympathizer, a strategy he would use often in his career. His fearless outspokenness and tactical brilliance allowed him to rise swiftly in political circles, and he was particularly prominent as a member of the House Committee on Un-American Activities. After serving in the Senate (1951–53) he became vice president under **Dwight D Eisenhower** in 1953 and was reelected in 1956. In 1959 on a visit to Moscow he achieved notoriety by his outspoken exchanges with **Nikita Khrushchev**. As the Republican presidential candidate in 1960, he lost the election to **John F Kennedy** by a tiny margin. Despite an emotional declaration that he was retiring from politics, he returned to win the presidential election in 1968 by a small margin, and he was reelected in 1972 by a large majority. His administration (1969–74) was marked by continuing controversy over the Vietnam War, especially the invasion of Cambodia (1970) and the heavy bombing of North Vietnam, which ended with the eventual signing of a cease-fire in 1973. Other dramatic foreign policy events were Nixon's initiation of a strategic arms limitation treaty with the USSR, his reopening of US relations with the People's Republic of China (1972), and his visit there, the first by a US president. During an official investigation into a break-in in June 1972 at the Democratic National Committee's headquarters in the Watergate building, Washington, Nixon lost credibility with the US people by at first claiming executive privilege for senior White House officials to prevent them being questioned, and by refusing to hand over tapes of relevant conversations. On August 9, 1974, after several leading members of his government had been found guilty of being involved in the Watergate scandal, he resigned, the first US president to do so, thus averting the threat of impeachment. In September 1974 he was given a full pardon by President **Gerald Ford**. In his memoirs (1978) and other works he sought to salvage his damaged reputation and rebuild his image as a statesman.

Nkomo, Joshua (Mqabuko Nyongolo) 1917–99 •*Zimbabwean nationalist and politician*• He was born in Semokwe, Matabeleland, and educated in Natal and at Fort Hare College, where he joined the African National Congress (ANC). He returned to Bulawayo as a social worker and became general secretary of the Rhodesian Railway African Employees Association in 1951. Elected chairman of the (Southern Rhodesian) African National Congress in 1951, he became its president in 1957, leaving the country for exile in 1959. When the ANC was banned, he became president of its successor, the National Democratic Party, but that, too, was banned. He then helped form the Zimbabwe African People's Union (ZAPU), of which he became president. His nonconfrontationist tactics and tendency to spend time outside Rhodesia led to a more radical group breaking away to form the Zimbabwe African National Union (ZANU). ZANU, led by **Robert Mugabe**, and ZAPU united to form the Patriotic Front in 1976. Mugabe became prime minister in 1980 and Nkomo, who still saw himself as the father of Zimbabwean nationalism, was disappointed to be offered only the post of minister of home affairs, from which he was dismissed in 1981. Violence in Matabeleland encouraged him into a period of further exile, but he returned and agreed to integrate his party into ZANU, the two merging to form ZANU-PF in 1988, making Zimbawe effectively a one-party state with Mugabe as president and Nkomo as vice president (1990–99).

Nkrumah, Kwame 1909–72 •*Ghanaian politician*• He was born in Nakroful, Gold Coast, and educated at Achimota College, Lincoln University, Pennsylvania, and the London School of Economics. He returned to Africa (1947) and in 1949 formed the nationalist Convention People's Party. In 1950 he was imprisoned for his part in calling strikes and was elected to parliament while still in jail. A year later he was released and became virtual prime minister. He was confirmed in power in the 1956 election and in 1957 was appointed the first prime minister of the independent Commonwealth State of Ghana. Called the "**Gandhi** of Africa," he was a significant leader, first of the movement against white domination, and then of Pan-African sentiment. Ghana became a republic in 1960. Legal imprisonment of political opponents for five years and more without trial, and interference with the judiciary in the treason trial (1963, when he dismissed the chief justice), heralded the successful referendum for a one-party state in 1964, in which the secrecy of the ballot was called into question. In 1966 his regime was overthrown by a military coup while he was in China. He sought refuge in Guinea, where he was appointed joint head of state. He died in Bucharest.

Noah •*Biblical character*• He is depicted as the son of Lamech. A "righteous man," he was given divine instruction to build an ark in which he, his immediate family, and a selection of animals were saved from a widespread flood over the Earth (Genesis 6:9). In the Table of Nations (Genesis 10), Noah's sons Japheth, **Ham** and Shem are depicted as the ancestors of all the nations on Earth.

Nobel, Alfred Bernhard 1833–96 •*Swedish chemist, manufacturer and founder of the Nobel Prizes*• He was born in Stockholm, the son of an engineer. He moved in his childhood to Russia, where his father was working on an underwater mine he had devised. He studied chemistry in Paris, worked in the US with the Swedish-born **John Ericsson**, and settled in Sweden in 1859. Like his father, he was an explosives expert, and in 1866 he invented a safe and manageable form of nitroglycerin, which he called "dynamite"; later, he invented smokeless gunpowder, and in 1875 gelignite. On the strength of these inventions, he created an industrial empire which manufactured many of his other inventions. He amassed a huge fortune, much of which he left to endow annual Nobel Prizes (first awarded in 1901) for physics, chemistry, physiology or medicine, literature and peace (a sixth prize, for economics, was instituted in his honor in 1969). The synthetic transuranic element nobelium was named after him.

Nobile, Umberto 1885–1978 •*Italian aviator*• Born in Lauro, he became an aeronautical engineer and built the airships *Norge* and *Italia*. He flew across the North Pole in the *Norge* with **Roald Amundsen** and **Lincoln Ellsworth** in 1926, but in 1928 he was wrecked in the *Italia* when returning from the North Pole, and was adjudged (1929) responsible for the disaster. In the US from 1936 to 1942, he later returned to Italy and was reinstated in the Italian air service.

Noble, Adrian Keith 1950– •*English stage director*• He studied at the University of Bristol and the Drama Centre in London, and worked for two years in community and young people's theater in Birmingham. He became an associate director of the Bristol Old Vic (1976–79), and joined the Royal Shakespeare Company as a resident director (1980). He became an associate director in 1982, and succeeded **Terry Hands** as artistic director in 1991. Among his recent productions are *The Family Reunion* (1999) and *The Seagull* (2000).

Noddack, Ida Eva Tacke, *née* **Tacke** 1896–1978 and **Walter Karl Friedrich** 1893–1960 •*German chemists* • Ida Tacke was born in Lackhausen and educated at the Technical University of Berlin-Charlottenburg. Walter Noddack was born in Berlin and educated at the University of Berlin. They worked together at the Physikalisch Technische Reichsanstalt and married in 1926. In 1935 they moved to the Institute of Physical Chemistry at the University of Freiburg. Walter taught at the University of Strasbourg, France, during World War II and they both ended their careers at the Institute of Geochemical Research, Bamberg, Germany. In 1925 they discovered rhenium (atomic number 75) by X-ray spectroscopy. The same year they announced the discovery of element 43, which they called masurium. Its existence was debated until 1937 when Carlo Perrier and **Emilio Segrè** demonstrated its presence in a sample of molybdenum which had been bombarded with deuterons, and named it technetium. In photochemistry the Noddacks investigated the physical properties of sensitizing coloring substances, photochemical problems in the human eye and other subjects.

Noel-Baker (of the City of Derby), Philip (John) Noel-Baker, Baron 1889–1982 •*English Labour politician and Nobel Prize winner*• Born in London, he captained the British Olympic team (1912) after a brilliant athletic and academic career at Cambridge, and in World War I commanded a Friends' ambulance unit. He served on the secretariat of the Peace Conference (1919) and of the League of Nations (1919–22), and was Member of Parliament for Coventry (1929–31), then for Derby from 1936. He was Cassel Professor of International Relations at London (1924–29) and Dodge lecturer at Yale (1934). He wrote a number of books on international problems, including a standard work, *The Arms Race* (1958). During and after World War II he held several junior ministerial posts. He was awarded the Nobel Peace Prize in 1959 and created a life peer in 1977. His son, Francis Edward Noel-Baker (1920–), was a Labour Member of Parliament.

Noether, (Amalie) Emmy 1882–1935 •*German mathematician*• Born in Erlangen, she studied at the Universities of Erlangen and Göttingen. As a woman she could not hold a full academic post, but worked at Göttingen in a semihonorary capacity until, expelled by the Nazis as a Jew, she emigrated to the US in 1933 to Bryn Mawr College and Princeton University. She was one of the leading figures in the development of abstract algebra, working in ring theory and the theory of ideals. The theory of Noetherian rings has been an important subject of later research, and she developed it to provide a neutral setting for problems in algebraic geometry and number theory.

Noguchi, Isamu 1904–88 •*US sculptor*• He was born in Los Angeles to a Japanese father and a US mother, and brought up in Japan. He studied medicine at Columbia University and settled in New York, where he attended sculpture classes. A Guggenheim Fellowship enabled him to study with **Constantine Brancusi** in Paris from 1927 to 1929. After returning to New York he made stylized sculptures of sheet metal, but from 1940 his work moved closer to surrealism, and he turned to slate and marble, for example in *Kouros* (1946, Metropolitan Museum of Art, New York City). From the mid-1940s he gained worldwide commissions for large-scale public sculptures, as in Peace Park, Hiroshima, and Fort Worth, Texas. Later work included the use of ceramics and stainless steel.

Noiret, Philippe 1930– •*French actor*• Born in Lille, he studied at the Centre Dramatique de l'Ouest and made his film debut in *Gigi* (1948). In 1953 he joined the Théâtre National Populaire and for a time was primarily a stage actor and cabaret performer. He embraced the cinema with a vengeance after 1960, playing key roles in such films as *Zazie dans le métro* (1960), *Les copains* (1964) and *Alexandre le bienheureux* (1967). His rare English-language films include *Lady L* (1965) and *Topaz* (1969). One of Europe's most distinguished and prolific film actors, he has won Best Actor César awards for *Le vieux fusil* (1976, *The Old Gun*) and *La vie et rien d'autre* (1989, *Life and Nothing But*). He has appeared in more than 100 films, including *Cinema paradiso* (1989) and *Il postino* (1994).

Noland, Kenneth 1924– •*US painter*• Born in Asheville, North Carolina, he trained at Black Mountain College there (1946–48). He was influenced initially by **Paul Klee** and **Henri Matisse**, and the New York action painters, but had developed his own kind of hard-edge minimalist abstract painting by the late 1950s. His style is characterized by large-scale circles, ovals or chevrons, and by horizontal stripes, as in *Via Blues* (1967, Rowan Collection, Pasadena). His "plaid" paintings date from c. 1971.

Nolde, Emil, *pseudonym of* **Emil Hansen** 1867–1956 •*German painter and printmaker*• Born in Nolde, he was one of the most important expressionist painters. He was briefly a member of the expressionist group *Die Brücke* (1906–07), but produced his own powerful style of distorted forms in his violent religious pictures such as *The Life of Christ* (1911–12). He also produced a large number of etchings, lithographs and woodcuts.

Nollekens, Joseph 1737–1823 •*English sculptor*• Born in London, from 1760 he spent ten years in Rome. He sculpted neoclassical busts of most of his famous contemporaries, including **Samuel Johnson** (1784, Westminster Abbey), **Charles James Fox** (1791, Holkham Hall, Norfolk) and **George III** (1773, Royal Society, London). He is also known for his statues of goddesses, including *Venus Tying Her Sandal* (1773).

Nono, Luigi 1924–90 •*Italian composer*• Born in Venice, he attended the Venice Conservatorio, studying for a time under **Bruno Maderna**. With Maderna, he and **Luciano Berio** helped to establish Italy in the forefront of contemporary music. Unlike them, however, Nono was a socially conscious and politically committed artist, which had a considerable influence on his music. He worked for a time at the electronic studio in Darmstadt, and though radically avant-garde in technique, his concern for artist-to-audience communication, and the readily understandable inspiration of pieces such as *La victoire de Guernica* (1954), prevented his work from degenerating into obscurity. *Il canto sospeso* (1956), based on the letters of victims of wartime oppression, brought him to international notice. Among his other compositions are *Polyfonica-monodia-ritmica* (1951), *Canto per il Vietnam* (1973), and the operas *Intolleranza* (1960–61, "Intolerance"), *Al gran sole carico d'amore* (1972–75, "In the Great Sun of Blooming Love") and *Prometeo* (1981–85).

Norden, Denis 1922– •*English scriptwriter and broadcaster*• Born in Hackney, London, he served in the RAF during World War II, and later teamed up with **Frank Muir** to write books and comedy scripts, including the successful radio series *Take It from Here* (1947–58) and *Bedtime with Braden* (1950–54). Several other series were written with or for **Jimmy Edwards**. Later Norden presented selected film clips of media mishaps on *It'll Be All Right on the Night* (1977–).

Noriega, General Manuel Antonio Morena 1940– •*Panamanian soldier and politician*• Born in Panama City, he was commissioned in Panama's National Guard in 1962 and rose to become Head of Intelligence (1970) and Chief of Staff (1982). As commander of the National Guard (1982–89), he eventually became de facto ruler of the country, in which there was growing evidence of undemocratic practices. He had been recruited by the CIA in the late 1960s and was supported by the US government until 1987, but in 1988 his indictment by a US grand jury on charges of drug trafficking made that association embarrassing. In 1989, an attempted coup against him failed, and US President **George Bush** was criticized for not supporting it. However, later that year, with relations rapidly deteriorating, Bush sent troops into Panama to arrest him. Noriega initially took refuge in the Vatican embassy but eventually surrendered and was taken to Miami for trial. In 1992 he was convicted of drug trafficking and racketeering, and he is serving a 30-year prison sentence.

Norman, Barry Leslie 1933– •*English journalist and broadcaster*• Born in London, the son of film director Leslie Norman (1914–93), he worked for various newspapers before specializing in the world of show business and hosting radio programs. He made his name as an influential film critic through the television series that began with *Film '73* (1973–81, 1983–98). He made various documentary series, including *The Hollywood Greats* (1977–79, 1984–85) and *Talking Pictures* (1988), and his publications include *100 Best Films* (1992) and *The Mickey Mouse Affair* (1995). A recipient of the British Academy of Film and Television Arts **Richard Dimbleby** award in 1981, he was given the honorary title of Commander, Order of the British Empire, in 1998.

Norman, Greg 1955– •*Australian golfer*• Born in Mount Isa, Queensland, he started playing golf when he was 15 years old, and turned professional in 1976. He has won two major titles—the 1986 and 1993 Open championships—but ironically retains the reputation of the eternal runner-up. The only player of modern times to have competed in a Grand Slam of playoffs, unfortunately he lost them all.

Norman, Jessye 1945– •*US soprano*• Born in Augusta, Georgia, she made her operatic debut at the Deutsche Oper, Berlin, in 1969 and at both La Scala and Covent Garden, London, in 1972. Her US debut was at the Hollywood Bowl (1972). She is widely admired in opera and concert music for her beauty of tone, breadth of register and her dynamic range. She has won four Grammies (1984, 1988, 1989, 1998).

Norrish, Ronald George Wreyford 1897–1978 •*English physical chemist and Nobel Prize winner*• Born in Cambridge, he studied at Emmanuel College, Cambridge, where became H O Jones Lecturer in Physical Chemistry in 1928. In 1937 he was promoted to Professor of Physical Chemistry and head of the department, a post he held until his retirement in 1965. He was one of the founders of modern photochemistry and also made advances in the area of chain reactions. His most important innovation (1945), in association with Sir **George Porter**, was flash photolysis. For this work Norrish was awarded the Nobel Prize for chemistry jointly with Porter and **Manfred Eigen** in 1967.

North, Frederick, 2nd Earl of Guilford, *known as* **Lord North** 1732–92 •*English statesman*• He entered parliament at the age of 22, became a lord of the treasury, Chancellor of the Exchequer and in 1770 prime minister. He was criticized both for failing to avert the Declaration of Independence by the North American colonies (1776) and for failing to defeat them in the subsequent war (1776–83). He resigned in 1782 and entered into a coalition with his former opponent, **Charles James Fox**, and served with him under the Duke of Portland (**William Bentinck**) in 1783. He succeeded to the earldom in 1790.

North, Oliver 1943– *•US soldier•* Born into a military family in San Antonio, Texas, he graduated from the US Naval Academy, Annapolis. During the Vietnam War he led a marines platoon, winning a Silver Star and Purple Heart, before returning home wounded. After working as an instructor and security officer, he was appointed a deputy director of the National Security Council by President **Ronald Reagan** in 1981. Here he played a key role in a series of controversial military and security actions. In 1986, when the Iran-Contra affair became public, he resigned, and in 1989 a Washington court found him guilty on 3 of 12 charges arising from the affair. He was given a three-year suspended jail sentence and fined $150,000, but he successfully appealed against this conviction, and in 1991 all charges were dropped.

“ ”

I thought using the Ayatollah's money to support the Nicaraguan resistance...was a neat idea.

1987 Testimony to the House Committee investigating arms sales to Iran, July 8.

North, Robert, *originally* **Robert North Dodson** 1945– *•British dancer and choreographer•* Born in Charleston, South Carolina, he joined the Royal Ballet School in 1965 and later took classes with the London Contemporary Dance School. Going on to become one of the founding members of London Contemporary Dance Theatre (1966), he spent 12 years with that company as a dancer and choreographer. Early work includes *Troy Game* (1974) and *Still Life* (1975). In 1981 he was made artistic director of Ballet Rambert, but was dismissed five years later. He was then ballet director of the Teatro Regio in Turin (1990–91) and of the Göteborg Ballet (1991–96) before becoming ballet director at the Arena di Verona (1997–99) and artistic director of Scottish Ballet in 1999.

Northcliffe, Lord *See* **Harmsworth, Alfred Charles William**

Northrop, John Howard 1891–1987 *•US biochemist and Nobel Prize winner•* Born in Yonkers, New York, and educated at Columbia University, he became Professor of Bacteriology at the University of California at Berkeley (1949–62). In 1930 he crystallized pepsin, the protein-digesting enzyme of the stomach, and went on to purify other macromolecules. He isolated the first bacterial virus, and was the first to equate the biological function of an enzyme with its chemical properties. He also discovered the fermentation process used in the manufacture of acetone. For their studies of methods of producing purified enzymes and virus products, Northrop, **Wendell Stanley** and **James Sumner** shared the 1946 Nobel Prize for chemistry.

Northrop, John Knudsen 1895–1981 *•US aircraft manufacturer•* Born in Newark, New Jersey, he became a cofounder and chief engineer of the Lockheed Aircraft Co of Burbank, California (1927–28). He was vice president and chief engineer of The Northrop Corporation, a subsidiary of Douglas Aircraft (1933–37), and became president and director of engineering of Northrop Aircraft Inc (1939–52). He was an engineering consultant from 1953. His company built many famous aircraft, including two very large all-wing types, the first propeller-driven and a later version jet-propelled.

Norton, Caroline Elizabeth Sarah, *née* **Sheridan** 1808–77 *•Irish writer and reformer•* She was born in London, the granddaughter of **Richard Brinsley Sheridan**. In 1827 she married a dissolute barrister, the Hon George Chapple Norton (1800–75), and bore him three sons. She took up writing to support the family, and in 1836 she separated from her husband, who brought an action of "criminal conversation" (adultery) against Lord **Melbourne**, obtained custody of the children and tried to obtain the profit from her books. Her spirited pamphlets led to improvements in the legal status of women in relation to infant custody (1839) and marriage and divorce (1857). She married the historian Sir William Stirling-Maxwell (1818–78) in 1877, but died soon afterward. Her books of verse include *The Sorrows of Rosalie* (1829) and *Voice from the Factories* (1836), an attack on child labor. She also published three novels.

Norton, Charles Eliot 1827–1908 *•US writer and scholar•* Born in Cambridge, Massachusetts, he was joint editor (with **James Russell Lowell**) of the *North American Review* (1864–68), and was a cofounder of *The Nation* (1865). He then became Professor of Art at Harvard (1873–97), where he instituted a course in the history of fine arts as related to society and general culture. A personal friend of **Thomas Carlyle**, **John Ruskin**, **Henry Wadsworth Longfellow**, **Ralph Waldo Emerson** and many other leading literary figures, he wrote on medieval church building, translated **Dante**'s *Divina Commedia* (1891–92), edited the poems of **John Donne** (1895) and **Anne Bradstreet** (1897), and the letters of Carlyle (1883–91).

Norton, Gale Ann 1954– *•US politician•* Born in Wichita, Kansas, she was educated at the University of Denver and subsequently embarked on a career in law. She was acclaimed the National Federalist Society's Young Lawyer of the Year in 1991. She went on to become Colorado Attorney General (1991–99) and ultimately secretary of the interior in the administration of **George W Bush** (2001).

Norton, Mary 1903–92 *•English children's novelist•* She was born in Leighton Buzzard, Bedfordshire. She published her first book in 1945, but it was *The Borrowers* (1952, Carnegie Medal), an enchanting story about tiny people living beneath the floorboards of a big house, which established her as one of the foremost children's writers of her generation. There were four sequels, the last being *The Borrowers Avenged* (1982).

Norton, Mary Teresa Hopkins, *née* **Hopkins** 1875–1959 *•US politician•* Born in Jersey City, New Jersey, she formed a nonsectarian daycare center for children of working women in 1912. She became the first woman to serve on the New Jersey State Democratic Committee, serving as either vice chair or chair from 1921 to 1944. From 1925 to 1951 she served in the US Congress, the first woman to be in that position on her own political strength. She was the first woman to head a congressional committee, chaired the Labor Committee in 1937, and fought successfully for the Fair Labor Standards Act.

Norton, Thomas 1532–84 *•English lawyer and poet•* Born in London, he was a successful lawyer and a zealous Protestant, and married a daughter of **Thomas Cranmer**. He translated **John Calvin**'s *Christianae religionis institutio* (1561). With **Thomas Sackville** he was joint author of the tragedy *Gorboduc*, which was performed before Queen **Elizabeth I** in 1562 and has some claim to be considered the first proper English tragedy.

Nostradamus, *also called* **Michel de Notredame** 1503–66 *•French physician and astrologer•* Born in St Rémy, Provence, he became doctor of medicine in 1529, and practiced in Agen, Lyons, and other places. He set himself up as a prophet in c. 1547. His *Centuries* of predictions in rhymed quatrains (two collections, 1555–58), expressed generally in obscure and enigmatic terms, brought their author a great reputation. **Charles IX** appointed him his physician-in-ordinary.

Nott, Sir John William Frederick 1932– *•English Conservative politician•* Born in Bideford, Devon, he was commissioned in the Second Gurkha Rifles and served in Malaysia (1952–56). He left the army to study law and economics at Trinity College, Cambridge (1957–59), and was called to the bar in 1959. He became a Member of Parliament in 1960, and was a junior treasury minister (1972–74) in the government of **Edward Heath**. In **Margaret Thatcher**'s administration he was Trade Secretary (1979–81), and then Defence Secretary during the Falklands War. He left the House of Commons, with a knighthood, in 1983 and worked in various posts in the private sector.

Nouri Said Pasha *See* **Es-Sa'id, Nuri**

Novalis, *pseudonym of* **Baron Friedrich Leopold von Hardenberg** 1772–1801 *•German Romantic poet and novelist•* Born in Oberwiederstadt, Saxony, he fell in love with a girl in 1795, in whose memory he wrote the prose lyrics of *Hymnen an die Nacht* (1800, Eng trans *Hymns to the Night*, 1948). He also published *Geistliche Lieder* (1799, Eng trans *Devotional Songs*, 1910). He left two philosophical romances, both incomplete, *Heinrich von Ofterdingen* (1802) and *Die Lehrlinge zu Sais* (1802, "The Apprentices of Sais"). He was known as "the Prophet of Romanticism."

Novatian 3rd century AD *•Roman Christian cleric•* Born in Rome, he was converted to Christianity and ordained a priest. Formerly a Stoic, in the aftermath of the persecution of **Decius** (AD 251), he challenged the papal policy of readmitting lapsed Christians to communion and formed instead his own sect (the Novatiani). The first theologian in Rome to write in Latin, Novatian is believed to have died in the persecution of **Valerian**. His sect survived until the 6th century.

Novello, Ivor, *originally* **David Ivor Davies** 1893–1951 *•Welsh actor, composer, songwriter and dramatist•* Born in Cardiff, the son of the singer Clara Novello Davies (1861–1943), he was educated at Magdalen College School, Oxford, where he was a chorister. His song "Keep the Home Fires Burning" was one of the best known of World War I. He first appeared on the regular stage in London in 1921 and enjoyed great popularity, his most successful and characteristic works being his "Ruritanian" musical plays such as *Glamorous Night* (1935) and *King's Rhapsody* (1949).

Novello, Vincent 1781–1861 *•English organist, composer and music publisher•* Born in London to an Italian father and English mother, in 1811 he founded the publishing house of Novello & Co. He was a founding member of the Philharmonic Society in 1813, and subsequently its pianist and conductor. His compositions include church music, and he was a painstaking editor of unpublished works. His son, Joseph Vincent Novello (1810–96), was also an organist and music publisher, and his daughter, Clara Anastasia Novello (1818–1908), had considerable success in Europe as a concert and operatic singer.

Novotný, Antonín 1904–75 *•Czechoslovak politician•* Born the son of a bricklayer in Letnany, near Prague, he became a Communist at the age of 17 and held various party jobs in the years before World War II. Arrested in 1941, he survived four years in a Nazi concentration camp. Following his release, he rose rapidly in the Czechoslovak Communist Party, becoming a member of the Central Committee in 1946. He played a leading part in the Communist takeover of the Czechoslovak government in 1948. Novotný became all-powerful first secretary of the party in 1953, and from 1958 to 1968 he was also president of the republic. By 1961 there was an economic recession, and his unpopularity forced him to make token concessions from 1962 onward, especially in the hope of placating the Slovaks, but he failed to satisfy his critics within the party. He was forced out, and was succeeded as first secretary by the reformist Slovak **Alexander Dubček** (1968), and was also forced to resign the presidency.

Noyce, Robert Norton 1927–90 *•US physicist and electronics engineer•* Born in Burlington, Iowa, he studied at MIT, and later joined **William Shockley**'s semiconductor laboratory. In 1957 he was cofounder of Fairchild Semiconductor in Silicon Valley, where he developed the planar integrated circuit, which led directly to the commercially feasible integrated circuit. With **Jack Kilby**, who worked on the microchip independently, he is regarded as the coinventor of the integrated circuit. He also cofounded the chip manufacturer Intel.

Noyes, Alfred 1880–1958 *•English poet•* Born in Staffordshire, he began writing verse as an undergraduate at Oxford, and on the strength of having a volume published in his final year, he left without taking a degree. This book, *The Loom of Years* (1902), which was praised by **George Meredith**, was followed by further well received volumes. The sea, and in particular its treatment in English poetry, was the subject of some of his most successful work, as in *Forty Singing Seamen* (1908) and the epic *Drake* (1908). He married an American, traveled in the US and became visiting Professor of Poetry at Princeton (1914–23). His trilogy *The Torchbearers* appeared between 1922 and 1930, praising men of science. He published literary essays, and also wrote plays, studies of **William Morris** and **Voltaire**, and an anecdotal memoir, *Two Worlds for Memory* (1953).

" "

Watch for me by moonlight;
I'll come to thee by moonlight, though hell should bar the way.

1907 "The Highwayman."

Noyes, Eliot 1910–77 *•US designer and architect•* Born in Boston, he came under the influence of **Walter Gropius**, **Marcel Breuer** and **Le Corbusier** when studying architecture, and it is not surprising that he was the most "European" of the prominent US designers working from the 1930s to the 1970s. In 1940 he set up and directed the department of industrial design at the Museum of Modern Art, New York. After working for the stage designer and architect Norman Bel Geddes (1893–1958), he established his own practice in 1947, working for major companies such as Westinghouse, Mobil and, most notably, IBM, for which he became consultant design director.

Nu, U, *originally* **Thakin Nu** 1907–95 *•Burmese politician•* Born in Wakema and educated at Rangoon University, in the 1930s he joined the Dobama Asiayone (Our Burma) Nationalist Organization. He was imprisoned by the British for sedition at the outbreak of World War II, during the Japanese occupation, and in 1942 was released to serve in Ba Maw's puppet government. He later founded the Anti-Fascist People's Freedom League (AFPFL), which collaborated with the British against the Japanese in 1945, and on independence in 1948 he became Burma's first prime minister. He held this post until 1962, when his parliamentary regime was overthrown by General **Ne Win**, and he was imprisoned until 1966 when he lived abroad in Thailand and India, organizing exiled opposition forces. He returned to Burma (Myanmar) in 1980, and in the same year became a Buddhist monk trainee in Rangoon. He helped found the National League for Democracy (1988).

Nuffield, William Richard Morris, 1st Viscount 1877–1963 *•English automobile magnate and philanthropist•* Born in Worcestershire, he started in the bicycle repair business and by 1910 was manufacturing prototypes of Morris Oxford cars at Cowley, in Oxford. The first British manufacturer to develop the mass production of cheap cars, he was raised to the peerage in 1934. He used part of his vast fortune to benefit hospitals, charities and Oxford University. In 1937 he endowed Nuffield College, Oxford, and he established the Nuffield Foundation for medical, scientific and social research in 1943.

Nujoma, Sam Daniel 1929– *•Namibian politician•* Born in Ongandjern and educated at a Finnish missionary school in Windhoek, he entered active politics as a cofounder of the South West Africa People's Organization of Namibia (SWAPO) in 1958. After being exiled in 1960 he set up a provisional headquarters for SWAPO in Dar es Salaam, Tanzania, and on his return to Namibia (1966) he was again arrested and expelled. He then established a military wing, the People's Liberation Army of Namibia (PLAN), in the mid-1960s, and his long struggle for Namibia's independence eventually bore fruit in 1989. He was elected president of the new republic in 1990 and was reelected in 1994 and 1999.

Numa Pompilius 8th–7th century BC *•Second of Rome's early kings•* According to tradition he ruled 715–673 BC. He is described as a peaceful ruler, and was credited with organizing the religious life of the community.

Núñez de Arce, Gaspar 1834–1903 *•Spanish poet, dramatist and politician•* Born in Valladolid, he held office in the government in 1883 and 1888. As a lyric poet he may be styled "the Spanish **Tennyson**," and among his poems are *Gritos del combate* (1875, "Cries of Battle"), *Última lamentación de Lord Byron* (1879, "Lord Byron's Last Lamentation") and *La Maruja* (1886). His plays include *La cuenta del Zapatero* (1859, "The Countess of Zapatero") and *El haz de leña* (1872, "The Bundle of Firewood").

Nunn, Trevor Robert 1940– *•English stage director•* Born in Ipswich, Suffolk, he graduated from Cambridge and joined the Belgrade Theatre, Coventry, as a trainee director before joining the Royal Shakespeare Company (1965). In 1968 he succeeded **Peter Hall** as the company's artistic director, and was joined as co-artistic director by **Terry Hands** ten years later. At the RSC he has directed many outstanding productions, and during his directorship (1968–86) two new theaters were opened in Stratford-upon-Avon: The Other Place (1974) and The Swan (1986). He directed several of **Andrew Lloyd Webber**'s musicals, as well as a number of operas at Glyndebourne. In 1997 he took over for Sir **Richard Eyre** as artistic director of the National Theatre and in 2001 announced that he would step down from the post in 2002.

Nureddin, *properly* **Nur ad-Din Abu al-Qasim Mahmud ibn 'Imad ad-Din Zangi**, *also known as* **al-Malik al-Adil ("the Just Ruler")** 1118–74 •*Sultan of Egypt and Syria*• He was the son of the Turkish atabeg **Zangi**, whom he succeeded as ruler of Aleppo (1146). He concentrated on the jihad, the holy war against the crusading Christian Franks, defeating and killing Prince Raymond of Antioch (1149) and completely extinguishing the most exposed Frankish state, the county of Edessa (1146–51). He aimed to unify the Muslim Middle East, conquering Damascus (1154) and Mosul (1170), while through his generals Shirkuh and **Saladin** he took control of Egypt and abolished the Fatimid caliphate. His empire began to disintegrate soon after his death, and it was left to Saladin, now independent, to carry on his mission.

Nureyev, Rudolf Hametovich 1938–93 •*Russian ballet dancer*• Born in Irkutsk, Siberia, he trained first as a folk dancer and then at the Kirov School in Leningrad (now St Petersburg), where he became principal dancer for the Kirov Ballet. While in Paris with them in 1961, he defected and obtained political asylum. An intelligent man with an impressive ability to express emotion through the body, he had many different roles, often appearing with **Margot Fonteyn**, with whom he made his Covent Garden debut in 1962. Theirs was a partnership which was to transform dance in the West. As a guest performer, he danced with most of the prominent companies of the world. He also had a successful career as a producer of full-length ballets and was artistic director of the Paris Opera (1983–89). Films in which he appeared include *Swan Lake* (1966), *Don Quixote* (1974) and *Valentino* (1977).

Nurmi, Paavo Johannes, *known as* **the Flying Finn** 1897–1973 •*Finnish athlete*• Born in Turku, he dominated long-distance running in the 1920s, winning nine gold medals at three Olympic Games (1920, 1924, 1928). From 1922 to 1926 he set four world records for 3,000 meters, bringing the time down to 8 minutes 20.4 seconds. He also established world records at six miles (1921, 29:7.1), one mile (1923, 4:10.4) and two miles (1931, 8:59.5). Disqualified in 1932 for alleged professionalism, he nevertheless remained a Finnish national hero.

Nurse, Sir Paul M(axime) 1949– •*English biologist and Nobel Prize winner*• He was born in Norwich, Norfolk, and studied at the Universities of Birmingham and East Anglia, with postdoctoral work at Bern, Edinburgh and Sussex. He became head of the Cell Cycle Laboratory of the Imperial Cancer Research Fund (ICRF) in 1984 and since 1996 has been the ICRF's director general. He was knighted in 1999, and in 2001 he shared the Nobel Prize for physiology or medicine with **Lee Hartwell** and **Tim Hunt** for their discoveries of key regulators of the cell cycle, allowing more accurate cancer diagnostics.

Nuttall, Thomas 1786–1859 •*US naturalist*• Born in Settle, Yorkshire, he emigrated to Philadelphia in 1808, where he took up botany, accompanied several scientific expeditions between 1811 and 1834, and discovered many new US plants. He wrote *Genera of North American Plants* (1818) and became curator of the botanical garden at Harvard (1822–32). While at Harvard he also turned his attention to ornithology, and published *A Manual of the Ornithology of the United States and Canada* (1832). His two-volume work *North American Silva* was published in 1842.

Nyerere, Julius Kambarage, *known as* **Mwalimu ("teacher")** 1922–99 •*Tanzanian politician*• Born in Butiama, Lake Victoria, he qualified as a teacher at Makerere College and, after a spell of teaching, studied at the University of Edinburgh. On his return in 1954, he reorganized the nationalists into the Tanganyika African National Union (of which he became president), entered the Legislative Council (1958) and in 1960 became chief minister. He became prime minister when Tanganyika was granted internal self-government (1961) and president when Tanganyika became a republic (1962). In 1964 he negotiated the union of Tanganyika and Zanzibar (which became Tanzania in October of the same year). He had genuine hopes of bringing a unique form of African socialism to his country, but his efforts were largely frustrated by economic difficulties, particularly following the debilitating war against the Ugandan dictator **Idi Amin** (1978–79). He gave up the presidency in 1985 but retained leadership of his party, Chama cha Mapinduzi (CCM, Revolutionary Party) until 1990, and remained one of Africa's most respected political figures. He wrote a number of political works, as well as Swahili translations of the plays of **Shakespeare**.

Nyman, Michael 1944– •*English pianist, composer and writer*• Born in London, he studied at the Royal Academy of Music and King's College London, and became a music critic (1968–78). He formed his own ensemble in 1977 to play his music, written in a minimalist vein, often with allusions to Baroque music woven in. He became a very successful composer of film soundtracks, including a large number for the filmmaker **Peter Greenaway**. His evocative score for **Jane Campion**'s *The Piano* (1993) became a best-seller. He has also written many works for chamber groups and symphony orchestras. His music for theater includes the opera *The Man Who Mistook His Wife for a Hat* (1986).

Nynia, St *See* **Ninian, St**

O

Oakley, Ann, *née* **Titmuss** 1944– •*British sociologist, writer, and feminist*• Educated at Somerville College, Oxford, she has been Professor of Sociology and Social Policy at the Institute of Education, University of London, since 1991. She is a prolific writer and her work focuses largely on gender roles. Her best-known work in recent years is *The Men's Room* (1988), which was made into a BBC television serial. Other works include *The Sociology of Housework* (1974) and *Essays on Women, Medicine and Health* (1994), as well as two books on which she collaborated with Juliet Mitchell, *The Rights and Wrongs of Women* (1976) and *What Is Feminism?* (1986).

Oakley, Annie, *originally* **Phoebe Anne Oakley Moses** 1860–1926 •*US sharpshooter and Wild West performer*• She was born near Woodland, Ohio, into a Quaker family and learned to shoot at an early age. She married Frank E Butler in 1880 after beating him in a shooting match. Together they formed a trick-shooting act, and from 1885 toured widely with Buffalo Bill's Wild West Show. A tiny woman just under five feet tall, she shot cigarettes from her husband's lips, and could shoot through the pips of a playing card tossed in the air (hence an "Annie Oakley" for a punched free ticket). Her life was fictionalized in the **Irving Berlin** musical comedy *Annie Get Your Gun* (1946), starring **Ethel Merman**.

Oaksey, 1st Baron *See* **Lawrence, Geoffrey**

Oasis •*British rock band*• Oasis (initially called the Rain) was formed in 1991 in their hometown of Manchester by the brothers Noel (1967–) and Liam Gallagher (1972–) on vocals, guitarist Paul Arthurs (1965–), bassist Paul McGuigan (1971–) and drummer Tony McCaroll, later replaced by Alan White (1972–). Fronted by the Gallagher brothers, who quickly established a controversial reputation for their belligerent behavior on- and offstage, Oasis became one of the most popular British rock bands of the 1990s. The band's albums, which have enjoyed success on both sides of the Atlantic, include *Definitely Maybe* (1994) and *(What's the Story) Morning Glory?* (1995).

Oates, Joyce Carol 1938– •*US writer*• Born in Millersport, New York, and educated at Syracuse University and the University of Wisconsin, she taught English at the University of Detroit (1961–67), then was appointed Professor of English at the University of Windsor, Ontario (1967–87). A prolific fiction writer and essayist, she published her first novel, *With Shuddering Fall*, in 1964. Violent and impressive in its social scope, her fiction challenges established ideas about the nature of human experience. *Them* (1969), her fourth novel, won a National Book award. Later novels include *You Must Remember This* (1989) and *What I Lived For* (1994).

Oates, Lawrence Edward Grace 1880–1912 •*English explorer*• Born in Putney, London, he was educated at Eton, but left school to serve in the South African War with the Inniskilling Dragoons. In 1910 he set out with Captain **Robert Scott**'s Antarctic expedition, and was one of the party of five to reach the South Pole (January 17, 1912). On the return journey the explorers were dangerously delayed and became weatherbound, and Oates, crippled by frostbite, walked out into the blizzard, deliberately sacrificing his life to enhance his comrades' chances of survival.

Oates, Titus 1649–1705 •*English conspirator*• Born in Oakham, he took Anglican orders, but was dismissed from his curacy for misconduct. In 1677 he concocted the Popish Plot, in which he infiltrated Jesuit seminaries pretending to be Catholic. In 1678 he told a magistrate, later found dead, of a Catholic plot to massacre Protestants, burn London, and assassinate **Charles II**, replacing him with his brother James, Duke of York (**James VII and II**). Oates was considered a hero, and his evidence led to 35 judicial murders. But after two years a reaction set in. In 1683 Oates was fined £100,000 for calling the Duke of York a traitor, and in May 1685 was sentenced to be imprisoned for life. He was set free in the revolution of 1688.

Obasanjo, Olusegun 1937– •*Nigerian soldier and politician*• He was born in Abeokuta and trained as an officer at Aldershot, England. He joined the Nigerian army in 1958, becoming a commander in 1963. Following the assassination of General Murtala Muhammad in 1976, he became head of state, but in elections held in 1979 was replaced by Shehu Shagari (1925–). Obasanjo was imprisoned under the rule of **Sani Abacha** and freed on the latter's death in 1998. His People's Democratic Party won the 1999 elections and he became president.

Oberth, Hermann Julius 1894–1990 •*German astrophysicist*• Born in Sibiu (Hermannstadt), Romania, he published his first book, *By Rocket to Interplanetary Space*, in 1923. In 1928 he was elected president of the German Society for Space Travel (Verein für Raumschiffahrt). He designed a manned rocket and space cabin for **Fritz Lang**'s film *Woman in the Moon* in 1929. In World War II he worked at the experimental rocket center at Peenemünde and later, from 1955 to 1961, he assisted **Wernher von Braun** in developing space rockets in the US.

Obote, (Apollo) Milton 1924– •*Ugandan politician*• Born in Lango, and educated in mission schools and Makerere College, Kampala, he was a founding member of the Kenyan African Union. He kept his political links with his home country and was a member of the Uganda National Congress (1952–60), being elected to the Legislative Council in 1957. He helped form the Uganda People's Congress (UPC) in 1960, became its leader and then leader of the Opposition during the Kiwanuka government of 1961–62. He became prime minister of a coalition government after the 1962 elections, but when fundamental differences emerged within the coalition, he staged a coup (1966), establishing himself as executive president. In 1971, however, his government was overthrown in a military coup led by **Idi Amin**. He went into exile in Tanzania and returned to Uganda with the Tanzanian army in 1979, regaining the presidency after elections in 1980. But he was once more overthrown by the military (July 1985) and went into exile again, this time in Zambia.

O'Brien, (Donal) Conor (Dermod David Donat) Cruise 1917– •*Irish historian, critic and politician*• Born into a strongly nationalist Dublin family, described in his *States of Ireland* (1973), he was educated at Trinity College, Dublin, and his doctoral dissertation was later published as *Parnell and His Party* (1957). His finest work is *To Katanga and Back* (1962), an autobiographical narrative of the Congo crisis of 1961 which he had seen as UN Secretary-General **Dag Hammarskjöld**'s representative in Katanga; the earlier tragedy of **Patrice Lumumba** formed the theme of his play *Murderous Angels* (1968). He was Irish Labour Teachda Dála (Member of Parliament) from 1969 to 1977, and was subsequently editor in chief of the *Observer* and a mordant political columnist, as well as the author of studies of **Albert Camus** and **Edmund Burke** (1992).

O'Brien, Edna 1932– •*Irish novelist, short-story writer and playwright*• Born in Tuamgraney, County Clare, she was educated at the Convent of Mercy, Loughrea, and at the Pharmaceutical College of Dublin, and practiced pharmacy briefly before becoming a writer. Her dominant themes are loneliness, guilt and loss, articulated in musical prose. Among her celebrated books are *The Country Girls* (1960), *The Lonely Girl* (1962), *Girls in Their Married Bliss* (1964), *August Is a Wicked Month* (1965) and *A Pagan Place* (1970). She has also published several collections of short stories. Recent novels include a collection of *The Country Girls Trilogy* with an epilogue (1986), *The High Road* (1988), *House of Splendid Isolation* (1994) and *Wild Decembers* (1999). She has also written a number of plays and screenplays, a book of verse, and some nonfiction.

O'Brien, Flann, *pseudonym of* **Brian O'Nolan** 1911–66 •*Irish writer*• He was born in Strabane, County Tyrone, and educated at University College Dublin, studying German, Irish and English, although much of his time was frittered away at billiards or in pubs. He founded *Blather*, whose six editions he wrote mainly himself, gave talks on literature on Irish radio, completed his eccentric but brilliant novel *At Swim-Two-Birds* in 1936, and joined the Irish Civil Service, which occupied him until his premature retirement in 1953. The publication of *At Swim-Two-Birds* in 1939 owed much to **Graham Greene**'s enthusiasm and led to the birth of the Flann O'Brien pseudonym. A year later, in 1940, came the debut of "Myles na Gopaleen," the pseudonym under which he contributed a column to the *Irish Times* for some 20 years. His second novel, *An béal bocht*, was published in Irish in 1941 (*The Poor Mouth*, 1973), and *The Third Policeman*, written and rejected in 1940, was published posthumously in 1967.

O'Brien, Kate 1897–1974 •*Irish playwright and novelist*• She was born in Limerick, County Limerick, and educated at University College Dublin. At 30 she began a career in London as a playwright, and in 1931 she published her prizewinning *Without My Cloak*, followed by *The Land of Spices* (1941), *That Lady* (1946) and *As Music and Splendour* (1958), among others. A remarkable observer of life, she suffered a profoundly unhappy marriage, and her novels are best understood by appreciation of her consciousness of a lesbian sexual identity. *Farewell Spain* (1937) and *My Ireland* (1962), in particular, reflect her deep knowledge of those countries.

Ó Cadhain, Máirtín, *anglicized name* **Martin Kane** 1906–70 •*Irish Gaelic short-story writer and novelist*• Born in Spiddal, Connemara, he was actively involved in the IRA and was interned during World War II. The second of five collections of short stories, *An braon broghach* (1948, Eng trans *The Hare Lip*, in *The Field Day Anthology of Irish Writing*, 1991), established him as a stern critic of accepted social conventions. The novel *Cré na cille* (1949, "The Clay of the Churchyard") is a commentary by the dead on the perfidies of the politicians in the "fledgling Free State." He was a staunch advocate of revolution, and had a strong influence on subsequent generations of writers.

O'Casey, Sean 1884–1964 •*Irish playwright*• Born in a poor part of Dublin, he picked up whatever education he could, and worked as a laborer and for nationalist organizations before beginning his career as a dramatist. His early plays, dealing with lowlife in Dublin—*Shadow of a Gunman* (1923) and *Juno and the Paycock* (1924)—were written for the Abbey Theatre, Dublin. Later he became more experimental and impressionistic. Other works include *The Plough and the Stars* (1926), *Cockadoodle Dandy* (1949) and *The Bishop's Bonfire* (1955). He also wrote essays, such as *The Flying Wasp* (1936). He was awarded the Hawthornden Prize in 1926. His autobiography appeared in six volumes (1939–54).

“ ”

There's no reason to bring religion into it. I think we ought to have as great a regard for religion as we can, so as to keep it out of as many things as possible.

1926 ***The Plough and the Stars****, act 1.*

Occam, William of *See* **Ockham, William of**

Ochoa, Severo 1905–93 •*US geneticist and Nobel Prize winner*• Born in Luarca, Spain, he graduated in medicine at Madrid in 1929 and worked at the University of Heidelberg and Oxford University before emigrating to the US, where he accepted posts at the Washington University School of Medicine in St Louis and at the New York University School of Medicine. Ochoa isolated two of the catalysts of the **Krebs** cycle, and this led him to study the energetics of carbon dioxide fixation in photosynthesis from 1948. He studied the enzyme later used for the first synthesis of artificial RNA, and in 1961 adopted **Marshall Nirenberg**'s approach to solving the amino acid genetic code. He also studied the direction of protein synthesis along the DNA (1965), and the first amino acid in a peptide sequence (1967). For his contributions to the elucidation of the genetic code he was awarded the 1959 Nobel Prize for physiology or medicine, jointly with **Arthur Kornberg**.

Ochs, Adolph Simon 1858–1935 •*US newspaper publisher*• Born in Cincinnati, Ohio, he entered the newspaper business at age 11 as an office boy for the *Knoxville Chronicle* in Tennessee. At the age of 20 he bought control of the *Chattanooga Times*, which became one of the leading journals in the South. He bought the failing *New York Times* in 1896 and served as its publisher until his death almost 40 years later. By rejecting the sensationalism of yellow journalism in favor of accurate, nonpartisan reporting, he turned the *Times* into one of the greatest newspapers in the world. He was also director of the Associated Press from 1900 to 1935.

Ochus *See* **Artaxerxes III**

Ockham or **Occam, William of**, *nicknamed* **the Venerable Inceptor** c. 1285–c. 1349 •*English philosopher, theologian and political writer*• Born in Ockham, Surrey, he entered the Franciscan order, studied theology at Oxford as an "inceptor" (beginner), but never obtained a higher degree—hence his nickname. He was summoned to Avignon by Pope **John XXII** to answer charges of heresy, and became involved in a dispute about Franciscan poverty which the Pope had denounced on doctrinal grounds. He fled to Bavaria (1328), was excommunicated, and remained under the protection of Emperor Louis of Bavaria until 1347. He died in Munich, probably of the Black Death. He published many works on logic while at Oxford and Avignon, notably the *Summa logicae*, *Quodlibeta septem* and commentaries on the *Sentences* of **Peter Lombard** and on **Aristotle**. He also published several important political treatises in the period 1333–47, generally directed against the papal claims to civil authority. His best-known philosophical contributions are his successful defense of nominalism against realism, and the philosophical principle of "Ockham's razor," that is, a theory should not propose the existence of anything more than is needed for its explanation. He was perhaps the most influential of later medieval philosophers.

O'Connell, Daniel, *known as* **the Liberator** 1775–1847 •*Irish political leader*• He was born near Cahirciveen, County Kerry. Called to the Irish bar in 1798, he agitated for the rights of Catholics, and in 1823 formed the Catholic Association, which successfully fought elections against the landlords. Elected Member of Parliament for County Clare in 1828, he was prevented as a Catholic from taking his seat, but was reelected in 1830, the Catholic Emancipation Bill having been passed in the meantime. He denounced the ministry of **Wellington** and **Robert Peel**, but in the face of a threatened prosecution (1831), he temporized, saved himself, and was made King's Counsel. At the general election of 1832 he became Member of Parliament for Dublin. In April 1840 he founded his famous Repeal Association for repeal of the 1801 Union with Great Britain. Yet the agitation languished until the appearance of the *Nation* in 1842 brought him the aid of the nationalists John Blake Dillon (1816–66), Charles Duffy (1816–1903) and James Mangan (1803–49). In 1843 he brought up repeal in the Dublin council, and carried it by 41 to 15. The agitation now leaped into prominence, but the Young Ireland party began to grow impatient with his tactics, and O'Connell allowed himself to outrun his better judgment. Wellington ordered 35,000 men into Ireland, and early in 1844, with his son and five of his chief supporters, O'Connell was imprisoned and fined for conspiracy to raise sedition. He opposed Peel's provincial "godless colleges," and it soon came to an open split between him and Young Ireland (1846). The potato famine followed next. A broken man, he left Ireland for the last time in January 1847, and died in Genoa on his way to Rome.

O'Connor, (Mary) Flannery 1925–64 •*US novelist*• Born in Savannah, Georgia, she was educated at Georgia State College for Women and the University of Iowa. She was brought up a Catholic in the "Christ-haunted" Bible belt of the Deep South, and in her work she homed in on the Protestant fundamentalists who dominated the region. Her characters seem almost grotesque and freakish, but she was describing her reality, and her heightened depiction of it is unforgettable. *Wise Blood* (1952), the first of her two novels, is a bizarre tragicomedy, and its theme of vocation is taken up again in her second, *The Violent Bear It Away* (1960). Regarded as one of the finest short-story writers of her generation, her work in that form can be found in *A Good Man Is Hard to Find and Other Stories* (1955) and *Everything That Rises Must Converge* (1965).

“ ”

I preach there are all kinds of truth, your truth and somebody else's. But behind all of them there is only one truth and that is that there's no truth.

1952 Hazel Motes. ***Wise Blood****, chapter 10.*

O'Connor, Frank, *pseudonym of* **Michael O'Donovan** 1903–66 •*Irish writer*• Born in Cork, County Cork, he was a member of the IRA in his teens (1921–22), fought in the Irish civil war and was imprisoned. He then worked as a railway clerk in Cork, and later as a librarian in Wicklow, Cork and Dublin. Although he wrote plays and some excellent literary criticism, his best medium was the short story. Representative titles are *Guests of the Nation* (1931), *Bones of Contention* (1936), *Crab Apple Jelly* (1944), *Travellers' Samples* (1956), and *My Oedipus Complex* (1963). He also wrote two volumes of memoirs, translations of Irish verse, a novel, *Dutch Interior* (1940), and a biography of **Michael Collins**, *The Big Fellow* (1937).

O'Connor, Sandra Day 1930– •*US jurist*• Born in El Paso, Texas, she studied law and was admitted to the bar in California. Taking up practice in Arizona, she became assistant attorney general there (1965–69) and then a state senator. She then became a superior court judge of Maricopa County (1974–79) and a judge of the Arizona Court of Appeals (1979–81) before being named an associate justice of the US Supreme Court (1981), the first woman to attain that office.

Octavia d. 11 BC •*Roman matron*• She was the sister of Emperor **Augustus**, distinguished for her beauty and womanly virtues. On the death of her first husband, Marcellus (40 BC), she consented to marry **Mark Antony**, to reconcile him and her brother, but in 32 Antony divorced her for **Cleopatra**. Noble, loyal and kind, she brought up Mark Antony's children by Cleopatra alongside her own.

Ó Dálaigh, Muireadhach Albanach c. 1180–c. 1250 •*Irish poet*• An outstanding character of his time, he is perhaps the only poet who has killed a tax collector (with an ax). Owing to this indiscretion, he had to flee his home in County Sligo and ended up in Scotland (hence "Albanach"). His poem on the death of his (probably Scottish) wife, beginning "I was robbed of my soul last night," is one of the most famous in Irish literature.

Odets, Clifford 1906–63 •*US playwright and actor*• Born in Philadelphia and educated in New York City, he joined the Group Theater, New York, in 1931, under whose auspices his early plays were produced. *Waiting for Lefty, Awake and Sing* and *Till the Day I Die* were all produced in 1935, and *Golden Boy* in 1937. The most important US playwright of the 1930s, his works are marked by a strong social conscience and grow largely from the conditions of the Depression of that time. He was also responsible for a number of film scenarios, including *None but the Lonely Heart* (1944, which he directed) and *The Big Knife* (1949).

“ ”

Go out and fight so life shouldn't be printed on dollar bills.

1935 Jacob. ***Awake and Sing****, act 1.*

Odo of Bayeux c. 1036–97 •*Anglo-Norman prelate*• He was Bishop of Bayeux. The half brother of **William the Conqueror**, he fought at the Battle of Hastings (1066) and was created Earl of Kent. He played a conspicuous part under William in English history, and was regent during his absences in Normandy, but left England after rebelling against **William II, Rufus**. He rebuilt Bayeux Cathedral, and may have commissioned the Bayeux Tapestry.

Odoacer or **Odovacar** AD 433–93 •*Germanic warrior, first barbarian king of Italy*• A leader of the Heruli, he was the German commander of the imperial guard in Rome. He participated in the revolution (AD 476) that drove Julius Nepos from the throne and gave Romulus the title of Augustus (known as **Romulus Augustulus**). He marched against Pavia (476), and Romulus abdicated in his favor, ending the western Roman Empire and making Odoacer king of Italy. His increasing power alarmed the Byzantine emperor Zeno, who encouraged **Theodoric the Great**, king of the Ostrogoths, to invade Italy (489). Odoacer retreated to Ravenna, where he finally capitulated in 493, and was assassinated at a banquet by Theodoric.

O'Donnell, Daniel 1961– •*Irish country singer*• Born in Kincasslagh, County Donegal, he established a reputation as a popular singer of sentimental ballads in an "easy listening" country style in his native Ireland before building an international following. He enjoyed his first chart success with "I Just Want to Dance with You" (1992) and subsequently released a series of albums that did well on both the pop and country charts, in defiance of their hostile reception from many critics.

Odovacar *See* **Odoacer**

O'Duffy, Eimar Ultan 1893–1935 •*Irish satirical playwright and novelist*• He was born in Dublin, educated at Stonyhurst (Jesuit) College in Lancashire and studied dentistry at University College Dublin. He embraced the new Irish revolutionary cultural nationalism under the influence of **Thomas MacDonagh** and Joseph Plunkett, who published and produced his first play, *The Walls of Athens*, and whose Irish Theatre also staged his *The Phoenix on the Roof* (1915). He broke with them on the Easter uprising of 1916, during which he was one of the couriers who tried to transmit the order countermanding it. His best play, *Bricriu's Feast* (1919), satirized Neo-Gaelicism, and his first novel, *The Wasted Island* (1919, revised edition 1929), is a valuable source on the origins of the uprising.

Oehlenschläger, Adam Gottlob 1779–1850 •*Danish poet and playwright*• Born in Vesterbro, he was the founder of Danish Romanticism, and was much influenced by **Goethe** and the **Schlegel** brothers. He is best known for writing 24 blank-verse historical tragedies, starting with *Hakon Jarl* (1807, "Earl Hakon"). He later wrote *Helge* (1814), a cycle of verse romances, and *Nordens guder* ("Gods of the North"), an epic ballad cycle. In 1849 he was publicly proclaimed the national poet of Denmark.

Oë Kenzaburo 1935– •*Japanese novelist and Nobel Prize winner*• He was born in Shikoku and educated at the University of Tokyo. His earliest fiction, influenced by **Abe Kobo**, attempts to come to terms with the bleak cultural landscape of postwar Japan. His first three novels were all published in 1958, but it was not until 1963 that Oë found an effective personal voice. In that year he visited Hiroshima and witnessed the delivery of his son, who was born with a major skull abnormality. *Kojinteki na taiken* (1964) was the first of his books to be published in English, as *A Personal Matter* (1968). His next book is perhaps his finest—*Man'en gannen no futtuboru* (1967, Eng trans *The Silent Cry*, 1974), about two brothers' search for their roots—and won Oë the **Tanizaki** prize. Four of his short novels of the 1970s were collected in translation as *Teach Us to Outgrow Our Madness* (1977). In the 1980s he began to explore new principles of organization for his fiction, drawing on social anthropology and philosophy, and published *The Crazy Iris and Other Stories of the Atomic Aftermath* (Eng trans 1985). One of Japan's most remarkable contemporary novelists, he was awarded the Nobel Prize for literature in 1994.

Oersted, Hans Christian 1777–1851 •*Danish physicist*• Born in Rudkøbing, Langeland, he had little formal education, but passed the entrance examination at the University of Copenhagen. The idea that nature's forces had a common origin resulted in his epochal discovery in 1820, as a professor at the University of Copenhagen, of the magnetic effect produced by an electric current. This paved the way for the electromagnetic discoveries of **André Ampère** and **Michael Faraday**, and the development of the galvanometer. He made an extremely accurate measurement of the compressibility of water, and succeeded in isolating aluminum for the first time in 1825.

Oerter, Al(fred) 1936– •*US athlete and discus thrower*• He was born in Astoria, New York. An outstanding Olympic competitor, he won four consecutive gold medals for the discus, at Melbourne (1956), Rome (1960), Tokyo (1964) and Mexico (1968), breaking the Olympic record each time. No other athlete has dominated an event so overwhelmingly for so long.

Offa d. 796 •*King of Mercia*• He succeeded his cousin Æthelbald (757), extended his dominion over Kent, Sussex, Wessex and East Anglia, and styled himself *rex Anglorum* in his charters. To protect his frontiers to the west against the Welsh, he built the great earthwork known as Offa's Dyke, stretching for 70 miles along the Welsh border. Overlord of all England south of the Humber, he was probably the most powerful English monarch before the tenth century. He founded a new archbishopric of Lichfield (788) with the sanction of Pope Hadrian I. His silver coinage remained standard until the 13th century. He had his son Ecgfrith anointed as king of Mercia (787), but Ecgfrith survived him by only a few months.

Offenbach, Jacques, *originally* **Jakob Eberst** 1819–80 •*German composer*• Born in Cologne, he composed many light, lively operettas, but is best known as the inventor of modern *opéra bouffe* (funny or farcical opera), examples of which are *Orphée aux enfers* (1858, "Orpheus in the Underworld"), *La belle Hélène* (1864), *Barbe-bleue* (1866, "Bluebeard") and *La vie Parisienne* (1866, "Parisian Life"). His one grand opera, *Les contes d'Hoffmann* ("The Tales of Hoffmann"), was produced posthumously in 1881.

Offiah, Martin 1966– •*English rugby league player*• Born in London, he began as a rugby union player with Rosslyn Park, representing England Students in the amateur code. He made the move to rugby league by signing for Widnes in September 1987, and by the following January had played for Great Britain. In January 1992 he joined Wigan, reinforcing that club's dominant position in the British game, and later played for the London Broncos and Salford City Reds. He made his 500th career try in 2001.

Ofili, Chris 1968– •*English artist*• Born in Manchester, he was educated at the Chelsea School of Art, the Hochschule der Kunst in Berlin and at the Royal College of Art in London. He has won acclaim for paintings incorporating a wide variety of influences, ranging from traditional African art to images drawn from popular culture and hip-hop music, and making use of such diverse materials as glitter, pins and even elephant dung. In 1998 he won the Tate Gallery's prestigious Turner Prize.

O'Flaherty, Liam 1897–1984 •*Irish writer*• Born on Inishmore, in the Aran Islands, he was educated at University College Dublin, fought in the British army during World War I, and later traveled in North America and Latin America. He returned to Ireland in 1921 and fought on the republican side in the Irish civil war. He went to London in 1922 to become a writer, and soon published his first novels, *Thy Neighbor's Wife* (1923) and *The Black Soul* (1924). *The Informer* (1926) won the James Tait Black Memorial Prize and was a popular success. Other books include *The Assassin* (1928), *Famine* (1937) and *Land* (1946).

Ogdon, John Andrew Howard 1937–89 •*English pianist and composer*• Born in Mansfield Woodhouse, Nottinghamshire, he studied at the Royal Manchester College of Music. In 1962 he was the joint winner (with **Vladimir Ashkenazy**) of the Moscow Tchaikovsky Competition. He had a powerful technique, a remarkable memory and a large repertoire in the virtuoso pianist-composer tradition, notably of **Franz Liszt**, **Ferruccio Busoni**, and others. His own works, which include a piano concerto, are part of that distinguished line. His career was interrupted by the onset of mental illness.

O'Hara, John 1905–70 •*US novelist and short-story writer*• He was born in Pottsville, Pennsylvania, which in his fiction becomes "Gibbsville," the setting of *Appointment in Samarra* (1934). O'Hara was notoriously irascible and hypersensitive. Unable to attend Yale University due to his father's death, he went to New York City to work as a critic and reporter. "Brash as a young man," wrote **John Updike**, "he became with success a slightly desperate braggart." Two of his works—*Butterfield 8* (1935) and *Pal Joey* (1940)—became film and stage successes. His short stories are obsessed with class, social privilege and feminist issues.

O'Hara, Maureen, *originally* **Maureen FitzSimons** 1920– •*Irish actress*• Born near Dublin, she joined the Abbey Players there at the age of 14. She made her Hollywood debut as the gypsy Esmerelda in *The Hunchback of Notre Dame* (1939), and over the next three decades appeared as a swashbuckling spitfire in such adventure films as *The Black Swan* (1942). Often cast as a fiery woman tamed by a man, she was a favorite costar of **John Wayne**, with whom she starred in *The Quiet Man* (1952), *McLintock* (1963) and *Big Jake* (1971), among others. She returned to the screen, little changed after a 20-year absence, in *Only the Lonely* (1991).

O'Higgins, Bernardo 1778–1842 •*Chilean revolutionary*• Born in Chillán, the illegitimate son of Ambrosio O'Higgins, an Irish-born governor of Chile and viceroy of Peru, he was educated in Peru and England. He played a major role in the Chilean struggle for independence, and was the first leader of the new Chilean state in 1817. However, his reforms aroused antagonism, particularly from the Church, the aristocracy and the business community, and he was deposed and exiled in 1823.

Ohlin, Bertil Gotthard 1899–1979 •*Swedish economist and politician, and Nobel Prize winner*• Born in Klippan and educated in Sweden and at Harvard in the US, he was professor at Copenhagen (1925–30) and at Stockholm (1930–65). He was a member of the Swedish parliament from 1938 to 1970 and leader of the Liberal Party from 1944 to 1967. He was awarded the 1977 Nobel Prize for economics, jointly with **James Meade**.

Ohm, Georg Simon 1787–1854 •*German physicist*• Born in Erlangen, Bavaria, he completed his studies at the University of Erlangen, and later became professor at the University of Nuremberg (1833–49) and Munich University (1849–54). "Ohm's law," relating voltage, current and resistance in an electrical circuit, was published in 1827, although neither this nor his work on the recognition of sinusoidal sound waves by the human ear (1843) received immediate recognition. The unit of electrical resistance is named after him.

Oistrakh, David Fyodorovich 1908–74 •*Russian violinist*• Born in Odessa, he studied at Odessa Conservatory, graduating in 1926. In 1928 he went to Moscow and began to teach at the conservatory there in 1934, being appointed a professor in 1939. He made concert tours in Europe and the US, and was awarded the Stalin Prize in 1945 and the Lenin Prize in 1960. His son Igor Davidovich (1931–), born in Odessa, is also a noted violinist.

O'Keeffe, Georgia 1887–1986 •*US painter*• Born in Sun Prairie, Wisconsin, she studied at the Art Institute of Chicago, 1905–06, and at the Art Students' League in New York City, 1907–08, where she met **Alfred Stieglitz**, whom she married in 1924. As early as 1915 she pioneered abstract art in the US (eg, *Blue and Green Music*, 1919) but later moved toward a more figurative style, painting flowers and architectural subjects, frequently with a surrealist flavor.

O'Kelly, Sean Thomas, *properly* **Seán Thomas Ó Ceallaigh** 1882–1966 •*Irish statesman*• Born in Dublin, he was a pioneer in the Sinn Fein movement and the Gaelic League. He fought in the Easter uprising (1916) and was imprisoned. Elected to the first Dáil in 1918, he became Speaker (1919–21). As an opponent of the Irish Free State, he became prominent in **de Valera**'s Fianna Fáil Party, and after serving in ministerial posts became president of the Irish Republic from 1945 to 1952, and again from 1952 to 1959.

Okri, Ben 1959– •*Nigerian novelist, poet and short-story writer*• He was born in Minna, but now lives in London, England. His first, precocious novel was *Flowers and Shadows* (1980), but it was not until 1987 and the publication of its successor, *Incidents at the Shrine*, that he achieved recognition. His third novel, *The Famished Road* (1991), won the Booker Prize; the sequel, *Songs of Enchantment*, followed in 1993. Subsequent novels include *Astonishing the Gods* (1995), *Birds of Heaven* (1995), *A Way of Being Free* (1996), *Dangerous Love* (1996) and *Infinite Riches* (1998).

“ ”

We feared the heartlessness of human beings, all of whom are born blind, few of whom ever learn to see.

1991 ***The Famished Road****, chapter 1.*

Olaf I Tryggvason c. 965–1000 •*King of Norway*• The great-grandson of **Harald I Halfdanarson** (Fair Hair), in the early 990s he took part in Viking expeditions to Britain, and was the leader of the Viking army that defeated the Anglo-Saxons at Maldon (991). He returned to harass England (994) under the king of Denmark, **Svein I Haraldsson** (Fork-Beard), and was converted to Christianity. He returned to Norway (995), where he seized the throne and attempted, with limited success, to convert Norway to Christianity by force. Five years later he was overwhelmed by a combined Danish and Swedish fleet at Svold (1000). When defeat became inevitable he leapt overboard and was never seen again.

Olaf II Haraldsson, St Olaf c. 995–1030 •*King of Norway*• He was the half brother of King **Harald III Sigurdsson** (Hardraade). He became a Viking mercenary in the Baltic and attacked England, Frisia and Spain. In England (1010) he took part in an attack on London when London Bridge was torn down with grappling irons ("London Bridge is falling down"). He was converted to Christianity in Normandy (1013), and returned to Norway (1014), where he seized the throne (1015) and tried to complete the conversion of Norway begun by **Olaf I Tryggvason**. In 1030, he was defeated and killed at Stiklestad. Within 12 months he was regarded as a national hero, and he was declared the patron saint of Norway in 1164. His feast day is July 29.

Olaf III Haraldsson, *called* **the Peaceful** d. 1093 •*King of Norway*• The son of **Harald III Sigurdsson** (Hardraade), he was at the Battle of Stamford Bridge in Yorkshire (1066) when his father was defeated and killed by King **Harold II** of England. He was allowed to return to Norway, and, after ruling jointly with his brother, Magnus II, became sole ruler (1069). His long reign was marked by unbroken peace and prosperity in Norway. He built churches and founded the city of Bergen. He was succeeded by his illegitimate son, **Magnus III** Olafsson (Barefoot).

Olav V 1903–91 •*King of Norway*• Born in England, he was the son and successor (1957) of **Haakon VII** and Maud, daughter of **Edward VII** of Great Britain. He was educated in Norway and at Balliol College, Oxford. An outstanding sportsman and Olympic yachtsman in his youth, he stayed in Norway when it was invaded by Germany (1940) and was appointed head of the Norwegian armed forces. Later he escaped with his father to England, returning in 1945. In 1929 he married Princess Martha of Sweden (1901–54). They had two daughters, and a son who succeeded to the Norwegian throne as **Harald V**.

Olcott, Henry Steel 1832–1907 •*US theosophist*• Born in Orange, New Jersey, he was a lawyer by training, but studied theosophy under Madame **Blavatsky** and was founding president of the Theosophical Society in 1875. He traveled to India and Ceylon as her partner (1879–84), but fell out with her in 1885. He opened schools for untouchables (scheduled castes) in India, and became an associate of **Annie Besant**.

Oldcastle, Sir John, *also called* **Lord Cobham** c. 1378–1417 •*English Lollard leader and knight*• Born in Herefordshire, he served under **Henry IV** on the Welsh marches. He acquired the title of Lord Cobham (1409) by marrying the heiress, fought in the Scottish and Welsh wars, and in France earned a European reputation for chivalry. A courageous man of principle, he was an able exponent of Lollard doctrine and had **John Wucliffe**'s works transcribed and distributed. He became an intimate friend of the Prince of Wales, the future **Henry V**, but after Henry's accession he was condemned as a heretic (1413). He escaped from the Tower of London and conspired with other Lollards to capture Henry and take control of London (1414), but was captured and eventually "hanged and burnt hanging."

Oldenburg, Claes Thure 1929– •*US sculptor*• Born in Stockholm, Sweden, he emigrated to the US in 1936, becoming a US citizen in 1953. He studied at Yale and the Art Institute of Chicago before moving to New York City (1956), where he became part of the milieu from which "happenings" and pop art developed. In 1962 he began to make giant versions of foodstuffs such as hamburgers, and the following year introduced soft sculptures of normally hard objects like light switches. His projects for colossal monuments in public places (eg, giant lipsticks in Piccadilly Circus, London) have occasionally been realized, as in the *Giant Clothespin* (1975) in Philadelphia. Since 1976 he has collaborated with his wife, the writer Coosje van Bruggen, to stage events and produce giant installations in Europe and the US.

Oldfield, Bruce 1950– •*English fashion designer*• Born in London, he taught art then studied fashion in Kent (1968–71) and in London (1972–73), after which he became a freelance designer. He showed his first collection in 1975 in London. His designs include evening dresses for royalty and screen stars, and ready-to-wear clothes. His publications include *Bruce Oldfield's Season* (1987, with Georgina Howell). He was given the honorary title Officer, Order of the British Empire, in 1990.

Oldham, Richard Dixon 1858–1936 •*Irish geologist and seismologist*• Born in Dublin, he was educated at Rugby and the Royal School of Mines and was a member of the Geological Survey of India (1878–1903). His important report on the Assam earthquake of June 1897 distinguished for the first time between primary and secondary seismic waves and was able to characterize many other phenomena of earthquake activity. He proved the generality of his notions about the different types of seismic waves with reference to six other earthquakes in *On the Propagation of Earthquake Motion to Great Distances* (1900) and laid the foundations of what is now one of the principal branches of geophysics. In 1906 he established from seismographic records the existence of the Earth's core.

Old Pretender, the *See* **Stuart, Prince James Francis Edward**

Olga, St c. 890–968 •*Russian princess and regent of Kiev*• The wife of Prince Igor of Kiev, as regent (945–64) she ruled Kiev firmly during the minority of her son, Svyatoslav. She was baptized at Constantinople (Istanbul) in c. 957 and, returning to Russia, worked hard for her new creed. She had little success in her lifetime but, subsequently sanctified, she played an important part in the development of Kievan Christianity. Her grandson was **Vladimir I (the Great)**. Her feast day is July 11.

Oliphant, Margaret, *née* **Wilson** 1828–97 •*Scottish novelist*• She was born in Wallyford, Midlothian, and moved to England with her family when she was 10 years old. Her first novel was written when she was just 16, but her first published work was *Passages in the Life of Mrs Margaret Maitland* (1849). In 1851 she began her lifelong connection with the Edinburgh publishers Blackwood and *Blackwood's Magazine*. In 1852 she married her cousin, Frances Oliphant, an artist, but she was widowed in 1859, and found herself £1,000 in debt with an extended family to support and educate. She went on to write almost a hundred novels, the best known of which are collectively known as *The Chronicles of Carlingford* (1863–76) and earned her the sobriquet: a "feminist **Trollope**."

Oliphant, Sir Mark (Marcus Laurence Elwin) 1901–2000 •*Australian nuclear physicist*• Born in Adelaide, he studied there and at Trinity College, Cambridge. Working at the Cavendish Laboratory in Cambridge with **Ernest Rutherford** and others, he discovered the tritium isotope of hydrogen in 1934, and in 1937 he became professor at the University of Birmingham. He worked on the Manhattan Project at Los Alamos (1943–45) to develop the nuclear bomb, but at the end of hostilities strongly argued against the US monopoly of atomic secrets. In 1946 he became the Australian representative of the UN Atomic Energy Commission. He was later appointed research professor at the University of Canberra (1950–63) and designed a proton synchrotron accelerator. From 1971 to 1976 he served as governor of South Australia. He was knighted in 1959.

Oliver, Jamie 1975– •*English television chef*• Born in Clavering, Essex, he studied at Westminster Catering College. After working in various restaurants in Britain and Europe, he was offered his own television series, *The Naked Chef*, in 1999, in which he failed to appear naked but offered attractive recipes for dishes such as fresh pasta and homemade bread. His Essex accent and tousle-haired manner of presentation delighted most critics, and he went on to publish several successful cookbooks including *Happy Days with the Naked Chef* (2001).

Oliver, King (Joe) 1885–1938 •*US cornetist, composer and bandleader*• He was born in Abend, Louisiana, and raised in New

Orleans. His first instrument was the trombone, and as a youth he played in various parade bands as well as in early jazz groups. He moved to Chicago, where in 1922 he formed his "Hot" Creole Jazz Band; featuring Oliver's cornet partnership with **Louis Armstrong**, the band made some of the finest recordings of the period. Some of his compositions, such as "Dippermouth Blues" and "Dr Jazz," are part of the standard traditional repertoire.

Olivetti, Adriano 1901–60 •*Italian manufacturer*• He was born in Ivrea. After a period in the US assimilating the methods of mass production, he returned to transform the manufacturing methods of the typewriter firm founded by his father, Camillo Olivetti (1868–1943). As well as greatly increasing production, he established a strong design policy which embraced products, graphics and the architecture of the company's buildings. His strong social concerns, for which he was widely noted, led him to provide housing and facilities of a high standard for his employees. The firm survived a period of stagnation in the 1970s to regain its primacy by exploiting modern technological advances in office equipment.

Olivier, Laurence Kerr, Baron Olivier of Brighton 1907–89 •*English actor, producer and director*• He was born in Dorking. His first professional appearance was in Chapman's *Byron* in 1924, and he joined the Old Vic Company in 1937. He played all the great Shakespearean roles, and his versatility was underlined by his virtuoso performance as a broken-down low comedian in *The Entertainer* (1957). After war service he became codirector of the Old Vic Company (1944); and he produced, directed and played in acclaimed films of *Henry V*, *Hamlet* and *Richard III*. He played memorable roles in several other films, including *Wuthering Heights* (1939), *Rebecca* (1940), *The Prince and the Showgirl* (which he directed, 1957), *Sleuth* (1972) and *Marathon Man* (1976). In 1962 he undertook the directorship of a new venture, the Chichester Festival, where he was highly successful; later the same year he was appointed director of the National Theatre, where among many successes he directed and acted a controversial but outstanding *Othello* (1964). He was director of the National Theatre until 1973, and then associate director for a year. After 1974 he appeared chiefly in films and in television productions (notably as Lord Marchmain in *Brideshead Revisited*, 1982, and as *King Lear* in 1983). He was divorced from his first wife, Jill Esmond, in 1960, and the following year he married **Joan Plowright**. Olivier was knighted in 1947, was made a life peer in 1970 and was awarded the Order of Merit in 1981.

Olmsted, Frederick Law 1822–1903 •*US landscape architect and writer*• Born in Hartford, Connecticut, he studied engineering and agriculture and published a notable series of travel books. In 1856 he was codesigner of Central Park, New York City, and he served as its chief architect. Among the other famous parks he created are Prospect Park in Brooklyn, the Emerald Necklace in Boston, and Jackson Park in Chicago. His object in park design was to provide the illusion of wildness and arcadian peace in the midst of the city, and his work is unequaled in US landscape architecture.

Olsen, Kenneth Harry 1926– •*US computer engineer and entrepreneur*• Born in Bridgeport, Connecticut, of Scandinavian parentage, he studied electrical engineering at MIT, and in 1956 established his own computer company, the Digital Equipment Corporation (DEC). DEC exploited a new niche in the growing computer industry—the market for minicomputers, or "interactive" machines, that were less expensive and easier to use than mainframes. Aided by brilliant engineers, such as Gordon Bell (1934–) from MIT, Olsen launched the first successful minicomputer in the early 1960s. In 1986 DEC was the second largest US computer company, behind IBM, but by 1992 the company was suffering heavy losses and stagnating sales, and Olsen was forced to resign as chief executive.

Olson, Charles John 1910–70 •*US poet*• Born in Worcester, Massachusetts, he was educated at Wesleyan University and at Yale and Harvard. During World War II he worked as a civil liberties activist, and in 1947 published *Call Me Ishmael*, ostensibly a study of **Herman Melville**, but one which strongly emphasizes Olson's concern for ethnic minorities and working-class solidarity. As director of Black Mountain College near Asheville, North Carolina (1951–56), Olson became nominal head of the "Black Mountain poets" (including **Robert Creeley**, Ed Dorn, and others). His most important work, *The Maximus Poems*, appeared in several volumes during his lifetime (1953–70, edited by George Butterick, 1983), but was left unfinished at his death. Olson's *Complete Shorter Poems* appeared in 1985.

“ ”

one loves only form,
and form only comes
into existence when
the thing is born.

*1953 **The Maximus Poems**, "I, Maximus of Gloucester, To You, 4."*

Olympias d. 316 BC •*Macedonian queen*• The wife of **Philip II** of Macedon, and mother of **Alexander the Great**, she was the daughter of King Neoptolemus of Epirus. When Philip divorced her and married Cleopatra, niece of Attalus, she left Macedonia and ruled Epirus by herself, supposedly instigating the murder of Cleopatra. After Alexander's death (323 BC) she returned to Macedonia, where she had his half brother and successor killed, and made Alexander's posthumous son, Alexander IV, king. Eventually **Cassander** besieged her in Pydna, and on its surrender put her to death.

Omar or **Umar** c. 581–644 •*Second caliph*• He was father of one of **Muhammad**'s wives, and succeeded **Abu Bakr** in 634. Through his generals he built up an empire comprising Persia (Iran), Syria and all North Africa. He was assassinated in Medina by a Persian slave.

Omar Khayyám c. 1048–c. 1122 •*Persian poet, mathematician and astronomer*• Born in Nishapuur, he was well educated in his hometown and in Balkh. In Samarkand he completed a seminal work on algebra, and he made the necessary astronomical observations for the reform of the Muslim calendar, collaborating on an observatory in Esfahan. On his return from a pilgrimage to Mecca he served at the court as an astrologer. As a poet he had attracted little attention until **Edward FitzGerald** translated and arranged the collection of *robáiyát*, or quatrains, attributed to him, in *The Rubáiyát of Omar Khayyám*, first published anonymously in 1859.

Omar, Mohammad 1962– •*Afghan religious and political leader*• Born into poverty in Nodeh, Uruzgan Province, he studied at several Pakistani Islamic schools and became a leading Muslim cleric, with the title mullah. He joined the jihad (holy war) against the Soviet occupation of Afghanistan in the 1980s, rising to the post of deputy chief commander of the Mujahideen guerrilla movement. In 1996 he was chosen as supreme commander of the religious militia movement called the Taliban and became the effective ruler of Afghanistan. In 2001 his refusal to surrender the Afghanistan-based terrorist leader **Osama bin Laden** to the US led to US-backed attacks on the country, precipitating the collapse of the Taliban regime.

Onassis, Aristotle Socrates 1906–75 •*Argentine-Greek ship owner*• He was born in Smyrna, Turkey, the son of a Greek tobacco importer. At the age of 16 he left Smyrna for Greece as a refugee, and from there went to Buenos Aires, where he made a fortune in tobacco and was Greek consul for a time. In 1925 he took Argentine and Greek citizenship. Buying his first ships in 1932, he built up one of the world's largest independent fleets, and was a pioneer in the construction of supertankers. His first marriage ended in divorce (1960), and after a long relationship with **Maria Callas**, in 1968 he married Jacqueline Bouvier Kennedy (see **Jackie Kennedy Onassis**).

Onassis, Jackie (Jacqueline) Kennedy, *née* **Lee Bouvier** 1929–94 •*US First Lady*• Born in Southampton, New York, she was a photographer with the *Washington Times-Herald* in 1952 before marrying **John F Kennedy** in 1953. During his presidency (1961–63), she supervised the restoration of the White House and wielded a powerful and widespread influence on fashion. After her husband's assassination she returned to private life, and in 1968 married the Greek shipping magnate **Aristotle Onassis**. She later worked with Viking Publications (1975–77), and Doubleday and Co as editor (1978–82).

“ ”

I felt like a moth hanging on the window pane.

*1961 On her first night in the White House, in **Newsweek**, January 1.*

Ondaatje, (Philip) Michael 1943– •*Canadian poet and novelist*• Born in Ceylon, he emigrated to Canada in 1962. Two decades later, he portrayed his aristocratic and eccentric relatives in the beguiling memoir, *Running in the Family* (1982). His first poetry was *The Dainty Monsters* (1967), followed by volumes such as the prize-winning *The Collected Works of Billy the Kid: Left Handed Poems* (1970). After his collected poems were published as *There's a Trick with a Knife I'm Learning to Do* (1979, published in the UK as *Rat Jelly and Other Poems*, 1980), he turned increasingly to prose. His novels include *Coming Through Slaughter* (1976), the hauntingly lyrical *The English Patient* (1991, filmed 1996), for which he shared the Booker Prize with **Barry Unsworth**, and *Anil's Ghost* (2000).

O'Neal, Shaquille Rashaun 1972– •*US basketball player*• Born in Newark, New Jersey, in his first season he transformed the Orlando Magic into a top team and was National Basketball Association (NBA) Rookie of the Year (1993). He played on the NBA All-Star team (1993) and the Dream Team II (1994). As center for Orlando in 1995, he was the NBA leading scorer with 2,315 points in 79 games. He played for the Orlando Magic from 1992 to 1996, when he joined the Los Angeles Lakers. He has released a number of rap albums and appeared in such films as *Blue Chips* (1994) and *Kazaam* (1996).

O'Neill, Eugene Gladstone 1888–1953 •*US playwright*• He was born in New York City, the third son of the popular actor James O'Neill (1847–1920). Following a fragmentary education and a year at Princeton University (1906–07), O'Neill took a clerical job, then signed on as a sailor on voyages to Australia, South Africa and elsewhere. He contracted tuberculosis while working as a reporter in Connecticut, and spent six months in a sanatorium (1912–13), where he began to write plays, the first being *The Web* (1914). He joined the Provincetown Players in 1915 and wrote a series of plays (including *Bound East for Cardiff*, 1916) based on life aboard a steamship. *Beyond the Horizon* (1920) was awarded the Pulitzer Prize. These works were followed during the next two years by *Exorcism* (1920), *Diff'rent* (1920), *The Emperor Jones* (1921), *Anna Christie* (1921; Pulitzer Prize), *The Hairy Ape* (1922) and *Desire Under the Elms* (1924). O'Neill then began experimenting in new dramatic techniques; in *The Great God Brown* (1926) he used masks to emphasize the differing relationships between a man, his family and his soul. *Strange Interlude* (1928; Pulitzer Prize), a marathon nine-act tragedy lasting five hours, uses a stream-of-consciousness technique with dramatic asides and soliloquies. In the same year he wrote *Lazarus Laughed*, a humanistic affirmation of his belief in the conquest of death. His trilogy *Mourning Becomes Electra* (1931), set at the end of the Civil War, is a restatement of the Orestean tragedy in terms of biological and psychological cause and effect. *Ah, Wilderness*, a nostalgic comedy, appeared in 1933, and *Days Without End* in 1934. For 12 years he released no more plays but worked on *The Iceman Cometh* (first performed in New York 1946; London, 1958) and *A Moon for the Misbegotten* (1947). The former, set in a bar, is a gargantuan, repetitive parable about the dangers of shattering illusions, and is considered one of his most important plays. *Long Day's Journey into Night* (first performed posthumously in 1956; Pulitzer Prize 1957) is probably O'Neill's masterpiece. Set in 1912, it describes one day in the life of the tragic Tyrone family, and is closely based on the playwright's early life. *A Touch of the Poet* (1957) and *Hughie* (1959, first performed 1964) were also published posthumously. He was awarded the Nobel Prize for literature in 1936, the first US dramatist to be thus honored.

O'Neill, Hugh, 2nd Earl of Tyrone c. 1540–1616 •*Irish rebel*• Born in Dungannon, the son of an illegitimate son of Conn O'Neill (c. 1484–c. 1559), a warlike Irish chieftain who was made Earl of Tyrone, he was invested with the title and estates c. 1597, but soon plunged into intrigues against **Elizabeth I**. As “the O'Neill” he spread insurrection all over Ulster, Connaught and Leinster (1587). Despite Spanish support, he was defeated in 1601–02 by **Charles Blount**, 8th Lord Mountjoy, at Kinsale and badly wounded. He plotted with Spain against **James VI and I**, and in 1607 fled to the Spanish Netherlands. He died in Rome.

O'Neill, Jonjo (John Joseph) 1952– •*Irish National Hunt jockey*• Born in Castletownroche, County Cork, he started as an apprentice jockey at The Curragh in Kildare, and later concentrated on National Hunt racing. Establishing a reputation for utter fearlessness and an astonishing ability to endure pain, he suffered innumerable broken bones, but fought on to become champion jockey twice, in 1977–78 and 1979–80. He set the then record of 149 winners in a season and won the Champion Hurdle on Sea Pigeon in 1980 and the Gold Cup on Dawn Run in 1986. He is now a racehorse trainer.

O'Neill (of the Maine), Terence (Marne) O'Neill, Baron 1914–90 •*Northern Irish statesman*• Born in County Antrim, he was a member of the Northern Ireland parliament (1946–70), holding various ministerial posts before becoming prime minister (1963–69). A supporter of closer cross-border links with the Republic, he angered many Unionists, and his acceptance in 1969 of civil rights for the Roman Catholic minority forced his resignation. O'Neill was made a life peer in 1970, and he continued to speak out on Northern Ireland issues.

O'Neill, Tip, *in full* **Thomas Philip O'Neill, Jr** 1912–94 •*US politician*• Born into an Irish Catholic family in Cambridge, Massachusetts, he was elected to the House of Representatives as a Democrat from Massachusetts in 1952. A canny and faithful member of his party, he became majority whip in 1971 and majority leader in 1973. He was Speaker of the House from 1977 to 1987.

“ ”

The Democratic Party has succeeded so well that many of its members are now Republicans.

Quoted in WAMU radio broadcast, Washington, March 29, 1995.

Onions, Charles Talbut 1873–1965 •*English scholar and lexicographer*• Born in Edgbaston, Birmingham, he was recruited to the staff of the *Oxford English Dictionary* by Sir **James Murray** in 1895. After the completion of that dictionary, he was commissioned to revise and complete the unfinished *Shorter Oxford English Dictionary*, which was published in 1933, and which he continued to revise and enlarge until 1959. His last great work was the *Oxford Dictionary of English Etymology* (1966), produced with the collaboration of **Robert Burchfield** and G W S Friedrichsen.

Onnes, Heike Kamerlingh *See* **Kamerlingh Onnes, Heike**

Ono, Yoko 1933– •*Japanese artist, writer, singer and campaigner for peace*• Born in Tokyo, she moved to the US after World War II and established a reputation as an avant-garde filmmaker, occasionally branching out into experimental music. She married **John Lennon** in 1969, and was criticized for her role in the **Beatles**' break-up (1970). She subsequently became Lennon's collaborator in the Plastic Ono Band and in various well-publicized peace protests. Her book *Grapefruit* (1970) and album *Approximately Infinite Universe* (1972) suggest she was more talented than detractors still claim. Since Lennon's murder, she has protected his unpublished work and continued to campaign for peace.

Ono No Komachi c. 810–c. 880 •*Japanese poet*• She was born probably in Kyoto. Like many of the other great figures of classical literature in Japan, she was a court poet, writing in a rarefied form of the vernacular—it was more common for men to write in a form of Chinese, which is why so much surviving classical Japanese literature is by women (see **Murasaki Shikibu**). She is known in Japan as one of the Six Poetic Geniuses, the supreme writer of the verse form *tanka*.

Onsager, Lars 1903–76 •*US chemical physicist and Nobel Prize winner*• Born in Christiania (Oslo), Norway, he was trained at the Technical University of Norway. He worked in Zurich with **Peter Joseph Wilhelm Debye** from 1926 to 1928 and then went to the US, where he spent the rest of his life. After periods at Johns Hopkins University, Brown University and Yale, he moved to the University of Miami as Distinguished University Professor. Onsager's work with Debye was on strong electrolytes, for which he developed an extension of the Debye-**Hückel** theory. However, he is best known for his pioneering work on the thermodynamics of irreversible processes, which he put on a sound basis. The fundamental equations in this field are called the reciprocal relations and are commonly known by his name. For this work he was awarded the Nobel Prize for chemistry in 1968.

Oort, Jan Hendrik 1900–92 •*Dutch astronomer*• Born in Franeker, he studied at the University of Groningen and then worked mainly at the Leiden Observatory (1924–70), becoming director there in 1945. He proved (1927) by observation that our galaxy is rotating and calculated the distance of the sun from the center of the galaxy. He also made the first calculation of the mass of galactic material interior to the sun's orbit. In 1932 he made the first measurement that indicated that there is dark matter in the galaxy. In 1946 he realized that the filamentary nebulae called the Cygnus Loop is a supernova remnant. In 1950 he extended Ernst Öpik's (1893–1985) suggestion concerning the huge circular reservoir of comets surrounding the solar system; this "Oort cloud" was the suggested source of long-period comets.

Oparin, Aleksandr Ivanovich 1894–1980 •*Russian biochemist*• Born near Moscow, he was educated at Moscow State University, and became head of plant biochemistry at Moscow University in 1929, and then director of the Bakh Institute of Biochemistry of the USSR Academy of Sciences. His thoughts on the origin of life in his *Proiskhozhdenie zhizni* (1924) received little attention until 1952, when **Harold Urey** used the Oparin-**Haldane** theory, that life slowly emerged from a primeval soup of biomolecules, as a basis for his generation of simple biomolecules. Oparin suggested that life was initiated by the slow binding together of molecules to form droplets, which then absorbed other biomolecules and spontaneously divided.

Opechancanough d. 1644 •*Native American chief of the Powhatan confederacy*• He succeeded **Powhatan**, the father of **Pocahontas** in 1618. Less peaceable than his predecessor, cunning and bitter, he attacked the white settlers of Virginia (1622). Years of reprisals and crop stealing by the whites had all but destroyed the livelihood of the Native Americans when Opechancanough led a renewed attack on the settlements in 1644. The chief, then in his nineties, was captured and killed, and the confederacy ceased to exist.

Ophuls or **Ophüls, Max**, *originally* **Max Oppenheimer** 1902–57 •*French film director*• Born in Saarbrücken, Germany, he chose French nationality in the plebiscite of 1934. He worked in films from 1930, in Germany, France, and the US. These included *Liebelei* (1932), *The Exile* (1947), *The Reckless Moment* (1949), *La ronde* ("The Round," 1950), and *Lola Montes* (1955).

Opie, Peter Mason 1918–82 and **Iona** 1923– •*British children's literature specialists*• They married in 1943 and the birth of their first child prompted them to study the folklore of childhood. This culminated in *The Oxford Dictionary of Nursery Rhymes* (1951), acknowledged widely for its scholarship as well as its sense of humor. Through their work on this they amassed the peerless Opie Collection of children's books which is now housed in the Bodleian Library, Oxford. In 1993 Iona published *The People in the Playground*.

Oppenheimer, (Julius) Robert 1904–67 •*US nuclear physicist*• Born in New York City, he studied at Harvard and Cambridge and under **Max Born** at the University of Göttingen, Germany. He returned to the US and established schools of theoretical physics at Berkeley and the California Institute of Technology (Caltech). His work included studies of electron-positron pairs, cosmic-ray theory and deuteron reactions. During World War II he was selected as leader of the atomic bomb project and set up the Los Alamos laboratory. After the war he became director of the Institute for Advanced Studies at Princeton University and continued to play an important role in US atomic energy policy from 1947, promoting peaceful uses of atomic energy and bitterly opposing development of the hydrogen bomb. In 1953 he was declared a security risk and was forced to retire from political activities.

Orbach, Susie 1946– •*British psychotherapist and feminist author*• Born in London, she studied in both London and New York and became a psychotherapist in 1972, cofounding the Women's Therapy Centre in London (1976) and the Women's Therapy Center Institute in New York (1981). Her book *Fat Is a Feminist Issue* (1976) addresses women's feelings about food, fat and femininity, and argues that the obsession with food that dieting induces actually makes women fat. Her later works include *Understanding Women* (1982, coauthored) and *Hungerstrike* (1985). She also worked as a television host and newspaper columnist.

Orbison, Roy 1936–88 •*US country/pop singer and songwriter*• Born in Vernon, Texas, he began playing on local radio stations at the age of eight, and had his first minor success with "Ooby Dooby" (1956). He found fame with such hit singles as "Only the Lonely" (1960) and "O! Pretty Woman" (1964). The deaths of his wife Claudette (1966) and two of his sons (1968) coincided with a low period in his career and he spent ten years in relative obscurity. However, in the late 1970s and early 1980s, a series of successful cover versions of his songs by other artists, and the patronage of a younger generation of musicians, helped to reverse his fortunes. In 1988 he became a member of the aging super-group the Traveling Wilburys, but he died later that year.

Orczy, Baroness (Emma Magdalena Rosilia Marie Josefa Barbara) 1865–1947 •*British novelist and playwright*• She was born in Tarnaörs, Hungary. Educated in Paris and Brussels, she then studied art in London, where she exhibited some of her work in the Royal Academy. *The Scarlet Pimpernel* (1905) was the first success in her long writing career. It was followed by many popular adventure romances, including *The Elusive Pimpernel* (1908) and *Mam'zelle Guillotine* (1940), which never quite attained the success of her early work.

Orellana, Francisco de c. 1500–49 •*Spanish explorer*• Born in Trujillo, he went to Peru with **Francisco Pizarro**. After crossing the Andes in 1541, he descended the Amazon River to its mouth. The river's original name was Rio Santa Maria de la Mar Dulce, but Orellana is said to have renamed it after an attack by a tribe in which he believed women were fighting alongside men.

Orff, Carl 1895–1982 •*German composer*• Born in Munich, he studied under Kaminski and in 1925 helped found the Günter school in Munich, where he subsequently taught. The influence of **Igor Stravinsky** is apparent in his compositions, which include three realizations of **Claudio Monteverdi**'s *Orfeo* (1925, 1931, 1941), an operatic setting of a 13th-century poem entitled *Carmina Burana* (1936, "Songs of Beuren"), *Die Kluge*, (1943, "The Clever Girl"), *Oedipus* (1958) and *Prometheus* (1968).

Orford, Earl of *See* **Walpole, Sir Robert**

Origen c. 185–c. 254 AD •*Christian scholar, theologian, and early Greek Father of the Church*• Born of Greek parents probably in Alexandria, he studied at the catechetical school there. He became head of the school (c. 211–32 AD), and was ordained in Palestine (c. 230), where he established a new school of literature, philosophy and theology in Caesarea. He was imprisoned and tortured during the persecution under **Decius** in 250. His views on the unity of God and speculations about the salvation of the Devil were condemned by Church councils in the 5th and 6th centuries. His many writings extended over nearly the whole of the Old and New Testaments, although his weighty *Hexapla*, the foundation of the textual criticism of the Scriptures, is mostly lost. His *Eight Books Against Celsus*, preserved in their entirety in Greek, constitute the greatest of early Christian apologies.

Orlando di Lasso *See* **Lassus, Orlando**

Orlando, Vittorio Emanuele 1860–1952 •*Italian politician*• Born in Palermo, Sicily, he became Professor of Law at the University of Palermo, and was elected to parliament in 1897, subsequently holding ministerial posts. At the height of the crisis following the disastrous defeat of the Italian forces at the Battle of Caporetto (Kobavid), he became prime minister, remaining in office until June 1919. His inability to force **Woodrow Wilson** and **Clemenceau** to honor the terms of the Treaty of London (1915) at the Paris peace talks, in addition to postwar economic dislocation and growing political violence, brought about his downfall. He initially made little attempt to resist **Mussolini**, but adopted a more openly anti-Fascist stance in 1925. After World War II he became a senator.

Orléans, Charles, Duc d' 1391–1465 •*French nobleman, poet and soldier*• Born in Paris, he married (1406) his cousin Isabella, widow of **Richard II** of England. In alliance with Bernard d'Armagnac, he did his best to avenge the murder of his father by the Duke of Burgundy. He held a high command at Agincourt (1415), and was captured and taken to England, where he lived for 25 years, composing courtly poetry in French and English. Ransomed in 1440, he returned to France, where he maintained a kind of literary court at Blois. His son became **Louis XII**.

Orléans, Jean Baptiste Gaston, Duc d' 1608–60 •*French nobleman and soldier*• Born at Fontainebleau, he was the third son of **Henry IV** of France. He was heir to **Louis XIII** until 1638 and conspired against **Cardinal Richelieu** on behalf of the queen mother, **Marie de Médicis**. He was lieutenant general of the kingdom during the minority of **Louis XIV**, but played a leading part in the Frondes. Spoiled, treacherous and unstable, he was exiled to his château at Blois.

Orléans, Louis Philippe Joseph, Duc d', *also called* **Philippe Égalité** 1747–93 •*French Bourbon prince*• Born in Saint-Cloud, the cousin of **Louis XVI**, he succeeded to the title on his father's death (1785). His hostility to **Marie Antoinette** caused him to live away from court. In 1787 he showed his liberalism against the king, and was sent by a *lettre-de-cachet* to his château of Villers-Cotterets. During the Revolution he was a forceful supporter of the Third Estate against the privileged orders, and in June 1789 he led the 47 nobles who seceded from their own order to join it. Although he joined the radical Jacobin Club (1791), he gradually lost influence and in 1792 renounced his title and adopted the name of Philippe Égalité. A member of the Convention, he voted for the death of Louis XVI. When his eldest son (afterward King **Louis Philippe**) rode with **Charles Dumouriez**, his commander, into the Austrian camp, Égalité was arrested with all the **Bourbon**s still in France, and was found guilty of conspiracy and guillotined.

Orléans, Philippe, Duc d' 1674–1723 •*Regent of France*• The son of the first Duke Philippe, and grandson of **Louis XIII**, he was born in Saint-Cloud. He showed courage at Steenkirk and Neerwinden (1692–93), and commanded successfully in Italy and Spain (1706–14). For some years he lived in exile from the court, spending his time in profligacy, the fine arts and chemistry. On **Louis XIV**'s death he became regent during the minority of **Louis XV** (1715–23). He was popular, but his adoption of John Law's financial plans led to disaster. He expelled **James Francis Stuart** from France, debarred the parliament of Paris from meddling with political affairs, and to appease the Jesuits, sacrificed the Jansenists.

Orm or **Ormin** fl. 1200 •*English monk and spelling reformer*• Born probably in Lincolnshire, he invented an orthography based on phonetic principles, in which he wrote the *Ormulum* (meaning "because Orm made it"), a series of homilies in verse on the gospel history.

Ormandy, Eugene, *real name* **Jenö Blau** 1899–1985 •*US conductor*• He was born in Budapest, Hungary, and studied violin at the Royal Academy there. While still a teenager, he toured Europe as a child prodigy. Having emigrated to the US in 1920, he became leader and then conductor of the Capitol cinema in New York, and in 1931, two years after becoming a US citizen, he was appointed conductor of the Minneapolis Symphony Orchestra. He became conductor of the Philadelphia Orchestra in 1936, remaining until shortly before his death. The last of his many recordings featured music by **Richard Strauss** and was released the year of his death.

Ormin *See* **Orm**

Orozco, José Clemente 1883–1949 •*Mexican painter*• Born in Zapotlán, Jalisco, he studied engineering and architectural drawing in Mexico City and from 1908 to 1914 studied art at the Academia San Carlos. His first exhibition was in Paris in 1925. One of the greatest mural painters of the 20th century, he decorated many public buildings in Mexico and the US. He was influenced by Byzantine mosaics (eg, *The Coming of Quetzalcoatl* and *The Return of Quetzalcoatl*, 1932–34, at Dartmouth College), and his powerful realistic style, verging on caricature, was a vehicle for revolutionary socialist ideas.

Orr, Bobby (Robert Gordon) 1948– •*US hockey player*• He was born in Parry Sound, Ontario, Canada. The highest goal scorer ever in North American National League Hockey, he played mainly with the Boston Bruins and became that city's greatest-ever sporting hero. During his career he changed the strategy of ice hockey by showing the defensive line could attack rather than just defend. By the time he moved to the Chicago Black Hawks in the 1976–77 season, six major leg operations had left him unable to stand the stress of major league hockey, and he played only a few games for Chicago before being compelled to retire in 1979.

Orrery, 1st Earl of *See* **Boyle, Roger**

Ortega Saavedra, Daniel 1945– •*Nicaraguan politician*• Born in La Libertad, Chontales, in 1963 he joined the Sandinista National Liberation Front (FSLN). He became national director of the FSLN in 1966, was imprisoned for seven years for urban guerrilla bank raids, and then, in 1979, played a major part in the overthrow of **Anastasio Somoza**. In 1985 he became president, but counterrevolutionary forces, the "Contras," with US support, threatened his government's stability. By 1989, however, there were encouraging signs of peace. He lost the 1990 general election to Violetta Chamorro (1919–).

Ortega y Gasset, José 1883–1955 •*Spanish critic, journalist and philosopher*• Born in Madrid, he studied at the University of Madrid (1898–1904), and was professor there from 1911. He also lived in South America and Portugal (1931–46). *Meditaciones del Quijote* (1914, Eng trans *Meditations on Quixote*, 1961) outlines national symbols in Spanish literature and compares them with those of others. His best-known work, *La rebelión de las masas* (1930, Eng trans *The Revolt of the Masses*, 1932), foreshadowed the Spanish civil war. Often mistakenly taken as a right-wing and elitist document, it is a masterly analysis of the 20th-century situation, in which the masses have revolted against minorities. He corrected any possible ambiguities inherent in this book in his posthumous *El hombre y la gente* (1957, Eng trans *Man and People*, 1957). His writing has radically influenced the majority of Spanish writers of his time and after.

Ortelius, Abraham Ortel 1527–98 •*Flemish geographer*• Born to German parents in Antwerp, he produced *Theatrum Orbis Terrarum* (1570, Eng trans *Epitome of the Theater of the Worlde*), the first great atlas.

Orton, Joe, *originally* **John Kingsley** 1933–67 •*English dramatist*• He was born in Leicester. After training as an actor at the Royal Academy of Dramatic Art in London, he turned to writing vivid, outrageous farces, beginning with *The Ruffian on the Stair* (1964) and *Entertaining Mr Sloane* (1964). Later plays include *Loot* (1966), *The Erpingham Camp* (1966) and *What the Butler Saw* (1969). He was murdered by his lover, Kenneth Halliwell, who subsequently killed himself.

Orwell, George, *pseudonym of* **Eric Arthur Blair** 1903–50 •*English novelist and essayist*• Born in Motihari, Bengal, he was educated in England at Eton, served in Burma in the Indian Imperial Police from 1922 to 1927 (later recalled in 1935 in the novel *Burmese Days*), and then literally went *Down and Out in Paris and London* (1933), making an occasional living as a tutor or bookshop assistant. In 1935 he became a small country shopkeeper, and published two novels, *A Clergyman's Daughter* (1935) and *Keep the Aspidistra Flying* (1936). He fought and was wounded in the Spanish civil war, and he developed his own brand of socialism in *The Road to Wigan Pier* (1937), *Homage to Catalonia* (1938) and *The Lion and the Unicorn* (1941). During World War II, he was war correspondent for the BBC and the *Observer*, and wrote for the *Tribune*. His intellectual honesty motivated his biting satire of communist ideology in *Animal Farm* (1945). It also prompted his terrifying prophecy for mankind in *Nineteen Eighty-Four* (1949): the triumph of the scientifically perfected servile state, the extermination of political freedom by thought control and an ideologically delimited basic language of *newspeak*. Other penetrating collections of essays include *Inside the Whale* (1940) and *Shooting an Elephant* (1950).

" "

If you want a picture of the future, imagine a boot stamping on a human face—for ever.

*1949 **Nineteen Eighty-Four**, part 3, chapter 3.*

Ory, Kid 1886–1973 •*US trombonist and bandleader*• Born in Louisiana, one of the first polyinstrumentalists, singers, and composers in jazz, he formed Kid Ory's Sunshine Orchestra in 1922, played with **Louis Armstrong**'s Hot Five and **Jelly Roll Morton**'s Red Hot Peppers, and took part in the New Orleans Revival from 1942. His compositions include "Muskrat Ramble."

Osborn, Henry Fairfield 1857–1935 •*US paleontologist and zoologist*• Born in Fairfield, Connecticut, he studied at Princeton and became Professor of Zoology at Columbia University and concurrently curator of vertebrate paleontology at the American Museum of Natural History (1891–1910). Retaining a research professorship at Columbia, he was president of the American Museum of Natural History from 1908 to 1933. Although known as an autocratic leader, he revolutionized museum display with innovative instructional techniques and the acquisition of spectacular specimens, especially dinosaurs. His many publications include *The Age of Mammals* (1910), *Man of the Old Stone Age* (1915) and *The Origin and Evolution of Life* (1917). His major scientific contribution was a vast monograph on *Proboscidea* (1935–42).

Osborne, John (James) 1929–94 •*English playwright and actor*• Born in London, he left Belmont College, Devon, at the age of 16 and became a copywriter for trade journals. Hating it, he turned to acting (1948) and by 1955 was playing leading roles in new plays at the Royal Court Theatre, London. There his fourth play, *Look Back in Anger* (1956, filmed 1958), and *The Entertainer* (1957, filmed 1960), with Sir **Laurence Olivier** playing Archie Rice, established Osborne as the leading young exponent of British social drama. The "hero" of the first, Jimmy Porter, the prototypical "Angry Young Man," and the pathetic, mediocre music-hall joker Archie Rice both echo the author's uncompromising hatred of outworn social and political institutions and attitudes. Among other works are *Inadmissible Evidence* (1965), *Time Present* and *The Hotel in Amsterdam* (both 1968), and the screenplay for *Tom Jones*, which won him an Academy Award (1963). He wrote his credo in *Declarations* (1957) and three volumes of autobiography (1981–1994).

Osborne, Thomas *See* **Leeds, Duke of**

Osbourne, Ozzy (John Michael) 1948– •*English rock musician*• He was born in Birmingham into a working-class family. After dropping out of school and spending time in jail for petty crimes, he began playing in rock bands in 1968. He helped to form a band ultimately dubbed Black Sabbath in 1969, which went on to achieve huge popularity and was a seminal influence on the development of heavy metal music. Lead singer of the band until leaving it in 1978 to pursue a solo career, he became notorious for his outrageous antics both on- and offstage. He has continued to release albums, and garnered a Grammy Award in 1993. His foray into "reality television," *The Osbournes* (debuting in 2001 on MTV), which features his family's domestic life in their Beverly Hills home, has been a surprise hit.

Osceola c. 1804–1838 •*Seminole leader*• Born probably in present-day Georgia, he moved into Florida Territory with his mother and is thought to have fought as a teenager against General **Andrew Jackson** in the first of the Seminole Wars. In the early 1830s he denounced treaties that required Native Americans to move west, and when his warriors killed an Indian agent (1835), the second of the Seminole Wars began. For two years he served as the military leader of the Seminole, leading guerilla attacks on US troops in Florida and avoiding capture by retreating deep into the Everglades. Their resistance was so fierce that the US lost 1,500 soldiers in the course of the war and spent at least $20 million, the most costly Indian war in US history. Osceola's frustrated opponent, General Thomas S Jesup, at last tricked him into a meeting under a flag of truce and arrested him (1837). He died in prison at Fort Moultrie, South Carolina.

O'Shane, Pat(ricia) 1941– •*Australian lawyer*• Born in Mossman, Queensland, the daughter of an Irish father and Aboriginal mother, she trained at the University of New South Wales, the first Aborigine to graduate in law there, and was called to the bar in 1976. She was head of the Ministry of Aboriginal Affairs in New South Wales from 1981 to 1986, when she became a magistrate in the local courts. She is known for her progressive attitude, as shown especially in decisions concerning women and Aboriginal people.

Oskar I 1799–1859 •*King of Sweden and Norway*• Born in Paris, he was the only son and successor (1844) of **Karl XIV Johan**. A liberal by temperament, though increasingly conservative after 1848, he sought to conciliate nationalist feelings in Norway, encouraged social and economic reforms, developed schools, railways, banks and industry, and pursued a policy of Scandinavian unity and Swedish neutrality.

Oskar II 1829–1907 •*King of Sweden and Norway*• He was born in Stockholm, the younger son of **Oskar I** and brother of **Karl XV**, whom he succeeded in 1872. A vigorous, intelligent man of a literary bent, his foreign policy was marked by admiration for the new German Empire of **Bismarck**, whose friendship he hoped would strengthen Sweden against Russia. He served as a mediator in international disputes, but found it impossible to keep the union of Norway and Sweden intact, and in 1905 surrendered the Crown of Norway to prince Karl of Denmark, elected king of Norway as **Haakon VII**. He was succeeded as king of Sweden by his son, **Gustav V**.

Osman I c. 1259–c. 1326 •*Founder of the Ottoman Empire*• Born in Bithynia, the son of a border chief, he founded a small Turkish state in Asia Minor called Osmanli (or Ottoman). On the overthrow of the Seljuk sultanate of Iconium in 1299 by the Mongols, he gradually subdued a great part of Asia Minor, his greatest success being the capture of Bursa.

Osmund, St d. 1099 •*Norman prelate*• He became Chancellor of England (1072) and helped compile the *Domesday Book*. Nephew and chaplain of **William the Conqueror**, he was Bishop of Salisbury from 1078, where he established the so-called Use of Sarum (a version of the Latin liturgy of worship). His feast day is December 4.

Ossian or **Oisín Mac Fhinn Mhic Cumhail Mhic Tréanmóir Uí Baoisne** 3rd century AD? •*Semilegendary Irish Gaelic poet and warrior*• The son of Fionn (Fingal), he served for many years in the *Fianna*, or sworn band of heroes, then he went to *Tír na n-Óg*, the land of perpetual youth, returning after 300 years to be converted to Christianity by St **Patrick**. Oral ballads, lyrics and prose ascribed to him were circulated in Ireland and Scotland, but the texts are probably from the 2nd century. The *Ossian* of **James Macpherson** supposes a coherence and royal status lacking in the original and was probably of Macpherson's own devising, since after Ossian's departure his father, Fionn, and his followers were finally defeated by the actual King of Ireland (or Tara), Cairbre Lifeachar.

Ossietzky, Carl von 1888–1938 •*German pacifist, writer, and Nobel Prize winner*• He was a reluctant conscript in the German army in World War I. The cofounder of *Nie wieder Krieg* ("No More War") in 1922, he became editor in 1927 of the weekly *Weltbühne*, in which his articles denounced German military leaders' secret rearmament activities. When **Hitler** became chancellor, he was sent to the Papenburg concentration camp. In the prison hospital he was awarded the 1935 Nobel Peace Prize. He died of tuberculosis under prison conditions in a private hospital.

Ossoli, Marchioness *See* **Fuller, (Sarah) Margaret**

Ostwald, (Friedrich) Wilhelm 1853–1932 •*German physical chemist and Nobel Prize winner*• Born in Riga, Latvia, he studied chemistry at the University of Dorpat (Tartu). After holding various posts as an assistant at Dorpat, he was appointed Professor of Chemistry at the Riga Polytechnic in 1881. In 1887 he moved to Leipzig as Professor of Physical Chemistry, taking early retirement in 1906. With **Jacobus Henricus van't Hoff** and **Svante August Arrhenius**, Ostwald is regarded as one of the founders of physical chemistry. At Dorpat he worked on the measurement of chemical affinity, and during his Riga period he used rates of reaction to study chemical affinity and he measured the affinity coefficients of many acids. In Leipzig he built up a great school of physical chemistry, and pursued studies of electrolytic conductivity (resulting in Ostwald's dilution law) and of the electromotive force of cells. His various books were very influential, and he founded the journals *Zeitschrift für physikalische Chemie* (1887) and *Annalen der Naturphilosophie* (1901). For his work on catalysis, he was awarded the Nobel Prize for chemistry in 1909.

O'Sullivan, Timothy H(enry) 1840-82 •*US photographer*• Born in New York City, he trained in **Mathew B Brady**'s gallery and was a key member of the team sent by Brady to make a photographic record of the Civil War. O'Sullivan's pictures of this period in US history include *Harvest of Death* (1863), depicting the dead after the Battle of Gettysburg. He left Brady in 1863 and joined Alexander Gardner (1821–82), contributing many photographs to his *Photographic Sketchbook of the War* (1965). He was chief photographer on the US Geological Exploration of the 40th parallel from Nevada to Colorado (1867–69) and in the early 1870s took part in the surveys of the Arizona and New Mexico deserts. He also took the first photographs of underground mines and in 1880 was appointed chief photographer for the treasury department.

Oswald, St c. 605–42 •*Anglo-Saxon king of Northumbria*• He was the second son of King Æthelfrith of Bernicia. He fled to Iona for safety when his father was overwhelmed by King **Edwin** (St Edwin) of Deira in 616, but after Edwin's death in 633, Oswald returned from Iona and fought his way to the throne of Northumbria (Deira and Bernicia) with a victory over King **Cadwallon** near Hexham in 634. He reestablished Christianity in Northumbria with the help of the Celtic monk **St Aidan**, whom he summoned from Iona to set up a bishopric on Lindisfarne, the Holy Isle, but was later killed by **Penda** of Mercia.

Oswald, Lee Harvey 1939–63 •*US assassin of President John F Kennedy*• Born in New Orleans, he was a Marxist and former US Marine who had lived for some time in the USSR (1959–62). On November 23, 1963, he was charged with the murder of President **Kennedy**, whom he was alleged to have shot from the sixth floor of the Texas School Book Depository as Kennedy passed by in a motorcade. Two days later, Oswald was shot dead by Jack Ruby (1911–67), who claimed to be avenging Jacqueline Kennedy (**Jackie Kennedy Onassis**). Claims were made that Oswald had links with the US Secret Service and with the Mafia. In 1979, the House Assassinations Committee decided that Kennedy "was probably assassinated as a result of a conspiracy."

Otho, Marcus Salvius AD 32–69 •*Roman emperor*• Formerly a close friend of Emperor **Nero** and ex-husband of Nero's consort, the empress Poppaea Sabina, from AD 58 until Nero's downfall (68), he governed in Spain, virtually as an exile from court. A supporter briefly of **Galba**, he rose against him (69) and became emperor in his place, only to find his own position immediately challenged by the governor of Lower Germany, **Aulus Vitellius**. In the brief civil war that followed, Otho was comprehensively defeated and committed suicide.

Otis, Elisha Graves 1811–61 •*US inventor*• Born in Halifax, Vermont, he became a master mechanic in a firm making bedsteads, and was put in charge of the construction of their new factory in Yonkers. The factory had several floors connected by a hoist, and Otis, knowing of the many serious accidents caused by runaway lifting platforms, designed in 1853 a spring-operated safety device which would hold the platform securely if there was any failure of tension in the rope. He patented the elevator and exhibited it in New York in 1854, after which orders came in rapidly for elevators to move passengers as well as goods.

O'Toole, Peter Seamus 1932– •*Irish actor*• Born in Connemara, he was a journalist and member of the submarine service, and a student at the Royal Academy of Dramatic Art, before joining the Bristol Old Vic, where he made his professional debut in *The Matchmaker* (1955). He made his film debut in *Kidnapped* (1959). West End success in *The Long and the Short and the Tall* (1959) and a season with the Royal Shakespeare Company (RSC) established his stage reputation, while his performance in *Lawrence of Arabia* (1962) made him an international film star. Adept at drama, comedy or musicals, he has tackled many of the great classical roles and is frequently cast as mercurial or eccentric characters. He was nominated seven times for Academy Awards, and his films include *The Lion in Winter* (1968), *Goodbye Mr Chips* (1969), *The Last Emperor* (1987) and *Fairytale—A True Story* (1997). He has published two autobiographies.

Ottey, Merlene 1960– •*Jamaican athlete*• She has won a record 14 world championship outdoor medals—the most by any female athlete—although she has never won an Olympic gold. Beaten on the line in Atlanta 1996, she had earlier lost the 1993 world 100-meter title by 0.001 seconds. Fired up, she went on to take the 1993 200-meter title, setting a then world-record time of 21.98 seconds.

Otto I (the Great) 912–73 •*Holy Roman Emperor*• The son of **Henry the Fowler**, he was crowned king of Germany in 936 and emperor in 962. Virtual founder of the kingdom of Germany, he brought the great tribal duchies under the control of the monarchy and made the Church the main instrument of royal government. He was married (930) to Edith, daughter of **Edward the Elder** and sister of **Athelstan** of England, and later (951) to St **Adelaide**. He preserved Germany from the Hungarian invasions by his great victory on the Lechfeld, near Augsburg (955), and reestablished imperial rule in Italy. He presided over a cultural revival, sometimes called the Ottonian renaissance.

Otto, Rudolf 1869–1937 •*German Protestant theologian and philosopher*• Born in Peine, Hanover, he became Professor of Systematic Theology at Göttingen (1904), and later held chairs at Breslau (1914) and Marburg (1917). His best-known work, *Das Heilige* (1917, "The Idea of the Holy"), explores the nonrational aspect of religion, termed "the numinous" (the deity or awareness of it), and was largely prompted by the work of both **Kant** and **Friedrich Schleiermacher**, and by his own study of non-Christian religions in the East.

Otway, Thomas 1652–85 •*English dramatist*• Born in Trotton, Sussex, he went to Christ Church, Oxford, in 1669, leaving without a degree in 1672. He failed utterly as an actor, but had some success with his tragedy *Alcibiades* (1675). In it the actress **Elizabeth Barry** made her first appearance, and Otway is said to have fallen in love with her. In 1676 theater manager Thomas Betterton (c. 1635–1710) accepted his *Don Carlos*, a good tragedy in rhyme. In 1678–79 he was in Flanders as a soldier. His coarse but diverting comedy, *Friendship in Fashion*, appeared in 1678, followed in 1680 by two tragedies, *The Orphan* and *Caius Marius*, and his one important poem, *The Poet's Complaint of His Muse*. His greatest work, *Venice Preserved, or a Plot Discovered* (1682), is a masterpiece of tragic passion. Later works include *The Atheist*, a feeble comedy, and *Windsor Castle* (1685), a poem addressed to the new king, **James VII and II**. He died in poverty. In 1719 a badly edited tragedy, *Heroick Friendship*, was published as his.

Ouida, *pseudonym of* **Marie Louise de la Ramée** 1839–1908 •*English novelist*• She was born in Bury St Edmunds. Her mother was English, her father French, and she was educated in Paris, then settled in London in 1857. "Ouida" was a childish mispronunciation of "Louise." Starting her career by contributing stories to magazines, in particular to *Bentley's Miscellany* (1859–60), her first success was *Held in Bondage* (1863), shortly followed by *Strathmore* (1865), both aimed at the circulating libraries. She was soon established as a writer of hot-house romances, and until her popularity waned in the 1890s, she was a best-selling author. From 1860 she spent much time in Italy, and in 1874 she settled in Florence, where she lived lavishly. She wrote almost 50 books, mainly novels, such as *Folle-Farine* (1871), which was praised by **Edward Bulwer Lytton**, and *A Village Commune* (1881)—but also animal stories, essays and tales for children. Eventually, her royalties dried up and she fell into debt; she spent her last years destitute in Viareggio.

Ouspensky, Peter 1878–1947 •*Russian philosopher*• He became a student of **Georgei Gurdjieff** in 1914, but eventually broke off relations with him in order to teach his own version of Gurdjieff's doctrine in London and the US. His works of fiction include *Strange Life of Ivan Osokin* (1947). His *In Search of the Miraculous* (1949) has been one of the most widely read religious books of the postwar period.

Overbeck, Johann Friedrich 1789–1869 •*German painter*• Born in Lübeck, he settled in Rome, where he allied himself with the like-minded **Peter von Cornelius**, Johann Gottfried Schadow (1764–1850), Julius Schnorr (1794–1872) and Philipp Veit (1793–

1877), who, because of the stress they laid on religion and moral significance, were nicknamed the Nazarenes.

Ovett, Steve 1955– •*English athlete*• Born in Brighton, Sussex, he launched, with **Sebastian Coe**, a new era of British dominance in middle-distance athletics. Gold medalist in the 800 meters at the 1980 Olympics, he also won a bronze in the 1,500 meters. He broke the world record at 1,500 meters (three times), at one mile (twice) and at two miles. An outspoken and sometimes controversial figure, he occasionally upset the press but remained generally popular with his fellow athletes and the spectators.

Ovid, *in full* **Publius Ovidius Naso** 43 BC–AD 17 •*Roman poet*• Born in Sulmo (Solmona), in the Abruzzi, he was trained as a lawyer in Rome, but devoted himself to poetry. Later acclaimed as the master of the elegiac couplet, he had his first literary success with a collection of love poems, the *Amores* ("Loves"), followed by *Heroides* ("Heroines"), imaginary love letters from ladies to their lords. The *Ars amandi* or *Ars amatoria* ("The Art of Love") appeared about 1 BC, followed by the *Remedia amoris* ("Cures for Love"). While writing his *Metamorphoses*, a collection of mythological tales in 15 books, he was banished by **Augustus** (AD 8), for some unknown reason, to Tomis (Constanza) on the Black Sea. He also wrote the *Tristia* ("Sorrows"), the four books of the *Epistolae ex Ponto* ("Letters from the Black Sea"), *Ibis*, written in imitation of **Callimachus**, and *Halieutica* ("Fishing Matters"), a poem extant only in fragments.

" "

Video meliora, proboque;
Deteriora sequor.
I see the better things, and approve; I follow the worse.

__Metamorphoses__, book 7, l. 20 (translated by Peter Green).

Owen, David Anthony Llewellyn Owen, Baron 1938– •*English politician*• He was born in Plymouth, and trained as a doctor before becoming Labour Member of Parliament for Plymouth in 1966. He was Minister of State at the Department of Health and Social Security (1974–76) and then at the Foreign and Commonwealth Office (1976–77) before becoming the youngest Foreign Secretary for over 40 years (1977–79). Owen was one of the so-called Gang of Four who broke away from the Labour Party to found the Social Democratic Party (SDP) in 1981. He succeeded **Roy Jenkins** as SDP leader in 1983. When in 1987 the Liberal leader, Sir **David Steel**, called for a merger of the party with the SDP, Owen resigned the leadership and persuaded a minority of members to join him in a breakaway, reconstituted SDP, but the party was dissolved in 1990. He retired from politics in 1991. From 1992 to 1995 he was cochairman (initially with **Cyrus R Vance**) of the international peace conference on the former Yugoslavia. He was made a life peer in 1992.

Owen, Sir Richard 1804–92 •*English zoologist and paleontologist*• Born in Lancaster, he studied medicine at Edinburgh and at St Bartholomew's Hospital, London, and became curator at the Royal College of Surgeons. In 1856 he was appointed superintendent of the natural history department of the British Museum and was instrumental in the establishment of the separate British Museum (Natural History), now the Natural History Museum, becoming its first director in 1881. He was the most prestigious zoologist of Victorian England and published 400 scientific papers as well as a number of important books, including *A History of British Fossil Reptiles* (1849–84). He named and reconstructed numerous celebrated fossils, including the dinosaur *Iguanodon* and the earliest bird, the *Archaeopteryx*. He coined the term "dinosaur" ("terrible lizard"). However, he remained implacably opposed to evolution.

Owen, Robert 1771–1858 •*Welsh social and educational reformer*• Born in Newtown, Montgomeryshire, at the age of 10 he started work in a draper's shop at Stamford, and by 19 had risen to be manager of a cotton mill in Manchester. In 1799 he married Anne Caroline, eldest daughter of Scottish industrialist and philanthropist David Dale (1739–1806), and bought from him the cotton mills and manufacturing village Dale had established with **Richard Arkwright** at New Lanark in Scotland. Here he established a model community with improved housing and working conditions, and built the Institute for the Formation of Character, a school (including the world's first day nursery and playground, and also evening classes) and a village store, the cradle of the cooperative movement. In 1813 he formed New Lanark into a new company with **Jeremy Bentham** and others. In *A New View of Society* (1813) he argued that character was formed by the social environment, and went on to found several cooperative Owenite communities, including one at New Harmony in Indiana (1825–28), but they were unsuccessful. In 1825 he ceased to be manager at New Lanark after disagreements with his partners, and in 1828 sold all his shares, after which the place went into obscurity.

Owen, Wilfred 1893–1918 •*English poet*• Born near Oswestry, Shropshire, he was educated at the Birkenhead Institute and at Shrewsbury Technical School, and worked as a pupil-teacher at Wyle Cop School. In 1913 he left England to teach English in Bordeaux at the Berlitz School of Languages. During World War I he suffered a concussion and trench fever and was sent to recuperate near Edinburgh, where he met **Siegfried Sassoon**, who helped him improve his poems. Posted back to France, he was killed in action a week before the armistice was signed. Only five of his poems were published while he was alive. His work was first collected in 1920 by Sassoon. His poetry expresses a horror of the cruelty and waste of war, and individual poems such as "Dulce et Decorum Est" and "Anthem for Doomed Youth" have shaped the attitude of many.

Owens, Jesse James Cleveland 1913–80 •*US track athlete*• He was born in Danville, Alabama. While competing for the Ohio State University team in 1935, he set three world records and equaled another (all within the space of an hour), including the long jump (26 ft 8¼ in), which lasted for 25 years. At the 1936 Olympics in Berlin he won four gold medals (100 meter, 200 meter, long jump, and 4×100-meter relay), which caused the German Nazi leader, **Adolf Hitler**, to leave the stadium. Back in the US, Owens gained no recognition for his feat and was reduced to running "freak" races against horses and dogs. Later he held an executive position with the Illinois Athletic Commission and attended the 1956 Olympics as President **Dwight Eisenhower**'s personal representative. In 1976 he was awarded the Presidential Medal of Freedom. He is considered the greatest sprinter of his generation.

" "

I let my feet spend as little time on the ground as possible. From the air, fast down, and from the ground, fast up.

Quoted in Colin Jarman __The Guinness Dictionary of Sports Quotations__ (1990).

Oxenstjerna or **Oxenstern, Count Axel Gustafsson** 1583–1654 •*Swedish statesman*• Born near Uppsala into one of Sweden's great families, he entered royal service in 1605 and helped achieve the smooth accession of **Gustav II Adolf** in 1611. From 1612 he was Gustav's chancellor and showed outstanding administrative and diplomatic ability, negotiating favorable peace treaties with Denmark (1613), Russia (1617) and Poland (1629). During the Thirty Years' War (1618–48) he governed Sweden when Gustav was absent on military expeditions. After the king's death in 1632, he became director of the Protestant League (1633). He was regent for Queen **Kristina** (1636–44), and continued to exercise authority in policymaking after she came of age.

Oz, Amos 1939– •*Israeli Hebrew-language writer*• He was born in Jerusalem and went to live on a kibbutz at the age of 14, where he taught in the school. His novels, which deal with historical and contemporary themes of guilt and persecution, include *Makom aber* (1966, Eng trans *Elsewhere, Perhaps*, 1973) and *Menuhah nekhonah* (1984, Eng trans *A Perfect Peace*, 1985). *Mikha'el sheli* (1972, Eng trans *My Michael*, 1972), described by the *New York Times* as "a modern Israeli *Madame Bovary*," is the book for which he is best known. *Kufsah shehorah* (Eng trans *Black Box*, 1988) appeared in 1988. His work has been widely translated (a process in which he has collaborated), and he has won many awards.

Özal, Turgut 1927–93 •*Turkish politician*• Born in Malatya and educated at Istanbul Technical University, he entered government service and in 1967 became Under-Secretary for State Planning. In 1979 joined the office of prime minister **Bülent Ecevit**, and in 1980 he was deputy to Prime Minister Bülent Ulusu, within the military regime of Kenan Evren. When political pluralism returned in 1983, Özal founded the Islamic, right-of-center Motherland Party (ANAP) and led it to victory that year. In the 1987 general election he retained his majority, and in 1989 became Turkey's first civilian president in 30 years. In the 1991 Gulf War, despite strong domestic criticism, he allowed Turkish bases to be used by the US Air Force in mounting attacks on Iraq and the occupation forces in Kuwait.

Ozawa, Seiji 1935– •*US conductor*• Born to Japanese parents in Manchuria, he studied piano in Tokyo and turned to composing and conducting after breaking both his index fingers in a rugby game. After further musical training in Paris and Berlin, he was appointed director of the Toronto Symphony (1965–69). The first Japanese conductor prominent in the West, he settled in the US and served as director of the San Francisco Symphony (1970–76) and the Boston Symphony Orchestra (1973–2002). In 2002, he became music director of the Vienna State Opera.

Ozbek, Rifat 1954– •*Turkish fashion designer*• Born in Istanbul, he began to study architecture at the University of Liverpool but, without completing the course, moved to St Martin's School of Art in London. Beginning with small collections, he now has a multimillion-dollar business and enjoys international acclaim, which has twice gained him the title of Designer of the Year (1989 and 1992). His vivid collections embrace myriad styles and display cross-cultural references.

Ozenfant, Amédée 1886–1966 •*French artist*• Born in St Quentin, he was the leader of the Purist movement in Paris and published a manifesto of Purism with **Le Corbusier** in 1919. From 1921 to 1925 they published an avant-garde magazine, *Esprit nouveau*. They also collaborated in writing *Après le Cubisme* (1918, "After Cubism") and *La peinture moderne* (1925, "Modern Painting"). Ozenfant's still lifes based on this theory reduce vases and jugs to a static counterpoint of two-dimensional shapes. He founded art schools in London (1935) and New York City (1938); his publications include *Art* (1928) and his diaries for the years 1931–34.

Ozick, Cynthia 1928– •*US novelist and short-story writer*• Born in New York City, she was educated at New York University and Ohio State University. She has said she began her first novel, *Trust* (1966), as an American writer and ended it six and a half years later as a Jewish one. Powerfully and originally expressing the Jewish ethos, her slight but significant œuvre includes *The Pagan Rabbi and Other Stories* (1971), *The Cannibal Galaxy* (1983) and *The Messiah of Stockholm* (1987). Her essays have been collected in volumes such as *Fame and Folly* (1996). More recent works include *The Puttermesser Papers* (1997).

Ozu, Yasujiro 1903–63 •*Japanese film director*• Born in Tokyo, he joined the industry as an assistant cameraman, became an assistant director and made his directorial debut with *Gakuso o idete* (1925, "Out of College"). Adept at many popular genres, he began to specialize from the 1930s in "home drama." A precise and rigorous cinematic stylist, his films offered gentle, compassionate portraits of everyday family life laced with humor and, latterly, underlying tragedy. A prolific filmmaker, his most widely seen work was made in the 1950s and includes *Ochazuke no aji* (1952, *The Flavor of Green Tea over Rice*), *Tokyo monogatari* (1953, *Tokyo Story*) and *Ohayo* (1959, *Good Morning!*).

P

Paar, Jack 1918–2004 •*US television host*• Born in Canton, Ohio, he began his career as a radio announcer and after World War II worked as a film actor and comedian. Having successfully filled in as a temporary host of **Jack Benny**'s radio show, he was invited in 1957 to host *The Tonight Show*, a late-night talk show that became one of the longest-running television programs. Interviewing both established stars and emerging talents in show business and politics, Paar effectively created the standard talk-show format and became a television icon watched by millions. After giving up his role as host in 1962 he hosted a weekly primetime variety show (1962–65) and in the late 1960s became a producer of primetime documentaries. He returned briefly as a talk show host in 1975 before retiring for good.

Paasikivi, Juho Kusti 1870–1956 •*Finnish statesman*• He was born in Tampere. He became Conservative prime minister after the civil war in 1918. He recognized the need for friendly relations with the USSR and took part in all Finnish-Soviet negotiations. He sought to avoid war in September 1939, conducted the armistice negotiations and became prime minister again in 1944. He succeeded **Carl Mannerheim** as president (1946–56).

Pabst, G(eorg) W(ilhelm) 1895–1967 •*German film director*• Born in Raudnitz, Bohemia, Austro-Hungary, he began directing in 1923 and developed a darkly realistic, almost documentary style in *Die Liebe der Jeanne Ney* (1927, "The Love of Jeanne Ney"). Other works, all examples of New Realism, include *Westfront 1918* (1930), *Kameradschaft* (1931, "Comradeship"), and he re-created the last days of **Hitler** in *Der letzte Akt* (1955, "The Last Act").

Pachelbel, Johann c.1653–1706 •*German composer and organist*• Born in Nuremberg, he held a variety of organist's posts before, in 1695, he returned to Nuremberg as organist of St Sebalds's Church. His works, which include six suites for two violins, and organ fugues, greatly influenced **J S Bach**.

Pacino, Al(fred James) 1940– •*US film actor*• Born in East Harlem, New York, he studied at the High School of Performing Arts and the Actors Studio, going on to win an Obie award for *The Indian Wants the Bronx* (1966) and a Tony for *Does a Tiger Wear a Necktie?* (1969). He received the first of his numerous Academy Award nominations for *The Godfather* (1972). Drawn to characters on an emotional knife-edge, he has made appearances in films like *Serpico* (1973), *The Godfather: Part II* (1974), *Dog Day Afternoon* (1975) and *Scarface* (1983). Absent from the screen after the failure of *Revolution* (1985), he returned in the thriller *Sea of Love* (1989), *Glengarry Glen Ross* (1992) and *Donnie Brasco* (1997). He finally won a Best Actor Academy Award for *Scent of a Woman* (1993) and made his directorial debut with *Looking for Richard* (1996). He has frequently returned to the stage.

Paderewski, Ignacy Jan 1860–1941 •*Polish pianist, composer, and patriot*• He was born in Kurylowka, Podolia. Beginning to play as a child of three, he studied in Warsaw, becoming a professor in the Warsaw Conservatory (1878), and a virtuoso pianist, appearing throughout Europe and the US. During World War I he used his popularity abroad to argue the case, particularly in the US, for Poland regaining its independence. In 1919 he became for a time prime minister of Poland, but he soon retired from politics, lived in Switzerland, and resumed concert work. He was elected president of Poland's provisional parliament in Paris in 1940, though poor health prevented his pursuing an active role.

Páez, José Antonio 1790–1873 •*Venezuelan revolutionary and political leader*• He was born near Aricagua, Venezuela. During the War of Independence he was chief Venezuelan commander under **Simón Bolívar**, winning victories that forced the withdrawal of the Spanish. In 1830 he became Venezuela's first president (1831), and he remained in control until 1846. He was a moderate dictator until his imprisonment (1847–50) and exile (1850–58), but when he returned to rule Venezuela again (1861–63), he was severely repressive.

Paganini, Niccolò 1782–1840 •*Italian violinist*• Born in Genoa, he gave his first concert in 1793 and began touring professionally in 1805. He later visited Austria, Germany, Paris and London (1828–31), where his dexterity and technical expertise acquired him an almost legendary reputation. He revolutionized violin technique, among his innovations being the use of stopped harmonics. He published six concertos and (1820) the celebrated *24 Capricci*.

Page, Sir Frederick Handley 1885–1962 •*English aircraft designer*• Born in Cheltenham, Gloucestershire, he founded the first British aircraft manufacturing firm, Handley-Page Ltd in 1909. His 0/400 (1915) was the first twin-engine bomber and saw service in World War I, and his Hampden and Halifax bombers were used in World War II. His civil aircraft include the Hannibal, Hermes and Herald transports. He was knighted in 1942.

Page, Geraldine 1924–87 •*US stage and screen actress*• Born in Missouri and trained at the Goodman Theater Dramatic School, Chicago, she made her New York debut in 1945, but it was not until her success in **Tennessee Williams**'s *Summer and Smoke* (1952) that she became established there. Credited with great versatility and sensitivity, her notable roles include Mother Miriam Ruth in *Agnes of God* (1982). She acted in many films, and won an Academy Award in 1985 for *The Trip to Bountiful*.

Pagels, Elaine 1943– •*US theologian*• As Professor of Religion at Princeton University, she is a recognized authority on the early Christian sect, the Gnostics. *The Gnostic Gospels* (1979) is a scholarly introduction to its ancient texts, and in *The Gnostic Paul* (1992) she examines historical sources, including the Nag Hammadi documents, and challenges the assumption that the Pauline letters were written to counter Gnosticism. Her other works include *Adam and Eve and the Serpent* (1988) and *The Origin of Satan* (1995).

Paget, Sir James 1814–99 •*English physician and pathologist*• Born in Great Yarmouth, Norfolk, he studied at St Bartholomew's Hospital, London, where he became full surgeon in 1861. One of the founders of modern pathology, he discovered the cause of trichinosis and described Paget's disease (an early indication of breast cancer) and Paget's disease of bone (osteitis deformans, a bone inflammation).

Paglia, Camille 1947– •*US academic, essay writer and media personality*• Born in Endicott, New York, she studied at Yale before becoming a teacher and lecturer at a number of institutions, latterly becoming Professor of Humanities and Media Studies (2000–) at Philadelphia College of Performing Arts (now called the University of the Arts). She has become renowned both for her powerful intellect and for her attempt not only to pour scorn on modern feminism, but also to promote her theory of women as the more powerful sex, whose destiny is neither to serve nor to demean men, but to rule them. Her publications include *Sexual Personae: Art and Decadence from Nefertiti to Emily Dickinson* (1990) and *Vamps and Tramps* (1995).

Pagnol, Marcel 1895–1974 •*French dramatist, filmmaker and scriptwriter*• He was born near Marseilles. His childhood in Provence informs his best work, the play trilogy *Marius* (1929, filmed 1931), *Fanny* (1931, filmed 1932) and *César* (1936, filmed two years earlier). He first became widely known with the memoir *Topaze* (1928), a satirical study of bourgeois bad faith, which was filmed five years later by Louis Gasneur. Provence and its warmth, both literal and human, is at the center of *La gloire de mon père* (1957, filmed 1990, *My Father's Glory*) and his other memoirs. The film *Jean de Florette* (1986), also set in Provence, was based on one of his stories, as was its sequel, *Manon des sources* (1986). In turn, both stories were based on Pagnol's own earlier film, *Manon des sources* (1952).

Pahlavi, Muhammad Reza 1919–80 •*Shah of Iran*• He succeeded on the abdication of his father, Reza Shah Pahlavi (1877–1944), in 1941. His reign was for many years marked by social reforms and a movement away from the old-fashioned despotic concept of the monarchy. Ambitious five-year plans (1963–72) enhanced agricultural and industrial development and increased literacy. Nationalization of the Western oil consortium (1973) boosted export revenue as oil prices increased. But in the later 1970s the economic situation deteriorated, and protest against Western-style "decadence" grew among the religious fundamentalists. Following several attempts at parliamentary reform, the shah, having lost control of the situation, left the country (1979), after which a revolutionary government was formed under Ayatollah **Khomeini**. When the ex-shah was admitted to the US for medical treatment, the Iranian government seized the US embassy in Tehran and held many of its staff hostage for over a year, demanding his return to Iran. He made his final residence in Egypt at the invitation of President **Sadat** and died there.

Paige, Elaine 1951– •*English actress and singer*• Born in Barnet, London, she joined the West End cast of *Hair* in 1969, but it was her performances in *Jesus Christ Superstar* (1972) and *Billy* (1974) that established her as an actress in musicals. She became a star as *Evita* (1978). In 1981 she played in *Cats*, and other musicals include *Chess* (1986), *Anything Goes* (1989), *Sunset Boulevard* (1996) and *The King and I* (2000–01).

Paige, Leroy Robert, *nicknamed* **Satchel** 1906–82 •*US baseball player*• Born in Mobile, Alabama, he established a reputation as the greatest pitcher in the Negro Leagues before finally being hired to play Major League baseball with the Cleveland Indians in 1948, helping them win the World Series that year and becoming the first African-American pitcher to play in the American League. Later in his career he played for St Louis and the Kansas City Athletics, ultimately retiring in 1965 after a last appearance for Kansas City at the age of 59.

Paine, Thomas 1737–1809 •*English-born American radical political writer*• He was born in Thetford, Norfolk, the son of a Quaker smallholder and corset maker. He worked at various jobs until in 1771 he became an exciseman, but he was dismissed as an agitator after fighting for an increase in pay. In London he met **Benjamin Franklin**, who in 1774 helped him to emigrate to America, where he settled in Philadelphia as a radical journalist. After the outbreak of the American Revolution (1775–83), he published a pamphlet, *Common Sense* (1776), which urged immediate independence. He served in the Continental army, issued a series of pamphlets supporting the colonial cause, and became secretary of the Congressional committee on foreign affairs (1777–79). He went to France in 1781, and published *Dissertations on Government* in 1786. He returned to England in 1787, where he published *The Rights of Man* (1791–92), a reply to **Edmund Burke**'s *Reflections on the French Revolution* (1790). In it he supported both the French Revolution and an overthrow of the British monarchy. He was indicted for treason, but escaped to Paris, was made a French citizen and became a member of the National Convention as the deputy for Pas-de-Calais (1792–93). A supporter of the Girondins, he opposed the execution of the king, thus falling afoul of **Robespierre**, who had Paine's French citizenship rescinded and arrested him (1793–94). After the Terror, he was released on the plea that he was a US citizen. Just before his arrest, he published Part I of his powerful attack on accepted religion, *The Age of Reason* (1794; Part II, written in prison, was published in 1796), alienating most of his friends, including **George Washington**. Following his release he remained in Paris, but in 1802 he returned to the US, where he was ostracized as an atheist and a freethinker. He died alone and in poverty.

" "

My country is the world, and my religion is to do good.

1791–92 ***The Rights of Man***.

Paisley, Bob 1919–96 •*English soccer coach and manager*• Born in Hetton-le-Hole, he is celebrated as perhaps the most successful club manager in British soccer history. After serving in the army in the desert campaigns of World War II, he joined Liverpool Football Club and won a championship medal in 1947. After his playing career finished, he was one of Liverpool's coaching staff for 20 years before succeeding **Bill Shankly** as manager. Under Paisley, Liverpool won the league championship six times, the European Cup thrice, the UEFA Cup once and also won three league cups. Only the Football Association Cup eluded him.

Paisley, Ian Richard Kyle 1926– •*Northern Irish clergyman and politician, founder of the Free Presbyterian Church of Ulster*• Born in Ballymena, and educated at South Wales Bible College and the Reformed Presbyterian Theological College, Belfast, he was ordained by his Baptist minister father in 1946 and founded his own denomination, the Free Presbyterian Church of Ulster, in 1951. In 1969 he entered the Northern Ireland parliament as Protestant Unionist Member of Parliament for Bannside, becoming leader of the Opposition in 1972. He cofounded the Democratic Unionist Party, and since 1970 has been Member of Parliament for Antrim North in the House of Commons and leader of the Democratic Unionists there. He has been a member of the European Parliament since 1979. The province's most vociferous opponent of Irish unification, he is the object of fanatical devotion from Ulster loyalists. His publications include *The Massacre of Bartholomew* (1974) and *Those Flaming Tennents* (1983).

Pal, Bipin Chandra 1858–1932 •*Indian nationalist and freedom fighter*• Though born into an orthodox Zamindar family in Sylhet (in Bangladesh), he opposed traditional orthodoxy and religious practices. He entered politics in 1877, and his association with the great reformist Brahma Samâj leader Keshub Chunder Sen (1838–84) drew him into this movement in 1880. He was also greatly influenced by **Bal Gangadhar Tilak**, **Lala Lajpat Rai** (with whom he formed the famous congressional trio "Lal, Pal and Bal") and **Aurobindo**. He launched a weekly journal, *Young India* (1902), through which he championed the cause of Indian freedom, advocating passive resistance and noncooperation. He spent the years between 1908 and 1911 in England, where he worked for India's freedom and published *Swaraj*.

Palach, Jan 1948–69 •*Czech philosophy student*• As a protest against the August 1968 invasion of Czechoslovakia by the Warsaw Pact forces, he set fire to himself in Václavské Námestí, Prague, on January 16, 1969. After his death five days later he became a hero and symbol of hope, and was mourned by thousands. In 1989 there were huge popular demonstrations in Prague to mark the 20th anniversary of his death.

Palestrina, Giovanni Pierluigi da c. 1525–94 •*Italian composer*• Born in Palestrina, he learned composition and organ playing in Rome, and in 1544 he became organist and *maestro di canto* at the cathedral of St Agapit, Palestrina. He was master of the Julian choir at St Peter's, for which he composed many fine masses from 1551, the first of several important appointments. His works include over 100 masses and a large number of motets, hymns and other liturgical pieces, as well as madrigals. His compositions show great skill in the handling of contrapuntal texture, and having in its original form no division into bars, his music is free-flowing and unhampered by rhythmic conventions.

Paley, William 1743–1805 •*English theologian*• Born in Peterborough, Cambridgeshire, he was Fellow and Tutor of Christ's College, Cambridge (1768–76), and became Archdeacon of Carlisle (1782) and Subdean of Lincoln (1795). He published *Principles of Moral and Political Philosophy* (1785), expounding a form of utilitarianism. In 1790 he published his most original work, *Horae Paulinae*, the aim of which was to disprove the hypothesis that the New Testament is a cunningly devised fable. It was followed in 1794 by his famous *Evidences of Christianity,* and in 1802 he published the widely popular *Natural Theology, or Evidences of the Existence and Attributes of the Deity.*

Palgrave, Francis Turner 1824–97 •*English poet and critic*• Born in Great Yarmouth, Norfolk, he was the eldest son of the historian Sir Francis Palgrave (1788–1861). He became a scholar of Balliol College, Oxford, and Fellow of Exeter College, and among various other appointments became Professor of Poetry at Oxford (1886–95). His works include *Idylls and Songs* (1854), *Essays on Art* (1866) and *Landscape in Poetry* (1897), but he is best known as the editor of the *Golden Treasury of Lyrical Poetry* (1875), *Sonnets and Songs of Shakespeare* (1877), selections from **Robert Herrick** (1877) and **Keats** (1885), and *Treasury of Sacred Song* (1889).

Palin, Michael Edward 1943– •*English actor and writer*• Born in Sheffield and educated at Oxford, he wrote for television shows such as *The Frost Report* (1966–67) and *Do Not Adjust Your Set* (1967–69) before joining the innovative *Monty Python's Flying Circus* (1969–74). He appeared with fellow members of the group in such films as *Monty Python and the Holy Grail* (1975) and *Monty Python's Life of Brian* (1977–79) and has been among the most successful of the team with a wide variety of solo ventures that include the comedy show *Ripping Yarns* (1976–80), children's novels such as *Small Harry and the Toothache Pills* (1981) and the globetrotting television documentary series *Around the World in 80 Days* (1989) and *Pole to Pole* (1992). Memorable film appearances include *A Fish Called Wanda* (1988) and *Fierce Creatures* (1996).

Palladio, Andrea, *originally* **Andrea di Pietro della Gondola** 1508–80 •*Italian architect*• He was born in Vicenza, and trained as a stonemason. He developed a modern Italian architectural style based on classical Roman principles, unlike the ornamentation of the Renaissance. This Palladian style was widely imitated all over Europe, in particular by **Inigo Jones** and **Christopher Wren**. Palladio's *Quattro libri dell' architettura* (1570, Eng trans *The Four Books of Architecture*, 1715) greatly influenced his successors.

Palme, (Sven) Olof 1927–86 •*Swedish politician*• Born in Stockholm, he was educated in the US at Kenyon College, and studied law at Stockholm University. He joined the Social Democratic Labor Party (SAP) in 1949 and became leader of its youth movement in 1955. After election to the Riksdag in 1956, he entered the government in 1963 and held several ministerial posts before assuming the leadership of the party and becoming prime minister in 1969. Although he lost his parliamentary majority in 1971, he managed to carry out major constitutional reforms, but was defeated in 1976 over taxation proposals to fund the welfare system. He was returned to power, heading a minority government, in 1982, and was reelected in 1985, but was shot and killed in Stockholm while walking home with his wife after a visit to a cinema.

Palmer, Arnold 1929– •*US golfer*• Born in Youngstown, Pennsylvania, he was one of the postwar golfing stars whose powerful, attacking golf technique introduced the game to millions throughout the world. He turned professional in 1955 after a brilliant amateur career, but won only eight majors. He was twice captain of the American Ryder Cup team. Arnie's Army, as his fans became known, flocked to see him play, and his back-to-back victories inspired his fellow Americans to travel and compete on the seaside courses of Great Britain.

Palmer, Samuel 1805–81 •*English landscape painter and etcher*• Born in London, he produced mainly watercolors in a mystical style derived from his friend **William Blake**. From 1826 to 1835 he lived in Shoreham, Kent, where he was surrounded by a group of friends who called themselves The Ancients. Palmer later visited Italy and began producing more academic, conventional work. He was thereafter forgotten until the Neo-Romantics—**Graham Sutherland**, John Minton (1917–57) and **Paul Nash**—rediscovered him during World War II, seeing in his work something essentially English but with overtones of surrealism.

Palmerston, Henry John Temple, 3rd Viscount 1784–1865 •*English statesman*• He was born in Westminster, and educated at the University of Edinburgh (1800) and Cambridge University (1803–06). In 1802 he succeeded his father as viscount and was elected Member of Parliament in 1807 for Newport (Wight). He was junior lord of the admiralty and secretary at war under **Spencer Perceval**, the Earl of **Liverpool**, **George Canning**, Frederick Ripon and the Duke of **Wellington** (1809–28). His official connection with the Tory Party ceased in 1828, and he entered the Foreign Office in Earl **Grey**'s Whig government in 1830. With England and France acting in concert, Palmerston took a leading part in securing the independence of Belgium, establishing the thrones of Maria of Portugal and **Isabella II** of Spain, and endeavoring, in alliance with both Austria and Turkey, to check Russian influence in the East. In 1841 Palmerston and the Whigs lost office on the question of free trade in corn, and under Lord **John Russell** in 1846 he again became foreign minister. His handling of events such as the revolutions in 1848 and the rupture between Spain and Great Britain, combined with his self-assertive character, brusque speech, and interference in foreign affairs, made him a controversial figure. In December 1851 Palmerston expressed to the French ambassador his approbation of the coup d'état of Louis-Napoleon (**Napoleon III**), without consulting either the premier or the queen, and Russell forced him to resign from the office of foreign secretary. He shattered the Russell administration soon after on a militia bill, refused office under the Earl of **Derby**, but was home secretary in the Earl of **Aberdeen**'s coalition (1852), whose fall (1855) brought him the premiership. Defeated in 1857 on **Richard Cobden**'s motion condemning the Chinese war, he appealed to the country and met the House of Commons with a greatly increased majority, but fell in February 1858 over the Conspiracy Bill. In June 1859 he again became prime minister, remaining in office till his death.

Paltrow, Gwyneth 1973– •*US actress*• Born in Los Angeles, she studied at the University of California. Early films included *Flesh and Bone* (1993), *Jefferson in Paris* (1995), *Seven* (1995) and *Emma* (1996), in which she played the title role. She received an Academy Award for Best Actress for *Shakespeare in Love* (1998). Subsequent films have included *The Talented Mr Ripley* (1999) and *The Royal Tenenbaums* (2001).

Pan Chao *See* **Ban Zhao**

Pancras, St d. 304 AD •*Greek Christian*• Born in Phrygia of Greek parents, he was baptized in Rome, but was killed in the **Diocletian** persecutions while still a child. One of the patron saints of children, his feast day is May 12.

Pandit *See* **Nehru, Jawaharlal**

Pandit, Vijaya Lakshmi, *née* **Swarup Kumari Nehru** 1900–90 •*Indian politician and diplomat*• Born in Allahabad, the sister of **Jawaharlal Nehru**, she was educated privately. She entered government service in 1935 and was local government and health minister (1937–39), and as a member of the Opposition was imprisoned in 1940 and 1941 for her nationalist campaigns. Leader of the Indian United Nations delegation (1946–48, 1952–53), she also held several ambassadorial posts (1947–51). She became the first woman president of the UN General Assembly in 1953, and then Indian high commissioner in London (1954–61).

Pandulf, Cardinal d. 1226 •*Italian prelate*• Born in Rome, he was the commissioner sent by **Innocent III** to King **John** of England after his excommunication to receive his submission (1213). He returned to England as papal legate (1218–21), was made Bishop of Norwich in 1218, and exercised great authority during the minority of **Henry III** (1299–1321).

Paṇini c. 6th century BC •*Indian grammarian*• He was the author of the *Aṣṭadhyayi* ("Eight Lectures"), a grammar of Sanskrit comprising 4,000 aphoristic statements which provide the rules of word formation and, to a lesser extent, sentence structure. His work has been reckoned by many to be the finest grammar ever written, but it is composed in a very condensed style and has required extensive commentary. It forms the basis of all later Sanskrit grammars.

Pankhurst, Adela Constantia 1885–1961 •*English suffragist*• She was the youngest daughter of **Emmeline Pankhurst**. She became involved in the movement for women's suffrage, but disagreements with her mother prompted her to sail for Australia.

There she helped direct the socialist-feminist movement with **Vida Goldstein** of the Women's Political Association.

Pankhurst, Christabel Harriette 1880–1958 •*English suffragist*• She was the eldest daughter of **Emmeline Pankhurst**. The militant campaigning that Christabel undertook with **Annie Kenney** in 1905 resulted in their arrest and stimulated a wave of militant action throughout the country with large-scale imprisonment and force-feeding of suffragists. She encouraged such tactics until 1914, when her efforts were channeled into meetings and tours in support of World War I. With the end of the war in 1918 and the granting of the vote to women over the age of 30, Christabel turned to preaching on Christ's Second Coming. She edited *The Suffragette* from 1912 to 1920 and wrote her political memoirs, *Unshackled: The Story of How We Won the Vote* (1959), at the very end of her life.

Pankhurst, Emmeline, *née* **Goulden** 1857–1928 •*English suffragist*• She was born in Manchester. In 1879 she married Richard Marsden Pankhurst (d. 1898), a radical Manchester barrister who had been the author of the first women's suffrage bill in Britain and of the 1870 and 1882 Married Women's Property Acts. In 1889 she founded the Women's Franchise League, and in 1903, with her daughter **Christabel Pankhurst**, the Women's Social and Political Union (WSPU), which fought for women's suffrage with extreme militancy. In 1894 she won the right for married women to vote in local elections, though not for Westminster offices. She was frequently imprisoned and underwent hunger strikes and force-feeding. She later joined the Conservative Party. Her 40-year campaign reached a peak of success shortly before her death, when the Representation of the People Act of 1928 was finally passed, establishing voting equality for men and women. She had three daughters: **Christabel**, **Sylvia** and **Adela**.

“ ”

Women never took a single step forward without being pushed back first of all by their opponents.

1912 Speech, January 14, during a tour of Canada.

Pankhurst, (Estelle) Sylvia 1882–1960 •*English suffragist*• She was the second daughter of **Emmeline Pankhurst**. Scholarships enabled her to study at both the Manchester Municipal School of Art and the Royal College of Art in London; at the same time she worked in London's East End for the Women's Social and Political Union. However, her relations with the union deteriorated, and in 1913 she left the East End branch. An irrepressible campaigner, she wrote extensively, advocating not only woman suffrage but also Ethiopian independence, socialism, and international and domestic issues.

Pan Ku *See* **Ban Gu**

Paolozzi, Sir Eduardo Luigi 1924– •*Scottish sculptor and printmaker*• Born in Leith, Edinburgh, of Italian parentage, he studied at Edinburgh College of Art and at the Slade School in London. He has held many teaching posts (in London, Hamburg and California, among other places). His early collages were inspired by surrealism, and his use of magazine cuttings in works such as *I Was a Rich Man's Plaything* (1947, Tate Modern) made him a pioneer of pop art. In the 1960s he made large sculptures in brightly painted metal, for example *The City of the Circle and the Square* (1963, Tate Modern). Other works incorporate waste material, such as oil cans. From the late 1970s he received public commissions, as for the Tottenham Court Road Underground mosaics (exhibited at the Royal Academy in 1986).

Papadopoulos, George 1919–99 •*Greek soldier and politician*• Born in Eleochorion, Achaia, he underwent army training in the Middle East and fought in Albania against the Italians before the German occupation of Greece in World War II. He was a member of the resistance during the occupation. In 1967 he led a coup against the government of King **Constantine II** and established a virtual military dictatorship. In 1973, following the abolition of the monarchy, he became president under a new republican constitution, but before the year was out he was himself ousted in another military coup. In 1974 he was arrested, tried for high treason and convicted, but his death sentence was commuted.

Papandreou, Andreas George 1919–96 •*Greek politician*• The son of **George Papandreou**, he was born on the island of Chios and educated at Athens University Law School, Columbia and Harvard. He served for two years in the US Navy, but returned to Greece as director of the Center for Economic Research in Athens (1961–64). His political activities led to imprisonment and exile after the military coup led by **George Papadopoulos** in 1967. He returned to Greece in 1974 and founded the Pan-Hellenic Liberation Movement, which later became PASOK (the Pan-Hellenic Socialist Movement). He was leader of the Opposition from 1977. In 1981 he became Greece's first socialist prime minister. During his ministry inflation was reduced, and Greece benefited from its membership of the EEC. Reelected in 1985, in 1988 a heart operation and his association with a young former flight attendant (whom he married following his divorce) created speculation and scandal, and PASOK was defeated. He was brought to trial on corruption charges but cleared in 1992, and his party was returned to power in 1993.

Papandreou, George 1888–1968 •*Greek politician*• Born in Salonika, he became a lawyer and moved into politics in the early 1920s. A left-of-center republican, he held office in several administrations before the war, and in 1942 he escaped from Greece during the German occupation and returned in 1944 to head a coalition government. Suspected by the army because of his socialist credentials, he remained in office for only a few weeks. He remained an important political figure, founding the Center Union Party in 1961, and returning as prime minister (1963, 1964–65). A disagreement with the young king **Constantine II** in 1965 led to his resignation, and in 1967, when a coup established a military regime, he was placed under house arrest. His son, **Andreas Papandreou**, then carried forward his political beliefs.

Papanicolaou, George Nicholas 1883–1962 •*US physiologist and microscopic anatomist*• Born in Kimi, Greece, he received his MD from the University of Athens (1904) and a PhD from the University of Munich (1910). He moved to the US in 1913, becoming assistant in pathology at the New York Hospital and, in 1914, assistant in anatomy at Weill Medical College of Cornell University. He became Professor of Clinical Anatomy at Cornell in 1924 and was Emeritus Professor from 1949. He noticed that he could identify cancer cells from scrapings from the cervixes of women with cervical cancer, and subsequently pioneered the technique, now known as the Pap smear, of microscopical examination of exfoliated cells for the early detection of cervical and other forms of cancer.

Papen, Franz von 1879–1969 •*German politician*• Born in Werl, Westphalia, he was military attaché in Mexico and Washington, chief of staff with a Turkish army, and took to center party politics. As chancellor under **Paul Hindenburg** in 1932 he suppressed the Prussian socialist government, and as **Hitler**'s vice chancellor (1933–34), he signed a concordat with Rome. He was ambassador to Austria (1936–38) and Turkey (1939–44) and was taken prisoner in 1945. He stood trial at Nuremberg in 1946 but was acquitted.

Papp, Joseph, *originally* **Yosl Papirofsky** 1921–91 •*US stage director and producer*• Born in Brooklyn, New York, he studied acting and directing in Hollywood under the GI Bill, then returned to New York and founded the Shakespeare Workshop at the Emmanuel Presbyterian Church on the Lower East Side (1952). They started performing free shows during the summer in Central Park (1954), which became the New York Shakespeare Festival (1960). A permanent open-air theater, the Delacorte, was built in the park for the company in 1962. In 1967 Papp founded the Public Theater, an off-Broadway house that staged classics as well as new works such as *Hair* (1967) and *A Chorus Line* (1975). He was director of the theaters at the Lincoln Center (1973–78).

Pappus of Alexandria 4th century AD •*Greek mathematician*• He wrote a mathematical *Collection* covering a wide range of geometrical problems, some of which contributed to the development of modern projective geometry. The work was of great importance for the historical understanding of Greek mathematics, covering the curves of a circle, the generalization of **Pythagoras**'s theorem to triangles that are not right-angled, and offering commentaries on **Euclid**'s *Elements* and **Ptolemy**'s *Almagest*.

Paracelsus, *real name* **Philippus Aureolus Theophrastus Bombastus von Hohenheim** 1493–1541 •*German alchemist and physician*• He was born in Einsieden, Switzerland. His name referred to the celebrated Roman physician **Celsus** and meant "beyond" or "better than" Celsus. He is said to have graduated in Vienna and taken his doctorate in Ferrara. He then spent many years exploring Europe, Russia and the Middle East, studying contemporary medical practices and the medical lore of the common people. In 1526 he was appointed town physician in Basel and lecturer in chemistry at the university. He raged against medical malpractices, criticized both the Catholic Church and the new Lutheran doctrines, and taught in German, not Latin. Having antagonized all the vested interests in the town, he had to flee (1528), and spent most of the rest of his life as an itinerant preacher and physician. However, his work became enormously influential, particularly through the emphasis he laid on observation and experiment and the need to assist—rather than hinder—natural processes. He stated that diseases had external causes and that every disease had its own characteristics, undertook careful studies of tuberculosis and silicosis, recognized that there was a connection between goiter and the minerals in drinking water and was the first to recognize congenital syphilis.

Pardo Bazán, Emilia, Condesa de 1851–1921 •*Spanish writer*• She was born in La Coruña, Spain, of an aristocratic Galician family, and later settled in Madrid. She was strongly influenced by the French naturalist writers, and this can be seen in her first novel, *Pascual Lopez* (1879). Her best-known books in this genre are *Los pazos de Ulloa* (1886, "The Manors of Ulloa") and *La madre naturaleza* (1887, "Mother Nature"), both set in the rural decadence of her native Galicia. Later novels such as *La quimera* (1905, "The Chimera") are unmistakably Modernist in atmosphere and psychology. Latterly she came under the influence of fin de siècle spiritualism and adopted more idealistic values. Besides her novels she published over 500 short stories, as well as poems, travel writing, critical and political works.

Paré, Ambroise c. 1510–90 •*French surgeon, "the father of modern surgery"*• He was born near Laval. In 1537 he joined the army as a surgeon, and became surgeon to **Henry II**, **Charles IX** and **Henry III**. He improved the treatment of gunshot wounds and substituted ligature of the arteries for cauterization with a red-hot iron after amputation. His *Cinq livres de chirurgie* (1562) and other writings exercised a great influence on surgery.

Paretsky, Sara 1947– •*US crime writer*• She was born in Eudora, Kansas, and educated at the University of Kansas and the University of Chicago. She worked for a research firm and as a marketing manager for an insurance company before becoming a full-time writer in 1986. That same year she cofounded Sisters in Crime, an organization devoted to promoting women crime writers. Her novels feature the feisty female detective V I Warshawski, who faces such diverse problems as toxic waste and antiabortionists. From these situations Paretsky looks at the nature of relationships between women, and at the line between the personal and professional. Her books include *Burn Marks* (1990), *Tunnel Vision* (1995) and *Hard Time* (1999).

Paris, Matthew c. 1200–59 •*English chronicler*• He entered the monastery of St Albans as a Benedictine monk in 1217 and succeeded **Roger of Wendover** as the abbey chronicler in 1236. He made two journeys to France and was sent on a mission to Norway on behalf of Pope **Innocent IV**. His *Chronica majora* is a revision of the earlier work of Roger of Wendover, with an additional 23 years of his own work, which establishes him as the finest chronicler of the 13th century. He also wrote biographies of abbots, and a book of *Additamenta*.

Park, Maud May, *née* **Wood** 1871–1955 •*US suffrage leader*• Born in Boston, Massachusetts, she was educated at Radcliffe College, and was cofounder and leader of Boston Equal Suffrage Association for Good Government. With Inez Haynes Gillmore (Irwin) (1873–1970) she founded the College Equal Suffrage League (from 1901), which aimed to involve young women in the fight for equality. An efficient, strong-minded campaigner, she helped to bring about the 19th Amendment (1920), which secured the vote for women. She became first president of the League of Women Voters (LWV) (1920–24).

Park, Mungo 1771–1806 •*Scottish explorer*• Born in Fowlshiels, in the Scottish Borders, he studied medicine at Edinburgh (1789–91). In 1795 his services were accepted by the African Association. After learning Mandingo at an English factory on the Gambia, he set off inland in December, finally reaching the Niger at Sego (Ségou) in July 1796. He pursued his way westward along its banks to Bammaku (Bamako), but fell ill and was eventually brought back to the factory by a slave trader. Park told his adventures in *Travels in the Interior of Africa* (1799), which at last made known the direction of flow of the Niger. He settled as a surgeon in Peebles, Scotland. In 1805 he undertook another journey to Africa but was drowned in a fight.

Park, Nick 1958– •*English animator*• Born in Lancaster, he studied communication arts at Sheffield, and animation at the National Film and Television School. Using painstaking stop-motion techniques and investing his plasticine characters with a rare fluidity and humanity, he made the short film *Creature Comforts* (1989), which won an Academy Award. Created over a period of six years, *A Grand Day Out* (1990) introduced the characters of inventor Wallace and his faithful dog Gromit. Subsequently they appeared in *The Wrong Trousers* (1993) and *A Close Shave* (1995), both of which also won Academy Awards and secured Park an international following.

Park Chung-Hee 1917–79 •*South Korean soldier and politician*• He was born in Sangmo-ri, in Kyongsang province, the son of a Buddhist farmer. He fought with the Japanese forces during World War II, but joined the South Korean army in 1946, becoming a major general by 1961, when he ousted the civilian government of Chang Myon in a bloodless coup. He was elected state president in December 1963, and embarked on a program of export-led industrial development based on strategic government planning and financial support, which attained "miracle" annual growth rates of 10 to 20 percent during the 1960s and 1970s. However, he ruled in an austere and authoritarian manner, imposing martial law in October 1972 and introducing restrictive "emergency measures" in May 1975. He was assassinated by the head of the Korean central intelligence service.

Parker, Alan 1944– •*English film director*• He was born in London and worked as a scriptwriter and on television before making his feature-film debut with the musical gangster pastiche *Bugsy Malone* (1976). This was followed by *Midnight Express* (1978), a brutal account of a young American incarcerated in a Turkish jail. He worked on *Birdy* (1985), *Angel Heart* (1987) and *Mississippi Burning* (1988) before moving into a lighter, more lyrical vein with the sentimental romance *Come See the Paradise* (1990) and the youth musical *The Commitments* (1991). Also a cartoonist and an irreverent critic of the British film establishment, he made the documentary, *A Turnip Head's Guide to the British Cinema*, in 1984. Later films include *Evita* (1996) and *Angela's Ashes* (1999).

Parker, Bonnie 1911–34 •*US thief and murderer*• Born in Rowena, Texas, she was the partner of **Clyde Barrow**. Despite their popular romantic image, they and their gang were responsible for a number of murders. The pair met in 1932, and shortly after, when Barrow was convicted of theft and sentenced to two years in jail, Parker smuggled a gun to him and he escaped. With their gang, Parker and Barrow continued to rob and murder until they were shot dead at a police roadblock in Louisiana. Their end was predicted by Parker in a poem, variously called *The Story of Bonnie and Clyde* and *The Story of Suicide Sal*.

Parker, Charlie (Charles Christopher), *known as* **Bird** 1920–55 •*US alto and tenor saxophonist, bandleader and composer*• Born in Kansas City, he learned to play baritone horn and alto saxophone while at school, frequenting the clubs and halls where jazz was played, and left school at 14 to practice and find casual work. In 1939 he went to New York, living by menial jobs but working out rhythmic and harmonic ideas which would form the basis of the bebop style. He worked from 1940 to 1942 with the Jay McShann Band, then joined the Earl Hines Band, where he began an important musical association with trumpeter **Dizzy Gillespie**. In 1945

Parker led the first of his influential bebop quintets, with Gillespie on trumpet. The harmonic and rhythmic advances of their music were rightly perceived as a sea change in jazz. Bebop was seen as a revolutionary style, although in retrospect it can be understood more as an evolution from the work of swing-era giants like **Lester Young**, **Coleman Hawkins** and **Charlie Christian**. His influence was not confined to saxophonists, but spread to players on every instrument. Despite addiction to heroin and alcohol and recurring mental illness, he continued to lead and record with the style-setting small groups of modern jazz, using trumpeters such as **Miles Davis** and pianists like Al Haig and Duke Jordan. His influence on the development of jazz cannot be overestimated, and many of his compositions, such as "Now's the Time" and "Ornithology," have become standard jazz works.

Parker, Dorothy, *née* **Rothschild** 1893–1967 •*US short-story writer and journalist*• She was born in West End, New Jersey, the daughter of a clothes salesman. Her mother died when she was five and her father remarried; Parker could barely contain her antipathy for her stepmother and refused to talk to her. She attended a private parochial school in New York City run by the Sisters of Charity, and Miss Dana's School in Morristown, New Jersey, where the typical girl was "equipped with a restfully uninquiring mind." She lasted only a few months, and her formal education ended in 1908 at the age of 14. She was a voracious reader, however, and in 1916 sold some of her poetry to the editor of *Vogue*, and was subsequently given an editorial position on the magazine, writing captions for fashion photographs and drawings. She then became drama critic of *Vanity Fair* (1917–20), where she met **Robert Benchley** and **Robert Sherwood** and formed with them the nucleus of the legendary Algonquin Hotel Round Table luncheon group in the 1920s. Famed for her spontaneous wit and acerbic criticism, she has had attributed to her many cruel wisecracks and backhanded compliments. She was at her most trenchant in stories and book reviews in the early issues (1927–33) of the *The New Yorker*, a magazine whose character she did much to form. Her short stories were collected in *Here Lies* (1939) and her reviews in *A Month of Saturdays* (1971). Her poems are included in *Not So Deep As a Well* (1930) and *Enough Rope* (1926), which became a bestseller. She also collaborated on several film scripts, including *A Star Is Born* (1937) and *The Little Foxes* (1941). Twice married (1917 and 1933), her public persona was not mirrored in her personal life. Both marriages foundered and there was a string of lacerating love affairs, abortive suicide attempts, abortions, debts and drinking bouts. She died alone in a Manhattan apartment with Troy, her poodle, at her side.

“ ”

Sorrow is tranquillity remembered in emotion.

1939 ***Here Lies**, "Sentiment."*

Parker, Matthew 1504–75 •*English prelate*• Born in Norwich, Norfolk, he became chaplain to Queen **Anne Boleyn** (1535), master of Corpus Christi College, Cambridge (1544), vice chancellor (1545) and dean of Lincoln. Deprived of his preferments by Queen **Mary I**, he was made Archbishop of Canterbury in 1559 by **Elizabeth I**. He took a middle road between Catholic and Puritan extremes, and revised the Thirty-Nine Articles of Anglican doctrine. Parker also made a revised translation of the Scriptures known as "the Bishops' Bible" (1572), and edited works by **Ælfric**, **Gildas**, **Asser**, **Matthew Paris**, **Thomas Walsingham** and **Giraldus Cambrensis**.

Parkes, Bessie Rayner 1829–1925 •*English feminist and editor*• Born into a Unitarian family, the great-granddaughter of **Joseph Priestley**, she formed a lifelong friendship with **Barbara Bodichon**, with whom she was a founding member of the women's movement. In 1858 Parkes bought the *Englishwoman's Journal*, which she edited with the help of Bodichon, **Emily Faithfull** and Jessie Boucherett, and the journal became the voice of the women's movement. In 1867 she married Louis Belloc, a French barrister, and became the mother of the future writers Marie Adelaide Belloc (1868–1947, later Mrs Lowndes) and **Hilaire Belloc**.

Parkes, Sir Henry 1815–96 •*Australian politician*• He was born near Kenilworth in Warwickshire, England. He fell under the influence of radical politics, and when his business failed he sailed in 1839 with his first wife to New South Wales, Australia. His ivory shop in Sydney was a focus of radical dissidents, and in 1850 he founded the *Empire* newspaper, which he edited until 1858. By 1854 he had become a member of the New South Wales (NSW) Legislative Council, and in the next 40 years he was rarely out of state parliament. He was NSW colonial secretary (1866–68), during which time he recruited, with the help of **Florence Nightingale**, the first trained nurses for the colony. He first became premier of NSW in 1872, a position he was to hold in five ministries for a total of 15 years. In the late 1880s he delivered his "Tenterfield Oration," which gave the necessary impetus to federalism. This led in 1891 to a meeting of the Australian colonies, which drafted a constitution, but Parkes, "the Father of Australian Federation," died before the establishment of the Commonwealth of Australia.

Parkinson, Cecil Edward Parkinson, Baron 1932– •*English Conservative politician*• He was born in Carnforth, Lancashire, and educated at the Royal Lancaster Grammar School and Emmanuel College, Cambridge. He became a Member of Parliament in 1970. In 1979 he was made a junior minister at the Department of Trade by **Margaret Thatcher** and, two years later, chairman of the Conservative Party. He became prominent as a close confidant of the prime minister and a member of her inner Cabinet during the Falklands War. After his successful direction of the 1983 general election campaign, his political future seemed secure until the publicity about an affair with his former secretary, Sara Keays, which had resulted in her pregnancy, forced his resignation. After a period on the back benches, he returned to the Cabinet as secretary of state for energy in 1987, and became secretary of state for transport in 1989. He surrendered office in the Cabinet reshuffle that followed **John Major**'s succession to the premiership in 1990. In 1992 he retired from politics and was made a life peer.

Parkinson, Cyril Northcote 1909–93 •*English political scientist, historian and writer*• He graduated from Emmanuel College, Cambridge, of which he became a Fellow in 1935. Professor of History at the University of Malaya (1950–58), and visiting professor at Harvard (1958), Illinois and California (1959–60), he wrote many works on historical, political and economic subjects, but achieved wider renown with his seriocomic tilt at bureaucratic malpractices, *Parkinson's Law, the Pursuit of Progress* (1957). Parkinson's Law—that work expands to fill the time available for its completion, and subordinates multiply at a fixed rate, regardless of the amount of work produced—has passed into the language.

Parkinson, James 1755–1824 •*English physician and amateur paleontologist*• In 1817 he gave the first description of paralysis agitans, or "Parkinson's disease" (shaking palsy, a disease characterized by shaking hands and rigidity of muscles). He had already (1812) described appendicitis and perforation, and was the first to recognize the latter condition as a cause of death.

Parkinson, Norman, *originally* **Ronald William Parkinson Smith** 1913–90 •*English photographer*• Born in London and educated at Westminster School, he opened his own studio in 1934 and became one of Great Britain's best-known portrait and fashion photographers. His style was primarily romantic, but some of his later portraits of the famous gave a clear insight into the sitter's personality. In the 1950s his advertising work took him all over the world, and he settled in Tobago in 1963.

Parkman, Francis 1823–93 •*US historian*• Born in Boston, he graduated from Harvard in 1844 and earned a law degree two years later. He then set out on a journey to the Western frontier, which he chronicled in his first book, *The California and Oregon Trail* (1849). Though hampered by a nervous disorder and near blindness, he became one of the most eminent US historians and an authority on the rise and fall of the French domination in America. His works include *The Pioneers of France in the New World* (1865), *La Salle and the Great West* (1869), *Frontenac and New France* (1877), *A Half-Century of Conflict* (1893) and *Montcalm and Wolfe* (1884).

Parks, Rosa Lee, *née* **McCauley** 1913– •*US civil rights activist*• Born in Tuskegee, Alabama, she worked as a seamstress and housekeeper and served as a secretary of the Montgomery,

Alabama, branch of the National Association for the Advancement of Colored People (NAACP) from 1943 to 1956. In December 1955 she was arrested and fined when she refused to give up her seat on a bus to a white man in Montgomery, choosing instead to disobey the segregated seating policies common in the South. This incident prompted **Martin Luther King, Jr**, and others to organize a citywide boycott of the bus company and file a federal suit challenging the constitutionality of the segregation laws. The boycott continued until the following year, when the Supreme Court declared the city's segregated seating policies unconstitutional.

Parmenides of Elea c. 515–c. 445 BC •*Greek philosopher*• Born in Southern Italy, he founded the Eleatic school (which included his pupils **Zeno** and **Melissus**). Little is known of his life, but he produced a remarkable philosophical treatise, *On Nature*, written in hexameter verse, which represents a radical departure from the cosmologies of his Ionian predecessors such as **Thales** and **Anaximander**. The first part is a sustained deductive argument about the nature of being, which argues for the impossibility of motion, plurality and change. He contrasts this "way of truth" with the "way of seeming" (apparently a more traditional cosmology) in the second part of the poem.

Parmigiano or **Parmigianino**, *properly* **Girolamo Francesco Maria Mazzola** 1503–40 •*Italian painter of the Lombard school*• Born in Parma, he first worked as a painter there, especially on the frescoes in San Giovanni Evangelista, but after 1523 he worked in Rome, whence he fled to Bologna when the city was sacked in 1527. At Bologna he painted his famous Madonna altarpiece for the nuns of St Margaret before returning to Parma in 1531. His work there includes *Madonna of the Long Neck* (c. 1535, Uffizi, Florence). Other well-known works include his *Vision of St Jerome* and *Self-Portrait in a Convex Mirror.*

Parnell, Charles Stewart 1846–91 •*Irish politician*• Born in Avondale, County Wicklow, he was the grandson of Sir John Parnell (1744–1801), who had been chancellor of the Irish Exchequer. He studied for four years at Magdalene College, Cambridge, but took no degree. He became high sheriff of County Wicklow (1874), and in 1875 he became a Member of Parliament supporting Home Rule. In 1877–78 he gained great popularity in Ireland with his audacious and deliberate obstruction of parliamentary tactics. In 1878 he devoted himself to agrarian agitation and was elected president of the Irish National Land League. In 1880 he became chairman of the Irish Parliamentary Party. The Land League was later declared illegal, and was revived in 1884 as the National League, with Parnell as president. In 1886, Parnell and his 85 fellow Irish Members of Parliament used their vote to help introduce **William Gladstone**'s Home Rule Bill, but failed to secure the legislation because of defections by Liberal Members of Parliament. When Salisbury took the issue to the country later the same year, he was returned with a Unionist majority of more than 100, causing Parnell to form an alliance with Gladstone. In 1889, Parnell was cleared of complicity in the murder of English politician Thomas Henry Burke (1829–82) and other organized outrages following the publication in *The Times* of letters purportedly written by him. In 1890 he was cited as co-respondent in a divorce case brought by Captain William Henry O'Shea (1840–1905) against his wife Katherine, and a decree was granted with costs against Parnell. The Irish members met to consider his position a week later, and eventually elected Justin McCarthy chairman in his place. Parnell also lost support in Ireland. He died suddenly in Brighton, five months after his marriage to Katherine O'Shea.

Parr, Catherine *See* **Catherine Parr**

Parr, Thomas, *known as* **Old Parr** c. 1483–1635 •*English centenarian*• He was born, according to tradition, in 1483. He was a Shropshire farm servant, and when 120 years old married his second wife, and till his 130th year performed all his usual work. In his 152nd year his fame had reached London, and he was induced to journey there to see **Charles I**, where he was treated at court so royally that he died. John Taylor (1580–1653), the "Water-poet," wrote his biography.

Parry, Sir (Charles) Hubert (Hastings) 1848–1918 •*English composer*• Born in Bournemouth, Hampshire, he was educated at Eton and Oxford. He became a professor at the Royal College of Music in 1883, and Professor of Music at Oxford in 1900. The composer of three oratorios, five symphonies, an opera, and many other works, his best-known works are the anthem "I Was Glad" (1902), and his unison chorus "Jerusalem" (1916). He published *Evolution of the Art of Music* (1896), a biography of **J S Bach** (1909) and *The Oxford History of Music*, vol 3 (1907).

Parsons, Sir Charles Algernon 1854–1931 •*Irish engineer*• Born in London, fourth son of the 3rd Earl of Rosse, he was educated at Dublin and Cambridge. In 1884 he developed the high-speed steam turbine, and built the first turbine-driven steamship, the *Turbinia*, in 1897. This caused a sensation at Queen Victoria's Diamond Jubilee Naval Review with its top speed of 35 knots, much faster than any other ship at that time. He was knighted in 1911, and was the first engineer to be admitted to the Order of Merit (1927).

Parsons, Louella Oettinger 1881–1972 •*US gossip columnist*• She was born in Freeport, Illinois. In 1910, she became a reporter for the *Chicago Tribune* and also wrote screenplays for silent films, publishing the book *How to Write for the Movies* in 1915. In New York from 1919 and Hollywood from 1926, she rose to prominence writing a daily syndicated Hollywood movie star gossip column. Feared within the film community for her influence, in time she could make or break a career. She also hosted a number of radio shows, including *Hollywood Hotel* (1934–38), and wrote the books *The Gay Illiterate* (1944) and *Tell It to Louella* (1961). She retired in 1964.

Parton, Dolly 1946– •*US country singer, songwriter and actress*• Born in Sevier County, Tennessee, the fourth of 12 children, she was a child television star. Her breakthrough came when she joined singer Porter Wagoner (1927–) on his television show in 1967. A string of hits followed, but their duo ended acrimoniously in 1974. She had her first big solo hit in 1970, and went on to become an international celebrity well beyond country music, as a pop singer, songwriter (her "I Will Always Love You" became a record-breaking hit for **Whitney Houston**) and actress, and made the most of her physical endowments. She moved back into country music settings in the 1990s. Her marriage to builder Carl Dean has lasted since 1966, and remains intensely private.

Partridge, Eric Honeywood 1894–1979 •*British lexicographer*• Born near Gisborne in New Zealand and educated at the University of Queensland and Oxford University, he was elected Queensland Traveling Fellow at Oxford after World War I. He was a lecturer at the Universities of Manchester and London (1925–27), wrote on French and English literature, and later made a specialized study of slang and colloquial language. His works in this field include the standard *Dictionary of Slang and Unconventional English* (1937) and *A Dictionary of the Underworld, British and American* (1950).

Pascal, Blaise 1623–62 •*French mathematician, physicist, theologian and man of letters*• He was born in Clermont-Ferrand, the son of the local president of the court of exchequer. When his mother died, the family moved to Paris (1630), where his father, a considerable mathematician, educated his children. By the age of 11 Pascal had worked out for himself in secret the first 23 propositions of **Euclid**, calling straight lines "bars" and circles "rounds." Inspired by the work of **Girard Desargues**, at 16 he published an essay on conics which **René Descartes** refused to believe was the work of a youth. Father and son collaborated on experiments to confirm **Evangelista Torricelli**'s theory, unpalatable to the schoolmen, that nature does not, after all, abhor a vacuum. They carried up to the Puy de Dôme two glass tubes containing mercury, inverted in a bath of mercury, and noted the fall of the mercury columns with increased altitude. This led to the invention of the barometer, the hydraulic press and the syringe. In 1647, he patented a calculating machine, later simplified by **Gottfried Leibniz**, built to assist his father in his accounts. In 1651 Pascal's father died, his sister, Jacqueline, entered the Jansenist convent at Port-Royal, and Pascal divided his time between mathematics and socializing. His correspondence with **Pierre de Fermat** in 1654 laid the foundations of probability theory. That year he had the first of two religious revelations, according to a note found sewn into his clothes. He joined his sister in her retreat, gave up mathematics and society almost completely and joined battle for the Jansenists against the Jesuits of the Sorbonne who had publicly denounced **Antoine Arnauld**, the Jansenist theologian and mathematician, as a heretic. In 18 anonymous pamphlets, the *Lettres provinciales* (1656–57), Pascal attacked the Jesuits' meaningless jargon, casuistry and moral laxity. This failed to save Arnauld, but undermined forever Jesuit authority and prestige. In 1658 Pascal's papers on the area of the cycloid heralded the invention of integral calculus. Notes for a casebook of Christian truths were discovered after his death and published as the *Pensées* in 1669.

“ ”

Le nez de Cléopâtre: s'il eût été plus court, toute la face de la terre aurait changé.
Cleopatra's nose: if it had been shorter the whole face of the earth would have been different.
c. 1654–62 ***Pensées****, no. 162 (translated by A Krailsheimer).*

Pasha, Arabi *See* **Ahmed Arabi**

Pasha, Nouri Said *See* **Es-Sa'id, Nuri**

Pasić, Nicola c. 1846–1926 •*Serbian statesman*• Born in Zajecar, he was condemned to death in 1883 for his part in the "Revolution of Zajecar," a plot against King Milan, but escaped to Austria, and on the accession of King **Peter I** became prime minister of Serbia (1891–92, 1904–05, 1906, and from 1908 almost continuously until 1918). He was instrumental in the creation of Yugoslavia, and was prime minister from 1921 to 1924 and 1924 to 1926.

Pasionaria, La *See* **Ibárruri Gómez, Dolores**

Pasmore, (Edwin John) Victor 1908–98 •*English artist*• Born in Chelsham, Warlingham, Surrey, he worked for the London County Council, attending evening classes at the Central School of Art, and was one of the founders of the Euston Road School of realist painters in London (1937). His *The Quiet River: The Thames at Chiswick* (1944, Tate Britain) is typical of this period. He became an art teacher and perfected a delicate style of landscape painting in which he was already turning from realism to a highly abstract style, culminating in works such as *Relief Construction in White, Black, Red and Maroon* (1957). In 1960 he exhibited at the Venice Biennale, and in 1966 took a house in Malta, reintroducing color and freer forms into his work.

Pasolini, Pier Paolo 1922–75 •*Italian critic, poet, novelist, film director and screenwriter*• Born and educated in Bologna, most of his childhood was spent in Casara della Delizia, in his mother's birthplace of Friuli. He became a Marxist following World War II, moved to Rome, wrote novels and also worked as a film scriptwriter and actor. Unheard of until the 1940s, he became notorious in the 1950s, principally through the publication of the first two parts of a projected trilogy, *Ragazzi di vita* (1955, Eng trans *The Ragazzi*, 1968) and *Una vita violenta* (1959, Eng trans *A Violent Life*, 1968). From 1961 he devoted himself to directing films, many based on literary sources, including *Il Vangelo secondo Matteo* (1964, *The Gospel According to Saint Matthew*), *Il decamerone* (1971, *The Decameron*) and *Salò, o, Le centoventi giornate di Sodoma* (1975, *Salo—The 120 Days of Sodom*). He was murdered during a sexual encounter with another man.

Passfield, Baron *See* **Webb, Sidney James**

Passmore, George *See* **Gilbert and George**

Pasternak, Boris Leonidovich 1890–1960 •*Russian lyric poet, novelist and translator*• Born in Moscow, the son of Leonid Pasternak (1862–1945), painter and illustrator of **Tolstoy**'s works, he studied law, then musical composition, abandoning both for philosophy at Marburg, Germany. A factory worker during World War I, and a librarian after it, he published three collections of verse between 1917 and 1923, and under the influence of his friend **Vladimir Mayakovsky** wrote the political poems on the Bolshevik uprising. Among his outstanding short stories are *Detstvo Lyuvers* (1922, Eng trans *The Childhood of Luvers*, 1945) and *Provest'* (1934, Eng trans *The Last Summer*, 1959), in which his imagery is at its freshest and most unexpected. Under **Stalin**, Pasternak became the official translator into Russian of **Shakespeare**, **Paul Verlaine**, **Goethe** and Heinrich von Kleist (1777–1811), but with **Khrushchev**'s misleading political "thaw," he caused an upheaval with his first novel, *Doktor Zhivago* (1957, Eng trans *Doctor Zhivago*, 1958), banned in Russia. A fragmentary, poet's novel, it describes with intense feeling the Russian revolution as it impinged upon one individual, who was both doctor and poet. Expelled by the Soviet Writers' Union, Pasternak had to take the unprecedented step of refusing the 1958 Nobel Prize for literature.

Pasteur, Louis 1822–95 •*French chemist*• Born in Dôle, he studied at Besançon and at the École Normale Supérieure, and held academic posts at Strasbourg, Lille and Paris, where in 1867 he became Professor of Chemistry at the Sorbonne. His principal work was in discovering that fermentations are essentially due to organisms, not spontaneous generation. He greatly extended **Theodor Schwann**'s research on putrefaction, and gave valuable rules for making vinegar and preventing wine disease, introducing in this work the technique of pasteurization, a mild and short heat treatment to destroy pathogenic bacteria. After 1865 his research into silkworm disease revived the silk industry in southern France; he also investigated injurious growths in beer, splenic fever, and fowl cholera. His germ theory of disease maintained that disease was communicable through the spread of microorganisms, the virulence of which could be reduced by exposure to air, by variety of culture, or by transmission through various animals. He demonstrated that sheep and cows vaccinated with the weakened bacilli of anthrax were protected from the harmful results of subsequent inoculation with the virulent bacterium; by the culture of antitoxic reagents, the prophylactic treatment of diphtheria, tubercular disease, cholera, yellow fever and plague was also found effective. In 1885 he introduced a similar treatment for hydrophobia (rabies). The Pasteur Institute, of which he became first director, was founded in 1888.

Patañjali fl. 2nd century BC •*Indian founder of the Yoga system of Hindu philosophy*• The four books of his *Yoga Sutra*, extant versions dating from the 3rd century AD but drawing on earlier traditions, expound the moral and physical disciplines considered necessary for attaining absolute freedom of the self. He is not to be confused, according to modern scholarship, with Patañjali the Grammarian (c. 140 BC), who wrote a substantial commentary on *Aṣṭadhyayi* (4th century BC), the Sanskrit grammar of **Paṇini**.

Pater, Walter Horatio 1839–94 •*English critic and essayist*• Born in London, he was educated at King's School, Canterbury, and Queen's College, Oxford, and became a Fellow of Brasenose College. His *Studies in the History of the Renaissance* (1873) displays the influence of the Pre-Raphaelites with whom he associated. His philosophic romance, *Marius the Epicurean* (1885), appealed to a wider audience. His *Imaginary Portraits* (1887) and *Appreciations* (1889), followed by *Plato and Platonism* (1893), established his position as a critic, but already people were beginning to talk of his influence as being unhealthy, in the sense that he advocated a cultivated hedonism. His influence on Oxford, however, was profound.

Paterson, A(ndrew) B(arton), *also called* **Banjo** 1864–1941 •*Australian bush poet and balladeer*• Born at Narrambla in Orange, New South Wales, he is best known for his verse "Waltzing Matilda," which he set to an old Scottish melody. It became the unofficial national anthem of Australia. Under the pseudonym "The Banjo" (the name of a bush racehorse), he contributed verse such as *Clancy of the Overflow* (1889), and *The Man From Snowy River* (1890) to the Sydney periodical the *Bulletin*. His verses were collected as *The Man From Snowy River, and Other Verses* (1895), followed by *Rio Grande's Last Race, and Other Verses* (1902), and his popular bush character appeared in *Saltbush Bill JP, and Other Verses* in 1917.

Pathé, Charles 1863–1957 •*French film pioneer*• Born in Paris, he founded the company Pathé Frères with his three brothers (1896), and introduced the newsreel to France (1909), the US (1910) and Great Britain, and the screen magazine *Pathé Pictorial*. The company developed Pathécolor, a hand-coloring stencil process, and became one of the world's largest film production organizations. In 1949 the company became Associated British Pathé Ltd.

Patmore, Coventry Kersey Dighton 1823–96 •*English poet*• Born in Woodford, Essex, he was an assistant librarian at the British Museum and was associated with the Pre-Raphaelite Brotherhood, with whom his verse was popular. His best-known work is *The Angel in the House* (4 vols, 1854), a poetic treatment of married love. After the death of his first wife in 1862, he converted to Roman Catholicism and from then his works had mystical or religious themes as in *The Rod, the Root, and the Flower* (1895).

“ ”

Those who know God know that it is quite a mistake to suppose that there are only five senses.

1895 ***The Rod, the Root, and the Flower**, "Aurea Dicta," no. 142.*

Paton, Alan 1903–88 •*South African writer and educator*• Born in Pietermaritzburg, he was educated at the University of Natal, and spent ten years as a schoolteacher. From 1935 to 1948 he was principal of the Diepkloof Reformatory for young offenders, where he became known for the success of his enlightened methods. From his deep concern with the racial problem in South Africa sprang the novel *Cry, the Beloved Country* (1948). His other novels were *Too Late the Phalarope* (1953) and *Ah, But Your Land Is Beautiful* (1981). Other writings include *Hope for South Africa* (1958), a political study written from the Liberal standpoint, and *Apartheid and the Archbishop* (1973). He was national president of the South African Liberal Party from 1953 to 1960.

Patou, Jean 1880–1936 •*French fashion designer*• He was born in Normandy, the son of a prosperous tanner, and he joined an uncle who dealt in furs in 1907. In 1912 he opened Maison Parry in Paris, and in 1913 sold his collection outright to an American buyer. After war service he successfully opened again as a couturier in 1919. He was noted for his designs for sports stars, actresses and society ladies, and for his perfume "Joy."

Patrick, St 5th century •*Christian apostle and patron saint of Ireland*• Born perhaps in South Wales, less probably at Boulogne-sur-Mer, or Kilpatrick near Dumbarton, his own Celtic name or nickname was Succat. According to legend, he was sold by pirates to an Antrim chief called Milchu when he was 15. After six years he escaped and went to France, where he became a monk. He was consecrated a bishop at 45, and in AD 432 it is thought he was sent by Pope **Celestine** as a missionary to Ireland. He converted his old master Milchu, and other chiefs, and after 20 years spent in missionary work, he fixed his see at Armagh (454). The only certainly authentic literary remains of the saint are his spiritual autobiography, *Confession*, and a letter addressed to Coroticus, a British chieftain who had taken some Irish Christians as slaves. His feast day is March 17.

Patten, Brian 1946– •*English poet and playwright*• He was born in Liverpool, Merseyside, and educated at Sefton Park Secondary, after which he worked as a reporter. With **Roger McGough** and **Adrian Henri** he shared the outstandingly successful *Penguin Modern Poets 10* (1967). Some of his best work can be found in his early poems, gathered in *Walking Out: The Early Poems of Brian Patten* (1970), and in the fine sequence *Notes to the Hurrying Man* (1969). He is never academically sententious; the bizarrely titled *The Eminent Professors and the Nature of Poetry as Enacted Out by Members of the Poetry Seminar One Rainy Evening* (1972) neatly captures his view of the literary world's pretensions. Later volumes include *Love Poems* (1981), *Storm Damage* (1988) and *Grinning Jack* (1990). He has also written for the theater and for children.

Patten, Chris(topher Francis) 1944– •*English Conservative politician*• After Balliol College, Oxford, he joined the Conservative Party's research department, and then, under **Edward Heath**, worked in the Cabinet and home offices. In opposition he was director of the research department (1974–79) and when the Conservatives returned to power in 1979, under **Margaret Thatcher**, he held a number of non-Cabinet posts, culminating in that of minister for overseas development in 1986. He replaced **Nicholas Ridley** as secretary of state for the environment in 1989. As chairman of the Conservative Party (1990–92) he organized a successful 1992 general election campaign but was not reelected. In the same year he was made governor of Hong Kong (1992–97). Since 1999 he has been a member of the European Commission.

Patterson, P(ercival) J(ames) 1935– •*Jamaican statesman and lawyer*• He was born in St Andrew and educated at the University of the West Indies and London School of Economics, being called to the bar in 1963. Having joined the People's National Party (PNP) in 1958, he was nominated to the Senate in 1967 and held various government posts before becoming prime minister when **Michael Norman Manley** resigned in 1992; he was elected to his first full term in 1993, and was reelected in 1997.

Patti, Adelina, *later* **Adelina Nicolini** 1843–1919 •*Italian soprano*• Born in Madrid, the daughter of a Sicilian tenor, she sang in New York at the age of seven, and made her debut there (1859). Her voice was an unusually high, rich, ringing soprano. In 1866 she married the Marquis de Caux, and, on her divorce in 1886, the Breton tenor Ernesto Nicolini (1834–98), followed in 1899 by the Swedish Baron Cederström. Her sister Carlotta (1840–89) was also a fine soprano.

Patton, George Smith, *known as* **Old Blood and Guts** 1885–1945 •*US soldier*• Born in San Gabriel, California, he graduated from West Point in 1909. In World War I he commanded a tank brigade on the Western Front. A major general by 1941, he became one of the most daring US combat commanders in World War II. He led the first US troops to fight in North Africa, playing a key role in the Allied invasion. In 1943 he commanded the US 7th Army in the Sicilian campaign. At the head of the 3rd Army, he swept across France and Germany in 1944–45 and reached the Czech frontier. He was fatally injured in a motor accident near Mannheim in occupied Germany.

Paul, St, *also known as* **Saul of Tarsus** d. c. 64/68 AD •*Christian missionary and martyr*• Born of Jewish parents at Tarsus in Cilicia, he was brought up to be a rabbi by Gamaliel at Jerusalem. A strenuous Pharisee, he took an active part in the persecution of Christians. He was on his way to Damascus on this mission when a vision of **Jesus** converted him into a fervent adherent of the new faith. After three years spent mainly in Damascus and partly in Arabia, he visited Jerusalem again, where Barnabas persuaded the Apostles of the genuineness of his conversion. He began to preach, but opposition to him was strong and he was compelled to live in retirement in Tarsus. After ten years, he was brought to Antioch by Barnabas, and began the first of three missionary journeys. On his return, he encountered controversy over the manner in which Gentiles and Jews were to be admitted to the Christian Church; this dispute led to the first apostolic council in Jerusalem (c. 49 or 50). Paul opposed **Peter** during the debate, and once the question was finally settled by a compromise, he addressed himself mainly to the Gentiles. Thousands of people became Christians through Paul's teaching. He returned to Jerusalem after his third missionary journey, but the fanaticism of the Jews against him led to disturbances, whereupon he was brought to Caesarea to be tried. Paul, invoking his right as a Roman citizen, "appealed to Caesar," and in the spring of 56 arrived in Rome, where he spent two years as a prisoner in his own hired house. He was executed under **Nero**, probably at the end of the two years' captivity, although according to tradition he escaped to visit Spain and other countries. The ancient Church recognized 13 of the New Testament Epistles as Paul's.

Paul, St Vincent de *See* **Vincent de Paul, St**

Paul 1754–1801 •*Emperor of Russia*• Born in St Petersburg, the second son of **Peter III** and **Catherine II (the Great)**, he succeeded his mother in 1796. His father's murder and his mother's neglect had exerted an unfortunate influence on his character. His earliest measures were the exile of the murderers and the pardon of Polish prisoners, including **Tadeusz Kościuszko**, but he soon revealed his violent temper, capriciousness and inconsistency. He suddenly declared for the allies against France, and sent an army of 56,000 men under Count **Suvorov** into Italy (1799). He sent a second army to cooperate with the Austrians, retired from the alliance, quarreled with England, and entered into close alliance with **Napoleon I**. After his convention with Sweden and Denmark, England sent a fleet into the Baltic under Lord **Nelson** to dissolve the coalition (1801). His own officers conspired to compel him to abdicate, and in a scuffle he was strangled.

Paul I 1901–64 •*King of Greece*• The son of **Constantine I**, brother and successor of **George II**, he was born in Athens and educated at the naval academy there. He was in exile with his father during his first deposition (1917–20). In 1922 he served with the Greek navy in the campaign against the Turks, but went into exile again (1923) when his brother George was deposed and a republic was proclaimed. In 1935 he returned to Greece with his brother, as Crown Prince. At the start of World War II he served with the Greek general staff in the Albanian campaign, and was a member of the Greek government in exile in London for the rest of the war. He succeeded to the throne on the death of his brother (1947), and his reign was seen as a symbol of Greek postwar recovery. He was succeeded by his son **Constantine II**.

Paul III, *originally* **Alessandro Farnese** 1468–1549 •*Italian pope*• Born in Canino, in the Papal States, he was made cardinal-deacon in 1493, and was elected pope in 1534. The first of the popes of the Counter Reformation, he issued the bull of excommunication and deposition against **Henry VIII** of England in 1538, and also the bull instituting the Order of the Jesuits in 1540. He summoned the Council of Trent in 1545.

Paul VI, *originally* **Giovanni Battista Montini** 1897–1978 •*Italian pope*• Born in Concesio, he graduated from the Gregorian University of Rome, was ordained in 1920, and entered the Vatican diplomatic service, where he remained until 1944. He was then made Archbishop of Milan, in which important diocese he became known for his liberal views. Made a cardinal in 1958, he was elected pope on the death of **John XXIII** in 1963, many of whose opinions he shared. He initiated important advances in the move toward Christian unity.

Paul, Alice 1885–1977 •*US feminist*• Born into a Quaker family in Moorestown, New Jersey, she was educated at Swarthmore College and at the University of Pennsylvania. Involved with the British suffragist movement while living in England, she became, on her return to the US, the leader of the National American Woman Suffrage Association (NAWSA) congressional committee. Although her tactics did much to publicize the cause, they proved too militant for her fellow NAWSA members, and she left the organization, founding and becoming leader of the National Women's Party. She used civil disobedience, hunger strikes, and pickets in the struggle to gain the vote for women, and after this goal was realized in the 19th Amendment (1920), continued to work for women's rights.

Paul, Jean *See* **Richter, Johann Paul Friedrich**

Pauli, Wolfgang 1900–58 •*Austrian-Swiss theoretical physicist and Nobel Prize winner*• Born in Vienna, he studied at the University of Munich, then worked at the University of Göttingen (1921–22) and with **Niels Bohr** at his institute in Copenhagen (1922–23) before becoming professor at the University of Hamburg (1923–28). In 1928 he moved to Zurich, became a Swiss citizen and was given a professorship at the Federal Institute of Technology. Pauli demonstrated that a fourth spin quantum number was required to describe the state of an atomic electron, and went on to formulate the Pauli exclusion principle (1924), which states that no two electrons in an atom can exist in exactly the same state, with the same quantum numbers. This earned him the 1945 Nobel Prize for physics. He suggested the existence of a low-mass neutral particle (1931), later discovered as the neutrino, and his studies in the early 1950s of quantum interactions paved the way for **Tsung-Dao Lee** and **Chen Ning Yang**'s discovery of parity nonconservation in 1956. In 1946 he became a naturalized US citizen.

Paulin, Tom 1949– •*English poet and critic*• Born in Leeds, Yorkshire, he grew up in Belfast and became one of Northern Ireland's leading writers. He won acclaim with his first book of poetry *A State of Justice* (1977), and subsequent publications have included *The Strange Museum* (1980), *Liberty Tree* (1983), *Fivemiletown* (1987), *Walking a Line* (1994), *The Wind Dog* (1999) and *The Invasion Handbook* (2001). He has also written for the stage and television and is well known as an arts pundit in the media.

Pauling, Linus Carl 1901–94 •*US chemist and Nobel Prize winner*• Born in Portland, Oregon, he was educated at Oregon State University and the California Institute of Technology (Caltech). After postdoctoral work in Munich, Zurich and Copenhagen, he was on the chemistry faculty at Caltech from 1927 to 1963, as full professor from 1931. His early work on crystal structures (1928) led to their rationalization in terms of ionic radii and greatly illuminated mineral chemistry. He then turned to the quantum-mechanical treatment of the chemical bond and made many important contributions, including the concept of the hybridization of orbitals, central to understanding the shapes of molecules. This period of his work generated two influential books: *Introduction to Quantum Mechanics* (1935, with E Bright Wilson) and *The Nature of the Chemical Bond* (1939). His interest in complex molecular structures led him into work in biology and medicine; he studied the structures of proteins and antibodies, and investigated the nature of serological reactions and the chemical basis of hereditary disease. He advocated the use of vitamin C in combating a wide range of diseases and infections, and his views sometimes generated controversy. He was also a controversial figure for his work in the peace movement and his criticism of nuclear deterrence policy. Pauling was awarded the Nobel Prize for chemistry in 1954 and the Nobel Peace Prize in 1962.

“ ”

Science is a search for truth—it is not a game in which one tries to best his opponent, to do harm to others.

1958 ***No More War.***

Paulinus d. 644 •*Roman Christian*• Born in Rome, he was a missionary to England in 601 with **Augustine of Canterbury**. Consecrated a bishop in 625, he went north with Princess Æthelburgh of Kent on her marriage to the pagan King **Edwin** of Northumbria. He baptized Edwin and all his court in York at Easter, 627, and was made Bishop, and later the first Archbishop of York (633). Edwin's murder by the pagan **Penda** of Mercia and **Cadwallon** of Wales in 633 drove him back to Kent, where he was appointed Bishop of Rochester.

Paulinus of Nola, St, *also called* **Pontius Meropius Anicius Paulinus** AD 353–431 •*French prelate*• Born in Bordeaux, he was baptized a Christian (c. 389 AD) and settled in Nola in Italy, where he became known for his charity and his rigid asceticism. He was consecrated Bishop of Nola (c. 409). He is remembered for his *Carmina* and for his epistles to **Augustine of Hippo**, **Jerome**, Sulpicius Severus, and Ausonius.

Paulinus, Pontius Meropius Anicius *See* **Paulinus of Nola, St**

Paulus, Friedrich 1890–1957 •*German soldier and tank specialist*• As commander of the 6th Army he capitulated to the Russians with the remnants of his army at the siege of Stalingrad in February 1943. Released from captivity in 1953, he became a lecturer on military affairs under the East German communist government.

Pausanias 5th century BC •*Spartan soldier and regent*• The nephew of **Leonidas**, he commanded the Greek forces at Plataea (479 BC), where the Persians were routed. He then compelled the Thebans to surrender the chiefs of the Persian party. Capturing the Cyprian cities and Byzantium (478), he negotiated with **Xerxes I** in the hope of becoming ruler under him of all Greece, and was twice recalled to Sparta for treachery. He tried to stir up the helots, was betrayed, and fled to a temple of Athena on the Spartan acropolis, where he was walled up and only taken out when dying of hunger (c. 470).

Pausanias 2nd century AD •*Greek geographer and historian*• Born probably in Lydia, he traveled through almost all Greece, Macedonia and Italy, and through part of Asia and Africa. From his observations and research he composed an *Itinerary* of Greece, describing the different parts of that country and the monuments of art. Intended as a guidebook, it is an invaluable source of information.

Pavarotti, Luciano 1935– •*Italian tenor*• He was born in Modena. He abandoned a career in teaching to become a singer, and won the international competition at the Teatro Reggio Emilia in 1961, making his operatic debut there as Rudolfo in *La Bohème* the same year. He performed with the La Scala tour of Europe in 1963–64 and in 1965 toured Australia with **Joan Sutherland** in *Lucia di Lammermoor.* He made his American debut at the Metropolitan Opera House, New York, in 1968. His voice and performance are very much in the powerful style of the traditional Italian tenor, and he is also internationally known as a concert performer. He has made many recordings, including joint performances with **José Carreras** and **Placido Domingo** as "The Three Tenors," and he appeared in the film *Yes, Giorgio* (1981). That year he won the Grammy award for best classical vocal soloist. In 1990, at the time of the soccer World Cup, he recorded the aria *Nessun dorma* ("Nobody Is Sleeping") from **Puccini**'s *Turandot*, which was used as the theme tune for the event.

Pavese, Cesare 1908–50 •*Italian novelist, poet, critic and translator*• Born in Piedmont, he was brought up in Turin. Among his various translations, that of **Herman Melville**'s *Moby-Dick* (1932) is regarded as a classic. A leader of the Italian postwar neorealist school, he was politically disillusioned and eventually committed suicide. His finest work is in novels like *La casa in collina* (1949, Eng trans *The House on the Hill*, 1961) and *La luna e i falò* (1950, Eng trans *The Moon and the Bonfire*, 1952), which express precisely and categorically his abhorrence of war and Fascism.

Pavlov, Ivan Petrovich 1849–1936 •*Russian physiologist and Nobel Prize winner*• Born near Ryazan, he studied natural sciences and medicine at St Petersburg, and from 1886 worked at the Military Medical Academy there. He later became Professor of Pharmacology (1890), Professor of Physiology (1895), and director of the Institute of Experimental Medicine (1913). He studied digestion in dogs, investigating the nervous control of salivation and the role of enzymes, and for this work was awarded the Nobel Prize for physiology or medicine in 1904. His most famous experiment showed that if a bell is sounded whenever food is presented to a dog, it will eventually begin to salivate when the bell is sounded without food being presented. This he termed a conditioned, or acquired, reflex, and it was the starting point for subsequent theories of animal and human behavior.

Pavlova, Anna 1881–1931 •*Russian ballerina*• Born in St Petersburg, she trained there at the Imperial Ballet School, and quickly became famous, creating roles in work by **Michel Fokine**, in particular *The Dying Swan* (1907). After traveling to Paris with **Sergei Diaghilev**'s Ballets Russes in 1909, she began touring all over the world with her own company. Among her best-known choreographies are *Snowflakes* (1915) and *Autumn Leaves* (1919). She did much to create the stereotyped image of the ballerina which persists today.

Paxman, Jeremy 1950– •*English journalist and broadcaster*• Born in Leeds, he was educated at Cambridge. He became a journalist in Northern Ireland before entering television as a host on current affairs programs including *Tonight* (1977–79), *Panorama* (1979–85), and *Newsnight* (1989–), and he has also served as master of ceremonies for a revived version of the quiz game *University Challenge* (1994–). His publications include *Friends in High Places* (1990) and *The English* (1998).

Paxton, Sir Joseph 1801–65 •*English gardener and architect*• Born in Milton-Bryant, near Woburn, he became superintendent of gardens for the Duke of Devonshire at Chiswick and Chatsworth (from 1826). He remodeled the gardens and designed a glass-and-iron conservatory at Chatsworth (1836–40). This became the model for his design of the building for the Great Exhibition of 1851 (it was later reerected as the Crystal Palace in Sydenham, and was destroyed by fire in 1936). He was Liberal Member of Parliament for Coventry from 1854.

Paxton, Steve 1939– •*US experimental dancer and choreographer*• Born in Tucson, Arizona, he trained in New York with **Merce Cunningham** and **José Limón**. An experimental composition course with musician Robert Dunn led to his involvement with the Judson Dance Theater, with which he performed works by **Yvonne Rainer**, **Trisha Brown** and others. He was also a founding member of the experimental Grand Union. In 1972 he invented the dance form known as contact improvisation, which has now been absorbed into the choreography of dancers the world over. Contact relies only on the performer's own weight to determine the shape of the dance, without any reliance on set steps.

Payne, (Geoffrey John) Nicholas 1945– •*English opera company director*• Born in London, he studied at Trinity College, Cambridge. His career in arts administration began with the finance department of the Royal Opera House (1968–70) and he subsequently worked for the Arts Council of Great Britain (1970–76), the Welsh National Opera (1976–82) and Opera North (1982–93). He became director of the Royal Opera in 1993 and of the English National Opera in 1998.

Payton, Walter, *nicknamed* **Sweetness** 1954–99 •*US football player*• Born in Columbia, Mississippi, he joined the Chicago Bears as a running back in 1975. Between then and his retirement in 1987 he established a National Football League rushing record of 16,726 yards, a record which stood until 2002, when it was broken by **Emmett Smith**. In one game (1977) he rushed for a record 275 yards. He scored 125 touchdowns between 1975 and 1987. In 1986, the Bears defeated the New England Patriots 46–10 to win the Super Bowl.

Paz, Octavio 1914–98 •*Mexican poet and Nobel Prize winner*• Born in Mexico City, he attended the National University of Mexico and identified with the republican side in the Spanish civil war. Diplomat (he was Mexican ambassador to India, 1962–68), essayist and editor, he is best known for his poetry, such as *Piedra de sol* (1957, Eng trans *Sun Stone*, 1963), written in ten volumes. Other works include a study of Mexican character and culture, *El laberinto de la soledad* (1950, revised edn 1959, Eng trans *The Labyrinth of Solitude*, 1962), *El arco y la lira* (1956, Eng trans *The Bow and the Lyre*, 1973) and *Vislumbres de la India* (1995, "Glimpses of India"). He was awarded the Nobel Prize for literature in 1990.

Paz Estenssoro, Víctor 1907–2001 •*Bolivian revolutionary and politician*• He was born in Tarija and educated at the University Mayor de St Andres, entering politics in the 1930s. He was the founder in 1941 of the left-wing Movimiento Nacionalista Revolucionario (MNR, National Revolutionary Movement), then went on to become its principal leader. He was exiled to Argentina (1946–51) but, following the 1952 revolution, he served as president (1952–56), and held office again from 1960 to 1964, when he was ousted by a military coup. After returning to Bolivia (1971) he failed to win election in 1979, but in 1985, after no candidate managed to achieve a majority, Congress elected him president. His main achievement in office (1985–90) was to reduce the raging inflation which had been crippling Bolivia's economy.

Peabody, George 1795–1869 •*US merchant, financier and philanthropist*• Born in South Danvers, Massachusetts, now called Peabody, he became a partner in a Baltimore dry-goods store in 1815. He established himself in London in 1837 as a merchant and banker, raising loans for US causes. In his lifetime he gave away a fortune for philanthropic purposes. He founded and endowed the Peabody Institutes in Baltimore and Peabody, and the Peabody Museums at Yale and Harvard. He also set up the Peabody Education Fund for the promotion of education in the southern US and built housing for workers in London.

Peacock, Thomas Love 1785–1866 •*English novelist and poet*• He was born in Weymouth, Dorset, and entered the service of the East India Company in 1819 after producing three satirical romances, *Headlong Hall* (1816), *Melincourt* (1817) and *Nightmare Abbey* (1818). *Crotchet Castle* (1831) concluded this series of satires. The framework of his satirical fictions is always the same—a company of humorists meet in a country house and display the sort of crotchets or prejudices which Peacock most disliked: the mechanical sort of political economy, morbid romance, the "march of science" and transcendental philosophy. The major poets of the Romantic school, including **Shelley**, one of Peacock's friends, are caricatured along with the Edinburgh Reviewers, who offer the extra target of being Scots. Other books include *Maid Marian* (1822) and *The Misfortunes of Elphin* (1829).

" "

Laughter is pleasant, but the exertion is too much for me.

*1818 **Nightmare Abbey**, chapter 5.*

Peake, Mervyn Laurence 1911–68 •*English writer and artist*• Born in south China, where his father was a missionary, he was educated at Tientsin Grammar School, Eltham College and the Royal Academy Schools. His first book was a children's story, *Captain Slaughterboard Drops Anchor* (1939), with his own illustrations. *The Craft of the Lead Pencil* (1946), a book on drawing, was published in the same year as his first novel, *Titus Groan*, the first part of a Gothic fantasy trilogy completed in *Gormenghast* (1950) and *Titus Alone* (1959). Another novel, *Mr Pye*, appeared in 1953. He published two volumes of verse, *Shapes and Sounds* (1941) and *The Glassblowers* (1950), and lighter sketches collected posthumously in *A Book of Nonsense* (1972). He illustrated several classics, notably *Treasure Island*, *The Hunting of the Snark* and *The Ancient Mariner*.

Peale, Charles Willson 1741–1827 •*US painter, naturalist and inventor*• Born in Queen Annes County, Maryland, he traveled to London in 1767, where he studied painting for two years under **Benjamin West**. He became known for his many portraits of the leading figures of the American Revolution, painted in a neoclassical style after the manner of **Jacques Louis David**. His works include the earliest known portrait of **George Washington** (1772). In 1775 he settled in Philadelphia, and from 1779 to 1780 was a Democratic member of the Pennsylvania Assembly. He established the first art gallery in the US in 1782.

Peano, Giuseppe 1858–1932 •*Italian mathematician*• Born in Cuneo, he was educated at the University of Turin, where he later taught. He did important work on differential equations and discovered continuous curves passing through every point of a square. He later moved to mathematical logic, and advocated writing mathematics in an entirely formal language, the symbolism he invented becoming the basis of that used by **Bertrand Russell** and **Alfred Whitehead** in their *Principia Mathematica*. He also promoted Interlingua, a universal language based on uninflected Latin.

Pears, Sir Peter Neville Luard 1910–86 •*English tenor*• Born in Farnham, Surrey, he was an organ scholar at Hertford College, Oxford, then studied singing (1933–34) at the Royal College of Music. He toured the US and Europe with his partner **Benjamin Britten**, and in 1943 joined Sadler's Wells. After the success of *Peter Grimes* (1945), he joined Britten in the English Opera Group, and was cofounder with him, in 1948, of the Aldeburgh Festival.

Pearse, Patrick 1879–1916 •*Irish writer, educator and nationalist*• Born in Dublin, he was the son of an English monumental sculptor and an Irish mother. A leader of the Gaelic revival, he joined the Gaelic League in 1895, became editor of its journal, and lectured in Irish at University College. In 1908 he founded a bilingual school, St Enda's, at Ranelagh. In 1915 he joined the Irish Republican Brotherhood. In the 1916 Easter uprising he was commander in chief of the insurgents, and was proclaimed president of the provisional government. After the revolt was quelled, he was arrested, court-martialed and then shot.

Pearson, Karl 1857–1936 •*English mathematician and scientist*• Born in London, he turned from the law to mathematics, becoming Professor of Applied Mathematics (1884) and Galton Professor of Eugenics (1911) at University College London. He published *The Grammar of Science* (1892) and works on eugenics, mathematics, and biometrics. He was a founder of modern statistical theory, and his work established statistics as a subject in its own right. He wrote *Life of Galton* (1914–30), and founded and edited the journal *Biometrika* (1901–36).

Pearson, Lester Bowles 1897–1972 •*Canadian statesman and Nobel Prize winner*• He was born in Newtonbrook, Ontario, and educated at the University of Toronto and Oxford University. He held various diplomatic and political appointments, among them assistant undersecretary of state for external affairs (1941), and ambassador to Washington (1945–46), and was a senior adviser at the Charter Conference of the UN in 1945 and was later leader of Canadian UN delegations. In 1952–53 he was president of the UN General Assembly, and in 1957 was awarded the Nobel Peace Prize. Leader of the Opposition party from 1958, he became prime minister in 1963, retaining power in 1965. He resigned as party leader and as prime minister in 1968.

Peary, Robert Edwin 1856–1920 •*US naval commander and explorer*• Born in Cresson Springs, Pennsylvania, he graduated from Bowdoin College and served in the navy's civil engineering corps. He made eight Arctic expeditions from 1886, exploring Greenland and the region later called Peary Land. In 1906 he reached 87° 6' N, and on April 6, 1909, attained the North Pole. His claim to be first to reach the North Pole was substantiated when Dr **Frederick Cook**'s own claim was discredited, although some doubt still exists regarding whether he reached the precise 90° position.

Pechstein, Max 1881–1955 •*German painter and printmaker*• Born in Zwickau, he studied in Dresden and joined the avant-garde group Die Brücke in 1906. In Berlin in 1908, he helped found the rival Neue Sezession. He developed a colorful style indebted to **Henri Matisse** and the fauvists; he visited the Pacific just before World War I, and while at Palau he painted figures in tropical settings, reminiscent of **Paul Gauguin**. He taught at the Berlin Academy from 1923 until he was dismissed by the Nazis in 1933; he was reinstated in 1945.

Peck, (Eldred) Gregory 1916–2003 •*US film actor*• Born in La Jolla, California, he acted for two years with the Neighborhood Playhouse in New York City before making his Broadway debut in *Morning Star* (1942). He made his cinema debut as a Russian guerrilla in *Days of Glory* (1944) and became one of the first major postwar film stars. Good-looking and soft-spoken, he portrayed men of action and everyday citizens distinguished by their sense of decency in films such as *Spellbound* (1945), *Twelve O'Clock High* (1949) and *The Gunfighter* (1950). He was nominated five times for an Academy Award, winning Best Actor for his role as a liberal Southern lawyer in *To Kill a Mockingbird* (1962). He also produced films. Later films include *The Omen* (1976) and *Cape Fear* (1991).

Peckinpah, Sam 1925–84 •*US film director*• Born in Fresno, California, he studied drama at Fresno State College and worked as a theater director, propman, assistant editor and actor before directing extensively for television. He made his film debut with the western *The Deadly Companions* (1961) and was to prove a master of the genre, revealing both the savagery and the lyricism of the Wild West in such films as *Ride the High Country* (1962) and his masterpiece *The Wild Bunch* (1969). Later films include *Straw Dogs* (1971) and *The Osterman Weekend* (1983).

Pedersen, Charles 1904–90 •*US chemist and Nobel Prize winner*• Born in Pusan, Korea, of Japanese-Norwegian extraction, he studied chemical engineering in the US (University of Dayton, Ohio) and took a master's degree in organic chemistry at MIT. The work for which he is best known was the accidental preparation of a cyclic polyether, a molecule shaped rather like a crown, given the name crown ether. Many compounds of this type bind alkali metal ions (sodium, potassium) very strongly, and their discovery initiated the study of guest-host chemistry and enhanced the understanding of which metal ions transport across membranes in living organisms. He retired in 1969 and shared the 1987 Nobel Prize for chemistry with **Donald Cram** and **Jean-Marie Lehn**.

Pedro I 1798–1834 •*Emperor of Brazil*• Born in Queluz, Portugal, the second son of John VI of Portugal, he fled to Brazil with his parents on **Napoleon I**'s invasion (1807), and became prince regent of Brazil on his father's return to Portugal (1821). He declared Brazilian independence in 1822 and was crowned as Pedro I in 1826, but his autocratic nature, dislike of parliamentary government, and his continued Portuguese connections annoyed his subjects. In 1831 he abdicated and withdrew to Portugal. He was Pedro IV of Portugal on the death of his father (1826), but abdicated within months in favor of his daughter, Donna Maria da Glória.

Pedro II 1825–91 •*Emperor of Brazil*• Born in Rio de Janeiro, he was the son of **Pedro I** and succeeded on his father's abdication in 1831, being crowned in 1841. Benevolent, popular, and distinguished by his love of learning and scholarly tastes, he reigned in peace until the 1889 revolution drove him to Europe. His remains were returned to Brazil in 1920.

Peel, Lady *See* **Lillie, Beatrice Gladys**

Peel, Sir Robert 1788–1850 •*English statesman and prime minister*• He was born near Bury, in Lancashire, educated at

Harrow and Christ Church, Oxford, and entered parliament in 1809 as Tory member for Cashel. In 1811 he was appointed undersecretary for the colonies, and became secretary for Ireland (1812–18). Known as "Orange Peel," he displayed strong anti-Catholic spirit, and was so fiercely attacked by **Daniel O'Connell** that he challenged him to a duel. In 1822 he became home secretary, working well with **George Canning**, foreign secretary, and devoting himself to the currency. However, when Canning formed a Whig-Tory ministry, Peel, along with the Duke of **Wellington** and others, withdrew from office over Catholic emancipation (1827). Paradoxically, when the death of Canning led to the Wellington-Peel government in 1829, it advocated the relief of the Roman Catholics. As home secretary Peel organized the London police force (the "Peelers" or "Bobbies"). In 1830 the Wellington-Peel ministry was succeeded by a Whig ministry under Earl **Grey**, which, in 1832, passed the Reform Bill. Peel opposed parliamentary reform and sought to hamper the new Liberalism. In November 1834 he accepted office as prime minister, but was replaced by Lord **Melbourne** in April 1835. The general election of 1841 was virtually a contest between free trade and protection, and protection won. The Conservative Party, headed by Peel, was returned to office. The Whigs wanted a fixed but moderate duty on foreign grain, and the Anti-Corn-Law League demanded a repeal, while Peel carried (1842) a modification of the sliding scale. Obliged to impose (1842) an income tax of 7 pence per pound of income, to be levied for three years, Peel revised the general tariff and either abolished or lowered the duties on several very important articles of commerce. He repressed Irish unrest and broke O'Connell's influence, but the potato blight in Ireland and the subsequent famine rendered cheap grain a necessity. **Richard Cobden** and the league redoubled their exertions. Peel informed his colleagues that the Corn Laws were doomed. Lord Stanley (afterward Earl of **Derby**), who replaced Peel, Lord George Bentinck, **Benjamin Disraeli** and others, formed a "no-surrender" Tory Party, but with the Duke of Wellington, Sir James Graham, the Earl of **Aberdeen**, **William Gladstone** and other eminent Conservatives, the laws were repealed. He retired in June 1846, yielding his place to a Whig administration under Lord **John Russell** to which he gave independent but general support. On June 29, 1850, he was thrown from his horse and died.

Peele, George c. 1558–96 •*English dramatist*• He was born in London and educated at Oxford. By 1581 he had moved to London, where for 17 years he lived a bohemian life as an actor, poet and playwright. He was one of those warned to repentance by **Robert Greene** in his *Groatsworth of Wit* (1592). Peele's plays include *The Arraignment of Paris* (1584), *Polyhymnia* (1590) and *Edward I* (1593), which contained slanders against Queen **Eleanor of Castile**. *The Old Wives' Tale* (1595) probably gave **Milton** the subject for his *Comus*.

Pei, I(eoh) M(eng) 1917– •*US architect*• He was born in Canton, China, and emigrated to the US in 1935, studying first at MIT and later with **Walter Gropius** at Harvard in the mid-1940s. He became a naturalized US citizen in 1954 and founded his own firm in 1955, becoming renowned for Modernist designs that feature elegant abstract shapes and vast interior spaces. His principal projects include Mile High Center in Denver (1955), the Kennedy Library (1979) in Boston and the glass pyramids at the Louvre in Paris (1988). He won the 1983 Pritzker Prize for architecture and was awarded the US Medal of Freedom in 1993.

" "

Let's do it right. This is for the ages.

1978 Quoted by J Carter Brown, Director, National Gallery of Art, Washington, in the ***Washington Post****, August 27, 1995. On his design for the gallery's East Building, which was soaring to an unbudgeted cost of $94.4 million.*

Peierls, Sir Rudolf Ernst 1907–95 •*British theoretical physicist*• Born in Berlin, Germany, and educated there, he studied under Arnold Sommerfeld (1868–1951) in Munich and **Werner Heisenberg** in Leipzig and became **Wolfgang Pauli**'s assistant in Zurich. Research at the University of Rome, Cambridge University and the University of Manchester followed, and he was appointed professor at the University of Birmingham in 1937. He became a British citizen in 1940. In 1963 he moved to Oxford University, and from 1974 to 1977 he was at the University of Washington, Seattle. He studied the theory of solids and analyzed electron motion in them, developed the theory of diamagnetism in metals, and in nuclear physics studied the interactions of protons and neutrons. During World War II, Peierls and **Otto Frisch** studied uranium fission and the accompanying neutron emission, publishing a report in 1940 that showed the possibility of producing an atomic bomb. The British government appointed Peierls to lead a group developing ways of separating uranium isotopes and calculating the efficiency of the chain reaction. The work was moved to the US as part of the combined Manhattan Project (1943). He was knighted in 1968.

Peirce, Charles Sanders 1839–1914 •*US philosopher, logician and mathematician*• Born in Cambridge, Massachusetts, the son of mathematician Benjamin Peirce (1809–80), he graduated from Harvard (1859) and began his career as a scientist, working for the US Coast and Geodetic Survey (1861, now the National Ocean Survey). He became a lecturer in logic at Johns Hopkins University (1879) but left (1894) to devote the rest of his life in seclusion to the private study of logic and philosophy. In his scientific work, he developed the theory of gravity measurement using pendulums, and made an early determination of the meter in terms of a wavelength of light. In philosophy, he was a pioneer in the development of modern, formal logic and the logic of relations, but he is best known as the founder of pragmatism, which he later named "pragmaticism" to distinguish it from the work of **William James**. His theory of meaning helped establish the new field of semiotics.

Pelagius c. 360–c. 420 AD •*British monk and heretic*• Born in Great Britain or Ireland, he settled in Rome (c. 400 AD), where he disputed with **Augustine of Hippo** on the nature of grace and original sin. His view that salvation could be achieved by the exercise of one's basically good moral nature (Pelagianism) was condemned as heretical by the councils in 416 and 418, and he was then excommunicated and banished from Rome.

Pelé, *pseudonym of* **Edson Arantes do Nascimento** 1940– •*Brazilian soccer player*• Born in Três Corações, Minas Gerais, he made his international debut at the age of 16, and in 1958 won his first World Cup medal, scoring twice in Brazil's win in the final over Sweden. He won another World Cup medal in 1970. For most of his senior career he played for Santos, of which he is now director (1993–), and in November 1969 he achieved the staggering mark of 1,000 goals in first-class soccer. In 1975 he signed a multimillion-dollar contract with the New York Cosmos, and led the team to the 1977 North American Soccer League Championship. He is considered one of the finest inside forwards in the history of the game.

Pelham, Henry c. 1695–1754 •*English statesman*• He took an active part in suppressing the Jacobite uprising of 1715, became secretary of war in 1724, and was a zealous supporter of **Robert Walpole**. He took office as prime minister in 1743. Notable events during his ministry (reconstructed in 1744 as the "Broad-Bottom administration") included the Austrian Succession War and the Jacobite uprising of 1745. His brother was **Thomas Pelham-Holles**.

Pelham-Holles, Sir Thomas, 1st Duke of Newcastle-under-Lyme 1693–1768 •*English statesman*• He was the brother of **Henry Pelham** and added the name Holles to his own on succeeding to the estates of his uncle John Holles in 1711. **George I** created him Earl of Clare (1714) and Duke of Newcastle (1715). A Whig and a supporter of **Robert Walpole**, he became secretary of state in 1724. In 1754 he succeeded his brother Henry as premier, but he retired in 1756. In July 1757 he was again premier, and was compelled to take William Pitt, later Earl of **Chatham**, into his ministry. In 1762 he was succeeded by the Earl of **Bute**.

Pelletier, Pierre Joseph 1788–1842 •*French chemist*• Born in Paris, he qualified as a pharmacist in 1810 and became professor and later assistant director at the School of Pharmacy in Paris, at the same time running a pharmacy and a chemical manufacturing business. His first research was on gum resins and other natural products such as amber and toad venom. He collaborated with **Joseph Bienaimé Caventou** (1817–21), and together they investigated the green pigment of leaves, naming it chlorophyll, and won international fame for their investigation of alkaloids. This research marked the beginning of alkaloid chemistry, led to more careful preparation of natural drugs and opened up the possibility of producing them synthetically.

Pelli, César 1926– *•US architect•* Born in Tucumán, Argentina, he was educated at the Universities of Tucumán and Illinois. Having emigrated to the US in 1952, he became a naturalized US citizen in 1964. He became a professor and dean at the Yale School of Architecture in 1977, in which year he also founded his own practice in New Haven, Connecticut. His most important buildings, many of which have a traditional character while using a range of modern materials, include the World Financial Center in New York (1985–87), Canary Wharf Tower in London (1990), the New Terminal at Washington National Airport (1998) and the Petronas Towers in Kuala Lumpur (1998).

Peltier, Jean Charles Athanase 1785–1845 *•French physicist•* Born in Ham, Picardy, he was largely self-taught. He published many of his investigations into phrenology, anatomy, microscopy, meteorology and electricity. A series of experiments led him in 1834 to observe that at the junction of two dissimilar metals, an electric current produced a rise or fall in temperature, depending on the direction of the current flow (the Peltier effect). This phenomenon was given new significance in the subsequent work of **James Joule** and Lord **Kelvin** on thermodynamics and thermoelectricity.

Pelton, Lester Allen 1829–1918 *•US inventor and engineer•* Born in Vermillion, Ohio, he was a carpenter when he joined the gold rush to California in 1849. He failed to strike it rich but became interested in the water wheels used to drive mining machinery, and devised an improved type of undershot wheel powered by a jet of water striking pairs of hemispherical cups. He was granted a patent in 1880, later selling the rights to the Pelton Water Wheel Company of San Francisco. Pelton wheels are now in use all over the world for high-head hydropower generation, at efficiencies approaching 90 percent.

Pen, Jean-Marie Le *See* **Le Pen, Jean-Marie**

Penda c. 577–655 *•King of Mercia•* A champion of paganism and scourge of Christian Northumbria, he was certainly in power by 628. He defeated (in alliance with the Welsh king, **Cadwallon**) **Edwin** (St Edwin) of Northumbria at Hatfield Chase (633), and attacked Northumbria again (642), defeating and killing King **Oswald** at Maserfeld (Old Oswestry). He also made inroads in Wessex and East Anglia. However, in another onslaught on Northumbria (655), he was defeated and killed by King Oswiu at the Battle of the Winwaed in Yorkshire.

Penderecki, Krzysztof 1933– *•Polish composer•* Born in Debica, he studied at the Kraków Conservatory and later taught there and in Essen. He achieved worldwide recognition for two innovative scores of the late 1960s: *Trenofiarom Hiroszimy* for 52 strings (1960, *Threnody to the Victims of Hiroshima*) and *The Passion According to St Luke* (1965). Several oratorios followed, as well as operas and other large-scale pieces, two symphonies, concertos and other works. Recent pieces include *Flute Concerto* (1992–93) and *Violin Concerto No. 2* (1995).

Penfield, Wilder Graves 1891–1976 *•Canadian neurosurgeon•* He was born in Spokane, Washington, and after undergraduate studies at Princeton, went to Oxford as a Rhodes scholar in 1914; the outbreak of World War I interrupted his studies. Wounded in the war, he returned to the US, where he finished his medical education at Johns Hopkins University. Further scientific study in Oxford and Spain prepared him for his experimental neurosurgical work. He moved to a neurosurgical appointment at McGill University in 1928, and was instrumental in founding the world-famous Montreal Neurological Institute, of which he became the first director (1934–60). His experimental work on animals and on the exposed brains of conscious human beings assisted in understanding the higher functions of the brain, the causes of brain diseases such as epilepsy, and the mechanisms involved in speech. He became a Canadian citizen in 1934.

Peniakoff, Vladimir, *nicknamed* **Popski** 1897–1951 *•Belgian soldier•* He was born in Belgium of Russian parentage and educated in England. He joined the British army and from 1940 to 1942 served with the Long Range Desert Group and the Libyan Arab Force. In October 1942, with the sanction of the army, he formed his own force, Popski's Private Army, which carried out spectacular raids behind the German lines. He was later decorated for bravery by Great Britain, France and Belgium.

Penn, William 1644–1718 *•English Quaker reformer and colonialist, founder of Pennsylvania•* He was born in London, the son of Admiral Sir William Penn (1621–70). He was dismissed from Christ Church, Oxford, for refusing to conform to the restored Anglican Church, and his father sent him to the Continent. He returned a polished man of the world, having served briefly in the Second Dutch War (1665–67). He studied law at Lincoln's Inn for a year, and in 1666 his father dispatched him to look after his estates in Cork. There he attended Quaker meetings, was imprisoned, and returned to England a convinced Quaker. In 1668 he was imprisoned in the Tower of London for writing *Sandy Foundation Shaken*, which attacked the ordinary doctrines of the Trinity. While in prison he wrote the most popular of his books, *No Cross, No Crown*, and *Innocency With Her Open Face*, which contributed to his liberation, obtained with the intervention of his father's friend, the Duke of York (the future **James VII and II**). In 1670 he was again imprisoned for preaching, and on his release visited the Netherlands and Germany for the advancement of Quakerism. Meanwhile, as one of the Quaker trustees of the American province of West Jersey, he had drawn up the settlers' celebrated "Concessions and Agreements" charter. In 1681 he obtained a grant of territory in North America, called "Pensilvania" in honor of his father, intending to establish a home for his coreligionists. He sailed with his emigrants for what is now Delaware in 1682. In November he held his famous interview with the Native Americans on the site of Philadelphia. He planned the city, and for two years governed the colony wisely and tolerantly, within the restrictions of Puritanism. He returned to England (1684–99) to help his persecuted Quaker brethren, and through his influence with James VII and II, in 1686 all persons imprisoned on account of their religious opinions (including 1,200 Quakers) were released. In 1699 he returned to Pennsylvania, where his constitution had proved unworkable and had to be much altered. He did something to mitigate the evils of slavery, but owned slaves himself. He departed for England in 1701. His last years were embittered by legal disputes, and he spent nine months in the Fleet Street debtors' prison (1708).

" "

Inquire often, but judge rarely, and thou wilt not often be mistaken.

*1693 **Some Fruits of Solitude**.*

Penney, William George, Baron 1909–91 *•English physicist•* Born in Sheerness, Kent, he was educated at the Universities of London and Wisconsin and at Cambridge University, became Professor of Mathematics at Imperial College, London, and worked at Los Alamos on the Manhattan (atomic bomb) project (1944–45). Later he was appointed director of the Atomic Weapons Research Establishment at Aldermaston (1953–59), and chairman of the UK Atomic Energy Authority (1964–67). He was the key figure in the UK's success in producing its own atomic (1952) and hydrogen bombs (1957). Knighted in 1952, he was created a life peer in 1967.

Penrose, Sir Roger 1931– *•English mathematical astronomer•* Born in Colchester, Essex, he was educated at University College London, and then obtained a doctorate at Cambridge. Since 1973 he has been Rouse Ball Professor of Mathematics at Oxford. He is known for his work on black holes, showing (jointly with **Stephen Hawking**) that once collapse of a very massive star at the end of its life has started, the formation of a black hole is inevitable. Penrose also put forward the hypothesis of cosmic censorship, proposing that there must be an event horizon around a black hole, isolating its physically unlawful behavior from the rest of the universe. He was knighted in 1994.

Penrose, Sir Roland Algernon 1900–84 *•English painter, connoisseur and art collector•* Born in London, he graduated from

Queen's College, Cambridge, in 1922, and lived in Paris from 1922 to 1935, when he began to collect Cubist and surrealist art. In 1936 he organized the International Surrealist Exhibition in London. He founded the Institute of Contemporary Arts, London, in 1947. Penrose's friendship with **Picasso** led him to writing Picasso's biography (1958).

Penzias, Arno Allan 1933– •*US astrophysicist and Nobel Prize winner*• Born in Munich, Germany, a refugee with his family from Nazi Germany, he was educated at Columbia University, New York, and joined the Bell Telephone Laboratories in 1961. In 1963 he and his colleague **Robert Wilson** were assigned the task of tracing the radio noise that was interfering with Earth-satellite-Earth communications, eventually discovering the residual relic of the intense heat that was associated with the birth of the universe following the hot big bang. This was the cosmic microwave background radiation predicted to exist by **George Gamow** and **Ralph Alpher** in 1948. In 1970, with Wilson and K B Jefferts, Penzias discovered the radio spectral line of carbon monoxide; this has since been used as a tracer of galactic gas clouds. Penzias and Wilson were awarded the Nobel Prize for physics in 1978, along with **Peter Kapitza**.

Pepin III (the Short) c. 715–68 •*King of the Franks*• The illegitimate son of **Charles Martel** and the father of **Charlemagne**, he founded the Frankish dynasty of the Carolingians. He was chosen king (751) in place of Childeric III, the last of the Merovingians. When Pope Stephen III was hard pressed by the Longobards, Pepin led an army into Italy (754), compelled the Lombard Aistulf to become his vassal, and laid the foundation of the temporal sovereignty of the popes (756). The rest of his life was spent in wars against Saxons and Saracens.

Pepys, Samuel 1633–1703 •*English diarist and admiralty official*• The son of a London tailor, he was educated at St Paul's School and Trinity Hall and Magdalene College, Cambridge. After the English civil war he lived in poor circumstances, but following the Restoration, through the patronage of the 1st Earl of **Sandwich**, his father's cousin, he rose rapidly in the naval service and became secretary to the admiralty in 1672. He lost his office and was imprisoned on account of his alleged complicity in the Popish Plot (1679), but was reappointed in 1684 and also became president of the Royal Society. At the revolution (1688) he was again removed from office. The celebrated diary, which ran from January 1, 1660, to May 31, 1669, is interesting both as the personal record (and confessions) of a man with an abounding love of life, and for the vivid picture it gives of contemporary life, including naval administration and court intrigue. The highlights are probably the Great Plague (1665–66), the Great Fire of London (1666) and the sailing up the Thames by the Dutch fleet (1665–67). The diary was written in cipher (a kind of shorthand), but was deciphered in 1825.

“ ”

Strange to say what delight we married people have to see these poor fools decoyed into our condition.

1665 Diary entry, December 25.

Perceval, Spencer 1762–1812 •*English statesman*• The son of the Earl of Egremont, he was born in London, educated at Harrow and at Trinity College, Cambridge, and was called to the bar in 1786. A Member of Parliament from 1796, he was solicitor general (1801), attorney general (1802), and chancellor of the exchequer (1807), before he became prime minister (1809–12). An efficient administrator, he had established his Tory government by the time he was shot dead by a bankrupt Liverpool broker, John Bellingham.

Percy, Sir Henry, *also known as* **Hotspur** 1364–1403 •*English nobleman*• He was the eldest son of Henry Percy, the earl of Northumberland, and was called "Hotspur" because of his fiery temper. His father had helped Henry of Lancaster (**Henry IV**) to the English throne but was dissatisfied with the king's lack of gratitude. Both father and son joined **Owen Glendower**'s rebellion against Henry IV, and Hotspur was killed in the defeat at Shrewsbury.

Percy, Thomas 1729–1811 •*English antiquary, poet and churchman*• Born in Bridgnorth and educated at Christ Church, Oxford, he became vicar of Easton Maudit in Northamptonshire (1753) and rector of Wilby (1756), and was later appointed chaplain to **George III**, then dean of Carlisle (1778) and Bishop of Dromore (1782). He published the first English version of a Chinese novel, *Hau Kiou Choaun* (1761, translated from the Portuguese), and, prompted by the success of **James Macpherson**'s spurious Ossianic translations, he also published, anonymously, *Runic Poetry Translated From the Icelandic Language* (1763). However, his fame rests on his *Reliques of Ancient English Poetry* (1765), which was largely compiled from a 17th-century manuscript of medieval ballads and other material found in a house in Shifnal, Shropshire, and much "restored" by him.

Percy, Walker 1916–90 •*US novelist*• Born in Birmingham, Alabama, he studied medicine, intending to make this his career, but had to abandon it when he contracted tuberculosis. His first and best novel, *The Moviegoer* (1961), won a National Book Award. He was a philosophical writer, and his novels are firmly grounded in his social observations as a liberal and unconventional Catholic Southerner. *Love in the Ruins* (1971) was subtitled "The Adventures of a Bad Catholic at a Time Near the End of the World." Other novels include *The Last Gentleman* (1966), *The Second Coming* (1980) and *The Thanatos Syndrome* (1987).

Perdita *See* **Robinson, Mary**

Pereira, Valdir *See* **Didi**

Perelman, S(ydney) J(oseph) 1904–79 •*US humorist*• He was born in Brooklyn, New York. Graduating from Brown University in 1925, he contributed to magazines until the publication of *Dawn Ginsbergh's Revenge* in 1929, which had the nation in stitches and secured the author's fame. He went to Hollywood and wrote scripts for, among others, the **Marx Brothers**. From 1931 much of his work was published first in the *New Yorker*. His writing is remarkable for its linguistic dexterity and ingenuity, and several modern sitting ducks sank under his humorous attacks. He is at his best in *Crazy Like a Fox* (1944), *Westward Ha! or, Around the World in 80 Clichés* (1948) and *The Swiss Family Perelman* (1950).

Peres, Shimon 1923– •*Israeli statesman and Nobel Prize winner*• Born in Wołożyn, Poland (now Valozhyn, Belarus), he emigrated with his family to Palestine (1934), and was raised on a kibbutz. He received most of his education in the US, studying at New York and Harvard Universities. After senior posts in the Israeli naval services and in the defense ministry, in 1959 he was elected to the Knesset. He was minister of defense (1974–77), and in 1977 became chairman of the Labor Party and leader of the Opposition until 1984, when he entered into a unique power-sharing agreement with the leader of the Consolidation Party (Likud), **Yitzhak Shamir**. Under this agreement, Peres was prime minister from 1984 to 1986, when Shamir took over. A new coalition began in 1988, but collapsed in 1990, when a government was formed by Shamir. In 1992 Peres was defeated for the Labor leadership by **Yitzhak Rabin** and Rabin went on to become prime minister that year. When Rabin was assassinated in 1995, Peres took over the premiership, but was defeated in elections in May 1996 by **Benjamin Netanyahu**. In 1994 he shared the Nobel Prize for peace with Rabin and **Yasser Arafat**.

Pérez de Cuéllar, Javier 1920– •*Peruvian diplomat*• Born in Lima, he studied at the University of Lima and embarked on a career in the Peruvian diplomatic service, representing his country at the first United Nations assembly in 1946 and as Peru's first ambassador to the USSR. He succeeded **Kurt Waldheim** as UN secretary-general in 1982. His patience and diplomacy secured notable achievements, particularly in his second term, including a ceasefire in the Iran-Iraq war and the achievement of independence for Namibia. He was succeeded as secretary-general in 1992 by **Boutros Boutros-Ghali**.

Perez Esquivel, Adolfo 1931– •*Argentine civil rights leader and Nobel Prize winner*• Born in Buenos Aires, he studied art and architecture and became a professor of art and a well-known sculptor. A devout Catholic, in 1974 he gave up his career to become head of the Service for Peace and Justice, a church-based network of organizations promoting social justice in Latin America by nonviolent means. He spoke out on behalf of the thousands who disappeared during the Argentine military junta's campaign against political dissidents, and was as a result imprisoned and tortured (1977–78). He was awarded the Nobel Peace Prize in 1980.

Pérez Galdós, Benito 1843–1920 •*Spanish novelist*• Born in Las Palmas, Canary Islands, he moved to Madrid as a student in 1861, and supported his family by writing. He was a prolific novelist and dramatist, and also wrote newspaper articles, travel diaries, criticism, and memoirs. He divided his novels, which are largely naturalistic in style, into categories in the manner of **Honoré de Balzac**, the principal two being the novels of contemporary Spanish life and the 46-volume historical series he called "*Episodios nacionales*." He is considered the greatest Spanish novelist after **Cervantes**, and his most admired book is the novel *Fortunata y Jacinta* (1886–87, Eng trans *Fortunata and Jacinta*, 1986).

Periander c. 625–585 BC •*Tyrant of Corinth*• He succeeded his father, **Cypselus**. Under him Corinth's power and position in the Greek world developed further, with great commercial prosperity, and he cultivated extensive links with foreign rulers. He is remembered by later tradition as an example of a repressive tyrant, yet he was also included in the canon of the Seven Wise Men of Greece. The tyranny came to an end soon after his death.

Pericles c. 490–429 BC •*Athenian statesman*• He was born into the aristocratic Alcmaeonid family in Athens. He came rapidly to the fore as a supporter of the new democracy. He helped prosecute the conservative **Cimon** in 463, who was subsequently ostracized, and with Ephialtes in 462/1, he brought in measures limiting the power of the old aristocratic Areopagus. When Ephialtes was murdered, Pericles became the dominant figure in Athenian politics, being elected 15 times to the office of *strategos* (general, but with political functions) between 451 (when he introduced a popular law which restricted citizenship) and his death. Athens under Pericles followed an expansionist policy in which the Delian League, founded to keep the defeated Persians away from Greece, was turned into an Athenian empire. Tribute was exacted from the former allies, and attempts to secede were crushed by force (notably Samos in 439). According to some accounts (but not **Thucydides**, the principal source), Pericles planned a grand Hellenic confederation to put an end to mutually destructive wars, which was frustrated by Spartan opposition. However, the historicity of this is doubtful. Athens and Sparta were almost continuously at war during these years, culminating in the Peloponnesian War, which broke out in 431. In 446 there was a peace in which Sparta recognized much of Athens's imperial ambition. During this respite, Pericles undertook a major building program that glorified Athens with the Parthenon, the Propylaea, and other buildings on the Acropolis. When war broke out again with Sparta in 431, Pericles advocated a policy of caution on land, allowing the invading Spartans to destroy the fields while the population was concentrated behind the strong city walls and the city's supply lines could be protected by the powerful Athenian navy. Thucydides puts into Pericles's mouth the famous funeral oration commemorating the victims of the first year of fighting. In 430 plague broke out in the city; the Athenians' patience broke and Pericles was removed from office. He was again elected *strategos*, but he died soon afterward, a victim himself of the plague. Thucydides said of Athens under Pericles that it was in fact a democracy but was in practice ruled by its first citizen. No other Athenian statesman before or since achieved such a dominant position.

“ ”

Famous men have the whole earth as their memorial.

*Quoted in Thucydides **History of the Peloponnesian War**, 2.43 (translated by R Warner, 1961).*

Perkins, Frances 1882–1965 •*US social reformer and politician*• She was born in Boston, Massachusetts, and was educated at Mount Holyoke College, Massachusetts. Later she visited various Chicago settlement houses, in particular Hull House, and grew convinced that the workers' conditions would be improved by practical deeds not political doctrines. Moving to New York, she became secretary of the New York Consumers' League (1910–12), then secretary of the Committee on Safety of the City of New York (1912–17), and helped to secure passage of state legislation that set factory safety standards, minimum wages and limited working hours. In 1918 she became the first woman member of the New York State Industrial Commission (chairman 1926, commissioner 1929). She joined the Democratic Party and for 30 years served as an expert on labor issues. She was appointed US secretary of labor (1933–45) by **Franklin D Roosevelt**, becoming the first US female Cabinet member.

Perl, Martin Lewis 1927– •*US physicist and Nobel Prize winner*• Born in New York, he was educated at Columbia University, began work in experimental particle physics in 1955 and became Professor of Physics at the Stanford Linear Accelerator Center from 1963. His work in the late 1970s established the existence of the elementary particle the tau lepton, and for this he shared the Nobel Prize for physics (1995) with **Frederick Reines**, discoverer of the neutrino.

Perlman, Itzhak 1945– •*Israeli violinist*• He was born in Tel Aviv, the son of Polish immigrants, and moved in 1958 to study at the Juilliard School, New York. He first played on US radio at age 10, at Carnegie Hall in 1963, and in London in 1968. Now one of the most highly acclaimed violinists of his time, he is noted for his brilliant technique and attention to detail.

Perón, (Maria) Eva Duarte De, *known as* **Evita** 1919–52 •*Argentine popular leader and social reformer*• The second wife of **Juan Perón**, she was born into a poor family in Los Toldos, Buenos Aires. She was a radio and stage actress before her marriage in 1945. She played a major part in her husband's successful presidential campaign the following year, and became a powerful political influence and mainstay of the Perón government. Meanwhile she used her position to press for women's suffrage by founding the Peronista Feminist Party in 1949, and by acquiring control of newspapers and businesses. As de facto minister of health and labor, she gained political support for her husband from among the working classes. Idolized by the populace, she founded the Eva Perón Foundation for the promotion of social welfare. After her death, support for her husband waned. When he was overthrown in 1955, her body was stolen and kept hidden until the early 1970s; it was repatriated by **Isabelita Perón** after Juan Perón's death in 1974. Her life story was the theme of a popular musical by **Andrew Lloyd-Webber** and **Tim Rice** (*Evita*, 1978), later filmed with **Madonna** in the lead role (1996).

Perón, Isabelita, *popular name of* **Maria Estela Martínez de Perón**, *née* **Cartas** 1931– •*Argentine politician*• She was born in La Rioja Province and adopted the name Isabel when she began her career as a dancer. She became the third wife of the deposed president Juan Perón in 1961, and lived with him in Spain until his triumphal return to Argentina as president in 1973, when she was made vice president. She took over the presidency at his death in 1974, but was ousted in a military coup in 1976 and placed under house arrest for five years. On her release in 1981 she settled in Madrid, and in 1988 she returned to Argentina.

Perón, Juan Domingo 1895–1974 •*Argentine soldier and statesman*• Born in Lobos, he joined the army in 1913, and took a leading part in the army revolt of 1943 which toppled the pro-Axis president, Ramón Castillo. He was well read, a hypnotic public speaker and a close student of **Benito Mussolini**; he developed a broad base of popular support, augmenting his rule with force. He organized the *descamisados*, a civilian paramilitary organization which, like both **Hitler**'s Brownshirts and Mussolini's Blackshirts, was drawn from the lower classes. Their affections were secured by his politically astute wife, **Eva Perón**. In 1945, senior army and navy officers, alarmed at Perón's mobilization of the masses, imprisoned him, but released him after thousands gathered in the public squares demanding his return. In 1946 after a populist campaign laced with strong nationalist and anti-American rhetoric, "El Líder" was elected president and set about building a corporatist state. He reduced the legislature and the judiciary to rubber stamps, tried to crush all opposition by any means including torture, and sought to modernize and industrialize the economy through large-scale government intervention and by nationalizing foreign-owned enterprises (including the railways). In 1955, with the economy in a shambles, he was deposed by the army and fled to Spain. Support for the Perónists continued, despite military opposition, and Perón triumphantly resumed the presidency in 1973. He died a year later, leaving his office to the vice president, his third wife, **Isabelita Perón**.

Perot, H(enry) Ross 1930– •*US billionaire and politician*• He was born in Texarkana, Texas. In 1962 he founded Electronic Data Systems (EDS), a computer services company, and after selling it to General Motors in 1984, he acquired interests in real estate, gas, and oil. Drawing on his vast fortune to buy media time, he ran for president as an independent in 1992 but was not elected. He later fought US ratification of the North American Free Trade Agreement. In 1996 he again ran for president as a third-party candidate.

Perrault, Charles 1628–1703 •*French writer*• Born in Paris, he studied law, and in 1663 he became a secretary or assistant to **Jean-Baptiste Colbert**. His poem, *Le siècle de Louis le Grand* (1687, "The Century of Louis XIV"), and **Nicolas Boileau**'s outspoken criticisms of it, opened up the dispute about the relative merits of the ancients and moderns. Perrault later contributed further works on the side of the moderns. All his writings would have been forgotten but for his eight inimitable fairy tales, the *Histoires ou contes du temps passé* (1697, Eng trans *Perrault's Popular Tales*, 1888), including "Belle au bois dormant" ("The Sleeping Beauty"), "Le petit chaperon rouge" ("Red Riding Hood") and "Barbe-Bleue" ("Bluebeard").

Perrin, Jean Baptiste 1870–1942 •*French physicist and Nobel Prize winner*• Born in Lille, Nord-Pas-de-Calais, he was educated at the École Normale Supérieure in Paris and from 1898 to 1940 was on the physical chemistry staff of the University of Paris. In 1940 he escaped to the US following Germany's invasion of France. His earliest work helped to establish the nature of cathode rays as negatively charged particles, but he is most remembered for his studies of Brownian movement. He demonstrated that the suspended particles which show Brownian motion essentially obey the gas laws, and he used such systems to determine a fairly accurate value for the Avogadro number. He was awarded the Nobel Prize for physics in 1926, and served as president of the French Academy of Sciences in 1938.

Perry, (Mary) Antoinette 1888–1946 •*US actress and director*• Born in Denver, Colorado, she had a long career on the stage from 1905 and as a director from 1928. In 1941 she founded the American Theater Wing. The annual Tony awards for theater on Broadway in New York are named after her.

Perry, Fred(erick John) 1909–95 •*US tennis player*• He was born in Stockport, Cheshire, England. His first sport was table tennis, at which he was world singles champion in 1929. He only took up lawn tennis when he was 19, and between 1933 and the end of 1936, when he turned professional, he won every major amateur title, including the Wimbledon singles three times, the US singles three times, and the Australian and French championships, and helped to keep the Davis Cup in Great Britain for four years. He was the first man to win all four major titles. He later took US citizenship (1938), and pursued a career in coaching, writing and broadcasting.

Perry, Matthew Calbraith 1794–1858 •*US naval officer*• He was born in Newport, Rhode Island, and in 1837 he was appointed commander of the *Fulton*, one of the first naval steamships. He was active in suppression of the slave trade on the African coast in 1843. In the Mexican War (1846–48) he captured several towns and took part in the siege of Veracruz. From 1852 to 1854 he led the naval expedition to Japan, forcing it to open diplomatic negotiations with the US and grant the first trading rights. He was the brother of **Oliver Hazard Perry**.

Perry, Oliver Hazard 1785–1819 •*US naval officer*• Born in South Kingston, Rhode Island, he entered the navy in 1799 and served in the Mediterranean during the Tripolitan War. In the War of 1812 he defeated a British squadron on Lake Erie (1813), a victory he reported with the famous message, "We have met the enemy and they are ours." He died of yellow fever on a mission to Venezuela. He was the brother of **Matthew Calbraith Perry**.

Perse, Saint-John *See* **Saint-John Perse**

Pershing, John Joseph, *known as* **Black Jack** 1860–1948 •*US soldier*• Born in Linn County, Missouri, he was a schoolteacher before he enrolled at West Point in 1880. He later served on frontier duty against the Sioux and Apaches (1886–98), in the Spanish-American War (1898), and during the Moro insurgencies in the Philippines (1903). In 1916 he led a US force into Mexico in an unsuccessful effort to track down **Pancho Villa**. As commander in chief (1917–18) of the American Expeditionary Force in Europe during World War I, he insisted that US troops should fight as a separate army under their own flag, and he led them effectively in the final battles of the war. From 1921 to 1924 he was US chief of staff.

Pertwee, Jon, *originally* **John Devon Roland Pertwee** 1919–96 •*English actor*• Born in London, he made his name during World War II in the radio series *HMS Waterlogged*, and his other radio successes included *The Navy Lark*. Among his films were *Knock on Wood* (1954), three *Carry On* pictures and *A Funny Thing Happened on the Way to the Forum* (1966). He was best known for his starring roles on television in *Doctor Who* (1970–74) and *Worzel Gummidge* (1979–82), which he re-created in *Worzel Gummidge Down Under* (1987, 1989).

Perugino, *properly* **Pietro di Cristoforo Vannucci** c. 1450–1523 •*Italian painter*• Born in Città della Pieve in Umbria, he established himself in Perugia (hence the nickname). In Rome, where he went about 1483, **Sixtus IV** employed him in painting the Sistine Chapel; his fresco *Christ Giving the Keys to Peter* is the best of those still visible, others having been destroyed to make way for **Michelangelo**'s *Last Judgment*. In Florence (1486–99), **Raphael** was his pupil. In Perugia (1499–1504) he adorned the Hall of the Cambio. After 1500 his art visibly declined. In his second Roman sojourn (1507–12) he, along with other painters, decorated the Stanze of the Vatican. One of his works there, the *Stanza del Incendio*, was the only fresco spared when Raphael was commissioned to repaint the walls and ceilings.

Perutz, Max Ferdinand 1914–2002 •*British biochemist and Nobel Prize winner*• Born in Vienna, Austria, he graduated from the university there and emigrated to the UK (1936), where he worked single-mindedly on the structure of hemoglobin at Cambridge. He became director of the Medical Research Council (MRC) Unit for Molecular Biology (1947–62) and from 1962 to 1979 he was director of the MRC Laboratory for Molecular Biology. In 1951 the presence of the alpha helix was predicted to occur in hemoglobin by Perutz, **Francis Crick** and Sir **Lawrence Bragg**, and Perutz later determined the hemoglobin structure to 5.5 angstroms. In further studies he predicted the detailed distribution of amino acids in hemoglobin (1964). He and **John Kendrew** were awarded the 1962 Nobel Prize for chemistry. Following this, Perutz studied numerous other aspects of hemoglobin.

Pestalozzi, Johann Heinrich 1746–1827 •*Swiss educator*• Born in Zurich, he devoted his life to the children of the very poor. Believing, like **Jean Jacques Rousseau**, in the moralizing virtue of agricultural occupations and a rural environment, he set up a residential farm school for waifs and strays on his estate at Neuhof in 1774; but owing to faulty domestic organization, it had to be abandoned after a five-year struggle (1780). In 1798 he opened his orphan school at Stanz, but at the end of eight months it too had to close. In partnership with others he opened a school of his own at Berthoud, and while there he published *How Gertrude Educates Her Children* (1801), the recognized exposition of the Pestalozzian method. In 1805 he moved his school to Yverdon and applied his method in a large secondary school, but his lack of ability in practical affairs resulted in the school's closure in 1825.

Pétain, (Henri) Philippe (Omer) 1856–1951 •*French soldier and statesman*• He was born in Cauchy-à-la-Tour of peasant parents. As a junior officer his confidential report was marked "If this officer rises above the rank of major it will be a disaster for France," but seniority brought him the military governorship of Paris. His defense of Verdun (1916) made him a national hero. As commander in chief in 1917, his appeasement policies virtually removed the French army from the war. Minister for war in 1934, he sponsored the ineffective Maginot Line and when France collapsed in early 1940, he succeeded **Paul Reynaud** as the head of the government, immediately arranging terms with the Germans. His administration at Vichy involved active collaboration with Germany, particularly through **Pierre Laval** and Marcel Deat (1894–1955). With the liberation of France (1944) Pétain was brought to trial, his death sentence for treason being commuted to life imprisonment on the Île d'Yeu. He died in captivity in 1951.

❝ ❞

They shall not pass.

This phrase came to symbolize the stubborn defense of Verdun against Ludendorf's siege, which cost 300,000 German and 400,000 French troops.

Peter, St, *originally* **Symeon** or **Simon bar Jona ("son of Jonah")** 1st century AD •*One of the 12 Apostles of Jesus*• He came from Bethsaida, but during the public ministry of **Jesus** had his house at Capernaum. Originally a fisherman, and brother of **Andrew**, he soon became the leader of the 12 Apostles, and was regarded by Jesus, who renamed him Cephas, or Peter ("rock"), with particular favor and affection. Despite his frailty at the time of the Crucifixion, when he denied Jesus three times, he was entrusted with the "keys of the Kingdom of Heaven." He was the first to baptize a Gentile convert. In Antioch he worked in harmony with **Paul** for a time, but the famous dispute (Galatians 2:11–21) led to the termination of Paul's ministry in that city. Peter's missionary activity seems to have extended to Pontus, Cappadocia, Galatia, Asia and Bithynia. That he suffered martyrdom is clear from John 21:18, 19, and is corroborated by ecclesiastical tradition: **Eusebius of Caesarea** says he was crucified with his head downward. Tradition from the end of the 2nd century suggests he died in Rome, and he is regarded by the Catholic Church as the first Bishop of Rome. The first epistle of Peter is usually accepted as genuine, but not the second. His feast day is June 29.

Peter I, *known as* **the Great** 1672–1725 •*Czar and emperor of Russia*• He was born in Moscow, the fourth son of the Czar **Alexis I Mikhailovich** by his second wife. He was made co-czar in 1682 with his mentally disabled half brother Ivan V (1666–96) on the death of their elder brother, Fyodor III, and under the regency of their sister, the Grandduchess Sophia (d. 1704). He became emperor in 1721. In 1689 he had his sister arrested and immured in a convent, and ruled on his own with his brother as a figurehead. In 1689 he married Eudoxia (1669–1731), the pious daughter of a boyar, by whom he had a son in 1690, the czarevitch Alexis (father of the future **Peter II**). In 1695 he served as a humble bombardier in the war against the Turks; in 1696 he captured the vital seaport of Azov; in 1697 he set off on a tour of Europe, whose main official purpose was to secure allies against the Turks. In the course of the 16-month journey he amassed knowledge of Western technology and hired thousands of craftsmen and military personnel to take back to Russia. He returned to Russia in the summer of 1698 to repress a revolt of the *streltsy* (regiments of musketeers), and Eudoxia, accused of conspiracy, was divorced and sent to a convent. Peter, often brutally and against the wishes of his people, set about the Westernization of Russia. In 1700, in alliance with Denmark and **Augustus II (the Strong)**, king of Poland and elector of Saxony, he launched the Great Northern War against Sweden (1700–21). Initially defeated, Peter ordered the church bells in Moscow melted down to make new cannons. He triumphed over the Swedish army in 1709 at the Battle of Poltava in Ukraine, and the 1721 Peace of Nystadt saw Sweden cede parts of Finland plus Ingria, Estonia and Latvia. In 1703 Peter had begun the construction of the new city and port of St Petersburg, which was designated as the capital of the empire. In 1712 he married his Lithuanian mistress, Catherine (the future **Catherine I**). In 1718 his son Alexis was imprisoned for suspected treason and died after torture. In 1723 Peter had Catherine crowned empress, and at his death she succeeded him without opposition. Peter had achieved during his reign a kind of cultural revolution that made Russia part of the general European state system for the first time in its history, and established it as a major power.

Peter II 1715–30 •*Czar of Russia*• The grandson of **Peter I** (the Great), and the son of the czarevich Alexis (1690–1718), he was born in St Petersburg and succeeded to the throne in 1727 on the death of his stepgrandmother, **Catherine I**. He died of smallpox on the day designated for his wedding. He was succeeded by the empress **Anna Ivanovna**, daughter of Peter the Great's half brother and co-czar, Ivan V.

Peter III 1728–62 •*Czar of Russia*• The grandson of **Peter I** (the Great) and the son of Peter's youngest daughter, Anna, and Charles Frederick, Duke of Holstein-Gottorp, he was born in Kiel. In 1742 he was declared heir presumptive to his aunt, the empress **Elizabeth Petrovna**, and in 1745 he married Sophia-Augusta von Anhalt-Zerbst (the future empress **Catherine II**). A weak and unstable man, and a great admirer of **Frederick II (the Great)**, he withdrew Russia's forces from the Seven Years' War as soon as he succeeded to the throne (1762), and restored East Prussia to Frederick. This enraged the army and aristocracy, and he was deposed (June 1762) by a group of nobles inspired by his wife Catherine and led by her lover, Count Orlov. He was strangled in captivity a few days later, and Catherine was proclaimed empress.

Peter I 1844–1921 •*King of Serbia*• The son of Prince Alexander Karadjordjević, he was born in Belgrade. He lived in exile for 45 years after his father's abdication (1858), fought in the French army in the Franco-Prussian War (1870–71), and was elected king of Serbia by the Serbian parliament (1903). In World War I he accompanied his army into exile in Greece (1916). He returned to Belgrade (1918) and was proclaimed titular king of the Serbs, Croats and Slovenes, although, because of his ill health, his second son, Alexander (1888–1934)—later Alexander I—was regent.

Peter II 1923–70 •*King of Yugoslavia*• Born in Belgrade, the son of Alexander I (1888–1934), he was at school in England when his father was assassinated (1934). His uncle, Prince Paul Karadjordjević (1873–1976), was regent until 1941 when he was ousted by pro-Allied army officers, who declared King Peter of age, and he assumed sovereignty. The subsequent German attack on Yugoslavia forced the king to go into exile within three weeks. He lost his throne when Yugoslavia became a republic (1945). From then on he lived mainly in California.

Peter the Hermit, *also called* **Peter of Amiens** c. 1050–c. 1115 •*French monk*• Born in Amiens, he served as a soldier, then became a monk. When **Urban II** launched the First Crusade at a council in Clermont in 1096, Peter traversed Europe, generating enthusiasm with vivid and emotive preaching. He rallied an army of 20,000 peasants, and led one section of the crusading army to Asia Minor, where it was defeated by the Turks at Nicaea. He later founded the monastery of Neufmoutier at Liée, Belgium.

Peters, Ellis, *pseudonym of* **Edith Mary Pargeter** 1913–95 •*English crime writer and novelist*• She lived in Shropshire. Always a prolific writer, she wrote a string of quietly successful detective novels under her pseudonym, many featuring Inspector Felse. Real success, however, came in her sixties when, reading about a historical incident in which the relics of St Winifred were moved to Shrewsbury Abbey, she hit upon the idea of Brother Cadfael, a medieval detective. *A Morbid Taste for Bones: A Mediaeval Whodunnit* (1977, as Ellis Peters) was an instant hit, and a series was born. The series was filmed for television starring Sir **Derek Jacobi** in the title role. She was also an accomplished translator of Czech-language literature.

Peterson, Oscar Emmanuel 1925– •*Canadian jazz pianist and composer*• He was born in Montreal, the son of immigrants from the West Indies. He studied piano from childhood and developed a phenomenal technique and driving style, comparable with that of **Art Tatum**, of whom he was an admirer and friend. From 1949 Peterson's work with the touring "Jazz at the Philharmonic" groups brought him international recognition. A prolific recording artist, his compositions include *Canadiana Suite* (1963), *Royal Suite* (1981) and *Africa Suite* (1983), written for ballet. He was made Commandeur, L'Ordre des Arts et des Lettres, in 1989 and has won numerous awards, including the IMC/UNESCO International Music Prize in 2000.

Peterson, Roger Tory 1908–96 •*US ornithologist and artist*• Born in Jamestown, New York, he studied art and design in New York City, then pursued an interest in ornithology while teaching in Massachusetts. In 1934 he published his *Field Guide to the Birds*, the first in a series of popular guides to the birds of North America and Mexico, illustrated with his own paintings.

Petipa, Marius 1818–1910 •*French dancer, ballet master and choreographer*• He was born in Marseilles. After touring France, Spain and the US as a dancer, he went to St Petersburg in 1847 to join the Imperial Theater. In 1858 he became the company's second ballet master, and four years later staged his first ballet, *Pharaoh's Daughter*, setting the style of *ballet à grand spectacle* which was to dominate Russian ballet for the rest of the century. In 1869 he became ballet master, and in the 34 years until his retirement in 1903 he created 46 original ballets, the most famous being **Tchaikovsky**'s *The Sleeping Beauty* (1890) and *Swan Lake* (1895).

Petit, Alexis Thérèse 1791–1820 •*French physicist*• Born in Vesoul, Haute-Saône, he became professor at the Lycée Bonaparte, and enunciated with Pierre Louis Dulong (1785–1838) the law of Dulong and Petit that states that for all elements the product of the specific heat and the atomic weight is the same.

Petit, Roland 1924– •*French choreographer and dancer*• Born in Paris, he began his studies at the Paris Opera under **Serge Lifar** at the age of nine, becoming the company's principal dancer (1943–44). Following a short period with the Ballets des Champs-Elysées, he founded his own troupe in 1948, Les Ballets de Paris de Roland Petit. From 1972 to 1997 he was artistic director of the Ballet National de Marseilles. He created many new ballets including *Le rossignol et la rose* (1944, "The Nightingale and the Rose"), a story by **Oscar Wilde** set to **Schumann**'s music; **Jean Anouilh**'s *Les demoiselles de la nuit* (1948, "The Young Ladies of the Night"); *Pink Floyd Ballet* (1972); *Nana* (1976) and *Marcel Proust Remembered* (1980). During the 1950s he was very active in the film industry, creating the ballet sequences in the film *Hans Christian Andersen* (1952), danced by his wife, Zizi Jeanmaire.

Petőfi, Sándor 1823–49? •*Hungarian poet*• He was born in Kiskőrös, and became an actor, soldier, then literary hack, but by 1844 had made his name as a poet, his most popular work being *János vitéz* (1845, "Janos the Hero"). His poetry broke completely with the old pedantic style, and, full of national feeling, began a new epoch in Hungarian literature. He also wrote a novel called *A hóhér kötele* (1846, "The Hangman's Rope").

Pétomane, Le *See* **Pujol, Joseph**

Petrarch, Francesco Petrarca 1304–74 •*Italian poet and scholar, one of the earliest and greatest of modern lyric poets*• Born in Arezzo, he was the son of an exiled Florentine notary. In 1312 his father went to Avignon, then the seat of the papal court, and there and in Bologna Francesco devoted himself with enthusiasm to the study of the classics, returning to Avignon after his father's death (1326). To obtain an income he became a churchman, and lived on the small benefices conferred by his many patrons. It was during this period (1327) that he first saw Laura (possibly Laure de Noves, married in 1325 to Hugo de Sade; she died, the mother of 11 children, in 1348). She inspired him with a passion which has become proverbial for its constancy and purity. Also at this time he began his friendship with the powerful Roman family of the Colonnas. As the fame of Petrarch's learning and genius grew, his position became one of unprecedented influence, and the most powerful sovereigns of the day competed for his presence at their courts. He traveled repeatedly in France, Germany and Flanders, searching for manuscripts. In Liège he found two new orations of **Cicero**, in Verona a collection of his letters, and in Florence an unknown portion of **Quintilian**. Invited by the Senate of Rome on Easter Sunday, 1341, he ascended the Capitol and was crowned poet laureate. In 1353, after the death of Laura and his friend Cardinal Colonna, he left Avignon and his country house at Vaucluse forever, disgusted with the corruption of the papal court. His remaining years were passed in various towns of northern Italy. Petrarch is considered the earliest of the great humanists of the Renaissance. It is as a poet that his fame has lasted for over five centuries, based on his *Canzoniere*, the Italian sonnets, madrigals, and songs that were almost all inspired by his unrequited passion for Laura.

Petrie, Sir (William Matthew) Flinders 1853–1942 •*English archaeologist and Egyptologist*• Born in Charlton, Kent, he was educated privately. He surveyed Stonehenge (1874–77), but turned from 1881 entirely to Egyptology, beginning by surveying the pyramids and temples of Giza and excavating the mounds of Tanis and Naucratis. The author of over 100 books, he became the first Edwards Professor of Archaeology at London (1892–1933), and continued excavating in Egypt and Palestine until well into his eighties.

Petronius Arbiter 1st century AD •*Roman satirist, author of the Satyricon*• He is usually supposed to be the voluptuary Gaius Petronius, whom **Tacitus** calls "arbiter elegantiae" at the court of **Nero**. He was governor of Bithynia for a time. The *Satyricon* ("Tales of Satyrs") is a long satirical romance in prose and verse, of which only parts of the 15th and 16th books still survive. The work depicts with wit, humor and realism the licentious life in southern Italy of the moneyed class. The favor Petronius enjoyed as Nero's aider and abettor and his entourage in every form of sensual indulgence aroused the jealousy of another confidant, Tigellinus, who procured his disgrace and banishment. Ordered to commit suicide, he cut open his veins.

“ ”

Abiit ad plures.
He has gone to the majority.

(ie He has died) ***Satyricon**, 42.*

Petrosian, Tigran Vartanovich 1929–84 •*USSR chess player*• He was born in Tbilisi, Georgia. He won the world championship from **Mikhail Botvinnik** in 1963 and made one successful defense, before losing it to **Boris Spassky** in 1969. His awkward, defensive style of chess earned him the nickname "Iron Tigran."

Petrovitch, Aleksis *See* **Alexis Petrovich**

Pettit, Bob (Robert E Lee) 1932– •*US basketball player*• Born in Baton Rouge, Louisiana, he enjoyed success in college basketball at Louisiana State University. In 1954, he began playing for the Milwaukee (later St Louis) Hawks. Superbly fit and among basketball's tallest centers (at six feet nine inches), he spent the next 11 years with the Hawks and inspired the team's NBA championship triumph of 1958. He was twice voted Most Valuable Player in the NBA (1956 and 1959). By the time of his retirement in 1965 he was the league's highest scorer (at 20,880) and the second highest rebounder (at 12,849).

Petty, Richard 1937– •*US racecar driver*• He was born in Level Cross, North Carolina. During more than three decades in stock-car racing (1958–92), he won 200 National Association for Stock Car Auto Racing (NASCAR) races, almost twice as many as any other driver at that time. His victories included a record of 7 Daytona 500 races and 7 NASCAR championships.

Pevsner, Antoine 1886–1962 •*French Constructivist sculptor and painter*• Born in Orël, Russia, he studied art in Kiev. He helped form the Suprematist Group in Moscow with **Kasimir Malevich**, **Vladimir Tatlin** and his brother, **Naum Gabo**. In 1920 he broke away from the Suprematists and issued the *Realist Manifesto* with his brother. This ultimately caused their exile from Russia, and he went to Paris. Several of his completely nonfigurative constructions (mainly in copper and bronze) are in the Museum of Modern Art, New York.

Pevsner, Sir Nikolaus Bernhard 1902–83 •*British art historian*• Born in Leipzig, Germany, he was a lecturer in art at the University of Göttingen until the Nazis came to power in 1933, when he fled to Great Britain and there became an authority on English architecture. His books include *An Enquiry Into Industrial Art in England* (1937), *Pioneers of the Modern Movement* (1936), and the very popular *An Outline of European Architecture* (1942), and he also became art editor for Penguin Books (1949). He was Slade Professor of Fine Art at Cambridge (1949–55). He also produced a series for Penguin Books, *The Buildings of England* (50 vols, 1951–74).

Pfeiffer, Michelle 1958– •*US film actress*• Born in Santa Ana, California, she began her career in television commercials before making her feature-film debut in *Falling in Love Again* (1980). Her first major commercial success was in *The Witches of Eastwick* (1987), and her delicate performance in *Dangerous Liaisons* (1988) brought her a Best Supporting Actress Academy Award nomination. She has consolidated her success with roles in *The Fabulous*

Baker Boys (1989), *The Russia House* (1990), *Batman Returns* (1992), *The Age of Innocence* (1994) and *What Lies Beneath* (2000).

Phalaris 6th century BC •*Greek tyrant of Acragas (Agrigentum) in Sicily*• He greatly embellished the city, and extended his sway over large districts in Sicily. After holding power for 16 years, he was overthrown and allegedly roasted alive in his own invention, the brazen bull.

Pheidias *See* **Phidias**

Phidias or **Pheidias** 5th century BC •*Greek sculptor, one of the major ancient Greek artists*• He was born in Athens, and received from **Pericles** a magnificent commission to execute the city's chief statues, becoming superintendent of all public works. He supervised the construction of the Propylaea and the Parthenon, designed the sculpture on the walls, and is thought to have made the gold-and-ivory *Athena* there, and the *Zeus* at Olympia (both lost) himself. Charged with appropriating gold from the statue and carving his own head on an ornament, he was accused of impiety, and disappeared from Athens.

Philby, Kim, *properly* **Harold Adrian Russell Philby** 1911–88 •*British double agent*• He was born in Ambala, India, the son of Arabist and explorer Harry St John Philby (1885–1960). He was educated at Westminster and Trinity College, Cambridge, where, like **Anthony Blunt**, **Donald Maclean** and **Guy Burgess**, he became a communist, and was recruited as a Soviet agent. He was employed by the British Secret Intelligence Service (MI6) and was head of anticommunist counterespionage (1944–46). In 1949–51 he was posted in Washington DC as chief liaison officer between MI6 and the CIA, but was asked to resign because of his earlier communist sympathies. He was a journalist in Beirut from 1956 until 1963, when he admitted his espionage and defected to the USSR. There he was granted citizenship and became a colonel in the KGB (Soviet Intelligence Service).

Philip, St 1st century AD •*One of the 12 Apostles of Jesus*• From Bethsaida, Galilee, he is mentioned in Mark 3:14 and Acts 1. John's Gospel relates that he led Nathanael to **Jesus** (1:43), was present at the feeding of the 5,000 (6:1) and brought some Greeks to meet Jesus (12:21). His later career is unknown, but traditions suggest he was martyred on a cross. He is not to be confused with Philip "the Evangelist" (Acts 6:5 and Acts 8). His feast day is May 1 (West) or November 14 (East).

Philip I 1052–1108 •*King of France*• The son of **Henry I**, he ruled from 1060. Although he increased royal wealth, his reign marked a low point in the prestige of the Capetian monarchy, largely due to his elopement with Bertrada, wife of Fulk of Anjou, a scandal which led to his excommunication. Extreme obesity caused him to allow his son **Louis VI** to administer the kingdom from 1104.

Philip II, *known as* **Philip Augustus** 1165–1223 •*First great Capetian king of France*• The son of **Louis VII**, he was born in Paris and crowned joint king in 1179. He succeeded his father (1180) and married Isabella of Hainault, the last direct descendant of the Carolingians. He supported the sons of **Henry II** of England against their father. **Richard I** and he set out on the Third Crusade (1190–91), but he soon returned to France and partitioned Richard's French territories with **John**. Richard's sudden return caused an exhausting war till 1199. In 1204 he conquered Normandy, Maine, Anjou and Touraine, with part of Poitou, and secured the overlordship of Brittany. The victory of Bouvines (1214) over the Flemish, the English, and the emperor Otto IV established his throne securely. His efficient, centralized government was based on royal officials controlling the feudal nobility, backed by the new university in Paris. Notre Dame remains a lasting monument of his attention to the fortification and layout of Paris.

Philip III (the Bold) 1245–85 •*King of France*• He was with his father, **Louis IX** (St Louis), at his death in Tunis (1270) and succeeded him to the throne. He fought several unlucky campaigns in Spain, the last of which, the attack on Aragon, caused his death from fever.

Philip IV (the Fair) 1268–1314 •*King of France*• Born at Fontainebleau, he succeeded his father, **Philip III (the Bold)**, in 1285. By his marriage to Queen Joanna of Navarre he acquired Navarre, Champagne and Brie. He overran Flanders, but was defeated by the Flemings at Courtrai (1302). His struggle with Pope Boniface VIII arose from his attempts to tax the French clergy. The king's reply to the papal bull *Unam Sanctam* was to send his minister William de Nogaret to seize Boniface, who escaped but died soon afterward (1303). After the short pontificate of Benedict XI, Philip procured the elevation of the pliant Frenchman, **Clement V** (1305), who came to reside at Avignon, thus beginning the 70-year "Babylonian captivity" of the papacy. Coveting the wealth of the Templars, Philip forced the pope to suppress the order (1312) and he appropriated their property. He fostered a strong central administration in France, encouraged French unity by summoning the Estates General and appointed capable ministers.

Philip VI, of Valois 1293–1350 •*First Valois king of France*• The son of Charles of Valois, younger brother of **Philip IV (the Fair)**, he became king on the death of **Charles IV** (1328). His right was denied by **Edward III** of England, son of Philip IV's daughter, who declared that females, though excluded by the Salic Law, could transmit their rights to their children. Thus began the Hundred Years' War with England in 1337. The French fleet was destroyed off Sluys (1340), and in 1346 Edward III landed in Normandy, and defeated Philip at Crécy, just as the Black Death was about to spread through France.

Philip II 382–336 BC •*King of Macedonia*• The father of **Alexander the Great**, he was born in Pella, and made himself king in 359 BC. He built up the army and pursued a policy of expansion and opportunism. He warred with most of Greece, made peace with the Athenians (346 BC), but was back at war with them (340) when he besieged Byzantium and Perinthus. In 339 the Amphicytyonic Council declared war against the Locrians of Amphissa, appointing Philip as their commander. The Athenians formed a league with the Thebans against him, but their forces were decisively defeated at Chaeronea (338), and Philip organized the Greek states in a federal league (the League of Corinth). His son Alexander the Great took over where Philip left off and conquered the Persian Empire.

Philip V 238–179 BC •*King of Macedonia in the Antigonid dynasty*• Adopted by Antigonus Doson whom he succeeded in 221 BC, he inherited a strong kingdom but, ambitious and active, he came into conflict with the growing power of Rome. He made an alliance with **Hannibal** (215) during the Second Punic War, which resulted in a first (indecisive) conflict with Rome (214–205). Conflict broke out again with Rome in the Second Macedonian War (200–196), which led to his defeat at Cynoscephalae (197). He was succeeded by his son Perseus.

Philip I (the Handsome) 1478–1506 •*King of Castile*• The son of Emperor **Maximilian I** and Mary of Burgundy, he was born at Bruges, and as Archduke of Austria and Duke of Burgundy he was married in 1496 to the Infanta of Spain, Juana ("Juana the Mad," 1479–1555), daughter of **Ferdinand the Catholic**, of Aragon, and **Isabella of Castile**. Isabella's death (1504) made Juana the queen of Castile, but Ferdinand declared himself her regent. In 1506 Philip went to claim the throne, but died in the same year, and Juana, who suffered from depression, was confined by her father. Their children were the Holy Roman emperors **Charles V** and his successor, **Ferdinand I**.

Philip II of Spain and **I of Portugal** 1527–98 •*King of Spain and of Portugal*• He was born in Valladolid, the only son of Emperor **Charles V**. In 1543 he married the Infanta Mary of Portugal, who died in 1546 giving birth to their son, **Don Carlos**. In 1554 he married **Mary I** (Mary Tudor) of England, but spent only 14 months in that country, where the marriage was not popular. In 1555–56 Charles abdicated the sovereignty of Spain, the Netherlands, and all Spanish dominions in Italy and the New World to Philip (king of Spain from 1556), who inherited an empire suffering from a serious financial crisis. Philip increasingly identified himself with the Spanish Inquisition, which he saw as useful both for combating heresy and for extending his control over his own dominions. He was involved in war against France and the papacy (1557–59), and against the Turks in the Mediterranean (1560), both wars necessitating a sharp increase in domestic taxation which served only to increase unrest. Mary Tudor died in 1558. Philip failed to secure the hand of her sister and successor, **Elizabeth I**, married Isabella of France (daughter of **Henry II**) in 1559 to seal the Valois-Habsburg peace, and in 1570 married as his fourth wife, his cousin Anna, daughter of the emperor **Maximilian II**, by whom he had a son, the future **Philip III**. At home, he faced threats from the Moriscos (converted Muslims) of Granada, and, more seriously, from the Netherlands, in open revolt from 1573. Abroad, Spain contributed to the Holy League against the Ottoman Turks, which, under the command of Philip's half brother, Don **John of Austria**, defeated the Ottoman fleet at Lepanto in 1571. In 1575, for the second time in Philip's reign, the Spanish crown was obliged to declare itself bankrupt, and in 1576 the discontented and unpaid Spanish troops in the Netherlands ran wild and sacked the city of Antwerp. In 1579 seven United Provinces of the Low Countries won independence. In 1580 Philip succeeded to the Portuguese throne. The increase in trade revenue from the New World in the 1580s resulted in a new prosperity and a more confident expansionist policy, and in 1588, the year after Sir **Francis Drake**'s sack of Cádiz, the great Armada was launched against England but was destroyed. The 1590s saw further revolt in Aragon (1591–92) and renewed financial crisis leading in 1596 to a third bankruptcy. Philip died two years later, leaving his empire divided, demoralized and economically depressed. The violence of his campaign against Protestants had destroyed all harmony within his dominions, while constant wars continued to deplete Spain's financial resources.

Philip III 1578–1621 •*King of Spain*• Born in Madrid, he was the son of **Philip II** (by his fourth marriage), whom he succeeded in 1598. Pious and indolent, he left government to his favorites, and devoted himself to hunting, bullfights and court entertainments. During his reign, agriculture and industry declined, and foreign wars (after 1618) drained the treasury. From 1609 to 1614, 275,000 Moriscos (Muslim converts to Christianity) were expelled from Spain with serious economic and demographic effects. He was succeeded by his son, **Philip IV**.

Philip IV 1605–65 •*King of Spain*• Born in Valladolid, he was the son and successor in 1621 of **Philip III**. A discerning patron of the arts (particularly of **Velázquez**), and a periodically remorseful debauchee, he left the administration of government to his favorite (*valido*), the Count-Duke of Olivares (1587–1645). Spain declined as a dominant European power during his reign. France declared open war (1635), in 1640 Portugal regained its independence, and the United Provinces confirmed theirs at the Treaty of Westphalia (1648). His daughter, Maria Theresa (1638–83), was the first wife of **Louis XIV** of France. He was succeeded by his four-year-old son, **Charles II**, the last of the Spanish Habsburgs.

Philip V 1683–1746 •*Duke of Anjou and first Bourbon king of Spain*• The grandson of **Louis XIV** of France, he was born at Versailles, and in 1700 succeeded to the Spanish throne under the will of **Charles II**. The prospect of a French prince ruling Spain precipitated the War of the Spanish Succession (1701–13). Spain lost Gibraltar and Minorca to the British, the Spanish Netherlands and Naples to Austria, and Sicily to the House of Savoy. Although vigorous in his youth, Philip became depressed, weary and eccentric under the domination of his second wife, Isabella Farnese of Parma, and her Italian favorite, Guilio Alberoni (1664–1752). In 1732 Oran was reconquered from the Moors and war with Austria (1733–36) regained Naples and Sicily. At Philip's death, Spain was involved in the War of the Austrian Succession (1740–48).

Philip I (the Arab) d. 249 AD •*Roman emperor*• Of Arab descent, he came to power (244) by causing the death of Gordian III. He celebrated the 1,000th anniversary of the founding of Rome with a mammoth staging of secular games (248), the last time they were celebrated in Roman history. His reign was plagued by usurpations, and he was killed in battle by **Decius**, who succeeded him.

Philip, Prince *See* **Edinburgh, Duke of**

Philip Neri, St *See* **Neri, St Philip**

Philip the Bold ("le Hardi") 1342–1404 •*Duke of Burgundy*• Born in Pontoise, the youngest son of John the Good, king of France, he fought at Poitiers (1356) and shared his father's captivity in England. He was made Duke of Burgundy in 1364, and married Margaret, heiress of Flanders, in 1369. In 1382 he subdued a Flemish rebellion at Roosebeke, and soon gained that country (1384–85). His wise government won the esteem of his new subjects. Following the insanity of his nephew, the French king, Charles VI, he became virtual ruler of France.

Philip the Good 1396–1467 •*Duke of Burgundy*• Born in Dijon, the grandson of **Philip the Bold**, he became Duke of Burgundy in 1419. Though he at first recognized **Henry V** of England as heir to the French Crown, he concluded a separate peace with the French (1435) and created one of the most powerful states in later medieval Europe, adding Brabant, Holland, Zeeland and Luxembourg (1430–43). **Jan van Eyck** was one of his court painters. A committed crusader, he maintained a fleet for operations against the Ottoman Turks.

Philip, *properly* **Metacomet** c. 1638–76 •*Native American leader*• Born on the lands of the Wampanoag people (now part of Massachusetts and Rhode Island), in 1662 he succeeded his older brother as chief. Called Philip or King Philip by the English, he led a confederation of tribes against the European settlers. King Philip's War (1675–76) raged throughout New England and was characterized by atrocities on both sides. Philip himself was shot after the final battle by one of his own braves, and his wife and nine-year-old son, along with hundreds of his people, were sold into slavery by the victorious colonists. His head was displayed on the fort at Plymouth, Massachusetts, for 25 years.

Philippa of Hainault c. 1314–69 •*Queen of England*• On her marriage to her second cousin **Edward III** at York (1327), she took Flemish weavers to England and made the French poet and historian **Jean Froissart** her secretary. She is said to have roused the English troops before the defeat of the Scots at Neville's Cross (1346), and to have interceded (1347) with Edward for mercy for the Burgesses of Calais. The Queen's College, Oxford, founded by Philippa's chaplain (1341), was named after her.

Philips, Ambrose c. 1674–1749 •*English poet*• Born in Shrewsbury, Shropshire, he was educated at St John's College, Cambridge, where he became a Fellow. He was Member of Parliament for Armagh, secretary to the Archbishop of Armagh, and registrar of the Prerogative Court. A friend of **Joseph Addison** and **Richard Steele**, he did hack writing, and gained a reputation with the *Winter-piece* in the *Tatler* and six pastorals in Tonson's *Miscellany* (1709). These were praised in the *Guardian* at **Pope**'s expense, and Pope's jealousy started a bitter feud. Of his plays only *The Distrest Mother* (1712) found favor with his contemporaries.

Philips, Katherine, *née* **Fowler**, *called* **the Matchless Orinda** 1631–64 •*English poet*• She was born in London, and at 16 married James Philips of Cardigan Priory. She is the first English woman poet to have her work published, and she received a dedication from **Jeremy Taylor** (*Discourse on the Nature, Offices and Measures of Friendship*, 1659). She translated **Pierre Corneille**'s *Pompée* and the greater part of his *Horace*. Her own poems, surreptitiously printed in 1663, were issued in 1667. She ran a literary salon, described in the *Letter of Orinda to Poliarchus* (1705). She died of smallpox on a visit to London.

Phillip, Arthur 1738–1814 •*English naval commander*• Born in London, he trained at Greenwich and joined the navy in 1755. He served in the Mediterranean with **George Byng**, and was at the taking of Havana. In 1787 he was appointed commander of the "First fleet" carrying convicts to Australia. He landed at Botany Bay on January 18, 1788, but chose Port Jackson instead for his penal colony settlement, establishing it on January 26 (Australia Day). He was founder and first governor of New South Wales.

Phillips, Mark Anthony Peter 1948– •*Equestrian and former husband of Princess Anne*• Born in Tetbury, Gloucestershire, he was educated at Marlborough and Sandhurst, joining the Queen's Dragoon Guards in 1969. In 1973 he married Princess **Anne**, but separated from her in 1989; they were divorced in 1992. A noted horseman, he was a regular member of the British Equestrian Team (1970–76), and won many team events, including the gold medal at the Olympic Games in Munich (1972). He has been consultant for the Gleneagles Mark Phillips Equestrian Centre in Scotland since 1992.

Phillips, Wendell 1811–84 •*US abolitionist*• Born in Boston, he graduated from Harvard in 1831 and was called to the bar in 1834. By 1837 he was the chief orator of the antislavery party, closely associated with **William Lloyd Garrison**. He called for defiance of the Fugitive Slave Law and argued that slaves deserved not only their freedom, but land, education and civil rights. He also championed the causes of temperance and the rights of women and of Native Americans.

“ ”

Revolutions are not made; they come.

1852 Speech, January 8.

Philo 2nd century AD •*Byzantine scientist*• He wrote a treatise on military engineering of which some fragments remain. He was probably the first to record the contraction of air in a globe over water when a candle is burned in it.

Philo Judaeus c. 20 BC–c. 40 AD •*Hellenistic Jewish philosopher*• He was born in Alexandria, Egypt, where he was a leading member of the Jewish community. A prolific author, his work brought together Greek philosophy and Jewish scripture, and greatly influenced subsequent Greek Christian theologians like **St Clement of Alexandria** and **Origen**. Most of his works consist of commentaries on the Pentateuch. In c. 40 AD he headed a deputation to the mad emperor **Caligula** to plead with him on behalf of Jews who refused to worship him, as he records in *De legatione*.

Phiz *See* **Browne, Hablot K(night)**

Phocion c. 397–318 BC •*Athenian soldier and politician*• Elected general 45 times, he commanded a division of the Athenian fleet at Naxos in 376 BC, and helped conquer Cyprus in 351 for **Artaxerxes III**. In 341 he crushed the Macedonian party in Euboea, and in 340 forced **Philip II** of Macedon to evacuate the Chersonesus, but advised Athens to make peace with him. The advice was not taken, but the disastrous Battle of Chaeronea in 338 proved its sense. Subsequently, he consistently opposed resistance to Macedonia. During a brief return to democracy in Athens, he was put to death on a charge of treason.

Phomvihane, Kaysone 1920–92 •*Laotian statesman*• Born in Savannakhet province and educated at the National University of Hanoi, he fought with the anti-French forces in Vietnam after World War II and joined the exiled Free Lao Front (Neo Lao Issara) nationalist movement in Bangkok in 1945. He later became leader of the communist Pathet Lao in 1955. He successfully directed guerrilla resistance to the incumbent rightist regime and in 1975 became prime minister of the newly formed People's Democratic Republic of Laos and general-secretary of the Lao People's Revolutionary Party. Initially he attempted to follow a radical socialist program of industrial nationalization and rural collectivization, but later began a policy of economic and political liberalization.

Photius c. 820–91 •*Byzantine prelate*• Born in Constantinople (Istanbul), Photius was hurried through holy orders and installed as Patriarch of Constantinople when Ignatius was deposed (858). In 862, however, Pope **Nicholas I** called a council at Rome to declare Photius's election invalid and reinstate Ignatius. In return, Photius assembled a council at Constantinople (867) which excommunicated Nicholas. Photius was then deposed and reinstated on several occasions, erased the *Filioque* clause from the Creed (879), and was finally exiled to Armenia (886). Among his surviving works are *Myriobiblon*, or *Bibliotheca*, a summary review of 280 works which Photius had read, the *Nomocanon*, a collection of the acts and decrees of the councils and ecclesiastical laws of the emperors, and a collection of letters. His feast day is February 6 (East).

Phryne 4th century BC •*Greek courtesan*• Born in Thespiae, Boeotia, she became enormously rich through her many lovers. Accused of profaning the Eleusinian mysteries, she was defended by the orator **Hyperides**, who threw off her robe in court, showing her loveliness, and so gained the verdict.

Piaf, Edith, *originally* **Edith Giovanna Gassion** 1915–63 •*French singer*• Born in Paris, she started her career by singing in the streets. Graduating to music halls and cabarets, she became known as Piaf, from the Parisian argot for "little sparrow," which suited her waiflike appearance. She appeared in stage plays and in films, but it was for her songs with their undercurrent of sadness and nostalgia, written by herself and songwriters such as **Jacques Prévert**, that she became well known, traveling widely in Europe and the US. After a severe illness she made a very successful but brief return to the stage in 1961, before recurring ill health led to her death two years later. Among her best-remembered songs are *Le Voyage du pauvre nègre, Mon légionnaire, Un monsieur m'a suivi dans la rue, La vie en rose*, and *Non, je ne regrette rien*. She was the daughter of the famous acrobat Jean Gassion.

Piaget, Jean 1896–1980 •*Swiss psychologist, a pioneer in the study of child intelligence*• Born in Neuchâtel, he studied zoology before turning to psychology and becoming Professor of Psychology at the University of Geneva (1929–54), director of the Centre d'Epistémologie Génétique and a director of the Institut des Sciences de l'Éducation. He is best known for his research on the development of cognitive functions (perception, intelligence, logic), for his intensive case-study methods of research, and for postulating stages of cognitive development. His books include *The Child's Conception of the World* (1926) and *The Early Growth of Logic in the Child* (1958).

Picabia, Francis 1879–1953 •*French Dadaist painter*• He was born in Paris. He was originally an Impressionist, but took part in every modern movement—Neoimpressionism, Cubism, Futurism, and finally, with **Marcel Duchamp**, Dadaism. His anti-art productions, often portraying imaginary machinery in satirical comparisons to the human condition, include *Parade amoureuse* (1917), *Infant Carburetor*, and many of the cover designs for the US anti-art magazine *291*, which he edited.

Picard, (Charles) Émile 1856–1941 •*French mathematician*• Born in Paris, he became professor at the Sorbonne (1886–97). Noted for his work in complex analysis and integral and differential equations, he investigated complex functions and wrote the definitive work of his generation on the theory of complex surfaces and integrals. Picard also introduced the method of successive approximations, a powerful technique for determining whether solutions to differential equations exist.

Picard, Jean 1620–82 •*French astronomer*• Born in La Flèche, Anjou, in 1645 he became professor in the Collège de France and helped to found the Paris observatory. He made the first accurate measurement of a degree of a meridian and thus arrived at an estimate of the radius of the Earth. He visited **Tycho Brahe**'s observatory on the island of Hven, and determined its latitude and longitude.

Picasso, Pablo 1881–1973 •*Spanish painter*• He was born in Málaga, Andalusia, the son of an art teacher, José Ruiz Blasco, and Maria Picasso y Lopez, whose maiden name he adopted. At the age of 14 he entered the academy at Barcelona; there he painted *Barefoot Girl* (1895). After two years he transferred to Madrid for more advanced study, and in 1898 he won a gold medal for *Customs of Aragon*. By now he was a master of the traditional forms of art, shown for example in his *Gypsy Girl on the Beach* (1898), and he quickly absorbed Neoimpressionist influences, as exemplified in *Longchamp* (1901), *The Blue Room* (1901), and other works. However, he soon began to develop his own idiom. The blue period (1902–04; referring to colors as well as mood), a series of striking studies of the poor in haunting attitudes of despair and gloom, gave way to the bright, life-affirming pink period (1904–06). Pink turned to brown in *La Coiffure* (1905–06) and the remarkable portrait of **Gertrude Stein** (1906). His interest in sculpture and his new enthusiasm for black art are fully reflected in the transitional *Two Nudes* (1906), which heralded his epoch-making break with tradition in *Les demoiselles d'Avignon* (1906–07), the first full-blown example of analytical Cubism, an attempt to render the three-dimensional on the flat picture surface without resorting to perspective. Nature was no longer to be copied, decorated or idealized, but exploited for creative ends. Its exclusive emphasis on formal, geometrical criteria contrasted sharply with the cult of color of the Fauvists, to whom he and **Georges Braque** for a time belonged, before the two joined forces in 1909 for their exploration of

Cubism through its various phases: analytic, synthetic, hermetic and rococo, in which collage, pieces of wood, wire, newspaper and string became media side by side with paint. The *Ma Jolie* series of pictures, after the music-hall song score which appears in them (1911–14), are examples of the last phase. From 1917 Picasso became associated with **Sergei Diaghilev**'s Ballets Russes, designing costumes and sets in both Cubist and neoclassical styles. The grotesque facial and bodily distortions of the *Three Dancers* (1925) foreshadows the immense canvas of *Guernica* (1937), which expressed Picasso's horror of the bombing of this Basque town during the civil war, of war in general and compassion and hope for its victims. During World War II Picasso was mostly in Paris, and after the liberation he joined the Communists. Picasso worked in a great variety of media, and was above all an innovator. As well as sculpture and painting, he produced constructions in metal, pottery, drawings, engravings, aquatints and lithographs.

“ ”

I paint objects as I think them, not as I see them.

Quoted in John Golding ***Cubism*** *(1959).*

Piccard, Auguste Antoine 1884–1962 •*Swiss physicist*• Born in Basel, Switzerland, he became a professor at Brussels in 1922 and held posts at the Universities of Lausanne, Chicago and Minnesota. With his brother **Jean Felix Piccard**, he ascended nearly 17 km (55,000 ft) by balloon (1931–32) into the stratosphere. In 1948 he explored the ocean depths off west Africa in a bathyscaphe constructed from his own design. His son Jacques, together with a US naval officer, Donald Walsh, established a world record by diving more than seven miles in the US bathyscaphe *Trieste* into the Marianas Trench of the Pacific Ocean in 1960.

Piccard, Jean Felix 1884–1963 •*US chemist*• Born in Basel, Switzerland, he was the twin brother of **Auguste Antoine Piccard**. He took a chemical engineering degree at the Swiss Institute of Technology in 1907, subsequently held a chair at New York, and became Professor Emeritus of Aeronautical Engineering at the University of Minnesota. His chief interest was in exploration of the stratosphere, and he designed and ascended (with his wife) in a balloon from Dearborn, Michigan, in 1934, to a height of 57,579 feet (17,550 meters), collecting valuable data concerning cosmic rays.

Pickering, William Hayward 1910–2004 •*US engineer and physicist*• Born in Wellington, New Zealand, he emigrated to the US in 1929, studied physics at the California Institute of Technology in 1936, and in 1944 joined the Jet Propulsion Laboratory there, where he developed the first telemetry system used in US rockets. He was director of the Jet Propulsion Laboratory from 1954 to 1976, and initiated the space exploration program that launched the first US satellite, *Explorer I*, in 1958. He supervised the Ranger lunar-impact flights in 1964–65, and the Mariner flights to Venus and Mars, which provided the first close-up photographs ever taken of the surface of another planet.

Pickford, Mary, *originally* **Gladys Mary Smith** 1893–1979 •*US actress*• Born in Toronto, Canada, in 1909 she made her first film, *The Violin Maker of Cremona*, directed by **D W Griffith**. Her beauty and her image of unsophisticated charm soon won her the title of “America's Sweetheart,” and she played the innocent heroine in many silent films, including *Rebecca of Sunnybrook Farm* (1917), *Pollyanna* (1920) and *Little Lord Fauntleroy* (1921). She won an Academy Award for her first talkie, *Coquette* (1929), and retired from the screen in 1933. She cofounded United Artists Film Corporation in 1919, the year in which she married **Douglas Fairbanks, Sr**, her second husband.

Pickup, Ronald Alfred 1940– •*English actor*• Born in Chester, he trained at the Royal Academy of Dramatic Art and made his London stage debut as Octavius in *Julius Caesar*, at the Royal Court Theatre (1964). He acted in more than 20 plays with the National Theatre Company at the Old Vic (1965–73). His many television roles include Randolph Churchill in *Jennie, Lady Randolph Churchill* (1974), **George Orwell** in *Orwell on Jura* (1983), Andrew Powell in *A Time to Dance* (1992), Daniel Byrne in *The Rector's Wife* (1994) and the title role in *King Henry IV* (1994). His films include *The Day of the Jackal* (1973), *The Thirty-Nine Steps* (1978) and *The Mission* (1986).

Pico Della Mirandola, Giovanni, Comte 1463–94 •*Italian philosopher and humanist*• Born in Mirandola, Ferrara, he studied in Italy and France, and settled later in Florence, where he came under the influence of **Marsilio Ficino**. In Rome he wrote his *Conclusiones* (1486), offering to dispute his 900 theses on logic, ethics, theology, mathematics and the *Kabbalah* against all comers, but the debate was forbidden by Pope Innocent VIII on the grounds that many of the theses were heretical. He wrote various Latin epistles and elegies, a series of florid Italian sonnets, *Heptaplus* (1490, a mystical interpretation of the Genesis creation myth), and some important philosophical works, including *De ente et uno* (1492, an attempt to reconcile Platonic and Aristotelian ontological doctrines).

Pieck, Wilhelm 1876–1960 •*East German politician*• Born near Berlin, the son of a laborer, he was active from an early age in socialist politics. In 1915 he helped found the Spartacus League and in 1918 the German Communist Party (KPD), leading the unsuccessful “Spartacus uprising” in Berlin in 1919. During the Weimar Republic, Pieck was elected as a Communist to the Reichstag in 1928, but was forced into exile in 1933 when **Hitler** came to power. He fled to Moscow where he became, in 1935, secretary of the Comintern. In 1945 he returned to Berlin in the wake of the Red Army and founded, in 1946, the dominant Socialist Unity Party (SED). From 1949 he served as president of the German Democratic Republic.

Pierce, Franklin 1804–69 •*14th President of the US*• Born in Hillsborough, New Hampshire, he studied law and was admitted to the bar in 1827. From 1829 to 1833 he was a member of the state legislature, the last two years as Speaker. In 1833 he was elected to Congress as a Jacksonian Democrat, and in 1837 to the US Senate. He resigned in 1842 to practice law, and in 1846 he volunteered for the Mexican War, rising to the rank of brigadier general. He was nominated in 1852 as a compromise candidate for the presidency and was elected by a generous margin over **Winfield Scott**. The events of his administration (1853–57) included the Gadsden Purchase from Spain, the expeditions of William Walker (1824–60) to Nicaragua and of others to Cuba, and, especially, the repeal of the Missouri Compromise and the passing of the Kansas-Nebraska Act, which led to bitter debates about the possible expansion of slavery, and contributed to the formation of the Republican Party. The unpopularity of this act led to his enforced retirement from politics, as he was passed over for the 1856 Democratic presidential nomination.

Piercy, Marge 1936– •*US author*• Born in Detroit, she studied at the University of Michigan and Northwestern University, and worked as an instructor and poet-in-residence before publishing her first collection of poetry, *Breaking Camp*, in 1968. Over a dozen collections followed. Her novels merge feminism, science fiction and social concerns and include *Woman on the Edge of Time* (1976), *City of Darkness, City of Light* (1996) and *Sleeping With Cats: A Memoir* (2002). She has lectured widely and worked as a public education policy adviser, and her many honors include the Paterson poetry prize (2000).

“ ”

On this twelfth day of my diet
I would rather die satiated
than slim.

1983 ***Stone, Paper, Knife****, “On Mental Corsets.”*

Piero della Francesca c. 1420–92 •*Italian painter*• Born in Borgo San Sepolcro, he also worked in Urbino, Ferrara, Florence and Rome, but by 1442 he was a town councilor at Borgo. A number of influences can be seen in his work, notably **Domenico Veneziano**, his teacher, but also **Masaccio**, **Leon Alberti** and **Paolo Uccello**. As a scientist and mathematician he developed a very precise and geometric attitude toward composition, which he wrote about in his treatise *On Perspective in Painting*. He also wrote a treatise on geometry. Complementing this is a subtle use of pale color and a concern for proportion and scale. **Perugino** and **Luca Signorelli** were both pupils of his, and through them his influence extends to the entire Italian school. His major work is a series of frescoes, titled *The Legend of the Holy Cross*, in the choir of San Francesco at Arezzo, painted c. 1452–66. Other works include the *Flagellation* (c. 1456–57) at Urbino.

Piero di Cosimo, *properly* **Piero di Lorenzo** c. 1462–c. 1521 •*Italian painter*• He was a pupil of Cosimo Rosselli, whose name he adopted. His later style was influenced by **Luca Signorelli** and **Leonardo da Vinci**, and among his best-known works are the mythological scene *The Battle of the Lapiths and Centaurs* (1486, National Gallery, London), *The Death of Procris* (c. 1500, National Gallery, London) and *Perseus and Andromeda* (c. 1515, Uffizi, Florence).

Pigalle, Jean Baptiste 1714–85 •*French sculptor*• Born in Paris, he became an extremely popular artist in his day, and was patronized by **Louis XV** and Madame de **Pompadour**. His works, in a style which reconciled the baroque and the classical traditions, include a statue of **Voltaire** (1776, Paris) and the tomb of Marshal **Maurice, Comte de Saxe**, in Strasbourg (1753–56). His *Vénus, l'amour et l'amitié* (1758) is in the Louvre, Paris.

Piggott, Lester Keith 1935– •*English jockey*• He was born in Wantage. He was champion jockey in England on 11 occasions, and in all he rode 30 Classic winners, including 9 Derbies. At five feet nine inches, Piggott was known as the "the Long Fellow," and had to diet rigorously to make the weight. When he retired from riding he became a trainer, but he was tried for tax irregularities (1987) and sentenced to three years' imprisonment. He was released on parole after one year, and resumed his career as a trainer. He eventually returned to riding and, after a gap of seven years, won the 2000 Guineas (his 30th Classic victory) at Newmarket in 1992. He is considered the most brilliant jockey since World War II.

Pilate, Pontius d. c. 36 AD •*Roman prefect of Judea and Samaria*• He presided at the trial of **Jesus** and ordered his crucifixion. Under his rule there were many uprisings, and **Vitellius** sent him to Rome to answer to Emperor **Tiberius** (36) on charges of rapacity and cruelty. **Eusebius of Caesarea** says that Pilate committed suicide; tradition makes him (or his wife) accept Christianity, and associates him with Pilatus in Switzerland. The so-called Acts of Pilate are not authentic.

Pilger, John Richard 1939– •*Australian journalist and documentary filmmaker*• Born in Sydney, he worked as a journalist in Australia before moving to the UK, where he joined the staff of the *Daily Mirror* (1963–85), making his name as a war correspondent and campaigning journalist. His first television documentaries were for *World in Action* (1970), before his own series, *Pilger* (from 1974), and, since 1978, single documentaries, such as *Do You Remember Vietnam?* (1978), *Year Zero—The Silent Death of Cambodia* (1979), *Death of a Nation* (1994)—about the slaughter in East Timor—and *The New Rulers of the World* (2001). He won the Journalist of the Year award twice (1967, 1979), the British Academy of Film and Television Arts Richard Dimbleby award (1991) and an Emmy award (1991).

Pilkington, Sir Alastair, *properly* **Sir Lionel Alexander Bethune Pilkington** 1920–95 •*English inventor*• Educated at Trinity College, Cambridge, he joined the family firm of glassmakers and in 1952 conceived the idea of float glass as a method of manufacturing plate glass without having to grind it to achieve a satisfactory finish. He led the team that successfully introduced the new technique of pouring glass straight from the furnace onto the surface of a bath of molten tin. It floats while cooling, the smooth surface of the tin giving the glass a perfect finish, allied to an extremely uniform thickness and an absence of defects.

Piłsudski, Józef 1867–1935 •*Polish soldier and statesman*• Born in Zulöw (now in Lithuania), he was sent to Siberia for five years in 1887, and on his return became leader of the Polish Socialist party. After further terms of imprisonment in Warsaw and St Petersburg, he escaped to Kraków and began to form a band of troops which fought on Austria's side at the beginning of World War I. In 1917, however, he disbanded his forces and was imprisoned in Magdeburg by the Germans. In 1918 Piłsudski became provisional president of a new Polish republic, and in 1920, now a marshal, he triumphed in a struggle with the Red Army to establish Poland's frontiers. In 1921 he temporarily retired, but in 1926 he returned to become minister of war, then premier. Although he resigned his premiership in 1928, he remained the real ruler of the country in his capacity of minister of war.

Pinchbeck, Christopher c. 1670–1732 •*English clockmaker and toymaker*• Born in London, he invented the gold-colored alloy of copper and zinc, "pinchbeck," for making imitation gold watches.

Pindar, *Greek* **Pindaros** c. 518–c. 438 BC •*Greek lyric poet*• Born nearThebes, Boeotia, he began his career as a composer of choral odes at 20 with a song of victory still extant (*Pythian Ode 10*, written 498 BC). He composed odes for the tyrants of Syracuse and Macedonia, as well as for the free cities of Greece. He wrote hymns to the gods, paeans, dithyrambs, odes for processions, mimic dancing songs, convivial songs, dirges, and odes in praise of princes. Of all these poems only fragments are extant, but his *Epinikia* ("Triumphal Odes") can be read in their entirety.

" "

Seek not, my soul, immortal life, but make the most of the resources that are within your reach.

***Pythia**, 3.109.*

Pindling, Sir Lynden Oscar 1930–2000 •*Bahamian statesman*• Educated in the Bahamas and at the University of London, he practiced as a lawyer before becoming centrally involved in politics, eventually as leader of the Progressive Liberal Party (PLP). He became prime minister in 1969 and led his country to full independence, within the Commonwealth, in 1973. The PLP, under Pindling, was reelected in 1977, 1982 and 1987. He was defeated in the 1992 general election by Hubert Alexander Ingraham.

Pine, Courtney 1964– •*English jazz saxophonist*• Born in London of Jamaican parents, he became the figurehead of the so-called British jazz boom of the late 1980s with the success of his debut album, *Journey to the Urge Within* (1986). His early music reflected his interest in soul, reggae and funk, while other projects have concentrated on a more purely defined jazz idiom, as in *Destiny's Dance (& the Image of Pursuance)* (1988). A powerful and charismatic performer, he broadened his range still further by incorporating hip-hop DJs in his live act and on *Modern Day Jazz Stories* (1996).

Pinero, Sir Arthur Wing 1855–1934 •*English playwright*• Born in London, he studied law, but in 1874 made his debut on the stage in Edinburgh, and in 1875 joined the Lyceum company. His first play, *£200 a Year*, appeared in 1877, followed by a series of comedies. In 1893, with *The Second Mrs Tanqueray*, generally reckoned his best, he began a period of realistic tragedies which were received with enthusiastic acclamation and made him the most successful playwright of his day. He was the author of some 50 plays, including *The Magistrate* (1885), *Dandy Dick* (1887), *The Profligate* (1889), *The Gay Lord Quex* (1899) and *Mid-Channel* (1909).

Pinker, Steven 1954– •*US psychologist*• Born in Montreal, Canada, he was educated at McGill University, Canada, and Harvard and subsequently accepted professorial posts at Stanford, MIT, and (since 2003) at Harvard. He established his reputation in experimental psychology through his exploration on cognition and language, as discussed in such books as *The Language Instinct* (1994), *How the Mind Works* (1997), *Words and Rules: The Ingredients of Language* (1999) and *The Blank Slate* (2002). Throughout his work he adopts a strictly evolutionary approach to human behavior and the development of the brain.

Pinkerton, Allan 1819–84 •*US detective*• He was born in Glasgow, Scotland, became a Chartist, and emigrated to the US in 1842, settling in Dundee, Illinois. He became a detective and deputy sheriff, and in 1850 founded the Pinkerton National Detective Agency in Chicago. He headed a federal intelligence network for General George B McClellan (1826–85) during the Civil War, and his agency later took a leading part in breaking up the Molly Maguires (a secret terrorist society) and in policing other labor disputes.

Pink Floyd •*English progressive rock band*• The band's name is derived from bluesmen Pink Anderson (1900–74) and Floyd Council (1911–76). The band was formed in 1965–66 by poet and singer Syd Barrett (originally Roger Barrett, 1946–), who dictated the nursery-rhyme surrealism of the early album, *Piper at the Gates of Dawn* (1967). After Barrett's departure the music became increasingly sententious and humorless, with guitarist David Gilmour (1944–), bassist and singer Roger Waters (1944–), keyboard player Richard Wright (1945–) and drummer Nick Mason (1945–) experimenting with long-form compositions and technology. *Dark Side of the Moon* (1973), *Wish You Were Here* (1975) and *The Wall* (1979) were all huge commercial successes. *The Division Bell* (1994) was well received, while the band's live show continued to grow ever more gargantuan.

Pinochet Ugarte, Augusto 1915– •*Chilean soldier and statesman*• He joined the army in 1933 and was a general by 1973. He was an instructor at Chile's senior military school, the Academy of War, from 1954 to 1964, when he became deputy director. He was made commander in chief of the armed forces in 1973 and in the same year led a coup which ousted and resulted in the death of the Marxist president, **Salvador Allende**. Pinochet took over the presidency, crushing all opposition. Despite widespread opposition to his harsh regime, and an assassination attempt, he announced in 1986 that he was considering remaining in office for another eight years. However, a plebiscite in October 1988, asking for support, produced a decisive "No." His presidency ended in March 1990, but he retained his military command until 1998, the year he was arrested in the UK at the request of Spain. He was ruled unfit to face extradition, and in 2000 returned to Chile. Facing charges relating to the cover-up of murder and kidnapping during his regime, it was later ruled that he was not fit to stand trial.

Pinsent, Matthew Clive 1970– •*English rower*• Born in Henley-on-Thames, Oxfordshire, he dominated world rowing through the 1990s in partnership with **Steve Redgrave**. Pinsent rowed for two winning Oxford University Boat Race crews (1990 and 1991) before he and Redgrave won the coxless pairs in the world championships in 1991. Further world championship golds followed in the coxless pairs in 1993, 1994 and 1995, as well as Olympic golds in 1992 and 1996. The pair also won gold medals in the coxless fours in the world championships in 1997, 1998 and 1999, and in the Olympic Games in 2000.

Pinter, Harold 1930– •*English dramatist*• Born in London, the son of an East End tailor of Portuguese-Jewish ancestry (da Pinta), he studied for a short time at the Royal Academy of Dramatic Art, and later at the Central School of Speech and Drama in London. He became a repertory actor and wrote poetry and later plays. His first London production, *The Birthday Party* (1959), was trounced by critics unused to his highly personal dramatic idiom. A superb verbal acrobat, he exposes and utilizes the illogical and inconsequential in everyday talk to induce an atmosphere of menace in *The Birthday Party*, or of claustrophobic isolation in *The Caretaker* (1958, filmed 1963). His television play *The Lover* (1963) won the Italia Prize. Other early plays include *The Collection* (television 1961, stage 1962), *The Dwarfs* (radio 1960, stage 1963), and *The Homecoming* (1965). His filmscripts include *The Servant* (1963) and *The Pumpkin Eaters* (1964). Later plays include *No Man's Land* (1975) and *Betrayal* (1978). He did not produce another full-length play until *Party Time* (1991), which was followed by *Moonlight* (1993). Three short pieces, under the title *Other Voices*, were shown at the National Theatre, London, in 1982 while Pinter was associate director there (1973–83). *One for the Road* (1984), *Mountain Language* (1988) and *A New World Order* (1990) deal with explicitly political themes. More recent filmscripts include *The French Lieutenant's Woman* (1981), from the novel by **John Fowles**, *The Handmaid's Tale* (1987), from the novel by **Margaret Atwood**, and *The Comfort of Strangers* (1990), from the novel by **Ian McEwan**.

Pinturicchio, *properly* **Bernardino di Betto Vagio** 1454–1513 •*Italian painter*• Born in Perugia, he helped **Perugino** with the frescoes in the Sistine Chapel at Rome, and himself painted frescoes in several Roman churches and in the Vatican library, as well as in Orvieto, Siena and elsewhere. His delight in brilliant color and ornamental detail is evident in these lavish decorative designs.

Pinza, Ezio, *originally* **Fortunio Pinza** 1892–1957 •*Italian bass*• He was born in Rome and studied at Bologna. His wide range extended from **Mozart** to **Wagner** and **Verdi**, and he sang in all the major opera houses of Europe and beyond, including the Metropolitan Opera in New York (often with **Bruno Walter**), where he became the most celebrated Don Giovanni of the postwar years. From 1948 he sang in Broadway musicals, most notably in *South Pacific*.

Pinzón, Vicente Yáñez c. 1460–c. 1524 •*Spanish explorer and discoverer of Brazil*• Born into a wealthy Andalusian family, he commanded the *Nina* in the first expedition of **Columbus** (1492). In 1499 he sailed on his own account, and in 1500 landed near Pernambuco on the Brazilian coast, which he followed north to the Orinoco river. He was made governor of Brazil by **Ferdinand the Catholic** and **Isabella of Castile**.

Piozzi, Hester Lynch, *previous married name* **Thrale**, *née* **Salusbury** 1741–1821 •*Welsh writer*• She was born in Bodvel, Caernarvonshire, and in 1763 married Henry Thrale, a prosperous Southwark brewer. Two years later Dr **Samuel Johnson** conceived an extraordinary affection for her. He lived in her house at Streatham Place for over 16 years, and her husband made him one of his four executors. Henry Thrale died in April 1781, leaving 12 children, and in 1784 she married the Italian musician Gabriel Piozzi. After extensive travels in Europe, the couple returned to England in 1787. She wrote poems and on hearing of Johnson's death while in Italy, published *Anecdotes of the Late Dr Johnson* (1786) and *Letters To and From the Late Dr Johnson* (1788).

Piper, John 1903–92 •*English artist*• Born in Epsom, his experiments in many media, including collage, led to a representational style which grew naturally from his abstract discipline. He designed sets for the theater, working with **W H Auden** and **Stephen Spender**, and for opera, working with his wife Myfanwy Evans (1911–97) and **Benjamin Britten**, and he collaborated with **John Betjeman** on books. He also made stained glass and painted a series of topographical pictures, such as the watercolors of *Windsor Castle* commissioned by **Elizabeth II** (1941–42), and dramatic pictures of war damage. He designed the stained glass for Coventry Cathedral.

Piquet, Nelson, *properly* **Nelson Souto Maior** 1952– •*Brazilian racecar driver*• Born in Rio de Janeiro, he changed his name so that his parents would not find out about his racing exploits. He was British Formula 3 champion in 1978, and Formula 1 world champion in 1981, 1983 (both with Brabham), and 1987 (with Williams). He won 20 races in 157 starts between 1978 and 1988.

Pirandello, Luigi 1867–1936 •*Italian dramatist, novelist and short-story writer, and Nobel Prize winner*• Born in Girgenti (Agrigento), Sicily, he studied philology at Rome and Bonn, becoming a lecturer in literature at Rome (1897–1922). After writing powerful and realistic novels and short stories, including *Il fu Mattia Pascal* (1904, rev edn 1921, Eng trans *The Late Mattia Pascal*, 1923) and *Si gira* (1916, Eng trans *Shoot!* 1926), he turned to the theater and quickly established his own extraordinary genre. Among his plays are *Sei personaggi in cerca d'autore* (1921, Eng trans *Six Characters in Search of an Author*, 1922) and *Come tu mi vuoi* (1930, Eng trans *As You Desire Me*, 1931). In 1925 he established a theater of his own in Rome and took his plays all over Europe. Many of his later plays have been filmed. He was awarded the Nobel Prize for literature in 1934.

Piranesi, Giambattista or **Giovanni Battista** 1720–78 •*Italian copper engraver and architect*• Born in Venice, he worked in Rome, producing innumerable etchings of the city both in ancient times and in his own day. His most imaginative work is perhaps the *Carceri d'invenzione*, a series of engravings of imaginary prisons.

Pire, (Dominique) Georges 1910–69 •*Belgian Dominican priest and Nobel Prize winner*• Born in Dinant, he lectured in moral philosophy at Louvain (1937–47) and was awarded the Croix de guerre for resistance work as priest and intelligence officer in World War II. After the war he devoted himself to helping refugees and displaced persons, and was awarded the 1958 Nobel Peace Prize for his project of "European villages," including the "Anne Frank village" in Germany for elderly refugees and destitute children.

Pirsig, Robert M 1928– •*US author*• Born in Minneapolis, Minnesota, he studied at the University of Minnesota and also attended Benares Hindu University in India. His first and best-selling novel was *Zen and the Art of Motorcycle Maintenance* (1974), an account of a trip by motorcycle across the US which explores the place of technology in the modern world and grapples with age-old philosophical conundrums. A long-awaited sequel was *Lila: An Inquiry Into Morals* (1992).

" "

That's the classical mind at work, runs fine inside but looks dingy on the surface.

*1974 **Zen and the Art of Motorcycle Maintenance**, part 3, chapter 26.*

Pisanello, Antonio, *real name* **Antonio Pisano** 1395–1455 •*Italian painter and medalist*• Born in Pisa, he was the foremost draftsman of his day. His drawings are marked by a naturalism which contrasts with the stylized manner of his great contemporary **Gentile da Fabriano** and became models for later Renaissance artists. Pisanello painted frescoes (all since destroyed) in the Doge's Palace at Venice (1415–20) and in the Lateran Basilica in Rome (1431–32). His surviving frescoes include the *Annunciation* (1423–24, Saint Fermo, Verona), and *St George and the Princess of Trebizond* (c. 1437–38, Santa Anastasia, Verona). Other surviving works include numerous precise drawings of costumes, birds, and animals. His most famous picture, however, is the *Vision of Saint Eustace*. He is also known as a portrait medalist, the greatest of his day.

Pisano, Andrea, *also called* **Andrea da Pontedera** c. 1270–1349 •*Italian sculptor*• Born in Pontedera, he became famous as a worker in bronze and marble, and settled in Florence, where he completed the earliest bronze doors of the Baptistery (1336), and in 1337 succeeded **Giotto** as chief artist in the cathedral. In 1347 he became chief artist in the cathedral at Orvieto, working on reliefs and statues.

Pisano, Giovanni c. 1250–c. 1320 •*Italian sculptor and architect*• He was the son of **Nicola Pisano**, and worked with him on the pulpit in Siena, on the fountain in Perugia, and then between 1284 and 1286 on a number of impressive, life-size statues for the façade of Siena Cathedral. He also sculpted figures for the entrance to the baptistery at Pisa (now in the Museo Nazionale), and made a number of free-standing Madonnas. His style is intensely dramatic and expressive, more dynamic than that of his father. He was one of the great sculptors of his day in the Italian Gothic tradition, and his innovation pointed the way to Renaissance sculptural ideals.

Pisano, Nicola c. 1225–c. 1284 •*Italian sculptor, architect and engineer*• Raised in Apulia, his first great work was the sculpted marble panels for the pulpit in the baptistery in Pisa, finished in 1260, whose powerful dramatic composition carved in high relief is in striking contrast to all earlier pulpit decoration. On a second pulpit, for the cathedral at Siena (1268), and on the Fontana Maggiore in Perugia (1278), he collaborated with his son, **Giovanni Pisano**. Although working in a traditional Gothic style, Nicola incorporated the forms of classical sculpture into his work.

Piscator, Erwin Friedrich Max 1893–1966 •*German theater director*• Born in Ulm, he joined the German Communist Party in 1918 and opened his own theater in Berlin in 1926. A major exponent of German political theater, he developed a style of agitprop which underlies the later epic theater. Among his more notable productions was *The Adventures of the Good Soldier Schweik*, adapted by **Bertolt Brecht** from the novel by **Jaroslav Hašek** (1927). He was in the Soviet Union from 1933 to 1936, and worked in the US (1938–51), where he became head of the Drama Department of the New School for Social Research, and where his adaptation of *War and Peace* was first produced (1942). In 1951 he decided to settle in West Germany, and from 1962 was director of the Freie Volksbuhne in Berlin.

Pisistratus, *Greek* **Peisistratos** c. 600–527 BC •*Tyrant of Athens*• He rose to power during the aristocratic factional quarrels that followed the reforms of **Solon**. His first two bids for power (c. 561 and c. 556 BC) failed, but eventually he established himself (c. 546) with support from other Greek states. He curbed aristocratic faction fighting, enforced a period of internal peace and stability, favored the peasantry of Attica, and was remembered as a popular ruler. At his death he transmitted his power to his sons Hippias and Hipparchus.

Pissarro, Camille 1830–1903 •*French Impressionist artist*• Born in St Thomas, West Indies, he went in 1855 to Paris, where he was much influenced by **Jean Corot**'s landscapes. In 1870 he lived in England for a short time, this being the first of several visits. Most of his works were painted in the countryside around Paris, and he lived in Pontoise from 1872 to 1884. In the next year he met **Paul Signac** and **Georges Seurat** and for the next five years adopted their divisionist style. Pissarro was the leader of the original Impressionists, and had considerable influence on **Cézanne** and **Paul Gauguin** at the beginning of their artistic careers. His famous painting of the *Boulevard Montmartre* by night (1897) is in the National Gallery, London.

Pitcairn, Robert c. 1745–70 •*English sailor*• He was a midshipman onboard the *Swallow* in July 1767, when he was the first to sight the island later called Pitcairn Island, which was to become the refuge of the *Bounty* mutineers, led by **Fletcher Christian**.

Pitman, Sir Isaac 1813–97 •*English educator and inventor of a shorthand system*• He was born in Trowbridge, Wiltshire. First a clerk, he became a schoolmaster, and issued his *Stenographic Sound Hand* (1837). Dismissed from Wotton because he had joined the New (Swedenborgian) Church, he established a Phonetic Institute for teaching shorthand in Bath (1839–43). In 1842 he brought out the *Phonetic Journal*, and in 1845 opened premises in London. His brother Benjamin Pitman (1822–1910) was the pioneer of shorthand in the US.

Pitman, Jenny (Jennifer Susan), *née* **Harvey** 1946– •*English National Hunt racehorse trainer*• Born in Hoby, Leicestershire, she married Richard Pitman in 1965 (separated 1978) and set up her first training stables with him. Since then her horses have won the Midland National, the Massey Fergusson Gold Cup, the Welsh National, the Cheltenham Gold Cup, the Hennessey Gold Cup and the Whitbread Trophy. Corbiere won the Grand National in 1983, while Royal Athlete won it in 1995. She has been declared the Piper-Heidsieck Trainer of the Year several times (1983–84, 1989–90) and the Golden Spurs Best National Hunt Trainer (1984).

Pitt, (William) Brad(ley) 1963– •*US actor*• He was born in Shawnee, Oklahoma, and studied journalism at the University of Michigan, leaving to pursue work as an actor. His testosterone-charged performances in early films such as *Thelma and Louise* (1991) and *True Romance* (1993) established him as a box-office draw and he subsequently appeared in high-grossing films such as *Interview With the Vampire* (1994), *Seven* (1996), *Fight Club* (1999) and *Troy* (2004).

Pitt, William or **Pitt the Elder** *See* **Chatham, 1st Earl of**

Pitt, William, *known as* **Pitt the Younger** 1759–1806 •*English statesman*• He was born in Hayes near Bromley, the second son of the Earl of **Chatham**. He graduated from Pembroke Hall, Cambridge, at the age of 17, and was called to the bar in 1780 but saw his career in the political field. He was elected for Appleby in 1781, soon making his mark as an orator. At the age of 23 he became chancellor of the exchequer and leader of the House of Commons in the ministry of Lord **Shelburne**, replacing **Charles James Fox**, who then became his bitter rival. When Shelburne resigned in 1783 the king offered Pitt the premiership but he declined, leaving it to **William Bentinck**, 3rd Duke of Portland. However, when Portland's government collapsed in December of the same year, Pitt decided to accept the challenge and, at the age of 24, became Britain's youngest prime minister. Pitt had clear ideas of what he wished to achieve. He wanted good relations with America, union with Ireland, a reduction in the national debt, reform of parliament, and reorganization of the East India Company. He did not achieve all his aims but, despite his inexperience and fierce opposition from Fox, made considerable progress. In 1801 the king refused to approve his bill to emancipate the Catholics and Pitt resigned in protest, but within three years he was persuaded to return in the face of a threatened invasion by **Napoleon I**. He formed a coalition with Russia, Austria and Sweden, and the French were defeated at Trafalgar (1805). Pitt was hailed as the savior of Europe, and his words of reply became immortal: "England has saved herself by her exertions, and will, I trust, save Europe by her example." He was dismayed when the coalition he had formed broke up and Napoleon triumphed against the Russians and Austrians at Austerlitz in 1805. He died nearly ten years before Napoleon's final defeat at Waterloo. Although Pitt was a popular national figure, his private life was comparatively sad and lonely. He had no close friends and did not marry. He died so heavily in debt that the House of Commons raised £40,000 to pay off his creditors.

" "

I think that I could eat one of Bellamy's veal pies.

1806 Attributed last words, January 23.

Pitt-Rivers, Augustus Henry Lane-Fox 1827–1900 •*English soldier and archaeologist*• He was born in Yorkshire. Educated at Sandhurst, he worked to improve army small-arms training and ultimately became a lieutenant general (1882). Having in 1880 inherited from his great-uncle, Lord Rivers, Wiltshire estates rich in Romano-British and Saxon remains, he devoted himself to archaeology, evolving a new scientific approach to excavation which became a model for later workers. His collections were presented to the Oxford Museum. In 1882 he became the first inspector of ancient monuments.

Pius IV, *originally* **Giovanni Angelo de' Medici** 1499–1565 •*Italian pope*• Born in Milan, he became Archbishop of Ragusa in 1547 and a cardinal in 1549 before being elected pope in 1559. He brought to a close the deliberations of the Council of Trent, and issued (1564) the Creed of Pius IV, or Tridentine Creed. He reformed the sacred college of cardinals, and established the Index of Forbidden Books. A notable patron of the arts, he built many public buildings and was patron to **Michelangelo**.

Pius V, St, *originally* **Michele Ghislieri** 1504–72 •*Italian pope*• Born in Cesena, he became a bishop in 1556 and a cardinal in 1557. As pope from 1566, he implemented the decrees of the Council of Trent (1545–63), excommunicated Queen **Elizabeth I** (1570), and inspired the Holy League (1571) against the Turks. The league's campaign culminated in the victory of the Christian fleet under Don **John of Austria** at the Battle of Lepanto in the Gulf of Corinth (1571). He was canonized in 1712, and his feast day is April 30.

Pius VI, *originally* **Giovanni Angelo Braschi** 1717–99 •*Italian pope*• Born in Cesena, Papal States, he became cardinal in 1773 and pope in 1775. To him Rome owes the drainage of the Pontine Marsh, the completion of St Peter's, the foundation of the New Museum of the Vatican, and the embellishment of the city. In the 1780s he went to Vienna, but failed to restrain the reforming emperor **Joseph II** from further curtailing papal privileges. Soon after came the French Revolution and the confiscation of Church property in France. The pope launched his thunders in vain, and then the murder of the French agent in Rome (1793) gave the Directory an excuse for the attack. **Napoleon I** took possession of the Legations, and afterward of the March of Ancona, and extorted (1797) the surrender of these provinces from Pius. The murder of a member of the French embassy in December was avenged by Alexandre Berthier's taking possession of Rome in 1798. Pius was called on to renounce his temporal sovereignty, and on his refusal was seized, and carried finally to Valence, where he died.

Pius VII, *originally* **Barnaba Gregorio Chiaramonti** 1742–1823 •*Italian pope*• Born in Cesena, Papal States, he became Bishop of Tivoli, and, already a cardinal, succeeded **Pius VI** in 1800. Rome was now restored to the papal authority, and the next year French troops were withdrawn from most of the papal territory. In 1801 Pius concluded a concordat with **Napoleon I**, which the latter altered by autocratic *Articles organiques*. In 1804 Napoleon compelled Pius to come to Paris to consecrate him as emperor, and soon after Pius's return the French seized Ancona and entered Rome. This was followed by the annexation (May 1809) of the Papal States to the French Empire. In June the pope excommunicated the robbers of the Holy See. Then he was removed to Grenoble, and finally to Fontainebleau, where he was forced to sign a new concordat and sanction the annexation. The fall of Napoleon (1814) allowed him to return to Rome, and the Congress of Vienna restored to him his territory.

Pius IX, *originally* **Giovanni Maria Mastai Ferretti**, *also called* **Pio Nono** 1792–1878 •*Italian pope*• Born in Sinigaglia, Papal States, he was made Archbishop of Spoleto (1827) and Bishop of Imola (1832). In 1840 he became a cardinal, and succeeded Gregory XVI in 1846. By the bull *Ineffabilis Deus* in 1854 he decreed the Immaculate Conception; his famous encyclical *Quanta Cura* and the *Syllabus of Errors* appeared in 1864. He also called the Vatican Council (1869–79), which proclaimed the infallibility of the pope.

Pius X, St, *originally* **Giuseppe Sarto** 1835–1914 •*Italian pope*• Born in Riese, near Venice, and ordained in 1858, he became Bishop of Mantua (1884) and cardinal and patriarch of Venice (1893) before being elected pope in 1903. He condemned theological modernism in his encyclical *Pascendi* in 1907, and revolutionary movements, but was a champion of social reforms (especially in the Catholic Action movement). He reformed the liturgy, recodified canon law, and was canonized in 1954.

Pius XI, *originally* **Ambrogio Damiano Achille Ratti** 1857–1939 •*Italian pope*• Born in Desio, near Milan, and ordained in 1879, he was a great linguist and scholar, and librarian of the Ambrosian (Milan) and Vatican libraries. He became Cardinal Archbishop of Milan in 1921. As pope from 1922, he signed the Lateran Treaty with **Mussolini** (1929), which brought into existence the Vatican state. He also broke new ground by appointing six Chinese bishops.

Pius XII, *originally* **Eugenio Pacelli** 1876–1958 •*Italian pope*• Born in Rome, he distinguished himself in the papal diplomatic service and as secretary of state to the Holy See before succeeding **Pius XI** in 1939. Under his leadership, the Vatican did much humanitarian work during World War II, notably for prisoners of war and refugees. There has been continuing controversy, however, over his attitude on the treatment of the Jews in Nazi Germany, critics arguing that he could have used his influence with Catholic Germany to prevent the massacres. In the postwar years the plight of the persecuted churchmen in the Communist countries, and the fate of Catholicism there, became his personal concern. He was widely respected as a distinguished scholar and as a man of immense moral authority.

Pizarro, Francisco c. 1478–1541 •*Spanish soldier and conqueror of Peru*• Born in Trujillo, he served under Gonsalvo di Cordova in Italy, and under **Vasco Núñez de Balboa**, discoverer of the Pacific Ocean. In 1526 Pizarro and **Diego de Almagro** sailed for Peru, where they collected information about the Incas. He returned to Spain for authority to undertake the conquest, which he received in 1529. He sailed again from Panama in 1531, Almagro following with reinforcements. The Spaniards began the march inland in May 1532, captured the Inca **Atahualpa** by treachery, and after extorting an enormous ransom (£3,500,000), put him to death (1533). He then marched to Cuzco, and was founding Lima and other cities on the coast when a Native American insurrection broke out. Both Cuzco and Lima were besieged, and his half brother Juan Pizarro (1505–36) was killed, but in spring 1537 Almagro returned from Chile, raised the Siege of Cuzco, and took possession of the city. Pizarro had no intention of allowing his rival to retain Cuzco. Too old to fight himself, he entrusted the command of his forces to his brothers, who defeated Almagro soon afterward. Followers of Almagro later attacked Pizarro's house in Lima and murdered him. His brother, Hernando Pizarro, was imprisoned for having beheaded Almagro at Cuzco.

Pizarro, Gonzalo c. 1506–48 •*Spanish soldier*• He accompanied his half brother **Francisco Pizarro** in the conquest of Peru, and in 1539 undertook an expedition to the east of Quito, enduring severe hardships. One of his lieutenants, **Francisco de Orellana**, deserted his starving comrades, discovered the whole course of the River Amazon, and returned to Spain; only 90 out of 350 Spaniards returned with Gonzalo in June 1542. On his return he discovered that his half brother had been assassinated in 1541. In 1544 the new viceroy arrived in Peru to enforce the "New Laws." The Spaniards, dismayed, entreated Gonzalo to protect their interests. He mustered 400 men, and defeated and killed the viceroy (1546). When news of this revolt reached Spain, Pedro de la Gasca, an able ecclesiastic, was sent to Peru as president to restore order. Gonzalo Pizarro met Gasca near Cuzco in April 1548, but his forces deserted him, and he gave himself up and was beheaded.

Plaatje, Sol Tshekisho 1876–1932 •*South African journalist, politician and literary figure*• One of the founders of Black nationalism, he first worked as a post office messenger and later a magistrates' court interpreter in Kimberley. He was in the town throughout the siege (1899–1900) during the Boer War and kept a lively diary of its events. After the war he founded and edited newspapers, wrote books, translated Shakespeare into Tswana, and was one of the founders of the South African Native National Congress (1912), later the ANC (African National Congress).

Planck, Max Karl Ernst 1858–1947 •*German theoretical physicist and Nobel Prize winner*• Born in Kiel, Schleswig-Holstein, he studied at the University of Munich and under **Gustav Kirchhoff** and **Hermann von Helmholtz** at the University of Berlin, where he succeeded the former in the professorship (1889–1926). His work on the law of thermodynamics and blackbody radiation led him to formulate the quantum theory (1900), which relied on **Ludwig Boltzmann**'s statistical interpretation of the second law of thermodynamics, and which assumed energy changes to take place in small discrete installments, or quanta. This successfully accounted for and predicted certain phenomena inexplicable in the classical Newtonian theory. **Albert Einstein**'s application of the quantum theory to light (1905) led to the theories of relativity, and in 1913 **Niels Bohr** successfully applied it to the problems of subatomic physics. Planck was awarded the Nobel Prize for physics (1918). In 1930 he was elected president of the Kaiser Wilhelm Institute, but resigned in 1937 in protest against the Nazi regime. He was eventually reappointed as president of the renamed Max Planck Institute.

Plante, Lynda La *See* **La Plante, Lynda**

Plantin, Christophe 1514–89 •*French printer*• Born in St Avertin near Tours, he settled as a bookbinder in Antwerp in 1549 and six years later began to print. His *Biblia Polyglotta* (1569–73, "Polyglot Bible"), his Latin, Hebrew and Dutch Bibles, and his editions of the classics are all famous. His printing houses in Antwerp, Leiden and Paris were carried on by his sons-in-law.

Plater, Alan Frederick 1935– •*English dramatist*• Born in Jarrow, Tyne and Wear, he trained as an architect, and his writing was first published in *Punch* (1958). Since 1960 he has built up an enormous body of work that reflects his working-class background, his political beliefs and his interest in jazz. He was a regular writer for the BBC series *Z Cars* (1963–65), and his many television plays include *Close the Coalhouse Door* (1968) and *The Land of Green Ginger* (1974). He is also responsible for the screen translations *The Good Companions* (1980) and *A Very British Coup* (1988) and has written film scripts such as *The Virgin and the Gypsy* (1969) and *Priest of Love* (1980). Equally prolific in other media, he has contributed to *The Guardian* and written the novels *Misterioso* (1987) and *The Beiderbecke Affair* (1985, from his television series of the same title).

Plath, Sylvia 1932–63 •*US poet*• Born in Boston, she was educated at Bradford High School and Smith College, where she suffered from depression and attempted suicide. She won a Fulbright Fellowship to Newnham College, Cambridge (1956), where she studied English and married **Ted Hughes**. After teaching in the US they settled in England (1959), but separated in 1962, a year before Sylvia committed suicide. Writing poetry from early childhood, she published her first volume, *A Winter Ship* (1960), anonymously, but put her name to the second, *The Colossus* (1960). After the birth of her second child she wrote a radio play, *Three Women* (1962), set in a maternity home. Her late poetry was published posthumously in *Ariel* (1965), *Crossing the Water* (1971) and *Winter Trees* (1972). Her only novel, *The Bell Jar* (1963), was published just before her death, under the pseudonym Victoria Lucas. *Collected Poems*, edited by Hughes, was published in 1982.

“ ”

Out of the ash
I rise with my red hair
And I eat men like air.

1965 ***Ariel**, "Lady Lazarus."*

Plato c. 428–c. 348 BC •*Greek philosopher*• He was born probably in Athens of a distinguished aristocratic family, but little is known of his early life. His works show the profound influence of **Socrates**, who converted Plato to philosophy after early attempts at poetry. Plato gives an account of Socrates' last days in 399 BC in three of his dialogues: the *Apology*, the *Crito* and the *Phaedo*. After Socrates' death, he and other disciples took temporary refuge at Megara with the philosopher **Eucleides**, and Plato then traveled widely in Greece, Egypt, southern Italy, where he encountered the Pythagoreans, and Sicily, where he became the friend and teacher of **Dion**, brother-in-law of **Dionysius the Elder** of Syracuse. Plato returned to Athens (c. 387), where he founded the Academy, which was named after the grove belonging to the hero Academus where the school was situated. It became a famous center for philosophical, mathematical and scientific research, and Plato himself presided over it for the rest of his life. He attempted to enter politics on two occasions, but was soon disillusioned with politicians and formed the conclusion that the only hope for the Greek cities was to trust in philosopher-kings, who have a knowledge of goodness and are able to lead others to goodness. He visited Sicily again on the death of Dionysius the Elder in 367, at Dion's request, to teach Dion's nephew **Dionysius the Younger** to become a philosopher-king, but Dionysius mistrusted Dion and had Plato banished. He returned to Athens and, despite a second visit in 361–60, his attempt to put principles into practice was a failure, as Plato himself went to great lengths to explain in his *Epistles*. Among Plato's pupils were **Aristotle**, who eventually founded the Peripatetic School at the Lyceum in Athens, **Speusippus**, Plato's successor as head of the Academy, and **Theophrastus**.

“ ”

It is not living, but living well, which we ought to consider most important.

***Crito**, 48b (translated by H North Fowler, 1923).*

Plautus, Titus Maccius or **Maccus** c. 250–184 BC •*Roman comic dramatist*• He was born in Sarsina, Umbria, and it is probable that he went to Rome while still young, and there learned his mastery of the most idiomatic Latin. He found work in connection with the stage, and then started a business in foreign trade. It failed, however, and he returned to Rome in such poverty that he had to work for a baker, turning a handmill. He probably began to write about 224 BC. He borrowed his plots to a large extent from the New Attic Comedy, and his plays show close familiarity with seafaring life and adventure, and an intimate knowledge of all the details of buying, selling and bookkeeping. About 130 plays were attributed to him in the time of **Aulus Gellius**, but **Marcus Terentius Varro** limited the genuine comedies to 21, and these so-called Varronian comedies are those which are now extant, the *Vidularia* ("The Rucksack Play") being fragmentary.

Player, Gary 1936– •*South African golfer*• He was born in Johannesburg. Small and slightly built, he nonetheless won three British Opens (1959, 1968, 1974), the US Masters three times (1961, 1974, 1978), the US Open once (1965), and the US Professional Golfers' Association title twice (1962, 1972). He also won the South African Open 13 times and the Australian Open 7 times. He won both the British and the American Seniors' Championship in 1988.

Playfair, William Henry 1789–1857 •*Scottish architect*• Born in London, he was brought up in Edinburgh. He designed many of Edinburgh's most prominent buildings, including the National Gallery of Scotland, the Royal Scottish Academy, the National Monument on Calton Hill, Surgeon's Hall and Donaldson's Hospital.

Pleasence, Donald 1919–95 •*English stage and film actor*• Born in Worksop, Nottinghamshire, he made his first appearance in Jersey in 1939, served in the RAF during World War II and returned to the stage in 1946. He worked at various repertory theaters, but scored a huge success as the malevolent tramp Davies in **Harold Pinter**'s *The Caretaker* (1960). After the 1960s, his London stage appearances were rare, but he made many television appearances and was in constant demand for film work, usually as a villain, as in *You Only Live Twice* (1967), in which he played James Bond's arch-enemy Blofeld, and in the horror film series *Halloween*, which started in 1978.

Plekhanov, Georgi Valentinovich 1856–1918 •*Russian revolutionary and Marxist philosopher*• Born in Gundalovka, he joined the Narodnist Populist movement as a student and led the first popular demonstration in St Petersburg (1876). In 1880 he left Russia and in 1883 founded the first Russian Marxist group (which became the Russian Social Democratic Workers' Party in 1898) in Geneva, where he spent the years 1883–1917 in exile. From 1889 to 1904 he was Russian delegate to the Second International. He was a major intellectual influence on **Lenin**, with whom he edited the journal *Iskra* (1900, "The Spark"). He argued that Russia would have to go through industrialization and capitalism before arriving at socialism, and in 1903 he supported the Mensheviks against Lenin's Bolsheviks. He returned to Russia in 1917, but denounced the October Revolution and moved to Finland. His commentaries on Marxist theory fill 26 volumes, and he is known as the father of Russian Marxism.

Plessner, Helmuth 1892–1985 •*German philosopher and social theorist*• Born in Wiesbaden, he studied zoology, medicine and philosophy at the Universities of Freiburg, Heidelberg and Berlin. He was professor at Cologne (1926–34), then moved to Groningen in Holland to escape the Nazis and became Professor of Sociology there (1934–42). Expelled during the Nazi occupation, he later became Professor of Philosophy there (1946–51), before returning to Germany in 1951. He helped found, with Max Scheler (1874–1928), the new discipline of "philosophical anthropology": humans are distinguished from animals by the "eccentric position" by which they can distance themselves from their own bodies through self-consciousness and can thus have access to experiences, expressions, language and institutions of a very different order of significance. He also wrote on social philosophy and the origins of Fascism in *Das Schicksal deutschen Geistes im Ausgang seiner bürgerlichen Epoche* (1935, "The Destiny of the German Spirit at the End of the Bourgeois Epoch").

Plimsoll, Samuel, *known as* **the sailors' friend** 1824–98 •*English social reformer*• He was born in Bristol. In 1854 he started business in the coal trade in London and soon began to interest himself in the dangers affecting the merchant navy. He entered parliament for Derby in 1868, but it was not until he had published *Our Seamen* (1873) and had made a public appeal that the Merchant Shipping Act (1876) was passed. This required every owner to mark on his ship a circular disk (the Plimsoll mark) with a horizontal line drawn through its center, down to which the vessel might be loaded. In 1890 he published *Cattle-ships*, exposing the cruelties and dangers of cattle shipping.

Pliny, Gaius Plinius Caecilius Secundus, *called* **the Younger** c. 62–c. 113 AD •*Roman writer and orator*• He was born in Novum Comum, and was the nephew and adopted son of **Pliny the Elder**. He wrote a Greek tragedy in his 14th year, and under **Quintilian**'s tuition became one of the most accomplished men of his time. His skill as an orator enabled him at 18 to plead in the forum, and he served as consul in AD 100, in which year he wrote his eulogy to **Trajan**. His second wife, Calpurnia, is fondly referred to in one of his most charming letters for the ways in which she sweetened his rather invalid life. His ten volumes of letters give an intimate picture of the upper class in the first century AD; above all, they show how the Romans regarded the early Christians and their "depraved and extravagant superstition."

Pliny, Gaius Plinius Secundus, *called* **the Elder** AD 23–79 •*Roman scholar*• He was born at Novum Comum (Como), where his wealthy Italian family had estates. He was educated in Rome, and at about age 23 entered the army and became colonel of a cavalry regiment, and a comrade of the future emperor **Titus**. He wrote a treatise on the throwing of missiles from horseback and compiled a history of the Germanic wars, later making a series of scientific tours. Returning to Rome in AD 52, he studied law, but withdrew to Como and devoted himself to reading and authorship. Apparently for the guidance of his nephew, he wrote his *Studiosus*, a treatise defining the culture necessary for the orator, and the grammatical work, *Dubius Sermo*. By **Nero** he was appointed procurator in Spain, and through his brother-in-law's death (71) became guardian of his sister's son, **Pliny the Younger**, whom he adopted. **Vespasian** was now emperor and became a close friend. Amid metropolitan distractions he worked assiduously, and by lifelong application, he filled 160 volumes of manuscript which, after using them for his universal encyclopedia in 37 volumes, *Historia Naturalis* (77), he bequeathed to his nephew. In 79 he was in command of the Roman fleet stationed off Misenum when the great eruption of Mount Vesuvius was at its height. Eager to witness the phenomenon as closely as possible, he landed at Stabiae (*Castellamare*), where the stifling vapors killed him. His *Historia Naturalis* alone of his many writings survives. Under that title the ancients classified everything of natural or nonartificial origin, and Pliny adds digressions on human inventions and institutions. His secondhand observations show no discrimination between the true and the false, between the marvelous and the probable, but he supplies information on an immense variety of subjects about which we would otherwise be ignorant.

Plotinus c. 205–70 AD •*Greek philosopher and founder of Neo-Platonism*• Born probably in Lycopolis, Egypt, of Roman parents, his intellectual background was Greek. He studied in Alexandria (under **Ammonius**) and in Persia (Iran), and settled in Rome (AD 244), where he became a popular lecturer, advocating asceticism and the contemplative life, though he seemed to live in style himself. His 54 works, produced between 253 and 270, were edited posthumously by his pupil **Porphyry**, who arranged them into six groups of nine books, or *Enneads*. They established the foundations of Neo-Platonism as a philosophical system, combining the doctrines of **Plato** with those of **Pythagoras**, **Aristotle** and the Stoics. He greatly influenced early Christian theology, and Neo-Platonism was the dominant philosophy in Europe for a thousand years, establishing a link between ancient and medieval thought.

Plowden, Lady Bridget Horatia, *née* **Richmond** 1910–2000 •*English educator*• Educated at Downe House, she was the first woman to chair the Central Advisory Council for Education, from 1963 to 1966, and subsequently became chairman of the Independent Broadcasting Authority (1975–80). Her report, *Children and Their Primary Schools* (1967), concentrated public attention on the relationship between the primary school and the home and social background of children. It argued that increased resources were needed for nursery education and for areas starved of new investment, and took child-centered approaches to their logical limits, insisting on the principle of complete individualization of the teaching/learning process. The *Plowden Report* marks a watershed in the development of English primary education. She was given the honorary title of Dame Commander, Order of the British Empire, in 1972.

Plowright, Joan Ann 1929– •*English actress and stage director*• She was born in Brigg, Lincolnshire, and trained at the Old Vic Theatre School. In 1956 she became a member of the English Stage Company at the Royal Court Theatre, London, where she played opposite **Laurence Olivier**, whom she married in 1961. She later appeared in plays by **John Osborne**, **Arnold Wesker** and others, and in 1963 joined the National Theatre in its first season. A talented classical actress, she is also an accomplished stage director. She has also worked in television and won two Golden Globe awards for Best Supporting Actress (1993) for the film *Enchanted April* and the miniseries *Stalin* (1992). Recent films include *The Scarlet Letter* (1995) and *Tea With Mussolini* (1999).

Plume, Thomas 1630–1704 •*English theologian*• Born in Maldon, Essex, he was educated in Chelmsford and at Christ's College, Cambridge. He was vicar of Greenwich from 1658 and archdeacon of Rochester from 1679. He endowed an observatory and the Plumian chair of astronomy and experimental philosophy at Cambridge, and bequeathed his extensive library to the town of Maldon, where it still exists intact.

Plutarch, *Greek* **Ploutarchos** c.46–c.120 AD •*Greek historian, biographer and philosopher*• He was born in Chaeroneia in Boeotia, of a wealthy and cultured family. He spent most of his later life there, but before that he studied philosophy in Athens and traveled in Italy and Egypt, building a circle of cultivated friends. His extant writings amount to about a half of his total output, and fall into two categories: the historical works and those which are grouped under the general heading of *Opera Moralia*. To the former belong his *Parallel Lives*, the work by which he is best known. These are biographies of 23 great Greek politicians and soldiers paired with 23 Roman lives that offer points of similarity, followed (in all but four cases) by a short comparison of each pair (regarded by some critics as spurious). They are of great historical value for the information they contain, which is often additional to that found in the narrative histories of Plutarch's particular time. The other and lesser known half of his writings—the *Moralia*—are a collection of short treatises, 60 or more (although certainly not all from Plutarch's hand) on various subjects, including *Ethics*, *Politics*, *History*, *Health* and *Philosophy*. The nine books of his *Symposiaca*, or "Table Talk," depict him as an amiable and genial companion, while his dialogue *Gryllus* reveals a remarkable sense of humor. Though not a profound thinker, Plutarch was a man of rare gifts, and he occupies a unique place in literature as the encyclopedist of antiquity.

Pocahontas, *Native American name* **Matoaka** 1595–1617 •*Native American princess*• Born near the future Jamestown, Virginia, she was the daughter of an American Indian chief, **Powhatan**. According to the English adventurer **John Smith**, she twice saved his life when he was at the mercy of her tribe, and she helped to maintain peace between the settlers and her people. Cajoled to Jamestown, Virginia (1612), she embraced Christianity, was baptized Rebecca (1613), married an English settler, John Rolfe (1613), and in 1616 went with him to England, where she was received by royalty. Having embarked for Virginia the following year, she died of smallpox off Gravesend. She left one son, and several Virginia families claim descent from her.

Po Chü-i, *See* **Bo Juyi**

Podgorny, Nikolai Viktorovich 1903–83 •*Soviet politician*• Born in Karklova, Ukraine, he held managerial, educational and ministerial posts connected with food supply. He joined the Communist Party (1930), and after World War II took a leading role in the economic reconstruction of the liberated Ukraine. He held various senior posts (1950–65), becoming a full member of the politburo in 1960. Following the dismissal of **Nikita Khrushchev** (1964), he became chairman of the Presidium and therefore titular head of state from 1965 until 1977, when he was replaced by **Leonid Brezhnev**.

Poe, Edgar Allan 1809–49 •*US poet and short-story writer*• Born in Boston, Massachusetts, he was orphaned in his third year, and was adopted by John Allan (1780–1834), a wealthy and childless merchant in Richmond, Virginia. He spent a year at the University of Virginia (1826) but after turning to gambling in an attempt to pay off his debts, he had a quarrel with his patron (Allan) and ran away to Boston. In 1827 he published his first volume of verse, *Tamerlane and Other Poems*, published a second volume, *Al Aaraaf* in 1829, and spent some time at West Point Military Academy, where he was dismissed in 1831 for deliberate neglect of duty. He went to New York City and brought out a third edition of his *Poems* (1831), which contained "Israfel," his earliest poem of value, and "To Helen." Next he turned to journalism and story writing and moved to Baltimore. His story "A MS. Found in a Bottle" won a prize in 1833. In 1835 he went to Richmond as assistant editor of the *Southern Literary Messenger* (1835–37), and the following year married his 13-year-old cousin Virginia Clemm. He left Richmond in 1837, returned briefly to New York, where he published *Narrative of Arthur Gordon Pym*, and established himself in Philadelphia in 1838. There he was coeditor of *Burton's Gentleman's Magazine* (1839–40) for which he wrote the well-known story "The Fall of the House of Usher," and he published *Tales of the Grotesque and Arabesque* (1839) in 1840. He resigned from *Burton's* in 1840, and went on to edit *Graham's Magazine* (1841–42), in which he published his pioneering detective story "The Murders in the Rue Morgue." In 1844 he returned again to New York, where he held various journalistic posts. His poem "The Raven" appeared first in the New York *Evening Mirror*, then in *The Raven and Other Poems* (both 1845), and won him immediate fame but not fortune. His wife died in 1847, and in November 1848 he attempted suicide. Recovering from alcohol addiction in 1849, he spent over two months in Richmond, lecturing there and at Norfolk, but died after being found in a wretched, delirious condition in Baltimore. The poems "The Bells" and "Annabel Lee," the tale "The Domain of Arnheim," and the bizarre philosophical prose poem *Eureka* (1848) were his last works of note.

" "

"Take thy beak from out my heart, and take thy form from off my door!"
Quoth the raven, "Nevermore."

1845 "The Raven," stanza 17. In ***American Review****, February.*

Poggio, Giovanni dal *See* **Giovanni di Paolo**

Pohl, Frederik 1919– •*US science-fiction writer*• He was born in Brooklyn, New York, and in 1938 became a founding member of a group of left-wing science-fiction writers called the Futurists, which included **Isaac Asimov**, among others. He served in the air force in World War II and later edited various science-fiction magazines (1953–69). He describes his own multifarious books as "cautionary literature," seeing science fiction as a kind of alarm signal. Of his vast output of novels, stories and anthologies, *The Space Merchants* (1953) and *Gladiator-at-Law* (1955), both written with C M Kornbluth, exemplify his social concern and strength as a storyteller.

Poincaré, Jules Henri 1854–1912 •*French mathematician*• Born in Nancy, he studied at the École Polytechnique, and became Professor of Mathematics in Paris in 1881. He created the theory of automorphic functions, non-Euclidean geometry and complex functions, and showed the importance of topological considerations in differential equations. Many of the basic ideas in modern topology—such as triangulation, homology, the Euler-Poincaré formula and the fundamental group—are due to him. In a paper on the three-body problem (1889), he opened up new directions in celestial mechanics and began the study of dynamical systems in the modern sense. In his last years he published several articles (later collected as books) on the philosophy of science and scientific method.

Poincaré, Raymond Nicolas Landry 1860–1934 •*French statesman*• He was born in Bar-le-Duc, the cousin of **Jules Poincaré**. He studied law, becoming a deputy (1887) and senator (1903), holding office in several ministerial posts. Elected prime minister (1912–13) and president (1913–20), he had some success at first, especially in foreign affairs, but when **Georges Clemenceau** became prime minister in 1917, he found himself sidelined, and was unable to influence decisions at the postwar peace conference. As prime minister once again (1922–24), he sought to enforce the terms of the Treaty of Versailles (notably the payment of reparations) against a recalcitrant Germany by occupying the Ruhr (1923–24). Although Germany was thus forced to negotiate, Poincaré had by then been defeated in the 1924 elections, and his successor as prime minister, **Édouard Herriot**, bowing to British and US pressure, conceded much of what Poincaré had hoped to achieve. He was brought back to power (1926–29), as prime minister and finance minister, to deal with a financial crisis; he stabilized the franc, inaugurating a brief period of prosperity before France succumbed to the Great Depression. He wrote on both literature and politics.

Poindexter, John Marlan 1936– •*US naval officer and political adviser*• Born in Washington, Indiana, he was educated at the US Naval Academy and California Institute of Technology (Caltech). He became chief of naval operations during the 1970s and was deputy head of naval educational training from 1978 to 1981. In 1985 he became President **Ronald Reagan**'s national security adviser. He resigned, together with his assistant, Lieutenant Colonel **Oliver North**, in 1986 in the aftermath of the Iran-Contra affair. Poindexter retired from the navy in 1987, and in 1990 was convicted by a federal court on charges of obstructing and lying to Congress. He was sentenced to six months in prison, but his sentence was overturned by the federal appeals court in 1991.

Poisson, Siméon Denis 1781–1840 •*French mathematical physicist*• Born in Pithiviers, Loiret, he was educated at the École Polytechnique and became the first Professor of Mechanics at the Sorbonne. He published extensively on mathematical physics, and his contributions to potential theory and the transformation of equations in mechanics by means of Poisson brackets have proved of lasting worth. He is also remembered for discovering the Poisson distribution, a special case of the binomial distribution in statistics.

Poitier, Sidney 1924– •*US actor and director*• Born in Miami, Florida, he was raised in the Bahamas and later studied at the American Negro Theater in New York. He appeared on stage before making his film debut in the documentary *From Whence Cometh My Help* (1949). His Hollywood debut followed in *No Way Out* (1950), and he gave strong performances in *Cry, the Beloved Country* (1952), *The Blackboard Jungle* (1955) and *The Defiant Ones* (1958). He won an Academy Award for *Lilies of the Field* (1963). Handsome and unassuming, he brought dignity to the portrayal of noble and intelligent characters in such films as *In the Heat of the Night* (1967) and *Guess Who's Coming to Dinner* (1967). He has also directed a number of comedies, including *Stir Crazy* (1980), and returned to acting after a ten-year absence in *Little Nikita* (1988) and *Shoot to Kill* (1988). Later television appearances include *To Sir With Love II* (1996).

Poitiers, Diane de *See* **Diane de Poitiers**

Polanski, Roman 1933– •*French-Polish film director, scriptwriter and actor*• Born in Paris, France, and brought up in Poland, he was an actor on radio and in the theater, attended the State Film School in Lodź (1954–59), and made a number of short films. His feature-length debut *Nóz w Wodzie* (1962, *Knife in the Water*) brought him international recognition and he has subsequently worked on films which often explore the nature of evil and personal corruption, including *Repulsion* (1965), *Cul de Sac* (1966) and *Rosemary's Baby* (1968). Later productions include *Chinatown* (1974), *Tess* (1979), *Frantic* (1988) and *Death and the Maiden* (1995). A traumatic life that includes the early death of his mother and the horrifying murder of his pregnant second wife, actress Sharon Tate, has been reflected in his creative work. On stage, he has directed *Lulu* (1974) and *Rigoletto* (1976) and acted in *Amadeus* (1981) and *Metamorphosis* (1988).

Polanyi, Michael 1891–1976 •*British physical chemist, social scientist and philosopher*• Born in Budapest, Hungary, he qualified in medicine at the University of Budapest in 1913 and studied physical chemistry at the Technische Hochschule, Karlsruhe. During World War I he was a medical officer in the Austrian army. From 1920 to 1923 he worked at the Kaiser Wilhelm Institute for Fiber Chemistry in Berlin, and then moved to the Institute of Physical Chemistry, where he worked on X-ray diffraction by fibers and began his studies of chemical kinetics. When **Hitler** rose to power in 1933, Polanyi accepted the chair of physical chemistry at the University of Manchester. There he was much involved in the development of transition state theory, but his interests were already moving to wider cultural and philosophical matters. He left physical chemistry and was given a personal chair in social studies in 1948. He became Senior Research Fellow of Merton College, Oxford, in 1958. His social and philosophical interests are best indicated by the titles of some of his books: *The Contempt of Freedom* (1940), *Full Employment and Free Trade* (1945), *Science, Faith and Society* (1946) and *Knowing and Being* (1969). His writings often met with suspicion and criticism in philosophical circles.

Pole, Reginald 1500–58 •*English Roman Catholic churchman*• Born in Stourton Castle, Staffordshire, he studied at Oxford, then in Padua, Italy. He was the son of Sir Richard Pole and Margaret, Countess of Salisbury (1473–1541). He gained **Henry VIII**'s favor, but lost it after opposing the king on divorce, and left for Italy, where he was made a cardinal (1536). In 1549 he was on the point of being elected pope, but on the election of Julius III lived quietly until the death of **Edward VI**. In 1554, during the reign of the Catholic Queen **Mary I**, he returned to England as papal legate, became one of her most powerful advisers, returned the country to Rome, and became Archbishop of Canterbury (1556). It is alleged that he was responsible for the hardening of Mary's attitude toward the Protestants.

Poliakoff, Stephen 1952– •*English dramatist*• Born in London, he studied at Cambridge. He achieved recognition with the plays *Hitting Town* and *City Sugar* (both 1975), which addressed the plight of the urban young in a Great Britain of concrete shopping arcades. Several plays followed on the same theme, but *Breaking the Silence* (1984), set in the aftermath of the Russian Revolution, is his finest work to date. Other stage plays include *Shout Across the River* (1978), *Coming Into Land* (1987) and *Remember This* (1999). His television plays include *Caught on a Train* (1980). He made his debut as a film director with *Hidden City* (1987), and both wrote and directed *Close My Eyes* (1991), based on *Hitting Town*.

Polignac, Auguste Jules Armand Marie, Prince de 1780–1847 •*French statesman*• He was born in Versailles. He was arrested for conspiring against **Napoleon I** (1804), became a peer at the **Bourbon** Restoration, and received the title of prince from the pope in 1820. English ambassador in 1823, he became head of the last Bourbon ministry in 1829, which decreed the St Cloud Ordinances that cost **Charles X** his throne (1830). Imprisoned until 1836, he then lived in exile in England, and returned to Paris in 1845.

Polk, James K(nox) 1795–1849 •*11th President of the US*• Born in Mecklenburg County, North Carolina, he was admitted to the bar in 1820. He was elected to Congress as a Democrat in 1825, becoming Speaker of the House in 1835 and advancing **Andrew Jackson**'s legislative aims. He served as governor of Tennessee (1839–41), and in 1844 he gained the Democratic nomination as a compromise candidate and was elected president, mainly because of his advocacy of the annexation of Texas. Congress voted to annex Texas just before Polk's inauguration in 1845, and when an effort to buy California from Mexico was rebuffed, the president forced hostilities by advancing the US Army to the Rio Grande, thus beginning the Mexican War. The capital was taken in 1847, and by the terms of peace the US acquired California and New Mexico. A strong leader who set himself major objectives and achieved them, Polk also succeeded in settling the Oregon boundary dispute with Great Britain. By the end of his term, however, he was exhausted and in poor health, and he died a few months after leaving office.

Polk, Leonidas 1806–64 •*US soldier*• Born in Raleigh, North Carolina, he was a cousin of **James K Polk**. He held a commission in the artillery, but resigned to study divinity and in 1831 received holy orders in the Episcopal church. From 1841 until his death he was Bishop of Louisiana, even when at the head of an army corps. In the Civil War (1861–65) he was made major general. At Belmont in November 1861, he was driven from his camp by **Ulysses S Grant**, but finally forced him to retire. At Shiloh and Corinth he commanded the first corps; promoted to lieutenant general, he conducted the retreat from Kentucky. After Chickamauga, where he commanded the right wing, he was relieved of his command; reappointed in December 1863, he opposed **William Sherman**'s march.

Pollaiuolo, Antonio 1429–98 •*Florentine goldsmith, medalist, metal caster and painter*• He cast sepulchral monuments in St Peter's in Rome for Popes **Sixtus IV** and Innocent VIII. His pictures are distinguished by their life and vigor. He was one of the first painters to study anatomy and apply it to art, and he was skilled in suggesting movement. His brother Piero (1443–96) worked with him.

Pollard, Albert Frederick 1869–1948 •*English historian*• Born in Ryde, Isle of Wight, he graduated from Oxford and became Professor of Constitutional History at the University of London (1903–31), founding in 1920 its Institute of Historical Research, and from 1908 to 1936 he was a Fellow of All Souls College, Oxford. Among his many historical works are biographies of *Henry VIII* (1902), *Thomas Cranmer* (1904) and *Wolsey* (1929). He also wrote *A Short History of the Great War* (1920) and *Factors in American History* (1925). The Historical Association was founded by him in 1906 and he was editor of *History* from 1916 to 1922.

Pollio, Gaius Asinius 76 BC–AD 4 •*Roman orator and soldier*• In the civil war against **Pompey** he sided with **Julius Caesar**; in 39 BC he commanded in Spain and, appointed by **Mark Antony** to settle the veterans on the lands assigned them, saved **Virgil**'s property from confiscation. He founded the first public library in Rome and was the patron of Virgil and **Horace**. Only a few fragments of his writings survive.

Pollock, (Paul) Jackson 1912–56 •*US artist*• Born in Cody, Wyoming, he was trained at the Art Students' League in New York and became the first exponent of tachism, or action painting, in the US. His art developed from surrealism to abstract art and the first drip paintings of 1947. This technique he continued with increasing violence and often on huge canvases, for example, *One*, which is 17 ft (5.2 m) long. Other striking works include *No. 32* and the black-and-white *Echo and Blue Poles*. He was killed in an automobile accident.

Polo, Marco 1254–1324 •*Venetian merchant, traveler and writer*• He was born of a noble Venetian merchant family. At the time of his birth, his father and uncle were on an expedition to Bokhara and Cathay (China). They were well received by **Kublai Khan**, who commissioned them as envoys to the pope to seek a hundred learned Europeans for the imperial court. They were unsuccessful in this commission (1269), and started out again in 1271, taking the young Marco with them. They arrived at the court of Kublai Khan in 1275, after traveling across Central Asia and through the Gobi Desert to Tangut and Shangtu. The emperor at first refused to allow the Polos to leave his court, but eventually they sailed to Persia, finally reaching Venice in 1295, and bringing with them the great wealth they had accumulated. In 1298 Marco commanded a galley at the Battle of Curzola, and after the Venetians' defeat he was taken prisoner for a year at Genoa. There he wrote an account of his travels, *Divisament dou monde*, either from memory (dictated to a fellow prisoner) or from notes which he had written for Kublai Khan. This account is one of the most important sources of our knowledge of China and the East before the 19th century. After his release (1298), he returned to Venice, where he spent the rest of his life.

“ ”

I have not told even the half of the things that I have seen.

c. 1320 On being accused of exaggeration in his accounts of China. Quoted in R H Poole and P Finch (eds) ***Newnes Pictorial Knowledge*** *(1950), volume 2.*

Pol Pot, *also known as* **Saloth Sar** 1925–98 •*Cambodian politician*• He was born in Kompong Thom province. After working on a rubber plantation in his early teens, he joined the anti-French resistance movement under **Ho Chi Minh** during the early 1940s, becoming a member of the Indo-Chinese Communist Party and Cambodian Communist Party in 1946. During the 1960s and early 1970s he led the pro-Chinese Communist Khmer Rouge in guerrilla activity against the Kampuchean governments of Prince **Sihanouk** and Lieutenant General Lon Nol, and in 1976, after the overthrow of Lon Nol, became prime minister. He proceeded brutally to introduce an extreme Communist regime which resulted in the loss of more than two million lives. The regime was overthrown by Vietnamese troops in January 1979, and Pol Pot took to the resistance struggle once more. The Khmer Rouge began to splinter in 1996, and in 1997 Pol Pot was arrested by an opposing faction. He died while under house arrest.

Polybius c. 205–c. 123 BC •*Greek historian*• Born in Megalopolis, Arcadia, he was one of the thousand noble Achaeans who, after the conquest of Macedonia in 168 BC, were sent to Rome and detained as political hostages in honorable captivity. He was the guest of Lucius Aemilius Paullus and became the close friend of his son, **Scipio Aemilianus**. In 151 the exiles were permitted to return to Greece, but Polybius rejoined Scipio, followed him in his African campaign, and was present at the destruction of Carthage in 146. The war between the Achaeans and Romans called him back to Greece, and, after the taking of Corinth by Rome (146), he procured favorable terms for the vanquished. In furtherance of his historical labors he traveled to Asia Minor, Egypt, upper Italy, southern France and Spain. His *History* covers the period 221–146. Of 40 books, only the first 5 are preserved complete.

Polycarp, St c. 69–c. 155 AD •*Greek Christian and one of the Apostolic Fathers*• He was Bishop of Smyrna during the little-known period between the Apostle **John**, who was his teacher in Ephesus, and his own disciple **Irenaeus**. The author of the *Epistle to the Philippians*, he visited Rome to discuss the timing of Easter, and was martyred on his return to Smyrna. His feast day is February 23.

Polyclitus 5th century BC •*Greek sculptor*• He was from Samos and was a contemporary of **Phidias**. A specialist in statues of muscular athletes, he is now best known for the lost bronze *Doryphorus* (Spear Bearer), a fragment of which is in the Uffizi Gallery, Florence. His works were often copied, and he was highly thought of by **Pliny**.

Polycrates d. c. 522 BC •*Tyrant of Samos*• He conquered several nearby islands and towns on the Asiatic mainland and was one of the most conspicuous and powerful Greek tyrants of his time. He made an alliance with Amasis II, king of Egypt, but later broke it by giving support to the Persian king **Cambyses II** in his invasion of Egypt. He successfully resisted an attack from Spartans, Corinthians and disaffected Samians, but was later lured to the mainland by Oroetes, a Persian satrap, seized, and crucified.

Pombal, Sebastião José de Carvalho e Mello, Marquês de 1699–1782 •*Portuguese statesman*• He was born near Coimbra. Appointed secretary for foreign affairs (1750), he showed resourcefulness in replanning Lisbon after the great earthquake (1755), and the following year was made prime minister. He opposed the tyranny of the Church and the Inquisition, and banished the Jesuits in 1759. He established elementary schools, reorganized the army, introduced fresh colonists into the Portuguese settlements and established West India and Brazil companies. The tyranny of the Inquisition was broken. Agriculture, commerce and finance were improved. In 1758 he was made Count of Oeyras, and in 1770 Marquês de Pombal. His power ended on the accession of Maria I (1777).

Pompadour, Jeanne Antoinette Poisson, Marquise de, *known as* **Madame de Pompadour** 1721–64 •*French courtier and mistress*• Born in Paris, possibly the child of Le Normant de Tournehem, a wealthy farmer general (of revenues), she was married in 1741 to his nephew, Le Normant d'Étiales. She caught the attention of King **Louis XV**, and was installed at Versailles and ennobled as Marquise de Pompadour. For 20 years she named her own favorites ministers of France and swayed the policy of the state, but her policy and wars were disastrous (the loss of Canada was blamed on her), and the ministry of the Duc de **Choiseul** was the only creditable portion of the reign. With Louis, she founded the École Militaire, the Place Louis XV (Place de la Concorde) and the royal porcelain factory at Sèvres. She was a lavish patron of poets and painters.

Pompey, *originally* **Gnaeus Pompeius Magnus**, *called* **the Great** 106–48 BC •*Roman soldier and politician*• At 17 he fought in the Social War against **Marius** and Cinna. He supported **Sulla**, and destroyed the remains of the Marian faction in Africa and Sicily. He extinguished the Marian party in Spain under Sertorius (76–71 BC), annihilated the remnants of the army of **Spartacus** and was popularly elected consul for the year 70. A member of the aristocratic party, he nevertheless carried a law restoring the tribunician power to the people. He cleared the Mediterranean Sea of pirates, defeated **Mithridates VI** of Pontus, Tigranes of Armenia, and Antiochus of Syria, subdued the Jews and captured Jerusalem, and entered Rome in triumph for the third time in 61. But now his star began to wane. Distrusted by the aristocracy, and second to **Julius Caesar** in popular favor, Pompey did not immediately secure Senate ratification of his acts in Asia. He and Caesar, with the plutocrat **Crassus**, formed the all-powerful "First Triumvirate." Pompey's acts in Asia were ratified, Caesar's designs were gained and Caesar's daughter, Julia, was married to Pompey. Jealousies arose, Julia died in 54 and Pompey returned to the aristocratic party. Caesar was ordered to lay down his office, which he consented to do if Pompey would do the same. The Senate insisted on unconditional resignation, otherwise he would be declared a public enemy. But crossing the Rubicon, Caesar defied the Senate and its armies. After his final defeat at Pharsalia in 48, Pompey fled to Egypt, where he was murdered. His younger son, Sextus, secured a fleet and ravaged the coasts of Italy, but in 36 he was defeated at sea by **Agrippa**, and in 35 slain at Mitylene.

Pompidou, Georges Jean Raymond 1911–74 •*French statesman*• Born in Montboudif in the Auvergne and trained as an administrator, he joined **de Gaulle**'s staff in 1944. He held similar opinions to those of de Gaulle, but was more moderate in his views. He filled various government posts from 1946, culminating in his appointment as prime minister in 1962. During the "Événements" of May 1968, Pompidou played a key role in defusing and resolving the political crisis, but was dismissed by his increasingly jealous patron, de Gaulle, soon after the parliamentary election held in June. However, in 1969, following de Gaulle's resignation, he was comfortably elected president and proceeded to pursue a somewhat more liberal and internationalist policy program. He died in office. The Centre Georges Pompidou (renamed Centre Beaubourg) in Paris was completed in his memory in 1978.

Ponce de León, Ernesto Zedillo *See* **Zedillo Ponce de León, Ernesto**

Ponce de León, Juan 1460–1521 •*Spanish explorer*• Born in San Servas, he was a court page, served against the Moors and became governor, first of part of Hispaniola, then (1510–12) of Puerto Rico. On a quest for the fountain of perpetual youth, he encountered Florida in April 1513, and was made governor. Failing to conquer his new subjects, he retired to Cuba and died there from a wound inflicted by a poisoned arrow.

Poniatowski, Stanisław *See* **Stanisław Poniatowski**

Ponte, Giacomo da *See* **Bassano, Jacopo da**

Pontedera, Andrea da *See* **Pisano, Andrea**

Pontiac c. 1720–69 •*Native American leader*• Born near the Maumee River in what is now Ohio, he became chief of the Ottawa. In 1763 he organized an uprising against the British garrisons, conducting an extended and ultimately unsuccessful siege of Detroit. Although Pontiac's forces captured several other forts, they were unable to match mounting British reinforcements, and the rebellion faltered by 1764. Pontiac was later murdered by a Native American from Illinois, causing a bitter intertribal war.

Pontormo, Jacopo da 1494–1552 •*Italian painter*• Of the Florentine school, he was influenced by **Leonardo da Vinci** and **Piero di Cosimo** and worked under **Andrea del Sarto**. His works included frescoes, notably of the Passion (1522–25), in the Certosa near Florence. The *Deposition* (c. 1525), which forms the altarpiece in a chapel in Santa Felicità, Florence, is probably his masterpiece, and is a prime example of the early Mannerist style. He also painted portraits.

Pop, Iggy, *originally* **James Newell Osterberg** 1947– •*US rock singer and songwriter*• Born in Ypsilanti, Michigan, he called himself Iggy after his first high school band, The Iguanas. Having headed The Stooges from 1969 to 1974, he collaborated with **David Bowie** on his best-selling solo albums *The Idiot* and *Lust for Life* (both 1977). Wild in appearance and performance, he had further success with such new wave albums as *New Values* (1979). Bowie returned to produce *Blah, Blah, Blah* in 1986 and Iggy Pop continued into the 1990s with *Brick by Brick* (1990), from which came the single "Candy." More recent albums have included *Skull Ring* (2003).

Pope, Alexander 1688–1744 •*English poet*• He was born in London, the son of a linen merchant. He was largely self-taught, which left gaps in his knowledge of literature. At the age of 3 he suffered his first serious illness, and at 12 he was crippled by a tubercular infection of the spine which accounted for his stunted growth (4 feet, 6 inches). He began writing at an early age. "Ode to Solitude" was completed in 1700, when he was 12. He wrote *The Pastorals* while a teenager and they were eventually published by Jacob Tonson in 1709. Metrically adept, they are remembered for his mastery of technique rather than their poetry. He produced his seminal work *An Essay on Criticism* (1711), and *The Rape of the Lock* (1712) confirmed him as a poetic force. With *Windsor Forest* (1713) his popularity was further enhanced and he became a favorite in London. **Joseph Addison** and **Jonathan Swift** were among his acquaintances, and he became a member of the Scriblerus Club. His persistent ambition was to translate **Homer**, and the first installment of the *Iliad* appeared in 1715; when completed in 1720 its genius was immediately acknowledged, though it bore flimsy resemblance to the original. During this time he also issued his *Works* (1717), a mix of odes, epistles, elegies and a translation of **Chaucer**'s *The House of Fame*. With the success of the *Iliad*, Pope was financially secure and was regarded as the senior figure of English letters. He bought a villa in Twickenham and lived there until his death. In 1726 he completed the *Odyssey*, following the failure of his edition of **Shakespeare** (1725), which Lewis Theobald (1688–1744) criticized for poor scholarship. Pope got his revenge in *The Dunciad* (1728), a mock-heroic satire, published anonymously, whose butt is "Dulness" in general and, in particular, all the authors whom he wanted to hold up to ridicule. It is not, however, confined to personal animus, and literary vices are likewise exposed and scorned. With Swift, **John Gay**, Lord Oxford, **John Arbuthnot** and **Henry, 1st Viscount Bolingbroke**, he arranged the publication of a *Miscellany* (3 vols, 1727–28). In 1733–34 he published his *Essay on Man* and wrote *Moral Essays* (1731–35).

“ ”

And wine can of their wits the wise beguile,
Make the sage frolic, and the serious smile.

1726 ***Odyssey****, book 14, l. 520–1.*

Pope-Hennessy, Sir John 1913–94 •*English art historian*• Born in London, he was educated at Balliol College, Oxford. He joined the staff of the Victoria and Albert Museum, London, in 1938, and subsequently held many academic and curatorial posts, including director of the Victoria and Albert Museum (1967–73), and of the British Museum (1974–76), before going to New York, where he worked at the Metropolitan Museum. He was a leading authority on Italian renaissance art, and his many books include studies of Sienese painting, **Paolo Uccello** and **Fra Angelico**, and a series of definitive volumes on Italian sculpture.

Popiełuszko, Jerzy (Alfons) 1947–84 •*Polish priest*• Born in Okopy, near Svchowola, Podlasie, he served in several Warsaw parishes after ordination and became an outspoken supporter of the Solidarity trade union, especially when it was banned in 1981. His sermons, regularly held in St Stanisław Kostka Church, were widely acclaimed. He resisted official moves to have him silenced, but was kidnapped and murdered by the secret police in October 1984, more than a year after the lifting of martial law. It was probably this tragedy more than any other event that, in a profoundly Catholic country, spelled the eventual demise of the Communist Party.

Pople, John A(nthony) 1925–2004 •*English chemist and Nobel Prize winner*• He was born in Burnham, Somerset, and educated at Trinity College, Cambridge. He lectured at Cambridge from 1954 to 1958, then moved to the US to teach, becoming Professor of Chemical Physics (later Natural Sciences) at the Carnegie-Mellon University in Pittsburgh (1964–93), as well as holding several other senior posts at US universities. His many honors included the Nobel Prize for chemistry (1998; with **Walter Kohn**) for his development of computational methods in quantum chemistry.

Popova, Lyubov Sergeyevna, *née* **Eding** 1889–1924 •*Russian painter and stage designer*• Born near Moscow, she studied in Paris (1912–13), then returned to Russia where she met **Vladimir Tatlin**, the founder of Soviet constructivism. In the year before her death she designed textiles for the First State Textile Print Factory, Moscow, where she was given a memorial exhibition in 1924. Her work was especially important for its exploration of abstract color values.

Popper, Sir Karl Raimund 1902–94 •*British philosopher*• Born in Vienna, Austria, he studied at the university there and associated with the Vienna Circle of philosophers, though he sharply criticized their logical positivism and their views, for example, on meaning and verification. He left Vienna in 1937 under the threat of German occupation, and after teaching in New Zealand (1937–45), was reader (1945–48) and later professor (1949–69) at the London School of Economics. His major work in scientific methodology, *Die Logik der Forschung* (1934, Eng trans *The Logic of*

Scientific Discovery, 1959), stressed the importance of falsifiability as a defining factor of true scientific theories, and contrasted these with "pseudosciences," like Marxism and psychoanalysis. He extended the critique of Marxism in *The Open Society and Its Enemies* (1945), a polemic directed against all philosophical systems with totalitarian political implications. He also attacked more generally the idea that historians and social scientists can discover large-scale laws of historical development, notably in *The Poverty of Historicism* (1957). His later works include *Conjectures and Refutations* (1963), *Objective Knowledge* (1972), and *The Self and Its Brain* (1977, with Sir **John Eccles**). Knighted in 1965, he held the rare distinction of being a Fellow of both the British Academy and the Royal Society.

❝ ❞

We may become the makers of our fate when we have ceased to pose as its prophets.

1945 ***The Open Society and Its Enemies****, introduction.*

Porphyry c. 232–c. 305 AD •*Neo-Platonist philosopher*• Born to Syrian parents, probably in Tyre, where he spent his boyhood, he studied at Athens and gained a reputation as a polymathic scholar. He went to Rome (c. 263 AD), where he became first a disciple of **Plotinus**, and later his biographer and editor. He is probably most important as a popularizer of Plotinus's thought, but his own works include a celebrated treatise *Against the Christians*, commentaries on **Plato**, Plotinus and **Aristotle**, *De abstinentia* (a tract on vegetarianism), and a moral address to his wife, Marcella. His most influential work was the *Isagoge*, a commentary on Aristotle's *Categories*, which was widely used in the Middle Ages.

Porritt, Sir Jonathon Espie 1950– •*English broadcaster, writer and environmentalist*• Born in London, he was educated at Eton and Magdalen College, Oxford. He was a teacher until 1984, when he became director of Friends of the Earth (FoE). He stood as a candidate for the Ecology Party and later the Green Party in the UK general elections in 1979 and 1983 and in the European elections in 1979 and 1984, without success. In the late 1980s he became a well-known environmental figure through his work at FoE, publications and regular television appearances. He resigned from FoE in 1990 to concentrate on his freelance career as a writer and broadcaster. His books include *The Coming of the Greens* (1988). He later became an adviser to **Charles**, Prince of Wales. He has been director of Forum for the Future since 1996, and chairman of the Sustainable Development Commission since 2000.

Porsche, Ferdinand 1875–1951 •*German car designer*• Born in Hafersdorf, Bohemia, he designed cars for Daimler and Auto Union, but set up his own independent studio in 1931. In 1934 he produced the plans for a revolutionary cheap car with a rear engine, to which the Nazis gave the name *Volkswagen* ("People's car") and which they promised to mass-produce for the German workers. After World War II the "Beetle," as it was known, became a record-breaking German export. He also designed the distinctive sports car that bears his name.

Porsena or **Porsenna, Lars** 6th century BC •*Etruscan ruler of Clusium*• According to Roman tradition he laid siege to Rome after the overthrow (510 BC) of **Tarquinius Superbus**, but was prevented from capturing the city by the heroism of Horatius Cocles in defending the bridge across the Tiber. However, this story may conceal a temporary occupation of Rome by Porsena.

Porta, Giacomo Della 1541–1604 •*Italian architect*• Born in Rome, he was a pupil of **Giacomo Vignola**, and is best known for the cupola of St Peter's and his work on the Palazzo Farnese, left unfinished by **Michelangelo**. He was also responsible for some of the fountains of Rome.

Portal (of Hungerford), Charles Frederick Algernon Portal, 1st Viscount 1893–1971 •*English air force officer*• Born in Hungerford, Berkshire, of an ancient Huguenot family, he joined the Royal Engineers in 1914 and served in the Royal Flying Corps (1915–18). Promoted to air vice marshal in 1937, he was director of organization at the Air Ministry (1937–38). In 1940 (April–October) he was commander in chief of Bomber Command before becoming chief of air staff (1940–46). He was controller of the Atomic Energy Authority (1946–51) and chairman of the British Aircraft Corporation (1960–68).

Porter, Cole 1891–1964 •*US composer*• Born in Peru, Indiana, he studied law at Harvard before deciding on a musical career. From his first hit on Broadway in 1929, he created a series of successful musical comedies, writing both lyrics and music for numerous classics of US popular song, such as "You Do Something to Me," "I Get a Kick out of You," "You're the Top" and "Just One of Those Things." In 1937 he was severely hurt in a riding accident, which left him in permanent pain, but he continued to compose, reaching the height of his success with *Kiss Me Kate* (1948) and *Can-Can* (1953). His style ranges from the unabashed romanticism of "Night and Day" (1932) to the droll wordplay and double entendres of "Too Darn Hot."

Porter, Eleanor, *née* **Hodgman** 1868–1920 •*US novelist*• She was born in Littleton, New Hampshire, and studied music at the New England Conservatory. In 1913 she published *Pollyanna*, the story of an orphaned girl who goes to live with her stern aunt, which was an immediate success and has retained its popularity ever since. A sequel, about the "glad child," *Pollyanna Grows Up*, was published in 1915, and two volumes of short stories, *The Tangled Threads* and *Across the Years*, appeared posthumously in 1924.

Porter (of Luddenham), George Porter, Baron 1920–2002 •*English physical chemist and Nobel Prize winner*• Born in Stainforth, Yorkshire, he studied at the University of Leeds and Cambridge. He became Professor of Physical Chemistry at Sheffield University in 1955, in 1963 transferring to the Firth Chair of Chemistry. In 1966 he was appointed Resident Professor and Director of the Royal Institution, where he remained until 1985. His research was mainly concerned with gaseous reactions, especially photochemical reactions, and with photochemistry generally. In the late 1940s, **Ronald Norrish** and Porter developed the technique of flash photolysis, which became important in the study of very rapid gas reactions. With **Manfred Eigen**, they were awarded the 1967 Nobel Prize for chemistry for this work. In later years Porter became prominent as a spokesman for science in the UK. He was knighted in 1972, admitted to the Order of Merit in 1989, and made a life peer in 1990.

Porter, Katherine Anne Maria Veronica Callista Russell 1890–1980 •*US writer*• Born in Indian Creek, Texas, she was brought up by a grandmother near Kyle, Texas. She worked as a reporter and actress, and went to Mexico (1920–22), where she took up Mexican causes. Her first collection of stories, *Flowering Judas*, was published in 1930. Later, in Paris, she wrote her first novel, *Hacienda* (1934). Back in the US, three short novels, published as *Pale Horse, Pale Rider* (1939), were a success. *Ship of Fools* (1962), a huge allegorical novel analyzing the German state of mind in the 1930s, was almost universally regarded as a failure. A volume of essays, *The Days Before*, appeared in 1952. Her *Collected Short Stories* (1965) won a Pulitzer Prize.

Porter, Peter Neville Frederick 1929– •*Australian poet and critic*• Born in Brisbane, he has lived in England since 1951 and has worked as a bookseller, journalist, clerk and advertising copywriter. His collections include *Once Bitten, Twice Bitten* (1961), *Words Without Music* (1968), *The Last of England* (1970) and *The Cost of Seriousness* (1978). He won the Whitbread award for *The Automatic Oracle* (1987). He has published two volumes of translation from Latin, *Epigrams by Martial* (1971) and *After Martial* (1972), showing an affection for the classics which is evident in his poem "On First Looking into Chapman's *Hesiod*" (1975). Later publications include *Possible Worlds* (1989) and *Millennial Fables* (1995).

Porter, Rodney Robert 1917–85 •*English biochemist and Nobel Prize winner*• Born in Newton-le-Willows, Lancashire, he studied there and with **Frederick Sanger** in Cambridge (1946–49), then worked at the National Institute for Medical Research (1949–60) and St Mary's Hospital Medical School in London (1960–67), before becoming Professor of Biochemistry at Oxford in 1967. He studied the biochemistry of antibodies, and was the first to propose the bilaterally symmetrical four-chain structure which is the basis of all immunoglobulins. **Gerald Edelman** carried out complementary studies in the US, and for this work they were jointly awarded the

Nobel Prize for physiology or medicine in 1972. In 1985 he was run over and killed while crossing a road.

Portillo, Michael 1953– •*English Conservative politician*• Born in Bushey, Hertfordshire, and educated at Harrow County School and Peterhouse, Cambridge, he joined the Conservative Research Department in 1976 and was elected Conservative Member of Parliament for Enfield Southgate in 1984. He became chief secretary of the treasury in 1992 and later served as secretary of state for employment (1994) and secretary of state for defense (1995–97). He was regarded as a potential future leader, but he lost his seat in the 1997 general election. Victory in a 1999 by-election led to his return to the House of Commons.

Portland, 3rd Duke of *See* **Bentinck, William Henry Cavendish**

Posidonius, *nicknamed* **the Athlete** c.135–c.51 BC •*Greek philosopher, scientist and polymath*• Born in Apamea, Syria, he studied at Athens as a pupil of **Panaetius**, spent many years in travel and scientific research in Europe and Africa, then settled in Rhodes, where he was head of the Stoic school, and later Rome (86 BC). There he became a friend of **Cicero** and other leading figures of the day. He wrote on a vast range of subjects, including geometry, geography, astronomy, meteorology, history and philosophy, although only fragments of his works survive. He made important contributions to the development of Stoic doctrines.

Post, Emily, *née* **Price** 1873–1960 •*US writer and socialite*• Born into a wealthy family in Baltimore, Maryland, she was educated in New York and married in 1892, but divorced after having two children. She then began a career writing novels and society journalism, but found lasting fame with *Etiquette in Society, in Business, in Politics and at Home* (1922), which became better known as *Etiquette: The Blue Book of Social Usage*. By the time of her death it had sold more than a million copies. She also wrote *How to Behave Though a Debutante* (1928) and a book about interior decorating, *The Personality of a House* (1930).

Post, Sir Laurens van der *See* **van der Post, Sir Laurens Jan**

Post, Wiley 1900–35 •*US pioneer aviator*• Born in Grand Saline, Texas, he toured the country as a mechanic, stunt parachutist and wingwalker in the early 1920s. On June 23, 1931, he left Roosevelt Field, New York City, in a Lockheed Vega monoplane with the Australian Harold Gatty (1903–57) as navigator, to fly around the world in 8 days, 15 hours and 51 minutes. (The previous record had been made by the Graf Zeppelin in 21 days.) In 1933 he made the first solo flight around the world, in 7 days, 18 hours and 49 minutes. He was killed in an air crash in Alaska.

Potemkin, Grigori Aleksandrovich 1739–91 •*Russian soldier and politician*• Born near Smolensk, of a noble but impoverished Polish family, he entered the Russian Horse Guards in 1755 and attracted the notice of **Catherine the Great** by his good looks. In 1774 he became her lover, and directed Russian policy. In charge of the newly acquired lands in the south, he made an able administrator, and constructed a fleet in the Black Sea. In the Second Turkish War (1787–92) he headed the army and took the credit for Count **Suvorov**'s victories (1791). He gained for Russia the Crimea and the north coast of the Black Sea, and he founded Sebastopol, Nikolaev and Yekaterinoslav (Dnipropetrovs'k).

Potok, Chaim (Herman Harold) 1929–2002 •*US novelist*• Born and educated in New York City, he studied there at Yeshiva University and the Jewish Theological Seminary. He was ordained a rabbi in 1954. After teaching in seminaries, he became scholar-in-residence at Har Zion Temple in Philadelphia (1959–63) and, later, special projects editor at the Jewish Publication Society. His novels explore the problems of Orthodox and Hasidic communities within an aggressively secular society, and include the controversial *My Name Is Asher Lev* (1972), in which the hero abandons his religious calling to become a painter, *The Book of Lights* (1982) and *Davita's Harp* (1985). In 1990 his troubled artist-hero reappeared in *The Gift of Asher Lev*. His *Wanderings* (1978) is a scholarly but personal history of the Jews.

Potter, (Helen) Beatrix 1866–1943 •*English author and illustrator of children's books*• She was born in Kensington, London, into a wealthy family. The atmosphere at home was oppressively quiet and Beatrix, supervised by nurses and educated by governesses, grew up a lonely town child longing for the country. She taught herself to draw and paint, and turned to sketching pet animals dressed as human beings in order to amuse younger children. The original version of *The Tale of Peter Rabbit* was enclosed with a letter to her ex-governess's child in 1893 and later published at her own expense, with fuller illustrations, in 1900, as was *The Tailor of Gloucester* (1902). When Frederick Warne took over publication in 1903, she had her first popular success with *The Tale of Squirrel Nutkin* (1903). In 1913, eight years after she had moved to a farm at Sawrey, near Lake Windermere (where six of her books are set), she married William Heelis, a Lake District solicitor. Thereafter she devoted herself almost entirely to farming and the National Trust (founded in 1895). *Johnny Town-Mouse* (1918) was her last book in the familiar style. She devised an elaborate cryptic diary whose code was later broken and published as *The Journal of Beatrix Potter 1881–1897* (1966). Beatrix Potter wrote with great realism and without sentimentality; the animal world she describes is constantly threatened by deceit, physical harm and death. She was the outstanding writer and artist of picture storybooks of her time, and her characters have become classics of children's literature.

Potter, Dennis Christopher George 1935–94 •*English dramatist*• He was born in Forest of Dean, Gloucestershire, and was educated at Oxford, working as a journalist and television critic before turning to writing plays. Although he wrote for the stage, he was primarily a television dramatist. Following *Vote, Vote, Vote for Nigel Barton* (1965), he wrote over 25 television plays and series. *Son of Man* (1969) was the first television screenplay that depicted Jesus as a man who struggled as much with his own doubts as with those opposed to his teaching. Other controversial plays include *Brimstone and Treacle* (1978), *The Singing Detective* (1986), *Blackeyes* (1989) and *Lipstick on Your Collar* (1993). He was also technically innovative: *Pennies From Heaven* (1978) required the actors to mime to popular songs of the 1920s and 30s, and *Blue Remembered Hills* (1979), a memory play, required the adult actors to impersonate children. His novel *Ticket to Ride* (1986) was adapted as the film *Secret Friends* (1992). The undisputed master of the serious television play, he completed two final dramas just before his death, *Karaoke* and *Cold Lazarus*, which were broadcast in 1996.

Potter, Stephen 1900–69 •*English writer and radio producer*• He joined the BBC in 1938, and was coauthor with **Joyce Grenfell** of the *How* series. He made his name with a series of comic books on the art of establishing personal supremacy by demoralizing the opposition: *Gamesmanship* (1947), *Lifemanship* (1950), *One-Upmanship* (1952) and *Supermanship* (1958).

“ ”

Each of us can, by ploy or gambit, most naturally gain the advantage.

*1950 **Lifemanship**.*

Poujade, Pierre 1920–2003 •*French political leader*• Born in Saint Céré, after serving in World War II, he became a publisher and bookseller there. In 1951 he was elected a member of the Saint Céré municipal council, and in 1954 he organized his Poujadist movement (a union for the defense of tradesmen and artisans) as a protest against the French tax system. His party had successes in the 1956 elections to the National Assembly, but disappeared in 1958. Poujade published his manifesto *J'ai choisi le combat* ("I Have Chosen Combat") in 1956.

Poulenc, Francis 1899–1963 •*French composer*• Born in Paris, he studied composition under Charles Koechlin (1867–1950), came under the influence of **Erik Satie**, and as a member of Les Six was prominent in the reaction against "Debussyesque" Impressionism. He wrote chamber music in a cool, limpid style, often for unusual combinations of instruments, and is also known for impressive stage works, especially the ballet *Les biches* (1923, "The Little Darlings") and the operas *Les mamelles de Tirésias* (1944, "The Breasts of Tiresias") and *Dialogues des Carmélites* (1953–56, "The Carmelites' Dialogues"). His cantata *Figure humaine* (1945) has as its theme the occupation of France. Perhaps his major contribution to music is his considerable output of songs, more romantic in outlook than his other compositions, which include *Poèmes de Ronsard* (1924) and *Fêtes galantes* (1943).

Pound, Ezra Weston Loomis 1885–1972 •*US poet, translator and critic*• He was born in Hailey, Idaho, and brought up in Wyncote, near Philadelphia. He graduated from the University of Pennsylvania in 1906, became an instructor at Wabash College in Crawfordsville, Indiana, and after four months left for Europe, traveling widely in Spain, Italy and Provence. He published his first collection of poems, *A lume spento* (1908, "With Tapers Quenched"), in Venice. In London he met **Ford Madox Ford**, **James Joyce** and **Wyndham Lewis**, and published *Personae* and *Exultations* in 1909, followed by a book of critical essays, *The Spirit of Romance* (1910). He was coeditor of *Blast* (1914–15), the magazine of the short-lived Vorticist movement, and London editor of the Chicago *Little Review* (1917–19), and in 1920 became Paris correspondent for *The Dial*. From 1924 he made his home in Italy. He became involved with fascist ideas and created resentment with antidemocracy broadcasts in the early stages of World War II. In 1945 he was escorted back to the US and indicted for treason. The trial did not proceed, however, as he was adjudged insane and placed in an asylum until 1958, when he returned to Italy. In addition to poetry, he wrote books on literature, music, art and economics, and translated many texts from Italian, French, Chinese and Japanese. As a poet of the imagist school at the outset of his career, he was a thoroughgoing experimenter, deploying much curious and often spurious learning, and **T S Eliot** regarded him as the motivating force behind modern poetry. *Homage to Sextus Propertius* (1919) and *Hugh Selwyn Mauberley* (1920) are among his most important early poems. His *Cantos*, a loosely knit series of poems, appeared first in 1917, continuing in many installments; his work in the classics and Chinese poetry are discernible in the Cantos form.

“ ”

Great literature is simply language charged with meaning to the utmost possible degree.

1931 ***How to Read****, part 2.*

Pountney, David Willoughby 1947– •*English opera director*• Born in Oxford, he studied at St John's College, Cambridge. He joined the Scottish Opera in 1970, becoming its director of productions from 1976 to 1980, and moved to the English National Opera to work in the same capacity from 1982 to 1994. As a freelance director he has staged guest productions for all the major British companies and several companies overseas, and is noted for his interpretations of **Janáček**, **Verdi**, **Smetana**, **Philip Glass** and others. He has also made numerous translations of opera from German, Italian, Russian and Czech.

Poussin, Nicolas 1594–1665 •*French painter*• Poussin was born in Les Andelys, Normandy. After struggling to make a living in Paris, he earned enough money to visit Rome in 1624, where he received commissions from Cardinal Francesco Barberini (1597–1679, nephew of the reigning pope, **Urban VIII**) and soon became rich and famous. Among the masterpieces dating from this period is *The Adoration of the Golden Calf*, now in the London National Gallery. In 1640 he was ordered by King **Louis XIII** and Cardinal **Richelieu** to return to France, where he was appointed painter-in-ordinary to the king. However, the types of work he was expected to carry out were unsuited to his abilities, and in 1643 he returned to Rome. He constructed his historical pictures with great deliberation and after much experimentation, even going so far as to make small clay models of his scenes to make sure the lighting was right. From this relentless search for perfection, he evolved the prototype for the History Picture, which was considered academically the highest form of art; painters strove to emulate Poussin's achievements for the next two centuries. His œuvre also includes biblical subjects, mythological works and, from his later years, landscapes. Among his most admired works are *The Inspiration of the Poet* (1636, Louvre, Paris), *The Rape of the Sabine Women* (1636–37, Metropolitan Museum of Art, New York), *The Arcadian Shepherds* (1638–39) and *Landscape With the Burial of Phocion* (1648, Louvre).

Powell, Adam Clayton, Jr 1908–72 •*US politician*• Born in New Haven, Connecticut, the son of the pastor of the Abyssinian Baptist Church in Harlem, New York, he earned a doctorate in divinity from Shaw University and succeeded his father as pastor in 1937. With the African-American population of New York solidly behind him, he served in the US House of Representatives (1945–67, 1969–71). He was the first to use the phrase "Black Power" (1966), and fought against segregation and for fair employment practices. He was stripped of his House seat in 1967 after being charged with the misuse of public funds and other improprieties, but the Supreme Court overturned his expulsion in 1969. He was voted out of office in 1970.

Powell, Anthony Dymoke 1905–2000 •*English novelist*• Born in London, the son of an army officer, he was educated at Eton and Balliol College, Oxford, where he met several other young writers, including **Evelyn Waugh** and **Graham Greene**. He worked in publishing and journalism before World War II, and by 1936 had published four satirical novels, among them *Afternoon Men* (1931) and *What's Become of Waring?* (1939). After the war he returned to reviewing books, wrote a biography of **John Aubrey** (1948), and began the series of novels he called *A Dance to the Music of Time*—12 volumes, beginning with *A Question of Upbringing* (1951), covering 50 years of British upper-middle-class life and attitudes. In this series the light, witty, satirical tone of the prewar novels developed into an intricate and disciplined interweaving of personal relationships, ironic, humorous, and with extraordinary scope and depth of vision. He won the James Tait Black Memorial Prize (1957) and W H Smith Literary award (1974). He later published a four-volume autobiography, *To Keep the Ball Rolling* (1976–82); two novels, *O, How the Wheel Becomes It!* (1983) and *The Fisher King* (1986); two volumes of criticism; and his *Journals* (1995–97).

Powell, Bud (Earl) 1924–66 •*US jazz pianist*• He was born in New York City. A jazz virtuoso, he was the most influential bebop piano stylist. He became interested in jazz as a teenager, joining the modern jazz movement in the 1940s with encouragement from **Thelonious Monk**. His mental instability brought periodic visits to mental hospitals, and a concomitant unevenness (and ultimate decline) in his creative powers. That instability was exacerbated by narcotics, and by the death of his brother, pianist Richie Powell, in a car accident in 1956 which also killed the brilliant trumpeter, Clifford Brown. He moved to Paris from 1959 to 1964, where he led a trio featuring American expatriate drummer Kenny Clarke, another bebop innovator. He died in New York.

Powell, Cecil Frank 1903–69 •*English physicist and Nobel Prize winner*• Born in Tonbridge, Kent, he was educated at Cambridge, and throughout his career he worked at the University of Bristol. A former pupil of **Ernest Rutherford** and **Charles Wilson**, Powell used specially developed photographic emulsions to study nuclear interactions and improved the techniques used to analyze nuclear particle tracks. In 1950 he was awarded the Nobel Prize for physics for his development of nuclear emulsions and his part in the discovery of the charged pion, a particle which had been predicted by **Hideki Yukawa** in 1935. In addition to his scientific work, he was one of the leaders of the movement to increase the social responsibility of scientists.

Powell, Colin Luther 1937– •*US soldier and statesman*• Born in New York City, the African-American son of Jamaican immigrants, he was educated at the City College of New York and received a commission in the US Army in 1958. He served in Vietnam, Korea and Europe, being much decorated and rising ultimately to the post of chairman of the Joint Chiefs of Staff (1989–93). He retired from the army in 1993 and in 2001 was appointed secretary of state by President **George W Bush**.

Powell, (John) Enoch 1912–98 •*English Conservative politician and scholar*• Born in Stechford, Birmingham, he was educated at Trinity College, Cambridge, becoming Professor of Greek at the University of Sydney (1937–39). He enlisted in World War II as a private in 1939, was commissioned in 1940 and rose to the rank of brigadier. In 1946 he joined the Conservative Party, and in 1950 entered parliament as Member of Parliament for Wolverhampton. He held offices including financial secretary to the treasury from 1957, resigning with **Peter Thorneycroft** over policy differences in 1958, and minister of health from 1960, resigning again over the appointment of Sir Alec Douglas-Home (Lord **Home**) as prime minister in 1963. His austere brand of intellectualism and his radical views on defense and foreign commitments made him a significant figure within his party. He created more general controversy with his outspoken attitude to nonwhite immigration and racial integration, especially with his 1968 "rivers of blood" speech. Because of his opposition to the Common Market, he did not stand for election in 1974, but returned to parliament as an Ulster Unionist from October 1974 until he was defeated in the 1987 general election. He published numerous academic and political works, including *Reflections of a Statesman* (1991). Other titles include *Collected Poems* (1990) and *The Evolution of the Gospel* (1994).

" "

History is littered with the wars which everybody knew would never happen.

1967 Speech to Conservative Party conference, October 19.

Powell, Michael 1905–90 •*English film director, scriptwriter and producer*• Born in Bekesbourne, near Canterbury, Kent, he began his film career at the studios of director Rex Ingram, where he learned every technical aspect of the filmmaking process. *Two Crowded Hours* (1931), his directorial debut, was one of two dozen "quota quickies" he made over six years. More prestigious assignments followed, and he was codirector on *The Thief of Baghdad* (1940) for **Alexander Korda**, who introduced him to the writer **Emeric Pressburger**, with whom he began a partnership that lasted until 1957. Known as "The Archers," they collaborated on such films as *The Life and Death of Colonel Blimp* (1943), *Black Narcissus* (1947) and *The Red Shoes* (1948), creating a body of work unique in its flamboyant use of color, expressionism and sensuality. After the partnership ended, Powell made the controversial *Peeping Tom* (1959), which was attacked for its "bad taste" and "sadism" but later reclaimed as a masterly commentary on the voyeurism of film. Often considered ahead of his time, he lived to see "The Archers" hailed as one of the most daring and distinctive forces in the history of British cinema.

Powhatan d. 1618 •*Native American chief*• The civil but energetic ruler of the Powhatan confederacy of New England tribes, despite considerable provocation he managed to maintain peace with the white settlers in Virginia. His favorite daughter, **Pocahontas**, was carried off by settlers in 1609, but married a white colonist with her father's consent. Powhatan was succeeded by his more warlike brother, **Opechancanough**.

Powys, John Cowper 1872–1963 •*English novelist, poet and essayist*• He was born in Shirley, Derbyshire, the son of a vicar; his mother was descended from **John Donne** and **William Cowper** and his brothers, T F Powys and Llewelyn Powys, were also novelists. He was brought up in the Dorset-Somerset countryside, and though he spent much of his later life in the US, his formative years greatly influenced his work. Educated at Sherborne and Corpus Christi College, Cambridge, he taught and lectured before becoming a prolific author. Of some 50 books, his best known are his novels, particularly *Wolf Solent* (1929), *A Glastonbury Romance* (1932), *Weymouth Sands* (1934) and *Owen Glendower* (1940). His reputation is the subject of much argument, but his standing is probably that of a cult author, rather than a widely recognized one.

Poynings, Sir Edward 1459–1521 •*English soldier and diplomat*• He took part in a rebellion against **Richard III**, escaped to the Continent and joined the Earl of Richmond (**Henry VII**), with whom he later returned to England. In 1493 he was governor of Calais, and in 1494 went to Ireland as deputy governor for Prince Henry (**Henry VIII**). His aim was to anglicize the government of Ireland. This he accomplished by means of the Statutes of Drogheda, known as Poynings' Law, to the effect that all Irish legislature had to be confirmed by the English privy council. This was not repealed until 1782. He was often abroad on diplomatic missions, and in 1520 he was present at the Field of the Cloth of Gold.

Poynter, Sir Edward John 1836–1919 •*English painter*• He was born of Huguenot ancestry in Paris, the son of the architect Ambrose Poynter (1796–1886). He studied (1853–54) in Rome and from 1856 to 1860 in Paris and elsewhere. He made designs for stained glass, and drawings on wood for various periodicals, and for **Edward Dalziel**'s projected illustrated Bible. This led to studies in Egyptian art, which resulted in his *Israel in Egypt* (1867). His watercolors are numerous. In 1871 he became Slade Professor at University College London. He was director of art at South Kensington (1876–81) and director of the National Gallery (1894–1905), and in 1896 was made president of the Royal Academy. Among his works are *The Visit of the Queen of Sheba to Solomon* (1891), a portrait of **Lillie Langtry** and *Nausicaa and Her Maidens* (1872–79).

Praagh, Dame Peggy Van *See* **Van Praagh, Dame Peggy**

Prasad, Rajendra 1884–1963 •*Indian statesman*• Born in Zeradei, Bihar, he left legal practice to become a follower of **Mahatma Gandhi**. A member of the Working Committee of the All-India Congress in 1922, he was president of the Congress several times between 1934 and 1948, and was the first president of the Republic of India from 1950 to 1962. He wrote several books, including *India Divided at the Feet of Mahatma Gandhi* and an autobiography, *Atma Katha* (1958).

Pratchett, Terry (Terence David John) 1948– •*English author*• Born in Beaconsfield, Buckinghamshire, his early career was spent as a journalist and press officer for the Central Electricity Generating Board (1980–87). His first fantasy novel, *The Carpet People*, appeared in 1971, and the first in the irrepressible Discworld series, *The Colour of Magic*, in 1983. Since then there have been numerous Discworld novels, including *Wyrd Sisters* (1988) and *The Last Hero* (2001).

Praxiteles 4th century BC •*Greek sculptor, one of the greatest Greek artists*• He was a citizen of Athens. His works, usually in marble, have almost all perished, though his *Hermes Carrying the Infant Dionysus* was found at Olympia in 1877. Several of his statues are known from Roman copies, for example *Aphrodite of Cnidos* (c. 350 BC, Vatican Museum, Rome), possibly the first female nude.

Pré, Jaqueline du *See* **du Pré, Jacqueline**

Pregl, Fritz 1869–1930 •*Austrian chemist and Nobel Prize winner*• Born in Laibach (Ljubljana, Slovenia), he studied medicine at Graz University and spent most of his working life there. Finding that traditional methods of analysis were useless when applied to the minute quantities of biochemical materials that he wished to investigate, he devised new techniques for microanalysis, including a scale accurate to 0.001 mg. His innovations were fundamental to the development of biochemistry and brought him the Nobel Prize for chemistry in 1923.

Prelog, Vladimir 1906–98 •*Swiss organic chemist and Nobel Prize winner*• Born in Sarajevo (now in Bosnia), he was educated at the Prague Institute of Technology and then worked as an industrial chemist before moving to the University of Zagreb. In 1941, when the Germans invaded Yugoslavia, he taught at the Federal Institute of Technology in Zurich, and was Professor of Chemistry (1950–76). Following his notable work in organic chemistry, and especially in stereochemistry, he shared the Nobel Prize for chemistry in 1975 with Sir **John Warcup Cornforth**.

Premadasa, Ranasinghe 1924–93 •*Sri Lankan statesman*• Born in a North Colombo slum, a member of the lowly dhobi (laundrymen's) caste, he was educated at St Joseph's College, Colombo. He joined the United National Party (UNP) in 1950 and, elected to Sri Lanka's parliament in 1960, he served successively as UNP chief whip (1965–68, 1970–77), minister of local government (1968–70) and leader of the House (1977–78) before becoming prime minister under President **Junius Jayawardene** in 1978. During ten years as prime minister, Premadasa implemented a popular housebuilding and poverty alleviation program, which provided the basis for his election as president in 1988. He faced mounting civil unrest, both in the Tamil north and Sinhala south, and deteriorating relations with India. He was assassinated by a suicide bomber thought to have been a member of the Tamil Tigers separatist group.

Preminger, Otto 1906–86 •*US film director and producer*• Born in Vienna, Austria, he studied law at the University of Vienna, then acted with **Max Reinhardt**, joined the Theater in der Josefstadt (1928) and became its director (1933). He directed his first film, *Die grosse Liebe*, in 1932. He emigrated to the US in 1935, becoming naturalized in 1943. After directing several Broadway productions he moved to Hollywood, first as an actor, then as a director, specializing in costume dramas and film noir thrillers. An independent filmmaker from 1952, he boldly tackled controversial themes such as drug addiction in *The Man With the Golden Arm* (1955), rape in *Anatomy of a Murder* (1959), Jewish repatriation in *Exodus* (1960), homosexuality in *Advise and Consent* (1962) and racism in *Hurry Sundown* (1966). Other notable films include *Carmen Jones* (1954), *Bonjour Tristesse* (1959) and *Porgy and Bess* (1959). The stereotype of the old-style autocratic film director, he was also a showman, craftsman and talent spotter who was prepared to fight antiquated notions of censorship in the Supreme Court. His later theatrical work includes *The Trial* (1953) and *Full Circle* (1973). He also acted in the film *Stalag 17* (1953) and the television series *Batman* (1966). His last film was *The Human Factor* (1979).

Prescott, John Leslie 1938– •*English Labour politician*• Born in Prestatyn, Clwyd, after leaving school he worked as a chef trainee and then served in the merchant navy (1955–63) before studying at Ruskin College, Oxford, and the University of Hull. He became a full-time officer of the National Union of Seamen (NUS) in 1968 and two years later entered the House of Commons as Labour Member in Parliament for Hull East. Although opposed to Britain's membership in the European Community, in 1975 he was elected to the European parliament and was leader of the Labour Group (1976–79). Never afraid to voice his feelings publicly, he has sometimes been openly critical of his party's leadership. A member of the Labour Party's Shadow Cabinet from 1983, he was spokesman for employment, energy and transport and deputy leader of the Labour Party under **Tony Blair** (1994–97). When Labour won a landslide victory in the 1997 general election, he was appointed deputy prime minister. He was also secretary of state for environment, transport and the regions (1997–2001) and is currently first secretary of state (2001–).

Presley, Elvis Aaron 1935–77 •*US popular singer*• He was born in Tupelo, Mississippi, began singing in his local church choir, then taught himself the rudiments of the guitar. He was discovered in 1953 by Sam Phillips (1923–2003), president of Sun Records in Memphis, Tennessee, who heard a record Presley had made privately for his mother. Sun sold Presley's contract to RCA in 1955, and by 1956 he was the most popular performer in the US and, before long, the world. Presley's unparalleled contribution to popular music sprang from his ability to combine white country and western with African-American rhythm and blues, the basic formula underpinning rock and roll. This, together with his overtly sexual style, made him controversial: moralists accused him of obscenity; racists attacked him for performing African-American music. Two years of national service with the US Army in West Germany did little to dim his popularity, though he produced few really outstanding records after the album *Elvis Is Back* (1960). The raw energy and sass of his 1950s classics were largely dissipated during the 1960s, when he was remolded as a middle-of-the-road popular icon. His appearances were mainly restricted to a succession of mediocre films made at the behest of his domineering manager, "Colonel" Tom Parker (1909–97), often with dreadful songs, although he still succeeded in turning out the occasional pop classic. He abandoned live performance altogether for seven years, until a celebrated television special in 1968, which suggested the old flame had not burned out entirely. In the 1970s he reemerged as a nightclub performer in Las Vegas, often performing twice a day, six days a week, to large audiences thrilled by the energy and showiness of his stage act. During his career he recorded over 450 original songs, as well as many by other artists, and he became the biggest-selling artist in history. Presley's greatest records were singles, not albums, and include: "Heartbreak Hotel" (1956), "Blue Suede Shoes" (1956), "Hound Dog" (1956), "Love Me Tender" (1956), "All Shook Up" (1957), "Jailhouse Rock" (1958), "Return to Sender" (1962), "In the Ghetto" (1969) and "Suspicious Minds" (1969). Suffering in his last years from ill health caused by obesity and narcotics, he died suddenly in 1977. Graceland, his home in Memphis, has become a shrine for his fans. The question of whether his middle name is spelled Aaron or Aron is often debated, but there is evidence that he preferred the spelling Aaron.

Pressburger, Emeric (Imre) 1902–88 •*Hungarian screenwriter*• Born in Miskolc and educated at Prague and Stuttgart, he worked as a journalist in Hungary and Germany before entering the film industry. Residing in Great Britain from 1935, he worked on various projects for Sir **Alexander Korda** before writing the thriller *The Spy in Black* (1939) for director **Michael Powell**. Together they formed "The Archers," one of the most innovative production units in the history of British cinema. As filmmakers they turned from the social realism typical of British cinema of the period, and embraced poetry, fantasy and sensuality. Among their most distinctive films are *The Life and Death of Colonel Blimp* (1943), *Black Narcissus* (1947) and *The Red Shoes* (1948). The partnership was dissolved in 1957. Working alone, Pressburger had directed *Twice Upon a Time* (1953) and subsequently wrote a number of short stories and novels, one of which was adapted for the film *Behold a Pale Horse* (1964). He reunited with Powell as the writer of the children's film *The Boy Who Turned Yellow* (1972).

Pretorius, Andries Wilhelminus Jacobus 1799–1853 •*Afrikaner leader*• Born in Graaff-Reinet, Cape Colony, he became a prosperous farmer and was one of the leaders of the Great Trek of 1837 into Natal. After Zulu atrocities, he defeated Dengaan's force of 10,000 at Blood River in 1838. He accepted British rule, but later led another trek across the Vaal River and made war against the British. Eventually (1852) the British recognized the Transvaal Republic (later the South African Republic), the new capital of which, Pretoria, was founded in 1855 and named after him.

Pretorius, Marthinus Wessels 1819–1901 •*Afrikaner soldier and statesman*• He became commandant general on succeeding his father, **Andries Pretorius**, in 1853. He was elected president of the South African Republic in 1857, and of the Orange Free State in 1859. Failing in his ambition to unite the two republics, he resigned the presidency of the Orange Free State in 1863. After the discovery of gold in Bechuanaland and diamonds in the Vaal River led to difficulties with the *Volksraad*, he resigned the presidency of the South African Republic in 1871. He fought against the British again in 1877, until the independence of the republic was recognized in 1881. He lived to see it extinguished in 1901 during the Second Boer War.

Prévert, Jacques 1900–77 •*French poet and screenwriter*• Born in Neuilly-sur-Seine, he was a shop worker who turned to writing after his military service. A member of the surrealist movement until he was expelled for irreverence, he first made his name as the author of humorous, anarchic "song poems" about street life in Paris, collected in *Paroles* (1946, Eng trans in part *Paroles: Selections*, 1958) and *Spectacle* (1951). A writer and performer with the agit-prop theater group Octobre, he wrote the screenplay for the group's film *L'affaire est dans le sac* (1932, "It's in the Bag"), after which he pursued a career as a screenwriter. With director **Marcel Carné**, he made films such as *Le jour se lève* (1939, "Daybreak"), as well as the masterpiece, *Les enfants du paradis* (1944, Eng trans 1968). In later years he collaborated with his brother, the director Pierre Prévert (1906–88), on short, animated films for children, and worked extensively for French television (1961–68).

Previn, André George 1929– •*US conductor and composer*• Born in Berlin, he emigrated to the US in 1938 and was naturalized in 1943. He studied music mainly in California and Paris and became musical director of the Houston Symphony Orchestra (1967–69), the London Symphony Orchestra (1968–79), the Pittsburgh Symphony Orchestra (1976–86), the Royal Philharmonic Orchestra (1985–87), and the Los Angeles Philharmonic Orchestra (1986–88). Since 1988 he has been a busy freelance conductor and chamber-music pianist. The composer of musicals, film scores and orchestral works, including a cello concerto (1967) and a guitar concerto (1971), he has achieved popular success through his work, bringing classical music to the attention of a wider public. He was given the honorary title Knight Commander, Order of the British Empire, in 1996.

“ ”

The basic difference between classical music and jazz is that in the former music is always greater than its performance—whereas the way jazz is performed is always more important than what is being played.

1967 Quoted in ***The Times*** *(London)*

Prévost, Abbé (Antoine François Prévost d'Exiles) 1697–1763 •*French novelist*• Born in Artois, he was educated by the Jesuits. He enlisted in the army at 16, but in 1720, following an unhappy love affair, he joined the Benedictines of St Maur and spent the next seven years in religious duties and in study. Around 1727 he fled France for six years, going first to London, where he started to write *Histoire de Cleveland,* and then to Holland (1729–31). He issued volumes 1–4 of *Mémoires d'un homme de qualité* (Eng trans *Memoirs of a Man of Quality,* 1938) in 1728 and volumes 5–6 in 1731. However, his reputation stands on the eighth volume, *Manon Lescaut* (Eng trans 1738), distinguished by its perfect simplicity and flowing, natural style. He employed himself in additional novels and translations, and went to London again, where he started *Le pour et contre* (1733–40, "Arguments For and Against"), a periodical review of life and letters, modeled on the British *Spectator.* In France by 1735, he was appointed honorary chaplain to the Prince de Conti. He went on to compile over a hundred volumes more.

Price, George 1919– •*Belize statesman*• Educated in Belize City and the US, in 1950 he founded the People's United Party (PUP) and called for the independence of Belize. Partial self-government was achieved in 1954, and Price became prime minister, continuing to lead his country until it achieved full independence in 1981. In 1984 PUP's 30 years of uninterrupted rule ended when the general election was won by the United Democratic Party (UDP), led by Manuel Esquivel (1940–), but Price unexpectedly returned to power in 1989 and remained there until 1993.

Price, Vincent Leonard 1911–93 •*US film actor*• Born in St Louis, Missouri, he established a career on the English stage and on Broadway before entering film in 1938. Though given mainly minor roles, in the 1940s he appeared in the major films *Laura* (1944) and *Dragonwyck* (1946). In 1960 he was cast by Roger Corman (1926–) as Roderick Usher in **Edgar Allan Poe**'s tale *The Fall of the House of Usher.* Instantly his star rose and he went on to major success in six more collaborations with Corman on Poe's horror tales, for which he is now best remembered. His last film appearance was as the elderly inventor in *Edward Scissorhands* (1991).

Prichard, Katharine Susannah 1883–1969 •*Australian writer*• Born in Levuka, on Ovalau, where her father was editor of the *Fiji Times*, in 1912 she went to London as a journalist. Her first novel, *The Pioneers* (1915), won the "colonial" section of a publisher's competition and was filmed in Australia the following year. Returning to Australia in 1916, she became a founding member of the Australian Communist Party (1920), and her socialist convictions colored much of her subsequent work, especially her powerful trilogy set in the West Australian goldfields, *The Roaring Nineties* (1946), *Golden Miles* (1948) and *Winged Seeds* (1950). Her last novel was *Subtle Flame* (1967). She also wrote poems, plays and short stories, and an autobiography, *Child of the Hurricane* (1963).

Pride, Charley 1938– •*US country singer*• Born in Sledge, Mississippi, he was the first African-American musician to become a major star in country music. **Chet Atkins** signed him to RCA in 1965, but his debut record was issued without publicity pictures. His singing won immediate favor, and he was able to surmount the color barrier implicit in country music. He went on to become one of its most successful performers.

Pride, Thomas d. 1658 •*English parliamentarian*• Born perhaps near Glastonbury, he was a London drayman or brewer. Then, at the beginning of the English civil war, became parliamentary captain, quickly rising to colonel. He commanded a brigade in Scotland, and when the House of Commons sought to effect a settlement with the king, he was appointed to expel its Presbyterian Royalist members. In "Pride's Purge" over 100 were excluded, and the House of Commons, reduced to about 80 members, proceeded to bring **Charles I** to justice. Pride sat among his judges, and signed the death warrant. He was later present at the battles of Dunbar (1650) and Worcester (1651).

Priest, Oscar Stanton De *See* **De Priest, Oscar Stanton**

Priestley, J(ohn) B(oynton) 1894–1984 •*English novelist, playwright and critic*• Born in Bradford, he was educated there and at Trinity Hall, Cambridge. He had already made a reputation with critical writings such as *The English Comic Characters* (1925) when the geniality of his novel *The Good Companions* (1929) gained him a wide popularity. It was followed by other novels, though not all of equal merit, including *Angel Pavement* (1930), *Let the People Sing* (1939) and *The Magicians* (1954). His reputation as a dramatist was established by *Dangerous Corner* (1932), *Time and the Conways* (1937), and other plays on space-time themes, as well as popular comedies such as *Laburnum Grove* (1933) and his psychological mystery, *An Inspector Calls* (1947). He was an astute, original and controversial commentator on contemporary society—*Journey Down the Rainbow* (1955), written with his archaeologist wife, **Jacquetta Hawkes**, was a jovial indictment of US life. In a serious vein, his collected essays, *Thoughts in the Wilderness* (1957), deal with both present and future social problems.

Priestley, Joseph 1733–1804 •*English clergyman and chemist*• Born in Fieldhead, Leeds, he spent four years at a dissenting academy in Daventry and in 1755 became minister at Needham Market. In 1758 he went to Nantwich, and in 1761 became a tutor at Warrington Academy. During visits to London he met **Benjamin Franklin**, who supplied him with books for his *History of Electricity* (1767). In 1767 he became minister of a chapel at Mill Hill, Leeds, where he took up the study of chemistry. In 1774, as literary companion, he accompanied Lord **Shelburne** on a Continental tour and also published *Letters to a Philosophical Unbeliever.* But at home he was branded an atheist in spite of his *Disquisition Relating to Matter and Spirit* (1777), affirming the hope of resurrection from revelation. He became minister of a chapel in Birmingham in 1780. His writings continued to cause controversy, and his reply to **Edmund Burke**'s *Reflections on the French Revolution* led a Birmingham mob to break into his house and destroy its contents (1791). He then settled in Hackney, London, and in 1794 moved to the US, where he was well received. He died in Northumberland, Pennsylvania, looking for the second coming of **Jesus**. Priestley was a pioneer in the chemistry of gases, and one of the discoverers of oxygen (see **Carl Wilhelm Scheele**).

Prigogine, Ilya, Vicomte 1917– •*Belgian theoretical chemist and Nobel Prize winner*• Born in Moscow, Russia, he moved to Belgium at the age of 12. He was educated at the Free University of Brussels, where he held a chair in chemistry from 1951 to 1987 and became emeritus professor. Since 1967 he has been director of the Ilya Prigogine Center for Statistical Mechanics, Thermodynamics and Complex Systems at the University of Texas, and since 1987 has also been associate director of studies at the École des Hautes Études en Sciences Sociales in France. Following the pioneering work of **Lars Onsager**, Prigogine continued the development of the thermodynamics of irreversible processes and discovered how to treat systems far from equilibrium. His methods are applicable to a wide range of chemical and biological systems. For this work he was awarded the Nobel Prize for chemistry in 1977.

Primakov, Yevgeny Maksimovich 1929– •*Russian politician and economist*• Born in Kiev, Ukraine, he was educated at the Moscow Institute of Oriental Studies and worked in Soviet broadcasting and on the Communist Party newspaper *Pravda* before his appointment as deputy director (1970) and subsequently director (1985) of the Institute of World Economic Affairs and International Relations. He was elected to the Congress of People's Deputies of the USSR in 1989 and that same year joined the central committee of the Communist Party. President **Gorbachev** made him his special envoy to the Gulf (1990–91), and he subsequently served as director of the Central Intelligence Service of the USSR, renamed the Foreign Intelligence Service of the Russian Federation (1991–96), and as minister of foreign affairs (1996–98). A hardliner, he was made prime minister under President **Boris Yeltsin** in 1998, but was dismissed the following year after resisting attempts to remove Communist members of his government.

Primo de Rivera (y Orbaneja), Miguel, Marqués de Estella 1870–1930 •*Spanish general and politician*• Born in Jerez de la Frontera, he served during the Spanish-American War (1898), and in Morocco (1909–13). Military governor of Cádiz (1915–19), Valencia (1919–22), and Barcelona (1922–23), he led a military coup d'état in 1923, inaugurating a dictatorship (1923–30). He brought the Moroccan War to an end in 1927, but soon afterward lost the support of the army, the ruling class, and King **Alfonso XIII**. He resigned in 1930.

Primus, Pearl 1919–94 •*US dancer, choreographer and teacher*• Born in Trinidad, West Indies, she moved with her family to New York City at the age of three. She studied medicine and anthropology at Columbia University before making her dance debut in 1941, and in 1944 she first appeared with her own group. She continued to present concerts and choreographed on Broadway, but her real direction lay in dance and anthropological research in Africa. She made her first extended study trip there in 1948. She earned a PhD in educational anthropology from New York University in 1978.

Prince, *in full* **Prince Rogers Nelson** 1958– •*US pop singer and composer*• Born in Minneapolis, Minnesota, he was raised in a musical family (he was named after the Prince Rogers Trio, a jazz band in which his father was a pianist). He was signed to Warner Brothers Records while still in his teens, and released his first album, *For You*, in 1978. Subsequent albums, including *Prince* (1979) and *Dirty Mind* (1980), attracted increasing controversy with their tendency to mix religious and overtly sexual themes. International success followed the release of *1999* (1982), and the film and album *Purple Rain* (1984) confirmed Prince as one of the US's most commercially successful artists. Other recordings have included *Sign "O" the Times* (1987), *Lovesexy* (1988) and *Come* (1994). For a time during the 1990s, Prince changed his name for a time to an unpronounceable symbol combining the signs for male and female, a move that led to his being universally referred to in the press as "the artist formerly known as Prince." More recent albums include *The Rainbow Children* (1996) and *Musicology* (2001).

Prince, Hal (Harold Smith) 1928– •*US stage director and producer*• Born in New York City, he took part in student productions at the University of Pennsylvania and became a stage manager on Broadway. His first production was *The Pajama Game* (1954), followed by *Damn Yankees* (1955), *West Side Story* (1957), **Stephen Sondheim**'s *A Funny Thing Happened on the Way to the Forum* (1963), *Fiddler on the Roof* (1964) and *Cabaret* (1968). He has maintained a long association with Sondheim, producing and directing many of the composer's shows. He also directed *Evita* (1978), *The Phantom of the Opera* (1986), *Kiss of the Spider Woman* (1990, 1993) and *Showboat* (1993, 1994). He is now one of the most successful producers and directors of stage musicals in the world.

Princip, Gavrilo 1895–1918 •*Serbian nationalist and revolutionary*• Born in Bosnia, he was a member of a secret Serbian terrorist organization known as the Black Hand, dedicated to the achievement of independence for the South Slav peoples from the Austro-Hungarian empire. On June 28, 1914, he and a group of young zealots assassinated the archduke **Franz Ferdinand** of Austria and his wife, Sophie, when they were on a visit to Sarajevo. The murder precipitated World War I, after Austria declared war on Serbia on July 28. Princip died in an Austrian prison.

Prior, Matthew 1664–1721 •*English poet and diplomat*• Born in Wimborne, Dorset, the son of a joiner, he was sent to Westminster School under the patronage of Lord Dorset, and from there he went with a scholarship to St John's College, Cambridge. He was first employed as secretary to the ambassador to The Hague. In Queen **Anne**'s time he turned Tory, and was instrumental in bringing about the Treaty of Utrecht (1713), for which dubious service he was imprisoned for two years (1715–17). His first work, a collaboration with Charles Montagu (Lord **Halifax**), was *The Hind and the Panther Transvers' to the Story of the Country and the City Mouse* (1687), a witty satire on **Dryden**'s *Hind and the Panther* (1685). He is best known as a poet of light occasional verse—mock lyrics such as *A Better Answer (to Chloe Jealous)*, and more seriously, *Lines Written in the Beginning of Mézeray's History of France*, a favorite with Sir **Walter Scott**.

“ ”

They never taste who always drink;
They always talk who never think.

1697 "Upon This Passage in Scaligerana."

Priscian, (Priscianus Caesariensis) fl. 500 AD •*Latin grammarian*• A native of Caesarea, he taught Latin at Constantinople (Istanbul) at the beginning of the 6th century. Besides his 18-volume *Institutiones grammaticae* ("Grammatical Foundations"), which was highly thought of in the Middle Ages, he wrote six smaller grammatical treatises and two hexameter poems.

Priscillian c. 340–85 AD •*Spanish Bishop of Ávila*• He was excommunicated by a synod at Saragossa in AD 380, and ultimately executed—the first case of capital punishment for heresy in the history of the Catholic Church. His doctrine, said to have been brought to Spain from Egypt, contained Gnostic and Manichaean elements, and was based on dualism. The Priscillianists were ascetics, eschewed marriage and animal food, and were said to hold strict truth obligatory only among themselves.

Pritchett, V S, *in full* **Sir Victor Sawdon Pritchett** 1900–97 •*English writer and critic*• He was born in Ipswich, Suffolk, educated at Dulwich College, London, and after working in the leather trade became a newspaper correspondent. He published his first novel, *Claire Drummer*, in 1929. His style is witty and idiosyncratic, his themes are satirical, and he was particularly interested in the fanaticism and guilt of the "puritan," as portrayed with increasing humor in the novels *Nothing Like Leather* (1935), *Dead Man Leading* (1937) and *Mr Beluncle* (1951). Highly regarded as a literary critic, he traveled and lectured widely. Among his critical works are *The Living Novel* (1946) and a biography of **Honoré de Balzac** (1973). He also wrote many volumes of short stories, and two autobiographical books. His *Complete Essays* was published in 1991. He was knighted in 1975.

Proclus c. 410–85 AD •*Greek Neo-Platonist philosopher*• Born in Constantinople (Istanbul) of aristocratic parents from Lycia, Asia Minor, he was educated in Lycia, Alexandria and then Athens, where he was a pupil of Syrianus, whom he succeeded to become the last head of **Plato**'s Academy. He was a champion of paganism above Christianity and theurgy above philosophy. His approach, based on **Plotinus**, combined the Roman, Syrian and Alexandrian schools of thought. His works were influential in the Middle Ages.

Procop or **Prokop, Andrew**, *also known as* **Procopius the Great** c. 1380–1434 •*Bohemian Hussite leader*• Originally a monk, he became a member of the conservative Utraquist Hussite movement and later the commander of the peasant Taborites. Under him the fearful raids into Silesia, Saxony and Franconia were carried out, and he repeatedly defeated German armies. He headed the internal conflict of the Taborites with the more moderate Calixtines, and was killed at Lipan, near Böhmischbrod.

Procopius c. 499–565 AD •*Byzantine historian*• Born in Caesarea, Palestine, he studied law and accompanied **Belisarius** on his campaigns. He was highly honored by **Justinian I**, and seems to have been appointed prefect of Constantinople (Istanbul) in 562. His principal works are his *Historiae* (on the Persian, Vandal and Gothic wars), *De aedificiis*, and *Anecdota* or *Historia arcana*, an attack on the court of Justinian and the empress **Theodora**.

Procopius the Great *See* **Procop, Andrew**

Prodi, Romano 1939– •*Italian politician*• Born in Scandiano, Italy, he was educated at the Catholic University of Milan and, after further studies in London and at Harvard, was a professor at the University of Bologna. He entered politics as minister for industry (1978–79). In 1996 he campaigned successfully against **Silvio Berlusconi** for the post of prime minister (1996–98), and while in office reduced the country's budget deficit, enabling Italy to gain entry into the European Monetary Union. Having lost power after the collapse of the coalition, Prodi was selected as president of the European Commission following the resignation of **Jacques Santer**.

Proesch, Gilbert *See* **Gilbert and George**

Profumo, John Dennis 1915– •*English politician*• Educated at Harrow and Oxford, he became a Conservative Member of Parliament in 1940. He held several government posts before becoming secretary of state for war in 1960. He resigned three years later during the scandal following his admission that he had earlier deceived the House of Commons about the nature of his relationship with **Christine Keeler**, who was at the time also involved with a Russian diplomat, Captain Yevgeny Ivanov. After his resignation, Profumo turned to charitable service, for which he was given the honorary title of Commander, Order of the British Empire, in 1975. *Scandal*, a film based on an account of his affair with Keeler, appeared in 1989.

Prokhorov, Aleksandr Mikhailovich 1916–2002 •*Russian physicist and Nobel Prize winner*• Born in Atherton, Queensland, Australia, of Russian émigré parents, he and his family returned to the USSR after the Russian Revolution, and he graduated from Leningrad (now St Petersburg) University in 1939. He took a junior post at the Lebedev Physical Institute, rising to become deputy director in 1968. In 1952, with his colleague **Nikolai Basov**, he used a beam of molecular ammonia to amplify electromagnetic radiation, and went on to describe a new way in which atomic systems could produce amplification of microwaves. This led to the development of the maser and eventually the laser. For this work he won the 1964 Nobel Prize for physics jointly with Basov and **Charles Townes**.

Prokofiev, Sergei Sergeyevich 1891–1953 •*Russian composer*• Born in Sontsovka, Ukraine, he was taught the piano by his mother, and studied with Glière from 1902, by which time he had already composed two operas. He entered the St Petersburg Conservatory in 1904 and remained there for 10 years, studying with Anatoli Liadov (1855–1914) and **Rimsky-Korsakov**. His compositions of this period, including his first two piano concertos and two piano sonatas, caused a furor among teachers and critics. In 1914 he visited London, where he heard **Stravinsky**'s music and met **Sergei Diaghilev**. He returned to St Petersburg and avoided war service by again enrolling at the conservatory. There he completed numerous works including piano sonatas, the opera *The Gambler* and the first of two violin concertos. In May 1918 he left Russia and remained in exile for 18 years, enjoying success in the US as a pianist, especially of his own works. In 1920 he moved to Paris, where he completed another opera, *The Fiery Angel* (1927), as well as a second version of *The Gambler* (Brussels, 1929), symphonies, piano concertos, and (for Diaghilev) a ballet entitled *The Prodigal Son*. All this time Prokofiev kept in touch with musical life in the USSR, to which he continued to feel emotionally and spiritually drawn. Finally, in 1936, he settled again in Moscow, his return unfortunately coinciding with the emergence of social realism as the political doctrine for the arts. His principal musical outlets proved to be ballet (*Romeo and Juliet* and *Cinderella*) and film scores, as well as further symphonies, sonatas, and a children's piece, *Peter and the Wolf* (1936). In 1941 he began work on the opera generally considered his greatest, *War and Peace*. In 1948 he was included among those named by the Communist Party Central Committee as composers of music "marked with formalist perversions" and "alien to the Soviet people." His last opera, *The Story of a Real Man*, was judged to be unsuitable by the Union of Composers, and was performed only after **Stalin** died, coincidentally on the same day as Prokofiev—March 5, 1953.

Prokop, Andrew *See* **Procop, Andrew**

Propertius, Sextus c. 48–c. 15 BC •*Roman elegiac poet*• Born probably in Asisium (Assisi), Italy, he was educated in Rome and became a poet. He won the favor of **Maecenas**, to whom he dedicated a book of his poems, and of **Augustus**. The central figure of his inspiration was his mistress, Cynthia, to whom he devoted his first book of poems, the only one published during his lifetime.

Prost, Alain 1955– •*French racecar driver*• Born in St Chamond, he had the talent to become a professional soccer player, but opted instead for racecar driving, and won his first Grand Prix in 1981. He was world champion four times (1985, 1986, 1989, 1993) and runner-up four times (1983, 1984, 1988, 1990). In 1987 he surpassed **Jackie Stewart**'s record of 27 Grand Prix wins, thus becoming the most successful driver in the history of the sport. He retired in 1994.

Protagoras c. 490–c. 420 BC •*Greek Sophist and teacher*• Born in Abdera in northeast Greece, he was the first and most famous of the Sophists who, for a fee, offered professional training in public life and in other skills. He became a friend of **Pericles** and was invited by him to draft a legal code for the new pan-Hellenic colony of Thurii. His works are almost entirely lost. Much of our information about him comes from **Plato**'s dialogues, one of which was named after him and portrays him memorably (and respectfully). His most famous maxim was "Man is the measure of all things," which is usually taken to imply a skeptical or relativistic view of human knowledge.

Proudhon, Pierre Joseph 1809–65 •*French journalist and political theorist*• Born in Besançon, he issued *Qu'est-ce que la propriété?* ("What Is Property?") in 1840, affirming the bold paradox "property is theft," because it involves the exploitation of others' labor. In 1846 he published his greatest work, *Système des contradictions économiques* (Eng trans *System of Economic Contradictions*, 1888). During the revolution of 1848 he was elected for the Seine district, and published several newspapers advocating his most advanced theories. Sentenced to three years' imprisonment, in March 1849 he fled to Geneva, but returned to Paris in June and gave himself up. In 1852 he was released, but in 1858 was again condemned to three years' imprisonment when his three-volume *De la justice dans la révolution et dans l'église* ("On Justice in the Revolution and the Church") was seized; he went to Belgium, and received an amnesty in 1860. A forerunner of **Karl Marx**, he emphasized liberty, equality and justice.

Proulx, E Annie, *pseudonym of* **Edna Ann Proulx** 1935– •*US author*• Born in Norwich, Connecticut, she studied at Concordia University, Montreal, and at the University of Virginia. She began her career as a freelance journalist, publishing her first collection of short stories, *Heart Songs*, in 1988. *The Shipping News* (1993), an evocative novel about a small town in Newfoundland, was a major success, winning a number of awards including the Pulitzer Prize in 1994, and was later successfully filmed (2001). Other books include *Accordion Crimes* (1996) and *Brokeback Mountain* (1998).

Proust, Joseph Louis 1754–1826 •*French analytical chemist*• Born in Angers, he studied pharmacy and chemistry in Paris, and spent most of his working life in Spain. In the early 1780s he conducted aerostatic experiments with Pilatre de Rozier and Jacques-Alexandre-César Charles, and in 1784 was one of the first people to make an ascent in a balloon. Proust made two significant advances in analytical chemistry: he developed the use of hydrogen sulfide as a reagent and he gave the results of his analyses in terms of percentage weights. By means of the percentages he realized that the proportions of the constituents in any chemical compound are always the same regardless of what method is used to prepare it. He announced this discovery, known as the law of definite proportions, in 1794. Not all his contemporaries accepted his findings, his principal adversary in a renowned controversy being **Claude Louis Berthollet**.

Proust, Marcel 1871–1922 •*French novelist*• Born in Auteuil, Paris, he was a semi-invalid all his life, and was cosseted by his mother. In the 1890s he moved in fashionable circles in Paris, and in 1896 he published a collection of stories and essays called *Les plaisirs et les jours* (Eng trans *Pleasures and Regrets*, 1948). In 1897 he became involved in the **Dreyfus** affair, in which he supported Alfred Dreyfus. But his mother's death in 1905, when he was 34 years old, caused him to withdraw from society and immure himself in a soundproof apartment, where he gave himself over entirely to introspection. Delving into the self below the levels of superficial consciousness, he set himself the task of transforming into art the realities of experience known to the inner emotional life. It is evident from the 13 volumes which make up *À la recherche du temps perdu* (*Remembrance of Things Past*), a series of autobiographical novels, that no detail escaped his observant eye. Influenced by the philosophy of **Henri Bergson**, he subjected experience to searching analysis in order to divine in it beauties and complexities that escape the superficial response of ordinary intelligence. Proust evolved a mode of communication by image, evocation and analogy for displaying his characters: not as a realist would see them, superficially, from the outside, but in terms of their concealed emotional life, evolving on a plane that has nothing to do with temporal limitations.

“ ”

Il n'y avait pas d'anormaux quand l'homosexualité était la norme.
There was nothing abnormal about it when homosexuality was the norm.
1920 ***À la recherche du temps perdu****, "Sodome et Gomorrhe."*

Prout, William 1785–1850 •*English physician*• Born in Horton, Gloucestershire, he studied medicine at the University of Edinburgh, then settled in London. From numerous analyses he deduced the famous Prout's hypothesis, which states that the atomic weights of all the elements are multiples of the atomic weight of hydrogen (1815). He was the first to analyze the constituents of urine, and he originated several of the revolutionary ideas attributed to **Justus von Liebig**; for example, that the various excretions (eg, urea, uric acid, carbonic acid) are derived from the waste or destruction of tissues which once formed a constituent part of the organism. He also discovered hydrochloric acid in healthy stomach juice (1823), and was the first to divide foodstuffs into carbohydrates, fats and proteins (1827).

Prud'hon, Pierre Paul 1758–1823 •*French painter*• Born in Cluny, he trained with engravers in Paris and, having won the Prix de Rome, went to Italy. Later patronized by the empresses of **Napoleon I**, he was made court painter, and among his best work is a portrait of the empress **Joséphine**. Many of his paintings had mythological and allegorical subjects and were commissioned for public buildings, such as his celebrated *Crime Pursued by Justice and Vengeance* (1808). He also designed furniture and interiors along classical lines.

Pryce, Jonathan 1947– •*Welsh actor*• Born in Holywell, Clwyd, he trained at the Royal Academy of Dramatic Art and acted with, among others, the Old Vic Company and Royal Shakespeare Company, winning a Tony award on Broadway for *Miss Saigon* (1989–91). On television, he played Gerd Heidemann in *Selling Hitler* (1991) and John Wroe in *Mr Wroe's Virgins* (1993). His films include *The Ploughman's Lunch* (1983), *Consuming Passions* (1987), *Carrington* (1995), for which he won a Cannes Film Festival Best Actor award, and *Very Annie-Mary* (1999).

Prynne, William 1600–69 •*English pamphleteer*• Born in Swanswick, near Bath, he graduated from Oriel College, Oxford, and was called to the bar. In 1633 he published his *Histrio-Mastix: The Players Scourge*, for which, on account of a supposed reflection on the virtue of Queen **Henrietta Maria**, he was sentenced in 1634 to have his book burned by the hangman, pay a fine of £5,000, be expelled from Oxford and Lincoln's Inn, lose both ears in the pillory, and suffer life imprisonment. Three years later, for attacking Archbishop **Laud**, he was branded on both cheeks with the letters *S L* ("seditious libeler"). He was released from prison on a warrant of the House of Commons (1640), and in 1648 became Member of Parliament for Newport, Cornwall. However, he opposed the Independents and **Charles I**'s execution, and was "purged" and imprisoned (1650–52). On **Cromwell**'s death he returned to Parliament and later became keeper of the Tower records. His best works were the *Calendar of Parliamentary Writs* and his *Records*.

Pryor, Richard 1940– •*US comedian*• Born in Peoria, Illinois, he served in the US Army before developing an act as a stand-up comic. He made his film debut in *The Busy Body* (1967). In the 1970s he developed into one of the US's most popular live entertainers, offering savagely witty, shockingly profane commentaries on the prejudices and injustices of the world. An award-winning scriptwriter for television, he released a number of best-selling albums, and his film career flourished too with roles in *Lady Sings the Blues* (1972), *Silver Streak* (1976) and *Blue Collar* (1978). He suffered from third-degree burns when he set fire to himself while freebasing, but recovered and appeared in later films including *Stir Crazy* (1980) and *Jo Jo Dancer, Your Life Is Calling* (1986), which he also directed. Despite suffering from multiple sclerosis, he continues to perform live, and returned to the screen in *Lost Highway* (1997).

Przewalski or **Przhevalski, Nikolai Mikhailovich** 1839–88 •*Russian traveler*• He was born near Smolensk, and from 1867 traveled in Mongolia, Turkestan and Tibet, reaching to within 160 miles (258 km) of Lhasa. He explored the upper Hwang Ho, reaching as far as Kiachta. During his travels he amassed a valuable collection of plants and animals, among them a wild camel and a wild horse, the latter now bearing his name.

Ptolemy I Soter c. 367–283 BC •*Egyptian king and soldier*• A son of Lagus, he was one of the greatest generals of **Alexander the Great**, upon whose death he obtained Egypt (323 BC). In 306 BC he was defeated by Demetrius Poliorcetes in a sea fight off Salamis in Cyprus, but still assumed the royal title (305 BC) and defended his territories against **Antigonus** (Monophthalmos) and Demetrius. In 304 BC he defended the Rhodians against Demetrius and received from them his title "Soter" ("Savior," or "Preserver"). Alexandria, his capital, became the center of commerce and Greek culture.

Ptolemy II Philadelphus 308–246 BC •*King of Egypt*• He was the son and successor (246 BC) of **Ptolemy I (Soter)**, and under him the power of Egypt attained its greatest height. He was generally successful in his external wars, founded the museum and library, purchased many valuable manuscripts of Greek literature, and attracted leading Greek intellectuals to his court. The Egyptian history of **Manetho** was dedicated to him.

Ptolemy, *Latin* **Claudius Ptolemaeus** c. 90–168 AD •*Egyptian astronomer and geographer*• He flourished in Alexandria. His "great compendium of astronomy" seems to have been denominated by the Greeks *megiste* ("the greatest"), from which the Arab name *Almagest*, by which it is generally known, was derived. His *Tetrabiblos syntaxis* is combined with another work called *Karpos*, or *Centiloquium*, because it contains a hundred aphorisms. Both treat astrological subjects. There is also a treatise on the fixed stars or a species of almanac, the *Geographia* and other works dealing with mapmaking, the musical scale and chronology. As astronomer and geographer, Ptolemy was the main influence on scientific thought down to the 16th–17th centuries, but he seems to have been not so much an independent investigator as a corrector and improver of the work of his predecessors. For example, in astronomy he depended largely on **Hipparchos**. However, as his works form the only remaining authority on ancient astronomy, the system they expound is called the *Ptolemaic System*. The Ptolemaic astronomy, handed on by Byzantines and Arabs, assumed that the Earth is the center of the universe, and that the heavenly bodies revolve around it. As a geographer, Ptolemy is the corrector of a predecessor, Marinus of Tyre. He also calculated the size of the Earth, and constructed a map of the world and other maps. His Earth-centered view of the universe dominated cosmological thought until swept aside by **Copernicus** in the 16th century.

Pucci, Emilio, Marchese di Barsento 1914–92 •*Italian fashion designer*• Born in Naples, he studied social sciences in Italy and the US, and was a member of Italy's Olympic ski team in 1934. He served in the Italian air force in World War II and in 1965 became a member of the Italian Parliament. He started designing ski clothes in 1947, and in 1950 opened his own couture house, creating casual, elegant, print dresses for women. He became renowned for his use of bold patterns and brilliant color.

Puccini, Giacomo (Antonio Domenico Michele Secondo Maria) 1858–1924 •*Italian composer of operas*• Born in Lucca, he was an organist and choirmaster there at the age of 19, his first extant compositions being written for use in the Catholic Church. He later attended the Milan Conservatorio (1880). His first opera, *Le Villi* (one-act version 1883, two-act version 1884, "The Wilis"), failed to secure a prize in the competition for which it was composed, but impressed Ricordi, the publisher, sufficiently to induce him to commission a second work, *Edgar*, which failed at its first performance in 1889. *Manon Lescaut* (1893) was his first great success, but it was eclipsed by *La Bohème* (1896, "Bohemian Life"). *Tosca* and *Madama Butterfly* (both 1900) have also remained popular favorites. His last opera, *Turandot*, was left unfinished at his death and was completed by his friend Franco Alfano (1875–1954). He was, perhaps, the last great representative of the Italian operatic tradition.

Pugachev, Yemelyan Ivanovich c. 1744–75 •*Russian Cossack soldier and pretender*• He fought in the Seven Years' War (1756–63) and in the war against Turkey (1769–74) before retiring to a lawless life in the south of Russia. In 1773 he proclaimed himself to be **Peter**

III, the assassinated husband of **Catherine the Great**, and began a reign of organized rebellion in the south. Catherine finally sent a proper army against him, and in a battle near Tsaritsyn (now Volgograd) he was defeated, captured and conveyed in an iron cage to Moscow, where he was executed.

Pugin, Augustus Welby Northmore 1812–52 •*English architect*• Born in London, the son of Augustus Pugin (1762–1832), a French architectural draftsman, and educated at Christ's Hospital School, he trained in his father's office. He was employed by Sir **Charles Barry** to make detailed drawings for the Houses of Parliament (1836–37), for which he designed and modeled a large part of the decorations and sculpture. A convert to Roman Catholicism, he designed several Roman Catholic churches, including the cathedral in Birmingham. He did much to revive Gothic architecture in England, and his aesthetic theories influenced a diverse range of architects and provided much of the foundation for the Arts and Crafts Movement.

Pujol, Joseph, *known as* **"Le Pétomane"** 1857–1945 •*French entertainer*• Born in Marseilles, he became a music-hall entertainer as a result of his capacity for breaking wind. He appeared in public in Marseilles in 1887, and in 1892 moved to Paris, where his unusual act topped the bill at the Moulin Rouge. In 1895 he opened his own theater, the Pompadour. Three years later he sued the Moulin Rouge for presenting a female "Pétomane," but before the case came to court she was exposed as a fraud, having concealed various whistles and bellows in her skirts. He retired from the stage in 1914 when the outbreak of World War I made his specialty act of mock artillery barrages seem inappropriate.

Pulitzer, Joseph 1847–1911 •*US newspaper proprietor*• He was born in Makó, Hungary, and was educated there before emigrating to join the US Army in 1864. Discharged the following year, he went penniless to St Louis, Missouri. There he became a reporter, was elected to the state legislature, and began to acquire newspapers, including the *New York World* (1883), which sealed his success. He endowed the Columbia University School of Journalism, and in his will established annual Pulitzer Prizes for literature, drama, music and journalism, which were first awarded in 1917.

" "

I want to talk to a nation, not to a select committee.

*1909 In **Pearson's Magazine**, March.*

Pullman, George Mortimer 1831–97 •*US inventor and businessman*• He was born in Brocton, New York. A cabinetmaker by trade, he became a contractor in Chicago and a storekeeper in Colorado before designing the railroad sleeping car named after him (patented in 1864 and 1865). The Pullman Palace Car Company was formed in 1867, and in 1880 he founded Pullman City for his workers, since absorbed by Chicago.

Pulu *See* **Tiglath-Pileser III**

Purcell, Edward Mills 1912–97 •*US physicist and Nobel Prize winner*• Born in Taylorville, Illinois, he studied at Purdue University, Illinois, and Harvard, where he later taught. During World War II he worked as a group leader at MIT's radiation laboratory. His research covered nuclear magnetism, radio astronomy, radar, astrophysics and biophysics. Independently of **Felix Bloch**, he developed nuclear magnetic resonance and was able to tune into resonances when nuclei were placed in a magnetic field. He was awarded the 1952 Nobel Prize for physics with Bloch for his work.

Purcell, Henry 1659–95 •*English composer*• He was born in London, the son of a court musician and Chapel Royal chorister. He was one of the "children of the chapel" from about 1669 to 1673, when he was apprenticed to the keeper—whom he ultimately succeeded in 1683—of the king's keyboard and wind instruments. In the meantime he had followed Matthew Locke (c. 1621–77) as "composer for the king's violins" (1677), and had been appointed organist at Westminster Abbey (1679) and the Chapel Royal (1682). In about 1680 he began writing incidental music for plays by **William Congreve**, **John Dryden**, **Aphra Behn**, and others, and from this time until his early death his output was prolific. Although his harpsichord pieces and his well-known set of trio sonatas for violins and continuo have retained their popularity, his greatest masterpieces are among his vocal and choral works. In his official capacity he produced a number of fine "welcome odes" in celebration of royal birthdays, and other occasions, as well as many anthems and services. In 1685 he wrote an anthem for the coronation of **James II** (**James VII and II**), and he wrote music for the coronation of **William III** four years later, as well as funeral music for Queen **Mary II** in 1694. He is credited with six operas, but of these only the first, *Dido and Aeneas*, written to a libretto by **Nahum Tate** in 1689, is opera in the true sense; it is now regarded as the first great English opera. His other operas consist essentially of spoken dialogue between the main characters interspersed with masques and other musical items. Purcell was writing at a time when the new Italian influence was first beginning to be felt in England, and his music includes superb examples of both this and the traditional English style, as well as of the French style. He was recognized in his own time, as now, as the greatest English composer of the age, but his fame declined after his death, and did not fully revive until the bicentenary of his death. Later English composers have done much to rehabilitate him by performance and adaptation of his music.

Purkinje or **Purkyne, Jan Evangelista** 1787–1869 •*Czech physiologist*• Born in Libochowitz, he trained for the priesthood, studied philosophy, and finally graduated in medicine. He rose to become professor at the University of Breslau and later in Prague. Much of his work centered on cell observations, and in 1837 he outlined the key features of the cell theory, describing nerve cells with their dendrites and nuclei, and Purkinje cells in the cerebellar cortex. In 1838 he observed cell division, and in the following year promoted the word "protoplasm" in the modern sense. He made improvements in histology and was interested in the peculiarities of the eyes, experimenting on the visual effects of pressure applied to the eyeball. The effect of being able to see the shadows of the retinal blood vessels in one's own eye is now known as Purkinje's figure.

Purkyne, Jan Evangelista *See* **Purkinje, Jan Evangelista**

Pusey, E(dward) B(ouverie) 1800–82 •*English theologian and leader of the Oxford Movement*• He was born in Pusey, Berkshire. He was educated at Eton and Christ Church, Oxford, was elected a Fellow of Oriel College, Oxford (1823), and while living in Germany (1825–27) acquainted himself with German theological teaching. In 1828 he was ordained deacon and priest, and was appointed Regius Professor of Hebrew at Oxford. He joined Cardinal **John Newman**, and they, with **John Keble**, became the leaders of the Oxford Movement (1833). Among Pusey's contributions to the *Tracts* were those on baptism and the Holy Eucharist, and in 1836 he commenced the *Oxford Library of the Fathers*, to which his chief contributions were translations of **Augustine**'s *Confessions* and works of **Tertullian**. In 1843 Pusey was suspended from preaching in Oxford for two years following his sermon asserting the presence of God in the Holy Eucharist, but at the first opportunity he reiterated his teaching. His numerous writings include *The Doctrine of the Real Presence* (1856–57), the series of three *Eirenicons* (1865–69), and a pamphlet titled *Collegiate and Professorial Teaching*. He spent large sums in helping to provide churches in East London and Leeds, and in founding sisterhoods.

Pushkin, Alexander Sergeyevich 1799–1837 •*Russian poet and writer*• Born in Moscow into an illustrious family, he attended the Lyceum at Tsarskoe Selo near St Petersburg, where his talent for poetry first emerged. In 1817 he entered government service, but because of his liberalism he was exiled in 1820 to the south. In 1824 he was dismissed and confined to his estate near Pskov, and did not return to Moscow until after the accession of **Nicholas I**. He married Natalia Goncharova in 1832, whose beauty attracted Baron Georges d'Anthès, a French royalist in the Russian service. Pushkin challenged him to a duel and was mortally wounded. Regarded as Russia's greatest poet, he had his first success with the romantic poem *Ruslan and Lyudmilla* (1820), followed by *The Prisoner of the Caucasus* (1822), *Fountain of Bakhchisarai* (1826), *Tzigani* (1827), and his masterpiece, *Eugene Onegin* (1828), a sophisticated novel in verse that was much imitated but never rivaled. Prolific for one whose life was so short, he also wrote lyric poems, essays, the blank verse historical drama *Boris Godunov* (1825), and, in 1830, the four "Little Tragedies": "Mozart and Salieri," "The Covetous Knight," "The Stone Guest" and "The Feast During the Plague."

Putin, Vladimir Vladimirovich 1952– •*Russian politician*• Born in Leningrad (now St Petersburg), he was educated at the Leningrad State University and spent 15 years as a foreign intelligence officer with the Committee for State Security (the KGB). In 1990 he retired and became an adviser to Anatoly Sobchak, the reforming mayor of St Petersburg, and by 1994 had become first deputy mayor. He went on to head (1998) the Federal Security Service (which replaced the KGB) and to become secretary of the influential Security Council. Impressed by Putin's intelligence and cool efficiency, President **Boris Yeltsin** identified him as his favored successor and made the then relatively unknown aide his prime minister in mid-1999. Putin won a strong popular following through his campaign against secessionist Chechen rebels later in the year (although it also attracted considerable criticism abroad). When Yeltsin resigned at the end of 1999, Putin replaced him as acting president; he subsequently won the presidential election in 2000 with a clear margin over rival Communist candidate **Gennady Zyuganov**.

Putnam, Frederic Ward 1839–1915 •*US archaeologist and ethnographer, the founder of archaeology in the US*• Born in Salem, Massachusetts, he trained as a zoologist, turning to archaeology on being appointed curator of the Peabody Museum at Harvard (1875–1909). He was Professor of American Archaeology and Ethnology at Harvard from 1887, and curator of anthropology at the American Museum of Natural History in New York City from 1894. The author of more than 400 articles, he was one of the first to study archaeological remains of Native Americans. The organizer of the anthropological exhibit at the 1893 Chicago Exposition, he helped found the Field Museum of Natural History in Chicago and the department of anthropology at the University of California at Berkeley (1903). For 25 years he also served as secretary of the American Association for the Advancement of Science.

Putnam, George Palmer 1814–72 •*US publisher*• Born in Brunswick, Maine, he went to London in 1840 and opened a branch bookshop selling US books. In 1848 he returned to the US and founded a book-publishing business, established in 1866 as the firm of G P Putnam & Sons (now G P Putnam's Sons). In 1853 he founded *Putnam's Monthly Magazine*. He was the grandnephew of **Israel Putnam**.

Putnam, Hilary 1926– •*US philosopher*• Born in Chicago, he held teaching positions at Northwestern University and Princeton, and was Professor of the Philosophy of Science at MIT (1961–65) and Professor of Philosophy at Harvard (1965–2000, then emeritus). Much of his early work was on problems arising out of physics, mathematics and logic, but he has gone on to work creatively in virtually all the main areas of philosophy. He has argued strongly for a conception of philosophy that makes it essential to a responsible view of the real world and our place in it. His main publications are *Philosophical Papers* (3 vols, 1975, 1975, 1979), *Meaning and the Moral Sciences* (1978), *Reason, Truth and History* (1982) and *Renewing Philosophy* (1992).

Putnam, Israel 1718–90 •*American Revolutionary soldier*• Born in Danvers, Massachusetts, he was a farmer before volunteering for military service in the French and Indian War (1755–63). As a captain he helped to repel a French invasion of New York, and was present at the Battle of Lake George (1755). In 1758 he was captured and tortured by Native Americans, and he was about to be burned alive when a French officer rescued him. In 1764 he helped rescue Detroit, but was then besieged by **Pontiac**. In 1775, after Concord, he was given command of the forces of Connecticut and distinguished himself at the Battle of Bunker Hill. He held the command at New York and at Brooklyn Heights (1776), where he was defeated by Viscount **Howe**. In 1777 he was appointed to the defense of the Highlands of the Hudson. He was a cousin of **Rufus Putnam**.

Putnam, Rufus 1738–1824 •*American Revolutionary general*• Born in Sutton, Massachusetts, he served against the French from 1757 to 1760, then settled as a farmer and millwright. In the American Revolution (1775–83) he served as an engineer, commanded a regiment, and in 1783 became brigadier general. In 1788 he founded Marietta, Ohio, and in 1789 he was appointed a judge of the Supreme Court of the Northwest Territory. From 1793 to 1803 he was surveyor general of the United States. He was a cousin of **Israel Putnam**.

Puttnam, David Terence Puttnam, Baron 1941– •*English filmmaker*• Born in Southgate, London, he produced his first feature film *S.W.A.L.K.* (1969) after a very successful background in advertising and photography. Subsequently he helped encourage new directorial talents with stylish, low-budget features such as *Bugsy Malone* (1976). *Chariots of Fire* (1981), which won four Academy Awards, epitomized the type of intelligent, humanist drama he wanted to make, and its international commercial appeal allowed him to progress to larger-scale films such as *Local Hero* (1983), *The Killing Fields* (1984) and *The Mission* (1986). A tireless spokesman and figurehead of the British film industry in the early 1980s, he was chairman and chief executive of Columbia Pictures (1986–88), but his antiestablishment stance led him to return to independent production with *Memphis Belle* (1990) and *Meeting Venus* (1991). Later films include *My Life So Far* (2000). He was knighted in 1995 and created a peer in 1997.

Puvis de Chavannes, Pierre 1824–98 •*French decorative, symbolic painter*• Born in Lyons, he painted murals of the life of St **Geneviève** (1898, Panthéon, Paris) and large allegorical works such as *Work* and *Peace*, hung along the staircase of the Musée de Picardie, Amiens. He created striking new images with paintings such as *The Poor Fisherman* (1881, Musée d'Orsay, Paris), which influenced younger painters and sculptors, such as **Georges Seurat** and **Aristide Maillol**, while his decorative style influenced **Paul Gauguin** and **Odilon Redon**.

Puyi (P'u-i), *personal name of* **Xuan Tong (Hsuan T'ung)** 1906–67 •*Last emperor of China and the first emperor of Manchuguo (Manchukuo, Manchuria)*• After the revolution of 1912 the young emperor was given a pension and a summer palace near Beijing (Peking). He became known as Henry P'u-i, but in 1932 he was called from private life to be provincial dictator of the Japanese puppet state of Manchuguo and (from 1934) emperor under the name of Kang De (K'ang Te). He was imprisoned by the Russians (1945–50) and subsequently by the Chinese Communists (1950–59), who undertook his political reeducation. After that he lived as a private citizen in Beijing until his death. The 1987 film *The Last Emperor* was based on his life.

Puzo, Mario 1920–99 •*US novelist*• Born in New York City and educated at Columbia University, he served in the US Air Force during World War II and worked for 20 years as an administrative assistant in government offices. His first novel was *The Dark Arena* (1955), but his breakthrough came with his novel about the Mafia, *The Godfather* (1969). The epic story of Don Corleone and his extended "family" of Sicilian immigrants, it became a bestseller, and was filmed by **Francis Ford Coppola** in 1972. This was followed by *The Last Don* (1996).

“ ”

A lawyer with a briefcase can steal more than a hundred men with guns.
*1969 **The Godfather**, book 1, chapter 1.*

Pym, Barbara Mary Crampton 1913–80 •*English novelist*• Born in Oswestry, Shropshire, she was educated at St Hilda's College, Oxford. For most of her adult life she worked at the International African Institute in London (1958–74). Her fiction is deliberately confined within narrow bounds, characteristically exploring the tragicomic lives of frustrated middle-class spinsters in a delicate, understated fashion. She published three novels in the 1950s, the best of which is *A Glass of Blessings* (1958), then lapsed into obscurity until, partly through the support of **Philip Larkin**, her *Quartet in Autumn* appeared in 1977. Four of her novels were published posthumously.

Pym, Francis Leslie Pym, Baron 1922– •*English politician*• Educated at Eton and Cambridge, he served in World War II and was awarded the Military Cross. A Conservative Member of Parliament from 1961, he gained political advancement through the whips' office before he was appointed secretary of state for Northern Ireland (1973–74). He spent two years as defense secretary (1979–81), and was appointed foreign secretary during the Falklands crisis of 1982. However, his comparatively gloomy assessments of economic prospects did not endear him to the prime minister, **Margaret Thatcher**, and he was dropped from the government following the Conservatives' 1983 landslide election victory. He accepted a life peerage in 1987. He published *The Politics of Consent* in 1984.

Pynchon, Thomas 1937– •*US novelist*• He was born in Glen Cove, New York, and educated at Cornell University. *V* (1963), his first novel, is a loose, episodic book, influenced by the Beat generation and by Pynchon's developing use of paranoia as a structural device, centering on a mysterious female principle at work in modern history. Seen by some as willfully obscure, by others as a swashbuckling experimentalist, he uses sprawling and loquacious language and fabulous structures in which the normal conventions of the novel have been largely abandoned. Subsequent publications include *The Crying of Lot 49* (1966) and *Gravity's Rainbow* (1973). *Vineland* (1990) appeared to return to an earlier, more freewheeling and satirical style and received mixed reviews. *Slow Learner* (1984) collected early stories, and he published *Mason & Dixon* in 1997.

Pyrrho or **Pyrrhon** c. 365–270 BC •*Greek philosopher and founder of the school of Skepticism*• Born in Elis, he traveled in Persia (Iran) and India with **Alexander the Great**, and returned to Elis where he effectively established the philosophical tradition later called Skepticism. His views were reported by his disciple Timon the Sillographer. He taught that humans can know nothing of the nature of things, and he recommended suspending judgment as an appropriate response, which would bring with it "an imperturbable peace of mind."

Pyrrhus c. 319–272 BC •*King of Epirus*• A general ranking with **Alexander the Great**, his second cousin, he is best known for his wars against the Romans in Italy. As king (from 307 BC) he lost his throne (302–297) but later emancipated Epirus from Macedonian control when the Tarentines asked for his support against Rome (281). He won battles on the River Siris (280) and at Asculum (279), after which he made the comment that led to a victory won at too great a cost being called a Pyrrhic victory. In 275 he resumed his war against the Romans, but was defeated by the consul Curius Dentatus near Beneventum. He was then forced to abandon Italy and return to Epirus, where he engaged in war with **Antigonus II Gonatas**, king of Macedonia. Next, he invaded the Peloponnese, where he failed to capture Sparta and was killed in a street fight in Argos.

Pythagoras c. 580–c. 500 BC •*Greek philosopher, mystic and mathematician*• He was probably born in Samos, although the traditions regarding his life are confused. About 530 he left Samos and settled in Croton, a Greek colony in southern Italy, where he attracted followers and established a community with its own rule of life. He may later have been exiled to Metapontum, where he died. Pythagoras left no writings, and his whole life is shrouded in myth and legend. Pythagoreanism was first a way of life rather than a philosophy. Its principal belief was in the immortality and transmigration (ie, reincarnation) of the soul, which is imprisoned in the body; by leading a pure life, the soul can eventually achieve its release from the body. Pythagoras is also associated with mathematical discoveries involving the chief musical intervals, the relations of numbers, the theorem on right triangles which bears his name, and with more fundamental beliefs about the understanding and representation of the world of nature through numbers. It is impossible to disentangle Pythagoras's own views from the later accretions of mysticism and Neo-Platonism, but he had a profound influence on **Plato** and on later philosophers, astronomers and mathematicians.

Q

Qaboos, Bin Said 1940– *•Sultan of Oman•* Born in Salalah, the son of Said bin Taimar, he was educated in England and trained at Sandhurst. He disagreed with the medieval views of his father, and, after five years under surveillance, overthrew him (1970) in a bloodless coup, the 14th descendant of the ruling dynasty of the Albusaid family. He proceeded to pursue more liberal and expansionist policies, while maintaining an international position of strict nonalignment.

Qaddafi or **Gaddafi, Muammar (Muhammad al-)** 1942– *•Libyan soldier and political leader•* Born into a nomadic family, he abandoned university studies to attend a military academy in 1963. He formed the Free Officers Movement that overthrew the regime of King Idris in 1969. Qaddafi became chairman of the Revolutionary Command Council, promoted himself to colonel (the highest rank in the revolutionary army) and became commander in chief of the Libyan armed forces. As effective head of state, he set about eradicating colonialism by expelling foreigners and closing down British and US bases. He also encouraged a religious revival and return to the fundamental principles of Islam. He has been president of Libya since 1977. A somewhat unpredictable figure, Qaddafi has openly supported violent revolutionaries in other parts of the world while following a unique blend of democratic and autocratic government at home, ruthlessly pursuing Libyan dissidents both at home and abroad. He waged a war in Chad, and in 1988 he saw his territory bombed by the US. He declared his unqualified support for Iraq's invasion of Kuwait in 1990, and found himself increasingly isolated after the UN's announcement at the end of the Gulf War that it would not entertain his formal participation in any future negotiations on the issue. More recently Qaddafi has turned his attention to Africa.

Qiu Jin (Ch'iu Chin) 1875–1907 *•Chinese feminist and revolutionary•* She left her family to study in Japan in 1904, where she became actively involved in radical Chinese student associations calling for the overthrow of the Manchu Qing (Ch'ing) dynasty. Returning to China in 1906, she founded a women's journal in which she argued that the liberation of women was an essential prerequisite for a strong China. In 1907 she was implicated in an abortive anti-Manchu uprising and was executed by the Qing authorities.

Quant, Mary 1934– *•English fashion designer•* Born in London, she studied at Goldsmiths College and launched her career in fashion design when she opened a small boutique in Chelsea in 1955. Two years later she married one of her partners, Alexander Plunkett Greene. Her clothes became extremely fashionable in the 1960s when the geometric simplicity of her designs, especially the miniskirt, and the originality of her colors became an essential feature of the "swinging Britain" era. In the 1970s she expanded into cosmetics and textile design. In 1990 she won the British Fashion Council's Hall of Fame award.

Quarles, Francis 1592–1644 *•English religious poet•* Born near Romford, Essex, he studied at Christ's College, Cambridge, and at Lincoln's Inn. He held various court and government posts and was secretary to Archbishop **Ussher** (c. 1629). Because he was a Royalist, his books and manuscripts were destroyed. He wrote abundantly in prose and verse, his *Emblems* (1635) being his best-known work, although *Hieroglyphikes of the Life of Man* (1638) was also popular. Other poetical works include *A Feast of Wormes* (1620), *The Historie of Samson* (1631) and *Divine Fancies* (1632). His prose work includes *Enchyridion* (1640, a book of aphorisms).

Quarton, *sometimes* **Charonton** or **Charrenton, Enguerrand** 15th century *•French painter•* Active in Avignon, he is the best-known late medieval French artist. Documents relating to six of his important paintings survive, one of which (for a coronation of the Virgin) is among the most comprehensive and interesting documents of early French art, since it includes the views both of the patron and the artist. Some have attributed to him the most famous of 15th-century French paintings, the *Pietà* of Villeneuve-lès-Avignon.

Quasimodo, Salvatore 1901–68 *•Italian poet and Nobel Prize winner•* Born in Syracuse, Sicily, he was a student of engineering, then a traveling inspector for the Italian State Power Board before taking up a career in literature and music. A Professor of Literature at the Milan Conservatorio, he wrote several volumes of poetry using both Christian and mythological allusions. His works include *Ed è subito sera* (1942, "And Suddenly It Is Evening") and *La terra impareggiabile* (1958, "The Matchless Earth"). He won the Nobel Prize for literature in 1959.

Quayle, Sir Anthony 1913–89 *•English actor and director•* Born in Ainsdale, Lancashire, he made his first stage appearance in 1931, and joined the Old Vic Company (1932–39). After six years' army service in World War II, he joined the Shakespeare Memorial Theatre Company at Stratford-upon-Avon as actor and theater director (1948–56). During his years there, he played 20 leading roles, directed 12 plays, and transformed a provincial repertory company into a theater of international standing, providing much of the groundwork for the creation of the Royal Shakespeare Company (1960). In 1982 he founded the Compass Theatre Company. He also had a successful film career, with roles in major films, including *The Guns of Navarone* (1961) and *Lawrence of Arabia* (1962). He was knighted in 1985.

Quayle, Dan (James Danforth) 1947– *•US Republican politician•* Born in Indianapolis, Indiana, into a rich newspaper-owning family, he studied political science, and was admitted to the Indiana bar in 1974. He was elected to the House of Representatives as a Republican in 1977 and to the Senate in 1981. He had little national reputation when, in 1988, he was chosen as the running mate of **George Bush** in an effort to add youth and good looks to the election campaign. His selection pleased the right wing of the party, which admired his conservative views on defense, fiscal and moral matters, but he was elsewhere strongly criticized by those who pointed to his relative lack of experience. During Quayle's vice presidency (1989–93), his sometimes ill-chosen remarks and actions served as a constant source of material for critical commentators and comedians.

Queen, Ellery, *pseudonym of* **Frederick Dannay** 1905–82 and **Manfred B Lee** 1905–71 *•US writers of crime fiction•* Both born in Brooklyn, New York, they were cousins. As businessmen they entered a detective-story competition, and won with *The Roman Hat Mystery* (1929). From then on they concentrated on detective fiction, using Ellery Queen both as pseudonym and as the name of their detective. Others of their very popular stories are *The Greek Coffin Mystery* (1932), *The Tragedy of X* (1940) and *Double, Double* (1950). They also wrote under the pseudonym Barnaby Ross, featuring the detective Drury Lane.

Queensberry, Sir John Sholto Douglas, 8th Marquis of 1844–1900 *•Scottish representative peer, and patron of boxing•* In 1867 he supervised the formulation by **John Graham Chambers** of new rules to govern boxing, since known as the Queensberry Rules. In 1895 he was unsuccessfully sued for criminal libel by **Oscar Wilde**, of whose friendship with his son, Lord **Alfred**

Douglas, he disapproved, and it was his allegations of homosexuality that led to Wilde's trial and imprisonment.

Queneau, Raymond 1903–76 •*French novelist, poet and painter*• He was born in Le Havre and educated at the Sorbonne. From 1938 he worked on *Encyclopédie de la Pléiade* and became its director for two decades (1955–75). His novels included *Le chiendent* (1933, Eng trans *The Bark Tree*, 1968), a witty reworking of **Descartes**, the untranslatable, punning verse novel *Chêne et chien* (1937) and *Zazie dans le métro* (1959, Eng trans *Zazie*, 1960). Queneau was a founding member of OuLiPo, the hermetic Ouvroir de Littérature Potentielle, a school of philosophy related to the "paraphysical science of imaginary solutions." His most famous book is *Exercices de style* (1947, Eng trans *Exercises in Style*, 1958), which gives a multiplicity of versions of exactly the same literary opening. His verse was published in *Cent mille milliards de poèmes* (1961, Eng trans *One Hundred Million Million Poems*, 1983). He also wrote as Sally Mara and published "her" *Œuvres complètes* in 1962.

Quennell, Sir Peter Courtney 1905–93 •*English biographer*• Born in London and educated at Balliol College, Oxford, he became Professor of English at Tokyo in 1930, and wrote *A Superficial Journey Through Tokyo and Peking* (1932). The author of several books of verse and a novel, and editor of *The Cornhill Magazine* (1944–51), he is best known for his biographical studies, which include **Byron** (1935, 1941), **John Ruskin** (1949), **Shakespeare** (1963), **Pope** (1968) and **Samuel Johnson** (1972). He edited many volumes of literary studies and wrote two autobiographical books. He was knighted in 1992.

Quercia, Jacopo Della c. 1367–1438 •*Italian sculptor*• He was born in Quercia Grossa, Siena, and spent some time in Lucca, where one striking example of his work in the cathedral is the tomb of Ilaria del Carretto (c. 1406). In direct contrast are the strongly dramatic reliefs for the doorway of the Church of San Petronio in Bologna, which he left unfinished at his death. His *Fonte Gaia* (1419) is in the Siena Museum, and between 1417 and 1431 he worked on the baptistery doors in Siena.

Quesada, Gonzalo Jiménez de c. 1497–1579 •*Spanish conquistador*• Born in Córdoba or Granada, he was appointed magistrate at Santa Marta, in present-day Colombia. In 1536 he conquered the rich territory of the Chibchas in the east, naming it New Granada, and its chief town Santa Fé de Bogotá. In 1569, during a later expedition in search of El Dorado, he reached the river Guaviare not far from the point where it meets the Orinoco.

Quesnel, Pasquier 1634–1719 •*French Jansenist theologian*• Born in Paris, he studied at the Sorbonne, and in 1662 became director of the Paris Oratory, where he wrote *Réflexions morales sur le Nouveau Testament* (1692, "Reflections on Morality in the New Testament"). Having refused to condemn Jansenism in 1684, he fled to Brussels, where his *Réflexions* were published (1687–94). The Jesuits were unceasing in their hostility, and Quesnel was flung into prison (1703), but escaped to Amsterdam. His book was condemned in the bull *Unigenitus* (1713).

Quezon (y Molina), Manuel Luis 1878–1944 •*Philippine statesman*• Born in Baler, Luzon, he studied at Manila, served with **Emilio Aguinaldo** during the insurrection of 1898 and in 1905 became governor of Tayabas. In 1909 he went to Washington as one of the resident Philippine commissioners and began to work for his country's independence. President of the Philippine Senate from 1916 to 1935, he was elected first president of the Philippine Commonwealth (1935). He established a highly centralized government and displayed great courage during the Japanese onslaught in 1941, refusing to evacuate to the US until appealed to by President **Franklin D Roosevelt**. The new capital of the Philippines on the island of Luzon is named after him.

Quiller-Couch, Sir Arthur 1863–1944 •*English writer*• Born in Bodmin, Cornwall, he was educated at Trinity College, Oxford, where he became a lecturer in classics (1886–87), and was later Professor of English Literature at Cambridge (1912). He edited the *Oxford Book of English Verse* (1900) and other anthologies, and published volumes of essays, criticism, poems and parodies, among them *From a Cornish Window* (1906), *On the Art of Writing* (1916), *Studies in Literature* and *On the Art of Reading* (1920). He is also remembered for a series of humorous novels set in a Cornish background, written under the pseudonym "Q."

“ ”

He that loves but half of Earth
Loves but half enough for me.

1896 "The Comrade."

Quimby, Harriet 1882–1912 •*US aviator and journalist*• Born in Arroyo Grande, California, she became the first woman to earn her pilot's license in 1911, eight years after the first flight of the **Wright** Brothers. She was also the first woman to fly across the English Channel, on April 12, 1912, which **Louis Blériot** had done for the first time in 1909.

Quincey, Thomas De *See* **De Quincey, Thomas**

Quincy, Josiah 1772–1864 •*US politician*• Born in Boston, he graduated from Harvard, and was called to the bar in 1793. He was a leading member of the Federal Party and, elected to Congress in 1804, distinguished himself as an orator. He denounced slavery and, in a remarkable speech, declared that the admission of Louisiana would be a sufficient cause for the dissolution of the union. Disgusted with the triumph of the Democrats and the War of 1812, he declined reelection to Congress. He was a member of the Massachusetts legislature, served as mayor of Boston from 1823 to 1828, and from 1829 to 1845 was president of Harvard.

Quine, William Van Orman 1908–2000 •*US philosopher and logician*• Born in Akron, Ohio, he was trained initially in mathematics, at Oberlin College in Ohio, then at Prague, Oxford and at Harvard, later becoming Professor of Philosophy at Harvard (1948–78). He was greatly influenced by **Rudolf Carnap**, the Vienna Circle of philosophers and the empiricist tradition generally, but went on to make his own distinctive and original contributions to philosophy. He is best known by such philosophical works as *Two Dogmas of Empiricism* (1951), *Word and Object* (1960) and *The Roots of Reference* (1973). In these he challenges the standard, sharp distinctions between analysis and synthetic truths and between science and metaphysics, and presents a systematic philosophy of language of his own, which successfully challenged the hitherto dominant linguistic philosophy of **Ludwig Wittgenstein** and **John Langshaw Austin**. Later publications include *From Stimulus to Science* (1995).

Quinet, Edgar 1803–75 •*French writer and politician*• Born in Bourg, he studied in Strasbourg, Geneva, Paris and Heidelberg, and through his early work won the friendship of Victor Cousin (1792–1867) and historian **Jules Michelet**. His reputation was established by *Ahasvérus* (1833), a kind of spiritual imitation of the ancient mysteries. Appointed Professor of Foreign Literature at Lyons in 1839, he was recalled to the Collège de France in Paris, where he joined Michelet in attacking the Jesuits, and his lectures caused so much excitement that the government suppressed them in 1846. During the 1848 revolution, Quinet took his place on the barricades, and in the National Assembly voted with the extreme left. After the coup d'état of 1851, he was exiled. He wrote the historical works *La révolution religieuse au XIXe siècle* (1857, "The Religious Revolution of the 19th Century"), *Histoire de mes idées* (1858, "History of My Ideas") and *La révolution* (1865). After the downfall of **Napoleon III**, he returned to Paris. He sat in the National Assemblies at Bordeaux and Versailles, and aroused great enthusiasm by his speeches.

Quinn, Anthony Rudolph Oaxaca 1915–2001 •*US actor*• Born in Chihuahua, Mexico, he worked at a variety of menial jobs before making his stage debut in *Clean Beds* (1936) and his film debut in *Parole!* (1936). In Hollywood from 1936, he played villains and supporting characters of all nationalities in numerous exotic adventure stories. His versatility and strength as an actor became more apparent in the 1950s when he starred in *La Strada* (1954), and received Best Supporting Actor Academy Awards for *Viva Zapata!* (1952) and *Lust for Life* (1956). He received a further nomination for *Zorba the Greek* (1964), *The Secret of Santa Vittoria* (1969) and *The Greek Tycoon* (1978). His stage work included *A Streetcar Named*

Desire (1950) and the musical *Zorba!* (1983–86). He also directed the film *The Buccaneer* (1958).

Quintilian, *properly* **Marcus Fabius Quintilianus** c. 35–c. 100 AD •*Roman rhetorician*• Born in Calagurris (Calahorra), Spain, he studied oratory in Rome, and returned there in 68 AD in the train of **Servius Sulpicius Galba**. He became eminent as a pleader, and more as a state teacher of the oratorical art, his pupils including **Pliny the Younger** and the great-nephews of **Domitian**. The emperor named him consul and gave him a pension. His reputation rests on his great work *Institutio Oratoria* ("Education of an Orator"), a complete system of rhetoric in 12 books, remarkable for its sound critical judgments, purity of taste, admirable form and the perfect familiarity it exhibits with the literature of oratory.

" "

Mendaces memorem esse oportere.
Liars need to have good memories.

***Institutio Oratoria**, 4.2.9.1 (translated by H E Butler, 1968).*

Quirk, (Charles) Randolph Quirk, Baron 1920– •*British grammarian and writer on language*• He was born in Lambfell on the Isle of Man and studied at University College London where, after a period as lecturer and professor at Durham (1954–60), he was appointed Professor of English (1960–81). He has also been director of the Survey of English Usage (1959–81). He has written widely on grammar, most notably in *A Comprehensive Grammar of the English Language* (1985). He was president of the British Academy (1985–89), and was knighted in 1985 and made a life peer in 1994.

Quiroga, Horacio 1878–1937 •*Uruguayan short-story writer and poet*• He was born in Salto. His life was a chapter of horrible accidents out of which he drew his inspiration to create a new genre: the mature horror story crossed with the animal fable. His father shot himself (probably), and so did his first wife and two of his children. He himself shot and killed a friend by accident at the turn of the century, and had to flee to Buenos Aires. He was a manic-depressive, subject to strange states of anxiety, tension, agitated depression and hypomania—all of which he tried to relieve through alcohol. He became a cotton planter in the Chaco region of Argentina, and no writer has evoked this uncanny wilderness with more accuracy. When he learned that he had cancer, he shot himself.

Quisling, Vidkun (Abraham Lauritz Jonsson) 1887–1945 •*Norwegian fascist leader*• Born in Fyresdal, he graduated from a military academy in 1911, and went on to serve as a military attaché in Russia and Finland (1918–21) and to work as a relief administrator in the USSR (1922–26). Quisling entered politics in 1929 and was minister of defense from 1931 to 1932. In 1933 he founded a new party, Nasjonal Samling (National Union), in imitation of the German National Socialist Party. However, the party met with little electoral success and disintegrated after 1936. He then turned to Germany, and made contact with various Nazi leaders, including **Hitler**. Following the German invasion of Norway in 1940, Quisling declared himself head of a government but won no support and was forced to step down six days later. It was from this point onward that his name became synonymous with "traitor." The German occupation authorities reluctantly allowed Quisling to head a puppet government from 1942 onward. At the end of World War II he was arrested, put on trial, and executed by firing squad in 1945.

R

Raab, Julius 1891–1964 •*Austrian statesman*• Born in St Pölten, he became an engineer and was a Christian Socialist member of the Austrian Diet (1927–34), and federal minister of trade and transport (1938). He retired from politics during the Nazi regime, and in 1945 was one of the founders of the People's Party, chairman of the party (1951–60), minister of economic reconstruction, and in 1953 was elected chancellor of Austria.

Rabelais, François 1483 or 1494–1553 •*French monk, physician and satirist*• He was born in or near the town of Chinon in the Loire Valley. He became a novice of the Franciscan order, and entered the monastery of Fontenay-le-Comte, where he had access to a large library. There he learned Greek, Hebrew and Arabic, studied all the Latin and French authors whose works he could find, and took an interest in medicine, astronomy, botany and mathematics. Later he joined the Benedictine order (1524). He studied medicine in Montpellier, and in 1532 became a physician in Lyons. There he began the series of books for which he is best known. In 1532 he wrote *Pantagruel*, in which serious ideas are set forth side by side with satirical comment and irreverent mockery, and in 1534 he wrote *Gargantua*. Both books were enormously successful, though disapproved of by the Church due to their irreverence. In 1533 and 1536 he traveled in Italy with Jean du Bellay, Bishop of Paris; from 1537 (when he took his doctorate) to 1538 he taught in Montpellier; and from 1540 to 1543 he was in the service of the cardinal's brother in Turin and France. In 1546 he published his *Tiers livre* ("Third Book"); it was again condemned, and he fled to Metz, but in 1548 became Jean du Bellay's physician in Rome. A *Quart livre* ("Fourth Book") appeared in part in 1548, and complete in 1552–53; it was again banned by the theologians. A professed fifth book, *L'isle sonante* (or *L'île sonnante*), perhaps founded on scraps and notes by Rabelais, appeared in 1562. The riotous license of his mirth has made Rabelais as many enemies as his wisdom has made him friends.

“ ”

Mieux est de ris que de larmes écrire
Pour ce que rire est le propre de l'homme.
It is better to write of laughter than of tears
For laughter is the basis of humankind.

1534 ***Gargantua**, Aux lecteurs.*

Rabi, Isidor Isaac 1898–1988 •*US physicist and Nobel Prize winner*• Born in Rymanow, Austria, he was a graduate of Cornell and Columbia Universities, and was professor at Columbia between 1937 and 1967. Rabi developed the resonance method for accurately determining the magnetic moments of fundamental particles, which won him the 1944 Nobel Prize for physics. He contributed to the development of radar and the nuclear bomb, and to the development of the laser and the atomic clock. He was one of the founders of the Brookhaven National Laboratory, and, as a member of UNESCO, he originated the movement that established CERN (Conseil Européen pour la Recherche Nucléaire) in Geneva.

Rabin, Yitzhak or **Itzhak** 1922–95 •*Israeli soldier and statesman, prime minister of Israel 1974–77 and 1992–95, and Nobel Prize winner*• He was born in Jerusalem and brought up in Tel Aviv. After studies at Kandoorie Agricultural High School, he embarked on an army career. During the war he took part in sabotage operations against the Vichy French in Lebanon and Syria. In 1954 he spent a year at Camberley Staff College in England. He fought in the "War of Independence" (1948–49) and represented the Israeli Defense Forces (IDF) at the armistice in Rhodes. He rose to become chief of staff in 1964, heading the armed forces during the Six-Day War of 1967. The credit for Israel's success in this war was due as much to Rabin as to the more widely acknowledged defense minister, **Moshe Dayan**. After serving as ambassador to the US (1968–73), he moved decisively into the political arena, becoming leader of the Labor Party and premier in 1974, but resigned this position in 1977. Appointed defense minister under the Likud coalition government (1984–90) of **Yitzhak Shamir** and **Shimon Peres**, in 1985 Rabin withdrew troops from Lebanon, which Israel had invaded three years earlier. However, he earned a name for harshness by his severe and at times uncharacteristically brutal handling of the Palestinian insurgents in the Gaza *intifada* of 1987. Rabin won back the leadership of the Labor Party and in 1992 was again prime minister of a center-left government that favored Palestinian self-government. In 1993, after secret talks in Oslo, he signed an accord with the PLO (Palestine Liberation Organization) granting self-rule to the Palestinians of Gaza and Jericho and stipulating a phased withdrawal of Israeli forces. In 1994 he signed a peace treaty with Jordan; the same year he was awarded the Nobel Peace Prize jointly with Shimon Peres and **Yasser Arafat**. In 1995 he signed a second accord agreeing to further troop withdrawals from the West Bank and further expansion of Palestinian self-rule on the West Bank. These concessions aroused extreme and often violent opposition in Israel. He was assassinated on November 4, 1995, and was succeeded as prime minister by Shimon Peres.

Rabuka, Sitiveni 1948– •*Fijian soldier and politician*• He was born in the village of Drekeniwai, north of Sura. After leaving the Queen Victoria School, he joined the Fijian army and was trained at Sandhurst in England. After serving with the UN peacekeeping force in Lebanon, he returned to Fiji with the rank of colonel. After the 1987 elections, which resulted in an Indian-dominated coalition government, he staged a coup which removed Prime Minister Kamisese Mara, and set up his own provisional government. The country was declared a republic, and in December Mara was reinstated, but Rabuka retained control of the security forces and internal affairs. He was prime minister from 1992 to 1999.

Rachmaninov, Sergei Vasilevich 1873–1943 •*Russian composer and pianist*• Born in Nizhny Novgorod, he studied at the St Petersburg Conservatory and later in Moscow. A distinguished performer, he traveled all over Europe on concert tours, visiting London in 1899. Having fled from the Russian Revolution, he settled in the US in 1918. Also an accomplished composer, he wrote operas, orchestral works and songs, but is best known for his piano music, which includes four concertos, the first three of which achieved great popularity. His style, largely devoid of national characteristics, epitomizes the lush romanticism of the later 19th century, which is still apparent in *Rhapsody on a Theme of Paganini* (1934) for piano and orchestra, a work of great craftsmanship which has remained a concert favorite.

Racine, Jean 1639–99 •*French dramatist and poet*• Born in La Ferté-Milon, he studied at the college of Beauvais and with the Jansenists at Port Royal. At 19 he went to study philosophy at the Collège d'Harcourt, where he wrote the first of many odes, *La nymphe de la Seine* (1660, "The Nymph of the River Seine"), on the marriage of **Louis XIV**, and made the acquaintance of **Jean de la Fontaine** and other men of letters. In 1664 his first play, *La Thébaïde, ou les frères ennemis* (Eng trans *The Fatal Legacy*, 1723), was acted by **Molière**'s company at the Palais Royal. His second, *Alexandre le grand* (1665, Eng trans *Alexander the Great*, 1714), was, after its sixth performance, played by rival actors, which led to a break with Molière. During the following ten years Racine produced his greatest works—*Andromaque* (1667, Eng trans *Andromache*, 1675); *Les plaideurs* (1668, Eng trans *The Litigants*, 1715); *Britannicus* (1669, Eng trans 1714); *Bérénice* (1670, Eng trans *Titus and Berenice*, 1701); *Bajazet* (1672, Eng trans *The Sultaness*, 1717); *Mithridate* (1673, Eng trans *Mithridates*, 1926); *Iphigénie* (1675, Eng trans *Achilles; or, Iphigenia in Aulis*, 1700); and *Phèdre* (1677, Eng trans *Phaedre and Hippolytys*, 1756), a marvelous representation of human agony. When the *troupe du roi* introduced a rival *Phèdre* by Jacques Pradon, supported by a powerful party, Racine retired from dramatic work, married in June 1677, and settled down to 20 years of domestic happiness. In 1677, jointly with **Nicolas Boileau**, he was appointed royal historian, and in 1689 and 1691 he wrote two plays on Old Testament themes: *Esther* for Madame de **Maintenon**'s schoolgirls at Saint-Cyr, and *Athalie*. Racine was greatly influenced by Greek drama, adopting its principles as well as its subjects.

Rackham, Arthur 1867–1939 •*English artist and book illustrator*• Born in London, he studied at the Lambeth School of Art. He became a watercolorist and book illustrator who was well known for his typically Romantic and grotesque pictures in books of fairy tales, including *Peter Pan* (1906) and his own *Arthur Rackham Fairy Book* (1933).

Radcliffe, Ann, *née* **Ward** 1764–1823 •*English romantic novelist*• She was born in London, and in 1789 published the first of her Gothic romances, *The Castles of Athlin and Dunbayne*, followed by *A Sicilian Romance* (1790), *The Romance of the Forest* (1791), *The Mysteries of Udolpho* (1794) and *The Italian* (1797). She traveled widely, and her journal reveals a keen eye for natural scenery and ruins. A sixth romance, *Gaston de Blondeville*, with a metrical tale, "St Alban's Abbey," and a short *Life*, was published in 1826. Her reputation among her contemporaries was considerable. She was praised by Sir **Walter Scott**, and she influenced writers such as **Byron**, **Shelley** and **Charlotte Brontë**. Her particular brand of writing prompted **Jane Austen**'s satire *Northanger Abbey*.

Radcliffe, John 1650–1714 •*English physician*• Born in Wakefield, Yorkshire, he studied at University College, Oxford. In 1684 he moved to London, where he soon became the most popular physician of his time. Despite being a Jacobite, he attended **William III** and Queen **Mary**. In 1713 he was elected Member of Parliament for Buckingham. He bequeathed the bulk of his large property to the Radcliffe Library, Infirmary and Observatory, all named after him, to University College, Oxford, and St Bartholomew's Hospital in London.

Radcliffe-Brown, Alfred Reginald 1881–1955 •*English social anthropologist*• He was born in Birmingham, and after studying at Cambridge carried out field research in the Andaman Islands (1906–08) and Australia (1910–11). Subsequently, he became Professor of Anthropology at Cape Town, Sydney, Chicago and Oxford. Along with **Bronisław Malinowski**, Radcliffe-Brown was the principal architect of modern social anthropology, but despite his early fieldwork his major contribution was more theoretical than ethnographic. Greatly influenced by the sociology of **Émile Durkheim**, he regarded social anthropology as the comparative study of "primitive" societies, whose aim was to establish generalizations about the forms and functioning of social structures. His *Structure and Function in Primitive Society* (1952) contains all the essentials of his theoretical program.

Radhakrishnan, Sir Sarvepalli 1888–1975 •*Indian philosopher and statesman*• Born in Tiruttani, Madras, he was educated at Madras Christian College. He was professor at the Universities of Mysore and Calcutta, and at Oxford, where he became Spalding Professor of Eastern Religions and Ethics in 1936. He also lectured in the US and in China. From 1931 to 1939 he was in Geneva as a member of the Committee of Intellectual Cooperation of the League of Nations. In 1946 he was chief Indian delegate to UNESCO, becoming its chairman in 1949. A member of the Indian Assembly in 1947, he was appointed first Indian ambassador (1949), then vice president of India (1952–62) and president (1962–67). He was appointed to the Order of Merit in 1963. He wrote scholarly philosophical works including *Indian Philosophy* (1927), and his Hibbert lectures of 1929, published as *An Idealist View of Life* (1932), is often thought to be his greatest work.

Radiguet, Raymond 1903–23 •*French novelist and poet*• He was born in Saint-Maur, and on moving to Paris, became known in literary circles at the age of 16. He became a protégé of **Jean Cocteau** and is best known for two stories, *Le diable au corps* (1923, "The Devil in the Flesh") and *Le bal du Comte d'Orgel* (1924, "The Count of Orgel's Ball"). Acclaimed as the "**Rimbaud** of the novel," he produced writing as austerely controlled as his personal behavior was erratic and unpredictable. The nature of love is his dominant theme, and his treatment of it in his fiction is comparable to the high moral conception of love in the tragedies of **Racine**.

Raeburn, Sir Henry 1756–1823 •*Scottish portrait painter*• Born near Edinburgh, he studied for two years in Rome (1785–87), then returned to Edinburgh and soon attained preeminence among Scottish artists. He was knighted by **George IV** in 1822, and appointed King's Limner for Scotland a few days before his death. His style was to some extent founded on that of Sir **Joshua Reynolds**, to which he brought a positive quality by means of bold brushwork and the use of contrasting colors. He painted the leading members of Edinburgh society, and among his sitters were Sir **Walter Scott**, **David Hume** and **James Boswell**. Among his best-known works is *The Reverend Robert Walker Skating* (1784, National Gallery, Edinburgh).

Raeder, Erich 1876–1960 •*German naval commander*• He joined the navy in 1894 and during World War I was Chief of Staff under Admiral **Franz von Hipper**. In 1928 he was promoted to admiral and became Commander in Chief of the navy, and rebuilt the fleet. In 1939 **Hitler** made him a grand admiral, but in 1943 he was relieved of his command for disagreements with Hitler over strategy. At the Nuremberg trials in 1946 he was sentenced to life imprisonment. He was released in September 1955.

Raffles, Sir (Thomas) Stamford 1781–1826 •*English colonial administrator and Oriental scholar*• Born off Port Morant, Jamaica, he was appointed to a clerkship in the East India House in 1795, and secretary at an establishment at Penang in 1805. In 1811 he accompanied an expedition against Java, and, on its capture, as Lieutenant Governor, completely reformed the internal administration. He later wrote a *History of Java* (1817). As Lieutenant Governor of Benkoelen in West Sumatra (1818–23), he formed a settlement at Singapore to counter Dutch influence, which rapidly grew into one of the more important trading centers in the East. He was closely involved in the establishment of the Zoological Society of London.

Rafsanjani, Hojatoleslam Ali Akbar Hashemi 1934– •*Iranian cleric and politician*• Born near Rafsanjan in southeastern Iran, he trained as a mullah from 1950 under Ayatollah **Ruholla Khomeini**. His friendship with Khomeini led him into opposition against Shah **Mohammed Reza Pahlavi** and brief imprisonment in 1963. During the 1970s he became wealthy from involvement in the construction business. Following the Islamic revolution of 1979–80 he became Speaker of the Iranian parliament (Majlis), emerging as an influential and pragmatic power broker between fundamentalist and technocrat factions within the ruling Islamic Republican Party, and he played a key role in securing an end to the Gulf War (1980–88). In August 1989, soon after the death of Ayatollah Khomeini, Rafsanjani became state president (1989–97).

Rafter, Pat 1972– •*Australian tennis player*• Born in Mount Isa, Queensland, he turned professional in 1991 and quickly established a reputation with his serve-and-volley game. He won his first Grand Slam event in 1997 with the US Open, successfully defending the title in 1998. Other highlights of his career have included dramatic Wimbledon men's singles finals in 2000, when he was beaten by **Pete Sampras**, and in 2001, which he narrowly lost to **Goran Ivanisevic**.

Raglan, Fitzroy James Henry Somerset, 1st Baron 1788–1855 •*English field marshal*• Born in Badminton, Gloucestershire, he served on the Duke of **Wellington**'s staff in the Peninsular War (1808–12), then fought at Waterloo (1815), losing his sword arm. Thereafter he sat in parliament as Member of Parliament for Truro and spent many years at the War Office. He was elevated to the peerage in 1852. In 1854 he headed an ill-prepared expeditionary force against the Russians in the Crimea, and won the Battle of

Alma, but lack of cohesion among the Allies prevented an effective follow-up. At Balaclava he gave the order that led to the disastrous Charge of the Light Brigade (1854). He won the Battle of Inkerman, but was blamed for the failure of the commissariat during the terrible winter of 1854–55. He died shortly before the storming of Sebastopol.

Rahner, Karl 1904–84 •*German Roman Catholic theologian*• Born in Freiburg im Breisgau, he joined the Society of Jesus in 1922 and was ordained a priest in 1932. Much influenced by the doctrines of **Thomas Aquinas**, he began his teaching career in Innsbruck in 1937. There, and later in Munich and Münster, his lectures and writings maintained a dialogue between traditional dogma and contemporary existential questions, based on the principle that grace is already present in human nature. He played a major role as consultant at the Second Vatican Council (1962–66). His works include *Theological Investigations* (1961–81) and the autobiographical interviews *I Remember* (1985).

Raine, Craig Anthony 1944– •*English poet*• He was born in Bishop Auckland, County Durham. He was educated at Oxford, where he has spent most of his life, apart from a short spell as poetry editor at Faber (1981). His first collection, *The Onion, Memory* (1978), established a characteristic method of attempting to "see" familiar things in new and unusual ways, which he developed in even greater depth in the "alien" viewpoint adopted in *A Martian Sends a Postcard Home* (1979). Later collections include *A Journey to Greece* (1979), *Rich* (1984), *History: The Home Movie* (1994) and a collection of essays, *Haydn and the Valve Trumpet* (1990). *1953* (1990) was a version of **Racine**'s drama *Andromaque*.

Rainer, Yvonne 1934– •*US experimental dancer, choreographer and filmmaker*• Born in San Francisco, she studied under **Martha Graham** in New York, then joined Anna Halprin's experimental summer course in California. On her return to New York she studied with **Merce Cunningham**, and enrolled in Robert Dunn's pioneering composition class along with **Trisha Brown**, **Steve Paxton**, **David Gordon** and **Lucinda Childs**. The radical Judson Dance Theater, for which she was a prolific choreographer, evolved out of these alternative sessions. Her signature piece, *Trio A* (1966, part of the larger work *The Mind Is a Muscle*), was designed for performance irrespective of age and level of training. In 1973, she turned from dance to filmmaking.

Rainey, Gertrude Pridgett, *known as* **Ma Rainey**, *née* **Pridgett** 1886–1939 •*US blues singer*• Born in Columbus, Georgia, she began her career as a singer with the Rabbit Foot Minstrels. She claimed that she first introduced blues into her act in 1902, after hearing a girl in Missouri sing a song about the man who had deserted her. She won a large following among African-American Southerners and toured with **Bessie Smith**, who was her protégée. Often called the "Mother of the Blues," she is considered to be the first of the great Black blues singers, with a style of singing that preserves the continuity from early African-American music to jazz. Her best-known songs include "See See Rider" and "Slow Driving Moan."

Rainey, Joseph Hayne 1832–87 •*US politician*• Born in Georgetown, South Carolina, he was a barber by trade. After the Civil War he served in the South Carolina state senate as a Republican. During Reconstruction Rainey became the first African American to be elected to the US House of Representatives (1870–79).

Rainey, Ma *See* **Rainey, Gertrude Pridgett**

Rainier III, *properly* **Rainier Louis Henri Maxence Bertrand de Grimaldi** 1923– •*Prince of Monaco*• Born in Monaco, he served in the French army during World War II and succeeded his grandfather Louis II in 1950. He is the twenty-sixth ruling prince of the House of Grimaldi, which was founded in 1297. In 1956 Rainier married the US film actress **Grace Kelly**, by whom he has a son, Prince Albert (1958–), the heir to the throne, and two daughters, Princess Caroline (1957–) and Princess Stephanie (1965–).

Rainwater, (Leo) James 1917–86 •*US physicist and Nobel Prize winner*• Born in Council, Idaho, he was educated at the California Institute of Technology (Caltech) and at Columbia University. During World War II he contributed to the Manhattan atomic bomb project. He became Professor of Physics at Columbia University (1952) and was director of the Nevis Cyclotron Laboratory (1951–53, 1956–61). At the time, there were two theories to describe the atomic nucleus: the concentric shell model and the "liquid drop" model. Rainwater produced a collective model combining the two ideas, and, with **Aage Bohr** and **Ben Roy Mottelson**, developed the theory and obtained experimental evidence in its support. The three shared the Nobel Prize for physics in 1975 for this work. Rainwater also worked with **Val Fitch** on studies of muonic X-rays.

Raitt, Bonnie 1949– •*US country blues singer and guitarist*• Born in Burbank, California, she worked with Freebo and with Bluesbusters (1969–71) before her eponymous debut album was released. She did not achieve mass appeal, perhaps because her records *Give It Up* (1972) and *Streetlights* (1974) had a less readily marketed flavor of jazz. However, she attained cult status with blues fans, particularly after her collaboration with **John Lee Hooker** on his album *The Healer* (1989). In the 1990s, however, she had a huge breakthrough in popularity in the US, winning Grammy awards.

Raiz, Gilles de Laval, Baron *See* **Retz, Gilles de Laval, Baron**

Rájá Rám Mohán Rái *See* **Rammohun Roy**

Rákóczi, Francis II 1676–1735 •*Hungarian nobleman and rebel leader*• He was born into a princely family of Hungary and Transylvania, and in 1703 led a Hungarian revolt against Austrian rule. He was hailed as a national hero, but his forces met with severe defeats (1708, 1710), and in 1711 he went into exile rather than accept a peace settlement. His later years were spent as a Carmelite monk.

Rakosi, Matyas 1892–1971 •*Hungarian politician*• He was active in the labor movement as a teenager and served in World War I, but spent most of the war years as a prisoner in Russia, joining the Hungarian Communist Party on his return home. He was commander of the Red Guard in **Béla Kun**'s Soviet Republic in 1919 and then fled to the USSR, where he became the secretary of Communist International. Returning to Hungary in 1924, he was imprisoned (1925–40, then returned to Moscow and led the Hungarian communist émigrés there. He came back to Budapest in 1945 as their general secretary. He was deeply implicated in the Stalinist purges, thus helping to provoke the 1956 Hungarian Uprising. He was then removed from office and, in 1962, expelled from the party.

Raleigh or **Ralegh, Sir Walter** 1552–1618 •*English courtier, navigator and poet*• He was born in Hayes Barton in Devon, studied briefly at Oxford, but left to volunteer for the Huguenot cause in France. In 1578 he joined a piratical expedition against the Spaniards organized by his half brother Sir Humphrey Gilbert (1537–83). He became a favorite of Queen **Elizabeth I**, who heaped favors on him. In 1585 he was appointed lord warden of the Stannaries and vice admiral of Devon and Cornwall, and entered parliament. From 1584 to 1589 he sent an expedition to America to take unknown lands in the queen's name, and dispatched an abortive settlement to Roanoke Island, North Carolina (1585–86). He later made unsuccessful attempts to colonize Virginia, and introduced tobacco and potatoes into Britain. Eclipsed as court favorite in 1587, he went to Ireland and became a close friend of the poet **Edmund Spenser**. On his return to England in 1592 he was committed to the Tower for a secret affair with Bessy Throckmorton, one of the queen's maids of honor, and for more than four years was excluded from the queen's presence; he and Bessy later married. In 1595, with five ships, he explored the coasts of Trinidad and sailed up the Orinoco, and in 1596 took part in the sack of Cádiz. In 1600 he became governor of Jersey, and in three years did much to promote the island's trade. He took little part in the dark intrigues at the end of Elizabeth's reign, but was arrested on July 17, 1603, and attempted suicide. He defended himself ably at his trial at Winchester, but even so he was condemned to death, and it was only on the scaffold that his sentence was commuted to life imprisonment. In the Tower of London, Raleigh spent his time studying and writing, and carrying out chemical experiments. In 1616 he was released to make an expedition to the Orinoco in search of a gold mine, but the mission was a failure. On his return in 1618, the suspended death sentence was invoked, and Raleigh was beheaded.

“ ”

I shall never be persuaded that God hath shut up all light of learning within the lantern of Aristotle's brain.

*1614 **The History of the World***

Ramakrishna Paramahasa, *originally* **Gadadhar Chatterjee** 1836–86 •*Indian mystic*• He was born in the Hooghly district of Bengal. A priest at Dakshineswar Kali temple, near Calcutta, he took instruction from several gurus, finally coming to believe in self-realization and God-realization, and that all religions were different paths to the same goal. His simple but effective retelling of traditional stories, and his personality, attracted the interest of Calcutta intellectuals, including **Vivekananda**, who became Ramakrishna's spiritual heir.

Raman, Sir Chandrasekhara Venkata 1888–1970 •*Indian physicist and Nobel Prize winner*• Born in Trichinopoly, Tamil Nadu, he was educated at the University of Madras, and became Professor of Physics at the University of Calcutta (1917–33). In 1930 he was awarded the Nobel Prize for physics for his work in demonstrating that the interaction of vibrating molecules with photons passing through altered the spectrum of the scattered light. This "Raman effect" became an important spectroscopic technique. He also researched the vibration of musical instruments and the physiology of vision. He was knighted in 1929.

Ramanuja 11th-12th century •*Tamil Brahmin philosopher*• He was born near Madras, southern India, and although little is known of his life, he holds an important position in Indian thought. Rejecting **Śankara**'s *advaita*, or nondualistic Vedanta, for *Viśishtadvaita* (which held that the soul was united with a personal god rather than absorbed into the Absolute), he prepared the way for the *bhakti*, or devotional strain of Hinduism that was taken up by **Madhva**, Nimbarka, Vallabha and **Caitanya**.

Ramanujan, Srinivasa 1887–1920 •*Indian mathematician*• Born in Eroda, Madras, he taught himself mathematics from an elementary textbook written in English. While working as a clerk, he devised over 100 remarkable theorems, which he sent to **Godfrey Hardy** at Cambridge. These included results on elliptic integrals, partitions and analytic number theory. Hardy was so impressed that he arranged for him to go to Cambridge in 1914. There Ramanujan published many papers, the most remarkable being an exact formula for the number of ways an integer can be written as a sum of positive integers. He was one of the most remarkable self-taught prodigies in the history of mathematics.

Ramaphosa, (Matamela) Cyril 1952– •*South African trade unionist and politician*• Born in Johannesburg, he became chairman of the all-Black South African Students' Organization in 1974, and after 11 months' detention (1974–75) became an articled clerk there and was active in the BPC (Black People's Convention). He graduated from the University of South Africa with a law degree in 1981. He later became general secretary of the National Union of Mineworkers (1982). He brought the NUM into COSATU (Congress of South African Trade Unions) and was elected secretary-general of the African National Congress (1991–96).

Rambaud, Patrick 1946– •*French author*• He was born in Paris and studied at the Lycée Condorcet there. A prolific journalist, scriptwriter, essayist and novelist, he cofounded *Actuel* magazine in 1970 and has garnered praise and awards for novels such as *Virginie Q* (1988) and *The Battle* (1997; Prix Goncourt), the latter a brutal narrative of the Napoleonic Wars. He is noted for his numerous parodies of other, mainly French, authors.

Rambert, Dame Marie, *stage name of* **Cyvia Rambam** 1888–1982 •*Polish-born British ballet dancer and teacher*• She was born in Warsaw. Sent to Paris to study medicine, she became involved in artistic circles and began to study eurhythmics. In 1913 she worked on **Igor Stravinsky**'s *Rite of Spring* with **Sergei Diaghilev**'s Ballets Russes. She moved to London and began to dance and teach. In 1930, ten years after opening her own dance studio, she formed the Ballet Club, a permanent producing and performing organization which featured dancer **Alicia Markova** and choreographer **Frederick Ashton**. She was particularly interested in promoting new ballets, and always encouraged her pupils to produce works; this led inevitably to occasional financial difficulties. Her company (which had become Ballet Rambert in 1935) had been expanding since the 1940s, but by 1966 was reduced to a small group which concentrated on new works and began to embrace modern dance techniques. It has since grown to become one of Great Britain's major touring contemporary dance companies, changing its name again, in 1987, to the Rambert Dance Company. Rambert was given the honorary title of Dame Commander, Order of the British Empire, in 1962.

Rambouillet, Catherine de Vivonne, Marquise de 1588–1665 •*French noblewoman*• She was born in Rome, the daughter of Jean de Vivonne, Marquis of Pisani. At the age of 12 she was married to the son of the Marquis de Rambouillet, who succeeded to the title in 1611. She disliked the morals and manners of the French court, and for 50 years she gathered together in the famous Hôtel de Rambouillet the talent and wit of the French nobility and literary world, including **Condé**, **François de Malherbe** and **Pierre Corneille**.

Rameau, Jean Philippe 1683–1764 •*French composer and musical theorist*• Born in Dijon, he became an organist, and in 1722 settled in Paris, where he published his *Traité de l'harmonie* (1722, "Treatise on Harmony"), a work of fundamental importance in the history of musical style. He wrote many operas, notably *Hippolyte et Aricie* (1733) and *Castor et Pollux* (1737), as well as ballets, harpsichord pieces (for which he is best known today), chamber music and vocal music.

Ramée, Pierre de la *See* **Ramus, Petrus**

Rameses II, *known as* **Rameses the Great**, *also spelled* **Ramesses** or **Ramses** 1304–1237 BC •*Egyptian pharaoh*• The third king of the 19th Dynasty, his reign marked the last zenith of Egyptian imperial power. His reign (c. 1292–1237 BC) is the most renowned in Egyptian history for temple building: he completed the mortuary temple of his father, Seti I, at Luxor and the colonnaded hall of the Karnak temple, and built the rock temples of Abu Simbel, dedicating the smaller one to his queen, Nefertari. His mummy was found at Deir-el-Bahari (1881).

Rameses III 1198–1167 BC •*Egyptian pharaoh*• He was the second king of the 20th Dynasty. He campaigned against the Philistines and other Sea Peoples and repeated the conquest of Ethiopia. He is sometimes identified with the Old Testament Pharaoh of the Exodus. His mummy was found at Bulak (1886).

Rammohun Roy or **Rájá Rám Mohán Rái** 1774–1833 •*Indian religious reformer*• Born in Burdwan, Bengal, of high Brahmin ancestry, he questioned his ancestral faith, and studied Buddhism in Tibet. He published various works in Persian, Arabic and Sanskrit, with the aim of eliminating idolatry, and he was influential in the abolition of suttee. He issued an English abridgment of the *Vedanta*, which provided a digest of the Veda. In 1820 he published *The Precepts of Jesus*, accepting the morality preached by **Jesus**, but rejecting his deity and miracles, and he wrote other pamphlets hostile both to Hinduism and to Christian Trinitarianism. In 1828 he began the Brahma Samaj Association, and in 1830 the emperor of Delhi bestowed on him the title of raja. In 1831 he visited England.

Ramón y Cajal, Santiago 1852–1934 •*Spanish physician, histologist and Nobel Prize winner*• Born in Petilla de Aragon, he graduated from the University of Saragossa in 1873. He joined the Army Medical Service and served in Cuba, where he contracted malaria and was soon discharged because of ill health. He returned to Saragossa for further anatomical training and in 1883 began his academic career as Professor of Anatomy at Valencia (1883–86), then as Professor of Histology at Barcelona (1886–92) and finally as Professor of Histology and Pathological Anatomy at Madrid (1892–1922). His major work was on the microstructure of the nervous system, and revealed how nerve impulses are transmitted to the brain. He made use of the specialized histological staining techniques of **Camillo Golgi**, and the two men shared the 1906 Nobel Prize for physiology or medicine.

Ramos, Fidel Valdez 1928– •*Philippine general and statesman*• Born in Manila, he was educated at the University of the Philippines and at West Point. He served with the US forces in the Korean War (1950–53) and in Vietnam, and was made chief of staff of the Philippine army in 1986. At the time, **Ferdinand Marcos** had used fraudulent means to claim victory over **Cory Aquino** in the general election. When Aquino challenged Marcos, Ramos supported her, and after she became president he served as her defense secretary (1988–92). He succeeded Aquino as president (1992–98).

Ramos-Horta, José 1949– •*East Timorese politician, campaigner and academic*• Born in Dili, he worked as a radio and television correspondent from 1969 to 1974. He was forced into exile shortly before the 1975 Indonesian invasion and spent the following years in international campaigning work and in studying throughout Europe and the US. He won the Nobel Peace Prize (1996; with **Carlos Ximenes Belo**) for his work toward a just and peaceful solution to the conflict in East Timor. He returned to Timor in 1999.

Ramphal, Sir Shridath Surrendranath, *also known as* **Sir Sonny Ramphal** 1928– •*Guyanese and Commonwealth lawyer and diplomat*• After studying law at King's College London, he was called to the bar in 1951. He returned to the West Indies, and from 1952 held increasingly responsible posts in Guyana and the West Indies before becoming Guyana's foreign minister and attorney general in 1972, and justice minister in 1973. During much of this time he sat in the Guyanan National Assembly. From 1975 to 1989 he was secretary-general of the Commonwealth.

Ramsay, Allan c. 1685–1758 •*Scottish poet*• Born in Leadhills, Lanarkshire, he was apprenticed to a wigmaker in Edinburgh (1704–09). By 1718 he had become known as a poet, having issued several short humorous satires printed as broadsides, and he had also written (1716–18) two additional cantos to the old Scots poem *Christ's Kirk on the Green*. He then started a business as a bookseller, and his new circulating library (1725) is thought to have been the first in Great Britain. His works include *Tartana, or the Plaid* (1718), *The Monk and the Miller's Wife* (1724), *The Tea-Table Miscellany* and *The Gentle Shepherd, A Pastoral Comedy* (1725), his most popular work. His eldest son was the painter **Allan Ramsay**.

Ramsay, Allan 1713–84 •*Scottish portrait painter*• He was born in Edinburgh, the eldest son of the poet **Allan Ramsay**. Trained in Italy, he was a distinguished portrait painter, working first in Edinburgh, but settling in London in 1762. His portrait of *Dr Richard Mead* (1747, Coram Foundation, London) is a fine example of his early period. In 1767, he was appointed portrait painter to **George III** (National Portrait Gallery, London, and work in Royal Collection). In his best works his painting is simple and delicate, and he was at his most impressive in his portraits of women, notably that of his wife (National Gallery of Scotland, Edinburgh).

Ramsay, Sir Bertram Home 1883–1945 •*Scottish naval officer*• Born in London into an old Scottish family, he served as a naval commander in World War I, resigned from the navy in 1938, but was recalled on the outbreak of World War II. He directed the Dunkirk evacuation of 338,000 Allied troops in May–June 1940, was deputy to Admiral **Andrew Cunningham** for the North African landings in 1942, and commanded the British naval forces for the Allied invasion of Sicily (1943). Reinstated on the active list as an admiral in 1944, he was Allied Naval Commander in Chief for the Normandy landings in 1944. He was killed in an aircraft accident near Paris.

Ramsay, James Andrew Broun *See* **Dalhousie, Marquis of**

Ramsay, Sir William 1852–1916 •*Scottish chemist and Nobel Prize winner*• He was born in Glasgow and studied at the Universities of Glasgow and Tübingen, becoming professor at University College, Bristol (1880–87) and University College London (1887–1913). In 1894, in conjunction with Lord John Kayleigh, he discovered argon. In 1895 he isolated a light inert gas resembling argon by boiling a mineral called cleivite. Spectroscopic analysis showed that this gas was helium, which Sir **Norman Lockyer** and Edward Frankland had discovered in the spectrum of the sun nearly 30 years earlier. Working with Morris William Travers (1872–1961), Ramsay found the green and yellow lines of krypton, the crimson of neon and the blue lines of xenon in 1898. Further research confirmed the inert nature of these gases and their atomic weights. In 1908 Ramsay obtained radon—discovered by **Frederich Ernst Dorn** in 1900—in sufficient quantities to show that it belonged to the same family as helium and the other inert gases. In 1904 he was knighted and awarded the Nobel Prize for chemistry.

Ramses *See* **Rameses**

Ramsey, Sir Alf(red) 1920–99 •*English soccer player and manager*• Born in Dagenham, Essex, he played defense for Southampton, Tottenham Hotspur and England before becoming a manager in 1955. Under his management, Ipswich Town won the First Division title in 1962. He was appointed manager of England in 1963 and led the team to their historic World Cup triumph in 1966. He lost the post of manager in 1974 when the team failed to qualify for the finals. He served briefly as manager of Birmingham City in 1977 and was knighted in 1967.

“ ”

You've beaten them once. Now go out and bloody beat them again.

1966 Addressing his players when the World Cup final went into extra time.

Ramsey, Arthur Michael, Baron 1904–88 •*English prelate, Archbishop of Canterbury*• Born in Cambridge, he was educated at Repton School (where the headmaster, Dr **Geoffrey Fisher**, was the man he would succeed as archbishop) and Magdalen College, Cambridge, where he was president of the Union (1926). He wrote his first book, *The Gospel and Catholic Church*, in 1936 and was appointed vicar at St Benet's, Cambridge, in 1938. He then became Professor of Divinity at Durham and a canon of the cathedral (1940), Regius Professor of Divinity at Cambridge (1950), Bishop of Durham (1952) and Archbishop of York (1956). As Archbishop of Canterbury (1961–74) he worked tirelessly for Church unity, making a historic visit to Pope **Paul VI** in the Vatican in 1966. He was an eminent scholar, and published many theological works. He was made a life peer in 1974.

Ramus, Petrus, *Latin name of* **Pierre de la Ramée** 1515–72 •*French humanist*• Born in Cuth, near Soissons, he became the servant of a rich scholar at the Collège de Navarre. Graduating at 23, he had great success as a lecturer on the Greek and Latin authors, and set out to reform the science of logic. His attempts were greeted with hostility from the Aristotelians, and his *Dialectic* (1543) was fiercely attacked by the scholars of the Sorbonne, Paris. But cardinals de Bourbon and Lorraine (**Charles Guise**) protected him. Forced to flee from Paris, he traveled in Germany and Switzerland, but he returned to France (1571) and was killed in the St Bartholomew's Day Massacre (1572). He wrote treatises on arithmetic, geometry and algebra, and was an early adherent of the Copernican system. His theories had considerable influence after his death, and the Ramist system of logic was adopted and taught throughout Europe.

Rancé, Armand Jean le Bouthillier de 1626–1700 •*French monk, the founder of the Trappists*• An accomplished but worldly priest, he became abbot of the Cistercian Abbey of La Trappe in 1662. Affected by the tragic deaths of two of his friends, he underwent a conversion, undertook a reform of his monastery and finally established what was practically a new religious order, its principles perpetual prayer and austere self-denial. Intellectual work was forbidden, and only manual labor was allowed to the monks.

Rand, Ayn 1905–82 •*US writer*• Born in St Petersburg, Russia, she emigrated to the US in 1926 and became a US citizen in 1931. Her best-known polemical novel *The Fountainhead* (1943), in which she advanced her characteristic themes of objectivism and freedom of the individual, established her popular reputation and was subsequently made into a film. Other publications included the novels *We Are the Living* (1936) and *Atlas Shrugged* (1957) and the journal *The Objectivist*, which she founded in 1962.

Randolph, A(sa) Philip 1889–1979 •*US African-American labor leader and civil rights activist*• He was born in Crescent City, Florida, the son of a clergyman, and studied at City College, New York. Initially a supporter of the Black nationalist Marcus Garvey, Randolph opposed the idea of economic separatism in his own journal, *The Messenger*. In 1925 he organized the Brotherhood of Sleeping Car Porters, the first Black union to gain major successes, including recognition by the Pullman Company. Among many other campaigns, he organized the March on Washington for Jobs and Freedom (August 28, 1963), at which **Martin Luther King** was the principal speaker.

Randolph, Edmund Jennings 1753–1813 •*US politician*• Born near Williamsburg, Virginia, he studied at the College of William and Mary and trained as a lawyer under his father. At the outbreak of the Revolution he became an aide-de-camp to **George Washington**. He served as a Virginia delegate to the Continental Congress (1779–82) and the Constitutional Convention (1787) as well as governor of Virginia (1786–88). Washington appointed him attorney general in 1789, and in 1794 Randolph was appointed secretary of state, but resigned over false charges of bribery in 1795 and was practically ruined. He resumed his law practice in Richmond and was chief counsel for **Aaron Burr** at his treason trial.

Randolph, John 1773–1833 •*US politician*• He was born in Cawsons, Virginia, and in 1799 he entered Congress, where he became distinguished for his wit and eccentricity. He was the Democratic leader of the House of Representatives, but quarreled with **Thomas Jefferson** and opposed the war of 1812; he also opposed the Missouri Compromise and nullification. From 1825 to 1827 he sat in the Senate, and in 1830 was appointed ambassador to Russia.

Ranjit Singh, *known as* **the Lion of the Punjab** 1780–1839 •*Sikh ruler*• In 1801 he succeeded his father, a Sikh chief, as ruler of Lahore (now in Pakistan), and directed all his energies to founding a kingdom which would unite all the Sikh provinces. With the help of an army trained by Western soldiers, including generals Ventura and Allard, he became the most powerful ruler in India. He was a firm ally of the British, the boundary between their territories having been amicably fixed at the Sutlej River. Soon after his death, the Sikh state collapsed amid chieftain rivalry.

Rank, J(oseph) Arthur, Baron 1888–1972 •*English film magnate*• Born in Hull, Humberside, he worked in his father's flour-milling business but developed an interest in films as a means of propagating the Gospel. He became chairman of many film companies and did much to promote the British film industry at a time when Hollywood and the US companies seemed to have gained a monopoly. A staunch and active supporter of the Methodist Church, he was keenly interested in social problems. He was raised to the peerage in 1957.

Ranke, Leopold von 1795–1886 •*German historian*• Born in Wiehe, Thuringia, he studied at Halle and Berlin. His early work was concerned with the Romance and Teutonic peoples in the Reformation period, and he criticized contemporary historians; as a result of this activity, he was appointed Professor of History at Berlin (1825–72). Among many other topics, he wrote on southern Europe in the 16th and 17th centuries (1827), the history of the papacy (1834–37), the Seven Years' War (1871), the revolutionary wars of 1791 to 1792 (1875), Venetian history (1878), a universal history (1881–88) and the history of Germany and France in the 19th century (1887), as well as biographies.

Rankin, Ian 1960– •*Scottish author*• He was born in Cardenden, Fife, and was educated at the University of Edinburgh. His first book was *The Flood* (1986), but it was with the introduction of the cynical, impatient and emotionally repressed Inspector Rebus that he made his reputation in books such as *Mortal Causes* (1994), *Black and Blue* (1997; Crime Writers Association Gold Dagger award), *The Hanging Garden* (1998) and *Set in Darkness* (2000).

Rankin, Jeannette 1880–1973 •*US feminist and pacifist*• Born near Missoula, Montana, she was educated at the University of Montana and the New York School of Philanthropy, and went on to become a social worker in Seattle (1909), where she involved herself in the women's rights movement. In 1914 she was appointed legislative secretary of the National American Woman Suffrage Association, and in 1916 was elected to the House of Representatives as a Republican, becoming the first woman to serve in Congress. During her two terms there (1917–19, 1941–43) she promoted labor reform, health care, and women's rights, and was the only member of Congress to vote against US participation in both world wars.

Rankine, William John MacQuorn 1820–72 •*Scottish engineer and scientist*• He was born in Edinburgh, and with **William Kelvin** and **Rudolf Clausius** he shaped the new science of thermodynamics, particularly by patenting an elaborate air engine with his friend James Robert Napier. Rankine introduced the terms "actual" (kinetic) and "potential" energy. Later he proposed an abstract "science of energetics" which sought to unify physics. In 1855 he was appointed to the chair of engineering at Glasgow. He was elected a Fellow of the Royal Society in 1853, and his works on the steam engine, machinery, shipbuilding and applied mechanics became standard textbooks. He also contributed to the theory of elasticity.

Ransom, John Crowe 1888–1974 •*US poet and critic*• Born in Pulaski, Tennessee, he studied at Vanderbilt University and at Oxford. From 1914 he taught English at Vanderbilt, where he gathered a group of students and colleagues, including **Allen Tate** and **Robert Penn Warren**, who contributed to the poetry magazine *The Fugitive* (1922–25) and shared an allegiance to the Southern agrarian ideal. Much of Ransom's poetry dates from this period, and his collections *Poems About God* (1919), *Chills and Fever* (1924) and *Two Gentlemen in Bonds* (1927) illustrate his aptitude as a balladist and elegist. His criticism includes *God Without Thunder* (1930) and *The New Criticism* (1941).

" "

Here lies a lady of beauty and high degree.
Of chills and fever she died, of fever and chills,
The delight of her husband, her aunts, an infant of three,
And of medicos marvelling sweetly on her ills.

1924 ***Chills and Fever**, "Here Lies a Lady."*

Ransome, Arthur Mitchell 1884–1967 •*English journalist and children's writer*• Born in Leeds, he was educated at Rugby, where he was a poor scholar and, by virtue of bad eyesight, inept at games. He worked as an office boy in a publishing house before graduating to ghostwriting, reviewing and writing short stories. He became a reporter for the *Daily News* and, in 1919, for the *Manchester Guardian*. Having learned Russian in 1913, he was sent to cover the revolution, and married **Trotsky**'s secretary, Evgenia Shelepin, with whom he fled from Russia, settling in the Lake District. He had been a published author for a quarter of a century before the appearance of *Swallows and Amazons* (1930), the first of 12 perennially popular novels featuring two families of adventurous but responsible children, who spend their school holidays reveling in the open air.

Rantzen, Esther Louise 1940– •*English television host and producer*• Born in Berkhamsted, Hertfordshire, and educated at Somerville College, Oxford, she joined the BBC in 1963, making sound effects for radio drama. Moving into research for *Man Alive* (1965–67), she joined *Braden's Week* (1968–72) as a reporter. From 1973 to 1994 she wrote, produced and hosted *That's Life*, a consumer program combining investigative journalism with a sequence of comical items. She has also campaigned against child abuse and drug addiction in several documentaries. In 1977 she married broadcaster Desmond Wilcox (1931–2000); their joint publications include *Baby Love* (1985). She is the moderator of her own television talk show, *Esther* (1994–).

Raphael, *properly* **Raffaello Santi** or **Sanzio** 1483–1520 •*Italian painter, one of the greatest artists of the Renaissance*• He was born in Urbino, the son of the poet-painter Giovanni Santi (d. 1494). From about 1500 he studied in Perugia under **Perugino**, and his early paintings show Perugino's influence. In 1505 he went to Siena, where he assisted **Pinturicchio**, then moved to Florence, where he studied the work of **Michelangelo** and **Leonardo da Vinci**. The

Borghese *Entombment* (1507) is an embodiment of all the new principles which Raphael acquired in Florence. Influenced by the style of **Fra Bartolommeo**, he completed the *Madonna del Baldacchino* in Florence. Some of the best work of his Florentine period was now produced: the small *Holy Family*, the *St Catherine*, the *Bridgewater* and *Colonna Madonnas*, the *Virgin and Sleeping Infant*, the large *Cowper Madonna*, the *Belle jardinière*, and the *Esterhazy Madonna*. In 1508 he went to Rome at the instigation of his relative **Donato Bramante**, then in high favor with Pope **Julius II**, who had laid the foundation of the new cathedral of St Peter, and who commissioned the redecoration of the papal chambers. Among Raphael's work there was the fresco series *The School of Athens*. Raphael divided his time between the labors of the Vatican and easel pictures. The use of pupils also enabled him to finish numerous works in the years 1511–14. He also painted the *Madonna of the Fish* (Madrid) and *Madonna della Sedia* (Florence), while in portraits such as *Altoviti* (Munich) and *Inghirami* (Florence) he rises to the perfect rendering of features and expression which finds its greatest triumph in the *Leo X* (Florence). **Leo X** selected Raphael to succeed Bramante as architect of St Peter's in 1514, and secured from him for the Vatican chambers the frescoes in the Camera dell' Incendio. He went with Leo X to Florence and Bologna, and there executed the *Sistine Madonna*, the *St Cecilia* of Bologna, and the *Ezechiel* of the Pitti, Florence. The labors subsequently completed were immense, including the *Spasimo*, the *Holy Family* and *St Michael* and the *Violin player*. His last work, the *Transfiguration*, was left unfinished when he died.

Rask, Rasmus Christian 1787–1832 •*Danish philologist*• Born on the island of Fyn, he mastered some 25 languages and dialects. Along with the works of **Franz Bopp** and **Jacob Grimm**, his *Essay on the Origin of the Ancient Scandinavian or Icelandic Tongue* (1818), in which he demonstrated the affinity of Icelandic to other European languages, opened up the science of comparative philology. He was one of the first to recognize that the Celtic languages are Indo-European, and, developing the work of the Swedish philologist Johan Ihre (1707–80), he anticipated Grimm in formulating the Germanic consonant shift described in what has become known as Grimm's Law.

Rasputin, Grigori Efimovich 1871–1916 •*Russian peasant and self-styled religious "elder" (starets)*• He was born in Pokrovskoye, Tobolsk. A member of the schismatic sect of *Khlysty* (flagellants), he arrived in St Petersburg at a time when mystical religion was fashionable, and obtained an introduction to the royal household. There he quickly gained the confidence of Czar **Nicholas II** and the empress **Alexandra** by his apparent ability to control through hypnosis the bleeding of the hemophiliac heir to the throne. However, he soon created a public scandal through his sexual and alcoholic excesses, and his political influence made him enemies. He was murdered by a clique of aristocrats who were loyal to the czar.

Rathbone, Eleanor Florence 1872–1946 •*English feminist and social reformer*• Born in Liverpool, she studied the classics at Somerville College, Oxford. A leader in the constitutional movement for female suffrage and an advocate of family allowances, she was an independent member of the Liverpool City Council from 1909, working in the housing campaign between the wars. She was elected as independent Member of Parliament for the Combined English Universities, fought to gain the franchise for Indian women, and denounced child marriage in India (*Child Marriage: The Indian Minotaur*, 1934).

Rathenau, Walther 1867–1922 •*German electrotechnician and industrialist*• Born in Berlin, he was head of the Allgemeine Elektrizitäts Gesellschaft (AEG), founded in 1883 by his father, and took responsibility for German war industries during World War I. As Minister of Reconstruction (1921) and Foreign Minister (1922), his attempts to negotiate a reparations agreement with the victorious Allies, and the fact that he was Jewish, made him extremely unpopular in nationalist circles, and he was murdered by extremists in the summer of 1922.

Rathke, Martin Heinrich 1793–1860 •*German biologist*• Born in Danzig (Gdansk, Poland), he studied medicine at the Universities of Göttingen and Berlin, and became Professor of Physiology at the Universities of Dorpat (now Tartu) in 1829 and Königsberg in 1835. In 1829 he discovered gill slits and gill arches in embryonic birds and mammals. "Rathke's pocket" is the name given to the small pit on the dorsal side of the oral cavity of developing vertebrates.

Ratsiraka, Didier 1936– •*Malagasy sailor and politician*• Born in Vatomandry, he served in the navy (1963–70) and was military attaché in Paris. Since independence in 1960 frequent clashes had occurred between the country's two main ethnic groups, the highland Merina and the coastal Cotiers. From independence in 1960 until 1972 the government had favored the Cotiers. In 1972 the army, representing the Merina, took control. A deteriorating economy and Cotier unrest led to the imposition of martial law in 1975, but this was lifted and, under a new constitution, Ratsiraka, who was a Cotier, was elected president. In 1976 he formed the Advance Guard of the Malagasy Revolution (AREMA), which became the nucleus of a one-party state. Although AREMA won overwhelming support in the Assembly elections of 1983 and 1989, discontent continued, particularly among the Merina. He was president until 1993.

Rattigan, Sir Terence Mervyn 1911–77 •*English playwright*• He was born in London, educated at Harrow and Oxford, and scored a considerable success with his comedy *French Without Tears* (1936). Best known among his other plays are *The Winslow Boy* (1946), based on the Archer Shee case, *The Browning Version* (1948), *The Deep Blue Sea* (1952), *Separate Tables* (1954) and *Ross* (1960), a fictional treatment of **T E Lawrence**. He was responsible for several successful films made from his own and other works.

" "

You can be in the Horseguards and still be common, dear.

1954 ***Separate Tables***.

Rattle, Sir Simon 1955– •*English conductor*• He was born in Liverpool. He won the Bournemouth International Conducting Competition at the age of 17, and made his London debut in 1976. Assistant conductor of the BBC Scottish Symphony Orchestra (1977–80), he was appointed principal conductor (1980–90) and music director (1990–98) of the City of Birmingham Symphony Orchestra. He was principal guest conductor of the Los Angeles Philharmonic Orchestra from 1981 to 1992. In 1991 he launched *Towards the Millennium*, a ten-year retrospective survey of 20th-century music. He is also principal conductor of the Orchestra of the Age of Enlightenment (1992–).

Rau, Johannes 1931– •*German politician*• Born in Wuppertal, in North Rhine-Westphalia, the son of a Protestant pastor, he began his career as a salesman for a church publishing company before being attracted to politics as a follower of **Gustav Heinemann**. He joined the Social Democratic Party (SPD) and was elected to the Diet of his home Land (state) in 1958. He served as chairman of the SPD's parliamentary group (1967–70), and as Minister of Science and Research in the Land (1970–78) before he became president in 1999.

Rauch, Christian Daniel 1777–1857 •*German sculptor*• Born in Arolsen, he practiced sculpture while serving as valet to **Frederick William III** of Prussia, and in 1804 went to Rome, where he came under the classicizing influence of **Antonio Canova** and Bertel Thorvaldsen (1770–1844), but his own style was naturalistic. From 1811 to 1815 he carved the recumbent effigy for the tomb of Queen **Louisa** at Charlottenburg. Other works include statues of **Dürer**, **Goethe**, **Schiller**, and **Kant**. His masterpiece was the equestrian statue of **Frederick the Great** (1851) in Berlin.

Rauschenberg, Robert 1925– •*US avant-garde artist*• Born in Port Arthur, Texas, of German and Indian descent, he studied art at the Kansas City Art Institute, in Paris, and at Black Mountain College, North Carolina. His collages and "combines" incorporate a variety of junk items (rusty metal, old tires, stuffed birds, fragments of clothing, etc.) splashed with paint. Sometimes categorized as a pop artist, his work has strong affinities with Dadaism and with the "ready-mades" of **Marcel Duchamp**.

Ravel, Maurice 1875–1937 •*French composer*• He was born in Ciboure in the Basque region, went to the Paris Conservatoire as a piano student in 1889, and later joined **Gabriel Fauré**'s composition class. His first orchestral piece, the overture *Schéhérazade*, had a hostile reception on its first performance in 1899, but he won recognition in the same year with the *Pavane pour une infante défunte* ("Pavane for a Dead Princess"), which is strongly redolent of his Basque background. At the height of his powers, he wrote a string quartet (1902–03), the exotic and beautiful *Introduction and Allegro* for a group of instruments including harp, and the piano pieces *Sonatine* (1905, "Little Sonata"), *Miroirs* (1905, "Mirrors"), *Ma mère l'oye* (1908, "Mother Goose") and *Gaspard de la nuit* (1908, "Gaspard of the Night"). In 1909 he began the music for the **Diaghilev** ballet *Daphnis et Chloé* ("Daphnis and Chloe"). He saw active service in World War I until he was discharged for health reasons. The choreographic poem *La Valse* was staged in 1920, and the opera *L'enfant et les sortilèges* ("The Child and His Spells), written to a libretto by **Colette**, in 1925. To this late period also belong the two piano concertos (1929–31), one for the left hand and written for the pianist Paul Wittgenstein (1887–1961), who had lost his right arm in the war, and *Boléro* (1928). In 1933 his mental faculties began to fail, and it was found that he had a brain tumor; he composed no more. His music is scintillating and dynamic; he defied the established rules of harmony with his unresolved sevenths and ninths and other devices, and his syncopation and strange sonorities.

Ravilious, Eric William 1903–42 •*English artist, designer and illustrator*• He studied at Eastbourne School of Art, London (1919–22), and at the Design School of the Royal College of Art (1922–25), where he was taught by **Paul Nash**. He designed printed patterns for J Wedgwood & Sons, but wood engraving was the center of his activity, and he was commissioned to illustrate many books, including *Twelfth Night* (1932) and *Elm Angel* (1930). During the late 1930s he turned increasingly to watercolor painting and color lithography. He was appointed official war artist in 1940 and was lost on air patrol off the coast of Iceland.

Ravi Shankar 1920– •*Indian musician*• He is widely regarded as India's most important musician, both as a virtuoso player of the sitar, and as a teacher and composer. His own early training as a dancer was followed by years of intensive musical study. He set up schools of Indian music, founded the National Orchestra of India, and by the mid-1950s his reputation had spread so widely that he became the first Indian instrumentalist to undertake an international tour. **George Harrison** was one of his pupils. He has written several film scores, the most notable being for **Satyajit Ray**'s trilogy, *Apu*.

Rawlings, Jerry John 1947– •*Ghanaian leader*• He was born in Accra. He was at the center of a peaceful coup in 1979, the intentions of which were to root out widespread corruption and promote "moral reform." After four months, Rawlings and his supporters returned power to a civilian government under an elected president, Hilla Limann. Despite being forcibly retired from the armed forces and sidelined by the civilian government, his popularity remained high, and he returned with his Armed Forces Revolutionary Council to seize power again at the end of 1981. He remained head of government, despite attempts to overthrow him twice in 1983 and again in 1987. After a referendum in 1992 voted for the return of constitutional government, Rawlings was elected president in multiparty elections. He retired in 2001.

Rawlings, Marjorie Kinnan 1896–1953 •*US novelist*• Born in Washington DC and educated at the University of Wisconsin, Madison, she worked as a journalist, editor and syndicated verse writer before devoting herself to full-time creative writing in 1928. She was awarded the O Henry Memorial award in 1933 for her short story "Gal Young Un." She published her first novel, *South Moon Under*, in the same year but is best remembered for her Pulitzer Prize–winning novel *The Yearling* (1938, later filmed), which describes a young boy's attachment to his pet fawn.

Rawsthorne, Alan 1905–71 •*English composer*• Born in Haslingden, Lancashire, he first studied dentistry, but developed an interest in music at the age of 20 and studied at the Royal Manchester College of Music. From 1932 to 1934 he taught at Dartington Hall, and settled in London in 1935. His works, forthright and polished, include symphonies, *Symphonic Studies* for orchestra (1939), concertos for piano and for violin, and choral and chamber music.

Ray, John 1627–1705 •*English naturalist*• Born in Black Notley, near Braintree, Essex, he was educated at Cambridge and became a Fellow of Trinity College in 1649, but lost his post in 1662 when he refused to take the oath to the Act of Uniformity after the Restoration. He then toured extensively in Europe (1662–66), studying botany and zoology. He originated the basic principles of plant classification into cryptogams, monocotyledons and dicotyledons in his pioneering *Catalogus plantarum Angliae* (1670) and *Methodus plantarum nova* (1682). His major work was *Historia generalis plantarum* (3 vols, 1686–1704), and his *Wisdom of God Manifested in the Works of the Creation* (1691) was immensely influential in its time. In his zoological work, he developed the most natural pre-Linnaean classification of the animal kingdom.

Ray, Man, *pseudonym of* **Emanuel Rabinovitch** 1890–1976 •*US painter, sculptor, photographer and filmmaker*• Born in Philadelphia, he studied art in New York, and became a major figure in the development of Modernism, establishing (with **Marcel Duchamp** and **Francis Picabia**), the New York Dadaist movement. He experimented with new techniques in painting and photography, moving to Paris, where he became interested in film. After working with **René Clair**, he made surrealist films like *Anemic Cinema* (1924) with **Marcel Duchamp**. During the 1930s he published and exhibited many photographs and "rayographs" (photographic images made without a camera), and returned to the US in 1940 to teach photography in Los Angeles.

Ray, Satyajit 1921–92 •*Indian film director*• Born in Calcutta, he graduated from Presidency College, Calcutta, Vishva-Bharati University, Shantiniketan, and worked as a commercial artist in an advertising agency while writing screenplays and attempting to finance his first film. With government support he eventually completed *Pather Panchali* (1955, *On the Road*), which was an international success. With *Aparajito* (1956, *The Unvanquished*) and *Apu Sansar* (1959, *The World of Apu*), it formed the Apu trilogy, an understated, affectionate portrait of social change in rural life. Later, he made documentaries and filmed tales from Indian folklore, such as *Devi* (1960, *The Goddess*), before tackling political themes such as famine in *Ashanti Sanket* (1973, *Distant Thunder*) and business ethics in *Jana-Arnaya* (1975, *The Middle Man*). He has frequently composed the music for his films, and worked in Hindi for the first time with *Shatranj Ke Khilari* (1977, *The Chess Players*). Later features include *Hirok Rajar Deshe* (1980, *The Kingdom of Diamonds*) and *Ghare-Baire* (1984, *The Home and the World*). He received a special Academy Award in 1992.

Rayburn, Sam(uel Taliaferro) 1882–1961 •*US legislator*• Born in Roane County, Tennessee, he grew up on a Texas farm and studied law. He was elected to the House of Representatives as a Democrat from Texas in 1913 and remained in Congress until his death, serving a record 17 years as Speaker of the House (1940–47, 1949–53, 1955–61). Though he did not consider himself an orator, he wielded political influence through a network of personal contacts and was influential in passing **Franklin D Roosevelt**'s New Deal.

Rayleigh, John William Strutt, 3rd Baron 1842–1919 •*English physicist and Nobel Prize winner*• Born near Maldon, Essex, he studied at Trinity College, Cambridge. He succeeded his father as third baron in 1873, and was appointed Professor of Experimental Physics at Cambridge (1879–84). He was appointed Professor of Natural Philosophy at the Royal Institution (1888–1905), president of the Royal Society (1905–08) and chancellor of Cambridge University in 1908. Rayleigh researched vibratory motion in both optics and acoustics, and with Sir **William Ramsay** he discovered argon (1894), for which he was awarded the Nobel Prize for physics in 1904. His research on radiation led to the Rayleigh-**Jeans** formula, which accurately predicts the long-wavelength radiation emitted by hot bodies.

Rayner, Claire Berenice 1931– •*English writer, broadcaster and journalist*• Raised and educated in London, she worked there as a nurse and midwife before becoming the medical correspondent for *Woman's Own* magazine. She was also the advice columnist for several national newspapers and on television and radio broadcasting, appearing on the BBC's *Breakfast Time*, *TV-am* (1985–92) and *Good Morning...with Anne & Nick*. Drawing on her medical knowledge and family experience, she has published over 75 advice books. She also writes fiction, both under her own name and as Sheila Brandon, and contributes to medical journals under the name Ann Lynton.

Rāzī, ar-, *Latin* **Rhazes** c. 865–923/932 •*Persian physician and alchemist*• Born in Baghdad, he wrote many medical works, some of which were translated into Latin and had considerable influence on medical science in the Middle Ages. He successfully distinguished smallpox from measles, and was considered the greatest physician of the Arab world.

Read, Sir Herbert 1893–1968 •*English art historian, critic and poet*• Born at Muscoates Grange, near Kirkbymoorside, North Yorkshire, he was educated in Halifax and at the University of Leeds. He became assistant keeper at the Victoria and Albert Museum in London (1922–31), Professor of Fine Art at the University of Edinburgh (1931–33) and editor of the *Burlington Magazine* (1933–39), and he held academic posts at Cambridge University, the Universities of Liverpool and London, and Harvard University. As an art critic he revived interest in the 19th-century Romantic movement and championed modern art movements in Great Britain. He was interested in industrial design, and was director of the first major British design consultancy, the Design Research Unit. His poetry included *Naked Warriors* (1919, based on his war experiences), and his other publications include *The Meaning of Art* (1931).

Reade, Charles 1814–84 •*English novelist and playwright*• He was born at Ipsden House, Oxfordshire, the youngest of 11 children. After five harrowing years at Iffley school, and six under two milder private tutors, in 1831 he earned a scholarship to Magdalen College, Oxford. He first wrote for the stage in 1850, and went on to produce 40 dramas. His novels include *Peg Woffington* (1852), *Hard Cash* (1863), *Foul Play* (1869, with Dion Boucicault), *A Terrible Temptation* (1871) and *A Woman-Hater* (1877). His masterpiece was his long historical novel of the 15th century, *The Cloister and the Hearth* (1861).

Reagan, Nancy Davis, *originally* **Anne Francis Robbins** 1923– •*First Lady of the US*• Born in New York City and educated at Smith College, Massachusetts, she was an actress under contract to MGM (1949–56), during which time she married **Ronald Reagan** in 1952. Her husband was US president from 1981 to 1989, and as First Lady she campaigned against substance abuse, winning numerous honors and awards. She was honorary chair of the "Just Say No" Foundation and the National Federation of Parents for Drug Free Youth.

" "

I'm more aware if somebody is trying to end-run him ... it just never occurs to him.

1988 On protecting her husband. In ***Time****, November 28.*

Reagan, Ronald Wilson 1911–2004 •*40th President of the US, and former film actor*• Born in Tampico, Illinois, he studied economics at Eureka College, Illinois. He moved to Hollywood, making his debut in *Love Is in the Air* (1937), and starred in 50 films, including *Bedtime for Bonzo* (1951) and *The Killers* (1964). During this period Reagan was a liberal Democrat and admirer of **Franklin D Roosevelt**. He became interested in politics when serving as president of the Screen Actors' Guild (1947–52), and moved increasingly toward Republicanism, particularly following his marriage in 1952 to Nancy Davis (see **Nancy Reagan**). He officially joined the Republicans in 1962. In 1966 Reagan was elected governor of California, and remained in the post for eight years. He unsuccessfully sought the Republican presidential nomination in 1968 and 1976. In 1980, however, after eventually capturing the party's nomination, he proceeded convincingly to defeat the incumbent, **Jimmy Carter**. His campaign stressed the need to reduce taxes, deregulate the economy and build up and modernize the US's defenses. He survived an attempted assassination in 1981 and, despite initial serious economic problems between 1981 and 1983, secured reelection by a record margin in 1984. During his second term, Reagan, the one-time hawk, despite advocating a new Strategic Defense ("Star Wars") Initiative of space-based military defense, became a convert to detente, holding four summit meetings with Soviet leader **Mikhail Gorbachev** between 1985 and 1988, and signing a treaty for the scrapping of intermediate nuclear forces. During 1986–87, however, the president's position was temporarily imperiled by the Iran-Contra Affair, which concerned illegal arms-for-hostages deals with Iran by senior members of his administration and the laundering of profits intended, equally illegally, to supply the anti-Marxist Contra guerrillas fighting in Nicaragua. As a result of the scandal, White House chief of staff **Donald Regan** and his national security adviser Rear Admiral **John Poindexter** were forced to resign, but Reagan escaped unscathed. Described as the "great communicator" for his accomplished use of modern media, Reagan had a unique, populist rapport with mainstream America and left office an immensely popular figure.

Réaumur, René Antoine Ferchault de 1683–1757 •*French natural philosopher*• Born in La Rochelle, he moved to Paris in 1703. In gathering the material required for the monumental *Description des arts et métiers* he acquired a wide knowledge of contemporary science and technology. He developed improved methods for producing iron and steel, and became one of the greatest naturalists of his age, publishing the first serious and comprehensive work of entomology. His thermometer of 1731 used a mixture of alcohol and water instead of mercury, and was calibrated with a scale (the Réaumur scale): 80 degrees between the freezing and boiling points of water.

Red Cloud, *Sioux name* **Mahpiua Luta** 1822–1909 •*Native American leader*• Born in north-central Nebraska, he proved his prowess as a warrior and became chief of the Oglala Sioux. He led the resistance to the Bozeman Trail, which crossed Native American lands in Nebraska, Wyoming and Montana. By carrying out raids on soldiers at frontier forts, he and his warriors forced the US government to abandon the trail in 1868. He signed a treaty with the US in 1869 and thereafter lived at peace with whites, and ended his days on a reservation in South Dakota.

Redding, Otis 1941–67 •*US soul singer*• He was born in Dawson, Georgia, and as a high school student in Macon, Georgia, he was so impressed by the success of **Little Richard** that he decided to become a full-time performer. His early work, including "Shout Bamalama" (1960), was heavily influenced by Richard's frantic jump-blues style. Despite several minor hits, he did not gain the widespread acceptance of US rock fans until an appearance at the Monterey pop festival in 1967. He died in a plane crash in December of that year. The posthumously released ballad "Dock of the Bay" became his first number-one US hit early in 1968. Several of his songs, including "I've Been Loving You Too Long" (1965), "Try a Little Tenderness" and "Mr Pitiful" (1965), are now regarded as soul classics.

Redford, (Charles) Robert 1937– •*US film actor and director*• Born in Santa Monica, California, he studied at the American Academy of Dramatic Art and made his film debut in *War Hunt* (1962). The long-running Broadway comedy *Barefoot in the Park* (1963) established him as a leading man, and the film version of the play (1967) brought him his first great success. His good looks and image of integrity made him popular in films including *Butch Cassidy and the Sundance Kid* (1969, with **Paul Newman**), *The Way We Were* (1973), *The Sting* (1973), *Out of Africa* (1985) and *Indecent Proposal* (1993). Other projects have reflected his interests in the American West, and in ecology and politics. In 1976 he produced and starred in *All the President's Men*, and in 1998, he directed and starred in *The Horse Whisperer*. He also directed *Ordinary People* (1980), for which he won an Academy Award, *A River Runs Through It* (1993), *Quiz Show* (1994) and other films.

Redgrave, Sir Michael Scudamore 1908–85 •*English stage and film actor*• Born in Bristol, Avon, the son of actor parents, he was educated at Clifton College, Bristol, and Magdalen College, Cambridge. He taught modern languages at Cranleigh School before taking up an acting career with Liverpool Repertory Company (1934–36). His sensitive, intellectual approach to acting was most successful in classical roles, including *Hamlet* (Old Vic and Elsinore, 1949–50), *Richard II* (1951) and *Uncle Vanya* (1963). Other plays in which he appeared include *Tiger at the Gates* (1955) and his own adaptation of *The Aspern Papers* (1959). He was equally successful in films, among them **Alfred Hitchcock**'s *The Lady Vanishes* (1938), *The Way to the Stars* (1945), *Mourning Becomes Electra* (1947, Academy Award nomination), *The Browning Version* (1951), *The Loneliness of the Long Distance Runner* (1962) and *Nicholas and Alexandra* (1971). He married the actress Rachel Kempson (1910–2003) in 1935, and their three children are all in the acting profession: **Vanessa**, Corin (1939–) and Lynn (1943–). He was knighted in 1959.

Redgrave, Sir Steve (Steven Geoffrey) 1962– •*English oarsman and sculler*• Born in Marlow, Buckinghamshire, he left school at 16 to begin his career in sculling, making his first international appearance in the world junior championships of 1979. In 1984 he moved into the coxed four, winning his first Olympic gold at Los Angeles in the same year. This was the beginning of a remarkable Olympic career in which he has won five gold medals at successive Games, an unprecedented achievement in world rowing and an unbeaten record in modern Olympic history. Nine times world champion, he also won a record three gold medals in the 1986 Commonwealth Games. His formidable partnership with **Matthew Pinsent** was characterized by exciting and powerful finishes. Redgrave and Pinsent were world coxless pairs champions in 1991, 1993, 1994 and 1995, Olympic champions in 1992 and 1996, and they set a world record time in Lucerne in 1994. Later they won gold medals in the coxless fours race in the 1997, 1998 and 1999 world championships, and captured the world's attention during their successful bid for a gold at the Olympic Games in Sydney in 2000. Redgrave was knighted in 2001.

Redgrave, Vanessa 1937– •*English actress*• She was born in London, the eldest daughter of Sir **Michael Redgrave** and actress Rachel Kempson (1910–2003). A student at the Central School of Speech and Drama (1954–57), she joined the Royal Shakespeare Company in the 1960s. Her first film, *Behind the Mask* (1958), was followed by many others, notably *Morgan* and *Blow-Up* (both 1966). Active in several media, she has proved herself one of the most distinguished performers of her generation. Her work in the theater includes *The Prime of Miss Jean Brodie* (1966), *The Lady from the Sea* (1976–77) and *Orpheus Descending* (1988–89). She received Academy Award nominations for *Morgan*, *Isadora* (1968), *Mary, Queen of Scots* (1971) and *The Bostonians* (1984), winning a Best Supporting Actress award for *Julia* (1977). On television she won an Emmy for *Playing for Time* (1980). Her later film appearances include *Prick Up Your Ears* (1987), *Howards End* (1992, Academy Award nomination) and *The Cradle Will Rock* (1999). She is also well known for her active support of left-wing and humanitarian causes.

Redman, Don(ald Matthew) 1900–64 •*US saxophonist, arranger and bandleader*• Born in Piedmont, West Virginia, he was able to play a wide range of wind instruments while still in school, and, after studies at music schools, including Boston Conservatory, began to work professionally as a clarinettist, alto saxophonist and arranger. His first achievement was the creation in the mid-1920s of a distinctive style for the **Fletcher Henderson** Orchestra. Redman's principles of swing-style orchestration later influenced nearly every important jazz composer of the era and are still respected in big-band music.

Redon, Odilon 1840–1916 •*French painter and lithographer*• Born in Bordeaux, he studied in Paris. He made many charcoal drawings and lithographs of imaginative power, including *Les yeux clos* (1890, "Closed Eyes," Musée d'Orsay, Paris). After 1900 he painted, mainly in pastel, pictures of flowers and portraits in intense color. His *Ophelia Among the Flowers* (c. 1905–08) is in the Tate Modern, London. A distinguished writer, he published his diaries (1867–1915) as *À soi-même* (1922), and his *Letters* were published in 1923. He is usually regarded as a forerunner of surrealism because of the use of dream images in his work.

Redpath, Anne 1895–1965 •*Scottish painter*• Born in Galashiels, Selkirkshire, she studied at Edinburgh Art College and lived in France from 1919 to 1934. One of the most important modern Scottish artists, her paintings in oil and watercolor, mainly of landscapes and still-lifes, show great richness of color and vigorous technique, notably *Altar at Chartres* (1964, Prudential Assurance, London). She was elected a member of the Royal Scottish Academy in 1952.

Redpath, Jean 1937– •*Scottish folk and traditional singer*• She was born in Edinburgh and became involved in folk music while studying at the university there. She emigrated to the US in 1961, where her pure voice and outstanding ability were quickly recognized. *The Scottish Fiddle* (1985) was an important recording, and she has made a special study of the songs of **Robert Burns**, which she has recorded in two separate projects, one using the controversial musical arrangements written by the US composer Serge Hovey. She continues to perform on the international circuit.

Reed, Sir Carol 1906–76 •*English film director*• Born in London and educated at King's School, Canterbury, he took to the stage (1924) and acted and produced for **Edgar Wallace** until 1930. He produced or directed such memorable films as *Kipps* (1941), *The Young Mr Pitt* (1942), *The Way Ahead* (1944), the Allied war documentary *The True Glory* (1945), and *The Fallen Idol* (1948), but is best remembered for his Cannes Film Festival prizewinning version of **Graham Greene**'s novel *The Third Man* (1949). *An Outcast of the Islands* (1952), based on a **Joseph Conrad** novel, and *Our Man in Havana* (1959) were additional successful literary adaptations. He won an Academy Award for *Oliver!* (1968).

Reed, Lou, *real name* **Louis Firbank** 1944– •*US rock singer, guitarist and songwriter*• Born on Long Island, New York, he initially gained fame as a member of the Velvet Underground, a band which was closely associated with **Andy Warhol** and his organization, The Factory. In 1972 he moved to England to record *Lou Reed* (1972). His 1973 album, *Transformer*, included "Walk on the Wild Side," a paean to transsexuality which somehow bypassed radio censorship to become the first major hit of his career. Subsequent albums have included *Rock 'n' Roll Animal* (1974), *New Sensations* (1984), *New York* (1989), *Magic and Loss* (1992) and *Set the Twilight Reeling* (1996). He reunited with fellow Velvet Underground founder John Cale (1940–) to create a tribute to Warhol, *Songs for 'Drella* (1990).

Reed, Walter 1851–1902 •*US army surgeon*• Born in Belroi, Virginia, he entered the medical corps in 1875, and was appointed Professor of Bacteriology at the Army Medical College, Washington, in 1893. Investigations carried out by him in 1900 proved that mosquitoes transmitted yellow fever, and his research led to the eventual eradication of the disease from Cuba.

Rees, Sir Martin John 1942– •*English astrophysicist*• Born in York, he was educated at Cambridge, and became a staff member of the Institute of Theoretical Astronomy there. He returned to Cambridge as Plumian Professor of Astronomy and Experimental Philosophy (1973–91) and director of the Institute of Astronomy (1977–82, 1987–91). Since 1992 he has been Royal Society Research Professor. Rees has made important contributions to the study of stellar systems and "dark matter," and his best-known work is in the study of active galactic nuclei. He demonstrated that the variations in brightness observed in quasars and active galaxies could be best understood if the nuclei contained gas which is outflowing at almost the speed of light. Observational evidence for this appeared in the 1970s. He became president of the Royal Astronomical Society in 1992, the year in which he was knighted. In 1995 he became Astronomer Royal.

Rees-Mogg, William Rees-Mogg, Baron 1928– •*English journalist*• Born in Bristol and educated at Charterhouse and Balliol College, Oxford, he joined the *Financial Times* in 1952 as assistant editor. In 1960 he moved to the *Sunday Times* and assumed the editorship of *The Times*, a post he held for 14 years. Having been vice chairman of the BBC and chairman of the Arts Council, he was appointed to head the new Broadcasting Standards Council (1988–93). A recent publication is *The Great Reckoning* (1991). He was made a life peer in 1988.

Reeve, Clara 1729–1807 •*English novelist*• Born in Ipswich, Suffolk, she wrote *The Champion of Virtue, A Gothic Story* (1777, renamed *The Old English Baron*), which was avowedly an imitation of **Horace Walpole**'s *The Castle of Otranto*. Her other novels include *The Two Mentors* (1783), *The Exiles* (1788), *Memoirs of Sir Roger de Clarendon* (1793), and *Destination* (1799). She also wrote a critical account of *The Progress of Romance* (1785).

Reeves, Keanu 1964– •*US actor*• He was born in Beirut, Lebanon, and studied at the Toronto High School for Performing Arts. He began his career on stage in Canada and moved to television and cinema in the mid-1980s, appearing in a diverse range of films, from comedies such as *Bill and Ted's Excellent Adventure* (1988) to action thrillers such as *Speed* (1994). Other notable films include *Dangerous Liaisons* (1988), *Point Break* (1991), *My Own Private Idaho* (1991), and in *The Matrix* triology (1998, 2003, 2003).

Regan, Donald Thomas 1918–2003 •*US politician*• Born in Cambridge, Massachusetts, he studied at Harvard. He switched allegiance from the Democrats to the Republicans in 1940, and during World War II reached the rank of lieutenant colonel. After the war he joined Merrill Lynch as a sales trainee and rose to become its president in 1968, building the company into the US's largest securities brokerage corporation. Attracted by his strong belief in supply-side free-market economics, President **Ronald Reagan** appointed him Secretary of the Treasury in 1981. He became White House chief of staff in January 1985, but was forced to resign two years later as a result of criticisms of his role in the 1985–86 Iran-Contra Affair.

“ ”

Mistaken in its assumptions, defective in its evidence and wrong in its conclusions.

1988 Of the congressional report faulting him on lack of direction and public disclosure of Iran-Contra arms sales. ***For the Record.***

Regiomontanus, *originally* **Johannes Müller** 1436–76 •*German mathematician and astronomer*• He took his name from his Franconian birthplace, Königsberg (*Mons Regius*), which is now Kaliningrad in Russia. In 1471 he settled in Nuremberg, where he was supported by the patrician Bernhard Walther. The two labored at the *Alphonsine Tables* and published *Ephemerides 1475–1506* (1473), a work used extensively by Christopher Columbus. Regiomontanus established the study of algebra and trigonometry in Germany and wrote on waterworks, burning glasses, weights and measures, and the quadrature of the circle.

Rego, Paula 1935– •*Portuguese artist*• Born in Lisbon, she studied at the Slade School of Art, London, then returned to Portugal. She has been influenced by an interest in folk and fairy tales, illustrative art and cartoon strips. Her early work used animals to express human behavior, but she then turned to human figures, collectively exploring issues such as power, gender stereotypes, sexuality and human emotions. These factors combine to give an eerie feel to her work that draws from surrealism. She has lived and worked in the UK since 1976.

Regulus or **Rule, St** 4th century AD •*Semilegendary monk*• Tradition holds that he was a monk of Constantinople or Bishop of Patras. In AD 347 he is said to have gone to Muckross or Kilrimont (afterward St Andrews), taking relics of **St Andrew** from the East.

Rehnquist, William 1924– •*US jurist*• Born in Milwaukee, Wisconsin, he studied political science at Stanford and Harvard, and law at the Stanford Law School. After 1952 he practiced law in Phoenix, Arizona, and became active in the Republican Party. In 1969 he was appointed head of the Office of Legal Counsel in the Justice Department by President **Richard Nixon**, and in this post supported such controversial measures as pretrial detention and wiretapping. He impressed Nixon, who appointed him associate justice of the Supreme Court in 1972. He duly emerged as the Court's most conservative member and in 1986 was appointed Chief Justice. Initially, the new Rehnquist Court differed little from its predecessor, but by 1989 a "new right" majority had been established by President **Ronald Reagan**, later helping to produce a series of conservative rulings on abortion and capital punishment.

Reich, Robert 1946– •*US government official*• Born in Scranton, Pennsylvania, he graduated from Dartmouth College in 1968 and was awarded a Rhodes scholarship to Oxford; he met fellow scholar and future US President **Bill Clinton** on the ship bound for England. He became a leading neoliberal economic theorist and a lecturer at Harvard (1981–1993), and he influenced Democratic policies with books such as *The Next American Frontier* (1983) and *The Work of Nations* (1991). As secretary of labor (1993–97) in the Clinton administration, he backed the North American Free Trade Agreement and called for higher minimum wages and tax incentives to discourage corporate layoffs. In an increasingly centrist administration, he served as a link to the labor movement and an advocate for the unemployed and underemployed. In 1997, he became University Professor at Brandeis University.

Reich, Steve 1936– •*US composer*• Born in New York, he has been strongly influenced by his training in drumming, his love of the music of **Stravinsky** and the pulse of jazz and the rhythms of African and Balinese music. He has written for a great variety of vocal and instrumental forces and timbres, and has used taped and electronic effects. Recent compositions are *The Cave* (1993) and *City Life* (1995).

Reichenbach, Hans 1891–1953 •*US philosopher of science*• Born in Hamburg, Germany, he became Professor of Philosophy at Berlin (1926–33), Istanbul (1933–38) and the University of California, Los Angeles (from 1938). He was an early associate of the Vienna Circle of logical positivists, and with **Rudolf Carnap** he founded the journal *Erkenntnis* ("Perception") in 1930. He made an important contribution to probability theory in which two truth tables are replaced by the multivalued concept "weight," and he wrote widely on logic and the philosophical bases of science.

Reichstein, Tadeus 1897–1996 •*Swiss chemist and Nobel Prize winner*• Born in Włocławek, Poland, he trained at the State Technical College, Zurich, returning there as an assistant to **Ružicka** and becoming associate professor there in 1937. He then moved to the University of Basel where he held a number of positions. His early academic work on carbohydrate chemistry led to the first synthesis of vitamin C (1933), independently of Sir **Norman Haworth**, as well as some sugars. From 1934 he also began synthesizing new steroids and isolating and identifying the life-maintaining natural steroids of the adrenal gland. For his outstanding work on the chemistry of the adrenal hormones, Reichstein received, with **Edward Kendall** and **Philip Hench**, the 1950 Nobel Prize for physiology or medicine.

Reid, Beryl 1919–96 •*English comedienne and actress*• Born in Hereford, she built a reputation as a variety entertainer and soubrette-cum-impressionist. The radio series *Educating Archie* (1952–56) established the comic character of schoolgirl Monica, and her other creations include Midlands teddy girl Marlene. She was a veteran of revues and pantomimes, and made her film debut in *Spare a Copper* (1940). Her long television career included such series as *The Girl Most Likely* (1957) and *The Secret Diary of Adrian Mole Aged 13¾* (1985), and straight roles in *The Rivals* (1970) and *Cracker* (1993). *The Killing of Sister George* (1965) established her as a serious actor and she won a Tony award for its Broadway production (1966), repeating her role on film in 1968. Her other films include *Star!* (1968) and *Entertaining Mr Sloane* (1970).

Reid, Sir Bob (Robert Paul) 1934– •*Scottish industrial executive*• Born in Cupar, Fife, the son of a butcher, he graduated from the University of St Andrews in 1956 and joined Shell, becoming chairman and chief executive of Shell UK in 1985. In 1988, as chairman of the British Institute of Management, he took a leading role in the reshaping of management education. From 1990 to 1995 he was chairman of British Rail. He is currently a deputy governor of the Bank of England (1997–) and chancellor of Robert Gordon University (1993–). He was knighted in 1990.

Reid, John 1947– •*Scottish Labour politician*• Born in Scotland, he was educated at Stirling University and worked as a researcher for the Labour Party before becoming political adviser to **Neil Kinnock** (1983–85). He organized Scottish trade unionists for Labour (1986–87) and in 1987 was elected Member of Parliament. After the Labour landslide of 1997, he became minister of state for defense (1997–98), minister for transport (1998–99), secretary of state for Scotland (1999–2000) and secretary of state for Northern

Ireland (2000–2002). He became leader of the House of Commons following **Robin Cook**'s resignation in 2003.

Reid, Thomas 1710–96 •*Scottish philosopher*• Born in Strachan, Kincardineshire, he was educated at Aberdeen, and became minister of New Machar in Aberdeenshire (1737) and Professor of Philosophy at Aberdeen (1751). He succeeded **Adam Smith** as Professor of Moral Philosophy at Glasgow (1764–80), and then retired to write. He was leader of the group known as the "Common Sense" or later the "Scottish" school, in opposition to the empirical philosophy of **David Hume**. Reid reasserted the existence of external objects by denying that simple "ideas" are our primary data. His best-known works include *Essays on the Intellectual Powers of Man* (1785) and *Essays on the Active Powers of Man* (1788).

Reiner, Fritz 1888–1963 •*US conductor*• He was born in Budapest, Hungary, and studied law and music at the University of Budapest. He conducted in Budapest and Dresden before moving to the US in 1922 to conduct the Cincinnati Symphony Orchestra. Reiner was head of the orchestra and opera departments at the Curtis Institute in Pennsylvania from 1931 to 1941, then was in charge of the Pittsburgh Orchestra (1938–48), conducted at the New York Metropolitan Opera (1949–53) and was musical director of the Chicago Symphony Orchestra (1953–63). His autocratic manner on the rostrum and in rehearsal gave him an awesome reputation, but the music he produced was far from cold and unyielding.

Reines, Frederick 1918–98 •*US physicist and Nobel Prize winner*• Born in Paterson, New Jersey, he was educated at the Steven's Institute of Technology in Hoboken, New Jersey, and at New York University. Between 1944 and 1959 he was a group leader at Los Alamos, and later taught at the Case Institute of Technology, Cleveland, and the University of California, Irvine (from 1966). Together with **Clyde Cowan, Jr**, he proved the existence of nature's most elusive particle, the neutrino. For his discovery of the neutrino he was awarded the Nobel Prize for physics jointly with **Martin Perl** in 1995.

Reinhardt, Django (Jean Baptiste) 1910–53 •*Belgian guitarist*• One of the first European jazz virtuosi, he was born in Liverchies to a family of Gypsy entertainers. Despite losing the use of two fingers of his left hand in a caravan fire, he developed an outstanding technique. After working as a cabaret player in Paris cafés, he joined violinist **Stephane Grappelli** in 1934 to form the Quintette du Hot Club de France, which established a distinctive French jazz style. In 1946 he joined the **Duke Ellington** Orchestra for a US tour, and became a powerful influence among swing-style guitarists.

Reinhardt, Max, *originally* **Max Goldmann** 1873–1943 •*Austrian theater manager*• He was born in Baden, Germany. An innovator in theater art and technique, his work often involved large-scale productions (for example, *The Miracle*, London 1911, which used over 2,000 actors). He cofounded the Salzburg Festival (1920), where he produced *Everyman* and *Faust* for the festivals of 1920 and subsequent years. He left Germany for the US in 1933, and opened a theater workshop in Hollywood.

Reiniger, Lotte 1899–1981 •*German film animator*• Born in Berlin, she studied design at **Max Reinhardt**'s theater school in 1916. She developed a special technique of silhouette animation and became a leading innovator in that art, utilizing her techniques in many films. She made the first-ever full-length animated feature film, *Die Abenteuer des Prinzen Achmed* (*The Adventures of Prince Achmed*) in 1926. She worked for the celebrated animation section of the National Film Board of Canada in the 1970s, and wrote a number of books on animation.

Reith (of Stonehaven), John Charles Walsham Reith, 1st Baron 1889–1971 •*Scottish engineer and pioneer of broadcasting*• Born in Stonehaven, Kincardineshire, and educated at Glasgow Academy and Gresham's School, Holt, he served an engineering apprenticeship and later entered the field of radio communication. The first general manager of the British Broadcasting Corporation in 1922, he was its director general from 1927 to 1938, before becoming Member of Parliament for Southampton (1940). He was the architect of public service broadcasting in the UK, and the BBC Reith Lectures on radio were instituted in 1948 in his honor.

Remarque, Erich Maria 1898–1970 •*US novelist*• Born in Osnabrück, Germany, he served in World War I, after which he published his famous war novel, *Im Westen nichts Neues* (1929, Eng trans *All Quiet on the Western Front*, 1929). He lived in Switzerland from 1929 to 1939, and published *Der Weg zurück* (1931, Eng trans *The Road Back*, 1931). In 1939 he emigrated to the US, and became a naturalized citizen, writing books that include *Arc de Triomphe* (1946, Eng trans *Arch of Triumph*, 1946) and *Die Nacht von Lissabon* (1962, Eng trans *The Night in Lisbon*, 1964).

Rembrandt, *properly* **Rembrandt Harmensz van Rijn** 1606–69 •*Dutch painter, the greatest northern European artist of his age*• He was born in Leiden. After working under Pieter Lastman in Amsterdam, he returned to his hometown and worked independently. He quickly achieved a high reputation as a portrait painter, and by 1628 had a pupil, **Gerard Dou**. Rembrandt excelled at group portraits of the burghers of Amsterdam after settling permanently there in 1631. In 1634 he married Saskia van Ulenburgh, who is featured in a number of paintings of the time. Other works from this period are *Rembrandt's Mother as the Prophetess Hannah* (1631, Rijksmuseum, Amsterdam), *The Anatomy Lesson of Doctor Tulp* (1632, Mauritshuis, The Hague), *The Entombment of Christ* (c. 1635, Hunterian Gallery, Glasgow), and *Belshazzar's Feast* (c. 1636, National Gallery, London). Rembrandt lived prosperously while Saskia was alive, and they had a son, Titus. In 1642 Rembrandt produced his most famous painting, *The Military Company of Captain Frans Banning Cocq* (better known as "The Night Watch," Rijksmuseum), a dramatically lit, dynamically composed group portrait of a local militia band. Saskia died the same year, and in spite of increasing fame, Rembrandt's financial situation declined over the next 25 years, and he narrowly avoided bankruptcy in 1656. From about 1647 he lived with Hendrickje Stoffels. There are about six portraits that have been identified with her, including a fine one in the National Gallery, London (c. 1659). In 1660 Titus and Hendrickje formed a company for dealing in art, and they employed Rembrandt, thereby affording him some financial relief. During these years he turned to biblical subjects, including *Christ and the Woman Taken in Adultery* (1644, National Gallery, London), *Susanna Surprised by the Elders* (c. 1647, Gemäldegalerie, Berlin), *Jacob Blessing the Sons of Joseph* (c. 1656, Cassel), and *The Return of the Prodigal Son* (c. 1669, Hermitage, St Petersburg). Also among his greatest achievements were his group portraits, notably the *Staalmeesters* (1662, "Officials of the Guild of Drapers," Rijksmuseum); his individual portraits, including the *Portrait of Jan Six* (1654, Rijksmuseum); and a superb series of self-portraits, as well as etchings and ink-and-wash drawings.

Remington, Philo 1816–89 •*US inventor*• Born in Litchfield, New York, he entered his father's small-arms factory, and for 25 years superintended the mechanical department. As president of the company from 1860, he perfected the Remington breech-loading rifle.

Remy or **Remigius, St**, *known as* **the Apostle of the Franks** c. 438–533 •*Frankish prelate*• He became Bishop of Rheims and, according to **Gregory of Tours**, he baptized **Clovis**, king of the Franks, in the Christian faith.

Renan, (Joseph) Ernest 1823–92 •*French philologist and historian*• Born in Tréguier, Brittany, he trained for the Church, but abandoned traditional faith after studying Hebrew and Greek biblical criticism. In 1850 he started work at the Bibliothèque Nationale and published *Averroès et l'Averroïsme* (1852, "Averroës and Averroism") and *Histoire générale des langues sémitiques* (1854, General History of the Semitic Languages"). His appointment as Professor of Hebrew at the Collège de France in 1861 was not confirmed until 1870 by the clerical party, especially after the appearance of his controversial *La vie de Jésus* (1863). It was the first of a series on the history of the origins of Christianity, which included books on the Apostles (1866) and **St Paul** (1869). Among his other works were books on **Job** (1858) and Ecclesiastes (1882).

“ ”

War is a condition of progress; the whip-cut that prevents a country from going to sleep and forces satisfied mediocrity to shake off its apathy.

1871 ***La réforme intellectuelle et morale.***

Rendell, Ruth Rendell, Baroness 1932– •*English detective-story writer*• She was born in London. She has written various detective stories featuring Chief Inspector Wexford (for example, *Shake Hands Forever*, 1975), and mystery thrillers (for example, *A Judgment in Stone*, 1977). Since 1986, she has also written psychological thrillers such as *King Solomon's Carpet* (1991) under the pen name of Barbara Vine. Later publications include a collection of short stories, *Blood Linen* (1995) and *Piranha to Scurfy* (2000). Several of her works have been adapted for the cinema and for television. She was created a life peer in 1997.

“ ”

I made the decision long ago that to be afraid would be to diminish my life.

1995 Interview in NPR broadcast, July 18.

René, (France-)Albert 1935– •*Seychelles politician*• Educated in the Seychelles, Switzerland, and at King's College London, he was called to the bar in 1957. He returned to the Seychelles and took up politics, establishing the Seychelles People's United Party (SPUP), a socialist group, in 1964. In 1970 he pressed for full independence for the Seychelles, while his contemporary, James Mancham of the Seychelles Democratic Party (SDP), favored integration with the UK. When independence was achieved in 1976, Mancham became president and René prime minister. In 1977, while Mancham was abroad, René staged a coup, made himself president and created a one-party state. He subsequently followed a nonnuclear policy of nonalignment and resisted attempts to remove him. He was elected in 1979, and reelected in 1984, 1989 and 1993.

Renfrew, (Andrew) Colin, Baron 1937– •*English archaeologist*• Born in Stockton-on-Tees, County Durham, he was educated at St John's College, Cambridge. His work has ranged widely and is essentially concerned with the nature of cultural change in early history. The origin, development and interaction of language, agriculture, urbanism, metallurgy, trade and social hierarchy are constant themes, pursued in such books as *Before Civilization* (1973) and *Archaeology and Language* (1987). Since 1981 he has been Professor of Archaeology at Cambridge. He has also contributed to several pioneering archaeological broadcasts, notably the BBC's *Chronicle* series. He was made a life peer in 1991.

Reni, Guido 1575–1642 •*Italian painter*• Born near Bologna, he studied under Denys Calvaert (c. 1545–1619) and **Ludovico Carracci**, and went to Rome in 1599 and again in 1605. *Aurora and the Hours* (1613) is usually regarded as his masterpiece. He was a prolific early painter of the classical style, although he was later criticized by **John Ruskin** for sentimental tendencies. He also produced some vigorous etchings.

Renner, Karl 1870–1950 •*Austrian statesman*• Born in Unter-Tannowitz, Bohemia, he trained as a lawyer, joined the Austrian Social Democrat Party, and became the first chancellor of the Austrian republic (1918–20). He was imprisoned as a Socialist leader following the brief civil war in 1934, but was chancellor again in 1945. He wrote political works and a national song. From 1946 until his death he was president of Austria.

Rennie, John 1761–1821 •*Scottish civil engineer*• He was born at Phantassie farm, East Linton, East Lothian, and after working as a millwright studied at the University of Edinburgh (1780–83). In 1784 he entered the employment of Messrs **Boulton** & **Watt**, and in 1791 established himself in London as an engineer and soon became famous as a bridge builder, constructing bridges at Kelso, Leeds, Musselburgh, Newton-Stewart, Boston, New Galloway, as well as Southwark and Waterloo bridges, and he planned London Bridge. He built many important canals, drained fens, designed the London docks and others at Blackwall, Hull, Liverpool, Dublin, Greenock and Leith, and improved harbors and dockyards at Portsmouth, Chatham, Sheerness and Plymouth.

Reno, Janet 1938– •*US politician and lawyer*• Born in Miami, Florida, she was educated at Cornell and Harvard Universities and was admitted to the Florida bar in 1963. After practicing for ten years she was appointed administrative assistant state attorney for the 11th Judiciary Circuit Florida, Miami (1973–76), then state attorney in Florida (1978–93). In 1993 she was nominated and confirmed as the US attorney general, the first woman in US history to hold this position.

Renoir, Jean 1894–1979 •*US film director*• Born in Paris, France, son of **Pierre-Auguste Renoir**, he won the croix de guerre in World War I. He turned from scriptwriting to filmmaking: his version of **Zola**'s *Nana* (1926), *La grande illusion* (1937, *Grand Illusion*), *La bête humaine* (1939, *The Human Beast*), *La carrozza d'oro* (1953, *The Golden Coach*), and *Le déjeuner sur l'herbe* (1959, *Picnic on the Grass*), all of which are among the masterpieces of the cinema. He left France in 1941 for the US and became a naturalized US citizen. His later films include *Le caporal épinglé* (1962, *The Elusive Corporal*) and *Le petit théâtre de Jean Renoir* (1969).

Renoir, Pierre-Auguste 1841–1919 •*French Impressionist painter*• Born in Limoges, he began at the age of 13 as a painter on porcelain, and later of fans. He made his first acquaintance with the work of **Antoine Watteau** and **François Boucher**, which was to influence his choice of subject matter as deeply as Impressionism was to influence his style. He entered the studio of Charles Gleyre (1806–74) in 1862 and began to paint in the open air about 1864. In 1874–79 and in 1882 he exhibited with the Impressionists his important, controversial picture of sunlight filtering through leaves, the *Moulin de la galette* (in the Louvre). He visited Italy in 1880 and during the next few years (1884–87) painted a series of *Bathers* in a more cold and classical style influenced by **Jean Ingres** and **Raphael**. He then returned to hot reds, orange and gold to portray nudes in sunlight, a style that he continued to develop until his death, although his hands were crippled by arthritis in his later years. His works include *The Umbrellas* (c. 1883, National Gallery, London) and *The Judgment of Paris* (c. 1914).

Renta, Oscar de la *See* **de la Renta, Oscar**

Repin, Ilya Yefimovich 1844–1930 •*Russian painter*• Born in Chuguyev, he and his family joined the Abramtsevo colony, a progressive community near Moscow, which is today considered the cradle of the modern movement in Russian art. Repin is possibly the most famous of the realist group the Wanderers, which had founded a new artistic code aimed at bringing art to the people. The major representative of naturalism in Russia during the second half of the 19th century, he gained popularity with paintings such as *The Reply of the Cossacks of Zaporoguus to Sultan Mahmoud IV* (1884), which his contemporaries saw as a symbol of the Russian people throwing off their chains, and also painted portraits of famous contemporaries.

Repton, Humphrey 1752–1818 •*English landscape designer*• Born in Bury St Edmunds, Suffolk, the natural successor to **Lancelot "Capability" Brown**, he completed the change from formal gardens of the early 18th century to the picturesque, and coined the phrase "landscape gardening." He drew designs for Uppark in Sussex and Sheringham Hall in Norfolk, and wrote *Observations on the Theory and Practice of Landscape Gardening* (1803).

Resnais, Alain 1922– •*French film director*• Born in Vannes, France, he began studying at the Institute of Advanced Cinematographic Studies in Paris, where he made a series of prize-winning short documentaries, including *Van Gogh* (1948, Academy Award), *Guernica* (1950) and *Nuit et brouillard* (1955, *Night and Fog*). His first feature film, *Hiroshima mon amour* (1959, "Hiroshima My Love"), intermingles the nightmare war memories of its heroine with her unhappy love for a Japanese soldier against the tragic background of contemporary Hiroshima. His next film, *L'année dernière à Marienbad* (1961, *Last Year at Marienbad*), illustrates his interest in the merging of past, present and future to the point of ambiguity. Works such as *Je t'aime, je t'aime* (1967) and *Mélo* (1985) had mixed receptions, although he enjoyed commercial success with the duo *Smoking* and *No Smoking* in 1993.

Respighi, Ottorino 1879–1936 •*Italian composer*• Born in Bologna, in 1913 he became Professor of Composition at the St Cecilia Academy in Rome. His works include nine operas, the symphonic poems *Fontane di Roma* (1916, "Fountains of Rome"), *Pini di Roma* (1924, "Pines of Rome"), *Gli uccelli* (1927, "The Birds") and *Feste romane* (1928, "Roman Festivals"), and the ballet *La boutique fan-*

tasque ("The FantasticToyshop"), produced by **Sergei Diaghilev** in 1919.

Restif or **Rétif de la Bretonne, Nicolas Edmé** 1734–1806 •*French writer*• He was born in Sacy, Yonne. His many voluminous and licentious novels, notably *Le pied de Fanchette* (1769, "Fauchette's Foot") and *Le paysan perverti* (1775, "The Corrupted Peasant"), give a vivid picture of 18th-century French life, and entitle him to be considered a forerunner of realism. His 16-volume work *Monsieur Nicolas* (1794–97, Eng trans 1930) is based loosely on his own life. He also wrote on social reform.

Retz or **Rais** or **Raiz, Gilles de Laval, Baron** 1404–40 •*French soldier and alleged murderer*• Born in Champtoceaux, France, he was a Breton of high rank who fought beside **Joan of Arc** at Orléans. He became marshal of France at the age of 25, but soon retired to his estates, where he is alleged to have indulged in satanism and orgies, kidnapping and killing 150 children. He was tried for heresy, and was hanged and burned at Nantes. His story is often connected with that of Bluebeard.

Reuter, Paul Julius Reuter, Baron von, *originally* **Israel Beer Josaphat** 1816–99 •*British journalist*• Born in Kassel, Germany, he was the founder of the first news agency. He changed his name to Reuter in 1844, and in 1849 formed in Aachen an organization for transmitting commercial news by telegraph and pigeon post. In 1851 he fixed his headquarters in London, and gradually his system spread to the remotest regions.

Reuther, Walter Philip 1907–70 •*US trade union leader*• He was born in Wheeling, West Virginia, and worked for Ford and in the USSR before helping to found the United Auto Workers' (UAW) union in 1935. He organized the automobile workers into what later became the largest union in the world, and fought against communist influence in trade unionism. He was UAW president from 1946 to 1970.

Revels, Hiram Rhoades 1822–1901 •*US politician and clergyman*• Born of free parents in Fayetteville, North Carolina, he was a minister of the African Methodist Episcopal Church who recruited three regiments of African-American troops during the Civil War and served as chaplain of an African-American regiment. Elected to the Mississippi state legislature in 1869, he was chosen the following year to complete **Jefferson Davis**'s last term in the Senate, becoming the first African-American senator (1870–71).

Revere, Paul 1735–1818 •*American patriot*• Born in Boston, he became a silversmith and copperplate printer and served as a lieutenant of artillery (1756). He was one of the raiders in the Boston Tea Party (1773), and was at the head of a secret society formed to keep watch on the British. On April 18, 1775, the night before the Battle of Lexington and Concord, he rode from Boston to Lexington and Lincoln, warning the people of Massachusetts that the British were on the move. His ride was celebrated in **Henry Wadsworth Longfellow**'s *The Midnight Ride of Paul Revere*.

Rexroth, Kenneth 1905–82 •*US poet, critic and father figure of the Beat Generation*• Born in South Bend, Indiana, he was largely self-educated. He worked as a manual laborer in the 1920s and became a prominent figure in the libertarian movement on the West Coast during the 1930s. He was a conscientious objector during World War II, serving as a hospital orderly in San Francisco; during this time he published his first book of verse, *In What Hour?* (1940). Other volumes include *The Signature of All Things* (1950), the quest-poem *The Dragon and the Unicorn* (1952) and *In Defense of the Earth* (1956). The best of his critical writing was published in *The Rexroth Reader* (1972).

Reyes, Alfonso 1889–1959 •*Mexican poet, critic, essayist and diarist*• Born in Monterrey, he became a diplomat, and was his country's ambassador to Argentina and Brazil. His poetry was influenced by European poets, especially **Mallarmé**, on whom he wrote *Mallarmé de nosotros* (1938, "Mallarmé Between Ourselves"). He spent many years in Spain and became one of the world's leading authorities on the Golden Age of Spanish literature. *Selected Essays* (1964) is a good introductory selection, while two important books on Mexico, *The Position of America* (1950) and *Mexico in a Nutshell* (1964), have been translated.

Reynaud, Paul 1878–1966 •*French statesman*• He was born in Barcelonnette. Originally a lawyer, he held many French government posts; he was influenced by **De Gaulle**'s advocacy of armored warfare, and he opposed appeasement. He was appointed prime minister in 1940 but the German onslaught led to his fall. He was replaced by **Philippe Pétain**, who sought an armistice. Reynaud was imprisoned by the Germans during the war. Afterward he reentered politics but without regaining his former influence, and lost his seat in 1962.

Reynolds, Albert 1932– •*Irish politician*• He was born in Rooskey, County Roscommon. In 1977 he became Fianna Fáil Member of Parliament for Longford-West Meath and was appointed minister for industry and commerce (1987–88) and finance (1988–91). Dismissed after an unsuccessful challenge to **Charles Haughey** (1991), he nevertheless won the party leadership by a large majority after Haughey's resignation (1992), and became prime minister (1992–94). In 1993 he entered into talks concerning the future of Northern Ireland with the British prime minister, **John Major**.

Reynolds, Burt 1936– •*US actor*• Born in Waycross, Georgia, he was a college football star before winning a scholarship to the Hyde Park Playhouse. He made his film debut in *Angel Baby* (1961) and was a regular performer in television series, including *Riverboat* (1959–60) and *Gunsmoke* (1962–65). The combination of a starring role in *Deliverance* (1972) and his decision to pose naked for *Cosmopolitan* magazine in 1972 consolidated his position as a top screen star. After the success of *Smokey and the Bandit* (1977) and *Hooper* (1978), his popularity declined in the 1980s. He found renewed popularity in the television series *Evening Shade* (1990–94), for which he received an Emmy award, and in 1997 was nominated for an Academy Award for his role in the film *Boogie Nights*.

Reynolds, Sir Joshua 1723–92 •*English portrait painter*• Born in Plympton Earls, near Plymouth, he settled in Plymouth Dock (now Devonport) in 1747. In Rome (1749–52) he studied **Raphael** and **Michelangelo**; while visiting the Vatican he caught a chill, which permanently affected his hearing. He then established himself in London and by 1760 was at the height of his fame. In 1764 he founded the Literary Club, of which **Samuel Johnson**, **David Garrick**, **Edmund Burke**, **Oliver Goldsmith**, **James Boswell** and **Richard Sheridan** were members. He was one of the earliest members of the Incorporated Society of Artists, and on the establishment of the Royal Academy (1768) was elected its first president. He was knighted in 1769. In 1784 he became painter to the king, and finished his painting of **Sarah Siddons** as the *Tragic Muse*, a work which exists in several versions. In 1789 his sight deteriorated, and he gave up painting. Reynolds' reputation rests largely on his portraits. These are notable for their power and expressiveness, and for the beauty of their coloring.

" "

A mere copier of nature never produces anything great.

*1770 **Discourses on Art**, no. 3, December 14.*

Rhazes *See* **Rāzī, ar-**

Rhee, Syngman 1875–1965 •*Korean statesman*• Born near Kaesong, he was imprisoned from 1897 to 1904 for campaigning for reform and a constitutional monarchy. Soon after his release he went to the US, then in 1910 he returned to Japanese-annexed Korea, and after the unsuccessful uprising of 1919 became president of the exiled Korean provisional government. On Japan's surrender in 1945, he returned to Korea, and in 1948 was elected president of the Republic of South Korea. He opposed the Korean truce of 1953, describing Korea's continued partition as an "appeasement of the Communists." Reelected for a fourth term as president in March 1960, he was obliged to resign in April after large-scale riots and the resignation of his cabinet, and went into exile.

Rheticus, *real name* **Georg Joachim von Lauchen** 1514–74 •*German astronomer and mathematician*• Born in Feldkirch, Austria, he became Professor of Mathematics at Wittenberg (1537). He is noted for his trigonometrical tables, some of which went to 15 decimal places. For a time he worked with **Copernicus**, and his own *Narratio prima de libris revolutionum Copernici* (1540, "The First Account of the Book on the Revolutions by Nicolaus Copernicus") was the first account of the Copernican theory.

Rhine, Joseph Banks 1895–1980 •*US psychologist, pioneer of parapsychology*• Born in Waterloo, Pennsylvania, he studied botany at Chicago, switched to psychology under William McDougall (1871–1938) at Duke University, and in 1937 became Professor of Psychology there. He cofounded the Parapsychology Laboratory there (1930), and the Institute of Parapsychology in Durham, North Carolina (1964). His laboratory-devised experiments involving packs of specially designed cards established the phenomenon of extrasensory perception and of telepathy on a statistical basis. He wrote *New Frontiers of the Mind* (1937) and *Extrasensory Perception* (1940).

Rhodes, Cecil John 1853–1902 •*South African statesman*• He was born in Bishop's Stortford, Hertfordshire. Sent to Natal because of his ill health, he subsequently made a fortune at the Kimberley diamond diggings, where he succeeded in amalgamating the several diamond companies to form the De Beers Consolidated Mines Company in 1888. He returned to England and studied at Oriel College, Oxford. He entered the Cape House of Assembly as member for Barkly. In 1890 he became prime minister of Cape Colony; but even before this he had become a ruling spirit in the extension of British territory in securing first Bechuanaland (later Botswana) as a protectorate (1884) and later (1889) the charter for the British South Africa Company, of which he was managing director until 1896, and whose territory was later to be known as Rhodesia. In 1896 he was forced to resign the Cape premiership in the aftermath of the **Jameson** Raid, but succeeded in quelling the Matabele rebellion by personal negotiations with the chiefs. Rhodes left a remarkable will which, besides making great benefactions to Cape Colony, founded scholarships at Oxford for Americans, Germans and members of the British Empire (later Commonwealth).

Rhys, Jean, *pseudonym of* **Gwen Williams** 1894–1979 •*British novelist*• She was born in the West Indies, her father a Welsh doctor and her mother a Creole. Educated at a convent in Roseau, Dominica, she moved to England in 1910 and joined a touring theater company. At the end of World War I, she married a Dutch poet, Max Hamer, and went to live on the Continent, spending many years in Paris. There she met writers and artists, including **Ernest Hemingway**, **James Joyce** and **Ford Madox Ford**. In 1927 she published *The Left Bank and Other Stories*, set mostly in Paris or in the West Indies of her childhood. Four novels followed: *Quartet* (originally published as *Postures*, 1928), *After Leaving Mr Mackenzie* (1930), *Voyage in the Dark* (1934) and *Good Morning Midnight* (1939). Her heroines were women attempting to live without regular financial support. After nearly 30 years she published in 1966 what was to become her best-known novel, *Wide Sargasso Sea*, which was based on the character of Rochester's mad wife in **Charlotte Brontë**'s *Jane Eyre*.

“ ”

I wanted to be black. I always wanted to be black ... Being black is warm and gay, being white is cold and sad.

1934 ***Voyage in the Dark****, chapter 1.*

Rhys Jones, Griff(ith) 1953– •*Welsh actor, writer, director and producer*• Born in Cardiff, he studied at Emmanuel College, Cambridge. His work has been mainly in comedy, beginning as a cowriter and actor in television series such as *Not the Nine O'Clock News* (1979–81) and *Alas Smith and Jones* (1982–87), the latter in collaboration with **Mel Smith**. He moved to the cinema with films such as *Morons from Outer Space* (1985) and *Wilt* (1989). He has worked extensively on radio and on stage, has directed opera at Covent Garden, and is a founder of the production company Talkback.

Rhys-Jones, Sophie *See* **Wessex, Sophie, Countess of**

Ribalta, Francisco de 1550–1628 •*Spanish painter*• Born in Castellón de la Plana, he studied in Rome and settled in Valencia. He was noted as a painter of historical subjects and for his use of chiaroscuro. His works include *The Last Supper* and *Christ Nailed to the Cross* (1582) in Madrid. His sons, José (1588–1656) and Juan (1597–1628), were also painters.

Ribbentrop, Joachim von 1893–1946 •*German Nazi politician*• Born in Wesel, he became a wine merchant. He joined the National Socialist Party in 1932, and as **Hitler**'s adviser in foreign affairs he was responsible in 1935 for the Anglo-German naval pact. The following year he was appointed ambassador to Great Britain, and then foreign minister (1938–45). He was captured by the British in 1945, condemned to death at Nuremberg and executed.

Ribera, Jusepe de, *called* **Lo Spagnoletto ("The Little Spaniard")** 1588–1656 •*Spanish painter and etcher*• Born in Játiva, he settled in Naples and became court painter there. He delighted in the horrible, often choosing such subjects as the martyrdom of the saints and painting them with a bold, unsympathetic style. Later works were calmer and more subtle, and include *The Immaculate Conception* and paintings of the Passion.

Ricardo, David 1772–1823 •*English political economist*• Born in London, he was a Dutch Jew by birth, and converted to Christianity on his marriage to Priscilla Ann Wilkinson, a Quaker, in 1793. In 1799 his interest in political economy was awakened by **Adam Smith**'s *Wealth of Nations*. His pamphlet, *The High Price of Bullion, A Proof of the Depreciation of Banknotes* (1809), was an argument in favor of a metallic basis of currency. In 1817 he published *Principles of Political Economy and Taxation*, a discussion of value, wages, rent, etc. In 1819 he became Radical Member of Parliament for Portarlington.

Ricci, Matteo 1552–1610 •*Italian founder of the Jesuit missions in China*• Born in Macerata, Papal States, he studied in Rome, was ordained in India (1580), and then went on to China (1582). His mastery of Chinese enabled him to write works that received much commendation from the Chinese literati. He was a successful missionary, although his methods aroused much controversy.

Ricci, Nina 1883–1970 •*Italian couturier*• Born in Turin, Italy, she became a dressmaker's apprentice at the age of 13, was in charge of an atelier by 18 and head designer at 20. In 1932 she opened her own Paris couture house with her jeweler husband, Louis. Her son Robert has managed the business since 1945. She became known for a high standard of workmanship that appealed to an elegant and wealthy clientele. She also made trousseaux for young brides-to-be. Her perfume, L'air du Temps, launched in 1948, is still highly popular worldwide.

Ricci, Sebastiano 1659–1734 •*Italian painter*• Born in Belluno, he was trained in Venice, where he fully assimilated the work of **Veronese** and developed a decorative style which was to influence **Giovanni Battista Tiepolo**. After extensive travel in Italy, he worked for two years (1701–03) in Vienna. In 1712 he traveled to England, via the Netherlands, with his nephew the painter Marco Ricci (1676–1730). The only complete work to survive from this time is a *Resurrection* in the apse of Chelsea Hospital chapel. He left England for Venice in 1716.

Riccio, David *See* **Rizzio, David**

Rice, Condoleezza 1954– •*US politician*• Born in Birmingham, Alabama, she was educated at the University of Denver and at Notre Dame and became a teacher in political science at Stanford University, California (1981–2001). She served as adviser on Soviet affairs in the government of **George Bush** (1989–91) and then returned to Stanford as its first female and first African-American provost. In 2001 she was appointed national security adviser by **George W Bush**.

Rice, Jerry Lee 1962– •*US football player*• Born in Starkville, Mississippi, his formidable catching skill was spotted early by his brothers, who threw him bricks as they helped their father, a mason, to build houses. He turned professional in 1985, joined the San Francisco 49ers, and by 1986 led the league with 86 catches. In 1987 he broke the National Football League (NFL) record when he caught 22 touchdown passes in just 12 games. He won many of the 1987 NFL awards. By 2001 he had 185 touchdowns. He helped lead the 49ers to three victories in the Super Bowl (1989, 1990, 1995), and joined the Oakland Raiders in 2001.

Rice, Sir Tim(othy Miles Bindon) 1944– •*English lyricist*• Born in Buckinghamshire, he studied law, but abandoned it to join the record company EMI. As a first musical contribution he wrote the lyrics to music by **Andrew Lloyd Webber** for *Joseph and the Amazing Technicolor Dreamcoat* (1968). The partnership went on to produce *Jesus Christ Superstar* (1971), *Evita* (1978) and *Cricket* (1986). Rice has also written *Chess* (1984), the film musical *Aladdin* (1992; Best Original Song Oscar 1993 for "A Whole New World"); *Beauty and the Beast* (1994), and *The Lion King* (1994). In addition to his television appearances and various publications, he has been chairman of the newly formed Foundation for Sport and the Arts since 1991. He was knighted in 1994.

Rice-Davies, Mandy (Marilyn) 1944– •*Welsh model and showgirl*• Born in Wales, the daughter of a police officer, she grew up in the West Midlands, where she worked in a department store before becoming a showgirl at Murray's Cabaret Club, London. There she met and befriended **Christine Keeler** and the osteopath **Stephen Ward**, who introduced her to influential London society. She was a witness at Ward's trial, and in reply to a suggestion that Lord Astor denied knowing her, she gave the celebrated retort: "He would, wouldn't he?" After the trial she moved to Israel, where she established two night clubs called Mandy. She later returned to live in London.

Rich, Adrienne Cecile 1929– •*US poet*• Born in Baltimore, Maryland, and educated at Radcliffe College, Cambridge, Massachusetts, she published her first volume of verse, *A Change of World* (1951), while she was still an undergraduate. It foreshadowed her emergence as the most forceful US woman poet since **Elizabeth Bishop** and **Sylvia Plath**. She was Professor of English and Feminist Studies at Stanford from 1986 to 1993. Later collections include *Snapshots of a Daughter-in-Law* (1963) and *The Will to Change* (1971). After her husband's suicide, Rich began to align herself more directly with the women's movement, and her prose became almost as influential as her verse. Her prose works include *Of Woman Born* (1976), *On Lies, Secrets, and Silence* (1979) and *Blood, Bread, and Poetry* (1986), and later verse includes *The Dream of a Common Language* (1978) and *Dark Fields of the Republic* (1995).

" "

Only where there is language is there world.

1969 ***Leaflets****, "The Demon Lover."*

Richard I, *known as* **Cœur de Lion ("the Lion Heart")** 1157–99 •*King of England*• He was born in Oxford, the third son of **Henry II** and **Eleanor of Aquitaine**. Of his ten-year reign he spent only a few months in England, and it is doubtful that he spoke English. For the rest of the time he was taking part in the crusades or, induced by his mother, in rebellion with his brothers Henry and Geoffrey against their father Henry II (1173 and 1189), on the second occasion in league with **Philip II** of France. Richard became king of England, Duke of Normandy and Count of Anjou on July 5, 1189. In 1190 he and Philip set out to join the Third Crusade. They spent the winter in Sicily, where the throne had recently been seized by the Norman **Tancred**; Tancred made his peace with Richard by giving up to him Richard's sister Johanna, the widowed queen, and by betrothing his daughter to Prince **Arthur**, Richard's nephew and heir. When in 1191 part of Richard's fleet was wrecked off Cyprus, the island's ruler, **Isaac I Comnenus**, treated the crews with hostility. Richard sailed back from Rhodes, defeated and deposed Isaac, and gave his crown to **Guy of Lusignan**. In Cyprus he married Berengaria of Navarre, and on June 8 landed near Acre, which surrendered. Richard's exploits, including his march to Joppa, two advances on Jerusalem (which he failed to regain), his capture of the fortresses in southern Palestine, and his rescue of Joppa, excited the admiration of Christendom. In September he concluded a three years' peace with **Saladin**, and set off alone on the journey home. Making his way in disguise through the dominions of his enemy, Leopold, Duke of Austria, he was recognized and was seized and handed over to the emperor **Henry VI** (1193), who demanded a heavy ransom for his release. Richard's subjects raised the money, and, despite his brother John's attempts to prevent him, he returned home in March 1194. John was forgiven, and Richard set off again for France, where he spent the rest of his life campaigning against Philip. The government of England was meanwhile entrusted to the justiciary **Hubert Walter**. Richard was killed while besieging the castle of Chalus, and was buried at Fontevrault.

Richard II 1367–1400 •*King of England*• Born in Bordeaux, France, the son of **Edward the Black Prince**, he succeeded his grandfather, **Edward III** in 1377 at the age of ten, and for a time his uncle, **John of Gaunt**, gained control. Richard's reign was characterized by a struggle between his own desire to act independently and the barons' concern to check his power. Richard showed great resolution and courage in facing the Peasants' Revolt of 1381, which had been caused largely by the introduction of the notorious poll tax to pay for war with France and the extravagance of the court. The men of Kent, led by **Wat Tyler**, ran riot pillaging and killing in London. They met the king at Smithfield (June 15), where, during the negotiations, Tyler was struck down, but Richard declared that he would grant them the concessions they demanded. From this time John of Gaunt exercised less power, and in 1386 he retired to live on the Continent. In 1385 Richard invaded Scotland and burned Edinburgh. Meanwhile his uncle, Thomas of Woodstock, Duke of Gloucester (1355–97), formed a baronial coalition in opposition to him. They impeached and executed several of his friends in the so-called Merciless Parliament of 1388. However, on May 3, 1389, Richard promptly declared himself of age, and for eight years he ruled as a moderate constitutional monarch. Later, he took a more despotic view of the monarchy, and he had a number of his enemies, including **Thomas Arundel**, arrested and executed or murdered. In 1398 several lords were banished, including John of Gaunt's son Henry Bolingbroke. The following year John died, and Henry succeeded him as Duke of Lancaster. Richard went over to Ireland in May, and Henry landed on July 4. Richard hurried back, submitted at Flint (August 19), and was put in the Tower. On September 29 he resigned the Crown, and the next day was deposed by parliament in favor of Lancaster, who succeeded as **Henry IV**. Richard was imprisoned in Pontefract Castle and died there, probably murdered, early in 1400.

Richard III 1452–85 •*King of England*• He was born in Fotheringay Castle. After the defeat and death of his father, Richard, 3rd Duke of **York**, in 1460, he was sent to Utrecht for safety; he returned to England after his brother Edward had won the Crown as **Edward IV** (1461), and was made Duke of Gloucester. When Edward went into exile in 1470, Richard went with him, and he helped bring about Edward's restoration the following year. He may have been implicated in the murder of Prince Edward, **Henry VI**'s son, after Edward's victory at Tewkesbury, and in the murder of Henry himself in the Tower. In 1472 Richard married Anne, the younger daughter of the Earl of Warwick. This alliance was resented by Richard's brother, the Duke of **Clarence**, who had married the elder sister and did not wish to share Warwick's extensive possessions. Clarence was impeached and put to death in the Tower in 1478. Richard has been suspected of his murder, but the evidence is inconclusive. In 1482 Richard commanded the army that invaded Scotland and captured Berwick. In 1483, while still in Yorkshire, he heard of King Edward's death, and learned that he himself had been designated guardian of Edward's 13-year-old son and heir, **Edward V**. On his way south, the Protector arrested the 2nd Earl Rivers and Lord Richard Grey, the uncle and stepbrother of the young king, and rallied the old nobility to his support. The dowager queen was induced to give up her other son, the little Duke of York, and he was put into the Tower together with his younger brother, the king. Richard is believed to have had his nephews murdered (though this has been disputed). Parliament sought Richard's accession to the throne, and on July 6, 1483, he was crowned, Rivers and Grey having been executed on June 25. Richard's principal supporter, Henry Stafford, 2nd Duke of Buckingham, changed sides soon after Richard's coronation and entered into a plot with the friends of Henry Tudor, Earl of Richmond (afterward **Henry VII**) and chief representative of the House of Lancaster, to achieve Richard's overthrow and proclaim Henry king. The attempted uprising collapsed, and Buckingham was executed on November 2. Henry landed at Milford Haven on August 7, 1485. Richard met him at Bosworth Field on August 22; he fought with courage, but in the end he lost his kingdom and his life.

Richard, Sir Cliff, *real name* **Harry Rodger Webb** 1940– •*English pop singer*• He was born in Lucknow, India, and taken to England at the age of eight. He began his professional career playing with the Dick Teague Group, and formed his own band, The Shadows (originally called The Drifters), in 1958. Following the success of "Living Doll" (1959), The Shadows were hailed as Great Britain's answer to US rock. Cliff Richard made a series of family musical films during the 1960s, including *Expresso Bongo* (1960), *The Young Ones* (1961) and *Summer Holiday* (1962). After be became a born-again Christian, his clean-cut image damaged his reputation with rock fans, but he became a British entertainment institution. He was knighted in 1995. In 1996 he took to the stage, playing the eponymous hero in *Heathcliff*.

Richard de Bury *See* **Aungerville, Richard**

Richards, Alun 1929– •*Welsh novelist, short-story writer and playwright*• Born in Pontypridd, Glamorgan, he was educated at University College, Swansea. He has published six novels, including *The Elephant You Gave Me* (1963) and *A Woman of Experience* (1969), and two collections of short stories (*Dai Country*, 1973, and *The Former Miss Merthyr Tydfil*, 1976). For much of his material he drew on his varied experiences working as a probation officer, a sailor and a teacher. Besides editing several short-story anthologies, he has written a book about Welsh rugby and many plays and adaptations for television, notably *The Onedin Line*.

Richards, Ceri 1903–71 •*Welsh artist*• Born in Dunvant, near Swansea, he studied at Swansea School of Art (1920–24) and at the Royal College of Art, London (1924–27). In 1932 he began making collages and constructions which showed the influence of **Max Ernst** and the surrealists generally. He joined the London Group in 1937, and taught at Chelsea School of Art (1945–55), at the Slade School of Art (1956–61) and at the Royal College (1961–62). In addition to his paintings, he designed opera sets, stained-glass windows and vestments. He won the Einaudi prize at the Venice Biennale in 1962.

Richards, Dickinson Woodruff 1895–1973 •*US physician and Nobel Prize winner*• Born in Orange, New Jersey, and educated at Yale, he specialized in cardiology, which he taught at Columbia University (1928–61). With **André Cournand**, Richards developed **Werner Forssman**'s technique of cardiac catheterization into an important procedure for studying blood pressure, oxygen tension and a variety of other physiological variables in health and disease. Their work led to a better understanding and treatment of shock, and provided the basis for much of modern cardiology. The three men shared the 1956 Nobel Prize for physiology or medicine. Richards was also an eloquent advocate for improved standards of medical care for the elderly and disadvantaged.

Richards, Frank, *pseudonym of* **Charles Hamilton** 1875–1961 •*English children's writer, author of the "Billy Bunter" series*• Born in London, he was educated privately and began to write stories for magazines and comics while still a schoolboy. He wrote for boys' magazines, particularly *The Gem* (1906–39) and *The Magnet* (1908–40), and produced many well-known school stories in book and play form, including the "Tom Merry" and "Billy Bunter" series.

Richards, Sir Gordon 1904–86 •*English jockey*• Born in Oakengates, Shropshire, he was the son of a coal miner. In 34 seasons (1921–54) he was champion jockey 26 times, and rode 4,870 winners. Toward the end of his career, in 1953, he finally rode his first Derby winner, Pinza; he was knighted in the same year. He took up training in 1954 after retiring from riding.

Richards, I(vor) A(rmstrong) 1893–1979 •*English scholar and literary critic, initiator of the so-called New Criticism movement*• Born in Sandbach, Cheshire, he studied psychology at Magdalene College, Cambridge. Later professor at Cambridge (1922–29), with **C K Ogden** he developed the idea of Basic English, and in 1924 published the influential *Principles of Literary Criticism*, followed by *Science and Poetry* (1925) and *Practical Criticism* (1929). In 1939 he left Cambridge to take up a professorship at Harvard (1939–63). There he taught **William Empson**, became a friend of **Robert Lowell, Jr**, and began himself to write poetry, publishing, among other collections, *Goodbye Earth and Other Poems* (1958).

" "

To be forced by desire into any unwarrantable belief is a calamity.

1924 ***Principles of Literacy Criticism***.

Richards, Keith *See* **Rolling Stones, The**

Richardson, Dorothy M(iller) 1873–1957 •*English novelist*• She was born in Abingdon, Oxfordshire, and after her mother's suicide in 1895 moved to London and worked as a teacher, clerk and dentist's assistant. She became a Fabian and had an affair with **H G Wells**, which led to a miscarriage and a near collapse in 1907. She started her writing career with works about the Quakers and **George Fox** (1914). Her first novel, *Painted Roofs* (1915), began a 12-volume sequence entitled *Pilgrimage*. She was the first exponent of the stream of consciousness style later made famous by **Virginia Woolf**.

Richardson, H(enry) H(andel), *pseudonym of* **Ethel Florence Lindesay Robertson**, *née* **Richardson** 1870–1946 •*Australian novelist and short-story writer*• She was born in Fitzroy, Melbourne, and after an unhappy childhood during which her father died insane, she traveled widely with her mother and studied music with distinction at the Leipzig Conservatory. She married a fellow student, John George Robertson, and moved to London, where her first novel, *Maurice Guest*, was published in 1908. Her major work was the trilogy *The Fortunes of Richard Mahoney* (1917–30). A later novel, *The Young Cosima* (1939), a study of the lives of **Franz Liszt**, **Richard Wagner** and Wagner's second wife, Cosima von Bülow, reflects her musical interests. She also wrote some short stories and an autobiography.

Richardson, H(enry) H(obson) 1838–86 •*US architect*• Born in Priestley Plantation, Louisiana, he was educated at Harvard and studied architecture in Paris. He initiated the Romanesque revival in the US, leading to a distinctively US style of architecture. He designed a number of churches, the Allegheny Co buildings in Pittsburgh and halls of residence at Harvard, and his range extended to private houses as well as railway stations and wholesale stores.

Richardson, Ian William 1934– •*Scottish actor*• He was born in Edinburgh and trained at the Royal College of Dramatic Art in Glasgow. His many plays with the Royal Shakespeare Company include *A Midsummer Night's Dream* (1962) and *Richard III* (1975). His other theater work includes Broadway appearances in *My Fair Lady* (1976) and *Lolita* (1981). He made his television debut in *As You Like It* (1962) and followed it with appearances in *Tinker, Tailor, Soldier, Spy* (1979), *The Winslow Boy* (1989) and as Francis Urquhart in *House of Cards* (1990), *To Play the King* (1993) and *The Final Cut* (1995). His film appearances include *Cry Freedom* (1987) and *Dark City* (1998).

Richardson, Miranda 1958– •*English actress*• Born in Southport, Merseyside, she studied at the Old Vic Theatre School, Bristol. She acted widely on stage before moving to the screen in films such as *Dance with a Stranger* (1985), *Enchanted April* (1992; Golden Globe award for Best Comedy Actress), *Damage* (1993; British Academy of Film and Television Arts award for Best Supporting Actress) and *Get Carter* (1999). Her extensive television work has included roles in *Blackadder* (1986–89) and *A Dance to the Music of Time* (1997).

Richardson, Sir Owen Willans 1879–1959 •*English physicist and Nobel Prize winner*• Born in Dewsbury, Yorkshire, he was educated at Cambridge, where at the Cavendish Laboratory he began his famous work on thermionics, a term he coined to describe the phenomenon of the emission of electricity from hot bodies. For this work he was awarded the Nobel Prize for physics in 1928. He was appointed Professor of Physics at King's College London in 1914, and from 1924 to 1944 was Yarrow Research Professor of the Royal Society.

Richardson, Sir Ralph David 1902–83 •*English actor*• Born in Cheltenham, Gloucestershire, he established his reputation with the Birmingham Repertory Company from 1926. He moved to the Old Vic Company (1930), taking many leading parts, including the title roles of **W Somerset Maugham**'s *Sheppey* (1930–32) and **J B**

Priestley's *Johnson over Jordan* (1938), and was codirector after his service in World War II. He played with the Stratford-on-Avon company (1952), and toured Australia and New Zealand (1955). His many stage appearances included *West of Suez* (1971), *The Cherry Orchard* (1978) and *The Understanding* (1982). His films include *Things to Come* (1936), *Anna Karenina* (1948), *Dr Zhivago* (1965), *Oh! What a Lovely War* (1969), *A Doll's House* (1973) and *Invitation to the Wedding* (1983).

Richardson, Samuel 1689–1761 •*English novelist*• Born in Mackworth, Derbyshire, he was apprenticed to a printer, married his master's daughter, and set up in business for himself in Salisbury Court, London. His first novel, *Pamela* (1740), is "a series of familiar letters ... published in order to cultivate the Principles of Virtue and Religion," and this was the aim of all his works. In his second novel, *Clarissa, or the History of a Young Lady* (7 vols, 1748), Richardson depicts the high life, of which he confessed he knew little, but the novel made Richardson famous, and he became acquainted with **Samuel Johnson** and **Edward Young** among others. His third novel, *Sir Charles Grandison* (1754), designed to portray the perfect gentleman, turns on the question of divided love. His work influenced writers such as **Jean Jacques Rousseau** and **Denis Diderot**, and the epistolary method was a means to suggest authenticity at a time when mere fiction was frowned upon.

Richelieu, Armand Jean Duplessis, Duc de, *known as* **Cardinal Richelieu** 1585–1642 •*French prelate and statesman*• He was born into a noble but impoverished family near Chinon, and was consecrated Bishop of Luçon, which was in the family's control, at the age of 22. In 1614 he became adviser to **Marie de Médicis**, in 1622 was made cardinal, and in 1624 became Minister of State under **Louis XIII**. In this capacity he made an alliance with Great Britain, which he strengthened by the marriage (1625) of the king's sister **Henrietta Maria** with **Charles I**. One of his principal aims was to destroy the political power of the Huguenots. La Rochelle was starved into submission (1628), and he destroyed Montauban, the last refuge of Huguenot independence. From 1629 he was Chief Minister and effective ruler of France. He sought to reduce the power of the **Habsburg**s by supporting the Protestants of the North and **Gustav II Adolf** of Sweden, to whom he gave a large subsidy, and the two treaties of Cherasco (1631) gave France a strategic supremacy. Meanwhile Richelieu successfully overcame a powerful conspiracy launched against him by the queen mother and others, and further intrigues and attempted rebellions were crushed with merciless severity. In July 1632 Richelieu seized the Duchy of Lorraine, and in 1635 entered the Thirty Years' War by declaring war on Spain. His policy soon led to the disorganization of the power of Spain, to the victories of Wolfenbüttel and Kempten over the imperialist forces in Germany and, later (in 1641), in Savoy, and to the ascendancy of the French party. At home the great French nobles continued to plot his downfall, and his safety lay in the king's helplessness without him. At the cost of high taxation and the suppression of constitutional government, Richelieu had built up the power of the French Crown and achieved for France a dominating position in Europe. Although he put what he thought were the interests of his country before personal ambition, he too often forgot in his methods the laws of morality and humanity.

“ ”

Wounds inflicted by the sword heal more easily than those inflicted by the tongue.

1688 ***Testament Politique***.

Richler, Mordecai 1931–2001 •*Canadian novelist*• Born in Montreal, he grew up in a Jewish working-class neighborhood and attended Sir George Williams College. His first novel, *The Acrobats* (1954), owed much to **Ernest Hemingway**, and he subsequently disowned it. In 1955 he published *Son of a Smaller Hero*, about a young man endeavoring to escape the Jewish ghetto and North American society in general. It was the first of several books for which he was accused of anti-Semitism. He achieved a breakthrough with *The Apprenticeship of Duddy Kravitz* (1959), about an endearing shyster, the same year he moved to England. Subsequent novels, such as *The Incomparable Auk* (1963), *Cocksure* (1968) and *Solomon Gursky Was Here* (1990), have enhanced his reputation as a bawdy humorist and vitriolic satirist.

Richter, Burton 1931– •*US particle physicist and Nobel Prize winner*• He was born in New York City and graduated from MIT. He then joined the high-energy physics laboratory at Stanford University, where he became professor in 1967. He was largely responsible for the Stanford Positron-Electron Accelerating Ring (SPEAR), an accelerator designed to collide positrons and electrons at high energies, and to study the resulting elementary particles. In 1974 he led a team which discovered the J/y hadron, a new heavy elementary particle which supported **Sheldon Glashow**'s hypothesis of charm quarks. Many related particles were subsequently discovered. He shared the 1976 Nobel Prize for physics with **Samuel Ting**, who had discovered the J/y almost simultaneously.

Richter, Charles Francis 1900–85 •*US seismologist*• He was born near Hamilton, Ohio. Educated at Stanford University and the California Institute of Technology (Caltech), he worked at the Carnegie Institute, where he met **Beno Gutenberg** and became interested in seismology. With Gutenberg he devised the Richter scale of earthquake strength (1927–35). In 1937 he returned to Caltech, where he spent the rest of his career.

Richter, Johann Paul Friedrich, *pseudonym* **Jean Paul** 1763–1825 •*German novelist and humorist*• He was born in Wunsiedel, northern Bavaria. From 1787 to 1796 he worked as a tutor and wrote, among other works, the satirical *Auswahl aus des Teufels Papieren* (1789, "Extracts from the Devil's Papers"), idylls such as *Dominie Wuz* (1793) and *Quintus Fixlein* (1796, translated by **Thomas Carlyle**, 1827), and the grand romances *Die unsichtbare Loge* (1793, Eng trans *The Invisible Lodge*, 1883) and *Campanerthal* (1797). *The Invisible Lodge* was his first literary success, and *Hesperus* (1795, Eng trans 1865) made him famous. For a few years he was widely idolized. He married in 1801 and three years later settled in Bayreuth. His later works include *Titan* (1800–03, Eng trans 1862), which he considered his masterpiece, and *Dr. Katzenbergers Badereise* (1809, "Dr. Katzenberger's Trip to the Spa"), the best of his satirico-humorous writings.

Richthofen, Manfred, Baron von 1882–1918 •*German airman*• Born in Schweidnitz, he joined the cavalry and then the German air force. During World War I, as commander of Fighter Group I ("Richthofen's Flying Circus"), he was noted for his high number (80) of aerial victories and was known as the "Red Baron." He was shot down behind British lines.

Rickert, Heinrich 1863–1936 •*German philosopher*• Born in Danzig (Gdansk, Poland), he became professor at Freiburg (1894) and Heidelberg (1916). He was a pupil of Wilhelm Windelband (1848–1915), and with him a founder of the Baden school of neo-Kantianism, which developed a distinctive theory of historical knowledge and the foundations of the social sciences. Rickert argued for a *Kulturwissenschaft* (science of culture) which could be an objective science of those universal concepts like religion, art and law that emerge from the multiplicity of individual cultures and societies. His views contrasted strongly with those of **Wilhelm Dilthey** and were a great influence on **Max Weber** and others.

Rickey, (Wesley) Branch, *nicknamed* **the Mahatma** 1881–1965 •*US baseball manager and administrator*• Born in Stockdale, Ohio, he profoundly influenced professional baseball. In 1919, as manager of the St Louis Cardinals, he introduced the farm system, whereby major league clubs linked themselves to lower-grade clubs to develop young players. This brought his team four world championships and made it the most profitable in baseball.

Rickman, Alan 1947– •*English actor*• Born in London to Irish-Welsh parents, he trained at the Royal Academy of Dramatic Art. He was spotted playing Valmont in *Les Liaisons Dangereuses* on Broadway by a Hollywood scout in 1985 and was hired to play Hans Gruber in the hugely successful action film *Die Hard*. He won a British Academy of Film and Television Arts Best Supporting Actor award for his Sheriff of Nottingham in *Robin Hood, Prince of Thieves* in 1991. His other films include *Truly, Madly, Deeply* (1991), *Sense and Sensibility* (1995), *Michael Collins* (1996) and *Galaxy*

Quest (1999). His television work includes *The Barchester Chronicles* (1982) and *Rasputin* (1996), for which he received an Emmy award. In 1996 he directed his first film, *The Winter Guest*.

Ricoeur, Paul 1913– •*French philosopher*• Born in Valence, Drôme, and educated at the Lycée de Rennes and at the University of Paris, he became professor successively at Strasbourg (1948–56), Paris-Nanterre (1956–70) and Chicago (1970). He was a pupil of **Gabriel Marcel**, and as a prisoner in World War II studied **Karl Jaspers**, **Martin Heidegger** and **Edmund Husserl**. Their influence is evident in his work, and he has published commentaries on Husserl. He has been an influential figure in both French and Anglo-US philosophy, engaging critically with various contemporary methodologies across a wide range of problems about the nature of language, interpretation, human action and will, freedom and evil.

Ride, Sally Kristen 1951– •*US astronaut, the first US woman in space*• Born in Los Angeles, she was educated at Stanford University, taking a doctoral degree in physics in 1978. In 1978 she was selected as an astronautical candidate by NASA (National Aeronautics and Space Administration), and she became a mission specialist on space shuttle flight crews, including a six-day flight of the orbiter Challenger in 1983. In 1987, her final year as an astronaut, she published a report to NASA on "Leadership—and America's Future in Space." Since 1989 she has been Professor of Physics at the University of California, San Diego, and director of the California Space Institute.

Ridgeway, John 1938– •*English transatlantic oarsman and explorer*• Educated at the Nautical College, Pangbourne, he served in the Merchant Navy before completing his national service. After two years at the Royal Military Academy, Sandhurst, he was commissioned into the Parachute Regiment and served worldwide. In 1966 he rowed across the Atlantic Ocean in 92 days from the US to Ireland with **Chay Blyth**. He then sailed the Atlantic Ocean singlehandedly to South America, led an expedition along the Amazon River, and another across the Chilean icecap.

Ridgway, Matthew B(unker) 1895–1993 •*US general*• Born in Fort Monroe, Virginia, he trained at West Point, then commanded the 82nd Airborne Division in Sicily (1943) and Normandy (1944). He commanded the 18th Airborne Corps in the Northwest Europe campaign (1944–45) and the US 8th Army in United Nations operations in Korea (1950). He replaced **Douglas MacArthur** as commander of US and UN forces in Korea and in occupied Japan (1951), and succeeded General **Eisenhower** as supreme Allied commander in Europe (1952–53). He later served as army chief of staff (1953).

Riding, Laura, *née* **Reichenfeld**, *later* **Laura Riding Jackson** 1901–91 •*US poet, critic, story writer, novelist and polemicist*• The daughter of an Austrian immigrant, she took courses at Cornell University, and married Louis Gottschalk, a history teacher there. Her first collection of poetry, *The Close Chaplet*, was published in England under the imprint of the Hogarth Press. She was the lover (1926–29) and then the literary associate (1929–39) of **Robert Graves**, with whom she lived in Mallorca, London and Rennes. In 1941 she married Schuyler Jackson, a minor poet and farmer. Her poetry is unlike any other poetry of the 20th century: based rhythmically on a four-accent line, it seeks to examine the reasons for human existence, and to establish the nature of human obligations.

" "

Art, whose honesty must work through artifice, cannot avoid cheating truth.

1975 ***Selected Poems: In Five Sets****, preface.*

Ridley, Nicholas c. 1500–55 •*English Protestant churchman*• Born near Haltwhistle, Northumberland, he studied at Cambridge, Paris and Louvain (1527–30). His various posts included chaplain to **Thomas Cranmer** and **Henry VIII**, Bishop of Rochester (1547) and Bishop of London (1550). He was an outspoken reformer, and helped Cranmer prepare the Thirty-Nine Articles. On the death of **Edward VI**, he denounced **Mary I** and **Elizabeth I** as illegitimate, and supported the cause of Lady **Jane Grey**. On Mary I's accession, he was imprisoned and executed.

Ridley (of Liddesdale), Nicholas Ridley, Baron 1929–93 •*English Conservative politician*• He was born in Newcastle upon Tyne, the son of the 3rd Viscount Ridley. He was educated at Eton and Oxford, and embarked on an industrial career, later turning to politics and becoming a Member of Parliament in 1959. He held various ministerial posts until 1983, when he entered the Cabinet of **Margaret Thatcher**. Regarded as one of her closest allies, he moved from the Department of Environment (1986–89), where he was responsible for introducing the generally unpopular community charge (poll tax), to the Department of Trade and Industry (1988–90). He resigned his office following a controversial magazine article in which he denounced federalist European ideas and German ambitions.

Ridolfo, Roberto di, *also called* **Roberto Ridolfi** 1531–1612 •*Florentine conspirator*• He was born in Florence and went to London on business. In 1570 he organized a Roman Catholic plot, supported by Spain, to marry **Mary Queen of Scots** to **Thomas Howard**, 4th Duke of Norfolk, and overthrow Queen **Elizabeth I**. The plot, which comprised the murder of Elizabeth and a Spanish invasion of England, was discovered when an emissary was seized. Ridolfo returned to Italy and in 1600 became a Florentine senator.

Rie, Dame Lucie, *née* **Gomperz** 1902–95 •*Austrian potter*• Born in Vienna, she trained at the Kunstgewerbeschule. In 1938 she and her husband moved to England, and from the end of World War II until 1960 she shared a workshop with Hans Coper (1920–81), producing ceramic jewelry and buttons while continuing her individual work. She pioneered the production of stoneware in an electric kiln, and produced stoneware, tin-glazed earthenware and porcelain pots throughout her working life with a precision and technical control that influenced many leading contemporary potters. Her work bridged the gap between the craft of pottery and the art of sculpture. She was given the honorary title of Dame Commander, Order of the British Empire, in 1991.

Riefenstahl, Leni (Helene Bertha Amalie) 1902–2003 •*German film director*• Born in Berlin, she studied fine art and ballet and became a professional dancer and actor. She appeared in some of the mountaineering films made by Arnold Fanck (1889–1974), and in 1931 she formed Riefenstahl Films and made her directorial debut with *Das blaue Licht* (1932, "The Blue Light"). She was appointed film adviser to the National Socialist Party by **Hitler**. Both her *Triumph des Willens* (1934, "Triumph of the Will"), a compelling record of the Nuremberg rally, and *Olympische Spiele 1936* (1936, "Olympiad") were propagandist documentaries of impressive technique. At the end of World War II she was interned by the Allies and held on charges of pro-Nazi activity, although these were subsequently dropped. She never fully went back to filmmaking, and became a photojournalist under the name of Helen Jacobs, covering the 1972 Olympic Games for the *Sunday Times*. She published her autobiography, *The Sieve of Time*, in 1993.

Riel, Louis 1844–85 •*Canadian politician and insurrectionist*• He was born in St Boniface, Manitoba. He succeeded his father as a leader of the Métis, of mixed Native American and French-Canadian ancestry, who were opposed to the incorporation of the Northwest Territories into the Dominion of Canada as well as to the encroachment of white, English-speaking settlers on their lands in Manitoba. He headed the Red River Rebellion in 1869–70, but the rebellion failed, and he was forced to flee to the US. On his return in 1873 he was elected to the House of Commons in Ottawa, but later barred from politics. In 1884 Riel responded to the pleas of the Métis in Saskatchewan and became involved in a second rebellion; it was suppressed, and he was hanged for treason.

Riemann, (Georg Friedrich) Bernhard 1826–66 •*German mathematician*• Born in Breselenz, he studied at Göttingen, where he was appointed Professor of Mathematics in 1859. His first publication (1851) was on the foundations of the theory of functions of a complex variable, including the result now known as the Riemann mapping theorem. In a later paper on Abelian functions (1857), he introduced the idea of Riemann surface to deal with multivalued algebraic functions; this was to become a key concept in the development of analysis. His famous lecture in 1854, "On the hypotheses that underlie geometry," first presented his notion of an *n*-dimensional curved space. These ideas were essential to the formulation of **Albert Einstein**'s theory of general relativity, and continue to play a vital role in theoretical physics. Riemann's name is also associated with the zeta function, which is central to the study of the distribution of prime numbers. The Riemann hypothesis is a famous unsolved problem concerning this function.

Riemerschmid, Richard 1868–1957 •*German architect and designer*• He was born in Munich, and in 1897, after varied experience, he founded *Werkstätten* (craft workshops) there. His early furniture resembled the linear freedom of art nouveau without the naturalistic decoration, whereas his designs of 1905 for the Deutsche Werkstätten in Dresden were functional, of simple construction and suitable for mass production. He was a founder and member of the Deutsche Werkbund (1907). His large output included buildings, furniture and interiors, glass and ceramics, cutlery, light fittings and graphics.

Rietveld, Gerrit Thomas 1888–1964 •*Dutch architect and furniture designer*• Born in Utrecht, he started his career as a woodworker. He attended night school, and began to design his own furniture, including the famous "red-blue" chair of 1918. The exploitation of space and its relation to physical objects were at the core of all Rietveld's work. The architectural equivalent of the chair was the Schröder House in Utrecht (1924), both also exhibiting the rectilinear quality and use of color associated with the De Stijl movement. He designed many buildings, and the culmination of his work is the building which houses the Van Gogh Museum, Amsterdam, completed posthumously in 1973.

Rieu, E(mile) V(ictor) 1887–1972 •*English editor and translator*• He was born in London. A classical scholar, he formed the habit of translating aloud to his wife, and it was her interest in *The Odyssey* that encouraged him to start on his own version. It was offered to **Allen Lane**, the founder of Penguin, and was published in 1946. It formed the cornerstone of the new Penguin Classics, of which Rieu became editor, and had sold over two million copies by 1964.

Rifkind, Sir Malcolm Leslie 1946– •*Scottish Conservative politician*• Born in Edinburgh, he was educated at the University of Edinburgh and became a lawyer and then a Member of Parliament (1974–97). Despite resigning from the Opposition front bench in protest of the antidevolution policy of his party, he was appointed Scottish office minister (1979–82) and foreign office minister (1982–86). After serving as the youngest-ever secretary of state for Scotland (1986–90), he became secretary of state for transport in 1990, defense secretary in 1992 and foreign secretary in 1995. He lost his seat in the 1997 election, and was knighted that year.

Rigg, Dame (Enid) Diana (Elizabeth) 1938– •*English actress*• She was born in Doncaster, South Yorkshire, and after studying at the Royal Academy of Dramatic Art, made her professional debut in *The Caucasian Chalk Circle* (1957). She appeared in repertory before joining the Royal Shakespeare Memorial Company (later the RSC) (1959–64). Her long and distinguished stage career includes *Twelfth Night* (1966) for the RSC, *The Misanthrope* (1973) at the National Theatre, and such later productions as *Medea* (1993–94, Tony award) and *Who's Afraid of Virginia Woolf?* (1996–97). On television, she won lasting fame as the leather-clad Emma Peel in *The Avengers* (1965–68). Her other television work includes her own series *Diana* (1973), *King Lear* (1983) and *Mother Love* (1989), for which she received a British Academy of Film and Television Arts award. Her films include *On Her Majesty's Secret Service* (1969) and *The Hospital* (1971). She was given the honorary title of Dame Commander, Order of the British Empire, in 1994.

Righi, Augusto 1850–1920 •*Italian physicist*• Born in Bologna, he was educated in his hometown, taught physics at various institutions including Padua, Palermo and Bologna. He invented an induction electrometer (1872) capable of detecting and amplifying small electrostatic charges, and his *L'ottica delle oscillazioni elettriche* (1897), which summarized his results, is considered a classic of experimental electromagnetism. By 1900 he had begun to work on X-rays and the **Zeeman** effect. In 1903 he wrote the first paper on wireless telegraphy.

Riley, Bridget Louise 1931– •*English painter*• Born in London, she studied at Goldsmiths College of Art (1949–52) and at the Royal College of Art (1952–55), holding her first one-woman show in London in 1962. A leading op artist, she manipulates overall flat patterns, originally in black and white but later in color, using repeated shapes or undulating lines, often creating an illusion of movement, as in *Fall* (1963) and *Winter Palace* (1981). She was the first English painter to win the major painting prize at the Venice Biennale (1968).

Rilke, Rainer Maria 1875–1926 •*Austrian lyric poet*• Born in Prague, he studied art history in Prague, Munich and Berlin. His early works include *Vom lieben Gott und Anderes* (1900, Eng trans *Stories of God*, 1931) and *Das Stundenbuch* (1905, Eng trans *Poems from the Book of Hours*, 1941), written after two journeys to Russia (1899–1900), where he met **Leo Tolstoy** and was influenced by Russian Pietism. In 1901 he married Klara Westhoff, a pupil of **Auguste Rodin**, whose secretary Rilke became in Paris, publishing *Auguste Rodin* (1903, Eng trans 1919). He also wrote *Neue Gedichte* (1907, 1908, "New Poems") and *Die Aufzeichnungen des Malte Laurids Brigge* (1910, Eng trans *Journal of My Other Self*, 1930), a key text of existentialism which prefigured such works as **Jean-Paul Sartre**'s *La nausée*. In 1923 he wrote his two major works, *Die Sonnette an Orpheus* (Eng trans *Sonnets to Orpheus*, 1936) and *Duineser Elegien* (Eng trans *Duino Elegies*, 1939). He is one of the most important figures in modern European literature.

Rimbaud, (Jean Nicolas) Arthur 1854–91 •*French poet*• He was born in Charleville, Ardennes. After a brilliant academic career at the Collège de Charleville, in 1870 he published his first book of poems and ran away to Paris. He soon returned to Charleville, where he lived as a writer and indulged in a life of leisure. There he published *Le bateau ivre* (1871, Eng trans *The Drunken Boat*, 1952) which, with its verbal eccentricities, daring imagery and evocative language, is among his most popular works. Soon after its publication in August 1871, **Paul Verlaine** invited him to Paris, where they became lovers. In Brussels in July 1873 he threatened to terminate the relationship; Verlaine shot and wounded him, and was imprisoned for attempted murder. From the summer of 1872, when the relationship with Verlaine was at its strongest, date many of his *Les illuminations* (Eng trans 1971), which most clearly state his poetic doctrine. These prose and verse poems show Rimbaud as a precursor of Symbolism, especially in his use of childhood, dream and mystical images. In 1873 he published *Une saison en enfer* (Eng trans *A Season in Hell*, 1939). He was bitterly disappointed at its cold reception, burned all his manuscripts, and at the age of 19 turned his back on literature and traveled. In 1886, Verlaine published *Les illuminations* as by the "late Arthur Rimbaud." Rimbaud knew of the sensation they caused and the reputation they were making for him, but reacted with indifference.

Rimington, Dame Stella 1935– •*English former director general of the Secret Service*• Born in London, she studied English at the University of Edinburgh, then joined MI5, evidently playing an important part in the F2 branch, which deals with domestic subversion. Toward the end of the 1980s she became director of counterterrorist activities, and was appointed director general of MI5 in 1992, the first woman to hold the post, and the first of either sex to be identified publicly. She retired in 1996.

Rimsky-Korsakov, Nikolai Andreyevich 1844–1908 •*Russian composer*• Born in Tikhvin, Novgorod, he was introduced in 1861 to **Mili Balakirev**, who became his friend and mentor, and in 1865 to **Mussorgsky**. In 1871 he became a professor at the St Petersburg Conservatory. In 1887–88 he produced his three great orchestral works, *Capriccio Espagnol*, *Easter Festival* and *Scheherazade*. He then turned to opera, in which his best-known works are *The Snow Maiden* (1882, *Snegurochka*), *Legend of Czar Saltan* (1900), *The Invisible City of Kitesh* (1906, *Skazaniye o nevidimom grade Kitezhe*) and *The Golden Cockerel* (1907, *Zolotoi petushok*), his last work, based on a satire against autocracy by **Alexander Pushkin** and banned at first from the Russian stage. His music is notable for its vitality and for its range of orchestral color. Constantly aware of his earlier technical shortcomings, he rewrote almost all his early work. He also edited and arranged the works of other composers, notably Mussorgsky's *Boris Godunov*. **Stravinsky** was his pupil. His autobiography, *My Musical Life*, was translated into English by Joffe in 1942.

“ ”

I have already heard it. I had better not go: I will start to get accustomed to it and finally like it.

Of the music of Debussy, when invited to a concert where it was to be performed. Quoted in Igor Stravinsky ***Chronicles of My Life*** *(1936).*

Ringan *See* **Ninian, St**

Ripken, Cal(vin Edwin), Jr 1960– •*US baseball player*• Born in Havre de Grace, Maryland, the son of a Baltimore Orioles coach, he grew up with the team, questioning players about strategy and taking part in batting practices while still in high school. He was drafted by the Baltimore Orioles in 1981 and became the team's shortstop in 1982. A heavy hitter and skillful fielder, he was named the American League's most valuable player in 1983 and 1991. In 1995 he broke **Lou Gehrig**'s 56-year-old record of 2,130 consecutive games played (1927–39), and amassed 2,632 before sitting one out in September 1998.

Riskin, Robert 1897–1955 •*US playwright and screenwriter*• He was born in New York City. After serving in the US Navy during World War I, he enjoyed success as a Broadway playwright before moving to Hollywood. From 1931 he was under contract to Columbia, where he collaborated with director **Frank Capra** on sparkling popular comedies which often celebrated the idealism of the common man as he triumphed over the cynicism of corrupt masters. He won an Academy Award for *It Happened One Night* (1934), and received further nominations for *Lady for a Day* (1933), *Mr Deeds Goes to Town* (1936) and *You Can't Take It with You* (1938). He also adapted **James Hilton**'s *Lost Horizon* (1937) for the screen; and as a producer, he formed the Overseas Motion Picture Bureau in 1942. Ill health forced his early retirement, but his body of work was honored with the Laurel award from the Writer's Guild of America in 1954.

Ritter, Johann Wilhelm 1776–1810 •*German physicist*• Born in Samitz, Silesia (now in Poland), he was trained as an apothecary before studying medicine at the University of Jena. He taught at Jena and at Gotha. While working in Jena in 1801 he discovered the ultraviolet rays in the spectrum, demonstrated that galvanic electricity was a manifestation of electricity (1800), made the first dry cell (1802), the first accumulator (1803), and was the first to propose an electrochemical series.

Ritts, Herb 1952–2002 •*US photographer*• Born in Los Angeles, he studied economics at Bard College before establishing his reputation as a celebrity photographer. Largely self-taught, his portraits were published in newspapers and leading fashion magazines such as *Vogue* and *Harpers Bazaar*. His celebrity subjects included **Nancy Reagan**, **Elizabeth Taylor**, **Mikhail Gorbachev**, **Jack Nicholson**, the **Dalai Lama**, **Tina Turner**, **Madonna**, and **Cindy Crawford**. His books include *Notorious* (1993).

Rivera, Diego 1886–1957 •*Mexican painter*• Born in Guanajuato, he won a travel scholarship to study in Madrid and Paris. He began a series of murals in public buildings in 1921, depicting the life and history (particularly the popular uprisings) of the Mexican people. From 1930 to 1934 he completed a number of frescoes in the US, mainly of industrial life. His art is a blend of folk art and revolutionary propaganda, as in *The Agrarian Leader Zapata* (1931, Museum of Modern Art, New York), with overtones of Byzantine and Aztec symbolism; it was a significant influence on the US realist art of the 1930s, especially on **Ben Shahn**. His mural *Man at the Crossroads* for the Rockefeller Center in New York (1933) was destroyed because it contained an apparent portrait of **Lenin**. Works of the 1940s and 1950s expounding his atheism and his views on war and peace likewise created a scandal and were similarly suppressed. He was married (twice) to **Frida Kahlo**, and on her death he donated her childhood home to Mexico City as a museum.

Rivera, Miguel *See* **Primo de Rivera (y Orbaneja), Miguel, Marqués de Estella**

Rivers, Augustus Pitt- *See* **Pitt-Rivers, Augustus**

Rivers, Joan, *originally* **Joan Alexandra Molinsky** 1933– •*US comedienne and writer*• Born in Larchmont, New York, she worked with the Chicago improvisational troupe Second City (1961–62), developing her prowess as an acid-tongued, stand-up comedienne. Success came with an appearance on *The Tonight Show* in 1965, and she made her Las Vegas debut in 1969. In 1978, she directed the film *Rabbit Test*, and in 1983 recorded the album *What Becomes a Semi-Legend Most*. She hosted the TV programs *That Show Starring Joan Rivers* (1968) and *The Joan Rivers Show* (1989–93), and was the regular guest host of *The Tonight Show* (1971–86).

Rix, Brian Norman Roger Rix, Baron 1924– •*English actor and manager*• Born in Cottingham, Humberside, he joined the **Donald Wolfit** Company (1943), appeared with the White Rose Players, Harrogate (1943–44), and served in the RAF (1944–47). He founded his own company, Rix Theatrical Productions, at Ilkley, Yorkshire (1948), forming a second company at the Hippodrome, Margate (1949). He had a great success with the farce *Reluctant Heroes* (1950), which ran at the Whitehall Theatre for four years, and became closely identified with the Whitehall farces which he both appeared in and managed during the 1950s and 1960s. In 1967 he moved to the Garrick Theatre. He has also produced and appeared in several films. In 1980 he left the theater to work for Mencap, a charity for the mentally handicapped, becoming its chairman in 1988. Also in that year, he returned to the Lyric to star in a revival of *Dry Rot* (1989). He was knighted in 1986, and raised to the peerage in 1992.

Rizzi, Carlo 1960– •*Italian conductor*• Born in Milan, he studied music at Milan and Siena. He made his debut in 1982, and in 1985 won the first **Toscanini** conductor's competition in Parma. Since the late 1980s he has conducted worldwide for companies including the Australian Opera Company, Netherlands Opera, Royal Opera, Deutsche Oper, Israel Philharmonic and Metropolitan Opera, New York. His numerous recordings include over ten complete operas and various orchestral works. He was musical director of the Welsh National Opera from 1992 to 2001.

Rizzio or **Riccio, David** c. 1533–66 •*Italian courtier and musician*• Born in Pancalieri, near Turin, he went to Scotland with the Duke of Savoy's embassy and entered the service of **Mary Queen of Scots** in 1561. He quickly became her favorite, and was made her French secretary (1564). He negotiated her marriage with **Darnley** (1565), with whom he was at first on good terms. Soon, however, Darnley suspected that Rizzio and Mary were lovers, and, with **James Douglas**, Earl of Morton, **William Ruthven** and others, entered into a plot to kill him. Rizzio was brutally murdered in the queen's antechamber at Holyroodhouse, Edinburgh.

Roach, Hal, *originally* **Harald Eugene Roach** 1892–1992 •*US film producer*• He was born in Elmira, New York. After a spell prospecting in Alaska, he entered the film industry as a stuntman and extra (1911). In 1915 he formed a production company to make short silent comedy films featuring **Harold Lloyd**. He became an expert in the mechanics of screen humor and slapstick, helping to foster the careers of **Will Rogers** and, most successfully, the partnership of **Stan Laurel** and **Oliver Hardy**. From 1928 he worked with sound and won Academy Awards for *The Music Box* (1932) and *Bored of Education* (1936). His range of full-length productions includes *Bonnie Scotland* (1935), *Way Out West* (1937), *Of Mice and Men* (1939) and *One Million B.C.* (1940), which he codirected. In 1984 he received a Special Academy Award.

Roach, Max(well) 1924– •*US jazz drummer and composer*• He was born in New Land, North Carolina. His mother was a gospel singer, and his early musical experiences were in church. He studied music formally for a time, and became involved with the evolution of bebop from 1942, playing in the quintets of **Dizzy Gillespie** and **Charlie Parker**. From the late 1950s he began to broaden the scope of his music, using free jazz, vocal music, symphony orchestras, percussion ensembles and elements from rap and hip-hop. He is an eloquent spokesman for African-American cultural and political movements, and a respected teacher.

Robards, Jason, Jr 1922–2000 •*US actor*• Born in Chicago, he studied at the American Academy of Dramatic Arts. Acclaimed for his performances in *The Iceman Cometh* (1956) and *Long Day's Journey into Night* (1958), he won a Tony award for *The Disenchanted* (1959) and gained a reputation as one of the US's finest actors, with a particular affinity for the works of **Eugene O'Neill**. His many theatrical appearances included *Moon for the Misbegotten* (1973) and *No Man's Land* (1993). He made his film debut in *The Journey* (1959) and developed into a reliable character actor, winning Best Supporting Actor Oscars for both *All the President's Men* (1976) and *Julia* (1977). His many television appearances include *Inherit the Wind* (1988), for which he won an Emmy award.

Robbe-Grillet, Alain 1922– •*French novelist*• Born in Brest, he was educated in Paris. His first novel, *Les gommes* (1953, Eng trans *The Erasers*, 1964), was controversial, and his subsequent work (*Dans le labyrinthe*, 1959, Eng trans *In the Labyrinth*, 1960, etc), established him as a leader of the *nouveau roman* ("new novel") group. He uses an unorthodox narrative structure and concentrates on a kind of external reality. He has also written film scenarios, for example, *L'année dernière à Marienbad* (1961, Eng trans in novel form and filmed as *Last Year at Marienbad*, 1962), and essays, *Pour un nouveau roman* (1963, Eng trans *Towards a New Novel*, 1965). Other publications include the novel *Projet pour une révolution à New York* (1970, "Project for a Revolution in New York"), *La belle captive* (written with **René Magritte**, 1976; adapted as a screenplay, 1983, "The Beautiful Prisoner") and *Les dernières jours de Corinthe* (1994, "The Last Days of Corinth").

" "

Le lecteur, lui non plus, ne voit pas les choses du dehors. Il est dans le labyrinthe aussi.

The reader [as well as the main character] does not view the work from outside. He too is in the labyrinth.

1959 ***Dans le labyrinthe.***

Robbia, Luca Della *See* **Della Robbia, Luca**

Robbins, Frederick Chapman 1916–2003 •*US physiologist, pediatrician and Nobel Prize winner*• Born in Auburn, Alabama, he trained at the University of Missouri and Harvard University Medical School. He served as intern at the Children's Hospital Medical Center, Boston (1941–42), and spent four years with the Army Medical Corps before returning to Boston to complete his pediatric training and join the Infectious Diseases Research Laboratory of the Children's Hospital. Robbins, **John Enders** and **Thomas Weller** had all worked on improving techniques for cultivating viruses. Their success led to quicker and cheaper means of diagnosis, and was also an important step in the development of a polio vaccine. For this work the three scientists were awarded the 1954 Nobel Prize for physiology or medicine.

Robbins, Harold, *pseudonym of* **Francis Kane** 1916–97 •*US novelist*• Born of unknown parentage in the Hell's Kitchen area of Manhattan, New York, he dropped out of high school at the age of 15, left his foster parents and worked in a grocery store. During the Depression he showed entrepreneurial flair by buying up crops and selling options to canning companies and the canning contracts to wholesale grocers. He was a millionaire by the time he was 20, but speculation in sugar before the outbreak of World War II lost him his fortune. He turned to writing in 1949; drawing on his knowledge of street life, high finance and Hollywood, he produced a series of escapist bestsellers, including *The Dream Merchants* (1949), *The Carpetbaggers* (1961), *Dreams Die First* (1977), *Descent for Xanadu* (1984) and *Tycoon* (1997).

Robbins, Jerome 1918–98 •*US dancer and choreographer*• Born in New York City, he danced with the American Ballet Theater for four years and in Broadway musicals before making his first choreographic piece, *Fancy Free* (1944). He joined the New York City Ballet in 1949, dancing principal roles in **George Balanchine** ballets and choreographing a total of nine ballets in ten years. During that time he also worked on Broadway in *The King and I* (1951), *Peter Pan* (1954) and *West Side Story* (1957), a unique achievement which combined the commercial theater with artistic skill. In order to free himself to experiment, he formed the small company Ballet: USA, out of which came *Moves*, a ballet without music (1959). Further Broadway successes included *Gypsy* (1959) and *Fiddler on the Roof* (1964). He returned to the New York City Ballet in 1969. After the death of Balanchine in 1983, he was made joint ballet master-in-chief with **Peter Martins**, holding that post until 1989. Blending classical ballet with more earthy folk styles, he was one of the US's most impressive choreographers. He won Academy Awards for the 1961 Hollywood version of *West Side Story.*

Robbins (of Clare Market), Lionel Charles Robbins, Baron 1898–1984 •*English economist*• Born in Sipson, Middlesex, he was Professor of Economics at the London School of Economics (1929–61), and directed the economic section of the War Cabinet. He resigned from the London School of Economics to become chairman of the *Financial Times* (1961–70). From 1961 to 1964 he chaired the Robbins Committee on the expansion of higher education in the UK. His best-known work is *An Essay on the Nature and Significance of Economic Science* (1932).

Robbins, Tim(othy Francis) 1958– •*US actor and director*• Born in West Covina, California, the son of a folksinger, he was raised in a politically active household and joined the avant-garde acting group Theater for the New City when he was 12. A drama major at UCLA, he was one of the founders of the experimental theater company the Actors' Gang in 1981, and worked extensively in mainstream film and television to subsidize the radical theater work that he often cowrote. Among his plays are *Slick Slack Griff Graff* (1985) and *Carnage: A Comedy* (1987). His film career progressed with roles as the dim-witted pitcher in the popular baseball comedy *Bull Durham* (1988), as the disturbed Vietnam veteran in *Jacob's Ladder* (1990) and as the murderous studio boss in *The Player* (1992). He directed and acted in the political satire *Bob Roberts* (1992) and also directed *Dead Man Walking* (1995), which won a Best Actress Academy Award for his off-screen partner, **Susan Sarandon**. He has also acted in *The Hudsucker Proxy* (1994), *The Shawshank Redemption* (1994) and *Arlington Road* (1998).

Robert I *See* **Bruce, Robert**

Robert II 1316–90 •*King of Scotland and founder of the Stewart dynasty*• The son of Walter Stewart and Marjory, only daughter of **Robert Bruce**, he twice acted as regent (1338–41, 1346–57) during the exile and captivity of **David II**. On David's death (1371) he became king by right of his descent from his maternal grandfather, Robert Bruce, and founded the royal **Stewart** dynasty. During his reign the kingdom was largely administered by his sons, but divisions were avoided, both over the succession and in relation to England, despite two English invasions (1384–85). His complicated matrimonial history, however, was to bring problems for later Stewart kings. The legitimacy of his first marriage to Elizabeth, daughter of Sir Adam Mure of Rowallan, was doubted on the grounds of their consanguinity. His second marriage (1355) was to Euphemia, Countess of Moray, and daughter of Hugh, Earl of Ross. A papal dispensation for the children of the first marriage was granted in 1347, and they were further recognized by an Act of Succession (1373).

Robert III c. 1340–1406 •*King of Scotland*• The eldest son of **Robert II** by his first marriage and originally called John, he was made Earl of Carrick (1368) and took the name Robert on his accession (1390). The issue of guardianship dominated politics since he was a permanent invalid, the result of a kick from a horse. The main contenders were his brother, Robert, Duke of **Albany** (c. 1340–1420), and his elder son, David, Duke of Rothesay (c. 1378–1402), who was appointed Lieutenant of Scotland by a general council in 1398. Rothesay's fall (1402), imprisonment and subsequent death at Falkland Castle brought Albany to an unrivaled position of power. Robert, anxious for the safety of his younger son, James (the future **James I**), sent him to France, but Robert died shortly after news arrived of James's capture by the English.

Robert Curthose c. 1054–1134 •*Duke of Normandy*• He was the eldest son of **William the Conqueror** and Matilda of Flanders. Although his father's successor, he was excluded from government and, after an unsuccessful revolt, was exiled to France. On William's death (1087) Robert succeeded to rule Normandy, while

England passed to the second son, **William II Rufus**. A protracted struggle between the two brothers gave William control of Normandy and was interrupted by Robert's courageous participation in the First Crusade (1096–1101). In his absence, his younger brother **Henry I** seized the English throne when Rufus died (1100). In 1106 Henry invaded Normandy, and Robert was captured at the Battle of Tinchebrai. He spent the rest of his life a prisoner.

Robert of Brunne *See* **Mannyng, Robert**

Roberts, Frederick Sleigh Roberts, 1st Earl 1832–1914 •*English field marshal*• Born in Cawnpore, India, he was educated at Clifton, Eton, Sandhurst and Addiscombe, and entered the Bengal Artillery in 1851. He was active during the Indian Mutiny (1857–58) and won the Victoria Cross at Khudagani in 1858. From 1885 to 1893 he was Commander in Chief in India. Made Lord Roberts of Kandahar and Waterford in 1892, he became field marshal, and Commander in Chief in Ireland in 1895. In 1899 he assumed chief command in the Second Boer War, relieved Kimberley, and made the great advance to Pretoria; he returned home in 1901 as Commander in Chief. Made an earl in 1901, he died while visiting troops in the field in France.

Roberts, Julia 1967– •*US film actress*• Born in Smyrna, Georgia, her earliest ambition was to be a veterinary surgeon, but she decided to study acting and at the same time joined a modeling agency. She gained recognition as the town beauty in *Mystic Pizza* (1988), and was nominated for a Best Supporting Actress Academy Award as the diabetic daughter of **Sally Field** in *Steel Magnolias* (1989). The success of *Pretty Woman* (1990) made her a star and added box-office appeal to *Flatliners* (1990) and *Sleeping with the Enemy* (1991). In 2000 she won the Best Actress Academy Award and a British Academy Film Award for *Erin Brockovich*.

Roberts, Kate 1891–1985 •*Welsh novelist and short-story writer*• She was born in Rhosgadfan, near Caernarfon, Gwynedd, and was educated at the University College of North Wales, Bangor. She then taught Welsh at Ystalyfera (1915–17) and Aberdare (1917–28). Sometimes described as "the Welsh **Chekhov**," she is generally regarded as the most distinguished prose writer in Welsh in the 20th century. Her work includes *O gors y bryniau* (1925, "From the Swamp of the Hills"), *Traed mewn cyffion* (1936, Eng trans *Feet in Chains*, 1977) and *Stryd y Glep* (1949, "Gossip Street").

Roberts, Michèle Brigitte 1949– •*English author*• Born to a French mother and an English father, she was brought up in London and studied at Somerville College, Oxford, and University College London. After working as a journalist for *Spare Rib* and other magazines, she published her first novel, *A Piece of the Night*, in 1978, following it with works such as *In the Red Kitchen* (1990), *Daughters of the House* (1992; W H Smith Literary award) and *The Looking Glass* (2001). Among her other works are poetry, plays and a television film, *Heavenly Twins* (1993).

Roberts, (Granville) Oral 1918– •*US evangelist and faith healer*• Born near Ada, Oklahoma, the son of a Pentecostal preacher and a half-Cherokee mother, he was ordained at the age of 18 in the Pentecostal Holiness Church. Flamboyant and enterprising, he gained a reputation for faith healing, and won wide support when he founded Oral Roberts University in Tulsa in 1967. By 1978 it had 3,800 students and assets of about $150 million. In 1981 Roberts also opened a medical center in Tulsa. From 1968 he preached by means of a weekly national television program, his own radio station and a mass-circulation monthly magazine. His writings include *How to Resist the Devil* (1989).

Roberts, Richard 1943– •*British molecular biologist and Nobel Prize winner*• He was born in Derby and educated at the University of Sheffield. He worked at Cold Spring Harbor Laboratory in New York from 1972, and since 1992 he has been research director at New England Biolabs in Beverly, Massachusetts. In 1977 he announced his intriguing discovery that genes contain sections of DNA (now known as "introns") which carry no genetic information. He shared the 1993 Nobel Prize for physiology or medicine with **Phillip Sharp**, who had independently come to the same conclusions at about the same time.

Roberts, Tom (Thomas William) 1856–1931 •*Australian landscape and portrait painter*• Born in Dorchester, England, he studied at the Royal Academy after a brief spell in Melbourne. On his return to Australia he formed, in 1886, with **Frederick McCubbin** and friends, the first artists' camp in Box Hill, Victoria. In 1888 he joined **Arthur Streeton** and Charles Conder (1868–1909) in Heidelberg, Victoria, to form the first indigenous Australian school of painting. Sixty-two of his paintings were exhibited in 1889 in the famous "9 x 5 Impression" exhibition. With Streeton, he camped at Sirius Cove on Sydney Harbor from 1891 to 1896, and there produced a sparkling series of harbor and beach scenes. He is most respected for his sensitive paintings of the Australian bush and pioneering life (for example, *Bailed Up*, 1895).

Robertson (of Port Ellen), George Islay Macneill Robertson, Baron 1946– •*Scottish Labour politician*• He was born in Port Ellen, Isle of Islay. Educated at the Universities of St Andrews and Dundee, he joined the Scottish Executive of the Labour Party in 1973 and became Member of Parliament for Hamilton in 1978. He was front bench spokesman for Scottish Affairs, Defense and then Foreign Affairs before becoming the principal Opposition spokesman on European Affairs (1984–93) and joining the Shadow Cabinet as principal spokesman for Scotland (1993–97). He entered **Tony Blair**'s Cabinet as Secretary of State for Defense (1997–99). In 1999 he became Secretary-General of NATO, and was made a life peer in the same year.

Robertson, Jeannie 1908–75 •*Scottish folksinger*• She was born in Aberdeen and was virtually unknown beyond the northeast of Scotland until discovered in 1953 by **Hamish Henderson**. Her huge repertoire of classic traditional ballads and other songs, passed down orally from generation to generation, together with her powerful and magnetic singing style, exerted a profound influence on the folk-music revival.

Robertson, Oscar Palmer 1938– •*US basketball player*• Born in Charlotte, Tennessee, he is often considered the most gifted offensive player in basketball history. Nicknamed the "Big O," he had a distinguished career in college basketball with the University of Cincinnati (1956–60), being named College Player of the Year three times. He served as co-captain of the 1960 US Olympic team, winning the gold medal, before turning professional with the Cincinnati Royals in 1961, in which year he was acclaimed Rookie of the Year and won the first of three All-Star Game Most Valuable Player awards (1961, 1964 and 1969). In 1962 he became the only player in the history of the NBA to average double figures in scoring, rebounding and assists. In 1970 he joined the Milwaukee Bucks, helping the team to its first NBA title that same season. By the time of his retirement in 1974 he was the NBA's all-time leader in career assists and free throws made.

Robertson, Sir William Robert 1860–1933 •*English field marshal*• He enlisted as a private in 1877 and rose to field marshal in 1920. In World War I he was Quarter-Master General (later Chief of General Staff) of the British Expeditionary Force, and became Chief of the Imperial General Staff from 1915 to 1918. He wrote his autobiography, *From Private to Field-Marshal* (1921).

Robeson, Paul (Bustill) 1898–1976 •*US singer and actor*• Born in Princeton, New Jersey, he was admitted to the bar before embarking on a stage career. Success as an actor was matched by popularity as a singer, and he appeared in works ranging from *Show Boat* to plays by **Eugene O'Neill** and **Shakespeare**. He was known particularly for his portrayal of Othello. He gave song recitals, notably of African-American spirituals, throughout the world, and appeared in numerous films. In the 1950s, his left-wing views caused him to leave the US, and he lived in England from 1958 to 1963, when he retired and returned to the US.

Robespierre, Maximilien Marie Isidore de 1758–94 •*French Revolutionary politician*• He was born at Arras, became a successful lawyer, and entered the Estates General (National Assembly) in 1789. He soon became immensely popular with the Paris commune and the extreme republican members of the Jacobin Club. His impartiality and support of democratic principles won him the nickname "Incorruptible." In 1792 he resigned his office as public accuser and petitioned for a revolutionary tribunal and a new convention. Elected to represent Paris at the National Convention, he emerged as leader of the Mountain (a group of Jacobin extremist Deputies), strenuously opposed to the Girondins, whom, with the support of **Georges Danton** and **Jean Paul Marat**, he helped to destroy. The murder of Marat the following year resulted in the proscription of the Girondins and Robespierre's election to the Committee of Public Safety. Robespierre and the Jacobins supported **Louis XVI**'s execution in 1793. With real power at his disposal for the first time, he purged the National Assembly of ultra-revolutionaries, introduced strict economic control, and embarked on the establishment of a form of welfare state. However, Robespierre's growing autocracy coincided with a new era of ascendancy for the French army that served to question the purpose of the Reign of Terror, and the prospect of Robespierre heading a dictatorship finally spurred his enemies into action. On July 27, 1794, he was denounced in the convention, and a deputy called for his arrest. He was apprehended by the National Guard, and the next day he and 21 of his supporters were guillotined without trial.

Robey, Sir George, *originally* **George Edward Wade** 1869–1954 •*English comedian*• Born in Herne Hill, London, he made a name for himself in musical shows such as *The Bing Boys* (1916) and later emerged as a **Shakespeare**an actor, playing Falstaff. Dubbed the "Prime Minister of Mirth," he was famous for his robust, often **Rabelais**ian humor, his bowler hat, long black collarless frock-coat, hooked stick and thickly painted eyebrows. He was knighted in 1954.

Robia, Luca Della *See* **Della Robbia, Luca**

Robin Hood c. 1250–c. 1350 •*Semilegendary English outlaw*• The hero of a group of old English ballads, the gallant and generous outlaw of Sherwood Forest, he is said to have spent his time under the greenwood tree with Little John, Will Scarlet, Friar Tuck and his merry men. Unrivaled with bow and quarterstaff, he gave generously to the poor and needy at the expense of proud abbots and rich knights, helping himself to their riches. The "rymes of Robyn Hood" are named in *Piers Plowman* (c. 1377) and the plays of Robin Hood in the *Paston Letters* (1473). Tradition made the outlaw into a political figure, a dispossessed Earl of Huntingdon and other characters, and in Sir **Walter Scott**'s *Ivanhoe* he is a Saxon holding out against the Normans; but there is no evidence that he was anything but the creation of popular imagination.

Robinson, Brooks 1937– •*US baseball player*• He was born in Little Rock, Arkansas. A highly proficient batter who hit more than 250 home runs and batted in over 1,300 runs, he is often considered to be the greatest third baseman of all time. He won the Gold Glove Award in that position for 16 consecutive years from 1960 and was named as the American League's Most Valuable Player (MVP) in 1960 and the Outstanding Player of the 1970 World Series.

Robinson, Edward G, *originally* **Emanuel Goldenberg** 1893–1973 •*US actor*• He was born in Bucharest, Romania, and emigrated to the US with his parents (1903). He studied at the American Academy of Dramatic Arts in New York City and worked in the theater until his career was interrupted by service in World War I. His first appearance in silent films was in *The Bright Shawl* (1923), and it was his vivid portrayal of the vicious gangster Rico in *Little Caesar* (1930) that brought him stardom. He played a succession of hoodlums and gangsters in films including *The Whole Town's Talking* (1935), *The Last Gangster* (1937) and *Key Largo* (1948), roles which his short squat appearance and wry humor made distinctive. His versatility as an actor is seen in his roles as the paranoid captain in *The Sea Wolf* (1941), a dogged insurance investigator in *Double Indemnity* (1944), a hen-pecked husband in *Scarlet Street* (1945) and the patriarch in *All My Sons* (1948). Off the screen he was a connoisseur of art.

Robinson, Edwin Arlington 1869–1935 •*US poet*• Born in Head Tide, Maine, he was brought up in Gardiner, Maine, which provided the background for "Tilbury Town," the fictional New England village of his best poetry. He was educated at Harvard, and made a name with an early collection of poetry, *The Children of the Night* (1897), followed by *Captain Craig* (1902), *The Town down the River* (1910) and *King Jasper* (1935). Poems such as "Miniver Cheevy" and "Richard Cory" are recognized as American classics. He won Pulitzer Prizes for his *Collected Poems* (1922), *The Man Who Died Twice* (1925) and *Tristram* (1927), one of his modern renditions of Arthurian legends.

“ ”

I shall have more to say when I am dead.

1920 ***The Three Taverns**, "John Brown."*

Robinson, (William) Heath 1872–1944 •*English artist, cartoonist and book illustrator*• Born in Hornsey Rise, London, he attended the Islington School of Art and the Royal Academy Schools in London. The first of many works illustrated by him was *Don Quixote* (1897); others include editions of *Arabian Nights* (1899), *Twelfth Night* (1908) and *Water Babies* (1915). His fame rests mainly on his humorous drawings, in which he satirizes the machine age with depictions of contraptions of absurd and fantastic design which are made to perform simple and practical operations, such as laying a table for dinner.

Robinson, Henry Crabb 1775–1867 •*English journalist and diarist*• He trained under a Colchester attorney (1790–95), then traveled in Germany, where he met **Goethe** and **Schiller**, and studied at the University of Jena. He joined *The Times* in 1807, and covered the Peninsular War as a war correspondent (1808–09); in this capacity he was the first of his kind. He worked as a lawyer from 1813 to 1828. He corresponded with major literary figures, including **Coleridge**, **Wordsworth**, **Charles Lamb** and **William Blake**, all of whom feature in his writings and correspondence. He was one of the founders of the University of London (1828).

Robinson, Henry Peach 1830–1901 •*English photographer*• Born in Ludlow, Shropshire, he opened a studio at Leamington Spa in 1857. He tired of formal portraiture and moved to "high art photography," often combining several separate images of costumed models and painted settings. Although criticized for artificiality, he had considerable influence until the end of the century. He was a founding member of the Linked Ring (1892), an association of photographers whose aims were artistic rather than technically accurate; this developed into the international Photo-Secession under **Alfred Stieglitz** and others.

Robinson, Jackie, *properly* **John Roosevelt Robinson** 1919–72 •*US baseball player*• Born in Cairo, Georgia, he was the first African-American player in major league baseball. After World War II he became a star infielder and outfielder for the Brooklyn Dodgers (1947–56). Known for his fierce competitiveness and skill at stealing home plate, he led the Dodgers to six National League pennants and one World Series victory (1955). He retired in 1956 with a lifetime batting average of .311. He was largely responsible for the acceptance of African-American athletes in professional sports, and wrote of the pressures on him in his autobiography *I Never Had It Made* (1972).

Robinson, Jancis 1950– •*English wine writer and broadcaster*• She was born and brought up in Carlisle. In 1984 she was the first journalist to become a member of the Institute of Masters of Wine, and in 1986 she was declared Wine Writer of the Year. She has been the *Financial Times* wine correspondent since 1989, and wrote *The Oxford Companion to Wine* (1994).

Robinson, Joan Violet, *née* **Maurice** 1903–83 •*English economist*• Born in Camberley, Surrey, and educated at Girton College, Cambridge, she married an economist, Austin Robinson, in 1926. After a brief period in India, she taught economics at Cambridge (1931–71) and in 1965 succeeded her husband as professor. She was one of the most influential economic theorists of her time and a leader of the Cambridge school, which developed macroeconomic theories of growth and distribution based on the work of **John Maynard Keynes**.

Robinson, John Arthur Thomas 1919–83 •*English Anglican prelate and theologian*• Born in Canterbury, he was a student and lecturer at Cambridge before his appointment as Bishop of Woolwich (1959–69). In 1963 he published *Honest to God*, which he described as an attempt to explain the Christian faith to modern humanity. It was highly successful, but it scandalized conservative elements in the Church, and adversely affected his prospects for further ecclesiastical advancement. He also made significant and more orthodox contributions to biblical studies in other publications, including *Redating the New Testament* (1976) and *The Priority of John* (1985, posthumous).

Robinson, Mary, *née* **Darby**, *known as* **Perdita** 1758–1800 •*English actress, poet and novelist*• She was born in Bristol. Between 1776 and 1780 she played Perdita and other **Shakespearean** roles at Drury Lane, and became mistress (1779) to the future **George IV**. Her prolific output as a writer included *Sappho and Phaon* (1796), two plays and several novels, including the best-selling *Vancenza* (1792).

Robinson, Mary, *née* **Bourke** 1944– •*Irish Labour politician and president*• Born in Ballina, County Mayo, she became Professor of Law at Trinity College, Dublin in 1969. As a member of the Irish Senate (1969–89), she campaigned for the rights of women and of single parents, and for the decriminalization of homosexuality. She was nominated for the presidency in 1990 by the Labour Party and unexpectedly defeated the Fianna Fáil candidate, Brian Lenihan (1930–96). As president, she gained the support of most of the Irish people. In 1993 she led a mission of reconciliation to Belfast, and met the Sinn Fein leader **Gerry Adams**, and in 1995 she visited Queen **Elizabeth II** in London. She stepped down in 1997 and became UN High Commissioner for Human Rights (1997–2002).

Robinson, Ray (Arthur Napoleon Raymond) 1926– •*Trinidad and Tobago politician*• Educated in Trinidad and at Oxford, he became a lawyer. On his return to the West Indies, he became politically active, and on independence in 1967 became deputy leader of the People's National Movement (PNM). In 1984 he formed a left-of-center coalition which became the National Alliance for Reconstruction (NAR), and which in the 1986 general election swept the PNM from power, making Robinson prime minister. Ousted in 1991, the NAR returned to power under Basdeo Panday in 1995, and in 1997 Robinson was elected president.

Robinson, Sir Robert 1886–1975 •*English chemist and Nobel Prize winner*• Born in Chesterfield, Derbyshire, he went to the Victoria University of Manchester in 1902 to study chemistry. He held a chair in organic chemistry in Sydney between 1912 and 1914, when he returned to Great Britain to take chairs in chemistry at Liverpool and later at St Andrews. He continued research on natural products and also developed many of his ideas on mechanistic organic chemistry. After holding positions at Manchester and University College London (1928–30), he became Waynflete Professor of Chemistry at Oxford, where he remained until 1955. During World War II he played an important role in the development of penicillin. He was a close friend of **Robert Maxwell**, and with his support founded a number of learned journals. He served on many government committees, was knighted in 1939, awarded the Order of Merit in 1949 and became president of the Royal Society in 1945. He received the Nobel Prize for chemistry in 1947.

Robinson, Sugar Ray, *originally* **Walker Smith** 1920–89 •*US boxer*• Born in Detroit, he gained the welterweight title in 1946 and won the middleweight championship five times between 1951 (when he knocked out Jake La Motta) and 1958 (when he defeated Carmen Basilio). His skill and speed brought him close to winning the world light heavyweight championship in 1952 despite a considerable physical disadvantage. He fought 202 professional bouts in his career and lost only 19, most of them when he was over 40.

Rob Roy, *Gaelic for* **Red Robert**, *properly* **Robert MacGregor** 1671–1734 •*Scottish outlaw*• He was born in Buchanan, Stirlingshire. As a young man he lived quietly grazing sheep at Balquhidder, but was forced to raise a private army to protect himself from the activities of outlaws. When these followers joined the Jacobite cause in the 1690s, he turned to plundering, and became an outlaw in 1712 when his lands were seized by the Duke of Montrose. Legends about him soon developed around Loch Katrine and Loch Lomond; they told of his hair's-breadth escapes, and of his generosity to the poor. Although he enjoyed the patronage of John, 2nd Duke of **Argyll**, he was arrested in 1727 and sentenced to be deported to a penal colony, but was pardoned. His life was romanticized in Sir **Walter Scott**'s *Rob Roy* (1818).

Robson, Dame Flora McKenzie 1902–84 •*English actress*• Born in South Shields, Tyne and Wear, she made her first professional appearance in 1921 and became famous for her mainly historical roles including Queen **Elizabeth I** in the film *Fire over England* (1937), and Thérèse Raquin in the play *Guilty* (1944), based on **Zola**'s story. Other memorable stage performances included **George Bernard Shaw**'s *Captain Brassbound's Conversion* (1948) and **Ibsen**'s *Ghosts* (1958). She was given the honorary title of Dame Commander, Order of the British Empire, in 1960.

Rocard, Michel 1930– •*French politician*• Born in the Paris suburb of Courbevoie, he was the son of a nuclear physicist who worked on the development of a French atomic bomb. He trained at the École National d'Administration, where he was a classmate of **Jacques Chirac**. He began his career in 1958 as an inspector of finances, and in 1967 became leader of the radical Unified Socialist Party (PSU), running as its presidential candidate in 1969 and being elected to the National Assembly in the same year. He joined the Socialist Party (PS) in 1973, emerging as leader of its moderate social democratic wing, and unsuccessfully challenged **François Mitterrand** for the party's presidential nomination in 1981. After serving in ministerial positions in the ensuing Mitterrand administration, he resigned in 1985 in opposition to the government's expedient introduction of proportional representation. In 1988, however, as part of a strategy termed the "opening to the center," Mitterrand appointed him prime minister, but replaced him with Mme **Edith Cresson** in 1991. He became a member of the European Parliament representing the Party of European Socialists in 1994.

Roche, Mazo de la *See* **de la Roche, Mazo**

Rochefoucauld, François *See* **La Rochefoucauld, François, 6th Duc de**

Rochester, John Wilmot, 2nd Earl of 1647–80 •*English courtier and poet*• Born in Ditchley, Oxfordshire, he was educated at Burford School and Wadham College, Oxford. He traveled in France and Italy, and then returned to the court of **Charles II**, where he was a prominent figure. He led a life of debauchery, yet wrote letters, satires (particularly "A Satyr Against Mankind," 1675), and bacchanalian and amatory songs and verses, and was a patron of the arts. Among the best of his poems are imitations of Horace and **Nicolas Boileau**, *Verses to Lord Mulgrave* and *Verses upon Nothing*.

“ ”

Since 'tis nature's law to change,
Constancy alone is strange.

"A Dialogue Between Strephon and Daphne," l. 31–2 (published 1691).

Rockefeller, John D(avison) 1839–1937 •*US oil magnate and philanthropist*• Born in Richford, New York, he worked in a small oil refinery at Cleveland, Ohio. In 1870 he founded the Standard Oil Co with his brother William (1841–1922), and this eventually gave him control of the US oil trade. He gave over $500 million in support of medical research and to universities and Baptist churches, and in 1913 he established the Rockefeller Foundation, avowedly "to promote the well-being of mankind." His son, John Davison, Jr (1874–1960), became chairman of the Rockefeller Institute of Medical Research and built the Rockefeller Center in New York (1939). He also restored colonial Williamsburg in Virginia. His grandsons included John Davison III (1906–78), who became chairman of the Rockefeller Foundation in 1952, and **Nelson Aldrich Rockefeller**.

Rockefeller, Nelson Aldrich 1908–79 •*US politician*• He was born in Bar Harbor, Maine, the grandson of industrialist **John D Rockefeller**. After graduating from Dartmouth College in 1930, he worked in the family businesses and philanthropic foundations. Entering politics as a liberal Republican, he served four terms as governor of New York (1958–73), and during the 1960s he made three unsuccessful attempts to win his party's presidential nomination. From 1974 to 1977 he was vice president under **Gerald R Ford**.

Rockingham, Charles Watson-Wentworth, 2nd Marquess of 1730–82 •*English statesman*• He became a leading Whig, but was dismissed from his appointments in 1762 when he opposed the policies of **Bute**. He became prime minister (1765–66, 1782) and died in office. He repealed the Stamp Act, and supported American independence.

Rockne, Knute Kenneth 1888–1931 •*US football coach*• Born in Voss, Norway, he was taken to the US as a child. He graduated from Notre Dame in 1914 and became head football coach there shortly after the end of World War I. He dominated US college football, having markedly changed the emphasis from sheer physical brawn to pace, elusiveness and ball handling, and built Notre Dame into a national collegiate football power, compiling a record of 105 wins, 12 losses and five draws. He died in an air crash.

Rockwell, Norman 1894–1978 •*US illustrator*• Born in New York City, he studied at the Art Students League there and became a magazine illustrator, selling his first cover painting to the *Saturday Evening Post* in 1916. His nostalgic anecdotal scenes of everyday small-town life in the US appeared on the cover of the *Post* for half a century, and through them he was enshrined in American popular culture. He also created patriotic posters and paintings during World War II, including his *Four Freedoms* series (1943).

Rodchenko, Aleksandr Mikhailovich 1891–1956 •*Russian painter, designer and photographer*• Born in St Petersburg, he studied at the Kazan Art School and met **Vladimir Tatlin** and the young Russian avant-garde. After the revolution he worked for the People's Commissariat of Enlightenment and taught in Moscow (1918–26). His most original works were abstract spatial constructions and documentary photographs of the new Communist society.

Roddenberry, Gene 1921–91 •*US scriptwriter, producer and director*• He was born in Texas and was a pilot before turning to writing, going on to work mainly in television. He is best known as the creator of the popular *Star Trek* series.

Roddick, Anita Lucia 1942– •*English retail entrepreneur*• Born in Brighton, East Sussex, she was educated at Maude Allen School for girls and studied at Newton Park College of Education, Bath. In 1976 she founded the Body Shop with her husband, Thomas Gordon Roddick, to sell cosmetics "stripped of the hype" and made from natural materials. The company has since established many stores in the UK and overseas. She lectures on environmental issues and conducts campaigns with Friends of the Earth, and in 1989 she won the UN environmental award.

Rodgers, Jimmie (James Charles) 1897–1933 •*US country music singer and songwriter*• Born in Meridian, Mississippi, he was known as "The Singing Brakeman" from the railway overalls he wore, and as "The Blue Yodeler" from his style of singing. He is regarded by many as the father of modern country music, and was its first solo star. He worked on the railway until he contracted tuberculosis in 1924, and recorded the historic first country sides for Ralph Peer in 1927; by 1928 he was famous. His music took in aspects of blues, jazz and even Hawaiian music, and his groundbreaking recordings (111 in all) have been immeasurably influential.

Rodgers, Richard 1902–79 •*US composer*• Born in New York City, he studied at Columbia University and the Institute of Musical Art (now the Juilliard School). He collaborated with the lyricist Lorenz Hart in a number of musicals including *Babes in Arms* (1937, which included "The Lady Is a Tramp"), *The Boys from Syracuse* (1938, which included "Falling in Love with Love") and *Pal Joey* (1940, which included "Bewitched, Bothered and Bewildered"). After Hart's death (1943), Rodgers worked on a series of hit musicals with **Oscar Hammerstein II**, notably *Oklahoma!* (1943, Pulitzer Prize), *Carousel* (1945), *South Pacific* (1949, Pulitzer Prize), *The King and I* (1951) and *The Sound of Music* (1959).

Rodgers (of Quarry Bank), William Thomas Rodgers, Baron 1928– •*English politician*• Born in Liverpool and educated at Oxford, he was elected a Labour Member of Parliament in 1962. He held a succession of posts in the Labour governments of the 1960s and 1970s, was a strong supporter of membership in the EC (European Community) and was concerned by the leftward tendency of his party. In 1981 he left the Labour Party to form the Social Democratic Party (SDP) with **Roy Jenkins**, **David Owen** and **Shirley Williams** (with whom he formed the "Gang of Four"). Although he lost his seat in the 1983 election, he continued to play an influential organizational role as SDP vice president (1982–87), directing the party's alliance with the Liberals. Despite expressing support for the SDP-Liberal merger of 1987–88, he formally withdrew from party politics in 1987. He was made a life peer in 1992.

Rodin, (François) Auguste (René) 1840–1917 •*French sculptor*• He was born in Paris, made three unsuccessful attempts to enter the École des Beaux-Arts, and from 1864 (the year in which he produced his first great work, *L'homme au nez cassé*, "The Man with the Broken Nose") until 1875 he worked in Paris and Brussels under the sculptor **Antoine Barye** and others. In 1875 he traveled in Italy, studying the work of **Donatello**, **Michelangelo** and others, and in 1877 made a tour of the French cathedrals. The Italian masters and the Gothic cathedrals both influenced Rodin's work considerably, as did his interest in the ancient Greeks, but the greatest influence on him was the current trend of Romanticism. In 1877 he exhibited anonymously at the Paris Salon *L'âge d'airain* ("The Age of Bronze"), which aroused controversy because of its realism. In 1879 he exhibited the more highly developed *Saint Jean Baptiste* ("St John the Baptist"). In 1880 he was commissioned by the government to produce the *Porte de l'enfer* ("The Gate of Hell"), inspired by **Dante**'s *Inferno*, for the Musée des Arts Décoratifs, and during the next 30 years he was primarily engaged in the 186 figures for these bronze doors. It was never completed, but many of his best-known works were originally conceived as part of the design of the doors, among them *Le baiser* (1898, "The Kiss") and *Le penseur* (1904, "The Thinker"). From 1886 to 1895 he worked on *Les bourgeois de Calais* ("The Burghers of Calais").

Rodman, Dennis Keith 1961– •*US basketball player*• Born in Trenton, New Jersey, he emerged as a formidable rebounder and defender playing for the Detroit Pistons (1986–93), the San Antonio Spurs (1993–95), the Chicago Bulls (1995–99) and the Los Angeles Lakers (1999). He became one of the most colorful characters in the game and led the league in field goal percentage in 1989 and was voted National Basketball Association Defensive Player of the Year in 1990.

Rodney (of Stoke-Rodney), George Brydges Rodney, 1st Baron c. 1718–92 •*English naval commander*• Born in London of an old Somerset family, he joined the navy in 1732, and in 1747 took part in Admiral **Edward Hawke**'s victory against the French off Cape Finisterre. In 1759 as rear admiral, he destroyed the flotilla assembled at Le Havre for the invasion of England. In 1761 he was appointed commander in chief on the Leeward Islands station, where in 1762 he captured Martinique, St Lucia and Grenada. He became commander in chief in Jamaica (1771–74) and in the Leeward Islands (1779–82), and captured a Spanish convoy off Cape Finisterre and defeated another squadron off Cape St Vincent (1780). In 1782 he gained a brilliant victory over the French off Dominica.

Rodrigo, Joaquín 1901–99 •*Spanish composer*• Born in Sagunto, near Valencia, he became totally blind at the age of three; in spite of this he learned to play the piano. He went to Paris to study with **Paul Dukas** and on returning to Spain was encouraged by **Manuel de Falla**, who nurtured in him a love of Spanish folk music and rhythms. In 1947 he was appointed Professor of Musical History at the University of Madrid. Much of his music involves the guitar, including his most frequently played work, the *Concierto de Aranjuez* (1939, *Aranjuez Concerto*). He also wrote concertos for the violin, the harp and the flute.

Roehm, Ernst *See* **Röhm, Ernst**

Roethke, Theodore 1908–63 •*US poet*• Born in Saginaw, Michigan, he was the son of a florist and often played in his father's greenhouses, an atmosphere later evoked in the horticultural imagery of his poems. He was educated at the University of Michigan and at Harvard, and was Professor of English at Washington University from 1948. It was not until the publication of his fourth collection, *The Waking* (1953, Pulitzer Prize), that he became widely known. His best poems are lyrical and inventive and reveal his grace in handling rhyme and meter. He was an alcoholic who suffered from periodic mental breakdowns, and he often reflected on his madness and despair in his poetry. **Robert Lowell** and others of the "Confessional" poets were influenced by him.

Roger of Taizé, *originally* **Roger Louis Schutz-Marsauche** 1915– •*Swiss founder of the Taizé Community*• Brother Roger was born in Provence, France, the son of a Protestant pastor. In 1940 he went to Taizé, a French hamlet between Cluny and Citeaux, to establish a community devoted to reconciliation and peace in Church and society. Since Easter 1949, when the first seven brothers took their vows, the community has attracted thousands of pilgrims, especially young people. His publications include *The Dynamic of the Provisional* (1965), *Violent for Peace* (1968) and several volumes of extracts from his journal. In 1992 he was awarded the Robert Schuman prize for his participation in the reconstruction of Europe.

Roger of Wendover d. 1236 •*English chronicler*• A Benedictine monk at the monastery of St Albans, he revised and extended the abbey chronicle from the creation to the year 1235, under the title *Flores historiarum* ("Flowers of History"). The section from 1188 to 1235 is believed to be Roger's firsthand account. The chronicle was later extended by **Matthew Paris**.

Rogers, Carl R(ansom) 1902–87 •*US psychotherapist, the originator of client-centered therapy*• Born in Oak Park, Illinois, he took his doctorate in psychology at Columbia University's Teachers College (1931), then worked as director of the child guidance center in Rochester, New York, and taught at the University of Chicago (1945–57). His research there on the one-to-one relationship in therapy is the subject of his book *Client-Centered Therapy* (1951). This form of psychotherapy attempts to elicit and resolve a person's problems by verbal means, but explicitly renounces attempts to talk the subject into accepting any doctrinaire interpretation of his or her symptoms, the procedure practiced by **Sigmund Freud** and his followers. Rogers was also a notable pioneer in carrying out systematic evaluations of the efficacy of psychotherapy.

Rogers, Ginger, *originally* **Virginia Katherine McMath** 1911–95 •*US actress and dancer*• Born in Independence, Missouri, she began her professional career as a dancer in vaudeville and switched from the stage to film after her successful appearance on Broadway in the **Gershwin** musical *Girl Crazy* in 1930. With her screen partner, **Fred Astaire**, she made a series of Hollywood film musicals, performing elaborate dance routines with exuberant grace. The ten films they made together, including *Top Hat* (1935) and *Swing Time* (1936), were enormously popular with audiences during the Depression. She also played dramatic roles in films such as *Kitty Foyle* (1940, Academy Award). She made her last film appearance in *Harlow* (1965). Her many stage appearances included *Hello Dolly!* (1965) on Broadway.

Rogers, Kenny 1938– •*US country and pop singer and actor*• He was born in Houston, Texas, in a poor housing project, and went on to become one of the most successful artists in modern music. He began his career in jazz bands before joining the New Christy Minstrels, then launched his own band, the First Edition, in a country-pop vein. He went solo in the mid-1970s, and began a sequence of immense hits with the country song "Lucille"; one, "The Gambler," was turned into a film, in which Rogers took the leading role.

Rogers (of Riverside), Richard George Rogers, Baron 1933– •*English architect*• Born in Florence, Italy, he studied at the Architectural Association in London and was a founder-member with **Norman Foster** and their wives of Team 4. Like Foster, he was concerned with advanced technology in architecture and pushed the limits of design. Two important works have caused widespread praise and controversy: the Beaubourg or Pompidou Center, Paris (1971–79, with Renzo Piano), a large open interior space clothed in highly colored surfaces; and Lloyds of London (1979–85), a masterful and dramatic exercise in steel and glass. Knighted in 1991, he was made a life peer in 1996.

Rogers, Will, *properly* **William Penn Adair Rogers** 1879–1935 •*US actor, rancher and humorist*• He was born in Oolagah, Indian Territory (Oklahoma), the son of a rancher. His colorful early life included travel to Buenos Aires and Johannesburg, and spells as a ranch hand and cowpuncher. The skills he acquired in riding and lariat throwing gained him employment from 1902 as "The Cherokee Kid" in a variety of Wild West shows. He also appeared at the St Louis World's Fair (1904) and starred in the musical *The Girl Rangers* (1907). He later became a regular attraction in the *Ziegfeld Follies* (1917–18). By this time his act had expanded to include homespun philosophy, wisecracking and rustic ruminations. He made a number of silent films, including *Laughing Bill Hyde* (1918), *Jubilo* (1919) and *Doubling for Romeo* (1921). The first of his many books, *The Cowboy Philosopher at the Peace Conference*, was published in 1919. He wrote a syndicated column from 1926, made frequent radio broadcasts, and came to personify the wisdom of the common man. He made his first sound film, *They Had to See Paris*, in 1929. *Will Rogers' Political Follies* (1929) illustrates his homely liberalism and cracker-barrel philosophy, and films like *State Fair* (1933) catapulted him to the top of movie popularity polls.

" "

You know everybody is ignorant, only on different subjects.

*1924 In the **New York Times**, August 31.*

Roget, Peter Mark 1779–1869 •*English physician and scholar and creator of Roget's Thesaurus*• He was the son of a Huguenot minister and studied medicine, becoming secretary of the Royal Society (1827–49) and Fullerian Professor of Physiology at the Royal Institution (1833–36). In his retirement he devoted his time to the conclusion of a linguistic project that he had been planning for some years. This was published as the *Thesaurus of English Words and Phrases* (1852) and made the name of Roget famous. In it English vocabulary is organized, not alphabetically as in conventional dictionaries, but according to concepts and themes.

Rohde, Ruth, *née* **Bryan** 1885–1954 •*US diplomat and feminist*• Born in Jacksonville, Illinois, she was educated at Monticello Female Academy and the University of Nebraska. In 1910 she married Reginald Owen, an English army major who was left an invalid after World War I. To support her family she entered politics as a Democrat in Florida, and in 1928 successfully ran for Congress, becoming the first congresswoman from the South. Defying accusations of ineligibility for Congress because of her marriage to a foreigner, her remarkable victory on feminist grounds resulted in an amendment to the Cable Act. In 1933 she was appointed US ambassador to Denmark, the first US diplomatic post ever held by a woman.

Röhm or **Roehm, Ernst** 1887–1934 •*German soldier and Nazi politician*• Born in Munich, he became an early supporter of **Hitler** and played a vital role in fostering good relations between the Nazi Party and the Bavarian authorities up until November 1923. He was the organizer and commander of the SA, or stormtroopers ("Brown Shirts"), during the mid-1920s and from 1931 to 1934; however, his plans to pursue policies independently of the NSDAP (German National Socialist Workers Party) and to increase the SA's power led to his summary execution on Hitler's orders.

Rohmer, Sax, *pseudonym of* **Arthur Sarsfield Ward** 1883–1959 •*English writer of mystery stories*• He was born in Birmingham and worked in London, first in commerce, then in journalism. He was interested in Egyptian antiquities and found literary fame with his sardonic "Fu Manchu," whose sinister and criminal schemes were featured in many spine-chilling tales, including *The Mystery of Dr Fu-Manchu* (1913), *The Yellow Claw* (1915), *Moon of Madness* (1927) and *Re-enter Dr Fu-Manchu* (1957).

Roh Tae Woo 1932– •*South Korean politician*• Born in the farming hamlet of Sinyong, in the southeastern region of Kyongsang, he was educated at the Korean Military Academy (1951–55), where he was a classmate of a future president, **Chun Doo-Hwan**. He fought briefly in the Korean War and was a battalion commander during the Vietnam War. He helped Chun seize power in the coup of 1979–80, retired from the army in 1981 and accepted positions in Chun's government. He was elected chairman of the ruling Democratic Justice Party in 1985, and in 1987, following serious popular disturbances, drew up a program of political reform that restored democracy to the country. He was elected president in 1987, and was succeeded by **Kim Young Sam** in 1992. In 1995 he was arrested on charges of accepting bribes in return for contracts, and apologized to the nation for his wrongdoing.

Rojas, Fernando de c. 1465–1541 •*Spanish novelist*• Born in Puebla de Montalbán of Jewish descent, he practiced law in Toledo and wrote a large part of one of the most influential dialogue novels in all European literature, *La Celestina* (1502). This sardonic and mock-moral tale of how a young gentleman makes use of a bawd (Celestina) to seduce a woman from a prestigious family presents many problems, textual and otherwise, and makes oblique reference to the enforced conversion of the Spanish Jews to Christianity.

Roland d. 778 •*Semilegendary French knight*• The hero of the *Chanson de Roland* (11th century, "The Song of Roland"), and the most celebrated of the Paladins of **Charlemagne**, he is said to have been Charlemagne's nephew, and the ideal of a Christian knight. The only evidence for his historical existence is a passage in **Einhard**'s *Life of Charlemagne*, which refers to Roland as having fallen at Roncesvalles, fighting against the Basques. **Matteo Maria Boiardo**'s *Orlando innamorato* and **Ludovico Ariosto**'s *Orlando furioso* depart widely from the old traditions.

Rolfe, Frederick William, *styled* **Baron Corvo** 1860–1913 •*English novelist and essayist*• He was born in London. A convert to Roman Catholicism, he felt his life was shattered by his rejection from the novitiate for the Roman priesthood at the Scots College in Rome, but it prompted his most famous work, *Hadrian VII* (1904), in which a comparable and obviously self-modeled "spoiled priest" is unexpectedly chosen for the papacy, institutes various reforms and is ultimately martyred. He contributed to the *Yellow Book* in the 1890s with *Stories Toto Told Me* (republished in book form, 1895) and is also remembered for *Chronicles of the House of Borgia* (1901) and the posthumous *The Desire and Pursuit of the Whole*, published in 1934.

Rolfe, John 1585–1622 •*English colonist in Virginia*• He emigrated from England to Jamestown, Virginia, in 1610 and discovered a method of curing tobacco which made possible export of the crop and thus helped establish the colony's lucrative tobacco trade. In 1614 he married **Pocahontas**, the daughter of a Powhatan chief, and two years later he took her to England. After her death he returned to Virginia and remarried.

Rolland, Romain 1866–1944 •*French musicologist, writer and Nobel Prize winner*• Born in Clamecy, Nièvre, he studied in Paris and at the French School in Rome, and in 1910 became Professor of the History of Music at the Sorbonne, Paris. In the same year he published *Beethoven*, the first of many works which also included biographies of **Michelangelo** (1906), **Tolstoy** (1911) and **Mahatma Gandhi** (1924). His ten-volume novel cycle *Jean-Christophe*, the hero of which is a musician, was written between 1904 and 1912, and in 1915 he was awarded the Nobel Prize for literature. In World War I he was unpopular for his pacifist and internationalist ideals. He lived in Switzerland until 1938, completing another novel cycle, a series of plays about the French Revolution, and numerous pieces of music criticism. On his return to France he became a mouthpiece of the opposition to Fascism and the Nazis.

Rolling Stones, The •*British rock group*• The group was formed in 1961 in London, and its original members were **Mick Jagger**, Keith Richards (1943–), Bill Wyman (1936–), Charlie Watts (1941–) and Brian Jones (1944–69). Initially in the shadow of the **Beatles**, their carefully cultivated rebellious image and greater reliance on rhythm and blues soon won them their own following. Although their uninhibited lifestyles often hit the headlines (with Jones dying from drug abuse and Jagger and Richards both convicted of possessing drugs), it was the quality of their compositions and the popularity of their stage act which ensured their continuing success. Controversy continued to surround them, with a murder taking place at their infamous Altamont concert in 1969. Jones was replaced shortly before his death by Mick Taylor, an outstanding blues guitarist, who was replaced in turn by the less subtle Ronnie Wood in 1976, while Bill Wyman was replaced by Darryl Jones. They remain the quintessential rock-and-roll band, and have recorded some of the classics of the genre in such singles as "Jumpin' Jack Flash" (1968) and "Honky Tonk Woman" (1969), and albums including *Beggar's Banquet* (1968), *Let it Bleed* (1969), *Sticky Fingers* (1971) and *Exile on Main Street* (1972).

Rollins, Sonny (Theodore Walter) 1930– •*US jazz saxophonist and composer*• Born in New York, he learned to play the piano and alto and tenor saxophone while at school. He worked and recorded with major bebop figures such as **Charlie Parker** and **Miles Davis** in the early 1950s, and emerged from the middle of that decade as an important and highly individual voice in the "hard bop" movement. His classic *Saxophone Colossus* (1956) is a landmark of the form. He is one of the most powerful jazz improvisers (on both tenor and soprano saxophones) to emerge in the post-Parker period. His use of calypso themes, such as his famous "St Thomas" and "Don't Stop the Carnival," reflects his mother's roots in the Virgin Islands. He took on some of the avant-garde directions of the 1960s, and experimented with jazz fusion in the 1970s, but returned to his roots in small-group acoustic jazz in the 1980s.

" "

America is deeply rooted in Negro culture: its colloquialisms, its humor, its music. How ironic that the Negro, who more than any other people can claim America's culture as his own, is being persecuted and repressed.

1958 Part of statement on sleeve of ***Freedom Suite.***

Rollo (Hrolf), *known as* **the Ganger ("Walker")** c. 860–c. 932 •*Viking founder of the duchy of Normandy*• The son of a Norse earl of Orkney (Rognvald of Möre), he became the leader of a band of mercenary Vikings foraging in France (911). In peace talks with King **Charles III** he was offered a large tract of land on the lower Seine in return for becoming Charles's vassal. This territory (Northmandy) was the nucleus of the future duchy of Normandy. One of his descendants was **William the Conqueror**. Rollo (Hrolf) is said to have been such a large man that no horse could carry him, hence his nickname.

Rolls, Charles Stewart 1877–1910 •*English car manufacturer and aviator*• Born in London and educated at Eton and Cambridge, he was the third son of the 1st Baron Llangattock. He experimented from 1895 with the earliest automobiles and in 1906 formed a partnership with **Henry Royce**. The same year he crossed the English Channel by balloon, and in 1910 made the first nonstop double crossing by airplane. He died in a plane crash shortly afterward. Rolls-Royce remains the manufacturer of some of the world's most famous automobile and aircraft engines.

Romano, Giulio *See* **Giulio Romano**

Romanov •*Family of Russian czars*• The family emigrated from (Slavonic) Prussia to the principality of Moscow. **Michael Romanov**, head of the family, was elected czar by the other Russian boyars (1613), and the czardom became hereditary in his house until 1762, when on the death of the Czaritza Elizabeth, the Duke of Holstein-Gottorp, son of **Peter I**'s daughter, succeeded as **Peter III**. Later czars were descended from him and his wife, **Catherine II (the Great)**.

Romberg, Sigmund 1887–1951 •*US composer of operettas*• Born in Nagy Kaniza, Hungary, he settled in the US in 1909, becoming a US citizen. He wrote more than 70 works, of which the most famous are *Blossom Time* (1921), *The Student Prince* (1924), *The Desert Song* (1926) and *The New Moon* (1928).

Romero y Galdames, Oscar Arnulfo 1917–80 •*Salvadorean Roman Catholic prelate and Nobel Prize winner*• He was born in Ciudad Barrios. Ordained in 1942, and, generally conservative in outlook, he was made bishop in 1970 and (to the dismay of the progressives) archbishop in 1977. Acts of political violence and repression of the poor made his public utterances and actions more outspoken. After thousands had died in a brutal persecution, he himself was murdered while preaching, one year after he was nominated for the Nobel Peace Prize by a large number of US and British parliamentarians.

Rommel, Erwin 1891–1944 •*German soldier*• He was born in Heidenheim. He served in World War I and became an instructor at the Dresden Military Academy, where he was an early Nazi sympathizer. He commanded **Hitler**'s headquarters guard, and displayed such skill while leading a panzer division during the invasion of France in 1940 that he was appointed to command the Afrika Corps. His spectacular successes against the attenuated Allied Eighth Army earned him the title "Desert Fox" and the admiration of his opponents. He drove the British back to El-Alamein, but in November 1942 was defeated there by **Montgomery** and retreated to Tunis. In March 1943 he was withdrawn, a sick man, from North Africa at **Mussolini**'s insistence. Hitler subsequently appointed him commander of the Channel defenses in France. Returning home wounded in 1944, he supported the July plot against Hitler's life. After its failure, he committed suicide.

Romney, George 1734–1802 •*English painter*• Born in Dalton-in-Furness, Lancashire, he specialized in portraiture from 1757, and was greatly influenced by Sir **Joshua Reynolds** and, to a lesser extent, by **Thomas Gainsborough**. He went to London in 1762. Most of the leading aristocratic and cultural figures of his day sat for him, including Emma, Lady **Hamilton**. His technique was ostentatiously fluent and elegant.

Romulus Augustulus, *properly* **Flavius Momyllus Romulus Augustus** 5th century •*Last Roman emperor of the West*• His father, Orestes, a Pannonian, established Augustus (the diminutive "Augustulus" was a nickname) as puppet emperor in AD 475–76, retaining all substantial power in his own hands. Orestes failed to conciliate the troops, who had helped him against the previous emperor, Julius Nepos, and was killed. Augustulus surrendered immediately to **Odoacer**, and was dismissed to a villa near Naples with an annual pension of 6,000 pieces of gold.

Ronaldo (Luiz Nazario da Lima) 1976– •*Brazilian soccer player*• Born in Bento Ribeiro, Rio de Janeiro, he lived in poverty before winning recognition as the best soccer player in the world in the 1990s. Having begun in Brazilian leagues in 1990, he joined PSV Eindhoven in 1994 and scored 55 goals in 56 games. In 1996 he transferred to Barcelona for a record fee and helped them to the Spanish League Cup and the European Cup Winners' Cup (1997) before moving to Inter Milan (1997) and Real Madrid (2002). As a star with Brazil, he won the Copa America in 1997 but disappointed in the World Cup final of 1998, which Brazil lost to France, having suffered a fit before the game.

Ronsard, Pierre de 1524–85 •*French poet*• Born in La Possonnière, he served the Dauphin and the Duc d'Orléans as page, and accompanied **James V** with his bride, Mary of Lorraine (**Guise**), to Scotland, and stayed there for three years. Despite the onset of partial deafness, he studied under the humanist **Jean Daurat**, at first with Jean Antoine de Baïf (1532–89) and later with **Joachim du Bellay** and Rémy Belleau (1528–77). His seven years of study produced *Odes* (1550), *Amours* (1552), *Bocage* (1554), *Hymnes* (1555), the conclusion of his *Amours* (1556) and the first collected edition of his poetry (1560). He subsequently wrote two bitter reflections on the state of France (1560–69, 1563), and in 1572, following the massacre of St Bartholomew, *La Franciade*, an unfinished epic. **Charles IX** heaped favors on Ronsard, who became the most important poet of 16th-century France, being the chief exemplar of the doctrines of the Pléiade, which aimed at raising the status of French as a literary language.

Röntgen or **Roentgen, Wilhelm Konrad von** 1845–1923 •*German physicist and Nobel Prize winner*• Born in Lennep, Prussia (now Remscheid, Germany), he studied at Zurich, and after teaching at the University of Strasbourg, he was appointed Professor of Physics successively at the Universities of Giessen (1879), Würzburg (1888), and Munich (1899–1919). At Würzburg in 1895 he discovered the electromagnetic rays which he called X-rays (known also as Röntgen rays), so called because of their unknown properties; for his work on them he was awarded the Rumford Medal in 1896, jointly with **Philipp Lenard**, and in 1901 the first Nobel Prize for physics. He also achieved important results on the heat conductivity of crystals, the specific heat of gases and the magnetic effects produced in dielectrics.

Rooney, Mickey, *originally* **Joe Yule, Jr** 1920– •*US entertainer*• Born in Brooklyn, New York, he appeared on stage as part of his parents' vaudeville act from the age of 15 months, and between 1927 and 1934 starred in about 80 Mickey McGuire short films. Small in stature and irrepressibly energetic, he sang, danced and acted, and played the all-American boy Andy Hardy in a series of films from *A Family Affair* (1937) to *Andy Hardy Comes Home* (1958) as well as numerous other films including *Babes in Arms* (1939) and *National Velvet* (1944). After wartime service in the army, his youthful persona was no longer to the public's taste, but he developed into a prolific and enduring character actor in films including *The Bold and the Brave* (1956) and *The Black Stallion* (1979). He won an Emmy award for a television film, *Bill* (1981), and found great success in the stage revue *Sugar Babies* (1979–85). He received special Academy Awards in 1938 and 1983. He has been married eight times.

Roosevelt, (Anna) Eleanor 1884–1962 •*US humanitarian and First Lady*• Born in New York City, the niece of **Theodore Roosevelt**, in 1905 she became the wife of **Franklin D Roosevelt**. She undertook extensive political activity during her husband's illness from polio, and in 1941 she became assistant director of the Office of Civilian Defense. She was a delegate to the UN Assembly in 1946, chair of the UN Human Rights Commission (1947–51) and US representative to the General Assembly (1946–52). She was also chair of the American UN Association. Her publications include *The Moral Basis of Democracy* (1940) and her autobiography (1962).

Roosevelt, Franklin D(elano), *also called* **FDR** 1882–1945 •*US Democratic statesman and 32nd President of the US*• A distant cousin of **Theodore Roosevelt**, he was born into a wealthy family in Hyde Park, New York, and was educated in Europe and at Harvard and Columbia Law Schools. He was admitted to the New York bar in 1907 and successively served as a state senator (1910–13) and as assistant secretary of the Navy (1913–20) before becoming the Democratic nominee for the vice presidency in 1920. Stricken by polio and paralyzed (1921–23), he was nonetheless elected governor of New York (1928–32). He defeated **Herbert Hoover** in the presidential election of 1932, in which the repeal of prohibition was a decisive issue. At once he was faced with a serious economic crisis, the Great Depression of 1933; he met this by launching his innovative New Deal program, which involved abandonment of the gold standard, devaluation of the dollar, agricultural price supports, and the passage of a Social Security Act (1935) which provided for unemployment and old age insurance. He also inculcated a new spirit of hope through his skillful and optimistic radio fireside chats. During the late 1930s he endeavored to avoid involvement in a European conflict, but on the outbreak of World War II he modified the US's neutrality in favor of the Allies (for example, by the Lend-Lease plan); eventually the country was brought fully into the conflict by Japan's attack on Pearl Harbor (December 1941). A conference with **Churchill** at sea produced the Atlantic Charter, a statement of peace aims; and there were other notable meetings with Churchill and **Stalin** at Tehran (1943) and Yalta (1945). He died three weeks before the Nazi surrender.

Roosevelt, Theodore, *nicknamed* **Teddy** 1858–1919 •*26th President of the US and Nobel Prize winner*• Born in New York City of Dutch and Scottish descent, he studied at Harvard, and after serving in New York politics became Assistant Secretary of the Navy. In 1898 he raised and commanded the volunteer cavalry known as the "Roughriders" in the Spanish-American War, returning to serve as governor of New York State (1898–1900). Elected vice president in 1900, he became president on the assassination of **William McKinley** (1901), and was reelected in 1904. During his presidency (1901–09), he strengthened the navy, initiated the construction of the Panama Canal, and introduced a Square Deal policy for enforcing antitrust laws. He received the Nobel Peace Prize in 1906 for his part in the negotiations that ended the Russo-Japanese War. He returned from a great hunting tour in Central Africa in time to take an active part in the elections of 1910, and created a split in the Republican Party, forming a "progressive" section with his supporters. As Progressive candidate for the presidency in 1912, he was defeated by **Woodrow Wilson**. After exploring the Rio Duvida, of Teodoro, in Brazil (1914), he campaigned vigorously during World War I in the cause of US intervention. He wrote on US ideals, ranching, hunting and zoology. He was an immensely popular president; the teddy bear is named after him.

Rorschach, Hermann 1884–1922 •*Swiss psychiatrist and neurologist*• Born in Zurich, he studied at the university there after deciding against a career in art. He devised a diagnostic procedure for mental disorders based upon the patient's interpretation of a series of standardized ink blots (the Rorschach test).

Rorty, Richard McKay 1931– •*US philosopher*• Born in New York City, he studied at the University of Chicago and Yale, and taught at Yale (1955–57), Wellesley College (1958–61) and Princeton (1961–82), before becoming a professor at the University of Virginia (1982–98) and Stanford (1998–). His *Philosophy and the Mirror of Nature* (1979) constituted a forceful and dramatic attack on the foundationalist, metaphysical aspirations of traditional philosophy. It was hailed by its supporters as the first major text in postanalytical philosophy, and was denounced by its opponents as unscholarly special pleading. He has subsequently attracted a wider readership among those interested in literary criticism, social theory and intellectual history generally, with works such as *Contingency, Irony and Solidarity* (1988) and *Objectivity, Relativism and Truth* (1991).

Rosa, Salvator 1615–73 •*Italian painter and poet*• Born near Naples, he worked in Rome, where his rebellious talents as a painter brought him fame. He made powerful enemies with his satires, and withdrew to Florence for nine years. After that he returned to Rome, where he died. He owes his reputation mainly to his wild and savage landscapes, although he also completed a number of etchings. His *Satires* were published in 1719.

Roscius, *in full* **Quintus Roscius Gallus** c.134–62 BC •*Roman comic actor*• Born into slavery, he became the greatest comic actor in Rome, and was freed by the dictator **Sulla**, with whom he was on close terms. He gave **Cicero** lessons in elocution, and wrote a treatise on eloquence and acting. When he was sued for 50,000 sesterces, Cicero defended him in his oration *Pro Q. Roscio Comoedo.*

Rose, Pete (Peter Edward) 1941– •*US baseball player and manager*• Born in Cincinnati, Ohio, he played with the Cincinnati Reds from 1963 to 1978, then went on to Philadelphia and Montreal before returning to the Reds as player-manager in 1984. In September 1985 he broke **Ty Cobb**'s 57-year-old record of career base hits (4,191). By the time he retired from playing in 1986 he had hit 4,256 base hits, an all-time record. He was manager of the Reds from 1987 to 1989, when an investigation into an alleged gambling offense led to his being banned from baseball for life.

Roseanne, *also known as* **Roseanne Barr**, *previously known as* **Roseanne Arnold** 1952– •*US comedienne*• Born into a Jewish family in Salt Lake City, Utah, she became a teenage mother and housewife, and later worked as a cocktail waitress. She moved to Los Angeles in 1985, and became a regular club and television performer before recording and writing *The Roseanne Barr Show* (1987). She subsequently starred in and wrote the popular television show *Roseanne* (1988–97). She has also appeared in such films as *She-Devil* (1989), *Even Cowgirls Get the Blues* (1994) and *Smoke* (1995), and has published books including *My Lives* (1994).

Rosebery, Archibald Philip Primrose, 5th Earl of 1847–1929 •*Scottish statesman*• He was born in London and was educated at Eton and Christ Church, Oxford. He succeeded his grandfather in 1868. From 1881 to 1883 he was Under-Secretary for the Home Department, and in 1884 became first Commissioner of Works. In 1886 and again from 1892 to 1894, he was Secretary for Foreign Affairs in the **Gladstone** administration. In 1889–90 and 1892 he was chairman of the London County Council. On Gladstone's retirement he became Liberal prime minister (1894). After his government had been defeated at the general election (1895), he remained leader of the Liberal Opposition until his resignation in 1896. In 1911 he was made Earl of Midlothian. He published several biographies and a collection called *Miscellanies* (2 vols, 1921). A devoted race driver, he won the Derby three times (1894, 1895, 1905).

Rosenberg, Alfred 1893–1946 •*German Nazi politician*• He was born in Estonia. An avid supporter of National Socialism, he joined the Nazis in 1920, edited their journals, for a time (1933) directed the party's foreign policy, and in 1934 was given control of its cultural and political education policy. In his *The Myth of the 20th Century* (1930) he expounded the extreme Nazi doctrines which he later put into practice in eastern Europe, for which crimes he was sentenced to death at Nuremberg in 1946.

Rosenberg, Isaac 1890–1918 •*English poet and artist*• Born in Bristol, the son of Jewish émigrés from Russia, he was educated at council schools in the East End of London, and was apprenticed as an engraver before studying art at the Slade School of Art. He went to South Africa in 1914 but returned to England the following year, enlisted in the army and was killed in action in France. His first collection, *Night and Day*, appeared in 1912, followed by *Youth* in 1915 and the posthumous *Poems* in 1922. Alhough he was revered by the cognoscenti, his reputation languished until the appearance in 1937 of his *Collected Works* (with a new edition in 1979).

“ ”

Death could drop from the dark
As easily as song.

1917 "Returning, We Hear the Larks."

Rosenberg, Julius 1918–53 and **Ethel**, *née* **Greenglass** 1915–53 •*US Communist spies*• Julius Rosenberg joined the Communist Party as a young man and graduated in electrical engineering. He and his wife, Ethel, were part of a transatlantic spy ring uncovered after the trial of **Klaus Fuchs** in Great Britain. Julius was employed by the US Army, and Ethel's brother, David Greenglass, at the nuclear research station at Los Alamos; all three were convicted of passing atomic secrets to the Soviet vice consul. Greenglass turned witness for the prosecution and saved his life. The Rosenbergs were sentenced to death in 1951 and, despite numerous appeals from many West European countries and three stays of execution, were executed at Sing Sing prison, New York. They were the first US citizens to be executed for espionage.

Rosenquist, James Albert 1933– •*US painter*• Born in Grand Falls, North Dakota, he studied at the Minneapolis School of Art (1948), the University of Minnesota (1952–54) and the Art Students League (1955). He began as an abstract painter but took to pop art in the mid-1960s, painting enlarged pieces of unrelated everyday objects, including *Horse Blinders* (1969, Ludwig Museum, Cologne). He is drawn to shiny surfaces and advertising logos, and the superimposition of one image on another in his work is often traced to the inspiration of his early employment as a billboard painter.

Rosenthal, Jack Morris 1931– •*English dramatist*• Born in Manchester and educated at the University of Sheffield, he began his professional writing with over 150 episodes of *Coronation Street* (1961–69). He was also a contributor to the influential satirical program *That Was the Week That Was* (1963). His warmly humorous television plays, dramatizing real-life stories, wartime nostalgia and Jewish domestic issues, include *The Evacuees* (1975), *Barmitzvah Boy* (1976), *Spend, Spend, Spend* (1977) and *London's Burning* (1986). He also wrote the film scripts *Lucky Star* (1980) and *Yentl* (1983) in collaboration with **Barbra Streisand**, and his stage work includes *Smash!* (1981) and *Our Gracie* (1983). Later television works include *Wide-Eyed and Legless* (1993) and *Moving Story* (1994). He is married to **Maureen Lipman**.

Rosenzweig, Franz 1886–1929 •*German theologian*• He was born in Kassel, to a Jewish family. He was on the point of converting from Judaism to Christianity when a religious experience in 1913 caused him to reaffirm his Jewishness and devote the rest of his life to the study and practice of Judaism. His major work was *Der Stern der Erlösung* ("The Star of Redemption"), begun while in active service in World War I and published in 1921. From 1922 he suffered progressive paralysis, but still collaborated with **Martin Buber** from 1925 on a new German translation of the Hebrew Bible. After his death his work exercised a profound influence on Jewish religious thought.

Ross, Betsy, *née* **Griscom** 1752–1836 •*US seamstress*• Born in Philadelphia, she was married to an Episcopal clergyman in 1773 and ran an upholstering business after his death in 1776. According to tradition, she was visited by **George Washington** and other patriots in June 1776 and asked to make a flag for the new nation. The design she suggested, the Stars and Stripes, was voted the national flag by the Continental Congress on June 14, 1777.

Ross, Diana, *professional name of* **Diane Earle** 1944– •*US pop singer and film actress*• She was born in Detroit, where she grew up in a poor housing project. With Florence Ballard and Mary Wilson, she formed the Primettes, later to become the Supremes. Their classic Tamla Motown hits "Baby Love" (1964) and "Stop! In the Name of Love" (1965) were characteristic of their style. In 1970 Ross began a solo career, both as singer and actress. She played the role of **Billie Holiday** in *Lady Sings the Blues* (1972) and later acted in *Mahogany* (1975) and *The Wiz* (1978). *Diana* (1980) and *Swept Away* (1984) are among her most acclaimed solo albums to date. In recent years, Ross has returned to her sanitized version of Holiday's style, having relaunched herself in 1990 as a jazz diva. Her television work includes the drama *Out of Darkness* (1994).

Ross, Harold Wallace 1892–1951 •*US editor*• He was born in Aspen, Colorado. After working as a reporter and editor, he founded the *New Yorker* in 1925. The magazine became legendary for its high standard of writing and attention to detail, as well as for its clever one-line cartoons. Known for his irascible temper and keen journalistic instincts, Ross drafted many gifted writers for the staff of the *New Yorker* and served as its editor until his death.

Ross, Sir James Clark 1800–62 •*Scottish explorer and naval officer*• Born in London, the son of a rich merchant, he first went to sea with his uncle, Sir **John Ross**, at the age of 12, conducting surveys of the White Sea and the Arctic, and assisting in Ross's first attempt to find the Northwest Passage in 1818, and accompanied William Parry (1790–1855) on four Arctic expeditions (1819–27). From 1829 to 1833 he was joint leader with his uncle of a private Arctic expedition, and in 1831 he located the magnetic North Pole. He led an expedition to the Antarctic (1839–43) on the *Erebus* and the *Terror*, during which he discovered Victoria Land and the volcano Mt Erebus. He was knighted on his return in 1843. He made a last expedition in 1848–49, searching for the ill-fated **Franklin** expedition in Baffin Bay. Ross Island, the Ross Sea and Ross's gull are named after him.

Ross, Sir John 1777–1856 •*Scottish explorer and naval officer*• Born at Inch manse in Wigtownshire, he joined the navy at the age of nine and served with distinction in the Napoleonic Wars. From 1812 he conducted surveys in the White Sea and the Arctic, leading an expedition in 1818, including his nephew Sir **James Clark Ross** and Sir **Edward Sabine**, in search of the Northwest Passage. He led another such expedition (1829–33) with his nephew, financed by the distilling magnate Sir Felix Booth, during which he discovered and named Boothia Peninsula, King William Land and the Gulf of Boothia.

Ross, John, *Cherokee name* **Kooweskoowe** or **Coowescoowe** 1790–1866 •*Native American leader and Cherokee chief*• Born near Lookout Mountain, Tennessee, the son of a Scottish father and a part-Cherokee mother, he was raised among the Cherokee but was taught by white tutors and attended an academy in Kingston, Tennessee. He served in a Cherokee regiment under General **Andrew Jackson** in the War of 1812. In 1820 the Cherokee adopted a republican form of government, and Ross sought to promote literacy and Christianity among his people in the hope that by establishing institutions parallel to those of the US, they could win toleration and statehood. He helped to write the constitution (1827) that established the Cherokee nation under the government of an elected chief, a senate, and a house of representatives. As chief of the eastern Cherokee (1828–39), he spent a decade resisting the campaign by the state of Georgia to take over Cherokee ancestral lands. He led a number of delegations to Washington and successfully brought the Cherokee's case before the US Supreme Court, which ruled in their favor in 1832. President **Jackson**, whom Ross and other Cherokee had served loyally in the Creek War, favored the policy of "Indian removal" and refused to enforce the Court's decree, and in 1838 the Cherokee were evicted from Georgia. Unwillingly Ross led his people on the Trail of Tears (1838–39), an 800-mile trek to Indian Territory in what is now Oklahoma, during which 4,000 Cherokee—almost a quarter of the nation—died of exhaustion, hunger, exposure and disease. Among those who perished on the journey was Ross's wife, Quatie. From 1839 until his death, Ross was chief of the eastern and western Cherokee, which were united in one nation in the new territory.

Ross, Mother *See* **Davies, Christian**

Ross, Sir Ronald 1857–1932 •*British physician and Nobel Prize winner, discoverer of the malaria parasite*• Born in Almara, Nepal, the son of an army officer, he studied medicine at St Bartholomew's Hospital in London and entered the Indian Medical Service in 1881. Investigating Sir **Patrick Manson**'s belief that malaria is transmitted through mosquito bites, Ross discovered the malaria parasite in the stomachs of mosquitoes that had bitten patients suffering from the disease, and by 1898 had worked out the life cycle of the malaria parasite for birds. He was knighted in 1911, and from 1926 he directed the Ross Institute in London. A gifted if eccentric mathematician who also wrote poetry and romances, his award of the 1902 Nobel Prize for physiology or medicine was contested by Giovanni Grassi (1854–1925), an Italian parasitologist who had independently and almost simultaneously worked out the life cycle of the human malaria parasite.

Rossellini, Isabella 1952– •*US actress and model*• Born in Rome, the daughter of **Ingrid Bergman** and **Roberto Rossellini**, she studied at the Academy of Fashion and Costume, Rome, and worked as a journalist, cosmetics model and costume designer. She first attracted major attention as a screen actress in the mid-1980s, notably as the victimized beauty Dorothy Vallens in the **David Lynch** film *Blue Velvet* (1986), and went on to star in *Wild at Heart* (1990) and *The Imposters* (1998).

Rossellini, Roberto 1906–77 •*Italian film director*• Born in Rome, he entered the film industry as a sound technician and editor before graduating by way of short films to his feature-length directorial debut with *La nave bianca* (1941). Immediately after World War II, his trilogy, *Roma città aperta* (1945, *Rome, Open City*), *Paisà* (1946, *Paisan*) and *Germania, Anno Zero* (1947, *Germany, Year Zero*), helped establish the neorealist movement with their raw, naturalistic depictions of everyday life. His affair with **Ingrid Bergman** (whom he later married, 1949–57) provoked worldwide condemnation, and the films they made together, such as *Stromboli* (1950) and *Viaggio in Italia* (1953, *Strangers*), were critically undervalued and sometimes banned. He enjoyed a popular success with *Il Generale della Rovere* (1959, *General della Rovere*) and spent his later years making television documentaries on historical figures. One of his daughters by Ingrid Bergman, **Isabella Rossellini**, is an actress.

Rossetti, Christina Georgina 1830–94 •*English poet*• Born in London, the sister of **Dante Gabriel Rossetti**, she was educated at home, and was to have been a governess, but retired because of ill health. Her grandfather printed a pamphlet by her before she was in her teens, and her earliest lyrics were published in the first issue of *The Germ* (1850) under the pseudonym Ellen Alleyne. *Goblin Market* (1862) was her best-known poem, and *The Prince's Progress* appeared in 1866 and *Sing Song: A Nursery Rhyme Book* in 1872. She was a devout Anglican, and her later works include *The Face of the Deep: A Devotional Commentary on the Apocalypse* (1892).

Rossetti, Dante Gabriel, *properly* **Gabriel Charles Dante Rossetti** 1828–82 •*English poet, painter and translator*• Born in London, he was the son of **Gabriele Rossetti** and brother of **Christina** and **William Rossetti**. He was educated at King's College School and attended Cary's Art Academy, and with **Holman Hunt** and **John Millais** he formed the Pre-Raphaelite Brotherhood. Throughout the 1840s he developed his poetry and painting, completing on canvas *The Girlhood of Mary Virgin* (1849) and *Ecce Ancilla Domini* (1850), both in Tate Britain, London. Like his sister Christina, several of his poems, for example, "The Blessed Damozel" appeared in *The Germ* (1850). He met Elizabeth Siddal (or Siddall) in 1849–50 and tutored her in her painting and writing, encouraging her to model for him. He married her in 1860. He met **John Ruskin** in 1854 and two years later **William Morris**, whom he manifestly influenced. In 1861 he published *The Early Italian Poets*, which consisted of translations from 60 poets. His wife's death in 1862 from an overdose of laudanum affected him deeply and his work became increasingly morbid. From 1869 he formed a liaison with Jane, the wife of William Morris, and she became his model during his sojourn at Kelmscott Manor (1871–74) and later, notably for *The Daydream* (1880, Victoria and Albert Museum, London). *Ballads and Sonnets*, with the sonnet sequence "The House of Life" and "The King's Tragedy," appeared in 1881. At odds with Victorian morality, his work is lush, erotic and medieval, romantic in spirit, and of abiding interest.

Rossetti, Gabriele 1783–1854 •*Italian poet and writer*• The father of **Christina Rossetti**, **Dante Gabriel Rossetti** and **William Michael Rossetti**, he was the curator of ancient bronzes in the Museum of Bronzes at Naples. He was a member of the provisional government set up by **Joachim Murat** in Rome (1813). After the restoration of **Ferdinand I** to Naples, he joined the Carbonari secret society and greeted the constitution demanded by the patriots in 1820 in a famous ode. On the overthrow of the constitution he went to London (1824), where he became Professor of Italian at the new University of London. He was also a student of **Dante**.

Rossetti, William Michael 1829–1919 •*English critic*• He was the son of **Gabriele Rossetti** and brother of **Christina** and **Dante Gabriel Rossetti**. He became one of the seven Pre-Raphaelite "brothers," and edited their manifesto *The Germ* (1850). He was art critic of *The Spectator* from 1850, wrote biographies of **Shelley** and **Keats**, and published editions of **Coleridge**, **Milton**, **William Blake** and **Walt Whitman**. Like all his family, he was devoted to the study of **Dante**, whose *Inferno* he translated. He also wrote memoirs of his brother (1895) and his sister (1904).

Rossini, Gioacchino Antonio 1792–1868 •*Italian operatic composer*• He was born in Pesaro. Taught to sing and play at an early age, in 1806 he began to study composition at the Liceo in Bologna. Tiring of the stern academic routine, he wrote several small-scale comic operas, among them *La scala di seta* (1812, "The Silken Ladder"), whose lively overture has remained popular although the opera itself was a failure. His first successes were *Tancredi* (1813) and *L'italiana in Algeri* (1813, "The Italian Girl in Algiers"). In 1816 his masterpiece, *Il barbiere de Seviglia* ("The Barber of Seville"), was received in Rome with enthusiasm despite a disastrous opening night. *Otello* (1816) has since been eclipsed by **Verdi**'s masterpiece. In 1817 *La cenerentola* ("Cinderella") was favorably received in Rome and *La gazza ladra* ("The Thieving Magpie") in Milan, and these were followed in Naples by *Armide* (1817), *Mosè in Egitto* (1818, "Moses in Egypt") and *La donna del lago* (1819, "The Lady of the Lake"). *Semiramide* (1823), the most advanced of his works, had only a lukewarm reception from the Venetians. Rossini was invited to become director of the Italian Theater in Paris, where he adapted several of his works to French taste: *Maometto II* (1820) as *Le siège de Corinth* (1826, "The Siege of Corinth"), *Mosè in Egitto* as *Moïse et pharaon* (1827), and the stage cantata *Il viaggio a Reims* (1825) as *Le Comte Ory* (1828, "Count Ory"). In 1829, what is arguably his greatest work, *Guillaume Tell* ("William Tell"), written in a nobler style than his Italian operas, was first performed. After 1829 Rossini wrote little music, and in 1836 he retired to Bologna and took charge of the Liceo, whose fortunes he revived. With **Donizetti** and **Bellini**, Rossini helped form the 19th-century Italian operatic style which became the inheritance of **Verdi**. Many of his works are still much performed.

“ ”

Monsieur Wagner a de beaux moments, mais de mauvais quart-d'heures!
Monsieur Wagner has good moments, but awful quarters of an hour!
1867 Quoted in Emile Naumann ***Italienische Tondichter*** *(1883).*

Rossiter, Leonard 1926–84 •*English actor*• Born in Liverpool, Merseyside, he was an insurance clerk before turning to the stage. Hawklike features, combined with expert timing and energetic attack, allowed him to portray the furtively sinister or the manically comic. His first film appearance in *A Kind of Loving* (1962) was followed by many others, including *Billy Liar* (1963). His notable stage work included *Banana Box* (1973), which was made into a television series, *Rising Damp* (1974–78), where his performance as the leering landlord Mr Rigsby brought widespread popularity. Later television appearances included *The Fall and Rise of Reginald Perrin* (1976–80).

Rostand, Edmond 1868–1918 •*French poet and dramatist*• He was born in Marseilles. He published *Les musardises* ("Dawdlings"), a volume of verse, in 1890, but rose to fame with *Cyrano de Bergerac* (1897, Eng trans 1898; also trans by **Anthony Burgess** for the film by Jean Paul Rappeneau, 1992), *L'aiglon* (1900, Eng trans 1900), *Chantecler* (1910, Eng trans 1910) and other plays in verse which eschewed the prevailing moods of naturalism and expressionism in favor of a lighter, more vivacious popular style.

Rostropovich, Mstislav Leopoldovich 1927– •*Russian cellist and conductor*• Born in Baku, he was awarded the Lenin prize in 1964, and left the USSR in 1974 with his wife, soprano Galina Vishnevskaya (1926–). He was musical director of the National Symphony Orchestra, Washington (1977–94), and joint artistic director of the Aldeburgh Festival in England. He was deprived of Soviet citizenship in 1978, although it was restored in 1990. **Benjamin Britten** was a close friend and wrote several cello works for him.

Rotblat, Sir Joseph 1908– •*British physicist, campaigner and Nobel Prize winner*• Born in Warsaw, Poland, he studied physics at the University of Warsaw. During World War II he worked on nuclear energy and weapons development at the University of Liverpool and Los Alamos, New Mexico, later teaching at St Bartholomew's Medical Hospital, London (1950–76). He was a founder, secretary-general (1957–73) and president (1988–97) of the Pugwash Conferences on Science and World Affairs, a forum for scientists wishing to promote nuclear disarmament, and won the Nobel Peace Prize in 1995 (jointly with the Pugwash organization) for his work in this area.

Roth, Henry 1906–95 •*US novelist*• He was born in Tysmenica in the Austro-Hungarian Empire, and was taken to the US as a baby. His childhood is fictionalized in *Call It Sleep* (1934), one of the classics of 20th-century US literature. During the Depression, Roth worked for the New Deal Works Progress Administration, then worked variously as a teacher, mental hospital assistant, duck farmer and machine tooler. *Shifting Landscape*, a collection of occasional pieces, was published in 1987. He took many years to complete his long-projected second novel, the second volume of which, *Mercy of a Rude Stream*, appeared in 1994.

Roth, Philip Milton 1933– •*US novelist*• Born in Newark, New Jersey, he grew up in a Jewish neighborhood and went to public schools. He attended Bucknell University as an undergraduate and received a master's degree from the University of Chicago. His early fiction deals largely with Jewish family life in Newark. His first book, *Goodbye, Columbus* (1959), a collection of short stories about a middle-class Jewish family, won the National Book Award. There followed two bleak, realistic novels, *Letting Go* (1962) and *When She Was Good* (1967). The publication of *Portnoy's Complaint* (1969), a sexually explicit, comedic novel, consisting of the narrator's confession to his psychiatrist, achieved both notoriety and critical acclaim. Roth has since produced a steady stream of novels in a variety of styles and genres, and won an abundance of awards, including the Pulitzer Prize and a second National Book Award. Nathan Zuckerman, a writer, is the central character in a series of novels, including *The Ghost Writer* (1979), *Zuckerman Unbound* (1981) and *The Anatomy Lesson* (1983), and its epilogue, *The Prague Orgy* (1985), collected in *Zuckerman Bound* (1985). Roth's namesake is the narrator of another group of novels, including *Patrimony* (1991), *Operation Shylock* (1993), and *The Plot Against America* (2004). His American trilogy, consisting of *American Pastoral* (1997), *I Married a Communist* (1998), and *The Human Stain* (2000), is constructed around key moments in recent American history.

Rothermere, 1st Viscount *See* **Harmsworth, Harold Sydney**

Rothko, Mark, *originally* **Marcus Rothkovitch** 1903–70 •*US painter*• Born in Dvinsk, Latvia, he emigrated with his family to the US in 1913 and later studied at Yale (1921–23). Largely self-taught as an artist, during the 1940s he was influenced by surrealism, but by the early 1950s had evolved his own peaceful and meditative form of abstract expressionism, staining huge canvases with rectangular blocks of pure color and later with somber reds and blacks. Among his works in this style, which was dubbed "color field painting," is *The Black and the Red* (1956). In 1958–59 he was commissioned to paint a series of murals for the Four Seasons Restaurant in the Seagram Building, New York, but he withheld them, and in 1969 donated a selection of them to the Tate Gallery, London (including *Black on Maroon*). On the day of their arrival in 1970 a cable from New York announced that he had been found dead in his studio.

Rothschild, Mayer Amschel 1744–1812 •*German financier*• Born in Frankfurt am Main, he was trained as a rabbi, but founded a business as a moneylender and became the financial adviser to the Landgrave of Hesse. The house received a heavy commission for transmitting money from the English government to the Duke of **Wellington** in Spain, paid the British subsidies to Continental princes and negotiated loans for Denmark between 1804 and 1812. At his death, the founder left five sons, all of whom were made barons of the Austrian Empire in 1822. Anselm Mayer (1773–1855), the eldest son, succeeded as head of the firm in Frankfurt; Solomon (1774–1855), established a branch in Vienna; Nathan Mayer (1777–1836), one in 1798 in London; Charles (1788–1855), one in Naples (discontinued in about 1861); and James (1792–1868), one in Paris. They negotiated many of the great government loans of the 19th century, and Nathan raised the house to be first among the banking houses of the world. He staked his fortunes on the success of Great Britain in her duel with **Napoleon**, and, receiving the first news of the outcome at Waterloo, sold and bought stock which brought him over £1 million profit. His son Lionel (1808–79) achieved much for the civil and political emancipation of the Jews in Great Britain. Lionel's son, Nathan (1840–1915), succeeded (1876) to his uncle Anthony's baronetcy (1846), and was made Baron Rothschild in 1885.

Rouault, Georges Henri 1871–1958 •*French painter and engraver*• Born in Paris, he was apprenticed to a stained-glass designer in 1885. He used glowing colors, outlined with black, to achieve a concise depiction of the clowns, prostitutes and biblical characters he chose as his subjects. He studied under **Gustave Moreau**, and in 1898 was made curator of the Moreau Museum, Paris. About 1904 he joined the Fauves, and in 1910 held his first one-man show. Many of his works were acquired by the art dealer Ambroise Vollard (1865–1939), who commissioned the series of large religious engravings *Miserere* and *Guerre*.

Roubillac or **Roubiliac, Louis François** 1702/1705–62 •*French sculptor*• Born in Lyons, he studied at Paris, and in the 1730s settled in London. His rococo statue of **Handel** for Vauxhall Gardens (1738, now in the Victoria and Albert Museum, London) first made him popular. His other most famous statues, also in a lively and informal style, are those of Sir **Isaac Newton** (1755) in Trinity College, Cambridge, and of **Shakespeare** (1758, now in the British Museum, London). Busts include **William Hogarth** (c. 1740, National Portrait Gallery, London), and **David Garrick** (1758, National Portrait Gallery). His first major commission in London was the Argyll monument in Westminster Abbey (1749).

Rous, (Francis) Peyton 1879–1970 •*US pathologist and Nobel Prize winner*• Born in Baltimore, Maryland, he was educated at Johns Hopkins University and Medical School, and held various posts at the Rockefeller Institute for Medical Research in New York City. From 1909 he began studying a sarcoma in chickens, which he demonstrated to have been caused by a virus. In the 1930s he discovered a rabbit tumor which was also caused by a virus, the first time that a virus was implicated in cancer. The discovery of many other oncogenic (cancer-causing) viruses from the 1950s made his early work more widely appreciated. He shared with **Charles B Huggins** the 1966 Nobel Prize for physiology or medicine.

Rousseau, Henri Julien Félix 1844–1910 •*French primitive painter*• Born in Laval, he joined the army at the age of about 18, but spent most of his life as a minor tax collector in the Paris toll office, hence his nickname *Le Douanier*. He retired in 1885 and spent his time painting and copying at the Louvre. From 1886 to 1898 he exhibited at the Salon des Indépendants and again from 1901 to 1910. Despite its denial of conventional perspective and color, his painting has a fierce reality more surrealist than primitive. He produced painstaking portraits, and painted dreams, such as the *Sleeping Gipsy* (1897), and exotic imaginary landscapes with trees and plants, which he had seen in the Jardin des Plantes.

Rousseau, Jean Jacques 1712–78 •*French political philosopher, educationist and author*• He was born in Geneva, Switzerland. He had no formal education, ran away to Italy and Savoy, and after an itinerant existence for a few years eventually became the lover and general factotum of Baronne Kouise de Varens (1733–41). In 1741 he moved to Paris, where he began to thrive, and began a lifelong association with an illiterate maidservant at his inn, Thérèse le Vasseur; together they had five children, all of whom he consigned to foundling hospitals, despite his later proclamations about the innocence of childhood. He became acquainted with **Voltaire** and **Denis Diderot**, and contributed articles on music and political economy to the *Encyclopédie*. In 1750 he made his name with a prize essay, *Discours sur les arts et sciences* (Eng trans *A Discourse on the Arts and Sciences*, 1752), which argued that civilization had corrupted our natural goodness and decreased our freedom; and in 1752 he triumphed with an operetta, *Le devin du village* (Eng trans *The Cunning Man*, 1766). He was now a celebrity, and in 1754 wrote *Discours sur l'origine et les fondements de l'inégalité parmi les hommes* ("Discourse on the Origin and Foundations of Inequality Among Men"), in which he attacked private property and argued that humans' perfect nature was corrupted by society. In 1762 he published his masterpiece, *Du contrat social* (Eng trans *A Treatise on the Social Contract*, 1764), in which every individual is made to surrender his rights totally to the collective "general will," which is the sole source of legitimate sovereignty and by definition represents the common good; the aberrant can then, in the sinister phrase, "be forced to be free" in their own interests. His text, with its slogan "Liberty, Equality, Fraternity," became the bible of the French Revolution and of progressive movements generally, though the main thesis is vulnerable to totalitarian misrepresentations. Also in 1762 he published his theory of education in the form of a novel, *Émile, ou de l'éducation* (Eng trans *Emilius and Sophia; or, A New System of Education*, 1762–73), a simple romance of a child reared apart from other children as an experiment. This work greatly influenced educationists such as **Johann Pestalozzi** and **Friedrich Froebel**, but so outraged the political and religious establishment that he fled to Switzerland. He moved to England in 1766 at the invitation of **David Hume** and went to live at Wootton Hall near Ashbourne in Derbyshire (1766–67), where he began writing his *Les confessions* (Eng trans *Confessions*, 1783–91), a remarkably frank work published posthumously (1782–89). He became mentally unstable at about this time, quarreled with his British friends (particularly Hume), developed a persecution complex, and fled back to France in 1767. In Paris from 1770 to 1778, he completed his *Confessions* and other works. He declined further, became seriously insane, and died in Ermenonville. In 1794 his remains were placed alongside those of Voltaire in the Panthéon in Paris.

Roussel, Albert 1869–1937 •*French composer*• Born in Tourcoing, he joined the navy and served in Indochina, but at the age of 25 he resigned his commission to study music in Paris, joining the Schola Cantorum in 1896 under **Vincent d'Indy**. A journey to India and the Far East gave him an interest in Asian music which, combined with the influence of **Stravinsky**, inspired the chorale *Évocations* (1912) and the opera *Padmâvati*, begun in 1914 and completed after World War I. Service in the war ruined his health, and after his discharge he largely retired into seclusion, devoting his time entirely to composition. His works include ballets, the best-known of which are *Bacchus et Ariane* (1931) and *Le festin de l'araignée* (1912, "The Spider's Feast"), four symphonies and numerous choral and orchestral works.

Roussel, Raymond 1887–1933 •*French fabulist*• He was born in Paris to a stockbroker father and an eccentrically artistic mother. He wrote verse at a young age and his first novel, *La doublure*, at the age of 10. His most important work is *Impressions d'Afrique* (1910, Eng trans *Impressions of Africa*, 1965), a surreal fantasy about parts of the continent he had never visited. The book is full of non sequiturs, quasi-documentary asides and free invention. It made a considerable impact on such US writers as **John Ashbery** and **Harry**

Mathews, who named their experimental journal after a later book of Roussel's, *Locus Solus*. He suffered from a heavy addiction to barbiturates, which is reflected in the astonishing pace and rhythmic freedom of his prose. He committed suicide.

Routledge, Patricia 1929– •*English actress*• Born in Birkenhead, Merseyside, she studied at the University of Liverpool and the Bristol Old Vic Theatre School, working widely in theater and winning a Tony award for Best Musical Actress in 1967. She later became well known in the role of Hyacinth Bucket (pronounced "Bouquet") in the television sitcom *Keeping Up Appearances* (1990–95) and has worked widely in film and radio drama, winning critical praise for her performances in **Alan Bennett**'s *Talking Heads* series (1988 and 1998).

Roux, Albert 1935– and **Michel André** 1941– •*French chefs and restaurateurs*• After training and working in Paris, the brothers moved to London and opened their first British restaurant, Le Gavroche, in 1967. They are both especially renowned for their patisserie, and in 1993 they were the only two restaurateurs in Great Britain to be awarded three Michelin stars. They appeared together on television in *At Home with the Roux Brothers* (1988), and have jointly written cookbooks.

Roux, (Pierre Paul) Émile 1853–1933 •*French bacteriologist*• Born in Confolens, Charente, he studied at the Universities of Clermont-Ferrand and Paris, where he became the assistant of **Louis Pasteur**, and in 1904 succeeded him as director of the Pasteur Institute. With Pasteur he tested the anthrax vaccine, and contributed much of the early work on the rabies vaccine. With Alexandre Yersin (1863–1943) he showed that the symptoms of diphtheria are caused by a lethal toxin produced by the diphtheria bacillus, and tested blood serum containing the antitoxin from horses on patients. As a result, the mortality rate fell dramatically. He also made important contributions to research on syphilis.

Rowbotham, Sheila 1943– •*English social historian and feminist*• Born in Leeds, she was educated at Oxford and became involved in the women's movement in the late 1960s. An active socialist, she wrote for several socialist papers and provoked controversy with *Beyond the Fragments: Feminism and the Making of Socialism* (1979, with Segal and Wainwright). Among her most important historical works are *Women, Resistance and Revolution* (1972) and *Woman's Consciousness, Man's World* (1973).

“ ”

There is no "beginning" of feminism in the sense that there is no beginning to defiance in women.

1972 ***Women, Resistance and Revolution****, chapter 1.*

Rowe, Nicholas 1674–1718 •*English poet and dramatist*• Born in Little Barford, Bedfordshire, he was educated at Westminster, London, and called to the bar, but from 1692 devoted himself to literature. Between 1700 and 1715 he produced eight plays, of which three were popular: *Tamerlane* (1702), *The Fair Penitent* (1703) and *The Tragedy of Jane Shore* (1714), followed by *The Tragedy of Lady Jane Grey* (1715). Lothario in *The Fair Penitent* was the prototype of Lovelace in **Samuel Richardson**'s *Clarissa*, and the name is still the eponym for a fashionable rake. Rowe translated **Lucan**'s *Pharsalia*, and his edition of **Shakespeare** (1709–10) contributed to the popularity of that author. He was undersecretary to the Duke of Queensberry from 1709 to 1711, and in 1715 was appointed poet laureate.

Rowland, Frank Sherwood 1927– •*US chemist and Nobel Prize winner*• Born in Delaware, Ohio, he studied at Ohio Wesleyan University and the University of Chicago and lectured at Princeton (1952–56) and the Universities of Kansas (1956–64) and California (1964–94). Among numerous honors, he received the Nobel Prize for chemistry (1995; with **Paul J Crutzen** and **Mario Molina**) for work on the role of chlorfluorocarbons in the catalytic destruction of atmospheric ozone.

Rowlandson, Thomas 1756–1827 •*English caricaturist*• Born in London, from the age of 15 he studied art in Paris, where he acquired a taste for high living and squandered a considerable legacy. In 1777 he returned to London to work as a portrait painter and turned to watercolor caricatures and book illustrations for authors including **Tobias Smollett**, **Laurence Sterne** and **Oliver Goldsmith**. He also engraved a popular series, *Tour of Dr Syntax in Search of the Picturesque* (1812, with sequels in 1820 and 1821); also *The English Dance of Death* (1815) and *The Dance of Life* (1816).

Rowley, William c. 1585–c. 1626 •*English actor and playwright*• Little is known about him except that he collaborated with **Thomas Dekker**, **Thomas Middleton**, **Thomas Heywood**, **John Webster**, **Philip Massinger** and **John Ford**. Four plays published under his name are extant: *A New Wonder, a Woman Never Vext* (1632), *All's Lost by Lust* (c. 1620, a tragedy), *A Match at Midnight* (1633) and *A Shoemaker, a Gentleman* (1638).

Rowling, J(oanne) K(athleen) 1965– •*English author*• She was born in Chipping Sodbury, Avon, studied at the University of Exeter, and began her career as a teacher of English and French. Her first children's book, *Harry Potter and the Sorcerer's Stone* (1997), set at the Hogwarts School of Witchcraft and Wizardry, was an immediate success and was followed by equally successful sequels. The lonely orphan Harry Potter became an international cult hero, and films of the first three Harry Potter novels were released in 2001, 2002, and 2004.

Rowling, Sir Wallace Edward 1927–95 •*New Zealand politician*• He was born in Motueka, South Island. After graduating from the University of Canterbury he joined the New Zealand army and served in the education corps before becoming active in the Labour Party. He entered parliament in 1962 and was finance minister in the administration of **Norman Kirk**. When Kirk died in 1974, Rowling succeeded him as prime minister until 1985. Rowling was knighted and became ambassador to the US (1985–88). From 1990 until his death he was president of the New Zealand Institute of International Affairs.

Rowntree, Joseph 1836–1925 •*English Quaker industrialist and reformer*• Born in York, he was the son of Joseph Rowntree, a Quaker grocer. With his brother, Henry Isaac (d. 1883), he became a partner in a cocoa firm in York in 1869, and built up welfare organizations for his employees. He was succeeded as chairman by his son **Seebohm Rowntree**.

Rowntree, (Benjamin) Seebohm 1871–1954 •*English manufacturer and philanthropist*• Born in York, the son of **Joseph Rowntree**, he was educated at the Friends' School in York and Owens College, Manchester. He became chairman of the family chocolate firm (1925–41), and introduced enlightened methods of worker participation. He devoted his life to the study of social problems and welfare, and wrote many books, including *Poverty: A Study of Town Life* (1901), *Poverty and Progress* (1941) and *Poverty and the Welfare State* (1951).

Rowse, Alfred Leslie 1903–97 •*English historian*• Born into a poor family in Tregonissey, near St Austell in Cornwall, he won a scholarship to Oxford and in 1925 became a Fellow of All Souls College. He wrote many works on English history, including *Tudor Cornwall* (1941), *The Use of History* (1946) and *The England of Elizabeth* (1950). He also wrote poetry, much of it on Cornwall, biographies of **Shakespeare** and **Christopher Marlowe**, and two volumes of autobiography, (1942, 1965). Later works include *All Souls in My Time* (1993) and *Historians I Have Known* (1995).

Roy, Arundhati 1961– •*Indian author*• Born in Shillong, she trained at the Delhi School of Architecture. She wrote two screenplays before producing her first novel, *The God of Small Things* (1997), a story of forbidden love set in the lushness of Kerala, which won the Booker Prize. She has written widely on environmental and nuclear issues.

Roy, Rammohun *See* **Rammohun Roy**

Royce, Sir (Frederick) Henry 1863–1933 •*English engineer*• Born near Peterborough, Cambridgeshire, he became interested in electricity and the engineering of motors, and founded the firm of Royce Ltd, mechanical and electrical engineers in Manchester (1884). He made his first car in 1904, and his meeting with **Charles Rolls** in that year led to the formation in 1906 of Rolls-Royce Ltd, automobile and aircraft engine builders. He later designed the aircraft engines that developed into the Merlin engines for Spitfires and Hurricanes in World War II.

Royden, (Agnes) Maud 1876–1956 •*English social worker and preacher*• Born in Liverpool and educated at Lady Margaret Hall, Oxford, she was prominent in the woman's suffrage movement. From 1917 to 1920 she was an assistant at the City Temple. She later helped to establish the Fellowship Services in Kensington. She published, among other titles, *Woman and the Sovereign State*, *The Church and Woman* and *Modern Sex Ideals*.

“ ”

The Church of England should no longer be satisfied to represent only the Conservative Party at prayer.

1917 Address to the Life and Liberty Movement, London, July 16.

Rozelle, (Alvin) Pete 1926–96 •*US football commissioner*• He was born in Los Angeles. In 1960 he became the commissioner for the National Football League (NFL). Holding this post for 29 years, he oversaw the expansion of the league from 12 to 28 teams, the amalgamation of the NFL with the American Football League, and the establishment of the Super Bowl as the sport's foremost attraction. He also negotiated the rights for the first league-wide television contract (1962). Hugely influential within the game until his retirement in 1989, he was enshrined in the Football Hall of Fame in 1985.

Rózsa, Miklós Nicholas 1907–95 •*Hungarian composer*• Born in Budapest, he graduated from the University of Leipzig in 1931. He composed symphonies and ballet music before being commissioned to write his first film score for *Knight Without Armour* (1937). He worked in Hollywood from 1940, where his use of jolting chords and pounding rhythms heightened the emotional impact of psychological melodramas and film noirs such as *Double Indemnity* (1944) and *The Killers* (1946). Later, he concentrated on lush accompaniments to historical epics, including *Quo Vadis* (1951) and *El Cid* (1961). His work outside the film industry is equally renowned; it includes a violin concerto (1953) written for **Jascha Heifetz** and a cello concerto (1968) for Janos Starker (1924–). He received Academy Awards for *Spellbound* (1945), *A Double Life* (1947) and *Ben Hur* (1959).

Rúa, Fernando de la *See* **de la Rúa, Fernando**

Rubbia, Carlo 1934– •*US physicist and Nobel Prize winner*• Born in Gorizia, Italy, and educated at the Universities of Pisa and Rome and Columbia University, from 1960 he worked at CERN (Conseil Européen pour la Recherche Nucléaire) in Geneva. He was head of the team that discovered the W and Z bosons which mediate the weak nuclear force, thus putting the unified theory of electromagnetic and weak forces (the electroweak theory) on a firm experimental footing. For this he shared the 1984 Nobel Prize for physics with **Simon van der Meer**. As director general of CERN (1989–93), he was the force behind the LEP (an electron-positron collider) and LHC (Large Hadron Collider) projects. He has been senior physicist of CERN since 1993.

Rubbra, Edmund 1901–86 •*English composer and music critic*• Born in Northampton, he studied at the University of Reading and the Royal College of Music. An interest in the polyphonic music of the 16th and 17th centuries is reflected in his characteristic contrapuntal style of composition, which he uses not only in works such as the "Spenser Sonnets" (1935), madrigals and masses (1945 and 1949), but also in his larger symphonic pieces, where he is more flexible in his interpretation of polyphonic principles. He wrote 11 symphonies, and chamber, choral and orchestral music, songs and works for various solo instruments. He was senior lecturer in music at Oxford (1947–68), and was made a Fellow of Worcester College in 1963, and Professor of Composition at the Guildhall School of Music (1961–74).

Rubens, Peter Paul 1577–1640 •*Flemish painter*• He was born in Siegen in Westphalia, studied from 1587 in Antwerp, and in 1600 went to Italy; in Venice he studied the works of **Titian** and **Veronese**. He next entered the service of Vincenzo Gonzago, Duke of Mantua, and in 1605 was dispatched on a mission to **Philip III** of Spain, thus beginning his career as a diplomat. On his return from Spain, he traveled in Italy; his paintings of this Italian period are much influenced by the Italian Renaissance, and already show the Rubens characteristics of vigorous composition and brilliant coloring. In 1608 he settled in Antwerp, and was appointed court painter to the archduke Albert (1609). Rubens was then approaching his artistic maturity, and his triptych *Descent from the Cross* (1611–14) in Antwerp Cathedral is usually regarded as his masterpiece. By this time he was famous, and pupils and commissions came in a steady stream, while he produced vast numbers of works, witnesses to his extraordinary energy and ability. In 1620 he was invited to France by **Marie de Médicis**, who was then engaged in decorating the Luxembourg Palace in Paris; and he undertook for her 21 large subjects on her life and regency. In 1628 he was dispatched on a diplomatic mission to **Philip IV** of Spain. He made the acquaintance of **Velázquez** in Madrid, and executed some 40 works, including five portraits of the Spanish monarch. In 1629 he was appointed envoy to **Charles I** of Great Britain, to negotiate for peace and, while he conducted a delicate negotiation with tact and success, he painted *Peace and War* (National Gallery, London) and also made sketches for the *Apotheosis* of **James VI and I** for the banqueting hall at Whitehall, completing the pictures on his return to Antwerp. In 1635 he designed the decorations which celebrated the entry of the Cardinal Infant Ferdinand into Antwerp as governor of the Netherlands and completed *The Crucifixion of St Peter* for the church of St Peter in Cologne. Rubens was a successful diplomat, a distinguished humanist, a man of wide erudition and culture, and in his own time was outstanding for versatility and for the power, spirit and vivacity of his artistic output.

Rubik, Ernö 1944– •*Hungarian architectural designer and inventor*• Born in Budapest, he studied architecture and industrial design at the Technical University in Budapest, and became a teacher at the School of Industrial Design there. He conceived the idea of his "Rubik cube" puzzle in 1974 and patented it the following year. By 1981 it had become a great international success and millions had been sold, many of them pirated. Although he has produced other puzzles, they have not caught the public imagination in the same way.

Rubinstein, Anton Grigorevich 1829–94 •*Russian pianist and composer*• Born in Vykhvatinets, Moldavia, he studied in Berlin and Vienna, and in 1848 settled in St Petersburg, where he taught music and took a part in founding the conservatory, of which he was director (1862–67, 1887–90). He undertook concert tours in Europe and the US, gaining widespread acclaim and lasting distinction for his technique and musical sensitivity. His compositions, which include operas, oratorios and piano concertos, have not retained their popularity, apart from some songs and melodious piano pieces. His brother Nikolai (1835–81) founded the Moscow Conservatory.

Rubinstein, Artur 1887–1982 •*US pianist*• Born in Łódź, Poland, he appeared in Berlin at the age of 12, and after further study with **Ignacy Paderewski**, began his career as a virtuoso, appearing in Paris and London in 1905 and visiting the US in 1906. After World War II he lived in the US, making frequent extensive concert tours. He took US citizenship in 1946, and was given the honorary title Knight Commander, Order of the British Empire, in 1977.

Rubinstein, Helena 1870–1965 •*US businesswoman*• Born in Kraków, Poland, she studied medicine and went to Australia in 1902, taking with her a facial cream made by her mother. When she found that it sold well, she opened a shop in Melbourne, studied dermatology in greater depth and launched her business in Europe. She opened her Maison de Beauté in London (1908) and Paris (1912), then went to the US and opened salons there. After World War II she built cosmetics factories all over the world and created a personal fortune of around $100 million. She remained active in the running of Helena Rubinstein Inc into her nineties, and in 1953 she established the Helena Rubinstein Foundation.

Rublev, Andrei fl. 1400 •*Russian painter*• Although little is known about his life or works, he is generally regarded as the greatest Russian icon painter. It is known that he became a monk, probably quite late in life, in the monastery of Troitse-Sergiev, and that he was an assistant of the Greek painter **Theophanes**, with whom he worked on the Kremlin in Moscow from 1405. In 1422 he returned to Troitse-Sergiev, where he is said to have completed his most famous work, the icon of the Old Testament Trinity, represented by three graceful angels. He was the subject of a highly acclaimed film portrait by **Andrei Tarkovsky** (1968).

Ruddock, Joan Mary 1943– •*Welsh antinuclear campaigner and politician*• She was born in Pontypool and educated in Wales and at Imperial College, London. She worked for Shelter, the national campaign for the homeless, between 1968 and 1973, and was then director of an Oxford housing aid center. In 1977 she joined the Manpower Services Commission, and was chairperson of the Campaign for Nuclear Disarmament (CND) from 1981. When she entered Parliament for Labour in 1987, she almost immediately became a member of the Opposition front bench. Her books include *The CND Story* (1983) and *Voices for One World* (1988).

Rude, François 1784–1855 •*French sculptor*• Born in Dion and trained in the classical tradition, he began as a smith, but later became known for his dramatic public monuments in Paris. His most famous works are the relief group *Le départ* (1836, meaning "the Departure of the Volunteers," known as the Marseillaise) on the Arc de Triomphe, and the statue of *Marshal Ney* in the Place de l'Observatoire (1853). His *Joan of Arc* (1852) is in the Louvre.

Rudolf I 1218–91 •*Uncrowned Holy Roman emperor, founder of the Habsburg dynasty*• He was the most powerful prince in Swabia when he was elected king of Germany (1273), although he was never crowned emperor. He attempted to restore the power of the monarchy by reclaiming lands and rights usurped by the princes since 1245. His victory at Durnkrüt on the Marchfeld (1278) over Ottokar II of Bohemia, who had occupied Austria and Styria, brought him control of these two duchies, which passed to his son **Albert I** and became the seat of Habsburg power.

Rudolf II 1552–1612 •*King of Hungary and of Bohemia, and Holy Roman emperor*• Born in Vienna, he ruled Hungary (1572–1608) and Bohemia (1575–1611) and became Holy Roman Emperor on the death of his father, **Maximilian II**, in 1576. Residing for most of his reign in Prague, he made the city a center for writers, artists and humanist scholars, including the astronomers **Tycho Brahe** and **Johannes Kepler**, and mystics such as **Giordano Bruno** and **John Dee**. His catholicizing policies provoked opposition among the Bohemian Protestants, who looked to his younger brother, **Matthias**, for support. He was shy and melancholy, and his mental instability became more pronounced in his later years, during which he was gradually superseded by Matthias.

Rudolph, Wilma Glodean 1940–94 •*US sprinter*• Born in Clarksville, Tennessee, the 20th of 22 children, she overcame childhood polio and came to prominence as a teenager as part of an athletics team known as the Tennessee Belles. As a 16-year-old she won a sprint relay bronze medal at Melbourne in the 1956 Olympic Games, and in the 1960 Olympics at Rome she won gold medals in the 100-meter, 200-meter and sprint relay events. She set a record in the 100-meters in 1961. She retired in 1964.

Ruether, Rosemary Radford 1936– •*US theologian*• Born in Minneapolis, she has been Professor of Applied Theology at Garrett-Evangelical Theological Seminary, Evanston, since 1976. She has written extensively on women and theological issues, analyzing the effects of male bias in official Church theology and seeking to affirm female aspects of religion and the importance of women's experience. Her books include *Mary: The Feminine Face of the Church* (1979), *Sexism and God-Talk* (1983) and *Gaia and God* (1992).

Ruïsdael or **Ruysdael, Jacob van** c. 1628–82 •*Dutch landscape painter*• Born in Haarlem, he was possibly a pupil of his father and uncle Salomon van Ruïsdael (c. 1600–70), a Haarlem landscape painter. He became a member of the Haarlem painters' guild in 1648, and in about 1655 moved to Amsterdam, thereafter traveling in Holland and Germany. One of the greatest landscape and seascape painters of the Dutch school, he excelled in dramatic skies and magnificent cloud effects. He is represented in the Rijksmuseum, Amsterdam (*The Jewish Cemetery*), the National Gallery, London (*Landscape with Ruins*), the Louvre (*Le coup de soleil*) and elsewhere. He was the teacher of **Meindert Hobbema**.

Ruiz, Juan c. 1283–c. 1350 •*Spanish author*• Nothing certain is recorded of his life, although his own autobiographical *Libro de buen amor* (*Book of Good Love*) claims that he was born at Alcalá de Henares, educated at Toledo, was a popular author of songs (some of which are in the book) and was archpriest of the village of Hita near Alcalá. The *Book*, regarded as the most important long medieval Spanish poem next to the 12th-century epic *El cantar de mio Cid*, is an ironic and ambiguous work in an esoteric tradition of late courtly love, with admixtures of other genres. It was an important influence on **Chaucer**.

“ ”

El amor siempre fabla mentiroso.
Love is always a liar.

c. 1330 ***Libro de buen amor****, stanza 161.*

Rule, St *See* **Regulus, St**

Rumford, Benjamin Thompson, Count 1753–1814 •*US administrator and scientist*• Born in Woburn, Massachusetts, he became a major in the Second New Hampshire regiment, but fled to England in 1776, possibly for political reasons. In 1784 he entered the service of Bavaria, where he became head of the Bavarian war department. It was here that he observed the immense heat generated by the boring of cannon, from which he deduced the relationship between the work done and the heat generated. He reported these findings to the Royal Society in 1798 in a classic paper of experimental science, *An Experimental Inquiry Concerning the Source of Heat Excited by Friction*. He invented the Rumford shadow photometer, designed the so-called Rumford oil lamp, and introduced the concept of the standard candle. He endowed two Rumford medals of the Royal Society, and two of the American Academy. In 1799 he left the Bavarian service, returned to London, and founded the Royal Institution.

Rumsfeld, Donald Henry 1932– •*US politician*• Born in Chicago, he was educated at Princeton University and served in the US Navy (1954–57) before entering politics. He was elected to the US House of Representatives in 1962, but resigned in 1969 to serve in senior posts in the **Nixon** administration. He was US ambassador to NATO (1973–74), White House chief of staff (1974–75) and secretary of defense (1975–77). Over the next 20 years he combined business activities with senior advisory and diplomatic roles, and in 2001 he was appointed secretary of defense for a second time by **George W Bush**.

Runcie, Robert Alexander Kennedy Runcie, Baron 1921–2000 •*English prelate and Archbishop of Canterbury*• He was educated at Oxford and served in the Scots Guards during World War II, for which he was awarded the Military Cross. He was ordained in 1951 and was Bishop of St Albans for ten years before being consecrated Archbishop of Canterbury (1980–91). His office was marked by a papal visit to Canterbury, the war with Argentina in the Falklands, continuing controversies over homosexuality and the role of women in the Church, his highly acclaimed chairmanship of the Lambeth conference and the captivity of his envoy **Terry Waite** in Beirut (1987–91). He was succeeded by **George Carey** in 1991, the year he was made a life peer.

Rundstedt, Karl Rudolf Gerd von 1875–1953 •*German soldier*• He was born in the Old Mark of Brandenburg. He served in World War I, and in 1938 commanded occupation troops in the Sudetenland, but was "purged" for his outspokenness about **Hitler**. Recalled in 1939, he directed the *Blitzkrieg* in Poland and France. In 1942 he commanded the Western Front stretching from Holland to the Italian frontier. His last great action was the Ardennes offensive (the Battle of the Bulge, 1944). In May 1945 he was captured by the Americans in Munich. Proceedings against him for war crimes were dropped because of ill health, and he was kept prisoner in Great Britain from 1946.

Runeberg, Johan Ludvig 1804–77 •*Finnish poet*• Born in Jakobstaed (Pietarsaari), he wrote in Swedish, and his style was much influenced by his studies of Finnish folk poetry. He taught at Helsinki (1830–37) and at Porvoo (1837–57). He wrote several volumes of lyric verse, and his major works were *Elgskyttarâe* ("The Elk Shooters," 1832), a Norse epic, *Kung Fjalar* (1844, Eng trans *King Fjalar*, 1904), and his collection of patriotic ballads, *Fänrik Ståls Sägner* (1848–60, "Tales of Ensign Stål," 2 vols), on the theme of Finland's war of independence (1808–09). It begins with "Vårt land" ("Our land"), which has become the Finnish national anthem. He also wrote epic poetry, plays, and religious pieces. He is considered the greatest Finnish poet and was a leader of the national Romantic school.

Runyon, (Alfred) Damon 1884–1946 •*US writer and journalist*• He was born in Manhattan, Kansas. After serving in the Spanish-American War (1898), he turned in 1911 to journalism. His first books were volumes of verse, but it was his racy short stories, written with liberal use of slang and angst, and depicting life in underworld New York and on Broadway, which won him popularity. His collection *Guys and Dolls* (1932) was adapted as a musical revue (1950). Other books include *Take It Easy* (1939), and the play, with Howard Lindsay, *A Slight Case of Murder* (1935). From 1941 he worked as a film producer.

Rupert, Prince, *also called* **Rupert of the Rhine** 1619–82 •*English cavalry officer*• Born in Prague, he was the third son of the Elector Palatine **Frederick V** and Elizabeth, daughter of **James VI and I** of Scotland and England, and nephew of **Charles I**. He fought against the Imperialists in the Thirty Years' War (1618–48) until he was taken prisoner at Vlotho. In 1642 he returned to England and was appointed General of the Horse by Charles I. He served the king with great loyalty and courage and was the ablest Royalist soldier, showing tactical skill and swiftness in cavalry actions, although at times his pursuit was too headlong. After his defeat at Naseby and surrender of Bristol (1645), Charles (who in 1644 had made him Duke of Cumberland and Commander in Chief), dismissed him. He later resumed his duties, but surrendered at Oxford to **Thomas Fairfax** (1646). Banished from England by parliament, he took command of the small Royalist fleet (1648) and preyed on English shipping; in 1650 Admiral **Robert Blake** attacked his squadron, burning or sinking most of his vessels. Rupert escaped to the West Indies, and in 1653 returned to France, where he chiefly lived until the Restoration. Thereafter he served under the Duke of York (the future **James VII and II**) against the Dutch, and took part in founding the Hudson's Bay Company (1670). One of the founders of the Royal Society, he produced beautiful mezzotints.

Rush, Geoffrey 1951– •*Australian actor*• Born in Toowoomba, he studied in Paris, and began his career with the Queensland Theatre Company. He made a number of films from the early 1980s and won rapturous praise for his portrayal of the pianist David Helfgott in *Shine* (1995), winning an Academy Award and a British Academy of Film and Television Arts award for Best Actor. He went on to appear in *Elizabeth* (1998) and *Shakespeare in Love* (1998), and continued to act and direct in theater.

Rushd, Ibn *See* **Averroës**

Rushdie, (Ahmed) Salman 1947– •*British novelist*• He was born in Bombay, India, and his family moved to Pakistan when he was 17. He was educated at the Cathedral School, Bombay, then at Rugby in England. He emigrated to Great Britain in 1965 and graduated from King's College, Cambridge, in 1968. He worked as an actor and an advertising copywriter before becoming a full-time writer. Writing in the tradition of **James Joyce**, **Günter Grass** and the South American "magic realists," he published his first novel, *Grimus*, in 1975, a muddled fable which sold poorly. With *Midnight's Children* (1981), a tour de force poised at the moment when India achieves independence, he emerged as a major international writer. It was awarded the Booker Prize. *Shame* (1983), a trenchant satire and a revisionist history of Pakistan and its leaders, was similarly conceived on a grand scale and was widely acclaimed. In *The Satanic Verses* (1988) he turned his attention toward Islam, in his familiar hyperbolic mode. The book was banned in India in 1988, and in 1989 **Ayatollah Khomeini** of Iran declared it blasphemous and issued a *fatwa*, or order of death, against him. Demonstrations followed, and copies of the book were burned in Bradford along with effigies of the author, who was forced into hiding under police protection. Despite having to remain in hiding, he has published *Haroun and the Sea of Stories* (1990, Writers' Guild award), *East, West* (1994) and *The Moor's Last Sigh* (1995, Whitbread Fiction award). More recent works include *The Ground Beneath Her Feet* (1999).

" "

To burn a book is not to destroy it. One minute of darkness will not make us blind.

1989 Book review in the ***Weekend Guardian,*** *October 14–15.*

Rushton, Willie (William George) 1937–96 •*English actor, cartoonist and broadcaster*• He was born in London and educated at Shrewsbury School. He completed his national service, and did not attend college. His public stage debut was in **Spike Milligan**'s *The Bedsitting Room* in 1961, the same year he helped to set up the satirical magazine *Private Eye*. He achieved his greatest fame on television (*That Was the Week That Was*, 1962–63) and on radio (*I'm Sorry I Haven't a Clue*, 1976–96). He also made a number of cameo film appearances, and wrote several humorous books. He was less well known for his cartoons, which he contributed to a wide range of periodicals.

Rusk, (David) Dean 1909–94 •*US politician*• Born in Cherokee County, Georgia, he was educated at Davidson College, North Carolina, and at Oxford, and in 1934 was appointed Associate Professor of Government and Dean of the Faculty at Mills College. After service in the army in World War II, he held various government posts, including that of deputy Undersecretary of State and Assistant Secretary for Far Eastern Affairs (1950–51). From 1961 he was Secretary of State in the **Kennedy** administration, in which capacity he played a major role in handling the Cuban missile crisis of 1962. He retained the post during the **Johnson** administration, retiring in 1969.

Ruskin, John 1819–1900 •*English author and art critic*• He was born in London, where he was tutored privately. In 1836 he went to Christ Church, Oxford, where he won the Newdigate prize for poetry. Shortly after graduating, he met **J M W Turner** and championed his painting in *Modern Painters* (1843–60). Along with *The Seven Lamps of Architecture* (1848) and *The Stones of Venice* (1851–53), this book established him as the major art and social critic of the day. In 1869 he became the first Slade Professor of Fine Art at Oxford. He settled at Coniston in the Lake District, and published various Slade lectures and *Fors Clavigera*, a series of papers addressed "To the Workmen and Labourers of Great Britain" (1871–84). He founded the St George's Guild—a nonprofit shop in Paddington Street in which members gave a tithe of their fortunes, the John Ruskin School at Camberwell, and the Whitelands College at Chelsea.

Russell, Anna, *properly* **Claudia Anna Russell-Brown** 1911– •*English singer and musical satirist*• Born in London, she studied singing and pursued an orthodox operatic career until she realized the possibilities of satire offered by opera and concert singing. She first appeared as a concert satirist of musical fads in New York in 1948, and has since achieved widespread fame in this medium.

Russell, Bertrand Arthur William Russell, 3rd Earl 1872–1970 •*English philosopher, mathematician, writer and Nobel Prize winner*• He was a controversial public figure throughout his long and extraordinarily active life. Born in Trelleck, Gwent, he was brought up by his grandmother, the widow of Lord **John Russell**. He took first-class honors in mathematics and philosophy at Trinity College, Cambridge, graduating in 1894. His most original contributions to mathematical logic and philosophy are generally agreed to belong to the period before World War I, as expounded in *The Principles of Mathematics* (1903), which argues that the whole of mathematics could be derived from logic, and the monumental *Principia Mathematica* (with **Alfred North Whitehead**, 1910–13), which worked out this program in a fully developed formal system and stands as a landmark in the history of logic and mathematics. Russell's famous theory of types and his theory of descriptions belong to this same period. **Ludwig Wittgenstein** went to Cambridge to be his student from 1912 to 1913. Russell wrote his first genuinely popular work in 1912, *The Problems of Philosophy*, which can still be read as a brilliantly stimulating introduction to the subject. Politics became his dominant concern during World War I, and his active pacifism caused his imprisonment (1918), during the course of which he wrote his *Introduction to Mathematical Philosophy* (1919). He now had to make a living by lecturing and journalism, and became a celebrated controversialist. He visited the USSR, where he met **Lenin**, **Trotsky** and **Gorky**, which sobered his early enthusiasm for Communism and led to the critical *Theory and Practice of Bolshevism* (1919). He also taught in Beijing (1920–21). In 1921 he married his second wife, Dora Black, and with her founded (in 1927) and ran a progressive school near Petersfield; he set out his educational views in *On Education* (1926) and *Education and the Social Order* (1932). In 1931 he succeeded his elder brother, John, 2nd Earl Russell, as 3rd Earl Russell. His second divorce (1934) and marriage to Patricia Spence (1936) helped to make controversial his book *Marriage and Morals* (1932); and his lectureship at City College, New York, was terminated in 1940 after complaints that he was an "enemy of religion and morality," although he later won substantial damages for wrongful dismissal. The rise of Fascism led him to renounce his pacifism in 1939, and he returned to England after World War II to be honored with an Order of Merit. He was awarded the Nobel Prize for literature in 1950. He had meanwhile continued publishing important philosophical work, mainly on epistemology, in such books as *The Analysis of Mind* (1921), *An Enquiry into Meaning and Truth* (1940) and *Human Knowledge: Its Scope and Limits* (1948), and in 1945 published the best-selling *History of Western Philosophy*. After 1949 he became increasingly preoccupied with the cause of nuclear disarmament, taking a leading role in CND (Campaign for Nuclear Disarmament) and later the Committee of 100, and engaging in a remarkable correspondence with various world leaders. In 1961 he was again imprisoned, with his fourth and last wife, Edith Finch, for his part in a sit-down demonstration in Whitehall. His last years were spent in North Wales, and he retained to the end his lucidity, independence of mind, and humor. The last major publications were his three volumes of *Autobiography* (1967–69).

“ ”

Mathematics possesses not only truth, but supreme beauty—a beauty cold and austere, like that of sculpture.

1903 ***The Principles of Mathematics***.

Russell, Bill (William Fenton) 1934– •*US basketball player and coach*• Born in Monroe, Louisiana, he distinguished himself as a defensive player with the University of San Francisco (1952–56) and subsequently became center with the Boston Celtics (1956–69). In 13 seasons he led the Celtics to a remarkable 11 NBA championships (1957–65, 1959–66 and 1968–69), earning an enduring reputation as the greatest defensive center in the history of the game. His head-to-head encounters with **Wilt Chamberlain** in particular acquired legendary status among fans. His other achievements included a gold medal as a member of the victorious US Olympic team in 1956 and five NBA Most Valuable Player awards (1958, 1961–63 and 1965). In 1967 he became the first African-American head coach in NBA history when he took over the Celtics as player-coach (1967–69).

Russell, Charles Taze, *known as* **Pastor Russell** 1852–1916 •*US religious leader, founder of the Jehovah's Witnesses*• Born in Pittsburgh, he was a Congregationalist and became a traveling preacher. In Pittsburgh in 1872 he founded the international Bible Students' Association (Jehovah's Witnesses), a group with specific views on prophecy and eschatology. He founded the journal *The Watchtower* in 1879.

Russell, Sir Frederick Stratten 1897–1984 •*English marine biologist*• Born in Doncaster, South Yorkshire, and educated at Cambridge, he joined the Plymouth Laboratory of the Marine Biological Association, of which he was director between 1946 and 1965. He is best known for his work on medusae, larval fish and zooplankton communities. By painstaking laboratory rearing, Russell succeeded in solving major taxonomic problems to link the medusa to the polyp phase for many species, and he established the Russell cycle of environmental changes in plankton communities. His work has potential applications in the assessment of changes in water circulation, and possibly climate change, in addition to predictions for commercially important fish populations. He was knighted in 1965.

Russell, Henry Norris 1877–1957 •*US astronomer*• Born in Pyster Bay, New York, after studies at Princeton and Cambridge, UK, he was appointed Professor of Astronomy at Princeton in 1905, and six years later director of the university observatory there. He developed with **Harlow Shapley** methods for the calculation of the orbits and dimensions of eclipsing binary stars and for the determination of the distances of double stars, and worked on the theory of stellar atmospheres. His most famous achievement was the formulation of the **Hertzsprung**-Russell diagram (1913) correlating the spectral types of stars with their luminosity, which became of fundamental importance for the theory of stellar evolution.

Russell, Jack (John) 1795–1883 •*English "sporting parson"*• He was born in Dartmouth, Devon, and educated at Oxford. He was perpetual curate of Swimbridge, near Barnstaple (1832–80), and master of foxhounds. He developed the West Country smooth-haired, short-legged terrier, named "Parson Russell" after him.

Russell, (Ernestine) Jane (Geraldine) 1921– •*US actress*• Born in Bemidji, Minnesota, she worked as a chiropodist's receptionist and photographer's model before studying acting. Her voluptuous figure brought her fame as the star of *The Outlaw* (1943), a Western whose notoriety resulted from the censor's concern over the amount of her cleavage exposed onscreen. She subsequently appeared in such films as *The Paleface* (1948) and *Gentlemen Prefer Blondes* (1953). As her film career faded, she appeared in cabaret, endorsed Playtex bras on television, and starred on Broadway in *Company* (1971) and in the television series *Yellow Rose* (1983).

Russell (of Kingston Russell), John Russell, 1st Earl 1792–1878 •*English statesman*• Born in London, the third son of the 6th Duke of Bedford, he studied at the University of Edinburgh, and in 1813 became a Member of Parliament. His strenuous efforts in favor of reform won many seats for the Liberals at the 1830 election, and he was one of the four members of Earl **Grey**'s ministry entrusted with the task of framing the first Reform Bill (1832). With the downfall of **Robert Peel** in 1835, he became home (and later colonial) secretary and leader of the Lower House. Immediately after the repeal of the Corn Laws in 1846, Russell became prime minister, at the head of a Whig administration (1846–52). In Lord **Aberdeen**'s coalition of 1852 he was foreign secretary and leader of the Commons again, but his inopportune Reform Bill (1854), the mismanagement of the Crimean campaign and his bungling of the Vienna conference combined to make him unpopular, and for four years he was out of office. In 1859 he returned as foreign secretary, under Lord **Palmerston**, and in 1861 was made Earl Russell. In 1865 he again became prime minister, but was defeated in June on his attempt to introduce another Reform Bill, and resigned.

Russell, Ken, *in full* **Henry Kenneth Alfred Russell** 1927– •*English film director*• Born in Southampton, he worked as a ballet dancer, actor and photographer before making short documentary films, and the BBC commissioned him to make musical biographies (1962–65) and pieces such as *Lotte Lenya Sings Kurt Weill* (1962). He turned to feature films with *French Dressing* (1963) and had international success with *Women in Love* (1969). His flamboyant style and musically inspired themes continued in *The Music Lovers* (1971) and *Mahler* (1974). Other productions include the films *The Devils* (1971), *Crimes of Passion* (1984), *The Rainbow* (1989) and *Mindbender* (1995), and on television *Lady Chatterley* (1993).

Russell, Lord William 1639–83 •*English politician*• The third son of William Russell, 5th Earl and 1st Duke of Bedford, at the Restoration he was elected a Member of Parliament. In 1674 he spoke against the actions of the Cabal, and became an active adherent of the Country Party. He led the attempt to exclude the Duke of York (later **James VII and II**) from the accession as a popish recusant. He was arrested with Robert Devereux, 2nd Earl of **Essex**, and **Algernon Sidney** for participation in the Rye House Plot, was found guilty of high treason by a stacked jury, and was beheaded.

Russell, Sir William Howard 1821–1907 •*Irish war correspondent*• Born near Tallaght, County Dublin, he was educated at

Trinity College, Dublin, then joined *The Times* in 1843. From the Crimea (1854–55) he wrote the famous dispatches (published in book form in 1856) about the sufferings of the soldiers during the winter of 1854–55, and in 1858 he witnessed the Indian Mutiny. He established the *Army and Navy Gazette* in 1860, and in 1861 the Civil War took him to the US. He covered various European conflicts during the 1860s and 1870s, and visited Egypt and the East (1874), and went to India (1877) as the private secretary of the Prince of Wales (**Edward VII**), and to South Africa (1879) with Viscount **Wolseley**. Among his books are *The Adventures of Dr Brady* (1868).

Russell, Willy (William) 1947– •*English playwright*• Born in Whiston, Merseyside, he became a teacher after several years of working in industry. He is one of the most frequently performed of contemporary British dramatists, and is best known for the highly successful stage play and film *Educating Rita* (1979), the musical *Blood Brothers* (1983) and the play *Shirley Valentine* (1986), also later filmed (1989). Russell is a founding member and director of Quintet Films and an honorary director of the Liverpool Playhouse.

" "

Of course I'm drunk—you don't really expect me to teach this stuff when I'm sober.

*1979 **Educating Rita**.*

Rutebeuf c. 1230–86 •*French epic poet*• Born in the Champenois, he lived in Paris and was the author of the semiliturgical drama *Miracle de Théophile* (c. 1260, a prototype of the Faust story), the *Dit de l'herberie* ("The Tale of the Herb Market"), a monologue by a quack doctor, full of comic charlatanesque rhetoric, and also several stories.

Ruth 12th century BC •*Biblical character*• She was a Moabite woman who had married one of the two sons of Elimelech and Naomi. When Naomi's husband and sons died, she resolved to return to her hometown of Bethlehem. Ruth insisted on accompanying her, believing that the God of Israel would protect them, and she later married a distant relative, the wealthy landowner Boaz. The story in the Book of Ruth can be interpreted as a parable of divine providence and devotion to duty, or as a reaction against teaching that forbids mixed marriages.

Ruth, Babe, *properly* **George Herman Ruth** 1895–1948 •*US baseball player*• Born in Baltimore, he started his career as a left-handed pitcher with the Boston Red Sox (1914–19), and became famous for his powerful hitting with the New York Yankees (1920–34). His 1927 season record of 60 home runs stood until 1961. In all he played in ten World Series, and hit 714 home runs, a record that stood for 30 years until it was surpassed by **Hank Aaron** in 1974. In 1935 he moved to the Boston Braves, and ended his career as coach for the Brooklyn Dodgers (1938). He is considered to be one of the greatest players in the history of the game.

Rutherford (of Nelson), Ernest Rutherford, 1st Baron 1871–1937 •*New Zealand physicist, the "father of nuclear physics," and Nobel Prize winner*• He was born in Brightwater, near Nelson, South Island. His first research projects were on magnetization of iron by high-frequency discharges (1894) and magnetic viscosity (1896). In 1895 he was admitted to the Cavendish Laboratory and Trinity College, Cambridge, on a scholarship. There he made the first successful wireless transmissions over two miles (3.2 km). Under the brilliant direction of **J J Thomson**, Rutherford discovered the three types of uranium radiation. In 1898 he became Professor of Physics at McGill University, Canada, where, with **Frederick Soddy**, he formulated the theory of atomic disintegration to account for the tremendous heat energy radiated by uranium. In 1907 he became professor at Manchester and there established that alpha particles were doubly ionized helium ions by counting the number given off with a counting device, which he jointly invented with the German physicist **Hans Geiger**. This led to a revolutionary conception of the atom as a miniature universe in which the mass is concentrated in the nucleus surrounded by planetary electrons. Rutherford's assistant, **Niels Bohr**, applied to this the quantum theory (1913), and the concept of the "Rutherford-Bohr atom" of nuclear physics was born. In 1919, in a series of experiments, he discovered that alpha-ray bombardments induced atomic transformation in atmospheric nitrogen, liberating hydrogen nuclei. The same year he succeeded Thomson to the Cavendish professorship at Cambridge and reorganized the laboratory, the world center for the study of *The Newer Alchemy* (1937). In 1920 he predicted the existence of the neutron, later discovered by his colleague, **James Chadwick**. He was awarded the Nobel prize for chemistry in 1908 and was president of the Royal Society from 1925 to 1930.

Rutherford, Dame Margaret 1892–1972 •*English theater and film actress*• Born in London, she gradually gained fame as a character actress and comedienne, with a gallery of eccentrics including Miss Prism in *The Importance of Being Earnest* (stage 1939, film 1952) and Madame Arcati in *Blithe Spirit* (stage 1941, film 1945). She was also an extremely successful Miss Marple in several films based on the novels of **Agatha Christie** from 1962, appearing with the actor Stringer Davis (1896–1973), whom she had married in 1945. She was given the honorary title of Dame Commander, Order of the British Empire, in 1967, and won an Academy Award as Best Supporting Actress for her part in *The V.I.P.'s* (1963).

Ruthven, William, 4th Baron Ruthven and **1st Earl of Gowrie** c. 1541–84 •*Scottish nobleman*• He was involved in the murder of **David Rizzio** (1566), and later was the custodian of **Mary Queen of Scots** during her captivity at Loch Leven (1567–68). He was made Earl of Gowrie in 1581. In 1582 he kidnapped the boy king **James VI** and took him to Castle Ruthven, near Perth; for this he was first pardoned and then ordered to leave the country. He was later beheaded at Stirling for his part in a conspiracy to take Stirling Castle.

Rutledge, John 1739–1800 •*US statesman and jurist* • Born into the Southern planter aristocracy in Charleston, South Carolina, he was a delegate to the Continental Congress (1774–76, 1782–83) and the Constitutional Convention (1787), where he championed slavery and argued for a strong central government. He later served as president (1776–78) and governor (1779–82) of South Carolina. From 1789 to 1791 he was an associate justice of the Supreme Court. He was named chief justice in 1795, but the Senate rejected the nomination, and he sat for only five months.

Ruysdael, Jacob van *See* **Ruïsdael, Jacob van**

Ruyter, Michiel Adriaanszoon de 1607–76 •*Dutch naval commander*• Born in Flushing, in the first Anglo-Dutch War (1652–54) he served with distinction under **Cornelis Tromp** against **Robert Blake** and **George Monk**, and in the second Anglo-Dutch War (1665–67) he defeated Monk in the Four Days' Battle off Dunkirk (1666). In 1667 he sailed up the River Medway, burned some of the English ships, and next sailed up the River Thames, and also attacked Harwich. In the war with France and England (1672–78), he attacked the French and English fleets in Solebay (May 28, 1672), and defeated Prince **Rupert** and d'Estrées (1673), thus preventing an English invasion. In 1675 he was mortally wounded in a battle off Sicily.

Ružička, Leopold Stephen 1887–1976 •*Swiss chemist and Nobel Prize winner*• Born in Vukovar, Croatia, he trained at the Technische Hochschule, Karlsruhe, studying the chemistry of the pyrethrins and other insecticides (1912), and continued this work at the Polytechnic in Zurich (1916). After a short stay in Utrecht (1926–29), he returned to Zurich as Professor of Organic and Inorganic Chemistry. He went on to study terpenes in great detail. In the 1930s he discovered their structural relationship to the steroids, which led him to enunciate in 1953 the rule by which the five-carbon units making up terpenes combine to form steroids. In 1935 he was able to announce the synthesis of the still undiscovered male hormones, testosterone and methyltestosterone. With **Adolf Butenandt**, he was awarded the 1939 Nobel Prize for chemistry.

Ryan, Desmond 1893–1964 •*Irish socialist and historian*• Born in London, the son of William Patrick Ryan (1867–1942), he grew up in the Dublin of the Irish Renaissance, vividly described in his autobiography of youth, *Remembering Sion* (1934). He was educated at **Patrick Pearse**'s school, St Enda's, became Pearse's secretary and fought in the General Post Office in the Easter Uprising (1916). He supported the Anglo-Irish Treaty but left Ireland in disgust at the civil war, and in London wrote novels, among them the hypnotically picaresque *St Eustace and theAlbatross* (1934), and penetrating analyses of **Eamon de Valera** and **John Devoy**. He returned to Dublin in the 1940s and produced in *The Rising* (1949) the definitive narrative of the Easter Uprising, and edited *Devoy's Post Bag* (1948, 1953, consisting of Fenian correspondence) as well as writing a biography of **James Stephens** (*The Fenian Chief*, published in 1957).

“ ”

The triumph of failure.

1949 Of the Irish uprising of 1916. ***The Rising****, closing words.*

Ryan, Elizabeth 1892–1979 •*US tennis player*• Born in Anaheim, California, she won 19 Wimbledon titles (12 doubles and 7 mixed doubles), a record which stood from 1934 until 1979, when it was surpassed by **Billie Jean King**. Six of her women's doubles titles were with **Suzanne Lenglen**.

Ryan, (Lynn) Nolan, Jr 1947– •*US baseball player*• Born in Refugio, Texas, he was measured as the fastest baseball pitcher of all time in 1974, throwing a fastball recorded at 100.8 mph. He played for the New York Mets (1966–71), California Angels (1972–79), Houston Astros (1980–88) and Texas Rangers (1989–93), retiring in 1993. He holds numerous major league all-time records, including most seasons pitched (27), most strikeouts (5,714) and most no-hitters (7).

Rydberg, (Abraham) Viktor 1828–95 •*Swedish writer and scholar*• He was born in Jönköping, and after a hard childhood and early struggles to gain an education, he worked as a journalist, wrote historical novels, including *Fribytaren på Östersjön* (1857, "Freebooter in the Baltic") and *Vapensmeden* (1891, "The Armorer"), and several volumes of biblical criticism. From 1884 to 1895 he was a professor at Stockholm University. The leading cultural figure of his day, he also wrote works on philosophy, philology and aesthetics, translated **Goethe**'s *Faust*, and published a mythological study, *Undersökningar i germanisk mytologi* (1886–89).

Ryder, Samuel 1859–1936 •*English businessman*• Born in Cheshire, the son of a nurseryman, he built up a prosperous business in St Albans, mainly through selling penny packets of seeds. In 1927 he donated the Ryder Cup, competed for between teams of British (now European) and US professional golfers.

Ryder (of Warsaw and Cavendish), Sue Ryder, Baroness 1923–2000 •*English philanthropist*• Born in Leeds, she was educated at Benenden School in Kent, joined the First Aid Nursing Yeomanry in World War II and worked with the Polish section of the Special Operations Executive in occupied Europe. As a result of her experiences she determined to establish a living memorial to the dead and to refugees and other oppressed people. The Sue Ryder Foundation (now called Sue Ryder Care), which was first established in 1953, now links 100 centers worldwide. In some countries projects function under the auspices of the Ryder-Cheshire Foundation, which links her work with that of **Leonard Cheshire**, whom she married in 1959.

Ryle, Gilbert 1900–76 •*English philosopher*• Born in Brighton, Sussex, he studied at Queen's College, Oxford, and became Waynflete Professor of Metaphysical Philosophy at Oxford (1945–68) after service in World War II. He was an influential defender of linguistic or "ordinary language" philosophy, and he helped make Oxford a center of philosophy in the English-speaking world in the postwar years. He was also editor of the journal *Mind* (1947–71). His first and best-known work is *The Concept of Mind* (1949), which aimed to exorcise "the ghost in the machine" in a behaviorist analysis directed against traditional Cartesian mind/body dualism. His other works include *Dilemmas* (1954) and *Plato's Progress* (1966).

Ryle, Sir Martin 1918–84 •*English physicist, radio astronomer and Nobel Prize winner*• Born in Brighton, Sussex, he was educated at Christ Church, Oxford. For the duration of the war he was involved in important research in the field of radar. At the end of the war he joined the Cavendish Laboratory in Cambridge, where he investigated the emission of radio waves from the sun and improved the low resolving power of radio telescopes. He then turned to studies of radio waves from deep space and found that the number of radio sources increased as their intensities decreased (1955), a result which pointed to an evolving universe starting with a "big bang." Ryle was one of the outstanding scientists of his generation. He was awarded a knighthood in 1966, was appointed to the first chair of radio astronomy at Cambridge in 1969, and in 1972 became Astronomer Royal. In 1974 he received the Nobel Prize for physics with his colleague **Antony Hewish**.

Rysbrack, (John) Michael c. 1693–1770 •*Flemish sculptor*• He was born possibly in Antwerp, and settled in London in 1720. Among his works in a classical style influenced by the baroque are the monument to Sir **Isaac Newton** in Westminster Abbey (1731) and a bronze equestrian statue of **William III** (1735, Bristol). Busts include **Alexander Pope** (1730, National Portrait Gallery, London), Sir **Robert Walpole** (1738, National Portrait Gallery) and Sir **Hans Sloane** (c. 1737, British Museum). His later monument to Admiral Edward Vernon (1763) in Westminster Abbey shows the influence of rococo style.

Ryzhkov, Nikolai Ivanovich 1929– •*Russian politician*• Born in the Urals industrial region, he began his working life as a miner before studying engineering at the Urals Polytechnic. He then worked his way up to become head of the giant Uralmash engineering conglomerate. A member of the Communist Party of the Soviet Union (CPSU) since 1956, in 1975 he went to Moscow to work as first deputy minister for heavy transport and machine building. Four years later, he became first deputy chairman of Gosplan, and in 1982 was inducted into the CPSU secretariat as head of economic affairs by **Yuri Andropov**. He was brought into the politburo by **Mikhail Gorbachev** in April 1985 and made prime minister in September. More cautious in his approach to reform than Gorbachev, he was viewed as a steadying and stable influence in overcoming the economic and constitutional problems that blighted Gorbachev's reformed USSR. He stepped down as prime minister in 1991.

S

Saadi *See* **Sádi**

Sa'adia, ben Joseph 882–942 •*Jewish philosopher, polemicist and scholar*•Born in Dilaz in al-Fayyum, he left Egypt (c. 905) and after a period in Palestine settled in Babylonia, where he became *gaon* (head) of the rabbinic Academy of Sura. He was one of the most important medieval Jewish thinkers and produced a Hebrew-Arabic dictionary, translated much of the Old Testament into Arabic and wrote treatises on Talmudic law and religious poetry, as well as a major philosophical work, *Kitāb al-amānāt wa al-i'tiqādāt* (935, "The Book of Beliefs and Opinions").

Saarinen, Eero 1910–61 •*US architect and furniture designer*• Born in Kirkknonummi, Finland, he emigrated at the age of 13 with his father, **Eliel Saarinen**, to the US. After studying sculpture in Paris and architecture at Yale University, he went into partnership with his father in 1937. He designed many public buildings in the US and Europe, including the Jefferson Memorial Arch in St Louis, the General Motors Technical Center in Warren, Michigan, the Columbia Broadcasting System headquarters in New York City, the US embassies in London and Oslo, the TWA terminal at New York's John F Kennedy Airport and Washington's Dulles International Airport.

Saarinen, (Gottlieb) Eliel 1873–1950 •*US architect*•He was born in Rantasalmi, Finland. The leading architect of his native country, he designed the Helsinki railway station (1904–14) before emigrating to the US in 1923, where he designed the buildings for the Cranbrook Academy of Art in Michigan, of which he became president (1932–48). An eloquent opponent of skyscrapers, he formed a partnership with his son, **Eero Saarinen**, and designed the Tabernacle Church of Christ in Columbus, Indiana, and Christ Lutheran Church in Minneapolis.

Sabatier, Paul 1854–1941 •*French chemist and Nobel Prize winner*• Born in Carcassonne, after secondary education at the École Normale Supérieure he taught briefly at a lycée in Nîmes and then moved to Paris to work with Marcellin Berthelot (1827–1907). He received his doctorate in 1880 and moved to Bordeaux for a year before taking an established post at Toulouse. He made a number of important discoveries in inorganic chemistry, and is best known for his discovery of catalyzed hydrogenation of unsaturated organic compounds, such as the conversion of ethene to ethane over reduced nickel. He received the Nobel Prize for chemistry in 1912.

Sabatini, Gabriela 1970– •*Argentine tennis player*• Born in Buenos Aires, she became at the age of 13 the youngest player to win the Under 18's Orange Bowl. After turning professional in 1985, she failed to fulfill her early promise, and won just one Grand Slam title (the 1990 US Open) and one Olympic silver medal (1988). She retired from the tour in October 1996.

Sabin, Albert Bruce 1906–93 •*US microbiologist*• Born in Białystok, Russia (now in Poland), he was educated at New York University, and in 1946 was appointed Research Professor of Pediatrics at the University of Cincinnati. After working on developing vaccines against dengue fever and Japanese B encephalitis, he became interested in the polio vaccine and attempted to develop a live attenuated vaccine (as opposed to **Jonas Salk**'s killed vaccine). In 1959, as the result of 4.5 million vaccinations, his vaccine was found to be completely safe. It presented a number of advantages over that of Salk, especially in affording a stronger and longer-lasting immunity and in being capable of oral administration.

Sabine, Sir Edward 1788–1883 •*Irish soldier, physicist, astronomer and explorer*• Born in Dublin and educated at Marlow and the Royal Military Academy at Woolwich, he was commissioned in the Artillery. He accompanied his lifelong friend Sir **James Clark Ross** as astronomer on **John Ross**'s expedition to find the Northwest Passage in 1818 and on William Parry's Arctic expedition of 1819–20. He conducted important pendulum experiments at Spitzbergen and in tropical Africa to determine the shape of the Earth (1821–23), and devoted the rest of his life to work on terrestrial magnetism. He made the important discovery that there is a correlation between variations in the Earth's magnetism and solar activity that follow a 10- to 11-year cycle. Sabine's gull is named after him. He was knighted in 1869.

Sacagawea, *also* **Sacajawea** c. 1786–c. 1812 •*Native American interpreter and guide*• Born in western Montana or eastern Idaho, a member of the Snake tribe of the Shoshone and known as Bird Woman, she was captured by the Hidatsas and sold to a Canadian trapper, Toussaint Charbonneau, whom she married (1804). Joining the **Lewis** and Clark Expedition as interpreters and guides, they traveled with the explorers from the Missouri River and guided them over the mountains to the Pacific Ocean. They obtained horses for the explorers from the Shoshone and left the expedition in about 1806, choosing to remain with the Wind River Shoshone tribe in Wyoming.

Sacco, Nicola 1891–1927 •*US anarchist*• He was born in Italy, and he and Bartolomeo Vanzetti (1888–1927) emigrated to the US and settled in Massachusetts, where Sacco worked in a shoe factory and Vanzetti peddled fish, and they became interested in radical politics. Arrested and brought to trial for robbing and killing a shoe-factory paymaster (1920), they were found guilty, although the evidence was conflicting and circumstantial. Worldwide protests and appeals for clemency led to an investigation, which upheld the verdict of the trial. The men were executed in the electric chair (1927). The case remained controversial for many years.

Sacher-Masoch, Leopold von 1836–95 •*Austrian lawyer and writer*• He was born in Lemberg, and wrote many short stories and novels, including *Der Don Juan von Kolomea* (1866), depicting the life of small-town Polish Jews. Sexual pleasure derived from receiving pain, which was a feature of his later works, was termed *masochism* after him.

Sachs, Julius von 1832–97 •*German botanist*• Born in Breslau (Wrocław, Poland), he studied at the University of Prague, and from 1868 held the post of Professor of Botany at the University of Würzburg. There he carried out important experiments on the influence of light and heat upon plants, and on the organic activities of vegetable growth. He established the mineral requirements of plants, observed the conversion of sugar into starch in chloroplasts, and investigated the role of enzymes. His *Lehrbuch der Botanik* (1868) and its English translation *Textbook of Botany* (1875) exerted widespread influence. He is regarded as the founder of modern plant physiology.

Sachs, Nelly Leonie 1891–1970 •*Swedish poet and playwright and Nobel Prize winner*• Born in Berlin of Jewish descent, she first published a book of stories, *Tales and Legends* (1921), and several volumes of lyrical poetry. With the rise of Nazi power, she studied Jewish religious and mystical literature, and in 1940 escaped to Sweden. After World War II she wrote plays and poetry on the theme of the anguish of the Jewish people. She was awarded the 1966 Nobel Prize for literature, jointly with the Israeli novelist **Shmuel Yosef Agnon**.

Sacks, Jonathan 1948– •*English rabbi*• Born in London and educated at Cambridge, he is a respected Jewish scholar and teacher and was principal of Jews' College, London, before succeeding

Immanuel Jakobovits as chief rabbi of Great Britain in 1991. His concern for the future of the Jewish faith and tradition in contemporary society is reflected in his published works, which include *Tradition in an Untraditional Age* (1990) and *Will We Have Jewish Grandchildren?* (1994).

Sacks, Oliver Wolf 1933– •*English neurologist and writer*•Born in London, he graduated from Oxford and studied for his medical degree at Middlesex Hospital. In 1960 he emigrated to the US, and after further studies became, in 1965, Professor of Clinical Neurology at Albert Einstein College of Medicine in New York City, where he also practices neurology. He has written extensively on his experiences with patients, chronicling neurological conditions such as autism, Tourette's syndrome, amnesia and colorblindness. His best-known works, *Awakenings* (1973) and *The Man Who Mistook His Wife for a Hat* (1985), are studies of neurological disorders couched in the form of narrative clinical tales. *Awakenings* was adapted as a film with the same title (1990), and by **Harold Pinter** as a play, *A Kind of Alaska* (1982). Later works include *An Anthropologist on Mars* (1995).

Sackville, Thomas, 1st Earl of Dorset 1536–1608 •*English poet and statesman*• Born in Buckhurst in Sussex, he studied law at Hart Hall, Oxford, and St John's College, Cambridge, and became a barrister. In 1558 he entered parliament. With **Thomas Norton** he produced the blank-verse tragedy *Ferrex and Porrex* (later called *Gorboduc*), which was acted (1560–61) before Queen **Elizabeth I**, who was Sackville's second cousin. This work is claimed to be the first play in blank verse. He also wrote the Induction and *The Complaint of Buckingham* for *A Mirror for Magistrates* (1563). His prodigality brought Sackville into disgrace, but he was later restored to political favor.

Sackville-West, V(ictoria Mary), *also called* **Vita** 1892–1962 •*English poet and novelist*• Born in Knole, Kent, she was educated privately. In 1913 she married the diplomat **Harold Nicolson**, and their marriage survived despite Nicolson's homosexuality and her own lesbian affair. In her *Orchard and Vineyard* (1921) and her long poem *The Land*, which won the 1927 Hawthornden Prize, she expresses her closeness to the countryside where she lived. Her prose works include the novels *The Edwardians* (1930), *All Passion Spent* (1931) and *No Signposts in the Sea* (1961); an account of her family in *Knole and the Sackvilles* (1947); and studies of **Andrew Marvell** and **Joan of Arc**. *Passenger to Tehran* (1926) records her years in Persia with her husband, and she was the model for **Virginia Woolf**'s *Orlando* (1928). She was a passionate gardener at her home at Sissinghurst in Kent (now owned by the National Trust).

Sadat, (Muḥammad) Anwar el- 1918–81 •*Egyptian soldier, politician and Nobel Prize winner*• Born in the Tala district of Egypt, he joined the army and was commissioned in 1938. Imprisoned in 1942 for contacts with the Germans in World War II, he continued to work for the overthrow of the British-dominated monarchy, and in 1952 was one of the group of officers who carried out the coup deposing King **Farouk I**. An ardent Egyptian nationalist and Muslim, he was editor of *Al-Jumhuriya* and *Al-Tahrir* in 1955–56, and held strong anti-Communist views. He became president of the United Arab Republic in 1970 after the death of **Gamal Abd al-Nasser**, at a time when Egypt's main preoccupation was the confrontation with Israel. He temporarily assumed the post of prime minister (1973–74), after which he sought diplomatic settlement of the conflict with Israel. He met the prime minister of Israel **Menachem Begin** in Jerusalem in December 1977 and at Camp David, US (1978), in which year he and Begin were jointly awarded the Nobel Peace Prize. Following criticism by other Arab statesmen and hard-line Muslims, he was assassinated by Muslim extremists while reviewing troops.

Sade, Donatien Alphonse François, Comte de, *known as* **Marquis de Sade** 1740–1814 •*French writer*• He was born in Paris, and became an army officer. In 1772 he was condemned to death at Aix for his cruelty and for sexual perversion. He made his escape, but was afterward imprisoned at Vincennes and in the Bastille, Paris, where he wrote works of sexual fantasy and perversion, including *Les 120 journées de Sodome* (1784, Eng trans *The 120 Days of Sodom*, 1954), *La philosophie dans le boudoir* (1793, Eng trans *The Bedroom Philosophers*, 1965) and *Les crimes de l'amour* (1800, Eng trans, in part, as *Quartet*, 1963). He died in a mental asylum at Charenton. "Sadism," the inflicting of pain for sexual pleasure, is named after him.

“ ”

Quand l'athéisme voudra des martyrs, qu'il le dise et mon sang est tout prêt.
When atheism wants martyrs, let it say so and my blood will be ready.
1797 ***La Nouvelle Justine***.

Sádi or **Saadi** or **Sa'adi**, *assumed name of* **Sheikh Muslih Addin** 1184?–1292? •*Persian poet*• A descendant of **Alī**, **Muhammad**'s son-in-law, he studied at Baghdad and traveled widely. Near Jerusalem he was taken prisoner by the Crusaders, but was ransomed. His works comprise 22 different kinds of writings in prose and verse, in Arabic and Persian, of which odes and dirges form the predominant part. The most celebrated writing is the *Gulistan* ("Rose Garden"), a kind of moral work in prose and verse, intermixed with stories, maxims, philosophical sentences and puns.

Saenredam, Pieter Jansz 1597–1665 •*Dutch painter*• Born in Assendelft, he studied painting in Haarlem. He was acquainted with the architect **Jacob van Campen** and may have been inspired by his architectural drawings to specialize in paintings of church interiors, a subject of which he is an acknowledged master. His paintings convey, in a distinctive high tonality, the subtle effects of light and atmosphere.

Sagan, Carl Edward 1934–96 •*US astronomer*• Born in New York City, he studied at Chicago and Berkeley, worked at Harvard, then moved to Cornell, becoming Professor of Astronomy and Space Science in 1970. He did work on the physics and chemistry of planetary atmospheres and surfaces, investigated the origin of life on Earth, and was an active member of the imaging team associated with the Voyager mission to the outer planets. In the 1960s he worked on the theoretical calculation of the Venus greenhouse effect, and after 1983 he studied the concept of nuclear winter. Sagan and James Pollack were the first to advocate that temporal changes on Mars were nonbiological and were in fact due to wind-blown dust. Through books and a television program, *Cosmos*, Sagan did much to interest the general public in science. His *Cosmic Connection* (1973) dealt with advances in planetary science; *The Dragons of Eden* (1977, Pulitzer Prize) and *Broca's Brain* (1979) helped to popularize recent advances in evolutionary theory and neurophysiology. He was president of the Planetary Society (1979–96) and was a strong proponent of SETI, the search for extraterrestrial intelligence.

Sagan, Françoise, *pseudonym of* **Françoise Quoirez** 1935– •*French novelist*• Born in Cajarc, Lot, she was educated at a convent in Paris and in private schools. At the age of 18 she wrote, in only four weeks, the best-selling *Bonjour tristesse* (1954, Eng trans 1955; filmed 1958), followed by *Un certain sourire* (1956, Eng trans *A Certain Smile*, 1956; filmed 1958), both strikingly direct testimonies of affluent adolescence, written with the economy of a remarkable literary style. Irony creeps into her third, *Dans un mois, dans un an* (1957, Eng trans *Those Without Shadows*, 1957), and moral consciousness takes over in her later novels, such as *Aimez-vous Brahms ...* (1959, Eng trans 1960; filmed 1961 as *Goodbye Again*).

Sager, Ruth 1918–97 •*US geneticist*• She earned a PhD in genetics from Columbia University in 1948 and worked as a research fellow in several institutions before becoming Professor of Biology at Hunter College (1966–75), then Professor of Cellular Genetics at Harvard (1975–88, then Emeritus Professor). Most of her experimental work used the single-celled alga *Chlamydomonas*, which she observed through numerous mutations, and in 1963 provided the clinching evidence that DNA existed in the cytoplasm. She postulated cytoplasmic inheritance (the inheritance of genes contained in the cell body or cytoplasm) in addition to the well-established inheritance of genes in the cell nucleus. She was elected to the National Academy of Sciences in 1977.

Sahib, Tippoo *See* **Tippoo Sahib**

Sahlins, Marshall David 1930– •*US cultural anthropologist*•

Born in Chicago, he was educated at Michigan and Columbia. He became Professor of Anthropology at Michigan in 1964, and was professor at the University of Chicago (1974–97, then emeritus). He has made major contributions in the field of Oceanic ethnography, cultural evolution, economic anthropology and the analysis of symbolism. In his early work, as in *Evolution and Culture* (1960), he presented a materialist and progressivist view of cultural evolution heavily influenced by the theory of Leslie White (1900–75). In *Culture and Practical Reason* (1976), however, he inverts this perspective, insisting on the autonomy of cultural systems.

Sainsbury (of Drury Lane), Alan John Sainsbury, Baron 1902–98 •*English retailer*• Born in Hornsey, Middlesex, and educated at Haileybury, he joined (1921) the family grocery business founded by his grandparents in 1869. From 1967 he was joint president of J Sainsbury, PLC with his younger brother, Sir Robert (1906–2000). His elder son, Baron John Davan Sainsbury of Preston Candover (1927–), has been president since 1992 (chairman 1969–92). Sir Robert's son, Baron David John Sainsbury of Turville (1940–), was chairman in 1992–98.

Sainte-Beuve, Charles Augustin 1804–69 •*French writer and critic*• Born in Boulogne-sur-Mer, he was educated at the Collège Charlemagne in Paris, and then studied medicine (1824–27). He was a contributor to the literary and political paper the *Globe*, and in 1827 he published a review praising the *Odes et ballades* of **Victor Hugo**, and the subsequent friendship with Hugo lasted until Sainte-Beuve's affair with Madame Hugo in 1834. In 1828 he published *Tableau de la poésie française au seizième siècle* ("Survey of 16th-Century French Poetry"). After the revolution of July 1830, he joined the staff of the *National*, the organ of extreme republicanism, and in 1835 he published his only novel, *Volupté* ("Voluptuousness"). He then lectured on the history of Port Royal at Lausanne (1837), and in book form these lectures contain some of his finest work. His many other literary works include *Portraits de femmes* (1844, "Portraits of Women") and, published posthumously, *M. de Talleyrand* (1870) and *Souvenirs et indiscrétions* (1872, "Recollections and Indiscretions").

Saint Denis, Ruth, *originally* **Ruth Dennis** 1879–1968 •*US dancer, director, choreographer and teacher*• Born in Somerville, New Jersey, she began performing in vaudeville at an early age and became known, first in Europe, for the exotic and colorful Eastern dances that were to characterize her work. She founded the Denishawn company school with her husband Ted Shawn (1891–1972) with him in Los Angeles in 1915 (later in New York), which was frequented by many Hollywood stars. In 1916 she choreographed the Babylonian dances for **D W Griffith**'s film *Intolerance*. The company toured the US until 1931, when the couple separated and the company was closed. She danced into her eighties, and published an autobiography, *An Unfinished Life*, in 1939.

Saint-Exupéry, Antoine de 1900–44 •*French novelist and airman*• Born in Lyons, he became a commercial airline pilot and wartime reconnaissance pilot. His philosophy of "heroic action," based on the framework of his experiences as a pilot, is expressed in his sensitive and imaginative *Courrier sud* (1929, "Southbound Mail"), *Pilote de guerre* (1942, Eng trans *Flight to Arras*, 1942) and other works. His most popular work is *Le petit prince* (1943, Eng trans *The Little Prince*, 1944), a touching allegory about a boy from another planet who befriends a pilot stranded in the desert. Saint-Exupéry was declared missing after a flight in World War II.

Saint-Gaudens, Augustus 1848–1907 •*US sculptor*• He was born in Dublin and was taken to the US as a baby. After training as a cameo cutter, he studied sculpture in Paris and later in Rome, where he was influenced by the work of the Italian Renaissance. He returned to the US in 1873 and became the foremost sculptor of his time. His major works include *Lincoln* (1887) in Lincoln Park, Chicago, *The Puritan* (1887, Deacon Chapin, in Springfield, Massachusetts), and the **Henry Adams** Memorial in Rock Creek Cemetery, Washington DC.

Saint John, Henry *See* **Bolingbroke, 1st Viscount**

Saint-John Perse, *pseudonym of* **Marie René Auguste Alexis Saint-Léger Léger** 1887–1975 •*French poet and diplomat and Nobel Prize winner*• Born in St Léger des Feuilles, an island near Guadeloupe, he studied at Bordeaux, and after many adventures in New Guinea and China, he entered the French foreign ministry in 1904. He became secretary-general in 1933, was dismissed in 1940 and fled to the US, where he became an adviser on French affairs to **Franklin D Roosevelt**. Symbolism was an influence on his earliest verse, and his blank verse utilizes a vocabulary of rare words. His best-known works include the long poem *Anabase* (1924; Eng trans *Anabasis* by **T S Eliot**, 1930), *Exil* (1942, "Exile"), *Pluies* (1944, "Rain") and *Chroniques* (1960, Eng trans 1961). He was awarded the Nobel Prize for literature in 1960.

Saint-Just, Louis Antoine Léon Florelle de 1767–94 •*French revolutionary*• He was born in Decize, studied law, and while in Paris began to write, producing in 1791 a revolutionary essay, *L'esprit de la Révolution et de la constitution de France*. He was elected to the Convention (1792), where he attracted notice by his fierce tirades against the king, and as a devoted follower of **Robespierre** was sent on missions to the armies of the Rhine and the Moselle. He joined the Committee of Public Safety and began the attacks on **Jacques Hébert** which were to send him to the guillotine with **Georges Danton**. In 1794 he led the attack on the Austrians at Fleurus. He was guillotined during the Thermidorian Reaction.

Saint Laurent, Louis Stephen 1882–1973 •*Canadian politician*• Born in Compton, Quebec, he became a lawyer and professor of law at the University of Laval, and in 1941 he entered the Dominion parliament as a Liberal. **Mackenzie King** appointed him minister of justice and, unlike other Quebec Liberals, he supported King on conscription in 1944 and was made secretary of state for external affairs in 1946. Saint Laurent became prime minister in 1948; he launched a social program that included the extension of the old-age pension plan and hospital insurance. Under his leadership, the Liberals were reelected in 1949 and 1953.

" "

Socialists are Liberals in a hurry.

Attributed. Quoted in Dale C Thomson ***Louis St. Laurent*** *(1967).*

Saint Laurent, Yves (Henri Donat Mathieu) 1936– •*French designer*• He was born in Oran, Algeria, and studied in Paris, graduating in modern languages. In 1955, after winning an international design competition, he was employed by **Christian Dior**, whom he succeeded in 1957. In 1962 he opened his own house, and launched the first of his Rive Gauche boutiques in 1966; by selling ready-to-wear clothes, he set a trend that many other designers were to follow. He announced his retirement in 2002.

Saint Leger, Anthony 1731/32–89 •*English soldier and racing enthusiast*• He was born in Grangemellan, Ireland, and educated at Eton and Cambridge. As a lieutenant colonel during the American Revolution, he was with General **James Wolfe** at Quebec. In 1776 he founded the classic St Leger Stakes at Doncaster, British racing's oldest classic.

Saint-Saëns, (Charles) Camille 1835–1921 •*French composer and music critic*• Born in Paris, he entered the Paris Conservatoire in 1848, and was a pupil of Benoist and **Fromental Elié Halévy**. He began his long and prolific career of composition with his prize-winning *Ode à Sainte Cécile* (1852, "Ode to St Cecilia"), and was a distinguished pianist and organist. Although conservative as a composer, he was a founder in 1871 of the Société Nationale de Musique, which was influential in encouraging the performance of works by young contemporary French composers. He wrote five symphonies; 13 operas, including his best known, *Samson et Dalila* (1877), four symphonic poems; five concertos for piano, three for violin and two for cello; *Carnaval des animaux* (1886, "Carnival of the Animals") for two pianos and orchestra; church music, including his *Messe solennelle* (1855, "Solemn Mass"); and chamber music and songs. His writings include *Au courant de la vie* (1914, "During a Lifetime").

Saint-Simon, Claude Henri de Rouvroy, Comte de 1760–1825 •*French social reformer and founder of French socialism*• Born in Paris, he served in the American Revolution (1776–83), and during the French Revolution he was imprisoned as an aristocrat. His first socialist ideas were expressed in *L'industrie* (1817), which he followed with works such as *L'organisateur* (1819) and his last and most important book, *Nouveau christianisme* (1825). In opposition to the destructive spirit of the Revolution, he sought a positive reorganization of society, with the feudal and military system being superseded by an industrial order, and the spiritual direction of society passing from the Church to men of science. He remained poor and would have died of starvation but for the support of friends and family.

Sakharov, Andrei Dimitriyevich 1921–89 •*Soviet physicist, dissident and Nobel Prize winner*• Born in Moscow, the son of a scientist, he graduated in physics from Moscow State University in 1942 and was awarded a doctorate for work on cosmic rays. He worked under **Igor Tamm** at the Lebdev Institute in Moscow, and took a leading part in the development of the Soviet hydrogen bomb. During the early 1960s he became increasingly estranged from the Soviet authorities when he campaigned for a nuclear test-ban treaty, peaceful international coexistence and improved civil rights within the USSR. In 1975 he was awarded the Nobel Peace Prize, and in 1980 was sent into internal exile in the "closed city" of Gorky (now Nizhny Novgorod). Here he undertook a series of hunger strikes in an effort to secure permission for his wife, **Yelena Bonner**, to receive medical treatment overseas. He was eventually released in 1986 and continued to campaign for improved civil rights.

Saki *See* **Munro, Hector Hubert**

Saladin, *properly* **Salah al-Din al-Ayyubi** 1138–93 •*Sultan of Egypt and Syria, and founder of a dynasty*• Born in Takrit on the Tigris, he entered the service of **Nureddin**, emir of Syria, and was made grand vizier of the Fatimid caliph (1169). In 1171 he made himself sovereign of Egypt, and on Nureddin's death he became sultan of Egypt and Syria (1175), conquered Mesopotamia, and received the homage of the Seljuk princes of Asia Minor. He defeated King Guy of Jerusalem and a united Christian army at Hattin near Tiberias, and then captured Jerusalem and almost every fortified place on the Syrian coast. This provoked the Third Crusade. After a two-year siege (1189–91), Acre was captured, while in 1191, **Richard I** defeated Saladin at Arsuf (1191), took Caesarea and Jaffa, and obtained a three years' treaty. Saladin died in Damascus, and his wise administration left a legacy of citadels, roads and canals.

Salam, Abdus 1926–96 •*Pakistani theoretical physicist and Nobel Prize winner*• Born in Jhang, Maghiana, Punjab, and educated at the University of the Punjab and Cambridge, he became Professor of Mathematics at the Government College Lahore (now in Pakistan) and at Punjab (1951–54). He lectured at Cambridge (1954–56) and then became Professor of Theoretical Physics at Imperial College of Science, Technology, and Medicine, London (1957–93). His concern for his subject in developing countries led to his setting up the International Center of Theoretical Physics in Trieste in 1964. In 1979 he was awarded the Nobel Prize for physics, with **Steven Weinberg** and **Sheldon Glashow**. Independently each had produced a single unifying theory of both the weak and electromagnetic interactions between elementary particles.

Salazar, António de Oliveira 1889–1970 •*Portuguese dictator*• Born near Coimbra, he was educated in a seminary and became a lecturer in economics at Coimbra. His economic expertise led to his ascendancy under the military dictatorship of General **Antonio Carmona** (1926–32). During the early 1930s he laid the foundations of the *Estado Novo* (New State) which he would dominate as dictator for over 35 years. The authoritarian and supposedly corporatist Salazarist state was underpinned by the army and the feared security police, the PIDE. His retrogressive economic policies made Portugal the poorest country in Europe, while greatly enhancing the wealth of its opulent oligarchy. The revolt of the army led to the downfall of the regime after his death.

Saleh, Ali Abdullah 1942– •*North Yemeni soldier and politician*• Born in Bayt al-Ahmar, North Yemen, he became a colonel in the army of the Yemen Arab Republic and took part in the 1974 coup when Colonel Ibrahim al-Hamadi seized power amid rumors that the monarchy was to be restored. Hamadi was assassinated in 1977 and Colonel Hussein al-Ghashmi took over, only to be killed by a South Yemen terrorist bomb in 1978. Against this background of death and violence, Saleh became president. Under his leadership, the war with South Yemen was ended and the two countries agreed to eventual reunion.

Salgado, Sebastião Ribeiro, Jr 1944– •*Brazilian photojournalist*• Born in Aimorés, Minas Gerais, he was educated at the University of São Paulo, Vanderbilt University and the University of Paris. He established his reputation as a photographer-reporter working in Europe, Africa and Latin America in the 1970s. His coverage of the drought in the Sahel in the mid-1980s attracted international attention, as did his photographs of manual labor taken around the world in the years 1986–92 and the ambitious *Migrations: Humanity in Transition* (1993–99).

Salieri, Antonio 1750–1825 •*Italian composer*• Born in Verona, he worked in Vienna for 50 years. A teacher of **Beethoven** and **Schubert**, he became court composer (1774) and Hofkapellmeister (1788), writing over 40 operas, an oratorio and masses. A rival of **Mozart**, he was later alleged to have poisoned him, although there is no substantive evidence of this.

Salinger, J(erome) D(avid) 1919– •*US novelist and short-story writer*• He was born in New York. He attended schools in Manhattan, and in 1934 his father enrolled him at Valley Forge Military Academy ("Pencey Prep" in *The Catcher in the Rye*). He left school at the age of 17, took a job as a dancing partner for wealthy spinsters on a cruise liner, then attended Columbia University, where his performance was said to be below average. His ambition was to become a writer, and after serving as an infantryman in World War II, he progressed from publishing in popular magazines to the *New Yorker*. *The Catcher in the Rye* (1951), his first novel (which sells 250,000 copies annually), made him the guru of disaffected youth. Its hero, Holden Caulfield, skips classes at his Pennsylvania boarding school and goes to New York, where he tries in vain to lose his virginity. Written in a slick and slangy first-person narrative, disrespectful to adults and authority, it provoked a hostile response from some critics. Other works include *Franny and Zooey* (1961), *Raise High the Roof Beam, Carpenters* and *Seymour: An Introduction* (both 1963). *Hapworth 16, 1924* (1997), his first published work in 34 years, had originally appeared in the *New Yorker* in 1965.

> "A confessional passage has probably never been written that didn't stink a little bit of the writer's pride in having given up his pride."
>
> *1963 **Seymour: An Introduction**.*

Salisbury, 1st Earl of *See* **Cecil, Robert**

Salisbury, 5th Marquis of *See* **Cecil, Robert Arthur James Gascoyne-**

Salisbury, John of *See* **John of Salisbury**

Salk, Jonas Edward 1914–95 •*US virologist*• Born in New York City, he was educated at New York University, obtaining his MD in 1939. He taught there and at other schools of medicine and public health, and in 1963 became director of the Salk Institute in San Diego, California. In 1954 he became known worldwide for his work on the Salk vaccine against poliomyelitis. His killed-virus vaccine had to overcome initial opposition, but a trial in 1954 showed that Salk's vaccination was 80 to 90 percent effective, and by the end of 1955 over seven million doses had been administered.

Salle, René Robert Cavalier, Sieur de La *See* **La Salle, René Robert Cavelier, Sieur de**

Sallust, *Latin* **Gaius Sallustius Crispus** 86–34 BC •*Roman historian and politician*• Born in Amiternum, in the Sabine country, he became tribune in 52 BC when he helped to avenge the murder of Clodius upon Milo and his party. In 50 BC he was expelled from the Senate and joined the cause of **Julius Caesar**; and in 47 BC he was made praetor and restored to senatorial rank. He served in Caesar's African campaign, and was left as governor of Numidia. His administration was marked by oppression and extortion, and from his gains he laid out famous gardens on the Quirinal and built the mansion which became an imperial residence for **Nerva**, **Vespasian** and **Aurelian**. In his retirement he wrote his histories, the *Bellum Catilinae*, the *Bellum Iugurthinum* and the *Historiarum libri quinque* (78–67 BC).

Salmond, Alex(ander Elliot Anderson) 1955– •*Scottish Nationalist politician*• Born in Linlithgow, West Lothian, he joined the Scottish National Party at the age of 19, while a student at the University of St Andrews. He graduated in economics and worked for the Royal Bank of Scotland before winning Banff and Buchan for the Scottish National Party (SNP) in the 1987 general election. He achieved a clear victory in the party's 1990 election of a successor to party leader Gordon Wilson (1938–). In the general election of 1997 the number of SNP MPs returned to Westminster rose from three to six. He stepped down as leader of the SNP in 2000.

Salome 1st century AD •*Judean princess*• She was the granddaughter of **Herod the Great** and daughter of Herodias by her first husband, Herod Philip, who was the brother of her second husband, **Herod Antipas**. She is identified by the historian **Josephus** as the girl in Mark 6:17–28 and Matthew 14:1–12 who danced before Herod Antipas and at her mother's instigation demanded the head of **John the Baptist**, who had denounced the marriage with Antipas. She is the subject of a play (1894) by **Oscar Wilde**, which in turn provided the libretto for an opera by **Richard Strauss** (1905).

Salten, Felix, *pseudonym of* **Siegmund Salzmann** 1869–1945 •*Austrian novelist and essayist*• He was born in Budapest, Hungary, and became a journalist and art critic at the age of 18. He is known especially for his animal stories, particularly *Bambi* (1929) which, in translation and as a film by **Walt Disney** (1941), achieved great popularity in the US and Great Britain. He also wrote *Florian* (1934, Eng trans *Florian: An Emperor's Horse*, 1934) and *Bambis Kinder* (1940, Eng trans *Bambi's Children*, 1940).

Salvator Rosa *See* **Rosa, Salvator**

Salviati, Cecchino, *originally* **Francesco de' Rossi** 1510–63 •*Italian painter*• Born in Florence, he was a pupil of **Andrea del Sarto** and a close friend of **Giorgio Vasari**. In about 1530 he traveled to Rome and entered the service of Cardinal Giovanni Salviati, whose name he adopted. He traveled extensively in Italy and executed decorative designs, painted portraits and designed tapestries in Rome, Venice and Florence. In 1554 he was called to the French court, but returned to Rome the following year. He is regarded as one of the major Italian Mannerist painters.

Samaranch, (Juan) Antonio 1920– •*Spanish sports administrator and diplomat*• He was born into a wealthy commercial family in Barcelona, had connections with the **Franco** family, and was a multimillionaire by the late 1960s. He entered politics, became minister of sport, ambassador to the USSR (1977–80), and president of the International Olympics Committee (1980–2001).

Samoset d. c. 1653 •*Native American leader*• He was chief of the Pemaquid band of Abnakis, who lived on Monhegan Island off the coast of present-day Maine. Having learned some English from fishermen in Maine, he spoke welcoming words to the Pilgrims in the Plymouth colony and introduced the colonists to **Squanto** and the chief Massasoit, both of the Wampanoag tribe. In 1625 he sold 12,000 acres of Pemaquid land to John Brown, thereby executing the first land transfer between a Native American and an Englishman.

Sampras, Pete 1971– •*US tennis player*• He was born in Washington DC. Four times winner of the US Open (1990, 1993, 1995–96) and seven times winner of Wimbledon (1993–95, 1997–2000), with 13 Grand Slam Championships, he is the game's most successful player. He is especially known for his powerful serves.

Samson •*Old Testament ruler*• He was the last of the 12 judges in the Book of Judges. The biblical account represents him not as a leader but as an individual whose deeds on behalf of Israel made him a popular hero. After a number of encounters with the Philistines he was lured into a trap by Delilah, who cut off his hair to reduce the strength that God had given him. Blinded by the Philistines, he took his revenge once his hair had grown again by bringing down the temple at Gaza.

Samuel 11th century BC •*Old Testament ruler and Hebrew prophet*• The son of Elkanah and his wife Hannah, he was an Ephraimite who was dedicated to the priesthood as a child. After the defeat of Israel and loss of the Ark of the Covenant to the Philistines, he endeavored to keep the tribal confederation together, moving in a circuit among Israel's shrines. He presided, apparently reluctantly, over **Saul**'s election as the first king of Israel, but later criticized Saul for assuming priestly prerogatives and disobeying divine instructions. Samuel finally anointed **David** as Saul's successor, rather than Saul's own son, Jonathan.

Samuelsson, Bengt Ingemar 1934– •*Swedish biochemist and Nobel Prize winner*• Born in Halmstad, he entered the medical school of Lund University, where he worked in the laboratory of Sune Bergström (1916–). In 1958 he moved to the Karolinska Institute in Stockholm. Samuelsson studied the biosynthesis of prostaglandins, substances that act as chemical messengers, and he and Bergström also investigated two groups of prostaglandins, one known as the E series, which lowers blood pressure and is used in treating circulatory diseases, and another, the F series, which raises blood pressure, and has been used to induce abortion. Samuelsson shared the 1982 Nobel Prize for physiology or medicine with Bergström and Sir **John Vane**.

Sanctorius (Santorio Santorio) 1561–1636 •*Italian physician*• Born in Justinopolis, Venetian Republic (Koper, Slovenia), he studied philosophy and medicine at Padua and practiced medicine in various places before settling in Venice in 1599. Professor of Theoretical Medicine at Padua from 1611, he is best known for his investigations into metabolism, consisting of an elaborate series of measurements of his own weight, food intake and excretia. He also invented instruments to measure humidity and temperature, a syringe for extracting bladder stones, and other devices. He was a friend of **Galileo**.

Sand, George, *pseudonym of* **Amandine Aurore Lucie Dupin, Baronne Dudevant** 1804–76 •*French novelist*• She was born in Paris, the illegitimate daughter of Marshal de Saxe, who died when she was still a child. She lived mostly with her grandmother, and inherited her property. At the age of 18 she married Casimir, Baron Dudevant, and had two children, but after nine years left him and went to Paris with her children to make her living writing literature in the Bohemian society of the period (1831). She scandalized bourgeois society for many years with her unconventional ways and her love affairs. Her first lover was Jules Sandeau (1811–83), from whose surname she took her pseudonym, and with whom she wrote a novel, *Rose et Blanche* (1831). She was always interested in poets and artists, including Prosper Mérimée (1803–70), **Alfred de Musset**, with whom she traveled in Italy, and **Chopin**, who was her lover for ten years. Later her attention turned to philosophers and politicians, such as priest and writer Félicité de Lamennais (1782–1854), the socialist Pierre Leroux, and the republican Michel de Bourges. After 1848 she settled down as the quiet "châtelaine of Nohant," and spent the rest of her life writing and traveling. Her work can be divided into four periods. When she first went to Paris, her candidly erotic novels, *Indiana* (1832), *Valentine* (1832), *Lélia* (1833) and *Jacques* (1834), emanated the Romantic extravagance of the time, and declared themselves against marriage. In the next period her philosophical and political teachers inspired the socialistic rhapsodies of *Spiridion* (1838, Eng trans 1842), *Consuelo* (1842–44, Eng trans 1846), *La Comtesse de Rudolstadt* (1843–45, Eng trans *The Countess of Rudolstadt*, 1847) and *Le meunier d'Angibault* (1845, Eng trans *The Miller of Angibault*, 1847). Between the two periods came the fine novel *Mauprat* (1837, Eng trans 1847). Then she began to turn toward the studies of rustic life, *La mare au diable* (1846, Eng trans *The Haunted Marsh*, 1848), *François le champi*, (1847–48, Eng trans *Francis the Waif*, 1889) and *La petite Fadette* (1849, Eng trans *Little Fadette*, 1850), which are considered her best works. The fourth period comprises the miscellaneous works of her last 20 years, some of them, such as *Les beaux messieurs de Bois-Doré* (1858, Eng trans *The Gallant Lords of Bois-Doré*, 1890), *Le Marquis de Villemer* (1860–61, Eng trans *The Marquis of Villemer*, 1871) and *Mademoiselle la Quintinie* (1863), being of high quality.

Sandburg, Carl 1878–1967 •*US poet*• Born in Galesburg, Illinois, of Swedish descent, after trying various jobs, fighting in the Spanish-American War and studying at Lombard College, he became a journalist in Chicago. His verse reflects the industrial US. Among his volumes of poetry are *Chicago Poems* (1915), *Corn*

Huskers (1918), *Smoke and Steel* (1920) and *Good Morning, America* (1928). His *Complete Poems* gained him the Pulitzer Prize in 1950. He published a collection of American folk songs and ballads in *The American Songbag* (1927). He also wrote an extensive *Life of Abraham Lincoln* (1926–39), which won a Pulitzer Prize.

Sanders, Barry 1968– •*US football player*• Born in Wichita, Kansas, he built a formidable reputation as a running back with Oklahoma State University, winning the Heisman Trophy in 1988 and breaking college records in rushing, scoring and touchdowns. He joined the Detroit Lions in 1989, in which year he was named Rookie of the Year, and went on to become NFL rushing leader four times (1990, 1994, 1996–97) and twice NFL Player of the Year (1991 and 1997). His career total of 15,269 yards made him the third-highest rusher of all time before his unexpected retirement at the end of the 1998 season.

Sanders, Deion 1967– •*US baseball and football player*• He was born in Fort Myers, Florida. Unusual in American sports, he plays both football and baseball. He made a record-breaking deal for $13 million when he left Super Bowl champions the San Francisco 49ers in 1995 and signed with the Dallas Cowboys. He played baseball for the New York Yankees (1988–90); the Atlanta Braves (1991–94); and the Cincinnati Reds (1994–95), whom he left for the San Francisco Giants.

Sanderson, Tessa (Theresa Ione) 1956– •*English sportswoman and television commentator*• Born in Wolverhampton, West Midlands, she first threw the javelin for Great Britain in 1974; together with her great rival **Fatima Whitbread**, she kept the country at the top of the event for the ensuing decade. She won three Commonwealth gold medals (1978, 1986 and 1990) and one Olympic gold medal at the Los Angeles games in 1984. In 1989 she became a sports newsreader for SkyTV.

Sandino, Augusto César 1895–1934 •*Nicaraguan revolutionary*• Born in Niquinohomo (La Victoria), he made the mountains of northern Nicaragua his stronghold and led guerrilla resistance to US occupation forces after 1926. After the withdrawal of the US Marines (1933), **Anastasio Somoza** arranged a meeting with him, apparently to discuss peace. This, however, was a ruse and Sandino was murdered on Somoza's orders near Managua. The Nicaraguan revolutionaries of 1979 (later known as the Sandinistas) regarded him as their principal hero.

Sands, Bobby (Robert) 1954–81 •*Northern Irish revolutionary*• Born in Belfast, he joined the IRA in 1972, and was sentenced to five years' imprisonment in 1973 for possession of guns. In 1977 he was sentenced to 14 years after the bombing of a furniture factory. On March 1, 1981, while at Long Kesh prison in Northern Ireland, he went on a hunger strike in protest against the authorities' refusal to consider him and his fellow IRA prisoners as political prisoners. On April 9 he was elected Westminster Member of Parliament for Fermanagh–South Tyrone in a by-election. He remained on hunger strike for 66 days and died on May 5.

Sandwich, Edward Montagu, 1st Earl of 1625–72 •*English naval commander*• In the English Civil War he fought on the parliamentary side as a soldier at Marston Moor (1644), sat in parliament (1645–48), shared the command of the fleet with **Robert Blake** from 1653, and fought in the first Anglo-Dutch War. On the restoration of the monarchy (1660), which he supported, he was appointed Admiral of the Narrow Seas. In the Dutch War with France and England (1672–78), he fought in the Battle of Southwold Bay, and was blown up with his flagship, the *Royal James*.

Sandwich, John Montagu, 4th Earl of 1718–92 •*English politician*• As First Lord of the Admiralty from 1748 to 1751 and 1771 to 1782, his ineptness contributed to British failures in the American Revolution. Notoriously corrupt, he was a member of Francis Dashwood's "Mad monks of Medmenham Abbey," and was involved in the persecution of his former friend, John Wilkes (1727–97). The Sandwich (now Hawaiian) Islands were named after him by Captain **Cook**. The sandwich is reputed to have been invented by him as a snack for eating at the gaming table.

Sanford, Katherine 1915– •*US medical researcher*• Born and educated in Wellesley, Massachusetts, she received her PhD from Brown University and then moved to the National Cancer Institute, where she spent her entire research career. She worked initially with Dr Virginia Evans and colleagues, developing tissue-culture techniques and examining ways of promoting cancerous transformations in cultured cells. Her cloning of a mammalian cell (the isolation of a single cell in order that it might propagate itself, producing a colony of identical cells) has become a vital tool for the detailed pathological study of cancer-causing mechanisms.

Sangallo, Antonio Giamberti da, the Younger 1485–1546 •*Italian architect and engineer*• Born in Florence, he was the most notable of a family of architects. He was a leading architect of the High Renaissance in Rome, designing the Palazzo Palma-Baldassini in Rome (c. 1520), and his masterpiece, the Palazzo Farnese, also in Rome (1534–46, completed by Michelangelo). He was also a military engineer, and designed the fortifications around Rome.

Sanger, Frederick 1918– •*English biochemist and Nobel Prize winner*• Born in Rendcombe, Gloucestershire, he was educated at Cambridge, and joined the staff of the Medical Research Council in Cambridge (1951–83). During the 1940s he devised methods of deducing the sequence of amino acids in the chains of the protein hormone insulin. For this he was awarded the Nobel Prize for chemistry in 1958. He then turned to RNA and DNA; eventually he was able to deduce the full sequence of bases in the DNA of the virus Phi X 174 and mitochondrial DNA. Such methods led to the determination of the full base sequence of the **Epstein**-Barr virus by 1984. For this work Sanger shared (with **Walter Gilbert** and **Paul Berg**) the 1980 Nobel Prize for chemistry, thereby becoming the first scientist to win two Nobel Prizes in this field. He was appointed to the Order of Merit in 1986.

Sanger, Margaret Louise, *née* **Higgins** 1883–1966 •*US social reformer and founder of the birth control movement*• Born in Corning, New York, and educated at Claverack College, she became a trained nurse, and married William Sanger in 1902. Appalled by some of her experiences as a nurse, she published in 1914 a radical feminist magazine, *The Woman Rebel*, which gave advice on contraception. In 1916 she founded the first American birth control clinic, in Brooklyn, New York, for which she was imprisoned. After a world tour, she founded the American Birth Control League in 1921. Her many books include *What Every Mother Should Know* (1917).

Sanguinetti, Julio María 1936– •*Uruguayan politician*• A member of the long-established progressive Colorado Party (PC), which had its origins in the civil war of 1836, he was elected to the assembly in 1962, later holding various ministerial posts. The oppressive regime of Juan Maria Bordaberry (1972–76) was forcibly removed, and military rule imposed before democratic government was restored in 1985. The 1966 constitution was restored with some modifications, and Sanguinetti was elected president. He took office in 1986, leading a government of national accord until the completion of his term in 1990. He was later reelected (1994–99).

Śankara c. 700–50 •*Hindu philosopher and theologian*• Born in Kalati, Kerala, he was the most famous exponent of *Advaita* (the *Vedanta* school of Hindu philosophy), and is the source of the main currents of modern Hindu thought. His thesis was that Brahma alone has true existence and the goal of the self is to become one with the Divine. This view, familiar to modern Westerners through the teaching of the Ramakrishna Mission, was strongly opposed by **Ramanuja** and his successors in the *Bhakti* tradition.

San Martín, José de 1778–1850 •*Argentine soldier and politician*• Born in Yapeyu, he played a large part in winning independence for Argentina, Chile and Peru. He was an officer in the Spanish army (1789–1812), but aided Buenos Aires in its struggle for independence (1812–14). He raised an army in Argentina (1814–16), which in January 1817 he led across the Andes into Chile, and with **Bernardo O'Higgins** defeated the Spanish at Chacabuco (1817) and Maipo (1818), thus achieving independence for Chile. In 1821, after creating a Chilean navy with Thomas Cochrane (1775–1860), he entered Lima and declared Peru's independence. He resigned in 1822 and died in exile in Boulogne.

Sansovino, *properly* **Andrea Contucci** 1460–1529 •*Italian sculptor and architect*• He was born in Monte San Savino, from which he derived his name, and worked in Florence, Portugal (at the court of John II) and in Rome. Some of his work survives, including, in Florence, the Corbinelli altar at Santo Spirito (c. 1486–91) and, at Santa Maria del Popolo in Rome, the tomb of Cardinal Ascanio Sforza (1505–09). He was also in charge of architecture at Loreto (c. 1513–27) and at San Savino.

Sansovino, Jacopo, *originally* **Jacopo Tatti** 1486–1570 •*Italian sculptor and architect*• Born in Florence, he was a pupil of **Sansovino**, and took his name. From 1529 he was state architect in Venice, where he did his best work. His most noteworthy works in architecture are the Libreria Vecchia, the Palazzo della Zecca and the Palazzo Corner, and in sculpture the two giants on the steps of the ducal palace.

Santa Anna, Antonio López de 1797–1876 •*Mexican soldier and statesman*• Born in Jalapa, he joined **Augustín de Iturbide** in 1821 in the struggle for Mexican independence, but in 1823 overthrew him, and in 1833 became president of Mexico. His reactionary policy resulted in the loss of Texas in 1836; he commanded the Mexican force at the siege and massacre of the Alamo, but was routed by Samuel Houston and imprisoned for eight months. In 1838 he lost a leg in the defense of Veracruz against the French. From 1841 to 1844 he was either president or the president's master; he was exiled in 1845 but recalled in 1846 to resume office during the war with the US, in which he was twice defeated. He was appointed president for life in 1853, but in 1855 was again overthrown, and went to Cuba. Under **Ferdinand Maximilian** he intrigued continually and in 1867, after the emperor's death, he tried to effect a landing; he was captured, and sentenced to death, but allowed to retire to New York.

Santander, Francisco de Paula 1792–1840 •*Colombian general and politician*• Born in Rosario de Cúcuta, New Granada, he was a revolutionary who fought for independence from Spain, and he served as vice president of Gran Colombia under **Simón Bolívar** (1821–28) until he was banished for his supposed complicity against Bolívar. In 1830 Gran Colombia was dissolved, and in 1832 Santander returned from exile and refounded the country as New Granada (comprising modern Colombia and Panama) and becoming its president (1832–37).

Santayana, George, *originally* **Jorge Augustín Nicolás Ruiz de Santayana** 1863–1952 •*Spanish-US philosopher, poet and novelist*• Born in Madrid, and educated from 1872 in the US, he taught at Harvard (from 1889) and was professor there (1907–12), but returned to Europe in 1912. He lived for some time in Oxford, but settled in Rome (1924) and spent his last years as the guest of a convent there. His writing career began as a poet with *Sonnets and Other Verses* (1894). He was also a successful novelist with *The Last Puritan* (1935), and a cultivated literary critic, aesthetician and essayist. Philosophy, however, became his main interest; his general outlook was naturalistic and materialistic, and he was critical of the transcendental claims of religion and of German idealism. He was also a skeptic, maintaining that knowledge of the external world depends on an act of "animal faith." But he was at the same time a Platonist in temperament and attitude, and was devoted to the institutions, if not the doctrines, of the Catholic Church. Santayana's philosophical works include *The Sense of Beauty* (1896), *Realms of Being* (4 vols, 1927–40) and *Platonism and the Spiritual Life* (1927).

“ ”

Those who cannot remember the past are condemned to repeat it.

1905–06 ***The Life of Reason.***

Santer, Jacques 1937– •*Luxembourg politician*• Born in Wasserbillig, he was educated at the Universities of Paris and Strasbourg and at the Institute of Political Studies in Paris. After graduating he became a lawyer at the Luxembourg Court of Appeal. As a Parti Chrétien-Social member he held several ministerial positions before becoming prime minister (1984–94). In 1995 he was elected president of the European Commission. He left this post in 1999 with the mass resignation of the commission and is currently a member of the European Parliament.

Sapir, Edward 1884–1939 •*US linguist and anthropologist*• Born in Lauenburg, Pomerania (now Poland), he went to the US with his family in 1889 and studied ethnology and American Indian languages at Columbia University. One of the founders of ethnolinguistics, he is best known for his work on the languages of the North American Indians, particularly his studies of the relationship between language and culture. His conclusions as to the effect that the grammatical structure and vocabulary of a language may have on the way its speakers perceive the world were developed by his pupil **Benjamin Lee Whorf**, and came to be known as the Sapir-Whorf hypothesis.

Sapper, *pseudonym of* **Herman Cyril McNeile** 1888–1937 •*English novelist and short-story writer*• Born in Bodmin, Cornwall, McNeile was educated at Cheltenham and at the Royal Military Academy at Woolwich. He joined the Royal Engineers as a regular in 1907 and was promoted to captain on the eve of World War I; he won the Military Cross and rose to lieutenant colonel before his retirement. He is remembered chiefly for the invention of Captain Hugh "Bulldog" (originally "Bull-Dog") Drummond, introduced in 1920 in an eponymous novel.

Sappho c. 610–c. 580 BC •*Greek lyric poet*• Born on the island of Lesbos, she seems to have been the center of a circle of women and girls, probably her pupils. Because her surviving poems express passionate love and admiration of females, the adjective "lesbian" has come to refer to female homosexuality. However, Sappho did marry and had a daughter, Cleis. Only two of her odes are extant in full, but many fragments have survived. The four-line sapphic stanza (used in Latin by **Catullus** and **Horace**) is named for her.

Sarah, *also spelled* **Sarai** 19th century BC •*Biblical character in the Old Testament*• Sarah, whose name means "princess" in Hebrew, was the wife of **Abraham** and mother of Isaac. She accompanied Abraham from Ur to Canaan (Genesis 12–23) and pretended to be Abraham's sister in front of the pharaoh in Egypt and Abimelech in Gerar, since her beauty and their desire for her might have endangered Abraham's life. Long barren, she eventually gave birth to Isaac in her old age, fulfilling God's promise that she would be the ancestor of nations (Genesis 17:16).

Saramago, José 1922– •*Portuguese author and Nobel Prize winner*• He was born in Azinhaga and worked for several years as a car mechanic before publishing his first novel, *The Land of Sin* (1947). International success came with the publication of *Baltasar and Blimunda* (1982), a love story set in 18th-century Portugal. Subsequent novels include *The Gospel According to Jesus Christ* (1991) and *All the Names* (1997). He has been a persistent critic of successive Portuguese governments. He won the Nobel Prize for literature in 1998.

Sarandon, Susan Abigail, *née* **Tomalin** 1946– •*US film actress*• Born in New York City, she studied drama at the Catholic University in Washington DC. She made her film debut in *Joe* (1970) and worked extensively in television and theater before graduating to more interesting roles in cinema, including Janet in *The Rocky Horror Picture Show* (1975). She received a Best Actress Award nomination for her role in *Atlantic City* (1980), but good work eluded her until her casting in *The Witches of Eastwick* (1987) and *Bull Durham* (1988). Increasingly in demand as a mature woman displaying strong sexuality, her subsequent triumphs include *White Palace* (1990), *Thelma and Louise* (1991), *Lorenzo's Oil* (1992) and *Dead Man Walking* (1995, Academy Award), directed by her offscreen companion **Tim Robbins**.

Sarasate, Pablo (Martin Melitón) 1844–1908 •*Spanish violinist and composer*• Born in Pamplona, he studied with distinction at the Paris Conservatoire, and in 1857 began to give concerts. A skilled performer in concertos, he was perhaps best at playing the Spanish dance music he composed. Various works were specially composed for him, including the *Symphonie espagnole* by Édouard Lalo (1823–92).

Sardanapalus *See* **Ashurbanipal**

Sargent, John Singer 1856–1925 •*US painter*• Born in Florence, Italy, the son of a US physician, he studied painting there and in

Paris. Most of his work, such as *Lord Ribblesdale* (1902, National Gallery, London), was, however, executed in England from 1885, where he became the most fashionable and elegant portrait painter of his age. To this period belongs his well-known *Carnation Lily, Lily, Rose* (1885–86, Tate Britain, London). In 1907 he exhibited with the English artists at the Venice Biennale. His early painting shows a French Impressionist influence, but Spanish art had a more lasting effect, and *Carmencita* is perhaps the best example of this. Visiting the US constantly, he worked on portraits and series of decorative paintings for public buildings, such as *The Evolution of Religion* for the Boston Public Library (1889–c. 1915). He also painted landscapes, and was an official war artist in World War I, producing *Gassed* (1818, Imperial War Museum, London) and other works.

Sargent, Sir (Harold) Malcolm Watts 1895–1967 •*English conductor*• Born in Stamford, Lincolnshire, he originally studied as an organist, first appearing as a conductor when his *Rhapsody on a Windy Day* was performed at a Promenade Concert in 1921. He was conductor of the Royal Choral Society from 1928, the Liverpool Philharmonic Orchestra (1942–48), and the BBC Symphony Orchestra (1950–57). From 1948 he directed the London (Henry Wood) Promenade Concerts. His fine conducting of choral music, as well as his sense of occasion and unfailing panache, won him great popularity at home and abroad.

Sargeson, Frank (Norris Frank Davey) 1903–82 •*New Zealand short-story writer and novelist*• Born in Hamilton, he made his name with collections of short stories such as *Conversations With My Uncle* (1936), *A Man and His Wife* (1940) and *That Summer and Other Stories* (1946), in which he satirized the provincial attitudes of his surroundings. His novels include *Memoirs of a Peon* (1965) and *Joy of the Worm* (1969). On account of his easy use of colloquial idioms and speech patterns, he is regarded as the founder of modern New Zealand writing.

Sarmiento, Domingo Faustino 1811–88 •*Argentine writer and politician*• An outspoken critic of the dictator Juan Manuel de Rosas (1793–1877) and the *caudillo* Juan Facundo Quiroga 1790–1835), he spent much of his early life in exile in Chile (1831–36, 1840–45, 1848–51), also traveling to Europe and the US. He later became his country's first civilian president (1868–74). An especially vigorous promoter of education and immigration, he was also a prolific and forceful writer. With Juan Bautista Alberdi (1810–84) and Bartolomé Mitre (1821–1906), he was one of the most important architects of modern Argentina.

Sarney (Costa), José 1930– •*Brazilian politician*• Born in Maranhao state, in 1956 he was elected to the state assembly. He became ARENA (National Renewal Alliance) governor of Maranhão in 1965 under **Humberto Castelo Branco**, and was a prominent senator during the 1970s, leading the Social Democratic Party (PDS) under Figueiredo. He was deputy to Tancredo Neves in the first civilian government in 21 years in 1985, and became president on Neves's sudden death. His attempt to retain the executive post during the 1987–88 Constituent Congress succeeded, but at enormous political and economic cost. He was succeeded in 1990 by Fernando Collor de Mello (1950–).

Saroyan, William 1908–81 •*US playwright and novelist*• He was born in Fresno, California, and was largely self-educated. He won literary fame with his first work, *The Daring Young Man on the Flying Trapeze* (1934), a volume of short stories. He continued to write unconventional and impressionistic stories, which were published in collections such as the autobiographical *My Name Is Aram* (1940). Idealistic and opposed to commercialism, he refused the Pulitzer Prize awarded in 1940 for his play *The Time of Your Life* (1939). Among his later works are several other plays, novels including *The Human Comedy* (1943) and memoirs.

Sarraute, Nathalie, *née* **Tcherniak** 1900–99 •*French writer*• She was born in Ivanovno-Voznesenk, Russia. Her parents settled in France when she was a child, and she was educated at the Sorbonne, graduating in arts and law. She then spent a year at Oxford (1922–23) and studied sociology in Berlin before establishing a law practice in Paris. Her first book was a collection of sketches on bourgeois life, *Tropismes* (1939, Eng trans *Tropisms*, 1964), in which she rejected traditional plot development and characterization in order to describe a world between the real and the imaginary. She developed this style in later novels, including *Le planétarium* (1959, Eng trans 1960) and *Ici* (1995, "Here"). She also wrote plays and essays.

Sarto, Andrea del, *properly* **d'Agnolo** 1486–1531 •*Italian painter*• He got his name from his father's trade of tailor. From 1509 to 1514 he was engaged by the Servites in Florence to paint a series of frescoes for their Church of the Annunciation, and a second series was next painted for the Recollets. In 1518 he went to Paris on the invitation of **Francis I**. He returned to Italy the next year with a commission to purchase works of art, but squandered the money and dared not return to France. Many of his most celebrated paintings, such as *Madonna of the Harpies* (1517), are in Florence.

Sartre, Jean-Paul 1905–80 •*French existentialist philosopher, dramatist, novelist and Nobel Prize winner*• Born in Paris, he studied at the Sorbonne and taught philosophy at Le Havre, Paris and Berlin (1934–35). He was taken prisoner in World War II (1941), and after his release became a member of the Resistance in Paris. In 1945 he emerged as the most prominent member of the left-wing, Left Bank intellectual life of Paris. In 1946, with **Simone de Beauvoir**, he founded and edited the avant-garde monthly *Les temps modernes* ("Modern Times"). His characteristic existentialist doctrines found full expression in his autobiographical novel *La nausée* (1938, Eng trans *Nausea*, 1949) and other fiction. The Nazi occupation provided the grim background to such plays as *Les mouches* (1943, Eng trans *The Flies*, 1946) and *Huis clos* (1944, Eng trans *In Camera*, 1946; also known as *No Exit* and *No Way Out*). His atheistic existentialist doctrines are outlined in *L'existentialisme est un humanisme* (1946, Eng trans *Existentialism and Humanism*, 1948) and are fully worked out in *L'être et le néant* (1943, Eng trans *Being and Nothingness*, 1956). Other notable works include the trilogy *Les chemins de la liberté* ("Paths of Freedom"). In 1964 he was awarded the Nobel Prize for literature, but he declined it. In the late 1960s he became closely involved in the opposition to US policies in Vietnam, and expressed support for the student rebellions of 1968. He wrote an autobiography, *Les mots* (1963, Eng trans *The Words*, 1964).

“ ”

L'Enfer, c'est les Autres.
Hell is other people.

1944 ***Huis Clos.***

Sassoon, Siegfried Louvain 1886–1967 •*English poet and novelist*• Born in Brenchley, Kent, he suffered experiences in World War I that made him detest war, and led to their fierce expression in *The Old Huntsman* (1917), *Counter-Attack* (1918) and *Satirical Poems* (1926). A semifictitious autobiography, *The Complete Memoirs of George Sherston* (1937), had as its first part *Memoirs of a Fox-Hunting Man* (1928, Hawthornden Prize 1929). *The Old Century* (1938), *The Weald of Youth* (1942) and *Siegfried's Journey 1916–20* (1945) are all autobiographical, and he also wrote a biography of **George Meredith** (1948). His later poems, including those in *Vigils* (1935) and *Sequences* (1956), are predominantly spiritual. His *Collected Poems* appeared in 1961.

Satie, Erik Alfred Leslie 1866–1925 •*French composer*• Born in Honfleur to French-Scottish parents, he worked as a café composer and studied under **Vincent d'Indy** and **Albert Roussel**. In his own work-ballads, lyric dramas, whimsical pieces and the ballet *Parade* (1917), he was in revolt against Wagnerism and orthodoxy in general, and had some influence on **Claude Debussy**, **Maurice Ravel** and others.

Saud, *in full* **Saud ibn Abd al-Aziz** 1902–69 •*King of Saudi Arabia*• He was the older son of **Ibn Abd al-Rahman al-Saud**, and succeeded him in 1953. His rule was characterized by inefficiency and corruption, and by financial disorder except for the periods when his brother **Faisal** served as finance minister. Eventually his brothers formed a group to press for reform, and a number of air force officers defected to Egypt, where they were supported by President **Nasser**. In 1964 the Council of Ministers deposed Saud and he agreed to pledge allegiance to his brother Faisal, who replaced him.

Saul 11th century BC •*Biblical ruler*• A Benjamite, the son of Kish, he was the first king elected by the Israelites; his name means "asked for." He conquered the Philistines, Ammonites and Amalekites, but became intensely jealous of **David**, his son-in-law, and was ultimately at odds with the priestly class. At length **Samuel** secretly anointed David king. Saul fell in battle with the Philistines at Mount Gilboa.

Saunders, Dame Cicely Mary Strode 1918– •*English founder of the modern hospice movement*• Born in Barnet, Greater London, she was educated at Roedean School and St Anne's College, Oxford, and trained at St Thomas's Hospital Medical School and the Nightingale School of Nursing. As founder (1967), medical director (1967–85) and chairman (1985–) of St Christopher's Hospice, Sydenham, she has promoted the principles of dying with dignity, maintaining that death is not a medical failure but a natural part of living and that its quality can be enhanced by sensitive nursing and effective pain control. She has received many awards for her pioneering work, including the Templeton Prize (1981) and the BMA Gold Medal (1987). She was given the honorary title of Dame Commander, Order of the British Empire, in 1980 and was awarded the Order of Merit in 1989.

Saunders, Jennifer 1958– •*English comedienne and actress*• Born in Sleaford, Lincolnshire, she trained at the Central School of Speech and Drama in London, where she met **Dawn French**. They formed a highly successful comedy duo, starting at the Comedy Store in London. In 1980 they joined the new Comic Strip club and later appeared on television in *The Comic Strip Presents* … films (1982–93), in series such as *Girls on Top* (1985–86), which they wrote with Ruby Wax, and in their own series, *French and Saunders* (1987–96). Away from the partnership, she wrote and starred (with **Joanna Lumley**) in *Absolutely Fabulous* (1992–95, 2001), winning an Emmy award for the script and a British Academy of Film and Television Arts award for her performance, and took a straight acting role in *Queen of the East* (1995).

Saussure, Ferdinand de 1857–1913 •*Swiss linguist*• Born in Geneva, he was appointed Professor of Indo-European Linguistics and Sanskrit at the University of Geneva in 1901, and also Professor of General Linguistics in 1907. His lectures on general linguistics constituted the first serious attempt to determine the nature of language as the object of which linguistics is the study and he is often described as the founder of modern linguistics. His *Course in General Linguistics* (1916; 5th edn 1955; English translation by Baskin, 1959) was compiled by two of his students after his death, mainly from lecture notes. As well as introducing the important dichotomy of *langue* (the system of language) and *parole* (an individual's actual speech), he pointed out that language can be viewed descriptively (synchronically) or historically (diachronically). His methodology inspired a great deal of the later work done by semiologists and structuralists.

Savage, Richard c.1697–1743 •*English poet*• He claimed to be the illegitimate child of Richard Savage, the fourth and last Earl Rivers, and the Countess of Macclesfield, but the story of his noble descent has been discredited. In 1727 he killed a man in a tavern brawl, and narrowly escaped the gallows. He led a dissipated life and was finally jailed for debt, and died there. He wrote a comedy, *Love in a Veil* (1718), in the dedication of which he asserted his parentage, and *The Tragedy of Sir Thomas Overbury* (1723), and at least one notable poem, *The Wanderer* (1729).

Savarin, (Jean) Anthelme Brillat- *See* **Brillat-Savarin, (Jean) Anthelme**

Savery, Thomas c. 1650–1715 •*English inventor and military engineer*• Born in Shilstone, Devonshire, he patented an invention for rowing vessels by means of paddle wheels (1696), and in 1698 developed the first practical high-pressure steam engine for pumping water from mines. It was superseded in 1712 by the much improved version designed in partnership with **Thomas Newcomen**.

Savile, George *See* **Halifax, 1st Marquis of**

Savile, Sir Henry 1549–1622 •*English scholar and courtier*• Born in Bradley, near Halifax, and educated at Brasenose College, Oxford, he became a Fellow of Merton College, Oxford, and was later appointed warden of Merton (1585), provost of Eton (1596) and Latin secretary and tutor in Greek to Queen **Elizabeth I**. Later he was one of the scholars appointed by King **James VI and I** to prepare the Authorized Version of the Bible. He translated part of the histories of **Tacitus** (1591) and the *Cyropaedia* of **Xenophon**. He also published the first edition of St **John Chrysostom** (1610–13). In 1619 he founded the Savilian chairs of mathematics and astronomy at Oxford.

Savile, Sir Jimmy (James Wilson Vincent) 1926– •*English broadcaster and charity worker*• Born in Leeds, Yorkshire, he became a miner, a ballroom manager with Mecca, then a radio disc jockey and television host, with regular appearances on *Top of the Pops* (1963–). An ebullient figure with an ostentatious lifestyle, he has used his celebrity status to work tirelessly for worthwhile causes, raising over £10 million to construct a National Spinal Injuries Centre at Stoke Mandeville Hospital, acting as a voluntary helper at Leeds Infirmary and Broadmoor Hospital, and running countless fundraising marathons. On television he has campaigned for car safety and was the host of *Jim'll Fix It* (1975–94), in which he helped to fulfill the special wishes of ordinary people. He was knighted in 1990.

Savimbi, Jonas Malheiro 1934–2002 •*Angolan soldier and nationalist*• Educated in Angola and at the University of Lausanne, he moved to Zambia and became a leader of the Popular Union of Angola. After a period with the Angolan National Liberation Front (FNLA), he broke away to form the National Union for the Total Independence of Angola (UNITA). Unable to agree with the leaders of the People's Movement for the Liberation of Angola (MPLA) and the FNLA, he continued the struggle against the MPLA from bases in the south of Angola, supported by South Africa and the US. Agreement to a ceasefire and democratic elections was finally achieved in Estoril in 1991, but when Savimbi lost the subsequent elections, the armed struggle broke out again. A further ceasefire began in 1995 with the confinement of UNITA troops. He was reported to have been shot dead by government forces in February 2002.

Savonarola, Girolamo 1452–98 •*Italian religious and political reformer*• He was born into a noble family in Ferrara, and in 1474 entered the Dominican order at Bologna. After initial failures he was soon acclaimed as a great and inspiring preacher and in 1489 he was called to Florence, where a humanist revival in art and literature was supported by **Lorenzo de' Medici**. When, after the intervention of **Charles VIII** of France, the Medici were expelled and a republic was established in Florence, Savonarola became its leader. The republic of Florence was to be a Christian commonwealth, of which God was the sole sovereign, and his Gospel the law; many flocked to the public square to fling down their costliest ornaments, which Savonarola's followers made into a huge "bonfire of vanities." His claim to the gift of prophecy led to his being cited (1495) to answer a charge of heresy in Rome, and when he failed to appear he was forbidden to preach, then excommunicated (1497). In the following year the Medici party came back into power. Savonarola was again forbidden to preach. He was tried for false prophecy and was hanged in Rome. His chief work is *The Triumph of the Cross*.

Sax, Antoine Joseph, *known as* **Adolphe Sax** 1814–94 •*Belgian musician and inventor*• He was born in Dinant, the son of a Brussels musical instrument maker. With his father he invented a valved brass wind instrument that he called the sax-horn (patented 1845), and also the saxophone, the saxtromba and the saxtuba. He moved to Paris to promote his inventions, and he was an instructor at the Paris Conservatoire, but he failed to make his expected fortune.

Saxe, Maurice, Comte de, *also called* **Marshal de Saxe** 1696–1750 •*Marshal of France*• Born in Goslar, the illegitimate son of **Augustus II**, at the age of 12 he ran off to join the army of the Duke of **Marlborough** in Flanders. He fought against the Turks in Hungary, and in 1726 against the Russians and Poles. In the War of the Polish Succession (1733–38) he opposed his half brother Augustus III, and in 1744, as marshal of France, he commanded the French army in Flanders. In 1745 he defeated the Duke of **Cumberland** at Fontenoy and retired two years later.

Saxe-Coburg-Gotha, Alfred Ernest Albert, Prince of 1844–1900 •*British prince*• He was born at Windsor Castle, the second son of Queen **Victoria**. He joined the Royal Navy (1858), and became commander in chief in the Mediterranean (1886–89) and at Devonport (1890–93). He was elected king of Greece (1862), but declined the dignity. He was created duke of Edinburgh (1866) and in 1874 married the Russian Grand Duchess Marie Alexandrovna (1853–1920), daughter of Czar **Alexander II** of Russia. In 1893 he succeeded his uncle as reigning duke of Saxe-Coburg-Gotha.

Saxo Grammaticus, *known as* **the Scholar** c. 1150–c. 1220 •*Danish chronicler*• Born on Sjaelland, he was secretary or clerk to Bishop Absalon of Roskilde. He compiled a monumental *Gesta Danorum*, a Latin history of legendary and historical kings of Denmark to 1186 (16 vols, probably written 1185–1216). He is remembered as the first national historian of Denmark.

Sayers, Dorothy L(eigh) 1893–1957 •*English detective-story writer*• She was born in Oxford and educated at Somerville College, Oxford. Beginning with *Whose Body?* (1923) and *Clouds of Witness* (1926), her novels tell the adventures of her hero Lord Peter Wimsey in various accurately observed milieux. Her other stories included *Strong Poison* (1930), *Gaudy Night* (1935), *Busman's Honeymoon* (1936) and *In the Teeth of the Evidence* (1939). She earned a reputation as a leading Christian apologist with two successful plays, *The Zeal of Thy House* (1937) and *The Devil to Pay* (1939), a series for broadcasting (*The Man Born to Be King*, 1943) and a closely reasoned essay, *The Mind of the Maker* (1941). A translation of **Dante**'s *Inferno* appeared in 1949 and of *Purgatorio* in 1955. *Paradiso* was left unfinished at her death, and was completed by her biographer, Barbara Reynolds.

Sayers, Gale 1943– •*US football player*• Born in Wichita, Kansas, he was the star running back with the Chicago Bears from 1965 to 1972. The holder of numerous records, he was elected to the sport's Hall of Fame in 1977. He once scored six touchdowns in one game (December 12, 1965). After retiring from the sport, he coached and became a computer company executive.

Scales, Prunella, *originally* **Prunella Margaret Rumney Illingworth** 1932– •*English actress*• Born in Sutton Abinger, Surrey, she appeared on Broadway in *The Matchmaker* (1955) and with the company at the Shakespeare Memorial Theatre (1956) before West End successes such as *Hay Fever* (1968). On television, she starred as Kate Starling in *Marriage Lines* (1963–66), Sybil Fawlty in *Fawlty Towers* (1975–79), Miss Elizabeth Mapp in *Mapp & Lucia* (1985–86), Sarah in *After Henry* (1988–92), **Elizabeth II** in *A Question of Attribution* (1991) and Mrs Tilston in *Searching* (1995). Her films include *An Awfully Big Adventure* (1995) and *Stiff Upper Lips* (1997). She is married to the actor **Timothy West**.

Scaliger, Joseph Justus 1540–1609 •*French scholar*• He was born in Agen, the son of Julius Caesar Scaliger (1484–1558). After studying at Bordeaux with his father, and in Paris, he acquired a surpassing mastery of the classics and eventually boasted a command of 13 languages, ancient and modern. While in Paris he became a Calvinist (1562) and from 1572 to 1574 he was professor at Calvin's College at Geneva. He then spent 20 years in France and there produced works which placed him at the head of European scholars. By his edition of Manilius and his *Opus de emendatione temporum* (1583) he founded modern chronology. From 1593 he held a chair at Leiden, and to his inspiration Holland owes her long line of scholars. His last years were embittered by controversy, especially with the Jesuits, who charged him with atheism and profligacy.

Scarfe, Gerald 1936– •*English cartoonist, caricaturist and animator*• Born in London, he studied art at St Martin's School, London, and freelanced cartoons for the *Daily Sketch* and *Punch*. He then worked for the satirical *Private Eye*, causing controversy with his *Annual* cover of **Harold Macmillan**. *The Sunday Times* refused to publish his commissioned caricature of **Winston Churchill**, but his work met with more approval in the US magazines *Life* and *Esquire*. He designed the animated sequences for the film, *Pink Floyd: The Wall* (1982). He is married to **Jane Asher**.

Scargill, Arthur 1938– •*English trade union leader*• Born in Leeds and educated in Yorkshire, he entered the mining industry at the age of 18 and was soon involved in politics, joining the Young Communist League in 1955 and the Labour Party in 1966. He was also active in the National Union of Mineworkers (NUM), becoming president from 1981 to 2002 (then honorary president). He constantly warned the union of the threat of massive pit closures, and in 1984 led them in a national strike. Its collapse ten months later raised doubts about his leadership tactics, but his predictions of closures and job losses proved to be correct. In 1992 he launched a resistance campaign against a new wave of proposed pit closures, and in January 1996 he broke away from the Labour party to form his own Socialist Labour Party.

“ ”

I speak of that most dangerous duo—President Ray-Gun and the plutonium blonde, Margaret Thatcher.

1984 Quoted in ***Time****, December 3.*

Scarlatti, Alessandro 1659–1725 •*Italian composer*• Born in Palermo, Sicily, he began his musical career in Rome, where in 1679 he produced his first opera, *Gli equivocinel sembiante*. This gained him the patronage of Queen **Kristina** of Sweden, whose maestro di cappella he became. He was later musical director at the Neapolitan court (1693–1703) and founder of the Neapolitan school of opera, writing nearly 120 works. About 70 of these survive, of which the best known is perhaps *Il tigrane* (1715). He also wrote 200 masses, 10 oratorios, 500 cantatas, and many motets and madrigals.

Scarlatti, (Giuseppe) Domenico 1685–1757 •*Italian composer*• Born in Naples, the son of **Alessandro Scarlatti**, he was the founder of the modern piano technique. From 1711 in Rome he was maestro di cappella to the Queen of Poland, for whom he composed several operas, and he also served in Lisbon from 1720 and Madrid from 1729. As choirmaster of St Peter's, Rome (1714–19), he wrote much church music. It is as a writer of harpsichord sonatas that Scarlatti is best remembered; he wrote over 550, which had an important effect on the development of the form.

Scarron, Paul 1610–60 •*French writer*• Born in Paris, he became an abbé, and in about 1634 paid an extended visit to Italy. In 1638 he began to suffer from an illness which ultimately left him paralyzed. He obtained a prebend in Mans (1643), but giving up all hope of remedy, returned to Paris in 1646 to write for a living. His metrical comedy, *Jodelet, ou le maître valet* (1645, "Jodelet; or, the Master Butler"), was a great success, and he followed it with a number of similar works. The burlesque predominates in most of his writing, but it is as the creator of the realistic novel that he is remembered. *Le roman comique* (1651–57, Eng trans *The Comical Romance*, 1665) was a reaction against the euphuistic and interminable novels of **Madeleine de Scudéry** and **Honoré d'Urfé**. In 1652 he married Françoise d'Aubigné (later Madame de **Maintenon**).

Scarry, Richard McClure 1919–94 •*US illustrator and children's writer*• Born in Boston, he was educated at the Boston Museum School of Fine Arts, and served in the US Army in the Mediterranean and North Africa. His popular children's books, with illustrations that are whimsical, humorous and detailed, teach young children about aspects of daily life. They include *What Do People Do All Day?* (1968) and *Hop Aboard, Here We Go!* (1972).

Schally, Andrew Victor 1926– •*US biochemist and Nobel Prize winner*• Born in Wilno, Poland (now Vilnius, Lithuania), he fled from Poland in 1939 and studied at the National Institute for Medical Research in London and McGill University in Montreal. He later worked at the Baylor Medical School (1957–62) and Tulane University (from 1962). While studying "releasing factors" from the hypothalamus which stimulate the release of hormones from the pituitary gland, Schally discovered an assay system for this in vitro (1955). Schally shared the 1977 Nobel Prize for physiology or medicine with **Roger Guillemin** and **Rosalyn Yalow**.

Schama, Simon Michael 1945– *•English historian and author•* Born in London, he studied at Christ's College, Cambridge. He taught at Cambridge (1966–76) and Oxford (1976–80) and later in the US, becoming a professor at Columbia University (1997–). He has specialized in Dutch history and art, and his books include *The Embarrassment of Riches: An Interpretation of Dutch Culture in the Golden Age* (1987), *Landscape and Memory* (1995), *Rembrandt's Eyes* (1999) and *A History of Britain* (2 vols, 2000–01), which he also adapted and presented as a television series (2000–01).

Scharnhorst, Gerhard Johann David von 1755–1813 *•German soldier and military reformer•* The son of a Hanoverian farmer, he fought in Flanders against the French (1793–95) and directed the training school for Prussian officers (1801). From 1807 he worked with **August von Gneisenau** to reform the Prussian army after its defeat by **Napoleon I**, thus making possible the defeat of Napoleon at Leipzig (1813). He also served as chief of staff under **Gebhard von Blücher**. He was fatally wounded fighting the French at Lützen.

Schaudinn, Fritz Richard 1871–1906 *•German zoologist and microbiologist•* Born in Röseningken, East Prussia, he studied at the University of Berlin, and became director of the department of protozoological research at the Institute for Tropical Diseases in Hamburg (1904). Schaudinn demonstrated the nature of tropical dysentery and discovered its cause. With the dermatologist Erich Hoffmann, he discovered the spirochete which causes syphilis (1905).

Schawlow, Arthur Leonard 1921–99 *•US physicist and Nobel Prize winner•* Born in Mount Vernon, New York, he studied at Toronto and Columbia (1949–51), where he worked with **Charles Townes**, and was later appointed Professor of Physics at Stanford University (1961–91, later emeritus). Townes and Schawlow collaborated to extend the maser principle to light, thereby establishing the feasibility of the laser, although it was **Theodore Maiman** who constructed the first working ruby laser in 1961. From the early 1970s Schawlow worked on the development of laser spectroscopy. With German-born physicist Theodor Hänsch, he was able to make precise measurements of the energy levels the electron can occupy in the hydrogen atom, allowing the value of the Rydberg constant to be determined with unprecedented accuracy. For this work Schawlow shared the 1981 Nobel Prize for physics with Nicolaas Bloembergen (1920–) and **Kai Siegbahn**.

Scheel, Walter 1919– *•West German statesman•* Born and educated in Solingen, he served in the Luftwaffe in World War II. After the war he went into business, joined the Free Democratic Party (FDP), and was elected to the Bundestag in 1953. In 1970 he negotiated treaties with the USSR and Poland, regarded as major advances in East-West relations. From 1969 to 1974 he was vice chancellor and foreign minister, and he became president (for five years) of the Federal Republic of Germany in 1974 on the resignation of **Gustav Heinemann**.

Scheele, Carl Wilhelm 1742–86 *•Swedish chemist•* He was born in Stralsund (now in Germany) and was apprenticed to an apothecary. In 1775, the year that he was elected to the Stockholm Royal Academy of Sciences, he moved to Köping. In the 1760s he began to investigate air and fire, and passed on information about his experiments to **Antoine Lavoisier**, who subsequently discovered the true nature of combustion and named the new flammable gas "oxigine." Scheele subsequently discovered a great many other substances, including hydrofluoric acid, chlorine, copper arsenide (known as Scheele's green), hydrogen sulfide, and many important organic acids. In 1781 he distinguished between two very similar minerals, plumbago (graphite) and molybdena, discovering the metal molybdenum in the process.

Schelling, Friedrich Wilhelm Joseph von 1775–1854 *•German philosopher•* Born in Leonberg, Württemberg, he studied at Tübingen and Leipzig, and taught at Jena (1798–1803), Würzburg (1803–08), Munich (until 1820, as secretary of the Royal Academy of Arts), Erlangen (1820–27), Munich again (1827–40) and Berlin (1841–46). His early work, influenced by **Kant** and **Johann Fichte**, culminated in the *Ideen zu einer Philosophie der Natur* (1797, Eng trans *Idealism and Philosophy of Nature*, 1978), and the *System des transzendentalen Idealismus* (1800, "System of Transcendental Idealism"), which examined the relation of the self to the objective world and argued that consciousness itself is the only immediate object of knowledge and that only in art can the mind become fully aware of itself. He thus became an important influence on romanticism.

Schepisi, Fred 1939– *•Australian film director•* Born in Melbourne, he intended to join the Catholic Church and spent 18 months in a monastery. Progressing to film directing through documentaries and commercials, his first major feature, *The Devil's Playground* (1976), won the Australian Film Institute Award for Best Film. After *The Chant of Jimmie Blacksmith* (1978), a true story of racism, he moved to the US, where his interest in myth and superstition was seen in *The Iceman* (1984). He enjoyed an international success with the comedy *Roxanne* (1987), while *Plenty* (1985) and *A Cry in the Dark* (1988) reveal his continuing concern with issues of class and social injustice. Later, less incisive films include *The Russia House* (1990), *Mr Baseball* (1992) and *Fierce Creatures* (1996).

Schiaparelli, Elsa 1890–1973 *•French fashion designer•* She was born in Rome, studied philosophy and lived in the US for a time, working as a film scriptwriter. In 1920 she and her daughter moved to Paris, where she designed and wore a black sweater knitted with a white bow that gave a *trompe l'œil* effect, which brought her orders from an American store and enabled her to start a business in 1929. Her designs were inventive and sensational, and she was noted for her use of color, including "shocking pink," and her original use of traditional fabrics.

Schiaparelli, Giovanni Virginio 1835–1910 *•Italian astronomer•* Born in Savigliano, Piedmont, he graduated at Turin in 1854 and became head of the Brera Observatory, Milan, from 1860. He worked on the relationship between meteors and comets and achieved the first identification of a meteoroid stream with a specific comet, the pair being the Perseids and comet Swift-Tuttle (1862 III). In 1877 he began observations of Mars, detecting linear markings on the surface, which he termed *canali* (ie, channels), and noticed that they changed as a function of the Martian season.

Schiele, Egon 1890–1918 *•Austrian painter•* Born in Tulln, he studied at the Vienna Academy of Art from 1906 to 1909. Much influenced by **Gustav Klimt**, he joined the Wiener Werkstätte, a craft studio which promoted the fashionable art nouveau style. He developed a personal form of Expressionism in which figures, often naked and emaciated and drawn with hard outlines, fill the canvas with awkward anguished gestures. In 1912 he was arrested and some of his work was destroyed by the police. He also painted intense and psychologically disturbing portraits.

Schiller, (Johann Christoph) Friedrich (von) 1759–1805 *•German dramatist, poet and historian•* He was born in Marbach on the Neckar. His father was an army surgeon in the service of the Duke of Württemberg. At the age of 13, he was obliged to attend the duke's military academy, finally qualified as a surgeon (1780) and was posted to a regiment in Stuttgart. His first play, the apparently anarchical and revolutionary *Die Räuber* (1781, Eng trans *The Robbers*, 1792), published at his own expense, was an instant success when it reached the stage at Mannheim (1782). Schiller absconded from his regiment to attend the performance and was arrested. In hiding at Bauerbach, he continued writing, and in 1784 he began a theatrical journal, *Die rheinische Thalia*, in which were first printed most of his play *Don Carlos*, many of his best poems, and the stories *Verbrecher aus verlorener Ehre* (1786, Eng trans *The Dishonored Irreclaimable*, 1826) and *Der Geisterseher* (1787–88, Eng trans *The Ghost-Seer, or Apparitionist*, 1795). In 1785 he was invited to Leipzig, and in Dresden, where the poet Christian Gottfried Körner (1756–1831) was living, he found rest from emotional excitement and financial worries. Here he finished *Don Carlos* (1787), which was written in blank verse, not prose, and was his first mature play. Among the results of his discussions with Körner and his circle are the poems *An die Freude* (c. 1788, "Ode to Joy"), later set to music by **Beethoven**, and *Die Künstler* (1789, "The Artists"). In 1788 he was appointed honorary Professor of History at Jena, and married, but his health broke down from overwork. He had been writing a history of the Thirty

Years' War, the letters on aesthetic education (1795) and the famous *Über naive und sentimentalische Dichtung* (1795–96, Eng trans *On Simple and Sentimental Poetry*, 1884), in which he distinguishes ancient from modern poetry by their different approaches to nature. His short-lived literary magazine, *Die Horen* (1795–97), was followed by the celebrated *Xenien* (1797, "Epigrams"); these were a collection of satirical epigrams in which his newly found friendship with **Goethe** found mutual expression. This inspired the great ballads (1797–98), *Der Taucher* ("The Diver"), *Der Ring des Polykrates* ("The Ring of Polykrates"), *Die Kraniche des Ibykus* ("The Cranes of Ibycus"), the famous *Das Lied von der Glocke* (completed in 1799, "Song of the Bell") and, under the influence of **Shakespeare**, the dramatic trilogy *Wallenstein* (1796–99), which is considered the greatest historical drama in the German language. This was followed by *Maria Stuart* (1800, translated by **Stephen Spender**, 1957), and a psychological study of the two queens, **Elizabeth I** and **Mary Queen of Scots**, in which Mary by her death gains a moral victory. He again alters history in *Die Jungfrau von Orleans* (1801, Eng trans *The Bride of Messina*, 1837), which portrays the relentless feud between two hostile brothers; and the half-legend of *Wilhelm Tell* (1804, Eng trans *William Tell*, 1825) is made by Schiller the basis of a dramatic manifesto for political freedom.

“ ”

Man kann den Menschen nicht verwehren,
Zu denken, was sie wollen.
One cannot prevent people from thinking what they please.

*1800 **Maria Stuart**, act I, scene 8.*

Schinkel, Karl Friedrich 1781–1841 •*German architect and painter*• Born in Neuruppin, Brandenburg, he was the state architect of Prussia from 1815 and a professor at the Berlin Royal Academy from 1820. He designed numerous military buildings, museums and churches in romantic-classical style and designed boulevards and squares in Berlin. He also attained distinction as a painter and illustrator.

Schlegel, August Wilhelm von 1767–1845 •*German scholar*• Born in Hanover, the brother of **Friedrich von Schlegel**, he studied theology at Göttingen, but soon turned to literature. In 1795 he settled in Jena, and in 1796 married a widow, Caroline Böhmer (1763–1809), who separated from him in 1803 and married **Friedrich von Schelling**. In 1798 he became Professor of Literature and Fine Art at Jena, and founded with his brother the literary journal *Das Athenäum*. In 1801–04 he lectured at Berlin. Most of the next 14 years he spent in the house of Madame de **Staël** at Coppet. From 1818 until his death he was Professor of Literature at Bonn. He translated 17 plays of **Shakespeare**, and also works by **Dante**, **Calderón**, **Cervantes** and **Luis de Camoëns**. He is regarded as a pioneer of the German Romantic movement.

Schlegel, (Karl Wilhelm) Friedrich von 1772–1829 •*German man of letters and critic*• He was born in Hanover, the brother of **August von Schlegel**. Educated at Göttingen and Leipzig, in 1798 he eloped with Dorothea (1763–1839), daughter of **Moses Mendelssohn** and mother of Philipp Veit (1793–1877), the religious painter; this experience inspired a notorious romance *Lucinde* (1799). He then joined his brother at Jena, and with him wrote and edited the literary journal *Das Athenäum*, a vehicle of the German Romantic movement. He studied Oriental languages at Paris (1802–04), and in 1808 published a pioneering work on Sanskrit and Indo-European linguistics. His best-known books are lectures, collected in the *Philosophy of History* (Eng trans 1835) and *History of Literature* (trans 1859).

Schleicher, Kurt von 1882–1934 •*German soldier and politician*• Born in Brandenburg, he was on the general staff during World War I. Politically active during **Heinrich Brüning**'s chancellorship, he succeeded **Franz von Papen** as chancellor. His failure to obtain either a parliamentary majority or emergency powers gave **Hitler** the opportunity to seize power in 1933. Schleicher and his wife were executed by the Nazis in 1934 on a trumped-up charge of treason.

Schleiermacher, Friedrich Ernst Daniel 1768–1834 •*German theologian and philosopher*• Born in Breslau, Lower Silesia (Wrocław, Poland), he studied philosophy and theology at the University of Halle. In 1796 he became a clergyman at the Charité, a Berlin hospital, and joined the literary and intellectual circles with which **Friedrich** and **August von Schlegel** and **Karl Wilhelm von Humboldt** were associated. He became a professor at Halle (1804–06) and Berlin (1810), and had a significant role in the union of the Lutheran and Reformed Churches in Prussia in 1817. His works include *Reden über die Religion* (1799, "On Religion: Speeches to Its Cultured Despisers"), *Monologen* (1800, "Soliloquies"), his major treatise *Der christliche Glaube* (1821–22, "The Christian Faith") and an influential life of Jesus, published posthumously. He is now regarded by many as the founder of modern Protestant theology.

Schlemmer, Oskar 1888–1943 •*German painter, sculptor, designer, dancer and theorist*• Born in Stuttgart, he was on the faculty of the Bauhaus from 1919 to 1933, where he developed his notions of theater as a mixture of color, light, form, space and motion. Using puppetlike human figures as the centerpiece, he called his experimental productions "architectonic dances." All were created between 1926 and 1929 except for the best-known *Triadic Ballet* (three versions: 1911, 1916 and 1922).

Schlesinger, John Richard 1926–2003 •*English actor and film, stage and opera director*• Born in London, he was a student at Oxford, where he joined the dramatic society and directed his first short film, *Black Legend* (1948). At the BBC (1956–61) he directed documentaries for the *Tonight* and *Monitor* series. He directed his first feature film, *A Kind of Loving*, in 1962, followed by *Billy Liar* (1963) and *Far From the Madding Crowd* (1967). He won an Academy Award for his first US film, *Midnight Cowboy* (1969). Later films include *Sunday, Bloody Sunday* (1971) and *Marathon Man* (1976). He also staged opera, and occasionally directed for television, notably *An Englishman Abroad* (1988), *A Question of Attribution* (1991) and *Cold Comfort Farm* (1995).

Schlick, Moritz 1882–1936 •*German philosopher*• Born in Berlin, he first studied physics at the Universities of Heidelberg, Lausanne and Berlin. He taught at Rostock and Kiel, and was Professor of Inductive Sciences at Vienna (1922–36), where he became a leader of the Vienna Circle of logical positivists. He elaborated their central verificationist theory of meaning and extended it to the field of ethics, which he argued was a factual science of the causes of human actions. His major works include *Allgemeine Erkenntnislehre* (1918, "General Theory of Knowledge") and *Fragen der Ethik* (1930, "Problems of Ethics"). He was murdered by a deranged student.

Schlieffen, Alfred, Count von 1833–1913 •*Prussian soldier*• He was born in Berlin. Chief of General Staff (1891–1905), he devised the Schlieffen Plan in 1895 on which German strategy was unsuccessfully based in World War I. In the event of a German war on two fronts, he envisaged a German breakthrough in Belgium and the defeat of France within six weeks by a colossal right-wheel flanking movement through Holland and then southward, cutting off Paris from the sea, meanwhile holding off any Russian intervention with a smaller army in the east.

Schliemann, Heinrich 1822–90 •*German archaeologist, excavator of Mycenae and Troy*• Born in Neubuckow, he went into business in Amsterdam (1842–46) and St Petersburg (1846–63), acquiring a considerable fortune and a knowledge of the principal modern and ancient European languages. At the age of 46 he retired to realize his childhood ambition of finding the site of Homeric Troy by excavating the mound of Hisarlik in Asia Minor. Excavations were begun in 1871–73. Assisted by the professional archaeologist Wilhelm Dörpfeld (1853–1940), he discovered nine superimposed city sites, one of which contained a considerable treasure. He also excavated the site of Mycenae (1876), and worked in Ithaca (1869 and 1878), at Orchomenos (1874–76, 1880) and at Tiryns (1884).

Schlüter, Poul Holmskov 1929– •*Danish politician*• After studying at the Universities of Aarhus and Copenhagen, he qualified as a barrister and Supreme Court attorney and was politically active at an early age, becoming leader of the youth movement of the Conservative People's Party (KF) in 1944. He was elected to parliament (*Folketinget*) in 1964 and ten years later became chairman of the KF, and prime minister from 1982 to 1993, heading a center-right coalition that survived the 1987 election but was reconstituted, with support from one of the minor center parties, Det Radikale Venstre, in 1988. After the election of 1990 the coalition consisted of only two parties: Schlüter's Conservative Party and the Danish Liberal Party, Venstre.

Schmidt, Helmut Heinrich Waldemar 1918– •*West German statesman*• Born in a working-class district of Hamburg, he was a group leader in the **Hitler** Youth organization, and won the Iron Cross for his service in the Wehrmacht in World War II. After the war he studied economics at the University of Hamburg and in 1947 became the first national chairman of the Socialist Student Leagues. He had joined the Social Democratic Party (SPD) in 1946, and entered the Bundestag in 1953. From 1969 to 1972 he was minister of defense. While he was minister of finance from 1972 to 1974, his financial policy consolidated the *Wirtschaftswunder* (economic miracle), giving Germany the most stable currency and economic position in the world. In 1974 he succeeded **Willy Brandt** as chancellor, and described his aim as the "political unification of Europe in partnership with the United States." He established himself as an energetic international statesman, and in 1977 emerged as the "hero of Mogadishu" after taking a firm stand against domestic and international terrorism. He was reelected chancellor in 1980, but was defeated in parliament in 1982. He retired from federal politics at the general election of 1983.

Schmidt, Maarten 1929– •*US astronomer*• Born in Groningen, the Netherlands, he was educated there and at Leiden, and moved to the US in 1959 to join the staff of the Hale Observatories. He is best known for his astounding results in the study of quasars. He studied the spectrum of an optically identified quasar and discovered that the peculiarities of its spectrum were caused by a massive **Doppler** red shift; it appeared to be receding from Earth at nearly 16 percent of the speed of light. Such high velocities are now interpreted to mean that quasars are distant objects, which must be as luminous as hundreds of galaxies in order to be visible on Earth. He also found that the number of quasars increases with distance from Earth, providing evidence for the big bang theory of the origin of the universe.

Schnabel, Artur 1882–1951 •*Austrian pianist and composer*• Born in Lipnik, he studied under Theodor Leschetizky and made his debut at the age of eight. He taught in Berlin, making frequent concert appearances throughout Europe and the US. When the Nazis came to power, he settled first in Switzerland, and from 1939 in the US. He was an authoritative player of a small range of German classics—notably **Beethoven**, **Mozart** and **Schubert**, and his compositions include a piano concerto, chamber music and piano works.

Schnabel, Julian 1951– •*US painter*• Born in New York City, he attracted attention in the 1980s with his expressionistic treatment of some of the grand themes of classical art—the crucifixion, mankind and nature. He uses thick paint, from which ghostly faces emerge, to convey a mood of loneliness and loss, as in *The Unexpected Death of Blinky Palermo in the Tropics* (1981, Stedelijk Museum, Amsterdam). Influenced by the work of **Antonio Gaudí**, he also applies paint to shards of crockery fixed to plywood, with menacing effect, as in *Humanity Asleep* (1982).

Schneiderman, Rose 1884–1972 •*US trade unionist, labor leader and social reformer*• Born in Poland, she emigrated to the US when she was eight. In 1904 she was elected to a union executive board, the highest position yet held by a woman in any US labor organization. After 1908 she worked mainly with the Women's Trade Union League. During **Franklin D Roosevelt**'s presidency, she was the only woman in the National Recovery Administration, and was appointed secretary of the New York State Department of Labor (1937–43).

Schnittke, Alfred 1934–98 •*Russian composer*• He was born in Engels near Saratov. In 1948 he moved to Moscow, trained as a choirmaster, and studied composition at the Moscow Conservatory (1953–58), where he taught from 1962 to 1972. His prolific output has attracted more Western attention than any Russian composer since **Dmitri Shostakovich**. His works include four symphonies and other orchestral works, numerous concertos, choral-orchestral works, ballets, film scores, and chamber, vocal and piano works.

Schnitzler, Arthur 1862–1931 •*Austrian dramatist and novelist*• Born in Vienna, he practiced as a physician there from 1885 before becoming a playwright. His highly psychological and often strongly erotic short plays and novels are set in Vienna and generally underline some social problem. *Anatol* (1893, Eng trans 1911) and *Reigen* (1900, Eng trans *Hands Around*, 1920; better known as *La Ronde*, the title of a 1959 translation) are cycles of one-act plays. Other notable works include *Der grüne Kakadu* (1899, Eng trans *The Green Cockatoo*, 1913) and *Flucht in die Finsternis* (1931, Eng trans *Flight Into Darkness*, 1931).

Schoenberg, Arnold Franz Walter 1874–1951 •*Austrian-born composer, conductor and teacher*• He was born in Vienna. He learned the violin as a boy but was largely self-taught. In his twenties he earned his living by orchestrating operettas, and from 1901 to 1903 he was in Berlin as conductor of a cabaret orchestra. The works of his first period were in the most lush vein of post-Wagnerian Romanticism and include the string sextet *Verklärte Nacht* (1899, "Transfigured Night"), a symphonic poem *Pelleas und Melisande* (1903) and the mammoth choral-orchestral *Gurrelieder* (1900–01; orchestrated by 1911). He was a notable teacher from his Berlin days until his last years, and his two most famous pupils, **Anton von Webern** and **Alban Berg**, joined him in Vienna in 1904. His search for a new and personal musical style began to show in such works as the First Chamber Symphony (1907) and the Second String Quartet (1908), which caused an uproar at their first Vienna performances because of their free use of dissonance. His works written before World War I, including *Erwartung* (1909, "Expectation") and *Pierrot Lunaire* (1912), were extremely chromatic in harmony, with tonality almost obscured, and they met with incomprehension and hostility. From 1915 to 1922 he worked on the text and music for an oratorio, *Die Jacobsleiter*, which remained unfinished. Gradually Schoenberg saw the need to harness his totally free chromatic style, and he logically evolved the discipline known as the twelve-note method—dodecaphony, or serialism; its first use was in the Piano Suite op. 25 (1921–23). This method was adopted by Webern and many others. Schoenberg himself used thematic serialism both strictly and freely, and in some later works departed from it entirely, even returning to tonality. In 1925 he succeeded **Ferruccio Busoni** as director of the composition master class at the Berlin Academy of the Arts. There he wrote his third String Quartet (*Variations for Orchestra*), a one-act opera, *Von Heute auf Morgen* ("From One Day to the Next"), a cello concerto and two acts of his greatest stage work, *Moses und Aaron* ("Moses and Aaron," unfinished). When the Nazis came to power he left Berlin for Paris, where he formally rejoined the Jewish faith. He set sail for the US in October, 1933, never to return to Europe. In America, Schoenberg suffered from bouts of ill health, money troubles, and general misunderstanding and neglect of his work. Yet after settling in Los Angeles (1934), he wrote much fine music, became a popular teacher at the University of California, taught privately, and wrote a number of valuable textbooks on composition. The Violin Concerto (1935–36) and fourth String Quartet are complex twelve-note works, while the Suite for Strings (1934) and a Hebrew setting of the *Kol Nidre* (1938) are more traditionally tonal. Sickness, financial cares and fear of neglect dogged Schoenberg's last years, but interest in his works was already increasing among a younger generation; a few years after his death his stature as a composer and teacher of immense influence was recognized.

" "

My music is not modern, it is merely badly played.

Quoted in C Rosen ***Schoenberg*** *(1976).*

Schongauer or **Schön, Martin** 1450–91 •*German painter and engraver*• He was born in Colmar, where his famous *Madonna of the Rose Garden* altarpiece shows Flemish influence, probably that of **Rogier van der Weyden**. Other religious paintings attributed to Schongauer have not been authenticated, but well over 100 of his engraved plates have survived, including *The Passion, The Wise and Foolish Virgins, Adoration of the Magi* and other religious subjects.

Schoonmaker, Thelma 1945– •*US film editor*• Raised in Africa, she is one of the leading editors in contemporary US cinema. She met **Martin Scorsese** at New York University, and was influential in helping create his distinctive visual style. She received an Academy Award for her work on *Raging Bull* (1980), and was also nominated for *Goodfellas* in 1990, and for the rock music documentary *Woodstock* in 1970. She was married to the director **Michael Powell** from 1984 until his death in 1990.

Schopenhauer, Arthur 1788–1860 •*German philosopher*• He was born in Danzig (Gdansk, Poland), where his father was a banker and his mother a novelist. The family moved to Hamburg in 1793. After his father's sudden death in 1805, he embarked on an academic education at Gotha, Weimar, Göttingen, Berlin and Jena. Throughout his unhappy life he was dark, distrustful, misogynistic and truculent. He reacted strongly against the post-Kantian idealist tradition represented by **Hegel**, **Johann Fichte** and **Friedrich von Schelling** and found his inspiration in the work of **Plato**, **Kant**, the ancient Indian philosophy of the *Vedas*, and **Goethe** (with whom he collaborated on the theory of colors). His major work was *Die Welt als Wille und Vorstellung* (1819, "The World as Will and Idea"), which included reflections on the theory of knowledge and its implications for the philosophy of nature, aesthetics and ethics. He emphasized the active role of the will as the creative but covert and irrational force in human nature, in a way that was greatly to influence **Nietzsche** and **Freud**, and he argued that art represented the sole kind of knowledge that was not subservient to the will. He took a teaching position in Berlin (1820) and combatively timed his lectures to coincide with those of Hegel, but he failed to attract students, his book was virtually ignored and he retired to live a bitter and reclusive life in Frankfurt am Main, accompanied for the most part only by his poodle. He continued his work, defiantly elaborating and defending the same basic ideas in such publications as *Über den Willen in der Natur* (1889, "On the Will in Nature"), *Die Beiden Grundprobleme der Ethik* (1841, "The Two Main Problems of Ethics") and a second edition of his major work (1844). In the end he achieved success with a collection of diverse essays and aphoristic writings published under the title *Parerga und Paralipomena* (1851); and he subsequently influenced not only philosophical movements, notably existentialism, but also a wide range of figures including **Richard Wagner**, **Leo Tolstoy**, **Marcel Proust** and **Thomas Mann**.

" "

Jede Trennung gibt einen Vorgeschmack des Todes—und jedes Wiedersehen einen Vorgeschmack der Auferstehung.

Every parting is a foretaste of death, and every reunion a foretaste of resurrection.

1851 ***Parerga und Paralipomena**, chapter 11.*

Schreiner, Olive 1855–1920 •*South African writer and feminist*• Born in Wittebergen Mission Station, Cape of Good Hope, the daughter of a German Methodist missionary and an English mother, she grew up largely self-educated, and at the age of 15 became a governess to a Boer family near the Karoo desert. She later lived in England (1881–89), where her novel *The Story of an African Farm* (1883) was published under the pseudonym "Ralph Iron." In her later works she was a passionate propagandist for women's rights, pro-Boer loyalty and pacifism. Other books include the polemical *Trooper Peter Halket* (1897), a sociological study titled *Woman and Labor* (1911) and her last novel, *From Man to Man* (1926).

Schrieffer, John Robert 1931– •*US physicist and Nobel Prize winner*• Born in Oak Park, Illinois, he studied electrical engineering and physics at MIT and the University of Illinois. He worked on superconductivity for his PhD under **John Bardeen**, and his collaboration with Bardeen and **Leon Cooper** led to the BCS (Bardeen-Cooper-Schrieffer) theory of superconductivity, for which all three shared the 1972 Nobel Prize for physics.

Schröder, Gerhard 1944– •*German politician*• Born in Mosenburg, Lippe, and educated at the University of Göttingen, he began a career in law, joined the Social Democratic Party (1963) and became national chairman of the Young Socialists (1976–80) and a member of the Bundestag (1980–86). He then rose through a succession of posts to become Social Democrat chancellor of Germany in 1998. As chancellor he distanced himself from the extreme left within his party and built a reputation as a modernizer with a somewhat less enthusiastic approach toward the European Union than his Christian Democrat predecessor, **Helmut Kohl**. He was reelected in 2002.

Schrödinger, Erwin 1887–1961 •*Austrian physicist and Nobel Prize winner*• Born in Vienna, he was educated at the University of Vienna. From 1920 he was a professor at Stuttgart (1920), Jena (1920–21), Breslau (1921) and Zurich (1921–27). He succeeded **Max Planck** as Professor of Physics at the University of Berlin before returning to Austria as professor at the University of Graz (1936–38). After the Anschluss, he fled to Dublin, where he worked at the Institute for Advanced Studies (1938–56), then returned to Austria as emeritus professor at Vienna. Schrödinger originated the science of wave mechanics as part of the quantum theory with his celebrated wave equation. **P A M Dirac** soon developed a more complete theory of quantum mechanics from their foundations, and for this work Schrödinger and Dirac shared the 1933 Nobel Prize for physics. Schrödinger's books include *What Is Life?* (1946).

Schubert, Franz Peter 1797–1828 •*Austrian composer*• He was born in Vienna. At the age of 11 he entered the Stadtkonvikt, a choristers' school attached to the court chapel. He played in the orchestra there, and wrote his first symphony (in D) for it (1813). In 1814 he became assistant master at his father's school; he continued to write music, among which were two fine early songs, the beautiful *Gretchen am Spinnrade* ("Gretchen at the Spinning Wheel") from **Goethe**'s *Faust*, and the powerful and sinister *Erlkönig*. In 1815 Schubert poured out a flood of over one hundred songs, including eight written on a single day, as well as other works. From 1817 he gave up teaching school, and lived a precarious existence in Vienna, earning a living by giving lessons. In 1818 the first public performance of Schubert's secular music included the overtures written in the style of **Rossini**, whom Schubert greatly admired. Schubert's veneration of **Beethoven** made him visit the coffee house that the older composer frequented, but he was too awestruck ever to approach him, except when Beethoven was sick, when he sent him his compositions. In 1822 he composed the Unfinished Symphony (no. 8), and the Wanderer Fantasy for piano (based on a theme from his song, *Der Wanderer*); about this time he began to be troubled by ill health, possibly syphilis. The song cycle *Die schöne Müllerin* ("Fair Maid of the Mill") and the incidental music to *Rosamunde* were written in 1823, the string quartets in A minor and D minor (including variations on a theme from his song *Der Tod und das Mädchen*, "Death and the Maiden") and the octet in F for wind and strings in 1824. In the last three years of his life Schubert wrote the *Winterreise* ("Winter Journey") song cycle and a posthumously published group of songs (not a cycle as such), *Schwanengesang* ("Swan Song"), the string quartet in G major, the string quintet in C, piano trios in B-flat and E-flat, the *moments musicaux* for piano, three piano sonatas, the fantasy in F minor for four hands, and a mass. The symphony in C major, formerly dated to 1828, is now thought to have been written three years earlier. He died on November 19, 1828, and was buried as near as possible to Beethoven's grave; later both composers were exhumed and reburied in the Central Cemetery in Vienna.

Schultz, Theodore William 1902–98 •*US economist and Nobel Prize winner*• Born in Arlington, South Dakota, and educated at South Dakota State University and the University of Wisconsin, he held professorships at Iowa State College (1930–43) and the University of Chicago (1943–72), and wrote *Transforming Traditional Agriculture* (1964). His work stressed the importance of the human factor in agriculture. He was awarded the Nobel Prize for economics in 1979 (with Sir **Arthur Lewis**). Later works include *The Economics of Being Poor* and *Origins of Increasing Returns* (both 1993).

Schulz, Charles M(onroe) 1922–2000 •*US cartoonist*• Born in Minneapolis, Minnesota, he learned cartooning from a correspondence course, and contributed cartoons to the *Saturday Evening Post* (1947). He is best known as the cartoonist of *Peanuts*

(1950–2000), featuring Charlie Brown (based on Schulz himself), Snoopy and Linus. In 1990 he was made Commandeur, L'Ordre des Arts et des Lettres.

Schumacher, Michael 1969– •*German racecar driver*• Born in Hürth-Hermuhlheim, he made a remarkable debut in the 1991 Belgium Grand Prix when he unexpectedly qualified in seventh place, and he joined the Bennetton team two weeks later. He won the Formula 1 world championship in 1994, 1995, 2000 and 2001. In 1996 he signed a $26-million contract with Ferrari.

Schuman, Robert 1886–1963 •*French statesman*• Born in Luxembourg, he was a member of the Resistance during World War II. He became prime minister in 1947 and 1948, and propounded the Schuman plan (1950) for pooling the coal and steel resources of western Europe. He was elected president of the Strasbourg European Assembly in 1958 and was awarded the Charlemagne Prize. He survived **de Gaulle**'s electoral reforms, being reelected to the National Assembly in 1958.

Schumann, Clara Josephine, *née* **Wieck** 1819–96 •*German pianist and composer*• Born in Leipzig, she was the daughter of a Leipzig piano teacher, Friedrich Wieck, who taught her to be a highly skilled concert pianist. She gave her first Gewandhaus concert when only 11, and the following year four of her polonaises were published. She married **Schumann** in 1840 and became his foremost interpreter. She undertook a concert tour of Russia (without him) in 1844. From 1856 she played regularly for the Royal Philharmonic Society in London, and from 1878 she was principal piano teacher at the Frankfurt am Main Conservatory. Her own compositions include piano music and songs. She was a close friend of **Brahms** during her husband's last illness and after his death.

Schumann, Robert Alexander 1810–56 •*German composer*• He was born in Zwickau in Saxony. He studied law at Leipzig and Heidelberg, but was always more interested in music. After hearing **Rossini**'s operas performed in Italy and **Paganini** playing at Frankfurt am Main, he persuaded his parents to allow him to study the piano. He wrote reviews and articles, including a significant one heralding the genius of the young **Chopin**. He managed to cripple a finger of his right hand with a finger-strengthening contraption that he had devised (1832), permanently ruining his prospects as a performer. His first compositions, the *Toccata in C*, *Paganini Etudes*, and *Intermezzi for Piano*, were published in 1833. In 1838 Schumann visited Vienna and came across the manuscript of **Schubert**'s C major symphony; Schumann sent it to **Mendelssohn**, who had it performed. By 1840, after his marriage to Clara Wieck (the future **Clara Schumann**), he had written his first songs, the Fool's Song in *Twelfth Night*, and the Chamisso songs *Frauenliebe und -Leben* ("Woman's Love and Life"). A flood of new songs and song cycles followed, including *Dichterliebe* ("Poet's Love"). These were followed by the A Minor Piano Concerto, the Piano Quintet, the choral *Paradise and the Peril*, the scenes from *Faust*, completed in 1848, the "Spring" Symphony in B-flat, and other works. In 1843 Schumann was appointed professor at the new Leipzig Conservatory. Increasing symptoms of mental illness prompted the move from Leipzig to Dresden. In 1847 the Symphony in C Major was completed and the death of his great friend Mendelssohn prompted him to write a set of reminiscences, first published in 1947. Revolution broke out in Dresden in 1849 when Prussian troops confronted republican revolutionaries, among them **Richard Wagner**. The Schumanns fled, but Robert wrote some stirring marches. His mental state allowed him one final productive phase in which he composed piano pieces, many songs and the incidental music to **Byron**'s *Manfred*. His appointment as musical director at Düsseldorf in 1850 saw a happy interlude and the composition of the *Rhenish* symphony, but his condition remained unstable, and in 1854 he threw himself into the Rhine, only to be rescued by fishermen. He died in an asylum two years later.

Schuschnigg, Kurt von 1897–1977 •*Austrian statesman*• He was born in Riva, South Tirol, and served in World War I. He was elected a Christian Socialist deputy in 1927 and was appointed minister of justice (1932) and minister of education (1933). After the murder of **Engelbert Dollfuss** in 1934, he succeeded as chancellor until March 1938, when **Hitler** annexed Austria. Imprisoned by the Nazis, he was liberated by US troops in 1945. He was a Professor of Political Science at Saint Louis University in the US (1948–67).

Schüssel, Wolfgang 1945– •*Austrian politician*• Born in Vienna, he studied law at the University of Vienna and, as deputy leader of the Austrian People's Party (OVP), became a member of the first house of the Austrian parliament (1979–89). He was federal minister of economic affairs in a coalition government (1989–95) and subsequently served as vice chancellor and federal minister for foreign affairs (1995–2000). He became chancellor of Austria in 2000.

Schütz, Heinrich 1585–1672 •*German composer*• Born in Köstritz, near Gera, he went to Venice in 1609 to study music, becoming a pupil of **Giovanni Gabrieli**. Returning to Germany in 1613, he was appointed Hofkapellmeister in Dresden (1617), where he introduced Italian music and styles, including madrigals, the use of continuo, and instrumentally accompanied choral compositions. He is therefore regarded by many as the founder of the Baroque school of German music. A visit to Italy in 1628 familiarized him with **Monteverdi**'s more recent musical developments, and from 1633 until his return to Dresden in 1641 he traveled between various courts. His compositions include much church music, notably four passion settings and "The Seven Words on the Cross" (1645, *Die sieben Worte Jesu Christi am Kreuz*), a German requiem and the first German opera, *Dafne*, produced in Torgau in 1627 and now lost.

Schuyler, Philip John 1733–1804 •*American general and politician*• Born in Albany, New York, he was a member of the colonial assembly from 1768 and a delegate to the Continental Congress of 1775, which appointed him one of the first four major generals. Besides acting as commissioner for Indian affairs and making treaties with the Six Nations, he sat in Congress (1777–81), was state senator for 13 years between 1780 and 1797, US senator in 1789–91 and 1797–98 and surveyor general of the state from 1782.

Schwann, Theodor 1810–82 •*German physiologist*• Born in Neuss, he was educated in Cologne and Berlin. He remained in Berlin for four years as the assistant of **Johannes Müller**, studying digestion and isolating the enzyme pepsin from the stomach lining. He later showed the role of yeast cells in producing fermentation. Schwann also discovered the cells—named the Schwann cells after him—that compose the sheath around peripheral nerve axons, and he showed an egg to be a single cell. His most renowned work, however, was on cell theory. In a major book of 1839, he contended that the entire plant or animal was comprised of cells, that cells have in some measure a life of their own, but that the life of the cells is also subordinated to that of the whole organism. This cell theory became pivotal to 19th-century biomedicine.

Schwartz, Delmore 1913–66 •*US poet, short-story writer and critic*• Born in Brooklyn, New York, he was educated at New York University. Writing lyrics, fiction, drama and criticism, he was associated with the *Partisan Review* group of writers (editor 1943–55), and was editor of *The New Republic* (1955–57). He was a profound ironist, and in 1960 he became one of the youngest winners of the Bollingen prize. His collections of verse include *Shenandoah* (1941) and *Summer Knowledge* (1959). His stories are collected in *The World Is a Wedding* (1948) and *Successful Love* (1961). **Saul Bellow** memorably portrayed him in *Humboldt's Gift* (1975).

Schwartz, Melvin 1932– •*US physicist*• Born in New York City, he was educated at Columbia University, where he later became professor of physics (1963–66). From 1966 he held professorships at Stanford University, but in the early 1980s he left academic research to work in the computer industry until 1991, when he became associate director of High Energy and Nuclear Physics at Brookhaven National Laboratory, before returning to Columbia University (1994–). He was awarded the 1988 Nobel Prize for physics jointly with **Leon Lederman** and **Jack Steinberger** for demonstrating the existence of the muon neutrino (1962).

Schwarzenberg, Karl Philipp, Prince of 1771–1820 •*Austrian general and diplomat*• He took part in the War of the Second Coalition (1792–1802). When Austria declared war on France in 1809 he participated in the unsuccessful campaign. After the peace treaty he pursued a diplomatic career until **Napoleon I** demanded that he serve as general of the Austrian contingent in the invasion of Russia in 1812. When Austria turned on Napoleon, Schwarzenberg was made generalissimo of the allied armies which won the battles of Dresden and Leipzig in 1813. In 1814 he helped occupy Paris.

Schwarzenegger, Arnold 1947– •*US film actor and politician*• He was born in Thal, near Graz in Austria. A bodybuilder and former Mr Universe, he made his film debut in *Hercules Goes to New York* (1969). Small roles followed, until his appearance in the documentary *Pumping Iron* (1977) revealed more of his highly competitive, yet playful personality. It was his physical prowess, though, that won him roles in such epics as *Conan the Barbarian* (1981), and his stardom was confirmed as the taciturn cyborg in *The Terminator* (1984). Schwarzenegger's most successful films include *Predator* (1987) and *Total Recall* (1990). Despite attempts to broaden his appeal in comedies like *Twins* (1988), he remains most popular in spectacular big-budget adventure stories like *Eraser* (1996). In 1986 he married television news anchorwoman Maria Shriver (1955–), the daughter of US public official R. Sargent Shriver (1915–) and philanthropist Eunice Kennedy Shriver (1921–), of the illustrious **Kennedy** family. A longtime supporter of the Republican party despite his relationship with the Kennedys, Schwarzenegger made his own entrance into politics in 2003 as a candidate in the California gubernatorial election that involved the recall of Governor Gray Davis (1942–). He was elected by a wide margin and inaugurated as governor of California in November 2003.

“ ”

Hasta la vista, baby.

1984 ***The Terminator.***

Schwarzkopf, Dame Elisabeth 1915– •*Austrian-British soprano*• Born in Jarotschin, she studied at the Berlin University for Music, making her debut there in 1938. Later, she sang in the Vienna State Opera (1944–48). She settled in Great Britain in 1948 and joined the Royal Opera, Covent Garden, London (1948–51), at first specializing in coloratura roles (notably as Zerbinetta in **Strauss**'s *Ariadne auf Naxos*) and only later appearing as a lyric soprano. She eschewed modern music, although she sang the first Anne Trulove in **Stravinsky**'s *The Rake's Progress* (1951) and **William Walton** wrote Cressida for her. She is chiefly celebrated for her performance in the central German repertory, in opera, especially **Mozart**, and in lieder. She was given the honorary title of Dame Commander, Order of the British Empire, in 1992.

Schwarzkopf, H Norman, *known as* **Stormin' Norman** 1934– •*US general*• Born in Trenton, New Jersey, into a military family, he became a cadet at the age of ten and joined the US Army after graduating from West Point. After distinguished service in the Vietnam War and in the 1986 US invasion of Grenada, he became a four-star general in 1988. He was given overall command of the coalition land forces in Operation Desert Shield and Desert Storm following the Iraqi invasion of Kuwait in November 1990, and led the offensive that in just 100 hours brought an end to the Gulf War with minimal casualties among the coalition forces. He retired from the army on his return from the Gulf in 1991 and became an international consultant on modern warfare.

Schwarzschild, Karl 1873–1916 •*German astronomer*• Born in Frankfurt am Main, he became interested in astronomy as a schoolboy and had published two papers on binary orbits by the time he was 16. Educated at the Universities of Strasbourg and Munich, he was appointed director of the Göttingen Observatory (1901) and the Astrophysical Observatory in Potsdam (1909). In 1916, while serving on the Russian front, he wrote two papers on **Einstein**'s general theory of relativity, giving the first solution to the complex partial differential equations of the theory. He also introduced the idea that when a star contracts under gravity, there will come a point at which the gravitational field is so intense that nothing, not even light, can escape. The radius to which a star of given mass must contract to reach this stage is known as the Schwarzschild radius. Stars that have contracted below this limit are now known as black holes.

Schweitzer, Albert 1875–1965 •*Alsatian medical missionary, theologian, musician, philosopher and Nobel Prize winner*• He was born in Kaysersberg, in Alsace, and brought up in Günsbach in the Münster valley, where he attended the local *Realgymnasium*, learned the organ in Paris, and studied theology and philosophy at Strasbourg, Paris and Berlin. In 1896 he resolved to live for science and art until he was 30 and then devote his life to serving humanity. In 1899 he obtained his doctorate on **Kant**'s philosophy of religion and became curate at St Nicholas Church, Strasbourg; in 1902, *Privatdozent* (private lecturer) at the university; and in 1903, principal of the theological college. In 1905 he published his authoritative study, *J S Bach, le musicien-poète* (1905, Eng trans by **Ernest Newman**, 1911), followed in 1906 by a notable essay on organ design. In 1913 he published *Geschichte der Leben-Jesu Forschung* (Eng trans *The Quest of the Historical Jesus*, 1910), which emphasized the role of **Jesus** as the herald of God's kingdom at hand and reduced the importance of the ethical teachings of Jesus. It marked a revolution in New Testament criticism. In addition to his internationally recognized work as musicologist, theologian and organist, he began to study medicine (1905), resigned as principal of the theological college (1906) and, when he had qualified in 1913, went with his new wife to set up a hospital to fight leprosy and sleeping sickness at Lambaréné, a deserted mission station on the Ogowe river in the heart of French Equatorial Africa. Except for his internment by the French (1917–18) as a German and periodic visits to Europe to raise funds for his mission by giving organ recitals, he made his self-built hospital the center of his paternalistic service to Africans, in a spirit "not of benevolence but of atonement." His newly discovered ethical principle "reverence for life" was fully worked out in relation to the defects of European civilization in *Verfall und Wiederaufbau der Kultur* (1923, Eng trans *The Decay and Restoration of Civilization*, 1923) and philosophically in *Kultur und Ethik* (1923, Eng trans 1923). He was awarded the Nobel Peace Prize in 1952.

“ ”

An optimist is a person who sees a green light everywhere, while the pessimist sees only the red stoplight. The truly wise person is colorblind.

1965 Quoted in CBS News tribute, January 14.

Schwenkfeld, Kaspar von c. 1490–1561 •*German reformer and mystic*• Born in Ossig, near Liegnitz, he studied at the Universities of Cologne and Frankfurt. He served at various German courts, and about 1525 became a Protestant, rejecting both **Luther**anism and Catholicism and aiming at "Reformation by the Middle Way." Some of his persecuted followers (most numerous in Silesia and Swabia) emigrated to Holland. In 1734, 40 families emigrated to England, and from there to Pennsylvania, where, as Schwenkfeldians, they maintained a distinct existence.

Schwimmer, Rosika 1877–1948 •*Hungarian feminist and pacifist*• Born in Budapest, she was active as a journalist in the Hungarian women's movement. She became vice president of the Women's International League for Peace and Freedom, and from 1918 to 1919 was Hungarian minister to Switzerland. In 1920, in order to escape the country's anti-Semitic leadership, she emigrated to the US, but was refused citizenship on the grounds of her pacifism.

Schwinger, Julian 1918–94 •*US physicist and Nobel Prize winner*• One of Harvard's youngest professors, he shared the 1965 Nobel Prize for physics with **Richard Feynman** and **Sin-Itiro Tomonaga**. He was one of the founders of quantum electrodynamics. He served as Professor of Physics at the University of California in Los Angeles from 1972 to 1980, and University Professor from 1980 until his death.

Schwitters, Kurt 1887–1948 •*German artist*• Born in Hanover, he studied at the Dresden Academy and painted abstract pictures before joining the Dadaists. His best-known contribution to the anarchic movement was *Merz*, his name for a form of collage made from everyday detritus: broken glass, tram tickets, scraps of paper. From 1920 he slowly built a three-dimensional construction (his "*Merzbau*") which filled his house until it was destroyed in an air raid in 1943. In 1937 he fled from the Nazi regime to Norway, and then to England.

Scipio Aemilianus Africanus, Publius Cornelius, *known as* **Scipio the Younger** 185–129 BC •*Roman general and politician*• He was a son of Lucius Aemilius Paullus, who conquered Macedon, but was adopted by his kinsman Publius Scipio, son of **Scipio Africanus** the Elder. He served in Spain under **Lucius Lucullus** (151 BC), and later as military tribune in the Third Punic War (149–146). He was elected consul in 147 and, although he did not qualify for the office, was given supreme command. **Polybius** records Scipio's famous Siege of Carthage, which fell and was sacked by Roman troops in 146. In 134 he held a second consulship and defeated the Numantines in a prolonged siege and with subsequent destruction of their city. He went on to take a leading role in Roman politics in opposition to his brother-in-law **Tiberius Gracchus**. He died suddenly in 129, perhaps murdered.

Scipio Africanus, Publius Cornelius, *known as* **Scipio the Elder** 236–183 BC •*Roman soldier and politician*• Hero of the Second Punic War (218–201 BC), he brought Spain under Roman control, expelling the Carthaginians led by **Hasdrubal**. He was elected consul in 205, and in 204 he sailed with 30,000 men to carry on the war in Africa, where his successes forced the Carthaginians to recall **Hannibal** from Italy. His victory at Zama in 202 ended the war. Scipio was granted the surname Africanus, and held a second consulship in 194. In 190 he and his brother Lucius defeated **Antiochus III** of Syria. Falling out of favor with the Senate, he retired to his estate in Campania. His daughter was Cornelia, mother of the Gracchi.

Scofield, (David) Paul 1922– •*English actor*• Born in Hurstpierpoint, Sussex, he was interested in amateur dramatics as a child, joined the Croydon Repertory School and studied at the London Mask Theatre before making his professional debut in *Desire Under the Elms* (1940). He appeared with various repertory companies before settling in London, where his early successes included *The Seagull* (1949) and *Time Remembered* (1954–55). His range continued to broaden in plays as diverse as *The Power and the Glory* (1956), *Expresso Bongo* (1958) and as Sir **Thomas More** in *A Man for All Seasons* (1960), which he repeated on Broadway (1962), winning a Tony Award. He made his first film, *That Lady*, in 1955 but has since made only rare film appearances, despite winning an Academy Award for the screen version of *A Man for All Seasons* (1966). Associate director of the National Theatre (1970–72), his later stage work includes *Amadeus* (1979), *Othello* (1980) and *John Gabriel Borkman* (1996). Recent films include *Quiz Show* (1994) and *The Crucible* (1996).

Scopas 4th century BC •*Greek sculptor*• Born on Paros, he moved to Athens and was the founder with **Praxiteles** of the later Attic school. He worked on the sculptures for the temple of Athena at Tegea and on the tomb of Mausolus at Halicarnassus. His work was noted for its depiction of strong emotion.

Scopes, John Thomas 1900–70 •*US educator*• Born in Salem, Illinois, he became a high-school teacher in Dayton, Tennessee, where he broke a state law by teaching **Charles Darwin**'s theory of evolution and was brought to trial. In the famous Scopes ("Monkey") Trial (1925), he was defended by **Clarence Darrow** in opposition to prosecuting attorney **W(illiam) J(ennings) Bryan** in a struggle between modern science and Christian fundamentalism. He was convicted and fined $100, but his conviction was overturned on a technicality.

Scorel, Jan van 1495–1562 •*Netherlandish painter*• Born in Schoorel, near Alkmaar, he studied painting in Amsterdam and, by 1517, was working in Utrecht. He went on to Venice, where he was much influenced by the work of **Giorgione**. After a pilgrimage to Jerusalem, he returned to Italy in 1521 and in Rome received the patronage of the Utrecht pope **Adrian VI**. He returned to Utrecht and stayed there, except for a journey to France in 1540. Much of his work was destroyed by the iconoclasts of the Reformation, but his surviving work demonstrates how much he was affected by the art of the south, combining the ideals of the Renaissance with the atmospheric traditions of Netherlandish art. His work had a great influence on subsequent Netherlandish painters.

Scorsese, Martin 1942– •*US film director*• Born in Queens, New York, as a student at New York University he made a number of short films. His first feature was *Who's That Knocking at My Door?* (1969), and he subsequently lectured, made commercials and served as an editor before returning to direction with *Boxcar Bertha* (1972). His work has sought to illuminate masculine aggression and sexual inequality, frequently questioning traditional US values, and with films such as *Taxi Driver* (1976) and *Raging Bull* (1980), he established himself as one of the foremost directors of his generation. In 1988 he achieved a long-held ambition to film **Nikos Kazantzakis**'s controversial novel *The Last Temptation of Christ*. His subsequent films include *Goodfellas* (1990), *Cape Fear* (1991), *The Age of Innocence* (1993) and *Casino* (1995).

Scott, Dred c. 1795–1858 •*US slave*• Born in Southampton County, Virginia, he made legal and constitutional history as the nominal plaintiff in a test case that sought to obtain his freedom on the grounds that he lived in the free state of Illinois—the celebrated Dred Scott Case (1848–57). The Supreme Court ruled against him, but he was soon emancipated, and became a hotel porter in St Louis, Missouri.

Scott, Sir George Gilbert 1811–78 •*English architect*• Born in Gawcott, Buckinghamshire, he was inspired by the Cambridge Camden Society and an article by **Augustus Pugin** (1840–41). He became the leading practical architect in the Gothic revival. Examples of his work are the Martyrs Memorial at Oxford (1841), St Nicholas at Hamburg (1844), St George's at Doncaster, the Home and Colonial Offices (from 1858), the Albert Memorial (1862–63), St Pancras station and hotel in London (1865), the University of Glasgow (1865), the chapels of Exeter and St John's Colleges, Oxford, and the Episcopal Cathedral in Edinburgh. In 1868 he was appointed Professor of Architecture at the Royal Academy.

Scott, Sir Giles Gilbert 1880–1960 •*English architect*• Born in London, he was educated at Beaumont College, Old Windsor. He won a competition in 1903 for the design of the Anglican Cathedral in Liverpool (consecrated 1924). Later designs include the new nave at Downside Abbey, the new buildings at Clare College, the new Bodleian Library at Oxford (1936–46) and the new Cambridge University Library (1931–34). He planned the new Waterloo Bridge (1939–45) and was responsible for the rebuilding of the House of Commons after World War II. He was the grandson of Sir **George Gilbert Scott**.

Scott, Michael 1907–83 •*English Anglican missionary and social and political activist*• He was educated at King's College, Taunton, and St Paul's College, Grahamstown, and served in a London East End parish and as a chaplain in India (1935–39). He was invalided out of the RAF in 1941, and served in various missions in South Africa (1943–50). He exposed the atrocities in the Bethal farming area and in the Transvaal, defended the Basutos against wrongful arrest, and brought the case of the dispossessed Herero tribe before the United Nations.

Scott, Paul Mark 1920–78 •*English novelist*• Born in London, he served in the British army (1940–43), and in the Indian army in India and Malaya (1943–46). His best-known work is *The Raj Quartet* (*The Jewel in the Crown*, 1966; *The Day of the Scorpion*, 1968; *The Towers of Silence*, 1971; *A Division of Spoils*, 1975). Set in the years 1939–47, the overlapping novels provide a vivid portrait of India during the last years of the Raj; they were adapted for television and brought Scott a late acclaim. *Staying On* (1977) was awarded the Booker Prize.

Scott, Sir Peter Markham 1909–89 •*English artist and ornithologist*• He was born in London, the son of **Robert Falcon Scott**, was educated at Cambridge, and became an enthusiastic hunter of wildfowl. He went on to the State Academy School at Munich and the Royal Academy of Art Schools in London to study painting, and became a professional artist, holding his first exhibition in 1933. He represented Great Britain in single-handed dinghy sailing at the 1936 Olympic Games, served with distinction with the Royal Navy in World War II, founded the Severn Wild Fowl Trust in 1948, explored in the Canadian Arctic in 1949, and was leader of several ornithological expeditions. Through television he helped to popularize natural history.

Scott, Ridley 1937– •*British film director*• Born in South Shields,

County Durham, he trained at the Royal College of Art, London, and began his career as a director of some 2000 acclaimed television commercials. He made his debut as a director of feature films with *The Duellists* (1978) and went on to huge popular success with the science-fiction thrillers *Alien* (1979) and *Blade Runner* (1982). Widely admired for the convincing reality of his fantasy settings, Scott also attracted acclaim for his mastery of lighting. Subsequent films have included *Legend* (1985), *Black Rain* (1989), the multiple-award-winning *Thelma and Louise* (1991), *Gladiator* (1999), which won an Oscar for Best Picture, and *Hannibal* (2000).

Scott, Robert Falcon 1868–1912 •*English explorer*• Born near Devonport, Devon, he joined the navy in 1881. In the *Discovery* he commanded the National Antarctic Expedition (1901–04), and discovered King Edward VII Land. In 1910 he embarked on his second expedition in the *Terra Nova*, and with a sledge party which consisted of **Edward Wilson**, **Lawrence Oates**, H R Bowers, Edgar Evans and himself, reached the South Pole on January 17, 1912, only to discover that the Norwegian expedition under **Roald Amundsen** had beaten them by a month. Delayed by blizzards and the sickness of Evans and Oates, who both died, the remaining members of the team eventually perished in the vicinity of One Ton Depot at the end of March, 1912, where their bodies and diaries were found by a search party eight months later. The Scott Polar Research Institute at Cambridge was founded in his memory. He was the father of Sir **Peter Markham Scott**.

Scott, Ronnie, *originally* **Ronald Schatt** 1927–96 •*English saxophonist and philosophical humorist*• Born in London, he learned his trade, like so many British jazzmen, on the transatlantic liners. He founded his own group in 1953, and his legendary London jazz club in Gerrard Street in 1959 (in Frith Street from 1965). The title of John Fordham's biography, *Let's Join Hands and Contact the Living* (1986), immortalizes a famous line delivered to an unresponsive audience.

Scott, Terry, *originally* **Owen John Scott** 1927–94 •*English actor*• Born in Watford, Hertfordshire, he began his career working with seaside repertory companies and in clubs and pantomime. He and Bill Maynard formed a comedy duo which appeared in a television sitcom, *Great Scott, It's Maynard* (1955), before he appeared in films such as *I'm All Right, Jack* (1959) and seven *Carry On* films. His string of television successes included *Hugh and I* (1962–66), with Hugh Lloyd, and three different series with **June Whitfield**: *Scott On-* (1969–74), *Happy Ever After* (1974–78) and *Terry and June* (1979–87).

Scott, Sir Walter 1771–1832 •*Scottish novelist and poet*• He was born in Edinburgh. As a young boy he contracted polio, which lamed his right leg for life, and he was sent to his grandfather's farm at Sandyknowe in Tweedale to recuperate, thus coming to know the Border country, which figures often in his work. He studied at the high school in Edinburgh (1779–83), and at the university. He entered his father's office as a law clerk, did well and rose to become a lawyer in 1792. His first publication consisted of rhymed versions of ballads by Gottfried Bürger in 1796. In 1799 he was appointed sheriff-depute of Selkirkshire. The ballad meanwhile absorbed all his literary interest: a translation of **Goethe**'s *Götz von Berlichingen* (1799) was followed by his first original ballads, *Glenfinlas* and *The Eve of St John*. His earlier raids into the western Borders, especially Liddesdale, to collect ballads led to the publication of his first major work, *The Minstrelsy of the Scottish Border* (vols 1 and 2, 1802; vol 3, 1803). The *Lay of the Last Minstrel* (1805), which grew from a ballad he had composed for the third volume of *The Minstrelsy*, made him the most popular author of the day. The other romances which followed—*Marmion* (1808) and *The Lady of the Lake* (1810)—enhanced his fame, but the lukewarm reception of *Rokeby* (1813), *The Lord of the Isles* (1815) and *Harold the Dauntless* (1817) turned his attention away from the ballad form and toward writing novels, going on to establish the form of the historical novel in Britain. In 1811 he bought some land and began to build his country seat, Abbotsford, near Galashiels, in the Borders. Meanwhile, in Edinburgh, the publishing firm which he had set up (although his involvement had not been made public) with **James Ballantyne** and his brother John following the success of *The Minstrelsy*, was expanding. However, Scott's and the firm's connections with publisher **Archibald Constable** and his London agents were to be their undoing: Scott lost all control over the financial side of the extensive publication program on which he now embarked. He was declared bankrupt, along with the Ballantynes and Constable, in 1826—in the middle of his great career as a novelist. Only following this bankruptcy did he publicly acknowledge the authorship of his novels, which had been published under the name of "The Author of *Waverley*." The Waverley novels fall into three groups: first, from *Waverley* (1814) to *The Bride of Lammermoor* (1819) and *A Legend of Montrose* (1819); next, from *Ivanhoe* (1820) to *The Talisman* (1825), the year before his bankruptcy; *Woodstock* (1826) opens the last period, which closes with *Castle Dangerous* and *Count Robert of Paris* (1832). He died at Abbotsford, and was buried in the ruins of Dryburgh Abbey.

“ ”

And come he slow, or come he fast,
It is but Death who comes at last.

*1808 **Marmion**, canto 2, stanza 30.*

Scott, Winfield 1786–1866 •*US general*• Born near Petersburg, Virginia, he was admitted to the bar in 1807, and obtained a commission as artillery captain in 1808. He became a national hero for his part in the War of 1812, rising from lieutenant colonel to brigadier general and distinguishing himself at the Battle of Lundy's Lane (1814). He commanded the war against the Seminoles and the Creeks in Florida (1835–37) and helped settle the disputed boundary line of Maine and New Brunswick (1839). He succeeded to the chief command of the army in 1841. In the Mexican War he took Vera Cruz (March 26, 1847), put **Antonio de Santa Anna** to flight and entered the Mexican capital (September 14). Known as "Old Fuss and Feathers" because of his insistence on military punctilio, he retained nominal command of the army until October 1861.

Scott-Thomas, Kristin 1960– •*English actress*• Born in Redruth, Cornwall, she studied at the École Nationale des Arts et Technique de Théâtre in Paris, and began her career in French television and films. Her English cinema career blossomed in the mid-1990s with films such as *Four Weddings and a Funeral* (1994; British Academy of Film and Television Arts award for Best Supporting Actress) and *Mission Impossible* (1996), and she made acclaimed appearances in *The English Patient* (1996) and *The Horse Whisperer* (1998).

Scriabin or **Skriabin, Aleksandr Nikolayevich** 1872–1915 •*Russian composer and pianist*• Born in Moscow, he studied at the Moscow Conservatory with **Rachmaninov** and **Nikolai Medtner**, and became Professor of Pianoforte (1898–1904). His compositions, which include a piano concerto, three symphonies, two symphonic poems, and ten sonatas, show an increasing reliance on extramusical factors (even colored light, as in *Prometheus* of 1910), and the influence of religion and theosophical ideas. Among his most widely played works is the *Poem of Ecstasy* (1908).

Scribe, (Augustin) Eugène 1791–1861 •*French dramatist*• He was born in Paris. After 1816 his productions became so popular that he established a theater workshop in which numerous *collaborateurs* turned out plays under his supervision. The best known are *Un verre d'eau* (1850, Eng trans *A Glass of Water*, 1851), *Adrienne Lecouvreur* (1848, Eng trans 1883) and *Bataille des dames* (1851, Eng trans *The Ladies' Battle!* 1851). Scribe also wrote novels and composed the libretti for 60 operas.

Scribner, Charles, *originally* **Scrivener** 1821–71 •*US publisher*• Born in New York, he graduated from Princeton in 1840, and in 1846 founded with Isaac Baker the New York publishing firm which became Charles Scribner's Sons in 1878. He founded *Scribner's Monthly* (1870–81), which reappeared as *The Century* (1881–1930) after it was bought by the Century Company. His three sons continued the business.

Scruton, Roger Vernon 1944– •*British political philosopher*• He was educated at Jesus College, Cambridge, and was called to the bar in 1978. He was Professor of Aesthetics at the University of London (1985–92) and Professor of Philosophy at Boston University (1992–95). He is politically conservative and has defended cultural tradition against aesthetic modernism. His publications include *Art and Imagination* (1974, 2nd edn 1982), *The Meaning of Conservatism* (1980), and *The Aesthetics of Music* (1997).

Scudamore, Peter 1958– •*English National Hunt jockey*• Educated at Belmont Abbey School, Hereford, he became the stable jockey of David Nicholson in 1978. He was champion jockey for the first time in the 1981–82 season and in 1985 rode his first winner for trainer Martin Pipe. Together they formed a partnership that was to dominate British racing for the next eight years. He was champion jockey for seven consecutive seasons (1986–93), breaking the season record with 221 wins in 1988–89. In 1993 he retired and turned to training.

Scudéry, Madeleine de 1608–1701 •*French novelist*• She was born in Le Havre. Left an orphan at six, she went to Paris in 1639 and with her brother was accepted into the literary society of Mme de **Rambouillet**'s salon. From 1644 to 1647 she was in Marseilles with her brother. She had begun her literary career with the romance *Ibrahim ou l'illustre Bassa* (1641, Eng trans *Ibrahim; or, The Illustrious Bassa*, 1652), and her most famous work was the ten-volume *Artamène, ou le Grand Cyrus* (1649–59, Eng trans *Artamenes, or the Grand Cyrus*, 1653–55), written with her brother. Her works were popular at the court because of their lampooning of public figures. She was satirized by **Molière** in *Les précieuses ridicules* (1659, "The Conceited Young Ladies").

Sculthorpe, Peter Joshua 1929– •*Australian composer*• Born in Launceston, Tasmania, he studied at the Melbourne University Conservatorium, and later in Oxford. Small-scale works, chamber music and the *Irkanda* series (1961) were followed by his four *Sun Music* pieces (1965, new recording 1996). In 1974 the Australian Opera performed his opera *Rites of Passage*, and in 1982 the Australian Broadcasting Corporation commissioned an opera for television, *Quiros*. *Sun Song* (1989), specially written for the Australian group Synergy, employs Aboriginal themes originally noted down by the French explorer Nicolas Baudin in the early 19th century. His work, though not prolific, is much influenced by the Australian landscape and he is a leading figure in promoting Australian music overseas.

Seaborg, Glenn Theodore 1912–99 •*US atomic scientist and Nobel Prize winner*• He was born in Ishpeming, Michigan, and educated at the University of California at Los Angeles and at Berkeley, where he taught and was chancellor from 1958 to 1961. His principal work was with **Enrico Fermi**'s team, which achieved the first chain reaction in uranium-235 in 1942. It was his laboratory which, in 1945, produced enough plutonium for the first atomic bomb. Seaborg and his team continued research on further transuranic elements and in 1944 synthesized americium and curium. In 1950, by bombarding these with alpha rays, they produced berkelium and californium. They later produced einsteinium, fermium, mendelevium and unnilhexium. In 1951 Seaborg shared the Nobel Prize for chemistry with **Edwin McMillan**. He was chairman of the US Atomic Energy Commission from 1961 to 1971.

Seaga, Edward Philip George 1930– •*Jamaican politician*• Born in Boston, Massachusetts, to Jamaican parents, he went to school in Kingston, Jamaica, returning to the US to study at Harvard University. He was on the staff of the University of the West Indies before moving into politics, joining the Jamaica Labour Party (JLP) and becoming its leader in 1974. In 1980 he and the JLP had a resounding and surprising win over **Michael Manley**'s People's National Party (PNP), and Seaga became prime minister. He called a snap election in 1983 and won all the assembly seats, but in 1989 Manley and the PNP returned to power with a landslide victory.

Seaman, Elizabeth Cochrane, *pseudonym* **Nellie Bly** 1867–1922 •*US journalist*• Born in Cochran's Mills, Pennsylvania, she adopted her pen name from a song popular when she was working as a journalist for the *Pittsburgh Dispatch*, and reported on issues of reform and taboo subjects such as divorce. Moving to New York, she worked for **Joseph Pulitzer**'s *World*, writing dramatic exposés of working conditions, women prisoners and other issues. She was given an assignment to travel around the world in less than 80 days, which she achieved in 1889. Her accounts of the expedition, which was undertaken by public transport, became front-page news.

Searle, John 1932– •*US philosopher*• Born in Denver, Colorado, he taught at Oxford (1956–59) and since 1959 has been Professor of Philosophy at the University of California at Berkeley. In such works as *Expression and Meaning* (1979), he expounded a distinctive approach to the study of language and its relation to mind, which has greatly influenced linguists and cognitive scientists as well as philosophers. He also wrote a famous account of the student riots in California, *The Campus War* (1971), and delivered the Reith Lectures on *Minds, Brains, and Science* in 1984.

Searle, Ronald William Fordham 1920– •*English cartoonist, painter and author*• He was born in Cambridge and studied at Cambridge School of Art. He drew his first cartoon for the *Cambridge Daily News* in 1935, and contributed a further 200 before moving on to magazines. In World War II he served in the Royal Engineers, painting camouflage; he was taken prisoner of war for over three years, and later published a book of sketches he made in Changi Camp. In 1956 he became staff theatrical caricaturist for *Punch* and in 1961 moved to Paris. He designed animated films like *Dick Deadeye* (1975), the animated sequences for *Those Magnificent Men in Their Flying Machines* (1965), and titles for features based on the St Trinian's schoolgirls, whom he created. His many publications include *Marquis de Sade Meets Goody Two-Shoes* (1994).

Sebastian, St d. 288 AD •*Roman Christian*• Born in Narbonne, France, to Roman parents, he is said to have been a captain of the Praetorian guard and a secret Christian. According to tradition, **Diocletian**, hearing that he favored Christians, ordered his death. But the archers did not quite kill him, and a woman named Irene nursed him back to life. When he criticized the tyrant for his cruelty, Diocletian had him beaten to death with rods. His feast day is January 20.

Sebastiano del Piombo, *properly* **Sebastiano Luciani** c. 1485–1547 •*Italian painter*• He was called del Piombo ("of the Seal") from his appointment in 1523 as sealer of briefs to Pope **Clement VII**. He studied under **Giovanni Bellini** and **Giorgione**, and went to Rome about 1510, where he worked in conjunction with **Michelangelo**. In 1519 he painted his masterpiece, the *Raising of Lazarus* (now in the National Gallery, London).

Secchi, Angelo 1818–78 •*Italian astronomer*• Born in Reggio Emilia, he joined the Society of Jesus in 1833 and in 1841 was made Professor of Physics and Astronomy at the Jesuit College in Loreto. In 1848 he became Professor of Astronomy at the Roman College of the Society, but he was expelled with all the Jesuits from Italy in the same year, and spent a brief exile in England and the US before returning to become director of the observatory of the Roman College in 1849. At the total solar eclipse in 1860, observed in Spain, he succeeded in photographing the prominences and the corona. Using an objective prism, he observed several thousand stellar spectra and divided the stars into three types—white, yellow and red—which corresponded roughly to their temperatures. He thus initiated the field of spectral classification.

Secombe, Sir Harry Donald 1921–2001 •*Welsh singer and entertainer*• Born in Swansea, he served in the army during World War II, and made his stage debut in *Revuedeville* (1947–48) before becoming a regular on the radio show *Variety Bandbox* (1947). He joined **Peter Sellers**, **Spike Milligan** and **Michael Bentine** in the radio program *The Goon Show* (1951–60). His stage appearances included *Pickwick* (1963) and *The Plumber's Progress* (1975). He was a popular singer with many albums to his credit, and his film appearances included *Oliver!* (1968). Later in his career he hosted the religious television series *Highway* (1983–93) and *Sunday Morning With Secombe* (1994). He was knighted in 1981.

Seddon, Richard John 1845–1906 •*New Zealand politician*• Born in Eccleston, Lancashire, England, he settled in New Zealand in 1866, and entered parliament in 1879. As prime minister (1893–1906) he led a Liberal Party government remembered for its social legislation, which included the introduction of old-age pensions (1898) and free secondary education (1903). His administration also saw the normalizing of relations with Australia, troop support of Britain in the Boer War, and annexation of the Cook Islands. As "King Dick" he dominated New Zealand politics from 1893 until his death in office.

Sedgwick, Adam 1785–1873 •*English geologist*• Born in Dent, Cumbria, he graduated in mathematics from Trinity College, Cambridge (1808), and became Woodwardian Professor of Geology there in 1818. In 1831 he began geological mapping in Wales and introduced the Cambrian system in 1835. Sedgwick became embroiled in controversy with **Roderick Impey Murchison**; the dispute was finally resolved with the introduction of the Ordovician system by Charles Lapworth (1842–1920). His best work was *British Palaeozoic Fossils* (1854).

Seeger, Pete 1919– •*US folksinger and songwriter*• Born in New York City, he studied sociology at Harvard University. In 1940, along with **Woody Guthrie**, he formed the Almanac Singers, whose repertoire of radical songs marked the start of the "protest" movement in contemporary folk music. Seeger's unpretentious singing style and homely banjo playing made him a popular solo artist, but his uncompromising political stance caused him to fall afoul of the House Un-American Activities Committee in the 1950s. He remained an activist on issues of ecology, politics and individual liberties. His best-known songs include "On Top of Old Smokey," "Where Have All the Flowers Gone?" and "Little Boxes," although his name will always be associated with "We Shall Overcome," which he adapted from a traditional song. He was influential in bringing about the US folk-music revival of the 1960s.

" "

Where have all the flowers gone?

1961 Title of song.

Seferis, George, *pseudonym of* **George Seferiades** 1900–71 •*Greek poet and diplomat and Nobel Prize winner*• Born in Smyrna in Asia Minor, he moved with his family to Athens in 1914. He studied law in Paris and London, and spent the rest of his life as a diplomat, serving as the Greek ambassador to London (1957–62). His first collection of poetry, *Strophe* ("Turning Point"), published in 1931, was an immediate success. His debt to Modernists such as **Ezra Pound** and **T S Eliot** became clear in *Mythistorima* (1935, "Myth History"), which contained some of the first free-verse poems in modern Greek. His later collections include *Hemerologhia katastromatos* ("Logbook") *I*, *II* and *III* (1940, 1944 and 1965). In 1963 he became the first Greek winner of the Nobel Prize for literature.

Segal, George 1924–2000 •*US sculptor*• Born in New York City, he studied at Cooper Union (1941) and the Pratt Institute of Design (1947), finally graduating from New York University in 1950 and Rutgers in 1963. Beginning as a painter, he turned to sculpture in the later 1950s and is best known for his plaster figures, including *Girl in a Doorway* (1969). Other works include *The Bowery* (1970) and *The Curtain* (1974).

Segar, Elzie Crisler 1894–1938 •*US cartoonist*• Born in Chester, Illinois, he took a correspondence course in cartooning and went to Chicago for the daily strip, *Charlie Chaplin's Comic Capers* (1916). In New York he started *Thimble Theater* (1919) for King Features, originally a burlesque on stage melodramas. The cast included heroine Olive Oyl, whose brother Castor encountered a one-eyed sailor named Popeye in January 1929. Popeye moved into Max Fleischer animated cartoons from 1933. He also popularized the hamburger, and added *jeep* and *goon* (from his characters Eugene the Jeep and Alice the Goon) to the English language.

Segovia, Andrés 1893–1987 •*Spanish guitarist*• Born in Linares, he was largely self-taught, and quickly gained an international reputation. Influenced by the Spanish nationalist composers, he evolved a revolutionary guitar technique that allowed the performance of a wide range of music, and many composers wrote works for him. In 1981 he was created Marquis of Salobrēna.

Segrè, Emilio 1905–89 •*US physicist and Nobel Prize winner*• Born in Rome, Italy, he was educated at the University of Rome. He remained at Rome, working with **Enrico Fermi**, but left Italy under **Mussolini**'s regime. He moved to the University of California at Berkeley and worked on the Manhattan atom bomb project during World War II. In 1937 Segrè discovered the first entirely synthetic element, technetium, and three years later was involved in the discoveries of astatine and plutonium (1940). In 1955 the research team led by Segrè discovered the antiproton, which had been predicted by **P A M Dirac**. For this work he shared the 1959 Nobel Prize for physics with **Owen Chamberlain**.

Seidler, Harry 1923– •*Australian architect*• Born in Vienna, Austria, he studied at the Vasa Institute in Vienna, and later at Harvard, where he studied under **Walter Gropius**. He worked in New York and later with **Oscar Niemeyer** in Brazil before setting up practice in Sydney in 1948. He has won many awards for public and private buildings, and has worked in Mexico and Hong Kong, and designed the Australian embassy in Paris. His application of modern building techniques was well demonstrated in his Maori Language Commission Centre and the award-winning Australia Square tower in Sydney.

Seifert, Jaroslav 1901–86 •*Czech poet and Nobel Prize winner*• He was born in Prague. His first collection, *Město v slzách* (1921, "City of Tears"), reflects on the human waste of World War I and urges a working-class revolution. In 1923 he moved to Paris and produced his second collection, *Samá láska* (1923, "All Love"). After the Nazi occupation, his patriotism emerged in *Přilba hlíny* (1945, "A Helmet of Earth"); his most memorable poems are those which evoke the four days in May 1945 when the citizens of Prague rose up against the remaining Nazi forces. *Morový sloup* (1977, Eng trans *The Prague Column*, 1979) was published abroad. He was awarded the Nobel Prize for literature in 1984.

Selacraig, Alexander *See* **Selkirk, Alexander**

Selby, Hubert, Jr 1928–2004 •*US novelist and short-story writer*• He was born in Brooklyn, New York. He enlisted in the US Merchant Marines in 1944, but was admitted to the hospital two years later with tuberculosis. He worked at a number of jobs until the publication of his controversial bestseller, *Last Exit to Brooklyn* (1964), a set of connected stories. It is a bleak and pitiless account of an urban hell characterized by violence, sexual brutality and drug abuse. Obscenity trials followed the book's publication. His other novels include *The Room* (1971), *Requiem for a Dream* (1978) and the short-story collection *Song of the Silent Snow* (1986).

Selden, John 1584–1654 •*English jurist, historian and antiquary*• Born near Worthing, Sussex, he studied at Oxford and London. He was an opponent of the divine right of kings, and was twice imprisoned for his views. In 1623 he was elected Member of Parliament for Lancaster, and in 1628 he helped draw up the Petition of Right, for which he was committed to the Tower. He entered the Long Parliament (1640) for Oxford University, and was appointed an admiralty commissioner (1644). His works include *Titles of Honour* (1614), which is still an authority, *Analecton Anglo-Britannicon* (1615) and *History of Tithes* (1618). He also wrote books on the Arundel Marbles (1624) and on Hebrew law (1634–50), besides posthumous tracts and treatises, of which the most valuable is his *Table Talk* (1689).

Seles, Monica 1973– •*US tennis player*• Born in Novi Sad (now in Serbia), she moved to the US in 1986. Turning professional at the age of 15, she has won the French Open three times (1990–92), the US Open twice (1991–92) and the Australian Open three times (1991–93). In 1992 she was defeated by **Steffi Graf** in the Wimbledon singles final. During a tournament in Hamburg in April 1993, she was injured in a knife attack by a member of the crowd and was unable to compete for over two years. After her return she won every match she played until in 1995 she was narrowly beaten by Graf in the US Open final. She became a US citizen in 1994.

Seleucus I Nicator ("the Conqueror") c. 358–281 BC •*Macedonian general, founder of the Seleucid dynasty*• After the death of **Alexander the Great** (323 BC), he rose from being governor of Babylonia (321) to being the ruler of an empire (312) which stretched from Asia Minor to India. He founded a new, more central capital at Antioch in northern Syria (300) and defeated two successive rivals, Antigonus I (301) and Lysimachus (281). Crossing into Europe to claim the throne of Macedonia, he was killed by Ptolemy Ceraunus, the son of **Ptolemy I Soter**. He was succeeded by his son **Antiochus I**.

Self, Will 1961– •*English author, critic and cartoonist*• Born in London, he was educated at Christ's College and Exeter College, Oxford, and went on to work as a freelance cartoonist and newspaper columnist. His distinctive writing style and offbeat approach to such subjects as gender, mental instability and death was further realized in *The Quantity Theory of Insanity* (1991) and other collections of short stories; in such novellas as *Cock and Bull* (1992); and in the novels *My Idea of Fun* (1993), *Great Apes* (1997) and *How the Dead Live* (2000).

" "

I think in retrospect that all those "alternative" modes of living were little more than exercises in arrested development.

1991 ***The Quantity Theory of Insanity and Five Supporting Propositions***, *"The Quantity Theory of Insanity."*

Selfridge, Harry Gordon 1858–1947 •*British merchant*• Born in Ripon, Wisconsin, and educated privately, he joined a trading firm in Chicago and brought new ideas and great organizing ability into the business. In 1892 he was made a junior partner. While visiting London in 1906, he bought a site on Oxford Street, which he used to build the large department store which bears his name (opened 1909). He took British nationality in 1937.

Seligman, Charles Gabriel 1873–1940 •*English anthropologist*• Born in London, he studied as a physician and later joined the Cambridge anthropological expedition to the Torres Straits (1898–99); he also carried out field research in New Guinea, Ceylon (Sri Lanka) and the Sudan. His principal works include *The Melanesians of British New Guinea* (1910), *The Veddas (Ceylon)* (1911) and *Pagan Tribes of the Nilotic Sudan* (1932), the last of these written jointly with his wife, Brenda, who collaborated in all his later research. He was appointed in 1913 to the first chair of ethnology at the University of London. He had a strong influence on the later work of both **Bronisław Malinowski** and Sir **Edward Evans-Pritchard**.

Selim I, the Grim 1467–1520 •*Ottoman sultan of Turkey*• In 1512 he dethroned his father, **Bayezit II**, and caused him, his own brothers, and nephews to be put to death. He declared war against Persia in 1514, and took Diyarbakir and Kurdistan. He later conquered Egypt (1517), Syria and the Hejaz and won from the sherif of Mecca the control of the holy cities of Mecca and Medina. He introduced new codes of criminal law, expanded trade, refined the recruitment of janissaries, completed the transfer of government from Edirne to Istanbul, and built a powerful new fleet. He was succeeded by his son, **Süleyman the Magnificent**.

Selim II 1524–74 •*Ottoman sultan of Turkey*• The son of **Süleyman the Magnificent**, whom he succeeded in 1566, he proved to be an indolent drunkard, controlled by the women of the harem. The government was run by his able grand vizier, Mehmed Sokollu. During his reign, a revolt in Yemen was successfully crushed (1569–70) and Cyprus was captured (1571). A naval force under Don **John of Austria** defeated the Turkish fleet at Lepanto (1571), but the victors did not follow up their success, and the Ottomans recaptured Tunisia (1574).

Selkirk or **Selacraig, Alexander** 1676–1721 •*Scottish sailor*• Born in Largo, Fife, he is said to have inspired **Daniel Defoe**'s *Robinson Crusoe*. In 1704 he joined the South Sea buccaneers. He quarreled with his captain, **William Dampier**, and at his own request was put ashore on the uninhabited island of Juan Fernández (1704). Having lived alone there for four years and four months, he was rescued by a physician, Thomas Dover (1660–1742). He returned to Largo in 1712, and at the time of his death was a lieutenant on a man-of-war.

Sella, Philippe 1962– •*French rugby union player*• He was born in Clairac and his home club was Agen. In 1993–94 he succeeded fellow Frenchman **Serge Blanco** as the most capped international player of all time with a record 111 caps. In the same period (1982–95) he was also France's most capped center. He retired from international tests after the 1995 World Cup.

Sellars, Peter 1958– •*US stage director*• Born in Pittsburgh, Pennsylvania, he was director of the Boston Shakespeare Company (1983–84), and director of the American National Theater at the Kennedy Center in Washington (1984–86), where his radical staging of **Sophocles**'s *Ajax* divided audiences and critics. He is internationally recognized as a daringly innovative director of opera, with productions including **Handel**'s *Orlando* (1981), in which Orlando was made into an astronaut, and *The Magic Flute* for Glyndebourne Opera, in which Sarastro was represented as leader of a hippie commune. In 1990 he was appointed director of the Los Angeles Festival and in 1991 directed his first film, *The Cabinet of Dr Ramirez*.

Sellers, Peter 1925–80 •*English actor and comedian*• He was born in Southsea, Hampshire. After a spell as a stand-up comic and impressionist, he moved into radio. His meeting with comedian **Spike Milligan** inspired the *Goon Show*. He made his film debut with *Penny Points to Paradise* (1951), the first of a run of successful British comedy films in the 1950s and 1960s which included *The Ladykillers* (1955), *I'm All Right Jack* (1959) and *Only Two Can Play* (1962). Two films with **Stanley Kubrick** established his international reputation: *Lolita* (1962) and *Dr Strangelove* (1963), in which he played three roles. He is perhaps best remembered as the incompetent French detective Inspector Clouseau in a series of films that began with *The Pink Panther* in 1963. He received an Academy Award nomination for *Being There* (1979).

Selwyn, George Augustus 1809–78 •*English prelate*• Born in Hampstead, London, he was educated at Eton and St John's College, Cambridge, where he rowed in the first university boat race (1829). In 1841 he was consecrated the first (and only) Bishop of New Zealand and Melanesia, of whose Church he played a large part in settling the constitution. In 1867 he was appointed Bishop of Lichfield, where on his initiative the first Diocesan Conference, in which the laity were represented, met in 1868. Selwyn College at Cambridge was founded in 1882 in his memory.

Selwyn-Lloyd, (John) Selwyn (Brooke), Baron 1904–78 •*English Conservative politician*• Born in the Wirral of Anglo-Welsh parentage and educated at Cambridge, he studied law and became a barrister in 1930. In 1936 he entered local government, and after service in World War II, became a Conservative Member of Parliament; he continued to practice law, becoming a King's Counsel in 1947. In 1951 he was appointed minister of state, and in 1954 became successively minister of supply and minister of defense. As foreign secretary in 1955, he defended **Anthony Eden**'s policy on Suez; he became chancellor of the exchequer (1960–1962), lord privy seal and leader of the House of Commons (1963–64) and speaker of the House of Commons (1971–76). He was created a life peer in 1976.

Selznick, David O(liver) 1902–65 •*US film producer*• Born in Pittsburgh, Pennsylvania, he worked for his father, Lewis J Selznick (1870–1933), in film distribution and promotion before becoming a producer, and was vice president in charge of production at RKO when the studio created such films as *King Kong* (1933). He was renowned for masterminding every aspect of a production and for the long detailed memos he sent to colleagues. In 1937 he formed his own production company, which produced *A Star Is Born* (1937) and *Gone With the Wind* (1939), for which he received an Academy Award. Other successes included *Rebecca* (1940), *Duel in the Sun* (1946), *The Third Man* (1949) and *A Farewell to Arms* (1957), which starred his second wife, the actress Jennifer Jones (1919–).

" "

If they will only do their job ... that is all that they are being overpaid for.

Of his stars, while filming The Garden of Allah. Quoted in Maria Riva ***Marlene Dietrich*** *(1992).*

Semenov, Nikolai Nikolayevich 1896–1986 •*Soviet physical chemist and Nobel Prize winner*• Born in Saratov, he graduated in 1917 from the University of Petrograd (now St Petersburg State University). From 1920 he worked at the Physico-Technical Institute there, becoming professor in 1928, and later director. From 1944 he was also professor at Moscow State University. He is best known for his contributions to chemical kinetics, particularly in connection with chain reactions. He investigated explosion limits and many other features of combustion, flames and detonation. Much of his work was parallel to that of **Cyril Hinshelwood**, with whom he shared the 1956 Nobel Prize for chemistry.

Semiramis 9th century BC •*Semilegendary queen of Assyria*•She is said to have been coveted by King Ninus of Assyria, who married her and fell under her spell. With him she is supposed to have founded Babylon.

Semmelweis, Ignaz Philipp 1818–65 •*Hungarian obstetrician*• Born in Buda (Budapest), he studied at the University of Pest and in Vienna. From 1845 he worked in the first obstetrical clinic of the Vienna General Hospital. He succeeded in reducing the mortality rate by initiating a strict regimen of washing hands and instruments in chlorinated lime solution between autopsy work and examining patients. However, there was much opposition to his ideas, and his later years were clouded by frustration and mental instability, and he died in a mental asylum. His ideas were idiosyncratic, but in the later bacteriological age he came to be seen as a pioneer of antiseptic obstetrics.

Senanayake, Don Stephen 1884–1952 •*Sri Lankan statesman*• He was born in Colombo and worked on his father's rubber estate. He entered the Legislative Council in 1922, founded the cooperative society movement in 1923 and was elected to the State Council in 1931, where he was minister of agriculture for 15 years. After independence he became Sri Lanka's first prime minister (1947–52), as well as minister of defense and external affairs. He died from a fall from his horse.

Sendak, Maurice Bernard 1928– •*US illustrator and writer of children's books*•Born in Brooklyn, New York, he was the son of poor Jewish immigrants from Poland. He attended Lafayette High School in New York and worked as a window dresser. He was commissioned by a publisher to illustrate *The Wonderful Farm* (1951) by Marcel Aymé, and followed it in 1956 with *Kenny's Window*, the first book for which he also wrote the text, and the more controversial *Where the Wild Things Are* (1963), which explored the fantasy world of mischievous Max. This was a great commercial success and won the Carnegie Medal. Other works include *In The Night Kitchen* (1970) and *We Are All in the Dumps With Jack and Guy* (1993).

Senebier, Jean 1742–1809 •*Swiss botanist, plant physiologist and pastor*• Born in Geneva, he was ordained pastor of the Protestant Church, Geneva, in 1765 and was librarian for the Republic of Geneva from 1773. Senebier was the first to demonstrate the basic principle of photosynthesis, his most important papers being *Action de la lumière sur la végétation* (1779, "Action of Sunlight on Vegetation") and *Expériences sur l'action de la lumière solaire dans la végétation* (1788, "Experiments on the Action of Sunlight on Vegetation"), and was also the first to establish a precise experimental method.

Seneca, Lucius Annaeus, *called* **Seneca the Younger** c. 4 BC–c. 65 AD •*Roman Stoic philosopher, statesman and tragedian*• Born in Corduba (Córdoba), Spain, the son of **Marcus Annaeus Seneca**, he began a career in politics and law in Rome in 31 AD. However, he was banished to Corsica (41–49) by Emperor **Claudius** on a charge of adultery with Claudius's niece Julia, and there wrote the three treatises *Consolationes*. Recalled to Rome in 49, he became the tutor of her son, the future emperor **Nero** and consul in 57, but he later withdrew from public life. In 65 he was implicated in the conspiracy of Piso and ordered to commit suicide. His writings include *Epistulae morales ad Lucilium* and the *Apocolocyntosis divi Claudii* (literally, "The Pumpkinification of the Divine Claudius"), a scathing satire. The publication in translation of his *Tenne Tragedies* (1581) was important in the evolution of English Elizabethan drama, which took from them the principal division into five acts.

“ ”

Utrumque enim vitium est, et omnibus credere et nulli.
It is equally unsound to trust everyone and to trust no one.

***Epistulae**, 3.4.*

Seneca, Marcus Annaeus, *called* **Seneca the Elder** c. 55 BC–c. 40 AD •*Roman rhetorician*• He was born in Corduba (Córdoba), Spain, and educated at Rome. In addition to a history of Rome, which is now lost, he wrote for his sons a collection of imaginary court cases, *Oratorum et rhetorum sententiae, Divisiones, Colores controversiae* (partly lost), and *Suasoriae*, a collection of earlier, rhetorical styles. He was the father of **Lucius Annaeus Seneca** and grandfather of **Lucan**.

Senghor, Léopold Sédar 1906–2001 •*Senegalese statesman and poet*• Educated in Dakar and at the Sorbonne in Paris, he taught classics in France from 1935, where he wrote poetry advocating the concept of "negritude." After World War II he sat in the French National Assembly (1946–58) and was a leader of the Senegalese independence movement. After independence in 1960, as leader of the Senegalese Progressive Union (UPS), he became the new nation's first president. In 1976 he reconstituted the UPS as the Senegalese Socialist Party (PS) and gradually the one-party political system which he had created became more pluralist. Senghor was reelected several times until his retirement in 1981. His successor was **Abdou Diouf**.

Senna, Ayrton 1960–94 •*Brazilian racecar driver*• Born in São Paulo, he made his Grand Prix debut in Brazil in 1984 with the Toleman team. He later drove for Lotus (1985–87), McLaren (1988–93) and Williams (1994). He was Formula One world champion in 1988, 1990, and 1991, but lost his title to **Nigel Mansell** in 1992. He was killed after crashing during the San Marino Grand Prix.

Sennacherib d. 681 BC •*King of Assyria*• He succeeded his father Sargon II in 705 BC. He sacked Babylon (689) and besieged Hezekiah unsuccessfully in Jerusalem. He rebuilt Nineveh, and undertook building projects for the embankment of the Tigris and for canals and water courses. He was succeeded by **Esarhaddon** after being killed by one of his sons.

Sennett, Mack, *originally* **Michell Sinott** 1880–1960 •*US film producer*• Born in Richmond, Quebec, he was a child singing prodigy. Hoping to pursue a career in opera, he also appeared on Broadway and in burlesque (1902–08). He joined Biograph Studios in 1908 and made his first film, *Baked in the Altar*, the same year. Under **D W Griffith**, he became a leading man and directed *The Lucky Toothache* (1910). By 1912 he had formed his own company, Keystone Co, in Los Angeles, and set about altering and defining the conventions of US screen comedy. He recruited **Charlie Chaplin**, Fatty Arbuckle and others, and made hundreds of short comedies which established a whole generation of players and a tradition of knockabout slapstick involving the Keystone Komics (1912), the Keystone Kops and the Sennett Bathing Beauties (1920). His feature films include *Tillie's Punctured Romance* (1914) and *Way Up Thar* (1935). He received a Special Academy Award in 1937.

Senusrit *See* **Sesostris**

Sequoyah, *also called* **George Guess** c. 1770–1843 •*Native American scholar*• Born in Tennessee, he was probably the son of an English trader but was raised by his part-Cherokee mother. He invented a Cherokee syllabary of 85 characters in 1826. He taught thousands of Cherokee to read and write and served as a political envoy for his people. His name was given to a genus of giant coniferous trees (*Sequoia*) and to a national park.

Serao, Matilde 1856–1927 •*Italian novelist and journalist*• Born in Patras, Greece, the daughter of a Greek father and an Italian mother, she graduated as a teacher in Naples. Her first novel of Neapolitan life was *Cuore infermo* (1881), after which she joined the Rome newspaper *Capitan Fracassa*. She enjoyed a huge success with her next romantic novel, *Fantasia* (1882), and this was followed by *Conquista di Roma* (1886, "Conquest of Rome"), *Riccardo Joanna* (1887), *All' erta, Sentinella!* (1889) and *Il paese di cuccagna* (1891, "The Land of the Cockayne").

Serling, Rod 1924–75 •*US science-fiction writer and television playwright*• He was born in Syracuse, New York. A combat paratrooper during World War II, he attended Antioch College and began writing radio scripts. He first wrote for television in 1951, and in 1955 won the first of six Emmy awards for his play *Patterns*. He created, wrote and hosted the popular anthology series *The*

Twilight Zone (1959–64). He also created *Night Gallery* (1970–73), was the author of over 200 television plays, and wrote the film script *Seven Days in May* (1964).

Serlio, Sebastiano 1475–1554 •*Italian architect and painter*• Born in Bologna, he studied there and in Rome. He moved to Venice in 1527, and in 1540 was called to France by **Francis I**. Especially influential was his treatise on Italian architecture, *Regole generali di architettura* (1537–51, and posthumously 1575). As master of works at Fontainebleau, his most important work was the Grand Ferrare (1541–48, demolished), where the pioneering use of an enclosed U-plan set the precedent for French townhouses in subsequent years. The quadrangular chateau at Ancy-le-Franc, Tonnerre (from 1546), was also noteworthy.

Serra, Junípero, *originally* **Miguel José Serra**, *called* **the Apostle of California** 1713–84 •*Spanish missionary*• Born on the island of Majorca, he studied at the cathedral school in Palma and entered the Franciscan order in 1730. He became a doctor of theology and lectured at the University of Palma until 1749, when he went to Mexico to proselytize among the Central American Indians. In 1767 he was sent to California. Known as the "walking friar," he was determined to follow the Franciscan injunction to travel on foot, despite an ulcerated leg that afflicted him for most of his life. He founded nine missions in upper California, including San Diego (1769), the first European settlement in California. He was beatified by **John Paul II** in 1985.

Serra, Richard 1939– •*US sculptor*• Born in San Francisco, he studied art at Berkeley and Yale, and from 1964 to 1966 studied in Paris and Florence, before settling in New York. In the late 1960s he produced a series of films and began manufacturing austere minimalist works from sheet steel, iron and lead, for example in *Shovel Plate Prop* (1969). Many of his works are of huge dimensions: notable are the long arcs of sheet metal which can span city squares and the cubic structures composed of massive metal plates balanced vertically against one another. Public commissions for such works have made him a controversial but highly influential artist.

Servetus, Michael 1511–53 •*Spanish theologian and physician*• Born in Tudela, he studied law in Toulouse, and worked largely in France and Switzerland. In his writings he denied the Trinity and the divinity of **Jesus**. He escaped the Inquisition but was burned in Geneva for heresy. He lectured on geography and astronomy, practiced medicine at Charlien and Vienna (1538–53), and discovered the pulmonary circulation of the blood, prefiguring **William Harvey**.

Service, Robert William 1874–1958 •*Canadian poet*• Born in Preston, England, he went to Canada, became a journalist, and served as an ambulance driver in World War I. His popular ballads, most notably "The Shooting of Dan McGrew," appeared in *Songs of a Sourdough* (1907), *Ballads of a Bohemian* (1920), *Rhymes of a Rebel* (1952) and *Carols of a Codger* (1954). He also wrote novels, of which *The House of Fear* (1927) is the most accomplished.

Servius Sulpicius Galba *See* **Galba, Servius Sulpicius**

Sesostris or **Senusrit** •*Egyptian monarch*• According to Greek legend, he invaded Libya, Arabia, Thrace and Scythia, subdued Ethiopia, placed a fleet on the Red Sea, and extended his dominion to India. He was possibly Sesostris I (c. 1980–1935 BC), II (c. 1906–1887 BC) and III (c. 1887–1849 BC) compounded into one hero.

Seth, Vikram 1952– •*Indian poet, novelist and travel writer*• He was born in Calcutta and educated at universities in England, the US and China. His first poetry collection was *Mappings* (1980). A travel book, *From Heaven Lake: Travels Through Sinkiang and Tibet*, appeared in 1983. His first novel, *The Golden Gate* (1986), was written in verse. His next novel was even more ambitious. At over 1,300 pages, *A Suitable Boy* (1993) is one of the longest single-volume novels in English, a love story with a large cast of characters set in post-independence India. The novel *An Equal Music* was published in 1999.

Seton, St Elizabeth Ann, *née* **Bayley** 1774–1821 •*US religious, and the first native-born saint of the US*• Born into New York upper-class society, she married at the age of 19 into a wealthy trading family, and in 1797 founded the Society for the Relief of Poor Widows with Small Children. In 1803 she herself was left a widowed mother of five. She converted to Catholicism from Episcopalianism, took vows, founded a Catholic elementary school in Baltimore, and in 1809 founded the first religious order in the US, the Sisters of Charity. She was canonized in 1975.

Seurat, Georges Pierre 1859–91 •*French artist*• He was born in Paris and studied at the École des Beaux-Arts. He developed the technique known as pointillism, in which the whole picture is composed of tiny rectangles of pure color which merge together when viewed from a distance. The technique was founded on the color theories of **Eugène Delacroix** and the chroma theory of chemist **Michel Eugène Chevreul**. He completed only seven canvases in this immensely demanding discipline, including *Un dimanche d'été à la Grande-Jatte* (1884–86, "Sunday Afternoon on the Island of La Grande Jatte," Chicago), *Les poseuses* (1887–88) and *Le cirque* (1891).

Seuss, Dr, *pseudonym of* **Theodor Seuss Geisel** 1904–91 •*US children's author and illustrator*• Born in Springfield, Massachusetts, he graduated from Dartmouth College, New Hampshire, in 1925, and after graduate study at Oxford, became a freelance cartoonist and illustrator. *And to Think That I Saw It on Mulberry Street* (1937) was the first of his many children's books, which are characterized by their engaging rhymed narratives and their imaginative, almost anarchic illustrations. His immensely popular stories include *The 500 Hats of Bartholomew Cubbins* (1938), *If I Ran the Zoo* (1950) and *Green Eggs and Ham* (1960). His story *How the Grinch Stole Christmas* (1957) was made into an animated television cartoon and has twice been made into a film (1957 and 2000), and he also wrote the screenplay for the cartoon *Gerald McBoing Boing* (1950), which won an Academy Award. In 1957 he began to write and draw a series of "Beginner Books," intended to help teach reading, for Random House, starting with *The Cat in the Hat* (1958) and *Yertle the Turtle* (1958). By 1970, 30 million copies had been sold in the US and Seuss had become synonymous with learning to read.

Severini, Gino 1883–1966 •*Italian artist*• Born in Cortona, he studied in Rome under **Giacomo Balla** from 1900 to 1906, then moved to Paris, where he worked as a pointillist. In 1910 he signed the first Futurist manifesto, associating with Balla and **Umberto Boccioni**, with whom he exhibited in Paris and London, including *Dynamic Hieroglyphic of the Bal Tabarin* (1912). After 1914 he evolved a personal brand of Cubism and Futurism in which he painted many striking nightclub scenes. In 1921 he reverted to a more representational neoclassical style, and after 1940 he adopted a decorative Cubist manner.

Severus, Lucius Septimius AD 146–211 •*Roman emperor*• The founder of the Severan dynasty, he was born near Leptis Magna in North Africa. After the murder of Publius Pertinax (AD 193), he was proclaimed emperor, defeated two rivals (195–197), campaigned in the East, took Byzantium, and defeated the Parthians (197–99). In 208 he marched to northern Britain to strengthen the frontier. He repaired the fortifications on Hadrian's Wall and was busy preparing a campaign into Scotland when he died at Eboracum (York). See also **Alexander Severus**.

Sévigné, Madame de, *née* **Marie de Rabutin-Chantal** 1626–96 •*French letter writer*• Born in Paris, she was orphaned at an early age and brought up by an uncle at the Abbaye de Livry, Brittany. She became a member of French court society, and after the marriage of her daughter in 1669, she began a series of letters to her which continued over 25 years. They recount the current news and events of the time of **Louis XIV** in great detail and in a natural colloquial style. The letters were published posthumously in 1725.

"

La grande amitié n'est jamais tranquille.
Great friendship is never peaceful.

1671 Letter to Mme de Grignan, September 16.

Seward, Anna, *known as* **the Swan of Lichfield** 1747–1809 •*English poet*• Born in Eyam Rectory, Derbyshire, she lived from the age of ten at Lichfield, where her father, himself a poet, became a canon. When he died in 1790, she continued to live on in the bishop's palace. Her "Elegy on Captain Cook" (1780) was commended by **Samuel Johnson**. She bequeathed all her poems to Sir **Walter Scott**, who published them in 1810 as *Poetical Works*.

Seward, William Henry 1801–72 •*US politician*• Born in Florida, New York, he was admitted to the bar at Utica in 1822. He was elected to the state senate in 1830 and won the governorship of New York State in 1838. During the 1850s he became a major spokesman for the antislavery movement and a leader of the Republican Party. Serving as an effective secretary of state under **Abraham Lincoln**, he took an uncompromising attitude toward French support for Archduke **Ferdinand Maximilian** as emperor of Mexico, which he saw as a breach of the Monroe Doctrine. Severely injured during the assassination of Lincoln, he recovered to remain secretary of state in President **Andrew Johnson**'s Cabinet. In 1867 he secured the purchase, for $7.2 million, of Alaska from Russia (known as Seward's folly) by persuading a reluctant Congress of its vast mineral wealth.

Sewell, Anna 1820–78 •*English novelist*• She was born in Great Yarmouth, Norfolk, and was an invalid for most of her life. In her youth she helped edit her mother's novels, which were popular at that time. Her only book is *Black Beauty, The Autobiography of a Horse* (1877), a work for children which was written as a plea for the more humane treatment of animals.

Sex Pistols •*English punk band*• The band was a product of the London King's Road punk scene in 1975, a counterblast to rock's perceived effeteness. After hearing Richard Hell and other New York punks, their opportunist manager, Malcolm McLaren (1946–), returned to the UK and recruited the sneering Johnny Rotten (originally John Lydon, 1956–) as vocalist, guitarist Steve Jones (1955–), bassist Glen Matlock (1956–), and drummer Paul Cook (1956–). Matlock was later replaced by the nihilistic Sid Vicious (originally John Simon Ritchie, 1957–79). During its brief existence the band offended many people and was often banned from appearing at its concert venues. Their only real album was *Never Mind the Bollocks* (1977), but they were hugely influential, and "Anarchy in the UK" (1976) remains a rock classic.

Sexton, Anne, *née* **Harvey** 1928–74 •*US poet*• Born in Newton, Massachusetts, she was a confessional poet in the mold of her teacher, **Robert Lowell**, and her friend, **Sylvia Plath**, with whom she is often associated. She wrote frankly about her personal experiences, including a nervous breakdown. She taught at Boston University (1969–71) and Colgate (1971–72). *To Bedlam and Part Way Back* (1962) was her first collection of poetry. Others include *Live or Die* (1966), *Love Poems* (1969), *The Book of Folly* (1972) and the posthumously published *The Awful Rowing Towards God* (1975) and *45 Mercy Street* (1976). She committed suicide.

“ ”

But suicides have a special language.
Like carpenters they want to know *which tools*.
They never ask *why build*.

1966 ***Live or Die****, "Wanting to Die."*

Sextus Empiricus 2nd century AD •*Greek philosopher and physician*• He was active at Alexandria and Athens, and is the main source of information for the Skeptical school of philosophy. Little is known of his life, but his surviving writings, *Outlines of Pyrrhonism* and *Against the Dogmatists*, had an enormous influence when they were rediscovered and published in Latin translations in the 1560s.

Seyfert, Carl Keenan 1911–60 •*US astronomer*• Born in Cleveland, Ohio, and educated at Harvard, he worked at the McDonald and Mount Wilson Observatories, then became associate Professor of Astronomy and Physics and director of Barnard Observatory, Vanderbilt University (1946–51). From 1951 he was Professor of Astronomy and director of the Arthur J Dyer Observatory. He is famous for his work on a special group of galaxies (named after him) which have very bright bluish starlike nuclei and are now thought to be the low-luminosity cousins of quasars.

Seymour, Edward, 1st Duke of Somerset, *known as* **Protector Somerset** c. 1506–52 •*English soldier and statesman*• The eldest son of Sir John Seymour and brother of **Jane Seymour**, he enjoyed high office under his brother-in-law, **Henry VIII**. He led the invading English army that devastated southern Scotland and Edinburgh in the "Rough Wooing" of 1543–44, after the Scots rejected a proposed marriage between Prince Edward (the future **Edward VI**) and the infant **Mary Queen of Scots**. At Henry's death in 1547, he was named Protector of England during the minority of Edward VI and was king in all but name. He defeated a Scottish army at Pinkie (1547), and furthered the Reformation with the first *Book of Common Prayer* (1549). Also in 1549, his younger brother **Thomas Seymour** was executed for attempting to marry Princess Elizabeth (the future Queen **Elizabeth I**), and soon he himself was indicted for "over-ambition." He was deposed by John Dudley, Earl of **Warwick** (1549), and eventually executed.

Seymour, Jane *See* **Jane Seymour**

Seymour, Lynn 1939– •*British dancer*• Born in Wainwright, Alberta, Canada, she trained in Vancouver, spending two years at the Royal Ballet School in London, and making her debut in 1956 with the Sadler's Wells branch of the company. She is best known for her passionate interpretations of the choreography of **Kenneth MacMillan** and **Frederick Ashton**. MacMillan cast her first in *The Burrow* (1958), after which she was frequently teamed with **Christopher Gable**. She was acclaimed in Ashton's *Five Brahms Waltzes in the Manner of Isadora Duncan* and *A Month in the Country* (both 1976). In 1978 she spent an unsuccessful season as director of the Bavarian Opera in Munich. She returned to the stage as Tatiana in *Onegin* and the mother in Gable's *A Simple Man* (both 1988). While best known as a dancer, she has choreographed several pieces.

Seymour (of Sudeley), Thomas Seymour, Baron c. 1508–49 •*English soldier and politician*• Son of Sir John Seymour and younger brother of **Edward Seymour**, Duke of Somerset, and brother-in-law of **Henry VIII** through Henry's marriage to **Jane Seymour**, he became high admiral of England in 1547, and in the same year married the dowager queen **Catherine Parr**, widow of Henry VIII. He schemed against his brother to marry **Edward VI** to Lady **Jane Grey**. After Catherine Parr's death in 1548, he tried to marry Princess **Elizabeth** of England, but was executed by his brother for treason.

Sforza, Carlo, Count 1873–1952 •*Italian statesman*• He was born in Montignoso. After a successful early career in the diplomatic service, he became foreign minister under **Giovanni Giolitti**, and in 1921 negotiated the Rapallo Treaty, which returned the strategically important port of Fiume to Yugoslavia; this ensured his unpopularity with the rightist extremists. He resigned when **Mussolini** assumed power the following year. He continued to lead the anti-Fascist opposition in the Senate until 1926, but then emigrated to France. In 1940 he fled the German occupation to live briefly in the UK and then the US, where he cultivated his involvement in a postwar administration, returning to his homeland after the war as a member of the provisional government. He served as foreign minister again under **Alcide de Gasperi**, and was a strong advocate of NATO until ill health forced his resignation in 1951.

Sforza, Francesco 1401–66 •*Duke of Milan*• The illegitimate son of Muzio Attendolo Sforza, he was the father of **Ludovico Sforza**. He sold his sword to the highest bidder, fighting for or against the pope, Milan, Venice and Florence. When he married the Duke of Milan's daughter in 1450, he became heir to the duchy; and before his death he had extended his power over Ancona, Pesaro, all Lombardy and Genoa.

Sforza, Ludovico, *also known as* **the Moor** 1452–1508 •*Duke of Milan and patron of Leonardo da Vinci*• The son of **Francesco Sforza**, he was born near Milan and acted as regent for his nephew Gian Galeazzo (1469–94) from 1476, but expelled him (1481) and gained the dukedom for himself. He made an alliance with **Lorenzo de' Medici** of Florence, and under his rule Milan underwent extensive civil and military engineering work and became the most glittering court in Europe. He helped to defeat the attempts of **Charles VIII** of France to secure Naples, but was expelled by **Louis XII** (1499) and imprisoned in France, where he died.

Shackleton, Sir Ernest Henry 1874–1922 •*British explorer*• Born in Kilkea, County Kildare, he was apprenticed in the Merchant Navy, and became a junior officer under Commander **Robert Scott**, on the *Discovery*, in the National Antarctic expedition of 1901–04. In 1908–09, in command of another expedition, he reached a point 97 miles (156.2 km) from the South Pole, which was at that time a record. During a further expedition (1914–16), his ship *Endurance* was crushed in the ice. By means of sledges and boats, he and his men reached Elephant Island, from where he and five others made a perilous voyage of 800 miles (1,288 km) to South Georgia and organized relief for those remaining on Elephant Island. He died in South Georgia while on a fourth Antarctic expedition, begun in 1922.

Shadwell, Thomas c. 1642–92 •*English dramatist*• Born at Broomhill House, Brandon, Suffolk, he was educated at Cambridge and at the Middle Temple, London. He achieved success with the first of his 13 comedies, *The Sullen Lovers* (1668). He also wrote three tragedies. **Dryden**, grossly assailed by him in the *Medal of John Bayes* (1682), heaped ridicule on him in *MacFlecknoe* ("Shadwell never deviates into sense") and as "Og" in the second part of *Absalom and Achitophel*. His works exhibit talent and comic force. He succeeded Dryden as poet laureate in 1689.

Shaffer, Peter Levin 1926– •*English dramatist*• He was born in Liverpool and studied at Cambridge. His plays are variations on the themes of genius and mediocrity, faith and reason, and the question of whether God, if he exists, is benevolent or not. These ideas form the intellectual core of *The Royal Hunt of the Sun* (1964), *Equus* (1973) and *Amadeus* (1979). Other plays include *The Private Ear* and *The Public Eye* (both 1962), *Black Comedy* (1965), *White Lies* (1967), *The Battle of Shrivings* (1970) and *The Gift of the Gorgon* (1992).

Shaftesbury, Anthony Ashley Cooper, 1st Earl of 1621–83 •*English politician*• Born in Wimborne St Giles, Dorset, he served with the Royalists in the English Civil War, and then joined the Parliamentarians. He was always suspected of Royalist sympathies, however, and in 1659 he was tried and imprisoned. On the eve of the Restoration, he was created Baron Ashley (1661), and from then until his elevation as the Earl of Shaftesbury in 1672, he was chancellor of the exchequer. He was a leading member of the movement to exclude the Roman Catholic Duke of York (**James VII and II**) from the throne, exploiting for his own purposes the fictitious Popish Plot allegedly uncovered by **Titus Oates**. He was subsequently tried for treason but acquitted, and moved to Amsterdam, where he died. He was satirized as "Achitophel" in **John Dryden**'s "Absalom and Achitophel" (1681).

Shaftesbury, Anthony Ashley Cooper, 3rd Earl of 1671–1713 •*English philosopher, politician and essayist*• He was born in London, and his early education was supervised by **John Locke** before he attended Winchester College. After he succeeded as 3rd Earl in 1699, he regularly attended the House of Lords until ill health forced him to abandon politics for literature (1702). He moved to Naples in 1711 and died there. He wrote essays on a wide range of philosophical and cultural topics, collected under the title *Characteristicks of Men, Manners, Opinions, Times* (3 vols, 1711). He is usually regarded as one of the principal English deists, and he argued that we possess a natural "moral sense" and natural affections directed to the good of the species and in harmony with the larger cosmic order.

Shaftesbury, Anthony Ashley Cooper, 7th Earl of 1801–85 •*English factory reformer and philanthropist*• Born in London and educated at Harrow and Christ Church, Oxford, he entered parliament in 1826. He took over the leadership of the factory reform movement in 1832 and piloted successive factory acts (1847, 1850, 1859) through the House of Commons, achieving the 10-hour day and the provision of lodging houses for the poor (1851). His Lunacy Act (1845) achieved considerable reform and his Coal Mines Act (1842) prohibited underground employment of women and of children under 13.

Shah, Eddy (Selim Jehane) 1944– •*English newspaper magnate and novelist*• He was born in Cambridge. He attended several schools and worked in theater and television before launching the *Sale and Altrincham Messenger* in 1974, and the *Stockport Messenger* in 1977. He grabbed national attention by confronting the unions over working practices, and arguably laid the foundations of the subsequent revolution in Fleet Street when he defeated a protracted strike. He launched *Today* in 1986, and was its chairman and chief executive until 1988. He also launched the ill-fated *Post* in 1988, which collapsed after a few months. His novels include *The Lucy Ghosts* (1992).

Shah Jahan 1592–1666 •*Mughal emperor*• Born in Lahore (now in Pakistan), he was in open revolt against his father, **Jahangir**, from 1624 until the latter's death in 1627. Disputes with the Sikhs of the Punjab led to defeats of the Mughal troops (1628, 1631), and Kandahar was lost (1653) to the Persians, but the emperor was able to consolidate his power in the Deccan. When he fell ill in 1658, his sons rebelled, and the victor was the third son, **Aurangzeb**, who became effective ruler of the empire, imprisoning Shah Jahan until his death. The Peacock Throne, the Taj Mahal, the Pearl Mosque, the Red Fort in Delhi, and the 98-mile Ravi Canal were among the achievements of his reign.

Shahn, Ben(jamin) 1898–1969 •*US painter*• Born in Kovno (Kaunas), Lithuania, he emigrated with his parents to New York in 1906. Studying painting at night school, he visited the European art centers (1922) and came under the influence of **Georges Rouault**. His didactic pictorial commentaries on contemporary events, such as his 23 satirical gouache paintings on the trial of the anarchists **Nicola Sacco** and Bartolomeo Vanzetti (1932, Museum of Modern Art, New York), and the 15 paintings of Tom Mooney, the Labor leader (1933), earned him the title of the "American **Hogarth**." In 1933 he worked with **Diego Rivera** on murals for Rockefeller Center, and later became one of the leading US realist painters.

Shaka c. 1787–1828 •*Zulu leader and founder of the Zulu nation*• An illegitimate son, he seized power from his half brother to become clan chief (1816). He organized a permanent army and conquered the Nguni peoples of modern Natal, exterminating many smaller clans, and built up a centralized, militaristic Zulu kingdom covering most of southern Africa. He became increasingly autocratic, to the point of insanity after the death (1827) of his mother Nandi, and was murdered by his half brothers.

Shakespeare, John c. 1530–1601 •*English glover and wool dealer*• Born in Snitterfield, near Stratford, Warwickshire, he was the father of **William Shakespeare**. After apprenticeship to a leathersmith and glove maker, he set up his own business in Stratford, which prospered. In 1559 he was elected burgess, and six years later became an alderman. In 1568 he was made bailiff (mayor) of Stratford and a justice of the peace. His wool business failed in 1577, but he managed to retain possession of his house. In 1592 he was rescued by his son William, whose earnings in the London theater were by then enough to restore the family's position.

Shakespeare, William 1564–1616 •*English playwright, poet and actor, the greatest English dramatist*• He was born in Stratford-upon-Avon in Warwickshire, the eldest son of **John Shakespeare**, a glover and wool dealer, and Mary Arden. He was most likely educated at Stratford Grammar School. During the winter of 1582–83 he married Anne Hathaway, a farmer's daughter who lived in Shottery, near Stratford. She was 26, and pregnant by him. Less than six months after their wedding, their first child, Susanna, was baptized in Stratford church. Early in 1585, Anne gave birth to twins: Hamnet, their only son (who died young), and Judith, their second daughter. With a wife and three children to maintain, and still dependent on his father, Shakespeare joined one of the London acting companies that had been touring in Stratford. By 1595 he had written several successful plays in all the forms of drama then popular, although the chronology and order of the early works is still disputed. They include histories, comedies, and the revenge tragedy *Titus Andronicus*. Between 1592 and 1594, when the theaters were closed by an outbreak of plague, Shakespeare turned to poetry, writing sonnets and two long narrative poems: *Venus and Adonis* (published April 18, 1593) and *The Rape of Lucrece* (published May 9, 1594). Both of these were dedicated to the 3rd Earl of **Southampton**, who was a patron of the arts. The 154 extant sonnets were probably written between 1592 and 1598, although they were not published until 1609, and the order in which he wrote them is not known. When the theaters reopened in 1594, Shakespeare joined the newly formed Lord Chamberlain's Men, and was entitled to a share of the profits. The company performed regularly at the court of Queen **Elizabeth I**. Shakespeare's considerable output of six comedies, five histories and one tragedy (*Romeo and Juliet*) between 1594 and 1598 took the London theater world by storm, and the language and the characters of the plays captured people's imaginations and entered their daily conversation. In 1599 the Chamberlain's Men dismantled the theater and used much of its material to build a new playhouse, called the Globe, on Bankside, south of the Thames. It was a bold and successful venture. The Globe's huge stage permitted the rapidity and continuity of action which the dramas of the day demanded and which Shakespeare was able to exploit in the plays he wrote for performance there. The Globe opened with *Henry V*, and its success was followed by *Julius Caesar*, *Twelfth Night*, *Hamlet* and *Othello*. When James I (**James VI and I**) succeeded to the English throne in 1603, he immediately conferred his own royal patronage on Shakespeare and his fellow sharers. They became the King's Men ("His Majesty's Servants") and were granted a patent. The darker tone of the plays that Shakespeare wrote in the early years of James's reign has led to speculation that these plays reflected some kind of personal and spiritual crisis. But nothing that is known about him amounts to a feasible explanation of why he wrote a succession of so-called problem plays (or dark comedies) and tragedies between 1602 and 1609: *All's Well That Ends Well*, *Measure for Measure*, *King Lear*, *Macbeth*, *Antony and Cleopatra*, *Timon of Athens*, *Coriolanus* and *Troilus and Cressida*. These plays were great popular successes at the Globe, and were also received with acclaim at court and when performed for wealthy and socially exclusive audiences in private halls and in the lawyers' Inns of Court. Meanwhile, Shakespeare was preparing to return to Stratford. Soon after writing *The Tempest*, he freed himself of his major commitment to the company by bringing forward **John Fletcher** to take over as the King's Men's chief dramatist. The company could stage any of his existing plays whenever they wished, and he was therefore able to spend more time in Stratford. By 1612 he had completed his withdrawal. He died at his home in Stratford on April 23, 1616. Two days later, he was buried in the church in which he had been christened. In 1623 a monument to him was erected in Holy Trinity Church. A few months later, the first collection of his plays, known as the First Folio, was published.

“ ”

What's in a name? That which we call a rose
By any other name would smell as sweet.

1595 Juliet. ***Romeo and Juliet****, act 2, scene 1, l. 85–6.*

Shalyapin, Fyodor Ivanovich *See* **Chaliapin, Feodor Ivanovich**

Shamir, Yitzhak, *originally* **Yitzhak Jazernicki** 1915– •*Israeli politician*• Born in Ruzhany (now in Belarus), he studied at Warsaw and Jerusalem. In his twenties, he became a founding member of the Stern Gang (Fighters for the Freedom of Israel), the Zionist terrorist group which carried out anti-British attacks on strategic targets and personnel in Palestine. He was arrested by the British (1941) and exiled to Eritrea (1946), but given asylum in France. He returned to the new State of Israel in 1948 and spent the next 20 years on the fringe of politics, later entering the Knesset (1973) and becoming foreign minister (1980–83), leader of the right-wing Likud Party and prime minister (1983). From 1984, he shared power in an uneasy coalition with the Israel Labor Party and its leader, **Shimon Peres**. In 1990 the "national unity" government collapsed, and in June 1992 Likud was defeated in the general election by the Labor Party, led by **Yitzhak Rabin**.

Shammai c. 1st century BC–1st century AD •*Jewish scholar and Pharisaic leader*• Apparently a native of Jerusalem, he was head of a famous school of Torah scholars, whose interpretation of Jewish law was often in conflict with the equally famous school led by **Hillel I**.

Shankly, Bill (William) 1913–81 •*Scottish soccer player and manager*• He won a Football Association Cup medal with Preston North End and five Scotland caps, and as a postwar manager he found success with Liverpool. With **Jock Stein** and Sir **Matt Busby**, he is considered one of the greatest soccer managers of recent times.

“ ”

Some people think football is a matter of life and death. I don't like that attitude. I can assure them it is much more serious than that.

Quoted in the ***Sunday Times****, October 4, 1981.*

Shannon, Claude Elwood 1916–2001 •*US applied mathematician*• He was born in Gaylord, Michigan, and educated at the University of Michigan and at MIT. A student of **Vannevar Bush**, the central concept of his work—that information can be treated like any other quantity and can be manipulated by a machine—had a profound impact on the development of computing. After graduating from MIT, he worked on information theory at the Bell Telephone Laboratories (1941–72). He wrote *The Mathematical Theory of Communications* (1949, with Warren Weaver).

Shao-chi, Liu *See* **Liu Shaoqi**

Shapiro, Karl Jay 1913–2000 •*US poet and critic*• Born in Baltimore, Maryland, he was educated at the University of Virginia, Charlottesville, and at Johns Hopkins University, Baltimore. He published his first collection of verse, *Poems*, in 1935, and his first major book, *V-Letter* (1944), during military service in World War II. This won him the Pulitzer Prize and was followed by *Essay on Rime* (1945) and *Trial of a Poet* (1947). He turned to freer verse forms and prose poetry, drawing on the unconscious as an inspiration, as in *The Bourgeois Poet* (1964). An influential critic, he rejected the Europeanism of **T S Eliot** and **Ezra Pound** in favor of a robust Americanism, his models being **Walt Whitman**, **William Carlos Williams** and **Randall Jarrell**, on whom he wrote an influential study (1967). He wrote one novel, *Edsel* (1971), a satire on academic life.

Shapley, Harlow 1885–1972 •*US astronomer*• Born in Nashville, Missouri, he studied astronomy at the University of Missouri and at Princeton (1911–14), and was appointed to the staff of the Mount Wilson Observatory in California (1914–21). There he established the distances of globular star clusters and discovered that the sun is near the edge of the stellar system and not at its center as had been the accepted view. Shortly afterward Shapley was appointed director of Harvard College Observatory (1921). His research includes the discovery of the first two dwarf galaxies, companions to our own galaxy, and investigations on the Magellanic Clouds.

Sharaff, Irene 1910–93 •*US costume designer*• Born in Boston, she studied art in New York and Paris, and began her career as a costume designer with the Civic Repertory Theater Company in 1929. She became a successful designer in Hollywood, contributing to such famous musicals as *Brigadoon* (1954), *Guys and Dolls* (1955), *West Side Story* (1961) and *Hello Dolly!* (1969). She was nominated for 16 Academy Awards and won five.

Sharman, Helen 1963– •*English chemist and astronaut*• Born in Sheffield, she trained as a chemist at the University of Sheffield. She joined the Anglo-Soviet Juno mission in May 1991 as the first-ever British astronaut, and flew on the *Soyuz TM-12* spacecraft 250 miles above the Earth to the Soviet *Mir* space station, where she worked for a week carrying out scientific and medical tests.

Sharon, Ariel 1928– •*Israeli general and politician*• Prominent in the War of Independence (1948) and Sinai Campaign (1956), in the Six-Day War of 1967, he recaptured the Milta Pass in the Sinai Peninsula. He left the army in 1973 but was recalled to fight in the Yom Kippur War. In the same year he helped to form the Likud (a coalition of right-wing parties led by the Herut [Freedom] Party), and was voted into the Knesset. As defense minister (1981–83) under **Menachem Begin**, Sharon planned Israel's invasion of Lebanon in 1982. He became leader of the right-wing Likud Party in 1999 and prime minister in 2001, and was reelected in 2003.

Sharp, Granville 1735–1813 •*English abolitionist*• He was born in Durham. He was active in the antislavery movement and, while defending a Black immigrant named James Sommersett (or Somerset), he won a legal decision that secured the freedom of any slave who set foot on British soil. He worked with **Thomas Clarkson** for the abolition of Black slavery, and developed a plan for a home for freed slaves in Sierra Leone.

Sharp, Phillip Allen 1944– •*US molecular biologist and Nobel Prize winner*• Born in Kentucky, he was educated at the University of Illinois. He was a postdoctoral Fellow at the California Institute of Technology (1969–71), and among other appointments became director of the MIT Center for Cancer Research (1985–91), head of its biology department (1991) and Institute Professor there (1999). He was also a cofounder of Biogen, where he became chairman of the scientific board in 1987. Sharp invented the mapping technique used extensively in the analysis of RNA molecules. This led to his discovery in 1977 that genes are split into several sections, separated by stretches of DNA known as introns, which appear to carry no genetic information. The discovery has prompted much research on how this phenomenon might be involved in genetic diseases and evolutionary processes. Sharp shared the 1993 Nobel Prize for physiology or medicine with **Richard Roberts**, who had discovered split genes at about the same time.

Sharpe, Tom (Thomas Ridley) 1928– •*English satirical novelist*• He was born in London. After graduating from Cambridge, he served in the Royal Marines and worked as a social worker, teacher and photographer before turning to full-time writing. Among his best novels, which combine farcical comedy and mild sexual titillation with an acute observation of English social manners and well-aimed satire, are *Porterhouse Blue* (1973) and *Blott on the Landscape* (1975). Further novels include *Wilt* (1976) and *The Midden* (1996).

Shastri, Lal Bahadur 1904–66 •*Indian politician*• Born in Benares, the son of a legal clerk, he joined **Mahatma Gandhi**'s independence movement at 16 and was seven times imprisoned by the British. He excelled as a Congress Party official and politician in the United Provinces and joined Nehru's Cabinet, becoming minister of transport (1957) and of commerce (1958) and home secretary (1960). Under the Kamaraj plan to invigorate the Congress Party at the popular level, he resigned with other Cabinet ministers in 1963; but he was recalled by Nehru in 1964, and succeeded him as prime minister in the same year.

Shaw, Anna Howard 1847–1919 •*US suffragist*• Born in Newcastle upon Tyne, she emigrated with her family to the US as a young child (1851). In 1880 she became the first woman to be ordained as a Methodist Protestant preacher, and in 1886 she graduated in medicine from Boston University. From 1904 to 1915 she was president of the National American Woman Suffrage Association. She was head of the Women's Committee of the Council of National Defense during World War I and published her autobiography, *The Story of a Pioneer*, in 1915.

Shaw, Artie, *originally* **Arthur Arshawsky** 1910– •*US bandleader and clarinettist*• Born in New York City, he took up writing and numerous music jobs before achieving success as a swing-band leader, notably with "Begin the Beguine" (1938), "Star Dust" (1940) and "Moonglow" (1941); he rivaled **Benny Goodman** as a clarinet soloist. He married eight times, and his wives included the actresses **Lana Turner**, **Ava Gardner** and Evelyn Keyes. He retired from performing in 1955.

Shaw, Fiona, *originally* **Fiona Bolton** 1958– •*Irish actress*• Born and brought up in Cork, she took a degree in philosophy and trained at the Royal Academy of Dramatic Art, making her debut in 1982. She went on to perform for the Royal Shakespeare Company, with roles including Madame de Volanges in *Les liaisons dangereuses* (1985) and Katharina in *The Taming of the Shrew* (1987), and became associated with highly emotional roles, notably the title roles in *Electra* and *Hedda Gabler*. A frequent collaborator with **Deborah Warner**, she played King Richard in *Richard II* in 1995.

Shaw, George Bernard 1856–1950 •*Irish dramatist and critic and Nobel Prize winner*• He was born in Dublin to Irish Protestant parents. After unhappy years at school and working for a firm of land agents, he left Ireland to follow his mother and sister to London. There he entered a long period of struggle and poverty, and five novels written between 1879 and 1883 were all rejected. He came under the influence of US economist Henry George (1839–97), whom he met in 1882, and the works of **Karl Marx**, and developed a belief in socialism which underlay all his future work. He joined the executive committee of the Fabian Society (1884–1911), for which he edited *Fabian Essays* (1889) and wrote many well-known socialist tracts. He made his first impact on the intellectual and social consciousness of his time as a music and drama critic, and produced the full-length studies *The Quintessence of Ibsenism* (1891) and *The Perfect Wagnerite* (1898). The rest of Shaw's life, especially after his marriage (1898) to the Irish heiress Charlotte Payne-Townshend, is mainly the history of his plays. His first was *Widowers' Houses*, begun in 1885 in collaboration with his friend William Archer. This was followed by *Mrs Warren's Profession* (1898), *Arms and the Man* (1898), *Candida* (1897) and *Three Plays for Puritans: The Devil's Disciple* (1897), *Caesar and Cleopatra* (1901) and *Captain Brassbound's Conversion* (1900). Shaw's long correspondence with the actresses **Ellen Terry** and Mrs Patrick **Campbell** also developed during these years, and his reputation was growing in England and abroad. This was reinforced by *Man and Superman* (1902), one of his greatest philosophical comedies, on the theme of the human quest for a purer religious approach to life. Other notable plays from this time are *John Bull's Other Island* (1904), *Major Barbara* (1905), *The Doctor's Dilemma* (1906) and two uniquely Shavian discussion plays, *Getting Married* (1908) and *Misalliance* (1910). These embrace a wide range of subject matter, from politics and statecraft to family life, prostitution and vaccination, and he sometimes fell afoul of the censors. In the years before the outbreak of World War I came two of his best-known plays, *Androcles and the Lion* (1912) and *Pygmalion* (1913), an antiromantic comedy which was later adapted as a musical play, *My Fair Lady*, in 1956 (filmed in 1964). After the war followed three of his greatest dramas: *Heartbreak House* (1919), *Back to Methuselah* (1921) and *Saint Joan* (1923). In 1931 he visited Russia, and the following year made a world tour with his wife. Greater perhaps than any of the plays written during the last years of his life are the two prose works: *The Intelligent Woman's Guide to Socialism and Capitalism* (1928) and *The Black Girl in Search of God* (1932), a modern *Pilgrim's Progress*. Of the later plays, only *The Apple Cart* (1929) has been regularly staged. He was awarded the Nobel Prize for literature in 1925.

" "

Martyrdom is the only way in which a man can become famous without ability.

1897 ***The Devil's Disciple****, act 3.*

Shawcross, Hartley William Shawcross, Baron 1902–2003 •*English jurist*• Born in Giessen, Germany, he was educated at Dulwich College. He was called to the bar at Gray's Inn in 1925 and was senior lecturer in law at Liverpool (1927–34). After service in World War II, he was attorney general (1945–51) and president of the Board of Trade (1951) in the Labour government. He established an international legal reputation for himself as chief British prosecutor at the Nuremberg Trials (1945–46) and was prosecutor in the **Klaus Fuchs** atom spy case (1950). Knighted in 1945, he was created a life peer in 1959.

Shawn, Ted (Edwin Myers) 1891–1972 •*US dancer and director*• Born in Kansas City, Missouri, in 1914 he met and married dancer and choreographer Ruth Saint Denis (1879–1968) in New York, and in 1915 they founded Denishawn, an influential dance school which was favored by the Hollywood studios. When the couple separated in 1931, Denishawn broke up, and Ted Shawn moved to a farm in Lee, Massachusetts; there he founded his own group, Ted Shawn and His Men Dancers, which toured for several years presenting dance inspired by Native American and Aboriginal work. In June 1941 the farm became the setting for Jacob's Pillow, an annual summer school and festival. His books include *The American Ballet* (1925) and *One Thousand and One Night Stands* (1960).

Shays, Daniel c. 1747–1825 •*American Revolutionary captain*• He was born probably in Hopkinton, Massachusetts. After serving in the American Army during the Revolution (1775–83), he returned to farming in Pelham, Massachusetts, but like many of his fellows, he found himself subjected to impossible economic demands. In 1786–87 he led a short-lived rural insurrection, known as Shays' Rebellion. It was crushed by state troops, but provided a major impetus to the drafting of the federal Constitution at the Constitutional Convention of 1787.

Sheba, Queen of *See* **Solomon**

Sheeler, Charles 1883–1965 •*US painter and photographer*• Born in Philadelphia, he studied at the Pennsylvania Academy of the Fine Arts, and during several trips to Europe (1904–09) was much influenced by the Cubist movement. From 1912 he worked as an industrial photographer, recording particularly the skyscrapers of Manhattan, and he collaborated on the film *Mannahatta* with **Paul Strand** (1920). In 1927 he was commissioned to photograph the building of the Ford Motor installation at River Rouge, Michigan, and was staff photographer at the New York Museum of Modern Art (1942–45).

Sheene, Barry Stephen Frank 1950–2003 •*English motorcycle racer*• Born in London, he made his racing debut in 1968, won the British 125-cc title in 1970. Despite a bad crash in 1975 at Daytona, which left him with fractures and a pin in his leg, he won the 500-cc world championship in 1976 to give Suzuki their first victory. He repeated it in 1977 and was runner-up in 1978. After another crash in 1982 at Silverstone, he retired to take up a career in broadcasting and business in Australia.

Shelburne, William Petty, 2nd Earl of 1737–1805 •*English politician*• Born in Dublin, the great-grandson of English economist Sir William Petty (1623–87), he studied at Christ Church, Oxford. He served in the army, entered parliament, succeeded his father to the earldom in 1761, was appointed president of the Board of Trade in 1763 and in 1766 secretary of state. When Lord **North**'s ministry fell in 1782, he declined to form a government, but became secretary of state under Charles, Marquis of **Rockingham**. When Rockingham died the same year, the king offered Shelburne the Treasury. **Charles Fox** resigned, and Shelburne introduced **William Pitt** the Younger into office as his chancellor of the exchequer, but this ministry fell when it was defeated by a coalition of Fox and North (February 1783).

Sheldon, Gilbert 1598–1677 •*English prelate*• Chaplain to **Charles I**, he was warden of All Souls, Oxford (1626–48), but was ejected by the Parliamentarians. At the Restoration in 1660, he was appointed Bishop of London, and in 1663 Archbishop of Canterbury. He built the Sheldonian Theatre in Oxford (1669).

Shelley, Mary Wollstonecraft, *née* **Godwin** 1797–1851 •*English writer*• She was born in London, the daughter of **William Godwin** and **Mary Wollstonecraft**. In 1814 she eloped with **Percy Bysshe Shelley**, and married him as his second wife in 1816. They lived abroad throughout their married life. Her first and most impressive novel was *Frankenstein, or the Modern Prometheus* (1818). After her husband's death in 1822 she returned from Italy to England with their son in 1823. *The Last Man* (1826) is a futuristic noble-savage romance of the ruin of human society by pestilence. In *Lodore* (1835) the story is told of Shelley's alienation from his first wife. Her last novel, *Falkner*, appeared in 1837. Of her occasional pieces of verse, the most remarkable is "The Choice." Her *Journal of a Six Weeks' Tour* (partly by Shelley) tells of their excursion to Switzerland in 1814, and *Rambles in Germany and Italy* (1844) describes tours of 1840–43. Her *Tales* were published in 1890, and two mythological dramas, *Proserpine* and *Midas*, in 1922.

" "

Everywhere I see bliss, from which I alone am irrevocably excluded.

1818 Frankenstein's monster. ***Frankenstein**, chapter 10.*

Shelley, Percy Bysshe 1792–1822 •*English lyric poet and writer, a leading figure in the Romantic movement*• He was born in Field Place, near Horsham in Sussex, and educated at Syon House Academy and Eton. He attended University College, Oxford, but was expelled for his contribution to a pamphlet called *The Necessity of Atheism*. He met and eloped with 16-year-old Harriet Westbrook, and lived for the next three years in York, in the Lake District, where he met **Robert Southey**, in Dublin, and at Lynmouth in Devon, where he set up a commune. At this time he wrote *Queen Mab* (1813), but it made little impact. He moved to London and there fell in love with the 16-year-old Mary Godwin (see **Mary Shelley**). They eloped in 1814, accompanied by her half sister, Jane "Claire" Clairmont, and were married after Harriet drowned herself in 1816. Meanwhile Shelley wrote an unfinished novella, *The Assassins* (1814), and published *Alastor* (1816). His son William was born in 1816, and he spent time with **Byron** at Lake Geneva. In 1818 he published *The Revolt of Islam*, and in the same year finally left England for Italy, where he was to spend the rest of his life. In 1819 came the major part of *Prometheus Unbound*, generally considered his masterpiece. The death of his son William in Rome devastated him, but he nevertheless completed the fourth part of *Prometheus*, *The Masque of Anarchy* (1819), inspired by the Peterloo massacre, "The Ode to the West Wind," "To Liberty" and "To Naples," "To a Skylark," "The Cloud," the intimate *Letter to Maria Gisborne* (1820) and *The Witch of Atlas*. These were followed by a series of prose pieces, a burlesque, *Adonais* (1821), an elegy on the death of Keats, and *Epipsychidion* (1821), the fruit of a platonic affair with a beautiful Italian heiress who was held in a convent. *Hellas* (1822), a verse drama inspired by the Greek war of independence, was his last work. Returning from a visit to Byron and **Leigh Hunt** at Livorno in August 1822, Shelley and his companions were drowned in a sudden squall. His body was cremated at Viareggio and his ashes taken to Rome.

Shen Gua (Shen Kua) 1031–95 •*Chinese administrator, engineer and scientist*• Born in Hangzhou, he made significant contributions to such diverse fields as astronomy, cartography, medicine, hydraulics and fortification. As director of the astronomical bureau from 1072, he improved methods of computation and the design of several observational devices; in 1075 he constructed a series of relief maps of China's northern frontier area and designed fortifications as defenses against nomadic invaders. In 1082, following the defeat of troops under his command, he was forced to resign from his government posts, and spent his last years writing *Brush Talks From Dream Brook*, a remarkable compilation of about 600 observations, now one of the most important sources of information on early Chinese science and technology.

Shenstone, William 1714–63 •*English poet*• Born near Halesowen, Worcestershire, he studied at Solihull Grammar School and Pembroke College, Oxford. In 1737 he published his best-known poem, "The School-mistress" (revised in 1742), which was written in imitation of **Edmund Spenser** and foreshadowed **Thomas Gray**'s *Elegy*. He published *The Judgement of Hercules* in 1741. His *Pastoral Ballad* (1755) was commended by Gray and **Samuel Johnson**.

Shepard, Alan Bartlett 1923–98 •*US astronaut, the first American in space*• Born in East Derry, New Hampshire, he graduated from the US Naval Academy in 1944 and served in the Pacific. He won his wings in 1947 and subsequently flew jet aircraft on test and training missions. On May 5, 1961, 23 days after **Yuri Gagarin**'s historic orbit of the earth, he was launched in "Freedom 7" on a ballistic suborbital trajectory to a height of 116 miles, controlling the whole 15-minute flight manually. He was director of astronaut training at NASA (1965–74), and commanded the Apollo 14 lunar mission in 1971.

Shepard, E(rnest) H(oward) 1879–1976 •*English artist and cartoonist*• He was born in London, the son of an architect, and studied at the Royal Academy Schools. After service in the Royal Artillery in World War I, he worked for *Punch*, and made his name with illustrations for children's books such as **A A Milne**'s *Winnie the Pooh* (1926) and **Kenneth Grahame**'s *The Wind in the Willows* (1931).

Shepard, Sam, *originally* **Samuel Shepard Rogers** 1943– •*US dramatist and actor*• Born in Fort Sheridan, Illinois, he studied agriculture at college for a year, joined a touring company, and then moved to New York City, where he worked in the avant-garde theater of the 1960s. His first plays, *Cowboy* and *The Rock Garden*, were written in 1964 and produced by Theater Genesis in New York, followed by *Dog* and *Rocking Chair* (both 1965) at La Mama. Subsequent works included a rock drama, *The Tooth of Crime*, *Buried Child* (1978), which won the Pulitzer Prize, *True West* (1980), *Fool for Love* (1983) and *A Lie of the Mind* (1985). He also appeared in films, and has written screenplays, including *Paris, Texas* (1984). He published a volume of short stories, *Cruising Paradise*, in 1996.

Shephard, Gillian, *née* **Watts** 1940– •*English Conservative politician*• Born in Norfolk and educated at Oxford, she began working as an education officer and schools inspector in Norfolk, later becoming a magistrate and entering local politics. She was elected Member of Parliament for South West Norfolk in 1987 and rose swiftly to enter the Cabinet in 1992 as secretary of state for employment. She was minister of agriculture, fisheries and food (1993–94) and then secretary of state for education and employment (1994–97) at a time of tense relations between the teaching profession and the government. She retained her seat in 1997 when Labour won the general election.

Sheppard, Jack 1702–24 •*English robber*• Born in Stepney, London, he committed the first of many robberies in 1720, and in 1724 was caught five times, and escaped four. He was eventually hanged at Tyburn in the presence of 200,000 spectators, and became the subject of many plays and ballads, tracts by **Daniel Defoe** and a novel by **William Ainsworth**.

Sher, Sir Antony 1949– •*British actor and writer*• Born in Cape Town, South Africa, he went to England in 1968 and studied at the Webber-Douglas Academy of Dramatic Art. He appeared in plays at the Royal Court Theatre, and joined the Royal Shakespeare Company (1982). In 1984 he gave a performance of macabre brilliance in the title role of **Bill Alexander**'s production of *Richard III*, and in 1992 he played the lead in Terry Hands' Royal Shakespeare Company production of *Tamburlaine the Great*. He has also appeared occasionally in television drama, notably in *The History Man* (1982). In his book *The Year of the King* (1985), he describes his work on *Richard III*. He illustrated the book himself, as he did his first novel, *Middlepost* (1988). He subsequently wrote a film script, *Changing Step* (1989), two more novels, and coauthored *Woza Shakespeare!* (1996, with Gregory Doran). He was given the honorary title Knight Commander, Order of the British Empire, in 2000.

Sheraton, Thomas 1751–1806 •*English furniture designer and writer*• Born in Stockton-on-Tees, Cleveland, he settled in London around 1790, but never had a workshop of his own. Although there is no extant furniture attributable to him, he achieved fame in his lifetime through his elegant neoclassical designs, influenced by **Thomas Chippendale** and **George Hepplewhite**. His major work, *The Cabinet-Maker and Upholsterer's Drawing Book*, was published in parts between 1791 and 1794. He was ordained in 1800.

Shere Ali 1825–79 •*Emir of Afghanistan*• He was the younger son of Dost Mohammed, whom he succeeded in 1863. Disagreements with his half brothers soon arose, which kept Afghanistan in anarchy; he fled to Kandahar, but regained possession of Kabul (1868) with assistance from the viceroy of India, Baron John Lawrence (1811–79). His refusal to receive a British mission (1878) led to war, and after severe fighting, he fled to Turkestan, where he died.

Sheridan, Philip Henry 1831–88 •*US soldier*• Born in Albany, New York, of Irish parentage, he commanded a Union division at the beginning of the Civil War (1861–65). In 1864 he was given command of the Army of the Shenandoah, turning the valley into a barren waste and defeating General **Robert E Lee**. He had a further victory at Five Forks in 1865, and was active in the final battles which led to Lee's surrender. He never lost a battle.

Sheridan, Richard Brinsley 1751–1816 •*Irish dramatist*• He was born in Dublin, the son of Thomas Sheridan (1719–88), author of a *Life of Swift*. His mother, Frances (1724–66), was also a writer. He was educated at Harrow, and in 1773 he married Elizabeth Linley. The couple settled in London to a life that was beyond their means, and Sheridan devoted time to dramatic composition. In 1775 *The Rivals* was successfully produced at Covent Garden, London, and in the same year appeared a poor farce called *St Patrick's Day* and also *The Duenna*. In 1776 Sheridan, with the aid of composer Thomas Linley (1732–95) and another friend, bought a half interest in Drury Lane Theatre for £35,000 from **David Garrick**, and in 1778 the remaining share for £45,000. His first production was a purified edition of **John Vanbrugh**'s *Relapse*, under the title *A Trip to Scarborough*. In 1777 he produced his most famous play, *The School for Scandal*, a satirical comedy of manners. *The Critic* (1779), teeming with sparkling wit, was his last dramatic effort, apart from a less successful tragedy, *Pizarro*. In 1780 he was elected Member of Parliament for Stafford, and became undersecretary for foreign affairs (1782) under Charles, Marquis of **Rockingham**, and afterward secretary of the treasury in the coalition ministry (1783). His parliamentary reputation dated from some great speeches in the impeachment of **Warren Hastings**. In 1794 he again electrified the House by a magnificent oration in reply to Lord Mornington's denunciation of the French Revolution. He remained the devoted friend and adherent of **Charles Fox** till Fox's death, and was also the defender and mouthpiece of the Prince Regent. In 1806 he was appointed treasurer of the navy. In 1812 he lost his seat. Meanwhile, the affairs of the theater had gone badly. The old building had to be closed as unfit to hold large audiences, and a new one, opened in 1794, was burned in 1809. This last calamity put the finishing touches on Sheridan's pecuniary difficulties, which had long been serious. He died in great poverty, but was given a magnificent funeral at Westminster Abbey.

Sherlock, Dame Sheila Patricia Violet 1918–2001 •*British physician*• She trained in medicine at the University of Edinburgh and was a Beit Research Fellow from 1942 to 1947. After a period at Yale University (1948), she became physician and lecturer in medicine at the Royal Postgraduate Medical School in London (1948–59), then Professor of Medicine at the Royal Free Hospital Medical School, London. She published extensively on liver function, structure and disease, and received numerous honorary degrees and fellowships. She worked for many medical organizations, and was given the honorary title of Dame Commander, Order of the British Empire, in 1978.

Sherman, William Tecumseh 1820–91 •*US soldier*• Born in Lancaster, Ohio, the brother of statesman John Sherman (1823–1900), he trained at West Point. At the outbreak of the Civil War, he was commissioned as a colonel (1861), and at Bull Run was promoted to brigadier general of volunteers. After the Battle of Shiloh (April 1862), he was made major general. In 1863, promoted to brigadier, he drove General **Joseph Johnston** out of Jackson, Mississippi; he joined **Ulysses S Grant** at Chattanooga, and soon after relieved **Ambrose Burnside** at Knoxville. In March 1864 he was appointed to the command of the southwest and drove Johnston to Atlanta, which was evacuated on September 1. He then marched to the sea with 65,000 men, destroying everything in his path and finally capturing the coastal town of Savannah. In February 1865 he reached Columbia. From there he moved on Goldsboro, fighting two battles on the way. On April 9 **Lee** surrendered, and Johnston made terms with Sherman. For four years he commanded the Mississippi division, and when Grant became president, he was made head of the army. In 1884, to make room for **Philip Sheridan**, he was retired on full pay.

“ ”

There is many a boy here today who looks on war as all glory, but, boys, it is all hell.

1880 Speech at Columbus, Ohio, August 11. Quoted in Lloyd Lewis ***Sherman: Fighting Prophet*** *(1932).*

Sherrington, Sir Charles Scott 1857–1952 •*English physiologist and Nobel Prize winner*• Born in London, after studying at Cambridge, he became a lecturer in physiology and later Waynflete Professor of Physiology at Oxford (1913–35). His career focused on the structure and function of the nervous system. His analysis of the reflexes is summarized in *The Integrative Action of the Nervous System* (1906), a book which constituted a significant landmark in modern neurophysiology. He described the reciprocal action by which the activity of one set of excited muscles is integrated with another set of inhibited muscles, and coined the word “synapse.” He also mapped the motor areas of the cerebral cortex of mammals, and produced an influential textbook on experimental physiology, *Mammalian Physiology* (1919). He was president of the Royal Society (1920–25) and shared the 1932 Nobel Prize for physiology or medicine with Lord **Adrian**.

Sher Shah (Sher Khan) c.1486–1545 •*Afghan ruler*• He was able to contest the supremacy of the Mughals in India, defeating

Emperor Hamayun at Chausa on the Ganges (1539) and forcing him into exile. An able administrator, he also built a new city at Delhi and a mausoleum at Sasaram in Bihar. His death in battle and the inefficiency of his successors allowed the Mughals to emerge triumphant.

Sherwood, Robert E(mmet) 1896–1955 •*US playwright and author*• Born in New Rochelle, New York, he wrote his first play while at Harvard. After service in World War I he became editor of *Life* (1924–28), and a member of the celebrated literary group known as the Algonquin Round Table. He won four Pulitzer Prizes, the first three for drama with *Idiot's Delight* (1936), *Abe Lincoln in Illinois* (1938) and *There Shall Be No Night* (1940). He later became President **Franklin D Roosevelt**'s chief speechwriter. He won his last Pulitzer Prize for his autobiographical *Roosevelt and Hopkins* (1949), which drew on his friendship with Roosevelt and with US administrator Harry L Hopkins (1890–1946). His screenplay, *The Best Years of Our Lives*, won an Academy Award in 1946.

Shetrup Akong Tarap *See* **Akong Tulku Rinpoche**

Shevardnadze, Eduard Amvrosevich 1928– •*Georgian and Soviet politician*• He was born in the Georgian village of Mamati. Having studied at the Kutaisi Institute of Education, he joined the Communist Party in 1948, and rose rapidly, entering the Georgian Ministry of the Interior in 1964. There he gained a reputation as a stern opponent of corruption, and he became Georgian Party secretary himself in 1972. He introduced imaginative agricultural reforms, and in 1978 was brought into the politburo as a candidate member. Having enjoyed longstanding connections with **Mikhail Gorbachev**, he was promoted to full politburo status and appointed foreign minister in 1985. He rapidly overhauled the Soviet foreign policy machine and, alongside Gorbachev, was responsible for the Soviet contribution to ending the Cold War. In 1992 he returned to Georgia where he became chairman of the Supreme Council and head of state (1992–95) and then president (1995–2003).

Shevchenko, Taras Grigorevich 1814–61 •*Ukrainian poet and prose writer*• Born a serf in Kirilovka (Kiev), he came to be considered the father of modern Ukrainian literature and the country's foremost 19th-century poet. He was adopted by a literary circle in St Petersburg, who bought his freedom in 1838. His early poems included Romantic ballads, love songs and historical subjects. He became professor at Kiev (1845), and founded an organization for radical social reforms. He was exiled to central Asia for ten years for working for Ukrainian independence, but was freed in 1857, although kept under surveillance.

Shields, Carol Ann 1935–2003 •*Canadian author and academic*• Born in Oak Park, Illinois, she moved to Canada in 1957, where she studied at the University of Ottawa. She combined professorships at several Canadian universities with her work as a writer, producing novels such as *The Republic of Love* (1992) and *The Stone Diaries* (1993), for which she received the Pulitzer Prize. *Larry's Party* (1997) won the Orange Prize in 1998. She also published numerous poems and short stories, and a biography of **Jane Austen** (2000).

Shi Huangdi (Shih Huang-ti) c. 259–210 BC •*Chinese emperor and founder of the Qin (Ch'in) dynasty*• The creator of the first unified Chinese empire (221 BC), he assumed the title of "first emperor," and greatly extended and consolidated the empire with the establishment of a centralized administration, the abolition of territorial feudal power, and far-reaching measures for standardization. He ordered a system of road construction and, using convict labor, linked together earlier fortifications to make the Great Wall (completed in 214 BC). In 1974, excavation of his tomb yielded several thousand terracotta soldiers and horses which had been buried with him.

Shinwell, Emmanuel Shinwell, Baron, *known as* **Manny Shinwell** 1884–1986 •*English Labour politician*• Born in Spitalfields, London, he began work as an errand boy in Glasgow at the age of 12. He was elected to the Glasgow Trades Council in 1911 and, as one of the "wild men of Clydeside," served a five months' prison sentence for incitement to riot in 1921. He entered parliament in 1931 and was appointed secretary of the Department of Mines (1924, 1930–31). In 1935 he defeated **Ramsay MacDonald** in one of the most bitterly contested British election battles of modern times. From 1942 he was chairman of the Labour Party committee which drafted the manifesto on which Labour won the 1945 election. As minister of fuel and power he nationalized the mines (1946), and the following year became secretary of state for war. From 1950 to 1951 he was minister of defense. Shinwell's considerable administrative ability outshone his prickly party belligerence and earned him the respect of **Churchill** and **Montgomery**. He was awarded a life peerage in 1970.

Shipley, Jenny (Jennifer Mary) 1952– •*New Zealand politician*• Born in Gore, New Zealand, she worked as a primary-school teacher and a farmer before joining the National Party in 1975 and becoming a Member of Parliament in 1987. Noted for her tough political style and widely regarded as New Zealand's version of **Margaret Thatcher**, she was appointed minister of social welfare (1990–93), women's affairs (1990–98), health (1993–96) and state services (1996–97), during which time she committed herself to making radical cuts in welfare payments. She became her country's first woman prime minister in 1997. In 1999, following defeat at the hands of a center-left coalition led by **Helen Clark**, she became leader of the opposition (1999–2001).

Shipton, Eric Earle 1907–77 •*English mountaineer*• He gained his early mountaineering experience during five expeditions to the mountains of East and Central Africa, climbing Kamet (25,447 ft) in 1931. He obtained much of his knowledge of the East during his terms as consul general in Kashgar (1940–42, 1946–48) and Kunming (1949–51). Between 1933 and 1951 he led or was a member of five expeditions to Mount Everest, and he contributed greatly to the successful **Hunt-Hillary** expedition of 1953.

Shipton, Mother, *originally* **Ursula Southiel** 1488–c. 1560 •*English witch*• She was born near Knaresborough, Yorkshire, and married a builder, Tony Shipton, at the age of 24. According to S Baker, who edited her "prophecies" (1797), she lived for more than 70 years. A book by Richard Head (1684) tells how she was carried off by the devil and bore him an imp. A small British moth, with wing markings resembling a witch's face, is named after her.

Shirakawa, Hideki 1936– •*Japanese materials scientist and Nobel Prize winner*• Born in Tokyo, he was educated at the Tokyo Institute of Technology, and joined the Institute of Materials Science at the University of Tsukuba in 1966. He received the Nobel Prize for chemistry (2000; with **Alan J Heeger** and **Alan G MacDiarmid**) for the discovery and development of conductive polymers, effectively allowing the birth of plastic electronics.

Shirley, James 1596–1666 •*English dramatist*• He was born in London and studied at St John's, Oxford, and St Catharine's, Cambridge. He then took orders and was appointed to an office in the Church at St Albans. Later, he converted to Catholicism, and taught (1623–24) in the grammar school there, but soon went to London and became a playwright. **Francis Beaumont**, **John Fletcher** and **Ben Jonson** were his models, but he has little of the grand Elizabethan manner. His chief plays include *The Lady of Pleasure* (1635), the most brilliant of his comedies; the tragedy *The Cardinal* (1641), which the author himself described as "the best of his flock"; and *The Traitor* (1631). As a masque writer he is second only to Jonson. He died as a result of the Great Fire of London.

Shirreff, Emily Anne Eliza 1814–97 •*English pioneer of women's education*• She was largely self-educated. With her sister, Maria Georgina Gray, she wrote *Thoughts on Self-Culture, Addressed to Women* (1850) and two novels, and she founded the National Union for the Higher Education of Women (1871). She was head of Girton College, Cambridge (1870–97), and published works on kindergartens and the **Froebel** system.

Shockley, William Bradford 1910–89 •*US physicist and Nobel Prize winner*• Born in London, the son of two US mining engineers, he was brought up in California and educated at the California and Massachusetts Institutes of Technology before starting work at the Bell Telephone Laboratories in 1936. During World War II he directed antisubmarine warfare research. Returning to Bell Telephone, he collaborated with **John Bardeen** and **Walter Brattain** in trying to produce semiconductor devices to replace thermionic valves, and they invented the point-contact transistor in 1947. A month later Shockley developed the junction transistor, and these devices led to the miniaturization of circuits in radio, television and computer equipment. Shockley, Bardeen and Brattain shared the Nobel Prize for physics in 1956.

Shoemaker, Willie (William Lee) 1931–2003 •*US jockey*• He was born in Fabens, Texas. In 1953 he rode a record 485 winners in a season. In the US his major successes included four Kentucky Derbies, five Belmont Stakes and two wins in the famous Preakness event at Baltimore. The first jockey to saddle more than 8,000 winners, he moved to Europe late in his career, proving equally successful there. He retired in 1990 with 8,833 wins.

Sholokhov, Mikhail Aleksandrovich 1905–84 •*Russian novelist, winner of the Nobel Prize for literature*• Born in Kruzhilin, he was educated at schools in Moscow, Boguchar and Veshenskaya. From 1920 to 1922 he served in the army, after which he had various occupations. He became a war correspondent during World War II. His literary career began with some 30 short stories written between 1923 and 1927, which demonstrate his rapid development into an original writer. His masterpiece is *Tikhy Don* (4 vols, 1928–40, rev edn 1953, Eng trans in 2 vols: *And Quiet Flows the Don* and *The Don Flows Home to the Sea*, 1934–40). Set in the years 1912–22, it is a monument to the Don Cossacks, offering a broad view of their life in times of peace and during the turbulent years of the civil war and revolution. He won the 1941 Stalin Prize and the 1965 Nobel Prize for literature.

Shore (of Stepney), Peter David Shore, Baron 1924–2001 •*English Labour politician*• Educated at Cambridge, he joined the Labour Party in 1948 and became a Member of Parliament in 1964. He was parliamentary private secretary to **Harold Wilson**, and held several government posts, including secretary of state for economic affairs (1967–69) and for the environment (1976–79). After holding various Opposition spokesperson posts, he became Shadow Leader of the Commons (1984–87). A persistent critic of European economic union, he launched a "No to Maastricht" campaign in 1992. He was awarded a life peerage in 1997.

Short, Clare 1946– •*English Labour politician*• Educated at Keele University and the University of Leeds, she joined the Home Office in 1970. She married a former Labour Member of Parliament, Alexander Ward Lyon (1931–93), in 1981 and became Member of Parliament for Birmingham Ladywood in 1983. Gradually gaining recognition, she has been an influential member of the National Executive Committee since 1988. She held a number of positions as Opposition spokesperson before entering **Tony Blair**'s Cabinet as international development secretary when Labour came to power in 1997, a position she resigned in 2003 over government policy on Iraq. In 1996 she was reunited with her son, whom she had given up for adoption in 1965.

Short, Nigel 1965– •*English chess player*• He became the world's youngest chess grand master, and Britain's youngest champion, at the age of 19. In January 1993 he defeated Dutchman Jan Timman to become the first British chess world championship challenger for over 100 years. Later that year he resigned from FIDE (Fédération Internationale des Echecs) and formed the Professional Chess Association with **Gary Kasparov**.

Shorter, Wayne 1933– •*US jazz saxophonist, bandleader and composer*• Born in Newark, New Jersey, he studied music at New York University. His first long association was with the **Art Blakey** Jazz Messengers (1959–63). For the next six years he worked with **Miles Davis** in his first experiments in electric jazz-rock fusion, then cofounded the quintet Weather Report, which performed from 1971 until the mid-1980s. Since then, Shorter has continued at the head of small combos. His solo albums include *Supernova* (1970), *Atlantis* (1986) and *The All-Seeing Eye* (1994).

Shostakovich, Dmitri Dmitriyevich 1906–75 •*Russian composer*• He was born in St Petersburg. He was taught to play the piano by his mother, and entered the conservatory in 1919. His First Symphony, performed in Leningrad and Moscow in 1926, attracted worldwide attention. His musical career falls into two broad periods—up to his Fifth Symphony, which was written in 1938 in response to savage Soviet criticism, and after it. He always attempted to support Soviet principles, and initially wrote mainly for the theater and films, notably the ballets *Zolotoi vek* (1930, *The Age of Gold*) and *Bolt* (1931, *The Bolt*), and the opera *Nos* (1927–28, performed 1930, *The Nose*). His music was at first highly successful, but the development of a more conservative attitude on the part of the Soviet government coincided with his own development of a more experimental outlook and led to official criticism of *The Nose*, his Second ("October") Symphony, and the ballet *Svetytoly ruchey* (1934–35, *Bright Stream*). His second opera, *Ledi Makbet Mtsenskogo uyezda* (1930–32, *Lady Macbeth of Mtsensk*, later revised in 1956 and performed in 1962 as *Katerina Izmaylova*), had to be withdrawn after violent press attacks on its decadence and its failure to observe the principles of "Soviet realism." He replied with his Fifth Symphony, described by a critic as "a Soviet artist's reply to just criticism," which achieved his rehabilitation and remains one of Shostakovich's most popular works. He composed prolifically in all forms, although he avoided stage works until after the death of **Stalin**. In 1943 he moved to Moscow and was appointed Professor of Composition at the conservatory. His Seventh Symphony (1941, "Leningrad," based on the Siege of Leningrad, which Shostakovich himself experienced) and his Eighth (1943) and Tenth (1953) Symphonies have achieved considerable popularity outside Russia. The Tenth uses the motif DSCH, based on his own initials. His Eleventh Symphony (1957), for which he was awarded a Lenin prize in 1958, is based on the events of the October Revolution of 1905; the Twelfth (1961) celebrates the 1917 Revolution; the Fifteenth Symphony, his last (1974), is purely instrumental. He also wrote two violin concertos, two cello concertos, two piano concertos, many vocal works, 15 string quartets, a piano quintet (which won the Stalin prize in 1940), two piano trios, and other chamber music, as well as songs. His son is the conductor and pianist Maxim Shostakovich (1938–).

Shriver, Pam 1962– •*US tennis player*• Born in Baltimore, Maryland, she is one of the most successful Grand Slam titleholders of all time. Between 1981 and 1992 she won 22 Grand Slam titles—21 doubles titles and one mixed title, the 1987 French Open with Emilio Sanchez. Twenty of her doubles titles were won in partnership with **Martina Navratilova**. She is coowner of the Baltimore Orioles baseball team.

Shula, Don(ald Francis) 1930– •*US football player and coach*• He was born in Grand River, Ohio. He played professional football before he became a coach in 1958. By the mid-1980s the teams he had coached in the NFL had amassed 250 victories. His most successful team was the Miami Dolphins, who won 100 games in 10 seasons and made him the first NFL coach with such a record.

Shull, Clifford G(lenwood) 1915–2001 •*US physicist and Nobel Prize winner*• Born in Pittsburgh, Pennsylvania, he was educated at the Carnegie Institute of Technology and New York University. He worked as a research physicist during World War II and later moved to Oak Ridge National Laboratory, Tennessee (1946–55). He lectured at MIT from 1955 to 1986. In 1994 he shared the Nobel Prize for physics, with Bertram Brockhouse (1918–) for the development of the neutron diffraction technique.

Shultz, George Pratt 1920– •*US politician*• Born in New York City, he studied at Princeton and was an artillery officer during World War II. After the war he taught economics at MIT (1946–57) and the University of Chicago (1957–68) before holding various posts in the **Nixon** administration. He was subsequently vice chairman of the giant Bechtel industrial corporation and economic adviser to President **Ronald Reagan** in 1980 before replacing **Alexander Haig** as secretary of state in 1982. He retained this post for the remainder of the Reagan administration, until 1989. A moderate, he acted as a counterweight to the hawkish defense secretary **Caspar Weinberger** and helped to improve US-Soviet relations in the period of détente that followed the accession of **Mikhail Gorbachev**. His greatest achievement was the 1987 Intermediate Nuclear Forces (INF) Treaty. As secretary of state, he also directed a campaign against international terrorism, backing the US bombing of Tripoli in 1986.

" "

Gardening ... is one of the most underrated aspects of diplomacy.

1993 On the need to meet people "on their own turf."

Turmoil and Triumph

Shuster, Joseph 1914–92 •*US cartoonist*• Born in Toronto, Canada, he was cocreator with **Jerry Siegel** of one of the world's most popular comic-book heroes, *Superman*.

Shute, Nevil, *pseudonym of* **Nevil Shute Norway** 1899–1960 •*English novelist*• Born in Ealing, Middlesex, he served in World War I and immediately afterward began an aeronautical career. He was chief calculator of the Airship Guarantee Company during the construction of the airship R100, in which he flew the Atlantic twice. He founded Airspeed Ltd, aircraft constructors, and became its managing director. He emigrated to Australia after World War II. His novels include *The Chequerboard* (1947), *No Highway* (1948), *A Town Like Alice* (1949), *Beyond the Black Stump* (1956) and *On the Beach* (1957), about an atomic war.

Sibbald, Sir Robert 1641–1722 •*Scottish physician and naturalist*• Born in Edinburgh, he studied there and at Leiden University. He founded a physic garden in Edinburgh in 1670, which formed the nucleus of the present-day Royal Botanic Garden. He founded the Royal College of Physicians of Edinburgh, and became the first Professor of Medicine at the University of Edinburgh in 1685. King **Charles II** commissioned him to undertake a survey of the natural history and archaeology of Scotland, his *Scotia Illustrata*, which was published in 1684. The genus *Sibbaldia* is named in his honor. He was knighted in 1682.

Sibelius, Jean Julius Christian 1865–1957 •*Finnish composer*• Born in Hämeenlinna (Tavastehus), he abandoned a legal career to study music. He was a passionate nationalist, and wrote a series of symphonic poems (eg, *Kullervo*, 1892; *Swan of Tuonela*, 1893) based on episodes in the Finnish oral epic *Kalevala*. A state grant enabled him to devote himself entirely to composition from 1897, and his seven symphonies, symphonic poems (notably *En Saga*, 1892, revised 1901; *Finlandia*, 1899; *Tapiola*, 1925–26) and violin concerto have established him as a major 20th-century composer both in Finland and internationally.

Sibley, Dame Antoinette 1939– •*English dancer*• Born in Bromley, Kent, she trained with the Royal Ballet and appeared as a soloist for the first time in 1956 in *Swan Lake*. A dancer of sensuality and beauty, her roles in **Frederick Ashton**'s *The Dream* (1964) and **Kenneth MacMillan**'s *Manon* (1974) are among her most celebrated, and she formed a famous partnership with **Anthony Dowell**. A knee injury forced an early retirement in 1976, but she was persuaded by Ashton to dance again five years later to great acclaim. In 1991 she became president of the Royal Academy of Dancing, and was given the honorary title of Dame Commander, Order of the British Empire, in 1996.

Sica, Vittorio De *See* **De Sica, Vittorio**

Sickert, Walter Richard 1860–1942 •*British artist*• Born in Munich, Germany, of mixed Dutch and Danish parentage, after three years on the English stage he studied at the Slade School and under **James McNeill Whistler**. While working in Paris, he was much influenced by **Degas**, and he used Degas's technique to illustrate London lowlife. He was a member of the New English Art Club, and about 1910 the Camden Town Group (later the London Group) was formed under his leadership. His famous interior *Ennui* belongs to this period. Both his painting and his writings on art have had great influence on later English painters.

Siddiqui, Kalim 1933–96 •*British Muslim leader and spokesman*• He was born near Hyderabad, India, and moved with his family to Pakistan after partition in 1947. He went to the UK in 1954 to pursue a career in journalism, and became increasingly involved in Muslim affairs, founding the Muslim Institute in London in 1972. After the Iranian Revolution of 1979, he became more radical, calling for a Muslim parliament and the publication of a Muslim manifesto. He was a strong supporter of the fatwa against **Salman Rushdie** (1989).

Siddons, Sarah, *née* **Kemble** 1755–1831 •*English actress*• She was born in Brecon, Wales, the eldest child of Roger Kemble (1721–1892), manager of a small traveling theatrical company, of which Sarah was a member from her earliest childhood. In 1773 she married her fellow actor, William Siddons. Her first appearance at Drury Lane in 1775, as Portia, was unremarkable, but her reputation grew quickly and she soon became the unquestioned queen of the English stage. In 1803 she followed her brother **John Philip Kemble** to Covent Garden, where she stayed until her farewell appearance as Lady Macbeth in 1812. Her gifts and her expressive and beautiful face, queenly figure and rich, flexible voice gave her great distinction as a tragic actress.

Sidgwick, Henry 1838–1900 •*English philosopher*• Born in Skipton, Yorkshire, he was educated at Rugby School and Cambridge, where he became Knightbridge Professor of Moral Philosophy (1883). His best-known work, *Methods of Ethics* (1874), contains a sophisticated and distinctive development of the utilitarian theories of **John Stuart Mill**. He was a founder and the first president of the Society for Psychical Research (1882). He was also active in promoting higher education for women and was involved in founding (1871) the precursor to Newnham College, Cambridge (1880). His wife, Eleanor Balfour (the sister of **Arthur James Balfour**), became principal of Newnham (1892–1910).

Sidmouth, Henry Addington, 1st Viscount 1757–1844 •*English politician*• Born in London, he was educated at Winchester and Brasenose College, Oxford. He became a Member of Parliament in 1783, and was elected Speaker of the House of Commons (1789–1801). When **William Pitt** the Younger resigned in 1801, he formed the administration which negotiated the Peace of Amiens in 1802. He was created Viscount Sidmouth in 1805 and held several Cabinet posts. As home secretary (1812–21) he took severe measures against Luddite rioters and suspended the Habeas Corpus Act; it was in his period of office that the Peterloo Massacre took place in Manchester in 1819.

Sidney or **Sydney, Algernon** c.1622–83 •*English politician*• Born probably in Penshurst, Kent, the grandnephew of Sir **Philip Sidney** and second son of the second Earl of Leicester, he was wounded during the English civil war at Marston Moor (1644), fighting on the parliamentary side. He was elected to the Long Parliament in 1645, but retired in 1653 on **Cromwell**'s usurpation of power. After the Restoration he lived on the Continent until 1677. He was always thought dangerous and unreliable, and in 1683 he was implicated in the Rye House Plot to kill **Charles II**, found guilty on slender evidence and beheaded.

Sidney, Sir Philip 1554–86 •*English poet and patron*• Born in Penshurst, Kent, he was the eldest son of Sir Henry Sidney (lord deputy of Ireland). He was educated at Shrewsbury School and Christ Church, Oxford, and from 1572 to 1575 he traveled and studied on the Continent. Returning to England, he was knighted in 1582 and appointed governor of Flushing in 1585. He spent his last year in the Netherlands, where he successfully plotted an attack on the town of Axel; he later led an assault on a Spanish convoy transporting arms to Zutphen, was shot in the thigh and died from the infection. His work, none of which was published in his lifetime, includes *Arcadia* (1590), *Astrophel and Stella* (1591) and *A Defence of Poetry* (1595). He bestowed patronage on a number of poets, notably **Edmund Spenser**.

“ ”

Poetry therefore, is an art of imitation … A speaking picture, with this end: to teach and delight.

1595 ***A Defence of Poetry.***

Sieff (of Brimpton), Israel Moses Sieff, Baron 1889–1972 •*English businessman*• Born in Manchester, he was educated at Manchester Grammar School and the University of Manchester. A schoolfellow of **Simon Marks**, together they developed the business called Marks and Spencer. He was joint managing director of the company from 1926 to 1967 and succeeded Lord Marks as chairman (1964–67). His younger son, Marcus Joseph (1913–2001), who took a life peerage in 1980 as Lord Sieff of Brimpton, was chairman of Marks and Spencer from 1972 to 1984, president 1984–85 and honorary president 1985–2001.

Siegbahn, Kai Mann Börje 1918– •*Swedish physicist and Nobel Prize winner*• He was born in Lund, the son of **Karl Siegbahn**, and was educated at Stockholm University, where he was Professor of Physics at the Royal Institute of Technology until 1954, and thereafter professor at Uppsala University (1954–84). In the early 1950s his studies on the energies of electrons emitted from solids exposed to X-rays revealed sharp peaks at energies which were characteristic of the materials. This technique became known as ESCA (electron spectroscopy for chemical analysis), and was later extended for use with liquids and gases. He shared the 1981 Nobel Prize for physics with Nicolaas Bloembergen (1920–) and **Arthur Schawlow** for his work in developing high-resolution electron spectroscopy.

Siegbahn, Karl Manne Georg 1886–1978 •*Swedish physicist and Nobel Prize winner*• Born in Örebro, he was educated at Lund University, and became a professor there (1920) and at Uppsala University (1923). From 1937 he was a professor at the Royal Academy of Sciences and director of the Nobel Institute for Physics at Stockholm University. Improving on previous techniques, he succeeded in producing X-rays of various wavelengths and penetrating power, the discovery of which reinforced **Aage Niels Bohr**'s shell model of the atom. He was awarded the Nobel Prize for physics in 1924. In the same year he showed that X-rays could be refracted, like light, by means of a prism.

Siegel, Jerry 1914–96 •*US cartoonist*• Born in Cleveland, Ohio, he met **Joseph Shuster** at high school, where they published their own science-fiction magazine. After a series of strips for various comic books, they created *Superman* for *Action Comics* in 1938. It became an instant success, leading to huge spinoffs in films and television.

Siemens, Ernst Werner von 1816–92 •*German electrical engineer*• He was born in Lenthe, Hanover. In 1834 he entered the Prussian artillery, and in 1844 took charge of the artillery workshops in Berlin. He developed the telegraphic system in Prussia, discovered the insulating property of gutta-percha, and devoted himself to making telegraphic and electrical apparatus. In 1847 he established factories for making telegraphy equipment in Berlin and elsewhere (in 1867 the business became known as Siemens Brothers). Besides devising numerous forms of galvanometers and other electrical instruments, he was one of the discoverers of the self-acting dynamo. He determined the electrical resistance of different substances, and the SI unit of electrical conductance was named after him. He was the brother of Sir **William Siemens**.

Siemens, Sir (Charles) William, *originally* **Karl Wilhelm Siemens** 1823–83 •*British electrical engineer*• He was born in Lenthe, Hanover, Germany, and was educated in Lübeck, Magdeburg, and Göttingen. In 1843 he visited England to introduce a process for electrogilding which he invented with his brother, **Ernst Werner von Siemens**, and in 1844 he patented his differential governor. He became a British citizen in 1859. As manager in England of the firm of Siemens Brothers, he was actively engaged in the construction of telegraphs, designed the steamship *Faraday* for cable laying, and in 1861 designed an open-hearth regenerative steel furnace which became the most widely used in the world. Other inventions included a water meter, pyrometer and bathometer. He was knighted in 1883.

Sieyès, Emmanuel Joseph, *called* **the Abbé Sieyès** 1748–1836 •*French cleric and political theorist*• Born in Fréjus, he studied theology. He became canon at Tréguier (1775), then chancellor and vicar general of Chartres (1788). His three pamphlets gained him popularity: *Vues sur les moyens d'exécution* (1788, "Views on the Methods of Execution"), *Essai sur les privilèges* (1788, "Essay on the Privileged") and, the most famous of all, *Qu'est-ce que le tiers-état?* (1789, "What Is the Third Estate?"). He was elected to the Estates General, and was one of the founders of the Jacobin club. As the French Revolution became more extreme, he withdrew from center stage, and became famous for his reply to the question as to what he had done during the revolution: "I survived." In 1799 he was a leading figure in the Brumaire coup that brought **Napoleon I** to power. He was exiled at the Restoration (1815) but returned to Paris in 1830, following the July Revolution.

Sigismund 1368–1437 •*Holy Roman emperor*• The younger son of Emperor **Charles IV**, he became king of Hungary (1387) as husband of Mary, daughter of Louis I (the Great), after defeating his Angevin rival Charles of Durazzo, king of Naples. He was also king of Bohemia (1419) and of Lombardy (1431). His dominions were continually eroded by Venetians, Angevins and Turks, who defeated him and his crusading allies at Nicopolis (1396). As emperor (from 1410) he failed to provide the safe conduct he had granted **Jan Huss**, which led to Huss being burned and ultimately to the Hussite wars (1420–33). A year before his death he negotiated a compromise settlement which allowed his return as king.

Sigismund III Vasa 1566–1632 •*King of Poland and of Sweden*• Born in Gripsholm, the Catholic son of King Johan III of Sweden and nephew of Sigismund II Augustus of Poland, he was elected to the Polish throne in 1587. In 1592 he succeeded his father as king of Sweden (1592–99), but before his coronation (1594), his uncle, the future **Karl IX**, promoted a convention renouncing Catholicism in Sweden, and after Sigismund's return to Poland, Karl ruled as regent. In 1598 he was defeated by Karl at Stångebro, and for several years he tried without success to regain the Swedish throne. In 1609 he invaded Russia in pursuit of the Russian crown and captured Moscow and Smolensk, causing his son Ladislas to be temporarily elected czar. He was succeeded in Poland by his son, Ladislas IV Vasa.

Signac, Paul 1863–1935 •*French artist*• He was born in Paris. He exhibited with the Impressionists in 1884 and was later associated with Henri Edmond Cross (1856–1910) and **Georges Seurat** in the Neoimpressionist movement. Signac, however, used mosaic-like patches of pure color, as compared with Seurat's pointillist dots. He published *D'Eugène Delacroix au Néo-impressionisme*, in which he sought to establish a scientific basis for his divisionist theories (1899).

Signorelli, Luca c. 1441–1523 •*Italian painter*• Born in Cortona, he worked, especially in frescoes, in Loreto, Rome, Florence, Siena, Cortona and Orvieto. Orvieto Cathedral contains his greatest works, the frescoes of *The Preaching of Anti-Christ* and *Last Judgment* (1499–1504), which display his great technical skill in the drawing of male nudes.

Sigurdsson, Sverrir *See* **Sverrir Sigurdsson**

Sihanouk, King Norodom 1922– •*Cambodian (Kampuchean) politician*• Educated in Vietnam and Paris, he was elected king of Cambodia in 1941. He negotiated the country's independence from France (1949–53) before abdicating (1955) in favor of his father so as to become an elected leader under the new constitution. As prime minister and, after his father's death (1960), head of state, he steered a neutral course during the Vietnam War. In 1970 he was deposed in a right-wing military coup led by the US-backed lieutenant general Lon Nol. Fleeing to Beijing (Peking), he formed a joint resistance front with **Pol Pot**, which successfully overthrew Lon Nol (1975), was ousted by the communist Khmer Rouge (1976), and led to the government-in-exile in North Korea, which sought to overthrow the Vietnamese-installed puppet regime in Cambodia. After the withdrawal of Vietnamese troops (1989), he was elected king in 1993.

Sikorski, Władysław 1881–1943 •*Polish statesman and soldier*• Born in Galicia, he joined the underground movement for Polish freedom from czarist rule. He served under General **Józef Piłsudski** (1867–1935) as head of the war department, and after the Treaty of Brest-Litovsk was imprisoned by the Austrians. In 1921 he became commander in chief and in 1922 was elected premier. After Piłsudski's coup d'état (1926), he retired to Paris. He returned to Poland in 1938 and advocated a strong alliance with Great Britain and France, and on the invasion of Poland became commander in chief of the Free Polish forces and leader in London of the Polish government-in-exile from June 1940. He was killed in an air crash over Gibraltar.

Sikorsky, Igor Ivan 1889–1972 •*US aeronautical engineer*• Born in Kiev, Ukraine, he began experimenting with building helicopters in 1909, and turned to aircraft, building and flying the first four-engine airplane in 1913. He emigrated to Paris (1918) and to the US (1919), where he founded the Sikorsky Aero Engineering Corporation (1923). He built several flying boats and in 1939 the first successful helicopter, the VS-300. He became a US citizen in 1928.

“ ”

The work of the individual still remains the spark that moves mankind ahead, even more than teamwork.

*Quoted in his **New York Times** obituary, October 27, 1972.*

Sillanpää, Frans Eemil 1888–1964 •*Finnish novelist and Nobel Prize winner*• He was born in Hämeenkyrö, of a peasant family, and the themes of his work reflect his background. His major books are *Hurskas kurjuus* (1919, "Meek Heritage"), a novel about the Finnish civil war, *Nuorena nukkunut* (1931, Eng trans *The Maid Silja*, 1931), about the collapse of traditional values in Finland, and *Ihmiset suviyössä* (1934, "People in the Summer Night"). He was the foremost Finnish writer of his time, and received the 1939 Nobel Prize for literature.

Sillitoe, Alan 1928– •*English novelist and short-story writer*• Born in Nottingham, he left school to work in a bicycle factory at the age of 14, and served as a wireless operator in the RAF (1946–49). He lived in France and Spain (1952–58), and began writing while convalescing from tuberculosis. He achieved a major success with his first novel, *Saturday Night and Sunday Morning* (1958), with its energetic young antihero, Arthur Seaton. The film based on the novel, for which he wrote the screenplay (1960), profoundly influenced the British film industry. The stories in *The Loneliness of the Long Distance Runner* (1959) were equally acclaimed. The outsider struggling in a brutal society is a recurring theme in his subsequent and more overtly political novels and stories, which include *Key to the Door* (1962), *Last Loves* (1991) and *Leonard's War* (1991). He has written plays and screenplays from his novels, several volumes of poems, plays, children's books and an autobiography.

Sills, Beverly, *originally* **Belle Miriam Silverman** 1929– •*US soprano*• Born in Brooklyn, New York, of Russian-Jewish descent, she had a varied and remarkable career as a child star and made her operatic debut in 1947. She later appeared with various US companies, including the New York City Opera (from 1955) and the Metropolitan Opera, as well as performing in Vienna and Buenos Aires (1967), at La Scala in Milan (1969), Covent Garden, London, and the Deutsche Oper Berlin (1970). An intelligent and dramatically gifted coloratura, she retired from the stage at the age of 50 to become general director of New York City Opera (1979–89), chairwoman of Lincoln Center (1994–2002), and chairwoman of the Metropolitan Opera (2002–). She published her autobiography, *Beverly*, in 1987.

Silvers, Phil, *originally* **Philip Silver** 1912–85 •*US comic actor*• Born in Brownsville, Brooklyn, New York, he made his Broadway debut in *Yokel Boy* (1939). After signing a contract with MGM, he appeared in supporting roles in films such as *Tom, Dick and Harry* (1941) and *Cover Girl* (1944). After World War II, he enjoyed notable Broadway hits with *High Button Shoes* (1947) and *Top Banana* (1951), for which he received a Tony Award. The television series *The Phil Silvers Show* (1955–59) earned him three Emmy Awards and established him irrevocably as Sergeant Bilko, "a Machiavellian clown in uniform," forever pursuing get-rich-quick schemes with fast-talking bravado. He achieved further Broadway success in *Do Re Me* (1960) and *A Funny Thing Happened on the Way to the Forum* (1972, Tony Award).

Silvia 1943– •*Queen of Sweden*• She was born in Heidelberg as Silvia Renate Sommerlath, the daughter of a West German businessman, Walther Sommerlath, and his Brazilian wife, Alice (*née* Soares de Toledo). In 1971 she was appointed chief hostess on the Organization Committee for the Olympic Games in Munich (1972), where she met Carl Gustaf (**Carl XVI Gustaf**), who was then heir to the Swedish throne. They were married (1976) and have three children, Crown Princess Victoria (1977–), Prince Carl Philip (1979–) and Princess Madeleine (1982–).

Sim, Alastair 1900–76 •*Scottish actor*• Born in Edinburgh and destined to follow in the family tailoring business, he was pulled elsewhere by his theatrical interests. Extensive stage work, including a season with the Old Vic, led to his film debut in *Riverside Murder* (1935). His lugubrious manner, distinctive features and inimitable vocal range made him a valued performer, and he was equally at home in comic or sinister characterizations. His numerous films include *Green for Danger* (1946), *The Happiest Days of Your Life* (1950), *Scrooge* (1951), *Laughter in Paradise* (1951) and *The Belles of St. Trinians* (1954). Onstage he enjoyed a long association with playwright James Bridie (1888–1951) and appeared in *The Tempest* (1962), *The Magistrate* (1969), *Dandy Dick* (1973) and many others.

Simak, Clifford Donald 1904–88 •*US science-fiction writer*• He was born in Milville, Wisconsin, of an immigrant Czech father and a US mother. During the Depression he entered journalism in Michigan and started publishing science-fiction stories in 1931. His major work was the story sequence *City* (1952), a chronicle in which dogs and robots take over a world abandoned by humans. He also wrote *Way Station* (1962) and *All Flesh Is Grass* (1965).

Sima Qian (Ssu-ma Ch'ien) c. 145–87 BC •*Chinese historian*• He succeeded his father, Sima Tan (Ssu-ma T'an), in 110 BC as grand astrologer, but incurred Emperor Wudi's wrath for taking the part of a friend who, in command of a military expedition, had surrendered to the enemy. Sima Qian was imprisoned for three years and castrated, but was gradually restored to favor. He is chiefly remembered for the *Shi Ji*, a history of China.

Sima Xiangru (Ssu-ma Hsiang-ju) 179–117 BC •*Chinese poet*• Born in Chengdu, Sichuan (Szechuan) province, he wrote the poem *Zi Xu Fu*, describing and denouncing the pleasures of the hunt, which holds an important place in Chinese literary history.

Simenon, Georges Joseph Christian 1903–89 •*French novelist*• He was born in Liège, Belgium, and at the age of 16 began work as a journalist on the *Gazette de Liège*. He moved to Paris in 1922 and became a prolific writer of popular fiction, writing under many pseudonyms. He also wrote more serious psychological novels, much admired but neglected in favor of almost a hundred short, economical novels featuring Jules Maigret, the dogged pipe-smoking detective, now known the world over, partly through film and television adaptations. The first two in the series were published in 1931: *M. Gallet décède* (Eng trans *The Death of Monsieur Gallet*, 1932) and *Le pendu de Saint-Pholien* (Eng trans *The Crime of Inspector Maigret*, 1933). In all, he published more than 500 novels and innumerable short stories.

Simeon Stylites, St AD 387–459 •*Syrian Christian ascetic*• Born in Sisan, Cilicia (near modern Aleppo, Syria), he became widely known as a miracle worker. In c. 420 AD, he established himself on top of a pillar about 65 feet (20 m) high in Telanessa, near Antioch, where he spent the rest of his life preaching to crowds. His many imitators were known as *stylites*. His feast day is January 5 (in Western churches) or September 1 (in Eastern churches).

Simnel, Lambert c. 1477–c. 1525 •*English pretender*• The son of a joiner, he bore a resemblance to **Edward IV**, and was carefully coached (1487) by an Oxford priest, Roger Symonds, before being set up in Ireland as, first, the younger son of Edward IV, and then as the Duke of **Clarence**'s son, Edward, Earl of Warwick (1475–99). Simnel achieved some success in Ireland and was crowned in Dublin as Edward VI (1487), but, landing in Lancashire with 2,000 German mercenaries, he was defeated at Stoke Field, Nottinghamshire (1487), and subsequently became a royal scullion and falconer.

Simon the Canaanite *See* **Simon the Zealot, St**

Simon the Zealot, St, *also called* **Simon Zelotes** and **Simon the Canaanite** 1st century AD •*One of the 12 Apostles of Jesus*• He may have belonged to the Jewish nationalist party (the Zealots). He is not mentioned in the New Testament after Pentecost, although traditions associate him with Edessa, the place of his death. In Western traditions he preached in Egypt before joining St **Jude** in Persia (Iran), where both were martyred. The Feast of St Simon and St Jude is October 28 (in Western churches) or August 21 (Eastern Orthodox).

Simon, Carly 1945– •*US composer and singer*• Born in New York City, she began her career in 1964, recording with her sister Lucy as the Simon Sisters. She received a Grammy for Best New Artist in 1971, the year of her hit songs "That's the Way I Always Heard It Should Be" and "Anticipation." Her single "Let the River Run" for the 1988 film *Working Girl* won an Academy Award for best original song in 1989. Among her other singles are "You're So Vain" and the James Bond film theme, "Nobody Does It Better."

Simon, Claude Henri Eugène 1913– •*French novelist and Nobel Prize winner*• Born in Tananarive, Madagascar, the son of a cavalry officer who was killed during World War I, he was raised by his mother in Perpignan, France. He was educated at the Collège Stanislas, Paris, and briefly at Oxford and Cambridge Universities, and studied painting before serving in the French cavalry. In World War II he joined the Resistance in Perpignan. The absence of story, time and punctuation is his hallmark, and his style is rich, sensuous and complex. *Le vent* (1957, Eng trans *The Wind*, 1959) and *La route des Flandres* (1960, Eng trans *The Flanders Road*, 1962) are his most important novels, both eloquently expressing his innate pessimism. In 1985 he was awarded the Nobel Prize for literature.

Simon, Sir Francis Eugene 1893–1956 •*German physicist*• Born in Berlin, he studied physics (1912) at the University of Munich. By 1927 he was professor at the University in Berlin, and in 1931 was appointed director of the Physical Chemistry Laboratory at the University of Breslau. With the rise of Nazism he left Germany for Oxford at the invitation of physicist Frederick Lindemann (Lord Cherwell). He verified experimentally the third law of thermodynamics, and under his guidance Oxford became one of the world's leading centers for the study of low-temperature physics. Involvement in the atomic energy and weapons project (1940–46) earned him the honorary title of Commander, Order of the British Empire (1946). He was elected a Fellow of the Royal Society in 1941, and knighted in 1954.

Simon, (Marvin) Neil 1927– •*US dramatist*• Born in New York City and educated at New York University, he achieved a hit with his first comedy, *Come Blow Your Horn* (1961). His stage works include the musical farce *Little Me* (1962), *Barefoot in the Park* (1963), *The Odd Couple* (1965), the musical *Promises, Promises* (1968), *The Prisoner of Second Avenue* (1972) and *The Sunshine Boys* (1972). Moving from New York to California, he had another hit with *California Suite* (1976). *Chapter Two* opened in 1977, and in 1979 his fourth musical, *They're Playing Our Song*, gave him another hit. Later he produced a semiautobiographical trilogy: *Brighton Beach Memoirs* (1983), *Biloxi Blues* (1985) and *Broadway Bound* (1986). More recent works include *Lost in Yonkers* (1991), which won him a Pulitzer Prize and a Tony Award, and *London Suite* (1995).

Simon, Paul 1941– •*US singer, songwriter and guitarist*• He was born in Newark, New Jersey. One of the finest pop lyricists in the US, Simon originally worked with Art Garfunkel (1941–) at the age of 15 (when they were known as Tom and Gerry), but he also pursued a solo career under various pseudonyms before "The Sound of Silence" (1965) brought the duo their first major success. In 1968 Simon's songs were used in the soundtrack of the film *The Graduate*, one of the first major films to incorporate rock music in this way. The duo's *Bridge Over Troubled Water* was the most successful album of the early 1970s. After separating from Garfunkel (1971), Simon returned to a solo career, releasing his album *Paul Simon* in 1972. Regular albums followed, including *Graceland* (1986), which featured the work of several South African musicians. One of his film roles was in **Woody Allen**'s *Annie Hall* (1977).

Simon, Richard 1638–1712 •*French theologian and biblical critic*• Born in Dieppe, he entered the Oratory in 1659. His criticisms of **Antoine Arnauld** caused great displeasure among the Port-Royalists, and the scandal caused by the liberalism of his *Histoire critique du Vieux Testament* (1678, "Critical History of the Old Testament"), in which he denied that **Moses** was the author of the Pentateuch, led to his expulsion from the order. Few writers of his age played a more prominent part in polemics. His suppressed *Histoire critique* (Eng trans 1682) often anticipates the later German rationalists and is the first work to treat the Bible as a literary product.

Simone, Nina, *professional name of* **Eunice Kathleen Waymon** 1933–2003 •*US singer, pianist and composer*• Born in Tryon, North Carolina, she was a gifted child pianist and her hometown raised cash for her musical education at the Juilliard School in New York City, although she later claimed that her classical ambitions were frustrated by racist attitudes. She became a nightclub singer in Atlantic City and began writing her own highly charged and often overtly political material in the early 1960s. Her first hit was **George Gershwin**'s "I Loves You, Porgy" in 1959, but later songs such as "Mississippi Goddam," a response to the racial murder of children, were more typical. In the later 1960s Simone left the US to live in Africa and then Europe.

Simonides of Ceos 556–468 BC •*Greek lyric poet*• Born on the island of Ceos, he celebrated the heroes and the battles of the Persian Wars in elegies, epigrams, odes and dirges. He won poetical contests 56 times, and his elegy on the heroes who fell at Marathon in 490 BC was preferred to that of **Aeschylus**, who had fought in the battle. Many stories and anecdotes about him circulated in antiquity, and he was noted for a fondness for money. A handful of epigrams in the Greek Anthology are all that survive of his work.

Simon Magus, *known as* **Simon the Magician** 1st century AD •*New Testament Samaritan sorcerer*• According to the New Testament (Acts 8), he became influential in Samaria through his magic. He was converted by the preaching of Philip the Evangelist and tried to buy the power of the Holy Spirit from **Peter** and **John** (hence the term "simony"). The apocryphal Acts of Peter (2nd century AD) describes the rivalry between Simon Magus and Simon Peter.

Simonov, Konstantin Mikhailovich 1915–79 •*Russian writer*• Born in Petrograd (now St Petersburg), he became a journalist and war correspondent in Mongolia (1934–38), and much of his best writing came out of his experiences in World War II, including his novel about the defense of Stalingrad, *Dni i nochi* (1945, Eng trans *Days and Nights*, 1945). He achieved a considerable reputation with his historical poem about Alexander Nevsky, his poems of World War II and the play *Russkye liudi* (1943, Eng trans *The Russians*, 1944).

Simpson, George Gaylord 1902–84 •*US paleontologist*• Born in Chicago and educated at the University of Colorado and at Yale, he joined the staff of the American Museum of Natural History in New York City in 1927, and from 1959 to 1970 taught at Harvard. He is considered one of the leading 20th-century paleontologists, and he proposed a classification of mammals which is now standard. Although mainly concerned with taxonomy, after World War II he devoted himself to demonstrating that the neo-Darwinian ideas of geneticists such as **Ernst Mayr** and **Theodosius Dobzhansky** could be reconciled with the paleontological evidence. His influential books were concerned with the fusion of paleontology and evolutionary genetics. Some of his ideas are presented in popular form in *The Meaning of Evolution* (1949).

Simpson, Helen de Guerry 1897–1940 •*British writer*• Born in Sydney, Australia, she gained notice for her novel *Boomerang* (1932), which despite its title had little Australian content. Her historical novel *Under Capricorn* (1937), a story of Sydney in the early 1800s, was filmed by **Alfred Hitchcock** in 1949, and nine further novels followed, including *Saraband for Dead Lovers* (1935), which was also filmed, and three in collaboration with **Clemence Dane**. Other writings include historical biographies.

Simpson, Sir James Young 1811–70 •*Scottish obstetrician and pioneer of anesthesia*• Born in Bathgate, West Lothian, he went to the University of Edinburgh at the age of 14, and became Professor of Midwifery in 1840. He originated the use of ether as an anesthetic in childbirth (1847) and, experimenting on himself and his assistants in the search for a better anesthetic, discovered the required properties in chloroform (November 1847). He championed its use against medical and religious opposition until its use on Queen **Victoria** at the birth of Prince **Leopold II** (1853) signaled general acceptance. He was made a baronet in 1866.

Simpson, John (Cody Fidler-) 1944– •*English broadcaster and author*• Born in Cleveleys, Lancashire, he studied at Magdalen College, Cambridge. He began his career in 1970 as a reporter and correspondent for BBC Radio, later moving to BBC television as world affairs editor (1988–). He is known for his reportage from the world's trouble spots, and his extensive journalistic experience has also included a stint as associate editor of the *Spectator* (1991–96). His publications include books on the Persian Gulf, Eastern Europe and South America.

Simpson, O(renthal) J(ames) 1947– •*US football player*• He was born in San Francisco. He played for the University of Southern California, turning professional with the Buffalo Bills (1969–77) and San Francisco 49ers (1978–79). He combined blistering pace with an astute strategical sense, and in 1973 established a record of 2,003 yards gained in rushing. After retiring from football he became a popular commentator and film actor. After the fatal stabbings of his former wife, Nicole Brown Simpson, and her friend Ronald Goldman in 1994, Simpson was charged with murder, and his televised trial became a media circus, which ended with his acquittal in 1995. The relatives of the victims brought a successful civil suit against him in 1996, charging him with wrongful death, and were awarded substantial damages.

“ ”

Absolutely 100 percent not guilty.

1994 Plea on arraignment for the murder of his estranged wife. Reported in the ***New York Times****, July 23.*

Simpson, Wallis, Duchess of Windsor, *née* **Bessie Wallis Warfield** 1896–1986 •*US socialite, wife of Edward, Duke of Windsor*• She was born in Blue Ridge Summit, Pennsylvania. She divorced her second husband, Ernest Simpson, in order to marry **Edward VIII**, who abdicated the throne (1936) to marry her (1937). Estranged from the British royal family, they lived in France and the Bahamas. After Edward's death she lived in Paris, virtually a recluse. She published her autobiography, *The Heart Has Its Reasons*, in 1956.

Sinatra, Frank (Francis Albert) 1915–98 •*US singer and film actor*• Born in Hoboken, New Jersey, he started his long and successful career as a recording artist singing with the bands of Harry James and **Tommy Dorsey** on radio, becoming a teen idol. He made his film debut in musicals in 1941, leading to films such as *Anchors Aweigh* (1945) and *On the Town* (1949). His appeal declined until he won an Academy Award as Best Supporting Actor for his role in *From Here to Eternity* (1953). This led to more film work, notably in *The Man With the Golden Arm* (1955), *Pal Joey* (1957), *The Manchurian Candidate* (1962) and *The Detective* (1968). His revival as an actor led to new singing opportunities, and he produced an impressive series of recordings (1956–65), notably the albums *For Swinging Lovers*, *Come Fly With Me* and *That's Life*. He was a top concert performer into the 1990s. He was married four times; his wives included **Ava Gardner** and **Mia Farrow**.

Sinclair, Sir Clive Marles 1940– •*English electronic engineer and inventor*• He attended St George's College, Weybridge, and worked in publishing before launching his own electronics research and manufacturing company, Sinclair Radionics Ltd (1958), which developed and successfully marketed a wide range of calculators, miniature television sets and personal computers. He later embarked on the manufacture of a small three-wheeled "personal transport" vehicle powered by a washing-machine motor and rechargeable batteries. It was widely condemned as unsafe and impractical, and its failure led to a period of retrenchment in Sinclair's business activities. He was knighted in 1983.

Sinclair, May (Mary Amelia) 1863–1946 •*English novelist*• Born in Rock Ferry, Cheshire, she was the daughter of a shipping magnate. She was educated at Cheltenham Ladies' College, and became an advocate of women's suffrage. She also took an interest in psychoanalysis, as revealed in some of her 24 novels. They include *The Divine Fire* (1904), *The Creators* (1910) and *The Dark Night* (1924). In books such as *The Life and Death of Harriett Frean* (1922) she adopted the stream-of-consciousness style of writing. She also wrote books on philosophical idealism.

Sinclair, Upton Beall 1878–1968 •*US novelist and social reformer*• Born in Baltimore, Maryland, he horrified the world with his exposure of meat-packing conditions in Chicago in his novel *The Jungle* (1906), which resulted in the passing by Congress of a Pure Food and Drug Bill. Later novels such as *Metropolis* (1908), *King Coal* (1917), *Oil!* (1927) and *Boston* (1928) were increasingly influenced by his socialist beliefs, and he was for many years prominent in California politics. He also wrote a monumental 11-volume series about Lanny Budd, including *Dragon's Teeth* (1942), which won the Pulitzer Prize.

Sinden, Sir Donald 1923– •*English actor*• He was born in Plymouth. After performing comedies for the armed forces on tour, he joined the Shakespeare Memorial Theatre company at Stratford-upon-Avon in 1946, and the Old Vic company in 1948. He alternated between classical roles with the Royal Shakespeare Company, such as Malvolio in *Twelfth Night* (1969, 1970), and lightweight comedy in the West End, and in later years turned to farce. During the 1950s he appeared in films during a five-year period, and for several seasons he played an English butler in the television comedy series *Two's Company*. He was knighted in 1997.

Singer, Isaac Bashevis 1904–91 •*US Yiddish writer and Nobel Prize winner*• He was born in Radzymin, Poland, the son of a rabbi and the brother of Esther and **Israel Joshua Singer**. He was educated at the Tachkemoni Rabbinical Seminary in Warsaw (1920–22), and worked for ten years as a proofreader and translator. He emigrated to the US in 1935, where he joined his brother working as a journalist. A firm believer in storytelling rather than commentary by the author, he set his novels and short stories among the Jews of Poland, Germany and the US, combining a deep psychological insight with dramatic and visual impact. He was awarded the Nobel Prize for literature in 1978. His novels include *The Magician of Lublin* (1960), *The Manor* (1967) and *Enemies: A Love Story* (1972). Among his short-story collections are *Gimpel the Fool and Other Stories* (1957) and *A Crown of Feathers* (1973). He also wrote a play, *Schlemiel the First* (1974), and many stories for children.

Singer, Isaac Merritt 1811–75 •*US inventor and manufacturer*• Born in Pittstown, New York, he patented a rock drill in 1839, a carving machine in 1849 and at Boston in 1852 an improved single-thread, chain-stitch sewing machine. He was sued by Elias Howe (1819–67) for infringement of patent for the so-called Howe needle, but despite having to pay compensation, he established the success of his Singer Manufacturing Company.

Singer, Israel Joshua 1893–1944 •*US Yiddish writer*• Born in Bilgorai, Poland, the brother of Esther and **Isaac Bashevis Singer**, he studied at the Rabbinical Yeshivah School in Warsaw. After World War I, he became a journalist in Kiev and emigrated to the US in 1933. His novels have been widely translated and include *Yoshe Kalt* (1933, Eng trans *The Sinner*), *The Brothers Ashkenazi* (1936), *The River Breaks Up* (1938) and *East of Eden* (1939).

Singh, V(ishwanath) P(ratap) 1931– •*Indian statesman*• Born in Allahabad, Uttar Pradesh, the son of an influential local raja, he was educated at the Universities of Pune and Allahabad. In 1971 he was elected to the Lok Sabha (federal parliament) as a representative of the Congress (I) Party. During the administrations of **Indira Gandhi** and **Rajiv Gandhi**, he served as minister of finance (1984–86) and minister of defense (1986–87). In 1987 he was ousted from the government and Congress (I) when he exposed the Bofors scandal, which involved payments for arms deals to senior officials closely connected with Rajiv Gandhi. He was elected prime minister in 1990, but in November of that year he was defeated on a vote of no confidence and was succeeded by Chandra Shekhar.

Siqueiros, David Alfaro 1896–1974 •*Mexican mural painter*• Born in Chihuahua, he was a revolutionary from his youth and fought in **Francisco Madero**'s revolution of 1910–11 which overthrew **Porfirio Díaz**. With **Diego Rivera** and **José Orozco**, he launched the review *El machete* in Mexico City in 1922, and painted the frescoes for the National Preparatory School there. He was frequently imprisoned for revolutionary activities. He was expelled from the US in 1932, and during the 1930s he worked in South America. In 1944 he founded the Center of Realist Art in Mexico City. One of the principal figures in 20th-century Mexican mural painting, his most-celebrated works include *From Porfirio's Dictatorship to the Revolution* (National History Museum).

Siraj-ud-Dawlah *See* **Suraja Dowlah**

Sirhan, Sirhan c. 1943– •*US assassin of Senator Robert Kennedy*• Born in Palestine, he was a refugee whose family settled in

Pasadena, California in 1956. Sirhan was angered by the pro-Israeli stance taken by Robert Kennedy in his campaign for the presidential nomination in 1968. On the night of June 5, 1968, he shot Kennedy in the head as the senator passed through the Ambassador Hotel in Los Angeles on his way to a victory press conference. He was found guilty of premeditated murder in the first degree and sentenced to life imprisonment.

Sisley, Alfred 1839–99 •*French Impressionist painter and etcher*• Born in Paris of English ancestry, he joined **Claude Monet** and **Renoir** in the studio of Charles Gleyre (1806–74) and was also influenced by **Camille Corot**. He painted mostly landscapes, particularly the valleys of the Seine, the Loire and the Thames, and was noted for his subtle treatment of skies.

Sisulu, Walter Max Ulyate 1912–2003 •*South African nationalist*• He was born in Transkei. After working as a laborer in Johannesburg and then running a real estate agency, he joined the African National Congress (ANC) in 1940, becoming treasurer of the Youth League in 1944. A leader of the Program of Action in 1949, he was elected secretary-general of the ANC in the same year. He resigned his post in 1954 because of banning orders, but continued to work underground. Captured in 1963, he was found guilty of treason and sentenced to life imprisonment (1964). He was released in 1989 and took responsibility for the party's internal organization after its legalization in 1990, becoming deputy president of the ANC in 1991, a position he held until the 1994 election.

Sithole, Reverend Ndabaningi 1920–2000 •*Zimbabwean clergyman and politician*• He was a prominent member of the National Democratic Party and the Zimbabwe African People's Union (ZAPU) before becoming president of the Zimbabwean African National Union (ZANU) in 1963. With **Abel Muzorewa**, he was regarded as one of the more moderate advocates of independence based on majority rule and in 1978 was party to an agreement with prime minister **Ian Smith** for an internal constitutional settlement. This was, however, rejected as insufficient by **Robert Mugabe** and **Joshua Nkomo**, and by the United Nations. When an internationally accepted settlement was achieved in 1979, Sithole's power and influence declined.

Sitsky, Larry 1934– •*Australian composer, pianist and teacher*• He was born to Russian parents in Tientsin, northern China, where he made his piano debut at the age of 11. He emigrated to Australia in 1951 and attended the New South Wales Conservatorium of Music until 1955, and later studied in England and the US. Returning to Australia, he held various teaching positions. He is a prolific writer in many genres, and his vocal compositions include *Fall of the House of Usher* (1965), *Lenz* (1970) and *The Golem* (1979), all to libretti by **Gwen Harwood**. Orchestral and instrumental works include *Concerto for Wind Quintet and Orchestra* (1971), *Twenty-two Paths of the Tarot: Concerto for Piano and Orchestra* (1991) and *Sphinx: Concerto for Cello and Orchestra* (1993).

Sitter, Willem de 1872–1934 •*Dutch astronomer and cosmologist*• Born in Sneek, Friesland, he studied mathematics at the University of Groningen, but later became an astronomer at Cape Town Observatory. He returned to Groningen working as the assistant to Jacobus Kapteyn (1851–1922), was appointed director and Professor of Astronomy at Leiden University in 1908, and from 1919 was also director of the observatory there. His interest in **Einstein**'s theory of general relativity led to its publicity in Great Britain and other English-speaking countries, with important consequences for cosmology.

Sitting Bull, *Indian name* **Tatanka Iyotake** c. 1834–90 •*Native American warrior, chief of the Dakota Sioux*• Born near Grand River, South Dakota, he was a leader in the Sioux War (1876–77), and led the massacre of General **Custer** and his men at the Battle of Little Big Horn (1876). He escaped to Canada but surrendered in 1881, and was forced onto the reservation at Standing Rock. He was featured in Buffalo Bill **Cody**'s Wild West Show (1885), and was killed attempting to evade the police in the Ghost Dance uprising (1890).

Sitwell, Dame Edith Louisa 1887–1964 •*English poet*• Born in Scarborough, Yorkshire, she was the sister of **Osbert** and **Sacheverell Sitwell**. She had an unhappy childhood until her governess introduced her to music and literature, in particular the poetry of **Algernon Charles Swinburne** and the Symbolists. She first attracted notice when she edited an anthology of new poetry, *Wheels* (1916–21). The first volume of her own poetry, *Façade* (1923), with **William Walton**'s music, was given a controversial public reading in London. It was followed by *Bucolic Comedies* (1923), *The Sleeping Beauty* (1924) and *Elegy for Dead Fashion* (1926), the last two written in an elegiac Romantic style. During World War II she denounced human cruelty in works such as *The Song of the Cold* (1945). Other works include *The English Eccentrics* (1933) and *The Queens and the Hive* (1962). Her autobiography, *Taken Care Of*, was published posthumously in 1965.

“ ”

I enjoyed talking to her, but thought *nothing* of her writing. I considered her "a beautiful little knitter."

1955 Of Virginia Woolf. Letter to Geoffrey Singleton, July 11.

Sitwell, Sir (Francis) Osbert 1892–1969 •*English writer*• Born in London, the brother of **Edith** and **Sacheverell Sitwell**, he was educated at Eton. He served in the Brigade of Guards in World War I, and in 1916 was invalided home. This provided him with the opportunity to satirize war and the types of people who prosper ingloriously at home. Many of his satirical poems were collected in *Argonaut and Juggernaut* (1919) and *Out of the Flame* (1923). After the war he narrowed his literary acquaintance to his sister and brother, **Ezra Pound**, **T S Eliot** and **Wyndham Lewis**. The object of the group was the regeneration of arts and letters, and in this pursuit the Sitwells acquired notoriety, Osbert not least by his novel *Before the Bombardment* (1927), which anatomized the grandees of Scarborough and by implication the social orders in general. He also wrote short stories and travel books, and is known for his five-volume autobiographical series, which begins with *Left Hand: Right Hand* (1944).

Sitwell, Sir Sacheverell 1897–1988 •*English writer and art critic*• Born in Scarborough, North Yorkshire, the younger brother of **Edith** and **Osbert Sitwell**, he was educated at Eton before becoming an officer in a Guards regiment, enjoying extensive travel abroad. After World War I the brothers toured Spain and Italy. Sacheverell's study of European art resulted in *Southern Baroque Art* (1924), *German Baroque Art* (1927) and *The Gothic North* (1929). A prolific writer, he published poetry and is best remembered for his mannered but lively travel books and eccentric cultural commentaries, such as *Monks, Nuns and Monasteries* (1965).

Sixtus IV, *originally* **Francesco della Rovere** 1414–84 •*Italian pope*• Born in Cella Ligura, Genoa, he was a famous Franciscan preacher. He became a cardinal in 1467 and pope in 1471. Although he fostered learning and built the Sistine Chapel and the Sistine Bridge, he compromised the moral authority of the papacy. His alliance with the Venetians in 1482 led to a general Italian war.

Skanderbeg, *originally* **George Castriota** or **Kastrioti**, *also known as* **Iskander Bey** c. 1403–68 •*Albanian national hero*• The son of a prince of Emathia, he was taken hostage by Turks at the age of seven and brought up as a Muslim. He became a favorite commander of Sultan Murad II. In 1443 he changed sides, renounced Islam, and drove the Turks from Albania. For 20 years he maintained the independence of Albania with only occasional support from Naples, Venice and the pope. After his death, however, Albanian opposition to the Turks collapsed.

Skeat, Walter William 1835–1912 •*English philologist*• Born in London and educated at King's College School and Christ's College, Cambridge, he became a Fellow in 1860 and in 1878 Professor of Anglo-Saxon. He was founder and first director of the Dialect Society (1873), and he contributed more than any scholar of his time to a sound knowledge of Middle English and English philology generally. He edited several important texts, notably *Piers Plowman* (1867–85). Other works include *Principles of English Etymology* (1887–91), *Chaucer* (6 vols, 1894–95), *Glossary of Tudor and Stuart Words* (1914) and papers on place names.

Skelton, John c. 1460–1529 •*English satirical poet*• Born in Norfolk, he studied at Oxford and Cambridge, and was created poet laureate by both. Later he was the tutor of Prince Henry (the future **Henry VIII**), took holy orders in 1498, and became rector of Diss in 1502, but seems to have been suspended in 1511 for having a mistress or wife. He produced translations and elegies in 1489, and became known for his satirical vernacular poetry, including *Colyn Cloute*, on corruptions of the Church, and *Why Come Ye Nat to Courte*, an invective against **Thomas Wolsey** for which Skelton had to take sanctuary at Westminster. Other works include *The Boke of Phyllyp Sparowe* and *The Tunnyng of Elynour Rummynge*.

Skinner, B(urrhus) F(rederic) 1904–90 •*US psychologist*• Born in Susquehanna, Pennsylvania, he was educated first at Hamilton College and then at Harvard, where he taught for many years (1931–36 and 1947–74). He also taught at the University of Minnesota (1936–45). He was the most consistent and radical proponent of behaviorism, developing and refining the ideas of **John Broadus Watson**, who advocated the study of behavior as the only possible road for a scientific psychology to travel. He invented the Skinner box, a chamber containing mechanisms for an animal to operate and an automatic device for presenting rewards. In education, his ideas led to the development and proliferation of programmed learning, a technique which seeks to direct teaching to the needs of each individual and to reinforce learning by regular and immediate feedback. He also wrote fiction, autobiography and philosophy.

“ ”

The real problem is not whether machines think but whether men do.
1969 ***Contingencies of Reinforcement***, *chapter 9.*

Skinner, James 1778–1841 •*Indian soldier*• Of Eurasian origin, he joined the army at the age of 15, was promoted to lieutenant for gallantry, but was dismissed by General Perron in 1803 because of his mixed origin. Under General Lord Lake, he formed Skinner's Horse, one of the most famous regiments in India. With the fabulous wealth of 30 years' looting, and several wives, he settled down to the life of a rich Mogul in Delhi. Always inclined to scholarship and philanthropy, he wrote books in flawless Persian, with decorations and numerous paintings by local artists, on the princes, castes and tribes of Hindustan. He also built a mosque, a temple and the Church of St James in Delhi.

Skobtsova, Maria 1891–1945 •*Russian Orthodox nun*• Born in Riga, she was the first woman to enroll at the Ecclesiastical Academy, St Petersburg. Escaping to France after the Revolution she worked with refugees and in 1932, despite having been divorced twice, became a nun. Unconventional and radical, she worked to feed and house those rejected by society. During World War II she worked with the Jews in Paris, and in 1943 she was arrested and sent to the Ravensbrück concentration camp, where she brought Christian light and hope despite appalling conditions. She was gassed on the eve of Easter in 1945.

Skram, (Bertha) Amalie, *née* **Alver** 1847–1905 •*Norwegian novelist*• She was born in Bergen, whose commercial life was the main setting for her work, and after divorcing her first husband in 1878 she worked as a critic and short-story writer. In 1884 she married Erik Skram, a Danish writer, and thereafter wrote a collection of novels in which she explored women's issues, and marriage in particular. Her best-known works include *Constance Ring* (1885, Eng trans 1988), the tetralogy *Hellemyrsfolket* (1887–98, "The People at Hellemyr") and *Forraadt* (1892, Eng trans *Betrayed*, 1987), *Professor Hieronimus* (1895, Eng trans 1899) and *På St Jørgen* (1895, "At St Jørgen's").

Skriabin, Aleksandr Nikolayevich *See* **Scriabin, Aleksandr Nikolayevich**

Slade, Felix 1790–1868 •*English antiquary and art collector*• Born in Halsteads, Yorkshire, he bequeathed his engravings and Venetian glass to the British Museum, and endowed professorships in art at Oxford and Cambridge. He also founded the Slade School of Art in London.

Sleep, Wayne Philip Colin 1948– •*English dancer and choreographer*• Born in Plymouth, he studied tap dancing and ballet as a child, joining the Royal Ballet School at the age of 12 and graduating into the company itself in 1966. Promoted to principal dancer in 1973, his small stature, extroverted personality and technical prowess led to leading roles in such ballets as **Frederick Ashton**'s *A Month in the Country* (1976) and **Kenneth MacMillan**'s *Manon* (1974). He also works on the musical stage, cinema and television. In 1980 he formed his own touring group, Dash, and later adapted his series *The Hot Shoe Show* (1983–84) into a fast-paced, eclectic live revue. He danced in and jointly choreographed the stage show *Bits and Pieces* in 1989.

Slessor, Kenneth Adolf 1901–71 •*Australian poet and journalist*• Born in Orange, New South Wales, he worked as a reporter, columnist and editor. He was an official war correspondent and covered the Battle of Britain and then followed the Australian Imperial Forces through the Near East and North Africa, and on to New Guinea. He contributed many poems to various periodicals; in 1924 he published *Thief of the Moon*, and in 1926 *Earth-Visitors*. *Darlinghurst Nights and Morning Glories* (1933), *Five Bells* (1939), and the best of his prose appeared in *Bread and Wine* (1970). He edited *Australian Poetry* (1945) and coedited the *Penguin Book of Australian Verse* (1958, rev edn 1961).

Slessor, Mary 1848–1915 •*Scottish missionary*• Born in Aberdeen, she worked as a mill girl in Dundee from childhood but, conceiving a burning ambition to become a missionary, persuaded the United Presbyterian Church to accept her for teaching in Calabar, Nigeria (1876). There she spent many years of devoted work among the local peoples, who called her Great Mother.

Slipher, Vesto Melvin 1875–1969 •*US astronomer*• Born in Mulberry, Indiana, he studied at the University of Indiana before working at the Lowell Observatory, Arizona, where he remained for over 50 years, becoming its director in 1926. The research which led to the discovery of the planet Pluto was carried out under his direction. Primarily a spectroscopist, his spectral studies revealed the presence of gaseous interstellar material. By measuring the **Doppler** shift in light reflected from the edges of planetary disks, he determined the periods of rotation of Uranus, Jupiter, Saturn, Venus and Mars in 1912. In his most important work, he extended this method to the Andromeda nebula, which was not yet perceived as an extragalactic object, and established that it is approaching the Earth at around 300 kilometers (186 miles) per second (1912). His results directed **Edwin Hubble** to the concept of the expanding universe.

Sloan, Alfred Pritchard, Jr 1875–1966 •*US industrialist and philanthropist*• Born in New Haven, Connecticut, he studied electrical engineering at MIT. From 1920 to 1924 he worked with **Pierre Du Pont** to reorganize and restructure General Motors. He became president in 1924 and chairman of the board from 1937 to 1956. A noted philanthropist, he founded the Alfred P Sloan Foundation in 1937 and the Sloan-Kettering Institute for Cancer Research in 1945.

Sloan, John 1871–1951 •*US artist*• Born in Lock Haven, Pennsylvania, he studied at Philadelphia Spring Garden Institute and Pennsylvania Academy of Fine Arts. Influenced by Robert Henri (1865–1929), he produced a series of etchings based on New York City life and became known as a member of the so-called Ashcan School. Notable paintings include *Wake of the Ferry* (1907), *Sunday, Women Drying Their Hair* (1912) and *McSorley's Bar* (1912).

Sloane, Sir Hans 1660–1753 •*British physician and naturalist*• Born in Killyleagh, County Down, he studied in London and in France, and settled in London as a physician. From 1685 to 1686 he was the physician of the governor of Jamaica, where he collected a herbarium of 800 species. He was secretary of the Royal Society (1693–1713), physician general of the army (1716) and first physician of **George II**. His museum and library formed the core collection of the British Museum.

Slovo, Joe 1926–95 •*South African lawyer, nationalist and Communist politician*• Born in Obelai, Lithuania, he emigrated in 1935 to South Africa, where he worked as a clerk before volunteering for service in World War II. After joining the South African Communist Party (SACP) in 1942, he qualified as a lawyer and defended many figures in political trials. He was a founding member of the Congress of Democrats in 1953. Charged in the treason trial of 1961, he escaped in 1963, and worked abroad for the African

National Congress (ANC) and SACP. In 1985 he became chief of staff of the military wing of the ANC, but resigned to become general secretary (1987–91) and later chairman of the SACP. He returned to South Africa in 1990 after the legalization of the SACP and was a major figure in the negotiations between the nationalist parties and the government. The first white member of the ANC's National Executive (from 1986), he was given a state funeral.

Sluter, Claus c. 1350–1405 •*Flemish sculptor*• He was born probably in Haarlem, and went to Dijon under the patronage of **Philip the Bold**, whose tomb he carved there (1384–1411, Dijon Museum). His chief works are the surviving porch sculptures (c. 1400) for the Carthusian house of Champmol near Dijon, and the fountain known as the *Well of Moses* (1395–1406) in the cloister of Champmol, where there is now a hospital. The realism of his style influenced the Italian Renaissance.

Sly Stone, *originally* **Sylvester Stewart** 1944– •*US rock singer and bandleader*• Born in Dallas, Texas, he recorded as part of the family group at the age of four. He moved to San Francisco in the 1960s, where he was a disc jockey and producer before forming Sly and The Family Stone in 1967. The band had a major hit with "Dance to the Music" in 1968, and went on to be one of the first groups to incorporate political themes into commercial dance music, notably *Stand* (1969). In the 1970s the band's sales declined, but its influence remained a powerful one.

Smalley, Richard Errett 1943– •*US chemist and Nobel Prize winner*• He was born in Akron, Ohio, and educated at the University of Michigan and Princeton University. He taught at various institutions and became director of the Rice Center for Nanoscale Science and Technology in 1996. He shared the Nobel Prize for chemistry (1996; with **Robert Curl** and **Harold Kroto**) for his role in the discovery of fullerenes.

Smalls, Robert 1839–1915 •*US soldier and politician*• Born into slavery in Beaufort, South Carolina, he was forced to join the Confederate navy during the Civil War, and he became a hero in the North when he commandeered a ship and delivered it into Union hands (May 1862). Serving then in the Union navy, he was promoted to the rank of captain (1863–66), becoming the highest-ranking African-American officer. He was elected to the South Carolina Senate (1871) and the US House of Representatives (1875–79, 1881–87), where he fought for civil rights.

Smart, Christopher 1722–71 •*English poet*• Born in Shipbourne near Tonbridge, he studied at Pembroke College, Cambridge. He settled to a precarious living in London, where **Samuel Johnson** assisted him in his monthly *Universal Visitor*. Smart's works include sacred poems, epigrams, birthday odes and occasional poems. He also wrote the *Hilliad* (1753), a satire on a quack doctor, several translations, and his most celebrated work, *A Song to David* (1763). His remarkable *Jubilate Agno* was not published until 1939.

Smeaton, John 1724–94 •*English civil engineer*• Born in Austhorpe, near Leeds, he was sent to London to study law at the age of 18. From about 1750, however, he worked as a mathematical-instrument maker. Elected a Fellow of the Royal Society in 1753, he won the Copley Medal for his research into the mechanics of waterwheels and windmills, and established his reputation with his novel design for the third Eddystone lighthouse (1756–59), which remained in use till 1877. Through systematic study and experiment he improved the atmospheric steam engine of **Thomas Newcomen**. His other chief engineering works include Ramsgate Harbour (1774), the Forth and Clyde Canal, and bridges at Coldstream and Perth.

Smellie, William 1740–95 •*Scottish editor, printer and antiquary*• Born in Edinburgh and educated at the city's high school, in 1765 he set up his own printing business and, with Andrew Bell and Colin MacFarquhar, produced the first edition of the *Encyclopaedia Britannica* (1768–71). A founder-member of the Society of Antiquities in 1780, he helped prepare the first statistical account of Scotland. **Robert Burns** described him as "that old Veteran in Genius, Wit and Bawdry." He printed the first edition of Burns's poems for the publisher William Creech.

Smetana, Bedřich 1824–84 •*Czech composer*• Born in Litomyšl, he studied in Prague. He conducted in Sweden (1856–59), and became conductor of the new National Theater in Prague (1866), for which his operas were composed. His compositions are intensely national in character and include nine operas, notably *Prodaná nevěsta* (1866, "The Bartered Bride") and *Dalibor* (1865–67), and many chamber and orchestral works, including a string quartet "From My Life" (1876) and a series of symphonic poems *Má Vlast* (1874–79, "My Country"). He became deaf in 1874.

Smiles, Samuel 1812–1904 •*Scottish writer and social reformer*• Born in Haddington, East Lothian, he studied medicine at Edinburgh, and later settled as a surgeon in Leeds. He became editor of the *Leeds Times*, secretary of the Leeds and Thirsk Railway (1845), and secretary of the Southeastern Railway (1854–66). His most celebrated work was *Self-Help* (1859), with its short lives of great men and the admonition "Do thou likewise," which made the ideal Victorian school prize. He wrote many other works on self-improvement, including *Character* (1871), *Thrift* (1875) and *Duty*.

Smirke, Sir Robert 1781–1867 •*English architect*• He was the son of the painter and book illustrator Robert Smirke (1752–1845). Architect to the Board of Works, his public buildings are usually classical, his domestic architecture Gothic. Covent Garden Theatre (1809) was his first great undertaking, and the British Museum (1823–47) his best known. He also designed the General Post Office (1824–29) and the College of Physicians (1825). His brother Sydney (1799–1877) completed the west wing of the British Museum and the reading room (1854), and rebuilt the Carlton Club (1857).

Smith, Adam 1723–90 •*Scottish economist and philosopher*• He was born in Kirkcaldy. He studied at Glasgow and Oxford, and from 1748 became one of the brilliant circle in Edinburgh which included **David Hume**, **John Home**, the jurist and historian Lord Hailes (1726–92), the preacher Hugh Blair (1718–1800) and the historian William Robertson (1721–93). In 1751 Smith became Professor of Logic at Glasgow, later moving to the chair of moral philosophy (1755–64). In 1759 he published his *Theory of Moral Sentiments*, based on Hume's doctrines. The essence of moral sentiments, Smith argued, was sympathy, like that of an impartial and well-informed spectator. While traveling as the tutor of Henry, the future 3rd Duke of Buccleuch (1746–1812), he met **Anne Robert Jacques Turgot**, **Jacques Necker** and others in Paris. In 1776 he witnessed the illness and death of his friend Hume and edited some of his papers. He also wrote a moving account of Hume's death. Soon after he went to London, where he became a member of the club to which **Joshua Reynolds**, **David Garrick** and **Samuel Johnson** belonged. In the same year (1776) he published a volume of five chapters, which he originally intended to be the first part of a complete theory of society in the tradition of Scottish moral philosophy, and to cover natural theology, ethics, politics and law. This single volume, *An Inquiry Into the Nature and Causes of the Wealth of Nations*, examined the consequences of economic freedom, and saw the division of labor as the main ingredient of economic growth, rather than land or money. At a public dinner, William Pitt the Elder (1st Earl of **Chatham**) invited Smith to be seated first, as "we are all your scholars." Smith returned to Edinburgh in 1778 as commissioner of customs; he died there and was buried in the Canongate churchyard. He was elected a Fellow of the Royal Society in 1767 and lord rector of the University of Glasgow in 1787.

“ ”

Consumption is the sole end and purpose of all production.
1776 ***An Inquiry Into the Nature and Causes of the Wealth of Nations.***

Smith, Alexander *See* **Adams, John**

Smith, Bessie (Elizabeth) 1894–1937 •*US blues singer*• Born in Chattanooga, Tennessee, her magnificent voice, blues-based repertoire and vivacious stage presence soon gained her recognition as one of the outstanding African-American performers of her day. Nicknamed the "Empress of the Blues," she made a series of recordings in the 1920s, accompanied by leading jazz musicians, including **Fletcher Henderson** and **Louis Armstrong**, and these are regarded as classic blues statements. In 1929 she had the leading role in a film, *St Louis Blues*. She died from injuries in a car crash.

Smith, David Roland 1906–65 •*US sculptor*• He was born in Decatur, Indiana. In 1925 he worked in the Studebaker car factory at South Bend and learned how to cut and shape metal. From 1926 he studied under the Czech abstract artist Jan Matulka at the Art Students' League in New York. His first welded-steel pieces, inspired by magazine photographs of similar work by **Picasso**, date from 1932, and during the rest of the decade he assimilated several avant-garde European styles, including cubism, surrealism and constructivism. His personal idiom developed from c. 1940, and during World War II he worked as a welder. His 15 bronze relief plaques, *Medals of Dishonour*, attacked violence and greed.

Smith, Delia 1941– •*English cooking writer and broadcaster*• She was born in Woking, Surrey, and left school at the age of 16. She began by writing for the *Daily Mirror* magazine (1969), where her future husband, Michael Wynn Jones, was deputy editor, and for the London *Evening Standard* (1972–85). Her first cookbook, *How to Cheat at Cooking* (1973), achieved wide popularity. She has since sold over ten million copies of her books, including those associated with her television broadcasts. She is a committed Christian and also writes religious books, including *A Journey Into God* (1980). She is also a major shareholder in the Norwich City Football Club.

Smith, Dodie, *pseudonym (until 1935)* **C L Anthony** 1896–1990 •*English playwright, novelist and theater producer*• Born in Manchester, she took up acting and a career in business. Her first play, *Autumn Crocus* (1930), was an instant success and enabled her to devote herself entirely to writing. Other plays include *Dear Octopus* (1938), *Letter From Paris* (adapted from *The Reverberator* by **Henry James**, 1952) and *I Capture the Castle* (adapted from her own novel, 1952). Other works include the highly popular children's book *The Hundred and One Dalmatians* (1956), and several autobiographical works.

Smith, E(dward) E(lmer), *nicknamed* **Doc** 1890–1965 •*US science-fiction writer*• He was born in Sheboygan, Wisconsin. A PhD in food chemistry was the basis of his writing nickname. He was an immensely popular creator of science-fiction space adventure stories in the pulp magazine era before World War II, and is widely regarded as the progenitor of "space opera." His best-known works are the multivolume sequences *Skylark* (begun 1928) and *Lensman* (begun 1948). The later *Family d'Alembert* series (begun 1964) appeared posthumously, and was completed by other writers.

Smith, Emmitt 1969– •*US football player*• Born in Pensacola, Florida, he played for Florida State University and (from 1990) the Dallas Cowboys. Considered one of the greatest running backs in National Football League (NFL) history, he was a member of three Super Bowl champion teams (1993, 1994, 1996), the NFL rushing leader four times (1991–93, 1995) and voted Most Valuable Player in both the league and the Super Bowl in 1993. In 2002, he established a new NFL rushing record (17,418 yards as of the start of the 2004 season), breaking the previous record of 16,726 yards set by **Walter Payton**.

Smith, Sir Francis Pettit 1808–74 •*English inventor of the screw propellor*• He was born in Hythe. In 1836 he took out a patent for the screw propellor, just ahead of **John Ericsson**. Smith built the first successful screw-propelled steamer, the *Archimedes* (1839), which eventually convinced the admiralty of the superiority of this type of ship, and in 1841–43 he built the first screw warship for the Royal Navy, the *Rattler*.

Smith, Frederick Edwin *See* **Birkenhead, 1st Earl of**

Smith, Gerrit 1797–1874 •*US reformer and philanthropist*• Born in Utica, New York, he was active in diverse reform movements, including Sunday observance, abstinence, vegetarianism, prison reform and women's suffrage. He became a prominent abolitionist in 1835, and supported **John Brown**'s (1800–59) antislavery campaigns.

Smith, Hamilton Othanel 1931– •*US molecular biologist and Nobel Prize winner*• Born in New York City, he graduated from Johns Hopkins Medical School, Maryland, where he later taught. In the 1970s he obtained enzymes from bacteria which would split genes to give genetically active fragments; these allowed the possibility of genetic engineering of a new kind. Smith went on to isolate type II enzymes, which would split a DNA strand at a specific and predictable site, allowing the nucleotide sequence of DNA to be established. He shared the 1978 Nobel Prize for physiology or medicine with **Werner Arber** and **Daniel Nathans**.

Smith, (Robert) Harvey 1938– •*English show jumper*• He was born in Yorkshire. After winning several British championships, he represented Great Britain in the 1968 and 1972 Olympics. With the increasing popularity of show jumping, Smith soon became a well-liked figure, typifying the blunt, bluff Yorkshireman. He wrote two books, *Show Jumping With Harvey Smith* (1979) and *Bedside Jumping* (1985).

Smith, Iain Crichton, *Gaelic* **Iain Mac A'Ghobhainn** 1928–98 •*Scottish poet and novelist*• Born on the island of Lewis, he was educated at the University of Aberdeen. His career as a writer ran in parallel with teaching in Clydebank, Dumbarton and Oban until 1977. Bilingual in Gaelic and English, his writing is rooted in the native culture but is sensible to the wider audience that English admits. His first collection of poems, *The Long River*, appeared in 1955. Five years later came *Burn Is Aran*, stories and poems in Gaelic which were highly praised. The novel *Consider the Lilies* (1968) is undoubtedly the best-known work from his prolific output. Focusing on the plight of an old woman who is evicted from her croft and betrayed by the Church, it portrays the harsh reality of Highland life.

Smith, Ian Douglas 1919– •*Rhodesian politician*• Born in Selukwe, he was educated at Rhodes University, South Africa. He was a fighter pilot in World War II and became a Member of Parliament in 1948. From 1953 he was a member of the United Federal Party, resigning in 1961 to become a member of the Rhodesian Front, which was dedicated to immediate independence for Rhodesia without African majority rule. He became prime minister in April 1964 and unilaterally declared independence in November 1965. Britain applied increasingly severe economic sanctions, but it was only in 1979 that majority rule was granted. Bishop **Abel Muzorewa**'s caretaker government appointed Smith minister without portfolio and a member of the Transitional Executive Council of 1978–79 to prepare for the transfer of power. He was elected a member of parliament in the government of **Robert Mugabe**, but was suspended from parliament in April 1987 because of his connections with South Africa.

“ ”

Let me say it again, I don't believe in black majority rule ever in Rhodesia. Not in a thousand years.

1976 Radio broadcast, March 20.

Smith, Ian McKenzie 1935– •*Scottish painter*• Born in Montrose, Angus, he studied at Gray's School of Art, Aberdeen (1953–58), became a teacher, then worked as an education officer. He was director of Aberdeen Art Gallery and Museums (1968–89), and was one of the first Scottish painters to adopt a style based on American minimal abstraction, whose intention is to evoke a meditative response.

Smith, John 1580–1631 •*English adventurer*• Born in Willoughby, Lincolnshire, he fought in France and Hungary, but was captured by the Turks and sold as a slave. He escaped to Russia and in 1607 joined an expedition to colonize Virginia. Saved from a Native American tribe by the chief's daughter **Pocahontas**, his experience in dealing with the tribal people led to his being elected president of the colony (1608–09), but he returned to England in 1609. In 1614 he was sent to New England and explored the coast. His works include *A Description of New England* (1616) and *The True Travels, Adventures, and Observations of Captaine John Smith* (1630).

Smith, John 1938–94 •*Scottish Labour politician*• Educated at Dunoon Grammar School and the University of Glasgow, where he studied law, he was called to the Scottish bar in 1967 and made a Queen's Counsel in 1983. He distinguished himself as a public speaker at an early age, winning the *Observer* Mace debating competition in 1962. He became a Member of Parliament in 1970 and served in the administrations of **Harold Wilson** and **James**

Callaghan, becoming trade secretary in 1978. From 1979 he was Opposition front-bench spokesman on trade, energy, employment and economic affairs. One of Labour's most respected politicians, he succeeded **Neil Kinnock** as Labour Party leader in 1992, but died suddenly of another heart attack in 1994.

Smith, Joseph 1805–44 •*US religious leader, regarded as the founder of the Mormon Church*• Born in Sharon, Vermont, he received his first call as a prophet in 1820. In 1823 he claimed that an angel told him of a hidden gospel written on golden plates, and in 1827 the sacred records were apparently delivered into his hands on a hill near Palmyra, New York. This, the Book of Mormon (1830), contains a postulated history of America to the fifth century of the Christian era, supposedly written by a prophet named Mormon. Despite ridicule and hostility, and sometimes open violence, "the new Church of Jesus Christ of Latter-day Saints" (founded in 1830) rapidly gained converts. In 1838 a general uprising took place in Missouri against the Mormons. In 1840 they moved to Illinois, and within three years the Mormons there numbered 20,000. Smith was an advocate of polygamy. He was shot dead by a mob who broke into Carthage jail, where he was under arrest on charges of conspiracy.

Smith, Logan Pearsall 1865–1946 •*British writer*• Born in Millville, New Jersey, in the US, and educated at Harvard and Oxford, he settled in England and took British citizenship in 1913. He produced critical editions of various authors, and published *Milton and His Modern Critics* (1941). He is best remembered for his delightful essays, collected in *All Trivia* (1933) and *Reperusals and Re-collections* (1936), and his short stories.

Smith, Dame Maggie (Margaret Natalie) 1934– •*English actress*• Born in Ilford, Essex, she was a student at the Oxford Playhouse School. After winning increasing critical esteem for her performances in *The Rehearsal* (1961) and *Mary, Mary* (1963), she joined the National Theatre. Her film debut in *Nowhere to Go* (1958) was followed by scene-stealing turns in such films as *The V.I.P.s* (1963) and *The Pumpkin Eater* (1964), but her tour de force was in *The Prime of Miss Jean Brodie* (1969, Academy Award). Her many film roles show a penchant for eccentric comedy and the portrayal of acidic spinsters, and include award-winning performances in *California Suite* (1978), *A Private Function* (1984, British Academy of Film and Television Arts Award for Best Actress), *A Room With a View* (1985) and *The Lonely Passion of Judith Hearne* (1987). In 1992 she played a wizened Wendy in *Hook*, and she returned to the stage as Lady Bracknell in *The Importance of Being Earnest*. More recent film work includes *Tea With Mussolini* (1999) and *Harry Potter and the Sorceror's Stone* (2001), *Harry Potter and the Chamber of Secrets* (2002) and *Harry Potter and the Prisoner of Azkaban* (2004). She was given the honorary title of Dame Commander, Order of the British Empire, in 1990.

Smith, Margaret Chase, *née* **Chase** 1897–1995 •*US Republican politician*• Born in Skowhegan, Maine, she worked as a teacher and then on a newspaper, marrying its publisher, Clyde Smith, in 1930. He became US Representative in Washington and when he died in 1940 she took over his position, becoming Maine's first congresswoman. Eight years later she became the first woman elected a US senator in her own right and the first woman to be elected to both houses of the US Congress. She served until 1973. In 1950 she became one of the first Republican senators to speak out against Senator **Joseph McCarthy**, and in 1964 she campaigned for the office of US president, the first woman to do so since **Victoria Woodhull** in 1872.

Smith, Mel(vyn Kenneth) 1952– •*English actor, writer and director*• Born in London, he studied at New College, Oxford. In the 1980s he moved into television as a comedy actor and writer for series such as *Not the Nine O'Clock News* (1979–81) and *Alas Smith and Jones* (1982–87), the latter in collaboration with **Griff Rhys Jones**. He has made feature films including *Morons From Outer Space* (1985) and *Wilt* (1989), and directed *Bean* (1997). With Griff Rhys Jones he is a founder of the production company Talkback.

Smith, Michael 1932–2000 •*Canadian biochemist and Nobel Prize winner*• Born in Blackpool, Lancashire, and educated at the University of Manchester, he moved to Canada in 1956. In 1966 he joined the University of British Columbia, and in 1978 he published his discovery of "site-specific mutagenesis," a technique which allows scientists to alter the genetic code through mutations induced at specific locations, whereas all previous methods of mutation had produced only random mutations. This new method has allowed the production of a whole new range of proteins with diverse functions. Smith was awarded the 1993 Nobel Prize for chemistry jointly with **Kary Mullis**.

Smith, Robyn 1943– •*US jockey*• She began her thoroughbred riding career in 1969. In 1972 she was the only American jockey of international standing, coming in seventh with 98 mounts and 20 percent of the winnings. She maintained her top US rank from 1972 to 1978. In 1973 she was the first woman jockey to win a stakes race when she rode North Sea to victory in the Paumonok Handicap. She married **Fred Astaire** in 1980.

Smith, Sir Ross MacPherson 1892–1922 •*Australian aviator*• Born in Semaphore, South Australia, he joined the Australian Imperial Forces and fought at Gallipoli, then transferred to the Australian Flying Corps (1916) and became its most decorated pilot. After World War I he flew a Handley-Page bomber from Cairo to Calcutta, a distance of nearly 2,400 miles and a record at that time. In 1919 the Australian government offered £10,000 for the first Australian-crewed plane to fly to Australia from England within 30 days. Ross and his elder brother Keith (1890–1955) flew from London in a Vickers Vimy biplane with two Australian engineers, arriving in Darwin 28 days later, a feat for which both brothers were knighted.

Smith, Stevie, *pseudonym of* **Florence Margaret Smith** 1902–71 •*English poet and novelist*• Born in Hull, Humberside, she moved with her family at the age of three to London, where she attended the North London Collegiate School for Girls before working for the Newnes publishing company. Her first novels, *Novel on Yellow Paper* (1936, an autobiographical monologue in conversational style), *Over the Frontier* (1938) and *The Holiday* (1949), were written on the advice of a publicist reacting to her poetry. Meanwhile her reputation as a humorous poet on serious themes was becoming established with *A Good Time Was Had by All* (1937) and *Not Waving but Drowning* (1957). She also wrote many reviews and critical articles, and produced a volume of the line drawings that often accompanied her poems, entitled *Some Are More Human Than Others* (1958).

Smith, Sydney 1771–1845 •*English clergyman, essayist and wit*• Born in Woodford, Essex, he was educated at Winchester and New College, Oxford. He was ordained (1794) and in 1802, with Francis Jeffrey, Francis Horner and **Henry Brougham**, he started the *Edinburgh Review*. He lived six years in London, where he made his mark as a preacher and a lecturer on moral philosophy at the Royal Institution (1804–06). His writings include 65 articles, collected in 1839 from the *Edinburgh Review* and *Peter Plymley's Letters* (1807–08), in favor of Catholic emancipation.

Smith, Sydney Goodsir 1915–75 •*Scottish poet*• Born in Wellington, New Zealand, he moved to Edinburgh in 1928 when his father, Sir Sydney Alfred Smith (1883–1969) was appointed Regius Professor of Forensic Medicine there. He studied at the University of Edinburgh and Oriel College, Oxford, and with such works as *Skail Wind* (1941), *Under the Eildon Tree* (1948, a modern love poem), *So Late Into the Night* (1952), *Orpheus and Eurydice* (1955) and *Figs and Thistles* (1959), he established a reputation as the best modern Lallans (lowland Scots) poet after **Hugh MacDiarmid**. He also wrote plays and a comic novel, *Carotid Cornucopius* (1947).

Smith, Theobald 1859–1934 •*US microbiologist and immunologist*• Born in Albany, New York, he was the greatest US bacteriologist of his generation. He received his medical degree from the Albany Medical College and was subsequently associated with several US institutions, including the Rockefeller Institute for Medical Research (1915–29). He studied both animal and human diseases, and first established the role of insects in the spread of disease when he showed that Texas cattle fever is spread by ticks. He distinguished the forms of bacillus causing human and bovine tuberculosis, laid the scientific foundations for a cholera vaccine, and also improved a number of vaccines.

Smith, Tommy (Thomas) 1967– •*Scottish jazz musician, composer and bandleader*• Born in Luton, Bedfordshire, to Scottish parents, he was brought up in Edinburgh and took up the saxophone at the age of 12. A teenage prodigy, he had done television and radio performances with internationally known musicians, as well as two records for Scottish labels, before he was 16. After studies in the US at Berklee College of Music, Boston, he brought his own quartet, Forward Motion, to play in Europe. In 1986 he became a member of vibraphone player Gary Burton's quintet. He soon became established as one of the brightest new jazz stars, playing wind synthesizer as well as saxophone, and leading a variety of groups.

Smith, W Eugene 1918–78 •*US photojournalist*• He was born in Wichita, Kansas, and worked for several magazines before becoming a war correspondent for *Life* magazine in 1942. Severely wounded at Okinawa in 1945, he did not photograph again until 1947, the year of his famous *The Walk to Paradise Garden* (showing two children walking away toward a sunlit forest clearing). He returned to *Life* and produced a series of eloquent photoessays (eg, *Country Doctor*, 1948; *Spanish Village*, 1951) which were to mark him as one of the most important photojournalists of his time. His last great work was a photographic record of a Japanese fishing village suffering the maiming effects of mercury poisoning from factory pollution: *Minimata: Life Sacred and Profane* (1973).

Smith, Sir William 1813–93 •*English lexicographer*• Born in London, he was educated at University College London. His great work was as editor and contributing author of the *Dictionary of Greek and Roman Antiquities* (1840–42), the *Dictionary of Greek and Roman Biography and Mythology* (1843–49) and the *Dictionary of Greek and Roman Geography* (1853–57). He also produced a *Dictionary of the Bible* (1860–63), a *Dictionary of Christian Antiquities* (1875–80) and a *Dictionary of Christian Biography and Doctrines* (1877–87). He was editor of *The Quarterly Review* from 1867 until his death.

Smith, William 1769–1839 •*English civil engineer and geologist*• Born in Churchill, Oxfordshire, he became an assistant to a surveyor in 1787 and he was later appointed an engineer with the Somerset Coal Canal (1794–99). In 1799 he produced a colored geological map of the country around Bath, and from 1799 he was a consultant engineer and surveyor, using fossils to aid his identification of strata. He produced the first geological map of England and 21 colored geological maps of the English counties (1819–24), assisted by his nephew John Phillips (1800–74). Smith is often regarded as the father of English geology and stratigraphy.

Smith, William Henry 1792–1865 •*English newsdealer*• He entered the newsdealer business of his father in the Strand, London, in 1812 and aided by his brother, Henry Edward Smith, expanded it into the largest in Great Britain by making extensive use of railways and fast carts for country deliveries. His son **William Henry Smith** took over the business and maintained its expansion.

Smith, William Henry 1825–91 •*English bookseller and politician*• Born in London, the son of **William Henry Smith**, he became his father's partner in a bookselling business in 1846. The business steadily expanded, and in 1849, they secured the privilege of selling books and newspapers at railway stations. Smith entered parliament in 1868, was financial secretary of the treasury (1874–77), first lord of the admiralty (1877–80) and secretary for war (1885). In the second **Salisbury** ministry he was first lord of the treasury and leader of the House of Commons until his death.

Smith, Zadie 1975– •*English author*• Born in London, the daughter of a Jamaican mother and an English father, she studied at King's College, Cambridge. Her first novel was *White Teeth* (2000), a warm and closely observed portrait of three families from three cultures over three generations, united in the London suburb of Willesden Green. It was an immediate bestseller, winning awards including the Whitbread prize for a first novel and the James Tait Black Memorial prize for fiction. Her second novel was *The Autograph Man*.

Smithson, James Louis Macie 1765–1829 •*English chemist*• He was born in Paris, the illegitimate son of Sir Hugh Smithson Percy, 1st Duke of Northumberland, and Elizabeth Macie. At first known as Macie, he changed his name in 1801 after the death of his mother. He was educated at Oxford, showing an early aptitude for mineralogy, and he was elected a Fellow of the Royal Society in 1787. Zinc carbonate was later named "smithsonite" after him. However, he is chiefly remembered for his bequest for the foundation "at Washington, under the name of the Smithsonian Institution, an Establishment for the increase and diffusion of knowledge among men."

Smithson, Robert 1938–73 •*US land artist*• Born in Passaic, New Jersey, he studied at the Art Students' League (1955–56) and at the Brooklyn Museum School. He took up minimalism in the 1960s, but is best known for such earthworks as the *Spiral Jetty on the Great Salt Lake, Utah* (1970). He was killed in a plane crash in Texas while engaged in aerial photography of one of his earthworks.

Smollett, Tobias George 1721–71 •*Scottish novelist*• Born on the farm of Dalquharn in the Vale of Leven, Dunbartonshire, he was educated at Dumbarton Grammar School and the University of Glasgow, where he took a degree in medicine. After sailing as surgeon's mate in the expedition to Carthagena against the Spanish in 1741, he practiced as a surgeon in London, but writing was his real interest. His first novels, *Roderick Random* (1748), modeled on **Alain Lesage**'s *Gil Blas* (1715), and *Peregrine Pickle* (1751), describe the adventures in love and war of an unprincipled hero. In 1753 he settled in Chelsea, editing the new *Critical Review*, which led to his imprisonment for libel in 1760, and writing his *History of England* (3 vols, 1757–58). After being ordered abroad for his health, he wrote the caustic *Travels in France and Italy* (1766), followed in 1769 by a coarse satire on public affairs, *The Adventures of an Atom*. *Humphrey Clinker* (1771), which is more kindly in tone and still a favorite, deals with the adventures of a party touring England and "North Britain."

Smuts, Jan Christian 1870–1950 •*South African statesman*• He was born in Malmesbury, Cape Colony, and educated at Christ's College, Cambridge. He entered the House of Assembly in 1907 and held several cabinet offices, succeeding **Louis Botha** as prime minister of the Union of South Africa (1919). Entrusted during World War I with operations in German East Africa, he was made a member of the Imperial War Cabinet. As minister of justice under **J B M Hertzog**, his coalition with the Nationalists in 1934 produced the United party, and he became prime minister in 1939.

Smyslov, Vasili Vasilevich 1921– •*Russian chess player*• Born in Moscow, he made chess his career after narrowly failing an audition for the Bolshoi Opera in 1950. After reaching a draw in a world championship match against **Mikhail Botvinnik** in 1954, which allowed the holder to retain his title, he beat him in 1957, but lost to him again in the 1958 rematch.

Smyth, Dame Ethel Mary 1858–1944 •*English composer*• Born in London, she studied at Leipzig. She composed a Mass in D minor, symphonies, choral works and operas, including *The Wreckers* (1906). A campaigner for women's suffrage, she composed the battle song of the Women's Social and Political Union (1911, "The March of the Women"), and was imprisoned for three months. She was given the honorary title of Dame Commander, Order of the British Empire, in 1922, and wrote the autobiographical *Female Pipings for Eden* (1933) and *What Happened Next* (1940).

Smythe, Reg, *originally* **Reginald Smith** 1917–98 •*English cartoon artist*• Born in Hartlepool, Cleveland, he became a regular soldier. After World War II he joined the Post Office and freelanced joke cartoons to the *Daily Mirror*, who invited him to contribute a regular joke for their new Northern edition in 1958. This became *Andy Capp*, the adventures of a cocky and idle layabout, more fond of beer than of his wife, Flo. It eventually became the first British cartoon strip to be syndicated worldwide. The strip was adapted as a stage musical and television series.

Smythson, Robert c. 1535–1614 •*English architect*• Trained as a mason, his first recorded work was at Longleat (1568), and his first major work was Wollaton Hall, Nottingham (1580–88), a lavish palace richly modeled and detailed. He developed a new vertical plan with the great hall set transversely, which revolutionized the spatial possibilities of contemporary buildings. Hardwick Hall, Derbyshire (1591–97), provides the quintessential Elizabethan house of state. Other buildings attributed to Smythson include Worksop Manor, Balborough and Bolsover Little Castle.

Snead, Sam (Samuel Jackson) 1912–2002 •*US golfer*• He was born in Ashwood, Virginia. Of the Majors, he won the Open championship once (1946), the Masters three times (1949, 1952, 1954) and the Professional Golfers' Association championship three times (1942, 1949, 1951). He had 81 US Tour victories, the last of which came at the age of 52 years 10 months, making him the oldest winner on the Tour.

Snell, George Davis 1903–96 •*US geneticist and Nobel Prize winner*• Born in Bradford, Massachusetts, he graduated from Dartmouth College, and worked at Harvard University and the University of Texas, where he demonstrated for the first time that X-rays can induce mutations in mammals. In 1933 he became assistant professor at Washington University, and in 1935 he joined the Jackson Laboratory in Bar Harbor, Maine. In the late 1930s he studied the genes responsible for rejection of tissue transplants in mice, later named the major histocompatibility complex (MHC). Snell, **Jean Dausset** and **Baruj Benacerraf** shared the 1980 Nobel Prize for physiology or medicine.

Snell, Peter 1938– •*New Zealand athlete*• Born in Opunake, Taranaki, he was a surprise winner of the Olympic 800 meters in 1960, and then went on to win gold medals in both the 800 and 1,500 meters in the 1964 Olympics. He also achieved the Commonwealth Games double in 1962 and set world records at 800 meters and one mile (twice), becoming his country's first athlete to run a mile in less than four minutes.

Snow, C(harles) P(ercy), Baron 1905–80 •*English novelist and physicist*• Born in Leicester, he was educated at Alderman Newton's School, then studied science at Leicester University College, and Christ's College, Cambridge, where he later taught (1935–45). He was chief of scientific personnel for the Ministry of Labour during World War II, and a Civil Service commissioner from 1945 to 1960. His major sequence of novels began with *Strangers and Brothers* (1940), which gave its name to the series as a whole. It was followed after the war by *The Light and the Dark* (1947) and *Time of Hope* (1949). *The Masters* (1951) stages the conflict aroused by the election of a new master in a Cambridge college, and *The New Men* (1954) poses the dilemma faced by scientists in the development of nuclear fission. Other books include *Corridors of Power* (1964) and *The Sleep of Reason* (1968). Several have been adapted for theater and television. His controversial *Two Cultures* (Rede Lecture, 1959) discussed the dichotomy between science and literature and his belief in closer contact between them. Created a life peer in 1964, he was made parliamentary secretary at the ministry of technology (1964–66) and lord rector of the University of St Andrews (1961–64). In 1950 he married the novelist **Pamela Hansford Johnson**.

Snow, John 1813–58 •*English anesthetist and epidemiologist*• Born in York, he was a young general practitioner when cholera first struck Great Britain in 1831–32, and his experience then convinced him that the disease was spread through contaminated water. He carried out brilliant epidemiological investigations during the cholera outbreaks of 1848 and 1854, tracing one local outbreak to a well in Soho into which raw sewage was seeping. Snow was also a pioneer anesthetist.

Snowdon, Antony Charles Robert Armstrong-Jones, 1st Earl of 1930– •*English photographer*• Born in London and educated at Eton and Cambridge, he was married to Princess Margaret (1960–78), and was created Earl of Snowdon in 1961. He became a freelance photojournalist in 1951 and an artistic adviser to many publications. He designed the aviary of London Zoo in 1965. A *Vogue* photographer since 1954, his informal portraits of the famous have often captured unusual facets of character, especially those taken during stage performances. More recently, he has sympathetically recorded the plight of the handicapped and disabled, both old and young, and has produced documentaries for television on similar themes.

Snyder, Gary Sherman 1930– •*US poet*• Born in San Francisco, he was educated at the University of California. Originally associated with the Beat poets, he showed great concern for the natural world and the values of simple living and hard physical work, earning his living as a lumberjack and forestry warden. He spent eight years in Japan studying Zen Buddhism (1958–66), and his writing is influenced by an interest in Asian religious practices and literary traditions, as is evident in *Myths and Texts* (1960) and the **Whitman**esque *Axe Handles* (1984). *Turtle Island* (1974) was awarded a Pulitzer Prize.

“ ”

After weeks of watching the roof leak
I fixed it tonight
by moving a single board.

1968 ***The Back Country***, *"Hitch Haiku."*

Snyder, Solomon Halbert 1938– •*US psychiatrist and pharmacologist*• Born in Washington, he studied medicine at Georgetown University (1962), and has held a number of teaching positions and professorships. From the mid-1960s Snyder investigated the biochemistry of nervous tissue, studying neurotransmitter substances and the ornithine decarboxylase enzyme, which is possibly involved in regulating RNA synthesis. His other major interest is in the effects of opiates and psychotropic drugs on the brain and the naturally occurring brain hormones, enkephalins and endorphins.

Soames, (Arthur) Christopher John, Baron Soames 1920–87 •*English Conservative politician*• Educated at Eton and Sandhurst, during World War II he served in the Middle East, Italy and France. In 1947 he married Mary, daughter of Sir **Winston Churchill**, and entered the House of Commons in 1950. He held junior ministerial posts under Churchill and Sir **Anthony Eden** before becoming war secretary in 1958 in **Harold Macmillan**'s administration and then agriculture minister (1960–64). He was ambassador to France (1968–72) and a member of the European Commission (1973–77). He was made a life peer in 1978 and, in 1979, was made lord president and leader of the House of Lords. He will be best remembered for his period as governor of Rhodesia (1979–80), in which he oversaw its transition to the independent state of Zimbabwe.

Soane, Sir John 1753–1837 •*English architect*• Born near Reading, Berkshire, he studied architecture under George Dance (the Younger) (1741–1806) and was an assistant to Henry Holland (1746–1806). He then spent 1777–80 in Italy, developing a restrained neoclassical style of his own. He designed the Bank of England (1788–1833, now destroyed), Dulwich College Art Gallery (1811–14) and his own house in Lincoln's Inn Fields, London, which he bequeathed to the nation as the Sir John Soane Museum.

Soares, Mário Alberto Nobre Lopes 1924– •*Portuguese politician*• Born in Lisbon and educated at the University of Lisbon and in the Faculty of Law at the Sorbonne, Paris, he was politically active in the democratic socialist movement from his early twenties and was imprisoned for his activities on several occasions. In 1968 he was deported, living mainly in Paris until 1974, by which time he had cofounded the Socialist Party (PS). In the same year he was elected to the Assembly and was soon brought into the government. He was prime minister (1976–78, 1983–85), and president (1986–96), Portugal's first civilian president for 60 years.

Socinus, Faustus, *Latin name of* **Fausto Paulo Sozini** 1539–1604 •*Italian religious reformer*• Born in Siena, the nephew of **Laelius Socinus**, and cofounder with his uncle of Socinianism, he studied theology at Basel, where he developed his uncle's anti-Trinitarian doctrines, arguing that human reason alone was the only solid basis of Protestantism. Later he became secretary to Duke Orsini in Florence (1563–75). In 1578, on the publication of his *De Jesu Christo Servatore*, he narrowly escaped assassination, and moved to Poland, where he became leader of an anti-Trinitarian church in Kraków. He was denounced by the Inquisition in 1590 and his possessions were confiscated. Destitute, he sought refuge in the village of Luclawice, where he died.

Socinus, Laelius, *also called* **Lelio Francesco Maria Sozini** 1525–62 •*Italian Protestant reformer*• He was born in Siena and studied law. Turning to biblical research, he settled in Zurich in 1548, and then traveled widely, meeting leading Protestant reformers including **John Calvin** and **Philip Melanchthon**. He developed an anti-Trinitarian doctrine that sought to reconcile Christianity with humanism, which profoundly influenced his nephew, **Faustus Socinus**.

Socrates 469–399 BC •*Greek philosopher*• He was born in Athens, the son of a stonemason (which he also became). In middle age he married Xanthippe, by whom he had three sons. He fought bravely as a hoplite in the Peloponnesian War and refused to cooperate with the Thirty Tyrants. He is represented as ugly, snub-nosed and with a paunch. He wrote nothing, founded no school and had no formal disciples, but along with **Plato** and **Aristotle** is one of the three great figures in ancient philosophy. His pivotal influence was such that all earlier Greek philosophy is classified as "pre-Socratic," and he was responsible for the shift of philosophical interest from speculations about the natural world and cosmology to ethics and conceptual analysis. The principal sources for his life are the dialogues of Plato, especially the *Apology*, *Crito* and *Phaedo*, which describe Socrates' trial, last days and death; in later dialogues he makes Socrates the mouthpiece for what were undoubtedly his own opinions. He held aloof from politics, guided by his "voice," which impelled him to philosophy and to the examination of conventional morality. The "Socratic method" was to ask for definitions of familiar concepts such as justice, courage and piety, to elicit contradictions in the responses of his interlocutors, and thus to demonstrate their ignorance, which he claimed to share. This unpopular activity no doubt contributed to the demands for his conviction for "impiety" and "corrupting the youth," and he was tried at the age of 70. He rejected the option of merely paying a fine, declined a later opportunity to escape from prison, and was sentenced to die by drinking hemlock.

" "

There is only one good, knowledge, and only one evil, ignorance.

*Quoted in Diogenes Laertius **Vitae Philosophorum**, 2.31 (translated by R D Hicks, 1950).*

Soddy, Frederick 1877–1965 •*English radiochemist and Nobel Prize winner*• Born in Eastbourne, Sussex, he studied at the University College of Wales, Aberystwyth, and at Oxford. In 1900 he was appointed demonstrator in chemistry at McGill University, Montreal, where he and **Ernest Rutherford** studied radioactivity. Working in London and Glasgow, he demonstrated that radium produces helium when it decays, and that uranium decays to radium. His principal achievement was the discovery of isotopes, which was of fundamental importance to all physics and chemistry. In 1921 he was awarded the Nobel Prize for chemistry. After his retirement he wrote on ethics, politics and economics, urging fellow scientists to restrict their research to areas which had peaceful applications.

Söderberg, Hjalmar 1869–1941 •*Swedish novelist and playwright*• Born in Stockholm, he wrote several collections of witty short stories, such as *Historietter* (1898, Eng trans *Selected Short Stories*, 1935), and novels of upper-middle-class life in Stockholm, including *Förvillelser* (1895, "Aberrations"), *Martin Bircks ungdom* (1901, Eng trans *Martin Birck's Youth*, 1930) and *Doktor Glas* (1905, Eng trans 1963). His plays included *Gertrud* (1905). In the last period of his life, he turned from fiction to religious scholarship.

Söderblom, Nathan 1866–1931 •*Swedish churchman and Nobel Prize winner*• Born in Trönö, near Söderhamn, he was educated at Uppsala, ordained in 1893, and became Professor of the History of Religion at Uppsala (1901) and Leipzig (1912). In 1914 he was appointed Archbishop of Uppsala and primate of the Swedish Lutheran Church. A leader in the ecumenical movement, he wrote several works on comparative religion and was the principal promoter of the Life and Work movement. He was awarded the Nobel Peace Prize in 1930.

Södergran, Edith 1892–1923 •*Finno-Swedish Expressionist poet*• The daughter of a peasant, she moved with her family to the Karelia peninsula, where the landscape and the people had a profound effect on her. After an unhappy love affair, she published *Dikter* (1916, "Poems"). This was followed by *Septemberlyran* (1918, "September Lyre"), *Rosenaltaret* (1919, "The Rose Altar") and the ironically titled *Fremtidens skugga* (1920, "The Shadow of the Future"), each of which attested to a growing sense of the poet as a prophetic, almost magical figure. She still exerts considerable influence on younger Swedish poets.

Söderström, Elisabeth Anna 1927– •*Swedish soprano*• Born in Stockholm, she studied at the Stockholm Opera School, and was engaged by the Royal Opera (1950). She made her debut at Glyndebourne in 1957, at the Metropolitan Opera Company in 1959 and at Covent Garden, London, in 1960, and subsequently sang in all the leading international opera houses, touring extensively in Europe, the US and the USSR. Her roles range from Nero in **Monteverdi**'s *Poppea* to roles in works by **Mozart**, **Tchaikovsky**, **Strauss**, **Debussy**, **Janáček** and **Benjamin Britten**.

Soeharto, Thojib N J *See* **Suharto, Thojib N J**

Soekarno, Ahmed *See* **Sukarno, Ahmed**

Sokolow, Anna 1912–2000 •*US dancer, choreographer and teacher*• Born in Hartford, Connecticut, she studied at the School of American Ballet and Metropolitan Opera Ballet School, and became one of **Martha Graham**'s original dancers (1930–38). She took up choreography in 1933, founded her own troupe and, in 1939, the first modern dance company in Mexico, called La Paloma Azul. In her choreographies for stage, television and film she was an uncompromising social critic. She also conducted pioneering collaborations with experimental jazz composers.

Soleri, Paolo 1919– •*Italian-US architect and urban planner*• Born in Turin, Italy, he earned a doctorate in architecture at the Torina Politècnico, then emigrated to the US in 1947 and studied with **Frank Lloyd Wright**. A visionary architectural designer, he has planned compact housing communities (*arcologies*, from *architecture* and *ecology*) which are designed to preserve the environment and conserve energy. Working in Arizona, where he established the Cosanti Foundation, he constructed his first experimental city (Arcosanti) in the 1970s.

Solomon c. 962–922 BC •*King of Israel*• The reign of Solomon, who was the second son of **David** and **Bathsheba**, is described in 1 Kings 1–11 and 2 Chronicles 1–10. It is characterized by expansion in trade and political contacts, by an elaborate building program, and by the centralization of authority in the crown. The major kingdoms of the Near East were all in a relatively weak state, and Solomon strengthened his army more as a warning than as an intention, and was free for most of his reign from the need to undertake extensive military campaigns. He built up a corps of chariots and founded chariot cities (1 Kings 10:26), of which those at Gezer, Megiddo and Hazor have been excavated. Solomon developed trade links with Phoenicia, Egypt, South Arabia, and in the north in Syria and Cilicia. He married Pharaoh's daughter, and developed relations with Hiram of Tyre. The principal building in Jerusalem was the temple and royal palace, both described in detail in 1 Kings. To finance this program, Solomon reorganized the administrative districts of Israel, reducing the old tribal loyalties and increasing revenues to the crown. He also subjugated the Canaanite population, drafting many of them into his workforce. Apart from his building, Solomon is famous especially for his wisdom; as a legendary wise man, several books were later attributed to him, including the Song of Solomon, the Wisdom of Solomon, Proverbs, and some of the Psalms. Among Solomon's contacts in the Arabian world was the queen of a country called Sheba, which makes its first appearance in history in this connection. **The Queen of Sheba** was the ruler of the Sabeans, a people who seem to have occupied a part of southwest Arabia (modern Yemen), though they are placed by some in north Arabia. She journeyed to Jerusalem to test the wisdom of Solomon and exchange extravagant gifts, such as spices, gold and jewels, although this may imply a trade pact. The story, as told in 1 Kings 10 and 2 Chronicles 9, can also be read in the Qur'an. According to later, Ethiopian tradition, the couple married and their son founded the royal dynasty of Ethiopia.

Solon c. 638–559 BC •*Athenian lawgiver*• He was born into an aristocratic Athenian family. He was elected archon in 594 BC, in a time of economic distress, and was appointed to reform the constitution. He set free all people who had been enslaved for debt, reformed the currency, admitted a fourth class (Thetes) to the citizenship, and set up a *Boulé* (council) of 400. He sought a compromise between democracy and oligarchy, and repealed the more stringent laws of Draco except those relating to murder. He wrote elegiac and iambic poetry, some of which survives, as a vehicle for his political and social observations. He died soon after his kinsman **Pisistratus** seized power.

Soloviev, Vladimir Sergeyevich 1853–1900 •*Russian philosopher, theologian and poet*• Born in Moscow, the son of the historian Sergei Mikhailovich Soloviev, he proposed a universal Christianity which would unite the Catholic and Orthodox churches, and attempted a synthesis of religious philosophy with science. His main works were *The Crisis of Western Philosophy* (1875), *Russia and the Universal Church* (1889) and *The Justification of the Good* (1898).

Solow, Robert Merton 1924– •*US economist and Nobel Prize winner*• Born in Brooklyn, New York, and educated at Harvard, he was a professor at MIT from 1949 to 1995 (now emeritus). He was awarded the 1987 Nobel Prize for economics for his "study of the factors which permit production growth and increased welfare." His publications include *The Labor Market as a Social Institution* (1990).

Solti, Sir Georg, *originally* **György Stern** 1912–97 •*British conductor*• Born in Budapest, Hungary, he appeared as a pianist at the age of 12, and entered the **Franz Liszt** Academy of Music, studying with **Béla Bartók**, **Ernst von Dohnanyi** and **Zoltán Kodály**. Anti-Semitic pressure forced him to leave in 1939 for Switzerland, where he achieved success as a pianist and conductor. Postwar appointments included musical directorships at the Munich Opera (1946–52) and Covent Garden (1961–71). Later, he conducted the Chicago Symphony Orchestra (1969–91), with which he toured extensively, and the London Philharmonic Orchestra (1979–83). He made a pioneering recording of **Richard Wagner**'s *Ring of the Nibelung* and conducted it at Salzburg and Bayreuth (1983). He was appointed artistic director of the Salzburg Easter Festival (1992–93). He took British nationality in 1972 and was the recipient of many international honors.

Solzhenitsyn, Aleksandr Isayevich 1918– •*Russian writer and Nobel Prize winner*• Born in Kislovodsk, he was brought up in Rostov, where he graduated in mathematics and physics. After distinguished service with the Red Army in World War II, he was imprisoned (1945–53) for his unfavorable comments on **Stalin**'s conduct of the war. Rehabilitated in 1956, his first novel, *Odin den' Ivana Denisovicha* (1962, Eng trans *One Day in the Life of Ivan Denisovich*, 1963), set in a prison camp, was acclaimed both in Russia and the West, but his denunciation in 1967 of the strict censorship in Russia led to the banning of his later novels, *Rakovyi korpus* (1968, Eng trans, 2 vols, *The Cancer Ward*, 1968–69) and *V kruge pervom* (1968, Eng trans *The First Circle*, 1968). He was awarded the Nobel Prize for literature in 1970, and afterward published *Arkhipelag Gulag* (3 vols, 1973–76, Eng trans *The Gulag Archipelago 1918–56*, 1974–78), a factual account of the Stalinist terror. In 1974 he was deported, settling in the US, and in 1994 returned to Russia. His memoirs, *Bodalsya telyonok s dubom* (1975), were published in translation in 1980 as *The Oak and the Calf*, and *Kak nam obustroit' Rossiyu?* (Eng trans *Rebuilding Russia*, 1991) in 1990.

" "

For us in Russia, communism is a dead dog, while, for many people in the West, it is still a living lion.

1979 In the ***Listener****, February 15.*

Somare, Michael Thomas 1936– •*Papua New Guinea politician*• Educated at Sogeri Secondary School, he was a teacher (1956–62) and a journalist (1966–68) before founding the pro-independence Pangu Pati (PP, Papua New Guinea Party) in 1967. He was elected to the House of Assembly a year later and in 1972 became chief minister. After independence in 1975 he was prime minister. He was forced to resign in 1980 in the wake of a government corruption scandal, but returned as prime minister (1982–85).

Somerville, Edith (Anna Oenone) 1858–1949 •*Irish novelist*• She was born in Corfu, and was taken as a baby to the family home of Drishane in Skibbereen, County Cork. Educated at Alexandra College, Dublin, she studied painting in London, Düsseldorf and Paris, and became a magazine illustrator. In 1886 she met her cousin, Violet Martin (pseudonym "Martin Ross") with whom she began a lasting literary partnership as "Somerville and Ross." They are known chiefly for a series of novels caricaturing the Irish. Beginning with *An Irish Cousin* (1889), they completed 14 works together, including *Some Experiences of an Irish R.M.* (1899), the success of which led to two sequels, *Further Experiences ...* (1908) and *In Mr Knox's Country* (1915). After Violet's death in 1915, Edith continued to write as "Somerville and Ross."

Somerville, Sir James Fownes 1882–1949 •*English naval commander*• As a specialist in radio communications he served in the Dardanelles (1915), and in the Grand Fleet (1915–18). As vice admiral in the Mediterranean, he sank the French ships at Oran (1940), shelled Genoa (1941), helped in the sinking of the *Bismarck* (1941), took part in the Malta convoy battle (1941) and, after the entry of the Japanese into the war, became commander in chief of the British fleet in the Indian Ocean. In 1945 he was promoted to admiral of the fleet.

Somerville, Mary, *née* **Fairfax** 1780–1872 •*Scottish mathematician and astronomer*• Born in Jedburgh, she was inspired by the works of **Euclid** and studied algebra and classics, despite strong disapproval from her family. From 1816 she lived in London, and in 1826 presented a paper on *The Magnetic Properties of the Violet Rays in the Solar Spectrum* to the Royal Society. In 1831 she published *The Mechanism of the Heavens*, her account for the general reader of **Pierre Simon Laplace**'s *Mécanique céleste*. This had great success and she wrote several further expository works on physics, physical geography and microscopic science. Somerville College (1879) at Oxford is named after her.

Somoza (García), Anastasio 1896–1956 •*Nicaraguan dictator*• Born in San Marcos, Nicaragua, he was educated there and in the US. As chief of the National Guard, he established himself in supreme power, deposed President Juan Bautista Sacasa and replaced him in 1937. Exiling most of his political opponents and amassing a huge personal fortune, he retained power until his assassination. His sons, Luis Somoza Debayle (1923–67) and Anastasio Somoza Debayle (1925–80), continued dynastic control of Nicaragua until the 1979 revolution.

Sondheim, Stephen Joshua 1930– •*US composer and lyricist*• Born in New York City, he saw little of his wealthy parents but was taken under the wing of **Oscar Hammerstein II**, who taught him to write lyrics. He wrote incidental music for *Girls of Summer* (1956) before providing the lyrics for **Leonard Bernstein**'s *West Side Story* (1957). The first shows for which he (somewhat unusually) wrote both the music and the lyrics were *A Funny Thing Happened on the Way to the Forum* (1962) and *Anyone Can Whistle* (1964). *Company* (1970, Tony award), about married life in New York, was followed by shows including *Follies* (1971, Tony award), *A Little Night Music* (1973, Tony award), *Sweeney Todd, The Demon Barber of Fleet Street* (1979, Tony award), *Sunday in the Park With George* (1984, Pulitzer Prize), *Assassins* (1991) and *Passion* (1994). His complex and eclectic musicals are regarded as classics of the genre.

Song Jiaoren (Sung Chiao-jen) 1882–1913 •*Chinese revolutionary and champion of parliamentary government*• He was one of the leading members of **Sun Yat-sen**'s revolutionary anti-Manchu organization, the Tongmenghui (T'ungmenghui, Alliance League), before 1911. On the establishment of a republic in 1912, the Tongmenghui was transformed into a political party, the Guomindang (Kuomintang, Nationalist Party). Song became its principal spokesman in the elections of 1912, which the Guomindang won, and he was heavily favored to become prime minister. His program, however, was a direct challenge to the hegemonic ambitions of the president, **Yuan Shikai**, and he was assassinated at Shanghai railway station by Yuan's henchmen.

Song Meiling *See* **Chiang Kai-shek**

Song Qingling (Soong Ch'ing-ling) 1892–1981 •*Chinese politician*• The daughter of Chinese merchant and Methodist missionary Charles Jones Soong (d. 1927), she married **Sun Yat-sen** in 1916. She played an increasingly active political role after his death (1925) and became associated with the left wing of the

Guomindang (Kuomintang). She was elected to the Central Executive Committee of the Guomindang (1926) and was a member of the left-wing Guomindang government established at Wuhan in 1927 in opposition to her brother-in-law **Chiang Kai-shek**. After the collapse of the Wuhan government, she spent two years in Moscow (1927–29). She returned to China from Hong Kong in 1937. In 1950 she was one of the three non-Communist vice chairmen of the new Chinese Communist Republic, and between 1976 and 1978 served as acting head of state.

Sonnino, (Giorgio) Sidney Sonnino, Baron 1847–1922 •*Italian diplomat and politician*• Born in Pisa of an English mother, he entered parliament in 1880 and occupied various ministerial posts. He was twice prime minister (1906, 1909–10), and as foreign minister was responsible, with Antonio Salandra (1853–1931), for bringing Italy into World War I on the side of the Allies. He was part of the Italian delegation to the postwar conference in Paris.

Son of Sam *See* **Berkowitz, David**

Sontag, Susan 1933– •*US writer and critic*• Born in New York City, she attended the University of Chicago and Harvard. Although she emerged first as an experimental fiction writer, as author of *The Benefactor* (1963) and *Death Kit* (1967), her main impact has been as a critic. Her influential books include *Against Interpretation* (1966), *On Photography* (1976) and *Illness as Metaphor* (1978), which she revised as *AIDS and Its Metaphors* (1989) to take AIDS into account. She has made four films, *Duet for Cannibals* (1964), *Brother Carl* (1971), *Promised Lands* (1974) and *Unguided Tour* (1983). Later publications include the novels *The Volcano Lover* (1992) and *In America* (2000), and a play, *Alice in Bed* (1993).

“ ”

Interpretation is the revenge of the intellect upon art.

1964 In ***The Evergreen Review****, December.*

Soong, T V (Tse-Ven) (Tzu-Wen Sung or **Ziwen Song)** 1894–1971 •*Chinese financier and politician*• Born in Shanghai, the son of Chinese merchant and Methodist missionary Charles Jones Soong (d. 1927), he studied at Harvard and Columbia Universities. His sister **Song Qingling** married **Sun Yat-sen**, and a second sister, Song Meiling (1897–2003), married **Chiang Kai-shek** in 1927. T V Soong provided the financial stability that made possible the 1926 Northern Expedition that reunited China under the Nationalists. He was finance minister of the Nationalist government at Guangzhou (Canton) (1925–27) and at Nanjing (Nanking) (1928–33), and was foreign minister from 1942 to 1945. He founded the Bank of China (1936). When the Nationalist government was overthrown in 1949, he went to the US.

Soong Ch'ing-ling *See* **Song Qingling**

Soper, Donald Oliver Soper, Baron 1903–98 •*English Methodist minister*• He was born in Wandsworth, London. Widely known for his open-air preaching, he was superintendent of the West London Mission (1936–78) and wrote many books on Christianity and social questions, particularly on international issues from the pacifist angle. He was president of the Methodist Conference in 1953, and was created a life peer in 1965.

Sophia 1630–1714 •*Electress of Hanover*• The youngest daughter of **Frederick V**, elector palatine, and **Elizabeth**, queen of Bohemia, she was born in The Hague. In 1658 she married Ernest Augustus, duke of Brunswick-Lüneburg, afterward (1692) elector of Hanover. She was the mother of **George I**.

Sophia Alekseyevna 1657–1704 •*Regent of Russia*• She was born in Moscow, the daughter of Czar **Alexis I Mikhailovich**. After the death of her brother, Czar Fyodor III (1682), her brothers Ivan and Peter were proclaimed joint czars, with Sophia as regent. Supported by her adviser and lover Prince Vasili V Gallitzin (or Golitsyn), she became the de facto ruler of Russia. During her regency a treaty of permanent peace was signed with Poland and treaties were also signed with Sweden and Denmark (1684) and with China (1689). However, unsuccessful campaigns against the Turks in the Crimea (1687, 1689) did much to discredit the regent, and she was removed from power by nobles in 1689. She spent the rest of her life in a convent in Moscow.

Sophocles c. 496–405 BC •*Athenian tragedian*• He was the son of Sophilus, a wealthy arms manufacturer of Colonus near Athens. He won his first dramatic victory at the Great Dionysia in 468, defeating **Aeschylus** apparently at his first attempt. He was twice elected *strategos* (general), once with **Pericles** in 440 (when they had to put down the revolt of Samos), and was appointed one of the commissioners to investigate the failure of the expedition to Sicily in 413. Unlike Aeschylus and **Euripides**, Sophocles is said to have declined invitations to live at royal courts. **Aristotle** regarded Sophocles as an innovator, for adding a third actor to the usual two, increasing the chorus from 12 to 15, and for giving each play in a trilogy its own theme and plot. The principal characteristics of his dramatic style concern the conflict of the individual and the state (most notably in *Antigone* and *Oedipus Tyrannus*), the action of individuals as showing their heroic stature, and the relation between an individual's character and behavior. Use of dialogue and dramatic irony are important elements in Sophocles' art. The play generally regarded as Sophocles' greatest is *Oedipus Tyrannus*, in which the apparently innocent Oedipus is gradually revealed as the murderer of his father and the husband of his mother, and suffers the fate imposed by his own sentence. Aristotle based his aesthetic theory of drama in the *Poetica* on this play, and from it **Sigmund Freud** derived the name and function of the Oedipus complex. In contrast to Aeschylean tragedy, where the plot is essentially static and the hero is virtually doomed from the beginning, in Sophocles' works the plot develops. Sophocles is said to have written 130 plays (of which 7 were spurious), and won the dramatic prize on 24 occasions with 96 plays. Seven of the tragedies have survived: *Ajax* (date uncertain), *Antigone* (441), *Oedipus Tyrannus* (c. 429), *Trachiniai* (c. 429, "Women of Trachis"), *Electra* (between 418 and 410), *Philoctetes* (409), and *Oedipus Coloneus* (produced 401, after his death). In addition, a papyrus discovered in modern times contains a large fragment of a satyr play, *Ichneutai* ("Trackers").

Sophonisba d. c. 203 BC •*Carthaginian noblewoman*• The daughter of a Carthaginian general, during the Second Punic War (218–202 BC) she married Syphax, king of Numidia, and urged him to join the Carthaginian side. In 203 BC he was defeated by a Roman army led by Rome's Numidian ally Masinissa, who took Sophonisba captive and married her. The Romans, fearful of Sophonisba's influence on him, objected to the marriage and Masinissa complied, but, according to **Livy**, sent her poison to prevent her being sent as a captive to Rome. **Corneille**, **Voltaire** and **Vittorio Alfieri** have written tragedies based on this story.

Sopwith, Sir Thomas Octave Murdoch 1888–1989 •*English aircraft designer and sportsman*• Born in London, he won the Baron de Forest Prize in 1910 for flying across the English Channel. In 1912 he founded the Sopwith Aviation Company at Kingston-on-Thames, London, where he designed and built many of the aircraft used in World War I, including the Pup and the Camel. He was chairman (later president) of the Hawker Siddeley Group (1935, 1963). A keen yachtsman, he competed for the America's Cup in 1934. He was knighted in 1953.

Sorabji, Cornelia 1866–1954 •*Indian lawyer*• The first female student at Decca College, Poona, she was awarded a British university scholarship, and attended Somerville College, Oxford, in 1888. Continuing her law studies at Lincoln's Inn, she became the first woman to take the Bachelor of Civil Law examination (1893), although women were not admitted to the English bar for 30 more years. She returned to India and took up the cause of women in purdah who were wards of the court, becoming their legal adviser in Assam, Orissa and Bihar in 1904. In 1923 she moved to Calcutta and practiced as a barrister. She published widely.

Soraya, *properly* **Princess Soraya Esfandiari Bakhtiari** 1932–2001 •*Queen of Persia*• Born in Esfahan of Persian and German parents, she was educated at Esfahan, and later in England and Switzerland. She became queen of Persia (Iran) on her marriage to **Muhammad Reza Pahlavi** (1951). The marriage was dissolved in 1958.

Sorbon, Robert de 1201–74 •*French churchman*• Born in Sorbon, near Rethels, he was educated in Rheims and Paris. He was the confessor of **Louis IX** and founded the college of the Sorbonne in Paris (c. 1257).

Sorel, Georges 1847–1922 •*French social philosopher*• Born in Cherbourg, Manche, he studied engineering but turned to philosophy and social theory, drawing on the works of **Nietzsche**, **Marx** and **Henri Bergson**. His best-known work is *Réflexions sur la violence* (1908, "Reflections on Violence"), in which he argued that socialism would only be achieved by confrontation and revolution. His work was read by political leaders as diverse as **Lenin** and **Mussolini**.

Sorley, Charles Hamilton 1895–1915 •*Scottish poet*• Born in Aberdeen, he was educated at King's College Choir School, and in 1908 he won a scholarship to Marlborough College. One of the first to enlist in 1914, he believed in the war as a necessary evil, as his poems show. In 1915 he went with his battalion to France, where he was killed by a sniper at the Battle of Loos. *Marlborough and Other Poems* was published posthumously by his family in 1916. Sorley left fewer than 40 complete poems, the best of which are unsentimental and direct. *The Collected Poems of Charles Hamilton Sorley* was edited in 1985.

Sosigenes fl. c. 40 BC •*Alexandrian astronomer*• He was an adviser to Julius Caesar in his reform of the calendar, introducing the leap year with an extra day every four years. This system remained in force in the West until the Gregorian reform of 1582.

Sotheby, John 1740–1807 •*English auctioneer and antiquary*• He was the nephew of Samuel Baker (d. 1778), who in 1744 founded at York Street, Covent Garden, London, the first sale room in Great Britain devoted exclusively to books, manuscripts and prints. He became a director of the firm (1780–1800) that became known as Leigh and Sotheby. In 1803 it was transferred to the Strand. The business was continued by his nephew, Samuel (1771–1842), and grandnephew, Samuel Leigh (1806–61).

Soto, Hernando or **Fernando de** c. 1500–42 •*Spanish explorer in America*• He was born into the nobility in Jerez de los Caballeros, Spain, but his family's fortunes were in decline, and he sailed to Central America in 1519. After helping **Francisco Pizzaro** conquer Peru, he was appointed governor of Cuba and Florida (1536). In 1539 he set out to explore Florida. Following illusory tales of gold and often clashing with Native American peoples, he and his soldiers traveled through much of the present-day American South. They became the first Europeans (1541) to see the Mississippi River, and when de Soto died of a fever, his body was sunk in the river to prevent its being desecrated by Native Americans.

Sottsass, Ettore, Jr 1917– •*Italian architect and designer*• Born in Innsbruck, Austria, he studied architecture in Turin. After serving in World War II he moved to Milan and set up his own design office in 1946, becoming involved in the postwar reconstruction of northern Italian towns. As an industrial designer he is associated from 1958 with the firm of Olivetti, for which he designed several typewriters and other office equipment. He departed from mainstream design in the 1970s, becoming a leader of the Memphis group (formed 1981).

Soult, Nicolas Jean de Dieu 1769–1851 •*French general*• Born in Saint-Amans-la-Bastide, Tarn, he was made general of division (April 1799) by **André Masséna**, and in 1804 Soult was appointed a marshal of France by **Napoleon I**. He led the French armies in the Peninsular War (1808–14) until defeated at Toulouse (1814). A skilled opportunist, he became a Royalist after Napoleon's abdication, but joined him again on his return from Elba and was made chief of staff. After Waterloo he rallied the wreck of the army at Laon, but agreed with **Lazare Carnot** as to the uselessness of further resistance. He was banished until 1819, when he was gradually restored to all his honors.

Souness, Graeme James 1953– •*Scottish soccer player and manager*• Born in Edinburgh, he joined Liverpool in 1978 after stints with Tottenham Hotspur and Middlesbrough, and brought the club league championships and European Cups. He played for the Italian club Sampdoria (1984–86), then returned home to become player-manager of the Rangers. He succeeded **Kenny Dalglish** as manager of Liverpool in 1991, and resigned in 1994. He has since managed a number of clubs, including Southampton and the Blackburn Rovers.

Souphanouvong, Prince 1902–95 •*Laotian statesman*• A half brother of Prince Souvanna Phouma, he was educated in Paris. After returning to Laos (1938) he founded the Chinese-backed Communist Pathet Lao (Land of the Lao), to fight first against French rule and then, from 1954, against the ruling Lao Issara and rightist forces. His pro-Vietnamese, Communist ties led to his imprisonment (1959–60). During the civil war in Laos in the 1960s, he and the Pathet Lao escaped to the hills. Following the declaration of a socialist republic (1975), he became president of the Lao People's Democratic Republic, retaining this largely ceremonial position until he retired in 1986.

Sousa, John Philip 1854–1932 •*US composer and bandmaster*• Born in Washington DC, he gained experience as a conductor of theater orchestras, and in 1880 he became conductor of the United States Marine Band. His own band, formed twelve years later, achieved an international reputation. He composed more than 100 popular marches, notably "Semper Fidelis" (1888) and "The Stars and Stripes Forever" (1887). He also composed ten comic operas. He is known as the inventor of the sousaphone, a large brass wind instrument resembling the tuba.

“ ”

Jazz will endure just as long as people hear it through their feet instead of their brains.

c. 1920 Attributed.

Soutar, William 1898–1943 •*Scottish poet*• Born in Perth, he was educated at Perth Academy. He was conscripted into the Royal Navy (1916–19), and contracted a form of spondylitis which confined him to bed for the last 13 years of his life. After demobilization he studied medicine and then English at Edinburgh. As an undergraduate he published his first volume of verse anonymously, as *Gleanings by an Undergraduate* (1923), followed by *Conflict* (1931). In 1933 he published his first volume of verse in Scots, *Seeds in the Wind*, for children. This was followed by his *Poems in Scots* (1935) and *Riddles in Scots* (1937), which gave him a permanent place in the Scottish literary revival. His remarkable *Diaries of a Dying Man* were published in 1954.

Southall, Ivan Francis 1921– •*Australian author*• Born in Canterbury, Victoria, he has written prolifically for children, including the escapist adventure series featuring airman Simon Black which began with *Meet Simon Black* (1950). His later books, which concentrate on more contemporary youth concerns, have won many awards, including *Ash Road* (1966) and *Let the Balloon Go* (1968, filmed in 1975). His World War II experiences, for which he received the Distinguished Flying Cross, led him to write a history of 461 Squadron, Royal Australian Air Force, *They Shall Not Pass Unseen* (1956), and biographies of air hero Keith Truscott and aviation pioneer **Lawrence Hargrave**. Other works include *Bread and Honey* (1970) and *Josh* (1971), which won the Carnegie Medal.

Southampton, Henry Wriothesley, 3rd Earl of 1573–1624 •*English soldier*• The son of Henry Wriothesley, the 2nd Earl, he was born in Cowdray, Sussex. He was a patron of poets, particularly of **Shakespeare**, who dedicated to him his *Venus and Adonis* (1593) and *The Rape of Lucrece* (1594) and, according to some scholars, addressed the sonnets to him. He accompanied Robert, 2nd Earl of **Essex**, to Cádiz (1596) and the Azores (1597), and took part in his rebellion. He revived *Richard II* in order to arouse anti-monarchic feeling, and was sentenced to death, but was released by **James VI and I** and restored to his peerage (1603). He was imprisoned in 1621 on charges of intrigue, and died while helping the Dutch against Spain.

Southcott, Joanna c. 1750–1814 •*English religious fanatic*• A farmer's daughter in Devon, she declared herself about 1792 to be the woman of Revelations, chapter 12, proclaiming the imminent arrival of Christ. She came to London and published *A Warning* (1803) and *The Book of Wonders* (1813–14). Her announcement that she was to give birth on October 19, 1814, to a second Prince of

Peace was received by her followers with devout reverence. But she fell into a coma and died of a brain tumor in December 1814.

Southerne, Thomas 1660–1746 •*Irish dramatist*• He was born in Oxmantown, County Dublin. From Trinity College, Dublin, he passed to the Middle Temple, London, and in 1682 began his career with *The Loyal Brother*. **Dryden** wrote the prologue and epilogue, and Southerne finished Dryden's *Cleomenes* (1692). He served a short time under the Duke of **Berwick** and, at his request, wrote the *Spartan Dame*. His best-known plays are *The Fatal Marriage* (1694) and *Oroonoko* (before 1696), based on **Aphra Behn**.

Southey, Robert 1774–1843 •*English poet and writer*• Born in Bristol, he was sent to Westminster School, but he was expelled in 1792 for his Jacobin sympathies and for denouncing whipping in the school magazine, and went on to Balliol College, Oxford. He met **Coleridge** in Bristol in 1794 and they wrote a topical drama together, *The Fall of Robespierre* (1794); Southey published a volume of *Poems* (1795) and an epic poem, *Joan of Arc* (1795). Also in 1795 he married Edith Fricker (d. 1838), whose elder sister Sara married Coleridge. After studying law he settled in Keswick. He became poet laureate in 1813. Many of his short poems are well known, such as "Holly Tree" and "After Blenheim." His other works include biographies—of *Nelson* (1813), *Wesley* (1820) and *Bunyan* (1830)—*A Vision of Judgment* (1821) and *The Doctor* (1834–47), a miscellany, which includes the nursery classic *The Three Bears*.

Soutine, Chaim 1893–1943 •*French artist*• Born in Smilovich, Lithuania, he studied at Vilno and moved to Paris in 1913. He is best known for his paintings of carcases, his series of *Choirboys* (1927) and the magnificent psychological study, *The Old Actress* (1924, Moltzau collection, Norway). After his death, his vivid colors and passionate handling of paint gained him recognition as one of the foremost Expressionist painters.

Souza, Madame de, *née* **Adelaïde Marie Emilie Filleul** 1761–1836 •*French novelist*• She was born in the Norman château of Longpré, and married the Comte de Flahaut (1785–1870). At the outbreak of the French Revolution (1789) she found refuge in Germany and England, and there learned of her husband's execution at Arras. She turned to writing, and in 1794 published her first book, *Adèle de Sénange* (1794). In 1802 she married the Marquis de Souza-Botelho (1758–1825). Later novels include *Charles et Marie* (1801).

Soyinka, Wole, *in full* **Akinwande Oluwole Soyinka** 1934– •*Nigerian dramatist, poet, novelist and Nobel Prize winner*• Born in Western Nigeria, he was educated in Abeokuta and Ibadan before moving to England to do research at the University of Leeds. His first play, *The Invention*, was performed at the Royal Court Theatre, London, in 1955. He returned to Ibadan in 1959, and productions of *The Swamp Dwellers* and *The Lion and the Jewel* immediately established him in the forefront of Nigerian literature. He founded the Masks amateur theater company (1960), and the professional Orisun Repertory (1964), companies which played an important part in his development of a new Nigerian drama, written in English but using the words, music, dance and pantomime of the traditional festivals. From 1967 to 1969 he was a political prisoner, and he later became Professor of Comparative Literature at the University of Ife (1976–85), and Professor of Africana Studies and Theater at Cornell University (1988–92). His writing is concerned with the tension between old and new in modern Africa, and includes his first novel, *The Interpreters* (1964), the poetic collection *A Shuttle in the Crypt* (1972), the mostly prose "prison notes," *The Man Died* (1973) and the play *The Beatification of Area Boy* (1995). He was awarded the Nobel Prize for literature in 1986.

Sozini, Fausto Paulo *See* **Socinus, Faustus**

Sozini, Lelio Francesco Maria *See* **Socinus, Laelius**

Spaak, Paul Henri 1899–1972 •*Belgian statesman*• He was born in Brussels, where he began to practice law in 1922. A socialist deputy for Brussels in 1932, he rose to become the first socialist premier of Belgium in 1938, but resigned the following year. He was foreign minister with the government-in-exile in London during World War II, and in 1946 was elected president of the first General Assembly of the United Nations. He was prime minister again in 1946 and from 1947 to 1949. He was in the forefront of the movement for European unity, and as foreign minister (1954–57), instrumental in helping to set up the EEC. He was secretary-general of NATO (1957–61), and foreign minister again from 1961 until his resignation from parliament in 1966.

Spacek, Sissy (Mary Elizabeth) 1949– •*US actress*• Born in Quitman, Texas, she studied at the Lee Strasberg Theater Institute. Her early films included *Badlands* (1974) and *Carrie* (1976). She received an Academy Award for Best Actress for her role as Loretta Lynn in *Coal Miner's Daughter* (1980), and further powerful performances followed in films such as *Crimes of the Heart* (1986), *Affliction* (1998) and *In the Bedroom* (2001).

Spacey, Kevin, *originally surnamed* **Fowler** 1959– •*US actor*• Born in South Orange, New Jersey, he studied at the Juilliard Drama School, New York, and began his career on stage. A versatile leading man, his film appearances include *Glengarry Glen Ross* (1992), *Seven* (1995), and *The Usual Suspects* (1995), for which he won an Academy Award for Best Actor in a Supporting Role. His portrayal of the frustrated family man Lester Burnham in *American Beauty* (1999) earned him an Academy Award for Best Actor in a Leading Role. More recent films include *The Shipping News* (2001) and *The Life of David Gale* (2003).

Spall, Timothy 1957– •*English actor*• Born in London, he studied at the Royal Academy of Dramatic Art. He was early associated with the director **Mike Leigh** in films such as *Life Is Sweet* (1990) and *Secrets and Lies* (1996), and has appeared, often in comic or burlesque roles, in films such as *Topsy Turvy* (1999) and *Rock Star* (2001). His television work has included parts in *Auf Wiedersehen Pet* (1983–84) and *Shooting the Past* (1999).

Spallanzani, Lazaro 1729–99 •*Italian biologist and naturalist*• Born in Scandiano in Modena, he studied law at Bologna and became a priest, and later rose to become Professor of Mathematics and Physics at Reggio University (1757), moving to Modena in 1763 and to the chair of natural history at the University of Pavia in 1769. He is remembered for his skills in experimental physiology. Deeply interested in reproduction, he set about disproving the long-established theory of spontaneous generation, showing in 1765 that broth, boiled thoroughly and hermetically sealed, remained sterile. He argued that gastric juice constituted the key digestive agent, was the first to observe blood passing from arteries to veins in a warm-blooded animal, and was successful in artificially inseminating amphibians, silkworms and a spaniel.

Spark, Dame Muriel Sarah, *née* **Camberg** 1918– •*Scottish novelist, short-story writer, biographer and poet*• Born in Edinburgh, the daughter of a Jewish engineer, she was educated there at James Gillespie's School for Girls and Heriot-Watt College. She was married in 1938 and spent some years in Central Africa. When the marriage failed, she returned to Britain in 1944 and worked in the Foreign Office; she remained in London after the war to become general secretary of the Poetry Society and editor of *Poetry Review* (1947–49). In 1951 she won a short-story competition with *The Seraph and the Zambesi*. Three years later she converted to Roman Catholicism, an event reflected in much of her later writing. Since the early 1960s she has lived mainly in New York and Italy. She is preeminently a novelist and short-story writer. *The Comforters* (1957) was hailed by **Evelyn Waugh** as "brilliantly original and fascinating" and her reputation grew steadily with the publication of *Memento Mori* (1959), *The Ballad of Peckham Rye* (1960) and *The Bachelors* (1961). She achieved public success with her sixth novel, *The Prime of Miss Jean Brodie* (1961), an eerie portrait of a schoolteacher with advanced ideas set on the eve of war in Europe. Later works include *The Girls of Slender Means* (1963), *The Mandelbaum Gate* (1965), *The Abbess of Crewe* (1974), *Loitering With Intent* (1981), *The Only Problem* (1984) and *A Far Cry From Kensington* (1988). Her stories were collected in 1967 and 1985, and the first volume of her autobiography, *Curriculum Vitae*, was published in 1992. She has also published a book for children, *The French Window and the Small Telephone* (1993), and has also written critical works. She was given the honorary title of Dame Commander, Order of the British Empire, in 1993.

" "

One's prime is elusive. You little girls, when you grow up, must be on the alert to recognize your prime at whatever time of your life it may occur. You must live it to the full.

*1961 **The Prime of Miss Jean Brodie**, chapter 1.*

Spartacus d. 71 BC *•Roman gladiator and rebel•* Born in Thrace, he was a shepherd who became a robber, but was captured and sold to a trainer of gladiators at Capua. In 73 BC he escaped and built an army of about 90,000 slaves and the dispossessed, with whom he defeated several Roman armies and devastated much of southern Italy. He was defeated by **Marcus Licinius Crassus** near the River Silarus in 71, and executed by crucifixion with his followers. The remnants of his army were annihilated by **Pompey** on his return from Spain.

Spassky, Boris Vasilevich 1937– *•Russian chess player•* He was born in Leningrad (now St Petersburg). He won the world championship from **Tigran Petrosian** in 1969, but lost, in his first defense, to **Bobby Fischer** in Reykjavík, Iceland, in 1972.

Spee, Count Maximilian von 1861–1914 *•German naval commander•* Born in Copenhagen, he joined the Imperial German Navy in 1878. In 1908 he became chief of staff of the North Sea Command. At the outbreak of World War I in 1914 he was in command of a commerce-raiding force in the Pacific Ocean. Off Coronel, Chile, he encountered an inferior British squadron and sank HMS *Good Hope* and *Monmouth.* He attempted an attack on British coaling and wireless stations in the Falklands, but six German ships were sunk by the British squadron under **Frederick Sturdee**. Von Spee and two of his sons went down with his flagship.

Speer, Albert 1905–81 *•German architect and Nazi government official•* He joined the National Socialist Party in 1931 and undertook architectural commissions for the party, becoming **Hitler**'s chief architect in 1934. In 1942 he was made minister of armaments; his talent for organization resulted in greatly improved industrial performance. Always more concerned with technology and administration than Nazi ideology, he openly opposed Hitler in the final months of the war, and was the only Nazi leader at the Nuremberg trials to admit responsibility for the regime's actions. He was sentenced to 20 years' imprisonment in Spandau fortress, and after his release in 1966 published *Inside the Third Reich* (1970) and *Spandau: The Secret Diaries* (1976).

Speight, Johnny 1920–98 *•English comic screenwriter•* Born in London, after World War II he began writing for such comic stars as **Frankie Howerd**, Arthur Haynes and **Morecambe and Wise**. He made his mark on television with the play *The Compartment* (1962), and the creation of the loud-mouthed, working-class bigot Alf Garnett in the controversial assault on sacred cows like religion and royalty, *Till Death Do Us Part* (1964–74). The series earned him Screenwriters' Guild Awards in 1966, 1967 and 1968, and the character was revived in another series, *In Sickness and in Health* (1985–86). His other television work includes *Spooner's Patch* (1979–82, cowritten with Ray Galton) and *The Nineteenth Hole* (1989). Among his publications are his autobiography, *For Richer, for Poorer* (1991).

Speke, John Hanning 1827–64 *•English explorer•* Born in Jordans, Ilminster, Somerset, he served with the Indian army in the Punjab. In 1854 he joined **Richard Francis Burton** in a hazardous expedition to Somaliland, and in 1857 the Royal Geographical Society sent them out to search for the equatorial lakes of Africa. Speke, while traveling alone, discovered the Victoria Nyanza and saw in it the headwaters of the Nile. In 1860 he returned with **James Grant**, explored the lake, and tracked the Nile flowing out of it. He was killed while hunting.

Spence, Sir Basil Urwin 1907–76 *•Scottish architect•* Born in India of Scots parents and educated at London and Edinburgh Schools of Architecture, he was twice mentioned in dispatches during World War II. In the postwar years, he gradually emerged as the leading British architect, with his fresh approach to new university buildings and conversions at Queen's College, Cambridge, Southampton, Sussex and other universities; his pavilions for the Festival of Britain (1951); the British Embassy in Rome; and his prize-winning designs for housing estates at Sunbury-on-Thames (1951). His best-known work is his prize design for the new Coventry Cathedral (1951), which boldly merged new and traditional structural methods.

Spence, Catherine Helen 1825–1910 *•Australian writer and feminist•* Born near Melrose, Scotland, she emigrated to Australia in 1839. She published the first novel of Australian life written by a woman (*Clare Morrison*, 1854) and wrote five more novels. A concern with social problems led her to make lecture tours of Great Britain and the US. She pressed for proportional representation in *A Plea for Pure Democracy* (1861), and she wrote Australia's first social studies textbook, *The Laws We Live Under* (1880). In 1897 she ran for election to the Federal Convention, becoming Australia's first woman candidate.

Spencer, Herbert 1820–1903 *•English evolutionary philosopher•* Born in Derby, he had a varied career as a railway engineer, teacher, journalist and assistant editor of *The Economist* (1848–53) before becoming a full-time writer. His particular interest was in evolutionary theory, which he expounded in *Principles of Psychology* in 1855, four years before **Charles Darwin**'s *The Origin of Species.* He also applied his evolutionary theories to ethics and sociology. An advocate of social Darwinism, he coined the phrase "survival of the fittest." His major work was the nine-volume *System of Synthetic Philosophy* (1862–93), which brought together metaphysics, ethics, biology, psychology and sociology.

Spencer, Sir Stanley 1891–1959 *•English painter•* Born in Cookham, Berkshire, he studied at the Slade School of Art, London, where he learned the linear drawing style which informs most of his work. Never part of any of the main movements in 20th-century British art, he remained an eccentric figure, tackling unfashionable religious subjects in his precise and distinctive style. These he transposed into his own local context at Cookham, especially in *The Resurrection* (1922–27). He was an official war artist in World War II. His best-known work is his decorative scheme of murals of army life for the Sandham Memorial Chapel, Burghclere (1926–32). His brother Gilbert (1892–1976) was also an artist.

Spencer Jones, Sir Harold *See* **Jones, Sir Harold Spencer**

Spender, Dale 1943– *•Australian feminist writer and teacher•* Born in Newcastle, New South Wales, Spender studied at the Universities of Sydney and London. The co-originator of the international database on women, *Women's International Knowledge: Encyclopedia and Data*, she worked as a lecturer and taught women's studies courses on the politics of knowledge and the intellectual aspects of sexism. As well as being the Australian representative for a number of international academic journals, she sat on the management committee of the Australian Society of Authors, and has edited several anthologies of literature, as well as the journal *Women's Studies International Forum.* Her books include *Man Made Language* (1981).

Spender, Sir Stephen 1909–95 *•English poet and critic•* Born in London, he was educated at University College Oxford. Left-wing in outlook, from 1939 to 1941 he was coeditor of *Horizon*, from 1953 to 1967 coeditor of *Encounter*, and was Professor of English at University College London (1970–77). He translated **Schiller**, **Rainer Maria Rilke** and **Federico García Lorca**, among others, besides writing much literary criticism. He relived his experiences in the Spanish civil war and World War II in *Poems From Spain* (1939), *Runes and Visions* (1941), *Poems of Dedication* (1941) and *The Edge of Darkness* (1949). Critical evaluations include *The Destructive Element* (1936), *Life and the Poet* (1942), *The Creative Element* (1944) and his first autobiography, *World Within World* (1951). His later work includes *The Year of the Young Rebels* (1969), *The Thirties and After* (1978) and *Chinese Journal* (with David Hockney, 1982). *Collected Poems 1930–85* was published in 1985, and his *Journals* (1939–83) in 1987. His acclaimed volume of poetry, *Dolphins*, was published in 1994.

Spengler, Oswald 1880–1936 *•German philosopher of history•* Born in Blankenburg, Harz, he studied at Halle, Munich and Berlin, and taught mathematics in Hamburg (1908) before devoting himself entirely to the compilation of the morbidly prophetic *Untergang des Abendlandes* (2 vols, 1918–22, Eng trans *The Decline of the West*, 1926–29), which argues, by analogy, that all civilizations or cultures are subject to the same cycle of growth and decay in accordance with predetermined "historical destiny."

Spenser, Edmund c. 1552–99 •*English poet*• He was born in London, the son of a gentleman tradesman, and educated at Merchant Taylors' School and Pembroke Hall, Cambridge. Shortly after leaving Cambridge (1576) he obtained a place in Robert Dudley, Earl of **Leicester**'s household, and this led to a friendship with Sir **Philip Sidney** and the Areopagus, a society of wits. His first original work, *The Shepheard's Calender* (1579), dedicated to Sidney, heralded the age of Elizabethan poetry. In 1580 he was appointed secretary to Lord Grey de Wilton, lord deputy in Ireland, and was rewarded for his involvement in crushing the Trim rebellion with Kilcolman Castle in Cork. He settled there (1586), but in 1589 visited London with Sir **Walter Raleigh**, who had seen the first three books of *The Faerie Queene* at Kilcolman and now carried him off to lay them at the feet of Queen **Elizabeth I**. Published in 1590, they were an immediate success, but a previous misdemeanor, the attack in *Mother Hubberd's Tale* on the proposed match between Elizabeth and the Duc d'Alençon, was not forgotten, and the poet returned to Ireland in 1591 a disappointed man. He later published his wry reflections on his visit in *Colin Clout's Come Home Again* (1595). *Complaints*, published in 1591, contains, besides his early work, the brilliantly colored but enigmatic *Muiopotmos, Mother Hubberd's Tale*, to which was now added a bitter satire on court favor, *The Early Tears of the Muses*, lamenting the lack of patronage; and his pastoral elegy for Sir Philip Sidney, which is so frigid as to put their friendship in question. In 1594 he married Elizabeth Boyle and celebrated his courtship in the sonnet sequence *Amoretti* and his wedding in the supreme marriage poem *Epithalamion*. He revisited London in 1596 with three more books of *The Faerie Queene*, which were published along with the *Four Hymns*. In the same year, he wrote *Prothalamion*. Kilcolman Castle was burned in the 1598 Irish uprising, but the Spensers escaped to Cork and from there to safety in London.

" "

And he that strives to touch the stars,
Oft stumbles at a straw.

1579 ***The Shepheard's Calender***, *"July," ll. 99–100.*

Speranza *See* **Wilde, Lady Jane Francesca**

Sperry, Roger Wolcott 1913–94 •*US neuroscientist and Nobel Prize winner*• Born in Hartford, Connecticut, he studied zoology at the University of Chicago, then worked at Harvard and the Yerkes Laboratory of Primate Biology (1941–46) and later at the University of Chicago (1946–52) and the California Institute of Technology (Caltech) (1954–84). He first made his name in the field of developmental neurobiology. In the 1950s and 1960s he pioneered the behavioral investigation of "split-brain" animals and humans, establishing that each hemisphere possessed specific higher functions, the left side controlling verbal activity and processes such as writing, reasoning, etc; whereas the right side is more responsive to music, face and voice recognition, etc. He shared the Nobel Prize for physiology or medicine in 1981 with **David Hubel** and **Torsten Wiesel**.

Speusippus c. 407–339 BC •*Greek philosopher*• He lived in Athens and was **Plato**'s nephew and his successor as head of the academy in 348 BC. He produced a large body of work, but only a few fragments survive. He was admired by **Aristotle**.

Spielberg, Steven 1946– •*US filmmaker*• Born in Cincinnati, Ohio, he enjoyed filmmaking from an early age, and became one of the youngest television directors at Universal Studios. A highly praised television film, *Duel* (1971), brought him the opportunity to direct for the cinema, and he followed this with a picaresque comic drama, *Sugarland Express* (1974). Since then, a succession of hits has made him the most commercially successful director ever. His films have explored primeval fears, as in *Jaws* (1975), or expressed childlike wonder at the marvels of this world and beyond, as in *Close Encounters of the Third Kind* (1977) and *E.T.* (1982). Other films include *Raiders of the Lost Ark* (1981), *Poltergeist* (1983), *Indiana Jones and the Temple of Doom* (1984) and *Gremlins* (1984). Later he concentrated on grand literary adaptations such as *The Color Purple* (1985) and *Empire of the Sun* (1987). Despite his commercial success, he did not win an Academy Award until 1994, when he was voted Best Director for *Schindler's List* (1993). That same year Spielberg cofounded the studio Dream Works SKG with Jeffrey Katzenberg (1951–) and David Geffen (1943–). More recent Spielberg films include *Saving Private Ryan* (1998, winner of five Academy Awards including Best Director), *A.I. Artificial Intelligence* (2001), *Catch Me If You Can* (2002) and *The Terminal* (2004).

Spillane, Mickey, *properly* **Frank Morrison Spillane** 1918– •*US mystery and detective novelist*• He was born in Brooklyn, New York. The author of almost 30 books, Spillane is a leading exponent of the sensational school of detective fiction. His first book, *I, the Jury* (1947), introduced Mike Hammer, a womanizing, hard-drinking, hard-fighting private investigator who punches his way with enormous relish through several books, including *Vengeance Is Mine!* (1950) and *The Body Lovers* (1967). The novels have inspired many films and a television series.

Spilsbury, Sir Bernard Henry 1877–1947 •*British pathologist*• Born in Leamington, Warwickshire, he studied physiology at Oxford, and specialized in what was then the new science of forensic pathology. He made his name at the trial of **Hawley Harvey Crippen** (1910), and was appointed pathologist to the Home Office. As an expert witness for the Crown, he was involved in many notable murder trials.

Spingarn, Joel Elias 1875–1939 •*US critic, author, and social reformer*• Born in New York City, he received a PhD from Columbia University in 1895 and taught comparative literature there until 1911, when he became an independent scholar. He is remembered chiefly for his work with the National Association for the Advancement of Colored People (NAACP), which he helped found in 1901 and headed as president (from 1930). The Spingarn Medal, established in 1914, is awarded every year to an African American who has reached high achievement in his or her field. He was also a founder of the publishing company Harcourt, Brace and Co (1919).

Spink, Ian 1947– •*Australian dancer, choreographer and director*• Born in Melbourne, he joined the Australian Ballet in 1969. In 1974 he went to perform with the Dance Company of New South Wales (now Sydney Dance Company). Moving to England in 1977, he formed the Ian Spink Group, and it was in partnership with **Siobhan Davies** and **Richard Alston** in Second Stride (founded in 1982) that he achieved his first success there, becoming sole artistic director in 1987. His work is both innovative and popular, and includes *Further and Further ...* , *Bosendorfer Waltzes*, *Weighing the Heart* (1987) and *Four Marys* (1992).

Spinola, Ambrogio, Marquis of Los Balbases 1539–1630 •*Genoese soldier*• In 1602 he raised and maintained 9,000 troops at his own expense and fought against Maurice, Count of Nassau, in the Spanish Netherlands. In the early stages of the Thirty Years' War, he served the Habsburg cause by subduing the Lower Palatinate. He was recalled to the Netherlands to fight once more against Maurice of Nassau, who, however, died of a fever while attempting to relieve Breda, which fell to Spinola in 1625. The event was commemorated in a famous painting by **Velázquez**.

Spínola, António Sebastião Ribeiro de 1910–96 •*Portuguese general and politician*• Born into a wealthy landed family, he fought on the side of General **Franco** during the Spanish civil war and was sent to Nazi Germany for training. As governor-general of Guinea-Bissau (1968–73), he endeavored to halt the independence movement through a combination of welfare and community projects and the latest counterinsurgency methods. When **António Salazar** fell in April 1974, the conservative Spínola became president as a compromise candidate. He proved a limited and naïve politician. Moreover, he clashed gravely with the Armed Forces Movement (MFA) over the granting of independence (July 1974) to Angola, Mozambique and Guinea. The ensuing power struggle led to his resignation in September 1974.

Spinoza, Benedict de, *Hebrew* **Baruch** 1632–77 •*Dutch philosopher and theologian*• He was born in Amsterdam into a Jewish émigré family that had fled from Portugal to escape Catholic persecution. His deep interest in the new astronomy and his radical ideas in theology and the philosophy of **Descartes** led to his expulsion from the Jewish community for heresy in 1656 and his persecution by **Calvin**ists. He became the leader of a small philosophical circle and made a living grinding and polishing lenses, moving in 1660 to Rijnsburg near Leiden, where he wrote his "Short Treatise on God, Man and His Well-Being" (c. 1662), the *Tractatus de intellectus emendatione* (1662, "Treatise on the Correction of the Understanding") and most of his geometrical version of Descartes's *Principia philosophiae* (1663). He moved in 1663 to Voorburg near The Hague and in 1670 to The Hague itself. The *Tractatus theologico-politicus* was published anonymously in 1670 and aroused great interest but was banned in 1674 for its controversial views on the Bible and Christian theology, including its advocacy of a strictly historical approach to the interpretation of biblical sources. He had sent **Gottfried Leibniz** his tract on optics in 1671, and Leibniz came to The Hague to visit him in 1676. But Spinoza was by then in an advanced stage of consumption, aggravated by the glass dust in his lungs, and he died the following year in Amsterdam, leaving no heir and few possessions. His major work was the *Ethics*, which was published posthumously in 1677. As the Latin title suggests (*Ethica ordine geometrico demonstrata*), this was a complete deductive metaphysical system, intended to be a proof of what is good for human beings derived with mathematical certainty from axioms, theorems and definitions. He rejects the Cartesian dualism of mind and matter in favor of a pantheistic God who is identified with the ultimate substance of the world—infinite, logically necessary and absolute—and has mind and matter as two of his attributes. Spinoza's work was first condemned as atheistical and subversive, but his reputation was restored by literary critics such as **Gotthold Lessing**, **Goethe** and **Coleridge** and later by professional philosophers, and he is now regarded as one of the great rationalist thinkers of the 17th century.

Spitz, Mark (Andrew) 1950– •*US swimmer*• Born in Modesto, California, he earned worldwide fame at the 1972 Olympics by winning seven gold medals, achieving a world record time in each event. He also won two golds in the 1968 Games, and set a total of 26 world records between 1967 and 1972. He turned professional in 1972.

Spock, Dr Benjamin McLane 1903–98 •*US pediatrician*• He was born in New Haven, Connecticut, and studied at both Yale (where he became a star oarsman and rowed in the 1924 Olympics) and Columbia. He qualified as a doctor, having trained in both pediatrics and psychiatry, and started a practice in Manhattan in 1933. He transformed the attitudes of the postwar generation on parenthood with his seminal book *The Common Sense Book of Baby and Child Care* (1946). In the 1960s he was an outspoken opponent of the Vietnam War, and was in turn accused of having been responsible for raising a weak and permissive generation of pacifists. In 1968 he was convicted on a charge of helping young men evade the draft, but appealed successfully and published *Dr Spock on Vietnam*. He continued his political interest with *Decent and Indecent: Our Personal Political Behavior* (1970), and helped form the People's Party, running for the US presidency in 1972 and the vice presidency in 1976.

“ ”

You know more than you think you do.

1946 ***The Common Sense Book of Baby and Child Care****, opening words.*

Spode, Josiah 1754–1827 •*English potter*• Born in Stoke-on-Trent, Staffordshire, he learned his trade in his father's workshops, and in 1770 founded a firm that manufactured pottery, porcelain and stoneware. He did much to popularize the willow pattern and became the foremost china manufacturer of his time. He was appointed potter to **George III** in 1806. After merging in 1833 with William Taylor Copeland, the firm also made numerous white imitation marble (*Parian*) figures.

Spoerli, Heinz 1941– •*Swiss dancer, choreographer and ballet director*• Born in Basel, he studied locally and at the School of American Ballet and the London Dance Centre before joining Basel Ballet (1960–63), Cologne Ballet (1963–66), Royal Winnipeg Ballet (1966–67), Les Grands Ballets Canadiens (1967–71) and Geneva Ballet (1971–73). He assumed directorship of Basel Ballet in 1973, gradually turning it into one of the most impressive of Europe's smaller dance ensembles. He is a prolific choreographer for companies throughout the Continent.

Spooner, William Archibald 1844–1930 •*English clergyman and educationist, after whom the spoonerism is named*• He was dean (1876–89) and warden (1903–24) of New College, Oxford. His name is associated with his own nervous tendency to transpose initial letters or half syllables, as in "a half-warmed fish" for "a half-formed wish." Many spoonerisms, such as "You must leave Oxford by the next town drain" are probably apocryphal.

Spottiswoode, William 1825–83 •*English mathematician and physicist*• Born in London, he was educated at Balliol College, Oxford, and in 1846 succeeded his father as head of the printing house of Eyre and Spottiswoode. Spottiswoode did original work on the polarization of light and electrical discharge in rarefied gases, using an early form of transformer. He wrote a series of original memoirs on the contact of curves and surfaces and the first elementary mathematical treatise on determinants (1851). He was elected a Fellow of the Royal Society in 1871 and was its president from 1878.

Sprague, Frank Julian 1857–1934 •*US electrical engineer and inventor*• Born in Milford, Connecticut, he graduated from the US Naval Academy in Annapolis, Maryland, in 1878 and served in the US Navy until 1883, after which he worked for a year with **Thomas Edison** before setting up the Sprague Electric Railway & Motor Company. He developed a new type of motor for street railways (trams), and by 1890 this had become so successful that his company was absorbed by the Edison General Electric Company. He turned to the manufacture of electric elevators, and as a result of his experience with them perfected in 1895 a system of control for multiple-unit trains, which he later developed into an automatic train control system.

Sprenger, Jacob 15th century •*German theologian*• A Dominican and Professor of Theology in Cologne, he compiled with Henricus Institor the famous *Malleus Maleficarum* (1489), which first formulated the doctrine of witchcraft, and assembled a textbook of procedure for witch trials. They were appointed inquisitors by Innocent VIII in 1484.

Spring, Dick (Richard) 1950– •*Irish Labour politician*• Born in Tralee and educated at Trinity College and King's Inns, Dublin, he worked as a lawyer before entering parliament as Labour Member of Parliament for Kerry North in 1981. In 1982 he became leader of the Labour Party and was appointed deputy prime minister, a post he held until 1987. As **John Bruton**'s deputy and foreign minister, he was instrumental in arranging the peace talks with Irish republican groups which led to the ceasefire of 1994. He has also played rugby union football for Ireland.

Spring, Howard 1889–1965 •*Welsh novelist*• Born in Cardiff, he became a newspaper reporter and literary critic, and established himself as a writer with his best-selling *Oh Absalom* (1938, renamed *My Son, My Son*). His other novels include *Fame Is the Spur* (1940), *Dunkerleys* (1946), *These Lovers Fled Away* (1955) and *Time and the Hour* (1957), and three autobiographical works (1939, 1942 and 1946).

Springfield, Dusty, *professional name of* **Mary O'Brien** 1939–99 •*English pop singer*• Born in Hampstead, London, she left the Lana Sisters to form The Springfields (1961), together with her brother Tom and Mike Hurst. Her first solo single was "I Only Want to Be With You" (1964), followed by "You Don't Have to Say You Love Me" (1966) and "Son of a Preacher Man" (1968), all of which were big hits. She performed little in the 1970s, but achieved renewed popularity with the theme song to the film *Scandal* (1989) and subsequent collaborations with The Pet Shop Boys.

Springsteen, Bruce 1949– •*US rock singer and guitarist*• He was born in Freehold, New Jersey. From the release of his first album, *Greetings From Asbury Park, NJ* (1973), he was hailed by critics and quickly developed a strong cult following, although it was not until the release of *Born to Run* (1975) that he met with major commercial success. His live performances were also highly acclaimed. Later albums included *Darkness on the Edge of Town* (1978), *The River* (1980), *Nebraska* (1982), *Born in the USA* (1984), *Tunnel of Love* (1987) and *Human Touch* (1992). By the mid-1980s he was the world's most popular white rock star, and he succeeded in combining his celebrity status with a populist style. He later returned to form with the stark acoustic set *The Ghost of Tom Joad* (1995).

Spry, Constance 1886–1960 •*English flower arranger and cookbook writer*• Born in Derby, she was educated in Ireland and, returning to England during World War I, became a welfare worker in London's East End. She began to work with flowers in the 1920s, opening flower shops and becoming chairman of the Constance Spry Flower School. She became joint principal, with Rosemary Hume, of the Cordon Bleu Cookery School in London and of the finishing school at Winkfield in Berkshire. She wrote *The Constance Spry Cookbook* (1956) with Rosemary Hume, as well as many books on flower arranging.

Spyri, Johanna 1827–1901 •*Swiss writer*• She was born near Zurich, the daughter of a doctor. She wrote to raise money for refugees of the Franco-Prussian War. *Heidi* (1880) is her best-known work; she also wrote other children's stories set in the Swiss Alps.

Squanto, *also called* **Tisquantum** d. 1622 •*Native American interpreter*• He was born into the Pawtuxet tribe near Plymouth, Massachusetts. An interpreter for the Wampanoag chief, Massasoit, he became known as a friend of the Pilgrims, teaching them how to plant corn and where to fish. He was taken from New England by English fishermen to be sold as a slave in Spain, but escaped to England and made his way back to America (1619). Because the Pawtuxets had been wiped out by disease, he joined the Wampanoags, whom he helped to conclude a peace treaty with the Pilgrims.

Squarcione, Francesco 1394–1474 •*Italian painter*• Credited as the founder of the so-called Paduan school, which was characterized by classical influences and a harsh approach to perspective, he was the teacher of many more famous painters, such as **Andrea Mantegna**. He painted panels and frescoes for the church of San Francesco in Padua, and was also a tailor and art dealer.

Ssu-ma Ch'ien *See* **Sima Qian**

Ssu-ma Hsiang-ju *See* **Sima Xiangru**

Staal, Marguerite Jeanne, Baronne de 1684–1750 •*French writer of memoirs*• She was born in Paris, the daughter of a poor Parisian painter. Her devotion to the interests of her employer, the Duchess of Maine, brought her two years in the Bastille, where she had a love affair with the Chevalier de Menil. In 1735 she married the Baron Staal. Her *Mémoires* (1755, Eng trans 1892) describes the world of the regency with intellect, observation and a subtle irony. Her *Œuvres complètes* ("Complete Works") appeared in 1821.

Staël, Madame de, *pseudonym of* **Anne Louise Germaine Necker, Baroness of Staël-Holstein** 1766–1817 •*French writer*• She was born in Paris, the only child of the financier and statesman **Jacques Necker**. In her girlhood she attended her mother's salon and turned to writing romantic comedies, tragedies, novels, essays and the celebrated *Lettres sur Rousseau* (1789). In 1786 she married Baron Eric Magnus of Staël-Holstein (1742–1802). She bore him three children, but the marriage was unhappy and she had many affairs. Her brilliant Parisian salon became the center of political discussion, but on the eve of the French Revolution, she left for Coppet, by Lake Geneva, in 1792. By 1795 she had returned to Paris, where she prepared for a political role, but was advised to return to Coppet. She published her famous *Littérature et ses rapports avec les institutions sociales* (Eng trans *The Influence of Literature Upon Society*, 1812) in 1800, followed by the novel *Delphine* (Eng trans 1903) in 1802. In December 1803, now a widow, she set out with her children for Germany, where she dazzled the Weimar court and met the German writers **Schiller**, **Goethe** and **August von Schlegel**. In 1805 she returned to Coppet and wrote *Corinne* (1807, Eng trans 1807), a romance which brought her fame throughout Europe. Her famous work *De l'Allemagne* (Eng trans *Germany*, 1813) was finished in 1810 and partly printed, when the whole impression was seized and destroyed, and she herself was exiled. She escaped secretly to Berne, and from there made her way to St Petersburg, Stockholm and (1813) London, where admiration reached its climax on the publication of *De l'Allemagne*. It revealed Germany to the French and made Romanticism—she was the first to use the word—acceptable to the Latin peoples. In 1816 she secretly married Albert de Rocca, an Italian officer in the French service, and returned to Paris, where she died. Her surviving son and daughter published her unfinished *Considérations sur la Révolution française* (1818, Eng trans *Considerations on the Principal Events of the French Revolution*, 1818), the *Dix années d'exil* (1821, Eng trans *Ten Years' Exile*, 1821) and her complete works (1820–21).

“ ”

En France, on étudie les hommes; en Allemagne, les livres.
In France, they study men; in Germany, books.

1810 ***De l'Allemagne***

Staël, Nicolas de 1914–55 •*French painter*• Born in St Petersburg, Russia, he studied in Brussels and worked in Paris. His paintings were at first abstract, and he made inspired use of rectangular patches of color, for example in *Marathon* (1948). His later pictures were more representational, as with his *Football Players*, and included landscapes, such as *The Roofs* (1952, Pompidou Center) and his vivid *Agrigente* (1954, private collection), which he painted just before he committed suicide.

Stafford, Jean 1915–79 •*US short-story writer and novelist*• She was born in Covina, California, and educated at the University of Colorado and Heidelberg, Germany. She married **Robert Lowell** against his family's wishes in 1940. *Boston Adventure*, her first novel, was published in 1944 to great acclaim, and *The Mountain Lion*, her second, appeared in 1947. Her stormy marriage to Lowell collapsed, and she underwent treatment for alcoholism and depression; the couple divorced in 1948. She published *The Catherine Wheel* in 1952, and during the 1960s she taught and published short stories, children's books and a series of interviews with the mother of **Lee Harvey Oswald**, *A Mother in History* (1966). One of the most admired short-story writers in the US, she won a Pulitzer Prize for her *Collected Stories* (1969).

Stafford-Clark, Max 1941– •*English stage director*• Born in Cambridge, he began his career in 1966 as associate director of the Traverse Theatre, Edinburgh. He became director of the Traverse Theatre Workshop Company (1970–74), after which he cofounded the Joint Stock Theatre Company. He became artistic director of the English Stage Company at the Royal Court Theatre, London, from 1979 until 1993, then was appointed artistic director of the Out of Joint Theatre Company. He published *Letters to George* in 1989.

Stagnelius, Erik Johan 1793–1823 •*Swedish Romantic poet*• The son of the Bishop of Kalmar, after graduating from Uppsala University, he became an unsalaried civil servant in Stockholm. He led a solitary life and suffered from ill health. His considerable output, all written within a decade, comprises epics, plays and lyric poetry, and were collected and published (1824–26) after his death. He was constantly torn between idealism and erotic sensualism, and contrasts dream and reality in a series of poems that include *Endymion*, *Narcissus* and *Till Natten* ("Ode to Night"). In other poems themes from nature symbolize the soul's longing for heaven, as in *Floden* ("The River") and *Flyttfåglarna* ("Migrant Birds"). Little known in his lifetime, he became the most influential of Swedish Romantics in succeeding generations.

Stahlberg, Kaarlo Juho 1865–1952 •*Finnish politician*• Having established his reputation as Professor of Law at the University of Helsinki and as a judge and a member of the Finnish Diet, in 1919 he drafted Finland's constitution and served as the republic's first president (1919–25). He was kidnapped by members of a pro-Fascist movement in 1930, and was narrowly defeated in the elections of 1931 and 1937.

Stair, James Dalrymple, 1st Viscount 1619–95 •*Scottish jurist*• He studied at the Universtiy of Glasgow, served in the Covenanting army, and, as regent in Philosophy, taught at Glasgow (1641–47).

After joining the bar (1648), he was recommended by General **George Monk** to **Cromwell** in 1659 for the office of a Lord of Session, and he advised Monk to call a free parliament (1660). He was created a Nova Scotia baronet in 1664, and in 1671 he was made president of the Court of Session and member of the Privy Council. When the Duke of York (later **James VII and II**) came to govern at Edinburgh in 1679, he retired to the country and worked on his famous *Institutions of the Law of Scotland*, still one of the most authoritative works on Scots law. Devoted to the cause of the Covenanters, he fled in 1682 to Holland. He returned with **William III**, was restored to the presidency and soon after was created Viscount Stair (1690).

Stalin, Joseph, *originally* **Iosif Vissarionovich Dzhugashvili** 1879–1953 •*Soviet revolutionary and leader*• Born near Tiflis (now Tblisi) in Georgia, the son of a shoemaker. He was educated for the priesthood at the Theological Seminary, but was expelled, probably for propagating Marxism. He joined the Bolshevik underground, was arrested and transported to Siberia, but escaped in 1904. The ensuing years witnessed his closer identification with revolutionary Marxism, his many escapes from captivity, his growing intimacy with **Lenin** and **Nikolai Bukharin**, his early disparagement of **Trotsky**, and his co-option, in 1912, to the illicit Bolshevik Central Committee. With the 1917 Revolution and the forcible replacement of the **Kerensky** government by Lenin and his supporters, Stalin was appointed commissar for nationalities and a member of the politburo. With his appointment as general secretary to the Central Committee in 1922, Stalin stealthily began to build up the power that would ensure his control of the situation after Lenin's death. When this occurred in 1924, he took over the reins, successfully testing his overriding authority in 1928 by engineering Trotsky's downfall. Stalin's reorganization of the USSR's resources, with its successive five-year plans, suffered many industrial setbacks and encountered consistently stubborn resistance in the field of agriculture, where the *kulaks*, or peasant proprietors, steadfastly refused to accept the principle of collectivization. The measures taken by the dictator to discipline those who opposed his will involved the death by execution or famine of up to ten million peasants (1932–33). The bloodbath which eliminated the Old Bolsheviks and the alleged right-wing intelligentsia was followed by a drastic purge of some thousands of the officer corps, who were accused of pro-German sympathies. In 1939 Stalin signed a nonaggression pact with **Hitler**, allowing him time to prepare for the German invasion he regarded as inevitable. In 1941 the Nazis' initial thrust into Russia was successful, but eventually, the German invasion was defeated by a war of attrition, The conferences at Tehran (1943), Yalta (1945) and Potsdam (1945) left Stalin in political control of most of Eastern Europe and an "iron curtain" cut off Soviet Russia and her satellites from the outside world. At the same time, he inaugurated a ruthless Cold War against all non-Communist countries, and at home his ruthless purge of all opposition continued. He died in mysterious circumstances; the official cause was said to be a brain hemorrhage. Stalin's cult of personality and the brutal purges of his rule were denounced after his death by **Nikita Khrushchev**. In 1961, by a vote of the Party Congress, Stalin's embalmed body was removed from the Mausoleum of Lenin and buried in an ordinary grave near the Kremlin.

“ ”

Communism fits Germany as a saddle fits a cow.

1944 In conversation with the Polish politician, Stanislaw Mikolajcik, August.

Stallone, Sylvester 1946– •*US film actor*• He was born in New York City. After a series of minor parts, he appeared in **Woody Allen**'s comedy *Bananas* (1971). Inspired by watching a **Muhammad Ali** fight in 1975, he wrote a screenplay about a boxer and made it a condition of selling the script that he would play the lead role. The success of *Rocky* (1976) catapulted him to stardom, giving him starring roles in the film's three sequels and leading to the role of John Rambo in *First Blood* (1982) and its two sequels. Later films include *Cliffhanger* (1992) and *Daylight* (1996).

Stamitz, Johann 1717–57 •*Bohemian violinist and composer*• Born in Deutschbrod (now Havlíckuv Brod, Czech Republic), he became a highly salaried court musician and concert master at Mannheim, and established the style of composition later known as the Mannheim school. His compositions include 74 symphonies, concertos for various instruments, chamber music and a mass. He developed the sonata form, introduced sharp contrasts into symphonic movements and wrote fine concerto music. His two sons, Carl Philipp Stamitz (1745–1801) and Anton Johann Baptista Stamitz (c. 1754–1809), were also musicians.

Standish, Myles c. 1584–1656 •*English soldier and colonist*• Born probably in Ormskirk, Lancashire, he served in the Netherlands, and in 1620 was hired by the Pilgrim Fathers to accompany them on the *Mayflower*. He was appointed military captain of the settlement at Plymouth, supervised the defenses, and negotiated with the Native Americans. In 1625 he went to London to negotiate ownership of their land. He became treasurer of Massachusetts (1644–49), and in 1631 was one of the founders of Duxbury, Massachusetts. **Henry Wadsworth Longfellow** and **James Russell Lowell** wrote about his exploits.

Stanford, Sir Charles Villiers 1852–1924 •*Irish composer*• Born in Dublin, he studied at Cambridge, Leipzig and Berlin, and became organist at Trinity College (1872–93), and a professor at the Royal College of Music (1882). As Cambridge Professor of Music (1887), he taught generations of young British composers. Among his works are choral settings of **Tennyson**'s *Revenge* (1886) and *Voyage of Maeldune* (1889); the oratorios *The Three Holy Children* (1885) and *Eden* (1891); the operas *The Veiled Prophet of Khorassan* (1881), *Shamus O'Brien* (1896) and *Much Ado About Nothing* (1901).

Stanford, (Amasa) Leland 1824–93 •*US philanthropist and politician*• Born in Watervliet, New York, he settled in San Francisco in 1856, became president of the Central Pacific Company, and was governor of California (1861–63) and a US senator from 1885. In memory of their only son, he and his wife founded and endowed Leland Stanford Junior University (Stanford University) at Palo Alto (1891).

Stanhope, Charles Stanhope, 3rd Earl Stanhope 1753–1816 •*English scientist and politician*• Born in London, the grandson of James, 1st Earl **Stanhope**, and educated at Eton and Geneva, he married Lady Hester Pitt, sister of **William Pitt** the Younger in 1774 and became a Member of Parliament in 1780. As a scientist he invented a microscope lens that bears his name, two calculating machines, the first hand-operated iron printing press, and a process of stereotyping. He also experimented with electricity and wrote *Principles of Electricity* (1779).

Stanhope, Lady Hester Lucy 1776–1839 •*English traveler*• The eldest daughter of **Charles Stanhope**, she went in 1803 to live with her uncle, **William Pitt** the Younger, and on his death (1806) received a pension of £1,200 from the king. Bored without the excitement of public life, she left England in 1810, traveled in the Levant, went to Jerusalem, camped with Bedouins in Palmyra, and in 1814 settled on Mount Lebanon. She adopted Middle Eastern manners, and was regarded by the local people as a kind of prophetess. Her last years were poverty-stricken on account of her reckless generosity.

Stanhope, James Stanhope, 1st Earl 1673–1721 •*English soldier and politician*• After a distinguished career in the field under the Duke of **Marlborough** in the War of the Spanish Succession (1701–14), he became leader of the Whig opposition in 1711. He helped to suppress the Jacobite uprising of 1715, and became chief minister under **George I** in 1717.

Stanhope, Philip Dormer *See* **Chesterfield, 4th Earl of**

Stanhope, Philip Henry Stanhope, 5th Earl 1805–75 •*English historian*• Born in Walmer, Kent, he studied at Oxford, entered parliament in 1830, was instrumental in passing the Copyright Act (1842), and was foreign undersecretary under Sir **Robert Peel** (1834–35) and secretary of the Indian Board of Control (1845–46). He was known as Lord Mahon until he succeeded to the earldom. His principal work is *A History of England 1713–83* (1836–54).

Stanislavsky, *professional name of* **Konstantin Sergeyevich**

Alekseyev 1863–1938 •*Russian actor, theater director and teacher*• Born in Moscow, he cofounded the Moscow Society of Art and Literature (1888) and in 1898 he helped found the Moscow Arts Theater. He gave up acting because of illness, but his teaching and his system of actor training were major contributions to 20th-century theater. The Method style derived from his teaching is characterized by improvisation, spontaneity and an emphasis on psychological realism, and has been widely practiced, especially in the US.

Stanisław I Leszczyński, *English* **Stanislas** or **Stanislaus** 1677–1766 •*King of Poland*• Born in Lemberg, he had the support of **Karl XII** of Sweden and defeated **Augustus II (the Strong)** to become king in 1704. However, after Karl's defeat at the Battle of Poltava in 1709, Stanisław was driven out by **Peter I (the Great)** to make room for Augustus again. His daughter Maria married **Louis XV** of France in 1725, a union which facilitated his reelection as king of Poland on Augustus's death in 1733. After losing the War of the Polish Succession, he formally abdicated in 1736. He died of burns in an accident.

Stanisław Poniatowski, *English* **Stanislas** or **Stanislaus** 1677–1762 •*Polish administrator and soldier*• He was the father of **Stanisław II Augustus Poniatowski**, the last king of Poland. He joined **Karl XII** of Sweden in supporting **Stanisław I Leszczyński**, and later under Augustus II and III was appointed to several administrative posts in Lithuania and Poland.

Stanisław II Augustus Poniatowski, *English* **Stanislas** or **Stanislaus** 1732–98 •*Last king of Poland*• The son of **Stanisław Poniatowski**, he became the lover of the empress **Catherine the Great**, and, largely through her influence, he was elected king (1764–95). After the first partition of Poland (1772) by Russia, Austria and Prussia, the intrigues of discontented nobles led to further foreign intervention, and a fruitless resistance was followed (1793) by a second partition. The Poles became desperate, a general uprising took place (1794), the Prussians were driven out, and the Russians were several times routed. When Austria became involved, **Kościuszko** was defeated, Warsaw was taken, the remainder of Poland was annexed by Russia, Prussia and Austria, and the Polish monarchy came to an end. Stanisłas resigned his crown (1795) and died in St Petersburg.

Stanley, Edward Geoffrey Smith *See* **Derby, 14th Earl of**

Stanley, Sir Henry Morton, *originally* **John Rowlands** 1841–1904 •*British-US explorer and journalist*• He was born in Denbigh, Wales. In 1859 he went as a cabin boy to New Orleans, where he was adopted by a merchant named Stanley. He served in the Confederate army and US Navy, contributed to several journals, and in 1867 joined the *New York Herald*. In October 1869 he received from *Herald* editor James Gordon Bennett (1841–1918) the laconic instruction, "Find **Livingstone**"; on his way he visited Egypt for the opening of the Suez Canal and traveled through Palestine, Turkey, Persia and India. On November 10, 1871, he "found" Livingstone at Ujiji in Tanganyika, and the two explored Lake Tanganyika. In 1872 and again in 1874 he returned to Africa, determined the shape of Lake Tanganyika, passed down the Lualaba to Nyangwé, and traced the Congo to the sea. Having published *Through the Dark Continent* (1878), in 1879 he again went to Africa to found, under the auspices of the Belgian king, the Congo Free State. He took part in the Congo Congress in Berlin (1884–85). In March 1886 he undertook an expedition for the rescue of **Emin Pasha**, in the course of which he discovered Lake Edward and Mount Ruwenzori (1888–89). He was naturalized as a British subject in 1892, and was a Unionist Member of Parliament for Lambeth (1895–1900).

Stanley, Wendell Meredith 1904–71 •*US biochemist and Nobel Prize winner*• Born in Ridgeville, Indiana, he was educated at the University of Illinois. He was a research fellow in Munich (1930–31) and in 1931 joined the Rockefeller Institute for Medical Research, Princeton, before holding a series of professorships at the University of California from 1940. He isolated the tobacco mosaic virus (1935) using the salt fractionation techniques of **John Howard Northrop**, and showed it to contain protein and nucleic acid (1936). He went on to characterize the physical and chemical properties of the virus, and determined the protein amino acid sequence (1960). Stanley also isolated other plant viruses and independently noted that viruses can cause cancer (1949). He shared the 1946 Nobel Prize for chemistry with Northrop and **James Sumner**.

Stanton, Edwin McMasters 1814–69 •*US lawyer and politician*• Born in Steubenville, Ohio, he was appointed US attorney general by President **James Buchanan** (1860), and later became secretary of war under **Abraham Lincoln** (1862), continuing in that post under **Andrew Johnson**. Outspoken and abrasive, he alienated Johnson by taking sides against him on the issue of Reconstruction and was suspended by the president (1867) but was reinstated by the Senate. When Johnson's impeachment failed, Stanton resigned (1868).

Stanton, Elizabeth Cady, *née* **Cady** 1815–1902 •*US social reformer*• She was born in Johnstown, New York. While studying law under her congressman father, she determined to readdress the inequality that she discovered in women's legal, political, and industrial rights, and in divorce law. In 1840 she married the lawyer and abolitionist Henry Brewster Stanton, insisting on dropping the word "obey" from the marriage vows. She accompanied him to the international slavery convention in London, where she encountered, with much indignation, a ruling that women delegates were excluded from the floor. In 1848, with **Lucretia Mott**, she organized the first women's rights convention at Seneca Falls, New York, which launched the women's suffrage movement, and she accepted the set of resolutions for the improvement of the status of women which Stanton had drawn up. Woman suffrage was included, although Mott allegedly did not agree. Stanton teamed up with **Susan B Anthony** in 1850, producing the feminist magazine *Revolution* (1868–70) and founding the National Woman Suffrage Movement in 1869. Stanton was president of the National Woman Suffrage Association (called from 1890 the National American Woman Suffrage Association) from 1869 to 1892. With Mott and **Matilda Joslyn Gage** she compiled three of the six volumes of the *History of Woman Suffrage* (1881–86). Stanton's daughter was the suffragette **Harriot Stanton Blatch**.

" "

Although woman has performed much of the labor of the world, her industry and economy have been the very means of increasing her degradation.

1881 ***History of Woman Suffrage**, vol. 1, chapter 1, "Preceding Causes."*

Stanwyck, Barbara, *originally* **Ruby Stevens** 1907–90 •*US actress*• Born in Brooklyn, New York, she worked from the age of 13. She became a dancer, and made her dramatic stage debut in *The Noose* (1926). Her first film was *Broadway Nights* (1927). Established as a major star in the 1930s, she is best remembered in roles as gutsy, pioneering women in Westerns such as *Annie Oakley* (1935) and *Union Pacific* (1939), or as sultry femmes fatales, as in *Double Indemnity* (1944). A durable leading lady, her range also extended to melodramas such as *Stella Dallas* (1937) and deft comic performances as in *The Lady Eve* (1941) and *Ball of Fire* (1941). Active in radio and television, she enjoyed a long-running series, *The Big Valley* (1965–69). She received a Special Academy Award in 1982.

Stapleton, Maureen 1925– •*US actress*• Born in Troy, New York, she made her Broadway debut in *The Playboy of the Western World* (1946). She won a Tony award for her role as Serafina in *The Rose Tattoo* (1951) which began a long association with the works of **Tennessee Williams**. Her numerous appearances on the stage include *The Gingerbread Lady* (1971, Tony) and *The Little Foxes* (1981). She received a Best Supporting Actress Academy Award nomination for her film debut in *Lonelyhearts* (1958) and subsequent nominations for *Airport* (1969) and *Interiors* (1978) before winning for *Reds* (1981). She won an Emmy for *Among the Paths to Eden* (1967) and subsequent nominations for films including *Miss Rose White* (1992).

Stapleton, Ruth, *née* **Carter** 1929–83 •*US evangelist and faith healer*• Born in Plains, Georgia, she was the younger sister of President **Jimmy Carter**, and is said to have been influential in his religious beliefs. Unlike many of her fellow Southern Baptists, she cooperated with other Christians, including Roman Catholics, and she used her graduate training in psychology in a remarkable ministry that stressed the necessity for inner healing. In the 1976 presidential campaign she addressed the National Press Club, Washington DC; it was said to be the first time that it heard a woman preacher.

Stark, Dame Freya Madeline 1893–1993 •*English writer and traveler*• Born in Paris, France, she spent her childhood in England and Italy before attending Bedford College, London University. She was a nurse on the Italian front during World War I, and afterward studied Arabic at the School of Oriental and African Studies in London, and was invited to Baghdad by the prime minister. There she worked at the *Baghdad Times* and mapped the Valley of the Assassins in Luristan, described in *Valley of the Assassins* (1934). During World War II she worked for the Ministry of Information in Aden and Cairo, and was the personal assistant of Lady Wavell, describing her experiences in *West Is East* (1945). She traveled extensively, financed by her writings, in Europe, Asia and the Middle East, and produced more than 30 travel books.

Stark, Harold Raynsford 1880–1972 •*US naval officer*• Born in Wilkes-Barre, Pennsylvania, he was educated at the US Naval Academy, Annapolis, and served in a destroyer flotilla (1914–15). He was chief of the Bureau of Ordnance (1934–37). Chief of Naval Operations from 1939 to 1942, he was relieved after the bombing of Pearl Harbor (December 1941) and became commander of the US Naval Forces in Europe (1942–43), with headquarters in London.

Stark, Johannes 1874–1957 •*German physicist and Nobel Prize winner*• Born in Schickenhof, he was educated at Munich and held numerous teaching posts before being appointed to chairs at the Universities of Aachen (1909), Greifswald (1917) and Würzburg (1920). He was awarded the Nobel Prize for physics in 1919. He later joined the Nazi Party and was rewarded with appointments to several prominent posts, but he did not hold these posts for long because of his quarrelsome nature and internal political struggles, and he retired in 1936. He discovered the Stark effect, concerning the splitting of spectrum lines by subjecting the light source to a strong electrostatic field, and also the **Doppler** effect in canal rays.

Starkey, David 1945– •*English historian and broadcaster*• Born in Kendal, Cumbria, he studied at Fitzwilliam College, Cambridge. He lectured at Cambridge (1970–72) and the London School of Economics (1972–98), publishing works on English (particularly Tudor) history. He has been a combative panelist on BBC Radio 4's *The Moral Maze* (1992–) and has written and hosted television series, including *Elizabeth* (2000) and *Six Wives of Henry VIII* (2001).

Starkie, Enid Mary 1897–1970 •*Irish critic of French literature*• Born in Killiney, County Dublin, the daughter of the classicist W J M Starkie and sister of the Hispanicist and gypsy lover, Walter Starkie, she was educated at Alexandra College, Dublin, Somerville College, Oxford, and the Sorbonne, where she wrote a doctoral thesis on Emile Verhaeren (1855–1916). She taught modern languages at Exeter and Oxford, wrote perceptively on **Baudelaire** (1933) and **André Gide** (1954), played a major part in establishing the poetic reputation of **Arthur Rimbaud** (1938) and crowned her work with two outstanding volumes on **Gustave Flaubert** (1967, 1971). She portrayed her early life in *A Lady's Child* (1941).

Starling, Ernest Henry 1866–1927 •*English physiologist*• Born in London, he studied at Guy's Hospital, where he was appointed lecturer in physiology. He moved to chairs at University College (1899–1927), and with Sir **William Bayliss** began a series of experiments on the nervous control of the viscera, in the course of which they discovered the pancreatic secretion *secretin* (1902), coining the word "hormone" to describe it. He did much to elucidate the physiology of the circulation and the mechanisms of cardiac activity, still known today as Starling's law of the heart, and his work on capillary function gave rise to Starling's equilibrium. He wrote many influential texts.

Starr, Bart 1934– •*US football player*• Born in Montgomery, Alabama, he joined the Green Bay Packers in 1956 and remained with them throughout his career (1956–71). Acclaimed as the leading quarterback of his generation, he led Green Bay to no less than five NFL titles and two Super Bowl victories between 1961 and 1967. He was named NFL Most Valuable Player in 1966 and Most Valuable Player in the Super Bowls I and II. His other achievements included a career passing total of 24,718 yards and 152 touchdowns and being a three-time NFL passing champion (1962, 1964 and 1966). He was also head coach of Green Bay (1975–83).

Starr, Ringo *See* **Beatles, The**

Statius, Publius Papinius c. 45–96 AD •*Roman poet*• Born in Naples, he won a poetry prize there, and went to Rome, where he flourished as a court poet and an improviser in the favor of **Domitian** until AD 94, when he retired to Naples. His major work was the *Thebaïs*, an epic in 12 books on the struggle between the Theban brothers Eteocles and Polyneices. His *Silvae*, or occasional verses, have freshness and vigor. He was admired by later poets, notably **Dante** and **Pope**.

Staudinger, Hermann 1881–1965 •*German chemist and Nobel Prize winner*• Born in Worms, he studied chemistry at the University of Halle and the Technical University at Darmstadt. He then became the assistant of Johannes Thiele in Strassburg (Strasbourg), where he discovered keten. After being appointed assistant professor at the Technical University at Karlsruhe, in 1910 he found a new and simpler way to synthesize isoprene, the basic unit of rubber. In 1912 he moved to the Federal Institute of Technology in Zurich, where he worked on the synthesis of natural products. During the 1930s he undertook the study of complex biological macromolecules, and in the 1940s he turned to molecular biology. He was awarded the Nobel Prize for chemistry in 1953 for his discoveries in the field of macromolecular chemistry. A research institute was established for Staudinger at the University of Freiburg in the 1940s, and he remained there until his retirement in 1956.

Stauffenberg, Count Claus von 1907–44 •*German soldier*• He was born in Bavaria. He was a colonel on the General Staff, and initially a supporter of **Hitler**, but he became alienated by Nazi brutality. He planted a bomb in the unsuccessful attempt to assassinate Hitler at his headquarters at Rastenburg on July 20, 1944. He was shot in the evening of the same day.

Stavisky, Serge Alexandre c. 1886–1934 •*French swindler*• Born in Kiev, Ukraine, he moved to Paris in 1900 and became a French citizen in 1914. He floated fraudulent companies, liquidating the debts of one with the profits of its successor. In 1933, he fled to Chamonix and probably committed suicide, but in the meantime the affair had revealed widespread corruption in the government and ultimately caused the downfall of two ministries. Stavisky was found guilty during a trial that ended in 1936 with the conviction of nine others.

Stead, Christina Ellen 1902–83 •*Australian novelist*• She was born in Rockdale, Sydney, the daughter of David George Stead, a leading English naturalist and writer. In 1928 she left Australia for Europe, where she lived in London and Paris. She went to live in Spain, but left at the outbreak of war and settled in the US, becoming a senior writer for MGM in Hollywood (1943). Her first novel to gain recognition was *Seven Poor Men of Sydney* (1934). *House of All Nations* (1938) took a critical look at the world of big finance, and her autobiographical novel, *The Man Who Loved Children* (1940), described suffocating family life under an egotistical father. Many of her short stories appeared in the *New Yorker*. She left the US in 1947 and settled in England, but finally returned to her homeland in 1974, in which year she was the first winner of the **Patrick White** Literary Award.

Steadman, Alison 1946– •*English actress*• Born in Liverpool, she studied drama at Loughton College, Essex, and began her career in repertory theater. She married the playwright **Mike Leigh** in 1973 and appeared in two of his early television plays, *Nuts in May* (1976) and *Abigail's Party* (1977). Later television work included *The Singing Detective* (1986) and *Selling Hitler* (1992). Her many films include *A Private Function* (1984), *Clockwise* (1986) and *Topsy-Turvy* (1999).

Stebbins, Emma 1815–82 •*US painter and sculptor*• She was born in New York City, where her amateur portraits of family and friends won her election as an associate of the National Academy of Design. Her sculptures include a bronze of the US educator and politician **Horace Mann**, in front of the State House in Boston, and *The Angel of the Waters* for the Bethesda Fountain in Central Park, New York City.

Stebbins, George Ledyard 1906–2000 •*US botanist*• Born in Lawrence, New York, he studied biology at Harvard University and spent his career at the University of California at Berkeley (1937–50) and Davis (1950–73), where he established the department of genetics. He was the first to apply modern ideas of evolution to botany, as expounded in his *Variation and Evolution in Plants* (1950). From the 1940s he used artificially induced polyploidy (the condition of having more than twice the basic number of chromosomes) to create fertile hybrids, a technique of value both in taxonomy and in plant breeding.

Steel (of Aikwood), David Martin Scott Steel, Baron 1938– •*Scottish politician, last leader of the Liberal Party*• Born in Kirkcaldy, Fife, he became a journalist and broadcaster, and was the youngest Member of Parliament when first elected in 1965. He sponsored a controversial bill to reform the laws on abortion (1966–67) and was active in the antiapartheid movement before succeeding Jeremy Thorpe (1929–) as leader of the Liberal Party in 1976. He led his party into an electoral pact with Labour (1977–78) and subsequently an alliance with the Social Democratic Party (SDP) (1981–88), but despite Steel's undoubted popularity, they won only 23 seats. After the 1987 general election he called for a merger of the Liberals and SDP; this took place in 1989 under the leadership of **Paddy Ashdown**, as Steel declined to seek the leadership. From 1999 to 2003 he was the presiding officer of the Scottish Parliament. He was awarded a knighthood in 1990 and a life peerage in 1997.

“ ”

[Margaret Thatcher] has turned the British bulldog into a Reagan poodle.

*1986 In **Time**, April 28.*

Steele, Sir Richard 1672–1729 •*Irish essayist, dramatist and politician*• Born in Dublin, he was educated at Charterhouse, where **Joseph Addison** was a contemporary, and Merton College, Oxford, after which he entered the army. His first venture in periodical literature, *The Tatler*, ran from 1709 to 1711, and concentrated on social and moral essays, with occasional articles on literature. With Addison he also founded *The Spectator* (1711–12) and *The Guardian* (1743). He briefly entered parliament (1713), but was expelled for supporting the Hanoverian cause. On the succession of **George I** he was awarded with the appointment of supervisor of Drury Lane Theatre, and a knighthood followed. Financial troubles caused him to retire to Wales (1722).

Steele, Tommy, *originally* **Thomas Hicks** 1936– •*English actor, singer and director*• Born in London, he achieved considerable success as a pop singer in the 1950s and 1960s, after making his stage debut in variety at the Empire Theatre, Sunderland (1956), and his London variety debut at the Dominion Theatre (1957). He continued to appear in musicals during the 1960s, most notably in *Half a Sixpence* (1963–64), had a one-man show in London (1979) and starred in and directed a stage adaptation of *Singin' in the Rain* at the London Palladium (1983). In 1992 he starred in and directed *Some Like It Hot*.

Steen, Jan 1626–79 •*Dutch painter*• Born in Leiden, he was a pupil of Adriaan van Ostade (1610–85) and Jan van Goyen (1596–1656). He joined the Leiden guild of painters in 1648 and next year went to The Hague until 1654, afterward following his father's trade as a brewer in Delft. He spent his last years as an innkeeper in Leiden. A versatile artist, he painted a wide range of religious, historical and mythological subjects. His best works are genre pictures depicting the everyday life of ordinary folk with rare insight and subtle humor. He also painted some fine portraits, and a well-known self-portrait depicting himself playing the lute (Lugano).

Steensen, Niels *See* **Steno, Nicolaus**

Stefan, Josef 1835–93 •*Austrian physicist*• Born near Klagenfurt, he became Professor of Physics at the University of Vienna in 1863. In 1866 he was appointed director of the Institute for Experimental Physics, and in 1879 he proposed Stefan's law (or the Stefan-**Boltzmann** law), stating that the amount of energy radiated from a black body is proportional to the absolute temperature, and he used this law to make the first satisfactory estimate of the sun's surface temperature. He also designed a diathermometer to measure heat conduction, and worked on the kinetic theory of heat and on the relationship between surface tension and evaporation (1886).

Stefánsson, Jón 1881–1962 •*Icelandic landscape painter*• Born in Sauðárkrókur in the north of Iceland, he was one of the three founders, with Ásgrímur Jónsson (1876–1958) and **Jóhannes Kjarval**, of modern art in Iceland. He went to Paris in 1908 and studied under **Henri Matisse**. A man of strong temperament, he painted landscapes on a grand scale, exploiting color with extraordinary luminosity.

Steichen, Edward Jean 1879–1973 •*US photographer*• Born in Luxembourg, he was taken as a child to the US, where he grew up in Michigan. He studied art in Milwaukee (1894–98) and worked as a painter and photographer in Europe until 1914. A member of the Linked Ring in England, he was noted for his nude studies. In 1902 he helped **Alfred Stieglitz** found the American Photo-Secession Group, and during World War I he commanded the photographic division of the US Army. In the 1920s he moved into fashion photography. He was head of US Naval Film Services during World War II and director of photography at the New York Museum of Modern Art (1945–1962), organizing the well-known exhibition *The Family of Man* in 1955.

Stein, Sir (Mark) Aurel 1862–1943 •*British archaeologist and explorer*• Born in Budapest, Hungary, he held educational and archaeological posts under the Indian government from 1900 to 1930, conducting a series of expeditions in Chinese Turkestan and Central Asia. His discoveries included the Cave of a Thousand Buddhas near Tan Huang, walled up since the 11th century. Later superintendent of the Indian Archaeological Survey (1910–29), he died at Kabul when about to begin an exploration of Afghanistan.

Stein, Charlotte von, *née* **von Schardt** 1742–1827 •*German writer*• She was a lady-in-waiting at the Weimar court, and in 1764 married Friedrich von Stein, the Duke of Saxe-Weimar's Master of the Horse. In 1775, she met **Goethe**, who fell in love with her. Their friendship was broken suddenly (1788), but was renewed before her death. She was the inspiration for many of his love poems and plays. She herself wrote works such as *Dido* (1792, published 1867), a prose tragedy lamenting the end of their affair.

Stein, Edith, *known as* **Sister Teresa Benedicta of the Cross** 1891–1942 •*German Carmelite philosopher*• Born in Breslau to a Jewish family, she was converted to Catholicism in 1922 and began interpreting the phenomenology she had learned under **Edmund Husserl** from a Thomistic point of view. She completed her project when she entered the Carmelite convent in Cologne in 1934, and for safety she transferred to the house in Echt, Holland, in 1938, where she wrote a phenomenological study of St John of the Cross. She was executed in Auschwitz concentration camp, together with other anti-Nazi priests and nuns. She was beatified in 1987.

Stein, Gertrude 1874–1946 •*US writer*• She was born in Allegheny, Pennsylvania, and spent her early years in Vienna, Paris and San Francisco. She studied psychology at Radcliffe College under William James, and medicine at Johns Hopkins University. She then settled in Paris, where she was absorbed into the world of experimental art and letters and came into contact with writers and artists including **Picasso** and **Matisse**. From 1907 she shared an apartment with her partner, Alice B Toklas (1877–1967). Stein sometimes attempted to apply the theories of abstract painting to her own writing, which led to a magnified reputation for obscurity and meaningless repetition. However, her first book, *Three Lives* (1908), reveals a sensitive ear for speech rhythms, and by far the larger part of her work is immediately comprehensible. The prose of *Tender Buttons* (1914) is repetitive, canonic and extremely musical, and she took a more ironic stance in the playfully titled *The Autobiography of Alice B. Toklas* (1933) and *Everybody's Autobiography* (1937). She wrote two libretti for operas with music by **Virgil Thomson**.

" "

Anyone who marries three girls from St Louis hasn't learned much.

Of Ernest Hemingway. Quoted in R Mellow ***Charmed Circle*** *(1974), chapter 16.*

Stein, Heinrich Friedrich Carl, Baron von 1757–1831 •*Prussian politician and German nationalist*• Born in Nassau, he entered the service of Prussia in 1780. During his tenure as secretary for trade (1804–07), he abolished the last relics of serfdom, created peasant proprietors, extirpated monopolies and hindrances to free trade, promoted municipal government and supported **Gerhard von Scharnhorst** in his plans for army reform. In 1812 he went to St Petersburg and built up the coalition against Napoleon. He liberalized the Prussian state, but at the same time fostered the myth of German destiny and aggressive nationalism, not least by founding the *Monumenta Germaniae Historica* in 1815.

Stein, Jock (John) 1922–85 •*Scottish soccer player and manager*• He was born in Burnbank, Lanarkshire. He became a great Scottish soccer team manager after an undistinguished playing career, managing first the unfashionable Fife club Dunfermline Athletic, which he led to victory in the Scottish Cup. A short successful spell with Hibernian followed, and in 1965 he took over Glasgow Celtic. In the next 13 years, Celtic won nine championships in a row, the League Cup on five consecutive occasions and several Scottish Cups. They also won the European Cup in 1967 and were finalists in 1970. Stein left Celtic in 1978 for a brief period as manager of Leeds United, but returned to Scotland to become national manager. Under him the Scottish team qualified for the World Cup Finals in Spain in 1982.

Stein, Rick (Christopher Richard) 1947– •*English television chef*• Born on a farm in Oxfordshire, he studied at New College, Oxford, and opened the Seafood Restaurant in Padstow, Cornwall, in 1975. His enthusiasm for fresh fish, simply cooked, has delighted audiences worldwide, and his cookbooks have become bestsellers. He has hosted a number of series for television, among them *Rick Stein's Seafood Lover's Guide* (2000).

Stein, William Howard 1911–80 •*US biochemist and Nobel Prize winner*• Born in New York City, he studied at Harvard and Columbia Universities, and joined the staff of the Rockefeller Institute, where he became Professor of Biochemistry in 1954. With **Stanford Moore**, he developed a column chromatographic method for the identification and quantification of amino acid mixtures in proteins and physiological tissues. They automated the analysis of the base sequence of RNA (1958), and studied a novel protease from streptococcus, showing that its molecular structure differed from that of the plant protease papain. This was the first example of the phenomenon called convergent evolution. Stein, Moore and **Christian Anfinsen** shared the Nobel Prize for chemistry in 1972.

Steinbeck, John Ernest 1902–68 •*US novelist and Nobel Prize winner*• Born in Salinas, California, he studied marine biology at Stanford University. *Tortilla Flat* (1935), his first novel of repute, is a faithful picture of the shifting *paisanos* of California, foreshadowing the solidarity which characterizes his major work, *The Grapes of Wrath* (1939), a study of the poor in the face of disaster and threatened disintegration. His journalistic grasp of significant detail and pictorial essence make this book a powerful plea for consideration of human values and common justice. It led to much-needed reform, and won the 1940 Pulitzer Prize. His other works include *In Dubious Battle* (1935), *Of Mice and Men* (1937), *The Moon Is Down* (1942), *The Pearl* (1947), *Burning Bright* (1950), *East of Eden* (1952) and *Winter of Our Discontent* (1961), as well as the light-hearted and humorous *Cannery Row* (1945) and *The Short Reign of Pippin IV* (1957). He won the Nobel Prize for literature in 1962.

" "

I know this—a man got to do what he got to do.

1939 ***The Grapes of Wrath****, chapter 18.*

Steinberg, Saul 1914–99 •*US artist*• He was born in Rîmnicu-Sarat, Romania, settled in the US in 1942, was naturalized and joined the US Navy in 1943. Soon after the end of World War II, he became a nationally known graphic artist and cartoonist. His witty and satirical drawings, which are filled with unexpected ideas and images and often include bizarre figures speaking forms of fantastic words, appeared regularly in the *New Yorker* magazine.

Steinberger, Jack 1921– •*US physicist*• Born in Bad Kissingen, Germany, he moved to the US in 1935, and was educated at the University of Chicago. He held professorships at Columbia University from 1950 to 1972, and from 1968 to 1986 was a staff member at CERN, the European center for nuclear research in Geneva, where he was a director from 1969 to 1972. He proved the existence of a neutral pion, measured the spin and parity of the charged pion, and established the existence of two distinct neutrino types. He was awarded the 1988 Nobel Prize for physics jointly with **Leon Lederman** and **Melvin Schwartz**. Since 1986 he has been Professor of Physics at the Scuola Normale Superiore, Pisa.

Steinem, Gloria 1934– •*US feminist and writer*• Born in Toledo, Ohio, she studied at Smith College in Northampton, Massachusetts. She became a journalist and emerged as a leading figure in the women's movement in the 1960s and early 1970s. A cofounder of Women's Action Alliance (1970) and the National Women's Political Caucus (1971), she was also founding editor of *Ms Magazine* (1972). Her published works include *Outrageous Acts and Everyday Rebellions* (1983) and *Revolution From Within: A Book of Self-Esteem* (1992).

Steiner, George 1929– •*US critic and scholar*• Born in Paris to Austrian-Jewish parents, he was educated at Chicago, Harvard, and Balliol College, Oxford, and taught at Princeton (1956–60), Cambridge (1961–), the University of Geneva (1974–94), and Oxford (1994–95). He sees literature as a part of a broader social and cultural context, and has made penetrating and controversial studies of the role and nature of language and the influences on it. His publications include *The Death of Tragedy* (1960), *Language and Silence* (1967), *After Babel* (1975)—regarded as his most important work—*Antigones* (1984) and *Real Presences* (1989).

Steiner, Max(imilian Raoul Walter) 1888–1971 •*US film score composer*• Born in Vienna, he was a student at the Imperial Academy there and developed into a child prodigy, his first operetta, *The Beautiful Greek Girl*, being performed in 1902. He was a conductor of musical comedies in London, Paris and Berlin, and in 1914 emigrated to New York, where he worked on Broadway. Moving to Hollywood to work at RKO, he was able to establish the power of music to enhance dramatic mood, seen most notably in *King Kong* (1933). At **Warner** Brothers from 1936, he contributed many vivid and full-blooded scores to some of the most enduring screen classics, among them *Casablanca* (1942) and *The Treasure of the Sierra Madre* (1948). He won Academy Awards for *The Informer* (1935), *Now Voyager* (1942) and *Since You Went Away* (1945).

Steiner, Rudolf 1861–1925 •*Austrian social philosopher, the founder of anthroposophy*• Born in Kraljevíc, Croatia, he studied science and mathematics, and edited **Goethe**'s scientific papers in Weimar (1889–96). He was temporarily influenced by **Annie Besant** and the Theosophists, and went on to found his own Anthroposophical Society in 1912 and establish his first Goetheanum, a school of "spiritual science," in Dornach, Switzerland. His aim was to integrate the psychological and practical aspects of life into an educational, ecological and therapeutic basis for spiritual and physical development. His first school was founded for the children of the Waldorf Astoria factory workers in 1919, the first of many hundreds of Waldorf or Steiner schools now operating. His system of anthroposophy has been influential in the realms of music, art, medicine and farming, and his work also inspired curative education as exemplified by the Camphill homes, schools and villages in Britain. His principal publications were *The Philosophy of Freedom* (1894, also translated as *The Philosophy of Spiritual Activity*), *Occult Science: An Outline* (1913) and *Story of My Life* (1924).

Steinitz, Wilhelm 1836–1900 •*Czech chess player*• He was born in Prague. From 1862 he settled in London for 20 years as a chess professional, supplementing his income as chess editor of *The Field*. After moving to New York, he won decisively in the 1886 match organized to decide the first official world champion. He defended his title successfully three times before losing it in 1894 to

Emanuel Lasker. He died impoverished in a New York mental asylum.

Steinway, Heinrich Engelhard, *originally* **Steinweg** 1797–1871 •*US piano maker*• Born in Wolfshagen, Germany, he fought in the Prussian army at the Battle of Waterloo (1815) and in 1836 established a piano factory in Brunswick. In 1850 he moved with his family to the US and established a business in New York, where he introduced many innovations into the instrument, such as a cast-iron frame.

Stella, Frank Philip 1936– •*US painter*• Born in Malden, Massachusetts, he studied at Phillips Academy and Princeton (1954–58). His earliest minimal paintings, symmetrical patterns of black stripes, date from 1959. He made a significant impression on younger artists such as **Donald Judd**.

Stendhal, *pseudonym of* **Henri Marie Beyle** 1783–1842 •*French novelist*• He was born in Grenoble, where he was educated at the École Centrale and wrote for the theater. A cousin offered him a post in the Ministry of War, and from 1800 he followed **Napoleon I**'s campaigns in Italy, Germany, Russia and Austria. Between wars he spent his time in Paris drawing rooms and theaters. When Napoleon fell he retired to Italy, adopted his pseudonym, and began to write books on Italian painting and on **Haydn** and **Mozart**, as well as copious journalism. After the 1830 revolution he was appointed consul at Trieste and Civitavecchia, but his health deteriorated and he returned to Paris. His recognized masterpieces, *Le rouge et le noir* (Eng trans *Red and Black*, 1898) and *La chartreuse de Parme* (Eng trans *The Charterhouse of Parma*, 1895), were published in 1830 and 1839, respectively. These are remarkable and original works, and were admired by **Honoré de Balzac**, although neither received great understanding during Stendhal's lifetime.

Stenmark, Ingemar 1956– •*Swedish champion skier*• Born in Tärnaby, he won the World Cup three years in succession (1976–78) and went on to become the most successful competitor in slalom and grand slalom ever recorded. He was World Master in 1978 and 1982 and won the Olympic gold medal at Lake Placid in 1980. He was the first man to win three consecutive slalom titles (1980–82). Between 1974 and 1989 he won a record 86 World Cup races. He retired in 1989.

Steno, Nicolaus, *also known as* **Niels Stensen** or **Steensen** 1638–86 •*Danish physician, naturalist and theologian*• Born in Copenhagen, he settled in Florence. He was appointed personal physician to the grand duke of Tuscany in 1666 and Royal Anatomist at Copenhagen in 1672. He became a priest in 1675, and gave up science on being appointed vicar-apostolic to North Germany and Scandinavia. He discovered Steno's duct of the parotid gland, and investigated the function of the ovaries. He also worked in crystallography (establishing Steno's law on crystal structure) and in geology and paleontology.

Stephen, St 1st century AD •*New Testament figure and the first Christian martyr*• All we know about him is from Acts 6–7. He was possibly a Hellenistic Jew, and was appointed by the Apostles to manage the finances and alms of the early Church. He was tried by the Sanhedrin for blasphemy and stoned to death. His feast day is December 26 (in the West) and December 27 (in the East).

Stephen I c. 977–1038 •*First king of Hungary*• Baptized by St Adalbert of Prague, he married Gisela, sister of Emperor Henry II, and succeeded to his father's dukedom in 997. He united Pannonia and Dacia, and was crowned king (1000). During a peaceful reign he organized a standing army, suppressed paganism, reformed the Church and endowed abbeys, and he laid the foundations of many institutions surviving to this day. He was canonized in 1083, and his feast day is August 16. He is the patron saint of Hungary.

Stephen c. 1097–1154 •*King of England*• He was the grandson of **William the Conqueror**. In 1114 he was sent to the court of his uncle, **Henry I** of England, who gave him Mortain in Normandy, and he acquired Boulogne by his marriage to Matilda, daughter of the Count of Boulogne. Stephen swore fealty to Henry's heir, his daughter **Matilda** (or the empress Maud), widow of the emperor **Henry V**, but on Henry's death (1135), Stephen took the crown himself. Although personally courageous and decisive, he was too genial to provide strong leadership. King **David I** of Scotland supported Matilda in two invasions, while Stephen antagonized Robert, Earl of Gloucester, an illegitimate son of Henry I, and also Bishop Roger of Salisbury. The ensuing civil war brought devastation to parts of the country. In 1141 Matilda imprisoned Stephen and was acknowledged queen; but London rose against her, and in November 1141 Stephen regained his liberty and his crown. In 1148 Matilda finally left England, but her son Henry of Anjou (**Henry II**) succeeded Stephen.

Stephen, Sir Leslie 1832–1904 •*English scholar and critic*• Born in London, he was the father of **Virginia Woolf** and **Vanessa Bell**. He was educated at Eton, King's College London and Trinity Hall, Cambridge, and ordained, but left the church in 1870 and became an agnostic. He published his reasons in *Essays on Free Thinking and Plain Speaking* (1873) and *An Agnostic's Apology* (1893). He helped found the *Pall Mall Gazette*, and was editor of the *Cornhill Magazine* (1871–82). He launched the *English Men of Letters* series with a biography of **Samuel Johnson** (1878), and in 1876 he published *The History of English Thought in the Eighteenth Century* (1876), which is generally regarded as his most important work.

Stephens, James Kenneth 1825–1901 •*Irish nationalist*• Born in Kilkenny, he became an active agent of the Young Ireland Party. Wounded during the uprising at Ballingarry (1848), he hid for three months in the mountains, and then escaped to France. In 1853 he journeyed around Ireland and founded the Irish Republican Brotherhood (Fenians) in 1858, of which he became the leader. He started the *Irish People* newspaper (1863) to urge armed rebellion and visited the US on fundraising missions. Deposed by the Fenians, he lived in the US, returning to Ireland in 1886.

Stephens, John Lloyd 1805–52 •*US archaeologist and traveler*• Born in Shrewsbury, New Jersey, and trained as a lawyer, he traveled extensively in the Levant, the Balkans, and central Europe before embarking with the architect and artist Frederick Catherwood (1799–1856) on an extended exploration of Mesoamerica in 1839–42. Their work founded the field of Mayan archaeology and they rediscovered the cities of Copan, Quirigua, Palenque, Uxmal and Chichen Itza, then unknown except to the local people. With Ephraim Squier (1821–88) they established American archaeology as a discipline in its own right.

Stephenson, George 1781–1848 •*English railway engineer*• Born in Wylam, near Newcastle, he became a fireman in a colliery while undergoing a rudimentary education at night school. In 1815 he invented, at the same time as **Humphry Davy**, a colliery safety lamp. In 1812 he had become enginewright at Killingworth Colliery, and there in 1814 he constructed his first locomotive, *Blucher*. In 1821 he was appointed engineer for the construction of the Stockton & Darlington mineral railway (opened September 1825), and in 1826 for the Liverpool & Manchester Railway, which, after considerable difficulties, was opened in September 1830. The previous October had seen the memorable contest of engines at Rainhill, resulting in the triumph of Stephenson's *Rocket* at 30 mph (48.3 kph). Thereafter he was engineer on the North Midland, Manchester & Leeds and Birmingham & Derby Railways, and many other railways in England.

Stephenson, Robert 1803–59 •*English mechanical and structural engineer*• He was born in Willington Quay, Northumberland, the son of **George Stephenson**. In 1823 he assisted his father in surveying the Stockton to Darlington Railway and, after three years in Colombia, he returned to manage his father's locomotive engine-works in Newcastle upon Tyne. He attained independent fame with his Britannia Tubular Bridge (1850), those at Conway (1848) and Montreal (1859), the High Level Bridge at Newcastle upon Tyne (1849) and others. He was a Member of Parliament for many years from 1847 and was buried in Westminster Abbey, London.

Steptoe, Patrick Christopher 1913–88 •*English gynecologist and reproduction biologist, pioneer of in vitro fertilization*• Born in Witney, Oxfordshire, he was educated in London at King's College and St George's Hospital Medical School. After military service, he specialized in obstetrics and gynecology, becoming senior obstetrician and gynecologist at the Oldham Hospitals in 1951. In 1980 he became medical director of the Bourn Hall Clinic in Cambridgeshire. He met **Robert Edwards** in 1968, and together they worked on the problem of in vitro fertilization of human embryos, which ten years later resulted in the birth of a baby after in vitro fertilization and implantation in her mother's uterus.

Stern, Isaac 1920–2001 •*US violinist*• Born in Kreminiecz, USSR, he was taken to the US as a child. He studied at the San Francisco Conservatory (1928–31) and made his recital debut in 1935 and his concert debut with the San Francisco Symphony Orchestra in 1936. He played subsequently as a soloist and in chamber music ensembles throughout the world. The recipient of numerous awards, he was regarded as one of the world's foremost violinists.

Stern, Otto 1888–1969 •*US physicist and Nobel Prize winner*• Born in Sohrau, Germany, and educated at the University of Breslau, he held posts at the Universities of Zurich, Frankfurt and Rostock and Hamburg. With the rise of the Nazis, he moved to the US, where he became Research Professor of Physics at the Carnegie Institute of Technology in Pittsburgh (1933–45). In collaboration with Walther Gerlach in 1920–21, he projected a beam of silver atoms through a nonuniform magnetic field and produced two distinct beams, thus proving the quantum theory prediction that an atom's magnetic moment can only be oriented in two fixed directions relative to an external magnetic field. For this work he was awarded the Nobel Prize for physics in 1943.

Sternberg, Josef Von *See* **Von Sternberg, Josef**

Sterne, Laurence 1713–68 •*Irish novelist*• He was born in Clonmel, County Tipperary, the son of an impoverished infantry ensign, and was educated at Jesus College, Cambridge. He was ordained in 1738, and was appointed to the living of Sutton-on-the-Forest and made a prebendary of York, where, in 1759, the first two volumes of *The Life and Opinions of Tristram Shandy* were published. These were well received, and further volumes appeared from 1761 to 1767. His health was now failing, and he lived mostly in France and Italy. *A Sentimental Journey Through France and Italy* appeared in 1768, shortly before he died in London of pleurisy. His novels display great mastery, and he developed the form of the novel as a channel for the utterance of the writer's own sentiments.

Stevens, Nettie Maria 1861–1912 •*US biologist*• Born in Cavendish, Vermont, she studied physiology at Stanford University and received a PhD from Bryn Mawr College, Pennsylvania (1903), where she later held research posts. Stevens was one of the first to explain the principle that sex is determined by particular chromosomes. She also studied sex determination in various plants and insects, demonstrating unusually large numbers of chromosomes in certain insects and the paired nature of chromosomes in mosquitoes and flies.

Stevens, Siaka Probin 1905–89 •*Sierra Leone politician*• He was born in Tolubu of mixed Christian and Muslim parentage, which helped him to understand both religions. After a period of study at Ruskin College, Oxford, in 1945, he helped found the Sierra Leone People's Party (APC) in 1951. The APC won the 1967 general election, but the result was disputed by the army and Stevens withdrew from the premiership. In 1968 an army revolt brought him back, and in 1971 he became Sierra Leone's first president. He established a one-party state and remained in power until his retirement at the age of 80.

Stevens, Stanley Smith 1906–73 •*US experimental psychologist*• Born in Ogden, Utah, he was educated at Harvard (gaining a PhD in 1933) and taught there from 1932 until his death. He made important contributions to the relatively new science of psychophysics and to our understanding of the sense of hearing. He also devised general theories and experimental techniques for the study of the scaling of sensory qualities (eg, loudness, brightness, pain).

Stevens, Wallace 1879–1955 •*US poet*• Born in Reading, Pennsylvania, he enrolled at Harvard (1897–1900) and afterward moved to New York, where he started out in journalism. He entered New York Law School in 1901 and at the age of 28 began working for various law firms, then joined an insurance company in Hartford, Connecticut. He wrote poetry in his spare time, and his first collection, *Harmonium*, was not published until 1923. Most of his early work, both poems and short stories, was published in *The Harvard Advocate*. Later works include *Ideas of Order* (1936), *The Man With the Blue Guitar* (1937), *Parts of a World* (1942) and *The Auroras of Autumn* (1950).

Stevenson, Adlai Ewing 1900–65 •*US Democratic politician and lawyer*• Born in Los Angeles, he was the grandson of another A E Stevenson (1835–1914), who was vice president of the US under **Grover Cleveland** (1893–97). He studied at Princeton, spent two years editing a family newspaper and then took up law practice in Chicago. From 1943 he took part in several European missions for the State Department and from 1945 served on US delegations to the foundation conferences of the United Nations Organization. In 1948 he was elected governor of Illinois. He ran against General **Eisenhower** as the Democratic presidential candidate in 1952 and 1956, but each time his urbane and intellectual campaign speeches had more appeal abroad than at home. He was US ambassador to the UN (1962–65).

" "

In America, any boy may become president. I suppose that's just one of the risks that he takes.

Attributed.

Stevenson, Juliet Anne Virginia 1956– •*English actress*• Born into an army family in Kelvedon, Essex, she joined the Royal Shakespeare Company in 1978, and the following year was made an RSC associate artist. Her many leading roles there include Titania and Hippolyta in *A Midsummer Night's Dream* (1981) and Madame de Tourvel in *Les Liaisons Dangereuses* (1985). At the Royal National Theatre, she has played the title role in *Hedda Gabler* (1989), and at the Royal Court and the West End she appeared in *Death and the Maiden* (1990, 1991). She has also appeared in films, including *Truly, Madly, Deeply* (1991), *The Trial* (1993) and *The Secret Rapture* (1994) and in a number of television roles.

Stevenson, Robert 1772–1850 •*Scottish engineer*• Born in Glasgow, he lost his father in infancy, and his mother married Thomas Smith, first engineer of the Northern Lighthouse Board. Stevenson took to engineering, and in 1796 succeeded his stepfather. During his 47 years' tenure in office he planned or constructed 23 Scottish lighthouses, employing the catoptric system of illumination, and invented intermittent, or flashing, lights. He also acted as a consulting engineer for roads, bridges, harbors, canals and railways.

Stevenson, Robert Louis Balfour 1850–94 •*Scottish writer*• He was born in Edinburgh, the grandson of **Robert Stevenson** and son of Thomas Stevenson, engineer of the Board of Northern Lighthouses. His childhood was afflicted by constant illness, and he suffered throughout his life from a chronic bronchial condition which may have been tuberculosis. He studied engineering briefly at the University of Edinburgh (1867), but transferred to law, becoming an advocate in 1875. He never practiced, however—his true inclination was for writing. His first major works, *Inland Voyage* (1878) and *Travels With a Donkey in the Cévennes* (1879), describe travels in Belgium and northern France undertaken to improve his health. It was in France that he met Fanny Osbourne, *née* Vandegrift (1840–1914), an American woman separated from her husband. He followed her to America and they married in 1880 after her divorce. The romantic adventure story *Treasure Island* brought him fame in 1883 and was followed by *Kidnapped* (1886), *Catriona* (1893) and *The Master of Ballantrae* (1889). *The Strange Case of Dr Jekyll and Mr Hyde* (1886) illustrates Stevenson's metaphysical interest in evil. Also written about this time were *The Black Arrow* (1888), the unfinished *Weir of Hermiston* (published posthumously in 1896) and *St Ives*, which was completed by Sir **Arthur Quiller Couch** in 1897. Stevenson's work as an essayist is seen at its best in *Virginibus Puerisque* (1881) and *Familiar Studies of Men and Books* (1882). *A Child's Garden of Verses* (1885) is a recollection of childhood in verse. In 1888 Stevenson set off with his family for the South Seas, famously visiting a leper colony and settling in Samoa, where he spent the last five years of his life on his estate of Vailima. With his stepson Lloyd Osbourne (1868–1947) he wrote *The Wrong Box* (1889), *The Wrecker* (1892) and *The Ebb Tide* (1894).

Stevenson, Ronald 1928– •*Scottish composer, pianist and writer on music*• Born in Blackburn, Lancashire, to Scottish parents, he studied at the Royal Manchester College of Music. Among his works are the 80-minute *Passacaglia on DSCH* for piano (1960–62), a piano concerto "The Continents" (1972), a violin concerto (1979), choral settings, many songs, ranging from settings of Scots to Japanese haiku. He promotes music as world-language, seeking in his works to embrace a large spectrum of international culture. He has composed for mentally handicapped children and played in geriatric homes. He has written widely on music and is an authority on **Ferruccio Busoni**.

Stevenson, William d. 1575 •*English scholar*• He entered Christ's College, Cambridge, in 1546, and became a Fellow, and is known to have staged plays there. He was probably the author of the earliest surviving English comedy, *Gammer Gurton's Needle* (1553), which is sometimes attributed to John Still or John Bridges.

Stewart, Andy (Andrew) 1933–94 •*Scottish comedian and singer*• Born in Glasgow, he entered show business as an impressionist, appearing in revue on the Edinburgh Festival Fringe singing "Ye Canna Shove Yer Granny Off a Bus." He went on to appear regularly on television, notably in the annual Hogmanay TV special, singing his own composition, "A Scottish Soldier." His own series, *The Andy Stewart Show*, followed (1963), and his radio shows included the series *17 Sauchie Street* and *Scotch Corner* (1952).

Stewart, Prince Charles Edward *See* **Stuart, Prince Charles Edward**

Stewart, Douglas Alexander 1913–85 •*Australian writer*• Born in Eltham, Taranaki, New Zealand, and educated at Victoria University of Wellington, his early books of lyric verse, *Green Lions* (1936) and *The White Cry* (1939), evoke his homeland. His first Australian verse was in *The Dosser in Springtime* (1946), in which he began to use ballad form, later put to dramatic effect in *Glencoe* (1947), a sequence on the Scottish massacre. He also wrote the classic radio drama *Fire in the Snow* (1939) on Captain **Scott**'s ill-fated Antarctic expedition. Later titles include *Back of Beyond* (1954) and *The Birdsville Track* (1955), on the life of the Australian interior. He also wrote a number of biographies.

Stewart, Sir Jackie (John Young) 1939– •*Scottish racecar driver*• Born in Dunbartonshire, he won the Dutch, German and US Grand Prix in 1968. He had been third in the world championships in 1965, his first season of Grand Prix racing, and he won the world title in 1969, 1971 and 1973. He retired at the end of the 1973 season. He was knighted in 2001.

Stewart, James *See* **Moray, James Stewart, 1st Earl of**

Stewart, Prince James Francis Edward *See* **Stuart, Prince James Francis Edward**

Stewart, Jimmy (James Maitland) 1908–97 •*US film actor*• Born in Indiana, Pennsylvania, he studied architecture at Princeton University before turning to acting, first on Broadway and later in Hollywood (from 1935). Tall, gangly, and with a distinctive drawl, he was at first cast as a naive idealist with integrity in films such as *You Can't Take It With You* (1938), *Mr. Smith Goes to Washington* (1939) and *Destry Rides Again* (1939). After distinguished service in World War II, he returned as the quintessential small-town man in *It's a Wonderful Life* (1946), and starred in the title role of *The Glenn Miller Story* (1953) before developing a more mature image as tough and resourceful heroes in Westerns and in thrillers such as *Rear Window* (1954), *Vertigo* (1958) and *Anatomy of a Murder* (1959). He won a Best Actor award for *The Philadelphia Story* (1940), and received an honorary award in 1984. His later work included *Fool's Parade* (1971).

Stieglitz, Alfred 1864–1946 •*US photographer*• Born in Hoboken, New Jersey, he studied in Berlin, traveling extensively in Europe before returning to New York in 1890. With **Edward Steichen** he founded the American Photo-Secession Group in 1902. He consistently influenced the development of creative photography as an art form through his magazine *Camera Work* (1903–17) and his gallery of modern art in New York. From 1910 he was an advocate of "straight" photography, which was dedicated to precision and clarity of image, especially in his studies of New York architecture (1910–16). He also executed portraits and studies of clouds (*Equivalents*, 1922–31).

Stiernhielm, Georg, *originally* **Georg Olofsson** 1598–1672 •*Swedish poet and linguist*• Born in Vika, he was known as the father of Swedish poetry. He was made a peer with the name of Stiernhielm in 1631, and held various government appointments. He was the first Swedish poet to write in hexameters, in *Hercules* (1658), an epic allegorical poem. He helped to reform and purify the Swedish language by studying Old Norse literature and incorporating the old vocabulary into modern Swedish.

Stifter, Adalbert 1805–68 •*Austrian novelist and painter*• Born in Oberplan, Bohemia, he studied in Vienna, and as private tutor to various aristocratic families had several unhappy love affairs. He settled in Linz and became an official in the Ministry of Education, but unhappiness and illness led him to commit suicide. His humanism and his love of traditional values pervade the short stories in collections such as *Der Condor* (1840, Eng trans *The Condor*, 1946), *Der Nachsommer* (1857, "The Indian Summer") and *Witiko* (1865–67), a heroic tale set in 12th-century Bohemia. He was also a considerable painter of city views.

Stigand d. 1072 •*English prelate*• Chaplain to King **Knut Sveinsson**, he was chief adviser to Knut's widow **Emma**. He was appointed chaplain by **Edward the Confessor**, and then Bishop of Elmham (1044), Bishop of Winchester (1047) and, uncanonically, Archbishop of Canterbury (1052). On the death of **Harold II** he supported **Edgar the Ætheling**. He was deprived of Canterbury and Winchester (1070) by **William the Conqueror**, whom he had helped to crown, and he died a prisoner at Winchester.

Stilicho, Flavius c. 365–408 AD •*Roman soldier*• Born a Vandal, he married Serena, niece of the emperor **Theodosius I**. In AD 394 he put **Flavius Honorius** on the throne of the Western Roman Empire, and ruled through him. On the death of Theodosius (394), **Alaric I** of the Visigoths invaded Greece and Italy, but was defeated by Stilicho at Pollentia (402) and Verona (403). Stilicho's proposed alliance with Alaric against the Vandals, Alans and Suevi was interpreted as treachery, and he was murdered at the command of Honorius.

Still, Clyfford 1904–80 •*US painter and printmaker*• Born in Grandin, North Dakota, he studied art at Washington State University. By about 1940 he had evolved a personal style, rejecting European ideas and employing the currently fashionable organic forms of biomorphism. He taught at the California School of Fine Arts, San Francisco, from 1946 to 1950.

Stiller, Mauritz 1883–1928 •*Swedish film director*• Born in Helsinki, Finland, of Finnish-Russian extraction, he settled in Sweden in 1909. In 1912 he began directing films for Svenska Bio. A leading figure of the Swedish silent cinema, he learned to combine his instinctive narrative technique with a dramatic force which proved right for the new medium. Of the 45 films he made in Sweden, *Herr Arnes pengar* (1919, *Sir Arne's Treasure*) and *Gösta Berlings saga* (1924, *The Story of Gösta Berling*) showed skill in producing cinematically the imaginative world of **Selma Lagerlöf**. His versatility is shown in *Erotikon* (1920), a sophisticated comedy about sexual rivalry which greatly influenced the comedies of **Ernst Lubitsch**. Stiller discovered **Greta Garbo** and took her to Hollywood in 1925, working there briefly until his death.

Stilwell, Joseph Warren, *nicknamed* **Vinegar Joe** 1883–1946 •*US soldier*• Born in Palatka, Florida, he graduated from West Point in 1904. In 1941 he became US military representative in China and in 1942 commander of the Fifth and Sixth Chinese Armies in Burma. He was also chief of staff under **Chiang Kai-shek**, for whom he planned the Ledo road (later known as the Stilwell road). In the Burma counteroffensive in 1943, he was commanding general of the US Forces in China, Burma and India, but he was recalled in 1944.

“ ”

This little book contains none of your damn business.

Note on flyleaf of 1906 diary. Quoted in Barbara Tuchman ***General Stilwell and the American Experience in China*** *(1970).*

Sting, *pseudonym of* **Gordon Matthew Sumner** 1951– •*English singer-songwriter and actor*• Born in Wallsend, Northumberland, he was a teacher before winning international fame as a singer-songwriter and bass player with the British rock trio the Police (1977–86). After the group split, Sting developed his solo career with such best-selling singles as "An Englishman in New York" (1990) and such albums as *Nothing Like the Sun* (1988), *Soul Cages* (1991) and *Brand New Day* (1999). He has also appeared in many films and is widely known as a campaigner to save Brazilian rain forests and support political prisoners around the world.

Stirling, Sir Archibald David 1915–90 •*Scottish soldier and creator of the Special Air Service*• Educated at Cambridge, he joined the Scots Guards at the outbreak of World War II. While convalescing from an injury, he formulated the idea of a small army within an army to make swift and secret raids deep behind enemy lines. The result was the SAS (Special Air Service Regiment), which quickly won a high reputation for its success in destroying aircraft and fuel dumps in German-held territory. In 1943 he was taken prisoner in Tunisia and was held in Colditz prison camp. On his release he left the army to settle in East Africa, and later moved to Hong Kong.

Stirling, James 1926–92 •*Scottish architect and town planner*• Born in Glasgow, his early designs in Britain include the History Faculty Building at Cambridge University (1964) and the Florey Building at Queen's College, Oxford (1966). His designs in Europe include the Neue Staatsgalerie in Stuttgart (1980–84), with its much-imitated curved glass entrance wall, and the Braun industrial complex in Melsungen (1992). His later work includes the Clore Gallery, an extension built onto the Tate Gallery, London, to house the Turner collection (1987). He also produced a controversial design for the redevelopment of the site at No. 1 Poultry in the City of London.

Stirling, Robert 1790–1878 •*Scottish clergyman and inventor*• Born in Cloag, Perthshire, and educated for the ministry at the Universities of Glasgow and Edinburgh, he was ordained in the Church of Scotland in 1816, and was minister of Galston, Ayrshire (1837–78). In the same year he patented a hot-air engine operating on what became known as the Stirling cycle, in which the working fluid (air) is heated at one end of the cylinder by an external source of heat. In spite of their greater efficiency, hot-air engines were superseded by the internal combustion engine and the electric motor, although some development work has been undertaken recently because of their nonpolluting characteristics.

Stirling, William Alexander, 1st Earl of c.1567–1640 •*Scottish poet and courtier*• Born in Alva, Clackmannanshire, he tutored young noblemen, and in 1613 he was attached to the household of Prince Charles (later **Charles I**). He had already published a collection of songs and madrigals in *Aurora* (1604); in 1614 he published part one of his huge poem *Doomesday*, (part two, 1637). From 1626 until his death he was secretary of state for Scotland. He was created Viscount (1630), Earl of Stirling (1633) and Earl of Dovan (1639), but he died insolvent in London. His tragedies include *Darius* (1603), *Croesus* (1604), *The Alexandrean Tragedy* (1605) and *Julius Caesar* (1607).

Stockhausen, Karlheinz 1928– •*German composer, regarded as a leader of the avant-garde*• Born in Mödrath, he was educated at the Universities of Cologne and Bonn. He joined the Musique Concrète group in Paris, and experimented with compositions based on electronic sounds. In Cologne, he helped found the electronic music studio (1953), and was appointed Professor of Composition at the Hochschule für Musik (1971). He has written orchestral, choral and instrumental works, including some which combine electronic and normal sonorities, such as *Kontakte* (1958–60, "Contact"), and parts of a large operatic cycle, *Licht* (1977– , "Light"). His *Helicopter Quartet* was premiered in 1995 in Washington.

Stockton, 1st Earl of *See* **Macmillan, Sir Harold**

Stockton, John Houston 1962– •*US basketball player*• Born in Spokane, Washington, he joined the Utah Jazz as a point guard in 1984 and was a member of both the 1992 and 1996 US Olympic gold medal-winning Dream Teams. From 1987 he led the NBA in assists for a record nine successive seasons, in the process becoming the all-time NBA leader in every major assist category. He also set a new NBA record for career steals (retiring with 3,265).

Stoker, Bram (Abraham) 1847–1912 •*Irish writer*• Born in Dublin, he was educated at Trinity College. He entered the Civil Service, but turned to literature, and joined Henry Irving in running the Lyceum Theatre in London from 1878 to 1905. He is best remembered for the classic vampire story *Dracula* (1897), and wrote a number of other novels dealing with futuristic and occult themes, including *The Jewel of the Seven Stars* (1903), *The Lady of the Shroud* (1909) and *The Lair of the White Worm* (1911).

Stokes, Sir George Gabriel 1819–1903 •*Irish mathematician and physicist*• Born in Skreen, Sligo, he graduated from Pembroke College, Cambridge, in 1841 and in 1849 became Lucasian Professor of Mathematics. From 1887 to 1892 he was Conservative Member of Parliament for Cambridge University. He used spectroscopy to determine the chemical compositions of the sun and stars, published a valuable paper on diffraction (1849), investigated X-rays, and formulated Stokes's law relating to the force opposing a small sphere in its passage through a viscous fluid. He is also remembered for his derivation of Stokes's theorem, which is used in vector calculus. He was made a baronet in 1889.

Stolypin, Pyotr Arkadevich 1862–1911 •*Russian statesman*• He was born in Dresden. After service in the ministry of the interior (from 1884) he became governor of Saratov province (1903–06), where he put down peasant uprisings and helped to suppress the revolutionary upheavals of 1905. As prime minister (1906–11) he introduced a series of agrarian reforms. In 1907 he suspended the Second Duma (national assembly) and arbitrarily limited the franchise. He was assassinated in Kiev.

Stone, Edward Durell 1902–78 •*US architect*• Born in Fayetteville, Arkansas, he founded his own architectural firm in New York City in 1936 and taught design and architecture at New York University (1935–40) and Yale (1946–51). His design (1937, with Philip Goodwin) for the Museum of Modern Art in New York City typifies the functional approach of the International style. Other notable buildings he designed are the US embassy in New Delhi (1954) and the Kennedy Center for the Performing Arts in Washington DC (opened 1971).

Stone, Irving, *originally* **Irving Tennenbaum** 1903–89 •*US novelist and playwright*• He was born in San Francisco, and studied political science at the University of California at Berkeley and worked as a saxophonist in a dance band. His *Lust for Life* (1934), based on the life of **Van Gogh**, became a bestseller. Other works include *Love Is Eternal* (1954, about **Abraham Lincoln**'s wife), *The Agony and the Ecstasy* (1961), a fictional life of **Michelangelo**, *Passions of the Mind* (1971, about **Sigmund Freud**), *The Origin* (1980, about **Charles Darwin**) and *Depths of Glory* (1985, about **Camille Pissarro**).

Stone, Isidor Feinstein 1907–89 •*US radical journalist*• Born in Philadelphia into a Jewish family, he studied at the University of Pennsylvania. As a journalist he took positions that were often unpopular, opposing American involvement in Korea and later in Vietnam, and criticizing the rise of militarism in Israel, a country he basically supported. He founded *I F Stone's Weekly*, which he ran with his wife, Esther, until 1971. He also wrote longer essays in *The New York Review of Books* and elsewhere. His last book was on the trial and death of **Socrates**.

Stone, Lucy 1818–93 •*US feminist*• Born in West Brookfield, Massachusetts, she studied at Oberlin College and soon started giving lectures on abolitionism and women's suffrage, calling the first national Women's Rights Convention at Worcester, Massachusetts, in 1850. She helped establish the American Woman Suffrage Association (1869) and founded the *Women's Journal* (1870), which she coedited with her husband, Henry Brown Blackwell, and which was later edited by their daughter, Alice Stone Blackwell (1857–1950).

Stone, Oliver 1946– •*US film director and screenwriter*• He was born in New York City and in 1967 saw active service in Vietnam, which made a deep impression on him. He won an Academy Award for the screenplay of *Midnight Express* (1978); his other scripts include *Conan the Barbarian* (1982), *Scarface* (1982) and

Year of the Dragon (1985). He won Academy Awards as best director for *Platoon* (1986) and *Born on the 4th of July* (1989), both dealing with the Vietnam War. Later films include *The Doors* (1991), a biography of rock star **Jim Morrison**; *JFK* (1991), an examination of the **Kennedy** assassination; and *Natural Born Killers* (1994), a controversial story of mass murder.

Stone, Sharon 1958– •*US actress*• Born in Meadville, Pennsylvania, she was a beauty queen and model before making her film debut in *Stardust Memories* (1980). Over the next ten years she pursued a career in minor film and television roles before appearing in the box-office hit *Total Recall* (1990). Her flamboyant performance in the erotic thriller *Basic Instinct* (1992) raised her to the status of sex symbol, and she consolidated her stardom in *Sliver* (1993), *The Specialist* (1994) and other films. She extended her range, playing a death-row inmate in *Last Dance* (1995) and earning a Best Actress Academy Award nomination as a drug-addicted showgirl in *Casino* (1995).

Stonehouse, John Thompson 1925–88 •*English politician*• Born in Southampton and educated at the London School of Economics, he served in the Royal Air Force (1944–47). He became active in the cooperative movement, working in Uganda and London (1952–57), and afterward became a Member of Parliament (1957). He was appointed minister of technology (1967–68) and minister of posts and telecommunications (1968–70). In 1974 he disappeared in Miami, Florida, and was feared drowned, but he reappeared in Australia, amid stories in the popular press of personal and financial problems. He was extradited to Britain in 1975 to face charges of fraud and embezzlement, and in 1976 he was imprisoned, being released for good behavior in 1979.

Stopes, Marie Charlotte Carmichael 1880–1958 •*British birth-control pioneer and paleobotanist*• Born in Edinburgh, she studied at University College London, and at the University of Munich, and in 1904 became the first female science lecturer at the University of Manchester, specializing in fossil plants and coal mining. In 1907 she lectured at Tokyo Imperial University (now the University of Tokyo), and with Professor Sakurai wrote a book titled *Plays of Old Japan, The No* (1913). In 1916, after the annulment of her first marriage, she began a crusade to disseminate information about these subjects. In 1918 her book, *Married Love*, caused a storm and was banned in the US. That year she married the aircraft manufacturer Humphrey Verdon Roe (1878–1949), with whom she opened the first British birth control clinic, in Holloway, London (1921). Her 70 books include *Contraception: Its Theory, History and Practice* (1923), *Sex and the Young* (1926) and a play, *Our Ostriches* (1923).

Stoppard, Miriam, *née* **Stern** 1937– •*English physician, writer and broadcaster*• Born in Newcastle upon Tyne, she trained as a doctor at the Royal Free Hospital School of Medicine in London and at King's College Medical School in Durham. After working in various hospitals, she became a research director for a pharmaceutical company, then entered television, appearing shows such as *So You Want to Stop Smoking?* (1981–82), *Baby & Co* (1984–87) and *Miriam Stoppard's Health and Beauty Show* (1988–). Her publications include *Miriam Stoppard's Book of Babycare* (1977), *Miriam Stoppard's Health and Beauty Book* (1988) and *The Breast Book* (1996), and she contributes to medical journals and women's magazines. From 1972 to 1992 she was married to the playwright **Tom Stoppard**.

Stoppard, Sir Tom, *originally* **Thomas Straussler** 1937– •*British dramatist*• Born in Zlín (now in the Czech Republic), he went to England in 1946 from India, his mother having married a British army officer after being widowed in Singapore during World War II. After attending schools in Nottingham and Yorkshire, Stoppard became a journalist in Bristol. He then went to London, where he worked as a freelance journalist and theater critic and wrote radio plays, including *The Dissolution of Dominic Boot* (1964). He made his name with *Rosencrantz and Guildenstern Are Dead* (premiered in 1966 at the Edinburgh Festival, staged at the National Theatre, London, in 1967, filmed in 1990). Built around the two "attendant lords" in **Shakespeare**'s *Hamlet*, the play hilariously examines the meaninglessness of life and questions the possibility of free will. His aim is a "perfect marriage between the play of ideas and farce": *Jumpers* (1972) is a farcical satire of logical positivism, and *Travesties* (1974) has **James Joyce**, **Lenin** and the Dadaist painter **Tristan Tzara** working together on an amateur production of **Oscar Wilde**'s *The Importance of Being Earnest*. His other plays include *The Real Inspector Hound* (1968), *Professional Foul* (1977, written for television and inspired by Amnesty International's Prisoner of Conscience Year), *The Real Thing* (1982), *Arcadia* (1993), *Indian Ink* (1995) and *The Invention of Love* (1997). In 1977 he collaborated with **André Previn** on a "play for actors and orchestra," *Every Good Boy Deserves Favor*. He has also written a novel, *Lord Malquist and Mr Moon* (1966), short stories, screenplays and film scripts, including *The Russia House* (1990) and *Shakespeare in Love* (1998), for which he shared an Academy Award with Marc Norman. He was knighted in 1997.

“ ”

Ambushing the audience is what theatre is all about.

1984 In ***Newsweek****, January 16.*

Storey, David Malcolm 1933– •*English dramatist and novelist*• He was born in Wakefield, Yorkshire. An art student and professional Rugby League player, he made a hit with his novel, *This Sporting Life* (1960). His later novels include *Pasmore* (1972), *Saville* (1976, Booker Prize) and *Present Times* (1984). His first play, *The Restoration of Arnold Middleton*, was staged at the Royal Court Theatre, London, in 1966. Subsequent plays include *In Celebration* (1969), *Home* (1970), *The Changing Room* (1971), *Cromwell* and *The Farm* (both 1973), *Life Class* (1974), *Sisters* (1978), *Early Days* (1980) and *Stages* (1992). He published a collection of poems, *Storey's Lives*, in 1992.

Storni, Alfonsina 1892–1938 •*Argentine feminist and poet*• Born in Sala Capriasca, Switzerland, she started work young as an actress with a traveling theatrical company, and in 1911 moved to Buenos Aires, Argentina, where she became a teacher and journalist. Her poetry is largely concerned with love and sexual passion. Her books include *La inquietud del rosal* (1916, "The Solicitude of the Rosebush"), *El dulce daño* (1918, "Sweet Injury"), *Languidez* (1921, "Languor") and *Mascarillo y trébol* (1938). She committed suicide on discovering that she was suffering from cancer. An edition of her verse appeared in 1961.

Storrier, Timothy Austin 1949– •*Australian figurative and landscape artist*• Born in Sydney, he studied at the National Art School there, and made working trips to central Australia, including Ayers Rock (1973) and Lake Eyre (1976), producing a series of vivid paintings. His delicate colors unite the harsh desert environment with symbolic or domestic trompe l'œil objects. He won the Sulman prize in 1968, and again in 1984 with *The Burn*. His travels to Egypt in that year resulted in his "Ticket to Egypt" exhibitions at the State Art Galleries of New South Wales and Western Australia (1986). His Sydney exhibition in 1989 included the powerful *Burning of the Gifts*.

Stoss or **Stozz, Veit** 1447–1533 •*German woodcarver and sculptor*• He was born probably in Nuremberg. For most of the period from 1477 to 1496 he was in Kraców, Poland, where he carved the high altar of the Marjacki Church. He returned to Nuremberg, and for the next 30 years worked in various churches there, including St Lorenz's, where his *Annunciation* can be seen. Despite the great size of many of his works, they all show great delicacy of form.

Stott, John Robert Walmsley 1921– •*English Anglican clergyman and writer*• Born in London, he graduated from Cambridge, and had a remarkable ministry at All Souls', Langham Place (in the heart of London's West End), as curate and then rector (1945–75). Widely acknowledged as a leading spokesman for Anglican Evangelicals, he has also had an effective ministry worldwide as a conference speaker, and was a royal chaplain from 1959 to 1991. Since 1991 he has been Extra Chaplain to the Queen. He was director of the London Institute for Contemporary Christianity (1982–86) and subsequently became its president. His many books include *Basic Christianity* (1958), *Issues Facing Christians Today* (1984) and *Why I Am a Christian* (2003).

Stout, Rex Todhunter 1886–1975 •*US detective-story writer*• He was born in Noblesville, Indiana. Before becoming a writer, he invented a school banking system that was installed in 400 cities throughout the US. His great creation is Nero Wolfe, the phenomenally fat private eye who, with the help of his confidential assistant, Archie Goodwin, got to the bottom of numerous mysteries, among them *The League of Frightened Men* (1935), *Black Orchids* (1942) and *A Family Affair* (1975).

Stow, John 1525–1605 •*English chronicler*• Born in London, he became a tailor in Cornhill, before devoting himself to antiquarian pursuits from about 1560. He became one of the best-known Elizabethan antiquaries. His principal works, which, for his time, are accurate and business-like, are his *Summary of English Chronicles* (1565), *Annals, or a General Chronicle of England* (1580) and the *Survey of London and Westminster* (1598), an account of their history, antiquities and government for six centuries. He also assisted in a second edition of **Raphael Holinshed**'s *Chronicles* (1585–87) and other editions of earlier writers.

Stow, (Julian) Randolph 1935– •*Australian novelist, poet and librettist*• He was born in Geraldton, Western Australia, worked as an anthropologist in Australia and Papua New Guinea, and subsequently taught at the Universities of Adelaide, Leeds (UK) and Western Australia. His first novel was *A Haunted Land* (1956), followed by *The Bystander* (1957), and *Tourmaline* (1963). In 1968 and 1969, while living in England, Stow wrote libretti for two music-theater works by the composer **Peter Maxwell Davies**: *Eight Songs for a Mad King* and *Miss Donnithorne's Maggot*. Other novels include *Visitants* (1979) and *The Suburbs of Hell* (1984). He also wrote a children's book, *Midnite* (1967), and a collection of verse, *A Counterfeit Silence* (1969).

Stowe, Harriet (Elizabeth) Beecher, *née* **Beecher** 1811–96 •*US novelist*• Born in Litchfield, Connecticut, she was the daughter of **Lyman Beecher**. She was brought up with puritanical strictness and joined her sister Catharine Beecher (1800–78) at the Connecticut Female Seminary at Hartford in 1824. In 1836 she married the Rev Calvin Ellis Stowe. She contributed sketches of southern life to *Western Monthly Magazine*, and won a short-story competition with *A New England Sketch* (1834). She became famous for her *Uncle Tom's Cabin* (1852), prompted by the passing of the Fugitive Slave Law, which immediately focused antislavery sentiment in the North. It was followed by a second antislavery novel, *Dred: A Tale of the Dismal Swamp* (1856). She lost popularity in Great Britain with *Lady Byron Vindicated* (1870), although the charges of incest with his half sister made against **Byron** in the book were later proven. She wrote a host of other works including fiction, biography and children's books. Her best works are those which deal with New England life, such as *Old Town Folks* (1869).

“ ”

The bitterest tears shed over graves are for words left unsaid and deeds left undone.

1865 ***Little Foxes****, chapter 3.*

Stozz, Veit *See* **Stoss, Veit**

Strabo c. 60 BC–c. 21 AD •*Greek geographer and Stoic*• Born in Amasia, Pontus, of Greek descent on his mother's side, he apparently spent his life in travel and study. He was at Corinth in 29 BC, he explored the Nile in 24 BC and seems to have settled at Rome after AD 14. Of his great historical work, *Historical Studies* (47 vols), only a few fragments survive, but his *Geographica* (17 vols) has survived almost complete, and is of great value for his extensive observations and copious references to his predecessors, **Eratosthenes**, **Polybius**, **Aristotle** and **Thucydides**. His name means "squint-eyed."

Strachey, Christopher 1916–75 •*English computer programmer and theorist*• Born in Hampstead, London, he studied mathematics and natural sciences at Cambridge, and then worked on radar. After World War II at Harrow, he did programming work on **Alan Turing**'s ACE computer at the National Physical Laboratory, and on the Manchester University Mark I. In 1952 he was appointed adviser to the National Research Development Corporation (NRDC), which placed him at the heart of the developing British computer industry. He made significant contributions in the areas of time-sharing, whereby several users could share one computer, and in denotational semantics, which sought to understand the meaning of computer languages in a mathematical way. He was one of the foremost computer architects and logicians of his day.

Strachey, (Giles) Lytton 1880–1932 •*English biographer*• Born in London, the son of an Indian civil engineer and soldier, he was educated at the University of Liverpool, where he studied history, and Trinity College, Cambridge. He was a book reviewer for the *Spectator* (1904–14), became a member of the Bloomsbury Group of writers and artists, and began his writing career as a critic with *Landmarks in French Literature* (1912). He was a conscientious objector during World War I. *Eminent Victorians* (1918) was a literary bombshell constituting, as it did, a vigorous, impertinent challenge to Victorian self-assurance. Its irony, mordant wit and the ruthless pinpointing of foible that was his method of evoking character transformed the genre. His later works include *Queen Victoria* (1921) and *Elizabeth and Essex: A Tragic History* (1928).

Stradella, Alessandro c. 1642–82 •*Italian composer*• He was born in Nepi, near Viterbo. His oratorio *San Giovanni Battista* (1675) influenced **Henry Purcell**, and in addition to dramatic oratorios he wrote operas and instrumental works of the concerto grosso type. It is said that he eloped from Venice to Turin with the mistress of one of the Contarini, who sent assassins to murder him. He was wounded, but recovered. He was eventually murdered in Genoa. His story has been the subject of operas, and F Marion Crawford (1854–1909) used it for his novel *Stradella* (1909).

Stradivari or **Stradivarius, Antonio** c. 1644–1737 •*Italian violin maker*• Born in Cremona, he was a pupil of **Niccolo Amati**. He experimented with the design of stringed instruments and perfected the Cremona type of violin, assisted by his sons Francesco (1671–1743) and Omobono (1679–1742). It is believed that he made over 1,000 violins, violas and violoncellos, of which around 650 still exist.

Strafford, Thomas Wentworth, 1st Earl of 1593–1641 •*English politician*• Born in London of a Yorkshire family with royal connections, he was knighted in 1611, and in 1614 became Member of Parliament for Yorkshire. He was originally an opponent of **Charles I** but in 1628 became a Royalist. In 1632 he was appointed Lord Deputy of Ireland, where he imposed firm rule, his aim being to make Charles "the most absolute prince in Christendom." In 1639 he became the king's principal adviser, and in this capacity was made Earl of Strafford and Lord Lieutenant of Ireland (1640). When he failed to suppress the rebellion in Scotland which had broken out as a result of Charles's policies toward the Scottish kirk (Bishops' Wars, 1639–40), he and Archbishop **Laud** were impeached by John Pym (1584–1643), leader of the Puritans in the Long Parliament, and he was executed.

Strand, Paul 1890–1976 •*US photographer*• Born in New York City, he studied under **Lewis W Hine**. He became a commercial photographer in 1912 and followed **Alfred Stieglitz** in his commitment to "straight" photography of precision and clarity in both landscape and close-up detail. He collaborated with **Charles Sheeler** in the documentary film *Mannahatta* (1920), and in 1933 was appointed chief of photography and cinematography in the government Secretariat of Education in Mexico. He made documentary films on social issues including *The Plow That Broke the Plains* (1936). His later work concentrated on still photography, in which he recorded life in many different parts of the world.

Strang, William 1859–1921 •*Scottish painter and etcher*• Born in Dumbarton, Strathclyde, he studied in London at the Slade School of Art from 1875, where he was taught and greatly influenced by **Alphonse Legros**. A prolific printmaker, he made over 750 etchings, drypoints, mezzotints, aquatints and woodcuts. Many consider his portraits to be his greatest achievement, and his sitters included **Rudyard Kipling** and **Thomas Hardy**. He illustrated several books, among them *Paradise Lost*, *Don Quixote*, *The Pilgrim's Progress* and *The Rime of the Ancient Mariner*.

Strasberg, Lee, *originally* **Israel Strassberg** 1901–82 •*US theater director, actor and teacher*• Born in Budzanow, Austria, he emigrated to the US in 1909 and became a professional actor in 1925. He gained a reputation with theTheater Guild of NewYork and helped form the GroupTheater in NewYork (1931), with which he evolved a technique which became known everywhere as "the Method" or "method acting." His teaching style owed much to the Russian director, **Stanislavsky**. As director of the Actors Studio in NewYork (1949–82), he taught **Marlon Brando**, **James Dean**, **Paul Newman** and others. In 1969 he established the Lee Strasberg Institute of Theater.

Strato or **Straton of Lampsacus** d. c. 269 BC •*Greek philosopher*• He succeeded **Theophrastus** as the third head of the Peripatetic school (from c. 287 to 269 BC) which **Aristotle** founded. His writings are lost, but had an original theory about the void, its distribution explaining differences in the weights of objects. He also denied any role of teleological, and hence theological, explanations in nature, which led naturally to the position **David Hume** called Stratonician atheism—the universe is ultimate, self-sustaining and needs no further external or divine explanation to account for it.

Stratton, Charles Sherwood, *called* **General Tom Thumb** 1838–83 •*US midget showman*• Born in Bridgeport, Connecticut, he stopped growing at six months of age and stayed 25 inches (63 cm) until his teens, eventually reaching 40 inches (101 cm). He was exhibited by the circus impresario **P T Barnum** from the age of five, and toured the US and Europe. In 1863 he married another midget, Lavinia Warren (1841–1919).

Strauss, David Friedrich 1808–74 •*German theologian*• Born in Ludwigsburg, Württemberg, he studied for the Church at Tübingen, where he also lectured on philosophy in the university as a disciple of **Hegel**. In his *Leben Jesu* (1835, Eng trans *The Life of Jesus Critically Examined* by **George Eliot**, 1846) he sought to prove the gospel history to be a collection of myths, and to detect a nucleus of historical truth free from every trace of supernaturalism. The book marks an epoch in New Testament criticism and raised a storm of controversy, and Strauss was dismissed from his post at Tübingen. His second great work, *Die christliche Glaubenslehre*, was a review of Christian dogma (1840–41). A new *Life of Jesus, Composed for the German People* (1864, Eng trans 1865), attempts to reconstruct a positive life of **Jesus**. In *Der alte und der neue Glaube* (1872, "The Old Faith and the New") Strauss endeavored to prove that Christianity as a system of religious belief is dead, and that a new faith must be built up out of art and the scientific knowledge of nature. He also wrote several biographies, and lectures on **Voltaire** (1870).

Strauss, Franz-Josef 1915–88 •*West German politician*• Born and educated in Munich, the son of a butcher, he served in the German army during World War II and in 1945 joined the Christian Democratic Union (CDU)'s Bavarian-based sister party, the Christian Social Union (CSU), being elected to the Bundestag (federal parliament) in 1949. He became leader of the CSU in 1961 and held a succession of ministerial posts. His career was seriously blighted when, for security purposes, he authorized a raid on the offices of the journal *Der Spiegel*, leading to his dismissal as minister of defense in 1962. During the 1970s he vigorously opposed the Ostpolitik initiative of the **Brandt** and **Schmidt** administrations. From 1978 he had success as the state premier of Bavaria, using this base to wield significant influence in the coalition government headed by Chancellor **Helmut Kohl**.

Strauss, Johann the Elder, *also known as* **Johann Strauss I** 1804–49 •*Austrian violinist, conductor, and composer*• Born in Vienna, he founded the Viennese Waltz tradition with composer Joseph Lanner (in whose quartet he played), a development from **Schubert**. He toured extensively in Europe with his own orchestra, played during Queen **Victoria**'s coronation celebrations (1838) and composed several marches, including the *Radetzky March* (1848) in honor of the general. He also composed many waltzes, but was eclipsed by his son, **Johann Strauss the Younger**.

Strauss, Johann the Younger, *also known as* **Johann Strauss II** 1825–99 •*Austrian violinist, conductor, and composer*• Born in Vienna, he was the son of **Johann Strauss the Elder**. He toured with his own orchestra, performing in London in 1869 and visiting the US in 1872. He composed over 400 waltzes, notably *The Blue Danube* (1867, *An der schönen blauen Donau*) and *Tales From the Vienna Woods* (1868, *Geschichten aus dem Wienerwald*), as well as polkas, marches, several operettas, including *Die Fledermaus* (1874, "The Bat"), and the concert piece *Perpetuum Mobile*. His brothers Josef (1827–70) and Eduard (1835–1916) were conductors, and Josef also composed waltzes.

Strauss, Levi c. 1829–1902 •*US clothing manufacturer*• Born in Germany, he emigrated to the US and lived in New York City before sailing around Cape Horn to California during the gold rush in 1850. He intended to become a prospector, but found a greater source of income when he began to sell trousers made of tent canvas to miners. He settled in San Francisco and founded Levi Strauss & Co to manufacture the trousers, which the miners called "Levi's." Ordering denim from New York, he dyed the fabric blue for uniformity and reinforced the pocket corners with copper rivets, creating what became the standard work trousers throughout the West of the 1860s and probably the most popular trousers in the world today.

Strauss, Richard 1864–1949 •*German composer*• Born in Munich, he began to compose at the age of six, and his first publications date from 1875. He began musical studies in Berlin the following year, and shortly afterward became assistant conductor under Hans von Bülow (1830–94) at Meiningen. There he was converted from the school of **Brahms**, under whose influence his early compositions had been written, to that of **Wagner** and **Liszt**, composing his first symphonic poems and succeeding von Bülow at Meiningen in 1885. After a period (1886–89) as assistant conductor at the Munich opera, he moved to Weimar. His symphonic poems include *Don Juan* (1889), *Tod und Verklärung* (1889, "Death and Transfiguration"), *Till Eulenspiegels lustige Streiche* (1895, "Till Eulenspiegel's Merry Pranks"), *Also sprach Zarathustra* (1895–96, "Thus Spake Zarathustra"), *Don Quixote* (1897) and *Ein Heldenleben* (1898, "A Hero's Life"). The first of his operas, *Guntram*, was produced at Weimar in 1894, and in the same year he became conductor of the Berlin Philharmonic Orchestra. His operas *Salome* (1905) and *Elektra* (1909), the first of his collaborations with the dramatic poet **Hugo von Hofmannsthal**, caused sensations by their erotic treatment of biblical and classical subjects. With Hofmannsthal he went on to compose the popular *Der Rosenkavalier* (1911) and *Ariadne auf Naxos* (1912, revised 1916). His work with Stefan Zweig (1881–1942) on *Die schweigsame Frau* (1935, "The Silent Woman") led him into difficulties with the Nazi government, which had previously appointed him president of the Reichsmusikkammer. He resigned the post, but his commanding position at the head of German musical life protected him from serious political reprisal. Indeed, he went on to produce three operas with Josef Gregor, *Friedenstag* (1938, "Day of Peace"), *Daphne* (1938) and *Die Liebe der Danae* (1938–40, "The Love of Danae"). After the completion of his last opera, *Capriccio* (to a libretto by Clemens Krauss, 1942), he turned to instrumental work and song: in 1943 he wrote *Metamorphosen*, an extended piece for 23 strings inspired by the wartime destruction of German cities, and finally a series of small-scale concerto and orchestral works and the valedictory *Vier letzte Lieder* (1948, "Four Last Songs").

Stravinsky, Igor Fyodorovich 1882–1971 •*Russian-born US composer*• Born in Oranienbaum, near St Petersburg, the son of a musician at the Imperial Opera, he studied law but became increasingly interested in musical composition, which he studied with **Rimsky-Korsakov**. **Sergei Diaghilev** heard Stravinsky's music and invited him to write a ballet on the legend of *The Firebird* (1910); his enchanting music was an instant success. A second ballet, *Petrushka* (1911), consolidated his international reputation, as did *The Rite of Spring* (1913). The **Hans Andersen** opera, *The Nightingale* (1914), was followed by the wartime "shoe-string" entertainments, *Renard* (1917) and *The Soldier's Tale* (1918), which aptly illustrate Stravinsky's adaptability. Essentially an experimenter, he then plunged headlong into neoclassicism. The ballets *Pulcinella* (1920), based on music by Giovanni Pergolesi (1710–36), *Apollo Musagetes* (1928), *The Card Game* (1937), *Orpheus* (1948) and the austere *Agon* (1957), using **Schoenberg**'s twelve-note system, exemplify this trend, as do the opera-oratorio *Oedipus Rex* (1927) and the magnificent choral *Symphony of Psalms* (1930). Stravinsky settled in France in 1934 and finally in the US, as an American citizen, in 1945. Other characteristic and outstanding works include the *Symphony in C Major* (1940); the opera *The Rake's Progress* (1951) for which **W H Auden** helped to write the libretto; the serial-music *In Memoriam Dylan Thomas* (1954); *The Flood* (1962), *Elegy for J.F.K.* (1964); *Variations* (1965); and *Requiem Canticles* (1966).

“ ”

My music is best understood by children and animals.

*1961 In the **Observer**, October 8.*

Straw, Jack (John Whitaker) 1946– •*English Labour politician*• Born in Buckhurst Hill, Essex, he studied at the University of Leeds, where from 1969 to 1971 he was president of the National Union of Students and displayed an early belief in law, order and stability. Elected to the Islington borough council (1971–78), he was called to the bar in 1972, and while practicing as a lawyer, became a deputy leader of the Inner London Education Authority (1973–74). On Labour's return to power in 1974, he became adviser to **Barbara Castle**, who was secretary of state for social services; then in 1976 he moved to be adviser to the environment secretary. After a couple of years with Granada Television, he became Member of Parliament for Blackburn (1979–). He joined the Shadow Cabinet in 1987 as principal Opposition spokesman on education (1987–92), on the environment (1992–94) and on home affairs (1994–97), and was appointed home secretary when Labour came to power in 1997. He is currently foreign secretary (2001–).

Streep, Meryl (Mary Louise) 1949– •*US actress*• Born in Summit, New Jersey, she graduated from Vassar College and Yale Drama School before making her New York stage debut in *The Playboy of Seville* (1969). Her film debut in *Julia* (1977), *The Deer Hunter* (1978) and *Kramer vs. Kramer* (1979, Academy Award) established her as a first-rank star. She has consistently expanded her range, showing sensitivity and a facility with accents in a series of acclaimed characterizations in films like *The French Lieutenant's Woman* (1981), *Sophie's Choice* (1982), for which she won a second Academy Award, *Silkwood* (1983), *Out of Africa* (1985), *Ironweed* (1987), *Postcards From the Edge* (1990), *Dancing at Lughnasa* (1998), *Adaptation* (2002) and *The Hours* (2002).

Street, George Edmund 1824–81 •*English architect*• Born in Woodford, Essex, he was the assistant of Sir **George Gilbert Scott**, and started his own practice in 1849. From his practice and influence emerged major figures like **William Morris** and **Philip Webb**. He restored Christ Church in Dublin, and designed Neogothic buildings, including the London Law Courts and scores of churches.

Street, Lady Jessie Mary Grey 1889–1970 •*Australian feminist and writer*• Born in Ranchi province of Chota Nagpur, northeast India, she was educated at private schools in England and at the University of Sydney. She became an early activist for the League of Nations, and in 1920 secretary of the National Council of Women, and later president of the Feminist Club. In 1929 she became founding president of the United Associations of Women, an umbrella group for the New South Wales feminist movement. She ran as Labor candidate in the federal election of 1943 and again in 1946, and in that year was the only woman delegate to the San Francisco conference which marked the beginnings of the United Nations Organization.

Streeter, Alison 1964– •*English swimmer*• Born in Surrey, she took up swimming to help her asthma, but has since racked up more English Channel crossings than any other person in the world. In 1988 she broke the world record, previously held by a man, for the fastest crossing from Scotland to Ireland, and she also set world records for the fastest swims around the Isle of Wight and around Jersey. In 2001 she swam the channel for the fortieth time, and she is the overall record holder for cross-channel swims.

Streeton, Sir Arthur Ernest 1867–1943 •*Australian landscape painter*• Born in Mount Duneed, Victoria, he studied at the National Gallery School in Melbourne and in 1886 joined **Frederick McCubbin** and **Tom Roberts** at their artists' camp at Box Hill, Victoria. In 1888, with Roberts and Charles Conder (1868–1909), he helped establish the Heidelberg school of painting, named after their camp near there. Purchases by the Art Gallery of New South Wales and by the National Gallery of Victoria confirmed Streeton's national reputation. In 1898 he went to London, and he exhibited at the Royal Academy in 1900. He visited Europe and his Italian pictures evoked **J M W Turner**'s use of light. Streeton also worked in France as an official war artist from 1914. He returned to Melbourne in 1924, where from 1929 he wrote art criticism for a local newspaper.

Street-Porter, Janet 1944– •*English television producer and host*• Born in London, she studied architecture for a year, then worked as a journalist before hosting television shows such as *Saturday Night People* (1978–80). She then turned to production, and her 1980s current affairs program *Network 7* won her a British Academy of Film and Television Arts award. In 1988 she became the BBC's first commissioning editor for youth programs, responsible for shows such as *Rapido*, then was promoted to head of youth and entertainment in 1991. Becoming head of independent production for BBC TV's entertainment group early in 1994, she left to become managing director of the new national cable television channel, LiveTV, but resigned suddenly in 1995. Since 1999 she has been editor of *The Independent on Sunday*.

Streicher, Julius 1885–1946 •*German journalist and politician*• Born in Fleinhausen, he was associated with **Hitler** in the early days of the National Socialist Party, taking part in the 1923 putsch. A ruthless persecutor of the Jews, he incited anti-Semitism through the newspaper *Der Stürmer*, which he founded and edited, and copies of which were widely displayed in prominent red boxes throughout the Reich. He was hanged at Nuremberg as a war criminal.

Streisand, Barbra, *originally* **Barbara Joan Rosen** 1942– •*US actress, director and singer*• Born in Brooklyn, New York, she made her New York debut in *Another Evening With Harry Stones* (1961) and had success on Broadway in *I Can Get It for You Wholesale* (1963) and *Funny Girl* (1964). Her 1965 television special, *My Name Is Barbra*, won five Emmy awards, and she has been the recipient of numerous Grammy awards, including five as best female vocalist. She repeated the success of *Funny Girl* in a film version (1968), earning an Academy Award for her first film appearance. She followed it with *Hello Dolly!* (1969), *The Way We Were* (1973), *A Star Is Born* (1976), which she produced, and *Nuts* (1987). She has won numerous awards as a top-selling recording artist and film actress, and diversified further in 1983 as the producer, director and cowriter of *Yentl*, in which she also acted and sang. She later acted in and directed *Prince of Tides* (1990) and *The Mirror Has Two Faces* (1996). In 1994 she ended a 27-year break from the mainstream concert stage with performances in Las Vegas and London.

Stresemann, Gustav 1878–1929 •*German politician and Nobel Prize winner*• He was born in Berlin. Entering the Reichstag in 1907 as a National Liberal, he rose to become leader of that party, and after World War I founded and led its successor, the German People's Party. He was chancellor of the new German (Weimar) Republic for a few months in 1923, when, and as minister of foreign affairs (1923–29), he pursued a policy of conciliation, and in 1925 negotiated the Locarno Pact of mutual security with **Aristide Briand** and **Austen Chamberlain**. He secured the entry of Germany into the League of Nations in 1926, and shared with Briand the 1926 Nobel Peace Prize for that year.

Stretton, Ross 1952– •*Australian ballet dancer and director*• Born in Canberra, he studied at the Australian Ballet School, Melbourne. After becoming principal artist in the Australian Ballet, he moved to the US in 1979 to join the Joffrey Ballet, subsequently appearing as guest dancer and then permanent member with the American Ballet Theater (1980–81). Since then he has guested with many other companies worldwide, and became director of the Australian Ballet in 1997 and director of the Royal Ballet in 2001.

Strijdom or **Strydom, Johannes Gerhardus** 1893–1958 •*South African statesman*• Born in Willowmore, Cape Province, he was educated at Stellenbosch and Pretoria, and took up law practice in the Transvaal. Elected Member of Parliament in 1929, he became leader of the extremists in the National Party. His two main political ends were establishing the policy of apartheid and setting up an Afrikaner Republic outside the Commonwealth. He succeeded **Daniel F Malan** as prime minister of South Africa from 1954 until shortly before his death.

Strindberg, (Johan) August 1849–1912 •*Swedish dramatist and novelist*• Born in Stockholm, he failed to complete his studies at Uppsala University. His personal life was turbulent and included three unsuccessful marriages and periods of severe persecution mania. He had a propensity for involvement in feuds and lived abroad for long periods, mainly in France and Italy. His first major play was *Mäster Olof* (1872, Eng trans 1915), a historical drama, a genre to which he was to return prolifically in the years around 1900 with, for instance, *Gustav Vasa* and *Erik XIV* (both 1899). His breakthrough came with a satirical novel about the art circles of Stockholm, *Röda rummet* (1879, Eng trans *The Red Room*, 1913), which created an uproar and is regarded as marking the arrival of both the modern realistic novel in Sweden and that of the naturalist movement. His later naturalist novel, *Hemsöborna* (1887, *The People of Hemsö*, 1959), his sunniest work, has become a popular classic. He produced two collections of short stories, *Giftas I* and *II* (1884–86, Eng trans *Getting Married*, 1913); a small incident in the first volume led to his trial on a charge of blasphemy, of which he was acquitted. He then published a bitter autobiography, *Tjänstekvinnans son* (1886, *The Son of a Servant*, 1913). In his major plays he combines naturalistic techniques with psychological analysis: *Fadren* (1887, Eng trans *The Father*, 1899), *Fröken Julie* (1888, Eng trans *Miss Julie*, 1918), and *Fordringsägare* (1889, Eng trans *The Creditors*, 1914). In the 1890s he experimented with the occult and pseudoscience, suffered a spiritual crisis verging on madness, and underwent a conversion influenced by the work of **Emanuel Swedenborg**. All of this is given dramatic expression in the trilogy *Till Damaskus* (1898–1904, *To Damascus*, 1913). His efforts to find a dramatic means of expressing inner reality in these and later plays, like *Drömspelet* (1902, Eng trans *A Dream Play*, 1929), mark him as a forerunner of expressionism and a major influence on modern theater.

Stroessner, Alfredo 1912– •*Paraguayan dictator*• Born in Encarnación, the son of a German immigrant, he took up military training at Asunción, then joined the army, was commissioned in 1932 and rose to become commander in chief in 1951. In conformity with Paraguay's long history of military governments, operating through the right-wing Colorado party, he became president in a coup d'état in 1954 which deposed Federico Chávez. He was reelected on seven occasions, despite his record on civil rights. In February 1989 he was ousted in a coup led by General Andrés Rodríguez (1923–97), and went into exile in Brazil.

Stroheim, Erich von, *originally* **Erich Oswald Stroheim** 1885–1957 •*Austrian film director and actor*• Born in Vienna, Austria, he was an officer in the Austrian cavalry (1902–09), then emigrated to the US and made his film debut with small parts in **D W Griffith**'s classics *Birth of a Nation* (1915) and *Intolerance* (1916). His first success as a film director was with *Blind Husbands* (1919), followed by *The Devil's Passkey* (1920), *Foolish Wives* (1922) and *Greed* (1923). His career was punctuated by furious rows with producers about his extravagance and arrogance, but he had box-office hits with *The Merry Widow* (1925) and *The Wedding March* (1928). In the 1930s he moved to France and starred as a sadistic Prussian officer in **Jean Renoir**'s *La grande illusion* (1937). He returned to Hollywood for *Sunset Boulevard* (1950, Academy Award nomination).

Strong, Sir Roy Colin 1935– •*English art historian and museum director*• Born in London and educated at Queen Mary College, London, and at the Warburg Institute, London, he became assistant keeper at the National Portrait Gallery, London, in 1959, then its director in 1967. He was also director of the Victoria and Albert Museum, London (1974–87) and has published books on art, literature and gardens. He was knighted in 1982.

Struve, Otto 1897–1963 •*US astronomer*• Born in Kharkov (now in Ukraine), the grandson of **Otto Wilhelm Struve**, he was educated at Kharkov State University, but in 1919 left Russia after the defeat of the antirevolutionary forces. He was offered a post at the Yerkes Observatory in 1921, where in 1932 he was appointed director. In 1939 he founded the McDonald Observatory of the University of Texas and was director of the Leuschner Observatory at the University of California from 1950. He was also the first director of the National Radio Astronomy Observatory (1959–62). Struve performed an immense volume of observational work on stars of various types, on the interstellar medium and on gaseous nebulae. He was president of the International Astronomical Union from 1952 to 1955.

Struve, Otto Wilhelm 1819–1905 •*Russian astronomer*• Born in Dorpat (now Tartu), the son of **Wilhelm Struve**, he went to the University of Dorpat, where he studied under his father and became assistant at the Pulkova Observatory. He remained on the staff of the Pulkova Observatory for the rest of his working life, finally as director in succession to his father (1862–89). Continuing his father's research on double stars, he discovered 500 new pairs. His own most important studies were his determination of the constant of precession and of the solar motion through space (1841). He took part in international projects such as the transits of Venus (1874), for which he organized 31 expeditions within and beyond the Russian empire.

Struve, (Friedrich Georg) Wilhelm 1793–1864 •*Russian astronomer*• Born in Altona, near Hamburg, Germany, he studied at the University of Dorpat (now Tartu) in Estonia (then part of the Russian empire) and he was later appointed Professor of Mathematics and Astronomy there (1816–39), also becoming director of Dorpat Observatory in 1818. At Dorpat he carried out a major program of double-star observations, published in a fundamental catalog of 3,112 double stars (1837). In 1837 he also measured the parallax of the star Vega. In 1835 he was summoned to superintend the building and equipping of a new observatory at Pulkova, near St Petersburg. Struve's astronomical research at Pulkova included work on the structure of the Milky Way (1847). He also supervised a huge geodetic survey, completed in 1860, extending from the Baltic Sea to the Caucasus Mountains. His son and assistant was **Otto Wilhelm Struve**.

Strydom, Johannes Gerhardus *See* **Strijdom, Johannes Gerhardus**

Stuart or **Stewart, Prince Charles Edward**, *known as* **the Young Pretender** and **Bonnie Prince Charlie** 1720–88 •*Claimant to the throne of England and Scotland*• He was the elder son of **James Francis Stuart**, the Old Pretender, and grandson of **James VII and II**. Born and educated in Rome, he became the center of Jacobite hopes. In 1744 he went to France to head the projected invasion of England, and after some delay landed in July 1745 with seven followers at Eriskay in the Hebrides. On August 19 he raised his father's standard in Glenfinnan, and the clansmen flocked to his support. Edinburgh surrendered, but the castle held out; and Charles kept court at Holyroodhouse, the palace of his ancestors. His army won a victory over Sir John Cope at Prestonpans (September 21), and on November 1 he left for London at the head of 6,500 men. He took Carlisle and advanced as far as Derby. Londoners became alarmed, with the cream of the British army engaged on the Continent. However, Charles was persuaded against his will to turn back because of lack of support in England, and although he won a further victory against the government forces at Falkirk on January 17, 1746, he suffered a crushing defeat at the hands of the Duke of **Cumberland**'s troops at Culloden Moor on April 16. The uprising was ruthlessly suppressed, and Charles was hunted in the highlands and islands for five months with a price on his head. He was helped by **Flora Macdonald** when, disguised as her maid, "Betty Burke," he crossed to Portree in June 1746. He was given hospitality at the French court until the Peace of Aix-la-Chapelle (1748) required his expulsion from France. He assumed the title of Charles III of Great Britain and retired to Florence. He died in Rome and was buried at Frascati, later at St Peter's.

Stuart or **Stewart, Prince James Francis Edward**, *known as* **the Old Pretender** 1688–1766 •*Claimant to the throne of Great Britain*• The only son of **James VII and II** and his second wife, **Mary of Modena**, he was born at St James's Palace, London. Six months later, he was taken by his fugitive mother to St Germain, where, on his father's death (1701), he was proclaimed his successor as **James III**. His attempt to land in Scotland (1708) failed and he returned to France to serve with the French in the Low Countries, distinguishing himself at Malplaquet (1709). He refused to renounce his Catholicism in order to be declared heir to Queen **Anne**. During John Erskine, Earl of **Mar**'s Jacobite rebellion, he landed at Peterhead (1715), but left six weeks later. Unable to return to France, he spent most of the rest of his life in Rome. In 1719 he had married Princess Clementina Sobieski (1702–35), who bore him two sons.

Stuart, Gilbert Charles 1755–1828 •*US painter*• Born in North Kingstown, Rhode Island, he studied under **Benjamin West** and became a fashionable portrait painter. In 1792 he returned to the US, and painted portraits of **Thomas Jefferson**, **James Madison**, **John Adams** and 124 of **George Washington**, including that which appears on the one-dollar bill. With **John Singleton Copley** he was regarded as a pioneer of classical American portraiture.

Stuart, James Ewell Brown, *known as* **Jeb Stuart** 1833–64 •*US Confederate soldier*• Born in Patrick County, Virginia, he graduated from West Point in 1854 and became a valued intelligence officer in the Confederate army during the Civil War, and the Confederacy's best-known cavalry commander, performing brilliantly in Pennsylvania, at Fredericksburg and Chancellorsville, and in the Wilderness Campaign. He was criticized at the Battle of Gettysburg, however, for arriving too late because he was off on a raid. He was mortally wounded at Yellow Tavern.

Stuart, John McDouall 1815–66 •*Australian explorer*• Born in Dysart, Fife, Scotland, he was educated at the Scottish Naval and Military Academy, Edinburgh. As a draftsman, he accompanied Captain Charles Sturt (1795–1869) on an expedition to central Australia (1844–45). Between 1855 and 1862 he made six expeditions to the interior and reached the "inland sea," Lake Eyre. He made three attempts to cross Australia from south to north, and on the first discovered the Finke River and the MacDonnell Ranges. His third attempt (1861–62) was successful. Mount Stuart is named after him.

“ ”

If this country is settled, it will be one of the finest Colonies under the Crown, suitable for the growth of any and everything.

1862 On reaching the sea at the Gulf of Carpentaria. Journal entry, July.

Stubbs, George 1724–1806 •*English painter and etcher*• Born in Liverpool, he became the most famous and original animal painter of his time. He was almost entirely self-taught. He specialized in horses, of which he had a thorough anatomical knowledge (he studied anatomy in York and in 1766 published his *Anatomy of the Horse*, for which he engraved his own plates), but also painted portraits, conversation pieces and rural scenes. His pictures of racehorses are distinguished from other animal paintings by masterly composition, as in *Whistlejacket* (1762, National Gallery, London), and a feeling for atmosphere, as in *Hambletonian* (1800, Mountstewart, Northern Ireland). He often painted wild animals, and experimented with enamel, as in *A Lion Devouring a Horse* (1769, Tate).

Sturdee, Sir Frederick Charles Doveton, 1st Baronet 1859–1925 •*English naval commander*• He joined the navy in 1871. As rear admiral in 1908, he commanded the *Invincible* in the action which wiped out the German squadron under **Graf von Spee** off the Falkland Islands in 1914. Thereafter he served with the Grand Fleet, including in the Battle of Jutland (1916). In 1921 he was promoted to Admiral of the Fleet.

Sture, Sten the Elder c. 1440–1503 •*Swedish regent*• On the death of his uncle, King **Karl VIII Knutsson** (1470), who had opposed the Kalmar Union and attempts to keep all the Scandinavian realms under one (Danish) monarch, he proclaimed himself regent. He strengthened his position by defeating his opponents in the Swedish Council and the Danish king **Christian I** at Brunkeberg (1471), and ruled for 27 years. In 1497 King Hans of Denmark and Norway resumed the struggle successfully and Sten relinquished power. In 1501 the Swedes rebelled against the Danes and Sten became regent again until his death.

Sturge, Joseph 1794–1859 •*English Quaker philanthropist and reformer*• Born in Elberton, Gloucestershire, he became a prominent campaigner against slavery in the British West Indies, which he helped to abolish in 1837. In 1841 he toured the US slave states with **John Greenleaf Whittier**, and later campaigned for the repeal of the Corn Laws and for the extension of adult suffrage and Chartism.

Sturgeon, William 1783–1850 •*English scientist*• Born in Whittington, North Lancashire, he became a shoemaker's apprentice, and in 1825 constructed the first practical electromagnet. This was followed by the first moving-coil galvanometer (1836) and various electromagnetic machines.

Sturges, Preston, *originally* **Edmund Preston Biden** 1898–1959 •*US screenwriter, film director and inventor*• Born in Chicago, and educated in the US and Europe, he enlisted in the Air Corps in 1917 and later worked in the cosmetics industry, inventing a "kiss-proof" lipstick, before making his mark as a dramatist (from 1927). He later moved to Hollywood and wrote screenplays such as *The Power and the Glory* (1933) and *The Good Fairy* (1935). A director from 1940, he enjoyed a brief run of successes with inventive, freewheeling comedies that combined wit, slapstick and social concerns. His notable films include *The Lady Eve* (1941), *Sullivan's Travels* (1941) and *Hail, the Conquering Hero* (1944). Commercial success eluded him thereafter, and he spent his last ten years in Paris. He received an Academy Award for the script of *The Great McGinty* (1940).

Sturluson, Snorri 1179–1241 •*Icelandic chieftain and historian*• He was born in Hvammur in western Iceland and acquired the estates of Borg and Reykholt. He was Lawspeaker of the Althing for 15 years from 1215 and became deeply involved in the turbulent politics of Iceland in the period which led to its loss of independence, first as an ally of King **Haakon IV Haakonsson** of Norway and then as his opponent. He was assassinated at Reykholt by one of the king's followers. He wrote two of the most important works of Icelandic literature, the *Prose Edda*, from which much of our knowledge of the Old Norse religion and myth derives, and *Heimskringla*, a history of the early kings of Norway.

Sturtevant, Alfred Henry 1891–1970 •*US geneticist*• Born in Jacksonville, Illinois, he studied at Columbia University, and from 1928 spent his career at the California Institute of Technology. As an undergraduate he drew up the first chromosome map of the fruit fly *Drosophila* in 1911, based on Morgan's suggestion that genes which are far apart on the same chromosome are more likely to be separated by the mechanism of recombination, or "crossing-over." Later, as part of Morgan's "fly room" group, he provided the mathematical background for genetic mapping experiments on *Drosophila*. Together with Morgan, **Hermann Müller** and C B Bridges, he established the basis for the chromosomal theory of heredity in *The Mechanism of Mendelian Inheritance* (1915).

Styron, William 1925– •*US novelist*• Born in Newport News, Virginia, he graduated from Duke University in Durham, North Carolina, in 1947. His first novel, *Lie Down in Darkness*, appeared in 1951. *Set This House on Fire* (1960) portrayed Americans in Europe after the war and was hugely successful in France. Unafraid of controversial topics, he has tackled racism in *The Confessions of Nat Turner* (1967) and the fate of Holocaust survivors in *Sophie's Choice* (1979). Subsequent works include *This Quiet Dust* (1982), *Darkness Visible: A Memoir of Madness* (1990) and *A Tidewater Morning* (1993).

Suárez, Francisco 1548–1617 •*Spanish philosopher and theologian*• Born in Granada, he entered the Society of Jesus (1564), was ordained (1572), taught theology at Segovia, Valladolid, Rome, Alcalá, Salamanca and Coimbra, and is considered by many to be the greatest scholastic philosopher after **Aquinas**. His *Disputationes Metaphysicae* was a very influential text in Catholic, and some Protestant, universities in the 17th and 18th centuries, and both **Descartes** and **Leibniz** studied it closely. He also wrote important studies on political theory, foreshadowing the modern doctrine of international law, and condeming the divine-right theories of kingship of **James VI and I**.

Suchet, David 1946– •*English actor*• Born in London, he trained at the London Academy of Music and Dramatic Art and acted extensively with the Royal Shakespeare Company (1973–79). He appeared on television as Edward Teller in *Oppenheimer* (1980), in the title role in *Blott on the Landscape* (1985) and as Inspector Japp in *Thirteen at Dinner* (1985) before playing the Belgian detective Hercule Poirot in *Agatha Christie's Poirot* (1989–97) and Adolf Verloc in *The Secret Agent* (1992). His film roles include *Greystoke: The Legend of Tarzan, Lord of the Apes* (1984) and *A Perfect Murder* (1998).

Suchet, Louis Gabriel, Duc d'Albufera da Valencia 1770–1826 •*French general*• Born in Lyons, he fought in Italy and Egypt and was made a general. He checked an Austrian invasion of the south of France (1800), took part in the campaigns against Austria (1805) and Prussia (1806), and, as generalissimo of the French army in Aragon, reduced the province to submission. He captured Tortosa in 1811, in 1812 he destroyed Blake's army at Sagunto, and by his capture of Valencia earned the title of Duc d'Albufera da Valencia. He was created a peer of France by **Louis XVIII**, but joined **Napoleon I** on the latter's return from Elba. Deprived of his peerage after Waterloo (1815), he did not return to court until 1819.

Suckling, Sir John 1609–42 •*English poet and dramatist*• He was born in Whitton, Middlesex, and educated at Trinity College, Cambridge. He lived at court in London, but involvement in political intrigue led him to flee the country, and he died (it is said by his own hand) in Paris. His plays include *Aglaura* (1637), and his major lyrics are included in the posthumously published *Fragmenta Aurea* (1646). It contains what is probably his most famous work, "Why So Pale and Wan, Fond Lover?"

“ ”

'Tis not the meat; but 'tis the appetite
Makes eating a delight.

c. 1638 Sonnet no. 2.

Sucre, Antonio José de 1793–1830 •*South American soldier, statesman and revolutionary*• Born in Cumana, Venezuela, he was **Simón Bolívar**'s lieutenant and first president (1826) of Bolivia, which he freed from Spanish rule by the victory of Aya Cucho (1824). He resigned after a rebellion in 1828. He fought for Colombia, winning the Battle of Giron (1829), and was assassinated on his way home from the Colombian Congress at Bogotá, of which he had been president. Sucre, the judicial capital of Bolivia, is named after him.

Su Dongpo (Su Tung-p'o), *pseudonym of* **Su Shi (Su Shih)** 1036–1101 •*Chinese painter, calligrapher, poet, philosopher and politician*• He was born in Mei-shan, now in Sichuan (Szechuan) province, into a family of peasant origins, which had only recently moved into the mandarinate. Su Dongpo's father as well as his own son were literati, collectively known as the three Su. Su Dongpo is almost unanimously referred to as one of the most prominent men of his time. Excelling in all branches of the arts, he epitomized the cultural ideal of 11th-century Chinese humanism, and was briefly prime minister before being exiled for holding views too aesthetically oriented and humanistic to serve the needs of the pragmatic Song (Sung) dynasty. Much of Chinese aesthetics derive from his writings and from his formulation of *wen ren hua* (literati painting).

Sue, (Marie Joseph) Eugène 1804–57 •*French novelist*• He was born in Paris, and served as a surgeon in Spain (1823) and at Navarino Bay (1827). He wrote a large number of Byronic novels, many of which were dramatized, idealizing the poor to the point of melodramatic absurdity, but they were nevertheless highly successful at the time. They had a profound influence on **Victor Hugo**, whose *Les misérables* has much in common with Sue's *Les mystères de Paris* (1843). Other novels include *Le Juif errant* (1845, "The Wandering Jew") and *Les mystères du peuple* (1849, "Mysteries of the People"). A republican deputy, he was driven into exile in 1851.

Suess, Eduard 1831–1914 •*Austrian geologist*• Born in London, England, he was the son of a German wool merchant of Jewish extraction. His parents moved to Prague (1843) and then to Vienna (1845) where he rose to great eminence at the university (1857–1901), becoming Professor of Geology. The greater part of his life was devoted to the study of the evolution of the features of the Earth's surface, particularly the problem of mountain building. His theory that there had once been a great supercontinent made up of the present southern continents was a forerunner of modern theories of continental drift. His four-volume book *Das Antlitz der Erde* (1885–1909, Eng trans *The Face of the Earth*, 1904–25) was his most important contribution, ranking alongside Sir **Charles Lyell**'s *Principles of Geology* and **Charles Darwin**'s *Origin of Species*. A man of varied interests and enthusiasms, he was a radical politician, an economist, an educationist and a geographer, and sat in the Austrian Lower House.

Suetonius, *in full* **Gaius Suetonius Tranquillus** c. 69–c. 140 AD •*Roman biographer and antiquary*• He was for a time a member of the imperial service (119–c. 122 AD) and secretary to the emperor **Hadrian**. His *De Vita Caesarum* (Eng trans *The Twelve Caesars* by **Robert Graves**, 1957) is an important historical source (though not always dependable without corroboration) and benefits from his access to the imperial archives and his contact with eyewitnesses. There survive also short biographies of **Virgil** and other Roman poets.

Sugar, Sir Alan Michael 1947– •*English entrepreneur*• Born in London, he was educated at Brooke House School, London. He founded AMSTRAD (the name is a contraction of Alan M Sugar Trading) in 1968. The company expanded rapidly during the personal-computer boom of the 1980s, but ran into problems with the slump at the end of that decade, losing, at one stage, £1 million per week. He has been chairman of the Tottenham Hotspur soccer club since 1991. He was knighted in 2000.

Suger c. 1081–1151 •*French prelate and politician*• Born near Paris, he was educated at the abbey of St Denis. As abbot of St Denis from 1122, he reformed the abbey and rebuilt its church in the first example of the Gothic style. **Louis VI** and **Louis VII** both employed him on diplomatic missions, and during Louis VII's absence on the Second Crusade, Suger served as regent. His *Life of Louis VI* is valuable for its contemporary view of the time.

Suharto or **Soeharto, Thojib N J** 1921– •*Indonesian soldier and statesman*• Born in Kemusu Argamulja, Java, he was educated for service in the Dutch colonial army. In 1943 he was given command of the Japanese-sponsored Indonesian army and in 1965 he became Indonesia's army chief of staff. He became a major political figure when the policies of President **Sukarno** led to a threat of civil war in 1965 and 1966, and assumed executive power in 1967, ordering the mass arrest and internment of alleged Communists. He became president in 1968, thereafter being reelected to office every five years. Suharto's virtual dictatorship saw an improvement in Indonesia's relations with her neighbors in Southeast Asia and the republic's return to membership in the United Nations. By 1970 the currency had stabilized, but his period in office was threatened by Islamic fundamentalist extremists and by the long-running civil war in East Timor, and he was driven from power in 1998.

Suk, Josef 1875–1935 •*Czech composer and violinist*• Born in Křecovice, he studied in Prague under **Antonín Dvořák**, whose daughter he married. He carried on his teacher's Romantic tradition through his violin *Fantaisie* (1903), the symphonic poem *Prague* (1904) and particularly his Second Symphony, *Asrael* (1905–06), in which he mourned the deaths of Dvořák and of his wife.

Sukarno or **Soekarno, Ahmed**, *known as* **Bung Karno** 1902–70 •*Indonesian statesman*• Born in Surabaya, Eastern Java, he was early identified with the movement for independence, forming the Partai National Indonesia in 1927. Imprisoned and exiled by the Dutch in Bandung (1929–31), he was freed by the Japanese (1942) and became the first president of the Indonesian Republic in 1945. His popularity with the people was gradually eroded as Indonesia suffered increasing internal chaos and poverty, while he and his government laid themselves open to charges of corruption. The abortive Communist coup of 1965 led to student riots and congressional criticism of Sukarno's alleged part in it, and the army eventually took over. Sukarno's absolute powers were gradually weakened, until finally in 1967 General **Thojib Suharto** took complete control.

Süleyman or **Sulaiman II** 1642–91 •*Ottoman sultan*• The son of Ibrahim I, he was born in Constantinople (Istanbul), and in 1687 succeeded his deposed brother **Mehmet IV** after 46 years of confinement. He was defeated by the Austrians (1688), but from 1689 his grand vizier, Mustafa Köprülü, drove the Austrians out of Bulgaria, Serbia and Transylvania, and retook Belgrade.

Süleyman the Magnificent 1494–1566 •*Ottoman emperor*• He succeeded his father **Selim I** in 1520 at a time when the empire was strong both on land and at sea. He himself was an experienced soldier and administrator, and was known to his own people as *Kanuni*, the "Lawgiver." He instituted a program of internal reforms aimed at securing higher standards of justice and administration and ensuring freedom of religion throughout the empire. He was an energetic patron of the arts, and literature as well as architecture and the visual arts flourished in Istanbul during his rule. He extended the bounds of his empire both to the east and west, capturing Belgrade in 1521 and Rhodes (from the Knights of St John) in 1522, and defeating the Hungarians in 1526. His advance to the west was finally checked in 1529 at the gates of Vienna, which he failed to take after a hard siege. In the east, he won territory from the Persians, made territorial gains in North Africa as far as Morocco, and took Aden on the Red Sea. Under **Barbarossa**, the Ottoman fleet was able to establish naval supremacy in the eastern Mediterranean and Aegean while also challenging the Portuguese in the east. They twice failed to capture Malta, but annexed Cyprus in 1570. Constant campaigning led Süleyman to withdraw increasingly from the active direction of government at home, a tendency which under his successors greatly weakened the empire in the long term. Nevertheless, during his reign Ottoman power abroad and Ottoman institutions and culture at home reached the peak of their achievement.

Sulla, Lucius Cornelius, *also called* **Felix ("Lucky")** 138–78 BC •*Roman politician and dictator*• His bitter feud with **Marius** began in Africa in 107 BC during the Jugurthine War. In 88 he chose to lead his army against the state rather than surrender to Marius his command of the war against Mithridates. He defeated **Mithridates VI**, and on his return to Rome (83), civil war broke out again when he used his forces to defeat the Marians and secure his own (illegal) position. Appointed dictator in 82, he set about reforming the state, and enacted a number of measures to boost the authority of the Senate. The cold-blooded ruthlessness of his dictatorship and the proscriptions were long remembered by later generations of Romans. He retired in 79.

Sullivan, Anne Mansfield *See* **Macy, Anne Mansfield Sullivan**

Sullivan, Sir Arthur Seymour 1842–1900 •*English composer*• He was born in London and studied music under William Sterndale Bennett (1816–75) and at the Leipzig Gewandhaus. He was organist and choirmaster of St Michael's, London, from 1861 to 1872, and became first principal of the National Training College (1871), later the Royal College of Music. His association with the theater, begun with his music to *Cox and Box* by John Morton (1811–91), with libretto by F C Burnand (1836–1917), was consolidated by his 18-year partnership with **W S Gilbert**, which produced the 14 comic "Savoy" operas from 1871, including *HMS Pinafore* (1878), *The Pirates of Penzance* (1880), *Iolanthe* (1882), *The Mikado* (1885) and *The Gondoliers* (1889). Sullivan also composed a *Te Deum* (1872), an opera, *Ivanhoe* (1891), cantatas, ballads and hymn tunes. His best-known songs include "Orpheus With his Lute," "The Lost Chord" and the tune for the hymn "Onward, Christian Soldiers."

Sullivan, Ed(ward Vincent) 1902–74 •*US newspaper columnist and broadcaster*• Born in New York City, he became a reporter with the *Port Chester Daily Item* (1918–19), and worked as a sports writer and columnist for a variety of publications before becoming a syndicated Broadway gossip columnist (1932–74). He was master of ceremonies for various theatrical events before moving into radio with *Ed Sullivan Entertains* (1942). Nationwide popularity followed him as the host of the television variety show *Toast of the Town*, which was later renamed *The Ed Sullivan Show* and ran from 1948 to 1971. He also wrote books and screenplays.

Sullivan, Louis Henry 1856–1924 •*US architect*• Born in Boston, he studied at MIT and at the influential Paris atelier of Joseph Auguste-Emile Vaudremer (1829–1914), and won the New Exposition building contract (1886) with **Dankmar Adler**. He was one of the first to design skyscrapers, such as the Wainwright building in St Louis (1890–91) and the Carson-Pirie-Scott building in Chicago (1899–1904). Because of his experimental, functional skeleton constructions of skyscrapers and office blocks, particularly the Gage building and Stock Exchange, Chicago (with Adler), he is often referred to as the Father of Modernism.

Sully, Maximilien de Béthune, Duc de, *also known as* **Baron de Rosny** 1560–1641 •*French financier*• The second son of the Huguenot Baron de Rosny, he was born in the château of Rosny near Mantes. He accompanied Henry of Navarre (the future **Henry IV**) in his flight from the French court (1576), took an active part in the war and helped decide the victory of Coutras (1587). At Ivry he captured the standard of Mayenne. He approved of Henry's conversion to Roman Catholicism in 1572, but he refused to become a Roman Catholic, and throughout the reign remained a trusted counselor. His first task was the restoration of the economy after 30 years of civil war, and he put the arsenals and fleet into good order. He was instrumental in arranging Henry's marriage to **Marie de Médicis** (1600). In 1606 he was created Duc de Sully. After Henry's assassination (1610) he had to resign, but was presented by Marie de Médicis with 300,000 livres, and retired to his estates, Rosny and Villebon.

Sully, Thomas 1783–1872 •*US painter*• Born in Horncastle, Lincolnshire, England, the son of actors, he and his family emigrated to Charleston, South Carolina, in 1792. He settled in Philadelphia in 1810. With a style influenced by **Gilbert Stuart** in the US and **Benjamin West** and **Sir Thomas Lawrence** in England, he painted elegant, exquisitely colored portraits and historical paintings. Subjects of his nearly 2,000 portraits include **Thomas Jefferson**, **James Madison** and Queen **Victoria**; his more than 500 historical works include *Washington Crossing the Delaware* (1818, Museum of Fine Arts, Boston).

Sully-Prudhomme, *pseudonym of* **René François Armand Prudhomme** 1839–1907 •*French poet and Nobel Prize winner*• Born in Paris, he studied science and developed an interest in philosophy which underlies most of his poetical works. He became one of the best known of the Parnassian poets. His early *Stances et poèmes* (1865, "Stanzas and Poems") was praised by **Charles-Augustin Sainte-Beuve**. Subsequent volumes include *Les épreuves* (1866, "Proofs"), *Croquis italiens* (1872, "Sketches of Italy"), *Impressions de la guerre* (1872, "Impressions of War"), *Les destins* (1872, "Destinies"), *La révolte des fleurs* (1874, "The Flowers' Revolution") and the didactic poems *La justice* (1878, "Justice") and *Le bonheur* (1888, "Happiness"). Other works include a metrical translation of book one by **Lucretius** (new edn 1886). He was awarded the first Nobel Prize for literature in 1901.

Sumner, Charles 1811–74 •*US politician*• Born in Boston, he graduated from Harvard, was admitted to the bar in 1834 and also studied jurisprudence in Europe (1837–40). He took little interest in politics until the threatened extensions of slavery over newly acquired territory. In 1848 he joined with others to form the Free Soil Party. In 1851 he was elected to the US Senate by the combined Free Soil and Democratic votes of the Massachusetts legislature, a post he held for life. Alone in the Senate as the uncompromising opponent of slavery, in 1856 he was struck on the head in the Senate chamber and was incapacitated for nearly four years. The secession of the southern states left the Republican Party in full control of both houses of Congress, and in 1861 Sumner was elected chairman of the Senate committee on foreign affairs. His criticisms of Grant's administration created a rift with leading Republican politicians, which was deepened by his support of **Horace Greeley** as candidate for the presidency in 1872.

Sumner, James Batcheller 1887–1955 •*US biochemist and Nobel Prize winner*• Born in Canton, Massachusetts, and educated at Harvard, he became Professor of Biochemistry (1929–55) at Cornell University, and director of the Laboratory of Enzyme Chemistry (1947–55). In 1926 he was first to crystallize an enzyme (urease), demonstrate its protein nature, and determine its kinetic and chemical properties. He raised and purified antibodies to urease (1933–34), and purified plant antibody-like globulins in 1938, thereby establishing a firm basis for the serological investigation of proteins. He also purified enzymes important for carrying out oxidative processes in the body. He shared the 1946 Nobel Prize for chemistry with **John Northrop** and **Wendell Stanley**.

Sumter, Thomas 1734–1832 •*American Revolutionary soldier*• He was born near Charlottesville, Virginia. In the American Revolution (1775–83) he opposed the British in South Carolina. He was defeated at Fishing Creek but gained a victory at Blackstock Hill (1780). He became a member of the US House of Representatives, and of the US Senate from 1801 to 1810. Fort Sumter was named after him.

Sung Chiao-jen *See* **Song Jiaoren**

Sun Yat-sen (Sun Yixian) or **Sun Zhongshan (Sun Chung-shan)** 1866–1925 •*Chinese revolutionary politician*• He was born in Zuiheng near Guangzhou (Canton), the son of a Christian farmer. He was brought up by his elder brother in Hawaii, and graduated in medicine at Hong Kong (1892). He visited Honolulu (1894) and founded his first political organization there, the Xing Zhong Hui (Revive China Society). After his first abortive uprising against the Manchus in Guangzhou in 1895, he lived in Japan, the US and Great Britain, studying Western politics and canvassing the support of the Chinese in these countries. After ten unsuccessful uprisings engineered by Sun from abroad, he was victorious in the revolution of 1911. In February 1912 China was proclaimed a republic with Sun as its provisional president, but he ceded to the northern general **Yuan Shikai**, who had forced the emperor's abdication. Yuan sought to make himself dictator, and Sun, opposing him from the south, was defeated and found himself again in exile. In 1916 Sun married **Song Qingling**, his former secretary. In 1923 he was back in Guangzhou and was elected president of the Southern Republic. With help from the Russians, Sun reorganized the Guomindang (Kuomintang) and established the Whampoa Military Academy under **Chiang Kai-shek**, who three years after Sun's death achieved the unification of China under a government inspired by Sun's *Three Principles of the People* (1927)—nationalism, democracy and social reform. During a conciliatory conference with other Chinese political leaders, he died of cancer in Beijing (Peking). Acknowledged by all political factions as the father of the Chinese Republic, he was reinterred in a mausoleum built in his honor in Nanjing (Nanking) in 1928. Sun was essentially empirical in his political teachings and rejected the communist dogma of the class war.

Sun Zhongshan *See* **Sun Yat-sen**

Suraja Dowlah or **Siraj-ud-Dawlah** c. 1732–57 •*Nabob of Bengal*• He came into conflict with the British over their fortification of Calcutta and marched on the city in 1756. Having captured Fort William, he confined his 146 prisoners in the military prison, the Black Hole (300 sq ft). The following morning there were 23 survivors. The British, under **Robert Clive**, joined forces with Suraja Dowlah's general, Mir Jafar, and defeated him at the Battle of Plassey in 1757. He fled to Murshidabad but was captured and executed.

Surman, John Douglas 1944– •*English jazz saxophonist and composer*• Born in Tavistock, Devon, he is one of the leading figures in European jazz. He played with Mike Westbrook (1936–) while still in school from 1958, and remained a part of his band for a decade. He formed his first group as leader that year, and was involved in various collaborations in the early 1970s, in a fiercely improvised, experimental jazz mode. At the same time, the English folk themes and multilayered soundscapes of *Westering Home* (1972) signaled the development of what became the dominant thread in his later music.

Surrey, Henry Howard, Earl of c. 1517–47 •*English courtier and poet*• The eldest son of **Thomas Howard**, 3rd Duke of Norfolk (1473–1554), he was born in Hunsdon, Hertfordshire. He accompanied **Henry VIII** to France in 1532, and served in Scotland, France and Flanders. He made enemies in high places, however, and in 1547 was charged with high treason, found guilty and executed. He is best remembered for his love poetry, in which he pioneered the use of blank verse and the Elizabethan sonnet form.

“ ”

Love, that doth reign and live within my thought,
And built his seat within my captive breast,
Clad in the arms wherein with me he fought,
Oft in my face he doth his banner rest.

"Love, that doth reign."

Surtees, John 1934– •*English racecar driver and motorcyclist*• Born in Westerham, Kent, he became the only man to win world titles on two and four wheels. He won the 350-cc motorcycling world title in 1958–60, and the 500-cc title in 1956 and 1958–60 (all on an MV Augusta). He then turned to car racing, and won the 1964 world title driving a Ferrari. He later became a racecar manufacturer.

Surtees, Robert Smith 1803–64 •*English journalist and novelist*• Born in Durham, where he was educated, he practiced as a lawyer and later became a justice of the peace and high sheriff of Durham County. He founded the *New Sporting Magazine* in 1831 where he introduced John Jorrocks, a sporting Cockney, whose adventures were later contained in *Jorrocks's Jaunts and Jollities* (1838) and in *Hillingdon Hall* (1845). Their influence on **Dickens**'s *Pickwick Papers* is conspicuous. His other great character, Mr Soapy Sponge, appears in *Mr Sponge's Sporting Tour* (1853).

“ ”

There is no secret so close as that between a rider and his horse.

Attributed.

Sutcliffe, Frank Meadow 1853–1941 •*English photographer*• Born near Whitby, Yorkshire, he made studies, from 1880, of the vanishing world of English farmhands and fishermen in Yorkshire, which brought him many awards from international exhibitions between 1881 and 1905. From the late 1890s he used the new lightweight Kodak cameras to capture spontaneous moments rather than formal poses.

Sutcliffe, Peter, *known as* **the Yorkshire Ripper** 1946– •*English murderer*• Born in Bingley, near Bradford, Sutcliffe was a truck driver. He murdered 13 women over five years in northern England and the Midlands until captured in January 1981. While his identity was unknown, he was dubbed the "Yorkshire Ripper." Several of his victims were prostitutes, and most were killed in the same way—their heads were beaten with a hammer and they were stabbed with a screwdriver. He was finally caught as police conducted a routine check on a prostitute and her client (Sutcliffe). He was found guilty of 13 murders and seven attempted murders in 1981 and was given a life sentence on each count.

Sutherland, Donald 1935– •*Canadian actor*• Born in St John, New Brunswick, he studied at the University of Toronto. His screen career burgeoned from the late 1960s with films such as *The Dirty Dozen* (1967), *M*A*S*H* (1970), *Klute* (1971) and *Don't Look Now* (1973), and he later appeared notably in *The Eagle Has Landed* (1977) and *Invasion of the Bodysnatchers* (1978). He has also worked widely in television. The actor **Kiefer Sutherland** is his son.

Sutherland, Graham Vivian 1903–80 •*English artist*• Born in London, he studied at Goldsmiths College School of Art, and worked mainly as an etcher until 1930. During the next ten years he made his reputation as a painter of Romantic, mainly abstract landscapes, with superb, if arbitrary, coloring. From 1941 to 1945 he was an official war artist. He produced several memorable portraits, including one of **W Somerset Maugham** (1949) and a controversial portrait of Sir **Winston Churchill** (1954), which was destroyed on the instructions of Lady Churchill. He also designed ceramics, posters and textiles: his large tapestry, *Christ in Glory*, was hung in the new Coventry Cathedral in 1962.

Sutherland, Dame Joan 1926– •*Australian soprano*• Born in Sydney, she made her debut there as Dido in **Henry Purcell**'s *Dido and Aeneas* (1947). She went to London in 1951 and joined the Royal Opera, Covent Garden, London (1952–88). She gained international fame in 1959 with her roles in **Donizetti**'s *Lucia di Lammermoor* ("The Bride of Lammermoor") and **Handel**'s *Samson*. Singing regularly in opera houses and concert halls all over the world, she retired in 1990 and now lives in Switzerland. She was appointed to the Order of Merit in 1991. In 1954 she married Richard Bonynge (1930–), who became her principal conductor and with whom she cowrote her autobiography, *The Joan Sutherland Album* (1986). He later became musical director of the Australian Opera Company (1976–85).

Sutherland, Kiefer 1966– •*US actor*• Born in Los Angeles, the son of **Donald Sutherland**, he made his stage debut at age nine and began appearing in films from the mid-1980s such as *The Lost Boys* (1987), *Flatliners* (1990), *A Few Good Men* (1992) and *Ring of Fire* (2000). His debut as a film director was *Truth or Consequences, N.M.* (1997). He has worked widely in television, most notably in *24* (2001–).

Sutherland, Margaret Ada 1897–1984 •*Australian composer*• Born in Adelaide, South Australia, she studied at the Melbourne Conservatorium of Music and at the age of 19 appeared as piano soloist with the New South Wales State Orchestra. She went in 1923 to study in Vienna and London, returning to Australia in 1925, where for many years she was active in music administration and promotional work. Recognition came late, but her Violin Concerto (1954) was warmly received and her opera, *The Young Kabbarli*, based on the life of **Daisy Bates**, was performed in 1965. She wrote a great deal of chamber music, and set a number of song cycles.

Sutherland, Robert Garioch *See* **Garioch, Robert**

Suttner, Bertha Félicie Sophie, Freifrau von, *née* **Kinsky** 1843–1914 •*Czech novelist and Nobel Prize winner*• She was born in Prague, of Bohemian descent, the daughter of an imperial general. In 1891 she founded a pacifist organization called the Austrian Society of Peace. Her journal, *Die Waffen nieder*, later published in book form (1889, Eng trans *Lay Down Your Arms, the Autobiography of Martha von Tilling*, 1892), shocked her readers by its pacifism. She wrote many other books on pacifism and from 1876 to 1896 corresponded with **Alfred Nobel** on the subject, which persuaded him to add provision for a peace award to the endowment in his will. She herself was awarded the Nobel Peace Prize in 1905.

Su Tung-p'o *See* **Su Dongpo**

Suvorov, Aleksandr Vasilevich, Count 1729–1800 •*Russian soldier*• Born in Moscow, he fought in the Seven Years' War (1756–63) and in Poland and Turkey, then aided the Austrians against the French in Italy (1799), winning several victories. Directed to join other Russian forces in Switzerland, he found them already defeated, and was forced into a winter retreat across the mountains to Austria.

Suyin, Han *See* **Han Suyin**

Suzman, Helen, *née* **Gavronsky** 1917– •*South African liberal politician*• She was born in Germiston, in the Transvaal, the daughter of a Lithuanian immigrant, and studied at the University of Witwatersrand, where she later lectured (1944–52). Deeply concerned about the apartheid system, she joined the Opposition United Party, later the Progressive and then the Democratic Party, and was elected to parliament in 1953. She gradually gained the respect of the Black community, including the African National Congress leader **Nelson Mandela**, and, as a member of the South African Institute of Race Relations, was a fierce opponent of apartheid. In 1978 she received the UN Human Rights award. She retired from parliament, after 36 uninterrupted years, in 1989.

Suzman, Janet 1939– •*British actress*• She was born in Johannesburg, South Africa, the niece of the antiapartheid campaigner **Helen Suzman**. Moving to England to complete her studies, she made her acting debut in *Billy Liar* at Ipswich in 1962. That year she joined the newly formed Royal Shakespeare Company and subsequently played roles such as Portia in *The Merchant of Venice* (1965) and Cleopatra in *Antony and Cleopatra* (1973). In the West End, she played the title role in *Hedda Gabler* (1977). As well as classical roles on television, she has played **Edwina Mountbatten** in *Mountbatten—The Last Viceroy* (1984) and Margaret, Duchess of Chester, in *The Secret Agent* (1992). Her films include *The Draughtsman's Contract* (1982) and *Leon the Pig Farmer* (1992).

Suzuki, Zenko 1911–2004 •*Japanese politician*• Born in Yamada, Honshu Iisland, he trained at the Japanese agriculture ministry's Academy of Fisheries during the 1930s. In 1947 he was elected to the Lower House of the Diet as a Socialist Party deputy, but moved to the Liberal Party in 1949 and then, on its formation in 1955, to the conservative Liberal Democratic Party (LDP). During the 1960s and 1970s he held a succession of ministerial and party posts. Following the death of his patron, Masayoshi Ohira, he succeeded to the dual positions of LDP president and prime minister in 1980. His premiership was marred by factional strife within the LDP, deteriorating relations with the US and opposition to his defense policy. He stepped down in 1982, but remained an influential LDP faction leader for some time.

Svedberg, Theodor 1884–1971 •*Swedish physical chemist and Nobel Prize winner*• Born in Fleräng, near Valbo, he went to Uppsala University in 1904 to study chemistry and was associated with that university for the next 45 years. Although beyond retirement age, he was director of the Gustaf Werner Institute of Nuclear Chemistry from 1949 to 1967. In the 1920s his interest in colloids led him to develop the ultracentrifuge as a means of following optically the sedimentation of particles too small to be seen in the ultramicroscope. His measurements of the molecular weights of proteins were particularly important, and for his work on the ultracentrifuge he received the 1926 Nobel Prize for chemistry. During World War II he developed a synthetic rubber. Svedberg's work at the Werner Institute involved the applications of a cyclotron in medicine, in radiation physics and in radiochemistry.

Svein I Haraldsson, "Fork-Beard" d. 1014 •*King of Denmark and of England*• He was the son of **Harald Gormsson** (Blue-Tooth), but rebelled against his father and deposed him (c. 986). He made several campaigns against England (from 994), each bribed away by King **Ethelred the Unready**. In 1013 with his son **Knut Sveinsson** (Canute), he forced King Ethelred to flee to Normandy. Svein took up the crown, but died five weeks later (February 1014).

Svein II Ulfsson, *sometimes known as* **Estridsson** d. 1074 •*King of Denmark*• The son of a regent of Denmark, Earl Ulf, and nephew of **Knut Sveinsson** (Canute), he was appointed regent of Denmark (1045) by King **Magnus I Olafsson** of Norway (and Denmark), and proclaimed king himself when Magnus died (1047). In 1069, after the conquest of England by **William the Conqueror**, Svein's army captured York, but he made peace with William (1070) and withdrew. Svein was a major informant for the historian **Adam of Bremen**.

Sverrir Sigurdsson c. 1150–1202 •*King of Norway*• Brought up in the Faroe Islands, he claimed to be the illegitimate son of Sigurd Haraldsson, "the Mouth" (d. 1155). Often called "the Usurper," he emerged from obscurity in 1179 to lay claim to the throne from **Magnus V Erlingsson**, whom he finally defeated and killed in 1184, becoming king in that year. He turned out to be one of Norway's greatest kings, strengthening the crown against both Church and nobles with the support of the freehold farmers. He commissioned one of the first Icelandic sagas: a biography of himself, *Sverris saga*.

Svevo, Italo, *pseudonym of* **Ettore Schmitz** 1861–1928 •*Italian novelist*• He was born in Trieste, of German-Jewish descent, educated primarily in Bavaria, and wrote in Italian. While working as a correspondence clerk in a Trieste bank, he wrote and published privately his first novel, *Una vita* (1892, Eng trans, *A Life*, 1963). It was followed in 1898 by *Senilità* (Eng trans *As a Man Grows Older*, 1932). Both novels failed, but in 1906 he met **James Joyce**, then teaching English in Trieste, who bolstered his confidence and promoted *La coscienza di Zeno* (Eng trans *The Confessions of Zeno*, 1930). Svevo won recognition in France and the rest of Europe, but died soon afterward in a car accident. His other novels include *La novella del buon vecchio e della bella fanciulla* (1929, Eng trans *The Nice Old Man and the Pretty Girl*, 1930) and *Il vecchione* (1967, Eng trans *The Grand Old Man*, 1968), which was incomplete at his death.

Svoboda, Ludvík 1895–1979 •*Czechoslovak soldier and politician*• He was born near Bratislava (now in Slovakia). He became commanding general of the Czechoslovak army corps attached to the Red Army in 1943, and helped liberate Košice, Brno and Prague from 1944 to 1945. In 1948 he joined the Communist Party and was minister of defense until 1950. In 1968, he succeeded the discredited **Antonín Novotný** as president. He supported the abortive reforms of **Alexander Dubček** and, after the hostile Soviet intervention in 1968, he traveled to Moscow to seek relaxation of the repressive measures imposed on the Czechoslovaks. He remained in office until 1975, when failing health forced his retirement.

Swan, Sir Joseph Wilson 1828–1914 •*English chemist, inventor and industrialist*• He was born near Sunderland, and after leaving school at 13 was apprenticed to a druggist, then in 1846 joined a pharmaceutical business in Newcastle. In 1856 he took out a patent for improving the wet-plate collodion photographic process, and the following year he invented high-speed bromide paper. The patent was bought by **George Eastman**, founder of Kodak, and helped to make photography cheaper and thus widely popular. By 1848 Swan was experimenting with carbonized paper filaments for electric lamps, but it was not until 1879 that he gave his first successful demonstration of a bulb. Within four years he was manufacturing 10,000 lamp bulbs a week, and in 1883, he amalgamated his business with **Thomas Alva Edison**, who had been granted a British patent in 1879, to form the Edison & Swan Electric Light Company. In searching for a better filament for his bulbs, Swan discovered the process that Hilaire Chardonnet (1839–1924) later adapted to make rayon. He was knighted in 1904.

Swanborough, Stella Isaacs, Baroness, *née* **Charnaud** 1894–1971 •*English pioneer of social services and WRVS founder*• Born in Constantinople (Istanbul), she returned to England with her family before World War I. In 1931 she married Rufus Isaacs, 1st Marquess of Reading (1860–1935), and the following year she began her volunteer work. She was invited by the home secretary in 1938 to form a women's organization to help with air-raid precautions. By the outbreak of World War II, the Women's Voluntary Service for Civil Defense was able to assist with the evacuation of women and children and with setting up canteens and services for troops. After the war, "for Civil Defense" was dropped from the title. (When "Royal" was added in 1966, it became widely known as the WRVS.) The WVS pioneered community service in the form of meals on wheels and home helps.

Swann, Donald 1923–94 •*Welsh composer and lyricist*• Born in Llanelli of an Anglo-Russian family, he was educated at Westminster School and Christ Church, Oxford. He began his writing career by contributing music to revues such as *Airs on a Shoestring* (1953). His long collaboration with **Michael Flanders** began in 1956, when he wrote the music, and Flanders the words and dialogue, for *At the Drop of a Hat*, followed by *At the Drop of Another Hat* in 1965. Their partnership ended in 1967 and after 1970 he became a frequent broadcaster on musical and other matters. He also wrote a musical fable for Christmas, three books of new carols, and his autobiography, *Swann's Way* (1991).

Swanson, Gloria, *originally* **Gloria May Josephine Svensson** 1897–1983 •*US actress*• Born in Chicago, after studying as a singer she entered the film industry as an extra and bit part player (1915). She became one of **Mack Sennett**'s bathing beauties before an association with director **Cecil B De Mille** brought her leading roles as chic sophisticates in the front line of the battle of the sexes. Her many silent features include *Male and Female* (1919), *The Affairs of Anatol* (1921) and *Manhandled* (1924). She survived the arrival of sound, receiving Academy Award nominations for *Sadie Thompson* (1928) and *The Trespasser* (1929). However, her film career gradually dwindled away despite a sensational comeback in *Sunset Boulevard* (1950). Never relinquishing her glamorous star status, she continued to appear on stage and television. Married six times, she published her autobiography, *Swanson on Swanson*, in 1980.

“ ”

Arriving Monday ... Arrange ovation.

*Transatlantic cable to Adolf Zukor. Quoted in the **New Yorker**, March 21, 1994.*

Swedenborg, Emanuel, *originally* **Swedberg** 1688–1772 •*Swedish mystic, theologian and scientist*• He was born in Stockholm, the son of a professor of theology at Uppsala. The family name was Swedberg, but was changed to Swedenborg when the family was ennobled in 1719. He studied at Uppsala, traveled widely in Europe, and returned to Sweden to be assessor at the Royal Board of Mines (1716–47). He wrote prolifically on technical and mathematical topics, followed by a long treatise, *Opera Philosophica et Mineralia* (1734, "Philosophical and Logical Works"), a mixture of metallurgy and metaphysical speculation on the creation of the world, and huge works on anatomy and physiology. In 1743–44 he had a religious crisis, recorded in his *Journal of Dreams*, which he interpreted as a direct vision of the spiritual world and which led him to resign his scientific post (1747) to expound his experiences and the mystical doctrines he based on them. He produced some 30 volumes of religious revelations in Latin, the best known being *Arcana Coelestia* (8 vols, 1749–56, "Heavenly Arcana"), *De Coelo et eius Mirabilibus et de Inferno* (1758, "On Heaven and Its Wonders and on Hell") and *Vera Christiana Religio* (1771, "The Christian Religion"). His followers organized a society in London known as the Church of the New Jerusalem (1787), which proliferated many further branches throughout the world (Swedenborgianism). He influenced **William Blake** and other writers, including the French Symbolists.

Swift, Graham 1949– •*English novelist and short-story writer*• He was born in London and educated at Cambridge University and the University of York. His writing is frequently preoccupied with history, memory, guilt and the natural world. His first novels, *The Sweet Shop Owner* (1980) and *Shuttlecock* (1981), were critically well received, and international acclaim arrived on publication of his third, the hugely successful *Waterland* (1983), which was shortlisted for the Booker Prize. In 1996 Swift won the Booker Prize and the James Tait Black Memorial Prize with *Last Orders*. Other books include *Out of This World* (1988) and *Ever After* (1992).

Swift, Jonathan 1667–1745 •*Anglo-Irish satirist and clergyman*• He was born in Dublin, to English parents, and educated at Kilkenny Grammar School and Trinity College, Dublin, where he obtained his degree only by "special grace" in 1685. Family connections helped him become secretary to the diplomat Sir **William Temple**, then resident at Moor Park, Farnham. He supported his patron on the side of the Ancients in the "Querelle des Anciens et des Modernes" which had spread to Great Britain from France. His contribution was the mock-epic *Battle of the Books*, published along with the much more powerful satire on religious dissension, *A Tale of a Tub*, in 1704. At Moor Park he first met Esther Johnson (1681–1728), then a child of eight, who from then on as pupil and lover or friend was to play an important role in his life and to survive for posterity in Swift's verse tributes and the *Journal to Stella* (1710–13), but it is uncertain if he ever married her. When Swift became vicar of Laracor near Dublin, "Stella" accompanied him. His visits to London were largely political, but he also visited the great figures in literary and aristocratic circles. Having been introduced to politics by Temple, he supported the Whigs, but his interest in the Church steered him toward the Tory Party. The friendship of **Robert Harley** assisted the change, which was resolved in 1710 when Harley returned to power. His *History of the Four Last Years of the Queen* [**Anne**] (1758) described the ferment of intrigue and pamphleteering during that period. The chief aims of the Tory Party were to secure the Establishment and end the war with France. The latter was powerfully aided by Swift's *On the Conduct of the Allies* (1713), one of the greatest pieces of pamphleteering. The death of Queen Anne (1714) disappointed all the hopes of Swift and his friends of the Scriblerus Club, founded in 1713. Swift accepted his "exile" to the deanery of St Patrick's Cathedral, Dublin, and from then on, except for two visits in 1726 and 1727, correspondence alone kept him in touch with London. Despite his loathing for Ireland, he threw himself into a strenuous campaign for Irish liberties, denied by the Whig government. On his first visit to London after the fall of the Tory ministry in 1714, he published the world-famous satire *Gulliver's Travels* (1726). In 1729 he published his ironical *A Modest Proposal*. His light verse now ranged from *The Grand Question Debated* (1729) to the *Verses on His Own Death* (1731), which, with its mixture of pathos and humor, ranks with the great satirical poems. He himself considered his *On Poetry; a Rhapsody* (1733) his best verse satire. The ironical *Directions to Servants* and *A Complete Collection of Genteel and Ingenious Conversation* followed in 1731. The satire in the first part of *Gulliver's Travels* is directed at political parties and religious dissension. The second part introduces deepening misanthropy, culminating in the king's description of mankind as "the most pernicious race of little odious vermin that Nature ever suffered to crawl upon the surface of the earth." The third part, a satire on inventors, is fun though less plausible. The last part, in the country of the Houyhnhnms, a race of horses governed only by reason, is a savage attack on humanity which points to the author's final mental collapse. Politics apart, Swift's influence was directed powerfully against the vogue of deistic science and modern invention and in favor of orthodoxy and good manners.

Swinburne, Algernon Charles 1837–1909 •*English poet and critic*• Born in London, he was educated partly in France and in England at Eton and Balliol College, Oxford, but left without taking a degree. He traveled on the Continent, where he came under the spell of **Victor Hugo**, visited **Walter Savage Landor** in Florence (1864), and on his return became associated with **Dante Gabriel Rossetti** and **William Morris**. After a breakdown due to heavy drinking and other excesses, he submitted to the care of his friend Theodore Watts-Dunton (1832–1914), in whose house he continued to live in semi-seclusion for the rest of his life. His first success was with *Atalanta in Calydon* (1865), a drama in the Greek form but modern in its spirit of revolt against religious acquiescence to the will of Heaven. However, it was the first of the series of *Poems and Ballads* (1866) which took the public by storm, although the uninhibited tone of certain passages affronted English puritanism. The second and third series (1878, 1889) were less successful. Meanwhile he found scope for his detestation of kings and priests in the struggle for Italian liberty. *Songs Before Sunrise* (1871) best expresses his fervent republicanism. A trilogy on **Mary Queen of Scots** was completed in 1881, and the following year *Tristram of Lyonesse*, an Arthurian romance in rhymed couplets, achieved a real success. His novel *Love's Cross Currents* (1877), published under the pseudonym Mrs H Manners, is a curiosity, but his critical works, above all his work on **Shakespeare** and his contemporaries, are stimulating.

" "

And the best and the worst of this is
That neither is most to blame
If you have forgotten my kisses
And I have forgotten your name.

1866 ***Poems and Ballads***, *"An Interlude."*

Swinney, John 1964– •*Scottish politician*• Born in Edinburgh and educated at the University of Edinburgh, he worked as a management consultant prior to joining the Scottish National Party and becoming Member of Parliament for Tayside North (1997–2001). He took his place in the newly formed Scottish parliament in 1999 and succeeded **Alex Salmond** as leader of the party and shadow leader in the Scottish parliament in 2000.

Swithin or **Swithun, St** d. 862 •*English ecclesiastic*• He was adviser to **Egbert** and was made Bishop of Winchester (852) by Ethelwulf. When the monks exhumed his body in 971 to bury it in the rebuilt cathedral, the removal, which was to have taken place on July 15, is said to have been delayed by violent rain. The belief therefore arose that if it rains on July 15, it will rain for 40 days more.

Sydenham, Thomas, *known as* **the English Hippocrates** 1624–89 •*English physician*• Born in Wynford Eagle, Dorset, he served in the Parliamentarian army during the civil war, and in 1647 went to Oxford, where he studied medicine at Wadham College. From 1655 he practiced in London. A great friend of such empiricists as **Robert Boyle** and **John Locke**, he urged doctors to become close observers at the bedside, where they would learn to distinguish specific diseases and through trial and error find specific remedies. He was much impressed with the capacity of Jesuit's bark (the active principle of which is quinine) to cure intermittent fever (malaria), and he believed that other such specific treatments might be found. He wrote *Observationes Medicae* (1667) and a treatise on gout (1683)—a disease from which he suffered, distinguished the symptoms of venereal disease (1675), recognized hysteria as a distinct disorder and gave his name to the mild convulsions of children, Sydenham's chorea (St Vitus's dance) and to the medicinal use of liquid opium, Sydenham's laudanum. By the time of his death, his reputation was growing and his vivid works, with their astute descriptions of diseases, were often reprinted and translated throughout the 18th century.

Sydney, Algernon *See* **Sidney, Algernon**

Sydow, Max Carl Adolf von 1929– •*Swedish actor*• Born in Lund, he studied at the Royal Academy in Stockholm and made his film debut in *Bara en mor* (1949). A member of various theatrical companies, he began a long association with director **Ingmar Bergman** at the Municipal Theater of Malmö. On film their many collaborations include *Det sjunde inseglet* (1957, *The Seventh Seal*), *Sasom in en spegel* (1961, *Through a Glass Darkly*) and *Skammen* (1968, *The Shame*). He made his US film debut as **Jesus** in *The Greatest Story Ever Told* (1965) and has spent many years as a character actor of international standing in films like *The Exorcist* (1973) and *Hannah and Her Sisters* (1986). He has also continued to appear on stage, and in 1988 he made his debut as a film director with *Katinka*.

Sykes, Eric 1923– •*English comedy writer and performer*• He was born in Oldham, near Manchester, and his wartime service in the RAF allowed him to perform in armed forces shows. He became a joke writer and progressed to full scripts, writing for such radio shows as *Educating Archie* (1950–54) and rising to become Britain's highest-paid scriptwriter. He starred in his own BBC television series, *Sykes* (1960–65, 1971–79). His stage performances include *Hatful of Sykes* (1979) and *Cinderella* (1981–82). He also appeared in films such as *Heavens Above!* (1963), *Those Magnificent Men in Their Flying Machines* (1964), *Monte Carlo or Bust!* (1969) and *Absolute Beginners* (1986). Almost totally deaf, he has written, directed and acted in the short, wordless comedies *The Plank* (1967) and *Rhubarb* (1970). Other television programs include *Curry and Chips* (1969) and *The Nineteenth Hole* (from 1989).

Sylvester II, *originally* **Gerbert of Aurillac** c. 940–1003 •*French pope*• Born in Aurillac, he became abbot of Bobbio (982) and Archbishop of Ravenna (988), and as pope (from 999) upheld the primacy of Rome against the separatist tendencies of the French Church. His erudition in chemistry, mathematics and philosophy led people to suspect him of being in league with the devil. He is said to have introduced Arabic numerals and to have invented clocks.

Symons, Arthur William 1865–1945 •*Welsh critic and poet*• Born of Cornish stock in Wales, he received little formal education. He did much to familiarize the British with the literature of France and Italy, especially the work of the French Symbolists. He translated **Gabriele d'Annunzio** (1902) and **Baudelaire** (1925). He wrote several volumes of lyrics and critical works, including *The Romantic Movement in English Poetry* (1909).

Symons, George James 1838–1900 •*English climatologist*• Born in Pimlico, London, he established a network of voluntary rainfall observers in 1860, which became the British Rainfall Organization. In 1863 he founded a circular which later became *Symons' Monthly Meteorological Magazine*. He was interested in instruments and invented the brontometer for recording the sequence of phenomena in thunderstorms, as well as organizing a comparison of thermometer screens which resulted in the Stevenson screen being accepted as the world standard. He compiled a catalog of over 60,000 meteorological books, and his comprehensive collection was bequeathed to the Royal Meteorological Society, for which he had served as secretary and president. On his death the Royal Meteorological Society opened a memorial fund, and the biennial gold medal provided from the proceeds is the society's highest award.

Synge, (Edmund) J(ohn) M(illington) 1871–1909 •*Irish dramatist*• Born near Dublin, he attended Trinity College, Dublin, and studied music in Germany. He then spent several years in Paris before settling among the people of the Aran Islands (1899–1902), who provided the material for plays including *Riders to the Sea* (1904), *The Well of the Saints* (1905) and his humorous masterpiece *The Playboy of the Western World* (1907), which was followed by *The Tinker's Wedding* (1909). He published *Poems and Translations*

(1909) and completed his last play, *Deirdre of the Sorrows* (published posthumously in 1910), while dying from Hodgkin's disease. He had a profound influence on the next generation of Irish playwrights and was a director of the Abbey Theatre, Dublin, from 1904.

Synge, Richard Laurence Millington 1914–94 •*English biochemist and Nobel Prize winner*• Born in Chester, Cheshire, he trained at Cambridge, and joined the Wool Industry Research Association in Leeds (1941–43), where he collaborated with **A J P Martin** on the development of partition chromatography and the mixture separation technique (1941), which revolutionized analytical chemistry. They also investigated mild protein hydrolysis and developed methods for the analysis of aldehydes and hydroxy-acids. They shared the Nobel Prize for chemistry in 1952 for their work. In 1944 Synge demonstrated the use of powdered cellulose for separating amino acids, and in 1948 he moved to the Rowett Research Institute, Aberdeen, where he showed the relation between the molecular weight of proteins and their dialyzability. From 1967 he worked at the Food Research Institute in Norwich.

Szasz, Thomas Stephen 1920– •*US psychiatrist*• Born in Budapest, Hungary, he went to the US in 1938 and received his MD from the University of Cincinnati in 1944. Since 1956 he has been Professor of Psychiatry at Syracuse University, New York (emeritus since 1990). He has written many books, most of which argue that all disease must be physical, that consequently the idea of "mental disease" is a myth, and that contemporary psychiatrists are often the agents of repression. His brand of individualism interprets all behavior as purposeful and intentional, and he argues that people should be allowed to do what they wish as long as they do not break the law, and that all psychiatric therapy should be contractual. A recent publication is *Cruel Compassion* (1994).

“ ”

Psychiatrists classify a person as neurotic if he suffers from his problems in living, and a psychotic if he makes others suffer.

1974 ***The Second Sin.***

Szent-György, Albert von Nagyrapolt 1893–1986 •*US biochemist and Nobel Prize winner*• Born in Budapest, Hungary, he lectured at the universities of Groningen, where he discovered hexuronic acid (vitamin C) in the adrenal cortex, and at Cambridge. He became professor at the University of Szeged (1931–45), where he crystallized vitamin C, and in consequence, vitamin B_2 (riboflavin). He was later appointed a professor at the University of Budapest (1945–47), director of the Institute of Muscle Research at Woods Hole, Massachusetts (1947–75), and scientific director of the National Foundation for Cancer Research, Massachusetts (1975). He also discovered the reducing system involved in the **Krebs** cycle (1935), and he made important contributions toward understanding muscular contraction, glycerinated fibers, allowing study of a physiologically active biochemical system (1948), and muscle relaxation (1953). He was awarded the Nobel Prize for physiology or medicine in 1937.

Szilard, Leo 1898–1964 •*US physicist*• Born in Budapest, Hungary, he studied there and in Berlin, working with **Max von Laue**. In 1933 he fled from Nazi Germany to England, and in 1938 emigrated to the US, where he began work on nuclear physics at Columbia University. On hearing of **Otto Hahn** and **Lise Meitner**'s fission of uranium (1938), he immediately approached **Albert Einstein** in order to write together to warn President **Franklin D Roosevelt** of the possibility of creating an atomic bomb. Together with **Enrico Fermi**, Szilard organized work on the first fission reactor, which operated in Chicago in 1942. He was a central figure in the Manhattan Project leading to the atomic bomb, and after World War II his research in molecular biology took the form of experimental work on bacterial mutations and theoretical work on aging and memory.

Szold, Henrietta 1860–1945 •*US Zionist leader*• Born in Baltimore, Maryland, she became a teacher, and cofounded the Jewish Publication Society of America, for which she edited the Jewish Yearbook (1892–1916). She became an ardent champion of Zionism, working to establish peace between Arabs and Jews and a binationalist state. In 1912 she founded the women's organization Hadassah and was its president until 1926. In 1927 she became the first woman to be elected to the World Zionist Organization, and in 1930 she went to live in Palestine. When the Nazis rose to power (1933) she founded Youth Aliyah, in order that Jewish children could escape the Holocaust.

Szymanowski, Karol 1883–1937 •*Polish composer*• Born in Tymoszowska, Ukraine, to Polish parents, he became director of the State Conservatory in Warsaw in 1926. Widely considered Poland's most distinguished composer since **Frédéric Chopin**, his works include operas, incidental music, symphonies, concertos, chamber music, piano music and many songs.

Szymborska, Wisława 1923– •*Polish poet and Nobel Prize winner*• She was born in Kórnik and educated at the Jagiellonian University, Cracow. She made her living as a book reviewer and translator during the period of Communist rule and contributed to samizdat publications such as *Arka*. Her many collections include *That's Why We're Alive* (1952), *People on the Bridge* (1986) and *View With a Grain of Sand* (1996). Her poems deal with the hard realities of Polish politics and the relationship with the Soviet Union, but her voice is often a pensive and lyrical one. She was awarded the Nobel Prize for literature in 1996.

Tabari, at-, *in full* **Abu Ja'far Muhammad ibn Jarir at-Tabari** 839–923 •*Arab historian*• Born in Amol, Persia, he traveled throughout the Middle East collecting scholarly material and wrote a major commentary on the Koran and a history of the world from creation until the early 10th century, which provided a basis for later historical and religious studies.

Tache, Edward *See* **Teach, Edward**

Tacitus, *in full* **Publius** or **Gaius Cornelius Tacitus** c. 55–120 AD •*Roman historian*• Born perhaps in Narbonese Gaul, he studied rhetoric in Rome, rose to eminence as a pleader in the Roman court, and in 77 AD married the daughter of **Agricola**, the conqueror of Britain. By 88 he was already praetor and a member of one of the priestly colleges. Under **Nerva** he became a consul (97). He established a great reputation as an orator, and 11 of **Pliny**'s letters were addressed to him. His major works are the 12-volume *Historiae* ("Histories"), of which only the first 4 books survive whole, and *Annales* ("Annals"), of which only 8 of the probable 18 books have survived.

“ ”

Miseram pacem vel bello bene mutari.
Even war is preferable to a shameful peace.

Annals, *book 3, chapter 44.*

Taeuber-Arp, Sophie, *née* **Taeuber** 1889–1943 •*Swiss painter and designer*• Born in Davos, she studied applied arts in Munich and Hamburg. From 1914 she worked in Zurich, and in 1915 she met **Jean Arp**, whom she married in 1922. In 1918 they drew up the Dada Manifesto and she modeled *Dada Head* (Pompidou Center, Paris). One of the most talented of the constructivist artists, she is best known for her distinctive rhythmic paintings for the Café l'Aubette (1928) at Strasbourg, on which she collaborated with Arp and **Theo van Doesburg**.

Taft, William Howard 1857–1930 •*27th President of the US*• Born in Cincinnati, Ohio, the son of President **Ulysses S Grant**'s secretary of war and attorney general, he studied at Yale and qualified as a lawyer in Cincinnati. In 1890 he became solicitor general for the US. In 1900 he was made president of the Philippine Commission, and in 1901 first civil governor of the islands. From 1904 to 1908 he was secretary of war for the US, and in 1906 provisional governor of Cuba. From 1909 to 1913 he was president of the US, continuing the antitrust policies of his predecessor, **Theodore Roosevelt**, but his conservatism alienated the progressive wing of the Republican Party, and he was defeated by **Woodrow Wilson** for a second term. From 1913 he was Professor of Law at Yale and from 1921 chief justice of the US Supreme Court.

Tagore, Rabindranath 1861–1941 •*Indian poet and philosopher and Nobel Prize winner*• Born in Calcutta, he studied law in England (1878–80). In 1901 he founded, near Bolpur, the Santiniketan, a communal school aiming to blend Eastern and Western philosophical and educational systems, which became Visva-Bharati University. His first book was a volume of poetry, *A Poet's Tale* (1878), followed by a novel, *Karuna*, and a drama, *The Tragedy of Rudachandra*. His major works include *Binodini* (1902, Eng trans 1964), the first modern novel by an Indian writer; *The Crescent Moon* (1913), poems about childhood; and his best-known play, *Chitra* (1914). He also wrote *My Reminiscences* (1917) and *My Boyhood Days* (1940). He received the Nobel Prize for literature in 1913, the first Asian to do so.

Tah-gah-jute *See* **Logan, James**

Tailleferre, Germaine, *originally* **Germaine Taillefesse** 1892–1983 •*French composer*• Born in Parc-St-Maur, near Paris, she studied at the Paris Conservatoire, taking lessons from **Maurice Ravel**. She became the only female member and longest surviving representative of the group known as Les Six with **Georges Auric**, **Louis Durey**, **Arthur Honegger**, **Darius Milhaud** and **Francis Poulenc**. Her works include *Concertino* for harp and orchestra (1926) and *Chansons françaises* (1930). In 1974 she published an autobiography, *Mémoires à l'emporte pièce*.

Taine, Hippolyte Adolphe 1828–93 •*French critic, historian and philosopher*• Born in Vouziers, Ardennes, he studied for a year in Paris before becoming an author. He made a reputation with his critical analysis of **La Fontaine**'s *Fables* (1853), followed by the *Voyage aux eaux des Pyrénées* (1855, "Journey to the Spas of the Pyrenees"). His positivism was strongly expressed in *Les philosophes français du dix-neuvième siècle* (1857, "French Philosophers of the Nineteenth Century"), *Philosophie de l'art* (1881, "Philosophy of Art") and *De l'intelligence* (1870, "On Intelligence"). His greatest work, *Les origines de la France contemporaine* (1875–94, "The Origins of Contemporary France"), constitutes a strong attack on the men and the motives of the Revolution.

Tait, Archibald Campbell 1811–82 •*Scottish Anglican prelate, and Archbishop of Canterbury*• Born in Edinburgh, he was brought up as a Presbyterian and educated at Edinburgh Academy, the University of Glasgow and Balliol College, Oxford. He entered the Church of England in 1836 and became an opponent of the Oxford Movement. He succeeded Dr **Thomas Arnold** as headmaster of Rugby (1842), became dean of Carlisle in 1849, and in 1856 Bishop of London. He condemned Bishop **Colenso**'s critical views on the accuracy of the Bible, but intervened on his side against attempts to have him deposed. In 1869 he was appointed Archbishop of Canterbury (the first Scotsman to hold the post), and helped to lull the strife caused by Irish disestablishment. He improved the organization of the church in the colonies, and presided over the 1878 Lambeth Conference. His biography was published in 1891 by his son-in-law, the future Archbishop of Canterbury, **Randall Thomas Davidson**.

Tait, Thomas Smith 1882–1952 •*Scottish architect*• Born in Paisley, Renfrewshire, he trained in Glasgow and on the Continent. He designed Adelaide House (1921–24), the *Daily Telegraph* office in London (1927) and St Andrew's House, Edinburgh (1934), and won the competition for the Hawkhead Infectious Diseases Hospital in Paisley (1932). He was controlling designer of the Glasgow Empire Exhibition of 1938 and was the most prominent Scots architect of the interwar period.

Takemitsu, Toru 1930–96 •*Japanese composer*• Born in Tokyo, he was self-taught and became one of the most significant composers in Japan. Between 1975 and 1983 he lectured extensively in the US, and in 1984 was composer in residence at the Aldeburgh Festival, England. His aim as a composer was always to "achieve a sound as intense as silence" and his music is subtle, even mystical. His output is huge and the titles of his works often suggest their mood: *Far Away* (1973), *Undisturbed Rest* (1952–59), *A Flock Descends into the Pentagonal Garden* (1977).

Takeshita, Noboru 1924–2000 •*Japanese statesman*• He was born in Kakeyamachi, in western Japan, the son of an affluent sake brewer. He trained as a kamikaze pilot during World War II. After his university years and a brief career as a schoolteacher, he was elected to the House of Representatives as a Liberal Democratic Party (LDP) deputy in 1958. Formerly a member of the powerful

Tanaka faction, he founded his own faction, the largest within the party, in 1987, and three months later was elected LDP president and prime minister. His administration was undermined by the uncovering of the Recruit-Cosmos insider share-dealing scandal, which, though dating back to 1986, forced the resignation of senior government ministers, including, eventually, Takeshita himself, in 1989.

Tal, Mikhail Nekhemevich 1936–92 •*Russian chess player*• He was born in Riga, Latvia. In 1960 he defeated **Mikhail Botvinnik** to become the youngest grand master to hold the world title until then. His withering stares over the board were held by opponents as attempts at hypnotism, but it is more likely that they succumbed to his unusually inventive style of attack.

Talbot, William Henry Fox 1800–77 •*English physicist and pioneer of photography*• Born in Melbury Abbas, Dorset, he was educated at Harrow and Trinity College, Cambridge. In 1838 he invented "photogenic drawing," a system of making photographic prints on silver chloride paper, in the same year as the invention of the daguerrotype by **Louis Daguerre**. In 1841 he patented the calotype, the first process for photographic negatives from which prints could be made. He also discovered a method of making instantaneous photographs, using electric spark illumination (the first use of flash photography), in 1851. His *Pencil of Nature* (1844) was one of the first photographically illustrated books to be published. He also wrote works on astronomy and mathematics. He became a Member of Parliament in 1833.

Talese, Gay 1932– •*US journalist*• Born in Ocean City, New Jersey, he became a reporter for the *New York Times* (1955–65), and wrote his first nonfiction "short stories" for *Esquire* magazine, beginning in 1963. **Tom Wolfe**, generally regarded as the pioneer of "new journalism," has recognized Talese as its true inventor. His new style reached maturity in his best-selling nonfiction novels, *The Kingdom and the Power* (1969) about the *New York Times*, and *Honor Thy Father* (1971), about the Mafia. Later works include *Unto the Sons* (1992).

Taliesin fl. c. 550 •*Welsh bard*• He is considered (with the mythical Merlin) one of the two great founders of the Welsh poetic tradition. He is named in the *Saxon Genealogies* appended to the *Historia Britonum* of **Nennius**, but later mythical material became attached to his legend. Although a mass of poetry, much of it of later date, has been ascribed to him, there are only eight heroic poems in the 13th-century *Book of Taliesin* thought to be written by him.

Talleyrand(-Périgord), Charles Maurice de, Prince of Benevento 1754–1838 •*French politician*• He was born in Paris. Educated for the Church, he was ordained (1779), appointed Bishop of Autun, elected to the Estates General (1789), and elected president of the Assembly (1790). He lived in exile in England and the US until after the fall of **Robespierre**. As foreign minister under the Directory (1797), he helped to consolidate **Napoleon I**'s position as consul for life (1802) and as emperor (1804); but alarmed by Napoleon's ambitions, he resigned in 1807, becoming leader of the anti-Napoleonic faction. He became minister of foreign affairs under **Louis XVIII**, representing France with great skill at the Congress of Vienna (1814–15). He then lived largely in retirement, but was **Louis Philippe**'s chief adviser at the July Revolution (1830), and was appointed ambassador to England (1830–34).

Tallien, Jean Lambert 1767–1820 •*French revolutionary*• Born in Paris, during the Revolution he made himself famous with his Jacobin broadsheets. He was conspicuous in the attack on the Tuileries and in the September massacres, was elected to the Convention (1792), and played a part in the downfall of the Girondins. On his mission to Bordeaux (1793) during the Terror, he quenched all opposition with the guillotine. He was recalled to Paris, and in 1794 was chosen president of the Convention; but **Robespierre** hated him, and Tallien, conspiring with the Comte de **Barras** and **Joseph Fouché**, brought about his eventual downfall. He was a member of the Council of Five Hundred under the Directory (1795–99) and accompanied **Napoleon I** to Egypt.

Tallis, Thomas c. 1505–85 •*English composer*• He was born in London. In 1575 **Elizabeth I** granted him, with **William Byrd**, a monopoly for printing music and music paper in England. He is considered "the father of English cathedral music," and one of the most distinguished contrapuntists of the English school, and an adaptation of his plainsong responses, and his setting of the Canticles in D minor, are still in use. He wrote much church music, including a motet in 40 parts, *Spem in alium*.

Tambo, Oliver 1917–93 •*South African politician*• Born in Bizana, Transkei, the son of a peasant farmer, at the age of 16 he traveled to Johannesburg to attend a school set up by the Community for the Resurrection, where he came under the influence of Father **Trevor Huddleston**. After graduating from the University of Fort Hare, he began a teacher's diploma course but was expelled for organizing a student protest, and in 1944 joined the African National Congress (ANC), being appointed vice president of its youth league. In 1956 he was imprisoned, and released the following year. ANC deputy president from 1958, when it was banned in 1960, he left South Africa and went to London to set up an external wing. With the continued imprisonment, until 1990, of **Nelson Mandela**, Tarnbo became acting ANC president in 1967, president in 1977 and national chairman from 1991.

Tamm, Igor Yevgenevich 1895–1971 •*Soviet physicist and Nobel Prize winner*• Born in Vladivostok, he was educated at the University of Edinburgh and at Moscow State University, and taught at the latter (1924–34) before moving to the Physics Institute of the Academy. Together with **Ilya Frank**, he developed a theory to describe the Cherenkov effect discovered by **Pavel Cherenkov**. They demonstrated that this radiation is due to a particle moving through a medium faster than the speed of light in the medium. Tamm shared the 1958 Nobel Prize for physics with Cherenkov and Frank for this work.

Tanaka, Kakuei 1918–93 •*Japanese statesman*• He was born into a bankrupt rural family in Futuda village, in western Japan. After training as a civil engineer and establishing a successful building contracting business, he was elected to Japan's House of Representatives in 1947. He rose swiftly within the dominant Liberal Democratic Party (LDP), becoming LDP president and prime minister (1972–74). He was arrested in 1976 on charges of accepting bribes from the Lockheed Corporation while in office, and eventually in 1983 was found guilty and sentenced to four years' imprisonment. He had resigned from the LDP in 1976, but remained an influential, behind-the-scenes faction leader. His appeal against the 1983 verdict was rejected by the High Court in 1987, but a further appeal was lodged. He died still fighting his appeals.

Tancred 1078–1112 •*Norman crusader*• He went on the First Crusade (1096–99) with **Bohemond I**, his uncle, and distinguished himself in many sieges. He established the great principality of Galilee (1099), but soon went to Antioch, where he ruled as regent. He is the hero of *Gerusalemme liberata* by **Tasso** (1593) and was the grandson of **Robert Guiscard**.

Tandy, Jessica 1907–94 •*US actress*• She was born in London and became a naturalized US citizen in 1954. She made her London debut in 1929, and on Broadway the following year. Establishing herself as a major stage star, she starred opposite **John Gielgud** in *Hamlet* (1934) and as Blanche Du Bois in *A Streetcar Named Desire* (1947). She appeared in a number of plays on Broadway with her second husband, Hume Cronyn (1911–2003). She acted in many films, and won an Academy Award for her title role in *Driving Miss Daisy* (1989).

Taney, Roger Brooke 1777–1864 •*US jurist*• Born in Calvert County, Maryland, he was educated at Dickinson College, Pennsylvania. He was admitted to the bar in 1799 and elected to the Maryland Senate in 1816. In 1831 he became attorney general, and in 1833 secretary of the treasury. The Senate, after rejecting his appointment as chief justice of the Supreme Court in 1835, confirmed it in 1836. His most famous decision was in the **Dred Scott** case (1857), when he ruled that the Missouri Compromise was unconstitutional and that African Americans were not citizens. Intended to put an end to antislavery agitation, this unjust and ill-considered ruling instead precipitated the Civil War.

Tange, Kenzo 1913– •*Japanese architect*• He was born and educated in Tokyo. His early buildings, such as the Hiroshima Peace Center (1949–55), owe a debt to tradition and **Le Corbusier**. He also designed the dramatic National Gymnasium for the 1964 Olympic Games, and the theme pavilion for the 1970 Osaka Exposition. Professor of Architecture at the University of Tokyo (1946–74), he has published several influential works, including *A Plan for Tokyo* (1960).

Tanguy, Yves 1900–55 •*US artist*• Born in Paris, France, he was mainly self-taught, and began to paint in 1922, joining the surrealists in 1926. In 1930 he traveled to Africa, and went to the US in 1939, becoming a US citizen in 1948. All his pictures are at the same time surrealist and nonfigurative, being peopled with numerous small objects or organisms, whose meaning and identity are unknown, suggesting the landscape of another planet.

Tang Yin (T'ang Yin), *also known as* **Tang Liujiu** 1470–1523 •*Chinese painter and poet*• Born in the Suzhou region of Jiangsu (Kiangsu) province, he passed the exams for the local government with distinction and found many benefactors, among them various masters of the Wu school of painting. At 28 he went to Beijing (Peking), but a scandal forced him to return home. In order to survive, he started painting in a popular and decorative style for the burghers of Suzhou: portraits, pretty women, erotica. He is counted among the Four Great Masters of the **Ming** dynasty.

Tanizaki Junichiro 1886–1965 •*Japanese novelist and playwright*• He was born and educated in Tokyo, where he studied Japanese literature at the Imperial University. After the earthquake of 1923, he removed to Kyoto-Osaka, which was to be the setting of his lengthy novel, *Sasameyuki* (1943–48, Eng trans *The Makioka Sisters*, 1957), a notable example of descriptive realism. From his first work onward, Tanizaki was concerned with the transformative power of the imagination; *Shisei* (1910, "Tattoo") is a story about a girl whose personality is changed by bodily decoration. *Bushuko hiwa* (1935) and *Yoshino kuzu* (1937) appeared together in English translation in 1982 as *The Secret History of the Lord of Musashi* and *Arrowroot*, respectively. He wrote a number of plays, literary essays and translations.

Tannhäuser, Der c. 1210–c. 1270 •*German poet and minnesinger*• He was probably from Bavaria. He was court poet to the ruler of Austria, and is thought to have traveled a great deal, including taking part in one of the crusades. He broke away from the previous rigid minnesang conventions, using humor, irony and even parody, as well as great sensuality in erotic passages. His name was linked with a legendary German knight in a popular 16th-century ballad. It tells of a man who seeks forgiveness for a life of pleasure, but, being refused absolution by the pope, returns to his former ways. The story was the basis for the opera by **Richard Wagner** (1845).

Tantia Topee, *real name* **Ramchandra Pandurangez** d. 1859 •*Indian soldier and rebel*• Born in Gwalior, he was **Nana Sahib**'s lieutenant in the Indian Mutiny (1857–58). He took part in the massacre of the British at Cawnpore (July 1857). With the Rani of Jhansi he occupied Gwalior and then held the field after his chief had fled. After marching through central India and Khandesh in an attempt to raise up the Marathas in revolt, he was betrayed, captured and executed.

Tàpies, Antoni 1923– •*Spanish painter*• He was born in Barcelona, and studied law there. A self-taught painter, he became a member of the Dau al Set (Die with the Seven) group of avant-garde artists and writers opposed to the **Franco** dictatorship. Inspired by surrealism, he made collages from everyday rubbish—rags, bits of string, torn canvas—splashed with paint and graffiti, as in *Upside-Down Hat* (1967, Pompidou Center, Paris). In 1957 he was a founder of the El Paso group, which championed Informalism. His first one-man show, in Barcelona (1951), was followed by numerous international exhibitions and prizes.

Tarantino, Quentin 1963– •*US director and screenwriter*• He was born in Knoxville, Tennessee, to a half-Irish, half-Cherokee mother and a father of Italian descent who was absent for most of his upbringing. He spent much of his childhood at the movies before working in a video store and training as an actor (he appears in his own films). One of his many scripts was made into his debut film as director, *Reservoir Dogs* (1993). In 1994 his second film, *Pulp Fiction*, won the Palme d'Or at the Cannes Film Festival. Characterized by brutality, violent escapism, and an intentional absence of morality, both films exist at the point where cruelty meets humor. He is also the original author of the story of **Oliver Stone**'s *Natural Born Killers* (1994). More recent films include *Kill Bill, Volume One* (2003) and *Kill Bill, Volume Two* (2004).

Tarbell, Ida M(inerva) 1857–1944 •*US reform journalist*• Born in Erie County, Pennsylvania, she was educated at Allegheny College and the Sorbonne (1891–94) and joined *McClure's Magazine* (1894–1906). Her explosive denunciation of **John D Rockefeller**'s fortune-building methods, *History of the Standard Oil Company* (published in book form in 1904), established women in the new "muckraking" journalism. She joined **Lincoln Steffens** and other *McClure's* writers in running the *American* magazine (1906–15), campaigning against corruption and big business interests. Her feminist writing includes *The Business of Being a Woman* (1912) and *The Ways of Women* (1915), and her history, *The Nationalizing of Business* (1936), was a standard work on American post–Civil War economic growth for 20 years.

Tareq Aziz 1936– •*Iraqi Ba'ath politician*• Born in Mosul and educated at the University of Baghdad, he worked as a journalist and an editor. Following a period in Syria with the Ba'ath press, he returned to Iraq and was elected to the Revolutionary Command Council General Affairs Bureau in 1972. Appointed foreign affairs minister in 1983, he became deputy prime minister in 1991. Following Iraq's invasion of Kuwait in 1990 and the war which followed, he emerged as Iraq's principal spokesman and apologist for President **Saddam Hussein**. Following the overthrow of the Hussein regime in 2003, he was arrested by the US forces.

Tarkenton, Fran(cis Asbury) 1940– •*US football player*• Born in Richmond, Virginia, he played for the Minnesota Vikings and New York Giants (1961–78), and gained 47,003 yards by passing, which was then a National Football League record. He later became a sports commentator and management consultant.

Tarkington, (Newton) Booth 1869–1946 •*US writer*• He was born in Indianapolis and studied at Purdue and Princeton Universities. Many of his novels are set in Indiana, but he is best known as the author of *Monsieur Beaucaire* (1900) and the "Penrod" books—*Penrod* (1914) and *Seventeen* (1916). His other works include a trilogy, *Growth* (1927), including *The Magnificent Ambersons* (1918), which won the Pulitzer Prize and was made into a successful film by **Orson Welles**; and *Alice Adams* (1921, Pulitzer Prize).

" "

An ideal wife is any woman who has an ideal husband.

1924 ***Looking Forward and Others****, "The Hopeful Pessimist."*

Tarkovsky, Andrei Arsenevich 1932–86 •*Russian filmmaker*• Born in Moscow, he studied Oriental languages and later attended the State Film School. His modest body of work gained him critical recognition as one of the cinema's true poets with a distinctive, slow-moving style that incorporated elliptical imagery and lengthy, enigmatic and often impenetrable subject material. He examined youth in *Ivanogo detstvo* (1962, *Ivan's Childhood*) and *Zerkalo* (1975, *Mirror*) while offering bleak visions of the future in *Solaris* (1972) and *Stalker* (1979). Later in exile in Paris, his final film, *Offret* (1986, *The Sacrifice*), featured a man willing to relinquish his own life and possessions to prevent an apocalypse.

Tarleton, Sir Banastre 1754–1833 •*English soldier*• Born in Liverpool, he served under Sir **Henry Clinton** and **Charles Cornwallis** in the American Revolution (1775–83). He defeated Colonel Abraham Buford at Waxham Creek (1780) and **Horatio Gates** at Camden, but was beaten by General Morgan at Cowpens. He held Gloucester until it capitulated (1782), and then returned to England. He was Member of Parliament for Liverpool (1790–1806, 1807–12).

Tarquinius Priscus, *in full* **Lucius Tarquinius Priscus** reigned 616–578 BC •*Traditionally the fifth king of Rome*• Of Etruscan origin, he is said to have modified the constitution, and to have begun the Servian agger and the Circus Maximus.

Tarquinius Superbus, *in full* **Lucius Tarquinius Superbus** reigned 534–510 BC •*Traditionally the seventh and last king of Rome*•

According to Roman tradition, his cruelty and the rape of **Lucretia** by his son Sextus provoked an uprising of the Roman people under **Lucius Junius Brutus**, his expulsion from Rome, and the establishment of the Republic. He is then said to have tried to reestablish himself in Rome with the help of **Lars Porsena** of Clusium, but died in exile.

Tasman, Abel Janszoon 1603–c. 1659 •*Dutch navigator*• He was born in Lutjegast, near Groningen. In 1642 he discovered Tasmania—named Van Diemen's Land until 1855—and New Zealand, and in 1643 Tonga and Fiji, having been dispatched in quest of the "Great South Land" by Antony Van Diemen (1593–1645), Governor-General of Batavia. He made a second voyage (1644) to the Gulf of Carpentaria and the northwest coast of Australia.

Tasso, Torquato 1544–95 •*Italian poet*• Born in Sorrento, he was sent (1560) to study law and philosophy at Padua, where he published his first work, a romantic poem, *Rinaldo* (1562, Eng trans 1792). At the court of Duke Alphonso II d'Este of Ferrara, he began his major work, the epic poem, *Gerusalemme liberata* (1580, Eng trans *Godfrey of Bouillon: The Recovery of Jerusalem*, 1600), a story of the First Crusade, which he completed in 1575. He later rewrote it as *Gerusalemme conquistata* (1593, "Jerusalem Conquered"). For the court theater he wrote the pastoral play, *Aminta* (1573, Eng trans 1591). In 1579 he was confined at Ferrara by order of the duke as insane, not, as is often alleged, for his love for the Princess Leonora, a story on which Lord **Byron** based his *Lament of Tasso*. In his seven years' confinement he wrote many verses and philosophical dialogues.

Tate, (John Orley) Allen 1899–1979 •*US poet*• Born in Winchester, Kentucky, he studied at Vanderbilt University, where he fell in with the group of poets led by **John Crowe Ransom** and known as "the Fugitives." He was editor (1944–46) of the influential *Sewanee Review* and taught at several universities. His collections of verse include *Mr Pope and Other Poems* (1928), *The Mediterranean and Other Poems* (1936) and *Winter Sea* (1945). Among his other writings are biographies and critical works such as *On the Limits of Poetry* (1948), which made him one of the leading exponents of New Criticism.

Tate, Sir Henry 1819–99 •*English sugar magnate, art patron and philanthropist*• Born in Chorley, Lancashire, he patented a method for cutting sugar cubes in 1872 and attained great wealth as a Liverpool sugar refiner. He founded the University Library at Liverpool and gave the British nation the Tate Gallery, Millbank, London, which was opened in 1897, and contained his own valuable private collection.

Tate, Nahum 1652–1715 •*Irish poet and dramatist*• Born in Dublin, he studied at Trinity College there. With Samuel **Johnson**'s approval, he wrote a number of "improved" versions of **Shakespeare**'s tragedies, substituting happy endings. With **John Dryden**'s help he wrote a second part to the poet's *Absalom and Achitophel* (1682), and with **Nicholas Brady** compiled a metrical version of the Psalms. "While Shepherds Watched Their Flocks by Night" is attributed to him, and he wrote the libretto of **Henry Purcell**'s *Dido and Aeneas* (1689). He succeeded **Thomas Shadwell** as poet laureate in 1692. His best-known work is *Panacea or a Poem on Tea* (1700).

Tati, Jacques, *pseudonym of* **Jacques Tatischeff** 1908–82 •*French actor, author and film producer*• Born in Le Pecq, Paris, he was a skilled rugby player in his youth and began his career in vaudeville with a wordless act in which he mimicked various sporting activities, an entertainment he continued in short films like *Oscar, champion de tennis* (1934). His first feature film as a director and performer was *Jour de fête* (1949, *The Big Day*). With *Les vacances de Monsieur Hulot* (1951, *Monsieur Hulot's Holiday*) and *Mon oncle* (1958, *My Uncle*), he perfected his best-known character of the pipe-smoking, lugubrious Hulot, forever beset by physical mishaps and confrontations with modern technology. His later films were less successful.

Tatian 2nd century AD •*Syrian Christian thinker*• He became a pupil of the martyr **Justin** at Rome and was converted to Christianity by him. After Justin's death in c. 165 AD he returned to Syria (c. 172), where he established, or was at least closely associated with, an ascetic religious community of Encratites, which fostered a heretical combination of Christianity and Stoicism. Only two of his many writings survive: the *Oratio ad Graecos* ("Speech to the Greeks"), a denunciation of the intellectualism of Greek culture, and the *Diatessaron* (literally "Out of Four"), a patchwork version of the four Gospels arranged as a continuous narrative.

Tatlin, Vladimir Yevgrafovich 1885–1953 •*Russian painter and designer*• Born in Moscow, he studied there in 1910 and exhibited with avant-garde artists such as **Natalia Goncharova** and **Mikhail Larionov** before going to visit Berlin and Paris. He founded Russian constructivism, a movement at first approved by the Soviet authorities, and he was commissioned to design the gigantic *Monument to the Third International*; the model was exhibited in 1920, but the monument itself was never built.

Tattersall, Richard 1724–95 •*English auctioneer*• He was born in Hurstwood, Lancashire. In London he entered the Duke of Kingston's service, became an auctioneer, and in 1776 set up auction rooms at Hyde Park Corner, which became a celebrated mart of thoroughbred horses and a great racing center. They were transferred to Knightsbridge in 1867.

Tatum, Art(hur) 1910–56 •*US jazz pianist*• Born in Toledo, Ohio, and largely self-taught, he became jazz music's first supreme keyboard virtuoso. Although nearly blind from birth, he was a professional musician from his teens. Moving to New York in 1932, he made solo recordings and club appearances which have hardly been equaled for technique, drive and improvisational ability. The most influential of the swing-style pianists, Tatum continued to work in the idiom until his death.

Tatum, Edward Lawrie 1909–75 •*US biochemist and Nobel Prize winner*• Born in Boulder, Colorado, he studied at the University of Wisconsin, and taught at Stanford University (1937–45, 1948–57), Yale (1945–48) and Rockefeller University, New York (1957–75). With **George Beadle** he demonstrated the role of genes in biochemical processes, and at Yale, he collaborated with **Joshua Lederberg** to show that bacteria reproduce by the sexual process of conjunction. All three shared the 1958 Nobel Prize for physiology or medicine.

Taufa'ahau, (Tupouto Tungi) Tupou IV 1918– •*King of Tonga*• The eldest son of Queen **Salote**, Tupou III, he was educated at Newington College and the University of Sydney. He became prime minister under his mother (1949), and on succeeding to the throne on his mother's death (1965), he assumed the designation King Taufa'ahau Tupou IV, sharing power with his brother, Prince Fatafehi Tu'ipelehake (1922–99), who became prime minister. King Taufa'ahau, while negotiating the country's independence within the Commonwealth (1970), remains the strongest supporter of the Western powers in the Pacific region.

Taussig, Helen Brooke 1898–1986 •*US pediatrician*• Born in Cambridge, Massachusetts, she received her MD from Johns Hopkins University in 1927 and later became the first woman to become a full professor there. With the cardiac surgeon **Alfred Blalock**, she pioneered the "blue baby" operations which heralded the beginnings of modern cardiac surgery. The babies were blue because of a variety of congenital anomalies, and Taussig was actively involved in the diagnosis and aftercare of the young patients on whom Blalock operated, and their joint efforts helped create a new specialty of pediatric cardiac surgery.

Tavener, Sir John Kenneth 1944– •*English composer*• Born and educated in London, he was first recognized as a composer with the cantata *The Whale* (1966), based on the story of **Jonah**. His mature work has been dominated by his conversion to the Greek Orthodox Church (1976), and the bulk of his output has been vocal music of liturgical character, including *Últimos ritos* (1972, "Last Rites"), for soloists, chorus, and orchestra, and a sacred opera, *Therese* (1979). His more recent works include *The Protecting Veil* (1987), for cello and strings, and *The Repentant Thief* (1990), for clarinet, percussion, and strings. He was knighted in 2000.

Taverner, John c. 1490–1545 •*English composer and organist*• Born in Boston, Lincolnshire, he was organist there and at Christ

Church, Oxford, and composed notable motets and masses. Accused of heresy, he was imprisoned by Cardinal **Wolsey**, but released, "being but a musitian."

Taverner, Richard c.1505–75 •*English writer*• He was patronized by Cardinal **Wolsey** and **Thomas Cromwell**, for whom he compiled *Taverner's Bible* (1539), a revision of *Matthew's Bible* by **John Rogers** (1537). On Cromwell's fall he was sent to the Tower of London, but was soon released, and found favor with **Henry VIII**.

Tavernier, Bertrand 1941– •*French film director*• Born in Lyons, he became a writer and critic before working as an assistant to director Jean-Pierre Melville. Following a decade as a freelance press agent and scriptwriter, he made his directorial debut with *L'horloger de Saint-Paul* (1973, *The Watchmaker of St Paul*). Telling well-rounded narratives with quiet professionalism, his eclectic body of work includes such period dramas as *Dimanche à la campagne* (1984, *Sunday in the Country*) and *La passion Béatrice* (1988), the chamber work *Daddy nostalgie* (1990, *These Foolish Things*) and edgy police stories like *L.627* (1992).

Tawney, R(ichard) H(enry) 1880–1962 •*English economic historian*• Born in Calcutta, he was educated at Rugby School and Balliol College, Oxford, of which he was elected a Fellow in 1918. He was severely wounded during World War I. After a period of social work in the East End of London, he became tutor, executive (1905–47) and president (1928–44) of the Workers' Educational Association. He was Professor of Economic History at London (1931–49), and wrote studies in English economic history, particularly of the Tudor and Stuart periods, including *Religion and the Rise of Capitalism* (1926), *Equality* (1931) and *Business and Politics Under James I* (1958).

Tayama Katai 1872–1930 •*Japanese writer*• He was born into a wealthy, upper-middle-class family, and sent to England to study. He is credited with inventing the *watakushi shosetsu* (I-novel), the most extreme product of Japanese naturalism, the dominant literary movement in the first half of the 20th century, in which realism is achieved by concentrating solely on the internal workings of the narrator's mind. In *Futon* (1907), his best and best-known work, nothing very much happens, except for the narrator losing his girlfriend; it is, instead, a long, intricately described account of his feelings and states of mind.

Taylor, A(lan) J(ohn) P(ercivale) 1906–90 •*English historian*• Born in Lancashire, he studied at Oriel College, Oxford. He was lecturer in modern history at the University of Manchester, Fellow of Magdalen College, Oxford (1938–76), and lecturer in international history at Oxford (1953–63). His major work was *The Struggle for Mastery in Europe 1848–1918* (1954). Other works include *The Origins of the Second World War* (1961) and *English History 1914–1945* (1965). He inspired many students, was a friend and biographer of Lord **Beaverbrook**, and wrote many essays and an autobiography, *A Personal History* (1983). In 1991 *Letters to Eva 1969–83* was published posthumously, a collection of love letters to his third wife.

" "

History gets thicker and thicker as it approaches recent times.

1965 ***English History 1914–1945.***

Taylor, (Winifred) Ann, *née* **Walker** 1947– •*British Labour politician*• Born in Motherwell, Scotland, and educated at the Universities of Bradford and Sheffield, she worked as an Open University tutor before entering parliament as Member of Parliament for Bolton West (1974–83). She held several posts in the areas of education, housing, and the environment, and was leader of the House of Commons (1997–98) and chief whip (1998–2001).

Taylor, Dame Elizabeth Rosemond 1932– •*US film actress*• She was born in London, England, to US parents, and moved with her family to Los Angeles (1939), where she made her screen debut at the age of ten. As a child star she made a number of films, including two "Lassie" stories (1943, 1946), *National Velvet* (1944), and *Little Women* (1949). She was first seen as an adult in *The Father of the Bride* (1950), and her career continued through the 1950s with films including *Cat on a Hot Tin Roof* (1958) and *Suddenly Last Summer* (1959). She was notable also for her many marriages, her first husband being Nick Hilton (m. 1950), her second the actor Michael Wilding (m. 1952), her third the producer **Mike Todd** (m. 1957), who was killed in an air crash the following year. She then married Eddie Fisher (1959), divorcing him in 1964. In 1960 she won her first Academy Award for *Butterfield 8*. The making of the spectacular epic *Cleopatra* (1962) provided the background to her well-publicized romance with her costar **Richard Burton**, whom she married for the first time in 1964. She made several films with Burton, including *Who's Afraid of Virginia Woolf?* (1966, Academy Award). Divorced from and remarried to Richard Burton, she was divorced from him again (1976), and married Senator John Warner (1978), from whom she separated in 1981. Her other films include *A Little Night Music* (1976) and *The Mirror Crack'd* (1981). After treatment for alcohol addiction, she resumed acting, mostly in television. She married Larry Fortensky in 1991, but filed for divorce in 1996. She was given the honorary title of Dame Commander, Order of the British Empire, in 2000.

" "

Some of my best leading men have been horses and dogs.

Attributed.

Taylor, Frederick W(inslow) 1856–1915 •*US engineer*• Born in Germantown, Pennsylvania, he studied at night while being employed at the Midvale steelworks in Philadelphia (1878–90), and obtained a degree in engineering from the Stevens Institute of Technology in 1883. He became chief engineer in 1889. He became chief engineer in 1889, having invented several devices and modified processes to increase efficiency, and then turned his attention to the part played by workers themselves, introducing time-and-motion study as an aid to efficient management, known as "Taylorism."

Taylor, Jeremy 1613–67 •*English theologian*• Born in Cambridge, he studied at Caius College, Cambridge, and became a Fellow of All Souls College, Oxford (1636), chaplain to Archbishop **Laud**, and in 1638 rector of Uppingham. During the civil war Taylor was imprisoned several times. In 1658 he got a lectureship at Lisburn, and at the Restoration the bishopric of Down and Connor. His many works, including *The Liberty of Prophesying* (1646) and the *52 Sermons* (1651–53), are considered some of the most eloquent sacred writings in the English language.

Taylor, Lawrence 1959– •*US football player*• Born in Williamsburg, Virginia, he emerged as one of the most formidable defensive players of his generation. He was recruited as an outside linebacker by the New York Giants in 1981 and made an immediate impact with 133 tackles, 9.5 sacks, eight passes defensed, two forced fumbles and an interception in his rookie season. Strong and fast, over the next 13 years he played a major role in getting the Giants to the playoffs six times and winning two Super Bowls (1986 and 1990). He was named the NFL's Most Valuable Player in 1986, in which year he achieved a career best of 20.5 sacks, 105 total tackles, five passes defensed and two forced fumbles. He retired because of injury in 1993.

Taylor, Sir Patrick Gordon 1896–1966 •*Australian pioneer aviator*• Born in Mosman, New South Wales, he served with the Royal Flying Corps during World War I, and received the Military Cross. He was associated with Sir **Charles Kingsford Smith** and **Charles Ulm** in many of their pioneering flights. In 1935, over the Tasman Sea with Kingsford Smith in his *Southern Cross*, one engine cut out and oil pressure was lost on another. Taylor spent the rest of the flight clambering across the wings every half-hour, transferring oil from the dead engine into the ailing one; for this he was awarded the George Cross.

Taylor, Paul Belville 1930– •*US modern-dance choreographer*• Born in Pittsburgh, Pennsylvania, he studied painting at college and trained as a swimmer. He first studied dance with **Merce Cunningham** (1953–54) and **Martha Graham** (1958–62). He began choreographing in 1956 and has developed an original, ebullient, lyrical style. Works include *Three Epitaphs* (1956), *Aureole* (1962), *Big*

Bertha (1971), *Esplanade* (1975), *Arden Court* (1981), *Speaking in Tongues* (1989), *Company B* (1991) and *Spindrift* (1993).

Taylor, Zachary 1784–1850 •*12th President of the US*• Born in Montebello, Virginia, he entered the army in 1808. He fought in several campaigns against the Native Americans and in the Mexican American War (1846–48). He emerged from the war as a hero, and was given the Whig presidential nomination. The main issues of his presidency (1849–50) were the status of the new territories and the extension of slavery there, but he died only 16 months after taking office. He was succeeded by **Millard Fillmore**.

Tchaikovsky, Pyotr Ilyich 1840–93 •*Russian composer*• He was born in Kamsko-Votkinsk in the Ural Mountains. His early musical talents were encouraged, but when the family moved to St Petersburg he started his working life as a minor civil servant. In 1862 he enrolled at the recently opened conservatory, but after three years he was engaged to teach harmony at his new conservatory in Moscow, which opened in 1866. His operas and second ("Little Russian") Symphony (1872) brought him into the public eye, and in 1875 his Piano Concerto in B-flat Minor had its premiere in Moscow. He married a pupil, Antonina Ivanovna Milyukova, despite his homosexual tendencies, but left her a month after the wedding in a state of nervous collapse (1877). After recuperation abroad he resigned from the conservatory and retired to the country to devote himself entirely to composition. At about the time of his marriage, Tchaikovsky received the moral and financial support of Nadezhda von Meck, the widow of a wealthy engineer; although they never met, they corresponded regularly until 1890. Her support enabled him to devote himself entirely to composition. Soon after his return to Russia from England in 1893, and after the first performance of his sixth ("Pathétique") Symphony, he died in St Petersburg. He was said to have died of cholera from drinking unboiled water (perhaps deliberately), but later research (by Alexandra Orlova), published in 1979, suggests that he may have committed suicide by swallowing poison, at the behest of a "court of honor," following his alleged relationship with a young male aristocrat. The melodiousness, colorful orchestration, and deeply expressive content of his music brought him then, and now, an enthusiastic following exceeding that of any other Russian composer. Tchaikovsky's introspective and melancholy nature is reflected in some of his symphonies and orchestral pieces, but much less in his ballet music: *Swan Lake* (1877), *The Sleeping Beauty* (1890) and *The Nutcracker* (1892), which have formed the core of the classical repertory. Other works include six symphonies, of which the last three are the best known, two piano concertos (a third was left uncompleted), a violin concerto, a number of tone poems including *Romeo and Juliet* (1870, dedicated to Balakirev) and *Italian capriccio*, songs and piano pieces. He also wrote chamber music, including a piano trio and three string quartets, and 11 operas, including *Eugene Onegin* (1879) and *The Queen of Spades* (1890).

Teach or **Tache** or **Thatch, Edward**, *known as* **Blackbeard** d. 1718 •*English pirate*• Born in Bristol, he was employed as a privateer against the Spanish during the War of the Spanish Succession (1701–13) and later turned to piracy, attacking Spanish and French vessels in the West Indies from his ship, *Queen Anne's Revenge*, a 40-gun warship. He formed an alliance with the governor of North Carolina and the state collector of taxes, giving them a percentage of the spoils in exchange for their protection. On November 22, 1718, he was shot dead and decapitated by Lieutenant Robert Maynard.

Teasdale, Sara, *née* **Trevor** 1884–1933 •*US poet*• Born in St Louis, Missouri, and educated at the Mary Institute and Hosmer Hall, in 1918 she was the first person to receive a Pulitzer Prize for poetry, for her collection *Love Songs* (1917). Much of her poetry is based on her own sheltered early life and unhappy marriage, and expresses the conflicting needs for independence and freedom, love and security. She wrote nine collections of poetry, two of which were published after her death, a suspected suicide.

Tebaldus *See* **Theobald**

Tebbit (of Chingford), Norman Beresford Tebbit, Baron 1931– •*English Conservative politician*• Born in Enfield, Middlesex, he left grammar school at 16 and began his career as a journalist. After national service in the RAF, he became an airline pilot. He was elected to parliament in 1970 and became noted for his radical, "New Right" convictions. Already an influential backroom strategist and junior minister, he was brought into the Cabinet of **Margaret Thatcher** as employment secretary in 1981 and trade and industry secretary in 1983. Noted for his robust invective and antiunion stance, he came to personify a new type of "Thatcherite" conservativism. His career, however, was partially checked by the injuries he and, in particular, his wife, Margaret, sustained as victims of the 1984 IRA bombing of the Grand Hotel, Brighton. He was appointed chancellor of the Duchy of Lancaster and Conservative Party chairman in 1985 and helped mastermind the 1987 general election victory. However, soon afterward, his relations with Thatcher cooled and he retired to the backbenches. In 1992 he decided not to contest his seat in the general election and was made a life peer.

Tecumseh 1768–1813 •*Shawnee chief*• Born in Old Piqua, Ohio, he became chief of the Shawnees. He joined his brother, "The Prophet," in an uprising against the whites, suppressed at Tippecanoe by **William Henry Harrison** (1811). He enlisted with the English, and commanded the Indian allies in the War of 1812 as brigadier general. He died fighting at the Thames River in Canada.

Tedder (of Glenguin), Arthur William Tedder, 1st Baron 1890–1967 •*Scottish marshal of the RAF*• He was born at Glenguin, Stirlingshire. He served in the Colonial Service and Royal Flying Corps during World War I. At the outbreak of World War II he was director general of research and development at the Air Ministry. From 1940 he organized the Middle East Air Force, later becoming deputy Supreme Commander under General **Eisenhower**. He was made marshal of the RAF (1945), created a baron in 1946, and in 1950 he became chancellor of Cambridge University and also a governor of the BBC.

Teilhard de Chardin, Pierre 1881–1955 •*French Jesuit theologian, paleontologist and philosopher*• Born at the castle of Sarcenat, he lectured in pure science at the Jesuit College in Cairo, and was ordained as a priest in 1911. He was a stretcher bearer during World War I, and subsequently became Professor of Geology (1918) at the Institut Catholique in Paris. He directed the 1929 excavations at the Choukoutien Peking Man site in China, and later worked in central Asia, Ethiopia, Java and Somalia, but his anthropological research did not conform to Jesuit orthodoxy, and he was forbidden by his religious superiors to teach and publish. From 1951 he lived and worked in the US. Posthumously published, his philosophical speculations employ the concept of "involution" to explain why *Homo sapiens* seems to be the only species which, in spreading over the globe, has resisted intense division into further species. *La phénomène humain* (written 1938–40, published 1955, Eng trans *The Phenomenon of Man*) is based on his scientific thinking and argues that humanity is a continuous process of evolution toward a perfect spiritual state; it is complementary to *Le milieu divin* (1957).

Te Kanawa, Dame Kiri Janette 1944– •*New Zealand soprano*• Born in Gisborne, Auckland, she won many prizes and awards in New Zealand and Australia before going to London, where she made her debut with the Royal Opera Company in 1970. She has since taken a wide range of leading roles at all the major opera houses and concert halls, and in 1981 sang at the wedding of **Charles** and **Diana**. In 1988 she made the first of her regular appearances in the Australian Broadcasting Corporation's *Opera in the Outback* concerts. She was given the honorary title of Dame Commander, Order of the British Empire, in 1982.

Teleki, Pál, Count 1879–1941 •*Hungarian statesman*• He was born in Budapest, where he became Professor of Geography at the university in 1919. Combining politics with an academic career, he was also in that year appointed foreign minister and, from 1920 to 1921, premier. Founder of the Christian National League and chief of Hungary's Boy Scouts, he was minister of education in 1938 and again premier (1939–41). When Germany marched against Yugoslavia through Hungary, he took his own life.

Telemann, Georg Philipp 1681–1767 •*German composer*• Born in Magdeburg, he taught himself music by learning to play a wide range of instruments (including the violin, recorder and zither, and later the shawm, oboe, flute and bass trombone) and studying the scores of the masters. He held several posts as Kapellmeister, and was musical director of the Johanneum at Hamburg from 1721 until his death. A prolific composer, he wrote church music, 46 passions, over 40 operas, oratorios, many songs, and much instrumental music. Ranked in his lifetime above his friend **J S Bach**, his popularity waned from his death until the 1930s.

Telford, Thomas 1757–1834 •*Scottish civil engineer*• Born in Westerkirk, Langholm, he was apprenticed to a stonemason at the age of 14. He found work at the Portsmouth dockyard in 1784 and in 1787 became surveyor of public works for Shropshire. His reputation was enhanced by his masonry arch bridge over the Severn at Montford (1790–92) and even more by the spectacular Pont-Cysyllte aqueduct and other works on the Ellesmere Canal (1793–1805). He constructed the Caledonian Canal (1803–23), more than 1,000 miles (1,609 km) of road, and 1,200 bridges, besides churches, manses, harbors, etc. Other works by him included the road from London to Holyhead, with the remarkable 579-foot-span (174-meter) wrought-iron Menai Suspension Bridge (1819–26), and the St Katherine's Docks (1824–28) in London. He was also responsible for draining large tracts of the fen country.

Tell, William 15th century •*Semilegendary Swiss patriot*• He was from Bürglen in Uri, and his name first occurs in a chronicle of 1470. A famous crossbow marksman, he reputedly saved his native district from Austrian oppression. Johannes von Müller (1752–1809), in his *History of Switzerland* (1786), records how Tell was compelled by the tyrannical Austrian governor, Hermann Gessler, to shoot an apple off his own son's head. Later, Tell killed the tyrant, and so initiated the movement which secured the independence of Switzerland. Similar tales are found in the folklore of many countries, and Tell may be pure legend.

Teller, Edward 1908–2003 •*US physicist*• Born in Budapest, Hungary, he studied at Karlsruhe, and the Universities of Munich and Göttingen, and under **Niels Bohr** at Copenhagen. He left Germany in 1933, lectured in London and Washington (1935), and contributed profoundly to the modern explanation of solar energy. He worked on the Manhattan atomic bomb project (1941–46), and joined **Robert Oppenheimer**'s theoretical study group at Berkeley, California. From 1963 to 1966 he was chairman of the Department of Applied Science at the University of California, Davis, then University Professor (1971–75). After Russia's first atomic test (1949), he was one of the architects of President **Harry S Truman**'s crash program to build and test (1952) the world's first hydrogen bomb. He repudiated any moral implications of his work.

“ ”

If there ever was a misnomer, it is "exact science." Science has always been full of mistakes; they require a genius to correct them. Of course, we do not see our own mistakes.

1991 ***Conversations on the Dark Secrets of Physics.***

Temin, Howard Martin 1934–94 •*US virologist and Nobel Prize winner*• Born in Philadelphia, he studied with **Renato Dulbecco** at the California Institute of Technology (Caltech). From 1969 he held various professorships at the University of Wisconsin. Temin formulated the "provirus" hypothesis that the genetic material of an invading virus is copied into the host cell DNA. In 1970 he isolated the enzyme reverse transcriptase (independently of **David Baltimore**), which enables new DNA to be inserted into the host cell. Viruses which contain this enzyme are retroviruses. Reverse transcriptase is used to make copies of specific genes, clones, and is widely used for genetic engineering. Temin shared the 1975 Nobel Prize for physiology or medicine with Dulbecco and Baltimore.

Temple, Frederick 1821–1902 •*English prelate and Archbishop of Canterbury*• Born in Santa Maura in the Ionian islands, and educated at Balliol College, Oxford, of which he became a mathematics lecturer and Fellow, he was principal of Kneller Hall Training College (1858–69), and headmaster of Rugby (1857–69). In 1885 he became Bishop of London and in 1897 Archbishop of Canterbury. He was responsible, with Archbishop Maclagen of York, for the "Lambeth Opinions" (1889), which attempted to solve some ritual controversies.

Temple, Shirley, *married name* **Shirley Temple Black** 1928– •*US child film actress and diplomat*• Born in Santa Monica, California, she was a precociously talented baby and appeared in a series of short films from the age of three-and-a-half. An unspoiled personality who sang, danced and did impressions, she captivated audiences during the Depression in films like *Curly Top* (1935) and *Dimples* (1936). Her appeal faded, however, and when attempts at an adult comeback floundered, she retired from the screen. Involved with Republican Party politics as Shirley Temple Black, she was appointed the US's representative to the United Nations General Assembly in 1969 and served as ambassador to Ghana (1974–76), White House chief of protocol (1976–1977) and ambassador to Czechoslovakia (1989–92). She received an honorary Academy Award in 1934. Her autobiography, *Child Star*, was published in 1988.

Temple, Sir William 1628–99 •*English diplomat and essay writer*• He was born in London and studied at Emmanuel College, Cambridge. A diplomat from 1655, he became ambassador at The Hague and negotiated the Triple Alliance (1668) against France. After the revolution he declined a political post in order to devote himself to literature. Among his works are *Miscellanea* (1679, 1692) and the famous essay "Upon the Ancient and Modern Learning." His essay style was a major influence on 18th-century writers, including **Jonathan Swift**, who was his secretary, and who published his letters (1700–03).

Temple, William 1881–1944 •*English prelate and Archbishop of Canterbury*• Born in Exeter, the son of **Frederick Temple**, he was educated at Oxford, where he became a Fellow of Queen's College (1904–10). He became ordained in 1908, was headmaster of Repton School (1910–14) and became a canon of Westminster in 1919. He then became successively Bishop of Manchester (1921–29), Archbishop of York (1929–42) and Archbishop of Canterbury (1942–44). He was an outspoken advocate of social reform, combining humanity with great administrative ability. His leadership was also seen in his chairmanship of the Doctrinal Commission of the Church of England and in his work for the Ecumenical Movement of Christian Union. His publications include *Church and Nation* (1915) and *Christianity and the Social Order* (1942).

“ ”

Personally, I have always looked upon cricket as organized loafing.

c. 1914 Address to parents of pupils at Repton School, Derbyshire.

Temple, William *See* **Bull, Phil**

Templer, Sir Gerald 1898–1979 •*English soldier*• Educated at Wellington College and Sandhurst, he served in World War I. In World War II he became commander of the Sixth Armored Division. He was vice-chief of the Imperial General Staff (1948–50), and chief of the Imperial General Staff (1955–58). As High Commissioner and Commander in Chief Malay Peninsula (1952–54), he frustrated the Communist guerrillas' offensive.

Templewood, 1st Viscount *See* **Hoare, Sir Samuel John Gurney**

ten Boom, Corrie 1892–1983 •*Dutch evangelist and author*• Born in the Netherlands, she worked as a watchmaker in her father's shop in Haarlem, and started clubs for teenage girls. The family's wartime role in helping 700 Jews escape the Germans led to their imprisonment in 1944. On unexpected release from Ravensbruck concentration camp in 1945, she carried out plans made with her sister Betsie (who did not survive) to establish a home for rehabilitating concentration camp victims in Holland and a home for refugees in Darmstadt, Germany.

Teniers, David the Elder 1582–1649 •*Flemish genre painter*• Born in Antwerp, he generally painted homely tavern scenes, rustic games, weddings and so on. His *Temptation of St Anthony* is well known.

Teniers, David the Younger 1610–90 •*Flemish genre painter*• The son of **David Teniers** the Elder, he quickly gained distinction, becoming court painter in Brussels (from 1647) to Archduke Leopold Wilhelm of Austria, governor of the Austrian Netherlands, and curator of his art collection. His 700 pictures possess to a superlative degree the qualities that mark his father's work.

Tenniel, Sir John 1820–1914 •*English cartoonist and illustrator*• Born in London, he was a self-trained artist, and was selected in 1845 to paint one of the frescoes (**Dryden**'s "St Cecilia") in the Houses of Parliament. He was on the staff of *Punch* for 50 years (1851–1901), succeeding **John Leech** as chief cartoonist in 1864. His most celebrated cartoon was "Dropping the Pilot" (1890), referring to **Bismarck**'s dismissal. His main claim to fame, however, are his delicate illustrations for **Lewis Carroll**'s *Alice's Adventures in Wonderland* (1865) and *Through the Looking-Glass* (published in December 1871, dated 1872). He also illustrated **Thomas Moore**'s *Lalla Rookh* (1861), and **Richard Barham**'s *Ingoldsby Legends* (1864), among others.

Tennyson, Alfred, Lord 1809–92 •*English poet*• He was born in Lincolnshire, the fourth son of the rector of Somersby. He was educated at Louth Grammar School, and in 1827 went to Trinity College, Cambridge. In 1829 he won a prize with the blank-verse poem "Timbuctoo," but his other early ventures in verse, *Poems Chiefly Lyrical* (1830) and *Poems* (1833), were slighted by the critics of the day as being too sentimental; the critics also failed to recognize a great poet in the first version of "The Lady of Shallott," "Oenone," "The Lotus-Eaters" and other poems in the 1833 volume. Nine years of revising these poems and adding fresh material resulted in the volume of *Poems* of 1842, which established Tennyson's fame. A greater achievement was the completion of the elegiac poem *In Memoriam* (1850). Also in 1850 he succeeded **William Wordsworth** as poet laureate and married Emily Sarah Sellwood. In 1853 he settled in a house on the Isle of Wight, Farringford, where he wrote "The Charge of the Light Brigade," and in 1868 built Aldworth in Sussex as a summer home. He was flattered by the homage of the entire nation from Queen **Victoria** downward, such was his popularity. He undertook short tours with his wife, but rarely left his Victorian England. After 1850 he devoted himself to the fashionable verse novelette: *Maud: A Monodrama* (1855), *Enoch Arden* (1864), and *Locksley Hall Sixty Years After* (1886). From 1859 to 1885 he published *Idylls of the King* (1859), a sequence of poems based on Arthurian legend that were extremely popular. In the 1870s he wrote a number of plays, of which *Becket*, produced by Sir **Henry Irving** in 1893, was the most successful. He continued to write poetry, and his last poem was a 16-line lyric written in 1889 while crossing from Lymington to the Isle of Wight, *Crossing the Bar*.

" "

For men may come and men may go,
But I go on for ever.

1855 "The Brook," l. 33–34.

Tenzing Norgay, *known as* **Sherpa Tenzing** 1914–86 •*Nepalese mountaineer*• Born in Tsa-chu, near Makalu, he made his first climb as a porter with a British expedition to Everest in 1935. In the years following, he climbed many of the Himalayan peaks, and on two later attempts on the ascent of Everest he reached 23,000 feet in 1938 and 28,215 feet in 1952. In 1953 he, with **Edmund Hillary**, succeeded in reaching the summit of Everest, and for this triumph he was awarded the George Medal. He was later appointed head of the Institute of Mountaineering and president of the Sherpa Association.

Terborch or **Terburg, Gerard the Younger** c. 1617–81 •*Dutch painter*• Born in Zwolle, he studied with his father. He was precociously talented, and his earliest dated drawing (now in the Rijksmuseum, Amsterdam) is from 1625. He visited England (1635), Italy (1640) and Germany, where he painted *The Peace Congress of Münster* (1648, National Gallery, London). From 1654 to his death he lived at Deventer, where he became burgomaster. He worked mostly on a small scale, producing genre pictures and fashionable portraits.

Terence, *properly* **Publius Terentius Afer** c. 195–159 BC •*Roman comic dramatist*• Born in Carthage, he became the slave of the Roman senator P Terentius Lucanus, who brought him to Rome, educated him, and freed him. His first play was the *Andria* (166 BC, "The Girl from Andros"). Its success introduced Terence to the most refined society of Rome and gained him the patronage of Laelius and **Scipio Aemilianus** the Younger. Six of his comedies are still extant: *Andria* (166 BC), *Hecyra* (165 BC, "Mother-in-Law"), *Heauton timoroumenos* (163 BC, "Self-Tormentor"), *Eunuchus* (161 BC), *Phormio* (161 BC), and *Adelphi* (160 BC, "Brothers"). They are Greek in origin and scene, and four of them are directly based on **Menander**. Many of his conventions and plot constructions were later used by **Molière**, **Richard Brinsley Sheridan**, and other European dramatists.

" "

Fortes Fortuna adiuvat.
Fortune favors the brave.

161 BC ***Phormio**, 203.*

Teresa or **Theresa of Ávila, St**, *also called* **Santa Teresa de Jesus** 1515–82 •*Spanish mystic, writer and first woman Doctor of the Church*• Born in Ávila, she entered a Carmelite convent there in 1533. She became well known for her asceticism and sanctity. To reestablish the ancient Carmelite rule, she founded the first of her 16 religious houses in 1562, and in 1568 helped St **John of the Cross** found the first community of reformed Carmelite friars. The most famous of her works are her autobiography, *Libro de la vida* (1562, "The Way of Perfection"), *Libro de las fundaciones* (1610, "The Book of Foundations"), which describes the journeys she made and the convents she founded or reformed, and *Las moradas* (1577, Eng trans *The Interior Castle*, 1852). She was canonized in 1622, and her feast day is October 15.

Teresa of Calcutta, Mother, *originally* **Agnes Gonxha Bojaxhiu** 1910–97 •*Roman Catholic nun, missionary, and Nobel Prize winner*• She was born in Skopje (now in Macedonia) to Albanian parents. She went to India in 1928, where she joined the Irish order of the Sisters of Loretto and taught at a convent school in Calcutta, taking her final vows in 1937. She became principal of the school, but in 1948 felt called to help the poor and left the convent to work alone in the slums. She undertook a weeklong course in basic nursing in Patna in the Indian state of Bihar. She was gradually joined in the slums by other nuns, and she opened her House for the Dying in 1952. Her religious order, the Order of the Missionaries of Charity, was founded in 1950 and became a pontifical congregation (answering directly to the pope) in 1956. The congregation now runs over 650 charity houses in 124 countries. In 1957 she started work with lepers and established a leper colony called Shanti Nagar ("Town of Peace") near Asansol in West Bengal. She was awarded the Pope John XXIII Peace Prize in 1971 and the Nobel Peace Prize in 1979 and was beatified in 2003.

Tereshkova, Valentina Vladimirovna 1937– •*Russian astronaut*• Born in Maslennikovo, she was the first woman to fly in space. She worked in a textile factory and qualified as a sports parachutist before training as a cosmonaut (1962). She was the solo crew member in the three-day *Vostok 6* flight of June 16. She was made a Hero of the Soviet Union, and became a member of the Central Committee of the Soviet Communist Party in 1971. Since 1992 she has chaired the Russian Association of International Cooperation.

Terkel, Studs (Louis) 1912– •*US writer and oral historian*• Born in New York City, he studied law at the University of Chicago. He acted in radio soap operas, worked as a disc jockey, a radio commentator and a television host, and has traveled worldwide conducting interviews. Described by **J K Galbraith** as "a national resource," he has published *Giants of Jazz* (1957), *Hard Times* (1970), which recalls the Depression, *Working* (1974), *American Dreams: Lost and Found* (1980), *The Good War: An Oral History of World War Two* (1984, Pulitzer Prize), and *Coming of Age* (1995).

Terman, Lewis Madison 1877–1956 •*US psychologist, pioneer of intelligence tests*• He was born in Johnson County, Indiana. At Stanford University he developed an English version of the **Binet-Simon** intelligence test and introduced Terman Group Intelligence

Tests into the US Army in 1920. He pioneered the use of the term IQ (Intelligence Quotient) in his *The Measurement of Intelligence* (1916).

Terry, Dame (Alice) Ellen 1848–1928 •*English actress*• Born in Coventry, she was the daughter of a provincial actor and the sister of **Fred Terry**. From 1862 she played in Bristol, and after a brief marriage to the painter **G F Watts** (1864) and a second retirement from the stage (1868–74) during which her two children by **E W Godwin**, Edith and **Edward Gordon Craig**, were born, she established herself as the leading Shakespearean actress in London, dominating the English and US theater (1878–1902) in partnership with **Henry Irving**. In 1903 she entered theater management and toured and lectured widely. **J M Barrie** and **George Bernard Shaw** wrote parts especially for her. She married Charles Kelly (Wardell) in 1876 and in 1907 the US actor, James Carew. She received the honorary title of Dame Commander, Order of the British Empire, in 1925.

Terry, Fred 1863–1933 •*English actor*• He was born in London, and was the brother of **Ellen Terry**. He played in the companies of **Herbert Beerbohm Tree**, **Johnston Forbes-Robertson** and **Henry Irving**, and established a reputation as a romantic actor. His sisters Kate (1844–1924), Marion and Florence were also actresses, as was his wife, **Julia Neilson**.

Terry-Thomas, *originally* **Thomas Terry Hoar-Stevens** 1911–90 •*English actor*• Born in Finchley, London, he was initially a buyer for a grocery firm, but drifted into showbusiness, appearing in cabaret, on radio and making his film debut as an extra in such productions as *Rhythm in the Air* (1936). After wartime service in the Royal Signal Corps, he worked as a standup comic in West End revues and television before returning to the cinema as upper-crust rogues and silly asses in comedies like *Carlton Browne of the FO* (1958) and *I'm All Right Jack* (1959). Gap-toothed and bowler-hatted, he became a favorite in Hollywood as a caricature of the Englishman in the 1960s with prominent roles in films like *Bachelor Flat* (1961) and *How to Murder Your Wife* (1965).

Tertullian, *in full* **Quintus Septimus Florens Tertullianus** c. 160–c. 220 AD •*North African Christian theologian*• Born in Carthage, he was brought up there as a pagan, then went to Rome, where he was converted to Christianity (c. 196 AD). His opposition to worldliness in the Church culminated in his becoming a leader of the Montanist sect c. 207, and his writings show increasing hostility to the Church. The first to produce major Christian works in Latin, he had a great influence on the development of ecclesiastical language, and also wrote against heathens, Jews and heretics. His style is vivid, vigorous and concise.

Tesla, Nikola 1856–1943 •*US physicist and electrical engineer*• Born in Smiljan, Croatia, he studied at the universities of Graz, Prague and Paris, emigrating to the US in 1884. He left the Edison Works at Menlo Park after quarreling with **Thomas Edison** and concentrated on his own inventions. Among his many projects, he improved dynamos and electric motors, invented the high-frequency Tesla coil and an air-core transformer. Firmly in favor of an alternating current (AC) electricity supply, by 1888 he had obtained patents on an AC system and in 1893 again demonstrated the feasibility of AC by lighting the 1893 Chicago World Columbian Exposition. He predicted wireless communication two years before **Guglielmo Marconi** developed it.

Tessin, Carl-Gustaf, Count 1695–1770 •*Swedish statesman, writer and art collector*• Son of **Nicodemus Tessin the Younger**, he led the anti-Russian Hat party which hoped to regain territory lost to Russia during **Karl XII**'s reign. He was elected leader of the Nobility Estate when the Hats gained a majority in 1738, and was responsible for the unsuccessful war against Russia in 1741. He gained the favor of king **Adolf Fredrik** and Queen Louisa Ulrika, and in 1746 was appointed Head of Chancellory and governor to the future king **Gustav III**, but his disapproval of their attempts to increase royal power caused him to retire from politics to write his memoirs, fables and didactic letters to the Crown Prince. His art collection forms the basis of the present National Museum and Royal Library in Stockholm.

Tessin, Nicodemus the Elder 1615–81 •*Swedish architect*• Born in Stralsund, Germany, he moved to Stockholm in 1636, where he entered the service of the Lord Chancellor, **Axel Oxenstjerna**, whose handsome castle Tidö, Västerås, he completed in 1645. He was then appointed royal architect in 1646, and city architect in Stockholm from 1661. After studying in Italy, France and Holland (1651–53), his commissions in Sweden included the *Wrangelska palatset* (1652–64), which now houses the Supreme Court in Stockholm; Kalmar Cathedral (started 1660); the Caroline Mausoleum in Riddarholm Church (1671); and the Bank of Sweden in Stockholm (1676). Most notable of all is the Palace of Drottningholm on Mälaren, completed by Tessin's son, **Nicodemus the Younger**.

Tessin, Nicodemus the Younger 1654–1728 •*Swedish architect*• Born in Nyköping, the son of **Nicodemus the Elder**, he finished his education with long periods in Rome (1673–78) and Paris (1678–80). His genius lay in his ability to borrow from baroque and French models and create a harmonious, uniquely northern, edifice. He was appointed royal architect in 1676 and succeeded his father as Stockholm city architect in 1682. He completed Drottningholm Palace and added the royal church (1690–99). Other notable structures include Steninge Castle (1694–98) and his own Tessin Palace (1696–1700), now the governor's palace. He designed ecclesiastical buildings such as Trinity Church, Karlskrona (1697–1747), and renovated others, notably Västerås Cathedral spire. His greatest achievement was the Royal Palace, Stockholm. He was the father of **Carl-Gustaf Tessin**.

Tetley, Glen 1926– •*US ballet dancer and choreographer*• Born in Cleveland, Ohio, he gave up medical studies to become a dancer and trained with **Hanya Holm** (1946–51). He shifted toward ballet, dancing with both the American Ballet Theater and as an original member of the Joffrey Ballet (1956). Working with the Netherlands Dance Theater during the 1960s, guest choreographing for Ballet Rambert, and a two-year contract with Stuttgart Ballet (1973–75) after **John Cranko**'s sudden death have given him a stronger hold and reputation in Europe. In 1986 he was commissioned by the National Ballet of Canada to choreograph *Alice*, a popular version of the **Lewis Carroll** tale. He subsequently became artistic director there. His ballets include *Pierrot lunaire* (1962), *La ronde* (1987) and *Oracle* (1994).

Tewfik Pasha, Mohammed 1852–92 •*Khedive of Egypt*• He was the eldest son of **Ismail Pasha** and succeeded on his abdication in 1879. The chief events of his reign were Arabi's insurrection (1882), the British intervention, the war with the Mahdi **Muhammad Ahmed** (1884–85), the pacification of the Sudan frontiers, and the improvement of Egypt under British administration. He was succeeded by his son **Abbas Hilmi Pasha**.

Tey, Josephine, *pseudonym of* **Elizabeth Mackintosh**, *who also wrote as* **Gordon Daviot** 1897–1952 •*Scottish crime and mystery writer*• She grew up in Inverness and trained as a physical education teacher. Her main invention, police inspector Alan Grant, tended to prefer cerebral rather than physical exercise. In *The Daughter of Time* (1952), she reopens the file on **Richard III**'s alleged murder of the little princes in the Tower of London; Grant conducts this masterpiece of retrospective investigation from his hospital bed. *Miss Pym Disposes* (1946) and *The Franchise Affair* (1948) were non-Grant mysteries, as was the popular *Brat Farrar* (1949, published in the US as *Come and Kill Me*, 1951).

Thackeray, William Makepeace 1811–63 •*English novelist*• He was born in Calcutta, India, where his father was in the service of the East India Company. His father died (1816) and his mother remarried, so Thackeray was sent home. He went to Trinity College, Cambridge (1829), but left without taking a degree. After spending much of his inheritance on traveling abroad, he began work as a journalist, and married Isabella Shawe (1836), who later gave birth to their first daughter, **Anne Thackeray Ritchie**. The birth of his third daughter, Harriett Marian (later the first wife of **Leslie Stephen**), permanently affected Mrs Thackeray's mind; the home was broken up and the children sent to their grandmother in Paris. His first publications, starting with *The Paris Sketchbook* (1840), and written under a number of pseudonyms (Wagstaff, Titmarsh, Fitz-Boodle, Yellowplush, Snob, etc), were comparative failures, although they included *The Yellowplush Papers*, *The Great Hoggarty Diamond* and *The Luck of Barry Lyndon*, all contributed to *Fraser's Magazine* (1841–44). His work on *Punch* from 1842 exploited the view of society as seen by the butler ("Jeames' Diary") and the great theme of English snobbery, and attracted attention. The great novels that were to follow—*Vanity Fair* (1847–48), *Pendennis* (1848), *Henry Esmond* (3 vols, 1852) and *The Newcomes* (1853–55), all, with the exception of *Henry Esmond*, monthly serials, established his fame. *Vanity Fair* is the first novel to give a view of London society with its mingling of rich parvenus and decadent upper class, through both of which the social climber, Becky Sharp, threads her way. The great historical novel, *Henry Esmond*, shows Thackeray's consuming love of the 18th century. Its sequel, *The Virginians* (1857–59), is not considered a success. *The Newcomes* shows a young love at the mercy of scheming relatives and mean-spirited rival suitors. Thackeray retired from *Punch* in 1854 and became the editor of the *Cornhill Magazine*, where much of his later work appeared. He also undertook lecturing tours at home and in the US, the fruit of which included *The English Humorists of the 18th Century* (1853) and *The Four Georges* (1860).

" "

If a man's character is to be abused, say what you will, there's nobody like a relation to do the business.

*1847–48 Miss Crawley. **Vanity Fair**, chapter 19.*

Thaddeus, St *See* **Judas, St**

Thais 4th century BC •*Greek courtesan*• She was born in Athens. Famous for her wit and beauty, she was, according to a doubtful legend, the mistress of **Alexander the Great**, whom she induced to burn down Persepolis. She had several children by Ptolemy Lagos.

Thalberg, Irving G(rant) 1899–1936 •*US film executive*• Born in New York City, he became a secretary at Universal Studios. He rose swiftly in the company to become general manager and later played a key role in the formation of MGM. As head of production, he was renowned for meticulous attention to detail and an obsessive devotion to his work. Among the films he helped put into production were *Grand Hotel* (1932), *Mutiny on the Bounty* (1935) and *Camille* (1936). He was married to the actress Norma Shearer (1900–83).

Thales c. 620–c. 555 BC •*Greek natural philosopher, astronomer and geometer*• He came from Miletus on mainland Ionia, Asia Minor. He is traditionally the founder of Greek, and therefore European, philosophy, and is important for having proposed the first natural cosmology, identifying water as the basis of the universe. He seems to have had wide-ranging practical and intellectual interests, with a reputation as a politician, engineer, geometer and astronomer. He was included in the traditional canon of "Seven Wise Men," and attracted various apocryphal anecdotes, for example, as the original absent-minded professor who would fall into a well while watching the stars. He left no writings, except possibly a nautical star guide.

Thant, U 1909–74 •*Burmese diplomat*• Born in Pantanaw, he became a schoolmaster under **Thakin Nu**, the future prime minister, whom he later succeeded as headmaster of Pantanaw National High School. He became a civil servant when Burma became independent in 1948 and became Burma's UN representative in 1957. As secretary-general of the UN (1962–71) after the death of **Dag Hammarskjöld**, he played a major diplomatic role during the Cuban Missile Crisis. He also formulated a plan to end the Congolese civil war (1962) and mobilized a UN peace-keeping force in Cyprus (1964).

Tharp, Twyla 1941– •*US dancer and choreographer*• Born in Portland, Indiana, she earned a degree in art history from Barnard College. She studied with **Martha Graham** and **Merce Cunningham**, and danced with the **Paul Taylor** Dance Company (1963–65) before founding her own small troupe in 1965. She became known for her ability to create modern dance with a popular appeal without losing either integrity or depth, and her early work was both structural and somber. But from *Eight Jelly Rolls* (1971, set to the jazz piano music of **Jelly Roll Morton**), she introduced a humorous, flippant note which charmed audiences. *Coupe*, a piece made to music by the Beach Boys (see **Brian Wilson**) for the Joffrey Ballet in 1973, was a notable success, as was *Push Comes to Shove* (1976), the first dance made by a US choreographer for the Russian star **Mikhail Baryshnikov**, then at the American Ballet Theater. Subsequent works include *Bach Partita* (1984), *Cutting Up* (1992, for Baryshnikov) and *Jump Start* (1995).

Tharpe, Sister Rosetta, *née* **Rubin** 1915–73 •*US gospel and blues singer*• Born in Cotton Plant, Arkansas, she sang and accompanied herself on electric guitar, switching without discomfort between sacred songs and very earthy blues material. With the important exception of **Mahalia Jackson**, she has been the most successful female gospel performer ever, with wartime hits like "Didn't It Rain" (1944). She recorded doggedly through her last years, despite losing a leg due to a thrombosis which also impaired her speech.

Thatch, Edward *See* **Teach, Edward**

Thatcher, Margaret Hilda Thatcher, Baroness, *née* **Roberts** 1925– •*English Conservative politician, the first woman to be prime minister of Great Britain (1979–90)*• She was born in Grantham, the daughter of Alderman Alfred Roberts, a grocer and lay Methodist minister. She was educated at Grantham High School and at Somerville College, Oxford, where she studied chemistry. In 1951 she married a wealthy businessman, Denis Thatcher (1915–2003). She went on to study law and was called to the bar in Lincoln's Inn in 1954. In 1959 she was elected Member of Parliament for Finchley, and after holding junior office, she became secretary of state for education and science (1970–74) and made herself widely unpopular by abolishing free milk for schoolchildren over the age of eight. In 1975 she replaced **Edward Heath** as leader of the Conservative Party to become the first woman party leader in British politics. The Conservative Party was elected to govern in May 1979 and devoted its energies to combating inflation, achieved at the cost of high unemployment (which doubled from 1979 to 1980) and reduced manufacturing output. Nonetheless, she was reelected with a majority of 144 in June 1983, her personal popularity having been greatly boosted by the recapture of the Falkland Islands from Argentina the previous year, and by the disarray in the opposition parties. In 1983 she was also elected a Fellow of the Royal Society. In their second term under her leadership, the Conservatives moved toward a more right-wing position, placing considerable emphasis on the market economy and the shedding of public-sector commitments through an extensive privatization program. Major legislation to reduce the power of the unions followed. A miners' strike that began in the early part of 1984 lasted for 12 months without success, because the government had foreseen it and taken extensive precautionary measures. In October 1984, an IRA bomb exploded at the Conservative Party Conference in Brighton, and she narrowly escaped being killed. Thatcher was returned for a third term in the 1987 general election with a majority of 102. After ten years in office she had established a personal political philosophy identified as Thatcherism, based on individualism, the operation of market forces, and minimum intervention by (and support from) the state in people's lives. In 1988 she became Britain's longest-serving prime minister of the century. From 1989 the tide of events turned decisively against her. The introduction of the community charge (popularly called the poll tax) was widely unpopular and led to public demonstrations. Her resistance to the growing influence of other EC member states over the British economy and to their plans for economic union led to the resignation of Chancellor **Nigel Lawson** and of Foreign Secretary **Geoffrey Howe** in 1990. Her leadership was challenged, and in November 1990, after a challenge in the first round of voting by Michael Heseltine, she resigned as leader and was succeeded by **John Major**. In 1992 she was created a life peer.

" "

There is no such thing as society. There are individual men and women, and there are families.

*1987 In **Woman's Own**, October 31.*

Thaw, John Edward 1942–2002 •*English actor*• Born in Manchester, he trained at the Royal Academy of Dramatic Art and worked in theater for much of the 1960s and 1970s. He became known to a wider audience as the hard-bitten detective Inspector

Jack Regan in the television series *The Sweeney* (1974–78), and scored further successes in the title parts of *Kavanagh QC* (1994–98) and *Inspector Morse* (1986–2001). His film work included *Cry Freedom* (1987). He was married to the actress **Sheila Hancock**.

Theaetetus c. 414–c. 369 BC •*Greek mathematician*• He was an associate of **Plato** at the Academy, whose work was later used by **Euclid** in Books X and XIII of the *Elements*. Plato named after him the dialogue *Theaetetus*, which was devoted to the nature of knowledge.

Themistocles c. 523–c. 458 BC •*Athenian politician and naval strategist*• He persuaded the Athenians to develop Piraeus as a port (493 BC) and use their rich silver deposits to expand their fleet (483). The fleet won a naval victory over the Persians, led by **Xerxes**, at Salamis (480), and laid the foundations of the Athenian maritime empire. The pro-Spartan faction in Athens plotted his downfall and he fled to Asia. **Artaxerxes I** of Persia received him with great favor and made him governor of Magnesia on the Maeander.

Thénard, Louis Jacques 1777–1857 •*French organic chemist and politician*• Born in La Louptière, the son of a peasant farmer, he went to Paris in search of an education. In 1798 he was appointed demonstrator at the École Polytechnique; he later succeeded Vauquelin in the chair at the Collège de France (1804), became dean of the Faculty of Sciences at Paris (1821) and was chancellor of the University of France (1845–1852). He also served two terms in the Chamber of Deputies. Thénard made many important discoveries in organic chemistry and prepared a wide range of esters. He investigated cobalt and its compounds, and from alumina and copper arsenate prepared a stable brilliant blue pigment (Thénard's blue) which was used in porcelain manufacture to replace the expensive pigments made from lapis lazuli. Between 1808 and 1811 he collaborated with **Joseph Louis Gay-Lussac** to study potassium, and they discovered boron (1808). In 1818 Thénard announced the discovery of hydrogen peroxide, perhaps his greatest achievement.

Theobald or **Tebaldus** d. 1161 •*English ecclesiastic*• Born near Bec, Normandy, France, he became a monk at Bec, then abbot (1137) and in 1138 became Archbishop of Canterbury. He crowned King **Stephen** in Canterbury, and after the latter's death eventually crowned **Henry II** (1154). He advanced his archdeacon, **Thomas à Becket**, to the chancellorship in 1155, and resisted all attempts by the monasteries to throw off episcopal jurisdiction.

Theocritus c. 310–250 BC •*Greek pastoral poet*• Born probably in Syracuse, Sicily, he was brought up on the island of Cos. The authenticity of some of his 30 extant bucolic poems has been disputed. He wrote a series of poems dealing with heroic legend, especially that of Heracles, and his famous 15th Idyll, *Syracusii* ("The Ladies of Syracuse"), is said to be copied from Sophron. His short pastoral poems, representing a single scene, came to be called Idylls *(eidullia)*. **Virgil** imitates him in his *Eclogues*, and **Tennyson** was influenced by him, as were the pastoral poets of the Renaissance.

Theodora c. 500–48 •*Byzantine empress*• The wife of **Justinian I**, she was the daughter of a circus bear tamer. An actress, she married Justinian in 525 and was empress from 527. As his most trusted counselor, she had enormous influence over government, and probably saved the throne during the Nika riots (532). She was very charitable, especially to women. There is a famous mosaic portrait of her in the Church of San Vitale, Ravenna.

Theodorakis, Mikis 1925– •*Greek composer*• Born in Khios, he studied at the Paris Conservatoire. His first ballet, *Antigone*, was produced in 1959 at Covent Garden, London. He returned to Greece (1961), and when the right-wing government took power in 1967, he was imprisoned and his music banned, but after worldwide appeals he was released (1970). Often inspired by the history, traditions, and folk tunes of Greece, his prolific musical output includes oratorios, ballets, song cycles, and music for film scores, the best known of which is *Zorba the Greek* (1965). He published an autobiography in 1986.

Theodore of Canterbury, St, *also called* **Theodore of Tarsus** c. 602–90 •*Greek prelate*• Born in Tarsus, Cilicia, to Greek parents, he was consecrated Archbishop of Canterbury by Pope Vitalian in 668. In Canterbury he established a Greek school and organized the administrative system of the English Church. His feast day is September 19.

Theodoric or **Theoderic the Great**, *known in Germany as* **Dietrich von Bern** c. 455–526 AD •*King of the Ostrogoths*• He founded the Ostrogothic monarchy. He became king (AD 475) and was later permitted by Emperor **Zeno** to take Italy from **Odoacer** (493). His reign secured for Italy tranquillity and prosperity. The Goths and the Romans remained distinct but harmonious nations, and religious freedom was permitted. His official letters show his great energy and enlightened zeal for his subjects' welfare. The judicial murders of **Boethius** and Symmachus, and acts of oppression against the Catholic Church, occurred during his last three years. To the Germans he is Dietrich von Bern, and one of the great heroes of legend, figuring in the *Nibelungenlied* ("Song of the Nibelungs").

Theodoric I d. 451 AD •*King of the Visigoths*• The son of **Alaric I**, he was elected king in AD 418. He betrayed the Romans (c. 421) and joined the Vandals. In 435 he attacked the Romans in Gaul and besieged Narbonne. He was forced to retreat to Toulouse, where he defeated a Roman army (439). On the invasion of **Attila** (451), he joined the Romans under **Aëtius**, and at Troyes commanded the right wing. He drove back the Huns under Attila but was killed.

Theodoric II d. 466 AD •*King of the Visigoths*• The son of **Theodoric I**, he rebelled against and assassinated his brother and predecessor Thorismund, taking the throne in AD 453. His initial policy was to spread Gothic dominion in Spain and Gaul through the Roman alliance. In 456 he broke his friendship with Rome and besieged Arles, but was forced by Emperor Majorian to make peace. In 462 he made another attempt in Gaul, but was defeated near Orléans (464). He was murdered by his brother Euric, who succeeded him.

Theodosius I (the Great) c. 347–95 AD •*Roman emperor*• The son of Theodosius the Elder (d. 367 AD), he was born in Cauca in northwest Spain. He was appointed by **Gratian** as his coemperor in the East (379). He campaigned against the Goths, but allowed them to settle within the Roman Empire (382). He secured peace with the Persian Sassanids by partitioning Armenia (c. 386). When the usurper **Magnus Maximus** expelled **Valentinian II** from Italy (387), Theodosius marched west and defeated and killed him at Aquileia (388). He was a devout Christian, and St **Ambrose** had great influence over him. In 392 Valentinian II was murdered, and in 394 Theodosius marched against the Franks and their puppet emperor, Eugenius. He defeated Eugenius, and for the remaining four months of his life ruled as sole Roman emperor. In 381 he affirmed the Nicene Creed, pursued heretics and pagans, and in 391 ordered the closing of all temples and banned all forms of pagan cult.

Theophanes the Greek c. 1370–c. 1405 •*Russian-Byzantine painter*• He was born probably in Greece, but active mainly in Russia. His early works in Constantinople (Istanbul) and the Crimea are lost, but his extant frescoes in the Church of Our Savior of the Transfiguration at Novgorod (from 1378) are some of the finest examples of Russian medieval art. He was also famous as a book illustrator (manuscripts in Moscow), and for his icons in Moscow (1395–1405).

Theophano c. 955–91 •*Byzantine princess and Holy Roman empress*• The daughter of the Byzantine emperor Romanus II, she married King **Otto II** in 972 in Rome as a symbol of the union of the Eastern and Western Empires. He ruled as Holy Roman emperor, with Theophano as empress, from 973 until his death in 983. She took an active role in politics, and with her mother-in-law **Adelaide** secured the throne for her son, **Otto III**, on his father's death, ruling as coregent from 983 to 991.

Theophrastus c. 372–c. 286 BC •*Greek philosopher*• Born in Eresus, Lesbos, he studied at Athens under **Plato** and became the close friend of **Aristotle**. He became head of the Peripatetic School (Lyceum) after Aristotle's death (322 BC) and is responsible for preserving many of Aristotle's works. Most of his own prolific output is lost, but surviving work includes important treatises on plants, reconstructed fragments of his history of the pre-Socratic philosophers, and the widely translated and imitated volume of *Characters*, containing 30 deft sketches of different moral types.

Theorell, (Axel) Hugo Teodor 1903–82 •*Swedish biochemist and Nobel Prize winner*• Born in Linköping, he studied medicine at the Karolinska Institute, Stockholm, held posts at Uppsala University (1930–36), and became director of the Nobel Institute of Biochemistry at Stockholm (1937–70). He crystallized myoglobin (the oxygen storage protein of muscle) and determined its molecular weight (1932). In Berlin in 1934 he separated the yellow coenzyme (flavine mononucleotide) from the protein and examined its properties. On his return to Uppsala he purified diphtheria antitoxin (1937) and went on to introduce fluorescence spectrometry. He was awarded the 1955 Nobel Prize for physiology or medicine.

Theresa of Ávila, St *See* **Teresa of Ávila, St**

Theresa of Calcutta, Mother *See* **Teresa of Calcutta, Mother**

Thérèse of Lisieux, St, *originally* **Marie Françoise Thérèse Martin**, *also called* **The Little Flower** *and* **St Theresa of the Child Jesus** 1873–97 •*French nun and virgin saint*• Born in Alençon, at the age of 15 she entered the Carmelite convent of Lisieux in Normandy, where she remained until her death from tuberculosis nine years later. She wrote an account of her childhood and later life which was edited and published posthumously as *Histoire d'une âme* (1898, "Story of a Soul"). Showing how the most ordinary person can attain sainthood by following her "little way" of simple, childlike, trusting Christianity, the book immediately gained great popularity. She was canonized in 1925, and in 1947 was associated with **Joan of Arc** as patron saint of France. Her feast day is October 1.

Theroux, Paul Edward 1941– •*US writer*• Born in Medford, Massachusetts, he has led a footloose life that is reflected in his literary output. *Waldo* (1969), his first novel, was followed by fictions based on three years spent in Africa. He subsequently taught at Singapore University (1968–71), a sojourn that resulted in a collection of short stories, *Sinning with Annie* (1976), and a novel, *Saint Jack* (1973, filmed 1979). Other novels, for example *The Family Arsenal* (1976) and *The London Embassy* (1982), have been based in London. *Millroy the Magician* (1993) was a quantum step, concentrating themes and ideas that have surfaced throughout his career. His extended rail journeys are recounted in *The Great Railway Bazaar: By Train Through Asia* (1975) and *The Old Patagonian Express: By Train Through the Americas* (1979). Other works include *The Mosquito Coast* (1981, James Tait Black Memorial Prize, filmed 1987) and *Fresh-Air Fiend* (2000).

Thesiger, Sir Wilfred Patrick 1910–2003 •*English explorer*• He was born in Addis Ababa, Abyssinia (now Ethiopia), where his father was British minister in charge of the legation. Educated at Eton and Oxford, in 1933 he returned to Abyssinia to hunt with the Danakil tribes, exploring the Sultanate of Aussa. In 1935 he joined the Sudan Political Service and while on leave traveled by camel across the Sahara to the Tibesti Mountains. He was transferred to the Sudan Defense Force and fought in Africa in World War II. From 1945 to 1950 he explored the Empty Quarter of southern Arabia and the borderlands of Oman, which he described in *Arabian Sands* (1959). From 1951 to 1958 he lived with the Marsh Arabs of Iraq and published *The Marsh Arabs* in 1964. He first traveled in East Africa in 1961, and returned to live with tribal peoples there from 1968 onwards. His autobiography, *The Life of My Choice*, was published in 1987, followed by *My Kenya Days* in 1994. He was knighted in 1995.

Thespis 6th century BC •*Greek poet, the reputed founder of Greek drama*• He came from Icaria, and is said to have won the first prize for tragedy at a festival in Athens in c. 534 BC. According to **Aristotle**, he used single actors to deliver speeches, in addition to the traditional chorus, the first to do so.

Thiers, (Louis) Adolphe 1797–1877 •*French statesman and historian*• Born in Marseilles, he studied law at Aix-en-Provence. He held many posts in the government of **Louis Philippe**, and was twice prime minister (1836, 1839). He supported **Napoleon III** in 1848, but was arrested and banished in the coup d'état of 1851. He was allowed, however, to return the next year. After the collapse of the empire during the Franco-Prussian War, he became head of the provisional government, suppressed the Paris Commune, and was elected first president of the Third Republic (1871–73). His most ambitious literary work was the 20-volume *L'histoire du consulat et de l'empire* (1845–62, "History of the Consulate and the Empire").

Thieu, Nguyen Van *See* **Nguyen Van Thieu**

Thirkell, Angela Margaret, *née* **Mackail** 1891–1961 •*English novelist*• Born in London, she was the granddaughter of Sir **Edward Burne-Jones**, and cousin of **Rudyard Kipling**. She wrote more than 30 novels set in Barsetshire, dealing with the descendants of characters from **Anthony Trollope**'s Barsetshire novels, including *Coronation Summer* (1937), *Growing Up* (1943) and *The Duke's Daughter* (1951). Her son was the novelist Colin MacInnes (1914–79).

Thistlewood, Arthur 1770–1820 •*English conspirator*• Born in Tupholme, Lincolnshire, he served in the army. Full of revolutionary ideas from his time in the US and France, he organized a mutiny at Spa Fields (1816) and in 1820 the Cato Street Conspiracy to murder Viscount **Castlereagh** and other ministers who were dining with Lord Harrowby. The conspirators were arrested, and Thistlewood, with four others, was convicted of high treason and was hanged and then publicly decapitated.

Thom, René Frédéric 1923– •*French mathematician*• Born in Montbéliard, he studied at the École Normale Supérieure, and worked at the Universities of Grenoble and Strasbourg, where he became professor. In 1958 he was awarded the Fields Medal (the mathematical equivalent of the Nobel Prize). His work has been in algebraic topology, where he helped to create the powerful theory known as cobordism theory, and on the singularity theory of differentiable manifolds, but he is best known for his book *Stabilité structurelle et morphogénèse* (1972, "Structural Stability and Morphogenesis"), which introduced catastrophe theory. This has been applied to widely differing situations, from the development of the human embryo to physical phenomena such as breaking waves.

Thomas, St 1st century AD •*One of the 12 Apostles of Jesus* • He is most prominent in **John**'s Gospel, where he is also called Didymus (the Twin), and where he is portrayed as doubting the Resurrection until he touches the wounds of the risen Christ (John 20). Early church traditions describe him subsequently as a missionary to the Parthians or a martyr in India. Many later apocryphal works bear his name. He is the patron saint of Portugal, and his feast day is December 21.

Thomas à Becket *See* **Becket, Thomas (à)**

Thomas à Kempis *See* **Kempis, Thomas à**

Thomas Aquinas, St *See* **Aquinas, St Thomas**

Thomas of Hereford, St *See* **Cantelupe, St Thomas de**

Thomas, (Martha) Carey 1857–1935 •*US feminist and educator*• Born in Baltimore, Maryland, into a Quaker family, she was educated privately and at Cornell University. She wanted to take a PhD at the newly founded Johns Hopkins University, but was allowed to attend only if she concealed herself behind a screen. Eventually the Swiss allowed her to take her PhD at Zurich (1882), and on her return she helped establish Bryn Mawr College for women in Philadelphia, being appointed its first dean. She was also Professor of English at Bryn Mawr, and later president (1894–1922). She was the first president of the National College Women's Equal Suffrage League in 1908, and later an active member of the National American Woman Suffrage Association.

Thomas, D(onald) M(itchell) 1935– •*English poet and novelist*• Born in Cornwall, he was educated in Australia and at New College, Oxford. He learned Russian while in national service, and has published numerous translations. His early poems, which range across science fiction, erotica, and evocations of his native Cornwall, were represented in *Selected Poems* (1983). His later poems include *The Puberty Tree: New and Selected Poems* (1992). His first two novels, *The Flute Player* (1979) and *Birthstone* (1980), have been overshadowed by the powerful, semifantastic meditation on Freudian psychology, *The White Hotel* (1981). His other fiction includes *Charlotte* (2000).

Thomas, (Edward) Donnall 1920– •*US physician and hematologist, and Nobel Prize winner*• Born in Mart, Texas, he studied at the University of Texas at Austin, then at the Harvard Medical School. After various posts, he joined the Mary Imogene Bassett Hospital in Cooperstown, where he worked on bone marrow transplantation. Becoming professor at the University of Washington School of Medicine, Seattle (1963–90, then emeritus), he used tissue-typing techniques and drugs which suppress the immune system to enable bone marrow transplants in the treatment of leukemia, aplastic anemia and certain genetic diseases. He joined the Fred Hutchinson Cancer Research Center in 1975, and shared the 1990 Nobel Prize for physiology or medicine with **Joseph Edward Murray**.

Thomas, Dylan Marlais 1914–53 •*Welsh poet*• Born in Swansea, he was the son of a schoolmaster. He worked for a time as a reporter and established himself with the publication of *Eighteen Poems* in 1934, in which year he moved to London, later settling permanently back in Wales at Laugharne (1949). In 1937 he married Caitlin Macnamara and published *Twenty-Five Poems*. His other works include *The Map of Love* (1939), *Portrait of the Artist as a Young Dog* (1940), *The World I Breathe* (1940), *Deaths and Entrances* (1946) and a scenario, *The Doctor and the Devils*. His *Collected Poems, 1934–52*, were published in 1952. From 1944 he worked intermittently on a radio "play for voices" about a Welsh seaside village, and in its first form it was called *Quite Early One Morning*. Thomas expanded it into *Under Milk Wood*, taking part in a reading of it in New York just before his death from chronic alcohol abuse. *Under Milk Wood* was immediately comprehensible, funny and fresh, with moments of lyric tenderness. It had a second success as a stage play and inspired a jazz suite by **Stan Tracey** (1965). In 1955 an unfinished novel, *Adventures in the Skin Trade*, was published.

“ ”

Straightfaced in his cunning sleep he pulls the legs of his dreams.

1954 ***Under Milk Wood.***

Thomas, (Philip) Edward, *pseudonym of* **Edward Eastaway** 1878–1917 •*British poet and nature writer*• Born in London to Welsh parents, he was educated at St Paul's School and Lincoln College, Oxford. He became a writer of reviews, critical studies, biographies and topographical works, but only realized his potential as a poet during active service in World War I. *Six Poems* was published in 1916. He died in action at Arras (April 1917) before the publication of *Poems* (1917), under his pseudonym. His poetry was rooted in the English tradition of nature poetry, but broke with the Georgian tradition in its lack of rhetoric and formality and in its emphasis on the austerity of Nature and solitariness of man.

Thomas, George Henry 1816–70 •*US general*• Born in Southampton County, Virginia, he trained at West Point. In the Civil War he joined the Union army in 1861, and in January 1862 won the Battle of Mill Springs. He saved the Battle of Stones River, and at Chickamauga again made victory a barren one for the Confederates (September 1863). In November 1863, he captured Mission Ridge. In 1864 he commanded the center in General **William Sherman**'s advance on Atlanta, was sent to oppose **John B Hood** in Tennessee in December and won the Battle of Nashville. He afterward commanded the military division of the Pacific.

Thomas, Margaret Haig, Viscountess Rhondda 1883–1958 •*Welsh feminist*• Born in London, she studied, briefly, at Somerville College, Oxford, before the time when women were allowed to graduate, and became a suffragist. On the death of her father (David Alfred Thomas, 1st Viscount **Rhondda**) in 1918, she attempted to take her seat in the House of Lords as Viscountess Rhondda, but was kept out after legal proceedings. In 1920 she founded *Time and Tide*, a weekly journal of politics and literature, publishing material which was boycotted elsewhere, such as **George Orwell**'s exposé of Stalinist repression in Republican Spain.

Thomas, Norman Mattoon 1884–1968 •*US socialist leader*• Born in Marion, Ohio, and educated at Bucknell University and Princeton, he studied theology and was ordained a Presbyterian minister, becoming pastor of East Harlem Church in New York City (1911–31). Horrified by the poverty he encountered, he became a pacifist and socialist. He founded and edited *The World Tomorrow* (1918–21), helped found the American Civil Liberties Union in 1920, worked as associate editor on the *Nation* weekly (1921–22), and was codirector of the League for Industrial Democracy (1922–37).

Thomas, R(onald) S(tuart) 1913–2000 •*Welsh poet and priest*• Born in Cardiff, and educated at the University College of North Wales, Bangor, he trained for the church and was ordained a priest in 1937, becoming rector of Manafon (1942–54), and vicar of Eglwyfach (1954–67) and of St Hywyn, Aberdaron (1967–78). He became noticed outside Wales with the publication of *Song at the Year's Turning* (1955). His later volumes include *Poetry for Supper* (1958), *Laboratories of the Spirit* (1976) and *Between Here and Now* (1981). He also wrote *Experimenting with an Amen* (1986) and *No Truce with the Furies* (1995). He published an autobiography, *Neb*, in 1985.

Thomas, Sidney Gilchrist 1850–85 •*English metallurgist*• Born in Canonbury, North London, and educated at Dulwich College, he also attended evening classes in chemistry at the Birkbeck Institution and studied metallurgy at the Royal School of Mines. In 1878 he announced that, with the help of his cousin **Percy Gilchrist** and Edward Martin, he had discovered how to remove phosphorus from steel by using dolomite for the furnace lining, together with an addition of lime. This method was described as the "basic **Bessemer** process" in Great Britain, but was always known as the "Thomas process" on the Continent. Within a few years, the same principles were applied to the Siemens open-hearth furnace.

Thompson, Benjamin *See* **Rumford, Benjamin Thompson, Count**

Thompson, Daley (Francis Morgan) 1958– •*English athlete*• Born in London, he became a specialist in the decathlon and won the gold medal at the Olympic Games of 1980 and 1984. He was victorious in the 1983 World Championships, but at Seoul in 1988 was affected by injury and came in fourth. He broke the world record four times between 1980 and 1984. He retired in 1992.

Thompson, Emma 1959– •*English actress*• Born in London and educated at Cambridge, she began her career with the Cambridge Footlights and asserted her dramatic capabilities in **John Byrne**'s television series *Tutti Frutti* (1987). She married **Kenneth Branagh** in 1989 (separated 1995), and appeared opposite him on stage in *Look Back in Anger* (1989) and in such films as *Henry V* (1989), *Peter's Friends* (1992) and *Much Ado About Nothing* (1993). Her other films include *Howards End* (1992), for which she received the Academy Award for Best Actress, *The Remains of the Day* (1993), *In the Name of the Father* (1993) and *Carrington* (1995). In 1996 she received an Academy Award for her adaptation of **Jane Austen**'s *Sense and Sensibility*, in which she starred as Elinor Dashwood. She subsequently appeared in *The Winter Guest* (1996) and *Love Actually* (2003).

Thompson, Flora Jane, *née* **Timms** 1876–1947 •*English writer*• Born in Juniper Hill, Oxfordshire, she left school at the age of 14 to work in the local post office, married young and wrote mass-market fiction to help support her increasing family. During her sixties she published the semiautobiographical trilogy *Lark Rise* (1939), *Over to Candleford* (1941) and *Candleford Green* (1943, combined as *Lark Rise to Candleford*, 1945). It is a remarkable feat of observation and memory, showing the erosion of rural society before modern industrialism.

Thompson, Francis 1859–1907 •*English poet*• Born in Preston, Lancashire, he was brought up in the Catholic faith and studied for the priesthood at Ushaw College. He then turned to medicine, but failed to graduate, and moved to London, where he became an opium addict. From this he was rescued by Wilfrid and **Alice Meynell**, to whom he had sent some poems for the magazine *Merry England*. His health was restored, and he wrote several poems in the 1890s, including the well-known *Hound of Heaven*, describing God's pursuit of the human soul. His works include *Sister Songs* and *New Poems* (1897). His *Essay on Shelley* (1909) and *Life of St Ignatius Loyola* (1909) appeared posthumously.

Thompson, Hunter S(tockton) 1939– •*US journalist*• Born in Louisville, Kentucky, he is an adherent of the "new journalism," and eschews objectivity. He was the first reporter to infiltrate the Hell's Angels and he rode with them for a year, which led to his being savagely beaten up and to *Hell's Angels: A Strange and Terrible Saga* (1966). The acme of the antiestablishment, he styled his unique brand of journalism "Gonzo" and produced a stream of outspoken, outrageous books, including *Fear and Loathing in Las Vegas* (1972), *Generation of Swine* (1988), *Songs of the Damned* (1990) and *Better Than Sex* (1993). Much of his work appeared originally in magazines, and since 1985 he has contributed a weekly column to the *San Francisco Examiner*.

Thompson, John Taliaferro 1860–1940 •*US soldier and inventor*• Born in Newport, Kentucky, he graduated in 1882 from the US Military Academy at West Point. In 1920 he invented the Thompson submachine-gun, known as the Tommy gun, which was a .45 caliber gun weighing 10 pounds (4.54 kg). It was first used for military purposes by the US Marines in Nicaragua in 1925.

Thomson, Alexander, *also known as* **Greek Thomson** 1817–75 •*Scottish architect*• Born in Balfour, Stirlingshire, the seventeenth of 20 children, he spent all his professional life in Glasgow. He was apprenticed to the architect John Baird, Sr (1836), and worked in partnership from 1857 to 1871 with his brother George Thomson. As he moved away from the restrictions of orthodox classicism to experiment with new techniques and materials, his prolific output included tenement blocks, terraces, and churches, as well as offices and warehouses. He became president of the Glasgow Institute of Architects in 1871, and published statements on the theoretical basis of his work.

Thomson, D(avid) C(ouper) 1861–1954 •*Scottish newspaper proprietor*• He was born in Dundee. At the age of 23 he left the family shipping firm to take charge of the newly acquired Dundee newspaper concern, which he owned and managed until his death. Its principal publications were the *Dundee Courier and Advertiser*, the *Sunday Post*, the *Scots Magazine* and *The People's Friend*, but it was known outside Scotland particularly for its many popular children's comics, such as the *Beano* and *Dandy*. Involved in local politics, he was also a governor of the university college of Dundee for 62 years.

Thomson, Derick S(mith), *Gaelic* **Ruaraidh MacThòmais** 1921– •*Scottish poet*• Born in Stornoway, Isle of Lewis, he was educated at the Nicolson Institute in Stornoway, the University of Aberdeen, Cambridge and North Wales before serving in the RAF during World War II. He taught at the Universities of Edinburgh, Aberdeen and Glasgow. In 1952 he founded, and remains the editor of, the Gaelic language quarterly *Gairm*, and helped set up the Gaelic Books Council in 1968. He has written important critical works on Gaelic poetry, compiled a *New English-Gaelic Dictionary* (1981); and edited *The Companion to Gaelic Scotland* (1983). Much of his own poetry is collected, in both Gaelic and his own English versions, in *Creachadh na clàrsaich* (1982, *Plundering the Harp—Collected Poems 1940–1980*).

Thomson, Elihu 1853–1937 •*US inventor*• Born in Manchester, England, he emigrated with his family to the US when he was a child and was educated in Philadelphia, where he was a chemistry teacher until he decided on a career as an inventor. He became one of the pioneers of the electrical manufacturing industry in the US, cooperating in 700 patented electrical inventions, which included the three-phase alternating-current generator and arc lighting. With **Edwin J Houston**, he founded the Thomson-Houston Electric Company (1883), which merged with **Thomas Edison**'s firm in 1892 to form the General Electric Company.

Thomson, Sir George Paget 1892–1975 •*English physicist and Nobel Prize winner*• The son of **J J Thomson**, he was born and educated in Cambridge, where he became a Fellow of Trinity College. He served in the Royal Flying Corps during World War I, was Professor of Physics at the University of Aberdeen (1922–30) and Imperial College, London (1930–52), and became master of Corpus Christi at Cambridge (1952–62). In 1927 Thomson and Alexander Reid were the first to notice that a beam of electrons could produce circular interference fringes, firm evidence for **Louis-Victor de Broglie**'s theory that moving particles have wave-like properties. In 1937 Thomson shared the Nobel Prize for physics with **Clinton J L Davisson** for the discovery of electron diffraction by crystals.

Thomson, Greek *See* **Thomson, Alexander**

Thomson, James 1700–48 •*Scottish poet*• Born in Ednam, Roxburghshire, he studied for the ministry, but abandoned his studies to seek his fortune as a writer in London. He published *Winter* (1726), *Summer* (1727), *Spring*, (1728) and *Autumn*, which appeared with the other three under the collective title *The Seasons* (1730). Substantially revised in 1744, it became a source book for much later bird poetry, and an influence on **Wordsworth**, **J M W Turner** and others. His tragedies include *Sophonisba* (1729), *Agamemnon* (1738), and *Coriolanus* (1748). "Britannia" (1729), which criticized Sir **Robert Walpole**'s foreign policy, secured him further patronage and the sinecure of surveyor general of the Leeward Isles (1744). *Alfred, a Masque* (1740) contains the song "Rule Britannia," also claimed by **David Mallet**. The **Spenser**ian *The Castle of Indolence* (1748) appeared a few weeks before his death.

“ ”

Welcome, kindred glooms!
Congenial horrors, hail!

1726 ***The Seasons***, *"Winter," l. 5–6.*

Thomson, James 1822–92 •*Scottish engineer*• Born in Belfast, Northern Ireland, he graduated from the University of Glasgow and became Professor of Civil Engineering at Queen's College, Belfast (1857), and Glasgow (1873–89). He also wrote papers on elastic fatigue, undercurrents and trade winds. He carried out important research on fluid dynamics, inventing or improving several types of water wheels, pumps and turbines. Over a long period he studied the effect of pressure on the freezing point of water, and its influence on the plastic behavior of ice and the movement of glaciers. He was the elder brother of Lord **Kelvin**.

Thomson, James, *occasional pseudonym* **B V** 1834–82 •*Scottish poet*• Born in Port Glasgow, he was educated in the Royal Caledonian Asylum orphanage, and trained as an army schoolmaster at the Royal Military Asylum, Chelsea, but was dismissed from army service for alcoholism (1862). He was a friend of **Charles Bradlaugh**, editor and owner of the *National Reformer*, and between 1862 and 1875 he contributed many somber poems to the paper, including *The City of Dreadful Night* (1874), his greatest work. He took a number of jobs, but ill health and depression drove him to narcotics and stimulants. His pseudonym—B V, Bysshe Vanolis—was partly from **Shelley**'s second name, partly from an anagram of **Novalis**.

Thomson, Sir J(oseph) J(ohn), *also called* **JJ** 1856–1940 •*English physicist, discoverer of the electron and Nobel Prize winner*• He was born in Cheetham Hill near Manchester, the son of a Scottish bookseller, and won a scholarship to Trinity College, Cambridge. In 1884 he was elected a Fellow of the Royal Society and succeeded Lord **Rayleigh** as Cavendish Professor of Experimental Physics, and in 1919 he was himself succeeded by his brilliant student **Ernest Rutherford**. Thomson's early theoretical work was concerned with the extension of **James Clerk Maxwell**'s electromagnetic theories. This led to the study of gaseous conductors of electricity and in particular the nature of cathode rays. Using **Wilhelm Röntgen**'s discovery of X-rays (1895), he showed that cathode rays were rapidly moving particles, and by measuring their speed and specific charge, the latter by two independent methods, he deduced that these "corpuscles" (electrons) must be nearly 2,000 times smaller in mass than the lightest known atomic particle, the hydrogen ion. This, the greatest revolution in physics since Sir **Isaac Newton**, was inaugurated by his lecture to the Royal Institution (1897). Thomson successfully studied the nature of positive rays (1911), and this work was crowned by the discovery of isotopes, which he demonstrated could be separated by deflecting positive rays in electric and magnetic fields—mass spectrometry. He was awarded the Nobel Prize for physics (1906), and was knighted in 1908. In 1936 he published *Recollections and Reflections*. He was one of the pioneers of nuclear physics.

Thomson, Joseph 1858–95 •*Scottish explorer*• Born near Thornhill, Dumfriesshire, he studied geology at the University of Edinburgh and then joined the Royal Geographical Society East-Central African expedition (1878–79), taking charge on the death of the leader. He was the first European to reach Lake Nyasa (Malawi) from the north and went on to Lake Tanganyika. In 1882 he was invited by the Royal Geographical Society to find a route through the Masai country from the coast via Mount Kilimanjaro to Lake Victoria. This took him across the Nijiri Desert through the Great Rift Valley, and led to his discovery of Lake Baringo and Mount Elgon. He later explored Sokoto in northwest Nigeria (1885) and the Upper Congo (1890), and also traveled in the Atlas Mountains of Morocco.

Thomson, Robert William 1822–73 •*Scottish engineer and inventor*• Born in Stonehaven, Grampian, he was intended for the Church but, rebelling against classical studies, educated himself in mathematics and other practical subjects. In 1845 he patented a vulcanized rubber pneumatic tire that was successfully tested in London, but was thought to be too expensive for general use. It had been quite forgotten by the time **John Boyd Dunlop** reinvented the pneumatic tire in 1888. Thomson patented the principle of the fountain pen, designed the first mobile steam crane, and patented a steam traction engine.

Thomson (of Fleet), Roy Herbert Thomson, 1st Baron 1894–1976 •*British newspaper and television magnate*• He was born in Toronto, Canada, the son of a Scottish barber, and was educated at Jarvis Collegiate, Toronto. After serving in the Canadian militia during World War I, he set up his own commercial transmitter at North Bay (1931), founding what later became the NBC network. He started more radio stations, acquired 28 Canadian and 6 US newspapers, which he turned over to his son in 1953, and settled in Edinburgh on acquiring his first British paper, *The Scotsman*, and associated publications. In 1957 he obtained a license for commercial television in Scotland, and in 1959 acquired Kemsley newspapers, which included the *Sunday Times*. In 1966 he acquired *The Times*. Both these papers were bought by **Rupert Murdoch** in 1981.

Thomson, Virgil 1896–1989 •*US composer and critic*• Born in Kansas City, Missouri, he was educated at Harvard and Paris. He set some of the writings of **Gertrude Stein** to music, and wrote operas, *Four Saints in Three Acts* (1934), first performed by a Black cast, and *The Mother of Us All* (1947), besides symphonies, ballets, choral, chamber and film music. His autobiography, *Virgil Thomson by Virgil Thomson*, was published in 1966, and his *Selected Letters* were published shortly before his death.

Thomson, William *See* **Kelvin, William Thomson, 1st Baron**

Thomson, Sir (Charles) Wyville 1830–82 •*Scottish oceanographer*• Born in Linlithgow, Lothian region, he studied at the University of Edinburgh. He held a number of teaching posts, becoming Professor of Natural History at the University of Edinburgh from 1870. His book *Depths of the Sea* (1877) was the first general textbook on oceanography, and he also investigated the mechanisms of evolution, deep-sea temperatures, the Gulf Stream and the continuity of chalk out to sea. He was director of the civilian staff aboard the HMS *Challenger* expedition (1872–76), and on its return was appointed director of the Challenger Expedition Commission, overseeing the analysis and reports of the results of the expedition. The Wyville Thomson Ridge was named after him, since he had predicted its existence from water temperature measurements. He was knighted in 1876.

Thoreau, Henry David 1817–62 •*US essayist and poet*• Born in Concord, Massachusetts, he graduated from Harvard in 1837, became a teacher in Concord, and lectured. He gave up teaching, and in about 1839 began his walks and studies of nature which became his main occupation, and made the voyage described in his *Week on the Concord and Merrimack Rivers* (1849). In 1845 he built himself a shanty in the woods by Walden Pond, near Concord, where he wrote much of the *Week*, his essay on **Thomas Carlyle**, and the classic, *Walden, or Life in the Woods* (1854). The remainder of his writings were published after his death. He then had various jobs, and his 1850 trip to Canada produced *A Yankee in Canada* (1866). He kept a daily journal (from 1835) of his walks and observations, from whose 30 volumes were published *Early Spring in Massachusetts* (1881), *Summer* (1884) and *Winter* (1887). Other publications are *Excursions in Field and Forest*, with a memoir by his friend **Ralph Waldo Emerson** (1863), *Poems of Nature* (1896), and a celebrated essay, *Civil Disobedience* (1849), provoked by his opposition to the Mexican War.

“ ”

Why level downward to our dullest perception always, and praise that as common sense?

1854 ***Walden, or Life in the Woods***, *"Conclusion."*

Thorfinn, *properly* **Thorfinnur Karesefni** fl. 1000 •*Icelandic explorer*• Around AD 1000 he led an expedition of colonists from Greenland that sailed along the northeast coasts of North America, which had previously been discovered and explored by **Leif the Lucky**. He attempted to found a Norse colony in an area called "Vínland" (Wineland), somewhere to the south of Newfoundland. The story is told in two Icelandic sagas, *Eiriks saga rauða* ("Saga of Eric") and *Grœnlendinga saga* ("Tale of the Greenlanders").

Thorndike, Dame (Agnes) Sybil 1882–1976 •*English actress*• She was born in Gainsborough, Lincolnshire, and although she trained as a pianist, she decided to enter the theater. After four years touring the US in Shakespearean repertory, she returned to England and became a prominent member of **Annie Horniman**'s Repertory Company in Manchester, and also worked in London at the Old Vic (1914–19). She eventually played a great variety of male and female roles, including the title role in the first English performance of **George Bernard Shaw**'s *Saint Joan* (1924). She was given the honorary title of Dame Commander, Order of the British Empire, in 1931. With her husband, Sir **Lewis Casson**, she wrote a biography of **Lilian Baylis**.

Thorneycroft (of Dunston), (George Edward) Peter Thorneycroft, Baron 1909–94 •*English Conservative politician*• He was educated at Eton and the Royal Marine Artillery, Woolwich, served as a regular artillery officer (1930–33), left the army to become a barrister, and entered parliament in 1938. President of the Board of Trade from 1951 to 1957, he was appointed chancellor of the exchequer in 1957, but, disagreeing with government financial policy, resigned after a year in office. He later held ministerial posts including secretary of state for defense (1964), but lost his parliamentary seat in the 1966 election. In 1967 he was created a life peer. He was chairman of the Conservative Party from 1975 to 1981.

Thornhill, Sir James 1675–1734 •*English painter*• Born in Melcombe Regis, Dorset, he was apprenticed to Thomas Highmore. He executed baroque paintings for the dome of St Paul's (c. 1710–17), the hall at Blenheim Palace, and his masterpiece, the Painted Hall at Greenwich Hospital (1707–c. 1727). He also painted occasional portraits, including those of **Isaac Newton** (1710, Trinity College, Cambridge), **Richard Steele**, and the robber **Jack Sheppard**. He founded a drawing school, and **William Hogarth**, who eloped with his daughter, was one of his pupils. He was knighted by **George I** (1720), becoming history painter to the king (1728). From 1722 he was Member of Parliament for Melcombe Regis. He was the first native-born painter to succeed as a full-time decorative artist in the face of foreign competition.

Thoroddsen, Jón, *originally* **Jón Thórðarson** 1818–68 •*Icelandic novelist and poet*• Born in Reykhólar, he studied law at Copenhagen, and wrote drinking songs in the style of **Carl Bellmann**. He was an avid reader of Sir **Walter Scott**, and used him as a model for his first novel, *Piltur og stúlka* (1850, "Boy and Girl"). It was the earliest novel produced in Iceland, and he is regarded as the father of the modern Icelandic novel. Its unfinished sequel, *Maður og kona* ("Man and Woman"), was published posthumously in 1876.

Thorpe, Sir (Thomas) Edward 1845–1925 •*English chemist, physicist and historian of science*• Born near Manchester, he was educated at Owens College, Manchester, and at the Universities of

Heidelberg and Bonn. After various professorial posts, he became government chemist, the first such appointment. He discovered several new compounds of chromium, sulfur and phosphorus, including phosphorus pentafluoride, which demonstrated that phosphorus could have a valence of five. He also carried out determinations of atomic weights that were more accurate than any others of the time. In collaboration with Sir Arthur Rücker, he made a magnetic survey of the British Isles. Thorpe is also remembered for his work in the history of science, particularly his biography of **Joseph Priestley**. He was knighted in 1909.

Thorpe, Ian 1982– •*Australian swimmer*• Born in Sydney, he proved his potential as a swimmer by qualifying for the Australian swimming team in 1997 at age 14. Nicknamed the "Thorpedo," he broke the world records for the 400-meter and 200-meter freestyle in 1999 and dominated the pool at the 2000 Olympic Games in Sydney, winning gold in the 400-meter freestyle (breaking his own record), silver in the 200-meter freestyle, and record-breaking golds in the 4 × 100-meter and 4 × 200-meter freestyle relays.

Thorpe, Jim (James Francis), *Native American name* **Wa-tho-huck ("Bright Path")** 1887–1953 •*US athlete*• Born in a one-room cabin in Prague, Oklahoma, of French, Irish and Native American descent, he began as a football player but later became one of the great all-around athletes of international sport, excelling at baseball, football and a range of athletic disciplines. In 1912 he won both the decathlon and the pentathlon at the Olympic Games in Stockholm, although he was subsequently disqualified on the grounds that he had played semiprofessional baseball (his medals were posthumously restored in 1982). He went on to play both major league baseball (1913–19) with the New York Giants, Cincinnati Reds and Boston Braves as well as pro football (1920–26 and 1928) and in 1950 was proclaimed Associated Press "Athlete of the Half Century."

Thothmes *See* **Thutmose III**

Thrale *See* **Piozzi, Hester Lynch**

Throckmorton, Francis 1554–84 •*English conspirator*• Son of the courtier John Throckmorton (d. 1580), he was apprehended in the act of writing in code to **Mary Queen of Scots** in an unsuccessful attempt to overthrow **Elizabeth I**. He confessed under torture and was executed at Tyburn.

Thucydides c. 460–c. 400 BC •*Greek historian*• Born near Athens, he suffered in the Athenian plague (c. 430 BC) but recovered. In the Peloponnesian War he commanded an Athenian squadron of ships at Thasos (424), but after losing the colony of Amphipolis to the Spartans (424 BC) he was condemned as a traitor, and retired to his Thracian estates. He lived in exile for 20 years (possibly visiting Sicily), and wrote his eight-volume *De Bello Peloponnesiaco* ("History of the Peloponnesian War"). According to tradition, he was assassinated. His account of the war ends in 411, but the *Hellenica* of **Xenophon** was written to continue Thucydides' narrative to the end of the war in 404.

Thumb, General Tom *See* **Stratton, Charles Sherwood**

Thurber, James Grover 1894–1961 •*US humorist and cartoonist*• Born in Columbus, Ohio, he attended Ohio State University. In the early 1920s he reported for various papers in the US and Europe, but in 1927 **E B White** introduced him to **Harold Ross**, editor of the *New Yorker*, and he was instantly appointed its managing editor. Unsuited to the job, he drifted into writing, but before leaving the staff altogether, he contributed regularly, humorous essays at first, then sketches. His drawings first appeared in *Is Sex Necessary?* (1929), which he coauthored with White. His books include *The Owl in the Attic and Other Perplexities* (1931), *The Seal in the Bedroom and Other Predicaments* (1932), *The Middle-Aged Man on the Flying Trapeze* (1935), and a fragmentary autobiography, *My Life and Hard Times* (1933). He was also a dramatist and appeared as himself in a brief run of *A Thurber Carnival* in 1960. He also wrote a number of short stories, of which *The Secret Life of Walter Mitty*, filmed with **Danny Kaye** (1946), is best known.

" "

Early to rise and early to bed makes a male healthy and wealthy and dead.
1939 "The Shrike and the Chipmunks," in ***The New Yorker****, February 18.*

Thurmond, (James) Strom 1902–2003 •*US politician*• Born in Edgefield, South Carolina, he became a lawyer and judge and fought in the US Army in World War II. He was governor of South Carolina (1947–51), and his opposition to civil rights legislation led him to run for president as the Dixiecrat candidate in 1948. A conservative and a militarist, he served in the Senate from 1954 until shortly before his death; he changed his affiliation from Democratic to Republican in 1964. From 1981 to 1987 and from 1995 to 2003 he was president pro tempore of the Senate.

Thurstan d. 1140 •*Norman prelate*• Born in Bayeux, he was made Archbishop of York in 1114. As archbishop, he struggled for primacy with Canterbury. On the invasion of King **David I** of Scotland (1137), he first persuaded him to accept a truce, and then collected forces at York and beat him at the Battle of the Standard (1138). A member of the Cluniac Order, he did much to help the growth of monasticism in the North and was involved in the foundation of Fountains Abbey (1132).

Thurstone, L(ouis) L(eon) 1887–1955 •*US psychologist*• He was born in Chicago. He studied at Cornell University and the University of Chicago, and taught at the Carnegie Institute of Technology (1915–23) and the University of Chicago (1927–52), becoming research professor and director of the Psychometric Laboratory at the University of North Carolina (1952–55). His academic work was devoted to the theory and practice of intelligence testing and the development of statistical techniques (especially multiple-factor analysis) to analyze the results. His battery of tests designed to measure the "Primary Mental Abilities" have enjoyed wide application, especially in the US.

Thutmose or **Tuthmosis I** fl. 1493–1482 BC •*King of Egypt*• He is believed to have come to the throne through marriage to Amhose, the sister of King Amenhotep I. He waged war in Nubia, where he extended Egyptian control into Kush beyond the Third Cataract, and in Syria, where he campaigned as far as the Euphrates. He constructed the fourth and fifth pylons (monumental gateways) at the Temple of Amun in Karnak, and erected a pair of granite obelisks, one of which still stands.

Thutmose or **Tuthmosis III**, *also called* **Thothmes** *and* **Tuthmose** d. 1426 BC •*Egyptian pharaoh of the 18th Dynasty*• The son of Thutmose II and father of **Amenhotep II**, he reigned jointly at first with Queen **Hatshepsut**, his aunt and stepmother, from c. 1501 BC, and by himself from 1479 to 1447. He invaded Syria, extended his territories to Carchemish on the Euphrates and made several invasions into Asia. He built the great temple of Amen at Karnak, restored others, and erected obelisks, including Cleopatra's Needle, taken to London (1878) by Sir **Erasmus Wilson**.

Tiberius, *in full* **Tiberius Julius Caesar Augustus**, *originally* **Tiberius Claudius Nero** 42 BC–AD 37 •*Second emperor of Rome*• He was the son of Tiberius Claudius Nero and of **Livia**. His father died when Tiberius was nine, and he succeeded his stepfather, the emperor **Augustus**, in AD 14. Almost the whole of his first 20 years of adulthood were spent on campaigns in Spain, Armenia, Gaul, Pannonia and Germany; he returned to Rome after crushing the Dalmatian revolt (9 BC). Tiberius was compelled (12 BC) to divorce his wife, Vipsania Agrippina, in order to marry **Julia**, **Agrippa**'s widow and the profligate daughter of Augustus. He retired to Rhodes (6 BC) where he devoted himself to study and astrology. Before his return (AD 2) Julia was banished to Pandataria (2 BC), and the deaths of the young princes Lucius and Gaius led Augustus to adopt Tiberius (AD 4) as imperial heir. He spent the next seven years in active service in north Germany, taking vengeance upon the Germans who had annihilated the army of **Varus** in AD 9. He succeeded Augustus in AD 14, but despite his eminent qualities and many services, he was not suited to the role of emperor. His rule began well, but was gradually eroded by suspicion and insecurity, which resulted in a growing number of treason trials and executions. He relied increasingly on the services of his friend the praetorian prefect Sejanus. In AD 26 he left Rome for Campania, and retired to the island of Capreae (Capri). Sejanus, in the meantime, assumed effective control in Rome until at last Tiberius became suspicious of his intentions and executed him (AD 31). His reign was blighted by internal conflicts: the murder of

Agrippa Postumus (AD 14), the mysterious death in the East of his heir, the popular Germanicus Caesar (AD 19), the alleged poisoning by Sejanus of Tiberius's own son Drusus (AD 23), the banishment of **Agrippina** (the Elder) and the death of her young sons Nero and Drusus (AD 31, AD 33). These events all but obliterated the memory of much good government earlier in his reign, and he died unmourned.

Tibullus, Albius c. 54–19 BC •*Roman elegiac poet*• He is believed to have been born in Gabii. In 30 BC **Augustus** commissioned Tibullus to crush a revolt in Aquitania, and although he served with distinction in the campaign, he never liked life as a soldier as much as he enjoyed Roman society. His gentle elegiac love poems to his mistresses persuaded **Quintilian** to place Tibullus at the head of Roman elegiac poets.

Ticknor, William Davis 1810–64 •*US publisher*• He was born in Lebanon, New Hampshire. He became a publisher in Boston in 1832, at first with John Allen, and then with James T Fields (1817–81). As Ticknor & Fields they published the *Atlantic Monthly* and the *North American Review*, and their office was frequented by **Ralph Waldo Emerson**, **Henry Wadsworth Longfellow**, **Nathaniel Hawthorne**, **Oliver Wendell Holmes**, **James Russell Lowell** and **John Greenleaf Whittier**. He was one of the first Americans to remunerate foreign authors.

Tieck, (Johann) Ludwig 1773–1853 •*German Romantic writer and critic*• He was born in Berlin and was educated at the Universities of Halle, Göttingen and Erlangen (1792–94). He produced a number of clever *Märchendramen* (dramatized versions of folktales), such as *Der gestiefelte Kater* (1797, "Puss in Boots"), and followed up this first success with the satire *Anti-Faust, oder Geschichte eines dummen Teufels* (1801, "Anti-Faust, or the Story of a Dim Devil"), the horror story *Der Runenberg* (1804, "The Rune Mountain"), and *Phantasus* (1812–17), a collection of traditional lore in story and drama. Besides supervising the completion of **August von Schlegel**'s translation of **Shakespeare**, he edited the doubtful plays and wrote a series of Shakespeare essays. He was also notable as a translator and a drama and literary critic.

Tiepolo, Giovanni Battista, *originally* **Giambattista Chiepoletto** 1696–1770 •*Italian decorative painter*• He was born in Venice, and was educated by an unknown artist named Lazzarini. His work is to be found in palaces and churches throughout Europe. Early examples include the Labia Palace at Venice and frescoes at Udine, Milan and Bergamo. In 1750 he began his most important decorative scheme, in the Archbishop's Palace at Würzburg. *An Allegory with Venus and Time* (National Gallery, London), part of a ceiling in the Contarini Palace, Venice, also belongs to this period (1750s). In 1761 **Charles III** of Spain called him to Madrid to work in the new Royal Palace, but the commission remained unfinished at his death. Tiepolo's compositions are full of movement and energy, as for example in *Antony and Cleopatra* at the Labia Palace, creating a sense of awe by the use of dramatically exaggerated foreshortening and subtle chiaroscuro. He was a superb draftsman, and his influence on **Francisco Goya** and on all subsequent decorative painting was enormous. The Courtauld Institute in London owns a rich collection of his work, including *Allegory of the Power of Eloquence* (c. 1725), *St Aloysius Gonzaga in Glory* (c. 1726), *The Adoration of the Magi* (c. 1726) and a series of religious paintings done in 1767.

Tiffany, Charles Lewis 1812–1902 •*US goldsmith and jeweler*• Born in Killingly, Connecticut, he began dealing in fancy goods in New York in 1837 and later founded Tiffany and Co. By 1883 he had become so successful that he was one of the largest manufacturers of silverware in the US. His work reflected current tastes with an accent on the traditional and historical. He held official appointments to 23 royal patrons, including the czar of Russia, Queen **Victoria** and the shah of Persia. Latterly, he marketed some of the art nouveau lamps made by his son, **Louis Comfort Tiffany**.

Tiffany, Louis Comfort 1848–1933 •*US glassmaker and interior decorator*• Born in New York City, the son of **Charles Lewis Tiffany**, he established a firm of interior decorators which became one of the most popular in New York by the early 1880s. He became better known, however, for his work in glass, and in 1892 he acquired glass furnaces at Cirona, New York. The first year's production went to museums, but the following year the first lamps were made available to the public, and by 1896 the first Favrile Glass (handmade) was offered for sale. Along with stained glass, furniture, fabrics, wallpaper and lamps, he produced goblets and glasses in the art nouveau style.

Tiglath-Pileser III, *also known as* **Pulu** 8th century BC •*King of Assyria*• A great empire builder, he ruled from 745 to 727 BC, and conquered the cities of north Syria and Phoenicia, including Damascus and Babylon.

Tikhonov, Nikolai Aleksandrovich 1905–97 •*Soviet politician*• He began his career as an assistant locomotive driver before training in the late 1920s at the Dnepropetrovsk Metallurgical Institute, where he met **Leonid Brezhnev**, then a Communist Party (CPSU) organizer. Tikhonov worked for two decades in the ferrous metallurgy industry before being appointed to various ministerial posts. He was inducted into the CPSU politburo as a full member in 1979 and appointed prime minister in 1980, a post which he held until 1985.

Tilak, Bal Gangadhar 1856–1920 •*Indian nationalist, scholar, and philosopher*• He was born in Ratnagiri. After teaching mathematics, he was owner and editor of two weekly newspapers. A militant member of the "extremist" wing within the Indian National Congress (and a member of the famous "Lal, Pal and Bal" trio), he was twice imprisoned by the British for his nationalist activities. He helped found the Home Rule League in 1914.

Tilden, Samuel Jones 1814–86 •*US politician*• Born in New Lebanon, New York, he was admitted to the bar. By 1868 he had become leader of the Democrats in the state, and he attacked and destroyed the Tweed Ring, bringing a civil suit against **William Marcy Tweed** to recover the money he had stolen in graft. In 1874 he was elected governor of New York on a reform ticket. As the Democratic candidate for president in 1876, he won more popular votes than **Rutherford B Hayes**, the Republican contender, but Hayes was the final victor by one electoral vote. Tilden returned to his career as a lawyer and on his death left much of his fortune to found a free library in New York City.

Tilley, Vesta, *stage name of* **Matilda Alice, Lady de Frece**, *née* **Powles** 1864–1952 •*English comedienne*• Born in Worcester, she first appeared as the Great Little Tilley, aged four, in Nottingham, and did her first male impersonation the following year. She adopted the name of Vesta Tilley and became, through her charm, vivacity and attention to sartorial detail, the most celebrated of all male impersonators. Of the many popular songs sung by her, "Burlington Bertie," "Following in Father's Footsteps," "Sweetheart May" and "Jolly Good Luck to the Girl who Loves a Soldier" are the best known. (1934).

Tillich, Paul Johannes 1886–1965 •*US Protestant theologian and philosopher*• Born in Starzeddel, Brandenburg, Germany, he became a Lutheran pastor (1912) and served as a military chaplain in the German army in World War I, later holding professorships in theology and philosophy at various German universities (1924–33). He was an early critic of **Hitler** and the Nazis and in 1933 was barred from German universities, the first non-Jewish academic "to be so honored," as he put it. He emigrated to the US, and taught at the Union Theological Seminary in New York (1933–55), Harvard Divinity School (1955–62) and Chicago Divinity School (1962–65), becoming a naturalized US citizen in 1940. In his main work, *Systematic Theology* (3 vols, 1951–63), he explains faith as a matter of "ultimate concern," with a reality transcending finite existence rather than a belief in a personal God, and this has led to oversimplified accusations of atheism or crypto-atheism. His influence on the development of theology has been very substantial, and his popular works, such as *The Courage to Be* (1952) and *Dynamics of Faith* (1957), have reached very large general readerships.

“ ”

Faith is the state of being ultimately concerned.

1957 ***Dynamics of Faith***

Tilly, Johann Tserklaes, Count von 1559–1632 •*Bavarian soldier*• Born at the castle of Tilly in Brabant, he was appointed in 1610 by Duke **Maximilian** of Bavaria to reorganize his army. Given the command of the Catholic League's army at the outbreak of the Thirty Years' War, he separated the armies of Mansfeld and of the Margrave of Baden, beat the latter at Wimpfen (1622), and expelled Christian of Brunswick from the Palatinate. Created a Count of the Empire, he defeated King **Christian IV** of Denmark at Lutter (1626), and with **Albrecht von Wallenstein** compelled him to sign the Treaty of Lübeck (1629). The next year he became Commander in Chief of the imperial forces, and stormed Magdeburg (1631). He was fatally wounded at Breitenfeld by the forces of **Gustav II Adolpho**.

Timon of Athens, *nicknamed* **the Misanthrope of Athens** 5th century BC •*Athenian nobleman*• He was a contemporary of **Socrates**. According to the comic writers who attacked him, he was disgusted with humankind on account of the ingratitude of his early friends, and lived a life of almost total seclusion. **Lucian** made him the subject of a dialogue. **Shakespeare**'s play *Timon of Athens* is based on the story.

Timothy, St fl. c. 50 AD •*Early Christian missionary*• The son of a Greek father and Jewish mother, he was a native of Lystra. He became one of St **Paul** 's protégés, entrusted with encouraging the persecuted churches of Thessalonica and Asia Minor. Praised by Paul for his loyalty, he is described as being affectionate but fearful. Tradition holds that he became Bishop of Ephesus, where he is said to have been martyred under **Domitian**. His feast day is January 22 (Greek Orthodox) or January 24 (Roman).

Timur, *also called* **Timur Lenk**, *Turkish for* **Timur the Lame**, *English* **Tamerlane** or **Tamburlaine** 1336–1405 •*Tatar conqueror*• Born in Kesh, near Samarkand, he proclaimed himself Mongol Khan in 1370. In a series of devastating wars (in which he sustained the wounds which gave him his nickname), he subdued nearly all of Persia from 1392 to 1396, Georgia, and the Tatar Empire, and conquered all the states between the River Indus and the lower Ganges with his army of nomadic Turks and Mongols. He won Damascus and Syria from the Mamluk sovereigns of Egypt, then defeated the Turks at Ankara (1402), taking Sultan **Bayezit I** prisoner. He died while marching to conquer China. He filled his capital, Samarkand, with splendid monuments.

Tinbergen, Jan 1903–94 •*Dutch economist and Nobel prize winner*• He was born in The Hague, the brother of **Nikolaas Tinbergen**. Educated at Leiden, he taught economics at the Erasmus University in Rotterdam (1933–73). He analyzed the Great Depression in the US in *Business Cycles in the US 1919–32* (1939), and was economic adviser to the League of Nations (1936–38). After World War II he directed the Netherlands Central Planning Bureau (1945–55). He shared the first Nobel Prize for economics in 1969 with **Ragnar Frisch**.

Tinbergen, Nikolaas 1907–88 •*Dutch ethologist and Nobel Prize winner*• He was born in The Hague, the brother of **Jan Tinbergen**. He studied zoology at Leiden University, and taught at Oxford (1949–74). With **Konrad Lorenz** he is considered to be the cofounder of ethology, the study of animal behavior in relation to the environment to which it is adapted. His best-known studies were on the three-spined stickleback and the herring gull, animals which perform many stereotyped or instinctive behavior patterns. His books include his classic *The Study of Instinct* (1951), *The Herring Gull's World* (1953), *Social Behavior in Animals* (1953) and *The Animal in Its World* (2 vols, 1972–73). In 1973 he published a controversial book *Autistic Children* (with his wife, Lies), in which he proposed a behavioral causation for autism. He shared the 1973 Nobel Prize for physiology or medicine with Lorenz and **Karl von Frisch**.

Tindale, William *See* **Tyndale, William**

Ting, Samuel Chao Chung 1936– •*US physicist and Nobel Prize winner*• Born in Ann Arbor, Michigan, he was raised in China and educated there and in Taiwan, and at the University of Michigan (1956–62). He then worked in elementary particle physics at CERN (Conseil Européen pour la Recherche Nucléaire) in Geneva, at Columbia University, at MIT, and elsewhere. In 1974 he was head of a team at the Brookhaven National Laboratory which directed protons onto a beryllium target, and a new product particle was observed and named the "J particle." At the same time, and independently, **Burton Richter** made the same discovery and named the particle "y." It is now named the "J/y particle," and for its discovery Ting and Richter shared the 1976 Nobel Prize for physics.

Ting Ling *See* **Ding Ling**

Tinguely, Jean 1925–91 •*Swiss sculptor*• He was born in Fribourg, and studied at the Basel Kunstgewerbeschule from 1941 to 1945. A pioneer of kinetic art, he worked in Paris from 1953 onward, exhibiting his "meta-mechanical" works. These moving metal constructions, or "junk mobiles," sometimes powered by small motors, often strike bottles or metal pans, and even make abstract drawings, for example *Monstranz* (1960, New York City). From about 1960 he began programming them to destroy themselves, as in *Hommage à New York* (Metropolitan Museum of Art, New York City). There is a large mobile by him in Basel Railway Station, and his *Fasnachts-Brunnen* (1977) is also in the town there.

Tintoretto, *properly* **Jacopo Robusti** 1518–94 •*Italian painter*• He was born probably in Venice, the son of a silk dyer, or *tintore* (hence his nickname of "Little Dyer"), but little is known of his life. He is supposed to have studied under **Titian**, but only for a short time. Except for visits to Mantua (1580, 1590–93), he lived all his life in Venice. Tintoretto pioneered the way from the classical to the baroque, evident in his early work, such as *The Miracle of the Slave* (1548). After 1556 he began to develop his mature style. *The Last Judgment*, *The Golden Calf* (both c. 1560) and *The Marriage of Cana* (1561) were followed by two masterpieces of perspective and lighting effects: *The Finding* and *The Removal of the Body of St Mark* (both c. 1562). Other notable late works are *The Origin of the Milky Way* (after 1570), the *Paradiso* (1588), famous for its colossal size, and his last version of *The Last Supper* (1592–94). Three of his seven children also became painters, including Marietta (1560–90), known as La Tintoretta.

Tippett, Sir Michael Kemp 1905–98 •*English composer*• Born in London, he studied at the Royal College of Music and from 1940 to 1951 was director of Music at Morley College. He first attracted attention with his chamber music and Concerto for Double String Orchestra (1939), but his oratorio, *A Child of Our Time* (1941), reflecting the political and spiritual problems of the 1930s and 1940s, won him wide recognition. A convinced pacifist, he went to prison for three months as a conscientious objector during World War II. He had considerable success with the operas *The Midsummer Marriage* (1952) and *King Priam* (1958). His other works include symphonies, a piano concerto (1957), the operas *The Knot Garden* (1966–70) and *The Ice Break* (1976), piano sonatas and an oratorio, *The Vision of St Augustine* (1963–65). Later compositions include *The Rose Lake* (1993) and *Caliban's Song* (1995). He was knighted in 1966 and was awarded the Order of Merit in 1983. He wrote books including *Those Twentieth-Century Blues* (1991), and *Tippett on Music* (1995).

Tippoo Sahib or **Tipú Sultán** c. 1749–99 •*Sultan of Mysore*• The son of **Haidar Ali**, he completely routed Bailey (1780, 1782) and Braithwaite (1782) during his father's wars with the British. In 1782 he succeeded his father as sultan of Mysore. An able general and administrator, he was cruel to enemies and lacked his father's wisdom. After the conclusion of peace between France and Great Britain, he agreed to a treaty (1784) confirming the status quo. Later he sent ambassadors to France (1787) to stir up a war with Great Britain, and, failing in this, in 1789 he invaded the protected state of Travancore. In the ensuing war (1790–92) the British, under Stuart and **Cornwallis**, were aided by the Marathas and the Nizam, and Tippoo was defeated (1792) and had to cede half his kingdom. After recommencing hostilities in 1799, he was killed during the siege of Seringapatam.

Tirpitz, Alfred Friedrich von 1849–1930 •*German admiral*• Born in Küstrin, Brandenburg, he joined the Prussian navy in 1865. He commanded the Asiatic squadron (1896–97), and as secretary of state for the Imperial German Navy (1897–1916), he raised a fleet to challenge British supremacy of the seas, and acted as its commander (1914–16). He advocated unrestricted submarine warfare, and resigned when this policy was initially opposed in government circles. He later sat in the Reichstag (1924–28).

Tiselius, Arne Wilhelm Kaurin 1902–71 •*Swedish chemist and Nobel Prize winner*• Born in Stockholm, he trained and worked at Uppsala University. He developed an accurate method for determining diffusion constants of proteins, important for analyzing ultracentrifuge sedimentation data (1934). He introduced protein analysis by moving boundary electrophoresis (1930–37), isolated bushy stunt and cucumber mosaic viruses (1938–39) and invented preparative electrophoresis (1943), electrokinetic filtration (1947) and other analytical techniques. From 1944 he developed methods for the chromatographic separation and identification of amino acids, sugars and other molecules. He worked with **Frederick Sanger** on the chemistry of insulin (1947) and with **Richard Synge** on chromatographic analysis (1950). Tiselius became vice president (1947–60) and president (1960–64) of the Nobel Foundation and was awarded the Nobel Prize for chemistry in 1948.

Tissot, James Joseph Jacques 1836–1902 •*French painter*• Born in Nantes, he studied in Paris, where he was influenced by **Degas**, and after the fall of the Commune took refuge in London in 1871–82, where he did caricatures for *Vanity Fair*, and painted fashionable social occasions, such as *The Ball on Shipboard* (1874, Tate Britain, London). In London his views of the River Thames earned him the title "the **Watteau** of Wapping." Traveling to Palestine in 1886, he produced a series of 300 watercolors of the life of Jesus, but his portraits of Victorian life remain his best-known work.

Titian, *properly* **Tiziano Vecellio** c. 1488–1576 •*Venetian painter*• Born in Pieve di Cadore in the Friulian Alps, he lived from the age of 10 with an uncle in Venice and studied under the mosaicists there, becoming a pupil of **Giovanni Bellini** and **Giorgione**. Bellini's influence is apparent in such early works as *Bishop Pesaro Before St Peter* (c. 1505). Titian assisted Giorgione with the paintings for the Fondaco dei Tedeschi (1508) and completed many of the works left unfinished at his death, for example *Noli me tangere* (c. 1510) and the *Sleeping Venus* (c. 1510), which was to serve as a model for Titian's more naturalistic *Venus of Urbino* (1538). Giorgione continued to be the chief influence on Titian's work. The first works definitely attributable to Titian alone are the three frescoes of scenes in the life of St Anthony at Padua (1511), the pastoral setting of *The Three Ages of Man* (c. 1515) and the masterly fusion of romantic realism and classical idealism achieved in his *Sacred and Profane Love* (c. 1515). After 1516 restrained postures and coloring give way to dynamic compositions in which bright colors are contrasted, and the classical intellectual approach gives way to sensuous, full-blooded treatment. *Assumption of the Virgin* (1516–18), *Madonna of the Pesaro Family* (1519–26), both in the Frari, Venice, and *St Peter Martyr* (destroyed in 1867) exemplify the beginnings of Titian's own revolutionary style. For the Duke of Ferrara he painted three great mythological subjects: *Feast of Venus* (c. 1515–18), *Bacchanal* (c. 1518) and the richly colored exuberant masterpiece *Bacchus and Ariadne* (1523). In sharp contrast is the finely modeled historical picture, *Presentation of the Virgin* (1534–38). In 1530 he met the emperor **Charles V**, of whom he painted many portraits, including the striking equestrian *Charles V at the Battle of Mühlberg* (1548), and by whom was ennobled. To this period also belongs *Ecce Homo* (1543) and portraits of the Farnese family, including Pope **Paul III** and his nephews (1545–46), painted on Titian's first visit to Rome. For **Philip II** of Spain he executed a remarkable series of mythological scenes, to which belong *Diana and Actaeon* (1559), *Diana and Callisto* (1559) and *Perseus and Andromeda* (c. 1556). To the poignant religious and mythological subjects of his last years belong *The Fall of Man* (c. 1570), *The Entombment* (1565), *Christ Crowned with Thorns* (c. 1570), *Madonna Suckling the Child* (1570–76), *Lucrezia and Tarquinius* (c. 1570) and the unfinished *Pietà* (1573–76). Titian was ceremoniously buried in the church of Santa Maria dei Frari, Venice. He revolutionized techniques in oil, and has been described as the founder of modern painting. His influence on later artists was profound.

Tito, *originally* **Josip Broz**, *also called* **Marshal Tito** 1892–1980 •*Yugoslav leader*• He was born near Klanjec, in Croatia. In World War I he served with the Austro-Hungarian Army, and, taken prisoner by the Russians, he adopted Communism and took part in the 1917 Revolution. In 1928 he was imprisoned in Yugoslavia for conspiring against the regime. In mid-1941 he organized partisan forces against the Axis conquerors of his country. In 1943 Tito established a provisional government at liberated Jajce in Bosnia, and following the expulsion of the remaining Axis forces, a new Yugoslav Federal Republic was declared in 1945. Effectively one-party elections followed, establishing the dominance of the Communist Party, with Tito serving as prime minister and, from 1953, as president. In 1948 the new Federal Republic broke with the Cominform (Communist Information Bureau) as a result of growing policy differences, **Stalin** viewing the successful system of decentralized profit-sharing workers' councils introduced by Tito as dangerously "revisionist." Thereafter, Tito became a leader of the nonaligned movement, pursuing a policy of "positive neutralism." He was made president-for-life in 1974 and proceeded to establish a unique system of collective, rotating leadership within the country during his later years.

Titus 1st century AD •*Greek Christian*• He was a companion of the Apostle **Paul**. He remained uncircumcised, an important factor in the Church's acceptance of Gentiles. Ecclesiastical tradition makes Titus "Bishop" of Crete.

Titus, Flavius Sabinus Vespasianus AD 39–81 •*Roman emperor*• The eldest son of **Vespasian**, on his father's accession to the throne (AD 69) he ended the Jewish war and captured Jerusalem (70). He had a liaison with **Berenice**, sister of **Herod Agrippa II**, and she accompanied him to Rome. There, however, the liaison between the son of the emperor and a Jewish woman was disapproved of, and he dismissed her. He assumed power in 79. Handsome, cultivated and universally popular in Rome, he completed the Colosseum, built baths, and lavished his generosity upon the sufferers from the eruption of Vesuvius (79), the three days' fire at Rome, and the pestilence. He died suddenly, but the suspicion that he had been poisoned by his brother and successor, **Domitian**, was probably unfounded.

Tizard, Dame Catherine Anne 1931– •*New Zealand politician*• Born in Auckland, she was a tutor in zoology at the University of Auckland for 20 years (1963–83), and was elected the first Labour mayor of Auckland in 1983. She resigned in 1990 on her appointment as New Zealand's first woman governor-general, a position she held until 1996. She has been active in most areas of public life, especially health, child care, education, the environment and the arts. She was given the honorary title of Dame Commander, Order of the British Empire, in 1984. She was married to the Right Honorable Bob Tizard PC (1924–), former deputy prime minister of New Zealand; their daughter Judith Ngaire Tizard (1956–) was elected Labour Member of Parliament for Panmure (1990–96).

Tocqueville, Alexis Charles Henri Maurice Clérel de 1805–59 •*French historian and political scientist*• Born in Verneuil, he was called to the bar in 1825. In 1831 he visited the US, and on his return published a penetrating political study, *De la démocratie en Amérique* (1835, "Democracy in America"), that made his name in Europe. He paid his first visit to England in 1833 and kept an extensive diary of his *Journeys to England and Ireland*. He became a member of the Chamber of Deputies (1839), and in 1849 was vice president of the Assembly and briefly minister of foreign affairs. After **Napoleon III**'s coup d'état he retired to his estate, where he wrote the first volume of *L'ancien régime et la révolution* (1856, "The Old Regime and the Revolution"), but he died before another volume could be completed.

" "

Il n'y a qu'un journal qui puisse venir déposer au même moment dans mille esprits la même pensée.

Only a newspaper can place at the same time in a thousand minds the same thought.

1835 ***De la démocratie en Amérique***
(Democracy in America), volume 2, part 2, chapter 6.

Todd (of Trumpington), Alexander Robertus Todd, Baron 1907–97 •*Scottish chemist and Nobel Prize winner*• Born in Glasgow, he studied at the University of Glasgow and at Frankfurt and Oxford. He spent two years in the medical chemistry department in Edinburgh, working on the chemistry of vitamin B, and then moved to the Lister Institute of Preventive Medicine in London. He held the chair of organic chemistry at Manchester from 1938 to 1944. His final post was as professor at Cambridge, where he remained until his retirement in 1971. The work for which he was awarded the Nobel Prize for chemistry in 1957 concerned the structure and synthesis of nucleotides, which was a necessary preliminary to **Francis Crick** and **James Watson**'s proposal of the double helix as the structure of DNA. Todd was elected to the Royal Society in 1942 and was later its president (1975–80). He was knighted in 1954 and was awarded the Order of Merit and made a life peer in 1977. A man of strong personality, he was known affectionately at Cambridge as Todd Almighty, later Lord Todd Almighty. As a trustee of various charities and as a member of many government committees, he played a substantial part in promoting scientific activity both in Great Britain and abroad.

Todd, Sir (Reginald Stephen) Garfield 1908–2002 •*Rhodesian politician*• Born in New Zealand, he was educated there and in South Africa. Having gone to Southern Rhodesia in 1934 as a missionary, he was elected to the Legislative Assembly (1946) and then to the leadership of the United Rhodesia Party (1953), which made him prime minister of Southern Rhodesia. He was removed from the leadership by an internal putsch because of his liberalism, and he helped form the overtly liberal Central African Party in 1959. The party failed in 1962, but he remained the spokesman for white liberalism, as a result of which he was restricted by the government under **Ian Smith** (1965–66, 1972–76). He supported **Joshua Nkomo** in the 1980 elections.

Todd, Mike (Michael), *originally* **Avrom Hirsh Goldbogen** 1909–58 •*US showman*• Born in Minneapolis, Minnesota, he started life as a fairgrounds attendant at the age of 9, but was already making his first fortune at 14 in sales promotion. In 1927 he went to Hollywood as a soundproofing expert, later putting on plays, musical comedies and films, including a jazz version of **Gilbert** and **Sullivan**, *The Hot Mikado* (1939). He perfected the three-dimensional film with Lowell Thomas and sponsored the "TODD-AO" wide-screen process, by which his best film, **Jules Verne**'s *Around the World in 80 Days* (1956), was made and presented, winning him an Academy Award. He married his third wife, the film actress **Elizabeth Taylor**, in 1957. He was killed in an air crash over New Mexico the following year.

Todd, Ron(ald) 1927– •*English trade union leader*• He was born in Walthamstow, London, the son of a market trader. After serving in the Far East with the Royal Marine commandos, he joined the Ford Motor Company in 1954 as a line worker and became a member of the country's largest trade union, the TGWU (Transport and General Workers' Union). He rose steadily from shop steward up to general secretary (1985–92). Although he was viewed as a staunch supporter of the then Labour Party leader **Neil Kinnock**, on many economic and social issues his union's and his own personal commitment to unilateral nuclear disarmament led to strains in the TGWU-Labour relationship.

Todd, Sweeney late 18th century •*English alleged murderer*• Known as the "Demon Barber of Fleet Street," he supposedly carried out his murders in 1780s' London. It has never been proved that he did in fact exist, although his story is well known. Using a revolving floor which had a barber's chair on each side of it, he is claimed to have swung unsuspecting clients into his cellar via the trap and then cut their throats. Their bodies were carried through a series of underground passages to a nearby bakery. There, Mrs Lovett is said to have used human flesh in her meat pies. Sawney Bean, a Scottish cannibal, may have been the source of the London tale, as may a French murderer who operated in Paris in 1800.

Tóibín, Colm 1955– •*Irish author*• Born in Wexford, he studied at University College Dublin, and lived and taught in Spain for five years before returning to Dublin to work as a journalist. His first novel, *The South* (1990), a love story set in Spain, was followed by books such as *The Story of the Night* (1998) and *The Blackwater Lightship* (2000). He has also edited several collections of fiction and published short stories and collected journalism.

Tojo, Hideki 1885–1948 •*Japanese soldier*• Born in Tokyo, in 1919 he was appointed military attaché in Germany. He served with the Kwantung army in Manchuria as chief of the Secret Police and chief of staff from 1937 to 1940. He became minister of war (1940–41), and from 1941 he was premier and dictator of Japan, resigning in 1944. Arrested, he attempted and failed to commit suicide. He was sentenced to death in 1948.

Tokugawa •*Dynasty of 15 Japanese shoguns*• They were the effective rulers of Japan for two and a half centuries. Ieyasu (1543–1616, shogun 1603–05) became an ally of the warlord Nobunaga, whose policy of unification he supported, but later a power struggle resulted in civil war. Ieyasu won and was appointed shogun (generalissimo) by the emperor (1603). He remained in practice the national leader of Japan until his death. His grandson, Iemitsu (shogun 1623–51), passed the three expulsion decrees (1633–39); aimed at the suppression of Christianity, they effectively closed Japan to foreign trade. Yoshimune (1716–45) drew up the Code of One Hundred Articles, embodying the Tokugawa legal reforms. The shogunate came to an end in 1867 with the resignation of Hitotsubashi Keiki.

Toledo Manrique, Alejandro 1946– •*Peruvian politician*• Born in Cabana, he was educated at the University of San Francisco and Stanford University in the US. An economist, he became minister of labor under President **Fernando Belaúnde**. Founder and president of the Partido Peru Posible (PP), he boycotted the 2000 presidential election, but went on to win the presidency in 2001.

Tolkien, J(ohn) R(onald) R(euel) 1892–1973 •*British philologist and writer*• Born in Bloemfontein, South Africa, he was educated at Merton College, Oxford, and became Professor of Anglo-Saxon there (1925–45), and of English Language and Literature (1945–59). His scholarly publications include an edition of *Sir Gawain and the Green Knight* (1925), and studies on **Chaucer** (1934) and *Beowulf* (1937). His interest in language and saga and his fascination with the land of faerie prompted him to write tales of a world of his own invention peopled by strange beings with their own carefully constructed language and mythology. These include *The Hobbit* (1937), a fascinating tale of the perilous journey of Bilbo Baggins to recover treasure from the sly dragon Smaug, and the more complex sequel, *The Lord of the Rings* (3 vols, 1954–55), in which Bilbo's nephew, Frodo, sets out to destroy a powerful but dangerous ring. Later works include *The Silmarillion* (posthumous, 1977).

“ ”

One Ring to rule them all, One Ring to find them
One Ring to bring them all and in the darkness bind them.
In the Land of Mordor where the Shadows lie.

1954 ***The Fellowship of the Ring****, epigraph and passim.*

Tolstoy, Count Leo Nikolayevich 1828–1910 •*Russian writer, aesthetic philosopher, moralist and mystic*• He was born on the family estate of Yasnaya Polyana in Tula province, and was educated privately. He studied law and Oriental languages at Kazan University, but returned to his estate, which he inherited in 1847, without graduating. According to his own account, the young Tolstoy led a dissolute life in town and played the gentleman farmer. Finally, in 1851, he accompanied his elder brother Nikolai to the Caucasus, where he joined an artillery regiment and there began his literary career. His first published work, *Istoria vcherashchnego dnya* (1851, "An Account of Yesterday"), was followed by the remarkable autobiographical trilogy *Detstvo* (1852, "Childhood"), *Otrochestvo* (1854, "Boyhood") and *Yunost* (1856, "Youth"). He received a commission at the outbreak of the Crimean War (1854) and commanded a battery during the defense of Sebastopol (1854–55). The horrors of war inspired *Tales of Army Life* and *Sevastopolskiye rasskazy* (1855–56, Eng trans *Sebastopol*, 1887), sketches which show the influence of **Stendhal**; afterwards he left the army, was welcomed into the literary circle in St Petersburg (1856), and traveled abroad. In 1862 he married Sophie Andreyevna Behrs and settled into domestic life, raising a family of 13 children. He settled on his Volga estate, devoting himself to the duties of a progressive landlord and to writing his greatest work, *Voina i mir* (1863–69, Eng trans *War and Peace*, 1866). This is both an epic and a domestic tale, a depiction of

Russia's struggle, defeat and victory over **Napoleon I**, set against the fortunes of two notable families, the Rostovs and the Bolkonskis. His second great work, *Anna Karenina* (1874–76), in which the passion felt by a married woman for a young army officer has tragic consequences for her, stems from Tolstoy's personal crisis between the claims of the creative novelist and the propagation of his own ethical code. This conflict found further expression in other works, including *Ispoved'* (1884, Eng trans *A Confession*, 1885). Christianity is purged of its mysticism and transformed into a severe asceticism based on the doctrine of nonresistance to evil. Other works in this vein, including *Tsarstvo Bozhie vnutri vas* (2 vols, 1893–94, Eng trans *The Kingdom of God Is Within You*, 1894), the play *Plody prosveshcheniya* (1889, Eng trans *The Fruits of Enlightenment*, 1891) and *Voskreseniye* (1899, Eng trans *Resurrection*, 1899), were considered so unorthodox that the Holy Synod excommunicated him (1901). In *Chto takoye iskusstvo?* (1898, Eng trans *What Is Art?* 1898) Tolstoy argued that only simple works, such as the parables of the Bible, constitute great art. Everything sophisticated, stylized and detailed, such as his own great novels, he condemned as worthless. Eventually he gave up his material possessions to his wife, who refused to participate in his asceticism, and lived as a peasant under her roof. Domestic quarrels made him leave home secretly one October night, accompanied only by his youngest daughter, Alexandra, and his personal physician, to seek refuge elsewhere. He died of pneumonia in a siding at Astapovo railway station. Tolstoy is best known as the consummate master of the psychological novel. Many of his works were illustrated by **Boris Pasternak**'s father, Leonid.

Tomba, Alberto, *nicknamed* **La Bomba** 1966– •*Italian alpine skier*• Born in Bologna, he became the superstar of skiing, characteristically winning from seemingly impossible positions. He regularly attracted thousands of chanting Italian fans to watch his phenomenal final runs. In his determination to win, he could make costly mistakes but always seemed able to make up the time. His many victories include being world champion (1996), Olympic champion (1988, 1992) and World Cup champion (1995).

Tombaugh, Clyde William 1906–97 •*US astronomer*• He was born in Streator, Illinois. Too poor to attend college, he built his own telescope, and in 1929 became an assistant at the Lowell Observatory, later studying at the University of Kansas. **Percival Lowell** had predicted the existence of an outermost planet, which he named Planet X, and Tombaugh joined the search team that was run by **Vesto Melvin Slipher**. Tombough devised the blink comparator which enabled him to detect if anything had moved in the sky between the taking of two celestial photographs, a few days apart. In 1930, he discovered Pluto in the constellation of Gemini. It was too faint to be the expected Planet X, and he spent another eight years looking, without success. In 1946 he became astronomer at the Aberdeen Ballistics Laboratories in New Mexico and was later appointed astronomer (1955–59), associate professor (1961–65) and professor (1965–73, then emeritus) at the University of New Mexico.

Tomlin, Lily (Mary Jean) 1939– •*US comedic actress*• Born in Detroit, Michigan, she was a premed student at Detroit's Wayne State University before dropping out to pursue a career performing in local cabaret and later moving to New York. Modestly active in all areas of showbusiness, she had her big break as part of television's *Laugh-In* (1960–72). She received an Academy Award nomination for a dramatic role in her film debut, *Nashville* (1975), and her subsequent, sporadic film appearances include *The Late Show* (1977), *All of Me* (1984), *Short Cuts* (1993) and *Tea with Mussolini* (1999).

Tomonaga, Sin-Itiro 1906–79 •*Japanese physicist and Nobel Prize winner*• Born in Kyoto, he was educated at Kyoto Imperial University, where he was a classmate of **Hideki Yukawa**. After graduating (1929), Tomonaga joined Yoshio Nishina at Riken, the Institute for Physical and Chemical Research in Tokyo (1932). In 1937 he moved to Leipzig in Germany to work with **Werner Heisenberg** on a model of the nucleus, returning to Riken in 1939. His most important work was a relativistic quantum description of the interaction between a photon and an electron, producing the theory of quantum electrodynamics, for which he shared the 1965 Nobel Prize for physics with **Richard Feynman** and **Julian Schwinger**.

Tompion, Thomas 1639–1713 •*English clockmaker*• Born possibly in Northill, Bedfordshire, he was apprenticed to a London clockmaker. In 1675, under the supervision of **Robert Hooke**, he made one of the first English watches equipped with a balance spring; this was subsequently gifted to **Charles II**. In 1676 he was appointed clockmaker for the newly opened Royal Observatory. Continuing to develop watch- and clock-making techniques, he patented the cylinder escapement in 1695 (with Edward Barlow), and branched out into barometers and sundials. He was known as the father of English watchmaking.

Tone, (Theobald) Wolfe 1763–98 •*Irish nationalist*• Born in Dublin, he studied there at Trinity College, and was called to the bar in 1789. In 1791 he published a pamphlet, *An Argument on Behalf of the Catholics of Ireland*, and helped found the Society of United Irishmen. In 1792 he became secretary of the Catholic Committee, which worked for the United Catholic Relief Act of 1793. In 1795 he left Ireland to avoid a charge of treason, and went (via the US) to Paris (1796). In September 1798 he embarked with a small French squadron, which after a fierce fight in Lough Swilly was captured. Tone was taken to Dublin, tried, and condemned to be hanged as a traitor, but cut his throat in prison.

Tonegawa, Susumu 1939– •*Japanese molecular biologist and Nobel Prize winner*• Born in Nagoya, he studied chemistry at Kyoto University, then joined the Department of Biology at the University of San Diego. In 1971 he accepted an appointment at the Institute for Immunology in Basel, Switzerland. Tonegawa applied the restriction enzyme and recombinant DNA techniques to resolve the origins of antibody diversity, showing that in the formation of antibody-manufacturing cells the genes undergo changes, allowing them to produce a new wide range of antibodies. In 1981 he returned to MIT, where he has applied the techniques of molecular biology to another aspect of the immune system—the action of the T-lymphocytes. He was awarded the 1987 Nobel Prize for physiology or medicine.

Tong, Xuan *See* **Puyi (P'u-i)**

Tonks, Henry 1862–1937 •*English artist*• Born in Solihull, after becoming a Fellow of the Royal College of Surgeons (1888), he gave up medicine for art. He studied under Frederick Brown, becoming his assistant at the Slade School of Art, joined the New English Art Club (1895), and was associated with **Walter Sickert** and **Philip Wilson Steer**. From 1918 to 1930 he was Slade Professor of Fine Art.

Topolski, Feliks 1907–89 •*British painter, draftsman and illustrator*• Born in Poland, he studied at Warsaw and in Italy and Paris, and went to England in 1935. From 1940 to 1945 he was an official war artist, and he was naturalized in 1947. His lively and sensitive drawings, depicting everyday life, appeared in books and periodicals, and he also designed for the theater. His publications include *Topolski's Chronicle* (1953–79, 1982–89), a draftsman's record of life in various countries, and *Shem, Ham and Japheth Inc.* (1971). His large paintings include the mural *The Coronation of Elizabeth II*, which is housed in Buckingham Palace.

Tormé, Mel(vin Howard) 1925–99 •*US jazz and popular singer, songwriter, arranger and novelist*• Born in Chicago, he studied piano and drums as a youngster, and led his own pop group, the Mel-Tones. He worked as an arranger after leaving the army in 1946, and began to build his reputation as a sophisticated singer of both jazz and pop music. His soft, slightly husky voice earned him the unwelcome nickname of "The Velvet Fog." He recorded classic albums with arranger Marty Paitch throughout his career, and worked regularly with pianist George Shearing from the early 1980s. He wrote hundreds of songs, as well as novels and books on music, including an autobiography and a biography of drummer Buddy Rich, and also both acted and produced for television.

Torquemada, Tomás de 1420–98 •*Spanish Dominican monk, and the first inquisitor general of Spain*• Born in Valladolid, he entered the Dominican Order, and was chosen to be a confessor of **Isabella of Castile** and **Ferdinand the Catholic** (1474). In 1482 he was appointed as one of the seven new inquisitors to continue the work of the recently founded (1480) Inquisition, and became inquisitor general in 1483. No evidence exists for attributing to Torquemada the evidently anti-Semitic philosophy of the early Inquisition, or responsibility for its excesses, but it is unquestionable that he was a major force behind the expulsion of the Jews from Spain in 1492, as well as being responsible for around 2,000 burnings.

Torres, Luis Vaez de fl. 1605–13 •*Spanish navigator*• Though regarded as Spanish, he may have been born in Brittany. He commanded one of three ships under **Pedro Fernandes de Queirós**. After parting from de Quiros, Torres sailed westward through the strait that now bears his name, between New Guinea and Australia, and sighted the tip of Cape York on the mainland of Australia, which he took to be another island.

Torricelli, Evangelista 1608–47 •*Italian physicist and mathematician*• Born probably in Faenza, in 1627 he went to Rome. His *Trattato del Moto* (1641) led **Galileo** to invite him to become his literary assistant, and on Galileo's death he was appointed Galileo's successor as professor at the Florentine Academy. He discovered that, because of atmospheric pressure, water will not rise above 33 feet in a suction pump. To him are owed the fundamental principles of hydromechanics, and in a letter to Ricci (1644) he gave the first description of a mercury barometer or "torricellian tube." He greatly improved both telescopes and microscopes, and published a large number of mathematical papers.

Torrijos Herrera, Omar 1929–81 •*Panamanian military ruler*• He came to power in a military coup in 1968 and was virtual dictator of Panama until his death, instituting social and economic reforms and suppressing political opposition. Fiercely nationalistic, he denounced US control of the Panama Canal, and in 1977 he concluded the treaty that provided for the transfer of the canal to Panamanian sovereignty.

Torrington, 1st Viscount *See* **Byng, George**

Tortelier, Paul 1914–90 •*French cellist, conductor and composer*• Born in Paris, he trained at the Conservatoire, and in 1931 made his debut there. His solo career began with the Concertgebouw, Amsterdam (1946), and with Sir **Thomas Beecham** in London (1947), and he subsequently toured worldwide. A leading soloist, he was also a distinguished teacher (his master classes were televised) and a composer of cello music and of the international anthem *The Great Flag* for the United Nations Organization. His son Yan Pascal (1947–) is a conductor and violinist.

Torvalds, Linus 1969– •*Finnish computer scientist*• Born in Helsinki, he studied at the University of Helsinki. In the early 1990s, while working as a research assistant, he developed a new version of the UNIX operating system which he intended as an improvement on Microsoft's MS-DOS, and dubbed LINUX. This was released onto the Internet as a free download, to acclaim from computer enthusiasts as well as support from a number of software companies including Netscape and Oracle. In 1997 Torvalds joined the Transmeta Corporation as a software developer.

Torvill, Jayne 1957– •*English ice skater*• Born in Nottingham, she started skating at the age of 10, and met **Christopher Dean** in 1975. The pair were six times British champions, World ice-dance champions (1981–84), and won the Olympic and European ice dance titles in 1984. They received a record 136 perfect "sixes" (the highest award a judge can give in ice skating). Their highly acclaimed performances included an interpretation of the music from **Ravel**'s *Bolero*. After retiring from competitive skating in 1984, they continued performing in their own ice show. In 1994 they returned to competitive ice dancing, gaining the British and European titles.

Toscanini, Arturo 1867–1957 •*Italian conductor*• Born in Parma, he won a scholarship to the conservatorio there at the age of nine. Initially a cellist, his earliest success as a conductor was in 1886, and he later conducted at La Scala, Milan (1898–1908), the Metropolitan Opera House, New York (1908–15), the New York Philharmonic Orchestra (1926–36), and at the Bayreuth (1930–31) and Salzburg (1934–37) festivals. He founded and became music director of the National Broadcasting Company Symphony Orchestra of America (1937–53). Always faithful to every detail of the musical score, he was possibly the most authoritarian, yet modest, conductor of his time.

Toulouse-Lautrec (-Monfa or **Montfa), Henri (Marie Raymond) de** 1864–1901 •*French painter and lithographer*• He was born into a wealthy aristocratic family in Albi. The first child of first cousins, he had increasingly severe physical problems, skeletal deformities and dwarfism that were almost certainly hereditary. He showed early promise as an artist, and from 1882 he studied under **Léon Bonnat** in Paris and in 1884 settled in Montmartre, the area which his paintings and posters were to make famous. His early paintings were mainly of sporting subjects. He was later influenced by his contact with the Impressionists and Post-impressionists, notably by **Degas**, but whereas Degas painted the world of ballet from a ballet-lover's theatrical point of view, Lautrec's studies of the cabaret stars, the prostitutes, the barmaids, the clowns and actors of Montmartre reveal an unfailing interest in the human being behind the purely professional function, as in *The Two Friends* (1894, Tate Collection). He disliked models, preferring to concentrate on the human form caught in a characteristic, often intimate posture by his superb draftsmanship regardless of chiaroscuro and background effects, as for example in *Le lit* and *La toilette* (1892 and 1896, Musée d'Orsay) and *Tête-à-tête Supper* (c. 1899, Courtauld Institute, London). His revolutionary poster designs, influenced by Japanese woodcuts which flatten and simplify the subject matter, demonstrate his gift for caricature, as in the posters of the music-hall star Aristide Bruant (1892) and **Yvette Guilbert** (1894). No one has portrayed so effectively the clientèle of these establishments as Toulouse-Lautrec in *Monsieur Boileau at the Café* (1892), and the *Moulin Rouge* paintings (1894). His works also depict fashionable society, as in *At the Races* (1899), and he executed remarkable portraits of his mother (1887), of **Van Gogh** in pastel (1887, Amsterdam) and a drawing of **Oscar Wilde** (1895). In 1895 he visited London, in 1896 Spain and in 1897 Holland. He was a heavy drinker and died from a paralytic stroke. Over 600 of his works are in the Musée Lautrec in Albi.

Tour, Georges de la *See* **La Tour, Georges de**

Tour, Maurice Quentin de la *See* **La Tour, Maurice Quentin de**

Touré, Kwam *See* **Carmichael, Stokely**

Tourneur, Cyril c. 1575–1626 •*English dramatist*• Little is known of his life. His fame rests on two plays, *The Revenger's Tragedy* (printed in 1607), which some critics believe was written by **Thomas Middleton** or **John Webster**, and the inferior *The Atheist's Tragedy*, printed in 1611.

Tourtel, Mary 1874–1948 •*English writer and illustrator*• Born in Canterbury, Kent, and educated at Canterbury Art School, she began her career in the 1890s and found lasting fame with her Rupert the Bear cartoon strip in the *Daily Express* (1920–35), after which time Rupert was carried on by Alfred Bestall (to 1965) and others.

Tourville, Anne Hilarion de Cotentin, Comte de 1642–1701 •*French naval commander*• Born in the Château Tourville, near Coutances, he inflicted a disastrous defeat on the English and Dutch off Beachy Head (1690). In 1692 Tourville sailed from Brest and defeated the English and Dutch, under Admiral Edward Russell, off Cape La Hogue. In 1693 he defeated an Anglo-Dutch fleet off Cape St Vincent, and also defeated Admiral **Rooke** in the Bay of Lagos, capturing or destroying a large part of the Smyrna fleet.

Toussaint Louverture, *originally* **François Dominique Toussaint** 1746–1803 •*Haitian revolutionary leader*• Born a slave in Saint Domingue (Haiti since 1804), but freed in 1777, he joined the insurgents in 1791, and by 1797 was effective ruler of the former colony. He drove out British and Spanish expeditions, and aimed at independence, but **Napoleon I** sent a new expedition to Saint Domingue and Toussaint was arrested and died in prison. His surname ("the opening") comes from his bravery in once making a breach in enemy ranks.

Tovey, Sir Donald Francis 1873–1940 •*English pianist, composer and writer on music*• Born in Eton College, Windsor, Berkshire, he studied there and at Balliol College, Oxford. He made his professional debut as a pianist in 1900, and in 1914 he became Professor of Music at Edinburgh, where he built up the Reid Symphony Orchestra. He composed an opera, *The Bride of Dionysus* (1907–08), a symphony, a piano concerto (1903), a cello concerto (1937, for **Pablo Casals**) and chamber music; but his fame rests largely on his writings, remarkable for great musical perception and learning, such as *Essays on Musical Analysis* (1935–39). He edited **Beethoven**'s sonatas, and edited and completed **J S Bach**'s *Art of Fugue*.

Tovey, John Cronyn Tovey, 1st Baron 1885–1971 •*English naval commander*• He distinguished himself as a destroyer captain in World War I, notably at the Battle of Jutland (1916). As Commander in Chief of the Home fleet (1941–43) he was responsible for the operations leading to the sinking of the German battleship *Bismarck*. He became Admiral of the Fleet in 1943.

Townes, Charles Hard 1915– •*US physicist and Nobel Prize winner*• Born in Greenville, South Carolina, he was educated at Furman University, then at Duke University and the California Institute of Technology (Caltech). During World War II he worked at the Bell Telephone Laboratories, designing radar bombing systems and navigational devices and making the first studies of the microwave spectra of gases. In 1948 he joined Columbia University, where he investigated the electrical and magnetic interaction between molecules and nuclei. In 1951 he passed a weak beam of microwaves through excited ammonia gas, triggering the ammonia molecules to emit their own intense, coherent microwave radiation. Thus he produced the first operational maser (Microwave Amplification by Stimulated Emission of Radiation), the forerunner of the laser. For his work Townes was joint winner of the Nobel Prize for physics with **Nikolai Basov** and **Aleksandr Prokhorov** in 1964. He was subsequently active in developing microwave and infrared astronomy techniques.

Townsend, Sir John Sealy Edward 1868–1957 •*Irish physicist*• Born in Galway, he graduated from Trinity College, Dublin, and in 1895 went to the Cavendish Laboratory in Cambridge. He became Wykeham Professor of Physics at Oxford in 1900. By 1897 he had determined the elementary electrical charge, and his main area of research continued to be the kinetics of ions and electrons in gases. After 1908 he concentrated on the study of the properties of electron clouds, investigating the electron's mean free path, which later had implications for quantum theory. He was knighted in 1941.

Townshend (of Rainham), Charles Townshend, 2nd Viscount, *nicknamed* **Turnip Townshend** 1674–1738 •*English statesman*• Born in Raynham Hall, Norfolk, he was educated at Eton and King's College, Cambridge. He entered public life as a Tory, but soon, as a disciple of Lord Somers (1651–1716), cooperated with the Whigs. He was one of the commissioners for the Union with Scotland (1707) and was joint plenipotentiary with the Duke of **Marlborough** at The Hague. Dismissed in 1712 on the formation of the **Harley** ministry, on the succession of **George I**, Townshend became Secretary of State. With **James Stanhope**, he formed a Whig ministry, which had **Robert Walpole**, his brother-in-law, for Chancellor of the Exchequer. In 1717 he became Lord Lieutenant of Ireland, and in 1721, Secretary of State. He retired in 1730, after which he became interested in agricultural improvement, proposing the use of turnips to improve crop rotation, and thus acquiring his nickname.

Toynbee, Arnold Joseph 1889–1975 •*English historian*• Born in London, he was educated at Winchester and Balliol College, Oxford. He served in the Foreign Office in both world wars and attended the Paris peace conferences (1919, 1946). He was Koraes Professor of Modern Greek and Byzantine History at London (1919–24) and director and research professor of the Royal Institute of International Affairs, London (1925–55). His major work was *History of the World* (10 vols, 1934–54), echoes of which reverberated through his controversial BBC Reith Lectures, *The World and the West* (1952). His numerous other works include *Greek Historical Thought* (1924) and *War and Civilization* (1951).

“ ”

America is a large, friendly dog in a very small room. Every time it wags its tail, it knocks over a chair.

1949 Letter, October 26.

Toyotomi, Hideyoshi *See* **Hideyoshi Toyotomi**

Tracey, Stan(ley William) 1926– •*British jazz pianist, bandleader and composer*• Born in London, he was largely self-taught. After working with dance orchestras such as the Roy Fox and Ted Heath Bands as well as with modern jazz groups in the 1950s, he was house pianist from 1960 to 1967 at Ronnie Scott's Club, Soho, accompanying many leading contemporary touring musicians. He developed a distinctive, angular, percussive keyboard style, rooted in **Thelonious Monk** and **Duke Ellington**, but with his own distinctive flavor. Since the mid-1960s he has led a succession of bands from quartets to 16-piece orchestras, has toured abroad and has written jazz suites such as *Under Milk Wood* (1965). His son, drummer Clark Tracey (1961–), is also an important jazz musician.

Tracy, Spencer Bonadventure 1900–67 •*US film actor*• Born in Milwaukee, Wisconsin, he attended the Northwestern Military Academy, Ripon College, and the American Academy of Dramatic Arts. He made his Broadway debut in *A Royal Fandango* (1923) and his feature film debut in *Up the River* (1930). Initially typecast as a tough guy and gangster, his acting skills and reliability eventually brought him more demanding roles, earning him a reputation as one of the screen's finest performers. Nominated nine times for an Academy Award, he won it for his performances in *Captains Courageous* (1937) and *Boy's Town* (1938). Other notable films include *Dr Jekyll and Mr Hyde* (1941), and *Judgment at Nuremberg* (1961). A long personal and professional association with **Katharine Hepburn** resulted in a series of comedies, including his final performance, in *Guess Who's Coming to Dinner* (1967).

Traherne, Thomas c.1636–74 •*English poet*• Born in Hereford, he studied at Brasenose College, Oxford, and became rector of Credenhill (1657) and chaplain (1667) to the Lord Keeper of the Great Seal, Sir Orlando Bridgeman. He wrote the anti-Catholic *Roman Forgeries* (1673) and *Christian Ethicks* (1675). His major work, *Centuries of Meditations* in prose, and many of his poems, were found in a notebook in a London bookstall in 1896, the former being first published in 1908, and the latter, as *Poetical Works*, in 1903. *Poems of Felicity* was published in 1910.

Trajan, *originally* **Marcus Ulpius Trajanus** c. 53–117 AD •*Roman emperor*• Born near Seville, he was adopted by **Nerva** as his colleague and successor (AD 97), and became sole ruler in 98. From 101 Trajan campaigned against the Dacians, and Dacia eventually became a Roman province (106). In 113 Trajan left Italy to campaign in the east, mainly against the Parthians. He made Armenia and Mesopotamia into Roman provinces, and captured the Parthian capital, Ctesiphon (115). Meanwhile uprisings took place in the rest of the empire, and he set sail for Italy, but died at Selinus in Cilicia. His reign saw the Roman Empire at its greatest extent, and the internal administration was excellent. The empire was covered in all directions by new military routes; canals, bridges and harbors were constructed; new towns built; the Pontine Marshes partially drained; and the magnificent Forum Trajani erected. He enjoyed great popularity in his lifetime and his reputation remained high after death, though under him the empire showed signs of economic breakdown.

Tranter, Nigel 1909–99 •*Scottish novelist and historian*• Born in Glasgow and educated at George Heriot's School in Edinburgh, he trained as an accountant before becoming a full-time writer in 1936. A prolific writer, he produced well over 130 books. His best-known novels are those on historical themes, most notably the trilogy on the life of **Robert the Bruce**, *The Steps to the Empty Throne* (1969), *The Path of the Hero King* (1970) and *The Price of the King's Peace* (1971). His nonfiction works include significant studies of Scottish castles and fortified houses.

Travers, Ben(jamin) 1886–1980 •*English dramatist and novelist*• Born in Hendon, London, he was educated at Charterhouse, served in the RAF in both world wars and was awarded the Air

Force Cross (1920). A master of light farce, he wrote to suit the highly individual comic talents of Ralph Lynn, Robertson Hare and Tom Walls in such pieces as *A Cuckoo in the Nest* (1925), *Rookery Nook* (1926) and *Plunder* (1928). His last work was a comedy, *The Bed Before Yesterday* (1976).

Travolta, John 1954– •*US actor*• Born in Englewood, New Jersey, he made his film debut in *The Devil's Rain* (1975). His role as the slow-witted Vinnie Barbarino in the television series *Welcome Back, Kotter* (1975–79) gained him national attention, and he received a Best Actor Academy Award nomination for *Saturday Night Fever* (1977). Boyishly handsome, he had his popularity confirmed with the success of the film *Grease* (1978). Subsequent films include *Staying Alive* (1983) and *Look Who's Talking* (1989). After a period out of the limelight, he made a welcome comeback as a hit man in *Pulp Fiction* (1994) and starred in a string of hit films including *Get Shorty* (1995), *Phenomenon* (1996) and *A Civil Action* (1998).

Tree, Sir Herbert (Draper) Beerbohm 1853–1917 •*English actor and manager*• He was born in London, and was the half brother of Sir **Max Beerbohm**. Following a commercial education in Germany, he became an actor, then took over the Haymarket Theatre (1887) and, with the box-office success of *Trilby* (1894), he built His Majesty's Theatre (1897). He founded the Royal Academy of Dramatic Art in 1904. A great character actor, he excelled in roles such as Svengali, Falstaff, Hamlet, Fagin, Shylock, Malvolio and Micawber. His wife, (Helen) Maud Holt (1864–1937), was also an accomplished actress; she is best remembered for the film *The Private Life of Henry VIII* (1932).

Tremain, Rose 1943– •*English author*• Born in London, she studied at the Sorbonne and at the University of East Anglia. She became a full-time writer in 1971, producing novels such as *Sadler's Birthday* (1976), *Restoration* (1989), *Sacred Country* (1992) and *Evangelista's Fan* (1994), and has written numerous short stories and several plays for radio. Among many awards she won the Whitbread prize in 1999 for *Music and Silence*.

Trench, Richard Chenevix 1807–86 •*Irish prelate, philologist and poet*• Born in Dublin and educated at Harrow and Trinity College, Cambridge, he became curate in 1841 to **Samuel Wilberforce**, and during 1835–46 published six volumes of poetry. In 1845 he became rector of Itchenstoke and in 1847 Professor of Theology at King's College London. In 1856 he became dean of Westminster and from 1864 to 1884 he was Archbishop of Dublin. In philology he popularized the scientific study of words, and the *New English Dictionary*, later the *Oxford English Dictionary*, was begun at his suggestion. His theological works include *Notes on the Parables of Our Lord* (1841).

Trevelyan, G(eorge) M(acaulay) 1876–1962 •*English historian*• Born in Welcombe, Warwickshire, he was educated at Harrow and Trinity College, Cambridge, of which he was elected master (1940–51). He served in World War I and was Regius Professor of Modern History at Cambridge (1927–40). He is best known for his *English Social History* (1944), a companion volume to his *History of England* (1926). Other works include studies of **Garibaldi** (1907, 1909, 1911) and **John Bright** (1913) and an autobiography (1949).

Trevino, Lee Buck 1939– •*US golfer*• Born in Dallas, Texas, he won six majors—the US Open twice (1968, 1971), the British Open twice (1971, 1972) and the US Professional Golfers' Association twice (1974, 1984)—but is the only man to hold the Open titles of America, Britain and Canada simultaneously. More than his victories, it was his ability to combine wisecracks with excellent golf that made him one of the game's most popular players.

Trevithick, Richard 1771–1833 •*English engineer and inventor*• He was born in Illogan, Redruth, Cornwall, and was educated locally. He became a mining engineer and devoted his life to the improvement of the steam engine. Between 1796 and 1801 he invented a steam carriage, which ran between Camborne and Tuckingmill, and which in 1803 was run from Leather Lane to Paddington via Oxford Street. From 1800 to 1815 he built several steam road carriages, the first steam railway locomotives and a large number of stationary steam engines. He later went to Peru and Costa Rica (1816–27), where his engines were introduced into the silver mines.

Trevor, William, *properly* **William Trevor Cox** 1928– •*Irish short-story writer, novelist and playwright*• Born in Mitchelstown, County Cork, he was educated at St Columba's College and Trinity College, Dublin. His first book was a novel, *A Standard of Behaviour* (1958), but although he has published a number of other novels, including *The Children of Dynmouth* (1976) and *Nights at the Alexandra* (1987), he is by inclination a short-story writer. He has lived in England for much of his life, but Ireland is the source of his inspiration. His superlative tales have been collected as *The Day We Got Drunk on Cake* (1967), *Angels at the Ritz* (1975) and *Family Sins* (1990). More recent works include *Felicia's Journey* (1994), which won Trevor the Whitbread Book of the Year award, and *After Rain and Other Stories* (1996). He has also written a number of plays and screenplays.

Trevor-Roper, Hugh Redwald, Baron Dacre of Glanton 1914–2003 •*English historian and controversialist*• Born in Glanton, Northumberland, he was educated at Charterhouse and Christ Church, Oxford, and won international fame for his vivid reconstruction of *The Last Days of Hitler* (1947). He was Regius Professor of Modern History at Oxford (1957–80) and wrote on a wide range of topics, including medieval Christendom, European witch hunting, the **John F Kennedy** assassination, the **Kim Philby** affair, the Scottish Enlightenment, and British devolution, and edited the **Goebbels** diaries (1978). He also received a great deal of publicity when he asserted the authenticity of diaries purporting to be those of **Hitler** that later proved to be fraudulent. He was master of Peterhouse College, Cambridge (1980–87), then made Honorary Fellow in 1987.

Trier, Lars von *See* **von Trier, Lars**

Trilling, Lionel 1905–75 •*US literary critic*• Born in New York City, he was educated at Columbia University, where he became Professor of English in 1948. A trenchant and influential writer, he held that culture was central to the human experience. In the tradition of **Matthew Arnold**, on whom he wrote a standard book (1939), his interests were wide-ranging, and his many publications include *The Liberal Imagination* (1950), *The Opposing Self* (1955), *Beyond Culture* (1965) and *Sincerity and Authenticity* (1972). His only novel, *The Middle of the Journey*, was published in 1947.

“ ”

The poet ... may be used as a barometer, but let us not forget that he is also part of the weather.

*1950 **The Liberal Imagination**.*

Trimble, (William) David 1944– •*Northern Irish politician and Nobel Prize winner*• Born in Belfast, he was educated at Queen's University there and worked as a barrister and university lecturer before serving as a member of the Northern Ireland Constitutional Convention (1975–76). A member of the Ulster Unionist Party, he was elected Member of Parliament in 1990 and became leader of the party in 1995. Variously respected and resented for his stern but also pragmatic approach to negotiations with nationalists in Northern Ireland, he shared the 1998 Nobel Peace Prize with SDLP leader **John Hume**. That same year he was appointed first minister of the reconstituted Northern Ireland Assembly. Trimble worked tirelessly to keep the peace process alive, his tactics including his own resignation (July 2001) as first minister of the Assembly.

Trinder, Tommy (Thomas Edward) 1909–89 •*English comedian and actor*• Born in Streatham, London, he first went on stage at the age of 12. A jaunty, cheerful performer, he was a master of ad lib and the quick retort, and happily performed without a script. His first big opportunity came in 1939 when he was invited to join the *Band Waggon* show at the London Palladium, and he went on to become well known, both as a standup comic in such revues as *Happy and Glorious* and as a leading man in films such as *Champagne Charlie* (1944). The self-confessed "Mr Woolworth of show-business" whose famous catchphrase was "You lucky people," he worked tirelessly during World War II, traveling to Italy, the Middle East and the Far East to entertain the troops. After the war he emceed the ITV show *Sunday Night at the London Palladium* (1954–58). He continued to perform into his late seventies. A soccer enthusiast, he was chairman of Fulham Football Club (1955–76).

Trintignant, Jean-Louis 1930– •*French actor*• Born in Port-St Esprit, he abandoned his legal studies to become an actor. His first major role, in *Responsabilité limitée* (1954), led to his film debut in the short *Peachinef* (1955), and his subsequent appearance in Roger Vadim's *Et Dieu créa la femme* (1956, *And God Created Woman*). His pale-skinned impassivity and sensitive eyes have lent themselves to the portrayal of romantic vulnerability and psychological disturbance. His career includes the internationally successful romance *Un homme et une femme* (1966, *A Man and a Woman*) and a variety of work for Europe's most distinguished directors including *Les biches* (1968, "The Does"), *Z* (1968) and *Il conformista* (1970, "The Conformist"). *Under Fire* (1983) marked a rare venture into English-language productions. He has also directed *Une journée bien remplie* (1972, "A Well-Filled Day") and *Le maître nageur* (1979, "The Lifeguard"). Later films include *Merci la vie* (1991), *Trois couleurs: rouge* (1994, "Three Colors: Red") and *Fiesta* (1995).

Troisi, Massimo 1953–94 •*Italian filmmaker*• Born in Naples, he was a well-known theater actor before finding national fame as part of the comedy group La Smorfia. He made his film debut in the comedy *Ricomincio da tre* (1981, "Beginning with Three") and soon became a guarantee of box-office success in feisty farces examining modern relationships. He worked sparingly for other directors, but won the Venice Film Festival Best Actor prize for his performance in *Che ora e?* (1989, "What Time Is It?"). Suffering with a heart that had been weakened by rheumatic fever as a child, he died 12 hours after completing *Il postino* (1994, "The Postman") in which his tender, poignant performance as a humble, lovestruck postman secured him a posthumous Academy Award nomination.

Trollope, Anthony 1815–82 •*English novelist*• He was born in London, educated (unhappily) at Harrow and Winchester, and with his family moved to Belgium, where his father, an unsuccessful lawyer and barrister, died. His mother, Frances Trollope (1780–1863), a woman of enviable energy, maintained the family by her prolific writing. He became a junior clerk in the General Post Office in London (1834) and was transferred to Ireland (1841). He left the Civil Service (1867), an important but idiosyncratic official whose achievements included the introduction in Great Britain of the pillar box for letters. His first novels, *The Macdermots of Ballycloran* (1847) and *The Kellys and the O'Kellys* (1848), were not successful, but with *The Warden* (1855), the first of the Barchester novels, came an inkling of his genius. It is the story of the struggle over Hiram's Hospital, and introduced into English fiction some of its most durable and memorable characters—Mr Harding, who recurs throughout the Barchester series, Archdeacon Grantly, and Bishop Proudie, who with his redoubtable wife dominates *Barchester Towers* (1857). The rest of the series are: *Doctor Thorne* (1858), *Framley Parsonage* (1861), *The Small House at Allington* (1864) and *The Last Chronicle of Barset* (1867). Interconnected by character and unified by their West Country setting in the imaginary town of Barchester, the novels are distinguished by their quiet comedy, slow pace and piquant detail. Trollope embarked on a second, more ambitious sequence (known collectively as the Palliser novels) with the publication in 1864 of *Can You Forgive Her?* Its sequel was *Phineas Finn* (1869), and others in the series are *The Eustace Diamonds* (1873), *Phineas Redux* (1874), *The Prime Minister* (1876), and *The Duke's Children* (1880). Several of his books were serialized in the *St Paul's Magazine*, which he edited (1867–70). His output was consequently prodigious and comprises 47 novels, travel books, biographies, plays, short stories and literary sketches. Other novels worthy of note include *The Three Clerks* (1858), *The Bertrams* (1859), *Orley Farm* (1862), *The Vicar of Bullhampton* (1870), *The Way We Live Now* (1875) and *Doctor Wortle's School* (1881). His *Autobiography* (1883) is an antidote to more romantic accounts of the literary life.

Tromp, Cornelis Maartenzoon 1629–91 •*Dutch naval commander*• He was the son of **Maarten Tromp**. He shared the glory of **Michiel de Ruyter**'s Four Days' Battle (1666) off Dunkirk, and won fame in the battles against the combined English and French fleets (June 7 and 14, 1673).

Tromp, Maarten Harpertszoon 1598–1653 •*Dutch admiral*• Born in Briel, he defeated a superior Spanish fleet off Gravelines in 1639, and the same year won the Battle of the Downs. Knighted by **Louis XIII** of France (1640) and by **Charles I** of England (1642), his encounter with **Robert Blake** in 1652 started the Anglo-Dutch Wars. Victorious off Dover, he was killed in an engagement with **George Monk** off Terheijde.

Trotsky, Leon, *alias of* **Lev Davidovich Bronstein** 1879–1940 •*Russian revolutionary*• He was born in Yanovka, Ukraine, and educated in Odessa. At the age of 19 he was arrested as a Marxist and was sent to Siberia. He escaped in 1902, joined **Lenin** in London, and in the abortive 1905 revolution became president of the St Petersburg Soviet. After escaping from a further exile period in Siberia, he became a revolutionary journalist among Russian émigrés in the West. He returned to Russia in 1917, joined the Bolshevik Party, and with **Lenin** played a major role in the October Revolution. As commissar for foreign affairs he conducted negotiations with the Germans for the peace treaty of Brest-Litovsk (1918). In the Russian civil war, as commissar for war, he created the Red Army of 5 million men from a nucleus of 7,000 men. On Lenin's death in 1924 Trotsky's influence began to decline. **Stalin**, who opposed his theory of permanent revolution, ousted him from the politburo, and he was exiled to Central Asia (1927), and then was expelled from the USSR (1929). He continued to agitate and intrigue as an exile in several countries. In 1937, having been sentenced to death in absentia by a Soviet court, he found asylum in Mexico City. There he was assassinated with an ice pick in 1940 by Ramon del Rio (alias Jacques Mornard). Ruthless, energetic, a superb orator and messianic visionary, in his later years he was the focus of those Communists, Soviet and otherwise, who opposed the endless opportunism of Stalin. He was a writer of power, wit and venom, and, in contrast to Stalin's "socialism in one country," he was an advocate of world revolution. His publications include *The Revolution Betrayed* (1937), *Stalin* (1948) and *Diary in Exile* (translated 1959), and remain influential in Western Marxist circles. In January 1989, as part of the policy of glasnost under **Mikhail Gorbachev**, it was revealed that Trotsky was murdered by the Soviet secret police. Trotsky's son, Sergei Sedov, who was shot dead in Moscow in 1937, was rehabilitated by the Soviet Supreme Court in 1988.

" "

Old age is the most unexpected of all things that happens to a man.

1935 ***Diary in Exile*** *(1959).*

Trudeau, Garry, *in full* **Garretson Beekman Trudeau** 1948– •*US cartoonist*• Born in New York City, he was a student at Yale in 1968 when he drew a comic strip featuring irreverent political and social satire, syndicated as *Doonesbury* in 1970. His work addresses social issues such as drug use and homelessness and fires salvos at intolerance and political hypocrisy. He won the Pulitzer Prize for editorial cartooning in 1975, and he has published many *Doonesbury* collections in book form.

Trudeau, Pierre Elliott 1919–2000 •*Canadian statesman*• Born in Montreal, he was called to the Quebec bar in 1944. In 1956 he was active in the short-lived *Rassemblement*, a group of left-wing opponents of **Maurice Duplessis**. From 1961 to 1965 he was Associate Professor of Law at the University of Montreal and in 1965, having rejected the New Democratic Party for the Liberal Party, was elected to the House of Commons. In 1966 he was appointed parliamentary secretary to the prime minister and in 1967, as minister of justice and attorney-general, he opposed the separation of Quebec from the rest of Canada. In 1968 he succeeded **Lester Pearson** as federal leader of the Liberal Party and prime minister. He then called a general election at which his party secured an overall majority. His government was defeated in 1979 but was returned to power in 1980. He retired from active politics in 1984 and published his memoirs in 1993.

Truffaut, François 1932–84 •*French film critic and director*• He was born in Paris. His early life as an unhappy child, reform school pupil and army deserter later formed elements of his more autobiographical works. His first film as director was the short *Une visite* (1955). A founding father of the French nouvelle vague ("new wave"), he made his feature debut with *Les quatre cents coups* (1959, "The 400 Blows"), a haunting study of deprived childhood that gained him an international reputation. His diverse work includes most of the popular genres, with films like *Jules et Jim* (1962), *Farenheit 451* (1966), *La nuit américaine* (1973, "Day for Night"), for which he received an Academy Award, and *Le dernier métro* (1980, "The Last Metro"). He acted in his own films and in *Close Encounters of the Third Kind* (1977). His many writings included an autobiography, *Les films de ma vie* (1975).

Truman, Harry S 1884–1972 •*33rd President of the US*• He was born in Lamar, Missouri, and educated in Independence, Missouri. After World War I, in which he served as an artillery captain on the Western Front, he became a judge in 1922 for the eastern district of Jackson County in Missouri, and in 1926 a presiding judge, a post he held until 1934, when Missouri elected him as a Democrat to the US Senate. He was elected vice president in 1944 and became president in April 1945 on the death of President **Franklin D Roosevelt**. He was reelected in 1948 in a surprise victory over Thomas E Dewey (1902–1971). During his presidency he made many historically important decisions, including dropping the first atom bombs on Hiroshima and Nagasaki; pushing through Congress a huge postwar loan to Great Britain (the **Marshall** Plan); making a major change in US policy toward the USSR, the Truman Doctrine of Communist containment and support for free peoples resisting subjugation; organizing the Berlin Airlift (1948–49); establishing NATO (1949); and sending US troops on behalf of the UN to withstand the Communist invasion of South Korea (1950). He also established the CIA. He did not run for reelection in 1952 and retired to Independence. Later he became a strong critic of the **Eisenhower** Republican administration.

Trumbull, John 1756–1843 •*American historical painter*• He was born in Lebanon, Connecticut. After service in the American Revolution, he began a series of celebrated war paintings, including *The Battle of Bunker Hill*, and a number of portraits of **George Washington**. He was later ambassador to London (1794–1804), and in 1817 painted four large historical pictures for the rotunda of the Capitol in Washington DC. The Trumbull Gallery at Yale was built to accommodate his collection of paintings (1832).

Truth, Sojourner, *originally* **Isabella Van Wagener** c. 1797–1883 •*US abolitionist*• Born a slave in Ulster County, New York, she gained her freedom, taking her surname from her previous master and becoming an ardent evangelist. In 1843 she felt called to change her name, and to fight against slavery and for women's suffrage. Preaching widely across the US, she drew large crowds with her infectious style of speaking. In 1850 she produced a biography, *The Narrative of Sojourner Truth*. She was appointed counselor to the freedmen of Washington by **Abraham Lincoln**, and continued to promote African-American rights, including educational opportunities, until her retirement in 1875.

Ts'ao Yü *See* **Cao Yu**

Tshombe, Moise Kapenda 1919–69 •*Congolese politician*• Educated in mission schools, he was a businessman who helped found the Confederation des Associations Tribales du Katanga in 1957. When Belgium granted the Congo independence in 1960, he declared the copper-rich province of Katanga independent and became its president. At the request of **Patrice Lumumba**, UN troops were called in to reintegrate the province, and Tshombe was forced into exile in 1963, returning in 1964. Forced into exile again after **Sese Seke Mobutu**'s 1966 coup, Tshombe was kidnapped in 1967 and taken to Algeria, where he died in custody.

Tsiolkovsky, Konstantin Eduardovich 1857–1935 •*Russian astrophysicist and rocket pioneer*• Born in the village of Izheskaye in the Spassk district, he was largely self-educated in science. Unaware of the work of **James Clerk Maxwell**, in 1881 he independently developed the kinetic theory of gases. By 1895 his published papers had suggested the possibility of space flight, three years later stressing the necessity for liquid-fuel rocket engines. In 1903 he published his seminal work, *Exploration of Cosmic Space by Means of Reaction Devices*, which established his reputation as the father of space flight theory. From 1911 he developed the basic theory of rocketry, and also multistage rocket technology (1929). He wrote a number of works of science fiction. Towards the end of his life the Soviet government became interested in space flight and his work began to be recognized.

Tubman, Harriet c. 1820–1913 •*US abolitionist*• Born in Dorchester County, Maryland, she escaped from slavery there (1849), and from then until the Civil War she was active in the slave escape route, a number of safe houses called the Underground Railroad, making a number of dangerous trips into the South and leading over 300 people to freedom. Famous among abolitionists, she counseled **John Brown** before his attempt to launch the Harpers Ferry weapons raid (1859). During the Civil War she was a Northern spy and scout.

Tubman, William V S 1895–1971 •*Liberian politician*• Educated in a Methodist seminary, he was a teacher, lawyer and Methodist preacher. He was elected for the True Whig Party, which protected the interests of the Americo-Liberian elite, and became a member of the Liberian Senate in 1922. In 1937 he was appointed deputy president of the Supreme Court and, in 1944, was chosen as president of Liberia, a post he retained until his death.

Tuchman, Barbara W(ertheim) 1912–89 •*US historian*• Born in New York City, she graduated from Radcliffe in 1933 and worked as a freelance journalist, traveling to Spain as a correspondent for the *Nation* in 1937. Later she became an independent scholar, writing histories praised for their narrative force and illuminating detail. Her best-known book is *The Guns of August* (1962, Pulitzer Prize), an account of the events that led to the outbreak of World War I. Other works include *The Proud Tower*, *Stilwell and the American Experience in China* (1971, Pulitzer Prize), *A Distant Mirror* (1978), and *The March of Folly* (1984).

""

Dead battles, like dead generals, hold the military mind in their dead grip.

*1962 **The Guns of August**, chapter 2.*

Tucker, Sophie, *professional name of* **Sonia Kalish**, *originally* **Sophie Abuza** 1884–1966 •*US singer and vaudeville entertainer*• Born in Russia, she made her debut in New York as a blackface comedienne and retained strong blues and jazz elements in her singing style. This style won her the title "the last of the red hot mamas." Like **Ethel Waters**, she made a significant contribution to perceptions of women in entertainment, and remained close to African-American composers like **Eubie Blake** and Shelton Brooks, who wrote her theme song "Some of These Days," the title of which she gave to her autobiography (1945).

Tudjman, Franjo 1922–99 •*Croatian politician and historian*• Born in Veliko Trgovise, Yugoslavia, he became in 1945 the youngest general in the Yugoslav federal army. In 1972 he was imprisoned during the purge of the Croatian nationalist movement and in 1981 was again sentenced to three years' imprisonment in the first major political trial since **Tito**'s death. A professor of modern history at the Faculty of Political Science at Zagreb, following the elections in 1990, as leader of the right-wing Croatian Democratic Union, he became president of Croatia. He declared the Republic of Croatia's independence from the Yugoslav federation (1992), but the republic soon found itself engaged in a brutal war against the Yugoslav federal army. While international recognition of the independence of the Republic of Croatia followed in 1991 and 1992, over a third of the republic still remained beyond the reach of Tudjman's government in Zagreb. He was reelected as president of Croatia in 1992 and 1997.

Tudor, Antony, *originally* **William Cook** 1908–87 •*English dancer, choreographer and teacher*• Born in London, he worked at Smithfield meat market there while studying dance with **Marie Rambert** (1928). In 1930 she made him stage manager/secretary of her Ballet Club, for whose company he later made several key pieces. His first was *Cross Garter'd* in 1931, followed by the celebrated *Lilac Garden* in 1936 and the moody *Dark Elegies* in 1937. That same year he and a number of other Rambert members formed their own group, Dance Theatre, known from 1938 to 1940 as London Ballet. **Agnes De Mille** persuaded Tudor and his friend Harold Laing to move to New York City, where Tudor was position staff choreographer with Ballet Theater (now American Ballet Theater) for ten years. The years following were spent primarily in teaching, as director of the Metropolitan Opera Ballet School, and tutoring at the Juilliard School of Music, New York, though he was a seasonal guest choregraher with both ABT and the Royal Swedish Ballet. He made *Echoing of Trumpets* in 1963 and *Shadowplay* in 1967, and in 1974 he returned to ABT to create *The Leaves Are Fading* (1975) and *The Tiller in the Fields* (1978). He is generally considered to be one of the great contemporary choreographers.

Tu Fu *See* **Du Fu**

Tukhachevsky, Mikhail Nikolayevich 1893–1937 •*Russian soldier and politician*• Born near Slednevo, he served as an officer in the Czarist Army in World War I, but became a member of the Communist Party in 1918. He commanded Bolshevik forces against the Poles under **Władysław Sikorski** and **Józef Piłsudski** in the Russo-Polish War (1920), against the White Russians (1919–20) and during the Kulak uprising of 1921. From 1926 he was chief of staff of the Red Army, which he was influential in transforming from a peasant army into a modern, mechanized force. He was created Marshal of the Soviet Union in 1935. In 1937 he was executed, an early victim of the great purge which decimated the Red Army's officer corps.

Tull, Jethro 1674–1741 •*English agriculturist*• He was born in Basildon, Berkshire, and educated at St John's College, Oxford. The inventor of a seed drill (1701), he introduced new farming methods in his native county, his chief innovation being the planting of seeds in rows. He wrote *The Horse-Hoing Husbandry* (1733).

Tupolev, Andrei Nikolayevich 1888–1972 •*Russian aeronautical engineer*• Born in Moscow, the son of a lawyer, he was educated at Moscow Higher Technical School, and was already working in a Moscow aircraft factory before the revolution. In the 1920s and 1930s he designed several bombers of world class, and even when imprisoned on false accusations of treason in 1937, he continued designing, and was therefore released in 1943. In 1955 he built the first Soviet civil jet, the Tu-104, and in 1968 he completed the first test flight of a supersonic passenger aircraft, the Tu-144.

Tura, Cosimo c. 1430–95 •*Italian artist*• Born in Ferrara, he was the leader, with Francesco del Cossa (c. 1435–77), of the Ferrarese school. He studied under **Francesco Squarcione** at Padua, and his metallic, tortured forms and unusual colors give a strange power to his pictures, which include the *Pietà* in the Louvre, Paris, and the *San Jerome* in the National Gallery, London.

Turenne, Henri de la Tour d'Auvergne, Vicomte de 1611–75 •*French soldier*• Born in Sedan, he was the second son of the Duc de Bouillon and Elizabeth of Nassau, **William I (the Silent**'s) daughter. Brought up in the Reformed faith, he fought first in the Dutch War of Independence (1625–30) under his uncle, Prince **Maurice of Nassau**. In the Thirty Years' War (1618–48) he fought with distinction for the armies of the Protestant alliance, and in 1641 became supreme commander. He captured Breisach (1638) and Turin (1640), and for the conquest of Roussillon from the Spaniards in 1642 was made a Marshal of France (1644). In the civil wars of the Fronde, Turenne at first joined the *frondeurs*, but then switched sides and saved the government of **Mazarin** and the young King **Louis XIV** by his campaigning (1652–53). In the Franco-Spanish War, he conquered much of the Spanish Netherlands and defeated the **Prince de Condé**, who had deserted to the *frondeurs*, at the Battle of the Dunes (1658). He won lasting fame for his campaigns in the United Provinces during the Dutch War (1672–75), but was killed while advancing along the Rhine at Sasbach.

Turgenev, Ivan Sergeyevich 1818–83 •*Russian novelist*• He was born in the province of Oryel, and after graduating from St Petersburg University went to Berlin to study philosophy, where he mingled with the radical thinkers of the day. He returned to Russia in 1841 to enter the civil service, but in 1843 abandoned this to take up literature. His tyrannical mother strongly disapproved, and she stopped his allowance. Until her death in 1850, when he came into his inheritance, he had to support himself by his writings. In 1850 he wrote his finest and best-known play, *A Month in the Country* (published 1869, staged 1872). *Zapiski okhotnika* (1852, Eng trans *A Sportsman's Sketches*), sympathetic studies of the peasant life, made his reputation, but were perceived by the government as an attack on serfdom. A notice praising **Nikolai Gogol** on his death in 1852 resulted in a two years' banishment to his country estates. After his exile he spent much time in Europe, writing several faithful descriptions of Russian liberalism. In his greatest novel, *Ottsy i dety* (1862, Eng trans *Fathers and Sons*, 1867), he portrayed the new generation, with its faith in science and lack of respect for tradition and authority. His popularity slumped in Russia but rose abroad, particularly in Great Britain, where the book was recognized as a major contribution to literature. Successive novels were *Dym* (1867, Eng trans *Smoke*, 1868) and *Nov'* (1877, Eng trans *Virgin Soil*, 1877). He also returned to the short story and to tales of the supernatural.

Turgot, Anne Robert Jacques 1727–81 •*French economist and politician*• Born in Paris of Norman ancestry, he was destined for the church but became a lawyer. Appointed intendant of Limoges in 1761, he introduced many reforms, including the abolition of compulsory labor on roads and bridges. Soon after the accession of **Louis XVI** (1774), he was appointed comptroller general of finance and at once he began to introduce wide reforms. He reduced expenditure and increased public revenue without imposing new taxes, established free trade in grain within France and removed the fiscal barriers between the provinces. He abolished the exclusive privileges of trade corporations and sought to break down the immunity from taxation enjoyed by the privileged classes, who pressed for his dismissal. Turgot was removed from office after only 20 months. His chief work, *Reflexions sur la formation et la distribution des richesses* (1766, Eng trans *Reflections on the Formation and Distribution of Wealth*), largely anticipated **Adam Smith**.

Turina, Joaquín 1882–1949 •*Spanish composer and pianist*• Born in Seville, he came under the influence of **Manuel de Falla** and the Spanish Nationalist composers. In 1905 he went to Paris to study at the Schola Cantorum, and became an important figure in French musical circles. Returning to Madrid in 1914, he was very active as a composer, pianist and critic until the Spanish civil war, in which he was a supporter of General **Franco**, curtailed his work. He wrote four operas, orchestral and chamber works, and piano pieces, the best of which combine strong Andalusian color and idiom with traditional forms.

Turing, Alan Mathison 1912–54 •*English mathematician*• Born in London, he studied mathematics at King's College, Cambridge, and also studied at the Institute for Advanced Study in Princeton. In 1936 Turing made an outstanding contribution to the development of computer science, outlining a theoretical universal machine (later called a Turing machine) and giving a precise mathematical characterization of the concept of computability. In World War II he worked in cryptography and on Colossus (a forerunner of the modern computer) before joining the National Physical Laboratory (1945), where he developed his Automatic Computing Engine (ACE). In 1948 he accepted a post at the University of Manchester, where he made contributions to the programming of the Manchester Mark I computer, researched some complicated theories in plant morphogenesis, and explored the problem of machine intelligence. Subsequently, harrassed and prosecuted for being gay, he committed suicide.

Turner, Ethel S(ibyl) 1872–1958 •*Australian novelist and children's author*• She was born in Doncaster, Yorkshire, England. She moved to Australia at the age of eight, and with her sister Lilian started *Iris*, a magazine for schoolgirls, later contributing children's pages to other publications under the name "Dame Durden." Her first book, *Seven Little Australians* (1894), is now a classic of Australian literature. It has been in print ever since publication, was filmed as early as 1939 and has been adapted for British and Australian television and as a stage musical. A sequel, *The Family at Misrule*, came out in 1895, and there followed a steady stream of juvenile books, short stories and verse.

Turner, Dame Eva 1892–1990 •*English opera singer*• Born in Oldham, Lancashire, she studied at the Royal Academy of Music and made her debut in the Carl Rosa Company chorus in 1916. During the 1920s she played many leading parts, including **Puccini**'s *Turandot* in 1926, a role for which she became famous. She traveled throughout Europe, pioneering the acceptance of the idea of a British prima donna, and made her US debut with the Chicago Opera in 1928. She later became visiting professor of voice at the University of Oklahoma (1949–59) and professor of singing at the Royal Academy of Music (1959–66).

Turner, John Napier 1929– •*Canadian politician*• Born in Richmond, England, he went to Canada with his family in 1932. After studying at the University of British Columbia and at Oxford, he practiced law in Britain, was called to the English bar, and later the bars of Quebec and Ontario, being made a Queen's Counsel in 1968. He entered the Canadian House of Commons in 1962 and was a junior minister in **Lester Pearson**'s government and later attorney general and finance minister under **Pierre Trudeau**. When Trudeau retired in 1984, Turner succeeded him as leader of the Liberal Party and prime minister. He lost the general election later the same year and became leader of the opposition. He resigned the leadership of his party in 1990.

Turner, J(oseph) M(allord) W(illiam) 1775–1851 •*English painter*• Born in London, at the age of 14 he entered the Royal Academy, and in the following year he was already exhibiting. At 18 he began touring England and Wales in search of material and made architectural drawings in the cathedral cities. For three years in the mid-1790s he joined forces with **Thomas Girtin**, the latter drawing the outlines and Turner washing in the color; between them they raised the art of watercolor to new heights of delicacy and charm. From 1796, he took up oils. In 1802 he visited the Louvre collections and was greatly attracted by **Titian** and **Nicolas Poussin**. More and more he became preoccupied with the delicate rendering of shifting gradations of light on such diverse forms as waves, shipwrecks, fantastic architecture and towering mountain ranges, conveying a generalized mood or impression of a scene, sometimes accentuated by a theatrically arbitrary choice of vivid color. Examples of his work from this period are *The Shipwreck* (1805), *Frosty Morning* (1813) and *Crossing the Brook* (1815). He also worked on engravings, the series *Liber Studiorum* (1807–19), which remained uncompleted and failed because he underpaid the engravers. He visited Italy several times between 1819 and 1840; there he completed the famous pictures of Venice, *The Fighting Téméraire* (1839) and *Rain, Steam and Speed* (1844), both in the National Gallery, London. Turner led a secretive private life; he never married, and when not staying with his patron, Lord Egremont at Petworth, he lived in London taverns. He died in a temporary lodging at Chelsea under the assumed name of Booth. He bequeathed 300 of his paintings and 20,000 watercolors and drawings to the nation. Turner's revolution in art foreshadowed Impressionism and found a timely champion in **John Ruskin**, whose *Modern Painters* (vol 1, 1843) helped turn the critical tide in Turner's favor.

Turner, Kathleen 1954– •*US film actress*• Born in Springfield, Missouri, she studied at the Central School of Speech and Drama in London. Her feature film debut was as the conniving wife in the contemporary film noir *Body Heat* (1981). Her stardom was consolidated with the popular romantic comedy *Romancing the Stone* (1984) and its sequel, *Jewel of the Nile* (1985). Other films include *Crimes of Passion* (1984), *Prizzi's Honor* (1985), *Peggy Sue Got Married* (1986, Best Actress Academy Award), *Who Framed Roger Rabbit?* (1988, as the voice of Jessica Rabbit), *V I Warshawski* (1991), and *Serial Mom* (1994). Her stage work includes *Cat on a Hot Tin Roof* (1989) and *Indiscretions* (1996).

Turner, Lana, *originally* **Julia Jean Mildred Frances Turner** 1920–95 •*US film actress*• Born in Wallace, Idaho, legend has it that as a teenager she was spotted sipping soda at a drugstore on Sunset Boulevard and asked if she would like to be in the movies. She duly appeared as an extra in *A Star Is Born* (1937) and was signed by MGM and promoted as "the sweater girl." She appeared opposite **Clark Gable** in *Honky Tonk* (1941), and later notable films included *The Postman Always Rings Twice* (1946) and *The Bad and the Beautiful* (1952). Later, she appeared on stage in a succession of glossy melodramas and also in television series such as *The Survivors* (1969) and *Falcon Crest* (1982–83). Her stormy private life, notably the murder of her lover by her daughter, Cheryl Crane, and her seven marriages, brought her some notoriety.

Turner, Nat 1800–31 •*US slave insurrectionist*• Born in Southampton County, Virginia, he learned to read, and in 1831 made plans for a slave uprising. Leading a force of eight, he succeeded in killing 51 whites, but as many as 100 slaves were killed, and the revolt quickly collapsed. Captured after six weeks in hiding, he was brought to trial and hanged at Jerusalem, Virginia.

Turner, Ted (Robert Edward) 1938– •*US entrepreneur and television broadcasting executive*• He was born in Cincinnati, Ohio, and educated at Brown University. He established the first television superstation, WTBS, in Atlanta in the mid-1970s, transmitting programs by satellite to cable networks around the country. In 1980 he created the Cable News Network (CNN), the first 24-hour news station. He bought the movie company MGM in 1985, and three years later he established a movie channel on television. In 1996 Time Warner Inc merged with the Turner Broadcasting System (TBS) to create the world's largest media company. He owns the Atlanta Braves baseball team and the Atlanta Hawks basketball team; also a yachtsman, he won the America's Cup race in 1977. He was married to **Jane Fonda** from 1991 to 2001.

Turner, Tina, *professional name of* **Annie Mae Bullock** 1938– •*US pop singer and film actress*• She was born in Nutbush, Tennessee. She met Ike Turner in a nightclub in St Louis, Missouri, and married him in 1958. Though the relationship was allegedly abusive, they were noted stage performers, and made hits like "River Deep, Mountain High" (1966), a classic example of producer Phil Spector's "wall of sound," before divorcing in 1978. She appeared in Ken Russell's *Tommy* (1974). Her career declined for a time, but her success in the film *Mad Max Beyond the Thunderdome* (1984) and the albums *Private Dancer* (1984), *Foreign Affair* (1989) and *Wildest Dreams* (1996) propelled her to huge stardom, and her powerful voice was still filling stadiums when she announced in 2000 that she was on her final tour.

Turner, William c. 1510–68 •*English clergyman, physician and naturalist*• Born in Morpeth, Northumberland, he became a Fellow of Pembroke Hall, Cambridge, and traveled extensively abroad, studying medicine and botany in Italy. He became the author of the first original English works on plants, including *Libellus de re Herbaria Novus* (1538), the first book in which localities for native British plants were recorded, and *Names of Herbes* (1548). His major work is *A New Herball*, published in three installments (1551–62), which demonstrated Turner's independence of thought and observation. He was dean of Wells (1550–53), left England during the reign of **Mary I**, but was restored to Wells in 1560. The basis he laid for "a system of nature" was developed by **John Ray** in the following century. He is known as the father of British botany.

Turpin, Dick (Richard) 1705–39 •*English robber*• He was born in Hempstead, Essex, and was a butcher's apprentice, smuggler, cattle thief, housebreaker, highwayman and horse thief. He was hanged at York for murder. His famous ride to York on his mare Black Bess, recounted in Harrison Ainsworth's *Rookwood* (1834), is now thought to have been done by "Swift John Nevison," who in 1676 is said to have robbed a sailor at Gadshill at 4 AM, and to have established an alibi by reaching York at 7:45 PM.

Tussaud, Marie, *née* **Grosholtz**, *known as* **Madame Tussaud** 1761–1850 •*Swiss modeler in wax*• Born in Strasbourg, she was apprenticed to her uncle, Dr Philippe Curtius, in Paris and inherited his wax museums after his death in 1794. After the Revolution, she attended the guillotine to take death masks from the severed heads. After a short imprisonment, she married a French soldier, François Tussaud, but separated from him in 1800 and went to England with her younger son. She toured Great Britain with her life-size portrait waxworks, and in 1835 set up a permanent exhibition in Baker Street, London, which was moved to Marylebone Road in 1884. The exhibition still contains some of her handiwork, notably **Marie Antoinette**, **Napoleon**, Sir **Walter Scott**, and **Burke and Hare** in the Chamber of Horrors.

Tutankhamun d. c. 1340 BC •*Egyptian pharaoh of the 18th Dynasty*• The son-in-law of **Akhenaten**, he became king at the age of 12 and died at 18. His magnificent tomb at Thebes was discovered in 1922 by Lord **Carnarvon** and **Howard Carter**.

Tuthmosis *See* **Thutmose**

Tutu, Desmond Mpilo 1931– •*South African Anglican prelate and Nobel Prize winner*• He was born in Klerksdorp in the Transvaal, the son of a primary school headmaster. He studied theology at the University of South Africa and King's College London. After working as a schoolteacher for about four years, he attended theological college and became an Anglican parish priest (1961). He rose rapidly to become Bishop of Lesotho (1976–78), secretary-general of the South African Council of Churches (1978–85), the first Black Bishop of Johannesburg (1985–86) and Archbishop of Cape Town (1986–96). A fierce opponent of apartheid, he repeatedly risked imprisonment for his advocacy of punitive international sanctions against South Africa, although he deplored the use of violence. He was awarded the Nobel Peace Prize in 1984, was appointed chancellor of the University of the Western Cape in Cape Town in 1988, and chaired the Truth and Reconciliation Commission from 1995 to 1999. His publications include *Crying in the Wilderness* (1982), *Hope and Suffering* (1983), *The Words of Desmond Tutu* (1989) and *The Rainbow People of God* (1994).

“ ”

Be nice to whites. They need you to rediscover their humanity.

*1984 In the **New York Times**, October 19.*

Tutuola, Amos 1920–97 •*Nigerian novelist*• Born in Abeokuta, he was educated at a Salvation Army school and later taught at Lagos High School. *The Palm-Wine Drinkard* (1952), his most popular book, written in a musical pidgin, deals with its hero's adventures among the "Deads" (the spirits of the departed). A more recent publication is *Pauper, Brawler and Slanderer* (1987).

Twain, Mark, *pseudonym of* **Samuel Langhorne Clemens** 1835–1910 •*US writer and journalist*• He was born in Florida, Missouri, and was first a printer (1847–55) and later a Mississippi riverboat pilot (1857–61). In his first writing he adopted his pen name from a well-known call of the man sounding the river in shallow places ("mark twain" meaning "by the mark two fathoms"). In 1861 he went to Carson City, Nevada, as secretary for his brother, who was in the service of the governor. For two years he edited the Virginia City *Territorial Enterprise* and in 1864 moved to San Francisco as a reporter. His first success was *The Celebrated Jumping Frog of Calaveras County* (1865), which was published as a book with other sketches in 1867. In 1867 he visited France, Italy and Palestine, gathering material for his *Innocents Abroad* (1869), which established his reputation as a humorist. After his return he was for a time editor of a newspaper in Buffalo, where he married the wealthy Olivia Landon. Later he moved to Hartford, Connecticut, and joined a publishing firm which failed, but largely recouped his losses by lecturing and writing. *Roughing It* (1872) is a humorous account of his Nevada experiences, while *The Gilded Age* (1873), written with **Charles Dudley Warner**, a novel which was later dramatized, exposes the readjustment period after the Civil War. He visited England for a lecture tour in 1872, and as a result wrote *The Prince and the Pauper* (1882) and *A Connecticut Yankee in King Arthur's Court* (1889). His two greatest masterpieces, *Tom Sawyer* (1876) and *Huckleberry Finn* (1884), are drawn from his own boyhood experiences, and give vivid accounts of life on the Mississippi frontier; other Twain favorites include *A Tramp Abroad* (1880). In 1883 he published *Life on the Mississippi*, an autobiographical account of his days as a riverboat pilot, which includes a famous attack on the influence of **Walter Scott**. From the 1890s to the end of his life, Twain was affected by financial problems. He tried to recover his fortunes by undertaking lecture tours in New Zealand, Australia, India and South Africa, but his difficulties intensified with the death of his wife (1904) and two of his daughters. His writing from these years has a more somber tone, notably in *The Man That Corrupted Hadleyburg* (1900) and *The Mysterious Stranger* (published posthumously in 1916). In these last years he dictated his autobiography to his secretary, A B Paine, and it was published in different versions.

Tweed, William Marcy, *nicknamed* **Boss Tweed** 1823–78 •*US criminal and politician*• Born in New York City, he trained as a chairmaker, became an alderman (1852–53), sat in Congress (1853–55), and was repeatedly elected to the state senate. One of the most notorious political bosses of the Tammany Society, he was made commissioner of public works for the city in 1870 and, as head of the Tweed Ring, controlled its finances. His gigantic frauds exposed in 1871, he was convicted, and died in a New York jail.

Twiggy, *originally* **Leslie Hornby**, *married name* **Twiggy Lawson** 1949– •*English model*• Born in London, she began her modeling career in 1966 and quickly shot to fame as a fashion model in newspapers and magazines worldwide. Her adolescent gaucheness was emphasized by the girlish 1960s mini dresses, pale tights and loon pants she modeled, and her short hair epitomized the boyish look in vogue at the time. She later proved she could sing, dance and act, and appeared in the films *The Boy Friend* (1971) and *The Blues Brothers* (1980).

Twombly, Cy 1928– •*US painter*• Born in Lexington, Virginia, he studied at the Boston Museum of Fine Arts School (1948–49), at the Art Students' League (1950–51) and at Black Mountain College (1951–52), going on to settle in Rome in 1957. His gestural, or "doodle," technique derives from surrealist belief in the expressive power of automatic writing to tap the unconscious.

Tyler, Anne 1941– •*US novelist and short-story writer*• She was born in Minneapolis, Minnesota. She graduated at 19 from Duke University, and later became a Russian bibliographer and assistant to the librarian, McGill University Law Library. Writing mainly of life in Baltimore or in Southern small towns, and concerned with the themes of loneliness, isolation and human interactions, she has had a productive career since her debut in 1964 with *If Morning Ever Comes*. Other significant titles include *Morgan's Passing* (1980), *The Accidental Tourist* (1985, filmed 1988), *Breathing Lessons* (1988, Pulitzer Prize) and *Ladder of Years* (1995).

Tyler, John 1790–1862 •*Tenth President of the US*• Born in Charles City County, Virginia, he was admitted to the bar in 1809, and having sat in the state legislature (1811–16), he entered Congress. In 1825 he was elected governor of Virginia, and in 1826 US senator. He resented the despotic methods by which **Andrew Jackson** overthrew the United States Bank, supported **Henry Clay**'s motion to censure the president, and in 1836 resigned his seat. In 1840 he was elected vice president. President **Harrison** died in 1841, a month after his inauguration, and Tyler became president. His administration (1841–45) was marked by the Ashburton Treaty and the annexation of Texas (1845). On the outbreak of the Civil War he adhered to the Confederate cause.

Tyler, Wat d. 1381 •*English rebel, leader of the Peasants' Revolt*• He was probably a tiler from Essex, chosen by a mob of peasants to be their spokesman after taking Rochester Castle (1381). Under him they moved to Canterbury, Blackheath and London. At a conference with **Richard II** at Smithfield, London, demanding an end to serfdom and greater freedom of labor, blows were exchanged and Tyler was wounded by William Walworth, mayor of London. Walworth had him dragged out from St Bartholomew's Hospital and beheaded.

Tylor, Sir Edward Burnett 1832–1917 •*English anthropologist*• Born in Camberwell, London, he went to the US in 1855 due to bad health, traveled with archaeologist Henry Christy (1810–65) to Mexico and published *Ahahuac*, an account of his journey, in 1861. His first major anthropological study, *Researches into the Early History of Mankind and the Development of Civilization*, appeared in 1865, and in 1871 he published his monumental *Primitive Culture* (2 vols). In this work he sought to show that human culture, above all in its religious aspect, is governed by definite laws of evolutionary development, such that the beliefs and practices of primitive nations may be taken to represent earlier stages in the progress of mankind. After the appearance of **Charles Darwin**'s *The Descent of Man* (1871), he was drawn to the view that cultural variation may be due to racial differences in mental endowment, as reflected in his general introductory work *Anthropology* (1881). He is widely regarded as the founder of the systematic study of human culture and from 1896 to 1909 was the first professor of anthropology at Oxford.

Tynan, Katharine 1861–1931 •*Irish poet and novelist*• Born in Clondalkin, County Dublin, she was a friend of **Parnell**, the **Meynell**s and the **Rossetti**s and a leading author of the Celtic literary revival. Her journalism established her reputation, but she also wrote some 18 volumes of verse, over a hundred novels, and around 40 other books, including five autobiographical works. Her *Collected Poems* appeared in 1930.

Tynan, Kenneth Peacock 1927–80 •*English theater critic*• He was born in Birmingham. While studying English at Magdalen College, Oxford, he became deeply involved in the theater, and his first book, *He That Plays the King* (1950), was a brilliant and provocative personal view of the current theater scene. He became drama critic for several publications, notably the *Observer* (1954–63), where he was one of the first to champion **John Osborne** and the other new playwrights of the time. He abandoned drama criticism to become literary manager of the National Theatre, London, (1963–69) under Sir **Laurence Olivier**. He also worked as an editor in films and television. A vigorous opponent of censorship, he later achieved some notoriety with his revue *Oh, Calcutta!* (1969), which featured much nudity.

“ ”

A critic is a man who knows the way but can't drive the car.

1966 In the ***New York Times Magazine****, January 9.*

Tyndale or **Tindale** or **Hutchins, William** c. 1494–1536 •*English translator of the Bible*• Born probably in Slymbridge in Gloucestershire, he was educated at Magdalen Hall, Oxford (1510–15) and became a chaplain and tutor, sympathetic to humanist learning. In 1523 he went to London to seek support for his project to translate the Scriptures into the vernacular. Bishop Cuthbert Tunstall having refused his support, Tyndale then went to Hamburg (1524), to Wittenberg, where he visited **Martin Luther**, and to Cologne (1525), where he began printing his English New Testament in the same year. This had not proceeded beyond the gospels of Matthew and Mark when the intrigues of Johann Cochlaeus forced Tyndale to flee to Worms, where he had 3,000 pocket-size New Testaments printed. The translation owed much to Luther and **Desiderius Erasmus**, much to his own scholarship and literary skill. Tunstall and the Archbishop of Canterbury, William Warham (1504–67), denounced the book, and hundreds of copies were burned. In 1531 he went to Antwerp and there probably (though possibly in Marburg) was published his *Pentateuch* (1530–31). An unauthorized revision of Tyndale's New Testament was made at Antwerp in August 1534, and in November Tyndale issued there his own revised version. One copy of his works was struck off on vellum for presentation to **Anne Boleyn**, under whose favor, apparently, a reprint of Tyndale's revised New Testament was printed in 1536 by T Godfray, the first volume of Holy Scripture printed in England. The emissaries of **Henry VIII** had often tried to get ahold of him, and in 1535 he was betrayed by Henry Philips, a Roman Catholic zealot, arrested in Antwerp, accused of heresy, imprisoned in the Castle of Vilvorde, tried there (1536), and on October 6 strangled and burned. His other original works were *The Parable of the Wicked Mammon* (1528), *The Obedience of a Christian Man*, his most elaborate book (1528), and *Practyse of Prelates* (1530). His *Works* were published in 1573.

Tyrone, 2nd Earl of *See* **O'Neill, Hugh**

Tyson, Mike (Michael Gerald) 1966– •*US boxer*• Born in New York City, he turned professional in 1985. He beat Trevor Berbick (1952–) for the World Boxing Council (WBC) version of the world heavyweight title in 1986, and added the World Boxing Association title in 1987, when he beat James Smith (1954–). In August 1987, he beat Tony Tucker (1958–) to become undisputed world champion, a title he held until February 1990, when he was defeated by James “Buster” Douglas. In 1992 he was sentenced to six years in jail for charges including rape; he served three years, and was released in 1995. In 1996 he beat **Frank Bruno** to reclaim the WBC title, which he then gave up later in the year. In 1997 he had his license revoked after biting off a piece of **Evander Holyfield**'s ear. He regained his license in 1998. In 1999 he was sentenced to a year's imprisonment for assault and was released on probation later that year.

Tzara, Tristan 1896–1963 •*Romanian poet*• He was born in Bucharest, but lived in Zurich during and shortly after World War I, and in Paris from 1920. One of the founders of Dadaism together with **Hans Arp**, **Hugo Ball** and others, the products of his involvement with the movement include the then revolutionary *Vingt-cinq poèmes* (1918, “25 Poems”) and *Sept manifestes Dada* (1924, “Seven Dadaist Manifestos”). After the movement moved its headquarters to Paris in 1920, he was an active participant in the movement's “happenings.” He became a card-carrying surrealist in 1929, producing *L'homme approximatif* (“The Approximate Man”) in 1930, but never recaptured the anarchic vitality of his early years.

Tyus, Wyomia 1945– •*US track and field athlete*• Born in Griffin, Georgia, she was a sprinter in high school and college, winning the 1962 Girls' American Athletic Union championships in the 100-yard dash, 50-yard dash and the 75-yard dash. At the 1964 Olympics, she won a gold medal in the 100 meters and a silver in the 4 × 100-meter relay. In the 1968 Olympics she won a second gold in the 100 meters, becoming the first athlete to win two consecutive gold medals in that event. She won another gold medal in the 4 × 100-meter relay. She is a founding member of the Women's Sports Foundation, which serves to promote women in all sports. She was elected to the National Track and Field Hall of Fame in 1980 and became a member of the International Women's Sports Hall of Fame in 1981.

Tz'u Hsi *See* **Cixi**

Tzu-Wen Sung *See* **Soong, T V**

U

U2 •*Irish rock band*• U2 was formed in 1978 at Dublin's Mount Temple School by vocalist Bono (Paul Hewson) (1960–), guitarist The Edge (David Evans) (1961–), drummer Larry Mullen (1961–) and bassist Adam Clayton (1960–). They made their recording debut in 1979 and had their first major success with the album *Boy* (1980) and the single "I Will Follow." The hard guitar-based rock of such albums as *October* (1981), *War* (1983) and *The Unforgettable Fire* (1984) established them as one of the world's top rock acts. Subsequent releases included *The Joshua Tree* (1987), *Rattle and Hum* (1988), *Achtung Baby* (1991) and *All That You Can't Leave Behind* (2000).

Uccello, Paolo c. 1396–1475 •*Florentine painter*• Born in Pratovecchio, near Florence, he belonged to the early Renaissance period, and was primarily concerned with developing the new science of perspective in painting, as in *The Flood* (c. 1450, Santa Maria Novella, Florence). He was originally apprenticed to **Lorenzo Ghiberti** but is more closely associated with the circle of **Donatello**. During his lifetime he became unfashionable with patrons and was forgotten until the 20th century, when abstract artists found their own concerns anticipated in his richly patterned compositions. Uccello's style is most evident in the three large-scale panels of the *Battle of San Romano* (1454–57, London, Paris and Florence), executed as decorations for the Palazzo Medici. He also painted in a Romantic style, as in *The Hunt in the Forest* (1468, Ashmolean, Oxford), where the horizontal arrangement draws the viewer's eye to a receding central point.

“ ”

O what a lovely thing this perspective is!

Attributed in Giorgio Vasari ***Lives of the Artists*** *(1568, translated by George Bull, 1965).*

Udall or **Uvedale, Nicholas** 1504–56 •*English dramatist*• Born in Hampshire, he was educated at Winchester and Corpus Christi College, Oxford, and became headmaster of Eton c. 1534, whose pupils soon learned of his predilection for corporal punishment. His dismissal in 1541 for indecent offenses did not affect his standing at the court. **Edward VI** appointed him prebendary of Windsor, and despite his great enthusiasm for the Reformation, he survived the reign of Queen **Mary I** without disfavor. He translated **Erasmus**, selections from the Great Bible, and Latin commentaries on the latter, but is chiefly remembered as the author of the comedy *Ralph Roister Doister*, written c. 1553 but not published until 1567, which influenced later English writers of comedies.

Udet, Ernst 1896–1941 •*German airman*• Born in Frankfurt, he was a leading German air ace in World War I, and from 1935 worked in the German air ministry. A *Luftwaffe* quartermaster general in World War II, he committed suicide in an air crash, having fallen afoul of the Gestapo. *The Devil's General*, a play by Carl Zuckmayer, is based on his life.

Udine, Giovanni da 1487–1564 •*Italian painter, decorative artist and architect*• Born in Udine, he joined the workshop of **Raphael** in Rome and became a specialist in a style of decoration called "grotesque," influenced by the graceful ornamental designs—employing fantastic animals, medallions, foliage and similar elements—that were being discovered in the excavations of ancient Rome. His decorative style rapidly spread throughout Europe and was especially popular during the neoclassical period of the 18th century.

Uemura, Naomi 1942–84 •*Japanese explorer and mountaineer*• Born in Tajima region, he studied agriculture at Meiji University, Tokyo, where he started climbing. After solo ascents of Mont Blanc, Kilimanjaro, Aconcagua and Mt McKinley, he reached the summit of Everest with Teruo Matsura in 1970, and so became the first person to reach the highest peaks on five continents. From 1977 to 1978 he spent a year living with the Inuit in the Canadian Arctic, traveling by dogsled up the coast of Greenland, and from Greenland to Alaska. He made a solo dogsled journey from Ellesmere Island to the North Pole, arriving on May 1, 1978, and was then airlifted to his base to undertake a north-south traverse of Greenland using 16 dogs. In the winter of 1981 he led the Japanese attempt to climb Mt Everest. In February 1984 he completed the first winter ascent of the West Buttress Route of Mt McKinley and is presumed to have died during the descent, though his body has not been found.

Uhle, Max 1856–1944 •*German archaeologist*• Trained as a philologist, he later transferred his allegiance to archaeology. From 1892 he undertook field research for the Universities of Pennsylvania and California, excavating on the Peruvian coast at Pachacamac and on Mochica and Chimu sites. He later extended his work into the highlands and to Bolivia, Ecuador, and Chile, making also a notable contribution to North American archaeology with his excavations of the Emeryville shell mound in San Francisco Bay. Influenced by the work of **Flinders Petrie** in Egypt, Uhle emphasized stratigraphic excavation, and his pioneering work in Peru and Bolivia revolutionized the field of archaeology.

Ulanova, Galina Sergeyevna 1910–98 •*Russian ballerina*• Born in St Petersburg, she studied there at the Petrograd State Ballet and made her debut in *Les sylphides* at the Kirov Theater in 1928. She joined the Bolshoi Ballet in 1944 and became the leading ballerina of the Soviet Union, winning the **Stalin** Prize four times and the **Lenin** Prize in 1957. She visited London in 1956 with the Bolshoi Ballet, when she gave a memorable performance in *Giselle*, perhaps her most famous role.

Ulbricht, Walter 1893–1973 •*East German Communist politician*• He was born in Leipzig. In 1928, after some years in Russia, he became Communist deputy for Potsdam. He left Germany when **Hitler** achieved power in 1933, spending the greater part of his exile in Russia. As Marshal **Georgi Zhukov**'s political adviser and head of the German Communist Party, he returned in 1945, and by 1950 had become deputy premier of the German Democratic Republic. The same year he was made secretary-general of the Communist Party, and was largely responsible for the sovietization of East Germany. He is remembered chiefly for building the Berlin Wall in 1961. He retired in 1971.

Ullman, Tracey 1959– •*English singer, comedienne and actress*• Born in Buckinghamshire, she went to stage school in London and had parts in musicals before her breakthrough as a comic in *Three of a Kind* (1981). Her singing career, consisting largely of cover versions, includes "Breakaway" and "They Don't Know" (**Neil Kinnock** and **Paul McCartney** appeared in the video). She returned to acting and received mixed critical reviews in Great Britain, but after moving to the US she starred in *The Tracey Ullman Show* (1987–90) and *Tracey Takes On …* (1996–99), both of which won several awards.

Ullmann, Liv Johanne 1939– •*Norwegian actress*• Born in Tokyo, Japan, she studied acting at the Webber-Douglas School in London before beginning her career with a repertory company in Stavanger, Norway. She made her film debut in *Fjols til fjells* (1957, *Fools in the Mountains*), but in her screen image, largely defined through a long professional and personal association with the Swedish director **Ingmar Bergman**, she laid bare the inner turmoil of women experiencing various emotional and sexual crises. Their films together include *Persona* (1966), *Viskningar och rop* (1972, *Cries and Whispers*), *Ansikte mot ansikte* (1975, *Face to Face*) and *Hostsonaten* (1978, *Autumn Sonata*). She made her Broadway debut in *A Doll's House* (1975), and has made regular theater appearances. She has worked extensively for the charity UNICEF and written two autobiographical works: *Changing* (1977) and *Choices* (1984). Her films as director include *Sofie* (1992) and *Enskilda Samtal* (1996).

Ulm, Charles Thomas Philippe 1898–1934 •*Australian pioneer aviator*• Born in Melbourne, Victoria, he fought with the Australian Imperial Forces at Gallipoli in 1915 and later qualified as a pilot. In 1927 he joined **Charles Kingsford Smith** in a record-breaking around-Australia flight, and in 1928 he was copilot with Kingsford Smith on the first flight across the Pacific Ocean and on the first trans-Tasman Sea flight. In 1929 they made a 13-day flight from Australia to England, a record Ulm lowered to 7 days (1933). In 1929 with Kingsford Smith he formed Australian National Airways, the first airline in Australia. While investigating the possibilities of regular airmail flights across the Pacific, he set out from California with two companions in his new twin-engine *Stella Australis*, but the plane vanished without a trace over the Hawaiian islands.

Ulrika Eleonora 1688–1741 •*Queen of Sweden*• The younger sister of **Charles XII**, she was born in Stockholm, married to Prince Frederick of Hesse (1715), and elected queen in 1718 after her brother's death. A new constitution, however, inaugurated the so-called Era of Liberty (1718–71) and saw the abolition of royal absolutism, giving power to the Riksdag (parliament). Ulrika was so displeased that she abdicated (1720) in favor of her husband, who ascended the throne as **Frederick I**.

Ulugh-Beg 1394–1449 •*Tatar prince and astronomer*• A grandson of **Timur** who drew learned men to Samarkand, he founded an observatory there in 1420, and between 1420 and 1437 prepared new planetary tables and a new star catalog, the latter being the first since that of **Ptolemy**. Positions were given with precision; this was the first time that latitude and longitude were measured to minutes of arc and not just degrees. He was ruler of Turkestan from 1447, and also wrote poetry and history. He was slain by a rebellious son.

Umar *See* **Omar**

Umar Pasha *See* **Omar Pasha**

Umberto I 1844–1900 •*King of Italy*• Born in Turin, the son and successor of **Victor Emmanuel II**, he distinguished himself at the Battle of Custozza (1866). In 1868 he married his cousin Margherita of Savoy and in 1878 succeeded his father. He is often portrayed as a model constitutional monarch who, despite his conservative sympathies and considerable pressure from reactionary politicians, rarely interfered in parliamentary affairs. In reality, he was content to block ministerial appointments and to use the royal prerogative, especially in matters concerning the army or foreign affairs. Despite a genuine concern for his subjects, manifest particularly at times of natural disaster, there were several attempts on his life (1878, 1897) before he was finally assassinated by an anarchist.

Unamuno, Miguel de 1864–1936 •*Spanish philosopher and writer*• Born in Bilbao to Basque parents, he was educated at the Instituto Vizcaino of Bilbao and the University of Madrid, and was Professor of Greek at Salamanca from 1892. He wrote mystic philosophy, historical studies, essays, books on travel, and austere poetry. Among his most important works are *Vida de Don Quijote y Sancho* (1905, Eng trans *The Life of Don Quixote and Sancho*, 1927), his novel *Niebla* (1914, Eng trans *Mist*, 1928), and a volume of religious poetry, *El Cristo de Velázquez* (1920, Eng trans *The Christ of Velasquez*, 1951). He was exiled as a republican to the island of Fuerteventura (1924–30) and reinstated at Salamanca on the founding of the republic (1931). Always a rebel and an individualist, though with the deepest faith in and interest of his country at heart, he was soon at variance with the socialist regime. The civil war was for him a nationalist struggle, and he denounced foreign interference.

Uncas c. 1588–c. 1683 •*Native American leader, first chief of the Mohegans*• Born into the Pequot people (in present-day Connecticut), he was frustrated in his efforts to become chief, and after leading an unsuccessful rebellion was forced into exile. With his followers he formed the Mohegans, siding with the British in the Pequot Wars (1638), and he later fought a series of wars with the Narragansett (1643–47).

Underhill, Evelyn 1875–1941 •*English poet and mystic*• Born in Wolverhampton, she was educated at King's College London and in 1921 became lecturer on the philosophy of religion at Manchester College, Oxford. She found her way intellectually from agnosticism to Christianity, and she wrote numerous books on mysticism, including *The Life of the Spirit* (1922), volumes of verse, and four novels. Underhill's *Mysticism* (1911) became a standard work.

Undset, Sigrid 1882–1949 •*Norwegian novelist and Nobel Prize winner*• She was born in Kalundborg, Denmark, the daughter of a noted Norwegian archaeologist. The problems facing young contemporary women shaped her early novels, including *Jenny* (1911). Her masterpiece, *Kristin Lavransdatter* (3 vols, 1920–22), which tells a graphic story of love and religion in 14th-century Norway, was followed by *Olav Audunssön* (4 vols, 1925–27) and *Den trofaste hustru* (1936, Eng trans *The Faithful Spouse*, 1937). She was awarded the Nobel Prize for literature in 1928. During World War II she was an exile in the US, an outspoken opponent of Nazism.

Ungaretti, Giuseppe 1888–1970 •*Italian poet*• Born in Alexandria, Egypt, he fought in the Italian army in World War I. From 1912 to 1914 he studied in Paris, and became Professor of Italian Literature at the University of São Paulo, Brazil (1936–42), and at the University of Rome (1942–58). The author of hermetic poems characterized by their symbolism, compressed imagery and modern verse structure, he had his first collection, *Il porto sepolto* ("The Buried Harbor"), published in 1916 with a preface by **Mussolini**. Among his collections is *Vita d'un uomo* (7 vols, 1942–61, "Life of a Man"), which includes *Il dolore* (1947, "Grief").

Ungaro, Emanuel Maffeolti 1933– •*French fashion designer*• He was born in Aix-en-Provence to Italian parents. Originally he trained to join the family tailoring business, but went instead to Paris in 1955, worked for a small tailoring firm, and later joined **Cristóbal Balenciaga**. In 1965 he opened his own house, with Sonia Knapp designing his fabrics. In 1968 he produced his first ready-to-wear lines.

Unitas, Johnny Constantine 1933–2002 •*US football player*• Born in Pittsburgh, Pennsylvania, he was one of the game's first television heroes. A quarterback, he signed with the Baltimore Colts in 1956. Two years later he led them to a championship victory against the New York Giants in overtime. The game was broadcast live and helped American football make its big television breakthrough. In 1973, at the age of 40, he joined the San Diego Chargers, but was injured after only three games and retired.

Universalis, Doctor *See* **Albertus Magnus, St**

Unna, Percy 1878–1950 •*Scottish environmental philanthropist*• Born in London, a civil engineer by profession, he became president of the Scottish Mountaineering Club in the mid-1930s. One of the first to appreciate the unique quality of Scottish mountain scenery, he compiled what are known as "Unna's Rules." These were guidelines for the conservation of the Scottish mountains, following the National Trust for Scotland's purchase of important mountain properties, such as Glencoe. He was a generous anonymous donor to the National Trust.

Unser, Al 1939– •*US racecar driver*• Born in Albuquerque, New Mexico, he has won the Indianapolis 500 four times—1970, 1971, 1978 and 1987. He was three times Indycar champion (1970, 1983 and 1985) and International Race of Champions (IROC) champion in 1978. He won the 24-hour Daytona race in 1985. His brother, Bobby Unser (1934–), was twice Indy champion (1968 and 1974) and IROC champion in 1975. His son, Al Unser, Jr (1962–), was Indy champion in 1990 and 1994 and IROC champion in 1986 and 1988, and he won Daytona in 1986 and 1987 and the Marlboro Challenge in 1989.

Unsworth, Barry (Foster) 1930– •*English novelist*• Born in Durham, he was the first of his family not to work in the coal mines. Educated at the University of Manchester, he traveled widely and held a variety of teaching posts. His first novel, *The Partnership* (1966), was followed by four more before *Pascali's Island* (1980), which was shortlisted for the Booker Prize and later filmed. His books often reflect on historical themes, and are set in locations which mirror his own wanderings, notably Turkey, Greece, and Italy. His major work is the novel *Sacred Hunger* (1992), an epic account of the 18th-century Atlantic slave trade, for which he was jointly awarded the Booker Prize, with **Michael Ondaatje**. Later novels include *Morality Play* (1995) and *Losing Nelson* (1999).

Updike, John Hoyer 1932– •*US novelist, poet and critic*• Born in Shillington, Pennsylvania, he studied at Harvard and the Ruskin School of Drawing and Fine Art in Oxford, England (1954–55). He then worked for the *New Yorker* (1955–57), the beginning of a long and fruitful relationship with the magazine that continues in his contributions of short stories, poems and book reviews. His status as one of the world's major writers is due largely to his fiction. Sophisticated, linguistically supple, fluent and inventive, his beat is the American middle class, his concerns those that dominated the 20th century: sex, marriage, adultery, divorce, religion, materialism. Among his best-known books are *The Centaur* (1963); the Rabbit series: *Rabbit, Run* (1960), *Rabbit Redux* (1971), *Rabbit Is Rich* (1981, Pulitzer Prize) and *Rabbit at Rest* (1990, Pulitzer Prize) —chronicling the life of a car salesman; *Couples* (1968); *The Coup* (1978); and *The Witches of Eastwick* (1984). More recent works include *Roger's Version* (1986) and *In the Beauty of the Lilies* (1996). *Self-Consciousness*, a memoir, was published in 1989, and his *Collected Poems 1953–1993* were published in 1993.

“ ”

The difficulty with humorists is that they will mix what they believe with what they don't; whichever seems likelier to win an effect.

1960 ***Rabbit, Run.***

Urbain, Georges 1872–1938 •*French chemist*• He was born in Paris and educated at the École de Physique et de Chimie in Paris and at the University of Paris. He was Professor of Analytical Chemistry at the Sorbonne from 1906 to 1928, when he became director of the Institut de Chimie de Paris. Between 1895 and 1912 he performed more than 200,000 fractional crystallizations, in which he separated the elements samarium, europium, gadolinium, terbium, dysprosium and holmium. In 1907 he discovered lutetium in ytterbium, previously thought to have been in a pure form, and in 1922 isolated hafnium at the same time as **George Charles de Hevesy** and Dirk Coster (1889–1950) working in Copenhagen. He also wrote on isomorphism and phosphorescence.

Urban II, *originally* **Odo of Lagery** c. 1035–99 •*French pope*•Born in Châtillon-sur-Marne, he became a monk at Cluny, and was made Cardinal Bishop of Ostia in 1078. As pope (1088–99), he introduced ecclesiastical reforms, drove foreign armies from Italy, and launched the First Crusade (1095).

Urban VIII, *originally* **Maffeo Barberini** 1568–1644 •*Italian pope*• Born in Florence, he became a cardinal (1606). Becoming pope in 1623, he supported Cardinal **Richelieu**'s policy against the Habsburgs in the Thirty Years' War, and carried out much ecclesiastical reform. A great scholar and supporter of the arts, he issued several condemnations of heresy, which included the writings of **Galileo** and **Cornelius Otto Jansen**.

Urey, Harold Clayton 1893–1981 •*US chemist and Nobel Prize winner*• Born in Walkerton, Indiana, he taught in rural schools and then studied at Montana State University and the University of California at Berkeley. In 1923–24 he worked with **Niels Bohr** in Copenhagen. From 1924 to 1929 he was an associate in chemistry at Johns Hopkins University, and from 1929 to 1945 he was on the chemistry faculty of Columbia University, New York. He worked in the Chemistry Department and the Institute for Nuclear Studies of the University of Chicago from 1945 to 1958, and thereafter continued to be scientifically active in retirement for many years at the University of California at La Jolla. Urey's earliest research was on atomic and molecular spectra and structure, but he is chiefly remembered for his discovery in 1932 of heavy hydrogen (deuterium), together with Ferdinand Brickwedde and George Murphy. Subsequently he made many studies of the separation of isotopes and isotopic exchange reactions. During World War II he was prominent in the attempts to separate uranium 235 for the atomic bomb. He later advocated an international ban on nuclear weapons. After 1945 his research interests moved to geochemistry and cosmochemistry. Among many awards, he received the Nobel Prize for chemistry in 1934.

“ ”

I thought it might have a practical use in something like neon signs.

c. 1934 Recalling his 1932 discovery of heavy water which proved critical to the development of the atomic bomb.

Urfé, Honoré d' 1568–1625 •*French writer*• Born in Marseilles, he fought in the religious wars of France and later settled in Savoy. He was the author of the pastoral romance, *Astrée* (1610–27, "Astrea"), which is regarded as the first French novel. He was killed at Villefranche-sur-Mer during the war between Savoy and Genoa.

Uris, Leon M(arcus) 1924–2003 •*US writer*• Born in Baltimore, Maryland, he dropped out of high school and joined the Marine Corps, taking part in battles in the Pacific. *Battle Cry* (1953) uses the experience to telling effect. *Exodus* (1958) remains the book by which he is best known. Depicting the early years of the state of Israel, it was made into a highly successful film. Subsequent works include *QBVII* (1970), *Trinity* (1976), *The Haj* (1984) and *Redemption* (1995).

Urquhart, Sir Thomas c. 1611–60 •*Scottish writer*• Born in Cromarty, he studied at King's College, Aberdeen, and traveled in France, Spain and Italy. On his return he took up arms against the Covenanting party in the north but was defeated and forced to flee to England, where he joined the court and was knighted in 1641. The same year he published his *Epigrams: Divine and Moral*. Returning north in 1642 he produced his *Trissotetras; Or a Most Exquisite Table for Resolving Triangles, etc* (1645), a study of trigonometry. He again took up arms in the royal cause, and was present at the Battle of Worcester (1651). In 1652 he published his *Pantochronochanon*, which traces the Urquhart family back to the biblical Adam, and *Ekskubalauron* (better known as *The Discoverie of a Most Exquisite Jewel*), in praise of the Scots nation. Other works include a brilliant translation of **Rabelais** (books 1 and 2, 1653; book 3 published posthumously). He is said to have died abroad, in a fit of mirth on hearing of the Restoration.

Ursula, St 4th century AD •*Semilegendary saint*• She is especially honored in Cologne, where she is said to have been killed with her 11,000 virgins by a horde of Huns on her journey home from a pilgrimage to Rome. She became the patron saint of many educational institutes, particularly the teaching order of the Ursulines. Her feast day is October 21.

Ussher or **Usher, James** 1581–1656 •*Irish prelate*• Born in Dublin, he was a scholar (1594) and Fellow (1599–1605) of Trinity College, Dublin. In 1605, he drew up the Articles of Doctrine for the Irish Protestant Church. In 1620 he was made Bishop of Meath, in 1623 Privy Councilor for Ireland, and in 1625 Archbishop of Armagh. He went to England (1640), and for about eight years was a preacher at Lincoln's Inn. Distinguished not only by his learning but also by his charity and good temper, he was **Calvin**istic in theology and moderate in his ideas of Church government. Of his numerous writings, the best known is the *Annales Veteris et Novi Testamenti* (1650–54), which fixed the Creation precisely at 4004 BC.

Ustinov, Sir Peter Alexander 1921–2004 •*British actor and playwright*• He was born in London, the son of White Russian parents, and first appeared on the stage in 1938. He had established himself as an accomplished artist by 1942, when four years' army service interrupted his career. As an actor in films such as *Spartacus* (1960) and *Death on the Nile* (1978), a film writer and producer, and a satirical comedian in broadcasting, he continued to build his reputation. A prolific playwright, his works are marked by a serious approach to human problems often presented with an acute sense of comedy. The most successful of his plays are *The Love of Four Colonels* (1951) and *Romanoff and Juliet* (1956). Among his other plays are *Photo Finish* (1962) and *Overheard* (1981). His other works include an autobiography, *Dear Me* (1977), the two novellas collected as *The Disinformer* (1989) and *The Old Man and Mr Smith* (1990). He wrote for *The European* newspaper, won many awards, and was knighted in 1990.

Utamaro, Kitagawa 1753–1806 •*Japanese painter and engraver*• Born and trained in Edo (Tokyo), he specialized in portraits of court ladies, in which the gracefulness of face, figure and flowing robes was depicted with precise detail. He also painted flowers, birds and fish, and used the technique of the *ukiyo-e* ("pictures of the floating world") school.

'Uthman c. 575–656 •*Third caliph*• He was elected in succession to Umar, in preference to **'Ali** (644). He established a commission of scholars who collected the revelations of **Muhammad** to produce the definitive version of the Koran. However, his administration was badly organized, and disagreements concerning the division of the gains made in the Muslim conquests gave rise to increased social tensions, culminating in a revolt in which he was killed.

Uticensis *See* **Cato, Marcus Porcius the Younger**

Utrillo, Maurice 1883–1955 •*French painter*• Born in Montmartre, Paris, he was the illegitimate son of the painter **Suzanne Valadon**. Adopted by the Spanish writer Miguel Utrillo, he began to paint at Montmagny in 1902, but it was the streets of Paris, particularly old Montmartre, and village scenes which were to provide him with most of his subjects. Despite acute alcoholism and drug addiction, and consequent sojourns in various nursing homes, his productivity was astonishing, and by 1925 he was famous. His White Period paintings of about 1908–14 are much sought after for their subtle coloring and sensitive feeling for atmosphere.

Uttley, Alison 1884–1976 •*English writer of children's stories*• Born on a farm in Derbyshire, she was widowed in 1930 and turned to writing to support herself and her young son. *The Country Child* (1931) was followed by a flood of books, mainly for children, which revealed her great love for and knowledge of the countryside and country lore. Many of her books were in the **Beatrix Potter** tradition, featuring much-loved characters such as Little Grey Rabbit and Sam Pig.

Utzon, Jørn 1918– •*Danish architect*• Born in Copenhagen, he was educated at the Royal Danish Academy. His buildings include the Sydney Opera House, the Kuwait House of Parliament and Paustian's House of Furniture (Copenhagen). In 1966 he won the competition for the design of the Zurich Schauspielhaus. He was awarded the Bund Deutscher Architekten's Ehrenplachette (1965), the gold medal of the Royal Institute of British Architects (1978), the Alvar Aalto Medal (1982), the Fritz Schumacher Prize (1988) and the Wolf Prize (1992, jointly).

Uvedale *See* **Udall**

V

Vajpayee, Atal Behari 1926– *•Indian politician•* Born in Gwalior, Madhya Pradesh, he was educated at Victoria (now Laximbai) College, Gwalior, and at the DAV College, Kanpur. He was arrested as a member of the Indian National Congress in 1942 and became a founding member of the Jana Sangh in 1951. He served as president of the Bharatiya Jana Sangh (1968–73) and (after a further period of detention) as leader of the Jana Sangh Parliamentary Party (1975–77). In 1980 he helped found the Bharatiya Janata Party, serving as its president (1980–86) and as leader of the Opposition (1993–98). He served briefly as prime minister of India in 1996 and again from 1998 to 2004.

Valadon, Suzanne 1869–1938 *•French painter•* The mother of **Maurice Utrillo**, she became an artist's model for **Renoir** and others. With the encouragement of **Toulouse-Lautrec**, **Degas** and **Cézanne**, she took up painting herself and excelled in her realistic treatment of nudes, portraits and figure studies, her work having some affinity with that of Degas.

Valdes, Peter *See* **Waldo, Peter**

Valdivia, Pedro de c. 1510–59 *•Spanish soldier•* Born near La Serena, Estremadura, he went to Venezuela (c. 1534) and then to Peru, where he became **Francisco Pizarro**'s lieutenant. He won renown at Las Salinas (1538), and was put in command of the expedition to Chile. He founded Santiago (1541) and other cities, including Concepción (1550) and Valdivia (1552). In 1559, while attempting to relieve Tucapel, he was captured and killed.

Valentine, St d. c. 269 AD *•Roman Christian priest•* He is said to have been executed during the persecutions under Claudius II (the Goth) but claims have been made for another St Valentine, supposedly Bishop of Turni, who was taken 60 miles to Rome for martyrdom. Neither Valentine is associated with romance. The custom of sending love letters on his feast day, February 14, originated in the late Middle Ages, when it was thought that this time of year was the birds' mating season.

Valentinian I AD 321–75 *•Roman emperor•* Born in Cibalis, Pannonia, the son of an army officer, he rose rapidly in rank under **Constantius** and **Julian**, and on the death of Emperor Jovian (AD 331–64) was chosen by the army as his successor. He resigned the East to his brother Valens, and he himself governed the West with watchful care, especially strengthening the Rhine fortification, until his death.

Valentino, *originally* **Valentino Garavani** 1933– *•Italian fashion designer•* Born in Rome, he studied fashion in Milan and Paris, then worked for Dessès and **Guy Laroche** in Paris. He opened his own house in Rome in 1959, achieving worldwide recognition with his 1962 show in Florence.

Valentino, Rudolph, *originally* **Rodolpho Alphonso Guglielmi di Valentina d'Antonguolla** 1895–1926 *•Italian-born US film actor, a great screen idol of the 1920s•* He was born in Castellaneta in southern Italy. He studied agriculture for a time, but emigrated to the US in 1913 and first appeared on the stage as a dancer. He moved to Hollywood and, after a number of parts as an extra, he made his first significant appearances as villains in *Out of Luck* (1919) and *Once to Every Woman* (1920). His first starring role was as Julio in *The Four Horsemen of the Apocalypse* (1921), in which his dark flashing eyes and erotic movements caused a sensation. Subsequent performances in *The Sheikh* (1921), *Blood and Sand* (1922), *The Young Rajah* (1922), *Monsieur Beaucaire* (1924), *The Eagle* (1925) and *The Son of the Sheikh* (1926) established him as the leading "screen lover" of the 1920s. He died suddenly in New York of peritonitis at the height of his fame, and his funeral was the occasion of wide public mourning.

Valerian, Publius Licinius c. 193–260 AD *•Roman emperor•* He was proclaimed emperor by the legions in Rhaetia after the murder of Gallus (AD 253), and assumed as colleague his eldest son, **Gallienus**. Throughout his reign trouble hovered on every frontier of the empire. Marching against the Persians, Valerian was completely defeated at Edessa (260). He was seized by King Shapur and died in captivity. He reportedly was stuffed and displayed as a trophy in a Persian temple.

Valéry, (Ambroise) Paul (Toussaint Jules) 1871–1945 *•French poet and writer•* Born in Sète, he settled in Paris in 1892, and, after publishing verse in the style of **Stéphane Mallarmé**, spent the next 20 years involved with mathematics and philosophical speculations. His new poetry was influenced by Symbolism, and he wrote *La jeune parque* (1917, "The Young Fate"), followed by the collection *Charmes ou poèmes* (1922). His prose works include *Soirée avec M. Teste* (1895, Eng trans *An Evening With Mr Teste*, 1925) and several aesthetic studies, such as *L'âme et la danse* (1924, Eng trans *Dance and the Soul*, 1951). A late, short play entitled *Le solitaire* ("The Solitary Man") foreshadows **Samuel Beckett**.

" "

La politique est l'art d'empêcher les gens de se mêler de ce qui les regarde.
Politics is the art of preventing people from taking part in affairs which concern them.

1943 ***Tel Quel 2***, *"Rhumbs."*

Vallière, Louise Françoise, Duchesse de la *See* **La Vallière, Louise Françoise, Duchesse de**

Vallotton, Felix 1865–1925 *•French painter•* Born in Lausanne, Switzerland, he studied at the Academy Julian with **Toulouse-Lautrec** and Charles Maurin. Early in his career he made engravings in the manner of **Jean François Millet**, **Rembrandt** and others. He was a member of the Nabis Symbolist movement, and one of the principal collaborators in *Le Revue Blanche* between 1894 and 1901. His most notable works were wood engravings, which were immensely popular and brought him immediate success. He is regarded as a forerunner of the generation of artist engravers which included such names as **Wassily Kandinsky**, **Edvard Munch** and **Aubrey Beardsley**. His striking images were later transferred to his oil painting.

Valois, Dame Ninette de, *stage name of* **Edris Stannus** 1898–2001 *•Irish ballerina•* Born in Blessington, County Wicklow, she made her stage debut in 1914. She subsequently appeared with the Beecham Opera Company and at Covent Garden. After a European tour with **Sergei Diaghilev** (1923–25), she partnered **Anton Dolin** in England and became director of ballet at the Abbey Theatre, Dublin. She was a founding member (1931) of the Camargo Society and the Vic-Wells Ballet (later Sadler's Wells Ballet and the Royal Ballet). She was artistic director of the Royal Ballet until 1963 and was regarded as a pioneer of British ballet. Her rarely performed choreographic works include *The Rake's Progress* (1935), *Checkmate* (1937) and *Don Quixote*. She was given the honorary title of Dame Commander, Order of the British Empire, in 1951, and was appointed to the Order of Merit in 1992.

Van Allen, James Alfred 1914– *•US physicist•* Born in Mount Pleasant, Iowa, he graduated from Iowa Wesleyan College in 1935 before becoming professor of physics and head of the Physics Department at the State University of Iowa (1951–85), where he is now Regent Distinguished Professor. During World War II he developed the radio proximity fuse, which guided explosive projectiles toward their targets and then detonated them. This work gained Van Allen expertise in the miniaturization of electronics, which he utilized in experiments carried out after the war into the properties of the Earth's upper atmosphere, particularly the measurement of cosmic ray intensity at high altitudes. He was involved in the launching of the US's first satellite, *Explorer I* (1958), which carried his cosmic ray detector. Such detectors later revealed the startling result that above a certain altitude there was much more high-energy radiation than previously expected, and satellite observations showed that the Earth's magnetic field traps high-speed charged particles in two zones known as the Van Allen belts. Van Allen was awarded the US National Medal of Science in 1987.

Vanbrugh, Sir John 1664–1726 •*English playwright and Baroque architect*• Born in London, the son of a tradesman and grandson of a Protestant refugee merchant from Ghent, he was educated in France, commissioned into Lord Huntingdon's regiment and suffered imprisonment in the Bastille, Paris, as a suspected spy (1690–1702). A staunch Whig, he became a leading spirit in society life and scored a success with his first comedy, *The Relapse* (1696), followed, again with success, by *The Provok'd Wife* (1697). *The Confederacy* (1705) was put on in the Haymarket, London, where **William Congreve** and Vanbrugh became theater managers. A playwright of the uninhibited Restoration comedy of manners period, he also achieved success as architect of Castle Howard (1702), and in 1705 he was commissioned to design Blenheim Palace at Woodstock. The immense baroque structure aroused the ridicule of **Jonathan Swift** and **Pope**. He was made comptroller of royal works in 1714 and Clarenceux king-of-arms (1705–25).

Van Buren, Martin 1782–1862 •*Eighth President of the US*• Born in Kinderhook, New York, he became a lawyer in 1803, then state attorney general (1816–19), senator (1821), governor of New York (1828), secretary of state (1829–31) and vice president (1833–37). He was a supporter of **Andrew Jackson** and a member of the group which evolved into the Democratic Party. His presidency (1837–41) was darkened by the financial panic of 1837 and, in response, he introduced the Independent Treasury system. He was defeated for reelection by the Whig Party in 1840. In 1848 he ran unsuccessfully for president as the candidate of the Free-Soil Party, which opposed the spread of slavery.

Vance, Cyrus R(oberts) 1917–2002 •*US lawyer and politician*• Born in Clarksburg, West Virginia, he served in the navy before practicing law, then held a number of government posts, and served as secretary of state under President **Carter**. He resigned in 1980 over the handling of the Iran hostage crisis involving US diplomats. In 1991 he was appointed UN special envoy in Yugoslavia, and the following year became cochairman with Lord **Owen** of the international peace conference on the former Yugoslavia (1992–93).

van Cleve, Joos *See* **Cleve, Joos van**

Van de Graaff, Robert J(emison) 1901–67 •*US physicist*• He was born in Tuscaloosa, Alabama. An engineering graduate of the University of Alabama (1923), he continued his studies at the Sorbonne, Paris (1924), where **Marie Curie**'s lectures inspired him to study physics. At Princeton in 1929 he constructed the first working model of an improved type of electrostatic generator (later to be known as the Van de Graaff generator). The charge was carried to a hollow metal sphere by means of an insulated fabric belt, allowing potentials of over a million volts to be achieved. At MIT Van de Graaff adapted his generator for use as a particle accelerator, which became a major research tool for atomic and nuclear physicists. The generator was also employed to produce high-energy X-rays, useful in the treatment of cancer.

Vanderbilt, Cornelius 1794–1877 •*US financier*• Born on Staten Island, New York, he bought a boat at the age of 16 and ferried passengers and goods between Staten Island and New York City. By 40 he had become the owner of steamers running to Boston and up the Hudson. In 1849, during the gold rush, he established a route from Lake Nicaragua to California, and during the Crimean War, a line of steamships to Havre. In 1862 he sold his ships and gradually obtained a controlling interest in a large number of railways. He gave a large sum of money to found Vanderbilt University in Nashville, Tennessee. William Henry Vanderbilt (1821–85), his eldest son, greatly extended the Vanderbilt system of railways.

Vanderbilt-Cooper, Gloria 1924– •*US artist, actress, model and fashion designer*• Born in New York, she was the subject of a sensational custody trial at the age of 10 between her mother, Gloria Morgan Vanderbilt, and her millionaire aunt Harry (Gertrude) Payne Whitney. Her aunt gained custody until Gloria was 14, at which age Gloria's estate was valued at some $4 million. In 1955 she made her professional acting debut in *The Time of Your Life* on Broadway, and also that year published the first of her six books, *Love Poems*. The winner of several design awards, she designs stationery, fabrics, clothing, household accessories, and she gave her name to the Vanderbilt perfume and jeans.

Van der Goes, Hugo *See* **Goes, Hugo van der**

van der Meer, Simon 1925– •*Dutch physicist and engineer and Nobel Prize winner*• Born in The Hague and educated at the Technical University, Delft, he worked at the Philips research laboratories in Eindhoven (1952–55) before becoming senior engineer (1956–90) for CERN (Conseil Européen pour la Recherche Nucléaire) in Geneva. He developed a method known as "stochastic cooling" to produce a higher intensity beam of antiprotons in accelerators than had been produced before. This technology made possible the experiments that led to the discovery of the field particles W and Z, which transfer the weak nuclear interaction. Van der Meer shared the 1984 Nobel Prize for physics with **Carlo Rubbia** for their separate contributions to this discovery.

van der Post, Sir Laurens Jan 1906–96 •*South African soldier, explorer, writer and philosopher*• He served with distinction in World War II in Ethiopia, the Western Desert, Syria and the Far East, where he was captured by the Japanese. On his release he joined **Louis Mountbatten**'s staff in Java. He went on to work for the British government on a variety of missions in Africa, and with the Kalahari Bushmen of southern Africa. A sensitive writer of lyrical insight, his books include *The Lost World of the Kalahari* (1958), *The Seed and the Sower* (1963, filmed as *Merry Christmas, Mr Lawrence*, 1983), *Yet Being Someone Other* (1982) and *The Voice of the Thunder* (1993). He was knighted in 1981.

van der Waals, Johannes Diderik *See* **Waals, Johannes Diderik van der**

van der Weyden, Rogier *See* **Weyden, Rogier van der**

Van de Velde, Henri *See* **Velde, Henri Clemens van de**

Van Doren, Carl Clinton 1885–1950 •*US critic and biographer*• Born in Hope, Illinois, he was the brother of **Mark Albert Van Doren**. He studied at the University of Illinois and at Columbia, where he lectured in English literature (1911–30). He was literary editor of the *Nation* (1919–22) and of the *Cambridge History of American Literature* (1917–21). He was also a distinguished biographer of **Thomas Love Peacock** (1911), **James Branch Cabell** (1925), **Jonathan Swift** (1930), **Sinclair Lewis** (1933) and **Benjamin Franklin** (1938, Pulitzer Prize, 1939). His critical studies include *The American Novel* (1921) and, with his brother, *American and British Literature Since 1890* (1925).

Van Doren, Mark Albert 1894–1972 •*US poet and critic*• The brother of **Carl Clinton Van Doren**, he was born in Hope, Illinois. He studied at the University of Illinois and at Columbia, where he taught from 1920 and became Professor of English in 1942. He served in the army during World War I, followed his brother to the editorship of the *Nation* (1924–28) and was awarded the Pulitzer Prize (1940) for his *Collected Poems* (1939). Later volumes include *The Mayfield Deer* (1941) and *Spring Birth* (1953). He collaborated with his brother on *American and British Literature Since 1890* (1925), edited the *Oxford Book of American Prose*, and also wrote critical studies and novels.

Van Dyck or **Vandyke, Sir Anthony** 1599–1641 •*Flemish painter*• Born in Antwerp, he studied painting under Hendrick van Balen (1575–1632) and **Rubens**. In 1618 he was admitted as master painter to the guild of St Luke at Antwerp and in 1620 was commissioned to paint Lady Arundel, wife of Thomas Howard, 2nd Earl of Arundel. Records show that on this visit to England (1620–21) he also executed a full-length portrait of **James VI and I** at Windsor. He was in Italy for much of the 1620s. At The Hague he painted the Prince of Orange (later **William III**) and his family. In 1632 he returned to London and was knighted by **Charles I**, who made him a painter-in-ordinary. Back in Holland on leave (1634–35), he painted Ferdinand of Austria and *The Deposition*. His flair for psychological accuracy in rendering the character of his sitters, always with a hint of flattery and in the most favorable settings, greatly influenced the British school of portraiture in the next century and imparted to posterity a thoroughly romantic glimpse of the Stuart monarchy. Among the best of these portraits are those depicting Charles I, Queen **Henrietta Maria** and the two royal children; the equestrian portrait of the king; the three aspects of the king (1637) to serve as a model for **Gian Lorenzo Bernini**'s sculpture (all at Windsor) and the magnificent *Le roi à la chasse*. He is regarded as one of the great masters of portraiture of the 17th century.

Van Dyke, Dick 1925– •*US actor and entertainer*• Born in West Plains, Missouri, he became a radio announcer in the US Air Force during World War II. He later toured as part of the nightclub act The Merry Mutes and as half of "Eric and Van." Moving into television, he acted as master of ceremonies on such programs as *Flair* (1960). His Broadway debut in *The Boys Against the Girls* (1959) was followed by *Bye, Bye Birdie* (1960–61), a role which won him a Tony Award and which he repeated on film (1963). His television series *The Dick Van Dyke Show* (1961–66) won him Emmy awards in 1962, 1964 and 1965. His subsequent films include *Mary Poppins* (1964) and *Chitty Chitty Bang Bang* (1968). After conquering alcoholism, he displayed his dramatic ability on film in *The Runner Stumbles* (1979). Subsequent television series have included *The Van Dyke Show* (1988).

Vane, Sir Henry 1613–62 •*English politician*• Born in Hadlow, Kent, he became a staunch Republican. In 1635 he sailed for New England. He was an unpopular governor of Massachusetts, and in 1637 he returned to England. In 1640 he entered the House of Commons and played a major part in securing the execution of the Earl of **Strafford**. Between 1643 and 1653 he was in effect the civilian head of the Parliamentary government. He was himself executed after the Restoration.

Vane, Sir John Robert 1927– •*English pharmacologist and Nobel Prize winner*• Born in Tardebigg, Worcestershire, he studied at Birmingham and Oxford before accepting pharmacology appointments at Yale (1953–55), the Royal College of Surgeons, London (1955–73), and the Wellcome Research Laboratories, Kent (1973–85). Working on adrenergic receptors of the nervous system and the role of the lung in drug uptake and metabolism, he devised a bioassay for the detection (1967) and characterization of labile and bioactive arachidonic acid (essential fatty acid) metabolites. He investigated the chemistry of prostaglandins and discovered a type which inhibits blood clots, and also illuminated the operation of aspirin in treating pain. For this work he shared with **Sune Bergström** and **Bengt Samuelsson** the 1982 Nobel Prize for physiology or medicine. He was knighted in 1984.

Van Gogh, Vincent Willem 1853–90 •*Dutch Postimpressionist painter, one of the pioneers of Expressionism*• He was born in Groot-Zundert, the son of a Lutheran pastor. At 16 he became an assistant (1869–76) with an international firm of art dealers in their shops in The Hague, London and Paris. An unrequited love affair with an English schoolmistress accentuated his inferiority complex and religious passion. He became an assistant master at Ramsgate and Isleworth (1876) and there trained unsuccessfully to become a Methodist preacher. In 1878 he became an evangelist for a religious society at the Belgian coal-mining center of Le Borinage (1878–80), where, first as a resident and later as an itinerant preacher, he practiced the Christian virtues with great zeal and gave away his possessions. In April 1881 he set off for Brussels to study art, but another unfortunate love affair, this time with a cousin, threw him off balance, and he eventually settled in The Hague, where he lived with his model Christien or "Sien," a prostitute. She appears in the drawing *Sorrow* (1882) and *Sien Posing* (1883). In his father's new parish at Nuenen he painted his dark, haunting, domestic scene of peasant poverty, *The Potato Eaters* (1885, Van Gogh Museum, Amsterdam), his first masterpiece, and *Boots* (1887, Museum of Art, Baltimore). His devoted brother Theo, now an art dealer, made it possible for him to continue his studies in Paris (1886–88) under Cormon, and there he met **Paul Gauguin**, **Henri Toulouse-Lautrec**, **Georges Seurat** and the art collector Tanguy, who is the subject, surrounded by Japanese woodcuts, of one of Van Gogh's remarkable portraits (1887–88). These new influences brightened his palette and on Lautrec's advice he left Paris to seek the intense colors of the Provençal landscape at Arles, the subject of many of his best works. There he also painted *Sunflowers* (1888), *The Bridge* (1888) and *The Chair and the Pipe* (1888) and invited Gauguin to found a community of artists. Gauguin's stay with him ended in a tragic quarrel in which Van Gogh, in remorse for having threatened Gaugin with a razor, cut off part of his own ear. Placed in an asylum at St Rémy (1889–90), he painted the grounds, the *Ravine* (1889, with increasingly frantic brushstrokes), the keeper and the physician. In 1890 he went to live at Auvers-sur-Oise near Paris. That year an exhaustive article appeared by A Aurier which at last brought Van Gogh some recognition. But on July 27, 1890, Van Gogh shot himself at the scene of his last painting, the foreboding *Cornfields With Flight of Birds*, and died two days later. Van Gogh's output included over 800 paintings and 700 drawings. He used color primarily for its emotive appeal, and he profoundly influenced the Fauves and other experimenters of 20th-century art.

“ ”

I cannot help it that my paintings do not sell. The time will come when people will see that they are worth more than the price of the paint.

1888 Letter to his brother Theo, October 24.

Van Meegeren, Han *See* **Meegeren, Han van**

Van Praagh, Dame Peggy (Margaret) 1910–90 •*English ballet dancer, teacher and producer*• Born in London, she joined the Ballet Rambert in 1933. She created many roles with that company, chiefly in works by **Antony Tudor**: *Jardin aux lilas* (1936, "Lilac Garden") and *Dark Elegies* (1937). She moved to Tudor's newly formed London Ballet in 1938 and introduced the idea of lunchtime performances during the Blitz. In 1941 she joined the Sadler's Wells Ballet as a dancer and teacher, and she worked as producer and assistant director with **Ninette de Valois** at the Sadler's Wells Theatre Ballet until 1956. She produced many ballets for BBC television and for international companies, and was founding artistic director of the Australian Ballet (1962–79). She was given the honorary title of Dame Commander, Order of the British Empire, in 1970.

Vansittart (of Denham), Robert Gilbert Vansittart, Baron 1881–1957 •*English diplomat*• Educated at Eton, he joined the diplomatic service in 1902 and served successively in Paris, Tehran, Cairo and Stockholm. He visited Germany in 1936, talked with **Hitler** and became the uncompromising opponent of Nazi Germany, warning that Britain should arm to meet the German menace. In 1938 his disagreement with **Neville Chamberlain**'s policy of appeasement led to his replacement by Sir Alexander Cadogan (1884–1968). He retired in 1941.

van't Hoff *See* **Hoff, Jacobus Henricus van't**

Van Vleck, John Hasbrouck 1899–1980 •*US physicist and Nobel Prize winner*• Born in Middletown, Connecticut, he studied at Wisconsin and Harvard and took up posts at the Universities of Minnesota and Wisconsin and finally at Harvard (1934–69). He largely founded the modern theory of magnetism. In the late 1920s and early 1930s his research in dielectric and magnetic susceptibilities culminated in his classic text, *The Theory of Electric and Magnetic Susceptibilities* (1932). He elucidated chemical bonding in crystals and studied the electric fields experienced by the electrons of an ion or atom due to its neighbors. These fields significantly affect the optical, magnetic and electrical properties of the material. During World War II he contributed to the exploitation of radar. In 1977 his pioneering research was recognized with the joint award of the Nobel Prize for physics, with **Philip Anderson** and Sir **Nevill Mott**.

Varda, Agnès 1928– •*French film writer and director*• Born in Brussels, Belgium, she was educated at the Sorbonne in Paris, and while studying art history at the École du Louvre, she took evening classes in photography and decided to make a career of it. She made her directorial debut with *La pointe courte* (1954), a film often cited as an early influence on the *nouvelle vague* (New Wave). Her work favored the documentary in such films as *Salut les cubains* (1963, *Salute to Cuba*), but she also cowrote the feature *Ultimo tango a Parigi* (1972, *Last Tango in Paris*). Other films include *Les cent et une nuits* (1994). Her marriage to the director Jacques Demy lasted from 1962 until his death in 1990, and she published her autobiography *Varda par Agnès* in 1994.

Vardon, Harry 1870–1937 •*British golfer*• He was born in Grouville, Jersey. He won the British Open championship six times, in 1896, 1898, 1899, 1903, 1911 and 1914. He also won the US Open in 1900, and the German Open in 1911. He turned professional in 1903, and is remembered for the fluency of his swing and his overlapping grip, which is still known as the Vardon grip.

Varèse, Edgard (Victor Achille Charles) 1885–1965 •*US composer*• Born in Paris of Italo-French parentage, he studied under **Albert Roussel**, **Vincent d'Indy** and **Charles Widor** in Paris, and later under **Ferruccio Busoni**. He settled in New York in 1915, where he founded the New Symphony Orchestra (1919) to promote the cause of modern music. In 1921 he founded the international Composers' Guild, a leading organization of progressive musicians. Almost entirely orchestral, his work often uses unconventional percussion instruments, and its abstract nature is reflected in titles like *Ionization* (1931).

Vargas, Getúlio (Dorneles) 1883–1954 •*Brazilian statesman*• Born in São Borja, after serving in the army and training as a lawyer, he was elected a federal deputy in 1923. He was minister of finance under Washington Luís Pereira de Souza and headed the Liberal Alliance ticket for the presidency in 1930. Defeated in the polls, he won the support of sufficient military force to govern with the army from 1930 to 1945. Ousted in 1945 by the army, he returned as constitutional president in 1951. Four years later, in the face of mounting opposition from the right wing, he committed suicide.

Vargas Llosa, Mario 1936– •*Peruvian novelist*• Born in Arequipa, he studied law and literature in Peru, then spent many years abroad as a student in Paris and Madrid, building up a reputation as a writer. He eventually returned to Lima shortly before the restoration of democratic government in Peru in 1980. *The Time of the Hero* (1962), his first novel, is a powerful social satire and so outraged the authorities that a thousand copies were publicly burned. *The Green House* (1965) brings to life Peruvian society in the days of the rubber boom. Subsequent novels include his masterpiece *Aunt Julia and the Scriptwriter* (1977, trans 1982), an energetic, inventive comedy with an autobiographical inspiration: the novelist's first wife, Julia, was his aunt by marriage. He has also written *The War at the End of the World* (1981), *The Real Life of Alejandro Mayta* (1984) and *In Praise of the Stepmother* (1990). He ran unsuccessfully for the presidency of Peru in 1990, having declined an offer of the premiership in 1984.

Varmus, Harold Elliot 1939– •*US molecular biologist and Nobel Prize winner*• Born in Oceanside, New York, he was educated at Harvard and Columbia University, New York, and has held various posts at the University of California Medical Center, San Francisco. In 1989 he was awarded the Nobel Prize for physiology or medicine (jointly with **Michael Bishop**) for his contribution to the discovery of oncogenes, normal cellular genes that control cellular growth.

Varro, Marcus Terentius 116–27 BC •*Roman scholar and writer*• He was born in Reate and studied at Athens. Politically opposed to **Julius Caesar**, he fought under **Pompey** in the civil war and was legate in Spain. He was pardoned by Caesar, who appointed him librarian, but under the second triumvirate **Mark Antony** placed his name on the list of the proscribed. **Augustus** later restored his property. His prose writings embraced oratory, history, jurisprudence, grammar, philosophy, geography and husbandry and include *Saturae Menippeae* ("Menippean Satires"), *De lingua Latina* ("On the Latin Language") and *De re rustica* ("Country Affairs"). His *Disciplinarum libri IX* was an encyclopedia of the liberal arts.

Varro, Publius Terentius c. 82–37 BC •*Roman poet*• He was called Atacinus, from his birth in the valley of the Atax in Narbonensian Gaul. He wrote satires and an epic poem on **Julius Caesar**'s Gallic Wars, called *Bellum Sequanicum*. His *Argonautica* was an adaptation of **Apollonius Rhodius**, and his erotic elegies pleased **Propertius**.

Varus, Publius Quintilius d. 9 AD •*Roman official*• As governor of Syria he suppressed the revolt of Judea (4 BC, also known as the War of Varus), and in AD 9 he was sent by **Augustus** to command forces in Germany. There **Arminius** destroyed three Roman legions (the "Varian Disaster"), and Varus killed himself.

Vasarely, Viktor 1908–97 •*French painter*• Born in Pecs, Hungary, he began as a medical student before studying art (1928–29) at the Mühely Academy (the "Budapest Bauhaus") under **László Moholy-Nagy**. He moved to Paris in 1930, and from about 1947 he painted abstract pictures using repeated geometrical shapes ("cinétisme"), which looked forward to the op art of the 1960s, as in *Supernovae* (1959–61). He also experimented with kinetic art. Exhibiting widely from the late 1940s, he won many prizes, including the Guggenheim Prize in New York (1964).

Vasari, Giorgio 1511–74 •*Italian artist and art historian*• Born in Arezzo, he studied under **Michelangelo**, and lived mostly in Florence and Rome. He was a greater architect than painter, but he is best known for his *Vite de' più eccellenti pittori, scultori, e architettori* (1550, "Lives of the Most Excellent Painters, Sculptors and Architects"), a book of biographies and of art criticism.

Vasco da Gama *See* **Gama, Vasco da**

Vassilou, Georgios Vassos 1931– •*Cypriot politician and businessman*• Born in Famagusta and educated at the Universities of Geneva, Vienna and Budapest, he embarked on a highly successful business career, eventually becoming a self-made millionaire. In 1988, believing that a fresh approach to the divisions in Cyprus was needed, he stood as an independent candidate for the presidency and won. As president, Vassilou worked consistently toward the reunification of the island, but he was defeated in the 1993 elections by **Glafkos Clerides** of the Democratic Rally (DISY) Party. Since then he has been leader of the United Democrats (formerly the Free Democrats Movement in Cyprus).

Vauban, Sébastien le Prestre de 1633–1707 •*French military engineer*• Born in Saint Léger, he enlisted under the 4th Prince de **Condé**, and served in Spain with him. By 1658 he was chief engineer under Viconte de **Turenne**. He introduced the effective method of approach by parallels at the Siege of Maestricht (1673), invented the socket bayonet (1687) and at the Siege of Philippsburg (1688), he introduced his ricochet batteries. In 1703 he became marshal of France. His *Dîme royale* (1707), in which he discussed the problem of taxation, was condemned and prohibited, and within a few weeks the disappointed Vauban was dead.

Vaughan, Henry 1622–95 •*Welsh religious poet*• Born in Newton-by-Usk, Breconshire, he entered Jesus College, Oxford, in 1638, and in 1646 he published *Poems, With the Tenth Satyre of Juvenal Englished.* He earned his medical degree and practiced as a physician, first in Brecon and then in Newton-by-Usk. In 1650 he printed his *Silex Scintillans* ("Sparkling Flint"), a volume of mystical and religious poems, and the collection *Olor Iscanus* was published in 1651. He also wrote prose (for example, *The Mount of Olives*, 1652) and *Thalia Rediviva: The Pastimes and Diversions of a Country Muse* (1678), a collection of elegies, translations and religious pieces published without authority by a friend.

Vaughan, Sarah Lois 1924–90 •*US jazz singer and pianist*• Born in Newark, New Jersey, as a child she sang gospel in church, and spent ten years studying the organ. Winning a talent competition in 1942 at the Apollo Theater, Harlem, she came to the attention of singer Billy Eckstine, and through him of **Earl Hines**, who promptly hired her as a singer and pianist. In 1944 she made her first recording, "I'll Wait and Pray," and launched a solo career the following year. By the early 1950s she was internationally acclaimed. She acquired the nickname "Sassy" and devoted increasing attention to a more commercial style, with lush orchestral backing, which dominated her work in the 1960s. She performed with small jazz ensembles again in the 1970s, utilizing her advanced harmonic knowledge, and continued to command a huge audience throughout her final decade.

Vaughan Williams, Ralph 1872–1958 •*English composer*• Born in Down Ampney, Gloucestershire, he studied with **Charles Stanford** at the Royal College of Music, **Max Bruch** in Berlin and **Maurice Ravel** in Paris. In touch from the start with the English choral tradition, he had his first success with *Sea Symphony* (1910), in which traditional choral styles were merged with a vigorously contemporary outlook. Under the influence of **Gustav Holst** he became a leader in the English folk-song movement, adding this tradition to the styles of Tudor church music, **Charles Parry** and Ravel. He was director of the Leith Hill Festival from 1905. Between *London Symphony* (1914) and *Pastoral Symphony* (1922) came a large number of works in all forms, including the ballad opera *Hugh the Drover* (1911–14). The ballet *Job* (1930) was notable for its concern with the moral issues of contemporary life, and it was followed by seven more symphonies, the opera *The Pilgrim's Progress* (1948–49) and numerous choral works. His versatility was demonstrated by his ability to provide music of equal quality for the stage (1909, **Aristophanes**'s *The Wasps*) and for films. In 1935 he was appointed to the Order of Merit.

“ ”

It takes perhaps a thousand poor musicians to produce one virtuoso.

*1954 In the **New York Times**, December 5.*

Vauquelin, Nicolas-Louis 1763–1829 •*French chemist*• Born in Saint-André-d'Hébertot, Normandy, he was an assistant to pharmacists in Rouen and Paris, where he met **Antoine François Fourcroy** with whom he collaborated throughout his life. From 1804 to 1809 he held the chair of applied chemistry at the Museum of Natural History, and from 1811 to 1822 he was Professor of Chemistry at the faculty of medicine of the University of Paris. He is chiefly remembered for the analyses of organic substances that he carried out with Fourcroy and for the discovery of chromium. He also found a new compound, beryllia (beryllium aluminum silicate), but the metal (later named beryllium) was not isolated until 1828 when **Friedrich Wöhler** and Antoine Bussy both prepared it. He was the first to isolate an amino acid, asparagine.

Vavilov, Nikolai Ivanovich 1887–1943 •*Russian botanist and plant geneticist*• Born in Moscow, he trained there and at the John Innes Horticultural Institute at Merton, Surrey. From his extensive travels he gathered the world's largest collection of seeds, building a collection of 40,000 species and varieties of wheat. In 1923 he established a network of 115 experimental stations across the USSR to sow the collection over the widest possible range. He published extensively, formulating the principle of diversity which postulates that, geographically, the center of greatest diversity represents the origin of a cultivated plant. His international reputation was challenged by the politico-scientific theories of **Trofim Lysenko**, who denounced him at a genetics conference (1937). Arrested in 1940, he died of starvation in a Siberian labor camp.

Veblen, Thorstein (Bunde) 1857–1929 •*US economist and social critic*• Born into a Norwegian immigrant family in Manitowoc County, Wisconsin, he grew up in an isolated farming community in Minnesota and studied at Carleton College and Johns Hopkins University before receiving a PhD in philosophy from Yale. In his major work, *The Theory of the Leisure Class* (1899), he held that feudal social divisions continued into modern times, with the lower classes laboring to support the leisure class, and he coined the term *conspicuous consumption*. The book became a classic text of US economics, and with his other writings it helped shape the terms of debate in his discipline.

Vega, Lope de, *in full* **Lope Félix de Vega Carpio** 1562–1635 •*Spanish dramatist and poet*• Born in Madrid, he was a student and graduate of Alcalá. He served in the Portuguese campaign of 1580, and in the Spanish Armada (1588). He became secretary to the Duke of Alva, Marquis of Malpica, and Marquis of Sarria. He took holy orders in 1614 and became an officer of the Inquisition. The more remarkable of his miscellaneous works are the *Rimas* (1604); *Peregrino en su patria* (1604, Eng trans *The Pilgrim of Casteele*, 1621), a romance; *Pastores de Belén* (1612), a religious pastoral; *Filomena* (1621) and *Circe* (1624), miscellanies in the style of **Cervantes**; *Corona Trágica* (1627, "Tragic Crown"), an epic on **Mary Queen of Scots**; and *Rimas de Tomé de Burguillos* (1634), a collection of lighter verse. He wrote about 2,000 historical and contemporary plays and dramas. Included in the roughly 500 that have survived are *Noche de San Juan* ("The Night of St John") and *El acero de Madrid*, the source of **Molière**'s *Le médecin malgré lui*.

Veil, Simone, *née* **Jacob** 1927– •*French politician and lawyer*• Born in Nice, she and her Jewish family were imprisoned in the Nazi concentration camps Auschwitz and Bergen-Belsen (1944). She studied law at the Institute d'Études Politiques in Paris then joined the Ministry of Justice in 1957, and became minister of health (1974–76), then of health and social security (1976–79) in the **Giscard d'Estaing** administration. She won the controversial legalization of abortion in 1974 and made contraception more easily available. In 1979 she became a Member of the European Parliament, becoming the first president (1979–82). An MEP until 1993, she received numerous honors for her work.

Velázquez or **Velásquez, Diego de Silva y** 1599–1660 •*Spanish painter who is among the greatest of the 17th century*• He was born in Seville. In 1613 he became the pupil of the painter and art historian Francisco Pacheco (1564–1654), whose daughter he married in 1618. In 1618 Velázquez set up his own studio. His early works were *bodegónes*, characteristically Spanish domestic genre pieces, of which *Old Woman Cooking Eggs* (1618, National Galleries of Scotland) is a typical example. In 1622 he tried his luck at court in Madrid and persuaded the poet **Luis de Góngora y Argote** to sit for him. The following year he achieved lifelong court patronage with his equestrian portrait (now lost) of **Philip IV**, who then had all other portraits of himself withdrawn. The other court artists accused Velázquez of being incapable of painting anything but heads. The king accordingly ordered a competition on a historical subject, which Velázquez won with his *Expulsion of the Moriscos by Philip III* (now also lost). In 1628 **Rubens** visited Madrid and befriended him. His advice and the palace collection of Italian art motivated Velázquez's visit to Italy (1629–31). His somber, austere, naturalistic style was transformed into the lightly modeled, more colorful styles of **Titian** and **Tintoretto**, as is apparent in his *Forge of Vulcan* (c. 1630) and *Joseph's Coat* (1630) and in the new type of portrait which Velázquez improvised, of the king (c. 1634) or his brother or son, in hunting costume with dog and landscape. The only surviving historical painting is his Baroque *Surrender of Breda* (c. 1634). Velázquez also painted many portraits of the royal children and of the court dwarfs (1644, 1655) and jester, nicknamed *Don Juan de Austria* (1652–59). In 1650 he was again in Rome to obtain art treasures for the king and there painted the portrait of Pope Innocent X and the two impressionistic *Views From Villa Medici*. He is best remembered for his three late masterpieces: *Las meniñas* (1656, "Maids of Honor"), in which the Infanta Margarita, her dwarf and attendants, and the artist himself with easel are grouped around a canvas in a large palace room hung with paintings; *Las hilanderas* (c. 1657, "The Tapestry Weavers") and the famous *Venus and Cupid*, known as the "Rokeby Venus" (c. 1658). Velázquez was appointed usher to the king's chamber (1627), superintendent of works (1643), palace chamberlain (1652) and was made a knight of the Order of Santiago (1658), the highest court award. His painting is distinguished for its unflattering realism, a remarkable achievement for a court painter.

Velázquez de Cuellar, Diego 1465–1524 •*Spanish soldier and colonialist*• He accompanied **Columbus** to Hispaniola in 1494, and in 1511 he conquered Cuba, of which he became governor from 1511 to 1524, and founded Havana. He sent out various expeditions of conquest, including in 1519 the Mexican expedition of **Hernán Cortés**.

Velde, Henri Clemens van de 1863–1957 •*Belgian architect, designer and teacher*• He was born in Antwerp. One of the originators of the art nouveau style, he started as a painter before pioneering the modern functional style of architecture. A disciple of **William Morris** and **John Ruskin** in the Arts and Crafts movement, he founded (with his pupil **Walter Gropius**) the Deutscher Werkbund movement in 1906 in Germany. He was a director of the Weimar School of Arts and Crafts, from which the Bauhaus sprang. His designs ranged beyond architecture to graphics, furniture, ceramics, metalwork and textiles. His works included the Werkbund Theater in Cologne, the Museum Kröller-Muller in Otterloo, the university library in Ghent, and the Belgian pavilions at the international exhibitions in Paris (1937) and New York (1939).

Vendôme, Louis Joseph, Duc de 1654–1712 •*French soldier*• Born in Paris, he served under Vicomte de **Turenne** in Germany and Alsace, in the Low Countries under the Duc de **Luxembourg**, and in Italy under Catinat. He captured Barcelona (1697), and enjoyed five years of self-indulgence before superseding the Duc de Villeroi in Italy in the War of the Spanish Succession (1701–14). He fought Prince **Eugène** (of Savoy) at Luzzara (1702) and Cassano (1705), finally defeating the Austrians in 1706. His defeat at Oudenarde by the Duke of **Marlborough** (July 1708) cost him his command. In 1710 he was sent to Spain to aid **Philip V**, whom he returned to Madrid, defeating the English at Brihuega, and the next day the Austrians at Villaviciosa. After a month of gluttony, even by his standards, he died.

Venizelos, Eleutherios 1864–1936 •*Greek statesman*• Born near Chania, Crete, he studied law in Athens, led the Liberal Party in the Cretan chamber of deputies and took a prominent part in the Cretan uprising against the Turks in 1896. As prime minister (1910–15) after the 1909 military coup, he restored law and order but excluded the Cretan deputies from the new parliament and promoted the Balkan League against Turkey (1912) and Bulgaria (1913). His sympathies with France and Britain at the outbreak of World War I clashed with those of King **Constantine I** and caused Venizelos to establish a provisional rival government at Salonika. In 1917 he forced the king's abdication. He secured further territories from Turkey at the Versailles Peace Conference, but he was heavily defeated in the general elections (1920), which brought the royalists and King Constantine back to power. He was prime minister again (1924, 1928–32, 1933).

Venn, John 1834–1923 •*English logician*• Born near Hull, Humberside, he became a Fellow of Caius College, Cambridge (1857). He developed **George Boole**'s symbolic logic and, in *Logic of Chance* (1866), the frequency theory of probability. He is best known for Venn diagrams, pictorially representing the relations between sets, though similar diagrams had been used by **Gottfried Leibniz** and **Leonhard Euler**.

Ventris, Michael George Francis 1922–56 •*English linguist*• He was born in Wheathampstead and was an architect by profession. As a teenager he became interested in the undeciphered Minoan scripts found on tablets excavated at palace sites in Crete. The earlier Linear A tablets had been found exclusively in Crete. Linear B tablets, of the late Minoan period, had appeared only at Knossos, but were beginning to turn up at Mycenaean sites in mainland Greece. His analysis proved that the language of Linear B was an early form of Greek. He was killed in a road accident shortly before the publication of his joint work, *Documents in Mycenaean Greek*, with John Chadwick (1920–98).

Venturi, Giovanni Battista 1746–1822 •*Italian physicist*• Born in Bibiano, near Reggio, he was ordained a priest at the age of 23, in 1773 became Professor of Geometry and Philosophy at the University of Modena, and later was appointed professor at Pavia. In addition to work on sound and colors, he published geological studies and kept in close touch with the work of **Daniel Bernoulli** and **Leonhard Euler** in fluid mechanics. He is remembered for his work on hydraulics (published 1797), particularly for the effect named after him (the decrease in the pressure of a fluid in a pipe where the diameter has been reduced by a gradual taper), which he first investigated in 1791.

Venturi, Robert Charles 1925– •*US architect*• Born in Philadelphia, he studied architecture at Princeton University. By the 1960s he was in reaction against the International style, and he began to create eclectic and playful designs that incorporated historical references and ornamentation for its own sake. He became a major figure in postmodernism and helped to establish the tenets of the movement with his 1966 book, *Complexity and Contradiction in Architecture*. With Stephen Izenour and his wife, **Denise Scott Brown**, he wrote the influential *Learning From Las Vegas* (1972), which praised the vitality of neon-lit, roadside Las Vegas architecture. His designs include the Vanna Venturi House in Philadelphia (1962) and the Sainsbury Wing of the National Gallery in London (opened 1991).

“ ”

[It is] drawing a mustache on a madonna.

*1977 On designing an addition to Oberlin College's 1917 Allen Memorial Art Museum. In the **New York Times**, January 30.*

Verdi, Giuseppe Fortunino Francesco 1813–1901 •*Italian composer*• He was born in Roncole, near Busseto, of humble rural origin, and much of his early musical education came from Provesi, organist of Busseto Cathedral. Subsidized by locals who admired his talent, he was sent to Milan, but was rejected by the conservatory because he was over age and was judged to be a poor pianist. Instead he studied profitably under Lavigna, *maestro al cembalo* at La Scala. On returning home he failed in his ambition to succeed Provesi as cathedral organist but was given a grant by the Philharmonic Society. Three years later he married the daughter of his friend and patron Barezzi, but both she and their two children died in the space of three years (1838–40). Verdi's first opera, *Oberto, conte di San Bonifacio*, was produced at La Scala in 1839, but it was with *Nabucco* (1842) that he achieved his first major success. In 1847 *I masnadieri* ("The Robbers," based on **Schiller**'s drama) was performed in London, with **Jenny Lind** in the cast. Of his other works up to 1850, only *Macbeth* (1847) and *Luisa Miller* (1849) are now regularly performed. *Rigoletto* (1851), *Il trovatore* (1853) and *La traviata* (1853) established his position as the leading Italian operatic composer of the day, and this was confirmed by *Simon Boccanegra* (1857) and *Un ballo in maschera* (1859, "A Masked Ball"). In all these works Verdi faced the opposition of the censors, especially when plots recalled current events. His next three works were all written for performance outside Italy: *La forza del destino* (1862, "The Force of Destiny," for St Petersburg), *Don Carlos* (1867, for Paris) and *Aïda* (1871, commissioned for the new opera house in Cairo, built in celebration of the Suez Canal). Apart from the *Requiem* (1873), written in commemoration of **Alessandro Manzoni**, there was a 16-year break in output until, in his old age, inspired by his literary collaborator **Arrigo Boito**, Verdi produced his two final masterpieces, *Otello* (1887) and *Falstaff* (1893). Both had their premieres at La Scala, ending nearly 20 years of feud with that theater. Apart from completing the *Quattro pezzi sacri* (1888–97, "Four Sacred Pieces"), Verdi never wrote again. His life coincided with the emergence of Italy as a nation, and he was an ardent nationalist, especially in his younger days. He took little active part in politics, and soon resigned his deputyship in the first Italian parliament (1860), although later in life he became a senator. Verdi's music is characterized by intimate tenderness as well as by moments of rousing splendor. He died in a Milan hotel in 1901. His funeral was accompanied by national mourning, and as his coffin passed by, the crowd spontaneously sang "Va, pensiero," the chorus of the exiled Hebrews from *Nabucco*.

Vergil *See* **Virgil**

Verlaine, Paul 1844–96 •*French poet*• He was born in Metz. He was educated at the Lycée Condorcet and entered the civil service. He mixed with the leading Parnassian poets and writers and took up their battle cry, "art for art's sake." The youthful morbidity of his first volume of poems, *Poèmes saturniens* (1866, "Saturnine Poems"), was criticized by **Charles Sainte-Beuve** as trying vainly to outdo **Baudelaire**. The evocation of the 18th century, provided the backdrop for his second work, *Fêtes galantes* (1869, Eng trans *Gallant Parties*, 1917), considered by many his finest poetical achievement. His love for 16-year-old Mathilde Mauté, whom he eventually married, was expressed in *La bonne chanson* (1870, "The Pretty Song"). The birth of a son did not resolve his marital difficulties, and he escaped (1872) to Flanders, Belgium and England, engaging in an affair with the fledgling poet **Arthur Rimbaud**, ten years his junior. Their friendship ended in Brussels in 1873, when Verlaine, drunk and desolate at Rimbaud's intention to leave him, shot him in the wrist. The police suspected immorality as a motive, and Verlaine was convicted and sentenced to two years' hard labor. *Romances sans paroles* (1874, Eng trans *Romances Without Words*, 1921) was written in Mons prison. He unsuccessfully attempted to enter a monastery on release, and he taught French at Stickney, Lincolnshire, and St Aloysius' College, Bournemouth (1875), where he completed his second masterpiece *Sagesse* (1881, "Wisdom"), full of the spirit of penitence and self-confession that appeared again in *Parallèlement* (1889, "In Parallel"). In 1877 he returned to France to teach English at the Collège of Notre Dame at Rethel. There he adopted a favorite pupil, Lucien Létinois, for whom he acquired a farm at Coulommes and whose death from typhus (1883) occasioned *Amour* (1888, "Love"). *Poètes maudits* (1884, "Accursed Poets"), comprising critical studies, was followed by the short stories *Louis Leclerc* and *Le poteau* (1886, "The Stake"), sacred and profane verse *Liturgies intimes* (1892, "Intimate Liturgies") and *Élégies* (1893). Verlaine is the master of a poetry which sacrificed all for sound and in which commonplace expressions take on a magic freshness.

Vermeer, Jan 1632–75 •*Dutch painter*• Born in Delft, he inherited his father's art dealership and painted purely for pleasure, though he may have studied under Carel Fabritius (1622–54). In 1653 he was admitted as master painter to the guild of St Luke, which he served as headman (1662–63, 1670–71). He gained some recognition in Holland in his lifetime, and his work was sought by collectors, but he made little effort to sell his paintings. His importance was only established in the late 19th century. Apart from a few portraits, *The Allegory of Faith*, *The Procuress* (1656, Dresden), *Christ in the House of Martha and Mary* and two views of Delft, he confined himself to painting small, detailed domestic interiors of his own house, spiced with an art dealer's furnishings and trappings. Fewer than 40 of his paintings are known, including the *Allegory of Painting* (c. 1665, Vienna), *Woman Reading a Letter* (c. 1662, Amsterdam), *Girl With a Pearl Earring* (The Hague), *Woman With a Water Jug* (c. 1658–60, New York) and *View of Delft* (c. 1660, The Hague). These paintings are notable for their use of perspective and treatment of the various tones of daylight. During World War II, forged Vermeers were produced by **Han van Meegeren**, who for some time deceived the experts.

Verne, Jules 1828–1905 •*French novelist*• He was born in Nantes, studied law, and from 1848 wrote opera libretti until the publication in 1863 of his novel *Cinq semaines en ballon* (Eng trans *Five Weeks in a Balloon*, 1870). In it he struck a new vein of fiction—exaggerating and often anticipating the possibilities of science and describing adventures carried out by means of scientific inventions. He greatly influenced the early science fiction of **H G Wells**. His best-known books, all of which have been translated, are *Voyage au centre de la terre* (1864, Eng trans *A Journey to the Center of the Earth*, 1872), *De la terre à la lune* (1865, Eng trans *From the Earth to the Moon*, 1873), *Vingt mille lieues sous les mers* (1869, Eng trans *Twenty Thousand Leagues Under the Sea*, 1873) and *Le tour du monde en quatre-vingts jours* (1873, Eng trans *Around the World in Eighty Days*, 1874).

Vernet, Antoine Charles Horace, *known as* **Carle** 1758–1835 •*French historical and animal painter*• Born in Bordeaux, the son of the marine painter Claude Joseph Vernet (1714–89), he went to Italy, where he decided to become a monk. Back in Paris, however, he took to painting horses again as well as the vast battle pieces of Marengo and Austerlitz (now at Versailles), for which **Napoleon I** awarded him the Legion of Honor.

Vernet, (Émile Jean) Horace 1789–1863 •*French battle painter*• Born in Paris, the son of **Antoine Vernet** and grandson of the marine painter Claude Joseph Vernet (1714–89), he became one of the great French military and sporting painters, and decorated the vast Constantine room at Versailles with battle scenes from Valmy, Wagram, Bouvines and *Napoleon at Friedland*. Other pictures include *The Wounded Trumpeter* (1819) in the Wallace Collection, London, and a portrait of **Napoleon I** in the National Gallery, London. His *Painter's Studio* depicts him in his favorite settings, surrounded by groups of people, boxing, playing instruments and leading horses.

Veronese, *pseudonym of* **Paolo Caliari** c. 1528–88 •*Venetian painter*• Born in Verona, from where he took his name, he was, along with **Titian** and **Tintoretto**, one of the greatest decorative artists of the 16th-century Venetian school. All his works are bravura displays of technical virtuosity that concentrate on rich costumes set off against sumptuous architectural frameworks. His first frescoes in the Doge's Palace and the Library of Saint Mark's in Venice were admired by Titian. In 1573, his *Feast in the House of Levi* (Venice) in which dwarves, animals, and other unlikely participants are introduced into the scene, brought him before the Inquisition for trivializing religious subjects. His major paintings include *The Adoration of the Magi* (1573, National Gallery, London) and *The Marriage Feast at Cana* (1562–63, Louvre, Paris). Other works include *The Triumph of Venice* on the ceiling of the Ducal Palace in Venice (c. 1585).

Veronica, St 1st century AD •*Semilegendary saint*• It is said that when she met **Jesus** and offered him her veil to wipe sweat from his brow, the divine features were miraculously imprinted upon the cloth. The veil is said to have been preserved in Rome from about 700, and was exhibited in St Peter's in 1933. Veronica may simply be a corruption of *vera icon*, "the true image" of Jesus.

Verrio, Antonio c. 1640–1707 •*Italian decorative painter*• Born in Lecce, he was established in Paris when he was persuaded (c. 1671) by **Charles II** to go to London and decorate Windsor Castle (1678–88). He succeeded Sir **Peter Lely** as court painter in 1684. He decorated the walls of Chatsworth and Burghley, where the Heaven Room is his masterpiece. He started work for **William III** at Hampton Court in 1699 and also decorated rooms for Queen **Anne**. He died at Hampton Court. His equestrian portrait of Charles II is in the Chelsea Hospital, London.

Verrocchio, Andrea del, *properly* **Andrea del Cione** c. 1435–c. 1488 •*Italian artist*• He was born in Florence and is best known as the teacher of **Leonardo da Vinci**. Although much of his work as goldsmith and sculptor has not survived, his bronze *David* (c. 1476, Bargello, Florence) is a milestone in the treatment of the standing male figure by Renaissance artists. With that of **Donatello** it is one of a trio which culminates in the genius of **Michelangelo**'s nude version. The equestrian monument to Bartolommeo Colleoni (1481–88) in Venice shows Verrocchio to be as capable of monumental public work of this kind as Donatello. Very little of his painting remains, a notable example being his *Baptism* (c. 1470, Uffizi, Florence).

Verwoerd, Hendrik Frensch 1901–66 •*South African politician*• He was born in Amsterdam, the Netherlands. He was educated at Stellenbosch, where he became Professor of Applied Psychology (1927) and Sociology (1933–37), and edited the nationalist *Die Transvaler* (1938–48). Exponent of the strict racial segregation policy of apartheid, Verwoerd was elected national leader in 1958 by the Nationalist Party parliamentary caucus. As sixth prime minister of South Africa he dedicated himself to the founding of a South African republic. After strong opposition to his policy of apartheid and an attempt on his life in 1960, South Africa broke from the commonwealth, becoming a republic in 1962, after which Verwoerd pursued a strict apartheid policy. He was assassinated in 1966 in the House of Assembly in Cape Town.

Very, Edward Wilson 1847–1910 •*US ordnance expert and inventor*• He served in the US Navy from 1867 to 1885, became an admiral, and in 1877 invented chemical flares (Very lights) for signaling at night.

Vesalius, Andreas 1514–64 •*Belgian anatomist, one of the first dissectors of human cadavers*• Born in Brussels, he studied in Paris, Louvain and Padua, where he took his degree. He was appointed Professor of Surgery at the University of Padua. In 1538 he published his six anatomical tables, still largely Galenist, and in 1541 he edited Galen's works. Comprehensive anatomizing enabled him to point out many errors in the traditional medical teachings derived from Galen. For instance, Vesalius insisted he could find no passage for blood through the ventricles of the heart, as Galen had assumed. His greatest work is the *De humani corporis fabrica* (1543, On the Structure of the Human Body"). With both its excellent descriptions and drawings of bones and the nervous system, the book set a completely new level of clarity and accuracy in anatomy. Many structures are described and drawn for the first time, for example, the thalamus. Vesalius became court physician of the emperor **Charles V** and his son **Philip II** of Spain.

Vespasian, Titus Flavius Vespasianus AD 9–79 •*Roman emperor*• Founder of the Flavian dynasty, he was born near Reate. In the reign of **Claudius** he commanded a legion in Germany and in Britain and was consul (AD 51) and then proconsul of Africa (c. 63). In 67 **Nero** sent him to subdue the Jews. When the struggle began between **Otho** and **Vitellius**, he was proclaimed imperator by the legions in the East, and on the death of Vitellius, he was appointed emperor. Leaving the war in Judea to his son **Titus**, he reached Rome in 70 and soon restored the government and finances to order. Bluff and popular, but astute and hard-working, he adopted a simple lifestyle. He embarked on an ambitious building program in Rome and extended and consolidated Roman conquests in Britain and Germany.

“ ”

Vae, puto deus fio.
Dear me, I must be turning into a god.

*79 Attributed last words. Quoted in Suetonius **Vespasian**, 23 (translated by Robert Graves, 1967).*

Vespucci, Amerigo 1451–1512 •*Spanish explorer after whom the continent of America was named*• Born in Florence, Italy, he was a contractor in Seville from 1495 to 1498 and provisioned one (or possibly two) of the expeditions of **Christopher Columbus**. Although not a navigator or pilot himself, in 1499 he promoted an expedition to the New World commanded by Alonso de Hojeda and sailed there in his own ship, in which he explored the coast of Venezuela. In 1505 he was naturalized in Spain, and in 1508, he was appointed pilot major of Spain. His name (Latinized as "Americus") was given to the American continents by the young German cartographer Martin Waldseemüller (c. 1480–c. 1521).

Vian, Sir Philip 1894–1968 •*English naval commander*• He was educated at the Royal Naval College, Dartmouth. In 1940, as captain of a destroyer flotilla on HMS *Cossack*, he penetrated Norwegian territorial waters to rescue 300 British from the German supply ship *Altmark*. He later played a leading role in the final destruction of the German battleship *Bismarck* (1941). He distinguished himself in the hazardous convoy operations for the relief of Malta (1941–42), took part in the assault landings in Sicily and Italy (1943) and Normandy (1944), and later commanded an aircraft carrier group in the Far East. He was Fifth Sea Lord (1946), and later Admiral of the Fleet.

Vicente, Gil c. 1470–c. 1537 •*Portuguese dramatist*• Born in Lisbon, he wrote 44 plays, 16 in Portuguese, 11 in Spanish and 17 using both languages. His early plays were religious, but gradually social criticism was added. His farces *Inês Pereira*, *Juiz da Beira* and the three *Autos das barcas* (*Inferno*, *Purgatório* and *Glória*, collective Eng trans *The Ship of Hell*, 1929) are his best. Considered to be the father of Portuguese drama, he displays great psychological insight, superb lyricism and a predominantly comical spirit.

Vicky, *pseudonym of* **Victor Weisz** 1913–66 •*British political cartoonist*• Born in Berlin, of Hungarian-Jewish extraction, he emigrated to the UK in 1935. He worked with the *News Chronicle*, the *Daily Mirror*, the *New Statesman* and the *Evening Standard*, and became a talented left-wing political cartoonist. He published collections of his work, including *Vicky's World* (1959) and *Home and Abroad* (1964).

Vico, Giambattista (Giovanni Battista) 1668–1744 •*Italian historical philosopher*• Born in Naples, he lived there for most of his life, apart from a period when he was a tutor with the Rocca family at the castle of Vatolla, south of Salerno (1686–95). Devoted to literature, history and philosophy, he became Professor of Rhetoric at Naples (1699). His published work was extremely wide-ranging, but his major work is the *Scienza nuova* (1725, "The New Science"), which presents an original, and often strikingly modern, view of the methods and presuppositions of historical inquiry. He explains the fundamental distinctions between scientific and historical explanation, rejects the idea of a single, fixed, human nature invariant over time, and argues that the recurring cyclical developments of history can only be understood by a study of the changing expressions of human nature through language, myth and culture. The work is now recognized as a landmark in European intellectual history.

Victor Emmanuel I 1759–1824 •*King of Sardinia*• The son of Victor Amadeus III (1726–96), he became king in 1802 on the abdication of his brother, Charles Emmanuel IV (1751–1819), and until 1814 lived at Cagliari in Sardinia, as his mainland possessions were in the hands of the French as a result of the war of 1793–96. After the Vienna Settlement (which awarded Genoa and the Ligurian coastal land to the Kingdom of Sardinia), he returned to Turin, where he fiercely rejected any legacy of French rule. Discontent grew, especially among those of his subjects who had supported the Napoleonic regime; it culminated in the liberal insurrection led by Annibale di Santarosa in 1821. Faced with mutiny, Victor Emmanuel abdicated in the same year in favor of his brother Charles Felix.

Victor Emmanuel II 1820–78 •*King of Sardinia and first king of Italy*• Born in Turin, he was the son of Charles Albert of Sardinia, who abdicated in his favor in 1849. Perhaps the most important act of his reign was the appointment (1852) of the Conte dí **Cavour** as his chief minister. In 1855 Sardinia joined the allies against Russia, and in 1857 diplomatic relations were broken off with Austria. He managed to defeat the Austrians at Montebello, Magenta and Solferino (1859); by the Treaty of Villafranca, Lombardy was ceded to Sardinia, and in 1860 Modena, Parma, the Romagna and Tuscany followed. Sicily and Naples were added by **Garibaldi**, while Savoy and Nice were ceded to France. In 1861 he was proclaimed king of Italy. In the Austro-Prussian War (1866), he allied with Prussia and added Venetia to his kingdom. After the withdrawal of the French garrison, he entered Rome in 1870, where he reigned as a strictly constitutional monarch.

Victor Emmanuel III 1869–1947 •*King of Italy*• The son of **Umberto I**, he was born in Naples. He became king in 1900 and generally ruled as a constitutional monarch with **Giovanni Giolitti** as premier, but he defied parliamentary majorities by bringing Italy into World War I on the side of the Allies (1915) and by offering **Mussolini** the premiership (1922). The king supported the dictator until the latter's fall (1944). Victor Emmanuel then retired from public life, leaving his son Umberto II (1904–83) as lieutenant general of the Realm, abdicated (1946) and died in exile in Egypt.

Victoria, *in full* **Alexandrina Victoria** 1819–1901 •*Queen of the United Kingdom of Great Britain and Ireland, and (from 1876) Empress of India*• She was born in Kensington Palace, London, the only child of Edward, Duke of Kent, fourth son of **George III**, and Victoria Maria Louisa of Saxe-Coburg, sister of **Leopold I** of Belgium. Her father died when she was still a baby, and Victoria became queen at the age of 18 on the death of her uncle, **William IV**, in 1837, and was crowned at Westminster on June 28, 1838. She quickly developed a grasp of constitutional principles and of the extent of her own prerogative, in which she had been carefully instructed in the many letters she received from her uncle Leopold. As a girl she had been almost constantly in the company of older people, instilling in her a precocious maturity and firmness of will that were now rapidly demonstrated. In her early formative years, Lord **Melbourne** was both her prime minister and her trusted friend and mentor. During the rest of her reign she was generally well disposed to the more conservative Melbourne and **Disraeli**, and less so to the more radical **Peel**, **Palmerston** and **Gladstone**. When Melbourne's government fell in 1839, she invited Peel to form a government, but she exercised her prerogative by setting aside the precedent which required her to dismiss the current ladies of the bedchamber. As a result, Peel resigned and the Melbourne administration was prolonged until 1841. On reaching marriageable age, the queen decided on Prince **Albert** of Saxe-Coburg and Gotha, with whom she was genuinely in love, and they were married in 1840. The marriage was happy and harmonious, and Albert's morals were uncharacteristically beyond reproach. Four sons and five daughters were born: of these the first, Victoria, the Princess

Royal, married Frederick III of Germany, and Albert Edward afterward became king as **Edward VII**. Their other children also formed important dynastic links by their marriages. Victoria was strongly influenced by Albert, and after his death in 1861 the stricken queen went into seclusion, which caused her to be temporarily unpopular. However, Disraeli, as prime minister from 1864, rekindled her interest in the Empire and repaid her confidence and affection by consolidating and extending her influence, acquiring for Great Britain a controlling interest in the Suez Canal, by having Victoria proclaimed Empress of India (1876), and by annexing the Transvaal in 1877. These events, and the celebratory Golden (1887) and Diamond (1897) Jubilees, restored her again to her subjects' favor. Her experience, shrewdness and innate political flair brought powerful influence to bear on the conduct of foreign affairs, as did the response to the country's policy made by her many relatives in the European royal houses. The royal couple visited the Scottish Highlands frequently, and Balmoral Castle was rebuilt to Albert's design. Victoria continued to grieve for Albert until her death. She died at Osborne House on the Isle of Wight, and was buried at Windsor.

" "

He speaks to Me as if I were a public meeting.

Of Gladstone. Attributed in G W E Russell ***Collections and Recollections*** *(1898).*

Vidal, Gore (Eugene Luther, Jr) 1925– •*US novelist, essayist and polemicist*• Born at the United States Military Academy in West Point, New York, he spent much of his childhood in Washington under the influence of his scholarly, witty and blind grandfather, Senator Thomas Gore. He was educated at Phillips Exeter Academy, but was a mediocre student, and in 1943 he joined the United States Army Reserve Corps. This gave him the material for his first novel, *Williwaw* (1946), published to some acclaim when he was just 19. Subsequent early novels, however, had a lukewarm reception. After a period as a television commentator he returned to the novel in 1964 with *Julian*, written in the voice of the emperor **Julian**, followed by a trilogy of books dealing with affairs of state—*Washington, DC* (1967), *Burr* (1973) and *1876* (1976). His liking for camp extravagance reached its apotheosis in the "apocalyptic" *Myra Breckenridge* (1968) and *Myron* (1974), "Myra's comeback." Since then his historical fiction has predominated. Even *Creation* (1981), his tour de force, was overshadowed by *Lincoln* (1984), an engrossing, meticulously researched, insightful portrait of the 16th president. In 1987 he published *Armageddon: Essays 1983–1987*, "random pieces" that reflect his ambivalent obsession with what he has called, with characteristic hauteur, "the land of the dull and the home of the literal." He published his memoirs, *Palimpsest*, in 1995.

Vidal de la Blache, Paul 1845–1918 •*French geographer*• Born in Pézenas, Hérault, and educated at the École Normale Supérieure in Paris, he taught at the University of Nancy (1872–77) and the École Normale Supérieure. He became the first Professor of Geography at the Sorbonne (1898–1918) and is regarded as the founder of modern French geography. He advocated a regional geography based on the intensive study of small physically defined regions such as the "pays" of France. He formulated the concept of possibilism.

Vidor, King Wallis 1894–1982 •*US film director*• Born in Galveston, Texas, he made his debut as the director of the documentary *Hurricane in Galveston* (1913). In Hollywood (from 1915), he worked as a writer and extra before directing a series of short films on juvenile crime and a feature, *The Turn of the Road* (1919). A successful mounting of *Peg o' My Heart* (1922) brought him a long-term contract with MGM. Showing an interest in social issues and the everyday struggles of the average American, his many films included *The Big Parade* (1925), *The Crowd* (1928) and *Our Daily Bread* (1934). His range of work also included Westerns, melodramas and historical epics. His autobiography, *A Tree Is a Tree*, was published in 1953. He also acted in *Love and Money* (1982). Nominated five times for an Academy Award, he received an honorary award in 1979.

Vieira, Antonio de 1608–97 •*Portuguese Jesuit missionary*• Born in Lisbon, he grew up in Brazil, where he attended the Jesuit College and became a missionary. He returned to Portugal after the restoration of independence (1640), was appointed court preacher (1641–52) to King John IV and became influential. In 1653 he returned to Brazil as Superior of Jesuit missions, but after years of conflict in which he defended the Indians against the colonists, he was expelled and sent back to Lisbon (1661). There he was put under house arrest and imprisoned by the Inquisition (1663–68). He subsequently went to Rome where he was well received, and in 1681 he was able to return with the Jesuits to Brazil. His letters give a clear picture of his time.

Vieira, João Bernardo 1939– •*Guinea-Bissau statesman*• Born in Bissau, he joined the African Party for the Independence of Portuguese Guinea and Cape Verde (PAIGC) in 1960, and in 1964 became a member of the political bureau during the war for independence from Portugal. After independence had been achieved in 1974, he served in the government of Luiz Cabral (1931–), but in 1980 he led the coup which deposed him. In 1984 Vieira became executive president. He was ousted in a coup in 1999.

Vigée Lebrun, (Marie) Élisabeth Louise, *née* **Vigée** 1755–1842 •*French painter*• She was born in Paris, the daughter of a painter, and her great beauty and the charm of her painting speedily made her work fashionable. Her portrait of **Marie Antoinette** (1779, Vienna) led to a lasting friendship with the queen, and she painted numerous portraits of the royal family. She left Paris for Italy at the outbreak of the Revolution, and after a triumphal progress through Europe, arrived in London in 1802, where she painted portraits of Lord **Byron** and others. One of her most admired paintings was *The Artist and Her Daughter* (1786, Louvre, Paris). Her *Memoires* were begun in 1835 and describe how she worked in her studio even when in labor.

Vignola, Giacomo Barozzi da 1507–73 •*Italian architect*• Born in Vignola, he studied in Bologna and became the leading Mannerist architect of his day in Rome. He designed the Villa di Papa Giulio for Pope Julius III and the Church of the Il Gesu in Rome, which, with its cruciform plan and side chapels, had a great influence on French and Italian church architecture. His other works included the Palazzo Farnese in Piacenza.

Vigny, Alfred Victor, Comte de 1797–1863 •*French writer*• He was born in Loches, Indre-et-Loire, and served in the Royal Guards (1814–28), retiring with a captaincy. His experiences provided the material for *Servitude et grandeur militaires* (1835, Eng trans *Military Servitude and Grandeur*, 1919), a candid commentary on the boredom and frustration induced by peacetime soldiering. He had already published some verse anonymously and *Poèmes antiques et modernes* (1826, "Ancient and Modern Poems," expanded edition 1829). He married an Englishwoman, Lydia Bunbury, in 1828, but his life was marred by domestic unhappiness. Much of his work reflects his disappointment and pessimism, particularly the romantic drama *Chatterton* (1835, Eng trans 1847), written for his love, the actress Marie Dorval. Other notable works include the historical novel *Cinq-Mars* (1826, Eng trans *Cinq-Mars; or, a Conspiracy Under Louis XIII*, 1847).

Vigo, Jean 1905–34 •*French filmmaker*• Born in Paris, he studied at the Sorbonne before his fascination with the camera led him to work as an assistant at Franco-Film. He made his debut with the iconoclastic documentary *À propos de Nice* (1930, "About Nice"). This was followed by the short film *Taris* (1931) and *Zéro de conduite* (1933, *Zero for Conduct*), which captured the anarchic spirit of rebellious youth. *L'Atalante* (1934) used arresting pyrotechnics to embellish a lyrical love story. Perennially in poor health, he died from leukemia shortly after the film's release.

Villa, Pancho (Francisco), *originally* **Doroteo Arangol** 1877–1923 •*Mexican revolutionary*• Born near San Juan del Río, Durango, the son of a field laborer, he had various modest occupations before the Mexican Revolution made him famous as a military commander. In a fierce struggle for control of the revolution, he and **Emiliano Zapata** were defeated (1915) by **Venustiano Carranza**, with whom Villa had earlier allied himself against the dictatorship of General **Victoriano Huerta**. Both Villa and Zapata withdrew to strongholds in north and central Mexico and continued to carry on guerrilla warfare. In 1916 Villa was responsible for the shooting of a number of US citizens in the town of Santa Isabel, as well as an attack on the city of Columbus, New Mexico, which precipitated the sending of a US punitive force by President **Woodrow Wilson**. He eventually made peace with the government (1920) but was murdered in Parral.

Villa-Lobos, Heitor 1887–1959 •*Brazilian composer and conductor*• Born in Rio de Janeiro, his first published composition was *Salon Waltz* (1908). He made an expedition up the Amazon to study folk music in 1915, after which he composed 12 symphonies, 16 string quartets, five operas and a number of large-scale symphonic poems on Brazilian subjects. He also wrote the music for several ballets. A meeting with **Darius Milhaud** in 1918 aroused his interest in modern music and led him to spend several years in Paris. He composed several *Chôros*, in popular Brazilian styles, following these with the series of suites *Bachianas brasileiras* (1930), in which he treats Brazilian-style melodies in the manner of **J S Bach**. In 1932 he became director of musical education for Brazil and in 1945 founded the Brazilian Academy of Music.

Villars, Claude Louis Hector, Duc de 1653–1734 •*French soldier*• He was born in Moulins. He fought in the Third Dutch War (1672–78), and in the War of the Spanish Succession (1701–14). He became marshal of France, and was commissioned to put down the Camisards (1704). He defended the northeastern frontier against the Duke of **Marlborough**, and in 1708 he defeated the attempts of Prince **Eugène** to penetrate into France. In 1709 he was sent to oppose Marlborough in the north, but at Malplaquet he was severely wounded. In 1711 he headed the last army France could raise, and with it attacked the British and Dutch at Denain (July 1712). He then defeated Prince Eugène and signed the Peace of Rastatt (1714). He fought admirably again in his 80s in the war of 1732–34 in Italy. He died in Turin.

Villehardouin, Geoffroi de c. 1160–1213 •*French nobleman and historian*• Born in the castle of Villehardouin in Aube, he participated in the Fourth Crusade (1199–1207) as one of its leaders. His *Conquête de Constantinople* ("Conquest of Constantinople")—he was present at the capture—which describes the events from 1198 to 1207, is one of the first examples of French prose.

Villella, Edward (Joseph) 1936– •*US ballet dancer*• Born in Long Island, New York, in 1957 he joined the New York City Ballet and danced in many works by **George Balanchine**, including *A Midsummer Night's Dream* (1962) and *Tarantella* (1964), which displayed his speed and high jumps, while **Jerome Robbins**'s *Watermill* (1972) showcased his contemplative control. He was artistic director of the Eglevsky Ballet Company (1979–84) and of Ballet Oklahoma (1983–86), and founding artistic director of the Miami City Ballet (1985–).

Villeneuve, Jacques 1971– •*Canadian racecar driver*• Born in St-Jean-sur-Richelieu, Quebec, the son of racecar driver Gilles Villeneuve who died in a Formula 1 crash in 1982, he raced in Italian Formula 3 until 1991. He won the PPG Indy Car World Series in 1995. He made his Formula 1 debut in 1996 with Williams Renault and that same season achieved his first win by taking the European Grand Prix. He won the Formula 1 championship in 1997 and joined the British American Racing team in 1999.

Villeneuve, Pierre Charles Jean Baptiste Sylvestre de 1763–1806 •*French naval commander*• Born in Valensoles, he commanded the rear division of the French navy at the Battle of the Nile (1798), saving his vessel and four others. In 1805 he took command of the fleet designed to invade England but was defeated by Lord **Nelson** off Cape Trafalgar. He was taken prisoner but released in 1806. On his way to report to **Napoleon I** in Paris, he committed suicide.

Villiers, George *See* **Buckingham, George Villiers, 2nd Duke of**

Villiers de l'Isle Adam, Auguste, Comte de 1838–89 •*French writer, pioneer of the Symbolist movement*• He was born in St Brieuc, Brittany, and claimed descent from the Knights of Malta. He dedicated his *Premières poésies* (1856–58, "First Poetic Works") to the Comte **de Vigny** but later developed into a considerable stylist in prose. His well-known short stories, *Contes cruels* (1883, "Cruel Stories") and *Nouveaux contes cruels* (1888, "New Cruel Stories"), are after the manner of **Edgar Allan Poe**. Hegelian idealism and Wagnerian Romanticism inspire his highly didactic novels and plays. The former include *L'Ève future* (1886, "Eve of the Future"), a satire on the materialism of modern science. The latter include his masterpiece, *Axel* (1885).

Villon, François, *originally* **François de Montcorbier** or **de Logos** 1431–after 1463 •*French poet*• Born in Paris, he took the surname of his guardian, Guillaume de Villon, who enabled him to study at university, to graduate (1449) and to become a Master of Arts (1452). In 1455 he had to flee from Paris after fatally wounding a priest in a street brawl, and he joined a criminal organization, the Brotherhood of the Coquille, which had its own secret jargon in which Villon was to write some of his ballades. He served several jail sentences, and his death sentence was commuted to banishment in January 1463. He left Paris and nothing further is known of him. The first printed edition of his works was published in 1489. The *Petit testament* comprises 40 octosyllabic octaves; the *Grand testament* comprises 172, bridged by 16 ballades and other verse forms.

Villon, Jacques, *real name* **Gaston Duchamp** 1875–1963 •*French painter*• Born in Damville, the half brother of **Marcel Duchamp** and **Raymond Duchamp-Villon**, he went to Paris in 1894 to study art, met **Toulouse-Lautrec**, and exhibited at the Salon d'Automne from 1904. He took up Cubism (c. 1911) and exhibited with **Fernand Léger** and others working in that style. He did not win international fame until after World War II.

Vincent, St d. 304 AD •*Spanish religious*• Born in Saragossa, he became a deacon, according to St **Augustine**. Under **Diocletian**'s persecutions, he was imprisoned and tortured at Valencia, where he died. His feast day is January 22.

Vincent de Paul, St c. 1581–1660 •*French priest and philanthropist*• Born in Pouy, Gascony, and educated by Franciscans in Dax, he was ordained in 1600. He was captured by corsairs (1605) and sold into slavery in Tunis but escaped to France (1607). He became almoner to **Henry IV**'s queen, forming associations for helping the sick, and in 1619 was made Almoner General of the galleys. In 1625 he founded the Congregation of Priests of the Missions (called "Lazarists" from their priory of St Lazare in Paris) and in 1634, the Foundling Hospital and the Sisterhood of Charity. He was canonized in 1737, and his feast day is September 27.

Vinci, Leonardo da *See* **Leonardo da Vinci**

Vine, Barbara *See* **Rendell, Ruth**

Vinogradsky, Boris *See* **Delfont (of Stepney), Bernard Delfont, Baron**

Viollet-Le-Duc, Eugène Emmanuel 1814–79 •*French architect and archaeologist*• Born in Paris, he studied in France and Italy and was the great restorer of ancient buildings in France, including the cathedrals of Notre Dame in Paris, Amiens, Laon, and the Château de Pierrefonds. He served as engineer in the defense of Paris and was an advanced republican politician. His best-known work was his great *Dictionnaire raisoné de l'architecture française du XIe au XVIe siècle* (1854–86, "Reasoned Dictionary of French Architecture From the XIth to the XVIth Century").

Virchow, Rudolf 1821–1902 •*German pathologist and politician*• Born in Schivelbein, Pomerania, he studied medicine in Berlin, then rose to become Professor of Pathological Anatomy at the University of Würzburg (1849–56). In 1845 he recognized leukemia and proceeded to study animal parasites, inflammation, thrombosis and embolism. In 1856 he returned to Berlin as Professor of Pathological Anatomy. Virchow argued that disease originated in cells or at least was the response of cells to abnormal circumstances. His suggestions led to much fertile work and founded modern pathology. His *Cellularpathologie* (1858) established that tumors and all other morbid structures contained cells derived from previous cells. He remained politically active, sitting as a liberal member of the Reichstag (1880–93).

Virgil or **Vergil**, *full name* **Publius Vergilius Maro** 70–19 BC •*Roman poet, one of the greatest of antiquity*• He was born in Andes near Mantua in Cisalpine Gaul and was educated at Cremona and Milan. At 16 he went to Rome to study rhetoric and philosophy. After the Battle of Philippi in 42 BC, his family estate seems to have been confiscated to provide land for the veterans of **Mark Antony** and Octavian (Emperor **Augustus**), but he went to Rome and was recompensed. He soon became one of the endowed court poets who received the patronage of **Gaius Cilnius Maecenas**, and in 37 his *Eclogues*, 10 pastorals modeled on those of **Theocritus**, were received with great enthusiasm. The same year, Virgil traveled with **Horace** to Brundisium, as recorded by Horace (*Satires*, bk. 1, no. 5). Soon afterward Virgil, now well-off from Maecenas's patronage, left Rome and moved to Campania, where he had a villa at Naples and a country house near Nola. In 30 he published the *Georgics*, or *Art of Husbandry*, in four books, confirming his position as the foremost poet of the age. The remaining 11 years of his life were devoted to a larger task, undertaken at the request of Emperor Augustus: the composition of a great national epic based on the story of Aeneas the Trojan, legendary founder of the Roman nation and of the Julian family. By 19 BC the *Aeneid* was nearly completed, and Virgil left Italy to travel in Greece and Asia, but he fell ill at Megara in central Greece, and died at Brundisium on his way home. At his own wish he was buried in Naples, on the road to Pozzuoli. The supremacy of Virgil in Latin poetry was immediate and almost unquestioned. His works were established classics even in his lifetime, and soon after his death they had become the textbooks of western Europe. His work has been translated and admired by generations of poets.

“ ”

Quidquid id est, timeo Danaos et dona ferentes.

Whatever it may be, I fear the Greeks, even when bearing gifts.

Spoken by Laocoon, a Trojan prince and priest of Apollo, warning the city against the wooden horse left by the Greeks.

***Aeneid**, book 2, line 49.*

Virtanen, Artturi Ilmari 1895–1973 •*Finnish biochemist and Nobel Prize winner*• Born in Helsinki, he was educated at the university there and eventually became Professor of Biochemistry at the University of Helsinki (1939–48). He studied the bacterial metabolism of sugars to form succinate and lactate, and observed the processes by which the root nodules of leguminous plants release nitrogenous substances. He also investigated the ways in which nitrogen is absorbed by legume root nodules and converted into other substances inside the plant (1938). For these discoveries he was awarded the Nobel Prize for chemistry (1945). Virtanen also worked on the nutritional requirements of plants and the plant biosynthesis of carotene and vitamin A.

Visconti, Gian Galeazzo 1351–1402 •*Milanese statesman*• He succeeded his father, Galeazzo II, as joint ruler (1378–85) with his uncle Bernabo, whom he put to death (1385). As duke (1385) he made himself master of northern Italy, bringing many independent cities into one state; arranged marriage alliances with England, France, Austria and Bavaria; and was a great arts patron.

Visconti, Luchino, *real name* **Count Don Luchino Visconti Di Morone** 1906–76 •*Italian stage and film director*• Born in Milan, an early interest in music and the theater led him to stage designing and the production of opera and ballet. His first film as director, *Ossessione* (1942, "Obsession"), took Italy by storm, in spite of trouble from the Fascist censors. In that film, and in *La terra trema* (1947, *The Earth Trembles*) and *Rocco e i suoi fratelli* (1960, *Rocco and His Brothers*), he showed the strict realism, formal beauty and concern with social problems which are the hallmarks of all his films. These include *Il gattopardo* (1963, *The Leopard*), *La caduta degli Dei* (1969, *The Damned*) and *Morte a Venezia* (1971, *Death in Venice*).

Vitellius, Aulus AD 15–69 •*Roman emperor*• He was proconsul in Africa (c. 61 AD) and was appointed by **Galba** to the command of the legions on the Lower Rhine (68). He was proclaimed emperor at Colonia Agrippinensis (Cologne) in 69, and he ended the reign of **Otho**. Many of his soldiers deserted when **Vespasian** was proclaimed emperor in Alexandria. Vitellius was defeated in two battles, dragged through the streets of Rome, and murdered. The only positive aspect of his rule was his initiation of free speech.

Vitruvius Pollio, Marcus 1st century AD •*Roman architect and military engineer*• A northern Italian in the service of **Augustus**, he wrote *De architectura* (before AD 27, "On Architecture"), which is the only Roman treatise on architecture still extant.

Vittorini, Elio 1908–66 •*Sicilian novelist, critic and translator*• Born in Syracuse, he educated himself despite great obstacles, and became founding editor of *Il politecnico* (1945–47) and *Il menabò* (1959–66), and a translator of modern US writers. *Conversazione in Sicilia* (1941, Eng trans *Conversation in Sicily*, 1949) is his metaphorical masterpiece. He was one of Italy's most influential authors, and he supported many younger writers.

Vitus, St early 4th century AD •*Sicilian Christian*• Born in Sicily, he was converted by his nurse Crescentia and her husband Modestus, with whom he was martyred under **Diocletian**. He was invoked against sudden death, hydrophobia and chorea (or St Vitus' Dance), and is sometimes regarded as the patron saint of comedians and actors. His feast day is June 15.

Vivaldi, Antonio Lucio 1678–1741 •*Italian violinist and composer*• Born in Venice, he was ordained in 1703, but gave up officiating, and was attached to the Conservatorio of the Ospedale della Pietà in Venice (1703–40). The 12 concertos of *L'estro armonico* (1712, "Harmonic Inspiration") gave him a European reputation, and *The Four Seasons* (1725, *Le quattro stagioni*), an early example of program music, was very popular. The composer of many operas, sacred music and over 450 concertos, he consolidated and developed the solo concerto, but he was forgotten after his death. **J S Bach** transcribed many of his concertos for the keyboard, and from the 19th century they were increasingly played. He was known as the "Red Priest" because of his red hair.

Vivekananda, *originally* **Narendranath Dutt** or **Datta** 1863–1902 •*Hindu missionary*• He was born in Calcutta and became the chief disciple of **Ramakrishna Paramahasa**. A highly educated representative of Vedanta as the universal religion at the Chicago Parliament of Religions (1893), he was a persuasive exponent of Hinduism in the West, and he proclaimed a reformed Hinduism with a social conscience in India. His organization of the now worldwide Ramakrishna Mission owed much to the methods of Christian missionaries.

Viviani, René 1862–1925 •*French statesman*• He was born in Sidi-bel-Abbès, Algeria. He was prime minister at the outbreak of World War I, and, in order to demonstrate France's peaceful intentions, he withdrew French forces from the German frontier. He was minister of justice (1915) and French representative at the League of Nations (1920).

Vladimir I, Saint, *called* **the Great** c. 956–1015 •*First Christian sovereign of Russia*• Born in Kiev, the son of Svyatoslav, Grand Prince of Kiev (d. 972), he became Prince of Novgorod (970) and seized Kiev from his brother (980) after his father's death, becoming ruler of Russia. Fierce and ambitious, he consolidated the Russian realm and extended its dominions into Lithuania, Galicia and Livonia, with Kiev as his capital. He made a pact with the Byzantine emperor **Basil II** (c. 987), marrying his sister and accepting Christianity, which he forced on many of his people. He encouraged education and reformed legal institutions. He died on an expedition against one of his sons. His feast day is July 15.

Vlaminck, Maurice de 1876–1958 •*French artist*• Born in Paris, he was largely self-taught and for a time was a racing cyclist. In about 1900, he began to work with **André Derain**. By 1905 he was one of the leaders of the Fauves, using typically brilliant color, as in *The Red Trees* (1906, Pompidou Center, Paris). From 1908 to 1914, however, he painted more realist landscapes under the influence of **Cézanne**. His palette was more somber after 1915, and his style more romantic, though still full of zest. After World War I he lived mainly in the country as a farmer.

“ ”

Good painting is like good cooking: it can be tasted, but not explained.

On Painting

Vleck, John Hasbrouck van *See* **Van Vleck, John Hasbrouck**

Vogel, Hans-Jochen 1926– •*German politician*• Born in Göttingen into a Catholic family and educated as a lawyer at the University of Munich, he became Social Democratic Party (SPD) Land (state) chairman in Bavaria in 1972 and was elected, in the same year, mayor of Munich. He was minister of housing and town planning (1972–74), and served in the **Schmidt** Cabinet as justice minister (1975–81) before being sent to West Berlin to serve as mayor and to clean up and overhaul the unpopular local party machine. An efficient, if somewhat colorless, party centrist, Vogel was Bundestag leader of the Opposition from 1983 to 1991 when his party was again defeated by the Christian Democrats under Chancellor **Kohl**. In June he replaced **Willy Brandt** as SPD chairman, a position he held until 1991.

Vogel, Sir Julius 1835–99 •*New Zealand statesman*• Born in London, he emigrated to Australia, where he founded a newspaper, moving to New Zealand in 1861. He was elected colonial treasurer there in 1869. He established a government public trust office (1872), improved immigration facilities and planned the introduction of trunk railways. He formed a government in 1872 and was premier (1873–75). He resigned in 1875 to devote himself to business, but he was again treasurer during the economic crisis in 1884.

Volstead, Andrew Joseph 1860–1947 •*US politician*• Born in Goodhue County, Minnesota, he practiced law and entered Congress as a Republican in 1903. He is best known for the Prohibition Act of 1919, named after him, which forbade the manufacture and sale of intoxicant liquors. This act, passed over President **Woodrow Wilson**'s veto, was intended to placate the influential temperance movement, which argued that alcohol contributed to crime and poverty, and to divert grain to food production in the wake of World War I. In fact, it proved impossible to enforce effectively and did little other than to create enormous profits for bootleggers and speakeasies and provide material for countless Hollywood gangster films. It was repealed in 1933.

Volta, Alessandro Giuseppe Anastasio, Count 1745–1827 •*Italian physicist and inventor*• Born in Como, he was appointed Professor of Physics at the university there (1775) and at Pavia (1778). In 1795 he became rector of the University of Pavia; he was dismissed in 1799 for political reasons and was later reinstated by the French. He invented the electrophorus (1775, the precursor of the induction machine), the condenser (1778), the candle flame collector of atmospheric electricity (1787) and the electrochemical battery, or "voltaic pile" (1800), which was the first source of continuous, or current, electricity. He also invented an "inflammable air" (hydrogen) electric pistol (1777). **Antoine Lavoisier** followed Volta's suggestion that the mixtures of air and hydrogen should be sparked over mercury (and not water), and identified the resultant to be water (1782). His name is given to the SI unit of electrical potential difference, the volt.

Voltaire, *pseudonym of* **François Marie Arouet** 1694–1778 •*French writer and historian, the embodiment of the 18th-century Enlightenment*• Born in Paris, he was educated by Jesuits and studied law but disliked it and turned instead to writing. He soon acquired notoriety as the author of a satire on his successful rival in the poetic competition for an Academy prize. In 1716, on suspicion of satirizing the regent, the Duc d'**Orléans**, he was banished for several months from Paris, and in 1717–18, a savage attack accusing the regent of all manner of crimes resulted in 11 months' imprisonment in the Bastille. There he rewrote his tragedy *Œdipe*, began a poem on **Henry IV** and assumed the name Voltaire. *Œdipe* was performed in 1718 and was triumphantly successful. The authorities refused to sanction the publication of "Henri IV" because it championed Protestantism and religious tolerance, so Voltaire had it printed secretly in Rouen (1723) and smuggled into Paris as "La Ligue, ou Henri le Grand." He was now famous and a favorite at court. He got into a quarrel with the Chevalier de Rohan-Chabot and circulated caustic epigrams about him; in the end he was once more thrown into the Bastille and was freed only on the condition that he would leave for England. There he remained for four years (1726–29), became acquainted with **Alexander Pope** and his circle, and familiarized himself with English literature. He was strongly attracted to **John Locke**'s philosophy, and he mastered the elements of **Isaac Newton**'s astronomical physics. Back in France, he laid the foundation of his great wealth by purchasing shares in a government lottery and by speculating in the corn trade. Having begun a relationship with Madame du Châtelet-Lomont (1706–49), he went to live with her at her husband's château of Cirey in Champagne (1734). Here he wrote dramas and poetry, several philosophical works, and scientific treatises. His *Princesse de Navarre*, performed on the occasion of the dauphin's marriage (February 1745), pleased **Louis XV** with its clever adulation; this and the patronage of Madame de **Pompadour** secured Voltaire appointments as official royal historian and gentleman-in-ordinary to the king. In 1750 Voltaire went to Berlin at the invitation of **Frederick II (the Great)**; he was appointed king's chamberlain with a pension of 20,000 francs and board in one of the royal palaces. There he caused offense with his satirical criticisms of Pierre de Maupertuis (1698–1759) in *Micromégas*, and in March 1753 Frederick and Voltaire parted, never to meet again. He settled in 1755 near Geneva and after 1758 at Ferney, four miles away. There he wrote his satirical short story *Candide*, his best-known work. In 1762 Voltaire published the first of his antireligious writings, which were to include didactic tragedies, biased histories, pamphlets and the *Dictionnaire philosophique* (1764). He became involved in the affair surrounding the judicial murder (1762) of Jean Calas, who had been falsely accused of killing one of his sons to keep him from becoming a Catholic. Voltaire was successful in establishing his innocence and in rescuing members of the Calas family from further punishment. This and similar efforts on behalf of victims of French fanaticism, for whom he provided a refuge at Ferney, won him widespread admiration. In 1778, at 84, he was welcomed back in Paris to stage his last tragedy, *Irène*. The excitement of this event brought on illness and his death. After the French Revolution, which his works and ideas helped to foster, his remains were reinterred in the Panthéon in Paris.

“ ”

Si Dieu n'existait pas, il faudrait l'inventer.

If God did not exist, it would be necessary to invent him.

Epîtres, *"A l'Auteur du Livre des Trois Imposteurs."*

---

von Braun, Wernher *See* **Braun, Wernher von**

von Euler, Ulf Svante *See* **Euler, Ulf Svante von**

Vo Nguyen Giap 1912– •*Vietnamese military leader*• Born in Quang Binh Province, he studied law at the University of Hanoi, and joined the Vietnamese Communist Party. He led the Viet Minh army in revolt against the French, leading to the decisive defeat of their garrison at Dien Bien Phu in 1954. As vice premier and defense minister of North Vietnam, he masterminded the military strategy that forced the US forces to leave South Vietnam (1973) and led to the reunification of Vietnam in 1975. He was a member of the Politburo from 1976 to 1982. He wrote *People's War, People's Army* (1961), which became a textbook for revolutionaries.

Von Klitzing, Klaus 1943– •*German physicist and Nobel Prize winner*• Born in Schroda, he was educated at the Technical University in Munich and at the University of Würzburg. He was appointed professor at the University of Munich in 1980, and in 1985 he became director of the **Max Planck** Institute, Stuttgart. In 1977 he presented a paper on two-dimensional electronic behavior in which the quantum Hall effect was clearly implied, causing a major revision of the theory of electric conduction in strong magnetic fields. For this work he was awarded the 1985 Nobel Prize for physics.

Vonnegut, Kurt, Jr 1922– •*US novelist*• Born in Indianapolis, Indiana, he was educated at Cornell and the University of Chicago and at the Carnegie Institute, Pittsburgh, then served in the US Army infantry (1942–45) and was given the Purple Heart. During the 1960s he emerged as one of the US's most influential, potent and provocative writers, a ribald commentator of the horrors of the century: holocaustal wars, the desperate state of the environment, and the dehumanization of the individual in a society dominated by science and technology. *Player Piano* (1952) was his first novel, and there were another three before *Slaughterhouse-Five* (1969), the central event of which is the destruction of Dresden during World War II, which the author witnessed as a prisoner of war. Later novels, including *Breakfast of Champions* (1973), *Deadeye Dick* (1982) and *Hocus Pocus* (1990), continued to satirize human folly in its various manifestations.

Von Neumann, John (Johann) 1903–57 •*US mathematician*• Born in Budapest, Hungary, he was educated in Berlin and Budapest, and taught at Berlin (1927–29), Hamburg (1929–30), and Princeton (1930–33) before becoming a member of the Institute for Advanced Study at Princeton (1933). In 1943 he worked on the Manhattan Project (atomic bomb) at Los Alamos, and in 1954 he joined the US Atomic Energy Commission. His best-known mathematical work was on the theory of linear operators, but he also gave a new axiomatization of set theory and formulated a precise description of quantum theory (1932). He designed some of the earliest computers, and his novel *The Theory of Games and Economic Behavior* (1944) contained a theory applicable both to games of chance and to games of pure skill, such as chess.

Von Sternberg, Josef, *originally* **Jonas Sternberg** 1894–1969 •*Austrian film director*• Born in Vienna, he worked in silent films in Hollywood in the 1920s as a scriptwriter, cameraman, and director, but he went to Germany to make his most famous film *Der blaue Engel* (1930, "The Blue Angel") with **Marlene Dietrich**. This was followed by six more Hollywood features in which she starred, the last being *The Devil Is a Woman* (1935).

von Sydow, Max Carl Adolf *See* **Sydow, Max Carl Adolf von**

von Trier, Lars 1956– •*Danish film director and screenwriter*• Born in Copenhagen, he was educated at the University of Copenhagen and trained at the Danish Film Institute. He established his reputation as Denmark's most talented film director with his debut feature, the horror-thriller *The Element of Crime* (1984), and became one of the founders of the Dogme movement, which argued for a simpler style of cinema. Among the films that followed was his masterpiece, the television series *The Kingdom* (1994), which made von Trier a household name in Denmark. His more recent films include *Breaking the Waves* (1996), which brought him an international audience, *The Idiots* (1998), which won the Palme d'Or at the Cannes Film Festival, and *Dancer in the Dark* (2000).

von Wolff, Christian *See* **Wolff, Christian von**

Voroshilov, Kliment Yefremovich 1881–1969 •*Soviet politician*• He was born near Dnepropetrovsk. A Bolshevik from 1903, his political activities led to his exile to Siberia. His military role in World War I and the 1917 Revolution led to his rapid promotion within the Communist Party. Appointed marshal of the Soviet Union in 1935, from 1925 to 1940 he was responsible for the modernization of the Red Army and its ultimate success in helping to defeat **Hitler**. He was president of the Soviet Union from **Stalin**'s death (1953) to 1960.

Vorster, John, *originally* **Balthazar Johannes Vorster** 1915–83 •*South African politician*• Born in Jamestown and educated at the University of Stellenbosch, he became a lawyer and was a leader of the extreme Afrikaner nationalist group, Ossewa Brandwag, in World War II. He was accepted into the National Party, becoming Member of Parliament for Nigel in 1953. In **Hendrik Verwoerd**'s government he was from 1961 minister of justice and responsible for several controversial measures. After the assassination of Verwoerd in September 1966, he was elected prime minister. Under him apartheid remained the official policy. In 1978 he resigned and was elected state president. The following year he resigned this position after an investigation by the Erasmus commission found him jointly responsible for a financial scandal.

Vortigern fl. 425–c. 450 AD •*British ruler*• He is reported by **Gildas**, **Bede** and **Nennius** to have invited the Saxons, led by **Hengist** and Horsa, into Britain to help him against the Picts, and to have married Hengist's daughter, Rowena.

Vouet, Simon 1590–1649 •*French painter*• Born in Paris, after 14 years in Italy he returned to France, where his religious and allegorical paintings and decorations in the Baroque style became very popular. A contemporary of **Nicolas Poussin**, who criticized him but was not a serious rival during his lifetime, he taught **Charles Le Brun** and Eustache Le Sueur (1617–55).

Voysey, Charles Francis Annesley 1857–1941 •*English architect and designer*• Born in London, he became a disciple of **John Ruskin** and **William Morris**. He designed traditional country houses influenced by the Arts and Crafts Movement, with accentuated gables, chimney stacks, buttresses and long sloping roofs. He was also an important designer of wallpaper, textiles, furniture and metalwork.

Vries, Hugo Marie de 1848–1935 •*Dutch botanist and geneticist*• Born in Haarlem, he studied at Leiden University and the Universities of Heidelberg and Würzburg and became Professor of Botany at the University of Amsterdam (1878–1918). From 1890 he studied heredity and variation in plants, significantly developing Mendelian genetics and evolutionary theory. His major work was *Die Mutationstheorie* (1901–03, "The Mutation Theory"). He described and correctly interpreted the phenomenon of plasmolysis, in which the cytoplasm in plant cells shrinks away from the walls, and introduced methods for studying plant cells which have become standard techniques.

Vries, Peter De *See* **De Vries Peter**

Vuillard, (Jean) Édouard 1868–1940 •*French artist*• Born in Cuiseaux, he shared a studio with **Pierre Bonnard** and was strongly influenced by **Paul Gauguin** and by the vogue for Japanese painting. Although his outlook was limited and mainly devoted to flower pieces and simple, intimate interiors, these are painted with an exquisite sense of light and color. He also produced murals for public buildings, such as the Théâtre des Champs-Elysées and Palais de Chaillot.

Vygotsky, Lev Semyonovich 1896–1934 •*Soviet psychologist*• Born in Orsha, he studied various social sciences at Moscow State University, then turned to psychology, and from 1924 until his death, he worked at the Institute of Psychology in Moscow. His theories of cognitive development, especially his view of the relationship between language and thinking, have strongly influenced both Marxist and Western psychology. He always emphasized the role of cultural and social factors in the development of cognition. His best-known work, *Thought and Language* (1934), is now a classic text in university courses in psycholinguistics.

Vyshinsky, Andrei Yanuarevich 1883–1954 •*Soviet jurist and politician*• Born in Odessa of Polish origin, he studied law at the University of Moscow but was debarred from a lectureship on account of his Menshevik revolutionary activities until 1921, when he left the Red Army. He was the notorious public prosecutor at the Metropolitan-Vickers trial (1933) and the subsequent state trials (1936–38) which removed **Stalin**'s rivals, Bukharin, **Karl Radek**, **Grigori Zinoviev**, **Lev Kamenev** and Sokolnikov. He was promoted to deputy foreign minister under **Vyacheslav Molotov** (1940) and was permanent Soviet delegate to the United Nations (1945–49, 1953–54), succeeding Molotov as foreign minister in 1949 until the death of Stalin (1953). He was the brilliant advocate of the disruptive Stalin-Molotov foreign policies and the author of many textbooks on Soviet law.

W

Waals, Johannes Diderik van der 1837–1923 •*Dutch physicist and Nobel Prize winner*• Born in Leiden, he went to the university there, graduating in 1865. After teaching physics at Deventer and The Hague, he studied again at Leiden, and became Professor of Physics at the University of Amsterdam (1877–1907). He convincingly accounted for many phenomena concerning vapors and liquids by postulating the existence of intermolecular forces and a finite molecular volume. He derived a new equation of state (the van der Waals equation) which agreed much more closely with experimental data and led to a Nobel Prize for physics (1910). The weak attractions between molecules (van der Waals forces) were named in his honor.

Waddington, David Charles Waddington, Baron 1929– •*English politician*• After studying at Oxford, where he was president of the Conservative Association, he qualified and practiced as a barrister but became a Member of Parliament in 1968. After a number of junior posts under **Margaret Thatcher**, he was made government chief whip in 1987, and in 1989 home secretary. A right-winger within his party, Waddington became one of the very few home secretaries openly to have supported the return of capital punishment. He was leader of the House of Lords from 1990 until his resignation from parliament in 1992. He was made a life peer in 1990 and from 1992 to 1997 was governor and commander in chief of Bermuda.

Wade, Sir Thomas Francis 1818–95 •*English diplomat and scholar*• Born in London, he became a member of the diplomatic corps in China and was the British ambassador in Peking (Beijing) from 1871–83. In 1888 he was appointed the first Professor of Chinese at Cambridge, holding this post until 1895. Among his works is the *Peking Syllabary* (1859), in which the Wade system of romanization is employed. This transliteration system was later modified by Wade's successor at Cambridge, Herbert Giles (1845–1935).

Wagner, Otto 1841–1918 •*Austrian architect and teacher*• He was a professor at the Vienna Academy (1894–1912), where his pupils included **Josef Hoffmann** and Joseph Olbrich (1867–1908). His most influential work, such as Karlsplatz Station (1898–99) and Am Steinhof Church (1905–07), was produced at the end of his career. Both exhibit flourishes of art nouveau tempered by traditional construction. In the main hall of K K Portsparkasse (savings bank) in Vienna (1904–06), he created what is universally regarded as the first example of modern architecture in the 20th century. He is considered to be the founder of modernism.

" "

The whole basis of the views of architecture prevailing today must be displayed by the recognition that the only possible point of departure for our artistic creation is modern life.

1895 ***Modern Architecture**, preface.*

Wagner, (Wilhelm) Richard 1813–83 •*German composer*• He was born in Leipzig and educated in Dresden and at the Leipzig Thomasschule. He wrote his Symphony in C in 1832, and his first completed opera was *Die Feen* ("The Fairies"), written in the style of **Carl Maria von Weber**'s *Oberon*. It was not, however, performed during his lifetime. His next work, *Das Liebesverbot* ("Forbidden Love," based on **Shakespeare**'s *Measure for Measure*), was produced in 1836 at Magdeburg, where Wagner had been appointed music director two years earlier. There he met Minna Planer, a member of the company, who became his wife in 1836. The Magdeburg opera soon went bankrupt, as did the theater at Königsberg, where Wagner found his next post. After a period as assistant conductor at Riga (1837–39), he resolved to try his luck in Paris with his partly finished opera based on **Bulwer Lytton**'s romance *Rienzi*. There, in spite of **Giacomo Meyerbeer**'s help, he barely made a living as a journalist and by undertaking hack operatic arrangements. He left Paris in 1842 with *Rienzi*—which he had finished in a debtors' prison—still unperformed, but now accepted for presentation at Dresden, where it scored a resounding success. *Der fliegende Holländer* (1843, "The Flying Dutchman") was also successful, and Wagner was shortly afterward appointed Kapellmeister at Dresden. There he conducted performances of Beethoven's Ninth Symphony and other works that became legendary. *Tannhäuser* was produced there in 1845. At this point Wagner began work on the theme that was to develop into the *Ring* cycle. He began with the poem for *Siegfrieds Tod* ("The Death of Siegfried," the future *Götterdämmerung*, "Twilight of the Gods"), which he completed in 1848, but by this time Wagner was deeply implicated in the revolutionary movement and barely escaped arrest by fleeing from Saxony. Aided financially by **Franz Liszt** at Weimar, he went first to Paris and later to Zurich. *Lohengrin* was eventually produced in Weimar by Liszt in 1850. During his exile Wagner again made a living by writing, and he completed the poem of the *Ring* cycle in 1852; the following year he began to write the music for *Das Rheingold* ("The Rhinegold"), followed by *Die Walküre* (1856, "The Valkyrie") and acts one and two of *Siegfried* (1857). This was interrupted (1857–59) by work on *Tristan und Isolde*, which was based on the old German version of the legend by **Gottfried von Strassburg**. Once again he sought to gain favor in Paris, and eventually **Napoleon III** called for a command performance of *Tannhäuser*, but the opera failed there. In 1861 he was allowed to return to Germany, but he still had a hard battle for recognition. *Tristan* was accepted at Vienna but abandoned as impracticable before it could be performed, and, now aged 50, pursued by creditors and vilified by critics, the composer was on the point of giving up in despair when the tide dramatically turned. The eccentric young king of Bavaria, **Ludwig II**, impressed by the pageantry of *Lohengrin*, read Wagner's *Ring* poem with its pessimistic preface. He summoned Wagner to his court and lavished hospitality on him. *Tristan* was staged with brilliant success at Munich in 1865, but Wagner's extravagance, political meddling, and preferential treatment aroused so much hostility that he was obliged to withdraw temporarily to the villa of Tribschen at Lucerne in Switzerland. Cosima, wife of the musical director **Hans von Bülow** and daughter of Liszt, had been having an affair with Wagner since 1863, and now left her husband and joined him; she eventually married him in 1870 after being divorced, Wagner's wife Minna having died in 1866. A son, Siegfried, was born to Wagner and Cosima in 1869. In Switzerland Wagner finished *Die Meistersinger* ("The Mastersingers"), his only nontragic drama, which scored a success in 1868. However, his greatest ambition, a complete performance of the *Ring*, was as yet unfulfilled. Productions in Munich of *Das Rheingold* in 1869 and *Die Walküre* in 1870 were against Wagner's wishes, as he had in mind an ideal theater of his own. Determined to fulfill his wish, he set about raising funds, and on a fraction of the required total plus a large amount of credit, he started the now famous theater at Bayreuth, which opened in 1876 with the first complete program of the *Ring* cycle. By 1874 Wagner and Cosima had moved to their new home at Bayreuth, Wahnfried, and he had completed work on *Götterdämmerung*, the final part of the *Ring* cycle. *Parsifal*, his last opera, was staged in 1882. The following year, he died in Venice from a heart attack. Wagner reformed the whole structure of opera. He wrote all his texts himself, completing the poem for each work before embarking on the music. Of great importance was his development of the leitmotiv.

Wagner, Robert John, Jr 1930– •*US actor*• Born in Detroit, Michigan, he attended Black-Foxe Military Institute and decided to become an actor. After a small role in *The Happy Years* (1950), he took charming juvenile leads in a succession of war, Western and adventure films. He was cast against type as a killer in *A Kiss Before Dying* (1956) and also played comedy in *The Pink Panther* (1963). However, his greatest popularity has been on television, where his boyish romantic appeal, suave manner and light humor were seen in his roles as a jewel thief in *It Takes a Thief* (1965–69), an ex-con man in *Switch* (1975–77) and a jet-set detective in *Hart to Hart* (1979–84). He was married to actress **Natalie Wood** from 1957 to 1962 and again from 1972 until her death in 1981. More recently, he has appeared in the *Austin Powers* series of films (1997, 1999, 2002).

Wain, John Barrington 1925–94 •*English critic and novelist*• Born in Stoke-on-Trent, Staffordshire, he studied at and was elected a Fellow of St John's College, Oxford, and lectured in English literature at the University of Reading (1947–55) before becoming a freelance author. His first four novels, beginning with *Hurry on Down* (1953), tilt at postwar British, particularly London, social values as viewed by a provincial. His debunking vigor and humor have affinities with those of **Kingsley Amis**. He also wrote poetry, and his *Poems 1949–1979* appeared in 1980. His other work includes plays and critical studies, and well as editing literary magazines. His later novels include *The Young Visitors* (1965), *Young Shoulders* (1982), *Comedies* (1990) and the children's book *Lizzie's Floating Shop* (1981). He was Professor of Poetry at Oxford (1973–88).

Waismann, Friedrich 1896–1959 •*Austrian philosopher*• Born in Vienna, he became a prominent member of the Vienna Circle, together with **Rudolf Carnap** and **Moritz Schlick**, but he modified the doctrines of logical positivism. He later taught at Cambridge and at Oxford. He argued that most empirical concepts have an "open texture," which means that we cannot completely foresee all the possible conditions in which they might properly be used, and that even empirical statements cannot therefore be verified strictly by observation. His works include *How I See Philosophy* (1968).

Waite, Terry (Terence Hardy) 1939– •*English religious adviser*• He was born in Cheshire and educated at the Church Army College, London, and privately in the US. He had lay training appointments as adviser in both the Anglican (1964–71) and Roman Catholic (1972–79) churches, and was adviser on Anglican Communion affairs to **Robert Runcie**, who was then Archbishop of Canterbury, in 1980. A man of great diplomatic skills, he undertook many overseas assignments, and in 1987, while making inquiries in Beirut about European hostages, he disappeared. Worldwide efforts to secure his release and that of his fellow hostages finally succeeded in 1991. He subsequently published an account of his experiences in the book *Taken on Trust* (1993).

“ ”

Politics come from man. Mercy, compassion, and justice come from God.

*1985 In **The Observer**, January 13.*

Waits, Tom 1949– •*US singer, songwriter, musician and actor*• Born in Pomona, California, he picked up on the beatnik literary ethos of the 1950s in his early music, and has been an idiosyncratic chronicler of the byways of American urban lowlife. He began singing in 1969, drawing on a cross section of musical influences which began to achieve a synthesis by the mid-1970s, culminating in *Heartattack and Vine* (1980). His next album, entitled *Swordfishtrombones* (1983), signaled a more surreal departure. From the late 1980s he devoted more time to work on film, both as a composer and an actor. Later albums include *Mule Variations* (1999).

Waitz, Grete 1953– •*Norwegian athlete*• She was born in Oslo. In 1975, she set a world record for the 3,000 meters (9:34.2, and later, in 1977, 8:46.6), and for more than a decade rivaled **Ingrid Kristiansen** as the world's greatest female distance runner. She has set a unique four world-best times for the marathon. In 1979, she became the first woman to run the New York marathon—a race she won eight times—in under two and a half hours. By 1983 she had brought her time down to 2:25.29. She won the marathon at the inaugural world championships in 1983.

Wajda, Andrzej 1926– •*Polish film director*• Born in Suwalki, Poland, he was a member of the Polish Resistance in World War II, and later studied art at the Kraków Academy of Fine Arts, and in the Łódź film school. His first feature film, *Pokolenie* (1954, *A Generation*), dealt with the effects of the war on disillusioned Polish youth. The results of war, the hollowness of the idea of military heroism, and the predicament of individuals caught up in political events were themes to which he was continually to return in such films as *Kanal* (1956), *Lotna* (1959) and *Landscape After the Battle* (1970). The two films for which he is now best known outside Poland are *Człowiek z marmaru* (1977, *Man of Marble*) and *Człowiek z zelaza* (1981, *Man of Iron*). His other films include romantic comedies, epics, and literary adaptations such as *The Wedding* (1972) and *Shadow Line* (1976). Also active in theater and television, he resided in France during the 1980s but returned to Poland and subsequently entered politics, serving as a senator (1989–91). His more recent films include *Korczak* (1990), *Nastazja* (1994) and *Miss Nobody* (1996).

Waksman, Selman Abraham 1888–1973 •*US biochemist and Nobel Prize winner*• Born in Priluka (now Priluki), Ukraine, he moved to the US in 1910 and became a US citizen in 1915, graduating in the same year from Rutgers University, where he spent most of his research life, becoming Professor of Microbiology (1930). From 1915 he worked on the microbial breakdown of organic substances in the soil, work that led to a new classification of microbes (1922) and methods for their scientific cultivation (1932). He discovered the anticancer drug actinomycin in 1941, the first antituberculosis drug, streptomycin (1944), and several other antibacterial agents. For these important discoveries he was awarded the Nobel Prize for physiology or medicine in 1952. He also worked extensively on marine bacteria and the enzyme alginase. His works include the autobiographical *My Life With the Microbes* (1954).

Walburga, St, *also spelled* **Walpurgis** or **Walpurga** c. 710–c. 779 •*English religious*• Born in Wessex, she joined **St Boniface** on his mission to Germany and became abbess of Heidenheim. Her relics were transferred (c. 870) to Eichstätt. Walpurgis Night (April 30) arose from the confusion between the day of the transfer of her remains (the night of May 1) and the popular superstitions regarding the flight of witches on that night. She was the sister of St Willibald (700–86). Her feast day is February 25.

Walcott, Derek Alton 1930– •*West Indian poet, dramatist and Nobel Prize winner*• Born in St Lucia, he was educated there and at Kingston, Jamaica. His first poems were published in Trinidad in 1948, followed by *Epitaph for the Young: XII Cantos* (1949). He founded the Trinidad Theatre Workshop in 1959, and has written and staged numerous plays, such as *The Joker of Seville* (1978). His early volumes of poetry include *In a Green Night* (1962), *Castaway* (1965) and *The Gulf* (1969); examples of his later works are *The Fortunate Traveler* and *Omeros* (both 1981). He was awarded the Nobel Prize for literature in 1992. A more recent work is *Tiepolo's Hounds* (2000). He has been visiting Professor of English at Boston University since 1985.

“ ”

The English language is nobody's special property. It is the property of the imagination: it is the property of the language itself.

*1992 Interviewed in George Plimpton (ed) **Writers at Work** (8th series, 1988).*

Wald, George 1906–97 •*US biochemist and Nobel Prize winner*• Born in New York City, he studied zoology at New York University and at Columbia University. Subsequently he worked at Harvard (1932–77). He established in 1935 that visual purple, the retinal pigment of the eye, is converted by light to a yellow compound which slowly changes to a colorless compound (vitamin A). In

1956 he made the key discovery that one isomer of vitamin A combines with the protein opsin to form visual purple (rhodopsin). He discovered a similar system using vitamin A_2 in fish, the visual mechanism common to the eyes of all known animals, and also established the nutritional relationship between vitamin A, night blindness and vitamin-deficient retinopathy. For these discoveries he shared the 1967 Nobel Prize for physiology or medicine with **Ragnar Granit** and **Haldan Hartline**.

Waldheim, Kurt 1918– •*Austrian statesman*• Born near Vienna, he served on the Russian front during World War II, but was wounded and then discharged (1942). On his return he studied in Vienna and entered the Austrian Foreign Service in 1945, becoming head of the personnel department at the Foreign Ministry (1951–55). He was minister and subsequently ambassador to Canada (1955–60) and director general of political affairs at the ministry (1960–64). From that year he was permanent representative at the UN, with a break (1968–70) to take the post of foreign minister. In 1972 he succeeded **U Thant** as secretary-general of the UN, a post he held until 1981. In 1986 he became president of Austria but allegations soon surfaced that, as a Nazi intelligence officer in World War II, he had some involvement in the transportation of Jews to death camps. As a result, he was defeated in elections in 1992. A US Justice Department report in 1994 confirmed that Waldheim had served as an officer in the German army and had been involved in atrocities against Jews, civilians and Allied soldiers during World War II.

Waldo or **Valdes, Peter** fl. 1175 •*French religious leader*• Born in Lyons, he became a preacher in Lyons in 1170 and practiced voluntary poverty. He was eventually excommunicated and banished from Lyons in 1184 with his followers, who, because of their vow of poverty, were known as "The Holy Paupers." They formed the Christian sect called the Waldenses.

Waldstein, Albrecht Wenzel Eusebius von *See* **Wallenstein, Albrecht Wenzel Eusebius von**

Wales, Prince of *See* **Charles, Prince of Wales**

Wales, Princess of *See* **Diana, Princess of Wales**

Wałesa, Lech 1943– •*Polish trade unionist and politician, and Nobel prize winner*• He was born in Popowo into a once affluent agricultural family. Following a technical education, he worked as an electrician at the **Lenin** Shipyard at Gdansk (1966–76) and became a trade union organizer, chairing the shipyard's strike committee in 1970. In 1980 he founded Solidarnośč (Solidarity), an independent trade union. Solidarnośč organized a series of strikes which, led by Wałesa, a charismatic and devout Catholic, drew widespread public support and forced substantial political and economic concessions from the Polish government during 1980–81. However, in December 1981 Solidarnośč was outlawed and Wałesa arrested, following the imposition of martial law by General **Wojciech Jaruzelski**. Wałesa was released in November 1982 and was awarded the Nobel Peace Prize in 1983. After leading a further series of crippling strikes during 1988, he negotiated the relegalization of Solidarnośč and the establishment of a new, semi-pluralist "socialist democracy." He became president following true elections in 1990, a position he retained until 1995, when he lost to Aleksander Kwasniewski (1954–).

Walker, Alice Malsenior 1944– •*US writer*• Born in Eatonville, Georgia, and educated at Spelman College, Atlanta, and Sarah Lawrence College, she later worked in voter registration campaigns before becoming a teacher and a lecturer. Her essay *In Search of Our Mother's Gardens* (1983) is an important rediscovery of an African-American female literary and cultural tradition. An accomplished poet, she is, however, better known for her novels, of which *The Color Purple* (1982) is her third and most popular. The winner of the 1983 Pulitzer Prize for fiction and later made into a successful film, it tells via letters the story of two sisters in the cruel, segregated world of the Deep South between the world wars. Later works include *The Temple of My Familiar* (1989), *Warrior Marks* (1993) and an autobiography, *The Same River Twice* (1997).

Walker, Mary Edwards 1832–1919 •*US physician*• She was educated at Syracuse Medical College and then joined her husband, Albert Miller, in a practice in New York State. She campaigned for rational dress for women and women's rights, revised marriage and divorce laws, and often wore male evening dress for her lectures. During the Civil War, she volunteered for army service, becoming the US Army's first female surgeon. She is the only woman to receive the Congressional Medal of Honor.

Walker, Peter Edward Walker, Baron 1932– •*English Conservative politician*• As a young man he was sufficiently successful in the city of London to have the wealth to pursue a political career, and became a Member of Parliament from 1961. He held ministerial posts under **Edward Heath**, and in **Margaret Thatcher**'s government was agriculture secretary (1979–83), energy secretary (1983–87) and secretary of state for Wales (1987–90). Regarded as a Conservative liberal, he was noted for his "coded criticisms" of some of the extreme aspects of Mrs Thatcher's policies. He retired from full-time politics in 1992 and was created a life peer.

Wall, Max, *originally* **Maxwell George Lorimer** 1908–90 •*English actor and comedian*• Born in London, he made his first stage appearance when he was 14. He made his first London appearance in 1925, as a dancer in *The London Revue*. He subsequently appeared in variety, revue, pantomime and radio. The radio program *Our Shed* (1946) helped to make him a star. Wall gradually perfected a laconic comedy routine, and was considered by many to be one of the most accomplished British comics of his time. In 1966 he appeared as Père Ubu in **Alfred Jarry**'s *Ubu Roi*. Subsequently, he specialized in the plays of **Samuel Beckett**. On television, he acted in the comedy series *Born and Bred* (1978, 1980), *Crossroads* and *Coronation Street*.

Wallace, Alfred Russel 1823–1913 •*English zoogeographer and pioneer of the theory of natural selection*• Born in Usk, Monmouthshire, he worked as a teacher in Leicester and as a surveyor in South Wales, then traveled and collected (1848–52) in the Amazon basin with **Henry Walter Bates**. He explored the Malay Archipelago (1854–62) and observed the significant demarcation, now known as Wallace's Line, between the areas supporting Asian and Australasian faunas. In 1855 he published his paper *On the Law Which Has Regulated the Introduction of New Species*. His memoir, sent to **Charles Darwin** in 1858 from the Moluccas, formed an important part of the Linnaean Society meeting which first promulgated the theory of evolution by means of natural selection, and hastened the publication of Darwin's *The Origin of Species*, a work later amplified by Wallace's *Darwinism* (1889). In his great *Geographical Distribution of Animals* (1879), *Island Life* (1880), and earlier work, Wallace contributed much to the scientific foundations of zoogeography. Other works include *The Wonderful Century* (1898), *Man's Place in the Universe* (1903) and *The World of Life* (1910). He was an outspoken advocate of socialism, pacifism, women's rights and other causes, and encapsulated his views in *Social Environment and Moral Progress* (1913).

Wallace, (Richard Horatio) Edgar 1875–1932 •*English writer*• He was found abandoned in Greenwich when nine days old and was brought up by a Billingsgate fish porter. He served in the army in South Africa, where he later became a journalist (1899), and in 1905 he published his first success, the adventure story *The Four Just Men*. Another early series in a different vein was set in West Africa and included *Bones* (1915). From then on he wrote prolifically—his output numbering over 170 novels and plays—and he is best remembered for his crime novels, such as *The Clue of the Twisted Candle* (1916). He became a scriptwriter in Hollywood, where he died while working on the screenplay of *King Kong* (1933). He published his autobiography, *People*, in 1926.

Wallace, George Corley 1919–98 •*US politician*• Born in Clio, Alabama, he served as a flight engineer in World War II and practiced law in Alabama before becoming involved in state Democratic politics. He served four terms as governor of Alabama (1963–67, 1971–79, 1983–87), earning notoriety in the early 1960s by seeking to block desegregation in the Alabama public schools. He ran for president as a member of the American Independent Party in 1968, capitalizing on white backlash to garner more votes than expected for a third-party candidate. In 1972 he was shot and paralyzed in an assassination attempt. His final term as governor was marked by a renunciation of his earlier racism.

Wallace, Jim (James Robert) 1954– •*Scottish Liberal Democratic politician*• Born in Annan, Dumfriesshire, he was educated at Annan Academy and at Cambridge University and the University of Edinburgh. He became a Member of Parliament in 1983 and went on to serve as a Liberal (and from 1988 Liberal Democratic) spokesman on various issues. He became leader of the Scottish Liberal Democratic Party in 1992 and deputy first minister of the Scottish parliament in 1999.

Wallace, Sir Richard 1818–90 •*English art collector and philanthropist*• Born in London, the illegitimate son of the 3rd Marquis of Hertford, he was a Member of Parliament from 1873 to 1885. In 1842 he inherited from his father a large collection of paintings and objets d'art later bequeathed (1897) by his widow to the British nation. These now comprise the Wallace Collection, housed in Hertford House, London, once his residence.

Wallace, Sir William, *also spelled* **Walays** *or* **Wallensis** c. 1274–1305 •*Scottish patriot*• He was the chief champion of Scotland's independence, born probably near Paisley. After he burned Lanark and defeated **Edward I**'s army at Stirling Bridge, the English were expelled from Scotland and the north of England was raided. In retaliation Edward invaded Scotland in 1298, meeting Wallace at Falkirk, where the Scots were this time defeated. Wallace eventually escaped to France in 1299 where he tried to enlist support. He returned in 1303, but in 1305 was arrested near Glasgow by Sir John Menteith, sheriff of Dumbarton. Taken to London, he was condemned and hanged, drawn and quartered. His quarters were sent to Newcastle, Berwick, Stirling and Perth.

Wallenberg, Raoul b. 1912 •*Swedish diplomat*• He was the nephew of the financier Marcus Laurentius Wallenberg (1864–1943). He earned a science degree at the University of Michigan in 1935 and from 1936 helped to run an import-export firm, which after 1939 involved business trips to Germany, Hungary and Nazi-occupied France. **Hitler**'s occupation of Hungary in 1944 put its 700,000-person Jewish population at immediate risk and the American War Refugee Board and the Swedish government sent Wallenberg to Budapest to initiate a rescue plan. He designed a Swedish protection passport (*Schutzpass*) and arranged "Swedish houses" offering Jews refuge. Through bribery, threats, blackmail or sheer strength of conviction and at great personal risk, he saved up to 100,000 Jews. When Soviet troops occupied Hungary in 1945, he was taken to Soviet headquarters and never returned. On insistent Swedish requests, Soviet authorities produced a document signed by Smoltsov, head of Ljubyanka prison hospital, stating that Wallenberg died of a heart attack in July 1947, but testimony of ex-prisoners suggested that he was still alive in the 1950s, and he was rumored to be still in prison in the 1970s. Wallenberg was made an honorary citizen of the US (1981), Canada (1985) and Israel (1986). A tree on the Avenue of the Righteous in Jerusalem was planted to honor his memory.

Wallenstein or **Waldstein, Albrecht Wenzel Eusebius von, Duke of Friedland and of Mecklenburg, Prince of Sagan** 1583–1634 •*Austrian soldier*• He was born in Hermanice in Bohemia, the son of a Czech nobleman, and was educated by Jesuits. He married a Bohemian widow, whose vast estates he inherited in 1614. In 1617 he commanded a force which he supplied to Archduke Ferdinand (later **Ferdinand II**) for use against Venice. At the outset of the Thirty Years' War (1618–48) he helped crush the Bohemian revolt (1618–20) under **Frederick V**, thereafter acquiring numerous confiscated estates and consolidating them into Friedland, of which he became duke in 1623. He was appointed commander in chief (1625) of all the imperial forces, and at Dessau Bridge (1626) defeated the army of Count Mansfeld. Establishing the peace in Hungary, he subdued (1627) Silesia, acquiring the dukedom of Sagan, joined Count von **Tilly** against **Christian IV**; was invested (1628) with the duchies of Mecklenburg, but encountered resistance in garrisoning the Hanse towns. In 1630, **Gustav II Adolf** of Sweden invaded northern Germany. The Catholic princes forced Ferdinand to dismiss Wallenstein (1630) and appoint Tilly commander in chief, although after Tilly's death Wallenstein was reinstated. His new army prevented the Swedish king from advancing on Ferdinand in Vienna. He was defeated in 1632 by Gustav Adolf at Lützen. Finally, his enemies persuaded the emperor to depose him again and denounce him. His intrigues led to an imperial proclamation of treason, resulting in his assassination by Irish mercenaries. The Wallenstein trilogy by **Schiller** is based on Wallenstein's career.

Waller, Edmund 1606–87 •*English poet and politician*• Born in Coleshill near Amersham, a cousin of **John Hampden**, he was a Member of Parliament in 1624, 1625 and 1627, and returned to the Long Parliament in 1640. In 1643, he was involved in a conspiracy ("Waller's Plot") against parliament on behalf of **Charles I**, arrested and expelled from the House. He avoided execution by abject confession and the payment of a £10,000 fine, and was banished. He lived mostly in France, entertaining impoverished exiles in Paris, his own banishment being revoked in 1651. His collected poems, reviving the heroic couplet and including "Go, lovely Rose," had been published in 1645 and was followed by *A Panegyric to My Lord Protector* (1655) and *To the King Upon His Majesty's Happy Return* (1660), addressed to **Cromwell** and **Charles II**, respectively.

Waller, Fats (Thomas Wright) 1904–43 •*US jazz pianist, composer and entertainer*• He was born in New York, the son of a Baptist preacher who encouraged him to play the organ for services as a child. A professional musician at 15, he gained experience as a theater organist and a movie-house and nightclub pianist. Influenced by stride pianist **James P Johnson**, who coached him, Waller began his recording career in 1922, and the first records by "Fats Waller and His Rhythm," featuring his novelty singing, were made in 1934. Waller wrote many jazz standards, such as "Honeysuckle Rose" (c. 1928) and "Ain't Misbehavin'" (1929).

" "

Madam, if you don't know by now, don't mess with it!

When asked what jazz was. Quoted in Marshall Stearns ***The Story of Jazz*** *(1956).*

Wallis, Sir Barnes Neville 1887–1979 •*English aeronautical engineer and inventor*• Born in Derbyshire, he won a scholarship to Christ's Hospital, London, then trained as a marine engineer at Cowes. He joined the Vickers Company in 1911, and subsequently designed for them the airship R100, which made its maiden flight in 1929 and successfully crossed the Atlantic. From 1923 he was chief designer of structures at Vickers Aviation, Weybridge, where he designed the Wellesley and Wellington bombers with their revolutionary geodetic fuselage structure, and the "bouncing bombs" used by the British to destroy the Möhne and Eder dams in Germany during World War II. He then became chief of aeronautical research and development for the British Aircraft Corporation at Weybridge (1945–71). In the early 1950s he was responsible for the design of the first variable-geometry (swing-wing) aircraft, the experimental Swallow. He was knighted in 1968.

Wallis, Samuel 1728–95 •*English explorer and naval officer*• From 1766 to 1768 he made a circumnavigation of the globe, and discovered Tahiti and the Wallis Islands.

Walpole, Horace, 4th Earl of Orford 1717–97 •*English writer*• Born in London, the son of Sir **Robert Walpole**, he was educated at Eton and at King's College, Cambridge, then undertook the Grand Tour, with the poet **Thomas Gray**. Returning to England in 1741, he became Member of Parliament for Callington, Cornwall. He exchanged his Cornish seat in 1754 for the family borough of Castle Rising, which he vacated in 1757 for the other family borough of King's Lynn. In 1747 he purchased, near Twickenham, the former coachman's cottage, which he gradually gothicized (1753–76) into the stuccoed and battlemented pseudocastle of Strawberry Hill, thus reversing the trend toward classical and Italianate design. He also established a private press on which some of his own works as well as **Lucan**'s *Pharsalia* and Gray's *Progress of Poesy* and *The Bard* were printed. He wrote essays and verse, and is at his best in such satires as the *Letter From Xo Ho to*

His Friend Lien Chi at Pekin (1757). His *Castle of Otranto* (1764) set the fashion for supernatural romance. However, his literary reputation rests chiefly on his letters, which deal, in the most vivacious way, with party politics, foreign affairs, art, literature and gossip.

Walpole, Sir Hugh Seymour 1884–1941 •*English novelist*• Born in Auckland, New Zealand, he was educated in England at Emmanuel College, Cambridge. He was intended for the Church but became a schoolmaster at a boys' prep school, then an author. His books, which were enormously popular during his lifetime, display a straightforward, flowing style, great descriptive power and a genius for evoking atmosphere which he unfortunately overworked at times, and which sometimes made his work open to parody. His many novels include *Mr Perrin and Mr Traill* (1911), based on his experience as a schoolteacher, *Fortitude* (1913), *The Dark Forest* (1916), *The Secret City* (1919, James Tait Black Memorial Prize), *The Cathedral* (1922), which owes much to **Anthony Trollope**, and *The Herries Chronicle* (1930–33).

Walpole, Sir Robert, 1st Earl of Orford 1676–1745 •*English Whig politician, the first prime minister of Great Britain*• He was born in Houghton in Norfolk, and educated at Eton and King's College, Cambridge. He was destined for the Church, and entered politics largely by accident when his two elder brothers died, leaving him the family estate and sufficient wealth to follow a political career. He entered the House of Commons in 1701 as the Whig member for Castle Rising, Norfolk, and in 1702 for King's Lynn. He was a formidable speaker and quickly rose in the ranks of his party during Queen **Anne**'s reign, appointed secretary for war in 1708 and treasurer of the Navy in 1710. During the Tory government that followed the Whig collapse in 1710, he was sent to the Tower for alleged corruption (1712), but was recalled by the new king, **George I**, who had succeeded to the throne in 1714, and was made a privy councilor and chancellor of the Exchequer (1715). George I could not speak English and gave up attending the proceedings of parliament, thereby leaving Walpole considerable freedom and discretion as leader of the government. Gradually Walpole established his supremacy, chairing, on the king's behalf, a small group of ministers that was the forerunner of the present-day cabinet. As a result, he came to be seen as England's first prime minister, although he himself rejected the title. He was knighted in 1725 and made Earl of Orford in 1742. He enjoyed good relations with the Prince of Wales, who became **George II**, and with his wife, Queen **Caroline**. In addition to his earldom, Walpole was presented with No. 10 Downing Street, which was to become the permanent London home of all future prime ministers.

Walpurgis, St *See* **Walburga, St**

Walsingham, Sir Francis c.1530–90 •*English statesman*• Born in Chislehurst, Kent, he was sent on an embassy to France in 1570–73 by **William Cecil**, Baron Burghley. He was then appointed one of the principal secretaries of state under **Elizabeth I**, sworn onto the Privy Council, and knighted. In 1578 he was sent on a mission to the Netherlands, in 1581 to France, and in 1583 to Scotland. He contrived an effective system of espionage at home and abroad, enabling him to reveal the **Babington** Plot, which implicated **Mary Queen of Scots** in treason, and to obtain, in 1587, details of some of the plans for the Spanish Armada. He favored the Puritan party. Elizabeth acknowledged his genius and important services, but kept him poor and without honors, and he died in poverty and debt.

Walsingham, Thomas d. c.1422 •*English chronicler and monk*• He was associated chiefly with St Albans abbey but for a time was prior of Wymondham. An authority on English history from 1377 until 1422, he compiled *Historia Anglicana, 1272–1422* (1863–64) and other works.

Walter, Bruno, *originally* **Bruno Walter Schlesinger** 1876–1962 •*US conductor*• Born in Berlin, Germany, he conducted at Cologne while still in his teens. He worked with **Mahler** in Hamburg and Vienna, directed the Munich Opera (1913–22), and became chief conductor of the Berlin Philharmonic Orchestra (1919). Leaving Nazi Germany in 1933 he went to France, then settled in the US, where he took US citizenship and became chief conductor of the New York Philharmonic Orchestra (1951). He was noted particularly for his interpretations of **Haydn**, **Mozart** and Mahler.

Walter, Hubert c. 1140–1205 •*English churchman and statesman*• He accompanied **Richard I** on the Third Crusade (1190–93). Appointed Archbishop of Canterbury in 1193, he helped to raise the ransom to secure Richard's release from captivity, and to contain the rebellion of the king's brother, **John**. He was made justiciar of England (1193–98) and was responsible for all the business of government. On John's accession (1199) he became chancellor.

Walter, Lucy, *also known as* **Mrs Barlow** 1630–58 •*English mistress of the future Charles II*• She was born probably in Dyfed, Wales, and met the future king in the Channel Islands when he was fleeing England in 1644 during the English civil war. In 1649 she bore him a son, James, Duke of **Monmouth**.

Walters, Julie 1950– •*English actress*• Born in Birmingham, she trained as a nurse before studying at the Manchester Polytechnic School of Theatre and working at the Liverpool Everyman Theatre. The role of the indomitable, working-class hairdresser in *Educating Rita* (1980) established her reputation, and she received an Oscar nomination when she repeated it in the 1983 film version. A skilled mimic, comedienne and versatile character actress, she has appeared on stage in *Macbeth* (1985) and *The Rose Tattoo* (1991). Other films include *Personal Services* (1986) and *Billy Elliot* (2000). She is also the author of *Babytalk* (1990), a frank and funny account of motherhood.

Walton, E(rnest) T(homas) S(inton) 1903–95 •*Irish physicist and Nobel Prize winner*• Born in Dungarvan, Waterford, he studied at Trinity College, Dublin, and in 1927 went to the Cavendish Laboratory, Cambridge, where he studied under **Ernest Rutherford**. He later became Professor of Natural and Experimental Philosophy at Trinity College, Dublin (1947–74). With Sir **John Cockcroft**, he produced the first artificial disintegration of a nucleus by bombarding lithium with protons in the first successful use of a particle accelerator. By studying the energies of the alpha particles produced, they were able to verify **Albert Einstein**'s theory of mass-energy equivalence, and were awarded the 1951 Nobel Prize for physics.

Walton, Izaak 1593–1683 •*English writer*• He was born in Stafford, the son of an alehouse keeper. In 1621 he settled as an ironmonger in London, where he became friends with **John Donne**. In 1626 he married a great-grandniece of **Thomas Cranmer**, and in 1647 Ann Ken, a half sister of the hymn writer **Thomas Ken**. He spent most of his time "in the families of the eminent clergymen of England." His later years were spent in Winchester. His most celebrated work is his *The Compleat Angler, or the Contemplative Man's Recreation*, which first appeared in 1653. His description of fishes, English rivers and rods and lines is interspersed with scraps of dialogue, moral reflections, old verses, songs and sayings and idyllic glimpses of country life. The anonymous *Arte of Angling* (1577), discovered in 1957, has been found to be one of his chief sources. Equally exquisite are his biographies of John Donne (1640), Sir Thomas Wotton (1651), Richard Hooker (1665), Richard Herbert (1670) and George Sanderson (1678).

Walton, Sir William Turner 1902–83 •*English composer*• Born in Oldham, Lancashire, he was a cathedral chorister at Christ Church, Oxford, before going to university in 1918. The same year, he wrote his first major work, a piano quartet, which was performed at the Salzburg festival of contemporary music in 1923. His *Façade* (1923), originally accompanied by declamatory verses by **Edith Sitwell**, subsequently reappeared as a pair of suites and as ballet music. *Belshazzar's Feast* (1931), a biblical cantata with a libretto by **Osbert Sitwell**, is a powerful work in which instrumentation for an augmented orchestra is contrasted with moving unaccompanied choral passages. His ballet music for *The Wise Virgins* (1940), based on pieces by **J S Bach**, contains a concert favorite in his orchestral arrangement of the aria *Sheep May Safely Graze*. During World War II he began composing incidental music for films and showed great flair for building up tension and atmosphere, as in **Laurence Olivier**'s *Henry V* (1944). Later works include the opera *Troilus and Cressida* (1954), a cello concerto (1956), a second symphony and a song cycle, *Anon in Love* (1960), *A Song for the Lord Mayor's Table* (1962) and a comic opera, *The Bear* (1967).

“ ”

I seriously advise all sensitive composers to die at the age of thirty-seven. I know I've gone through the first halcyon period, and am just about ripe for my critical damnation.

1939 Letter.

Wanamaker, Sam 1919–93 •*US actor and director*• Born in Chicago, he worked with summer stock companies there as an actor and director (1936–39), and made his New York stage debut in 1942. After serving in World War II he returned to acting in New York (1946). He made his London debut in **Clifford Odets**'s *Winter Journey* (1952), which he also directed, and remained based in England, directing and acting in several plays. He was appointed director of the New Shakespeare Theatre, Liverpool (1957), and he joined the Shakespeare Memorial Theatre company at Stratford-upon-Avon (1959). He continued to direct on both sides of the Atlantic Ocean, but concentrated latterly upon his ambition to build a replica of **Shakespeare**'s Globe Theatre near its original site on London's Bankside, which opened in 1996, three years after his death. The Bear Garden Museum, founded by Wanamaker and displaying exhibits from Shakespeare's era, is nearby.

Wang, An 1920–90 •*US physicist and computer company executive*• Born in Shanghai, he graduated in science from Jiao Tong University in Shanghai (1940), and in 1945 emigrated to the US, where he studied applied physics at Harvard. Possessing technological genius and entrepreneurial ability, he invented magnetic core memories for computers, and in 1951 founded Wang Laboratories in Boston, Massachusetts, which, through the success of Wang's electronic calculator, went on to become a leading manufacturer of minicomputers. However, in 1992 the company filed for bankruptcy. He was a leading philanthropist in Boston.

Wang Ching-wei *See* **Wang Jingwei**

Wang Jingwei (Wang Ching-wei) 1883–1944 •*Chinese politician*• An associate of **Sun Yat-sen**, he studied in Japan, where he joined Sun's revolutionary party, and from 1917 became his personal assistant. In 1927 he was appointed head of the new Guomindang (Kuomintang) government at Wuhan, and in 1932 became the party's president, with his main rival for control of the Guomindang, **Chiang Kai-shek**, in charge of the military. In 1938, after the outbreak of war with Japan, Wang became head of a puppet regime ruling the Japanese-occupied areas.

Wankel, Felix 1902–88 •*German mechanical engineer*• Born in Luhran, he was employed in various engineering works before opening his own research establishment in 1930, devoting himself to the development of an alternative configuration to the conventional piston-and-cylinder internal-combustion engine. After many trials he produced a successful prototype engine in 1956, with a curved equilateral triangular rotor in a fat figure-eight-shaped chamber. Continuing problems with the sealing of the rotor have prevented its large-scale adoption.

Warbeck, Perkin c. 1474–99 •*Flemish impostor*• Pretender to the English throne, he was born in Tournai. He appeared in 1490 claiming to be Richard, Duke of York, the younger of the two sons of **Edward IV** murdered in the Tower. The Irish and the French, under **Charles VIII**, supported him, and in July 1495 he landed in Kent. In Scotland, **James IV** married him to a daughter of the Earl of Huntly. In 1498 he attempted to besiege Exeter, but later surrendered, was thrown into the Tower, and executed.

Warburg, Otto Heinrich 1883–1970 •*German biochemist and Nobel Prize winner*• Born in Freiburg, Baden, he was educated at the Universities of Berlin and Heidelberg, and served with distinction during World War I. He worked at the Kaiser Wilhelm (later **Max Planck**) Institute in Berlin from 1913, becoming director there in 1953. He was the first to discover the important role of iron in nearly all cells. In 1926 he demonstrated that oxygen uptake by yeast is inhibited by carbon monoxide and determined that carboxyhemoglobin is a heme protein. He also discovered the role of riboflavin in the oxidation of glucose compounds by a yeast preparation, and he showed the efficiency with which the green alga *Chlorella* produces oxygen from the absorption of red light (1923). The gas manometer developed by Warburg in 1926 was crucial to the discoveries of **Hans Krebs** and others. Warburg also engaged in cancer research. He was awarded the 1931 Nobel Prize for physiology or medicine. In 1944 he was offered a second Nobel Prize, which, as a Jew, he was prevented from accepting by **Hitler**.

Ward, Dame Barbara Mary *See* **Jackson (of Lodsworth), Baroness**

Ward, Mrs Humphry *See* **Ward, Mary Augusta**

Ward, Sir Joseph George 1856–1930 •*New Zealand statesman*• Born in Melbourne, he entered parliament in 1887 and held many prominent posts, including minister of public health (the first in the world). He was Liberal prime minister from 1906 to 1912 and from 1928 to 1930. With **William Ferguson Massey** he represented New Zealand at the Paris Peace Conference (1919).

Ward, Mary 1585–1645 •*English religious reformer*• The founder of a Catholic society for women, modeled on the Society of Jesus in 1609, she and her devotees founded schools and taught in them, giving up the cloistered existence and the habit of nuns. These innovations were questioned, and Pope **Urban VIII** at last called her to Rome and suppressed her society in 1630. She was allowed to return to England in 1639. Her institute was fully restored in 1877 and became the model for modern Catholic women's institutes.

Ward, Mary Augusta, *known as* **Mrs Humphry Ward**, *née* **Arnold** 1851–1920 •*English novelist*• She was born in Hobart, Tasmania, the granddaughter of **Thomas Arnold** and niece of **Matthew Arnold**. Her family returned to Great Britain (1856), and after attending private boarding schools she joined them in Oxford in 1867. In 1872 she married Thomas Humphry Ward (1845–1926), a Fellow and tutor of Brasenose College, Oxford, and she became secretary at Somerville College, Oxford (1879), before moving to London in 1881. A children's story, *Milly and Olly* (1881), *Miss Bretherton* (1884), a slight novel, and a translation (1885) of **Henri Amiel**'s *Journal intime* preceded her greatest success, the best-selling spiritual romance *Robert Elsmere* (1888), which inspired the philanthropist Passmore Edwards to found the Tavistock Square settlement for the London poor in 1897. Her later novels, all on social or religious issues, include *Sir George Tressady* (1896) and *The Case of Richard Meynell* (1911). She was both an enthusiastic social worker and an antisuffragist, becoming the first president of the Anti-Suffrage League in 1908.

Ward, Stephen 1913–63 •*English painter and osteopath*• He was a London osteopath who was at the center of the Profumo scandal in 1963. He introduced **Christine Keeler** to **John Profumo** and provided information that disproved Profumo's denial of involvement made in the House of Commons. He became the establishment scapegoat for the whole affair and was tried on charges of living on immoral earnings. He committed suicide before a verdict was reached. Also an accomplished painter, he included members of the royal family among his subjects.

Warhol, Andy, *originally* **Andrew Warhola** 1928–87 •*US pop artist and filmmaker*• Born in Pittsburgh, Pennsylvania, to Czech parents, he worked as a commercial designer before becoming in 1961 a pioneer of pop art with colorful reproductions of familiar everyday objects (for example, *100 Soup Cans* and *Green Coca-Cola Bottles*, 1962). His first films (such as *Sleep*, 1963) endeavored to eliminate the individuality of the filmmaker by use of a fixed camera viewpoint without sound. In later sound production from his Greenwich Village “film factory,” his avant-garde style employed continual violent changes of visual and aural perspective within long single scenes, typified by *Chelsea Girls* (1967). After 1968, when he was shot and wounded by Valerie Solanas, his films were controlled by his former assistant and cameraman with much more commercial exploitation of Warhol's cult reputation, as in *Flesh* (1968) and *Trash* (1969). In the 1970s Warhol turned to portrait painting, still attempting to suppress artistic individuality by painting in series, as in the ten Mao portraits of 1972.

“ ”

In the future everybody will be world famous for fifteen minutes.

Quoted in Andy Warhol, Kasper König, Pontus Hultén and Olle Granath eds., ***Andy Warhol*** *(1968).*

Warlock, Peter, *pseudonym of* **Philip Arnold Heseltine** 1894–1930 •*English musicologist and composer*• Born in London, he met **Frederick Delius** in 1910 and in 1916, Bernard van Dieren (1884–1936), both of whom had a great musical influence on him. His friendship with **D H Lawrence** is also reflected in his music. His works include the song cycle *The Curlew* (1920–22), *Serenade* (1923), dedicated to Delius, the orchestral suite *Capriol* (1926), many songs, often in the Elizabethan manner, and choral works. He wrote *Frederick Delius* (1923, under his original name) and *The English Ayre* (1926).

Warmerdam, Cornelius 1915–2001 •*US pole vaulter*• Born in Long Beach, California, he was the first man to break the 15-foot (4.57-meter) landmark (1941). Seven times the world record holder, he set a new standard in the sport. Using a bamboo pole, he set records during World War II that were not bettered until the next decade. His career-best indoor vault of 15 feet 8 inches (4.78 meters), set in 1943, was not beaten for more than 14 years. The development of more flexible fiberglass poles since the 1950s have led to dramatic improvements in vaulting records, but in his own time his achievements were exceptional.

Warner, Deborah 1959– •*English theater director*• Born in Oxford, she was educated at St Clare's College, Oxford, then at the Central School of Speech and Drama. She founded the KickTheatre Company in 1980, and was its artistic director (1980–86) before becoming resident director at the Royal Shakespeare Company (1987–89) and associate director of the Royal National Theatre (1989–98). She won the *Evening Standard* and Laurence Olivier awards for direction in 1988 for her acclaimed *Electra*, which was revived in 1992. She also won an Olivier award for her production of **Ibsen**'s *Hedda Gabler* at the Abbey Theatre in Dublin in 1991. Her controversial production of **Beckett**'s *Footfalls* (1994) was followed by a version of **Shakespeare**'s *Richard II* in which **Fiona Shaw** played the monarch.

Warner, Jack Leonard, *originally* **Jack Leonard Eichelbaum** 1892–1978 •*US film producer*• Born in Canada, in London, Ontario, he was the youngest son of a large and impoverished immigrant family. A boy soprano and inveterate performer, he embarked upon a show-business career, later joining his brothers Harry, Albert and Samuel in the exhibition and distribution of motion pictures in Pennsylvania. Building a nationwide company, they moved into production with *Perils of the Plains* (1910) and built a studio of their own in Los Angeles (1919). The Warners were the first to introduce sound, in *Don Juan* (1926) and *The Jazz Singer* (1927). The sensational popularity of the latter made Warner Brothers into a major studio, home to such stars as **Bette Davis**, **James Cagney** and **Humphrey Bogart**. As a tough head of production, Warner supervised such films as *Yankee Doodle Dandy* (1942), *My Fair Lady* (1964) and *Camelot* (1967) but eventually sold his interest and the name to the Canadian company Seven Arts. He wrote two autobiographies (1965, 1975).

Warner, Marina Sarah 1946– •*English literary critic and writer*• Born in London and educated at Lady Margaret Hall, Oxford, she was the Paul Getty Scholar at the Getty Centre for the History of Art and the Humanities (1987–88) and the Tinbergen Professor at Erasmus University, Rotterdam (1990–91). She was Young Writer of the Year in 1969, and winner of the Fawcett prize in 1986 and of the Commonwealth Writers' prize (Eurasia) in 1989. In 1994 she delivered the Reith Lectures, later published as *Managing Monsters* (1994). Other publications include *Alone of All Her Sex: The Myth and Culture of the Virgin Mary* (1976), *Monuments and Maidens* (1985) and *Mermaids in the Basement* (1993).

Warner, Rex 1905–86 •*English writer*• Born in Birmingham, he studied classics at Wadham College, Oxford. He was a specialist in classical literature and taught before turning to writing. *The Wild Goose Chase* (1937), *The Professor* (1938) and *The Aerodrome* (1941) established his reputation as a writer concerned with the problems of the individual involved with authority. *Men of Stones* (1949) explores the nature of totalitarianism. He was perhaps best known for his later historical novels such as *The Young Caesar* (1958), *Imperial Caesar* (1960) and *Pericles the Athenian* (1963). He was a poet of sensuous quality (*Poems*, 1931) and also a translator of Greek classics.

Warner, Sylvia Townsend 1893–1978 •*English novelist*• She was born in Harrow, London, studied music, and was one of the four editors of the ten-volume *Tudor Church Music* (1923–29). She published seven novels, four volumes of poetry, essays and eight volumes of short stories. A gifted writer, she produced works which range widely in theme, locale and period. Significant titles are *Lolly Willowes* (1926), *Mr Fortune's Maggot* (1927), *Summer Will Show* (1936), *After the Death of Don Juan* (1938) and *The Corner That Held Them* (1948).

Warnock, (Helen) Mary Warnock, Baroness, *née* **Wilson** 1924– •*English philosopher and educator*• She was born in Winchester and studied at Oxford, where she became a fellow in philosophy at St Hugh's College (1949–66, 1976–84). She was headmistress of Oxford High School (1968–72) and mistress of Girton College, Cambridge (1985–91), and has contributed to or chaired important committees of inquiry into issues such as environmental pollution (1979–84), animal experiments (1979–85), human fertilization (1982–84) and teaching standards (1990). Her publications include *Education: A Way Forward* (1979), *A Question of Life* (1985) and *Teacher Teach Thyself* (The Dimbleby Lecture, 1985). She was awarded a life peerage in 1985.

Warr, 3rd or 12th Baron De la *See* **De la Warr, 3rd or 12th Baron**

Warren, Earl 1891–1974 •*US politician and jurist*• Born in Los Angeles and educated at the University of California, he practiced law in California and was then admitted to the bar. An active Republican, he became governor of California (1943–53) and chief justice of the US Supreme Court in 1953. The Warren Court (1953–69) was responsible for the landmark decision in *Brown v. Board of Education of Topeka* (1954), which outlawed school segregation, and for *Miranda v. Arizona* (1966), which ruled that criminal suspects be informed of their rights before being questioned by the police. Warren was chairman of the federal commission (the Warren Commission, 1963–64) that investigated the assassination of President **John F Kennedy** and found that the killing was not part of a domestic or foreign conspiracy.

" "

We conclude that in the field of public education the doctrine of "separate but equal" has no place.

1954 Ruling to declare segregated schools unconstitutional, May 17.

Warren, Robert Penn 1905–89 •*US novelist and poet*• Born in Guthrie, Kentucky, he was educated at Vanderbilt, the University of California at Berkeley and Yale University. Professor of English at Louisiana (1934–42) and Minnesota (1942–50), he was Professor of Drama (1951–56) and of English (1962–73) at Yale. He established an international reputation with his Pulitzer Prize–winning political novel about the governor of a Southern state, *All the King's Men* (1946, filmed 1949), in which the demagogue Willie Stark closely resembles Governor **Huey Long**. Other works include *Night Rider* (1939), *The Cave* (1959), *Wilderness* (1961), the story of a Jew in the Civil War, and *Meet Me in the Green Glen* (1971). He also published some volumes of short stories and verse, including *Promises* (1957, Pulitzer Prize), *Selected Poems, Old and New, 1923–66* (1966), *Or Else* (1974) and *Rumor Verified* (1981).

Warwick, Dionne, *also spelled* **Warwicke** 1940– •*US soul and pop singer*• Born in East Orange, New Jersey, to a musical family which includes Cissy and **Whitney Houston**, she was discovered by songwriters Burt Bacharach and Hal David, who wrote "Anyone Who Had a Heart," "Walk on By" (1964), "I Say a Little Prayer" (1967) and "Do You Know the Way to San Jose" (1968) for her, among other songs. She was less successful after splitting from Bacharach and David, but had a number-one hit with the Spinners on "Then Came You" (1974).

Warwick, John Dudley, Duke of Northumberland and **Earl of** 1502–53 •*English soldier and statesman*• Son of lawyer and privy councillor Edmund Dudley (c. 1462–1510), he served under **Edward Seymour**, Duke of Somerset, in his Scottish campaigns. Made Earl of Warwick in 1546, he was appointed joint regent for **Edward VI** and high chamberlain of England in 1547. As virtual ruler of England he was created Duke of Northumberland in 1551 and brought about the downfall and eventual execution of Somerset (1550–52). He married his fourth son, Lord Guildford, to Lady **Jane Grey**, and proclaimed her queen on the death of Edward VI in 1553, but was executed on the accession of **Mary I**.

Warwick, Richard Neville, Earl of, *known as* **the Kingmaker** 1428–71 •*English soldier and statesman*• As a boy he married the daughter of the Earl of Warwick and so at 21 succeeded to the earldom. He acquired the earldom of Salisbury in his own right when his father died in 1460. Consequently he had so much land and wealth that during the Wars of the Roses he held the balance between the Yorkist and Lancastrian factions. He first supported the Yorkists and established the son of Richard, Duke of York, as **Edward IV**, supplanting **Henry VI**. But Edward resented Warwick as the "power behind the throne" and forced him into exile in France. In 1460 he returned to England, now supporting the Lancastrian cause; he compelled Edward to leave the country so that he could reinstate Henry VI. Edward soon returned, however, and routed Warwick's forces at Barnet in March 1471. The "kingmaker" was killed in the battle.

Warwick, Robert Rich, 2nd Earl of 1587–1658 •*English colonialist*• He played a large role in the early history of the American colonies, and managed New England, Bermudas and Providence companies. In 1628 he got the patent of the Massachusetts Bay colony and in 1635 founded the settlement of Saybrook, Connecticut. A Puritan, he fought for the parliamentary side as Admiral of the Fleet (1642–49) during the English civil war. In 1643 he was nominated head of a commission for the government of the colonies. Warwick in Rhode Island was named after him.

Washington, Booker T(aliaferro) 1856–1915 •*US educator*• He was born a slave in Franklin County, Virginia, and was educated at the Hampton Institute before becoming a teacher, writer and speaker on African-American issues. In 1881 he was appointed principal of the newly opened Tuskegee Institute, Alabama, and built it into a major center of African-American education. The foremost African-American leader in the late 19th century, he encouraged Blacks to focus on economic equality rather than fight for social or political equality. He was strongly criticized by **William Du Bois**, and his policies were repudiated by the 20th-century civil rights movement. He is the author of *Up From Slavery* (1901) and *The Story of My Life and Work* (1900, as *An Autobiography*, 1901).

“ ”

In all things that are purely social we can be as separate as the fingers, yet one as the hand in all things essential to mutual progress.

1895 "The Atlanta Exposition Address," in ***Up From Slavery*** *(1901), chapter 14.*

Washington, Denzel 1954– •*US film actor*• Born in Mount Vernon, New York, he studied acting with the American Conservatory Theater in San Francisco, then returned to New York and worked with the Shakespeare in the Park ensemble and in a number of off-Broadway productions. He made his film debut in *Carbon Copy* (1981) and had a starring role in the popular television series *St Elsewhere* (1982–88). He played **Steve Biko** in *Cry Freedom* (1987) and won an Academy Award for Best Actor in a Supporting Role for *Glory* (1989) and one for Best Actor in a Lead Role for *Training Day* (2001). Others films of his include *Malcolm X* (1992), *Philadelphia* (1993) and *The Hurricane* (1999).

Washington, Dinah, *pseudonym of* **Ruth Jones** 1924–63 •*US jazz and rhythm-and-blues singer*• She was born in Tuscaloosa, Alabama, and was apprenticed to the Sara Martin gospel singers, but she made a gradual (though never complete) switch to jazz, joining the **Lionel Hampton** band in 1943 and shortly thereafter making her first recordings as leader. She later divided her activities between lucrative rhythm-and-blues sessions and more taxing improvisation sessions with the likes of trumpeter Clifford Brown. Plagued by alcoholism, she died at the age of 38.

Washington, George 1732–99 •*First President of the US*• He was born in Bridges Creek, Westmoreland County, Virginia, of immigrant English stock from Northamptonshire. George's father, Augustine, died while his son was still a boy, leaving a large family and inadequate means. George seems to have been a healthy, sober-minded boy, and the story of his honest admission to cutting down a cherry tree with a hatchet is probably the invention of his biographer, Mason Weems. He had an informal education, worked as a surveyor, and first fought in the campaigns of the French and Indian War (1754–58). He then managed the family estate at Mount Vernon, Virginia, and entered politics, representing his county in the House of Burgesses (1758–74). When he showed an interest in the growing dispute of the colonies with the British Crown, he was chosen to represent Virginia in the first (1774) and second (1775) Continental Congresses, and took an active part in them. He was neither orator nor writer, but in plain common sense and in the management of affairs he excelled. As an American soldier of national reputation, he was the inevitable choice as commander in chief of the Colonial army (1775). Washington set about an ambitious program of recruitment and training, and under his leadership a half-armed body of men managed to coop up a well-equipped British army in Boston and to force their evacuation (1776); the retreat from Concord and the slaughter at Bunker Hill were largely due to the incompetence of the English commander. The only able English commander was **Charles Cornwallis**, and he was hampered by the stupidity of his superior. Following reverses in the New York area, Washington made a remarkable retreat through New Jersey, inflicting notable defeats on the enemy at Trenton and Princeton (1777). He suffered reverses at Brandywine and Germantown but held his army together through the winter of 1777–78 at Valley Forge, near Philadelphia. France entered the war on the American side in 1778, and with the assistance of the Comte de **Rochambeau**, Washington forced the defeat and surrender of Cornwallis at Yorktown in 1781, which virtually ended the War of Independence. Washington resigned his commission in 1783 and retired to Mount Vernon, where he sought to secure a strong government by constitutional means. In 1787 he presided over the convention of delegates from 12 states at Philadelphia which formulated the Constitution; and the government under this Constitution began in 1789 with Washington as first chief magistrate, or president. The new administration was a strong consolidated government; parties were formed, led by Washington's two most trusted advisers, **Thomas Jefferson** and **Alexander Hamilton**, whom he appointed as his secretary of state and treasury secretary, respectively. In 1793 Washington was elected to a second term, but by this time considerable differences had developed between Jefferson's Democratic Republicans and Hamilton's Federalists. Washington tended to favor the Federalists; in the face of fierce personal attacks from the Republicans, he retired from the presidency in 1797. He died at Mount Vernon on December 14, 1799. The federal capital of the United States, in the planning of which he was associated, was named after him.

Waterhouse, John William 1847–1917 •*English painter*• He was born in Rome and painted classical stories, under the influence of the Pre-Raphaelites. Among his pictures are *Ulysses and the Sirens* (1892), *The Lady of Shalott* (1888, Tate Britain, London) and *Hylas and the Nymphs* (1897, Royal Academy, London).

Waterhouse, Keith Spencer 1929– •*English novelist, dramatist, humorist and journalist*• Born in Leeds, he first came to critical and popular attention with *Billy Liar* (1959), a whimsical novel about a working-class dreamer. The following year it became the basis of a successful play, on which he collaborated with **Willis Hall**. Waterhouse has since written various humorous novels, the best of which are *Jubb* (1963), *Office Life* (1978) and *Maggie Muggins, or Spring in Earl's Court* (1981). Other plays include *Jeffrey Bernard Is Unwell* (1989). Later works include *Unsweet Charity* (1992), a novel, *City Lights* (1994), and *Streets Ahead* (1995).

Waters, Ethel, *née* **Howard** 1896–1977 •*US jazz singer and actress*• Born in Chester, Pennsylvania, she made her first recordings in 1921, then later worked with **Duke Ellington**, **Benny Goodman** and others. From the late 1930s she turned to acting, notably in *Cabin in the Sky* (1943). Growing up in the North gave her a less secure blues feel than either **Bessie Smith** or Ma Rainey

(**Gertrude Rainey**), and she was much influenced by white vaudevillians. However, her vocal improvisations made a considerable impact on **Ella Fitzgerald**. Her autobiography, *His Eye Is on the Sparrow* (1951), is a powerfully moving narrative documenting her religious faith.

Waters, Muddy, *real name* **McKinley Morganfield** 1915–83 •*US blues singer, composer and guitarist*• Born in Rolling Fork, Mississippi, he learned to play the harmonica as a child, and the guitar in his teens. He was first recorded in a classic Delta blues style in 1941 by Alan Lomax (see entry at **John Avery Lomax**), but moved to Chicago in 1943 and became the crucial figure in the development of the electric urban blues style. He gained his first national success with "Rollin' Stone" (1950). In that same year he put together a band consisting of Little Walter, Otis Spann and Jimmy Rogers, which was to have a profound influence not only on other blues musicians, but also on the white rhythm-and-blues artists of the mid-1960s. The band's best-known singles include "I've Got My Mojo Working" (1957) and "Hoochie Coochie Man" (1954). His earthy, rough-hewn vocals and electrifying guitar work won him a large white audience from the late 1950s, but his 1960s and early 1970s recordings varied in quality. *Hard Again* (1977) and *I'm Ready* (1978) signaled a late resurgence in his music.

Watkins, Vernon Phillips 1906–67 •*Welsh poet*• Born in Maesteg, Glamorgan, he was educated at Magdalen College, Cambridge. For much of his life he lived at Pennard, Gower, and the shoreline there often provided illustrative material for his poetry. He published eight collections of verse during his lifetime, including *Ballad of Mari Lwyd* (1941), *Death Bell* (1954) and *Affinities* (1962). Regarded as one of the greatest Welsh poets in English, as well as one of the most unusual, he was long overshadowed by his friend **Dylan Thomas**.

Watson, James Dewey 1928– •*US biologist and Nobel Prize winner*• Born in Chicago, he studied zoology at the University of Chicago, and as a postgraduate at Indiana University he studied under **Hermann Müller** and **Salvador Luria**. He spent the period 1951–53 at the Cavendish Laboratory in Cambridge, UK, and from 1955 taught at Harvard. He was director of the Cold Spring Harbor Laboratory in New York (1968–94), then president (1994–), and he has also served as director of the National Center for Human Genome Research (1989–92). While in Cambridge in 1951, Watson worked with **Francis Crick** on the structure of DNA, the biological molecule in cells which carries genetic information. They published their model of a two-stranded helical molecule in 1953, showing that each strand consists of a series of the nucleotide bases wound around a common center, with the strands linked together by hydrogen bonds. For this work, Watson was awarded the 1962 Nobel Prize for physiology or medicine jointly with Crick and **Maurice Wilkins**. He wrote a personal account of the discovery of the DNA structure in *The Double Helix* (1968), and the textbooks *The Molecular Biology of the Gene* (1965) and *Recombinant DNA* (1984).

Watson, John Broadus 1878–1958 •*US psychologist*• He was born in Greenville, South Carolina. As a professor at Johns Hopkins University (1908–20), he was a leading exponent of behaviorism, holding that a scientific psychology could only study what was directly observable, that is, behavior. His most important work is *Behavior—An Introduction to Comparative Psychology* (1914). He later resigned from Johns Hopkins and became an advertising executive.

Watson, Thomas c. 1557–92 •*English lyric poet*• Born in London, he was educated at Oxford and studied law in London. Coming to **Christopher Marlowe**'s aid in a street fight, he killed a man in 1589. He is best known for English sonnets such as *Hecatompathia or Passionate Century of Love* (1582) and *The Tears of Fancie* (1593), and his sonnets were probably studied by **Shakespeare**. He also translated classics into Latin and English, including **Sophocles**, **Torquato Tasso**, and Italian madrigals.

Watson, Tom (Thomas Sturges) 1949– •*US golfer*• He was born in Kansas City, Missouri. Through the mid-1970s and early 1980s Watson, with **Jack Nicklaus**, dominated world golf, winning the US Open, two Masters tournaments and five British Opens. He was the US Player of the Year on six occasions and in 1993 captained the US Ryder Cup team to victory.

Watson-Watt, Sir Robert Alexander 1892–1973 •*Scottish physicist*• Born in Brechin, Angus, he was educated at the Universities of Dundee and St Andrews, and worked in the meteorological office, the Department of Scientific and Industrial Research and the National Physical Laboratory before becoming scientific adviser to the Air Ministry in 1940. By 1935 he had perfected a shortwave-radio system called "Radio Detecting And Ranging," or radar, that could locate airplanes. He was knighted for this work in 1942. In 1958 he published *Three Steps to Victory*.

Watt, James 1736–1819 •*Scottish engineer and inventor*• He was born in Greenock, Strathclyde, and was educated by his mother and at the local grammar school. He was the mathematical instrument maker for the University of Glasgow from 1757 to 1763. He was also employed on surveys for the Forth and Clyde Canal (1767), and worked on the improvement of harbors and the deepening of the Forth and Clyde Rivers. In 1763–64 a model of **Thomas Newcomen**'s steam engine was sent to his workshop for repair. He easily put it into order, and seeing the defects in the working of the machine, he hit upon the expedient of the separate condenser. This was probably the greatest single improvement ever made to the reciprocating steam engine, enabling its efficiency to increase to about three times that of the old atmospheric engines. He entered into a partnership with Matthew Boulton (1728–1809) in 1774, and began manufacturing the new engine. Watt's soon superseded Newcomen's machine as a pumping engine, and between 1781 and 1785 he obtained patents for the sun-and-planet motion, the expansion principle, the double-acting engine, the parallel motion, a smokeless furnace and the governor. He described a steam locomotive in one of his patents (1784). The modern scientific unit of power, the watt, is named after him, and horsepower, the original unit of power, was first experimentally determined and used by him in 1783.

Watteau, (Jean) Antoine 1684–1721 •*French painter*• Born in Valenciennes, he ran away to Paris in 1702 and worked as a scene painter at the Opera and as a copyist. After 1712 his early canvases were mostly military scenes, but it was the mythological *Embarquement pour l'îsle de Cythère* which won him membership in the academy (1717). While staying at the castle of Montmorency, he painted his *Fêtes galantes*, quasi-pastoral idylls in court dress which became fashionable in high society. His last great work depicted the interior of the shop of his art-dealer friend Gersaint, drawn from nature and intended as a signboard, but in fact it was the most classical and the most perfectly composed of his paintings. Essentially aristocratic in conception, Watteau's paintings fell into disfavor during the French Revolution, and it was not until the end of the 19th century that they regained popularity. He is now regarded as a forerunner of the Impressionists in his handling of color and study of nature. He influenced and was imitated by many later artists, most notably **Jean Honoré Fragonard** and **François Boucher**.

Watts, George Frederick 1817–1904 •*English painter*• Born in London, he formed his style after the Venetian masters and became known for his penetrating portraits of notables, 150 of which he presented to the National Portrait Gallery in 1904. These represent his best work, but in his lifetime his moral and allegorical pieces enjoyed enormous popularity, and monochrome reproductions of *Sir Galahad*, *Love Triumphant*, *Hope* and so on adorned the walls of countless late Victorian middle-class homes. He also executed some sculpture, including *Physical Energy* (Kensington Gardens). In 1864 he married **Ellen Terry**, but parted from her within a year.

Watts, Isaac 1674–1748 •*English hymnwriter*• Born in Southampton, he succeeded an independent minister in Mark Lane, London, in 1702 and became eminent as a preacher. His hymns and psalms are contained in *Horae Lyricae* (1706), *Hymns and Spiritual Songs* (1707–09) and *Psalms of David Imitated* (1719), and include "Jesus shall reign where'er the sun," "When I survey the wondrous cross" and "O God, our help in ages past."

Waugh, Alec (Alexander Raban) 1898–1981 •*English novelist and travel writer*• Born in London, the brother of **Evelyn Waugh**, he was educated at Sherborne, but was involved in a homosexual scandal there and left in 1915 to become a cadet in the Inns of Court Officers Training Corps at Sandhurst. He spent two years in training before being posted to a machine-gun unit in France, just in time for Passchendaele. In seven and a half weeks he wrote his first book, the autobiographical *Loom of Youth* (1917), in which he expressed the bitterness and love he felt for his school. It was an immediate success, but it was tainted with notoriety and has overshadowed worthy successors: *Wheels Within Wheels* (1933), *Where the Clock Chimes Twice* (1952) and various travel books, the most popular being *Island in the Sun* (1956). He wrote several autobiographical volumes, including *The Best Wine Last* (1978).

Waugh, Auberon Alexander 1939–2001 •*English journalist and novelist*• He was born in Pixton Park, Dulverton, Somerset, the eldest son of **Evelyn Waugh**. He did his National Service in the Royal Horse Guards and was sent to Cyprus, where he accidentally shot himself, losing a lung, his spleen, several ribs and a finger; he denied speculation that he had been fired on by his own troops. Completing his education at Oxford, he got a job on the *Daily Telegraph* in 1960, the same year he published his first novel, *The Foxglove Saga*. Four more novels followed. He contributed to most national papers and to the *New Statesman*, the *Spectator* and *Private Eye* (1970–86). He was editor (1986–2000), then editor in chief (2000–01) of the *Literary Review*. A later publication was *Way of the World* (1994).

Waugh, Evelyn Arthur St John 1903–66 •*English writer*• He was born in Hampstead, London, the younger brother of **Alec Waugh**. He was educated at Lancing and Hertford College, Oxford, where he studied modern history but with little application. He became a schoolmaster (1925–27), and attempted suicide. The experience gave him the material for *Decline and Fall* (1928), his first and immoderately successful novel. It made him the talk of the town, for, its comic genius apart, it was obviously a roman à clef. After a brief and unsuccessful marriage, he spent a few years traveling. He contributed variously to newspapers, particularly the *Daily Mail*, published the social satire *Vile Bodies* (1930) and two travel books, *Labels* (1930) and *Remote People* (1931). In 1930 he became a Roman Catholic, an event which he regarded as the most important in his life. Between 1932 and 1937 he visited British Guiana (Guyana), Brazil, Morocco and Abyssinia (Ethiopia), and he cruised in the Mediterranean. After he married Laura Herbert (1937), he settled at Piers Court, Stinchcombe, Gloucestershire, and published *Scoop* (1938), a newspaper farce in which the wrong correspondent is sent to cover the civil war in the African Republic of Ishmaelia. Further travels to Hungary and Mexico followed before the outbreak of World War II, which Waugh spent in a variety of postings as a junior officer. During the war he published four books, including *Put Out More Flags* (1942) and *Brideshead Revisited* (1945), a nostalgic, highly wrought evocation of halcyon days at Oxford. This period also inspired "The Sword of Honor" trilogy—*Men at Arms* (1952), *Officers and Gentlemen* (1955) and *Unconditional Surrender* (1961). Other books published during this period include *The Loved One* (1947), *Helena* (1950) and *The Ordeal of Gilbert Pinfold* (1957), a painfully personal but fictionalized account of a middle-aged writer's mental collapse. In 1964 he published *A Little Learning*, intended as the first of several volumes of an autobiography he never completed. He was revered as a wit and a stylist and one of the 20th century's greatest comic novelists. *The Diaries of Evelyn Waugh* were published in 1976 and his *Letters*, edited by Mark Amory, in 1980. He was the father of **Auberon Waugh**.

" "

Words should be an intense pleasure, just as leather should be to a shoemaker.

1950 In the ***New York Times****, November 19.*

Wavell, Archibald Percival Wavell, 1st Earl 1883–1950 •*English soldier*• Born in Winchester and trained at Sandhurst, he served in the Second Boer War (1899–1902) and on the Indian frontier (1908). He was wounded in 1916 and lost the sight of one eye. He became chief of staff under Viscount **Allenby** in Palestine, and from 1938 to 1941 he was commander in chief of British forces in the Middle East. He conquered Abyssinia, but was defeated by **Rommel** in North Africa. He became commander in chief in 1941 and supreme commander of Allied forces in the Southwest Pacific (1942). From 1943 to 1947, during the difficult years that preceded the transfer of power, he was viceroy in India. He became field marshal and viscount (1943) and earl (1947), and published *Generals and Generalship* (1941) and an anthology of poetry (1944).

Wayne, John, *originally* **Marion Michael Morrison** 1907–79 •*US film actor*• Born in Winterset, Iowa, he had a succession of small parts in low-budget films and serials which eventually led to stardom in *Stagecoach* (1939). Known as "Duke," he went on to make over 80 films, typically starring in Westerns as a tough but warm-hearted gunfighter or lawman, or in war films. He gave notable performances in, among others, *Red River* (1948), *The Searchers* (1956), *True Grit* (1969, Academy Award) and *The Shootist* (1976), his final film and one of his best.

Waynflete, William of *See* **William of Waynflete**

Wearing, Gillian 1963– •*English artist*• Born in Birmingham, she studied at the Chelsea School of Art and Goldsmiths College, London. Her work concentrates mainly on photography and video, with pieces such as *Signs That Say What You Want Them to Say and Not Signs That Say What Someone Else Wants You to Say* (1992–93), a series of photographs in which passers-by write their thoughts on cards, and *Sixty-Minute Silence* (1997), a video film of a group of police officers remaining posed and motionless, which was part of a Turner Prize–winning exhibition. Subsequent work has included *Drunk* (1999), a video installation featuring homeless alcoholics.

Weatherill, (Bruce) Bernard Weatherill, Baron 1920– •*British politician*• After service in World War II, he became managing director of his family's chain of menswear shops, and entered parliament as a Conservative Member of Parliament in 1964. He served as an Opposition whip, then as a treasury minister, before being appointed deputy speaker (1979), and then speaker (1983–92), a position he relinquished to **Betty Boothroyd**. He was made a life peer in 1992.

Weaver, Sigourney (Susan Alexandra) 1949– •*US film and stage actress*• Born in New York City, she studied English at Stanford University and drama at Yale. Entering the acting profession in off-Broadway plays, she made her film debut with a tiny role in *Annie Hall* (1977). She achieved major success with her portrayal of Ripley in the *Alien* series (1979, 1986, 1992 and 1997). She gave equally powerful performances in *Gorillas in the Mist* (1988) and *Death and the Maiden* (1994), and revealed a flair for comedy in *Ghostbusters* (1984) and *Working Girl* (1988). Her frequent stage appearances include *Old Times* (1981) and *The Merchant of Venice* (1986).

Webb, (Martha) Beatrice, *née* **Potter** 1858–1943 •*English social reformer, social historian and economist*• She was born in Gloucester, and was largely self-educated. She undertook social work in London and wrote the book *The Co-operative Movement in Great Britain* (1891). She began to research labor unions and working-class economic conditions, which led to her meeting (1890) **Sidney Webb**, later Baron Passfield. They married in 1892, forming a partnership that was dedicated to Fabian Socialist values and to a radical approach to social reform. Together they established the London School of Economics and Political Science (1895) and became highly influential in society. Their joint publications include *Soviet Communism: A New Civilization?* (1935).

" "

All along the line, physically, mentally, morally, alcohol is a weakening and deadening force, and it is worth a great deal to save women and girls from its influence.

1917 ***Health of Working Girls****, chapter 10.*

Webb, Karrie 1974– •*Australian golfer*• Born in Ayr, Queensland, she began playing golf at age eight and turned professional in 1994. She won the Women's British Open a year later and by the end of her first season had added another four major tournament titles. She reclaimed the Women's British Open in 1997, among other titles, and was soon being described as women's golf's equivalent of

Tiger Woods. In 2001, with victory in the Ladies Professional Golf Association championship, she became the youngest woman to complete a Grand Slam of all four of the modern-day majors.

Webb, Matthew 1848–83 •*English swimmer*• Born in Dawley, Shropshire, he was the first person to swim the English Channel. He trained as a seaman and became a master mariner before becoming a professional swimmer in 1875. In August 1875, he swam from Dover to Calais in 21¾ hours. He was drowned attempting to swim the Niagara rapids.

Webb, Philip 1831–1915 •*English architect and designer*• He was born in Oxford. After his training he joined the practice of **George Edmund Street** (1852), where he met **William Morris**, who joined Street briefly in 1856. Thus began a long association, with Webb becoming a central figure in the Arts and Crafts Movement and its offshoots. He designed furniture, metalwork and stained glass for Morris's firm, as well as animals and birds for textiles, and in architectural practice on his own from 1858, he designed several important houses such as the Red House, Bexley, for William and Jane Morris (1859) and Standen, East Grinstead (1891).

Webb, Sidney James, Baron Passfield 1859–1947 •*English social reformer, social historian and economist*• He was born in London, the son of an accountant, and in 1885 graduated with a Bachelor of Laws degree from the University of London. He was instrumental in establishing the London School of Economics and Political Science (1895), where he was a Professor of Public Administration (1912–27). An active member of the Labour Party, he entered parliament in 1922 and held several administrative posts between 1924 and 1931. He was also a founder of the Fabian Society (1884). In 1892 he married Beatrice Potter (see **Beatrice Webb**), and they worked together for social reform.

Webber, Andrew Lloyd *See* **Lloyd-Webber, Andrew Lloyd Webber, Baron**

Weber, Carl Maria Friedrich von 1786–1826 •*German composer and pianist*• Born near Lübeck, his second opera, *Das Waldmädchen* (1800), was produced at Freiburg before he was 14, and was afterward remodeled as *Silvana*. He became conductor of the opera at Breslau (Wrocław, Poland) in 1804, but ran into debt, was charged with embezzlement and ordered to leave the country in 1810. In 1813 he settled in Prague as opera Kapellmeister, and was invited by the king of Saxony to direct the German opera at Dresden (c. 1816). As founder of German Romantic opera, notably *Der Freischütz* (1821, "The Freeshooter"), *Euryanthe* (1823) and *Oberon* (1826), he was the forerunner of **Richard Wagner**. He also wrote several orchestral works, piano, chamber and church music, and many songs.

Weber, Max 1864–1920 •*German sociologist*• Born in Erfurt, he was educated at the Universities of Heidelberg, Berlin and Göttingen and taught at Berlin from 1892, Freiburg from 1894 and Heidelberg from 1897. He accepted a chair of sociology in Vienna in 1918, and in 1919 he took over the chair of sociology at Munich. Regarded as one of the founders of sociology, Weber is best known for his work *Die protestantische Ethik und der Geist des Kapitalismus* (1904, Eng trans *The Protestant Ethic and the Spirit of Capitalism*, 1930).

Webern, Anton Friedrich Wilhelm von 1883–1945 •*Austrian composer*• Born in Vienna, he was one of **Arnold Schoenberg**'s first musical disciples and made wide use of twelve-note technique, which led to hostile demonstrations when his works were first performed. They include a symphony, three cantatas, *Four Pieces for Violin and Pianoforte* (1910), *Five Pieces for Orchestra* (1911–13), a concerto for nine instruments and songs. His work has had great influence on many later composers. The Nazis banned his music, so he worked as a proofreader during World War II. He was accidentally shot dead by a US soldier near Salzburg.

Webster, Ben(jamin Francis) 1909–73 •*US jazz saxophonist*• Born in Kansas City, Missouri, he began his professional career as a pianist before turning to the saxophone in the early 1930s. He quickly established himself as a leading instrumentalist of the swing era and worked in many of the leading bands of the period, including that of **Fletcher Henderson** in New York. His **Coleman Hawkins**–influenced style blossomed in the music of **Duke Ellington**. He became a soloist much in demand after leaving the band and a mainstay of the famous Jazz at the Philharmonic touring packages.

Webster, Daniel 1782–1852 •*US lawyer and politician*• Born in Salisbury, New Hampshire, he was called to the bar in 1805 and served in the US House of Representatives (1813–17). Settling in Boston as a lawyer in 1816, he became famous as an orator, returned to Congress in 1823 and in 1827 was elected to the Senate. His career was marked by a reverence for established institutions. When the Whig Party triumphed in 1840, he was called into Benjamin Harrison's cabinet as secretary of state (1841–43). Under President **John Tyler** he negotiated the Webster-Ashburton Treaty (1842) with Great Britain. He resigned from the cabinet in 1843. In 1844 he refused his party's nomination for president and supported **Henry Clay**. In 1850 he voiced his abhorrence of slavery and, unwilling to break up the Union to abolish it, supported compromise measures. Under President **Millard Fillmore**, he was recalled as secretary of state (1850–52) to settle differences with England. His speeches were published in 1851.

Webster, John c. 1580–c. 1625 •*English dramatist*• He is supposed to have been at one time clerk of St Andrews, Holborn, London. In *Lady Jane* and *The Two Harpies* (both lost) he collaborated with **Thomas Dekker**, **Michael Drayton**, **Henry Chettle** and others, and in 1604 he made some additions to *The Malcontent* of **John Marston**. His other collaborations with Dekker include the *Famous History of Sir Thomas Wyat*, *Westward Hoe* and *Northward Hoe* (all 1607). He is best known, however, for his two tragedies, *The White Devil* (1612) and *The Duchess of Malfi* (1623). He was not popular in his own day, and his stature was first recognized by **Charles Lamb**.

“ ”

They that sleep with dogs shall rise with fleas.

1612 ***The White Devil****, act 5, scene 1.*

Webster, Noah 1758–1843 •*US lexicographer*• Born in West Hartford, Connecticut, he graduated from Yale and, after a stint as a teacher, was admitted to the bar in 1781. He soon, however, resumed teaching and published the first part of *A Grammatical Institute of the English Language* (1783), which became very popular. He later published *A Compendious Dictionary of the English Language* (1806), an English grammar (1807) and the great *American Dictionary of the English Language* (2 vols, 1828), now *Webster's New International Dictionary of the English Language*. He was a fervent nationalist, and his efforts to standardize US spelling and grammar were informed by his vision of the US as a nation distinct from Britain by historical destiny.

Weddell, James 1787–1834 •*English navigator*• Born in Ostend, Belgium, on his principal voyage (1822–23) he penetrated to 74°15' south by 34°17' west in Antarctica. Weddell Sea and Weddell Quadrant there are named after him, as is a type of seal which he found.

Wedekind, Frank 1864–1918 •*German dramatist*• Born in Hanover, the son of a doctor and an actress, he grew up in Switzerland but returned to Germany, where he was an actor and cabaret singer as well as a writer. He won fame with *Erdgeist* (1895, Eng trans *Earth Spirit*, 1914), *Frühlings Erwachen* (1891, first performed 1906, Eng trans *The Awakening of Spring*, 1909; better known as *Spring Awakening*, the title of the 1980 translation), *Die Büchse der Pandora* (1903, first performed 1918, Eng trans *Pandora's Box*, 1918) and other unconventional tragedies which foreshadowed the emergence of the expressionist movement in both their themes and performance styles. He was imprisoned in 1899 after publishing satirical poems in *Simplicissimus* in Munich.

Wedgwood, Josiah 1730–95 •*English potter*• Born in Burslem, Staffordshire, he worked in the family pottery business, became a partner in a Staffordshire firm in 1754, and patented a cream-colored ware (Queen's ware) in 1763. He emulated antique models, producing the unglazed blue Jasper ware with its raised designs in white and the black basalt ware. His products and their imitations were named after him (Wedgwood ware). From 1775 he employed **John Flaxman** as designer.

Wedgwood, Dame (Cicely) Veronica 1910–97 •*English historian*• Born in Stocksfield, Northumberland, she studied at Lady Margaret Hall, Oxford, and specialized in 17th-century history. Her publications include the biographies *Strafford* (1935), *Oliver Cromwell* (1939) and *William the Silent* (1944, James Tait Black Memorial Prize), as well as *The Thirty Years' War* (1938), *The King's War* (1958) and *The Trial of Charles I* (1964). A more recent work is a collection of essays, *History and Hope* (1987). She was given the honorary title of Dame Commander, Order of the British Empire, in 1968 and appointed to the Order of Merit in 1969.

Weems, Mason Locke, *known as* **Parson Weems** 1759–1825 •*US clergyman and author*• Born in Anne Arundel County, Maryland, he became an itinerant evangelist and bookseller whose laudatory fictionalized biography of **George Washington** (first published in 1800) was popular for decades. The 1806 edition contains the apocryphal story of Washington's chopping down his father's cherry tree.

Wegener, Alfred Lothar 1880–1930 •*German meteorologist and geophysicist*• Born in Berlin and educated at the Universities of Heidelberg, Innsbruck and Berlin, he first worked as an astronomer. In 1906 he joined a Danish expedition to northeast Greenland and learned the techniques of polar travel. On his return he became a lecturer in astronomy and meteorology at the University of Marburg. After World War I he joined the German Marine Observatory in Hamburg and was also Professor of Meteorology in Graz, Austria (1924). *Die Entstehung der Kontinente und Ozeane* ("The Origin of Continents and Oceans"), first published in 1915, is based on his observations that the continents may once have been joined into one supercontinent (Pangaea) which later broke up, the fragments drifting apart to form the continents as they are today. Wegener provided historical, geological, geomorphological, climatic and paleontological evidence, but at that time no logical mechanism was known by which continents could drift, and the hypothesis remained controversial until the 1960s, when the structure of oceans became understood.

Weierstrass, Karl Theodor Wilhelm 1815–97 •*German mathematician*• Born in Ostenfelde and educated at the Universities of Bonn and Münster, he became a professor at Berlin University in 1856. He became famous for his lectures, in which he gave a systematic account of analysis with previously unknown rigor, basing complex function theory on power series, in contrast to the approach of **Augustin-Louis Cauchy** and **Bernhard Riemann**. He made important advances in the theory of elliptic and Abelian functions, constructed the first accepted example of a continuous but nowhere-differentiable function, and showed that every continuous function could be uniformly approximated by polynomials. Many of his most profound ideas grew out of his attempts to present a completely systematic, self-contained account of contemporary mathematics.

Weigel, Helene 1900–71 •*German actress-manager*• Born in Austria, she began her acting career in Frankfurt but went to Berlin (1923) and met **Bertolt Brecht**, whom she married (1929). She accompanied him in his exile from Germany (1933–48). On their return to East Berlin (1948), she and Brecht cofounded and ran the Berliner Ensemble, regarded as one of the great world theater companies. She became a leading exponent of Brecht's work, took control of the Berliner Ensemble after his death in 1956, and was instrumental in furthering his influence internationally.

Weil, André 1906–98 •*French mathematician*• Born in Paris, he studied at the University of Paris, and spent two years in India and some time in Strasbourg (1933–40), the US (1941–42, 1947–58) and Brazil (1945–47) before settling at Princeton University in 1958. He worked on number theory, algebraic geometry and topological group theory, was one of the founders of the **Bourbaki** group, and wrote on the history of mathematics. Weil did much to extend the theory of algebraic geometry to varieties of any dimension and to define them over fields of arbitrary characteristics. The brother of **Simone Weil**, he was one of the most brilliant mathematicians of the 20th century.

Weil, Simone 1909–43 •*French philosopher and mystic*• Born in Paris into a Jewish intellectual family, she had a brilliant academic career, and subsequently taught philosophy in schools (1931–38), worked for an anarchist trade union and in a factory, shared her wages with the unemployed, and lived in poverty. She fought against General **Franco** in the Spanish civil war and then moved to England, where she died of anorexia. In her profound theological thinking she concluded that God, who certainly existed and exists, withdrew himself from the universe after creating it; humanity is obliged to withdraw itself likewise from material considerations, and thus return to God. She is seen at her best in her *Cahiers* (1951–56, Eng trans *Notebooks*, 1956) and in *Seventy Letters* (1965). Other influential books include *L'attente de Dieu* (1949, Eng trans *Waiting for God*, 1959) and *L'enracinement* (1949–50, Eng trans *The Need for Roots*, 1955). Although she has been accused of overparadoxicality, she increasingly and successfully strove to make herself clear to her readers, eschewing all pretension.

" "

Tous les péchés sont des tentatives pour combler des vides.
All sins are attempts to fill voids.

1947 ***La Pesanteur et la Grâce.***

Weill, Kurt 1900–50 •*US composer*• Born in Dessau, Germany, he studied under **Engelbert Humperdinck** and **Ferruccio Busoni**, and early works included chamber music, two symphonies (1921, 1933) and some stage works. He achieved fame with *Die Dreigroschenoper*, **Bertolt Brecht**'s modernization of **John Gay**'s *Beggar's Opera*, in 1928. Other works of that time included *Aufstieg und Fall der Stadt Mahagonny* (1927–29, "Rise and Fall of the City of Mahagonny"), *Die sieben Todsünden* (1933, "Seven Deadly Sins"), both with Brecht, and *Der Silbersee* (1933). A refugee from the Nazis, he settled in the USA in 1934, becoming a US citizen in 1943. In all his works Weill was influenced by jazz idioms, and his later songs, operas and musical comedies, many of which contain elements of social criticism. Later pieces for the US stage include *Street Scene* (1946) and *Lost in the Stars* (1949).

Weinberg, Steven 1933– •*US physicist and Nobel Prize winner*• Born in New York City, he was educated at Cornell and Princeton Universities and held appointments at Columbia University, the University of California at Berkeley, MIT and Harvard before becoming Josey Regental Professor of Science at the University of Texas in 1982. In 1967 he unified the electromagnetic and weak nuclear forces and predicted a new interaction due to neutral currents, whereby a chargeless particle is exchanged, giving rise to a force between particles. This was duly observed in 1973, giving strong support to the theory (now called the Weinberg-Salam theory). As the work was independently developed by Weinberg and **Abdus Salam**, and subsequently extended by **Sheldon Glashow**, all three shared the 1979 Nobel Prize for physics. *The Quantum Theory of Fields* is a recent publication (1995–2000).

Weinberger, Caspar Willard 1917– •*US politician*• Born in San Francisco, after military service (1941–45) he trained and worked as a lawyer before entering politics as a member of the California state legislature in 1952. He served as finance director (1968–69) in the California administration of **Ronald Reagan** and then moved to Washington, becoming secretary of health, education and welfare (1973–75) in the **Nixon** and **Ford** administrations. Following a period in private industry, he was appointed defense secretary by President Reagan with the mandate to oversee a major military build-up. This he successfully did, developing such high-profile projects as the Strategic Defense Initiative. A hawk with respect to East-West issues, Weinberger opposed the rapprochement with the USSR during the final years of the Reagan administration and resigned in 1987. He published *Fighting for Peace* in 1990 and has been chairman of *Forbes Magazine* since 1993.

Weir, Dame Gillian Constance 1941– •*New Zealand organist and harpsichordist*• Born in Martinborough, Wellington, she studied at the Royal College of Music, London, where she won an international organ competition in 1964. In 1965 she made her international debut as a concert organist at the Royal Festival Hall, London, and has since appeared with leading orchestras under

Claudio Abbado, Sir **Charles Mackerras** and others. She had her own BBC television series, *The King of Instruments*, and is a regular writer, commentator and adjudicator, as well as a consultant on organ design. She was given the honorary title of Dame Commander, Order of the British Empire, in 1996.

Weir, Judith 1954– •*Scottish lecturer and composer*• Born in Cambridge to Scottish parents, she was taught by **John Tavener**, Robin Holloway and **Olivier Messiaen**. She was educated at King's College, Cambridge, and was composer in residence at the Royal Scottish Academy of Music (1988–91). She had notable success with her operas *The Black Spider* (1984), *A Night at the Chinese Opera* (Kent Opera, 1987) and *The Vanishing Bridegroom* (Scottish Opera, 1990). Other vocal works include *The Consolations of Scholarship* (1985), *Lovers, Learners and Libations* (1987), *Missa del Cid* (1988) and *Heaven Ablaze* (1989), with two pianos and eight dancers. Her instrumental works include keyboard music, a string quartet (1990), and *Sederunt Principes* (1987, for chamber orchestra), among others.

Weir, Peter Lindsay 1944– •*Australian film director*• Born in Sydney and educated at the University of Sydney, his early films *Michael* (1970) and *Homesdale* (1971) both won the Australian Film Institute Grand Prix. His feature film debut, *The Cars That Ate Paris* (1974), and the dreamlike ghost story *Picnic at Hanging Rock* (1975) established his reputation. *The Last Wave* (1977) illustrated his fascination with the clash between ancient and modern cultures. Since then he has looked increasingly to international projects, bringing his imaginative flair, sensitivity, and atmosphere of mystery to such films as *The Year of Living Dangerously* (1982), *Dead Poets Society* (1989) and *Fearless* (1993).

Weissmuller, Johnny (Peter John), *originally* **Jonas Weismuller** 1903–84 •*US swimmer and actor*• Born in Freidorf, Romania, he emigrated with his family to the US in 1908. He was the first man to swim 100 meters in under one minute and 440 yards (402 meters) in less than five minutes. Undefeated from 1921 to 1928, he won a total of five Olympic gold medals. After turning professional in 1932, he modeled swimwear. His physique, swimming prowess and popularity won him the film role of Tarzan in 19 films (1932–48).

Weizmann, Chaim Azriel 1874–1952 •*Russian chemist and Zionist leader and first president of Israel*• Born in Motol (near Pinsk, now in Belarus), of humble Jewish parentage, he began his scientific education at the gymnasium in Pinsk and later moved to Darmstadt (1893–94), Berlin, Fribourg and Geneva, where he produced a number of commercially profitable patents on dyestuffs. By this time he was already an important figure in the Zionist movement. In 1904 he moved to Manchester where he continued his work on dyestuffs and commenced a series of studies of fermentation. In 1912 he found a bacterium, *Clostridium acetobutylium*, which would convert carbohydrate into acetone. This process was of great importance in World War I, as acetone is used in large quantities to plasticize the propellant cordite. Partly out of gratitude for the development of the acetone process, the government agreed to the Balfour Declaration promising British help in establishing a Jewish homeland. The Daniel Sieff (later Weizmann) Institute of Science in Rehovot was founded in 1934 and Weizmann continued his research there. In 1948 he became the first president of Israel and his scientific work ceased.

Weizsäcker, Richard, Freiherr von 1920– •*West German politician*• Born in Stuttgart, the son of a baron-diplomat who was tried at Nuremberg, he was educated at Berlin, Oxford, Grenoble and Göttingen Universities. During World War II he served in the Wehrmacht, and after the war he worked as a professional lawyer and was active in the German Protestant Church, becoming president of its congress (1964–70). A member of the conservative Christian Democratic Union (CDU) from 1954, he served as a deputy in the Bundestag from 1969, as CDU deputy chairman (1972–79) and, from 1981, as a successful mayor of West Berlin before being elected federal president in May 1984. A cultured, centrist Christian Democrat, he urged Germans never to forget the lessons of the Nazi era. Weizsacker finally stepped down as president in 1994, after the maximum 10 years, amid enthusiastic tributes from all sides.

Welch, Raquel, *originally* **Raquel Tejada** 1940– •*US actress*• Born in Chicago, as a child she studied ballet and began entering beauty contests as a teenager. A model, waitress and television "weather girl" before making her film debut in *A House Is Not a Home* (1964), she was launched as a curvaceous sex symbol after her scantily clad appearance in *One Million Years B.C.* (1966). She displayed comedic ability in *The Three Musketeers* (1973), for which she received a Best Actress Golden Globe Award. A nightclub entertainer and best-selling author of health and beauty books and videos, she has also found some success on stage, notably in the Broadway musical *Woman of the Year* (1982). She returned to the cinema for the first time since 1977 in *Naked Gun 33⅓: The Final Insult* (1994).

Weldon, Fay, *originally* **Franklin Birkinshaw** 1931– •*English novelist, television screenplay writer and polemicist*• Born in Alvechurch, Worcestershire, she attended the University of St Andrews. She became a successful advertising copywriter before publishing her first novel, *The Fat Woman's Joke* (1967). Her recurring themes include the nature of women's sexuality and experience in a patriarchal world. Her novels include *The Life and Loves of a She-Devil* (1983), in which an ugly and rejected heroine seeks retribution, *Puffball* (1980), which looks at pregnancy and womanhood, and *The Cloning of Joanna May* (1989, televised 1992), which considers genetic engineering. A number of her novels have been televised. More recent works include *The Bulgari Connection* (2001).

Welensky, Sir Roy 1907–91 •*Rhodesian politician*• Born in Salisbury, Southern Rhodesia, he was educated in local schools and then started work on the railways at the age of 14. He became leader of the Railway Workers' Union in Northern Rhodesia in 1933, by which time he had also been heavyweight boxing champion (1926–28). Elected to the Northern Rhodesia Legislative Council in 1938, he founded the Northern Rhodesia Labour Party in 1941 and became chairman of the unofficial opposition in 1946. A strong supporter of the proposed Federation of Rhodesia and Nyasaland, he was elected to its first parliament. He succeeded Sir **Godfrey Huggins** (Lord Malvern) as prime minister in 1956, a post he held until the federation's breakup at the end of 1963. Although considered a champion of white rule, he was strongly opposed to Southern Rhodesia's UDI (Unilateral Declaration of Independence).

Welland, Colin 1934– •*English playwright and actor*• Born in Liverpool, he studied at Goldsmiths College, London, and worked as an art teacher from 1958 to 1962. In the early 1960s he began taking stage and film roles, and won a British Academy of Film and Television Arts award for Best Supporting Actor in *Kes* (1969). He wrote the screenplays for *Yanks* (1978) and *Chariots of Fire* (1980) and has written widely for television, including the plays *Say Goodnight to Grandma* (1973) and *Roll On Four O'Clock* (1981).

Weller, Thomas Huckle 1915– •*US virologist and Nobel Prize winner*• Born in Ann Arbor, Michigan, he studied at the University of Michigan and Harvard University Medical School under **John Enders**. During World War II he conducted research into tropical diseases, and after the war Enders invited Weller and **Frederick Robbins** to join him at the newly created Infectious Diseases Research Laboratory at Children's Hospital, Boston. Weller and his colleagues developed new techniques for cultivating the poliomyelitis virus which made it possible for other workers to develop the polio vaccine. For this achievement Weller, Enders and Robbins shared the 1954 Nobel Prize for physiology or medicine. Weller also isolated the causative agents of chickenpox, shingles and German measles, and discovered a new viral etiology of congenital damage, a virus he named "cytomegalovirus." In 1954 he was named Strong Professor and head of the Department of Tropical Public Health at Harvard, a post he held until 1981.

Welles, (George) Orson 1915–85 •*US film director and actor*• Born in Kenosha, Wisconsin, he appeared at the Gate Theatre, Dublin (1931), returned to America, became a radio producer (1934), and founded the Mercury Theater (1937). His 1938 radio production of **H G Wells**'s *War of the Worlds* was so realistic that it caused panic in the US. He wrote, produced, directed and acted in *Citizen Kane* (1941), a revolutionary landmark in cinema technique, and produced and directed a screen version of **Booth Tarkington**'s *The*

Magnificent Ambersons (1942). His later work, giving ample rein to his unpredictable talents, includes his individual film versions of *Macbeth* (1948), *Othello* (1951), **Franz Kafka**'s *The Trial* (1962) and *Chimes at Midnight* (1965, based on **Shakespeare**'s Falstaff character). As an actor, the most notable of his varied and memorable stage and film performances was as Harry Lime in *The Third Man* (1949).

" "

A film is never really good unless the camera is an eye in the head of a poet.
1958 "Un ruban de rêves" in L'Express, June 5. Reprinted in English in ***International Film Annual****, no. 2.*

Wellington, Arthur Wellesley, 1st Duke of, *known as* **the Iron Duke** 1769–1852 •*Irish-born soldier and statesman*• He was born in Dublin, the son of an Irish peer. He studied at Chelsea, Eton and Brussels, and in a military school in Angers. In 1787 he was appointed to an ensign's commission in the 73rd Foot, and after service in other regiments was promoted to the rank of captain. He also served as aide-de-camp for two lord lieutenants of Ireland and was member for Trim in the Irish parliament (1790–95). He took command of the 33rd Foot, and in 1797 his regiment was sent to India. He was dispatched to deal with **Tippoo Sahib** of Mysore and, as brigade commander under General George Harris (1746–1829), did admirable work throughout the Seringapatam expedition and as subsequent administrator of the conquered territory. His campaigns against Holkar and Scindia resulted in the capture of Poona (1803), the breaking of Maratha power at Ahmednagar and Assaye, and final victory at Argaum. On his return home he was knighted (1805). He was elected MP for Rye (1806–09), and appointed Irish secretary in 1807. He was released from his parliamentary duties to accompany the Copenhagen expedition the same year, and defeated the Danes at Sjaelland. In 1808 he was sent to help the Portuguese against the French in the Peninsular War, winning victories at Roliça and Vimeiro. He resumed his parliamentary post, but **John Moore**'s retreat on La Coruña sent him back, in 1809, to assume chief command on the Peninsula. Talavera (July 1809) was nearly a blunder, but it was quickly retrieved, and Wellesley was elevated to the peerage (as Viscount Wellington) after his victory. Salamanca (July 1812) was a decisive victory and, although there were minor setbacks, ultimately the French were driven out of Spain and brought to submission at Toulouse in 1814. Made Duke of Wellington and heaped with honors, after the first Treaty of Paris he was appointed ambassador to **Louis XVIII**, the newly restored king of France. He remained in Paris until the Congress of Vienna, where for a brief period he served as Viscount **Castlereagh**'s replacement. On learning of **Napoleon I**'s escape from Elba, Wellington hastened from the Congress to take command of the scratch force (which he called "an infamous army") mustered to oppose him. After the defeat of **Blücher** and his supporting forces at Ligny, Wellington took up opposition on the well-reconnoitered field of Waterloo, where the French were routed on June 18, 1815. Following this he was appointed commander in chief during the occupation of France (1815–18). In 1818 he returned to politics, joining the **Liverpool** administration as master general of the ordnance. In 1826 he was made constable of the Tower, and in 1827 commander in chief, an office in which he was confirmed for life in 1842. He had represented Great Britain at the Congress of Aix-la-Chapelle (1818) and the Congress of Verona (1822), and in 1826 was sent to Russia by **George Canning** to negotiate binding Britain, France and Russia to impose recognition of Greek autonomy on Turkey; the Duke disapproved of Canning's foreign policy so strongly that he resigned, but with Canning's death in 1827 and the collapse of the nebulous Goderich administration, he became prime minister. In general, Wellington's political policy was to refrain from weakening established authority and to avoid foreign entanglements, since Britain did not now possess an army adequate to enforce her will. In the political crisis of 1834 Wellington again formed a government, and in Peel's temporary absence abroad he acted for all the secretaries of state. With Peel's return to power in 1841, Wellington joined his cabinet, but without an appointment. He retired from public life in 1846. He was buried in St Paul's Cathedral.

Wells, Allan 1952– •*Scottish athlete*• Born in Edinburgh, the most successful Scottish sprinter since **Eric Liddell**, he was initially more noteworthy as a long jumper, achieving his first Scottish title when he won the under-15 championship in that event. It was not until 1976 that he concentrated on sprinting. Two years later he won Commonwealth gold in the 100 meters. In the Moscow Olympics of 1980 he became the oldest winner to date of the 100 meters, and in the 1982 Commonwealth Games won the 100 and 200 meters.

Wells, H(erbert) G(eorge) 1866–1946 •*English novelist, short-story writer and popular historian*• Born in Bromley, Kent, he became a draper's apprentice, then a pupil teacher at the Midhurst Grammar School, where he won a scholarship to the Normal School of Science, South Kensington, and studied biology under **T H Huxley**. He then lectured until the success of his short stories allowed him to concentrate full-time on writing. Idealistic, impatient and dynamic, he threw himself into contemporary issues—free love, Fabianism, progressive education, scientific theory, world government (he was an early agitator for a League of Nations) and human rights. His private life was no less restless than his public—he was married twice and had numerous affairs, notably with women who were feminists and intellectuals, including Elizabeth von Arnim and **Rebecca West**. He achieved fame as a novelist with *The Time Machine* (1895), an allegory set in the year 802701 describing a two-tiered society. It pioneered English science fiction and was followed by *The Invisible Man* (1897), *The War of the Worlds* (1898) and *The First Men in the Moon* (1901). He also wrote some of the best-known English comic novels—*Love and Mr Lewisham* (1900), *Kipps* (1905) and *The History of Mr Polly* (1910). His other works include *The Outline of History* (1920), which enjoyed a vast circulation, *The Shape of Things to Come* (1933), a plea to confront Fascism before it was too late, and the despairing *Mind at the End of Its Tether* (1945). *Experiment in Autobiography* (1934) contains a striking self-portrait and studies of friends and contemporaries.

Wells, John Campbell 1936–98 •*English actor, dramatist, humorist and director*• Born in Ashford, Kent, he studied French and German at Oxford and taught both languages at Eton (1961–63) while contributing material for revues at the Edinburgh Festival. He was a coeditor of the satirical magazine *Private Eye* (1964–67), and continued writing for the magazine throughout his life, most notably the supposed diary of Mrs Wilson, **Harold Wilson**'s wife, and the Dear Bill letters, the hypothetical correspondence of Denis Thatcher, husband of **Margaret Thatcher**. He wrote a number of plays for the theater, including *Anyone for Denis* (1981), in which Wells played the title role. He was also highly regarded as a translator of plays and opera from French and German. He directed a revival of *The Mikado* in 1989. His publications include *Princess Caraboo: Her True Story* (1994).

Wells-Barnett, Ida, *née* **Wells** 1862–1931 •*US journalist and activist*• Born to slave parents in Holly Springs, Mississippi, she became a teacher before turning to journalism. In 1895 she married Ferdinand Lee Barnett, the editor of the *Chicago Conservator*. She was an active campaigner against lynching and chronicled crimes in a pamphlet entitled *Southern Horrors* (1892). She was also one of two women who signed a call for the formation of the NAACP (National Association for the Advancement of Colored People) and, on her own, founded the first African-American woman suffrage organization, entitled the Alpha Suffrage Club of Chicago.

Welty, Eudora 1909–2001 •*US novelist and short-story writer*• She was born in Jackson, Mississippi, and educated at the Mississippi State College for Women, the University of Wisconsin and the Columbia University School of Business. A publicity agent with the Works Progress Administration in Mississippi, she traveled extensively in the state and took numerous photographs, which were later published as *One Time, One Place: Mississippi in the Depression: A Snapshot Album* (1971). During World War II she was on the staff of the *New York Review of Books*. She started writing short stories with "Death of a Traveling Salesman" (1936), and published several collections from 1941 to 1954. She also wrote five novels, mostly drawn from Mississippi life including *The Robber Bridegroom* (1942) and *The Optimist's Daughter* (1972). Among her many accolades, she received two Guggenheim Fellowships, three **O Henry** Awards, the

Pulitzer Prize and the National Medal for Literature. Her autobiography, *One Writer's Beginnings*, was published in 1984.

Wenceslas or **Wenceslaus, St**, *also called* **Good King Wenceslas** c. 907–29 •*Bohemian Prince-Duke and patron saint of Bohemia*• Born in Stochov, he was raised as a Christian by his grandmother. When he came of age (c. 924) he was free of his pagan mother's protectorate and could encourage German missionaries to come to Bohemia. He put his duchy under the protection of **Henry the Fowler** of Germany, and was murdered by his pagan brother Boleslaw. He was regarded as a symbol of Czech nationalism. His feast day is September 28.

Wenders, Wim 1945– •*German film director*• Born in Düsseldorf, he studied medicine and philosophy, then attended Munich's Cinema and Television College (1967–70), where he made his first short film, *Schauplätze* (1967). He made his feature debut with *Summer in the City* (1970). Concerned with the influence of American culture on postwar German society, his work deals with isolation and alienation, often involving journeys in search of enlightenment. These themes are especially evident in *Alice in den Stadten* (1974, *Alice in the Cities*) and *Der Stand den Dinge* (1982, *The State of Things*). He has been frequently honored by the Cannes Film Festival, winning the International Critics Award for *Im Lauf der Zeit* (1976, *Kings of the Road*), the Golden Palm for *Paris, Texas* (1984) and Best Director for *Der Himmel über Berlin* (1987, *Wings of Desire*). Recent films include *Until the End of the World* (1991) and *The End of Violence* (1997).

Wenner-Gren, Axel Leonard 1881–1961 •*Swedish financier, industrialist and philanthropist*• He founded AB Electrolux in 1919, which he owned until 1956. Through Electrolux he also launched the Platen-Munter refrigerator. He owned Svenska Cellulosa AB from 1934 to 1941 and had interests in AB Bofors, but from 1930 onward he spent most of his time developing business interests abroad. During his lifetime and in his will he donated vast sums to institutions for scientific research, the best known of which are the Wenner-Gren Institut for experimental biology (1937, part of Stockholm University), the Wenner-Gren Foundation for anthropological research, established in New York in 1941, and above all the Wenner-Gren Center, an international scientific research center set up in Stockholm in 1962.

Wentworth, Charles Watson *See* **Rockingham, Charles Watson-Wentworth**

Wentworth, Thomas *See* **Strafford, 1st Earl of**

Wergeland, (Jacobine) Camilla *See* **Collett, (Jacobine) Camilla**

Werner, Abraham Gottlob 1749–1817 •*German geologist*• Born in Wehrau, Silesia (now in Poland), he gave his name to the Wernerian (or Neptunian) theory of deposition. In essence Werner advocated that crystalline igneous rocks were formed by direct precipitation from sea water, as part of his overall system of strata from the crystalline "primitive rocks," succeeded by the "transition rocks"—resting on highly inclined strata—the flat-lying and well-stratified "floetz rocks" and finally the poorly stratified alluvial series. The Plutonists, led by **James Hutton**, were able to demonstrate the intrusive nature of such rocks. Werner was one of the great geological teachers of his time and many scholars, including **Goethe**, studied with him.

Wernicke, Carl 1848–1905 •*German neurologist and psychiatrist*• Born in Tarnowitz, Upper Silesia (now in Poland), he qualified in medicine at the University of Breslau (Wrocław, Poland), and in 1874 he published *Der aphasische Symptomencomplex* ("The Aphasic Syndrome"). The form of aphasia, loss of speech, which he described was marked by a severe defect in the understanding of speech, and it became known as sensory aphasia. This was in contrast to the motor aphasia proposed by **Paul Broca**. From postmortem studies on his patients' brains, Wernicke showed that his type of aphasia was typically localized in the left temporal lobe, now known as Wernicke's area. He established a clinic in Berlin specializing in diseases of the nervous system, moving to Breslau in 1885 and in 1904 to Halle, where he died as a result of an accident.

Wertheimer, Max 1880–1943 •*German psychologist and philosopher*• He was born in Prague. After studying there and in Berlin and Würzburg, he conducted experiments in perception (1912) with **Kurt Koffka** and **Wolfgang Köhler** which led to the founding of the Gestalt school of psychology. He was a professor at Berlin and Frankfurt, but he left Germany for the US in 1933 at the Nazi assumption of power and taught at the New School for Social Research in New York City (1933–43).

Wesker, Arnold 1932– •*English dramatist*• He was born in London's East End, of Jewish immigrant parents, and left school at 14. His family background and attempts to earn a living are important ingredients of such plays as the Kahn family trilogy, *Chicken Soup With Barley, Roots* and *I'm Talking About Jerusalem* (1958–60). *Roots* is an aesthetic recipe for all he attempted to put into practice by taking art to the workers through his Centre-42 (1961–70), which was situated in an old locomotive shed in Camden Town, London, and which was heavily involved with the trade union movement. Other plays include *Chips With Everything* (1962), *The Four Seasons* (1965) and *Love Letters on Blue Paper* (1978), originally written for television in 1976. He also wrote the essay collection *Fears of Fragmentation* (1970) and *Words—As Definitions of Experience* (1976). A one-woman play, *Annie Wobbler* (1984), was well received, and his plays were collected in five volumes in 1989–90, but so far his reputation rests firmly on his earliest works. Recent works include the plays *Wild Spring* (1992) and *Tokyo* (1994), and the autobiography *As Much As I Dare* (1994).

Wesley, Charles 1707–88 •*English hymnwriter, evangelist and founder of Methodism*• He was born in Epworth, Lincolnshire. He studied at Christ Church, Oxford, where he experienced spiritual renewal, which led him in 1729 to form a small group of fellow students, nicknamed the Holy Club, or the Oxford Methodists, who were later joined by his brother **John Wesley**. Ordained in 1735, he accompanied John to Georgia as secretary to Governor **James Oglethorpe**, but returned to England in 1738. After another spiritual experience in 1738, when he found himself "at peace with God," he became an evangelist and wrote over 5,500 hymns, including "Jesu, Lover of My Soul," "Hark, the Herald Angels Sing," "Love Divine, All Loves Excelling" and "Christ the Lord Is Ris'n Today."

Wesley, John 1703–91 •*English evangelist and founder of Methodism*• He was born in Epworth, Lincolnshire, where his father was rector. He studied at Oxford, was ordained deacon in 1725 and priest in 1728. He was much influenced by the spiritual writings of **William Law**, and became the leader of a small dedicated group which had gathered around his brother **Charles Wesley**. The group was nicknamed the Holy Club and the Oxford Methodists, a name later adopted by John for the adherents of the great evangelical movement which developed from it. They were joined in 1730 by James Hervey and **George Whitefield**. When their father died (1735), John and Charles went on a missionary journey to Georgia, but they aroused the hostility of the colonists and returned to England (1738). John had been influenced by Moravians on the voyage out, and now he met Peter Böhler and attended society meetings. At one of these, held in Aldersgate Street, during the reading of **Martin Luther**'s preface to the Epistle to the Romans, he experienced an assurance of salvation which convinced him that he must bring the same to others. But his unwonted zeal alarmed and angered most of the parish clergy, who closed their pulpits against him; this intolerance, Whitefield's example, and the needs of the masses drove him into the open air at Bristol (1739). John founded the first Methodist chapel in Bristol, and in London he bought the ruinous foundry in Moorfields, which he used to preach in and as his headquarters. During his itineraries, 10,000 to 30,000 people would wait patiently for hours to hear him. He gave his strength to working-class neighborhoods, and most of his converts were colliers, miners, foundrymen, weavers, and day laborers in towns. He traveled 250,000 miles and preached 40,000 sermons, yet he also achieved an enormous amount of literary work, producing grammars, extracts from the classics, histories, abridged biographies, collections of psalms, hymns and tunes, his own sermons and journals. He also founded the *Methodist Magazine* (1778). He founded charitable institutions at

Newcastle and London and Kingswood School in Bristol. Wesley broke with the Moravians in 1745. He was determined to remain loyal to the Church of England and urged his followers to do the same; although he ordained one of his assistants (**Francis Asbury**) for work in the US, he always regarded Methodism as a movement within the Church, and it remained so during his lifetime. His journeys and spiritual odyssey were recorded in his *Journal*.

Wesley, Mary, *pseudonym of* **Mary Aline Siepmann**, *née* **Farmar** 1912–2002 •*English novelist*• She was born in Englefield Green, Berkshire. She wrote two children's books before publishing her first adult novel, *Jumping the Queue*, in 1983, at the age of 70. After that, she produced a succession of books dealing with middle-class mores, each written with ironic, detached amusement and taking an unblinkered though compassionate look at sexual values. One of the best known is *The Camomile Lawn* (1984), which considers sexual and emotional relationships in the turmoil of World War II. It was made into a television series in 1991.

Wessel, Horst 1907–30 •*German National Socialist*• He was born in Bielefeld. He was the composer of the Nazi anthem "Die Fahne hoch," known as the Horst Wessel song.

Wessex, Prince Edward, Earl of, *in full* **Edward Antony Richard Louis** 1964– •*British prince*• The third son of Queen **Elizabeth II**, he was educated at Gordonstoun and then spent several months as a house tutor in New Zealand at Wanganui Collegiate School. After studying history at Jesus College, Cambridge, he joined the Royal Marines (1986) but left the following year and began a career in the theater as a production assistant with **Andrew Lloyd Webber**'s Really Useful Theatre Company. In 1993 he set up his own production company, Ardent Productions. In 1999 he married and took the title Earl of Wessex, with his wife, Sophie Rhys-Jones, becoming **Sophie Wessex**.

Wessex, Sophie, Countess of, *née* **Rhys-Jones** 1965– •*British countess and public relations consultant*• Born in Oxford, she attended West Kent College girls' school and worked as a barmaid, press officer, and holiday representative before setting up her own public relations company, R-J H, with her business partner, Murray Harkin, in 1996. She married Prince **Edward** in 1999 and changed her name to Sophie Wessex, but she continued to pursue an independent career.

Wesson, Daniel Baird 1825–1906 •*US gunsmith*• He was born in Worcester, Massachusetts. With Horace Smith (1808–93) he devised a new type of repeating mechanism for small arms (1854) and founded the firm of Smith & Wesson in Springfield, Massachusetts, in 1857.

West, Benjamin 1738–1820 •*British painter*• Born in Springfield, Pennsylvania, he showed early promise as a portraitist and was sent on a sponsored visit to Italy. On his return in 1763, he was induced to settle in London. **George III** was his patron for 40 years. The representation of modern instead of classical costume in his best-known picture, *The Death of General Wolfe* (1771), was an innovation in English historical painting.

West, Mae 1893–1980 •*US vaudeville performer and film actress*• Born in Brooklyn, New York, she made her debut on Broadway in 1911, exploiting her voluptuousness in roles of sultry sexual innuendo. Noted for her wit, she wrote many of the plays she starred in, such as *Sex* (1926) and *Diamond Lil* (1928), which was later filmed as *She Done Him Wrong* with **Cary Grant** (1933). Her other films include *I'm No Angel* (1933), *Klondike Annie* (1936) and *My Little Chickadee* (1940). She returned to the screen in 1970 in *Myra Breckenridge*. The "Mae West," an inflatable life jacket, is affectionately named after her.

“ ”

When I'm good I'm very very good, but when I'm bad I'm better.

1933 ***I'm No Angel***

West, Morris Langlo 1916–99 •*Australian novelist and playwright*• Born in St Kilda, Victoria, he trained for the priesthood but left before taking vows. After war service he published his first novel, *Moon in My Pocket* (1945), which dealt with the conflicts facing a Catholic novitiate. In 1955 he left Australia for Italy, where his fourth novel, *Children of the Sun* (1957), a tale of Neapolitan slum urchins, attracted attention. *The Devil's Advocate* (1959, James Tait Black Memorial Prize, filmed 1977) became an international best-seller, and his subsequent books were eagerly awaited. They include prize-winning novels such as *The Shoes of the Fisherman* (1963), *Summer of the Red Wolf* (1971), *The Ringmaster* (1991), *Vanishing Point* (1996) and *A View From the Ridge* (1996). He dramatized several of his works.

West, Dame Rebecca, *pseudonym of* **Cecily Isabel Andrews**, *née* **Fairfield** 1892–1983 •*Irish novelist and critic*• She was born in County Kerry and educated at George Watson's Ladies College. She trained for the stage in London, where she adopted (1912) the pseudonym Rebecca West, the heroine of **Ibsen**'s *Rosmersholm*, which she had once played and who is characterized by a passionate will. She was involved with the suffragists from an early age, joined the staff of the *Freewoman* (1911) and became a political writer on the *Clarion*, a socialist newspaper (1912). Her love affair with **H G Wells** began in 1913 and lasted for ten turbulent years, during which time they had a son. Her first published book was a critical study of **Henry James** (1916). Her second, a novel, *The Return of the Soldier* (1918), describes the homecoming of a shell-shocked soldier. After the final break with Wells she went to the US, where she lectured and formed a long association with the *New York Herald Tribune*. In 1930 she married Henry Maxwell Andrews, a banker, and they lived in Buckinghamshire until his death in 1968. She published eight novels, including *Harriet Hume* (1929), *The Thinking Reed* (1936) and the largely autobiographical *The Fountain Overflows* (1957). Her last (unfinished) novel was *Cousin Rosamund* (1988). In the mid-1930s she made several trips to the Balkans that resulted in her masterful analysis of Yugoslav politics and history, *Black Lamb and Grey Falcon* (2 vols, 1941). During World War II she supervised BBC broadcasts to Yugoslavia, and she attended the Nuremberg war crimes trials (1945–46). From this and other cases came *The Meaning of Treason* (1949) and *A Train of Powder* (1955). Witty, incisive and combative, she was described by **George Bernard Shaw** as handling a pen "as brilliantly as ever I could and much more savagely."

West, Jerry (Jerome Alan) 1938– •*US basketball player, coach and general manager*• Born in Chelyan, West Virginia, he earned a reputation in college basketball as a guard with West Virginia University (1956–60) before being recruited by the Los Angeles Lakers. Nicknamed "Mister Clutch," over the next 14 years he became one of the highest-scoring players in the history of the NBA, breaking numerous records. Having led the LA Lakers to the NBA title as a player in 1972, he took them to another six championship titles as coach, general manager and ultimately executive vice president (1980, 1982, 1985, 1987–88 and 2000). He entered the NBA Hall of Fame in 1979 and also led the US Olympic team to the gold medal in 1960.

West, Rosemary *See* **West, Fred**

West, Thomas *See* **De la Warr, 3rd or 12th Baron**

West, Timothy 1934– •*English actor*• Born in Bradford, West Yorkshire, the son of actor Lockwood West, he started as an assistant stage manager at Wimbledon Theatre (1956) and went on to appear in many West End and Royal Shakespeare Company productions. His many television roles include Mortimer in *Edward II* (1970), the title role in *Edward the Seventh* (1975), Bounderby in *Hard Times* (1977), Wolsey in *Henry VIII* (1979), **Winston Churchill** in *Churchill and the Generals* (1979), Bradley Hardacre in *Brass* (1983, 1990) and Lord Reith in *Reith to the Nation* (1993). A later stage appearance was as Falstaff in the English Touring Company's production of **Shakespeare**'s *Henry IV*, parts I and II (1996–97). He is married to **Prunella Scales**.

Westinghouse, George 1846–1914 •*US engineer*• Born in Central Bridge, New York, he ran away from school to fight for the North in the Civil War, then served for a short time in the US Navy. In 1865 he took out the first of his more than 400 patents, for a railway steam locomotive. His most important invention was the air-brake system he patented in 1869, which became known as the Westinghouse air brake, which greatly increased the speed at which trains could safely travel. He later became a pioneer in the use of alternating current for distributing electric power, founding the Westinghouse Electrical Company in 1886 and attracting **Nikola Tesla** to work with him. In 1895 he successfully harnessed the power of the Niagara Falls to generate sufficient electricity for the town of Buffalo, 22 miles (35.4 km) away.

Westmoreland, William Childs 1914– •*US soldier*• Born in Spartanburg County, South Carolina, he graduated from West Point in 1936 and saw action in North Africa and Europe during World War II, and later in the Korean War. As the senior military commander of US forces in Vietnam (1964–68), General Westmoreland favored the strategy of escalating US involvement in the Vietnam War. After the Tet Offensive he was replaced as commander, and he returned to the US, where he served as army chief of staff (1968–72).

Weston, Edward 1886–1958 •*US photographer*• Born in Highland Park, Illinois, he established his own studio in Glendale, California (c. 1910), moving to Mexico in 1923. He became recognized as a Modernist, emphasizing sharp images and precise definition, and in 1932 joined **Ansel Adams** and others in forming the "straight photography" purists' Group f/64, in California. His close-up studies of inanimate objects such as shells and vegetables exemplified his vision of detailed form and the richness of his control of tone. He produced notable landscapes of the Mohave Desert and in 1937, with the first-ever award of a Guggenheim Fellowship to a photographer, traveled widely throughout the western states of the US. He followed this with a long tour of the southern and eastern states to illustrate an edition of **Walt Whitman**'s *Leaves of Grass*.

Westwood, Vivienne 1941– •*English fashion designer*• Born in London, she was a primary school teacher in early adulthood, then turned her attention to clothes design on meeting Malcolm McLaren, manager of the **Sex Pistols**. They established a shop in London and became known as the leading creators of punk clothing. Their designs, using rubber, leather and bondage gear, were influenced by the paraphernalia of pornography. Since her split from McLaren in 1983, she has become accepted by the mainstream, and was Designer of the Year in 1990 and 1991. She was Professor of Fashion at the Vienna Academy of Applied Arts (1989–91).

Weyden, Rogier van der, *real name* **Rogier de la Pasture** 1400–64 •*Flemish painter*• After the death of **Jan van Eyck** in 1441, he was the most important Early Netherlandish painter. Very little is known of his life, and even his identity has been disputed. Between 1435 and 1449 he was in Brussels, where he was appointed painter to the city. Patronized by the Burgundian court, his famous *Last Judgment* was painted for Chancellor Rolin. Akin to that of other members of the Early Netherlandish school in its meticulous attention to detail, Weyden's work is distinguished by its ability to convey drama and emotion.

Weygand, Maxime 1867–1965 •*French soldier*• He was born in Brussels. As chief of staff under **Ferdinand Foch** (1914–23), he served in World War I, and later became commander in chief of the army (1931). Retired in 1935, he was recalled in 1939 and in May 1940 he replaced Maurice Gamelin (1872–1958) as commander in chief, but it was too late for him to do much more than recommend an armistice. The Vichy government sent him as its delegate to North Africa, but he was recalled and imprisoned in Germany until the end of World War II. In 1948 he was brought before the High Court for his role in 1940, but the case was dropped and he retired into obscurity.

Wharton, Edith Newbold, *née* **Jones** c. 1861–1937 •*US novelist and short-story writer*• Born in New York into a wealthy and aristocratic family, she was educated at home and in Europe. In 1885 she married Edward Wharton, a friend of the family, and they traveled widely before settling in Paris in 1907. Her husband, however, was mentally unbalanced, and they were divorced in 1913. It was *The House of Mirth* (1905), a tragedy about a beautiful and sensitive girl who is destroyed by the very society her upbringing has designed her to inhabit, that established her as a major novelist. Many other works followed, almost 50 in all, including short stories, travel books and volumes of verse, but she is known principally as a novelist of manners, a witty, satirical, and keen observer of society. Her most uncharacteristic novel is *Ethan Frome* (1911), which deals partly with her unhappy marriage. Important later works are *The Age of Innocence* (1920), *The Children* (1928) and *Hudson River Bracketed* (1929). Socially gregarious, she formed a durable friendship with **Henry James**. Her approach to her work is discussed in *The Writing of Fiction* (1925). *A Backwards Glance* (1934) is her revealing autobiography.

“ ”

If I were shabby no one would have me: a woman is asked out as much for her clothes as for herself.

1905 ***The House of Mirth**, chapter 1.*

Wheatley, Phillis c. 1753–85 •*African-American poet*• Born in Africa, possibly Senegal, she was shipped to the slave market in Boston, Massachusetts, as a child (1761) and sold as a maidservant to the family of a Boston tailor, who educated her with the rest of his family. She studied Latin and Greek, and started writing poetry in English at the age of 13. She published *Poems on Various Subjects, Religious and Moral* (1783) and visited England that year, to huge popular interest, although some doubted her poems' authenticity. A *Collected Works* appeared in 1988.

Wheatstone, Sir Charles 1802–75 •*English physicist*• He was born in Gloucester, and first became known as a result of his work in acoustics. He invented the concertina in 1829, and in 1834 was appointed Professor of Experimental Physics at King's College London. In 1837 he and Sir William Cooke (1806–79) took out a patent for an electric telegraph, and in conjunction with the new London & Birmingham Railway Company, they installed a demonstration telegraph line about a mile (1.6 km) long. By 1852 more than 4,000 miles (6,436 km) of telegraph line were in operation throughout Britain. Wheatstone built the first printing telegraph in 1841, and in 1845 devised a single-needle instrument. In 1838, in a paper to the Royal Society (of which he had become a Fellow in 1836), he explained the principle of the stereoscope (later improved by **David Brewster**). He also invented a sound magnifier, for which he introduced the term "microphone." He was knighted in 1868.

Wheeler, Sir (Robert Eric) Mortimer 1890–1976 •*English archaeologist*• Born in Glasgow and educated at Bradford and London, he became director of the National Museum of Wales (1920) and director of the London Museum (1926–44). He carried out notable excavations in Great Britain at Verulamium (St Albans) and Maiden Castle, and from 1944 to 1947 was director general of archaeology in India working to particular effect at Mohenjo-daro and Harappa. He then became Professor of the Archaeology of the Roman Provinces at the newly founded Institute of Archaeology in London (1948–55). Knighted in 1952, he was well known for spirited popular accounts of his subject, in books and on television.

Whicker, Alan Donald 1925– •*English broadcaster and journalist*• Born in Cairo, he was commissioned in the Devonshire Regiment during World War II and served with the Army Film and Photo Unit. Thereafter, he was a war correspondent, reporting on the Inchon landings in Korea before joining the BBC (1957–68), where he worked on the *Tonight* program (1957–65) and began his *Whicker's World* documentary series in 1958. Television's most traveled man, he has broadcast on the rich and famous, as well as the exotic and extraordinary aspects of everyday lives in all parts of the world. He has received numerous awards, including the **Richard Dimbleby** award (1977). Later works for television include *Whicker's Miss World* (1993). His books include *Some Rise by Sin* (1949), the autobiography *Within Whicker's World* (1982) and *Whicker's World Down Under* (1988).

Whillans, Don(ald Desbrow) 1933–85 •*English mountaineer*• Born in Salford, he became one of the best-known figures in British mountaineering. His partnership with **Joe Brown** led to many higher-standard routes being put up on rock faces in the Peak District and North Wales. Whillans also climbed extensively in Scotland and the Alps, where he put up several new routes. From 1960 he concentrated on big expeditions, including the first ascent of the south face of Annapurna in the Himalayas (1970).

Whipple, Fred Lawrence 1906– •*US astronomer*• Born in Red Oak, Iowa, he studied at UCLA and became Professor of Astronomy at Harvard in 1945. An expert on the solar system (his *Earth, Moon and Planets* published in 1941 is a standard text), he is known especially for his work on comets. He was also the first to define the term "micrometeorite" and used the rate of decay of meteors as an indicator of the temperature profile of the atmosphere. With Fletcher Watson he was responsible for Harvard's two-station meteor program. He was the prime mover behind the production and use of the Baker Super-Schmidt meteor cameras, and he was a pioneer in the use of these cameras to observe the decay of satellite orbits. His meteoroid bumper shield was used to dissipate the energy of impacting dust particles on the Giotto mission to **Halley**'s comet, which confirmed his "dirty snowball" model. His publications include *The Mystery of Comets* (1985).

Whipple, George Hoyt 1878–1976 •*US pathologist and Nobel Prize winner*• Born in Ashland, New Hampshire, he studied at Yale and Johns Hopkins Universities. In 1914 he was appointed director of the Hooper Foundation for Medical Research at the University of California, and in 1921 Professor of Pathology and Dean of Medicine at the University of Rochester in New York. His research there laid the groundwork for **George Minot** and **William Murphy**'s successful treatment of pernicious anemia with liver (1926), until then a fatal disease, and the three men shared the 1934 Nobel Prize for physiology or medicine.

Whistler, James (Abbott) McNeill 1834–1903 •*US artist*• Born in Lowell, Massachusetts, he spent five years of his boyhood in St Petersburg (Leningrad), where his father, an engineer, was engaged on a railway project for the czar. After briefly returning home he left the US, never to return, and went to study art in Paris. He was deeply impressed by **Gustave Courbet** and later by the newly discovered **Katsushika Hokusai**, and he exhibited at the *Salon des réfusés*. London subsequently became the center of his activities, and he became celebrated as a portraitist. **John Ruskin**'s vitriolic criticism of his contributions to the Grosvenor Gallery exhibition of 1877 (Ruskin accused him of "flinging a pot of paint in the public's face") provoked the famous lawsuit in which Whistler was awarded a farthing's worth of damages. His feelings on the subject are embodied in his *The Gentle Art of Making Enemies* (1890). A recalcitrant rebel at a time when the sentimental Victorian subject picture was still de rigueur, Whistler conceived his paintings, even the portraits, as experiments in color harmony and tonal effect; the famous portrait of his mother (1871–72), now in the Louvre, was originally exhibited at the Royal Academy as *An Arrangement in Grey and Black*, and evening scenes such as the well-known *Old Battersea Bridge* (1872–75) were called "nocturnes." His etchings, especially his "Thames" set, succeed in imparting beauty to some of the more unpromising parts of the London riverside.

" "

A picture is finished when all trace of the means used to bring about the end has disappeared.

1890 ***The Gentle Art of Making Enemies.***

Whitaker, Pernell, *nicknamed* **Sweet Pea** 1964– •*US boxer*• Born in Norfolk, Virginia, he is reckoned to be the world's best pound-for-pound fighter (ie, if all boxers were the same height and size, he would be the champion). Of his 37 contests he won 35, lost one and drew one. His outstanding technique made him a star of the 1984 Olympics, where he won the lightweight gold medal. He has won titles at a range of weights: lightweight, light-welter, welter and light-middle.

Whitbread, Fatima, *originally* **Fatima Vedad** 1961– •*English javelin thrower*• Abandoned by her parents as a baby and brought up in a children's home in east London, she was adopted by her physical education teacher and trainer, former British international javelin thrower Margaret Whitbread. Traditionally considered too short at 5 feet 5 inches (1.67 meter) to excel at the javelin, in 1985 she became the first woman to throw a javelin over 76 meters. She set a then world record of over 77 meters the following year. She took the world championship title in Rome in 1987 and the Olympic silver medal in 1988.

White, Edward Douglass 1845–1921 •*US jurist*• Born in Lafourche Parish, Louisiana, he fought in the Confederate army, was captured and paroled, and became a lawyer in New Orleans. He served in the Louisiana state senate and on the state supreme court as well as in the US Senate (1891–94). As associate justice of the US Supreme Court from 1894, he formulated the White doctrine, declaring that territories under US sovereignty did not receive all the constitutional protections extended to the states. As chief justice of the Supreme Court (1910–21) he presided over antitrust cases against Standard Oil and other companies, and he asserted that the Sherman Antitrust Act does not outlaw all restraints on competition, but only "unreasonable" ones.

White, Ellen Gould, *née* **Harmon** 1827–1915 •*US Seventh-day Adventist leader*• Born in Gorham, Maine, she was converted to Adventism in 1842 through the preaching of **William Miller**. In 1846 she married an Adventist minister, James White. She was said to have experienced during her lifetime "two thousand visions and prophetic dreams." With the official establishment of the Seventh-day Adventist Church in 1863, she became leader, and her pronouncements were regarded as the "spirit of prophecy." Through more than 60 written works, she still dominates the denomination.

White, E(lwyn) B(rooks) 1899–1985 •*US essayist, children's novelist, poet and parodist*• Born in Mount Vernon, New York, in Westchester County, he graduated from Cornell University. He began his long association with the *New Yorker* in 1925, and did as much to make its name as it did his. His reputation rests on his three best-selling novels for children (*Stuart Little*, 1945; *Charlotte's Web*, 1952; and *The Trumpet of the Swan*, 1970); the essays he wrote in the column "One Man's Meat"; his collaboration with **James Thurber** on *Is Sex Necessary? Or Why You Feel the Way You Do* (1929); *The Elements of Style* (1959); a long article entitled "Here Is New York"; and a peerless parody of **Ernest Hemingway** entitled "Across the Street and Into the Grill."

White, Gilbert 1720–93 •*English naturalist and clergyman*• Born in Selborne, Hampshire, he was educated at Oriel College, Oxford (1739–43). He took holy orders in 1747 and obtained the sinecure college living of Moreton Pinkney, Northamptonshire (1758). His fame is based on his *Natural History and Antiquities of Selborne* (1789), a natural history of a parish comprising the journal for a whole year and resulting from a series of letters written by White. In its original form, dealing only with the natural history of Selborne, the journal was completed in 1769, but the inclusion of additional letters on antiquarian and parish subjects delayed its publication for almost 20 years. White's thrush is named after him.

White, Marco Pierre 1961– •*English chef and restaurateur*• Born in Leeds, the son of an English father and Italian mother, he left school and home when he was 16 years old and worked his way to London, where his passionate enthusiasm persuaded **Albert Roux** to give him a job at Le Gavroche when White walked in off the street. Roux was his mentor and guide, but he has also worked for and learned from Nico Ladenis (1934–) and **Raymond Blanc**. Albert Roux provided backing to help him open his own restaurant, Harveys, in 1987, and White was awarded three Michelin stars between 1988 and 1995, becoming the youngest and first British chef to do so. In 1992 he opened The Canteen Restaurant, and Quo Vadis in 1996, a restaurant noted for its interior designed by **Damien Hirst**.

White, Patrick Victor Martindale 1912–90 •*Australian novelist and Nobel Prize winner*• Born in London, into an old Australian pastoralist family, he was educated at Cheltenham College and then worked in Australia for two years before going to King's College, Cambridge. After war service in the RAF he wrote *Happy Valley* (1939), *The Living and the Dead* (1941) and *The Aunt's Story* (1946), and then bought a farm near Sydney and settled in Australia. He achieved international success with *The Tree of Man* (1954), a symbolic novel about a small community in the Australian bush. In 1957 he published *Voss*, an allegorical account, in religious terms, of a grueling attempt to cross the Australian continent. This was followed by works such as *The Solid Mandala* (1966) and *The Twyborn Affair* (1979). He also published short stories and plays, including *Four Plays* (1965) and *Signal Driver* (1981). His own "self-portrait," *Flaws in the Glass* (1981), describes the background to his supposedly "ungracious" receipt of the Nobel Prize for literature in 1973. With the proceeds of the prize he established the Patrick White Literary Award, which makes an annual grant to an older Australian writer whose work has not received appropriate critical or financial recognition.

White, Richard Grant 1821–85 •*US Shakespearean scholar*• Born in New York City, he studied medicine and law before becoming a journalist. His Shakespearean studies included criticisms on **John Payne Collier**'s folio emendations (*Shakespeare's Scholar*, 1854) and two editions (1857–65, 1883) of the *Works*. His other publications included *Words and Their Uses* (1870), *Everyday English* (1881) and *England Without and Within* (1881). His son was the architect **Stanford White**.

White, Stanford 1853–1906 •*US architect*• Born in New York City, he learned architecture under H H Richardson and afterward lived in Paris. In 1879 he and two old friends formed the architectural firm of **McKim**, Mead & White, which was to design some of the most important buildings in US architectural history. A man of prodigious creative energy and eclectic tastes, White was often responsible for the interior design and decoration of their buildings. He used a Renaissance style in his two surviving works in New York, the Washington Arch and the Century Club. He designed the old Madison Square Garden in 1889, commissioning for the cupola a statue of Diana that shocked New York with its nudity, and building for himself in the tower a notorious private apartment that he used for his satyrlike amusements. He was finally shot and killed there by a jealous husband.

White, T(erence) H(anbury) 1906–64 •*English novelist*• Born in Bombay, India, he was educated at Cheltenham College and Queens' College Cambridge. Until 1936 he was a master at Stowe, and he later lived in a gamekeeper's cottage near the school. Always a keen sportsman, he was an ardent falconer and fisherman, and his work is imbued with his knowledge and love of nature. He wrote more than 25 books, but he is best known for his interpretation of the Arthurian legend, a tetralogy known collectively as *The Once and Future King* (1958), the first part of which, *The Sword in the Stone* (1937), is a children's classic. A fifth volume, found among his papers, was published as *The Book of Merlyn* (1977). *Mistress Masham's Repose* (1947) is another notable children's book. His adult works include *The Goshawk* (1951), *The Master* (1957) and *The Book of Beasts* (1954), translated from a 12th-century Latin bestiary.

Whitefield, George 1714–70 •*English evangelist, one of the founders of Methodism*• Born in the Bell Inn, Gloucester, he went to Pembroke College, Oxford, as a servitor at 18. The **Wesley**s had already laid the foundations of Methodism at Oxford, and Whitefield became an enthusiastic evangelist. In 1738 he followed John Wesley to Georgia and was appointed minister at Savannah. He returned to England in 1739 to be admitted to priest's orders. He was actively opposed by his fellow churchmen, but when the parish pulpits were denied him he preached in the open air. He returned to Georgia and made extensive preaching tours. About 1741, differences on predestination led to his separation as a rigid Calvinist from John Wesley as an Arminian. His supporters built him a chapel in Bristol and the Moorfields "Tabernacle" in London. Many of his adherents followed the Countess of **Huntingdon** in Wales and formed Calvinistic Methodists, so she appointed him her chaplain and built and endowed many chapels for him. He made seven evangelistic visits to America, and he spent the rest of his life in preaching tours through England, Scotland (1741) and Wales.

Whitehead, Alfred North 1861–1947 •*English mathematician and idealist philosopher*• Born in London, he was educated at Sherborne and Trinity College, Cambridge, where he was senior lecturer in mathematics until 1911. He became Professor of Applied Mathematics at Imperial College, London (1914–24), and Professor of Philosophy at Harvard (1924–37). Extending the Booleian symbolic logic in a highly original *Treatise on Universal Algebra* (1898), he contributed a remarkable memoir to the Royal Society, *Mathematical Concepts of the Material World* (1905). Profoundly influenced by **Giuseppe Peano**, he collaborated with his former pupil at Trinity, **Bertrand Russell**, in the *Principia Mathematica* (1910–13), the greatest single contribution to logic since **Aristotle**. In his Edinburgh Gifford Lectures, "Process and Reality" (1929), he attempted a metaphysics comprising psychological as well as physical experience. More popular works include *Adventures of Ideas* (1933).

Whitelaw, Billie 1932– •*English actress*• Born in Coventry, West Midlands, she made her London debut in **Georges Feydeau**'s *Hotel Paradiso* (1956), and joined the National Theatre (1964), appearing in **Samuel Beckett**'s one-act *Play*. She joined the Royal Shakespeare Company (1971) and returned to Beckett in 1973 to play Mouth in *Not I*. Other noted Beckett interpretations include a revival of *Happy Days* at the Royal Court (1979). She has played many other modern roles on stage, and appeared on television and in several films, including *The Omen* (1976) and *The Krays* (1990).

Whitelaw, Willie (William Stephen Ian) Whitelaw, 1st Viscount 1918–99 •*Scottish Conservative politician*• Born in Edinburgh, he was educated at Winchester and Cambridge, served in the Scots Guards during and after World War II, and first became a Conservative Member of Parliament in 1955. Secretary of state for Northern Ireland (1972–73) and for employment (1973–74), he was home secretary for four years before being made a viscount in 1983 and was leader of the Lords until 1988. During the 1975 Conservative leadership contest, his loyalty to **Edward Heath**, which persuaded him not to stand directly against him in the first ballot, is thought to have allowed **Margaret Thatcher** to win in the second ballot. As her deputy, however, he displayed the same loyalty and was one of her closest advisers in the Falklands War and general election campaigns.

Whiteley, Brett 1939–92 •*Australian artist*• Born in Paddington, Sydney, he studied in Sydney until a scholarship enabled him to go to Italy. He was represented in the 1961 Whitechapel Gallery exhibition. He worked in New York from 1967 to 1969 and continued to travel and exhibit abroad regularly, painting in an abstract expressionist style. He won many prestigious awards. His colors are typically ochers, creamy whites, and reddish browns, recalling the hot Australian landscape, with a hint of eroticism, violence and death. He was also an animal painter.

Whiteman, Paul 1891–1967 •*US bandleader*• He was born in Denver, Colorado. He became famous in the 1920s as a pioneer of sweet style, as opposed to the traditional classical style jazz. His band employed such brilliant exponents of true jazz as the trumpeter **Bix Beiderbecke**, and Whiteman became popularly regarded as the inventor of jazz itself rather than of a deviation from true jazz style. He was responsible for **George Gershwin**'s experiments in symphonic jazz, commissioning the *Rhapsody in Blue* for a concert in New York in 1924.

Whiteread, Rachel 1963– •*English sculptor*• Born in London, she trained at Brighton Polytechnic and the Slade School, and won a scholarship to Berlin (1992–93). She takes casts from objects bearing traces of human existence, such as bathtubs, old mattresses, shelves, mortuary slabs and even whole rooms, capturing the space in and around them and transforming them into ghostly icons. Thus, the inside of a hot water bottle becomes *Torso* (1991). She also molds in rubber, as with *Orange Bath* (1996). In 1993–94 she became the most talked-about sculptor for decades when, sponsored by Tarmac Structural Repairs, she cast an entire disused house in East London. *House*, together with *Room* (1993), and her exhibitions in Eindhoven, Sydney, Venice and Paris, made her the clear favorite and the winner of the 1993 Turner Prize. Since 1994 she has also worked using resin. In 1996 her cast of a library, with rubber and fiberglass pages bolted onto the outside, was unveiled as the *Holocaust Memorial* in the Judenplatz, Vienna.

Whitfield, June Rosemary 1925– •*English comic actress*• Born in Streatham, London, she graduated from the Royal Academy of Dramatic Art and worked in revues, musicals and pantomimes as a foil to some of the top comedians in show business before enjoying her own success in the long-running radio series *Take It From Here* (1953–60) as Eth Glum. She has been an indispensable part of television light entertainment in such series as *Beggar My Neighbour* (1966–67), and a long professional association with **Terry Scott** resulted in the series *Scott on ...* (1969–73) and *Terry and June* (1979–87). Her film appearances include *Carry on Nurse* (1959) and *Jude* (1996); stage appearances include *An Ideal Husband* (1987) and *Babes in the Wood* (1990). She has recently revived her television career by appearing in **Jennifer Saunders**'s popular comedy series, *Absolutely Fabulous* (1992–95, 2001), and the drama *Family Money* (1997).

Whitlam, (Edward) Gough 1916– •*Australian statesman*• Educated at the University of Sydney, after war service in the Royal Australian Air Force he became a barrister. He entered politics in 1952 and led the Australian Labor Party (1967–77), forming the first Labor government since 1949. His administration (1972–75) was notable for its radicalism: ending conscription and withdrawing Australian troops from the Vietnam War, recognizing Communist China, relaxing the restrictions on nonwhite immigrants, abolishing university fees and creating Medibank (the state-funded healthcare system). He was controversially dismissed by the Governor-General **John Kerr** in 1975 after the Senate had blocked his money bills; Labor lost the subsequent election. Whitlam went on to become Australian ambassador to UNESCO in Paris (1983–86) and a member of its executive board (1985–89).

Whitman, Walt(er) 1819–92 •*US poet*• Born in West Hills, Long Island, New York, he was raised in Brooklyn from about the age of four, and worked first as an office boy (in a lawyer's, a doctor's and finally a printer's office). He then became an itinerant teacher in country schools. He returned to printing, wrote an earnest temperance novel, *Franklin Evans, or The Inebriate* (1842), and in 1846 became editor of the *Brooklyn Eagle*, a Democratic paper. This and his other numerous press engagements did not last long. In 1848, he traveled with his brothers to New Orleans, where he worked briefly on the New Orleans *Crescent* before returning to Brooklyn as a journalist (1848–54). He seemed unable to find expression for his emotions until he hit on the curious, irregular, recitative measures of *Leaves of Grass* (1855). Originally a small 12-poem folio of 95 pages published anonymously with the author's portrait in work clothes enigmatically facing the title page, it grew in the eight succeeding editions (until 1891–92) to nearly 440 pages. The untitled poem that introduced the first edition was later called "Song of Myself" (1881). **Ralph Waldo Emerson**, in a letter to Whitman, praised the first collection as "the most extraordinary piece of wit and wisdom that America has yet contributed." The 1860 edition added the "Calamus" sequence of 45 poems, considered by many to be a poetic celebration of Whitman's apparent homosexuality. *Leaves of Grass*, along with his prose work, *Specimen Days and Collect* (1882–83), constitutes Whitman's main lifework as a writer. In 1862, he was summoned to his brother who had been wounded at Fredericksburg in the Civil War, and he subsequently became a volunteer nurse in the Washington hospitals of the Northern and Southern armies. The exposure, exertion, and drain of those few years left him a shattered and prematurely aged man. In 1865 he received a government clerkship but was dismissed by Secretary **Harlan** as the author of "an indecent book" (*Leaves of Grass*); however, he obtained a similar post almost immediately. In 1873 he suffered a paralytic stroke and left Washington for Camden, New Jersey, where he spent the rest of his life. The poetry in his last collection of poems and prose, *Good-Bye, My Fancy* (1891), was reprinted in the final edition of *Leaves of Grass*. Many of his poems for *Leaves of Grass* are now considered American classics, such as the sequence *Drum Taps* (1865–66), which contains the elegies "When Lilacs Last in the Courtyard Bloom'd" and "O Captain! My Captain!," written in memory of the assassinated **Abraham Lincoln**.

" "

Do I contradict myself?
Very well then I contradict myself,
(I am large, I contain multitudes.)

1855 ***Leaves of Grass**, "Song of Myself," section 51.*

Whitney, Anne 1821–1915 •*US sculptor*• She was born in Watertown, Massachusetts. Her early works, created in Boston, reflect her interest in social justice. Following the Civil War, she traveled and studied extensively in Europe and continued sculpting well into her eighties. At the age of 72, she anonymously entered a competition to create a memorial to US statesman **Charles Sumner**. Her sculpture won, but the honor was withdrawn when it was discovered that she was a woman. At least 100 of her works have been cataloged and are owned by such institutions as the Smithsonian and the National Collection of Fine Arts.

Whitney, Eli 1765–1825 •*US inventor*• Born in Westborough, Massachusetts, he was educated at Yale and went to Georgia as a teacher. Finding a patron in Mrs Nathaniel Greene, the widow of a general, he stayed on her plantation, studied law and set to work to invent a cotton gin for separating cotton fiber from the seeds. His machine was stolen, and lawsuits in defense of his rights consumed all his profits and the $50,000 voted him by the state of South Carolina. In 1798 he got a government contract for the manufacture of firearms, and he subsequently made a fortune in this business.

Whitney, Gertrude Vanderbilt, *née* **Vanderbilt** 1875–1942 •*US sculptor and patron of the arts*• She was born into a wealthy family in New York City and married Harry Payne Whitney (1872–1930), a financier, in 1896. She trained at the Art Students League of New York and in Paris. During World War I she established a hospital and worked as a nurse, which became the inspiration for the two panels *Victory Arch* (1918–20) and *The Washington Heights War Memorial* (1921), both in New York City. Other works include the *Aztec Fountain* (1912) and *Titanic Memorial* (1914–31). In 1930 Whitney donated her collection of 500 works of 20th-century art and bought 100 more to found the Whitney Museum of Modern Art in Greenwich Village, which opened in 1931.

Whitney, Josiah Dwight 1819–96 •*US geologist*• Born in Northampton, Massachusetts, he graduated from Yale and in 1840 joined the New Hampshire Survey. He worked in Michigan from 1847 to 1849, and in the Lake Superior region. Following his studies of mining problems in Illinois, he published *Mineral Wealth of the United States* (1854). He was appointed professor at the University of Iowa in 1855, state geologist of California in 1860 and professor at Harvard in 1865. He produced important work on the *Auriferous Gravels of the Sierra Nevada* (1879–80), in which he recognized that the gold deposits were not marine deposits as had been supposed, but were the products of erosion and deposition of preexisting gold-bearing mineral veins. He also wrote on the *Climate Changes of Later Geological Time* (1880, 1882). Mount Whitney in southern California is named in his honor.

Whitney, William Dwight 1827–94 •*US philologist*• Brother of **Josiah Dwight Whitney**, he studied at Williams and Yale, and in Germany prepared an edition of the *Atharva Veda Sanhita* (1856). In 1854 he became a professor of Sanskrit at Yale, and in 1870 also of comparative philology. He was an office-bearer of the American Oriental Society, edited numerous Sanskrit texts and contributed to the great Sanskrit dictionary of Otto von Böhtlingk and Rudolph Roth (1855–75). Among his works were *Language and the Study of Language* (1867), *Material and Form in Language* (1872), *Life and Growth of Language* (1876), *Essentials of English Grammar* (1877) and *Mixture in Language* (1881). He was the editor of the 1864 edition of *Webster's Dictionary* and editor in chief of the *Century Dictionary and Cyclopedia* (1889–91).

Whittier, John Greenleaf 1807–92 •*US Quaker poet and abolitionist*• Born near Haverhill, Massachusetts, he was largely self-educated. In 1829 he entered journalism, and in 1831 published *Legends of New England*, a collection of poems and stories. In 1840 he settled at Amesbury, a village near his birthplace, and devoted himself to the cause of emancipation. His later works include the collection *In War Time* (1864), which contains the well-known ballad "Barbara Frietchie."

Whittington, Dick (Richard) c. 1358–1423 •*English merchant and philanthropist*• He was the youngest son of Sir William Whittington of Pauntley, Gloucestershire. As a young man he was apprenticed to a prosperous London merchant, and in 1393 became an alderman and sheriff. In 1397 he took over as mayor of London at the previous incumbent's death, and was mayor again three times, in 1398, 1406 and 1419. He became a Member of Parliament in 1416. He traded with and loaned money to **Henry IV** and **Henry V**. He built a library at Greyfriars and left his fortune to a trust which provided for the building of a library at Guildhall, the rebuilding of Newgate Prison, and the foundation of a college and almshouse (now at East Grinstead). The legend of his cat is an accepted part of English folklore, dating from the early 17th century.

Whittle, Sir Frank 1907–96 •*English aeronautical engineer and inventor*• Born in Coventry, Warwickshire, he joined the RAF as an apprentice (1923), and studied at the RAF College, Cranwell, and at Cambridge (1934–37). He conceived the idea of trying to develop a replacement for the conventional internal combustion plane engine, researching jet propulsion before 1930, while he was still a student. After a long fight against official inertia, his engine was first flown successfully in a Gloster aircraft in May 1941, about two years after the world's first flights of both turbojet and rocket-powered aircraft had taken place in Germany. He was knighted in 1948.

Whitworth, Kathy (Kathrynne Ann) 1939– •*US golfer*• Born in Monahans, Texas, she turned professional in 1958 and over the next 30 years went on to establish herself as the most successful of all women golfers. She captured the US Ladies' Professional Golf Association (LPGA) Championship four times (1967, 1971, 1975 and 1982), and during her career she notched up a record 88 tour wins, including six majors and all the leading women's events on the US circuit, with the sole exception of the US Open. She was the LPGA Player of the Year seven times (1966–69 and 1971–73) and headed the table of money-winners eight times between 1965 and 1973.

Whorf, Benjamin Lee 1897–1941 •*US linguist*• Born in Winthrop, Massachusetts, he was a chemical engineer and fire prevention officer by profession and studied linguistics and Native American languages in his spare time. Influenced by **Edward Sapir**'s teachings at Yale University (1931–32), he developed Sapir's insights into the influence of language on people's perception of the world into what became known as the Sapir-Whorf hypothesis.

Whymper, Edward 1840–1911 •*English wood engraver and mountaineer*• Born in London, he was trained as an artist in wood, but became more famous for his mountaineering. In 1860–69 he conquered several hitherto unscaled peaks of the Alps, including the Matterhorn. In 1867 and 1872 he made many geological discoveries in North Greenland. His travels in the Andes (including ascents of Chimborazo) took place in 1879–80. He illustrated his books *Scrambles Amongst the Alps* (1871, 1893) and *Travels Amongst the Great Andes* (1892).

Wicliffe, John *See* **Wycliffe, John**

Widdecombe, Ann Noreen 1947– •*English Conservative politician*• Born in Bath, she was educated at a convent there and at the University of Birmingham and at Oxford. She worked for Unilever (1973–75) and as an administrator at the University of London (1975–87) before entering parliament on her third attempt in 1987. She then served as a parliamentary undersecretary of state at the Department of Social Security (1990–93) and at the Department of Employment (1993–94) before becoming minister for employment (1994–95) and minister for the home office (1995–97). Well known for her outspoken right-wing views, she was considered by some a politician in the mold of **Margaret Thatcher**. She kept her seat in the Conservative electoral disaster of 1997 and subsequently served as shadow health minister (1997–99) and as shadow home secretary (1999–2001). Her publications include the novel *The Clematis Tree* (2000).

Wieman, Carl E(dwin) 1951– •*US physicist and Nobel Prize winner*• Born in Corvallis, Oregon, he studied at MIT and Stanford University. From 1977 he worked as a research scientist at the Universities of Michigan and Colorado, becoming Professor of Physics at the University of Colorado in 1987. Among numerous professional awards he received the Nobel Prize for physics (2001; with **Wolfgang Ketterle** and **Eric A Cornell**) for the achievement of Bose-Einstein condensation in dilute gases at very low temperatures, effectively creating a new state of matter.

Wien, Wilhelm Carl Werner Otto Fritz Franz 1864–1928 •*German physicist and Nobel Prize winner*• Born in Gaffken in East Prussia, he attended the Universities of Göttingen, Berlin and Heidelberg. He was appointed to professorships at the Universities of Aachen (1896), Giessen (1899), Würzburg (1899) and finally Munich (1920). His chief contribution was on blackbody radiation, in which he advanced the work of **Ludwig Boltzmann** (1884) to show that the wavelength at which maximum energy is radiated is inversely proportional to the absolute temperature of the body (1893). He cleared the way for **Max Planck** to resolve the observed distribution of all frequencies with the quantum theory (1900), and in 1911 was awarded the Nobel Prize for physics. His subsequent research covered hydrodynamics, X-rays and cathode rays.

Wiener, Norbert 1894–1964 •*US mathematician*• Born in Columbia, Missouri, he studied zoology at Harvard and philosophy at Cornell University, and in Europe studied with **Bertrand Russell** at Cambridge and the University of Göttingen. He was later appointed Professor of Mathematics at MIT (1932–60), where he worked on stochastic processes and harmonic analysis, inventing the concepts later called the Wiener integral and Wiener measure. During World War II he studied mathematical communication theory applied to predictors and guided missiles, and his study of feedback in the handling of information by electronic devices led him to compare this with analogous mental processes in animals in *Cybernetics, or Control and Communication in the Animal and the Machine* (1948) and other works.

Wiesel, Elie(zer) 1928– •*US writer and Nobel Prize winner*• Born in Sighet, Romania, he was a teenager during World War II and was imprisoned in both Auschwitz and Buchenwald, where his parents and a sister perished. After the war he became a journalist and a US citizen (1963). His first novel, *Night* (1958), is an autobiographical account of the horrors of the death camps, and in his subsequent novels, stories and plays he continued his effort to memorialize the Holocaust. Since 1976 Wiesel has been Andrew W Mellon Professor in the Humanities at Boston University, where he is also Professor of Religious Studies. In 1986 he was awarded the Nobel Peace Prize.

Wiesel, Torsten Nils 1924– •*Swedish neurophysiologist and Nobel Prize winner*• Born in Uppsala, he studied medicine at the Karolinska Institute in Stockholm, and then went to the US, working initially at Johns Hopkins University Medical School in ophthalmology and then at Harvard Medical School where he held several professorships. With **David Hubel** he studied the way in which the brain processes visual information, and they demonstrated that there is a hierarchical processing pathway, of increasingly sophisticated analysis, of visual information by nerve cells. In 1981 Wiesel and Hubel shared the Nobel Prize for physiology or medicine with **Roger Sperry**. He joined Rockefeller University as head of the laboratory of neurobiology in 1983, becoming president in 1992.

Wiggin, Kate Douglas, *née* **Smith** 1856–1953 •*US novelist*• Born in Philadelphia, she moved to San Francisco to organize the first free kindergarten school in the West (1878). She wrote novels for both adults and children, but was more successful with the latter. *Rebecca of Sunnybrook Farm* (1903) is probably her best-known book, although the *Penelope* exploits (which were adult seminovels), *The Birds' Christmas Carol* (1888) and *Mother Carey's Chickens* (1911) were all popular.

Wigglesworth, Michael 1631–1705 •*American poet and clergyman*• Born in Yorkshire, England, he was taken to Massachusetts Bay colony at the age of seven, and educated at Harvard. Fellow and tutor at Harvard from 1652 to 1654, and again from 1697 to 1705, he was ordained to the ministry of the Puritan Church in Malden around 1656. His epic poem, the first American epic, "Day of Doom" (1662), takes a lengthy and somewhat pessimistic view of the Day of Judgment. He wrote a shorter poem intended for edification in 1669: "Meat out of the Eater, or Meditations Concerning the Necessity, End and Usefulness of Afflictions unto God's Children." His *Diary* was published in 1951.

Wightman, Hazel Hotchkiss 1886–1974 •*US tennis player*• Born in Healdsburg, California, she began tournament play in 1902 and introduced more active play for women, employing volley and net play for the first time. She also challenged the restrictive women's dress of the day. She won the national triple of the singles, the doubles and the mixed doubles in 1909, 1910 and 1911. In 1919 she promoted international competitions for women, and in the 1920s began teaching. A donated vase to the United States Lawn Tennis Association became known as the Hazel Hotchkiss Wightman Trophy. She published *Better Tennis* in 1933.

Wigman, Mary, *originally* **Marie Wiegmann** 1886–1973 •*German dancer, choreographer and teacher*• Born in Hanover, she studied eurhythmics with the Swiss composer Émile Jaques-Dalcroze (1865–1951) and assisted **Rudolf von Laban** during World War I. She subsequently made her name as a soloist, but her ensemble dances were landmarks in the German Expressionist style. She opened several schools in Germany from 1920, and, through her star pupil **Hanya Holm**, in the US; the Nazis later closed the German schools. The most famous German dancer of her era, she exerted a great influence on European modern dance. She opened another school in West Berlin in 1949.

Wigner, Eugene Paul 1902–95 •*US theoretical physicist and Nobel Prize winner*• He was born in Budapest, Hungary, and educated at Berlin. He moved to the US in 1930, and apart from two years at the University of Wisconsin (1936–38), he worked at Princeton University throughout his academic career. Wigner made a number of important contributions to nuclear physics and quantum theory. In 1927 he introduced the idea of parity conservation in nuclear interactions, and in the 1930s he demonstrated that the strong nuclear force has very short range. He is especially known for the Breit-Wigner formula (devised with US physicist Gregory Breit, 1899–1981), which describes resonant nuclear reactions, and the Wigner theorem concerning the conservation of the angular momentum of electron spin. His name is also given to the most important class of mirror nuclides (Wigner nuclides). Wigner's calculations were used by **Enrico Fermi** in building the first nuclear reactor in Chicago (1942), and he received the Nobel Prize for physics in 1963 for his work in furthering quantum mechanics and nuclear physics.

Wilberforce, Samuel 1805–73 •*English prelate*• The third son of **William Wilberforce**, he was born in Clapham, London. In 1826 he graduated from Oriel College, Oxford, and was ordained in 1828. In 1840 he became rector of Alverstoke, canon of Winchester and chaplain to **Albert**, the Prince Consort, and in 1845 Dean of Westminster and Bishop of Oxford. He took part in the controversies of the Renn Hampden, Gorham, *Essay and Reviews*, and **John Colenso** cases. Instrumental in reviving Convocation (1852), he instituted Cuddesdon Theological College (1854). The charm of his many-sided personality and his social and oratorical gifts earned him the nickname of "Soapy Sam." He edited *Letters and Journals of Henry Martyn* (1837) and wrote with his brother, Robert, the life of their father (1838). He also wrote books, including a *History of the Protestant Episcopal Church in America* (1844). Bishop of Winchester from 1869, he was killed by a fall from his horse. Of his sons, Ernest Roland (1840–1908) and Albert Basil Orme (1841–1916) became prominent churchmen.

Wilberforce, William 1759–1833•*English philanthropist and reformer*• He was born in Hull and educated at St John's College, Cambridge. In 1780 he was elected a Member of Parliament for Yorkshire and became a close friend of **William Pitt**, the Younger, while remaining independent of any party. In 1784–85, during a tour on the Continent, he was converted to evangelical Christianity. In 1788, supported by **Thomas Clarkson** and the Quakers, he began a 19-year campaign for the abolition of the slave trade in the British West Indies, which he finally achieved in 1807. He next sought to secure the abolition of slavery itself, but declining health compelled him to retire from parliament. He died one month before the Slavery Abolition Act was passed. Wilberforce was a central figure in the Clapham Sect of Evangelicals for a long time. He published *A Practical View of Christianity* in 1797, helped to found the *Christian Observer*, and promoted many schemes for the welfare of the community. He was buried in Westminster Abbey.

Wilcox, Ella Wheeler 1850–1919 •*US journalist and verse writer*• Born in Johnstown Center, Wisconsin, she had completed a novel before she was ten, and she later wrote at least two poems a day. The most successful of her many volumes of verse was *Poems of Passion* (1883). She also wrote a great deal of fiction and contributed essays to many periodicals. Her *Story of a Literary Career* (1905) and *The World and I* (1918) were autobiographical.

Wilde, Lady Jane Francesca, *known as* **Speranza**, *née* **Elgee** 1826–96 •*Irish poet and hostess*• Born in Dublin, she was an ardent nationalist and contributed poetry and prose to the *Nation* from 1845 under the pen name "Speranza." In 1851 she married Sir **William Wilde**; their son was **Oscar Wilde**. Her salon was the most famous in Dublin. After her husband's death she moved to London and published several works on folklore, including *Ancient Legends of Ireland* (1887).

Wilde, Oscar Fingal O'Flahertie Wills 1854–1900•*Irish playwright, novelist, essayist, poet and wit*• Born in Dublin, his parents were **William Wilde** and **Jane Francesca Wilde**. Educated at Trinity College, Dublin (1871–74) and Magdalen College, Oxford (1874–78), he was sympathetic toward the Pre-Raphaelites, contemptuous of conventional morality, and sexually ambiguous. He was also an accomplished Classicist, and won the Newdigate prize at Oxford in 1878 for the poem "Ravenna." Wilde's first collection of poetry was published in 1881, the year in which he was ridiculed in **Gilbert** and **Sullivan**'s *Patience* as an adherent of the cult of "Art for Art's sake." The next year he embarked on a tour of the US where, when asked if he had anything to declare, he allegedly replied, "Only my genius." In 1884 he married Constance Lloyd, the daughter of an Irish barrister, and had two sons, for whom he wrote the classic children's fairy stories *The Happy Prince and Other Tales* (1888). His only novel, *The Picture of Dorian Gray* (1891), was modeled on his presumed lover, the poet John Gray, and was originally published in *Lippincott's Magazine* (1890). More fairy stories appeared in 1891 in *A House of Pomegranates*. In this year he also published *Lord Arthur Savile's Crime and Other Stories* and a second play, *The Duchess of Padua*, an uninspired verse tragedy. Over the next five years he built his dramatic reputation, first with *Lady Windermere's Fan* (1892), followed by *A Woman of No Importance* (1893), *An Ideal Husband* (1895) and his masterpiece, *The Importance of Being Earnest* (1895). *Salomé*, originally written in French (1893), was refused a production license in France because it featured biblical characters, but it appeared in 1894 in an English translation by Lord **Alfred Douglas**. By then, it was commonly known that Wilde was gay, and the 8th Marquis of **Queensbury**, father of Lord Alfred, left a card at Wilde's club addressed "To Oscar Wilde posing as a Somdomite" (sic). Wilde took it that he meant "ponce and Sodomite" and sued for libel. He lost the case, and was himself prosecuted and imprisoned (1895) for homosexuality. In 1905 his bitter reproach to Lord Alfred was published in part as *De Profundis*. Released in 1897, he went to France. *The Ballad of Reading Gaol* was published in 1898. He also wrote literary essays and *The Soul of Man Under Socialism* (1891) a riposte to **George Bernard Shaw**. His last years were spent wandering and idling on the Continent, and he died in Paris.

" "

The play was a great success, but the audience was a disaster.

1892 Attributed comment after the poor reception of ***Lady Windermere's Fan***.

Wilde, Sir William Robert Wills 1815–76 •*Irish oculist, aurist and topographer*• Born in Castlerea, County Roscommon, he studied at London, Berlin and Vienna, and returning to Dublin, he served as medical commissioner on the Irish Census (1841 and 1851), publishing a major medical report, *The Epidemics of Ireland* (1851). He also wrote on ocular and aural surgery, pioneered the operation for mastoiditis, invented an ophthalmoscope and founded St Mark's Ophthalmic Hospital. His topographical works include *The Beauties of the Boyne and the Blackwater* (1849). He published a major catalog of the holdings of the Royal Irish Academy and was apparently fluent in Gaelic. He married (1851) Jane Francesca Elgee (**Wilde**), famous as the poet "Speranza." He was named Queen **Victoria**'s Irish oculist in ordinary.

Wilder, Billy, *originally* **Samuel Wilder** 1906–2002 •*US filmmaker*• Born in Sucha, Austria, he studied law at the University of Vienna, then worked as a journalist and crime reporter before making his film debut in Germany as the cowriter of *Menschen am Sonntag* (1929, *People on Sunday*). In Paris he codirected *Mauvaise Graine* (1933, "Bad Seed") before moving to Hollywood and embarking on a fruitful collaboration with writer Charles Brackett (1892–1969). Their scripts include *Ninotchka* (1939) and *Ball of Fire* (1941). A US citizen from 1934, he made his directorial debut in the US with *The Major and the Minor* (1942), then began a distinguished career as the creator of incisive dramas, acerbic comedies and bittersweet romances, winning multiple Academy Awards for *The Lost Weekend* (1945), *Sunset Boulevard* (1950) and *The Apartment* (1960). His many popular successes include *Double Indemnity* (1944), *The Seven-Year Itch* (1955) and *Some Like It Hot* (1959). He made seven films with actor **Jack Lemmon**. He worked with writer I A L Diamond (1920–88) from 1957.

Wilder, Laura Ingalls 1867–1957 •*US children's writer*• Born in Pepin, Wisconsin, she was a farm woman all her life, and it was not until she was in her sixties, when her daughter suggested that she write down her childhood memories, that her evocative "Little House" series began to appear. *Little House in the Big Woods* (1932) achieved instant popularity in the US and was followed by the sequels *Little House on the Prairie* (1935), *Little Town on the Prairie* (1941) and *These Happy Golden Years* (1943). The television series *Little House on the Prairie* (1974–83) is based on her books.

Wilder, Thornton Niven 1897–1975 •*US writer and playwright*• Born in Madison, Wisconsin, he was educated at Yale and served in both world wars, becoming a lieutenant colonel in 1944. He started his career as a teacher of English at Lawrenceville Academy (1921–28) and the University of Chicago (1930–37). His first novel, *The Cabala*, appeared in 1926. Set in contemporary Rome, it established the cool atmosphere of sophistication and detached irony that was to permeate all his books. These include *The Bridge of San Luis Rey* (1927, a bestseller and winner of the Pulitzer Prize), *Heaven's My Destination* (1935) and *The Ides of March* (1948). His first plays were literary rather than dramatic, but in 1938 he produced *Our Town*, a successful play that evokes without scenery or costumes a universal flavor of provincial life. This was followed in 1942 by *The Skin of Our Teeth*, an amusing yet profound fable of humanity's struggle to survive. Both these plays were awarded the Pulitzer Prize. His later plays include *The Matchmaker* (1954), *Theophilus North* (1974) and, in 1964, the musical *Hello Dolly!*, based on *The Matchmaker*.

Wilfrid or **Wilfrith, St** 634–709 •*English prelate*• Born in Northumbria, he trained at Lindisfarne. He upheld the replacement of Celtic with Roman religious practices at the Synod of Whitby (664), and was made Bishop of Ripon and Bishop of York (c. 665). When Archbishop Theodore divided Northumbria into four sees in 678, Wilfrid appealed to Rome, the first British churchman to do so. Pope Agatho decided in his favor, but King Ecgfrid imprisoned him. He escaped to Sussex but was allowed to return by the new king, Aldfrith, in 686.

Wilhelm I 1797–1888 •*Seventh king of Prussia and first German emperor*• The second son of **Frederick William III**, he was born in Berlin. In 1814 he entered Paris with the allies, and during the king's absence in Russia he directed Prussian military affairs. In 1829 he married Princess Augusta of Saxe-Weimar and became heir presumptive (1840). During the Revolution of 1848 his attitude toward the people made him unpopular, and he was obliged to leave Prussia for London, but he returned to subdue disaffection in Baden (1849). He was appointed regent (1858) for his ailing brother, **Frederick William IV**, and when he succeeded in 1861, he made plain his intention of consolidating the throne and strengthening the army. Despite parliamentary disapproval, Prince **Bismarck** was placed at the head of the ministry. In 1864 Prussia and Austria defeated Denmark and in 1866 Prussia defeated Austria in the struggle for supremacy over the German states. In 1870 France and Prussia went to war; France was defeated. In 1871 Wilhelm was proclaimed German emperor. An Austro-German alliance of 1871 was strengthened (1873) by the adhesion of the czar. The rapid rise of socialism in Germany led to severe repressive measures, and several attempts were made on the emperor's life.

Wilhelm II 1859–1941 •*German emperor and king of Prussia*• He was born in Berlin, the eldest son of Prince Frederick, later Frederick III, and of Victoria, the daughter of Great Britain's Queen **Victoria**. He received a strict military and academic education at the Kassel gymnasium and the University of Bonn, taking part in military exercises despite a deformed left arm. A military enthusiast, he had a deep conviction of the divine right of the **Hohenzollern**s. He was intelligent if somewhat temperamental. Emperor of Germany and king of Prussia from 1888 until 1918, he quarreled with and dismissed (1890) **Bismarck**. A long spell of personal rule followed, but in 1908 he suffered a nervous breakdown, which greatly lessened his influence on policymaking in the last ten years of his reign. Wilhelm's speeches revolved around German imperialism. In 1896 he sent a telegram to President **Kruger** of South Africa congratulating him on the suppression of the **Jameson** raid. He also backed Admiral **von Tirpitz**'s plans for a large German navy to match the British, and as an ally of Turkey he encouraged German economic penetration into the Middle East. He supported immoderate demands on Serbia after the assassination of the Archduke **Franz Ferdinand** at Sarajevo (1914), but he made strenuous efforts to avoid the world war he saw as imminent. Political power passed from him to the generals, and during World War I he became a mere figurehead, contrary to the popular image of him as a great warlord. The defeat of Germany forced him to abdicate (November 9, 1918) and flee the country. He and his family settled first at Amerongen, then at Doorn near Arnheim, where he wrote his *Memoirs 1878–1918* (translated 1922) and ignored the Nazi "liberation" (1940) of the Netherlands. He also wrote *My Early Life* (1926). In 1881 he married Princess Augusta Victoria of Schleswig-Holstein, by whom he had six sons and one daughter. After her death in 1921, he married Princess Hermine of Reuss.

Wilhelmina Helena Pauline Maria of Orange-Nassau 1880–1962 •*Queen of the Netherlands*• Born in The Hague, she succeeded her father, William III, in 1890 at a very early age, and until 1898 her mother, Queen Emma, acted as regent. Queen Wilhelmina fully upheld the principles of constitutional monarchy, especially winning the admiration of her people during World War II. Though compelled to seek refuge in Great Britain, she steadfastly encouraged Dutch resistance to the German occupation. In 1948, in view of the length of her reign, she abdicated in favor of her daughter **Juliana**. She wrote *Lonely but Not Alone* (1960), which revealed her profound religious sentiments.

Wilkes, Sir Maurice Vincent 1913– •*English computer scientist*• Born in Dudley, West Midlands, he was educated at Cambridge. He conducted research in physics at the Cavendish Laboratory, and directed the Mathematical (later Computer) Laboratory at Cambridge (1946–80), where he became known for his pioneering work with the EDSAC (Electronic Delay Storage Automatic Calculator), intended to provide a useful and reliable computing service. Besides important software advances, Wilkes also performed fundamental work on processor controls (microprogramming). After 1980 Wilkes became a computer engineer for the Digital Equipment Corporation until 1986. His publications include *Computing Perspectives* (1995). He was knighted in 2000.

Wilkie, Sir David 1785–1841 •*Scottish painter*• Born in Cults manse in Fife, he was sent to study at the Trustees' Academy in Edinburgh. The great success of *The Village Politicians* (1806) caused him to settle in London. His fame mainly rests on his genre pictures in the Dutch style, such as the *Card Players*, *Village Festival* (1811), *Reading the Will* (1811), *The Penny Wedding* (1818) and others. Later he changed his style, sought to emulate the depth and richness of coloring of the old masters, and chose more elevated historical subjects, like *John Knox Preaching Before the Lords of Congregation* (1832). He also painted portraits and was successful as an etcher. In 1823 he was appointed King's Limner in Scotland, and in 1830 painter-in-ordinary to King **William IV**.

Wilkins, Sir George Hubert 1888–1958 •*Australian explorer*• He was born in Mt Bryan East, and first went to the Arctic in 1913. In 1919 he flew from England to Australia, then spent from 1921 to 1922 in the Antarctic. After his return he collected material in Central Australia on behalf of the British Museum, London. In 1926 he returned to the Arctic, and in 1928 was knighted for a pioneer flight from Alaska to Spitsbergen, over polar ice. In 1931 he undertook a further expedition, this time with the submarine *Nautilus*, but an attempt to reach the North Pole under the ice was unsuccessful.

Wilkins, Maurice Hugh Frederick 1916– •*British physicist and Nobel Prize winner*• Born in New Zealand and educated at St John's College, Cambridge, he did research on uranium isotope separation at the University of California in 1944. He joined the Medical Research Council's Biophysics Research Unit at King's College London in 1946, becoming director 1970–72 and professor of biophysics (1970–81), now emeritus. **Francis Crick** and **James Watson** deduced their double helix model of DNA from Wilkins and **Rosalind Franklin**'s X-ray data of DNA fibers, and Crick, Watson and Wilkins were awarded the 1962 Nobel Prize for physiology or medicine for this work.

Wilkins, Roy 1901–81 •*US social reformer and civil rights leader*• Born in St Louis, Missouri, he graduated from the University of Minnesota in 1923 and for eight years edited the *Kansas City Call*, the leading African-American newspaper of the day. He joined the National Association for the Advancement of Colored People (NAACP) in 1931 and rose to become its executive director (1965–77). He was a major force behind school desegregation and the 1964 Civil Rights Act.

Wilkinson, Ellen Cicely 1891–1947 •*English feminist and Labour politician*• Born in Manchester, she was an early member of the Independent Labour Party and an active campaigner for women's suffrage. In 1924 she became Labour Member of Parliament for Middlesbrough East. Losing this seat in 1931, she reentered parliament in 1935 as Member of Parliament for Jarrow. In 1940 she became parliamentary secretary to the Ministry of Home Security, and in 1945 minister of education, the first woman to hold such an appointment.

Wilkinson, Sir Geoffrey 1921–96 •*English chemist and Nobel Prize winner*• He was born in Springside, near Manchester, and studied at Imperial College, London. During World War II he worked on the Canadian branch of the atomic bomb project with the National Research Council of Canada. He then moved to the Lawrence Radiation Laboratory of the University of California at Berkeley, and was appointed assistant professor at Harvard (1951). From 1955 to 1988 he was Professor of Inorganic Chemistry at Imperial College. While at Harvard he studied ferrocene and discovered that it had a type of structure entirely new to chemistry. This led to new lines of research in organic, inorganic and theoretical chemistry, and to the development of new catalysts used in industry and pharmaceutical manufacture. Wilkinson coauthored (with F A Cotton) a pioneering textbook, *Advanced Inorganic Chemistry* (1962), and was knighted in 1976. In 1973 he shared the Nobel Prize for chemistry with **Ernst Fischer**.

Willard, Emma, *née* **Hart** 1787–1870 •*US educator, a pioneer of higher education for women*• Born in Berlin, Connecticut, and educated at Berlin Academy (1802–03), she married Dr John Willard (d. 1825) in 1809. In 1814 she opened Middlebury Female Seminary, offering an unprecedented range of subjects, in order to prepare women for college. Unsuccessful in gaining funding for her school, she moved to Troy, New York, where she received financial help. The school developed fast, and she wrote several highly regarded history textbooks. Her campaign for equal educational opportunities for women paved the way for coeducation.

Willard, Frances Elizabeth Caroline 1839–98 •*US temperance campaigner*• Born in Churchville, New York, she studied at the Northwestern Female College, Evanston, Illinois, and became a professor of Aesthetics there. In 1874 she became secretary of the Women's Christian Temperance Union and edited the *Chicago Daily Post*. She helped found the International Council of Women.

William I (of England) *See* **William the Conqueror**

William II (Rufus) c. 1056–1100 •*King of England*• He was the second surviving son of **William the Conqueror**, whom he succeeded in 1087. The Norman nobles in England rebelled against him in favor of his eldest brother, Robert, Duke of Normandy, but Rufus suppressed the rebellion with the support of the English people after making false promises of a relaxation of the forest laws and of fiscal burdens. He appointed **Anselm** as Archbishop of Canterbury, though he later quarreled with Anselm over the liberties of the Church. Rufus warred with Robert in Normandy, but peace was made (1091), and in 1096 the duchy was mortgaged to him. In 1098 he conquered Maine, but failed to hold the whole of it. Rufus invaded Wales three times. He was killed by an arrow while hunting in the New Forest, but whether his death was an accident has never been established. He was largely responsible for the Norman Conquest of the north of England.

William III, *also called* **William of Orange** 1650–1702 •*Stadtholder of the United Provinces of the Netherlands, and king of Great Britain and Ireland*• Born in The Hague, he was the posthumous son of William II (1626–50) of Orange and Mary (1631–60), eldest daughter of **Charles I** of Great Britain. Following the assassination of the grand pensionary, **Jan De Witt**, he was chosen stadtholder of the Netherlands in 1672. An inexperienced soldier, he defied all odds and was able to halt the advance of the French army and negotiate favorable peace terms at Nijmegen in 1678. Great Britain, an ally of France, was forced out of the war following a highly successful propaganda campaign linking the French alliance with British fears of Catholicism and arbitrary government. In 1677, in an attempt to retrieve the situation, **Charles II** agreed to a marriage between William and **Mary**, eldest daughter of James, Duke of York (**James VII and II**). When James became king of Scotland and England (1685), his policy of Catholicization provided William with the opportunity for invading his father-in-law's kingdoms in the name of his wife. He landed at Torbay on November 5, 1688, ostensibly to protect the Protestant religion and traditional parliamentary liberties, but he was more concerned to mobilize British resources in money and manpower for the Continental war effort. James then fled to France, and William and Mary were crowned in February 1689. The successive defeats of James's supporters at Killiecrankie (July 1689) and on the Boyne (1690) and the surrender of Limerick (1691) effectively ended Jacobite resistance, and William turned his attention to the Continental war, which was ended indecisively at the Peace of Ryswick (1697). Never popular in Great Britain, William found his position materially weakened by the death of Mary in 1694. His reign nevertheless brought stability at home after a period of considerable political unrest. He transferred control of the standing army to parliament (1698) and introduced greater freedom of the press (1695). He died after a fall when his horse stumbled over a molehill. He was succeeded by Mary's sister, Queen **Anne**.

“ ”

People in Parliament occupy themselves with private animosities and petty quarrels, and think little of the national interest.

1699 Letter, January.

William IV, *known as* **the Sailor King** 1765–1837 •*King of Great Britain*• The third son of **George III**, he was born at Buckingham Palace, London. He joined the navy (1779), and in 1789 was made Duke of Clarence. From 1790 to 1811 he lived with the actress **Dorothy Jordan**, who bore him ten children, but in 1818 he married Adelaide (1792–1849), eldest daughter of the Duke of Saxe-Meiningen. Their two daughters died in infancy. With the Duke of York's death (1827), the Duke of Clarence became heir presumptive to the throne, to which he succeeded on the death of his eldest brother, **George IV**, in 1830. A Whig up to his accession, he turned Tory, and did much to obstruct the passing of the first Reform Act (1832), but then accepted a succession of liberal reforms. He was succeeded by his niece, **Victoria**.

William I (the Silent) 1533–84 •*Prince of Orange*• He became the first of the hereditary stadtholders of the United Provinces of the Netherlands in 1572. He joined the aristocratic protest of the oppressive and antiheretic policies of **Philip II** of Spain, and eventually organized an army against the Duke of **Alva**, Philip's regent in the Netherlands. After initial reverses, he began the recovery of the coastal towns, and he became the leader of the northern provinces, united in the Union of Utrecht (1579) in revolt against Spain in the Eighty Years' War. He was assassinated in Delft by a Spanish agent. His nickname comes from his ability to keep secret **Henry II** of France's scheme to massacre all the Protestants of France and the Netherlands, confided to him when he was a French hostage (1559).

William I 1143–1214 •*King of Scotland*• He was the grandson of **David I** and brother of **Malcolm IV**, whom he succeeded in 1165. He continued the consolidation of Scotland as a feudal kingdom and defended it from the Angevin kings of England, but was forced to pay **Henry II** explicit homage for Scotland and his other lands (1174). This was revoked by **Richard I** (1189) in return for payment of 10,000 marks. He enjoyed a reputation for personal piety and was buried in the abbey church at Arbroath, which he had founded in 1178.

William of Auvergne, *also known as* **William of Paris** and **Guillaume d'Auvergne** c. 1180–1249 •*French philosopher and theologian*• Born in Aurillac, Aquitaine, he became a professor of Theology at the University of Paris (1225) and was Bishop of Paris (1228–49). His most important work is the monumental *Magisterium divinale* (1223–40, "The Divine Teaching"), and his main achievement was the attempted integration of classical Greek and Arabic philosophy with Christian theology.

William of Auxerre c. 1140–1231 •*French theologian and philosopher*• Born in Auxerre, he became a master of theology and was for many years an administrator at the University of Paris. In 1230 he was sent as French envoy to Pope **Gregory IX** to advise on dissension in the university, and he pleaded the cause of the students against King **Louis IX**. His main publication is the *Summa aurea in quatuor libros sententiarum* ("Golden Compendium on the Four Books of Sentences"), a commentary on early and medieval Christian thought tending to emphasize the value of philosophy and rational analysis as a tool for Christian theology.

William of Malmesbury c. 1090–c. 1143 •*English chronicler and monk*• Born probably near Malmesbury, Wiltshire, he became a Benedictine monk in the monastery at Malmesbury, and eventually librarian and precentor. He took part in the council at Winchester against King **Stephen** in 1141. His *Gesta pontificum* is an ecclesiastical history of the bishops and chief monasteries of England to 1123. The *Gesta regum Anglorum* provides a lively history of the kings of England from the Saxon invasion to 1126, and the *Historia novella* brings the narrative to 1142. Other works are an account of the church at Glastonbury and lives of St **Dunstan** and St **Wulfstan**.

William of Orange *See* **William III**

William of Paris *See* **William of Auvergne**

William of Waynflete 1395–1486 •*English prelate*• Educated probably at New College, Oxford, he became the provost of Eton in 1443, Bishop of Winchester in 1447 and in 1448 founded Magdalen College, Oxford. Involved in the negotiations which ended **Jack Cade**'s 1450 rebellion, he played an important role, as a Lancastrian, advising **Henry VI** in the Wars of the Roses. He was lord chancellor (1456–60).

William of Wykeham or **Wickham** 1324–1404 •*English churchman and statesman*• Born in Wickham, Hampshire, perhaps the son of a serf, he rose in the service of **Edward III** to become keeper of the Privy Seal (1363), bishop of Winchester (1367) and twice chancellor of England (1367–71, 1389–91). He founded New College, Oxford, and Winchester College. He has been called the "father of the public school system," and he established (though he did not invent) perpendicular architecture.

William the Conqueror, *also called* **William the Bastard** 1027–87 •*King of England as William I from 1066*• He was born in Falaise, the bastard son of Robert, Duke of Normandy, and a tanner's daughter called Arlette. On his father's death in 1035 he was accepted as duke by the nobles, but his youth was passed in difficulty and danger. In 1051 he visited his cousin, **Edward the Confessor**, king of England, and may well have received the promise of the English succession. He married Matilda, daughter of Baldwin V, Count of Flanders, in 1053. In the next ten years William repulsed two French invasions, and in 1063 conquered Maine. It is probable that in 1064 Harold Godwinsson (later **Harold II**) was at his court and swore to help him to gain the English Crown on Edward's death. When, however, Edward died in 1066, Harold himself became king. William laid his claim to the English throne before the pope and western Christendom. The pope approved his claim, and William invaded England on September 28, immediately taking the towns of Pevensey and Hastings. At the Battle of Hastings (or Senlac), on October 14, 1066, Harold was defeated and killed, and William was crowned king of England in Westminster Abbey on Christmas Day. The west and north of England were subdued in 1068; the following year the north rebelled, and William devastated the country between York and Durham. English government under William assumed a more feudal aspect, the old national assembly becoming a council of the king's tenants in chief, and all title to land was derived from his grant. In 1086 he ordered the compilation of the Domesday Book, which contains details of the land settlement. The church was also reformed and feudalized. William's rule was successful despite several revolts which occurred even after 1069. In 1070 there was a rebellion in the Fen Country, and under the leadership of **Hereward the Wake**, the rebels for some time held out on the Isle of Ely. English exiles were sheltered by the Scottish king, **Malcolm III Canmore**, who occasionally plundered the northern shires, but William in 1072 compelled Malcolm to do him homage at Abernethy. In 1073 he was forced to reconquer Maine. Having entered on a war with **Philip I** of France in 1087, William burned Mantes. As he rode through the burning town his horse stumbled, and he received an injury, of which he died at Rouen on September 9; he was buried in the abbey he had founded at Caen. He left Normandy to his son Robert, and England to his other surviving son, **William II**.

Williams, Sir Bernard Arthur Owen 1929–2003 •*English philosopher*• Educated at Balliol College, Oxford, he taught in London and Oxford before becoming a professor of philosophy at Bedford College, London (1964–67). He became a professor of philosophy at Cambridge (1967) and provost of King's College, Cambridge (1979). He held many visiting positions at universities in the US, Australia and Africa, and in 1987 emigrated to become Professor of Philosophy at the University of California, Berkeley. He returned to the UK to become Professor of Philosophy at Oxford (1990–96). His philosophical work was wide-ranging, with particularly influential contributions to moral philosophy in works such as *Morality: An Introduction to Ethics* (1972). He chaired the Committee on Obscenity and Film Censorship, which produced the Williams Report in 1979. He was married (1955–74) to the politician **Shirley Williams** and was knighted in 1999.

Williams, Betty 1943– •*Irish peace activist and Nobel Prize winner*• Born in Belfast, a Roman Catholic, she founded with **Mairead Corrigan-Maguire** the Northern Ireland Peace Movement (the "Peace People") in 1976. They shared the 1976 Nobel Peace Prize.

Williams, Cicely Delphine 1893–1992 •*British pioneer in maternal and child health*• Born in Kew Park, Jamaica, into a plantation-owning family, she attended Somerville College, Oxford, then qualified as a doctor at King's College Hospital (1923). She joined the Colonial Medical Service in the Gold Coast in 1929, and gave a vivid description in the *Lancet* (1935) of the condition kwashiorkor (a disease in newly weaned children caused by protein deficiency). She was in Singapore in 1942 when the Japanese invaded; imprisoned in Changi, she survived incarceration in cages with the dead and the dying. She later became the first head of Mother and Child Health (1948–52) in the World Health Organization, Geneva, and lectured in more than 70 countries, promoting breastfeeding and combined preventive and curative medicine.

Williams, Edward, *pseudonym* **Iolo Morganwg** 1747–1826 •*Welsh poet and antiquary*• Born in Llancarfan, Glamorgan, he worked there as a stonemason and became a poet in Welsh and English. He had links with 18th-century radicalism, mingling its ideas with Romantic exaltation of the Welsh past, and he established neo-Druidic cults and celebrations in Wales. He published collected poems purportedly by the 14th-century poet Dafydd ap

Gwilym, which in fact were his own work; other material from the Welsh past with varying degrees of authenticity was published posthumously. A brilliant forger whose deceptions far outlived his own time, he prolonged, revived and reinvigorated ancient and modern Welsh culture.

Williams, Esther Jane 1922– •*US swimmer and film actress*• Born in Inglewood, California, near Los Angeles, she became a record-breaking swimmer, was selected for the canceled 1940 Olympics, and entered the fringes of show business as part of a San Francisco Aquacade in 1940. Seen by a Hollywood talent scout, she signed with MGM and made her film debut in *Andy Hardy's Double Life* in 1942. Beginning with *Bathing Beauty* (1944) she specialized in films designed to showcase her aquatic abilities. A top box-office attraction, she appeared in several films including *Neptune's Daughter* (1949), *Jupiter's Darling* (1955) and *The Big Show* (1961). She later designed a range of swimwear, promoted swimming pools and worked as a sports commentator. In 1994, she hosted *That's Entertainment III*, a nostalgic celebration of MGM's past.

Williams, Sir Frederic Calland 1911–77 •*English electrical engineer*• Born in Romily, Cheshire, he studied at the University of Manchester and at Oxford. During World War II he was recognized as a world authority on radar. He became a professor of electrical engineering at Manchester in 1946 and is chiefly known for his development of the Williams tube, the first successful electrostatic random access memory for the digital computer. This enabled him, with his collaborator **Tom Kilburn**, to operate the world's first stored-program computer in June 1948. Williams was knighted in 1976.

Williams, Fred(erick Ronald) 1927–82 •*Australian landscape painter and etcher*• Born in Richmond, Victoria, he studied in London at the Chelsea and Central Schools of Art. Although he painted distinguished portraits, his considerable reputation lies in his landscapes, where his personal vision, use of color and sense of scale brought him recognition as the most significant painter of the Australian landscape since Sir **Arthur Streeton**, acknowledged when their work was shown together at an exhibition held at the National Gallery of Victoria in 1970. He won the Wynne Prize in 1966 and 1976.

Williams, (Hiram) Hank 1923–53 •*US country singer and songwriter*• He was born in Mount Olive, Alabama. Inspired by **Jimmie Rodgers** and Roy Acuff, he won a talent contest in 1937, and had his own local radio show. The war interrupted his career, but he signed to the Acuff-Rose publishing agency as a songwriter in 1946 and had his first big hit in 1949 with "Lovesick Blues." Despite continuing problems with alcohol, drugs and failing health, he became country music's biggest star. He wrote and sang some of the genre's greatest songs, including "Cold, Cold Heart," "Hey, Good Lookin'" and "I'm So Lonesome I Could Cry." He died of alcohol-related heart disease while traveling to a New Year's Day show in Ohio. His son, Hank Williams, Jr (1949–), also became a leading country singer.

" "

You got to have smelt a lot of mule manure before you can sing like a hillbilly.
*Quoted in **Rolling Stone**, 1969.*

Williams, Jody 1950– •*US campaigner*• Born in Rutland, Vermont, she studied at Johns Hopkins University and worked in educational and medical aid projects for a number of Central American countries. She cofounded the International Campaign to Ban Landmines in 1992, which sought to bring to public attention the minefield casualty rate of some 26,000 people a year, primarily civilians, in more than 60 countries worldwide. The campaign paved the way for the Oslo Treaty of 1997 calling for a ban on the development, trade, and use of the weapons. In 1997 she and the campaign were jointly awarded the Nobel Peace Prize.

Williams, John Christopher 1941– •*Australian classical guitarist*• Born in Melbourne, Victoria, he trained at the Accademia Musicale Chigiana di Siena, Italy, and at the Royal College of Music, London. He became a leading international figure on classical guitar and has been responsible for commissioning a great deal of contemporary compositions for the instrument. He tours widely, giving solo recitals and performing in chamber groups and as soloist with international orchestras. He has also performed in rock (notably with the group Sky, 1979–84), jazz and folk contexts, and has taken a number of recordings into the pop charts.

Williams, John (Towner) 1932– •*US composer of film music*• Born in Floral Park on Long Island, New York, he trained at the Juilliard School of Music and began his career as a jazz pianist. In the late 1950s he started composing for television, turning to film in the 1960s. He began his long professional association with **Steven Spielberg** in 1974, and his work includes the Oscar-winning orchestrations of *Fiddler on the Roof* (1971), *Jaws* (1975), *Star Wars* (1977), *E.T.* (1982) and the Harry Potter films (2001, 2002, 2004).

Williams, Kenneth 1926–88 •*English actor and comedian*• Born in London, he made his London debut as Slightly in *Peter Pan* in 1952. He later starred in comedies and in such revues as *Share My Lettuce* (1957), *Pieces of Eight* (1959) and *One Over the Eight* (1961). He became well known in such radio series as *Round the Horne* and *Stop Messing About*, in which his affected style of speech and rich, punctilious enunciation made him instantly recognizable. He made several films, appearing regularly in the *Carry On* series of comedies.

Williams, Mary Lou 1910–81 •*US jazz pianist, arranger and composer*• Born in Atlanta, Georgia, and brought up in Pittsburgh, she interrupted her high school studies to become a touring show pianist. Her outstanding qualities as an arranger brought her work from **Duke Ellington** (for whom she arranged the well-known *Trumpets No End*), **Earl Hines** and **Benny Goodman**, among others. She later embraced the bebop style as well as writing several sacred works, such as "Mary Lou's Mass" (1970). Her *Waltz Boogie* (1946) was one of the first jazz pieces in 3/4 time.

Williams, Michael 1935–2001 •*English actor*• Born in Manchester, he made his West End debut as Bernard Fuller in *Celebration* (1961) and had a long career with the Royal Shakespeare Company. On television, he played Mike in *A Fine Romance* (1980–82), N V Standish in *Double First* (1988), Billy Balsam in *September Song* (1993–95) and Barry Masefield in *Conjugal Rites* (1993–94). He was married to the actress Dame **Judi Dench**.

Williams, Raymond 1921–88 •*Welsh critic and novelist*• Born in Pandy, Gwent, the son of a railway signalman, he was educated at Cambridge. He wrote *Culture and Society* (1958), which required socialists to seek inspiration in figures like **Edmund Burke**, **Robert Southey**, and **Thomas Carlyle**. He opened up questions of mass readership and cultural and ethical values in *The Long Revolution* (1966). He was made a Fellow of Jesus College, Cambridge, in 1961 and was Professor of Drama there from 1974 to 1983. He was active in New Left intellectual movements, producing the *May Day Manifesto* (1968), but his novels *Border Country* (1960) and *Loyalties* (1985) underline the significance of Welsh consciousness for him. Of his many major works in socioliterary criticism, *The Country and the City* (1973) was possibly the most inspirational.

Williams, Robbie (Robert Peter) 1974– •*English pop singer*• Born in Stoke-on-Trent, Staffordshire, he achieved stardom as a singer with the teenage boy band Take That (1991–95), with whom he had eight number-one singles. In 1995 he sensationally left the band and concentrated on a solo career, with hit singles including "Angels" (1997), "Let Me Entertain You" (1998), "Millennium" (1998) and "Rock DJ" (2000), as well as with the albums *Life Thru a Lens* (1998) and *Sing When You're Winning* (2000).

Williams, Robin 1951– •*US film actor*• Born in Chicago, Illinois, he was a student of acting at the Juilliard School in New York, and later settled in California, developing into a nimble-witted stand-up comic with a restless, inventive mind and a gift for improvisation. Roles in the television series *Happy Days* and *Mork and Mindy* (1978–82) brought him national popularity, and he made his big screen debut in *Popeye* (1980). His cinema career struggled until he received Best Actor Academy Award nominations for *Good Morning, Vietnam* (1987), *Dead Poets Society* (1989) and *The Fisher King* (1991). Films like *Mrs Doubtfire* (1993) and *The Birdcage* (1996) have confirmed his comedy genius, and he has shown his dramatic abilities in *Seize the Day* (1986), *Awakenings* (1990) and *Good Will Hunting* (1997), for which he won an Academy Award. More recent films include *Jakob the Liar* (1999) and *One Hour Photo* (2002).

Williams, Roger c. 1604–83 •*American colonist and clergyman*• Born in London, he was educated at Charterhouse and Pembroke College, Cambridge. He took Anglican orders, became an extreme Puritan and emigrated in 1630 to the Massachusetts Bay colony. He refused to participate in the Church in Boston, believing it had not separated from the English Church. He moved to Salem where, after challenging the authority of the Puritan magistrates over matters of personal conscience, he was persecuted and eventually banished. He took refuge with Native Americans, then purchased land from them on which he founded the city of Providence in 1636, establishing the first Baptist church in the US in 1639. His colony of Rhode Island was a model of democracy and religious freedom. He went to England in 1643 and 1651 to procure a charter for it and served as its president (1654–57). His works include *The Bloudy Tenent of Persecution for Cause of Conscience* (1644) and *The Bloudy Tenent Yet More Bloudy by Mr Cotton's Endeavour to Wash It White in the Blood of the Lamb* (1652).

Williams, Serena 1981– •*US tennis player*• Born in Saginaw, Michigan, she and her older sister **Venus Williams** were acknowledged as the dominant forces in women's tennis at the beginning of the 21st century. Coached in tennis by her father from the age of four, in 1999 she won the US Open singles. She went on to win numerous doubles titles in partnership with Venus, including Olympic gold in 2000. She lost to her sister in the singles semifinals at Wimbledon in 2000, but defeated her in 2002, when they also won the doubles title.

Williams, Shirley Vivien Teresa Brittain Williams, Baroness 1930– •*English politician*• The daughter of **Vera Brittain**, she studied at Oxford. She first became a Labour Member of Parliament in 1964, holding ministerial posts before being appointed secretary of state for prices and consumer protection (1974–76), then for education and science (1976–79). She was a cofounder of the Social Democratic Party (SDP) in 1981 and became the party's first elected Member of Parliament later that year. She became president of the SDP the following year, but lost her seat in the 1983 general election. In 1988 she joined the newly merged Social and Liberal Democratic Party (SLDP). Her first husband was the philosopher **Bernard Williams** (married 1955–74) and married again in 1998. She was a professor of elective politics at Harvard (1998–2000) and is the leader of the liberal democrats in the House of Lords. She was awarded a life peerage in 1993.

Williams, Ted 1918–2002 •*US baseball player*• Born in San Diego, California, he won acclaim as one of the greatest hitters in baseball history as a star with the Boston Red Sox in the 1940s and 1950s. Despite missing nearly five full seasons through injury and military service in World War II and Korea, he hit 521 home runs and won two Triple Crowns (1942, 1947), two Most Valuable Player awards (1946, 1949) and six American League batting championships.

Williams, Tennessee, *originally* **Thomas Lanier** 1911–83 •*US playwright*• Born in Columbus, Mississippi, the son of a traveling salesman, he had an itinerant college education, finally receiving a degree from the University of Iowa in 1938. He worked at various menial jobs before recognition of his literary talent came in 1940, when he received a Rockefeller Fellowship for his first play, *Battle of Angels*. In 1943 he signed a six-month contract with MGM, later canceled when he submitted a script that became *The Glass Menagerie*. This play, which in 1945 earned him the New York Drama Critics' Circle Award, introduced him as an important US playwright. He was awarded the Pulitzer Prize in 1948 for *A Streetcar Named Desire*, and again in 1955 for *Cat on a Hot Tin Roof*. He continued with *Suddenly Last Summer* (1958), *Sweet Bird of Youth* (1959) and *The Night of the Iguana* (1961). In addition to his plays, he published poetry collections and short stories. He wrote one novel, *The Roman Spring of Mrs Stone* (1950), and the scripts for several films, including *Baby Doll* (1956). *Where I Live: Selected Essays* (1978) is autobiographical.

“ ”

I have always depended on the kindness of strangers.

1947 Blanche. ***A Streetcar Named Desire****, scene 11.*

Williams, Venus 1980– •*US tennis player*• Born in Lynwood, California, she and her younger sister, **Serena Williams**, emerged as the leading forces on the women's circuit at the beginning of the 21st century. Coached by her father from the age of four, she reached the final of the US Open in 1997. Her first Grand Slam singles victory came in 2000 when she won the Wimbledon title. She added the US Open and the Olympic singles titles that same year. A second Wimbledon singles title followed in 2001. Her many doubles titles in partnership with Serena have included an Olympic gold medal in 2000.

Williams, William Carlos 1883–1963 •*US poet, novelist and cultural historian*• Born in Rutherford, Connecticut, with French, Jewish, Basque and British antecedents, he was educated in Switzerland and Paris, then took his MD at the University of Pennsylvania, Philadelphia. There he met both **Ezra Pound** and **Hilda Doolittle** ("HD"), both of whom had a considerable impact on his developing interest in poetry. His early volumes, such as *The Tempers* (1913) and *Sour Grapes* (1921), steered him toward the simple free-verse idiom, with its focus on immediate physical detail, which would characterize his work. He reached creative maturity with *Spring and All* (1923) and his ironic *The Great American Novel* (1923). *In the American Grain* (1925) was a brilliant study of American myths. In 1937 he published *White Mule* (1937), the first in a trilogy of novels completed by *In the Money* (1940) and *The Build-Up* (1952). He is best known for his poetic masterpiece *Paterson*, a vast synoptic study of a real American town, begun in 1946. Williams's objectivist credo "No ideas but in things" became a major tenet of modernist writing. He won the Pulitzer Prize for *Pictures From Breughel* (1962). His *Autobiography* appeared in 1951.

Williamson, David Keith 1942– •*Australian playwright*• Born in Melbourne, Victoria, he graduated in mechanical engineering from Monash University, Melbourne, but turned to writing plays and scripts for films and television. His first works to receive recognition were *The Removalists* (1971) and *Don's Party* (1973). Other successes include *The Club* (1977), *The Perfectionist* (1982) and *Sons of Cain* (1985). Some of his stage works have subsequently been filmed, and he has also written other film scripts, including those for *Gallipoli* (1981), *Phar Lap* (1983) and *Money and Friends* (1992).

Williamson, Henry 1895–1977 •*English writer*• He was born in Bedfordshire, and after service in World War I became a journalist, but he turned to farming in Norfolk and eventually settled in a cottage on Exmoor. He wrote several semiautobiographical novels, including his long series *A Chronicle of Ancient Sunlight* (1951–69). He is best known, however, for his classic nature stories, starting with *The Peregrine's Saga* (1923). He achieved enduring fame with *Tarka the Otter* (1927, Hawthornden Prize) and *Salar the Salmon* (1935). His trenchant antiwar novel *A Patriot's Progress* (1930) was much admired, but his support for Sir **Oswald Mosley** and **Hitler** greatly damaged his reputation. He wrote two autobiographical works (1929, 1958), and a biography of his friend **T E Lawrence** (1941).

Williamson, Malcolm Benjamin Graham Christoper 1931–2003 •*Australian composer*• Born in Sydney, he studied under **Eugène Goossens** and **Elizabeth Lutyens**, and went to England in 1953. His operas include *Our Man in Havana* (1963), *The Violins of Saint-Jacques* (1966) and *The Red Sea* (1972). He wrote for television and films, including *The Happy Prince* (1965) and *Julius Caesar Jones* (1966), and composed ballets, orchestral works, vocal, choral and piano music, and "cassations," often involving the audience. He was made Master of the Queen's Music in 1975.

Willibrord, St 658–739 •*English monk*• Born in Northumbria, he trained in Ripon Abbey. After working in Ireland, he and 11 others left for the Netherlands as missionaries in 690. Responsible for converting much of the Netherlands to Christianity, the Merovingian and Carolingian Frankish kings legitimized his work in Friesland. Willibrord visited Rome about 692 and 695, and was made Archbishop of the Frisians, based in Utrecht, in 694. In 700 he founded the monastery of Echternach in Luxembourg. His feast day is November 7.

Willis, Bruce 1955– •*US actor*• Born in Penn's Grove, New Jersey, he worked as a security guard and played in a blues band before studying drama at Montclair State College and making his off-Broadway debut in *Heaven and Earth* (1977). An extra in films including *The Verdict* (1982), he became a star as the wisecracking David Addison in the television series *Moonlighting* (1985–89), for which he received an Emmy award. *Die Hard* (1988) established him as a movie star, and he has pursued an erratic career, alternating action-man roles with more sensitive character parts in films like *Mortal Thoughts* (1991), *Pulp Fiction* (1994) and *Nobody's Fool* (1994). Other films include *Die Hard With a Vengeance* (1995), *Twelve Monkeys* (1995) and *The Sixth Sense* (1999).

Willis, Norman David 1933– •*English trade union leader*• Educated at Ruskin and Oriel Colleges, Oxford, he worked for two years for the Transport and General Workers' Union (TGWU) before national service (1951–53). He returned to the TGWU in increasingly senior positions before being appointed assistant general secretary of the Trades Union Congress (TUC) in 1974. He succeeded **Len Murray** as general secretary (1984–93). As a moderate, he frequently provoked a hostile reaction from leftist union leaders.

Willis, Thomas 1621–73 •*English physician, one of the founders of the Royal Society*• Born in Great Bedwyn, Wiltshire, he studied at Oxford, and briefly served in the Royalist army in the British civil war. He was one of the small group of natural philosophers including **Robert Boyle** who met in Oxford in 1648–49 and who in 1662 were to become founding members of the Royal Society of London. He became Sedleian Professor of Natural Philosophy at Oxford (1660–75), but his fame and wealth derived from a fashionable medical practice in London. His *Cerebri anatome, cui accessit nervorum descriptio et usus* (1664, "Anatomy of the Brain, With a Description of the Nerves and Their Function") was the principal study of brain anatomy of its time. He was also a pioneer of the clinical and pathological analysis of diabetes and the first to recognize that spasm of the bronchial muscles was the essential characteristic of asthma.

Willkie, Wendell 1892–1944 •*US politician*• Born in Elwood, Indiana, he became first a lawyer and later an industrialist. Having removed his support from the Democratic to the Republican cause in 1940, he was nominated as presidential candidate by the Republican Party and was narrowly defeated in the election of that year. In 1941–42 he traveled the world representing the president. An opponent of isolationism, he was leader of the left-wing element in his party.

Wills, William John 1834–61 •*Australian surveyor and explorer*• He was born in Totnes, Devon, England, and trained in medicine. He arrived in Victoria in 1852 as a surveyor and became second-in-command of **Robert O'Hara Burke**'s ill-fated expedition to cross the continent of Australia from south to north. They set off from Melbourne and reached the edge of the Gulf of Carpentaria, but then ran out of food, ate their camels, and continued on foot. Wills and Burke reached their supply depot at Cooper's Creek seven hours after the support party had left, but died of starvation in terrible conditions at the end of June 1861; only **John King** survived the expedition.

Wills Moody, Helen Newington, *née* **Wills** 1905–98 •*US tennis player*• Born in Centreville, California, she dominated women's tennis from the retirement of **Suzanne Lenglen** in 1926 until the outbreak of World War II, winning eight singles finals at Wimbledon and seven US championships. She also won gold medals in the women's singles and doubles at the 1924 Olympics. While she was married (1929–37) she added her husband's name to her own. Her great rivalry with Helen Jacobs (1908–97) drove her to continue to play during the 1938 Wimbledon final, despite being severely handicapped by injury.

Wilmore, Michael *See* **Mac Liammóir, Mícheál**

Wilson, Alexander 1766–1813 •*US ornithologist*• Born in Paisley, Renfrewshire, Scotland, he worked as a weaver from the age of 13, and published *Poems* (1790) and *Watty and Meg* (1792). He was prosecuted for a libelous poem against the mill owners, which he denied writing, but he was jailed for 18 months. In 1794 he emigrated to the US and became a schoolteacher. He decided to devote himself to ornithology and made several journeys across the US, collecting species and drawing them. In 1806 he was employed on the US edition of *Rees's Cyclopaedia*, and he prevailed on the publisher to undertake an illustrated *American Ornithology* (7 vols, 1808–14); the eighth and ninth volumes were completed after his death. Wilson's storm petrel and Wilson's phalarope were named in his honor. He is regarded as the founder of American ornithology.

Wilson, A(ndrew) N(orman) 1950– •*English novelist, biographer, critic and journalist*• Born in Stone, Staffordshire, he was educated at Rugby and Oxford. Since publishing his first novel, *The Sweets of Pimlico* (1977), he has maintained a prolific output. Many of his earlier novels were comedies of manners, but works such as *The Healing Art* (1980) and *Wise Virgin* (1982) deal with specific moral issues. His biographies include *Sir Walter Scott* (1980), *Milton* (1983), *Tolstoy* (1987), the controversial *Jesus* (1992) and *The Rise and Fall of the House of Windsor* (1993). He was literary editor of the *Evening Standard* from 1990 to 1997.

Wilson, Sir Angus Frank Johnstone 1913–91 •*English writer*• Born in Bexhill, Sussex, the son of an English father and a South African mother, he was educated at Westminster School and Merton College, Oxford. He joined the staff of the British Museum library in London in 1937. He began writing in 1946 and rapidly established a reputation with his brilliant collection of short stories, *The Wrong Set* (1949), satirizing the more aimless sections of prewar middle-class society. The novels *Hemlock and After* (1952) and *Anglo-Saxon Attitudes* (1956) were both best-sellers, and his later novels, including *The Old Men in the Zoo* (1961), *Late Call* (1965) and *No Laughing Matter* (1967), an ambitious family chronicle of the egocentric Matthews family spanning the 20th century, also received critical acclaim. His later novels include *As If by Magic* (1973) and *Setting the World on Fire* (1980). He also wrote one play, *The Mulberry Bush* (1955). He was Professor of English Literature at the University of East Anglia from 1966 to 1978.

“ ”

All fiction is for me a kind of magic and trickery—a confidence trick, trying to make people believe something is true that isn't.

1957 In ***The Paris Review****, no. 17.*

Wilson, August 1945– •*US playwright*• Born in Pittsburgh into an African-American working-class family, he dropped out of high school. He began to write poetry in his twenties, then turned to drama. His powerful, richly colloquial plays draw on jazz, the blues and African-American idiom and folk culture for their inspiration. In the 1980s he began an ambitious cycle chronicling the lives of African Americans in the 20th century, with each play focusing on a different decade. He has twice been awarded the Pulitzer Prize for drama, for *Fences* in 1987 and *The Piano Lesson* in 1990. His other works include *Ma Rainey's Black Bottom* (1984), *Joe Turner's Come and Gone* (1986) and *Seven Guitars* (1995).

Wilson, Brian 1942– •*US pop and rock musician and composer*• He was born in Hawthorne, California, and was the creative force behind The Beach Boys, the most successful American group of the 1960s. Their early surfing hits gave way to more ambitious projects from *Pet Sounds* (1966) onward, the most famous of which, the fabled *Smile* album, was never made in its projected form. Wilson gave up most performing and retreated to the studio in the wake of a nervous breakdown in 1964, which marked the beginning of a long history of mental disturbance. His involvement in the band and in music became increasingly sporadic, but he returned with a solo album, *Love and Mercy*, in 1988. He sang on Van Dyke Parks's *Orange Crate Art* (1995) and also on the soundtrack to a documentary film about him, *I Just Wasn't Made for These Times* (1995).

Wilson, Charles Thomson Rees 1869–1959 •*Scottish pioneer of atomic and nuclear physics, and Nobel Prize winner*• He was born in Glencorse, near Edinburgh. Educated at Manchester and at Cambridge, where he later became Professor of Natural Philosophy

(1925–34), he was noted for his study of atmospheric electricity, one byproduct of which was the successful protection from lightning of Britain's wartime barrage balloons. His greatest achievement was to devise the cloud chamber method of marking the track of alpha particles and electrons. The principle was also used by **Donald Glaser** to develop the bubble chamber. In 1927 he shared with **Arthur Compton** the Nobel Prize for physics.

Wilson, Edmund 1895–1972 •*US literary critic, social commentator and novelist*• Born in Red Bank, New Jersey, he was educated at Princeton and became a journalist with *Vanity Fair*, editor of the *New Republic* (1926–31), and chief book reviewer for the *New Yorker*. A lively, waspish critic of other writers, his own fiction, of which *Memoirs of Hecate Country* (1946) is the most notable example, is largely forgotten. However, few critics have caused such a stir as he, and he was more listened to than most. *Axel's Castle* (1931), a study of Symbolist literature, is a landmark, but *To the Finland Station* (1940), an account of the origins of the Bolshevik Revolution, and *The Wound and the Bow* (1941), a study of the relation between psychic malaise and creativity, are no less significant. In *Patriotic Gore: Studies in the Literature of the Civil War* (1962), Wilson surveyed in detail the writers of the period. Over a wide-ranging oeuvre and argumentative life he published on many subjects and in a variety of forms, encompassing plays, articles, correspondence and, in *The Scrolls From the Dead Sea* (1955), for which he learned Hebrew, a contentious but illuminating guide to a complex subject. Various memoirs detailing his life have appeared. He married four times; his third marriage was to the novelist **Mary McCarthy**.

Wilson, Edmund Beecher 1856–1939 •*US zoologist and embryologist*• Born in Geneva, Illinois, he studied at Yale and Johns Hopkins Universities, and after several teaching posts became Da Costa Professor of Zoology at Columbia University in New York. His research was concerned with cell lineage and the formation of tissues from precursor cells; his major contribution was to show the importance of the chromosomes, particularly the sex chromosomes, in heredity and cell structure. His *Cell in Development and Inheritance* (1896, 1925) was instrumental in the synthesis of cytology and Mendelian genetics. He is considered to be one of the founders of modern genetics.

Wilson, Edward Adrian 1872–1912 •*English physician, naturalist and explorer*• Born in Cheltenham, Gloucestershire, he first went to the Antarctic with **Robert Scott** on the *Discovery* (1900–04). In 1910 he returned to the Antarctic on the *Terra Nova* as chief of the expedition's scientific staff. One of the party of five that reached the South Pole just after the Norwegian **Roald Amundsen**, he died with the others on the return journey.

Wilson, Edward Osborne 1929– •*US biologist*• Born in Birmingham, Alabama, he studied there and at Harvard, where he became Baird Professor of Science (1976–94) and Curator of Entomology (1972–97, now honorary) at the Museum of Comparative Zoology. He has been a major figure in the development of sociobiology. His early research on the social behavior, communication and evolution of ants resulted in the publication of *The Insect Societies* (1971), in which he outlines his belief that the same evolutionary forces have shaped the behaviors of insects and other animals, including humans. His book *Sociobiology: The New Synthesis* (1975) was acclaimed for its detailed compilation and analysis of social behavior in a wide range of animals. In this work, too, he stated his controversial claim that the genes control a range of human behaviors, including aggression, homosexuality, altruism and differences between the sexes. His books include *On Human Nature* (1978) and *The Ants* (1990, with B Hölldobler), both of which won Pulitzer Prizes, and *The Diversity of Life* (1992).

Wilson (of Rievaulx), (James) Harold Wilson, Baron 1916–95 •*English Labour politician*• Born in Huddersfield, he was educated there, in Cheshire and at Oxford, where he became a lecturer in economics in 1937. In 1943–44 he was director of economics and statistics at the Ministry of Fuel and Power. Becoming Member of Parliament for Ormskirk in 1945, in 1947 he became successively secretary for overseas trade and president of the Board of Trade until his resignation on the tide of Bevanism in April 1951. In 1951 and 1955 he was reelected Member of Parliament for Huyton. The youngest cabinet minister since **William Pitt** the Younger, after 1956, when he headed the voting for the Labour shadow cabinet, he became the principal Opposition spokesman on economic affairs. An able and hard-hitting debater, in 1963 he succeeded **Hugh Gaitskell** as leader of the Labour Party, becoming prime minister in 1964 with a precariously small majority and being reelected in 1966 with comfortably large support. His government's economic plans were badly affected at home by the balance of payments crisis, leading to severe restrictive measures. Abroad he was faced with the Rhodesian problem (increasingly severe economic sanctions being applied) and continued intransigence from **de Gaulle** over Great Britain's proposed entry into the Common Market. His party lost power in the 1970 general election, and he became leader of the Opposition, but led the Labour Party back into government in 1974, resigning as party leader two years later. He was knighted in 1976 and made a life peer in 1983. Although he cultivated a homely, man-of-the-people public image, he was noted for his skill as a debater, and is considered to have been one of the shrewdest political operators of the 20th century. His *Memoirs* were published in 1986.

“ ”

A week is a long time in politics.

1964 Comment to lobby correspondents, October. As such meetings are off the record, there is no exact source for this famous phrase.

Wilson, Sir Henry Hughes 1864–1922 •*Irish field marshal*• He was born in Edgeworthstown, County Longford, and served in Burma (1884–87) and South Africa (1899–1901). He became director of military operations at the War Office (1910–14), and by the end of World War I was chief of the Imperial General Staff. Promoted to field marshal and made a baronet (1919), he resigned from the army in 1922 and became a Member of Parliament. His implacable opposition to the leaders of Sinn Fein led to his assassination on the doorstep of his London home.

Wilson, John Dover 1881–1969 •*English Shakespearean scholar*• Born in London and educated at Cambridge, he spent some years as a teacher, lecturer and royal inspector of adult education, then held professorships at King's College London (1924–35) and at Edinburgh (1935–45). He is best known for his Shakespearean studies, particularly on the problems in *Hamlet*. From 1921 till 1966 he was editor of the New Shakespeare series. His works include *What Happens in Hamlet* (1935) and *Shakespeare's Sonnets—An Introduction for Historians and Others* (1963).

Wilson, Kenneth Geddes 1936– •*US theoretical physicist and Nobel Prize winner*• Born in Waltham, Massachusetts, he was educated at Harvard and Caltech. After working at CERN (Conseil Européen pour la Recherche Nucléaire), in Geneva (1962–63), he moved to Cornell University, where he became professor of physics in 1971, later holding the same position at The Ohio State University (1988–). He applied ingenious mathematical methods to the understanding of the magnetic properties of atoms. He later used similar methods in the study of phase changes between liquids and gases, and in alloys. He proposed that the properties of a system of large numbers of interacting atoms could be predicted from observations of individual atoms, and for this work he was awarded the Nobel Prize for physics in 1982. More recently, he has applied his technique to the strong nuclear force that binds quarks in the nucleus.

Wilson, Richard, *originally* **Ian Colquhoun Wilson** 1936– •*Scottish actor and director*• Born in Greenock, Renfrewshire, he worked as a research scientist before training at the Royal Academy of Dramatic Art. His many television comedy roles include Jeremy Parsons in *A Sharp Intake of Breath* (1978–80) and Victor Meldrew in *One Foot in the Grave* (1990–2000). He was also in the television dramas *Selling Hitler* (1991), *The Life and Times of Henry Pratt* (1992) and *Under the Hammer* (1994), and has appeared in films such as *A Passage to India* (1984) and *Whoops Apocalypse* (1986). In the theater, he has worked extensively as an actor and director.

Wilson, Robert 1941– •*US epic theater maker, director and designer*• He was born in Waco, Texas, and trained as a painter in

Texas, Paris and New York. He developed a sense of visual impact that became evident in his subsequent career as a flamboyant postmodern creator of theatrical spectacle. He mixes a combination of movement, contemporary music and exciting imagery, often in very long performances (some have reached 12 hours). His set designs have been exhibited in major museums. His work includes *The Life and Times of Sigmund Freud* (1969), *The Life and Times of Joseph Stalin* (1973), *Death, Destruction and Detroit* (1979) and *The CIVIL WarS* (conceived 1984), one of the most ambitious theatrical events ever proposed and still to be mounted in full. He has collaborated with **Tom Waits**, most notably on the pop operas *The Black Rider* (1990) and *Alice* (1992).

Wilson, Robert Woodrow 1936– •*US physicist and Nobel Prize winner*• Born in Houston, Texas, he was educated at Rice University and the California Institute of Technology (Caltech). He then joined Bell Laboratories in New Jersey and became head of the radiophysics research department (1976–94). There he collaborated with **Arno Allan Penzias** in using a large radio telescope designed for communication with satellites; they detected in 1964 a radio noise background which came from all directions. **Robert Dicke** and **Phillip Peebles** suggested that this radiation is the residual radiation from the Big Bang at the universe's creation. Such a cosmic background radiation had been predicted to exist by **George Gamow**, **Ralph Alpher**, **Hans Bethe** and Robert Herman in 1948. Wilson and Penzias (jointly with **Peter Kapitza**) shared the 1978 Nobel Prize for physics for their work. In 1970 he continued his collaboration with Penzias and they discovered (with K B Jefferts) the 2.6-millimeter-wavelength radiation from interstellar carbon monoxide.

Wilson, Teddy (Theodore Shaw) 1912–86 •*US pianist, bandleader and arranger*• One of the most influential stylists of the swing era of the late 1930s, he was born in Austin, Texas, and studied music briefly at Talladega College, Alabama. As a teenager he worked in Chicago with major artists **Louis Armstrong** and clarinettist Jimmy Noone, among others. With his move to New York in 1933 to join the **Benny Carter** Orchestra, his career as a pianist and arranger was firmly established. He led many studio groups accompanying the singer **Billie Holiday**, and these recordings show his elegant, graceful style at its best.

Wilson, (Thomas) Woodrow 1856–1924 •*28th President of the US, and Nobel Prize winner*• Born in Staunton, Virginia, he studied at Princeton and Johns Hopkins Universities. He then practiced law, lectured at Bryn Mawr and Princeton, became president of Princeton in 1902, and governor of New Jersey in 1911. In 1912 and 1916, as Democratic candidate, he was elected president of the United States. Wilson's administration, ending in tragic failure and his own physical breakdown, is memorable for the Prohibition and women's suffrage amendments to the Constitution, trouble with Mexico, US participation in World War I, his part in the peace conference, his "fourteen points" plan for peace, which led to the Armistice, his championship of the League of Nations, and the Senate's rejection of the Treaty of Versailles, which led to his breakdown. He wrote *History of the American People* (1902) and other works, and was awarded the 1919 Nobel Peace Prize.

Winchilsea, Anne Finch, Countess of, *née* **Kingsmill** 1661–1720 •*English poet*• Born in Sidmonton near Southampton, she was the daughter of Sir William Kingsmill. In 1684 she married Heneage Finch, Earl of Winchilsea (from 1712). Her longest poem, a Pindaric ode called *The Spleen*, was printed in 1701, and her *Miscellany Poems* was printed in 1713. She was a friend of **Pope**, **Jonathan Swift** and **John Gay**, and her nature poems were admired by **Wordsworth** in his *Lyrical Ballads*.

Winckelmann, Johann Joachim 1717–68 •*German archaeologist*• Born in Stendal, in Prussian Saxony, he studied the history of art, published a treatise on the imitation of the antique (1754), and was librarian to a cardinal in Rome (1755). In 1758 he examined the remains of Herculaneum, Pompeii, and Paestum, and went to Florence. He wrote a treatise on ancient architecture (1762), the epoch-making *Geschichte der Kunst des Altertums* (1764, "History of the Art of Antiquity"), and *Monumenti Antichi Inediti* (1766). He was murdered in Trieste.

Windaus, Adolf Otto Reinhold 1876–1959 •*German chemist and Nobel Prize winner*• Born in Berlin, he commenced medical studies at the University of Berlin in 1895, but both there and subsequently at the University of Freiburg he became increasingly interested in chemistry. In 1915 he moved to the University of Göttingen, where he remained for the rest of his professional life. His most important research was on the structure of cholesterol, and in the 1920s he turned to a study of vitamin D, which is structurally related to cholesterol. For his work on cholesterol and vitamins he was awarded the Nobel Prize for chemistry in 1928.

Winfrey, Oprah Gail 1954– •*US actress and talk-show host*• Born in Kosciusko, Mississippi, she was a contestant in the Miss Black America Pageant in 1971 before securing a job cohosting the evening news on WTVF-TV in Nashville, Tennessee. She then became the cohost of *Baltimore Is Talking* (1977–84) and hosted *A.M. Chicago* in 1984. The following year saw the program retitled *The Oprah Winfrey Show* (1985–). Her film debut in *The Color Purple* (1985) resulted in an Academy Award nomination, and she has appeared in such television dramas as *The Women of Brewster Place* (1990), produced through her company, Harpo Productions. She has won numerous awards. She is also the first woman to own and produce her own talk show and the first African American to own a large television studio.

Wingate, Orde Charles 1903–44 •*English soldier, leader of the Chindits*• He served with the Sudan Defense Force from 1928 to 1933 in Palestine and Transjordan. In the Burma theater in 1942, realizing that the only answer to penetration was counter-penetration, he obtained sanction to organize the Chindits, specially trained jungle fighters. Supplied by air, they thrust far behind the enemy lines, gravely disrupting the entire supply system. Wingate was killed in a plane crash in Burma.

Winkler, Hans-Günther 1926– •*German show jumper*• Born in Wuppertal-Barmen, Westphalia, he is the only man to have won five Olympic gold medals at show jumping (the team golds in 1956, 1960, 1964 and 1972, and the individual title in 1956). He had previously won the individual world title in 1954 and 1955.

Winnemucca, Sarah 1844–91 •*Native American activist and educator*• Born of Northern Paiute descent near the Humboldt River, western Nevada, she was used as an interpreter during the Snake War (1866) because she knew English. In 1872 the Paiutes were relocated to the Malheur reservation in Oregon, where she assisted reservation agent Samuel Parrish with his agricultural programs and was an interpreter and teacher. Parrish's replacement refused to pay the Paiute for their agricultural labor, which led to the Bannock War. She was again used as an interpreter and peacemaker, but the Paiute were forced onto another reservation. She wrote *Life Among the Paiutes: Their Wrongs and Claims*. She established a school for Native American children, and in 1994 she was inducted into the National Women's Hall of Fame.

Winston of Hammersmith, Robert Maurice Lipson Winston, Baron 1940– •*English obstetrician and gynecologist*• He was educated at the University of London and began his career as a registrar at Hammersmith Hospital, London (1970–74). His subsequent years of lecturing and research in Britain and abroad culminated in a professorship of fertility studies at Imperial College, London (1997–). Among many professional posts he was appointed chair of the House of Lords Select Committee on Science and Technology (1999–). He has been the host of several popular BBC television series, including *The Human Body* (1998) and *Superhuman* (2000), and has published widely. He was made a life peer in 1995.

Winters, (Arthur) Yvor 1900–68 •*US critic and poet*• Born in Chicago, he was educated there and at the University of Colorado and at Stanford, and in 1949 was appointed Professor of English at Stanford. A versifier whose *Collected Poems* were published in 1960, he is remembered primarily as a quirky, irascible critic, opposed to the Expressionists and with a sharp eye for detail. Significant books are *In Defense of Reason* (1947) and *The Function of Criticism* (1957).

Winterson, Jeanette 1959– •*English author*• She was born in Manchester and educated at St Catherine's College, Oxford. Her first novel, *Oranges Are Not the Only Fruit* (1985), charting the rebellious adolescence of a girl adopted into a Pentecostal family, won the Whitbread Prize and was made into a celebrated television drama (1990). Other novels include *The Passion* (1987), *Sexing the Cherry* (1989), *Written on the Body* (1992) and *The Power Book* (2000). She has also published essays, short stories and a children's book, *The King of Capri* (2001).

" "

I asked why he was a priest and he said that if you have to work for anybody an absentee boss is best.

1987 ***The Passion****, chapter 1.*

Winthrop, John 1588–1649 •*English colonialist*• Born in Groton, Suffolk, he was appointed governor of the Massachusetts Bay Colony in 1629. He was periodically reelected, and probably had more influence than anyone else in forming the political institutions of the northern states of America. The first part of his *Journal* was published in 1790, and the whole in 1825–26.

Winthrop, John 1606–76 •*English colonialist*• Born in Groton, Suffolk, son of **John Winthrop** (1588–1649), he emigrated to colonial America in 1631, landing in Boston, and became a magistrate in Massachusetts. In 1635 he went to Connecticut, and he founded New London in 1646. In 1657 he was elected governor of Connecticut, and, except for one year, held that post until his death. He obtained from **Charles II** a charter uniting the colonies of Connecticut and New Haven, and, under that charter, was named first governor.

Winthrop, John, *known as* **Fitz-John** 1639–1707 •*Anglo-American soldier and colonial administrator*• Born in Ipswich, Massachusetts, he was the son of **John Winthrop** (1606–76). He served under **George Monk** in the parliamentary army (1660), and settled in Connecticut in 1663. He was a commander against the Dutch, the Native Americans and the French. He was governor of Connecticut from 1698.

Wisdom, Sir Norman 1915– •*English comedian*• Born in London, he made his stage debut in 1946. In 1948 he appeared in variety shows at the London Casino, thereafter appearing regularly at the London Palladium. His earliest film success was as a slapstick comedian in *Trouble in Store* (1953). Such films as *Man of the Moment* (1955), *Just My Luck* (1958), *On the Beat* (1962), *Sandwich Man* (1966) and *What's Good for the Goose* (1969) followed. On television, he is best known for series such as *A Little Bit of Wisdom* (1974–76). Popular as a comic in the US too, he made a film there, *The Night They Raided Minsky's*, in 1968. His book, *Don't Laugh at Me: An Autobiography*, was published in 1992. He was knighted in 2000.

Wise, Ernie *See* **Morecambe and Wise**

Wiseman, Nicholas Patrick Stephen 1802–65 •*English prelate and cardinal*• Born in Seville, Spain, of an Irish family, he entered the English College in Rome, was ordained in 1825, and became rector of the college from 1828 to 1840. He established the *Dublin Review* (1836), and in 1840, he was named coadjutor vicar-apostolic and president of St Mary's College at Oscott. In 1850 he was appointed the first Archbishop of Westminster and a cardinal, arousing religious indignation which resulted in the Ecclesiastical Titles Assumption Act; in response he published his conciliatory *Appeal to the Reason and Good Feeling of the English People* (1850). One of his best-known works was a novel, *Fabiola* (1854).

Wishart, George c. 1513–46 •*Scottish reformer*• He was born in Pitarrow, Kincardineshire. As a schoolmaster in Montrose (1538), he incurred a charge of heresy for teaching the Greek New Testament, and he then went to Cambridge, where he met the reformer **Hugh Latimer**. He preached the Lutheran doctrine of justification in several places, but, at the insistence of Cardinal **David Beaton**, he was arrested in 1546 and burned at St Andrews on March 1. **John Knox** was first inspired by Wishart.

Witherspoon, John 1723–94 •*American clergyman and theologian*• Born in Gifford, Lothian, Scotland, he was minister at Beith and then Paisley, and in 1768 emigrated to America, where he became president of the College of New Jersey (now Princeton University) from 1768 to 1794. He taught several future leaders in American public life, including President **James Madison**, whose coauthorship of *The Federalist* papers bore the influence of his teacher's Calvinist social and political thought. He was a representative of New Jersey to the Continental Congress (1776–82), and he helped frame the American Declaration of Independence (1776).

Witt, Jan de 1625–72 •*Dutch statesman*• Born in Dort, the son of Jacob de Witt, he was one of the deputies sent by the States of Holland in 1652 to Zeeland to dissuade that province from adopting an Orange policy. In 1653 he was made grand pensionary. The Orange Party, during the war between England and Holland, strove to increase the power of the young prince (afterward **William III**); the Republican (or oligarchic) Party, made up of the nobles and the wealthier burgesses, with de Witt at their head, sought to abolish the office of stadtholder. In 1654, on the conclusion of the war, a secret article in the treaty drawn up between de Witt and **Cromwell** deprived the House of Orange of all state offices. After the restoration of **Charles II**, de Witt favored France.

Wittgenstein, Ludwig Josef Johann 1889–1951 •*Austrian-born British philosopher*• He was born in Vienna, and was educated at home until the age of 14, then at an Austrian school for three years. He went on to study mechanical engineering at Berlin (1906–08) and at Manchester (1908–11). There his reading of **Bertrand Russell**'s *The Principles of Mathematics* (1903) turned his attention to mathematics; in 1911 he abandoned his engineering research and moved to Cambridge to study mathematical logic under Russell (1912–13). He served in World War I as an artillery officer in the Austrian army and was taken prisoner on the Italian front in 1918. Throughout the war he had continued to work on problems in logic, carrying his notebooks around with him in his rucksack, and in the POW camp near Monte Cassino he completed his first work, the only one published in his lifetime, and sent it to Russell in England. It was eventually published in 1921 under the title *Logisch-philosophische Abhandlung* (and then in 1922, with a parallel German-English text and an introduction by Russell, as *Tractatus Logico-Philosophicus*). This was a novel, rather startling work, consisting of a series of numbered, aphoristic remarks centered on the nature and limits of language. Meaningful language, he conceived, must consist in "atomic propositions" that are pictures of the facts of which the world is composed. On this criterion we must discard as literally meaningless much of our conventional discourse, including judgments of value, and many of the claims of speculative philosophy. And since the limits of language are also the limits of thought, he reaches the portentous conclusion that "what we cannot speak about we must be silent about." This template for a logically foolproof language, a perfect instrument for meaningful assertion, appeared to represent a kind of terminus, and Wittgenstein now turned away from philosophy to find another vocation. He gave away the money he had inherited and lived a simple ascetic life, working as an elementary schoolteacher in Austrian country districts (1920–26), a gardener's assistant in a monastery, and an amateur architect and builder commissioned by one of his sisters. In the late 1920s he was sought out by various philosophers who had found inspiration in the *Tractatus*. He revived his philosophical interests and returned to Cambridge in 1929. He was appointed Professor of Philosophy in 1939, but he was unable to take up the position until 1945, at the end of World War II, during which he had served as a medical orderly. After two years he resigned and went to live in Ireland for a time. At Cambridge his philosophy began to take quite a new direction. He attracted a group of devoted pupils, and through his lectures and the circulation of his students' notes, he came to exert a powerful influence on philosophy throughout the English-speaking world. The work of this second period of his philosophical career is best summarized in the posthumous *Philosophical Investigations* (1953), a discursive and often enigmatic work which rejects most of the assumptions and conclusions of the *Tractatus*. In the *Investigations* Wittgenstein no longer tries to reduce language to a perfect logical model, but rather points to the variety, open-endedness and subtlety of everyday language, and explores the actual communicative and social functions of different modes of speech, or "language games." He died of cancer in Cambridge in 1951; since then there has been a continuous stream of posthumously edited publications from his prolific notebooks and manuscripts, including *Remarks on the Foundations of Mathematics* (1956), *The Blue and Brown Books* (1958), *Philosophische Bemerkungen* (1964) and *On Certainty* (1969).

“ ”

Der Tod ist kein Ereignis des Lebens. Den Tod erlebt man nicht.
Death is not an event in life: we do not live to experience death.

1921 ***Tractatus Logico-Philosophicus****, prop 6.4311 (translated by Pears and McGuinness).*

Wittig, Georg 1897–1987 •*German chemist and Nobel Prize winner*• Born in Berlin, he went to the University of Tübingen in 1916, but soon left to serve in World War I. In 1920 he recommenced the study of chemistry for a degree at the University of Marburg, where he later joined the staff. He also held appointments at the Technical University of Brunswick (1932) and the Universities of Freiburg, Tübingen, and Heidelberg. He is most famous for a serendipitous discovery that some ylides (organometallic compounds containing both positive and negative charges) react smoothly with aldehydes and ketones, with the creation of an olefinic double bond. This procedure has been of enormous value in the laboratory synthesis of numerous important compounds, including vitamin A, vitamin D, steroids and prostaglandin precursors. For this work he shared the 1979 Nobel Prize for chemistry with Herbert Brown (1912–).

Władysław IV, *English* **Ladislas** 1595–1648 •*King of Poland*• The son of **Sigismund III Vasa** of Sweden, he was born in Kraków. He proved popular after his father's haughtiness. His reign (1632–48) was also peaceful, since Poland remained neutral during the Thirty Years' War. He crushed the Cossack rebellions (1637–38), initiating ten years of peace in Ukraine.

Wodehouse, Sir P(elham) G(renville) 1881–1975 •*English novelist*• Born in Guildford, Surrey, he became a US citizen in 1955. He was educated at Dulwich College, London, and worked for the Hong Kong and Shanghai Bank for two years before beginning to earn a living as a journalist and story writer. In the US before World War I, he sold a serial to the *Saturday Evening Post,* and for a quarter of a century almost all his books appeared first in that magazine. He made his name with *Piccadilly Jim* (1917), but World War II blighted his reputation. Captured by the Germans at Le Touquet, he was interned then released but not allowed to leave Germany. Foolishly he agreed to make broadcasts for the Germans, and though they were harmless, he was branded as a traitor. Eventually his name was cleared, but he made the US his home. His copious oeuvre includes over 100 books, but he is best known as the creator of Bertie Wooster and his legendary valet, Jeeves. Of his many felicitous titles, *Right Ho, Jeeves* (1934), *Quick Service* (1940) and *The Mating Season* (1949) stand out.

Wogan, Terry (Michael Terence) 1938– •*Irish broadcaster and writer*• Born in Limerick, he joined Radio Telefis Éireann (1963) as an announcer, and from 1965 hosted various BBC radio programs, including *The Terry Wogan Show* (1969–72). Resident in England from 1969, he became popular as the host of BBC Radio 2's *Breakfast Show* (1972–84, 1993–). Active on television in many capacities, he hosted the game show *Blankety Blank* (1977–81), *You Must Be Joking* (1981) and *The Eurovision Song Contest.* He began a regular talk show in 1982 which later became a thrice-weekly fixture (1985–92). He has written several books including *Is It Me?* (2000).

Wöhler, Friedrich 1800–82 •*German chemist*• Born in Eschersheim, he was educated at the Universities of Marburg and Heidelberg and qualified as a doctor of medicine in 1823, but he never practiced. He taught chemistry at industrial schools in Berlin (1825–31) and Kassel (1831–36), and became Professor of Chemistry at Göttingen in 1836, remaining there until his death. One of the formative experiences of his life was the year he spent with **Jöns Jacob Berzelius** in Stockholm, which led to a lifelong friendship. His friendship with **Justus von Liebig** was equally important to him, and from their common interest in cyanates came Wöhler's most famous discovery. In 1828 he attempted to prepare ammonium cyanate from silver cyanate and ammonium chloride, but instead obtained urea. Equally important was his preparation of aluminum in 1827. The Danish scientist **Hans Oersted** claimed to have extracted the metal from alumina in 1825, but it is doubtful whether the metal he obtained was pure aluminum. Wöhler used a different procedure, and the product (still extant) is essentially pure metal. For this work he was honored by **Napoleon III**.

Wolf, Hugo 1860–1903 •*Austrian composer*• Born in Windischgräz, Styria, he studied at the Vienna Conservatory, then earned a meager living by teaching and conducting. From 1884 to 1888 he was music critic of the *Wiener Salonblatt.* His best compositions came after 1888 and include the Mörike set of 53 songs (1888), settings of poems by **Goethe** (1888–89), the *Italienisches Liederbuch* ("Italian Songbook") of Heyse and Emanuel von Geibel (1889–90) and three sonnets of Michelangelo (1897). He also wrote an opera, *Der Corregidor* (1895, "The Mayor"), and other works. In 1897 he went insane, and was confined from 1898 in the asylum at Steinhof, near Vienna, where he died.

Wolfe, James 1727–59 •*English general*• Born in Kent, he was the eldest son of General Edward Wolfe (1685–1759). In 1745–46 he served against the Scottish Jacobites at Falkirk and Culloden. In 1758, as colonel, Pitt the Elder (the Earl of **Chatham**) gave him the command of a brigade in the expedition against Cape Breton under General **Jeffrey Amherst**, and he was mainly responsible for the capture of Louisburg (1758). Pitt gave Wolfe command of the expedition for the capture of Quebec, and, as major general in command of 9,000 men, Wolfe landed below Quebec in June 1759. The attack on **Montcalm**'s strong position foiled Wolfe until on September 13 he reached the Plains of Abraham by scaling the cliffs at a poorly guarded point. After a short struggle Quebec capitulated, and its fall decided the fate of Canada. Wolfe died in the hour of victory.

Wolfe, Thomas Clayton 1900–38 •*US novelist*• He was born in Asheville, North Carolina, and educated at the University of North Carolina and at Harvard. After an abortive start as a playwright, in 1925 he embarked on a turbulent affair with Mrs Aline Bernstein, a maternal figure who did much to encourage his writing, particularly his first novel, *Look Homeward, Angel* (1929), which was patently autobiographical. The massive, shapeless manuscript of *Of Time and the River* (1935), its sequel, was honed into shape by Max Perkins, his editor at Scribner's. Both these novels feature Eugene Gant, Wolfe's alter ego. *The Web and the Rock* (1939) and *You Can't Go Home Again* (1940) were published posthumously. Prolix, careless, bombastic and overambitious, he nevertheless wrote vividly of people and places. Some assert that his best work is to be found in the stories in *From Death to Morning* (1935).

Wolfe, Tom (Thomas Kennerly) 1931– •*US journalist, pop critic and novelist*• Born in Richmond, Virginia, he graduated from Washington and Lee University and received his doctorate from Yale University. Later he worked as a reporter for the *Springfield Union*, the *Washington Post* and the *New York Herald Tribune*. He is a proponent of New Journalism, and his style is distinctive, clever and narcissistic. A fashion leader and follower, he has written a number of books with eye-catching titles: *The Electric Kool-Aid Acid Test* (1968), about **Ken Kesey** and the Merry Pranksters, and *The Kandy-Kolored Tangerine-Flake Streamline Baby* (1965). Other works include *The Right Stuff (1979), The Bonfire of the Vanities* (1988) and *Hooking Up* (2000).

Wolfenden, John Frederick Wolfenden, Baron 1906–85 •*English educator and governmental adviser on social questions*• Born in Halifax, Yorkshire, he was a Fellow and tutor in philosophy at Magdalen College, Oxford (1929–34), headmaster of Uppingham (1934–44) and Shrewsbury (1944–50), and vice chancellor of the University of Reading from 1950. He is best known as the chairman of the royal commission on homosexuality and prostitution (the Wolfenden Report, 1959), which called for the legalization of private homosexual acts between consenting adults aged 21 and over. This recommendation became law under the Sexual Offenses Act of 1967. He was made a life peer in 1974.

Wolff or **Wolf, Christian von** 1679–1754 •*German philosopher*• Born in Breslau, Silesia (now Wrocław, Poland), he studied at the

Universities of Breslau, Jena and Leipzig and was a pupil of **Gottfried Leibniz**, on whose recommendation he was appointed Professor of Mathematics at the University of Halle (1707). In a turbulent career he was a professor at Marburg (1723–40) and also became chancellor of Halle (1743). He was made Baron of the Empire by the Elector of Bavaria. Wolff published widely in philosophy, theology, mathematics and the natural sciences, but his main intellectual achievement was to systematize and popularize the philosophy of Leibniz, in works such as *Philosophia prima sive ontologia* (1729). His work gave rationalism a further great impulse in the German tradition, and he is usually regarded as the German spokesman of the Enlightenment in the 18th century.

Wolfit, Sir Donald 1902–68 •*English actor-manager*• Born in Newark, Nottinghamshire, he began his stage career in 1920 and made his first London appearance in *The Wandering Jew* (1924). Forming his own company (1937), he played **Shakespeare** in the provinces, and during World War II he instituted the first London season of "Lunchtime Shakespeare" during the Battle of Britain. Known especially for his portrayal of Shakespearean heroes and of **Ben Jonson**'s Volpone, he also appeared in several films and on television. His autobiography, *First Interval*, appeared in 1954, and he was knighted in 1957.

Wolfram von Eschenbach c. 1170–c. 1220 •*German poet*• Born near Anspach, Bavaria, he lived some time at the court of the Count of Thuringia. His epic *Parzival* (Eng trans 1894), with the history of the Grail as its main theme, is one of the most notable poems of the Middle Ages. From it Wagner derived the libretto of his opera *Parsifal*. He also wrote *Taglieder* (lyrics), seven love songs, a short epic titled *Willehalm* and two fragments called *Titurel*.

Wolfson, Sir Isaac 1897–1991 •*Scottish businessman and philanthropist*• Born and educated in Glasgow, he left school early and became a traveling salesman. He joined Great Universal Stores in 1932 and became managing director in 1934. In 1955 he set up the Wolfson Foundation for the advancement of health, education and youth activities in the UK and the Commonwealth. He also founded Wolfson College, Oxford, in 1966. In 1973, University College, Cambridge, was renamed Wolfson College after a grant from the foundation. He was active in Jewish causes. His son, Leonard (1927–), is now a life peer.

Wollstonecraft, Mary, *later* **Mary Godwin** 1759–97 •*Anglo-Irish feminist and writer*• Born in London, she obtained work with a publisher (1788) as a translator and became acquainted with a group of political writers and reformers known as the English Jacobins, among whom was her future husband, **William Godwin**. In 1790 she wrote *A Vindication of the Rights of Man* and in 1792 produced her controversial *A Vindication of the Rights of Woman*, which advocated equality of the sexes and equal opportunities in education. In Paris in 1792 to collect material for her *View of the French Revolution* (vol 1, 1794), she met a US timber merchant, Captain Gilbert Imlay, by whom she had a daughter, Fanny, who committed suicide in 1816. Deserted by him, Mary herself tried to commit suicide. In 1797 she married Godwin and gave birth to a daughter, Mary (the future **Mary Wollstonecraft Shelley**), but died soon afterward.

" "

I do not wish them to have power over men; but over themselves.

1792 Of women. ***A Vindication of the Rights of Woman****, part 1, chapter 4.*

Wolseley, Garnet Joseph, Viscount 1833–1913 •*British field marshal*• He was born in Golden Bridge House, County Dublin. Entering the army in 1852, he served in the Burmese War (1852–53), the Crimean War (where he lost an eye), the Indian Uprising (1857–59), and the Chinese War (1860). In 1870 he put down the Red River rebellion under **Louis Riel**, and he commanded in the Ashanti War (1873–74). After several senior posts in India, Cyprus, South Africa and Egypt, he was commander in chief of the expedition to Egypt in 1882, and he was made general in the same year. He commanded the Sudan expedition in 1884 that arrived too late to save General **Gordon** at Khartoum. From 1890 to 1895 he was commander in chief of the entire army when he carried out several reforms and mobilized forces for the Boer War (1899–1902). His extensive writings include a novel, *Marley Castle* (1877), *The Decline and Fall of Napoleon* (1895) and his memoir, *Story of a Soldier's Life* (1903–04).

Wolsey, Thomas c. 1475–1530 •*English cardinal and politician*• He was born in Ipswich, the son of a prosperous butcher and grazier. He studied at Magdalen College, Oxford. Having been ordained in 1498, he was given the living at Lymington in Somerset; influence later brought him the post of secretary and domestic chaplain to the Archbishop of Canterbury. With the primate's death in 1502, Wolsey was endowed with the chaplaincy of Calais, where his ability brought him to the notice of **Henry VII**. Appointed a chaplain to the king (1507), his skill and ability brought him the lucrative deanery of Lincoln, and with the accession of **Henry VIII**, Wolsey strove to render himself indispensable. In 1513 Wolsey accompanied Henry to France. His conduct of the negotiations between Henry and **Francis I** brought him the bishopric of Lincoln, the archbishopric of York (1514) and a cardinalate (1515). In the same year, he was made lord chancellor and was awarded by Henry the administration of the see of Bath and Wells and the temporalities of the wealthy abbey of St Alban's. Deep in the king's confidence, he had attained a position more powerful than that enjoyed by any minister of the Crown since **Thomas à Becket**. As the controller of England's foreign policy, he lent support to France and Germany alternately, entering into a secret alliance with the emperor **Charles V** against Francis I, always seeking to improve England's position, but this policy ultimately proved unsuccessful. His aim in England was absolute monarchy with himself behind the throne. He established Cardinal's College (Christ Church) at Oxford and a grammar school at Ipswich. Wolsey's downfall originated in his prevarication and evasiveness over the question of Henry's divorce from **Catherine of Aragon**, which provoked the king's anger and aroused the enmity of the **Anne Boleyn** faction and of many other enemies outraged by the cardinal's haughtiness. His outmoded assertion of the ecclesiastical right to dominate secular policy was unacceptable to the powerful aristocracy of the countinghouse bred by the new spirit of mercantilism. Prosecuted under the statute of praemunire in 1529, the cardinal had to surrender the Great Seal and retire to Winchester. Impeachment by the House of Lords was followed by the forfeiture of all his property to the Crown. Arrested again on a charge of high treason, he died while journeying from his York diocese to London.

Wonder, Stevie, *real name* **Steveland Judkins** 1950– •*US soul, pop and rock singer and instrumentalist*• Born in Saginaw, Michigan, a premature baby, he was blinded permanently by receiving too much oxygen in the incubator. He played the harmonica from an early age and was signed to Motown Records in 1961. His first album, *Little Stevie Wonder: The 12-Year-Old Genius* (released when he was actually 13), was an immediate success. Most of his early recordings followed the orthodox Motown sound, but "Where I'm Coming From" (1971) moved toward progressive rock. During the 1970s he became one of the most proficient users of synthesizer technology and developed musically to the point where he was widely regarded as among the important popular composers of the era. His music ranged from the up-tempo rock of "Superstition" and the social commentary of "Living in the City" to the simple balladry of "I Just Called to Say I Love You." One of America's best-loved entertainers, his most noteworthy albums have included *Talking Book* (1972), *Innervisions* (1973), *Songs in the Key of Life* (1976) and *Hotter Than July* (1980). Later albums include *Characters* (1987), *Jungle Fever* (1991) and *At the Close of a Century* (1999).

Woo, John 1948– •*Chinese film director*• Born in Guangzhou (Canton), he studied at Matteo Ricci College, Hong Kong. He made his mainstream directorial debut in the Chinese cinema in 1973 with *The Young Dragons*, thereafter producing a string of highly successful action films such as *Run, Tiger, Run* (1985). His reputation for slick, stylized violence was sealed with *The Killer* (1989), and he moved to Hollywood in the early 1990s to direct such films as *Hard Target* (1993), *Replacement Killers* (1998) and *Mission: Impossible 2* (2000).

Wood, Edward Frederick Lindley *See* **Halifax, 1st Earl of**

Wood, Grant 1892–1942 •*US artist*• Born on a farm in Anamosa, Iowa, he studied at the Art Institute of Chicago and served in the camouflage division of the army in World War I, returning to Iowa after the war to teach art in Cedar Rapids. In 1928 he went to Munich to execute a commission for a stained-glass window and was deeply impressed by the 15th-century Flemish and German primitive art he saw there. Under its influence he began to paint the life of the rural Midwest in an expressive and sharply detailed style. He is best known for stark portraits such as *American Gothic* (1930) and *Daughters of the Revolution* (1932).

Wood, Haydn 1882–1959 •*English composer and violinist*• Born in Slaithwaite, Yorkshire, he studied at the Royal College of Music and worked for a time in music halls with his wife, Dorothy Court, for whom he wrote a large number of ballads. Of these, the best known is "Roses of Picardy" (1916). Concentrating on more serious composition, he wrote prolifically for orchestra, brass band, chamber music groups and voices.

Wood, Mrs Henry, *née* **Ellen Price** 1814–87 •*English novelist*• Born in Worcester, the daughter of a manufacturer, she suffered a spinal disease which confined her to bed or a sofa for most of her life. She married Henry Wood and lived in France for 20 years, but returned to England with him in 1860 and settled in Norwood. After his death in 1866, she moved to London and wrote for magazines. Her second published novel, *East Lynne* (1861), had immense success. She never rose above the commonplace in her many novels, but she showed some power in the analysis of character in her anonymous *Johnny Ludlow* stories (1874–80).

Wood, Sir Henry Joseph 1869–1944 •*English conductor*• Born in London, he founded with Robert Newman the Promenade Concerts, which he conducted annually from 1895 until his death. He composed operettas and an oratorio, *Saint Dorothea* (1889), but his international reputation was gained as conductor of the Queen's Hall symphony and promenade concerts. He was knighted in 1911. In 1938 he published *My Life of Music*.

Wood, John the Elder, *known as* **Wood of Bath** c. 1705–54 •*English architect*• He was responsible for many of the best-known streets and buildings of Bath, such as the North and South Parades, Queen Square, the Circus, Prior Park and other houses. His son John the Younger (d. 1782) designed the Royal Crescent and the Assembly Rooms.

Wood, Natalie, *originally* **Natasha Gurdin** 1938–81 •*US film actress*• Born in San Francisco, she began her many film appearances at age five in the wartime melodrama *Happy Land* (1943). In 1955 she appeared in the highly influential *Rebel Without a Cause* (1955), earning a Best Supporting Actress Academy Award nomination. She was also in the popular western, *The Searchers* (1956). *Marjorie Morningstar* (1958) saw her graduate to stardom, followed by *Splendor in the Grass* (1961) and *West Side Story* (1961). Her career slowed during the 1970s, and in 1981 she drowned mysteriously with a high blood-alcohol level after being reported missing from her yacht. She was married to actor **Robert Wagner**.

Wood, Victoria 1953– •*English comedienne and writer*• Born in Prestwich, Lancashire, she studied drama at the University of Birmingham and began singing her own comic songs on local radio and television while still a student. After winning the television talent show *New Faces* (1975), she gained a regular singing spot on *That's Life* (1976). Her first play, *Talent* (1978), was adapted for television (1979). Her television series include *Wood and Walters* (with **Julie Walters**, 1981–82), *Victoria Wood—As Seen on Television* (1984–87) and *An Audience With Victoria Wood* (1988, British Academy award). She has made frequent stage tours and published several books, including *Mens Sana in Thingummy Doodah* (1990).

Woodbridge, Todd 1971– •*Australian tennis player*• Born in Sydney, he turned professional in 1988, and as a right-handed player in partnership with the left-handed **Mark Woodforde**, he formed one of the most successful men's doubles teams in tennis history. Known as the Woodies, the pair took five consecutive Wimbledon doubles titles (1993–97). Other victories included a gold medal in the 1996 Olympic Games. They won the world doubles championship in 1992 and 1996.

Wooden, John (Robert) 1910– •*US college basketball player and coach*• Born in Martinsville, Indiana, he had a notable career as a highschool and college basketball player playing for Martinsville High School and Purdue University and being named College Player of the Year in 1932, but he is best known as the most successful coach in college basketball history. After early experience as a coach with Indiana State University and elsewhere, he served as head coach at UCLA (1948–75), guiding the team to 10 national championships, including seven in a row. He was named the US Basketball Writers Association Coach of the Year six times between 1964 and 1973 and is one of only two men enshrined in the Basketball Hall of Fame as both player and coach.

Woodforde, Mark 1965– •*Australian tennis player*• Born in Adelaide, South Australia, he formed one of the most successful doubles teams in tennis history in partnership with **Todd Woodbridge**. A left-hander, he won the US Open doubles title with **John McEnroe** in 1989 and went on, with Woodbridge, to win five consecutive Wimbledon doubles titles (1993–97) as well as gold in the 1996 Olympic Games and the world doubles championship in 1992 and 1996.

Woodhull, Victoria, *née* **Claflin** 1838–1927 •*US reformer*• Born in Homer, Ohio, she was one of a large family which earned a living by giving fortune-telling and medicine shows, and performed a spiritualist act with her sister, Tennessee (1846–1923). From 1853 to 1864 she was married to Dr Canning Woodhull. In 1868 she went with Tennessee to New York, where they persuaded the rich **Cornelius Vanderbilt** to set them up as stockbrokers. At this time they became involved with a socialist group called Pantarchy and began to advocate its principles of free love, equal rights and legal prostitution. A vigorous speaker, Victoria won support from the leaders of the women's suffrage movement and became the first woman nominated for the presidency. In 1877 she moved to London, with Tennessee. Her publications include *The Human Body the Temple of God* (1890, with Tennessee).

Woods, Donald 1933–2001 •*South African journalist and campaigner*• Born in Elliotdale, he studied law at the University of Cape Town and worked as editor of the *Daily Dispatch* (1965–77), in which position he was an active opponent of the apartheid regime. While under house arrest, he published the book *Biko* (1978), about the imprisonment and murder of the activist **Steve Biko**, which became an international bestseller and the subject of the film *Cry Freedom* (1987). Woods was forced into exile in England and continued to lecture on racism there and abroad, publishing his final book, *Rainbow Nation Revisited*, in 2000.

Woods, Tiger, *real name* **Eldrick Woods** 1976– •*US golfer*• Born in Cypress, California, he was the first man to win both the US junior amateur and US amateur titles. The nickname "Tiger" is a tribute to a Vietnam colleague of his father. He retained the amateur title for a record three years in a row, and his outstanding amateur career included both Walker Cup (1995) and Eisenhower (1994) appearances. Having turned professional in August 1996, in 1997 he became the youngest winner of the US Masters. He continues to win numerous events, including the British Open (2000), the US Open (2000, 2002), the US PGA Championship (1999, 2000) and the US Masters (2001, 2002).

Woodville, Elizabeth c. 1437–92 •*Queen of England*• The eldest daughter of Sir Richard Woodville, 1st Earl **Rivers**, she married Sir John Grey, who was killed at St Albans (1461). In 1464 she was married privately to **Edward IV**, and was crowned in 1465. When Edward fled to Flanders (1470), she sought sanctuary in Westminster. The rise to wealth and power of her numerous family contributed to the animosity within the Yorkist dynasty. In 1483 her sons, **Edward V** and Richard, Duke of York, were murdered (the Princes in the Tower). After the accession of **Henry VII** (1485) her rights as dowager queen were restored, but soon she had to retire to the Abbey of Bermondsey, where she died. Her eldest daughter, Elizabeth of York (1465–1503), married Henry in 1486.

Woodward, Edward (Albert Arthur) 1930– •*English actor*• Born in Croydon, Surrey, he trained at the Royal Academy of

Dramatic Art. His films include *Becket* (1963), *Young Winston* (1971), *The Wicker Man* (1973), *Breaker Morant* (1980) and *Champions* (1983). He starred on television in the title role of *Callan* (1967–73), as Robert McCall in *The Equalizer* (1985–90) and as Nev in *Common as Muck* (1994), and was the host of the crime-reconstruction drama series *In Suspicious Circumstances* (1991–94).

Woodward, Joanne 1930– •*US film and television actress*• Born in Thomasville, Georgia, she appeared on Broadway and in numerous television dramas before Twentieth Century Fox cast her in a minor Western, *Count Three and Pray* (1955). She won a Best Actress Academy Award for her performance as a schizophrenic in *The Three Faces of Eve* (1957), followed by notable performances in *No Down Payment* (1957), *The Long Hot Summer* (1958) and *The Stripper* (1963). She was acclaimed again in *Rachel, Rachel* (1968), directed by her husband, **Paul Newman**, and later in *Mr and Mrs Bridge* (1990) and *Philadelphia* (1993).

Woodward, Robert Burns 1917–79 •*US chemist and Nobel Prize winner*• Born in Boston, he studied chemistry at MIT. He then moved to Harvard (1937) and by 1944 had become associate professor, working on the chemistry of the antimalarial drug quinine and the new wonder drug penicillin. For the next 20 years he executed the syntheses of an array of biological compounds. His feel for the art and architecture of constructing complex molecules was astounding. He was also famous for his lectures. He was awarded the Nobel Prize for chemistry in 1965 for the totality of his work in the art of synthetic chemistry, structure determination and theoretical analysis. Woodward and the Swiss chemist Albert Eschenmoser (1925–) set out to synthesize vitamin B_{12}; in the course of this work Woodward conceived the idea that molecular orbitals could affect the products obtained in cyclization reactions, and he invited a young Harvard theoretician, **Roald Hoffmann**, to collaborate. This led eventually to the Woodward-Hoffmann rules for the conservation of orbital symmetry. Unfortunately Woodward died from a heart attack before the award of a Nobel Prize for chemistry for this work. He received almost every honor and award possible for an organic chemist, and the pharmaceutical company Ciba-Geigy established the Woodward Research Institute in Basel in his memory.

Woolf, Leonard Sidney 1880–1969 •*English publisher and writer*• Born in London, he was educated at St Paul's School and Trinity College, Cambridge. He worked in the Ceylon Civil Service (1904–11), and his early novels, such as *The Village and the Jungle* (1913), have Ceylon as a background. In 1916 he joined the Fabian Society and in 1917, along with his wife **Virginia Woolf**, he founded the Hogarth Press; the two became the center of the so-called Bloomsbury Group. His works include *Socialism and Co-operation* (1921), *After the Deluge* (1931, 1939) and *Principia Politica* (1953). He published his autobiography in five volumes (1960–69).

Woolf, (Adeline) Virginia, *née* **Stephen** 1882–1941 •*English novelist, critic and essayist*• She was born in London, the daughter of Sir **Leslie Stephen**, and was close to her sister, **Vanessa Bell**. Taught at home by her parents and governesses, she received an uneven education. In 1891 she started the *Hyde Park Gate News*, which appeared weekly until 1895 and included her first efforts at fiction. Her father died in 1904 and the family moved to Bloomsbury, where they formed the nucleus of the Bloomsbury Group, comprising—among others—**John Maynard Keynes**, **E M Forster**, **Roger Fry**, **Duncan Grant** and **Lytton Strachey**: philosophers, writers and artists. A year later she became a reviewer for the *Times Literary Supplement*, an association that lasted until just before her death. She married **Leonard Woolf** in 1912 and her first novel, *The Voyage Out*, was published in 1915. It was favorably received and, although it was a realistic novel, it contained hints of the lyricism which would later become her hallmark. By this time, her health was already poor and she suffered from recurring bouts of depression; she had attempted suicide in 1913. In 1917 she and Leonard formed the Hogarth Press. Its first publication was *Two Stories* (1917), one by each of the founders. They went on to publish works by other modern writers, including **Katherine Mansfield** and **T S Eliot**. Woolf's second novel, *Night and Day*, appeared in 1919. *Jacob's Room* followed in 1922 and marked a turning point in her fiction, showing her experimenting with narrative and language. It was well received and made her a celebrity. In 1923 she published the essay "Mr Bennett and Mrs Brown" in the *Nation and Athenaeum*. An attack on the "Georgian novelists" **Arnold Bennett**, **John Galsworthy** and **H G Wells**, the essay can be read as her own aesthetic manifesto. Regarded as a major figure in the Modernist movement, she continued to make a significant contribution to the development of the novel. In six years she published the three novels that have made her one of the 20th century's great writers: *Mrs Dalloway* (1925), *To the Lighthouse* (1927) and *The Waves* (1931), noted for their impressionistic, stream-of-consciousness style. Her most commercially successful novel, *Orlando* (1928), which describes the fantastic life of an aristocratic poet as he travels through four centuries, changing sex on the way, was dedicated to her intimate friend, **Vita Sackville-West**. Her work took its toll on her health, and although she wrote prolifically, she was beset by deep depression and debilitating headaches. Throughout the 1930s she worked on the novel *The Years*, which was published in 1937. A year later *Three Guineas*, provisionally entitled "Professions for Women," was published. This was intended as a sequel to *A Room of One's Own* (1929), a long essay which is still regarded as a feminist classic and in which Woolf stated that "A woman must have money and a room of her own if she is to write fiction." Her last novel, the experimental *Between the Acts*, was published posthumously in 1941, after she had forced a large stone into her pocket and drowned herself in the River Ouse, near her home at Rodmell in Sussex. She is, with **James Joyce** (whose novel *Ulysses* the Hogarth Press declined to publish), regarded as one of the great innovators of the novel in English.

“ ”

Never did I read such tosh.

*1922 On James Joyce's **Ulysses**. Letter to Lytton Strachey, April 24.*

Woolley, Sir (Charles) Leonard 1880–1960 •*English archaeologist*• Born in London, he was educated at New College, Oxford, and conducted excavations at Carchemish (1912–14), Al'Ubaid, and Tell el-Amarna, and subsequently directed the important excavations (1922–34) at Ur in Mesopotamia, which in 1926 uncovered gold and lapis lazuli in the royal tombs. He was knighted in 1935, and from 1943 to 1946 was archaeological adviser to the War Office. He wrote several popular accounts of his work, notably *Digging Up the Past* (1930).

Woolworth, Frank Winfield 1852–1919 •*US businessman*• He was born in Rodman, Jefferson County, New York. In 1873, after several years as a farm worker, he became a shop assistant. His employers backed his proposal to open a store in Utica for five-cent goods only (1879). This failed, but later the same year a second store, in Lancaster, Pennsylvania, selling ten-cent goods as well, was successful. In partnership with his employers, his brother, and cousin, from 1905 he began building a large chain of similar stores, and by the time he died the F W Woolworth company controlled over a thousand stores, reaching Great Britain in 1910.

Worde, Wynkyn de d. c. 1535 •*English printer*• He was born in Alsace. A pupil of **William Caxton**, he succeeded to his stock-in-trade in Westminster in 1491. In 1500 he moved to Fleet Street. He made great improvements in printing and creating new type, including the use of italic, and printed hundreds of books.

Wordsworth, Dorothy 1771–1855 •*English writer*• Born in Cockermouth, Cumberland, the only sister of **William Wordsworth**, she was his constant companion, and accompanied him on his travels. Her *Journals* show that her keen observation and sensibility provided a good deal of poetic imagery for both her brother and his friend **Coleridge**—more than that, they regarded her as the embodiment of that joy in nature which it was their object to depict. In 1829 she suffered a breakdown from which she never fully recovered. Her *Recollections of a Tour Made in Scotland AD 1803* (1874) is a classic.

Wordsworth, William 1770–1850 •*English poet*• He was born in Cockermouth, Cumberland, and was orphaned at an early age. He was sent to Hawkshead in the Lake District for board and education, and then attended St John's College, Cambridge (1787–91), where he was exposed to agnostic and revolutionary ideas. A walking tour through France and Switzerland in 1790 showed him a France still optimistic from their revolution, before disillusionment had set in. Two immature poems belong to this period—*An Evening Walk* and *Descriptive Sketches*, both published in 1793. Leaving Cambridge without a profession, he stayed for a little over a year in Blois. There he had an affair with Annette Vallon, which produced an illegitimate daughter, Ann Caroline, and is reflected in *Vaudracour and Julia* (c. 1804, published 1820). He returned to England when war with France was declared, but the depressing poem *Guilt and Sorrow* from this period shows that he was still passionate about social justice. For a time he fell under the spell of **William Godwin**'s philosophic anarchism, but the unreadable *Borderers* reveals that by 1795 he was turning his back on both the French Revolution and on Godwinism. With the help of his sister **Dorothy Wordsworth** and **Samuel Taylor Coleridge**, who had renounced his revolutionary ardor somewhat earlier, he discovered his true vocation—that of the poet exploring the lives of common people living in contact with divine nature and untouched by the rebellious spirit of the times. The Wordsworths and Coleridge settled in Somerset (1797), and from this close association resulted *Lyrical Ballads* (1798), the first manifesto of the new poetry, which opened with Coleridge's "Ancient Mariner" and concluded with Wordsworth's "Tintern Abbey." This alliance ended when the Wordsworths moved to Grasmere after a visit to Germany with Coleridge, and Wordsworth married Mary Hutchinson (1802). Modestly provided for by a legacy of £900, he embarked on a long period of routine work and relative happiness broken only by family misfortunes—the death of his sailor brother John (1805), which may have inspired the "Ode to Duty," and Dorothy's mental breakdown. Meanwhile **Napoleon** I's ambitions had completely destroyed the poet's revolutionary sympathies, as the patriotic sonnets sent to the *Morning Post* at about the time of the Peace of Amiens (1802–03) and afterward show. Apart from the sonnets, this was Wordsworth's most inspired period. The additions to the third edition of *Lyrical Ballads* (1801) contained the grave pastoral *Michael*, *Ruth* and four of the exquisite *Lucy* poems. The first of his tours in Scotland (1803), recorded perfectly by Dorothy, yielded some fine poems, including *The Solitary Reaper*. The great poem he was now contemplating, *The Recluse*, was never finished, but *The Prelude*, the record of the poet's mind, was read to Coleridge in 1805. It remained unpublished until after Wordsworth's death. Two volumes of poems appeared in 1807, the product of five years of intense activity. The ode "Intimations of Immortality" is only the loftiest of a number of masterpieces, including the patriotic sonnets, "Affliction of Margaret," "Memorials of a Tour in Scotland," "Ode to Duty," and many others. He succeeded **Robert Southey** as poet laureate in 1843.

" "

I wandered lonely as a cloud
That floats on high o'er vales and hills,
When all at once I saw a crowd,
A host, of golden daffodils;
Beside the lake, beneath the trees,
Fluttering and dancing in the breeze.

1804 "I wandered lonely as a cloud," stanza 1 (published 1807).

Worlock, Derek John Harford 1920–96 •*English Roman Catholic prelate*• Born in London, he was educated at St Edmund's College, Ware, and was ordained as a priest in 1944. He was the private secretary of the Archbishop of Westminster (1945–64), then became a rector in London (1964–65). He was Bishop of Portsmouth (1965–76) and served several ecclesiastical councils before becoming Archbishop of Liverpool in 1976. He wrote a number of religious books, including two in collaboration with the Anglican Bishop of Liverpool, **David Sheppard**, *Better Together* (1988) and *With Christ in the Wilderness* (1990).

Worrall, Denis John 1935– •*South African politician*• Born in Benoni, he was educated at the University of Cape Town and Cornell University, where he subsequently taught political science. He held a succession of academic posts during the 1960s and 1970s and also worked as a journalist before being elected a National Party (NP) senator in 1974 and Member of Parliament in 1977. In 1987 he resigned from the NP and in 1988 he established the Independent Party (IP). In 1989 the IP merged with other white opposition parties to form the reformist Democratic Party (DP), which advocated dismantlement of the apartheid system and universal adult suffrage. A coleader of the DP, Worrall was elected to parliament from 1989 to 1994.

Worth, Irene 1916–2002 •*US actress*• Born in Nebraska, she spent some years as a teacher before making her professional debut with a US touring company in 1942, appearing on Broadway a year later. In 1944 she moved to London. Equally at home on both sides of the Atlantic Ocean, she created the role of Celia Copplestone in **T S Eliot**'s *The Cocktail Party* at the Edinburgh Festival (1949). She joined the Old Vic in 1951, and moved to the Royal Shakespeare Company at Stratford-upon-Avon (1960). From then on she gave memorable performances in most of the major leading roles. Her role in *Lost in Yonkers* in New York (1991) won her a Tony award, and she went on to star in the 1993 film version. In 1989 she received an Obie award for outstanding achievement in the theater.

Wotton, Sir Henry 1568–1639 •*English traveler, diplomat, scholar and poet*• Born in Boughton Malherbe, Kent, he was educated at Winchester and Oxford, then spent the next seven years in Bavaria, Austria, Italy, Switzerland and France. On his return he became the confidant of Robert Devereux, 2nd Earl of **Essex**. Following Essex's downfall (1601), Wotton went to France, then to Italy, and was sent by Ferdinand, Duke of Florence, on a secret mission to **James VI** of Scotland. James later knighted him and employed him as ambassador. He returned to England a poor man in 1624, was made provost of Eton, and took orders. His tracts, letters and so on were collected as *Reliquiae Wottonianae* (1651). It was Wotton who described an ambassador as an honest man sent abroad to lie for the good of his country.

Wouk, Herman 1915– •*US novelist*• Born in New York City, the son of Jewish immigrants, he attended Columbia University and wrote radio scripts. He served in the US Navy in the South Pacific in World War II, later using his experience in his classic war novel, *The Caine Mutiny* (1951). It won the Pulitzer Prize and became a successful play and film. Later books—*Marjorie Morningstar* (1955) and *Youngblood Hawke* (1962)—also sold well. *The Winds of War* (1971) and *War and Remembrance* (1978) became popular television serials in 1983 and 1989, respectively.

Wovoka, *also known as* **Jack Wilson** c. 1858–1932 •*Native American religious leader*• Born into the Paiute tribe near Walter Lake, Nevada, he was the son of a religious mystic, and at the age of 14, after the death of his father, he went to live and work on the ranch of a local white family. He had a religious vision in late 1888 that prompted him to found the messianic Ghost Dance religion. He promised that if Native Americans lived peacefully and performed the Ghost Dance ritual, whites would disappear, the buffalo would return and the dead would rise. He won followers among many tribes, especially the Sioux, but after the massacre at Wounded Knee, South Dakota (1890), when many were killed wearing "ghost shirts" from which they expected supernatural protection, the movement came to an end.

Wozniak, Steve (Stephen) 1950– •*US computer pioneer and entrepreneur*• Born in San Jose, California, he studied at the University of California and became an engineer with Hewlett-Packard (1973–76). With **Steve Jobs** he developed and built the Apple II computer in Jobs's garage, later cofounding the Apple Computer Company and leading the revolution in personal computing. Wozniak left the company in 1985 and went on to pursue his interest in teaching computer skills to children.

Wray, Fay 1907–2004 •*US actress*• Born near Cardston, Alberta, in Canada, and raised in Los Angeles, she made an early film debut in *Blind Husbands* (1919) and appeared in many small roles before starring in *The Wedding March* (1928). After *King Kong* (1933), she specialized in distressed damsels screaming for help. She retired from the screen in 1942 but returned for a handful of matronly character parts before finally appearing in *Dragstrip Riot* (1958). She later wrote plays and acted on television in *Gideon's Trumpet* (1980). Her autobiography, *On the Other Hand*, was published in 1989.

Wren, Sir Christopher 1632–1723 •*English architect*• Born in East Knoyle, Wiltshire, he was the son of Dr Christopher Wren, dean of Windsor. He was educated at Westminster and Wadham College, Oxford, distinguished himself in physics and mathematics, and helped to perfect the barometer. In 1657 he became Professor of Astronomy at Gresham College in London, but in 1661 returned to Oxford as Savilian Professor of Astronomy. Before leaving London, Wren had, with **Robert Boyle**, John Wilkins and others, laid the foundation of the Royal Society. The first work built from a design by Wren was the chapel at Pembroke College, Cambridge (1663), and from 1663–66 he designed the Sheldonian Theatre at Oxford and the library of Trinity College, Cambridge. The Great Fire of London (1666) presented him with a unique opportunity to redesign the whole city, embracing wide streets and magnificent quays, but his design was never implemented. In 1669 he was appointed surveyor general and was chosen as the architect for the new St Paul's (1675–1710) and for more than 50 other churches in place of those destroyed by the fire. He also designed the Royal Exchange Greenwich Observatory, the Ashmolean Museum at Oxford, additions to Hampton Court, Buckingham House, Marlborough House and the western towers and north transept of Westminster Abbey. He was buried in St Paul's, where his monument reads *Si monumentum requiris, circumspice* ("If you seek a monument, look around you").

Wren, P(ercival) C(hristopher) 1885–1941 •*English novelist*• Born in Devon, he was successively a teacher, journalist, explorer and soldier in the French Foreign Legion, which provided him with the background for *Beau Geste* (1924), the first of his romantic adventure novels. The book spawned a thousand sequels, among them his own *Beau Sabreur* (1926), and *Beau Ideal* (1928). Among his many other books are *Valiant Dust* (1932) and *The Uniform of Glory* (1941), but none approached the success of *Beau Geste*.

Wright, Frances or **Fanny**, *also known as* **Frances Darusmont** 1795–1852 •*US reformer and abolitionist*• Born in Dundee, Scotland, the heiress to a large fortune, she emigrated to the US in 1818 and toured widely, publishing *Views of Society and Manners in America* in 1821. In the company of the reformer **Marie Joseph Lafayette**, she founded a short-lived community for freed slaves at Nashoba in western Tennessee. Settling in New York in 1829, she published with **Robert Dale Owen** a socialist journal, *Free Enquirer*. One of the early suffragists, she campaigned vigorously against religion and for the emancipation of women.

Wright, Frank Lloyd 1867–1959 •*US architect*• Born in Richland Center, Wisconsin, he studied civil engineering at the University of Wisconsin. After setting up in architectural practice in Chicago, he became known for low-built prairie-style bungalows like Chicago's Robie House, but he soon launched into more daring and controversial designs that exploited modern technology and Cubist spatial concepts. He designed his own home, Taliesin, at Spring Green, Wisconsin (1911), and another home and school, Taliesin West, near Phoenix, Arizona (1938). His best-known public buildings include the earthquake-proof Imperial Hotel in Tokyo (1916–20), the "Fallingwater" weekend retreat at Mill Run, near Pittsburgh (1936), the Johnson Wax office block in Racine, Wisconsin (1936), Florida Southern College (1940) and the Guggenheim Museum of Art in New York (1959). He was an innovator in the field of open planning. He also designed furniture and textiles and is considered one of the outstanding architects of the 20th century. He wrote an *Autobiography* (1932) and numerous other works.

> “ ”
> The physician can bury his mistakes, but the architect can only advise his client to plant vines.
>
> *1953 In the **New York Times**, October 4.*

Wright, Joseph, *nicknamed* **Wright of Derby** 1734–97 •*English genre and portrait painter*• He spent his whole life in his native town, except for a few years spent in London, Bath, and Italy. His fireside portrait groups often show unusual light effects. His industrial works include the depiction of experiments made by candlelight (for example, *Experiment With the Air Pump*, 1768, London).

Wright, Judith Arundell 1915–2000 •*Australian poet*• Born in Armidale, New South Wales, she was brought up on a sheep farm and educated at the University of Sydney. *The Moving Image* (1946) was her first collection, after which she was an industrious poet, critic, anthologist, editor and short-story writer. Her main volumes of poetry are *Woman to Man* (1949), *The Gateway* (1953), *The Two Fires* (1955), *Birds* (1962), *City Sunrise* (1964), *The Other Half* (1966), *Alive* (1973) and *Fourth Quarter and Other Poems* (1976). *The Cry for the Dead* (1981) is about the impact of European immigration on the Aboriginals, and a collection of essays on Aboriginal culture, *Born of the Conquerors*, was published in 1991. In 1993 she became the first Australian to receive the Queen's Medal for poetry.

Wright, Orville 1871–1948 and **Wilbur** 1867–1912 •*US aviation pioneers*• Orville was born in Dayton, Ohio, and Wilbur near Millville, Indiana. They operated a bicycle shop together and were self-taught inventors, becoming the first to fly in a heavier-than-air machine (December 17, 1903), at Kitty Hawk, North Carolina. Encouraged by this, they patented their flying machine and formed an aircraft production company (1909). In 1915 Orville sold his interests in the business in order to devote himself to research.

Wright, Peter 1916–95 •*English intelligence officer*• Born in Chesterfield, Derbyshire, he farmed before joining the Admiralty's Research Laboratory during World War II. He worked for MI5 (counterintelligence) from 1955, and, on his retirement in 1976, bought a sheep ranch in Tasmania and wrote his autobiography, *Spycatcher* (1987). In it, he alleged that Sir Roger Hollis, the former director general of MI5, had been a Soviet double agent, the so-called Fifth Man, and that elements within MI5 had tried to overthrow the **Wilson** government during the mid-1960s. Attempts by the **Thatcher** government to suppress both the publication and the distribution of the book were unsuccessful.

Wright, Sir Peter Robert 1926– •*English ballet director*• Born in London, he made his debut as a professional dancer with the Ballets Jooss in 1944. He danced with a number of companies from the late 1940s, becoming a freelance choreographer and teacher from the late 1950s with modern works as well as classics such as *Giselle*, *The Sleeping Beauty*, *Coppelia* and *The Nutcracker*. He has produced various West End musicals and revues and worked extensively in television, and among many other posts was director of the Sadler's Wells Royal Ballet (now the Birmingham Royal Ballet) from 1977 to 1995.

Wright, Richard Nathaniel 1908–60 •*US novelist, short-story writer and critic*• Born on a plantation in Mississippi, the grandson of slaves, he was abandoned by his father at age five, received a poor education, and was subjected to ill-treatment by his relatives and to religious fanaticism. During the Depression he left the South, became a journalist and joined the progressive Writers' Project. *Uncle Tom's Children*, a volume of short stories, appeared in 1938. By this time Wright had joined the Communist Party, consequently becoming a pessimistic humanist; but he left it in 1942. A naturalist and later in Paris an existentialist who was acquainted with **Jean-Paul Sartre**, he wrote *Native Son* (1940), a novel about an African-American youth who murders a white woman and is sent to the electric chair. *Native Son* was followed by *Black Boy* (1945), a harrowing autobiography, and the novel *The Outsider* (1953).

Wu, Chien-Shiung 1912–97 •*US physicist*• Born in Shanghai, China, she studied at National Center University in China, and from 1936 at University of California, Berkeley. From 1946 she worked at Columbia University, New York. In 1956 Wu and her colleagues tested **Tsung-Dao Lee** and **Chen Ning Yang**'s hypothesis that parity is not conserved in weak decays, and they observed the emission of electrons preferentially in one direction, thus proving that parity was not conserved. This was later explained by the V-A theory of weak interactions proposed by **Richard Feynman** and **Murray Gell-Mann**.

Wu Cheng'en (Wu Ch'eng-en) 16th century •*Chinese writer*• Born in Shanyang, Huaian (now Jiangsu [Kiangsu] province), he was the author of the novel *Xiyou zhi* (1593, Eng trans *Monkey*, 1942), based on the pilgrimage of **Xuan Zang**.

Wulfstan, St c. 1009–95 •*Anglo-Saxon prelate*• Born in Long Itchington, near Warwick, he was educated at the Abbey of Peterborough. He was appointed Bishop of Worcester in 1062. At the Norman Conquest of 1066 he made submission to **William the Conqueror**, and later supported **William II Rufus**. He preached at Bristol against the slave trade practiced by merchants there, putting an end to it. He helped to compile the *Domesday Book*, and he may have written part of the *Anglo-Saxon Chronicle*. He was canonized in 1203, and his feast day is January 19.

Wulfstan d. 1023 •*Anglo-Saxon prelate and writer*• He was Bishop of London (996–1002), Archbishop of York from 1002, and also Bishop of Worcester (1003–16). He was the author of homilies in the vernacular, including a celebrated address to the English, *Sermo Lupi ad Anglos*.

Wundt, Wilhelm Max 1832–1920 •*German physiologist and psychologist, founder of experimental psychology*• Born in Neckarau, Baden, he studied at the University of Heidelberg and in 1875 became Professor of Physiology at Leipzig. He made studies of the nervous system and the senses, the relations of physiology and psychology, logic and other subjects, seeking to understand the consciousness by means of its experiences. He published *Vorlesungen über die Menschen und Thierseele* (1863, "Lectures on the Mind of Humans and Animals"), a book on ethics (1886), *Grundriss der Psychologie* (1896, "Outlines of Psychology"), and *Völkerpsychologie* (10 vols, 1900–20, "Ethnic Psychology").

Wyatt, Sir Thomas 1503–42 •*English poet and courtier*• Born in Allington, Kent, he studied at St John's College, Cambridge. He published nothing in his lifetime, but has served as an exemplar for English love poets. His best work consists of his lyrics and sonnets, and he was regarded as the most important of all the English poets who imitated—and then added to—Italian models.

Wycherley, William c. 1640–1716 •*English dramatist*• Born in Clive, near Shrewsbury, he was sent to France as a youth, left Queen's College, Oxford, without a degree, and entered the Middle Temple. His *Love in a Wood, or St James's Park*, a brisk comedy based on Charles Sedley's *Mulberry Garden*, was acted and well-received in 1671. The Duke of **Buckingham** gave him a commission in a regiment, **Charles II** made him a present of £500 and he served for a short time in the fleet. *The Gentleman Dancing-master* (1672), a clever farcical comedy of intrigue, was followed by *The Country Wife* (1675), Wycherley's coarsest but strongest play, and *The Plain Dealer* (1677), both based on plays by **Molière**. A little after 1679 Wycherley married the young widowed Countess of Drogheda. She died a few years later, leaving him all her fortune, a bequest which involved him in a lawsuit whereby he was reduced to poverty and cast into the Fleet prison for some years. **James VII and II**, having seen a representation of *The Plain Dealer*, paid his debts and gave him a pension of £200 a year. Nevertheless Wycherley's money troubles continued to the end of his life.

“ ”

Wit is more necessary than beauty; and I think no young woman ugly that has it, and no handsome woman agreeable without it.

*1675 **The Country Wife**, act 1, scene 1.*

Wycliffe, John, *also spelled* **Wycliff, Wyclif, Wicliffe** or **Wiclif** c. 1329–84 •*English religious reformer*• He was born near Richmond, Yorkshire. He distinguished himself at Oxford, where he taught philosophy, was master of Balliol College (1360), then became rector of Fillingham, which he exchanged in 1368 for Ludgershall, Buckinghamshire. He became rector of Lutterworth (1374), and was sent to Bruges to discuss ecclesiastical abuses with ambassadors from the pope. His strenuous activity gained him support among the nobles and the London citizenry. In 1376 he wrote *De Dominio Divino*, expounding the doctrine that all authority is founded in grace and that wicked rulers (whether secular or ecclesiastical) thereby forfeited their right to rule. His maintenance of a right in the secular power to control the clergy was offensive to the bishops, who summoned him before the archbishop in St Paul's in 1377. Pope **Gregory XI** banned him, and urged that he be made to answer before the archbishop and the pope. When at last proceedings were undertaken, at Lambeth in 1378, the prosecution had little effect upon Wycliffe's position. The whole fabric of the Church was in the same year shaken by the Great Schism and the election of an antipope. Wycliffe now began to attack the constitution of the Church, declaring it would be better without pope or prelates. He denied the priestly power of absolution and the whole system of enforced confession, penances and indulgence, and asserted the right of every man to examine the Bible for himself. He began to write in English instead of Latin, and by issuing popular tracts became a leading English prose writer. He organized a body of itinerant preachers, his "poor priests," who spread his doctrines throughout the country, and began the first English translation of the Bible. His 1380 attack on the central dogma of transubstantiation was more dangerous. Archbishop Courtenay convoked a council (1382) and condemned Wycliffite opinions. His followers were arrested, and all compelled to recant, but for some unknown reason he himself was not judged. He withdrew from Oxford to Lutterworth, and his work in the next two years continued to insist on inward religion, although he attacked the established practices of the Church only so far as he thought they had degenerated into mere mechanical uses. The influence of his teaching continued up to the Reformation, and his supporters came to be derisively known as "Lollards" (from a Dutch word meaning "mumblers"). **Jan Huss** was avowedly his disciple. Forty-five articles extracted from his writings were condemned as heretical by the Council of Constance (1414), which ordered his bones to be dug up and burned and cast into the River Swift—a sentence executed in 1428.

Wyeth, Andrew Newell 1917– •*US painter*• Born in Chadds Ford, Pennsylvania, he studied under his father, the book illustrator N C Wyeth (1882–1945). His soberly realistic photographic paintings, usually executed with tempera and watercolor rather than oils, often focus on landscapes, as in *April Wind* (1952, Hartford, Connecticut), using off-center compositions in order to give a sense of haunting unease, as in *Christina's World* (1948, Museum of Modern Art, New York City).

Wykeham, William of *See* **William of Wykeham**

Wyler, William 1902–81 •*US film director*• Born in Mülhausen, Germany (now Mulhouse, France), he directed his first film, *Crook Buster*, in 1925. Over the next five years he made many Westerns before undertaking more prestigious productions, usually involving star actors and noted literary sources. He became renowned for his obsessively meticulous approach to composition, performance and narrative structure, and his many films include *These Three* (1936), *Wuthering Heights* (1939), *The Little Foxes* (1941), *The Collector* (1965) and *Funny Girl* (1968). He served as a major in the US Army Air Corps (1942–45) and helped form the committee to defend the First Amendment in 1947. He received Academy Awards for *Mrs. Miniver* (1942), *The Best Years of Our Lives* (1946) and *Ben Hur* (1959). He retired in 1972.

Wyman, Bill *See* **Rolling Stones, The**

Wyman, Jane, *originally* **Sarah Jane Fulks** 1914– •*US actress*• Born in St Joseph, Missouri, she was a child actress, and made her first breakthrough as a radio singer. It was not until her performance in the film *The Lost Weekend* (1945) that she was recognized as a serious actress. She was nominated for an Academy Award for *The Yearling* (1946), and she won one for *Johnny Belinda* (1948), in which she played a deaf-mute character. She acted in many films, and starred in the television soap opera *Falcon Crest* in the 1980s. She was married to **Ronald Reagan** from 1940 to 1948.

Wyndham, Sir Charles, *originally* **Charles Culverwell** 1837–1919 •*English actor-manager*• Born in Liverpool, he trained as a doctor before his first appearance on the stage in New York City in 1861. He left the stage temporarily to enlist in the Union army as a surgeon during the Civil War. His London debut followed in 1866, and in 1899 he built and managed Wyndham's Theatre, which opened with another successful revival of *David Garrick*.

Wyndham, John, *pseudonym of* **John Wyndham Parkes Lucas Beynon Harris** 1903–69 •*English science-fiction writer*• He was born in Knowle, Warwickshire. As a child he was fascinated by the stories of **H G Wells**, and in the late 1920s he began to write science-fiction tales for popular magazines, showing a much greater regard for literary style and moral and philosophical values than was common in this field. In 1951 he published his most successful novel, *The Day of the Triffids*, which describes the fortunes of the blinded survivors of a thermonuclear explosion who are threatened by the triffids, intelligent vegetable beings hostile to human beings. His other novels include *The Kraken Wakes* (1953, in the US, *Out of the Deeps*), *The Chrysalids* (1955, in the US, *Rebirth*), *The Midwych Cuckoos* (1957), *The Trouble With Lichen* (1960) and *Chocky* (1968). *Consider Her Ways* (1961) and *Seeds of Time* (1969) are collections of short stories.

Wynette, Tammy, *professional name of* **Virginia Wynette Pugh** 1942–98 •*US country singer*• She was born in Tupelo, Mississippi, and raised in Alabama. She married five times, the third time to singer George Jones (1931–) in 1969. Their string of hit duets continued beyond their divorce in 1975, and the troubled marriage is often said to have added fuel to her most famous solo hits, "D-I-V-O-R-C-E" (1970) and "Stand by Your Man" (1971). She had a surprise pop hit in 1992 with "Justified and Ancient," a collaboration with the British techno-pop group KLF. In 1995, she and Jones released *One*, their first new album together since the late 1970s.

Wynkyn de Worde *See* **Worde, Wynkyn de**

Wyss, Johann Rudolf 1781–1830 •*Swiss writer*• He was born in Bern. Professor of Philosophy at Bern from 1805, he was the author of the Swiss national anthem, "Rufst du mein Vaterland" ("You Call, My Fatherland"), and collected Swiss folktales. He is best known for his connection with *Der schweizerische Robinson* (4 vols, 1812–27, Eng trans *The Swiss Family Robinson*, 1814–28), which he completed and edited for his father, Johann David Wyss (1743–1818).

Wyszyński, Stefan 1901–81 •*Polish prelate and cardinal*• Born in Zuzela, near Warsaw, he was educated at Wjocjawek seminary and Lublin Catholic University. He was a professor at the Higher Seminary, Włocławek (1930–39), and founded the Catholic Workers university there (1935). During World War II he was associated with the Resistance movement during the German occupation of Poland. In 1945 he became rector of Włocławek seminary, in 1946 Bishop of Lublin and in 1949 Archbishop of Warsaw and Gniezno and primate of Poland. He was made a cardinal in 1952. In 1953, following his indictment of the Communist campaign against the Church, he was suspended from his ecclesiastical functions and imprisoned. Freed after the "bloodless revolution" of 1956, he agreed to a reconciliation between Church and State under the "liberalizing" **Gomułka** regime, but relations became increasingly strained.

XYZ

Xanthippe 5th century BC •*Wife of Socrates*• The traditional description of her as a quarrelsome and shrewish wife made her name proverbial.

Xavier, St Francis *See* **Francis Xavier, St**

Xenakis, Iannis 1922–2001 •*French composer*• Born of Greek parentage in Braila, Romania, he studied engineering in Athens and worked as an architect for **Le Corbusier** in Paris, then turned to musical composition (1954) with *Metastasis* for orchestra. He developed a highly complex style which incorporated mathematical concepts of chance and probability (so-called stochastic music) as well as electronic techniques in mainly instrumental and orchestral works.

Xenocrates c.395–314 BC •*Greek philosopher and scientist*• Born in Chalcedon on the Bosporus, he was a pupil of **Plato** and in 339 BC succeeded **Speusippus** as head of the academy Plato had founded. He is recorded as traveling with **Aristotle** after Plato's death in 348 BC. He wrote prolifically on natural science, astronomy and philosophy, but only fragments of this output survive.

Xenophanes c. 570–c. 480 BC •*Greek philosopher, poet and religious thinker*• Born in Colophon, Ionia, Asia Minor, where he probably lived until the Persian conquest of the region (546 BC). He seems then to have wandered around the Mediterranean. He wrote poetry, fragments of which survive, and seems to have been an independent and original thinker, though later traditions tried to claim him as a member either of the Ionian or the Eleatic school. He attacked the anthropomorphism of popular religion and **Homer**ic mythology (pointing out that each race credits the gods with its own physical characteristics, and that animals would do the same), posited by way of reaction a single deity who somehow energizes the world ("without toil he shakes all things by the thought of his mind"), and made some bold speculations about the successive inundations of the Earth based on the observation of fossils.

Xenophon c. 435–c. 354 BC •*Greek historian, essayist and soldier*• He was born in Attica, the son of Gryllus, an Athenian knight, and a disciple of **Socrates**. He was a skilled soldier and inspirational leader of his armies, and saw action in several campaigns, before returning to Scillus, near Olympia with his wife Philesia and his two sons. He spent the next 20 years there, but the breakup of Spartan ascendancy after the Battle of Leuctra (371) drove him from his retreat when Elis reclaimed Scillus. The Athenians, who had now joined the Spartans against Thebes, repealed the sentence of banishment against him, but he settled and died in Corinth. His writings give the impression of having been composed with great singleness of purpose, modesty and love of truth. They can be categorized into four groups: (1) historical—the *Hellenica* (Eng trans *History of My Times*, 1966, the history of Greece for 49 years, serving as a continuation of Thucydides), *Anabasis* (Eng trans *The March Upcountry*, 1947, the story of the expedition with Cyrus) and *Encomium of Agesilaus*; (2) technical and didactic—*De Praefectura Equestri* ("On Horsemanship"), the *Hipparchicus* ("Guide for a Cavalry Commander") and the *Cynegeticus* ("Guide to Hunting"); (3) politico-philosophical—*Respublica Lacedaemoniorum* ("Constitution of the Lacedaemons"), *Cyropaedia* ("The Education of Cyrus," a historical romance) and *The Revenues* (on Athenian finance); (4) ethico-philosophical—*Memorabilia Socratis* (sketches and dialogues illustrating the life and character of his master), *Symposium* (Eng trans 1970), *Oeconomicus* (Eng trans 1970), *Hieron* and *Apologia* (Eng trans *Socrates' Defense Before the Jury*, 1965).

Xerxes I c. 520–465 BC •*King of Persia*• He succeeded his father, **Darius I**, in 486 BC. He subdued the rebellious Egyptians, then (484) marched on Greece with a vast army drawn from all parts of the empire. A bridge consisting of a double line of boats was built across the Hellespont, and a canal was cut through Mount Athos. His immense force reached Thermopylae, then destroyed Athens, but was defeated in the naval battle of Salamis (480). He withdrew to the Hellespont, but his hopes of conquest died with the fall of his general, Mardonius, at Plataea (479). He then withdrew to Persia (Iran), where he added monuments to his capital at Persepolis. Xerxes was later murdered by Artabanus.

X-et *See* **Erixson, Sven**

Ximénes or **Jiménez de Cisneros, Francisco** 1436–1517 •*Spanish prelate and statesman*• Born in Castile, he was educated at Alcalá, Salamanca and Rome. Ordained in Rome, his papal nomination was refused by the Archbishop of Toledo and he was imprisoned for six years. On his release, he joined a Franciscan monastery, but soon became confessor to Queen **Isabella of Castile**. Three years later he replaced the Archbishop of Toledo who had once incarcerated him, and on Isabella's death, and in the absence of her husband, **Ferdinand** the Catholic, wielded great influence over the country's affairs, introducing beneficial fiscal reforms and obsessively persecuting the Moors. When Ferdinand died in 1516, Ximénes became regent, but he died traveling to meet his new emperor, **Charles V**.

Xuan Zang (Hsüan Tsang) 602–64 •*Chinese Buddhist traveler*• Born in Henan (Honan), he became a Buddhist monk in 620 and made a pilgrimage through China and India, traveling 40,000 miles in 16 years. His books graphically describe the Buddhist world of his time, and his travels form the basis for **Wu Cheng'en**'s book *Monkey*.

Yahya Khan, Agha Muhammad 1917–80 •*Pakistani soldier*• Born in Chakwal town, in Jhelum district, he was educated at the University of the Punjab and the Indian Military Academy, Dehra Dun. He fought with the British 8th Army during World War II and afterward rose to become chief of the army general staff (1957–62). He supported General **Ayub Khan**'s successful coup in 1958, became army commander in chief in 1966 and in 1969 replaced Ayub Khan as military ruler. In 1970 he sanctioned the country's first national elections based on universal suffrage, but his mishandling of the Bangladesh separatist issue led to civil war and the dismemberment of the republic in 1971. After defeat by India in the Bangladesh war, Yahya Khan resigned and was sentenced to five years' house arrest.

Yale, Elihu 1649–1721 •*English colonial administrator and benefactor*• He was born in Boston, Massachusetts, to English parents. They returned to Great Britain in 1652, and he was educated in London. In 1672 he went to India in the service of the East India Company, becoming governor of Madras in 1687. He lived in England from 1699, and donated money to a collegiate school established (1701) at Saybrook, Connecticut. The school later moved to New Haven, and in 1718 it took the name of Yale College in his honor. In 1887 it became Yale University.

Yale, Linus 1821–68 •*US inventor and manufacturer*• He was born in Salisbury, New York, and set up business as a locksmith in Shelburne Falls, Massachusetts. He invented various types of locks, including the small cylinder Yale locks, by which his name is known.

Yalow, Rosalyn, *née* **Sussman** 1921– •*US biophysicist and Nobel Prize winner*• Born in New York City, she studied at Hunter College, New York, and at the University of Illinois. She taught physics at

Hunter College until 1950, in 1947 becoming consultant to the Radioisotope Unit at the Bronx Veterans Administration (VA) Hospital. From 1950 she collaborated on diabetes research with Solomon Berson, in the process developing radioimmunoassay (RIA), an ultrasensitive method of measuring concentrations of substances in the body. They suggested that, in adult diabetics, antibodies which inactivate injected insulin are formed. In 1977, for her work on RIA, Yalow shared the Nobel Prize for physiology or medicine with **Roger Guillemin** and **Andrew Schally**.

Yamagata Aritomo 1838–1922 •*Japanese soldier and statesman*• Born in Hagi, he was made commanding officer of the Kiheitai in 1863. He went on to become vice minister of war (1871), army minister (1878), home minister (1883–89) and was Japan's first prime minister (1889–91 and 1898–1900). His modernization of the military system led to Japanese victories in the Sino-Japanese War (1894–95) and the Russo-Japanese War (1904–05)—for which he was made Prince, or *Koshaku*—and the emergence of Japan as a significant force in world politics. From 1903 he alternated with Ito Hirobumi as president of the Privy Council until the latter's death (1909), when he became the dominant senior statesman. His interference in the marriage of the crown prince in 1921 led to his public censure, and he died in disgrace the following year.

Yamamoto, Isoroku, *originally surnamed* **Takano** 1884–1943 •*Japanese naval officer*• Educated at the Naval Academy, Etajima, he was wounded in the Battle of Tsushima in the Russo-Japanese war (1904–05). He studied at Harvard (1917–19) and became naval attaché in Washington (1926–28). He became chief of the aviation department of the Japanese navy in 1935, and vice navy minister from 1936 to 1939. He was opposed to the Japanese entry into World War II. As admiral (1940) and commander in chief of the Combined Fleet (1939–43), he planned and directed the attack on Pearl Harbor in December 1941. His forces were defeated at the Battle of Midway (June 1942), and he was killed when his plane was shot down over the Solomon Islands.

Yang, Chen Ning 1922– •*US physicist and Nobel Prize winner*• Born in Hofei, China, he was educated in Kuming before gaining a scholarship to the University of Chicago in 1945 to work under **Edward Teller**. He became a professor at the Institute for Advanced Studies, Princeton (1955–65), and from 1965 was director of the Institute for Theoretical Physics at New York State University, Stony Brook. In 1956 with **Tsung-Dao Lee**, he concluded that the quantum property known as parity was unlikely to be conserved in weak interactions. This was confirmed later that year by a group of physicists headed by **Chien-Shiung Wu**. For this prediction Lee and Yang were awarded the 1957 Nobel Prize for physics.

Yang Shangkun (Yang Shang-k'un) 1907–98 •*Chinese politician*• The son of a wealthy Sichuan (Szechuan) province landlord, he joined the Chinese Communist Party (CCP) in 1926 and studied in Moscow (1927–30). He took part in the Long March (1934–35) and the Liberation War (1937–49), and became an alternate member of the CCP's secretariat in 1956, but during the Cultural Revolution (1966–69) he was purged for alleged revisionism. He was subsequently rehabilitated in 1978 and in 1982 was inducted into the CCP's politburo and military affairs commission. A year later he became a vice chairman of the State Central Military Commission and in 1988 was elected state president, a position he held until 1993. He was viewed as a trusted supporter of **Deng Xiaoping** and had strong personal ties with senior military leaders.

Yates, Dornford, *pseudonym of* **Cecil William Mercer** 1885–1960 •*English novelist*• He was born in London, educated at Harrow and Oxford, and was called to the bar before achieving great popularity with two entertaining series of novels: one of international adventure, including such titles as *Blind Corner* (1927), and one of primarily humorous banter, about the character Berry Pleydell and his rich, indolent circle, for instance, *Berry and Co* (1920). A prolific author, he was a nephew of **Anthony Hope**, whose work may well have influenced him.

Yeager, Chuck (Charles Elwood) 1923– •*US test pilot*• Born in Myra, West Virginia, he enlisted in the US Air Force in 1941, graduated as a fighter pilot in 1943, and during combat missions won 12 victories. On October 14, 1947, he flew the Bell X-1 rocket research aircraft to a level speed of more than 670 mph, thus "breaking the sound barrier," and in the Bell X-1A he flew at more than twice the speed of sound (1953). He was commander of the US Air Force Aerospace Research Pilot School and commanded the Fourth Fighter Bomber Wing.

Yeats, Jack B (John Butler) 1870–1957 •*Irish cartoonist and Impressionist painter*• Born in London, he was the son of the artist John Butler Yeats (1839–1922) and brother of **W B Yeats**. Educated in County Sligo, he sketched horses for *Paddock Life* magazine (1891), then drew cartoons for *Cassell's Saturday Journal*, among others (1892). In 1894 he created the first cartoon strip version of Sherlock Holmes, *Chubblock Homes*, as well as many strips featuring horses and show business. He wrote and illustrated children's books beginning with *James Flaunty* (1901), and he drew many other strips until 1918, when he concentrated on painting, playwriting and writing.

Yeats, W(illiam) B(utler) 1865–1939 •*Irish poet and winner of the Nobel Prize for literature*• He was born in Sandymount, a Dublin suburb. His father was the artist John Butler Yeats (1839–1922). His mother came from Sligo, where Yeats spent much time as a child. When he was two, the family moved to London, but they returned to Ireland in 1881 and lived in Howth, near Dublin. In 1884 he enrolled in the Metropolitan School of Art in Dublin, and his first lyrics were published in *The Dublin University Review* (1885). He was preoccupied with mysticism and the occult, and helped found the Dublin Hermetic Society in 1885. He also pursued his interest in Irish mythology, the source of much of his poetry. In 1886 his first volume of verse, *Mosada: A Dramatic Poem*, was published. He returned to London the following year with his family and contributed to anthologies of Irish poets and edited *Fairy and Folk Tales of the Irish Peasantry* (1888). He began to have poems accepted by English magazines; two American newspapers appointed him their literary correspondent; and his circle of friends widened to include **William Morris**, **George Bernard Shaw**, **Oscar Wilde** and others. In 1889 he met and fell in love with the ardent Irish nationalist **Maud Gonne**. Despite repeated offers from him (until 1903), she refused to marry him. Also in 1889 he published *The Wanderings of Oisin and Other Poems*, which was well reviewed and established him as a literary figure. However, he became increasingly homesick and returned to Ireland in 1891. A year later he published *John Sherman* and *Dhoya* (1892), two stories on Celtic themes suggested by his father, and the play *The Countess Kathleen* (1892), a Celtic drama rich in imagery and inspired by Maud Gonne. He also became a founding member of the Irish Literary Society. In 1893 he published *The Celtic Twilight*, a collection of stories and legends. His drama *The Land of Heart's Desire* (1894) began regular production in London in 1894. Meanwhile, Yeats worked on his collected *Poems* (1895), which elevated him to the ranks of the major poets. In 1896 he met Lady **Gregory**, the mistress of an estate at Coole in Galway, where he set and composed many of his finest poems. With her encouragement, he helped found the Irish Literary Theatre in 1899, promoting playwrights such as **J M Synge** and contributing his own plays for performance (for instance, his most successful play, *Cathleen ni Houlihan* [1902], a propaganda play with Maud Gonne in the title role, which it is thought may have sparked the Easter uprising of 1916). This theater became the Irish National Theatre, which opened the Abbey Theatre in Dublin in 1904. In 1903, after learning that Maud Gonne had married John MacBride, Yeats went to America. (MacBride was executed in the aftermath of the 1916 uprising, and Yeats remembered him and others in his famous poem, "Easter 1916.") *The Collected Works in Prose and Verse* in eight volumes was published in 1906, and he worked on *The Player Queen* for the actress Mrs **Patrick Campbell**. It premiered at the Abbey Theatre in 1919. His last attempt to write poetic drama using legends as a source appeared in *The Green Helmet and Other Poems* (1910), and in 1914 he published *Responsibilities*. In 1917 he married Georgie Hyde-Lees. Together they shared an interest in psychical research which, along with Hyde-Lee's automatic writing, influenced Yeats's later work, including *The Wild Swans at Coole* (1919) and the prose *A Vision* (1925). *Michael Robartes and the Dancer* (1921) preempted the outbreak of the civil war, and it was seven years before he published his next collection of poems. During the intervening years he was engaged in playwriting and politics (he became a member of the Irish senate in 1922, on the foundation of the Irish Free State), and in 1923 was awarded the Nobel Prize for literature. In 1928 he moved to Rapallo in Italy and in that year published *The Tower*, a dark vision of the future exquisitely expressed which, with the powerful collection *The Winding Stair* (1933), is generally regarded as his best poetic work. Yeats was very much a grand literary and public figure, although his reputation was slightly tainted by his flirtation with fascism. He moved to Cap Martin, Alpes Maritimes, in 1938, where he died. His body was returned to Ireland in 1948 and buried in County Sligo.

“ ”

The innocent and the beautiful
Have no enemy but time.

1927 "In Memory of Eva Gore-Booth and Con Markiewicz," l. 24–5. Collected in ***The Winding Stair and Other Poems*** *(1933).*

Yeltsin, Boris Nikolayevich 1931– •*Russian statesman*• Born in Sverdlovsk (now Yekaterinburg) and educated at the same Urals Polytechnic as **Nikolai Ryzhkov**, he began his career in the construction industry. He joined the Communist Party of the Soviet Union (CPSU) in 1961 and was appointed first secretary of the Sverdlovsk region in 1976. He was inducted into the CPSU's Central Committee (CC) in 1985 by **Mikhail Gorbachev** and was appointed Communist Party chief in Moscow in the same year. Yeltsin, a blunt-talking, hands-on reformer, rapidly set about renovating the corrupt "Moscow machine" and was elected a candidate member of the CPSU politburo in 1986; in 1987, at a CC plenum, after he had bluntly criticized party conservatives, he was downgraded to a lowly administrative post. He returned to public attention in 1989 by being elected to the new Congress of USSR People's Deputies. In 1990 he was elected president of the Russian Federation. He played a high-profile role in the resistance against the failed attempt to depose Gorbachev as president. In 1996 Yeltsin was reelected, but throughout his presidency he suffered recurring bouts of ill health, and underwent heart bypass surgery in the year of his reelection. He resigned in 1999 and was replaced by **Vladimir Putin**.

Yentob, Alan 1947– •*English broadcaster and administrator*• He was born in Manchester, the son of a Sephardic Jewish immigrant. He studied at the Universities of Grenoble and Leeds, and worked at Bush House for the BBC World Service. He moved to television as an assistant director in arts, began making programs, and became head of music and arts in 1985. In 1988 he became controller of BBC2, in 1993 controller of BBC1, in 1997 director of television and in 2000 BBC director of entertainment, drama and films.

Yerkes, Charles Tyson 1837–1905 •*US railway financier*• Born in Philadelphia, he made and lost several fortunes, and in 1899 was forced to sell out in Chicago after allegations of political chicanery. In London in 1900 he headed the consortium that built the London Underground. In 1892 he presented the Yerkes Observatory to the University of Chicago.

Yesenin, Sergei Aleksandrovich 1895–1925 •*Russian peasant poet*• Born in the Ryazan district to a peasant family, in his remarkable first collection of poetry, *Radunitsa* (1915, "Memorial Service"), there was nothing antipathetic to Bolshevism, but his second, *Goluben* (1918), and some subsequent ones, tried—fatally to their integrity—to come to terms with it. His greatest poetry was written after he had rejected Bolshevism and had become an alcoholic and hooligan, wandering about Russia and elsewhere in a haze of riotous living which became legendary. In 1922 he married the dancer **Isadora Duncan**, with whom he was unable to exchange a word, as she knew no Russian and he knew no English. In his later collections such as *Moskva kabatskaya* (1924, "Moscow Tavern") and *Rus' sovetskaya* (1925, "Soviet Russia"), his poetry took on new dimensions in its expression of his regrets for the death of his hopes for himself and for Russia. He hanged himself after writing a suicide note in his own blood. The Communists suppressed his work for many years after his death, but in the 1960s it was revived, with great success.

Yevtushenko, Yevgeni Aleksandrovich 1933– •*Russian poet*• Born in Zima, Siberia, he moved to Moscow with his mother in 1944. His work did not attract much attention until the publication of *Trety sneg* (1955, "Third Snow"), *Shosse entuziastov* (1956, "Highway of the Enthusiasts") and *Obeshchaniye* (1957, "The Promise") made him a spokesman for the young post-**Stalin** generation. His long poem *Stantsya Zima* ("Zima Junction") prompted criticism, as did *Babi Yar* (1962), which attacked anti-Semitism in Russia as well as Nazi Germany. Travel abroad inspired poems such as those published in *Vzmakh ruki* (1962, "A Wave of the Hand"). He publicly supported **Aleksandr Solzhenitsyn** on his arrest in 1974. His later work includes *Love Poems* (1977) and the novel *Yagodnye mesta* (1982, Eng trans *Wild Berries*, 1984). **Shostakovich** set five of his poems to music, including *Babi Yar*, as his Thirteenth Symphony.

“ ”

I love sport because I love life, and sport is one of the basic joys of life.

1966 In ***Sports Illustrated****, December 19.*

Yoakam, Dwight 1956– •*US country singer*• Born in Pikeville, Kentucky, he studied drama in Ohio, and has acted in both stage plays and films. He took a proselytizing stance against the homogenized commercialization of early 1980s country music, and was established as a leading figure in the so-called new traditionalist or new country movement with the release of his debut album, *Guitars, Cadillacs, Etc, Etc* (1986), and its successor, *Hillbilly Deluxe* (1987). Both were defiant champions of the driving, hard-edged honky-tonk sound that had disappeared from the sanitized Nashville scene. Further albums include *This Time* (1992), *Gone* (1995) and *Tomorrow's Sounds Today* (2000).

Yonge, Charlotte Mary 1823–1901 •*English novelist*• Born in Otterbourne, Hampshire, she achieved great popular success with *The Heir of Redclyffe* (1853) and its successors, publishing some 120 volumes of fiction, High Church in tone. She devoted part of the profits from her *Heir of Redclyffe* to fitting out the missionary schooner *Southern Cross* for Bishop **George Selwyn**, and the profits from the *Daisy Chain* (£2,000) she gave to build a missionary college in New Zealand. She also published historical, biographical, and other works, and edited the girls' magazine *Monthly Packet* from 1851 to 1890.

York, Prince Andrew, Duke of, *in full* **Andrew Albert Christian Edward** 1960– •*British prince*• The second son of Queen **Elizabeth II** and Prince Philip, Duke of **Edinburgh**, he was educated at Gordonstoun School, Scotland, Lakefield College, Ontario, and the Royal Naval College, Dartmouth. He was commissioned in the Royal Navy, qualifying as a helicopter pilot and serving in the Falklands War (1982). In 1986 he married Sarah Margaret Ferguson (see Duchess of **York**) and was made Duke of York. They have two children: Princess Beatrice (1988–) and Princess Eugenie (1990–). They were divorced in 1996.

York, Richard, 3rd Duke of 1411–60 •*English nobleman and claimant to the English throne*• The father of **Edward IV**, **Richard III**, and George, Duke of **Clarence**, he loyally served the weak-minded **Henry VI** in Ireland and France, and was appointed Protector during his illnesses (1454–56), but he was always in conflict with the king's wife, **Margaret of Anjou**, and her Lancastrian forces. In 1460 he marched on Westminster and claimed the Crown, was promised the succession and appointed Protector again, but was killed in an uprising by Lancastrian forces at Wakefield.

York, Sarah, Duchess of, *nicknamed* **Fergie**, *née* **Sarah Margaret Ferguson** 1959– •*British member of the Royal Family*• She was born in London, the second daughter of Major Ronald Ferguson of the Life Guards. Her parents were divorced and her mother later married an Argentinian polo player. After a brief career in publishing, Sarah married Prince Andrew, Duke of **York**, in 1986. They had two daughters, Beatrice (1988–) and Eugenie (1990–). They were separated in 1992 amid intense press publicity about the marriage, and were divorced in 1996. Since then she has written books for children and her autobiography, *My Story* (1996), and has gained celebrity status in the US.

York, Susannah, *originally* **Susannah Yolande-Fletcher** 1941–

•*English actress*• Born in London, she was brought up in Scotland and studied at the Royal Academy of Dramatic Art in London. She worked in repertory theater and pantomime before becoming one of the quintessential faces of the 1960s, making her film debut in *Tunes of Glory* (1960). She followed this with more than 50 pictures, including *Tom Jones* (1963), *A Man for All Seasons* (1968), *The Killing of Sister George* (1968), *They Shoot Horses, Don't They?* (1969) and *Just Ask for Diamond* (1988). She played the eponymous hero's mother in the *Superman* films of the 1980s, and she has also written screenplays and children's stories. Her stage appearances include the title role in *Hedda Gabler* in New York (1981).

Yorkshire Ripper *See* **Sutcliffe, Peter**

Yoshida Shigeru 1878–1967 •*Japanese statesman*• Born in Tokyo and educated at Tokyo Imperial University, he served as a diplomat and ambassador in several capitals. As a fervent advocate of Japanese surrender, he was imprisoned (June 1945) for this view in the closing stages of World War II. He was released (September 1945) under the US occupation and was appointed foreign minister. After Ichiro Hatoyama was removed by the US authorities from public office, Yoshida stepped into his shoes as leader of the Liberal Party. As prime minister (1946–47, 1949–54), he was instrumental in the socioeconomic development of postwar Japan and in fostering relations with the West. In 1954, Hatoyama forced him out of office and Yoshida later withdrew from politics.

Yoshihito 1879–1926 •*Emperor of Japan*• Born in Tokyo, the only son of Emperor **Mutsuhito**, he succeeded his father on the imperial throne in 1912. His 14-year reign saw the emergence of Japan as a great world power. Unlike his father, however, he took little part in active politics, for his mental health deteriorated (1921). In the last five years of his life, Crown Prince **Hirohito** was regent. Japanese custom accorded Yoshihito the posthumous courtesy title, Taisho Tenno.

Young, Andrew Jackson, Jr 1932– •*US clergyman, politician and civil rights leader*• Born in New Orleans, he was educated at Howard University and Hartford Theological Seminary. Ordained a minister in 1955, he became a leading figure in the civil rights movement. He served as executive director of the Southern Christian Leadership Conference (1964–70) and in 1972 was elected to the US House of Representatives as a Democrat from Georgia. He represented the US in the United Nations (1977–79) and later became mayor of Atlanta (1982–89).

Young, Brigham 1801–77 •*US Mormon leader*• Born in Whitingham, Vermont, he became a carpenter, painter and glazier in Mendon, New York. He first saw the *Book of Mormon* in 1830, and in 1832, converted by a brother of **Joseph Smith**, was baptized and began to preach near Mendon. In 1835 he was appointed to the Quorum of the Twelve Apostles of the Mormon Church, directed the settlement at Nauvoo, Illinois, and in 1844 succeeded Joseph Smith as president. When the Mormons were driven from Nauvoo, he led them to Utah (1847), where they founded Salt Lake City. In 1850 President **Fillmore** appointed Brigham Young governor of Utah Territory, but the Mormon practice of polygamy caused growing concern, and in 1857 a new governor was sent with a force of US troops under **Albert Sidney Johnston** to suppress it.

Young, Chic (Murat Bernard) 1901–73 •*US cartoonist*• Born in Chicago, he studied at the Art Institute of Chicago and joined Newspaper Enterprise Association, creating his first strip, *Affairs of Jane*, in 1920. His best-known strip is *Blondie* (1930), featuring the millionaire's daughter, Blondie Boopadoop, who developed into a suburban housewife and mother of two. Twenty-eight films were based on the strip, as were radio and television series.

Young, Cy, *properly* **Denton True Young** 1867–1955 •*US baseball pitcher*• Born in Gilmore, Ohio, he recorded a total of 511 victories between 1890 and 1911, a record that remains unequaled. He is commemorated by the annual Cy Young award to the most successful pitcher in the US major leagues. In 1904 he pitched the first "perfect game" in baseball, that is, one in which no opposing batter reached first base on either a hit or a walk.

Young (of Graffham), David Ivor Young, Lord 1932– •*English Conservative politician and businessman*• He was educated at Christ's College, Finchley, and University College London, where he took a law degree. He qualified as a solicitor and became a business executive, pursuing a successful industrial career until his talents were recognized by Sir Keith Joseph (1918–94) and **Margaret Thatcher**, who persuaded him to become director of the Centre for Policy Studies, a right-wing think tank (1979–82). He was chairman of the Manpower Services Commission (MSC) (1981–84), then was made a life peer and brought into the Thatcher cabinet, from 1985 as employment secretary. In 1989 he moved out of the political center and returned to commerce. He was chairman of the International Council of Jewish Social and Welfare Services (1981–84) and in 1993 became chairman of the Central Council for Jewish Community Services.

Young, Edward 1683–1765 •*English poet*• Born in Upham rectory, near Winchester, he was educated at Winchester and at New College and Corpus Christi College, Oxford. In 1719 he produced a tragedy, *Busiris*, at Drury Lane; his second tragedy, *The Revenge*, was produced in 1721, and his third and last, *The Brothers*, in 1753. His satires, *The Love of Fame, the Universal Passion* (1725–28), brought financial reward as well as fame, and for *The Instalment* (1726), a poem addressed to Sir **Robert Walpole**, he received a pension of £200. In 1724 Young took orders, in 1727 he was appointed a royal chaplain, and in 1730 he became rector of Welwyn. *The Complaint, or Night Thoughts on Life, Death and Immortality* (1742–45), usually known as *Night Thoughts*, was occasioned by his wife's death and other sorrows, and has many lines which have passed into proverbial use.

Young, Francis Brett 1884–1954 •*English novelist*• Born in Halesowen, Worcestershire he became a physician and spent a period as a ship's doctor but achieved celebrity as the author of *Portrait of Clare* (1927), which won the James Tait Black Memorial Prize. From then on he wrote a succession of novels of leisurely charm, characterized by a deep love of his native country. Noteworthy titles are *My Brother Jonathan* (1928), *Far Forest* (1936) and *Portrait of a Village* (1951). He also wrote short stories and poetry, including *Poems 1916–1918* (1919) and *The Island* (1944), a history of England told in historically appropriate verse forms.

Young, Lester Willis, *known as* **Prez** 1909–59 •*US tenor saxophonist and occasional clarinettist*• Born in Woodville, Mississippi, he first played alto saxophone in a family band, but changed to tenor saxophone in 1927 and worked with a succession of bands in the Midwest. He joined the newly formed **Count Basie** Orchestra in 1934 for a time, rejoining it in 1936. The band's rise to national prominence in the late 1930s brought Young recognition as an innovative soloist whose light tone and easy articulation marked a break from the baroque swing-style saxophone, and inspired such modernists as **Charlie Parker** and Dexter Gordon. Around this time, Young accompanied singer **Billie Holiday** on several important recording sessions. During the 1950s, his dependence on alcohol became marked, and his later performances diminished in creative power.

Young, Neil 1945– •*Canadian singer and songwriter*• Born in Toronto, he moved to Los Angeles, where he cofounded the influential country-rock group Buffalo Springfield, and later was part of a "supergroup" with Dave Crosby, Stephen Stills and Graham Nash. His albums *After the Gold Rush* (1970) and *Harvest* (1972) were best-sellers, but he turned away from their commercial country-rock vein on denser, darker records in the rest of the decade. His distinctive guitar style influenced the punk and grunge movements, but he has continually shifted stylistic ground, taking in country, rhythm and blues, early rock and roll, and even electronic music. Unlike many of his contemporaries, he has retained his credibility with both critics and audiences.

Young, Sheila 1950– •*US speed skater and cyclist*• Born in Birmingham, Michigan, she won her first two speed-skating titles, the US national outdoor competition and the North American outdoor championship, in 1970. In 1971 she defended both titles and won the Amateur Bicycle League of America women's national sprint title. In 1976 she won three medals at the Winter Olympics: gold in the 500-meter, silver in the 1,500-meter and bronze in the 1,000-meter speed-skating events. She was a founding member of the Women's Sports Foundation and has served on numerous boards, including the US Cycling Federation and the Special Olympics International. She was the US Olympic Committee's Sportswoman of the Year in 1981 and is in the International Women's Sports Hall of Fame.

Young, Thomas 1773–1829 •*English physicist, physician and Egyptologist*• Born in Milverton, Somerset, he studied medicine at the Universities of London, Edinburgh, and Göttingen and at Cambridge, and became a physician in London in 1800. In 1801 he was appointed Professor of Natural Philosophy at the Royal Institution and held several public offices related to science and navigation. He became best known in the 19th century for his wave theory of light, and he combined the wave theory of **Christiaan Huygens** and **Isaac Newton**'s theory of colors to explain the interference phenomenon produced by ruled gratings, thin plates, and the colors of the rainbow. He also did valuable work in insurance, hemodynamics and Egyptology and made a fundamental contribution to the deciphering of the inscriptions on the Rosetta stone.

Young, Whitney Moore, Jr 1921–71 •*US civil rights leader*• Born in Lincoln Ridge, Kentucky, he began his career as a social worker and university professor. As executive director of the National Urban League (1961–71), he sought to improve education, housing, and job opportunities for African Americans in the inner city. In 1963 he developed a "domestic Marshall Plan," much of which was incorporated into antipoverty legislation under President **Lyndon B Johnson**.

Younger (of Leckie), Sir George Younger, 1st Viscount 1851–1929 •*Scottish Conservative politician*• Born in Alloa and educated at Edinburgh Academy and the University of Edinburgh, he left college at the age of 17 to run the family brewery after his father died. He was president of the Scottish Conservative and Unionist Association in 1904. Member of Parliament for Ayr Burghs (1906–22), he was chairman of the (British) Conservative Party organization (1916–23) and helped run the "Coupon" general election of 1918, ensuring the return of many Conservatives. In 1922 he was central in breaking up the **Lloyd George** coalition government and replacing it with the Conservative governments of **Andrew Bonar Law** and **Stanley Baldwin**. He was made a peer in 1923. In the tradition of his uncle, William McEwan, he combined a career as a politician with that of a successful brewer.

Younger (of Prestwick), George Kenneth Hotson Younger, Baron 1931– •*Scottish Conservative politician*• Born in Winchester into a family with deep roots in Scottish Conservatism, and educated at Oxford, he became manager and director of the family brewing business. He was Member of Parliament for Ayr from 1964 to 1992, Scottish Conservative Whip (1965–67) and chairman of the Scottish Conservative Party (1974–75). He was junior minister at the Scottish Office (1970–74), then secretary of state for Scotland (1979–86). In this post he built up the Scottish Development Agency and attracted high-technology industry to Scotland to balance the collapse of traditional manufacturing sectors. He was defense secretary from 1986 to 1989 and since 1991 has been chairman of the Bank of Scotland Group. He was made a life peer in 1992.

Younghusband, Dame Eileen Louise 1902–81 •*English social work pioneer*• Born in London, she studied at the London School of Economics, where she taught from 1929 to 1957. During World War II she worked for the National Association of Girls' Clubs, directed courses for the British Council for Social Welfare, and set up one of the first Citizens Advice Bureaus. Later she compiled reports on social work training and social work (1947, 1951) and was principal adviser to the National Institute for Social Work Training (1961–67).

Younghusband, Sir Francis Edward 1863–1942 •*British explorer*• Born in Murree, India, he explored Manchuria in 1886 and on the way back discovered the route from Kashgar into India via the Mustagh Pass. In 1902 he went on the expedition which opened up Tibet to the Western world. A British resident in Kashmir (1906–09), he wrote much on India and Central Asia. He was deeply religious and founded the World Congress of Faiths in 1936.

Yourcenar, Marguerite, *pseudonym of* **Marguerite de Crayencour** 1903–87 •*French novelist and poet*• Born in Brussels, Belgium, and educated at home in a wealthy and cultured household, her first poems were privately printed in her teens. Her novels, many of them historical reconstructions, include *Les mémoires d'Hadrien* (1941, Eng trans *Memoirs of Hadrian*, 1954) and *L'œuvre au noir* (1968, Eng trans *The Abyss*, 1976). She also wrote the long prose poem *Feux* (1939, Eng trans *Fires*, 1981) and an autobiography (1977). She emigrated to the US in 1939, but was later given French citizenship by presidential decree, and in 1980, she became the first woman writer to be elected to the Académie Française.

“ ”

Que le Dieu qui nous tue nous vienne en aide!
God who kills us, come to our rescue!

1963 ***Qui n'a pas son Minotaure?****, part 3.*

Yrigoyen, Hipólito *See* **Irigoyen, Hipólito**

Yuan Shikai (Yüan Shih-k'ai) 1859–1916 •*Chinese politician and soldier*• He was born in Henan (Honan) province. He served in the army and became imperial adviser, but he remained neutral during the Boxer Rebellion (1898–1900). As a result, his army survived intact and he won the gratitude of the foreign powers. On the death of his patron, the Empress Dowager **Cixi** (1908), he was removed from influence, but was recalled after the successful Chinese Revolution of 1911. He became the first president of the republic (1912–16), but lost support by procuring the murder of the parliamentary leader of the Guomindang (Kuomintang) and making war on them. He accepted Japan's Twenty-One Demands, and proclaimed himself emperor (1915) but was forced to abdicate.

Yukawa, Hideki, *originally* **Hideki Ogawi** 1907–81 •*Japanese physicist and Nobel Prize winner*• Born in Tokyo, he was educated at Kyoto and Osaka Imperial Universities. He returned to Kyoto as Professor of Theoretical Physics (1939–50), and he later became director of the Kyoto Research Institute for Fundamental Physics (1953–70). In 1935 he suggested that a strong short-range attractive interaction between neutrons and protons would overcome the electrical repulsion between protons. The existence of the intermediate particles which propagate the interaction was confirmed by **Cecil Powell**'s discovery in 1947 of the p-meson, or pion. For his work on quantum theory and nuclear physics, he was awarded the Nobel Prize for physics in 1949, becoming the first Japanese to be so honored.

Zachariadis, Nikos 1903–73 •*Greek political leader*• The son of a tobacco worker, he was one of the many Greeks who were forced to leave Anatolia in 1923 after the Second Greco-Turkish War and who became Communists. He was secretary-general of the Communist Party of Greece (KKE) from 1931 to 1941. Imprisoned during World War II in the Dachau concentration camp, he lived to return home in 1945 to direct Communist opposition to the British-backed Greek government and resumed his post as secretary-general of the KKE. He succeeded Markos Vafiadis (1906–92) as commander of the Democratic Army in 1949.

Zacharias, Basileios *See* **Zaharoff, Sir Basil**

Zadkine, Ossip 1890–1967 •*French sculptor*• He was born in Smolensk, Russia, studied in Sunderland and at the London Polytechnic, and settled in Paris in 1909. There he developed an individual style, making effective use of the play of light on concave surfaces, as in *The Three Musicians* (1926), *Orpheus* (1948, carved from a tree trunk), and the war memorial in Rotterdam, entitled *The Destroyed City* (1952).

Zaharias, Babe (Mildred Ella), *née* **Didrikson** 1914–56 •*US golfer and athlete*• She was born in Port Arthur, Texas. She was on the All-American basketball team (1930–32), then turned to track events and won two gold medals (javelin and 80-meter sprint) at the 1932 Olympics in Los Angeles. She also broke the world record in the high jump but was disqualified for using the new Western Roll technique. Excelling also in swimming, tennis and rifle shooting, she turned to golf in 1934, and won the US National Women's Amateur Championship in 1946 and the British Ladies' Amateur Championship in 1947. She went on to win the US Women's Open three times (1948, 1950, 1954).

Zaharoff, Sir Basil, *originally* **Basileios Zacharias** 1850–1936 •*French armaments magnate and financier*• Born in Anatolia, Turkey, to Greek parents, he was educated in Istanbul and England. He entered the munitions industry in the 1880s and became a shadowy but influential figure in international politics and finance, amassing a huge fortune. He became a French citizen in 1913, and was knighted by the British in 1918 for his services to the Allies in World War I. He donated large sums of money to universities and other institutions.

Zahir Shah, King Mohammed 1914– •*King of Afghanistan*• Educated in Kabul and Paris, he succeeded to the throne in 1933 after the assassination of his father, Nadir Shah. His reign was characterized by a concern to preserve neutrality and promote gradual modernization. He became a constitutional monarch in 1964, but, in 1973, while in Italy receiving medical treatment, he was overthrown in a republican coup led by his cousin, General Daud Khan, following a three-year famine. He then lived in exile in Rome and remained a popular symbol of national unity for some moderate Afghan opposition groups. He returned to Afghanistan in 2002 as a private citizen.

Zamenhof, (Lazarus) Ludwig 1859–1917 •*Polish oculist and philologist*• He was born in Bialystok. He invented Esperanto ("One who hopes") as an international language to promote world peace. In 1893, a formal organization was established, and annual conferences were held from 1905. Zamenhof translated many well-known works into Esperanto, such as the plays of **Shakespeare**, **Molière** and **Goethe**, and his *Fundamento de Esperanto* (Eng trans *Basis of Esperanto*, 1979) was published in 1905.

Zamyatin, Yevgeni Ivanovich 1884–1937 •*Russian writer*• He was born in Lebedyan, Tambov Province. In 1914 he wrote a novella, *Na kulichkakh* ("At the World's End"), satirizing the life of army officers in a remote garrison town, and he was tried but ultimately acquitted of "maligning the officer corps." A naval architect by training, he spent 18 months in Glasgow and the north of England during World War I designing and supervising the building of ice-breakers for Russia. He returned to Russia, to St Petersburg, in 1917 and participated in various cooperative literary projects, but he was repeatedly attacked as "a bourgeois intellectual." Zamyatin refused to tailor his art to political dogma, and in 1920 wrote *My* (Eng trans *We*, 1924), a dystopian fantasy prophesying **Stalin**ism and the failure of the revolution. Its influence on **Aldous Huxley**'s *Brave New World* (1932) is striking, and it was read by **George Orwell** before he wrote *Nineteen Eighty-Four* (1949). His best stories are contained in *The Dragon*, first published in English in 1966. He left Russia in 1931, and he settled for exile in Paris, where he died.

Zangwill, Israel 1864–1926 •*English writer*• Born in London, he went to school in Plymouth and Bristol but was mainly self-taught, and graduated with honors from the University of London. After teaching, he became a journalist and was editor of the comic journal *Ariel*, in which he published the witty tales collected as *The Bachelors' Club* (1891) and *The Old Maids' Club* (1892). A leading Zionist, he wrote poems, plays and essays and became widely known for his novels on Jewish themes, including *Children of the Ghetto* (1892) and *Ghetto Tragedies* (1894). Other works include the plays *The Revolted Daughter* (1901) and *We Moderns* (1925).

Zanuck, Darryl F(rancis) 1902–79 •*US film producer*• Born in Wahoo, Nebraska, he became a scriptwriter for Warner Brothers (1924) and cofounder of Twentieth Century Pictures (1933), becoming vice president of that company and, after its merger with Fox Films (1935), of Twentieth Century Fox Films Corporation. Among his many successful films are *The Jazz Singer* (1927, the first "talkie"), *Little Caesar* (1930), *The Grapes of Wrath* (1940), *How Green Was My Valley* (1941), *The Robe* (1953), *The Longest Day* (1962) and *The Sound of Music* (1965). He retired in 1971.

Zapata, Emiliano 1879–1919 •*Mexican revolutionary*• Born in Anencuilio, Morelos, the son of a mestizo peasant, he became a local peasant leader. After the onset of the Mexican Revolution, he occupied estates by force and mounted a program for the return of land to the Indians in the areas he controlled. He initially supported **Francisco Madero**, and with a small force of men was largely responsible for toppling the dictatorship of **Porfirio Díaz**. Along with **Pancho Villa**, he subsequently fought the **Carranza** government. Meanwhile, he continued to implement agrarian reforms in the southern area under his control. He was eventually lured to his death at the Chinameca hacienda in Morelos.

Zapolya, Stephen d. 1499 •*Hungarian soldier*• He gained renown as a military leader under **Matthias I Hunyadi** by his defeat of the Turks and his conquest of Austria, of which he was made governor (1485). He was the father of John Zapolya, king of Hungary from 1526.

Zapotocky, Antonin 1884–1957 •*Czech trade unionist and politician*• A stonemason from Kladno, he was active in the socialist youth movement from 1900 and in the Socialist Party from 1907. In 1921 he helped found the Communist Party. Imprisoned during World War II, he emerged in 1945 to become the president of the revolutionary trade-union organization that played a key role in seizing power in 1948. He was appointed prime minister and succeeded **Klement Gottwald** to the presidency in 1953. His responsibility for the purges was probably less than Gottwald's, but despite the moderation of old age, he lost much of the opportunity to make amends.

Zappa, Frank (Francis Vincent) 1940–93 •*US rock guitarist, singer and composer*• He was born in Baltimore into a family of Sicilian Greek origin, who moved to the West Coast in 1949. He began his career as a drummer, then turned to guitar. Zappa was a multifarious and highly unpredictable talent in rock music, and he explored musical areas well beyond the genre's normal boundaries. He established his reputation as a major iconoclast with his group The Mothers of Invention from 1966, and he continued to build a vast experimental musical edifice throughout his life, ranging from catchy pop to avant-garde composition, much of which was issued on his own record labels.

Zaradusht *See* **Zoroaster**

Zarathustra *See* **Zoroaster**

Zatopek, Emil 1922–2000 •*Czech athlete and middle-distance runner*• He was born in the Moravian town of Koprivnice. After many successes in Czechoslovak track events, he won the gold medal for the 10,000 meters at the 1948 Olympics in London. For the next six years, despite an astonishingly labored style, he proved himself to be the greatest long-distance runner of his time, breaking 13 world records. At the 1952 Olympics in Helsinki, he retained his gold medal in the 10,000 meters and also won the 5,000 meters and the marathon. His wife and fellow athlete, Dana Zatopekova, also won an Olympic gold medal (for the javelin) in 1952.

" "

An athlete cannot run with money in his pockets. He must run with hope in his heart and dreams in his head.

*Quoted by Christopher Brasher in **The Observer**, September 12, 1982.*

Zedillo Ponce de León, Ernesto 1951– •*Mexican politician*• Born in Mexico City, he studied at the National Polytechnic Institute and earned a PhD in economics at Yale (1981). He went to work for the Banco de Mexico and helped devise a successful program to manage Mexico's enormous foreign debt. A member of the Institutional Revolutionary Party (PRI), he served as budget and planning minister under President Salinas from 1988, promoting the NAFTA free-trade agreement with the US and Canada, and as education minister from 1992. Taking office as president of Mexico in 1994, he promptly triggered an economic crisis by devaluing the peso. But he also proved unexpectedly sympathetic to democratic reforms, overhauled the corrupt justice system, signed a peace pact (1996) with the Zapatista rebels and made sweeping electoral reforms designed to bring about fairness. He was succeeded by **Vicente Fox Quesada** in 2000.

Zeeman, Pieter 1865–1943 •*Dutch physicist and Nobel Prize winner*• Born in Zonnemaire, Zeeland, he studied with **Hendrik Lorentz** at the University of Leiden. He became a lecturer at Leiden in 1897 and in 1900 was appointed Professor of Physics at the University of Amsterdam. In 1896 he studied light sources in a magnetic field and deduced that the resultant broadening of spectral emission lines was due to the splitting of spectrum lines into two or three components. This phenomenon became known as the Zeeman effect. Zeeman also investigated the absorption and motion of electricity in fluids, magnetic fields on the solar surface, the **Doppler** effect and the effect of nuclear magnetic moments on spectral lines. In 1902 he shared with Lorentz the Nobel Prize for physics for the discovery and explanation of the Zeeman effect.

Zeffirelli, Franco 1923– •*Italian stage, opera and film director*• Born and educated in Florence, he began his career as an actor and theater-set and costume designer (1945–51). His first opera production, *La Cenerentola* (1953), at La Scala, Milan, was followed by a brilliant series of productions in Italy and abroad, culminating in *Lucia di Lammermoor, Cavelleria rusticana* and *I Pagliacci* at Covent Garden, London (1959), and an outstanding *Falstaff* at the New York Metropolitan Opera House (1964). His stage productions include *Romeo and Juliet* at the Old Vic, London (1960), and *Who's Afraid of Virginia Woolf?* (Paris 1964, Milan 1965). He has also filmed lively and spectacular versions of *The Taming of the Shrew* (1966) and *Romeo and Juliet* (1968), and produced film versions of the operas *La traviata* (1983) and *Otello* (1986). Recent films include *Tea With Mussolini* (1999). Turning to politics, he was elected as a member of the right-wing Forza Italia in 1994.

Zeiss, Carl 1816–88 •*German optician and industrialist*• Born in Weimar, in 1846 he established the factory at Jena which became noted for the production of lenses, microscopes, field glasses, and the like. His business was organized on a system whereby the workers had a share in the profits.

Zemeckis, Robert 1952– •*US film director*• Born in Chicago, Illinois, he studied film at the University of Southern California and became an editor of television news and commercials. His talent was spotted by **Steven Spielberg**, who was executive producer on Zemeckis's directorial debut, *I Wanna Hold Your Hand* (1978). He followed this with the brash comedy *Used Cars* (1980) and the sweeping high adventure *Romancing the Stone* (1984). His later films—*Back to the Future* (1985), its two sequels, and *Who Framed Roger Rabbit?* (1988)—showed him to be a master of popular entertainment. He won a Best Director Academy Award for *Forrest Gump* (1994). More recent films include *Cast Away* (2000).

Zeno of Citium c. 334–c. 265 BC •*Greek philosopher, the founder of Stoicism*• He was born in Citium, Cyprus, went to Athens as a young man (c. 315 BC) and attended **Plato**'s Academy and other schools there. He then set up his own school (c. 300) in the *Stoa poikile* ("painted porch"), which gave the Stoics their name. He had a formative role in the development of Stoicism as a distinctive and coherent philosophy. None of his many treatises survive, but his main contribution seems to have been in the area of ethics. He supposedly committed suicide.

Zeno of Elea c. 490–c. 420 BC •*Greek philosopher and mathematician*• He was a native of Elea, a Greek colony in southern Italy, where he lived all or most of his life, and was a disciple of Parmenides of Elea. In defense of his monistic philosophy against the Pythagoreans, he devised his famous paradoxes, which purported to show the impossibility of motion and of spatial division by showing that space and time could be neither continuous nor discrete. The paradoxes are "Achilles and the Tortoise," "The Flying Arrow," "The Stadium" and "The Moving Rows."

Zenobia 3rd century AD •*Queen of Palmyra*• Probably of Arab descent, she married the Bedouin Odaenathus, lord of the city, who was recognized by **Gallienus** as governor of the East (AD 264). On the eve of her husband's murder (c. 267), she conquered Egypt (269) and much of Asia Minor (270), declaring her son the Eastern emperor. **Aurelian** defeated her in battle, besieged Palmyra, and captured her in 272. She blamed the war on her secretary, **Longinus**; he was beheaded and Palmyra destroyed. Strikingly beautiful, Zenobia married a Roman senator and was presented with large possessions near Tivoli, where, with her two sons, she passed the rest of her life in comfort and splendor.

Zephaniah 7th century BC •*Old Testament prophet*• He made his prophecies during the reign of King Josiah of Judah. His account of a coming "Day of Wrath" inspired the medieval Latin hymn *Dies Irae*.

Zephaniah, Benjamin Obadiah Iqbal 1958– •*English poet*• Born in Black River, Jamaica, he emigrated with his family to England at the age of two, settling in Handsworth, Birmingham. Sent to a reform school at the age of 14 and subsequently imprisoned for two years, he published his first book of poetry, *Pen Rhythm*, in 1982. Among those that followed were *The Dread Affair* (1985) and *Refugee Boy* (2001). He has established a reputation as a leading popularizer of poetry, performing regularly at festivals and on television and radio.

Zeppelin, Count Ferdinand von 1838–1917 •*German army officer*• Born in Constance, Baden, he served in the Civil War in the Union Army, and in the Franco-Prussian War (1870–71). From 1897 to 1900 he constructed his first airship (a dirigible balloon of the rigid type) named a "zeppelin," which first flew on July 2, 1900.

Zetterling, Mai 1925–94 •*Swedish actress and director*• Born in Vasteras, Sweden, she made both her stage and screen debuts at the age of 16. Her first major role was in the influential Swedish film *Hets* (1944; US *Torment*, UK *Frenzy*). She played in many British and US films before turning her attention to directing with her debut film, the award-winning documentary *The War Game* (1963), which she cowrote with her husband, David Hughes. She directed a number of feature films in Sweden and also wrote novels.

Zhao Ziyang (Chao Tzu-yang) 1918– •*Chinese statesman*• The son of a wealthy Henan (Honan) Province landlord, he joined the Communist Youth League in 1932 and worked underground as a Chinese Communist Party (CCP) official during the Liberation War (1937–49). He then rose to prominence implementing land reform in Guangdong (1951–62), becoming the province's CCP first secretary in 1964. He was dismissed during the 1966–69 Cultural Revolution, paraded through Guangzhou in a dunce's cap and sent to Nei Menggu (Inner Mongolia). Rehabilitated in 1973 he became the Communist Party's first secretary of China's largest province, Sichuan, in 1975. Here he introduced radical and successful market-oriented rural reforms, which attracted the eye of **Deng Xiaoping** and led to his induction into the CCP politburo as a full member in 1979 and to his appointment as prime minister a year later. As premier he oversaw the implementation of a radical new market socialist and open door economic program, and in 1987 he replaced the disgraced **Hu Yaobang** as CCP general secretary. However, in 1989, he was controversially dismissed for his allegedly over-liberal handling of student pro-democracy demonstrations in Beijing. He was placed under house arrest for five months.

Zhivkov, Todor 1911–98 •*Bulgarian statesman*• Born and educated in Sofia, he became a printer and joined the (illegal) Communist Party in 1932. He fought with the Bulgarian Resistance in 1943 and took part in the Sofia coup d'état that overthrew the pro-German regime in 1944. He became first secretary of the Bulgarian Communist Party (BCP) in 1954, prime minister in 1962 and, as chairman of the Council of State in 1971, became effectively the president of the People's Republic. His period in office was characterized by unquestioned loyalty to the USSR and caution and conservatism in policymaking, which led to mounting economic problems in the 1980s. He was eventually ousted in 1989 in a committee-room coup and, with his health failing, was subsequently expelled from the BCP and placed under house arrest, pending trial. In 1992 his seven-year prison sentence was commuted to detention under house arrest.

“ ”

If I had to do it over again, I would not even be a communist. And if Lenin were alive today, he would say the same thing.

1990 In the ***Sunday Times****, December 9.*

Zhou Enlai (Chou En-lai) 1898–1975 •*Chinese statesman*• Born into a family of the mandarin gentry in Jiangsu (Kiangsu) Province near Shanghai, he was educated at an American missionary college in Tianjin (Tientsin) and studied in Japan (1917–18) and Paris (1920–24), where he became a founding member of the overseas branch of the Chinese Communist Party (CCP). He married Deng Yingchao (Teng Ying-ch'ao) (b. 1903) in 1924 and was an adherent to the Moscow line of urban-based revolution in China, organizing

Communist cells in Shanghai and an abortive uprising in Nanchang in 1927. He served as head of the political department of the Whampoa Military Academy in Canton. In 1935, at the Zunyi conference, Zhou supported the election of **Mao Zedong** as CCP leader and remained a loyal ally during the next 40 years. Between 1937 and 1946 he served as a liaison officer between the CCP and **Chiang Kai-shek**'s Nationalist government. In 1949 he became prime minister, an office he held until his death. Zhou, standing intermediate between the opposing camps of **Liu Shaoqi** and Mao Zedong, served as a moderating influence, restoring orderly progress after the Great Leap Forward (1958–60) and the Cultural Revolution (1966–69). He was the architect of the Four Modernizations program in 1975 and played a key role in foreign affairs. He averted an outright border confrontation with the USSR by negotiation with **Aleksei Kosygin** in 1969 and was the principal advocate of détente with the US during the early 1970s.

Zhu De (Chu Te or **Teh)** 1886–1976 •*Chinese soldier and politician*• The son of a wealthy Sichuan (Szechuan) Province landlord, he joined the **Sun Yat-sen** Revolution (1911). He later took part in the Nanchang Army Revolt (1927), from which he formed the Chinese Red Army. He was elected commander in chief of the Fourth Army and led it in the famous Long March (1934–36). Working closely with **Mao Zedong**, Zhu devised the successful tactic of mobile guerrilla warfare, leading the Communist military forces during the Second Sino-Japanese War (1937–45). He became supreme commander of the renamed People's Liberation Army, which expelled the Nationalists from mainland China during the civil war of 1946–49. He was made a marshal in 1955 and served as head of state and chairman of the Standing Committee of the National People's Congress (1975–76).

Zhukov, Georgi Konstantinovich 1896–1974 •*Soviet general*• He was born to peasant parents in Strelkovka, Kaluga region. In 1918 he joined the Red Army. An expert in armored warfare, he commanded the Soviet tanks in Outer Mongolia in 1939, and in 1941 became army chief of staff. In December 1941 he led the Siege of Moscow, and in February 1943 his counteroffensive was successful at Stalingrad (Volgograd). In command of the First Byelo-Russian Army in 1944–45, he captured Warsaw and conquered Berlin. On May 8, 1945, on behalf of the Soviet high command, he accepted the German surrender. After the war he became commander in chief of the Russian zone of Germany, in 1955 became minister of defense, and in 1957 he supported **Nikita Khrushchev** against the **Malenkov-Molotov** faction. He was dismissed by Khrushchev in 1957.

Zhu Rongji 1928– •*Chinese politician*• Born in Changsha, Hunan Province, into a family of intellectuals, he was educated at Qinghua University and became a member of the Chinese Communist Party (CCP) in 1949. By 1957 he had risen to a senior position in the State Economic Commission. After criticizing the policies of Chairman **Mao** in 1958, he was forced to work as a teacher prior to political rehabilitation in 1962. His career suffered once more during the Cultural Revolution of the 1970s, but he returned to take up senior economic posts and in 1987 joined the Central Committee of the CCP. He served as mayor of Shanghai and, with the support of President **Deng Xiaoping**, joined the politburo of the CCP in 1992 and became the chief architect of economic reform in China through the 1990s. In 1998 he succeeded **Li Peng** as Chinese prime minister, in which post he massively reduced China's bureaucracy and continued his efforts to reorganize the economy and open it up to Western investment. He was succeeded by Wen Jiabao in 2003.

Zia, (Begum) Khaleda 1945– •*Bangladeshi politician*• She was educated at Surendranath College, Dinajpur, and married General **Ziaur Rahman** in 1960. After his assassination in 1981, she became leader of the Bangladesh Nationalist Party (BNP) in 1982. In 1990, when President **Hossain Mohammad Ershad** was forced to resign, elections were called, and from 1991 to 1996 Khaleda Zia served as the first woman prime minister of Bangladesh. In 1996 she relinquished power to a caretaker government and was defeated by Sheikh Hasina in the general election. She returned to power in 2001.

Zia ul-Haq, Mohammed 1924–88 •*Pakistani soldier and politician*• He was born in Jalandhar, into a strict, middle-class Punjabi-Muslim family, and fought in Burma, Malaya and Indonesia during World War II. He became army chief of staff in 1976 and led the military coup against **Zulfikar Ali Bhutto** in July 1977, becoming president in September 1978. He proceeded to introduce a new policy of Islamization and a freer-market economic program. Zia's opposition to the Soviet invasion of Afghanistan in December 1979 drew support from the US, and, from 1981, he began to engineer a gradual return to civilian government. He lifted martial law in December 1985. He was killed in a dubious accident three years later.

Ziaur Rahman 1935–81 •*Bangladeshi soldier and politician*• He played an important part in the civil war and the eventual emergence of the state of Bangladesh. He was appointed chief of the army staff after the assassination of the ruling sheikh **Mujibur Rahman** in 1975 and became the dominant figure within the military. President of Bangladesh from 1977 until his death, he led a government which was military in character, even after the election of 1978 confirmed his popularity. He was assassinated in Dhaka.

Zidane, Zinedine 1972– •*French soccer player*• Born in Marseilles, France, of Algerian origin, he became one of the most talented attacking midfielders in the world in the 1990s. He played for Cannes and Bordeaux before transferring to Juventus in 1996 and winning two Italian league titles (1997, 1998) with them. Having made his debut for France in 1994, he became a French hero as part of the national team that won the World Cup in 1998, clinching victory in the final against Brazil with two headed goals. France also captured the European championship in 2000. He was FIFA (Fédération Internationale de Football Association) Footballer of the Year in 1998 and 2000. He currently plays for Real Madrid (2001–).

Ziegfeld, Florenz 1869–1932 •*US theater manager*• Born in Chicago, the son of the president of Chicago Musical College, he devised and perfected the US revue spectacle, based on the *Folies Bergère*. His *Follies of 1907* was the first of an annual series that continued until 1931 and made his name synonymous with extravagant theatrical production. The *Follies* featured a chorus line of some of the most beautiful women in the US, all personally chosen by Ziegfeld, whose aim was to "glorify the American girl." He also supervised the choice of music, costumes and stage effects, and directed the production of each number. The result was a popularization of revue and new standards of artistry and production. The *Follies* also helped the careers of such stars as Eddie Cantor, **Fanny Brice** and **W C Fields**. His wide range of other musical productions included *The Red Feather, Kid Boots, Sally* (1920), *Show Boat* (1927) and the US production of *Bitter Sweet*.

Ziegler, Karl 1898–1973 •*German chemist and Nobel Prize winner*• Born in Helsa (Oberhessen), he taught at Marburg from 1920 and at Heidelberg from 1936, and in 1943 he was appointed director of the **Max Planck** Carbon Research Institute at Mülheim. With Giulio Natta (1903–79) he was awarded the Nobel Prize for chemistry in 1963 for research on long-chain polymers that lead to new developments in industrial materials.

Zimmermann, Arthur 1864–1940 •*German politician*• Born in East Prussia, after posts in the diplomatic service and foreign office, he became foreign secretary (1916–17). In January 1917 he sent the famous Zimmermann telegram to the German minister in Mexico with the terms of an alliance between Mexico and Germany by which Mexico was to attack the United States with German and Japanese assistance in return for the US states of New Mexico, Texas and Arizona. This telegram finally brought the hesitant US government into the war against Germany.

Zinkernagel, Rolf 1944– •*Swiss immunologist and Nobel Prize winner*• He was born in Basel and after graduating from the university there, he went as a visiting Fellow to the John Curtin School of Medical Research, Australian National University, Canberra. There in 1973 he collaborated with **Peter Doherty** on research into the human immune system that led to their jointly being awarded the 1996 Nobel Prize for physiology or medicine. Since 1992 he has been head of the Institute of Experimental Immunology at the University of Zurich.

Zinnemann, Fred 1907–97 •*Austrian film director*•Born in Vienna, he studied film in Paris, moved to Hollywood in 1929, and began directing features. Often concerned with conflicts of conscience and the moral dilemmas of reluctant heroes, his films include *The Search* (1948), *High Noon* (1952), *The Nun's Story* (1959) and *Julia* (1977). He received Best Director Academy Awards for *From Here to Eternity* (1953) and *A Man for All Seasons* (1966). He received further Academy Awards for the short film *That Mothers Might Live* (1938) and the documentary *Benjy* (1951). His last film was *Five Days One Summer* (1982).

Zinoviev, Grigori Yvseyevich 1883–1936 •*Russian politician*• Born in Yelisavetgrad (now Kirovohrad), Ukraine, he was from 1917 to 1926 a leading member of the Soviet government. A letter allegedly written by him to the British Communist Party in 1924 was used in the election campaign to defeat **Ramsay MacDonald**'s first Labour government. In 1927 Zinoviev suffered expulsion, and in 1936 death, having been charged with conspiring with **Trotsky** and **Lev Kamenev** to murder **Sergei Kirov** and **Stalin**. In 1988 he was posthumously rehabilitated.

Zoë 980–1050 •*Empress of the Eastern Roman Empire*• She was the daughter of the Byzantine emperor Constantine VIII. In 1028 she married Romanus III but had him murdered in 1034 and made her paramour emperor as Michael IV. When his successor, Michael V, was deposed (1042), she became joint empress with her sister **Theodora**, and married her third husband, Constantine IX.

Zoffany, John 1733–1810 •*British portrait painter*• Born in Frankfurt am Main, Germany, he settled in London in 1758 after studying art in Rome. Securing royal patronage, he painted many portraits and conversation pieces. He was a founding member of the Royal Academy in 1768. He traveled in Italy (1772–79), and later was a portraitist in India (1783–90).

Zog I, *originally* **Ahmed Bey Zogu** 1895–1961 •*King of the Albanians*• Born in central Albania, the son of a highland tribal chieftain, he was educated in Constantinople (Istanbul). He became head of the clan at the age of 12, growing up in an atmosphere of tribal feuds, and in 1912, when Albania declared her independence, Zog took a blood oath to defend it. As the outstanding nationalist leader, he formed a republican government (1922) and was its premier, president and commander in chief, proclaiming himself king in 1928. When Albania was annexed by the Italians (1939), he went to Great Britain, then Egypt, then France in 1955. His son, Leka (1939–), was proclaimed king in exile on his father's death.

Zohr, Ibn *See* **Avenzoar**

Zola, Émile 1840–1902 •*French novelist*• He was born in Paris, the son of an Italian engineer. He entered the publishing house of Hachette as a clerk, and soon became an active journalist. His first short stories were published as *Contes à Ninon* (1864, "Stories for Ninon"), and other collections followed. In the later years of the empire he formed a sort of informal society along with **Gustave Flaubert**, **Alphonse Daudet**, **Edmond** and **Jules de Goncourt**, and **Ivan Turgenev**, out of which grew the naturalist school of fiction. His first major novel, *Thérèse Raquin* (1867), a powerful picture of remorse, belongs to this school. Later he began the series of novels called *Les Rougon-Macquart*, a collection of some 20 volumes, all connected by the appearance of the same or different members of one family. These include *Nana* (1880), *Germinal* (1885), *La terre* (1887, "Earth") and *La bête humaine* (1890, "The Beast in Man"). In order to describe the human condition effectively, Zola mastered the technical details of many professions, occupations and crafts, as well as the history of recent events in France: this is seen, for example, in *L'œuvre* (concerning art and literature), *La terre* (the peasantry), *Germinal* (mining), *La bête humaine* (railways), *Le rêve* (church ritual), and other works. In 1898 Zola espoused the cause of **Alfred Dreyfus**, indicting the military authorities in his pamphlet *J'accuse* ("I accuse"). He was sentenced to prison but escaped for a year to England and was welcomed back a hero. He died in Paris, accidentally suffocated by charcoal fumes.

" "

J'accuse.
I accuse.

1898 Title of open letter to the president of France regarding the Dreyfus case.

Zoroaster, *Greek form of* **Zarathustra**, *modern form* **Zaradusht**, *originally* **Spitama** c. 630–c. 553 BC •*Persian religious leader and prophet, the founder or reformer of Zoroastrianism*• Born probably in Rhages, Persia (Iran), he appears as a historical person only in the earliest portion of the *Avesta*, the sacred book of Zoroastrianism. As the center of a group of chieftains, he carried on a political, military, and theological struggle for the defense or wider establishment of a holy agricultural state against Turanian and Vedic aggressors. He apparently had visions of Ahura Mazda, which led him to preach against polytheism. The keynote of his system is that the world and history demonstrate the struggle between Ormuzd and Ahriman (the creator or good spirit, and the evil principle, the devil), in which at the end good will triumph.

Zuckerman (of Burnham Thorpe), Solly Zuckerman, Baron 1904–93 •*British zoologist*• Born in Cape Town, South Africa, he taught at Oxford from 1932, and during World War II investigated the biological effects of bomb blasts. He became Professor of Anatomy at Birmingham (1946–68) and secretary of the Zoological Society of London in 1955. He was chief scientific adviser to the British government from 1964 to 1971. The results of his research on baboons at the London Zoo were published in two influential books, *The Social Life of Monkeys and Apes* (1932) and *Functional Affinities of Man, Monkeys and Apes* (1933). The first primatologist to consider that such studies could provide insights into the origins and behavior of human beings, he proposed that sex was the original social bond. Knighted in 1956, Zuckerman was awarded a life peerage in 1971, and he published his autobiography in 1978.

Zukor, Adolph 1873–1976 •*US film executive*• Born in Hungary, he emigrated to America in 1889. His success as a fur trader enabled him to invest in nickelodeons and build a small distribution network. Recognizing the potential of celebrity in attracting audiences to the cinema, he founded the Famous Players Company and was instrumental in establishing the star system. Among those he helped promote were **Mary Pickford**, **Rudolph Valentino** and **Gloria Swanson**. In 1916 he became president of the Famous Players-Lasky Corporation, which became Paramount Pictures in 1927. Zukor received a special Academy Award in March 1949 as "the man who has been called the father of the feature film in America."

Zúñiga, Alonso de Ercilla y *See* **Ercilla y Zúñiga, Alonso de**

Zurbarán, Francisco 1598–1662 •*Spanish religious painter*• Born in Fuente de Cantos in Andalusia, he spent most of his life in Seville, where he was appointed city painter, and court painter to **Philip IV** in 1638. He also specialized in religious themes, particularly saints' lives. In Madrid he painted mythological and historical subjects. He came to be called "the Spanish **Caravaggio**."

Zuse, Konrad 1910–95 •*German computer pioneer*• Born in Berlin, he was educated at the Berlin Institute of Technology before joining the Henschel Aircraft Company in 1935. In the following year, he began building a calculating machine in his spare time, a task which occupied him until 1945. He built a number of prototypes, the most historic being the Z3, which was the first operational general-purpose program-controlled calculator. Zuse built up his own firm, Zuse KG, until it was bought out by another firm in the 1960s, and he became honorary professor at the University of Göttingen in 1966.

Zweig, George 1937– •*US physicist*• Born in Moscow, he was educated at the University of Michigan and Caltech, and then worked at CERN (Conseil Européen pour la Recherche Nucléaire) in Geneva (1963–64) before returning to Caltech, where he became a professor in 1967. Independently of **Murray Gell-Mann**, he developed the theory of quarks as the fundamental physical building blocks. They suggested that three types exist, although there are now believed to be six types of quark.

Zwingli, Huldreich or **Ulrich**, *Latin* **Ulricus Zuinglius** 1484–1531 •*Swiss reformer*• Born in Wildhaus, St Gall, he studied at Bern, Vienna and Basel, and was ordained in 1506. He taught himself Greek, and twice went as field-chaplain of the Glarus mercenaries to war in Italy, taking part in the battles of Novara (1513) and Marignano (1515). He was elected preacher at the Grossmünster in Zurich (1518), rousing the council to forbid admittance within the city to Bernhardin Samson, a seller of indulgences. He stopped Zurich from joining (1521) the other cantons in their alliance with France. The Bishop of Constance sent his vicar general (1523), but he could not stop the city from adopting the Reformed doctrines as set forth in Zwingli's 67 theses. A second disputation followed (1523), with the result that holy images and the Mass were swept away. On Easter Sunday 1525 he dispensed the sacrament in both kinds, and the Reformation spread widely over Switzerland. At Marburg in 1529 he conferred with other Protestant leaders, and there disagreed with **Martin Luther** over the Eucharist, a dispute which eventually split the Protestant Church. He rejected every form of local or corporeal presence, whether by transubstantiation or consubstantiation. The progress of the Reformation aroused bitter hatred in the forest cantons, five of which formed an alliance (1528). Zurich declared war (1529) on account of the burning alive of a Protestant pastor seized on neutral territory, and in October 1531, the forest cantons made a sudden dash on Zurich with 8,000 men, to be met at Cappel by 2,000, including Zwingli. The men of Zurich were completely defeated, with Zwingli among the dead. Zwingli preached the Reformed doctrines as early as 1516, the year before the appearance of Luther's theses. He regarded original sin as a moral disease rather than as punishable sin or guilt. He maintained the salvation of unbaptized infants, and he believed in the salvation of the virtuous. On predestination he was as Calvinistic as **John Calvin**. With less fire and power than Luther, he was the most open-minded and liberal of the Reformers. Zwingli's *Opera* fill four folios (1545), the chief being the *Commentarius de Vera et Falsa Religione* (1525).

Zyuganov, Gennady Andreyevich 1944– •*Russian Communist politician*• Born in Mymrino Village, Orel Region, he was educated at the Orel Pedagogical Institute and then worked as a teacher. In 1967 his interest in trade union legislation took him into politics, first as a local organizer for the Communist Party and in 1983 as head of propaganda in Moscow. In 1989 he joined the politburo, and he became secretary of the Communist Party of the Russian Federation in 1992. Elected to the state duma in 1993, he emerged as the main Communist leader in parliament. Although he lost to **Boris Yeltsin** in the 1996 presidential election, he continued to attract large numbers of voters who regretted the passing of the Communist regime in Russia.